Goldmine

standard catalog of® • 7th Edition

American RECORDS 1948-1991

Martin Popoff

Published by

Krause Publications, a division of F+W Media, Inc.
700 East State Street • Iola, WI 54990-0001
715-445-2214 • 888-457-2873
www.krausebooks.com

To order books or other products call toll-free 1-800-258-0929.

ISSN: 1523-7257
ISBN-13: 978-1-4402-1131-7
ISBN-10: 1-4402-1131-0

Cover Design by Shawn Williams
Designed by Stacy Bloch
Edited by Dan Brownell

Printed in United States of America

CONTENTS

ACKNOWLEDGMENTS

First (and again), I'd like to thank all the record folks I've dealt with over the years, and especially those who specifically applied their expertise to this edition of the book. Instrumental in helping overhaul this edition has been my board of advisors, namely Akim Boldireff, Stephen Braitman, and Jack Cusenza. Their expertise was tantamount to me mounting the challenge to rock 'n' roll through these massive tomes of scholarly reference. Also Rick Broomfield of Mr. Retro (a.k.a. Ric Collectibles) here in Toronto has graciously helped with a supply of records to photograph and Dan Campbell's keen eye has helped tighten things even further.

Also, I also want to thank those people at Krause Publications, past and present, who helped make this seventh edition a reality, namely Paul Kennedy, Dan Brownell, Peter Lindblad, Stacy Bloch, Steve Duberstein, and Tammy Kuhnle.

Finally, last but not least, I'd like to thank my family, who allow me this record 'n' music obsession—I'm getting rid of some of it... chipping away... I promise!

Martin Popoff

THE GOLDMINE BOARD OF ADVISORS

Akim Boldireff

Akim Boldireff is widely considered Toronto, Canada's foremost record man. Full-time buyer, seller, appraiser, and Cheap Trick, Queen, and Sparks appreciator, Akim has collected and even sometimes resold many of the finest rock 'n' roll artifacts that have passed through Eastern Canada and the American Midwest. His biannual record shows in Toronto have, in recent years, eclipsed the London, Ontario, show as the best gatherings of vinyl obsessors in the nation, with more ambitious plans in the offing for the 2010 shows. Akim is widely reputed in the industry as an honest broker and fair remunerator when it comes to acquiring collections. He can be reached at sonictemple@sympatico.ca.

Stephen Braitman

Stephen M.H. Braitman started writing about music as a young teenager in Los Angeles and has since reviewed and interviewed many of his favorite recording artists. He has been publisher and editor of numerous magazines and newspapers based in the San Francisco Bay Area, including *Musician's News*, *City Arts Monthly*, *Key This Week*, *Rolling Your Own*, *Entertainment News*, and *SF Live*. Stephen was a contributing writer for *Alternative Press* for ten years, and wrote for many other publications, including the *Los Angeles Times*, *Marin Independent Journal*, *New Times*, *Antique Trader*, *Sunset*, *San Francisco Chronicle*, *New York Times*, *San Francisco Focus*, and *Electronic Musician*, among others. Stephen is a major collector of records and music paraphernalia, owning tens of thousands of LPs, CDs, 45s, photographs, magazines, and other memorabilia. His collection has been used as an archival resource for many organizations, including Rhino Records, Sundazed, Ace (U.K.), and MCA Records. He was a major contributor of posters and flyers for the publication of the popular book The Art of Rock (Abbeville Press). Photographs from his archive are featured in the noted series by Paul Williams about Bob Dylan's performing career. He has written a column on rare 45 rpm picture sleeves for *Goldmine* magazine. He also is a music analyst for Gracenote, Inc., the digital media company. And, he is a certified music appraiser. See www.musicappraisals.com for more information.

Jack Cusenza

Jack Cusenza is a longtime collector who initially focused on the vinyl he enjoyed and bought in the early '60s, with an emphasis on '50s and '60s rock, but he's expanded in the past 20 years to include a large portion of the '70s and some artists from the '80s. Eventually and in stages, Jack has added much jazz, C&W, pop, and soundtrack recordings to his vast collection, along with the odd bootleg, picture disc, and promotional item. He obtained most of his LPs and 45s weekly from an established network of contacts, vendors, and local sellers in Michigan and a few shops outside of Michigan. Recently, though, he has begun buying and selling online. Jack is an enthusiastic purchaser of all things record-related. He can be reached at myvinyltunes@aol.com

Martin Popoff

Martin Popoff has written 29 books on hard rock, heavy metal, and classic rock, his first for Krause Publications being the *Goldmine® Heavy Metal Record Price Guide*. His stewardship with the more general Goldmine guides began with the 7th edition of the *Goldmine® Price Guide To 45 RPM Records*. Martin also contributes to *Guitar World*, *Lollipop*, *Goldmine* magazine, *Record Collector*, bravewords.com, lollipop.com and hardradio.com, with many record label band bios and liner notes to his credit as well. Raised in Trail, British Columbia, Canada, Martin went on to complete an MBA, work for Xerox, then co-own a graphic design and print brokering firm before becoming a full-time rock critic in 1998. Gillan, Max Webster, Deep Purple, ZZ Top, and Black Sabbath are his favorite five bands of all time. His collection consists of approximately 12,000 LPs, 15,000 CDs, 3,000 45s, 1,400 backstage passes and 2,900 autographed items. Martin currently resides in Toronto and can be reached through martinp@inforamp.net or www.martinpopoff.com. His website includes detailed information on the 24 or so books of his that are currently in print.

INTRODUCTION

Welcome to the seventh edition of the *Goldmine® Standard Catalogue of American Records*.

We thank you for your support of the first six editions as we strive to create the world's most comprehensive guide to cataloguing and valuing your (American-issued) vinyl.

Record collecting continues to grow as a new generation of buyers discovers vinyl. In the two years since the publication of the sixth edition, we've seen countless articles about the resurgence in vinyl, both used and new, as well as bigger crowds attending record shows. Indeed, it is almost impossible to keep up with all the vinyl releases in a given year, whether new or reissues, but we try! So if this is the first time you've picked up this book, welcome and dig in!

What's New For 2010?

The changes from the 6th edition to the 7th edition fall into a few loose categories, namely photography, price changes, typos/corrections/added notes, and the inclusion and deletion of artists, based on, well, older artists who were wobbly as actually being considered collectible, becoming less so over time—I think we can all agree on that, at least as a huge generalization. Perhaps a few comments are in order. And yes, if much of the following commentary seems familiar, sure, many of these ideas were first established in the revamp of the recent *Goldmine® Price Guide to 45 RPM Records*, 7th Edition as well as the *Goldmine® Record Album Price Guide*, 6th Edition. Anyway, bear with me and this spot of repetition—the same concepts generally still apply, economic crash and partial recovery notwithstanding!

On the topic of photography, we've endeavored to provide a plethora of new shots, spanning many genres, eras, price points, and along the way, even basing our decision to use a certain shot on things like quality of the artwork or amusing kitsch value. There is also consideration given to things readers might not think about, like the desire to have artists representing each letter of the alphabet for an even spread throughout the book. You have no idea what goes on behind the scenes.

Also, if you haven't noticed already, this book contains both 45s and LPs. It's a bit of a quirk, but in the area of 45s, we continue the tradition of shooting picture sleeves only—they just make a better photograph, although all of us around here... sure, we love the academic value of all that obscure info on an actual label, and we are well aware that most of the most expensive 45s in the world are non-picture sleeve.

With respect to price changes, look closely, and you will see that many prices have changed, upward or downward, from the previous edition. We will deal with pricing in more detail later, but quickly, general effects on pricing continue to include eBay and the effect of a "more perfect market" given the existence of the Internet, than what was the case, say, pre-1996 (and more like 2000), the current tough economic times, the aging of some subsets of collectors and the ushering in of younger collector types, and finally artists becoming more in vogue or more out of vogue.

With respect to added notes, fixed bits etc., what we've tried to do is catch typos, reduce the amount of missing or disputed info (i.e. question marks), and add a few more helpful notes with respect to other artists associated with a listed artist—the proverbial "Also see."

The most material or far-reaching change to the book is deciding, given a static page count, which artists to include and which to delete to make room for what we are considering "more relevant" artists. First on the new inclusions. The mandate of these books is to strike some sort of balance between the serious collector and/or dealer, and the casual potential buyer of the book with the proverbial "I found these records in my parents' attic; I wonder if they are worth anything?" story.

Yet probably the biggest change from the previous edition, in fact, has more to do with the expansion of our date parameters. The rationale behind picking 1948 to 1991 was this: those years cover the natural life of the LP in America, and pretty much the 45 as well. Sure there was vinyl after that, but it was a whole different product. It wouldn't have taken much effort to bring it up to the current day, but consider this an intermediate step for the 1975 used last time, a date which always felt a bit arbitrary. Please note as well, there are in fact records from the years after 1991. The rule was that if an artist's first album fell within those dates, then his entire catalogue was included.

Now, back to which artists to include... we tend to lean toward the serious collector. We think that's healthy. We want it to be a good book. Fortunately, the only nods one needs to provide to satisfy the requirements of the casual buyer revolves around two things: name recognition and the concept of "commons" or cheap, not-all-that-collectible records.

Here's what we've decided on that front (and stay with me, because it's a little complicated). First off, we've removed quite a few easy listening, classical, verging on classical and "bad pop" (contentious idea, I know), artists from the '50s and '60s who are also not collectible and who are also quite forgotten, i.e. have low name recognition. In this respect, part of the mandate was roughly like this: let's not remove Ray Conniff and Henry Mancini and Guy Lombardo, but let's remove their no-name equivalents. Our entire board of directors was in agreement on this, and even going so far as to say that all uncollectible easy listening-type material from decades ago, could go. So that, roughly, constitutes the main removals, the unanimous decision, or the general rule being that if it's easy listening that few have heard of or remember and no one collects, it could come out. We tried to retain country and jazz listings (and really, somewhat unsatisfyingly, no changes have been made with respect to intensifying or diminishing children's records, comedy, spoken word or oddball) and also any "soft rock" that simply escaped the scalpel because it was of a more modern era.

Now, in terms of additions, we've tried to strengthen a few areas. First, we've tried to relocate and re-evaluate oldies that somehow got dropped along the years that have indeed "stood the test of time," either critically or as collectible, from the fields of rock 'n' roll, jazz, pop, and even country. But more extensively, we've tried to modernize in all areas, reflecting the natural age shift that happens in the collectibles market, namely older collectors eventually losing interest, divesting and dying, taking with them certain artists that very few concern themselves with any more (see above re: deletion criteria, and for an even more graphic example of this phenomenon—parallel with the collectability of film stars from the '20s and '30s and '40s).

But our modernization has inclined us toward including artists who are quite uncollectible, i.e. with a lot of "commons," and maybe no collectible records at all. Why? Well, back to the attic. Nowadays, that guy is more likely to find Human League and Crowded House and Cinderella records up there versus Perry Como. So these types of artists are retained from the previous edition or are coming back or are coming in for the first time. And along with modernization, we've automatically bolstered listings for heavy metal, progressive rock, new wave and post-punk.

Essentially, a broad mandate was exercised toward putting dollar value aside a bit, and saying, if it's an act from those last years of vinyl before the CD took over, it should go in, especially if they had a modicum of fame or success at some point, i.e. they at least have a few threads in the cultural fabric of the music world. There's that nod to name recognition again. Billy Idol was a clear add, but I wavered and ultimately declined to list Icehouse or Icicle Works.

There you go. In general, call it a subtle modernization, and without the snobbery of being too concerned about covering too many common or cheap records. Another note I might add, is that we found ourselves in the fortunate position of having the artists we wanted to delete being much longer listings/entries than those we wanted to add. This means that the number of artists added is double or triple the number that we have removed.

LP Market Trends For 2010

In general, all specific peaks and valleys considered, the record market as a whole is flat. Many parts of the market have stabilized. We've discussed most of these areas in previous editions, but essentially little has changed—these still see a lot of activity:

– **Near-mint, mint, and sealed LPs.** One thing that the growth of eBay has shown is that albums in truly near-mint condition, especially original editions from the 1950s through the 1970s, are extremely hard to find.

Condition has always meant a lot when it came to records. Today, it means more than ever. Perhaps a new generation of record buyers has been spoiled by the quiet, efficient sound coming from a compact disc or a digital file and won't tolerate the pops and ticks that sometimes are audible on even the best-pressed records. You'll find that some of the prices in this year's book, though still reflecting an average of many sources, may be low on certain items. Along those lines, some of the prices I've seen for sealed vintage LPs border on the obscene.

There are sound reasons to be wary of sealed albums, especially older ones. But that hasn't stopped prices from going sky-high on some of them: A couple years back, a sealed original mono copy of Pet Sounds by the Beach Boys traded for over $1,500 and a sealed stereo copy of The Beatles (The White Album) has sold for over $1,400. The only thing extraordinary about them is that they were, presumably, never opened. Like I say though, be wary. A sealed LP can be a re-seal, but even without that issue, even if a record is sealed, the cover could have any manner of damage from mashed corners to unreported delete marks, bends, and warps. Perhaps more necessary than with any other type of purchase, this is the type of transaction you want to conduct in person at a record show, given that average photography misses some of these things.

– **"Audiophile" LPs.** Albums that appeal to the audience that appreciates good sound quality are hotter than ever.

This does not only apply to the records of the 1980s and 1990s that were specially licensed and marketed to appeal to this small subset of collectors. True, albums on the DCC Compact Classics label from the 1990s are almost uniformly collectible, with near-mint copies of many titles trading for three figures routinely. And many albums on the Mobile Fidelity, Nautilus, and Direct Disc labels are in that range. Condition is even more important when it comes to these records, including consideration around stickers used to seal some of them, the plastic sleeves they came in, and, of course, the condition of the covers.

Today, many audiophiles are paying closer attention to more mainstream albums. Indeed, the work of certain cutting engineers—the people who "translate" the sound of a master tape to the record—are becoming sought-after by this group. Often the only way these desirable pressings can be identified is by checking the trail-off wax of the albums. So far, this trend hasn't crossed over to the vast majority of record collectors, who still value a general first pressing over a specific one. But it's something we are watching closely.

– **Albums from the 1990s and early 2000s.** We noted in the 6th Edition that some albums from the "dark ages" of vinyl were becoming very collectible and very expensive. Not only has this not changed, but it's affected even more albums—some of which were still common in retail stores as recently as two years ago. We have seen no letup in demand for vinyl LPs released from about 1991 to the present day. Indeed, many of the values listed for these records—some of which almost never show up for sale anywhere—are conservative, even for those with three-figure values attached. The "hysterical" or "hype" element around some of these releases stems, unsurprisingly, from the fact that many of the new vinyl issues from the CD and mp3 age are pressed in very limited quantities. Huge acts such as Metallica, already have a complicated discography for their records re-visited since the big switchover to CDs in 1990.

– **Hot Genres.** As one generation of record collectors passes the torch to the next, unsurprisingly, those new collectors collect what they connect with. Ergo, sort of pre-1965 artists continue to fall off the radar, even as hot spots continue to build to their record of established high prices, in some cases, continuing to march upward. Still, genres with more activity tend to begin with garage and psych, with progressive rock, punk and metal continuing to prove strong.

– **Commons.** Quite simply, with the reduction of brick-and-mortar stores out there, along with the fact that most folks who were inclined to do a record purge and switch to CD or mp3 have now done so years ago, even commons in good condition are selling for solid prices, to generalize, in the $6 to $15 range. Artists who have proven their worth, stood the test of time… their records are constantly finding homes, and stores price them accordingly, knowing they will move. This is more of an LP story than one for 45, however.

– **Bootlegs.** In closing, board member Stephen Braitman chimes in on what he considers hot areas in LP collecting this year, namely bootlegs, late '60s/early '70s psych and folk Capitol releases, original vinyl releases from the late '80s and '90s that were missed the first time around (and are much cheaper than the "180 gram audiophile reissues"), and finally punk releases pre-1985.

45 RPM Market Trends

Some of this has been touched upon in the previous section, but a few general comments are in order, much of this being information we've retained to reiterate for you from the previous edition of this book (if it reads a little familiar, that's why—also the case with some other "standard" sections throughout these front bits!).

In general, 45s remain the most avidly collected musical format in the world. And the condition of those discs is more important than ever.

We've taken the step of using only the Near Mint price as a space-saving device. But this change also reflects a continuing trend in the marketplace. More and more collectors are seeking copies of 45s that are as close to perfect as possible, and they are willing to pay for them. But they are less willing to pay the Near Mint price, or anything close to it, for records with any discernible flaws whatsoever. Even the VG+ price is more than they are willing to pay for a nice, but not quite perfect, record.

Only a small fraction of the 45s that survive today are in Near Mint condition. That fraction is somewhat larger with records from the 1980s and later; it is smaller with records from the 1970s; and it's still smaller with records from the 1950s and 1960s. This is why the values for the records in this book, even for common artists, may seem high. Depending on the record, perhaps two to five percent of all copies are in Near Mint condition. In some cases, Near Mint examples simply are not known to exist!

I'm tempted to say that, if somehow one were able to find every copy of a 45 that still exists, the results would follow a bell curve, with very few Near Mint copies, very few truly trashed copies (these, by definition, have been trashed, i.e. gone to landfill), and most copies coming in around VG. But from experience, it seems that we're on a downward slope, with most copies trashed; fewer copies in VG; still fewer in VG+; and extremely few in the NM category. At the very best, the distribution might be a modified bell curve, with more space under the "poor" section than under "Near Mint."

In other words: For many collectors, more so than ever before, if it's not perfect, it's not for me—at any price.

Going beyond condition, here are some of the areas of 45 rpm collecting that are hot since the last edition:

– **Soul music of all kinds, especially from the 1960s and 1970s, especially the "Northern Soul" category.** We mentioned in the last edition a record label from Washington, D.C. called Shrine. It's called "the world's most collectible record label" by soul aficionados, as the 45s released by the label are almost uniformly rare, yet almost uniformly sought-after. By now, it may be the most collectible 45 rpm label, period.

– **Picture sleeves, especially from the 1950s and 1960s.** This includes the often promo-only inserts that were included inside otherwise ordinary company sleeves. This is an area where documentation is just starting. Paper goods is a hot market, and this kind of completism crosses over into the paper goods area.

– **"Holy Grails," or the rarest records by collectible artists.** The most obvious example is Elvis Presley 45s on Sun, which remain hot as the more common parts of his catalog cool off. It's hard to over-emphasize this. Dealers say, "People always want the best records." Or "good records." Weird statement, but it's true. The high marks just keep getting higher, but the good, strong mid-to-high stuff can languish or see declines. Strange.

– **Punk.** In more of a holding pattern, but holding up quite well. In fact, I might add that post-punk has taken over much of the buzz.

– **Surf and garage music of the 1960s.** There is still plenty of demand for these.

– **The Beatles.** The more unusual a record is, the better, but anything in near-mint condition will sell. We've even seen prices that far exceed those in this book for the rarest items.

And some areas that are trending in the opposite direction:

– **Doo-Wop**. Very few 45s in this category have increased in value recently. There are still some die-hard collectors of the genre, but some are dying, and fewer new aficionados are coming in to replace them.

– **Elvis Presley.** Unless it's already rare, it's not going up in value.

– **UK limited edition 45 pressings.** Most UK pressings are between 500 and 1,000 and are sold out in the pre-order stage. An example of this is the latest Muse 7", which had a wholesale of $4.50 and the demand is so huge that the item is commanding $30 in the marketplace.

– **Fan club 7" pressings by Pearl Jam, REM, etc.** These are very collectible and sought after. Many bands are providing these goodies via their fan club sites to thank their fans.

– **Exclusive 7" releases to promote Record Store Day** in the spring in North America yielded some great releases by Elvis Costello, Oasis, and Morrisey.

– **New Wave of British Heavy Metal.** Although values have increased in many corners of the metal realm, prices for this very specific area seems to have peaked in the mid to late '90s.

– **Finally, funk and reggae continue to be hot!**

In closing, one trend I wish would expand, and it was mentioned in the last edition as well, is that more of today's music would appear on 7-inch singles. It may not be a huge market, but it is a market, and it is not being served right now. Sure, there's a bit of life there in terms of supply, and undoubtedly, because there is really not much being issued, these records will trend upwards for many years to come.

The eBay Effect

In general, eBay has not been kind to "old-line" record collecting. Items once believed to be rare are found to be more common than expected, thus their values have stayed the same or, in some cases, even declined since earlier editions of this book.

At the same time, eBay has had a positive effect on the values in some areas, especially modern jazz and vinyl albums of the 1991 to the present. Demand in these areas is much greater than once believed, and, as discussed, supply is necessarily much more limited since the day when, as the saying goes, "there were 100 artists selling a million records and now there are a million artists selling a hundred records" (other issues are at hand in that statement, but it partly applies to our discussion here as well).

You could theoretically use eBay as one's sole determinant of market value, and indeed, some people do. But you'd miss a large part of the market that still happens elsewhere. It would be like determining the price of everything by going to only one place. We look at as many sources as possible, thus the Goldmine® Standard Catalog of American Records remains vital to your enjoyment of collecting vinyl albums, not to mention the fact that it provides a handy overview of an artist's output, including labels, catalogue numbers, and other vital information. As a general rule of thumb in the use of this book: the higher the price you see quoted for a specific LP or 45, the more prudent it would be to check other sources for corroboration or consensus.

HOW TO USE THIS BOOK

The prices in this book are taken from many sources, both online and off, and from the advice of many correspondents, including our board of directors. It is only a guide; it is not holy writ. When using the prices in this book, to use another famous disclaimer, "Your mileage may vary." And at a minimum, the numbers we provide should scream out to you whether an artist is collectible or not, as well as a relative idea of which items by that artist might warrant the time and effort of further research. In other words, the price you see should at least provide a handy dandy guideline, but it can also serve as a "red flag" that might prompt you—based on the dollars involved—to make sure a second and third opinion is secured.

That said, we at least can tell you what is in each listing and what it means. We have decided to emphasize some areas that seem to confuse the most readers, so those who do understand how to use the listings based on a casual glance of these listings, please bear with us.

Records in this book, (except for the odds and sods-type sections after the letter Z), are listed alphabetically by artist. The artist's name is in BOLD CAPITAL LETTERS. They are mostly alphabetized the way our computer did (last name first, etc.), so blame anything that seems out of order on that.

In some cases, we know that the artist name was used by several different performers. When we don't know for sure which are which, we have left them together. When we do know with some certainty, we have separated them.

In most but not all cases, the most collectible is listed first, usually with the number (1) in parentheses following it. The exceptions are those artists whose fame or number of records overshadows any other performer with the same name, or those who rarely used "The" in front of their name, such as Eagles, Outlaws, and Pretenders. The rest of the performers with the same name will be arranged alphabetically by record label and will be followed by the appropriate parenthetical number – (2), (3), (4), and so on. Finally, those for which we don't know where they go are listed with a (U) for Unknown after the name.

Underneath some artists are cross-references or other information we feel is helpful. Cross-references to other artists are in CAPITAL LETTERS.

Then we have grouped the record listings by label, with the labels listed alphabetically. Under each record label are the individual listings in numerical, not necessarily chronological, order.

Each line starts with a check box, which you can use to keep track of what you have. Then comes the record number. Then comes, in some cases, a couple letters enclosed in [brackets]. These designate something special about the record as follows:

[B]: the album is listed as stereo, but some of the tracks are in mono (the "B" means "both" stereo and mono);

[DJ]: some sort of promotional copy, usually for radio stations, and not meant for public sale;

[EP]: a 12-inch extended play album, usually with only four to six tracks. It is normally no more than half the length of a regular album. Rarely used to describe 12-inch records before the 1980s; before that, it refers to similar 7-inch records;

[M]: mono record (all 12-inch records released in either mono only or in both mono and stereo before 1968);

[P]: the album is listed as stereo, but only part of it is "true" two-channel stereo;

[PD]: picture disc (graphics actually appear as part of the record and not merely on the label area; these also are usually identified as such below the listing);

[Q]: quadraphonic record (mostly from the years 1972-1976, these were usually remixed, sometimes radically, to play on systems with four separate speakers);

[R]: the album is listed as stereo, but actually is all, or almost all, rechanneled or "fake" stereo (called "Duophonic" by Capitol or "Enhanced for Stereo" or "Simulated Stereo" by Decca); these almost always are less sought-after than the same material in "true mono";

[S]: stereo record (again, for those discs pressed in both mono and stereo). If we're not sure of an album's "true" stereo content, or if we know an album is all, or almost all, true stereo, we use "S";

[10]: a 10-inch album, most of which are from the early years of LPs, 1948-1954, and are quite difficult to find in top condition;

[(x)]: where x is a number: the number of records in a set.

[PS]: picture sleeve, as in 45 talk for when a record has a picture sleeve or note. In past editions, the attendant price was considered to be for the sleeve alone. We thought long and hard about this. Given that there is practically no market of sellers and buyers for such an animal, we now consider the price listed to cover both the record and sleeve, namely the item as intended. Think about it, do some shopping… it's a policy that stands up.

You'll next find the title of the record listed as best as we can determine. Sometimes, discerning the actual title of a record isn't as straightforward as you might think. For LPs, titles can be listed differently on the front cover, back cover, label, and spine (as an example, there a good four spellings for rock 'n' roll, and the confusion is so bad, these spellings may differ from front to spine!).

After that information is the year of release of the record, based on record label information or chart data. Sometimes, this differs from a year listed on a record itself. When in doubt, believe in the years WE list and NOT those on the record, unless you have an additional source OTHER THAN a year on the record label or jacket that proves us incorrect.

Finally, each line ends with an approximate value in Near Mint condition. Something to think about before you deem numbers we've provided as being too high—Near Mint is a hard grade to achieve. Additionally, old records don't get "mintier" as time goes on; they all, in fact, get less mintier—just like all record collectors!

Some records have an additional line of type underneath the listing, in italics. That denotes something about the item listed above it, such as who also is on the record, or color of label, or color of vinyl.

In the back section, after the letter Z, records are sorted differently. We have broken these sections into "Original Cast Recordings," "Soundtracks," "Television Records," and "Various Artists Collections."

Within each of these categories, these are arranged alphabetically by the title of the release, ignoring "A," "An," and "The." Albums that begin with a number are sorted as if the number was spelled out.

Underneath each title are the applicable releases, arranged alphabetically and numerically by label. (Thus the original version is not necessarily listed first!) Those lines start with a check box, then are followed by the label and number listed together. Any applicable abbreviations—the same as used in the A-Z section—follow; then the year of release; then the pricing information. Finally, some items have more information below the listing in italics.

SELLING RECORDS

By far the most often asked question over the years has been some variation of the following:

How do I sell my records and get the most for them?

First, here's the Reader's Digest version of the answer to the question.

You will get more for your records if you can sell them directly to someone who wants what you have (a collector), rather than selling to someone who is going to turn around and re-sell them (a dealer).

A corollary to the first line of advice above: The prices in this book are RETAIL prices—what collectors might pay for these from a seller. They are NOT a dealer's buying prices!

If you want to sell all your records at once to the same person, whether that person is a dealer or collector, expect to get much less per item for them, no matter what condition or genre they are.

The more time you spend on the project, the more you'll likely get for each record.

Now, some more details. First, buy this book and use it. You are better off working from a position of knowing what you have rather than guessing. As discussed, use the prices not as definitive answers, but red flags for things that should be the subject of more research, opinion, or consensus.

So yes, look through it and see if you have anything that is more valuable than the average. If not, or if your records and covers are "well loved" (say, VG condition or worse), it probably isn't worth your time to work hard to sell them. Be kind to a friend: Give them to someone who collects records. Or sell them at your next garage/rummage sale for 10 cents or a quarter each. Or donate them to Goodwill, the Salvation Army, the St. Vincent de Paul Society, or some other charity with a thrift shop, and get a tax receipt. But don't throw them away! We never recommend that unless your records are in truly poor condition. But if you must… recycle responsibly!

Maybe your stash has some records of above-average value, or maybe you actually took good care of your records and they are still in VG+ condition or better. You can do either of two things:

— sell them to a dealer;

— sell them yourself, directly to collectors.

What to expect when selling to a dealer. As we already mentioned, the prices in this book are NOT dealer's prices; they are collector's prices. Also, please note that the prices in this book are a guide and not sent down from on high. You are in for a rude awakening if you expect to get these prices from a dealer.

For something genuinely rare, you might get 40 to 60 percent of the "book value." For many of these, all a dealer has to do is pick up the phone and call the right customer, and the record is sold. For less expensive records, though, don't expect to get more than 10 to 25 percent of the "book value." The less valuable a record is, the lower the percentage of the retail price a dealer will give you for it. Sellers, even those who only sell online, have overhead costs they have to recover, such as inventory, rent, utilities, postage and packing fees, employees, insurance, taxes, listing fees, bandwidth, and many more things that a dealer has to recoup in order to stay in business. Some dealers won't even try to get records from people who say they consulted a price guide, because these sellers sometimes get delusions about what they deserve for their records. If this happens to you, don't say we didn't warn you.

Sometimes, the hardest part of selling to a dealer is finding one. Most large cities, and many smaller ones, have used record stores, although numbers are greatly down from even five years ago. The best way to find them in your area is to look in your local Yellow Pages. Depending on who published the phone book, used record stores are found either under the heading "Records, Tapes and Compact Discs – Retail" or "Compact Discs, Tapes and Records – Retail."

Just because you've found that store (or stores) doesn't mean they will buy your records. From a dealer's standpoint, common records are almost literally a dime a dozen. You might get only a token amount for a pile of records if all of them are fairly common, regardless what this price guide says. But if the alternative is between getting something for them or getting nothing for them, you'll probably be happy with the result. And you no longer have the records in your way.

What to expect when selling to a collector. In the era of online auctions, this is a more appealing alternative than it used to be. Regardless what method you use, it will take longer and require more patience than selling to a dealer. Plus, if you will be selling through the mail, you'll have some additional costs, most notably for good packaging and postage. But it can be worth the effort.

It takes work to sell your records directly to someone who wants them for a collection. We do not have lists of record collectors that you can contact. Finding collectors is up to you.

Before the Internet, you basically had two options for doing it yourself to reach the collector's market: Setting up at record shows/fairs, or advertising in record collecting magazines. And both still have their place.

For a seller, the record show is a great place to meet other collectors and dealers, get ideas and advice, and see some records you might not see anywhere else. Also, some high-value deals still take place at shows. If you like the direct interaction and the wheeling and dealing—and can resist the temptation to add to your own inventory or collection with the proceeds—then selling at a record show may be for you.

Record collecting magazines have shrunk in recent years, but they remain a viable outlet for certain kinds of collectibles. Indeed, only one significant record collecting magazine remains in the United States, and that is *Goldmine*. It is best for selling middle- to higher-priced items that allow you to make up for the cost of the ad and still make money. And, as most serious collectors read *Goldmine* at least occasionally, an ad letting them know of your existence can pay dividends. It serves a smaller, but more targeted, audience than an online auction.

Goldmine is published by F+W Media; if you've never seen it, you can find it at many major bookstores and independent record shops, or a sample copy can be obtained by calling 800-258-0929. More details are available at goldminemag.com.

For most people with an accumulation of records who want to "eliminate the middleman," online has been the way to go since the late 1990s. And the most popular site for this action is eBay (www.ebay.com).

Online selling seems to draw two widely different audiences. One is much the same as a stand-alone record store, except on a global scale rather than a regional one. Browsers who know next to nothing about record collecting and the relative scarcity of the listed pieces are common. These are people who can sometimes be fooled into paying too much for a common record if they get caught up in "auction fever," where the thrill of the hunt can override their rational knowledge that the item can be had cheaper somewhere else or with a bit more patience at eBay.

The other audience drawn to online sales is the hyper-specialist, and this is often where items can justifiably go for much more than in a retail store. Thanks to search engines, a fan of, say, Elvis Costello can type in the words "Elvis Costello" and find nothing but the Elvis Costello-related material. People who specialize in one artist will usually pay more—sometimes a lot more—than someone who collects a broader range of artists. Because they are specialists, though, they also know which items are common, so they don't get taken on the easy stuff.

As a seller, you are reaching a larger audience than you would in a record collecting magazine, but a much less targeted one. The Internet seems to be a good place to sell lower-priced items that might take up valuable space in an expensive print ad. But many more valuable items fetch less online than they do through more traditional means.

To do the best at selling online:

– Use the *Goldmine® Grading Guide* provided in this book. Don't say that your records are in "good condition," because "good" is a low grade… unless, of course, they really are in only "good" condition.

– Grade your records conservatively, and mention any flaws with them in your description.

– Always mention the record label and number of any record you sell. I am amazed at how many auctions lack this basic, and vital, information.

– Take a picture of, or scan, everything you sell, and post those images with your auctions. If possible, use multiple images. Photos can tell the potential buyer more than your words will.

– That said, don't alter your images in any way or steal someone else's better images! Your buyers probably won't deal with you again when they find out that your "pristine" record or sleeve has serious flaws.

– Answer all of your customers' questions, no matter how arcane or trivial they may seem. It could be the difference between a sale and no sale.

– Make your minimum bid the lowest amount you'll be willing to take for the item. Many items sell for only the minimum.

– However, if you really want to sell, don't set that minimum too high. It is better to start an auction low and watch the action send an item to new heights than to put a high minimum on an item. If you feel queasy, use a hidden reserve price, below which you won't sell the item.

– Charge a reasonable amount for shipping. It is expected that buyers will pay for shipping. But don't try to make a profit at it, either. If you charge more than what the Postal Service or your private shipper of choice charges to send an item, explain why.

– Once you sell the items, pack them well. Some customers will have specific requests on how they want an item sent. Listen to them!

Remember, too, that with tens of thousands of records for sale at any given time, approximately half of all records on eBay receive no bids at all. In addition to not following the advice for sellers listed above, it's possible that no one wanted to buy your record during the time your record was posted. Maybe at another time, you'll get bidders.

GRADING YOUR RECORDS

Nothing is more important in determining the value of your records than their condition! Yes, their relative rarity and demand is important, but a collector or dealer will pay much more for a record in Near Mint condition than one in Very Good Minus condition.

However, I've found that most people with collections or accumulations have an inflated sense of the condition of their discs. I don't know how many times I've heard people who think they know what they are talking about tell me, "My records are all Mint!" Sure, and I've got some oceanfront property in Arizona to sell you.

The truth is that most records, especially from before the 1970s, are not in anything close to Mint or Near Mint condition. That is why a collector will pay a premium for such a disc if he or she has to have it.

This book lists values for records in Near Mint condition. Records in lesser condition are worth a fraction of the Near Mint prices.

For most collectors, Very Good is the lowest grade for which they will pay more than bargain-bin prices. And some won't even do that. Lower-grade records are only good as placeholders, until a better copy comes along, or as examples of truly rare records that are difficult to find in any condition.

Most of the time, LPs are sold with two grades, one for the record and one for the cover. In this book, we list only one grade, however, because with some exceptions, albums without covers are worthless, and covers without the accompanying record are worthless. If an album is graded VG for the cover and VG+ for the record, add the two values together and divide by 2 to get a rough estimate of the value of a "mixed grade" LP.

Most records are graded visually. This is because most record dealers have lots of records—hundreds of thousands in some cases—and they don't have the time to play their entire stock. That said, some defects are easy to see, such as scratches and warps. Others are subtle, such as groove wear from using a cheap or poorly aligned tone arm. It has been our experience that older LPs (1950s to about 1971) tend to play better than they look, and newer LPs (at least until 1989) tend to play worse than they look.

When grading your records, do so under a strong light. Look at everything carefully, and then assign a grade based on your overall observations.

Some records will be worthy of a higher grade, except for defects such as writing, tape, or minor seam splits. Always mention these when selling a record! For some collectors, they will be irrelevant, but for others, they will be a deal-breaker. For all, they are important to know. Also note that sophisticated collectors are sometimes looking for a better sleeve to "marry" to the decent condition record they have currently housed in a trashed sleeve, and vice versa.

Also, some LPs were made for promotional purposes only. Again, always mention if a record is a promo copy when advertising it for sale! Certain promo designations tend to lower the value of a record (sawcuts, punches, cut corners and other cut-out marks), while others tend to raise the value (white labels). The gold stamp? Still debatable or often inconsequential.

One of the obstacles to the further growth of record collecting is poor grading and a lack of consensus as to what constitutes a "Very Good Plus" or "Near Mint" record or cover. Over the years, the *Goldmine® Grading Guide* has tried to standardize this. It is now the most widely used guide for the buying and selling of vinyl albums; many eBay auctions and stand-alone websites swear by it. But we recognize that there are many variables to grading a record. As a seller, you are better off grading conservatively and surprising the buyer with a better record than was expected, than by grading based on wishful thinking and losing a customer.

That said, here are the standard grades for record albums, from best to worst.

THE GOLDMINE GRADING GUIDE

Mint (M)

These are absolutely perfect in every way. Often rumored but rarely seen, Mint should never be used as a grade unless more than one person agrees that the record or sleeve truly is in this condition. There is no set percentage of the Near Mint value these can bring; it is best negotiated between buyer and seller.

Near Mint (NM or M-)

A good description of a NM record is "it looks like it just came from a retail store and it was opened for the first time." In other words, it's nearly perfect. Many dealers won't use a grade higher than this, implying (perhaps correctly) that no record or sleeve is ever truly perfect.

NM records are shiny, with no visible defects. Writing, stickers or other markings cannot appear on the label, nor can any "spindle marks" from someone trying to blindly put the record on the turntable. Major factory defects also must not be present; a record and label obviously pressed off center is not Near Mint. If played, it will do so with no surface noise. (NM records don't have to be "never played"; a record used on an excellent turntable can remain NM after many plays if the disc is properly cared for.)

NM covers have no creases, ring wear, or seam splits of any kind.

These are high standards, and they are not on a sliding scale. A record or sleeve from the 1950s must meet the same standards as one from the 1990s or 2000s to be Near Mint! It's estimated that no more than 2 to 4 percent of all records remaining from the 1950s and 1960s are truly Near Mint. This is why they fetch such high prices, even for more common items. Do not assume your records are Near Mint. They must meet these standards to qualify!

In the 45 world, NM picture sleeves also, as above, "have no creases, ring wear or seam splits of any kind." It should look as if it never housed a record. This is a great reason to remove your 45s from their picture sleeves and keep them separate. Just keeping the 45 inside the sleeve will cause damage than can reduce the grade of the sleeve.

Very Good Plus (VG+) or Excellent (E)

A good description of a VG+ record is "except for a couple minor things, this would be Near Mint." Most collectors, especially those who want to play their records, will be happy with a VG+ record, especially if it is toward the high end of the grade (sometimes called VG++ or E+).

VG+ records may show some slight signs of wear, including light scuffs or very light scratches that do not affect the listening experience. Slight warps that do not affect the sound are OK. Minor signs of handling are OK, too, such as telltale marks around the center hole, but repeated playing has not misshapen the hole. There may be some very light ring wear or discoloration, but it should be barely noticeable.

VG+ covers should have only minor wear. A VG+ cover might have some very minor seam wear or a split (less than one inch long) at the bottom, the most vulnerable location. Also, a VG+ cover may have some defacing, such as a cut-out marking. Covers with cut-out markings can never be considered Near Mint.

Very Good (VG)

Many of the imperfections found on a VG+ record are more obvious on a VG record. That said, VG records — which usually sell for no more than 25 percent of a NM record—are among the biggest bargains in record collecting, because most of the "big money" goes for more perfect copies. For many listeners, a VG record or sleeve will be worth the money.

VG records have more obvious flaws than their counterparts in better shape. They lack most of the original gloss found on factory-fresh records. Groove wear is evident on sight, as are light scratches deep enough to feel with a fingernail. When played, a VG record has surface noise, and some scratches may be audible, especially in soft passages and during a song's intro and ending. But the noise will not overpower the music otherwise. Minor writing, tape, or a sticker can detract from the label. Many collectors who have jukeboxes will use VG records in them and not think twice. They remain a fine listening experience, just not the same as if it were in better shape.

VG covers will have many signs of human handling. Ring wear in the middle or along the edges of the cover where the edge of a record would reside, is obvious, though not overwhelming. Some more creases might be visible. Seam splitting will be more obvious; it may appear on all three sides, though it won't be obvious upon looking. Someone might have written on it or stamped a price tag on it, too.

Lower Grades

Good (G), Good Plus (G+) or Very Good Minus (VG–) records go for 10 to 15 percent of the Near Mint value, if you are lucky.

Good does not mean bad! The record still plays through without skipping, so it can serve as filler until something better comes along. But it has significant surface noise and groove wear, and the label is worn, with significant ring wear, heavy writing, or obvious damage caused by someone trying to remove tape or stickers and failing miserably. A Good to VG– cover has ring wear to the point of distraction, has seam splits obvious on sight and may have even heavier writing, such as, for example, huge radio station letters written across the front to deter theft.

If the item is common, it's probably better to pass it up. But if you've been seeking it for a long time, get it cheap and look to upgrade.

Poor (P) and Fair (F) records go for 0 to 5 percent of the Near Mint value, if they go at all. More likely, they end up going in the trash. Records are cracked, impossibly warped, or skip and/or repeat when an attempt is made to play them. Covers are so heavily damaged that you almost want to cry. Only the most outrageously rare items ever sell for more than a few cents in this condition—again, if they sell at all.

Sealed Albums

Still-sealed albums can—and do—bring even higher prices than listed in the book.

However, one must be careful when paying a premium for sealed LPs of any kind for several reasons:

1. They may have been re-sealed;
2. The records might not be in Near Mint condition;
3. The record inside might not be the original pressing or the most desirable pressing;
4. Most bizarre of all, the wrong record might be inside. I've had this happen to me; I opened a sealed album by one MCA artist only to find a record by a different MCA artist inside! Fortunately, I didn't pay a lot for that sealed LP. I would have been quite upset if I had.

Sealed Singles

Very few 45s were ever sold "sealed" at retail the way an LP usually is. Two exceptions are the Pink Floyd single "When the Tigers Broke Free" and the Grateful Dead's grey vinyl edition of "Touch of Grey." If still sealed, these can bring even higher prices than listed in the book, assuming none of the signs of abuse that detract from the condition of the picture sleeve. Yes, sealed records can be in a lower grade than Near Mint!

Some 7-inch EPs definitely were sold sealed, especially in the 1960s. I've sometimes come across copies that were open but still had shrink wrap on them.

One must be careful when paying a premium for sealed 45s of any kind for several reasons:

1. They probably were re-sealed, as with very rare exceptions, 45s were never sold sealed at retail. (In the 1970s, there were distributors who stuck "oldies" in plastic bags or on cardboard backing, then sealed them; this was done to distinguish them from new releases, and few collectors find them exciting as sealed objects.)
2. As with LPs, the record inside might not be in Near Mint condition.
3. Also as with LPs, the record inside might not be the original pressing or the most desirable pressing.

RECORDS NOT LISTED IN THIS BOOK

Obviously—or at least I hope it's obvious to you—no book of even 1,300+ pages could possibly list every record ever made.

From the first time we compiled this book, we've had to make decisions about what we could include and what we couldn't, based upon the space available. The two biggest areas where we chose to limit our listings the most fit into the categories of imports and promotional copies.

Imports

The *Goldmine® Standard Catalog of American Records* lists only those vinyl LPs and 45s manufactured in the United States or, in a few instances, manufactured in other countries, but specifically for release in the United States. Any record that fits the following criteria is an import, and you won't find it in the book:

– LPs on the Parlophone label by any artist, at least before 2000. Parlophone, best known as the Beatles' British label, was not used as a label in the United States until very recently.

– LPs that have the letters "BIEM," "GEMA" or "MAPL" on them.

– LPs that say anywhere on the label or cover, "Made in Canada," "Made in the UK," "Made in Germany," etc.

We have chosen not to list records from Great Britain, Canada, Japan, or any other nation for logistical reasons: Where do you start, and where do you stop?

Unfortunately, we realize that there is a lack of reliable information on the value of non-U.S. records, especially published in the United States. Please don't contact us seeking information on non-U.S. records; we cannot help.

Also unfortunately, there are few general rules about the value of an import as compared to an American edition. Some import albums, especially well-made Japanese imports that still have their "obi strip," can go for much more than the U.S. counterpart. Others seem to attract little interest in the States.

One rule that is just as true of imports as it is with U.S. records: Those discs that are originals in the best condition will sell for more than reissues and those in less than top-notch shape.

Promotional Copies

Basically, a promotional record is any copy of a record not meant for retail sale. Different labels identify these in different ways: The most common method on LPs is to use a white label instead of the regular-color label and/or to add words such as the following:

"Demonstration—Not for Sale"
"Audition Record"
"For Radio-TV Use Only"
"Promotional Copy"

Some labels, of course, used colors other than white; still others used the same labels as their stock copies, but added a promotional disclaimer to the label.

Most promotional albums have the same catalog number as the regular release, except for those differences.

Sometimes, regular stock copies have "Demonstration—Not for Sale" or "Promo" rubber stamped on the cover; these are known as "designate promos" and are not of the same cachet as true promotional records. Treat these as stock copies that have been defaced. Exceptions are noted in the listings.

All of this is mentioned as a means of identification. As a rule, we do not list promotional records separately in this book, nor are we interested in doing so. There are exceptions, which we will list below. But we feel that the precious space in this book is better used for unique commercially available records rather than for thousands upon thousands of promotional copies.

Most promotional LPs sell for approximately the same as a stock copy of the same catalog number. That has been our experience. However, there are certain exceptions. Those are the kinds of promos that you'll find documented in this book, and which we plan to continue to document. These include:

— Colored vinyl promos.

— Promos in special numbering series, such as Columbia albums with an "AS" or "CAS" prefix; Warner Bros, albums with a "PRO" or "PRO-A-" prefix; Capitol albums with a "PRO" or "SPRO" prefix; Mercury albums with an "MK" prefix; and other similar series on other labels.

— Promos that are somehow different than the released versions, either because of changes in the cover or changes in the music between the promo LP and the regular stock LP.

— Promos pressed on special high-quality vinyl; these were popular in the 1980s and can bring a premium above stock copies of the same titles.

Other Records Not Listed

Unfortunately, it's impossible to assume that because a record isn't listed in a price guide that it has no value. There remain a lot of undocumented records out there that are collectible for different reasons, or would be collectible if they were more widely known. We are always interested in learning about records that ought to be listed because they have significant value, and not simply because they are missing from the book.

Some areas of records that are under-represented in this book deserve special mention.

— **Children's records.** Most records that were marketed to children have some collectibility, especially if they have a legitimate tie-in to either a popular television show or to the Walt Disney empire. Some are listed in this book, but others are difficult to list because it's hard to define the "artist" under whom some of the ensemble pieces should be listed.

The challenge in collecting children's records is finding them in near-mint condition. Kids generally trashed anything they owned, and that included the records they played.

— **Jazz LPs.** To find more complete listings for jazz performers, we recommend the Goldmine® Jazz Album Price Guide, 2nd Edition, published in 2004. This book is now out of print, but can be purchased through Amazon or eBay.

— **Classical LPs.** About 98 percent of all classical albums are worth less than their original list price. Some of the other 2 percent are in this book. We have no interest in continuing a classical artist's discography beyond the bounds we've already set—basically RCA Victor Living Stereo "shaded dogs" and Mercury Living Presence stereo LPs. Mono versions of the same albums (with an LM- prefix on RCA Victor, for example) are generally not listed because they have a mere fraction of the value of the stereo counterpart.

—**Spoken-word LPs.** Few have significant collector value. They are usually quite rare, but there is relatively little demand for them.

FROM MY COLD, DEAD HANDS

by Martin Popoff

OK, Charlton Heston was talking about his rifle, but as my research has found, many people haven't thought much further than this when pondering the fate of their record collections. You see, a buddy and I were talking about what would happen with our stuff—rooms full of it—if either of us got torn to bits in a car crash, or suffered some other less dramatic premature death as a result of entering our, ahem, advanced years.

And it didn't take long to come up with a pact, and why a pact was needed. See, the problem is this. Are we really so egocentric and blind that automatically, we figure our kids, in my case, young enough that he's barely into music, are going to adopt our collections and slake of this hobby as deeply and as passionately as we have? Second, assuming it's "to be sold," by whom? Our wives? To whom? A dealer? eBay? Who has the time? How in th' heck are they supposed to have a clue that my Fields record is worth a lot more than her personal fave, Elton John's Greatest Hits?

That last thought led to a cringing ponder of a future where one of the dozen or so dealers and/or record store owners we know swoops in and slaps down $5,000 in cash to a hurried and bereaving wife, and there ya go, this junk is off my to-do list. Get it?

Not really, as I found out asking folks this very question. Still, despite few seeing the implications of deciding the above obvious answers, there's something positively cheery and grounded in the way collectors approach this problem. Ergo, here goes a sampling of responses, a few of them somewhat practical, some amusing, some poignant, some defiantly oblivious… but that's life!

• "I still haven't grown out of collecting, but with all my major favorite artists getting older as well and a relative lack of interest in the newer bands, there is not as much that I want (my bank account sez Thank God!). I'm never bored of it; I just regret these days, what with family/business and other recreational activities that I don't have the time to enjoy all of what I have already purchased and continue to buy. At 52, the question of my own mortality comes up in my mind occasionally, but not as it relates to the collection. My parents on their passing left a small collection of old Italian/opera, etc. 78s that are my charge now and I fully intend to catalog them someday and investigate their worth. So too my collection will be passed onto my children and so on. I hope."

• "Hopefully by then I'll have kids and if they show interest in my music and collection then obviously it will go to them. If not then depending on what the times will be like, that will determine whether it gets sold on eBay or thrown in the garbage. Sometimes I feel like I can't stop buying, and I feel the only way to stop is to just get rid of everything. But I really can't do that. If I get rid of my collection, I might as well just get rid of myself. My collection is part of who I am and it's something that makes me happy."

• "Music is a huge part of my life, it has truly shaped who I am today, but I have really not thought that far ahead. A couple of years ago, my grandmother sold her house that she had lived in for the past 50 years. The amount of stuff that she had amassed over those years was staggering, and it got to the point where we were just looking to throw away most of it. I'm sure when my time comes, my kids will curse me for the cleaning job that I'll be leaving behind for them."

• "No way. I still obsess about it. Music and collecting have been such defining points in my life thus far. It is my historical documentation on where I have been musically. It is my feeble attempt at owning that history, hanging on tight to it, and not letting it go. I don't see it ever ending."

• "My collection will probably be buried with me when I go. I have not met or known anyone that I can trust with my whole collection. And to say this is just a phase I'm going through would be a lie."

• "You know, I have thought about this many times. I'm not sure, but I expect I will give them to my oldest son, who is also into music. He's more into dark and ambient techno versus the stuff I listen to, but he's also a DJ on the side, and I've given him some classic rock in the past to spin. I think Kansas went over real well at the bowling alley lounge he used to spin at. That said, I expect to hang onto them for several more years. Sometimes there's a sense of guilt. Like, what in the hell am I doing with all these records that I will never have the time to listen to? I still have them though. As stated earlier, I will probably will them to my son. Or possibly sell them when the time is right? Not sure yet. When I was younger I sold several albums to the used record store because I needed the money at the time. Also, I went through a rough job layoff a few years back and sold several CDs. My thought process was kinda like that ol' 'You can't take it with you.' Anyway, I regret selling many of them and wish I had them back."

• "It goes away only when I die; I will give it to my son and advise him how much I enjoy it and the relics that I collect."

• "Hopefully to my son; he is six now and his favourite album now is U.D.O.'s Dominator, and so it gives me some hope."

• "I have often thought about what I would do with it all if I knew I was going to depart. A few choices are possible. May leave it all for the wife in case she needs cash at some point. Maybe some prize pieces would be left to someone who would keep and cherish the stuff—if anybody at that time would. Or sell it all for a Kiss coffin and be buried in that. That way I can say I took it all with me."

• "I have many times contemplated selling my stuff. You kind of weigh the options in your head or talk yourself into it. You say, 'Well it just sits there; I'm the only one who sees it. I could get a Les Paul guitar or a TV and that is useful, so I have parted with some major stuff to get other things. I'll tell you though, after you do it, it hurts. It's like a divorce almost; it's a hard thing to do. Something about your collection feeds your soul. It gives you comfort; it gives you joy. Other people just think you're nuts for having it but they don't get it. It gives you something not everyone has, something in the heart. Passion, love for the music, band or whatever it may be. Its something you should take thought on before you part with stuff—you may not ever get it back. There will always be TVs and guitars and cars, but there won't always be a costume or a stage-worn fire helmet."

• "That is a question I've asked myself for years. I have a great nephew that has shown signs of being careful with his belongings, and he is heavily into music. My wife will be my independent executor when I pass, but I'll see that he gets my records, books and other musical memorabilia when she passes."

• "A few years ago I thought about getting rid of all my records because they take up so much space in my house! Thankfully I have a wife that understands how valuable these things are and she quickly adjusted my mindset when she heard me talk about getting rid of them. I will never get rid of my records."

• "Had a guilt trip about the "evils" of rock 'n' roll put on me when attending church in the '80s and sold my records. Soon after I re-collected them all plus more."

• "It's a very poignant question, and one that any collector has to ponder no matter what their particular vice is. 'Has it been worth it? You know you can't take any of these things with you when you die, right?' As much as I enjoy collecting, I also find it stifling and at times downright destructive. I think of the time spent looking for music, waiting for albums to come out, and the money spent on them... wow. At times I feel like I can't stop; definitely an addiction. It would be fine if I was the only person it affected, but I also have a family to be concerned about. On the other hand, collecting has allowed me to keep my sanity and have a passion outside of police work (which can suck the life out of you if you let it). The love of heavy music is a bond I share with my son, and we enjoy talking about and reviewing music. We especially love going to shows, and do so whenever we get a chance. So, I rationalize my collection by stating that I'm not in debt because of it, and there are certainly much more destructive addictions to have, such as gambling, alcohol, drugs, etc. You know, I still get that same feeling I did as a kid when a new Maiden or Slayer album drops. How do you describe it? I'm much older now, and certainly more jaded musically, but I never want to lose that feeling I had as a kid. It's magic, plain and simple."

• "I always tell people I want to be cremated with my record collection. Realistically; I have no idea. I would likely give it away to some of my collector friends who have some interest. Many of my friends have no interest in my vinyl... especially those who have helped me move the last few times."

• "I have never gotten bored with collecting. I don't consider myself "obsessive" with it but it's definitely part of who I am. I always think that someone who doesn't have a hobby, something they enjoy doing outside of work or day-to-day life must be really bored. I have been collecting for over 25 years and I don't see myself stopping."

• "My brother and my friend Alex will have it after I perish. My brother will sell off the CDs and Alex is a musician who will appreciate it. This is all with the approval of my fiancé, soon-to-be wife. My friend Pete, who plays trombone in jazz outfits can have my collection of swing and my collection of classical music, which in vinyl is quite impressive."

• "I love the music and it calms me, especially hard rock. After two heart surgeries and a stroke, there is an irony of hard rock satiating a need and calming me, but it does. It makes me feel alive. I will never part with my treasures. Beside it took too long to collect it and what then would I blog about?"

• "I always thought I would let my pals go through it and just have what they want, but now I suppose the responsible thing to do would be let my old lady and/or daughter sell it for the bread."

• "I've been thinking about this a lot lately. Now that I have a kid and need to take things like space and finances more seriously, having a zillion CDs, records and tapes lying around the house seems absurd at times... like, all the time. I'm a bit of a neurotic collector, but I have so much damn music I will never listen to again. Truth is, I just like having it, looking at the spines of the CDs, knowing it's there, having it 'for reference,' which really doesn't mean much anymore—it's just an excuse to not sell the stuff."

• "When I was younger—and you always hear people romanticizing this—I'd sit back with the liner notes, read along with the lyrics, all that. Now I need to combine listening to new music with dishes, going from point A to point B on the bus or just working. I just don't need to own the stuff anymore. Having said that, collecting is fun (when it doesn't take over your life); it's a fun hobby. Everyone's time, money and space goes to something. There's just something about record collecting that gets harder to justify as we get older."

• "A friend of my dad's passed away recently and he had over 15,000 albums (mostly 78s) including all the Louis Armstrong recordings—an absolutely amazing collection. They were looking at selling it or donating it to a museum."

• "I haven't thought about it. I have no kids and will probably not have any, so I guess I will pass it on to my niece. Or maybe have it burned with me and spread over the Lake of Neuchatel in Switzerland, where I was born."

• "I am not tired of my collection at all. I rediscover it on a very regular basis. I dust off a few albums every week and they are part of who I am. I have never sold, exchanged, threw away one single album. They are all part of my collection and if one went missing, it would kill it. I feel that all my albums are related, linked in a strange kind of way. Weird."

• "It'll go to a friend of mine. He and my wife already know."

• "My ideal is to inherit it to one of my nephews who happen to love this type of music as much as I do."

• "I truly believe that every fan has their own desert island selection comprised of the closer and more meaningful music to each person. I know for sure I will never get rid of certain albums, but as you know, forever is a long time (laughs)."

• "If I ever have children I would bequeath my collection to one of them. Or maybe I could get some money if they ever became really valuable. But if I never have children, I would probably give them to a library, or find someone that really wants them. Maybe I'll be buried with my Kiss records. But no, I would pass them on to someone who I would trust to take care of them and enjoy them. I don't get bored with it though—collecting music is a never-ending journey."

• "Who knows what the world of record buying will look like when I die. My first instinct would be to pass my records along to any family-members who are nascent music/record-freaks. I guess I'd like to imagine my kids being interested, like me, in the discovery of new sounds and music. After family, I'd give records to interested friends. After that, I guess I'd aim to sell the collection (whole) to an independent record store, to be sold in the physical store. After that, I'd just be interested in liquidating and leaving the proceeds to my family. I think about this all the time, but I think worrying about the decadence and bloat of things I enjoy is just something I am disposed towards worrying about. These feelings have never compelled me to sell everything, but they have compelled me to pare down. This goal may eventually lead to opening my own brick-and-mortar store."

• "I really don't know what to do with my collection when I die. No one in my family will want to deal with it. I have one friend that I know would appreciate it, but he's ten years older than me. He'll probably kick the bucket before I do. I'll probably have to sit down and write out some instructions for my sister on what pieces are valuable and which aren't. She could at least cash in on some items on eBay. Kind of sad that all the time, money, and effort I've spent on this stuff and there's really no one I know that would truly treasure it."

• "Been on the other end of this death/record collection issue actually. An uncle, old timey rock'n' roller who put out a few records on his own label in the '50s kicked the bucked, only in his 50s—too much pills over the years; pretty rock 'n' roll. Scads and scads of vinyl, CDs, box sets, mostly jazz, country, old time rock 'n' roll. Since he had no kids, the loot got divided up by three remaining siblings, and my mom's cut became mine. Got most of the jazz, since it's more up my alley than the country and bluegrass. I figure, when I discover a great album from his collection (Grant Green—Carryin' On, and Horace Silver Quartet's The Jody Grind are now favorites of mine), he'd be happy someone discovered 'em. Lots of Jerry Lee Lewis…one of his heroes. One of the siblings was selling great jazz CDs (Coltrane, Miles, Dolphy) at a garage sale, $2. Imagine the horror. When you leave your stuff behind, reality is the commodities will be sold. You can't really expect someone to keep a thousand albums around just to remind 'em of your rocker self. I will have to deal with my old man's huge sports collection one day (balls, pucks, programs, cards, etc.) and I dread it! I love to watch sports, but fussing with the minutia of it does not interest me in the least. I'd rather fuss with someone's rock 'n' roll collection. Which makes me believe, blood or not, you are better to give your music collection to someone into music. Or liquidate it yourself before you go to that great gig in the sky. My new view of my collection—the material needs to earn its keep. No room for copycat bands with albums that don't stand out."

• "I can't really say what will happen to my collection; I have no children that I know of. And if I did, chances are they may not appreciate it as I do. However I do have a friend I might pass a few on to. And I plan on showing my wife how to get rid of them. You know… who to call and stuff."

• "I sometimes tire of it, you know, the collecting, the struggle of it. But on the other hand, it has given me every emotion one could think of! And without it, well I just wouldn't be me. It has helped me through the best and worst times of my life, even though everything in life is temporary in one way or another. As for now, my collection is mine and I love it! I only hope that when the time comes the next owner(s) like it as much as I do."

• "My wife says that most of my stuff is 'useless.' How fooled is she?! I suppose my older son would want some of the stuff, but on CD. The 'cool' stuff is supposed to go to my best buddy, Javi. If he would have to sell some to make money for my wife, he would know the best way to do so."

• "I will never stop collecting and I would never consider ever getting rid of my collection."

• "I guess my kids (if I have any) or a couple of my friends will inherit this gigantic pile of plastic and vinyl. Hopefully it goes to someone who will appreciate it and take care of it. Yes, it's kind of crazy when you think about it. The thrill is in the hunt in collecting, but with music it's not just collecting. I think of it as pieces of art that have a life that can go on forever. Like paintings and other forms of art, there will always be great art produced, but some of it for numerous reasons will be passed by only to be discovered and validated later on (which I find fascinating). I've been collecting for about 20 years now, and haven't once gotten bored of it. In fact it's what I spend the most money on, and the one material thing that keeps me happy."

• "I have pondered this as many times as I have moved, thankfully only a few times, and feel the taxation of space. What a cruel thing to leave behind a large collection to my heirs who might not care, let alone know the value of rarities amongst the general population of 2,200 records. As I get older, I feel my emotional attachment waning but it has never been tested. I sometime wish somebody would come and haul it all away for a buck an album but then I see the value of selling one at a time online, possibly realizing some of its worth. Perhaps it will supplement my income when I retire and give me something to do, as it always has. I have a gnawing feeling that I can't take it with me and could convert 40 or 50 years of hunting music into some spendin' cabbage at Tim Horton's in the coming years. Maybe I will donate it all to some library for others to enjoy; those bootlegs may be hard to get rid of though. Not bored so far but the most curious thing is always wanting the next one. Some days I peruse 2,200 album and 2,000 CDs and hundreds of digital downloads and I can't quite find the one to play so I have to get something new. It's always about the next one you get. I drank the same way and now I don't drink anymore. Music collecting never got me into the same kind of trouble. I guess that's why I trust it and continue to do it. I never have sold off anything of mine. I even survived many parties without having a cherished album stolen. I had a buddy that got religion and sold off some of his collection to me and others—strange though, soon enough he started to collect again. Powerful. I can't take it with me and that might be my saddest thought of the end of life, the end of the music. What would I have done with all that time if I hadn't been into collecting and listening to music on a daily basis? I might have had a wife and children, traveled more, had a career?"

• "This used to really bother me. For a long time I was terrified at the thought of losing my stuff or having it stolen....so ingrained these items had become into my psyche. Collecting can bear quite the psychological weight and I think people like us share similar psychological profiles due to having similar life experiences/personality types which predispose us to viewing the world through a similar lens. Part of me thinks collecting borders on a spiritual issue—it's some attempt by a spirit to grasp hold of eternity and transcend time by holding onto the past as if the future needs to be feared. I don't think most collectors are with-it enough to see it that way, but anyways that's my perspective. It's also another way for men to relive their childhood/youth, and our society has loads of ways for men to do that, some more socially acceptable than others. While in our minds we understand our lives are transitory but we still want to deny that it's not, and have some idealized perspective of the past as somehow more worthy and interesting than the present—a real nutzo idea that can be very seductive to the mind. "Some collect due to greed/not knowing when to stop. Some have so much, it's embarrassing, more than they will ever be able to listen to in a lifetime. So why do they have all of it? I ask them this and get no answer, maybe a shrug. Either they don't know themselves well enough or they don't want to spill the beans, as if I'm going to judge them for their neuroses. Enjoyment equals sharing the experience with others, not jamming yourself full of product in some misguided notion that you are going to achieve intellectual nirvana or something. I think people who have trouble letting go of the past or who have a penchant for nostalgia are seriously predisposed to be collectors, collectors of anything—it doesn't matter what it is, newspapers to spoons to CDs. At least from my own experience, I used to think buying all this would bring me some form of mental solace but it never did. If you do it for the wrong reasons, it can be very empty. And all this physical clutter can really disorganize the mind. From Sweden to Canada to the US, it's odd having been in the homes of so many hardcore record collectors and noticing how eerily similar they are—crammed full, hardly anywhere to step, complete absence of any form of sensible organization of material, simply overwhelming, an unbridled mess. And this included my own home at one time."

• "When I have children, I'd like the idea of placing it in storage or trust until they're old enough to handle it themselves. I'd love to create some sort of provision whereby they're prohibited from selling off more than ten percent of the catalog. I simply cannot stand the idea of having it broken up and sold for short-term gain. Show them who's boss! I dunno, I'd like the collection to be held as a testament to my eclecticism and dedication. If I have to donate it to some college or institution for archiving, I might do that as well. I think of the adage commonly attributed to a nameless Buddhist monk: 'You think you own your possessions, but in truth they own you.' However, I can insist that I've never gotten tired or bored of collecting music. I may be overwhelmed and burdened (spatially and temporally) by the sheer volume in my possession and the very real possibility that I might never even get a chance to play them all in my lifetime, but that is no contradiction or negation of my love. I'm grateful and humbled by my desire to be a part of music history, to catch a firefly or two (or 21,000) and observe its glow."

THE WORLD'S BIGGEST RECORD COLLECTION

by Martin Popoff

Pittsburgh's Paul Mawhinney has been an old-school record man all his life, but now into his 70s and in fragile health, he's been forced to confront the idea of his life's work (known as "The World's Greatest Record Collection" all over the Internet) finding a new home, or worse, not. Mawhinney's story hit the mainstream a couple years back when an eBay bid for his collection came to light at just over the $3 million reserve price. But the deal fell through (the bid was a hoax), and ever since it's been one setback after another. The Library of Congress was talked about, as was the University of Texas and even a few schemes around an independent museum. But to date, all ideas have hit roadblocks and prospective buyers have scattered leaving broken promises in their wake, really, too much for Mawhinney to handle, as he looks for something positive to happen so he can leave some financially security for his wife and kids.

So what's Paul got? Well, there's no question that there's a lot of junk and duplicates and things that shouldn't be junk, but are just so woefully forgotten, they qualify as junk to almost all who might potentially care. There is indeed a wild west gathering of around half a million albums (down, apparently, from one million), not catalogued, along with posters, furniture, racks, old cylinder systems, cassettes, 78 recorders, thousands of 78s, antique furniture, indeed anything a massive accumulator of things related to this business invariably ends up with. From this stash, Paul is a willing seller, and dealers and serious collectors have been showing up regularly (by appointment) at his Record Rama Sound Archive in 8,000 square feet of industrial space in Pittsburgh to spend thousands.

But most intriguing is Mawhinney's singles and EP collection, comprising about 1.5 million pieces (again, there are duplicates), but with about half that number fully catalogued using his own MusicMaster system, of which there was a print version published back in 1983, comprising, at that point, 200,000 listings for records from 1947 to 1982. This is where Paul sees most of the value in what he's done, the recorded proof of all this weight that he has thus far been adamant not to break up. He values the word "archive" like a scholar, and has stayed faithful to the concept, at least as it pertains to singles (many LPs and CDs are in the database as well), and has indeed kept updating it over the years. And to be clear, there are two components here that Mawhinney figures are laden with value, both for different reasons—the discographical work and then, well, all those classified 7" records.

But what does he like about singles? "That's the history of American recorded sound and I'll tell you why," begins Paul. "Because a lot, awful lot of that material has never been put on an album. In the early days, the '50s and the '60s, there were a lot of releases that never got past the single stage—the groups never even did an album. The rhythm and blues and the doo-wop stuff... a lot of that never saw the light of day on albums. So that's why the singles are so important. You know, I have a lot of people that don't believe the Library of Congress's statement that I have 83 percent of the music that's not on any CD in on this country. They did a survey and that is what gives that to me. (Note: the key finding of the survey is that 17 percent of all the music released from 1944 to 1966 is not available in CD—it is assumed Paul is claming he's got 100 percent of that music—but this gets considerably muddied when you include album and non-American music). Everybody has albums. There are albums everywhere. I get offered album collections every day, even now. But the singles are much more difficult, and the early ones from the '50s and '60s are damned difficult. I have some really rare Beach Boys-related things, Beatles-related things, Elvis-related things—the Beatles and Elvis are over 1,000 records each. I have a tremendous amount, because I collected everything. In the early days a lot of people didn't save any of the black music, or R&B—they just collected the pop stuff."

But the most important material in here, academically speaking, comes from all those forgotten artists, really, the kinds of things that got the Library of Congress interested (yes, one of the deals that fell through). And then, like I say, there's a couple of components—the music right there on plastic and the cataloguing work of that music, searchable, in context with the times.

"It would be wonderful to let people know that the singles collection is untouched," says Paul, summarizing and keying in, again, on the part of this he is most proud of, the archive. "That is in my work life. And I would love to save that, preserve it for future generations, and I would love to find somebody who is interested sincerely in saving this collection past my life. I would like to see it go on. Because you're never going to get another collection equal to it. A lot of the records you will never find anywhere else."

Er, how much space would the singles take up? "Well, I have 8,000 square feet, and I would say that takes up about half of it. That's doing it with plenty of... you could probably pack it a lot tighter than that if you didn't have it work in it. If you have to work in it and have access, then you're going to need at least 4,000." Of note, Paul had been working out of two locations, the warehouse and the store, but, "I'm working now out of what used to be just the archive. I boxed everything else and moved it into that, and I'm still maintaining the archive, the way I did. So as I said, I have about 8,000 square feet, now. I had 16,400 (laughs)."

"I would say the minimum value would be $2 million," ponders Paul, asked for his latest price on this huge stack of wax. "But what I would like to see is someone to come in and just buy everything that I have, and I would say $3 million would be a realistic number. I've never really asked for what the stuff is worth, because I had an appraisal for $50.5 million that the Anderson company did in 1999, so $3 million is barely 5 percent. So yeah, $3 million is nothing for what they're going to get. There is probably $30 million worth of singles alone."

After so many deals gone sour, there's a streak of sadness to this tale, and Paul is all too aware that it revolves around huge swaths of American culture that so few people care about anymore, let alone collect or get up the gumption to catalogue. The collecting of any given musical genre waxes and wanes, and he's all too aware that tens of thousands of the records in his unique archive have fallen completely off the radar in terms of interest. Yet many still are gems waiting to be rediscovered, or indeed discovered for the first time, outside of the handful of folks that were there at the brief life of some of these acts. In any event, stay tuned to Goldmine magazine for developments concerning Paul and his commendable life work, an American cultural archive that, if there's any justice in the world, should show up in a museum or university to be preserved for generations to come.

More Must-Haves for Your Library

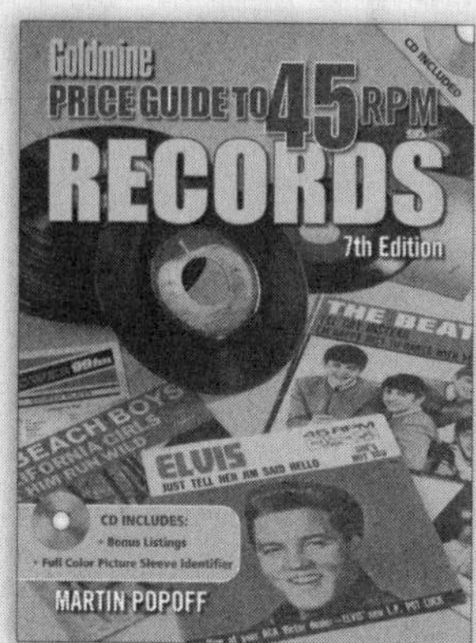

Do you know what your 45 RPM collection is worth? An easy way to get the answer, which could be a value more than what you thought, is to add this popular record guide to your library. With 80,000 listings, including artist, label and variation information, and a bonus CD with an additional 20,000 listings not included in the book, you can't go wrong with this record reference. 760 p

Item#Z3764 • $32.99

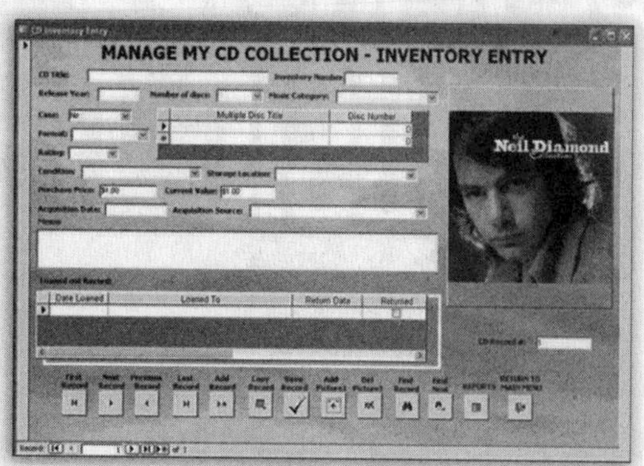

There's nothing better than having a great selection of music, but sometimes the collection can become a challenge to inventory and even harder to locate the CDs when you're looking for them. All of that can be corrected quickly and easily when you have the CD Collections software from Manage My Collectibles. With space to inventory your CDs by the details that are most important to you, you can use this CD to check your inventory before adding to the collection.

Format-CD

Item#Z8759 • $29.95

In this single record reference you'll gain the essential details to help you identify and price 70,000 albums released since 1948, by hundreds of artists and groups. The alphabetical organization, easy-to-follow listings and large-size photographs of album covers make for easy and accurate identification of LPs. Don't settle for anything less, get the Standard in record references. 688 p.

Item#Z5020 • $26.99

Selling your "stuff" online might seem like a daunting task, but with this book in hand you can learn the ropes from one of the best dealers in the world of online auctions. You'll learn which sites are the best for buying and selling, how to avoid scams, which promotions and perks are worth pursuing, and what you can do to organize your online business and boost profits. 304 p

Item#582-4 • $14.95

Number	Title (A Side/B Side)	Yr	NM

A

A.B. SKHY

45s

MGM

Number	Title (A Side/B Side)	Yr	NM
❑ K 14086	Camel Back/Just What I Need	1969	8.00
❑ K 14086 [PS]	Camel Back/Just What I Need	1969	12.00

Albums

MGM

Number	Title (A Side/B Side)	Yr	NM
❑ SE-4628	A.B. Skhy	1969	15.00
❑ SE-4676	Ramblin' On	1970	15.00

A.F.O. EXECUTIVES WITH TAMI LYNN

Albums

A.F.O.

Number	Title (A Side/B Side)	Yr	NM
❑ 5002 [M]	A Compendium	1962	150.00

ABACO DREAM

45s

A&M

Number	Title (A Side/B Side)	Yr	NM
❑ 1081	Life and Death in G and A/ Cat Woman	1969	8.00
❑ 1160	Another Night of Love/ Chocolate Pudding	1970	8.00

ABAD, MARCUS Maybe the same person as TONY ALAMO (2).

45s

LITTLE MARK

Number	Title (A Side/B Side)	Yr	NM
❑ 1937	Little Yankee Girl/Big Coal Man	196?	10.00

ABBA Also see BJORN AND BENNY.

12-Inch Singles

ATLANTIC

Number	Title (A Side/B Side)	Yr	NM
❑ DSKO 81 [DJ]	Dancing Queen (same on both sides)	1976	25.00
❑ DSKO 202 [DJ]	Voulez-Vous (6:05) (same on both sides)	1979	20.00
❑ DMD 308 [DJ]	Lay All Your Love on Me/ The Day Before You Came	1980	20.00
❑ DMD 329 [DJ]	The Visitors (Long)/(Short)	1981	15.00

POLYDOR

Number	Title (A Side/B Side)	Yr	NM
❑ 859789-1	Dancing Queen/ Take a Chance on Me	1992	10.00

45s

ATLANTIC

Number	Title (A Side/B Side)	Yr	NM
❑ PR 380 [DJ]	Happy New Year (mono/stereo)	1980	12.00
❑ PR 390 [DJ]	Happy New Year	1980	12.00
—One-sided promo			
❑ 3035	Waterloo/Watch Out	1974	5.00
❑ 3035 [PS]	Waterloo	1974	15.00
—Sleeve is promo only			
❑ 3209	Honey Honey/Dance (While the Music Still Goes On)	1974	5.00
❑ 3240	Hasta Manana/Ring Ring	1975	5.00
❑ 3265	SOS/Man in the Middle	1975	5.00
❑ 3310	I Do, I Do, I Do, I Do, I Do/ Bang-a-Boomerang	1975	5.00
❑ 3315	Mamma Mia/Tropical Loveland	1976	5.00
❑ 3346	Fernando/Rock Me	1976	4.00
❑ 3346	Fernando/Tropical Loveland	1976	4.00
❑ 3372	Dancing Queen/That's Me	1976	4.00
❑ 3387	Knowing Me, Knowing You/ Happy Hawaii	1977	4.00
❑ 3387 [PS]	Knowing Me, Knowing You/ Happy Hawaii	1977	7.00
❑ 3434	Money, Money, Money/ Crazy World	1977	4.00
❑ 3434 [PS]	Money, Money, Money/ Crazy World	1977	7.00
❑ 3449	The Name of the Game/ I Wonder (Departure)	1977	4.00
❑ 3457	Take a Chance on Me/ I'm a Marionette	1978	4.00
❑ 3457 [PS]	Take a Chance on Me/ I'm a Marionette	1978	6.00
❑ 3574	Does Your Mother Know/ Kisses of Fire	1979	4.00
❑ 3574 [PS]	Does Your Mother Know/ Kisses of Fire	1979	6.00
❑ 3609	Voulez-Vous/Angeleyes	1979	4.00
❑ 3609 [PS]	Voulez-Vous/Angeleyes	1979	7.00
❑ 3629	Chiquitita/Lovelight	1979	4.00
❑ 3630	Chiquitita (Spanish Version)/ I Have a Dream (Spanish Version)	1979	5.00
❑ 3652	Gimme! Gimme! Gimme! (A Man After Midnight)/ The King Has Lost His Crown	1980	4.00
❑ 3776	The Winner Takes It All/Elaine	1980	4.00
❑ 3806	Super Trouper/The Piper	1981	4.00
❑ 3806 [PS]	Super Trouper/The Piper	1981	4.00

Abba, "Voulez-Vous," Atlantic 3609, 1979, $5.

Number	Title (A Side/B Side)	Yr	NM
❑ 3826	On and On and On/Lay All Your Love on Me	1981	4.00
❑ 3889	When All Is Said and Done/ Should I Laugh or Cry	1982	3.00
❑ 3889 [PS]	When All Is Said and Done/ Should I Laugh or Cry	1982	3.00
❑ 4031	The Visitors/Head Over Heels	1982	3.00
❑ 4031 [PS]	The Visitors/Head Over Heels	1982	3.00
❑ 89881	One of Us/Should I Laugh or Cry	1983	3.00
❑ 89881 [PS]	One of Us/Should I Laugh or Cry	1983	4.00
❑ 89948	The Day Before You Came/ Cassandra	1982	3.00

CBS INTERNATIONAL

Number	Title (A Side/B Side)	Yr	NM
❑ DAS 40001 [DJ]	Estoy Sonando/Conociendome, Conociendote	1980	20.00
❑ DAS 40002 [DJ]	Fernando/Al Andar	1980	20.00
❑ DAS 40003 [DJ]	Dame! Dame! Dame!/Gracias Por La Musica	1980	20.00

—The above three are in Spanish, pressed in the U.S. for Hispanic markets; we don't know if stock copies exist

Albums

ATLANTIC

Number	Title (A Side/B Side)	Yr	NM
❑ PR 300 [DJ]	Abba	1978	30.00
❑ PR 432 [DJ]	A Collection of Hits	1982	30.00
❑ PR 436 [(2)DJ]	The Abba Special	1983	50.00
❑ SD 16000	Voulez-Vous	1979	10.00
❑ SD 16009	Greatest Hits, Vol. 2	1979	12.00
❑ SD 16023	Super Trouper	1980	10.00
❑ SD 18101	Waterloo	1974	12.00
❑ SD 18146	Abba	1975	12.00
❑ SD 18189	Greatest Hits	1976	12.00
❑ SD 18207	Arrival	1977	12.00
❑ SD 19114	Greatest Hits	1977	10.00
❑ SD 19115	Arrival	1977	10.00
❑ SD 19164	The Album	1978	10.00
❑ SD 19332	The Visitors	1981	10.00
❑ 80036 [(2)]	The Singles — The First Ten Years	1982	15.00
❑ 80142	I Love Abba	1984	10.00
❑ 81675	Abba Live	1986	12.00

CBS INTERNATIONAL

Number	Title (A Side/B Side)	Yr	NM
❑ DAL 40301	Gracias Por La Musica	1980	40.00

—Spanish-language versions of some of their hits, this LP was pressed in the U.S.

K-TEL

Number	Title (A Side/B Side)	Yr	NM
❑ NU 9510	The Magic of Abba	1978	15.00

NAUTILUS

Number	Title (A Side/B Side)	Yr	NM
❑ NR-20	Arrival	1981	30.00
—Audiophile vinyl			

POLYDOR

Number	Title (A Side/B Side)	Yr	NM
❑ 5499701	The Album	2008	20.00

ABBEY TAVERN SINGERS, THE

45s

HANNA-BARBERA

Number	Title (A Side/B Side)	Yr	NM
❑ 498	Off to Dublin in the Green/ The Gallant Forty Twa'	1966	8.00

Albums

V.I.P.

Number	Title (A Side/B Side)	Yr	NM
❑ 402 [M]	We're Off to Dublin in the Green	1966	40.00
❑ S-402 [S]	We're Off to Dublin in the Green	1966	50.00

ABBOTT, BILLY, AND THE JEWELS

45s

PARKWAY

Number	Title (A Side/B Side)	Yr	NM
❑ 874	Groovy Baby/Come On Dance with Me	1963	20.00
❑ 905	It Isn't Fair/Hey, Good Lookin'	1964	20.00

ABC

12-Inch Singles

MCA

Number	Title (A Side/B Side)	Yr	NM
❑ 54055	Say It (5 versions)	1991	8.00

MERCURY

Number	Title (A Side/B Side)	Yr	NM
❑ PRO 371 [DJ]	Be Near Me (same on both sides)	1985	8.00
❑ PRO 397 [DJ]	How to Be a Zillionaire (4 versions)	1985	8.00
❑ MDS-4023	The Look of Love (Part 3 — Dance 7:37)/(Remix Dub)	1982	12.00

Except when noted otherwise, VG = 25% of NM, and VG+ = 50% of NM. (Example: VG = $2.00, VG+ = $4.00 and NM = $8.00.)

Number	Title (A Side/B Side)	Yr	NM
❑ 811329-1	Poison Arrow/Theme from Mantrap (2 mixes)	1983	8.00
❑ 870102-1	King Without a Crown (2 versions)/The Look of Love (Live)/Poison Arrow (Live)/All of My Heart (Live)	1988	10.00
❑ 876397-1	The Real Thing (LP Version) (Frankie Knuckles Mix) (May Day Mix)	1989	8.00
❑ 884052-1	Be Near Me (2 mixes)/What's Your Destination	1985	8.00
❑ 884382-1	How to Be a Zillionaire (5:22) (6:05)/Tower of London (5:58)	1985	8.00
❑ 884714-1	Vanity Kills/ABC Megamix	1986	10.00
❑ 888726-1	When Smokey Sings (4 versions)/Chicago Part 1 & Part 2	1987	8.00
❑ 888894-1	The Night You Murdered Love (4 versions)/Minneapolis	1987	8.00

45s

COLLECTABLES

Number	Title (A Side/B Side)	Yr	NM
❑ 4262	The Look of Love/Poison Arrow	199?	3.00
—Reissue			
❑ 4846	When Smokey Sings/Be Near Me	199?	3.00
—Reissue			

MERCURY

Number	Title (A Side/B Side)	Yr	NM
❑ PRO 546-7 [DJ]	The Night You Murdered Love (Radio Edit) (same on both sides)	1987	6.00
❑ PRO 580-7 [DJ]	King Without a Crown (same on both sides)	1987	6.00
❑ 76168	The Look of Love (Part One)/Theme from Mantrap	1982	3.00
❑ 76168 [PS]	The Look of Love (Part One)/Theme from Mantrap	1982	4.00
❑ 810340-7	Poison Arrow/Tears Are Not Enough	1983	3.00
❑ 810340-7 [PS]	Poison Arrow/Tears Are Not Enough	1983	4.00
❑ 814631-7	That Was Then But This Is Now/Vertigo	1983	3.00
❑ 814631-7 [PS]	That Was Then But This Is Now/Vertigo	1983	4.00
❑ 814876-7	The Look of Love (Part One)/Poison Arrow	1983	3.00
—Reissue			
❑ 870102-7	King Without a Crown/The Look of Love	1988	3.00
❑ 870102-7 [PS]	King Without a Crown/The Look of Love	1988	3.00
❑ 880626-7	Be Near Me/A To Z	1985	3.00
❑ 880626-7 [PS]	Be Near Me/A To Z	1985	3.00
❑ 884382-7	(How to Be a) Millionaire/Tower of London	1985	3.00
❑ 884382-7 [PS]	(How to Be a) Millionaire/Tower of London	1985	3.00
❑ 884714-7	Vanity Kills/Judy's Jewels	1986	3.00
❑ 884714-7 [PS]	Vanity Kills/Judy's Jewels	1986	3.00
❑ 888604-7	When Smokey Sings/Chicago	1987	3.00
❑ 888604-7 [PS]	When Smokey Sings/Chicago	1987	3.00
❑ 888783-7	The Night You Murdered Love/Minneapolis	1987	3.00
❑ 888783-7 [PS]	The Night You Murdered Love/Minneapolis	1987	3.00

Albums

MERCURY

Number	Title (A Side/B Side)	Yr	NM
❑ SRM-1-4059	The Lexicon of Love	1982	10.00
❑ R 143756	Alphabet City	1987	12.00
—BMG Direct Marketing edition			
❑ 814661-1	Beauty Stab	1984	10.00
❑ 822890-1	The Lexicon of Love	1984	8.00
—Reissue			
❑ 824904-1	How to Be a Zillionaire	1985	10.00
❑ 832391-1	Alphabet City	1987	10.00
❑ 838646-1	Up	1989	10.00

ABDUL, PAULA

12-Inch Singles

VIRGIN

Number	Title (A Side/B Side)	Yr	NM
❑ DMD 1171 [DJ]	Knocked Out (7:03) (3:43) (4:58) (6:31)	1988	12.00
❑ 1239 [DJ]	(It's Just) The Way That You Love Me (12" Remix) (Radio Edit) (Dub) (Houseafire Mix)	1988	10.00
❑ 1262 [DJ]	Straight Up (6:52) (4:57) (7:10) (6:38)	1988	10.00
❑ DMD 1300 [DJ]	Forever Your Girl (3 versions)/Next to You/Straight Up (Kevin Saunderson Club Mix)	1989	10.00
❑ 1352 [DJ]	Cold Hearted (Extended Version 6:50) (House Mix 6:41)//(Dubstramental 5:41) (Percapella 4:00)/One or the Other	1989	10.00
❑ DMD 1370 [DJ]	Cold Hearted (Quiverin' 12") (7" Edit) (Chillin' Bass Dub) (Acapella) (Instrumental)	1989	8.00
❑ 1398 [DJ]	Opposites Attract (6 versions)	1989	10.00
❑ 1687 [(2)DJ]	Vibeology (8 versions)/The Promise of a New Day (12" Mix)	1991	15.00
❑ 1768 [DJ]	Vibeology (House 12") (Underground Mix) (Silky Sax Dub) (Underground Sax Dub)	1991	10.00
❑ SPRO-11016 [(2)DJ]	Crazy Cool (Deep Dish's Crazy Cool Remix) (Strike Vocal Mix) (Dub Fire Cool Dub) (Bad Boy Bill House Mix) (Bad Boy Dub) (Sharam Crazy Journey)	1995	20.00
❑ 38493	My Love Is for Real (3 versions)/Didn't I Say I Love You	1995	8.00
❑ 38497 [(2)]	My Love Is for Real (9 versions)	1995	15.00
❑ 38510	Crazy Cool (Bad Boy Bill House Mix) (Strike's Dub) (Deep Dish's Crazy Cool Remix)/The Choice Is Yours (Edit)	1995	10.00
❑ 96107	Vibeology (Hurley's House 7:04) (Hurley's Underground 5:27) (Silky Sax Dub 5:42) (Underground Sax Dub 4:58)	1991	10.00
❑ 96546	Cold Hearted (Extended Version) (House Mix) (Dubstramental) (Percapella)/One or the Other	1989	10.00
❑ 96565	Forever Your Girl (3 versions)/Next to You/Straight Up	1989	8.00
❑ 96594	Straight Up (6:52) (4:57) (7:10)	1988	8.00
❑ 96614	(It's Just) The Way That You Love Me (12" Remix)/(7" Dub) (Houseafire Mix)	1988	10.00
❑ 96661	Knocked Out (Extended) (Instrumental) (Radio Edit) (TKO Dub)	1988	12.00

45s

VIRGIN

Number	Title (A Side/B Side)	Yr	NM
❑ S7-18850	Crazy Cool/The Choice Is Yours	1995	3.00
❑ S7-18877	Forever Your Girl/(It's Just) The Way That You Love Me	1995	3.00
❑ 38493	My Love Is for Real/Didn't I Say I Love You	1995	2.00
❑ 38493 [PS]	My Love Is for Real/Didn't I Say I Love You	1995	2.00
❑ 98584	Will You Marry Me/Goodnight, My Love	1992	4.00
❑ 98683	Blowing Kisses in the Wind/Spellbound	1991	4.00
❑ 98737	Vibeology/Vibeology (House Mix)	1991	4.00
❑ 98752	The Promise of a New Day/The Promise of a New Day (West Coast 12")	1991	4.00
❑ 98828	Rush, Rush/Rush, Rush (Dub Mix)	1991	4.00
❑ 99158	Opposites Attract/One or the Other	1989	2.00
❑ 99158 [PS]	Opposites Attract/One or the Other	1989	2.00
❑ 99196	Cold Hearted/One or the Other	1989	2.00
❑ 99196 [PS]	Cold Hearted/One or the Other	1989	2.00
❑ 99230	Forever Your Girl/Next to You	1989	2.00
❑ 99230 [PS]	Forever Your Girl/Next to You	1989	2.00
❑ 99256	Straight Up/Straight Up (Power Mix)	1988	3.00
❑ 99256	Straight Up/Cold Hearted	1988	4.00
❑ 99282	(It's Just) The Way That You Love Me/(It's Just) The Way That You Love Me (Dub)	1988	3.00
—Second pressing on orange labels			
❑ 99282	(It's Just) The Way That You Love Me/(It's Just) The Way That You Love Me (Dub)	1988	4.00
—Originals on black labels			
❑ 99282 [PS]	(It's Just) The Way That You Love Me/(It's Just) The Way That You Love Me (Dub)	1988	4.00
❑ 99329	Knocked Out/(Instrumental)	1988	3.00
❑ 99329 [PS]	Knocked Out/(Instrumental)	1988	3.00

Albums

VIRGIN

Number	Title (A Side/B Side)	Yr	NM
❑ IP-8128	Spellbound	1991	25.00
—Columbia House edition; the only U.S. vinyl of this LP			
❑ 90943	Forever Your Girl	1988	10.00
❑ 91362	Shut Up and Dance	1990	12.00
—Blue print on cover			
❑ 91362	Shut Up and Dance	1990	12.00
—Purple print on cover			
❑ 91362	Shut Up and Dance	1990	12.00
—Red print on cover			
❑ 91362	Shut Up and Dance	1990	12.00
—Yellow print on cover			

ABRAMS, MISS, AND THE STRAWBERRY POINT SCHOOL THIRD GRADE CLASS

45s

A&M

Number	Title (A Side/B Side)	Yr	NM
❑ 1263	Floating Away/Wonder	1971	5.00

REPRISE

Number	Title (A Side/B Side)	Yr	NM
❑ 0928	Mill Valley/The Happiest Day of My Life	1970	4.00
❑ 0928 [PS]	Mill Valley/The Happiest Day of My Life	1970	5.00
❑ 0971	Buildin' a Heaven on Earth/This Time of Life	1970	4.00
❑ 1098	Green Grass/Sweet Summertime	1972	4.00
❑ 1136	I Never Asked/Wonder	1972	4.00
❑ 1322	America (Let's Get Started Again)/Running in the Green Grass	1975	4.00
—This one by Miss Abrams' "Fourth Grade Class"			
❑ 1322 [PS]	America (Let's Get Started Again)/Running in the Green Grass	1975	7.00

Albums

REPRISE

Number	Title (A Side/B Side)	Yr	NM
❑ MS 2098	Abrams, Miss, and the Strawberry Point School Third Grade Class	1972	12.00

ABSTRACTS, THE

45s

POMPEII

Number	Title (A Side/B Side)	Yr	NM
❑ 66679	Smell the Incense/See the Birdies	1968	20.00

Albums

POMPEII

Number	Title (A Side/B Side)	Yr	NM
❑ 6002 [M]	The Abstracts	1968	80.00
—Stereo cover with "DJ Copy Monaural" sticker; white label promo record			
❑ SD 6002 [S]	The Abstracts	1968	40.00

AC/DC Also see GEORDIE.

12-Inch Singles

ATLANTIC

Number	Title (A Side/B Side)	Yr	NM
❑ PR 419 [DJ]	Let's Get It Up (same on both sides)	1983	15.00
❑ PR 530 [DJ]	Flick of the Switch/Guns for Hire	1983	15.00
❑ PR 645 [DJ]	Jailbreak (same on both sides)	1984	15.00
❑ PR 750 [DJ]	Danger (same on both sides)	1985	15.00
❑ PR 754 [DJ]	Shake Your Foundations (same on both sides)	1985	15.00
❑ PR 2207 [DJ]	Heatseeker (same on both sides)	1988	12.00
❑ PR 2283 [DJ]	That's the Way I Want to Rock 'n' Roll (same on both sides)	1988	10.00

45s

ATCO

Number	Title (A Side/B Side)	Yr	NM
❑ 7068	High Voltage/It's a Long Way to the Top	1976	8.00
❑ 7086	Problem Child/Let There Be Rock	1977	8.00
❑ 8886	Mistress For Christmas/Moneytalks	1990	6.00
❑ 8886 [PS]	Mistress For Christmas/Moneytalks	1990	6.00
—U.K. import			
❑ 98881	Moneytalks/Borrowed Time	1990	5.00

ATLANTIC

Number	Title (A Side/B Side)	Yr	NM
❑ 3499	Rock 'N' Roll Damnation/Kick in the Teeth	1978	6.00
❑ 3553	Whole Lotta Rosie/Hell Ain't a Bad Place to Be	1979	6.00
❑ 3617	Highway to Hell/Night Prowler	1979	6.00
❑ 3644	Touch Too Much/Walk All Over You	1980	5.00
❑ 3761	You Shook Me All Night Long/Have a Drink on Me	1980	5.00
❑ 3787	Back in Black/What Do You Do for Money Honey	1980	5.00
❑ 3894	Let's Get It Up/Snowballed	1982	4.00
❑ 3894 [PS]	Let's Get It Up/Snowballed	1982	7.00
❑ 4029	For Those About to Rock We Salute You/T.N.T.	1982	4.00
❑ 4029 [PS]	For Those About to Rock We Salute You/T.N.T.	1982	8.00
❑ 89098	The Way I Wanna Rock 'N' Roll/Kissin' Dynamite	1988	3.00
❑ 89136	Heatseeker/Go Zone	1988	3.00
❑ 89136 [PS]	Heatseeker/Go Zone	1988	4.00
❑ 89377	You Shook Me All Night Long/She's Got Balls	1986	4.00
❑ 89425	Who Made Who/Guns for Hire (Live)	1986	3.00

Number	Title (A Side/B Side)	Yr	NM
❑ 89425 [PS]	Who Made Who/Guns for Hire (Live)	1986	6.00
❑ 89532	Danger/Back in Business	1985	3.00
❑ 89532 [PS]	Danger/Back in Business	1985	6.00
❑ 89614	Jailbreak/Show Business	1984	3.00
❑ 89614 [PS]	Jailbreak/Show Business	1984	6.00
❑ 89722	Flick of the Switch/Badlands	1983	3.00
❑ 89774	Guns for Hire/Landslide	1983	4.00
❑ 89774 [PS]	Guns for Hire/Landslide	1983	7.00
Albums			
ATCO			
❑ SD 36-142	High Voltage	1976	12.00
❑ SD 36-151	Let There Be Rock	1977	12.00
❑ 91413	The Razors Edge	1990	15.00
ATLANTIC			
❑ LAAS-001 [DJ]	Live at the Atlantic Studios	1977	60.00
—This album has been counterfeited			
❑ PR 562 [DJ]	Flick of the Switch Interview Album	1983	40.00
❑ SD 11111	For Those About to Rock We Salute You	1981	10.00
❑ SD 16018	Back in Black	1980	10.00
❑ SD 16033	Dirty Deeds Done Dirt Cheap	1981	10.00
❑ SD 19180	Powerage	1978	10.00
❑ SD 19212	If You Want Blood You've Got It	1978	10.00
❑ SD 19244	Highway to Hell	1979	10.00
❑ 80100	Flick of the Switch	1983	10.00
❑ 80178 [EP]	74 Jailbreak	1984	6.00
❑ 81263	Fly on the Wall	1985	10.00
❑ 81650	Who Made Who	1986	10.00
❑ 81828	Blow Up Your Video	1988	10.00
EASTWEST			
❑ 61780	Ballbreaker	1995	22.00
EPIC			
❑ E 80200 [EP]	74 Jailbreak	2003	10.00
❑ E 80201	High Voltage	2003	12.00
❑ E 80202	Dirty Deeds Done Dirt Cheap	2003	12.00
❑ E 80203	Let There Be Rock	2003	12.00
❑ E 80204	Powerage	2003	12.00
❑ E 80205	If You Want Blood You've Got It	2003	12.00
❑ E 80206	Highway to Hell	2003	12.00
❑ E 80207	Back in Black	2003	12.00
❑ E 80208	For Those About to Rock We Salute You	2003	12.00
❑ E 80209	Flick of the Switch	2003	12.00
❑ E 80210	Fly on the Wall	2003	12.00
❑ E 80211	Who Made Who	2003	12.00
❑ E 80212	Blow Up Your Video	2003	12.00
❑ E 80213	The Razors Edge	2003	25.00
❑ E2 90553 [(2)]	AC/DC Live	2003	15.00
❑ 90643 [(16)]	AC/DC	2003	200.00
—Box set with 15 albums on 16 LPs in black slipcase			

AC/DC, *If You Want Blood You've Got It*, Atlantic SD 19212, 1978, **$10.**

ACADEMICS, THE

Number	Title (A Side/B Side)	Yr	NM
45s			
ANCHO			
❑ 100	At My Front Door/Darla, My Darling	1957	80.00
❑ 101	Too Good to Be True/Heavenly Love	1957	100.00
—Reissue of Anchor 101			
ANCHOR			
❑ 101	Too Good to Be True/Heavenly Love	1957	1000.
—Original edition			
ELMONT			
❑ 1001/2	Drive-In Movie/Something Cool	1958	60.00

ACCENTS, THE
Several different groups.

Number	Title (A Side/B Side)	Yr	NM
45s			
ACCENT			
❑ 1036	Voice of the Boyous/Where Will You Be	1956	30.00
❑ 1037	The Name Song/This Ole Body	1956	30.00
BANGAR			
❑ 605	Wherever There's a Will/Howlin' for My Baby	1964	15.00
❑ 629	Searchin'/You Don't Love Me	1964	15.00
❑ 648	Road Runner/Why	1965	15.00
BRUNSWICK			
❑ 55100	Wiggle Waggle/Dreamin' and Schemin'	1958	15.00
❑ 55123	I Give My Heart to You/Ching-a-Ling	1959	15.00
C-R-C			
❑ 1017	I've Got Better Things to Do/Then He Starts to Cry	1964	20.00
—Featuring Sandi			
CHALLENGE			
❑ 59254	Tell Me/Better Watch Out Boy	1964	15.00
❑ 59294	Sweet Talk/Tell Me	1965	12.00
CHARTER			
❑ 1017	I've Got Better Things to Do/Then He Starts to Cry	1964	15.00
—Featuring Sandi			
COMMERCE			
❑ 5012	Tell Me/Better Watch Out Boy	1964	20.00
CORAL			
❑ 62151	Autumn Leaves/Anything You Want Me to Be	1959	15.00
GARRETT			
❑ 4008	Wherever There's a Will/Howlin' for My Baby	1964	20.00
❑ 4014	Road Runner/Why	1965	20.00
JERDEN			
❑ 728	Linda Lou/Stickey	1964	12.00
—Featuring Ron Peterson			
JUBILEE			
❑ 5353	Red Light/22 Del Rio Ave.	1958	15.00
KARATE			
❑ 529	He's the One/On the Run	1966	15.00
LIBERTY			
❑ 55813	I Really Love You/What Do You Want to Do (Little Darlin')	1965	12.00
M-PAC!			
❑ 7216	New Girl/Do You Need a Good Man	1964	20.00
MERCURY			
❑ 72154	Enchanted Garden/Tell Me Now	1963	10.00
ONE-DERFUL			
❑ 4833	You Better Think Again/Who You Gonna Love	1965	20.00
RCA VICTOR			
❑ 74-0127	Love Is a Many-Splendored Thing/Yours Until Tomorrow	1969	6.00
SULTAN			
❑ 5500	Rags to Riches/Where Can I Go?	1961	60.00
VEE JAY			
❑ 484	Our Wonderful Love/A Hundred Walkin' Cats	1963	8.00

ACE

Number	Title (A Side/B Side)	Yr	NM
45s			
ANCHOR			
❑ 21000	How Long/Sniffin' About	1975	5.00
❑ 21001	No Future in Your Eyes/I'm a Man	1975	5.00
❑ 21002	Rock & Roll Runaway/Know How It Feels	1975	5.00
❑ 21004	You're All That I Need/(B-side unknown)	1976	5.00
Albums			
ANCHOR			
❑ ANCL-2001	Five-a-Side (An Ace Album)	1975	12.00
❑ ANCL-2013	Time for Another	1975	12.00
❑ ANCL-2020	No Strings	1977	12.00

ACE, JOHNNY

Number	Title (A Side/B Side)	Yr	NM
45s			
DUKE			
❑ 102	My Song/Follow the Rule	1952	80.00
❑ 107	Cross My Heart/Angel	1953	60.00
❑ 112	The Clock/Ace's Wild	1953	60.00
❑ 118	Saving My Love for You/Yes Baby	1953	40.00
❑ 128	Please Forgive Me/You've Been Gone So Long	1954	40.00
❑ 132	Never Let Me Go/Burley Cutie	1954	40.00
❑ 136	Pledging My Love/No Money	1954	40.00
❑ 144	Anymore/How Can You Be So Mean	1955	40.00
❑ 148	So Lonely/I'm Crazy	1956	30.00
❑ 154	Still Love You So/Don't You Know	1956	30.00

Except when noted otherwise, VG = 25% of NM, and VG+ = 50% of NM. (Example: VG = $2.00, VG+ = $4.00 and NM = $8.00.)

A

Number	Title (A Side/B Side)	Yr	NM
FLAIR			
❑ 1015	Midnight Hours Journey/Trouble and Me	1953	150.00
—B-side by Earl Forrest			
7-Inch Extended Plays			
DUKE			
❑ LP 71	Pledging My Love/Never Let Me Go/Saving My Love for You//The Clock/Cross My Heart/So Lonely	196?	60.00
—Jukebox issue; small hole, plays at 33 1/3 rpm			
❑ LP 71 [PS]	Memorial Album	196?	60.00
❑ 80	Pledging My Love/Saving My Love for You//Angel/Please Forgive Me	1955	150.00
❑ 80 [PS]	Memorial Album	1955	150.00
❑ 81	The Clock/Never Let Me Go//Cross My Heart/My Song	1955	150.00
❑ 81 [PS]	Tribute to Johnny Ace	1955	150.00
Albums			
ABC DUKE			
❑ DLPX-71	Memorial Album	1974	20.00
DUKE			
❑ DLP-70 [10]	Memorial Album for Johnny Ace	1955	1200.
—VG value 400; VG+ value 800			
❑ DLP-71 [M]	Memorial Album for Johnny Ace	1956	500.00
—With no playing card on front cover			
❑ DLP-71 [M]	Memorial Album for Johnny Ace	1961	200.00
—With playing card on front cover			
❑ DLP-71 [M]	Memorial Album for Johnny Ace	1961	4000.
—Playing card cover; red vinyl; VG value 2000; VG+ value 3000			
❑ LP-71 [R]	Memorial Album for Johnny Ace	196?	50.00
—Orange label; trail-off number is "LRS-71"			
MCA			
❑ 27014	Memorial Album	1983	8.00

ACE, SONNY

Number	Title (A Side/B Side)	Yr	NM
45s			
ATLANTIC			
❑ 2364	Wooleh Booleh/Chili Peppers	1966	10.00

ACE SPECTRUM

Number	Title (A Side/B Side)	Yr	NM
12-Inch Singles			
ATLANTIC			
❑ DSKO 77	Live and Learn (5:50) (same on both sides)	1976	30.00
45s			
ATLANTIC			
❑ 3012	Don't Send Nobody Else/Don't Let Me Be Lonely Tonight	1974	50.00
❑ 3281	Trust Me/I Just Want to Spend the Night with You	1975	25.00
❑ 3296	Without You/Keep Holding On	1975	40.00
❑ 3353	Live and Learn/Just Like in the Movies	1976	20.00
Albums			
ATLANTIC			
❑ SD 7299	Inner Spectrum	1974	20.00
❑ SD 18143	Low Rent Rendezvous	1975	20.00
❑ SD 18185	Just Like in the Movies	1976	20.00

ACKLES, DAVID

Number	Title (A Side/B Side)	Yr	NM
45s			
ELEKTRA			
❑ 45634	Down River/L.A. Route and Chicago	1968	8.00
❑ 45676	That's No Reason to Cry/Subway to the Country	1970	8.00
❑ 45712	One Night Stand/Be My Friend	1971	6.00
❑ 45797	Love's Enough/American Gothic	1972	6.00
❑ 45810	Oh California/One Night Stand	1972	6.00
Albums			
COLUMBIA			
❑ KC 32466	Five & Dime	1973	12.00
ELEKTRA			
❑ EKS-74022	David Ackles	1968	15.00
❑ EKS-74060	Subway to the Country	1970	12.00
❑ EKS-75032	American Gothic	1972	12.00

ACKLIN, BARBARA

Number	Title (A Side/B Side)	Yr	NM
45s			
BRUNSWICK			
❑ 55319	Fool, Fool, Fool (Look in the Mirror)/Your Sweet Loving	1967	8.00
❑ 55355	I've Got You Baby/Old Matchmaker	1967	8.00
❑ 55379	Love Makes a Woman/Come and See My Baby	1968	8.00
❑ 55388	Just Ain't No Love/Please Sunrise Please	1968	8.00
❑ 55388 [PS]	Just Ain't No Love/Please Sunrise Please	1968	15.00
❑ 55399	Am I the Same Girl/Be By My Side	1969	8.00
❑ 55412	Seven Days of Night/Raggedy Ride	1969	8.00
❑ 55421	After You/More Ways Than One	1969	8.00
❑ 55433	Is It Me/Someone Else's Arms	1970	8.00
❑ 55440	I Did It/I'm Living with a Memory	1970	8.00
❑ 55447	I Can't Do My Thing/Make the Man Love You	1971	8.00
❑ 55465	Lady, Lady, Lady/Stop, Look and Listen	1971	8.00
❑ 55486	I Call It Trouble/Love You Are Mine Today	1972	8.00
❑ 55501	I'm Gonna Bake a Man/I Call It Trouble	1973	6.00
CAPITOL			
❑ 3892	Raindrops/Here You Come Again	1974	5.00
❑ 4013	Special Loving/You Gave Him Everything, But I Gave Him Love	1974	5.00
❑ 4061	Give Me Some of Your Sweet Love/Fire Love	1975	5.00
SPECIAL AGENT			
❑ 203	I'm Not Mad Anymore/(B-side unknown)	196?	1200.
Albums			
BRUNSWICK			
❑ BL 754129	Great Soul Hits	1967	25.00
❑ BL 754137	Love Makes a Woman	1968	20.00
❑ BL 754148	Seven Days of Night	1969	20.00
❑ BL 754156	Someone Else's Arms	1970	20.00
❑ BL 754166	I Did It	1971	20.00
❑ BL 754187	I Call It Trouble	1972	20.00
CAPITOL			
❑ ST-11377	A Place in the Sun	1975	12.00

ACORNS, THE

Number	Title (A Side/B Side)	Yr	NM
45s			
UNART			
❑ 2006	Angel/I'm Gonna Stick to You	1958	20.00
❑ 2015	Please Come Back/Your Name and Mine	1959	20.00

ACTION, THE

Number	Title (A Side/B Side)	Yr	NM
45s			
CAPITOL			
❑ 5949	Never Ever/24th Hour	1967	8.00

ACUFF, ROY

Number	Title (A Side/B Side)	Yr	NM
45s			
CAPITOL			
❑ F2385	What Will I Do/Tied Down	1953	25.00
❑ F2460	Lonesome Joe/Is It Love or Is It Lies?	1953	25.00
❑ F2548	Don't Say Goodbye/Sixteen Chickens and a Tambourine	1953	25.00
❑ F2642	Swamp Lily/Sweep Around Your Own Back Door	1953	25.00
❑ F2738	Rushing Around/Whoa Mule	1954	25.00
❑ F2820	Sunshine Special/I Closed My Heart's Door	1954	25.00
❑ F2901	I'm Planting a Rose/Streamlined Heartbreaker	1954	25.00
❑ F3064	Don't Judge Your Neighbors/Thief Upon the Tree	1955	25.00
❑ F3115	That's What Makes the Juke Box Play/Night Spots	1955	25.00
❑ F3209	Little Moses/Oh Those Tombs	1955	25.00
COLUMBIA			
❑ 2-357	Lonesome Old River Blues/It's Just About Time	1949	40.00
—Microgroove 33 1/3 rpm 7-inch single			
❑ 2-483	The Day They Laid Mary Away/It's All Right Now	1950	40.00
—Microgroove 33 1/3 rpm 7-inch single			
❑ 4-20792	A Plastic Heart/Your Address Unknown	1951	30.00
❑ 4-20804	Pliney Jane/Baldknob, Arkansas	1951	30.00
❑ 4-20828	Doug MacArthur/In the Shadow of the Smokies	1951	30.00
❑ 4-20858	Advice to Joe/When My Money Ran Out	1951	30.00
❑ 4-20877	Just Friends/Thy Burdens Are Greater Than Mine	1952	25.00
❑ 4-20912	Ten Little Numbers/My Tears Don't Show	1952	25.00
❑ 4-20951	Cheating/Don't Hang Your Dirty Linen on the Line	1952	25.00
❑ 4-21018	Wonder Is All I Do/She Isn't Guaranteed	1952	25.00
DECCA			
❑ 9-29748	Crazy Worried Mind/Along the China Coast	1955	20.00
❑ 9-29935	Goodbye Mr. Brown/Mother Hold Me Tight	1956	20.00
—With Kitty Wells			
❑ 9-30141	I Like Mountain Music/It's Hard to Love	1956	20.00
ELEKTRA			
❑ 45515	That's the Man I'm Looking For/(B-side unknown)	1978	5.00
❑ 46515	Freight Train Blues/Don't Worry 'Bout the Walk	1979	5.00
❑ 47040	I Can't Help It (If I'm Still in Love with You)/Cold, Cold Heart	1980	5.00
❑ 47480	Smokey Mountain Memories/What Have They Done to the Trains	1982	5.00
❑ 69937	Fireball Mail/The Stage	1982	5.00
—B-side by Boxcar Willie			
HICKORY			
❑ 1073	Once More/I Don't Care (If You Don't Love Me)	1958	15.00
❑ 1081	The One I Love (Is Gone)/Searchin' for Happiness	1958	15.00
❑ 1090	So Many Times/They'll Never Take Her Love from Me	1958	15.00
❑ 1097	Come and Knock (On the Door of My Heart)/My Love Came Back to Me	1959	15.00
❑ 1106	Nero Played His Fiddle/Write Me Sweetheart	1959	15.00
❑ 1113	Don't Know Why/Thanks for Not Telling Me	1960	12.00
❑ 1134	Mountain Guitar/Till No Longer You Care (For Me)	1960	12.00
❑ 1142	Streamlined Cannon Ball/Time Will Make You Pay	1961	12.00
❑ 1149	Little Mary/Lost John, He's Gone	1961	12.00
❑ 1160	Six More Days/Willie Boy, The Crippled Boy	1962	12.00
❑ 1178	Wabash Cannonball/Old Age Pension Check	1962	12.00
❑ 1191	Fireball Mail/The Great Speckled Bird	1962	12.00
❑ 1206	Don't Make Me Go to Bed and I'll Be Good/Pins and Needles (In My Heart)	1963	12.00
❑ 1223	The Great Titanic/The Birmingham Jail	1963	12.00
❑ 1244	Low and Lonely/Wabash Cannonball	1964	10.00
❑ 1271	Do You Wonder Why/Things That Might Have Been	1964	10.00
❑ 1291	Freight Train Blues/All the World Is Lonely Now	1965	10.00
❑ 1316	Life to Go/Rising Sun	1965	10.00
❑ 1331	I'm Planning a Rose/Tennessee Central	1965	10.00
❑ 1365	Pan American/Don't Tell Mama	1966	10.00
❑ 1394	Golden Treasure/Lost Highway	1966	10.00
❑ 1424	Kaw-Liga/Couldn't Believe It Was True	1966	10.00
❑ 1479	I Love You Because/I'm Movin' On	1967	10.00
❑ 1497	I'll Go On Alone/Uncle Pen	1967	10.00
❑ 1519	Don't Be Angry/The Nearest Thing to Heaven Is You	1968	10.00
❑ 1581	Life to Go/Each Season Changes You	1970	8.00
❑ 1627	Somebody Touched Me/Carry Me Back to the Mountains	1972	8.00
❑ 1636	A Pale Horse and His Ride/Sing a Country Song	1972	8.00
❑ 1644	Satisfied Mind/Just a Friend	1973	8.00
HICKORY/MGM			
❑ 314	Back in the Country/Jole Blon	1974	6.00
❑ 319	Old Time Sunshine Song/This World Can't Stand Long	1974	6.00
❑ 336	Back Down to Atlanta/A Most Reasonable Guy	1974	6.00
❑ 341	Fireball Mail/Roof Top Lullaby	1975	6.00
❑ 348	A Whole Month of Sundays/I Can't Find a Train	1975	6.00
❑ 355	That's Country/Take Me Home, Country Roads	1975	6.00
❑ 362	Walk a Mile in Your Neighbor's Shoes/Waltz in the Wind	1975	6.00
7-Inch Extended Plays			
COLUMBIA			
❑ H 4-3 [PS]	Songs of the Smoky Mountains	195?	15.00
—Fold-open sleeve for 6-1230 and 6-1231			
❑ 6-1230	Wreck on the Highway/Fire Ball Mail//Wait for the Light to Shine/Low and Lonely	195?	15.00
—Alternate numbers are "H 4-3-1" and "H 4-3-4"			

Except when noted otherwise, VG = 25% of NM, and VG+ = 50% of NM. (Example: VG = $2.00, VG+ = $4.00 and NM = $8.00.)

Number	Title (A Side/B Side)	Yr	NM
❑ 6-1231	Precious Jewel/Pins and Needles//Wabash Cannon Ball/Freight Train Blues	195?	15.00
—Alternate numbers are "H 4-3-2" and "H 4-3-3"			
❑ B-2803	Wabash Cannon Ball/The Precious Jewel//Freight Train Blues/Wreck on the Highway	195?	15.00
❑ B-2803 [PS]	Roy Acuff (Hall of Fame Series)	195?	15.00
Albums			
CAPITOL			
❑ T 617 [M]	Songs of the Smoky Mountains	1955	60.00
❑ DT 1870 [R]	The Best of Roy Acuff	1963	20.00
❑ T 1870 [M]	The Best of Roy Acuff	1963	30.00
❑ DT 2103 [R]	The Great Roy Acuff	1964	15.00
❑ T 2103 [M]	The Great Roy Acuff	1964	25.00
❑ ST 2276 [S]	The Voice of Country Music	1965	40.00
❑ T 2276 [M]	The Voice of Country Music	1965	30.00
COLUMBIA			
❑ CL 9004 [10]	Songs of the Smoky Mountains	1949	200.00
❑ CL 9010 [10]	Old Time Barn Dance	1949	150.00
❑ CL 9013 [10]	Songs of the Saddle	1950	150.00
❑ FC 39998	Columbia Historic Edition	1985	10.00
ELEKTRA			
❑ E-C 10-1-78 [DJ]	An Interview with Roy Acuff	1978	25.00
HARMONY			
❑ HL 7082 [M]	Great Speckled Bird	1958	25.00
❑ HL 7294 [M]	That Glory Bound Train	1961	20.00
❑ HL 7342 [M]	The Great Roy Acuff	196?	15.00
❑ HL 7376 [M]	Waiting for My Call to Glory	196?	15.00
HICKORY			
❑ LPM-H-101 [M]	Once More It's Roy Acuff	1961	30.00
❑ LPM-109 [M]	King of Country Music — All-Time Greatest Hits	1962	25.00
❑ LPM-113 [M]	Roy Acuff — Star of the Grand Ole Opry	1963	25.00
❑ LPM-114 [M]	The World Is His Stage	1963	25.00
❑ LPM-115 [M]	Roy Acuff Sings American Folk Songs	1963	25.00
❑ LPM-117 [M]	Hand-Clapping Gospel Songs	1963	25.00
❑ LPM-119 [M]	Country Music Hall of Fame	1964	20.00
❑ LPM-125 [M]	Great Train Songs	1965	20.00
❑ LPM-134 [M]	Roy Acuff Sings Hank Williams	1966	40.00
❑ LPS-134 [S]	Roy Acuff Sings Hank Williams	1966	40.00
❑ LPS-139	Famous Opry Favorites	1967	20.00
❑ LPS-145	Living Legend	1968	20.00
❑ LPS-147	Treasury of Country Hits	1969	20.00
❑ LPS-156	Roy Acuff Time	1970	20.00
❑ DT-90698 [R]	Great Train Songs	1965	25.00
—Capitol Record Club edition			
❑ T-90704 [M]	King of Country Music — All-Time Greatest Hits	1966	25.00
—Capitol Record Club edition			
❑ ST-91297	Famous Opry Favorites	1967	25.00
—Capitol Record Club edition			
METRO			
❑ M 508 [M]	Roy Acuff	1965	15.00
❑ MS 508 [R]	Roy Acuff	1965	10.00
MGM			
❑ E-3707 [M]	Favorite Hymns	1958	50.00
❑ E-4044 [M]	Hymn Time	1962	25.00
❑ SE-4044 [R]	Hymn Time	196?	20.00
ROUNDER			
❑ SS-23	1936-1939: Steamboat Whistle Blues	1985	10.00
❑ SS-24	1939-1941: Fly Birdie Fly	1985	10.00

ACUFF, ROY, JR.

Number	Title (A Side/B Side)	Yr	NM
45s			
HICKORY			
❑ 1349	Baby Just Said Goodbye/Wabash Cannonball	1965	10.00
❑ 1371	Stand Tall/You Won't Ever See Me Here Again	1966	10.00
❑ 1398	I Wish It Were Me/Turn That Frown Upside Down	1966	10.00
❑ 1425	Looks Like the Sun Ain't Gonna Shine/Victim of Circumstances	1966	12.00
—As "Roy Junior"			
❑ 1456	The Lament of the Cherokee Reservation Indian/The Luckiest Guy in the World	1967	12.00
❑ 1476	As Long As I Live/You, You, You, You	1967	10.00
❑ 1505	My World Has Stopped/Follow Your Drum	1968	10.00
❑ 1515	Blue Train (Of the Heartbreak Line)/Thru the Windows of Your House	1968	10.00
❑ 1535	The Guy Who Played Bass (So Well in Harlin Mason's Band)/The Luckiest Guy in the World	1969	10.00
❑ 1551	Looks Like Baby's Gone/Through the Windows of Your Mind	1969	10.00
❑ 1583	Back Down to Atlanta/Outlaw	1970	8.00
❑ 1597	Running/Street Singer	1971	8.00
HICKORY/MGM			
❑ 321	California Lady/Take Me Back	1974	6.00
❑ 331	Don't Worry 'Bout the Mule/Precious Memories	1974	6.00
❑ 344	Good Morning Country Rain/Sittin' Around the Campfire	1975	6.00
❑ 351	Good Time and T-Bird Wine/Turpentine Blues	1975	6.00
❑ 358	Baby, Maybe, Some Day/When She's Thirty	1975	6.00

ACUFF, ROY, JR., AND SUE THOMPSON

Number	Title (A Side/B Side)	Yr	NM
45s			
HICKORY			
❑ 1542	Thoughts/Are You Teasing Me	1969	10.00
❑ 1558	Talk Back Trembling Lips/Till I Can't Take It Anymore	1970	8.00
❑ 1573	Don't Let the Stars Get In Your Eyes/Why You Been Gone	1970	8.00

AD LIBS, THE

Probably all the same group.

Number	Title (A Side/B Side)	Yr	NM
45s			
AGP			
❑ 101	New York in the Dark/Human	1968	100.00
BLUE CAT			
❑ 102	The Boy from New York City/Kicked Around	1965	15.00
❑ 114	Ask Anybody/He Ain't No Angel	1965	10.00
❑ 119	On the Corner/Oo-Wee Oh Me Oh My	1965	10.00
❑ 123	Just a Down Home Girl/Johnny My Boy	1966	10.00
CAPITOL			
❑ 2944	Love Me/Know All About You	1970	6.00
JOHNNIE BOY			
❑ 01	Santa's On His Way/I Stayed Home (New Year's Eve)	19??	8.00
KAREN			
❑ 1527	Think of Me/Every Boy and Girl	1966	20.00
PHILIPS			
❑ 40461	Don't Ever Leave Me/You're in Love	1967	8.00
SHARE			
❑ 101	You're Just a Rolling Stone/Show a Little Appreciation	1969	8.00
❑ 104	Giving Up/Appreciation	1969	8.00
❑ 106	The Boy from New York City/Nothing Worse Than Being Alone	1969	8.00

ADAM AND THE ANTS

Number	Title (A Side/B Side)	Yr	NM
12-Inch Singles			
EPIC			
❑ AS 973 [DJ]	Los Rancheros/Physical	1980	12.00
❑ 48-01061	Antmusic/Don't Be Square (Be There)	1981	15.00
❑ 49-02193	Stand and Deliver/Beat My Guest	1981	12.00
45s			
EPIC			
❑ AE7 1236 [DJ]	Stand and Deliver/Beat My Guest	1981	3.00
❑ AE7 1236 [PS]	Stand and Deliver/Beat My Guest	1981	3.00
❑ 19-02042	Antmusic/Don't Be Square (Be There)	1981	5.00
Albums			
EPIC			
❑ AE 1331 [DJ]	Adam and the Ants	1981	10.00
—Five-song promo-only sampler			
❑ NJE 37033	Kings of the Wild Frontier	1981	12.00
❑ PE 37033	Kings of the Wild Frontier	1985	8.00
—Budget-line reissue			
❑ ARE 37615	Prince Charming	1981	10.00
❑ PE 37615	Prince Charming	1984	8.00
—Budget-line reissue			
❑ FE 38698	Dirk Wears White Sox	1983	10.00
—First U.S. issue of U.K. debut			
❑ PE 38698	Dirk Wears White Sox	1984	8.00
—Budget-line reissue			

ADAM, MIKE AND TIM

Number	Title (A Side/B Side)	Yr	NM
45s			
PRESS			
❑ 9728	Little Baby/You're the Reason Why	1964	10.00

ADAM'S APPLES

Number	Title (A Side/B Side)	Yr	NM
45s			
BRUNSWICK			
❑ 55330	Don't Take It Out on This World/Don't You Want Me Home	1967	100.00
❑ 55367	You Are the One I Love/Stop Along the Way	1968	50.00

ADAMS, ART

Number	Title (A Side/B Side)	Yr	NM
45s			
CHERRY			
❑ 1004	Rock Crazy Baby/Indian Joe	1960	100.00
❑ 1018	Dancing Doll/She Don't Live Here Anymore	1960	100.00

ADAMS, BILLY

Number	Title (A Side/B Side)	Yr	NM
45s			
AMY			
❑ 893	You and Me/Go (Go On, Get Out of Here Now)	1963	12.00
APT			
❑ 25072	My Happiness/Big M	1962	12.00
CAPITOL			
❑ 4308	Count Every Star/Peggy's Party	1959	25.00
❑ 4373	Can't Get Enough/The Gods Were Angry With Me	1960	25.00
DECCA			
❑ 30724	Baby I'm Bugged/Short Hair and Turtle Neck Sweater	1958	30.00
DOT			
❑ 15689	You Heard Me Knocking/True Love Will Come Your Way	1958	30.00
FERN			
❑ 807	Darling Take My Hand/Tender Years	1961	25.00
❑ 808	Tattle Tale/Born to Be a Loser	1961	25.00
❑ 812	Rip Van Winkle/Sleep Baby Sleep	1961	25.00
❑ 813	Comic Strip/Call Me	1961	25.00
HOME OF THE BLUES			
❑ 239	Looking for My Baby/Had the Blues	1962	10.00
❑ 242	My Happiness/Big M	1962	20.00
NAU VOO			
❑ 802	You've Gotta Have a Duck Tail/Walking Star	1959	100.00
❑ 805	Return of the All American Boy/That's My Baby	1959	75.00
❑ 808	Blue Eyed Ella/Fun House	1959	75.00
QUINCY			
❑ 932	Rock Pretty Mama/(B-side unknown)	195?	1500.
SUN			
❑ 389	Got My Mojo Workin'/Betty and Dupree	1964	20.00
❑ 391	Trouble in My Mind/Lookin' for Mary Ann	1964	20.00
❑ 394	Reconsider Baby/Ruby Jane	1964	20.00
❑ 401	Open the Door, Richard/Rock Me Baby	1966	20.00

ADAMS, BRYAN

Number	Title (A Side/B Side)	Yr	NM
12-Inch Singles			
A&M			
❑ SP-12014	Let Me Take You Dancing/(Instrumental)	1979	40.00
—This is for the U.S. pressing with the "A&M Disco" label; Canadian editions with the same number go for between 50 and 75 percent of this price			
❑ SP-12162 [DJ]	Christmas Time (4:06)/Reggae Christmas (2:47)	1985	15.00
❑ SP-17250 [DJ]	This Time (LP Version)//I'm Ready (Extended 5:23)/Take Me Back (Live 6:52)	1983	15.00
❑ SP-17296 [DJ]	Run to You (same on both sides)	1984	10.00
❑ SP-17303 [DJ]	Somebody (Single Version) (Album Version)	1985	15.00
❑ SP-17318 [DJ]	Heaven/Heaven (Live)/Kids Wanna Rock (Live)	1985	15.00
❑ SP-17325 [DJ]	Summer of '69 (same on both sides)	1985	7.00
❑ SP-17341 [DJ]	One Night Love Affair (same on both sides)	1985	10.00
❑ SP-17358 [DJ]	It's Only Love (LP Version)/(Live Version)	1985	15.00
—With Tina Turner			
❑ SP-17515 [DJ]	Only the Strong Survive (Album Version)(Live Version)/Victim of Love	1987	20.00

A

45s

A&M

Number	Title (A Side/B Side)	Yr	NM
❑ 31458 0422 7	Please Forgive Me/ Cuts Like a Knife	1993	5.00
❑ 31458 0476 7	All for Love/(Instrumental)	1993	4.00
—With Rod Stewart and Sting			
❑ 31458 1194 7	Have You Ever Really Loved a Woman?/Low Life	1995	5.00
❑ 75021 1567 7	(Everything I Do) I Do It for You/ (Everything I Do) I Do It for You (Long)	1991	8.00
❑ 75021 1576 7	Can't Stop This Thing We Started/(Everything I Do) I Do It for You	1991	5.00
❑ 31458 1578 7	The Only Thing That Looks Good On Me Is You/Hey Elvis	1996	4.00
❑ 31458 1578 7 [PS]	The Only Thing That Looks Good On Me Is You/Hey Elvis	1996	8.00
❑ 31458 1862 7	Let's Make a Night to Remember/Star	1996	5.00
❑ 2163	Let Me Take You Dancing/ Don't Turn Away	1979	30.00
❑ 2163 [DJ]	Let Me Take You Dancing (stereo/mono)	1979	12.00
❑ 2220	Hidin' from Love/Wait and See	1980	10.00
❑ 2220 [DJ]	Hidin' from Love (stereo/mono)	1980	6.00
❑ 2249	Give Me Your Love/ Wait and See	1980	10.00
❑ 2249 [DJ]	Give Me Your Love (stereo/mono)	1980	5.00
❑ 2359	Lonely Nights/Don't Look Now	1981	10.00
❑ 2359 [DJ]	Lonely Nights (stereo/mono)	1981	6.00
❑ 2409	Coming Home/Fits Ya Good	1982	8.00
❑ 2531	Cuts Like a Knife/ One Good Reason	1983	—
—Unreleased on this number?			
❑ 2533	This Time/One Good Reason	1983	—
—Unreleased on this number?			
❑ 2536	Straight from the Heart/ One Good Reason	1983	4.00
❑ 2536 [PS]	Straight from the Heart/ One Good Reason	1983	4.00
❑ 2553	Cuts Like a Knife/Lonely Nights	1983	4.00
❑ 2553 [PS]	Cuts Like a Knife/Lonely Nights	1983	4.00
❑ 2574	This Time/Fits Ya Good	1983	4.00
❑ 2574 [PS]	This Time/Fits Ya Good	1983	5.00
❑ 2606	The Best Was Yet to Come /I'm Ready	1983	4.00
❑ 2686	Run to You/I'm Ready	1984	3.00
❑ 2686 [PS]	Run to You/I'm Ready	1984	4.00
❑ 2701	Somebody/Long Gone	1984	3.00
❑ 2701 [PS]	Somebody/Long Gone	1984	4.00
❑ 2722 [DJ]	Diana (same on both sides)	1985	—
—Unreleased?			
❑ 2729	Heaven/Heaven "Live"	1985	3.00
❑ 2729 [PS]	Heaven/Heaven "Live"	1985	4.00
❑ 2739	Summer of '69/ The Best Was Yet to Come	1985	3.00
❑ 2739 [PS]	Summer of '69/ The Best Was Yet to Come	1985	3.00
❑ 2770	One Night Love Affair/ Lonely Nights	1985	3.00
❑ 2770 [PS]	One Night Love Affair/ Lonely Nights	1985	3.00
❑ 2791	It's Only Love/The Only One	1985	3.00
—A-side with Tina Turner			
❑ 2791 [PS]	It's Only Love/The Only One	1985	3.00
—A-side: With Tina Turner			
❑ 2798	Christmas Time/ Reggae Christmas	1985	—
—Canceled; reassigned to 8651			
❑ 2921	Heat of the Night/Another Day	1987	3.00
❑ 2921 [PS]	Heat of the Night/Another Day	1987	3.00
❑ 2921 [DJ]	Heat of the Night (4:21) (same on both sides)	1987	8.00
—A 5:07 version appeared on the stock 45s			
❑ 2948	Hearts on Fire/ The Best Is Yet to Come	1987	3.00
❑ 2948 [PS]	Hearts on Fire/ The Best Is Yet to Come	1987	3.00
❑ 2964	Victim of Love/Into the Fire	1987	3.00
❑ 2964 [PS]	Victim of Love/Into the Fire	1987	3.00
❑ 8645	Straight from the Heart/ Cuts Like a Knife	1985	3.00
—"A&M Memories" reissue			
❑ 8651	Christmas Time/ Reggae Christmas	1985	5.00
—Red custom label; green vinyl			
❑ 8651 [PS]	Christmas Time/ Reggae Christmas	1985	6.00
—"Package" sleeve			
❑ 8651 [PS]	Christmas Time/ Reggae Christmas	1986	5.00
—Sleeve with winter scene			
❑ 8652	Run to You/Somebody	1985	3.00
—"A&M Memories" reissue			
❑ 8653	Heaven/Summer of '69	1985	3.00
—"A&M Memories" reissue			
❑ 8654	One Night Love Affair/ It's Only Love	1985	3.00
—"A&M Memories" reissue; B-side with Tina Turner			
❑ 8677	Heat of the Night/Victim of Love	199?	3.00
—"A&M Memories" reissue			
❑ 8709	Can't Stop This Thing We Started/This Time	199?	3.00
—"A&M Memories" reissue on white label, pink and black print and "Collectables" logo on side			
❑ 8710	(Everything I Do) I Do It for You/ Hearts on Fire	199?	3.00
—"A&M Memories" reissue; white label with pink and black print and "Collectables" logo on side			

Albums

A&M

Number	Title	Yr	NM
❑ SP-3100	Bryan Adams	198?	8.00
—Budget-line reissue of 4800			
❑ SP-3154	You Want It, You Got It	198?	8.00
—Budget-line reissue of 4864			
❑ SP-3288	Cuts Like a Knife	198?	8.00
—Budget-line reissue of 4919			
❑ SP-3907	Into the Fire	1987	8.00
❑ SP-4800	Bryan Adams	1980	12.00
❑ SP-4864	You Want It, You Got It	1981	12.00
❑ SP-4919	Cuts Like a Knife	1984	8.00
—Reissue without the "6" in the catalog number			
❑ SP-6-4919	Cuts Like a Knife	1983	10.00
—Original with "6" as part of the catalog number			
❑ SP-5013	Reckless	1984	8.00
❑ SP-5327 [(2)]	Waking Up the Neighbours	1991	20.00
—Columbia House edition; the only U.S. vinyl of this LP			
❑ SP-17231 [EP]	Cuts	1983	25.00
—Promo-only four-song sampler from "Cuts Like a Knife" LP			
❑ SP-17321 [DJ]	Retail Sampler	1985	30.00
—10-song collection, a sort of "greatest hits" compilation to that time; promo only			
❑ R 151540	Reckless	1984	10.00
—RCA Music Service edition			
❑ R 153919	Into the Fire	1987	10.00
—BMG Direct Marketing edition			

ADAMS, CLIFF

45s

DOT

Number	Title (A Side/B Side)	Yr	NM
❑ 16385	Funny Kind of Feeling/ Keep Off My Mountain	1962	10.00

ADAMS, FAYE

45s

ATLANTIC

Number	Title (A Side/B Side)	Yr	NM
❑ 1007	Sweet Talk/Watch Out, I Told You	1953	50.00

HERALD

Number	Title (A Side/B Side)	Yr	NM
❑ 416	Shake a Hand/ I've Got to Leave You	1953	30.00
—Black vinyl			
❑ 416	Shake a Hand/ I've Got to Leave You	1953	100.00
—Red vinyl			
❑ 419	I'll Be True/Happiness to My Soul	1953	25.00
❑ 423	Say a Prayer/Every Day	1954	25.00
❑ 429	Somebody, Somewhere, Someday/Crazy Mixed-Up World	1954	25.00
❑ 434	Hurts Me to My Heart/ Ain't Gonna Tell	1954	25.00
❑ 439	I Owe My Heart to You/Love Ain't Nothin' to Play With	1954	25.00
❑ 444	Anything for a Friend/Your Love Has My Heart Burning	1955	25.00
❑ 450	You Ain't Been True/ My Greatest Desire	1955	25.00
❑ 457	Angels Tell Me/Tag Along	1955	25.00
❑ 462	No Way Out/Same Old Me	1955	25.00
❑ 470	Teen-Age Heart/Witness to the Crime	1956	25.00
❑ 480	Takin' You Back/ Don't Forget to Smile	1956	25.00
❑ 489	Anytime, Anyplace, Anywhere/ The Hammer Keeps Knockin'	1956	25.00
❑ 512	Shake a Hand/I'll Be True	1958	20.00

IMPERIAL

Number	Title (A Side/B Side)	Yr	NM
❑ 5443	Keeper of My Heart/So Much	1957	20.00
❑ 5456	Johnny Lee/You're Crazy	1957	20.00
❑ 5471	I Have a Twinkle in My Eye/ Someone Like You	1957	20.00
❑ 5525	When We Kiss/Everything	1958	20.00

LIDO

Number	Title (A Side/B Side)	Yr	NM
❑ 603	That's All Right/It Made Me Cry	1960	12.00
❑ 606	It Can't Be Wrong/ I Waited So Long	1960	12.00

SAVOY

Number	Title (A Side/B Side)	Yr	NM
❑ 1606	Cry, You Crazy Heart/ Step Up and Rescue Me	1960	12.00
❑ 4357	Sinner Man/God	197?	5.00

WARWICK

Number	Title (A Side/B Side)	Yr	NM
❑ 590	Shake a Hand/ It Hurts to My Heart	1960	12.00
❑ 620	Johnny, Don't/Obey My Rules	1961	12.00
❑ 638	It Can't Be Wrong/ It's Nice to Know	1961	12.00

Albums

COLLECTABLES

Number	Title	Yr	NM
❑ COL-5122	Golden Classics	1988	10.00

WARWICK

Number	Title	Yr	NM
❑ W 2031 [M]	Shake a Hand	1961	600.00

ADAMS, JERRI

45s

COLUMBIA

Number	Title (A Side/B Side)	Yr	NM
❑ 4-40279	Alone Together/Two's a Crowd When Only One's in Love	1954	15.00
❑ 4-40415	Guess I Had Too Much to Dream Last Night/ Snow Dreams	1955	15.00
❑ 4-40615	Happiness Is a Thing Called Joe/Take My Hand, Show Me the Way	1955	15.00
❑ 4-40690	If I Forget You/Walk Fast	1956	15.00
❑ 4-40888	A Little Bit of Kindness/ Suddenly (The Meeting)	1957	12.00
❑ 4-40992	Looking for Someone to Love/ I'm All Right Now	1957	12.00
❑ 4-41111	Every Night About This Time/ My Heart Tells Me	1958	12.00

FRATERNITY

Number	Title (A Side/B Side)	Yr	NM
❑ F-874	Ivory Tower/All Around This Heart	1961	10.00

7-Inch Extended Plays

COLUMBIA

Number	Title	Yr	NM
❑ B-9162	(contents unknown)	1956	12.00
❑ B-9162 [PS]	It's Cool Inside, Vol. 2	1956	12.00

ADAMS, JOHNNY

45s

ARIOLA AMERICA

Number	Title (A Side/B Side)	Yr	NM
❑ 7701	After All the Good Is Gone/ Chasing Rainbows	1978	5.00
❑ 7718	Selfish/One Fine Day	1978	5.00

ATLANTIC

Number	Title (A Side/B Side)	Yr	NM
❑ 2834	More Than One Way/You Got Your Kind of Life to Live	1971	10.00
❑ 2887	Salt of the Earth/I'll Carry You	1972	10.00
❑ 2905	I Wish It Would Rain/ You're a Lady	1972	10.00

GAMMA

Number	Title (A Side/B Side)	Yr	NM
❑ 101	Best of Luck to You/Sharing You	197?	6.00

GONE

Number	Title (A Side/B Side)	Yr	NM
❑ 5147	Going to the City/I'm Grateful	1964	50.00

HEP ME

Number	Title (A Side/B Side)	Yr	NM
❑ 132	Spanish Harlem/Feel the Beat, Feel the Heat	197?	8.00
❑ 137	After All the Good Is Gone/ Chasing Rainbows	197?	8.00
❑ 147	Love Me Now/I Only Wanna Be with You	197?	6.00
❑ 160	I Believe in You/It Only Rains on Me	197?	6.00
❑ 162	I Live My Whole World at Night/ (There's) No Gettin' Over Me	197?	8.00

MODERN

Number	Title (A Side/B Side)	Yr	NM
❑ 1036	No In Between/ Don't Wait Too Long	1967	15.00
❑ 1044	One Day/Your Kind of Love	1967	15.00

PACEMAKER

Number	Title (A Side/B Side)	Yr	NM
❑ 240	A Place Called Home/ Spunky Onions	1965	20.00
❑ 249	When I'll Stop Loving You/ A Man Will Shed a Few Tears	1965	20.00
❑ 255	Let Them Talk/Operator	1965	20.00

PAID

Number	Title (A Side/B Side)	Yr	NM
❑ 105	Love Me Now/I Only Want to Be with You	1980	6.00
❑ 117	I'm Afraid to Let You Into My Life/Hell Yes I Cheated	1981	6.00

RIC

Number	Title (A Side/B Side)	Yr	NM
❑ 961	I Won't Cry/Who Are You	1959	25.00
❑ 963	Come On/Nowhere to Go	1959	25.00
❑ 966	Bells Are Ringing/ Teach Me to Forget	1960	20.00
❑ 971	Let the Wind Blow/ Someone for Me	1960	20.00
❑ 976	You Can Make It If You Try/ Closer to You	1960	20.00
❑ 980	Wedding Day/O, So Nice	1961	20.00
❑ 983	I Solemnly Promise/ Life Is Just a Struggle	1961	20.00

Except when noted otherwise, VG = 25% of NM, and VG+ = 50% of NM. (Example: VG = $2.00, VG+ = $4.00 and NM = $8.00.)

Number	Title (A Side/B Side)	Yr	NM
❑ 986	A Losing Battle/Who's Gonna Love You	1962	20.00
❑ 992	Showdown/Tra La La	1962	20.00
RON			
❑ 995	I Want to Do Everything for You/Lonely Drifter	196?	15.00
❑ 996	Cold, Cold Heart/Coming 'Round the Mountain	196?	15.00
SSS INTERNATIONAL			
❑ 750	Release Me/You Make a New Man Out of Me	1968	15.00
❑ 770	Reconsider Me/If I Could See You One More Time	1969	15.00
❑ 780	I Can't Be All Bad/In a Moment of Weakness	1969	15.00
❑ 787	Proud Woman/Real Live Livin' Hurtin' Man	1970	12.00
❑ 797	Georgia Mountain Dew/Real Live Livin' Hurtin' Man	1970	12.00
❑ 809	I Won't Cry/I Want to Walk Through This Life with You	197?	12.00
❑ 831	South Side of Soul Street/Something Worth Leaving For	197?	12.00
❑ 865	Too Much Pride/I Don't Worry Myself	197?	10.00
❑ 867	Kiss the Hurt Away/Something Worth Leaving For	197?	10.00
❑ 870	Born to Love You/You're a Bad Habit Baby	197?	10.00
❑ 873	How Can I Prove I Love You/Just Call Me Darling	197?	10.00
WATCH			
❑ 1906	Release Me/You Make a New Man Out of Me	1968	30.00
❑ 6330	I Brought It On Myself/I Believe I'll Find Happiness	196?	40.00
❑ 6333	A Part of Me/Some Day	196?	40.00
Albums			
ANALOGUE PRODUCTIONS			
❑ APP 028	Johnny Adams Sings Doc Pomus — The Real Me	199?	20.00
ARIOLA AMERICA			
❑ SW 50038	After All the Good Is Gone	1978	15.00
CHELSEA			
❑ CHL 525	Stand By Me	1977	25.00
HEP ME			
❑ 159	Christmas in New Orleans	197?	15.00
ROUNDER			
❑ 2044	From the Heart	1984	12.00
❑ 2049	After Dark	1986	12.00
❑ 2059	Room with a View of the Blues	1988	12.00
❑ 2095	Walking on a Tightrope	1989	12.00
SSS INTERNATIONAL			
❑ 5	Heart and Soul	1969	20.00

ADAMS, MIKE, AND THE RED JACKETS

Number	Title (A Side/B Side)	Yr	NM
Albums			
CROWN			
❑ CST-255 [S]	Twist Contest	1962	30.00
❑ CST-312 [S] *—Black vinyl*	Surfer's Beat	1963	30.00
❑ CST-312 [S] *—Red vinyl*	Surfer's Beat	1963	100.00
❑ CLP-5255 [M]	Twist Contest	1962	25.00
❑ CLP-5312 [M]	Surfer's Beat	1963	25.00

ADAMS, NANCY

Number	Title (A Side/B Side)	Yr	NM
45s			
BUENA VISTA			
❑ 495	Love/Robin Hood	1974	8.00
MEGA			
❑ 0076	I'm Leaving You/Pretty Lies	1972	8.00
MGM			
❑ 14059	California Dream Boy/One Tiny Taco	1969	10.00
RCA VICTOR			
❑ 47-8354	You've Got to Show Me/Somebody's in My Orchard	1964	12.00
❑ 47-8410	Lipstick Paint a Smile on Me/I Wanna Hear It from You	1964	12.00
❑ 47-8529	Nothing Is Too Good for You/Give It a Go	1965	12.00
❑ 47-8599	Love Is/Little Gold Screw	1965	12.00
❑ 47-8650	I'm Gonna Build a Fence/Go On!	1965	12.00
Albums			
MEGA			
❑ M31-1018	Nancy Adams and the Deer Creek Fundamentalists	1972	20.00

ADAMS, RICHIE

Number	Title (A Side/B Side)	Yr	NM
45s			
BELTONE			
❑ 1001	No Mistakin' It/The Right Way	1961	15.00
❑ 1011	Two Initials (In a Heart)/What Took You So Long	1961	15.00
CONGRESS			
❑ 217	I Understand/Lookin' for the Blues	1964	15.00
❑ 226	Are You Changing/The King	1964	15.00
❑ 232	Slippin' Away/What Am I	1965	15.00
❑ 248	Every Window in the City/I Ain't Gonna Make It Without You	1965	15.00
❑ 256	Road to Nowhere/I Can't Escape from You	1965	60.00
IMPERIAL			
❑ 5806	Something Inside of Me Died/I Got Eyes	1962	15.00
❑ 5838	My Prayer of Love/Pakistan	1962	15.00
❑ 5856	It's Worth It/Test of Love	1962	15.00
MCA			
❑ 41182	The Best of the Rest of Our Lives/Warm	1980	4.00
MGM			
❑ 13629	You Were Mine/Better Off Without You	1966	10.00
P.I.P.			
❑ 6519	Mamacita/Lisa Lisa	1976	4.00
RIBBON			
❑ 6910	Lonely One/Tell Me Baby Did You Wait	1960	12.00
❑ 6913	Back to School/Don't Go, My Love, Don't Go	1960	12.00

ADAMS, RUSH

Number	Title (A Side/B Side)	Yr	NM
45s			
KING			
❑ 1270	Counterfeit Heart/Crying for the Carolines	1953	20.00
❑ 1284	No One to Cry To/I'm Sorry Dear	1953	20.00
❑ 1321	Bluebirds Singing in the Rain/Just One Kiss Goodnight	1954	20.00
❑ 1330	Arizona/Then I'll Be Happy	1954	20.00
MGM			
❑ K11834	It Was So Beautiful/Love Can Make an Earthquake	1954	20.00
❑ K11873	All of You/I Go Out of My Mind	1954	20.00
❑ K11953	Only for You/The Rose in Her Hair	1955	20.00
❑ K12051	How Can I Forget/At Last We're Alone	1955	20.00
❑ K12145	I Love You to the Point of No Return/Love Plays the Strings of a Banjo	1955	20.00
❑ K12228	The Birds and the Bees/My Buddy's Girls	1956	15.00
❑ K12299	The Best Things in Life Are Free/The Crazy Lips	1956	15.00
VIRGO			
❑ 1001	Perfection/Lover (Do You Really, Really Love Me)	1959	15.00
ZEPHYR			
❑ 70-014	Dancing in the Streets/Kisses	1957	20.00

ADDEO, NICKY

Number	Title (A Side/B Side)	Yr	NM
45s			
EARLS			
❑ 1533	Gloria/Bring Back Your Heart	19??	10.00
MELODY			
❑ 1417	Where There Is Love/You Can Depend on Me	1964	25.00
REVELATION			
❑ 7-101	Danny Boy/A Lovely Way to Spend An Evening	1964	500.00
SAVOY			
❑ 200 *—Black vinyl*	Gloria/Bring Back Your Heart	1963	200.00
❑ 200 *—Green vinyl*	Gloria/Bring Back Your Heart	1963	300.00
❑ 200 *—Red vinyl*	Gloria/Bring Back Your Heart	1963	400.00
SELSOM			
❑ 104	Over the Rainbow/Fool #2	1965	200.00

ADDERLEY, CANNONBALL

Number	Title (A Side/B Side)	Yr	NM
45s			
BLUE NOTE			
❑ 1737	Autumn Leaves (Part 1)/Autumn Leaves (Part 2)	1959	10.00
❑ 1738	Somethin' Else (Part 1)/Somethin' Else (Part 2)	1959	10.00
❑ 1739	One for Daddy-O (Part 1)/One for Daddy-O (Part 2)	1959	10.00
CAPITOL			
❑ 2064	Oh Babe/Games	1967	6.00
❑ 2299	Hamba Nami/Gumba Gumba	1968	6.00
❑ 2399	Zorba/Sweet Emma	1969	6.00
❑ 2698	Country Preacher/Hummin'	1970	5.00
❑ 2798	Marabi/Oh Babe	1970	5.00
❑ 2939	The Price You Got to Pay to Be Free/Run Away Sunshine	1970	5.00
❑ 3041	Down in Black Bottom/Get Up Off Your Knees	1971	5.00
❑ 5281	Goodbye Charlie/Little Boy with Sad Eyes	1964	8.00
❑ 5374	Matchmaker/Chavaleh	1965	8.00
❑ 5457	Shake a Lady/Cyclops	1965	8.00
❑ 5648	Money in the Pocket/Hear Me Talking to You	1966	6.00
❑ 5736	Sticks/Cannon's Theme	1966	6.00
❑ 5798	Mercy, Mercy, Mercy/Games	1966	7.00
❑ 5877	Why Am I Treated So Bad/I'm On My Way	1967	6.00
❑ 5968	Walk Tall/Do, Do, Do	1967	6.00
FANTASY			
❑ 706	Inside Straight/Saudade	1973	5.00
MERCURY			
❑ 71712	Limehouse Blues/Stars Fell on Alabama	1960	10.00
RIVERSIDE			
❑ 415	Things Are Getting Better (Part 1)/Things Are Getting Better (Part 2)	1958	12.00
❑ 428	Poor Butterfly (Part 1)/Poor Butterfly (Part 2)	1958	12.00
❑ 432	This Year (Part 1)/This Year (Part 2)	1959	12.00
❑ 442	Jeanine (Part 1)/Jeanine (Part 2)	1959	12.00
❑ 443	The Word Song/Sassier	1959	12.00
❑ 454	Sack of Woe (Part 1)/Sack of Woe (Part 2)	1960	10.00
❑ 457	African Waltz/Kelly Blue	1961	10.00
❑ 465	The Chant (Part 1)/The Chant (Part 2)	1961	10.00
❑ 4501	The Uptown/Something Different	1962	8.00
❑ 4509	Gemini (Part 1)/Gemini (Part 2)	1962	8.00
❑ 4528	Blue Brass Groove/This Here	1963	8.00
❑ 4541	The Jive Samba/Lillie	1963	8.00
❑ 4562	Brother John/Tengo Tango	1964	8.00
❑ 4573	Nippon Soul/Tengo Tango	1964	8.00
Albums			
AMBASSADOR			
❑ S-98053	The Love Album	197?	15.00
BLUE NOTE			
❑ BN-LA169-F *—Reissue*	Somethin' Else	1973	12.00
❑ LT-169 *—Another reissue*	Somethin' Else	1981	10.00
❑ BLP-1595 [M] *—Regular version; W. 63rd St. address on label*	Somethin' Else	1958	120.00
❑ BLP-1595 [M] *—"Deep groove" version; W. 63rd St. address on label*	Somethin' Else	1958	250.00
❑ BLP-1595 [M] *—"New York, USA" address on label*	Somethin' Else	1963	30.00
❑ BLP-1595 [M] *—Classic Records reissue on 200-gram vinyl*	Somethin' Else	2002	30.00
❑ BLP-1595C [(2)] *—"Comparison Pack"; contains both the mono and stereo versions of the LP; Classic Records issue on 200-gram vinyl*	Somethin' Else	2002	50.00
❑ BST-1595 [S] *—Regular version; W. 63rd St. address on label*	Somethin' Else	1959	100.00
❑ BST-1595 [S] *—"Deep groove" version; W. 63rd St. address on label*	Somethin' Else	1959	150.00
❑ BST-1595 [S] *—Classic Records reissue on 200-gram vinyl*	Somethin' Else	2002	30.00
❑ ST-46338 *—Audiophile reissue*	Somethin' Else	1997	20.00
❑ BST-81595 *—"The Finest in Jazz Since 1939" label*	Somethin' Else	1984	10.00
❑ BST-81595 *—Classic Records reissue on 180-gram vinyl*	Somethin' Else	199?	30.00
❑ BST-81595 [S] *—"New York, USA" address on label*	Somethin' Else	1963	25.00
❑ BST-81595 [S] *—With "A Division of Liberty Records" on label*	Somethin' Else	1966	20.00
CAPITOL			
❑ ST-162	Cannonball in Person	1968	20.00
❑ SKAO-404	Country Preacher	1970	25.00
❑ ST-484	Experience in E, Tensity, Dialogues	1970	40.00
❑ SWBB-636 [(2)]	The Price You Got to Pay to Be Free	1971	100.00
❑ STBB-697 [(2)]	Walk Tall/Quiet Nights	1971	20.00

A

Number	Title (A Side/B Side)	Yr	NM
SWBO-812 [(2)]	Cannonball Adderley and Friends	1971	20.00
SWBO-846 [(2)]	The Black Messiah	1972	100.00
ST 2203 [S]	Domination	1964	25.00
T 2203 [M]	Domination	1964	20.00
ST 2216 [S]	Fiddler on the Roof	1965	25.00
T 2216 [M]	Fiddler on the Roof	1965	20.00
ST 2284 [S]	Live Session	1965	25.00
T 2284 [M]	Live Session	1965	20.00
SM-2399	Cannonball Adderley — Live!	1976	10.00
ST 2399 [S]	Cannonball Adderley — Live!	1965	25.00
T 2399 [M]	Cannonball Adderley — Live!	1965	20.00
ST 2531 [S]	Great Love Themes	1966	25.00
T 2531 [M]	Great Love Themes	1966	20.00
ST 2617 [S]	Why Am I Treated So Bad?	1966	20.00
T 2617 [M]	Why Am I Treated So Bad?	1966	15.00
SM-2663	Mercy, Mercy, Mercy!	1976	10.00
ST 2663 [S]	Mercy, Mercy, Mercy!	1967	15.00
ST-8-2663 [S]	Mercy, Mercy, Mercy!	1969	20.00
—Capitol Record Club edition			
T 2663 [M]	Mercy, Mercy, Mercy!	1967	20.00
ST 2822 [S]	74 Miles Away — Walk Tall	1967	20.00
T 2822 [M]	74 Miles Away — Walk Tall	1967	40.00
ST-2877	Cannonball Adderley and the Bossa Rio Sextet with Sergio Mendes	1968	25.00
—Reissue of 8 of the 10 tracks from Riverside 9455			
SKAO 2939	The Best of Cannonball Adderley	1968	15.00
—Black label with colorband			
ST 2987	Accent on Africa	1968	20.00
ST-11008	Fiddler on the Roof	1972	15.00
—Reissue of 2216			
SABB-11120 [(2)]	The Soul of the Bible	1973	120.00
—Reproductions exist			
ST-11121	Happy People	1973	40.00
SVBB-11233 [(2)]	Cannonball Adderley and Friends	1974	15.00
—Reissue of 812			
ST-11484	Music, You All	1975	15.00
SM-11817	Cannonball Adderley and Friends, Vol. 1	1978	10.00
SM-11838	Cannonball Adderley and Friends, Vol. 2	1978	10.00
SN-16002	The Best of Cannonball Adderley	1979	8.00
SN-16153	Mercy, Mercy, Mercy!	1981	8.00
—Budget-line reissue			
SKAO-80404	Country Preacher	1970	30.00
—Capitol Record Club edition			
SKAO-502939	The Best of Cannonball Adderley	1976	15.00
—Columbia House edition; orange labels			
DOBRE			
1008	Cannonball, Vol. 1	1977	12.00
EMARCY			
EMS-2-404 [(2)]	Beginnings	1976	20.00
MG-36043 [M]	Julian "Cannonball" Adderley	1955	80.00
MG-36063 [M]	Julian "Cannonball" Adderley and Strings	1956	80.00
MG-36077 [M]	In the Land of Hi-Fi	1956	100.00
MG-36110 [M]	Sophisticated Swing	1957	70.00
MG-36135 [M]	Cannonball's Sharpshooters	1958	60.00
MG-36146 [M]	Jump for Joy	1958	80.00
SR-80017 [S]	Jump for Joy	1958	60.00
EVEREST ARCHIVE OF FOLK & JAZZ			
FS-261	Cannonball Adderley and John Coltrane	1973	12.00
—Abridged reissue of Limelight 86009			
FS-291	Cannonabll Adderley with Sergio Mendes	197?	12.00
FANTASY			
FSP 2 [DJ]	Musical Highliights from Big Man	1975	30.00
OJC-032	Things Are Getting Better	1982	10.00
OJC-035	Cannonball Adderley Quintet in San Francisco	1982	10.00
OJC-105	Know What I Mean?	1984	10.00
OJC-142	Cannonball Adderley Sextet In New York	1985	10.00
OJC-258	African Waltz	1987	10.00
OJC-306	The Cannonball Adderley Quintet Plus	1988	10.00
OJC-361	Portrait of Cannonball	1989	10.00
OJC-435	Nippon Soul	1990	15.00
F-9435	Inside Straight	1973	20.00
F-9445	Love, Sex and the Zodiac	1974	100.00
F-9455	Pyramid	1974	40.00
F-9505	Lovers	1975	40.00
F-79004 [(2)]	Phenix	1975	25.00
F-79006 [(2)]	Big Man	1976	20.00
LANDMARK			
LLP-1301	The Cannonball Adderley Collection Vol. 1: Them Dirty Blues	1985	10.00
LLP-1302	The Cannonball Adderley Collection Vol. 2: Cannonball's Bossa Nova	1985	10.00
LLP-1303	The Cannonball Adderley Collection Vol. 3: Jazz Workshop Revisited	1985	10.00
LLP-1304	The Cannonball Adderley Collection Vol. 4: Cannonball and the Poll-Winners	1985	10.00
LLP-1305	The Cannonball Adderley Collection Vol. 5: At the Lighthouse	1985	10.00
LLP-1306	The Cannonball Adderley Collection Vol. 6: Cannonball Takes Charge	1985	10.00
LLP-1307	The Cannonball Adderley Collection Vol. 7: Cannonball in Europe	1985	10.00
LIMELIGHT			
LM 82009 [M]	Cannonball and Coltrane	1964	25.00
—Reissue of Mercury 20449			
LS 86009 [S]	Cannonball and Coltrane	1964	20.00
—Reissue of Mercury 60134			
MERCURY			
MG-20449 [M]	Cannonball Adderley Quintet in Chicago	1959	50.00
MG-20530 [M]	Jump for Joy	1960	40.00
—Reissue of EmArcy 36146			
MG-20531 [M]	Cannonball's Sharpshooters	1960	40.00
—Reissue of EmArcy 36135			
MG-20616 [M]	Cannonball En Route	1961	50.00
MG-20652 [M]	The Lush Side of Cannonball Adderley	1961	40.00
—Reissue of EmArcy 36063			
SR-60134 [S]	Cannonball Adderley Quintet in Chicago	1960	40.00
SR-60530 [S]	Jump for Joy	1960	30.00
SR-60531 [S]	Cannonball's Sharpshooters	1960	30.00
SR-60616 [S]	Cannonball En Route	1961	40.00
SR-60652 [R]	The Lush Side of Cannonball Adderley	1961	25.00
MILESTONE			
M-9030	Cannonball Adderley in New Orleans	197?	20.00
M-9106	The Sextet	198?	15.00
M-47001 [(2)]	Eight Giants	1973	15.00
M-47029 [(2)]	The Japanese Concerts	1975	25.00
M-47039 [(2)]	Coast to Coast	1976	25.00
M-47053 [(2)]	What I Mean	1979	15.00
M-47059 [(2)]	Alabama/Africa	1982	15.00
PABLO LIVE			
2308238	What Is This Thing Called Soul	1984	12.00
PICKWICK			
SPC-3128	I Got It Bad and That Ain't Good	196?	10.00
SPC-3255	Quiet Nights of Quiet Stars	196?	10.00
—Reissue of eight of the 10 tracks on Riverside 9455; co-credited to Sergio Mendes			
RIVERSIDE			
RLP 12-269 [M]	Portrait of Cannonball	1958	100.00
RLP 12-286 [M]	Things Are Getting Better	1959	100.00
RLP 12-303 [M]	Cannonball Takes Charge	1959	100.00
RLP 12-311 [M]	Cannonball Adderley Quintet in San Francisco	1959	80.00
RLP 12-322 [M]	Them Dirty Blues	1960	80.00
RLP 344 [M]	Cannonball Adderley Quintet at the Lighthouse	1960	50.00
RLP 355 [M]	Cannonball Adderley and the Poll-Winners	1960	50.00
RLP 377 [M]	African Waltz	1961	50.00
RLP 388 [M]	Cannonball Adderley Quintet Plus	1961	50.00
RLP 404 [M]	Cannonball Adderley Sextet In New York	1962	50.00
RLP 416 [M]	Cannonball's Greatest Hits	1962	50.00
RLP 433 [M]	Know What I Mean?	1962	40.00
RLP 444 [M]	Jazz Workshop Revisited	1963	40.00
RLP 455 [M]	Cannonball's Bossa Nova	1963	40.00
RLP 477 [M]	Nippon Soul — Recorded in Concert in Tokyo	1964	40.00
RM 499 [M]	Cannonball in Europe	1964	40.00
RLP 1128 [S]	Things Are Getting Better	1959	80.00
RLP 1148 [S]	Cannonball Takes Charge	1959	80.00
RLP 1157 [S]	Cannonball Adderley Quintet in San Francisco	1959	60.00
RLP 1170 [S]	Them Dirty Blues	1960	60.00
RS 3038	The Best of Cannonball Adderley	1968	25.00
RS 3041	Planet Earth	1969	40.00
6051	Know What I Mean?	197?	15.00
—Reissue of 9433			
6062	Cannonball Adderley Quintet in San Francisco	197?	15.00
—Reissue of 1157			
6108	Cannonball Adderley Sextet In New York	197?	15.00
—Reissue of 9404			
6122	Things Are Getting Better	197?	15.00
—Reissue of 1128			
RS 9344 [S]	Cannonball Adderley Quintet at the Lighthouse	1960	40.00
RS 9355 [S]	Cannonball Adderley and the Poll-Winners	1960	40.00
RS 9377 [S]	African Waltz	1961	40.00
RS 9388 [S]	Cannonball Adderley Quintet Plus	1961	40.00
RS 9404 [S]	Cannonball Adderley Sextet In New York	1962	40.00
RS 9416 [S]	Cannonball's Greatest Hits	1962	40.00
RS 9433 [S]	Know What I Mean?	1962	40.00
RS 9444 [S]	Jazz Workshop Revisited	1963	40.00
RS 9455 [S]	Cannonball's Bossa Nova	1963	40.00
RS 9477 [S]	Nippon Soul — Recorded in Concert in Tokyo	1964	40.00
RS 9499 [S]	Cannonball in Europe	1964	30.00
SAVOY			
MG-12018 [M]	Presenting Cannonball	1955	150.00
—Band pictured on cover			
MG-12018 [M]	Presenting Cannonball	196?	80.00
—Cannonballs pictured on cover with band members merely listed			
SAVOY JAZZ			
SJC-401	Presenting Cannonball	1985	12.00
—Reissue of Savoy 12018			
SJL-1195	Discoveries	1987	15.00
SJL-2206 [(2)]	Spontaneous Combustion	1976	15.00
SEARS			
SPS-460	Jump for Joy	196?	15.00
TRIP			
TLP-5573 [M]	In the Land of Hi-Fi	197?	15.00
WING			
SRW-16362 [S]	Cannonball Adderley Quintet	196?	20.00
WONDERLAND/RIVERSIDE			
RLP 1435 [M]	A Child's Introduction to Jazz	196?	50.00
—Adderley narrates an album introducing the works of such artists as Armstrong, Monk, Waller, etc.			

ADDERLEY, CANNONBALL AND NAT

Albums

Number	Title (A Side/B Side)	Yr	NM
LIMELIGHT			
LM 82032 [M]	Them Adderleys	1966	50.00
LS 86032 [S]	Them Adderleys	1966	50.00

ADDERLEY, NAT

Albums

Number	Title (A Side/B Side)	Yr	NM
A&M			
LP-2005 [M]	You, Baby	1968	25.00
—Mono is promo only			
SP-3005 [S]	You, Baby	1968	15.00
SP9-3005	You, Baby	1983	15.00
—"Audio Master Plus" reissue			
SP-3017	Calling Out Loud	1969	15.00
ATLANTIC			
1439 [M]	Autobiography	1965	15.00
SD 1439 [S]	Autobiography	1965	20.00
1460 [M]	Sayin' Something	1966	15.00
SD 1460 [S]	Sayin' Something	1966	20.00
1475 [M]	Live at Memory Lane	1967	20.00
SD 1475 [S]	Live at Memory Lane	1967	15.00
CAPITOL			
SVBB-11025 [(2)]	Cannonball Adderley Presents Soul Zodiac	1972	100.00
EMARCY			
MG-36091 [M]	Introducing Nat Adderley	1955	80.00
MG-36100 [M]	To the Ivy League from Nat	1956	80.00
FANTASY			
OJC-255	Branching Out	1987	10.00
—Reissue of Riverside 12-285			
OJC-363	The Work Song	198?	10.00
—Reissue of Riverside 1167			
OJC-648	In the Bag	1991	12.00
—Reissue of Jazzland 975			
GALAXY			
5120	Little New York Midtown Music	197?	10.00
JAZZLAND			
JLP-47 [M]	Naturally!	1961	30.00
JLP-75 [M]	In the Bag	1962	30.00
JLP-947 [S]	Naturally!	1961	40.00
JLP-975 [S]	In the Bag	1962	40.00
LITTLE DAVID			
LD 1012	Hummin'	1975	12.00
MILESTONE			
MSP-9009	Natural Soul	1968	15.00
MSP-9016	The Scavenger	1968	15.00
47047 [(2)]	Work Songs	197?	12.00
PRESTIGE			
10090	Double Exposure	1974	12.00
RIVERSIDE			
RLP 12-285 [M]	Branching Out	1958	50.00
RLP 12-301 [M]	Much Brass	1959	50.00

Except when noted otherwise, VG = 25% of NM, and VG+ = 50% of NM. (Example: VG = $2.00, VG+ = $4.00 and NM = $8.00.)

A

Number	Title (A Side/B Side)	Yr	NM
❑ RLP 12-318 [M]	The Work Song	1960	40.00
❑ RLP-330 [M]	That's Right!	1960	30.00
❑ RM-474 [M]	Little Big Horn!	1964	30.00
❑ RLP-1143 [S]	Much Brass	1959	50.00
❑ RLP-1167 [S]	The Work Song	1960	50.00
❑ 6041	The Work Song	197?	12.00
—Reissue			
❑ RS-9330 [S]	That's Right!	1960	40.00
❑ RS-9474 [S]	Little Big Horn!	1964	40.00
SAVOY			
❑ MG-12021 [M]	That's Nat	1955	80.00
SAVOY JAZZ			
❑ SJL-1128	That's Nat	198?	10.00
—Reissue of Savoy 12021			
STEEPLECHASE			
❑ SCS-1059	Don't Look Back	198?	10.00
THERESA			
❑ TR-117	On the Move	198?	10.00
❑ TR-122	Blue Autumn	1987	10.00
WING			
❑ MGW-60000 [M]	Introducing Nat Adderley	1956	50.00

ADDRISI, DICK

45s

Number	Title (A Side/B Side)	Yr	NM
VALIANT			
❑ 742	You're Bad/Excuse Me	1966	12.00

ADDRISI BROTHERS, THE

45s

Number	Title (A Side/B Side)	Yr	NM
BELL			
❑ 45434	Somebody Found Her/Who Do You Think I Am	1974	4.00
BRAD			
❑ 003	I'll Be True/Everybody's Happy	1958	35.00
BUDDAH			
❑ 566	Slow Dancin' Don't Turn Me On (Short)/Slow Dancin' Don't Turn Me On (Long)	1977	5.00
❑ 579	Does She Do It Like She Dances/Baby, Love Is a Two-Way Street	1977	4.00
❑ 587	Never My Love/Emergency	1977	4.00
COLUMBIA			
❑ 45521	We've Got to Get It On Again/You Make It All Worthwhile	1972	5.00
❑ 45610	One Last Time/I Can Feel You	1972	5.00
❑ 45705	Lifetime/I Can Count on You	1972	5.00
DEL-FI			
❑ 4116	Cherrystone/Lilies Grow High	1959	30.00
❑ 4120	Saving My Kisses/Un Jarro	1959	30.00
❑ 4125	It's Love/Back to the Old Salt Mine	1959	30.00
❑ 4130	Gonna See My Baby/Ven Ami	1959	25.00
ELEKTRA			
❑ 47203	Honey Come Home/Red-Eye Flight	1981	4.00
IMPERIAL			
❑ 5715	What a Night for Love/Poor Little Girls	1960	20.00
POM POM			
❑ 4160	The Dance Is Over/Socialite	1962	25.00
PRIVATE STOCK			
❑ 45,012	Wait for Me/You Made All the Difference	1975	4.00
SCOTTI BROTHERS			
❑ 500	Ghost Dancer/Ghost Dancer	1979	4.00
❑ 500 [PS]	Ghost Dancer/Ghost Dancer	1979	6.00
—Promo-only title sleeve			
❑ 506	As Long As the Music Keeps Playing/(B-side unknown)	1979	4.00
VALIANT			
❑ 720	Mr. Love/Side by Side	1965	12.00
❑ 6047	Love Me Baby/The Way You Look at Him	1964	12.00
❑ 6058	C'mon Home Baby/Little Miss Sad	1964	15.00
WARNER BROS.			
❑ 5268	The Dance Is Over (Dance with Me)/Sleeping Beauty	1962	15.00
❑ 7249	Time to Love/Good News	1968	10.00

Albums

Number	Title (A Side/B Side)	Yr	NM
BUDDAH			
❑ BDS-5694	Addrisi Brothers	1977	10.00
COLUMBIA			
❑ KC 31296	We've Got to Get It On Again	1972	12.00

ADELPHIS, THE

45s

Number	Title (A Side/B Side)	Yr	NM
RIM			
❑ 2020	Darlin' It's You/Kathleen	1958	100.00
—Artist's name spelled correctly as "Adelphis"			
❑ 2020	Darlin' It's You/Kathleen	1958	150.00
—Artist's name listed as "Adelphies"			

ADLIBS, THE

Not to be confused with THE AD LIBS, this is a British group.

45s

Number	Title (A Side/B Side)	Yr	NM
INTERPHON			
❑ 7717	Neighbour, Neighbour/Lovely Ladies	1965	10.00

ADMIRAL TONES, THE

45s

Number	Title (A Side/B Side)	Yr	NM
FELSTED			
❑ 8563	Rocksville, Pa./Hey Hey Pretty Baby	1959	30.00
FUTURE			
❑ 1006	Rocksville, Pa./Hey Hey Pretty Baby	1959	60.00

ADMIRALS, THE

45s

Number	Title (A Side/B Side)	Yr	NM
KING			
❑ 4772	Oh Yes/Left with a Broken Heart	1955	250.00
❑ 4782	Close Your Eyes/Give Me Love	1955	250.00
❑ 4792	It's a Sad, Sad Feeling/Ow	1955	50.00
—With Lucky Millinder			

ADMIRATIONS, THE

More than one group.

45s

Number	Title (A Side/B Side)	Yr	NM
ATOMIC			
❑ 12871	Dear Lady/Memories Are Here to Stay	195?	200.00
BRUNSWICK			
❑ 55332	Hey Mama/Lonely Street	1967	20.00
HULL			
❑ 1202	Moonlight/Ain't It Funny	1965	200.00
KELLWAY			
❑ 108	Over the Rainbow/In My Younger Days	196?	10.00
MERCURY			
❑ 71521	The Bells of Roja Rita/Little Bo Poop	1959	40.00
❑ 71883	To the Aisle/Hey Senorita	1962	200.00
ONE-DERFUL			
❑ 4849	Wait Till I Get to Know You/(Instrumental)	1967	25.00
❑ 4851	Don't Leave Me/All for You	1967	25.00

ADORABLES, THE

45s

Number	Title (A Side/B Side)	Yr	NM
GOLDEN WORLD			
❑ 4	Daddy Please/Deep Freeze	1964	25.00
❑ 10	School's All Over/Be	1964	25.00
❑ 25	Ooh Boy!/Devil in His Eyes	1965	80.00
PEACOCK			
❑ 1924	The Drive/Baby, Come and Get It	1963	12.00

ADRIAN AND THE SUNSETS

45s

Number	Title (A Side/B Side)	Yr	NM
SUNSET			
❑ 602	Breakthrough/Cherry Pie	1963	40.00
❑ 602 [PS]	Breakthrough/Cherry Pie	1963	120.00

Albums

Number	Title (A Side/B Side)	Yr	NM
SUNSET			
❑ 63-601 [M]	Breakthrough	1963	80.00
—Black vinyl			
❑ 63-601 [M]	Breakthrough	1963	150.00
—Multi-color vinyl			
❑ SD 63-601 [S]	Breakthrough	1963	150.00
—Black vinyl			
❑ SD 63-601 [S]	Breakthrough	1963	300.00
—Multi-color vinyl			

ADVANCEMENT, THE

Albums

Number	Title (A Side/B Side)	Yr	NM
PHILIPS			
❑ PHS 600328	The Advancement	1969	75.00

ADVENTURERS, THE (1)

45s

Number	Title (A Side/B Side)	Yr	NM
COLUMBIA			
❑ 42227	Rock and Roll Uprising/My Mama Done Told Me	1961	40.00

Albums

Number	Title (A Side/B Side)	Yr	NM
COLUMBIA			
❑ CL 1747 [M]	Can't Stop Twistin'	1961	60.00
❑ CS 8547 [S]	Can't Stop Twistin'	1961	80.00

ADVENTURERS, THE (U)

45s

Number	Title (A Side/B Side)	Yr	NM
BLUE ROCK			
❑ 4071	Something Bad (Is Happening)/Nobody Can Save Me	1968	8.00
CAPITOL			
❑ F-4292	Rip Van Winkle/Trail Blazer	1959	15.00
COMPASS			
❑ 7010	Easy Baby/(These Days) A Good Girl Is So Hard to Find	1967	8.00
MECCA			
❑ A-11	2 O'Clock Express/Shaggin'	1960	40.00
MIRACLE			
❑ 1	2 O'Clock Express/October Days	1960	20.00

AEROSMITH

Also see JOE PERRY PROJECT; WHITFORD-ST. HOLMES.

12-Inch Singles

Number	Title (A Side/B Side)	Yr	NM
COLUMBIA			
❑ CAS 2333 [DJ]	Dream On (Live) (same on both sides?)	1986	15.00
❑ CAS 9965 [DJ]	Falling in Love (Is Hard on the Knees) (5 versions)	1997	10.00
GEFFEN			
❑ PRO-A-2382 [DJ]	Let the Music Do the Talking (same on both sides)	1986	10.00
❑ PRO-A-2401 [DJ]	Shela (same on both sides)	1986	10.00
❑ PRO-A-2882 [DJ]	Dude (Looks Like a Lady) (4 versions)	1987	8.00
❑ PRO-A-3138 [DJ]	Rag Doll (Extended Vacation Mix) (Rockapella) (Dub)	1988	15.00
❑ PRO-A-3810 [DJ]	Love in an Elevator (3 versions)	1989	10.00
❑ PRO-A-4117 [DJ]	The Other Side (LP Version) (Matt Dike Honky Tonk Version) (Club Mix)//Theme from "Wayne's World"/My Girl	1990	12.00
❑ 20751	Dude (Looks Like a Lady)/Simoriah//Once Is Enough/The Movie	1987	10.00

45s

Number	Title (A Side/B Side)	Yr	NM
COLUMBIA			
❑ 38-08536	Chip Away the Stone/S.O.S.	1989	4.00
❑ 10034	Train Kept a-Rollin'/Spaced	1974	6.00
❑ 10105	S.O.S. (Too Bad)/Lord of the Thighs	1975	6.00
❑ 10155	Sweet Emotion/Pandora's Box	1975	5.00
❑ 10206	Walk This Way/Round and Round	1975	6.00
❑ 10253	Toys in the Attic/You See Me Crying	1975	6.00
❑ 10278	Dream On/Somebody	1975	5.00
—Contains the full-length version of A-side			
❑ 10359	Last Child/Combination	1976	5.00
❑ 10407	Home Tonight/Pandora's Box	1976	5.00
❑ 10449	Walk This Way/Uncle Salty	1976	5.00
❑ 10516	Back in the Saddle/Nobody's Fault	1977	5.00
❑ 10637	Draw the Line/Bright, Light, Fright	1977	5.00
❑ 10699	Kings and Queens/Critical Mass	1978	5.00
❑ 10727	Get It Up/Milk Cow Blues	1978	5.00
❑ 10802	Come Together/Kings and Queens	1978	5.00
❑ 10880	Chip Away the Stone (Studio)//S.O.S./Chip Away the Stone (Live)	1979	6.00
❑ 11181	Remember (Walking in the Sand)/Bone to Bone (Coney Island White Fish Boy)	1980	5.00
❑ 45894	Dream On/Somebody	1973	6.00
—Contains a remixed, edited version of A-side			
❑ 46029	Pandora's Box/Same Old Song and Dance	1974	6.00
❑ 78499	Falling in Love (Is Hard on the Knees)/Fall Together	1997	4.00
—Small hole			
❑ 78499 [PS]	Falling in Love (Is Hard on the Knees)/Fall Together	1997	4.00
❑ 78569	Hole in My Soul/Falling Off	1997	4.00
❑ 78569 [PS]	Hole in My Soul/Falling Off	1997	5.00

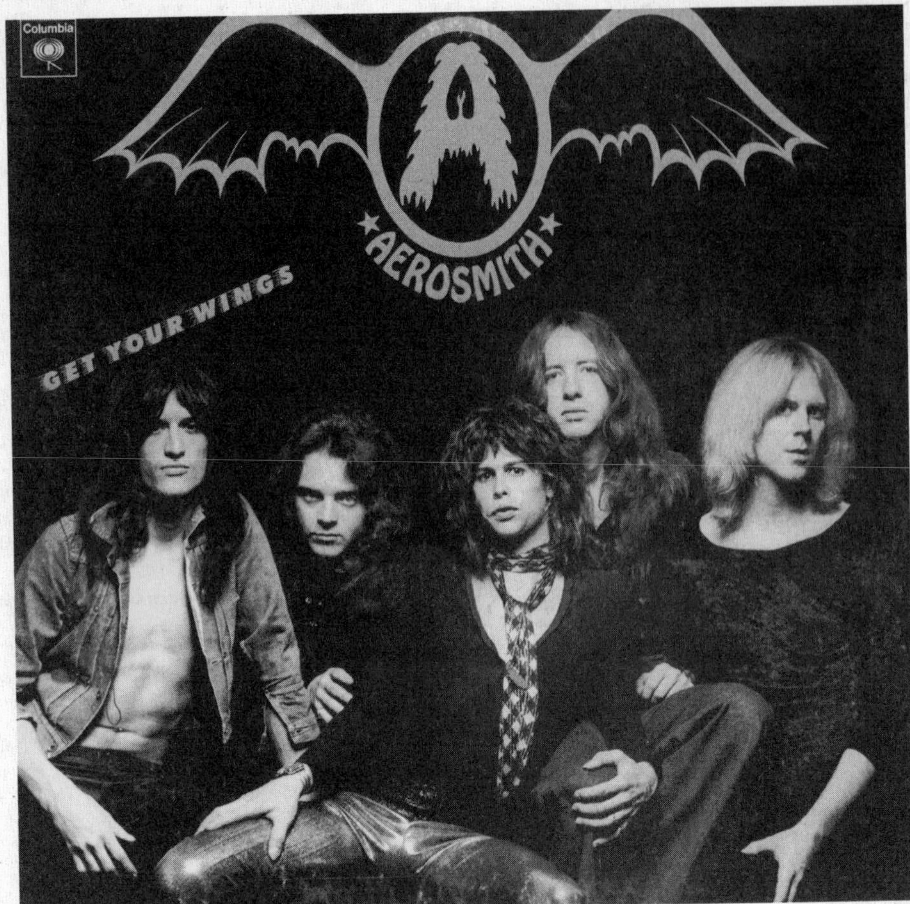

Aerosmith, *Get Your Wings*, Columbia KC 32847, 1974, **$12.**

Number	Title (A Side/B Side)	Yr	NM
❑ 78952	I Don't Want to Miss a Thing/ Animal Crackers//Taste of India (Rock Remix)	1998	4.00
❑ 78952 [PS]	I Don't Want to Miss a Thing/ Animal Crackers//Taste of India (Rock Remix)	1998	5.00
❑ 79572	Jaded/Angel's Eye	2001	3.00

GEFFEN

Number	Title (A Side/B Side)	Yr	NM
❑ 19143	Livin' on the Edge/Don't Stop	1993	3.00
❑ 19256	Cryin'/Walk On Down	1993	3.00
❑ 19264	Amazing/Fever	1993	3.00
❑ 19267	Crazy/Gotta Love It	1994	3.00
❑ 19377	Blind Man/Head First	1994	3.00
❑ 19927	The Other Side/My Girl	1990	3.00
❑ 19946	What It Takes/ Monkey on My Back	1990	3.00
❑ 22845	Love in an Elevator/ Young Lust	1989	3.00
❑ 22845 [PS]	Love in an Elevator/ Young Lust	1989	5.00
❑ 27915	Rag Doll/St. John	1988	3.00
❑ 27915 [PS]	Rag Doll/St. John	1988	5.00
❑ 28240	Dude (Looks Like a Lady)/ Simoriah	1987	3.00
❑ 28240 [PS]	Dude (Looks Like a Lady)/ Simoriah	1987	5.00
❑ 28249	Angel/Girl Keeps Coming Apart	1987	3.00
❑ 28249 [PS]	Angel/Girl Keeps Coming Apart	1987	4.00
❑ 28814	Shela/Gypsy Boots	1986	4.00
❑ 28814 [PS]	Shela/Gypsy Boots	1986	5.00

Albums

COLUMBIA

Number	Title (A Side/B Side)	Yr	NM
❑ A3S 187 [DJ]	Pure Gold from Rock 'n' Roll's Golden Boys	1976	60.00
—Promo-only compilation of the first three albums			
❑ JC 32005	Aerosmith	1977	8.00
❑ KC 32005	Aerosmith	1973	12.00
—Light blue cover, most (if not all) of which say "Featuring 'Dream On'" on front			
❑ KC 32005	Aerosmith	1973	15.00
—Orange cover with correct title "Walking The Dog"			
❑ KC 32005	Aerosmith	1973	20.00
—Orange cover with back cover typo "Walking The Dig"			
❑ PC 32005	Aerosmith	1976	10.00
—Without bar code			
❑ PC 32005	Aerosmith	1984	8.00
—With bar code			
❑ JC 32847	Get Your Wings	1977	8.00
❑ KC 32847	Get Your Wings	1974	12.00
❑ KCQ 32847 [Q]	Get Your Wings	1974	25.00
❑ PC 32847	Get Your Wings	1976	10.00
—Without bar code			
❑ PC 32847	Get Your Wings	1984	8.00
—With bar code			
❑ JC 33479	Toys in the Attic	1977	10.00
❑ PC 33479	Toys in the Attic	1975	12.00
—Without bar code			
❑ PC 33479	Toys in the Attic	1984	8.00
—With bar code			
❑ PCQ 33479 [Q]	Toys in the Attic	1975	25.00
❑ JC 34165	Rocks	1976	10.00
—Some copies have "Rocks" in quotes on the cover, others don't; no difference in value			
❑ PC 34165	Rocks	1976	12.00
—Without bar code. Some copies have "Rocks" in quotes on the cover, others don't; no difference in value			
❑ PC 34165	Rocks	1984	8.00
—With bar code			
❑ PCQ 34165 [Q]	Rocks	1976	25.00
❑ JC 34856	Draw the Line	1977	12.00
❑ PC 34856	Draw the Line	198?	8.00
❑ PC2 35564 [(2)]	Live! Bootleg	1978	15.00
❑ FC 36050	Night in the Ruts	1979	10.00
❑ PC 36050	Night in the Ruts	1984	8.00
❑ FC 36865	Aerosmith's Greatest Hits	1980	10.00
❑ PC 36865	Aerosmith's Greatest Hits	1984	8.00
❑ FC 38061	Rock in a Hard Place	1982	10.00
❑ PC 38061	Rock in a Hard Place	1984	8.00
❑ FC 40329	Classics Live	1986	10.00
❑ FC 40855	Classics Live, Vol. 2	1987	10.00
❑ FC 44487	Gems (1973-1982)	1989	10.00
❑ C 62088	Just Push Play	2001	15.00
❑ C 87025	Honkin' on Bobo	2004	15.00

GEFFEN

Number	Title (A Side/B Side)	Yr	NM
❑ GHS 24091	Done with Mirrors	1985	8.00
❑ GHS 24162	Permanent Vacation	1987	10.00
❑ GHS 24254	Pump	1989	10.00
❑ GHS 24254	Pump	2008	20.00

AESOP'S FABLES

45s

ATCO

Number	Title (A Side/B Side)	Yr	NM
❑ 6508	Girl, I've Got News for You/ Yes I'm Back	1967	8.00
❑ 6523	Take a Step/What's a Man to Do	1967	8.00
❑ 6565	Slow and Easy/The Truth	1968	8.00

CADET CONCEPT

Number	Title (A Side/B Side)	Yr	NM
❑ 7011	Temptation 'Bout to Get Me/ What Is Love	1969	8.00
❑ 7016	I'm Gonna Make You Love Me/ They Go Out and Get It	1968	8.00
❑ 7016	And When It's Over/ What Is Love	1969	8.00

Albums

CADET CONCEPT

Number	Title (A Side/B Side)	Yr	NM
❑ LPS-323	In Due Time	1969	50.00

AFDEM, JEFF, AND THE SPRINGFIELD FLUTE

Albums

BURDETTE

Number	Title (A Side/B Side)	Yr	NM
❑ 5162	Something	1969	40.00

AFFECTION COLLECTION, THE

45s

EVOLUTION

Number	Title (A Side/B Side)	Yr	NM
❑ 1004	Girl/I'll Be There	1969	12.00
❑ 1013	Watch Her Walk/I Don't Mind	1969	12.00

UNITED ARTISTS

Number	Title (A Side/B Side)	Yr	NM
❑ 50268	In Apple Blossom Time/Time Rests Heavy on My Hands	1968	10.00

Albums

EVOLUTION

Number	Title (A Side/B Side)	Yr	NM
❑ 2007	The Affection Collection	1969	20.00

AFFINITY

Albums

PARAMOUNT

Number	Title (A Side/B Side)	Yr	NM
❑ PAS-5027	Affinity	1970	25.00

AFGHAN WHIGS

45s

MONO CAT 7

Number	Title (A Side/B Side)	Yr	NM
❑ 004	Mr. Superlove/You My Flower	1993	4.00
—B-side by Ass Ponys			
❑ 004 [PS]	Mr. Superlove/You My Flower	1993	4.00

SUB POP

Number	Title (A Side/B Side)	Yr	NM
❑ 32	I Am the Sticks/White Trash Party	1989	20.00
❑ 32 [PS]	I Am the Sticks/White Trash Party	1989	20.00
—Sub Pop Singles Club, April 1989 (#6)			
❑ 84	Sister Brother/Hey Cuz	1990	10.00
❑ 84	Sister Brother/Hey Cuz	1990	10.00
—First 2,000 on red vinyl			
❑ 84 [PS]	Sister Brother/Hey Cuz	1990	5.00
❑ 142	Conjure Me/My World Is Empty	1992	10.00
—Lavender vinyl			
❑ 142	Conjure Me/My World Is Empty	1992	10.00
—White vinyl			
❑ 142 [PS]	Conjure Me/My World Is Empty	1992	10.00

Albums

COLUMBIA

Number	Title (A Side/B Side)	Yr	NM
❑ C 69450	1969	1998	12.00

SUB POP

Number	Title (A Side/B Side)	Yr	NM
❑ 60	Up In It	1990	12.00
❑ 60	Up In It	1990	25.00
—First pressings have orange vinyl and a different sleeve than the black vinyl version			
❑ 130	Congregation	1992	20.00
—Import only; made in Germany (no U.S. vinyl)			
❑ 238	Gentlemen	1993	12.00
❑ 353	Black Love	1996	12.00

ULTRASUEDE

Number	Title (A Side/B Side)	Yr	NM
❑ 001	Big Top Halloween	1988	50.00
—Approximately 2,000 copies were made			

AFRICA

45s

ODE

Number	Title (A Side/B Side)	Yr	NM
❑ ZS7-116	Here I Stand/Widow	1969	8.00
❑ ZS7-126	From Africa with Love/ Savin' All My Love	1969	8.00

AFRIQUE

45s

MAINSTREAM

Number	Title (A Side/B Side)	Yr	NM
❑ 5542	Soul Makossa/Hot Mud	1973	5.00
❑ 5547	Kumbo Coming/Hot Mud	1973	5.00

Except when noted otherwise, VG = 25% of NM, and VG+ = 50% of NM. (Example: VG = $2.00, VG+ = $4.00 and NM = $8.00.)

Number	Title (A Side/B Side)	Yr	NM
Albums			
MAINSTREAM			
❑ S-394	Soul Makossa	1973	12.00

AGAPE

Number	Title (A Side/B Side)	Yr	NM
Albums			
MARK			
❑ MRS-2170	Gospel Hard Rock	1971	120.00
RENRUT			
❑ 101	Victims of Tradition	1972	120.00

AGE OF REASON, THE

Number	Title (A Side/B Side)	Yr	NM
Albums			
GEORGETOWNE			
❑ (no #)	The Age of Reason	1969	150.00

AGGREGATION, THE

Number	Title (A Side/B Side)	Yr	NM
45s			
LHI			
❑ 1209	Sunshine Superman/ Maharish	1968	30.00
Albums			
LHI			
❑ 12008	Mind Odyssey	1967	400.00

AGNOSTIC FRONT

Number	Title (A Side/B Side)	Yr	NM
Albums			
COMBAT			
❑ 3022	One Voice	1992	15.00
❑ 8204	Liberty and Justice for...	1987	12.00
COMBAT CORE			
❑ CC 8046	Victim in Pain	1986	15.00
❑ CC8049	Cause for Alarm	1986	15.00
EPITAPH			
❑ 86536	Something's Gotta Give	1998	12.00
❑ 86567	Riot Riot Upstart	1999	12.00
IN EFFECT			
❑ 3001	Live at CBGB's	1989	12.00

AGRATI, DON
See DON GRADY.

AHBEZ, EDEN

Number	Title (A Side/B Side)	Yr	NM
45s			
DEL-FI			
❑ 4131	Tobago/The Old Boat	1959	15.00
Albums			
DEL-FI			
❑ DFLP-1211 [M]	Eden's Island	1960	150.00
❑ DFST-1211 [S]	Eden's Island	1960	200.00

AKENS, JEWEL

Number	Title (A Side/B Side)	Yr	NM
45s			
AMERICAN INT'L			
❑ 110	When Something Is Wrong with My Baby/I Just Can't Turn My Habit into Love	196?	6.00
CAPEHART			
❑ 5007	(Dancing) The Mashed Potatoes/Wee Bit More of Your Lovih'	1962	12.00
COLGEMS			
❑ 66-1009	Little Bitty Pretty One/ Born a Loser	1967	10.00
❑ 66-1025	It's a Sin to Tell a Lie/ You Better Move On	1968	8.00
CREST			
❑ 1098	(Dancing) The Mashed Potatoes/ Wee Bit More of Your Lovin'	1962	10.00
ERA			
❑ 104	Buenos Aires/Mississippi Syrup Sopper	1969	6.00
❑ 3141	The Birds and the Bees/ Tic Tac Toe	1964	15.00
❑ 3142	Georgie Porgie/ Around the Corner	1965	10.00
❑ 3147	You Sure Know How to Hurt a Guy/It's the Only Way to Fly	1965	10.00
❑ 3154	You Don't Need a Crowd/I've Arrived	1965	10.00
❑ 3156	A Slice of the Pie/ You Better Believe It	1965	10.00
❑ 3164	My First Lonely Night/Mama Take Your Daughter Back	1966	10.00
❑ 3207	A Slice of the Pie/A Land Where Animals Are People	1969	8.00
MDM			
❑ 191	Christine/Please God	1988	4.00
—As "Jewel Akens, Mr. Birds and Bees"			

Number	Title (A Side/B Side)	Yr	NM
Albums			
ERA			
❑ EL-110 [M]	The Birds and the Bees	1965	30.00
❑ ES-110 [S]	The Birds and the Bees	1965	100.00

AKKERMAN, JAN
Also see BRAINBOX; FOCUS.

Number	Title (A Side/B Side)	Yr	NM
45s			
ATLANTIC			
❑ 3478	Crackers/(B-side unknown)	1978	4.00
Albums			
ATCO			
❑ SD 7032	Tabernakel	1974	12.00
ATLANTIC			
❑ SD 18210	Eli	1977	10.00
❑ SD 19159	Jan Akkerman	1978	10.00
SIRE			
❑ SAS 7407	Profile	1973	15.00

ALADDINS, THE

Number	Title (A Side/B Side)	Yr	NM
45s			
ALADDIN			
❑ 3275	Remember/Cry Baby Cry	1955	200.00
❑ 3298	I Had a Dream Last Night/ Get Off My Feet	1955	200.00
❑ 3314	All My Life/So Long, Farewell, Bye Bye	1956	200.00
❑ 3358	Help Me/Lord, Show Me	1957	200.00
FRANKIE			
❑ 6	Dot, My Love/My Charlene	1958	400.00
WITCH			
❑ 109	Please Love Me/Munch	1962	50.00
❑ 111	Our Love Will Be/Simple Simon	1962	50.00

ALAIMO, CHUCK

Number	Title (A Side/B Side)	Yr	NM
45s			
MGM			
❑ 12449	Leap Frog/That's My Desire	1957	15.00
❑ 12508	Local 60-6/How I Love You	1957	15.00
❑ 12589	Where's My Baby/Lovers Again	1957	15.00
❑ 12636	Hop in My Jalop/Rockin' in G	1958	15.00

ALAIMO, STEVE
Also see THE REDCOATS; THE UNKNOWNS.

Number	Title (A Side/B Side)	Yr	NM
45s			
ABC			
❑ 10805	So Much Love/Truer Than True	1966	12.00
❑ 10833	Happy/On the Beach	1966	12.00
❑ 10873	Pardon Me (It's My First Day Alone)/Savin' All My Love	1966	12.00
❑ 10917	You Don't Love Me/You Don't Know Like I Know	1967	10.00
ABC-PARAMOUNT			
❑ 10540	Love's Gonna Live Here/ Let Her Go	1964	12.00
❑ 10553	Love Is a Many Splendored Thing/Fade Out	1964	12.00
❑ 10580	I Don't Know/That's What Love Will Do	1964	12.00
❑ 10605	Happy/Everybody Knows But Her	1964	12.00
❑ 10620	Real Live Girl/Need You	1965	12.00
❑ 10643	Laughing on the Outside/ Tomorrow Is Another Day	1965	12.00
❑ 10680	Cast Your Fate to the Wind/ Mais Oui	1965	12.00
❑ 10712	Blowin' in the Wind/ Lady of the House	1965	12.00
❑ 10764	Bright Lights Big City/Once a Day	1966	12.00
ATCO			
❑ 6512	New Orleans/Ooh Poo Pah Doo	1967	8.00
❑ 6560	Cuando Yo Vuelvo Ami Tierra/ Todavia	1968	10.00
❑ 6561	Denver/I Do	1968	8.00
❑ 6589	1 x 1 Ain't 2/My Friend	1968	8.00
❑ 6620	Thank You for the Sunshine Days/Watching the Trains Go	1968	8.00
❑ 6659	I'm Thankful/Afetr the Smoke Is Gone	1969	8.00
—With Betty Wright			
❑ 6710	One Woman/And Then I Tripped Over Your Goodbye	1969	8.00
❑ 6732	Melissa/Smilin' in My Sleep	1970	6.00
❑ 6797	Can't You See/(On the) Wild Side of Life	1971	6.00
CHECKER			
❑ 981	Big Bad Beulah/ I Cried All the Way Home	1961	12.00
❑ 989	All Night Long/I'm Thankful	1961	12.00
❑ 998	The Waiting's So Hard/ You Got Me Whistling	1961	12.00
❑ 1006	Mashed Potatoes/Mashed Potatoes (Part 2)	1962	12.00
❑ 1018	My Friend/Going Back to Mary	1962	12.00
❑ 1024	Cry Myself to Sleep/ One Good Reason	1962	12.00
❑ 1032	Every Day I Have to Cry/ Little Girl	1962	12.00
❑ 1042	A Lifetime of Loneliness/ It's a Long, Long Way to Happiness	1963	12.00
❑ 1047	Don't Let the Sun Catch You Cryin'/I Told You So	1963	12.00
❑ 1054	Michael—Pt. 1/Michael—Pt. 2	1963	12.00
DADE			
❑ 1800	Home by Eleven /I Wanna Kiss You	1959	50.00
❑ 1805	Love Letters/You Can Fall in Love	1959	50.00
DICKSON			
❑ 6444/5	Blue Fire/My Heart Never Said Goodbye	1960	20.00
ENTRANCE			
❑ 7501	When My Little Girl Is Smiling/ Gemini	1971	5.00
❑ 7503	Thorn in Our Roses/ Nobody's Fool	1971	5.00
❑ 7507	Amerikan Music/Nobody's Fool	1972	5.00
❑ 7513	Sand in My Pocket/Gemini	1972	5.00
IMPERIAL			
❑ 5699	My Heart Never Said Goodbye/ Blue Fire	1960	15.00
❑ 5717	Unchained Melody/ It Happens Ev'ry Time	1961	15.00
❑ 66003	Gotta Lotta Love/Happy Pappy	1963	12.00
LIFETIME			
❑ 6112/3	Jelly/The Girl Can't Help It	1957	80.00
MARLIN			
❑ 6064	I Want You to Love Me/ Blue Skies	1959	30.00
❑ 6065	The Weekend's Over/ Girls! Girls! Girls!	1959	25.00
❑ 6067	She's My Baby/Should I Care?	1959	25.00
❑ 6103	Spooky/The Redcoats Are Coming	1961	30.00
—As "Count Stephen"			
TONE LATINO			
❑ 5051	Yo No Se Que Voy A Hacer Sin Ti/No Quiero Dejaria Ya	1970	8.00
7-Inch Extended Plays			
ABC			
❑ LP-ABCS-531	Where the Action Is/Sweet Little Sixteen/500 Miles//Papa's Got a Brand New Bag/Personality/ Blowin' in the Wind	1966	20.00
—Jukebox issue; small hole, plays at 33 1/3 rpm			
❑ LP-ABCS-531 [PS]	Where the Action Is	1966	20.00
CHECKER			
❑ EP-5135	Don't Cry/I Wake Up Crying// Cry/Don't Let the Sun Catch You Crying	1963	80.00
❑ EP-5135 [PS]	(title unknown)	1963	80.00
Albums			
ABC-PARAMOUNT			
❑ 501 [M]	Starring Steve Alaimo	1965	40.00
❑ S-501 [S]	Starring Steve Alaimo	1965	50.00
❑ 531 [M]	Where the Action Is	1965	40.00
❑ S-531 [S]	Where the Action Is	1965	50.00
❑ 551 [M]	Steve Alaimo Sings and Swings	1966	40.00
❑ S-551 [S]	Steve Alaimo Sings and Swings	1966	50.00
CHECKER			
❑ LP-2981 [M]	Twist with Steve Alaimo	1962	150.00
❑ LP-2983 [M]	Mashed Potatoes	1962	150.00
❑ LP-2986 [M]	Every Day I Have to Cry	1963	150.00
CROWN			
❑ CST-382 [R]	Steve Alaimo	1963	15.00
❑ CLP-5382 [M]	Steve Alaimo	1963	25.00

ALAMO, TONY (1)
Former Big Band singer.

Number	Title (A Side/B Side)	Yr	NM
45s			
MGM			
❑ K11380	Merry Christmas Darling/ It's Christmas Time	1952	20.00
PORT			
❑ 70012	Fabulous/For All We Know	1960	15.00

ALAMO, TONY (2)
Real name: Bernie LaZar Hoffman. Also a controversial evangelist with his own ministry.

Number	Title (A Side/B Side)	Yr	NM
45s			
ALAMO			
❑ 334	Something/Dreamer	1986	4.00
—With Kim Morris			
❑ 334 [PS]	Something/Dreamer	1986	4.00

A

Number	Title (A Side/B Side)	Yr	NM

ALAN, LEE

45s

LEE ALAN PRESENTS

❑ (no #)	A Trip to Miami	1964	500.00

—Interviews with the Beatles; a giveaway with Lee Alan's two-page story of his trip ($200 NM)

ALBERT, MORRIS

45s

AUDIO LATINO

❑ AL-577	"Dime" Feelings/Christine	1975	5.00

—Pronounced "DEE-may," this is the Spanish version of "Feelings"

RCA

❑ GB-10937	Feelings/Memories	1977	3.00

—Gold Standard Series

❑ PB-10958	Never Let You Go/Conversation	1977	3.00
❑ PB-11089	Someone, Somehow/ So Good to Me	1977	3.00

RCA VICTOR

❑ PB-10279	Feelings/This World Today Is a Mess	1975	4.00
❑ PB-10437	Sweet Loving Man/Christine	1975	4.00
❑ PB-10626	Summer in Paris/She's My Girl	1976	4.00
❑ PB-10706	Memories/The Same Things	1976	4.00

Albums

RCA VICTOR

❑ APL1-1018	Feelings	1975	8.00
❑ APL1-1496	Morris Albert	1976	8.00

ALBERT, THE

Albums

PERCEPTION

❑ 9	The Albert	1971	20.00

ALBERTS, AL Also see FOUR ACES.

45s

COLUMBIA

❑ 42737	Fly Me to the Moon/Before Tomorrow Is Yesterday	1963	8.00

CORAL

❑ 62035	Things I Didn't Say/ God's Greatest Gifts	1958	10.00
❑ 62061	My Love/Willingly	1958	10.00
❑ 62083	How Soon/ Love Is the Tomorrow	1959	10.00
❑ 62090	How Soon/Taking a Chance on Love	1959	10.00
❑ 62113	By You/High School	1959	10.00

DECCA

❑ 28807	Please Tell Me/Endless	1953	15.00

MGM

❑ 12836	Imagination/Handful of Gold	1959	10.00
❑ 12884	South of the Border/ No Love But Your Love	1960	10.00
❑ 12922	Handful of Gold/ Blue Bird of Happiness	1960	10.00

PRESIDENT

❑ 711	Don't Wait for the Hearse/ Heaven Needed an Angel	1961	8.00
❑ 712	Only on Sunday/Heaven Needed an Angel	1961	8.00
❑ 715	Blue O'Clock in the Morning/ Till Then (I'll Never Again)	1962	8.00
❑ 719	Fly Me to the Moon/Before Tomorrow Is Yesterday	1963	12.00

SWAN

❑ 4067	Oh My Papa/Alone	1961	10.00
❑ 4191	Mr. Sandman/ Summertime in Venice	1964	10.00

VEE JAY

❑ 568	One Has My Name, The Other Has My Heart/Mala Femina	1963	15.00

Albums

CORAL

❑ CRL 57259 [M]	A Man Has Got to Sing	1959	25.00
❑ CRL 757259 [S]	A Man Has Got to Sing	1959	30.00

ALBISTON, TONY

45s

BOGUS

❑ 1001/2	Mount Shasta/ Old Fashioned Couple	1960	200.00

ALCATRAZZ

45s

ROCSHIRE

❑ 95047	Island in the Sun/ Hiroshima Mon Amour	1983	10.00
❑ 95047 [PS]	Island in the Sun/ Hiroshima Mon Amour	1983	12.00

Albums

CAPITOL

❑ ST-12385	Disturbing the Peace	1985	20.00
❑ ST-12477	Dangerous Games	1986	20.00

ROCSHIRE

❑ 22016	No Parole from Rock 'n' Roll	1983	25.00
❑ 22020	Live Sentence	1984	20.00

ALDA, ALEX Actually Nick Massi of THE FOUR SEASONS.

45s

ONE WAY

❑ 224	The Ballad of Mr. Nixon/ Little Pony	1976	5.00

TOPIX

❑ 6007 [DJ]	Little Pony (one-sided)	1961	100.00

ALDEN AND THE ONE-NIGHTERS

45s

RCA VICTOR

❑ 47-7490	Love-O-Meter/Theme from Love-O-Meter	1959	30.00

ALDRICH, RONNIE

7-Inch Extended Plays

LONDON PHASE 4

❑ SBG 68	Blowin' in the Wind/Do It Again/ Time//Mas Que Nada/Theme from "The Fox"/Something Here in My Heart	1968	10.00

—Jukebox issue; small hole, plays at 33 1/3 rpm

❑ SBG 68 [PS]	This Way "In"	1968	10.00

Albums

LONDON

❑ LL 3348 [M]	The Romantic Pianos of Ronnie Aldrich	1964	12.00
❑ LL 3383 [M]	Christmas with Ronnie	1964	10.00

LONDON PHASE 4

❑ 22 [(2)]	Love Story	1971	15.00
❑ SP-44007 [S]	Melody and Percussion for Two Pianos	1961	15.00
❑ SP 44018 [S]	Ronnie Aldrich and His Two Pianos	1962	15.00
❑ SP-44029 [S]	The Magnificent Pianos of Ronnie Aldrich	1963	15.00
❑ SP-44042 [S]	The Romantic Pianos of Ronnie Aldrich	1964	15.00
❑ SP 44051 [S]	Christmas with Ronnie	1964	15.00
❑ SP-44062 [S]	Magic Moods	1965	12.00
❑ SP-44070 [S]	That Aldrich Feeling	1966	12.00
❑ SP-44081 [S]	All-Time Piano Hits	1967	12.00
❑ SP-44092 [S]	Two Pianos in Hollywood	196?	10.00
❑ SP-44108 [S]	For Young Lovers	196?	10.00

ALEXANDER, ARTHUR

45s

BUDDAH

❑ 492	Every Day I Have to Cry Some/ Everybody Needs Somebody to Love	1975	5.00
❑ 522	Sharing the Night Together/ She'll Throw Stones at You	1976	5.00
❑ 602	Sharing the Night Together/ She'll Throw Stones at You	1978	4.00

DOT

❑ 45-126	You Better Move On/Anna	196?	10.00

—Reissue; black label

❑ 45-126	You Better Move On/Anna	1969	7.00

—Reissue; multi-color label

❑ 16309	You Better Move On/ A Shot of Rhythm and Blues	1962	20.00
❑ 16357	Where Have You Been (All My Life)/Soldier of Love	1962	20.00
❑ 16387	Anna/I Hang My Head and Cry	1962	20.00
❑ 16425	You're the Reason/ Go Home Girl	1963	15.00
❑ 16454	I Wonder Where You Are Tonight/Dream Girl	1963	15.00
❑ 16509	Pretty Girls Everywhere/ Baby Baby	1963	15.00
❑ 16554	Where Did Sally Go/ Keep Her Guessin'	1963	15.00
❑ 16616	Black Knight/Ole John Amos	1964	12.00
❑ 16737	Detroit City/You Don't Care	1965	12.00

JUDD

❑ 1020	Sally Sue Brown/The Girl That Radiates That Charm	1960	50.00

—As "June Alexander"

MONUMENT

❑ 1060	I Need You Baby/ Spanish Harlem	1968	8.00

MUSIC MILL

❑ 1012	Hound Dog Man's Gone/ So Long Baby	1977	6.00

SOUND STAGE 7

❑ 2556	The Other Woman/ (Baby) For You	1965	10.00
❑ 2572	Turn Around (And Try Me)/ Show Me the Road	1966	10.00
❑ 2619	Set Me Free/Love's Where Life Begins	1968	8.00
❑ 2626	Bye Bye Love/Another	1969	8.00
❑ 2652	Glory Road/Cry Like a Baby	1970	8.00

WARNER BROS.

❑ 7571	I'm Comin' Home/It Hurts to Want It So Bad	1972	6.00
❑ 7633	Mr. John/You Got Me Knockin'	1972	6.00
❑ 7658	Burning Love/It Hurts to Want It So Bad	1972	6.00

7-Inch Extended Plays

DOT

❑ DLP-434	You Better Move On/Hey! Baby/Funny How Time Slips Away//Lover Please/The Wanderer/You're the Reason	1962	50.00

—Jukebox issue; small hole, plays at 33 1/3 rpm

❑ DLP-434 [PS]	You Better Move On	1962	50.00

Albums

DOT

❑ DLP 3434 [M]	You Better Move On	1962	100.00
❑ DLP 25434 [S]	You Better Move On	1962	160.00

WARNER BROS.

❑ BS 2592	Arthur Alexander	1972	25.00

ALEXANDER, JOE, AND THE CUBANS With a pre-Chess CHUCK BERRY in the band.

45s

BALLAD

❑ 1008	Oh Maria/I Hope These Words Will FInd You Well	1954	1500.

ALEXANDER, JUNE See ARTHUR ALEXANDER.

ALEXANDER, MAX

45s

CAPROCK

❑ 116	Little Rome/Rock, Rock, Rock Everybody	1959	200.00

ALEXANDER AND THE GREATS

45s

ARVEE

❑ 5064	Swanee Stomp/Waterlogged	1963	40.00

LIMELIGHT

❑ 3040	Do the Mustang/ Hot Dang Mustang	1964	40.00

ALEXANDER'S TIMELESS BLOOZBAND

45s

KAPP

❑ 967	Maybe Baby/Power of Your Love	1969	12.00

MATAMAT

❑ 101	Love So Strong/Horn Song	1967	20.00

UNI

❑ 55044	Love So Strong/Horn Song	1967	15.00

Albums

SMASK

❑ 1001 [M]	Alexander's Timeless Bloozband	1967	200.00

UNI

❑ 73021	For Sale	1968	25.00

ALEXANDRIA, LOREZ

45s

ABC-PARAMOUNT

❑ 10594	That Far Away Look/Little Boat	1966	12.00

ARGO

❑ 5367	I Ain't Got Nothin' But the Blues/ Early in the Morning	1960	15.00
❑ 5371	I Almost Lost My Mind/ Don't Explain	1960	15.00
❑ 5432	Baltimore Oriole/Mother Earth	1963	15.00

KING

❑ 5189	You're My Thrill/I'm Gonna Sit Right Down and Write Myself a Letter	1959	20.00
❑ 5206	Love Is Just Around the Corner/ Ain't Misbehavin'	1959	20.00
❑ 5253	Just You, Just Me/ Don't Blame Us	1959	20.00

PZAZZ

❑ 001	I'm Wishin'/Endless	1968	12.00
❑ 003	Didn't We/The One You Love Is You	1968	12.00
❑ 017	Santa Is Here/Nonchalantly	1968	12.00

Except when noted otherwise, VG = 25% of NM, and VG+ = 50% of NM. (Example: VG = $2.00, VG+ = $4.00 and NM = $8.00.)

Number	Title (A Side/B Side)	Yr	NM
❑ 025	Hey Jude/I Don't Want to Hear It Anymore	1969	12.00
❑ 046	My Way/Hello There Girl	1969	12.00

Albums

ABC IMPULSE!

Number	Title (A Side/B Side)	Yr	NM
❑ AS-62	Alexandria the Great	1968	20.00
—Reissue of Impulse! AS-62			
❑ AS-76	More of the Great Lorez Alexandria	1968	20.00
—Reissue of Impulse! AS-76			

ARGO

Number	Title (A Side/B Side)	Yr	NM
❑ LP-663 [M]	Early in the Morning	1960	70.00
❑ LPS-663 [S]	Early in the Morning	1960	100.00
—With the Ramsey Lewis Trio			
❑ LP-682 [M]	Sing No Sad Songs for Me	1961	70.00
❑ LPS-682 [S]	Sing No Sad Songs for Me	1961	100.00
❑ LP-694 [M]	Deep Roots	1962	70.00
❑ LPS-694 [S]	Deep Roots	1962	100.00
❑ LP-720 [M]	For Swingers Only	1963	70.00
❑ LPS-720 [S]	For Swingers Only	1963	100.00

CADET

Number	Title (A Side/B Side)	Yr	NM
❑ LPS-682	Sing No Sad Songs for Me	1966	25.00
—Reissue of Argo 682			

DISCOVERY

Number	Title (A Side/B Side)	Yr	NM
❑ DS-782	How Will I Remember You?	1978	60.00
❑ DS-800	A Woman Knows	1979	50.00
❑ DS-826	Lorez Alexandria Sings Johnny Mercer	1981	25.00
❑ DS-905	Harlem Butterfly (Sings the Songs of Johnny Mercer Vol. 2)	1984	20.00

IMPULSE!

Number	Title (A Side/B Side)	Yr	NM
❑ A-62 [M]	Alexandria the Great	1964	40.00
❑ AS-62 [S]	Alexandria the Great	1964	50.00
❑ A-76 [M]	More of the Great Lorez Alexandria	1965	40.00
❑ AS-76 [S]	More of the Great Lorez Alexandria	1965	50.00

KING

Number	Title (A Side/B Side)	Yr	NM
❑ 542 [M]	This Is Lorez	1956	200.00
—Black label, crownless "King"			
❑ 565 [M]	Lorez Sings Prez	1956	200.00
—Black label, crownless "King"			
❑ 657 [M]	The Band Swings, Lorez Sings	1959	200.00
—Black label, crownless "King"			
❑ S-657 [S]	The Band Swings, Lorez Sings	1959	300.00
—Dark blue label, crownless "King"			
❑ 676 [M]	Singing Songs Everyone Knows	1959	200.00
—Black label, crownless "King"			

MCA

Number	Title (A Side/B Side)	Yr	NM
❑ 29000	Alexandria the Great	198?	10.00
—Reissue of ABC Impulse! AS-62			

PZAZZ

Number	Title (A Side/B Side)	Yr	NM
❑ LP-320	Didn't We	1968	50.00
❑ LP-324	In a Different Bag	1969	30.00

TREND

Number	Title (A Side/B Side)	Yr	NM
❑ TR-538	Tangerine (Sings the Songs of Johnny Mercer Vol. 3)	1986	15.00
❑ TR-547	Dear to My Heart	1988	15.00

ALFI AND HARRY

45s

LIBERTY

Number	Title (A Side/B Side)	Yr	NM
❑ 55008	The Trouble with Harry/Little Beauty	1955	25.00
❑ 55016	The Word Game Song/Persian on Excursion	1956	25.00
❑ 55066	Safari/Cloding Time	1957	25.00

ALHONA, RICHIE

45s

FANTASY

Number	Title (A Side/B Side)	Yr	NM
❑ 553	One Desire/Young Boy, Young Girl	1961	12.00
—Black vinyl			
❑ 553	One Desire/Young Boy, Young Girl	1961	30.00
—Red vinyl			
❑ 553 [PS]	One Desire/Young Boy, Young Girl	1961	30.00
❑ 556	Mama, Mama/The Pagan	1961	12.00
❑ 561	The Fool/Teenager Teenager	1962	12.00

ALICE IN CHAINS

12-Inch Singles

COLUMBIA

Number	Title (A Side/B Side)	Yr	NM
❑ CAS 2095 [DJ]	We Die Young/It Ain't Like That/Killing Yourself	1990	22.00
—Promo-only three-song single predating their first LP			

45s

COLUMBIA

Number	Title (A Side/B Side)	Yr	NM
❑ CS7-04013 [DJ]	Bleed the Freak (Live)/Put You Down (Live)	1991	20.00
—White label with no label name			
❑ 74820	Angry Chair/Brother	1993	20.00
—Cassette only			
❑ 78176	Grind/Nutshell	1995	15.00
—Deleted on day of issue			

Albums

COLUMBIA

Number	Title (A Side/B Side)	Yr	NM
❑ CAS 2192 [EP]	We Die Young	1990	50.00
—Five-song promo-only issue predating their first LP			
❑ C2 57804 [(2)]	Jar of Flies/Sap	1994	25.00
—Two cassette/CD EP releases in one vinyl package			
❑ C2 67248 [(2)]	Alice in Chains	1995	25.00

ALICE JEAN AND THE MONDELLOS

See THE MONDELLOS.

ALIOTTA-HAYNES-JEREMIAH

45s

AMPEX

Number	Title (A Side/B Side)	Yr	NM
❑ 11012	Pitter Patter/(B-side unknown)	1970	8.00
—As "Aliotta Haynes"			
❑ 11026	Tomorrow's Another Day/One Night Stand	1971	8.00
—As "Aliotta Haynes"			

SNOW QUEEN

Number	Title (A Side/B Side)	Yr	NM
❑ 1000	Lake Shore Drive (L.S.D.)/Snow Queen	1973	20.00

Albums

AMPEX

Number	Title (A Side/B Side)	Yr	NM
❑ A-10108	Aliotta-Haynes Music	1970	20.00
—As "Aliota-Haynes"			
❑ A-10119	Aliotta-Haynes-Jeremiah	1970	20.00

BIG FOOT

Number	Title (A Side/B Side)	Yr	NM
❑ 714	Lake Shore Drive	1978	25.00

LITTLE FOOT

Number	Title (A Side/B Side)	Yr	NM
❑ 711	Slippin' Away	1977	20.00

ALIVE AND KICKING

45s

ROULETTE

Number	Title (A Side/B Side)	Yr	NM
❑ 7078	Tighter, Tighter/Sunday Morning	1970	5.00
❑ 7087	Just Let It Come/Mother Carey's Chicken	1970	5.00
❑ 7094	London Bridge/You Gave Me Something	1971	5.00
❑ 7113	Good Ole Lovin' Back Home/Jordan	1971	5.00

Albums

ROULETTE

Number	Title (A Side/B Side)	Yr	NM
❑ SR 42052	Alive and Kicking	1970	20.00

ALL AMERICAN RUMBLERS, THE

Albums

GONE

Number	Title (A Side/B Side)	Yr	NM
❑ LP-5006 [M]	Destination Dixie	1959	50.00

ALL NIGHT WORKERS, THE

45s

CAMEO

Number	Title (A Side/B Side)	Yr	NM
❑ 420	Honey and Wine/God Bless the Child	1966	40.00

MERCURY

Number	Title (A Side/B Side)	Yr	NM
❑ 72833	The Collector/Misery	1968	30.00

ROUND SOUND

Number	Title (A Side/B Side)	Yr	NM
❑ RS-1	Don't Put All Your Eggs in One Basket/Why Don't You Smile	1983	500.00
—Lou Reed and John Cale co-wrote the B-side of this record			

ALL-NITERS, THE

45s

ERIE

Number	Title (A Side/B Side)	Yr	NM
❑ 001	Hey Baby/Talk to Me	1966	25.00
❑ 002	Hello (Lonely One)/Girl Don't Go	1966	25.00

GMA

Number	Title (A Side/B Side)	Yr	NM
❑ 1	Summertime Blues/You Talk Too Much	1965	40.00

ALL STARS, THE

Albums

GRAMOPHONE

Number	Title (A Side/B Side)	Yr	NM
❑ 20192	Boogie Woogie	196?	50.00

ALLAN, CHAD

Member of the early GUESS WHO.

45s

MALA

Number	Title (A Side/B Side)	Yr	NM
❑ 12033	Thru the Looking Glass/Ramon's Hourglass	1968	6.00

REPRISE

Number	Title (A Side/B Side)	Yr	NM
❑ 1003	On the Back Step/West Coast Girl	1971	6.00

ALLAN, DAVIE, AND THE ARROWS

45s

CUDE

Number	Title (A Side/B Side)	Yr	NM
❑ 101	War Path/Beyond the Blue	1963	100.00

GET HIP

Number	Title (A Side/B Side)	Yr	NM
❑ GH-209	The Born Losers Theme/The Glory Stompers	1997	2.00
❑ GH-209 [PS]	The Born Losers Theme/The Glory Stompers	1997	2.00

MARC

Number	Title (A Side/B Side)	Yr	NM
❑ 3223	War Path/Beyond the Blue	1963	50.00

MGM

Number	Title (A Side/B Side)	Yr	NM
❑ 14299	It's the Little Things You Do/Haven't You Heard	1971	8.00
❑ 14374	Head Over Heels/Here It Comes	1972	8.00
❑ 14432	Dawn of the 7th Cavalry/Little Big Horn	1972	8.00
❑ 14560	And Evil Did Too/Pleasure Girl	1973	8.00
❑ 14650	Apache '73/Run of the Arrow	1973	8.00

MRC

Number	Title (A Side/B Side)	Yr	NM
❑ 0901	Stoked on Surf/Flashback	1984	5.00

PRIVATE STOCK

Number	Title (A Side/B Side)	Yr	NM
❑ 45,001	Touch Too Much/We Can Make It Together	1974	6.00

SIDEWALK

Number	Title (A Side/B Side)	Yr	NM
❑ 1	Apache '65/Blue Guitar	1965	20.00

TOWER

Number	Title (A Side/B Side)	Yr	NM
❑ 116	Apache '65/Blue Guitar	1965	15.00
❑ 133	Moon Dawg '65/Dance the Freddie	1965	12.00
❑ 142	Baby Ruth/I'm Looking Over a Four Leaf Clover	1965	12.00
❑ 158	Space Hop/Granny Goose	1965	12.00
❑ 267	Wild Angels Theme/UFO	1966	12.00
❑ 295	Blue's Theme/Bongo Party	1966	12.00
—As "The Arrows featuring Davie Allen"			
❑ 341	Devil's Angels/Cody's Theme	1967	12.00
❑ 381	Cycle-Delic/Blue Rides Again	1967	12.00
❑ 446	Wild in the Streets/Shape of Things to Come	1968	12.00

Albums

TOWER

Number	Title (A Side/B Side)	Yr	NM
❑ DT 5002 [R]	Apache '65	1965	30.00
❑ T 5002 [M]	Apache '65	1965	40.00
❑ DT 5043 [R]	The Wild Angels	1966	20.00
❑ T 5043 [M]	The Wild Angels	1966	30.00
❑ DT 5056 [R]	The Wild Angels, Vol. II	1967	20.00
❑ T 5056 [M]	The Wild Angels, Vol. II	1967	30.00
❑ DT 5074 [R]	Devil's Angel	1967	20.00
❑ T 5074 [M]	Devil's Angel	1967	30.00
❑ DT 5078 [R]	Blues Theme	1967	40.00
❑ T 5078 [M]	Blues Theme	1967	50.00
❑ DT 5083 [R]	Mondo Hollywood	1968	20.00
❑ T 5083 [M]	Mondo Hollywood	1968	30.00
❑ DT 5094 [R]	Cycle-Delic Sounds	1968	50.00
❑ T 5094 [M]	Cycle-Delic Sounds	1968	100.00

ALLAN & THE FLAMES

45s

CAMPBELL

Number	Title (A Side/B Side)	Yr	NM
❑ 225	Winter Wonderland/Till The End Of Time	1960	50.00

COLONIAL

Number	Title (A Side/B Side)	Yr	NM
❑ 7006	Winter Wonderland/'Till The End of Time	1960	50.00

ALLEN, BILLY

45s

EL DORADO

Number	Title (A Side/B Side)	Yr	NM
❑ 505	Butterfly/Oo Wee Baby	1957	20.00
—As "Bill Allen"			

IMPERIAL

Number	Title (A Side/B Side)	Yr	NM
❑ 5500	Please Give Me Something/Since I Have You	1958	100.00

ALLEN, DAVE

Albums

INTERNATIONAL ARTISTS

Number	Title (A Side/B Side)	Yr	NM
❑ 11	Color Blind	1969	60.00
—Original pressing			
❑ 11	Color Blind	1979	20.00
—Repressing with "RE2" and "Masterfonics" in dead wax			

ALLEN, DAYTON

Albums

GRAND AWARD

Number	Title (A Side/B Side)	Yr	NM
❑ GA 33-424 [M]	Why Not?	1960	25.00

Except when noted otherwise, VG = 25% of NM, and VG+ = 50% of NM. (Example: VG = $2.00, VG+ = $4.00 and NM = $8.00.)

A

ALLEN, JASON

45s

HIT

Number	Title (A Side/B Side)	Yr	NM
❑ 226	Everybody Loves a Clown/ You've Got Your Troubles	1965	8.00

—B-side by the Spades

ALLEN, JESSE

45s

Number	Title (A Side/B Side)	Yr	NM
ALADDIN			
❑ 3129	Rock This Morning/Gonna Move Away from Town	1953	200.00
BAYOU			
❑ 011	Dragnet/Take It Easy	1953	100.00
CORAL			
❑ 65078	My Suffering/Let's Party	1952	200.00
IMPERIAL			
❑ 5256	Gotta Call That Number/ Gonna Tell My Mama	1953	200.00
—With Audrey Walker			
❑ 5285	Sittin' and Wonderin'/ I Wonder What's the Matter	1954	250.00
❑ 5303	What a Party/The Things I'm Gonna Do	1954	200.00
❑ 5315	Rockin' and Rollin'/ I Love You So	1954	200.00

ALLEN, JIMMY, AND TOMMY BARTELLA

45s

Number	Title (A Side/B Side)	Yr	NM
AL-BRITE			
❑ 1300	When Santa Comes Over The Brooklyn Bridge/ What Would You Like To Have For Christmas?	1959	40.00

ALLEN, LEE

45s

Number	Title (A Side/B Side)	Yr	NM
ALADDIN			
❑ 3334	Shimmy/Rockin' at Cosmos	1956	25.00
EMBER			
❑ 1027	Walkin' with Mr. Lee/ Promenade	1957	25.00
❑ 1031	Strollin' with Mr. Lee/ Boppin' at the Hop	1958	20.00
❑ 1039	Tic Toc/Chuggin'	1958	20.00
❑ 1047	Jim Jam/Short Circuit	1958	20.00
❑ 1057	Cat Walk/Creole Alley	1959	20.00
❑ 1082	Twistin' with Mr. Lee/ Twist Around the Clock	1962	15.00
LOST-NITE			
❑ 416	Walkin' with Mr. Lee/Promenade	197?	5.00
—Reissue			

7-Inch Extended Plays

Number	Title (A Side/B Side)	Yr	NM
EMBER			
❑ 103	Walkin' with Mr. Lee/ Teen Dream//Promenade/ Big Horn Special	1958	200.00
❑ 103 [PS]	Walkin' with Mr. Lee	1958	200.00

Albums

Number	Title (A Side/B Side)	Yr	NM
EMBER			
❑ ELP-200 [M]	Walkin' with Mr. Lee	1958	500.00
—Red label			
❑ ELP-200 [M]	Walkin' with Mr. Lee	1959	200.00
—White "logs" label			
❑ ELP-200 [M]	Walkin' with Mr. Lee	1961	100.00
—Red and black label			

ALLEN, MILTON

45s

Number	Title (A Side/B Side)	Yr	NM
RCA VICTOR			
❑ 47-6994	Love A Love A Lover/Just Look, Don't Touch, She's Mine	1957	30.00
❑ 47-7116	Don't Bug Me Baby/Jamboree	1957	50.00

ALLEN, RAY

45s

Number	Title (A Side/B Side)	Yr	NM
DCP			
❑ 1007	He Don't Love You Anymore/ Please Make Up Your Mind	1964	15.00
❑ 1103	No Top Suit/Yesterday Is Sweetheart But Today's a Souvenir	1964	15.00
MALA			
❑ 504	That Is My Love/Bluebirds Over the Mountain	1965	12.00
❑ 522	Dondi/That Is My Love	1966	12.00
PARAMOUNT			
❑ 0207	Yonkers U.S.A./Did-ja Hear Me People	1973	6.00
❑ 0215	Yes Sir Mr. President (Wounded Knee)/(Instrumental)	1973	6.00
ROULETTE			
❑ 4721	Torna/Al Di La	1967	10.00
❑ 4737	Hey Ben Go Fly a Kite/Roselina	1967	10.00

Albums

Number	Title (A Side/B Side)	Yr	NM
PARAMOUNT			
❑ PAS-6060	Ray Allen and the Yonkers Children's Chorus	1973	15.00

ALLEN, RAY, AND THE UPBEATS

45s

Number	Title (A Side/B Side)	Yr	NM
BLAST			
❑ 204	Peggy Sue/La Bamba	1962	30.00
SINCLAIR			
❑ 1004	Sweet Lorraine/Let Them Talk	1961	50.00

Albums

Number	Title (A Side/B Side)	Yr	NM
BLAST			
❑ BLP-6804 [M]	A Tribute to Six	1962	120.00

ALLEN, REX

45s

Number	Title (A Side/B Side)	Yr	NM
BUENA VISTA			
❑ F-341	Lazy River/Say One for Me	1959	15.00
❑ F-342	I Couldn't Care Less/ Pretty Irish Girl	1959	15.00
❑ F-347	The Little Old Church in the Valley/Morgen	1959	15.00
❑ F-351	Staying Young/Forever and Ever	1959	15.00
❑ F-355	Barefoot Country Boy/ Conversation with a Mule	1960	15.00
❑ F-358	The Lilacs Grow High/ I'm the Man	1960	15.00
❑ F-363	Charro Bravo/I Love You So Much It Hurts	1960	15.00
❑ F-370	Dodie Ann/Pretty Irish Girl	1960	15.00
DECCA			
❑ 9-27876	Ragtime Melody/Tuck Me to Sleep in My Old 'Tucky Home	1951	25.00
❑ 9-27952	The Waltz of the Roses/As Long As the River Flows On	1952	20.00
❑ 9-28146	Till the Well Goes Dry/Rack Up the Balls Boys	1952	20.00
❑ 9-28341	Jambalaya (On the Bayou)/ The Two-Faced Clock	1952	20.00
❑ 9-28446	No One Will Ever Know/ Hootin' and Howlin'	1952	20.00
❑ 9-28556	Knocking on the Door/ Why My Darlin' Why	1953	15.00
❑ 9-28758	Crying in the Chapel/ I Thank the Lord	1953	20.00
❑ 9-28897	To Be Alone/If God Can Forgive You, So Can I	1953	20.00
❑ 9-28933	Where Did My Snowman Go?/ Why Daddy?	1953	20.00
❑ 9-28998	He Played the Steel Guitar/ Somewhere	1954	20.00
❑ 9-29111	Bringing Home the Bacon/ I Could Cry My Heart Out	1954	15.00
❑ 9-29168	In the Chapel in the Moonlight/ Chapel of Memories	1954	15.00
❑ 9-29297	You Took My Name/ I'm Learning to Live	1954	20.00
❑ 9-29397	Tomorrow's Another Day to Cry/L-O-N-E-S-O-M-E Letter Blues	1955	15.00
❑ 9-29586	That's What Makes the Juke Box Play/Pedro Gonzales, Tennessee Lopez	1955	20.00
❑ 9-29610	Daddy, You Know What/ The Albino Stallion	1955	15.00
❑ 9-29729	The Last Round-Up/ I'm a Young Cowboy	1955	15.00
❑ 9-29871	The Last Frontier/Sky Boss	1956	12.00
❑ 9-30066	Trail of the Lonesome Pine/ Nothin; to Do	1956	12.00
❑ 9-30204	Drango/Little White Horse	1957	12.00
❑ 9-30205	Westward Ho the Wagons/ Wringle Wrangle	1957	12.00
❑ 9-30364	Money, Marbles and Chalk/ Flowers of San Antone	1957	12.00
❑ 9-30511	Blue Dream/Blue Light Waltz	1957	12.00
❑ 9-30651	Knock, Knock, Rattle /Invitation to the Blues	1958	25.00
❑ 9-30833	I Know the Reason Why/ The Mystery of His Way	1959	12.00
❑ 9-31039	Take Me Lord/Sheltered in the Arms of the Old Rugged Cross	1959	12.00
❑ 32072	A Waltz That Never Ends/A Woman (Can Change a Man)	1967	8.00
❑ 32322	Tiny Bubbles/Jose Villa Lobo Alfredo Thomaso Vincente Lopez	1968	6.00
❑ 32401	Bummin' Around/When I Leave This World Behind	1968	6.00
❑ 32467	It Happens Over and Over Again/Sai Finis	1969	6.00
❑ 732612	Ain't That Beautiful Singing/ A Voice	1970	6.00
❑ 9-46390	I've Got So Many Million Years (I Can't Count 'Em)/ Is He Satisfied	1952	20.00
❑ 9-88161	Where Did My Snowman Go?/ Why Daddy?	1953	15.00
—Yellow label "Children's Series" release			
❑ 9-88161 [PS]	Where Did My Snowman Go?/ Why Daddy?	1953	30.00
HACIENDA			
❑ WWA 01	I Gotta Have My Baby Back/ My Confession	196?	15.00
❑ WW 002	Lonesome Letter Blues/ Love Gone Cold	196?	15.00
MCA			
❑ 41071	So Long Duke/ At the Rainbow's End	1979	6.00
MERCURY			
❑ 5573-X45	The Roving Kind/ Wresk of the John B.	1950	25.00
❑ 5597-X45	Sparrow in the Tree Top/ Always You	1951	25.00
❑ 5619-X45	I'm a Sentimental Fool/ Ten More Miles to Go	1951	25.00
❑ 5647-X45	Mister and Mississippi/ Lonely Little Robin	1951	25.00
❑ 5713-X45	Angel to Joe/Cowpoke	1951	25.00
❑ 6297-X45	I Ain't Gonna Cry No More/ You Drifted	1951	25.00
❑ 6349-X45	Naggin'/Albuquerque Polka	1951	25.00
❑ 70373	True Blue Lou-Lou-Lou/ Save a Little Corner in Your Heart for Me	1954	20.00
❑ 71844	Marines, Let's Go/ Heartaches of a Fool	1961	10.00
❑ 71997	Don't Go Near the Indians/ Touched So Deeply	1962	10.00
❑ 72071	Only the Hangman/ Johnny Travers	1962	8.00
❑ 72095	Roll Up Your Sleeve/ Oohin' and Aahin'	1963	8.00
❑ 72137	Silver Spoon Lonely Me/To-Ra	1963	8.00
❑ 72205	Tear After Tear/ I'm Just Killing Time	1964	8.00
❑ 72205 [PS]	Tear After Tear/ I'm Just Killing Time	1964	15.00
MUSICOR			
❑ 1132	Take It Back and Change It for a Boy/Rodeo Twist	1965	8.00
WARNER BROS.			
❑ 5891	Jawbreaker/Change Me	1967	7.00

Albums

Number	Title (A Side/B Side)	Yr	NM
BUENA VISTA			
❑ BV-3307 [M]	Rex Allen Sings 16 Golden Hits	1961	40.00
DECCA			
❑ DL 8402 [M]	Under Western Skies	1956	50.00
❑ DL 8776 [M]	Mister Cowboy	1959	40.00
❑ DL 75011 [S]	The Smooth Country Sound of Rex Allen	1968	20.00
❑ DL 75205	The Touch of God's Hand	1970	20.00
❑ DL 78776 [S]	Mister Cowboy	1959	60.00
HACIENDA			
❑ WWLP-101 [M]	Rex Allen Sings	1960	200.00
MERCURY			
❑ MG-20719 [M]	Faith of a Man	1962	25.00
❑ MG-20752 [M]	Rex Allen Sings and Tells Tales	1963	25.00
❑ SR-60719 [S]	Faith of a Man	1962	30.00
❑ SR-60752 [S]	Rex Allen Sings and Tells Tales	1963	30.00

ALLEN, RICHIE

45s

Number	Title (A Side/B Side)	Yr	NM
ERA			
❑ 3058	Blue Holiday/Goochie Bamba	1961	20.00
IMPERIAL			
❑ 5683	Stranger from Durango/Redskin	1960	20.00
❑ 5701	Sally Ann/Why Did It End	1960	15.00
—As "Dickie Allen"			
❑ 5720	Haunted Guitar/ In a Persian Market	1961	20.00
❑ 5846	Mr. Hobbs (Theme)/ Comin' Back to You	1962	15.00
❑ 5865	Not So Quiet/A Touch of Blue	1962	15.00
❑ 5872	Cave Man/Room 304	1962	20.00
❑ 5885	Kick Off/Undercurrent	1962	20.00
❑ 5917	Butterscotch/Sunday Picnic	1963	15.00
❑ 5929	Foot Stomp U.S.A./ Skag Along Pete	1963	20.00
❑ 5941	Surf Beater/The Rising Surf	1963	15.00
❑ 5984	The Quiet Surf/Ballad of the Surf	1963	15.00
TOWER			
❑ 273	Stranger from Durango/ Nothing Good	1966	12.00

Except when noted otherwise, VG = 25% of NM, and VG+ = 50% of NM. (Example: VG = $2.00, VG+ = $4.00 and NM = $8.00.)

Number	Title (A Side/B Side)	Yr	NM
Albums			
IMPERIAL			
❑ LP-9212 [M]	Stranger from Durango	1962	40.00
❑ LP-9229 [M]	The Rising Surf	1963	80.00
❑ LP-9243 [M]	Surfer's Slide	1963	80.00
❑ LP-12212 [S]	Stranger from Durango	1962	50.00
❑ LP-12229 [S]	The Rising Surf	1963	150.00
❑ LP-12243 [S]	Surfer's Slide	1963	150.00

ALLEN, RONNIE

Number	Title (A Side/B Side)	Yr	NM
45s			
DAPT			
❑ 205	Flip You Over/Ronnie's Swanee	1961	40.00
SAN			
❑ 208	Juvenile Delinquent/ River of Love	1959	80.00
❑ 209	High School Love/ (B-side unknown)	1959	80.00
❑ 300	Gonna Get My Baby/ (B-side unknown)	1959	80.00

ALLEN, TONY Also see THE ORIGINALS (4).

Number	Title (A Side/B Side)	Yr	NM
45s			
ALADDIN			
❑ 3403	Time Won't Wait on You/ Holy Smoke, Baby	1957	20.00
BETHLEHEM			
❑ 3002	Come-A, Come-A Baby/ Just Like Before	1961	12.00
❑ 3004	It Hurts Me So/The Trakey-Doo	1962	12.00
DIG			
❑ 104	It Hurts Me So/Check Yourself	1955	20.00
❑ 109	I Found An Angel/I'm Dreaming	1956	50.00
EBB			
❑ 115	Come Back/Why in the World	1957	20.00
IMPERIAL			
❑ 5523	Strange Talk/Call My Name	1958	15.00
❑ 5547	Forgive Me/Rockin' Shoes	1958	15.00
JAMIE			
❑ 1143	Train of Love/God Gave Me You	1959	15.00
KENT			
❑ 364	Dreaming/Be My Love, Be My Love	1961	12.00
SPECIALTY			
❑ 560	Nite Owl/I	1955	50.00
❑ 570	Check Yourself Baby/ Especially	1956	30.00
TAMPA			
❑ 157	Be My Love, Be My Love/ Tell Me	195?	30.00
—As "The Wonders"			
ULTRA			
❑ 104	It Hurts Me So/Check Yourself	1955	30.00
UNITED ARTISTS			
❑ 50190	Now Is Forever/Triple Cross	1967	8.00
Albums			
CROWN			
❑ CST-240 [S]	Rock and Roll with Tony Allen	1961	100.00
❑ CLP-5231 [M]	Rock and Roll with Tony Allen	1960	100.00
—Black label			
❑ CLP-5231 [M]	Rock and Roll with Tony Allen	1961	60.00
—Gray label			

ALLEN, WOODY

Number	Title (A Side/B Side)	Yr	NM
Albums			
BELL			
❑ 6008	The Wonderful Wacky World of Woody Allen	1967	20.00
CAPITOL			
❑ ST 2986	The Third Woody Allen Album	1968	25.00
CASABLANCA			
❑ NBLP2-7145 [(2)]	Woody Allen: Stand-Up Comic 1964-1968	1979	15.00
—Compilation of material from Colpix and Capitol LPs (different from either UA collection)			
COLPIX			
❑ CP 488 [M]	Woody Allen 2	1965	30.00
❑ SCP 488 [R]	Woody Allen 2	1965	25.00
❑ CP 518 [M]	Woody Allen	1964	30.00
UNITED ARTISTS			
❑ UA-LA849-J2 [(2)]	Woody Allen: Stand-Up Comic 1964-1968	1977	20.00
—Compilation of material from Colpix and Capitol LPs (different from UA 9968)			
❑ UAS 9968 [(2)]	Woody Allen: The Nightclub Years	1972	20.00
—Compilation of material from Colpix and Capitol LPs			

ALLENS, ARVEE See RITCHIE VALENS.

ALLEY CATS, THE

Number	Title (A Side/B Side)	Yr	NM
45s			
EPIC			
❑ 9778	Lily of the West/I Should Have Stayed at Home Tonight	1965	12.00
PHILLES			
❑ 108	Puddin N' Tain (Ask Me Again, I'll Tell You the Same)/ Feel So Good	1962	25.00
PHILLES/COLLECTABLES			
❑ 3201	Puddin' and Tain/ Then He Kissed Me	1985	6.00
—Red vinyl; part of box set "Phil Spector Wall of Sound Series Vol. 2"; B-side by the Crystals			
❑ 3201	Puddin' and Tain/Then He Kissed Me	1986	5.00
—Black vinyl; B-side by the Crystals			
WHIPPET			
❑ 202	This Thing Called Love/ Spang-a-Lang	1957	20.00
❑ 209	Snap, Crackle and Pop/ Last Night	1958	20.00

ALLIES, THE

Number	Title (A Side/B Side)	Yr	NM
45s			
REPRISE			
❑ 0674	I Would Love You/ The Sound of Children	1968	20.00
VALIANT			
❑ 748	I'll Sell My Soul/Burning Glass	1966	40.00

ALLIN, GG

Number	Title (A Side/B Side)	Yr	NM
45s			
BLACK & BLUE			
❑ (no #)	GG's Xmas Song/ Santa Claus Is Dead	198?	10.00
—B-side by Algae Afterbirth			
❑ (no #) [PS]	GG's Xmas Song/ Santa Claus Is Dead	198?	10.00
—B-side by Algae Afterbirth			
Albums			
ALIVE			
❑ 0001	Brutality and Bloodshed for All	199?	10.00
❑ 0012	Terror in America	199?	10.00
BLACK & BLUE			
❑ (# unknown)	Eat My Fuc	1988	12.00
—Reissue of Blood LP of the same name			
❑ (# unknown)	Banned in Boston	1989	12.00
❑ 006053-X	Always Was, Is and Always Shall Be	1985	50.00
—Reissue of Orange original			
BLOOD			
❑ (# unknown)	Eat My Fuc	198?	50.00
—Hand-decorated plain cover			
HOMESTEAD			
❑ HMS-069	You Give Love a Bad Name	1987	12.00
ORANGE			
❑ (# unknown)	Always Was, Is and Always Shall Be	1980	100.00

ALLISON, GENE

Number	Title (A Side/B Side)	Yr	NM
45s			
CHAMPION			
❑ 1008	Goodbye My Love/ If Things Don't Change	196?	12.00
❑ 1019	Now We're Together/ Understand	196?	12.00
CHEROKEE			
❑ 1022	You Gonna Be Sorry/ I Know I Can Make It	196?	15.00
DECCA			
❑ 30185	You're My Baby/ Somebody Somewhere	1957	15.00
MONUMENT			
❑ 876	Ev'rybody's Got a Little Problem/Now Hear This	1965	8.00
REF-O-REE			
❑ 703	Having a Party/ Almost Sundown	196?	10.00
❑ 709	I Understand/ Somebody Somewhere	196?	10.00
❑ 727	How Long's the Train Been Gone/You Can Make It If You Try & Have Faith	196?	10.00
❑ 729	I Understand/Almost Sundown	196?	10.00
VEE JAY			
❑ 256	You Can Make It If You Try/ Hey, Hey, I Love You	1957	20.00
❑ 273	Have Faith/My Heart Remembers	1958	15.00
❑ 286	I Don't Know Why/ Let's Sit and Talk	1958	15.00
❑ 299	Everything Will Be Alright/ I'm a Fool Wanting You	1958	15.00
❑ 305	Tell Me the Truth/ Reap What You Sow	1959	15.00
❑ 317	Everybody But Me/ I Believe in Myself	1959	15.00
❑ 329	I'll Be Waiting for You/ Let There Be Women	1959	15.00
❑ 341	Why Do You Treat Me So Cold/ Oh Yeah I'm in Love	1960	15.00
❑ 365	Ask/Tell Me Sugar Baby	1960	15.00
Albums			
VEE JAY			
❑ LP-1009 [M]	Gene Allison	1959	300.00
—Maroon label			
❑ LP-1009 [M]	Gene Allison	196?	100.00
—Black label, oval or brackets logo			

ALLISON, KEITH

Number	Title (A Side/B Side)	Yr	NM
45s			
AMY			
❑ 11024	Who Do You Love/Don't Want Nobody But You	1968	12.00
COLUMBIA			
❑ 43619	Look at Me/I Ain't Blaming You	1966	12.00
❑ 43619 [PS]	Look at Me/I Ain't Blaming You	1966	25.00
❑ 43900	Action/Glitter and Gold	1966	12.00
❑ 44028	Louise/Freeborn Man	1967	12.00
❑ 44028 [PS]	Louise/Freeborn Man	1967	25.00
❑ 44853	Birds of a Feather/ To Know Her Is to Love Her	1969	10.00
❑ 45115	Everybody/Wednesday's Child	1970	10.00
WARNER BROS.			
❑ 5681	Sweet Little Rock and Roller/ The Girl Can't Help It	1965	12.00
❑ 5681 [PS]	Sweet Little Rock and Roller/ The Girl Can't Help It	1965	25.00
Albums			
COLUMBIA			
❑ CL 2641 [M]	Keith Allison In Action	1967	25.00
❑ CS 9441 [S]	Keith Allison In Action	1967	25.00

ALLISON, LUTHER

Number	Title (A Side/B Side)	Yr	NM
45s			
GORDY			
❑ 7128	The Little Red Rooster/ Raggedy and Dirty	1973	5.00
❑ 7137	Part Time Love/Now You Got It	1974	5.00
Albums			
DELMARK			
❑ DS-625	Love Me, Mama	1969	25.00
GORDY			
❑ G-964	Bad News Is Coming	1973	10.00
❑ G-967	Luther's Blues	1974	10.00
❑ G-974	Night Life	1976	10.00

ALLISONS, THE (1) British male duo.

Number	Title (A Side/B Side)	Yr	NM
45s			
COLUMBIA			
❑ 42034	Words/Blue Tears	1961	10.00
LONDON			
❑ 1977	Are You Sure/ There's One Thing More	1961	10.00
❑ 1977 [PS]	Are You Sure/ There's One Thing More	1961	25.00
SMASH			
❑ 1749	Lessons in Love/Oh My Love	1962	10.00

ALLISONS, THE (2) American girl group.

Number	Title (A Side/B Side)	Yr	NM
45s			
TIP			
❑ 1011	Surfer Street/Money	1963	40.00

ALLMAN, DUANE Of THE ALLMAN BROTHERS BAND and THE ALLMAN JOYS.

Number	Title (A Side/B Side)	Yr	NM
Albums			
CAPRICORN			
❑ 2CP 0108 [(2)]	An Anthology	1972	20.00
❑ 2CP 0139 [(2)]	An Anthology, Vol. II	1974	20.00
POLYDOR			
❑ PD-1-6338	The Best of Duane Allman	1981	12.00
❑ 827563-1	The Best of Duane Allman	1984	8.00

ALLMAN, DUANE AND GREGG Of THE ALLMAN BROTHERS BAND and THE ALLMAN JOYS.

Number	Title (A Side/B Side)	Yr	NM
45s			
BOLD			
❑ 200	Morning Dew/Morning Dew	1973	10.00

Gregg Allman, *Laid Back*, Capricorn CP 0116, 1973, **$12.**

Number	Title (A Side/B Side)	Yr	NM
❑ 200 [DJ]	Morning Dew/Morning Dew	1973	20.00
—Promo on red vinyl			
Albums			
BOLD			
❑ 33-301	Duane and Gregg Allman	197?	18.00
—Non-gatefold cover			
❑ 33-301	Duane and Gregg Allman	1972	25.00
—Gatefold cover			

ALLMAN, GREGG Of THE ALLMAN BROTHERS BAND and THE ALLMAN JOYS. Also see ALLMAN AND WOMAN.

Number	Title (A Side/B Side)	Yr	NM
12-Inch Singles			
EPIC			
❑ EAS 1173 [DJ]	Can't Get Over You (same on both sides?)	1988	8.00
45s			
CAPRICORN			
❑ 0035	Midnight Rider/ Multi-Colored Lady	1973	5.00
❑ 0042	Don't Mess Up a Good Thing/ Please Call Home	1974	4.00
❑ 0053	Midnight Rider/Don't Mess Up a Good Thing	1975	4.00
—Back to Back Hits series			
❑ 0279	Cryin' Shame/One More Try	1977	4.00
EPIC			
❑ 06998	I'm No Angel/Lead Me On	1987	4.00
❑ 07215	Can't Keep Running/ Anything Goes	1987	3.00
❑ 07430	Evidence of Love/ Anything Goes	1987	3.00
❑ 08041	Slip Away/Every Hungry Woman	1988	3.00
7-Inch Extended Plays			
CAPRICORN			
❑ S CP 0116	Queen of Hearts/Please Call Home//Don't Mess Up a Good Thing/Midnight Rider	1973	10.00
—Jukebox issue; small hole, plays at 33 1/3 rpm			
❑ S CP 0116 [PS]	Laid Back	1973	15.00
—Part of "Little LP" series (LLP #237)			
Albums			
CAPRICORN			
❑ CP 0116	Laid Back	1973	12.00
❑ 2CP 0141 [(2)]	The Gregg Allman Tour	1974	15.00
❑ CP 0181	Playin' Up a Storm	1977	12.00
EPIC			
❑ FE 40531	I'm No Angel	1987	10.00
❑ OE 44033	Just Before the Bullets Fly	1988	10.00

ALLMAN, SHELDON

Number	Title (A Side/B Side)	Yr	NM
45s			
HIFI			
❑ 593	Walk on the Ground/ Radioactive Mama	1960	12.00
ORIGINAL SOUND			
❑ 25	Heartbreak Boulevard/ Little Black Things	1963	10.00

ALLMAN AND WOMAN GREGG ALLMAN and CHER.

Number	Title (A Side/B Side)	Yr	NM
45s			
WARNER BROS.			
❑ 8504	Love Me/Move Me	1977	5.00
Albums			
WARNER BROS.			
❑ BSK 3120	Two the Hard Way	1977	10.00

ALLMAN BROTHERS BAND, THE Also see ALLMAN AND WOMAN; THE ALLMAN JOYS; DUANE ALLMAN; DUANE AND GREGG ALLMAN; GREGG ALLMAN; DICKIE BETTS; THE HOUR GLASS.

Number	Title (A Side/B Side)	Yr	NM
45s			
ARISTA			
❑ 0555	Angeline/So Long	1980	4.00
❑ 0584	Mystery Woman/ Hell and High Water	1981	4.00
❑ 0618	Straight from the Heart/Leavin'	1981	4.00
❑ 0618 [PS]	Straight from the Heart/Leavin'	1981	6.00
❑ 0643	Two Rights/Never Knew How Much	1981	4.00
CAPRICORN			
❑ 0003	Ain't Wastin' Time No More/ Melissa	1972	5.00
❑ 0007	Melissa/Blue Sky	1972	5.00
❑ 0014	One Way Out/Standback	1972	5.00
❑ 0027	Ramblin Man/Pony Boy	1973	5.00
❑ 0036	Jessica/Come and Go Blues	1973	5.00
❑ 0050	Ain't Wastin' Time No More/ Blue Sky	1974	4.00
—Back to Back Hits series			
❑ 0051	Ramblin Man/Jessica	1974	4.00
—Back to Back Hits series			
❑ 0246	Nevertheless/Louisiana Lou and Three Card Monty John	1975	4.00
❑ 0320	Crazy Love/Just Ain't Easy	1979	4.00
❑ 0326	Can't Take It With You/ Sail Away	1979	4.00
❑ 8003	Black Hearted Woman/ Every Hungry Woman	1970	6.00
❑ 8011	Revival (Love Is Everywhere)/ Leave My Blues at Home	1971	5.00
❑ 8014	Whipping Post/Midnight Rider	1971	5.00
EPIC			
❑ 73504	Good Clean Fun/Seven Turns	1990	4.00
7-Inch Extended Plays			
ATLANTIC			
❑ SD 7-2-805	Black Hearted Woman/Revival (Love Is Everywhere)// Whipping Post/Midnight Rider	1973	15.00
—Jukebox issue; small hole, plays at 33 1/3 rpm			
❑ SD 7-2-805 [PS]	Beginnings	1973	15.00
CAPRICORN			
❑ S CP 0111	Come and Go Blues/ Wasted Words//Jessica	1973	12.00
—Jukebox issue; small hole, plays at 33 1/3 rpm			
❑ S CP 0111 [PS]	Brothers and Sisters	1973	12.00
—Part of "Little LP" series (LLP #229)			
Albums			
ARISTA			
❑ AL 9535	Reach for the Sky	1980	10.00
❑ AL 9564	Brothers of the Road	1981	10.00
ATCO			
❑ SD 33-308	The Allman Brothers Band	1969	15.00
❑ SD 33-342	Idlewild South	1970	15.00
❑ SD 2-805 [(2)]	Beginnings	1973	20.00
CAPRICORN			
❑ 2CP 0102 [(2)]	Eat a Peach	1972	15.00
❑ CPN2 0102 [(2)]	Eat a Peach	198?	12.00
❑ CX4 0102 [(2)Q]	Eat a Peach	1974	30.00
❑ CP 0111	Brothers and Sisters	1973	12.00
❑ CPN 0111	Brothers and Sisters	198?	8.00
❑ 2CP 0131 [(2)]	The Allman Brothers Band at Fillmore East	1974	15.00
❑ CPN2 0131 [(2)]	The Allman Brothers Band at Fillmore East	198?	12.00
❑ CX4 0131 [(2)Q]	The Allman Brothers Band at Fillmore East	1974	30.00
❑ 2CX 0132 [(2)]	Beginnings	1974	15.00
❑ CPN2 0132 [(2)]	Beginnings	198?	12.00
❑ CP 0156	Win, Lose or Draw	1975	10.00
❑ CPN 0156	Win, Lose or Draw	198?	8.00
❑ 2CX 0164 [(2)]	The Road Goes On Forever	1975	12.00
❑ 2CX 0177 [(2)]	Wipe the Windows, Check the Oil, Dollar Gas	1976	12.00
❑ CPN 0196	The Allman Brothers Band	1978	10.00
❑ CPN 0197	Idlewild South	1978	10.00
❑ CPN 0218	Enlightened Rogues	1979	10.00
❑ 2-802 [(2)M]	The Allman Brothers Band at Fillmore East	1971	80.00
—Promo only; sticker on front cover says "Promotional DJ Copy Monaural Not for Sale"			
❑ SD 2-802 [(2)S]	The Allman Brothers Band at Fillmore East	1971	20.00
EPIC			
❑ E 46144	Seven Turns	1990	15.00
MOBILE FIDELITY			
❑ 1-157 [(2)]	Eat a Peach	1984	200.00
—Audiophile vinyl			
❑ 1-213	Brothers and Sisters	1994	30.00
—Audiophile vinyl			
NAUTILUS			
❑ NR-30 [(2)]	The Allman Brothers Band at Fillmore East	1982	100.00
—Audiophile vinyl			
POLYDOR			
❑ PD-1-6339	The Best of the Allman Brothers Band	1981	10.00
❑ 823273-1 [(2)]	The Allman Brothers Band at Fillmore East	1984	10.00
❑ 823653-1	The Allman Brothers Band	1984	8.00
❑ 823654-1 [(2)]	Eat a Peach	1984	10.00
❑ 823708-1	The Best of the Allman Brothers Band	1984	8.00
—Reissue of PD-1-6339			

Number	Title (A Side/B Side)	Yr	NM
❑ 825092-1	Brothers and Sisters	1985	8.00
❑ 839417-1 [(6)]	Dreams	1989	40.00

ALLMAN JOYS, THE Early ALLMAN BROTHERS BAND.

45s

DIAL

Number	Title (A Side/B Side)	Yr	NM
❑ 4046	Spoonful/You Deserve Each Other	1966	40.00

Albums

DIAL

Number	Title (A Side/B Side)	Yr	NM
❑ DL 6005	Early Allman	1973	15.00

ALLSUP, TOMMY

45s

GRT

Number	Title (A Side/B Side)	Yr	NM
❑ 38	I'll See Him Through/Snowbird	1971	6.00

Albums

GRT

Number	Title (A Side/B Side)	Yr	NM
❑ 20004	Tommy Allsup and the Tennessee Saxes Play the Hits of Tammy Wynette	1970	20.00

METROMEDIA

Number	Title (A Side/B Side)	Yr	NM
❑ MM 1004	Tommy Allsup and the Nashville Survey Play the Hits of Charley Pride	1969	25.00

REPRISE

Number	Title (A Side/B Side)	Yr	NM
❑ R 6182 [M]	Tommy Allsup Plays the Buddy Holly Songbook	1965	40.00
❑ RS 6182 [S]	Tommy Allsup Plays the Buddy Holly Songbook	1965	50.00

ALMA-KEYS, THE

45s

KISKI

Number	Title (A Side/B Side)	Yr	NM
❑ 2056	Please Come Back to Me/Jumpin' Twist	1962	300.00

ALMOND, JOHNNY

45s

DERAM

Number	Title (A Side/B Side)	Yr	NM
❑ 85052	Music Machine to R.K./Solar Level	1969	8.00

Albums

DERAM

Number	Title (A Side/B Side)	Yr	NM
❑ DES 18030	Music Machine	1969	15.00

ALMOND, MARC

12-Inch Singles

CAPITOL

Number	Title (A Side/B Side)	Yr	NM
❑ V-15418	Tears Run Rings (Just Rite Mix) (Just Rite Edit)// (Acid Tears Dub)/ Everything I Want Love to Be	1988	8.00
❑ V-15597	Desperate Hours (4 versions)	1990	8.00

SIRE

Number	Title (A Side/B Side)	Yr	NM
❑ PRO-A-5332 [DJ]	My Hand Over My Heart (7:12) (5:03)/Deadly Serenade// Money for Love (6:21) (4:51)/ Night and No Morning	1991	12.00
❑ 40234	Jacky (Youth Remix) (Alpine Dub)//Deep Night/ A Love Outgrown	1991	8.00

45s

CAPITOL

Number	Title (A Side/B Side)	Yr	NM
❑ B-44240	Tears Run Rings/Everything I Want Love to Be	1988	3.00
❑ B-44240 [PS]	Tears Run Rings/Everything I Want Love to Be	1988	3.00

Albums

CAPITOL

Number	Title (A Side/B Side)	Yr	NM
❑ C1-91042	The Stars We Are	1988	10.00
❑ C1-94404	Enchanted	1990	15.00

ALPERT, DORE See HERB ALPERT.

ALPERT, HERB

12-Inch Singles

A&M

Number	Title (A Side/B Side)	Yr	NM
❑ 75021 2356 1	North on South St. (7 versions)	1991	8.00
❑ 75021 2359 1	Jump Street (Brighton Daze Remix Radio Edit 3:58) (LP Version 4:46) (Brighton Daze Extended Remix 6:30) (Brighton Daze Remix 6:31) (Ubiquity Mix 6:57)	1991	8.00
❑ SP-12022	Rise/Aranjuez (Mon Amour)	1979	20.00
—Clear vinyl in plastic sleeve			
❑ SP-12032	Rotation/(B-side unknown)	1979	15.00
—Clear vinyl in plastic sleeve			
❑ SP-12034	Beyond (4:14) (6:00)	1980	15.00
—Clear vinyl in plastic sleeve			
❑ SP-12042	Manhattan Melody/Besame Mucho	1981	8.00
❑ SP-12078	Red Hot (3:45) (6:31)	1983	12.00
—Red vinyl			
❑ SP-12145	"8" Ball (Dance Mix)/ (LP Version)	1985	8.00
❑ SP-12226	Keep Your Eye on Me (Extended Version)/Our Song	1987	6.00
❑ SP-12231	Diamonds (3 versions)	1987	6.00
❑ SP-12316	3 O'Clock Jump (Album Version) (12" Version) (Dub Street Mix)	1989	6.00
❑ SP-17127 [DJ]	Kamali (Edit) (LP)	1980	8.00
❑ SP-17163 [DJ]	Magic Man (3:45) (5:33)	1981	10.00
❑ SP-17197 [DJ]	Push and Pull/Fandango// Route 101/Love Me the Way I Am	1982	8.00
—Promo-only four-song sampler			
❑ SP-17210 [DJ]	Fandango (Specially Mixed Version) (same on both sides)	1982	8.00
❑ SP-17237 [DJ]	Garden Party (3:51)/(5:16)	1983	6.00
❑ SP-17499 [(3)DJ]	Making Love in the Rain (5:53) (Remix 5:50)//Diamonds (Cool Summer Mix 6:16) (Cool Summer Dance Mix 5:51) (Instrumental 5:23) (Dub Version 4:20) (7" Edit 3"50)//Keep Your Eye on Me (Extended Version 5:53)/Our Song (3:54)	1987	30.00
—Promo-only set; Record 1 is on red vinyl, Record 2 is on clear vinyl, Record 3 is on blue vinyl; comes in wide cardboard sleeve with no writing except "SP 17499" on spine			

Allman and Woman, *Two the Hard Way*, Warner 3120, 1977, **$10.**

45s

A&M

Number	Title (A Side/B Side)	Yr	NM
❑ 714	Dina/You're Doin' What You Did with Me with Him	1963	10.00
—As "Dore Alpert"			
❑ 729	I'd Do It All Again/ Special Kind of Love	1964	8.00
—As "Dore Alpert"			
❑ 1231	I Need You/The Lady in My Life	1988	3.00
❑ 1446	3 O'Clock Jump/Kalimba	1989	3.00
❑ 2107	Foreign Natives/Mama Way	1979	4.00
—With Hugh Masekela			
❑ 2151	Rise/Aranjuez (Mon Amour)	1979	4.00
❑ 2202	Rotation/Angelina	1979	4.00
❑ 2202 [PS]	Rotation/Ange lina	1979	5.00
❑ 2221	Street Life/1980	1980	4.00
❑ 2221 [PS]	Street Life/1980	1980	5.00
❑ 2246	Beyond/Keep It Goin'	1980	4.00
❑ 2246 [PS]	Beyond/Keep It Goin'	1980	4.00
❑ 2268	Kamali/Interlude (For Erica)	1980	4.00
❑ 2289	Reach for the Stars/ Interlude (For Erica)	1980	4.00
❑ 2356	Magic Man/Fantasy Island	1981	4.00
❑ 2356 [PS]	Magic Man/Fantasy Island	1981	5.00
❑ 2375	Manhattan Melody/You Smile, The Song Begins	1981	4.00
❑ 2422	Route 101/Angel	1982	4.00
❑ 2422 [PS]	Route 101/Angel	1982	5.00
❑ 2426	Fandango/The Lonely Bull	1982	—
—Unreleased?			
❑ 2441	Fandango/Coco Loco	1982	4.00
❑ 2515	Love Me the Way I Am (Quiereme Tal Como Say)/ California Blues	1982	4.00
❑ 2562	Garden Party/Oriental Eyes	1983	4.00
❑ 2573	Sundown/Garden Party	1983	4.00
❑ 2593	Red Hot/Sundown	1983	4.00
❑ 2621	Oriental Eyes/Sundown	1984	4.00
❑ 2632	We Could Be Flying/ Come What May	1984	4.00
—With Lani Hall			
❑ 2757	"8" Ball/Lady Love	1985	3.00
❑ 2757 [PS]	"8" Ball/Lady Love	1985	4.00
❑ 2779	You Are the One/Lady Love	1985	3.00
—With Brenda Russell			
❑ 2779 [PS]	You Are the One/Lady Love	1985	4.00
❑ 2802	African Flame/Lady Love	1985	3.00
❑ 2915	Keep Your Eye on Me/ Our Song	1987	3.00
❑ 2915 [PS]	Keep Your Eye on Me/ Our Song	1987	3.00

Number	Title (A Side/B Side)	Yr	NM
2929	Diamonds/African Flame	1987	3.00
2929 [PS]	Diamonds/African Flame	1987	5.00
2949	Making Love in the Rain/ Rocket to the Moon	1987	3.00
2949 [PS]	Making Love in the Rain/ Rocket to the Moon	1987	3.00
2973	Our Song/African Flame	1987	3.00

ANDEX

Number	Title (A Side/B Side)	Yr	NM
4036	Summer School/Hully Gully	1959	10.00
—As "Herbie Alpert Sextet"			

CARNIVAL

Number	Title (A Side/B Side)	Yr	NM
701	Tell It to the Birds/ Fallout Shelter	1962	10.00
—As "Dore Alpert"			

CAROL

Number	Title (A Side/B Side)	Yr	NM
700	Sweet Georgia Brown/ Vipers Blues	1961	10.00

DOT

Number	Title (A Side/B Side)	Yr	NM
16396	Fallout Shelter/Tell It to the Birds	1962	10.00
—As "Dore Alpert"			

RCA VICTOR

Number	Title (A Side/B Side)	Yr	NM
47-7918	Gotta Get a Girl/Dreamland	1961	12.00
—As "Dore Alpert"			
47-7988	Little Lost Lover/Won't You Be My Valentine	1962	12.00
—As "Dore Alpert"			

Albums

A&M

Number	Title	Yr	NM
SP-3714	Rise	1980	8.00
—Reissue of 4790			
SP-3717	Beyond	1980	8.00
SP-3728	Magic Man	1981	8.00
SP-3731	Fandango	1982	8.00
SP-4591	Just You and Me	1976	10.00
SP-4790	Rise	1979	10.00
SP-4949	Blow Your Own Horn	1983	8.00
SP-5082	Wild Romance	1985	8.00
SP-5125	Keep Your Eye on Me	1987	8.00
SP-5209	Under a Spanish Moon	1988	8.00
SP-5273	My Abstract Heart	1989	8.00
75021 5345 1	North on South Street	1991	12.00

MOBILE FIDELITY

Number	Title	Yr	NM
1-053	Rise	1981	25.00
—Audiophile vinyl			

ALPERT, HERB, AND THE TIJUANA BRASS

12-Inch Singles

A&M

Number	Title (A Side/B Side)	Yr	NM
SP-12104	Bullish (3:58)/(5:49)	1984	8.00

45s

A&M

Number	Title (A Side/B Side)	Yr	NM
703	The Lonely Bull (El Solo Torro)/ Acapulco 1922	1962	10.00
—With pale brown label and no horn logo			
705	Marching Through Madrid/ Struttin' with Maria	1963	8.00
711	Mexican Corn/Let It Be Me	1963	8.00
721	Spanish Harlem/A-Mer-I-Ca	1963	8.00
732	Mexican Drummer Man/ Great Manolete	1963	8.00
742	The Mexican Shuffle/ Numero Cinco	1964	8.00
751	All My Loving/El Presidente	1964	8.00
755	South of the Border/ Up Cherry Street	1965	6.00
760	Whipped Cream/Las Mananitas	1965	6.00
767	El Garbanzo/Mae	1965	6.00
775	Taste of Honey/ Third Man Theme	1965	6.00
787	Zorba the Greek/Tijuana Taxi	1965	6.00
792	What Now My Love/ Spanish Flea	1966	6.00
792 [PS]	What Now My Love/ Spanish Flea	1966	10.00
805	The Work Song/Plucky	1966	6.00
805 [PS]	The Work Song/Plucky	1966	10.00
813	Flamingo/So What's New	1966	6.00
813 [PS]	Flamingo/So What's New	1966	10.00
823	Mame/Our Day Will Come	1966	6.00
823 [PS]	Mame/Our Day Will Come	1966	10.00
840	Wade in the Water/ Mexican Road Race	1967	5.00
840 [PS]	Wade in the Water/ Mexican Road Race	1967	8.00
850	Casino Royale/Wall Street Rag	1967	5.00
850 [PS]	Casino Royale/Wall Street Rag	1967	8.00
860	The Happening/ Town Without Pity	1967	5.00
860 [PS]	The Happening/ Town Without Pity	1967	8.00
870	A Banda/Miss Frenchy Brown	1967	5.00
870 [PS]	A Banda/Miss Frenchy Brown	1967	8.00
890	Carmen/A Love So Fine	1967	5.00
890 [PS]	Carmen/A Love So Fine	1967	8.00
925	Cabaret/Slick	1968	5.00
925 [PS]	Cabaret/Slick	1968	8.00
929	This Guy's in Love with You/ A Quiet Tear	1968	5.00
929 [PS]	This Guy's in Love with You/ A Quiet Tear	1968	8.00
960	Yo Doy Ese Amor (This Guy's in Love with You)/ A Love So Fine	1968	6.00
964	To Wait for Love/Bud	1968	5.00
964 [PS]	To Wait for Love/Bud	1968	8.00
1001	My Favorite Things/ The Christmas Song	1968	6.00
1001 [PS]	My Favorite Things/ The Christmas Song	1968	10.00
1015	She Touched Me/ My Favorite Things	1969	5.00
1028	Monday, Monday/ Treasure of San Miguel	1969	5.00
1043	Zazueira/Treasure of San Miguel	1969	5.00
1043 [PS]	Zazueira/Treasure of San Miguel	1969	6.00
1065	Without Her/Sandbox	1969	5.00
1065 [PS]	Without Her/Sandbox	1969	6.00
1094	Ob-La-Di, Ob-La-Da/Girl Talk	1969	5.00
1100	Marjorine/Warm	1969	5.00
1102	Marjorine/Ob-La-Di, Ob-La-Da	1969	5.00
1143	You Are My Life/ Good Morning Mr. Sunshine	1969	5.00
1143 [PS]	You Are My Life/ Good Morning Mr. Sunshine	1969	6.00
1159	The Maltese Melody/ Country Lake	1969	5.00
1194	Brasilia/Love Potion #9	1970	4.00
1225	Jerusalem/Strike Up the Band	1970	4.00
1225 [PS]	Jerusalem/Strike Up the Band	1970	5.00
1237	The Bell That Couldn't Jingle/ Las Mananitas	1970	5.00
1261	Summertime/Hurt So Bad	1971	4.00
1261 [PS]	Summertime/Hurt So Bad	1971	6.00
1284	Montezuma's Revenge/Darlin'	1971	4.00
1337	Without Her/Zazuiera	1972	4.00
1337 [PS]	Without Her/Zazuiera	1972	6.00
1420	Last Tango in Paris/ Fire and Rain	1973	4.00
1423	The Nicest Things Happen/ Last Tango in Paris	1973	4.00
1526	Fox Hunt/I Can't Go On Living, Baby, Without You	1974	4.00
1542	You Smile, the Song Begins/ Save the Sunlight	1974	4.00
1688	Coney Island/Ratatouille	1975	4.00
1714	El Bimbo/Catfish	1975	4.00
1762	The Whistle Song (Whistlestar)/Carmine	1975	4.00
1852	Promenade/Musique	1976	4.00
1962	African Summer/You in Me	1977	4.00
2655	Bullish/Oriental Eyes	1984	4.00
—As "Herb Alpert Tijuana Brass"			
2655 [PS]	Bullish/Oriental Eyes	1984	4.00
2690	Struttin' on Five/ Blow Your Own Horn	1984	4.00
—As "Herb Alpert Tijuana Brass"			

7-Inch Extended Plays

A&M

Number	Title (A Side/B Side)	Yr	NM
SP-401	The Lonely Bull/Acapulco 1922/Struttin' with Maria// Never on Sunday/A Quiet Tear/Tijuana Sauerkraut	196?	12.00
—Jukebox issue; small hole, plays at 33 1/3 rpm			
SP-401 [PS]	The Lonely Bull	196?	12.00
SP-403	A-Me-Ri-Ca/Surfin' Senorita/ Crea Mi Amor//Mexican Corn/Swinger from Seville/ Winds of Barcelona	1964	12.00
—Jukebox issue; small hole, plays at 33 1/3 rpm			
SP-403 [PS]	Herb Alpert's Tijuana Brass Vol. 2	1964	12.00
SP 408	Mexican Shuffle/Up Cherry Street/All My Loving//South of the Border/I've Grown Accustomed to Her Face/ Hello, Dolly	1965	12.00
—Stereo jukebox issue; small hole, plays at 33 1/3 rpm			
SP 408 [PS]	South of the Border	1965	12.00
SP 410	Taste of Honey/Green Peppers/Whipped Cream// Bittersweet Samba/Lollipops and Roses/El Garbanzo	1965	10.00
—Jukebox issue; small hole, plays at 33 1/3 rpm			
SP 410 [PS]	Whipped Cream and Other Delights	1965	10.00
SP 412	3rd Man Theme/Cinco De Mayo/Tijuana Taxi//And the Angels Sing/Spanish Flea/ A Walk in the Black Forest	1966	10.00
—Jukebox issue; small hole, plays at 33 1/3 rpm			
SP 412 [PS]	Going Places!	1966	10.00
SP 414	What Now My Love/Freckles/ Plucky//Memories of Madrid/ So What's New/Brasilia	1966	10.00
—Jukebox issue; small hole, plays at 33 1/3 rpm			
SP 414 [PS]	What Now My Love	1966	10.00
SP 424	Gotta Lotta Livin' to Do/Lady Godiva/Bo-Bo//Miss Frenchy Brown/In a Little Spanish Town/Wade in the Water	1966	10.00
—Jukebox issue; small hole, plays at 33 1/3 rpm			
SP 424 [PS]	Casino Royale	1966	10.00
SP 434	A Banda/"Bud"/Love So Fine// With a Little Help from My Friends/Cowboys and Indians/Carmen	1967	10.00
—Jukebox issue; small hole, plays at 33 1/3 rpm			
SP 434 [PS]	Herb Alpert's Ninth	1967	10.00
SP 446	A Beautiful Friend/Cabaret/ Panama//Slick/She Touched Me/The Robin	1968	10.00
—Jukebox issue; small hole, plays at 33 1/3 rpm			
SP 446 [PS]	The Beat of the Brass	1968	10.00

Albums

A&M

Number	Title	Yr	NM
LP-101 [M]	The Lonely Bull	1962	20.00
—Originals on yellowish label with brown print			
LP-101 [M]	The Lonely Bull	1963	15.00
—Second pressings with brown label and A&M logo at top			
LP-101 [M]	The Lonely Bull	1964	12.00
—Third pressing with brown label and A&M logo at left			
SP-101 [S]	The Lonely Bull	1962	25.00
—Original editions had this number			
LP-103 [M]	Herb Alpert's Tijuana Brass, Vol. 2	1963	15.00
—Brown label with A&M logo at top			
LP-103 [M]	Herb Alpert's Tijuana Brass, Vol. 2	1964	12.00
—Brown label with A&M logo at left			
SP-103 [S]	Herb Alpert's Tijuana Brass, Vol. 2	1963	20.00
—Original issues had this number			
LP-108 [M]	South of the Border	1964	12.00
SP-108 [S]	South of the Border	1964	20.00
—Original issues had this number			
LP-110 [M]	Whipped Cream & Other Delights	1965	10.00
LP-112 [M]	Going Places	1965	10.00
LP-114 [M]	What Now My Love	1966	10.00
LP-119 [M]	S.R.O.	1966	10.00
LP-124 [M]	Sounds Like	1967	10.00
LP166 [M]	Christmas Album	1968	25.00
—Mono is white label promo only			
SP-3101	The Lonely Bull	198?	8.00
—Reissue			
SP-3113	Christmas Album	198?	8.00
—Reissue of SP-4166			
SP-3157	Whipped Cream & Other Delights	198?	8.00
—Reissue			
SP-3263	South of the Border	1984	8.00
SP-3264	Going Places	1984	8.00
—Reissue			
SP-3265	What Now My Love	1984	8.00
SP-3266	The Beat of the Brass	1984	8.00
—Reissue			
SP-3267	Greatest Hits	1984	8.00
—Reissue			
SP-3268	Solid Brass	1984	8.00
SP-3269	Greatest Hits, Vol. 2	1984	8.00
SP-3521 [(2)]	Foursider	1973	12.00
SP-3620	You Smile — The Song Begins	1974	10.00
SP-4101 [S]	The Lonely Bull	1962	15.00
SP-4103 [S]	Herb Alpert's Tijuana Brass, Vol. 2	1963	15.00
SP-4108 [S]	South of the Border	1964	15.00
SP-4110 [S]	Whipped Cream & Other Delights	1965	12.00
SP-4112 [S]	Going Places	1965	12.00
SP-4114 [S]	What Now My Love	1966	12.00
SP-4119 [S]	S.R.O.	1966	12.00
SP-4124 [S]	Sounds Like	1967	12.00
SP-4134	Herb Alpert's Ninth	1967	10.00
SP-4146	The Beat of the Brass	1968	10.00
SP-4166 [S]	Christmas Album	1968	12.00
SP-4190	Warm	1969	10.00
SP-4228	The Brass Are Comin'	1969	10.00
SP-4245	Greatest Hits	1970	10.00
SP-4314	Summertime	1971	10.00
SP-4341	Solid Brass	1972	10.00
SP-4521	Coney Island	1975	10.00
SP-4627	Greatest Hits, Vol. 2	1976	10.00
SP-5022	Bullish	1984	8.00
SP-6011 [(2)]	Foursider	197?	10.00
—Reissue			
LP-9004 [DJ]	The Best from Herb Alpert & The Tijuana Brass	196?	15.00
—Promo-only compilation			
ST-90073 [S]	South of the Border	1964	20.00
—Capitol Record Club edition			

Number | Title (A Side/B Side) | Yr | NM

❑ T-90074 [M] Herb Alpert's Tijuana Brass, Vol. 2 1964 20.00
—Capitol Record Club edition
❑ ST-90387 [S] Whipped Cream & Other Delights 1965 15.00
—Capitol Record Club edition
❑ ST-90507 [S] Going Places 1965 20.00
—Capitol Record Club edition
❑ T-90507 [M] Going Places 1965 15.00
—Capitol Record Club edition
❑ T-90655 [M] What Now My Love 1966 12.00
—Capitol Record Club edition
❑ SW-93870 Summertime 197? 12.00
—Capitol Record Club edition

LONGINES SYMPHONETTE
❑ LWS-500 [(5)] Treasury of Herb Alpert and the Tijuana Brass 196? 25.00
—Also contains music by the Baja Marimba Band; records are individually numbered from 500 through 504

ALPERT, HERB/HUGH MASEKELA Also see each artist's individual listings.

45s

HORIZON
❑ 115 Skokiaan/African Summer 1978 4.00
❑ 115 [PS] Skokiaan/African Summer 1978 5.00
❑ 116 Lobo/African Summer 1978 4.00

Albums

A&M
❑ SP-3150 Herb Alpert/Hugh Masekela 198? 8.00
❑ SP-4727 Main Event 1978 10.00

HORIZON
❑ 728 Herb Alpert/Hugh Masekela 1978 10.00

ALTAIRS, THE GEORGE BENSON was a member.

45s

AMY
❑ 803 If You Love Me/Groove Time 1960 20.00

ALTON AND JIMMY

45s

SUN
❑ 323 Have Faith in My Love/No More Crying the Blues 1959 25.00

ALVANS, THE

45s

MAY
❑ 102 Love Is a Game/What Can It Be 1961 150.00

ALVIN, DANNY

Albums

JAZZOLOGY
❑ 8 [M] Danny Alvin and the Kings of Dixieland 1964 20.00
❑ S-8 [S] Danny Alvin and the Kings of Dixieland 1964 20.00

STEPHENY
❑ MF-4002 [M] Club Basin Street 1957 50.00

ALVIN, DAVE

45s

EPIC
❑ 34-07394 Every Night About This Time/Brother on the Line 1987 4.00

Albums

EPIC
❑ FE 40921 Romeo's Escape 1987 10.00

ALVIN AND BILL

45s

FERNWOOD
❑ 124 Typing Jive/How Long 1960 60.00

AMAZING RHYTHM ACES

45s

ABC
❑ 12078 Third Rate Romance/Mystery Train 1975 5.00
❑ 12142 Amazing Grace (Used to Be Her Favorite Song)/Beautiful Lie 1975 4.00
❑ 12202 Same Ol' Me/The End Is Not in Sight 1976 4.00
❑ 12242 Dancin' the Night Away/If I Just Knew What to Say 1976 4.00
❑ 12272 Two Can Do It Too/Living in a World Unknown 1977 4.00
❑ 12287 Just Between You and Me and the Wall/Never Been to the Islands 1977 4.00
❑ 12359 Burning the Ballroom Down/All That I Had Left (With You) 1978 4.00
❑ 12369 Ashes of Love/All That I Had Left (With You) 1978 4.00
❑ 12454 Lipstick Traces (On a Cigarette)/Whispering in the Night 1979 4.00

COLUMBIA
❑ 10983 Love and Happiness/Homestead in My Heart 1979 4.00

WARNER BROS.
❑ 49543 Living on Borrowed Time/What Kind of Love Is This 1980 4.00
❑ 49600 I Musta Died and Gone to Texas/Give Me Flowers While I'm Living 1980 4.00

Albums

ABC
❑ D-913 Stacked Deck 1975 20.00
❑ D-940 Too Stuffed to Jump 1976 15.00
❑ AB-1005 Toucan Do It Too 1977 15.00
❑ AA-1063 Burning the Ballroom Down 1978 15.00
❑ AA-1123 The Amazing Rhythm Aces 1979 20.00

COLUMBIA
❑ JC 36083 The Amazing Rhythm Aces 1979 12.00
—Reissue of ABC 1123

WARNER BROS.
❑ BSK 3476 How the Hell Do You Spell Rythum? 1980 12.00

AMBASSADORS, THE (1) Male vocal group from Philadelphia.

45s

ARCTIC
❑ 147 I Really Love You/I Can't Believe You Love Me 1969 12.00
❑ 150 Ain't Got the Love of One Girl/Music Makes You Wanna Dance 1969 10.00
❑ 153 Storm Warning/I Dig You Baby 1969 10.00
❑ 156 Can't Take My Eyes Off You/A.W.O.L. 1969 10.00

ATLANTIC
❑ 2442 (I've Got to Find) Happiness)/I'm So Proud of My Baby 1967 10.00
❑ 2491 Good Love Gone Bad/Happiness 1968 10.00
❑ 2547 We Got Love/Never Get Tired of Loving You 1968 10.00

Albums

ARCTIC
❑ ALPS-1005 Soul Summit 1969 25.00

AMBASSADORS, THE (2) British band known as The Saints in the U.K.

45s

DOT
❑ 16528 Surfin' John Brown/Big Breaker 1963 30.00

AMBASSADORS, THE (U) More than one group. Some of these may go with (1) above.

45s

CUCA
❑ 1022 Christmas Polka/Little Drummer Boy 1960 12.00

SOUND STAGE 7
❑ 2588 If You Don't Know (You Better Ask Somebody)/There's Something on My Baby's Mind 1967 10.00

TIME
❑ 1007 El Grippo/Can't Believe Ya 1959 15.00

TIMELY
❑ 1001 Darling I'm Sorry/Willa-Bea 1954 400.00

UPTOWN
❑ 734 I Need Someone/Bear With Me 1965 25.00

AMBOY DUKES, THE Also see CACTUS; TED NUGENT.

45s

DISCREET
❑ 1199 Sweet Revenge/Ain't It the Truth 1974 8.00
—As "Ted Nugent and the Amboy Dukes"

MAINSTREAM
❑ 676 Baby Please Don't Go/Psalms of Aftermath 1968 12.00
❑ 684 Journey to the Center of the Mind/Mississippi Murderer 1968 15.00
❑ 693 You Talk Sunshine, I Breathe Fire/Scottish Tea 1968 12.00
❑ 700 Prodigal Man/Good Natured Emma 1969 12.00
❑ 704 For His Namesake/Loaded for Bear 1969 12.00
❑ 711 Flight of the Byrd/Ivory Castles 1969 12.00

Albums

DISCREET
❑ DS 2181 Call of the Wild 1974 15.00
—As "Ted Nugent and the Amboy Dukes"
❑ DS 2203 Tooth, Fang and Claw 1974 15.00
—As "Ted Nugent and the Amboy Dukes"

MAINSTREAM
❑ S-414 Dr. Slingshot 1975 15.00
❑ S-421 Ted Nugent and the Amboy Dukes 1976 30.00
—Reissue of early material
❑ S-2-801 [(2)] Journeys and Migrations 1974 30.00
—Reissue of 6112 and 6118
❑ S-6104 [S] The Amboy Dukes 1967 40.00
❑ S-6112 Journey to the Center of the Mind 1968 40.00
❑ S-6118 Migration 1968 40.00
❑ S-6125 The Best of the Original Amboy Dukes 1969 30.00
❑ 56104 [M] The Amboy Dukes 1967 80.00

POLYDOR
❑ 24-4012 Marriage on the Rocks/Rock Bottom 1970 25.00
❑ 24-4035 Survival of the Fittest/Live 1971 25.00
—As "Ted Nugent and the Amboy Dukes"

AMBROSE SLADE See SLADE.

AMBROSIA

12-Inch Singles

WARNER BROS.
❑ PRO-A-1024 [DJ]For Openers//Kid No More/How Can You Love Me 1982 10.00

45s

FULL MOON
❑ 49654 Outside/I Can't Tell You Why 1981 5.00
—B-side by Eagles

SCEPTER
❑ 12373 Shine On/Listen To Her Sing 1973 8.00

20TH CENTURY
❑ 2207 Holdin' On to Yesterday/Make Us All Aware 1975 5.00
❑ 2244 Nice, Nice, Very Nice/Lover Arrive 1975 4.00
❑ 2310 Can't Let a Woman/The Brunt 1976 4.00
❑ 2327 Magical Mystery Tour/Cowboy Star 1977 5.00

WARNER BROS.
❑ 8640 How Much I Feel/Ready for Amarillo 1978 4.00
—With white label
❑ 8640 How Much I Feel/Ready for Amarillo 1978 5.00
—With "Burbank..." palm trees label
❑ 8699 Life Beyond L.A./Angola 1978 4.00
❑ 8817 If Heaven Could Find Me/Apothecary 1979 4.00
❑ 29937 Feelin' Alive Again/For Openers 1982 4.00
❑ 29996 How Can You Love Me/Still Not Satisfied 1982 4.00
❑ 49225 Biggest Part of Me/Livin' on My Own 1980 4.00
❑ 49508 You're the Only Woman (You & I)/Shape I'm In 1980 4.00
❑ 49590 Cryin' in the Rain/No Big Deal 1980 4.00

Albums

NAUTILUS
❑ NR-23 Life Beyond L.A. 1981 30.00
—Audiophile vinyl

20TH CENTURY
❑ T-434 Ambrosia 1975 10.00
—New cover without black border
❑ T-434 Ambrosia 1975 12.00
—Original cover with black border
❑ T-510 Somewhere I've Never Traveled 1976 10.00
—Standard cover
❑ T-510 Somewhere I've Never Traveled 1976 12.00
—Fold-open cover in the shape of a pyramid

WARNER BROS.
❑ BSK 3135 Life Beyond L.A. 1978 10.00
❑ BSK 3181 Ambrosia 1978 8.00
—Reissue of 20th Century 434
❑ BSK 3368 One Eighty 1980 10.00
❑ BSK 3638 Road Island 1982 10.00

AMECHE, JIM

45s

DELTONE
❑ 5016 The First Christmas Tree (Part 1)/The First Christmas Tree (Part 2) 1964 10.00

Except when noted otherwise, VG = 25% of NM, and VG+ = 50% of NM. (Example: VG = $2.00, VG+ = $4.00 and NM = $8.00.)

A

Number	Title (A Side/B Side)	Yr	NM
RIC			
❑ 137	The First Christmas Tree (Part 1)/The First Christmas Tree (Part 2)	1964	10.00
❑ 137 [PS]	The First Christmas Tree (Part 1)/The First Christmas Tree (Part 2)	1964	12.00

AMELIO, JOHNNY

45s

Number	Title (A Side/B Side)	Yr	NM
BLUE MOON			
❑ 405	Jugue/Downbeat	1957	150.00
❑ 408	Jo-Ann, Jo-Ann/I'll Forever Love You	1958	100.00
❑ 410	Jugue/Jo-Ann, Jo-Ann	1958	80.00

AMEN CORNER

45s

Number	Title (A Side/B Side)	Yr	NM
DERAM			
❑ 7521	Run, Run, Run/High in the Sky	1968	10.00
❑ 85014	Gin House Blues/I Know	1967	12.00
❑ 85021	Nema/World of Broken Hearts	1967	12.00
IMMEDIATE			
❑ 5013	If Paradise Is Half As Nice/Hey Hey Girl	1968	10.00

AMERICA

45s

Number	Title (A Side/B Side)	Yr	NM
AMERICAN INT'L.			
❑ 700	California Dreamin'/See It My Way	1979	5.00
—B-side by FDR			
❑ 700 [PS]	California Dreamin'/See It My Way	1979	5.00
CAPITOL			
❑ 4752	Only Game in Town/High in the City	1979	4.00
❑ 4777	All My Life/One Morning	1979	4.00
❑ 4817	All Around/1960	1980	4.00
❑ 4915	You Could've Been the One/Catch That Train	1980	4.00
❑ 4950	One in a Million/Hangover	1980	4.00
❑ B-5142	You Can Do Magic/Even the Score	1982	4.00
❑ B-5177	Right Before Your Eyes/Inspector Mills	1982	3.00
❑ B-5177 [PS]	Right Before Your Eyes/Inspector Mills	1982	3.00
❑ B-5236	The Border/Sometimes Lovers	1983	3.00
❑ B-5236 [PS]	The Border/Sometimes Lovers	1983	3.00
❑ B-5275	Cast the Spirit/My Dear	1983	3.00
❑ B-5398	Special Girl/Unconditional Love	1984	3.00
❑ B-5430	(Can't Fall Asleep to a) Lullaby/Fallin' Off the World	1984	3.00
WARNER BROS.			
❑ 7555	A Horse with No Name/Everyone I Meet Is From California	1972	6.00
❑ 7580	I Need You/Riverside	1972	5.00
❑ 7580 [PS]	I Need You/Riverside	1972	6.00
❑ 7641	Ventura Highway/Saturn Nights	1972	5.00
❑ 7650	A Horse with No Name/I Need You	1973	4.00
—"Back to Back Hits" series			
❑ 7670	Don't Cross the River/To Each His Own	1972	5.00
❑ 7694	Only in Your Heart/Moon Song	1973	5.00
❑ 7725	Muskrat Love/Cornwall Blank	1973	5.00
❑ 7760	Rainbow Song/Willow Tree Lullaby	1973	5.00
❑ 7785	She's Gonna Let You Down/Green Monkey	1974	5.00
❑ 7839	Tin Man/In the Country	1974	5.00
❑ 8014	Tin Man/In the Country	1974	4.00
❑ 8048	Lonely People/Mad Dog	1974	5.00
❑ 8048 [PS]	Lonely People/Mad Dog	1974	6.00
❑ 8086	Sister Golden Hair/Midnight	1975	5.00
❑ 8118	Daisy Jane/Tomorrow	1975	5.00
❑ 8157	Woman Tonight/Bell Tree	1975	5.00
❑ 8212	Today's the Day/Hideaway (Part 2)	1976	5.00
❑ 8238	Amber Cascades/Who Loves You	1976	5.00
❑ 8285	She's Beside You/She's a Liar	1976	5.00
❑ 8373	God of the Sun/Down to the Water	1977	5.00
❑ 8397	Don't Cry Baby/Monster	1977	5.00

Albums

Number	Title (A Side/B Side)	Yr	NM
CAPITOL			
❑ SO-11950	Silent Letter	1979	10.00
❑ SOO-12098	Alibi	1980	10.00
❑ ST-12209	View from the Ground	1982	10.00
❑ ST-12277	Your Move	1983	10.00
❑ ST-12370	Perspective	1984	10.00
❑ ST-12422	In Concert	1985	10.00
❑ SN-16275	Alibi	1982	8.00
❑ SN-16350	View from the Ground	1985	8.00
❑ SN-16361	Your Move	1985	8.00
WARNER BROS.			
❑ BS 2576	America	1971	25.00
—First pressings omit "A Horse with No Name"			
❑ BS 2576	America	1972	12.00
—With "A Horse with No Name" mentioned on front cover; green label			
❑ BS 2576	America	1972	15.00
—Transitional edition includes "A Horse with No Name" but doesn't mention it on the front cover			
❑ BS 2655	Homecoming	1972	12.00
❑ BS 2728	Hat Trick	1973	12.00
❑ BS 2808	Holiday	1974	12.00
❑ BS4 2808 [Q]	Holiday	1974	20.00
❑ BS 2852	Hearts	1975	12.00
❑ BS4 2852 [Q]	Hearts	1975	20.00
❑ BS 2894	History/America's Greatest Hits	1975	12.00
❑ BS 2932	Hideaway	1976	12.00
❑ BSK 3017	Harbor	1977	12.00
❑ BSK 3110	History/America's Greatest Hits	1977	10.00
—Reissue of BS 2894 with "Burbank" palm trees label (later white labels are $8 NM)			
❑ BSK 3136	America/Live	1977	12.00

AMERICAN BEATLES, THE

45s

Number	Title (A Side/B Side)	Yr	NM
BYP			
❑ 1001	She's Mine/Theme of the American Beetles	1964	20.00
—As "The American Beetles"			
ROULETTE			
❑ 4550	You Did It to Me/Don't Be Unkind	1964	15.00
❑ 4559	School Days/Hey Hey Girl	1964	15.00
—As "The American Beetles"			

AMERICAN BLUES, THE

Early incarnation of ZZ TOP.

45s

Number	Title (A Side/B Side)	Yr	NM
AMY			
❑ 997	Your Love Is True/Say So	1967	25.00
KARMA			
❑ 1001	If I Were a Carpenter/(B-side unknown)	1967	40.00

Albums

Number	Title (A Side/B Side)	Yr	NM
KARMA			
❑ 1001	The American Blues Is Here	1967	400.00
UNI			
❑ 73044	The American Blues Do Their Thing	1968	60.00

AMERICAN BLUES EXCHANGE, THE

Albums

Number	Title (A Side/B Side)	Yr	NM
TAYL			
❑ TLS-1	Blueprints	1969	400.00

AMERICAN BREED, THE

Members of this band later formed RUFUS.

45s

Number	Title (A Side/B Side)	Yr	NM
ACTA			
❑ 802	I Don't Think You Know/Give Two Young Lovers a Chance	1967	8.00
❑ 804	Step Out of Your Mind/Same Old Thing	1967	10.00
❑ 808	Don't Forget About Me/Short Skirts	1967	8.00
❑ 811	Bend Me, Shape Me/Mindrocker	1967	12.00
❑ 821	Green Light/Don't It Make You Cry	1968	8.00
❑ 821 [PS]	Green Light/Don't It Make You Cry	1968	20.00
❑ 824	Ready, Willing and Able/Take Me If You Want Me	1968	8.00
❑ 827	Anyway You Want Me/Master of My Fate	1968	8.00
❑ 830	Private Zoo/Keep the Faith	1968	8.00
❑ 833	Hunky Funky/Enter Her Majesty	1969	8.00
❑ 836	Room at the Top/Walls	1969	8.00
❑ 837	Cool It/The Brain	1969	8.00
PARAMOUNT			
❑ 0040	Can't Make It Without You/When I'm With You	1970	6.00
❑ 100	Bend Me, Shape Me/Step Out of Your Mind	197?	6.00

Albums

Number	Title (A Side/B Side)	Yr	NM
ACTA			
❑ 8002 [M]	The American Breed	1967	20.00
❑ 8003 [M]	Bend Me, Shape Me	1968	20.00
❑ 8006 [M]	Pumpkin, Powder, Scarlet & Green	1968	50.00
—Stock label; the cover is the same as stereo but with a "Monaural" sticker attached			
❑ 8008 [M]	Lonely Side of the City	1969	50.00
—In stereo cover with "Monaural" sticker; record is regular yellow label			
❑ 38002 [S]	The American Breed	1967	25.00
❑ 38003 [S]	Bend Me, Shape Me	1968	25.00
❑ 38006 [S]	Pumpkin, Powder, Scarlet & Green	1968	20.00
❑ 38008 [S]	Lonely Side of the City	1969	20.00

AMERICAN DREAM, THE

45s

Number	Title (A Side/B Side)	Yr	NM
AMPEX			
❑ 11001	Goodnews/I Ain't Searchin'	1970	10.00
❑ 11001 [PS]	Goodnews/I Ain't Searchin'	1970	15.00

Albums

Number	Title (A Side/B Side)	Yr	NM
AMPEX			
❑ A-10101	The American Dream	1970	20.00
—Produced by Todd Rundgren			

AMERICAN EAGLE

45s

Number	Title (A Side/B Side)	Yr	NM
DECCA			
❑ 32788	Family/Gospel	1971	8.00
❑ 32833	Ballad of a Well-Known Gun/On the Rack	1971	10.00

Albums

Number	Title (A Side/B Side)	Yr	NM
DECCA			
❑ DL 75258	American Eagle	1971	20.00

AMERICAN FOUR, THE

With Arthur Lee, future leader of LOVE.

45s

Number	Title (A Side/B Side)	Yr	NM
SELMA			
❑ 2001	Luci Baines/Soul Food	1964	50.00

AMERICAN REVOLUTION, THE

Albums

Number	Title (A Side/B Side)	Yr	NM
FLICK DISC			
❑ FL-45,002 [M]	The American Revolution	1968	50.00
—White label promo in stereo cover with "Not for Sale DJ Monaural" sticker on front			
❑ FLS-45,002 [S]	The American Revolution	1968	25.00

AMERICAN SPRING

Formed by ex-members of THE HONEYS. Also see SPRING.

45s

Number	Title (A Side/B Side)	Yr	NM
COLUMBIA			
❑ 45834	Fallin' in Love/Shyin' Away	1973	30.00
❑ 45834 [PS]	Fallin' in Love/Shyin' Away	1973	60.00

AMES, APRIL

45s

Number	Title (A Side/B Side)	Yr	NM
UNICAL			
❑ 7M-0004	Oh My Johnny Boy/You Are My Sunshine	195?	12.00
ZEPHYR			
❑ ZR 70-013	Imagination/A Smile Will Go a Long, Long Way	1957	12.00

AMES, ED

Also see THE AMES BROTHERS.

45s

Number	Title (A Side/B Side)	Yr	NM
HELLO LYNDON			
❑ RPKM-4426	Hello, Lyndon!/Hello, Lyndon! (Chorus)	1964	25.00
❑ RPKM-4426 [PS]	Hello, Lyndon!/Hello, Lyndon! (Chorus)	1964	50.00
—Promotional item for Lyndon Johnson's 1964 election campaign			
RCA VICTOR			
❑ 47-6791	The Bean Song/I'd Give You the World	1957	12.00
—As "Eddie Ames"			
❑ 47-8231	My Love Is Yours/Somewhere	1963	8.00
❑ 47-8245	Before I Kiss the World Goodbye/They Were You	1963	8.00
❑ 47-8320	It Only Takes a Moment/The Time Has Come	1964	8.00
❑ 47-8393	Give Me Back My Life/Monica (Love Theme from "The Carpetbaggers")	1964	8.00
❑ 47-8483	Try to Remember/Love Is Here to Stay	1964	8.00
❑ 47-8547	Dio Mio/Weaver, Weaver	1965	8.00
❑ 47-8700	Pretty Is/Melinda	1965	8.00
❑ 47-8752	River Boy/A Man and a Woman	1965	8.00
❑ 47-8871	Gone/There's a Time for Everything	1966	8.00
❑ 47-9002	My Cup Runneth Over/It Seems a Long, Long Time	1966	8.00
❑ 47-9178	One Little Girl at a Time/Time, Time	1967	6.00
❑ 47-9249	Ballad of the War Wagon/Time, Time	1967	6.00
❑ 47-9319	Let Me So Love/When the Snow Is On the Roses	1967	6.00

Except when noted otherwise, VG = 25% of NM, and VG+ = 50% of NM. (Example: VG = $2.00, VG+ = $4.00 and NM = $8.00.)

Number	Title (A Side/B Side)	Yr	NM
❑ 47-9400	Who Will Answer/My Love Is Gone from Me	1967	6.00
❑ 47-9400 [PS]	Who Will Answer/My Love Is Gone from Me	1967	12.00
❑ 47-9517	Apologize/The Wind Will Change Tomorrow	1968	6.00
❑ 47-9589	I'll Stay Lonely/All My Love's Laughter	1968	6.00
❑ 47-9647	Kiss Her Now/Gloves, Pictures, Dreams (Doors, Mirrors and Heartaches)	1968	6.00
❑ 47-9682	Away in a Manger/Carry the Lord to Jerusalem	1968	—
—Unreleased			
❑ 47-9726	Changing, Changing/Six Words	1969	6.00
❑ 47-9864	Chippewa Town/Sing Away the World	1970	6.00
❑ 74-0156	2001/Son of a Travelin' Man	1969	6.00
❑ 74-0253	Love of the Common People/Leave Them a Flower	1969	6.00
❑ 74-0296	Thing Called Love/Today Is the First Day of the Rest of Our Lives	1969	6.00
❑ 74-0329	Honey, What's the Matter/Three Good Reasons	1970	5.00
❑ 74-0398	The Answer Is/Sweet, Sweet Reason	1970	5.00
❑ 74-0498	More Than Ever Before/The Day	1971	5.00
❑ 74-0551	He Gives Us All His Love/Angelica	1971	5.00
❑ 74-0678	And I Love You So/The Ship	1972	4.00
❑ 74-0726	Distant Drums/Blue Side of Lonesome	1972	4.00
❑ 74-0800	Lost Horizon/Question Me an Answer	1972	4.00
❑ 74-0883	Butterflies Are Free/The World Is a Circle	1973	4.00
❑ SP-45-188 [DJ]	The Ballad Of The Christmas Donkey/Let It Snow! Let It Snow! Let It Snow!	1968	8.00

Albums

RCA CAMDEN

Number	Title	Yr	NM
❑ ACL1-0244	Do You Hear What I Hear?	1973	12.00
❑ CAS-2536	Ed Ames	1972	12.00
❑ CAS-2598	Somewhere, My Love	1972	12.00

RCA VICTOR

Number	Title	Yr	NM
❑ ANL1-1780	Pure Gold	1976	10.00
❑ LPM-2781 [M]	Opening Night	1963	12.00
❑ LSP-2781 [S]	Opening Night	1963	15.00
❑ ANL1-2891	The Impossible Dream	1978	10.00
❑ LPM-2944 [M]	The Ed Ames Album	1964	12.00
❑ LSP-2944 [S]	The Ed Ames Album	1964	15.00
❑ LPM-3390 [M]	My Kind of Songs	1965	12.00
❑ LSP-3390 [S]	My Kind of Songs	1965	15.00
❑ LPM-3460 [M]	It's a Man's World	1965	12.00
❑ LSP-3460 [S]	It's a Man's World	1965	15.00
❑ LPM-3636 [M]	More I Cannot Wish You	1966	10.00
❑ LSP-3636 [S]	More I Cannot Wish You	1966	12.00
❑ LPM-3774 [M]	My Cup Runneth Over	1967	10.00
❑ LSP-3774 [S]	My Cup Runneth Over	1967	12.00
❑ LPM-3834 [M]	Time, Time	1967	12.00
❑ LSP-3834 [S]	Time, Time	1967	10.00
❑ LPM-3838 [M]	Christmas with Ed Ames	1967	15.00
❑ LSP-3838 [S]	Christmas with Ed Ames	1967	12.00
❑ LPM-3913 [M]	When the Snow Is On the Roses	1967	12.00
❑ LSP-3913 [S]	When the Snow Is On the Roses	1967	10.00
❑ LPM-3961 [M]	Who Will Answer? And Other Songs of Our Time	1968	15.00
❑ LSP-3961 [S]	Who Will Answer? And Other Songs of Our Time	1968	10.00
❑ LPM-4028 [M]	Apologize	1968	20.00
❑ LSP-4028 [S]	Apologize	1968	10.00
❑ LSP-4079	The Hits of Broadway and Hollywood	1968	10.00
❑ LSP-4128	A Time for Living, A Time for Hope	1969	10.00
❑ LSP-4172	The Windmills of Your Mind	1969	10.00
❑ LSP-4184	The Best of Ed Ames	1969	10.00
❑ LSP-4249	Love of the Common People	1969	10.00
❑ LSP-4381	Sing Away the World	1970	10.00
❑ LSP-4385	Christmas Is the Warmest Time of the Year	1970	20.00
❑ LSP-4453	The Songs of Bacharach and David	1971	10.00
❑ LSP-4634	Ed Ames	1972	15.00
❑ LSP-4683	Ed Ames Remembers Jim Reeves	1972	15.00
❑ LSP-4808	Songs from "Lost Horizon"	1973	15.00
❑ VPS-6023 [(2)]	This Is Ed Ames	1970	20.00

AMES, NANCY

45s

ABC

Number	Title (A Side/B Side)	Yr	NM
❑ 11100	On Green Dolphin Street/Something's Gotten Hold of My Heart	1968	6.00

EPIC

Number	Title (A Side/B Side)	Yr	NM
❑ 9845	Shake a Hand/Funny Thing About It	1965	8.00
❑ 9874	I've Got a Lot of Love (Left in Me)/Friends and Lovers Forever	1965	8.00
❑ 9885	Dear Hearts and Gentle People/Friends and Lovers Forever	1966	8.00
❑ 10003	He Wore the Green Beret/War Is a Card Game	1966	8.00
❑ 10056	I Don't Want to Talk About It/Cry Softly	1966	12.00
❑ 10149	Love's Like Wine/My Story Book	1967	8.00

LIBERTY

Number	Title (A Side/B Side)	Yr	NM
❑ 55548	Bonsoir Cher/Cu Cu Rru Cu Cu Paloma	1963	10.00
❑ 55598	An Elizabethan Ballad (Part 1)/An Elizabethan Ballad (Part 2)	1963	10.00
❑ 55737	Malaguena Salerosa/Cu Cu Ru Cu Cu Paloma	1964	10.00
❑ 55762	It Scares Me/Let Tonight Linger On	1965	10.00

7-Inch Extended Plays

EPIC

Number	Title	Yr	NM
❑ 5-26197	As Time Goes By/You've Changed/Now Is the Hour//You'll Never Know/How Deep Is the Ocean (How High Is the Sky)/Speak Low	1967	10.00
—Jukebox issue; small hole, plays at 33 1/3 rpm			
❑ 5-26197 [PS]	As Time Goes By	1967	10.00

Albums

EPIC

Number	Title	Yr	NM
❑ LN 24189 [M]	Latin Pulse	1966	12.00
❑ LN 24197 [M]	As Time Goes By	1967	12.00
❑ LN 24238 [M]	Spiced with Brazil	1967	12.00
❑ BN 26189 [S]	Latin Pulse	1966	15.00
❑ BN 26197 [S]	As Time Goes By	1967	15.00
❑ BN 26238 [S]	Spiced with Brazil	1967	15.00
❑ BN 26378	Nancy Ames at the Americana	1968	12.00

LIBERTY

Number	Title	Yr	NM
❑ LRP-3276 [M]	The Incredible Nancy Ames	1963	15.00
❑ LRP-3299 [M]	Portrait of Nancy	1963	15.00
❑ LRP-3329 [M]	I Never Will Marry	1964	15.00
❑ LRP-3369 [M]	This Is the Girl That Is	1964	15.00
❑ LRP-3400 [M]	Let It Be Me	1965	15.00
❑ LST-7276 [S]	The Incredible Nancy Ames	1963	20.00
❑ LST-7299 [S]	Portrait of Nancy	1963	20.00
❑ LST-7329 [S]	I Never Will Marry	1964	20.00
❑ LST-7369 [S]	This Is the Girl That Is	1964	20.00
❑ LST-7400 [S]	Let It Be Me	1965	20.00

SUNSET

Number	Title	Yr	NM
❑ SUM-1109 [M]	The Versatile Nancy Ames	196?	12.00
❑ SUS-5109 [S]	The Versatile Nancy Ames	196?	15.00

AMESBURY, BILL

45s

CAPITOL

Number	Title (A Side/B Side)	Yr	NM
❑ 4287	I Remember/Lucky Day	1976	4.00

CASABLANCA

Number	Title (A Side/B Side)	Yr	NM
❑ NEB 0001	Virginia (Touch Me Like You Do)/That Close to Me	1974	5.00
❑ NEB 0101	Rock My Roll/She's in Love	1974	5.00
❑ 813	Frog Man Bradley/She's in Love	1974	5.00
❑ 832	Every Girl in the World Tonight/(B-side unknown)	1975	6.00

Albums

CAPITOL

Number	Title	Yr	NM
❑ ST-11528	Can You Feel It	1976	12.00

CASABLANCA

Number	Title	Yr	NM
❑ NB 9005	Jus' a Taste of the Kid	1974	12.00

AMISH, THE

Albums

SUSSEX

Number	Title	Yr	NM
❑ SUX-7016	The Amish	1972	25.00

AMMONS, GENE

45s

ARGO

Number	Title (A Side/B Side)	Yr	NM
❑ 5417	I Can't Stop Loving You/My Babe	1962	10.00

DECCA

Number	Title (A Side/B Side)	Yr	NM
❑ 9-28094	Old Folks/I'll Walk Alone	1952	15.00
❑ 9-28222	Breezy/Somewhere Along the Way	1952	15.00

PRESTIGE

Number	Title (A Side/B Side)	Yr	NM
❑ 112	The Happy Blues (Part 1)/The Happy Blues (Part 2)	196?	10.00
❑ 140	Blue Greens and Beans (Part 1)/Blue Greens and Beans (Part 2)	196?	10.00
❑ 166	Woofin' and Tweetin' (Part 1)/Woofin' and Tweetin' (Part 2)	196?	10.00
❑ 176	Hit the Jug/Canadian Sunset	196?	10.00
❑ 189	Ol' Man River/Exactly Like You	196?	10.00
❑ 201	Miss Lucy/Namely You	196?	10.00
❑ 206	The Breeze and I/Uptight	196?	10.00
❑ 214	Twisting the Jug (Part 1)/Twisting the Jug (Part 2)	1962	12.00
❑ 226	I Sold My Heart to the Junkman/Moonglow	1962	10.00
❑ 227	Anna/Pagan Love Song	1962	10.00
❑ 229	Ca' Purange (Part 1)/Ca' Purange (Part 2)	196?	10.00
❑ 245	Molto Mato Grosso (Part 1)/Molto Mato Grosso (Part 2)	196?	10.00
❑ 253	On the Street of Dreams/You'd Be So Nice to Come Home To	196?	10.00
❑ 276	Let It Be You/Seed Shack	196?	10.00
❑ 294	Tuby/Love I've Found You	196?	10.00
❑ 319	The Party's Over/I Wanna Be Loved	196?	10.00
❑ 336	Velvet Soul/Stranger in Town	196?	10.00
❑ 371	Angel Eyes (Part 1)/Angel Eyes (Part 2)	196?	8.00
❑ 390	Seed Shack/Canadian Sunset	196?	8.00
❑ 403	Rock Roll/Sock	196?	8.00
❑ 441	Don't Go to Strangers/Carbow	196?	8.00
❑ 707	Jungle Soul (Part 1)/Jungle Soul (Part 2)	196?	6.00
❑ 713	Bye Bye/Let It Be	1951	15.00
❑ 717	I Wanna Be Loved/Gravy	1951	15.00
❑ 721	La Vie En Rose/Who Put the Sleeping Pills in Rip Van Winkle's Coffee	195?	15.00
❑ 721	Angel Eyes (Part 1)/Angel Eyes (Part 2)	196?	6.00
❑ 729	Jungle Boss (Part 1)/Jungle Boss (Part 2)	196?	6.00
❑ 731	I Can't Give You Anything But My Love/Sweet Jennie Lou	195?	15.00
❑ 734	Didn't We/Son of a Preacher Man	1970	6.00
❑ 735	Jug/Around About One A.M.	195?	15.00
❑ 737	Jungle Strut/Madame Queen	197?	6.00
❑ 741	Blue & Sentimental/Chabootie	195?	15.00
❑ 742	Jug Eyes/He's a Real Gone Guy	197?	6.00
❑ 745	Something/The Black Cat	197?	6.00
❑ 753	My Way/Chicago Breakdown	197?	6.00
❑ 754	Hot Stuff/When the Saints Go Marching In	195?	15.00
❑ 757	Lady Sings the Blues/Play Me	1973	6.00
❑ 805	Wow/When I Dream of You	195?	15.00
❑ 844	Jug/La Vie En Rose	195?	12.00
❑ 845	Bye Bye/I Can't Give You Anything But Love	195?	12.00
❑ 907	Cara Mia/Count Your Blessings	195?	12.00
❑ 910	This Is Always/I've Had My Last Affair	195?	12.00
❑ 911	Sock/Blue Roller	195?	12.00
❑ 916	What I Say/Our Love Is Here to Stay	195?	12.00
❑ 921	Undecided/Until the Real Thing Comes Along	195?	12.00

UNITED

Number	Title (A Side/B Side)	Yr	NM
❑ 137	Street of Dreams/The Beat	1954	15.00
❑ 149	Red Top/Just Chips	1955	15.00
❑ 164	Stairway to the Stars/Jim Dog	1955	15.00
❑ 175	Big Slam (Part 1)/Big Slam (Part 2)	1955	15.00
❑ 185	Traveling Light/Fuzzy	1956	15.00

Albums

ANALOGUE PRODUCTIONS

Number	Title	Yr	NM
❑ AP 038 [M]	The Soulful Moods of Gene Ammons	199?	30.00
—180-gram reissue of Moodsville 28			

ARGO

Number	Title	Yr	NM
❑ 697 [M]	Dig Him	1962	60.00
❑ S-697 [S]	Dig Him	1962	50.00
❑ 698 [M]	Just Jug	1962	50.00
❑ S-698 [S]	Just Jug	1962	40.00

CADET

Number	Title	Yr	NM
❑ CA-783 [S]	Makes It Happen	197?	15.00
—Yellow and pink label (reissue)			
❑ LP-783 [M]	Makes It Happen	1967	40.00
❑ LPS-783 [S]	Makes It Happen	1967	20.00
—Fading blue label (original)			
❑ 2CA-60038 [(2)]	Early Visions	1975	15.00

CHESS

Number	Title	Yr	NM
❑ LP 1442 [DJ]	Soulful Saxophone	1959	150.00
—White label promo; multicolor swirl vinyl			
❑ LP 1442 [M]	Soulful Saxophone	1959	70.00
—Black vinyl			
❑ CH2-92514 [(2)]	Early Visions	198?	12.00
—Reissue of Cadet 60038			

Number	Title (A Side/B Side)	Yr	NM
EMARCY			
❑ EMS-2-400 [(2)]	The "Jug" Sessions	1976	20.00
❑ MG-26031 [10]	With or Without	1954	150.00
ENJA			
❑ 3093	Gene Ammons in Sweden	1981	15.00
FANTASY			
❑ OJC-013	The Happy Blues	198?	10.00
❑ OJC-014	All-Star Sessions	1982	10.00
❑ OJC-129	Jammin' in Hi-Fi	198?	10.00
❑ OJC-192	Blue Gene	1985	10.00
❑ OJC-211	Jammin' with Gene	1986	10.00
❑ OJC-244	Funky	1987	10.00
❑ OJC-297	Boss Tenor	1988	10.00
❑ OJC-351	Bad! Bossa Nova	198?	10.00
❑ OJC-395	Live in Chicago	198?	10.00
❑ OJC-651	The Big Sound	1991	12.00
❑ OJC-6005	Gene Ammons' Greatest Hits, Vol. 1: The Sixties	1988	12.00
MOODSVILLE			
❑ MVLP-18 [M]	Nice and Cool	1961	80.00
—Originals have green label			
❑ MVLP-18 [M]	Nice and Cool	1965	40.00
—Second editions have blue label with trident at right			
❑ MVLP-28 [M]	The Soulful Moods of Gene Ammons	1963	80.00
—Originals have green label			
❑ MVLP-28 [M]	The Soulful Moods of Gene Ammons	1965	40.00
—Second editions have blue label with trident at right			
❑ MVST-28 [S]	The Soulful Moods of Gene Ammons	1963	80.00
PRESTIGE			
❑ PRLP-107 [10]	Gene Ammons	1951	300.00
❑ PRLP-112 [10]	Tenor Sax Favorites, Vol. 1	1951	300.00
❑ PRLP-127 [10]	Gene Ammons Favorites, Vol. 2	1952	300.00
❑ PRLP-149 [10]	Gene Ammons Favorites, Vol. 3	1953	300.00
❑ PRLP-211 [10]	Gene Ammons Jazz Session	1955	300.00
❑ MPP-2514	Blue Groove	1982	12.00
❑ PRLP-7039 [M]	Hi Fidelity Jam Session	1956	150.00
❑ PRLP-7039 [M]	The Happy Blues	1960	80.00
—Retitled version of "Hi Fidelity Jam Session"			
❑ PRLP-7050 [M]	Gene Ammons All Star Session	1956	150.00
—Compilation of Prestige 107 and 127			
❑ PRLP-7050 [M]	Woofin' and Tweetin'	1960	80.00
—Retitled version of "Gene Ammons All Star Session"			
❑ PRLP-7060 [M]	Jammin' with Gene	1956	150.00
❑ PRLP-7060 [M]	Not Really the Blues	1960	80.00
—Retitled version of "Jammin' with Gene"			
❑ PRLP-7083 [M]	Funky	1957	150.00
—Originals have yellow label, "W. 50th St., NYC" address			
❑ PRLP-7110 [M]	Jammin' in Hi-Fi with Gene Ammons	1957	150.00
—Originals have yellow label, "W. 50th St., NYC" address			
❑ PRLP-7132 [M]	The Big Sound	1958	150.00
—Originals have yellow label, "W. 50th St., NYC" address			
❑ PRLP-7146 [M]	Blue Gene	1958	80.00
—Originals have yellow label, Bergenfield, N.J. address			
❑ PRLP-7176 [M]	The Twister	1960	100.00
—Originals have yellow label, Bergenfield, N.J. address; reissue of 7110			
❑ PRLP-7180 [M]	Boss Tenor	1960	80.00
—Originals have yellow label, Bergenfield, N.J. address			
❑ PRST-7180 [S]	Boss Tenor	1960	60.00
—Originals have silver label			
❑ PRLP-7192 [M]	Jug	1960	100.00
—Originals have yellow label, Bergenfield, N.J. address			
❑ PRST-7192 [S]	Jug	1960	80.00
—Originals have silver label			
❑ PRST-7192 [S]	Jug	1972	30.00
—Reissue; trident logo at top			
❑ PRLP-7201 [M]	Groove Blues	1961	80.00
—Originals have yellow label, Bergenfield, N.J. address			
❑ PRLP-7208 [M]	Up Tight!	1961	80.00
—Originals have yellow label, Bergenfield, N.J. address			
❑ PRST-7208 [S]	Up Tight!	1961	60.00
—Originals have silver label			
❑ PRLP-7238 [M]	Twistin' the Jug	1962	80.00
—Originals have yellow label, Bergenfield, N.J. address			
❑ PRST-7238 [S]	Twistin' the Jug	1962	60.00
—Originals have silver label			
❑ PRLP-7257 [M]	Bad! Bossa Nova	1962	60.00
—Originals have yellow label, Bergenfield, N.J. address; some copies have a cover calling this "Jungle Soul! (ca' purange)"			
❑ PRST-7257 [S]	Bad! Bossa Nova	1962	50.00
—Originals have silver label			
❑ PRLP-7270 [M]	Preachin'	1963	60.00
—Originals have yellow label, Bergenfield, N.J. address			
❑ PRST-7270 [S]	Preachin'	1963	70.00
—Originals have silver label			
❑ PRLP-7275 [M]	Soul Summit, Vol. 2	1963	60.00
—Originals have yellow label, Bergenfield, N.J. address			
❑ PRST-7275 [S]	Soul Summit, Vol. 2	1963	70.00
—Originals have silver label			
❑ PRLP-7287 [M]	Late Hour Special	1964	40.00
—Originals have yellow label, Bergenfield, N.J. address			
❑ PRST-7287 [S]	Late Hour Special	1964	50.00
—Originals have silver label			
❑ PRLP-7320 [M]	Velvet Soul	1964	60.00
—Originals have yellow label, Bergenfield, N.J. address			
❑ PRLP-7320 [M]	Velvet Soul	1965	40.00
—Blue label with tridenr at right			
❑ PRST-7320 [S]	Velvet Soul	1964	80.00
—Originals have silver label			
❑ PRST-7320 [S]	Velvet Soul	1965	50.00
—Blue label with tridenr at right			
❑ PRLP-7369 [M]	Angel Eyes	1965	50.00
—Originals have blue label with trident at right			
❑ PRST-7369 [S]	Angel Eyes	1965	60.00
—Originals have blue label with trident at right			
❑ PRLP-7400 [M]	Sock!	1966	50.00
—Originals have blue label with trident at right			
❑ PRST-7400 [S]	Sock!	1966	60.00
—Originals have blue label with trident at right			
❑ PRLP-7445 [M]	Boss Soul!	1967	50.00
—Originals have blue label with trident at right			
❑ PRST-7445 [S]	Boss Soul!	1967	50.00
—Originals have blue label with trident at right			
❑ PRLP-7495 [M]	Gene Ammons Live in Chicago	1967	50.00
—Originals have blue label with trident at right			
❑ PRST-7495 [S]	Gene Ammons Live in Chicago	1967	40.00
—Originals have blue label with trident at right			
❑ PRLP-7534 [M]	Boss Tenor	1967	50.00
—Reissue of 7180; originals have blue label with trident at right			
❑ PRST-7534 [S]	Boss Tenor	1967	30.00
—Reissue of 7180; originals have blue label with trident at right			
❑ PRST-7552	Jungle Soul	1968	40.00
—Reissue of 7257			
❑ PRST-7654	The Happy Blues — Jam Session, Vol. 1	1969	25.00
—Second reissue of 7039			
❑ PRST-7708	The Best of Gene Ammons for Beautiful People	1969	20.00
❑ PRST-7739	The Boss Is Back!	1970	30.00
❑ PRST-7774	The Best of Gene Ammons	1970	20.00
❑ P-7862	Night Lights	1985	12.00
❑ PRST-10006	Black Cat	1970	30.00
—Original on purple label			
❑ PRST-10006	Black Cat	1973	25.00
—Second edition on green label			
❑ PRST-10010	Chase!	1970	30.00
❑ P-10021	Brother Jug	1970	40.00
❑ P-10022	My Way	197?	20.00
❑ P-10023	The Boss Is Back	197?	20.00
—Reissue of 7739			
❑ P-10040	Free Again	1972	25.00
❑ PRST-10058	Got My Own	1973	25.00
❑ P-10070	Big Bad Jug	1973	40.00
❑ P-10078	Gene Ammons and Friends at Montreux	1973	15.00
❑ P-10080	Brasswind	1974	25.00
❑ P-10084	Greatest Hits	1974	30.00
❑ P-10093	Goodbye	1975	20.00
❑ P-24021 [(2)]	Jug and Dodo	1972	20.00
❑ P-24036 [(2)]	Juganthology	197?	20.00
❑ P-24058 [(2)]	The Gene Ammons Story: The 78 Era	197?	20.00
❑ P-24071 [(2)]	The Gene Ammons Story: Organ Combos	197?	25.00
❑ P-24079 [(2)]	The Gene Ammons Story: Gentle Jug	197?	20.00
❑ P-24098 [(2)]	The Big Sound of Gene Ammons	1981	20.00
ROOTS			
❑ 1002	Swinging the Jugg	1976	20.00
SAVOY			
❑ SJL-1103	Red Top	1976	12.00
❑ MG-14033 [M]	Golden Saxophone	1961	50.00
STATUS			
❑ 18	Nice & Cool	197?	15.00
TRIP			
❑ TLP-5578 [M]	Light, Bluesy and Moody	197?	12.00
UPFRONT			
❑ UPF-116	Nothing But Soul	1968	15.00
—Reissue of Vee-Jay material			
VEE JAY			
❑ LP-3024 [M]	Juggin' Around	1961	80.00
❑ LPS-3024 [S]	Juggin' Around	1961	80.00
WING			
❑ MGW-12156 [M]	Light, Bluesy and Moody	1963	20.00
—Reissue of EmArcy 10-inch LP			
❑ SRW-16156 [R]	Light, Bluesy and Moody	1963	15.00

AMMONS, GENE, AND TOM ARCHIA

Number	Title (A Side/B Side)	Yr	NM
45s			
CHESS			
❑ 1445	Boppin' With Santa/Talk Of The Town	1950	—
—Unknown on 45 rpm			

AMMONS, GENE, AND RICHARD "GROOVE" HOLMES

Number	Title (A Side/B Side)	Yr	NM
Albums			
PACIFIC JAZZ			
❑ PJ-32 [M]	Groovin' with Jug	1961	80.00
❑ ST-32 [S]	Groovin' with Jug	1961	60.00

AMMONS, GENE, AND JAMES MOODY

Number	Title (A Side/B Side)	Yr	NM
Albums			
PRESTIGE			
❑ P-10065	Chicago Concert	1973	30.00

AMMONS, GENE, AND SONNY STITT

Number	Title (A Side/B Side)	Yr	NM
45s			
PRESTIGE			
❑ 709	Blues Up and Down/You Can Depend On Me	1951	20.00
❑ 748	Stringin' the Jugs (Part 1)/Stringin' the Jugs (Part 2)	195?	15.00
❑ 877	New Blues Up and Down (Part 1)/New Blues Up and Down (Part 2)	195?	12.00
Albums			
CADET			
❑ LP-785 [M]	Jug and Sonny	1967	40.00
❑ LPS-785 [S]	Jug and Sonny	1967	25.00
—Fading blue label			
❑ LPS-785 [S]	Jug and Sonny	197?	15.00
—Yellow and pink label (reissue)			
CHESS			
❑ LP 1445 [M]	Jug and Sonny	1960	80.00
❑ CH-91549	Jug and Sonny	198?	10.00
PRESTIGE			
❑ PRLP-107 [10]	Gene Ammons vs. Sonny Stitt: Battle of the Saxes	1951	250.00
❑ PRLP-7234 [M]	Soul Summit	1962	50.00
❑ PRST-7234 [S]	Soul Summit	1962	40.00
❑ PRLP-7454 [M]	Soul Summit	1967	20.00
❑ PRST-7454 [S]	Soul Summit	1967	15.00
❑ PRST-7606	We'll Be Together Again	1969	40.00
❑ PRST-7823	Blues Up and Down Vol. 1	1969	20.00
❑ PRST-10019	You Talk That Talk!	1970	40.00
❑ P-10100	Together Again for the Last Time	197?	20.00
VERVE			
❑ V-8426 [M]	Boss Tenors	1962	30.00
❑ V6-8426 [S]	Boss Tenors	1962	25.00
❑ V-8468 [M]	Boss Tenors in Orbit	1962	30.00
❑ V6-8468 [S]	Boss Tenors in Orbit	1962	25.00
❑ 2V6S-8812 [(2)S]	Prime Cuts	1972	20.00

AMON DUUL

Number	Title (A Side/B Side)	Yr	NM
Albums			
PROPHESY			
❑ PHS-1003	Amon Duul	1969	50.00

AMON DUUL II

Number	Title (A Side/B Side)	Yr	NM
45s			
LIBERTY			
❑ 56196	Soda Shop Rock/Archangel's Thunderbird	1970	6.00
UNITED ARTISTS			
❑ XW419	Pigman/Mozambique	1974	5.00
Albums			
ATCO			
❑ SD 36-108	Hijack	1975	15.00
❑ SD 36-119	Made in Germany	1976	15.00
UNITED ARTISTS			
❑ UA-LA017-F	Wolf City	1973	18.00
❑ UA-LA198-F	Viva La Trance	1974	18.00
❑ UAS-5586	Carnival in Babylon	1972	18.00
❑ UAS-9954 [(2)]	Dance of the Lemmings	1971	22.00

AMY AND THE JARRETTS

Number	Title (A Side/B Side)	Yr	NM
45s			
HIT			
❑ 151	I Know Johnny Loves Me/Tobacco Road	1964	10.00
—B-side by the Roamers			

ANACOSTIA

Number	Title (A Side/B Side)	Yr	NM
12-Inch Singles			
TABU			
❑ 494	Ain't Nothing To It (5:39)/Anything for You (7:55)	1978	25.00
45s			
COLUMBIA			
❑ 3-10203	All I Need/One Less Morning	1975	5.00
❑ 4-45685	On and Off (Part 1)/(Part 2)	1972	6.00
❑ 4-45820	Thick and Thin/I Just Wander	1973	6.00
MCA			
❑ 40838	I Can't Stop Loving Her/What Kind of Love	1977	6.00
ROULETTE			
❑ 7300	Love Is Never Wrong/(B-side unknown)	1980	8.00

Except when noted otherwise, VG = 25% of NM, and VG+ = 50% of NM. (Example: VG = $2.00, VG+ = $4.00 and NM = $8.00.)

A

Number	Title (A Side/B Side)	Yr	NM
TABU			
❑ 5506	Ain't Nothing To It/ Anything for You	1978	5.00
Albums			
MCA			
❑ 2269	Anacostia	1977	12.00

ANASTASIA

Number	Title (A Side/B Side)	Yr	NM
45s			
LAURIE			
❑ 3066	Time Bomb/That's My Kind of Love	1960	25.00
STASI			
❑ 1000	Every Road I Walk Along/ Bicycle Hop	196?	200.00
❑ 1001	Seven Days a Week/ Nothing Beats My Girl	196?	150.00

ANCIENT GREASE

Number	Title (A Side/B Side)	Yr	NM
Albums			
MERCURY			
❑ SR-61305	Women and Children First	1970	30.00

ANDANTES, THE

Number	Title (A Side/B Side)	Yr	NM
45s			
DOT			
❑ 16495	My Baby's Gone/No Yo Ru	1963	25.00
V.I.P.			
❑ 25006	If You Were Mine/ (Like a) Nightmare	1964	4000.
—One of the rarest of all Motown-related 45s. VG 2000; VG+ 3000			

ANDERS, BERNIE

Number	Title (A Side/B Side)	Yr	NM
45s			
KING			
❑ 4833	My Heart Believes/ Too Late I Learned	1955	50.00

ANDERS & PONCIA

Number	Title (A Side/B Side)	Yr	NM
45s			
KAMA SUTRA			
❑ 240	So It Goes/Virgin of the Night	1967	12.00
WARNER BROS.			
❑ 7271	Take His Love/ I'm Beginning to Touch You	1969	8.00
❑ 7294	Make a Change (To Something Better)/Lucky	1969	8.00
Albums			
WARNER BROS.			
❑ WS 1778	The Anders & Poncia Album	1969	30.00

ANDERSEN, ERIC

Number	Title (A Side/B Side)	Yr	NM
45s			
ARISTA			
❑ 0121	Ol' 55/Can't Get You Out of My Life	1975	4.00
❑ 0141	Be True to You/(B-side unknown)	1975	4.00
COLUMBIA			
❑ 45637	Is It Really Love at All/Pearl's Goodtime Blues	1972	5.00
❑ 45730	Blue River/More Often Than Not	1972	5.00
WARNER BROS.			
❑ 7231	Think About It/So Hard to Fall	1968	6.00
❑ 7408	Lie with Me/Secrets	1970	6.00
❑ 7435	Sittin' in the Sunshine/ Sunshine & Flowers	1970	6.00
❑ 7459	Born Again/Rocky Mountain Red	1971	6.00
Albums			
ARISTA			
❑ AL 4033	Be True to You	1975	10.00
❑ AL 4075	Sweet Surprise	1976	10.00
❑ AL 4128	The Best Songs	1977	10.00
COLUMBIA			
❑ KC 31062	Blue River	1972	10.00
❑ PC 31062	Blue River	197?	8.00
—Reissue			
VANGUARD			
❑ VSD 7/8 [(2)]	The Best of Eric Andersen	1971	15.00
❑ VSD 6540	A Country Dream	1969	15.00
❑ VRS 9157 [M]	Today Is the Highway	1965	15.00
❑ VRS 9206 [M]	'Bout Changes and Things	1966	15.00
❑ VSD 79157 [S]	Today Is the Highway	1965	20.00
❑ VSD 79206 [S]	'Bout Changes and Things	1966	20.00
❑ VSD 79236	'Bout Changes and Things, Take 2	1968	15.00
❑ VSD 79271	More Hits from Tin Can Alley	1969	15.00
WARNER BROS.			
❑ WS 1748	Avalanche	1968	15.00
❑ WS 1806	Eric Andersen	1969	15.00

Jon Anderson, *Olias of Sunwillow*, Atlantic SD 18180, 1976, **$12.**

ANDERSON, BROTHER JAMES

Number	Title (A Side/B Side)	Yr	NM
45s			
SUN			
❑ 406	I'm Gonna Move in the Room with the Lord/My Soul Needs Resting	1967	50.00

ANDERSON, ELTON

Number	Title (A Side/B Side)	Yr	NM
45s			
CAPITOL			
❑ 4762	Sick and Tired/Life Problem	1962	15.00
❑ 4830	Shed So Many Tears/ That's How It's Been	1962	15.00
LANOR			
❑ 507	Humpty Dumpty Heart/ Don't Touch Me Baby	1962	15.00
❑ 509	Sick and Tired/Life Problem	1962	20.00
❑ 514	I Love You So/(Sorry) I'm Gonna Have to Pass	1963	15.00
❑ 516	The Crawl (Part 1)/(Part 2)	1963	15.00
❑ 518	Bye Bye Little Angel/ Don't Touch Me Baby	1963	15.00
MERCURY			
❑ 71542	Secret of Love/Cool Down Baby	1959	20.00
❑ 71643	Walking Alone/Crying Blues	1960	20.00
❑ 71777	Please Accept My Love/ I Love You, Cheri	1961	20.00
TREY			
❑ 1002	Want a Come Back Home /I Love You	1959	25.00
❑ 1011	Secret of Love/Cool Down Baby	1959	25.00
VIN			
❑ 1001	Roll On Train/ Shed So Many Tears	1958	30.00

ANDERSON, ERNESTINE

Number	Title (A Side/B Side)	Yr	NM
45s			
MERCURY			
❑ 71354	My Man/Wrap Your Troubles in Dreams	1958	10.00
❑ 71423	I Don't See Me in Your Eyes Anymore/Be Mine	1959	10.00
❑ 71500	I Can Dream, Can't I/ I Heard You Cried Last Night	1959	10.00
❑ 71536	Call Me Darling/ My Love Will Last	1959	10.00
❑ 71559	There Are Such Things/ You, You, You	1960	8.00
❑ 71604	A Kiss to Build a Dream On/ Come On Baby, Let's Go	1960	8.00
❑ 71772	A Lover's Question/ That's All I Want from You	1961	8.00
❑ 71919	See See Rider/Mound Bayou	1961	8.00
❑ 71960	Hurry Hurry/After the Lights Go Down Low	1962	8.00
SUE			
❑ 10-004	You Deserve the Best/ You're Not the Guy for Me	1968	6.00
❑ 115	I Pity the Fool/ You're Not the Guy for Me	1964	25.00
❑ 793	Keep an Eye on Love/ Continental Mind	1963	25.00
❑ 803	The Best Is Yet to Come/ Will I Find My Love Today	1964	8.00
Albums			
CONCORD JAZZ			
❑ CJ-31	Hello Like Before	1977	20.00
❑ CJ-54	Live from Concord to London	1978	30.00
❑ CJ-109	Sunshine	1980	20.00
❑ CJ-147	Never Make Your Move Too Soon	1982	20.00
❑ CJ-214	Big City	1983	20.00
❑ CJ-263	When the Sun Goes Down	1985	20.00
❑ CJ-319	Be Mine Tonight	1987	20.00

A

Anderson Bruford Wakeman Howe, "Brother of Mine," Arista 9852 1989, **$3.**

Number	Title (A Side/B Side)	Yr	NM
MERCURY			
❑ MG-20354 [M]	Hot Cargo	1958	60.00
❑ MG-20400 [M]	Ernestine Anderson	1959	40.00
❑ MG-20492 [M]	Fascinating Ernestine	1959	50.00
❑ MG-20496 [M]	My Kinda Swing	1959	60.00
❑ MG-20582 [M]	Moanin'	1960	40.00
❑ SR-60074 [S]	Ernestine Anderson	1959	100.00
❑ SR-60171 [S]	Fascinating Ernestine	1959	80.00
❑ SR-60175 [S]	My Kinda Swing	1959	80.00
❑ SR-60242 [S]	Moanin'	1960	50.00
SUE			
❑ LP 1015 [M]	The New Sound of Ernestine Anderson	1963	20.00
WING			
❑ MGW-12281 [M]	My Kinda Swing	1964	15.00
❑ SRW-16281 [S]	My Kinda Swing	1964	20.00

ANDERSON, JESSE

45s

Number	Title (A Side/B Side)	Yr	NM
CADET			
❑ 5554	True Love Express/ You're Only a Woman	1967	10.00
❑ 5588	Get Loose When You Get Loose/Swing Too High	1968	10.00
JEWEL			
❑ 835	Help Wanted/ Send Me Some Loving	1972	8.00
THOMAS			
❑ 805	I Got a Problem/Mighty Mighty	1970	15.00
❑ 807	Let Me Back In/ Readings in Astrology	1970	10.00

ANDERSON, JON

12-Inch Singles

Number	Title (A Side/B Side)	Yr	NM
ATLANTIC			
❑ PR 376 [DJ]	Some Are Born (same on both sides?)	1980	20.00

45s

Number	Title (A Side/B Side)	Yr	NM
ATLANTIC			
❑ 3356	Flight of the Moorglade/ To the Runner	1976	5.00
—Member of Yes			
❑ 3774 [DJ]	Some Are Born (same on both sides)	1980	5.00
—May be promo only			
❑ 3795 [DJ]	Heart of the Matter (same on both sides)	1981	5.00
—May be promo only			
❑ 4054 [DJ]	Surrender (same on both sides)	1982	5.00
—May be promo only			
❑ 89997	All in a Matter of Time/Olympia	1982	4.00
COLUMBIA			
❑ 38-07766	Hold On to Love/Sundancing	1988	4.00
ELEKTRA			
❑ 69580	Easier Said Than Done/ Day of Days	1985	5.00
—Black vinyl			
❑ 69580	Easier Said Than Done/ Day of Days	1985	10.00
—Green vinyl			

Albums

Number	Title (A Side/B Side)	Yr	NM
ATLANTIC			
❑ SD 16021	Song of Seven	1980	10.00
❑ SD 18180	Olias of Sunhillow	1976	12.00
❑ SD 19355	Animation	1982	10.00
COLUMBIA			
❑ BFC 40910	In the City of Angels	1988	10.00
ELEKTRA			
❑ 60469	3 Ships	1985	12.00

ANDERSON, LALE

45s

Number	Title (A Side/B Side)	Yr	NM
KING			
❑ 5478	(A Ship Will Come) Ein Schiff Wird Kommen/Manchmal Traum Ich Vom Kornfeld	1961	10.00

ANDERSON, LAURIE

12-Inch Singles

Number	Title (A Side/B Side)	Yr	NM
WARNER BROS.			
❑ PRO-A-2465 [DJ]	Language Is a Virus (same on both sides)	1986	8.00
❑ PRO-A-7508 [DJ]	In Our Sleep (Trance Mix) (Instrumental Mix) (Single Mix)/ Poison (3 versions)	1995	12.00
❑ 49888	O Superman/Walk the Dog	1981	10.00

45s

Number	Title (A Side/B Side)	Yr	NM
ONE TEN			
❑ (# unknown)	O Superman/Walk the Dog	1981	10.00
❑ (# unknown) [PS]	O Superman/Walk the Dog	1981	10.00
WARNER BROS.			
❑ 19961	Baby Doll/The Dream Before	1990	—
—Cassette only			
❑ 28677	Language Is a Virus/White Lily	1986	4.00
❑ 49876	O Superman/Walk the Dog	1981	5.00
—7-inch 33 1/3 RPM record			
❑ 49876 [PS]	O Superman/Walk the Dog	1981	5.00
—Includes sleeve and lyric sheet			

Albums

Number	Title (A Side/B Side)	Yr	NM
WARNER BROS.			
❑ WBMS-134-2 [(2)DJ]	Home of the Brave Interview	1986	30.00
—Part of the Warner Bros. Music Show series			
❑ PRO-A-2123 [EP]	Selections from Mister Heartbreak	1984	8.00
—Promo-only sampler with three songs (Excellent Birds/Sharkey's Day/Sharkey's Night)			
❑ PRO-A-2229 [DJ]	Selections from United States Live	1984	12.00
—Promo-only sampler with eight tracks			
❑ BSK 3674	Big Science	1982	10.00
❑ 25077	Mister Heartbreak	1984	10.00
❑ 25077 [DJ]	Mister Heartbreak	1984	15.00
—"Quiex II" audiophile pressing			
❑ 25192 [(5)]	United States Live	1984	40.00
—Boxed set			
❑ 25400	Home of the Brave (Soundtrack)	1986	10.00
❑ 25900	Strange Angels	1989	12.00

ANDERSON, LEROY

45s

Number	Title (A Side/B Side)	Yr	NM
DECCA			
❑ 9-16000	Sleigh Ride/Promenade	1952	20.00
❑ 9-16005	The Syncopated Clock/ The Waltzing Cat	1952	15.00
❑ 9-16021	China Doll/Penny Whistle Song	1953	15.00
❑ 9-16041	A Christmas Festival/ (B-side unknown)	195?	15.00
❑ 25581	Clarinet Candy/Lazy Moon	1962	8.00
❑ 9-27875	Blue Tango/Belle of the Ball	1951	15.00
❑ 9-28037	The Penny Whistling Song/ Horse and Buggy	1952	15.00
❑ 9-28168	Plink, Plank, Plunk/Serenata	1952	15.00
❑ 9-28300	Fiddle-Faddle/ A Trumpeter's Holiday	1952	15.00
❑ 9-28429	Sleigh Ride/Saraband	1952	15.00
❑ 9-28776	China Doll/Phantom Regiment	1953	15.00
❑ 9-28881	The Typewriter/The Girl in Satin	1953	15.00
❑ 9-29050	Serenade/Jazz Pizzicato-Jazz Legato	1954	12.00
❑ 9-29206	Bugler's Holiday/Summer Skies	1954	12.00
❑ 9-29319	Sandpaper Ballet/ Song of the Bells	1954	12.00
❑ 9-30403	Bluebells of Scotland/ Forgotten Dreams	1957	10.00
❑ 9-40201	The Syncopated Clock/ The Waltzing Cat	1951	15.00

7-Inch Extended Plays

Number	Title (A Side/B Side)	Yr	NM
DECCA			
❑ ED 2313	(contents unknown)	195?	8.00
❑ ED 2313 [PS]	Christmas Carols	195?	8.00
❑ ED 2315	Angels In Our Fields Abiding/ Pastores A Belen/O Come, O Come, Emmanuel/I Saw Three Ships//It Came Upon a Midnight Clear/The Coventry Carol/March of the Kings	195?	8.00
❑ ED 2315 [PS]	(title unknown)	195?	12.00

Albums

Number	Title (A Side/B Side)	Yr	NM
DECCA			
❑ DL 4335 [M]	New Music of Leroy Anderson	1962	15.00
❑ DL 7509 [10]	Leroy Anderson Conducts His Own Compositions, Vol. 1	195?	30.00
❑ DL 7519 [10]	Leroy Anderson Conducts His Own Compositions, Vol. 2	195?	30.00

Except when noted otherwise, VG = 25% of NM, and VG+ = 50% of NM. (Example: VG = $2.00, VG+ = $4.00 and NM = $8.00.)

Number	Title (A Side/B Side)	Yr	NM
❑ DL 8121 [M]	Blue Tango and Other Favorites	1955	20.00
❑ DL 8193 [M]	Christmas Carols	1955	20.00
❑ DL 8865 [M]	Leroy Anderson Conducts Leroy Anderson	1958	15.00
❑ DL 8925 [M]	Christmas Festival	1959	12.00
❑ DL 8954 [M]	Leroy Anderson Conducts His Music	1959	20.00
❑ DL 9749 [M]	Leroy Anderson "Pops" Concert	195?	20.00
❑ DL 74335 [S]	New Music of Leroy Anderson	1962	20.00
❑ DL 78865 [S]	Leroy Anderson Conducts Leroy Anderson	1958	20.00
❑ DL 78925 [S]	Christmas Festival	1959	15.00
❑ DL 78954 [S]	Leroy Anderson Conducts His Music	1959	25.00
MCA			
❑ 531	Leroy Anderson Conducts His Music	197?	12.00
—Reissue of Decca 78954; black label with rainbow			
❑ 555	Leroy Anderson Conducts Leroy Anderson	197?	12.00
—Reissue of Decca 78665; black label with rainbow			
PICKWICK			
❑ SPC-1036	Christmas Festival	197?	15.00

ANDERSON, MARTY

Number	Title (A Side/B Side)	Yr	NM
45s			
HIT			
❑ 216	One Dyin' and a-Buryin'/I'm Henry VIII, I Am	1965	10.00
—B-side by the Chords (2)			

ANDERSON, MILDRED

Number	Title (A Side/B Side)	Yr	NM
45s			
BLUESVILLE			
❑ 804	Person to Person/Connections	1960	15.00
Albums			
BLUESVILLE			
❑ BVLP-1004 [M]	Person to Person	1960	50.00
—Blue and silver label			
❑ BVLP-1004 [M]	Person to Person	1964	25.00
—Blue label with trident logo			
❑ BVLP-1017 [M]	No More in Life	1961	50.00
—Blue and silver label			
❑ BVLP-1017 [M]	No More in Life	1964	25.00
—Blue label with trident logo			

ANDERSON, SONNY

Number	Title (A Side/B Side)	Yr	NM
45s			
IMPERIAL			
❑ 5634	Yes, I'm Gonna Love You/Lonely, Lonely Train	1959	50.00
❑ 5689	Our Love Could Never Be/Fool	1960	50.00

ANDERSON, VICKI

Also see JAMES BROWN.

Number	Title (A Side/B Side)	Yr	NM
45s			
BROWNSTONE			
❑ 4202	I'm Too Tough for Mr. Big Stuff/Sound Funky	1971	6.00
❑ 4204	I'll Work It Out/In the Land of Milk and Honey	1971	6.00
❑ 4307	Don't Throw Your Love in the Garbage Can/In the Land of Milk and Honey	1972	6.00
DELUXE			
❑ 6201	Wide Awake in a Dream/Nobody Cares	1966	8.00
FONTANA			
❑ 1527	Never, Never Let You Go (Part 1)/Never, Never Let You Go (Part 2)	1965	12.00
KING			
❑ 6066	You Send Me/Unchain My Heart	1967	8.00
❑ 6091	Think/Nobody Cares	1967	10.00
—A-side: With James Brown			
❑ 6109	Tears of Joy/If You Don't Give Me	1967	8.00
❑ 6138	That Feelin' Is Real/Baby Don't You Know	1967	8.00
❑ 6152	You've Got the Power/What the World Needs Now Is Love	1968	10.00
—A-side: With James Brown			
❑ 6221	What the World Needs Now Is Love/I'll Work It Out	1969	8.00
❑ 6251	The Answer to Mother Popcorn (I Got a Mother for You)/I'll Work It Out	1969	8.00
❑ 6274	Wide Awake in a Dream/I Want to Be in the Land of Milk and Honey	1969	8.00
❑ 6293	Let It Be Me/Baby, Don't You Know	1970	10.00
—A-side: With James Brown			
❑ 6314	Never Find a Love Like Mine/No More Heartaches, No More Pain	1970	8.00
❑ 6377	Message from the Soul Sisters Part 1/Yesterday	1971	8.00
SMASH			
❑ 1985	I Love You/Nobody Cares	1965	10.00
TUFF			
❑ 420	I Can't Stop Loving You/I Lost a Good Man	1964	10.00

ANDERSON BRUFORD WAKEMAN HOWE

Number	Title (A Side/B Side)	Yr	NM
45s			
ARISTA			
❑ 9852	Brother of Mine/Vultures	1989	3.00
❑ 9898	Quartet-I'm Alive/Let's Pretend	1989	5.00
Albums			
ARISTA			
❑ 90126	Anderson Bruford Wakeman Howe	1989	8.00

ANDREWS, CHRIS

Number	Title (A Side/B Side)	Yr	NM
45s			
ATCO			
❑ 6385	Yesterday Man/Too Bad You Don't Want Me	1965	10.00
❑ 6414	Something On My Mind/To Whom It May Concern	1966	10.00
RCA VICTOR			
❑ 47-9746	Pretty Belinda/Maker of Mistakes	1969	8.00

ANDREWS, JIMMY

Number	Title (A Side/B Side)	Yr	NM
45s			
BLUE JAY			
❑ 5003/4	Big City Playboy/Happy Guy	196?	1500.

ANDREWS, LEE, AND THE HEARTS

Number	Title (A Side/B Side)	Yr	NM
45s			
ARGO			
❑ 1000	Tear Drops/The Girl Around the Corner	1957	50.00
CASINO			
❑ 110	Baby, Come Back/I Wonder	1958	30.00
❑ 452	Try the Impossible/Nobody's Home	1958	200.00
—All-black label			
❑ 452	Try the Impossible/Nobody's Home	1958	600.00
—With playing cards on label			
CHESS			
❑ 1665	Long Lonely Nights/The Clock	1957	15.00
—All-blue label			
❑ 1665	Long Lonely Nights/The Clock	1957	40.00
—Sliver-top "chess pieces" label			
❑ 1675	Tear Drops/The Girl Around the Corner	1957	20.00
—All-blue label (if a "chess pieces" label exists, we aren't aware of it)			
CRIMSON			
❑ 1002	Oh My Love/Island of Love	1967	8.00
❑ 1009	Nevertheless/Island of Love	1967	8.00
❑ 1015	I've Had It/Little Bird	1968	8.00
GOTHAM			
❑ 318	Bluebird of Happiness/Show Me the Meringue	1956	200.00
❑ 320	Lonely Room/Leona	1956	300.00
❑ 321	Just Suppose/It's Me!	1956	300.00
GRAND			
❑ 156	Teardrops/The Girl Around the Corner	1962	12.00
❑ 157	Long Lonely Nights/The Clock	1962	12.00
LANA			
❑ 110	Long Lonely Nights/The Clock	196?	6.00
❑ 111	Try the Impossible/Nobody's Home	196?	6.00
❑ 112	Teardrops/The Girl Around the Corner	196?	6.00
—Lana records are reissues			
LOST-NITE			
❑ 104	The Fairest/Much Too Much	196?	6.00
❑ 106	The Bells of St. Mary/Much Too Much	196?	6.00
❑ 108	The White Cliffs of Dover/Much Too Much	196?	6.00
❑ 110	Maybe You'll Be There/Baby Come Back	196?	6.00
❑ 135	The Bluebird of Happiness/Show Me the Meringue	196?	6.00
❑ 136	Lonely Room/Leona	196?	6.00
❑ 137	Just Suppose/It's Me	196?	6.00
❑ 176	Teardrops/The Girl Around the Corner	196?	6.00
❑ 190	Long Lonely Nights/The Clock	196?	6.00
❑ 193	Try the Impossible/Nobody's Home	196?	6.00
❑ 216	All I Ask Is Love/Maybe You'll Be There	196?	6.00
❑ 234	Glad to Be Here/Why Do I	196?	6.00
—All the above Lost-Nite records (three-digit numbers) are reissues			
❑ 1001	Cold Gray Dawn/All You Can Do	1968	8.00
❑ 1004	Oh My Love/Can't Do Without You	1968	8.00
❑ 1005	Quiet As It's Kept/Island of Love	1968	8.00
—The above three are NOT reissues			
MAIN LINE			
❑ 102	Long Lonely Nights/The Clock	1957	200.00
—Black label, Philadelphia address on label			
❑ 102	Long Lonely Nights/The Clock	1957	400.00
—Green label, no address			
❑ 102	Long Lonely Nights/The Clock	1962	30.00
—Black label, no address			
❑ 105	Teardrops/The Girl Around the Corner	1962	12.00
PARKWAY			
❑ 860	I'm Sorry, Pillow/Gee, But I'm Lonesome	1962	15.00
❑ 866	Looking Back/Operator	1963	15.00
RAINBOW			
❑ 252	Maybe You'll Be There/Baby Come Back	1954	400.00
—Black vinyl			
❑ 252	Maybe You'll Be There/Baby Come Back	1954	800.00
—Red vinyl			
❑ 252	Maybe You'll Be There/Baby Come Back	1962	10.00
—Reissue with large print			
❑ 256	White Cliffs of Dover/Much Too Much	1954	1500.
—Yellow label original			
❑ 256	White Cliffs of Dover/Much Too Much	1962	10.00
—Blue label reissue			
❑ 259	The Bells of St. Mary's/The Fairest	1954	600.00
—Yellow label original			
❑ 259	The Bells of St. Mary's/The Fairest	1962	10.00
—Blue label reissue			
RCA VICTOR			
❑ 47-8929	Quiet As It's Kept/You're Taking a Long Time Coming Back	1966	10.00
SWAN			
❑ 4065	I Miss You So/I've Got to Cry	1960	100.00
❑ 4076	A Night Like This/You Gave to Me	1961	150.00
❑ 4087	P.S. I Love You/I Cried	1961	200.00
UNITED ARTISTS			
❑ 123	Try the Impossible/Nobody's Home	1958	25.00
❑ 136	Why Do I/Glad to Be Here	1958	20.00
❑ 151	Maybe You'll Be There/All I Ask Is Love	1958	20.00
❑ 162	Boom/Just Suppose	1959	20.00
❑ 592	Try the Impossible/Nobody's Home	1963	15.00
Albums			
COLLECTABLES			
❑ COL-5003	Gotham Recording Sessions	1982	12.00
❑ COL-5028	Biggest Hits	198?	12.00
LOST-NITE			
❑ LLP-1 [10]	The Best of Lee Andrews and the Hearts, Vol. 1	1981	12.00
—Red vinyl; in die-cut cover with sticker			
❑ LLP-2 [10]	The Best of Lee Andrews and the Hearts, Vol. 2	1981	12.00
—Red vinyl; in die-cut cover with sticker			
❑ LP-101 [M]	Biggest Hits	1964	50.00
—Black vinyl			
❑ LP-101 [M]	Biggest Hits	1964	100.00
—Yellow vinyl			
❑ LP-113 [M]	Lee Andrews and the Hearts Live	1965	50.00

ANDREWS, PATTY

Also see THE ANDREWS SISTERS.

Number	Title (A Side/B Side)	Yr	NM
45s			
CAPITOL			
❑ F3159	Without Love/Where To, My Love?	1955	12.00
❑ F3228	Suddenly There's a Valley/Booga-Da-Woog	1955	12.00
❑ F3268	I'll Forgive You/The Rains Came Down	1955	12.00
❑ F3344	Daybreak Blues/I Never Will Marry	1956	12.00
❑ F3403	Friendship Ring/Music Drives Me Crazy	1956	12.00
❑ F3495	Too Old to Rock and Roll/Broken	1956	15.00

Number	Title (A Side/B Side)	Yr	NM
DECCA			
9-27569	Too Young/Gotta Find Somebody to Love	1951	15.00

ANDREWS, RUBY

Number	Title (A Side/B Side)	Yr	NM
45s			
ABC			
12215	I Got a Bone to Pick with You/I Don't Know How to Love You	1976	8.00
12257	Queen of the Disco/A Little Fixin' Up (Will Keep Him From Messin' Up)	1977	8.00
12286	I Wanna Be Near You/Cinderella	1977	8.00
ICHIBAN			
90-228	I Got What I Want at Home/To the Other Woman	1990	5.00
ZODIAC			
1001	Let's Get a Groove Going On (Part 1)/(Part 2)	1967	100.00
1003	Johnny's Gone Away/I Just Can't Get Enough	1967	80.00
1004	Casonova (Your Playing Days Are Over)/I Just Don't Believe It	1967	10.00
1006	Hey Boy Take a Chance on Love/Come to Me	1967	20.00
1007	You Can Run (But You Can't Hide)/Wonderful Nite	1968	15.00
1010	The Love I Need/Just Loving You	1968	300.00
1012	I Let Him Take Me (In His Arms)/I Guess That Don't Make Me a Loser	1968	12.00
1015	You Made a Believer (Out of Me)/Where Have You Gone	1969	12.00
1016	Help Yourself (Lover)/All the Way	1969	12.00
1017	Everybody Saw You/Can You Get Away	1970	12.00
1020	You Ole Boo Boo You/Gotta Break Away	1971	10.00
1022	Hound Dog/Away from the Crowd	1971	10.00
1023	Whatever It Takes to Please You (Part 1)/(Part 2)	1971	10.00
1024	My Love Is Coming Down/Good 'n' Plenty	1971	10.00
1032	You Got to Do the Same Thing/Didn't I Fool You	197?	10.00
Albums			
ABC			
AB-1002	Genuine Ruby	1977	15.00
ICHIBAN			
1104	Kiss This	1991	15.00
ZODIAC			
ZS 1001	Everybody Saw You	1970	80.00

ANDREWS SISTERS, THE

Also see PATTY ANDREWS; BING CROSBY.

Number	Title (A Side/B Side)	Yr	NM
45s			
CAPITOL			
F-3567	Crazy Arms/I Want to Linger	1956	12.00
F-3583	A Child's Christmas Song/Silver Bells	1956	15.00
F-3658	Rum and Coca Cola/No Baby	1957	12.00
F-3707	Give Me Back My Heart/Stars, Stars	1957	12.00
F-3784	By His Word/I'm Goin' Home	1957	12.00
F-3869	One Mistake/Melancholy Moon	1957	12.00
F-3965	Torero/Sunshine	1958	12.00
F-4144	I've Got an Invitation to a Dance/My Love Is a Kitten	1959	10.00
DECCA			
9-23605	Bei Mir Bist Du Schoen/Joseph! Joseph!	1950	15.00
9-23606	Hold Tight, Hold Tight/Well Alright	1950	15.00
9-23607	Beat Me Daddy, Eight to the Bar/Scrub Me Mama with a Boogie Beat	1950	15.00
9-23608	(I'll Be With You) In Apple Blossom Time/Rhumba Boogie	1950	15.00
—The above four comprise a box set (9-23) originally issued on 78s			
9-23608	(I'll Be With You) In Apple Blossom Time/Rhumba Boogie	1955	12.00
—Black label, star under the first "C" of "Decca"			
23722	Christmas Island/Winter Wonderland	1960	10.00
—With Guy Lombardo and His Royal Canadians; color bars label			
9-23722	Christmas Island/Winter Wonderland	1950	15.00
—With Guy Lombardo and His Royal Canadians; lines label			
9-23722	Christmas Island/Winter Wonderland	1955	12.00
—With Guy Lombardo and His Royal Canadians; star label			
9-24705	I Can Dream, Can't I?/The Wedding of Lili Marlene	1950	20.00
—78 released in 1949			
9-24748	Merry Christmas Polka/Christmas Candles	1950	20.00
—With Guy Lombardo and His Royal Canadians; from "Album No. A-9-95"; 78 released in 1949			
9-27007	I Wanna Be Loved/I've Just Got to Get Out of the Habit	1950	15.00
9-27115	Can't We Talk It Over/There Will Never Be Another You	1950	15.00
9-27202	The Glory of Love/A Rainy Day Refrain	1950	15.00
—With Guy Lombardo and His Royal Canadians			
9-27242	Jing-a-Ling/Parade of the Wooden Soldiers	1950	15.00
9-27251	I'd Like to Hitch a Ride with Santa Claus/(Sweet Angie) The Christmas Tree Angel	1950	15.00
9-27252	A Bushel and a Peck/Guys and Dolls	1950	15.00
9-27310	Sleigh Ride/Telephone Song	1950	20.00
9-27349	Go West, Young Man/Along the Navaho Trail	1950	15.00
9-27414	A Penny a Kiss — A Penny A Hug/Zing Zing, Zoom Zoom	1951	15.00
9-27421	Between Two Trees/I Wish I Knew	1951	15.00
9-27432	Three O'Clock in the Morning/Lullaby of Broadway	1951	15.00
9-27537	I Remember Mama/My Mom	1951	15.00
9-27635	It Never Entered My Mind/I'm in Love Again	1951	15.00
9-27652	Night on the Waters/Dimples and Cherry Cheeks	1951	15.00
9-27700	How Many Times/I Used to Love You	1951	15.00
—With Tommy Dorsey and His Orchestra			
9-27715	Can We Talk It Over/There Will Never Be Another You	1951	15.00
9-27757	Carioca/Daddy	1951	15.00
9-27760	Lying in the Way/Love Is Such a Cheat	1951	15.00
9-27834	Nobody's Darling But Mine/Goodbye, Darling	1951	15.00
9-27858	The Three Bells/The Windmill Song	1951	15.00
9-27878	Blonde Sailor/All the World to Me	1951	15.00
9-27894	Down in the Valley/Red River Valley	1951	15.00
9-27910	I'm on a Seesaw of Love/Play Me a Hurtin' Tune	1951	15.00
—With Guy Lombardo and His Royal Canadians			
9-27979	Wondering/Poor Whip-Poor-Will	1952	15.00
9-28042	Why Worry/That Ever Lovin' Rag	1952	15.00
9-28116	Dreams Come Tumbling Down/Music Lessons	1952	15.00
9-28143	Linger Awhile/Wabash Blues	1952	15.00
—With Russ Morgan and His Orchestra			
9-28163	Where Is Your Wandering Mother Tonight/Hang Your Head in Shame	1952	15.00
—A-side with Red Foley			
9-28276	Idle Chatter/One for the Wonder	1952	15.00
9-28294	Isle of Golden Dreams/Nalani	1952	12.00
9-28295	Kings Serenade/Cockeyed Mayor of Kannakakai	1952	12.00
9-28296	Fair Hawaii/Ke Kali Nei Au	1952	12.00
9-28297	Good Night, Aloha/Malihini Mele	1952	12.00
—Above 4 with Alfred Apaka and His Orchestra			
9-28342	Adios/Carmen's Boogie	1952	15.00
9-28480	Don't Be That Way/Sing, Sing, Sing	1952	12.00
9-28481	Piccolo Pete/If I Had a Boy Like You	1952	12.00
9-28482	East of the Sun/In the Mood	1952	12.00
9-28483	Old Don Juan/The Mambo Man	1952	12.00
9-28492	No Deposit, No Return/You Blew Me a Kiss	1952	12.00
9-28680	Fugue for Tinhorns/Now That I'm in Love	1953	15.00
9-28773	You Too, You Too?/Tegucigalpa	1953	15.00
9-28929	This Little Piggie Went to Market/Love Sends a Little Gift of Roses	1953	15.00
9-29149	My Love, The Blues and Me/There's a Rainbow in the Valley	1954	15.00
9-29995	Rum and Coca Cola/Jack, Jack, Jack	1956	12.00
DOT			
16433	Pistol Packin' Mama/Ti-Pi-Tin	1963	8.00
16497	Mr. Bass Man/My Midnight Prison	1963	8.00
16962	A Man and a Woman/Song from "Come September"	1966	7.00
KAPP			
309	One, Two, Three, Four/I've Got to Pass Your House	1959	12.00
MCA			
60012	Beer Barrel Polka/Pennsylvania Polka	1973	4.00
60040	Boogie Woogie Bugle Boy/Rum and Coca-Cola	1974	4.00
60041	Bei Mir Bist Du Schoen/(I'll Be With You) In Apple Blossom Time	1974	4.00
60042	Don't Sit Under the Apple Tree/I Can Dream, Can't I?	1974	4.00
65016	Take Me Out to the Ball Game/In the Good Old Summertime	1973	4.00
65020	Christmas Island/Winter Wonderland	1973	4.00
—With Guy Lombardo and His Royal Canadians; black label with rainbow			
65020	Christmas Island/Winter Wonderland	1980	3.00
—With Guy Lombardo and His Royal Canadians; blue label with rainbow			
PARAMOUNT			
0257	Rum and Coca-Cola/Pennsylvania Polka	1973	5.00
7-Inch Extended Plays			
DECCA			
ED 2006	I Can Dream, Can't I?/I Wanna Be Loved//I Don't Know Why/Jealous	195?	15.00
ED 2006 [PS]	The Andrews Sisters, Vol. 1	195?	15.00
DOT			
DLP 567	Tennessee Waltz/Careless Hands/Cold, Cold Heart//I'm Thinking Tonight of My Blue Eyes/Bouquet of Roses/Your Cheatin' Heart	1963	12.00
—Jukebox issue; small hole, plays at 33 1/3 rpm			
DLP 567 [PS]	Great Country Hits	1963	12.00
DLP 807	A Man and a Woman/Everybody Wants to Be Loved/Theme from "Come September"//Is It Really Over/I Forgot More Than You'll Ever Know/Satin Doll	1967	10.00
—Jukebox issue; small hole, plays at 33 1/3 rpm			
DLP 807 [PS]	Great Performers	1967	10.00
Albums			
ABC			
4003	Sixteen Great Performances	1975	12.00
CAPITOL			
T 790 [M]	The Andrews Sisters in Hi-Fi	1957	30.00
T 860 [M]	Fresh and Fancy Free	1957	30.00
T 973 [M]	The Dancing Twenties	1957	30.00
DT 1924 [R]	The Hits of the Andrews Sisters	1963	12.00
T 1924 [M]	The Hits of the Andrews Sisters	1963	20.00
DECCA			
DL 4019 [M]	Curtain Call	1956	30.00
DL 5065 [10]	Tropical Songs	1950	40.00
DL 5120 [10]	The Andrews Sisters	1951	40.00
DL 5155 [10]	Club 15	1951	40.00
DL 5264 [10]	Berlin Songs	1951	40.00
DL 5282 [10]	Christmas Cheer	1950	40.00
—Also see "Crosby, Bing"			
DL 5306 [10]	I Love to Tell the Story	1952	40.00
DL 5423 [10]	My Isle of Golden Dreams	1953	40.00
DL 5438 [10]	Sing, Sing, Sing	1953	40.00
DL 8354 [M]	Jingle Bells	1956	30.00
DL 8360 [M]	The Andrews Sisters — By Popular Demand	1957	30.00
DOT			
DLP 3406 [M]	The Andrews Sisters' Greatest Hits	1962	15.00
DLP 3452 [M]	Great Golden Hits	1962	15.00
DLP 3529 [M]	Present	1963	12.00
DLP 3567 [M]	Great Country Hits	1963	12.00
DLP 3632 [M]	The Andrews Sisters Go Hawaiian	1964	12.00
DLP 25406 [S]	The Andrews Sisters' Greatest Hits	1962	20.00
DLP 25452 [S]	Great Golden Hits	1962	20.00
DLP 25529 [S]	Present	1963	15.00
DLP 25567 [S]	Great Country Hits	1963	15.00
DLP 25632 [S]	The Andrews Sisters Go Hawaiian	1964	15.00
HAMILTON			
HLP 124 [M]	Pennsylvania Polka	196?	12.00
HLP 12124 [S]	Pennsylvania Polka	196?	15.00
MCA			
739	Near You	198?	8.00
—Reissue of Vocalion album			

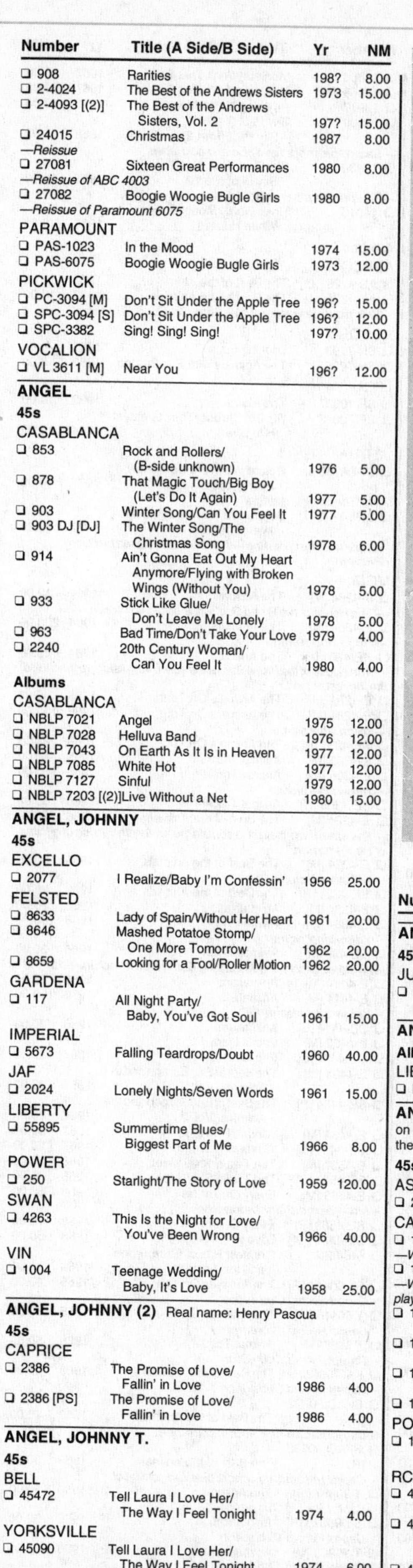

Number	Title (A Side/B Side)	Yr	NM
❑ 908	Rarities	198?	8.00
❑ 2-4024	The Best of the Andrews Sisters	1973	15.00
❑ 2-4093 [(2)]	The Best of the Andrews Sisters, Vol. 2	197?	15.00
❑ 24015	Christmas	1987	8.00
—Reissue			
❑ 27081	Sixteen Great Performances	1980	8.00
—Reissue of ABC 4003			
❑ 27082	Boogie Woogie Bugle Girls	1980	8.00
—Reissue of Paramount 6075			
PARAMOUNT			
❑ PAS-1023	In the Mood	1974	15.00
❑ PAS-6075	Boogie Woogie Bugle Girls	1973	12.00
PICKWICK			
❑ PC-3094 [M]	Don't Sit Under the Apple Tree	196?	15.00
❑ SPC-3094 [S]	Don't Sit Under the Apple Tree	196?	12.00
❑ SPC-3382	Sing! Sing! Sing!	197?	10.00
VOCALION			
❑ VL 3611 [M]	Near You	196?	12.00

ANGEL

45s

Number	Title (A Side/B Side)	Yr	NM
CASABLANCA			
❑ 853	Rock and Rollers/ (B-side unknown)	1976	5.00
❑ 878	That Magic Touch/Big Boy (Let's Do It Again)	1977	5.00
❑ 903	Winter Song/Can You Feel It	1977	5.00
❑ 903 DJ [DJ]	The Winter Song/The Christmas Song	1978	6.00
❑ 914	Ain't Gonna Eat Out My Heart Anymore/Flying with Broken Wings (Without You)	1978	5.00
❑ 933	Stick Like Glue/ Don't Leave Me Lonely	1978	5.00
❑ 963	Bad Time/Don't Take Your Love	1979	4.00
❑ 2240	20th Century Woman/ Can You Feel It	1980	4.00

Albums

Number	Title (A Side/B Side)	Yr	NM
CASABLANCA			
❑ NBLP 7021	Angel	1975	12.00
❑ NBLP 7028	Helluva Band	1976	12.00
❑ NBLP 7043	On Earth As It Is in Heaven	1977	12.00
❑ NBLP 7085	White Hot	1977	12.00
❑ NBLP 7127	Sinful	1979	12.00
❑ NBLP 7203 [(2)]	Live Without a Net	1980	15.00

ANGEL, JOHNNY

45s

Number	Title (A Side/B Side)	Yr	NM
EXCELLO			
❑ 2077	I Realize/Baby I'm Confessin'	1956	25.00
FELSTED			
❑ 8633	Lady of Spain/Without Her Heart	1961	20.00
❑ 8646	Mashed Potatoe Stomp/ One More Tomorrow	1962	20.00
❑ 8659	Looking for a Fool/Roller Motion	1962	20.00
GARDENA			
❑ 117	All Night Party/ Baby, You've Got Soul	1961	15.00
IMPERIAL			
❑ 5673	Falling Teardrops/Doubt	1960	40.00
JAF			
❑ 2024	Lonely Nights/Seven Words	1961	15.00
LIBERTY			
❑ 55895	Summertime Blues/ Biggest Part of Me	1966	8.00
POWER			
❑ 250	Starlight/The Story of Love	1959	120.00
SWAN			
❑ 4263	This Is the Night for Love/ You've Been Wrong	1966	40.00
VIN			
❑ 1004	Teenage Wedding/ Baby, It's Love	1958	25.00

ANGEL, JOHNNY (2) Real name: Henry Pascua

45s

Number	Title (A Side/B Side)	Yr	NM
CAPRICE			
❑ 2386	The Promise of Love/ Fallin' in Love	1986	4.00
❑ 2386 [PS]	The Promise of Love/ Fallin' in Love	1986	4.00

ANGEL, JOHNNY T.

45s

Number	Title (A Side/B Side)	Yr	NM
BELL			
❑ 45472	Tell Laura I Love Her/ The Way I Feel Tonight	1974	4.00
YORKSVILLE			
❑ 45090	Tell Laura I Love Her/ The Way I Feel Tonight	1974	6.00

The Angels, "I Adore Him"/"Thank You and Good Night," Smash 1854, 1963, **$60.**

ANGEL, MARIAN

45s

Number	Title (A Side/B Side)	Yr	NM
JUBILEE			
❑ 5508	It's Gonna Be Alright/ Tomorrow's Fool	1965	10.00

ANGELOU, MAYA

Albums

Number	Title (A Side/B Side)	Yr	NM
LIBERTY			
❑ LRP-3028 [M]	Miss Calypso	1958	50.00

ANGELS, THE (1) At least two other groups used this name, on the Cameo, Gee, Grand and Tawny labels; those are outside the scope of this publication. Female vocal group.

45s

Number	Title (A Side/B Side)	Yr	NM
ASCOT			
❑ 2139	Irresistible/Cotton Fields	1963	12.00
CAPRICE			
❑ 107	'Til/A Moment Ago	1961	20.00
—With semicircular "Caprice" logo			
❑ 107	'Til/A Moment Ago	1961	30.00
—With horizontal "Caprice" logo; B-side listed as "A Moment Ago" but plays "Cotton Fields"			
❑ 112	Cry Baby Cry/ That's All I Ask of You	1962	20.00
❑ 116	Everybody Loves a Lover/ Blow Joe	1962	15.00
❑ 118	You Should Have Told Me/ I'd Be Good for You	1962	15.00
❑ 121	Cotton Fields/A Moment Ago	1963	15.00
POLYDOR			
❑ 14222	You're All I Need to Get By/ Poppa's Side of the Bed	1974	5.00
RCA VICTOR			
❑ 47-9129	I Had a Dream I Lost You/ What to Do	1967	10.00
❑ 47-9246	Go Out and Play/ You'll Never Get to Heaven (If You Break My Heart)	1967	10.00
❑ 47-9404	You're the Cause of It/With Love	1967	10.00
❑ 47-9541	The Medley: Moments to Remember-Theme from A Summer Place-One Summer Night/If I Didn't Love You	1968	10.00
❑ 47-9612	But for Love/The Man with the Green Eyes	1968	10.00
❑ 47-9681	Merry Go Round/So Nice (Samba De Verao)	1968	10.00
SMASH			
❑ 1834	My Boyfriend's Back/ (Love Me) Now	1963	16.00
❑ 1854	I Adore Him/Thank You and Goodnight	1963	15.00
❑ 1854 [PS]	I Adore Him/Thank You and Goodnight	1963	60.00
❑ 1870	Wow Wow Wee (He's the Boy for Me)/ Snowflakes and Teardrops	1964	15.00
❑ 1885	Little Beatle Boy/Java	1964	20.00
❑ 1915	Jamaica Joe/Dream Boy	1964	15.00
❑ 1915 [PS]	Jamaica Joe/Dream Boy	1964	60.00
❑ 1931	World Without Love/ The Boy from Crosstown	1964	15.00
❑ 1931 [PS]	World Without Love/ The Boy from Crosstown	1964	80.00
❑ 810325-7	My Boyfriend's Back/ Thank You and Goodnight	1983	4.00
—Reissue in stereo			

Albums

Number	Title (A Side/B Side)	Yr	NM
ASCOT			
❑ AM 13009 [M]	The Angels Sing — Twelve of Their Greatest Hits	1964	25.00
❑ ALS 16009 [S]	The Angels Sing — Twelve of Their Greatest Hits	1964	30.00
CAPRICE			
❑ LP 1001 [M]	...And the Angels Sing	1962	120.00
❑ SLP 1001 [S]	...And the Angels Sing	1962	200.00
COLLECTABLES			
❑ COL-5085	My Boyfriend's Back: Golden Classics	198?	10.00

Number	Title (A Side/B Side)	Yr	NM
SMASH			
❑ MGS-27039 [M]	My Boyfriend's Back	1963	40.00
❑ MGS-27048 [M]	A Halo to You	1964	40.00
❑ SRS-67039 [S]	My Boyfriend's Back	1963	60.00
❑ SRS-67048 [S]	A Halo to You	1964	60.00

—Some copies distributed with Netherlands Philips 842 948 edition vinyl instead of US.

ANGELS, THE (2)
Male vocal group.

45s

Number	Title (A Side/B Side)	Yr	NM
GEE			
❑ 1024	Glory of Love/It's You I Love Best	1956	60.00
GRAND			
❑ 115	Wedding Bells/ Times Have Changed	1954	50.00
—With address on label			
❑ 115	Wedding Bells/ Times Have Changed	1954	400.00
—With no address on label			
❑ 121	A Lovely Way to Spend An Evening/You're Still My Baby	1954	50.00
—With address on label			
❑ 121	A Lovely Way to Spend An Evening/You're Still My Baby	1954	500.00
—With no address on label			
LOST-NITE			
❑ 323	Wedding Bells Are Ringing in My Ears/Times Have Changed	197?	5.00
❑ 327	A Lovely Way to Spend An Evening/You're Still My Baby	197?	5.00
—Reissue			

ANGELS, THE (3)
Different male vocal group than (2). Also see THE SAFARIS.

45s

Number	Title (A Side/B Side)	Yr	NM
TAWNY			
❑ 101	A Lover's Poem (To Him)/ A Lover's Poem (To Her)	1959	40.00

ANGELS, THE (U)

45s

Number	Title (A Side/B Side)	Yr	NM
CAMEO			
❑ 250	You Turn Me On/ Raining Teardrops	1963	15.00

ANGIE AND THE CHICKLETTES

45s

Number	Title (A Side/B Side)	Yr	NM
APT			
❑ 25080	Treat Him Tender Maureen (Now That Ringo Belongs to You)/Tommy	1965	30.00

ANGLO-AMERICANS, THE

45s

Number	Title (A Side/B Side)	Yr	NM
CHATTAHOOCHIE			
❑ 705	The Music Never Stops/ Are You Ready for This?	1966	30.00

ANGLOS, THE

45s

Number	Title (A Side/B Side)	Yr	NM
ORBIT			
❑ 201	Incense/You're Fooling Me	1965	50.00
—Steve Winwood is on this record, his first			
SCEPTER			
❑ 12204	Since You've Been Gone/ A Small Town Boy	1967	20.00

ANGRY SAMOANS

45s

Number	Title (A Side/B Side)	Yr	NM
BAD TRIP			
❑ 019	Dope on the Scarecrow/Heroin	1995	6.00
❑ 019 [PS]	Dope on the Scarecrow/Heroin	1995	6.00

—A "tribute" (?) to dead Dead-man Jerry Garcia, written and recorded in 1987! 900 copies were pressed.

7-Inch Extended Plays

Number	Title (A Side/B Side)	Yr	NM
HOMOPHOBIC			
❑ HOMO-02	Stupid Jerk/Time to Fuck/ The Todd Killings// They Saved Hitler's Cock	1982	10.00
—As "The Queer Pills"			
❑ HOMO-02 [PS]	Stupid Jerk/Time to Fuck/ The Todd Killings// They Saved Hitler's Cock	1982	10.00
—As "The Queer Pills" with "Angry Samoans" rubber-stamp			
❑ HOMO-02 [PS]	Stupid Jerk/Time to Fuck/ The Todd Killings// They Saved Hitler's Cock	1982	15.00
—As "The Queer Pills" without "Angry Samoans" rubber-stamped on it			

Albums

Number	Title (A Side/B Side)	Yr	NM
BAD TRIP			
❑ (# unknown)	Back from Samoa	1982	30.00
❑ 001 [EP]	Different World/Unhinged + 4	1986	50.00
❑ 002	The Mistaken	1987	50.00
—As "The Mistaken"; 1,000 copies made			
❑ 201 [EP]	Inside My Brain	1981	25.00
❑ 201 [EP]	Inside My Brain	1981	50.00
—Original with heavy gray cardboard cover			
PVC			
❑ 6915	Yesterday Started Tomorrow	1987	15.00
❑ 8955	Inside My Brain	1987	15.00
—Reissue			
❑ 8965	STP Not LSD	1988	12.00

ANIMALS, THE
Includes "Eric Burdon and the Animals." Also see ERIC BURDON; ERIC BURDON AND WAR; ALAN PRICE; HILTON VALENTINE.

12-Inch Singles

Number	Title (A Side/B Side)	Yr	NM
I.R.S.			
❑ SP-70969 [DJ]	The Night (same on both sides)	1983	10.00

45s

Number	Title (A Side/B Side)	Yr	NM
ABKCO			
❑ 4025	House of the Rising Sun/Bring It On Home to Me	1973	8.00
—Contains the full-length version of A-side			
❑ 4026	We Gotta Get Out of This Place/ It's My Life	1973	4.00
❑ 4037	Don't Let Me Be Misunderstood/ Talkin' About You	1973	4.00
❑ 4038	I'm Cryin'/Boom Boom	1973	4.00
I.R.S.			
❑ 9920	The Night/No John No	1983	5.00
❑ 9923	Love Is For All Time/It's Too Late	1983	5.00
JET			
❑ XW-1070	Fire on the Sun/Riverside County	1977	6.00
MGM			
❑ CS-11-5	Celebrity Scene: The Animals	1967	80.00
—Box set of five singles (13791-13795). Price includes box, all 5 singles, jukebox title strips, bio. Records are sometimes found by themselves, so they are also listed separately.			
❑ KGC 178	Gonna Take You Back to Walker/Baby Let Me Take You Home	196?	8.00
—Reissue label			
❑ KGC 179	The House of the Rising Sun/ I'm Crying	196?	10.00
—Reissue label; A-side, despite being labeled 2:58, actually plays 4:29			
❑ KGC 180	Don't Let Me Be Misunderstood/Boom Boom	196?	8.00
—Reissue label			
❑ KGC 181	We Gotta Get Out of This Place/ Don't Bring Me Down	196?	8.00
—Reissue label			
❑ KGC 182	It's My Life/Inside Looking Out	196?	8.00
—Reissue label			
❑ 13242	Gonna Send You Back to Walker (Gonna Send You Back to Georgia)/Baby, Let Me Take You Home	1964	15.00
❑ 13264	The House of the Rising Sun/ Talkin' About You	1964	15.00
❑ 13264 [PS]	The House of the Rising Sun/ Talkin' About You	1964	30.00
❑ 13274	I'm Crying/Take It Easy Baby	1964	15.00
❑ 13274 [PS]	I'm Crying/Take It Easy Baby	1964	25.00
❑ 13298	Boom Boom/Blue Feeling	1964	15.00
❑ 13298 [PS]	Boom Boom/Blue Feeling	1964	25.00
❑ 13311	Don't Let Me Be Misunderstood/ Club A-Go-Go	1964	15.00
❑ 13339	Bring It On Home to Me/ For Miss Caulker	1965	12.00
❑ 13339 [PS]	Bring It On Home to Me/ For Miss Caulker	1965	25.00
❑ 13382	We Gotta Get Out of This Place/ I Can't Believe It	1965	12.00
❑ 13414	It's My Life/I'm Going to Change the World	1965	12.00
❑ 13468	Inside-Looking Out/ You're On My Mind	1966	12.00
❑ 13514	Don't Bring Me Down/Cheating	1966	12.00
❑ 13582	See See Rider/She'll Return It	1966	10.00
—Starting here, records are by "Eric Burdon and the Animals"			
❑ 13636	Help Me Girl/ That Ain't Where It's At	1966	10.00
❑ 13721	When I Was Young/ A Girl Called Sandoz	1967	10.00
❑ 13769	San Franciscan Nights/ Good Times	1967	10.00
❑ 13769 [PS]	San Franciscan Nights/ Good Times	1967	25.00
❑ 13791	Don't Bring Me Down/ When I Was Young	1967	12.00
❑ 13792	See See Rider/Hey Gyp	1967	12.00
❑ 13793	Inside-Looking Out/ Help Me Girl	1967	12.00
❑ 13794	San Franciscan Nights/ Good Times	1967	12.00
❑ 13795	It's All Meat/ The Other Side of This Life	1967	12.00
❑ 13868	Monterey/Ain't That So	1967	10.00
❑ 13868 [PS]	Monterey/Ain't That So	1967	25.00
❑ 13917	Anything/It's All Meat	1968	10.00
❑ 13939	Sky Pilot (Part 1)/ Sky Pilot (Part 2)	1968	8.00
—Second pressings have blue and gold labels			
❑ 13939	Sky Pilot (Part 1)/ Sky Pilot (Part 2)	1968	10.00
—First pressings have black labels			
❑ 14013	River Deep, Mountain High/ White Houses	1968	8.00

Albums

Number	Title (A Side/B Side)	Yr	NM
ABKCO			
❑ AB-4226 [(2)]	The Best of the Animals	1973	12.00
❑ AB-4324 [M]	The Best of the Animals	1987	10.00
—With alternate version of "We Gotta Get Out of This Place"			
ACCORD			
❑ SN-7193	Looking Back	1981	8.00
❑ SN-7235	The Animals with Eric Burdon	1982	8.00
I.R.S.			
❑ SP 70037	The Ark	1983	10.00
❑ SP 70043	Rip It to Shreds: Their Greatest Hits Live	1984	10.00
JET/UA			
❑ JT-LA790-H	Before We Were So Rudely Interrupted	1977	10.00
—As "The Original Animals"			
❑ JT-LA790-H	Before We Were So Rudely Interrupted	1977	100.00
—White label test pressing with promo letter signed by Danny Goldberg			
MGM			
❑ E-4264 [M]	The Animals	1964	30.00
—"The House of the Rising Sun" is the edited 45 version			
❑ E-4264 [M]	The Animals	1964	200.00
—Yellow label promo			
❑ SE-4264 [R]	The Animals	1964	25.00
—"The House of the Rising Sun" is the edited 45 version (rechanneled, like the rest of the LP)			
❑ E-4281 [M]	The Animals On Tour	1965	30.00
❑ E-4281 [M]	The Animals On Tour	1965	100.00
—Yellow label promo			
❑ SE-4281 [R]	The Animals On Tour	1965	25.00
❑ E-4305 [M]	Animal Tracks	1965	40.00
❑ E-4305 [M]	Animal Tracks	1965	150.00
—Yellow label promo			
❑ SE-4305 [R]	Animal Tracks	1965	30.00
❑ E-4324 [M]	The Best of the Animals	1966	20.00
—This album was the first to contain the full-length version of "House of the Rising Sun."			
❑ E-4324 [M]	The Best of the Animals	1966	80.00
—Yellow label promo			
❑ SE-4324 [R]	The Best of the Animals	1966	25.00
❑ E-4384 [M]	Animalization	1966	25.00
❑ E-4384 [M]	Animalization	1966	100.00
—Yellow label promo			
❑ SE-4384 [P]	Animalization	1966	30.00
—All stereo except "Inside Looking Out," which is rechanneled.			
❑ E-4414 [M]	Animalism	1966	25.00
❑ E-4414 [M]	Animalism	1966	100.00
—Yellow label promo			
❑ SE-4414 [S]	Animalism	1966	30.00
❑ E-4433 [M]	Eric Is Here	1967	15.00
❑ SE-4433 [S]	Eric Is Here	1967	20.00
❑ E-4454 [M]	The Best of Eric Burdon and the Animals, Vol. 2	1967	20.00
❑ SE-4454 [P]	The Best of Eric Burdon and the Animals, Vol. 2	1967	20.00
❑ E-4484 [M]	Winds of Change	1967	20.00
❑ SE-4484 [S]	Winds of Change	1967	25.00
❑ E-4537 [M]	The Twain Shall Meet	1968	20.00
❑ SE-4537 [S]	The Twain Shall Meet	1968	25.00
❑ E-4553 [M]	Every One of Us	1968	50.00
—Mono is promo only (yellow label)			
❑ SE-4553 [S]	Every One of Us	1968	25.00
❑ SE-4591 [(2)]	Love Is	1968	50.00
❑ SE-4602	Greatest Hits of Eric Burdon and the Animals	1969	15.00
❑ ST 90414 [R]	The Animals On Tour	1965	40.00
—Capitol Record Club edition			
❑ T 90414 [M]	The Animals On Tour	1965	50.00
—Capitol Record Club edition			
❑ T 90571 [M]	Animal Tracks	1965	50.00
—Capitol Record Club edition			
❑ KAO 90622 [M]	The Best of the Animals	1966	40.00
—Capitol Record Club edition			
❑ SKAO 90622 [R]	The Best of the Animals	1966	40.00
—Capitol Record Club edition; black label			
❑ SKAO 90622 [R]	The Best of the Animals	1969	30.00
—Capitol Record Club edition; blue and gold label			
❑ T 90687 [M]	The Animals	1966	50.00
—Capitol Record Club edition			
❑ ST 90923 [P]	Animalization	1966	50.00
—Capitol Record Club edition			
❑ T 90923 [M]	Animalization	1966	50.00
—Capitol Record Club edition			

Except when noted otherwise, VG = 25% of NM, and VG+ = 50% of NM. (Example: VG = $2.00, VG+ = $4.00 and NM = $8.00.)

Number	Title (A Side/B Side)	Yr	NM
❑ T-91156 [M]	The Best of Eric Burdon and the Animals, Vol. 2	1967	30.00

—Capitol Record Club edition

Number	Title (A Side/B Side)	Yr	NM
❑ ST-91550 [S]	Every One of Us	1968	40.00

—Capitol Record Club edition; black label

PICKWICK

Number	Title (A Side/B Side)	Yr	NM
❑ SPC-3330	The Early Animals with Eric Burdon	1971	8.00

POLYDOR

Number	Title (A Side/B Side)	Yr	NM
❑ 829091-1 [M]	Animalization	1986	8.00

SCEPTER CITATION

Number	Title (A Side/B Side)	Yr	NM
❑ CTN-18026	The Best of the Animals	1972	8.00

SPRINGBOARD

Number	Title (A Side/B Side)	Yr	NM
❑ SPB-4025	The Best of the Animals	1972	8.00
❑ SPB-4065	The Night Time Is the Right Time	1973	8.00

WAND

Number	Title (A Side/B Side)	Yr	NM
❑ WDS-690	In the Beginning	1970	10.00

ANIMATED EGG, THE

Albums

ALSHIRE

Number	Title (A Side/B Side)	Yr	NM
❑ SF-32700	The Animated Egg	1967	100.00

ANITA AND TH' SO-AND-SO'S

See ANITA KERR SINGERS.

ANKA, PAUL

45s

ABC-PARAMOUNT

Number	Title (A Side/B Side)	Yr	NM
❑ 45-PRO-104	(You Can) Share Your Love/I Talk to You (On the Telephone)	1958	30.00

—Evidently a custom pressing for Paul Anka's fan club

Number	Title (A Side/B Side)	Yr	NM
❑ S 296-1 [S]	(All of a Sudden) My Heart Sings/(B-side unknown)	1959	40.00
❑ S 296-2 [S]	(titles unknown)	1959	40.00
❑ S 296-3 [S]	C'est Si Bon/Comme Ci, Comme Ca	1959	40.00
❑ S 296-4 [S]	Melodie D'Amour/I Miss You So	1959	40.00
❑ S 296-5 [S]	I Love Paris/If You Love Me, Really Love Me	1959	40.00

—The above five are jukebox singles excerpting the LP "My Heart Sings"

Number	Title (A Side/B Side)	Yr	NM
❑ 9831	Diana/Don't Gamble with Love	1957	20.00
❑ 9855	I Love You, Baby/Tell Me That You Love Me	1957	30.00
❑ 9880	You Are My Destiny/When I Stop Loving You	1958	20.00
❑ 9907	Crazy Love/Let the Bells Keep Ringing	1958	20.00
❑ 9937	Midnight/Verboten!	1958	20.00
❑ 9956	Just Young/So It's Goodbye	1958	20.00
❑ 9956 [PS]	Just Young/So It's Goodbye	1958	—

—Rumored to exist, but without conclusive evidence, we will delete this from future editions

Number	Title (A Side/B Side)	Yr	NM
❑ 9987 [M]	(All of a Sudden) My Heart Sings/That's Love	1958	20.00
❑ S-9987 [S]	(All of a Sudden) My Heart Sings/That's Love	1958	50.00
❑ 10011 [M]	I Miss You So/Late Last Night	1959	15.00
❑ 10011 [PS]	I Miss You So/Late Last Night	1959	25.00
❑ S-10011 [S]	I Miss You So/Late Last Night	1959	50.00
❑ 10022 [M]	Lonely Boy/Your Love	1959	15.00
❑ S-10022 [S]	Lonely Boy/Your Love	1959	50.00
❑ 10040 [M]	Put Your Head on My Shoulder/Don't Ever Leave Me	1959	15.00
❑ 10040 [PS]	Put Your Head on My Shoulder/Don't Ever Leave Me	1959	25.00
❑ S-10040 [S]	Put Your Head on My Shoulder/Don't Ever Leave Me	1959	50.00
❑ 10064 [M]	It's Time to Cry/Something Has Changed Me	1959	15.00
❑ 10064 [PS]	It's Time to Cry/Something Has Changed Me	1959	25.00
❑ S-10064 [S]	It's Time to Cry/Something Has Changed Me	1959	50.00
❑ 10082 [M]	Puppy Love/Adam and Eve	1960	15.00
❑ 10082 [PS]	Puppy Love/Adam and Eve	1960	25.00
❑ S-10082 [S]	Puppy Love/Adam and Eve	1960	50.00
❑ 10106 [M]	My Home Town/Something Happened	1960	15.00
❑ 10106 [PS]	My Home Town/Something Happened	1960	25.00
❑ S-10106 [S]	My Home Town/Something Happened	1960	50.00
❑ 10132 [M]	Hello Young Lovers/I Love You in the Same Old Way	1960	15.00
❑ 10132 [PS]	Hello Young Lovers/I Love You in the Same Old Way	1960	25.00
❑ S-10132 [S]	Hello Young Lovers/I Love You in the Same Old Way	1960	50.00
❑ 10147 [M]	Summer's Gone/I'd Have to Share	1960	15.00
❑ 10147 [PS]	Summer's Gone/I'd Have to Share	1960	20.00
❑ S-10147 [S]	Summer's Gone/I'd Have to Share	1960	50.00
❑ 10163	Rudolph, the Red-Nosed Reindeer/I Saw Mommy Kissing Santa Claus	1960	25.00
❑ 10168 [M]	The Story of My Love/Don't Say You're Sorry	1960	15.00
❑ 10168 [PS]	The Story of My Love/Don't Say You're Sorry	1960	25.00
❑ S-10168 [S]	The Story of My Love/Don't Say You're Sorry	1960	50.00
❑ 10169	It's Christmas Everywhere/Rudolph, the Red-Nosed Reindeer	1960	16.00
❑ 10169 [PS]	It's Christmas Everywhere/Rudolph, the Red-Nosed Reindeer	1960	25.00
❑ 10194	Tonight My Love, Tonight/I'm Just a Fool Anyway	1961	12.00
❑ 10194 [PS]	Tonight My Love, Tonight/I'm Just a Fool Anyway	1961	25.00
❑ 10220	Dance On Little Girl/I Talk to You	1961	12.00
❑ 10220 [PS]	Dance On Little Girl/I Talk to You	1961	25.00
❑ 10239	Kissin' on the Phone/Cinderella	1961	12.00
❑ 10239 [PS]	Kissin' on the Phone/Cinderella	1961	25.00
❑ 10279	Loveland/The Bells at My Wedding	1961	12.00
❑ 10282	The Fools Hall of Fame/Far from the Lights of Town	1961	12.00
❑ 10311	I'd Never Find Another You/Uh Huh	1962	10.00
❑ 10338	I'm Coming Home/Cry	1962	10.00

BARNABY

Number	Title (A Side/B Side)	Yr	NM
❑ 2027	You're Some Kind of Friend/Why Are You Leaning on Me, Sir	1971	6.00

BUDDAH

Number	Title (A Side/B Side)	Yr	NM
❑ 252	Do I Love You/So Long City	1971	5.00
❑ 294	Everything's Been Changed/Jubilation	1972	5.00
❑ 314	Something Good Is Coming/Life Song	1972	5.00
❑ 337	While We're Still Young/This Is Your Song	1973	5.00
❑ 349	Hey Girl/You and Me Today	1973	5.00

COLUMBIA

Number	Title (A Side/B Side)	Yr	NM
❑ 03897	Hold Me 'Til the Mornin' Comes/This Is the First Time	1983	3.00
❑ 03897 [PS]	Hold Me 'Til the Mornin' Comes/This Is the First Time	1983	4.00
❑ 04187	Gimme the Word/No Way Out	1983	3.00

—A-side: With Karla DeVito

Number	Title (A Side/B Side)	Yr	NM
❑ 04407	Second Chance/Walk a Fine Line	1984	3.00
❑ 07358	No Way Out/Just for Once	1987	3.00

—A-side: Paul Anka and Julia Migenas; B-side: Migenas solo

EPIC

Number	Title (A Side/B Side)	Yr	NM
❑ 50298	You/Make It Up to Me in Love	1976	4.00

—With Odia Coates

ERIC

Number	Title (A Side/B Side)	Yr	NM
❑ 197	It's Time to Cry/Crazy Love	197?	4.00
❑ 197 [PS]	It's Time to Cry/Crazy Love	197?	5.00
❑ 198	(All of a Sudden) My Heart Sings/My Home Town	197?	4.00
❑ 198 [PS]	(All of a Sudden) My Heart Sings/My Home Town	197?	5.00
❑ 199	You Are My Destiny/Let the Bells Keep Ringing	197?	4.00
❑ 199 [PS]	You Are My Destiny/Let the Bells Keep Ringing	197?	5.00
❑ 200	Diana/Don't Gamble with Love	197?	4.00
❑ 200 [PS]	Diana/Don't Gamble with Love	197?	5.00
❑ 201	Lonely Boy/I Miss You So	197?	4.00
❑ 201 [PS]	Lonely Boy/I Miss You So	197?	5.00
❑ 202	Puppy Love/Adam & Eve	197?	4.00
❑ 202 [PS]	Puppy Love/Adam & Eve	197?	5.00
❑ 203	Put Your Head on My Shoulder/Summer's Gone	197?	4.00
❑ 203 [PS]	Put Your Head on My Shoulder/Summer's Gone	197?	5.00
❑ 204	Tonight My Love, Tonight/Dance On Little Girl	197?	4.00
❑ 204 [PS]	Tonight My Love, Tonight/Dance On Little Girl	197?	4.00

—All of the above Eric singles are reissues; all of the picture sleeves have the same photo on both sides, with the only difference between them the different song titles

FAME

Number	Title (A Side/B Side)	Yr	NM
❑ XW-345	Flashback/Let Me Get to Know You	1973	4.00

RCA

Number	Title (A Side/B Side)	Yr	NM
❑ PB-11351	Lovely Lady/Brought Up in New York	1978	4.00
❑ PB-11351 [PS]	Lovely Lady/Brought Up in New York	1978	5.00
❑ PB-11395	This Is Love/I'm By Myself Again	1978	4.00
❑ PB-11662	As Long As We Keep Believing/Headlines	1979	4.00
❑ PB-11957	Rainbow/After All	1980	—

—Unreleased

Number	Title (A Side/B Side)	Yr	NM
❑ PB-12184	We Love Each Other/Think I'm in Love Again	1981	3.00
❑ PB-12225	I've Been Waiting for You All My Life/Think I'm in Love Again	1981	3.00
❑ PB-12262	Lady Lay Down/You're Still a Part of Me	1981	3.00

RCA VICTOR

Number	Title (A Side/B Side)	Yr	NM
❑ 37-7977	Love Me Warm and Tender/I'd Like to Know	1962	25.00

—"Compact Single 33" (small hole, plays at LP speed)

Number	Title (A Side/B Side)	Yr	NM
❑ 47-7977	Love Me Warm and Tender/I'd Like to Know	1962	10.00
❑ 47-7977 [PS]	Love Me Warm and Tender/I'd Like to Know	1962	20.00
❑ 47-8030	A Steel Guitar and a Glass of Wine/I Never Knew Your Name	1962	10.00
❑ 47-8030 [PS]	A Steel Guitar and a Glass of Wine/I Never Knew Your Name	1962	20.00
❑ 47-8068	Every Night (Without You)/There You Go	1962	10.00
❑ 47-8068 [PS]	Every Night (Without You)/There You Go	1962	20.00
❑ 47-8097	Eso Beso (That Kiss!)/Give Me Back My Heart	1962	10.00
❑ 47-8097 [PS]	Eso Beso (That Kiss!)/Give Me Back My Heart	1962	20.00
❑ 47-8115	Love (Makes the World Go 'Round)/Crying in the Wind	1962	10.00
❑ 47-8115 [PS]	Love (Makes the World Go 'Round)/Crying in the Wind	1962	20.00
❑ 47-8158	Think About It/At Night	1963	—

—Unreleased

Number	Title (A Side/B Side)	Yr	NM
❑ 47-8170	Remember Diana/At Night	1963	10.00
❑ 47-8170 [PS]	Remember Diana/At Night	1963	20.00
❑ 47-8195	Hello Jim/You've Got the Nerve to Call This Love	1963	10.00
❑ 47-8195 [PS]	Hello Jim/You've Got the Nerve to Call This Love	1963	20.00
❑ 47-8237	Wondrous Are the Ways of Love/Hurry Up and Tell Me	1963	10.00
❑ 47-8237 [PS]	Wondrous Are the Ways of Love/Hurry Up and Tell Me	1963	20.00
❑ 47-8272	Did You Have a Happy Birthday/For No Good Reason at All	1963	10.00
❑ 47-8272 [PS]	Did You Have a Happy Birthday/For No Good Reason at All	1963	20.00
❑ 47-8311	From Rocking Horse to Rocking Chair/Cheer Up	1964	8.00
❑ 47-8311 [PS]	From Rocking Horse to Rocking Chair/Cheer Up	1964	15.00
❑ 47-8349	My Baby's Comin' Home/No, No	1964	8.00
❑ 47-8349 [PS]	My Baby's Comin' Home/No, No	1964	15.00
❑ 47-8396	In My Imagination/It's Easy to Say	1964	8.00
❑ 47-8396 [PS]	In My Imagination/It's Easy to Say	1964	15.00
❑ 47-8441	Cindy Go Home/Ogni Volta	1964	8.00
❑ 47-8441 [PS]	Cindy Go Home/Ogni Volta	1964	15.00
❑ 47-8493	Sylvia/Behind My Smile	1965	8.00
❑ 47-8595	The Loneliest Boy in the World/Dream Me Happy	1965	8.00
❑ 47-8595 [PS]	The Loneliest Boy in the World/Dream Me Happy	1965	30.00
❑ 47-8662	Every Day a Heart Is Broken/As If There Were No Tomorrow	1965	8.00
❑ 47-8764	Truly Yours/Oh, Such a Stranger	1965	8.00
❑ 47-8839	I Wish/I Went to Your Wedding	1966	8.00
❑ 47-8893	I Can't Help Loving You/Can't Get Along Very Well Without Her	1966	8.00
❑ 47-9032	Poor Old World/I'd Rather Be a Stranger	1966	8.00
❑ 47-9128	Until It's Time for You to Go/Would You Still Be My Baby	1967	8.00
❑ 47-9228	A Woman Is a Sentimental Thing/That's How Love Goes	1967	8.00
❑ 47-9457	Can't Get You Out of My Mind/When We Get There	1968	8.00
❑ 47-9648	Goodnight My Love/This Crazy World	1968	8.00
❑ 47-9767	Happy/Can't Get You Out of My Mind	1969	8.00
❑ 47-9846	Midnight Mistress/Before It's Too Late-This Land Is Your Land	1970	8.00
❑ 74-0126	In the Still of the Night/Pickin' Up the Pieces	1969	8.00
❑ 74-0164	Sincerely/Next Year	1969	8.00

Annette, "O Dio Mio," Buena Vista 354, **$30.**

Number	Title (A Side/B Side)	Yr	NM
❑ 47-8662 [PS]	Every Day a Heart Is Broken/As If There Were No Tomorrow	1965	30.00
❑ VP1-2502 [S]	Young, Alive and In Love/Young and Foolish	1962	40.00
❑ VP2-2502 [S]	Younger Than Springtime/You Make Me Feel So Young	1962	40.00
❑ VP3-2502 [S]	This Life of Mine/Life Is Just a Bowl of Cherries	1962	40.00
❑ VP4-2502 [S]	I Love Life/Aren't You Glad You're You?	1962	40.00
❑ VP5-2502 [S]	Falling in Love with You/You're Just in Love	1962	40.00
—The above five are 33 1/3 rpm, small hole jukebox singles excerpting the LP "Young, Alive and In Love"			
❑ GB-10180	Diana/Put Your Head on My Shoulders	1975	4.00
—Gold Standard Series			
❑ GB-10181	Puppy Love/Lonely Boy	1975	4.00
—Gold Standard Series			
❑ GB-10182	You Are My Destiny/Tonight, My Love, Tonight	1975	4.00
—Gold Standard Series			
RPM			
❑ 472	I Confess/Blau-Wile Deveest Fontaine	1956	80.00
❑ 499	I Confess/Blau-Wile Deveest Fontaine	1957	30.00
UNITED ARTISTS			
❑ XW-454	(You're) Having My Baby/Papa	1974	4.00
❑ XW-569	One Man Woman/One Woman Man//Let Me Get to Know You	1974	4.00
—A-side: With Odia Coates			
❑ XW-615	I Don't Like to Sleep Alone/How Can Anything Be Beautiful After You	1975	4.00
❑ XW-615 [PS]	I Don't Like to Sleep Alone/How Can Anything Be Beautiful After You	1975	4.00
❑ XW-685	(I Believe) There's Nothing Stronger Than Our Love/Today I Became a Fool	1975	4.00
❑ XW-737	Times of Your Life/Water Runs Deep	1975	4.00

Number	Title (A Side/B Side)	Yr	NM
❑ XW-737 [PS]	Times of Your Life/Water Runs Deep	1975	4.00
❑ XW-789	Anytime (I'll Be There)/Something About You	1976	4.00
❑ XW-911	Happier/Closing Doors	1976	4.00
❑ XW-945	I'll Help You/Never Gonna Fall in Love Like I Fell in Love with You	1977	4.00
❑ XW-972	My Best Friend's Wife/Never Gonna Fall in Love Like I Fell in Love with You	1977	4.00
❑ XW-1018	Tonight/Everybody Ought to Be in Love	1977	4.00
❑ XW-1157	(You're) Having My Baby//One Man Woman/One Woman Man	1978	3.00
—Reissue			
❑ XW-1158	I Don't Like to Sleep Alone/Times of Your Life	1978	3.00
—Reissue			
7-Inch Extended Plays			
ABC-PARAMOUNT			
❑ A-240	Down by the Riverside/You Belong to Me//Waiting for You/Walkin' My Baby Back Home	1958	25.00
❑ A-240 [PS]	Paul Anka, Vol. 1	1958	25.00
❑ C-296	So It's Goodbye/Les Filles de Paris//Melodie D'Amour/Autumn Leaves	1959	25.00
❑ C-296 [PS]	My Heart Sings	1959	25.00
❑ A-323	Diana/Puppy Love//Put Your Head on My Shoulder/Lonely Boy	1960	25.00
❑ A-323 [PS]	Four Songs from Paul Anka Sings His Big 15	1960	25.00
RCA VICTOR			
❑ VLP 2575	Teach Me Tonight/Let's Fall in Love//Let's Sit This One Out/I'll See You in My Dreams	1962	15.00
—Jukebox issue; small hole, plays at 33 1/3 rpm			
❑ VLP 2575 [PS]	Paul Anka	1962	15.00

Number	Title (A Side/B Side)	Yr	NM
Albums			
ABC-PARAMOUNT			
❑ 240 [M]	Paul Anka	1958	50.00
❑ 296 [M]	My Heart Sings	1959	30.00
❑ S-296 [S]	My Heart Sings	1959	50.00
❑ 323 [M]	Paul Anka Sings His Big 15	1960	50.00
❑ S-323 [R]	Paul Anka Sings His Big 15	196?	30.00
❑ 347 [M]	Paul Anka Swings for Young Lovers	1960	30.00
❑ S-347 [S]	Paul Anka Swings for Young Lovers	1960	40.00
❑ 353 [M]	Anka at the Copa	1960	30.00
❑ S-353 [S]	Anka at the Copa	1960	40.00
❑ ABC 360 [M]	It's Christmas Everywhere	1960	30.00
❑ ABCS 360 [S]	It's Christmas Everywhere	1960	40.00
❑ 371 [M]	Strictly Instrumental	1961	30.00
❑ S-371 [S]	Strictly Instrumental	1961	40.00
❑ 390 [M]	Paul Anka Sings His Big 15, Vol. 2	1961	30.00
❑ S-390 [S]	Paul Anka Sings His Big 15, Vol. 2	1961	40.00
❑ 409 [M]	Paul Anka Sings His Big, Big 15, Vol. III	1962	25.00
❑ S-409 [S]	Paul Anka Sings His Big, Big 15, Vol. III	1962	30.00
❑ 420 [M]	Diana	1962	25.00
❑ S-420 [S]	Diana	1962	30.00
ACCORD			
❑ SN-7117	She's a Lady	1981	8.00
BUDDAH			
❑ BDS 5093	Paul Anka	1971	12.00
❑ BDS 5114	Jubilation	1972	12.00
❑ BDS 5622 [(2)]	This Is Anka	1974	15.00
❑ BDS 5667 [(2)]	The Essential Paul Anka	1974	15.00
COLUMBIA			
❑ FC 38442	Walk a Fine Line	1983	8.00
❑ FC 39323	Paul Anka Live	1984	8.00
LIBERTY			
❑ LN-10000	Paul Anka: His Best	1980	8.00
—Budget-line reissue			
❑ LN-10001	The Times of Your Life	1980	8.00
—Budget-line reissue			
❑ LN-10149	Feelings	1982	8.00
—Budget-line reissue			
❑ LN-10220	The Painter	1983	8.00
—Budget-line reissue			
PAIR			
❑ PDL2-1129 [(2)]	Songs I Write and Sing	1986	12.00
PICKWICK			
❑ PTP-2087 [(2)]	Paul Anka Way	197?	10.00
❑ SPC-3508	Puppy Love	1975	8.00
❑ SPC-3523	She's a Lady	1975	8.00
RANWOOD			
❑ 8203	The Very Best of Paul Anka	1981	8.00
RCA CAMDEN			
❑ ACL1-0616	My Way	1974	8.00
RCA VICTOR			
❑ ANL1-0896	Remember Diana	1975	10.00
❑ ANL1-1054	She's a Lady	1975	10.00
❑ ANL1-1584	Paul Anka Sings His Favorites	1976	10.00
❑ ANL1-2482	Songs I Wish I'd Written	1977	10.00
❑ LPM-2502 [M]	Young, Alive and In Love!	1962	15.00
—With portrait of Paul Anka on back cover			
❑ LPM-2502 [M]	Young, Alive and In Love!	1962	25.00
—With portrait of Paul Anka on front cover			
❑ LSP-2502 [S]	Young, Alive and In Love!	1962	20.00
—With portrait of Paul Anka on back cover			
❑ LSP-2502 [S]	Young, Alive and In Love!	1962	30.00
—With portrait of Paul Anka on front cover			
❑ LPM-2575 [M]	Let's Sit This One Out	1962	20.00
❑ LSP-2575 [S]	Let's Sit This One Out	1962	25.00
❑ LPM-2614 [M]	Our Man Around the World	1963	20.00
❑ LSP-2614 [S]	Our Man Around the World	1963	25.00
❑ LPM-2691 [M]	Paul Anka's 21 Golden Hits	1963	20.00
❑ LSP-2691 [S]	Paul Anka's 21 Golden Hits	1963	25.00
—LPM/LSP-2691 has re-recorded versions of ABC-Paramount hits			
❑ LPM-2744 [M]	Songs I Wish I'd Written	1963	15.00
❑ LSP-2744 [S]	Songs I Wish I'd Written	1963	20.00
❑ AFL1-2892	Listen to Your Heart	1978	10.00
❑ LPM-2996 [M]	Excitement on Park Avenue	1964	15.00
❑ LSP-2996 [S]	Excitement on Park Avenue	1964	20.00
❑ AFL1-3382	Headlines	1979	10.00
❑ LPM-3580 [M]	Strictly Nashville	1966	15.00
❑ LSP-3580 [S]	Strictly Nashville	1966	20.00
❑ AYL1-3808	Paul Anka's 21 Golden Hits	1980	8.00
—"Best Buy Series" reissue			
❑ LPM-3875 [M]	Paul Anka Live	1967	15.00
❑ LSP-3875 [S]	Paul Anka Live	1967	20.00
❑ AFL1-3926	Both Sides of Love	1981	10.00
❑ LSP-4142	Goodnight My Love	1969	15.00
❑ LSP-4203	Sincerely	1969	15.00
❑ LSP-4250	Life Goes On	1969	15.00
❑ LSP-4300	Paul Anka 70s	1970	15.00

A

Number	Title (A Side/B Side)	Yr	NM
RHINO			
❑ RNLP-70220	The Best of Paul Anka (14 Original Hits, 1957-1961)	1986	10.00
RIVIERA			
❑ 0047 [M]	Paul Anka and Others	1959	150.00
	—With Paul Anka's RPM recordings plus tracks by other artists		
SIRE			
❑ SASH-3704 [(2)]	Paul Anka Gold	1974	15.00
❑ SBK 6043 [(2)]	The Vintage Years 1957-1961	1978	12.00
UNITED ARTISTS			
❑ UA-LA314-G	Anka	1974	10.00
❑ UA-LA367-G	Feelings	1975	10.00
❑ UA-LA569-G	Times of Your Life	1975	10.00
❑ UA-LA653-G [Q]	The Painter	1976	12.00
	—All copies are quadraphonic		
❑ UA-LA746-H	The Music Man	1977	10.00
❑ UA-LA922-H	Paul Anka: His Best	1978	10.00

ANKA, PAUL/GEORGE HAMILTON IV/JOHNNY NASH

Also see each artist's individual listings.

Number	Title (A Side/B Side)	Yr	NM
45s			
ABC-PARAMOUNT			
❑ 9974	The Teen Commandments/If You Learn to Pray	1958	25.00

ANN-MARGRET

Also see JOHN GARY; AL HIRT.

Number	Title (A Side/B Side)	Yr	NM
45s			
ARIOLA			
❑ 7511	Love Rush/For You	1979	6.00
AVCO EMBASSY			
❑ 4547	Today/Today	1970	15.00
	—B-side by Lenny Stack		
LHI			
❑ 1	It's a Nice World to Visit/You Turned My Head Around	1969	6.00
❑ 2	Chico/Sleep in the Grass	1969	6.00
	—With Lee Hazlewood		
❑ 5	The Dark End of the Street/Victims of the Night	1969	6.00
	—With Lee Hazlewood		
❑ 11	Walk Out of My Mind/Hangin' In	1970	6.00
	—With Lee Hazlewood		
MCA			
❑ 41186	Love Rush/For You	1980	5.00
❑ 41223	Midnight Message/For You	1980	5.00
RCA VICTOR			
❑ 37-7857	I Ain't Got Nobody/Lost Love	1961	25.00
	—"Compact Single 33" (small hole, plays at LP speed)		
❑ 37-7894	I Just Don't Understand/I Don't Hurt Anymore	1961	25.00
	—"Compact Single 33" (small hole, plays at LP speed)		
❑ 37-7952	It Do Me So Good/Gimme Love	1961	25.00
	—"Compact Single 33" (small hole, plays at LP speed)		
❑ 47-7857	I Ain't Got Nobody/Lost Love	1961	12.00
❑ 47-7894	I Just Don't Understand/I Don't Hurt Anymore	1961	15.00
❑ 47-7894 [PS]	I Just Don't Understand/I Don't Hurt Anymore	1961	25.00
❑ 47-7952	It Do Me So Good/Gimme Love	1961	10.00
❑ 47-7952 [PS]	It Do Me So Good/Gimme Love	1961	25.00
❑ 47-7986	What Am I Supposed to Do/Let's Stop Kidding Each Other	1962	10.00
❑ 47-7986 [PS]	What Am I Supposed to Do/Let's Stop Kidding Each Other	1962	25.00
❑ 47-8061	Jim Dandy/I Was Only Kidding	1962	10.00
❑ 47-8061 [PS]	Jim Dandy/I Was Only Kidding	1962	25.00
❑ 47-8130	No More/So Did I	1963	10.00
❑ 47-8130 [PS]	No More/So Did I	1963	25.00
❑ 47-8168	Bye Bye Birdie/Take All the Kisses	1963	10.00
❑ 47-8168 [PS]	Bye Bye Birdie/Take All the Kisses	1963	25.00
❑ 47-8295	Hey Little Star/Man's Favorite Sport	1963	10.00
❑ 47-8446	He's My Man/Someday Soon	1964	10.00
❑ 47-8446 [PS]	He's My Man/Someday Soon	1964	30.00
❑ 47-8734	Mister Kiss Kiss Bang Bang/What Did I Have That I Don't Have Now	1965	10.00
❑ 47-9013	The Swinger/You've Come a Long Way from St. Louis	1966	10.00
❑ VP1-2551 [S]	Jim Dandy/Thirteen Men	1962	40.00
❑ VP2-2551 [S]	Rock and Roll Waltz/There'll Be Some Changes Made	1962	40.00
❑ VP3-2551 [S]	Make Love to Me/Tell Me, Tell Me	1962	40.00
❑ VP4-2551 [S]	C'est Si Bon/Please Don't Talk About Me When I'm Gone	1962	40.00
❑ VP5-2551 [S]	Inka Dinka Doo/Begin the Beguine	1962	40.00
	—The above five are 33 1/3 rpm, small hole jukebox singles excerpting the LP "The Vivacious One"		
Albums			
LHI			
❑ S-12007	The Cowboy and the Lady	1969	40.00
	—With Lee Hazlewood		
MCA			
❑ 3226	Ann-Margret	1980	12.00
RCA VICTOR			
❑ LPM-2399 [M]	And Here She Is...	1961	30.00
❑ LSP-2399 [S]	And Here She Is...	1961	40.00
❑ LPM-2453 [M]	On the Way Up	1961	30.00
❑ LSP-2453 [S]	On the Way Up	1961	40.00
❑ LPM-2551 [M]	The Vivacious One	1962	30.00
❑ LSP-2551 [S]	The Vivacious One	1962	40.00
❑ LPM-2659 [M]	Bachelor's Paradise	1963	30.00
❑ LSP-2659 [S]	Bachelor's Paradise	1963	40.00
❑ LPM-3710 [M]	Songs from The Swinger and Others	1966	60.00
❑ LSP-3710 [S]	Songs from The Swinger and Others	1966	80.00

ANNETTE

Also see FRANKIE AVALON AND ANNETTE FUNICELLO.

Number	Title (A Side/B Side)	Yr	NM
45s			
BUENA VISTA			
❑ 336	Jo Jo the Dog Faced Boy/Love Me Forever	1959	15.00
❑ 336	Jo Jo the Dog Faced Boy/Lonely Guitar	1959	20.00
❑ 339	Wild Willie/Lonely Guitar	1959	15.00
❑ 339 [PS]	Wild Willie/Lonely Guitar	1959	30.00
❑ 344	Especially for You/My Heart Became of Age	1959	15.00
❑ 349	First Name Initial/My Heart Became of Age	1959	15.00
❑ 349 [PS]	First Name Initial/My Heart Became of Age	1959	30.00
❑ 354	O Dio Mio/It Took Dreams	1960	15.00
❑ 354 [PS]	O Dio Mio/It Took Dreams	1960	30.00
❑ 359	Train of Love/Tell Me Who's the Girl	1960	15.00
❑ 359 [PS]	Train of Love/Tell Me Who's the Girl	1960	40.00
❑ 362	Pineapple Princess/Luau Cha Cha Cha	1960	15.00
❑ 362 [PS]	Pineapple Princess/Luau Cha Cha Cha	1960	30.00
❑ 369	Talk to Me Baby/I Love You Baby	1960	15.00
❑ 369 [PS]	Talk to Me Baby/I Love You Baby	1960	30.00
❑ 374	Dream Boy/Please, Please Signore	1961	15.00
❑ 374 [PS]	Dream Boy/Please, Please Signore	1961	30.00
❑ 375	Indian Giver/Mama, Mama Rosa (Where's the Spumoni)	1961	15.00
❑ 375 [PS]	Indian Giver/Mama, Mama Rosa (Where's the Spumoni)	1961	30.00
❑ 384	Hawaiian Love Talk/Blue Muu Muu	1961	15.00
❑ 384 [PS]	Hawaiian Love Talk/Blue Muu Muu	1961	50.00
❑ 388	Dreamin' About You/Strummin' Song	1961	15.00
❑ 388 [PS]	Dreamin' About You/Strummin' Song	1961	30.00
❑ 392	That Crazy Place From Outer Space/Seven Moons (Of Batalayre)	1962	15.00
	—B-side by Danny Saval and Tom Tryon		
❑ 392 [PS]	That Crazy Place From Outer Space/Seven Moons (Of Batalayre)	1962	40.00
❑ 394	The Truth About Youth/I Can't Do the Sum	1962	15.00
❑ 394 [PS]	The Truth About Youth/I Can't Do the Sum	1962	40.00
❑ 400	My Little Grass Shack/Hukilau	1962	15.00
❑ 405	He's My Ideal/Mr. Piano Man	1962	15.00
❑ 405 [PS]	He's My Ideal/Mr. Piano Man	1962	30.00
❑ 407	Bella Bella Florence/Canzone d'Amoure	1962	15.00
	—With Marcochi		
❑ 407 [PS]	Bella Bella Florence/Canzone d'Amoure	1962	150.00
❑ 414	Teenage Wedding/Walkin' and Talkin'	1962	20.00
❑ 414 [PS]	Teenage Wedding/Walkin' and Talkin'	1962	600.00
❑ 427	Treat Him Nicely/Promise Me Anything	1963	15.00
❑ 427 [PS]	Treat Him Nicely/Promise Me Anything	1963	60.00
❑ 431	Merlin Jones/The Scrambled Egghead	1964	12.00
	—With Tommy Kirk		
❑ 431 [PS]	Merlin Jones/The Scrambled Egghead	1964	30.00
❑ 432	Custom City/Rebel Rider	1964	20.00
❑ 432 [PS]	Custom City/Rebel Rider	1964	60.00
❑ 433	Muscle Beach Party/I Dream About Frankie	1964	15.00
❑ 433 [PS]	Muscle Beach Party/I Dream About Frankie	1964	30.00
❑ 436	Bikini Beach Party/The Clyde	1964	15.00
❑ 436 [PS]	Bikini Beach Party/The Clyde	1964	40.00
❑ 437	The Wah-Watusi/The Clyde	1964	12.00
❑ 438	Something Borrowed, Something Blue/How Will I Know My Love	1965	15.00
❑ 438 [PS]	Something Borrowed, Something Blue/How Will I Know My Love	1965	80.00
❑ 440	The Monkey's Uncle/How Will I Know My Love	1965	12.00
	—With the Beach Boys backing up		
❑ 440 [PS]	The Monkey's Uncle/How Will I Know My Love	1965	20.00
❑ 442	The Boy to Love/No One Else Could Be Prouder	1965	12.00
❑ 450	No Way to Go But Up/Crystal Ball	1966	12.00
❑ 475	The Computer Wore Tennis Shoes/Merlin Jones	1970	8.00
DISNEYLAND			
❑ 102	How Will I Know My Love/Don't Jump to Conclusions	1958	30.00
❑ 102 [PS]	How Will I Know My Love/Don't Jump to Conclusions	1958	50.00
❑ 114	That Crazy Place in Outer Space/Gold Doubloons and Pieces of Eight	1958	40.00
	—B-side: "Theme from the Hardy Boys"		
❑ 118	Tall Paul/Ma, He's Making Eyes at Me	1959	20.00
❑ 786	That Crazy Place From Outer Space/Happy Glow	196?	10.00
	—No artist credit on label, but A-side is the same recording as Disneyland 114		
EPIC			
❑ 9829	Baby Needs Me Now/Moment of Silence	1965	25.00
	—With Cecil Null		
STARVIEW			
❑ 3001	The Promised Land/In Between and Out of Love	1983	10.00
❑ 3001 [PS]	The Promised Land/In Between and Out of Love	1983	10.00
TOWER			
❑ 326	What's a Girl to Do/When You Get What You Want	1967	30.00
Albums			
BUENA VISTA			
❑ BV-3301 [M]	Annette	1959	120.00
❑ BV-3302 [M]	Annette Sings Anka	1960	100.00
❑ BV-3303 [M]	Hawaiiannette	1960	75.00
❑ BV-3304 [M]	Italiannette	1960	75.00
❑ BV-3305 [M]	Dance Annette	1961	75.00
❑ BV-3312 [M]	The Story of My Teens	1962	75.00
❑ BV-3313 [M]	Teen Street	1962	75.00
❑ BV-3314 [M]	Muscle Beach Party	1963	75.00
❑ STER-3314 [S]	Muscle Beach Party	1963	150.00
❑ BV-3316 [M]	Beach Party	1963	60.00
❑ STER-3316 [S]	Beach Party	1963	100.00
❑ BV-3320 [M]	Annette on Campus	1964	50.00
❑ STER-3320 [S]	Annette on Campus	1964	100.00
❑ BV-3324 [M]	Annette at Bikini Beach	1964	50.00
❑ STER-3324 [S]	Annette at Bikini Beach	1964	100.00
❑ BV-3325 [M]	Annette's Pajama Party	1964	40.00
❑ STER-3325 [S]	Annette's Pajama Party	1964	100.00
❑ BV-3327 [M]	Annette Sings Golden Surfin' Hits	1964	100.00
❑ STER-3327 [S]	Annette Sings Golden Surfin' Hits	1964	150.00
❑ BV-3328 [M]	Something Borrowed, Something Blue	1964	60.00
❑ STER-3328 [P]	Something Borrowed, Something Blue	1964	100.00
❑ BV-4037	Annette Funicello	1972	50.00
RHINO			
❑ RNDF-206	The Best of Annette	1984	12.00
❑ RNLP-702 [PD]	The Best of Annette	1984	25.00

ANNETTE / HAYLEY MILLS

Number	Title (A Side/B Side)	Yr	NM
Albums			
DISNEYLAND			
❑ DL-3508 [M]	Annette and Hayley Mills (Singing 10 of Their Greatest All-Time Hits)	1964	1000.
	—TV offer; issued with paper jacket. Though the cover says "Buena Vista Records Presents," the label is the yellow Disneyland label		

Except when noted otherwise, VG = 25% of NM, and VG+ = 50% of NM. (Example: VG = $2.00, VG+ = $4.00 and NM = $8.00.)

ANNIE AND THE ORPHANS

45s

CAPITOL

Number	Title (A Side/B Side)	Yr	NM
❑ 5144	My Girl's Been Bitten by the Beatle Bug/A Place Called Happiness	1964	20.00
❑ 5144 [PS]	My Girl's Been Bitten by the Beatle Bug/A Place Called Happiness	1964	25.00

ANONYMOUS

Albums

A-MAJOR

Number	Title (A Side/B Side)	Yr	NM
❑ AMLS-1002	Inside the Shadow	1976	250.00

ANT, ADAM

12-Inch Singles

EPIC

Number	Title (A Side/B Side)	Yr	NM
❑ AE 1556 [DJ]	Hello I Love You/Desperate But Not Serious/Goody Two Shoes	1982	10.00
❑ AE 1593 [DJ]	Friend or Foe/Desperate But Not Serious	1983	10.00
❑ 49-05261	Vive Le Rock (2 versions)/Greta X	1985	8.00

MCA

Number	Title (A Side/B Side)	Yr	NM
❑ L33-18134 [DJ]	Room at the Top (Extended Version 6:45) (B-side version unknown)	1990	10.00
❑ L33-18436 [DJ]	Rough Stuff (4 versions)	1990	6.00
❑ L33-18466 [DJ]	Rough Stuff (Alternative Mix)/(Alternative Dub)	1990	7.00
❑ 23964	Room at the Top (3 versions)	1989	10.00
❑ 24035	Rough Stuff (Extended)/(Dub)	1990	6.00

45s

CAPITOL

Number	Title (A Side/B Side)	Yr	NM
❑ S7-18393	Wonderful/Goes Around	1995	4.00

EPIC

Number	Title (A Side/B Side)	Yr	NM
❑ 34-03367	Goody Two Shoes/Crackpot History	1982	4.00
❑ ENR-03529	Goody Two Shoes/(B-side blank)	1983	8.00
—One-sided budget release			
❑ 34-03688	Desparate But Not Serious/Place in the Country	1983	4.00
❑ ENR-03762	Desparate But Not Serious/(B-side blank)	1983	8.00
—One-sided budget release			
❑ 34-04337	Strip/Yours, Yours, Yours	1984	3.00
❑ 34-04337 [PS]	Strip/Yours, Yours, Yours	1984	4.00
❑ 34-04461	Puss 'N Boots/Kiss the Drummer	1984	3.00
❑ 34-04461 [PS]	Puss 'N Boots/Kiss the Drummer	1984	4.00
❑ 15-05538	Goody Two Shoes/Crackpot History	1984	3.00
—"Golden Oldies" reissue			
❑ 34-05574	Vive Le Rock/Greta X	1985	3.00
❑ 34-05574 [PS]	Vive Le Rock/Greta X	1985	4.00

MCA

Number	Title (A Side/B Side)	Yr	NM
❑ 53679	Room at the Top/Bruce Lee	1989	3.00
❑ 79042	Rough Stuff/Bright Lights Black Leather	1990	3.00

Albums

EPIC

Number	Title (A Side/B Side)	Yr	NM
❑ ARE 38370	Friend or Foe	1982	10.00
❑ FE 39108	Strip	1984	10.00
❑ BFE 40159	Vive Le Rock	1985	8.00

MCA

Number	Title (A Side/B Side)	Yr	NM
❑ 6315	Manners & Physique	1989	10.00

ANT TRIP CEREMONY

Albums

C.R.C.

Number	Title (A Side/B Side)	Yr	NM
❑ 2129	24 Hours	1970	750.00
—Originals have thick cover and black vinyl			

ANTELL, PETE

45s

BOUNTY

Number	Title (A Side/B Side)	Yr	NM
❑ 103	The Times They Are a-Changin'/Yesterrday and Tomorrow	1965	15.00

CAMEO

Number	Title (A Side/B Side)	Yr	NM
❑ 234	Night Time/Something About You	1962	20.00
❑ 264	You in Disguise/Keep It Up	1963	15.00

NEW VOICE

Number	Title (A Side/B Side)	Yr	NM
❑ 818	Wanting/Warm Smoke	1967	10.00

ANTHEM

Albums

BUDDAH

Number	Title (A Side/B Side)	Yr	NM
❑ BDS-5071	Anthem	1971	20.00

ANTHONY, LAMONT

See LAMONT DOZIER.

ANTHONY, MARK

45s

LA BELLE

Number	Title (A Side/B Side)	Yr	NM
❑ 779	Mama's Twistin' with Santa/Music from Studio "D"	1962	12.00

ANTHONY, NICK

45s

ABC-PARAMOUNT

Number	Title (A Side/B Side)	Yr	NM
❑ 9919	More Than Ever/You're Real Keen, Jelly Bean	1958	20.00
❑ 9985	Forbidden Love/My Baby's Gone	1958	20.00

ANTHONY, RAY

45s

CAPITOL

Number	Title (A Side/B Side)	Yr	NM
❑ F794	Sitting by the Window/Dixie	1949	15.00
❑ F819	I'll See You In My Dreams/My Baby Is Blue	1950	12.00
❑ F859	Count Every Star/Bamboo	1950	12.00
❑ F923	Sentimental Me/Spaghetti Rag	1950	12.00
❑ F933	Where in the World/Candy & Cake	1950	12.00
❑ F945	Why/Little Peach from East Orange	1950	12.00
❑ F958	In the Mood/Way Down Yonder	1950	12.00
❑ F968	Autumn Nocturne/Tenderly	1950	12.00
❑ F979	Count Every Star/The Darktown Strutters Ball	1950	12.00
❑ F1001	Roses/National Emblem March	1950	12.00
❑ F1020	The Girl That I Marry/They Say It's Wonderful	1950	12.00
❑ F1040	Skip to My Lou/Scattered Toys	1950	12.00
❑ F1051	Francie/Mama Teach Me to Do the Charleston	1950	12.00
❑ F1073	Lazy Old Tune/Lackawanna Local	1950	12.00
❑ F1107	Star Dust/Young Man with a Horn	1950	12.00
❑ F1131	Can Anyone Explain/Shy Coach	1950	12.00
❑ F1169	Dixie Doodle/All of a Sudden (My Heart Sings)	1950	12.00
❑ F1190	Harbor Lights/Nevertheless (I'm in Love with You)	1950	12.00
❑ F1196	A Marshmallow World/Where Do I Go from You	1950	15.00
❑ F1249	My Heart Is Out of Town/Harlem Nocturne	1950	12.00
❑ F1280	Autumn Leaves/Mr. Anthony's Boogie	1950	12.00
❑ F1310	The Night Is Young and You're So Beautiful/All Anthony No Cleopatra	1950	12.00
❑ F1352	Be My Love/I Wonder What's Become of Sally	1951	12.00
❑ F1367	More Than I Care to Remember/Columbia, The Gem of the Ocean	1951	12.00
❑ F1490	I'll Never Know Why/Faithfully Yours	1951	12.00
❑ F1502	Mr. Anthony's Blues/Cooks Tour	1951	12.00
❑ F1522	These Things I Offer You (For a Lifetime)/Here's To Your Illusions	1951	12.00
❑ F1556	Villa/Melancholy Rhapsody	1951	12.00
❑ F1574	Believing You/One Dance with You	1951	12.00
❑ F1583	My Truly, Truly Fair/Pretty Eyed Baby	1951	12.00
❑ F1622	Star Dust/Man with a Horn	1951	12.00
❑ F1654	Tenderly/Autumn Nocturne	1951	12.00
❑ F1664	What Is This Thing Called Love/Harlem Nocturne	1951	12.00
❑ F1678	As Time Goes By/At Last	1954	10.00
—Reissue			
❑ F1679	Mr. Anthony's Boogie/I Wonder What's Become of Sally	1954	10.00
—Reissue			
❑ F1723	I Love the Sunshine in Your Smile/You Blew Out the Flame	1951	12.00
❑ F1739	Mary Rose/Ho Ho	1951	12.00
❑ F1758	The Fox/Rollin' Home	1951	12.00
❑ F1810	Deep Night/With All My Heart and Soul	1951	12.00
❑ F1824	Undecided/Just a Moment More	1951	12.00
❑ F1835	My Concerto/I'll Remember April	1951	12.00
❑ F1857	Brother Fats/I Remember Harlem	1951	12.00
❑ F1884	Honeydriper/Busman's Holiday	1951	12.00
❑ F1912	At Last/I'll See You in My Dreams	1952	10.00
❑ F1956	Bermuda/Broken Hearted	1952	10.00
❑ F1957	Singin' in the Rain/I Let a Song Go Out of My Heart	1952	10.00
❑ F1973	I Hear a Rhapsody/For Dancers Only	1952	10.00
❑ F2002	There Are Such Things/Moonlight Savings Time	1952	10.00
❑ F2058	Trumpet Boogie/You're Driving Me Crazy	1952	10.00
❑ 6F-2085	Slaughter on Tenth Avenue (Part I)/Slaughter on Tenth Avenue (Part II)	1952	10.00
—Has a maroon rather than purple label			
❑ F2104	As Time Goes By/Scatterbrain	1952	10.00
❑ F2194	Make Believe Dreams/Loaded with Love	1952	10.00
❑ F2207	Marilyn/Randles Island	1952	20.00
❑ F2251	Bunny Hop/Blow, Man, Blow	1952	12.00
❑ F2293	Idaho/People in Love	1952	10.00
❑ F2327	On the Trail/Street Scene	1953	10.00
❑ F2349	You're a Heartbreaker/Wild Horses	1953	10.00
❑ F2393	True Blue Lou/They Didn't Believe Me	1953	10.00
❑ F2427	The Hokey Pokey/Bunny Hop	1953	12.00
❑ F2451	Piccadilly Circus/Thunderbird	1953	10.00
❑ F2488	When the Saints Go Marching In/That's My Weakness Now	1953	10.00
❑ F2532	Jersey Bounce/I Guess It Was You All the Time	1953	10.00
❑ F2562	Dragnet/Dancing in the Dark	1953	15.00
❑ F2637	Sound Off/Another Dawn, Another Day	1953	10.00
❑ F2678	O Mein Papa (O! My Papa)/Secret Love	1953	10.00
❑ F2699	Tuxedo Junction/In the Mood	1954	10.00
❑ F2728	Sign Post/Air Express	1954	10.00
❑ F2777	Dance My Heart/Somewhere Beyond Tonight	1954	10.00
❑ F2860	I Don't Hurt Anymore/Cat Dancin'	1954	10.00
❑ F2896	Skokiaan/Say Hey	1954	10.00
❑ F2936	A Woman's World/Jambo	1954	10.00
❑ F3029	Heat Wave/Juke Box Special	1955	10.00
❑ F3096	Sluefoot/Something's Gotta Give	1955	10.00
❑ F3147	Learning the Blues/Mmmm Marie	1955	10.00
❑ F3176	Pete Kelly's Blues/D.C. 7	1955	10.00
❑ F3261	Flip Flop/Hurricane Anthony	1955	10.00
❑ F3319	Bullfighter Lament/Rockin' Thru Dixie	1955	10.00
❑ F3335	Madeira/Show Me the Way to Go Home	1955	10.00
❑ F3416	Chubasco (Mexican Storm Song)/Sleepwalker	1956	8.00
❑ F3500	I Am in Love/I Love You Samantha	1956	8.00
❑ F3593	Love Is Just Around the Corner/Danciong Lovers	1956	8.00
❑ F3646	Calypso Dance/Plymouth Rock	1957	8.00
❑ F3676	The Incredible Shrinking Man/This Could Be the Night	1957	8.00
❑ F3739	Lonely Trumpet/Cello-Phane	1957	8.00
❑ F3897	Till There Was You/Big Record	1958	8.00
❑ F4041	Peter Gunn/Tango for Two	1958	10.00
❑ F4176	Walkin' to Mother's/Bunny Hop	1959	10.00
❑ F4227	Fly Now Pay Later/707	1959	8.00
❑ F4275	Room 45/Stockholm Blues	1959	8.00
❑ 4358	Just in Time/Tres Chic	1960	8.00
❑ 4440	Atsa Nice-a/You Know It, You Know It	1960	8.00
❑ 4513	Gurney Slade Theme/Return to Me	1961	8.00
❑ 4603	Moliendo Café/Champs Elysses	1961	8.00
❑ 4728	Bunny Hop Twist/Tequila with a Twist	1962	8.00
❑ 4742	Worried Mind/Al Di La	1962	8.00
❑ 4834	I Almost Lost My Mind/Trouble in Mind	1962	8.00
❑ 4876	Let Me Entertain You/Wishing Star	1962	8.00
❑ 4972	Heartaches/Mexican Market Day	1963	6.00
❑ 5026	Toys in the Attic/Oh Steal Away	1963	6.00
❑ 5070	Candy Wrapper/Mr. Novak	1963	6.00
❑ 5149	Let's All Do the Swim/Everybody Do the Swim	1964	6.00
❑ 5320	Lady Bird/Tiger Tail	1964	6.00
❑ 5418	Skunk in a Trunk/Sabor Ami	1965	6.00
❑ 5468	Seventh Son/Meeting Over Yonder	1965	6.00
❑ 5589	It's Such a Happy Day/Bah-Yoop	1966	6.00

Except when noted otherwise, VG = 25% of NM, and VG+ = 50% of NM. (Example: VG = $2.00, VG+ = $4.00 and NM = $8.00.)

Number	Title (A Side/B Side)	Yr	NM
❑ 5654	Goodbye My Love/Merci Cherie	1966	6.00
❑ 5714	Danke Schoen/ Huapango Mexicana	1966	6.00
❑ 5836	Gallant Men/Around the World	1967	5.00

7-Inch Extended Plays

CAPITOL

Number	Title (A Side/B Side)	Yr	NM
❑ EAP 1-373	I Wonder What's Become of Sally/Mr. Anthony's Boogie// The Man with the Horn/ Mr. Anthony's Blues	195?	12.00
❑ EAP 1-373 [PS]	(title unknown)	195?	12.00
❑ EAP 2-373	For Dancers Only/Harlem Nocturne//Tenderly/Stardust	195?	12.00
❑ EAP 2-373 [PS]	(title unknown)	195?	12.00
❑ EBF 373 [PS]	(title unknown)	195?	12.00

—Gatefold cover for some versions of 1-373 and 2-373

Number	Title (A Side/B Side)	Yr	NM
❑ EAP 1-406	Slaughter on Tenth Avenue// On the Trail/Street Scene	195?	12.00
❑ EAP 1-406 [PS]	Ray Anthony Concert	195?	12.00
❑ 1-476	Tuxedo Junction/Chattanooga Choo Choo//Ida/ Moonlight Serenade	195?	10.00
❑ 2-476	Serenade in Blue/Elmer's Tune//In the Mood/ I Know Why	195?	10.00
❑ EBF 476 [PS]	I Remember Glenn Miller	195?	10.00

—Two-pocket cover

Number	Title (A Side/B Side)	Yr	NM
❑ EAP 1-504	Cooks Tour/Idaho//Jersey Bounce/Thunderbird	1955	10.00
❑ EAP 1-504 [PS]	Ray Anthony Plays for Dancing	1955	10.00
❑ EAP 1-563	Golden Horn/Amor//The Birth of the Blues/The Brave Bulls	195?	10.00
❑ EAP 1-563 [PS]	Golden Horn, Part 1	195?	10.00
❑ EAP 1-597	Sluefoot/Dream//Something's Gotta Give/Thunderbird	195?	10.00
❑ EAP 1-597 [PS]	Daddy Long Legs	195?	10.00
❑ EAP 1-1181	Peter Gunn/Fallout//Walkin' to Mothers/Dreamsville	1959	12.00
❑ EAP 1-1181 [PS]	Peter Gunn	1959	12.00
❑ MA1-1587	Dragnet/Peter Gunn Theme// Slaughter on Tenth Avenue	196?	10.00

—Jukebox issue; small hole, plays at 33 1/3 rpm

Number	Title (A Side/B Side)	Yr	NM
❑ MA1-1587 [PS]	Ray Anthony	196?	10.00
❑ SXA-1783	I Almost Lost My Mind/Don't Let the Sun Catch You Cryin'/ Midnight Flyer//Prayers/ Long Lonely Nights/ Trouble in Mind	1962	10.00

—Jukebox issue; small hole, plays at 33 1/3 rpm

Number	Title (A Side/B Side)	Yr	NM
❑ SXA-1783 [PS]	I Almost Lost My Mind	1962	10.00
❑ SU-2457	Everybody Loves Somebody/ A Taste of Honey/Red Roses for a Blue Lady//Are You Lonesome Tonight/You've Lost That Lovin' Feelin'/ Dear Heart	1965	10.00

—Jukebox issue; small hole, plays at 33 1/3 rpm

Number	Title (A Side/B Side)	Yr	NM
❑ SU-2457 [PS]	Dream Dancing Today	1965	10.00

RANWOOD

Number	Title (A Side/B Side)	Yr	NM
❑ RLP-8033	Are You Sincere/Rainin' in My Heart/Soul Serenade//Tuff/ Kansas City/Creole Love Call	197?	8.00

—Jukebox issue; small hole, plays at 33 1/3 rpm

Number	Title (A Side/B Side)	Yr	NM
❑ RLP-8033 [PS]	Now	197?	8.00

Albums

AERO SPACE

Number	Title (A Side/B Side)	Yr	NM
❑ RA 1007	Around the World	197?	10.00
❑ RA 1028	Let's Go Dancing	197?	12.00

—Green vinyl; Arthur Murray promotional item; add 25 percent if certificate for a free dance lesson is included

CAPITOL

Number	Title (A Side/B Side)	Yr	NM
❑ H 258 [10]	Fox Trots	195?	40.00
❑ H 292 [10]	Houseparty Hop	195?	40.00

—Reissue of L 292; purple label; "This Album Contains 8 Selections" on upper right back cover

Number	Title (A Side/B Side)	Yr	NM
❑ L 292 [10]	Houseparty Hop	195?	50.00

—Original issue; maroon label; "In addition to the selections listed, this long playing record contains: PERDIDO - WAGON WHEELS" under the title on back cover

Number	Title (A Side/B Side)	Yr	NM
❑ H 362 [10]	Campus Rumpus	195?	50.00
❑ H 476 [10]	I Remember Glenn Miller	1954	40.00
❑ T 563 [M]	Golden Horn	1955	15.00
❑ T 723 [M]	Dream Dancing	1956	15.00
❑ T 749 [M]	Jam Session at the Tower	1956	40.00
❑ T 831 [M]	Star Dancing	1957	15.00
❑ T 866 [M]	Young Ideas	1957	15.00
❑ T 917 [M]	Moments Together	1958	15.00
❑ T 969 [M]	The Dream Girl	1958	15.00
❑ T 1028 [M]	Dancing Over the Waves	1958	15.00
❑ T 1066 [M]	Ray Anthony Plays Steve Allen	1958	15.00
❑ T 1200 [M]	Sound Spectacular	1959	15.00
❑ ST 1252 [S]	More Dream Dancing	1959	15.00
❑ T 1252 [M]	More Dream Dancing	1959	12.00
❑ ST 1304 [S]	Like Wild!	1959	15.00
❑ T 1304 [M]	Like Wild!	1959	12.00
❑ T 1371 [M]	Arthur Murray Favorites — Fox Trots	1960	12.00

Anthrax, "Soldiers of Metal," Megaforce MRS-01, 1983, **$25.**

Number	Title (A Side/B Side)	Yr	NM
❑ ST 1420 [S]	Dancing Alone Together	1960	15.00

—Black colorband label, Capitol logo at left

Number	Title (A Side/B Side)	Yr	NM
❑ ST 1420 [S]	Dancing Alone Together	1962	12.00

—Black colorband label, Capitol logo at top

Number	Title (A Side/B Side)	Yr	NM
❑ T 1420 [M]	Dancing Alone Together	1960	12.00

—Black colorband label, Capitol logo at left

Number	Title (A Side/B Side)	Yr	NM
❑ T 1420 [M]	Dancing Alone Together	1962	10.00

—Black colorband label, Capitol logo at top

Number	Title (A Side/B Side)	Yr	NM
❑ ST 1421 [S]	The New Ray Anthony Show	1960	15.00
❑ T 1421 [M]	The New Ray Anthony Show	1960	12.00
❑ T 1477 [M]	The Hits of Ray Anthony	1960	12.00
❑ ST 1608 [S]	Dream Dancing Medley	1961	15.00
❑ T 1608 [M]	Dream Dancing Medley	1961	12.00
❑ ST 1668 [S]	Twist with Ray Anthony	1961	15.00
❑ T 1668 [M]	Twist with Ray Anthony	1961	12.00
❑ ST 1752 [S]	Worried Mind	1962	15.00
❑ T 1752 [M]	Worried Mind	1962	12.00
❑ ST 1783 [S]	I Almost Lost My Mind	1962	15.00
❑ T 1783 [M]	I Almost Lost My Mind	1962	12.00
❑ ST 1917 [S]	Smash Hits of '63	1963	15.00
❑ T 1917 [M]	Smash Hits of '63	1963	12.00
❑ ST 2043 [S]	Charade and Other Top Themes	1964	15.00
❑ T 2043 [M]	Charade and Other Top Themes	1964	12.00
❑ ST 2150 [S]	My Love, Forgive Me	1964	15.00
❑ T 2150 [M]	My Love, Forgive Me	1964	12.00
❑ ST 2188 [S]	Swim, Swim, C'mon, Let's Swim	1964	15.00
❑ T 2188 [M]	Swim, Swim, C'mon, Let's Swim	1964	12.00
❑ ST 2457 [S]	Dream Dancing Today	1966	15.00
❑ T 2457 [M]	Dream Dancing Today	1966	12.00
❑ ST 2530 [S]	Hit Songs to Remember	1966	15.00
❑ T 2530 [M]	Hit Songs to Remember	1966	12.00
❑ M-11978	Fox Trots	1979	10.00

CIRCLE

Number	Title (A Side/B Side)	Yr	NM
❑ CLP-96	Sweet and Swingin' 1949-1953	1987	10.00

HINDSIGHT

Number	Title (A Side/B Side)	Yr	NM
❑ HSR-240	Young Man with a Horn	1988	10.00

RANWOOD

Number	Title (A Side/B Side)	Yr	NM
❑ R.8033	Now	197?	10.00

—Cover uses "R." prefix, label uses "RLP" prefix

Number	Title (A Side/B Side)	Yr	NM
❑ 8059	Love Is for the Two of Us	197?	10.00
❑ 8083	I Get the Blues When It Rains	197?	10.00
❑ 8153	Golden Hits	197?	10.00

ANTHONY, RAYBURN

45s

SUN

Number	Title (A Side/B Side)	Yr	NM
❑ 333	Alice Blue Gown/St. Louis Blues	1959	20.00
❑ 339	There's No Tomorrow/Who's Gonna Shoe Your Pretty Foot	1960	20.00
❑ 373	Big Dream/How Well I Know	1962	20.00

ANTHONY, TONY

45s

HERALD

Number	Title (A Side/B Side)	Yr	NM
❑ 533	Peek-a-Boo/Lonely One	1959	30.00

ANTHONY AND THE SOPHOMORES

Also see THE DYNAMICS (3).

45s

ABC

Number	Title (A Side/B Side)	Yr	NM
❑ 10844	Heartbreak/I'll Go Through Life Loving You	1966	20.00

ABC-PARAMOUNT

Number	Title (A Side/B Side)	Yr	NM
❑ 10737	Gee (But I'd Give the World)/ It Depends On You	1965	20.00
❑ 10770	Get Back to You/Wild for Her	1966	20.00

GRAND

Number	Title (A Side/B Side)	Yr	NM
❑ 163	Embraceable You/ Beautiful Dreamer	1963	60.00

JAMIE

Number	Title (A Side/B Side)	Yr	NM
❑ 1330	Serenade (From The Student Prince)/Work Out	1967	15.00
❑ 1340	One Summer Night/Work Out	1967	15.00

JASON SCOTT

Number	Title (A Side/B Side)	Yr	NM
❑ 18	Embraceable You/Beautiful Dreamer	1978	4.00

MERCURY

Number	Title (A Side/B Side)	Yr	NM
❑ 72103	Play Those Oldies Mr. D.J./ Clap Your Hands	1963	60.00
❑ 72168	Swingin' at the Chariot/ Better Late Than Never	1963	30.00

Aphrodite's Child, *(The Apocalypse of John)*, Vertigo VEL-2-500, 1972, **$20.**

Number	Title (A Side/B Side)	Yr	NM
ANTHRAX			
12-Inch Singles			
ISLAND			
❑ PR 2015 [DJ]	Islands (same on both sides)	1987	12.00
❑ PR12-6635 [DJ]	Got the Time (unknown versions)	1990	15.00
45s			
MEGAFORCE			
❑ MRS-01	Soldiers of Metal/Howling Furies	1983	25.00
❑ MRS-01 [PS]	Soldiers of Metal/Howling Furies	1983	25.00
Albums			
ISLAND			
❑ PR 2563 [DJ]	Statements of Euphoria	1988	15.00
—Promo-only interview album			
❑ 90480	Spreading the Disease	1985	8.00
❑ 90584	Among the Living	1987	8.00
❑ 90685 [EP]	I'm the Man	1987	8.00
❑ 91004	State of Euphoria	1988	8.00
❑ 846480-1	Persistence of Time	1990	15.00
❑ 848804-1	Attack of the Killer B's	1991	15.00
MEGAFORCE			
❑ MRS-05 [EP]	Armed & Dangerous	1985	10.00
❑ MRI-469	Fistful of Metal	1983	10.00
❑ CAROL-1382 [EP]	Armed & Dangerous	198?	6.00
—Reissue of 5			
❑ CAROL-1383	Fistful of Metal	198?	8.00
—Reissue of 469			
ANTI NOWHERE LEAGUE			
12-Inch Singles			
GWR			
❑ 7198 [DJ]	Crime (LP Version) (Edit)	1987	15.00
Albums			
GWR			
❑ 1238	The Perfect Crime	1987	15.00
WXYZ			
❑ COPE 4	We Are ... The League	1982	15.00
❑ FEP 1301 [EP]	I Hate...People	1982	14.00

Number	Title (A Side/B Side)	Yr	NM
ANTIQUES, THE			
45s			
LASALLE			
❑ 0069	Go for Yourself/(B-side unknown)	196?	1200.
ANTISEEN			
45s			
AJAX			
❑ 007	Two Headed Dog/Cause I Love You	1990	5.00
—Blue vinyl (all copies)			
❑ 007 [PS]	Two Headed Dog/Cause I Love You	1990	5.00
SUB POP			
❑ 174	We Got This Far (Without You)/(We Will Not) Remember	1992	7.50
—Clear magenta vinyl			
❑ 174 [PS]	We Got This Far (Without You)/(We Will Not) Remember	1992	7.50
—#49 in Sub Pop Singles Club series			
7-Inch Extended Plays			
AJAX			
❑ 003	(contents unknown)	1988	8.00
—Black vinyl			
❑ 003	(contents unknown)	1988	12.50
—Red vinyl; 300 made			
❑ 003 [PS]	Blood of Freaks	1988	8.00
—Regular sleeve			
❑ 003 [PS]	Blood of Freaks	1988	12.50
—Poster sleeve; 300 made (issued with red vinyl record)			
DEATH TRAIN			
❑ 001	(contents unknown)	1985	20.00
—Second pressing, with corrected address on labels			
❑ 001	(contents unknown)	1985	40.00
—First pressing, with wrong address crossed out on labels			
❑ 001 [PS]	Drastic	1985	30.00
❑ 002	(contents unknown)	1986	10.00
❑ 002 [PS]	N.C. Royalty	1986	10.00
—White sleeve, no lyrics			

Number	Title (A Side/B Side)	Yr	NM
❑ 002 [PS]	N.C. Royalty	1986	15.00
—Orange sleeve with lyrics			
❑ 002 [PS]	N.C. Royalty	1986	20.00
—Blue/green sleeve with lyrics			
TPOS PRODUCTIONS			
❑ 038	(contents unknown)	1989	7.50
❑ 038 [PS]	WXCI Live Radio Broadcast	1989	7.50
Albums			
BONA FIDE/CHOPPER			
❑ (# unknown)	Honor Among Thieves	1987	12.00
REPO			
❑ (# unknown)	The Raw Shit	1986	12.00
—Pink vinyl			
ANTOINETTE			
45s			
PARKWAY			
❑ 932	There He Goes/Little Things Mean a Lot	1964	12.00
ANTWINETTES, THE			
45s			
RCA VICTOR			
❑ 47-7398	Johnny/Kill It	1958	40.00
ANVIL			
12-Inch Singles			
ENIGMA			
❑ EPRO-135 [DJ]	Blood on the Ice (same on both sides)	1988	8.00
Albums			
ENIGMA/METAL BLADE			
❑ ST-73267	Strength of Steel	1987	15.00
❑ 7-73336	Pound for Pound	1988	15.00
AORTA			
45s			
ATLANTIC			
❑ 2545	Strange/Shape of Things to Come	1968	20.00
COLUMBIA			
❑ 44870	Strange/Ode to Missy Mztsfpklk	1969	10.00
HAPPY TIGER			
❑ 567	Sandcastles/Willie Jean	1970	15.00
Albums			
COLUMBIA			
❑ CS 9785	Aorta	1969	30.00
HAPPY TIGER			
❑ HT-1010	Aorta 2	1970	40.00
APHRODITE'S CHILD			
45s			
PHILIPS			
❑ 40536	Other People/Plastics Nevermore	1968	20.00
❑ 40587	End of the World/You Always Stand in My Way	1969	20.00
POLYDOR			
❑ 15005	Magic Mirror/I Want to Live	1969	8.00
VERTIGO			
❑ 107	Babylon/Break	1973	6.00
Albums			
VERTIGO			
❑ VEL-2-500 [(2)]	666 (The Apocalypse of John)	1972	20.00
APOLLO 100			
45s			
ATCO			
❑ 7001	Dan the Banjo Man/Tidal Wave	1974	6.00
MEGA			
❑ 0050	Joy/Exercise in A Minor	1971	5.00
❑ 0069	Symphony #4, 2nd Movement/Reach for the Sky	1972	4.00
❑ 0080	Minuet for a Funky Lady/Telstar	1972	4.00
Albums			
MEGA			
❑ 31-1010	Joy	1972	10.00
APPALACHIANS, THE			
45s			
ABC-PARAMOUNT			
❑ 10419	Bony Maronie/It Takes a Man	1963	10.00
❑ 10464	Big Betty/Hilly-Billy-Ding-Dong-Choo-Choo	1963	8.00
❑ 10498	Lawdy Miss Clawdy/Over Yonder	1963	8.00

Except when noted otherwise, VG = 25% of NM, and VG+ = 50% of NM. (Example: VG = $2.00, VG+ = $4.00 and NM = $8.00.)

Number	Title (A Side/B Side)	Yr	NM

APPALOOSA

Albums

COLUMBIA

Number	Title (A Side/B Side)	Yr	NM
❑ CS 9819	Appaloosa	1969	15.00

—Produced by Al Kooper

APPELL, DAVE See THE APPLEJACKS (1).

APPLE PIE MOTHERHOOD BAND, THE

45s

ATLANTIC

Number	Title (A Side/B Side)	Yr	NM
❑ 2477	Flight Path/Long Live Apple Pie	1968	8.00

Albums

ATLANTIC

Number	Title (A Side/B Side)	Yr	NM
❑ SD 8189	The Apple Pie Motherhood Band	1968	25.00
❑ SD 8233	Apple Pie	1969	25.00

APPLEJACKS, THE (1) Essentially Dave Appell. The below includes his "solo" records.

45s

B.T. PUPPY

Number	Title (A Side/B Side)	Yr	NM
❑ 554	The Son of a Preacher Man/ Girl of the Skies	1970	8.00

—As "Dave Appell"

CAMEO

Number	Title (A Side/B Side)	Yr	NM
❑ 110	Love in the Jungle/ Chitter Chatter Baby	1957	20.00
❑ 132	Dinner with Drac/ No Name Theme	1958	25.00
❑ 138	Moonlight Serenade/Walk On	1958	20.00
❑ 149	Mexican Hat Rock/ Stop! Red Light	1958	16.00
❑ 149	Mexican Hat Rock/ Sophisticated Swing	1958	20.00
❑ 155	Rocka-Conga/Am I Blue	1958	16.00

—Later pressings have correct A-side title

Number	Title (A Side/B Side)	Yr	NM
❑ 155	Rocka-Tonga/Am I Blue	1958	20.00

—First pressing contains a typographical error on A-side

Number	Title (A Side/B Side)	Yr	NM
❑ 158	Bunny Hop/Night Train Stroll	1959	16.00
❑ 170	Circle Dance/Love Scene	1959	16.00
❑ 177	The Untouchables/ Memories Are Made of This	1960	16.00
❑ 184	Theme from The Young Ones/ September Song	1960	15.00

—As "Dave Appell and His Orchestra"

Number	Title (A Side/B Side)	Yr	NM
❑ 203	Mexican Hat Twist/ Let's Continental	1961	15.00
❑ 207	Happy Jose/Noivous	1961	15.00

—As "Dave Appell and His Orchestra"

Number	Title (A Side/B Side)	Yr	NM
❑ 222	Struttin' in the Summertime/ Any Time	1962	15.00
❑ 248	Hippies Waltz/Back in 60 Seconds	1963	15.00
❑ 283	Hot Toddy/Dance of the Hours	1963	15.00
❑ 321	She Loves You/Bongo Beach	1964	15.00

—As "Dave Appell and The Applejacks (Featuring Joe Sher on Drums)"

DECCA

Number	Title (A Side/B Side)	Yr	NM
❑ 9-29218	Smarter/My Heart Will Wait for You	1954	20.00
❑ 9-29330	Sweet Patootie Pie/Reunion	1954	20.00

PRESIDENT

Number	Title (A Side/B Side)	Yr	NM
❑ 1005	Ring Around My Baby/ Love Express	1956	20.00
❑ 1006	Teenage Meeting/Ooh Baby Ooh	1956	20.00
❑ 1011	Rock and Roll Story/ Rainbow of Love	1956	20.00

TONE-CRAFT

Number	Title (A Side/B Side)	Yr	NM
❑ 200	Ookey-Ook/Honey	1955	20.00

—As "Dave Appell and the Applejacks"

Number	Title (A Side/B Side)	Yr	NM
❑ 202	Where Is My Love/Alrighty	1955	20.00

—As "Dave Appell and the Applejacks"

Albums

CAMEO

Number	Title (A Side/B Side)	Yr	NM
❑ C-1004 [M]	Alone Together	1958	50.00

—As "Dave Appell"

APPLEJACKS, THE (2) British band.

45s

LONDON

Number	Title (A Side/B Side)	Yr	NM
❑ 9658	Baby Jane/Tell Me When	1964	12.00
❑ 9681	Like Dreamers Do/ Everybody Fall Down	1964	15.00
❑ 9709	You're the One for Me/ Send Me Love	1964	12.00
❑ 9709	You're the One for Me/ Three Little Words	1964	12.00

APPLETREE THEATRE CO.

45s

VERVE FORECAST

Number	Title (A Side/B Side)	Yr	NM
❑ 5071	Hightower Square/ Who Do You Think I Am	1967	12.00

April Wine, *The Nature of the Beast*, Capitol SOO-12125, 1981, **$10.**

Number	Title (A Side/B Side)	Yr	NM
❑ 5082	Lotus Flower/What a Way to Go	1968	12.00

Albums

VERVE FORECAST

Number	Title (A Side/B Side)	Yr	NM
❑ FTS-3042	Playback	1968	50.00

—RICK NELSON appears on this album

APPRECIATIONS, THE

45s

JUBILEE

Number	Title (A Side/B Side)	Yr	NM
❑ 5525	Afraid of Love/ Far from Your Love	1966	12.00

SPORT

Number	Title (A Side/B Side)	Yr	NM
❑ 108	There's a Place in My Heart/She Never Really Believed Me	1967	100.00
❑ 112	It's Better to Cry/ Gimme Back My Soul	1967	200.00

APRIL WINE

12-Inch Singles

CAPITOL

Number	Title (A Side/B Side)	Yr	NM
❑ SPRO-9069 [DJ]	This Could Be the Right One (same on both sides)	1984	10.00
❑ SPRO-9110 [DJ]	Sons of the Pioneers (same on both sides)	1984	10.00
❑ SPRO-9468 [DJ]	Rock Myself to Sleep (same on both sides)	1985	10.00

45s

BIG TREE

Number	Title (A Side/B Side)	Yr	NM
❑ 133	You Could Have Been a Lady/ Teacher	1972	6.00
❑ 142	Bad Side of the Moon/ Believe in Me	1972	5.00
❑ 15006	Come On Along/ I'm on Fire for You Baby	1974	5.00
❑ 16010	Just Like That/Weeping Willow	1973	5.00
❑ 16036	Oowatanite/(B-side unknown)	1975	5.00

CAPITOL

Number	Title (A Side/B Side)	Yr	NM
❑ 4660	Roller/Right Down to It	1978	4.00
❑ 4728	Get Ready for Love/Comin' Right Down on Top of Me	1979	4.00
❑ 4802	Before the Dawn/Say Hello	1979	4.00
❑ 4828	I Like to Rock/Babes in Arms	1980	4.00
❑ 4859	Lady's Man/Tonite	1980	4.00
❑ 4975	Just Between You and Me/ Big City Girls	1981	4.00
❑ 4975 [PS]	Just Between You and Me/ Big City Girls	1981	5.00

—Regular sleeve

Number	Title (A Side/B Side)	Yr	NM
❑ 4975 [PS]	Just Between You and Me/ Big City Girls	1981	8.00

—Fold-out poster sleeve

Number	Title (A Side/B Side)	Yr	NM
❑ A-5001	Sign of the Gypsy Queen/ Crash and Burn	1981	4.00
❑ A-5001 [PS]	Sign of the Gypsy Queen/ Crash and Burn	1981	5.00
❑ B-5133	Enough Is Enough/ Ain't Got Your Love	1982	4.00
❑ B-5133 [PS]	Enough Is Enough/ Ain't Got Your Love	1982	5.00
❑ B-5153	If You See Kay/Blood Money	1982	5.00
❑ B-5168	Tell Me Why/ Runners in the Night	1982	4.00
❑ B-5319	This Could Be the Right One/ Really Don't Want Your Love	1984	3.00
❑ B-5319 [PS]	This Could Be the Right One/ Really Don't Want Your Love	1984	4.00
❑ B-5506	Rock Myself to Sleep/ All It Will Ever Be	1985	3.00

LONDON

Number	Title (A Side/B Side)	Yr	NM
❑ 245	Shot Down/(B-side unknown)	1976	5.00
❑ 255	You Won't Dance with Me/ Shot Down	1976	5.00
❑ 265	I'm Alive/Rock and Roll Is a Vicious Game	1977	5.00

Albums

AQUARIUS

Number	Title (A Side/B Side)	Yr	NM
❑ AQR 504	Electric Jewels	1973	15.00
❑ AQR 505	Live	1974	15.00

The Archies, *Everything's Archie*, Calendar KES-103, 1969, **$25.**

Number	Title (A Side/B Side)	Yr	NM
ATLANTIC			
❑ SD 19303	Stand Back	1981	10.00
—Reissue of Big Tree 89506			
BIG TREE			
❑ BTS 2012	April Wine	1972	20.00
❑ 89506	Stand Back	1975	15.00
CAPITOL			
❑ SPRO-9632/3 [DJ]	Summer Tour 1981	1981	20.00
—Promo-only sampler			
❑ ST-11852	First Glance	1979	12.00
❑ ST-12013	Harder...Faster	1979	10.00
❑ SOO-12125	The Nature of the Beast	1981	10.00
❑ ST-12218	Power Play	1982	10.00
❑ ST-12311	Animal Grace	1984	10.00
❑ SN-16245	First Glance	1982	8.00
—Budget-line reissue			
❑ SN-16322	Harder...Faster	1984	8.00
—Budget-line reissue			
❑ SN-16344	Power Play	1984	8.00
—Budget-line reissue			
❑ SN-16379	The Nature of the Beast	1986	8.00
—Budget-line reissue			
❑ C1-48418	Walking Through Fire	1988	12.00
LONDON			
❑ PS 675	The Whole World's Goin' Crazy	1976	15.00
❑ PS 699	Live at the El Mocambo	1977	15.00
AQUARIANS			
45s			
UNI			
❑ 55124	Abela/Jungle Grass	1969	6.00
Albums			
UNI			
❑ 73053	Jungle Grass	1969	15.00

Number	Title (A Side/B Side)	Yr	NM
AQUATONES, THE			
45s			
FARGO			
❑ 1001	You/She's the One for Me	1958	25.00
❑ 1002	Say You'll Be Mine/So Fine	1958	25.00
❑ 1003	Our First Kiss/The Drive-In	1958	25.00
❑ 1005	My Treasure/My One Desire	1959	25.00
❑ 1015	Every Time/There's a Long, Long Trail	1960	25.00
❑ 1016	Wanted/Crazy for You	1961	25.00
❑ 1022	My Treasure/Say You'll Be Mine	1962	25.00
❑ 1111	My Darling/For You, For You	1960	20.00
Albums			
FARGO			
❑ 3001 [M]	The Aquatones Sing	1964	500.00
RELIC/FARGO			
❑ 5033 [M]	The Aquatones Sing	198?	8.00
ARBORS, THE			
45s			
CARNEY			
❑ 1011	A Symphony for Susan/ Love Is the Light	1966	25.00
DATE			
❑ 1529	A Symphony for Susan/ Love Is the Light	1966	10.00
❑ 1546	Dreamer Girl/Just Let It Happen	1967	10.00
❑ 1561	Graduation Day/I Win the Whole Wide World	1967	10.00
❑ 1570	Love for All Seasons/ With You Girl	1967	10.00
❑ 1581	Valley of the Dolls/ You Are the Music	1967	10.00
❑ 1581 [PS]	Valley of the Dolls/ You Are the Music	1967	25.00
❑ 1601	That's the Way It Is/ Graduation Day	1968	10.00
❑ 1638	The Letter/Most of All	1969	12.00
❑ 1645	I Can't Quit Her/Lovin' Tonight (Maybe Tonight)	1969	10.00

Number	Title (A Side/B Side)	Yr	NM
❑ 1651	Touch Me/Motet	1969	10.00
❑ 1672	Julie I Tried/Okalona River Bottom Band	1970	10.00
MERCURY			
❑ 72456	Anybody Here for Love/The Girl with the Heather Green Eyes	1965	12.00
Albums			
DATE			
❑ TEM 3003 [M]	A Symphony for Susan	1967	15.00
❑ TEM 3011 [M]	Valley of the Dolls	1967	20.00
❑ TES 4003 [S]	A Symphony for Susan	1967	15.00
❑ TES 4011 [S]	Valley of the Dolls	1967	15.00
❑ TES 4017	The Arbors Featuring I Can't Quit Her and The Letter	1969	15.00
ARCHERS, THE			
45s			
LAURIE			
❑ 3207	Hey Rube/Unwind It	1963	15.00
SUMMER			
❑ 502	Motorcycle Michael/Golden Girl	196?	30.00
ARCHIBALD			
45s			
IMPERIAL			
❑ 5212	Early Morning Blues/ Great Big Eyes	1953	1500.
❑ 5358	Stack-O-Lee (Part 1)/ Stack-O-Lee (Part 2)	1955	100.00
❑ 5563	Stack-A-Lee/Whispering Hope	1959	50.00
ARCHIES, THE Also see RON DANTE.			
12-Inch Singles			
CULT			
❑ 0595	Sugar Sugar (Julian Beeston Remix '99) (Pistel Remix '99)	2000	6.00
45s			
CALENDAR			
❑ 63-1006	Bang-Shang-a-Lang/ Truck Driver	1968	8.00
❑ 63-1006 [PS]	Bang-Shang-a-Lang/ Truck Driver	1968	16.00
❑ 63-1007	Feelin' So Good (S.K.O.O.B.Y.-D.O.O.)/ Love Light	1968	8.00
❑ 63-1007 [PS]	Feelin' So Good (S.K.O.O.B.Y.-D.O.O.)/ Love Light	1968	25.00
❑ 63-1008	Sugar Sugar/Melody Hill	1969	10.00
KIRSHNER			
❑ SP-45-218 [DJ]	Sunshine (same on both sides)	1970	15.00
—Promo-only number			
❑ 63-1009	Sunshine/Over and Over	1970	8.00
❑ 63-5002	Jingle Jangle/Justine	1969	8.00
❑ 63-5003	Who's Your Baby/Senorita Rita	1970	8.00
❑ 63-5009	Everything's Alright/ Together We Two	1970	8.00
❑ 63-5011	Throw a Little Love My Way/ This Is Love	1971	8.00
❑ 63-5014	A Summer Prayer for Peace/ Maybe I'm Wrong	1971	8.00
❑ 63-5014 [PS]	A Summer Prayer for Peace/ Maybe I'm Wrong	1971	16.00
❑ 63-5018	Love Is Living in You/ Hold On to Lovin'	1972	8.00
❑ 63-5021	Strangers in the Morning/ Plum Crazy	1972	8.00
Albums			
ACCORD			
❑ SN-7149	Straight A's	1981	10.00
CALENDAR			
❑ KES-101	The Archies	1968	25.00
❑ KES-103	Everything's Archie	1969	25.00
51 WEST			
❑ 16002	The Archies	1979	10.00
KIRSHNER			
❑ KES-103 [DJ]	Everything's Archie Box	1969	100.00
—Box with LP, photos, press kit and buttons			
❑ KES-105	Jingle Jangle	1969	25.00
❑ KES-107	Sunshine	1970	25.00
❑ KES-109	The Archies Greatest Hits	1970	25.00
❑ KES-110	This Is Love	1971	30.00
ARDELLS, THE			
45s			
EPIC			
❑ 9621	Eefananny/Lonely Valley	1963	15.00
❑ 9621 [PS]	Eefananny/Lonely Valley	1963	30.00
—Title sleeve with lyrics			
MARCO			
❑ 102	Every Day of the Week/Roll On	1961	30.00

Except when noted otherwise, VG = 25% of NM, and VG+ = 50% of NM. (Example: VG = $2.00, VG+ = $4.00 and NM = $8.00.)

Number	Title (A Side/B Side)	Yr	NM
SELMA			
❑ 4001	Seven Lonely Nights/ You Can Fall in Love	1963	25.00

ARDEN, TONI

Number	Title (A Side/B Side)	Yr	NM
45s			
BONFIRE			
❑ 1501	Don't You Come Home Bill Bailey/I'll Say It Again	197?	6.00
COLUMBIA			
❑ 1-377	I Can Dream, Can't I?/ A Little Hug, a Little Kiss	1949	30.00
—Microgroove 33 1/3 rpm 7-inch single, small hole			
❑ 1-560 (?)	Mother, Mother, Mother/Rain	1950	30.00
—Microgroove 33 1/3 rpm 7-inch single, small hole			
❑ 1-630 (?)	Why/Tonight	1950	30.00
—Microgroove 33 1/3 rpm 7-inch single, small hole			
❑ 1-760 (?)	Can't We Talk It Over/ Only a Moment Ago	1950	30.00
—Microgroove 33 1/3 rpm 7-inch single, small hole			
❑ 1-830 (?)	My Tears Won't Dry/ And You'll Be Home	1950	30.00
—Microgroove 33 1/3 rpm 7-inch single, small hole			
❑ 1-937	Every Moment of My Life/I'm Praying to St. Christopher	1950	30.00
—Microgroove 33 1/3 rpm 7-inch single, small hole			
❑ 4-39003	My Tears Won't Dry/ And You'll Be Home	1950	20.00
❑ 4-39080	Every Moment of My Life/I'm Praying to St. Christopher	1950	20.00
❑ 4-39117	My Man/Playing Our Song	1950	20.00
❑ 4-39208	Chante Moi/So Deep in Love	1951	15.00
❑ 4-39271	Too Young/Too Late Now	1951	15.00
❑ 4-39348	Little Child/Come Back to Sorrento	1951	15.00
❑ 4-39427	Wonder Why/Dark Is the Night	1951	15.00
❑ 4-39525	The Day Isn't Long Enough/ I'll Hold You In My Heart	1951	15.00
❑ 4-39577	Once/Never	1951	15.00
❑ 4-39650	Heart of Stone/There's Always My Heart	1952	15.00
❑ 4-39737	Kiss of Fire/I'm Yours	1952	15.00
❑ 4-39766	Blow Out the Candle/ Where Did the Night Go	1952	15.00
❑ 4-39768	Take My Heart/Tell Your Tale, Nightingale	1952	15.00
❑ 4-39810	Remembering/ One Love Too Many	1952	15.00
❑ 4-39878	Take a Chance/ Sweet Forgiveness	1952	15.00
❑ 4-39911	Kiss/It's Not Their Heartache	1953	15.00
❑ 4-39978	It's Only My Heart/F'r Instance	1953	15.00
❑ 4-40019	All I Desire/Lover's Waltz	1953	15.00
—With the Four Lads			
❑ 4-40081	I Forgot More Than You'll Ever Know/Any More	1953	15.00
❑ 4-40125	Take Me Now/I Wish I Knew	1953	15.00
❑ 4-40196	In Paris and In Love/ Cry, My Heart	1954	15.00
❑ 4-40225	Three Coins in the Fountain/ When the Rolling Mountains Meet the Rolling Sea	1954	15.00
DECCA			
❑ 25542	Arrivederci Roma/Non Dimenticar	196?	8.00
❑ 25586	Come Back to Sorrento/ Senza Mama E Namurato	196?	8.00
❑ 9-30180	Little by Little/Without Love	1957	10.00
❑ 9-30291	Like a Baby/An Empty Heart	1957	10.00
❑ 9-30396	It Takes Only One/Good Morning, Mister Love	1957	10.00
❑ 9-30507	Like You/Can You Blame Me	1957	10.00
❑ 9-30563	King Size Love/Queen of Tears	1958	10.00
❑ 9-30628	Padre/All at Once	1958	12.00
❑ 9-30732	You're Not Losing a Daughter Mama/If Your Heart Doesn't Dance	1958	10.00
❑ 9-30765	Desire Me/The Window	1958	10.00
❑ 9-30832	Just for Once/Why, Why, Why (Zon, Zon, Zon)	1959	10.00
❑ 9-30951	Only with You (You Are Me, I Am You)/Your Touch	1959	10.00
❑ 9-30986	Besame Mucho/Anna	1959	10.00
❑ 9-31025	The Village of St. Bernadette/ Feeling Foolish in Brazil	1959	10.00
❑ 9-31139	Na Voce Na Chittara (E'o Poco E Luna) (I Only Know I Love You)/No, No, Nevermore	1960	8.00
❑ 31576	In the Summer of His Years/ My Heart Is a Chapel	1963	8.00
❑ 31694	Quando, Quando, Quando/ It's True, It's True	1964	8.00
❑ 7-34175 [S]	Just Say I Love Him/ Anema E Core	196?	12.00
❑ 7-34176 [S]	Come Prima/Summertime in Venice	196?	12.00
❑ 7-34177 [S]	Padre/Quando, Quando, Quando	196?	12.00
❑ 7-34178 [S]	Al Di La/Retorna a Me	196?	12.00
❑ 7-34179 [S]	Guaglione/Mama	196?	12.00
—The above five are small hole, 33 1/3 rpm jukebox singles			
RCA VICTOR			
❑ 47-6142	Beware/I'll Step Aside	1955	12.00
❑ 47-6346	Are You Satisfied/I Forgot to Remember to Forget	1956	15.00
❑ 47-6536	Believe in Love/ How Sweet My Love	1956	12.00
Albums			
DECCA			
❑ DL 4375 [M]	Italian Gold	196?	12.00
❑ DL 8651 [M]	Miss Toni Arden	1957	30.00
—Black label, silver print			
❑ DL 8765 [M]	Sing a Song of Italy	1958	25.00
—Black label, silver print			
❑ DL 8875 [M]	Besame	1959	20.00
—Black label, silver print			
❑ DL 74375 [S]	Italian Gold	196?	15.00
❑ DL 78765 [S]	Sing a Song of Italy	1959	30.00
—Maroon label, silver print			
HARMONY			
❑ HL 7212 [M]	Exciting Toni Arden	196?	20.00

AREA CODE 615

Number	Title (A Side/B Side)	Yr	NM
45s			
POLYDOR			
❑ 14012	Why Ask Why/Ruby	1969	6.00
❑ 14215	Stone Fox Chase/Sligo	1973	5.00
Albums			
POLYDOR			
❑ 24-4002	Area Code 615	1969	25.00
❑ 24-4025	A Trip in the Country	1970	25.00

ARENA BRASS, THE

Number	Title (A Side/B Side)	Yr	NM
7-Inch Extended Plays			
EPIC			
❑ 5-26039	The Lonely Bull/Desafinado/ Spanish Harlem//Eso Beso (That Kiss)/Tequila/La Virgen De La Macarena	1962	10.00
—Jukebox issue; small hole, plays at 33 1/3 rpm			
❑ 5-26039 [PS]	The Lonely Bull	1962	10.00
Albums			
EPIC			
❑ LN 24039 [M]	The Lonely Bull	1962	12.00
❑ BN 26039 [S]	The Lonely Bull	1962	15.00

ARGENT

Rod Argent's group after THE ZOMBIES broke up. Rod Argent's group after THE ZOMBIES broke up. Also see RUSS BALLARD.

Number	Title (A Side/B Side)	Yr	NM
45s			
DATE			
❑ 1659	Liar/Schoolgirl	1970	10.00
EPIC			
❑ 10718	Rejoice/Sweet Mary	1971	6.00
❑ 10746	Celebration/Kingdom	1971	6.00
❑ 10852	Hold Your Head Up/ Closer to Heaven	1972	8.00
❑ 10919	Tragedy/He's a Dynamo	1972	5.00
❑ 10972	God Gave Rock and Roll To You/Christmas for the Free	1973	5.00
❑ 11019	It's Only Money, Part 2/ Losing Hold	1973	5.00
❑ 11137	Man for All Seasons/ Music from the Spheres	1974	5.00
❑ 50025	The Coming of Kohoutek/ Thunder and Lightning	1974	5.00
Albums			
EPIC			
❑ BN 26525	Argent	1970	20.00
—Yellow label			
❑ BN 26525	Argent	1973	12.00
—Orange label			
❑ E 30128	A Ring of Hands	1971	20.00
—Yellow label			
❑ KE 30128	A Ring of Hands	1973	12.00
—Orange label			
❑ KE 31556	All Together Now	1972	20.00
—Yellow label			
❑ KE 31556	All Together Now	1973	12.00
—Orange label			
❑ KE 32195	In Deep	1973	20.00
—Orange label			
❑ KE 32195	In Deep	1973	25.00
—Yellow label			
❑ PEQ 32195 [Q]	In Deep	1974	30.00
❑ PE 32573	Nexus	1974	20.00
—Orange label			
❑ PEG 33079 [(2)]	Encore — Live in Concert	1975	20.00
—Orange labels			
❑ PE 33422	Circus	1975	20.00
—Orange label			
❑ PE 33955	Anthology	1976	15.00
—Orange label			
❑ PE 33955	Anthology	1979	10.00
—Dark blue label			
UNITED ARTISTS			
❑ UA-LA560-G	Counterpoint	1975	12.00

ARGOSY

Featuring Roger Hodgson, later of SUPERTRAMP, with ELTON JOHN on piano and NIGEL OLSSON on drums.

Number	Title (A Side/B Side)	Yr	NM
45s			
CONGRESS			
❑ C-6013	Mr. Boyd/Imagine	1969	150.00

ARGYLES, THE (1)

See THE HOLLYWOOD ARGYLES.

ARGYLES, THE (2)

Number	Title (A Side/B Side)	Yr	NM
45s			
BALLY			
❑ 1030	Moonbeam/ Every Time You Smile	1957	40.00

ARIELS, THE

Number	Title (A Side/B Side)	Yr	NM
45s			
BRENT			
❑ 7060	Feels Like I'm Cryin'/I Love You	1967	60.00

ARISTOCATS, THE

Number	Title (A Side/B Side)	Yr	NM
Albums			
HIFI			
❑ J-610 [M]	Boogie and Blues	1959	30.00
❑ JS-610 [S]	Boogie and Blues	1959	40.00

ARISTOCRATS, THE

Number	Title (A Side/B Side)	Yr	NM
45s			
ARGO			
❑ 5275	Maid of the Mist/Vagabonds	1957	25.00
ESSEX			
❑ 366	Believe Me/I'm Waiting for Ships	1954	60.00

ARKADE

Number	Title (A Side/B Side)	Yr	NM
45s			
ABC DUNHILL			
❑ 4247	Sing Out the Love (In My Heart)/ Susan	1970	6.00
❑ 4268	The Morning of Our Lives/ Rhythm of the People	1971	6.00
❑ 4268 [PS]	The Morning of Our Lives/ Rhythm of the People	1971	10.00
❑ 4277	Where You Lead/ Sentimental Lisa	1971	6.00
❑ 4286	Fool's Way of Lovin'/ The Morning of Our Lives	1971	6.00

ARLINGTON, BRUCE

Number	Title (A Side/B Side)	Yr	NM
45s			
KING			
❑ 5918	You Made Me Cry/ How Could You Know	1964	30.00

ARMAGEDDON (1)

Number	Title (A Side/B Side)	Yr	NM
Albums			
AMOS			
❑ 73075	Armageddon	1970	25.00

ARMAGEDDON (2)

With KEITH RELF, ex-member of THE YARDBIRDS; his last material before his death. Also see CAPTAIN BEYOND.

Number	Title (A Side/B Side)	Yr	NM
Albums			
A&M			
❑ SP-4513	Armageddon	1975	20.00

ARMATRADING, JOAN

Number	Title (A Side/B Side)	Yr	NM
12-Inch Singles			
A&M			
❑ SP-12184 [DJ]	Kind Words (2 versions)/ Figure of Speech	1986	6.00
❑ SP-17229 [DJ]	(I Love It When You) Call Me Names/Drop the Pilot	1983	6.00
❑ SP-17311 [DJ]	Temptation (7" Version)/ (Album Version)	1985	6.00
❑ SP-17386 [DJ]	Kind Words (And a Real Good Heart) (same on both sides)	1986	6.00
❑ SP-17414 [DJ]	Angel Man (same on both sides)	1986	6.00
❑ SP-17654 [DJ]	Shouting Stage (same on both sides?)	1988	6.00
45s			
A&M			
❑ 1235	Living for You/I Really Must Be Going	1988	4.00
❑ 1452	Lonely Lady/Together in Words and Music	1973	4.00
❑ 1865	Love and Affection/Help Yourself	1976	5.00
❑ 1898	Down to Zero/Like Fire	1976	4.00
❑ 1914	Water with the Wine/People	1977	4.00

Number	Title (A Side/B Side)	Yr	NM
❑ 1994	Show Some Emotion/No Way Out	1977	4.00
❑ 2018	Warm Love/No Way Out	1978	4.00
❑ 2102	Bottom to the Top/Your Letter	1978	4.00
❑ 2113	Barefoot and Pregnant/Your Letter	1979	4.00
❑ 2210	Rosie/Show Some Emotion	1979	4.00
❑ 2224	He Wants Up/Show Some Emotion	1980	4.00
❑ 2240	Me Myself I/Friends	1980	4.00
❑ 2262	Is It Tomorrow Yet/Ma-Me-O-Beach	1980	4.00
❑ 2381	Weakness in Me/Crying	1981	4.00
❑ 2400	I Wanna Hold You/Crying	1982	4.00
❑ 2538	Drop the Pilot/Business Is Business	1983	4.00
❑ 2538 [PS]	Drop the Pilot/Business Is Business	1983	5.00
❑ 2564 [DJ]	(I Love It When You) Call Me Names (same on both sides)	1983	5.00
—Stock copies do not exist			
❑ 2622	Frustration/Heaven	1984	4.00
❑ 2712	Temptation/Talking to the Wall	1985	4.00
❑ 2751	Love Grows/Thinking Man	1985	4.00
❑ 2837	Kind Words (And a Real Good Heart)/Figure of Speech	1986	4.00
❑ 2837 [PS]	Kind Words (And a Real Good Heart)/Figure of Speech	1986	5.00
❑ 2868	Angel Man/Rivers on Fire	1986	4.00

7-Inch Extended Plays

A&M

Number	Title (A Side/B Side)	Yr	NM
❑ 2391 [DJ]	*Me Myself & I/Tall in the Saddle/Show Some Emotion/Love and Affection/Rosie/Back to the Night/People	1980	5.00
—White label, small hole, plays at 33 1/3 rpm			
❑ 2391 [PS]	Free Joan Armatrading	1980	5.00

Albums

A&M

Number	Title (A Side/B Side)	Yr	NM
❑ SP-3141	Back to the Night	1980	8.00
—Reissue			
❑ SP-3227	Whatever's For Us	1984	8.00
—Reissue			
❑ SP-3228	Joan Armatrading	1984	8.00
—Reissue			
❑ SP-3273	Show Some Emotion	1984	8.00
—Reissue			
❑ SP-3302 [EP]	How Cruel	1979	8.00
❑ SP-4382	Whatever's For Us	1974	12.00
❑ SP-4525	Back to the Night	1975	12.00
❑ SP-4588	Joan Armatrading	1976	10.00
❑ SP-4663	Show Some Emotion	1977	10.00
❑ SP-4732	To the Limit	1978	10.00
❑ SP-4809	Me Myself I	1980	10.00
❑ SP-4876	Walk Under Ladders	1981	10.00
❑ SP-4912	The Key	1983	10.00
❑ SP-4987	Track Record	1984	10.00
❑ SP-5040	Secret Secrets	1985	10.00
❑ SP-5130	Sleight of Hand	1986	10.00
❑ SP-5211	The Shouting Stage	1988	10.00
❑ 75021 5298 1	Hearts and Flowers	1990	15.00
❑ SP-8414 [DJ]	Joan Armatrading Live at the Bijou Café	1977	20.00
—Promo-only "Superstars Radio Network" issue			
❑ SP-12400 [EP]	How Cruel	1984	6.00
—Reissue			

ARMORED SAINT

12-Inch Singles

CHRYSALIS

Number	Title (A Side/B Side)	Yr	NM
❑ AS 2009 [DJ]	Take a Turn (same on both sides)	1985	10.00
❑ VAS 2213 [DJ]	Over the Edge (same on both sides)	1986	10.00
❑ VAS 2767 [DJ]	Isolation (same on both sides)	1987	10.00

Albums

CHRYSALIS

Number	Title (A Side/B Side)	Yr	NM
❑ FV 41476	March of the Saint	1984	10.00
❑ BFV 41516	Delirious Nomad	1985	10.00
❑ BFV 41601	Raising Fear	1987	10.00

ENIGMA/METAL BLADE

Number	Title (A Side/B Side)	Yr	NM
❑ 72301 [EP]	Live: Saints Will Conquer	1988	10.00

METAL BLADE

Number	Title (A Side/B Side)	Yr	NM
❑ MBR 1009 [EP]	Armored Saint	1983	50.00

ARMS, RUSSELL

45s

EPIC

Number	Title (A Side/B Side)	Yr	NM
❑ 5-9083	The "Point of View" Song/The Touch	1954	12.00
❑ 5-9109	Not As a Stranger/Don't Be Afraid to Fall in Love	1955	12.00
❑ 5-9136	Nobody Knows/Methinks	1955	12.00

ERA

Number	Title (A Side/B Side)	Yr	NM
❑ 1018	Is There a Heaven/I Saw a Star	1956	10.00
❑ 1026	Cinco Robles (Five Oaks)/The World Is Made of Liza	1956	15.00
❑ 1033	Share My Love/Evangeline	1957	12.00
❑ 1040	The Bridge of San Angelo/Where Can a Wanderer Go	1957	12.00
❑ 1048	I Wonder Where's My Darlin'/I'm Tired of Pride	1957	12.00
❑ 1059	Hasta La Vista/Walkin' By Your Window	1957	12.00
❑ 1078	Blue Hawaii/Der Glockenspiel	1958	12.00
❑ 3053	Cinco Robles (Five Oaks)/The World Is Made of Lisa	1961	10.00

Albums

ERA

Number	Title (A Side/B Side)	Yr	NM
❑ EL-20013 [M]	Where Can a Wanderer Go	1957	25.00

ARMSTRONG, BRICE, AND THE AMERICAN GHOULS

45s

DUCHESS

Number	Title (A Side/B Side)	Yr	NM
❑ 1020	The Fright Before Christmas/Happy Ghoul Tide	1962	20.00

ARMSTRONG, JIMMY

45s

BROTHERS THREE

Number	Title (A Side/B Side)	Yr	NM
❑ 1001	You're Getting Next to Me Baby/Going to the Well Too Many Times	196?	400.00

ENJOY

Number	Title (A Side/B Side)	Yr	NM
❑ 1016	Count the Tears/I'm Going to Lock My Heart	1964	20.00

JET SET

Number	Title (A Side/B Side)	Yr	NM
❑ 768	I Won't Believe It Till I See It/I'm About to Say Goodbye	196?	40.00

SHRINE

Number	Title (A Side/B Side)	Yr	NM
❑ 0102	I'm About to Say Goodbye/Mystery	1965	200.00
❑ 105	It's Gonna Take Love/I Believe I'll Love You	1965	
—Canceled			

STOP

Number	Title (A Side/B Side)	Yr	NM
❑ 105	Close to You/Hanging Out with Early Bird	1965	200.00

ARMSTRONG, LOUIS Also see BING CROSBY; ELLA FITZGERALD.

45s

A&M

Number	Title (A Side/B Side)	Yr	NM
❑ 3010	What a Wonderful World/Game of Love	1988	4.00
—B-side by Wayne Fontana and the Mindbenders			
❑ 3010 [PS]	What a Wonderful World/Game of Love	1988	4.00
—"Good Morning Vietnam" sleeve			

ABC

Number	Title (A Side/B Side)	Yr	NM
❑ 10982	What a Wonderful World/Cabaret	1967	8.00
❑ 11075	Hellzapoppin'/The Sunshine of Love	1968	6.00
❑ 11126	Hello Brother/The Sunshine of Love	1968	6.00

AMSTERDAM

Number	Title (A Side/B Side)	Yr	NM
❑ 85013	We Shall Overcome/(Instrumental)	1970	6.00
❑ 85016	Give Peace a Chance/The Creator Has a Master Plan	1970	8.00
❑ 85017 [DJ]	Here Is My Heart For Christmas/His Father Wore Long Hair	1970	10.00
❑ 85019	Everybody's Talkin'/(B-side unknown)	1970	5.00
❑ 85021	What a Wonderful World/His Father Wore Long Hair	1971	5.00

AUDIO FIDELITY

Number	Title (A Side/B Side)	Yr	NM
❑ 097	Ain't Gonna Give Nobody None of My Jelly Roll/Frankie & Johnny	196?	8.00
❑ 173	Bill Bailey/The Creator Has a Master Plan	1971	6.00
❑ AFSD 5924-1 [S]	Bourbon Street Parade/Washington and Lee Swing	1960	10.00
—Jukebox issue; small hole, plays at 33 1/3 rpm			
❑ AFSD 5924-2 [S]	(contents unknown)	1960	10.00
—Jukebox issue; small hole, plays at 33 1/3 rpm			
❑ AFSD 5924-3 [S]	(contents unknown)	1960	10.00
—Jukebox issue; small hole, plays at 33 1/3 rpm			
❑ AFSD 5924-4 [S]	Sheik of Araby/Wolverine Blues	1960	10.00
—Jukebox issue; small hole, plays at 33 1/3 rpm			
❑ AFSD 5924-5 [S]	Sweet Georgia Brown/Limehouse Blues	1960	10.00
—Jukebox issue; small hole, plays at 33 1/3 rpm			

AVCO EMBASSY

Number	Title (A Side/B Side)	Yr	NM
❑ 4562	Miller's Cave/You Can Have Her	1971	6.00

BRUNSWICK

Number	Title (A Side/B Side)	Yr	NM
❑ 55318	Daydream/Northern Boulevard Blues	1967	6.00
❑ 55328	Louie's Dream/Step Down, Brother, Next Case	1967	6.00
❑ 55350	Rosie/You'll Never Walk Alone	1967	6.00
❑ 55360	Happy Time/Willkomen	1968	6.00
❑ 55380	Talk to the Animals/I Will Wait for You	1968	6.00
❑ 55395	I Believe/Sunrise, Sunset	1968	6.00
❑ 55457	I Believe/You'll Never Walk Alone	1971	5.00
❑ 55474	Willkomen/Sunrise, Sunset	1972	5.00
❑ 55534	'Twas the Night Before Christmas/(B-side unknown)	1976	8.00

BUENA VISTA

Number	Title (A Side/B Side)	Yr	NM
❑ F-465	Ten Feet Off the Ground/'Bout Time	1968	15.00
❑ F-465 [PS]	Ten Feet Off the Ground/'Bout Time	1968	25.00
❑ F-466	The Bare Necessities/Louis	1968	15.00
❑ F-469	Bibbidi-Bobbidi-Boo/Zip-a-Dee-Doo-Dah	1968	15.00
❑ F-470	Heigh-Ho/When You Wish Upon a Star	1968	15.00
❑ F-471	The Ballad of Davy Crocket/Chim-Chim-Cheree	1968	20.00
❑ F-489	When You Wish Upon a Star/Zip-a-Dee-Doo-Dah	1972	10.00

COLUMBIA

Number	Title (A Side/B Side)	Yr	NM
❑ 40587	A Theme from the Threepenny Opera (Mack the Knife)/Back O' Town Blues	1956	15.00
❑ 40662	When the Red, Red Robin Comes Bob, Bob, Bobbin' Along/Six Foot Four	1956	12.00
❑ 40711	The Faithful Hussar/Six Foot Four	1956	12.00
❑ 41471	Mack the Knife/The Faithful Hussar	1959	10.00

CONTINENTAL

Number	Title (A Side/B Side)	Yr	NM
❑ 1001	The Night Before Christmas/When the Saints Go Marching In	1971	5.00
❑ 1001 [PS]	The Night Before Christmas/When the Saints Go Marching In	1971	5.00
—With sticker: "Only 25 cents with purchase" of one of four brands of cigarette			
❑ 1001 [PS]	The Night Before Christmas/When the Saints Go Marching In	1971	6.00
—With sticker: "Free with purchase" of six-pack of Fresca			

DECCA

Number	Title (A Side/B Side)	Yr	NM
❑ 27059	New Orleans Function (Part 1)/New Orleans Function (Part 2)	1950	20.00
❑ 27113	La Vie En Rose/C'est Si Bon	1950	20.00
❑ 27187	That's for Me (Part 1)/Russian Lullaby (Part 2)	1950	12.00
❑ 27188	That's for Me (Part 2)/Russian Lullaby (Part 1)	1950	12.00
❑ 27189	Fine and Dandy/I Surrender Dear (Part 2)	1950	12.00
❑ 27190	Baby Won't You Please Come Home/I Surrender Dear (Part 1)	1950	12.00
❑ 27191	Panama (Part 1)/Bugle Call Rag (Part 3)	1950	12.00
❑ 27192	Panama (Part 2)/Bugle Call Rag (Part 2)	1950	12.00
❑ 27193	New Orleans Function (Part 1)/Bugle Call Rag (Part 1)	1950	12.00
❑ 27194	New Orleans Function (Part 2)/My Bucket's Got a Hole In It	1950	12.00
❑ 27254	Sit Down You're Rockin' the Boat/That's What the Man Said	1950	20.00
❑ 27481	If/You're Just in Love	1951	15.00
❑ 27616	Unless/That's for Me	1951	15.00
❑ 27720	(When We Are Dancing) I Get Ideas/A Kiss to Buid a Dream On	1951	15.00
❑ 27816	Because of You/Cold, Cold Heart	1951	15.00
❑ 27899	When It's Sleepy Time Down South/It's All in the Game	1952	15.00
—With Gordon Jenkins and His Orchestra			
❑ 27931	You're the Apple of My Eye/Big Butter and Egg Man	1952	15.00

Except when noted otherwise, VG = 25% of NM, and VG+ = 50% of NM. (Example: VG = $2.00, VG+ = $4.00 and NM = $8.00.)

A

Number	Title (A Side/B Side)	Yr	NM
9-28076	Indian Love Call/Jeannine	1952	15.00
—With Gordon Jenkins and His Orchestra			
28095	Royal Garden Blues (Part 2)/ Muskrat Ramble (Part 1)	1952	12.00
28096	Royal Garden Blues (Part 1)/ Muskrat Ramble (Part 2)	1952	12.00
—Above two with Edward "Kid" Ory			
28097	Lover/Black and Blue	1952	12.00
28098	Mahogany Hall Stomp/ Since I Fell for You	1952	12.00
28099	I Cried for You (Part 1)/ Tea for Two (Part 2)	1952	12.00
28100	I Cried for You (Part 2)/ Tea for Two (Part 1)	1952	12.00
—Above two with Velma Middleton			
28101	Stars Fell on Alabama (Part 1)/ Stars Fell on Alabama (Part 2)	1952	12.00
28102	Boff Boff/C Jam Blues	1952	12.00
28103	Body and Soul (Part 1)/ How High the Moon (Part 2)	1952	12.00
28104	Body and Soul (Part 2)/ How High the Moon (Part 1)	1952	12.00
—Above two with Barney B			
28105	On the Sunny Side of the Street (Part 1)/That's My Desire (Part 2)	1952	12.00
28106	On the Sunny Side of the Street (Part 2)/That's My Desire (Part 1)	1952	12.00
28107	High Society/Baby Won't You Please Come Home	1952	12.00
28108	Steak Face (Part 1)/ Steak Face (Part 2)	1952	12.00
28169	Back Home Again in Indiana (Part 1)/Way Down Yonder in New Orleans (Part 2)	1952	12.00
28170	Back Home Again in Indiana (Part 2)/Way Down Yonder in New Orleans (Part 1)	1952	12.00
28171	The Hucklebuck/Stardust (Part 2)	1952	12.00
28172	Baby It's Cold Outside/ Stardust (Part 1)	1952	12.00
28173	Honeysuckle Rose/ That's a Plenty	1952	12.00
28174	My Monday Date (Part 1)/ My Monday Date (Part 4)	1952	12.00
28175	My Monday Date (Part 2)/ My Monday Date (Part 3)	1952	12.00
28176	Big Daddy Blues/ You Can Depend on Me	1952	12.00
28177	Kiss of Fire/Delicado	1952	15.00
28306	Once in a While/Confessin'	1952	15.00
28372	That's My Desire/ Baby It's Cold Outside	1952	15.00
28394	Takes Two to Tango/ I Laughed at Love	1952	15.00
28443	White Christmas/ Winter Wonderland	1952	15.00
28524	Chlo-E/Listen to the Mocking Bird	1953	15.00
28628	Your Cheatin' Heart/ Congratulations to Someone	1953	15.00
28704	April in Portugal/Ramona	1953	15.00
28803	The Dummy Song/ Sittin' in the Sun	1953	15.00
28943	'Zat You, Santa Claus?/ Cool Yule	1953	15.00
28995	The Gypsy/I Can't Afford to Miss This Dream	1954	15.00
29102	Basin Street Blues (Part 1)/ Basin Street Blues (Part 2)	1954	15.00
29117	On a Coconut Island/ To You Sweetheart Aloha	1954	15.00
29153	The Whiffenpoof Song/ Bye and Bye	1954	15.00
—With Gordon Jenkins and His Orchestra			
29256	Skokiaan (Part 1)/ Skokiaan (Part 2)	1954	15.00
29280	Muskrat Ramble/ Someday You'll Be Sorry	1954	15.00
29352	Trees/Spooks	1954	15.00
29421	Sincerely/Pledging My Love	1955	15.00
29546	Pretty Little Missy/Baby Your Sleep Is Showing	1955	15.00
29694	Only You (And You Alone)/ Moments to Remember	1955	15.00
29710	Christmas Night in Harlem/ Christmas in New Orleans	1955	15.00
29921	Lazy Bones/Easy Street	1956	12.00
—With Gary Crosby			
30091	Blueberry Hill/ That Lucky Old Sun	1956	12.00
30188	This Younger Generation/In Pursuit of Happiness	1957	10.00
30309	The Prisoner's Song/ You're a Heavenly Thing	1957	10.00

Number	Title (A Side/B Side)	Yr	NM
30624	Nobody Knows the Trouble I've Seen/When You're Smiling	1958	10.00
30771	I Love Jazz/Mardi Gras March	1958	10.00
30860	I'll String Along with You/ On My Way (Out on My Traveling Shoes)	1959	10.00
30980	Only You (And You Alone)/ Onkel Satchmo's Lullaby	1960	10.00
DOT			
15941	The Five Pennies Saints/ Just the Blues	1959	10.00
—With Danny Kaye			
15991	Battle Hymn of the Republic/ Lullaby in Ragtime	1959	10.00
—With Red Nichols			
KAPP			
573	Hello, Dolly!/A Lot of Livin' to Do	1964	6.00
573 [PS]	Hello, Dolly!/A Lot of Livin' to Do	1964	10.00
597	I Still Get Jealous/Someday	1964	6.00
597 [PS]	I Still Get Jealous/Someday	1964	10.00
901	You Are Woman, I Am Man/ Life of the Party	1968	6.00
977	Kinda Love Song/Someday	1969	6.00
2145	That's All I Want the World to Remember Me By/Hello, Dolly!	1971	5.00
MCA			
MSS-35147	What a Wonderful World/ America the Beautiful	1989	10.00
—B-side by the San Francisco Boys Chorus			
MSS-35147 [PS]	What a Wonderful World/ America the Beautiful	1989	10.00
—Special item for the Environmental Defense Fund			
53321	What a Wonderful World/ Dream a Little Dream of Me	1988	5.00
—Reissue			
MERCURY			
72338	So Long Dearie/ Pretty Little Missy	1964	8.00
72338 [PS]	So Long Dearie/ Pretty Little Missy	1964	12.00
72371	By and By/Faith	1964	8.00
72495	Circle of Your Arms/ Short But Sweet	1965	8.00
72574	Mame/Tin Roof Blues	1966	8.00
72593	Cheesecake/Bye 'N' Bye	1966	8.00
MGM			
12809	Someday You'll Be Sorry/ The Beat Generation	1959	12.00
RCA VICTOR			
47-4004	Rockin' Chair/ Save It, Pretty Mama	1950	15.00
47-4005	Ain't Misbehavin'/ Pennies from Heaven	1950	15.00
47-4006	Saint James Infirmary/ Back o' Town Blues	1950	15.00
UNITED ARTISTS			
50251	No Time Is Good Goodbye Time/We're a Home	1968	6.00
50617	We Have All the Time in the World/Pretty Little Missy	1969	6.00
VERVE			
10154	Top Hat, White Tie and Tails/ East of the Sun	1958	12.00
10182	Nobody Knows the Troubles I've Seen/That Old Feeling	1959	12.00

7-Inch Extended Plays

Number	Title (A Side/B Side)	Yr	NM
ABC			
EP-ABCS-650	Cabaret/Dream a Little Dream of Me/The Sunshine of Love/ /Hello Brother/Fantastic That's You/I Guess I'll Get the Papers and Go Home	1967	10.00
—Jukebox issue; small hole, plays at 33 1/3 rpm			
EP-ABCS-650 [PS]	What a Wonderful World	1967	10.00
COLUMBIA			
5-1192	Walkin' My Baby Back Home/ You Rascal You// All of Me/Shine	195?	20.00
—Alternate numbers are "B-1523-1" and "B-1523-2"			
B-1523 [PS]	Louis Armstrong Spotlight	195?	20.00
—Contains record 5-1192			
B-2540	*Mack the Knife/Ain't Misbehavin'/St. Louis Blues	1958	20.00
B-2540 [PS]	Louis Armstrong (Hall of Fame Series)	1958	20.00
DECCA			
ED 2012	Kiss of Fire/I'll Walk Alone// Takes Two to Tango/ Sit Down, You're Rocking the Boat	195?	15.00
ED 2012 [PS]	Louis Armstrong, Vol. 1	195?	15.00
ED 2126	Basin Street Blues/ Otchi-Tchor-Ni-Ya	195?	15.00
ED 2126 [PS]	The Glenn Miller Story	195?	15.00
ED 2496	When Did You Leave Heaven/ You're a Heavenly Thing// I Married an Angel/A Sinner Kissed an Angel	195?	12.00
ED 2496 [PS]	(title unknown)	195?	12.00
KAPP			
KBS 969	Hello, Dolly!/Blueberry Hill/ Be My Life's Companion// I Still Get Jealous/Hey, Look Me Over/You Are Woman, I Am Man	1964	10.00
—Jukebox issue; small hole, plays at 33 1/3 rpm			
KBS 969 [PS]	Hello, Dolly!	1964	10.00

Albums

Number	Title	Yr	NM
ABC			
S-650	What a Wonderful World	1968	30.00
ACCORD			
SN-7161	Mr. Music	1982	10.00
AMSTERDAM			
AMS 12009	Louis Armstrong and His Friends	1970	15.00
AUDIO FIDELITY			
AFLP-1924 [M]	Louie and the Dukes of Dixieland	1960	30.00
AFLP-1930 [M]	Louis Armstrong Plays King Oliver	1960	30.00
AFLP-2128 [M]	Ain't Gonna Give Nobody None of My Jelly Roll	1964	15.00
AFLP-2132 [M]	The Best of Louis Armstrong	1964	15.00
AFSD-5924 [S]	Louie and the Dukes of Dixieland	1960	40.00
AFSD-5930 [S]	Louis Armstrong Plays King Oliver	1960	40.00
AFSD-6128 [S]	Ain't Gonna Give Nobody None of My Jelly Roll	1964	20.00
AFSD-6132 [S]	The Best of Louis Armstrong	1964	20.00
AFSD-6241	Louis Armstrong	196?	15.00
BIOGRAPH			
C-5	Great Soloists	1973	12.00
C-6	Louis Armstrong Plays the Blues	1973	12.00
BLUEBIRD			
AXM2-5519 [(2)]	Young Louis (1932-1933)	1984	12.00
5920-1-RB [(2)]	Pops: The 1940s Small Band Sides	1987	15.00
8310-1-RB	What a Wonderful World	1988	10.00
9759-1-RB	Louis Armstrong & His Orchestra 1932-33: Laughin' Louie	1989	12.00
BRUNSWICK			
BL 58004 [10]	Armstrong Classics	1950	100.00
BL 754136	I Will Wait for You	1968	15.00
BUENA VISTA			
BV-4044	Disney Swings the Satchmo Way	1968	40.00
CHIAROSCURO			
2002	Snake Rag	1977	12.00
2003	Great Alternatives	1977	12.00
2006	Sweetheart	1977	12.00
COLUMBIA			
CL 591 [M]	Louis Armstrong Plays W.C. Handy	1954	60.00
—Maroon label, gold print (original)			
CL 591 [M]	Louis Armstrong Plays W.C. Handy	1955	40.00
—Red and black label with six "eye" logos			
CL 708 [M]	Satch Plays Fats	1955	40.00
—Red and black label with six "eye" logos			
CL 840 [M]	Ambassador Satch	1956	40.00
CL 851 [M]	The Louis Armstrong Story, Vol. 1: Louis Armstrong and His Hot Five	1956	30.00
—Red and black label with six "eye" logos; reissue of 4383			
CL 851 [M]	The Louis Armstrong Story, Vol. 1: Louis Armstrong and His Hot Five	197?	12.00
—Orange label			
CL 852 [M]	The Louis Armstrong Story, Vol. 2: Louis Armstrong and His Hot Seven	1956	30.00
—Red and black label with six "eye" logos; reissue of 5484			
CL 853 [M]	The Louis Armstrong Story, Vol. 3: Louis Armstrong and Earl Hines	1956	30.00
—Red and black label with six "eye" logos; reissue of 4385			
CL 853 [M]	The Louis Armstrong Story, Vol. 3: Louis Armstrong and Earl Hines	197?	12.00
—Orange label reissue			
CL 854 [M]	The Louis Armstrong Story, Vol. 4: Louis Armstrong Favorites	1956	30.00
—Red and black label with six "eye" logos; reissue of 4386			
CL 1077 [M]	Satchmo the Great	1957	30.00
CL 2638 [M]	Louis Armstrong's Greatest Hits	1967	20.00

Number	Title (A Side/B Side)	Yr	NM
ML 4383 [M]	The Louis Armstrong Story, Vol. 1: Louis Armstrong and His Hot Five	1951	50.00
—Green label, gold or silver print			
ML 4384 [M]	The Louis Armstrong Story, Vol. 2: Louis Armstrong and His Hot Seven	1951	50.00
—Green label, gold or silver print			
ML 4385 [M]	The Louis Armstrong Story, Vol. 3: Louis Armstrong and Earl Hines	1951	50.00
—Green label, gold or silver print			
ML 4386 [M]	The Louis Armstrong Story, Vol. 4: Louis Armstrong Favorites	1951	50.00
—Green label, gold or silver print			
CL 6335 [10]	Louis Armstrong Plays W.C. Handy, Vol. 2	1955	40.00
CS 9438 [R]	Louis Armstrong's Greatest Hits	1967	12.00
PC 9438 [R]	Louis Armstrong's Greatest Hits	198?	8.00
—Budget-line reissue			
G 30416 [(2)]	The Genius of Louis Armstrong, Vol. 1	1971	15.00
COLUMBIA JAZZ MASTERPIECES			
CJ 40242	Louis Armstrong Plays W.C. Handy	1986	10.00
CJ 40378	Satch Plays Fats	1986	10.00
COLUMBIA MUSICAL TREASURIES			
P4M 5676 [(4)]	40 Greatest Hits	197?	20.00
COLUMBIA SPECIAL PRODUCTS			
JCL 708 [M]	Satch Plays Fats	196?	12.00
—"Special Collector's Series" reissue			
DECCA			
DX 108 [(2)M]	Satchmo at Symphony Hall	1954	75.00
—Black labels, silver print			
DX 155 [(4)M]	Satchmo, A Musical Autobiography	1956	100.00
—Black labels, silver print			
DXM 155 [(4)M]	Satchmo, A Musical Autobiography	1960	40.00
—Black labels with color bars			
DXB 183 [(2)M]	The Best of Louis Armstrong	196?	30.00
DL 4137 [M]	Satchmo's Golden Favorites	1961	20.00
DL 4227 [M]	I Love Jazz	1962	20.00
DL 4230 [M]	Satchmo, A Musical Autobiography, 1926-1927	1962	25.00
DL 4245 [M]	King Louis	1962	20.00
DL 4330 [M]	Satchmo, A Musical Autobiography, 1928-1930	1962	25.00
DL 4331 [M]	Satchmo, A Musical Autobiography, 1930-1934	1962	25.00
DL 5225 [10]	New Orleans to New York	1950	75.00
DL 5279 [10]	New Orleans Days	1950	75.00
DL 5280 [10]	Jazz Concert	1950	75.00
DL 5401 [10]	Satchmo Serenades	1952	75.00
DL 5532 [10]	Latter-Day Louis	1954	75.00
DL 5536 [10]	Louis Armstrong-Gordon Jenkins	1954	75.00
DXSB 7183 [(2)R]	The Best of Louis Armstrong	196?	15.00
DL 8037 [M]	Satchmo at Symphony Hall, Vol. 1	1954	40.00
—Black label, silver print			
DL 8037 [M]	Satchmo at Symphony Hall, Vol. 1	1960	15.00
—Black label with color bars			
DL 8038 [M]	Satchmo at Symphony Hall, Vol. 2	1954	40.00
—Black label, silver print			
DL 8038 [M]	Satchmo at Symphony Hall, Vol. 2	1960	15.00
—Black label with color bars			
DL 8041 [M]	Satchmo at Pasadena	1954	40.00
—Black label, silver print			
DL 8041 [M]	Satchmo at Pasadena	1960	15.00
—Black label with color bars			
DL 8126 [M]	Satchmo Sings	1955	40.00
—Black label, silver print			
DL 8126 [M]	Satchmo Sings	1960	15.00
—Black label with color bars			
DL 8168 [M]	Louis Armstrong at the Crescendo, Vol. 1	1955	40.00
—Black label, silver print			
DL 8169 [M]	Louis Armstrong at the Crescendo, Vol. 2	1955	40.00
—Black label, silver print			
DL 8211 [M]	Satchmo Serenades	1956	40.00
—Black label, silver print			
DL 8211 [M]	Satchmo Serenades	1960	15.00
—Black label with color bars			
DL 8283 [M]	New Orleans Jazz	1956	40.00
—Black label, silver print			
DL 8283 [M]	New Orleans Jazz	1960	15.00
—Black label with color bars			
DL 8284 [M]	Jazz Classics	1956	40.00
—Black label, silver print			
DL 8284 [M]	Jazz Classics	1960	15.00
—Black label with color bars			
DL 8327 [M]	Satchmo's Collector's Items	1957	40.00
—Black label, silver print			

Number	Title (A Side/B Side)	Yr	NM
DL 8327 [M]	Satchmo's Collector's Items	1960	15.00
—Black label with color bars			
DL 8329 [M]	New Orleans Nights	1957	40.00
—Black label, silver print			
DL 8329 [M]	New Orleans Nights	1960	15.00
—Black label with color bars			
DL 8330 [M]	Satchmo on Stage	1957	40.00
—Black label, silver print			
DL 8330 [M]	Satchmo on Stage	1960	15.00
—Black label with color bars			
DL 8488 [M]	Louis and the Angels	1957	40.00
—Black label, silver print			
DL 8488 [M]	Louis and the Angels	1960	15.00
—Black label with color bars			
DL 8741 [M]	Louis and the Good Book	1960	15.00
—Black label with color bars			
DL 8781 [M]	Louis and the Good Book	1958	40.00
—Black label, silver print			
DL 8840 [M]	Satchmo in Style	1958	40.00
—Black label, silver print			
DL 8840 [M]	Satchmo in Style	1960	15.00
—Black label with color bars			
DL 8963 [M]	Satchmo, A Musical Autobiography, 1923-1925	1960	25.00
DL 9225 [M]	Rare Items (1935-1944)	196?	20.00
DL 9233 [M]	Young Louis the Sideman (1924-1927)	196?	20.00
DL 74137 [R]	Satchmo's Golden Favorites	1961	12.00
DL 74227 [R]	I Love Jazz	1962	12.00
DL 74245 [R]	King Louis	1962	12.00
DL 74330 [R]	A Musical Autobiography, 1928-1930	1962	12.00
DL 78963 [R]	Satchmo, A Musical Autobiography, 1923-1925	196?	12.00
DL 79225 [R]	Rare Items (1935-1944)	196?	12.00
DL 79233 [R]	Young Louis the Sideman (1924-1927)	196?	12.00
DISNEYLAND			
STER-1341	The Wonderful World of Walt Disney	1971	20.00
—Reissue of Buena Vista 4044			
EVEREST			
3312 [R]	In Memoriam	1971	10.00
EVEREST ARCHIVE OF FOLK & JAZZ			
258	Louis "Satchmo" Armstrong	197?	12.00
312	Louis Armstrong, Vol. 2	197?	10.00
GNP CRESCENDO			
9050	Pasadena Concert, Vol. II	1987	10.00
11001 [(2)]	An Evening with Louis Armstrong	1977	15.00
HARMONY			
HS 11316	Louis Armstrong	197?	12.00
KH 31236	The Louis Armstrong Saga	1971	12.00
IAJRC			
LP-29	Oregon State Fair, 1960	198?	10.00
JOLLY ROGER			
5009 [10]	Louis Armstrong	1954	50.00
KAPP			
KL-1364 [M]	Hello, Dolly!	1964	12.00
KS-3364 [S]	Hello, Dolly!	1964	15.00
MCA			
538	Hello, Dolly!	197?	10.00
—Reissue of Kapp LP			
1300	Louis and the Good Book	197?	10.00
—Reissue of Decca 8741			
1301	Young Louis the Sideman	197?	10.00
—Reissue of Decca 9233			
1304	Back in New York	197?	10.00
1306	Louis with Guest Stars	197?	10.00
1312	Swing That Music!	197?	10.00
1316	Satchmo Serenades	197?	10.00
—Reissue of Decca 8211			
1322	Satchmo's Collector's Items	197?	10.00
—Reissue of Decca 8327			
1334	Satchmo For Ever!	197?	10.00
1335	Old Favorites	197?	10.00
2-4013 [(2)]	Louis Armstrong at the Crescendo	197?	12.00
—Reissue of Decca 8168/8169 in one sleeve			
2-4035 [(2)]	The Best of Louis Armstrong	197?	12.00
—Reissue of Decca 7183			
2-4057 [(2)]	Satchmo at Symphony Hall	197?	12.00
—Reissue of Decca 108			
10006 [(4)]	Satchmo, A Musical Autobiography	197?	25.00
—Reissue of Decca 155			
25204	What a Wonderful World	1988	10.00
—Reissue of ABC 650			
42328	Louis Armstrong of New Orleans	1990	12.00
MERCURY			
MG-21081 [M]	Louis Armstrong Sings Louis Armstrong	1965	12.00
SR-61081 [S]	Louis Armstrong Sings Louis Armstrong	1965	15.00
METRO			
M-510 [M]	Hello, Louis	1965	12.00

Number	Title (A Side/B Side)	Yr	NM
MS-510 [S]	Hello, Louis	1965	15.00
MILESTONE			
2010	Early Portrait	1969	10.00
47017 [(2)]	Louis Armstrong and King Oliver	197?	12.00
MOSAIC			
MQ8-146 [(8)]	The Complete Decca Studio Recordings of Louis Armstrong and the All-Stars	199?	150.00
PABLO			
2310941	Mack the Knife	1990	12.00
PAIR			
PDL2-1042 [(2)]	The Jazz Legend	1986	12.00
PAUSA			
9018	The Greatest of Louis Armstrong	1983	10.00
RCA VICTOR			
LPT 7 [10]	Louis Armstrong Town Hall Concert	1951	80.00
LJM-1005 [M]	Louis Armstrong Sings the Blues	1954	50.00
LPM-1443 [M]	Town Hall Concert Plus	1957	50.00
LPM-2322 [M]	A Rare Batch of Satch	1961	25.00
LPM-2971 [M]	Louis Armstrong in the '30s/in the '40s	1964	20.00
LSP-2971(e) [R]	Louis Armstrong in the '30s/in the '40s	1964	12.00
VPM-6044 [(2)]	July 4, 1900/July 6, 1971	1971	20.00
RIVERSIDE			
RLP 12-101 [M]	The Young Louis Armstrong	195?	40.00
—Blue label			
RLP 12-101 [M]	The Young Louis Armstrong	1956	80.00
—White label, blue print			
RLP 12-122 [M]	Louis Armstrong 1923	195?	40.00
—Blue label			
RLP 12-122 [M]	Louis Armstrong 1923	1956	80.00
—White label, blue print			
RLP-1001 [10]	Louis Armstrong Plays the Blues	1953	100.00
RLP-1029 [10]	Louis Armstrong with King Oliver's Creole Jazz Band 1923	1953	100.00
SEAGULL			
LG-8206	Greatest Hits: Live in Concert	198?	12.00
STORYVILLE			
4012	Louis Armstrong and His All-Stars	1980	10.00
SWING			
SW-8450	Louis and the Big Bands	1984	10.00
TIME-LIFE			
STL-J-01 [(3)]	Giants of Jazz	1978	20.00
STBB-22 [(2)]	Big Bands: Louis Armstrong	1985	15.00
VANGUARD			
VSD 91/92 [(2)]	Essential Louis Armstrong	1977	15.00
VMS 73129	Essential Louis Armstrong, Vol. 1	1986	8.00
VERVE			
MGV-4012 [M]	Louis Under the Stars	1957	50.00
MGV-4012 [S]	Louis Under the Stars	199?	25.00
—180-gram reissue; distributed by Classic Records			
V-4012 [M]	Louis Under the Stars	1961	20.00
V6-4012 [S]	Louis Under the Stars	1961	15.00
MGV-4035 [M]	I've Got the World on a String	1959	50.00
MGVS-4035	I've Got the World on a String	199?	25.00
—Classic Records reissue			
V-4035 [M]	I've Got the World on a String	1961	20.00
V6-4035 [S]	I've Got the World on a String	1961	15.00
MGVS-6044 [S]	Louis Under the Stars	1960	40.00
MGVS-6101 [S]	I've Got the World on a String	1960	40.00
V-8569 [M]	The Essential Louis A.	1963	12.00
V6-8569 [S]	The Essential Louis A.	1963	15.00
V-8595 [M]	The Best of Louis Armstrong	1964	15.00
V6-8595 [S]	The Best of Louis Armstrong	1964	15.00
SW-90658 [S]	The Best of Louis Armstrong	1964	20.00
—Capitol Record Club edition			
VOCALION			
VL 3851 [M]	Here's Louis Armstrong	196?	15.00
VL 73851 [R]	Here's Louis Armstrong	196?	10.00
VL 73871 [R]	The One and Only Louis Armstrong	1968	10.00
WING			
SR-16381	Great Louis	196?	10.00

ARMSTRONG, LOUIS, AND SIDNEY BECHET

Albums

Number	Title (A Side/B Side)	Yr	NM
JOLLY ROGER			
5029 [M]	Louis Armstrong and Sidney Bechet	195?	40.00

ARMSTRONG, LOUIS, AND DUKE ELLINGTON

Also see each artist's individual listings.

Albums

Number	Title (A Side/B Side)	Yr	NM
MOBILE FIDELITY			
2-155 [(2)]	The Great Reunion	1984	80.00
—Audiophile vinyl			

Number	Title (A Side/B Side)	Yr	NM
PICKWICK			
❑ PC-3033	Louis Armstrong and Duke Ellington	196?	10.00
ROULETTE			
❑ RE-108 [(2)]	The Duke Ellington-Louis Armstrong Era	1973	15.00
❑ R 52074 [M]	Together for the First Time	1961	25.00
❑ SR 52074 [S]	Together for the First Time	1961	20.00
❑ R 52103 [M]	The Great Reunion	1963	20.00
❑ SR 52103 [S]	The Great Reunion	1963	25.00

ARMSTRONG, LOUIS/AL HIRT

Number	Title (A Side/B Side)	Yr	NM
Albums			
MURRAY HILL			
❑ 930633 [(4)]	Louis Armstrong and Al Hirt Play Dixieland Trumpet	197?	20.00

ARMSTRONG, LOUIS, AND THE MILLS BROTHERS

Also see each artist's individual listings.

Number	Title (A Side/B Side)	Yr	NM
45s			
DECCA			
❑ 28984	My Walking Stick/Marie	1953	15.00
Albums			
DECCA			
❑ DL 5509 [10]	Louis Armstrong and the Mills Brothers	1954	60.00

ARMSTRONG, LOUIS, AND OSCAR PETERSON

Also see each artist's individual listings.

Number	Title (A Side/B Side)	Yr	NM
Albums			
VERVE			
❑ MGVS-6062 [S]	Louis Armstrong Meets Oscar Peterson	1960	40.00
❑ MGV-8322 [M]	Louis Armstrong Meets Oscar Peterson	1959	50.00
❑ V-8322 [M]	Louis Armstrong Meets Oscar Peterson	1961	20.00
❑ V6-8322 [S]	Louis Armstrong Meets Oscar Peterson	1961	15.00

ARNAZ, DESI

Number	Title (A Side/B Side)	Yr	NM
45s			
COLUMBIA			
❑ 4-39937	I Love Lucy/There's a Brand New Baby	1953	40.00
RCA VICTOR			
❑ 47-2865	Tabu/Cuban Pete	1949	15.00
❑ 47-2866	Babalu/Brazil	1949	15.00
❑ 47-2867	Tico Tico/Peanut Vendor	1949	15.00
—The above three comprise a box set			
Albums			
RCA VICTOR			
❑ LPM-3096 [10]	Babalu!	1954	120.00

ARNDT, BILL

Number	Title (A Side/B Side)	Yr	NM
45s			
HIT			
❑ 21	Breaking Up Is Hard to Do/Sealed with a Kiss	1962	8.00
—B-side by Dick Swift			

ARNELL, GINNY

Number	Title (A Side/B Side)	Yr	NM
45s			
DECCA			
❑ 31104	Carnival/We	1960	15.00
❑ 31190	Look Who's Talkin'/Tell Me What You Said	1960	15.00
MGM			
❑ K13146	I'm Crying Too/Trouble's Back in Town	1963	12.00
❑ K13177	Dumb Head/How Many Times Can One Heart Break	1963	12.00
❑ K13226	He's My Little Devil/I Wish I Knew What Dress to Wear	1964	12.00
❑ K13248	Let Me Make You Smile Again/Yesterday's Memories	1964	12.00
❑ K13309	Just Like a Boy/Portrait of a Fool	1965	12.00
❑ K13362	B-I-L-L Why/A Little Bit of Love Can Hurt	1965	10.00
❑ K13403	I'm Gettin' Mad/I'm So Afraid of Loving You	1965	10.00
WARWICK			
❑ 671	No One Cares/Tribute to You	1961	25.00
❑ 680	Married to You/He Likes Me Better Than Rock and Roll	1962	20.00
Albums			
MGM			
❑ E-4228 [M]	Meet Ginny Arnell	1964	25.00
❑ SE-4228 [S]	Meet Ginny Arnell	1964	40.00

ARNO, AUDREY

Number	Title (A Side/B Side)	Yr	NM
45s			
DECCA			
❑ 31238	La Pachanga/Bei Mir Ist Nix Amore So Im Vorubergehn	1961	10.00

ARNOLD, BILLY BOY See BILLY BOY.

ARNOLD, CALVIN

Number	Title (A Side/B Side)	Yr	NM
45s			
IX CHAINS			
❑ 7009	Satisfy My Woman/You'll Do It	1975	10.00
❑ 7013	I'm Your Friendly Neighborhood Freak (Part 1)/(Part 2)	1975	10.00
SONDAY			
❑ 6005	Think I Better Rest/Portrait of a Step-Daddy	197?	8.00
SOUND STAGE 7			
❑ 45-2506	After the Love Has Gone/(B-side unknown)	1977	40.00
VENTURE			
❑ 605	Funky Way/Snatchin' Back	1967	10.00
❑ 610	Scoobie Doo/Lovely Way to Go	1968	15.00
❑ 626	Mama in Law/Miniskirt	1968	10.00
❑ 634	Just a Matter of Time/You Got to Live for Yourself	1969	10.00

ARNOLD, P.P.

Number	Title (A Side/B Side)	Yr	NM
45s			
ATLANTIC			
❑ 2674	Bury Me Down by the River/Give a Hand, Take a Hand	1969	6.00
IMMEDIATE			
❑ 1901	The First Cut Is the Deepest/Speak to Me	1967	10.00
❑ 5006	If You Think You're Groovy/It Hurts Me Badly	1968	10.00
Albums			
IMMEDIATE			
❑ Z12 52016	Kafunta	1968	15.00

ARNOLD, VANCE, AND THE AVENGERS See JOE COCKER.

ARRIBIANS, THE

Number	Title (A Side/B Side)	Yr	NM
45s			
J.O.B.			
❑ 1116	To Look at a Star/Working and Gambling	1958	800.00

ARROGANTS, THE

Number	Title (A Side/B Side)	Yr	NM
45s			
LUTE			
❑ 6226	Mirror Mirror/Canadian Sunset	1963	30.00

ARROWS, THE See DAVIE ALLAN AND THE ARROWS.

ARS NOVA

Number	Title (A Side/B Side)	Yr	NM
45s			
ATLANTIC			
❑ 2625	Sunshine and Shadows/Walk on the Sand	1969	6.00
ELEKTRA			
❑ 45627	Pavan for My Lady (Fall Winter Summer and Spring)/Zoroaster	1968	8.00
❑ 45631	Fields of People/March of the Mad Duke's Circus	1968	8.00
Albums			
ATLANTIC			
❑ SD 8221	Sunshine and Shadows	1969	22.00
ELEKTRA			
❑ EKS-74020	Ars Nova	1968	22.00

ART BEARS

Number	Title (A Side/B Side)	Yr	NM
45s			
RALPH			
❑ RR 7904	Rats & Monkeys/Collapse	1979	6.00
❑ RR 7904 [PS]	Rats & Monkeys/Collapse	1979	6.00
Albums			
RALPH			
❑ RR 7905	Winter Songs	1979	20.00

ART OF LOVIN'

Number	Title (A Side/B Side)	Yr	NM
45s			
MAINSTREAM			
❑ 687	Good Times/You've Got the Power	1968	25.00
Albums			
MAINSTREAM			
❑ S-6113	Art of Lovin'	1968	300.00

ARTHUR

Number	Title (A Side/B Side)	Yr	NM
Albums			
LHI			
❑ 12000	Dreams and Images	1968	75.00

ARTISTICS, THE

Number	Title (A Side/B Side)	Yr	NM
45s			
BRUNSWICK			
❑ 55301	I'm Gonna Miss You/Hope We Have	1966	8.00
❑ 55315	Girl I Need You/Glad I Met You	1967	8.00
❑ 55326	Love Song/I'll Always Love You	1967	8.00
❑ 55342	The Chase Is On/One Last Chance	1967	8.00
❑ 55353	You Make Me Happy/Nothing But Heartaches	1967	8.00
❑ 55370	Hard to Carry On/Trouble, Heartaches and Pain	1968	8.00
❑ 55384	Lonely Old World/You Left Me	1968	8.00
❑ 55404	Walking Tall/What Happened	1969	8.00
❑ 55416	Price of Love/Yesterday's Girl	1969	8.00
❑ 55431	Just Another Heartache/Ain't It Strange	1970	8.00
❑ 55444	(I Want You To) Make My Life Over/Sugar Cane	1971	8.00
❑ 55477	Being in Love/It's Those Little Things That Count	1972	8.00
❑ 55493	She's Heaven/Look Out I'm Gonna Get You	1973	8.00
OKEH			
❑ 7177	I Need Your Love/What'll I Do	1963	10.00
❑ 7193	Get My Hands on Some Lovin'/I'll Leave It Up to You	1964	10.00
❑ 7217	In Another Man's Arms/Patty Cake	1965	10.00
❑ 7232	This Heart of Mine/I'll Come Running	1965	10.00
❑ 7243	Loveland/So Much Love in My Heart	1966	10.00
Albums			
BRUNSWICK			
❑ BL 54123 [M]	I'm Gonna Miss You	1967	25.00
❑ BL 754123 [S]	I'm Gonna Miss You	1967	25.00
❑ BL 754139	The Articulate Artistics	1968	25.00
❑ BL 754153	What Happened	1969	25.00
❑ BL 754168	I Want You to Make My Life Over	1970	25.00
❑ BL 754195	Look Out	1973	20.00
OKEH			
❑ OKM-12119 [M]	Get My Hands on Some Lovin'	1967	80.00
❑ OKS-14119 [S]	Get My Hands on Some Lovin'	1967	80.00

ARZACHEL

Number	Title (A Side/B Side)	Yr	NM
Albums			
ROULETTE			
❑ SR 42036	Arzachel	1969	150.00

ASCOTS, THE More than one group.

Number	Title (A Side/B Side)	Yr	NM
45s			
ACE			
❑ 650	I'm Touched/Perfect Love	1962	25.00
ARROW			
❑ 736	Easier Said Than Done/Is It Really You	1958	30.00
BETHLEHEM			
❑ 3046	Hip Talk/She Did	1962	15.00
DUAL-TONE			
❑ 1120	Acapulco Run/The Gladiator	1963	60.00
J&S			
❑ 1628/9	What Love Can Do/Everything Will Be Alright	1958	30.00
KING			
❑ 5679	I Don't Care One Bit/Tonight	1962	30.00
SUPER			
❑ 102	Monkey See, Monkey Do/You Can't Do That	1966	20.00
❑ 103	Midnight Hour/Midnight Hour (Part 2)	1966	20.00
❑ 104	Put Your Arms Around Me/Sookie Sookie	1966	20.00

ASGAERD

Number	Title (A Side/B Side)	Yr	NM
45s			
THRESHOLD			
❑ 67010	Friends/Children of a New Born Age	1972	10.00

Albums

THRESHOLD

Number	Title (A Side/B Side)	Yr	NM
THS 6	In the Realm of Asgaerd	1972	20.00

ASH, DANIEL

12-Inch Singles

BEGGARS BANQUET

Number	Title (A Side/B Side)	Yr	NM
2754-1-RD	This Love//Heaven Is Waiting/Coming Down (Slow Version)	1991	8.00
2776-1-RDAB [DJ]	This Love (Midnight Mix)/(Single Mix)	1991	12.00

Albums

BEGGARS BANQUET

Number	Title (A Side/B Side)	Yr	NM
3014-1-R	Coming Home	1991	15.00

ASHE, CLARENCE

45s

ABC-PARAMOUNT

Number	Title (A Side/B Side)	Yr	NM
45-10698	Don't Open the Door on Monday Morning/Close to You	1965	12.00

CHESS

Number	Title (A Side/B Side)	Yr	NM
1896	Trouble I've Had/Dancing in a Dream World	1964	15.00

J&S

Number	Title (A Side/B Side)	Yr	NM
1466	Trouble I've Had/Dancing in a Dream World	1964	25.00
1469	If I Could Only Lie/Why Have I Had So Much Trouble	1964	20.00
1470/1	Everything Happens to Me/New Broom Sweeps Good	1964	15.00
1472	Row Row Row Your Love/In the Middle of the Night	1965	15.00
1475/6	Don't Open the Door on Monday Morning/Close to You	1965	15.00

ASHES

45s

VAULT

Number	Title (A Side/B Side)	Yr	NM
924	Is There Anything I Can Do/Every Little Prayer	1966	12.00
936	Dark on You Now/Roses Gone	1967	12.00
973	Homeward Bound/Sleeping Serenade	1971	10.00

Albums

VAULT

Number	Title (A Side/B Side)	Yr	NM
125	Ashes	1971	100.00

—Recorded in 1968 but released in 1971

ASHFORD, NICK Also see ASHFORD AND SIMPSON.

45s

ABC

Number	Title (A Side/B Side)	Yr	NM
11260	Let's Go Get Stoned/Dead End Kids	1970	6.00

VERVE

Number	Title (A Side/B Side)	Yr	NM
10463	I Don't Need No Doctor/Young Emotions	1966	10.00
10493	When I Feel the Need/Young Emotions	1967	10.00
10599	California Soul/Young Emotions	1968	8.00

ASHFORD AND SIMPSON Also see NICK ASHFORD; VALERIE SIMPSON.

12-Inch Singles

CAPITOL

Number	Title (A Side/B Side)	Yr	NM
V-8528	Street Corner/Make It Work Again	1982	10.00
V-8558	High Rise (6:05)/(Instrumental)	1983	8.00
V-8570	It's Much Deeper (3:47) (6:30)	1983	8.00
V-8612	Solid (Special Club Mix 6:12)/(Dub Version 5:51)	1984	10.00
V-8623	Outta the World (6:05)/(6:16)	1985	8.00
V-8641	Babies (unknown versions)	1985	8.00
SPRO-9020/1 [DJ]	It's Much Deeper (3:47) (6:30)	1983	10.00
SPRO-9951 [DJ]	Nobody Walks in L.A. (same on both sides?)	1986	10.00
V-15243	Count Your Blessings/Side Effect	1986	8.00
V-15259	What Becomes of Love (Edit) (LP)/It's a Rush	1986	8.00
V-15272	Nobody Walks in L.A. (3 versions)/Way Ahead	1986	8.00
V-15448	I'll Be There for You/Way Ahead	1989	8.00
V-15487	Cookies and Cake (5 versions)	1989	7.00

ORPHEUS

Number	Title (A Side/B Side)	Yr	NM
V-72289	Hungry for Me Again (Edit) (LP) (Instrumental)	1990	10.00

WARNER BROS.

Number	Title (A Side/B Side)	Yr	NM
PRO-A-837 [DJ]	Nobody Knows (6:35) (same on both sides)	1979	20.00
DWBS 8874	Found a Cure (7:00)/You Always Could	1979	12.00

45s

CAPITOL

Number	Title (A Side/B Side)	Yr	NM
B-5109	Street Corner/Make It Work Again	1982	3.00
B-5109 [PS]	Street Corner/Make It Work Again	1982	3.00
B-5146	Love It Away/Street Opera (Part 2)	1982	3.00
B-5190	I'll Take the Whole World On/Mighty Mighty Love	1982	3.00
B-5250	High-Rise/(Instrumental)	1983	3.00
B-5250 [PS]	High-Rise/(Instrumental)	1983	3.00
B-5284	It's Much Deeper/Working Man	1983	3.00
B-5284 [PS]	It's Much Deeper/Working Man	1983	3.00
B-5310	I'm Not That Tough/Side Effect	1984	3.00
B-5310 [PS]	I'm Not That Tough/Side Effect	1984	3.00
B-5397	Solid/Solid (Dub Version)	1984	3.00
B-5397 [PS]	Solid/Solid (Dub Version)	1984	3.00
B-5435	Outta the World/Outta the World (Dub)	1985	3.00
B-5435 [PS]	Outta the World/Outta the World (Dub)	1985	3.00
B-5468	Babies/Street Corner	1985	3.00
B-5468 [PS]	Babies/Street Corner	1985	3.00
B-5598	Count Your Blessings/Side Effect	1986	3.00
B-5598 [PS]	Count Your Blessings/Side Effect	1986	3.00
B-5637	What Becomes of Love/It's a Rush	1986	3.00
B-5666	Nobody Walks in L.A./Way Ah Way Ahead	1987	3.00
B-44326	I'll Be There for You/Way Ahead	1989	3.00
B-44326 [PS]	I'll Be There for You/Way Ahead	1989	3.00
B-44404	Cookies and Cake/(B-side unknown)	1989	4.00

HOPSACK & SILK

Number	Title (A Side/B Side)	Yr	NM
96-398	Been Found/I Remember All	1996	3.00

—With Maya Angelou

WARNER BROS.

Number	Title (A Side/B Side)	Yr	NM
7745	(I'd Know You) Anywhere/I'm Determined	1973	4.00
7781	Have You Ever Tried It/Time	1974	4.00
7811	Main Line/Don't Fight It	1974	4.00
8030	Everybody's Got to Give It Up/Over to Where You Are	1974	4.00
8070	Bend Me/Ain't Nothin' But a Name	1975	4.00
8179	It'll Come, It'll Come, It'll Come/Caretaker	1976	4.00
8216	Somebody Told a Lie/It Came to Me	1976	4.00
8286	Tried, Tested and Found True/Believe in Me	1976	4.00
8337	So So Satisfied/Maybe I Can Find It	1977	4.00
8391	Over and Over/It's You	1977	4.00
8453	Send It/Couldn't Get Enough	1977	4.00
8514	Don't Cost You Nothing/Let Love Use Me	1978	4.00
8571	By Way of Love's Express/Too Bad	1978	4.00
8651	It Seems to Hang On/Too Bad	1978	4.00
8710	Is It Still Good to Ya/As Long As It Holds You	1978	4.00
8775	Flashback/Ain't It a Shame	1979	4.00
8870	Found a Cure/You Always Could	1979	4.00
49099	Nobody Knows/Crazy	1979	4.00
49269	Love Don't Make It Right/Finally Got to Me	1980	4.00
49269 [PS]	Love Don't Make It Right/Finally Got to Me	1980	5.00
49594	Happy Endings/Make It to the Sky	1980	4.00
49646	Get Out Your Handkerchief/You Never Left Me Alone	1980	4.00
49805	It Shows in the Eyes/Enough	1981	4.00
49867	I Need Your Light/It's the Long Run	1981	4.00

Albums

CAPITOL

Number	Title (A Side/B Side)	Yr	NM
ST-12207	Street Opera	1982	8.00
ST-12282	High Rise	1983	8.00
ST-12366	Solid	1984	8.00
ST-12469	Real Love	1986	8.00
C1-46946	Love Or Physical	1989	10.00

WARNER BROS.

Number	Title (A Side/B Side)	Yr	NM
BS 2739	Gimme Something Real	1973	10.00
BS 2789	I Wanna Be Selfish	1974	10.00
BS 2858	Come As You Are	1976	10.00
BS 2992	So So Satisfied	1977	10.00
BS 3088	Send It	1977	10.00
BSK 3219	Is It Still Good to Ya	1978	10.00
BSK 3357	Stay Free	1979	10.00
HS 3458	A Musical Affair	1980	10.00
2BS 3524 [(2)]	Performance	1981	12.00

ASHKAN

Albums

SIRE

Number	Title (A Side/B Side)	Yr	NM
SES-97107	In from the Cold	1970	40.00

ASHLEY, DEL See DAVID GATES.

ASHLEY, JOHN

45s

CAPEHART

Number	Title (A Side/B Side)	Yr	NM
5006	Little Lou/I Need Your Lovin'	1961	50.00

DOT

Number	Title (A Side/B Side)	Yr	NM
15775	Born to Rock/Pickin' on the Wrong Chicken	1958	50.00
15878	My Story/Let the Good Times Roll	1958	15.00

INTRO

Number	Title (A Side/B Side)	Yr	NM
6097	Bermuda/Let Yourself Go Go Go	196?	30.00

SILVER

Number	Title (A Side/B Side)	Yr	NM
1002	I Want to Hear It from You/Seriously in Love	1959	25.00
1005	Cry of the Wild Goose/One Love	1960	25.00

ASHLEY, LEON

45s

ASHLEY

Number	Title (A Side/B Side)	Yr	NM
22	Ain't Gonna Worry/Illusions of Life	1969	10.00
100	Our Old Love Song/She Picked Me Up	197?	8.00
350	If Love Has Died/How Can We Divide These Little Hearts	197?	8.00
666	Lean On Me/I Ain't Got Over You Yet	197?	8.00
764	The Weakness of a Man/Most Men	197?	8.00
768	Before You Were Mine/Su-Sow	197?	8.00
2003	Laura (What's He Got That I Ain't Got)/With the Help of the Wine	1967	10.00
2003	Laura/With the Help of the Wine	1967	15.00
	—Some early copies have no subtitle on A-side		
2025	Anna, I'm Taking You Home/Curtain of Sadness	1967	10.00
2075	Mental Journey/All I Can Stand	1968	10.00
4000	Flower of Love/Prayers Can't Reach Me	1968	10.00
4317	By Loving Me/Ease Up	197?	6.00
	—Reissue		
5323	Dear Willie/Letter from Luckenbach	197?	8.00
7000	While Your Lover Sleeps/That's Alright	1968	10.00
7600	I'll Be There/If I Could See Over the Mountain	197?	8.00
9000	Walkin' Back to Birmingham/It's All Over But the Crying	1969	10.00
35001	A Life for a Wife/The Bees Are Making Honey	197?	6.00
35003	Tell Him Daddy Said Hello/Brace Up and Face It	197?	6.00
35004	Happy Loving You/Love Me or Leave Me	197?	6.00
35005	Mama's Ten/Keeping Her Memory Alive	197?	6.00
35008	There Ain't No Easy Way/Losing Man	197?	6.00
35010	Ease Up/Until Dawn	197?	6.00
35011	Not a Single Thing About Her (That I'd Change)/Before the Next Teardrop Falls	197?	6.00
35012	The Well's Not Dry/Guess I've Just Love You Too Long	197?	6.00
35013	Love Fits Me Better/Off and Running	197?	6.00

DOT

Number	Title (A Side/B Side)	Yr	NM
16649	You Gave Me a Reason to Live/You've Got a Heartbreak	1964	15.00

GOLDBAND

Number	Title (A Side/B Side)	Yr	NM
1096	Just in Her Teens/Prize Possession	1960	40.00
1104	He'll Never Go/I Was King of the Universe	1960	25.00
1124	You Win Again/Not Going Home	1962	20.00

GUSTO

Number	Title (A Side/B Side)	Yr	NM
GT4-2041	Laura (What's He Got That I Ain't Got)/Flower of Love	197?	6.00

—Reissue

IMPERIAL

Number	Title (A Side/B Side)	Yr	NM
5759	The Longest Walk/Teenage Angel	1961	20.00

Except when noted otherwise, VG = 25% of NM, and VG+ = 50% of NM. (Example: VG = $2.00, VG+ = $4.00 and NM = $8.00.)

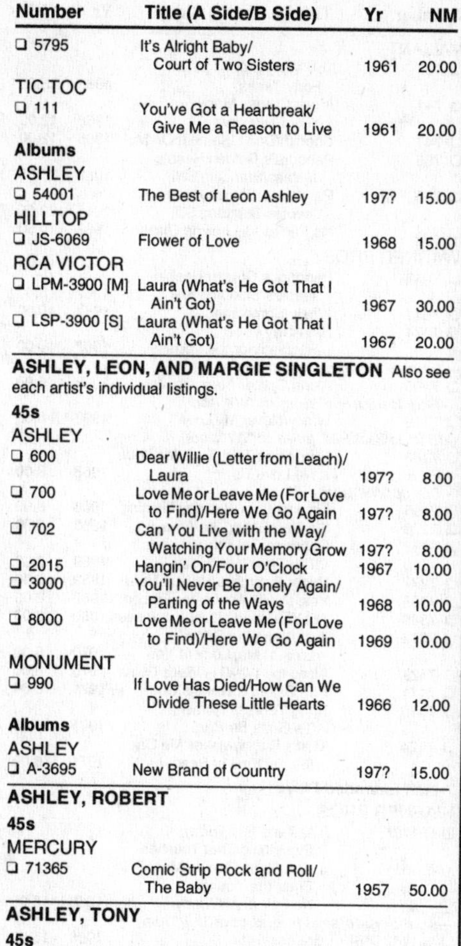

Number	Title (A Side/B Side)	Yr	NM
❑ 5795	It's Alright Baby/ Court of Two Sisters	1961	20.00
TIC TOC			
❑ 111	You've Got a Heartbreak/ Give Me a Reason to Live	1961	20.00
Albums			
ASHLEY			
❑ 54001	The Best of Leon Ashley	197?	15.00
HILLTOP			
❑ JS-6069	Flower of Love	1968	15.00
RCA VICTOR			
❑ LPM-3900 [M]	Laura (What's He Got That I Ain't Got)	1967	30.00
❑ LSP-3900 [S]	Laura (What's He Got That I Ain't Got)	1967	20.00

ASHLEY, LEON, AND MARGIE SINGLETON Also see each artist's individual listings.

Number	Title (A Side/B Side)	Yr	NM
45s			
ASHLEY			
❑ 600	Dear Willie (Letter from Leach)/ Laura	197?	8.00
❑ 700	Love Me or Leave Me (For Love to Find)/Here We Go Again	197?	8.00
❑ 702	Can You Live with the Way/ Watching Your Memory Grow	197?	8.00
❑ 2015	Hangin' On/Four O'Clock	1967	10.00
❑ 3000	You'll Never Be Lonely Again/ Parting of the Ways	1968	10.00
❑ 8000	Love Me or Leave Me (For Love to Find)/Here We Go Again	1969	10.00
MONUMENT			
❑ 990	If Love Has Died/How Can We Divide These Little Hearts	1966	12.00
Albums			
ASHLEY			
❑ A-3695	New Brand of Country	197?	15.00

ASHLEY, ROBERT

Number	Title (A Side/B Side)	Yr	NM
45s			
MERCURY			
❑ 71365	Comic Strip Rock and Roll/ The Baby	1957	50.00

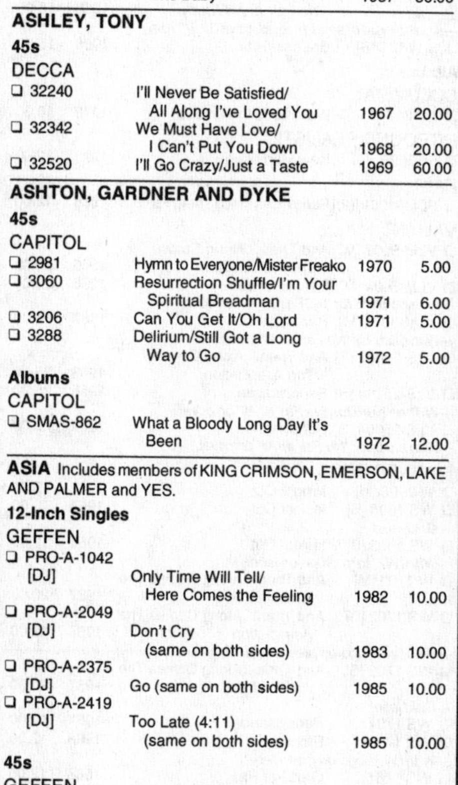

ASHLEY, TONY

Number	Title (A Side/B Side)	Yr	NM
45s			
DECCA			
❑ 32240	I'll Never Be Satisfied/ All Along I've Loved You	1967	20.00
❑ 32342	We Must Have Love/ I Can't Put You Down	1968	20.00
❑ 32520	I'll Go Crazy/Just a Taste	1969	60.00

ASHTON, GARDNER AND DYKE

Number	Title (A Side/B Side)	Yr	NM
45s			
CAPITOL			
❑ 2981	Hymn to Everyone/Mister Freako	1970	5.00
❑ 3060	Resurrection Shuffle/I'm Your Spiritual Breadman	1971	6.00
❑ 3206	Can You Get It/Oh Lord	1971	5.00
❑ 3288	Delirium/Still Got a Long Way to Go	1972	5.00
Albums			
CAPITOL			
❑ SMAS-862	What a Bloody Long Day It's Been	1972	12.00

ASIA Includes members of KING CRIMSON, EMERSON, LAKE AND PALMER and YES.

Number	Title (A Side/B Side)	Yr	NM
12-Inch Singles			
GEFFEN			
❑ PRO-A-1042 [DJ]	Only Time Will Tell/ Here Comes the Feeling	1982	10.00
❑ PRO-A-2049 [DJ]	Don't Cry (same on both sides)	1983	10.00
❑ PRO-A-2375 [DJ]	Go (same on both sides)	1985	10.00
❑ PRO-A-2419 [DJ]	Too Late (4:11) (same on both sides)	1985	10.00
45s			
GEFFEN			
❑ 28745	Too Late/Wishing	1986	3.00
❑ 28872	Go/After the War	1985	3.00
❑ 28872 [PS]	Go/After the War	1985	3.00
❑ 29475	The Smile Has Left Your Eyes/ Lying to Yourself	1983	4.00
❑ 29475 [PS]	The Smile Has Left Your Eyes/ Lying to Yourself	1983	4.00
❑ 29571	Don't Cry/Daylight	1983	4.00
❑ 29571 [PS]	Don't Cry/Daylight	1983	4.00
❑ 29871	Sole Survivor/ Here Comes the Feeling	1982	4.00
❑ 29871 [PS]	Sole Survivor/ Here Comes the Feeling	1982	4.00
❑ 29970	Only Time Will Tell/Time Again	1982	4.00
❑ 29970 [PS]	Only Time Will Tell/Time Again	1982	4.00
❑ 50040	Heat of the Moment/Ride Easy	1982	4.00
❑ 50040 [PS]	Heat of the Moment/Ride Easy	1982	5.00
Albums			
GEFFEN			
❑ GHS 2008	Asia	1982	8.00
—White label with pinstripes			
❑ GHS 2008 [DJ]	Asia	1982	20.00
—Promo on "Quiex II" vinyl			
❑ GHS 4008	Alpha	1983	8.00
—White label with pinstripes			
❑ GHS 4008 [DJ]	Alpha	1983	20.00
—Promo on "Quiex II" vinyl			
❑ GHS 24072	Astra	1985	8.00
❑ GHS 24298	Then and Now	1990	12.00

Asleep at the Wheel, *Framed*, MCA 5131, 1980, **$10.**

ASLEEP AT THE WHEEL

Number	Title (A Side/B Side)	Yr	NM
45s			
ARISTA			
❑ 2045	Keepin' Me Up Nights/ Pedernales Stroll	1990	3.00
❑ 2122	That's the Way Love Is/Beat Me, Daddy (Eight to the Bar)	1990	3.00
❑ 2178	Dance With Who Brung You/ Quittin' Time	1991	3.00
❑ 12425	(Get Your Kicks on) Route 66/ Black and White Rag	1992	4.00
CAPITOL			
❑ 4115	The Letter That Johnny Walker Read (Part 1)/(Part 2)	1975	5.00
❑ 4187	Bump Bounce Boogie/ Fat Boy Rag	1975	5.00
❑ 4238	Nothin' Takes the Place of You/ Tonight the Bartender Is on the Wrong Side of the Bar	1976	5.00
❑ 4319	Route 66/Shout Wa Hey	1976	5.00
❑ 4357	Miles and Miles of Texas/ Blues for Dixie	1976	5.00
❑ 4393	The Trouble with Lovin' Today/ Ragtime Annie	1977	5.00
❑ 4438	Somebody Stole His Body/ Let's Face Up	1977	5.00
❑ 4601	Ghost Dancer/Louisiana	1978	5.00
❑ 4659	Texas Me & You/ One O'Clock Jump	1978	5.00
❑ 4725	Choo Choo Ch'Boogie/ Too Many Bad Habits	1979	5.00
CAPITOL NASHVILLE			
❑ S7-18844	Lay Down Sally/Hightower	1995	4.00
EPIC			
❑ 06671	Way Down Texas Way/ String of Pars	1987	3.00
❑ 06671 [PS]	Way Down Texas Way/ String of Pars	1987	4.00
❑ 07125	House of Blue Lights/ Big Foot Stomp	1987	3.00
❑ 07610	Boogie Back to Texas/ Tulsa Straight Ahead	1987	3.00
❑ 07659	Blowin' Like a Bandit/ String of Pars	1987	3.00
❑ 07966	Walk On By/Sugarfoot Rag	1988	3.00
❑ 08087	Hot Rod Lincoln/String of Pars	1988	3.00
❑ 08461	House of Blue Lights/ Blowin' Like a Bandit	1988	3.00
—Reissue			
❑ 8-50024	You and Me Instead/ Don't Ask Me Why	1974	5.00
❑ 8-50045	Choo Choo Ch'Boogie/Our Names Aren't Mentioned	1974	5.00
❑ 68620	Chattanooga Choo Choo/ Sugarfoot Rag	1989	3.00
LIBERTY			
❑ S7-17715	Red Wing/Bring It On Down to My House	1993	4.00
❑ S7-17970	Blues for Dixie/Got a Letter from My Kid Today	1993	4.00

The Association, *The Association*, Warner Bros. WS 1800, 1969, **$12.**

Number	Title (A Side/B Side)	Yr	NM
MCA			
❑ 51020	Cool as a Breeze/Don't Get Caught Out in the Rain	1980	4.00
UNITED ARTISTS			
❑ XW-245	Take Me Back to Tulsa Before You Stop Loving Me	1973	6.00
❑ XW-344	Daddy's Advice/ Drivin' Nails in My Coffin	1973	6.00

Albums

Number	Title (A Side/B Side)	Yr	NM
ARISTA			
❑ AL-8550	Keepin' Me Up Nights	1990	12.00
CAPITOL			
❑ ST-11441	Texas Gold	1975	12.00
❑ ST-11548	Wheelin' and Dealin'	1976	12.00
❑ ST-11620	The Wheel	1977	12.00
❑ SW-11726	Collision Course	1978	12.00
❑ ST-11945	Served Live	1979	12.00
❑ SN-16306	Served Live	1984	8.00
—Budget-line reissue			
CAPITOL SPECIAL MARKETS			
❑ SL-8138	Drivin'	1980	12.00
DOT/MCA			
❑ 39036	Asleep at the Wheel	1985	10.00
EPIC			
❑ KE 33097	Asleep at the Wheel	1974	15.00
❑ PE 33097	Asleep at the Wheel	197?	8.00
—Reissue			
❑ BG 33782 [(2)]	Fathers and Sons	1974	25.00
—With Bob Wills			
❑ EG 33782 [(2)]	Fathers and Sons	197?	12.00
—Reissue			
❑ BFE 40681	10	1987	8.00
❑ FE 44213	Western Standard Time	1988	8.00
LIBERTY			
❑ LN-10296	Comin' Right At Ya!	1986	8.00
—Budget-line reissue			
MCA			
❑ 742	Framed	1982	8.00
—Reissue of 5131			
❑ 5131	Framed	1980	10.00
UNITED ARTISTS			
❑ UA-LA038-F	Comin' Right At Ya!	1973	20.00

ASSEMBLED MULTITUDE, THE

45s

Number	Title (A Side/B Side)	Yr	NM
ATLANTIC			
❑ 2737	Overture from Tommy (A Rock Opera)/Mud	1970	4.00
❑ 2764	Woodstock/Mr. Peppercorn	1970	4.00
❑ 2780	Medley from "Superstar" (A Rock Opera)/Where the Wood Bine Twineth	1971	4.00
❑ 2870	Godfather Waltz/Mac Arthur Park	1972	4.00

Albums

Number	Title (A Side/B Side)	Yr	NM
ATLANTIC			
❑ SD 8262	The Assembled Multitude	1970	12.00

ASSOCIATION, THE

45s

Number	Title (A Side/B Side)	Yr	NM
COLUMBIA			
❑ 45602	Indian Wells Woman/ Darling Be Home Soon	1972	5.00
❑ 45654	Come the Fall/ Kicking the Gong Around	1972	5.00
ELEKTRA			
❑ 47094	Dreamer/You Turn the Light On	1980	4.00
❑ 47146	Small Town Lovers/ Across the Persian Gulf	1981	4.00
JUBILEE			
❑ 5505	Babe I'm Gonna Leave You/ Baby Can't You Hear Me Call Your Name	1965	25.00
MUMS			
❑ 6016	Names, Tags, Numbers & Labels/Rainbows Bent	1973	4.00
RCA VICTOR			
❑ PB-10217	One Sunday Morning/ Life Is a Carnival	1975	4.00
VALIANT			
❑ 730	Too Many Mornings/ Forty Times	1965	15.00
❑ 741	Along Comes Mary/ Your Own Love	1966	12.00
❑ 747	Cherish/Don't Blame It On Me	1966	12.00
❑ 755	Pandora's Golden Heebie Jeebies/Standing Still	1966	10.00
❑ 755 [PS]	Pandora's Golden Heebie Jeebies/Standing Still	1966	20.00
❑ 758	No Fair at All/Looking Glass	1967	10.00
WARNER BROS.			
❑ 7040	Pandora's Golden Heebie Jeebies/Standing Still	1967	8.00
❑ 7041	Windy/Sometime	1967	10.00
❑ 7074	Never My Love/ Requiem for the Masses	1967	10.00
—A picture sleeve is rumored to exist			
❑ 7105	Along Comes Mary/Cherish	1968	8.00
—"Back to Back Hits" series on "W7" label			
❑ 7119	Windy/Never My Love	1968	8.00
—"Back to Back Hits" series on "W7" label			
❑ 7163	Everything That Touches You/ We Love Us	1968	8.00
—Orange "WB" label			
❑ 7195	Time for Livin'/Birthday Morning	1968	8.00
❑ 7229	Six Man Band/Like Always	1968	8.00
❑ 7267	Goodbye Columbus/ The Time It Is Today	1969	8.00
❑ 7277	Under Branches/Hear in Here	1969	8.00
❑ 7305	Yes, I Will/I Am Up for Europe	1969	8.00
❑ 7349	Are You Ready/Dubuque Blues	1969	8.00
❑ 7372	Just About the Same/ Look at Me, Look at You	1970	6.00
❑ 7429	Along the Way/Traveler's Guide	1970	6.00
❑ 7471	P.F. Sloan/Traveler's Guide	1971	6.00
❑ 7515	Bring Yourself Home/ It's Gotta Be Real	1971	6.00
❑ 7524	That's Racin'/Makes Me Cry (Funny Kind of Song)	1971	6.00

7-Inch Extended Plays

Number	Title (A Side/B Side)	Yr	NM
WARNER BROS.			
❑ S 1767	The Time It Is Today/ Everything That Touches You/Along Comes Mary// Enter the Young/ No Fair at All/Windy	1968	15.00
—Jukebox issue; small hole, plays at 33 1/3 rpm			
❑ S 1767 [PS]	Greatest Hits	1968	15.00

Albums

Number	Title (A Side/B Side)	Yr	NM
COLUMBIA			
❑ KC 31348	Waterbeds in Trinidad	1972	10.00
HITBOUND/REALISTIC			
❑ 51-3022	New Memories	1983	12.00
PAIR			
❑ PDL2-1061 [(2)]	Songs That Made Them Famous	1986	12.00
VALIANT			
❑ VLM-5002 [M]	And Then...Along Comes The Association	1966	20.00
❑ VLM-5004 [M]	Renaissance	1966	20.00
—With no blurb for "No Fair at All" on cover			
❑ VLM-5004 [M]	Renaissance	1967	15.00
—With blurb for "No Fair at All" on cover			
❑ VLS-25002 [S]	And Then...Along Comes The Association	1966	25.00
❑ VLS-25004 [S]	Renaissance	1966	25.00
—With no blurb for "No Fair at All" on cover			
❑ VLS-25004 [S]	Renaissance	1967	20.00
—With blurb for "No Fair at All" on cover			
WARNER BROS.			
❑ W 1696 [M]	Insight Out	1967	15.00
❑ WS 1696 [S]	Insight Out	1967	20.00
—Gold label			
❑ WS 1696 [S]	Insight Out	1968	12.00
—With "W7" logo on green label			
❑ W 1702 [M]	And Then...Along Comes The Association	1967	20.00
❑ WS 1702 [S]	And Then...Along Comes The Association	1967	12.00
—With "W7" logo on green label			
❑ WS 1702 [S]	And Then...Along Comes The Association	1967	20.00
—Gold label			
❑ WS 1704	Renaissance	1967	12.00
❑ WS 1733	Birthday	1968	12.00
—With "W7" logo on green label			
❑ WS 1767	Greatest Hits	1968	12.00
—With "W7" logo on green label			
❑ WS 1767	Greatest Hits	197?	8.00
—Any later pressing (LP in print until the late 1980s)			
❑ WS 1786	Goodbye Columbus	1969	12.00
—With "W7" logo on green label			
❑ WS 1800	The Association	1969	12.00
—With "W7" logo on green label			
❑ 2WS 1868 [(2)]	The Association "Live"	1970	15.00
❑ WS 1927	Stop Your Motor	1971	12.00

Except when noted otherwise, VG = 25% of NM, and VG+ = 50% of NM. (Example: VG = $2.00, VG+ = $4.00 and NM = $8.00.)

A

Number	Title (A Side/B Side)	Yr	NM
❑ ST-91317 [S]	Insight Out	1967	25.00
—Capitol Record Club edition			
❑ ST-91586	Greatest Hits	1968	20.00
—Capitol Record Club edition			
❑ STBO-93249 [(2)]	The Association "Live"	1970	20.00
—Capitol Record Club edition			

ASTORS, THE

45s

STAX

Number	Title (A Side/B Side)	Yr	NM
❑ 139	What Can It Be/Just Enough to Hurt Me	1963	80.00
❑ 170	Candy/I Found Out	1965	25.00
❑ 179	Mystery Woman/ In the Twilight Zone	1965	25.00
❑ 232	Daddy Didn't Tell You/ More Power to You	1967	12.00

ASTRO JETS, THE

45s

IMPERIAL

Number	Title (A Side/B Side)	Yr	NM
❑ 5760	Hide and Seek/Boom-A-Lay	1961	20.00

ASTRONAUTS, THE (1) Best known as a surf-instrumental group.

45s

RCA VICTOR

Number	Title (A Side/B Side)	Yr	NM
❑ 47-8194	Baja/Kuk	1963	20.00
❑ 47-8224	Hot Doggin'/Everyone But Me	1963	20.00
❑ 47-8224 [PS]	Hot Doggin'/Everyone But Me	1963	60.00
❑ 47-8298	Competition Coupe/Surf Party	1963	20.00
❑ 47-8364	Go Fight for Her/ Swim Little Mermaid	1964	20.00
❑ 47-8419	Main Title from Ride the Wild Surf/Around and Around	1964	20.00
❑ 47-8463	I'm a Fool/Can't You See I Do	1964	20.00
❑ 47-8499	Almost Grown/My Sin Is Pride	1965	20.00
❑ 47-8545	Tomorrow's Gonna Be Another Day/Razza Matazz	1965	20.00
❑ 47-8628	It Doesn't Matter Anymore/ The La La La Song	1965	20.00
❑ 47-8885	In My Car/Main Street	1966	15.00
❑ 47-9109	I Know You Rider/Better Things	1967	15.00

Albums

RCA VICTOR

Number	Title (A Side/B Side)	Yr	NM
❑ PRM-183 [M]	Rockin' with the Astronauts	1965	30.00
—Promo only			
❑ LPM-2760 [M]	Surfin' with the Astronauts	1963	60.00
❑ LSP-2760 [S]	Surfin' with the Astronauts	1963	80.00
❑ LPM-2782 [M]	Everything Is A-OK!	1964	50.00
❑ LSP-2782 [S]	Everything Is A-OK!	1964	60.00
❑ LPM-2858 [M]	Competition Coupe	1964	60.00
❑ LSP-2858 [S]	Competition Coupe	1964	80.00
❑ LPM-2903 [M]	The Astronauts Orbit Kampus	1964	40.00
❑ LSP-2903 [S]	The Astronauts Orbit Kampus	1964	50.00
❑ LPM-3307 [M]	The Astronauts Go, Go, Go	1965	30.00
❑ LSP-3307 [S]	The Astronauts Go, Go, Go	1965	40.00
❑ LPM-3359 [M]	Favorites for You from Us	1965	30.00
❑ LSP-3359 [S]	Favorites for You from Us	1965	40.00
❑ LPM-3454 [M]	Down the Line	1966	30.00
❑ LSP-3454 [S]	Down the Line	1966	40.00
❑ LPM-3733 [M]	Travelin' Men	1967	50.00
❑ LSP-3733 [S]	Travelin' Men	1967	30.00

ASTRONAUTS, THE (1) / THE LIVERPOOL FIVE

Albums

RCA VICTOR

Number	Title (A Side/B Side)	Yr	NM
❑ PRS-251 [S]	Stereo Festival	1967	100.00
—Special-prodcuts edition			

ASTRONAUTS, THE (U)

45s

JAN ELL

Number	Title (A Side/B Side)	Yr	NM
❑ 459	Geneva Twist/Take 17	1962	30.00

LUNEY

Number	Title (A Side/B Side)	Yr	NM
❑ 100	Ridge Route/Blast Off	1962	30.00

MERCURY

Number	Title (A Side/B Side)	Yr	NM
❑ 71675	Alabama Jubilee/Gadabout	1960	12.00

PALLADIUM

Number	Title (A Side/B Side)	Yr	NM
❑ 610	Come Along Baby/ Trying to Get to You	1962	100.00

TRIAL

Number	Title (A Side/B Side)	Yr	NM
❑ 3521	Farewell/Chili Charlene	1960	200.00

VANRUS

Number	Title (A Side/B Side)	Yr	NM
❑ 1000	Ski Lift/Blues Beat	1962	30.00

ASYLUM CHOIR LEON RUSSELL and MARC BENNO.

45s

SHELTER

Number	Title (A Side/B Side)	Yr	NM
❑ 7313	Straight Brother/ Tryin' to Stay Alive	1971	8.00

SMASH

Number	Title (A Side/B Side)	Yr	NM
❑ 2186	Soul Food/Welcome to Hollywood	1968	8.00
—As "Asylum Choir"			
❑ 2204	Indian Style/Icicle Star Tree	1969	8.00
—As "Asylum Choir"			

Albums

MCA

Number	Title (A Side/B Side)	Yr	NM
❑ 684	Asylum Choir II	1979	8.00
—Reissue of Shelter 52010			

SHELTER

Number	Title (A Side/B Side)	Yr	NM
❑ SR 2120	Asylum Choir II	1974	12.00
—Reissue of 8910			
❑ SW-8910	Asylum Choir II	1971	15.00
❑ 52010	Asylum Choir II	1977	10.00
—Reissue of 2120			

SMASH

Number	Title (A Side/B Side)	Yr	NM
❑ SRS-67107	Look Inside the Asylum Choir	1968	30.00
—Front cover has a roll of toilet paper			
❑ SRS-67107	Look Inside the Asylum Choir	197?	15.00
—Front cover has a photo of Leon and Marc			

ATKINS, CHET

45s

COLUMBIA

Number	Title (A Side/B Side)	Yr	NM
❑ AE7 1776 [DJ]	East Tennessee Christmas/ Winter Wonderland	1983	4.00
❑ CS7 2712 [DJ]	Sails/My Song	1987	4.00
❑ CS7 2712 [PS]	Sails/My Song	1987	4.00
❑ 03984	Run Don't Walk/Walk Me Home	1983	3.00
❑ 04859	The Boot and the Stone/ Sunrise	1985	3.00
❑ 05662	Please Stay Tuned/Some Leather and Lace	1985	3.00
❑ 06165	The Official Beach Music/Alicia	1986	3.00
❑ 07929	I Still Can't Say Goodbye/ The Mockingbird	1988	3.00

RCA

Number	Title (A Side/B Side)	Yr	NM
❑ PB-10901	La Chicana/Four in the Morning	1977	4.00
—With Danny Davis and Floyd Cramer			
❑ PB-11071	Me and My Guitar/Cascade	1977	4.00
❑ PB-11892	Blind Willie/Dance with Me	1980	4.00
❑ PB-12064	I Can Hear Kentucky Calling Me/Strawberry Man	1980	4.00
❑ PB-12263	Orange Blossom Special/ Ready for the Times to Get Better	1981	4.00

RCA VICTOR

Number	Title (A Side/B Side)	Yr	NM
❑ 37-7971	Jingle Bells/Jingle Bell Rock	1961	25.00
—"Compact Single 33"; small hole, plays at 33 1/3 rpm			
❑ 47-4377	In the Mood/Sweet Bunch of Daisies	1951	25.00
❑ 47-4491	Goodbye Blues/Rainbow	1952	25.00
❑ 47-4684	Spanish Fandango/ Your Mean Little Heart	1952	25.00
❑ 47-4896	Meet Mr. Callaghan/ Chinatown, My Chinatown	1952	25.00
❑ 47-4922	Gallopin' on the Guitar/ (B-side unknown)	1952	25.00
❑ 47-4931	Tennessee Rag/My Little Girl	1952	25.00
❑ 47-5010	Midnight/Rustic Dance	1952	25.00
❑ 47-5100	Guitar Polka/Dream Train	1952	20.00
—With Rosalie Allen			
❑ 47-5181	Fig Leaf Rag/High Rockin' Swing	1953	20.00
❑ 47-5300	Country Gentlemen/The Bells of St. Mary's	1953	20.00
❑ 47-5484	Three O'Clock in the Morning/ City Slicker	1953	20.00
❑ 47-5565	Barber Shop Rag/Centipede Boogie	1953	20.00
❑ 47-5638	Wildwood Flower/Simple Simon	1954	20.00
❑ 47-5650	Georgia Camp Meeting/ Jealous Hearted Me	1954	20.00
—With Minnie Pearl			
❑ 47-5704	Downhill Drag/Kentucky Derby	1954	20.00
❑ 47-5813	San Antonio Rose/Mister Misery	1954	20.00
—With Red Kirk			
❑ 47-5956	Mr. Sandman/Set a Spell	1954	20.00
❑ 47-6108	Hey Mr. Guitar/ Unchained Melody	1955	15.00
❑ 47-6199	Somebody Stole My Gal/ Shine On Harvest Moon	1955	15.00
❑ 47-6314	Christmas Carols/Jingle Bells	1955	15.00
❑ 47-6366	Jean's Song/Honey	1955	15.00
❑ 47-6550	Cecilia/The Lady Loves	1956	15.00
❑ 47-6796	Trambone/Blue Echo	1957	15.00
❑ 47-6808	Tricky/Peanut Vendor	1957	15.00
—With the Rhythm Rockers			
❑ 47-6919	Martinique/Dig These Blues	1957	15.00
—With the Rhythm Rockers			
❑ 47-7048	Hidden Charms/ Colonial Ballroom	1957	15.00
❑ 47-7589	Boo Boo Stick Beat/ Django's Castle	1959	12.00
❑ 47-7684	One Mint Julep/Teensville	1960	12.00
❑ 47-7747	Slinkey/Rainbow's End	1960	12.00
❑ 47-7796	Hocus Pocus/Theme from The Dark at the End of the Stairs	1960	12.00
❑ 47-7847	The Slop/Hot Mocking Bird	1961	12.00
❑ 47-7891	Man of Mystery/Windy and Warm	1961	12.00
❑ 47-7971	Jingle Bells/Jingle Bell Rock	1961	12.00
❑ 47-8029	Down Home/Melissa	1962	12.00
❑ 47-8246	Guitar Country/Waitin' for the Evening Train	1963	12.00
—With the Anita Kerr Quartet			
❑ 47-8342	Freight Train/Dobro	1964	12.00
❑ 47-8492	Travelin'/Cloudy and Cool	1965	10.00
❑ 47-8590	Yakety Axe/Letter Edged in Black	1965	10.00
❑ 47-8781	From Nashville with Love/ Rhythm Guitar	1966	10.00
❑ 47-8829	Tennessee Waltz/ Country Gentleman	1966	10.00
❑ 47-8927	Prissy/La Fiesta	1966	10.00
❑ 47-9116	Charlie Brown/What'd I Say	1967	10.00
❑ 47-9578	Huntin' Boots/Blue Angel	1968	8.00
❑ 47-9672	Light My Fire/Mrs. Robinson	1968	8.00
❑ 47-9725	Theme from Zorba the Greek/ Those Were the Days	1969	6.00
❑ 47-9824	Love Beads/Passion Flower	1969	6.00
❑ 47-9827	Steeplechase Lane/Love Beads	1970	5.00
❑ 47-9890	Tennessee Stud/ Cannonball Rag	1970	5.00
—With Jerry Reed			
❑ 47-9956	Snowbird/Chaplain in New Shoes	1971	5.00
❑ 48-0062	Guitar Waltz/Barber Shop Rag	1949	25.00
—Second pressings: Green label, black vinyl			
❑ 48-0062	Guitar Waltz/Barber Shop Rag	1949	50.00
—Originals on green vinyl			
❑ 48-0089	Dance of the Goldenrod/Telling My Troubles to My Old Guitar	1949	25.00
—Second pressings: Green label, black vinyl			
❑ 48-0089	Dance of the Goldenrod/Telling My Troubles to My Old Guitar	1949	50.00
—Originals on green vinyl			
❑ 48-0142	Centipede Boogie/ Wednesday Night Waltz	1949	25.00
—Second pressings: Green label, black vinyl			
❑ 48-0142	Centipede Boogie/ Wednesday Night Waltz	1949	50.00
—Originals on green vinyl			
❑ 48-0173	One More Chance/ Old Buck Dance	1950	25.00
—Originals on green vinyl			
❑ 48-0173	One More Chance/ Old Buck Dance	1950	25.00
—Second pressings: Green label, black vinyl			
❑ 48-0329	Main Street Breakdown/Under the Hickory Nut Tree	1950	25.00
—Second pressings: Green label, black vinyl			
❑ 48-0329	Main Street Breakdown/ Under the Hickory Nut Tree	1950	50.00
—Originals on green vinyl			
❑ 48-0367	Boogie Man Boogie/Was Bitten By the Same Bug Twice	1950	25.00
—Second pressings: Green label, black vinyl			
❑ 48-0367	Boogie Man Boogie/Was Bitten By the Same Bug Twice	1950	50.00
—Originals on green vinyl			
❑ 48-0402	The Birth of the Blues/Confusin'	1950	25.00
—Second pressings: Green label, black vinyl			
❑ 48-0402	The Birth of the Blues/Confusin'	1950	50.00
—Originals on green vinyl			
❑ 48-0428	Indian Love Call/Music in My Heart	1951	25.00
—Second pressings: Green label, black vinyl			
❑ 48-0428	Indian Love Call/ Music in My Heart	1951	50.00
—Originals on green vinyl			
❑ 48-0439	My Life with You/ A Trinket of Shiny Gold	1951	25.00
—With the Carter Sisters			
❑ 48-0440	You're Always Brand New/ Mountain Melody	1951	25.00
❑ 48-0471	Jitterbug Waltz/My Crazy Heart	1951	25.00
❑ 48-0500	Crazy Rhythm/Hybrid Corn	1951	25.00
❑ 74-0236	Delilah/Ode to Billie Joe	1969	5.00
—With Arthur Fiedler and the Boston Pops			
❑ 74-0536	Black Magic Woman/ Wabash Blues	1971	5.00
❑ 74-0696	Red, White and Blue Medley/ Kentucky	1972	5.00
❑ 74-0775	Nashtownville/ Jerry's Breakdown	1972	5.00
—With Jerry Reed			
❑ 74-0914	Ruby, Are You Mad at Your Man/Somewhere, My Love	1973	4.00
❑ 47-7847 [PS]	The Slop/Hot Mocking Bird	1961	20.00
❑ APBO-0146	Fiddlin' Around/Paramaribo	1973	4.00
❑ VP-1-2450 [S]	I Ain't Gonna Work Tomorrow/ Never on Sunday	196?	15.00
—Jukebox issue; small hole, plays at 33 1/3 rpm			
❑ VP-2-2450 [S]	Tuxedo Junction/Give the World a Smile	196?	15.00
—Jukebox issue; small hole, plays at 33 1/3 rpm			

Number	Title (A Side/B Side)	Yr	NM
❑ VP-3-2450 [S]	I'm a Pilgrim/Salty Dog Drag	196?	15.00
—Jukebox issue; small hole, plays at 33 1/3 rpm			
❑ VP-4-2450 [S]	Steel Guitar Rag/Trambone	196?	15.00
—Jukebox issue; small hole, plays at 33 1/3 rpm; the above 4 came in a box originally, which is worth at least as much as any of the discs			
❑ PB-10046	The Entertainer/Dizzy Fingers	1974	4.00
❑ PB-10346	The Night Atlanta Burned/ Old Folks of Okracoke	1975	4.00
—As "The Atkins String Co."			
❑ PB-10448	Sonora/Mostly Mozart	1975	4.00
—As "The Atkins String Co."			
❑ PB-10614	Frog Kissin'/Bill Cheatham	1976	4.00

7-Inch Extended Plays

RCA VICTOR

Number	Title (A Side/B Side)	Yr	NM
❑ LPC-124	Theme from "The Dark at the Top of the Stairs"/Theme from "Picnic"//Limelight/ Meet Mister Callaghan	1961	15.00
—"Compact Double 33"; small hole, plays at 33 1/3 rpm			
❑ LPC-124 [PS]	Chet Atkins Plays Great Movie Themes	1961	20.00
❑ 547-0141	Gallopin' Guitar/Stephen Foster Medley//St. Louis Blues/Hangover Blues	1952	20.00
—One record of 2-EP set EPB 3079			
❑ 547-0142	Black Mountain Rag/Lover, Come Back to Me//The 3rd Man Theme/Imagination	1952	20.00
—One record of 2-EP set EPB 3079			
❑ 547-0535	South/Indiana//A Gay Ranchero/Frankie and Johnnie	1954	15.00
—One record of 2-EP set EPB 1090			
❑ 547-0536	Alabama Jubilee/Have You Ever Been Lonely (Have You Ever Been Blue?)//Caravan/ The Birth of the Blues	1954	15.00
—One record of 2-EP set EPB 1090			
❑ EPA-588	Pagan Love Song/Sunrise Serenade//Beautiful Ohio/ Avalon	1954	20.00
❑ EPA-588 [PS]	Chet Atkins and His Guitar	1954	20.00
❑ EPA-594	Tweedlee Dee/(The Wallflower) Dance with Me Henry//Cherry Pink and Apple Blossom White/Darling, Je Vous Aime Beaucoup	1955	20.00
❑ EPA-594 [PS]	Pickin' the Hits	1955	20.00
❑ EPA-685	Arkansaw Traveler/ Londonderry Air//Ochi Chornya/La Golondrina	1955	20.00
❑ EPA-685 [PS]	Chet Atkins in 3 Dimensions Vol. 1: Folk	1955	20.00
❑ EPA-686	Blues in the Night/Tenderly// Little Rock Getaway/Tip-Toe Through the Tulips with Me	1955	20.00
❑ EPA-686 [PS]	Chet Atkins in 3 Dimensions Vol. 2: Popular	1955	20.00
❑ EPA-687	Minuet and Prelude/ Intermezzo//Schon Rosmarin/Minute Waltz	1955	20.00
❑ EPA-687 [PS]	Chet Atkins in 3 Dimensions Vol. 3: Classical	1955	20.00
❑ EPA-796	Indian Love Call/Memphis Blues//St. Louis Blues/ Black Mountain Rag	1956	20.00
❑ EPA-796 [PS]	Stringin' Along with Chet Atkins	1956	20.00
❑ 547-0919	Oh By Jingo/Indian Love Call// Alice Blue Gown/The 3rd Man Theme	1956	20.00
—One record of 2-EP set EPB 1236			
❑ 547-0920	Memphis Blues/12th Street Rag//Gallopin' Guitar/ St. Louis Blues	1956	20.00
—One record of 2-EP set EPB 1236			
❑ EPB 1090 [PS]	A Session with Chet Atkins	1954	20.00
—Cover for 2-EP set (547-0535, 547-0536)			
❑ EPB 1236 [PS]	Stringin' Along with Chet Atkins	1956	20.00
❑ EAP 1-1383	Swedish Rhapsody/Liza// Petite Waltz/Unchained Melody	1956	15.00
❑ EAP 1-1383 [PS]	Finger-Style Guitar, Vol. 1	1956	15.00
❑ EPA 2-1383	Heartaches/Glow Worm// Malaguena/Waltz in A Flat	1956	15.00
❑ EPA 2-1383 [PS]	Finger-Style Guitar, Vol. II	1956	15.00
❑ VLP 2450	Salty Dog Drag/Trambone/ The Girl Friend of the Whirling Dervish//I'm a Pilgrim/Steel Guitar Rag/Give the World a Smile	196?	15.00
—Jukebox issue; small hole, plays at 33 1/3 rpm			
❑ VLP 2450 [PS]	Down Home	196?	15.00
❑ VLP-2549	Yellow Bird/The Banana Boat Song/Montego Bay// Moon Over Miami/ Come to the Mardi Gras/ The Enchanted Sea	1962	15.00
—Jukebox issue; small hole, plays at 33 1/3 rpm			
❑ VLP-2549 [PS]	Caribbean Guitar	1962	15.00
❑ EPB 3079 [PS]	Chet Atkins' Gallopin' Guitar	1952	20.00
—Cover for 2-EP set (547-0141, 547-0142)			
❑ VLP 3316	Josephine/It Don't Mean a Thing/Rose Ann//Travelin'/ Wimoweh/Say It with Soul	196?	15.00
—Jukebox issue; small hole, plays at 33 1/3 rpm			
❑ VLP 3316 [PS]	My Favorite Guitars	196?	15.00
❑ VLP-3531	I Feel Fine/Can't Buy Me Love/ Michelle//A Hard Day's Night/ She's a Woman/ She Loves You	1966	15.00
—Jukebox issue; small hole, plays at 33 1/3 rpm			
❑ VLP-3531 [PS]	Chet Atkins Picks On the Beatles	1966	15.00
❑ VLP 3558	Yakety Axe/Josephine/ White Silver Sands// Oh Lonesome Me/Freight Train/Cloudy and Cool	196?	12.00
—Jukebox issue; small hole, plays at 33 1/3 rpm			
❑ VLP 3558 [PS]	The Best of Chet Atkins, Vol. 2	196?	12.00
❑ EPA-4194	Say "Si Si"/Villa//Yankee Doodle Dandy/You're Just in Love	1958	15.00
❑ EPA-4194 [PS]	Chet Atkins at Home	1958	15.00
❑ EPA-4343	In the Good Old Summertime/ Bill Bailey//Sweet Bunch of Daisies/John Henry	1959	15.00
❑ EPA-4343 [PS]	Hum and Strum Along with Chet	1959	15.00
❑ EPA-5052	The Poor People of Paris (Jean's Song)/Chinatown, My Chinatown//San Antonio Rose/Country Gentleman	195?	15.00
❑ EPA-5052 [PS]	Chet Atkins (Gold Standard Series)	1958	15.00

Albums

COLUMBIA

Number	Title (A Side/B Side)	Yr	NM
❑ FC 38536	Work It Out with Chet Atkins C.G.P.	1983	10.00
❑ PC 38536	Work It Out with Chet Atkins C.G.P.	1985	8.00
—Budget-line reissue			
❑ PC 39003	East Tennessee Christmas	1983	10.00
❑ FC 39591	Stay Tuned	1985	10.00
❑ FC 40256	Street Dreams	1986	8.00
❑ FC 40593	Sails	1987	8.00
❑ FC 44323	Chet Atkins, C.G.P.	1989	8.00

DOLTON

Number	Title (A Side/B Side)	Yr	NM
❑ BLP-16506 [M]	Play Guitar with Chet Atkins	1967	25.00
❑ BST-17506 [S]	Play Guitar with Chet Atkins	1967	30.00

PAIR

Number	Title (A Side/B Side)	Yr	NM
❑ PDL2-1047 [(2)]	Tennessee Guitar Man	1985	12.00
❑ PDL2-1115 [(2)]	Guitar for All Seasons	1986	12.00

RCA CAMDEN

Number	Title (A Side/B Side)	Yr	NM
❑ CAL-659 [M]	Chet Atkins and His Guitar	196?	15.00
❑ CAS-659(e) [R]	Chet Atkins and His Guitar	1964	12.00
❑ CAL-753 [M]	Guitar Genius	196?	15.00
❑ CAS-753(e) [R]	Guitar Genius	196?	12.00
❑ CAL-981 [M]	Music from Nashville, My Home Town	1966	12.00
❑ CAS-981 [S]	Music from Nashville, My Home Town	1966	15.00
❑ CAL-2182 [M]	Chet	1967	12.00
❑ CAS-2182 [S]	Chet	1967	15.00
❑ CAS-2296	Relaxin' with Chet	1969	12.00
❑ CAS-2523	Chet 'n Boots	1972	12.00
❑ CAS-2555	Nashville Gold	1972	12.00
❑ CAS-2600	Finger Pickin' Good	1973	10.00
❑ ACL1-7042	Love Letters	197?	10.00

RCA RED SEAL

Number	Title (A Side/B Side)	Yr	NM
❑ LM-2870 [M]	The "Pops" Goes Country	1966	15.00
❑ LSC-2870 [S]	The "Pops" Goes Country	1966	20.00
—Above two with the Boston Pops Orchestra, Arthur Fiedler, conductor			
❑ LSC-3104	Chet Picks On the Pops	1969	15.00
—With the Boston Pops Orchestra, Arthur Fiedler, conductor			

RCA VICTOR

Number	Title (A Side/B Side)	Yr	NM
❑ APL1-0159	Alone	1973	12.00
❑ APD1-0329 [Q]	Superpickers	1974	20.00
❑ APL1-0329	Superpickers	1974	12.00
❑ APL1-0545	Chet Atkins Picks On Jerry Reed	1974	12.00
❑ APL1-0645	Chat Atkins Goes to the Movies	1973	12.00
❑ ANL1-0981	Chet Atkins Picks the Best	1975	10.00
❑ LPM-1090 [M]	A Session with Chet Atkins	1954	60.00
—Red cover			
❑ LPM-1090 [M]	A Session with Chet Atkins	1961	20.00
—Woman and guitars cover			
❑ LSP-1090(e) [R]	A Session with Chet Atkins	1967	10.00
❑ LPM-1197 [M]	Chet Atkins in Three Dimensions	1956	50.00
—Black-and-white guitar cover			
❑ LPM-1197 [M]	Chet Atkins in Three Dimensions	1961	20.00
—Red guitar cover			
❑ LSP-1197(e) [R]	Chet Atkins in Three Dimensions	1967	10.00
❑ APL1-1233	The Night Atlanta Burned	1975	12.00
❑ LPM-1236 [M]	Stringin' Along with Chet Atkins	1956	50.00
—Orange cover			
❑ LPM-1236 [M]	Stringin' Along with Chet Atkins	1961	20.00
—Full-color cover			
❑ LSP-1236(e) [R]	Stringin' Along with Chet Atkins	1967	10.00
❑ LPM-1383 [M]	Finger Style Guitar	1956	50.00
—Chet's face not visible on cover			
❑ LPM-1383 [M]	Finger Style Guitar	1961	20.00
—Chet's face visible on cover			
❑ LSP-1383(e) [R]	Finger Style Guitar	1962	12.00
❑ LPM-1544 [M]	Chet Atkins at Home	1957	50.00
—Title in block letters on cover			
❑ LPM-1544 [M]	Chet Atkins at Home	1961	20.00
—Title in script on cover			
❑ LSP-1544(e) [R]	Chet Atkins at Home	1967	10.00
❑ LPM-1577 [M]	Hi-Fi in Focus	1957	20.00
—Guitar on cover			
❑ LPM-1577 [M]	Hi-Fi in Focus	1957	50.00
—No guitars on cover			
❑ LSP-1577(e) [R]	Hi-Fi in Focus	196?	10.00
❑ ANL1-1935	Christmas with Chet Atkins	1976	8.00
—Reissue of LSP-2423			
❑ APL1-1985	The Best of Chet Atkins	1975	12.00
❑ LPM-1993 [M]	Chet Atkins in Hollywood	1959	30.00
—Night-time cover			
❑ LPM-1993 [M]	Chet Atkins in Hollywood	1961	20.00
—Daylight "blonde" cover			
❑ LSP-1993 [S]	Chet Atkins in Hollywood	1959	50.00
—Night-time cover			
❑ LSP-1993 [S]	Chet Atkins in Hollywood	1961	30.00
—Daylight "blonde" cover			
❑ LPM-2025 [M]	Hum & Strum Along	1959	25.00
—Add $10 NM if instruction book is included			
❑ LSP-2025 [S]	Hum & Strum Along	1959	40.00
—Add $10 NM if instruction book is included			
❑ LPM-2103 [M]	Mister Guitar	1959	30.00
—Lone guitar on cover			
❑ LPM-2103 [M]	Mister Guitar	1961	20.00
—Guitar and woman on cover			
❑ LSP-2103 [S]	Mister Guitar	1959	50.00
—Lone guitar on cover			
❑ LSP-2103 [S]	Mister Guitar	1961	30.00
—Guitar and woman on cover			
❑ LPM-2161 [M]	Teensville	1960	30.00
—Title overlaps cover photo			
❑ LPM-2161 [M]	Teensville	1961	20.00
—Title in black strip at top of cover photo			
❑ LSP-2161 [S]	Teensville	1960	50.00
—Title overlaps cover photo			
❑ LSP-2161 [S]	Teensville	1961	30.00
—Title in black strip at top of cover photo			
❑ LPM-2175 [M]	The Other Chet Atkins	1960	20.00
❑ LSP-2175 [S]	The Other Chet Atkins	1960	30.00
❑ LPM-2232 [M]	Chet Atkins' Workshop	1961	20.00
❑ LSP-2232 [S]	Chet Atkins' Workshop	1961	30.00
❑ LPM-2346 [M]	The Most Popular Guitar	1961	20.00
❑ LSP-2346 [S]	The Most Popular Guitar	1961	30.00
❑ AHL1-2405	My Guitar	1977	12.00
❑ LPM-2423 [M]	Christmas with Chet Atkins	1961	20.00
❑ LSP-2423 [S]	Christmas with Chet Atkins	1961	30.00
❑ LPM-2450 [M]	Down Home	1962	20.00
❑ LSP-2450 [S]	Down Home	1962	25.00
❑ CPL1-2503	A Legendary Performer	1977	12.00
❑ LPM-2549 [M]	Caribbean Guitar	1962	20.00
❑ LSP-2549 [S]	Caribbean Guitar	1962	25.00
❑ LPM-2601 [M]	Back Home Hymns	1962	20.00
❑ LSP-2601 [S]	Back Home Hymns	1962	25.00
❑ LPM-2616 [M]	Our Man in Nashville	1963	20.00
❑ LSP-2616 [S]	Our Man in Nashville	1963	25.00
❑ LPM-2678 [M]	Travelin'	1963	20.00
❑ LSP-2678 [S]	Travelin'	1963	25.00
❑ LPM-2719 [M]	Teen Scene	1963	20.00
❑ LSP-2719 [S]	Teen Scene	1963	25.00
❑ LPM-2783 [M]	Guitar Country	1964	15.00
❑ LSP-2783 [S]	Guitar Country	1964	20.00
❑ LPM-2887 [M]	The Best of Chet Atkins	1964	15.00
❑ LSP-2887 [S]	The Best of Chet Atkins	1964	20.00
❑ LPM-2908 [M]	Progressive Pickin'	1964	15.00
❑ LSP-2908 [S]	Progressive Pickin'	1964	20.00
❑ LPM-3079 [10]	Chet Atkins' Gallopin' Guitar	1952	150.00
❑ LPM-3169 [10]	Stringin' Along with Chet Atkins	1953	100.00
❑ AHL1-3302	The First Nashville Guitar Quartet	1979	12.00
❑ LPM-3316 [M]	My Favorite Guitars	1965	15.00
❑ LSP-3316 [S]	My Favorite Guitars	1965	20.00
❑ LPM-3429 [M]	More of That "Guitar Country"	1965	15.00
❑ LSP-3429 [S]	More of That "Guitar Country"	1965	20.00
❑ AHL1-3505	The Best of Chet On The Road...Live	1980	12.00
❑ LPM-3531 [M]	Chet Atkins Picks On the Beatles	1966	25.00
❑ LSP-3531 [S]	Chet Atkins Picks On the Beatles	1966	30.00

Except when noted otherwise, VG = 25% of NM, and VG+ = 50% of NM. (Example: VG = $2.00, VG+ = $4.00 and NM = $8.00.)

Number	Title (A Side/B Side)	Yr	NM
❑ LPM-3558 [M]	The Best of Chet Atkins, Vol. 2	1966	12.00
❑ LSP-3558 [S]	The Best of Chet Atkins, Vol. 2	1966	15.00
❑ LPM-3647 [M]	From Nashville with Love	1966	12.00
❑ LSP-3647 [S]	From Nashville with Love	1966	15.00
❑ LPM-3728 [M]	It's a Guitar World	1967	30.00
❑ LSP-3728 [S]	It's a Guitar World	1967	12.00
❑ AYL1-3741	The First Nashville Guitar Quartet	1981	8.00
—"Best Buy Series" reissue			
❑ LPM-3818 [M]	Chet Atkins Picks the Best	1967	30.00
❑ LSP-3818 [S]	Chet Atkins Picks the Best	1967	12.00
❑ LPM-3885 [M]	Class Guitar	1967	30.00
❑ LSP-3885 [S]	Class Guitar	1967	12.00
❑ LPM-3992 [M]	Solo Flights	1968	50.00
❑ LSP-3992 [S]	Solo Flights	1968	12.00
❑ LPM-4017 [M]	Hometown Guitar	1968	80.00
❑ LSP-4017 [S]	Hometown Guitar	1968	15.00
❑ AHL1-4044	Still Country — After All These Years	1981	10.00
❑ LSP-4061	Solid Gold '68	1968	15.00
❑ LSP-4135	Lover's Guitar	1968	15.00
❑ LSP-4244	Solid Gold '69	1969	12.00
❑ LSP-4331	Yestergroovin'	1970	12.00
❑ LSP-4396	Me & Jerry	1971	15.00
—With Jerry Reed			
❑ LSP-4464	For the Good Times	1971	15.00
❑ AHL1-4724	Great Hits of the Past	1983	10.00
❑ LSP-4754	Chet Atkins Picks the Hits	1973	15.00
❑ AHL1-5495	Collector's Series	1985	10.00
❑ VPS-6030 [(2)]	This Is Chet Atkins	1972	15.00
❑ VPXS-6079 [(2)]	Now & Then	1972	15.00
TIME-LIFE			
❑ STW-117	Country Music	1981	12.00

ATKINS, CHET, AND LES PAUL
Also see each artist's individual listings.

45s

Number	Title (A Side/B Side)	Yr	NM
RCA			
❑ PB-11330	I'm Your Greatest Fan/Hot Toddy	1978	4.00
RCA VICTOR			
❑ PB-10642	Moonglow/Avalon	1976	5.00

Albums

Number	Title (A Side/B Side)	Yr	NM
RCA VICTOR			
❑ APL1-1167	Chester and Lester	1976	12.00
❑ APL1-2786	Guitar Monsters	1978	12.00
❑ AYL1-3682	Chester and Lester	1980	8.00
—"Best Buy Series" reissue			

ATKINS, CHET, AND HANK SNOW
Also see each artist's individual listings.

45s

Number	Title (A Side/B Side)	Yr	NM
RCA VICTOR			
❑ 47-5995	Silver Bell/Old Spinning Wheel	1954	20.00
❑ 47-6558	Reminiscing/New Spanish Two-Step	1956	15.00
❑ 47-9803	Wheels/Difficult	1969	8.00

ATKINS, CHET, AND DOC WATSON
Also see each artist's individual listings.

45s

Number	Title (A Side/B Side)	Yr	NM
RCA			
❑ PB-12138	Medley-Tennessee Rag & Beaumont Rag/On My Way to Canaan's Land	1981	4.00

Albums

Number	Title (A Side/B Side)	Yr	NM
RCA VICTOR			
❑ AHL1-3701	Reflections	1980	10.00

ATKINSON, SANDY

45s

Number	Title (A Side/B Side)	Yr	NM
HIT			
❑ 37	Mama Sang a Song/Big Girls Don't Cry	1962	8.00
—B-side by the Chellows			

ATLANTA DISCO BAND, THE

45s

Number	Title (A Side/B Side)	Yr	NM
ARIOLA AMERICA			
❑ 7611	Bad Luck/Ole Goat	1975	5.00
❑ 7615	Do What You Feel/I Am Trying	1976	5.00
SCORPIO			
❑ 5000	Bad Luck/Ole Goat	1975	7.00

Albums

Number	Title (A Side/B Side)	Yr	NM
ARIOLA AMERICA			
❑ SW-50004	Bad Luck	1975	10.00

ATLANTA RHYTHM SECTION
Formed by ex-members of THE CANDYMEN and CLASSICS IV.

12-Inch Singles

Number	Title (A Side/B Side)	Yr	NM
COLUMBIA			
❑ 1271 [DJ]	Alien//Homesick/Quinella	1981	10.00
POLYDOR			
❑ PRO 121 [DJ]	Back Up Against the Wall/Doraville//Large Time/Angel (What in the World's Come Over Us)	1979	15.00
—Four-song promo-only sampler from "Are You Ready!"			

45s

Number	Title (A Side/B Side)	Yr	NM
COLUMBIA			
❑ 18-02471	Alien/Southern Exposure	1981	4.00
DECCA			
❑ 32928	All in Your Mind/Can't Stand It No More	1972	8.00
❑ 32948	Earnestine/Another Man's Woman	1972	8.00
❑ 33051	Back Up Against the Wall/It Must Be Done	1973	8.00
MCA			
❑ 40059	Cold Turkey, Tennessee/Conversation	1973	6.00
❑ 40719	All in Your Mind/Earnestine	1977	5.00
POLYDOR			
❑ 2001	Spooky/It's Only Music	1979	4.00
❑ 2039	Back Up Against the Wall/Large Time	1980	4.00
❑ 2079	Conversation/Indigo Passion	1980	4.00
❑ 2125	Putting My Faith in Love/I Ain't Much	1980	4.00
❑ 2142	Silver Eagle/Strictly R & R	1981	4.00
❑ 14248	Doraville/Who Are You Going to Run To	1974	4.00
❑ 14262	Angel (What in the World's Come Over Us)/Help Yourself	1975	4.00
❑ 14273	Get Your Head Out of Your Heart/Jesus Hearted People	1975	4.00
❑ 14289	Bless My Soul/Crazy	1975	4.00
❑ 14323	Jukin'/Beautiful Dreamer	1976	4.00
❑ 14339	Free Spirit/Police Police	1976	4.00
❑ 14373	So In to You/Everybody Gotta Go	1977	4.00
❑ 14397	Neon Nites/Don't Miss the Message	1977	4.00
❑ 14411	Dog Days/Cuban Crisis	1977	4.00
❑ 14459	Imaginary Lover/Silent Treatment	1978	4.00
❑ 14484	I'm Not Gonna Let It Bother Me Tonight/Ballad of Lois Malone	1978	4.00
❑ 14504	Champagne Jam/Great Escape	1978	4.00
❑ 14568	Do It or Die/My Song	1979	4.00
❑ 14582	Spooky/It's Only Music	1979	4.00
—Unreleased?			

Albums

Number	Title (A Side/B Side)	Yr	NM
COLUMBIA			
❑ FC 37550	Quinella	1981	10.00
❑ PC 37550	Quinella	1982	8.00
—Budget-line reissue			
DECCA			
❑ DL 75265	Atlanta Rhythm Section	1972	25.00
❑ DL 75390	Back Up Against the Wall	1973	25.00
MCA			
❑ 2-4114 [(2)]	Atlanta Rhythm Section	1977	12.00
—Combines the two Decca LPs into one package			
MOBILE FIDELITY			
❑ 1-038	Champagne Jam	1981	40.00
—Audiophile vinyl			
POLYDOR			
❑ PD 6027	Third Annual Pipe Dream	1974	10.00
❑ PD 6041	Dog Days	1975	10.00
❑ PD-1-6060	Red Tape	1976	10.00
❑ PD-1-6080	A Rock and Roll Alternative	1977	10.00
❑ PD-1-6134	Champagne Jam	1978	10.00
❑ PD-1-6200	Underdog	1979	10.00
❑ PD-2-6236 [(2)]	Are You Ready!	1979	12.00
❑ PD-1-6285	The Boys from Doraville	1980	10.00

ATLANTIC SOUNDS, THE

45s

Number	Title (A Side/B Side)	Yr	NM
ATLANTIC			
❑ 2468	Blast Off/Pata Pata	1967	30.00
❑ 2492	I Gotta Keep On Gwine/L. David Sloane	1968	12.00

ATLANTICS, THE
More than one group.

45s

Number	Title (A Side/B Side)	Yr	NM
COLUMBIA			
❑ 42877	Greensleeves/Bombera	1963	20.00
❑ 43023	War of the World/Bow Man	1964	20.00
FARO			
❑ 613	Flame of Love/Tracy	1964	15.00
—B-side by Barry White			
LINDA			
❑ 103	Boo-Hoo-Hoo/Everything Is Gonna Be All Right	1961	25.00
❑ 107	Remember the Night/Flame of Love	1962	80.00
RAMPART			
❑ 614	Let Me Call You Sweetheart/Home on the Range	1964	12.00
❑ 643	Beaver Shot/Fine, Fine, Fine	1965	10.00
❑ 647	Slopp Dance/Sonny and Cher	1965	10.00

ATOMIC ROOSTER

45s

Number	Title (A Side/B Side)	Yr	NM
ELEKTRA			
❑ 45727	Tomorrow Night/Play the Game	1971	5.00
❑ 45745	Devil's Answer/The Rock	1971	5.00
❑ 45766	Save Me/Never to Lose	1972	5.00
❑ 45800	Stand By Me/Never to Lose	1972	5.00

Albums

Number	Title (A Side/B Side)	Yr	NM
ELEKTRA			
❑ EKS-74094	Death Walks Behind You	1971	20.00
❑ EKS-74109	In Hearing Of Atomic Rooster	1971	20.00
❑ EKS-75039	Made in England	1972	20.00
❑ EKS-75074	Atomic Rooster IV	1973	15.00

ATTILA
BILLY JOEL was a member.

Albums

Number	Title (A Side/B Side)	Yr	NM
BACK-TRAC			
❑ P 18808	Attila	1985	10.00
EPIC			
❑ E 30030	Attila	1970	30.00

ATTITUDES

45s

Number	Title (A Side/B Side)	Yr	NM
DARK HORSE			
❑ 8404	Sweet Summer Music/If We Want To	1977	4.00
❑ 8452	Good News/In a Stranger's Arms	1977	4.00
❑ 10004	Ain't Love Enough/The Whole World's Crazy	1975	5.00
❑ 10004 [PS]	Ain't Love Enough/The Whole World's Crazy	1975	12.00
❑ 10008	Lend a Hand/Honey Don't Leave L.A.	1976	5.00
❑ 10011	Sweet Summer Music/If We Want To	1976	5.00

Albums

Number	Title (A Side/B Side)	Yr	NM
DARK HORSE			
❑ DH 3021	Good News	1977	10.00
❑ SP-22008	Attitudes	1976	12.00

ATTRACTIONS, THE

45s

Number	Title (A Side/B Side)	Yr	NM
BELL			
❑ 659	Destination You/Find Me	1967	20.00
❑ 674	New Girl in the Neighborhood/That Girl Is Mine	1967	20.00
❑ 690	Why Shouldn't a Man Cry/Some of Your Time	1967	20.00
JUNE BUG			
❑ 697/8	You Don't Know, Boy/Think Back	1966	25.00

ATWELL, WINIFRED

45s

Number	Title (A Side/B Side)	Yr	NM
COLUMBIA			
❑ 43472	Snow Bells/Flea Circus	1965	6.00

ATWOOD THE ELECTRIC ICEMAN
Actually the SIR DOUGLAS QUINTET with Atwood Allen.

45s

Number	Title (A Side/B Side)	Yr	NM
UNI			
❑ 55216	Bossier City/Michoacan	1970	6.00

AUDIENCE

45s

Number	Title (A Side/B Side)	Yr	NM
ELEKTRA			
❑ 45732	Indian Summer/It Brings a Tear	1971	5.00
❑ 45756	I Put a Spell on You/Nancy	1971	5.00
❑ 45788	Stand By the Door/Seven Sore Bruises	1972	5.00

Albums

Number	Title (A Side/B Side)	Yr	NM
ELEKTRA			
❑ EKS-74100	House on the Hill	1971	16.00
❑ EKS-75026	Lunch	1972	16.00

AUDIO TWO

12-Inch Singles

Number	Title (A Side/B Side)	Yr	NM
FIRST PRIORITY			
❑ 3205	On the Road Again/Get Your Mother Off	1990	40.00

Albums

Number	Title (A Side/B Side)	Yr	NM
FIRST PRIORITY			
❑ 90907	What More Can I Say?	1988	80.00
❑ 91358	I Don't Care — The Album	1990	80.00

A

AUDREY

45s

PLUS

Number	Title (A Side/B Side)	Yr	NM
❑ 104	Dear Elvis/Dear Elvis (Part 2)	1956	80.00

—Black vinyl; a red vinyl pressing has been reported but is unconfirmed

AUGER, BRIAN, TRINITY

Includes "Brian Auger's Oblivion Express."

45s

ATCO

Number	Title (A Side/B Side)	Yr	NM
❑ 6593	This Wheel's On Fire/ A Kind of Love-In	1968	8.00

—With Julie Driscoll

Number	Title (A Side/B Side)	Yr	NM
❑ 6611	Black Cat/In and Out	1968	8.00
❑ 6629	Shadows of You/Road to Cairo	1968	8.00

—With Julie Driscoll

Number	Title (A Side/B Side)	Yr	NM
❑ 6656	A Day in the Life/ Bumpin' On Sunset	1969	8.00
❑ 6685	Save the Country/Light My Fire	1969	8.00
❑ 6685	Save the Country/The Flesh Failures (Let the Sun Shine In)	1969	8.00
❑ 6685 [DJ]	Save the Country (long/short versions)	1969	12.00

RCA VICTOR

Number	Title (A Side/B Side)	Yr	NM
❑ 74-0381	I Wanna Take You Higher/ Listen Here	1970	6.00
❑ 74-0579	Maria's Wedding/Trouble	1971	5.00

—Group becomes "Oblivion Express"

Number	Title (A Side/B Side)	Yr	NM
❑ 74-0735	Second Wind/ Freedom Jazz Dance	1972	5.00
❑ APBO-0085	Happiness Is Just Around the Bend/Inner City Blues	1973	5.00
❑ APBO-0282	Straight Ahead/Beginning Again	1974	5.00

Albums

ATCO

Number	Title (A Side/B Side)	Yr	NM
❑ 33-258 [M]	Open	1968	20.00

—White label promo; no stock copies were issued in mono

Number	Title (A Side/B Side)	Yr	NM
❑ SD 33-258 [S]	Open	1968	12.00
❑ SD 33-273	Definitely What!	1969	12.00
❑ SD 2-701 [(2)]	Streetnoise	1969	20.00

CAPITOL

Number	Title (A Side/B Side)	Yr	NM
❑ DT-136 [R]	Jools & Brian	1969	12.00

—American issue of pre-Atco material

HEADFIRST

Number	Title (A Side/B Side)	Yr	NM
❑ 9702	Search Party	1981	15.00

POLYDOR

Number	Title (A Side/B Side)	Yr	NM
❑ PD-1-6505	Genesis	1975	12.00

RCA VICTOR

Number	Title (A Side/B Side)	Yr	NM
❑ AFL1-0140	Closer To It	197?	8.00

—Reissue

Number	Title (A Side/B Side)	Yr	NM
❑ APL1-0140	Closer To It	1973	10.00
❑ AFL1-0454	Straight Ahead	197?	8.00

—Reissue

Number	Title (A Side/B Side)	Yr	NM
❑ CPL1-0454	Straight Ahead	1974	10.00
❑ CPL1-0645	Live Oblivion	1974	10.00
❑ APL1-1210	Reinforcements	1975	10.00
❑ CPL2-1230 [(2)]	Live Oblivion, Vol. 2	1976	15.00
❑ AFL1-2249	The Best of Brian Auger	1977	10.00
❑ ANL1-2481	Live Oblivion	1977	8.00

—Reissue

Number	Title (A Side/B Side)	Yr	NM
❑ LSP-4372	Befour	1970	10.00
❑ AFL1-4462	Brian Auger's Oblivion Express	197?	8.00

—Reissue

Number	Title (A Side/B Side)	Yr	NM
❑ LSP-4462	Brian Auger's Oblivion Express	1971	10.00

—Starting here, group is "Oblivion Express"

Number	Title (A Side/B Side)	Yr	NM
❑ LSP-4540	A Better Land	1971	10.00
❑ AFL1-4703	Second Wind	197?	8.00

—Reissue

Number	Title (A Side/B Side)	Yr	NM
❑ LSP-4703	Second Wind	1972	10.00

SPRINGBOARD

Number	Title (A Side/B Side)	Yr	NM
❑ SPB-4044	Brian Auger	1973	8.00

—Reissue of early material

WARNER BROS.

Number	Title (A Side/B Side)	Yr	NM
❑ BS 2981	Happiness Heartaches	1977	10.00
❑ BSK 3153	Encore	1978	10.00

AUGUST, JAN

45s

MERCURY

Number	Title (A Side/B Side)	Yr	NM
❑ 1245-X45	The Christmas Song/White Christmas	195?	12.00
❑ 5106-X45	Intermezzo/Oye Negra	1950	15.00

—78 originally issued in 1948

Number	Title (A Side/B Side)	Yr	NM
❑ 5395-X45	Besame Mucho/Jan's Jam	1950	12.00

—Note: Earlier 5000-series 45s by Jan August, other than those listed, may exist

Number	Title (A Side/B Side)	Yr	NM
❑ 5399-X45	Bewitched/Blue Prelude	1950	12.00

—With Jerry Murad's Harmonicats

Number	Title (A Side/B Side)	Yr	NM
❑ 5400-X45	The Old Piano Roll Blues/Spain	1950	12.00
❑ 5423-X45	A Day at the Seashore/ Egyptian Ella	1950	12.00
❑ 5470-X45	Clair de Lune/Scheherazade	1950	12.00
❑ 5478-X45	You've Got Me Crying Again/ My Silent Love	1950	12.00
❑ 5483-X45	Deep Night/Where Do I Go from Here	1950	12.00
❑ 5497-X45	Little Gray Home/Down by the Old Mill Stream/Meet Me Tonight in Dreamland	1950	12.00
❑ 5556-X45	Babalu/Tango of Roses	1950	12.00
❑ 5589-X45	Perfidia/Jan's Cucaracha	1951	12.00
❑ 5654-X45	Dizzy Fingers/Two Lonely Hearts	1951	12.00
❑ 5723-X45	San Antonio Rose/Oriental Blues	1951	12.00
❑ 5781-X45	Ma Belle/Hot Lips	1952	12.00
❑ 5859-X45	Delicado/Just One of Those Things	1952	12.00
❑ 5900-X45	Meet Mister Callaghan/ Wish You Were Here	1952	12.00

—With Jerry Murad's Harmonicats

Number	Title (A Side/B Side)	Yr	NM
❑ 30000-X45	Malaguena/Miserlou	1957	8.00

—"Celebrity Series" reissue

Number	Title (A Side/B Side)	Yr	NM
❑ 30001-X45	Where or When/Jalousie	1957	8.00

—"Celebrity Series" reissue

Number	Title (A Side/B Side)	Yr	NM
❑ 30002-X45	Scheherazade/Clair de Lune	1957	8.00

—"Celebrity Series" reissue

Number	Title (A Side/B Side)	Yr	NM
❑ 30003-X45	Intermezzo/Oye Negra	1957	8.00
❑ 70056-X45	Ti-Pi-Tin/Finesse	1953	10.00
❑ 70078-X45	Song of Lola/Habanera	1953	10.00
❑ 70144-X45	Rhumba Bells/Jamboree	1953	10.00
❑ 70206-X45	Night and Day/ Dancing in the Dark	1953	10.00
❑ 70228-X45	Cow Cow Blues/Martha	1953	10.00
❑ 70250-X45	Petite Ballerina/Prince Igor	1953	10.00
❑ 70320-X45	Esplanada/Silhouettes	1954	10.00
❑ 70357-X45	Circle in the Square/Nobody Wants to Go Home	1954	10.00
❑ 70498-X45	Mambo Is In the Air/ The Love Nest	1954	10.00
❑ 70541-X45	The Crazy Julius (Part 1)/ (Part 2)	1955	10.00
❑ 70608-X45	Naughty Ghost/Chiqui Chiqui	1955	10.00
❑ 70711-X45	Bach Mambo/Minuet in Mambo	1955	10.00
❑ 70726-X45	I Never Knew/Skater's Waltz	1955	10.00
❑ 70875-X45	Dominique/Lovers and Lollipops	1956	8.00
❑ 71012-X45	Desert Sunrise/ Nickelodeon Tango	1956	8.00
❑ 71211-X45	The Twilight Theme/ Somehow You Know	1957	8.00
❑ 71743	What Is This Thing Called Love/ Me and My Shadow	1960	8.00
❑ 71964	Canadian Capers/ The Volga Boat Man	1962	7.00

7-Inch Extended Plays

MERCURY

Number	Title (A Side/B Side)	Yr	NM
❑ SR-610-C	Flight of the Bumble Bee/Clair De Lune/Humoresque// Fantasy Impromptu/Minuet (in G)/Moonlight Sonata	196?	10.00

—Jukebox issue; small hole, plays at 33 1/3 rpm

Number	Title (A Side/B Side)	Yr	NM
❑ SR-610-C [PS]	Jan August Styles the Great Pop Piano Classics	196?	10.00
❑ EP-1-3005	(contents unknown)	195?	8.00
❑ EP-1-3005 [PS]	Piano Poetry	195?	8.00
❑ EP-1-3017	Misirlou/Oye Negra// Malaguena/Jalousie	195?	8.00
❑ EP-1-3017 [PS]	Piano Rhythm	195?	8.00
❑ EP-1-3022	Dancing in the Dark/September Song//Nola/Night and Day	195?	8.00
❑ EP-1-3022 [PS]	More Favorites	195?	8.00
❑ EP-1-3027	(contents unknown)	195?	8.00
❑ EP-1-3027 [PS]	Exotic Piano Rhythms	195?	8.00
❑ EP-1-3064	Dark Eyes/Intermezzo// Zigeuner/Hungarian Rhapsody	195?	8.00
❑ EP-1-3064 [PS]	Dark Eyes	195?	8.00

Albums

MERCURY

Number	Title (A Side/B Side)	Yr	NM
❑ MG 20072 [M]	Jan August Plays Songs to Remember	1955	25.00
❑ MG 20078 [M]	Music for the Quiet Hour	1955	25.00
❑ MG 20147 [M]	Piano Roll Blues	1955	25.00
❑ MG 20160 [M]	Christmas Favorites	1955	25.00
❑ MG 20272 [M]	Cocktails and Conversation	195?	20.00
❑ MG 20273 [M]	Keyboard Waltzes	195?	20.00
❑ MG 20274 [M]	Latin Rhythms	195?	20.00
❑ MG 20408 [M]	Cha Cha Charm	1959	15.00
❑ MG 20513 [M]	Jan August Plays Great Piano Hits	195?	15.00
❑ MG 20618 [M]	Accent!	1961	15.00
❑ MG 20659 [M]	Jan August Styles the Great Pop Piano Classics	196?	15.00
❑ MG 20667 [M]	Jan August Styles the Great International Hits	196?	15.00
❑ MG 20744 [M]	Jan August Plays a Collection of 27 Popular Classical Melodies	196?	15.00
❑ MG 25087 [10]	Piano Favorites	195?	30.00
❑ MG 25136 [10]	Piano Poetry	195?	30.00
❑ SR 60082 [S]	Cha Cha Charm	1959	20.00
❑ SR 60189 [S]	Jan August Plays Great Piano Hits	195?	20.00
❑ SR 60618 [S]	Accent!	1961	20.00
❑ SR 60659 [S]	Jan August Styles the Great Pop Piano Classics	196?	20.00
❑ SR 60667 [S]	Jan August Styles the Great International Hits	196?	20.00
❑ SR 60744 [S]	Jan August Plays a Collection of 27 Popular Classical Melodies	196?	20.00

WING

Number	Title (A Side/B Side)	Yr	NM
❑ MGW 12129 [M]	Music for the Quiet Hour	196?	12.00
❑ MGW 12175 [M]	Christmas Favorites	196?	12.00
❑ MGW 12254 [M]	The Piano Wizardry of Jan August	196?	12.00
❑ SRW 16129 [R]	Music for the Quiet Hour	196?	10.00
❑ SRW 16254 [R]	The Piano Wizardry of Jan August	196?	10.00

AUGUST AND DENEEN

45s

ABC

Number	Title (A Side/B Side)	Yr	NM
❑ 11082	We Go Together/Can't Get You Out of My Head	1968	60.00

AUM

Albums

FILLMORE

Number	Title (A Side/B Side)	Yr	NM
❑ Z 30002	Resurrection	1970	30.00

SIRE

Number	Title (A Side/B Side)	Yr	NM
❑ SES-97007	Bluesvibes	1969	50.00

AUSTIN, BILL

45s

HIT

Number	Title (A Side/B Side)	Yr	NM
❑ 05	Shout/Dr. Feelgood	1962	8.00

—B-side by Jim Porter

Number	Title (A Side/B Side)	Yr	NM
❑ 06	Dear One/If a Woman Answers	1962	8.00
❑ 11	Shout! Shout! (Knock Yourself Out)/Hide 'Nor Hair	1962	8.00

—B-side by Herbert Hunter

Number	Title (A Side/B Side)	Yr	NM
❑ 82	You Can Never Stop Me Loving You/Blue Velvet	1963	8.00

—B-side by Fred York

Number	Title (A Side/B Side)	Yr	NM
❑ 105	You Don't Know Me/ Talking About My Baby	1964	8.00

—B-side by Harvey Frolic

AUSTIN, DONALD

45s

EASTBOUND

Number	Title (A Side/B Side)	Yr	NM
❑ 603	Crazy Legs/Nan Zee	1973	8.00
❑ 608	Sex Plot/Can't Understand the Strain	1973	8.00

Albums

EASTBOUND

Number	Title (A Side/B Side)	Yr	NM
❑ EB-9005	Crazy Legs	1973	30.00

AUSTIN, GENE

45s

FRATERNITY

Number	Title (A Side/B Side)	Yr	NM
❑ 779	My Blue Heaven/Lonesome Road	1957	10.00

RCA VICTOR

Number	Title (A Side/B Side)	Yr	NM
❑ 47-6880	Too Late/That's Love	1957	12.00
❑ 47-6880 [PS]	Too Late/That's Love	1957	20.00
❑ 47-6969	I Could Write a Book/ A Porter's Love Song to a Chambermaid	1957	10.00
❑ 47-7117	I'm Not the Braggin' Kind/Wonder	1957	10.00

7-Inch Extended Plays

RCA VICTOR

Number	Title (A Side/B Side)	Yr	NM
❑ EPA-4057	(contents unknown)	1957	12.00
❑ EPA-4057 [PS]	The Gene Austin Story	1957	12.00

Albums

DECCA

Number	Title (A Side/B Side)	Yr	NM
❑ DL 8433 [M]	My Blue Heaven	1957	40.00

DOT

Number	Title (A Side/B Side)	Yr	NM
❑ DLP 3300 [M]	Great Hits	1960	20.00
❑ DLP 25300 [S]	Great Hits	1960	25.00

FRATERNITY

Number	Title (A Side/B Side)	Yr	NM
❑ F-1006 [M]	Gene Austin and His Lonesome Road	1957	20.00

RCA VICTOR

Number	Title (A Side/B Side)	Yr	NM
❑ LPM-1549 [M]	Restless Heart	1957	40.00
❑ LPM-2490 [M]	My Blue Heaven	1961	25.00
❑ LPM-3200 [10]	My Blue Heaven	1953	60.00
❑ VPM-6065 [(2)]	This Is Gene Austin	1972	20.00

Except when noted otherwise, VG = 25% of NM, and VG+ = 50% of NM. (Example: VG = $2.00, VG+ = $4.00 and NM = $8.00.)

AUSTIN, PATTI

12-Inch Singles

Number	Title (A Side/B Side)	Yr	NM
CTI			
OJL-4	Love Me by Name (same om both sides?)	1979	15.00
GRP			
4010	Through the Test of Time (4 versions)	1990	8.00
4013	Soldier Boy (3 versions)	1991	8.00
4019	Reach (7:41) (3:48) (9:48)	1992	6.00
QWEST			
PRO-A-2076 [DJ]	It's Gonna Be Special (Dance Remix 6:30)/(Single Edit 4:14)	1984	8.00
PRO-A-2144 [DJ]	Rhythm of the Street (Edit) (LP Version)	1984	6.00
PRO-A-2339 [DJ]	The Heat of Heat (Edit) (LP Version)	1986	6.00
PRO-A-2516 [DJ]	Gettin' Away with Murder (Edit) (LP Version)	1986	10.00
PRO-A-3271 [DJ]	Smoke Gets in Your Eyes (same on both sides?)	1988	10.00
20222	Rhythm of the Street (6:09)/It's Gonna Be Special (6:30)	1984	8.00
20235	Shoot the Moon/Rhythm of the Street	1984	8.00
20361	Honey for the Bees (2 versions) Hot! In the Flames of Love	1985	8.00
20462	The Heat of Heat (4 versions)	1986	6.00

45s

Number	Title (A Side/B Side)	Yr	NM
ABC			
11104	Music to My Heart/Love 'Em and Leave 'Em Kind of Love	1968	15.00
COLUMBIA			
45337	Are We Ready for Love/Now That I Know What Loneliness Is	1971	5.00
45410	Black California/All Good Gifts-Day by Day	1971	5.00
45499	God Only Knows/Can't Forget the One I Love	1971	5.00
45592	Day by Day/Didn't Say a Word	1972	5.00
45785	Come to Him/Turn On the Music	1973	5.00
45906	Being with You/Take a Closer Look	1973	5.00
CORAL			
62455	He's Good Enough for Me/Earl	1965	20.00
62471	I Wanna Be Loved/A Most Unusual Boy	1965	20.00
62478	Someone's Gonna Cry/You'd Better Know What You're Getting	1966	100.00
62491	Take Your Time/Take Away the Pain Stain	1966	20.00
62500	Leave a Little Love/My Lovelight Ain't Gonna Shine	1966	20.00
62511	Got to Check You Out/What a Difference a Day Makes	1967	20.00
62518	Only All the Time/Oh How I Need You Joe	1967	20.00
62541	I'll Keep Loving You/You're Too Much a Part of Me	1967	20.00
62548	(I've Given) All My Love/Why Can't We Try It Again	1968	20.00
CTI			
7	In My Life (Part 1)/In My Life (Part 2)	1973	5.00
—With Jerry Butler			
33	Say You Love Me/In My Life	1976	4.00
41	We're in Love/Golden Oldies	1977	4.00
51	Love Me by Name/You Fooled Me	1978	4.00
59	What's at the End of the Rainbow/In My Life	1978	4.00
9600	Body Language/People in Love	1980	4.00
9601	I Want You Tonight/Love Me Again	1980	4.00
QWEST			
27718	Smoke Gets In Your Eyes/How Long Has This Been Goin' On?	1988	3.00
27718 [PS]	Smoke Gets In Your Eyes/How Long Has This Been Goin' On?	1988	3.00
28573	Only a Breath Away/Summer Is the Coldest Time of Year	1986	3.00
28659	Gettin' Away with Murder/Anything Can Happen Here	1986	3.00
28788	The Heat of Heat/Hot in the Flames of Love	1986	3.00
28935	Honey for the Bees/Hot in the Flames of Love	1985	3.00
29136	All Behind Us Now/Fine Fine Fella (Got to Have You)	1984	4.00
29234	Shoot the Moon/Change Your Attitude	1984	4.00
29305	Rhythm of the Street/Solero	1984	4.00
29373	It's Gonna Be Special/Solero	1984	4.00
29618	How Do You Keep the Music Playing/same (Long Version)	1983	4.00
—With James Ingram			
29727	Every Home Should Have One/Solero	1983	4.00
49754	Do You Love Me/Solero	1981	4.00
49854	Every Home Should Have One/Solero	1981	5.00
50036	Baby, Come to Me/Solero	1982	4.00
—With James Ingram			
UNITED ARTISTS			
50520	The Family Tree/Magical Boy	1969	8.00
50588	I Will Wait for You/Big Mouth	1969	8.00
50640	Your Love Made a Difference in Me/It's Easier to Laugh Than Cry	1970	8.00

Albums

Number	Title	Yr	NM
CTI			
5001	End of a Rainbow	1976	10.00
5006	Havana Candy	1977	10.00
7086	Live at the Bottom Line	1979	10.00
JZ 36503	Body Language	1980	10.00
PZ 36503	Body Language	198?	8.00
—Budget-line reissue			
GRP			
GR-9603	Love Is Gonna Getcha	1990	10.00
QWEST			
QWS 3591	Every Home Should Have One	1981	8.00
23974	Patti Austin	1984	8.00
25276	Gettin' Away with Murder	1985	8.00
25698	The Real Me	1988	8.00

AUSTIN, SIL

45s

Number	Title (A Side/B Side)	Yr	NM
JERRI			
104	Disco Lady/Disco Music	197?	6.00
JUBILEE			
5153	Stagecoach/Volleyball	1954	15.00
5162	Shuffle Board/Sil's Loose	1954	15.00
5178	Crossfire (Part 1)/(Part 2)	1955	15.00
MERCURY			
30080-X45	Danny Boy/The Hungry Eye	196?	8.00
—"Celebrity Series" reissue			
70963-X45	Slow Walk/Wildwood	1956	15.00
71027-X45	Birthday Party/The Last Time	1957	15.00
71077-X45	Seven Days in Barcelona/Pretend	1957	15.00
71115-X45	He's a Real Gone Guy/Dues Day	1957	15.00
71196-X45	Fall Out/Green Blazer	1957	15.00
71305-X45	Hey Eula/Rainstorm	1958	12.00
71361-X45	Riff Raff/The Chamber	1958	12.00
71408-X45	Applesauce/Vernice Cha Cha	1958	12.00
71442-X45	Danny Boy/Hungry Eye	1959	12.00
71496-X45	Summertime/Ruby	1959	12.00
71543-X45	September Song/Gone Again	1959	12.00
71578	One More Time/Satisfied, Satisfied	1960	10.00
71627	Say Lou/Girl with a Foxy Frame	1960	10.00
71693	Why Not/When My Dreamboat Comes Home	1960	10.00
71808	The Continental Stroll (Part 1)/(Part 2)	1961	10.00
71977	Golden Twist/Tippin' In	1962	10.00
72238	Back in Your Own Back Yard/Nature Boy	1964	10.00
SEW CITY			
102	Big Boss Man/Sil's Concerto	196?	7.00
SSS INTERNATIONAL			
747	Honey/Lover's Holiday	1968	6.00
792	Massachusetts/Tara's Theme	1970	6.00
WING			
90075-X45	Titanic/Sil's Groove	1956	15.00

Albums

Number	Title	Yr	NM
MERCURY			
MG-20237 [M]	Slow Walk Rock	1957	70.00
MG-20320 [M]	Everything's Shakin'	1958	70.00
MG-20424 [M]	Sil Austin Plays Pretty for the People	1959	40.00
MG-20576 [M]	Soft, Plaintive and Moody	1960	40.00
MG-20663 [M]	Golden Saxophone Hits	1961	25.00
MG-20755 [M]	Folk Songs	1963	15.00
MG-20925 [M]	Sil Austin Plays Pretty Melodies of the World	1964	20.00
MG-21126 [M]	Sil Austin Plays Pretty for the People Again	1967	20.00
SR-60096 [S]	Sil Austin Plays Pretty for the People	1959	60.00
—Black label			
SR-60096 [S]	Sil Austin Plays Pretty for the People	1965	20.00
—Red label, white "MERCURY" at top			
SR-60096 [S]	Sil Austin Plays Pretty for the People	1974	10.00
—"Chicago styline" label			
SR-60236 [S]	Soft, Plaintive and Moody	1960	60.00
SR-60663 [S]	Golden Saxophone Hits	1961	30.00
SR-60755 [S]	Folk Songs	1963	20.00
SR-60925 [S]	Sil Austin Plays Pretty Melodies of the World	1964	25.00
SR-61126 [S]	Sil Austin Plays Pretty for the People Again	1967	20.00
SSS INTERNATIONAL			
4	Honey Sax	1969	15.00
8	Soft Soul with Strings	1970	15.00
14	Sil and Silver Screen	1971	15.00
23	Songs of Gold	1971	15.00
WING			
SRW-16227 [S]	Everything's Shakin'	196?	15.00
SRW-16369 [S]	Sil Austin Again Plays Pretty for the People	196?	15.00

AUTOGRAPH

12-Inch Singles

Number	Title (A Side/B Side)	Yr	NM
RCA			
JR-13941 [DJ]	Turn Up the Radio (Radio Guitar Mix) (same on both sides)	1984	12.00
JR-14023 [DJ]	My Girlfriend's Boyfriend Isn't Me (same on both sides)	1985	10.00
JR-14062 [DJ]	Send Her to Me (same on both sides)	1985	10.00
JW-14131 [DJ]	Night Teen & Non Stop//Turn Up the Radio/Send Her to Me	1985	10.00
JR-14195 [DJ]	Blondes in Black Cars (same on both sides)	1985	8.00
JR-14279 [DJ]	That's the Stuff (same on both sides)	1986	8.00
JR-14316 [DJ]	We're An American Band (same on both sides)	1986	8.00

45s

Number	Title (A Side/B Side)	Yr	NM
RCA			
5240-1-R	She Never Looked That Good to Me/Dance All Night	1987	3.00
PB-13953	Turn Up the Radio/Thrill of Love	1984	4.00
PB-13953 [PS]	Turn Up the Radio/Thrill of Love	1984	6.00
PB-14055	Send Her to Me/All I'm Gonna Take	1985	4.00
PB-14231	Blondes in Black Cars/Built for Speed	1985	4.00
PB-14278	That's the Stuff/Six String Fever	1986	4.00

Albums

Number	Title	Yr	NM
RCA			
5796-1-R	Loud and Clear	1987	8.00
RCA VICTOR			
AFL1-5423	Sign In Please	1984	8.00
AFL1-7009	That's the Stuff	1985	8.00

AUTOSALVAGE

45s

Number	Title (A Side/B Side)	Yr	NM
RCA VICTOR			
47-9506	Parahighway/Rampant Generalities	1968	12.00

Albums

Number	Title	Yr	NM
RCA VICTOR			
LPM-3940 [M]	Autosalvage	1968	150.00
LSP-3940 [S]	Autosalvage	1968	100.00

AUTRY, GENE

45s

Number	Title (A Side/B Side)	Yr	NM
CHALLENGE			
1009	No Back Door to Heaven/You're the Only Good Thing	1957	12.00
1010	Rudolph, the Red-Nosed Reindeer/Here Come Santa Claus	1957	12.00
—Re-recordings of originals on Columbia			
59030	Rudolph, the Red-Nosed Reindeer/Here Come Santa Claus	1958	12.00
59030 [PS]	Rudolph, the Red-Nosed Reindeer/Here Come Santa Claus	1958	30.00
COLUMBIA			
4-56	Rudolph, the Red-Nosed Reindeer/If It Doesn't Snow on Christmas	1951	20.00
—Yellow label, red print; second number on label is 90049			

Gene Autry, "Poppy the Puppy," Columbia 4-122, 1952, **$25.**

Number	Title (A Side/B Side)	Yr	NM
❑ 4-56 [PS]	Rudolph, the Red-Nosed Reindeer/If It Doesn't Snow on Christmas	1951	25.00
—Sleeve was manufactured with a hole in the middle			
❑ 4-68	Peter Cottontail/ Funny Little Bunny	1950	20.00
—Yellow label, red print; second number on label is 90063			
❑ 4-68 [PS]	Peter Cottontail/ Funny Little Bunny	1950	25.00
—Sleeve was manufactured with a hole in the middle			
❑ 4-75	Frosty the Snow Man/When Santa Claus Gets Your Letter	1951	20.00
—Yellow label, red print; second number on label is 90072			
❑ 4-75 [PS]	Frosty the Snow Man/When Santa Claus Gets Your Letter	1951	25.00
—Sleeve was manufactured with a hole in the middle			
❑ 4-84	Here Comes Santa Claus/ He's a Chubby Little Fellow	1951	20.00
—Yellow label, red print; second number on label is 90088			
❑ 4-84 [PS]	Here Comes Santa Claus/He's a Chubby Little Fellow	1951	25.00
—Sleeve was manufactured with a hole in the middle			
❑ 4-103	Sonny the Bunny/ Bunny Round-Up	1952	20.00
—Yellow label, red print; second number on label is 90110			
❑ 4-121	Thirty-Two Feet — Eight Little Tails/(Hedrock, Coco and Joe) The Three Little Dwarfs	1952	20.00
—Yellow label, red print; second number on label is 90135			
❑ 4-121 [PS]	Thirty-Two Feet — Eight Little Tails/(Hedrock, Coco and Joe) The Three Little Dwarfs	1952	25.00
—Sleeve was manufactured with a hole in the middle			
❑ 4-122	Poppy the Puppy/He'll Be Coming Down the Chimney (Like He Always Did Before)	1952	20.00
—Yellow label, red print; second number on label is 90136			
❑ 4-122 [PS]	Poppy the Puppy/He'll Be Coming Down the Chimney (Like He Always Did Before)	1952	25.00
—Sleeve was manufactured with a hole in the middle			
❑ 2-127	Bible on the Table/ I Lost My Little Darlin'	1949	50.00
—Microgroove 33 1/3 rpm 7-inch single, small hole			
❑ 4-148	Smokey the Bear/ Back in the Saddle Again	1953	15.00
—Yellow label, red print; second number on label is 90168			
❑ 4-148 [PS]	Smokey the Bear/ Back in the Saddle Again	1953	20.00
—All sleeves have a hole in the middle			
❑ 4-150	Merry Texas Christmas, You All!/The Night Before Christmas (In Texas, That Is)	1953	15.00
—Yellow label, red print; second number on label is 90172			
❑ 4-150 [PS]	Merry Texas Christmas, You All!/The Night Before Christmas (In Texas, That Is)	1953	20.00
—Sleeve was manufactured with a hole in the middle			
❑ J 4-172	Where Did My Snowman Go?/ Freddie, the Little Fir Tree	1954	15.00
❑ J 4-172 [PS]	Where Did My Snowman Go?/ Freddie, the Little Fir Tree	1954	20.00
❑ 4-176	Santa Claus Is Comin' to Town/ Up on the Housetop (Ho! Ho! Ho!)	1954	15.00
—Yellow label, red print			
❑ 4-176 [PS]	Santa Claus Is Comin' to Town/ Up on the Housetop (Ho! Ho! Ho!)	1954	20.00
❑ 2-210 (?)	Ellie Mae/Sun Flower	1949	40.00
—Microgroove 33 1/3 rpm single			
❑ 2-258	My Empty Heart/I Wish I Had Stayed Over Yonder	1949	40.00
—Microgroove 33 1/3 rpm single			
❑ 4-262	Round, Round the Christmas Tree/Merry Christmas Waltz	1955	15.00
—Yellow label, red print			
❑ 4-262 [PS]	Round, Round the Christmas Tree/Merry Christmas Waltz	1955	20.00
❑ 4-293	Everyone's a Child at Christmas/You Can See Old Santa Claus	1956	15.00
—Yellow label, red print			
❑ 4-293 [PS]	Everyone's a Child at Christmas/You Can See Old Santa Claus	1956	20.00
❑ 2-336	Santa, Santa, Santa/ He's a Chubby Little Fellow	1949	40.00
—Microgroove 33 1/3 rpm single			
❑ 2-350	When the Silver Colorado Turns to Gold/Whirlwinds	1949	40.00
—Microgroove 33 1/3 rpm single			
❑ 2-370 (?)	Riders in the Sky/ Cowboy Trademarks	1949	40.00
—Microgroove 33 1/3 rpm single			
❑ 1-375	Rudolph, the Red-Nosed Reindeer/If It Doesn't Snow on Christmas	1949	40.00
—Microgroove 33 1/3 rpm single			
❑ 6-375	Rudolph, the Red-Nosed Reindeer/If It Doesn't Snow on Christmas	1950	25.00
—Reissue on 45 of a single originally on 33 1/3 Microgroove single			
❑ 2-421	Mule Train/A Cowboy's Serenade	1950	40.00
—Microgroove 33 1/3 rpm single			
❑ 2-484	Poison Ivy/A New Star Is Shining	1950	40.00
—Microgroove 33 1/3 rpm single			
❑ 2-550 (?)	Take Me Back to My Boots and Saddle/Dust	1950	40.00
—Microgroove 33 1/3 rpm single			
❑ 1-575	Peter Cottontail/Funny Little Bunny	1950	40.00
—Microgroove 33 1/3 rpm single			
❑ 1-630 (?)	Roses/The Roses I Picked for Our Wedding	1950	40.00
—Microgroove 33 1/3 rpm single			
❑ 1-741 (?)	Blue Canadian Rockies/Onteora	1950	40.00
—Microgroove 33 1/3 rpm single			
❑ 6-741 (?)	Blue Canadian Rockies/Onteora	1950	25.00
❑ 1-742	Frosty the Snow Man/When Santa Claus Gets Your Letter	1950	40.00
—Microgroove 33 1/3 rpm single			
❑ 6-742	Frosty the Snow Man/When Santa Claus Gets Your Letter	1950	20.00
❑ 1-767	Goodnight Irene/ Texans Never Cry	1950	40.00
—Microgroove 33 1/3 rpm single			
❑ 6-767	Goodnight Irene/ Texans Never Cry	1950	25.00
❑ 1-810 (?)	Little Johnny Pilgrim/ Guffy the Goofy Gobbler	1950	40.00
—Microgroove 33 1/3 rpm single			
❑ 6-810 (?)	Little Johnny Pilgrim/ Guffy the Goofy Gobbler	1950	25.00
❑ 2-901	Rose Colored Memories/Let Me Cry on Your Shoulder	1950	40.00
—Microgroove 45 1/3 rpm 7-inch single, small hole			
❑ 6-901	Rose Colored Memories/Let Me Cry on Your Shoulder	1950	30.00
—Original 45 issue of 20763			
❑ 38-06189	The Statue in the Bay/ God Bless America	1986	4.00
❑ 4-20047	You Are My Sunshine /It Makes No Difference Now	1951	25.00
—Reissue of 78 rpm single from 1948, which itself was a reissue			
❑ 4-20084	Back in the Saddle Again/ Tumbling Tumbleweeds	1951	25.00
—Reissue of 78 rpm single from 1948, which itself was a reissue			
❑ 4-20377	Here Comes Santa Claus (Down Santa Claus Lane)/ An Old-Fashioned Tree	1950	20.00
—Reissue on 45 of a single originally on 78			
❑ 20709	I Love You Because/ The Last Straw	1950	25.00
❑ 20727	That Silver Haired Daddy of Mine/Mississippi Valley Blues	1950	25.00
—Reissue of 78 rpm material			
❑ 20763	Rose Colored Memories/Let Me Cry on Your Shoulder	1950	25.00
❑ 20775	The Statue in the Bay/The Place Where I Worship	1951	20.00
❑ 20814	At Mail Call Today/I'll Be Back	1951	20.00
—Reissue of Columbia 37041 (78)			
❑ 20865	When It's Springtime in the Rockies/I Don't Want to Set the World on Fire	1951	20.00
❑ 20899	Heartsick Soldier on Heartbreak Ridge/ I'm Learning to Live	1952	15.00
❑ 20904	Am I a Pastime/I Was Just Walking Out the Door	1952	15.00
❑ 20929	Diesel Smoke, Dangerous Curves/Stop Your Gambling	1952	15.00
❑ 21035	I've Lived a Lifetime for You/ Story Book of Love	1952	15.00
❑ 21144	Love Is So Misleadin'/ Don't Send Your Love	1953	15.00
❑ 21207	Bimbo/Roly Poly	1954	15.00
❑ 21229	Angels in the Sky/ A Voice in the Choir	1954	15.00
❑ 21252	Closing the Book/My Lazy Day	1954	15.00
❑ 21269	20-20 Vision/You're the Only Good Thing	1954	15.00

Except when noted otherwise, VG = 25% of NM, and VG+ = 50% of NM. (Example: VG = $2.00, VG+ = $4.00 and NM = $8.00.)

Number	Title (A Side/B Side)	Yr	NM
❑ 21280	I'm a Fool to Care/ A Broken Promise Means a Broken Heart	1954	15.00
❑ 21304	When He Grows Tired of You/ It Just Don't Seem Like Home	1954	15.00
❑ 21329	Barney the Bashful Bullfrog/ Little Peter Pumpkin Eater	1954	15.00
❑ 21358	I'm Innocent/You're an Angel	1955	15.00
❑ 21481	You've Got to Take the Bitter with the Sweet/ Two Cheaters in Love	1956	15.00
❑ 21527	God's in the Saddle/If Today Were the End of the World	1956	15.00
❑ 33023	Back in the Saddle Again/ Tumbling Tumbleweeds	196?	8.00
—"Hall of Fame" reissue; red and black label			
❑ 13-33165	Rudolph, the Red-Nosed Reindeer/Here Comes Santa Claus	198?	3.00
—Reissue; gray label			
❑ 4-33165	Rudolph, the Red-Nosed Reindeer/Here Comes Santa Claus	1969	5.00
—"Hall of Fame" reissue; red and black label			
❑ 4-33165 [DJ]	Rudolph, the Red-Nosed Reindeer/Here Comes Santa Claus	1969	10.00
—"Promotion Copy Not for Sale" on red and black label above catalog number			
❑ 4-33165 [PS]	Rudolph, the Red-Nosed Reindeer/Here Comes Santa Claus	1969	12.00
—Possibly promo-only sleeve issued for the 20th anniversary of the original release of "Rudolph"			
❑ 38610	Rudolph, the Red-Nosed Reindeer/If It Doesn't Snow on Christmas	1951	15.00
—Second 45 issue of this song			
❑ 38907	Frosty The Snowman/When Santa Claus Gets Your Letter	1951	15.00
—Second 45 issue of this song			
❑ 3-39086	My Heart Cries for You/ Teardrops from My Eyes	1950	30.00
—Microgroove 33 1/3 rpm single			
❑ 4-39086	My Heart Cries for You/ Teardrops from My Eyes	1950	20.00
❑ 39217	Sonny the Bunny/Bunny Roundup Time	1951	20.00
❑ 39347	Crime Will Never Pay/ Gold Can Buy Anything	1951	15.00
❑ 39371	Mr. and Mississippi/ How Long Is Forever	1951	15.00
❑ 39405	Old Soldiers Never Die/ God Bless America	1951	15.00
❑ 39461	Frosty the Snow Man/An Old-Fashioned Tree	1951	12.00
❑ 39462	When Santa Claus Gets Your Letter/He's a Chubby Little Fellow	1951	12.00
❑ 39463	Rudolph, the Red-Nosed Reindeer/Here Comes Santa Claus (Down Santa Claus Lane)	1951	12.00
❑ 39464	Santa, Santa, Santa/If It Doesn't Snow on Christmas	1951	12.00
❑ 39542	Poppy the Puppy/He'll Be Coming Down the Chimney (Like He Always Did Before)	1951	15.00
❑ 39543	Thirty-Two Feet — Eight Little Tails/(Hedrock, Coco and Joe) The Three Little Dwarfs	1951	15.00
❑ 39808	Don't Believe a Word They Say/ God's Little Candles	1952	15.00
❑ 39876	The Night Before Christmas Song/Look Out the Window	1952	15.00
—With Rosemary Clooney			
❑ 40092	Where Did My Snowman Go?/ Freddie the Little Fir Tree	1953	15.00
❑ 40135	I Wish My Mom Would Marry Santa Claus/Sleigh Bells	1953	15.00
❑ 40167	Easter Morning/The Horse with the Easter Bonnet	1954	15.00
❑ 40589	Round, Round the Christmas Tree/Merry Christmas Tree	1955	15.00
❑ 40790	Everyone's a Child at Christmas/You Can See Old Santa Claus	1956	15.00
❑ 40931	Johnny Reb and Billy Yank/ Happy Little Island	1957	12.00
❑ 40960	Half Your Heart/Darlin' What More Can I Do	1957	12.00
❑ 44632	Back in the Saddle Again/ Home on the Range	1968	8.00
CRICKET			
❑ CX-6	Rudolph, the Red-Nosed Reindeer/Tinker Town Santa Claus	196?	12.00
—B-side by the Cricketones			

Number	Title (A Side/B Side)	Yr	NM
MISTLETOE			
❑ 801	Rudolph, The Red-Nosed Reindeer/Up On The House Top	196?	8.00
❑ 801 [PS]	Rudolph, The Red-Nosed Reindeer/Up On The House Top	196?	12.00
REPUBLIC			
❑ 001	Back in the Saddle Again/ The Last Round-Up	1977	5.00
❑ 326	Rudolph the Red-Nosed Reindeer/Here Comes Santa Claus	1976	4.00
❑ 1405	Rudolph the Red-Nosed Reindeer/Here Comes Santa Claus	1969	8.00
❑ 2001	Nine Little Reindeer/Buon Natale (Means Merry Christmas)	1959	12.00
❑ 2001 [PS]	Nine Little Reindeer/ Buon Natale (Means Merry Christmas)	1959	12.00
❑ 2002	Santa's Comin' in a Whirlybird/ Jingle Bells	1959	12.00
7-Inch Extended Plays			
COLUMBIA			
❑ B-270 [PS]	Merry Christmas with Gene Autry	195?	25.00
—Gatefold cover for 2-EP set (5-1067 and 5-1068)			
❑ 5-1067	Frosty the Snow Man/ When Santa Claus Gets Your Letter//If It Doesn't Snow on Christmas/Here Comes Santa Claus	195?	25.00
—Alternate numbers are B-270-1 and B-270-4			
❑ 5-1068	He's a Chubby Little Fellow/ An Old Fashioned Tree// Rudolph the Red-Nosed Reindeer/Santa, Santa, Santa	195?	25.00
—Alternate numbers are B-270-2 and B-270-3			
❑ B-2612	Rudolph the Red-Nosed Reindeer/Frosty the Snow Man//When Santa Claus Gets Your Letter/Here Come Santa Claus (Down Santa Claus Lane)	195?	20.00
❑ B-2612 [PS]	Children's Christmas (Hall of Fame Series)	195?	20.00
❑ B-2806	Mexicali Rose/Tumbling Tumbleweeds//Back in the Saddle Again/You Are My Sunshine	195?	20.00
❑ B-2806 [PS]	Gene Autry (Hall of Fame Series)	195?	20.00
Albums			
CBS SPECIAL PRODUCTS			
❑ P 18737	Golden Hits	1985	10.00
❑ P 18963	His Golden Hits	1985	10.00
❑ P 18964	Famous Favorites	1985	10.00
CHALLENGE			
❑ CHL-600 [M]	Christmas with Gene Autry	1958	50.00
COLUMBIA			
❑ CL (# unk) [10]	Easter Favorites	1949	150.00
❑ CL 677 [M]	Gene Autry and Champion — Western Adventures	1955	120.00
❑ CS 1035	Gene Autry's Country Music Hall of Fame Album	1970	15.00
❑ CL 1575 [M]	Gene Autry's Greatest Hits	1961	30.00
—Red and black label with six "eye" logos			
❑ CL 2547 [10]	Merry Christmas with Gene Autry	1954	120.00
—"House Party Series" release			
❑ CL 2568 [10]	Easter Favorites	1955	120.00
—"House Party Series" issue			
❑ CL 6020 [10]	Gene Autry's Western Classics	1949	150.00
❑ CL 6137 [10]	Merry Christmas	1950	150.00
❑ JL 8001 [10]	Gene Autry at the Rodeo	1949	150.00
❑ JL 8009 [10]	Stampede	1949	150.00
❑ JL 8012 [10]	Champion	1950	150.00
❑ HL 9001 [10]	Gene Autry's Western Classics, Vol. 1	1949	150.00
❑ HL 9002 [10]	Gene Autry's Western Classics, Vol. 2	1949	150.00
COLUMBIA SPECIAL PRODUCTS			
❑ P 15766	Christmas Favorites	1981	12.00
❑ P 15767	Everyone's a Child at Christmas	1981	12.00
GRAND PRIX			
❑ KS-X11 [S]	The Original Gene Autry Sings Rudolph the Red-Nosed Reindeer and Other Christmas Favorites	1961	20.00
❑ KX-11 [M]	The Original Gene Autry Sings Rudolph the Red-Nosed Reindeer and Other Christmas Favorites	1961	15.00

Number	Title (A Side/B Side)	Yr	NM
GUSTO			
❑ 1038	Christmas Classics	1978	10.00
HARMONY			
❑ HL 7332 [M]	Gene Autry's Great Western Hits	1965	30.00
❑ HL 7376 [M]	Back in the Saddle Again	1966	20.00
❑ HL 7399 [M]	Gene Autry Sings	1966	20.00
❑ HL 9505 [M]	Gene Autry and Champion — Western Adventures	1959	30.00
❑ HL 9550 [M]	The Original Rudolph the Red-Nosed Reindeer and Other Children's Christmas Favorites	1964	25.00
❑ HS 11199 [R]	Gene Autry Sings	1966	15.00
❑ HS 11276 [R]	Back in the Saddle Again	1966	15.00
❑ HS 14450 [R]	The Original Rudolph the Red-Nosed Reindeer and Other Children's Christmas Favorites	1964	12.00
MELODY RANCH			
❑ 101 [M]	Melody Ranch	1965	40.00
MURRAY HILL			
❑ 897296 [(4)]	Melody Ranch Radio Show	197?	60.00
—Compilation of some of Gene's radio shows in a box set			
RCA VICTOR			
❑ LPM-2623 [M]	Gene Autry's Golden Hits	1962	30.00
❑ LSP-2623 [S]	Gene Autry's Golden Hits	1962	40.00
REPUBLIC			
❑ 6011	South of the Border, All American Cowboy	1976	20.00
❑ 6012	Cowboy Hall of Fame	1976	20.00
❑ RLP 6018 [M]	Christmas with Gene Autry	1976	12.00

AVALANCHES, THE

Number	Title (A Side/B Side)	Yr	NM
45s			
WARNER BROS.			
❑ 5407	Baby, It's Cold Outside/ Avalanche	1964	15.00
Albums			
WARNER BROS.			
❑ W 1525 [M]	Ski Surfin'	1963	40.00
❑ WS 1525 [S]	Ski Surfin'	1963	60.00

AVALON, FRANKIE

Number	Title (A Side/B Side)	Yr	NM
45s			
AMOS			
❑ 127	The Star/Woman Cryin'	1969	5.00
BOBCAT			
❑ 04103	Such a Miracle/You're the Miracle	1983	4.00
CHANCELLOR			
❑ 11FX 1	Christmas Holiday/ Dear Gesu Bambino	196?	20.00
❑ C-1 [DJ]	Shy Guy/Too Young to Love	1959	40.00
—Promo-only record made for "Acnecare"			
❑ 1004	Cupid/Jivin' with the Saints	1957	20.00
❑ 1006	Shy Guy/Teacher's Pet	1957	20.00
❑ 1011	Dede Dinah/Ooh La La	1958	15.00
❑ 1016	You Excite Me/Darlin'	1958	15.00
❑ 1021	Ginger Bread/Blue Betty	1958	15.00
❑ 1021 [PS]	Ginger Bread/Blue Betty	1958	40.00
❑ 1026	I'll Wait for You/What Little Girl	1958	15.00
❑ 1026 [PS]	I'll Wait for You/What Little Girl	1958	40.00
❑ 1031 [M]	Venus/I'm Broke	1959	20.00
❑ 1031 [PS]	Venus/I'm Broke	1959	40.00
❑ S-1031 [S]	Venus/I'm Broke	1959	40.00
❑ 1036 [M]	Bobby Sox to Stockings/ A Boy Without a Girl	1959	12.00
—Reissues have black labels			
❑ 1036 [M]	Bobby Sox to Stockings/ A Boy Without a Girl	1959	20.00
—Originals have pink labels			
❑ 1036 [PS]	Bobby Sox to Stockings/ A Boy Without a Girl	1959	40.00
❑ S-1036 [S]	Bobby Sox to Stockings/ A Boy Without a Girl	1959	40.00
❑ 1040 [M]	Just Ask Your Heart/Two Fools	1959	15.00
❑ 1040 [PS]	Just Ask Your Heart/Two Fools	1959	30.00
❑ S-1040 [S]	Just Ask Your Heart/Two Fools	1959	40.00
❑ 1045 [M]	Why/Swingin' on a Rainbow	1959	15.00
❑ 1045 [PS]	Why/Swingin' on a Rainbow	1959	30.00
—Blue background, different picture from Chancellor 1040			
❑ 1045 [PS]	Why/Swingin' on a Rainbow	1959	40.00
❑ 1045 [PS]	Why/Swingin' on a Rainbow	1959	40.00
—Red background, same picture as on Chancellor 1040			
❑ S-1045 [S]	Why/Swingin' on a Rainbow	1959	40.00
❑ 1048	Don't Throw Away All Those Teardrops/Talk, Talk, Talk	1960	15.00
❑ 1048 [PS]	Don't Throw Away All Those Teardrops/Talk, Talk, Talk	1960	30.00
❑ 1052	Where Are You/Tuxedo Junction	1960	15.00
❑ 1052 [PS]	Where Are You/Tuxedo Junction	1960	30.00
❑ 1056	Togetherness/Don't Let Love Pass You By	1960	15.00
❑ 1056 [PS]	Togetherness/Don't Let Love Pass You By	1960	30.00
❑ 1065	A Perfect Love/The Puppet Song	1960	15.00
❑ 1065 [PS]	A Perfect Love/The Puppet Song	1960	30.00

Except when noted otherwise, VG = 25% of NM, and VG+ = 50% of NM. (Example: VG = $2.00, VG+ = $4.00 and NM = $8.00.)

A

Number	Title (A Side/B Side)	Yr	NM
❑ 1071	All of Everything/Call Me Anytime	1961	12.00
❑ 1071 [PS]	All of Everything/Call Me Anytime	1961	25.00
❑ 1077	Who Else But You/Gotta Get a Girl	1961	12.00
❑ 1081	Voyage to the Bottom of the Sea/Summer of '61	1961	12.00
❑ 1081 [PS]	Voyage to the Bottom of the Sea/Summer of '61	1961	25.00
❑ 1087	True, True Love/Married	1961	10.00
❑ 1087 [PS]	True, True Love/Married	1961	20.00
❑ 1095	Sleeping Beauty/The Lonely Bit	1961	10.00
❑ 1095 [PS]	Sleeping Beauty/The Lonely Bit	1961	20.00
❑ 1101	After You've Gone/If You Don't Think I'm Leaving	1962	10.00
❑ 1101 [PS]	After You've Gone/If You Don't Think I'm Leaving	1962	20.00
❑ 1107	You Are Mine/Ponchinello	1962	10.00
❑ 1107	You Are Mine/Italiano	1962	12.00
❑ 1107 [PS]	You Are Mine/Ponchinello	1962	20.00
❑ 1114	Venus/I'm Broke	1962	10.00
❑ 1115	A Miracle/Don't Let Me Stand in Your Way	1962	10.00
❑ 1115 [PS]	A Miracle/Don't Let Me Stand in Your Way	1962	20.00
❑ 1125	Dance the Bossa Nova/Welcome Home	1962	10.00
❑ 1125 [PS]	Dance the Bossa Nova/Welcome Home	1962	20.00
❑ 1131	My Ex-Best Friend/First Love Never Dies	1963	10.00
❑ 1134	Come Fly with Me/Girl Back Home	1963	10.00
❑ 1135	Cleopatra/Heartbeats	1963	10.00
❑ 1139	Beach Party/Don't Stop Now	1963	15.00
DE-LITE			
❑ 907	Beauty School Dropout/Midnight Lady	1978	4.00
❑ 907 [PS]	Beauty School Dropout/Midnight Lady	1978	5.00
❑ 1578	Venus/Venus (Disco Version)	1976	4.00
❑ 1578 [PS]	Venus/Venus (Disco Version)	1976	8.00
❑ 1582	Thank You for That Extra Sunrise/It's His Game	1976	4.00
❑ 1584	It's Never Too Late/Where ILeave Off (And You Begin)	1976	4.00
❑ 1589	Midnight Lady/Does She Wonder Where I Am	1977	4.00
❑ 1591	Splish Splash/When I Said I Love You	1977	4.00
❑ 1595	Roses Grow Beyond the Wall/Midnight Lady	1977	4.00
METROMEDIA			
❑ 181	Come On Back to Me Baby/Empty	1970	5.00
❑ 192	Heart of Everything/I Want You Near Me	1970	5.00
REGALIA			
❑ 5508	I'm in the Mood for Love/It's the Same Old Dream	1972	5.00
REPRISE			
❑ 0697	Dancing on the Stars/But I Do	1968	8.00
❑ 0796	Don't You Do It/It's Over	1968	8.00
❑ 0826	For Your Love/Why Don't They Understand	1969	8.00
UNITED ARTISTS			
❑ 728	Again/Don't Make Fun of Me	1964	10.00
❑ 748	My Love Is Here to Stay/New-Fangled, Jingle-Jangle, Swimming Suit from Paris	1964	10.00
❑ 748 [PS]	My Love Is Here to Stay/New-Fangled, Jingle-Jangle, Swimming Suit from Paris	1964	20.00
❑ 800	Moon River/Every Girl Should Get Married	1964	10.00
❑ 895	There'll Be Rainbows Again/I'll Take Sweden	1965	10.00
"X"			
❑ 0006	Trumpet Sorrento/The Rock	1954	50.00
❑ 0026	Trumpet Tarantella/Dormi, Dormi	1954	50.00
7-Inch Extended Plays			
CHANCELLOR			
❑ B-5000	Shy Guy/The One I Love//Trumpet Instrumental/Undecided	1959	50.00
❑ B-5000 [PS]	The Young Frankie Avalon	1959	50.00
❑ A-5002	Too Young to Love/Into Each Life Some Rain Must Fall//Pretty Eyed Baby/I Can't Begin to Tell You	1959	50.00
❑ A-5002 [PS]	The Young Frankie Avalon	1959	50.00
"X"			
❑ EXA-20	Trumpet Taarantella/Dormi, Dormi (Sleep, My Darling)//Trumpet Sorrento/The Book	1954	50.00
❑ EXA-20 [PS]	Very Young Man with a Horn	1954	50.00
Albums			
ABC			
❑ ABCX-805 [R]	16 Greatest Hits	1974	12.00
CHANCELLOR			
❑ CHL 5001 [M]	Frankie Avalon	1958	50.00
	—Pink label		
❑ CHL 5001 [M]	Frankie Avalon	1959	40.00
	—Black label		
❑ CHL 5002 [M]	The Young Frankie Avalon	1959	40.00
	—Black label		
❑ CHL 5002 [M]	The Young Frankie Avalon	1959	50.00
	—Pink label		
❑ CHLS 5002 [S]	The Young Frankie Avalon	1959	50.00
	—Black label		
❑ CHLS 5002 [S]	The Young Frankie Avalon	1959	60.00
	—Pink label		
❑ CHLX 5004 [M]	Swingin' on a Rainbow	1959	40.00
❑ CHLXS 5004 [S]	Swingin' on a Rainbow	1959	50.00
❑ CHL 5011 [M]	Summer Scene	1960	30.00
❑ CHLS 5011 [S]	Summer Scene	1960	40.00
❑ CHL 5018 [M]	A Whole Lotta Frankie	1961	30.00
❑ CHL 5022 [M]	And Now About Mr. Avalon	1961	30.00
❑ CHLS 5022 [S]	And Now About Mr. Avalon	1961	40.00
❑ CHL 5025 [M]	Italiano	1962	30.00
❑ CHLS 5025 [S]	Italiano	1962	40.00
❑ CHL 5027 [M]	You're Mine	1962	30.00
❑ CHLS 5027 [S]	You're Mine	1962	40.00
❑ CHL 5031 [M]	Frankie Avalon's Christmas Album	1962	30.00
❑ CHLS 5031 [S]	Frankie Avalon's Christmas Album	1962	40.00
❑ CHL 5032 [M]	Cleopatra Plus 13 Other Great Hits	1963	30.00
❑ CHLS 5032 [S]	Cleopatra Plus 13 Other Great Hits	1963	40.00
❑ 69801 [M]	Young and In Love	1960	40.00
	—LP without the box		
❑ 69801 [M]	Young and In Love	1960	80.00
	—LP in felt cover and 3-D portrait, all in box		
DE-LITE			
❑ 2020	Venus	1976	15.00
❑ 9504	You're My Life	1977	15.00
EVEREST			
❑ 4187	Greatest Hits	1982	10.00
LIBERTY			
❑ LN-10193	Songs from Muscle Beach Party	1981	8.00
	—Budget-line reissue		
MCA			
❑ 27096	The Best of Frankie Avalon	1985	8.00
METROMEDIA			
❑ MD-1034	I Want You Near Me	1970	15.00
SUNSET			
❑ SUS-5244	Frankie Avalon	1969	15.00
TRIP			
❑ 1621	16 Greatest Hits of Frankie Avalon	1977	10.00
UNITED ARTISTS			
❑ UA-LA450-F	The Very Best of Frankie Avalon	1975	12.00
❑ UAL-3371 [M]	Songs from Muscle Beach Party	1964	25.00
❑ UAL-3382 [M]	Frankie Avalon's 15 Greatest Hits	1964	20.00
❑ UAS-6371 [S]	Songs from Muscle Beach Party	1964	30.00
❑ UAS-6382 [S]	Frankie Avalon's 15 Greatest Hits	1964	25.00

AVALON, FRANKIE AND FABIAN

Number	Title (A Side/B Side)	Yr	NM
Albums			
MCA			
❑ 27097	The Greatest of Frankie Avalon and Fabian	1985	10.00

AVALON, FRANKIE, AND ANNETTE FUNICELLO

Also see each artist's individual listings.

Number	Title (A Side/B Side)	Yr	NM
45s			
PACIFIC STAR			
❑ 569	(Together We Can Make a) Merry Christmas/The Night Before Christmas	1981	5.00
	—Red vinyl		
❑ 569 [PS]	(Together We Can Make a) Merry Christmas/The Night Before Christmas	1981	5.00

AVALONS, THE

Number	Title (A Side/B Side)	Yr	NM
45s			
ALADDIN			
❑ 3336	I Miss You/Love Me	1956	30.00
CASINO			
❑ 108	You Do Something to Me/You Can Count on Me	1959	200.00
DICE			
❑ 90/91	Louella/You Broke Our Hearts	1958	150.00
GROOVE			
❑ 0141	Chains Around My Heart/Och! She Flew	1956	150.00
	—Black vinyl		
❑ 0141	Chains Around My Heart/Och! She Flew	1956	500.00
	—Green vinyl		
❑ 0174	It's Funny But It's True/Sugar Sugar	1956	150.00
LOST-NITE			
❑ 215	Hearts Desire/Ebbtide	196?	5.00
	—Reissue		
NPC			
❑ 302	Begin the Beguine/Malanese	1964	25.00
ROULETTE			
❑ 4568	Is It the End/Many Things from Your Window	1964	12.00
UNART			
❑ 2007	Hearts Desire/Ebbtide	1958	120.00

AVANT-GARDE, THE

Game-show host CHUCK WOOLERY was in this group.

Number	Title (A Side/B Side)	Yr	NM
45s			
COLUMBIA			
❑ 44388	Yellow Beads/Honey and Gall	1967	8.00
❑ 44590	Naturally Stoned/Honey and Gall	1968	8.00
❑ 44701	Fly with Me/Revelations	1968	8.00
	—While not issued with a picture sleeve, some stock copies came with a lyric insert. Triple the value if this is included.		

AVANTIS, THE

Probably more than one group.

Number	Title (A Side/B Side)	Yr	NM
45s			
ARGO			
❑ 5436	Keep On Dancing/I Want to Dance	1963	15.00
ASTRA			
❑ 1006	Gypsy Surfer/Wax 'Em Down	1963	40.00
CHANCELLOR			
❑ 1144	Gypsy Surfer/Wax 'Em Down	1963	25.00
IKON			
❑ 115	Too Much/Mid-Night Blues	196?	25.00
PEPPER			
❑ 435	You Got a Funny Way/One Man's Poison	196?	12.00
REGENCY			
❑ 108	Do the Surfin' Granny/Surfin' Granny	1964	40.00
❑ 110	Phantom Surfer/Lucille	1964	40.00

AVENGERS

Number	Title (A Side/B Side)	Yr	NM
45s			
CD PRESENTS			
❑ 006	Paint It Black/Thin White Line	1983	6.00
	—Red vinyl		
❑ 006 [PS]	Paint It Black/Thin White Line	1983	6.00
DANGERHOUSE			
❑ SFD 400	We Are the One//I Believe in Me/Car Crash	1977	60.00
	—Red vinyl		
❑ SFD 400	We Are the One//I Believe in Me/Car Crash	1977	80.00
	—Black vinyl		
❑ SFD 400 [PS]	We Are the One//I Believe in Me/Car Crash	1977	60.00
	—Target cover (goes with red vinyl record)		
❑ SFD 400 [PS]	We Are the One//I Believe in Me/Car Crash	1977	80.00
	—Crucifix cover (goes with black vinyl record)		
Albums			
CD PRESENTS			
❑ 007	Avengers	1983	20.00
	—Black vinyl		
❑ 007	Avengers	1983	30.00
	—Red vinyl		
GO			
❑ 005	Avengers	1983	120.00
LOOKOUT!			
❑ 217	The Avengers Died for Your Sins	1999	10.00
WHITE NOISE			
❑ 002 [EP]	Avengers	1978	50.00

AVENGERS VI, THE

Number	Title (A Side/B Side)	Yr	NM
Albums			
MARK 56			
❑ 536	Good Humor Presents Real Cool Hits	1966	250.00
	—Custom pressing for the Good Humor ice cream company		

AVERAGE WHITE BAND

12-Inch Singles

TRACK

Number	Title (A Side/B Side)	Yr	NM
❑ 58831	The Spirit of Love (5 versions)	1988	8.00

45s

ARISTA

Number	Title (A Side/B Side)	Yr	NM
❑ 0515	Let's Go Round Again/Shine	1980	4.00
❑ 0553	For You, For Love/Whatcha 'Gonna Do for Me	1980	4.00
❑ 0580	Into the Night/(B-side unknown)	1980	4.00
❑ 0679	Easier Said Than Done/ (B-side unknown)	1982	4.00
❑ 1022	Cupid's in Fashion/ (B-side unknown)	1982	4.00

ATLANTIC

Number	Title (A Side/B Side)	Yr	NM
❑ 3044	Nothing You Can Do/I Just Can't Give You Up	1974	4.00
❑ 3229	Pick Up the Pieces/Work to Do	1974	5.00
❑ 3261	Cut the Cake/Person to Person	1975	4.00
❑ 3285	If I Ever Lose This Heaven/ High Flyin' Woman	1975	4.00
❑ 3304	School Boy Crush/ Groovin' the Night Away	1975	4.00
❑ 3354	Queen of My Soul/ Would You Stay	1976	4.00
❑ 3363	Soul Searching/ Love of Your Own	1976	4.00
❑ 3388	Cloudy/Love Your Life	1977	4.00
❑ 3402	Get It Up/Keepin' It To Myself	1977	4.00
—With Ben E. King			
❑ 3427	A Star in the Ghetto/ What Is Soul?	1977	4.00
—With Ben E. King			
❑ 3444	Fool for You Anyway/ The Message	1977	4.00
—With Ben E. King			
❑ 3481	Your Love Is a Miracle/One Look	1978	4.00
❑ 3500	Big City Lights/She's a Dream	1978	4.00
❑ 3563	Walk On By/Too Late to Cry	1979	4.00
❑ 3581	Feel No Fret/Fire Burning	1979	4.00
❑ 3614 [DJ]	When Will You Be Mine (same on both sides)	1979	4.00
—May be promo only			

MCA

Number	Title (A Side/B Side)	Yr	NM
❑ 40168	This World Has Music/ The Jugglers	1973	5.00
❑ 40196	Twilight Zone/How Can You Go Home	1974	5.00

Albums

ARISTA

Number	Title (A Side/B Side)	Yr	NM
❑ AB 9523	Shine	1980	10.00
❑ AB 9594	Cupid's in Fashion	1981	10.00

ATLANTIC

Number	Title (A Side/B Side)	Yr	NM
❑ SD 2-1002 [(2)]	Person to Person	1977	12.00
❑ QD 7308 [Q]	Average White Band	1975	20.00
❑ SD 7308	Average White Band	1974	10.00
❑ SD 18140	Cut the Cake	1975	10.00
❑ SD 18179	Soul Searching	1976	10.00
❑ SD 19105	Benny and Us	1977	10.00
—With Ben E. King			
❑ SD 19116	Average White Band	1977	8.00
—Reissue			
❑ SD 19162	Warmer Communications	1978	10.00
❑ SD 19207	Feel No Fret	1979	10.00
❑ SD 19266	Vol. VIII	1980	10.00

MCA

Number	Title (A Side/B Side)	Yr	NM
❑ 345	Show Your Hands	1973	25.00
❑ 475	Put It Where You Want It	1975	10.00
—Reissue of MCA 345			

MOBILE FIDELITY

Number	Title (A Side/B Side)	Yr	NM
❑ 1-245	Average White Band	1996	20.00
—Audiophile vinyl			

TRACK

Number	Title (A Side/B Side)	Yr	NM
❑ 58830	Aftershock	1988	10.00

AVONS, THE (1) Male vocal group.

45s

ASTRA

Number	Title (A Side/B Side)	Yr	NM
❑ 1023	Baby/Whisper (Softly)	1966	30.00
—Reissue of Hull material			

HULL

Number	Title (A Side/B Side)	Yr	NM
❑ 717	Our Love Will Never End/ I'm Sending S.O.S.	1956	50.00
—Red label			
❑ 717	Our Love Will Never End/ I'm Sending S.O.S.	1956	200.00
—Black label			
❑ 722	Baby/Bonnie	1957	150.00
❑ 726	You Are So Close to Me/ Gonna Catch You Nappin'	1958	120.00
❑ 728	What Will I Do/Please Come Back to Me	1958	120.00
❑ 731	What Love Can Do/On the Island	1958	120.00
❑ 744	Whisper (Softly)/ If I Just (Had My Way)	196?	80.00
—Brown label			
❑ 744	Whisper (Softly)/ If I Just (Had My Way)	1961	100.00
—Pink label			
❑ 744	Whisper (Softly)/ If I Just (Had My Way)	1961	100.00
—White label			
❑ 754	A Girl to Call My Own/The Grass Is Greener on the Other Side	1962	80.00
—Brown label			
❑ 754	A Girl to Call My Own/The Grass Is Greener on the Other Side	1962	150.00
—White label			

Albums

HULL

Number	Title (A Side/B Side)	Yr	NM
❑ HLP-1000 [M]	The Avons	1960	700.00

AVONS, THE (U)

45s

ABET

Number	Title (A Side/B Side)	Yr	NM
❑ 9419	Talk to Me/Got to Get Used to You	1967	8.00

EXCELLO

Number	Title (A Side/B Side)	Yr	NM
❑ 2296	Since I Met You Baby/ He's My Hero	1968	8.00

GROOVE

Number	Title (A Side/B Side)	Yr	NM
❑ 58-0022	Oh, Gee Baby/ Push a Little Harder	1963	15.00
❑ 58-0022 [PS]	Oh, Gee Baby/ Push a Little Harder	1963	30.00
❑ 58-0033	Words Written on Water/ Rolling Stone	1964	12.00
❑ 58-0039	Whatever Happened to Our Love/Tonight Kiss Your Baby Goodbye	1964	12.00

MERCURY

Number	Title (A Side/B Side)	Yr	NM
❑ 71618	We Fell in Love/Pickin' Petals	1960	15.00

REF-O-REE

Number	Title (A Side/B Side)	Yr	NM
❑ 700	Tell Me Baby/ A Sample of My Love	196?	20.00

SOUND STAGE 7

Number	Title (A Side/B Side)	Yr	NM
❑ 2561	Be Good to Your Baby/ Just As Long As I Live	1966	10.00

AWESOME DRE AND THE HARDCORE COMMITTEE

12-Inch Singles

BENTLEY

Number	Title (A Side/B Side)	Yr	NM
❑ 12000	You Can't Hold Me Back (3:45)/ Committing Rhymes (4:30)	1989	15.00

PRIORITY

Number	Title (A Side/B Side)	Yr	NM
❑ PVL 7274	Frankly Speaking (2 versions)/ Executioner Style (2 versions)	1989	10.00

Albums

BENTLEY

Number	Title (A Side/B Side)	Yr	NM
❑ 12001	You Can't Hold Me Back	1989	20.00

AXE

12-Inch Singles

ATCO

Number	Title (A Side/B Side)	Yr	NM
❑ PR 515 [DJ]	Heat in the Street (same on both sides)	1983	7.00

MCA

Number	Title (A Side/B Side)	Yr	NM
❑ L33-1863 [DJ]	Living on the Edge (same on both sides?)	1980	10.00

45s

ATCO

Number	Title (A Side/B Side)	Yr	NM
❑ 7408	Now or Never/Video Inspiration	1982	4.00
❑ 99823	I Think You'll Remember Tonight/ Let the Music Come Back	1983	4.00
❑ 99850	Heat in the Street/ (B-side unknown)	1983	5.00
❑ 99975	Rock 'n' Roll Party in the Streets/(B-side unknown)	1982	5.00

MCA

Number	Title (A Side/B Side)	Yr	NM
❑ 41073	Hang On/How Come I Love You	1979	5.00
❑ 41137	Life's Just an Illusion/How Come I Love You	1979	5.00
❑ 41229	Let Me Know/I Can't Help Myself	1980	5.00

Albums

ATCO

Number	Title (A Side/B Side)	Yr	NM
❑ SD 38-148	Offering	1982	8.00
❑ 90099	Nemesis	1983	8.00

MCA

Number	Title (A Side/B Side)	Yr	NM
❑ 3171	Axe	1979	10.00
❑ 3224	Living on the Edge	1980	10.00

AXTON, HOYT

45s

A&M

Number	Title (A Side/B Side)	Yr	NM
❑ 1437	Sweet Misery/ Less Than the Song	1973	5.00
❑ 1497	When the Morning Comes/ Billie's Theme	1974	5.00
❑ 1541	Boney Fingers/Theme from Buster and Billie	1974	5.00
❑ 1607	Boney Fingers/Life Machine	1974	5.00
❑ 1607 [PS]	Boney Fingers/Life Machine	1974	6.00
❑ 1657	Nashville/Speed Trap	1974	5.00
❑ 1683	Lion in the Winter/No No Song	1975	5.00
❑ 1713	In a Young Girl's Mind/ Southbound	1975	5.00
❑ 1811	Flash of Fire/Paid in Advance	1976	4.00
❑ 1864	Evangelina/Jealous Man	1976	5.00

BRIAR

Number	Title (A Side/B Side)	Yr	NM
❑ 100	Georgia Hoss Soldier/ Drinking Gourd	1961	15.00

CAPITOL

Number	Title (A Side/B Side)	Yr	NM
❑ 3121	Alice in Wonderland/ Have a Nice Day	1971	6.00
❑ 3167	California Women/ Ease Your Pain	1971	6.00
❑ 3259	Speed Traps/Hey, Mr. Pilot Man	1972	6.00

COLGEMS

Number	Title (A Side/B Side)	Yr	NM
❑ 66-1005	San Fernando/ Ten Thousand Sunsets	1967	10.00
❑ 66-1005 [PS]	San Fernando/ Ten Thousand Sunsets	1967	20.00

COLPIX

Number	Title (A Side/B Side)	Yr	NM
❑ 802	Soldier's Last Letter/Speed Trap	1966	10.00

COLUMBIA

Number	Title (A Side/B Side)	Yr	NM
❑ 44810	Snowblind Friend/ It's All Right Now	1969	7.00
❑ 44850	Way Before the Time of Towns/ It's All Right Now	1969	7.00

ELEKTRA

Number	Title (A Side/B Side)	Yr	NM
❑ 47133	Flo's Yellow Rose/ Lion in the Winter	1981	4.00

HORIZON

Number	Title (A Side/B Side)	Yr	NM
❑ 2	Grizzly Bear/Gypsy Woman	1963	10.00
❑ 6	The Happy Song/ We'll Sing in the Sunshine	1963	10.00
❑ 351	Greenback Dollar/ Crawdad Song	1962	15.00
❑ 360	Grizzly Bear/Gypsy Woman	1963	12.00
❑ 361	This Little Light/ Thunder 'N' Lightnin'	1963	12.00
❑ 362	One More Round/ Greenback Dollar	1963	12.00

JEREMIAH

Number	Title (A Side/B Side)	Yr	NM
❑ 1000	Della and the Dealer/ In a Young Girl's Mind	1979	4.00
❑ 1001	A Rusty Old Halo/ Gotta Keep Rollin'	1979	4.00
❑ 1003	Wild Bull Rider/Torpedo	1979	4.00
❑ 1005	Evangelina/So Hard to Give It All Up	1980	4.00
❑ 1006	Boozers Are Losers (When the Benders Don't End)/Politicians	1980	4.00
❑ 1008	Where Did the Money Go/ Smile As You Go By	1980	4.00
❑ 1011	The Devil/Jealous Man	1981	4.00
❑ 1012	Win This One/Ease Your Pain	1981	4.00
❑ 1014	She's Too Lazy to Be Crazy/ You Do Not Tango	1982	4.00
❑ 1015	There Stands the Glass/James Dean and the Junkman	1982	4.00
❑ 1016	Pistol Packin' Mama/Fearless the Wonderdog	1982	4.00
❑ 1017	Warm Stones and Wild Flowers/Don't Fence Me In	1983	4.00
❑ 1018	If You're a Cowboy/ I Collect Hearts	1983	4.00

MCA

Number	Title (A Side/B Side)	Yr	NM
❑ 40711	You're the Hangnail in My Life/ Never Been to Spain	1977	4.00
❑ 40731	Little White Moon/ Funeral of the King	1977	5.00

20TH FOX

Number	Title (A Side/B Side)	Yr	NM
❑ 6648	Five Dollar Bill/Smoky	1966	10.00

VEE JAY

Number	Title (A Side/B Side)	Yr	NM
❑ 604	L.A. Town/Double Double Dare	1964	12.00
❑ 619	Bring Your Lovin'/Tiger in the Closet	1964	12.00
❑ 659	Hush Hush Sweet Charlotte/ After You've Gone	1965	10.00

A

Number	Title (A Side/B Side)	Yr	NM
Albums			
A&M			
❑ SP-3155	Life Machine	198?	8.00
—Budget-line reissue			
❑ SP-3182	Road Songs	198?	8.00
—Budget-line reissue			
❑ SP-4376	Less Than a Song	1973	10.00
❑ SP-4402	Life Machine	1974	10.00
❑ SP-4510	Southbound	1975	10.00
❑ SP-4571	Fearless	1976	10.00
❑ SP-4669	Road Songs	1977	10.00
ACCORD			
❑ SN-7197	Heartbreak Hotel	1982	10.00
ALLEGIANCE			
❑ AV-5023	Down and Out	1984	10.00
BRYLEN			
❑ BN 4400	Double Dare	1982	12.00
CAPITOL			
❑ ST-788	Joy to the World	1971	12.00
❑ SMAS-850	Country Anthem	1971	12.00
COLUMBIA			
❑ CS 9766	My Griffin Is Gone	1969	15.00
❑ KC 33103	My Griffin Is Gone	1975	10.00
❑ PC 33103	My Griffin Is Gone	1979	8.00
—Budget-line reissue			
EXODUS			
❑ EX-301 [M]	Hoyt Axton Sings Bessie Smith	1966	20.00
❑ EXS-321 [M]	Saturday's Child	1966	20.00
—Cover says stereo, record plays mono			
HORIZON			
❑ WP-1601 [M]	The Balladeer	1962	25.00
—Black label			
❑ WP-1601 [M]	Greenback Dollar	1963	20.00
—Black label; two fewer songs than "The Balladeer"			
❑ WP-1601 [S]	The Balladeer	1962	30.00
—Same number as mono, but with blue label			
❑ WP-1601 [S]	Greenback Dollar	1963	25.00
—Blue label; two fewer songs than "The Balladeer"			
❑ SWP-1613 [S]	Thunder 'N Lightnin'	1963	30.00
❑ WP-1613 [M]	Thunder 'N Lightnin'	1963	25.00
❑ SWP-1621 [S]	Saturday's Child	1963	30.00
❑ WP-1621 [M]	Saturday's Child	1963	25.00
JEREMIAH			
❑ JH-5000	A Rusty Old Halo	1979	12.00
❑ JH-5001	Where Did the Money Go?	1980	12.00
MCA			
❑ 647	Snow Blind Friend	198?	8.00
—Budget-line reissue			
❑ 648	Free Sailin'	198?	8.00
—Budget-line reissue			
❑ 2263	Snow Blind Friend	1977	10.00
❑ 2319	Free Sailin'	1978	10.00
SURREY			
❑ S-1005 [M]	Mr. Greenback Dollar Man	1965	20.00
❑ SS-1005 [S]	Mr. Greenback Dollar Man	1965	25.00
VEE JAY			
❑ LP-1098 [M]	Hoyt Axton Explodes!	1964	25.00
❑ LPS-1098 [R]	Hoyt Axton Explodes!	1964	20.00
❑ LP-1118 [M]	The Best of Hoyt Axton	1965	20.00
❑ LPS-1118 [S]	The Best of Hoyt Axton	1965	25.00
❑ LP-1126 [M]	Greenback Dollar	1965	20.00
❑ LPS-1126 [S]	Greenback Dollar	1965	25.00
❑ LP-1127 [M]	Saturday's Child	1965	20.00
❑ LPS-1127 [S]	Saturday's Child	1965	25.00
—Reissue of Horizon 1621			
❑ LP-1128 [M]	Thunder 'N Lightnin'	1965	20.00
❑ LPS-1128 [S]	Thunder 'N Lightnin'	1965	25.00
—Reissue of Horizon 1613			
VEE JAY INTERNATIONAL			
❑ VJS-2-1005 [(2)]	Gold	1974	20.00
—Compilation of older Vee Jay material			
❑ LP-6001	Long Old Road	1977	15.00
VEE JAY/DYNASTY			
❑ VJS-7306	Bessie Smith… My Way	1974	15.00

AYALA, HANK, AND THE MATADORS

Number	Title (A Side/B Side)	Yr	NM
45s			
BACK BEAT			
❑ 530	Betty Jo/Handsome	1960	12.00
❑ 530 [PS]	Betty Jo/Handsome	1960	40.00

AYERS, ROY Includes "Roy Ayers Ubiquity."

Number	Title (A Side/B Side)	Yr	NM
12-Inch Singles			
COLUMBIA			
❑ CAS 2804 [DJ]	I'm the One (Extended Version 7:18) (Extended Radio 5:35) (Instrumental 8:23)	1987	6.00
❑ 44-05115	In the Dark (5:51)/Love Is in the Feel	1984	8.00
❑ 44-05330	Hot (6:03)/(Dub)	1985	8.00
GROOVETOWN			
❑ 64361	Naste (5 versions)	1995	6.00
ICHIBAN			
❑ 12 PO 14 [DJ]	Fast Money (same on both sides)	1989	6.00
❑ 12 PO 23 [DJ]	Suave/And Then We Were One	198?	10.00
45s			
COLUMBIA			
❑ 38-04653	In the Dark/Love Is in the Feel	1984	3.00
❑ 38-04821	Poo Poo La La/Sexy Sexy Sexy	1985	3.00
❑ 38-05613	Slip n' Slide/Can I See You	1985	3.00
❑ 38-05752	Hot/Virgo	1985	3.00
❑ 38-05874	Programmed for Love/For You	1986	3.00
ICHIBAN			
❑ 149	Fast Money/(Instrumental)	1987	4.00
❑ 157	D.C. City/(Instrumental)	1987	4.00
POLYDOR			
❑ 2020	Fever/I Wanna Feel It	1979	4.00
❑ 2037	Don't Stop the Feeling/Don't Hide Your Love	1979	4.00
❑ 2066	What You Won't Do for Love/Shack Up, Pack Up, It's Up (When I'm Gone)_	1980	4.00
❑ 2138	Rock Your Roll/Sigh & Feel the Vibration	1981	4.00
❑ 2154	Love Fantasy/Baby Bubba	1981	4.00
❑ 2185	There's a Master Plan/Land of Fruit and Honey	1981	4.00
❑ 2198	Turn Me Loose/Ooh	1982	4.00
❑ 2204	Fire Up the Funk/Let's Stay Together	1982	4.00
❑ 14078	Pretty Brown Skin/He Gives Us All His Love	1971	5.00
❑ 14111	He's a Superstar (Part 1)/He's a Superstar (Part 2)	1972	5.00
❑ 14165	Will Your Soul Be Free (Henceforth)/Rhythms of Your Mind	1973	5.00
❑ 14171	Red, Black and Green/Will Your Soul Be Free (Henceforth)	1973	5.00
❑ 14275	Magic Lady/No Question	1975	4.00
❑ 14294	Way of the World/2000 Black	1975	4.00
❑ 14316	Mystic Voyage/(B-side unknown)	1976	4.00
❑ 14337	The Golden Rod/Tongue Power	1976	4.00
❑ 14349	You and Me My Love/Hey-Uh-What You Say Come On	1976	4.00
❑ 14370	Vibrations/Domelo (Give It to Me)	1977	4.00
❑ 14379	Searching/Come Out and Play	1977	4.00
❑ 14415	Running Away/Cincinnati Growl	1977	4.00
❑ 14451	Freaky Deaky/You Came Into My Life	1978	4.00
❑ 14477	Let's Do It/Melody Maker	1978	4.00
❑ 14509	Get On Up, Get On Down/And Don't You Say No	1978	4.00
❑ 14573	Love Will Bring Us Back Together/Leo	1979	4.00
Albums			
ATLANTIC			
❑ 1488 [M]	Virgo Vibes	1967	20.00
❑ SD 1488 [S]	Virgo Vibes	1967	15.00
❑ SD 1514	Stoned Soul Picnic	1968	20.00
❑ SD 1538	Daddy Bug	1969	20.00
❑ SD 1692	Daddy Bug & Friends	1976	12.00
COLUMBIA			
❑ FC 39422	In the Dark	1984	10.00
ICHIBAN			
❑ ICH-1028	Drive	198?	10.00
❑ ICH-1040	Wake Up	198?	10.00
POLYDOR			
❑ PD 5022	He's Coming	1972	12.00
❑ PD 5045	Red, Black and Green	1973	12.00
❑ PD 6016	Virgo Red	1973	12.00
❑ PD 6032	Change Up the Groove	1974	10.00
❑ PD 6046	A Tear to a Smile	1975	10.00
❑ PD 6057	Mystic Voyage	1976	10.00
❑ PD-1-6070	Everybody Loves the Sunshine	1976	10.00
❑ PD-1-6078	Red, Black and Green	1976	10.00
—Reissue of 5045			
❑ PD-1-6091	Vibrations	1977	10.00
❑ PD-1-6108	Lifeline	1977	10.00
❑ PD-1-6126	Let's Do It	1978	10.00
❑ PD-1-6159	You Send Me	1978	10.00
❑ PD-1-6204	Fever	1979	10.00
❑ PD-1-6246	No Stranger to Love	1979	10.00
❑ PD-1-6301	Love Fantasy	1980	10.00
❑ PD-1-6327	Africa, Center of the World	1981	10.00
❑ PD-1-6348	Feeling Good	1982	10.00
UNITED ARTISTS			
❑ UAL-3325 [M]	West Coast Vibes	1964	20.00
❑ UAS-6325 [S]	West Coast Vibes	1964	25.00

AYERS, ROY, AND WAYNE HENDERSON

Number	Title (A Side/B Side)	Yr	NM
12-Inch Singles			
POLYDOR			
❑ PRO 071 [DJ]	Heat Of the Beat (7:06) (same on both sides)	1978	12.00
45s			
POLYDOR			
❑ 2114	You Make Me Feel Like (Rockin' with You)/Million Dollar Baby (Feel So Real)	1980	4.00
❑ 2127	Weekend Lover/Thank You, Thank You	1980	—
—Canceled			
❑ 14523	Heat of the Beat/No Deposit No Return	1978	4.00
❑ 14545	Ooh Baby/Step Into Our Life	1979	4.00
❑ 14559	No Deposit No Return/Step Into Our Life	1979	4.00
Albums			
POLYDOR			
❑ PD-1-6179	Step Into Our Life	1978	10.00
❑ PD-1-6276	Prine Time	1980	10.00

AYLER, ALBERT

Number	Title (A Side/B Side)	Yr	NM
Albums			
ESP-DISK'			
❑ ESP-3030	Prophecy	1975	15.00

AZALEAS, THE

Number	Title (A Side/B Side)	Yr	NM
45s			
ROMULUS			
❑ 3001	Hands Off/One Drummer Can't Keep Time	1963	30.00

AZTECA

Number	Title (A Side/B Side)	Yr	NM
45s			
COLUMBIA			
❑ 45762	Peace Everybody/Mamita Linda	1973	6.00
❑ 45808	Ain't Got No Special Woman/Can't Take the Funk Out of Me	1973	6.00
❑ 45962	Night in Nazca/Whatcha Gonna Do	1973	5.00
Albums			
COLUMBIA			
❑ CQ 31776 [Q]	Azteca	1974	20.00
❑ KC 31776	Azteca	1972	12.00
❑ KC 32451	Pyramid of the Sun	1973	12.00

AZTECS, THE

Number	Title (A Side/B Side)	Yr	NM
45s			
WORLD ARTISTS			
❑ 1029	Da Doo Ron Ron/Hi-Hel Sneakers	1964	12.00
Albums			
WORLD ARTISTS			
❑ WAM-2001 [M]	Live at the Ad Lib Club of London	1964	60.00
—Features Beatles on the cover endorsing the band			

AZTEX

Number	Title (A Side/B Side)	Yr	NM
45s			
STAFF			
❑ (# unknown)	I Said Move/(B-side unknown)	196?	2500.

B

B. BUMBLE AND THE STINGERS

Number	Title (A Side/B Side)	Yr	NM
45s			
DYMO			
❑ 13	Pollywog/Slumber Party	196?	10.00
ERA BACK TO BACK HITS			
❑ 038	Bumble Boogie/Angel Baby	197?	6.00
—B-side by Rosie and the Originals			
ERIC			
❑ 297	Nut Rocker/Bumble Boogie	197?	4.00
GOLDIES 45			
❑ 2465	Bumble Boogie/School Day Blues	1973	5.00
❑ 2466	Nut Rocker/Nautilus	1973	5.00
GOLDISC			
❑ 3106	Nut Rocker/Bumble Boogie	198?	4.00
HI OLDIES			
❑ 409	Nut Rocker/Nautilus	197?	5.00
HIGHLAND			
❑ 2001	Bumble Boogie/School Day Blues	196?	10.00

Except when noted otherwise, VG = 25% of NM, and VG+ = 50% of NM. (Example: VG = $2.00, VG+ = $4.00 and NM = $8.00.)

Number	Title (A Side/B Side)	Yr	NM
MERCURY			
❑ 72614	Green Hornet Theme/Flight of the Hornet	1966	10.00
❑ 72665	Silent Movies/Twelfth Street Rag	1967	10.00
OLDIES 45			
❑ 37	Nut Rocker/Nautilus	1964	8.00
❑ 065	Nut Rocker/Baby I Love You	197?	5.00
—B-side by Joe Weaver and the Don Juans			
RENDEZVOUS			
❑ 140	Bumble Boogie/School Day Blues	1961	20.00
❑ 151	Boogie Woogie/Near You	1961	15.00
❑ 160	Bee Hive/Caravan	1961	15.00
❑ 166	Nut Rocker/Nautilus	1962	15.00
❑ 174	Rockin-On-And-Off/Mashed #5	1962	12.00
❑ 179	Apple Knocker/The Moon and the Sea	1962	12.00
❑ 182	Dawn Cracker/Scales	1962	12.00
❑ 186	12th Street Rag/Canadian Sunset	1962	12.00
❑ 192	Baby Mash/Night Time Madness	1962	12.00
❑ 210	In the Mood/Chicken Chow Mein	1963	12.00
TRIAD			
❑ 778	Chariots from the Stars/Funky Mud	197?	6.00
WAX			
❑ 13	Pollywog/Slumber Party	196?	8.00
—"Wax" in large sideways print			
❑ 13	Pollywog/Slumber Party	196?	10.00
—"Wax" in small vertical print			

B-52'S, THE

12-Inch Singles

Number	Title (A Side/B Side)	Yr	NM
MCA			
❑ MCA8P-(# unk) [DJ]	(Meet) The Flintstones (4 versions)	1994	10.00
—As "The BC-52's"			
REPRISE			
❑ PRO-A-3626 [DJ]	Channel Z (7" Remix 4:10) (Album Version 4:49) (12" Rock Mix 6:20) (12" Rock Dub 5:34)	1989	12.00
❑ PRO-A-5852 [DJ]	Revolution Earth (CO2 Mix 8:35) (PPM Dub 6:52) (Vibe Tribe Version 4:53) (LP Version 5:49)	1992	8.00
❑ PRO-A-9288-A [DJ]	Debbie (Edge Factor Club Mix) (Edge Factor Instrumental) (Tea Dance Dub) (Album Version)	1998	10.00
❑ PRO-A-9332 [DJ]	Time Capsule Megamixes (Hot Mix Club Megamix 5:08) (Hot Mix Radio Megamix 5:04) (Hot Tracks Club Megamix 11:20) (Hot Tracks Radio Megamix 3:57)	1998	10.00
❑ 21318	Love Shack (12" Remix 7:57) (12" Instrumental 7:46) (12" Mix 6:07) (Big Radio Mix 5:31)/Channel Z (12" Rock Mix 6:22)	1989	12.00
❑ 21441	Roam (7" Remix 5:11) (Radio Mix 4:13) (12" Remix 8:17)/Bushfire	1989	7.00
❑ 40561	Good Stuff (12" Mix 7:51) (Remix Edit 3:54) (Schottische Mix 3:41)/Bad Influence	1992	8.00
❑ 40594	Tell It Like It T-I-Is (5 versions)/The World's Green Laughter	1992	6.00
❑ 40642	Revolution Earth (3 versions)/Is That You Mo-Dean	1992	6.00
WARNER BROS.			
❑ PRO-A-836 [DJ]	Rock Lobster (Edit)//Dance This Mess Around/Planet Claire	1979	20.00
—With two-page biographical insert			
❑ PRO-A-890 [DJ]	Private Idaho/Party Out of Bounds (Instrumental)	1979	12.00
❑ PRO-A-927 [DJ]	Give Me Back My Man/Strobe Light	1980	12.00
❑ PRO-A-1016 [DJ]	Mesopotamia/Deep Sleep/Cake	1982	12.00
❑ PRO-A-2045 [DJ]	Legal Tender/Whammy Kiss/Song for a Future Generation	1983	10.00
❑ 20509	Summer of Love (Summer Party Mix 6:04) (Love Dub 7:47) (Single Edit 3:58)	1986	8.00
❑ 20588	Girl from Ipanema Goes to Greenland (Extended Mix 8:56) (Single Edit 3:58) (12" Mix 7:05) (Dub 7:02)	1986	12.00

45s

Number	Title (A Side/B Side)	Yr	NM
DB			
❑ 52	Rock Lobster/52 Girls	1978	30.00
❑ 52 [PS]	Rock Lobster/52 Girls	1978	30.00
MCA			
❑ 54839	(Meet) The Flintstones (Fred's Edit)/(Barney's Edit)	1994	4.00
—As "The BC-52's"			
REPRISE			
❑ 18895	Good Stuff/Bad Influence	1992	4.00
❑ 19430	Love Shack/Roam	199?	3.00
—Reissue			
❑ 19938	Deadbeat Club/Planet Claire (Live)	1990	3.00
❑ 22667	Roam/Bushfire	1990	4.00
❑ 22817	Love Shack/Channel Z	1989	3.00
❑ 22817 [PS]	Love Shack/Channel Z	1989	3.00
WARNER BROS.			
❑ GWB 0416	Rock Lobster/Private Idaho	198?	3.00
—Back to Back Hits reissue			
❑ 28561	Summer of Love/Housework	1986	3.00
❑ 28561 [PS]	Summer of Love/Housework	1986	3.00
❑ 29561	Song for a Future Generation/Trism	1983	3.00
❑ 29561 [PS]	Song for a Future Generation/Trism	1983	3.00
❑ 29579	Legal Tender/Moon 83	1983	3.00
❑ 29971	Mesopotamia/Throw That Beat in the Garbage Can	1982	3.00
❑ 49173	Rock Lobster/6060-842	1980	4.00
❑ 49173 [PS]	Rock Lobster/6060-842	1980	6.00
❑ 49212	Planet Claire/There's a Moon in the Sky (Called the Moon)	1980	4.00
❑ 49212 [PS]	Planet Claire/There's a Moon in the Sky (Called the Moon)	1980	6.00
❑ 49537	Private Idaho/Party Out of Bounds	1980	4.00
❑ 49537 [PS]	Private Idaho/Party Out of Bounds	1980	6.00
❑ 49717	Lava/Quiche Lorraine	1981	10.00
❑ 50064	Deep Sleep/Nip It in the Bud	1982	4.00

Albums

Number	Title (A Side/B Side)	Yr	NM
REPRISE			
❑ 25854	Cosmic Thing	1989	12.00
❑ 44519 [(2)]	Time Capsule — The Mixes	1998	15.00
—Numbered as if it were a 12-inch single, this contains remixes of seven songs from the "best of" CD compilation, so we've listed it under LPs; issued in orange vinyl cover			
WARNER BROS.			
❑ BSK 3355	The B-52's	1979	10.00
❑ BSK 3471	Wild Planet	1980	12.00
—Originals have red custom labels (deduct 33% for later pressings)			
❑ MINI 3596 [EP]	Party Mix	1981	12.00
❑ MINI 3641 [EP]	Mesopotamia	1982	8.00
❑ 23819	Whammy!	1983	10.00
❑ 25504	Bouncing Off the Satellites	1986	10.00
❑ R 154582	Bouncing Off the Satellites	1986	12.00
—RCA Music Service edition			

B.J. AND THE GEMINIS

45s

Number	Title (A Side/B Side)	Yr	NM
ATCO			
❑ 6364	Scratch My Back Part 1/Scratch My Back Part 2	1965	25.00

B.R.A.T.T.S., THE

45s

Number	Title (A Side/B Side)	Yr	NM
TOLLIE			
❑ 9024	Secret Weapon (The British Are Coming)/Jealous Kinda Woman	1964	20.00

B.T. EXPRESS

12-Inch Singles

Number	Title (A Side/B Side)	Yr	NM
COAST TO COAST			
❑ AS 1494 [DJ]	Keep It Up (Long) (Short)	1982	15.00
❑ 4Z9-02631	Let Yourself Go/Cowboy Dancer	1981	8.00
❑ 4Z9-03247	Star Child (Spirit of the Night) (7:26)/This Must Be the Night for Love (7:26)	1982	15.00
COLUMBIA			
❑ AS 403 [DJ]	Shout It Out (stereo/mono)	1977	15.00
❑ 43-60518	Let Me Be the One/Midnight Beat	1981	15.00
KING DAVIS			
❑ 3661	Cover Girl (Radio Version) (Club Version)	1985	12.00
ROADSHOW			
❑ 233 [DJ]	Can't Stop Groovin' Now, Wanna Do It Some More (5:54) (stereo/mono)	1976	50.00

45s

Number	Title (A Side/B Side)	Yr	NM
COAST TO COAST			
❑ ZS5-02630	Let Yourself Go/Cowboy Dancer	1981	4.00
❑ ZS5-02994	Keep It Up/Dancin' Dreams	1982	4.00
❑ ZS4-03246	Star Child (Spirit of the Night)/This Must Be the Night for Love	1982	4.00
COLUMBIA			
❑ 3-10346	Can't Stop Groovin' Now, Wanna Do It Some More/Herbs	1976	4.00
❑ 3-10399	Energy to Burn/Make Your Body Move	1976	4.00
❑ 3-10582	Funky Music (Don't Laugh at My Funk)/We Got It Together	1977	4.00
❑ 3-10649	Shout It Out/Ride On B.T.	1977	4.00
❑ 3-10752	You Got Something/What You Do in the Dark	1978	4.00
❑ 1-11200	Heart of Fire/Better Late Than Never	1980	4.00
❑ 1-11249	Give Up the Funk (Let's Dance)/Better Late Than Never	1980	4.00
❑ 1-11336	Does It Feel Good/Have Some Fun	1980	4.00
❑ 11400	Stretch/Just Want to Hold You	1980	4.00
ROADSHOW			
❑ 7001	Express/Express (Disco Mix)	1975	4.00
❑ 7003	Give It What You Got/Peace Pipe	1975	4.00
❑ 7005	Close to You/(B-side unknown)	1975	4.00
SCEPTER			
❑ 12395	Do It ('Til You're Satisfied)/(Long Version)	1974	5.00

Albums

Number	Title (A Side/B Side)	Yr	NM
COAST TO COAST			
❑ FZ 38001	Keep It Up	1982	10.00
COLLECTABLES			
❑ COL-5190	Golden Classics: Express	198?	10.00
COLUMBIA			
❑ PC 34178	Energy to Burn	1976	10.00
❑ PCQ 34178 [Q]	Energy to Burn	1976	15.00
❑ PC 34702	Function at the Junction	1977	10.00
❑ JC 35078	Shout!	1978	10.00
❑ JC 36333	B.T. Express 1980	1980	10.00
❑ JC 36923	Greatest Hits	1980	10.00
ROADSHOW			
❑ 41001	Non-Stop	1975	12.00
ROADSHOW/SCEPTER			
❑ 5117	Do It ('Til You're Satisfied)	1974	12.00

B-52'S, THE

12-Inch Singles

Number	Title (A Side/B Side)	Yr	NM
REPRISE			
❑ PRO5852 [DJ]	Revolution Earth (4 versions)	1992	8.00
WARNER BROS.			
❑ PRO2045 [DJ]	Legal Tender/Whammy Kiss/Future Generation	1983	10.00
❑ PRO890 [DJ]	Private Idaho/Party Out of Bounds (Instrumental)	1979	12.00
❑ PRO927 [DJ]	Give Me Back My Man/Strobe Light	1980	12.00

BABE RUTH

45s

Number	Title (A Side/B Side)	Yr	NM
CAPITOL			
❑ 4219	Say No More/Elusive	1976	4.00
HARVEST			
❑ 3553	Wells Fargo/Theme from "For A Few Dollars More"	1973	5.00

Albums

Number	Title (A Side/B Side)	Yr	NM
CAPITOL			
❑ ST-11515	Kids Stuff	1976	20.00
HARVEST			
❑ SW-11151	First Base	1973	40.00
❑ ST-11275	Amar Caballero	1974	30.00
❑ ST-11367	Babe Ruth	1975	15.00
❑ ST-11451	Stealin' Home	1975	15.00

BABIES, THE

45s

Number	Title (A Side/B Side)	Yr	NM
ABC DUNHILL			
❑ 4148	I Wanna Testify/Party Time	1968	12.00
DUNHILL			
❑ 4085	You Make Me Feel Like Someone/The Hand of Fate	1967	16.00

The Bachelors, "I Believe," London 9672, 1964, **$25.**

Number	Title (A Side/B Side)	Yr	NM
❑ 4085 [PS]	You Make Me Feel Like Someone/The Hand of Fate	1967	30.00
❑ 4101	I'm Not Asking for the World/Goodbye My Love, Goodbye	1967	15.00

BABY

45s

Number	Title (A Side/B Side)	Yr	NM
CHELSEA			
❑ 3057	Where Did All the Money Go/(B-side unknown)	1976	5.00
❑ 3068	Fallen Angel/Baton Rouge	1977	5.00

Albums

Number	Title (A Side/B Side)	Yr	NM
CHELSEA			
❑ CHL-517	Where Did All the Money Go	1976	16.00
LONE STARR			
❑ 9782	Baby	1974	25.00

BABY BUGS, THE

45s

Number	Title (A Side/B Side)	Yr	NM
VEE JAY			
❑ 594	Bingo/Bingo's Bongo Bingo Party	1964	25.00
❑ 594 [PS]	Bingo/Bingo's Bongo Bingo Party	1964	75.00

BABY DOLLS, THE

45s

Number	Title (A Side/B Side)	Yr	NM
BOOM			
❑ 60002	I Will Do It ('Cause He Wants Me To)/Now That I've Lost You	1966	10.00
GAMBLE			
❑ 213	Please Don't Rush Me/There You Are	1968	8.00
HOLLYWOOD			
❑ 1111	Got to Get You Into My Life/Why Can't I Make Him Like You	1960	40.00
MASKE			
❑ 103	Go Away Baby/I'm Lonely	1960	50.00
❑ 701	Thanks, Mr. DJ/What a Wonderful Love	1961	120.00
RCA VICTOR			
❑ 47-7296	Tutti Frutti/Cause I'm in Love	1958	15.00
WARNER BROS.			
❑ 5086	Hey Baby/Quiet	1959	12.00

BABY EARL AND THE TRINI-DADS

45s

Number	Title (A Side/B Side)	Yr	NM
S.P.Q.R.			
❑ 3317	Everybody Do the Ska/Back Slop	1964	25.00

BABY GRAND

45s

Number	Title (A Side/B Side)	Yr	NM
ARISTA			
❑ 0293	Bring Me Your Broken Heart/Lady of My Dreams	1977	5.00
❑ 0312	Never Enough/Lady of My Dreams	1978	5.00
❑ 0374	Walk Away Renee/Much Too Much	1978	5.00
❑ 0394 [DJ]	All Night Long (same on both sides)	1979	5.00
—May be promo only			

Albums

Number	Title (A Side/B Side)	Yr	NM
ARISTA			
❑ AL 4148	Baby Grand	1977	20.00

BABY HUEY

45s

Number	Title (A Side/B Side)	Yr	NM
BREAKTHROUGH			
❑ 1001	Just Being Careful/(B-side unknown)	196?	1500.
CURTOM			
❑ 1939	Mighty Mighty Children/Mighty Mighty Children (Part 2)	1969	10.00
❑ 1962	Hard Times/Listen to Me	1971	10.00
SATELLITE			
❑ 2013	Messin' with the Kid/Monkey Man	196?	20.00
U.S.A.			
❑ 801	Messin' with the Kid/Just Being Careful	196?	20.00

Albums

Number	Title (A Side/B Side)	Yr	NM
CURTOM			
❑ CRS-8007	The Living Legend	1970	40.00

BABY JANE AND THE ROCKABYES

45s

Number	Title (A Side/B Side)	Yr	NM
PORT			
❑ 3013	Heartbreak Shop/Dance Till My Feet Get Tired	1964	30.00
UNITED ARTISTS			
❑ 505	If You Wanna/Oh Johnny	1962	20.00
❑ 560	How Much is That Doggie in the Window/My Boy John	1963	20.00
❑ 593	Get Me to the Church on Time/Hickory Dickory Dock	1963	15.00

BABY RAY

45s

Number	Title (A Side/B Side)	Yr	NM
IMPERIAL			
❑ 66216	There's Something On Your Mind/House on Soul Hill	1966	15.00
❑ 66232	Elvira/Just Because	1967	15.00
❑ 66256	Your Sweet Love/Yours Until Tomorrow	1967	15.00

Albums

Number	Title (A Side/B Side)	Yr	NM
IMPERIAL			
❑ LP-9335 [M]	Where Soul Lives	1967	25.00
❑ LP-12335 [S]	Where Soul Lives	1967	30.00

BABY RAY AND THE FERNS

An early production of FRANK ZAPPA.

45s

Number	Title (A Side/B Side)	Yr	NM
DONNA			
❑ 1378	How's Your Bird/The World's Greatest Sinner	1963	200.00

BABYLON A.D.

Albums

Number	Title (A Side/B Side)	Yr	NM
ARISTA			
❑ AL 8580	Babylon A.D.	1989	10.00

BABYS, THE

Also see JOHN WAITE; BAD ENGLISH.

12-Inch Singles

Number	Title (A Side/B Side)	Yr	NM
CHRYSALIS			
❑ CHS 8-PDJ [DJ]	Head First (same on both sides)	1979	10.00

45s

Number	Title (A Side/B Side)	Yr	NM
CHRYSALIS			
❑ 2132	If You've Got the Time/Head Above the Waves	1976	6.00
❑ 2173	Isn't It Time/Give Me Your Love	1977	5.00
❑ 2201	Silver Dreams/And If You Could See Me Cry	1978	5.00
❑ 2279	Every Time I Think of You/Head First	1978	5.00
❑ 2279	Every Time I Think of You/Please Don't Leave Me Here	1979	4.00
❑ 2323	Head First/California	1979	4.00
❑ 2398	Back on My Feet Again/Turn Around in Tokyo	1980	4.00
❑ 2398 [PS]	Back on My Feet Again/Turn Around in Tokyo	1980	6.00
❑ 2425	Midnight Rendezvous/Love Is Just a Mystery	1980	4.00
❑ 2467	Turn and Walk Away/Darker Side of Town	1980	4.00
❑ 2495	Postcard/Too Far Gone	1981	5.00
❑ S7-18918	Back on My Feet Again/Hot Child in the City	1996	3.00
—B-side by Nick Gilder			

Albums

Number	Title (A Side/B Side)	Yr	NM
CHRYSALIS			
❑ CHR 1129	The Babys	1976	12.00
❑ CHR 1150	Broken Heart	1977	10.00
❑ CHR 1195	Head First	1979	10.00
❑ CHR 1267	Union Jacks	1980	10.00
❑ CHR 1305	On the Edge	1980	10.00
❑ CHR 1351	Anthology	1981	10.00
❑ PV 41129	The Babys	1983	8.00
—Reissue of 1129			
❑ PV 41150	Broken Heart	1983	8.00
—Reissue of 1150			
❑ FV 41195	Head First	1983	8.00
—Reissue of 1195			
❑ PV 41267	Union Jacks	1983	8.00
—Reissue of 1267			
❑ PV 41305	On the Edge	1983	8.00
—Reissue of 1305			
❑ PV 41351	Anthology	198?	8.00
—Reissue of 1351			

Except when noted otherwise, VG = 25% of NM, and VG+ = 50% of NM. (Example: VG = $2.00, VG+ = $4.00 and NM = $8.00.)

Number	Title (A Side/B Side)	Yr	NM

BACHELORS, THE (1) British Invasion male vocal group. Several other groups used this name, on the Aladdin, Epic, Mercury, MGM, National, Poplar, Royal Roost and Smash labels; those are outside the scope of this publication.

45s

LONDON

Number	Title (A Side/B Side)	Yr	NM
❑ 9584	Charmaine/Old Bill	1963	12.00
❑ 9623	Faraway Places/ Is There a Chance	1964	12.00
❑ 9632	Whispering/ No Light in the Window	1964	12.00
❑ 9639	Diane/Happy Land	1964	12.00
❑ 9639	Diane/I Believe	1964	15.00
❑ 9672	I Believe/Sweet Lullaby	1964	12.00
❑ 9672 [PS]	I Believe/Sweet Lullaby	1964	25.00
❑ 9693	I Wouldn't Trade You for the World/Beneath the Willow Tree	1964	12.00
❑ 9693 [PS]	I Wouldn't Trade You for the World/Beneath the Willow Tree	1964	25.00
❑ 9724	No Arms Can Ever Hold You/ Oh Samuel, Don't Die	1964	12.00
❑ 9762	Marie/You Can Tell	1965	10.00
❑ 9793	Chapel in the Moonlight/ The Old Wishing Well	1965	10.00
❑ 9793 [PS]	Chapel in the Moonlight/ The Old Wishing Well	1965	20.00
❑ 9828	Love Me with All of Your Heart/ There's No Room in My Heart	1966	10.00
❑ 20010	Can I Trust You/My Girl	1966	10.00
❑ 20018	Walk with Faith in Your Heart/ Queen Molly Malone of Ireland	1966	10.00
❑ 20027	Marta/Oh How I Miss You	1967	8.00
❑ 20033	Learn to Live Without You/ 3 O'Clock Flamingo Street	1967	8.00
❑ 20051	Punky's Dilemma/It's a Beautiful Day	1968	8.00
❑ 20063	Love Is All/The Colours of Love	1970	6.00
❑ 20071	Diamonds Are Forever/ Where There's a Heartache	1971	6.00

Albums

LONDON

Number	Title (A Side/B Side)	Yr	NM
❑ PS 353 [S]	Presenting the Bachelors	1964	30.00
❑ PS 393 [P]	Back Again	1964	20.00
—"I Wouldn't Trade You for the World" is rechanneled.			
❑ PS 418 [S]	No Arms Can Ever Hold You	1965	20.00
❑ PS 435 [P]	Marie	1965	20.00
—"Marie" is rechanneled			
❑ PS 460 [S]	Hits of the 60's	1966	20.00
❑ PS 491 [P]	The Bachelors' Girls	1966	15.00
—"Marie" is rechanneled			
❑ PS 518 [P]	Golden All Time Hits	1967	15.00
❑ PS 528 [S]	Bachelors '68	1968	12.00
❑ PS 611	Under and Over	1972	10.00
❑ LL 3353 [M]	Presenting the Bachelors	1964	15.00
❑ LL 3393 [M]	Back Again	1964	15.00
❑ LL 3418 [M]	No Arms Can Ever Hold You	1965	15.00
❑ LL 3435 [M]	Marie	1965	15.00
❑ LL 3460 [M]	Hits of the 60's	1966	15.00
❑ LL 3491 [M]	The Bachelors' Girls	1966	12.00
❑ LL 3518 [M]	Golden All Time Hits	1967	15.00
❑ LL 3528 [M]	Bachelors '68	1968	20.00

BACHELORS, THE (2) American male vocal group.

45s

ALADDIN

Number	Title (A Side/B Side)	Yr	NM
❑ 3210	Pretty Baby/ Can't Help Loving You	1953	2500.

ROYAL ROOST

Number	Title (A Side/B Side)	Yr	NM
❑ 620	I Found Love/You've Lied	1952	300.00

BACHELORS, THE (U) None of these are group (1), though some could be group (2).

45s

EPIC

Number	Title (A Side/B Side)	Yr	NM
❑ 9369	Do the Madison/Bachelor's Club	1960	12.00

MERCURY

Number	Title (A Side/B Side)	Yr	NM
❑ 8159	Yesterday's Roses/Hereafter	1949	300.00

MGM

Number	Title (A Side/B Side)	Yr	NM
❑ 12668	Sometimes/Teenage Memory	1958	20.00

NATIONAL

Number	Title (A Side/B Side)	Yr	NM
❑ 104	From Your Heart/ A Million Teardrops	1957	25.00
❑ 115	Today, Tomorrow, Forever/ I Want a Girl	1957	25.00

POPLAR

Number	Title (A Side/B Side)	Yr	NM
❑ 101	After/You Know, I Know (I Love You)	1957	50.00

SMASH

Number	Title (A Side/B Side)	Yr	NM
❑ 1723	The Day I Met You/ Hey Little Girl	1961	12.00

Bachman-Turner Overdrive, *Best of B.T.O. (So Far)*, Mercury SRM-1-1101, 1976, **$10.**

BACHMAN, RANDY Also see GUESS WHO; BACHMAN-TURNER OVERDRIVE; IRONHORSE.

45s

POLYDOR

Number	Title (A Side/B Side)	Yr	NM
❑ 14478	Is the Night Too Cold for Dancing/ Maybe Again	1978	6.00

Albums

POLYDOR

Number	Title (A Side/B Side)	Yr	NM
❑ PD-1-6141	Survivor	1978	12.00

BACHMAN-TURNER OVERDRIVE Also see BRAVE BELT; THE GUESS WHO. Earlier material appears in the Goldmine Standard Catalog of American Records 1950-1975. Also see RANDY BACHMAN; GUESS WHO.

45s

COMPLEAT

Number	Title (A Side/B Side)	Yr	NM
❑ 127	For the Weekend/ Just Look at Me Now	1984	4.00
❑ 133	My Sugaree/ Service with a Smile	1984	4.00
❑ 137	My Sugaree/(B-side unknown)	1985	4.00

MERCURY

Number	Title (A Side/B Side)	Yr	NM
❑ 73383	Gimmie Your Money Please/ Little Gandy Dancer	1973	5.00
❑ 73417	Blue Collar/Hold Back the Water	1973	5.00
❑ 73457	Let It Ride/Tramp	1974	4.00
❑ 73487	Takin' Care of Business/ Stonegates	1974	4.00
❑ 73622	You Ain't Seen Nothin' Yet/ Free Wheelin'	1974	4.00
❑ 73656	Roll On Down the Highway/ Sledgehammer	1975	4.00
❑ 73683	Hey You/Flat Broke Love	1975	4.00
❑ 73724	Down to the Line/She's a Devil	1975	4.00
❑ 73724 [PS]	Down to the Line/She's a Devil	1975	8.00
❑ 73766	Take It Like a Man/Woncha Take Me for a While	1976	4.00
❑ 73784	Looking Out for #1/ Find Out About Love	1976	4.00
❑ 73843	Gimme Your Money Please/ Four Wheel Drive	1976	4.00
❑ 73903	Freeways/ My Wheels Won't Turn	1977	4.00
❑ 73926	Shotgun Rider/Down, Down	1977	4.00
❑ 73951	Life Still Goes On (I'm Lonely)/ Just for You	1977	4.00
❑ 73987	Down the Road/A Long Time for a Little While	1978	4.00
❑ 74046	Heaven Tonight/Heartaches	1979	4.00
❑ 74062	End of the Line/Jamaica	1979	4.00

Albums

COMPLEAT

Number	Title (A Side/B Side)	Yr	NM
❑ CPL1-1010	Bachman-Turner Overdrive	1984	8.00

MCA/CURB

Number	Title (A Side/B Side)	Yr	NM
❑ 5760	Live! Live! Live!	1986	8.00

MERCURY

Number	Title (A Side/B Side)	Yr	NM
❑ SRM-1-673	Bachman-Turner Overdrive	1973	12.00
—Red label			
❑ SRM-1-673	Bachman-Turner Overdrive	1974	10.00
—Chicago skyline label			
❑ SRM-1-696	Bachman-Turner Overdrive II	1973	12.00
—Red label			
❑ SRM-1-696	Bachman-Turner Overdrive II	1974	10.00
—Chicago skyline label			
❑ SRM-1-1004	Not Fragile	1974	10.00
❑ SRM-1-1027	Four Wheel Drive	1975	10.00
❑ SRM-1-1067	Head On	1975	10.00
❑ SRM-1-1101	Best of B.T.O. (So Far)	1976	10.00
❑ SRM-1-3700	Freeways	1977	10.00
❑ SRM-1-3713	Street Action	1978	10.00
❑ SRM-1-3748	Rock N' Roll Nights	1979	10.00
❑ 822786-1	Best of B.T.O. (So Far)	1984	8.00
—Reissue of 1101			

BACHS, THE

Albums

ROTO

Number	Title (A Side/B Side)	Yr	NM
❑ PR-1044	Out of the Bachs	1968	4000.
—VG value 2000, VG+ value 3000			

B

Bad Company, "Rock 'n' Roll Fantasy," Swan Song 70119, 1979, **$6.**

Number	Title (A Side/B Side)	Yr	NM
BACK BEAT			
45s			
LAURIE			
❑ 3092	Rock and Roll Symphony, 1st and 2nd Movements	1961	20.00
BACK PORCH MAJORITY, THE			
45s			
EPIC			
❑ 9689	Friends/Hand-Me-Down Things	1964	10.00
❑ 9754	Hey Nelly Nelly/ Ol' Dan Tucker	1965	10.00
❑ 9769	Smash Flops/Jack O'Diamonds	1965	10.00
❑ 9769 [PS]	Smash Flops/Jack O'Diamonds	1965	15.00
❑ 9809	Good-Time Joe/Ramblin' Man	1965	10.00
❑ 9850	The Mighty Mississippi/ Song of Hope	1965	10.00
❑ 9879	Second Hand Man/That's the Way It's Gonna Be	1965	10.00
❑ 10036	Honey and Wine/ Brother John	1966	8.00
❑ 10079	Once Again/Slippery Sal and Dirty Dan, the Oyster Man	1966	8.00
❑ 10129	Southtown U.S.A./ This Little Light	1967	8.00
Albums			
EPIC			
❑ LN 24134 [M]	Live from Ledbetter's	1965	15.00
❑ LN 24149 [M]	Riverboat Days	1965	15.00
❑ LN 24184 [M]	That's the Way It's Gonna Be	1966	15.00
❑ LN 24319 [M]	Willy Nilly Wonder of Illusion	1967	20.00
❑ BN 26134 [S]	Live from Ledbetter's	1965	20.00
❑ BN 26149 [S]	Riverboat Days	1965	20.00
❑ BN 26184 [S]	That's the Way It's Gonna Be	1966	20.00
❑ BN 26319 [S]	Willy Nilly Wonder of Illusion	1967	15.00

Number	Title (A Side/B Side)	Yr	NM
BACK STREET CRAWLER			
7-Inch Extended Plays			
ATCO			
❑ PR 247 [DJ]	Hoo Doo Woman/All the Girls Are Crazy//Survivor/ The Band Plays On	1975	6.00
—Small hole, plays at 33 1/3 rpm			
❑ PR 247 [PS]	Back Street Crawler	1975	8.00
Albums			
ATCO			
❑ SD 36-125	The Band Plays On	1975	12.00
❑ SD 36-138	2nd Street	1976	12.00
EPIC			
❑ PE 34900	Crawler	1977	10.00
—Epic titles as "Crawler"			
❑ JE 35482	Snake, Rattle and Roll	1978	10.00
BACKUS, JIM			
45s			
DICO			
❑ 101	I Was a Teenage Reindeer/ The Office Party	1959	20.00
DORE			
❑ 899	Dirty Old Man/Frigid	1974	5.00
JUBILEE			
❑ 5330	Delicious!/I Need a Vacation	1958	15.00
—As "Jim Bakus and Friend"			
❑ 5351	Cave Man/Why Don't You Go Home for Christmas	1958	12.00
❑ 5361	Cave Man/Rock on the Roof	1959	12.00
Albums			
RCA VICTOR			
❑ LPM-1362 [M]	Mr. Magoo in Hi-Fi	1957	50.00

Number	Title (A Side/B Side)	Yr	NM
BACON, GAR			
45s			
BATON			
❑ 248	There's Gonna Be Rockin' Tonight/Y-I-O-U	1957	60.00
❑ 250	Justice/Pucker Up	1958	40.00
DALE			
❑ 105	Chains of Love/Mary Jane	1957	25.00
❑ 108	Dutch Treat/I'll Never Fail You	1958	30.00
OKEH			
❑ 7115	Marshall, Marshall/ Too Young to Love	1959	20.00
RKO UNIQUE			
❑ 395	Lonesome Wail/ You and Your Love	1957	20.00
BACON FAT			
Albums			
BLUE HORIZON			
❑ BH-4807	Grease One for Me	1970	25.00
BAD BOY			
45s			
UNITED ARTISTS			
❑ XW1063	Shake Me Up/Thinking of You	1977	5.00
❑ XW1118	I've Had Enough/Disco	1978	5.00
Albums			
UNITED ARTISTS			
❑ UA-LA781-G	The Band That Milwaukee Made Famous	1977	12.00
❑ UA-LA869-H	Back to Back	1978	12.00
BAD BOYS, THE			
45s			
WARNER BROS.			
❑ 5605	The Owl and the Pussycat/ That's What I'll Do	1965	12.00
BAD BRAINS			
45s			
BAD BRAINS			
❑ 001	Pay to Cum/Stay Close to Me	1980	40.00
—Black vinyl; colored vinyl versions are not originals			
❑ 001 [PS]	Pay to Cum/Stay Close to Me	1980	40.00
—With lyric insert; some reissues have a Xerox copy of the original picture sleeve			
CAROLINE			
❑ (# unknown)	Banned in D.C./At the Movies/ Pay to Cum	1990	6.00
❑ (# unknown) [PS]	Banned in D.C./At the Movies/ Pay to Cum	1990	6.00
MAVERICK			
❑ 1001 [DJ]	God of Love/Longtime	1995	5.00
—Red vinyl			
❑ 1001 [PS]	God of Love/Longtime	1995	5.00
—Numbered limited edition			
SST			
❑ 065	House of Suffering/ (B-side blank)	1986	10.00
❑ 065 [PS]	House of Suffering	1986	15.00
Albums			
BAD BRAINS			
❑ 003 [EP]	I and I Survive/Destroy Babylon	1983	40.00
CAROLINE			
❑ CAROL-1375	Quickness	1989	15.00
❑ CAROL-1613	Rock for Light	1990	16.00
—Reissue of PVC 8917 with three bonus tracks			
❑ CAROL-1617	The Youth Are Getting Restless	1990	16.00
IMPORTANT			
❑ 003 [EP]	I and I Survive/Destroy Babylon	1983	20.00
MAVERICK			
❑ 45882	God of Love	1995	18.00
PVC			
❑ 8917	Rock for Light	1983	15.00
ROIR			
❑ 8223	Bad Brains	1997	15.00
—First issued in the early 1980s on cassette only, this is a limited vinyl reissue			
SST			
❑ 065	I Against I	1986	15.00
—No back cover bar code			
❑ 065	I Against I	199?	10.00
—With back cover bar code			
❑ 160	Live	1988	16.00
❑ 228 [10]	Spirit Electricity	1991	10.00
VICTORY			
❑ VR 64 [10]	The Omega Sessions	1997	15.00

Except when noted otherwise, VG = 25% of NM, and VG+ = 50% of NM. (Example: VG = $2.00, VG+ = $4.00 and NM = $8.00.)

BAD COMPANY
Also see FREE, PAUL RODGERS; THE FIRM.

12-Inch Singles

ATLANTIC

Number	Title (A Side/B Side)	Yr	NM
❑ PR 959 [DJ]	This Love (same on both sides)	1986	8.00
❑ PR 999 [DJ]	That Girl (same on both sides?)	1987	8.00
❑ 2409 [DJ]	No Smoke Without a Fire (same on both sides)	1988	8.00

45s

ATCO

Number	Title (A Side/B Side)	Yr	NM
❑ 98463	This Could Be the One/How About That	1992	4.00

ATLANTIC

Number	Title (A Side/B Side)	Yr	NM
❑ 88939	Shake It Up/Dangerous Age	1989	4.00
❑ 88939 [PS]	Shake It Up/Dangerous Age	1989	4.00
❑ 89035	No Smoke Without a Fire/Love Attack	1988	4.00
❑ 89035 [PS]	No Smoke Without a Fire/Love Attack	1988	4.00
❑ 89299	That Girl/If I'm Sleeping	1987	4.00
❑ 89355	This Love/Tell It Like It Is	1986	4.00
❑ 89355 [PS]	This Love/Tell It Like It Is	1986	4.00

ATLANTIC OLDIES SERIES

Number	Title (A Side/B Side)	Yr	NM
❑ 94936	If You Needed Somebody/Holy Water	1993	4.00

—"Reissue" of two hits that had not appeared on a U.S. vinyl 45 before

SWAN SONG

Number	Title (A Side/B Side)	Yr	NM
❑ 70015	Can't Get Enough/Little Miss Fortune	1974	6.00
❑ 70101	Movin' On/Easy on My Soul	1974	5.00
❑ 70103	Good Lovin' Gone Bad/Whiskey Bottle	1975	5.00
❑ 70106	Feel Like Makin' Love/Wild Fire Woman	1975	6.00
❑ 70108	Young Blood/Do Right by Your Woman	1976	5.00
❑ 70109	Honey Child/Fade Away	1976	4.00
❑ 70112	Burnin' Sky/Everything I Need	1976	4.00
❑ 70119	Rock 'N' Roll Fantasy/Crazy Circles	1979	5.00
❑ 70119 [PS]	Rock 'N' Roll Fantasy/Crazy Circles	1979	6.00
❑ 71000	Gone, Gone, Gone/Take the Time	1979	5.00
❑ 71000 [PS]	Gone, Gone, Gone/Take the Time	1979	6.00
❑ 99966	Electricland/Untie the Knot	1982	5.00
❑ 99966 [PS]	Electricland/Untie the Knot	1982	5.00

Albums

ATCO

Number	Title (A Side/B Side)	Yr	NM
❑ 91371	Holy Water	1990	15.00

ATLANTIC

Number	Title (A Side/B Side)	Yr	NM
❑ 81625	10 from 6 (The Best of Bad Company)	1986	10.00
❑ 81684	Fame and Fortune	1987	10.00
❑ 81884	Dangerous Age	1988	10.00

SWAN SONG

Number	Title (A Side/B Side)	Yr	NM
❑ SS 8410	Bad Company	1974	10.00
❑ SS 8413	Straight Shooter	1975	10.00
❑ SS 8415	Run with the Pack	1976	10.00
❑ SS 8500	Burnin' Sky	1977	10.00
❑ SS 8501	Bad Company	1977	8.00
❑ SS 8502	Straight Shooter	1977	8.00
❑ SS 8503	Run with the Pack	1977	8.00
❑ SS 8506	Desolation Angels	1979	10.00
❑ 90001	Rough Diamonds	1982	10.00

BAD ENGLISH
Also see JOHN WAITE; THE BABYS.

45s

COLLECTABLES

Number	Title (A Side/B Side)	Yr	NM
❑ 4627	Price of Love/Possession	199?	3.00

—Reissue

EPIC

Number	Title (A Side/B Side)	Yr	NM
❑ 34-68946	Forget Me Not/Lay Down	1989	3.00
❑ 34-69082	When I See You Smile/Rockin' Horse	1989	4.00
❑ 34-73094	Price of Love/The Restless Ones	1989	4.00
❑ 34-73398	Possession/Tough Times Don't Last	1990	4.00

Albums

EPIC

Number	Title (A Side/B Side)	Yr	NM
❑ OE 45083	Bad English	1989	12.00

BAD MANNERS

12-Inch Singles

PORTRAIT

Number	Title (A Side/B Side)	Yr	NM
❑ 4R9-05020	That'll Do Nicely (Remix) (Single Version)/Exodus	1984	12.00
❑ 4R9-05099	My Girl Lollipop (3 versions)	1984	15.00
❑ 4R9-05274	What the Papers Say (Extended Version) (LP Version)	1985	12.00
❑ 4R9-05343	Bang the Drum All Day (3 versions)/Saturday Night	1985	12.00

Badfinger, *Ass*, Apple SW-3411, 1973, **$20.**

45s

BLUE BEAT

Number	Title (A Side/B Side)	Yr	NM
❑ 010	Christmas Time Again/Skinhead Love Affair	198?	8.00
❑ 010 [PS]	Christmas Time Again/Skinhead Love Affair	198?	10.00

—U.K. import

PORTRAIT

Number	Title (A Side/B Side)	Yr	NM
❑ 37-04602	My Girl Lollipop (My Boy Lollipop)/Falling Out of Love	1984	5.00
❑ 37-05725	What the Papers Say/Louie Louie	1985	5.00
❑ 37-05725 [PS]	What the Papers Say/Louie Louie	1985	5.00

Albums

MCA

Number	Title (A Side/B Side)	Yr	NM
❑ 5218	Bad Manners	1981	15.00
❑ 5415	Klass	1983	15.00

PORTRAIT

Number	Title (A Side/B Side)	Yr	NM
❑ BFR 39413	Forging Ahead	1984	12.00
❑ BFR 40070	Mental Notes	1985	12.00

BAD RELIGION

45s

SYMPATHY FOR THE RECORD INDUSTRY

Number	Title (A Side/B Side)	Yr	NM
❑ SFTRI 158	Atomic Garden/(no B-side)	1991	4.00

—With etched B-side

Number	Title (A Side/B Side)	Yr	NM
❑ SFTRI 158 [PS]	Atomic Garden	1991	4.00
❑ SFTRI 232	American Jesus/Stealth	1993	3.00
❑ SFTRI 232 [PS]	American Jesus/Stealth	1993	4.00
❑ SFTRI 326	Stranger Than Fiction/Markovian Process	1994	3.00
❑ SFTRI 326 [PS]	Stranger Than Fiction/Markovian Process	1994	3.00

UNPLAYABLE

Number	Title (A Side/B Side)	Yr	NM
❑ 87079	Punk Rock Song//The Universal Cynic/The Dodo	1996	5.00

—Gray marbled vinyl, small hole

Number	Title (A Side/B Side)	Yr	NM
❑ 87079 [PS]	Punk Rock Song//The Universal Cynic/The Dodo	1996	5.00

7-Inch Extended Plays

EPITAPH

Number	Title (A Side/B Side)	Yr	NM
❑ (# unknown)	Yesterday/Frogger/Bad Religion//Along the Way/New Leaf	1985	25.00
❑ (# unknown) [PS]	Back to the Known	1985	25.00
❑ 1072	Bad Religion/Politics/Sensory Overload//Slaves/Drastic Actions/World War III	1981	100.00

—Red vinyl issues with the title "SUFFER" on the label are bootlegs

Number	Title (A Side/B Side)	Yr	NM
❑ 1072 [PS]	Bad Religion	1981	100.00

Albums

ATLANTIC

Number	Title (A Side/B Side)	Yr	NM
❑ 82658	Stranger Than Fiction	1994	25.00

—Issued on red vinyl

Number	Title (A Side/B Side)	Yr	NM
❑ 82870	The Gray Race	1996	20.00

—Issued on gray vinyl

Number	Title (A Side/B Side)	Yr	NM
❑ 83094	No Substance	1998	20.00
❑ 83303	The New America	2000	15.00

EPITAPH

Number	Title (A Side/B Side)	Yr	NM
❑ EPI-BRLP-1	How Could Hell Be Any Worse?	1982	100.00

—Original edition with lyric sheet. Some copies have personal notes or autographs scribbled on the inner sleeves by the band members; these can bring significantly more than this.

Number	Title (A Side/B Side)	Yr	NM
❑ EPI-BRLP-2	Into the Unknown	1983	200.00
❑ 86404	Suffer	1988	15.00
❑ 86406	No Control	1989	15.00
❑ 86407	How Could Hell Be Any Worse?	1989	25.00

—Reissue of Epitaph BRLP-1

Number	Title (A Side/B Side)	Yr	NM
❑ 86409	Against the Grain	1990	15.00
❑ 86416	Generator	1992	15.00
❑ 86420	Recipe for Hate	1993	15.00
❑ 86443	All Ages	1995	12.00
❑ 86635	The Process of Belief	2002	15.00
❑ 86694	The Empire Strikes First	2004	12.00

BADD BOYS, THE

Number	Title (A Side/B Side)	Yr	NM
45s			
EPIC			
❑ 10119	Never Going Back to Georgia/River Deep Mountain High	1967	50.00
❑ 10165	Folks in a Hurry/I Told You So	1967	60.00

BADFINGER

Also see GEORGE HARRISON AND FRIENDS.

Number	Title (A Side/B Side)	Yr	NM
45s			
APPLE			
❑ 1803	Maybe Tomorrow/And Her Daddy's a Millionaire	1969	20.00
—By "The Iveys"; without star on label			
❑ 1803	Maybe Tomorrow/And Her Daddy's a Millionaire	1969	30.00
—By "The Iveys"; with star on label			
❑ 1815	Come and Get It/Rock of All Ages	1969	6.00
❑ 1815	Come and Get It/Rock of All Ages	1969	8.00
—With Capitol logo on B-side bottom			
❑ 1822	No Matter What/Carry On Till Tomorrow	1970	6.00
❑ 1822	No Matter What/Carry On Till Tomorrow	1970	20.00
—With star on A-side label			
❑ 1841	Day After Day/Money	1971	6.00
❑ 1841	Day After Day/Money	1971	20.00
—With star on A-side label			
❑ 1841 [DJ]	Day After Day/Money	1971	120.00
—White label			
❑ 1844	Baby Blue/Flying	1972	6.00
❑ 1844 [DJ]	Baby Blue/Flying	1972	120.00
—White label			
❑ 1844 [PS]	Baby Blue/Flying	1972	15.00
❑ 1864	Apple of My Eye/Blind Owl	1973	6.00
❑ P-1864 [DJ]	Apple of My Eye (mono/stereo)	1973	25.00
APPLE/AMERICOM			
❑ 1803P/M-300	Maybe Tomorrow/And Her Daddy's a Millionaire	1969	600.00
—By "The Iveys"; four-inch flexidisc sold from vending machines			
CAPITOL			
❑ S7-17487	Baby Blue/Day After Day	1993	6.00
—Blue vinyl			
❑ S7-17487	Baby Blue/Day After Day	1993	7.00
—Black vinyl			
ELEKTRA			
❑ 46022	Lost Inside Your Love/Come Down Hard	1979	5.00
❑ 46025	Love Is Gonna Come At Last/Sail Away	1979	5.00
RADIO			
❑ 3793	Hold On/Passin' Time	1981	5.00
❑ 3815	I Got You/Rock and Roll Contract	1981	5.00
❑ 3833	Because I Love You/Too Hung Up on You	1981	5.00
WARNER BROS.			
❑ 7801	I Miss You/Shine On	1974	6.00
Albums			
APPLE			
❑ ST-3355	Maybe Tomorrow	1969	2000.
—As "The Iveys"; album not released in US; price is for an LP slick, which does exist			
❑ ST 3364	Magic Christian Music	1970	20.00
❑ ST 3364	Magic Christian Music	1970	30.00
—With Capitol logo on Side 2 bottom			
❑ SKAO 3367	No Dice	1970	30.00
❑ SW 3387	Straight Up	1971	60.00
❑ SW 3411	Ass	1973	20.00
ELEKTRA			
❑ 6E-175	Airwaves	1979	12.00
RADIO			
❑ RR 16030	Say No More	1981	10.00
RYKO ANALOGUE			
❑ RALP 10189	Day After Day	1990	20.00
—Limited edition on clear vinyl with obi			
WARNER BROS.			
❑ BS 2762	Badfinger	1974	15.00
❑ BS 2827	Wish You Were Here	1974	15.00

BADGER

Number	Title (A Side/B Side)	Yr	NM
Albums			
ATCO			
❑ SD 7022	One Live Badger	1973	16.00
EPIC			
❑ KE 32831	White Lady	1974	15.00

BADLANDS

Also see BLACK SABBATH; OZZY OSBOURNE; KISS.

Number	Title (A Side/B Side)	Yr	NM
45s			
ATLANTIC			
❑ 88888	Dreams in the Dark/Hard Driver	1989	4.00
Albums			
ATLANTIC			
❑ 81966	Badlands	1989	10.00
CMH			
❑ 6254	Badlands	198?	10.00

BAEZ, JOAN

Number	Title (A Side/B Side)	Yr	NM
45s			
A&M			
❑ 1334	Song of Bangladesh/Prison Trilogy (Billy Rose)	1972	5.00
❑ 1334 [PS]	Song of Bangladesh/Prison Trilogy (Billy Rose)	1972	10.00
❑ 1362	In the Quiet Morning/To Bobby	1972	4.00
❑ 1362 [PS]	In the Quiet Morning/To Bobby	1972	8.00
❑ 1393	Love Song to a Stranger/Tumbleweed	1972	4.00
❑ 1454	The Best of Friends/Mary Call	1973	4.00
❑ 1472	Less Than the Song/Windrose	1973	4.00
❑ 1516	Forever Young/Guantanamera	1974	4.00
❑ 1703	Blue Sky/Dida	1975	4.00
❑ 1737	Diamonds and Rust/Winds of the Old Days	1975	5.00
❑ 1802	Please Come to Boston/Love Song to a Stranger	1976	4.00
❑ 1820	Never Dreamed You'd Leave in Summer/Children and All That Jazz	1976	4.00
❑ 1884	Caruso/Time Is Passing Us By	1976	4.00
❑ 1906	O Brother/Still Waters at Night	1977	4.00
DECCA			
❑ 32890	Silent Running/Rejoice in the Sun	1971	6.00
GUARDIAN			
❑ S7-19727	No Mermaid/Diamonds and Rust	1997	3.00
PHILCO-FORD			
❑ HP-36	There But For Fortune/Pack Up Your Sorrows	1969	20.00
—4-inch plastic "Hip Pocket Record" with color sleeve			
PORTRAIT			
❑ 70006	I'm Blowing Away/The Altar Boy and the Sheep	1977	4.00
❑ 70009	Time Rag/Miracles	1977	4.00
❑ 70032	Light a Light/Michael	1979	4.00
RCA VICTOR			
❑ 74-0568	The Ballad of Sacco and Vanzetti/Here's to You	1971	6.00
VANGUARD			
❑ SPV-6	Maria Dolores/Plane Wreck at Los Gatos (Deportee)	1971	4.00
—Small hole, plays at 33 1/3 rpm			
❑ SPV-6 [PS]	Maria Dolores/Plane Wreck at Los Gatos (Deportee)	1971	4.00
—The above single and sleeve were a bonus single included with the album "Blessed Are..."; as it is sometimes found apart from the LP, we've made a separate listing, but it was never sold separately at the time			
❑ 35012	Banks of the Ohio/Old Blue	1962	8.00
❑ 35013	Lonesome Road/Pal of Mine	1962	8.00
❑ 35018	What Have They Done to the Rain/Danger Waters	1963	8.00
❑ 35023	We Shall Overcome/What Have They Done to the Rain	1963	8.00
❑ 35026	Medley: With God on Our Side/Railroad Bill//Rambler Gambler	1964	8.00
❑ 35031	There But for Fortune/Daddy You Been On My Mind	1965	8.00
❑ 35031 [PS]	There But for Fortune/Daddy You Been On My Mind	1965	30.00
❑ 35040	Pack Up Your Sorrows/Swallow Song	1966	8.00
❑ 35046	Little Drummer Boy/Cantique de Noel	1966	10.00
❑ 35055	Be Not Too Hard/The North	1967	8.00
❑ 35088	Love Is Just a Four-Letter Word/Love Minus Zero-No Limit	1969	8.00
❑ 35092	If I Knew/Rock Salt and Nails	1969	8.00
❑ 35098	Four Days Gone/Hickory Wind	1969	8.00
❑ 35103	No Expectations/One Day at a Time	1970	6.00
❑ 35106	Sweet Sir Galahad/The Ghetto	1970	6.00
❑ 35114	Carry It On/Rock Salt and Nails	1970	6.00
❑ 35138	The Night They Drove Old Dixie Down/When Time Is Stolen	1971	8.00
❑ 35145	Let It Be/Poor Wayfaring Stranger	1971	6.00
❑ 35148	Will the Circle Be Unbroken/Just a Closer Walk with Thee	1972	5.00
❑ 35158	Blessed Are/The Brand New Tennessee Waltz	1972	5.00
Albums			
A&M			
❑ SP-3103	Come From the Shadows	198?	8.00
—Budget-line reissue			
❑ SP-3233	Diamonds and Rust	198?	8.00
—Budget-line reissue			
❑ SP-3234	The Best of Joan C. Baez	198?	8.00
—Budget-line reissue			
❑ SP-3614	Gracias A La Vida	1974	12.00
❑ SP-3704 [(2)]	From Every Stage	1976	12.00
❑ SP-4339	Come From the Shadows	1972	10.00
❑ SP-4390	Where Are You Now, My Son?	1973	10.00
❑ SP-4527	Diamonds and Rust	1975	10.00
❑ SP-4603	Gulf Winds	1976	10.00
❑ SP-4668	The Best of Joan C. Baez	1977	10.00
❑ SP-6506 [(2)]	From Every Stage	198?	10.00
—Reissue			
❑ QU-54339 [Q]	Come From the Shadows	1974	20.00
❑ QU-54527 [Q]	Diamonds and Rust	1975	20.00
BOOK-OF-THE-MONTH			
❑ 40-5711 [(4)]	Satisfied Mind	1979	25.00
—With booklet			
GOLD CASTLE			
❑ D1-71309	Recently	1989	12.00
—Reissue of 171 009			
❑ D1-71321	Diamonds and Rust in the Bullring	1989	12.00
❑ D1-71324	Speaking of Dreams	1989	12.00
❑ 171009	Recently	1988	10.00
MOBILE FIDELITY			
❑ 1-238	Diamonds and Rust	1996	60.00
—Audiophile vinyl			
NAUTILUS			
❑ NR-12	Diamonds and Rust	1980	40.00
—Audiophile vinyl			
PORTRAIT			
❑ PR 34697	Blowin' Away	1977	10.00
❑ JR 35766	Honest Lullaby	1979	10.00
SQUIRE			
❑ SQ-33001 [M]	The Best of Joan Baez	1963	20.00
VANGUARD			
❑ VSD-41/42 [(2)]	The Joan Baez Ballad Book	1972	12.00
❑ VSD-49/50 [(2)]	The Contemporary Ballad Book	1974	12.00
❑ VSD-79/80 [(2)]	The Love Song Album	197?	12.00
❑ VSD-105/6 [(2)]	The Country Music Album	1979	12.00
❑ VSD-2077 [S]	Joan Baez	1960	25.00
❑ VSD-2097 [S]	Joan Baez, Vol. 2	1961	25.00
❑ VSD-2122 [S]	Joan Baez In Concert	1962	25.00
❑ VSD-2123 [S]	Joan Baez In Concert, Part 2	1963	25.00
❑ VSD-6560/1 [(2)]	The First 10 Years	1970	15.00
❑ VSD-6570/1 [(2)]	Blessed Are...	1971	15.00
—Add 50 percent if bonus 7-inch single, "Maria Dolores"/"Plane Wreck at Los Gatos (Deportee)," and its special sleeve are still in the package			
❑ VRS-9078 [M]	Joan Baez	1960	20.00
❑ VRS-9094 [M]	Joan Baez, Vol. 2	1961	20.00
❑ VRS-9112 [M]	Joan Baez In Concert	1962	20.00
❑ VRS-9113 [M]	Joan Baez In Concert, Part 2	1963	20.00
❑ VRS-9160 [M]	Joan Baez/5	1964	15.00
❑ VRS-9200 [M]	Farewell, Angelina	1965	15.00
❑ VRS-9230 [M]	Noel	1966	15.00
❑ VRS-9240 [M]	Joan	1967	15.00
❑ VSQ-40001/2 [(2)Q]	Blessed Are	1973	25.00
❑ VSQ-40032 [Q]	Hits/Greatest & Others	1973	20.00
❑ VMS-73107	The Joan Baez Ballad Book, Vol. 1	1985	10.00
❑ VMS-73115	The Joan Baez Ballad Book, Vol. 2	1985	10.00
❑ VMS-73119	The Night They Drove Old Dixie Down	198?	10.00
❑ VSD-79160 [S]	Joan Baez/5	1964	20.00
❑ VSD-79200 [S]	Farewell, Angelina	1965	20.00
❑ VSD-79230 [S]	Noel	1966	20.00
❑ VSD-79240 [S]	Joan	1967	20.00
❑ VSD-79275	Baptism	1968	20.00
❑ VSD-79306/7 [(2)]	Any Day Now	1969	25.00
❑ VSD-79308	David's Album	1969	12.00
❑ VSD-79310	One Day at a Time	1970	12.00
❑ VSD-79313	Carry It On	1971	25.00
—Soundtrack album			
❑ VSD-79332	Hits/Greatest & Others	1973	10.00
❑ VSD-79446/7	Very Early Joan	1981	12.00

BAG, THE

Number	Title (A Side/B Side)	Yr	NM
45s			
DECCA			
❑ 32279	Nobody's Child/Nickels 'N Dimes	1968	8.00
❑ 32409	Down and Out/Up in the Mornin'	1968	8.00
❑ 32463	Red, Purple and Blue/I Want You By My Side	1969	8.00

Except when noted otherwise, VG = 25% of NM, and VG+ = 50% of NM. (Example: VG = $2.00, VG+ = $4.00 and NM = $8.00.)

Number	Title (A Side/B Side)	Yr	NM
Albums			
DECCA			
❑ DL 75057	Real	1968	15.00

BAGDASARIAN, ROSS

Real name of DAVID SEVILLE, who also invented THE CHIPMUNKS.

Number	Title (A Side/B Side)	Yr	NM
45s			
CORAL			
❑ 60544	Come On-a My House/Oh Beauty	1951	30.00
❑ 60597	The Girl with the Tambourine/He Says Mu-Humm	1951	25.00
IMPERIAL			
❑ 66379	Jone-Cone-Phone/Spanish Pizza	1969	10.00
❑ 66414	You've Got Me on a Merry-Go-Round/You Better Open Your Eyes	1969	10.00
LIBERTY			
❑ 55013	The Bold and the Brave/See a Teardrop Fall	1956	20.00
❑ 55193	Judy/Maria from Madrid	1959	16.00
❑ 55239	Lotta Bull/(B-side unknown)	1959	16.00
❑ 55275	Lazy Lovers/One Finger Waltz	1960	16.00
❑ 55462	Armen's Theme/Russian Roulette	1962	15.00
❑ 55557	Cecelia/Gotta Get to Your House	1963	15.00
❑ 55619	Lucy, Lucy/Scalliwags and Sinners	1963	15.00
❑ 55810	La Noche/Naval Maneuver	1965	12.00
❑ 55837	Come On-a My House/Gotta Get to Your House	1965	12.00
❑ 56004	Walking Birds of Carnaby/Red Wine	1967	12.00
❑ 56043	Yallah/Naval Maneuver	1968	—
—Unreleased			
❑ 56048	When I Look in Your Eyes/Sands of Time	1968	12.00
❑ 56165	I Treasure Thee/Lie Lie	1969	12.00
MERCURY			
❑ 70254	Let's Have a Merry, Merry Christmas/Hey Brother, Pour the Wine	1953	25.00
Albums			
LIBERTY			
❑ LRP-3451 [M]	The Crazy, Mixed-Up World of Ross Bagdasarian	1966	40.00
❑ LST-7451 [S]	The Crazy, Mixed-Up World of Ross Bagdasarian	1966	50.00

BAGELS, THE

Number	Title (A Side/B Side)	Yr	NM
45s			
WARNER BROS.			
❑ 5420	I Wanna Hold Your Hair/Yeah, Yeah, Yeah, Yeah	1964	15.00

BAGGYS, THE

Number	Title (A Side/B Side)	Yr	NM
45s			
PIPELINE			
❑ 501	El Surfer/El Seagull	1963	40.00

BAILEY, DIANE

Number	Title (A Side/B Side)	Yr	NM
45s			
SWAN			
❑ 4079	Golden Idol/Someone Else's Hands	1961	12.00
❑ 4086	True Blue Love/There's a Time	1961	12.00

BAILEY, J.R.

Number	Title (A Side/B Side)	Yr	NM
45s			
CALLA			
❑ 158	Love Won't Wear Off/(Instrumental)	1968	6.00
MALA			
❑ 12015	Hold Back the Dawn/Too Late	1968	8.00
MAM			
❑ 3635	I'll Always Be Your Lover/Not Too Long Ago	1974	5.00
❑ 3639	Everything I Want I See in You/I Can't See Me Without You	1974	5.00
MIDLAND INT'L			
❑ PB-10305	The Entertainer (If They Could Only See Me Now)/You Pass My Love (Like a Moving Train)	1975	5.00
RCA			
❑ PB-10799	Super Loser/Love Still Remains	1976	5.00
SPRING			
❑ 3038	I'm Still in Love with You/(B-side unknown)	1984	4.00
TOY			
❑ 3801	Love, Love, Love/(B-side unknown)	1972	6.00
❑ 3805	After Hours/(B-side unknown)	1972	6.00
UNITED ARTISTS			
❑ XW-1215	Alone in the Morning/Stella by Starlight	1978	4.00
Albums			
MAM			
❑ 9	Just Me 'N' You	1974	12.00

BAILEY, PEARL

Number	Title (A Side/B Side)	Yr	NM
45s			
COLUMBIA			
❑ 4-43588	Mame/If My Friends Could See Me Now	1966	7.00
DECCA			
❑ 31667	I Was a Little Too Lonely/I'd Rather Be Rich	1964	7.00
MERCURY			
❑ 70926	I Can't Rock and Roll to Save My Soul/The Gypsy Goofed	1956	15.00
RCA VICTOR			
❑ 74-0435	Mama, a Rainbow/Two by Two	1971	5.00
❑ 74-0510	Close to You/A House Is Not a Home	1971	5.00
ROULETTE			
❑ 4016	Bill Bailey, Won't You Please Come Home/C'est Magnifique	1957	12.00
❑ 4167	I Got Rhythm/Summertime	1959	12.00
❑ 4206	Jingle Bells (Cha Cha Cha)/Five Pound Box of Money	1959	20.00
❑ 4233	New Shoes/Not Now John	1960	10.00
❑ 4279	Ain't Misbehavin'/Bill Bailey, Won't You Please Come Home	1960	10.00
❑ 4415	Gee Baby (Ain't I Good to You)/You Gotta Dance	1962	8.00
❑ 4781	Look At That Face/Was It a Necessary Evil	1967	6.00
7-Inch Extended Plays			
COLUMBIA			
❑ B-2570	Tired/Legalize My Name//That's Good Enough for Me/It's a Woman's Prerogative	195?	10.00
❑ B-2570 [PS]	Pearl Bailey (Hall of Fame Series)	195?	10.00
Albums			
COLUMBIA			
❑ CL 985 [M]	The Definitive Pearl Bailey	1957	25.00
❑ CL 6099 [10]	Pearl Bailey Entertains	1950	50.00
CORAL			
❑ CRL 56068 [10]	Say Si Si	1953	50.00
❑ CRL 56078 [10]	I'm with You	1954	50.00
❑ CRL 57037 [M]	Pearl Bailey	1957	40.00
❑ CRL 57162 [M]	Cultured Pearl	1958	40.00
MERCURY			
❑ MG-20187 [M]	The One and Only Pearl Bailey Sings	1956	40.00
❑ MG-20277 [M]	The Intoxicating Pearl Bailey	1957	40.00
PROJECT 3			
❑ PR 5022 SD	The Real Pearl	1968	15.00
RCA VICTOR			
❑ LSP-4529	Pearl's Pearls	1971	15.00
ROULETTE			
❑ SR 5004	Songs of the Bad Old Days	1976	12.00
❑ R-25012 [M]	Pearl Bailey A Broad	1957	30.00
—Black label original			
❑ SR-25012 [R]	Pearl Bailey A Broad	196?	12.00
❑ R-25016 [M]	Pearl Bailey Sings for Adults Only	1959	20.00
—Originals have a white label with colored spokes			
❑ SR-25016 [S]	Pearl Bailey Sings for Adults Only	1959	25.00
—Originals have a white label with colored spokes			
❑ R-25037 [M]	St. Louis Blues	1958	30.00
—Black label original			
❑ SR-25037 [S]	St. Louis Blues	1959	30.00
—Originals have a white label with colored spokes			
❑ R-25063 [M]	Pearl Bailey Sings Porgy and Bess and Other Gershwin Melodies	1959	20.00
—Originals have a white label with colored spokes			
❑ SR-25063 [S]	Pearl Bailey Sings Porgy and Bess and Other Gershwin Melodies	1959	25.00
—Originals have a white label with colored spokes			
❑ R-25101 [M]	More Songs for Adults Only	1960	20.00
—Originals have a white label with colored spokes			
❑ SR-25101 [S]	More Songs for Adults Only	1960	25.00
—Originals have a white label with colored spokes			
❑ R-25116 [M]	Songs of the Bad Old Days	1960	20.00
—Originals have a white label with colored spokes			
❑ SR-25116 [S]	Songs of the Bad Old Days	1960	25.00
—Originals have a white label with colored spokes			
❑ R-25125 [M]	Naughty But Nice	1960	20.00
—Originals have a white label with colored spokes			
❑ SR-25125 [S]	Naughty But Nice	1960	25.00
—Originals have a white label with colored spokes			
❑ R-25144 [M]	The Best of Pearl Bailey	1961	20.00
—Originals have a white label with colored spokes			
❑ SR-25144 [S]	The Best of Pearl Bailey	1961	25.00
—Originals have a white label with colored spokes			
❑ SR-25144 [S]	The Best of Pearl Bailey	1964	15.00
—Orange and yellow "roulette wheel" label			
❑ R-25155 [M]	Pearl Bailey Sings Songs of Harold Arlen	1961	20.00
—Originals have a white label with colored spokes			
❑ SR-25155 [S]	Pearl Bailey Sings Songs of Harold Arlen	1961	25.00
—Originals have a white label with colored spokes			
❑ R-25167 [M]	Happy Sounds	1962	20.00
—Originals have a white label with colored spokes			
❑ SR-25167 [S]	Happy Sounds	1962	25.00
—Originals have a white label with colored spokes			
❑ R-25181 [M]	Come On, Let's Play with Pearlie Mae	1962	20.00
—Originals have a white label with colored spokes			
❑ SR-25181 [S]	Come On, Let's Play with Pearlie Mae	1962	25.00
—Originals have a white label with colored spokes			
❑ R-25195 [M]	All About Good Little Girls and Bad Little Boys	1963	20.00
—Originals have a pink and orange label			
❑ SR-25195 [S]	All About Good Little Girls and Bad Little Boys	1963	25.00
—Originals have a pink and orange label			
❑ R-25222 [M]	C'est La Vie	1963	20.00
—Originals have a pink and orange label			
❑ SR-25222 [S]	C'est La Vie	1963	25.00
—Originals have a pink and orange label			
❑ R-25259 [M]	The Risque World of Pearl Bailey	1964	15.00
❑ SR-25259 [S]	The Risque World of Pearl Bailey	1964	20.00
❑ R-25271 [M]	Songs by James Van Heusen	1964	15.00
❑ SR-25271 [S]	Songs by James Van Heusen	1964	20.00
❑ R-25300 [M]	For Women Only	1965	15.00
❑ SR-25300 [S]	For Women Only	1965	20.00
VOCALION			
❑ VL 3621 [M]	Gems by Pearl Bailey	1958	25.00

BAILEY, THOMAS

Number	Title (A Side/B Side)	Yr	NM
45s			
FEDERAL			
❑ 12559	Fran/Just Won't Move	1969	12.00
❑ 12567	Wish I Was Back/Percy's Place	1970	100.00

BAINES, VICKI

Number	Title (A Side/B Side)	Yr	NM
45s			
LOMA			
❑ 2078	We Can Find True Love/Sweeter Than Sweet Things	1967	12.00
PARKWAY			
❑ 957	Losing You/Got to Run	1965	25.00
❑ 966	Country Girl/Are You Kidding	1966	100.00

BAJA MARIMBA BAND, THE

Also includes records as "Julius Wechter and the Baja Marimba Band."

Number	Title (A Side/B Side)	Yr	NM
45s			
A&M			
❑ XMAS 1 [DJ]	The 12 Days Of Christmas/My Favorite Things	1968	12.00
—B-side by We Five			
❑ XMAS 1 [PS]	The 12 Days Of Christmas/My Favorite Things	1968	15.00
—B-side by We Five			
❑ 816	The Telephone Song/Portuguese Washerwoman	1966	5.00
❑ 824	Ghost Riders in the Sky/Sabor A Mi	1966	5.00
❑ 833	The Cry of the Wild Goose/Spanish Moss	1967	5.00
❑ 833 [PS]	The Cry of the Wild Goose/Spanish Moss	1967	8.00
❑ 843	Georgy Girl/Cabeza Arriba (Heads Up)	1967	5.00
❑ 862	Along Comes Mary/Wall Street Rag	1967	4.00
❑ 862 [PS]	Along Comes Mary/Wall Street Rag	1967	5.00
❑ 892	Foul Play/The Sounds of Silence	1967	4.00
❑ 913	Fiddler on the Roof/Sunday Mornin'	1968	4.00
❑ 937	Brasilia/Yes Sir, That's My Baby	1968	4.00
❑ 937 [PS]	Brasilia/Yes Sir, That's My Baby	1968	7.00
❑ 975	Little Prayer/Do You Know the Way to San Jose	1968	4.00
—Artist credit: "Julius Wechter & The Baja Marimba Band"			
❑ 1005	Flyin' High/Les Bicyclettes de Belsize	1968	4.00

Except when noted otherwise, VG = 25% of NM, and VG+ = 50% of NM. (Example: VG = $2.00, VG+ = $4.00 and NM = $8.00.)

Number	Title (A Side/B Side)	Yr	NM
❑ 1047	Big Red/Ruby '68	1969	4.00
❑ 1078	I'll Marimba You/I Don't Wanna Walk Without You	1969	4.00

—Artist credit: "Julius Wechter & The Baja Marimba Band"

Number	Title (A Side/B Side)	Yr	NM
❑ 1126	Fresh Air/Wave	1969	4.00
❑ 1136	Can You Dig It Part 1/ Can You Dig It Part 2	1969	4.00
❑ 1186	Picasso Summer/Samba Nuevo	1970	4.00
❑ 1281	Spanish Flea/As Time Goes By	1971	4.00

—Artist credit: "Julius Wechter & The Baja Marimba Band"

ALMO

Number	Title (A Side/B Side)	Yr	NM
❑ 201	Comin' In the Back Door/ December's Child	1963	8.00
❑ 203	Moonglow & Theme from Picnic/Acapulco 1922	1964	6.00
❑ 206	Pedro's Pouch/Wincle Lamoyan Coan	1964	6.00
❑ 207	Up Cherry Street/Woody Woodpecker Song	1964	6.00
❑ 211	Baja Ska/Samba De Orfeu	1964	6.00
❑ 216	Juarez/Guacamole	1965	6.00
❑ 218	Goin' Out the Side Door/ Brasilia	1965	6.00
❑ 228	Yellow Bird/For Animals Only	1966	6.00
❑ 231	(How Much Is That) Doggie in the Window/ Puff (The Magic Dragon)	1966	6.00

BELL

Number	Title (A Side/B Side)	Yr	NM
❑ 45339	Theme from "Deep Throat"/ Do You Want to Dance	1973	5.00
❑ 45376	Anytime of the Year/Taco Belle	1973	4.00

Albums

A&M

Number	Title (A Side/B Side)	Yr	NM
❑ LP-104 [M]	Baja Marimba Band	1964	10.00
—Reissue with A&M logo at left			
❑ LP-104 [M]	Baja Marimba Band	1964	12.00
—Original pressing with A&M logo at top			
❑ SP-104 [S]	Baja Marimba Band	1964	15.00
—Original number; has A&M logo at top			
❑ LP-109 [M]	Baja Marimba Band Rides Again	1965	10.00
❑ SP-109 [S]	Baja Marimba Band Rides Again	1965	15.00
—Original issues had this number			
❑ SP-113 [M]	For Animals Only	1965	10.00
❑ SP-118 [M]	Watch Out!	1966	10.00
❑ SP-123 [M]	Heads Up	1967	10.00
❑ SP-3523 [(2)]	Foursider	1972	12.00
❑ SP-4104 [S]	Baja Marimba Band	1964	12.00
—Reissue; has A&M logo at left			
❑ SP-4109 [S]	Baja Marimba Band Rides Again	1965	12.00
❑ SP-4113 [S]	For Animals Only	1965	12.00
❑ SP-4118 [S]	Watch Out!	1966	12.00
❑ SP-4123 [S]	Heads Up	1967	12.00
❑ SP-4136	Fowl Play	1968	10.00
❑ SP-4150	Do You Know the Way to San Jose?	1968	10.00
❑ SP-4167	Those Were the Days	1969	10.00
❑ SP-4200	Fresh Air	1969	10.00
❑ SP-4248	Greatest Hits	1970	10.00
❑ SP-4298	As Time Goes By	1971	10.00

BAKER, B.J.

45s

DECCA

Number	Title (A Side/B Side)	Yr	NM
❑ 732487	The Melody Man/Anywhere	1969	8.00

BAKER, BOBBY

45s

SWAN

Number	Title (A Side/B Side)	Yr	NM
❑ 4037	Baby Blue Eyes/Hush Our Secret	1959	15.00

BAKER, CHARLES

45s

HIT

Number	Title (A Side/B Side)	Yr	NM
❑ 159	Where You Been/Sha La La	1964	15.00

—B-side by the Beasts

BAKER, CHARLIE

45s

LIBERTY

Number	Title (A Side/B Side)	Yr	NM
❑ 55226	Star of Wonder/You Crack Me Up	1959	25.00

MUNRAB

Number	Title (A Side/B Side)	Yr	NM
❑ 106	Star of Wonder/You Crack Me Up	1959	150.00

BAKER, DONNIE, AND THE DEMENSIONALS

45s

RAINBOW

Number	Title (A Side/B Side)	Yr	NM
❑ 219	Drinkin' Pop Sodee-Odee (Pop Pop)/Sleepy Time Gal	1953	60.00
—Black vinyl			
❑ 219	Drinkin' Pop Sodee-Odee (Pop Pop)/Sleepy Time Gal	1953	150.00
—Red vinyl			

BAKER, GEORGE, SELECTION

45s

COLOSSUS

Number	Title (A Side/B Side)	Yr	NM
❑ 112	Little Gren Bag/ Pretty Little Dreamer	1970	5.00
❑ 117	Dear Ann/Fly	1970	4.00
❑ 124	I Wanna Love You/Impressions	1970	4.00

WARNER BROS.

Number	Title (A Side/B Side)	Yr	NM
❑ 8115	Paloma Blanca/Dreamboat	1975	4.00
❑ 8207	Baby Blue/Morning Sky	1976	4.00

Albums

COLOSSUS

Number	Title (A Side/B Side)	Yr	NM
❑ CS-1002	Little Green Bag	1970	20.00

WARNER BROS.

Number	Title (A Side/B Side)	Yr	NM
❑ BS 2905	Paloma Blanca	1975	15.00

BAKER, GINGER, 'S AIR FORCE

Includes records credited only to Ginger Baker. Also see BLIND FAITH; CREAM.

45s

ATCO

Number	Title (A Side/B Side)	Yr	NM
❑ 6750	Man of Constant Sorrow/Doin' It	1970	5.00
❑ 6816	Atunde! (We Are Here) Part 1/ Atunde! (We Are Here) Part 2	1971	5.00

Albums

ATCO

Number	Title (A Side/B Side)	Yr	NM
❑ SD 33-343	Ginger Baker's Air Force 2	1971	12.00
❑ SD 2-703 [(2)]	Ginger Baker's Air Force	1970	20.00
❑ SD 7012	Stratavarious	1972	12.00

AXIOM

Number	Title (A Side/B Side)	Yr	NM
❑ 539864-1	Middle Passage	1990	15.00

CELLULOID

Number	Title (A Side/B Side)	Yr	NM
❑ CEL-6126	Horses and Trees	1986	10.00

POLYDOR

Number	Title (A Side/B Side)	Yr	NM
❑ 3504 [(2)]	Ginger Baker At His Best	1973	15.00

SIRE

Number	Title (A Side/B Side)	Yr	NM
❑ SASD-7532	Eleven Sides of Baker	1977	10.00

BAKER, KENNY

45s

ORBIT

Number	Title (A Side/B Side)	Yr	NM
❑ 541	Goodbye Little Star/ I'm Gonna Love You	1959	20.00

BAKER, LAVERN

45s

ATLANTIC

Number	Title (A Side/B Side)	Yr	NM
❑ 1004	How Can You Leave a Man Like This/Soul on Fire	1953	50.00
❑ 1030	I Can't Hold Out Any Longer/ I'm Living My Life for You	1954	40.00
❑ 1047	Tweedlee Dee/Tomorrow Night	1954	40.00
❑ 1057	Bop-Ting-a-Ling/That's All I Need	1955	40.00
❑ 1075	Play It Fair/That Lucky Old Sun	1955	40.00
❑ 1087	Get Up Get Up (You Sleepyhead)/ My Happiness Forever	1956	25.00
❑ 1093	Fee Fee Fi Fo Fum/ I'll Do the Same for You	1956	25.00
❑ 1104	I Can't Love You Enough/Still	1956	25.00
❑ 1116	Jim Dandy/Tra La La	1956	25.00
❑ 1136	Jim Dandy Got Married/ The Game of Love	1957	25.00
❑ 1150	Humpty Dumpty Heart/ Love Me Right	1957	25.00
❑ 1163	St.Louis Blues/Miracles	1957	25.00
❑ 1176	Substitute/Learning to Love	1958	25.00
❑ 1189	Harbor Lights/Whipper Snapper	1958	25.00
❑ 2001	It's So Fine/Why Baby Why	1958	25.00
❑ 2007	I Cried a Tear/Dix-A-Billy	1958	25.00
❑ 2021	I Waited Too Long/You're Teasing Me	1959	20.00
❑ 2033	So High So Low/If You Love Me	1959	20.00
❑ 2041	Tiny Tim/For Love of You	1959	20.00
❑ 2048	Shake a Hand/Manana	1960	20.00
❑ 2059	Wheel of Fortune/ Shadows of Love	1960	15.00
❑ 2067	A Help-Each-Other Romance/ How Often	1960	15.00
—With Ben E. King			
❑ 2077	Bumble Bee/My Time Will Come	1960	15.00
❑ 2090	You're the Boss/I'll Never Be Free	1961	15.00
—With Jimmy Ricks			
❑ 2099	Saved/Don Juan	1961	15.00
❑ 2109	I Didn't Know I Was Crying/ Hurtin' Inside	1961	15.00
❑ 2119	Hey, Memphis/Voodoo Voodoo	1961	15.00
❑ 2137	Must I Cry Again/ No Love So True	1962	12.00
❑ 2167	See See Rider/ The Story of My Love	1962	12.00
❑ 2186	Trouble in Mind/Half of Your Love	1963	12.00
❑ 2203	Itty Bitty Girl/Oh, Johnny Oh, Johnny	1963	12.00
❑ 2234	You'd Better Find Yourself Another Fool/Go Away	1964	10.00
❑ 2267	Fly Me to the Moon/ Ain't Gonna Cry No More	1965	10.00

ATLANTIC OLDIES SERIES

Number	Title (A Side/B Side)	Yr	NM
❑ 13001	See See Rider/Jim Dandy	196?	5.00
—Originals have gold and black labels			
❑ 13002	I Cried a Tear/Saved	196?	5.00
—Originals have gold and black labels			

BRUNSWICK

Number	Title (A Side/B Side)	Yr	NM
❑ 55285	Let Me Belong to You/ Pledging My Love	1965	8.00
❑ 55287	Think Twice/ Please Don't Hurt Me	1965	8.00
—With Jackie Wilson			
❑ 55291	One Monkey (Don't Stop the Show)/Baby	1966	8.00
❑ 55297	Batman to the Rescue/ Call Me Darling	1966	10.00
❑ 55311	Nothing Like Being in Love/ Wrapped, Tied and Tangled	1967	8.00
❑ 55341	Born to Lose/I Need You So	1967	8.00
❑ 55408	I'm the One to Do It/Baby	1969	6.00

KING

Number	Title (A Side/B Side)	Yr	NM
❑ 4556	Trying/Snuff Dipper	1952	50.00
—B-side by Todd Rhodes			
❑ 4583	Must I Cry Again/Hog Maw and Cabbage Slaw	1952	50.00
—B-side by Todd Rhodes			
❑ 4601	Lost Child/Thunderball Boogie	1953	50.00
—B-side by Todd Rhodes			

7-Inch Extended Plays

ATLANTIC

Number	Title (A Side/B Side)	Yr	NM
❑ 566	(contents unknown)	1956	100.00
❑ 566 [PS]	Tweedle Dee	1956	100.00
❑ 588	*Jim Dandy/Still/Play It Fair/ Tra La La	1957	80.00
❑ 588 [PS]	Jim Dandy	1957	100.00
❑ 617	I Cried a Tear/Dix-a-Billy// I Waited Too Long/You're Teasing Me	1958	80.00
❑ 617 [PS]	I Cried a Tear	1958	100.00

Albums

ATCO

Number	Title (A Side/B Side)	Yr	NM
❑ SD 33-372	Her Greatest Recordings	1971	12.00

ATLANTIC

Number	Title (A Side/B Side)	Yr	NM
❑ 1281 [M]	LaVern Baker Sings Bessie Smith	1958	120.00
—Black label			
❑ 1281 [M]	LaVern Baker Sings Bessie Smith	1960	30.00
—Red and purple label, "fan" logo in white			
❑ 1281 [M]	LaVern Baker Sings Bessie Smith	1963	20.00
—Red and purple label, "fan" logo in black			
❑ SD 1281 [S]	LaVern Baker Sings Bessie Smith	1959	150.00
—Green label			
❑ SD 1281 [S]	LaVern Baker Sings Bessie Smith	1960	40.00
—Green and blue label, "fan" logo in white			
❑ SD 1281 [S]	LaVern Baker Sings Bessie Smith	1963	25.00
—Green and blue label, "fan" logo in black			
❑ 8002 [M]	LaVern	1956	250.00
—Black label			
❑ 8002 [M]	LaVern	1960	30.00
—Red and purple label, "fan" logo in white			
❑ 8002 [M]	LaVern	1963	20.00
—Red and purple label, "fan" logo in black			
❑ 8007 [M]	LaVern Baker	1957	250.00
—Black label			
❑ 8007 [M]	LaVern Baker	1960	30.00
—Red and purple label, "fan" logo in white			
❑ 8007 [M]	LaVern Baker	1963	20.00
—Red and purple label, "fan" logo in black			
❑ 8030 [M]	Blues Ballads	1959	200.00
—Black label			
❑ 8030 [M]	Blues Ballads	1960	30.00
—Red and purple label, "fan" logo in white			
❑ 8030 [M]	Blues Ballads	1960	150.00
—White "bullseye" label			
❑ 8030 [M]	Blues Ballads	1963	20.00
—Red and purple label, "fan" logo in black			
❑ 8036 [M]	Precious Memories	1959	200.00
—Black label			
❑ 8036 [M]	Precious Memories	1960	30.00
—Red and purple label, "fan" logo in white			
❑ 8036 [M]	Precious Memories	1960	150.00
—White "bullseye" label			
❑ 8036 [M]	Precious Memories	1963	20.00
—Red and purple label, "fan" logo in black			
❑ SD 8036 [S]	Precious Memories	1959	300.00
—Green label			

Except when noted otherwise, VG = 25% of NM, and VG+ = 50% of NM. (Example: VG = $2.00, VG+ = $4.00 and NM = $8.00.)

Number	Title (A Side/B Side)	Yr	NM
❑ SD 8036 [S]	Precious Memories	1960	40.00
—Green and blue label, "fan" logo in white			
❑ SD 8036 [S]	Precious Memories	1960	200.00
—White "bullseye" label			
❑ SD 8036 [S]	Precious Memories	1963	25.00
—Green and blue label, "fan" logo in black			
❑ 8050 [M]	Saved	1961	100.00
—Red and purple label, "fan" logo in white			
❑ 8050 [M]	Saved	1963	20.00
—Red and purple label, "fan" logo in black			
❑ SD 8050 [S]	Saved	1961	150.00
—Green and blue label, "fan" logo in white			
❑ SD 8050 [S]	Saved	1963	25.00
—Green and blue label, "fan" logo in black			
❑ 8071 [M]	See See Rider	1962	100.00
—Red and purple label, "fan" logo in white			
❑ 8071 [M]	See See Rider	1963	20.00
—Red and purple label, "fan" logo in black			
❑ SD 8071 [S]	See See Rider	1962	150.00
—Green and blue label, "fan" logo in white			
❑ SD 8071 [S]	See See Rider	1963	25.00
—Green and blue label, "fan" logo in black			
❑ 8078 [M]	The Best of LaVern Baker	1963	150.00
—Red and purple label, "fan" logo in black			
❑ 90980	LaVern Baker Sings Bessie Smith	1989	12.00
—Reissue of SD 1281			
BRUNSWICK			
❑ BL 754160	Let Me Belong to You	1970	20.00

BAKER, MICKEY "GUITAR" Also see MICKEY AND SYLVIA.

Number	Title (A Side/B Side)	Yr	NM
45s			
ATLANTIC			
❑ 2042	Third Man Theme/Baia	1959	12.00
KING			
❑ 5951	Side Show/Steam Roller	1964	10.00
❑ 5979	Do What You Do/Night Blue	1965	10.00
MGM			
❑ 12418	Spinnin' Rock Boogie/Tricky	1957	20.00
RAINBOW			
❑ 288	Shake Walkin'/Greasy Spoon	1955	30.00
❑ 299	Bandstand Stomp/ Rock with a Sock	1955	30.00
❑ 303	Old Devil Moon/Guitarambo	1955	30.00
SAVOY			
❑ 867	Guitar Mambo/Riverboat	1952	50.00
❑ 874	Love Me Baby/Oh Happy Day	1953	50.00
Albums			
ATLANTIC			
❑ 8035 [M]	The Wildest Guitar	1959	150.00
—Black label			
❑ 8035 [M]	The Wildest Guitar	1960	50.00
—Red and purple label, "fan" logo in white			
❑ SD 8035 [S]	The Wildest Guitar	1959	250.00
—Green label			
❑ SD 8035 [S]	The Wildest Guitar	1960	80.00
—Green and blue label, "fan" logo in white			
KICKING MULE			
❑ 140	The Jazz Rock Guitar of Mickey Baker	1978	12.00
❑ 142	The Blues and Jazz Guitar of Mickey Baker	1978	12.00
KING			
❑ 839 [M]	But Wild	196?	80.00
—Blue label with crown			
❑ 839 [M]	But Wild	1963	400.00
—Black label, no crown			
❑ S-839 [R]	But Wild	196?	40.00

BAKER, PENNY, AND THE PILLOWS

Number	Title (A Side/B Side)	Yr	NM
45s			
WITCH			
❑ 123	Bring Back the Beatles/ Gonna Win Him	1964	20.00
❑ 123 [PS]	Bring Back the Beatles/ Gonna Win Him	1964	20.00

BAKER, RONNIE

Number	Title (A Side/B Side)	Yr	NM
45s			
LAURIE			
❑ 3128	My Story/I Want to Be Loved	1962	60.00
❑ 3164	Land of Love/Time Told Me	1963	20.00
❑ 3250	See You in September/ Young at Heart	1964	20.00

BAKER, SAM, AND NANCY COHEN

Number	Title (A Side/B Side)	Yr	NM
45s			
HIT			
❑ 125	Once Upon a Time/ No Particular Place to Go	1964	8.00
—B-side by Sammie Moore			

BAKER, SHARI

Number	Title (A Side/B Side)	Yr	NM
45s			
HIT			
❑ 175	Don't Forget I Still Love You/ My World's a Blue World	1965	8.00
—B-side by Ed Hardin			

BAKER, YVONNE Also see THE SENSATIONS.

Number	Title (A Side/B Side)	Yr	NM
45s			
JAMIE			
❑ 1290	What a Difference Love Makes/ Funny What Time Can Do	1965	12.00
MODERN			
❑ 1055	A Woman Needs a Man/ My Baby Needs Me	196?	10.00
PARKWAY			
❑ 140	You Didn't Say a Word/ To Prove My Love Is True	1967	100.00

BAKER GURVITZ ARMY, THE

Number	Title (A Side/B Side)	Yr	NM
45s			
ATCO			
❑ 7043	People/(B-side unknown)	1976	5.00
JANUS			
❑ 248	4 Phil/Help Me	1975	5.00
Albums			
ATCO			
❑ SD 36-123	Elysian Encounters	1975	10.00
❑ SD 36-137	Hearts On Fire	1976	10.00
JANUS			
❑ JXS-7015	The Baker Gurvitz Army	1975	12.00

BAKER SISTERS, THE

Number	Title (A Side/B Side)	Yr	NM
45s			
MERCURY			
❑ 70839	Too Many Teardrops/ Break the String	1956	20.00
❑ 70980	Little Monster/One By One	1956	20.00
❑ 71074	Trinidaddy/Careless Love	1957	20.00
UNIQUE			
❑ 324	Last Bus Home/If You're Ever Gonna Leave Me	1956	15.00

BAKER TWINS, THE

Number	Title (A Side/B Side)	Yr	NM
45s			
CAMEO			
❑ 324	He's No Good/Words Written on Water	1964	20.00

BALANCE

Number	Title (A Side/B Side)	Yr	NM
45s			
PORTRAIT			
❑ 24-02177	Breaking Away/It's So Strange	1981	4.00
❑ 24-02608	Falling in Love/ Fly Through the Night	1981	4.00
❑ 24-02826	American Dream/ I'm Through Loving You	1982	4.00
❑ 24-03083	Slow Motion/Is It Over	1982	4.00
Albums			
PORTRAIT			
❑ NFR 37357	Balance	1981	8.00
❑ ARR 38019	In for the Count	1982	8.00

BALDRY, LONG JOHN

Number	Title (A Side/B Side)	Yr	NM
45s			
A&M			
❑ 974	When the Sun Comes Shining Through/Wise to the Ways of the World	1968	8.00
❑ 1041	It's Too Late Now/ Long and Lonely Nights	1969	8.00
ASCOT			
❑ 2229	Bring My Baby Back to Me/ Cuckoo	1967	10.00
❑ 2236	Only a Fool Breaks His Own Heart/Let Him Go	1967	10.00
EMI AMERICA			
❑ 8018	You've Lost That Lovin' Feelin'/ Baldry's Out	1979	4.00
—A-side: With Kathi McDonald			
❑ 8018 [PS]	You've Lost That Lovin' Feelin'/ Baldry's Out	1979	6.00
❑ 8024	A Thrill Is a Thrill/Find You	1979	4.00
UNITED ARTISTS			
❑ 50141	Bring My Baby Back to Me/ Cuckoo	1967	10.00
WARNER BROS.			
❑ 7098	Hey Lord You Made the Night Too Long/Let the Heartaches Begin	1967	8.00
❑ 7184	Hold Back the Daybreak/Since I Lost You Baby	1968	6.00
❑ 7506	Don't Try to Lay No Boogie-Woogie on the King of Rock N Roll/Mr. Rubin	1971	6.00
❑ 7516	Don't Try to Lay No Boogie-Woogie on the King of Rock N Roll/same (Part 2)	1971	6.00
❑ 7597	Iko Iko/You Can't Judge a Book by Its Cover	1972	6.00
❑ 7617	Mother Ain't Dead/You Can't Judge a Book by Its Cover	1972	6.00
Albums			
ASCOT			
❑ AM-13022 [M]	Long John's Blues	1965	50.00
❑ AS-16022 [R]	Long John's Blues	1965	40.00
CASABLANCA			
❑ NBLP 7012	Good to Be Alive	1975	12.00
❑ NBLP 7035	Welcome to the Club	1976	12.00
EMI AMERICA			
❑ SW-17015	Baldry's Out	1979	10.00
❑ SW-17038	Long John Baldry	1980	10.00
UNITED ARTISTS			
❑ UAS-5543 [M]	Long John's Blues	1971	12.00
—Reissue of Ascot 13022			
WARNER BROS.			
❑ WS 1921	It Ain't Easy	1971	15.00
❑ BS 2614	Everything Stops for Tea	1973	12.00

BALDWIN, CLIVE

Number	Title (A Side/B Side)	Yr	NM
45s			
MERCURY			
❑ 73680	Now It's Paul McCartney, Stevie Wonder, Alice Cooper, Elton John/The Disco Rag	1975	8.00

BALIN, MARTY Also see BODACIOUS D.F.; JEFFERSON AIRPLANE; JEFFERSON STARSHIP.

Number	Title (A Side/B Side)	Yr	NM
45s			
CHALLENGE			
❑ 9146	Nobody But You/ You Made Me Fall	1962	50.00
❑ 9156	I Specialize in Love/ You're Alive with Love	1962	50.00
EMI AMERICA			
❑ 8084	Hearts/Freeway	1981	4.00
❑ 8084 [PS]	Hearts/Freeway	1981	5.00
❑ 8093	Atlanta Lady (Something About Your Love)/Lydia	1981	4.00
❑ 8153	What Love Is/Will You Forever	1983	4.00
❑ 8153 [PS]	What Love Is/Will You Forever	1983	5.00
❑ 8160	Do It for Love/Heart of Stone	1983	4.00
❑ 8160 [PS]	Do It for Love/Heart of Stone	1983	5.00
Albums			
EMI AMERICA			
❑ SPRO-9673 [DJ]	Balin	1981	20.00
—Red vinyl			
❑ ST-17054	Balin	1981	10.00
❑ ST-17088	Lucky	1983	10.00

BALL, KENNY

Number	Title (A Side/B Side)	Yr	NM
45s			
BELL			
❑ 45412	Make Love to Me/ Smile, Smile, Smile	1973	5.00
DECCA			
❑ 32083	Greenback Theme/Red Square	1967	8.00
❑ 32104	Rosie/Harmonize	1967	8.00
—With Max Bygraves			
GUYDEN			
❑ 2054	Samantha/I Still Love You All	1961	15.00
JERDEN			
❑ 776	900 Miles/(I Wonder) What Becomes of Life	1965	20.00
KAPP			
❑ KJB-11	Midnight in Moscow/The Green Leaves of Summer	1964	6.00
❑ KJB-11 [PS]	Midnight in Moscow/The Green Leaves of Summer	1964	10.00
❑ 442	Midnight in Moscow/ American Patrol	1962	12.00
❑ 451	March of the Siamese Children/ Villa	1962	10.00
❑ 460	The Green Leaves of Summer/ I Shall Not Be Moved	1962	10.00
❑ 483	So Do I/All Through the Night	1962	10.00
❑ 494	The Payoff/Coronet Chop Suey	1962	10.00
❑ 509	Sukiyaki/Hazelmere	1963	10.00

B

Number	Title (A Side/B Side)	Yr	NM
❑ 509	Sukiyaki/Nuages	1963	10.00
❑ 531	55 Days at Peking/Rondo	1963	10.00
❑ 554	Heartaches/High Hopes	1963	10.00
❑ 581	From Russia with Love/ Acapulco 1922	1964	10.00
Albums			
JAZZOLOGY			
❑ 65	In Concert in the USA, Vol. 1	1979	10.00
❑ 66	In Concert in the USA, Vol. 2	1979	10.00
KAPP			
❑ KL-1276 [M]	Midnight in Moscow	1962	20.00
❑ KL-1285 [M]	It's Trad	1962	20.00
❑ KL-1294 [M]	Recorded Live	1962	20.00
❑ KL-1314 [M]	More	1963	15.00
❑ KL-1340 [M]	Big Ones	1963	15.00
❑ KL-1348 [M]	Washington Square and the Best of Kenny Ball	1964	15.00
❑ KL-1392 [M]	For the Jet Set	1964	15.00
❑ KS-3276 [S]	Midnight in Moscow	1962	20.00
❑ KS-3285 [S]	It's Trad	1962	20.00
❑ KS-3294 [S]	Recorded Live	1962	20.00
❑ KS-3314 [S]	More	1963	20.00
❑ KS-3340 [S]	Big Ones	1963	20.00
❑ KS-3348 [S]	Washington Square and the Best of Kenny Ball	1964	20.00
❑ KS-3392 [S]	For the Jet Set	1964	20.00

BALLACK, ROBERT JOHN

45s

Number	Title (A Side/B Side)	Yr	NM
ROULETTE			
❑ 7122	Sweet Sounds of Music/I'm Comin' to Get You	1972	5.00
❑ 7133	Ain't No Use/Givin' Up Givin' You Up	1972	5.00

BALLADEERS, THE

45s

Number	Title (A Side/B Side)	Yr	NM
DEL-FI			
❑ 4123	Morning Star/Tom Gets the Last Laugh	1959	20.00
❑ 4127	Durant Jail/Turtle Dove	1959	20.00
❑ 4138	Hurtin'/Roll Call Company "J"	1960	20.00
ERA			
❑ 3069	A Long Way from Home/ Wedding John Doe	1962	15.00
Albums			
DEL-FI			
❑ DFLP-1204 [M]	Alive-O!	1959	40.00
❑ DFST-1204 [S]	Alive-O!	1959	60.00

BALLADS, THE

45s

Number	Title (A Side/B Side)	Yr	NM
VEE JAY			
❑ 714	I Can't See Your Love (Vocal)/ (Instrumental)	1966	25.00
VENTURE			
❑ 615	God Bless Our Love/My Baby Knows How to Love Her Man	1968	15.00
❑ 615	God Bless Our Love/My Baby Knows How to Love Her Man	1968	20.00
—Original pressings call the group "The Ballards"			
❑ 625	I Love You Yeah/You're the One	1968	15.00
❑ 630	Goodnight My Love/ Hey Diddle Diddle	1969	15.00
❑ 637	The Gift of Love/I Wish I Knew	1969	15.00

BALLARD, FLORENCE

Former member of THE SUPREMES.

45s

Number	Title (A Side/B Side)	Yr	NM
ABC			
❑ 11074	Goin' Out of My Head/ It Doesn't Matter How I Say It	1968	30.00
❑ 11144	Love Ain't Love/Forever Faithful	1968	30.00
❑ 11144 [PS]	Love Ain't Love/Forever Faithful	1968	80.00

BALLARD, FRANK

Albums

Number	Title (A Side/B Side)	Yr	NM
PHILLIPS INTERNATIONAL			
❑ 1985 [M]	Rhythm-Blues Party	1962	5000.
—VG value 2500; VG+ value 3750			

BALLARD, HANK, AND THE MIDNIGHTERS

Includes records credited only to Hank Ballard. Also see THE MIDNIGHTERS; THE ROYALS (1).

45s

Number	Title (A Side/B Side)	Yr	NM
CHESS			
❑ 2111	Love, Why Is It Taking You So Long/I'm a Junkie for My Baby's Love	1971	6.00
KING			
❑ S-7 1619 [S]	Let's Go Again (Where We Went Last Night)/ These Young Girls	196?	30.00
—Jukebox single; 33 1/3 rpm, small hole			
❑ S-7 1620 [S]	I Must Be Crazy/ Move - Move - Move	196?	30.00
—Jukebox single; 33 1/3 rpm, small hole			
❑ S-7 1621 [S]	Hoochi Coochi Coo/Mona Lisa	196?	30.00
—Jukebox single; 33 1/3 rpm, small hole			
❑ S-7 1622 [S]	Summertime/ Don't Go I Love You	196?	30.00
—Jukebox single; 33 1/3 rpm, small hole			
❑ S-7 1623 [S]	Finger Poppin' Time/ Let's Go, Let's Go, Let's Go	196?	40.00
—Jukebox single; 33 1/3 rpm, small hole			
❑ 5171	Teardrops on Your Letter/ The Twist	1959	30.00
❑ 5195 [M]	Kansas City/I'll Keep You Happy	1959	25.00
❑ S-5195 [S]	Kansas City/I'll Keep You Happy	1959	50.00
❑ 5215 [M]	Sugaree/Rain Down Tears	1959	25.00
❑ S-5215 [S]	Sugaree/Rain Down Tears	1959	50.00
❑ 5245	Cute Little Ways/ A House with No Windows	1959	25.00
❑ 5275	I Could Love You/Never Knew	1959	25.00
❑ 5289	Look at Little Sister/ I Said I Wouldn't Beg You	1959	25.00
❑ 5312	The Coffee Grind/Waiting	1960	25.00
❑ 5341	Finger Poppin' Time/I Love You, I Love You So-o-o	1960	25.00
❑ 5400	Let's Go, Let's Go, Let's Go/ If You'd Forgive Me	1960	25.00
❑ 5430	The Hoochi Coochi Coo/ I'm Thinking of You	1960	20.00
❑ 5459	Let's Go Again (Where We Went Last Night)/ Deep Blue Sea	1961	20.00
❑ 5491	The Continental Walk/ What Is This I See	1961	20.00
❑ 5491 [PS]	The Continental Walk/ What Is This I See	1961	80.00
❑ 5510	The Switch-A-Roo/The Float	1961	15.00
❑ 5513	The Big Frog/Doin' Everything	1961	15.00
—B-side by Henry Moore			
❑ 5535	Nothing But Good/ Keep On Dancing	1961	15.00
❑ 5550	Big Red Sunset/Can't You See — I Need a Friend	1961	15.00
❑ 5578	Do You Remember/ I'm Gonna Miss You	1961	15.00
❑ 5593	Do You Know How to Twist/ Broadway	1962	15.00
❑ 5601	It's Twistin' Time/Autumn Breeze	1962	15.00
❑ 5635	Good Twistin' Tonight/I'm Young	1962	15.00
❑ 5655	I Want to Thank You/Excuse Me	1962	15.00
❑ 5677	Dream World/When I Need You	1962	15.00
❑ 5693	Shaky Mae/I Love and Care for You	1962	15.00
❑ 5703	Bring Me Your Love/ She's the One	1962	15.00
❑ 5713	All the Things in Life That Please You/The Rising Tide	1963	15.00
❑ 5719	The House on the Hill/ That Low-Down Move	1963	15.00
❑ 5729	Christmas Time for Everyone But Me/Santa Claus Is Coming	1963	15.00
❑ 5746	How Could You Leave Your Man Alone/Walkin' and Talkin'	1963	15.00
❑ 5798	Those Lonely, Lonely Feelings/ It's Love, Baby	1963	15.00
❑ 5821	Buttin' In/I'm Leavin'	1963	15.00
❑ 5835	Don't Let Temptation Turn You Around/Have Mercy, Have a Little Pity	1964	15.00
❑ 5860	Don't Fall in Love with Me/ I'm So Mad with You	1964	15.00
❑ 5884	I Don't Know How to Do But One Thing/These Young Girls	1964	15.00
❑ 5901	Stay Away from My Baby/She's Got a Whole Lot of Soul	1964	15.00
❑ 5931	Daddy Rolling Stone/ What's Your Name	1964	15.00
❑ 5954	Let's Get the Show on the Road/A Winner Never Quits	1964	15.00
❑ 5963	One Monkey Don't Stop No Show/What Can I Tell You	1964	15.00
❑ 5974	The Handwriting on the Wall/ I Done It	1964	15.00
❑ 5996	Poppin' the Whip/You, Just You	1965	12.00
❑ 6001	I'm Just a Fool and Everybody Knows/Do It Zulu Style	1965	12.00
❑ 6018	Sloop and Slide/My Sun Is Going Down	1966	12.00
❑ 6031	I'm Ready/Togetherness	1966	12.00
❑ 6055	I Was Born to Move/ He Came Alone	1966	12.00
❑ 6092	Here Comes the Hurt/ Dance Till It Hurt Cha	1967	12.00
❑ 6119	You're in Real Good Hands/ Unwind Yourself	1967	12.00
❑ 6131	Funky's Soul Train/ Which Way Should I Turn	1967	12.00
❑ 6177	I'm Back to Stay/Come On Wit' It	1968	12.00
❑ 6196	How You Gonna Get Respect (When You Haven't Cut Your Process Yet)/Teardrops on Your Letter	1968	10.00
—As "Hank Ballard Along With The Dapps"			
❑ 6215	You're So Sexy/Thrill on the Hill	1969	10.00
—As "Hank Ballard Along With The Dapps"			
❑ 6228	Are You Lonely for Me Baby/ With Our Sweet Lovin' Self	1969	10.00
❑ 6244	Butter Your Popcorn/ Funky Soul Train	1969	15.00
❑ 6246	Come On with It/Blackenized	1969	15.00
❑ 6332	Work With Me Annie/Sexy Ways	1970	10.00
PEOPLE			
❑ 604	Teardrops on Your Letter/ Annie Had a Baby	1972	5.00
❑ 606	With Your Sweet Lovin' Self/ Finger Poppin' Time	1972	5.00
POLYDOR			
❑ 14128	Finger Poppin' Time/ From the Love Side	1972	5.00
❑ 14166	Going to Get a Thrill/ (B-side unknown)	1973	—
—Canceled?			
SILVER FOX			
❑ 23	Sunday Morning Coming Down/ Love Made a Fool of Me	1970	6.00
STANG			
❑ 5053	Let's Go Streaking/ Let's Go Streaking (Part 2)	1974	5.00
❑ 5058	Hey There Sexy Lady/ (Instrumental)	1975	5.00
❑ 5061	Let's Go Skinny Dipping/ Love On Love	1975	5.00
7-Inch Extended Plays			
KING			
❑ 435	Teardrops on Your Letter/ The Twist//Cute Little Ways/ House with No Windows	1959	120.00
❑ 435 [PS]	Singin' and Swingin', Vol. 1	1959	120.00
❑ 436	(contents unknown)	1959	120.00
❑ 436 [PS]	Singin' and Swingin', Vol. 2	1959	120.00
Albums			
KING			
❑ 618 [M]	Singin' and Swingin'	1959	250.00
❑ 674 [M]	The One and Only Hank Ballard	1959	250.00
—Brown cover			
❑ 674 [M]	The One and Only Hank Ballard	1960	150.00
—Green cover			
❑ 700 [M]	Mr. Rhythm and Blues	1960	150.00
❑ 740 [M]	Spotlight on Hank Ballard	1961	150.00
❑ KS-740 [S]	Spotlight on Hank Ballard	1961	300.00
❑ 748 [M]	Let's Go Again	1961	120.00
❑ 759 [M]	Dance Along	1961	120.00
❑ 781 [M]	The Twistin' Fools	1962	100.00
❑ 793 [M]	Jumpin' Hank Ballard	1962	100.00
❑ 815 [M]	The 1963 Sound of Hank Ballard	1963	100.00
❑ 867 [M]	Biggest Hits	1963	100.00
❑ 896 [M]	A Star in Your Eyes	1964	100.00
❑ 913 [M]	Those Lazy, Lazy Days	1965	70.00
❑ 927 [M]	Glad Songs, Sad Songs	1965	70.00
❑ 950 [M]	24 Hit Tunes	1966	60.00
❑ 981 [M]	24 Great Songs	1968	40.00
❑ KSD-1052	You Can't Keep a Good Man Down	1969	50.00

BALLARD, KENNY

45s

Number	Title (A Side/B Side)	Yr	NM
GENIE			
❑ 101	Lady of Stone/(B-side unknown)	196?	30.00
KAPP			
❑ 602	Mr. Magic/Oh How I Cried	1964	25.00
ROULETTE			
❑ 4716	Your Letter/I'm Losing You	1966	15.00

BALLARD, RUSS

Member of ARGENT.

12-Inch Singles

Number	Title (A Side/B Side)	Yr	NM
EMI AMERICA			
❑ SPRO-9406 [DJ]	The Fire Still Burns (7" Version)/(LP Version)	1985	6.00
EPIC			
❑ 429 [DJ]	Cast the Spirit/Dancer	1978	12.00
45s			
EMI AMERICA			
❑ 8204	Voices/Living Without You	1984	4.00
❑ 8204 [PS]	Voices/Living Without You	1984	4.00
❑ 8217	Two Silhouettes/Playing with Fire	1984	4.00

Except when noted otherwise, VG = 25% of NM, and VG+ = 50% of NM. (Example: VG = $2.00, VG+ = $4.00 and NM = $8.00.)

Number	Title (A Side/B Side)	Yr	NM
❑ 8275	The Fire Still Burns/Hold On	1985	3.00
❑ 8275 [PS]	The Fire Still Burns/Hold On	1985	3.00

EPIC

Number	Title (A Side/B Side)	Yr	NM
❑ 50085	You Can Do Voodoo/ Danger Zone Part 2	1975	4.00
❑ 50211	Winning/Here I Am	1976	4.00
❑ 50542	Treat Her Right/ What Does It Take	1978	4.00
❑ 50883	On the Rebound/ Riding with the Angels	1980	4.00
❑ 51002	Breakdown/Rock and Roll Lover	1981	4.00

Albums

EMI AMERICA

Number	Title	Yr	NM
❑ ST-17108	Russ Ballard	1984	8.00
❑ ST-17162	The Fire Still Burns	1985	8.00

EPIC

Number	Title	Yr	NM
❑ KE 33252	Russ Ballard	1974	10.00
❑ PE 34093	Winning	1976	10.00
❑ JE 35035	At the Third Stroke	1978	10.00
❑ JE 36186	Russ Ballard & the Barnet Dogs	1980	10.00
❑ JE 36993	Into the Fire	1981	10.00

BALLARDS, THE See THE BALLADS.

BALLIN' JACK

45s

COLUMBIA

Number	Title (A Side/B Side)	Yr	NM
❑ 45312	Super Highway/Only a Tear	1971	5.00
❑ 45464	Ballin' the Jack/Hold On	1971	5.00
❑ 45698	Playin' the Game/ I'm the One You Need	1972	4.00

MERCURY

Number	Title (A Side/B Side)	Yr	NM
❑ 73401	Thunder/Try to Relax	1973	5.00
❑ 73429	Sunday Morning/This Song	1973	5.00

Albums

COLUMBIA

Number	Title	Yr	NM
❑ C 30344	Ballin' Jack	1971	10.00
❑ KC 31468	Buzzard Luck	1972	10.00

MERCURY

Number	Title	Yr	NM
❑ SRM-1-672	Special Pride	1973	10.00

BALLOON FARM, THE

45s

LAURIE

Number	Title (A Side/B Side)	Yr	NM
❑ 3405	A Question of Temperature/ Hurtin' for Your Lovin'	1967	10.00
	—Second pressing corrects A-side spelling		
❑ 3405	A Question of Tempature/ Hurtin' for Your Lovin'	1967	20.00
	—First pressing has misspelled A-side		
❑ 3445	Hurry Up Sundown/ Farmer Brown	1968	10.00

BALTIMORE AND OHIO MARCHING BAND, THE

45s

JUBILEE

Number	Title (A Side/B Side)	Yr	NM
❑ 5592	Lapland/Condition Red	1967	6.00
❑ 5614	The B&O Marching Band Song/ The Wanderer	1968	5.00
❑ 5644	Sgt. Crunch/Typsy Gypsy	1968	5.00
❑ 5672	Little Arrows/(B-side unknown)	1969	5.00

Albums

JUBILEE

Number	Title	Yr	NM
❑ JGS-8008	Lapland	1968	15.00

BALTINEERS, THE

45s

LOST-NITE

Number	Title (A Side/B Side)	Yr	NM
❑ 113	Moments Like This/New Love	196?	8.00
	—Reissue		
❑ 114	Tears in My Eyes/Joe's Calypso	196?	8.00
	—Reissue		

TEENAGE

Number	Title (A Side/B Side)	Yr	NM
❑ 1000	Moments Like This/New Love	1956	300.00
❑ 1002	Tears in My Eyes/Joe's Calypso	1956	300.00

BANANA AND THE BUNCH

45s

WARNER BROS.

Number	Title (A Side/B Side)	Yr	NM
❑ 7621	My True Life Blues/ Vanderbilt's Lament	1972	5.00
❑ 7626	Back in the U.S.A./ My True Life Blues	1972	5.00

Albums

WARNER BROS.

Number	Title	Yr	NM
❑ BS 2626	Mid Mountain Ranch	1972	12.00

BAN-LONS, THE

45s

FIDELITY

Number	Title (A Side/B Side)	Yr	NM
❑ 4051	Highest Mountain/Hey Baby	1959	200.00
❑ 4056	I Like It/Hey Good Lookin'	1959	200.00

BANANA BOYS

45s

UNI

Number	Title (A Side/B Side)	Yr	NM
❑ 55194	Come Into My Life/ What Will Your Mama Say	1970	10.00

BANANA SPLITS, THE

45s

DECCA

Number	Title (A Side/B Side)	Yr	NM
❑ 32391	We're the Banana Splits/ Wait Til Tomorrow	1968	12.00
❑ 32429	The Tra-La-La Song (One Banana, Two Banana)/ Toy Piano Melody	1968	12.00
❑ 32429 [PS]	The Tra-La-La Song (One Banana, Two Banana)/ Toy Piano Melody	1968	25.00
❑ 32536	Pretty Painted Carousel/ Long Live Love	1969	12.00
❑ 32536 [PS]	Pretty Painted Carousel/ Long Live Love	1969	25.00

7-Inch Extended Plays

KELLOGG'S/HANNA-BARBERA

Number	Title (A Side/B Side)	Yr	NM
❑ 34578	The Tra La La Song/That's the Pretty Part of You//It's a Good Day for a Parade/The Very First Kid on My Block	1969	20.00
❑ 34578 [PS]	Kellogg's Presents The Banana Splits, Vol. 1	1969	20.00
❑ 34579	Doin' the Banana Split/I Enjoy Being a Boy (In Love with You)/ /The Beautiful Calliopa/Let Me Remember You Smiling	1969	20.00
❑ 34579 [PS]	Kellogg's Presents The Banana Splits, Vol. 2	1969	20.00

Albums

DECCA

Number	Title	Yr	NM
❑ DL 75075	We're the Banana Splits	1969	200.00

BANBARRA

45s

UNITED ARTISTS

Number	Title (A Side/B Side)	Yr	NM
❑ XW-734	Shack Up Part 1/Shack Up Part 2	1975	4.00

BANCHEE

45s

ATLANTIC

Number	Title (A Side/B Side)	Yr	NM
❑ 2708	I Just Don't Know/Train of Life	1970	10.00

POLYDOR

Number	Title (A Side/B Side)	Yr	NM
❑ 14104	Searcher's Life//3/4 Song	1971	10.00

Albums

ATLANTIC

Number	Title	Yr	NM
❑ SD 8240	Banchee	1969	50.00
	—With insert		

POLYDOR

Number	Title	Yr	NM
❑ 24-4066	Thinkin'	1971	50.00

BAND, THE Also see RICK DANKO; BOB DYLAN; RONNIE HAWKINS AND THE HAWKS; LEVON AND THE HAWKS; LEVON HELM; ROBBIE ROBERTSON.

45s

CAPITOL

Number	Title (A Side/B Side)	Yr	NM
❑ 2269	The Weight/I Shall Be Released	1968	8.00
	—First pressing credits "Jaime Robbie Robertson, Rick Danko, Richard Manuel, Garth Hudson, Levon Helm"		
❑ 2635	Up on Cripple Creek/The Night They Drove Old Dixie Down	1969	6.00
❑ 2705	Rag Mama Rag/ The Unfaithful Servant	1969	6.00
❑ 2705 [PS]	Rag Mama Rag/ The Unfaithful Servant	1969	6.00
❑ 2870	Time to Kill/The Shape I'm In	1970	6.00
❑ 3199	Life Is a Carnival/ The Moon Struck One	1971	6.00
❑ 3433	Don't Do It/Rag Mama Rag	1972	5.00
❑ 3500	Hang Up My Rock & Roll Shoes/Caledonia Mission	1972	5.00
❑ 3758	Ain't Got No Home/Get Up Jake	1973	5.00
❑ 3828	Third Man Theme/W.S. Walcott Medicine Show	1974	5.00
❑ 4230	Ophelia/Hobo Jungle	1976	4.00
❑ 4316	Twilight/Acadian Driftwood	1976	4.00
❑ 4361	Georgia on My Mind/The Night They Drove Old Dixie Down	1976	4.00
❑ 58876	The Shape I'm In/ Life Is a Carnival	2000	5.00

WARNER BROS.

Number	Title (A Side/B Side)	Yr	NM
❑ 8592	Out of the Blue/The Well	1978	4.00

Albums

CAPITOL

Number	Title	Yr	NM
❑ STAO-132	The Band	1969	15.00
	—Lime green label		
❑ STAO-8-0132	The Band	1969	100.00
	—Capitol Record Club edition with black rainbow label; we don't know if any standard versions of this album exist with this label		
❑ SW-425	Stage Fright	1970	10.00
	—Without tear-off wraparound cover		
❑ SW-425	Stage Fright	1970	15.00
	—Includes tear-off wraparound cover		
❑ SMAS-651	Cahoots	1971	15.00
❑ SKAO 2955	Music from Big Pink	1968	25.00
	—Black label with colorband		
❑ SKAO 2955	Music from Big Pink	1969	15.00
	—Lime green label		
❑ SKAO 2955	Music from Big Pink	1971	15.00
	—Red label, purple "C" logo at top		
❑ SABB-11045 [(2)]	Rock of Ages	1972	20.00
❑ SW-11214	Moondog Matinee	1973	10.00
	—Without tear-off wraparound cover		
❑ SW-11214	Moondog Matinee	1973	15.00
	—Includes tear-off wraparound cover		
❑ ST-11440	Northern Lights-Southern Cross	1975	12.00
❑ ST-11553	The Best of the Band	1976	12.00
❑ SO-11602	Islands	1977	12.00
❑ SKBO-11856 [(2)]	Anthology	1978	15.00
❑ SN-16003	Cahoots	1980	8.00
	—Budget-line reissue		
❑ SN-16004	Moondog Matinee	1980	8.00
	—Budget-line reissue		
❑ SN-16005	Northern Lights-Southern Cross	1980	8.00
	—Budget-line reissue		
❑ SN-16006	Stage Fright	1980	8.00
	—Budget-line reissue		
❑ SN-16007	Islands	1980	8.00
	—Budget-line reissue		
❑ SN-16008	Rock of Ages, Vol. 1	1980	8.00
	—Budget-line reissue		
❑ SN-16009	Rock of Ages, Vol. 2	1980	8.00
	—Budget-line reissue		
❑ SN-16010	Anthology, Vol. 1	1980	8.00
	—Budget-line reissue		
❑ SN-16011	Anthology, Vol. 2	1980	8.00
	—Budget-line reissue		
❑ SN-16296	The Band	198?	8.00
	—Budget-line reissue		
❑ SN-16331	The Best of the Band	198?	8.00
	—Budget-line reissue		

MOBILE FIDELITY

Number	Title	Yr	NM
❑ 1-039	Music from Big Pink	1981	50.00
	—Audiophile vinyl		

RHINO HANDMADE

Number	Title	Yr	NM
❑ RHM1-7801 [(3)]	The Last Waltz	2003	60.00
	—Box set with remixed version of the album, booklet, facsimiles of tickets, posters and other ephemera, many bonus photos, and a reproduction of the cover signed by Robbie Robertson		

WARNER BROS.

Number	Title	Yr	NM
❑ PRO-A-737 [DJ]	The Last Waltz Sampler	1978	20.00
❑ 3WS 3146 [(3)]	The Last Waltz	1978	20.00

BAND OF ANGELS

45s

MUMS

Number	Title (A Side/B Side)	Yr	NM
❑ ZS8 6035	He's Not There/So Hard Living Without You	1975	6.00

BAND WITHOUT A NAME, THE

45s

SIDEWALK

Number	Title (A Side/B Side)	Yr	NM
❑ 913	Theme from "Thunder Alley"/ Time After Time	1967	20.00

TOWER

Number	Title (A Side/B Side)	Yr	NM
❑ 246	Turn On Your Love Light/ Perfect Girl	1966	15.00
❑ 246 [PS]	Turn On Your Love Light/ Perfect Girl	1966	30.00

BANDS OF GOLD

45s

SMASH

Number	Title (A Side/B Side)	Yr	NM
❑ 2058	It's Over/You Won't Change Me	1966	25.00

BANDWAGON, THE Also includes records credited to "Johnny Johnson and the Bandwagon."

45s

BELL

Number	Title (A Side/B Side)	Yr	NM
❑ 902	Sweet Inspiration/ Pride Comes Before Fall	1970	6.00
❑ 953	(Blame It) On the Pony Express/Never Let Her Go	1971	6.00

EPIC

Number	Title (A Side/B Side)	Yr	NM
❑ 10255	Baby Make Your Own Sweet Music/On the Day We Fell in Love	1967	8.00
❑ 10352	Breakin' Down the Walls of Heartache/Dancin' Master	1968	8.00
❑ 10412	I Ain't Lying/You	1968	8.00
	—Artist credit: "Johnny Johnson and the Bandwagon"		

Number	Title (A Side/B Side)	Yr	NM
❑ 10442	Don't Let It In/When Love Has Gone Away	1969	8.00
❑ 10473	You Blew Your Cool (And Lost Your Fool)/Let's Hang On	1969	8.00

—Artist credit: "Johnny Johnson and the Bandwagon"

Albums

EPIC

Number	Title (A Side/B Side)	Yr	NM
❑ BN 26426	Johnny Johnson and the Bandwagon	1969	20.00

BANG

45s

CAPITOL

Number	Title (A Side/B Side)	Yr	NM
❑ 3304	Questions/Future Shock	1972	5.00
❑ 3386	Keep On/Redman	1972	4.00
❑ 3474	No Sugar Tonight/Idealist Realist	1972	4.00
❑ 3622	Must Be Love/Love Sonnet	1973	4.00
❑ 3816	Feels Nice/Slow Down	1974	4.00

Albums

CAPITOL

Number	Title (A Side/B Side)	Yr	NM
❑ ST-11015	Bang	1972	25.00
❑ SMAS-11110	Mother/Bow to the Music	1972	25.00
❑ ST-11190	Music	1973	30.00

BANG TANGO

12-Inch Singles

MCA

Number	Title (A Side/B Side)	Yr	NM
❑ L33-17854 [DJ]	Attack of Life (same on both sides?)	1989	6.00

45s

MCA

Number	Title (A Side/B Side)	Yr	NM
❑ 53753	Breaking Up a Heart of Stone/Don't Stop Now	1989	4.00

Albums

MCA

Number	Title (A Side/B Side)	Yr	NM
❑ 6300	Psycho Cafe	1989	10.00

WORLD OF HURT

Number	Title (A Side/B Side)	Yr	NM
❑ WEP 1000 [EP]	Live Injection	1989	15.00

BANGLES

12-Inch Singles

COLUMBIA

Number	Title (A Side/B Side)	Yr	NM
❑ AS 1883 [DJ]	Hero Takes a Fall (same on both sides)	1984	12.00
❑ AS 1939 [DJ]	Going Down to Liverpool (same on both sides)	1984	12.00
❑ CAS 2249 [DJ]	Manic Monday (3:03) (same on both sides)	1986	12.00
❑ CAS 2334 [DJ]	If She Knew What She Wants (same on both sides)	1986	12.00
❑ CAS 2453 [DJ]	Walk Like an Egyptian (same on both sides)	1986	10.00
❑ 44-05935	Walk Like an Egyptian (Extended Dance Mix)/(Dub Mix) (A Cappella Mix)	1986	8.00
❑ 44-06760	Walking Down Your Street (Extended Dance Mix)/(Dub Mix) (Instrumental Mix)	1986	8.00
❑ 44-08170	In Your Room (12-Inch Extended Version) (7-Inch Remix) (12-Inch Instrumental) (7-Inch Single Version)	1988	6.00

DEF JAM

Number	Title (A Side/B Side)	Yr	NM
❑ CAS 2857 [DJ]	Hazy Shade of Winter (with intro)/(without intro)	1987	8.00
❑ 44-07540	Hazy Shade of Winter (4 versions)	1987	8.00

FAULTY PRODUCTS

Number	Title (A Side/B Side)	Yr	NM
❑ DJ 1000 [DJ]	The Real World (same on both sides)	1983	50.00

45s

COLUMBIA

Number	Title (A Side/B Side)	Yr	NM
❑ 38-04479	Hero Takes a Fall/Where Were You When I Needed You	1984	5.00
❑ 38-04479 [PS]	Hero Takes a Fall/Where Were You When I Needed You	1984	7.00
❑ 38-04634	Going Down to Liverpool/Dover Beach	1984	5.00
❑ 38-04770	Hero Takes a Fall (Remix)/Tell Me	1985	10.00
❑ 38-04770 [PS]	Hero Takes a Fall (Remix)/Tell Me	1985	10.00
❑ 38-05757	Manic Monday/In a Different Light	1986	3.00

—A-side written by Prince under pseudonym "Christopher"

Number	Title (A Side/B Side)	Yr	NM
❑ 38-05757 [PS]	Manic Monday/In a Different Light	1986	3.00
❑ 38-05886	If She Knew What She Wants/Not Like You	1986	3.00
❑ 38-05886 [PS]	If She Knew What She Wants/Not Like You	1986	3.00
❑ 38-06257	Walk Like an Egyptian/Angels Don't Fall in Love	1986	3.00
❑ 38-06674	Walking Down Your Street/Let It Go	1987	3.00
❑ 38-06674 [PS]	Walking Down Your Street/Let It Go	1987	3.00
❑ 38-08090	In Your Room/Bell Jar	1988	3.00
❑ 38-08090 [PS]	In Your Room/Bell Jar	1988	3.00
❑ 38-08385	Manic Monday/Hazy Shade of Winter	1988	3.00

—Gray label "Golden Oldies" reissue

Number	Title (A Side/B Side)	Yr	NM
❑ 38-08386	Walk Like an Egyptian/Walking Down Your Street	1988	3.00

—Gray label "Golden Oldies" reissue

Number	Title (A Side/B Side)	Yr	NM
❑ 38-68533	Eternal Flame/What I Meant to Say	1989	3.00
❑ 38-68744	Be with You/Let It Go	1989	3.00
❑ 38-73791	Eternal Flame/What I Meant to Say	1991	3.00

—Reissue

DEF JAM

Number	Title (A Side/B Side)	Yr	NM
❑ 38-07630	Hazy Shade of Winter/She's Lost You	1987	3.00

—B-side by Joan Jett and the Blackhearts

Number	Title (A Side/B Side)	Yr	NM
❑ 38-07630 [PS]	Hazy Shade of Winter/She's Lost You	1987	3.00

Albums

COLUMBIA

Number	Title (A Side/B Side)	Yr	NM
❑ CAS 2270 [DJ]	Interchords	1986	25.00

—Promo-only interview album

Number	Title (A Side/B Side)	Yr	NM
❑ BFC 39220	All Over the Place	1984	12.00
❑ PC 39220	All Over the Place	1986	8.00

—Reissue with new prefix and longer bar code

Number	Title (A Side/B Side)	Yr	NM
❑ BFC 40039	Different Light	1986	12.00
❑ FC 40039	Different Light	1986	8.00

—Reissue with new prefix; "02" added to bar code on back cover

Number	Title (A Side/B Side)	Yr	NM
❑ OC 44056	Everything	1988	10.00

FAULTY PRODUCTS

Number	Title (A Side/B Side)	Yr	NM
❑ FEP 1302 [EP]	Bangles	1982	20.00

I.R.S.

Number	Title (A Side/B Side)	Yr	NM
❑ SP-70506 [EP]	Bangles	1983	12.00

—Reissue of Faulty Products EP

BANGOR FLYING CIRCUS

45s

ABC DUNHILL

Number	Title (A Side/B Side)	Yr	NM
❑ 4220	Come On People/A Change in Our Lives	1969	6.00
❑ 4223	Mama Don't You Know/Someday I'll Find	1970	6.00

Albums

ABC DUNHILL

Number	Title (A Side/B Side)	Yr	NM
❑ DS-50069	Bangor Flying Circus	1969	15.00

BANKS, BESSIE

45s

BLUE CAT

Number	Title (A Side/B Side)	Yr	NM
❑ 106	Go Now/It Sounds Like My Baby	1965	10.00

SPOKANE

Number	Title (A Side/B Side)	Yr	NM
❑ 4009	Do It Now/(You Should Have Been a) Doctor	1963	15.00

TIGER

Number	Title (A Side/B Side)	Yr	NM
❑ 102	Go Now/It Sounds Like My Baby	1964	20.00

VERVE

Number	Title (A Side/B Side)	Yr	NM
❑ 10519	I Can't Make It (Without You Baby)/Need You	1967	8.00

VOLT

Number	Title (A Side/B Side)	Yr	NM
❑ 4112	Ain't No Easy Way/Try to Leave Me If You Can	1974	6.00

WAND

Number	Title (A Side/B Side)	Yr	NM
❑ 163	Do It Now/(You Should Have Been a) Doctor	1964	12.00

BANKS, DARRELL

45s

ATCO

Number	Title (A Side/B Side)	Yr	NM
❑ 6471	Here Come the Tears/I've Got That Feeling	1967	25.00
❑ 6484	Angel Baby Don't You Leave Me/Look Into the Eyes of a Fool	1967	25.00

COTILLION

Number	Title (A Side/B Side)	Yr	NM
❑ 44006	I Wanna Go Home/Love of My Woman	1968	10.00

REVILOT

Number	Title (A Side/B Side)	Yr	NM
❑ 201	Open the Door to Your Heart/Our Love Is In the Pocket	1966	15.00
❑ 203	Somebody (Somewhere) Needs You/Baby Whatcha Got (For Me)	1966	15.00

VOLT

Number	Title (A Side/B Side)	Yr	NM
❑ 4014	Just Because Your Love Has Gone/I'm the One Who Loves You	1969	10.00
❑ 4026	Beautiful Feeling/No One Blinder	1969	10.00

Albums

ATCO

Number	Title (A Side/B Side)	Yr	NM
❑ 33-216 [M]	Darrell Banks Is Here	1967	25.00
❑ SD 33-216 [S]	Darrell Banks Is Here	1967	30.00

VOLT

Number	Title (A Side/B Side)	Yr	NM
❑ VOS-6002	Here to Stay	1969	25.00

BANKS, DICK

45s

LIBERTY

Number	Title (A Side/B Side)	Yr	NM
❑ 55145	Dirty Dog/Too Late	1958	40.00
❑ 55507	Just Like You/Be Faithful to Me	1962	20.00

BANKS, DOUG

45s

ARGO

Number	Title (A Side/B Side)	Yr	NM
❑ 5483	I Just Keep Dancing/Baby Since You Went Away	1964	60.00

GUYDEN

Number	Title (A Side/B Side)	Yr	NM
❑ 2082	Ain't That Just Like a Woman/Never Say Goodbye	1963	60.00

BANKS, EDDIE

45s

JOSIE

Number	Title (A Side/B Side)	Yr	NM
❑ 804	Sugar Diabetes/Rock-a-Bye Blues	1956	40.00

BANKS, HOMER

45s

GENIE

Number	Title (A Side/B Side)	Yr	NM
❑ 1000	Hooked by Love/Lady of Stone	1966	50.00

MINIT

Number	Title (A Side/B Side)	Yr	NM
❑ 32000	A Lot of Love/Fighting to Win	1966	25.00
❑ 32008	Do You Know What/60 Minutes of Your Love	1966	25.00
❑ 32020	Hooked by Love/Lady of Stone	1967	25.00

BANKS, PETER

Albums

CAPITOL/SOVEREIGN

Number	Title (A Side/B Side)	Yr	NM
❑ SMAS-11217	Two Sides of Peter Banks	1973	15.00

BANNED, THE

45s

FONTANA

Number	Title (A Side/B Side)	Yr	NM
❑ 1604	My Life Is My Own/Nothing Matters But You	1967	10.00
❑ 1616	It Couldn't Happen Here/Annie Went to Ohio	1968	10.00
❑ 1616 [PS]	It Couldn't Happen Here/Annie Went to Ohio	1968	20.00
❑ 1621	Goodbye, Groovy, Goodbye/A Blanket of Sound	1968	10.00

BANTAMS, THE

45s

DECCA

Number	Title (A Side/B Side)	Yr	NM
❑ 31040	My Swing Is Broke/Windows of Blue	1959	15.00

WARNER BROS.

Number	Title (A Side/B Side)	Yr	NM
❑ 5695	Follow Me/Meet Me Tonight Little Girl	1966	10.00
❑ 5868	Good Lovin' Girl/I'm So Lucky	1966	10.00

Albums

WARNER BROS.

Number	Title (A Side/B Side)	Yr	NM
❑ W 1625 [M]	Beware the Bantams	1966	20.00
❑ WS 1625 [S]	Beware the Bantams	1966	25.00

BAR-KAYS, THE

12-Inch Singles

BASIX

Number	Title (A Side/B Side)	Yr	NM
❑ 1309	Old School Mega Mix/Out of My Mind	1994	8.00

MERCURY

Number	Title (A Side/B Side)	Yr	NM
❑ PRO 296-1 [DJ]	Dirty Dancer (same on both sides)	1984	6.00
❑ MDS-4024	Do It (Let Me See You Shake) (Original Mix) (Instrumental)	1982	8.00
❑ 818631-1	Freakshow on the Dance Floor/Lovers Should Never Fall in Love	1984	8.00
❑ 870018-1	Don't Hang Up (4 versions)	1987	8.00
❑ 872103-1	Struck by You (Extended 12-Inch Mix) (Dub Mix) (Acapella) (7-Inch Mix)/Your Place or Mine	1989	7.00

Except when noted otherwise, VG = 25% of NM, and VG+ = 50% of NM. (Example: VG = $2.00, VG+ = $4.00 and NM = $8.00.)

Number	Title (A Side/B Side)	Yr	NM
❑ 872955-1	Animal (4 versions)/Time Out	1989	7.00
❑ 880255-1	Sexomatic (3 versions)	1984	8.00
❑ 880966-1	Your Place or Mine (Club Version) (Dub Version)	1985	8.00
❑ 884232-1	Banging the Walls (2 versions)/Gina	1985	8.00
❑ 888837-1	Certified True (3 versions)/ It Be That Way Sometimes	1987	7.00
45s			
HIGH STACKS			
❑ 9801	Body Fine/Hey Rufus!	1999	3.00
—B-side by Rufus Thomas; artist listed as "The Barkays"			
MERCURY			
❑ 73833	Shake Your Rump to the Funk/ Summer of Our Love	1976	4.00
❑ 73888	Too Hot to Stop (Pt. 1)/ Bang Bang (Stick 'Em Up)	1977	4.00
❑ 73915	Spellbound/You're So Sexy	1977	4.00
❑ 73971	Let's Have Some Fun/Cozy	1977	4.00
❑ 73994	Attitudes/Can't Keep My Hands Off You	1978	4.00
❑ 74039	I'll Dance/Angel Eyes	1978	4.00
❑ 74048	Shine/Are You Being Real	1979	4.00
❑ 76015	Move Your Boogie Body/ Love's What It's All About	1979	4.00
❑ 76036	Today is the Day/Loving You Is My Occupation	1980	4.00
❑ 76088	Boogie Body Land/Running In and Out of My Life	1980	4.00
❑ 76097	Body Fever/Deliver Us	1981	4.00
❑ 76123	Hit and Run/Say It Through Love	1981	4.00
❑ 76143	Freaky Behavior/Backseat Driver	1982	4.00
❑ 76187	Do It (Let Me See You Shake)/ Feels Like I'm Falling in Love	1982	4.00
❑ 810435-7	She Talks to Me with Her Body/ Anticipation	1983	4.00
❑ 818631-7	Freakshow on the Dance Floor/ Lovers Should Never Fall in Love	1984	4.00
❑ 870018-7	Don't Hang Up/Contagious	1988	3.00
❑ 870018-7 [PS]	Don't Hang Up/Contagious	1988	3.00
❑ 870214-7	Many Mistakes/Contagious	1988	3.00
❑ 872102-7	Struck by You/Your Place or Mine	1989	3.00
❑ 872102-7 [PS]	Struck by You/Your Place or Mine	1989	3.00
❑ 872954-7	Animal/Time Out	1989	3.00
❑ 872954-7 [PS]	Animal/Time Out	1989	3.00
❑ 880045-7	Dirty Dancer/(Instrumental)	1984	3.00
❑ 880255-7	Sexomatic/Sexomatic (Bonus Beats)	1984	3.00
❑ 880966-7	Your Place or Mine/ (Instrumental)	1985	3.00
❑ 884232-7	Banging the Walls/Gina	1985	3.00
❑ 888837-7	Certified True/It Be That Way Sometimes	1987	3.00
STAX			
❑ 3216	Holy Ghost/Monster	1978	5.00
VOLT			
❑ 148	Soul Finger/Knucklehead	1967	8.00
❑ 154	Give Everybody Some/ Don't Do That	1967	6.00
❑ 158	A Hard Day's Night/ I Want Someone	1968	6.00
❑ 4007	Copy Cat/In the Middle	1968	6.00
❑ 4011	Don't Stop Dancing/ Don't Stop Dancing (Part 2)	1969	6.00
❑ 4019	Midnight Cowboy/ A.J. The Housefly	1969	6.00
❑ 4033	Song and Dance/I Thank You	1970	6.00
❑ 4050	Montego Bay/Humpin'	1971	5.00
❑ 4073	Son of Shaft/Song and Dance	1972	5.00
❑ 4081	Dance, Dance, Dance/ Memphis at Sunrise	1972	5.00
❑ 4092	You're the Best Thing That Ever Happened to Me/ You're Still My Brother	1973	5.00
❑ 4097	God Is Watching/It Ain't Easy	1973	5.00
Albums			
ATCO			
❑ SD 33-289	Soul Finger	1968	25.00
MERCURY			
❑ SRM-1-1099	Too Hot to Stop	1976	10.00
❑ SRM-1-1181	Flying High on Your Love	1977	10.00
❑ SRM-1-3732	Light of Life	1978	10.00
❑ SRM-1-3781	Injoy	1979	10.00
❑ SRM-1-3844	As One	1980	10.00
❑ SRM-1-4028	Nightcruising	1981	10.00
❑ SRM-1-4065	Propositions	1982	10.00
❑ 818478-1	Dangerous	1984	10.00
❑ 824727-1	Banging the Wall	1985	10.00
❑ 830305-1	Contagious	1987	10.00
❑ 836774-1	Animal	1989	10.00
STAX			
❑ 4106	Money Talks	1978	10.00
❑ 4130	Gotta Groove	1979	10.00
❑ MPS-8510	Cold Blooded	1981	10.00
❑ MPS-8542	The Best of the Bar-Kays	1988	10.00
VOLT			
❑ 417 [M]	Soul Finger	1967	40.00
❑ S-417 [S]	Soul Finger	1967	40.00
❑ 6004	Gotta Groove	1969	30.00
❑ 6011	Black Rock	1971	25.00
❑ VOS-8001	Do You See What I See	1972	25.00
❑ 9504	Cold Blooded	1974	25.00

BARA, TONY

Number	Title (A Side/B Side)	Yr	NM
45s			
ATCO			
❑ 6172	Rambling/Long Gone Mare	1960	12.00

BARBARA AND THE BELIEVERS

Number	Title (A Side/B Side)	Yr	NM
45s			
CAPITOL			
❑ 5866	When You Wish Upon a Star/ What Can Happen to Me Now	1967	16.00

BARBARA AND THE BOYS

Number	Title (A Side/B Side)	Yr	NM
45s			
DOT			
❑ 15794	Hooty Sapperticker/Cobra	1958	15.00

BARBARA AND THE BROWNS

Number	Title (A Side/B Side)	Yr	NM
45s			
STAX			
❑ 150	Big Party/You Belong to Her	1964	20.00
❑ 158	Please Be Honest with Me/ In My Heart	1964	15.00
❑ 164	I Don't Want Trouble/My Lover	1965	15.00

BARBARIANS, THE

Number	Title (A Side/B Side)	Yr	NM
45s			
JOY			
❑ 290	Hey Little Bird/You've Got to Understand	1964	50.00
LAURIE			
❑ 3308	Are You a Boy or Are You a Girl/ Take It or Leave It	1965	20.00
❑ 3321	Susie Q/What the New Breed Say	1965	20.00
❑ 3326	Moulty/I'll Keep On Seeing You	1965	20.00
Albums			
LAURIE			
❑ LLP-2033 [M]	Are You a Boy or Are You a Girl?	1966	100.00
❑ SLP-2033 [S]	Are You a Boy or Are You a Girl?	1966	100.00
RHINO			
❑ RNLP 008	The Barbarians	1979	12.00

BARBARY, RICHARD

Number	Title (A Side/B Side)	Yr	NM
45s			
A&M			
❑ 1019	Call On Me/Like You, Babe	1969	6.00
SPRING			
❑ 701	Get Right/When Johnny Comes Marching Home	1967	8.00
Albums			
A&M			
❑ SP-3010	Soul Machine	1969	20.00

BARBEES, THE

Early version of THE VELVELETTES.

Number	Title (A Side/B Side)	Yr	NM
45s			
STEPP			
❑ 236	The Wind/Que Pasa	1963	200.00

BARBER, CHRIS

Number	Title (A Side/B Side)	Yr	NM
45s			
ATLANTIC			
❑ 2016	Hush-a-Bye/ You Don't Understand	1959	12.00
LAURIE			
❑ 3022	Petite Fleur/Wild Cat Blues	1958	15.00
❑ 3022 [PS]	Petite Fleur/Wild Cat Blues	1958	25.00
❑ 3026	Rugged Cross/Thriller Rag	1959	12.00
❑ 3057	Swanee River/ Lonesome	1960	12.00
❑ 3154	It Looks Like a Big Night Tonight/King Kong	1963	12.00
LONDON			
❑ 9571V	The Loneliness of the Long Distance Runner/ Valley of Roses	1963	12.00
Albums			
ATLANTIC			
❑ 1292 [M]	Here Is Chris Barber	1959	40.00
COLPIX			
❑ CP-404 [M]	Chris Barber Plays "Trad"	1959	30.00
GHB			
❑ GHB-40 [M]	Collaboration	1967	15.00
LAURIE			
❑ 1001 [M]	Petite Fleur	1959	40.00
❑ LLP-1003 [M]	Trad Jazz Vol. 1	1960	30.00
❑ LLP-1009 [M]	Chris Barber's "American" Jazz Band	1962	30.00

BARBIERI, GATO

Number	Title (A Side/B Side)	Yr	NM
12-Inch Singles			
A&M			
❑ AM-8397 [DJ]	I Want You (Edited Version 3:58) (Long Version 5:53)	1976	12.00
❑ AM-8458 [DJ]	Ruby, Ruby/Sunride/Nostalgia/ Adios (all edited)	1977	10.00
—Promo-only sampler			
❑ SP-17027 [DJ]	Poinciana (Edit) (same on both sides)	1978	10.00
❑ SP-17037 [DJ]	Latin Lady (Edit) (same on both sides)	1978	10.00
45s			
A&M			
❑ 1857	I Want You/(B-side unknown)	1976	5.00
❑ 1885	Fiesta/Behind the Rain	1976	5.00
❑ 1916	Don't Cry Rochelle/Europa (Earth's Cry Heaven's Smile)	1977	4.00
❑ 2006	Midnight Tango/Nostalgia	1978	4.00
❑ 2066	Poinciana (Song of the Tree)/ Evil Eyes	1978	4.00
❑ 2141	Firepower/Lions Also Cry	1979	4.00
❑ 2189	Secret Fiesta/Sophia	1979	4.00
UNITED ARTISTS			
❑ XW-175	Last Tango in Paris/ Return Tango	1973	4.00
Albums			
A&M			
❑ SP-3029	Fire and Passion	1970	25.00
❑ SP-9-3029	Fire and Passion	1984	15.00
—"Audio Master Plus" reissue			
❑ SP-3188	Euphoria	198?	8.00
—Reissue of 4774			
❑ SP-3247	Caliente!	198?	8.00
—Reissue of 4597			
❑ SP-4597	Caliente!	1976	10.00
❑ SP-4655	Ruby, Ruby	1977	10.00
❑ SP-4710	Tropico	1978	10.00
❑ SP-4774	Euphoria	1979	10.00
ABC IMPULSE!			
❑ AS-9248	Chapter One — Latin America	1973	20.00
❑ AS-9263	Chapter Two — Hasta Siempre	1974	20.00
❑ ASD-9279	Chapter Three — Viva Emiliano Zapata	1974	20.00
❑ ASD-9303	Chapter Four — Alive in New York	1975	20.00
BLUEBIRD			
❑ 6995-1-RB	Third World Revisited	1988	12.00
DOCTOR JAZZ			
❑ W2X 39204 [(2)]	Gato...Para Los Amigos	1985	12.00
❑ FW 40183	Apasionado	1986	10.00
ESP-DISK'			
❑ 1049	In Search of the Mystery	1968	40.00
FANIA			
❑ JM 608	Gato = Bahia	1982	12.00
FLYING DUTCHMAN			
❑ BDL1-0550	Yesterdays	1974	12.00
❑ BDL1-1147	El Gato	1976	12.00
❑ BXL1-2826	3rd World	1978	10.00
—Reissue of 10117			
❑ BXL1-2827	Fenix	1978	10.00
—Reissue of 10144			
❑ BXL1-2828	El Pampero	1978	10.00
—Reissue of 10151			
❑ BXL1-2829	Under Fire	1978	10.00
—Reissue of 10156			
❑ BXL1-2830	Bolivia	1978	10.00
—Reissue of 10158			
❑ AYL1-3815	3rd World	1980	8.00
—Budget-line reissue			
❑ AYL1-3816	Yesterdays	1980	8.00
—Budget-line reissue			
❑ AYL1-3817	El Gato	1980	8.00
—Budget-line reissue			
❑ FD 10117	3rd World	1970	20.00
❑ FD 10144	Fenix	1972	20.00
❑ FD 10151	El Pampero	1973	20.00
❑ FD 10156	Under Fire	1973	20.00
❑ FD 10158	Bolivia	1973	25.00
❑ FD 10165	The Legend of Gato Barbieri	1974	20.00
MCA			
❑ 29002	Chapter Two — Hasta Siempre	1981	8.00
—Reissue of Impulse 9263			

B

Number	Title (A Side/B Side)	Yr	NM
❑ 29003	Chapter Four — Alive in New York	1981	10.00
—Reissue of Impulse 9303			
QUINTESSENCE			
❑ QJ-25281	Gato Barbieri	1979	10.00
—Reissue of 1974 recordings			
UNITED ARTISTS			
❑ UA-LA045-F	Last Tango in Paris	1973	15.00

BARBIERI, GATO & DOLLAR BRAND

Albums

Number	Title (A Side/B Side)	Yr	NM
ARISTA FREEDOM			
❑ AL 1003	Confluence	1975	15.00

BARBOUR, KEITH

45s

Number	Title (A Side/B Side)	Yr	NM
BARNABY			
❑ 2036	A Pound of Peaches/ Music Sweet Music	1971	5.00
EPIC			
❑ 10486	Echo Park/Here I Am Losing You	1969	6.00
❑ 10575	Bake Me a Woman/ If I Could Only Touch You	1970	6.00
❑ 10598	Alicia/Sweet Mary Sunday	1970	6.00
❑ 10652	In the Quiet of Your Love/My God and I	1970	6.00

Albums

Number	Title (A Side/B Side)	Yr	NM
EPIC			
❑ BN 26485	Echo Park	1969	20.00

BARBRA AND NEIL

BARBRA STREISAND and NEIL DIAMOND.

45s

Number	Title (A Side/B Side)	Yr	NM
COLUMBIA			
❑ 3-10840	You Don't Bring Me Flowers/ (Instrumental)	1978	5.00

BARCLAY JAMES HARVEST

45s

Number	Title (A Side/B Side)	Yr	NM
HARVEST			
❑ 3501	Thank You/Medicine Man	1972	5.00
MCA			
❑ 40690	Rock 'N' Roll Star/ Polk Street Rag	1977	4.00
❑ 40795	Hymn/Our Kid's Kid	1977	4.00
POLYDOR			
❑ 14546	Loving Is Easy (Fantasy)/ Turning in Circles	1979	4.00
❑ 15104	Crazy City/Child of the Universe	1975	4.00
❑ 15118	Titles/(B-side unknown)	197?	4.00
SIRE			
❑ 4105	Early Morning/Mr. Sunshine	1969	8.00
❑ 4112	Brother Thrush/Poor Wages	1969	8.00

Albums

Number	Title (A Side/B Side)	Yr	NM
HARVEST			
❑ SW-11145	Baby James Harvest	1973	15.00
MCA			
❑ 2234	Octoberon	1976	10.00
❑ 2302	Gone to Earth	1977	10.00
POLYDOR			
❑ PD-1-6173	XII	1978	10.00
❑ PD-1-6267	Eyes of the Universe	1980	10.00
❑ PD-6508	Everyone Is Everybody Else	1974	12.00
❑ PD-6517	Time Honoured Ghosts	1975	12.00
SIRE			
❑ SI-4904	Back Again	1971	15.00
❑ SI-5904	Other Short Stories	1972	15.00
❑ SES-97026	Barclay James Harvest	1970	20.00

BARD, ANNETTE

One of THE TEDDY BEARS.

45s

Number	Title (A Side/B Side)	Yr	NM
IMPERIAL			
❑ 5643	What Difference Does It Make/ Alibi	1960	50.00

BARDS, THE (1)

45s

Number	Title (A Side/B Side)	Yr	NM
BURDETTE			
❑ 103	I Want You/Freedom Catcher	1971	8.00
CAPITOL			
❑ 2041	The Jabberwocky/ Never Too Much Love	1967	10.00
❑ 2148	The Owl and the Pussycat/ The Light of Love	1968	10.00
❑ 2148 [PS]	The Owl and the Pussycat/ The Light of Love	1968	20.00
JERDEN			
❑ 907	Good Time Charlie's Got the Blues/Tunesmith	1969	12.00
PARROT			
❑ 337	Good Time Charlie's Got the Blues/Tunesmith	1969	10.00
❑ 344	Our Love/Jubilation	1970	10.00
❑ 351	Day by Day/Wadda Wadda	1970	10.00
PICCADILLY			
❑ 224	The Owl and the Pussycat/ The Light of Love	1966	20.00
❑ 232	The Jabberwocky/My Generation	1966	12.00
❑ 242	Our Love/Jubilation	1967	12.00

BARDS, THE (2)

45s

Number	Title (A Side/B Side)	Yr	NM
DAWN			
❑ 208	I'm a Wine Drinker/ Easy Going Baby	1954	250.00
❑ 209	Gravy/Avalon	1954	250.00

BARE, CHARLIE

45s

Number	Title (A Side/B Side)	Yr	NM
HIT			
❑ 178	Do-Wacka-Do/Ode to the Little Brown Shack Out Back	1965	8.00
—B-side by Johnny Singer			
❑ 189	King of the Road/Look of Love	1965	8.00
—B-side by Connie Dee			

BARGE, GENE

45s

Number	Title (A Side/B Side)	Yr	NM
CHECKER			
❑ 839	Way Down Home/Country	1954	30.00
❑ 1110	Fine Twine/The "In" Crowd	1965	10.00
LEGRAND			
❑ 1006	Thinking of You/Autumn Leaves	1961	40.00
PARAMOUNT			
❑ 0160	Love Theme from "The Godfather"/Gina	1972	5.00

Albums

Number	Title (A Side/B Side)	Yr	NM
CHECKER			
❑ LP-2994 [M]	Dance with Daddy G	1965	50.00

BARIN, PETE

45s

Number	Title (A Side/B Side)	Yr	NM
SABINA			
❑ 504	So Wrong/Broken Heart	1962	50.00
❑ 512	Loneliest Guy in the World/ Look Out for Cindy	1962	30.00

BARITONES, THE

45s

Number	Title (A Side/B Side)	Yr	NM
DORE			
❑ 501	After School Rock/ Sentimental Baby	1958	40.00

BARKER, DELBERT

45s

Number	Title (A Side/B Side)	Yr	NM
KING			
❑ 4951	That's a Sin/ No Good, Robin Hood	1956	30.00
❑ 5008	Wild Heart/There Must Be a Way	1957	30.00
❑ 5031	Amanda/Broken Heart	1957	30.00
❑ 6042	It Can't Last Long/Color Me Gone	1966	10.00

BARKER, FRANCINE

45s

Number	Title (A Side/B Side)	Yr	NM
COLUMBIA			
❑ 4-44614	Don't You Know Love When You See It/Mr. D.J.	1968	8.00
❑ 4-44614 [PS]	Don't You Know Love When You See It/Mr. D.J.	1968	12.00
❑ 4-44771	Angels in the Sky/A Love You Can Depend On	1969	10.00
❑ 4-44910	Traces/Angels in the Sky	1969	12.00

BARKER BROTHERS, THE

45s

Number	Title (A Side/B Side)	Yr	NM
DECCA			
❑ 9-30753	Well All Right... Friday Night/ How Can You Tell If It's Love	1958	30.00
❑ 9-30811	Lovin' Honey/Sunbeam	1959	30.00
KENT			
❑ 302	Hey Little Mama/I'm in Love with My Teacher	1958	100.00
RCA VICTOR			
❑ 47-8405	Shh, Don't Wake Me Up/ I Gotta Know	1964	20.00
VALIANT			
❑ 6018	Drifter/Tonight, Baby, Tonight	1962	12.00

BARNABY BYE

45s

Number	Title (A Side/B Side)	Yr	NM
ATLANTIC			
❑ 2984	I Think I'm Gonna Like It/ Dreamer	1973	5.00
❑ 3244	Take Me With You/Blonde	1975	5.00
❑ 3266	Can't Live This Way/ Happy Was the Day We Met	1975	5.00

Albums

Number	Title (A Side/B Side)	Yr	NM
ATLANTIC			
❑ SD 7273	Room to Grow	1973	12.00
❑ SD 18104	Touch	1974	12.00

BARNES, BENNY

45s

Number	Title (A Side/B Side)	Yr	NM
D			
❑ 1052	Gold Records in the Snow/ Happy Little Blue Bird	1959	60.00
HALL-WAY			
❑ 1203	A Bar with No Beer/Headed for Heartbreak	1964	10.00
❑ 1207	It's Good to Be Home/ For a Minute There	1965	10.00
KAPP			
❑ 859	A Bar with No Beer/ Headed for Heartbreak	1967	8.00
❑ 912	Sweet Suzannah/ It's My Mind That's Broken	1968	8.00
MEGA			
❑ 0071	Woman, Leave My Mind Alone/ I'm Just Here to Get My Baby Off My Mind	1972	5.00
MERCURY			
❑ 71048	Poor Man's Riches/ Those Who Know	1957	20.00
❑ 71057	Poor Old Me/Penalty	1957	20.00
❑ 71119	Nickels Worth of Dreams/ Mine All Mine	1957	20.00
❑ 71188	King for a Day/Your Old Stand By	1957	20.00
❑ 71284	Moon Over My Shoulder/ Lonely Street	1958	25.00
❑ 71552	Beggar to a King/ The Fastest Gun Alive	1959	20.00
❑ 71600	That-a Boy Willie/Token of Love	1960	20.00
❑ 71637	Pretty Little Girl/ Message in the Wind	1960	20.00
❑ 71717	You're Still on My Mind/I Think I'll Take a Walk and Disappear	1960	20.00
❑ 71806	Yearning/Go On, Go On	1961	20.00
❑ 71896	The World's Worst Loser/ I Changed My Mind	1961	20.00
MUSICOR			
❑ 1100	Let Me Live As Long As I Can/ Tea Leaves Don't Lie	1965	8.00
❑ 1127	Have We Really Tried/ Heartache's Comin'	1965	8.00
❑ 1169	Diesel Smoke/ That's How I Need You	1966	8.00
❑ 1194	Stand By Your Window/ You're Not There	1966	8.00
❑ 1223	What's the Matter with Me/ Third Time Down	1966	8.00
❑ 1247	I'm Her Lover/Same Old Boat	1967	8.00
❑ 1277	Let One Call Do It All/ Rosanna Martin	1967	8.00
PLAYBOY			
❑ 5808	I've Got Some Gettin' Over You to Do/I'll Drink to That	1977	8.00
❑ 6084	Little Brown Paper Bag Blues/ (B-side unknown)	1976	8.00
RCA VICTOR			
❑ 47-9830	An Old Memory Got in My Eye/ You're Everywhere	1970	6.00
❑ 74-0271	Pressure Cooker/ To the Ones I Love	1969	6.00
STARDAY			
❑ 236	Once Again/No Fault of Mine	1956	30.00
❑ 262	Poor Man's Riches/ Those Who Know	1956	30.00
❑ 401	You Gotta Pay/Heads You Win	1958	25.00

BARNES, BILL

45s

Number	Title (A Side/B Side)	Yr	NM
COLUMBIA			
❑ 4-43491	Repeat After Me/Sloop John B.	1965	8.00
❑ 4-43491 [PS]	Repeat After Me/Sloop John B.	1965	15.00

BARNES, BILLY

45s

Number	Title (A Side/B Side)	Yr	NM
LIBERTY			
❑ 55421	Until/To Prove My Love	1962	25.00

Number	Title (A Side/B Side)	Yr	NM
TAHOE			
❑ 2532	Road of Love/ There's a Lion Out There	196?	30.00
UNITED ARTISTS			
❑ 148	You'd Have to Fall in Love/ If You But Knew	1958	20.00
❑ 157	I'm Coming to See You/ What Am I Supposed to Do	1959	20.00
❑ 218	Home Again/I Wish I Didn't Love You So	1960	20.00
❑ 311	C.C. Rider/Here Am I	1961	20.00

BARNES, DENA

Number	Title (A Side/B Side)	Yr	NM
45s			
INFERNO			
❑ 2002	Who Am I/(B-side unknown)	196?	250.00

BARNES, GEORGE

Number	Title (A Side/B Side)	Yr	NM
45s			
DECCA			
❑ 30398	Tammy/Around the World	1957	20.00
MERCURY			
❑ 71968	Transville/Spooky	1962	30.00

BARNES, J.J.

Number	Title (A Side/B Side)	Yr	NM
45s			
BUDDAH			
❑ 120	Evidence/I'll Keep Coming Back	1969	15.00
CONTEMPO			
❑ 7003	How Long/The Erroll Flynn	1977	5.00
GROOVESVILLE			
❑ 1006	Baby Please Come Back Home/Chains of Love	1967	15.00
❑ 1008	Now That I Got You Back/ Forgive Me	1967	15.00
❑ 1009	Easy Living/(B-side unknown)	1967	16.00
INVASION			
❑ 1001	My Baby/(You Still) My Baby	1970	10.00
KABLE			
❑ 437	Won't You Let Me Know/My Love Came Tumbling Down	1960	50.00
MAGIC TOUCH			
❑ 1000	To An Early Grave/Cloudy Days	1970	10.00
MICKAY'S			
❑ 3004	Just One More Time/Hey Child, I Love You	1963	80.00
❑ 4472	Get a Hold of Yourself/ Lonely No More	1964	80.00
PERCEPTION			
❑ 546	Just a Living Doll/Touching You	1974	6.00
REVILOT			
❑ 216	Hold On to It/Now She's Gone	1968	15.00
❑ 218	I'll Keep Coming Back/ Sad Day a-Comin'	1968	15.00
❑ 222	Our Love Is in the Pocket/All Your Goodies Are Gone	1968	80.00
❑ 225	So-Called Friends/ Now She's Gone	1968	15.00
RIC-TIC			
❑ 106	Please Let Me In/ I Think I Found a Love	1965	15.00
❑ 110	Real Humdinger/ I Ain't Gonna Do It	1966	15.00
❑ 115	Day Tripper/ Don't Bring Me Bad News	1966	15.00
❑ 117	Deeper in Love/Say It	1966	15.00
RICH			
❑ 1005	Won't You Let Me Know/My Love Came Tumbling Down	1960	100.00
❑ 1737	Won't You Let Me Know/My Love Came Tumbling Down	1962	25.00
RING			
❑ 101	She Ain't Ready/ Poor-Unfortunate Me	1964	25.00
SCEPTER			
❑ 1266	Just One More Time/Hey Child, I Love You	1964	30.00
VOLT			
❑ 4027	Got to Get Rid of You/Snowflakes	1969	15.00
Albums			
VOLT			
❑ VOS-6001	Rare Stamps	1969	30.00
—With Steve Mancha			

BARNES, SIDNEY

Number	Title (A Side/B Side)	Yr	NM
45s			
BLUE CAT			
❑ 125	I Hurt on the Other Side/ Switchy Walk	1966	150.00
CHESS			
❑ 2094	Baloney/Old Times	1970	10.00
PARACHUTE			
❑ 521	Hold On I'm Coming/ Your Love Is So Good to Me	1978	4.00
RED BIRD			
❑ 10-039	You'll Always Be in Style/ I'm So Glad	1965	40.00
❑ 10-054	I Hurt on the Other Side/ Switchy Walk	1966	40.00
Albums			
PARACHUTE			
❑ 9009	Footstomp'n Music	1978	12.00

BARNES, TAWANDA

Number	Title (A Side/B Side)	Yr	NM
45s			
A&M			
❑ 1141	(You Better) Find Someone to Love/You Don't Mean It	1969	25.00

BARNETT, BILLY

Not the same person as "Billy Barnette" who recorded for Parkway and Mt. Vernon in the early 1960s.

Number	Title (A Side/B Side)	Yr	NM
45s			
TEX			
❑ 105	Tired of Your Honky-Tonk Love/One Day Nearer Home	1957	250.00

BARNETTE, BILLY

See BILLY JOE BURNETTE. Not the same person as BILLY BARNETT.

BARNUM, H.B.

Number	Title (A Side/B Side)	Yr	NM
45s			
CAPITOL			
❑ 2036	Baby, Love Me/ The Bad Luck's on Me	1967	12.00
❑ 2139	Vaya Con Dios/ What Did Sister Do	1968	10.00
❑ 2317	Happiness/ It's Just a Game, Love	1968	10.00
❑ 5391	I'm a Man/The Record	1965	12.00
❑ 5440	Gimme Some/Don't Forget 127th Street	1965	12.00
❑ 5477	I Can't Help It/Dance with Me	1965	12.00
❑ 5748	Gotta Go/Nobody Wants to Hear Nobody's Trouble	1966	12.00
❑ 5932	Heartbreaker/ Searchin' for My Soul	1967	20.00
DECCA			
❑ 32892	Run to Daylight/Howard Hardsell	1971	5.00
—B-side by Tom Patchett and Jay Tarses			
ELDO			
❑ 111	Lost Love/Hallelujah	1960	15.00
IMPERIAL			
❑ 5530	Blue Moon/Tia-Juana	1958	40.00
❑ 66011	Backstage/Rented Tuxedo	1964	12.00
❑ 66046	Skakiaan (Skokiaan)/Ska Drums	1964	12.00
❑ 66063	Calpyso Blues/Three Room Flat	1964	12.00
❑ 66074	Eternal Love/So What	1964	12.00
RCA VICTOR			
❑ 47-7960	Baby Baby Baby (All the Time)/ How Many More Times	1961	15.00
❑ 47-8014	Call On Me/Oh My Achin' Back	1962	15.00
❑ 47-8112	Lonely Hearts/It Hurts Too Much to Cry	1962	60.00
UNITED ARTISTS			
❑ XW338	Theme from "5 on the Back Hand Side"/Keep It Comin'	1973	5.00
Albums			
CAPITOL			
❑ ST 2278 [S]	Golden Boy	1965	20.00
❑ T 2278 [M]	Golden Boy	1965	15.00
❑ ST 2289 [S]	Big Hits of Detroit	1965	20.00
❑ T 2289 [M]	Big Hits of Detroit	1965	15.00
❑ ST 2583 [S]	Pop and Ice Cream Sodas	1966	20.00
❑ T 2583 [M]	Pop and Ice Cream Sodas	1966	15.00

BARON, ELLIOTT

Number	Title (A Side/B Side)	Yr	NM
45s			
GOLDEN WORLD			
❑ 11	Man to Man/The Spare Rib	1964	200.00

BARONS, THE

Several different groups.

Number	Title (A Side/B Side)	Yr	NM
45s			
BELLAIRE			
❑ 103	The Bandit/Wanderin'	1963	20.00
BROWNFIELD			
❑ 1035	Hope I Please You/Don't Burn It	196?	50.00
DART			
❑ 126	Lonely Loretta/Lula Mae	1959	25.00
❑ 134	Perfect Love/Until the Thirteenth Chime	1960	25.00
DECCA			
❑ 29293	Exactly Like You/ Forget About Me	1954	120.00
❑ 48323	A Year and a Day/ My Baby's Gone	1954	120.00
DEMON			
❑ 1520	Gravel Gert/The Fight	1959	15.00
EPIC			
❑ 9586	Don't Go Away (Pretty Little Girl)/Pledge of a Fool	1963	30.00
❑ 9747	Lucky Star/Remember Rita	1964	150.00
❑ 10093	Don't Go Away (Pretty Little Girl)/Pledge of a Fool	1966	15.00
IMPERIAL			
❑ 5343	Eternally Yours/Boom Boom	1955	120.00
❑ 5343	Eternally Yours/Boom Boom	1955	300.00
—Red vinyl, probably promo only			
❑ 5359	I Know I Was Wrong/My Dream, My Love	1955	120.00
❑ 5370	Cold Kisses/Searching for You	1955	120.00
❑ 5383	So Long My Darling/ Crying for You Baby	1956	120.00
❑ 5397	Don't Walk Out/Once in a Lifetime	1956	80.00
❑ 66057	Silence/I Just Go Wild Inside	1964	15.00
RCA VICTOR			
❑ 47-9034	Since You're Gone/My Smile Is Bigger (Than Your Smile)	1966	25.00
SPARTAN			
❑ 400	I've Been Hurt/ Willow Weep for Me	196?	15.00
TENDER			
❑ 511	Drawbridge/(B-side unknown)	1958	15.00

BAROQUE ENSEMBLE OF THE MERSEYSIDE KAMMERMUSIKGESELLSCHAFT, THE

Number	Title (A Side/B Side)	Yr	NM
45s			
ELEKTRA			
❑ 45602	You've Got to Hide Your Love Away/Ticket to Ride	1966	12.00
Albums			
ELEKTRA			
❑ EKL-306 [M]	The Baroque Beatles Book	1966	25.00
❑ EKS-7306 [S]	The Baroque Beatles Book	1966	30.00

BAROQUES, THE

Number	Title (A Side/B Side)	Yr	NM
45s			
CHESS			
❑ 2001	Mary Jane/Iowa, A Girl's Name	1967	15.00

BARRABAS

Number	Title (A Side/B Side)	Yr	NM
45s			
ATCO			
❑ 7027	Hi Jack/Susie Wong	1975	5.00
❑ 7036	Mellow Blue (Long)/Checkmate	1975	5.00
❑ 7059	Desperately/If	1976	5.00
POLYDOR			
❑ 14267	Hi Jack	1974	—
—Unreleased			
Albums			
ATCO			
❑ SD 36-110	Barrabas	1974	10.00
❑ SD 36-118	Heart of the City	1975	10.00
❑ SD 36-136	Watch Out	1976	10.00
RCA VICTOR			
❑ LSP-4861	Wild Safari	1973	12.00

BARRACUDA

Number	Title (A Side/B Side)	Yr	NM
45s			
RCA VICTOR			
❑ 47-9660	The Dance of St. Francis/ Lady Fingers	1968	20.00
❑ 47-9660 [PS]	The Dance of St. Francis/ Lady Fingers	1968	40.00
❑ 47-9743	Julie (The Song I Sing Is To You)/ Sleeping Out the Storm	1969	12.00

BARRACUDAS, THE

Number	Title (A Side/B Side)	Yr	NM
Albums			
JUSTICE			
❑ JLP-143	A Plane View	1968	250.00

Except when noted otherwise, VG = 25% of NM, and VG+ = 50% of NM. (Example: VG = $2.00, VG+ = $4.00 and NM = $8.00.)

BARRAN, BOB

Number	Title (A Side/B Side)	Yr	NM
45s			
SILVER STREAK			
❑ 311	Tom Tom Rock/ Mother Goose Hop	1960	150.00

BARRETT, RICHARD

Number	Title (A Side/B Side)	Yr	NM
45s			
ATLANTIC			
❑ 2142	Some Other Guy/Tricky Dicky	1962	15.00
—As "Richie Barrett"			
CRACKERJACK			
❑ 4012	Summer's Love/ Let Me Down Easy	1963	15.00
GONE			
❑ 5056	Come Softly to Me/ Walking Through Dreamland	1959	30.00
—With the Chantels			
❑ 5060	Summer's Love/All Is Forgiven	1959	30.00
—With the Chantels			
METRO			
❑ 20006	Lovable/Only One Way	1959	15.00
MGM			
❑ 12616	Smoke Gets In Your Eyes/ Remember Me	1958	30.00
❑ 12659	Body and Soul/The Party	1958	30.00
SEVILLE			
❑ 104	Dream On/I Am Yours	1960	15.00
20TH FOX			
❑ 150	Lovely One/The Snake and the Bookworm	1959	15.00

BARRETT, SUSAN

Number	Title (A Side/B Side)	Yr	NM
45s			
PHILIPS			
❑ 40147	Between Two Loves/Chico's Girl	1963	25.00
❑ 40247	The Love We Never Knew/ No One But You	1964	25.00
RCA VICTOR			
❑ 47-8888	A Grain of Sand/She Gets Everything She Wants	1966	20.00
❑ 47-9017	Walking Happy/How Can You Hold On to a Dream	1966	20.00
❑ 47-9296	What's It Gonna Be/ It's No Secret	1967	50.00
❑ 47-9384	Sunny/Ev'ry Time We Say Goodbye	1967	20.00
Albums			
CAPITOL			
❑ T 1266 [M]	Mixed Emotions	1959	50.00
RCA VICTOR			
❑ LPM-3738 [M]	Susan Barrett	1967	40.00
❑ LSP-3738 [S]	Susan Barrett	1967	30.00

BARRETT, SYD

Member of the earliest incarnation of PINK FLOYD.

Number	Title (A Side/B Side)	Yr	NM
7-Inch Extended Plays			
CAPITOL			
❑ NR-58186	Terrapin/Octopus// Baby Lemonade/ Effervescent Elephant	1994	10.00
—Pink vinyl			
❑ NR-58186 [PS]	Crazy Diamond	1994	10.00
Albums			
CAPITOL			
❑ C1-91206	Opel	1989	20.00
HARVEST			
❑ SABB-11314 [(2)]	The Madcap Laughs/Barrett	1974	25.00

BARRI, STEVE

Cohort of P.F. SLOAN. Also see THE FANTASTIC BAGGYS; THE GRASS ROOTS; THE IMAGINATIONS (2); THE INNER CIRCLE; THE LIFEGUARDS (2); PHILIP AND STEPHAN; THE RALLY PACKS; THE RINCON SURFSIDE BAND; THE STREET CLEANERS; THEMES INC.; WILLIE AND THE WHEELS.

Number	Title (A Side/B Side)	Yr	NM
45s			
RONA			
❑ 1003	Down Around the Corner/ Please Let It Be You	1961	40.00
❑ 1004	I Want Your Love/ Story of the Ring	1961	40.00
❑ 1005	Two Different Worlds/ Don't Run Away from Love	1962	40.00
❑ 1006	Never Before/ Whenever You Kiss Me	1962	40.00

BARRIX, BILLY

Number	Title (A Side/B Side)	Yr	NM
45s			
CHESS			
❑ 1662	Cool Off Baby/Almost	1958	10000.
—This record has been counterfeited; most of these are obvious on sight because neither the typeface nor the blue color matches original Chess 45s of the era, the fake label is glossy and originals aren't, and the publisher information at 3 o'clock is flush left on the originals and centered on the fake. VG 5000; VG+ 7500			

BARRON KNIGHTS, THE

Number	Title (A Side/B Side)	Yr	NM
45s			
DECCA			
❑ 32160	Lazy Fat People/In the Night	1967	10.00
EPIC			
❑ 9835	Pop Go the Workers Part 1/Part 2	1965	12.00
❑ 50755	The Topical Song/ The Big V-asectomy	1979	5.00
MERCURY			
❑ 73302	Nothin' Doin'/You're All I Need	1972	5.00
❑ 73302 [PS]	Nothin' Doin'/You're All I Need	1972	10.00

BARRY, GENE

Number	Title (A Side/B Side)	Yr	NM
45s			
FELSTED			
❑ 8648	Moonlight Gambler/Red Silk Stockings and Green Perfume	1961	12.00
Albums			
RCA VICTOR			
❑ LPM-2975 [M]	The Star of "Burke's Law" Sings of Love and Things	1964	25.00
❑ LSP-2975 [S]	The Star of "Burke's Law" Sings of Love and Things	1964	30.00

BARRY, JAY

Number	Title (A Side/B Side)	Yr	NM
45s			
ABC-PARAMOUNT			
❑ 10154	A Picture of You/Sherry	1960	15.00
❑ 10226	Love Bank/Love Spell	1961	15.00

BARRY, JEFF

Also see THE RAINDROPS.

Number	Title (A Side/B Side)	Yr	NM
45s			
A&M			
❑ 1422	Walkin' in the Sun/Whatcha Wanna Do	1973	5.00
BELL			
❑ 45140	Sweet Saviour/Love Has Never Let Me Down	1971	6.00
DECCA			
❑ 31037	Never Never/It Won't Hurt	1959	20.00
❑ 31089	Lenore/Why Does the Feeling Go Away	1960	20.00
RCA VICTOR			
❑ 47-7477	It's Called Rock & Roll/ Hip Couples	1959	25.00
❑ 47-7797	The Face from Outer Space/ Lovely Lips	1960	25.00
❑ 47-7821	All You Need Is a Quarter/ Teen Quartet	1960	25.00
RED BIRD			
❑ 10-026	I'll Still Love You/Our Love Can Still Be Saved	1965	16.00
UNITED ARTISTS			
❑ 440	We Got Love Money Can't Buy/ Welcome Home	1962	16.00
❑ 50529	Much Too Young/Where It's At	1969	8.00
Albums			
A&M			
❑ SP-4393	Walkin' in the Sun	1973	15.00

BARRY, JOHN

Number	Title (A Side/B Side)	Yr	NM
45s			
CAPITOL			
❑ F4212	Snap 'N Whistle/Long Long	1959	15.00
COLUMBIA			
❑ 43320	A Man Alone/Barbara's Theme	1965	8.00
❑ 43360	The Knack (And How to Get It)/ The Knack (And How to Get It)	1965	10.00
—B-side by Johnny DeLittle			
❑ 43544	The Chase/Saturday Night Philosopher	1966	10.00
❑ 43801	Theme from Born Free/ Goldfinger	1966	10.00
❑ 43951	Wednesday's Child/ Sleep Well, My Darling	1966	10.00
❑ 44167	You Only Live Twice/The Girl with the Sun in Her Hair	1967	8.00
❑ 44721	The Lion in Winter/To Rome	1968	8.00
❑ 44891	Midnight Cowboy/Fun City	1969	6.00
❑ 45062	On Her Majesty's Secret Service/We Have All the Time in the World	1970	6.00
❑ 45140	Theme from "The Appointment"/ The More Things Change	1970	6.00
DECCA			
❑ 31815	A Man Alone (Jazz Version)/ A Man Alone (Latin Version)	1965	10.00
EPIC			
❑ 10865	The Persuaders/The Girl with the Sun in Her Hair	1972	6.00
KING			
❑ 5495	Black Stockings/ Get Lost Jack Frost	1961	15.00
MERCURY			
❑ 72261	From Russia with Love/007	1964	12.00
MGM			
❑ 13591	Born Free/Elsa at Play	1966	8.00
20TH FOX			
❑ 472	Theme from "Man in the Middle"/Barney's Blues	1964	12.00
UNITED ARTISTS			
❑ 581	James Bond Theme/ March of the Mandarins	1963	15.00
❑ 581 [PS]	James Bond Theme/ March of the Mandarins	1963	50.00
❑ 743	Big Shield/Zulu Stomp	1964	10.00
❑ 791	Goldfinger/Troubadour	1964	10.00
❑ 863	From Russia with Love/ James Bond Theme	1965	10.00
WARNER BROS.			
❑ 7230	Highway 101/Petula	1968	6.00
Albums			
BULLDOG			
❑ BDL-1036	Bond by Barry	198?	10.00
COLUMBIA			
❑ C 1003	Ready When You Are, Mr. J.B.	1970	10.00
❑ CL 2493 [M]	Great Movie Sounds of John Barry	1966	15.00
❑ CL 2708 [M]	You Only Live Twice	1967	15.00
❑ CS 9293 [S]	Great Movie Sounds of John Barry	1966	20.00
❑ CS 9508 [S]	You Only Live Twice	1967	20.00
UNITED ARTISTS			
❑ UAL 3424 [M]	Goldfinger and Other Favorites	1965	12.00
❑ UAS 6424 [S]	Goldfinger and Other Favorites	1965	15.00

BARRY, LEN

Former member of THE DOVELLS.

Number	Title (A Side/B Side)	Yr	NM
45s			
AMY			
❑ 11026	4-5-6 (Now I'm Alone)/ Funky Night	1968	6.00
❑ 11037	You're My Picasso, Baby/ Christopher Columbus	1968	6.00
❑ 11047	The Child Is Born/Wouldn't It Be Beautiful	1968	6.00
BUDDAH			
❑ 284	Just the Two of Us/Diggin' Life	1972	5.00
❑ 284 [PS]	Just the Two of Us/Diggin' Life	1972	6.00
CAMEO			
❑ 303	Jim Dandy/Don't Come Back	1964	12.00
❑ 318	Little White House/ Hearts Are Trump	1964	12.00
DECCA			
❑ 31788	Lip Sync (To the Tongue Twisters)/At the Hop '65	1965	10.00
❑ 31827	1-2-3/Bullseye	1965	15.00
❑ 31889	Like a Baby/Happiness (Is a Girl Like You)	1966	10.00
❑ 31923	Somewhere/It's a Crying Shame	1966	10.00
❑ 31969	It's That Time of the Year/ Happily Ever After	1966	10.00
❑ 32011	I Struck It Rich/Love Is	1966	10.00
❑ 32054	Would I Love You/You Baby	1966	10.00
MERCURY			
❑ 72299	Let's Do It Again/Happy Days	1964	12.00
PARAMOUNT			
❑ 0206	Heaven Plus Earth/ I'm Marching to the Music	1973	5.00
PARKWAY			
❑ 969	Little White House/ Hearts Are Trump	1966	8.00
RCA VICTOR			
❑ 47-9150	Our Song/The Moving Finger Writes	1967	8.00
❑ 47-9275	All Those Memories/ Rainy Side of the Street	1967	8.00
❑ 47-9348	The ABC's of Love/ Come Rain or Shine	1967	8.00

Number	Title (A Side/B Side)	Yr	NM
❑ 47-9464	Sweet and Funny/I Like the Way	1968	8.00
SCEPTER			
❑ 12251	Put Out the Fire/ Spread It On Like Butter	1969	8.00
❑ 12263	Keem-O-Sabe/This Old World	1969	8.00
❑ 12284	Bob & Carol & Ted & Alice/In My Present State of Mind	1970	6.00
7-Inch Extended Plays			
DECCA			
❑ 7-34346	1-2-3/Would I Love You?/ Lip Sync (To the Tongue Twisters)//Bullseye/ Treat Her Right/I.O.U.	1965	20.00
—Stereo jukebox issue; small hole, plays at 33 1/3 rpm			
❑ 7-34346 [PS]	1-2-3	1965	20.00
Albums			
BUDDAH			
❑ BDS-5105	Ups & Downs	1972	15.00
DECCA			
❑ DL 4720 [M]	1-2-3	1965	30.00
❑ DL 74720 [P]	1-2-3	1965	40.00
—"Lip Sync" is rechanneled			
RCA VICTOR			
❑ LPM-3823 [M]	My Kind of Soul	1967	25.00
❑ LSP-3823 [S]	My Kind of Soul	1967	20.00

BARRY, SANDRA

Number	Title (A Side/B Side)	Yr	NM
45s			
PARKWAY			
❑ 943	We Were Lovers/The End of the Line	1965	15.00
❑ 954	Question/You Can Take It from Me	1965	15.00

BARRY AND BARRY See BARRY McGUIRE AND BARRY KANE.

BARRY AND THE TAMERLANES Also see BARRY DeVORZON.

Number	Title (A Side/B Side)	Yr	NM
45s			
VALIANT			
❑ 703	I Wonder What She's Doing Tonight/Roberta	1965	12.00
❑ 6034	I Wonder What She's Doing Tonight/Don't Go	1963	20.00
❑ 6040	Roberta/Butterfly	1964	15.00
❑ 6046	Lucky Guy/I Don't Want to Be Your Clown	1964	15.00
❑ 6050	A Date with Judy/Pretty Things	1964	15.00
❑ 6059	Gee/Don't Cry Cindy	1964	15.00
Albums			
VALIANT			
❑ LP-406 [M]	I Wonder What She's Doing Tonight	1963	150.00
❑ LPS-406 [S]	I Wonder What She's Doing Tonight	1963	300.00

BARTEL, JON, THING

Number	Title (A Side/B Side)	Yr	NM
Albums			
CAPITOL			
❑ ST-274	The Jon Bartel Thing	1969	25.00

BARTEL, LOU

Number	Title (A Side/B Side)	Yr	NM
45s			
ABC-PARAMOUNT			
❑ 9801	Natural, Natural Baby/ My Idea of Heaven	1957	25.00
❑ 9877	Blue Moon/I'm Gonna Kiss My Baby Goodnight	1957	25.00
APOLLO			
❑ 473	I Pray/(Zoom) Give Me Your Tonight	1954	150.00

BARTHOLOMEW, DAVE

Number	Title (A Side/B Side)	Yr	NM
45s			
DECCA			
❑ 48216	Tra La La/Teejim	1951	120.00
IMPERIAL			
❑ 5210	Who Drank the Beer While I Was in the Rear/ The Rest of My Life	1952	120.00
—Dave Bartholomew records on Imperial before 5210 are unconfirmed on 45 rpm			
❑ 5249	No More Black Nights/Air Tight	1953	120.00
❑ 5273	Texas Hop/When the Saints Go Marchin' In Boogie	1954	150.00
❑ 5308	Cat Music/Jump Children	1954	120.00
❑ 5322	Another Mule/ I Want to Be with Her	1955	50.00
❑ 5350	Every Night, Every Day/ Four Winds	1955	50.00
❑ 5373	Shrimp and Gumbo/An Old Cowhand from a Blues Band	1956	40.00
❑ 5390	Would You/Turn Your Lamp Down Low	1956	40.00
❑ 5408	Lovin' You/Three Time Loser	1956	30.00
❑ 5438	The Monkey/The Shuffling	1957	25.00
❑ 5460	How Could You/Barrel House	1957	25.00
❑ 5481	Hard Times (The Slop)/ Cinderella	1957	25.00
❑ 5560	Button Blues/Short Subjects	1959	20.00
❑ 5702	I Cried/Somebody New	1960	20.00
❑ 5714	People Are Talking/Yeah, Yeah	1961	20.00
❑ 5803	I'm Walkin'/Going to the River	1962	15.00
❑ 5835	A Sunday Kind of Love/ Honky Tonk Trumpet	1962	15.00
KING			
❑ 4482	Sweet Home Blues/Twins	1951	150.00
❑ 4508	In the Alley/I'll Never Be the Same	1952	200.00
❑ 4523	Lawdy, Lawdy, Lawd (Part 1)/ Lawdy, Lawdy, Lawd (Part 2)	1952	150.00
❑ 4544	My Ding-a-Ling/Bad Habit	1952	250.00
❑ 4559	The Golden Rule/ Mother Knows Best	1952	100.00
❑ 4585	High Flying Woman/ Stormy Weather	1953	100.00
Albums			
BROADMOOR			
❑ BR-1201	Dave Bartholomew's New Orleans Jazz Band	1981	15.00
IMPERIAL			
❑ LP-9162 [M]	Fats Domino Presents Dave Bartholomew	1961	100.00
❑ LP-9217 [M]	New Orleans House Party	1963	100.00
❑ LP-12076 [S]	Fats Domino Presents Dave Bartholomew	1961	150.00
❑ LP-12217 [S]	New Orleans House Party	1963	150.00

BARTLEY, CHRIS

Number	Title (A Side/B Side)	Yr	NM
45s			
BUDDAH			
❑ 93	I'll Take the Blame/ Baby I'm Yours	1969	25.00
❑ 115	I Know We Can Work It Out/ (My Baby's) One Wonderful Girl AKA Sugar Baby	1969	50.00
MUSICOR			
❑ 1437	Tomorrow Keeps Shining on Me/A Man, a Woman	1971	50.00
VANDO			
❑ DV-101	The Sweetest Thing This Side of Heaven/Love Me Baby	1967	15.00
❑ 3000	Baby, It's Wonderful/ I'll Be Loving You	1967	20.00
❑ 3002	You Get Next to My Heart/ For You	1968	20.00
❑ 14000	Truer Words Were Never Spoken/This Feeling You Give Me	1968	30.00
❑ 14001	I Found a Goodie/ Be Mine Forever	1968	30.00
Albums			
VANDO			
❑ VA-60000 [M]	The Sweetest Thing This Side of Heaven	1967	50.00
❑ VAS-60000 [S]	The Sweetest Thing This Side of Heaven	1967	40.00

BARTON, EILEEN

Number	Title (A Side/B Side)	Yr	NM
45s			
CORAL			
❑ 9-60592	Cry/Hold Me Just a Little Longer, Daddy	1951	20.00
❑ 9-60651	Wishin'/When You're Near Me	1952	20.00
❑ 9-60691	To Be Loved by You/Wrong	1952	20.00
❑ 9-60775	Rhode Island Red/En-Thuz-E-Uz-E-As-M	1952	12.00
—With Teresa Brewer			
❑ 9-60927	Pretend/Too Proud to Cry	1953	15.00
❑ 9-60986	Pot Luck/A Pretty Girl Milking Her Cow	1953	15.00
❑ 9-61019	I Ain't Gonna Do It/Toys	1953	15.00
❑ 9-61057	Anytime, Anywhere/Toys	1953	15.00
❑ 9-61109	Don't Ask Me Why/ Away Up There	1953	15.00
❑ 9-61146	Jesse James/Signpost	1954	15.00
❑ 9-61175	Bright Eyed and Bushy Tailed/ Twilight Time in Tennessee	1954	20.00
—With Jimmy Wakely			
❑ 9-61185	Sway/When Mama Calls	1954	15.00
❑ 9-61227	A Husband/A Wife	1954	12.00
—With Johnny Desmond			
❑ 9-61247	And Then/I Have to Tell You	1954	15.00
❑ 9-61293	Without Love/Happy Birthday, My Darling	1954	15.00
❑ 9-61324	Punch/This-a-Way, That-a-Way	1954	20.00
—With Jimmy Wakely			
❑ 9-61337	The Year We Fell in Love/ I Don't Want to Mambo Polka	1955	12.00
—With Lawrence Welk			
❑ 9-61344	I Wish You'd Fall in Love with Me/On a Lonely Walk	1955	12.00
❑ 9-61377	How Ja-Do, How Ja-Do, How Ja-Do (If I Knew You Were Comin' I'd've Baked a Cake)/ Fujiyama Mama	1955	12.00
❑ 9-61413	How Could You Forget Me/ He Asked Me	1955	12.00
❑ 9-61459	Here I Am in Love Again/ Apollo Umberto Silvano	1955	12.00
❑ 9-61530	Cry Me a River/Come Home	1955	12.00
❑ 9-61585	Teenage Heart/My Social Hot Dog	1956	12.00
❑ 9-61609	Too Close for Comfort/ The Scene of the Crime	1956	12.00
❑ 9-61657	I'll Be Laughing at My Tears/ Spring It Was	1956	12.00
❑ 9-61695	Then I'll Be Tired of You/ Dumayerry	1956	12.00
CREST			
❑ 1107	You Say You Love Me/Oh, Love	1962	8.00
MERCURY			
❑ 5392-X45	If I Knew You Were Comin' I'd've Baked a Cake/ Poco, Loco in the Coco	1950	40.00
MGM			
❑ K12758	If I Knew You Were Comin' (I'd've Baked a Cake)/ When Love Happens to You	1959	10.00
NATIONAL			
❑ 9103-X45	If I Knew You Were Comin' I'd've Baked a Cake/ Poco, Loco in the Coco	1950	50.00
❑ 9109-X45	Honey, Honeymoon with Me/ Dixieland Fall	1950	30.00
❑ 9112-X45	May I Take Two Giant Steps?/ If You Saw What I Saw	1950	30.00
❑ 9123-X45	Baby Me/What Will Be, Will Be	1950	30.00
❑ 9137-X45	I Met Him at One O'Clock/ Tell Me	1951	30.00
❑ 9152-X45	The Syncopated Clock/ Lock the Barn Door	1951	30.00
20TH CENTURY FOX			
❑ 417	The Earth Stood Still/ Patty Cake, Patty Cake	1963	8.00

BARTON, ERNIE

Number	Title (A Side/B Side)	Yr	NM
45s			
PHILLIPS INTERNATIONAL			
❑ 3528	Stairway of Love/ Raining the Blues	1958	20.00
❑ 3541	Open the Door Richard/ Shut Your Mouth	1959	150.00

BARY, HENRY

Number	Title (A Side/B Side)	Yr	NM
45s			
HIT			
❑ 228	One, Two, Three/ Get Off of My Cloud	1965	12.00
—B-side by the Jalopy Five			

BASH, OTTO

Number	Title (A Side/B Side)	Yr	NM
45s			
HDS			
❑ 2008	My Babe/Straighten Up and Fly Right	1956	20.00
RCA VICTOR			
❑ 47-6426	Later Alligator/Lookout Mountain	1956	25.00
❑ 47-6585	The Elvis Blues/Later	1956	50.00

BASIC BLACK AND PEARL

Number	Title (A Side/B Side)	Yr	NM
45s			
POLYDOR			
❑ 15111	There'll Come a Time, There'll Come a Day/He's a Rebel	1975	5.00

BASIE, COUNT

Number	Title (A Side/B Side)	Yr	NM
45s			
BRUNSWICK			
❑ 55344	Bright Lights, Big City/ Mercy, Mercy, Mercy	1967	6.00
❑ 55352	Green Onions/Hang On Sloopy	1967	6.00
CAPITOL			
❑ S7-57888	Jingle Bells/Let It Snow! Let It Snow! Let It Snow!	1992	4.00
—B-side by Lena Horne			
CLEF			
❑ 89070	Blee Blop Blues/Small Hotel	1953	15.00
❑ 89086	Tippin' on the QT/Bread	1953	15.00
❑ 89101	Count's Organ Blues/Basie Beat	1954	15.00

B

Number	Title (A Side/B Side)	Yr	NM
89102	K.C. Organ Blues/Stan Shorthair	1954	15.00
89112	Basie Goes Wess/Softly, With Feeling	1954	15.00
89120	Cherry Point/Right On	1954	15.00
89126	You for Me/Slow But Sure	1955	15.00
89131	Two for the Blues/Soft Drink	1955	15.00
89137	Stereophonie/I Feel Like a New Man	1955	15.00
89147	Ska-Di-De-Dee-Oo/16 Men Swinging	1955	15.00
89149	Every Day/The Comeback	1955	15.00
89151	The Comeback (Part 1)/The Comeback (Part 2)	1955	15.00
89167	Teach Me Tonight/My Baby Upsets Me	1956	12.00
89169	Big Red/Smack Dab in the Middle	1956	12.00
89171	Amazing Love/Magic	1956	12.00
89172	April in Paris/Party Blues	1956	12.00
COLUMBIA			
1-709	Bluebeard Blues/Golden Bullet	1950	30.00
	—Microgroove 7-inch, 33 1/3 rpm single		
6-709	Bluebeard Blues/Golden Bullet	1950	20.00
1-930 (?)	Danny Boy/Neal's Deal	1950	30.00
	—Microgroove 7-inch, 33 1/3 rpm single		
6-930 (?)	Danny Boy/Neal's Deal	1950	20.00
39406	Little Pony/Beaver Junction	1951	20.00
DOT			
17201	Hay Burner/That Warm Feeling	1969	5.00
MERCURY			
89014	Paradise Squat/Hot Nail Boogie	1953	20.00
89028	Goin' to Chicago/Sent for You Yesterday and Here You Come Today	1953	20.00
89033	I Want a Little Girl/Oh, Lady Be Good	1953	20.00
89061	Song of the Islands/Royal Garden Blues	1953	20.00
OKEH			
6895	Jump the Blues Away/Wiggle Woogie	1952	20.00
RCA VICTOR			
47-2915	Cheek to Cheek/Bran' New Dolly	1949	20.00
47-2990	Did You See Jackie Robinson Hit That Ball?/Shoutin' Blues	1949	40.00
47-3032	She's a Wine-O/Slider	1949	20.00
47-3065	Rocky Mountain Blues/Walking Slow Behind You	1949	20.00
47-3107	St. Louis Baby/Normania	1949	20.00
REPRISE			
0240	I Left My Heart in San Francisco/Walk Don't Run	1963	10.00
20170	I Can't Stop Loving You/Nice & Easy	1963	10.00
ROULETTE			
4040	Lil' Darlin'/The Kid from Red Bank	1957	10.00
4088	Going to Chicago Blues/Swingin' the Blues	1958	10.00
4109	M Squad Theme/Late Late Show	1958	10.00
4124	Jumpin' at the Woodside/Rusty Dusty Blues	1958	10.00
4166	Rat Race/The Big Walk	1959	10.00
4226	How Am I to Know/It Had to Be You	1960	10.00
4286	Ol' Man River Part 1/Ol' Man River Part 2	1960	10.00
4403	The Basie Twist/Trot	1962	12.00
4409	Song of the Islands/Summertime	1962	10.00
4465	Basie's Jingle Bells/Lullabye of Birdland	1962	10.00
UNITED ARTISTS			
50002	Double-O-Seven/Kingston Calypso	1966	8.00
VERVE			
10318	All of Me/On the Road to Mandalay	1964	8.00
10329	Li'l Ol' Groove Maker/Pleasingly Plump	1964	8.00
10350	My Kind of Town/Watermelon Man	1965	8.00
89177	Only Forever/Move	1957	12.00

7-Inch Extended Plays

Number	Title (A Side/B Side)	Yr	NM
CLEF			
EP-195	Cash Box/Tom Whaley//Jack and Jill/Basie Talks	195?	20.00
EP-195 [PS]	Count Basie Big Band	195?	25.00
COLUMBIA			
B-2555	*One O'Clock Jump/I'm Gonna Move to the Outskirts of Town/Queer Street/The King	195?	12.00
B-2555 [PS]	Count Basie (Hall of Fame Series)	195?	12.00

Albums

Number	Title (A Side/B Side)	Yr	NM
ABC			
4001	16 Great Performances	1974	12.00
AC-30004	The ABC Collection	1976	12.00
ABC IMPULSE!			
AS-15 [S]	Count Basie and the Kansas City Seven	1968	12.00
IA-9351 [(2)]	Retrospective Sessions	1978	12.00
ABC-PARAMOUNT			
ABC-570 [M]	Basie's Swingin' — Voices Singin'	1966	20.00
ABCS-570 [S]	Basie's Swingin' — Voices Singin'	1966	25.00
ACCORD			
SN-7183	Command Performance	1981	10.00
ALAMAC			
QSR-2412	Count Basie and His Orchestra 1937	198?	10.00
AMERICAN RECORDING SOCIETY			
G-401 [M]	Count Basie	1956	40.00
G-402 [M]	The Band That Swings the Blues	1956	40.00
G-422 [M]	Basie's Best	1957	40.00
G-435 [M]	Mainstream Jazz Swing	1957	40.00
BASF			
25111 [(2)]	Basic Basie	1973	15.00
BOOK-OF-THE-MONTH CLUB			
91-6545 [(3)]	The Early Years	1982	25.00
	—Alternate number: P3-16389		
BRIGHT ORANGE			
XBO-702	Count Basie Featuring B.B. King	196?	20.00
BRUNSWICK			
BL 54012 [M]	Count Basie	1957	40.00
BL 58019 [10]	Basie's Best	195?	100.00
BL 754127	Basie's in the Bag	196?	15.00
BULLDOG			
BDL-2020	20 Golden Pieces of Count Basie	1980	12.00
CLEF			
MCG-120 [10]	Count Basie and His Orchestra Collates	1953	250.00
MCG-146 [10]	Count Basie Sextet	1954	250.00
MGC-148 [10]	Count Basie Big Band	1954	250.00
MGC-626 [M]	Count Basie Dance Session #1	1954	100.00
MGC-633 [M]	Basie Jazz	1954	100.00
MGC-647 [M]	Count Basie Jazz Session #2	1955	100.00
MGC-666 [M]	Basie	1955	100.00
MGC-685 [M]	The Count	1956	80.00
MGC-706 [M]	The Swinging Count	1956	60.00
MGC-722 [M]	The Band of Distinction	1956	60.00
MGC-723 [M]	Basie Roars Again	1956	60.00
MGC-724 [M]	The King of Swing	1956	60.00
MGC-729 [M]	Basie Rides Again!	1956	60.00
MGC-749 [M]	Basie in Europe	1956	—
	—Canceled; released as Verve 8199		
COLISEUM			
41003 [M]	The Happiest Millionaire	1968	40.00
51003 [S]	The Happiest Millionaire	1968	15.00
COLUMBIA			
CL 754 [M]	Classics	1955	60.00
CL 901 [M]	Blues By Basie	1956	40.00
CL 997 [M]	One O'Clock Jump	1956	40.00
CL 2560 [10]	Basie Bash	1956	80.00
CL 6079 [10]	Dance Parade	1949	100.00
G 31224 [(2)]	Suoer Chief	1972	15.00
COLUMBIA JAZZ MASTERPIECES			
CJ 40608	The Essential Count Basie, Vol. 1	1987	10.00
CJ 40835	The Essential Count Basie, Vol. 2	1987	10.00
CJ 44150	The Essential Count Basie, Vol. 3	1988	10.00
COLUMBIA JAZZ ODYSSEY			
PC 36824	Blues By Basie	1981	8.00
COLUMBIA SPECIAL PRODUCTS			
P 14355	The Count	198?	8.00
COMMAND			
33-905 [M]	Broadway Basie's...Way	1966	12.00
RS 905 SD [S]	Broadway Basie's...Way	1966	15.00
33-912 [M]	Hollywood... Basie's Way	1967	15.00
RS 912 SD [S]	Hollywood... Basie's Way	1967	12.00
CQ-40004 [Q]	Broadway Basie's...Way	1972	20.00
DAYBREAK			
2005	Have a Nice Day	1971	12.00
DECCA			
DXB 170 [(2)M]	The Best of Count Basie	196?	25.00
DL 5111 [10]	Count Basie at the Piano	1950	120.00
DXSB 7170 [(2)R]	The Best of Count Basie	196?	15.00
DL 8049 [M]	Count Basie and His Orchestra	1954	50.00
DL 78049 [R]	Count Basie and His Orchestra	196?	12.00
DOCTOR JAZZ			
FW 39520	Afrique	1985	10.00
	—Reissue of Flying Dutchman 10138		
DOT			
DLP-25902	Straight Ahead	1969	15.00
DLP-25938	Standing Ovation	1969	15.00
EMARCY			
MG-26023 [10]	Jazz Royalty	1954	70.00
EMUS			
ES12011	Basie at Birdland	197?	10.00
EPIC			
LG 1021 [10]	The Old Count and the New Count — Basie	1954	70.00
LN 1117 [10]	Rock the Blues	1955	70.00
LN 3107 [M]	Lester Leaps In	1955	50.00
	—With Lester Young		
LN 3168 [M]	Let's Go to Prez	1955	50.00
	—With Lester Young		
LN 3169 [M]	Basie's Back in Town	1955	50.00
EVEREST ARCHIVE OF FOLK & JAZZ			
FS-318	Savoy Ballroom 1937	197?	10.00
FANTASY			
OJC-379	Basie Big Band Montreux '77	1989	10.00
	—Reissue of Pablo Live 2308 209		
OJC-416	88 Basie Street	198?	12.00
OJC-449	Kansas City 6	1990	12.00
	—Reissue of Pablo 2310 871		
OJC-600	Kansas City 3/For the Second Time	1991	12.00
	—Reissue of Pablo 2310 878		
FLYING DUTCHMAN			
FD 10138	Afrique	1972	30.00
FORUM			
F-9032 [M]	Kansas City Suite	196?	12.00
SF-9032 [S]	Kansas City Suite	196?	15.00
	—Reissue of Roulette 52056		
F-9060 [M]	One More Time	196?	12.00
SF-9060 [S]	One More Time	196?	15.00
	—Reissue of Roulette 52024		
F-9063 [M]	Not Now — I'll Tell You When	196?	12.00
SF-9063 [S]	Not Now — I'll Tell You When	196?	15.00
	—Reissue of Roulette 52044		
GROOVE MERCHANT			
2001	Evergreens	1972	12.00
HAPPY TIGER			
1007	Basie on the Beatles	196?	25.00
HARMONY			
HL 7229 [M]	Basie's Best	1960	15.00
HS 11371	Just in Time	1970	12.00
IMPULSE!			
A-15 [M]	Count Basie and the Kansas City Seven	1962	30.00
AS-15 [S]	Count Basie and the Kansas City Seven	1962	40.00
INTERMEDIA			
QS-5028	The Deacon	198?	10.00
QS-5039	The Classic Count	198?	10.00
JAZZ ARCHIVES			
JA-16	The Count at the Chatterbox, 1937	198?	10.00
JA-41	At the Famous Door, 1938-1939	198?	10.00
JAZZ MAN			
5006	Ain't It the Truth	198?	10.00
JAZZ PANORAMA			
1803 [10]	Count Basie and Lester Young	1951	100.00
MCA			
718	16 Greatest Performances	198?	8.00
4050 [(2)]	The Best of Count Basie	197?	12.00
4108 [(2)]	Good Morning Blues	197?	12.00
4130 [(2)]	Retrospective Sessions	198?	10.00
4163 [(2)]	Showtime	198?	10.00
29003	Count Basie and the Kansas City Seven	198?	8.00
29004	Straight Ahead	198?	8.00
29005	Standing Ovation	198?	8.00
42324	One O'Clock Jump	1990	12.00
MCA/IMPULSE!			
5656	Count Basie and the Kansas City Seven	1986	8.00
MERCURY			
MGC-120 [10]	Count Basie and His Orchestra Collates	1952	220.00
MG-25105 [10]	Count Basie and His Kansas City Seven	1952	100.00
METRO			
M-516 [M]	Count Basie	1965	15.00
MS-516 [S]	Count Basie	1965	12.00
MGM			
GAS-126	Count Basie (Golden Archive Series)	1970	15.00

Number	Title (A Side/B Side)	Yr	NM
MOBILE FIDELITY			
❑ 1-129	Basie Plays Hefti	1985	80.00
—Audiophile vinyl			
❑ 1-237	April in Paris	1995	40.00
—Audiophile vinyl			
MOSAIC			
❑ MR12-135 [(12)]	The Complete Roulette Live Recordings of Count Basie and His Orchestra	199?	200.00
❑ MQ15-149 [(15)]	The Complete Roulette Studio Recordings of Count Basie and His Orchestra	199?	250.00
PABLO			
❑ 2310709	The Bosses	1974	12.00
❑ 2310712	For the First Time	1974	12.00
❑ 2310718	Basie Jam	1975	15.00
❑ 2310745	Basie and Zoot	1976	20.00
❑ 2310750	Basie Jam/Montreux '75	1976	12.00
❑ 2310756	Basie Big Band	1975	20.00
❑ 2310767	I Told You So	1976	12.00
❑ 2310786	Basie Jam #2	1977	15.00
❑ 2310797	Prime Time	1977	12.00
❑ 2310840	Basie Jam #3	1979	12.00
❑ 2310852	The Best of Basie	1980	10.00
❑ 2310859	Kansas City Shout	1980	12.00
—With Joe Turner and Eddie "Cleanhead" Vinson			
❑ 2310871	Kansas City 6	198?	12.00
❑ 2310874	Farmers Market Barbecue	1982	10.00
❑ 2310891	Me & You	1983	10.00
❑ 2310901	88 Basie Street	1984	20.00
❑ 2310919	Mostly Blues...And Some Others	1987	10.00
❑ 2310920	Fancy Pants	1987	10.00
❑ 2310924	Count Basie Get Together	1987	10.00
❑ 2310925	Basie and His Friends	1988	12.00
❑ 2405408	The Best of the Count Basie Band	198?	10.00
PABLO LIVE			
❑ 2308207	Basie Big Band Montreux '77	1977	12.00
❑ 2308209	Basie Jam/Montreux '77	1977	12.00
❑ 2308246	Live in Japan, 1978	198?	10.00
PABLO TODAY			
❑ 2312112	On the Road	1980	10.00
❑ 2312126	Kansas City 5	198?	10.00
❑ 2312131	Warm Breeze	198?	10.00
PAIR			
❑ PDL2-1045 [(2)]	Basic Basie	1986	12.00
PAUSA			
❑ 7105	High Voltage	198?	10.00
PICKWICK			
❑ PC-3028 [M]	His Hits of the 60's	196?	15.00
❑ SPC-3028 [S]	His Hits of the 60's	196?	12.00
❑ SPC-3500	Everything's Coming Up Roses	197?	10.00
PRESTIGE			
❑ 24109 [(2)]	Reunions	197?	12.00
QUINTESSENCE			
❑ 25151	Everything's Coming Up Roses	197?	10.00
RCA CAMDEN			
❑ CAL-395 [M]	The Count	1958	25.00
❑ CAL-497 [M]	Basie's Basement	1959	25.00
❑ CAL-514 [M]	Count Basie in Kansas City	1959	25.00
RCA VICTOR			
❑ LPV-514 [M]	Count Basie in Kansas City	1965	25.00
❑ LPM-1112 [M]	Count Basie	1955	50.00
❑ AFM1-5180	Kansas City Style	1985	10.00
REPRISE			
❑ R-6070 [M]	This Time by Basie! Hits of the 50's and 60's	1963	20.00
❑ R9-6070 [S]	This Time by Basie! Hits of the 50's and 60's	1963	25.00
❑ R-6153 [M]	Pop Goes the Basie	1965	15.00
❑ RS-6153 [S]	Pop Goes the Basie	1965	20.00
ROULETTE			
❑ RB-1 [(2)M]	The Count Basie Story	1960	40.00
❑ SRB-1 [(2)S]	The Count Basie Story	1960	50.00
❑ RE-102 [(2)]	Echoes of an Era (The Count Basie Years)	1971	15.00
❑ RE-107 [(2)]	Echoes of an Era (The Vocal Years)	1971	15.00
❑ RE-118 [(2)]	The Best of Count Basie	1971	15.00
❑ RE-124 [(2)]	Kansas City Suite/Easin' It	1973	15.00
❑ SR 42009	Fantail	1968	15.00
❑ SR 42015	The Kid from Red Bank	1968	15.00
❑ R 52003 [M]	Basie	1958	50.00
—White label with colored "spokes"			
❑ R 52003 [M]	Basie	1964	30.00
—Orange and yellow "roulette wheel" label			
❑ R 52003 [M]	Basie	2003	30.00
—200-gram vinyl reissue; distributed by Classic Records			
❑ SR 52003 [S]	Basie	1958	60.00
—Black vinyl; white label with colored "spokes"			
❑ SR 52003 [S]	Basie	1958	150.00
—Red vinyl; white label with colored "spokes"			
❑ SR 52003 [S]	Basie	1964	40.00
—Orange and yellow "roulette wheel" label			
❑ R 52011 [M]	Basie Plays Hefti	1958	30.00
❑ SR 52011 [S]	Basie Plays Hefti	1958	30.00
❑ R 52024 [M]	One More Time	1959	30.00
❑ SR 52024 [S]	One More Time	1959	30.00
❑ R 52028 [M]	Breakfast, Dance & Barbeque	1959	30.00
❑ SR 52028 [S]	Breakfast, Dance & Barbeque	1959	30.00
❑ R 52032 [M]	Chairman of the Board	1959	30.00
❑ SR 52032 [S]	Chairman of the Board	1959	30.00
❑ R 52036 [M]	Dance Along with Basie	1959	30.00
❑ SR 52036 [S]	Dance Along with Basie	1959	30.00
❑ R 52044 [M]	Not Now — I'll Tell You When	1960	25.00
❑ SR 52044 [S]	Not Now — I'll Tell You When	1960	30.00
❑ R 52051 [M]	String Along with Basie	1960	25.00
❑ SR 52051 [S]	String Along with Basie	1960	30.00
❑ R 52056 [M]	Benny Carter's Kansas City Suite	1960	25.00
❑ SR 52056 [S]	Benny Carter's Kansas City Suite	1960	30.00
❑ R 52065 [M]	Basie at Birdland	1961	25.00
❑ SR 52065 [S]	Basie at Birdland	1961	30.00
❑ R 52081 [M]	The Best of Basie	1962	15.00
❑ SR 52081 [S]	The Best of Basie	1962	20.00
❑ R 52086 [M]	The Legend	1962	20.00
❑ SR 52086 [S]	The Legend	1962	25.00
❑ R 52089 [M]	The Best of Basie, Vol. 2	1962	15.00
❑ SR 52089 [S]	The Best of Basie, Vol. 2	1962	20.00
❑ R 52099 [M]	Count Basie in Sweden	1963	20.00
❑ SR 52099 [S]	Count Basie in Sweden	1963	25.00
❑ R 52106 [M]	Easin' It	1963	20.00
❑ SR 52106 [S]	Easin' It	1963	25.00
❑ R 52111/3 [(2)M]	The World of Count Basie	1964	40.00
❑ SR 52111/3 [(2)S]	The World of Count Basie	1964	50.00
❑ R 52113 [M]	Back with Basie	1964	20.00
❑ SR 52113 [S]	Back with Basie	1964	25.00
SOLID STATE			
❑ SS-18032	Basie Meets Bond	1968	15.00
—Reissue of United Artists LP			
TIME-LIFE			
❑ STBB-08 [(2)]	Big Bands: Count Basie	1983	15.00
❑ STL-J-22 [(3)]	Giants of Jazz	1982	20.00
UNITED ARTISTS			
❑ UAL-3480 [M]	Basie Meets Bond	1966	25.00
❑ UAS-6480 [S]	Basie Meets Bond	1966	30.00
UPFRONT			
❑ UPF-142	Count Basie and His Orchestra	1969	12.00
VEE JAY			
❑ VJS-3054	I Got Rhythm	198?	12.00
VERVE			
❑ VSP-12 [M]	Inside Basie, Outside	1966	15.00
❑ VSPS-12 [S]	Inside Basie, Outside	1966	20.00
❑ VE-2-2517 [(2)]	16 Men Swinging	197?	12.00
❑ VE-2-2542 [(2)]	Paradise Squat	197?	12.00
❑ UMV-1-2619	Count Basie at Newport	198?	10.00
❑ UMV-1-2641	April in Paris	198?	10.00
❑ MGVS-6024 [S]	Count Basie at Newport	1960	50.00
❑ MGV-8012 [M]	April in Paris	1957	50.00
❑ V-8012 [M]	April in Paris	1961	20.00
❑ MGV-8018 [M]	Basie Roars Again	1957	50.00
—Reissue of Clef 723			
❑ V-8018 [M]	Basie Roars Again	1961	20.00
❑ MGV-8070 [M]	The Count	1957	50.00
—Reissue of Clef 120			
❑ V-8070 [M]	The Count	1961	20.00
❑ MGV-8090 [M]	The Swinging Count!	1957	50.00
—Reissue of Clef 706			
❑ V-8090 [M]	The Swinging Count!	1961	20.00
❑ MGV-8103 [M]	The Band of Distinction	1957	50.00
—Reissue of Clef 722			
❑ V-8103 [M]	The Band of Distinction	1961	20.00
❑ MGV-8104 [M]	The King of Swing	1957	50.00
—Reissue of Clef 724			
❑ V-8104 [M]	The King of Swing	1961	20.00
❑ MGV-8108 [M]	Basie Rides Again!	1957	50.00
—Reissue of Clef 729			
❑ V-8108 [M]	Basie Rides Again!	1961	20.00
❑ MGV-8199 [M]	Basie in London	1957	50.00
❑ V-8199 [M]	Basie in London	1961	20.00
❑ MGV-8243 [M]	Count Basie at Newport	1958	50.00
❑ V-8243 [M]	Count Basie at Newport	1961	20.00
❑ V6-8243 [S]	Count Basie at Newport	1961	20.00
❑ MGV-8291 [M]	Hall of Fame	1958	50.00
❑ V-8291 [M]	Hall of Fame	1961	20.00
❑ V-8407 [M]	The Essential Count Basie	1961	15.00
❑ V6-8407 [S]	The Essential Count Basie	1961	20.00
❑ V-8511 [M]	On My Way and Shoutin' Again!	1963	15.00
❑ V6-8511 [S]	On My Way and Shoutin' Again!	1963	20.00
❑ V-8549 [M]	Li'l Ol' Groovemaker...Basie!	1963	20.00
❑ V6-8549 [S]	Li'l Ol' Groovemaker...Basie!	1963	25.00
❑ V-8563 [M]	More Hits of the 50's and 60's	1963	20.00
❑ V6-8563 [S]	More Hits of the 50's and 60's	1963	25.00
❑ V-8596 [M]	Verve's Choice — Best of Count Basie	1964	15.00
❑ V6-8596 [S]	Verve's Choice — Best of Count Basie	1964	20.00
❑ V-8597 [M]	Basie Land	1964	15.00
❑ V6-8597 [S]	Basie Land	1964	20.00
❑ V-8616 [M]	Basie Picks the Winners	1965	15.00
❑ V6-8616 [S]	Basie Picks the Winners	1965	20.00
❑ V-8659 [M]	Basie's Beatle Bag	1966	30.00
❑ V6-8659 [S]	Basie's Beatle Bag	1966	40.00
❑ V-8687 [M]	Basie's Beat	1967	20.00
❑ V6-8687 [S]	Basie's Beat	1967	15.00
❑ V6-8783	Basie	1969	15.00
❑ V6-8831	The Newport Years	1973	12.00
❑ 821291-1	Basic Basie	198?	12.00
❑ 825194-1	High Voltage (Basic Basie Vol. 2)	198?	10.00

BASIE, COUNT, AND SAMMY DAVIS, JR.

Number	Title (A Side/B Side)	Yr	NM
45s			
VERVE			
❑ 10349	She's a Woman/You're Nobody 'Til Somebody Loves You	1965	6.00
Albums			
VERVE			
❑ V-8605 [M]	Our Shining Hour	1965	15.00
❑ V6-8605 [S]	Our Shining Hour	1965	20.00

BASIE, COUNT, AND BILLY ECKSTINE

Number	Title (A Side/B Side)	Yr	NM
Albums			
ROULETTE			
❑ SR 42017	Count Basie and Billy Eckstine	1968	15.00
—Reissue			
❑ R 52029 [M]	Basie/Eckstine, Incorporated	1959	30.00
❑ SR 52029 [S]	Basie/Eckstine, Incorporated	1959	40.00

BASIE, COUNT, AND DUKE ELLINGTON

Number	Title (A Side/B Side)	Yr	NM
Albums			
ACCORD			
❑ SN-7200	Heads of State	1982	10.00

BASIE, COUNT, AND MAYNARD FERGUSON

Number	Title (A Side/B Side)	Yr	NM
Albums			
ROULETTE			
❑ R 52117 [M]	Big Band Scene '65	1965	20.00
❑ SR 52117 [S]	Big Band Scene '65	1965	25.00

BASIE, COUNT, AND DIZZY GILLESPIE

Number	Title (A Side/B Side)	Yr	NM
Albums			
PABLO			
❑ 2310833	The Gifted Ones	1979	10.00
VERVE			
❑ V-8560 [M]	The Count Basie Band and the Dizzy Gillespie Band at Newport	1963	20.00
❑ V6-8560 [S]	The Count Basie Band and the Dizzy Gillespie Band at Newport	1963	25.00

BASIE, COUNT, AND THE MILLS BROTHERS

Number	Title (A Side/B Side)	Yr	NM
Albums			
DOT			
❑ DLP-25838	The Board of Directors	1968	15.00

BASIE, COUNT, AND OSCAR PETERSON

Number	Title (A Side/B Side)	Yr	NM
Albums			
PABLO			
❑ 2310722	"Satch" and "Josh"	1975	12.00
❑ 2310802	Satch and Josh Again	1978	10.00
❑ 2310843	Night Rider	1979	10.00
❑ 2310896	The Timekeepers	198?	12.00
❑ 2310923	Yessir, That's My Baby	1987	10.00

BASIE, COUNT, AND JOE WILLIAMS

Number	Title (A Side/B Side)	Yr	NM
45s			
CLEF			
❑ 89152	Alright, Okay, You Win/When the Sun Goes Down	1955	15.00
❑ 89162	April in Paris/Roll 'Em Pete	1956	15.00
Albums			
CLEF			
❑ MGC-678 [M]	Count Basie Swings/Joe Williams Sings	1955	50.00
ROULETTE			
❑ R 52021 [M]	Memories Ad Lib	1959	30.00
❑ SR 52021 [S]	Memories Ad Lib	1959	40.00
❑ R 52033 [M]	Everyday I Have the Blues	1959	30.00
❑ SR 52033 [S]	Everyday I Have the Blues	1959	40.00
❑ R 52054 [M]	Just the Blues	1960	30.00
❑ SR 52054 [S]	Just the Blues	1960	40.00
❑ R 52093 [M]	Back to Basie and Blues	1963	25.00
❑ SR 52093 [S]	Back to Basie and Blues	1963	30.00
VANGUARD			
❑ VRS-8508 [M]	A Night at Count Basie's	1955	50.00

Number	Title (A Side/B Side)	Yr	NM
VERVE			
❑ MGV-2016 [M]	The Greatest! Count Basie Swings/Joe Williams Sings Standards	1956	50.00
❑ UMV-2650	The Greatest	1981	10.00
❑ MGVS-6006 [S]	The Greatest! Count Basie Swings/Joe Williams Sings Standards	1960	40.00
❑ MGV-8063 [M]	Count Basie Swings/Joe Williams Sings	1957	40.00
—Reissue of Clef 678			
❑ V-8488 [M]	Count Basie Swings/Joe Williams Sings	1962	25.00
—Reissue of 8063			
❑ V6-8488 [R]	Count Basie Swings/Joe Williams Sings	1962	12.00

BASIE, COUNT; JOE WILLIAMS; LAMBERT, HENDRICKS AND ROSS

Albums

Number	Title (A Side/B Side)	Yr	NM
ROULETTE			
❑ R 52018 [M]	Sing Along with Basie	1959	20.00
❑ SR 52018 [S]	Sing Along with Basie	1959	25.00

BASIL, TONI

12-Inch Singles

Number	Title (A Side/B Side)	Yr	NM
CHRYSALIS			
❑ AS 1615 [DJ]	Nobody/Rock On	1983	10.00
❑ 4V9-42708	Street Beat (Special Club Mix)/(Beat Dub)	1983	8.00
❑ 4V9-42824	Suspense/(Dub)	1984	8.00
RAZOR & TIE			
❑ 80750	Mickey (4 versions)	1999	10.00

45s

Number	Title (A Side/B Side)	Yr	NM
A&M			
❑ 791	Breakaway/I'm 28	1966	200.00
CHRYSALIS			
❑ 2638	Mickey/Thief on the Loose	1982	3.00
❑ 2638 [PS]	Mickey/Thief on the Loose	1982	3.00
❑ 2665	Mickey (Spanish)/Thief on the Loose	1982	5.00
❑ 2665 [PS]	Mickey (Spanish)/Thief on the Loose	1982	5.00
❑ VS4-03537	Shoppin' from A to Z/Time After Time	1983	3.00
❑ VS4-03537 [PS]	Shoppin' from A to Z/Time After Time	1983	3.00
❑ VS4-03539	Mickey/Thief on the Loose	1983	4.00
—Reissue of 2638, but harder to find			
❑ VS4 42711	Street Beat/(B-side unknown)	1983	3.00
❑ VS4 42753	Over My Head/Best Performance	1983	3.00
❑ VS4 42753 [PS]	Over My Head/Best Performance	1983	3.00
RAZOR & TIE			
❑ 93018-07507	Mickey (Radio Remix)/Mickey ("Killa Klub" Edit)	1999	4.00

Albums

Number	Title (A Side/B Side)	Yr	NM
CHRYSALIS			
❑ CHR 1410	Word of Mouth	1982	12.00
❑ FV 41410	Word of Mouth	1983	10.00
—Reissue of 1410			
❑ PV 41410	Word of Mouth	1986	8.00
—Reissue with new prefix			
❑ FV 41449	Toni Basil	1983	10.00
❑ PV 41449	Toni Basil	1986	8.00
—Reissue with new prefix			

BASILE, VINNIE

45s

Number	Title (A Side/B Side)	Yr	NM
DAVY JONES			
❑ 661	Gypsy Girl/Girl	1968	25.00

BASKERVILLE HOUNDS, THE

45s

Number	Title (A Side/B Side)	Yr	NM
AVCO EMBASSY			
❑ 4504	Hold Me/Here I Come, Miami	1968	10.00
BUDDAH			
❑ 17	Caroline/Last Night on the Back Porch	1967	10.00
DOT			
❑ 17004	Space Rock, Part 1/Space Rock, Part 2	1967	10.00
❑ 17017	Debbie/Jackie's Theme	1967	10.00
❑ 17037	Baby, Am I Losing/Never on Sunday	1967	10.00
TEMA			
❑ 125	Debbie/Jackie's Theme	1966	15.00
❑ 128	Space Rock, Part 1/Space Rock, Part 2	1966	15.00
❑ 131	Christmas Is Here (But Not For Long)/Make Me Your Man	1966	15.00
❑ 131 [PS]	Christmas Is Here (But Not For Long)/Make Me Your Man	1966	50.00
❑ 132	All You Had to Do Was Ask/Who Does She Love	1967	15.00
❑ 135	Hold Me/Here I Come, Miami	1967	15.00

Albums

Number	Title (A Side/B Side)	Yr	NM
DOT			
❑ DLP-3823 [M]	The Baskerville Hounds (Featuring Space Rock, Part 2)	1967	100.00
❑ DLP-25823 [S]	The Baskerville Hounds (Featuring Space Rock, Part 2)	1967	100.00

BASS, FONTELLA

45s

Number	Title (A Side/B Side)	Yr	NM
BOBBIN			
❑ 134	I Don't Hurt Anymore/Brand New Love	1962	15.00
❑ 140	Honey Bee/Bad Boy	1963	15.00
CHECKER			
❑ 1097	Don't Mess Up a Good Thing/Baby, What You Want Me to Do	1965	10.00
—With Bobby McClure			
❑ 1111	You'll Miss Me (When I'm Gone)/Don't Jump	1965	10.00
—With Bobby McClure			
❑ 1120	Rescue Me/Soul of the Man	1965	15.00
—Light blue label with red and black checkers			
❑ 1120	Rescue Me/Soul of the Man	1965	20.00
—Red label with "Checker" vertically on left			
❑ 1120	Rescue Me/Soul of the Man	1966	10.00
—Fading light blue label, no checkers			
❑ 1131	Recovery/Leave It in the Hands of Love	1965	10.00
❑ 1137	I Surrender/I Can't Rest	1966	10.00
❑ 1147	Safe and Sound/You'll Never Ever Know	1966	10.00
❑ 1183	Lucky in Love/Sweet Lovin' Daddy	1967	10.00
EPIC			
❑ 50341	Soon as I Touched Him/You Can Betcha in Love	1977	4.00
PAULA			
❑ 360	Who You Gonna Blame/Hold On This Time	1972	5.00
❑ 367	I Need to Be Loved/I Want Everyone to Know	1972	5.00
❑ 376	It Sure Is Good/I'm Leaving the Choice to You	1973	5.00
❑ 389	Home Wrecker/Now That I've Found a Good Thing	1973	5.00
❑ 393	Talking About Freedom/It's Hard to Get Back In	1974	5.00

Albums

Number	Title (A Side/B Side)	Yr	NM
CHECKER			
❑ LP-2997 [M]	The "New" Look	1966	60.00
—Blue label with red and black checkers			
❑ LP-2997 [M]	The "New" Look	1967	30.00
—Blue and white label			
❑ LPS-2997 [S]	The "New" Look	1966	80.00
—Blue label with red and black checkers			
❑ LPS-2997 [S]	The "New" Look	1967	40.00
—Blue and white label			
PAULA			
❑ LPS-2203	Free	1971	12.00

BASS, FONTELLA, AND TINA TURNER

Also see each artist's individual listings.

45s

Number	Title (A Side/B Side)	Yr	NM
VESUVIUS			
❑ 1002	This Would Make Me Happy/Poor Little Fool	1963	25.00

BASS, MARTHA AND FONTELLA

Albums

Number	Title (A Side/B Side)	Yr	NM
SOUL NOTE			
❑ SN-1006	From the Root to the Source	197?	12.00

BASSEY, SHIRLEY

45s

Number	Title (A Side/B Side)	Yr	NM
COLUMBIA			
❑ 40848	Tonight My Heart Is Crying/If I Had a Needle and Thread	1957	15.00
EPIC			
❑ 9303	As I Love You/Kiss Me Honey, Honey Kiss Me	1959	12.00
MERCURY			
❑ 874412-7	No Tengo Nada (I Who Have Nothing)/Sin Ti (Without You)	1989	3.00
MGM			
❑ 12919	'S Wonderful/The Party's Over	1960	12.00
UNITED ARTISTS			
❑ 0146	Diamonds Are Forever/This Is My Love	1973	4.00
—Silver Spotlight Series issue			
❑ XW211	Never, Never, Never/Day by Day	1973	4.00
❑ XW318	This Is My Life/Make the World a Little Younger	1973	4.00
❑ 363	Reach for the Stars/You'll Never Know	1961	10.00
❑ XW387	Davy/The Trouble with Hello	1974	4.00
❑ 404	I'll Get By/Climb Ev'ry Mountain	1962	10.00
❑ 421	Climb Ev'ry Mountain/Where Are You	1962	10.00
❑ 503	What Kind of Fool Am I/What Now My Love	1962	10.00
❑ XW508	Goldfinger/How Can I Tell	1974	4.00
❑ XW509	Never, Never, Never (Grande, Grande, Grande)/Something	1974	4.00
❑ 511	Above All Others/As Long As He Needs Me	1962	10.00
❑ 681	Theme from "The Victors"/How Can You Tell	1964	8.00
❑ 699	I Who Have Nothing/Imagination	1964	8.00
❑ XW717	Send In the Clowns/Living	1975	4.00
❑ 790	Goldfinger/Strange How Love Can Be	1964	10.00
❑ XW854	Everything That Touches You/If I Never Sing Another Song	1976	4.00
❑ 872	No Regrets/See-Saw Dreams	1965	8.00
❑ XW923	What I Did for Love/Feeling	1976	4.00
❑ 956	It's Yourself/Secrets	1965	8.00
❑ X1303	Copacabana/This Is My Life (La Vita)	1979	4.00
❑ X1308	Moonraker-Main Title/Moonraker-End Title	1979	4.00
❑ 50031	Don't Take the Lovers from the World/Take Away	1966	6.00
❑ 50071	Give Me Your Love/Who Could Love Me	1966	6.00
❑ 50099	The Liquidator/Sunshine	1966	6.00
❑ 50105	I (Who Have Nothing)/Shirley	1966	6.00
❑ 50125	The Impossible Dream/They	1967	—
—Unreleased			
❑ 50129	The Impossible Dream/Do I Look Like a Fool	1967	6.00
❑ 50229	Big Spender/Dangerous Games	1967	6.00
❑ 50312	Funny Girl/This Is My Life (La Vita)	1968	—
—Unreleased			
❑ 50459	Funny Girl/This Is My Life (La Vita)	1968	5.00
❑ 50502	Medley: Goin' Out of My Head-You Go to My Head/I Must Know	1969	5.00
❑ 50544	Does Anybody Miss Me/We	1969	5.00
❑ 50606	Fa Fa Fa (Live for Today)/A Bus That Never Comes	1969	5.00
❑ 50682	Sea and Sand/What About Today	1970	4.00
❑ 50698	Something/What Are You Doing the Rest of Your Life	1970	4.00
❑ 50770	Breakfast in Bed/Pieces of Dreams	1971	4.00
❑ 50833	For All We Know/What's Done Is Done	1971	4.00
❑ 50845	Diamonds Are Forever/For the Love of Him	1971	4.00
❑ 50961	And I Love You So/Jezebel	1972	4.00

Albums

Number	Title (A Side/B Side)	Yr	NM
APPLAUSE			
❑ APLP 1005	Shirley Bassey	1982	10.00
EPIC			
❑ LN 3834 [M]	The Bewitching Shirley Bassey	1962	20.00
LIBERTY			
❑ LWB-111 [(2)]	Live at Carnegie Hall	198?	10.00
❑ LWB-715 [(2)]	Greatest Hits	198?	10.00
❑ LW-847	Yesterdays	198?	8.00
❑ LM-1013	Something Else	198?	8.00
❑ LN-10012	The Magic Is You	1980	8.00
❑ LN-10104	The Best of Shirley Bassey	1980	8.00
❑ LN-10180	I, Capricorn	198?	8.00
❑ LN-10252	Greatest Hits	198?	8.00
❑ LN-10262	Shirley Means Bassey	198?	8.00
MERCURY			
❑ 838033-1	La Mujer	1989	12.00
MGM			
❑ E-3862 [M]	The Fabulous Shirley Bassey	1960	20.00
❑ SE-3862 [S]	The Fabulous Shirley Bassey	1960	25.00
❑ E-4301 [M]	Golden Sound	1965	12.00
❑ SE-4301 [S]	Golden Sound	1965	15.00
PAIR			
❑ PDL2-1057 [(2)]	Sassy Bassey	1986	12.00

Except when noted otherwise, VG = 25% of NM, and VG+ = 50% of NM. (Example: VG = $2.00, VG+ = $4.00 and NM = $8.00.)

PHILIPS

Number	Title (A Side/B Side)	Yr	NM
❑ PHM 200168 [M]	Spectacular Shirley Bassey	1965	12.00
❑ PHS 600168 [S]	Spectacular Shirley Bassey	1965	15.00

PICKWICK

Number	Title (A Side/B Side)	Yr	NM
❑ SPC-3303	How About You	197?	10.00

SPRINGBOARD

Number	Title (A Side/B Side)	Yr	NM
❑ SPB-4045	This Is My Life	197?	8.00

UNITED ARTISTS

Number	Title (A Side/B Side)	Yr	NM
❑ UA-LA055-F	Never, Never, Never	1973	10.00
❑ UA-LA111-H2 [(2)]	Live at Carnegie Hall	1973	15.00
❑ UA-LA214-G	Nobody Does It Like Me	1974	10.00
❑ UA-LA542-G	Good, Bad But Beautiful	1975	10.00
❑ UA-LA605-G	Love, Life and Feelings	1976	10.00
❑ UA-LA715-H2 [(2)]	Greatest Hits	1976	15.00
❑ UA-LA751-H	You Take My Heart Away	1977	10.00
❑ UA-LA847-H	Yesterdays	1977	10.00
❑ UA-LA926-H	The Magic Is You	1978	10.00
❑ LM-1013	Something Else	1979	10.00
❑ UAL 3169 [M]	Shirley Bassey	1962	15.00
❑ UAL 3237 [M]	Shirley Bassey Sings the Hits from "Oliver"	1962	15.00
❑ UAL 3419 [M]	Shirley Bassey Belts the Best	1965	12.00
❑ UAL 3463 [M]	In Person	1965	12.00
❑ UAL 3545 [M]	Shirley Means Bassey	1966	12.00
❑ UAL 3565 [M]	And We Were Lovers	1967	12.00
❑ UAS 5565	I, Capricorn	1971	10.00
❑ UAS 5643	And I Love You So	1972	10.00
❑ UAS 6169 [S]	Shirley Bassey	1962	20.00
❑ UAS 6237 [S]	Shirley Bassey Sings the Hits from "Oliver"	1962	20.00
❑ UAS 6419 [S]	Shirley Bassey Belts the Best	1965	15.00
❑ UAS 6463 [S]	In Person	1965	15.00
❑ UAS 6545 [S]	Shirley Means Bassey	1966	15.00
❑ UAS 6565 [S]	And We Were Lovers	1967	15.00
❑ UAS 6675	This Is My Life	1969	12.00
❑ UAS 6713	Does Anybody Miss Me?	1969	12.00
❑ UAS 6765	Shirley Bassey Is Really "Something"	1970	10.00
❑ UAS 6797	Something Else	1971	10.00

BASTILLES, THE

45s

PHILIPS

Number	Title (A Side/B Side)	Yr	NM
❑ 40453	Tenderly/Vengeance	1967	20.00

BATCHELOR, RUTH

45s

PARKWAY

Number	Title (A Side/B Side)	Yr	NM
❑ 852	Mr. Principal/Lemon Drops Lolly Pops	1962	15.00

BATDORF & RODNEY

45s

ARISTA

Number	Title (A Side/B Side)	Yr	NM
❑ 0132	You Are a Song/Another Part of Me	1975	4.00
❑ 0159	Somewhere in the Night/Ain't It Like Home	1975	4.00

ASYLUM

Number	Title (A Side/B Side)	Yr	NM
❑ 11011	All I Need/Between the Ages	1972	5.00
❑ 11012	Home Again/Between the Ages	1972	5.00

ATLANTIC

Number	Title (A Side/B Side)	Yr	NM
❑ 2850	Oh My Surprise/Farm	1972	5.00
❑ 2863	Can You See Him/Never See His Face Again	1972	5.00

BATISTE, ROSE

45s

GOLDEN WORLD

Number	Title (A Side/B Side)	Yr	NM
❑ 33	Sweetheart Darling/That's What He Told Me	1966	30.00

REVILOT

Number	Title (A Side/B Side)	Yr	NM
❑ 204	I Miss My Baby/Hit and Run	1967	200.00
❑ 206	I Still Wait for You/Come Back in a Hurry	1967	150.00

RIC-TIC

Number	Title (A Side/B Side)	Yr	NM
❑ 105	Holding Hands/That's What He Told Me	1965	300.00

BATORS, STIV

12-Inch Singles

BOMP!

Number	Title (A Side/B Side)	Yr	NM
❑ BMP 12-136	Story in Your Eyes/Have Love, Will Travel	1987	12.00
❑ BEP-1202	Too Much to Dream/Make Up Your Mind	1980	20.00

45s

BOMP!

Number	Title (A Side/B Side)	Yr	NM
❑ 124	It's Cold Outside/The Last Year	1979	10.00
❑ 124 [PS]	It's Cold Outside/The Last Year	1979	15.00
❑ 128	Not That Way Anymore/Circumstantial Evidence	1979	8.00
❑ 128 [PS]	Not That Way Anymore/Circumstantial Evidence	1979	8.00
❑ X-128 [DJ]	Not That Way Anymore/Circumstantial Evidence	1979	15.00

Albums

BOMP!

Number	Title (A Side/B Side)	Yr	NM
❑ 4015	Disconnected	1980	20.00
❑ 4043 [10]	Disconnected	1993	15.00

—Reissue of 4015 on 10-inch vinyl

Number	Title (A Side/B Side)	Yr	NM
❑ 4046 [10]	L.A. L.A.	1993	15.00

BATS, THE (1)

45s

HBR

Number	Title (A Side/B Side)	Yr	NM
❑ 445	Big Bright Eyes/Nothing at All	1965	10.00

PARROT

Number	Title (A Side/B Side)	Yr	NM
❑ 40013	Listen to My Heart/You Look Good Together	1967	10.00

BATS, THE (U)

45s

FLAME

Number	Title (A Side/B Side)	Yr	NM
❑ 5155	Batmobile/Batusi	1966	40.00

BATTERED ORNAMENTS

Albums

HARVEST

Number	Title (A Side/B Side)	Yr	NM
❑ SKAO-422	Mantle-Piece	1970	75.00

BATTIN, SKIP

Mamber of later versions of THE BYRDS.

45s

AURORA

Number	Title (A Side/B Side)	Yr	NM
❑ 159	The Dating Game Theme/Night Time Girl	1966	15.00

GROOVE

Number	Title (A Side/B Side)	Yr	NM
❑ 58-0055	Searchin'/She Acts Like We Never Have Met	1965	40.00
❑ 58-0065	Ten Feet Tall/What's Mine Is Mine	1965	40.00

SIGNPOST

Number	Title (A Side/B Side)	Yr	NM
❑ 70010 [DJ]	Ballad of Dick Clark (mono/stereo)	1973	6.00

—May be promo only

Albums

SIGNPOST

Number	Title (A Side/B Side)	Yr	NM
❑ SP 8408	Skip Battin	1972	12.00

BAUM, ALLEN

45s

RED ROBIN

Number	Title (A Side/B Side)	Yr	NM
❑ 124	My Kinda Woman/Too Much Competition	1954	400.00

BAXTER

45s

PARAMOUNT

Number	Title (A Side/B Side)	Yr	NM
❑ 0194	Give It All/197 Three	1973	8.00

Albums

PARAMOUNT

Number	Title (A Side/B Side)	Yr	NM
❑ PAS-6050	Baxter	1973	20.00

BAXTER, DUKE

45s

MERCURY

Number	Title (A Side/B Side)	Yr	NM
❑ 73107	Absolute Zero/Wings of Love	1970	15.00

VMC

Number	Title (A Side/B Side)	Yr	NM
❑ 740	Everybody Knows Matilda/I Ain't No Schoo Boy	1969	8.00
❑ 749	Superstition Bend/Crosstown Woman She Set Me Free	1969	10.00
❑ 750	Don't Hurt Me/(B-side unknown)	1969	15.00

Albums

VMC

Number	Title (A Side/B Side)	Yr	NM
❑ VS-138	Everybody Knows Matilda	1969	20.00

BAXTER, LES

45s

A/S

Number	Title (A Side/B Side)	Yr	NM
❑ 4511	La La La/Girl on the Boulevard	1970	5.00
❑ 4515	Soolaimon/A Taste of Soul	1970	5.00

AMERICAN INT'L.

Number	Title (A Side/B Side)	Yr	NM
❑ 143	Dunwich/Necronomicon	1970	5.00
❑ 145	Dock at Papeete/Bora Bora	1970	5.00

CAPITOL

Number	Title (A Side/B Side)	Yr	NM
❑ F1299	Somewhere, Somehow, Someday/Tamberina	1950	15.00
❑ F1381	The Roving Kind/So Long	1951	15.00
❑ F1390	Zing Zing Zoom Zoom/When You Return	1951	15.00
❑ F1493	Because of You/Unless	1951	15.00
❑ F1546	Roller Coaster/On Top of the Ferris Wheel	1951	15.00
❑ F1584	Vanity/The World Is Mine	1951	15.00
❑ F1596	How Many Times/Bacoa	1951	15.00
❑ F1681	Because of You/Blue Tango	195?	12.00
❑ F1731	Longing for You/Sarah Kelly from Plumb Nelly	1951	15.00
❑ F1760	Somewhere, Somehow, Someday/Because of You	1951	12.00
❑ F1773	You'll Know/Stay Awhile	1951	12.00
❑ F1785	Be Mine Tonight/California Moon	1951	15.00
❑ F1818	When/If You've Forgotten Me	1951	15.00
❑ F1839	I Remember You Love/I Only Have One Life to Live	1951	15.00
❑ F1873	Jalousie/Shrimp Boats	1951	15.00
❑ F1887	Somebody's Been Beatin' My Time/I Can't Help It	1951	15.00
❑ F1966	Blue Tango/Please Mr. Sun	1952	12.00
❑ F2005	Festival/Invitation	1952	12.00
❑ F2018	Wondering/God's Little Candles	1952	12.00
❑ F2053	Green Grow the Lilacs/A Day Away from You	1952	12.00
❑ F2102	I'm Yours/Kiss of Fire	1952	12.00
❑ F2106	Lonely Wine/Lost in Meditation	1952	12.00
❑ F2117	Tears/Please Say You Love Me	1952	12.00
❑ F2143	Auf Wiedersehn Sweetheart/Padam Padam	1952	12.00
❑ F2205	Till the End of the World/The Two-Faced Clock	1952	12.00
❑ F2225	Quiet Village/Indian Summer	1952	12.00
❑ F2274	Yours/Flute Salad	1952	12.00
❑ F2275	Santa Claus' Party/Hang Your Wishes on the Tree	1952	12.00
❑ F2328	Vieni, Vieni/As Long As You Care	1953	12.00
❑ F2374	Aprin in Portugal/Suddenly	1953	12.00
❑ F2375	The Lord Is My Shepherd/My Name Is God	1953	12.00
❑ F2405	No More Goodbyes/Dance of the Flutes	1953	12.00
❑ F2457	A Little Love/Ruby	1953	12.00
❑ F2479	I Love Paris/Gigi	1953	12.00
❑ F2568	Tropicana/Julie	1953	12.00
❑ F2579	Cornflakes/Elaine	1953	12.00
❑ F2632	Love Theme from The Robe/Manhattan	1953	12.00
❑ F2705	Atlantis/The Flirtation Waltz	1954	12.00
❑ F2748	If You Were Mine/Douchka	1954	12.00
❑ F2799	Venezuela/Sea Song	1954	12.00
❑ F2845	The High and the Mighty/More Love Than Your Love	1954	12.00
❑ F2918	Romantic Rio/When You're in Love	1954	12.00
❑ F2950	Midnight on the Cliffs/Dream Rhapsody	1954	12.00

—With Leonard Pennario

Number	Title (A Side/B Side)	Yr	NM
❑ F3002	Earth Angel (Will You Be Mine)/Happy Baby	1954	12.00
❑ F3040	I Ain't Mad at You/Blue Mirage	1955	12.00
❑ F3055	Unchained Melody/Medic	1955	12.00
❑ F3120	Walke the Town and Tell the People/I'll Never Stop Loving You	1955	12.00
❑ F3195	Toy Tiger/Shrike	1955	12.00
❑ F3259	Song of the Bayou/Monika	1955	12.00
❑ F3291	The Trouble with Harry/Havana	1955	12.00
❑ F3336	The Poor People of Paris/Theme from "Helen of Troy"	1956	15.00
❑ F3404	Tango of the Drums/Sinner Man	1956	10.00
❑ F3478	Foreign Interlude/Melodia Loca	1956	10.00
❑ F3526	Giant/There's Never Been Anyone Else But You	1956	10.00
❑ F3573	The Left Arm of Buddah/What Happens in Buenos Aires	1956	10.00
❑ F3599	Dream Rhapsody/Midnight on the Cliffs	1956	10.00
❑ F3606	Stealin'/I'd Love to Fall Asleep	1956	10.00

—With Line Renaud

Number	Title (A Side/B Side)	Yr	NM
❑ F3624	Clown on the Eiffel Tower/Woman's Devotion	1957	10.00
❑ F3653	Rain on My Window/I Dance When I Walk	1957	10.00
❑ F3704	Blue Echo/Designing Woman	1957	10.00
❑ F3728	The Lonely Whistler/Ruby Lips	1957	10.00
❑ F3768	La Panse/Manhattan	1957	10.00
❑ F3798	Search for Paradise/Ricordate Marcellino	1957	10.00
❑ F3841	Invisible Boy/I Never Had a Dream Like This Before	1957	10.00
❑ F3887	A Farewell to Arms/The Dance from Bonjour Tristesse	1958	10.00
❑ F4011	Love Song from Houseboat/Lily of Laguna	1958	10.00
❑ F4032	Dance, Everyone, Dance/A Chance Is All I Ask	1958	10.00

B

Number	Title (A Side/B Side)	Yr	NM
❑ F4091	Come Prima/ My Heart's in Portugal	1958	10.00
❑ F4206	Tell Me, Margarita/ Piccolissima Serenata	1959	10.00
❑ F4249	Sabre Dance/Milord	1959	10.00
❑ 4322	Prelude & Ben-Hur Theme/ Till Tomorrow	1959	10.00
❑ 4374	Boomada/Cochi Baba	1960	10.00
❑ 4489	Pepe/Dolce Par Niente	1960	10.00
❑ 4523	Angelina/Follow Me	1961	10.00

GNP CRESCENDO

Number	Title (A Side/B Side)	Yr	NM
❑ 313	Linin' Track/Baion	1964	8.00
❑ 382	And We Were Lovers/ Balan Samba	1967	8.00
❑ 399	Live for Life/Free Again	1967	8.00
❑ 425	Flame Tree/Girl from Uganda	1969	6.00

RCA VICTOR

Number	Title (A Side/B Side)	Yr	NM
❑ 47-3305	Toujours Moi/Fame	1949	20.00
❑ 47-3306	Jet/Tzezane	1949	20.00
❑ 47-3307	L'Ardente Nuit/Possession	1949	20.00

—RCA sides by "Leslie Baxter and His Orchestra"

REPRISE

Number	Title (A Side/B Side)	Yr	NM
❑ 0243	How Shall I Send Thee/ Have Yourself a Merry Little Christmas	1963	20.00
—B-side by Frank Sinatra			
❑ 20120	Theme from "The Manchurian Candidate"/The Manchurian Beat	1962	10.00
❑ 20120 [PS]	Theme from "The Manchurian Candidate"/The Manchurian Beat	1962	50.00
❑ 20159	Theme from "How the West Was Won"/Theme from "Lawrence of Arabia"	1963	10.00
❑ 20165	Sail Away Ladies/Due Bonita Bandera	1963	10.00

7-Inch Extended Plays

CAPITOL

Number	Title (A Side/B Side)	Yr	NM
❑ EAP 1-447	April in Portugal/Blue Tango// Ruby/Quiet Village	195?	15.00
❑ EAP 1-447 [PS]	Blue Tango	195?	15.00
❑ EAP 1-474	Little White Lies/Miss You// Nevertheless/Mine	195?	12.00
❑ EAP 1-474 [PS]	Thinking of You, Part 1	195?	12.00
❑ EAP 2-474	Thinking of You/Speak Low// With My Eyes Wide Open I'm Dreaming/The Nearness of You	195?	12.00
❑ EAP 2-474 [PS]	Thinking of You, Part 2	195?	12.00
❑ EBF-474 [PS]	Thinking of You	195?	12.00
—Gatefold sleeve with some versions of 1-474 and 2-474			
❑ EAP 1-494	(contents unknown)	195?	15.00
❑ EAP 1-494 [PS]	Invitation	195?	15.00
❑ EAP 1-599	Blue Mirage (Don't Go)/Lonely Wine//Unchained Melody/ If You've Forgotten Me	195?	12.00
❑ EAP 1-599 [PS]	Blue Mirage	195?	12.00
❑ EAP 1-672	*Wake the Town and Tell the People/The Shrike/Toy Tiger/ I'll Never Stop Loving You	1955	12.00
❑ EAP 1-672 [PS]	Wake the Town and Tell the People	1955	12.00
❑ EAP 1-730	The Poor People of Paris/ Theme from "Helen of Troy"// The Trouble with Harry/ If You Can Dream	1956	12.00
❑ EAP 1-730 [PS]	The Poor People of Paris	1956	12.00

Albums

CAPITOL

Number	Title (A Side/B Side)	Yr	NM
❑ H (# unknown) [10]	Music for Peace of Mind	1953	80.00
❑ DT 288 [R]	Ritual of the Savage (Le Sacre Du Sauvage)	196?	12.00
❑ H 288 [10]	Le Sacre Du Sauvage	1952	80.00
❑ T 288 [M]	Le Sacre Du Sauvage	1954	40.00
❑ T 390 [M]	Music Out of the Moon/ Music for Peace of Mind	1954	40.00
❑ H 474 [10]	Thinking of You	1954	50.00
❑ T 474 [M]	Thinking of You	1954	40.00
❑ LAL 486 [M]	The Passions	1954	40.00
❑ T 594 [M]	Kaleidoscope	1955	40.00
❑ T 655 [M]	Tamboo!	1955	40.00
❑ T 733 [M]	Caribbean Moonlight	1956	40.00
❑ T 774 [M]	Skins!	1957	40.00
❑ T 780 [M]	'Round the World	1957	40.00
❑ T 843 [M]	Midnight on the Cliffs	1957	40.00
❑ T 868 [M]	Ports of Pleasure	1957	40.00
❑ T 968 [M]	Space Escapade	1958	40.00
❑ T 1012 [M]	Selections from "South Pacific"	1958	40.00
❑ T 1088 [M]	Love Is a Fabulous Thing	1958	40.00
❑ T 1117 [M]	African Jazz	1958	40.00
❑ DT 1388 [R]	Baxter's Best	1960	15.00
❑ SM-1388	Baxter's Best	197?	8.00
❑ T 1388 [M]	Baxter's Best	1960	30.00
❑ ST 1537 [S]	Jewels of the Sea	1961	30.00
❑ T 1537 [M]	Jewels of the Sea	1961	25.00
❑ ST 1661 [S]	The Sensational Les Baxter	1962	30.00
❑ T 1661 [M]	The Sensational Les Baxter	1962	25.00
❑ ST 1846 [S]	The Original Quiet Village	1963	25.00
❑ T 1846 [M]	The Original Quiet Village	1963	20.00
❑ H 2000 [10]	Music Out of the Moon	1953	80.00
❑ T 10015 [M]	La Femme	1956	40.00
❑ M-11702	Ritual of the Savage	1977	10.00
❑ SQBO-90984 [(2)]	The Sounds of Adventure	1967	30.00
—Capitol Record Club exclusive			

GNP CRESCENDO

Number	Title (A Side/B Side)	Yr	NM
❑ GNP-2036 [M]	Brazil Now	1967	15.00
❑ GNPS-2036 [S]	Brazil Now	1967	12.00
❑ GNPS-2042	Love Is Blue	1968	12.00
❑ GNPS-2047	Aftrican Blue	1969	12.00
❑ GNPS-2053	Moon Rock	1969	12.00

PICKWICK

Number	Title (A Side/B Side)	Yr	NM
❑ PC-3011 [M]	The Fabulous Sounds of Les Baxter	196?	15.00
❑ SPC-3011 [S]	The Fabulous Sounds of Les Baxter	196?	15.00
❑ PC-3048 [M]	I Could Have Danced All Night	196?	15.00
❑ SPC-3048 [S]	I Could Have Danced All Night	196?	12.00

REPRISE

Number	Title (A Side/B Side)	Yr	NM
❑ R-6036 [M]	Voices in Rhythm	1961	15.00
❑ R9-6036 [S]	Voices in Rhythm	1961	20.00
❑ R-6048 [M]	The Primitive and the Passionate	1962	15.00
❑ R9-6049 [S]	The Primitive and the Passionate	1962	20.00
❑ R-6079 [M]	Academy Award Winners '63	1963	15.00
❑ R9-6079 [S]	Academy Award Winners '63	1963	20.00
❑ R-6100 [M]	The Soul of the Drums	1963	15.00
❑ R9-6100 [S]	The Soul of the Drums	1963	20.00

BAXTER, RONNIE

45s

ATCO

Number	Title (A Side/B Side)	Yr	NM
❑ 6093	Drivin' Me Out of My Mind/ Afraid of Love	1957	40.00

GONE

Number	Title (A Side/B Side)	Yr	NM
❑ 5036	Someone to Love Me/ Gates of Heaven	1958	30.00
❑ 5041	Gates of Heaven/ Prisoner of Love	1958	30.00
❑ 5050	Is It Because/I Finally Found You	1958	30.00
❑ 5058	Is It Because/I Finally Found You	1959	30.00
❑ 5084	It's Magic/If You Let Me	1960	25.00

MARK-X

Number	Title (A Side/B Side)	Yr	NM
❑ 8001	It's Magic/If You Let Me	1959	12.00

BAY CITY 5 See LUIGI MARTINI AND THE BAY CITY 5.

BAY CITY ROLLERS

45s

ARISTA

Number	Title (A Side/B Side)	Yr	NM
❑ 0120	Bye Bye Baby/It's for You	1975	10.00
❑ 0149	Saturday Night/Marlina	1975	4.00
❑ 0149 [PS]	Saturday Night/Marlina	1975	6.00
❑ 0170	Money Honey/Maryanne	1976	4.00
❑ 0170 [PS]	Money Honey/Maryanne	1976	8.00
❑ 0185	Rock and Roll Love Letter/ Shanghai'd in Love	1976	4.00
❑ 0193	Don't Stop the Music (Long)/ Don't Stop the Music (Short)	1976	6.00
❑ 0205	I Only Want to Be with You/ Write a Letter	1976	4.00
❑ 0216	Yesterday's Hero/My Lisa	1976	4.00
❑ 0233	Dedication/Rock N' Roller	1977	4.00
❑ 0233 [PS]	Dedication/Rock N' Roller	1977	5.00
❑ 0256	You Made Me Believe in Magic/ Dance Dance Dance	1977	4.00
❑ 0272	The Way I Feel Tonight/ Love Power	1977	5.00
❑ 0272	The Way I Feel Tonight/ Sweet Virginia	1977	5.00
❑ 0363	Where Will I Be Now/ If You Were My Woman	1978	4.00
❑ 0476	Turn On the Radio/ Hello and Welcome Home	1979	4.00
—As "The Rollers"			

BELL

Number	Title (A Side/B Side)	Yr	NM
❑ 45169	Keep On Dancing/Alright	1972	10.00
❑ 45274	Manana/I Heard You Singing Your Song	1972	15.00
❑ 45481	Shang-a-Lang/(B-side unknown)	1974	15.00
❑ 45607	Summerlove Sensation/ (B-side unknown)	1974	15.00
❑ 45618	All of Me Loves All of You/ The Bump	1974	15.00

Albums

ARISTA

Number	Title (A Side/B Side)	Yr	NM
❑ AL 4049	Bay City Rollers	1975	10.00
❑ AL 4071	Rock N' Roll Love Letter	1976	10.00
❑ AL 4093	Dedication	1976	10.00
❑ AB 4158	Greatest Hits	1977	10.00
❑ AB 4194	Strangers in the Wind	1978	10.00
❑ AB 4241	Elevator	1979	10.00
—As "The Rollers"			
❑ AB 7004	It's a Game	1977	10.00

BAY RIDGE, THE

45s

ATLANTIC

Number	Title (A Side/B Side)	Yr	NM
❑ 2431	Back Track/I Can't Get Her Out of My Mind	1967	10.00

BAYOU BOYS, THE

45s

CHECKER

Number	Title (A Side/B Side)	Yr	NM
❑ 765	Dinah/Bambalays	1952	150.00

BAYSIDERS, THE

45s

EVEREST

Number	Title (A Side/B Side)	Yr	NM
❑ 19366	Over the Rainbow/My Bonnie	1960	15.00
❑ 19386	Trees/Look for the Silver Lining	1960	15.00
❑ 19393	The Bells of St. Mary's/ Comin' Thru the Rye	1961	15.00

Albums

EVEREST

Number	Title (A Side/B Side)	Yr	NM
❑ BRST-1124 [S]	Over the Rainbow	1961	300.00
❑ LPBR-5124 [M]	Over the Rainbow	1961	200.00

BAZUKA, TONY CAMILLO'S

45s

A&M

Number	Title (A Side/B Side)	Yr	NM
❑ 1666	Dynomite Part 1/Dynomite Part 2	1975	4.00
❑ 1744	Bazuka Limited/Love Explosion	1975	4.00
❑ 1840	Theme from "Policeman"/ Walkin' Tall	1976	4.00

VENTURE

Number	Title (A Side/B Side)	Yr	NM
❑ 110	(C'est) Le Rock/ Rock the Night Away	1979	4.00

Albums

A&M

Number	Title (A Side/B Side)	Yr	NM
❑ SP-3406	Tomy Camillo's Bazuka	1975	10.00

BE-BOP DELUXE

45s

HARVEST

Number	Title (A Side/B Side)	Yr	NM
❑ 4151	Sister Seagull/Maid in Heaven	1975	4.00
❑ 4244	Crying to the Sky/ Ships in the Night	1976	4.00
❑ 4571	Panic in the World/ Blue As a Jewel	1978	4.00

Albums

CAPITOL

Number	Title (A Side/B Side)	Yr	NM
❑ SPRO-8486 [DJ]	Sunburst Finish	1975	25.00
—Specially banded version for radio			
❑ SN-16022	Sunburst Finish	1980	8.00
—Reissue of Harvest 11478			
❑ SN-16023	Drastic Plastic	1980	8.00
—Reissue of Harvest 11750			
❑ SN-16024	Futurama	1980	8.00
—Reissue of Harvest 11432			
❑ SN-16025	Axe Victim	1980	8.00
—Reissue of Harvest 11689			
❑ SN-16026	Modern Music	1980	8.00
—Reissue of Harvest 11575			

HARVEST

Number	Title (A Side/B Side)	Yr	NM
❑ SPRO-8531 [DJ]	Be-Bop's Biggest	1978	30.00
—Promo-only compilation			
❑ ST-11432	Futurama	1975	10.00
❑ ST-11478	Sunburst Finish	1975	10.00
❑ ST-11575	Modern Music	1976	10.00
❑ SKBB-11666 [(2)]	Live! In the Air Age	1977	12.00
❑ SM-11689	Axe Victim	1977	10.00
—Their first UK album; first US issue has "SM" prefix			
❑ SW-11750	Drastic Plastic	1978	10.00
❑ SKBO-11870 [(2)]	The Best Of & The Rest Of Be-Bop Deluxe	1979	12.00

BEACH, BILL

45s

KING

Number	Title (A Side/B Side)	Yr	NM
❑ 4940	Peg Pants/You're Gonna Like My Baby	1956	150.00

Except when noted otherwise, VG = 25% of NM, and VG+ = 50% of NM. (Example: VG = $2.00, VG+ = $4.00 and NM = $8.00.)

B

BEACH BOYS, THE Also see GLEN CAMPBELL; BRUCE JOHNSTON; BRIAN WILSON; BRIAN WILSON AND MIKE LOVE.

12-Inch Singles

CAPITOL

Number	Title (A Side/B Side)	Yr	NM
❑ SPRO-9711/2 [DJ]	Rock 'n' Roll to the Rescue/ Good Vibrations	1986	10.00
❑ SPRO-9796 [DJ]	California Dreamin' (same on both sides?)	1986	10.00

CARIBOU

Number	Title (A Side/B Side)	Yr	NM
❑ AS 557 [DJ]	Here Comes the Night (Remix) (Instrumental)	1979	15.00
—Blue vinyl			
❑ 2Z8 9028	Here Comes the Night/ (Instrumental)	1979	10.00
—Issued in generic "Disco Single" sleeve			
❑ 2Z8 9028 [DJ]	Here Comes the Night (Long) (Short)	1979	12.00

45s

BROTHER

Number	Title (A Side/B Side)	Yr	NM
❑ 1001	Heroes and Villains/ You're Welcome	1967	12.00
❑ 1001 [PS]	Heroes and Villains/ You're Welcome	1967	100.00
—Not to be confused with Capitol 5826, which is a completely different sleeve			

BROTHER/REPRISE

Number	Title (A Side/B Side)	Yr	NM
❑ 0101	Wouldn't It Be Nice/Sloop John B	1973	5.00
—"Back to Back Hits" series			
❑ 0102	God Only Knows/Caroline, No	1973	5.00
—"Back to Back Hits" series			
❑ 0103	Good Vibrations/ Heroes and Villains	1973	5.00
—"Back to Back Hits" series			
❑ 0104	Darlin'/Wild Honey	1973	5.00
—"Back to Back Hits" series			
❑ 0105	Friends/Be Here in the Morning	1973	5.00
—"Back to Back Hits" series			
❑ 0106	Do It Again/Cottonfields	1973	5.00
—"Back to Back Hits" series			
❑ 0107	I Can Hear Music/Bluebirds Over the Mountain	1973	5.00
—"Back to Back Hits" series			
❑ 0118	Rock and Roll Music/It's O.K.	1977	4.00
—"Back to Back Hits" series			
❑ 0894	Add Some Music to Your Day/ Susie Cincinnati	1970	8.00
❑ 0929	Slip On Through/ This Whole World	1970	10.00
❑ 0957	It's About Time/ Tears in the Morning	1970	20.00
❑ 0998	Cool, Cool Water/Forever	1971	80.00
❑ 1015	Long Promised Road/Deirdre	1971	20.00
❑ 1047	Long Promised Road/'Til I Die	1971	20.00
❑ 1058	Surf's Up/Don't Go Near the Water	1971	50.00
❑ 1091	You Need a Mess of Help to Stand Alone/Cuddle Up	1972	30.00
❑ 1101	Marcella/Hold On Dear Brother	1972	30.00
❑ 1138	Sail On Sailor/Only With You	1972	10.00
❑ 1156	California Saga (On My Way to Sunny Californ-I-A)/ Funky Pretty	1973	10.00
❑ 1310	I Can Hear Music/ Let the Wind Blow	1974	10.00
❑ 1321	Child of Winter (Christmas Song)/Susie Cincinnati	1974	50.00
❑ 1321 [DJ]	Child Of Winter (Christmas Song) (mono/stereo)	1974	25.00
❑ 1325	Sail On Sailor/Only With You	1975	8.00
❑ 1336	Wouldn't It Be Nice/Caroline, No	1975	12.00
❑ 1354	Rock and Roll Music/ The T M Song	1976	4.00
❑ 1368	It's O.K./Had to Phone Ya	1976	4.00
❑ 1375	Everyone's In Love with You/ Susie Cincinnati	1976	4.00
❑ 1389	Honkin' Down the Highway/ Solar System	1977	4.00
❑ 1394	Peggy Sue/Hey Little Tomboy	1978	4.00

CANDIX

Number	Title (A Side/B Side)	Yr	NM
❑ 301	Surfin'/Luau	1961	200.00
—Label says "Distributed by Era Records Sales, Inc."			
❑ 301	Surfin'/Luau	1961	300.00
—No mention of Era Records on label			
❑ 331	Surfin'/Luau	1962	200.00

CAPITOL

Number	Title (A Side/B Side)	Yr	NM
❑ 2028	Wild Honey/Wind Chimes	1967	12.00
❑ 2068	Darlin'/Here Today	1967	12.00
❑ 2068 [PS]	Darlin'/Here Today	1967	20.00
❑ 2160	Friends/Little Bird	1968	12.00
❑ 2239	Do It Again/Wake the World	1968	12.00
❑ 2360	Bluebirds Over the Mountain/ Never Learn Not to Love	1968	12.00
❑ 2432	I Can Hear Music/All I Want to Do	1969	12.00

The Beach Boys, "Help Me Rhonda," Capitol 5395, 1965, **$40.**

Number	Title (A Side/B Side)	Yr	NM
❑ 2530	Break Away/Celebrate the News	1969	12.00
❑ 2765	Cottonfields/The Nearest Faraway Place	1970	20.00
❑ PRO 2936/7	Salt Lake City/Amusemant Parks U.S.A.	1965	200.00
—"Courtesy of Downtown Salt Lake City Stores" promotional item			
❑ 3924	Surfin' U.S.A./ The Warmth of the Sun	1974	5.00
❑ 4093	Little Honda/Hawaii	1975	5.00
❑ 4110	Barbara Ann/Little Honda	1975	5.00
❑ 4334	Be True to Your School/ Graduation Day	1976	5.00
❑ 4777	Surfin' Safari/409	1962	25.00
❑ 4777 [PS]	Surfin' Safari/409	1962	80.00
❑ 4880	Ten Little Indians/County Fair	1962	30.00
❑ 4880 [PS]	Ten Little Indians/County Fair	1962	200.00
❑ 4932	Surfin' U.S.A./Shut Down	1963	25.00
—Version 2: Chuck Berry listed as composer of "Surfin' U.S.A."			
❑ 4932	Surfin' U.S.A./Shut Down	1963	25.00
—Version 1: Brian Wilson listed as composer of "Surfin' U.S.A."			
❑ 5009	Surfer Girl/Little Deuce Coupe	1963	25.00
❑ A-5030	The Beach Boys Medley/ God Only Knows	1981	5.00
❑ 5069	Be True to Your School/ In My Room	1963	25.00
❑ 5096	Little Saint Nick/ The Lord's Prayer	1963	30.00
—Orange and yellow swirl label			
❑ 5096	Little Saint Nick/ The Lord's Prayer	1969	18.00
—Red and orange "target" label			
❑ 5096	Little Saint Nick/ The Lord's Prayer	1972	15.00
—Orange label with "Capitol" at bottom of label			
❑ 5096	Little Saint Nick/ The Lord's Prayer	1978	5.00
—Purple label			
❑ 5096	Little Saint Nick/ The Lord's Prayer	1982	5.00
—Black label with colorband			
❑ 5118	Fun, Fun, Fun/ Why Do Fools Fall in Love	1964	20.00
—A-side songwriter listed as "Brian Wilson-Mike Love"			
❑ 5118	Fun, Fun, Fun/Why Do Fools Fall in Love	1964	25.00
—A-side songwriter listed as "Brian Wilson"			
❑ 5118 [PS]	Fun, Fun, Fun/Why Do Fools Fall in Love	1964	40.00
❑ 5174	I Get Around/Don't Worry Baby	1964	25.00
—Orange and yellow swirl label			
❑ 5174	I Get Around/Don't Worry Baby	1969	12.00
—Red and orange "target" label			
❑ 5174	I Get Around/Don't Worry Baby	1972	8.00
—Orange label with "Capitol" at bottom			
❑ 5174	I Get Around/Don't Worry Baby	1978	5.00
—Purple label			
❑ 5174	I Get Around/Don't Worry Baby	1982	5.00
—Black label with colorband			
❑ 5174 [PS]	I Get Around/Don't Worry Baby	1964	40.00
❑ 5245	When I Grow Up (To Be a Man)/ She Knows Me Too Well	1964	25.00
❑ 5245 [PS]	When I Grow Up (To Be a Man)/ She Knows Me Too Well	1964	40.00
—With blue border			
❑ 5245 [PS]	When I Grow Up (To Be a Man)/ She Knows Me Too Well	1964	50.00
—With green border			
❑ 5306	Dance, Dance, Dance/ The Warmth of the Sun	1964	25.00
❑ 5306 [PS]	Dance, Dance, Dance/ The Warmth of the Sun	1964	120.00
❑ 5312	The Man with All the Toys/ Blue Christmas	1964	30.00
❑ 5372	Do You Wanna Dance/ Please Let Me Wonder	1965	20.00
❑ 5372 [PS]	Do You Wanna Dance/ Please Let Me Wonder	1965	40.00
❑ 5395	Help Me, Rhonda/Kiss Me, Baby	1965	25.00
❑ 5395 [PS]	Help Me, Rhonda/Kiss Me, Baby	1965	40.00
❑ 5464	California Girls/Let Him Run Wild	1965	25.00
—Orange and yellow swirl label			
❑ 5464	California Girls/Let Him Run Wild	1969	10.00
—Red and orange "target" label			
❑ 5464	California Girls/Let Him Run Wild	1973	8.00
—Orange label with "Capitol" at bottom of label			
❑ 5464	California Girls/Let Him Run Wild	1978	5.00
—Purple label			

Except when noted otherwise, VG = 25% of NM, and VG+ = 50% of NM. (Example: VG = $2.00, VG+ = $4.00 and NM = $8.00.)

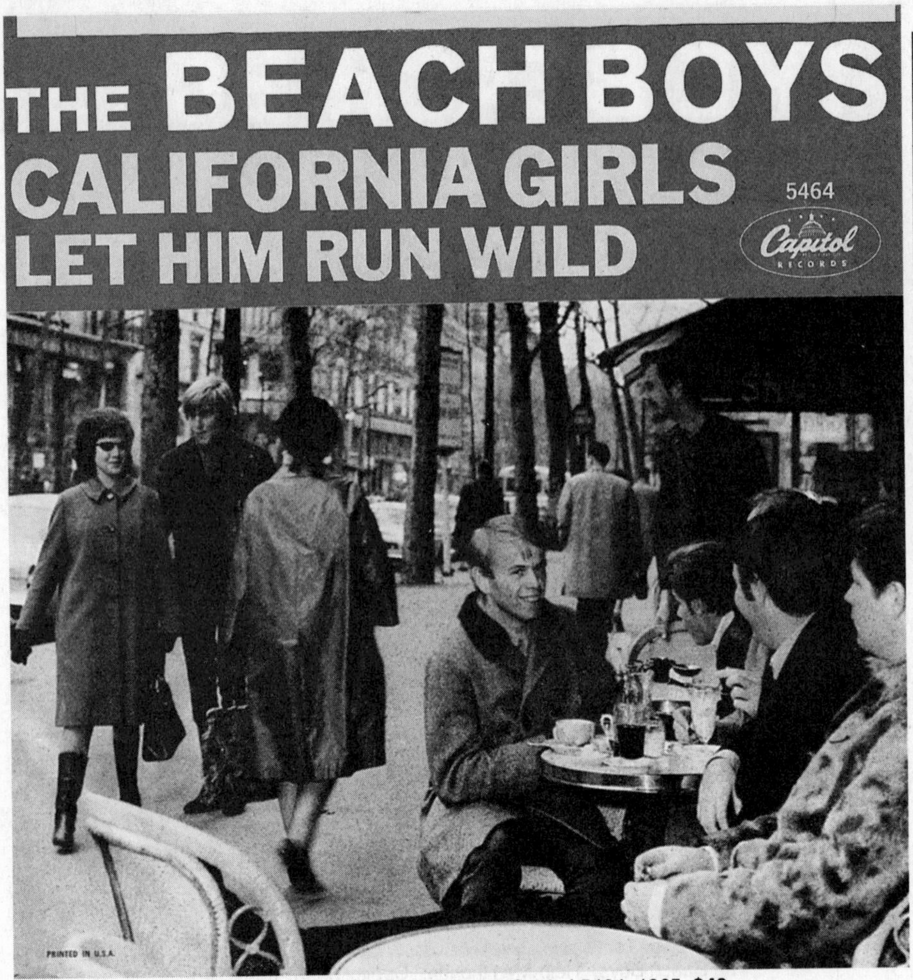

The Beach Boys, "California Girls," Capitol 5464, 1965, **$40.**

Number	Title (A Side/B Side)	Yr	NM
❑ 5464 [PS]	California Girls/Let Him Run Wild	1965	40.00
❑ 5540	The Little Girl I Once Knew/ There's No Other (Like My Baby)	1965	20.00
❑ 5540 [PS]	The Little Girl I Once Knew/ There's No Other (Like My Baby)	1965	40.00
❑ 5561	Barbara Ann/Girl Don't Tell Me	1965	20.00
❑ 5561 [PS]	Barbara Ann/Girl Don't Tell Me	1965	150.00
—Glossy finish			
❑ 5561 [PS]	Barbara Ann/Girl Don't Tell Me	1965	200.00
—Non-glossy finish			
❑ B-5595	Rock and Roll to the Rescue/ Good Vibrations (Live in London)	1986	3.00
❑ B-5595 [PS]	Rock and Roll to the Rescue/ Good Vibrations (Live in London)	1986	4.00
❑ 5602	Sloop John B/ You're So Good to Me	1966	20.00
—Orange and yellow swirl label			
❑ 5602	Sloop John B/ You're So Good to Me	1969	10.00
—Red and orange "target" label			
❑ 5602	Sloop John B/ You're So Good to Me	1973	8.00
—Orange label with "Capitol" at bottom of label			
❑ 5602	Sloop John B/ You're So Good to Me	1978	5.00
—Purple label			
❑ 5602 [PS]	Sloop John B/ You're So Good to Me	1966	30.00
❑ B-5630	California Dreamin'/Lady Liberty	1986	3.00
❑ 5676	Good Vibrations/ Let's Go Away for Awhile	1966	20.00
❑ 5676 [PS]	Good Vibrations/ Let's Go Away for Awhile	1966	30.00
❑ 5706	Wouldn't It Be Nice/ God Only Knows	1966	20.00
—Even though it has a higher number, this single was released before "Good Vibrations."			
❑ 5826 [PS]	Heroes and Villains	1967	400.00
—U.S. picture sleeve for unreleased record. This sleeve, however, was exported and used in other countries.			
❑ S7-17521	409/Punchline	1993	4.00
❑ S7-17522	Be True to Your School/ Things We Did Last Summer	1993	4.00
❑ S7-17523	Do You Wanna Dance/ Ruby Baby	1993	4.00
❑ S7-18205	Merry Christmas, Baby/ Santa's Beard	1994	4.00
—Green vinyl			
❑ S7-19765	The Man with All the Toys/We Three Kings of Orient Are	1997	3.00
❑ B-44297	Don't Worry Baby/ Tequila Dreams	1989	4.00
—A-side: With the Everly Brothers; B-side by Dave Grusin			
❑ B-44297 [PS]	Don't Worry Baby/ Tequila Dreams	1989	10.00
❑ S7-57886	Frosty the Snowman/ Little Saint Nick	1992	5.00
—Originals on black vinyl			
❑ S7-57886	Frosty the Snowman/ Little Saint Nick	1993	4.00
—Second pressing on green vinyl			
❑ 58745	Child of Winter (Christmas Song)/Winter Symphony	1998	4.00
❑ 58746	Christmas Is Here Again/ Auld Lang Syne	1998	4.00
❑ 58747	I'll Be Home for Christmas/Little Saint Nick (Alternate Version)	1998	4.00
❑ 7PRO-79789 [DJ]	Still Cruisin' (same on both sides)	1989	60.00
—Vinyl is promo only			
❑ 7PRO-79841 [DJ]	Somewhere Near Japan (same on both sides)	1989	60.00
—Vinyl is promo only			

CAPITOL CUSTOM

Number	Title (A Side/B Side)	Yr	NM
❑ (no #)	Spirit of America/Boogie Woodie	1963	200.00
❑ (no #) [PS]	Spirit of America/Boogie Woodie	1963	600.00
—Promo for KFWB and opening day of Wallich's Music City South Bay store			

CAPITOL STARLINE

Number	Title (A Side/B Side)	Yr	NM
❑ 6059	Be True to Your School/ In My Room	1965	15.00
—Originals have green swirl labels			
❑ 6060	Ten Little Indians/ She Knows Me Too Well	1965	15.00
—Originals have green swirl labels			
❑ 6081	Help Me, Rhonda/ Do You Wanna Dance?	1966	15.00
—Originals have green swirl labels			
❑ 6094	Surfin' U.S.A./Shut Down	1966	15.00
—Originals have green swirl labels			
❑ 6095	Surfin' Safari/409	1966	15.00
—Originals have green swirl labels			
❑ 6105	Dance, Dance, Dance/ The Warmth of the Sun	1967	12.00
—Originals have red and white "target" labels			
❑ 6106	Fun, Fun, Fun/ Why Do Fools Fall in Love	1967	12.00
—Originals have red and white "target" labels			
❑ 6107	Surfer Girl/Little Deuce Coupe	1967	12.00
—Originals have red and white "target" labels			
❑ 6132	Good Vibrations/Barbara Ann	1968	12.00
—Originals have red and white "target" labels			
❑ 6204	When I Grow Up (To Be a Man)/ She Knows Me Too Well	197?	5.00
—Originals have grayish labels			
❑ 6205	Wendy/Little Honda	197?	5.00
—Originals have grayish labels			
❑ 6259	Barbara Ann/Little Honda	1978	4.00
—Originals have grayish labels			
❑ 6277	Little Saint Nick/ The Lord's Prayer	1981	3.00
—Originals have blue labels			
❑ 6280	I Get Around/Don't Worry Baby	1981	3.00
—Originals have blue labels			
❑ 6289	California Girls/Let Him Run Wild	1981	3.00
—Originals have blue labels			
❑ 6295	Sloop John B/You're So Good to Me	1981	3.00
—Originals have blue labels			

CARIBOU

Number	Title (A Side/B Side)	Yr	NM
❑ 02633	Come Go with Me/ Don't Go Near the Water	1981	3.00
❑ 04913	Getcha Back/Male Ego	1985	3.00
❑ 04913 [PS]	Getcha Back/Male Ego	1985	3.00
❑ 05433	It's Gettin' Late/It's OK	1985	3.00
❑ 05433 [PS]	It's Gettin' Late/It's OK	1985	3.00
❑ 05624	She Believes in Love Again/ It's Just a Matter of Time	1985	3.00
❑ 05624 [PS]	She Believes in Love Again/ It's Just a Matter of Time	1985	3.00
❑ 9026	Here Comes the Night/Baby Blue	1979	4.00
❑ 9029	Good Timin'/Love Surrounds Me	1979	4.00
❑ 9030	Lady Lynda/Full Sail	1979	4.00
❑ 9031	It's a Beautiful Day/Sumahama	1979	4.00
❑ 9032	Goin' On/Endless Harmony	1980	4.00
❑ 9033	Livin' with a Heartache/ Santa Ana Winds	1980	4.00
❑ 9034	School Day (Ring! Ring! Goes the Bell)/When Girls Get Together	1980	—
—Not known to exist			
❑ 9034 [DJ]	School Day (Ring! Ring! Goes the Bell) (same on both sides)	1980	250.00

CRITIQUE

Number	Title (A Side/B Side)	Yr	NM
❑ 99392	Happy Endings/California Girls	1987	3.00
—A-side with Little Richard			
❑ 99392 [PS]	Happy Endings/California Girls	1987	5.00
—Both the Beach Bosy and Little Richard are on the sleeve			

ELEKTRA

Number	Title (A Side/B Side)	Yr	NM
❑ 69385	Kokomo/Tutti-Frutti	1988	3.00
—B-side by Little Richard			

ERA BACK TO BACK HITS

Number	Title (A Side/B Side)	Yr	NM
❑ 042	Surfer Girl/The Freeze	197?	8.00
—A-side is from the Hite Morgan sessions; B-side by Tony & Jo			
❑ 043	Surfin'/Surfin' Safari	197?	8.00
—Both sides from the Hite Morgan sessions			

FBI

Number	Title (A Side/B Side)	Yr	NM
❑ 7701	East Meets West/Rhapsody	1986	20.00
—With Frankie Valli and the Four Seasons			

ODE

Number	Title (A Side/B Side)	Yr	NM
❑ 66016	Wouldn't It Be Nice/The Times They Are a-Changing	1971	30.00
—B-side by Merry Clayton			

SUB POP

Number	Title (A Side/B Side)	Yr	NM
❑ 363	I Just Wasn't Made for These Times/Wouldn't It Be Nice// Here Today	1996	5.00
—Newly released versions from the Pet Sounds box set			
❑ 363 [PS]	I Just Wasn't Made for These Times/Wouldn't It Be Nice// Here Today	1996	5.00
—Not seam sealed (folded piece of cardboard)			

X

Number	Title (A Side/B Side)	Yr	NM
❑ 301	Surfin'/Luau	1961	1000.

Except when noted otherwise, VG = 25% of NM, and VG+ = 50% of NM. (Example: VG = $2.00, VG+ = $4.00 and NM = $8.00.)

Number	Title (A Side/B Side)	Yr	NM

7-Inch Extended Plays

CAPITOL

❑ SXA-1981 Your Summer Dream/Our Car Club/Surfer Girl//Catch a Wave/In My Room/Hawaii 1963 150.00
—Jukebox issue; small hole, plays at 33 1/3 rpm
❑ SXA-1981 [PS] Surfer Girl 1963 150.00
❑ SXA-2027 Keep an Eye on Summer/Fun, Fun, Fun/The Warmth of the Sun//Why Do Fools Fall in Love/In the Parking Lot/Don't Worry Baby 1964 120.00
—Jukebox issue; small hole, plays at 33 1/3 rpm
❑ SXA-2027 [PS] Shut Down, Vol. 2 1964 120.00
❑ DU 2269 Kiss Me, Baby/Don't Hurt My Little Sister/In the Back of My Mind//I'm So Young/Good to My Baby/She Knows Me Too Well 1965 80.00
—Jukebox issue; small hole, plays at 33 1/3 rpm
❑ DU 2269 [PS] The Beach Boys Today! 1965 80.00
❑ DU-2545 Surfin' U.S.A./Surfer Girl/Little Deuce Coupe//Fun, Fun, Fun/In My Room/Little Honda 1966 80.00
—Jukebox issue; small hole, plays at 33 1/3 rpm; red and white target "Starline" label
❑ DU-2545 [PS] Best of the Beach Boys 1966 80.00
❑ R-5267 Wendy/Don't Back Down//Little Honda/Hushabye 1964 60.00
❑ R-5267 [PS] 4-By the Beach Boys 1964 60.00

Albums

ASYLUM

❑ R 113793 Surf's Up 1972 150.00
—RCA Record Club edition, pressed with wrong labels

BROTHER

❑ ST 9001 [R] Smiley Smile 1967 15.00
—"Title for this album by Barry Turnbull" on back cover
❑ ST 9001 [R] Smiley Smile 1967 20.00
—No mention of Barry Turnbull on cover
❑ T 9001 [M] Smiley Smile 1967 30.00
—"Title for this album by Barry Turnbull" on back cover
❑ T 9001 [M] Smiley Smile 1967 40.00
—No mention of Barry Turnbull on cover

BROTHER/REPRISE

❑ 2MS 2083 [(2)] Carl and the Passions "So Tough"/Pet Sounds 1972 30.00
❑ 2MS 2083 [(2)DJ] Carl and the Passions "So Tough"/Pet Sounds 1972 50.00
—White label promo
❑ MS 2118 Holland 1973 15.00
—Includes bonus stock-copy EP, "Mount Vernon and Fairway," in picture sleeve, taped to back cover
❑ MS 2118 [DJ] Holland 1973 40.00
—White label promo; includes bonus white-label promo EP, "Mount Vernon and Fairway," in picture sleeve, taped to back cover
❑ MS 2118 [DJ] Holland 1973 500.00
—Test pressing with "We Got Love," deleted from promos and stock copies
❑ 2MS 2166 [(2)] Wild Honey & 20/20 1974 15.00
❑ 2MS 2167 [(2)] Friends & Smiley Smile 1974 15.00
❑ MS 2197 [M] Pet Sounds 1974 20.00
❑ MS 2223 Good Vibrations — Best of the Beach Boys 1975 12.00
❑ MS 2251 15 Big Ones 1976 12.00
❑ MSK 2258 Love You 1977 12.00
❑ MSK 2268 M.I.U. Album 1978 12.00
❑ MSK 2280 Good Vibrations — Best of the Beach Boys 1978 10.00
❑ RS-6382 Sunflower 1970 25.00
❑ RS-6382 [DJ] Sunflower 1970 50.00
—White label promo
❑ RS 6453 Surf's Up 1971 20.00
❑ RS 6453 [DJ] Surf's Up 1971 40.00
—White label promo
❑ 2RS 6484 [(2)] The Beach Boys In Concert 1973 20.00
❑ 2RS 6484 [(2)DJ] The Beach Boys In Concert 1973 40.00
—White label promo
❑ SKAO-93352 Sunflower 1970 200.00
—Capitol Record Club edition
❑ R 113793 Surf's Up 1972 25.00
—RCA Record Club edition
❑ R 130223 15 Big Ones 1976 15.00
—RCA Record Club edition
❑ R 223569 [(2)] The Beach Boys In Concert 1973 25.00
—RCA Record Club edition

CAPITOL

❑ SKAO-133 20/20 1969 15.00
—"Starline" label
❑ SKAO-133 20/20 1969 20.00
—Black label with colorband
❑ SKAO-8-0133 20/20 1969 30.00
—Capitol Record Club edition; black label
❑ SKAO-8-0133 20/20 1970 40.00
—Capitol Record Club edition; lime label
❑ SWBB-253 [(2)] Close-Up 1969 30.00
—Reissue of "Surfin' U.S.A." and "All Summer Long" in one package; black labels with colorband
❑ SWBB-253 [(2)] Close-Up 1970 40.00
—Lime labels
❑ ST-442 Good Vibrations 1970 20.00
—Lime label (original)
❑ ST-442 Good Vibrations 1972 25.00
—Red or orange label
❑ ST-8-0442 Good Vibrations 1970 30.00
—Capitol Record Club edition
❑ STBB-500 [(2)] All Summer Long/California Girls 1970 20.00
—Lime labels; "Special Double Play" pack; two separate LPs (abridged versions of "All Summer Long" and "Summer Days [And Summer Nights!!]") bound together
❑ STBB-500 [(2)] All Summer Long/California Girls 1971 25.00
—Red labels; "Special Double Play" pack; two separate LPs (abridged versions of "All Summer Long" and "Summer Days [And Summer Nights!!]") bound together
❑ SF-501 All Summer Long 1970 10.00
—Individual record from above set
❑ SF-8-0501 All Summer Long 1971 10.00
—Capitol Record Club edition
❑ SF-502 California Girls 1970 10.00
—Individual record from above set
❑ SF-8-0502 California Girls 1971 10.00
—Capitol Record Club edition
❑ STBB-701 [(2)] Fun, Fun, Fun/Dance, Dance, Dance 1970 20.00
—Lime labels; "Special Double Play" pack; two separate LPs (abridged versions of "Shut Down, Vol. 2" and "The Beach Boys Today!") bound together
❑ STBB-701 [(2)] Fun, Fun, Fun/Dance, Dance, Dance 1971 25.00
—Red labels; "Special Double Play" pack; two separate LPs (abridged versions of "Shut Down, Vol. 2" and "The Beach Boys Today!") bound together
❑ SF-702 Fun, Fun, Fun 1971 10.00
—Individual record from above set
❑ SF-8-0702 Fun, Fun, Fun 1971 10.00
—Capitol Record Club edition
❑ SF-703 Dance, Dance, Dance 1971 10.00
—Individual record from above set
❑ SF-8-0703 Dance, Dance, Dance 1971 10.00
—Capitol Record Club edition
❑ DT 1808 [R] Surfin' Safari 1962 25.00
—With only the "Duophonic" banner at top
❑ DT 1808 [R] Surfin' Safari 1962 80.00
—With "Capitol Full Dimensional Stereo" banner under the "Duophonic" banner
❑ SM-1808 [R] Surfin' Safari 197? 10.00
❑ T 1808 [M] Surfin' Safari 1962 40.00
❑ SM-1890 [S] Surfin' U.S.A. 197? 10.00
❑ ST 1890 [S] Surfin' U.S.A. 1963 50.00
❑ T 1890 [M] Surfin' U.S.A. 1963 40.00
❑ SM-1981 [S] Surfer Girl 197? 10.00
❑ ST 1981 [S] Surfer Girl 1963 50.00
—With reference to "their other new single record, 'Little Deuce Coupe'" in liner notes
❑ ST 1981 [S] Surfer Girl 1963 50.00
—With reference to The Four Freshmen in liner notes
❑ T 1981 [M] Surfer Girl 1963 40.00
—With reference to "their other new single record, 'Little Deuce Coupe'" in liner notes
❑ T 1981 [M] Surfer Girl 1963 40.00
—With reference to The Four Freshmen in liner notes
❑ SM-1998 [S] Little Deuce Coupe 197? 10.00
❑ ST 1998 [S] Little Deuce Coupe 1963 40.00
❑ T 1998 [M] Little Deuce Coupe 1963 40.00
❑ ST 2027 [P] Shut Down, Vol. 2 1964 40.00
❑ T 2027 [M] Shut Down, Vol. 2 1964 40.00
❑ ST 2110 [S] All Summer Long 1964 30.00
—With "Don't Back Down" correctly listed on front cover
❑ ST 2110 [S] All Summer Long 1964 50.00
—With "Don't Break Down" erroneously listed on front cover
❑ T 2110 [M] All Summer Long 1964 30.00
—With "Don't Back Down" correctly listed on front cover
❑ T 2110 [M] All Summer Long 1964 50.00
—With "Don't Break Down" erroneously listed on front cover
❑ SM-2164 The Beach Boys' Christmas Album 197? 10.00
❑ ST 2164 [S] The Beach Boys' Christmas Album 1964 50.00
❑ T 2164 [M] The Beach Boys' Christmas Album 1964 50.00
❑ SM-2198 Beach Boys Concert 197? 10.00
❑ STAO 2198 [S] Beach Boys Concert 1964 30.00
—With bound-in booklet
❑ STAO-8-2198 [S] Beach Boys Concert 196? 80.00
—Capitol Record Club edition
❑ TAO 2198 [M] Beach Boys Concert 1964 30.00
—With bound-in booklet
❑ DT 2269 [R] The Beach Boys Today! 1965 25.00
❑ DT-8-2269 [R] The Beach Boys Today! 1965 80.00
—Capitol Record Club edition
❑ T 2269 [M] The Beach Boys Today! 1965 30.00
❑ DT 2354 [R] Summer Days (And Summer Nights!!) 1965 25.00
—With "Duophonic" banner
❑ DT 2354 [R] Summer Days (And Summer Nights!!) 1965 50.00
—With "New Improved Full Dimensional Stereo" banner
❑ T 2354 [M] Summer Days (And Summer Nights!!) 1965 30.00
❑ DMAS 2398 [R] Beach Boys Party! 1965 25.00
—Without sheet of photos
❑ DMAS 2398 [R] Beach Boys Party! 1965 30.00
—With sheet of photos
❑ MAS 2398 [M] Beach Boys Party! 1965 30.00
—Without sheet of photos
❑ MAS 2398 [M] Beach Boys Party! 1965 40.00
—With sheet of photos
❑ DT 2458 [R] Pet Sounds 1966 30.00
❑ T 2458 [M] Pet Sounds 1966 40.00
❑ DT 2545 [P] Best of the Beach Boys 1966 12.00
—Black "The Star Line" label
❑ DT 2545 [P] Best of the Beach Boys 1966 15.00
—Black label with colorband
❑ DT 2545 [P] Best of the Beach Boys 1967 15.00
—Red and white "Starline" label
❑ DT 2545 [P] Best of the Beach Boys 1970 12.00
—Green "Starline" label
❑ DT 2545 [P] Best of the Beach Boys 1973 10.00
—Orange label, "Capitol" on bottom
❑ DT 2545 [P] Best of the Beach Boys 1978 10.00
—Purple label, large Capitol logo
❑ DT 2545 [P] Best of the Beach Boys 1983 10.00
—Black label, print in colorband
❑ T 2545 [M] Best of the Beach Boys 1966 15.00
—Black "The Star Line" label
❑ T 2545 [M] Best of the Beach Boys 1966 20.00
—Black label with colorband
❑ T 2545 [M] Best of the Beach Boys 1967 30.00
—Red and white "Starline" label
❑ T/DT 2580 Smile Booklet 1966 300.00
—Printed for insertion into unreleased "Smile" LP; counterfeits exist
❑ T/DT 2580 Smile 1966 1000.
—Unreleased; price is for cover slick, which has been counterfeited
❑ DT 2706 [P] Best of the Beach Boys, Vol. 2 1967 15.00
—Red and while "Starline" label
❑ DT 2706 [P] Best of the Beach Boys, Vol. 2 1970 12.00
—Green "Starline" label
❑ DT 2706 [P] Best of the Beach Boys, Vol. 2 1973 10.00
—Orange label, "Capitol" on bottom
❑ DT 2706 [P] Best of the Beach Boys, Vol. 2 1978 10.00
—Purple label, large Capitol logo
❑ T 2706 [M] Best of the Beach Boys, Vol. 2 1967 25.00
❑ DTCL 2813 [(3)R] The Beach Boys Deluxe Set 1967 50.00
—Maroon border on box; custom pressings of LPs with "DTCL" prefixes
❑ DTCL-8-2813 [(3)R] The Beach Boys Deluxe Set 1967 150.00
—Capitol Record Club edition; blue border on box; custom pressings of LPs with "DTCL" prefixes
❑ TCL 2813 [(3)M] The Beach Boys Deluxe Set 1967 250.00
—Black border on box; albums have "T" prefixes
❑ ST 2859 [S] Wild Honey 1967 20.00
❑ T 2859 [M] Wild Honey 1967 40.00
❑ ST-8-2891 [R] Smiley Smile 1968 300.00
—Capitol Record Club edition
❑ DKAO 2893 Stack-o-Tracks 1968 50.00
—Without sheet music booklet
❑ DKAO 2893 Stack-o-Tracks 1968 100.00
—With sheet music booklet
❑ DKAO-8-2893 Stack-o-Tracks 1968 200.00
—Capitol Record Club edition
❑ ST 2895 Friends 1968 25.00
❑ DKAO 2945 [P] The Best of the Beach Boys, Vol. 3 1968 15.00
—Black label with colorband
❑ DKAO 2945 [P] The Best of the Beach Boys, Vol. 3 1969 20.00
—"Starline" label
❑ PRO 3133 [DJ] Silver Platter Service from Hollywood: The Beach Boys Christmas Special 1964 200.00
❑ SY-4572 [R] Surfin' Safari 197? 12.00
—Orange label, Capitol logo at bottom; reissue of DT-1808 with completely different back cover and the words "... A Collector's Item ... Special Collections of Classic Hit Recordings by the Brightest Stars ..."
❑ SVBB-11307 [(2)] Endless Summer 1974 20.00
—Orange labels, "Capitol" on bottom; with poster
❑ SVBB-11307 [(2)] Endless Summer 1978 15.00
—Purple labels, large Capitol logo
❑ SVBB-11307 [(2)] Endless Summer 1983 12.00
—Black labels, print in colorband
❑ SVBB-11307 [(2)] Endless Summer 1988 12.00
—Purple labels, small Capitol logo
❑ SVBB-11384 [(2)] Spirit of America 1975 15.00
—Orange labels, "Capitol" on bottom
❑ SVBB-11384 [(2)] Spirit of America 1978 12.00
—Purple labels, large Capitol logo

Except when noted otherwise, VG = 25% of NM, and VG+ = 50% of NM. (Example: VG = $2.00, VG+ = $4.00 and NM = $8.00.)

B

Number	Title (A Side/B Side)	Yr	NM
❑ SVBB-11384 [(2)]	Spirit of America	1983	10.00

—Black labels, print in colorband

Number	Title (A Side/B Side)	Yr	NM
❑ SVBB-11384 [(2)]	Spirit of America	1988	10.00

—Purple labels, small Capitol logo

Number	Title (A Side/B Side)	Yr	NM
❑ ST-11584	Beach Boys '69 (The Beach Boys Live in London)	1976	12.00
❑ SN-12011	Beach Boys '69 (The Beach Boys Live in London)	1979	10.00
❑ SVBB-12220 [(2)]	Sunshine Dream	1982	12.00
❑ ST-12293	Rarities	1983	15.00
❑ STBK-12396 [(2)]	Made in U.S.A.	1986	12.00
❑ N-16012 [M]	Surfin' Safari	1980	8.00
❑ SN-16013 [S]	Little Deuce Coupe	1980	8.00
❑ SN-16014 [S]	Surfer Girl	1980	8.00
❑ SN-16015 [S]	Surfin' U.S.A.	1980	8.00
❑ SN-16016 [S]	All Summer Long	1980	8.00
❑ DN-16017 [R]	California Girls	1980	8.00
❑ SN-16018 [P]	Fun, Fun, Fun	1980	8.00

—Reissue of "Shut Down, Vol. 2"

Number	Title (A Side/B Side)	Yr	NM
❑ DN-16019 [R]	Dance, Dance, Dance	1981	8.00
❑ SN-16134	Beach Boys '69 (The Beach Boys Live in London)	1981	8.00
❑ SN-16156 [M]	Pet Sounds	1981	8.00
❑ SN-16157	Friends	1981	8.00
❑ SN-16158 [M]	Smiley Smile	1981	8.00
❑ SN-16159 [S]	Wild Honey	1981	8.00
❑ DN-16272 [R]	Beach Boys Party!	1982	8.00
❑ N-16273	Be True to Your School	1983	8.00
❑ DN-16318 [R]	Best of the Beach Boys, Vol. 2	1984	8.00
❑ C1-21241 [S]	Pet Sounds	1999	15.00

—True stereo version on heavyweight vinyl

Number	Title (A Side/B Side)	Yr	NM
❑ C1-29628 [S]	Surfer Girl	1994	15.00
❑ C1-29629 [M]	Shut Down, Vol. 2	1994	15.00
❑ C1-29630 [S]	Little Deuce Coupe	1994	15.00
❑ C1-29631 [S]	All Summer Long	1994	15.00
❑ C1-29632 [M]	The Beach Boys Today!	1994	15.00
❑ C1-29633 [M]	Summer Days (And Summer Nights!!)	1994	15.00
❑ C1-29634	Beach Boys '69 (The Beach Boys Live in London)	1994	15.00
❑ C1-29635 [M]	Smiley Smile	1994	15.00
❑ C1-29636 [S]	Wild Honey	1994	15.00
❑ C1-29637	Friends	1994	15.00
❑ C1-29638	20/20	1994	15.00
❑ C1-29640 [M]	Beach Boys Party!	1994	15.00
❑ C1-29641	Stack-o-Tracks	1994	15.00
❑ C1-29661 [M]	Surfin' Safari	1994	15.00
❑ C1-48421 [M]	Pet Sounds	1994	15.00
❑ C1-48422 [S]	Surfin' U.S.A.	1994	15.00
❑ 09463-51370-1-9 [(2)]	Pet Sounds	2006	30.00

—Limited two-record edition; one record is on yellow vinyl and contains the original mono mix; the other is on green vinyl and contains the 2003 stereo mix

Number	Title (A Side/B Side)	Yr	NM
❑ C1-90427	Beach Boys Concert	1994	15.00
❑ C1-91318 [R]	Best of the Beach Boys	1988	12.00

—Purple label, small Capitol logo

Number	Title (A Side/B Side)	Yr	NM
❑ C1-92639	Still Cruisin'	1989	12.00
❑ R 123946	Best of the Beach Boys	197?	15.00

—RCA Music Service edition

Number	Title (A Side/B Side)	Yr	NM
❑ R 133854	The Beach Boys' Christmas Album	197?	15.00

—RCA Music Service edition

Number	Title (A Side/B Side)	Yr	NM
❑ R 223559 [(2)]	Endless Summer	197?	25.00

—RCA Music Service edition

Number	Title (A Side/B Side)	Yr	NM
❑ R 233593 [(2)]	American Summer	1975	25.00

—RCA Music Service exclusive

Number	Title (A Side/B Side)	Yr	NM
❑ SF-500501	All Summer Long	1971	10.00

—Columbia Record Club edition

Number	Title (A Side/B Side)	Yr	NM
❑ SF-500502	California Girls	1971	10.00

—Columbia Record Club edition

Number	Title (A Side/B Side)	Yr	NM
❑ DT-502545 [P]	Best of the Beach Boys	197?	15.00

—Columbia Record Club edition

Number	Title (A Side/B Side)	Yr	NM
❑ DT-502706 [P]	Best of the Beach Boys, Vol. 2	197?	15.00

—Columbia Record Club edition

Number	Title (A Side/B Side)	Yr	NM
❑ SVBB-511307 [(2)]	Endless Summer	197?	25.00

—Columbia Record Club edition

Number	Title (A Side/B Side)	Yr	NM
❑ SVBB-511384 [(2)]	Spirit of America	1975	20.00

—Columbia Record Club edition

CAPITOL SPECIAL MARKETS

Number	Title (A Side/B Side)	Yr	NM
❑ SLB-6994 [(2)]	Golden Years of the Beach Boys	1975	20.00
❑ SL-8114	Beach Boys Super Hits	1978	10.00
❑ SLB-8134 [(2)]	The Beach Boys	1980	20.00
❑ SL-9431	Good Vibrations from the Beach Boys	1986	15.00

—Special issue for Sunkist

CARIBOU

Number	Title (A Side/B Side)	Yr	NM
❑ JZ 35752	L.A. (Light Album)	1979	10.00
❑ JZ 35752 [DJ]	L.A. (Light Album)	1979	15.00

—White label promo

Number	Title (A Side/B Side)	Yr	NM
❑ PZ 35752	L.A. (Light Album)	1980	8.00

—Budget-line reissue

Number	Title (A Side/B Side)	Yr	NM
❑ FZ 36283	Keepin' the Summer Alive	1980	10.00
❑ FZ 36283 [DJ]	Keepin' the Summer Alive	1980	15.00

—White label promo

Number	Title (A Side/B Side)	Yr	NM
❑ Z2X 37445 [(2)]	Ten Years of Harmony (1970-1980)	1981	12.00
❑ BFZ 39946	The Beach Boys	1985	10.00
❑ PZ 39946	The Beach Boys	1988	8.00

—Budget-line reissue

DCC COMPACT CLASSICS

Number	Title (A Side/B Side)	Yr	NM
❑ LPZ-2006 [M]	Pet Sounds	1995	120.00

—Audiophile vinyl

ERA

Number	Title (A Side/B Side)	Yr	NM
❑ HTE-805 [M]	The Beach Boys' Biggest Beach Hits	1969	15.00

—Also contains non-Beach Boys filler

EVEREST

Number	Title (A Side/B Side)	Yr	NM
❑ 4108 [M]	Rare Early Recordings	1981	8.00

GATEWAY

Number	Title (A Side/B Side)	Yr	NM
❑ GSLP-10104 [M]	Surfing with the Beach Boys, the Marketts and the Frogmen	1979	8.00

MOBILE FIDELITY

Number	Title (A Side/B Side)	Yr	NM
❑ 1-116	Surfer Girl	1984	30.00

—Audiophile vinyl

ORBIT

Number	Title (A Side/B Side)	Yr	NM
❑ OR 688 [M]	The Beach Boys' Greatest Hits 1961-1963	1972	12.00

—Also contains non-Beach Boys filler

PAIR

Number	Title (A Side/B Side)	Yr	NM
❑ PDL2-1068 [(2)]	For All Seasons	1986	15.00
❑ PDL2-1084 [(2)]	Golden Harmonies	1986	15.00

PICKWICK

Number	Title (A Side/B Side)	Yr	NM
❑ PTP-2059 [(2)]	High Water	1973	12.00
❑ SPC-3221	Summertime Blues	1970	10.00
❑ SPC-3269	Good Vibrations	1971	10.00
❑ SPC-3309	Wow! Great Concert!	1972	10.00
❑ SPC-3351	Surfer Girl	1973	10.00
❑ SPC-3562	Little Deuce Coupe	1975	10.00

READER'S DIGEST

Number	Title (A Side/B Side)	Yr	NM
❑ RBA-178 [(4)]	Their Greatest Hits and Finest Performances	1989	50.00

—Box set

SCEPTER CITATION

Number	Title (A Side/B Side)	Yr	NM
❑ CTN-18004 [M]	The Best of the Beach Boys (1961-1963)	1972	12.00

—Also contains non-Beach Boys filler

SEARS

Number	Title (A Side/B Side)	Yr	NM
❑ SPS-609	Summertime Blues	1970	50.00

SPRINGBOARD

Number	Title (A Side/B Side)	Yr	NM
❑ SPB-4021 [M]	The Beach Boys 1961	1977	8.00

—Also contains non-Beach Boys filler

SUNDAZED

Number	Title (A Side/B Side)	Yr	NM
❑ LP 5005 [B]	Lost & Found!	1991	12.00

—Colored vinyl (red, yellow and light blue are known); first LP issue of the 1961 sessions from the master tapes; three tracks are stereo

TIME-LIFE

Number	Title (A Side/B Side)	Yr	NM
❑ SRNR-03 [(2)]	The Beach Boys: 1963-1967	1986	15.00

—2 LPs in box with fold-open liner notes; second cover has a portrait of the Beach Boys

Number	Title (A Side/B Side)	Yr	NM
❑ SRNR-03 [(2)]	The Beach Boys: 1963-1967	1986	25.00

—2 LPs in box with fold-open liner notes; original cover portrays the Beach Boys surfing

WAND

Number	Title (A Side/B Side)	Yr	NM
❑ WDS-688 [M]	The Beach Boys' Greatest Hits 1961-1963	1972	12.00

—Also contains non-Beach Boys filler

BEACH BOYS, THE (2)

No relation to the group that became famous.

45s

KAPP

Number	Title (A Side/B Side)	Yr	NM
❑ 289	Bathing Beauty/On the Beach at Sunset	1959	25.00

BEACH BUMS, THE

Early BOB SEGER.

45s

ARE YOU KIDDING ME?

Number	Title (A Side/B Side)	Yr	NM
❑ 1010	Florida Time/The Ballad of the Yellow Beret	1966	60.00

—B-side credited to "D. Dodger"

BEACH GIRLS, THE

45s

DYNO VOX

Number	Title (A Side/B Side)	Yr	NM
❑ 202	Goin' Places/Skiing in the Snow	1965	25.00

VAULT

Number	Title (A Side/B Side)	Yr	NM
❑ 905	He's My Surfin' Guy/Bobby's the Boy	1963	30.00

BEACH NUTS, THE

45s

BANG

Number	Title (A Side/B Side)	Yr	NM
❑ 504	Out in the Sun (Hey-O)/Someday Soon	1965	50.00

CORONADO

Number	Title (A Side/B Side)	Yr	NM
❑ 131	Surf Ride '65/The Last Ride	1965	50.00
❑ 131 [PS]	Surf Ride '65/The Last Ride	1965	60.00

BEACON STREET UNION, THE

45s

MGM

Number	Title (A Side/B Side)	Yr	NM
❑ 13865	South End Incident/Speed Kills	1967	10.00
❑ 13935	Blue Suede Shoes/Four Hundred and Five	1968	10.00
❑ 14012	May I Light Your Cigarette/Mayola	1968	10.00

Albums

MGM

Number	Title (A Side/B Side)	Yr	NM
❑ E-4517 [M]	The Eyes of the Beacon Street Union	1967	30.00
❑ SE-4517 [S]	The Eyes of the Beacon Street Union	1967	25.00
❑ E-4568 [M]	The Clown Died in Marvin Gardens	1968	50.00

—May be promo only (yellow label)

Number	Title (A Side/B Side)	Yr	NM
❑ SE-4568 [S]	The Clown Died in Marvin Gardens	1968	25.00

BEAGLES, THE

45s

ERA

Number	Title (A Side/B Side)	Yr	NM
❑ 3132	Let's All Sing Like the Birdies Sing/Deep in the Heart of Texas	1964	15.00
❑ 3132 [PS]	Let's All Sing Like the Birdies Sing/Deep in the Heart of Texas	1964	25.00

HIT

Number	Title (A Side/B Side)	Yr	NM
❑ 113	Can't Buy Me Love/White on White	1964	12.00

—B-side by Fred York

BEALE STREET BOYS, THE

45s

OBA

Number	Title (A Side/B Side)	Yr	NM
❑ 101	Next Christmas/There's Nothing Greater Than A Prayer	1960	60.00

BEAN, YOUNG BILLY

See BILLY BURNETTE.

BEANS

45s

AVALANCHE

Number	Title (A Side/B Side)	Yr	NM
❑ 36011	Bleecker Street Rain/Honky Tonk Refrigerator	1972	8.00

Albums

AVALANCHE

Number	Title (A Side/B Side)	Yr	NM
❑ 9200	Beans	1971	20.00

BEAR, EDWARD

See EDWARD BEAR under "E" — it's a group, not a person.

BEARD, DEAN

45s

ATLANTIC

Number	Title (A Side/B Side)	Yr	NM
❑ 1137	On My Mind Again/Rakin' and Scrapin'	1957	40.00
❑ 1162	Party Party/Stand By Me	1957	40.00
❑ 1182	Take Time to Love Me/Hold Me Close	1958	30.00

CANDIX

Number	Title (A Side/B Side)	Yr	NM
❑ 341	The Day That I Lost You/Villa Acuna	1962	12.00

CHALLENGE

Number	Title (A Side/B Side)	Yr	NM
❑ 59033	Egad, Charlie Brown/Keeper of the Key	1958	25.00
❑ 59048	Holding On to a Memory/Little Lover	1959	25.00

EDMORAL

Number	Title (A Side/B Side)	Yr	NM
❑ 1011	On My Mind Again/Rakin' and Scrapin'	1956	150.00

JOED

Number	Title (A Side/B Side)	Yr	NM
❑ 715	Coffee Break/Tropical Nights	1962	25.00

SIMS

Number	Title (A Side/B Side)	Yr	NM
❑ 299	(Are There) Honkytonks in Heaven/Pocketful of Stardust	1966	10.00

WINSTON

Number	Title (A Side/B Side)	Yr	NM
❑ 1063	I Don't Know How/The Red Rose	1962	12.00

Number	Title (A Side/B Side)	Yr	NM
❑ 1073	Don't Let the Stars Get In Your Eyes/That's How It Gets Sun Up	1963	12.00
❑ 1075	Smile Pretty for Me Temper/ To Me	1963	12.00

—With Bill Graham

BEARFOOT

45s

EPIC

Number	Title (A Side/B Side)	Yr	NM
❑ 11018	Right On/Mark Twain	1973	5.00

Albums

EPIC

Number	Title (A Side/B Side)	Yr	NM
❑ KE 32146	Bearfoot	1973	12.00

BEARS, THE

Also see ADRIAN BELEW; KING CRIMSON.

12-Inch Singles

I.R.S.

Number	Title (A Side/B Side)	Yr	NM
❑ L33-17371 [DJ]	Trust (3 versions)	1987	10.00
❑ L33-17523 [DJ]	Aches and Pains/Talking About Music Is Like Whisting About Chickens	1988	10.00

45s

I.R.S.

Number	Title (A Side/B Side)	Yr	NM
❑ 53197	Trust (Mix 106)/Save Me	1987	3.00
❑ 53197 [PS]	Trust (Mix 106)/Save Me	1987	3.00

Albums

I.R.S.

Number	Title (A Side/B Side)	Yr	NM
❑ 42011	The Bears	1987	12.00
❑ 42139	Rise and Shine	1988	10.00

BEASLEY, JIMMY

45s

MODERN

Number	Title (A Side/B Side)	Yr	NM
❑ 991	Ella Jane/No Love for Me	1956	25.00
❑ 996	Don't Feel Sorry for Me/ Little Coquette	1956	25.00
❑ 1009	My Happiness/Jambalaya	1956	25.00
❑ 1014	Near You/I'm So Blue	1956	25.00
❑ 1018	Thinking of You/ You Were Fooling	1956	25.00
❑ 1021	Johnny's House Party (Part 1)/ Johnny's House Party (Part 2)	1957	25.00
❑ 1023	I Want My Baby/We Three	1957	25.00

BEAST

45s

EVOLUTION

Number	Title (A Side/B Side)	Yr	NM
❑ 1028	Communication/Move Mountain	1970	6.00

Albums

COTILLION

Number	Title (A Side/B Side)	Yr	NM
❑ SD 9012	Beast	1969	15.00

EVOLUTION

Number	Title (A Side/B Side)	Yr	NM
❑ 2017	Beast	1970	15.00

BEASTIE BOYS

12-Inch Singles

CAPITOL

Number	Title (A Side/B Side)	Yr	NM
❑ SPRO 12872 [DJ]	Intergalactic (LP Version) (Acappella) (Instrumental) (Strawberry Bath and Jelly Soles Instrumental Version)	1998	12.00
❑ SPRO 13506 [DJ]	Body Movin' (LP Version) (Instrumental) (Kut Masta Kurt Remix) (Acappella) (Kut Masta Kurt Remix Instrumental)	1998	12.00
❑ SPRO 13520 [DJ]	Body Movin' (LP Version) (Acappella) (Fatboy Slim Remix) (Instrumental)	1998	15.00
❑ SPRO-13870 [DJ]	Alive (LP Version 3:51) (Acapella 3:08) (Instrumental 3:44)	1999	10.00
❑ SPRO-13873 [DJ]	Alive at Yauch's House (2 versions)	2000	12.00
❑ V-15483	Shake Your Rump/Hey Ladies/ 33% God/Dis Yourself in 89	1989	10.00

—Also known as the "Love American Style" EP

Number	Title (A Side/B Side)	Yr	NM
❑ V-15523	Shadrach/Caught in the Middle of a 3-Way Mix/And What You Give Is What You Get/Car Thief/Some Dumb Cop Gave Me Two Tickets Already/Your Sister's Def	1989	12.00

—Also known as the "An Exciting Evening at Home with Shadrach, Meshach and Abednego" EP

Number	Title (A Side/B Side)	Yr	NM
❑ Y-15827	Pass the Mic/Dub the Mic// Drunken Praying Mantis Style/Pass the Mic (Pt. 2, Skills to Pay Bills)/Netty's Girl [unlisted track]	1992	15.00
❑ Y-15836	Jimmy James (Single Version) (LP Version) (Original Original Version)/ The Maestro/Boomin' Granny/Drinkin' Wine	1992	12.00
❑ Y-15847	So What 'Cha Want (Single Version) (Soul Assassin Remix Version) (Butt Naked Version) (All the Way Live Freestyle Version)/The Skills to Pay the Bills/Groove Holmes (2 versions)	1992	12.00
❑ Y-15944	Gratitude/Stand Together (Live at French's Tavern, Sydney, Australia)/Finger Licken' Good (Government Cheese Remix)/Gratitude (Live at Budokon)/Honkey Rink	1992	12.00
❑ SPRO-18631 [DJ]	Ch-Check It Out (Clean Version) (Explicit Version) (Instrumental) (Explicit Acappella)	2004	12.00
❑ SPRO-18687 [DJ]	Ch-Check It Out (Clean) (Explicit) (Just Blaze A Cappella Explicit) (Just Blaze Remix Clean) (Just Blaze Remix Explicit) (Just Blaze Remix Instrumental)	2004	10.00
❑ Y-58171	Get It Together/(Instrumental)	1994	10.00
❑ Y-58185	Get It Together (5 versions)/ Resolution Time/Sabotage/ Dope Little Song	1994	10.00
❑ Y-58226	Sure Shot (LP Version) (European B-Boy Mix) (Large Professor Mix) (Nardone Mix)/The Vibes/ Son of Neck Bone	1994	10.00
❑ Y 58705	Intergalactic (LP Version) (Prisoners of Technology/ TMS 1 Remix) (Strawberry Bath & Jelly Souls Instrumental Version) (Fuzzy Logic Remix) (Instrumental)/ Hail Sagan (Special K)	1998	10.00
❑ Y 58740	Body Movin' (LP Version) (Fatboy Slim Remix) (Acappella) (Instrumental)/ Peanut Butter and Jelly/Dr. Lee Ph.D ("Instrumental" Dub Mix)	1998	10.00
❑ SPRO-79181 [DJ]	Pass the Mic/Pass the Mic Pt. 2 (Skills to Pay Bills)	1992	12.00
❑ SPRO 79226 [DJ]	Professor Booty (same on both sides)	1992	12.00
❑ SPRO 79269/70 [DJ]	Get It Together (Buck Wild Clean Remix) (LP Version Clean) (A.B.A. Remix Clean) (Buck Wild Instrumental) (Buck Wild Remix) (LP Version) (A.B.A. Remix) (A.B.A. Instrumental)	1994	15.00
❑ SPRO-79320/1 [DJ]	Get It Together (LP Version) (Instrumental)	1994	10.00
❑ SPRO 79412/3 [DJ]	Sure Shot (Large Professor Remix Clean) (LP Version Clean) (Pruins / European B-Boy Mix Clean) (Nardone Mix Clean) (Pruins / European B-Boy Mix Instrumental) (Large Professor Remix) (LP Version) (Pruins / European B-Boy Mix) (Nardone Mix) (Large Professor Instrumental)	1994	15.00
❑ SPRO-79559/65 [DJ]	Finger Licken Good (2 versions)/Gratitude (2 versions)	1992	20.00
❑ SPRO-79627 [DJ]	Root Down (Free Zone Mix Clean) (Prince Paul Balloon Mix Clean) (LP Version Clean)/ (Free Zone Mix) (PP Balloon Mix) (LP Version)	1995	12.00

DEF JAM

Number	Title (A Side/B Side)	Yr	NM
❑ DJ 002	Rock Hard/Beastie Groove// The Party's Getting Rough/ Beastie Groove (Instrumental)	1985	100.00

—Immediately withdrawn from sale because of the unauthorized use of a sample from an AC/DC song

Number	Title (A Side/B Side)	Yr	NM
❑ CAS 2554 [DJ]	(You Gotta) Fight for Your Right (To Party!)/Girls	1987	15.00
❑ 44-05292	She's On It/Slow and Low	1986	10.00
❑ 44-05369	Hold It Now, Hit It (LP Version) (Instrumental) (Acapulco)	1986	10.00
❑ 44-05958	It's the New Style (vocal and instrumental)/Paul Revere (vocal and instrumental)	1986	12.00
❑ 44-06726	She's Crafty (2 versions?)	1987	12.00

GRAND ROYAL

Number	Title (A Side/B Side)	Yr	NM
❑ GR 064	Shake Your Rump/Hey Ladies/ 33% God/Dis Yourself in 89	1999	6.00

—Also known as the "Love American Style" EP; reissue

Number	Title (A Side/B Side)	Yr	NM
❑ GR 069	Body Movin' (Movin' in Kent Mix) (Micky Finn Remix) (Deep in Kent Anti-Vocal Remix)	1999	8.00

45s

CAPITOL

Number	Title (A Side/B Side)	Yr	NM
❑ S7-18042	Get It Together/Futterman's Rule	1994	5.00

—White vinyl

Number	Title (A Side/B Side)	Yr	NM
❑ S7-18125	Sure Shot (Clean Version)/ Sabotage (Clean Version)	1994	5.00

—Blue vinyl

Number	Title (A Side/B Side)	Yr	NM
❑ S7-18578	Root Down/Ricky's Theme	1995	5.00
❑ S7-19973	Intergalactic/ Peanut Butter & Jelly	1998	4.00
❑ B-44454	Hey Ladies/Shake Your Rump	1989	5.00
❑ B-44472	Shadrach/And What You Give Is What You Get	1989	6.00
❑ 58816	Alive/Big Shot (Live)	1999	3.00
❑ 7PRO-79698	Hey Ladies (same on both sides)	1989	10.00

—Originally issued as a promo only; 44454 came later

DEF JAM

Number	Title (A Side/B Side)	Yr	NM
❑ CS7 2264 [DJ]	Slow and Low (same on both sides)	1986	12.00
❑ 38-05683	She's On It/Slow and Low	1985	5.00
❑ 38-05683 [PS]	She's On It/Slow and Low	1985	5.00
❑ 38-05864	Hold It Now, Hit It/Hold It Now, Hit It (Acapulco)	1986	6.00
❑ 38-06341	It's the New Style/Paul Revere	1986	6.00
❑ 38-06595	(You Gotta) Fight for Your Right (To Party!)/Paul Revere	1987	6.00
❑ 38-06675	She's Crafty/ No Sleep Till Brooklyn	1987	6.00
❑ 38-06675 [PS]	She's Crafty/ No Sleep Till Brooklyn	1987	10.00
❑ 38-07020	Brass Monkey/Posse in Effect	1987	5.00
❑ 38-08388	(You Gotta) Fight for Your Right (To Party!)/She's On It	1988	3.00

—"Golden Oldies" reissue

7-Inch Extended Plays

RAT CAGE

Number	Title (A Side/B Side)	Yr	NM
❑ MOTR 21	*Beastie Boys/Transit Cop/ Jimi/Holy Snappers/Riot Fight/Ode to.../Michelle's Farm/Egg Raid on Mojo	1982	20.00
❑ MOTR 21 [PS]	Polly Wog Stew	1982	20.00

Albums

CAPITOL

Number	Title (A Side/B Side)	Yr	NM
❑ C1-22940 [(4)]	The Sounds of Science	2000	150.00

—Boxed set with hardbound booklet; released a year after a similar CD compilation

Number	Title (A Side/B Side)	Yr	NM
❑ C1-28599 [(2)]	Ill Communications	1994	20.00
❑ C1 37716 [(2)]	Hello Nasty	1998	20.00
❑ SPRO 79461 [(2)DJ]	Hip Hop Sampler	1994	50.00

—Promo-only compilation of remixes and rarities; 1,250 copies were pressed; only the Side 1 number is listed above (the other three sides are numbered SPRO-79463, SPRO-79472 and SPRO-79473); this album has been counterfeited; there are several differences; most notably that authentic copies have gatefold sleeves, and the counterfeits have single-pocket sleeves

Number	Title (A Side/B Side)	Yr	NM
❑ SPRO 79461 [(2)DJ]	Hip Hop Sampler	1994	50.00

—This album has been counterfeited; there are several differences, most notably that authentic copies have gatefold sleeves, and the counterfeits have single-pocket sleeves

Number	Title (A Side/B Side)	Yr	NM
❑ C1-84571 [(2)]	To the 5 Boroughs	2004	30.00
❑ C1-91743	Paul's Boutique	1989	15.00

—Single gatefold edition

Number	Title (A Side/B Side)	Yr	NM
❑ C1-92844	Paul's Boutique	1989	25.00

—Multi-gatefold edition (number on record is 91743, the same as single gatefold edition)

Number	Title (A Side/B Side)	Yr	NM
❑ C1-98938 [(2)]	Check Your Head	1992	50.00

DEF JAM

Number	Title (A Side/B Side)	Yr	NM
❑ BFC 40238	Licensed to Ill	1986	20.00
❑ FC 40238	Licensed to Ill	1986	15.00

—Second pressing, with "02" added to bar code on back cover

B

Number | Title (A Side/B Side) | Yr | NM

GRAND ROYAL
❑ GR 003 Some Old Bullshit 1994 15.00
❑ GR 006 [(2)] Ill Communication 1994 25.00
❑ GR 013 The In Sound from Way Out! 1996 80.00
—Original editions were limited to 5,000 and have a sticker indicating this on the back cover
❑ GR 013 The In Sound from Way Out! 1999 25.00
—Second editions were not limited and have no sticker on the back cover
❑ GR 018 [EP] Root Down 1995 15.00
—Black vinyl
❑ GR 018 [EP] Root Down 1995 30.00
—Blue vinyl
❑ GR 026 [EP] Aglio E Olio 1995 15.00
❑ GR 061 [(2)] Hello Nasty 1998 25.00
—Limited edition on yellow vinyl
❑ GR 065 [(2)] Paul's Boutique 1999 20.00
—Reissue of original multi-gatefold edition
❑ GR 066 [(2)] Check Your Head 1998 25.00
—Vinyl reissue of Capitol 98938
❑ GR 071 [EP] Scientists of Sound 2000 12.00
—Remix album

RAT CAGE
❑ 026 [EP] Cookypuss 1983 40.00

BEASTS, THE

45s

HIT
❑ 159 Sha La La/Where You Been 1964 15.00
—B-side by Charles Baker

BEAT BROTHERS, THE

45s

MGM
❑ 13201 Nick Nack Hully Gully/ Lantern Hully Gully 1963 16.00

BEAT MERCHANTS, THE

45s

TOWER
❑ 127 So Fine/You Were Made for Me 1965 15.00
—B-side by Freddie and the Dreamers

BEAT OF THE EARTH, THE

Albums

ARDISH
❑ AS-001 The Beat of the Earth 1968 300.00
❑ AS-0001 The Beat of the Earth 1968 400.00

BEATIN' PATH, THE

45s

FONTANA
❑ 1583 The Original Nothing People/ I Waited So Long 1967 20.00

BEATLE BUDDIES, THE

Albums

DIPLOMAT
❑ D-2313 [M] The Beatle Buddies 1964 15.00
❑ DS-2313 [S] The Beatle Buddies 1964 20.00

BEATLE-ETTES, THE

45s

ASSAULT
❑ 1893 Yes, You Can Hold My Hand/ Yes, You Can Hold My Hand (Part 2) 1964 20.00

JAMIE
❑ 1270 Dance, Beatle, Dance/We Were Meant to Be Married 1964 20.00

JUBILEE
❑ 5472 Only Seventeen/Now We're Together 1964 20.00

BEATLES, THE Also see PETE BEST; GEORGE HARRISON; JOHN LENNON; PAUL McCARTNEY; RINGO STARR.

12-Inch Singles

(NO LABEL)
❑ (no #) [DJ] Merry Christmas and Happy New Year 1965 500.00
—Promo item from KYA Radio, San Francisco; B-side is blank

45s

(NO LABEL)
❑ MBRF-55551 Decade 1974 —
—A clever bootleg of radio spots for the Beatles' back catalog, compiled without authorization by two former Capitol employees.

APPLE
❑ Promo-1970 [DJ] Dialogue from the Beatles' Motion Picture "Let It Be" 1970 60.00
❑ 2056 Hello Goodbye/I Am the Walrus 1971 10.00
—Without star on A-side label
❑ 2056 Hello Goodbye/I Am the Walrus 1971 30.00
—With star on A-side label
❑ 2056 Hello Goodbye/I Am the Walrus 1975 20.00
—With "All Rights Reserved" disclaimer
❑ 2138 Lady Madonna/The Inner Light 1971 10.00
—Without star on A-side label
❑ 2138 Lady Madonna/The Inner Light 1971 30.00
—With star on A-side label
❑ 2138 Lady Madonna/The Inner Light 1975 20.00
—With "All Rights Reserved" disclaimer
❑ 2276 Hey Jude/Revolution 1968 10.00
—With "Mfd. by Apple" on label
❑ 2276 Hey Jude/Revolution 1968 15.00
—Original: With small Capitol logo on bottom of B-side label
❑ 2276 Hey Jude/Revolution 1975 20.00
—With "All Rights Reserved" disclaimer
❑ 2490 Get Back/Don't Let Me Down 1969 10.00
—With "Mfd. by Apple" on label
❑ 2490 Get Back/Don't Let Me Down 1969 10.00
—Original: With small Capitol logo on bottom of B-side label
❑ 2490 Get Back/Don't Let Me Down 1975 20.00
—With "All Rights Reserved" disclaimer
❑ 2531 The Ballad of John and Yoko/ Old Brown Shoe 1969 10.00
—With "Mfd. by Apple" on label
❑ 2531 The Ballad of John and Yoko/ Old Brown Shoe 1969 10.00
—Original: With small Capitol logo on bottom of B-side label
❑ 2531 The Ballad of John and Yoko/ Old Brown Shoe 1975 20.00
—With "All Rights Reserved" disclaimer
❑ 2531 [PS] The Ballad of John and Yoko/ Old Brown Shoe 1969 100.00
❑ 2654 Something/Come Together 1969 10.00
—With "Mfd. by Apple" on label
❑ 2654 Something/Come Together 1969 100.00
—Original: With small Capitol logo on bottom of B-side label
❑ 2654 Something/Come Together 1975 20.00
—With "All Rights Reserved" disclaimer
❑ 2764 Let It Be/You Know My Name (Look Up My Number) 1970 10.00
—With "Mfd. by Apple" on label
❑ 2764 Let It Be/You Know My Name (Look Up My Number) 1970 12.00
—Original: With small Capitol logo on bottom of B-side label
❑ 2764 Let It Be/You Know My Name (Look Up My Number) 1975 20.00
—With "All Rights Reserved" disclaimer
❑ 2764 [PS] Let It Be/You Know My Name (Look Up the Number) 1970 100.00
❑ 2832 The Long and Winding Road/ For You Blue 1970 10.00
—With "Mfd. by Apple" on label
❑ 2832 The Long and Winding Road/ For You Blue 1970 20.00
—Original: With small Capitol logo on bottom of B-side label
❑ 2832 The Long and Winding Road/ For You Blue 1975 20.00
—With "All Rights Reserved" disclaimer
❑ 2832 [PS] The Long and Winding Road/ For You Blue 1970 100.00
❑ 5112 I Want to Hold Your Hand/ I Saw Her Standing There 1971 10.00
—Without star on label
❑ 5112 I Want to Hold Your Hand/ I Saw Her Standing There 1971 30.00
—With star on label
❑ 5112 I Want to Hold Your Hand/ I Saw Her Standing There 1975 20.00
—With "All Rights Reserved" disclaimer on label
❑ 5150 Can't Buy Me Love/ You Can't Do That 1971 10.00
—Without star on A-side label
❑ 5150 Can't Buy Me Love/ You Can't Do That 1971 30.00
—With star on A-side label
❑ 5150 Can't Buy Me Love/ You Can't Do That 1975 15.00
—With "All Rights Reserved" disclaimer on label
❑ 5222 A Hard Day's Night/ I Should Have Known Better 1971 10.00
—Without star on A-side label
❑ 5222 A Hard Day's Night/ I Should Have Known Better 1971 30.00
—With star on A-side label
❑ 5222 A Hard Day's Night/ I Should Have Known Better 1975 15.00
—With "All Rights Reserved" disclaimer
❑ 5234 I'll Cry Instead/I'm Happy Just to Dance with You 1971 10.00
—Without star on A-side label
❑ 5234 I'll Cry Instead/I'm Happy Just to Dance with You 1971 30.00
—With star on A-side label
❑ 5234 I'll Cry Instead/I'm Happy Just to Dance with You 1975 15.00
—With "All Rights Reserved" disclaimer
❑ 5235 And I Love Her/If I Fell 1971 10.00
—Without star on A-side label
❑ 5235 And I Love Her/If I Fell 1971 30.00
—With star on A-side label
❑ 5235 And I Love Her/If I Fell 1975 15.00
—With "All Rights Reserved" disclaimer
❑ 5255 Matchbox/Slow Down 1971 10.00
—Without star on A-side label
❑ 5255 Matchbox/Slow Down 1971 30.00
—With star on A-side label
❑ 5255 Matchbox/Slow Down 1975 15.00
—With "All Rights Reserved" disclaimer
❑ 5327 I Feel Fine/She's a Woman 1971 10.00
—Without star on A-side label
❑ 5327 I Feel Fine/She's a Woman 1971 30.00
—With star on A-side label
❑ 5327 I Feel Fine/She's a Woman 1975 15.00
—With "All Rights Reserved" disclaimer
❑ 5371 Eight Days a Week/I Don't Want to Spoil the Party 1971 10.00
—Without star on A-side label
❑ 5371 Eight Days a Week/I Don't Want to Spoil the Party 1971 30.00
—With star on A-side label
❑ 5371 Eight Days a Week/I Don't Want to Spoil the Party 1975 15.00
—With "All Rights Reserved" disclaimer
❑ 5407 Ticket to Ride/Yes It Is 1971 10.00
—Without star on A-side label
❑ 5407 Ticket to Ride/Yes It Is 1971 30.00
—With star on A-side label
❑ 5407 Ticket to Ride/Yes It Is 1975 15.00
—With "All Rights Reserved" disclaimer
❑ 5476 Help!/I'm Down 1971 10.00
—Without star on A-side label
❑ 5476 Help!/I'm Down 1971 30.00
—With star on A-side label
❑ 5476 Help!/I'm Down 1975 15.00
—With "All Rights Reserved" disclaimer
❑ 5498 Yesterday/Act Naturally 1971 10.00
—Without star on A-side label
❑ 5498 Yesterday/Act Naturally 1971 30.00
—With star on A-side label
❑ 5498 Yesterday/Act Naturally 1975 15.00
—With "All Rights Reserved" disclaimer
❑ 5555 We Can Work It Out/Day Tripper 1971 10.00
—Without star on A-side label
❑ 5555 We Can Work It Out/Day Tripper 1971 30.00
—With star on A-side label
❑ 5555 We Can Work It Out/Day Tripper 1975 15.00
—With "All Rights Reserved" disclaimer
❑ 5587 Nowhere Man/What Goes On 1971 10.00
—Without star on A-side label
❑ 5587 Nowhere Man/What Goes On 1971 30.00
—With star on A-side label
❑ 5587 Nowhere Man/What Goes On 1975 15.00
—With "All Rights Reserved" disclaimer
❑ 5651 Paperback Writer/Rain 1971 10.00
—Without star on A-side label
❑ 5651 Paperback Writer/Rain 1971 30.00
—With star on A-side label
❑ 5651 Paperback Writer/Rain 1975 15.00
—With "All Rights Reserved" disclaimer
❑ 5715 Yellow Submarine/Eleanor Rigby 1971 10.00
—Without star on A-side label
❑ 5715 Yellow Submarine/Eleanor Rigby 1971 30.00
—With star on A-side label
❑ 5715 Yellow Submarine/Eleanor Rigby 1975 15.00
—With "All Rights Reserved" disclaimer
❑ 5810 Penny Lane/Strawberry Fields Forever 1971 10.00
—Without star on A-side label
❑ 5810 Penny Lane/Strawberry Fields Forever 1971 30.00
—With star on A-side label
❑ 5810 Penny Lane/Strawberry Fields Forever 1975 15.00
—With "All Rights Reserved" disclaimer
❑ 5964 All You Need Is Love/ Baby, You're a Rich Man 1971 10.00
—Without star on A-side label
❑ 5964 All You Need Is Love/ Baby, You're a Rich Man 1971 30.00
—With star on A-side label
❑ 5964 All You Need Is Love/ Baby, You're a Rich Man 1975 15.00
—With "All Rights Reserved" disclaimer
❑ 58348 Baby It's You/I'll Follow the Sun// Devil in Her Heart/Boys 1995 4.00
—All 4 tracks from BBC sessions
❑ 58348 [PS] Baby It's You/I'll Follow the Sun//Devil in Her Heart/Boys 1995 4.00
❑ 58497 Free as a Bird/Christmas Time (Is Here Again) 1995 4.00
—Small center hole; all with large hole were "dinked" somewhere other than when manufactured and have little, if any, value
❑ 58497 [PS] Free as a Bird/Christmas Time (Is Here Again) 1995 4.00
❑ 58544 Real Love/Baby's in Black (Live) 1996 3.00
—Small center hole; all with large hole were "dinked" somewhere other than when manufactured and have little, if any, value
❑ 58544 [PS] Real Love/Baby's in Black (Live) 1996 3.00

APPLE/AMERICOM
❑ 2276/M-221 Hey Jude/Revolution 1969 300.00
—Four-inch flexi-disc sold in vending machines; "Hey Jude" is edited to 3:25

Except when noted otherwise, VG = 25% of NM, and VG+ = 50% of NM. (Example: VG = $2.00, VG+ = $4.00 and NM = $8.00.)

Number	Title (A Side/B Side)	Yr	NM
❑ 2490/M-335	Get Back/Don't Let Me Down	1969	1000.
—Four-inch flexi-disc sold in vending machines			
❑ 2531/M-382	The Ballad of John and Yoko/ Old Brown Shoe	1969	800.00
—Four-inch flexi-disc sold in vending machines			
❑ 5715	Yellow Submarine/Eleanor Rigby	1969	2000.
—Four-inch flexi-disc sold in vending machines. VG 1000; VG+ 1500			

ATCO

Number	Title (A Side/B Side)	Yr	NM
❑ 6302	Sweet Georgia Brown/Take Out Some Insurance On Me Baby	1964	200.00
❑ 6308	Ain't She Sweet/Nobody's Child	1964	50.00
—With "Vocal by John Lennon" on left of label			
❑ 6308	Ain't She Sweet/Nobody's Child	1964	60.00
—With "Vocal by John Lennon" under "The Beatles"			
❑ 6308 [PS]	Ain't She Sweet/Nobody's Child	1964	500.00
—Sleeves with black and green print are reproductions			

ATLANTIC

Number	Title (A Side/B Side)	Yr	NM
❑ OS-13243	Ain't She Sweet/ Sweet Georgia Brown	1983	10.00
—"Oldies Series"			

BACKSTAGE

Number	Title (A Side/B Side)	Yr	NM
❑ 1112 [DJ]	Like Dreamers Do/ Love of the Loved	1982	25.00
—Promotional 45 from "Oui" magazine			
❑ 1122 [DJ]	Love of the Loved/Memphis	1983	25.00
—Promotional picture disc			
❑ 1133 [DJ]	Like Dreamers Do/ Three Cool Cats	1983	25.00
—Promotional picture disc			
❑ 1155 [DJ]	Crying, Waiting, Hoping/ Take Good Care of My Baby	1983	25.00

BEATLES FAN CLUB

Number	Title (A Side/B Side)	Yr	NM
❑ (1964)	Season's Greetings from the Beatles	1964	300.00
—Tri-fold soundcard			
❑ (1965)	The Beatles Third Christmas Record	1965	80.00
—Flexi-disc			
❑ (1965) [PS]	The Beatles Third Christmas Record	1965	100.00
❑ (1966)	Everywhere It's Christmas	1966	150.00
—Postcard			
❑ (1967)	Christmastime Is Here Again	1967	150.00
—Postcard			
❑ (1968) H-2041	The Beatles 1968 Christmas Record	1968	60.00
—Flexi-disc			
❑ (1968) H-2041 [PS]	The Beatles 1968 Christmas Record	1968	70.00
❑ (1969) H-2565	Happy Christmas 1969	1969	40.00
—Flexi-disc			
❑ (1969) H-2565 [PS]	Happy Christmas 1969	1969	60.00

CAPITOL

Number	Title (A Side/B Side)	Yr	NM
❑ 2056	Hello Goodbye/I Am the Walrus	1967	30.00
—Original: Orange and yellow swirl, without "A Subsidiary Of"... in perimeter label print; publishing credited to "Comet" (we're not sure which came first)			
❑ 2056	Hello Goodbye/I Am the Walrus	1967	30.00
—Original: Orange and yellow swirl, without "A Subsidiary Of"... in perimeter label print; publishing credited to "Maclen" (we're not sure which came first)			
❑ 2056	Hello Goodbye/I Am the Walrus	1968	50.00
—Orange and yellow swirl label with "A Subsidiary Of" in perimeter print			
❑ 2056	Hello Goodbye/I Am the Walrus	1969	20.00
—Red and orange "target" label with Capitol round logo			
❑ 2056	Hello Goodbye/I Am the Walrus	1969	60.00
—Red and orange "target" label with Capitol dome logo			
❑ 2056	Hello Goodbye/I Am the Walrus	1976	6.00
—Orange label with "Capitol" at bottom			
❑ 2056	Hello Goodbye/I Am the Walrus	1978	8.00
—Purple label; label has reeded edge			
❑ 2056	Hello Goodbye/I Am the Walrus	1983	6.00
—Black label with colorband			
❑ 2056	Hello Goodbye/I Am the Walrus	1988	5.00
—Purple label; label has smooth edge			
❑ 2056 [PS]	Hello Goodbye/I Am the Walrus	1967	100.00
❑ P 2056 [DJ]	Hello Goodbye/I Am the Walrus	1967	250.00
—Light green label promo			
❑ 2138	Lady Madonna/The Inner Light	1968	30.00
—Original: Orange and yellow swirl, without "A Subsidiary Of"... in perimeter label print			
❑ 2138	Lady Madonna/The Inner Light	1968	50.00
—Orange and yellow swirl label with "A Subsidiary Of" in perimeter print			
❑ 2138	Lady Madonna/The Inner Light	1969	20.00
—Red and orange "target" label with Capitol round logo			
❑ 2138	Lady Madonna/The Inner Light	1969	60.00
—Red and orange "target" label with Capitol dome logo			
❑ 2138	Lady Madonna/The Inner Light	1976	6.00
—Orange label with "Capitol" at bottom			
❑ 2138	Lady Madonna/The Inner Light	1978	8.00
—Purple label; label has reeded edge			
❑ 2138	Lady Madonna/The Inner Light	1983	6.00
—Black label with colorband			
❑ 2138	Lady Madonna/The Inner Light	1988	5.00
—Purple label; label has smooth edge			

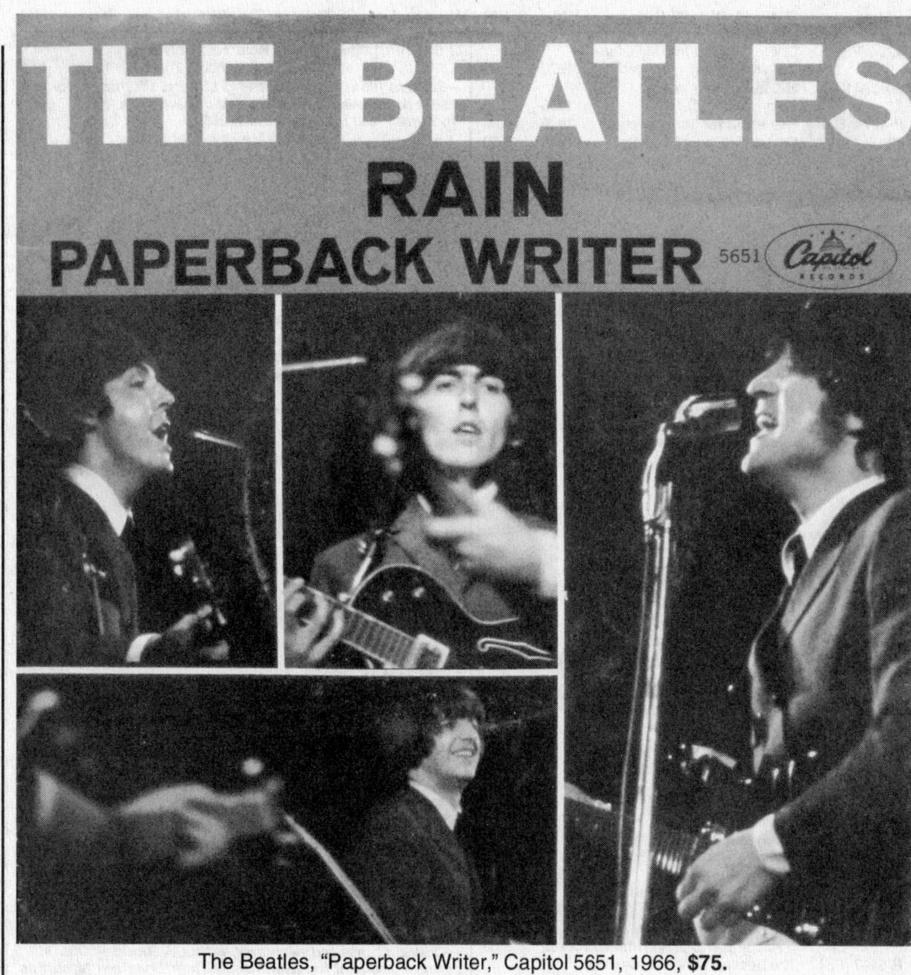

The Beatles, "Paperback Writer," Capitol 5651, 1966, **$75.**

Number	Title (A Side/B Side)	Yr	NM
❑ 2138 [PS]	Lady Madonna/The Inner Light	1968	20.00
—"Beatles Fan Club" insert that was issued with above sleeve. Originals are glossy.			
❑ 2138 [PS]	Lady Madonna/The Inner Light	1968	100.00
❑ P 2138 [DJ]	Lady Madonna/The Inner Light	1968	200.00
—Light green label promo			
❑ 2276	Hey Jude/Revolution	1976	6.00
—Orange label with "Capitol" at bottom			
❑ 2276	Hey Jude/Revolution	1978	8.00
—Purple label; label has reeded edge			
❑ 2276	Hey Jude/Revolution	1983	6.00
—Black label with colorband			
❑ 2276	Hey Jude/Revolution	1988	5.00
—Purple label; label has smooth edge			
❑ 2490	Get Back/Don't Let Me Down	1976	6.00
—Orange label with "Capitol" at bottom			
❑ 2490	Get Back/Don't Let Me Down	1978	8.00
—Purple label; label has reeded edge			
❑ 2490	Get Back/Don't Let Me Down	1983	6.00
—Black label with colorband; "Get Back" replaced by LP version as on Let It Be			
❑ 2490	Get Back/Don't Let Me Down	1988	5.00
—Purple label; label has smooth edge; "Get Back" replaced by LP version as on Let It Be			
❑ 2531	The Ballad of John and Yoko/ Old Brown Shoe	1976	—
—Orange label with "Capitol" at bottom; should exist, but not known to exist			
❑ 2531	The Ballad of John and Yoko/ Old Brown Shoe	1978	6.00
—Purple label; label has reeded edge			
❑ 2531	The Ballad of John and Yoko/ Old Brown Shoe	1983	7.00
—Black label with colorband			
❑ 2531	The Ballad of John and Yoko/ Old Brown Shoe	1988	6.00
—Purple label; label has smooth edge			
❑ 2654	Something/Come Together	1976	6.00
—Orange label with "Capitol" at bottom			
❑ 2654	Something/Come Together	1978	6.00
—Purple label; label has reeded edge			
❑ 2654	Something/Come Together	1983	6.00
—Black label with colorband			
❑ 2654	Something/Come Together	1988	5.00
—Purple label; label has smooth edge			
❑ 2764	Let It Be/You Know My Name (Look Up My Number)	1976	6.00
—Orange label with "Capitol" at bottom			
❑ 2764	Let It Be/You Know My Name (Look Up My Number)	1978	8.00
—Purple label; label has reeded edge			
❑ 2764	Let It Be/You Know My Name (Look Up My Number)	1983	6.00
—Black label with colorband			
❑ 2764	Let It Be/You Know My Name (Look Up My Number)	1988	5.00
—Purple label; label has smooth edge			
❑ 2832	The Long and Winding Road/ For You Blue	1976	6.00
—Orange label with "Capitol" at bottom			
❑ 2832	The Long and Winding Road/ For You Blue	1978	8.00
—Purple label; label has reeded edge			
❑ 2832	The Long and Winding Road/ For You Blue	1983	6.00
—Black label with colorband			
❑ 2832	The Long and Winding Road/ For You Blue	1988	5.00
—Purple label; label has smooth edge			
❑ 4274	Got to Get You Into My Life/ Helter Skelter	1976	6.00
—Original: Orange label with "Capitol" at bottom, George Martin's name not on label			
❑ 4274	Got to Get You Into My Life/ Helter Skelter	1976	10.00
—Orange label with "Capitol" at bottom, George Martin's name is on label			
❑ 4274	Got to Get You Into My Life/ Helter Skelter	1978	6.00
—Purple label; label has reeded edge			
❑ 4274	Got to Get You Into My Life/ Helter Skelter	1983	6.00
—Black label with colorband			
❑ 4274	Got to Get You Into My Life/ Helter Skelter	1988	5.00
—Purple label; label has smooth edge			

B

Number	Title (A Side/B Side)	Yr	NM
❑ 4274 [PS]	Got to Get You Into My Life/ Helter Skelter	1976	5.00
❑ P-4274 [DJ]	Got to Get You Into My Life (mono/stereo)	1976	40.00
❑ P-4274 [DJ]	Helter Skelter (mono/stereo)	1976	40.00
❑ 4347	Ob-La-Di, Ob-La-Da/Julia	1976	8.00
—Original: Orange label with "Capitol" at bottom			
❑ 4347	Ob-La-Di, Ob-La-Da/Julia	1978	8.00
—Purple label; label has reeded edge			
❑ 4347	Ob-La-Di, Ob-La-Da/Julia	1983	6.00
—Black label with colorband			
❑ 4347	Ob-La-Di, Ob-La-Da/Julia	1988	5.00
—Purple label; label has smooth edge			
❑ 4347 [PS]	Ob-La-Di, Ob-La-Da/Julia	1976	8.00
—Sleeves are individually numbered; very low numbers (under 1000) can fetch premium prices			
❑ P-4347 [DJ]	Ob-La-Di, Ob-La-Da (mono/stereo)	1976	40.00
❑ 4506 [PS]	Girl/You're Going to Lose That Girl	1977	15.00
—Sleeve for a single that was never pressed			
❑ P-4506 [DJ]	Girl (mono/stereo)	1977	200.00
—Promo only; all colored vinyl versions are counterfeits			
❑ 4612	Sgt. Pepper's Lonely Hearts Club Band-With a Little Help from My Friends/ A Day in the Life	1978	8.00
—Original: Purple label; label has reeded edge			
❑ 4612	Sgt. Pepper's Lonely Hearts Club Band-With a Little Help from My Friends/A Day in the Life	1983	6.00
—Black label with colorband			
❑ 4612	Sgt. Pepper's Lonely Hearts Club Band-With a Little Help from My Friends/A Day in the Life	1988	5.00
—Purple label; label has smooth edge			
❑ 4612 [PS]	Sgt. Pepper's Lonely Hearts Club Band-With a Little Help from My Friends/A Day in the Life	1978	20.00
❑ P-4612 [DJ]	Sgt. Pepper's Lonely Hearts Club Band-With a Little Help from My Friends (mono/stereo)	1978	40.00
❑ B-5100	The Beatles' Movie Medley/ Fab Four on Film	1982	50.00
—Stock copy; not officially released, but some got out by mistake			
❑ B-5100 [PS]	The Beatles' Movie Medley/ Fab Four on Film	1982	20.00
❑ PB-5100 [DJ]	The Beatles' Movie Medley/ Fab Four on Film	1982	25.00
❑ B-5107	The Beatles' Movie Medley/I'm Happy Just to Dance with You	1982	5.00
❑ B-5107 [PS]	The Beatles' Movie Medley/I'm Happy Just to Dance with You	1982	5.00
❑ 5112	I Want to Hold Your Hand/ I Saw Her Standing There	1964	30.00
—Third pressings credit "Gil Music" as B-side publisher			
❑ 5112	I Want to Hold Your Hand/ I Saw Her Standing There	1964	35.00
—Second pressing credits "George Pincus and Sons" as B-side publisher			
❑ 5112	I Want to Hold Your Hand/ I Saw Her Standing There	1964	40.00
—First pressing credits "Walter Hofer" as B-side publisher			
❑ 5112	I Want to Hold Your Hand/ I Saw Her Standing There	1968	60.00
—Orange and yellow swirl label with "A Subsidiary Of" in perimeter print			
❑ 5112	I Want to Hold Your Hand/ I Saw Her Standing There	1969	25.00
—Red and orange "target" label, round logo			
❑ 5112	I Want to Hold Your Hand/ I Saw Her Standing There	1969	60.00
—Red and orange "target" label, dome logo			
❑ 5112	I Want to Hold Your Hand/ I Saw Her Standing There	1976	10.00
—Orange label, "Capitol" logo on bottom			
❑ 5112	I Want to Hold Your Hand/ I Saw Her Standing There	1978	15.00
—Purple label			
❑ 5112	I Want to Hold Your Hand/ I Saw Her Standing There	1984	5.00
—20th anniversary reissue; black print on perimeter of label (1964 pressings are white)			
❑ 5112	I Want to Hold Your Hand/ I Saw Her Standing There	1994	5.00
—30th anniversary reissue; has "7243-8-58123-7-8" engraved in record's trail-off area			
❑ 5112 [PS]	I Want to Hold Your Hand/ I Saw Her Standing There	1964	100.00
—Die-cut, crops George Harrison's head in photo			
❑ 5112 [PS]	I Want to Hold Your Hand/I Saw Her Standing There	1964	100.00
—Straight cut, shows all of George Harrison's head			
❑ 5112 [PS]	I Want to Hold Your Hand/ WMCA Good Guys	1964	2000.
—Giveaway from New York radio station with photo of WMCA DJs on rear			
❑ 5112 [PS]	I Want to Hold Your Hand/ I Saw Her Standing There	1984	6.00
—Same as 1964 sleeve except has "1984" in small print, and Paul McCartney's cigarette is airbrushed out			
❑ 5112 [PS]	I Want to Hold Your Hand/ I Saw Her Standing There	1994	4.00
—Same as 1964 sleeve except "Reg. U.S. Pat. Off." has periods (1964s do not). Also came with a plastic sleeve with a "30th Anniversary" and UPC stickers (add 25%)			
❑ 5150	Can't Buy Me Love/ You Can't Do That	1964	30.00
—Original: Orange and yellow swirl, without "A Subsidiary Of"... in perimeter label print			
❑ 5150	Can't Buy Me Love/ You Can't Do That	1968	50.00
—Orange and yellow swirl label with "A Subsidiary Of" in perimeter print			
❑ 5150	Can't Buy Me Love/ You Can't Do That	1969	25.00
—Red and orange "target" label, dome logo			
❑ 5150	Can't Buy Me Love/ You Can't Do That	1969	60.00
—Red and orange "target" label, round logo			
❑ 5150	Can't Buy Me Love/ You Can't Do That	1976	6.00
—Orange label with "Capitol" at bottom			
❑ 5150	Can't Buy Me Love/ You Can't Do That	1978	15.00
—Purple label			
❑ 5150 [PS]	Can't Buy Me Love/ You Can't Do That	1964	800.00
—One of the rarest Beatles picture sleeves. Numerous counterfeits exist; if in doubt, see an expert.			
❑ 5150	Can't Buy Me Love/ You Can't Do That	1964	2000.
—Yellow and black vinyl (unauthorized); value is conjecture. VG 1000; VG+ 1500			
❑ 5150	Can't Buy Me Love/ You Can't Do That	1964	4000.
—Yellow vinyl (unauthorized); value is conjecture. VG 2000; VG+ 3000			
❑ B-5189	Love Me Do/P.S. I Love You	1982	5.00
—Original: Orange and yellow swirl label, black print			
❑ B-5189	Love Me Do/P.S. I Love You	1983	6.00
—Black label with colorband			
❑ B-5189	Love Me Do/P.S. I Love You	1988	4.00
—Purple label; label has smooth edge			
❑ B-5189 [PS]	Love Me Do/P.S. I Love You	1982	5.00
❑ PB-5189 [DJ]	Love Me Do (same on both sides)	1982	15.00
❑ 5222	A Hard Day's Night/I Should Have Known Better	1964	30.00
—Orange and yellow swirl, without "A Subsidiary Of"... in perimeter label print; second version credited only "Maclen" as publishers			
❑ 5222	A Hard Day's Night/I Should Have Known Better	1964	30.00
—Original: Orange and yellow swirl, without "A Subsidiary Of"... in perimeter label print; first version credited both "Unart" and "Maclen" as publishers			
❑ 5222	A Hard Day's Night/I Should Have Known Better	1968	50.00
—Orange and yellow swirl with "A Subsidiary Of"... on perimeter print in white			
❑ 5222	A Hard Day's Night/I Should Have Known Better	1968	100.00
—Orange and yellow swirl with "A Subsidiary Of"... on perimeter print in black			
❑ 5222	A Hard Day's Night/I Should Have Known Better	1969	20.00
—Red and orange "target" label with Capitol round logo			
❑ 5222	A Hard Day's Night/I Should Have Known Better	1969	60.00
—Red and orange "target" label with Capitol dome logo			
❑ 5222	A Hard Day's Night/I Should Have Known Better	1976	6.00
—Orange label with "Capitol" at bottom			
❑ 5222	A Hard Day's Night/I Should Have Known Better	1978	15.00
—Purple label			
❑ 5222 [PS]	A Hard Day's Night/I Should Have Known Better	1964	100.00
❑ 5234	I'll Cry Instead/I'm Happy Just to Dance with You	1964	40.00
—Original: Orange and yellow swirl, without "A Subsidiary Of"... in perimeter label print			
❑ 5234	I'll Cry Instead/I'm Happy Just to Dance with You	1968	60.00
—Orange and yellow swirl label with "A Subsidiary Of" in perimeter print			
❑ 5234	I'll Cry Instead/I'm Happy Just to Dance with You	1969	20.00
—Red and orange "target" label with Capitol round logo			
❑ 5234	I'll Cry Instead/I'm Happy Just to Dance with You	1969	70.00
—Red and orange "target" label with Capitol dome logo			
❑ 5234	I'll Cry Instead/I'm Happy Just to Dance with You	1976	6.00
—Orange label with "Capitol" at bottom			
❑ 5234	I'll Cry Instead/I'm Happy Just to Dance with You	1978	15.00
—Purple label			
❑ 5234 [PS]	I'll Cry Instead/I'm Happy Just to Dance with You	1964	150.00
❑ 5235	And I Love Her/If I Fell	1964	30.00
—Original: Orange and yellow swirl, without "A Subsidiary Of"... in perimeter label print; publishers listed as "Maclen" only			
❑ 5235	And I Love Her/If I Fell	1964	30.00
—Original: Orange and yellow swirl, without "A Subsidiary Of"... in perimeter label print; publishers listed as "Unart" and "Maclen"			
❑ 5235	And I Love Her/If I Fell	1968	50.00
—Orange and yellow swirl with "A Subsidiary Of"... on perimeter print in white			
❑ 5235	And I Love Her/If I Fell	1968	75.00
—Orange and yellow swirl with "A Subsidiary Of"... on perimeter print in black			
❑ 5235	And I Love Her/If I Fell	1969	20.00
—Red and orange "target" label with Capitol dome logo			
❑ 5235	And I Love Her/If I Fell	1969	60.00
—Red and orange "target" label with Capitol round logo			
❑ 5235	And I Love Her/If I Fell	1976	6.00
—Orange label with "Capitol" at bottom			
❑ 5235	And I Love Her/If I Fell	1978	15.00
—Purple label			
❑ 5235 [PS]	And I Love Her/If I Fell	1964	120.00
❑ 5255	Matchbox/Slow Down	1964	30.00
—Original: Orange and yellow swirl, without "A Subsidiary Of"... in perimeter label print			
❑ 5255	Matchbox/Slow Down	1968	50.00
—Orange and yellow swirl label with "A Subsidiary Of" in perimeter print			
❑ 5255	Matchbox/Slow Down	1969	20.00
—Red and orange "target" label with Capitol round logo			
❑ 5255	Matchbox/Slow Down	1969	60.00
—Red and orange "target" label with Capitol dome logo			
❑ 5255	Matchbox/Slow Down	1976	6.00
—Orange label with "Capitol" at bottom			
❑ 5255	Matchbox/Slow Down	1978	15.00
—Purple label			
❑ 5255 [PS]	Matchbox/Slow Down	1964	150.00
❑ 5327	I Feel Fine/She's a Woman	1964	30.00
—Original: Orange and yellow swirl, without "A Subsidiary Of"... in perimeter label print			
❑ 5327	I Feel Fine/She's a Woman	1968	50.00
—Orange and yellow swirl label with "A Subsidiary Of" in perimeter print			
❑ 5327	I Feel Fine/She's a Woman	1969	20.00
—Red and orange "target" label with Capitol dome logo			
❑ 5327	I Feel Fine/She's a Woman	1969	60.00
—Red and orange "target" label with Capitol round logo			
❑ 5327	I Feel Fine/She's a Woman	1976	6.00
—Orange label with "Capitol" at bottom			
❑ 5327	I Feel Fine/She's a Woman	1978	15.00
—Purple label			
❑ 5327 [PS]	I Feel Fine/She's a Woman	1964	80.00
❑ 5371	Eight Days a Week/I Don't Want to Spoil the Party	1965	30.00
—Original: Orange and yellow swirl, without "A Subsidiary Of"... in perimeter label print			
❑ 5371	Eight Days a Week/I Don't Want to Spoil the Party	1968	50.00
—Orange and yellow swirl label with "A Subsidiary Of" in perimeter print			
❑ 5371	Eight Days a Week/I Don't Want to Spoil the Party	1969	20.00
—Red and orange "target" label with Capitol round logo			
❑ 5371	Eight Days a Week/I Don't Want to Spoil the Party	1969	60.00
—Red and orange "target" label with Capitol dome logo			
❑ 5371	Eight Days a Week/I Don't Want to Spoil the Party	1976	6.00
—Orange label with "Capitol" at bottom			
❑ 5371	Eight Days a Week/I Don't Want to Spoil the Party	1978	15.00
—Purple label			
❑ 5371 [PS]	Eight Days a Week/I Don't Want to Spoil the Party	1965	25.00
—Die-cut sleeve			
❑ 5371 [PS]	Eight Days a Week/I Don't Want to Spoil the Party	1965	75.00
—Straight-cut sleeve			
❑ 5407	Ticket to Ride/Yes It Is	1965	30.00
—Original: Orange and yellow swirl, without "A Subsidiary Of"... in perimeter label print			
❑ 5407	Ticket to Ride/Yes It Is	1968	50.00
—Orange and yellow swirl with "A Subsidiary Of"... on perimeter print in white			
❑ 5407	Ticket to Ride/Yes It Is	1968	100.00
—Orange and yellow swirl with "A Subsidiary Of"... on perimeter print in black			
❑ 5407	Ticket to Ride/Yes It Is	1969	20.00
—Red and orange "target" label with Capitol round logo			
❑ 5407	Ticket to Ride/Yes It Is	1969	60.00
—Red and orange "target" label with Capitol dome logo			
❑ 5407	Ticket to Ride/Yes It Is	1976	6.00
—Orange label with "Capitol" at bottom			
❑ 5407	Ticket to Ride/Yes It Is	1978	15.00
—Purple label			
❑ 5407 [PS]	Ticket to Ride/Yes It Is	1965	100.00
❑ B-5439 [PS]	Leave My Kitten Alone/ Ob-La-Di, Ob-La-Da	1985	50.00
—Sleeve for a record that was never released, not even as a promo			
❑ 5476	Help!/I'm Down	1965	30.00
—Original: Orange and yellow swirl, without "A Subsidiary Of"... in perimeter label print			
❑ 5476	Help!/I'm Down	1968	50.00
—Orange and yellow swirl with "A Subsidiary Of"... on perimeter print in white			

Except when noted otherwise, VG = 25% of NM, and VG+ = 50% of NM. (Example: VG = $2.00, VG+ = $4.00 and NM = $8.00.)

Number	Title (A Side/B Side)	Yr	NM
❑ 5476	Help!/I'm Down	1968	100.00
—Orange and yellow swirl with "A Subsidiary Of"... on perimeter print in black			
❑ 5476	Help!/I'm Down	1969	20.00
—Red and orange "target" label with Capitol round logo			
❑ 5476	Help!/I'm Down	1969	60.00
—Red and orange "target" label with Capitol dome logo			
❑ 5476	Help!/I'm Down	1976	6.00
—Orange label with "Capitol" at bottom			
❑ 5476	Help!/I'm Down	1978	15.00
—Purple label			
❑ 5476 [PS]	Help!/I'm Down	1965	75.00
❑ 5498	Yesterday/Act Naturally	1965	30.00
—Original: Orange and yellow swirl, without "A Subsidiary Of"... in perimeter label print			
❑ 5498	Yesterday/Act Naturally	1968	50.00
—Orange and yellow swirl with "A Subsidiary Of"... on perimeter print in white			
❑ 5498	Yesterday/Act Naturally	1968	100.00
—Orange and yellow swirl with "A Subsidiary Of"... on perimeter print in black			
❑ 5498	Yesterday/Act Naturally	1969	20.00
—Red and orange "target" label with Capitol round logo			
❑ 5498	Yesterday/Act Naturally	1969	60.00
—Red and orange "target" label with Capitol dome logo			
❑ 5498	Yesterday/Act Naturally	1976	6.00
—Orange label with "Capitol" at bottom			
❑ 5498	Yesterday/Act Naturally	1978	15.00
—Purple label			
❑ 5498 [PS]	Yesterday/Act Naturally	1965	100.00
❑ 5555	We Can Work It Out/Day Tripper	1965	30.00
—Original: Orange and yellow swirl, without "A Subsidiary Of"... in perimeter label print			
❑ 5555	We Can Work It Out/Day Tripper	1968	50.00
—Orange and yellow swirl label with "A Subsidiary Of" in perimeter print			
❑ 5555	We Can Work It Out/Day Tripper	1969	20.00
—Red and orange "target" label with Capitol round logo			
❑ 5555	We Can Work It Out/Day Tripper	1969	60.00
—Red and orange "target" label with Capitol dome logo			
❑ 5555	We Can Work It Out/Day Tripper	1969	1500.
—Red and white "Starline" label (mispress)			
❑ 5555	We Can Work It Out/Day Tripper	1976	6.00
—Orange label with "Capitol" at bottom			
❑ 5555	We Can Work It Out/Day Tripper	1978	15.00
—Purple label			
❑ 5555 [PS]	We Can Work It Out/Day Tripper	1965	60.00
❑ 5587	Nowhere Man/What Goes On	1966	25.00
—Original: Orange and yellow swirl, without "A Subsidiary Of"... in perimeter label print; composers of B-side listed as "John Lennon-Paul McCartney"			
❑ 5587	Nowhere Man/What Goes On	1966	50.00
—Orange and yellow swirl, without "A Subsidiary Of"... in perimeter label print; B-side composers listed as "Lennon-McCartney-Starkey"			
❑ 5587	Nowhere Man/What Goes On	1968	50.00
—Orange and yellow swirl label with "A Subsidiary Of" in perimeter print			
❑ 5587	Nowhere Man/What Goes On	1969	20.00
—Red and orange "target""target" label with Capitol round logo			
❑ 5587	Nowhere Man/What Goes On	1969	60.00
—Red and orange "target" label with Capitol dome logo			
❑ 5587	Nowhere Man/What Goes On	1976	6.00
—Orange label with "Capitol" at bottom			
❑ 5587	Nowhere Man/What Goes On	1978	15.00
—Purple label			
❑ 5587 [PS]	Nowhere Man/What Goes On	1966	40.00
❑ B-5624	Twist and Shout/There's a Place	1986	5.00
—Black label with colorband			
❑ B-5624	Twist and Shout/There's a Place	1988	5.00
—Purple label; label has smooth edge			
❑ P-B-5624 [DJ]	Twist and Shout (same on both sides)	1986	15.00
❑ 5651	Paperback Writer/Rain	1966	25.00
—Original: Orange and yellow swirl, without "A Subsidiary Of"... in perimeter label print			
❑ 5651	Paperback Writer/Rain	1968	50.00
—Orange and yellow swirl with "A Subsidiary Of"... on perimeter print in white			
❑ 5651	Paperback Writer/Rain	1968	100.00
—Orange and yellow swirl with "A Subsidiary Of"... on perimeter print in black			
❑ 5651	Paperback Writer/Rain	1969	20.00
—Red and orange "target" label with Capitol round logo			
❑ 5651	Paperback Writer/Rain	1969	60.00
—Red and orange "target" label with Capitol dome logo			
❑ 5651	Paperback Writer/Rain	1976	6.00
—Orange label with "Capitol" at bottom			
❑ 5651	Paperback Writer/Rain	1978	15.00
—Purple label			
❑ 5651 [PS]	Paperback Writer/Rain	1966	75.00
❑ 5715	Yellow Submarine/Eleanor Rigby	1966	25.00
—Original: Orange and yellow swirl, without "A Subsidiary Of"... in perimeter label print; print on perimeter is white			
❑ 5715	Yellow Submarine/Eleanor Rigby	1966	50.00
—Orange and yellow swirl, without "A Subsidiary Of"... in perimeter label print; print on perimeter is yellow (mispress)			
❑ 5715	Yellow Submarine/Eleanor Rigby	1968	50.00
—Orange and yellow swirl label with "A Subsidiary Of" in perimeter print			
❑ 5715	Yellow Submarine/Eleanor Rigby	1969	20.00
—Red and orange "target" label with Capitol dome logo			

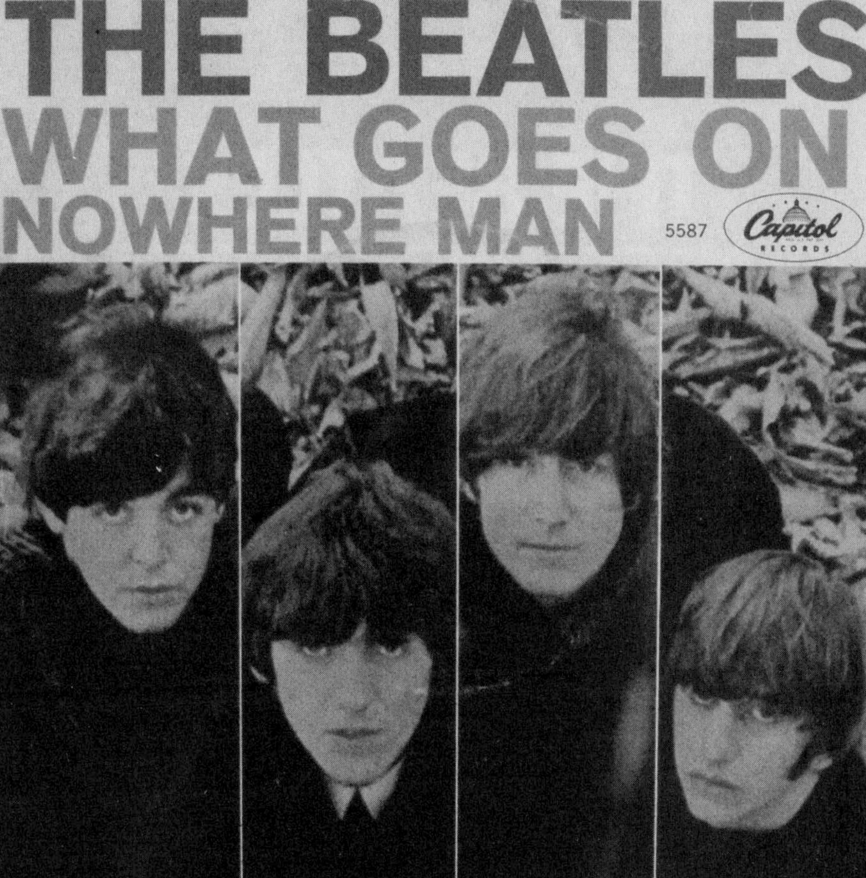

The Beatles, "Nowhere Man," Capitol 5587, 1966, **$40.**

Number	Title (A Side/B Side)	Yr	NM
❑ 5715	Yellow Submarine/Eleanor Rigby	1969	60.00
—Red and orange "target" label with Capitol round logo			
❑ 5715	Yellow Submarine/Eleanor Rigby	1976	6.00
—Orange label with "Capitol" at bottom			
❑ 5715	Yellow Submarine/Eleanor Rigby	1978	15.00
—Purple label			
❑ 5715 [PS]	Yellow Submarine/Eleanor Rigby	1966	100.00
❑ 5810	Penny Lane/Strawberry Fields Forever	1967	25.00
—Original: Orange and yellow swirl, without "A Subsidiary Of"... in perimeter label print; "Penny Lane" time listed as 3:00			
❑ 5810	Penny Lane/Strawberry Fields Forever	1967	30.00
—Orange and yellow swirl, without "A Subsidiary Of"... in perimeter label print; "Penny Lane" time listed as 2:57			
❑ 5810	Penny Lane/Strawberry Fields Forever	1968	50.00
—Orange and yellow swirl label with "A Subsidiary Of" in perimeter print			
❑ 5810	Penny Lane/Strawberry Fields Forever	1969	20.00
—Red and orange "target" label with Capitol round logo			
❑ 5810	Penny Lane/Strawberry Fields Forever	1969	60.00
—Red and orange "target" label with Capitol dome logo			
❑ 5810	Penny Lane/Strawberry Fields Forever	1976	6.00
—Orange label with "Capitol" at bottom			
❑ 5810	Penny Lane/Strawberry Fields Forever	1978	15.00
—Purple label			
❑ 5810 [PS]	Penny Lane/Strawberry Fields Forever	1967	100.00
❑ P 5810 [DJ]	Penny Lane/Strawberry Fields Forever	1967	300.00
—Light green promo; most copies have an extra trumpet solo at the end of "Penny Lane"			
❑ P 5810 [DJ]	Penny Lane/Strawberry Fields Forever	1967	600.00
—Light green promo; a few copies have no trumpet solo at the end of "Penny Lane"			

Number	Title (A Side/B Side)	Yr	NM
❑ 5964	All You Need Is Love/Baby, You're a Rich Man	1967	25.00
—Original: Orange and yellow swirl, without "A Subsidiary Of"... in perimeter label print			
❑ 5964	All You Need Is Love/Baby, You're a Rich Man	1968	50.00
—Orange and yellow swirl label with "A Subsidiary Of" in perimeter print			
❑ 5964	All You Need Is Love/Baby, You're a Rich Man	1969	20.00
—Red and orange "target" label with Capitol round logo			
❑ 5964	All You Need Is Love/Baby, You're a Rich Man	1969	75.00
—Red and orange "target" label with Capitol dome logo			
❑ 5964	All You Need Is Love/Baby, You're a Rich Man	1976	6.00
—Orange label with "Capitol" at bottom			
❑ 5964	All You Need Is Love/Baby, You're a Rich Man	1978	15.00
—Purple label			
❑ 5964 [PS]	All You Need Is Love/Baby, You're a Rich Man	1967	40.00
❑ P 5964 [DJ]	All You Need Is Love/Baby, You're a Rich Man	1967	250.00
—Light green label promo			
❑ S7-17488	Birthday/Taxman	1994	4.00
—Green vinyl			
❑ S7-17488	Birthday/Taxman	1994	50.00
—Black vinyl "error" pressing			
❑ S7-17688	She Loves You/I'll Get You	1994	4.00
—Red vinyl			
❑ S7-17689	I Want to Hold Your Hand/This Boy	1994	4.00
—Clear vinyl			
❑ S7-17690	Can't Buy Me Love/You Can't Do That	1994	4.00
—Gren vinyl			
❑ S7-17691	Help!/I'm Down	1994	4.00
—White vinyl			
❑ S7-17692	A Hard Day's Night/Things We Said Today	1994	4.00
—White vinyl			

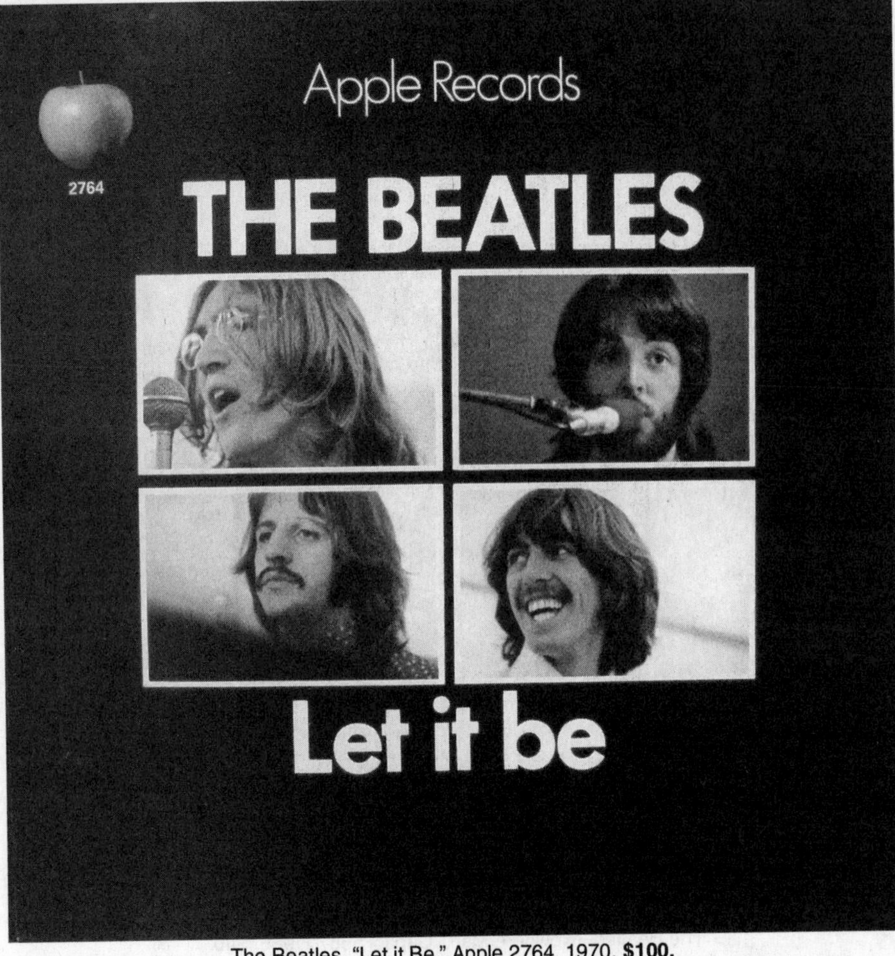

The Beatles, "Let it Be," Apple 2764, 1970, **$100.**

Number	Title (A Side/B Side)	Yr	NM
❑ S7-17693	All You Need Is Love/Baby You're a Rich Man	1994	4.00
—Pink vinyl			
❑ S7-17694	Hey Jude/Revolution	1994	4.00
—Blue vinyl			
❑ S7-17695	Let It Be/You Know My Name (Look Up My Number)	1994	4.00
—Yellow vinyl			
❑ S7-17696	Yellow Submarine/Eleanor Rigby	1994	4.00
—Yellow vinyl			
❑ S7-17697	Strawberry Fields Forever/Penny Lane	1994	4.00
—Red vinyl			
❑ S7-17698	Something/Come Together	1994	4.00
—Blue vinyl			
❑ S7-17699	Twist and Shout/There's a Place	1994	4.00
—Pink vinyl			
❑ S7-17700	Here Comes the Sun/Octopus's Garden	1994	4.00
—Gold/orange vinyl			
❑ S7-17701	Sgt. Pepper's Lonely Hearts Club Band-With a Little Help from My Friends/A Day in the Life	1994	4.00
—Clear vinyl			
❑ S7-18888	Norwegian Wood/If I Needed Someone	1995	150.00
—Green vinyl; 1,000 pressed, given by Collectors' Choice Music to buyers of Beatles reissue LPs			
❑ S7-18889	You've Got to Hide Your Love Away/I've Just Seen a Face	1996	4.00
—Gold/orange vinyl			
❑ S7-18890	Magical Mystery Tour/The Fool on the Hill	1996	4.00
—Yellow vinyl			
❑ S7-18891	Across the Universe/Two of Us	1996	4.00
—Clear vinyl			
❑ S7-18892	While My Guitar Gently Weeps/Blackbird	1996	4.00
—Blue vinyl			
❑ S7-18893	It's All Too Much/Only a Northern Song	1996	4.00
—Blue vinyl			
❑ S7-18894	Nowhere Man/What Goes On	1996	4.00
—Green vinyl			

Number	Title (A Side/B Side)	Yr	NM
❑ S7-18895	We Can Work It Out/Day Tripper	1996	4.00
—Pink vinyl			
❑ S7-18896	Lucy in the Sky with Diamonds/When I'm 64	1996	4.00
—Red vinyl			
❑ S7-18897	Here, There and Everywhere/Good Day Sunshine	1996	4.00
—Yellow vinyl			
❑ S7-18898	The Long and Winding Road/For You Blue	1996	4.00
—Blue vinyl			
❑ S7-18899	Got to Get You Into My Life/Helter Skelter	1996	4.00
—Gold/orange vinyl			
❑ S7-18900	Ob-La-Di, Ob-La-Da/Julia	1996	4.00
—Clear vinyl			
❑ S7-18901	Yesterday/Act Naturally	1996	4.00
—Pink vinyl			
❑ S7-18902	Paperback Writer/Rain	1996	4.00
—Red vinyl			
❑ S7-19341	Norwegian Wood (This Bird Has Flown)/If I Needed Someone	1996	3.00
❑ S7-56785	Love Me Do/P.S. I Love You	1992	4.00
❑ S7-56785	Love Me Do/P.S. I Love You	1992	30.00
—Small pressing on red vinyl "by mistake"			
❑ 72133	Roll Over Beethoven/Please Mister Postman	1964	50.00
—Orange and yellow swirl; Canadian release that was heavily imported to the U.S.			
❑ 72144	All My Loving/This Boy	1964	50.00
—Orange and yellow swirl; Canadian release that was heavily imported to the U.S.			
❑ 72144	All My Loving/This Boy	1971	100.00
—Canadian number with U.S. labels (red and orange "target" label)			
❑ 7PRO-79551/2 [DJ]	Love Me Do/P.S. I Love You	1992	25.00
❑ 7PRO-79551/2 [PS]	Love Me Do/P.S. I Love You	1992	25.00
CAPITOL STARLINE			
❑ 6061	Twist and Shout/There's a Place	1965	120.00
—Green swirl label			
❑ 6062	Love Me Do/P.S. I Love You	1965	120.00
—Green swirl label			

Number	Title (A Side/B Side)	Yr	NM
❑ 6063	Please Please Me/From Me to You	1965	120.00
—Green swirl label			
❑ 6064	Do You Want to Know a Secret/Thank You Girl	1965	120.00
—Green swirl label			
❑ 6065	Roll Over Beethoven/Misery	1965	120.00
—Green swirl label			
❑ 6065	Roll Over Beethoven/Misery	1971	30.00
—Red and orange "target" label			
❑ 6066	Boys/Kansas City	1965	80.00
—Green swirl label			
❑ 6066	Boys/Kansas City	1971	30.00
—Red and orange "target" label			
❑ 6278	I Want to Hold Your Hand/I Saw Her Standing There	1981	20.00
—Originals have blue labels			
❑ 6279	Can't Buy Me Love/You Can't Do That	1981	8.00
—Originals have blue labels			
❑ 6281	A Hard Day's Night/I Should Have Known Better	1981	8.00
—Originals have blue labels			
❑ 6282	I'll Cry Instead/I'm Happy Just to Dance with You	1981	8.00
—Originals have blue labels			
❑ 6283	And I Love Her/If I Fell	1981	8.00
—Originals have blue labels			
❑ 6284	Matchbox/Slow Down	1981	8.00
—Originals have blue labels			
❑ 6286	I Feel Fine/She's a Woman	1981	8.00
—Originals have blue labels			
❑ 6287	Eight Days a Week/I Don't Want to Spoil the Party	1981	8.00
—Originals have blue labels			
❑ 6288	Ticket to Ride/Yes It Is	1981	8.00
—Originals have blue labels			
❑ 6290	Help!/I'm Down	1981	8.00
—Originals have blue labels			
❑ 6291	Yesterday/Act Naturally	1981	8.00
—Originals have blue labels			
❑ 6293	We Can Work It Out/Day Tripper	1981	8.00
—Originals have blue labels			
❑ 6294	Nowhere Man/What Goes On	1981	8.00
—Originals have blue labels			
❑ 6296	Paperback Writer/Rain	1981	8.00
—Originals have blue labels			
❑ 6297	Yellow Submarine/Eleanor Rigby	1981	8.00
—Originals have blue labels			
❑ 6299	Penny Lane/Strawberry Fields Forever	1981	8.00
—Originals have blue labels			
❑ 6300	All You Need Is Love/Baby You're a Rich Man	1981	8.00
—Originals have blue labels			
CAPITOL/EVATONE			
❑ 420826cs	All My Loving/You've Got to Hide Your Love Away	1982	10.00
—Flexi-disc issued as giveaway by The Musicland Group; "Musicland" version			
❑ 420826cs	All My Loving/You've Got to Hide Your Love Away	1982	20.00
—Flexi-disc issued as giveaway by The Musicland Group; "Discount" version			
❑ 420826cs	All My Loving/You've Got to Hide Your Love Away	1982	25.00
—Flexi-disc issued as giveaway by The Musicland Group; "Sam Goody" version			
❑ 420827cs	Magical Mystery Tour/Here Comes the Sun	1982	10.00
—Flexi-disc issued as giveaway by The Musicland Group; "Musicland" version			
❑ 420827cs	Magical Mystery Tour/Here Comes the Sun	1982	20.00
—Flexi-disc issued as giveaway by The Musicland Group; "Discount" version			
❑ 420827cs	Magical Mystery Tour/Here Comes the Sun	1982	25.00
—Flexi-disc issued as giveaway by The Musicland Group; "Sam Goody" version			
❑ 420828cs	Rocky Raccoon/Why Don't We Do It in the Road?	1982	10.00
—Flexi-disc issued as giveaway by The Musicland Group; "Musicland" version			
❑ 420828cs	Rocky Raccoon/Why Don't We Do It in the Road?	1982	20.00
—Flexi-disc issued as giveaway by The Musicland Group; "Discount" version			
❑ 420828cs	Rocky Raccoon/Why Don't We Do It in the Road?	1982	25.00
—Flexi-disc issued as giveaway by The Musicland Group; "Sam Goody" version			
❑ 830771 X	Till There Was You/Three Cool Cats	1983	6.00
—Flexi-disc issued as giveaway with a book			
❑ 1214825cs	German Medley	1983	60.00
—Flexi-disc given away by House of Guitars in New York			

Except when noted otherwise, VG = 25% of NM, and VG+ = 50% of NM. (Example: VG = $2.00, VG+ = $4.00 and NM = $8.00.)

B

Number	Title (A Side/B Side)	Yr	NM

CICADELIC/BIODISC

❑ 001 — A Hard Day's Night Open End Interview — 1990 — 15.00
—Limited edition of 700; lower numbers increase value substantially
❑ 001 — A Hard Day's Night Open End Interview — 1990 — 30.00
—"Records Etc." pressing
❑ 002 — Help! Open End Interview — 1990 — 5.00
❑ 002 [PS] — Help! Open End Interview — 1990 — 5.00

COLLECTABLES

❑ 1501 — I'm Gonna Sit Right Down and Cry Over You/Roll Over Beethoven — 1982 — 3.00
❑ 1501 [PS] — I'm Gonna Sit Right Down and Cry Over You/Roll Over Beethoven — 1982 — 3.00
❑ 1502 — Hippy Hippy Shake/Sweet Little Sixteen — 1982 — 3.00
❑ 1502 [PS] — Hippy Hippy Shake/Sweet Little Sixteen — 1982 — 3.00
❑ 1503 — Lend Me Your Comb/Your Feets Too Big — 1982 — 3.00
❑ 1503 [PS] — Lend Me Your Comb/Your Feets Too Big — 1982 — 3.00
❑ 1504 — Where Have You Been All My Life/Mr. Moonlight — 1982 — 3.00
❑ 1504 [PS] — Where Have You Been All My Life/Mr. Moonlight — 1982 — 3.00
❑ 1505 — A Taste of Honey/Besame Mucho — 1982 — 3.00
❑ 1505 [PS] — A Taste of Honey/Besame Mucho — 1982 — 3.00
❑ 1506 — Till There Was You/Everybody's Trying to Be My Baby — 1982 — 3.00
❑ 1506 [PS] — Till There Was You/Everybody's Trying to Be My Baby — 1982 — 3.00
❑ 1507 — Kansas City-Hey Hey Hey Hey/Ain't Nothing Shakin Like the Leaves on a Tree — 1982 — 3.00
❑ 1507 [PS] — Kansas City-Hey Hey Hey Hey/Ain't Nothing Shakin Like the Leaves on a Tree — 1982 — 3.00
❑ 1508 — To Know Her Is To Love Her/Little Queenie — 1982 — 3.00
❑ 1508 [PS] — To Know Her Is To Love Her/Little Queenie — 1982 — 3.00
❑ 1509 — Falling in Love Again/Sheila — 1982 — 3.00
❑ 1509 [PS] — Falling in Love Again/Sheila — 1982 — 3.00
❑ 1510 — Be-Bop-a-Lula/Hallelujah I Love Her So — 1982 — 3.00
❑ 1510 [PS] — Be-Bop-a-Lula/Hallelujah I Love Her So — 1982 — 3.00
❑ 1511 — Red Sails in the Sunset/Matchbox — 1982 — 3.00
❑ 1511 [PS] — Red Sails in the Sunset/Matchbox — 1982 — 3.00
❑ 1512 — Talkin' Bout You/Shimmy Shake — 1982 — 3.00
❑ 1512 [PS] — Talkin' Bout You/Shimmy Shake — 1982 — 3.00
❑ 1513 — Long Tall Sally/I Remember You — 1982 — 3.00
❑ 1513 [PS] — Long Tall Sally/I Remember You — 1982 — 3.00
❑ 1514 — Ask Me Why/Twist and Shout — 1982 — 3.00
❑ 1514 [PS] — Ask Me Why/Twist and Shout — 1982 — 3.00
❑ 1515 — I Saw Her Standing There/Can't Help It "Blue Angel" — 1982 — 3.00
—B-side is actually "Reminiscing"
❑ 1515 [PS] — I Saw Her Standing There/Can't Help It "Blue Angel" — 1982 — 3.00
❑ 1516 — I'll Try Anyway/I Don't Know Why I Do (I Just Do) — 1987 — 10.00
—Despite label credit to The Beatles, both are Peter Best recordings
❑ 1517 — She's Not the Only Girl in Town/More Than I Need Myself — 1987 — 10.00
—Despite label credit to The Beatles, both are Peter Best recordings
❑ 1518 — I'll Have Everything Too/I'm Checking Out Now Baby — 1987 — 10.00
—Despite label credit to The Beatles, both are Peter Best recordings
❑ 1519 — How'd You Get to Know Her Name/If You Can't Get Her — 1987 — 10.00
—Despite label credit to The Beatles, both are Peter Best recordings
❑ 1520 — Cry for a Shadow/Rock and Roll Music — 1987 — 5.00
—Despite label credit to The Beatles, B-side is a Peter Best recording
❑ 1521 — Let's Dance/If You Love Me Baby — 1987 — 6.00
—Despite label credit to The Beatles, A-side is a Tony Sheridan solo recording
❑ 1522 — What'd I Say/Sweet Georgia Brown — 1987 — 6.00
—Despite label credit to The Beatles, A-side is a Tony Sheridan solo recording
❑ 1523 — Ruby Baby/Ya Ya — 1987 — 6.00
—Despite label credit to The Beatles, both are by Tony Sheridan without the Fab Four
❑ 1524 — Why/I'll Try Anyway — 1987 — 6.00
—Despite label credit to The Beatles, B-side is a Peter Best recording

DECCA

❑ 31382 — My Bonnie/The Saints — 1962 — 15000.
—By "Tony Sheridan and the Beat Brothers"; black label with color bars (all-black label with star under "Decca" should be a counterfeit). VG 7500; VG+ 11,250
❑ 31382 [DJ] — My Bonnie/The Saints — 1962 — 3000.
—By "Tony Sheridan and the Beat Brothers"; pink label, star on label under "Decca". VG 1,000; VG+ 2,000

EVA-TONE

❑ 830771X [DJ] — Til There Was You/Three Cool Cats (both on same side) — 1983 — 6.00
—Red plastic flexidisc; issued as giveaway with a Beatles price guide

MGM

❑ 13213 — My Bonnie (My Bonnie Lies Over the Ocean)/The Saints (When the Saints Go Marching In) — 1964 — 40.00
—The Beatles with Tony Sheridan; no reference to LP on label
❑ 13213 — My Bonnie (My Bonnie Lies Over the Ocean)/The Saints (When the Saints Go Marching In) — 1964 — 50.00
—The Beatles with Tony Sheridan; LP number on label
❑ 13213 [DJ] — My Bonnie (My Bonnie Lies Over the Ocean)/The Saints (When the Saints Go Marching In) — 1964 — 300.00
—The Beatles with Tony Sheridan
❑ 13213 [PS] — My Bonnie (My Bonnie Lies Over the Ocean)/The Saints (When the Saints Go Marching In) — 1964 — 120.00
—The Beatles with Tony Sheridan
❑ 13227 — Why/Cry for a Shadow — 1964 — 150.00
—The Beatles with Tony Sheridan
❑ 13227 [DJ] — Why/Cry for a Shadow — 1964 — 250.00
—The Beatles with Tony Sheridan
❑ 13227 [PS] — Why/Cry for a Shadow — 1964 — 400.00
—The Beatles with Tony Sheridan

OLDIES 45

❑ 149 — Do You Want to Know a Secret/Thank You Girl — 1964 — 15.00
❑ 150 — Please Please Me/From Me to You — 1964 — 15.00
❑ 151 — Love Me Do/P.S. I Love You — 1964 — 15.00
❑ 152 — Twist and Shout/There's a Place — 1964 — 15.00

SWAN

❑ 4152 — She Loves You/I'll Get You — 196? — 20.00
—Black label, silver print, "Don't Drop Out" not on label, smaller numbers in trailoff area
❑ 4152 — She Loves You/I'll Get You — 196? — 50.00
—White label, red or maroon print, same as above
❑ 4152 — She Loves You/I'll Get You — 1963 — 600.00
—Semi-glossy white label/blue printing
❑ 4152 — She Loves You/I'll Get You — 1963 — 600.00
—Semi-glossy white label/red print; "Don't Drop Out" not on label
❑ 4152 — She Loves You/I'll Get You — 1963 — 650.00
—Flat white label/red print, "Don't Drop Out" not on label
❑ 4152 — She Loves You/I'll Get You — 1963 — 650.00
—Semi-glossy white label/red print, "Don't Drop Out" on label
❑ 4152 — She Loves You/I'll Get You — 1964 — 30.00
—Black label, silver print, "Don't Drop Out" on label
❑ 4152 — She Loves You/I'll Get You — 1964 — 40.00
—Black label, silver print, "Don't Drop Out" not on label
❑ 4152 — She Loves You/I'll Get You — 1964 — 50.00
—Black label, silver print, "Produced by George Martin" on both labels
❑ 4152 — She Loves You/I'll Get You — 1964 — 50.00
—Black label, silver print, "Produced by George Martin" on only one label
❑ 4152 [DJ] — She Loves You/I'll Get You — 1963 — 450.00
—Thin print, "Don't Drop Out" on label
❑ 4152 [DJ] — She Loves You/I'll Get You — 1963 — 500.00
—Flat white label, no "Don't Drop Out" on label
❑ 4152 [DJ] — She Loves You/I'll Get You — 1963 — 500.00
—Thick print, no "Don't Drop Out" on label
❑ 4152 [DJ] — I'll Get You (one-sided) — 1964 — 600.00
❑ 4152 [PS] — She Loves You/I'll Get You — 1964 — 120.00
❑ 4182 — Sie Liebt Dich (She Loves You)/I'll Get You — 1964 — 150.00
—White label, "(She Loves You)" under "Sie Liebt Dich," wide red print
❑ 4182 — Sie Liebt Dich (She Loves You)/I'll Get You — 1964 — 150.00
—White label, "Sie Liebt Dich (She Loves You)" on one line
❑ 4182 — Sie Liebt Dich (She Loves You)/I'll Get You — 1964 — 150.00
—White label, "(She Loves You)" under "Sie Liebt Dich," narrow print
❑ 4182 — Sie Liebt Dich (She Loves You)/I'll Get You — 1964 — 175.00
—White label, "(She Loves You)" under "Sie Liebt Dich," wide orange print
❑ 4182 [DJ] — Sie Liebt Dich (She Loves You)/I'll Get You — 1964 — 400.00
—White label, "(She Loves You)" under "Sie Liebt Dich"
❑ 4182 [DJ] — Sie Liebt Dich (She Loves You)/I'll Get You — 1964 — 450.00
—White label, "Sie Liebt Dich (She Loves You)" on one line

TOLLIE

❑ 9001 — Twist and Shout/There's a Place — 1964 — 50.00
—Yellow label, black print, "TOLLIE" stands alone
❑ 9001 — Twist and Shout/There's a Place — 1964 — 50.00
—Yellow label, black print, black "tollie" in box
❑ 9001 — Twist and Shout/There's a Place — 1964 — 50.00
—Yellow label, green print, "tollie" lowercase
❑ 9001 — Twist and Shout/There's a Place — 1964 — 50.00
—Yellow label, black print, black "TOLLIE" in thin box
❑ 9001 — Twist and Shout/There's a Place — 1964 — 60.00
—Black label, silver print
❑ 9001 — Twist and Shout/There's a Place — 1964 — 60.00
—Yellow label, black print, purple "tollie" in box
❑ 9001 — Twist and Shout/There's a Place — 1964 — 60.00
—Yellow label, blue print
❑ 9001 — Twist and Shout/There's a Place — 1964 — 75.00
—Yellow label, black print, "TOLLIE" in brackets
❑ 9001 — Twist and Shout/There's a Place — 1964 — 80.00
—Yellow label, green print, "TOLLIE" uppercase
❑ 9001 — Twist and Shout/There's a Place — 1964 — 80.00
—Yellow label, purple print
❑ 9008 — Love Me Do/P.S. I Love You — 1964 — 50.00
—Yellow label, blue/green print
❑ 9008 — Love Me Do/P.S. I Love You — 1964 — 50.00
—Yellow label, black print (any logo or print variation)
❑ 9008 — Love Me Do/P.S. I Love You — 1964 — 60.00
—Black label, silver print
❑ 9008 [DJ] — Love Me Do/P.S. I Love You — 1964 — 400.00
❑ 9008 [PS] — Love Me Do/P.S. I Love You — 1964 — 150.00

UNITED ARTISTS

❑ SP-2357 [DJ] — A Hard Day's Night Theatre Lobby Spot — 1964 — 1500.
❑ UAEP 10029 [DJ] — A Hard Day's Night Open End Interview — 1964 — 1500.
❑ ULP-42370 — Let It Be Radio Spots — 1970 — 1200.

VEE JAY

❑ (no #) [PS] — We Wish You a Merry Christmas and a Happy New Year — 1964 — 80.00
—Used with any Vee Jay or Tollie Beatles single in 1964-65 holiday season
❑ Spec. DJ No. 8 — Ask Me Why/Anna — 1964 — 10000.
—Though it doesn't fit into any known Vee Jay numbering system (other "Spec. DJ No." records are rumored, but none are confirmed), this is an authentic 1964 promotional release. VG 5000; VG+ 7500
❑ 498 — Please Please Me/Ask Me Why — 1963 — 900.00
—Correct spelling; number is "VJ 498"; thick print
❑ 498 — Please Please Me/Ask Me Why — 1963 — 1500.
—Misspelled "The Beattles"; number is "VJ 498"
❑ 498 — Please Please Me/Ask Me Why — 1963 — 1600.
—Correct spelling; number is "#498"
❑ 498 — Please Please Me/Ask Me Why — 1963 — 1600.
—Misspelled "The Beattles"; number is "#498"
❑ 498 [DJ] — Please Please Me/Ask Me Why — 1963 — 1100.
—Misspelled "The Beattles"
❑ 498 — Please Please Me/Ask Me Why — 1963 — 2000.
—Correct spelling; number is "VJ 498"; brackets label. VG 1000; VG+ 1500
❑ 522 — From Me to You/Thank You Girl — 1963 — 600.00
—Black rainbow label; "Vee Jay" in oval
❑ 522 — From Me to You/Thank You Girl — 1963 — 800.00
—Plain black label
❑ 522 — From Me to You/Thank You Girl — 1963 — 900.00
—Black rainbow label; "VJ" in brackets
❑ 522 [DJ] — From Me to You/Thank You Girl — 1963 — 500.00
❑ 581 — Please Please Me/From Me to You — 1964 — 45.00
—Plain black label with two horizontal lines
❑ 581 — Please Please Me/From Me to You — 1964 — 50.00
—Black rainbow label, oval logo
❑ 581 — Please Please Me/From Me to You — 1964 — 60.00
—Plain black label, "VEE JAY" stands alone
❑ 581 — Please Please Me/From Me to You — 1964 — 60.00
—Plain black label, oval logo
❑ 581 — Please Please Me/From Me to You — 1964 — 60.00
—Black rainbow label, brackets logo
❑ 581 — Please Please Me/From Me to You — 1964 — 65.00
—Plain black label, "VJ" stands alone
❑ 581 — Please Please Me/From Me to You — 1964 — 75.00
—Plain black label, brackets logo
❑ 581 — Please Please Me/From Me to You — 1964 — 75.00
—Yellow label
❑ 581 — Please Please Me/From Me to You — 1964 — 160.00
—White label
❑ 581 — Please Please Me/From Me to You — 1964 — 250.00
—Purple label
❑ 581 [DJ] — Please Please Me/From Me to You — 1964 — 600.00
—White label, blue print; "Promotional Copy" on label
❑ 581 [DJ] — Please Please Me/From Me to You — 1964 — 900.00
—White label, blue print; no "Promotional Copy" on label
❑ 581 [PS] — Please Please Me/From Me to You — 1964 — 500.00
❑ 581 [PS] — Please Please Me/From Me to You — 1964 — 2500.
—Special "The Record That Started Beatlemania" promo-only sleeve. VG 1250; VG+ 1875

B

Number	Title (A Side/B Side)	Yr	NM
❑ 587	Do You Want to Know a Secret/ Thank You Girl	1964	40.00

—Black rainbow label, brackets logo

❑ 587 Do You Want to Know a Secret/ Thank You Girl 1964 45.00

—Plain black label with two horizontal lines; "VJ" in brackets

❑ 587 Do You Want to Know a Secret/ Thank You Girl 1964 50.00

—Black rainbow label, oval logo

❑ 587 Do You Want to Know a Secret/ Thank You Girl 1964 50.00

—Plain black label; "VEE JAY" stands alone

❑ 587 Do You Want to Know a Secret/ Thank You Girl 1964 65.00

—Plain black label; "Vee Jay" in oval

❑ 587 Do You Want to Know a Secret/ Thank You Girl 1964 65.00

—Plain black label; "VJ" in brackets

❑ 587 Do You Want to Know a Secret/ Thank You Girl 1964 65.00

—Plain black label; "VJ" stands alone

❑ 587 Do You Want to Know a Secret/ Thank You Girl 1964 65.00

—Yellow label

❑ 587 [DJ] Do You Want to Know a Secret/ Thank You Girl 1964 600.00

❑ 587 [PS] Do You Want to Know a Secret/ Thank You Girl 1964 120.00

—Any copy of this claiming to be a "Promotional Copy" is a fake

7-Inch Extended Plays

CAPITOL

❑ SXA-2047 It Won't Be Long/This Boy/All My Loving//Don't Bother Me/ All I've Got to Do/I Wanna Be Your Man 1964 400.00

—Stereo jukebox edition; small hole, plays at 33 1/3 rpm

❑ SXA-2047 [PS] Meet the Beatles 1964 600.00

—With all jukebox title strips intact (deduct 33 percent if missing, deduct less if material is there but not intact)

❑ SXA-2080 Thank You Girl/Devil in Her Heart/Money (That's What I Want)//Long Tall Sally/I Call Your Name/Please Mister Postman 1964 400.00

—33 1/3 rpm, small hole jukebox edition

❑ SXA-2080 [PS] The Beatles' Second Album 1964 600.00

—With all jukebox title strips intact (deduct 33 percent if missing, deduct less if material is there but not intact)

❑ SXA-2108 I'll Cry Instead/And I Love Her/ Slow Down//If I Fell/Tell Me Why/Matchbox 1964 400.00

—33 1/3 rpm, small hole jukebox edition

❑ SXA-2108 [PS] Something New 1964 600.00

—With all jukebox title strips intact (deduct 33 percent if missing, deduct less if material is there but not intact)

❑ EAP 1-2121 Roll Over Beethoven/This Boy// All My Loving/ Please Mr. Postman 1964 100.00

❑ EAP 1-2121 [PS] Four by the Beatles 1964 300.00

❑ PRO-2548/9 [DJ] Open End Interview with the Beatles 1964 800.00

—33 1/3 rpm, small hole. Authentic copies have colorband along outside of label.

❑ PRO-2548/9 [PS] Open End Interview with the Beatles 1964 1000.

—Contains script for interview. Authentic copies are glossy and have a die-cut thumb tab.

❑ PRO-2598/9 [DJ] The Beatles Second Album Open End Interview 1964 800.00

—33 1/3 rpm, small hole; interview plus three songs from the LP

❑ PRO-2598/9 [PS] The Beatles Second Album Open End Interview 1964 1000.

—Contains script for interview

❑ R-5365 Honey Don't/I'm a Loser// Mr. Moonlight/Everybody's Trying to Be My Baby 1965 80.00

❑ R-5365 [PS] 4-By the Beatles 1965 200.00

POLYDOR

❑ PRO 1113-7 [DJ] Ain't She Sweet/Cry for a Shadow//My Bonnie/ The Saints 1994 25.00

❑ PRO 1113-7 [PS] Backbeat 1994 25.00

—Picture sleeve for above sampler

VEE JAY

❑ 1-903 Misery/Taste of Honey// Ask Me Why/Anna 1964 40.00

—Black rainbow label, oval logo

❑ 1-903 Misery/Taste of Honey// Ask Me Why/Anna 1964 90.00

—Black rainbow label, brackets logo, all titles the same size

❑ 1-903 Misery/Taste of Honey// Ask Me Why/Anna 1964 125.00

—Black rainbow label, brackets logo, "Ask Me Why" in much larger print

❑ 1-903 Misery/Taste of Honey// Ask Me Why/Anna 1964 125.00

—Plain black label, oval logo

Number	Title (A Side/B Side)	Yr	NM
❑ 1-903	Misery/Taste of Honey// Ask Me Why/Anna	1964	150.00

—Plain black label, "VEE JAY" stands alone

❑ 1-903 Misery/Taste of Honey// Ask Me Why/Anna 1964 200.00

—Plain black label, brackets logo

❑ 1-903 [DJ] Misery/Taste of Honey// Ask Me Why/Anna 1964 300.00

—White and blue label, "Ask Me Why" in much larger print

❑ 1-903 [DJ] Misery/Taste of Honey//Ask Me Why/Anna 1964 400.00

—White and blue label, all titles the same size

❑ 1-903 [PS] Souvenir of Their Visit to America 1964 60.00

—Cardboard sleeve

❑ 1-903 [PS] Souvenir of Their Visit to America 1964 8000.

—"Ask Me Why/The Beatles" plugged on promo-only sleeve. VG 4000; VG+ 6000

Albums

APPLE

❑ SBC-100 [M] The Beatles' Christmas Album 1970 400.00

—Fan club issue of the seven Christmas messages; very good counterfeits exist

❑ SWBO-101 [(2)] The Beatles 1968 200.00

—Numbered copy; includes four individual photos and large poster (included in value); because the white cover shows ring wear so readily, this is an EXTREMELY difficult album to find in near-mint condition; second pressing labels have Side 1, Song 5 correctly listed as "The Continuing Story of Bungalow Bill"; VG value 37.50; VG+ value 75

❑ SWBO-101 [(2)] The Beatles 1968 400.00

—Numbered copy; includes four individual photos and large poster (included in value); because the white cover shows ring wear so readily, this is an EXTREMELY difficult album to find in near-mint condition; first pressing label has Side 1, Song 5 incorrectly listed as "Bungalow Bill"; VG value 60; VG+ value 120

❑ SWBO-101 [(2)] The Beatles 197? 60.00

—Un-numbered copy; includes four individual photos and large poster (included in value)

❑ SWBO-101 [(2)] The Beatles 1975 70.00

—With "All Rights Reserved" on labels; title in black on cover; photos and poster of thinner stock than originals

❑ SW-153 [P] Yellow Submarine 1969 50.00

—With Capitol logo on Side 2 bottom. "Only a Northern Song" is rechanneled.

❑ SW-153 [P] Yellow Submarine 1971 20.00

—With "Mfd. by Apple" on label

❑ SW-153 [P] Yellow Submarine 1975 25.00

—With "All Rights Reserved" on label

❑ SO-383 Abbey Road 1969 20.00

—With "Mfd. by Apple" on label; "Her Majesty" IS listed on the label

❑ SO-383 Abbey Road 1969 20.00

—With "Mfd. by Apple" on label; "Her Majesty" is NOT listed on the label

❑ SO-383 Abbey Road 1969 40.00

—With Capitol logo on Side 2 bottom; "Her Majesty" IS listed on both the jacket and the label

❑ SO-383 Abbey Road 1969 75.00

—With Capitol logo on Side 2 bottom; "Her Majesty" is NOT listed on either the jacket or the label

❑ SO-383 Abbey Road 1975 25.00

—With "All Rights Reserved" on label, either in black print or in light print along label edge (both versions exist)

❑ SO-385 [DJ] The Beatles Again 1970 8000.

—Prototype covers with "The Beatles Again" on cover; not released to the general public. This is NOT a standard issue! VG value 4000; VG+ value 6000

❑ SW-385 Hey Jude 1970 20.00

—With "Mfd. by Apple" on label; label calls the LP "Hey Jude"

❑ SW-385 Hey Jude 1970 25.00

—Label calls the LP "The Beatles Again"; record is "SW-385"

❑ SW-385 Hey Jude 1970 40.00

—Label calls the LP "The Beatles Again"; record is "SO-385" (this could be found in retail stores as late as 1973)

❑ SW-385 Hey Jude 1970 75.00

—With Capitol logo on Side 2 bottom; label calls the LP "Hey Jude"

❑ SW-385 Hey Jude 1975 25.00

—With "All Rights Reserved" on label; label calls the LP "Hey Jude"

❑ SKBO-3403 [P] The Beatles 1962-1966 1973 30.00

—Custom red Apple labels. "Love Me Do" and "I Want to Hold Your Hand" are rechanneled; "She Loves You," "A Hard Day's Night," "I Feel Fine" and "Ticket to Ride" are mono; "From Me to You," "Can't Buy Me Love" and everything else is stereo.

❑ SKBO-3403 [P] The Beatles 1962-1966 1975 50.00

—Custom red Apple labels with "All Rights Reserved" on labels

❑ SKBO-3404 [B] The Beatles 1967-1970 1973 30.00

—Custom blue Apple labels. "Hello Goodbye" and "Penny Lane" are mono, all others stereo.

❑ SKBO-3404 [B] The Beatles 1967-1970 1975 50.00

—Custom blue Apple labels with "All Rights Reserved" on labels

❑ SPRO 11206/7 [EP] Anthology 2 Sampler 1996 150.00

—Promo-only collection sent to college radio stations

❑ C1-8-31796 [(2)] Live at the BBC 1994 50.00

❑ AR-34001 Let It Be 1970 25.00

—Red Apple label; originals have "Bell Sound" stamped in trail-off area, counterfeits do not

❑ C1-8-34445 [(3)] Anthology 1 1995 40.00

—All copies distributed in the U.S. were manufactured in the U.K. with no distinguishing marks (some LPs imported directly from the U.K. have "Made in England" stickers, which can be removed easily)

❑ C1-8-34448 [(3)] Anthology 2 1996 40.00

Number	Title (A Side/B Side)	Yr	NM
❑ C1-8-34451 [(3)]	Anthology 3	1996	30.00
❑ C1-97036 [B]	The Beatles 1962-1966	1993	25.00

—Custom red Apple labels; red vinyl; all copies pressed in U.K; U.S. versions have a bar-code sticker over the international bar code on back cover. "Love Me Do," "Please Please Me," "From Me to You" and "She Loves You" are mono; all others are stereo.

❑ C1-97039 The Beatles 1967-1970 1993 25.00

—Custom blue Apple labels; blue vinyl; all copies pressed in U.K.; U.S. versions have a bar-code sticker over the international bar code on back cover

APPLE FILMS

❑ KAL 004 [DJ] The Yellow Submarine (A United Artists Release) 1969 2000.

—One-sided LP with radio spots for movie; VG value 1000; VG+ value 1500

APPLE/CAPITOL

❑ (no #) [(10)] The Beatles Special Limited Edition 1974 1200.

❑ (no #) [(17)] The Beatles 10th Anniversary Box Set 1974 2000.

—VG value 1000; VG+ value 1500

❑ ST 2047 [P] Meet the Beatles! 1968 40.00

—With Capitol logo on Side 2 bottom

❑ ST 2047 [P] Meet the Beatles! 1971 20.00

—With "Mfd. by Apple" on label

❑ ST 2047 [P] Meet the Beatles! 1975 25.00

—With "All Rights Reserved" on label

❑ ST 2080 [P] The Beatles' Second Album 1968 40.00

—With Capitol logo on Side 2 bottom

❑ ST 2080 [P] The Beatles' Second Album 1971 20.00

—With "Mfd. by Apple" on label

❑ ST 2080 [P] The Beatles' Second Album 1975 25.00

—With "All Rights Reserved" on label

❑ ST 2108 [S] Something New 1968 40.00

—With Capitol logo on Side 2 bottom

❑ ST 2108 [S] Something New 1971 20.00

—With "Mfd. by Apple" on label

❑ ST 2108 [S] Something New 1975 25.00

—With "All Rights Reserved" on label

❑ STBO 2222 [(2)P] The Beatles' Story 1968 50.00

—With Capitol logo on bottom of B-side of both records

❑ STBO 2222 [(2)P] The Beatles' Story 1971 30.00

—With "Mfd. by Apple" on labels

❑ STBO 2222 [(2)P] The Beatles' Story 1975 40.00

—With "All Rights Reserved" on labels

❑ ST 2228 [P] Beatles '65 1968 40.00

—With Capitol logo on Side 2 bottom

❑ ST 2228 [P] Beatles '65 1971 20.00

—With "Mfd. by Apple" on label

❑ ST 2228 [P] Beatles '65 1975 25.00

—With "All Rights Reserved" on label

❑ ST 2309 [P] The Early Beatles 1969 40.00

—With Capitol logo on Side 2 bottom

❑ ST 2309 [P] The Early Beatles 1971 20.00

—With "Mfd. by Apple" on label

❑ ST 2309 [P] The Early Beatles 1975 25.00

—With "All Rights Reserved" on label

❑ ST 2358 [P] Beatles VI 1969 40.00

—With Capitol logo on Side 2 bottom

❑ ST 2358 [P] Beatles VI 1971 20.00

—With "Mfd. by Apple" on label

❑ ST 2358 [P] Beatles VI 1975 25.00

—With "All Rights Reserved" on label

❑ SMAS 2386 [P] Help! 1969 40.00

—With Capitol logo on Side 2 bottom

❑ SMAS 2386 [P] Help! 1971 20.00

—With "Mfd. by Apple" on label

❑ SMAS 2386 [P] Help! 1975 25.00

—With "All Rights Reserved" on label

❑ ST 2442 [S] Rubber Soul 1969 40.00

—With Capitol logo on Side 2 bottom

❑ ST 2442 [S] Rubber Soul 1971 20.00

—With "Mfd. by Apple" on label

❑ ST 2442 [S] Rubber Soul 1975 25.00

—With "All Rights Reserved" on label

❑ ST 2553 [P] Yesterday and Today 1969 40.00

—With Capitol logo on Side 2 bottom

❑ ST 2553 [P] Yesterday and Today 1971 20.00

—With "Mfd. by Apple" on label

❑ ST 2553 [P] Yesterday and Today 1975 25.00

—With "All Rights Reserved" on label

❑ ST 2553 [S] Yesterday and Today 1971 25.00

—With "Mfd. by Apple" on label; all 11 tracks are in true stereo. Check for a triangle in the record's trail-off area.

❑ ST 2576 [S] Revolver 1969 40.00

—With Capitol logo on Side 2 bottom

❑ ST 2576 [S] Revolver 1971 20.00

—With "Mfd. by Apple" on label

❑ ST 2576 [S] Revolver 1975 25.00

—With "All Rights Reserved" on label

❑ SMAS 2653 [S] Sgt. Pepper's Lonely Hearts Club Band 1969 40.00

—With Capitol logo on Side 2 bottom

❑ SMAS 2653 [S] Sgt. Pepper's Lonely Hearts Club Band 1971 25.00

—With "Mfd. by Apple" on label

Except when noted otherwise, VG = 25% of NM, and VG+ = 50% of NM. (Example: VG = $2.00, VG+ = $4.00 and NM = $8.00.)

Number	Title (A Side/B Side)	Yr	NM
❑ SMAS 2653 [S]	Sgt. Pepper's Lonely Hearts Club Band	1975	25.00

—With "All Rights Reserved" on label

❑ SMAL 2835 [P] Magical Mystery Tour 1969 40.00
—With Capitol logo on Side 2 bottom; with 24-page booklet
❑ SMAL 2835 [P] Magical Mystery Tour 1971 20.00
—With "Mfd. by Apple" on label; with 24-page booklet
❑ SMAL 2835 [P] Magical Mystery Tour 1975 25.00
—With "All Rights Reserved" on label; with 24-page booklet

ATCO

❑ 33-169 [M] Ain't She Sweet 1964 200.00
❑ 33-169 [M] Ain't She Sweet 1964 1000.
—White label promo
❑ SD 33-169 [P] Ain't She Sweet 1964 400.00
—Tan and purple label; all four Beatles tracks are rechanneled
❑ SD 33-169 [P] Ain't She Sweet 1969 500.00
—Yellow label

AUDIO RARITIES

❑ AR-2452 [M] The Complete Silver Beatles 1982 15.00
—Contains 12 Decca audition tracks

AUDIOFIDELITY

❑ PD-339 [M] First Movement 1982 30.00
—Contains eight Decca audition tracks; picture disc
❑ PHX-339 [M] First Movement 1982 12.00
—Contains eight Decca audition tracks

BACKSTAGE

❑ 2-201 [(2)M] Like Dreamers Do 1982 40.00
—Gatefold package, individually numbered (numbers under 100 increase value significantly)
❑ 2-201 [(2)M] Like Dreamers Do 1982 50.00
—Non-gatefold package
❑ BSR-1111 [DJ] Like Dreamers Do 1982 50.00
—Gray vinyl promo in white sleeve
❑ BSR-1111 [DJ] Like Dreamers Do 1982 50.00
—White vinyl promo in white sleeve
❑ BSR-1111 [(3)M]Like Dreamers Do 1982 60.00
—Two picture discs (10 of 15 Decca audition tracks on one, interviews on the other) and one white-vinyl record (same contests as musical picture disc)
❑ BSR-1111 [(3)M]Like Dreamers Do 1982 100.00
—Same as above, except colored-vinyl LP is gray
❑ BSR-1165 [PD] The Beatles Talk with Jerry G. 1982 25.00
—Picture disc
❑ BSR-1175 [PD] The Beatles Talk with Jerry G., Vol. 2 1983 25.00
—Picture disc

CAPITOL

❑ (no #) [(18)] The Beatles Collection Platinum Series 1984 800.00
❑ BC-13 [(14)] The Beatles Collection 1978 250.00
—American versions have "EMI" and "BC-13" on box spine; imports go for less
❑ SWBO-101 [(2)] The Beatles 1976 30.00
—Orange label; with photos and poster
❑ SWBO-101 [(2)] The Beatles 1978 30.00
—Purple label, large Capitol logo; with photos and poster (some copies have four photos as one perforated sheet)
❑ SWBO-101 [(2)] The Beatles 1983 40.00
—Black label, print in colorband; with photos and poster (some copies have four photos as one perforated sheet)
❑ SW-153 [P] Yellow Submarine 1976 12.00
—Orange label
❑ SW-153 [P] Yellow Submarine 1978 10.00
—Purple label, large Capitol logo
❑ SW-153 [P] Yellow Submarine 1983 15.00
—Black label, print in colorband
❑ SJ-383 Abbey Road 1984 30.00
—New prefix; black label, print in colorband
❑ SO-383 Abbey Road 1976 12.00
—Orange label
❑ SO-383 Abbey Road 1978 10.00
—Purple label, large Capitol logo
❑ SO-383 Abbey Road 1983 15.00
—Black label, print in colorband
❑ SJ-385 Hey Jude 1984 30.00
—New prefix; black label, print in colorband
❑ SW-385 Hey Jude 1976 12.00
—Orange label (all Capitol label versions call the LP "Hey Jude")
❑ SW-385 Hey Jude 1978 10.00
—Purple label, large Capitol logo
❑ SW-385 Hey Jude 1983 50.00
—Black label, print in colorband
❑ ST 2047 [P] Meet the Beatles! 1964 120.00
—Black label with colorband; "Beatles!" on cover in tan to brown print; some labels have "ASCAP" after every title except "I Want to Hold Your Hand"; other labels have "ASCAP" after every title except "I Want to Hold Your Hand," "I Saw Her Standing There" and "I Wanna Be Your Man"; still other labels have "ASCAP" after every title except "I Want to Hold Your Hand" and "I Wanna Be Your Man"; back cover adds "Produced by George Martin" to lower left
❑ ST 2047 [P] Meet the Beatles! 1964 150.00
—Black label with colorband; "Beatles!" on cover in tan to brown print; label has "ASCAP" after every title except "I Want to Hold Your Hand" (BMI); no producer credit on back cover (this is the second edition of this LP)
❑ ST 2047 [P] Meet the Beatles! 1964 400.00
—Black label with colorband; "Beatles!" on cover in tan to brown print; "ASCAP" and "BMI" credits are missing on the label; no producer credit on back cover (this is the first edition of the LP)
❑ ST 2047 [P] Meet the Beatles! 1965 75.00
—Black label with colorband; "Beatles!" on cover in green print; most of these have "Produced by George Martin" on lower left of back cover; many of these have a label giving "BMI" credit to every song except "Don't Bother Me" and "Till There Was You"
❑ ST 2047 [P] Meet the Beatles! 1968 50.00
—Black colorband label; border print adds "A Subsidiary of Capitol Industries Inc."
❑ ST 2047 [P] Meet the Beatles! 1969 40.00
—Lime green label
❑ ST 2047 [P] Meet the Beatles! 1976 12.00
—Orange label
❑ ST 2047 [P] Meet the Beatles! 1978 10.00
—Purple label, large Capitol logo
❑ ST 2047 [P] Meet the Beatles! 1983 15.00
—Black label, print in colorband
❑ ST-8-2047 [P] Meet the Beatles! 1969 200.00
—Capitol Record Club edition; lime green label
❑ ST-8-2047 [P] Meet the Beatles! 1969 500.00
—Capitol Record Club edition; black label with colorband
❑ T 2047 [M] Meet the Beatles! 1964 150.00
—Black label with colorband; "Beatles!" on cover in tan to brown print; some labels have "ASCAP" after every title except "I Want to Hold Your Hand"; other labels have "ASCAP" after every title except "I Want to Hold Your Hand," "I Saw Her Standing There" and "I Wanna Be Your Man"; still other labels have "ASCAP" after every title except "I Want to Hold Your Hand" and "I Wanna Be Your Man"; most of the back covers add "Produced by George Martin" to lower left
❑ T 2047 [M] Meet the Beatles! 1964 200.00
—Black label with colorband; "Beatles!" on cover in tan to brown print; label has "ASCAP" after every title except "I Want to Hold Your Hand" (BMI); no producer credit on back cover (this is the second edition of this LP)
❑ T 2047 [M] Meet the Beatles! 1964 400.00
—Black label with colorband; "Beatles!" on cover in tan to brown print; no producer credit on back cover; "ASCAP" and "BMI" credits are missing on the label (this is the first edition of the LP)
❑ T 2047 [M] Meet the Beatles! 1965 100.00
—Black label with colorband; "Beatles!" on cover in green print; most of these have "Produced by George Martin" on lower left of back cover; many of these have a label giving "BMI" credit to every song except "Don't Bother Me" and "Till There Was You"
❑ ST 2080 [P] The Beatles' Second Album 1964 100.00
—Black label with colorband. "She Loves You," "I'll Get You" and "You Can't Do That" are rechanneled
❑ ST 2080 [P] The Beatles' Second Album 1968 50.00
—Black colorband label; border print adds "A Subsidiary of Capitol Industries Inc."
❑ ST 2080 [P] The Beatles' Second Album 1969 40.00
—Lime green label
❑ ST 2080 [P] The Beatles' Second Album 1976 12.00
—Orange label
❑ ST 2080 [P] The Beatles' Second Album 1978 10.00
—Purple label, large Capitol logo
❑ ST 2080 [P] The Beatles' Second Album 1983 15.00
—Black label, print in colorband
❑ ST-8-2080 [P] The Beatles' Second Album 1964 500.00
—Capitol Record Club edition; black label with colorband
❑ ST-8-2080 [P] The Beatles' Second Album 1969 300.00
—Capitol Record Club edition; lime green label
❑ T 2080 [M] The Beatles' Second Album 1964 180.00
❑ ST 2108 [S] Something New 1964 80.00
—Black label with colorband
❑ ST 2108 [S] Something New 1968 50.00
—Black colorband label; border print adds "A Subsidiary of Capitol Industries Inc."
❑ ST 2108 [S] Something New 1969 40.00
—Lime green label
❑ ST 2108 [S] Something New 1976 12.00
—Orange label
❑ ST 2108 [S] Something New 1978 10.00
—Purple label, large Capitol logo
❑ ST 2108 [S] Something New 1983 15.00
—Black label, print in colorband
❑ ST-8-2108 [S] Something New 1964 300.00
—Capitol Record Club edition; black label with colorband
❑ ST-8-2108 [S] Something New 1969 150.00
—Capitol Record Club edition; lime green label
❑ ST-8-2108 [S] Something New 1969 300.00
—Longines Symphonette edition (will be stated on label); lime green label
❑ T 2108 [M] Something New 1964 150.00
❑ STBO 2222 [(2)P] The Beatles' Story 1964 150.00
—Black label with colorband. Some of the musical snippets are rechanneled.
❑ STBO 2222 [(2)P] The Beatles' Story 1968 80.00
—Black colorband label; border print adds "A Subsidiary of Capitol Industries Inc."
❑ STBO 2222 [(2)P] The Beatles' Story 1969 50.00
—Lime green label
❑ STBO 2222 [(2)P] The Beatles' Story 1976 20.00
—Orange label
❑ STBO 2222 [(2)P] The Beatles' Story 1978 20.00
—Purple label, large Capitol logo
❑ STBO 2222 [(2)P] The Beatles' Story 1983 40.00
—Black label, print in colorband
❑ TBO 2222 [(2)M] The Beatles' Story 1964 200.00
❑ ST 2228 [P] Beatles '65 1964 80.00
—Black label with colorband. "She's a Woman" and "I Feel Fine" are rechanneled.
❑ ST 2228 [P] Beatles '65 1968 50.00
—Black colorband label; border print adds "A Subsidiary of Capitol Industries Inc."
❑ ST 2228 [P] Beatles '65 1969 40.00
—Lime green label
❑ ST 2228 [P] Beatles '65 1976 12.00
—Orange label
❑ ST 2228 [P] Beatles '65 1978 10.00
—Purple label, large Capitol logo
❑ ST 2228 [P] Beatles '65 1983 15.00
—Black label, print in colorband
❑ T 2228 [M] Beatles '65 1964 120.00
❑ ST 2309 [P] The Early Beatles 1965 100.00
—Black label with colorband. "Love Me Do" and "P.S. I Love You" are rechanneled.
❑ ST 2309 [P] The Early Beatles 1968 50.00
—Black colorband label; border print adds "A Subsidiary of Capitol Industries Inc."
❑ ST 2309 [P] The Early Beatles 1969 40.00
—Lime green label
❑ ST 2309 [P] The Early Beatles 1976 12.00
—Orange label
❑ ST 2309 [P] The Early Beatles 1978 10.00
—Purple label, large Capitol logo
❑ ST 2309 [P] The Early Beatles 1983 25.00
—Black label, print in colorband
❑ T 2309 [M] The Early Beatles 1965 200.00
❑ ST 2358 [M] Beatles VI 1983 15.00
—Black label, print in colorband; plays in mono despite label designation
❑ ST 2358 [M] Beatles VI 1988 80.00
—Purple label, small Capitol logo; plays in mono despite label designation
❑ ST 2358 [P] Beatles VI 1965 75.00
—Black label with colorband; with song titles listed in correct order on back cover. "Yes It Is" is rechanneled.
❑ ST 2358 [P] Beatles VI 1965 80.00
—Black label with colorband; with "See label for correct playing order" on back cover
❑ ST 2358 [P] Beatles VI 1968 50.00
—Black colorband label; border print adds "A Subsidiary of Capitol Industries Inc."
❑ ST 2358 [P] Beatles VI 1969 40.00
—Lime green label
❑ ST 2358 [P] Beatles VI 1976 12.00
—Orange label
❑ ST 2358 [P] Beatles VI 1978 10.00
—Purple label, large Capitol logo
❑ ST-8-2358 [P] Beatles VI 1965 500.00
—Capitol Record Club edition; black label with colorband
❑ ST-8-2358 [P] Beatles VI 1969 400.00
—Capitol Record Club edition; lime green label
❑ T 2358 [M] Beatles VI 1965 100.00
—With song titles listed in correct order on back cover
❑ T 2358 [M] Beatles VI 1965 120.00
—With "See label for correct playing order" on back cover
❑ MAS 2386 [M] Help! 1965 150.00
❑ SMAS 2386 [P] Help! 1965 75.00
—Black label with colorband. Has incidental music by George Martin. "Ticket to Ride" is rechanneled.
❑ SMAS 2386 [P] Help! 1968 50.00
—Black colorband label; border print adds "A Subsidiary of Capitol Industries Inc."
❑ SMAS 2386 [P] Help! 1969 40.00
—Lime green label
❑ SMAS 2386 [P] Help! 1976 12.00
—Orange label
❑ SMAS 2386 [P] Help! 1978 10.00
—Purple label, large Capitol logo
❑ SMAS 2386 [P] Help! 1983 15.00
—Black label, print in colorband
❑ SMAS-8-2386 [P] Help! 1965 400.00
—Capitol Record Club edition; black label with colorband; no "8" on cover
❑ SMAS-8-2386 [P] Help! 1965 600.00
—Capitol Record Club edition; black label with colorband; with "8" on cover
❑ SMAS-8-2386 [P] Help! 1969 200.00
—Capitol Record Club edition; lime green label; no "8" on cover
❑ SMAS-8-2386 [P] Help! 1969 400.00
—Capitol Record Club edition; lime green label; with "8" on cover
❑ SMAS-8-2386 [P] Help! 197? 700.00
—Longines Symphonette edition; with "Mfd. by Longines" and "8" on cover
❑ ST 2442 [S] Rubber Soul 1965 60.00
—Black label with colorband
❑ ST 2442 [S] Rubber Soul 1968 50.00
—Black colorband label; border print adds "A Subsidiary of Capitol Industries Inc."
❑ ST 2442 [S] Rubber Soul 1969 40.00
—Lime green label

Number | Title (A Side/B Side) | Yr | NM

❑ ST 2442 [S] Rubber Soul 1976 12.00
—Orange label
❑ ST-8-2442 [S] Rubber Soul 1965 300.00
—Capitol Record Club edition; black label with colorband
❑ ST-8-2442 [S] Rubber Soul 1969 200.00
—Capitol Record Club edition; lime green label
❑ ST-8-2442 [S] Rubber Soul 1969 250.00
—Longines Symphonette edition (will be stated on label); lime green label
❑ SW 2442 [S] Rubber Soul 1978 10.00
—Purple label, large Capitol logo
❑ SW 2442 [S] Rubber Soul 1983 15.00
—Black label, print in colorband
❑ T 2442 [M] Rubber Soul 1965 120.00
❑ ST 2553 [P] Yesterday and Today 1966 80.00
—Trunk cover; black label with colorband (all later variations have the trunk cover). "I'm Only Sleeping," "Dr. Robert" and "And Your Bird Can Sing" are rechanneled.
❑ ST 2553 [P] Yesterday and Today 1966 1000.
—"Second state" butcher cover (trunk cover pasted over original cover)
❑ ST 2553 [P] Yesterday and Today 1966 1500.
—"Third state" butcher cover (trunk cover removed, leaving butcher cover intact); cover will be about 3/16-inch narrower than other Capitol Beatles LPs; value is highly negotiable depending upon the success of removing the paste-over
❑ ST 2553 [P] Yesterday and Today 1966 8000.
—"First state" butcher cover (never had other cover on top); cover will be the same size as other Capitol Beatles LPs; VG value 4000; VG+ value 6000
❑ ST 2553 [P] Yesterday and Today 1968 50.00
—Black colorband label; border print adds "A Subsidiary of Capitol Industries Inc."
❑ ST 2553 [P] Yesterday and Today 1969 40.00
—Lime green label
❑ ST 2553 [P] Yesterday and Today 1976 12.00
—Orange label; it's possible that this and all future pressings have all 11 tracks in true stereo, but we don't know.
❑ ST 2553 [P] Yesterday and Today 1978 10.00
—Purple label, large Capitol logo
❑ ST 2553 [P] Yesterday and Today 1983 15.00
—Black label, print in colorband
❑ ST-8-2553 [P] Yesterday and Today 1966 300.00
—Capitol Record Club edition; black label with colorband
❑ ST-8-2553 [S] Yesterday and Today 1969 150.00
—Capitol Record Club edition; lime green label; all 11 tracks are in true stereo! (We don't know if the same is true of the black label version.)
❑ T 2553 [M] Yesterday and Today 1966 150.00
—Trunk cover
❑ T 2553 [M] Yesterday and Today 1966 1000.
—"Second state" butcher cover (trunk cover pasted over original cover)
❑ T 2553 [M] Yesterday and Today 1966 1200.
—"Third state" butcher cover (trunk cover removed, leaving butcher cover intact); cover will be about 3/16-inch narrower than other Capitol Beatles LPs; value is highly negotiable depending upon the success of removing the paste-over; VG value 400; VG+ value 800
❑ T 2553 [M] Yesterday and Today 1966 4000.
—"First state" butcher cover (never had other cover on top); cover will be the same size as other Capitol Beatles LPs; VG value 2000; VG+ value 3000
❑ ST 2576 [S] Revolver 1966 100.00
—Black label with colorband
❑ ST 2576 [S] Revolver 1968 50.00
—Black colorband label; border print adds "A Subsidiary of Capitol Industries Inc."
❑ ST 2576 [S] Revolver 1969 40.00
—Lime green label
❑ ST 2576 [S] Revolver 1970 300.00
—Red label with "target" Capitol at top (same design as lime green label)
❑ ST 2576 [S] Revolver 1976 12.00
—Orange label
❑ ST-8-2576 [S] Revolver 1966 400.00
—Capitol Record Club edition; black label with colorband
❑ ST-8-2576 [S] Revolver 1969 120.00
—Capitol Record Club edition; lime green label
❑ ST-8-2576 [S] Revolver 1973? 200.00
—Longines Symphonette edition; orange label (a very late issue, as the club closed in 1974)
❑ SW 2576 [S] Revolver 1978 10.00
—Purple label, large Capitol logo
❑ SW 2576 [S] Revolver 1983 15.00
—Black label, print in colorband
❑ T 2576 [M] Revolver 1966 200.00
❑ 2653 Sgt. Pepper's Lonely Hearts Club Band Cut-Out Inserts 1967 3.00
❑ 2653 Sgt. Pepper's Lonely Hearts Club Band Special Inner Sleeve 1967 15.00
—Red-pink psychedelic sleeve only issued with 1967 (mono and stereo) editions
❑ MAS 2653 [M] Sgt. Pepper's Lonely Hearts Club Band 1967 300.00
❑ SMAS 2653 [S] Sgt. Pepper's Lonely Hearts Club Band 1967 100.00
—Black label with colorband
❑ SMAS 2653 [S] Sgt. Pepper's Lonely Hearts Club Band 1968 60.00
—Black colorband label; border print adds "A Subsidiary of Capitol Industries Inc."
❑ SMAS 2653 [S] Sgt. Pepper's Lonely Hearts Club Band 1969 50.00
—Lime green label
❑ SMAS 2653 [S] Sgt. Pepper's Lonely Hearts Club Band 1976 12.00
—Orange label
❑ SMAS 2653 [S] Sgt. Pepper's Lonely Hearts Club Band 1978 10.00
—Purple label, large Capitol logo. Many copies from 1978 had a "The Original Classic" sticker on shrink wrap; it was added at the time of the release of the bomb movie version of Sgt. Pepper. Double the value if the sticker is still there.
❑ SMAS 2653 [S] Sgt. Pepper's Lonely Hearts Club Band 1983 15.00
—Black label, print in colorband; some of these had "The Original Classic" stickers, too. Add $10 to value if it is there.
❑ MAL 2835 [M] Magical Mystery Tour 1967 300.00
—With 24-page book bound into center of gatefold
❑ SMAL 2835 [P] Magical Mystery Tour 1967 100.00
—Black label with colorband; with 24-page booklet. "Penny Lane," "Baby You're a Rich Man" and "All You Need Is Love" is rechanneled, as is the second half of "I Am the Walrus" (every "stereo" version of "Walrus" is this way)
❑ SMAL 2835 [P] Magical Mystery Tour 1968 60.00
—Black colorband label; border print adds "A Subsidiary of Capitol Industries Inc."; with 24-page booklet
❑ SMAL 2835 [P] Magical Mystery Tour 1969 50.00
—Lime green label; with 24-page booklet
❑ SMAL 2835 [P] Magical Mystery Tour 1976 12.00
—Orange label; with 24-page booklet
❑ SMAL 2835 [P] Magical Mystery Tour 1978 10.00
—Purple label, large Capitol logo; this edition did not come with booklet
❑ SMAL 2835 [P] Magical Mystery Tour 1983 15.00
—Black label, print in colorband; no booklet
❑ SKBO-3403 [P] The Beatles 1962-1966 1976 20.00
—Red labels
❑ SKBO-3403 [P] The Beatles 1962-1966 1976 30.00
—Blue labels (error pressing)
❑ SKBO-3404 [B] The Beatles 1967-1970 1976 20.00
—Blue labels
❑ SPRO-8969 Rarities 1978 50.00
—Purple label, large Capitol logo; part of the U.S. box set The Beatles Collection (BC-13)
❑ SKBO-11537 [(2)] Rock 'n' Roll Music 1976 25.00
❑ SMAS-11638 The Beatles at the Hollywood Bowl 1977 20.00
—Originals with embossed title and ticket on front cover
❑ SMAS-11638 The Beatles at the Hollywood Bowl 1980 15.00
—Second pressing without embossed title and ticket
❑ SMAS-11638 The Beatles at the Hollywood Bowl 1989 40.00
—With UPC code on back cover
❑ SMAS-11638 [DJ] The Beatles at the Hollywood Bowl 1977 500.00
—Advance tan label promo in plain white jacket
❑ SKBL-11711 [(2)P] Love Songs 1977 20.00
—With booklet and embossed, leather-like cover. "P.S. I Love You" and "Yes It Is" are rechanneled.
❑ SKBL-11711 [(2)P] Love Songs 1988 30.00
—With booklet, but without embossed cover
❑ SEAX-11840 [PD] Sgt. Pepper's Lonely Hearts Club Band 1978 20.00
—Picture disc; deduct 25% for cut-outs
❑ SEBX-11841 [(2)] The Beatles 1978 50.00
—White vinyl; with photos and poster (with number "SEBX-11841" on each)
❑ SEBX-11842 [P] The Beatles 1962-1966 1978 40.00
—Red vinyl
❑ SEBX-11843 [B] The Beatles 1967-1970 1978 40.00
—Blue vinyl
❑ SEAX-11900 [PD] Abbey Road 1978 40.00
—Picture disc; deduct 25% for cut-outs
❑ SW-11921 [P] A Hard Day's Night 1979 12.00
—Purple label, large Capitol logo
❑ SW-11921 [P] A Hard Day's Night 1983 15.00
—Black label, print in colorband
❑ SW-11921 [P] A Hard Day's Night 1988 25.00
—Purple label, small Capitol logo
❑ SW-11922 Let It Be 1979 15.00
—Purple label, large Capitol logo; with poster and custom innersleeve
❑ SW-11922 Let It Be 1983 15.00
—Black label, print in colorband; add 33% if poster is included
❑ SW-11922 Let It Be 1988 25.00
—Purple label, small Capitol logo; add 20% if poster and custom innersleeve are included
❑ SN-12009 [DJ] Rarities 1979 300.00
—Green label; withdrawn before official release; all known copies have a plain white sleeve
❑ SHAL-12060 [B] Rarities 1980 15.00
—Same as above, with errors deleted and "Produced by George Martin" added to back cover
❑ SHAL-12060 [B] Rarities 1980 20.00
—Black label with colorband. First pressing says that "There's a Place" debuts in stereo (false) and that the screaming at the end of "Helter Skelter" was a "classic Lennon statement" (it's actually Ringo).
❑ SV-12199 Reel Music 1982 10.00
—Standard issue with 12-page booklet
❑ SV-12199 [DJ] Reel Music 1982 20.00
—Yellow vinyl promo; plain white cover with 12-page booklet
❑ SV-12199 [DJ] Reel Music 1982 40.00
—Yellow vinyl promo; numbered back cover with 12-page booklet
❑ SV-12245 [P] 20 Greatest Hits 1982 20.00
—Purple label, large Capitol logo. "Love Me Do" and "She Loves You" are rechanneled, the other 18 tracks are stereo
❑ SV-12245 [P] 20 Greatest Hits 1983 20.00
—Black label, print in colorband
❑ SV-12245 [P] 20 Greatest Hits 1988 25.00
—Purple label, small Capitol logo
❑ SN-16020 Rock 'n' Roll Music, Vol. 1 1980 10.00
❑ SN-16021 Rock 'n' Roll Music, Vol. 2 1980 10.00
❑ C1-46435 [M] Please Please Me 1995 12.00
—New prefix; Apple logo on back cover
❑ CLJ-46435 [M] Please Please Me 1987 20.00
—Black label, print in colorband; first Capitol version of original British LP
❑ CLJ-46435 [M] Please Please Me 1988 25.00
—Purple label, small Capitol logo
❑ C1-46436 [M] With the Beatles 1995 12.00
—New prefix; Apple logo on back cover
❑ CLJ-46436 [M] With the Beatles 1987 20.00
—Black label, print in colorband; first Capitol version of original British LP
❑ CLJ-46436 [M] With the Beatles 1988 25.00
—Purple label, small Capitol logo
❑ C1-46437 [M] A Hard Day's Night 1995 12.00
—New prefix; Apple logo on back cover
❑ CLJ-46437 [M] A Hard Day's Night 1987 20.00
—Black label, print in colorband; first Capitol version of original British LP
❑ CLJ-46437 [M] A Hard Day's Night 1988 25.00
—Purple label, small Capitol logo
❑ C1-46438 [M] Beatles for Sale 1995 12.00
—New prefix; Apple logo on back cover
❑ CLJ-46438 [M] Beatles for Sale 1987 20.00
—Black label, print in colorband; first Capitol version of original British LP
❑ CLJ-46438 [M] Beatles for Sale 1988 25.00
—Purple label, small Capitol logo
❑ C1-46439 [S] Help! 1995 12.00
—New prefix; Apple logo on back cover
❑ CLJ-46439 [S] Help! 1987 20.00
—Black label, print in colorband; first Capitol version of original British LP
❑ CLJ-46439 [S] Help! 1988 25.00
—Purple label, small Capitol logo
❑ C1-46440 [S] Rubber Soul 1995 12.00
—New prefix; Apple logo on back cover
❑ CLJ-46440 [S] Rubber Soul 1987 20.00
—Black label, print in colorband; first Capitol version of original British LP
❑ CLJ-46440 [S] Rubber Soul 1988 25.00
—Purple label, small Capitol logo
❑ C1-46441 [S] Revolver 1995 12.00
—New prefix; Apple logo on back cover
❑ CLJ-46441 [S] Revolver 1987 20.00
—Black label, print in colorband; first Capitol version of original British LP
❑ CLJ-46441 [S] Revolver 1988 25.00
—Purple label, small Capitol logo
❑ C1-46442 [S] Sgt. Pepper's Lonely Hearts Club Band 1988 25.00
—New number; purple label, small Capitol logo
❑ C1-46442 [S] Sgt. Pepper's Lonely Hearts Club Band 1995 12.00
—With Apple logo on back cover
❑ C1-46443 [(2)] The Beatles 1988 50.00
—New number; purple label, small Capitol logo; with photos and poster (some copies have four photos as one perforated sheet)
❑ C1-46443 [(2)] The Beatles 1995 20.00
—With Apple logo on back cover
❑ C1-46445 [P] Yellow Submarine 1988 25.00
—New number; purple label, small Capitol logo
❑ C1-46445 [P] Yellow Submarine 1995 12.00
—Reissue has the British liner notes, which include a review of the White Album.
❑ C1-46446 Abbey Road 1988 25.00
—New number; purple label, small Capitol logo
❑ C1-46446 Abbey Road 1995 12.00
—Apple logo restored to back cover on reissue
❑ C1-46447 Let It Be 1995 12.00
—New number (the only 1995 reissue with a completely new number)
❑ C1-48062 [P] Magical Mystery Tour 1988 25.00
—New number; purple label, small Capitol logo; no booklet
❑ C1-48062 [P] Magical Mystery Tour 1992 12.00
—With Apple logo on back cover; reissue restores booklet to package
❑ C1-90435 [P] The Beatles 1962-1966 1988 30.00
—New number; purple labels, small Capitol logo
❑ C1-90438 [B] The Beatles 1967-1970 1988 30.00
—New number; purple labels, small Capitol logo
❑ C1-90441 [P] Meet the Beatles! 1988 25.00
—New number; purple label, small Capitol logo
❑ C1-90442 Hey Jude 1988 25.00
—New number; purple label, small Capitol logo
❑ C1-90443 [S] Something New 1988 25.00
—New number; purple label, small Capitol logo
❑ C1-90444 [P] The Beatles' Second Album 1988 25.00
—New number; purple label, small Capitol logo

Number	Title (A Side/B Side)	Yr	NM
❑ C1-90445 [M]	Beatles VI	1988	25.00
—New number; purple label, small Capitol logo; plays in mono despite label designation			
❑ C1-90446 [P]	Beatles '65	1988	25.00
—New number; purple label, small Capitol logo			
❑ C1-90447 [P]	Yesterday and Today	1988	25.00
—New number; purple label, small Capitol logo; stereo content uncertain			
❑ C1-90452 [S]	Revolver	1988	25.00
—New number; purple label, small Capitol logo			
❑ C1-90453 [S]	Rubber Soul	1988	25.00
—New number; purple label, small Capitol logo			
❑ C1-90454 [P]	Help!	1988	25.00
—New number; purple label, small Capitol logo			
❑ C1-91135 [(2)B]	Past Masters Vol. 1 and 2	1988	25.00
—Some early tracks are in mono, but "This Boy," "She's a Woman." "Yes It Is," and "The Inner Light" are in stereo.			
❑ BBX1-91302 [(14)]	The Beatles Deluxe Box Set	1988	300.00
CICADELIC			
❑ 1960	Moviemania	1987	12.00
❑ 1961	Not a Second Time	1987	12.00
❑ 1962	Things We Said Today	1986	12.00
❑ 1963	All Our Loving	1986	12.00
❑ 1964	East Coast Invasion	1985	12.00
❑ 1965	Round the World	1986	12.00
❑ 1966	West Coast Invasion	1985	12.00
❑ 1967	From Britain with Beat!	1987	12.00
❑ 1968	Here, There and Everywhere	1988	12.00
CLARION			
❑ 601 [M]	The Amazing Beatles and Other Great English Group Sounds	1966	100.00
❑ SD 601 [P]	The Amazing Beatles and Other Great English Group Sounds	1966	200.00
—All four Beatles tracks are rechanneled			
GREAT NORTHWEST			
❑ GNW 4007	Beatle Talk	1978	10.00
❑ GNW 4007	Beatle Talk	1978	50.00
—Columbia Record Club edition; "CRC" on spine			
HALL OF MUSIC			
❑ HM-1-2200 [(2)M]	Live 1962, Hamburg, Germany	1981	50.00
—Only American LP with the original Europoean contents — "I Saw Her Standing There," "Twist and Shout," "Ask Me Why" and "Reminiscing" replace the four songs listed with the Lingasong issue			
I-N-S RADIO NEWS			
❑ DOC-1 [DJ]	Beatlemania Tour Coverage	1964	1500.
—Promo-only open-end interview with script in plain white jacket; VG value 750; VG+ value 1125			
LINGASONG			
❑ LS-2-7001 [(2)DJ]	Live at the Star Club in Hamburg, Germany, 1962	1977	40.00
—Promo on black vinyl; "D.J. Copy Not for Sale" on labels			
❑ LS-2-7001 [(2)DJ]	Live at the Star Club in Hamburg, Germany, 1962	1977	200.00
—Promo only on red vinyl			
❑ LS-2-7001 [(2)DJ]	Live at the Star Club in Hamburg, Germany, 1962	1977	300.00
—Promo only on blue vinyl			
❑ LS-2-7001 [(2)R]	Live at the Star Club in Hamburg, Germany, 1962	1977	20.00
—American version contains "I'm Gonna Sit Right Down and Cry," "Where Have You Been All My Life," "Till There Was You," and "Sheila," not on imports			
LLOYDS			
❑ ER-MC-LTD	The Great American Tour — 1965 Live Beatlemania Concert	1965	600.00
—Another interview album from the Ed Rudy people, with a live Beatles show in the background and the songs poorly overdubbed by the Liverpool Lads			
METRO			
❑ M-563 [M]	This Is Where It Started	1966	100.00
—Reissue of MGM album with two of the "others" tracks deleted			
❑ MS-563 [R]	This Is Where It Started	1966	150.00
—In stereo cover			
❑ MS-563 [R]	This Is Where It Started	1966	200.00
—In mono cover with "Stereo" sticker			
MGM			
❑ E-4215 [M]	The Beatles with Tony Sheridan and Their Guests	1964	200.00
—Without "And Guests" on cover			
❑ E-4215 [M]	The Beatles with Tony Sheridan and Their Guests	1964	250.00
—With "And Guests" on cover			
❑ SE-4215 [R]	The Beatles with Tony Sheridan and Their Guests	1964	600.00
—With "And Guests" on cover			
❑ SE-4215 [R]	The Beatles with Tony Sheridan and Their Guests	1964	800.00
—Without "And Guests" on cover			
MOBILE FIDELITY			
❑ BC-1 [(13)]	The Beatles Collection	1982	500.00
❑ 1-023	Abbey Road	1979	50.00
—Audiophile vinyl			

The Beatles, "I'll Cry Instead," Capitol 5234, 1964, **$150.**

Number	Title (A Side/B Side)	Yr	NM
❑ 1-047 [P]	Magical Mystery Tour	1980	60.00
—Audiophile vinyl; yes, this contains the rechanneled stereo versions of "Penny Lane," "Baby You're a Rich Man" and "All You Need Is Love"			
❑ 2-072 [(2)]	The Beatles	1982	50.00
—Audiophile vinyl; not issued with photos or poster			
❑ 1-100 [S]	Sgt. Pepper's Lonely Hearts Club Band	1985	40.00
—Audiophile vinyl			
❑ UHQR 1-100 [S]	Sgt. Pepper's Lonely Hearts Club Band	1982	300.00
—Ultra High Quality release with special cover; numbered edition of 5,000; numbers under 100 fetch even more			
❑ 1-101 [P]	Please Please Me	1986	40.00
—Audiophile vinyl; British version of album. "Love Me Do" and "P.S. I Love You" are rechanneled.			
❑ 1-102 [S]	With the Beatles	1986	150.00
—Audiophile vinyl; British version of album. Limited run because of a damaged stamper that was not replaced.			
❑ 1-103 [S]	A Hard Day's Night	1987	40.00
—Audiophile vinyl; British version of album			
❑ 1-104 [S]	Beatles for Sale	1986	40.00
—Audiophile vinyl; British version of album			
❑ 1-105 [S]	Help!	1985	40.00
—Audiophile vinyl; British version of album			
❑ 1-106 [S]	Rubber Soul	1985	40.00
—Audiophile vinyl; British version of album			
❑ 1-107 [S]	Revolver	1986	40.00
—Audiophile vinyl; British version of album			
❑ 1-108 [P]	Yellow Submarine	1987	60.00
—Audiophile vinyl			
❑ 1-109	Let It Be	1987	40.00
—Audiophile vinyl; gatefold cover			
❑ 1-109	Let It Be	1987	200.00
—Audiophile vinyl; regular cover			
ORANGE			
❑ ORC-12880 [DJ]	The Silver Beatles	1985	300.00
—Test pressing; white cover with title sticker			
❑ ORC-12880 [DJ]	The Silver Beatles	1985	400.00
—Test pressing; full cover cover slick folded around a white cover. Both contain all 15 Decca audition tracks			
PBR INTERNATIONAL			
❑ 7005/6 [(2)]	The David Wigg Interviews (The Beatles Tapes)	1978	80.00
—Blue vinyl			

Number	Title (A Side/B Side)	Yr	NM
❑ 7005/6 [(2)]	The David Wigg Interviews (The Beatles Tapes)	1980	60.00
—Black vinyl			
PHOENIX			
❑ PHX-352 [M]	Silver Beatles, Vol. 1	1982	12.00
—Contains seven Decca audition tracks			
❑ PHX-353 [M]	Silver Beatles, Vol. 2	1982	12.00
—Contains seven Decca audition tracks (different seven than Phoenix 352)			
❑ P20-623	20 Hits, Beatles	1983	20.00
—With 12 Decca audition tracks, four Beatles/Tony Sheridan tracks, and four Tony Sheridan solo tracks			
❑ P20-629	20 Hits, Beatles	1983	20.00
—With 20 live Hamburg tracks			
PICKWICK			
❑ PTP-2098 [(2)M]	The Historic First Live Recordings	1980	18.00
—Same contents as Lingasong LP, plus "Hully Gully"			
❑ SPC-3661 [M]	The Beatles' First Live Recordings, Vol. 1	1979	12.00
❑ SPC-3662 [M]	The Beatles' First Live Recordings, Vol. 2	1979	12.00
❑ BAN-90051 [M]	Recorded Live in Hamburg, Vol. 1	1978	30.00
❑ BAN-90061 [M]	Recorded Live in Hamburg, Vol. 2	1978	30.00
❑ BAN-90071 [M]	Recorded Live in Hamburg, Vol. 3	1978	40.00
POLYDOR			
❑ 24-4504 [P]	The Beatles — Circa 1960 — In the Beginning Featuring Tony Sheridan	197?	40.00
—Some copies of the record contain only the title "The Beatles -- In the Beginning"			
❑ 24-4504 [P]	The Beatles — Circa 1960 — In the Beginning Featuring Tony Sheridan	1970	25.00
—Originals have gatefold cover			
❑ PD-4504 [P]	The Beatles — Circa 1960 — In the Beginning Featuring Tony Sheridan	1981	12.00
—Reissue without gatefold cover			
❑ SKAO-93199 [P]	The Beatles — Circa 1960 — In the Beginning Featuring Tony Sheridan	1970	40.00
—Capitol Record Club edition			

B

Number	Title (A Side/B Side)	Yr	NM
❑ 825073-1 [P]	The Beatles — Circa 1960 — In the Beginning Featuring Tony Sheridan	1988	20.00

—Reissue with new number

RADIO PULSEBEAT NEWS

Number	Title (A Side/B Side)	Yr	NM
❑ 2	The American Tour with Ed Rudy	1964	100.00

—Yellow label; some copies came with a special edition of Teen Talk magazine (add 50%)

Number	Title (A Side/B Side)	Yr	NM
❑ 2	The American Tour with Ed Rudy	1980	25.00

—Blue label; authorized reissue with Beatles' photo on cover

Number	Title (A Side/B Side)	Yr	NM
❑ 3	1965 Talk Album — Ed Rudy with New U.S. Tour	1965	150.00

—"The Beatles" in black print under front cover photo (other versions appear to be bootlegs)

RAVEN/PVC

Number	Title (A Side/B Side)	Yr	NM
❑ 8911	Talk Downunder	1981	10.00
❑ 8911 [DJ]	Talk Downunder	1981	80.00

—Promo only in white cover with title sticker. Label reads "For Radio Play Only"

SAVAGE

Number	Title (A Side/B Side)	Yr	NM
❑ BM-69 [M]	The Savage Young Beatles	1964	150.00

—Orange label; no legitimate copy says "Stereo" on cover

Number	Title (A Side/B Side)	Yr	NM
❑ BM-69 [M]	The Savage Young Beatles	1964	1500.

—Yellow label, glossy orange cover

SILHOUETTE

Number	Title (A Side/B Side)	Yr	NM
❑ SM-10004 [PD]	Timeless	1981	20.00

—Picture disc with all interviews

Number	Title (A Side/B Side)	Yr	NM
❑ SM-10004 [PD]	Timeless	1981	25.00

—Picture disc with interviews plus remakes of "Imagine" and "Let It Be" (by non-Beatles)

Number	Title (A Side/B Side)	Yr	NM
❑ SM-10010 [PD]	Timeless II	1982	20.00

—Picture disc with mostly interviews

Number	Title (A Side/B Side)	Yr	NM
❑ SM-10013	The British Are Coming	1984	15.00

—Interview album with numbered sticker (very low numbers increase the value)

Number	Title (A Side/B Side)	Yr	NM
❑ SM-10013	The British Are Coming	1984	80.00

—Same as above, but on red vinyl

Number	Title (A Side/B Side)	Yr	NM
❑ SM-10013 [DJ]	The British Are Coming	1984	40.00

—White label promo; no numbered sticker

Number	Title (A Side/B Side)	Yr	NM
❑ SM-10015	Golden Beatles	1985	15.00
❑ SM-10015	Golden Beatles	1985	80.00

—Gold vinyl

Number	Title (A Side/B Side)	Yr	NM
❑ PD-83010 [PD]	The British Are Coming	1985	30.00

—Picture disc

STERLING

Number	Title (A Side/B Side)	Yr	NM
❑ 8895-6481	I Apologize	1966	300.00

—Same as above, but without photo

Number	Title (A Side/B Side)	Yr	NM
❑ 8895-6481	I Apologize	1966	400.00

—One-sided LP with John Lennon's "apology" for supposed anti-Christian remarks; includes photo

UNITED ARTISTS

Number	Title (A Side/B Side)	Yr	NM
❑ UA-Help-A/B [DJ]	United Artists Presents Help!	1965	1500.

—Radio spots for movie; VG value 500; VG+ value 1000

Number	Title (A Side/B Side)	Yr	NM
❑ UA-Help-INT [DJ]	United Artists Presents Help!	1965	2000.

—Open-end interview with script (red label); VG value 1000; VG+ value 1500

Number	Title (A Side/B Side)	Yr	NM
❑ UA-Help-Show [DJ]	United Artists Presents Help!	1965	3000.

—One-sided interview with script (blue label); VG value 1500; VG+ value 2250

Number	Title (A Side/B Side)	Yr	NM
❑ SP-2359/60 [DJ]	United Artists Presents A Hard Day's Night	1964	2000.

—Open-end interview with script; VG value 1000; VG+ value 1500

Number	Title (A Side/B Side)	Yr	NM
❑ SP-2362/3 [DJ]	United Artists Presents A Hard Day's Night	1964	1500.

—Radio spots for movie

Number	Title (A Side/B Side)	Yr	NM
❑ UAL 3366 [M]	A Hard Day's Night	1964	200.00

—With "I Cry Instead" listing

Number	Title (A Side/B Side)	Yr	NM
❑ UAL 3366 [M]	A Hard Day's Night	1964	250.00

—With "I'll Cry Instead" listing

Number	Title (A Side/B Side)	Yr	NM
❑ UAL 3366 [M]	A Hard Day's Night	1964	3000.

—White label promo

Number	Title (A Side/B Side)	Yr	NM
❑ UAS 6366 [P]	A Hard Day's Night	1964	200.00

—With "I Cry Instead" listing

Number	Title (A Side/B Side)	Yr	NM
❑ UAS 6366 [P]	A Hard Day's Night	1964	250.00

—With "I'll Cry Instead" listing. Has incidental music by George Martin. All eight Beatles tracks are rechanneled; Martin's are in true stereo.

Number	Title (A Side/B Side)	Yr	NM
❑ UAS 6366 [P]	A Hard Day's Night	1964	12000.

—Pink vinyl; only one copy known, probably privately (and secretly) done by a pressing-plant employee; VG value 6000; VG+ value 9000

Number	Title (A Side/B Side)	Yr	NM
❑ UAS 6366 [P]	A Hard Day's Night	1968	50.00

—Pink and orange label

Number	Title (A Side/B Side)	Yr	NM
❑ UAS 6366 [P]	A Hard Day's Night	1970	50.00

—Black and orange label

Number	Title (A Side/B Side)	Yr	NM
❑ UAS 6366 [P]	A Hard Day's Night	1971	20.00

—Tan label

Number	Title (A Side/B Side)	Yr	NM
❑ UAS 6366 [P]	A Hard Day's Night	1975	20.00

—Tan label with "All Rights Reserved" in perimeter print

Number	Title (A Side/B Side)	Yr	NM
❑ UAS 6366 [P]	A Hard Day's Night	1977	20.00

—Sunrise label. Note: Any of the variations from 1968 on can have titles of songs incorrectly listed as "I Cry Instead" and "Tell Me Who," or only one can be wrong, or neither can be wrong. No difference in value at this time.

Number	Title (A Side/B Side)	Yr	NM
❑ ST-90828 [P]	A Hard Day's Night	1964	750.00

—Capitol Record Club edition

Number	Title (A Side/B Side)	Yr	NM
❑ T-90828 [M]	A Hard Day's Night	1964	1500.

—Capitol Record Club edition; VG value 750; VG+ value 1125

UNITED DISTRIBUTORS

Number	Title (A Side/B Side)	Yr	NM
❑ UDL-2333 [M]	Dawn of the Silver Beatles	1981	50.00

—With numbered registration card (deduct 20% if missing)

Number	Title (A Side/B Side)	Yr	NM
❑ UDL-2333 [M]	Dawn of the Silver Beatles	1981	60.00

—Hand-stamped numbers on back cover and label; contains 10 Decca audition tracks

Number	Title (A Side/B Side)	Yr	NM
❑ UDL-2382 [M]	Lightning Strikes Twice	1981	60.00

—Side 1 has five Beatles' Decca audition tracks; Side 2 has live Elvis Presley performances from 1955

VEE JAY

Number	Title (A Side/B Side)	Yr	NM
❑ DX(S)-30	The Beatles vs. The Four Seasons Poster	1964	300.00
❑ DX-30 [(2)M]	The Beatles vs. The Four Seasons	1964	800.00

—Combines "Introducing the Beatles" with "Golden Hits of the Four Seasons" (Vee Jay 1065)

Number	Title (A Side/B Side)	Yr	NM
❑ DXS-30 [(2)S]	The Beatles vs. The Four Seasons	1964	3000.

—Combines "Introducing the Beatles" with "Golden Hits of the Four Seasons" (Vee Jay 1065); VG value 1500; VG+ value 2250

Number	Title (A Side/B Side)	Yr	NM
❑ 202 [M]	Hear the Beatles Tell All	1964	300.00

—Without "PRO" prefix on label

Number	Title (A Side/B Side)	Yr	NM
❑ PRO 202 [DJ]	Hear the Beatles Tell All	1964	18000.

—White label promo with blue print; VG value 6000; VG+ value 12000

Number	Title (A Side/B Side)	Yr	NM
❑ PRO 202 [M]	Hear the Beatles Tell All	1964	200.00

—With "PRO" prefix on label

Number	Title (A Side/B Side)	Yr	NM
❑ PRO 202 [M]	Hear the Beatles Tell All	1979	10.00

—Authorized reissue; every copy with the word "Stereo" on the front cover is this edition, though the record still plays in mono (no 1964 copies have "Stereo" on the cover)

Number	Title (A Side/B Side)	Yr	NM
❑ PRO 202 [PD]	Hear the Beatles Tell All	1987	20.00

—Shaped picture disc with same recordings as the black vinyl versions

Number	Title (A Side/B Side)	Yr	NM
❑ LP 1062 [M]	Introducing the Beatles	1964	250.00

—Song titles cover; with "Please Please Me" and "Ask Me Why"; plain Vee Jay logo on solid black label

Number	Title (A Side/B Side)	Yr	NM
❑ LP 1062 [M]	Introducing the Beatles	1964	250.00

—Song titles cover; with "Please Please Me" and "Ask Me Why"; brackets Vee Jay logo with colorband (most common authentic version)

Number	Title (A Side/B Side)	Yr	NM
❑ LP 1062 [M]	Introducing the Beatles	1964	300.00

—Song titles cover; with "Please Please Me" and "Ask Me Why"; oval Vee Jay logo on solid black label

Number	Title (A Side/B Side)	Yr	NM
❑ LP 1062 [M]	Introducing the Beatles	1964	300.00

—Song titles cover; with "Please Please Me" and "Ask Me Why"; oval Vee Jay logo with colorband

Number	Title (A Side/B Side)	Yr	NM
❑ LP 1062 [M]	Introducing the Beatles	1964	800.00

—Song titles cover; with "Love Me Do" and "P.S. I Love You"; oval Vee Jay logo with colorband only!

Number	Title (A Side/B Side)	Yr	NM
❑ LP 1062 [M]	Introducing the Beatles	1964	1000.

—Blank back cover; with "Please Please Me" and "Ask Me Why"; oval Vee Jay logo with colorband only!

Number	Title (A Side/B Side)	Yr	NM
❑ LP 1062 [M]	Introducing the Beatles	1964	1000.

—Song titles cover; with "Please Please Me" and "Ask Me Why"; brackets Vee Jay logo on solid black label

Number	Title (A Side/B Side)	Yr	NM
❑ LP 1062 [M]	Introducing the Beatles	1964	1200.

—Blank back cover; with "Love Me Do" and "P.S. I Love You"; oval Vee Jay logo with colorband only!; VG value 400; VG+ value 800

Number	Title (A Side/B Side)	Yr	NM
❑ LP 1062 [M]	Introducing the Beatles	1964	4000.

—"Ad back" cover; with "Love Me Do" and "P.S. I Love You"; oval Vee Jay logo with colorband only!; VG value 1500; VG+ value 2750

Number	Title (A Side/B Side)	Yr	NM
❑ SR 1062 [B]	Introducing the Beatles	1964	2500.

—Blank back cover; with "Love Me Do" and "P.S. I Love You"; oval Vee Jay logo with colorband only!

Number	Title (A Side/B Side)	Yr	NM
❑ SR 1062 [B]	Introducing the Beatles	1964	8000.

—Song titles cover; with "Love Me Do" and "P.S. I Love You"; oval Vee Jay logo with colorband only!; VG value 3000; VG+ value 5500; This album has been heavily counterfeited; please check the label of your copy before contacting the author. If the words "Introducing the Beatles" are above the center hole of the record, and the words "The Beatles" are below, it is automatically a counterfeit and almost worthless.

Number	Title (A Side/B Side)	Yr	NM
❑ SR 1062 [B]	Introducing the Beatles	1964	12000.

—"Ad back" cover; with "Love Me Do" and "P.S. I Love You" (both mono); oval Vee Jay logo with colorband only!; VG value 4000; VG+ value 8000

Number	Title (A Side/B Side)	Yr	NM
❑ SR 1062 [S]	Introducing the Beatles	1964	1500.

—Song titles cover; with "Please Please Me" and "Ask Me Why"; brackets Vee Jay logo with colorband

Number	Title (A Side/B Side)	Yr	NM
❑ SR 1062 [S]	Introducing the Beatles	1964	1600.

—Song titles cover; with "Please Please Me" and "Ask Me Why"; oval Vee Jay logo with colorband

Number	Title (A Side/B Side)	Yr	NM
❑ SR 1062 [S]	Introducing the Beatles	1964	1600.

—Song titles cover; with "Please Please Me" and "Ask Me Why"; plain Vee Jay logo on solid black label

Number	Title (A Side/B Side)	Yr	NM
❑ LP 1085 [M]	Jolly What! The Beatles and Frank Ifield on Stage	1964	250.00

—Man in Beatle wig cover; originals have printing on spine and a dark blue/purple background (counterfeits have a black background and no spine print)

Number	Title (A Side/B Side)	Yr	NM
❑ LP 1085 [M]	The Beatles and Frank Ifield on Stage	1964	5000.

—Portrait of Beatles cover; counterfeits are poorly reproduced and have no spine print; VG value 2000; VG+ value 3500

Number	Title (A Side/B Side)	Yr	NM
❑ SR 1085 [B]	Jolly What! The Beatles and Frank Ifield on Stage	1964	500.00

—Man in Beatle wig cover; "Stereo" on both cover and label. "From Me to You" is mono.

Number	Title (A Side/B Side)	Yr	NM
❑ SR 1085 [B]	The Beatles and Frank Ifield on Stage	1964	12000.

—Portrait of Beatles cover; "Stereo" on both cover and label; VG value 4000; VG+ value 8000

Number	Title (A Side/B Side)	Yr	NM
❑ LP 1092 [M]	Songs, Pictures and Stories of the Fabulous Beatles	1964	500.00

—See above; brackets Vee Jay logo with colorband

Number	Title (A Side/B Side)	Yr	NM
❑ LP 1092 [M]	Songs, Pictures and Stories of the Fabulous Beatles	1964	500.00

—See above; oval Vee Jay logo on solid black label

Number	Title (A Side/B Side)	Yr	NM
❑ LP 1092 [M]	Songs, Pictures and Stories of the Fabulous Beatles	1964	500.00

—See above; plain Vee Jay logo on solid black label

Number	Title (A Side/B Side)	Yr	NM
❑ LP 1092 [M]	Songs, Pictures and Stories of the Fabulous Beatles	1964	500.00

—All copies have gatefold cover with 2/3 width on front; also, all copies have "Introducing the Beatles" records. Oval Vee Jay logo with colorband.

Number	Title (A Side/B Side)	Yr	NM
❑ VJS 1092 [S]	Songs, Pictures and Stories of the Fabulous Beatles	1964	2400.

—See above; brackets Vee Jay logo with colorband; VG value 800; VG+ value 1600

Number	Title (A Side/B Side)	Yr	NM
❑ VJS 1092 [S]	Songs, Pictures and Stories of the Fabulous Beatles	1964	2400.

—See above; plain Vee Jay logo on solid black label. NOTE: Any non-gatefold copy or any copy called "Songs and Pictures of the Fabulous Beatles" is a counterfeit; VG value 800; VG+ value 1600

Number	Title (A Side/B Side)	Yr	NM
❑ VJS 1092 [S]	Songs, Pictures and Stories of the Fabulous Beatles	1964	2400.

—All copies have gatefold cover with 2/3 width on front; also, all copies have "Introducing the Beatles" records. Oval Vee Jay logo with colorband; VG value 800; VG+ value 1600

BEATSTALKERS, THE

45s

PRESS

Number	Title (A Side/B Side)	Yr	NM
❑ 5001	Left, Right, Left/ Get a Better Hold On	1966	15.00

BEAU BRUMMELS, THE

Also see RON ELLIOTT; SAL VALENTINO.

45s

AUTUMN

Number	Title (A Side/B Side)	Yr	NM
❑ 8	Laugh, Laugh/Still in Love with You Baby	1965	12.00

—Tan label

Number	Title (A Side/B Side)	Yr	NM
❑ 8	Laugh, Laugh/Still in Love with You Baby	1965	15.00

—White label

Number	Title (A Side/B Side)	Yr	NM
❑ 10	Just a Little/They'll Make You Cry	1965	15.00
❑ 16	You Tell Me Why/I Want You	1965	8.00
❑ 20	Don't Talk to Strangers/ In Good Time	1965	8.00
❑ 24	Good Time Music/Sad Little Girl	1965	8.00

RHINO

Number	Title (A Side/B Side)	Yr	NM
❑ RNOR 4506	Laugh, Laugh/Just a Little	1984	4.00
❑ RNOR 4506 [PS]	Laugh, Laugh/Just a Little	1984	4.00

WARNER BROS.

Number	Title (A Side/B Side)	Yr	NM
❑ 5813	One Too Many Mornings/ She Reigns	1966	8.00
❑ 5848	Fine with Me/Here We Are Again	1966	8.00
❑ 7014	Don't Make Promises/ Two Days 'Til Tomorrow	1967	8.00
❑ 7079	Magic Hollow/Lower Level	1967	8.00
❑ 7204	Are You Happy/Lift Me	1968	6.00
❑ 7218	I'm a Sleeper/Long Walking Down to Misery	1968	6.00
❑ 7260	Cherokee Girl/Deep Water	1969	6.00
❑ 8119	You Tell Me Why/ Down to the Bottom	1975	5.00

Albums

ACCORD

Number	Title (A Side/B Side)	Yr	NM
❑ SN-7175	Just a Little	1982	10.00

AUTUMN

Number	Title (A Side/B Side)	Yr	NM
❑ LP 103 [M]	Introducing the Beau Brummels	1965	50.00
❑ SLP 103 [S]	Introducing the Beau Brummels	1965	60.00
❑ LP 104 [M]	The Beau Brummels, Vol. 2	1965	40.00
❑ SLP 104 [S]	The Beau Brummels, Vol. 2	1965	50.00

JAS

Number	Title (A Side/B Side)	Yr	NM
❑ 5000	Original Hits of the Beau Brummels	1976	15.00

POST

Number	Title (A Side/B Side)	Yr	NM
❑ 6000	The Beau Brummels Sing	196?	15.00

RHINO

Number	Title (A Side/B Side)	Yr	NM
❑ RNLP-101	The Best of the Beau Brummels	1981	10.00
❑ RNLP-102	Introducing the Beau Brummels	1981	10.00
❑ RNLP-104	From the Vaults	1981	12.00
❑ RNLP-70171	The Best of the Beau Brummels (Golden Archive Series)	1986	10.00

SUNDAZED

Number	Title (A Side/B Side)	Yr	NM
❑ LP 5088	North Beach Legends	2001	12.00
❑ LP 5089	Gentle Wanderin' Ways	2001	12.00

VAULT

Number	Title (A Side/B Side)	Yr	NM
❑ LP-114 [M]	Best of the Beau Brummels	1967	25.00
❑ SLP-114 [S]	Best of the Beau Brummels	1967	25.00
❑ SLP-121	Beau Brummels, Vol. 44	1968	25.00

Except when noted otherwise, VG = 25% of NM, and VG+ = 50% of NM. (Example: VG = $2.00, VG+ = $4.00 and NM = $8.00.)

Number	Title (A Side/B Side)	Yr	NM
WARNER BROS.			
❑ W 1644 [M]	Beau Brummels '66	1966	20.00
❑ WS 1644 [S]	Beau Brummels '66	1966	25.00
❑ W 1692 [M]	Triangle	1967	20.00
❑ WS 1692 [S]	Triangle	1967	25.00
❑ WS 1760	Bradley's Barn	1968	25.00
❑ BS 2842	The Beau Brummels	1975	20.00

BEAU-K'S, THE

Number	Title (A Side/B Side)	Yr	NM
45s			
MERCURY			
❑ 72157	Packin' Up/Forget Me Not	1963	10.00
❑ 72224	A Rose and a Star/What Else Could I Do But Cry	1963	10.00

BEAU-MARKS, THE

Number	Title (A Side/B Side)	Yr	NM
45s			
MAINSTREAM			
❑ 688	Clap Your Hands/Daddy Said	1968	10.00
PORT			
❑ 70029	Little Miss Twist/Lovely Little Lady	1962	15.00
RUST			
❑ 5035	School Is Out/Classmates	1961	20.00
❑ 5050	I'll Never Be the Same/Tender Years	1962	20.00
SHAD			
❑ 5017	Clap Your Hands/Daddy Said	1960	20.00
❑ 5021	Cause We're in Love/Billy Went a-Walkin'	1960	20.00
TIME			
❑ 1032	Oh Joan/Rockin' Blues	1961	30.00

BEAUMONT, JIMMY
Of THE SKYLINERS.

Number	Title (A Side/B Side)	Yr	NM
45s			
BANG			
❑ 510	Tell Me/I Feel Like I'm Falling in Love	1965	20.00
❑ 525	I Never Loved Her Anyway/You Got Too Much Going for You	1966	30.00
COLPIX			
❑ 607	The End of a Story/Baion Rhythms	1961	30.00
GALLANT			
❑ 3007	Please Send Me Someone to Love/There Is No Other Love	196?	20.00
❑ 3012	Love Is a Dangerous Game/Just a Little Closer	196?	12.00
MAY			
❑ 112	Ev'rybody's Cryin'/Camera	1961	25.00
❑ 115	I Should Have Listened to Mama/Juarez	1962	25.00
❑ 120	Never Say Goodbye/I'm Gonna Try My Wings	1962	25.00
❑ 136	I'll Always Be in Love with You/Give Her My Best	1963	25.00

BEAUREGARDE

Number	Title (A Side/B Side)	Yr	NM
45s			
INTERNATIONAL ARTISTS			
❑ 123	Popcorn Popper/Mama Never Taught Me How to Jelly Roll	1968	25.00
Albums			
EMPIRE			
❑ (no #)	Beauregarde	1969	100.00
SOUND			
❑ 7104	Beauregarde	1969	80.00

BEAUTIFUL PEOPLE, THE

Number	Title (A Side/B Side)	Yr	NM
45s			
ROULETTE			
❑ 7001	Green Tambourine/Rainbow Tree	1968	—

BEAUTIFUL SOUTH, THE

Number	Title (A Side/B Side)	Yr	NM
12-Inch Singles			
ELEKTRA			
❑ ED5444 [DJ]	You Keep It All In (Single Version) (same on both sides)	1990	5.00
❑ ED 5444 [DJ]	You Keep It All In (Single Version) (same on both sides)	1990	7.00
45s			
ARK 21			
❑ S7-19942	Don't Marry Her/Mirror	1998	5.00
Albums			
ELEKTRA			
❑ 60917	Welcome to the Beautiful South	1989	15.00

BEAVER, PAUL

Number	Title (A Side/B Side)	Yr	NM
Albums			
RAPTURE			
❑ 11111	Perchance to Dream	196?	50.00

BEAVER AND KRAUSE

Number	Title (A Side/B Side)	Yr	NM
45s			
WARNER BROS.			
❑ 7414	People's Park/Salute to the Vanishing Bald Eagle	1970	6.00
❑ 7485	Walkin' By the River/The Saga of the Blue Beaver	1971	6.00
❑ 7642	Bluebird Canyon Stomp/Real Slow Drag	1972	6.00
Albums			
LIMELIGHT			
❑ 86069	Ragnarok — Electronic Funk	1969	30.00
WARNER BROS.			
❑ WS 1850	In a Wild Sanctuary	1969	15.00
❑ WS 1909	Gandharva	1970	15.00
❑ BS 2624	All Good Men	1972	15.00

BEAVERS, JACKEY

Number	Title (A Side/B Side)	Yr	NM
45s			
CHECKER			
❑ 1102	Jack-a-Rue/Silly Boy	1965	20.00
—As "Jackey Beaver"			
❑ 1119	I Want Somebody/Slingshot	1965	20.00
—As "Jackey Beaver"			
DADE			
❑ 2041	Tryin' to Get Back to You Girl/(Part 2)	197?	10.00
MAINSTREAM			
❑ 713	When Something Is Wrong with My Baby/We're Not Too Young to Fall in Love	1969	60.00
REVILOT			
❑ 208	Love That Never Grows Old/I Need My Baby	1967	1000.
SOUND STAGE 7			
❑ ZS7 1502	Someday We'll Be Together/Lover Come Back	1971	20.00
❑ ZS7 1506	Singing a Funky Song (For My Baby)/Hey Girl (I Can't Stand to See You Go)	1972	10.00
❑ 2649	Hey Girl (I Can't Stand to See You Go)/Hold On	1969	12.00
❑ 2662	You Can Have Her/(B-side unknown)	1970	15.00

BEAVERS, THE

Number	Title (A Side/B Side)	Yr	NM
45s			
CAPITOL			
❑ F3956	Sack Dress/Rockin' at the Drive-In	1958	25.00
❑ F4015	The Road to Happiness/Low As I Can Be	1958	20.00

BECK, BECKY LEE

Number	Title (A Side/B Side)	Yr	NM
45s			
CHALLENGE			
❑ 59272	I Want a Beatle for Christmas/Puppy Dog	1964	20.00

BECK, BOBBY

Number	Title (A Side/B Side)	Yr	NM
45s			
ABC-PARAMOUNT			
❑ 10099	Isle of Capri/Swinging on a Chandelier	1960	20.00
❑ 10148	The Door Is Always Open/You Got All My Love	1960	20.00

BECK, JEFF
Includes the Jeff Beck Group, of whom ROD STEWART was lead singer. Also see BECK, BOGERT AND APPICE; THE YARDBIRDS.

Number	Title (A Side/B Side)	Yr	NM
45s			
EPIC			
❑ 34-05595	Gets Us All in the End/You Know We Know	1985	4.00
❑ 10157	Beck's Bolero/Hi-Ho Silver Lining	1967	16.00
❑ 10218	Rock My Plimsoul/Tally Man	1967	16.00
❑ 10390	Blues De Luxe/Ol' Man River	1968	12.00
❑ 10484	Jailhouse Rock/Plynth (Water Down the Drain)	1969	12.00
❑ 10814	Got the Feeling/Situation	1971	10.00
❑ 10938	Definitely Maybe/Hi Ho Silver Lining	1973	10.00
❑ 50112	Constipated Duck/You Know What I Mean	1975	6.00
❑ 50276	Come Dancing/Head for Backstage Pass	1976	4.00
❑ 50914	Too Much to Lose/The Final Peace	1980	4.00
Albums			
ACCORD			
❑ SN-7141	Early Anthology	1981	10.00
EPIC			
❑ AS 151 [DJ]	Everything You Always Wanted to Hear by Jeff Beck But Were Afraid to Ask For	1977	20.00
—Promo-only sampler			
❑ A2S 850 [(2)DJ]	Then and Now	1981	25.00
—Promo-only sampler			
❑ BN 26413	Truth	1973	10.00
—Orange label			
❑ BN 26413 [M]	Truth	1968	40.00
—Mono is promo only with stereo number; cover has "Mono" sticker covering the word "Stereo"			
❑ BN 26413 [S]	Truth	1968	15.00
—Yellow label			
❑ PE 26413	Truth	198?	8.00
—Reissue with new prefix			
❑ BN 26478	Beck-Ola	1969	15.00
—Yellow label			
❑ BN 26478	Beck-Ola	1973	10.00
—Orange label			
❑ PE 26478	Beck-Ola	197?	8.00
—Reissue with new prefix			
❑ PE 30973	Rough and Ready	198?	8.00
—Budget-line reissue			
❑ EQ 30993 [Q]	Rough and Ready	1972	20.00
❑ KE 30993	Rough and Ready	1971	15.00
—Yellow label			
❑ KE 30993	Rough and Ready	1973	10.00
—Orange label			
❑ EQ 31331 [Q]	Jeff Beck Group	1972	20.00
❑ KE 31331	Jeff Beck Group	1972	15.00
—Yellow label			
❑ KE 31331	Jeff Beck Group	1973	10.00
—Orange label			
❑ PE 31331	Jeff Beck Group	198?	8.00
—Budget-line reissue			
❑ PE 33409	Blow by Blow	1975	10.00
—Orange label, no bar code on cover			
❑ PE 33409	Blow by Blow	198?	8.00
—Reissue with dark blue label and bar code on cover			
❑ PEQ 33409 [Q]	Blow by Blow	1975	20.00
❑ BG 33779 [(2)]	Truth/Beck-Ola	1975	12.00
❑ PE 33849	Wired	1976	10.00
—Orange label, no bar code on cover			
❑ PE 33849	Wired	1979	8.00
—Reissue with dark blue label; with or without bar code on cover			
❑ PEQ 33849 [Q]	Wired	1976	20.00
❑ PE 34433	Jeff Beck with the Jan Hammer Group Live	1977	10.00
—Orange label, no bar code on cover			
❑ PE 34433	Jeff Beck with the Jan Hammer Group Live	198?	8.00
—Reissue with dark blue label and bar code on cover			
❑ FE 35684	There and Back	1980	10.00
❑ PE 35684	There and Back	1985	8.00
—Budget-line reissue			
❑ FE 39483	Flash	1985	10.00
❑ HE 43409	Blow by Blow	1980	30.00
—Half-speed mastered edition			
❑ HE 43849	Wired	198?	30.00
—Half-speed mastered edition			
❑ FE 44313	Jeff Beck's Guitar Shop	1989	15.00

BECK, JEFF, AND ROD STEWART
Also see each artist's individual listings.

Number	Title (A Side/B Side)	Yr	NM
45s			
EPIC			
❑ 34-05416	People Get Ready/Back on the Street	1985	3.00
❑ 34-05416 [PS]	People Get Ready/Back on the Street	1985	3.00

BECK, JOE

Number	Title (A Side/B Side)	Yr	NM
45s			
POLYDOR			
❑ 14384	Dr. Lee/Stand Up and Be Someone	1977	4.00
Albums			
CTI			
❑ 8002	Beck & Sanborn	1979	10.00
—Reissue of Kudu 21 with new title			
CTI/CBS ASSOCIATED			
❑ FZ 40805	Beck & Sanborn	1987	10.00
KUDU			
❑ 21	Beck	1975	12.00
POLYDOR			
❑ PD-1-6092	Watch the Time	1976	10.00

BECK, BOGERT & APPICE
Also see JEFF BECK; VANILLA FUDGE; CACTUS.

45s

Number	Title (A Side/B Side)	Yr	NM
EPIC			
❑ 10998	I'm So Proud/Oh to Love You	1973	8.00
❑ 11027	Lady/Oh to Love You	1973	8.00

Albums

Number	Title (A Side/B Side)	Yr	NM
EPIC			
❑ CQ 32140 [Q]	Beck, Bogert & Appice	1973	20.00
❑ KE 32140	Beck, Bogert & Appice	1973	10.00
—Orange label			
❑ KE 32140	Beck, Bogert & Appice	1973	15.00
—Yellow label			
❑ PE 32140	Beck, Bogert & Appice	198?	8.00
—Budget-line reissue			

BECKER, GLORIA

45s

Number	Title (A Side/B Side)	Yr	NM
REAL			
❑ 1304	Sixteen Pounds (Housewife's Lament)/Adios to Mexico City	1956	20.00
—A-side is a parody of "Sixteen Tons"			

BECKHAM, BOB

45s

Number	Title (A Side/B Side)	Yr	NM
DECCA			
❑ 30617	Tomorrow/I'm Tired of Everyone But You	1958	12.00
❑ 30861	Just As Much As Ever/Your Sweet Love	1959	12.00
❑ 31029	Crazy Arms/Beloved	1959	12.00
❑ 31029 [PS]	Crazy Arms/Beloved	1959	20.00
❑ 31089	Only the Broken Hearted/Mais Oui	1960	10.00
❑ 31132	Two Wrongs Don't Make a Right/Nothing Is Forever	1960	10.00
❑ 31132 [PS]	Two Wrongs Don't Make a Right/Nothing Is Forever	1960	20.00
❑ 31163	Meet Me Halfway/One More Time	1960	10.00
❑ 31239	Forget It/Like a Fool	1961	10.00
❑ 31285	How Soon (Will I Be Seeing You)/I'm Wondering	1961	10.00
❑ 31337	10,000 Teardrops (And One Broken Heart)/Just Friends	1961	10.00
❑ 31391	I Cry Like a Baby/I'll Take My Chances	1962	8.00
❑ 31432	Building Memories/Memory Mountain	1962	8.00
❑ 31493	Footprints/Midnight	1963	8.00
❑ 31547	Grabbing at Rainbows/My Heart Would Know	1963	8.00
❑ 31607	Helpless/I'll Be Around	1964	8.00
MONUMENT			
❑ 1018	Cherokee Strip/You Really Know How to Hurt a Guy	1967	6.00
❑ 1030	Lily White/Look at Them	1967	6.00
SMASH			
❑ 1990	Slowly Dying/It's My Heart	1965	8.00

BECKY AND THE LOLLIPOPS

45s

Number	Title (A Side/B Side)	Yr	NM
EPIC			
❑ 9736	I Don't Care (What They Say)/My Boyfriend	1964	12.00

BED BUGS, THE

45s

Number	Title (A Side/B Side)	Yr	NM
LIBERTY			
❑ 55679	Yeah Yeah/Lucy Lucy	1964	25.00

BEDLAM
Includes RAINBOW and BLACK SABBATH drummer Cozy Powell.

Albums

Number	Title (A Side/B Side)	Yr	NM
CHRYSALIS			
❑ CHR-1048	Bedlam	1973	25.00

BEE, MOLLY

45s

Number	Title (A Side/B Side)	Yr	NM
CAPITOL			
❑ F2258	Tennessee Tango/Kids Who Pay	1952	25.00
❑ F2285	I Saw Mommy Kissing Santa Claus/Willy Claus (Little Son of Santa Claus)	1952	20.00
❑ F2339	Honky Tonk Mountain/Nobody's Lonesome for Me	1953	20.00
❑ F2396	What'll He Do/Dancing with Someone	1953	20.00
❑ F2494	Doggie on the Highway/I'll Tell My Mommy	1953	20.00
❑ F2567	God Bless Us All/This Is My Dog	1953	20.00
❑ F2741	Remember Me/Pine Tree Pine Over Me	1954	20.00
❑ F2790	Stuffy/In the Pyrenees	1954	20.00
❑ F3865	Magic Mirror/I'm Going Steady with a Dream	1957	15.00
❑ F3968	Don't Look Back/Please Don't Talk About Me When I'm Gone	1958	15.00
❑ F4064	Five Points of a Star/After You've Gone	1958	15.00
CORAL			
❑ 9-61357	I Won't Grow Up/False Alarm	1955	20.00
DOT			
❑ 15453	Sweet Shoppe Sweetheart/From the Wrong Side of Town	1956	20.00
❑ 15517	Since I Met You Baby/I'll Be Waiting for You	1956	20.00
GRANITE			
❑ 509	She Kept On Talkin'/Baby You Got It	1974	7.00
❑ 515	Right or Left at Oak Street/I Got a Man	1975	7.00
❑ 524	California Country/(B-side unknown)	1975	7.00
❑ 531	I Can't Live in the Dark Anymore/(B-side unknown)	1975	7.00
LIBERTY			
❑ 55438	Just for the Record/Lyin' Again	1962	12.00
❑ 55543	All My Love, All My Life/She's New to You	1963	12.00
❑ 55569	I Was Only Kidding/He's My True Love	1963	12.00
❑ 55631	Some Tears Fall Dry/Johnny Liar	1963	12.00
❑ 55691	Our Secret/He Doesn't Want You	1964	12.00
MGM			
❑ 13356	Keep It a Secret/Single Girl Again	1965	10.00
❑ 13411	Together Again/I'm Gonna Change Everything	1965	10.00
❑ 13491	Losing You/Miserable Me	1966	10.00
❑ 13537	How's the World Treating You/It Keeps Right On a-Hurtin'	1966	10.00
❑ 13694	Almost Persuaded/Heartbreak U.S.A.	1967	10.00
❑ 13770	You Win Again/I Hate to See Me Go	1967	10.00

Albums

Number	Title (A Side/B Side)	Yr	NM
ACCORD			
❑ 7901	Sounds Fine to Me	1982	10.00
CAPITOL			
❑ T 1097 [M]	Young Romance	1958	40.00
GRANITE			
❑ 1002	Good Golly Ms. Molly	1974	12.00
MGM			
❑ E-4303 [M]	It's Great, It's Molly Bee	1965	20.00
❑ SE-4303 [S]	It's Great, It's Molly Bee	1965	25.00
❑ E-4423 [M]	Swingin' Country	1967	20.00
❑ SE-4423 [S]	Swingin' Country	1967	25.00

BEE BEE TWINS, THE

45s

Number	Title (A Side/B Side)	Yr	NM
LIBERTY			
❑ 55173	The Night Before Christmas/Yuletide Tango	1958	15.00

BEE GEES
Also see BARRY GIBB; MAURICE GIBB; ROBIN GIBB.

12-Inch Singles

Number	Title (A Side/B Side)	Yr	NM
POLYDOR			
❑ PRO 1068-1 [DJ]	Paying the Price of Love (Jellybean Dub Mix #1) (Edit) (Ocean Drive Dub)	1993	12.00
❑ 859165-1	Paying the Price of Love (Ocean Drive Mix 6:09) (Jellybean Mix #1 6:09) (Jellybean Mix #1 Dub Vibe 6:09)/Decadance (Classic House Mix 8:42)	1993	6.00
RSO			
❑ PRO 209 [DJ]	The Woman in You (5:43) (same on both sides)	1983	12.00
❑ RS 853 [DJ]	You Should Be Dancing (B-side blank)	1976	150.00
—This is for the U.S. white label promo, not for the Canadian issue			
❑ RPO 1029 [DJ]	He's a Liar (Special Dance Version)/(Instrumental)	1981	10.00
UNIVERSAL			
❑ 587696-1	This Is Where I Came In (DJ Domino Remix) (DJ Domino Remix Edit) (LP Version)/(same on both sides)	2001	8.00
WARNER BROS.			
❑ PRO-A-2822 [DJ]	You Win Again (Fade) (same on both sides)	1987	8.00
❑ PRO-A-2918 [DJ]	E.S.P. (Edit) (Remix No Guitars) (Extra Sensory House Vocal) (E.S. Piano Dub)	1987	10.00
❑ PRO-A-3753 [DJ]	One (12" Club Mix) (Dub Mix) (Remix Edit) (12" Dance Version)	1989	12.00
❑ 20760	You Win Again (Extended Remix)/Backtafunk	1987	8.00

45s

Number	Title (A Side/B Side)	Yr	NM
ATCO			
❑ 6487	New York Mining Disaster 1941 Have You Seen My Wife, Mr. Jones/I Can't See Nobody	1967	10.00
❑ 6487	New York Mining Disaster 1941/I Can't See Nobody	1967	12.00
❑ 6487 [DJ]	New York Mining Disaster 1941/I Can't See Nobody	1967	25.00
—Artist not listed on label.			
❑ 6503	To Love Somebody/Close Another Door	1967	10.00
❑ 6521	Holiday/Every Christian Lion Hearted Man Will Show You	1967	10.00
❑ 6532	(The Lights Went Out in) Massachusetts/Sir Geoffrey Saved the World	1967	10.00
❑ 6548	Words/Sinking Ships	1968	10.00
❑ 6570	Jumbo/The Singer Sang His Song	1968	8.00
❑ 6603	I've Gotta Get a Message to You/Kitty Can	1968	8.00
❑ 6639	I Started a Joke/Kilburn Towers	1969	8.00
❑ 6657	First of May/Lamplight	1969	8.00
❑ 6682	Tomorrow Tomorrow/Sun in My Morning	1969	8.00
❑ 6682 [DJ]	Tomorrow Tomorrow (Short Version 3:04)/(Long Version 4:02)	1969	12.00
—On white label with no promo markings			
❑ 6702	Don't Forget to Remember/The Lord	1969	10.00
❑ 6741	If Only I Had My Mind on Something Else/Sweetheart	1970	8.00
❑ 6752	I.O.I.O./Then You Left Me	1970	8.00
❑ 6795	Lonely Days/Man for All Seasons	1971	6.00
❑ 6824	How Can You Mend a Broken Heart/Country Woman	1971	6.00
❑ 6847	Don't Wanna Live Inside Myself/Walking Back to Waterloo	1971	6.00
❑ 6871	My World/On Time	1972	5.00
❑ 6896	Run to Me/Road to Alaska	1972	5.00
❑ 6909	Alive/Paper Mache, Cabbages and Kings	1972	5.00
EMMC			
❑ (no #)	A Personal Message from the Bee Gees/The Rescue of Bonnie Prince Wally	1979	10.00
—Official Bee Gees Fan Club record; small hole, plays at 33 1/3 rpm			
POLYDOR			
❑ 31457 1006 7	Alone/How Deep Is Your Love	1997	3.00
RSO			
❑ RP 106 [DJ]	Sgt. Pepper's Lonely Hearts Club Band/With a Little Help from My Friends (stereo/mono)	1978	15.00
—As "Lonely Hearts Club Band" (Bee Gees with Peter Frampton and Paul Nicholas); promo only			
❑ 401	Saw a New Morning/My Life Has Been a Song	1973	6.00
❑ 404	Wouldn't I Be Someone/Elisa	1973	6.00
❑ 408	Mr. Natural/It Doesn't Matter Much to Me	1974	6.00
❑ 410	Throw a Penny/I Can't Let Go	1974	6.00
❑ 501	Charade/Heavy Breathing	1974	6.00
❑ 510	Jive Talkin'/Wind of Change	1975	4.00
❑ 515	Nights on Broadway/Edge of the Universe	1975	4.00
❑ 515 [DJ]	Nights on Broadway (Stereo Short Version 2:52)/(Mono Short Version 2:52)	1975	8.00
❑ 519	Fanny (Be Tender With My Love)/Country Lanes	1975	4.00
❑ 853	You Should Be Dancing/Subway	1976	4.00
❑ 859	Love So Right/You Stepped Into My Life	1976	4.00
❑ 867	Boogie Child/Lovers	1976	4.00
❑ 880	Edge of the Universe/Words	1977	4.00
❑ 882	How Deep Is Your Love/Can't Keep a Good Man Down	1977	4.00
❑ 885	Stayin' Alive/If I Can't Have You	1977	4.00
❑ 889	Night Fever/Down the Road	1978	4.00

Except when noted otherwise, VG = 25% of NM, and VG+ = 50% of NM. (Example: VG = $2.00, VG+ = $4.00 and NM = $8.00.)

Number	Title (A Side/B Side)	Yr	NM
❑ 907	She's Leaving Home/Oh! Darling	1978	4.00
—B-side by Robin Gibb solo			
❑ 913	Too Much Heaven/ Rest Your Love on Me	1978	4.00
❑ 913 [DJ]	Rest Your Love on Me (stereo/mono)	1979	12.00
—Promo of B-side, sent to country radio			
❑ 913 A [DJ]	Too Much Heaven (Stereo 3:15)/(Mono 3:15)	1978	10.00
—Both sides have edited versions			
❑ 918	Tragedy/Until	1979	4.00
❑ 918 [DJ]	Tragedy (Stereo 4:32)/ (Mono 3:42)	1979	10.00
—Promo only; both sides are shorter than the 5:01 stock copy			
❑ 925	Love You Inside Out/I'm Satisfied	1979	4.00
❑ 1066	He's a Liar/(Instrumental)	1981	3.00
❑ 1067	Living Eyes/I Still Love You	1981	3.00
❑ 8001	Come On Over/Jive Talkin'	1980	4.00
—Reissue series; first time on 45 for A-side			
❑ 8003	You Should Be Dancing/ Love So Right	1980	3.00
—Reissue series			
❑ 8009	Stayin' Alive/ How Deep Is Your Love	1980	3.00
—Reissue series			
❑ 8010	To Love Somebody/How Can You Mend a Broken Heart	1980	3.00
—Reissue series			
❑ 8011	Lonely Days/Words	1980	3.00
—Reissue series			
❑ 8012	Nights on Broadway/ Boogie Child	1980	3.00
—Reissue series			
❑ 8019	More Than a Woman/ Night Fever	1980	4.00
—Reissue series; first time on 45 for A-side			
❑ 8022	Tragedy/Love You Inside Out	1980	3.00
—Reissue series			
❑ 8030	Too Much Heaven/ Rest Your Love on Me	1980	3.00
—Reissue series			
❑ 813173-7	The Woman in You/Stayin' Alive	1983	3.00
❑ 813173-7 [PS]	The Woman in You/Stayin' Alive	1983	6.00
❑ 815235-7	Someone Belonging to Someone/I Love You Too Much	1983	3.00
❑ 815235-7 [PS]	Someone Belonging to Someone/I Love You Too Much	1983	6.00
WARNER BROS.			
❑ PRO-S-2858 [DJ]	You Win Again (Edit) (same on both sides)	1987	10.00
❑ 22733	You Win Again/ Will You Ever Let Me	1989	5.00
❑ 22899	One/Wing and a Prayer	1989	3.00
❑ 22899 [PS]	One/Wing and a Prayer	1989	3.00
❑ 28139	E.S.P./Overnight	1987	3.00
❑ 28139 [PS]	E.S.P./Overnight	1987	4.00
❑ 28351	You Win Again/Backtafunk	1987	3.00
❑ 28351 [PS]	You Win Again/Backtafunk	1987	3.00
7-Inch Extended Plays			
ATCO			
❑ SD 37-264	Where Are You/Spicks and Specks/Playdown//Second Hand People/Monday's Rain/ Tint of Blue	1968	25.00
—Jukebox single; small hole, plays at 33 1/3 rpm			
❑ SD 37-264 [PS]	Rare, Precious & Beautiful	1968	25.00
Albums			
ATCO			
❑ 33-223 [M]	Bee Gees' 1st	1967	30.00
❑ SD 33-223	Bee Gees' 1st	1969	10.00
—Yellow label reissue			
❑ SD 33-223 [S]	Bee Gees' 1st	1967	20.00
—Brown and purple label original			
❑ 33-233 [M]	Horizontal	1968	30.00
❑ SD 33-233	Horizontal	1969	10.00
—Yellow label reissue			
❑ SD 33-233 [S]	Horizontal	1968	20.00
—Brown and purple label original			
❑ 33-253 [M]	Idea	1968	50.00
—White label promo only			
❑ SD 33-253	Idea	1969	10.00
—Yellow label reissue			
❑ SD 33-253 [S]	Idea	1968	20.00
—Brown and purple label original			
❑ 33-264 [M]	Rare, Precious & Beautiful	1968	30.00
—White label promo only			
❑ SD 33-264	Rare, Precious & Beautiful	1969	10.00
—Yellow label reissue			
❑ SD 33-264 [R]	Rare, Precious & Beautiful	1968	15.00
—Brown and purple label original			
❑ 33-292 [M]	Best of Bee Gees	1969	30.00
—White label promo only			
❑ SD 33-292 [S]	Best of Bee Gees	1969	12.00
❑ 33-321 [M]	Rare, Precious & Beautiful, Vol. 2	1970	30.00
—White label promo only			
❑ SD 33-321 [R]	Rare, Precious & Beautiful, Vol. 2	1970	12.00

Number	Title (A Side/B Side)	Yr	NM
❑ SD 33-327	Cucumber Castle	1970	12.00
❑ 33-353 [M]	2 Years On	1971	30.00
—White label promo only; "DJ Copy Monaural" sticker on cover			
❑ SD 33-353 [S]	2 Years On	1971	12.00
❑ SD 2-702 [(2)]	Odessa	1969	40.00
—Red felt cover			
❑ SD 2-702 [(2)]	Odessa	1969	80.00
—Record club editions with plain red cover			
❑ SD 7003	Trafalgar	1971	12.00
❑ SD 7012	To Whom It May Concern	1972	12.00
MOBILE FIDELITY			
❑ 1-263	Trafalgar	1996	40.00
—Audiophile vinyl			
NAUTILUS			
❑ NR-17	Spirits Having Flown	1981	30.00
❑ NR-42	Living Eyes	1982	100.00
—Record was never released; value is for test pressings			
PICKWICK			
❑ BAN-90011 [R]	Turn Around, Look at Me	1978	8.00
—Reissue of Australian recordings			
❑ BAN-90021 [R]	Monday's Rain	1978	8.00
—Reissue of Australian recordings			
❑ BAN-90031 [R]	Take Hold of That Star	1978	8.00
—Reissue of Australian recordings			
❑ BAN-90041 [R]	Peace of Mind	1978	8.00
—Reissue of Australian recordings; tracks on this LP were making their first appearance in the U.S.			
RSO			
❑ SMP-1 [DJ]	The Words and Music of Maurice, Barry and Robin Gibb	1979	50.00
—Promo-only publisher's sampler			
❑ PRO 033 [DJ]	Saturday Night Fever Special Disco Versions	1978	50.00
—Promo-only sampler; contains an otherwise unavailable extended version of "Stayin' Alive"			
❑ SO 870 [M]	Life in a Tin Can	1973	60.00
—Mono is white label promo only; cover has red "d/j copy monaural" sticker on front; Side 1 master number is "SO-14153"; Side 2 master number is "SO-14154"			
❑ SO 870 [S]	Life in a Tin Can	1973	10.00
—Side 1 master number is "ST-SO-722677"; Side 2 master number is "ST-SO-722678"			
❑ SO 874	Best of Bee Gees	1973	10.00
—Reissue of Atco SD 33-292			
❑ SO 875	Best of Bee Gees, Vol. 2	1973	10.00
❑ PUB-1000 [DJ]	Unichappell Publisher's Sampler	1980	50.00
❑ RPO 1008 [DJ]	Select Disco Cuts from "Spirits Having Flown"	1979	30.00
❑ RS-1-3003	Children of the World	1976	10.00
❑ RS-1-3006	Bee Gees Gold, Vol. One	1976	10.00
❑ RS-1-3007	Odessa	1976	10.00
—Condensed version of Atco original			
❑ RS-1-3024	Main Course	1977	8.00
❑ RS-1-3041	Spirits Having Flown	1979	10.00
—Some pressings have a cardboard innersleeve, others a paper innersleeve. No difference in value.			
❑ RS-1-3042 [PD]	Spirits Having Flown	1979	15.00
❑ RS-1-3098	Living Eyes	1981	10.00
❑ RS-2-3901 [(2)]	Here At Last...Bee Gees...Live	1977	12.00
❑ RS-2-4200 [(2)]	Bee Gees' Greatest	1979	12.00
❑ SO 4800	Mr. Natural	1974	10.00
❑ SO 4807	Main Course	1975	10.00
❑ 823274-1 [(2)]	Here At Last...Bee Gees...Live	1984	10.00
❑ 823658-1	Children of the World	1984	8.00
❑ 823659-1	Bee Gees Gold, Vol. One	1984	8.00
❑ 825390-1 [(2)]	Bee Gees' Greatest	1984	10.00
—Gatefold replaced by single-pocket cover			
WARNER BROS.			
❑ 25541	E.S.P.	1987	10.00
❑ 25887	One	1989	12.00

BEE JAY

Number	Title (A Side/B Side)	Yr	NM
45s			
CLOCK			
❑ 1743	I'll Go On/There's No One for Me	1962	25.00

BEEFEATERS, THE Early version of THE BYRDS.

Number	Title (A Side/B Side)	Yr	NM
45s			
ELEKTRA			
❑ 45013	Please Let Me Love You/ Don't Be Long	1964	500.00
❑ 45013 [DJ]	Please Let Me Love You/ Don't Be Long	1964	250.00

BEEHIVES, THE

Number	Title (A Side/B Side)	Yr	NM
45s			
KING			
❑ 5881	I Want to Hold Your Hand/ She Loves You	1964	15.00

BEES, THE At least two different groups.

Number	Title (A Side/B Side)	Yr	NM
45s			
FINCH			
❑ 506	So Jealous/(B-side unknown)	196?	75.00

Number	Title (A Side/B Side)	Yr	NM
IMPERIAL			
❑ 5314	Toy Bell/Snatchin' Back	1954	200.00
❑ 5320	I Want to Be Loved/ Get Away Baby	1954	300.00
LIVERPOOL			
❑ 62225	Voices Green and Purple/ (B-side unknown)	1966	80.00
❑ 62225 [PS]	Voices Green and Purple/ (B-side unknown)	1966	100.00
MIRWOOD			
❑ 5503	She's An Artist/Leave Me Be	1965	25.00

BEETHOVEN SOUL

Number	Title (A Side/B Side)	Yr	NM
45s			
DOT			
❑ 17031	Good Time Gal/ The Walls Are High	1967	8.00
Albums			
DOT			
❑ DLP-3821 [M]	Beethoven Soul	1967	25.00
❑ DLP-25821 [S]	Beethoven Soul	1967	25.00

BEETLES, THE

Number	Title (A Side/B Side)	Yr	NM
45s			
BLUE CAT			
❑ 115	Ain't That Love/Welcome to My Heart	1965	15.00
—Also issued as "The Bouquets"			

BEGINNING OF THE END, THE

Number	Title (A Side/B Side)	Yr	NM
45s			
ALSTON			
❑ 4595	Funky Nassau- Part 1/ Funky Nassau - Part 2	1971	5.00
❑ 4599	Hey Pretty Girl/Monkey Tamarind	1971	4.00
❑ 4604	Come Down Baby - Part 1/ Come Down Baby - Part 2	1971	4.00
❑ 4605	Gee Whiz, It's Christmas/ Surrey Ride	1971	4.00
❑ 4607	Doin' the Funky Do/Fishman	1972	4.00
Albums			
ALSTON			
❑ SD 33-379	Funky Nassau	1971	20.00

BEL-AIRE GIRLS, THE

Number	Title (A Side/B Side)	Yr	NM
Albums			
EVEREST			
❑ STBR-1081 [S]	The Bel-Aire Girls Sing Along with the Teen-Agers	1960	80.00
❑ LPBR-5081 [M]	The Bel-Aire Girls Sing Along with the Teen-Agers	1960	60.00

BEL-AIRE POPS ORCHESTRA, THE

Number	Title (A Side/B Side)	Yr	NM
Albums			
LIBERTY			
❑ LRP-3414 [M]	Jan and Dean's Pop Symphony No. 1	1965	120.00
❑ LST-7414 [S]	Jan and Dean's Pop Symphony No. 1	1965	200.00

BEL-AIRES, THE (1)

Number	Title (A Side/B Side)	Yr	NM
45s			
CROWN			
❑ 126	Cherry Pie/Tick Tock	1954	50.00
FLIP			
❑ 303	This Paradise/Let's Party Awhile	1954	50.00
—Blue label			
❑ 303	This Paradise/Let's Party Awhile	1954	100.00
—Maroon label			
❑ 304	White Port and Lemon Juice/ This Is Goodbye	1955	100.00

BEL-AIRES, THE (U)

Number	Title (A Side/B Side)	Yr	NM
45s			
DECCA			
❑ 30631	My Yearbook/Rockin' An' Strollin'	1958	30.00
MERCURY			
❑ 71763	Knock Knock Knock (Knocking on My Door)/Wear My Class Ring on a Ribbon	1961	12.00
NU SOUND			
❑ 1022	Palmeras/Pony Rock	1962	12.00

BELAFONTE, HARRY

Number	Title (A Side/B Side)	Yr	NM
45s			
CAPITOL			
❑ F856	Whispering/Sometimes I Feel Like a Motherless Child	1950	40.00
❑ F1018	A Farewell to Arms/ I Still Get a Thrill	1950	30.00

Harry Belafonte, "Mama Look at Bubu," RCA Victor 47-6830, 1957, **$25.**

Number	Title (A Side/B Side)	Yr	NM
COLUMBIA			
❑ 18-02396	Forever Young/Something to Hold On To	1981	4.00
GEFFEN			
❑ 27859	Day-O/Main Titles	1988	3.00
—B-side: instrumental from the "Beetlejuice" soundtrack			
❑ 27859 [PS]	Day-O/Main Titles	1988	3.00
JUBILEE			
❑ 5158	Venezuela/Annabelle Lee	1954	20.00
RCA VICTOR			
❑ 47-4676	A-Roving/Chimney Smoke	1952	15.00
❑ 47-4892	Man Smart (Woman Smarter)/ Jerry	1952	15.00
❑ 47-5051	Scarlet Ribbons (For Her Hair)/ Shenandoah	1952	15.00
❑ 47-5210	Springfield Mountain/ Gomen-Nasai	1953	15.00
❑ 47-5311	Matilda, Matilda/Suzanne	1953	15.00
❑ 47-5617	Hold 'Em Joe/ I'm Just a Country Boy	1954	15.00
❑ 47-5722	Pretty As A Rainbow/ Acorn in the Meadow	1954	15.00
❑ 47-5722 [PS]	Pretty As A Rainbow/ Acorn in the Meadow	1954	30.00
❑ 47-5872	John Henry/(B-side unknown)	1954	15.00
❑ 47-6249	Troubles/Hello Everybody	1955	12.00
❑ 47-6458	The Blues Is Man (Part 1)/ The Blues Is Man (Part 2)	1956	12.00
❑ 47-6663	Jamaica Farewell/Once Was	1956	12.00
❑ 47-6663 [PS]	Jamaica Farewell/Once Was	1956	25.00
❑ 47-6735	Mary's Boy Child/Venezuela	1956	12.00
❑ 47-6735 [PS]	Mary's Boy Child/Venezuela	1956	25.00
❑ 47-6771	Banana Boat (Day-O)/Star-O	1956	12.00
❑ 47-6771 [PS]	Banana Boat (Day-O)/Star-O	1956	25.00
❑ 47-6780	John Henry/Tol' My Captain	1956	10.00
❑ 47-6781	Mo Mary/Lord Randall	1956	10.00
❑ 47-6782	Man Piaba/The Fox	1956	10.00
❑ 47-6782 [PS]	Man Piaba/The Fox	1956	20.00
❑ 47-6783	Man Smart (Woman Smarter)/ Chimney Smoke	1956	10.00
❑ 47-6784	Unchained Melody/A-Roving	1956	10.00
❑ 47-6785	Jump Down-Spin Around/In That Great Gettin' Up Mornin'	1956	10.00
❑ 47-6786	Will His Love Be Like His Rum?/ Dolly Dawn	1956	10.00
❑ 47-6787	Hosanna/I Adore Her	1956	10.00
❑ 47-6788	Come Back Liza/Brown Skin Girl	1956	10.00
❑ 47-6789	Water Boy/Noah	1956	10.00
❑ 47-6790	Danny Boy/Take My Mother Home	1956	10.00
❑ 47-6790 [PS]	Danny Boy/Take My Mother Home	1956	20.00
❑ 47-6830	Mama Look a Boo Boo (Shut Your Mouth - Go Away)/ Don't Ever Love Me	1957	12.00
—Same recording as above, but new A-side title			
❑ 47-6830	Mama Look at Bubu/ Don't Ever Love Me	1957	12.00
❑ 47-6830 [PS]	Mama Look at Bubu/ Don't Ever Love Me	1957	25.00
❑ 47-6885	Island in the Sun/ Cocoanut Woman	1957	10.00
❑ 47-7176	The Marching Saints/ Did You Hear About Jerry?	1958	8.00
❑ 47-7289	Ain't That Love/ The Waiting Game	1958	8.00
❑ 47-7425	I Heard the Bells on Christmas Day/Mary, Mary	1958	8.00
❑ 47-7425 [PS]	I Heard the Bells on Christmas Day/Mary, Mary	1958	15.00
❑ 47-7445	Gotta Travel On/Tarrytown	1959	8.00
❑ 47-7491	Darlin' Cora/Turn Around	1959	8.00
❑ 47-7550	Fifteen/'Round the Bay of Mexico	1959	8.00
❑ 47-7681	March Down to Jordan/ Oh Freedom	1960	8.00
❑ 47-8513	Hallelujah I Love You So/ In the Even' Mama	1965	6.00
❑ 47-8717	Little Bit of Rain/Roll On, Buddy	1965	6.00
❑ 47-9075	Hurry Sundown/ Mama Look At Bubu	1967	6.00
❑ 47-9263	Sunflower/A Strange Song	1967	6.00
❑ 47-9406	Annie Love/I'm Just a Country Boy	1967	6.00
❑ 47-9542	By the Time I Get to Phoenix/ Sleep Late, My Lady Friend	1968	6.00
❑ 74-0145	Lullabye/The Train Song	1969	5.00
—With Miriam Makeba			
❑ 74-0428	Circle 'Round the Sun/ Something in the Way She Moves	1971	5.00
❑ 74-0628	Women/Pastures of Plenty	1971	5.00
❑ 47-6783 [PS]	Man Smart (Woman Smarter)/ Chimney Smoke	1956	20.00
❑ 47-6784 [PS]	Unchained Melody/A-Roving	1956	20.00
❑ 47-7550 [PS]	Fifteen/'Round the Bay of Mexico	1959	15.00
❑ 47-9263 [PS]	Sunflower/A Strange Song	1967	10.00
❑ 447-0320	Suzanne/Matilda, Matilda!	195?	10.00
—Black label, dog on top			
❑ 447-0321	Shenandoah/Scarlet Ribbons	195?	10.00
—Black label, dog on top			
❑ 447-0321 [PS]	Shenandoah/Scarlet Ribbons	195?	20.00
❑ 447-0322	Hold 'Em Joe/I'm Just a Country Boy	195?	10.00
—Black label, dog on top			
❑ 447-0323	Mary's Boy Child/Venezuela	195?	10.00
—Black label, dog on top			
❑ 447-0324	Banana Boat (Day-O)/ Jamaica Farewell	195?	10.00
—Black label, dog on top			
❑ 447-0325	Mama Look A Boo Boo/ Don't Ever Love Me	195?	10.00
—Black label, dog on top			
❑ APBO-0093	Morningside/So Close	1973	4.00
❑ SP-45-181 [DJ]	By the Time I Get to Phoenix/ Sleep Late, My Lady Friend	1968	12.00
—Promo-only number			
7-Inch Extended Plays			
CAPITOL			
❑ EAP-1-619	Close Your Eyes/Sometimes I Feel Like a Motherless Child// I Still Get a Thrill/Deep As the River	1955	15.00
❑ EAP-1-619 [PS]	Close Your Eyes	1955	15.00
JUBILEE			
❑ EP 5006	Simple, Simple, Simple/ Annabelle Lee//Venezuela/ Only One Like Me	195?	20.00
❑ EP 5006 [PS]	Ballads by Belafonte	195?	20.00
RCA VICTOR			
❑ SPD-24 [PS]	The Best of Belafonte	1956	20.00
—Box for 10-EP set plus liner-note booklet			
❑ SP-45-67	Cocoanut Woman/A Woman Is a Sometime Thing//Turn Around/In the Evenin' Mama	1959	20.00
❑ SP-45-67 [PS]	RCA Victor Presents a Harry Belafonte Preview Album	1959	20.00
❑ LPC-127	Day-o/Jamaica Farewell// Man Smart (Woman Smarter)/Shenandoah	1961	10.00
—"Compact 33 Double"; small hole, plays at 33 1/3 rpm			
❑ LPC-127 [PS]	Belafonte at Carnegie Hall Highlights	1961	10.00
❑ 547-0404	Mark Twain/Man Piaba// Mo Mary/Lord Randall	1954	10.00
—Record 1 of 2-EP set EPB 1022			
❑ 547-0405	John Henry/Tol' My Captain// Soldier, Soldier/ The Next Big River	1954	10.00
—Record 2 of 2-EP set EPB 1022			
❑ EPA 412	Shenandoah/Scarlet Ribbons (For Her Hair)//Man Smart (Woman Smarter)/Jerry (This Timber Got to Roll)	1952	15.00
—Black label, outline of dog at right			
❑ EPA 412	Shenandoah/Scarlet Ribbons (For Her Hair)//Man Smart (Woman Smarter)/Jerry (This Timber Got to Roll)	1954	10.00
—Black label, white dog at top			
❑ EPA 412 [PS]	Harry Belafonte Sings "Man Smart" and Other Folk Songs	1952	12.00
❑ EPA 559	Delia/The Fox//Kalenda Rock/ The Drummer and the Cook	195?	12.00
❑ EPA 559 [PS]	Harry Belafonte	195?	12.00
❑ EPA 693	Take My Mother Home// Unchained Melody/Matilda	1955	12.00
❑ EPA 693 [PS]	Belafonte, Act 1	1955	12.00
❑ EPA 694	Sylvie//In That Great Gettin' Up Mornin'/Jump Down, Spin Around	1955	12.00
—With dog on label			
❑ EPA 694	Sylvie//In That Great Gettin' Up Mornin'/Jump Down, Spin Around	1955	15.00
—No dog on label			
❑ EPA 694 [PS]	Belafonte, Act 2	1955	12.00
❑ EPA 695	Noah//Suzanne (Every Night When the Sun Goes Down)/ Waterboy	1955	10.00
❑ EPA 695 [PS]	Belafonte, Act 3	1955	10.00

Except when noted otherwise, VG = 25% of NM, and VG+ = 50% of NM. (Example: VG = $2.00, VG+ = $4.00 and NM = $8.00.)

Number	Title (A Side/B Side)	Yr	NM
❑ EPA 768	Day O/Will His Love Be Like His Rum?//Jamaica Farewell/Dolly Dawn	1956	12.00
❑ EPA 768 [PS]	Calypso	1956	12.00
❑ 547-0899	Day-O/I Do Adore Her//Brown Skin Girl/Dolly Dawn	1956	10.00
—Record 1 of 2-EP set EPB 1248			
❑ 547-0900	Jamaica Farewell/Will His Love Be Like His Rum?//Star O/Hosanna	1956	10.00
—Record 2 of 2-EP set EPB 1248			
❑ EPB 1022 [PS]	"Mark Twain" and Other Folk Favorites	1954	20.00
—Two-pocket jacket for two-EP set			
❑ EPB 1248 [PS]	Calypso	1956	20.00
—Two-pocket jacket for two-EP set			
❑ EPA 1-1402	Merci Bon Dieu//The Drummer and the Cook/Danny Boy	1956	12.00
❑ EPA 1-1402 [PS]	An Evening with Belafonte, Vol. 1	1956	12.00
❑ EPA 2-1402	Cu Cu Ru Cu Cu/Paloma//Hava Negela/When the Saints Go Marching In	1956	12.00
❑ EPA 2-1402 [PS]	An Evening with Belafonte, Vol. 2	1956	12.00
❑ EPA 3-1402	Come Oh My Love//Eden Was Like This/Shenandoah	1956	12.00
❑ EPA 3-1402 [PS]	An Evening with Belafonte, Vol. 3	1956	12.00
❑ EPA 1-1505	Haiti Cherie/Love, Love Alone//Lucy's Door/Scratch, Scratch	1957	10.00
❑ EPA 1-1505 [PS]	Belafonte Sings of the Caribbean, Vol. 1	1957	10.00
❑ EPA 2-1505	(contents unknown)	1957	10.00
❑ EPA 2-1505 [PS]	Belafonte Sings of the Caribbean, Vol. 2	1957	10.00
❑ VLP 2449	Midnight Special/Crawdad Hole//Gotta Travel On/Mule Skinner	1962	50.00
—Jukebox issue; small hole, plays at 33 1/3 rpm; Bob Dylan plays harmonica on the first track			
❑ VLP 2449 [PS]	The Midnight Special	1962	50.00
❑ EPA-4084	Island in the Sun/Cocoanut Woman//Lead Man Holler	1957	12.00
❑ EPA-4084 [PS]	Island in the Sun	1957	12.00
❑ EPA 4217	Cordella Brown/Judy Drownded//Lead Man Holler/Angelique-O	1958	12.00
❑ EPA 4217 [PS]	Ballads by Belafonte	1958	12.00
❑ 599-9126	Day-O/I Do Adore Her//Jamaica Farewell/Will His Love Be Like His Rum?	1956	8.00
—Side 1 and 20 of 10-EP set SPD-24			
❑ 599-9127	Dolly Dawn/Star O//The Jack-Ass Song/Hosanna	1956	8.00
—Side 2 and 19 of 10-EP set SPD-24			
❑ 599-9128	Come Back Liza/Brown Skin Girl//Man Smart (Woman Smarter)/Matilda	1956	8.00
—Side 3 and 18 of 10-EP set SPD-24			
❑ 599-9129	Waterboy/Suzanne (Every Night When the Sun Goes Down)//Troubles/In That Great Gettin' Up Mornin'	1956	8.00
—Side 4 and 17 of 10-EP set SPD 24			
❑ 599-9130	Noah/Jump Down, Spin Around//Take My Mother Home	1956	8.00
—Side 5 and 16 of 10-EP set SPD-24			
❑ 599-9131	Sylvie//Scarlet Ribbons (For Her Hair)/Unchained Melody	1956	8.00
—Side 6 and 15 of 10-EP set SPD-24			
❑ 599-9132	Mark Twain/Tol' My Captain//Man Piaba/The Drummer and the Cook	1956	8.00
—Side 7 and 14 of 10-EP set SPD-24			
❑ 599-9133	John Henry/Kalenda Rock//The Fox/Soldier, Soldier/The Next Big River	1956	8.00
—Side 8 and 13 of 10-EP set SPD-24			
❑ 599-9134	Mo Mary/Lord Randall//Delia/Shenandoah	1956	8.00
—Side 9 and 12 of 10-EP set SPD-24			
❑ 599-9135	Jerry (The Timber Got to Roll)/The Blues Is Man - Part I//Acorn in the Meadow/Hello Everybody	1956	8.00
—Side 10 and 11 of 10-EP set SPD-24			

Albums

COLUMBIA

Number	Title (A Side/B Side)	Yr	NM
❑ FC 37489	Loving You Is Where I Belong	1981	10.00

DCC COMPACT CLASSICS

Number	Title (A Side/B Side)	Yr	NM
❑ LPZ-2039	Jump Up Calypso	1997	60.00
—Audiophile vinyl			

EMI

Number	Title (A Side/B Side)	Yr	NM
❑ E1-92247	Belafonte '89	1989	12.00

EMI MANHATAN

Number	Title (A Side/B Side)	Yr	NM
❑ E1-46971	Paradise in Gazankulu	1988	12.00

PAIR

Number	Title (A Side/B Side)	Yr	NM
❑ PDL2-1060 [(2)]	The Belafonte Song Book	1986	12.00

RCA CAMDEN

Number	Title (A Side/B Side)	Yr	NM
❑ ACL1-0502	Abraham, Martin and John	1974	10.00
❑ CAS-2599	Harry	1972	10.00

RCA CUSTOM EDITION

Number	Title (A Side/B Side)	Yr	NM
❑ DRL1-0068	I Wish You a Merry Christmas	1973	15.00
—Reissue of LSP-2424 with two tracks deleted			

RCA VICTOR

Number	Title (A Side/B Side)	Yr	NM
❑ APL1-0094	Play Me	1973	12.00
❑ ANL1-0979	Pure Gold	1975	10.00
❑ LOP-1006 [M]	Belafonte Sings the Blues	1958	30.00
—Original issue			
❑ LPM-1022 [M]	"Mark Twain" and Other Folk Favorites	1954	50.00
❑ LSP-1022(e) [R]	"Mark Twain" and Other Folk Favorites	196?	12.00
❑ LPM-1150 [M]	Belafonte	1955	50.00
❑ LSP-1150(e) [R]	Belafonte	196?	12.00
❑ AFL1-1248	Calypso	1977	10.00
—Reissue with new prefix			
❑ LPM-1248 [M]	Calypso	1956	30.00
❑ LSP-1248(e) [R]	Calypso	196?	12.00
❑ LPM-1402 [M]	An Evening with Belafonte	1957	25.00
❑ LSP-1402(e) [R]	An Evening with Belafonte	1960	12.00
—Dog on top			
❑ LSP-1402(e) [R]	An Evening with Belafonte	1969	10.00
—Orange label			
❑ ANL1-1434	An Evening with Belafonte	1976	10.00
—Reissue of LSP-1402			
❑ LPM-1505 [M]	Belafonte Sings of the Caribbean	1957	30.00
❑ LSP-1505(e) [R]	Belafonte Sings of the Caribbean	196?	12.00
❑ LOC-1507 [M]	Porgy and Bess	1959	20.00
❑ LSO-1507 [S]	Porgy and Bess	1959	25.00
—With Lena Horne			
❑ LPM-1887 [M]	To Wish You a Merry Christmas	1958	25.00
❑ LSP-1887 [S]	To Wish You a Merry Christmas	1958	40.00
❑ LPM-1927 [M]	Love Is a Gentle Thing	1959	20.00
❑ LSP-1927 [S]	Love Is a Gentle Thing	1959	25.00
❑ LPM-1972 [M]	Belafonte Sings the Blues	1959	20.00
—Reissue of LOP-1006			
❑ LSP-1972	Belafonte Sings the Blues	199?	25.00
—Classic Records reissue on audiophile vinyl			
❑ LSP-1972 [S]	Belafonte Sings the Blues	1959	25.00
❑ LPM-2022 [M]	My Lord What a Mornin'	1960	20.00
❑ LSP-2022 [S]	My Lord What a Mornin'	1960	25.00
❑ LPM-2194 [M]	Swing Dat Hammer	1961	20.00
❑ LSP-2194 [S]	Swing Dat Hammer	1961	25.00
❑ LPM-2309 [M]	At Home and Abroad	1961	20.00
❑ LSP-2309 [S]	At Home and Abroad	1961	25.00
❑ ANL1-2324	The Midnight Special	1976	10.00
—Reissue of LSP-2449			
❑ LPM-2388 [M]	Jump Up Calypso	1961	20.00
❑ LSP-2388 [S]	Jump Up Calypso	1961	25.00
❑ LPM-2449 [M]	The Midnight Special	1962	30.00
❑ LSP-2449 [S]	The Midnight Special	1962	40.00
—The above LP features Bob Dylan on harmonica on the title track, his first appearance on record			
❑ CPL1-2469	A Legendary Performer	1977	10.00
❑ LPM-2574 [M]	The Many Moods of Belafonte	1962	20.00
❑ LSP-2574 [S]	The Many Moods of Belafonte	196?	20.00
—"Stereo" on black label, "RCA Victor" in white			
❑ LSP-2574 [S]	The Many Moods of Belafonte	1962	25.00
—"Living Stereo" on label, "RCA Victor" in silver			
❑ LSP-2574 [S]	The Many Moods of Belafonte	1969	12.00
—Orange label			
❑ LPM-2626 [M]	To Wish You a Merry Christmas	1962	20.00
—Reissue of LPM-1887 with new cover and one additional track			
❑ LSP-2626 [S]	To Wish You a Merry Christmas	1962	25.00
❑ LPM-2695 [M]	Streets I Have Walked	1963	20.00
❑ LSP-2695 [S]	Streets I Have Walked	1963	25.00
❑ LPM-2953 [M]	Ballads, Blues and Boasters	1964	15.00
❑ LSP-2953 [S]	Ballads, Blues and Boasters	1964	20.00
❑ LPM-3415 [M]	An Evening with Belafonte/Mouskouri	1966	15.00
❑ LSP-3415 [S]	An Evening with Belafonte/Mouskouri	1966	20.00
—With Nana Mouskouri			
❑ LPM-3420 [M]	An Evening with Belafonte/Makeba	1965	15.00
❑ LSP-3420 [S]	An Evening with Belafonte/Makeba	1965	20.00
—With Miriam Makeba			
❑ LPM-3571 [M]	In My Quiet Room	1966	12.00
❑ LSP-3571 [S]	In My Quiet Room	1966	15.00
❑ LPM-3658 [M]	Calypso in Brass	1967	12.00
❑ LSP-3658 [S]	Calypso in Brass	1967	15.00
❑ LPM-3779 [M]	Belafonte on Campus	1967	12.00
❑ LSP-3779 [S]	Belafonte on Campus	1967	15.00
❑ AYL1-3801(e) [R]	Calypso	1980	8.00
❑ AYL1-3860(e) [R]	Pure Gold	1980	8.00
❑ LPM-3938 [M]	Belafonte Sings of Love	1968	15.00
❑ LSP-3938 [S]	Belafonte Sings of Love	1968	15.00
❑ LSP-4255	Homeward Bound	1969	15.00
❑ LSP-4301	By Request	1970	12.00
❑ LSP-4481	Warm Touch	1971	12.00
❑ LSP-4521	Calypso Carnival	1971	12.00
❑ LOC-6006 [(2)M]	Belafonte at Carnegie Hall	1959	25.00
❑ LSO-6006 [(2)S]	Belafonte at Carnegie Hall	1959	100.00
❑ LSO-6006 [(2)S]	Belafonte at Carnegie Hall	1996	40.00
—Classic Records reissue on audiophile vinyl			
❑ LOC-6007 [(2)M]	Belafonte Returns to Carnegie Hall	1960	20.00
❑ LSO-6007 [(2)]	Belafonte Returns to Carnegie Hall	1996	40.00
—Classic Records reissue on audiophile vinyl			
❑ LSO-6007 [(2)S]	Belafonte Returns to Carnegie Hall	1960	50.00
—The above LP also has tracks by Odetta, Miriam Makeba and The Chad Mitchell Trio (the latter for the first time on record)			
❑ LOC-6009 [(2)M]	Belafonte at the Greek Theatre	1964	20.00
❑ LSO-6009 [(2)S]	Belafonte at the Greek Theatre	1964	50.00
❑ VPS-6024 [(2)]	This Is Harry Belafonte	1970	15.00
❑ VPSX-6077 [(2)]	Belafonte Live	1972	15.00

TIME-LIFE

Number	Title (A Side/B Side)	Yr	NM
❑ SLGD-17 [(2)]	Legendary Singers: Harry Belafonte	1986	15.00

BELAIRS, THE

45s

ARVEE

Number	Title (A Side/B Side)	Yr	NM
❑ A-5034	Mr. Moto/Little Brown Jug	1961	40.00
❑ A-5054	Volcanic Action/Runaway	1962	30.00

BELEW, ADRIAN

Member of THE BEARS; KING CRIMSON; also briefly guitarist for FRANK ZAPPA and DAVID BOWIE.

12-Inch Singles

ATLANTIC

Number	Title (A Side/B Side)	Yr	NM
❑ 3324 [DJ]	I Am What I Am/Men in Helicopters/Young Lions	1990	6.00

45s

ATLANTIC

Number	Title (A Side/B Side)	Yr	NM
❑ 88904	Oh Daddy/Peaceable Kingdom	1989	3.00
❑ 88904 [PS]	Oh Daddy/Peaceable Kingdom	1989	3.00

Albums

ATLANTIC

Number	Title (A Side/B Side)	Yr	NM
❑ 81959	Mr. Music Head	1989	10.00
❑ 82099	Young Lions	1990	12.00

ISLAND

Number	Title (A Side/B Side)	Yr	NM
❑ IL 9751	Lone Rhino	1982	12.00
❑ 90108	Twang Bar King	1983	10.00
❑ 90551	Desire Caught by the Tail	1986	10.00

BELFAST GYPSIES, THE

Also see THEM.

45s

LOMA

Number	Title (A Side/B Side)	Yr	NM
❑ 2051	Gloria's Dream/Secret Police	1966	15.00
❑ 2060	Portland Town/People, Let's Freak Out	1966	15.00

BELL, ARCHIE, AND THE DRELLS

12-Inch Singles

BECKET

Number	Title (A Side/B Side)	Yr	NM
❑ BKD-501	Any Time Is Right (5:25)/Why Didja Do Me (5:05)	1981	12.00

PHILADELPHIA INT'L

Number	Title (A Side/B Side)	Yr	NM
❑ ASD 375 [DJ]	Glad You Could Make It (5:36)/There's No Other Like You (4:45)	1977	20.00

PHILADELPHIA INT'L.

Number	Title (A Side/B Side)	Yr	NM
❑ 4Z8 3701	Strategy/We Got 'Um Dancin'	1979	12.00

45s

ATLANTIC

Number	Title (A Side/B Side)	Yr	NM
❑ 2478	Tighten Up/Tighten Up — Part 2	1968	8.00
❑ 2478	Tighten Up/Dog Eat Dog	1968	12.00
❑ 2534	I Can't Stop Dancing/You're Such a Beautiful Child	1968	7.00
❑ 2559	Do the Choo Choo/Love Will Rain on You	1968	7.00
❑ 2583	(There's Gonna Be A) Showdown/Go for What You Know	1968	7.00
❑ 2612	I Love My Baby/Just a Little Closer	1969	7.00
❑ 2644	Girl You're Too Young/Do the Hand Jive	1969	7.00
❑ 2663	My Balloon's Going Up/Giving Up Dancing	1969	7.00
❑ 2693	A World Without Music/Here I Go Again	1969	7.00
❑ 2721	Don't Let the Music Slip Away/Houston, Texas	1970	7.00
❑ 2744	I Wish/Get from the Bottom	1970	7.00
❑ 2769	Wrap It Up/Deal with Him	1970	7.00
❑ 2793	I Just Want to Fall in Love/Love at First Sight	1971	6.00

Except when noted otherwise, VG = 25% of NM, and VG+ = 50% of NM. (Example: VG = $2.00, VG+ = $4.00 and NM = $8.00.)

Number	Title (A Side/B Side)	Yr	NM
❑ 2829	Let the World Know/ Archie's in Love	1971	6.00
❑ 2855	Green Power/ I Can't Face You Baby	1972	6.00
BECKET			
❑ 45-4	Any Time Is Right/ (B-side unknown)	1981	4.00
EAST WEST			
❑ 2048	She's My Woman/ The Yankee Dance	1968	7.00
GLADES			
❑ 1707	Dancing to Your Music/ Count the Ways	1973	6.00
❑ 1711	Ain't Nothing for a Man in Love/ You Never Know What's On a Woman's Mind	1973	6.00
❑ 1718	Girls Grow Up Faster Than Boys/ Love's Gonna Rain on You	1973	6.00
OVIDE			
❑ 228	Tighten Up/Dog Eat Dog	1967	60.00
PHILADELPHIA INT'L			
❑ 3605	Nothing Comes Easy/Right Here Is Where I Want to Be	1976	5.00
❑ 3615	Everybody Have a Good Time/ I Bet I Can Do That Dance You're Doin'	1977	5.00
❑ 3632	Glad You Could Make It/ There's No Other Like You	1977	5.00
❑ 3637	I've Been Missing You/It's Hard Not to Love You	1977	5.00
❑ 3651	Old People/On the Radio	1978	5.00
PHILADELPHIA INT'L.			
❑ 3710	Strategy/We Got 'Um Dancin'	1979	5.00
TSOP			
❑ 4767	I Could Dance All Night/ King of the Castle	1975	5.00
❑ 4774	The Soul City Walk/ King of the Castle	1975	5.00
❑ 4775	Let's Groove (Part 1)/ Let's Groove (Part 2)	1976	5.00
WMOT			
❑ 03057	Touchin' You/(Instrumental)	1982	5.00
Albums			
ATLANTIC			
❑ 8181 [M]	Tighten Up	1968	50.00
❑ SD 8181 [S]	Tighten Up	1968	30.00
❑ SD 8204	I Can't Stop Dancing	1968	30.00
❑ SD 8226	There's Gonna Be a Showdown	1969	30.00
PHILADELPHIA INT'L.			
❑ PZ 34323	Where Will You Go When the Party's Over	1976	10.00
❑ PZ 34855	Hard Not to Like It	1977	10.00
❑ JZ 36096	Strategy	1979	10.00
TSOP			
❑ PZ 33844	Dance Your Troubles Away	1975	10.00

BELL, CARL, AND THE NORVAIRS

Number	Title (A Side/B Side)	Yr	NM
45s			
LAURIE			
❑ 3014	Birth of the Beat/Open House in Your Heart	1958	25.00

BELL, FREDDIE, AND THE BELL BOYS

Number	Title (A Side/B Side)	Yr	NM
45s			
MERCURY			
❑ 70919	Stay Loose, Mother Goose/ All Right, OK, You Win	1956	20.00
❑ 71075	Take the First Train Out of Town/Hey There You	1957	20.00
❑ 71105	Rockin' Is My Business/ You're Gonna Be Sorry	1957	40.00
TEEN			
❑ 101	Hound Dog/Move Me Baby	1955	50.00
❑ 103	Old Town Hall/5-10-15 Hours	1955	30.00
WING			
❑ 90066	Giddy Up a Ding Dong/ I Said It and I'm Glad	1956	40.00
❑ 90082	The Hucklebuck/ Rompin' and Stompin'	1956	40.00
Albums			
MERCURY			
❑ MG-20289 [M]	Rock and Roll... All Flavors	1957	200.00
20TH FOX			
❑ TF-4146 [M]	Bells Are Swinging	1964	25.00
❑ TFS-4146 [S]	Bells Are Swinging	1964	30.00

BELL, MADELINE
Also see BLUE MINK.

Number	Title (A Side/B Side)	Yr	NM
45s			
ASCOT			
❑ 2156	You Don't Love Me No More/ Don't Cross Over to My Side of the Street	1964	10.00
❑ 2180	Don't Cry My Heart/Daytime	1965	10.00
BRUT			
❑ 808	All That Love Went to Waste/ A Touch of Class	1973	5.00
MOD			
❑ 1007	I'm Gonna Make You Love Me/ Picture Me Gone	1967	12.00
PHILIPS			
❑ 40517	I'm Gonna Make You Love Me/ Picture Me Gone	1968	8.00
❑ 40539	Finding You, Loving You/Doing Things Together with You	1968	6.00
❑ 40582	Step Inside Love/What I'm Supposed to Do	1969	6.00
PYE			
❑ 71061	I Always Seem to Wind Up Loving You/Your Smile	1976	4.00
Albums			
PHILIPS			
❑ PHS 600271	I'm Gonna Make You Love Me	1968	12.00

BELL, MAGGIE
Also see STONE THE CROWS.

Number	Title (A Side/B Side)	Yr	NM
45s			
ATLANTIC			
❑ 3018	After Midnight/Souvenirs	1974	5.00
❑ 3040	Caddo Queen/Oh My My	1974	5.00
SWAN SONG			
❑ 70105	Wishing Well/Comin' On Strong	1975	5.00
❑ 99907	Here, There and Everywhere/ Put Angels Around You	1983	4.00
—With Bobby Whitlock			
❑ 99907 [PS]	Here, There and Everywhere/ Put Angels Around You	1983	4.00
—With Bobby Whitlock			
Albums			
ATLANTIC			
❑ SD 7293	Queen of the Night	1974	12.00
SWAN SONG			
❑ SS 8412	Suicide Sal	1975	12.00

BELL, TRUDY

Number	Title (A Side/B Side)	Yr	NM
45s			
PHILIPS			
❑ 40021	Willie/This Friend of Mine	1962	12.00
❑ 40055	I Remember Jimmy/A Promise and a Kiss Goodnight	1962	12.00

BELL, VINCENT

Number	Title (A Side/B Side)	Yr	NM
45s			
DECCA			
❑ 32224	Eleanor/Goin' Out of My Head	1967	6.00
❑ 32418	California Summer/A Sinner Kissed An Angel	1968	6.00
❑ 32483	Good Morning Starshine/ Because of You	1969	5.00
❑ 32530	Les Bicyclettes De Belsize/ The Ballad of John and Yoko	1969	5.00
❑ 32659	Airport Love Theme/ Marilyn's Theme	1970	5.00
❑ 32695	Darling Lili/Nikki	1970	5.00
INDEPENDENT			
❑ 102	Quicksand/(B-side unknown)	1960	40.00
MUSICOR			
❑ 1068	Just a Little Kiss/ Baker Street Mystery	1965	12.00
VERVE			
❑ 10308	Shindig/Whistle Stop	1963	12.00
Albums			
DECCA			
❑ DL 4938 [M]	Pop Goes the Electric Sitar	1967	20.00
❑ DL 74938 [S]	Pop Goes the Electric Sitar	1967	15.00
❑ DL 75212	Airport Love Theme	1970	15.00
MUSICOR			
❑ MM-3009 [M]	51 Motion Picture Favorites	1963	15.00
❑ MS-3009 [S]	51 Motion Picture Favorites	1963	20.00
❑ MM-3047 [M]	Big 16 Guitar Favorites	1965	15.00
❑ MS-3047 [S]	Big 16 Guitar Favorites	1965	20.00
VERVE			
❑ V-8574 [M]	Whistle Stop	1964	15.00
❑ V6-8574 [S]	Whistle Stop	1964	20.00

BELL, WILLIAM

Number	Title (A Side/B Side)	Yr	NM
12-Inch Singles			
WRC			
❑ 12204	Headline News/ Let Him Pay the Band	1986	10.00
45s			
ATLANTIC			
❑ 13154	Everyday Will Be Like A Holiday/Winner	197?	4.00
—Oldies Series reissue			
KAT FAMILY			
❑ 03502	Bad Time to Break Off/The Truth in Your Eyes	1983	4.00
❑ 03995	Playing Hard to Get/ The Truth in Your Eyes	1983	4.00
MERCURY			
❑ 73839	Tryin' to Love Two/If Sex Was All We Had	1976	5.00
❑ 73922	Coming Back for More/You I Absolutely Positively Love	1977	4.00
❑ 73961	Your Love Keeps Me Goin'/ Easy Comin' Out	1977	4.00
STAX			
❑ 0005	Private Number/Love-Eye-Tis	1968	5.00
—With Judy Clay			
❑ 0015	I Forgot to Be Your Lover/ Bring the Curtains Down	1968	6.00
❑ 0017	Left-Over Love/My Baby Specializes	1968	5.00
—With Judy Clay			
❑ 0032	My Whole World Is Falling Down/All God's Children Got Soul	1969	5.00
❑ 0038	My Kind of Girl/Happy	1969	5.00
❑ 0043	Love's Sweet Sensation/ Strung Out	1969	5.00
—With Mavis Staples			
❑ 0044	I Can't Stop/I Need You Woman	1969	5.00
—With Carla Thomas			
❑ 0054	Born Under a Bad Sign/A Smile Can't Hide a Broken Heart	1969	5.00
❑ 0067	All I Have to Do Is Dream/Leave the Girl Alone	1970	5.00
—With Carla Thomas			
❑ 0070	Lonely Soldier/Let Me Ride	1970	5.00
❑ 0092	A Penny for Your Thoughts/Till My Back Ain't Got No Bone	1971	5.00
❑ 0106	All for the Love of a Woman/ I'll Be Home	1971	5.00
❑ 116	You Don't Miss Your Water/ Formula of Love	1961	20.00
❑ 128	Any Other Way/Please Help Me I'm Falling	1962	20.00
❑ 0128	If You Really Love Him/Save Us	1972	5.00
❑ 132	I Told You So/ What'Cha Gonna Do	1963	15.00
❑ 135	Just As I Thought/ I'm Waiting on You	1963	15.00
❑ 138	Somebody Mentioned Your Name/What Can I Do to Forget	1963	15.00
❑ 141	I'll Show You/Monkeying Around	1963	15.00
❑ 146	Don't Make Something Out of Nothing/Who Will It Be Tomorrow	1964	12.00
❑ 0157	Livin' on Borrowed Time/ The Man in the Street	1973	5.00
❑ 174	Crying All By Myself/ Don't Stop Now	1965	12.00
❑ 0175	You've Got the Kind of Love I Need/I've Got to Go On Without You	1973	5.00
❑ 191	Share What You Got/ Marching Off to War	1966	10.00
❑ 0198	All I Need Is Your Love/ Gettin' What You Want	1974	5.00
❑ 199	Soldier's Goodbye/ Never Like This Before	1966	10.00
❑ 212	Everybody Loves a Winner/ You're Such a Sweet Thing	1967	8.00
❑ 0221	Get It While It's Hot/Nobody Walks Away from Love Unhurt	1974	5.00
❑ 227	One Plus One/Eloise (Hang On In There)	1967	8.00
❑ 237	Everyday Will Be Like a Holiday/Ain't Got No Girl	1967	8.00
❑ 248	A Tribute to a King (Otis Redding)/Every Man Oughta Have a Woman	1968	6.00
WRC			
❑ 202	I Don't Want to Wake Up (Feelin' Guilty)/Whatever You Want (You Got It)	1986	5.00
—With Janice Bulluck			
❑ 204	Headline News/ Let Him Pay the Band	1986	5.00

Except when noted otherwise, VG = 25% of NM, and VG+ = 50% of NM. (Example: VG = $2.00, VG+ = $4.00 and NM = $8.00.)

Number	Title (A Side/B Side)	Yr	NM
Albums			
KAT FAMILY			
❑ FZ 38643	Survivor	1983	10.00
MERCURY			
❑ SRM-1-1146	Coming Back for More	1977	10.00
❑ SRM-1-1193	It's Time You Took Another Listen	1978	10.00
STAX			
❑ 719 [M]	Soul of a Bell	1967	40.00
❑ S-719 [S]	Soul of a Bell	1967	50.00
❑ ST-2014 [M]	Bound to Happen	1969	50.00
—Mono is promo only			
❑ STS-2014 [S]	Bound to Happen	1969	30.00
❑ STS-2037	Wow...	1971	30.00
❑ STS-3005	Phases of Reality	1973	20.00
❑ STS-5502	Relating	1974	20.00
❑ MPS-8541	The Best of William Bell	1988	10.00
WRC			
❑ WL-3007	On a Roll	1986	12.00

BELL HOPS, THE
Probably two different groups.

Number	Title (A Side/B Side)	Yr	NM
45s			
BARB			
❑ 100	Angela/Ring Dang Doo Ting-a-Ling	1958	25.00
❑ 101/2	Teenage Years/Carmella	1958	25.00
DECCA			
❑ 48208	For the Rest of My Life/It Would Take a Million Years	1951	100.00
❑ 48239	I'm All Yours/Where Is Love	1951	100.00
TIN PAN ALLEY			
❑ 153	Please Don't Say No to Me/ Merchant Street Blues	1956	150.00

BELL NOTES, THE

Number	Title (A Side/B Side)	Yr	NM
45s			
AUTOGRAPH			
❑ 204	Little Girl in Blue/ Too Young or Too Old	1960	25.00
CLOCK			
❑ 71889	There She Goes/ My Pledge to You	1961	20.00
MADISON			
❑ 136	Shortnin' Bread/ To Each His Own	1960	20.00
❑ 141	Real Wild Child/Friendly Star	1960	20.00
TIME			
❑ 1004	I've Had It/Be Mine	1958	30.00
—First pressing on blue labels			
❑ 1004	I've Had It/Be Mine	1959	25.00
—Later pressings on red labels			
❑ 1010	Old Spanish Town/She Went Thataway	1959	25.00
❑ 1013	That's Right/Betty Dear	1959	25.00
❑ 1015	You're a Big Girl Now/ Don't Ask Me Why	1959	25.00
❑ 1017	White Buckskin Sneakers and Checkerboard Socks/No Dice	1959	25.00
7-Inch Extended Plays			
TIME			
❑ TEP-100	I've Had It/Be Mine//Dream Street/A Sad Guitar	1959	100.00
❑ TEP-100 [PS]	I've Had It	1959	100.00

BELL TONES, THE

Number	Title (A Side/B Side)	Yr	NM
45s			
RAMA			
❑ 170	Heart to Heart/The Wedding	1955	200.00

BELLAMY, DAVID
One-half of THE BELLAMY BROTHERS.

Number	Title (A Side/B Side)	Yr	NM
45s			
WARNER BROS.			
❑ 8123	Baby, You're Not a Legend/ Nothin' Heavy	1975	5.00

BELLAND & SOMERVILLE

Number	Title (A Side/B Side)	Yr	NM
45s			
BARNABY			
❑ 2009	Sure Seems a Lot Like Sunday/ When She's Lovin'	1969	8.00

BELLES, THE

Number	Title (A Side/B Side)	Yr	NM
45s			
HIT			
❑ 83	Sally Go 'Round the Roses/ Be My Baby	1963	8.00
—B-side by the Georgettes			
❑ 96	You Don't Have to Be a Baby to Cry/There! I've Said It Again	1963	8.00
—B-side by Fred York			
❑ 101	The Boy Next Door/As Usual	1964	8.00
—B-side by Betty Williams			

BELLS, THE (1)
Canadian band with male and female lead singers.

Number	Title (A Side/B Side)	Yr	NM
45s			
MGM			
❑ 14533	Child of Mine/He Was Me, He Was You	1973	4.00
❑ 14624	Love Once Removed/ The Singer	1973	4.00
POLYDOR			
❑ 15016	Fly Little White Dove, Fly/ Follow the Sun	1970	4.00
❑ 15023	Stay Awhile/Sing a Song of Freedom	1971	5.00
❑ 15025	Je Vais Rester/Blanc Petit Ois Eau Blanc	1970	4.00
❑ 15027	I Love You Lady Dawn/Rain	1971	4.00
❑ 15029	She's a Lady/ Sweet Sounds of Music	1971	4.00
❑ 15031	To Know You Is To Love You/ For Better For Worse	1971	4.00
❑ 15036	Oh My Love/You You You	1972	4.00
❑ 15039	Lord, Don't You Think It's Time/ Easier Said Than Done	1972	4.00
❑ 15063	Kris Collection/Simple Song of Freedom	1973	4.00
Albums			
POLYDOR			
❑ 24-4510	Fly, Little White Dove, Fly	1971	15.00
❑ 24-5503	Love, Luck & Lollypops	1972	15.00

BELLS, THE (2)
Male vocal group.

Number	Title (A Side/B Side)	Yr	NM
45s			
RAMA			
❑ 166	What Can I Tell Her Now/ Let Me Love You, Love You	1955	500.00

BELLTONES, THE

Number	Title (A Side/B Side)	Yr	NM
45s			
GRAND			
❑ 102	Estelle/Promise Love	1954	4000.
—VG 2000; VG+ 3000			
LOST-NITE			
❑ 319	Estelle/Promise Love	197?	5.00
—Reissue			

BELLUS, TONY

Number	Title (A Side/B Side)	Yr	NM
45s			
ERA BACK TO BACK HITS			
❑ 048	Robbin' the Cradle/ Rockin' Little Angel	197?	5.00
—B-side by Ray Smith			
KING			
❑ 5973	Mustang/Goodbye Baby, Goodbye	1964	12.00
NRC			
❑ 023	Robbin' the Cradle/Valentine Girl	1959	20.00
—Available with the letters "NRC" with no background, with the title of the song in either orange or blue letters; also with each letter of "NRC" in a background box. No difference in value.			
❑ 035	Hey Little Darlin'/Only Your Heart	1959	20.00
❑ 040	Little Dreams/Young Girls	1959	20.00
❑ 045	Hey Little Darlin'/Young Girls	1959	20.00
❑ 051	The End of My Love/ The Echo of An Old Song	1960	20.00
—Available on both white and tan labels, no difference in value			
❑ 051 [PS]	The End of My Love/ The Echo of An Old Song	1960	50.00
❑ 058	The Great Pretender/Give Me a Heart	1960	20.00
SHI-FI			
❑ 60	Seven Flags/Robbin' the Cradle	196?	50.00
❑ 60 [PS]	Seven Flags/Robbin' the Cradle	196?	50.00
—Special promotional item for "Tony Bellus' Seven Flags" International Cafe & Lounge in Kankakee, IL			
Albums			
NRC			
❑ LPA-8 [M]	Robbin' the Cradle	1960	100.00
—Black label			
❑ LPA-8 [M]	Robbin' the Cradle	1960	200.00
—Blue label			
SHI-FI			
❑ LP-11 [M]	Gems of Tony Bellus	196?	60.00

BELMONTS, THE
Also see DION AND THE BELMONTS; BUDDY SHEPPARD AND THE HOLIDAYS.

Number	Title (A Side/B Side)	Yr	NM
45s			
DOT			
❑ 17173	Reminiscing/She Only Wants to Do Her Thing	1968	15.00
❑ 17257	Have You Heard-The Worst That Could Happen/ Answer Me My Love	1969	15.00
LAURIE			
❑ 3080	We Belong Together/ Such a Long Way	1961	30.00
❑ 3631	A Brand New Song/Story Teller	1975	5.00
❑ 3698	Medley/You're the Only Girl for Me	198?	5.00
—B-side by Ernie Maresca			
SABINA			
❑ 502	I Need Some One/ That American Dance	1961	25.00
❑ 503	Hombre/I Confess	1962	25.00
❑ 505	Come On Little Angel/ How About Me	1962	20.00
—Greenish label			
❑ 505	Come On Little Angel/ How About Me	1962	25.00
—Black label			
❑ 507	Diddle-Dee-Dum (What Happens When Your Love Has Gone)/Farewell	1962	20.00
❑ 509	Ann Marie/Ac-Cent-Tchu-Ate the Positive	1963	20.00
❑ 513	Let's Call It a Day/Walk On Boy	1963	20.00
❑ 517	More Important Things to Do/ Walk On Boy	1963	20.00
❑ 519	C'mon Everybody/Why	1964	20.00
❑ 521	Summertime/Nothing in Return	1964	20.00
SABRINA			
❑ 500	Tell Me Why/ Smoke from Your Cigarette	1961	25.00
❑ 501	Searching for a New Love/Don't Get Around Much Anymore	1961	25.00
STRAWBERRY			
❑ 106	Cheek to Cheek/Voyager	1976	5.00
SURPRISE			
❑ 1000	Tell Me Why/ Smoke from Your Cigarette	1961	100.00
UNITED ARTISTS			
❑ 809	Wintertime/I Don't Know Why, I Just Do	1965	20.00
❑ 904	(Then) I Walked Away/Today My Love Has Gone Away	1965	20.00
❑ 966	I Got a Feeling/To Be with You	1965	20.00
❑ S7-19769	Wintertime/Please Come Home for Christmas	1997	4.00
—B-side by Dion on The Right Stuff			
❑ 50007	Come with Me/ You're Like a Mystery	1966	25.00
Albums			
BUDDAH			
❑ BDS-5123	Cigars, Acapella, Candy	1972	50.00
DOT			
❑ DLP-25949	Summer Love	1969	30.00
SABINA			
❑ SALP-5001 [M]	The Belmonts' Carnival of Hits	1962	150.00
STRAWBERRY			
❑ 6001	Cheek to Cheek	1978	15.00

BELVIN, ANDY

Number	Title (A Side/B Side)	Yr	NM
45s			
ATCO			
❑ 6289	Travelin' Mood/Flip Flip	1964	12.00
CANDIX			
❑ 338	Walking the Blues/Prettiest Girl	1962	20.00
VAULT			
❑ 908	Travelin' Mood/Flip Flop	1964	15.00

BELVIN, JESSE
Also see THE CLIQUES; JESSE AND MARVIN.

Number	Title (A Side/B Side)	Yr	NM
45s			
ALADDIN			
❑ 3431	Let Me Dream/Sugar Doll	1958	40.00
CASH			
❑ 1056	Dry Your Tears/Beware	1957	25.00
—Orange and black label			
❑ 1056	Dry Your Tears/Beware	1957	100.00
—Black and silver label			
CLASS			
❑ 267	I'm Confessin'/Deep in My Heart	1960	25.00
HOLLYWOOD			
❑ 1059	Betty My Darling/Dear Heart	1956	400.00
IMPACT			
❑ 23	Tonight My Love/ Looking for Love	1962	15.00
JAMIE			
❑ 1145	Goodnight My Love (Pleasant Dreams)/My Desire	1959	20.00
KENT			
❑ 326	Sentimental Reasons/Senorita	1959	25.00

Except when noted otherwise, VG = 25% of NM, and VG+ = 50% of NM. (Example: VG = $2.00, VG+ = $4.00 and NM = $8.00.)

Pat Benatar, "All Fired Up," Chrysalis 43268, 1988, **$3.**

Number	Title (A Side/B Side)	Yr	NM
KNIGHT			
❑ 2012	Little Darling/Deacon Dan Tucker	1959	40.00
MODERN			
❑ 45x1005	Goodnight My Love (Pleasant Dreams)/Let Me Love You Tonight	1956	40.00
❑ 45x1005	Goodnight My Love (Pleasant Dreams)/I Want You With Me Xmas	1956	50.00
❑ 1013	I Need You So/Senorita	1957	30.00
❑ 1015	By My Side/Don't Close the Door	1957	30.00
❑ 1020	Sad and Lonesome/I'm Not Free	1957	30.00
❑ 1025	You Send Me/Summertime	1957	30.00
❑ 1027	My Satellite/Just to Say Hello	1957	30.00
MONEY			
❑ 208	I'm Only a Fool/ Trouble and Misery	1955	60.00
RCA VICTOR			
❑ 47-7310	Volare/Ever Since We Met	1958	20.00
❑ 47-7387	Funny/Pledging My Love	1958	20.00
❑ 47-7469	Guess Who/My Girl Is Just Enough Woman for Me	1959	20.00
❑ 47-7543	Here's a Heart/ It Could've Been Worse	1959	20.00
❑ 47-7596	Give Me Love/I'll Never Be Lonely Again	1959	20.00
❑ 47-7675	Something Happens to Me/The Door Is Always Open	1960	20.00
❑ 47-8040	Guess Who/Funny	1962	15.00
❑ 61-7469	Guess Who/My Girl Is Just Enough Woman for Me	1959	50.00
—"Living Stereo" (large hole, plays at 45 rpm)			
RECORDED IN HOLLYWOOD			
❑ 120	Dream Girl/Hang Your Tears Out to Dry	1951	600.00
❑ 412	Love Comes Tumbling Down/ (B-side unknown)	1953	400.00
SPECIALTY			
❑ 435	Confusin' Blues/Baby Don't Go	1952	80.00
❑ 550	Gone/One Little Blessing	1955	50.00
❑ 559	Where's My Girl/ Love, Love of My Life	1955	50.00
Albums			
CROWN			
❑ CLP-5145 [M]	The Casual Jesse Belvin	1959	70.00
—Black label			
❑ CLP-5145 [M]	The Casual Jesse Belvin	196?	15.00
—Gray label			
❑ CLP-5187 [M]	The Unforgettable Jesse Belvin	1959	70.00
—Black label			
❑ CLP-5187 [M]	The Unforgettable Jesse Belvin	196?	15.00
—Gray label			
RCA CAMDEN			
❑ CAL-960 [M]	Jesse Belvin's Best	1966	12.00
❑ CAS-960 [S]	Jesse Belvin's Best	1966	15.00
RCA VICTOR			
❑ LPM-2089 [M]	Just Jesse Belvin	1959	40.00
❑ LSP-2089 [S]	Just Jesse Belvin	1959	60.00
❑ LPM-2105 [M]	Mr. Easy	1960	30.00
❑ LSP-2105 [S]	Mr. Easy	1960	40.00
SPECIALTY			
❑ SP-7003	The Blues Balladeer	1990	15.00

BEN, LA BRENDA

Number	Title (A Side/B Side)	Yr	NM
45s			
GORDY			
❑ 7009	Camel Walk/The Chaperone	1962	50.00
❑ 7021	I Can't Help It, I Gotta Dance/ Just Be Yourself	1963	50.00
MOTOWN			
❑ 1033	Camel Walk/Chaperone	1962	400.00

BENATAR, PAT

Number	Title (A Side/B Side)	Yr	NM
12-Inch Singles			
CHRYSALIS			
❑ CHS-20-PDJ [DJ]	We Live for Love (Specially Mixed for Rock Radio 3:35) (same on both sides)	1980	10.00
❑ CHS-23-PDJ [DJ]	You Better Run (Specially Mixed) (same on both sides)	1980	10.00
❑ CHS-44-PDJ [DJ]	Shadows of the Night (same on both sides)	1982	8.00
❑ VAS 1164 [DJ]	All Fired Up (Edit) (LP Version)	1988	12.00
❑ VAS 1374 [DJ]	Let's Stay Together (12" Mix) (Dub Mix) (12" Edit)	1988	10.00
❑ AS 1616 [DJ]	Little Too Late/Anxiety (Get Nervous)	1983	12.00
❑ AS 1745 [DJ]	Love Is a Battlefield (Long) (Short)	1983	8.00
❑ AS 1924 [DJ]	We Belong (3:40) (same on both sides)	1984	12.00
❑ AS 1996 [DJ]	Ooh Ooh Song (same on both sides)	1984	12.00
❑ VAS 2031 [DJ]	Temporary Heroes (Special Re-Mix for Radio 4:22) (Single Version 4:00)	1985	15.00
❑ VAS 2098 [DJ]	Invincible (Theme from The Legend of Billie Jean) (same on both sides)	1985	8.00
❑ VAS 2157 [DJ]	Sex as a Weapon (4:15) (same on both sides)	1985	8.00
❑ VAS 2267 [DJ]	Le Bel Age (Edit 4:15) (LP Version 5:10)	1986	8.00
❑ VAS 2292 [DJ]	Big Life (same on both sides)	1986	8.00
❑ 4V9 42734	Love Is a Battlefield (Extended Version) (Instrumental)	1983	10.00
❑ 4V9 42878	Invincible (Theme from The Legend of Billie Jean) (Extended Remix 5:29) (Instrumental 4:23)	1985	8.00
❑ 4V9 42917	Sex as a Weapon (Extended Version 6:13) (Instrumental 4:48)	1985	10.00
DREAMWORKS			
❑ PRO-A-5113 [DJ]	Love Is a Battlefield (unknown versions)	1998	15.00
—With Queen Latifah; from the movie soundtrack of "Small Soldiers"			
45s			
CHRYSALIS			
❑ 2373	If You Think You Know How to Love Me/(B-side unknown)	1979	8.00
❑ 2395	Heartbreaker/ My Clone Sleeps Alone	1979	4.00
❑ 2395 [PS]	Heartbreaker/ My Clone Sleeps Alone	1979	6.00
❑ 2419	We Live for Love/So Sincere	1980	4.00
❑ 2419 [PS]	We Live for Love/So Sincere	1980	6.00
❑ 2450	You Better Run/Out-A Touch	1980	3.00
❑ 2464 [PS]	Hit Me with Your Best Shot/ Prisoner of Love	1980	4.00
❑ 2464	Hit Me with Your Best Shot/ Prisoner of Love	1980	3.00
❑ 2487 [PS]	Treat Me Right/Never Wana Leave You	1981	4.00
❑ 2487	Treat Me Right/Never Wana Leave You	1981	3.00
❑ 2529 [PS]	Fire and Ice/Hard to Believe	1981	4.00
❑ 2529	Fire and Ice/Hard to Believe	1981	3.00
❑ 2555 [PS]	Promises in the Dark/Evil Genius	1981	4.00
❑ 2555	Promises in the Dark/Evil Genius	1981	3.00
❑ 2647 [PS]	Shadows of the Night/The Victim	1982	4.00
❑ 2647	Shadows of the Night/The Victim	1982	3.00
❑ 03536	Little Too Late/Fight It Out	1983	3.00
❑ 03536 [PS]	Little Too Late/Fight It Out	1983	3.00
❑ 03541	Shadows of the Night/The Victim	1983	4.00
❑ S7-17490	Somebody's Baby/Crying	1993	3.00
❑ S7-17592	Everybody Lay Down/ Promises in the Dark (Live)	1993	3.00
❑ S7-18301	Hit Me with Your Best Shot/ Heartbreaker	1995	3.00
❑ S7-18302	Shadows of the Night/ Little Too Late	1995	3.00
❑ S7-18913	Please Come Home for Christmas/True Love	1995	3.00
❑ 42688	Looking for a Stranger/I'll Do It	1983	3.00
❑ 42688 [PS]	Looking for a Stranger/I'll Do It	1983	4.00
❑ 42732	Love Is a Battlefield/ Hell Is For Children	1983	3.00
❑ 42732 [PS]	Love Is a Battlefield/ Hell Is For Children	1983	3.00
❑ 42826	We Belong/Suburban King	1984	3.00
❑ 42826 [PS]	We Belong/Suburban King	1984	4.00
❑ 42843	Ooh Ooh Song/ La Cancion Ooh Ooh	1984	3.00
❑ 42843 [PS]	Ooh Ooh Song/ La Cancion Ooh Ooh	1984	3.00
❑ 42877	Invincible (Theme from The Legend of Billie Jean)/ (Instrumental)	1985	3.00
—Note slightly altered subtitle			
❑ 42877	Invincible (Theme from Legend of Billie Jean)/(Instrumental)	1985	4.00

Number	Title (A Side/B Side)	Yr	NM
❑ 42877 [PS]	Invincible (Theme from The Legend of Billie Jean)/ (Instrumental)	1985	4.00
❑ 42927	Sex as a Weapon/Red Vision	1985	3.00
❑ 42927 [PS]	Sex as a Weapon/Red Vision	1985	4.00
❑ 42968	Le Bel Age/Walking in the Underground	1986	3.00
❑ 43268	All Fired Up/Cool Zero	1988	3.00
❑ 43268 [PS]	All Fired Up/Cool Zero	1988	3.00
❑ 43301	Don't Walk Away/Lift 'Em On Up	1988	3.00
❑ 43314	Let's Stay Together/Wide Awake in Dreamland	1988	3.00
❑ 43314 [PS]	Let's Stay Together/Wide Awake in Dreamland	1988	3.00

TRACE

Number	Title (A Side/B Side)	Yr	NM
❑ 5293	Day Gig/Last Saturday	1976	30.00

Albums

CHRYSALIS

Number	Title (A Side/B Side)	Yr	NM
❑ CHR 1236	In the Heat of the Night	1979	8.00
❑ CHE 1275	Crimes of Passion	1980	8.00
❑ CHE 1275	Crimes of Passion	1980	30.00
—Error pressing: White label (not a promo) with photo of Pat leaning on a barre, as on regular copies, but with no blue at all, and with no butterfly or "Chrysalis" on label			
❑ CHR 1346	Precious Time	1981	8.00
❑ CHR 1396	Get Nervous	1982	8.00
❑ F1-21715	Best Shots	1989	12.00
❑ FV 41236	In the Heat of the Night	1983	6.00
—Reissue of 1236			
❑ FV 41275	Crimes of Passion	1983	6.00
—Reissue of 1275			
❑ FV 41346	Precious Time	1983	6.00
—Reissue of 1346			
❑ FV 41396	Get Nervous	1983	6.00
—Reissue of 1396			
❑ FV 41444	Live from Earth	1983	8.00
❑ FV 41471	Tropico	1984	8.00
❑ FV 41507	Seven the Hard Way	1985	8.00
❑ FV 41628	Wide Awake in Dreamland	1988	8.00

MOBILE FIDELITY

Number	Title (A Side/B Side)	Yr	NM
❑ 1-057	In the Heat of the Night	1981	25.00
—Audiophile vinyl			

BENDER, FREDDIE

45s

PARKWAY

Number	Title (A Side/B Side)	Yr	NM
❑ 876	Miss Daisy De Lite/ Let's Twist Again	1963	15.00

BENET, VICKI

45s

DECCA

Number	Title (A Side/B Side)	Yr	NM
❑ 30044	Sam's Song (The Happy Tune)/ Tea for Two	1956	15.00

LIBERTY

Number	Title (A Side/B Side)	Yr	NM
❑ 55100	After My Laughter Came Tears/ Always in My Heart	1957	15.00
❑ 55186	Heartstring Melody/Love Me	1959	12.00

Albums

DECCA

Number	Title (A Side/B Side)	Yr	NM
❑ DL 8233 [M]	Woman of Paris	1956	40.00
❑ DL 8381 [M]	The French Touch	1957	40.00
❑ DL 8987 [M]	Vicki Benet a Paris	1959	30.00
❑ DL 78987 [S]	Vicki Benet a Paris	1959	40.00

LIBERTY

Number	Title (A Side/B Side)	Yr	NM
❑ LRP-3103 [M]	Sing to Me of Love	1960	25.00
❑ LST-7103 [S]	Sing to Me of Love	1960	30.00

BENNETT, BOYD

45s

KING

Number	Title (A Side/B Side)	Yr	NM
❑ 1201	Precious Little Sweetheart/ Wasting My Time	1953	50.00
❑ 1413	Waterloo/I've Had Enough	1954	35.00
❑ 1432	Poison Ivy/You Upset Me Baby	1955	35.00
❑ 1443	Everlovin'/Boogie at Midnight	1955	35.00
❑ 1470	Seventeen/Little Old You-All	1955	25.00
—Blue label			
❑ 1470	Seventeen/Little Old You-All	1955	35.00
—Maroon label			
❑ 1475	Tennessee Rock and Roll/ Oo, Oo, Oo	1955	25.00
❑ 1494	My Boy-Flat Top/ Banjo Rock and Roll	1955	25.00
❑ 4853	Desperately/The Most	1955	25.00
❑ 4874	Right Around the Corner/ Partners for Life	1956	25.00
❑ 4903	Blue Suede Shoes/ Mumbles Blues	1956	25.00
❑ 4925	Let Me Love You/Groovy Age	1956	25.00
❑ 4953	Hit That Jive, Jack/Rabbit-Eye Pink and Charcoal Black	1956	25.00
❑ 4985	Rockin' Up a Storm/ A Lock of Your Hair	1956	25.00
❑ 5021	I'm Moving On/Big Jay Shuffle	1957	25.00
❑ 5049	Big Boy/Put the Chain on the Door	1957	25.00
❑ 5097	Sentimental Journey/ Boy Meets Girl	1957	25.00
❑ 5113	Signed, Sealed and Delivered/ Her Momma Doesn't Think It's Right	1958	25.00
❑ 5115	Click Clack/Move	1958	25.00
❑ 5282	High School Hop/ Cool Disc Jockey	1959	25.00
❑ 5374	Seventeen/My Boy Flat Top	1960	25.00
❑ 5738	Teenage Years/Hear Me Talking	1963	15.00

MERCURY

Number	Title (A Side/B Side)	Yr	NM
❑ 71409	Tight Tights/Tear It Up	1959	20.00
❑ 71479	Boogie Bear/A Boy Can Tell	1959	20.00
❑ 71537	Naughty Rock and Roll/ Lover's Night	1959	20.00
❑ 71605	It's Wonderful/Amo, Amas, Amat	1960	20.00
❑ 71648	Seventeen/Sarasota	1960	20.00
❑ 71724	Hershey Bar/Big Junior	1960	20.00
❑ 71813	Coffee Break/The Brain	1961	20.00

7-Inch Extended Plays

KING

Number	Title (A Side/B Side)	Yr	NM
❑ 377	(contents unknown)	1956	200.00
❑ 377 [PS]	Boyd Bennett	1956	300.00
❑ 383 [PS]	Rock & Roll with Boyd Bennett & the Rockets	1956	300.00
❑ 383	Right Around the Corner/The Most//My Boy - Flat Top/ Tennessee Rock and Roll	1956	200.00

Albums

KING

Number	Title (A Side/B Side)	Yr	NM
❑ 395-594 [M]	Boyd Bennett	1955	4000.
—VG value 1500; VG+ value 2750			

BENNETT, CLIFF, AND THE REBEL ROUSERS

45s

ABC

Number	Title (A Side/B Side)	Yr	NM
❑ 10842	Got to Get You Into My Life/ Baby Each Day	1966	15.00

AMY

Number	Title (A Side/B Side)	Yr	NM
❑ 930	If Only You'd Reply/Three Rooms with Running Water	1965	15.00

ASCOT

Number	Title (A Side/B Side)	Yr	NM
❑ 2146	Everybody Loves a Lover/ My Old Stand By	1964	15.00

CAPITOL

Number	Title (A Side/B Side)	Yr	NM
❑ 4621	I'm in Love with You/ You've Got What I Like	1961	50.00
❑ 5309	One Way Love/ I'm in Love with You	1964	15.00

BENNETT, JOE, AND THE SPARKLETONES

45s

ABC-PARAMOUNT

Number	Title (A Side/B Side)	Yr	NM
❑ 9837	Black Slacks/ Boppin' Rock Boogie	1957	30.00
❑ 9867	Penny Loafers and Bobby Socks/Rocket	1957	30.00
❑ 9885	Cotton Pickin' Rocker/ I Dig You Baby	1958	30.00
❑ 9929	Little Turtle/We've Had It	1958	30.00
❑ 9959	Do the Stop/Late Again	1958	30.00

PARIS

Number	Title (A Side/B Side)	Yr	NM
❑ 530	Bayou Rock/Beautiful One	1959	30.00
❑ 537	Boys Do Cry/What the Heck	1959	25.00
❑ 546	Softly/What the Heck	1960	25.00

Albums

MCA

Number	Title (A Side/B Side)	Yr	NM
❑ 1553	Black Slacks	1983	15.00

BENNETT, TONY

45s

BRUT

Number	Title (A Side/B Side)	Yr	NM
❑ 813	All That Love Went to Waste/ Some of These Days	1973	6.00
❑ 813 [PS]	All That Love Went to Waste/ Some of These Days	1973	6.00

COLUMBIA

Number	Title (A Side/B Side)	Yr	NM
❑ AE 28 [DJ]	My Favorite Things/ I Love the Winter Weather	1970	8.00
❑ AE 28 [PS]	My Favorite Things/ I Love the Winter Weather	1970	12.00
—Theme Song for 1970 Christmas Seals Campaign			
❑ 1-640 (?)	The Boulevard of Broken Dreams/I Wanna Be Loved	1950	25.00
—Microgroove 7-inch 33 1/3 rpm single			
❑ 1-670 (?)	Let's Make Love/I Can't Give You Anything But Love, Baby	1950	25.00
—Microgroove 7-inch 33 1/3 rpm single			
❑ 1-800 (?)	Sing You Sinners/Kiss You	1950	25.00
—Microgroove 7-inch 33 1/3 rpm single			
❑ 6-800 (?)	Sing You Sinners/Kiss You	1950	20.00
❑ 38-06138	Why Do People Fall in Love/ Moments Like This	1986	3.00
❑ 38-07658	White Christmas/All of My Life	1987	3.00
❑ 38-07658 [PS]	White Christmas/All of My Life	1987	3.00
❑ 31272 [S]	(contents unknown)	1961	12.00
❑ 31273 [S]	(contents unknown)	1961	12.00
❑ 31274 [S]	(contents unknown)	1961	12.00
❑ 31275 [S]	(contents unknown)	1961	12.00
❑ 31276 [S]	(contents unknown)	1961	12.00
❑ 31563 [S]	(contents unknown)	1962	12.00
❑ 31564 [S]	(contents unknown)	1962	12.00
❑ 31565 [S]	(contents unknown)	1962	12.00
❑ 31566 [S]	(contents unknown)	1962	12.00
❑ 31567 [S]	(contents unknown)	1962	12.00
—Anyone who can fill in these gaps — the above 10 all are Columbia "Stereo 7" singles — please let us know.			
❑ 39187	Once There Lived a Fool/ I Can't Give You Anything But Love, Baby	1951	15.00
❑ 39209	Beautiful Madness/ Valentino Tango	1951	15.00
❑ 3-39209	Beautiful Madness/ Valentino Tango	1951	25.00
—Microgroove 7-inch 33 1/3 rpm single			
❑ 39362	Because of You/ I Won't Cry Anymore	1951	12.00
❑ 39449	Cold, Cold Heart/ While We're Young	1951	12.00
❑ 39555	Blue Velvet/Solitaire	1951	12.00
❑ 39635	Silly Dreamer/ Since My Love Has Gone	1952	12.00
❑ 4-39695	Sleepless/Somewhere Along the Way	1952	12.00
❑ 39745	Here in My Heart/I'm Lost Again	1952	12.00
❑ 39764	Have a Good Time/ Please My Love	1952	12.00
❑ 39815	You Could Make Me Smile Again/Roses of Yesterday	1952	12.00
❑ 39824	Because of You/ I Won't Cry Anymore	1952	10.00
❑ 39825	The Boulevard of Broken Dreams/I Wanna Be Loved	1952	10.00
❑ 39826	Once There Lived a Fool/ The Valentine Tango	1952	10.00
❑ 39827	Cold, Cold Heart/ While We're Young	1952	10.00
❑ 39910	Congratulations to Someone/ Take Me	1953	12.00
❑ 39964	I'm the King of Broken Hearts/ No One Will Ever Know	1953	12.00
❑ 40004	Someone Turned the Moon Upside Down/I'll Go	1953	12.00
❑ 40048	Rags to Riches/Here Comes That Heartache Again	1953	12.00
❑ 40121	Stranger in Paradise/Why Does It Have to Be Me	1953	12.00
❑ 40169	There'll Be No Teardrops Tonight/My Heart Won't Say Goodbye	1954	12.00
❑ 40213	Until Yesterday/Please Driver, Once Around the Park Again	1954	12.00
❑ 40272	Cinnamon Sinner/ Take Me Back Again	1954	12.00
❑ 4-40311	Not As a Stranger/ Madonna, Madonna	1954	12.00
❑ 40376	Funny Thing/My Pretty Shoo-Gah	1954	12.00
❑ 40427	It's Too Soon to Know/ Close Your Eyes	1955	10.00
❑ 40491	What Will I Tell My Heart/ Punch and Judy Love	1955	10.00
❑ 40523	May I Never Love Again/ Don't Tell Me Why	1955	10.00
❑ 40567	How Can I Replace You/ Tell Me That You Love Me	1955	10.00
❑ 40598	Come Next Spring/ Afraid of the Dark	1955	10.00
❑ 40632	Sing You Sinners/Capri in May	1956	10.00
❑ 40667	Can You Find It in Your Heart/ Forget Her	1956	10.00
❑ 40726	From the Candy Store on the Corner to the Chapel on the Hill/Happiness Street (Corner Sunshine Square)	1956	10.00
❑ 40770	The Autumn Waltz/Just in Time	1956	10.00
❑ 40849	One Kiss Away from Heaven/ Sold to the Man with the Broken Heart	1957	10.00
❑ 40907	One for My Baby (And One More for the Road)/ No Hard Feelings	1957	10.00
❑ 40965	In the Middle of An Island/I Am	1957	10.00
❑ 41032	Ca, C'est L'amour/I Never Felt More Like Falling in Love	1957	10.00
❑ 41086	Love Song from Beauty and the Beast/Weary Blues From Waitin'	1957	10.00
❑ 41127	You're So Right for Me/ Alone at Last	1958	10.00

B

Number	Title (A Side/B Side)	Yr	NM
❑ 41157	Crazy Rhythm/The Beat of My Heart	1958	10.00
❑ 41172	Young and Warm and Wonderful/Now I Lay Me Down to Sleep	1958	10.00
❑ 41237	Firefly/The Night That Heaven Fell	1958	10.00
❑ 41237 [PS]	Firefly/The Night That Heaven Fell	1958	20.00
❑ 41298	Love, Look Away/Blue Moon	1958	10.00
❑ 41341	It's So Peaceful in the Country/Being True to One Another	1959	10.00
❑ 41381	The Cool School/You'll Never Get Away from Me	1959	10.00
❑ 41434	Smile/You Can't Love 'Em All	1959	10.00
❑ 41520	Climb Ev'ry Mountain/Ask Anyone in Love	1959	10.00
❑ 41595	I'll Bring You a Rainbow/Ask Me (I Know)	1960	8.00
❑ 41691	Put On a Happy Face/Baby, Talk to Me	1960	8.00
❑ 41770	Till/I Am	1960	8.00
❑ 41860	Marriage-Go-Round/Somebody	1960	8.00
❑ 41874	Ramona/Follow Me	1960	8.00
❑ 41965	The Best Is Yet to Come/Marry Young	1961	8.00
❑ 42003	Toot Toot Tootsie (Goodbye)/I'm Coming Virginia	1961	8.00
❑ 42135	Close Your Eyes/Rules of the Road	1961	8.00
❑ 42219	Tender Is the Night/Comes Once in a Lifetime	1961	8.00
❑ 42332	I Left My Heart In San Francisco/Once Upon a Time	1962	8.00
❑ 42332 [PS]	I Left My Heart In San Francisco/Once Upon a Time	1962	15.00
❑ 42395	Candy Kisses/Have I Told You Lately That I Love You	1962	8.00
❑ 42634	I Wanna Be Around/I Will Live My Life for You	1962	8.00
❑ 42779	The Good Life/Spring in Manhattan	1963	8.00
❑ 42820	This Is All I Ask/True Blue Lou	1963	8.00
❑ 42886	Don't Wait Too Long/Limehouse Blues	1963	8.00
❑ 42931	The Little Boy/The Moment of Truth	1963	8.00
❑ 42996	When Joanna Loved Me/The Kid's a Dreamer	1964	8.00
❑ 42996 [DJ]	When Joanna Loved Me (same on both sides)	1964	20.00
—Promo only on red vinyl			
❑ 42996 [PS]	When Joanna Loved Me/The Kid's a Dreamer	1964	20.00
—Promo-only title sleeve with red vinyl issue; no number on sleeve			
❑ 43073	It's a Sin to Tell a Lie/A Taste of Honey	1964	8.00
❑ 43141	Who Can I Turn To (When Nobody Needs Me)/Waltz for Debby	1964	8.00
❑ 43202	The Best Thing to Be Is a Person/The Brightest Smile in Town	1964	8.00
❑ 43220	If I Ruled the World/Take the Moment	1965	6.00
❑ 43331	Fly Me to the Moon (In Other Words)/How Insensitive	1965	6.00
❑ 43431	The Shadow of Your Smile/I'll Only Miss Her When I Think of Her	1965	6.00
❑ 43508	Song from The Oscar/Baby Dream Your Dream	1966	6.00
❑ 43508 [PS]	Song from The Oscar/Baby Dream Your Dream	1966	10.00
❑ 43715	Georgia Rose/The Very Thought	1966	6.00
❑ 43768	A Time for Love/Touch the Earth	1966	6.00
❑ 43954	What Makes It Happen/Country Girl	1966	6.00
❑ 43954 [DJ]	What Makes It Happen/Country Girl	1966	15.00
—Orange-vinyl promo issue			
❑ 44154	Keep Smiling at Trouble/Days of Love	1967	5.00
❑ 44258	For Once in My Life/How Do You Say Auf Wiedersehn	1967	6.00
❑ 44443	The Glory of Love/A Fool of Fools	1968	5.00
❑ 44510	Yesterday I Heard the Rain/Sweet Georgie Fame	1968	5.00
❑ 44584	Hushabye Mountain/Hi-Ho	1968	5.00
❑ 44688	Where Is Love/My Favorite Things	1968	5.00
❑ 44755	People/They All Laughed	1969	5.00
❑ 44824	Whoever You Are, I Love You/A Place Over the Sun	1969	5.00
❑ 44855	What the World Needs Now Is Love/Play It Again Sam	1969	5.00
❑ 44947	I've Gotta Be Me/A Lonely Place	1969	5.00
❑ 45032	MacArthur Park/Before We Say Goodbye	1969	5.00
❑ 45073	Little Green Apples/Coco	1970	5.00
❑ 45109	Something/Eleanor Rigby	1970	5.00
❑ 45157	Everybody's Talkin'/Think How It's Gonna Be	1970	5.00
❑ 45205	Something/Think How It's Gonna Be	1970	5.00
❑ 45255	I'll Begin Again/I Do Not Know a Day I Did Not Love You	1970	5.00
❑ 45316	(Where Do I Begin) Love Story/I'll Begin Again	1971	5.00
❑ 45376	I Want to Be Happy/Tea for Two	1971	5.00
❑ 45411	More and More/I'm Losing My Mind	1971	5.00
❑ 45449	Walkabout/How Beautiful Is Night	1971	5.00
❑ 45493	Remind Me/The Riviera	1971	5.00
❑ 45523	Somewhere Along the Line/The Summer Knows	1972	5.00
❑ 45573	Twilight World/Easy Come, Easy Go	1972	5.00
❑ 45613	Love/Maybe This Time	1972	5.00
❑ 38-79658	New York State of Mind/Don't Cry Baby	2001	3.00
—A-side with Billy Joel			
❑ JZSP 112321 [DJ]	Love Theme from "The Sandpiper" (The Shadow of Your Smile) (same on both sides)	1965	8.00
—Black vinyl promo			

IMPROV

Number	Title (A Side/B Side)	Yr	NM
❑ 6976	There's Always Tomorrow (Theme Song for the United Way)/I Wish I Were in Love Again	197?	4.00

MGM

Number	Title (A Side/B Side)	Yr	NM
❑ 14607	My Love/(B-side unknown)	1973	4.00

VERVE

Number	Title (A Side/B Side)	Yr	NM
❑ 10690	Living Together, Growing Together/The Good Things in Life	1972	4.00
❑ 10702	O Solo Mio/The Good Things in Life	1973	4.00
❑ 10714	Tell Her It's Snowing/If I Could Go Back	1973	4.00

7-Inch Extended Plays

COLUMBIA

Number	Title (A Side/B Side)	Yr	NM
❑ B-314 [PS]	Because of You	195?	20.00
—Gatefold cover for 2-EP set (5-1003 and 5-1004)			
❑ 7-823	Blue Velvet/Rags to Riches/Because of You//It Amazes Me/Firefly/I Left My Heart in San Francisco	196?	10.00
—"Special Coin Operator Release"; small hole, plays at 33 1/3 rpm			
❑ 7-823 [PS]	Tony Bennett at Carnegie Hall	196?	10.00
❑ 5-1003	Because of You/The Boulevard of Broken Dreams//I Won't Cry Anymore/Cold, Cold Heart	195?	20.00
—Alternate numbers are "B-314-1" and "B-314-4"			
❑ B-1842	Stranger in Paradise/Why Does It Have to Be Me//Rags to Riches/Congratulations to Someone	195?	15.00
❑ B-1842 [PS]	Tony Bennett Spotlite	195?	15.00
❑ B-2582	*One for My Baby/I Can't Give You Anything But Love/Solitaire/Once There Lived a Fool	1959	10.00
❑ B-2582	Tony Bennett (Hall of Fame Series)	1959	10.00
❑ 7-8800	I Wanna Be Around/The Good Life/Let's Face the Music and Dance//Once Upon a Summertime/Someone to Love/Quiet Night	1964	10.00
—"Special Coin Operator Release"; small hole, plays at 33 1/3 rpm			
❑ 7-8800 [PS]	I Wanna Be Around	1964	10.00
❑ 7-9085	Who Can I Turn To (When Nobody Needs Me)/Wrap Your Troubles in Dreams (And Dream Your Troubles Away)/Autumn Leaves//The Brightest Smile in Town/Listen, Little Girl/The Best Thing to Be Is a Person	1964	10.00
—"Special Coin Operator Release"; small hole, plays at 33 1/3 rpm			
❑ 7-9085 [PS]	Who Can I Turn To	1964	10.00
❑ 7-9173	I Left My Heart in San Francisco/I Wanna Be Around/Quiet Nights of Quiet Stars/The Good Life/A Taste of Honey/The Best Is Yet to Come	1964	10.00
—"Special Coin Operator Release"; small hole, plays at 33 1/3 rpm			
❑ 7-9173 [PS]	Tony Bennett's Greatest Hits Vol. III	1964	12.00
❑ B-9382	*These Foolish Things/I Can't Give You Anything But Love/Boulevard of Broken Dreams/I'll Be Seeing You	1957	10.00
❑ B-9382 [PS]	Tony	1957	10.00
❑ ZTEP 26851/2	Because of You/In the Middle of an Island/Cold, Cold Heart//From Rags to Riches/Come Next Spring/Can You Find It in Your Heart	1957	25.00
—Coca-Cola promotional item			
❑ ZTEP 26851/2 [PS]	Tony Bennett Autographed Edition of Hits	1957	25.00
—Coca-Cola promotional item			

Albums

COLUMBIA

Number	Title (A Side/B Side)	Yr	NM
❑ GP 14 [(2)]	Love Songs	1969	15.00
❑ C2L 23 [(2)M]	Tony Bennett at Carnegie Hall	1962	20.00
❑ CL 621 [M]	Cloud Seven	1955	40.00
❑ C2S 823 [(2)S]	Tony Bennett at Carnegie Hall	1962	25.00
❑ CL 938 [M]	Tony	1956	30.00
❑ CL 1079 [M]	The Beat of My Heart	1957	30.00
❑ CL 1186 [M]	Long Ago and Far Away	1958	30.00
❑ CL 1229 [M]	Tony's Greatest Hits	1958	30.00
❑ CL 1292 [M]	Blue Velvet	1958	30.00
❑ CL 1301 [M]	Hometown, My Hometown	1959	25.00
❑ CL 1429 [M]	To My Wonderful One	1960	25.00
❑ CL 1446 [M]	Tony Sings for Two	1960	25.00
❑ CL 1471 [M]	Alone Together	1960	25.00
❑ CL 1535 [M]	More Tony's Greatest Hits	1961	20.00
❑ CL 1559 [M]	A String of Harold Arlen	1961	20.00
❑ CL 1658 [M]	My Heart Sings	1961	20.00
❑ CL 1763 [M]	Mr. Broadway	1962	15.00
❑ CL 1869 [M]	I Left My Heart in San Francisco	1962	15.00
❑ CL 1905 [M]	Tony Bennett at Carnegie Hall Vol. 1	1963	15.00
❑ CL 2000 [M]	I Wanna Be Around	1963	15.00
❑ CL 2056 [M]	This Is All I Ask	1963	15.00
❑ CL 2141 [M]	The Many Moods of Tony	1964	15.00
❑ CL 2175 [M]	When Lights Are Low	1964	15.00
❑ CL 2285 [M]	Who Can I Turn To	1964	15.00
❑ CL 2343 [M]	If I Ruled the World — Songs for the Jet Set	1965	12.00
❑ CL 2373 [M]	Tony's Greatest Hits, Vol. III	1965	12.00
❑ CL 2472 [M]	The Movie Song Album	1966	12.00
❑ CL 2507 [10]	Alone at Last with Tony Bennett	1955	60.00
❑ CL 2550 [10]	Because of You	1956	60.00
❑ CL 2560 [M]	A Time for Love	1966	12.00
❑ CL 2653 [M]	Tony Makes It Happen!	1967	15.00
❑ CL 2773 [M]	For Once in My Life	1967	30.00
❑ CL 6221 [10]	Because of You	1952	80.00
❑ CS 8107 [S]	Hometown, My Hometown	1959	40.00
❑ CS 8226 [S]	To My Wonderful One	1960	40.00
❑ CS 8242 [S]	Tony Sings for Two	1960	40.00
❑ CS 8262 [S]	Alone Together	1960	40.00
❑ CS 8335 [S]	More Tony's Greatest Hits	1961	25.00
❑ CS 8359 [S]	A String of Harold Arlen	1961	25.00
❑ CS 8458 [S]	My Heart Sings	1961	25.00
❑ CS 8563 [S]	Mr. Broadway	1962	20.00
❑ CS 8652 [R]	Tony's Greatest Hits	1962	15.00
❑ CS 8669 [S]	I Left My Heart in San Francisco	1962	20.00
❑ PC 8669	I Left My Heart in San Francisco	198?	8.00
—Reissue with new prefix			
❑ CS 8705 [S]	Tony Bennett at Carnegie Hall Vol. 1	1963	20.00
❑ CS 8800 [S]	I Wanna Be Around	1963	25.00
❑ CS 8856 [S]	This Is All I Ask	1963	20.00
❑ CS 8941 [S]	The Many Moods of Tony	1964	20.00
❑ CS 8975 [S]	When Lights Are Low	1964	20.00
❑ CS 9085 [S]	Who Can I Turn To	1964	20.00
❑ CS 9143 [S]	If I Ruled the World — Songs for the Jet Set	1965	15.00
❑ CS 9173 [S]	Tony's Greatest Hits, Vol. III	1965	15.00
❑ CS 9272 [S]	The Movie Song Album	1966	15.00
❑ CS 9360 [S]	A Time for Love	1966	15.00
❑ CS 9453 [S]	Tony Makes It Happen!	1967	15.00
❑ CS 9573 [S]	For Once in My Life	1967	15.00
❑ CS 9678	Yesterday I Heard the Rain	1968	15.00
❑ CS 9739	Snowfall: The Tony Bennett Christmas Album	1968	12.00
❑ CS 9814	Tony Bennett's Greatest Hits, Vol. IV	1969	15.00
❑ CS 9882	I've Gotta Be Me	1969	15.00
❑ CS 9980	Tony Sings the Great Hits of Today!	1970	12.00
❑ C 30240	All Time Hall of Fame Hits	1971	12.00
❑ PC 30240	All Time Hall of Fame Hits	197?	10.00
—Reissue with new prefix			
❑ C 30280	Tony Bennett's "Something"	1971	12.00
❑ C 30558	Love Story	1971	12.00
❑ C 31219	Summer of '42	1972	12.00
❑ KC 31460	With Love	1972	12.00
❑ KG 31494 [(2)]	Tony Bennett's All-Time Greatest Hits	1972	15.00
❑ CG 33612 [(2)]	I Left My Heart in San Francisco/Tony Sings the Great Hits of Today!	1975	15.00

Except when noted otherwise, VG = 25% of NM, and VG+ = 50% of NM. (Example: VG = $2.00, VG+ = $4.00 and NM = $8.00.)

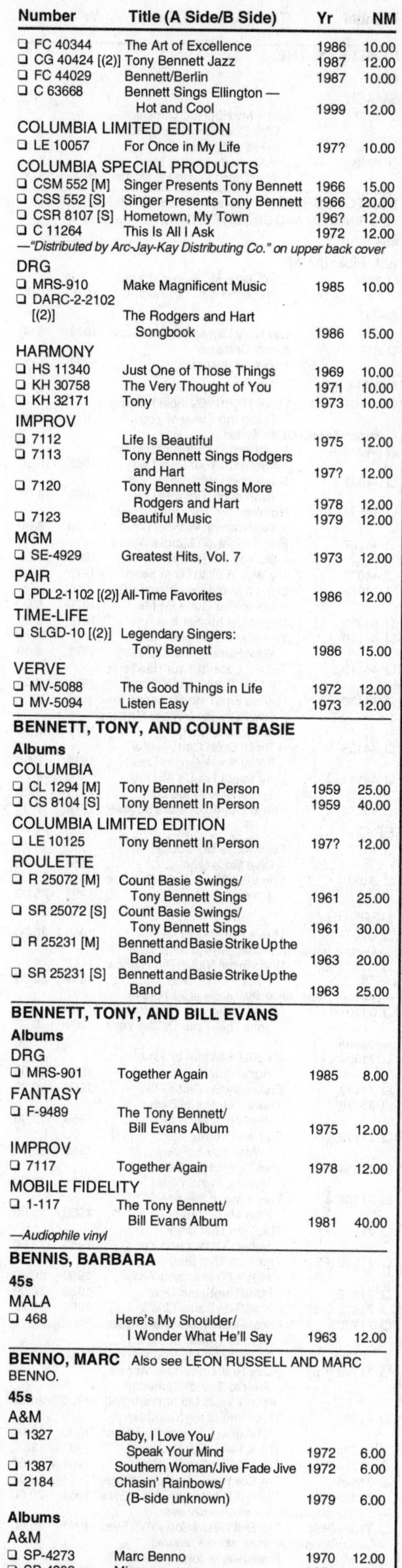

Number	Title (A Side/B Side)	Yr	NM
❑ FC 40344	The Art of Excellence	1986	10.00
❑ CG 40424 [(2)]	Tony Bennett Jazz	1987	12.00
❑ FC 44029	Bennett/Berlin	1987	10.00
❑ C 63668	Bennett Sings Ellington — Hot and Cool	1999	12.00

COLUMBIA LIMITED EDITION

Number	Title (A Side/B Side)	Yr	NM
❑ LE 10057	For Once in My Life	197?	10.00

COLUMBIA SPECIAL PRODUCTS

Number	Title (A Side/B Side)	Yr	NM
❑ CSM 552 [M]	Singer Presents Tony Bennett	1966	15.00
❑ CSS 552 [S]	Singer Presents Tony Bennett	1966	20.00
❑ CSR 8107 [S]	Hometown, My Town	196?	12.00
❑ C 11264	This Is All I Ask	1972	12.00

—"Distributed by Arc-Jay-Kay Distributing Co." on upper back cover

DRG

Number	Title (A Side/B Side)	Yr	NM
❑ MRS-910	Make Magnificent Music	1985	10.00
❑ DARC-2-2102 [(2)]	The Rodgers and Hart Songbook	1986	15.00

HARMONY

Number	Title (A Side/B Side)	Yr	NM
❑ HS 11340	Just One of Those Things	1969	10.00
❑ KH 30758	The Very Thought of You	1971	10.00
❑ KH 32171	Tony	1973	10.00

IMPROV

Number	Title (A Side/B Side)	Yr	NM
❑ 7112	Life Is Beautiful	1975	12.00
❑ 7113	Tony Bennett Sings Rodgers and Hart	197?	12.00
❑ 7120	Tony Bennett Sings More Rodgers and Hart	1978	12.00
❑ 7123	Beautiful Music	1979	12.00

MGM

Number	Title (A Side/B Side)	Yr	NM
❑ SE-4929	Greatest Hits, Vol. 7	1973	12.00

PAIR

Number	Title (A Side/B Side)	Yr	NM
❑ PDL2-1102 [(2)]	All-Time Favorites	1986	12.00

TIME-LIFE

Number	Title (A Side/B Side)	Yr	NM
❑ SLGD-10 [(2)]	Legendary Singers: Tony Bennett	1986	15.00

VERVE

Number	Title (A Side/B Side)	Yr	NM
❑ MV-5088	The Good Things in Life	1972	12.00
❑ MV-5094	Listen Easy	1973	12.00

BENNETT, TONY, AND COUNT BASIE

Albums

COLUMBIA

Number	Title (A Side/B Side)	Yr	NM
❑ CL 1294 [M]	Tony Bennett In Person	1959	25.00
❑ CS 8104 [S]	Tony Bennett In Person	1959	40.00

COLUMBIA LIMITED EDITION

Number	Title (A Side/B Side)	Yr	NM
❑ LE 10125	Tony Bennett In Person	197?	12.00

ROULETTE

Number	Title (A Side/B Side)	Yr	NM
❑ R 25072 [M]	Count Basie Swings/ Tony Bennett Sings	1961	25.00
❑ SR 25072 [S]	Count Basie Swings/ Tony Bennett Sings	1961	30.00
❑ R 25231 [M]	Bennett and Basie Strike Up the Band	1963	20.00
❑ SR 25231 [S]	Bennett and Basie Strike Up the Band	1963	25.00

BENNETT, TONY, AND BILL EVANS

Albums

DRG

Number	Title (A Side/B Side)	Yr	NM
❑ MRS-901	Together Again	1985	8.00

FANTASY

Number	Title (A Side/B Side)	Yr	NM
❑ F-9489	The Tony Bennett/ Bill Evans Album	1975	12.00

IMPROV

Number	Title (A Side/B Side)	Yr	NM
❑ 7117	Together Again	1978	12.00

MOBILE FIDELITY

Number	Title (A Side/B Side)	Yr	NM
❑ 1-117	The Tony Bennett/ Bill Evans Album	1981	40.00

—Audiophile vinyl

BENNIS, BARBARA

45s

MALA

Number	Title (A Side/B Side)	Yr	NM
❑ 468	Here's My Shoulder/ I Wonder What He'll Say	1963	12.00

BENNO, MARC

Also see LEON RUSSELL AND MARC BENNO.

45s

A&M

Number	Title (A Side/B Side)	Yr	NM
❑ 1327	Baby, I Love You/ Speak Your Mind	1972	6.00
❑ 1387	Southern Woman/Jive Fade Jive	1972	6.00
❑ 2184	Chasin' Rainbows/ (B-side unknown)	1979	6.00

Albums

A&M

Number	Title (A Side/B Side)	Yr	NM
❑ SP-4273	Marc Benno	1970	12.00
❑ SP-4303	Minnows	1971	12.00

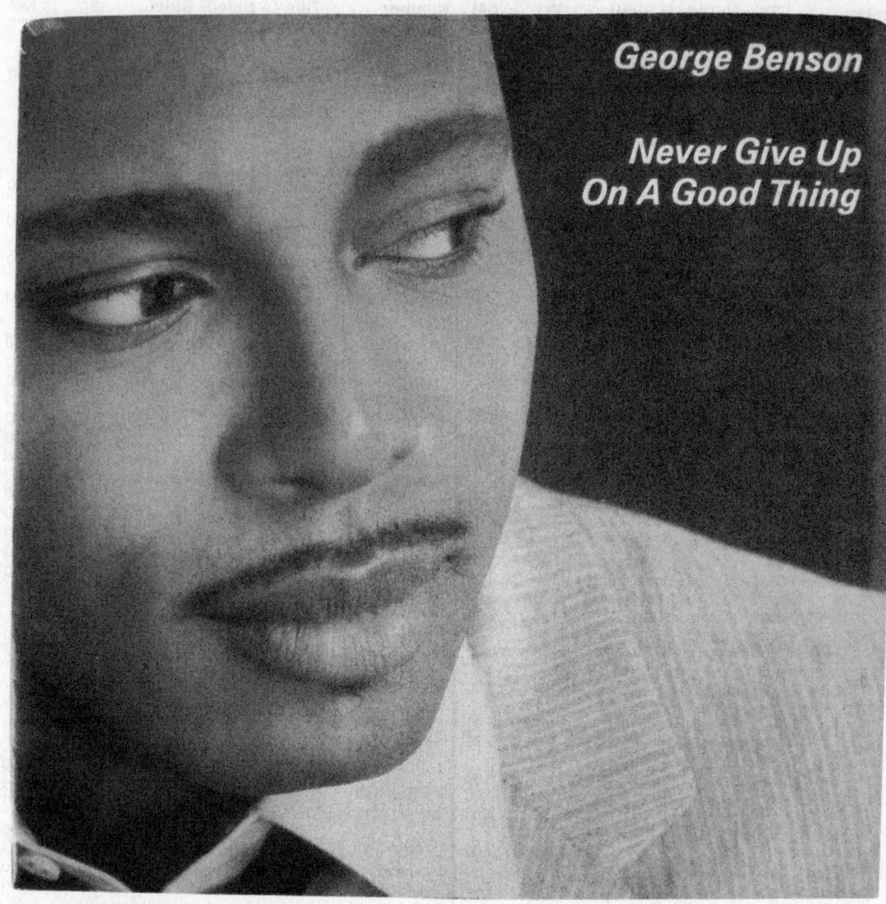

George Benson, "Never Give up on a Good Thing," Warner Bros. 50005, 1981, **$4.**

Number	Title (A Side/B Side)	Yr	NM
❑ SP-4364	Ambush	1972	12.00
❑ SP-4767	Lost in Austin	1979	10.00

BENNY AND THE BEDBUGS

45s

DCP

Number	Title (A Side/B Side)	Yr	NM
❑ 1008	The Beatle Beat/ Roll Over Beethoven	1964	15.00
❑ 1008 [PS]	The Beatle Beat/ Roll Over Beethoven	1964	25.00

BENSON, GEORGE

Also see THE ALTAIRS.

12-Inch Singles

VERVE

Number	Title (A Side/B Side)	Yr	NM
❑ 01028 [DJ]	El Barrio (Maw Mix 7:14) (Instrumental 5:02) (LP Version 8:29) (+1 more?)	2000	12.00
❑ 561788-1	The Ghetto (El Barrio) (4 versions)	2000	8.00

WARNER BROS.

Number	Title (A Side/B Side)	Yr	NM
❑ PRO-A-2026 [DJ]	Inside Love (So Personal) (5:13) (7:03) (4:08)	1983	10.00
❑ PRO-A-2251 [DJ]	20/20 (Extended Dance Mix 6:32) (same on both sides)	1984	8.00
❑ PRO-A-2617 [DJ]	Shiver (Extended) (7" Version) (Dub)/Love Is Here Tonight	1986	8.00
❑ PRO-A-3454 [DJ]	Good Habit (Remix) (Radio Version)	1988	7.00
❑ PRO-A-3722 [DJ]	Here, There and Everywhere (Edit) (Instrumental Edit)	1989	10.00
❑ PRO-A-6237 [DJ]	Love of My Life (same on both sides)	1993	10.00
❑ PRO-A-6242 [DJ]	Kiss and Make Up/My Heart Is Dancing/Got to Be There/ I'll Be Good to You	1993	10.00
❑ PRO-A-6365 [DJ]	I'll Be Good to You (Edit) (LP Version)	1993	8.00
❑ 20110	Inside Love (So Personal) (2 versions)/In Search of a Dream	1983	6.00
❑ 20572	Shiver (3 versions)/ Love Is Here Tonight	1986	7.00
❑ 20640	Teaser (3 versions)/ Did You Hear Thunder	1987	7.00
❑ 21115	Twice the Love (Guitar Love Mix) (Guitar Love Edit) (Club Love Edit) (Club Love Dub)	1988	8.00

45s

A&M

Number	Title (A Side/B Side)	Yr	NM
❑ 1003	Chattanooga Choo Choo/The Shape of Things to Come	1968	6.00
❑ 1057	Don't Let Me Lose This Dream Part 1/Part 2	1969	6.00
❑ 1076	Jackie All/My Woman's Good to Me	1969	6.00
❑ 1124	My Cherie Amour/Tell It Like It Is	1969	6.00
❑ 1128	I Got a Woman Part 1/ I Got a Woman Part 2	1969	6.00
❑ 8395	Golden Slumbers-You Never Give Me Your Money (Medley)/(B-side unknown)	1971	6.00

—May be promo only

ARISTA

Number	Title (A Side/B Side)	Yr	NM
❑ 0251	The Greatest Love of All/ Ali's Theme	1977	4.00

—B-side by Michael Masser

Number	Title (A Side/B Side)	Yr	NM
❑ 0251 [PS]	The Greatest Love of All/ Ali's Theme	1977	6.00

COLUMBIA

Number	Title (A Side/B Side)	Yr	NM
❑ 43684	Summertime/Ain't That Peculiar	1966	10.00
❑ 43998	The Man from Toledo/ Georgia Stick	1967	10.00

CTI

Number	Title (A Side/B Side)	Yr	NM
❑ 25	Supership/My Latin Brother	1975	6.00

Number	Title (A Side/B Side)	Yr	NM
❑ 30	Summertime & 2001 (Part 1)/ Summertime & 2001 (Part 2)	1977	5.00
❑ 47	Hold On, I'm Comin'/Gone	1978	5.00

GROOVE

Number	Title (A Side/B Side)	Yr	NM
❑ 0024	It Should Have Been Me #2/ She Makes Me Mad	1954	40.00

PRESTIGE

Number	Title (A Side/B Side)	Yr	NM
❑ 317	Just Another Sunday/ Shadow Dancers	1964	12.00

WARNER BROS.

Number	Title (A Side/B Side)	Yr	NM
❑ 8209	This Masquerade/Lady	1976	5.00
❑ 8268	Breezin'/Six to Four	1976	4.00
❑ 8360	Everything Must Change/ The Wind and I	1977	4.00
❑ 8377	Gonna Love You More/ Valdez in the Country	1977	4.00
❑ 8542	On Broadway/We As Love	1978	4.00
❑ 8542 [PS]	On Broadway/We As Love	1978	5.00
❑ 8604	Lady Blue/California P.M.	1978	4.00
❑ 8604 [PS]	Lady Blue/California P.M.	1978	5.00
❑ 8759	Love Ballad/You're Never Too Far from Me	1979	4.00
❑ 8759 [PS]	Love Ballad/You're Never Too Far from Me	1979	5.00
❑ 8843	Unchained Melody/ Before You Go	1979	4.00
❑ 27537	Good Habit/Stephanie	1989	3.00
❑ 27658	Twice the Love/(Instrumental)	1989	3.00
❑ 27658 [PS]	Twice the Love/(Instrumental)	1989	3.00
❑ 27780	Let's Do It Again/Let Go	1988	3.00
❑ 27780 [PS]	Let's Do It Again/Let Go	1988	3.00
❑ 28410	Did You Hear Thunder/Teaser	1987	3.00
❑ 28523	Shiver/Love Is Here Tonight	1986	3.00
❑ 28640	Kisses in the Moonlight/Open Your Eyes (Instrumental)	1986	3.00
❑ 28640 [PS]	Kisses in the Moonlight/Open Your Eyes (Instrumental)	1986	3.00
❑ 28969	New Day/No One Emotion	1985	3.00
❑ 29042	I Just Wanna Hang Around You/Beyond the Sea (La Mer)	1985	3.00
❑ 29120	20-20/Shark Bite	1984	4.00
❑ 29120 [PS]	20-20/Shark Bite	1984	4.00
❑ 29442	In Your Eyes/Never Too Far to Fall	1983	4.00
❑ 29563	Lady Love Me (One More Time)/Being with You	1983	4.00
❑ 29649	Inside Love (So Personal)/ In Search of a Dream	1983	4.00
❑ 29649 [PS]	Inside Love (So Personal)/ In Search of a Dream	1983	4.00
❑ 49051	Hey Girl/Welcome Into My World	1979	4.00
❑ 49505	Give Me the Night/ Dinorah, Dinorah	1980	4.00
❑ 49505 [PS]	Give Me the Night/ Dinorah, Dinorah	1980	5.00
❑ 49570	Love Dance/Love X Love	1980	4.00
❑ 49637	Midnight Love Affair/ Turn Off the Lamplight	1980	4.00
❑ 49846	Turn Your Love Around/ Nature Boy	1981	4.00
❑ 49846 [PS]	Turn Your Love Around/ Nature Boy	1981	4.00
❑ 50005	Never Give Up on a Good Thing/Livin' Inside Your Love	1982	4.00
❑ 50005 [PS]	Never Give Up on a Good Thing/Livin' Inside Your Love	1982	4.00

Albums

A&M

Number	Title (A Side/B Side)	Yr	NM
❑ SP-3014	Shape of Things to Come	1969	20.00
—Brown label			
❑ SP-3014	Shape of Things to Come	1976	12.00
—Silvery label with fading "A&M" logo			
❑ SP9-3014	Shape of Things to Come	1983	15.00
—"Audio Master Plus" reissue			
❑ SP-3020	Tell It Like It Is	1969	20.00
—Brown label			
❑ SP-3020	Tell It Like It Is	1976	12.00
—Silvery label with fading "A&M" logo			
❑ SP9-3020	Tell It Like It Is	1984	15.00
—"Audio Master Plus" reissue			
❑ SP-3028	The Other Side of Abbey Road	1970	25.00
—Brown label			
❑ SP-3028	The Other Side of Abbey Road	1976	12.00
—Silvery label with fading "A&M" logo			
❑ SP9-3028	The Other Side of Abbey Road	1984	15.00
—"Audio Master Plus" reissue			
❑ SP-3203	The Best of George Benson	1983	10.00

COLUMBIA

Number	Title (A Side/B Side)	Yr	NM
❑ CL 2525 [M]	The Most Exciting New Guitarist on the Jazz Scene Today — It's Uptown	1966	20.00
❑ CL 2613 [M]	The George Benson Cook Book	1967	20.00
❑ CS 9325	The Most Exciting New Guitarist on the Jazz Scene Today — It's Uptown	1976	10.00
—Orange label			
❑ CS 9325 [S]	The Most Exciting New Guitarist on the Jazz Scene Today — It's Uptown	1966	20.00
—Red "360 Sound" label			
❑ PC 9325	The Most Exciting New Guitarist on the Jazz Scene Today — It's Uptown	198?	8.00
—Reissue with new prefix			
❑ CS 9413	The George Benson Cook Book	1976	10.00
—Orange label			
❑ CS 9413 [S]	The George Benson Cook Book	1967	20.00
—Red "360 Sound" label			
❑ PC 9413	The George Benson Cook Book	198?	8.00
—Reissue with new prefix			
❑ CG 33569 [(2)]	Benson Burner	1976	12.00

CTI

Number	Title (A Side/B Side)	Yr	NM
❑ 6009	Beyond the Blue Horizon	1971	12.00
❑ 6015	White Rabbit	1972	12.00
❑ 6033	Body Talk	1973	12.00
❑ CTSQ-6033 [Q]	Body Talk	1973	20.00
❑ 6045	Bad Benson	1974	12.00
❑ 6062	Good King Bad	1976	12.00
❑ 6069	Benson & Farrell	1976	12.00
❑ 6072	George Benson In Concert — Carnegie Hall	1976	12.00
❑ 8009	White Rabbit	198?	10.00
❑ 8014	Take Five	198?	10.00
❑ 8030	Cast Your Fate to the Wind	1982	10.00
❑ 8031	Summertime: In Concert	198?	10.00

FANTASY

Number	Title (A Side/B Side)	Yr	NM
❑ OJC-461	The New Boss Guitar of George Benson	1990	12.00
—Reissue of Prestige 7310			

MOBILE FIDELITY

Number	Title (A Side/B Side)	Yr	NM
❑ 1-011	Breezin'	1979	60.00
—Audiophile vinyl			

POLYDOR

Number	Title (A Side/B Side)	Yr	NM
❑ PD-1-6084	Blue Benson	1976	10.00

PRESTIGE

Number	Title (A Side/B Side)	Yr	NM
❑ PRLP-7310 [M]	The New Boss Guitar of George Benson	1964	30.00
❑ PRST-7310 [S]	The New Boss Guitar of George Benson	1964	40.00
❑ 24072 [(2)]	George Benson & Jack McDuff	1976	15.00

VERVE

Number	Title (A Side/B Side)	Yr	NM
❑ V6-8749	Giblet Gravy	1968	20.00
❑ V6-8771	Goodies	1969	20.00

WARNER BROS.

Number	Title (A Side/B Side)	Yr	NM
❑ BS 2919	Breezin'	1976	10.00
—With "Contains This Masquerade" on front cover			
❑ BS 2919	Breezin'	1976	15.00
—With no mention of "This Masquerade" on front cover			
❑ BSK 2983	In Flight	1977	10.00
❑ BSK 3111	Breezin'	1977	8.00
—Reissue of 2919			
❑ 2WS 3139 [(2)]	Weekend in L.A.	1978	12.00
❑ 2BSK 3277	Livin' Inside Your Love	1979	12.00
❑ HS 3453	Give Me the Night	1980	10.00
❑ 2HS 3577 [(2)]	The George Benson Collection	1981	12.00
❑ 23744	In Your Eyes	1983	10.00
❑ 25178	20/20	1985	10.00
❑ 25475	While the City Sleeps…	1986	10.00
❑ 25705	Twice the Love	1988	10.00
❑ 25907	Tenderly	1989	12.00
❑ 26295	Big Boss Band	1990	15.00

BENSON, GEORGE, AND EARL KLUGH

45s

WARNER BROS.

Number	Title (A Side/B Side)	Yr	NM
❑ 27975	Since You're Gone/ Love Theme from "Romeo and Juliet"	1988	3.00
❑ 27975 [PS]	Since You're Gone/ Love Theme from "Romeo and Juliet"	1988	4.00
❑ 28244	Dreamin'/Love Theme from "Romeo and Juliet"	1987	3.00

Albums

WARNER BROS.

Number	Title (A Side/B Side)	Yr	NM
❑ 25580	Collaboration	1987	10.00

BENSON, JANE

45s

ATCO

Number	Title (A Side/B Side)	Yr	NM
❑ 6151	Growing Up/Surrendering	1959	15.00

BENT BOLT AND THE NUTS

45s

MGM

Number	Title (A Side/B Side)	Yr	NM
❑ 13635	Mechanical Man/Sweet and Sour	1966	8.00
❑ 13635 [PS]	Mechanical Man/Sweet and Sour	1966	10.00

BENTLEYS, THE

45s

SMASH

Number	Title (A Side/B Side)	Yr	NM
❑ 1967	She's My Hot Rod Queen/ Why Does Everybody Want to Hold My Baby	1965	25.00
❑ 1988	Did Anybody Lose a Tear/ Why Didn't I Listen to Mother	1965	25.00

BENTON, BROOK

Also see THE SANDMEN (2); DINAH WASHINGTON AND BROOK BENTON.

45s

ALL PLATINUM

Number	Title (A Side/B Side)	Yr	NM
❑ 2364	Can't Take My Eyes Off You/ Weekend with Feathers	1976	5.00

BRUT

Number	Title (A Side/B Side)	Yr	NM
❑ 810	Lay Lady Lay/A Touch of Class	1973	5.00
❑ 816	South Carolina/ (B-side unknown)	1973	5.00

COTILLION

Number	Title (A Side/B Side)	Yr	NM
❑ 13107	Rainy Night in Georgia/Nothing Takes the Place of You	197?	4.00
—Part of "Atlantic Oldies Series"			
❑ 44007	I Just Don't Know What to Do with Myself/Do Your Own Thing	1968	8.00
❑ 44031	She Knows What to Do with 'Em/Touch 'Em with Love	1969	8.00
❑ 44034	Nothing Can Take the Place of You/Woman Without Love	1969	8.00
❑ 44057	Rainy Night in Georgia/Where Do You Go from Here	1969	10.00
❑ 44072	My Way/A Little Bit of Soap	1970	6.00
❑ 44078	Don't It Make You Want to Go Home/I've Gotta Be Me	1970	6.00
❑ 44093	Shoes/Let Me Fix It	1970	6.00
❑ 44110	Whoever Finds This, I Love You/Heaven Help Us All	1971	6.00
❑ 44119	Take a Look at Your Hands/ If You Think God Is Dead	1971	6.00
❑ 44130	Please Send Me Someone to Love/She Even Woke Me Up to Say Goodbye	1971	6.00
❑ 44138	A Black Child Can't Smile/ If You Think God Is Dead	1971	6.00
❑ 44141	Soul Santa/Let Us All Get Together with the Lord	1971	8.00
❑ 44152	Movin' Day/Poor Make Believer	1972	6.00

EPIC

Number	Title (A Side/B Side)	Yr	NM
❑ 9177	Love Made Me Your Fool/ Give Me a Sign	1956	25.00
❑ 9199	The Wall/All My Love Belongs to You	1957	25.00

MERCURY

Number	Title (A Side/B Side)	Yr	NM
❑ C7071 [S]	I Love Paris/All of Me	196?	20.00
—Jukebox issue, small hole, plays at 33 1/3 rpm			
❑ C7072 [S]	Blues in the Night/I Didn't Know What Time It Was	196?	20.00
—Jukebox issue, small hole, plays at 33 1/3 rpm			
❑ 30101	Merry Christmas, Happy New Year/This Time Of The Year	196?	8.00
—Reissue			
❑ 71394	It's Just a Matter of Time/ Hurtin' Inside	1959	15.00
❑ 71443	Endlessly/So Close	1959	15.00
❑ 71478	Thank You Pretty Baby/ With All of My Heart	1959	15.00
❑ 71512	So Many Ways/ I Want You Forever	1959	15.00
❑ 71554	This Time of the Year/ Nothing in the World	1959	15.00
❑ 71558	This Time of the Year/ How Many Times	1959	15.00
❑ 71566	The Ties That Bind/ Hither, Thither and Yon	1960	12.00
❑ 71566 [PS]	The Ties That Bind/ Hither, Thither and Yon	1960	20.00
❑ 71652	Kiddio/The Same One	1960	12.00
❑ 71652 [PS]	Kiddio/The Same One	1960	20.00
❑ 71722	Fools Rush In (Where Angels Fear to Tread)/Someday You'll Want Me to Want You	1960	12.00
❑ 71722 [PS]	Fools Rush In (Where Angels Fear to Tread)/Someday You'll Want Me to Want You	1960	20.00
❑ 71730	This Time of the Year/Merry Christmas, Happy New Year	1960	12.00
❑ 71774	Think Twice/For My Baby	1961	12.00
❑ 71774 [PS]	Think Twice/For My Baby	1961	20.00
❑ 71820	The Boll Weevil Song/Your Eyes	1961	12.00
❑ 71820 [PS]	The Boll Weevil Song/Your Eyes	1961	20.00
—Back of sleeve has six albums pictured			
❑ 71820 [PS]	The Boll Weevil Song/Your Eyes	1961	25.00
—Back of sleeve has three albums pictured			
❑ 71859	Frankie and Johnny/It's Just a House Without You	1961	12.00

Number	Title (A Side/B Side)	Yr	NM
❑ 71859 [PS]	Frankie and Johnny/It's Just a House Without You	1961	20.00
❑ 71903	Revenge/Really Really	1961	12.00
❑ 71903 [PS]	Revenge/Really Really	1961	20.00
❑ 71912	Shadrack/The Lost Penny	1961	12.00
❑ 71912 [PS]	Shadrack/The Lost Penny	1961	20.00
❑ 71925	Walk on the Wild Side/ Somewhere in the Used to Be	1962	10.00
❑ 71925 [PS]	Walk on the Wild Side/ Somewhere in the Used to Be	1962	20.00
❑ 71962	Hit Record/Thanks to the Fool	1962	10.00
❑ 71962 [PS]	Hit Record/Thanks to the Fool	1962	20.00
—Blue background with orange title banner			
❑ 71962 [PS]	Hit Record/Thanks to the Fool	1962	30.00
—All-orange background with different photo			
❑ 72009	Two Tickets to Paradise/ It's Alright	1962	—
—Unreleased			
❑ 72024	Lie to Me/With the Touch of Your Hand	1962	10.00
❑ 72024 [PS]	Lie to Me/With the Touch of Your Hand	1962	20.00
❑ 72055	Hotel Happiness/ Still Waters Run Deep	1962	10.00
❑ 72055 [PS]	Hotel Happiness/ Still Waters Run Deep	1962	20.00
❑ 72099	I Got What I Wanted/ Dearer Than Life	1963	10.00
❑ 72099 [PS]	I Got What I Wanted/ Dearer Than Life	1963	20.00
❑ 72135	My True Confession/ Tender Years	1963	10.00
❑ 72135 [PS]	My True Confession/ Tender Years	1963	20.00
❑ 72177	Two Tickets to Paradise/ Don't Hate Me	1963	10.00
❑ 72177 [PS]	Two Tickets to Paradise/ Don't Hate Me	1963	20.00
❑ 72214	You're All I Want for Christmas/ This Time of the Year	1963	10.00
❑ 72214 [PS]	You're All I Want for Christmas/ This Time of the Year	1963	25.00
❑ 72230	Going, Going, Gone/ After Midnight	1963	10.00
❑ 72230 [PS]	Going, Going, Gone/ After Midnight	1963	20.00
❑ 72266	Too Late to Turn Back Now/ Another Cup of Coffee	1964	10.00
❑ 72266 [PS]	Too Late to Turn Back Now/ Another Cup of Coffee	1964	20.00
❑ 72303	A House Is Not a Home/ Come On Back	1964	10.00
❑ 72303 [PS]	A House Is Not a Home/ Come On Back	1964	20.00
❑ 72333	Lumberjack/Don't Do What I Did (Do What I Say)	1964	10.00
❑ 72333 [PS]	Lumberjack/Don't Do What I Did (Do What I Say)	1964	20.00
❑ 72365	Do It Right/Please, Please Make It Easy	1964	10.00
❑ 72365 [PS]	Do It Right/Please, Please Make It Easy	1964	20.00
❑ 72398	Special Years/Where There's a Will (There's a Way)	1965	10.00
❑ 72446	Love Me Now/A-Sleepin' at the End of the Bed	1965	10.00
❑ 872796-7	It's Just a Matter of Time/ Hurtin' Inside	1989	4.00
❑ 872798-7	Endlessly/So Many Ways	1989	4.00
MGM			
❑ 14440	If You've Got the Time/ You Take Me Home Honey	1972	5.00
OKEH			
❑ 7058	The Kentuckian Song/Ooh	1955	25.00
❑ 7065	Bring Me Love/Some of My Best Friends	1956	25.00
OLDE WORLD			
❑ 1100	Makin' Love Is Good for You/ Better Times	1977	5.00
❑ 1107	Soft/Glow Love	1978	5.00
POLYDOR			
❑ 2015	I Cried for You/Love Me a Little	1979	4.00
RCA VICTOR			
❑ 47-8693	Mother Nature, Father Time/ You're Mine	1965	10.00
❑ 47-8693 [PS]	Mother Nature, Father Time/ You're Mine	1965	20.00
❑ 47-8768	Where There's Life/Only a Girl Like You	1965	10.00
❑ 47-8830	Too Much Good Lovin'/ A Sailor Boy's Love Song	1966	10.00
❑ 47-8879	Break Her Heart/In the Evening in the Moonlight	1966	10.00
❑ 47-8944	Where Does a Man Go to Cry/ The Roach Song	1966	10.00
❑ 47-8995	So True in Life, So True in Love/ If You Only Knew	1966	10.00

Number	Title (A Side/B Side)	Yr	NM
❑ 47-9031	Our First Christmas Together/ Silent Night	1966	12.00
❑ 47-9096	Wake Up/All My Love Belongs to You	1967	8.00
❑ 47-9105	Keep the Faith Baby/ Going to Soulsville	1967	8.00
❑ 47-7489	Only Your Love/ If Only I Had Known	1959	30.00
REPRISE			
❑ 0611	You're the Reason I'm Living/ Laura (Tell Me What He's Got That I Ain't Got)	1967	8.00
❑ 0649	Glory of Love/Weakness in a Man	1967	8.00
❑ 0676	Instead (Of Loving You)/ Lonely Street	1968	8.00
STAX			
❑ 0231	Winds of Change/ I Keep Thinking to Myself	1974	5.00
VIK			
❑ 0285	I Wanna Do Everything for You/ Come On Be Nice	1957	20.00
❑ 0311	A Million Miles from Nowhere/ Devoted	1957	20.00
❑ 0325	Because You Love Me/ Crinoline Skirt	1958	20.00
❑ 0336	Crazy in Love with You/ I'm Coming Back to You	1958	20.00

7-Inch Extended Plays

Number	Title (A Side/B Side)	Yr	NM
MERCURY			
❑ SR-632-C	Hotel Happiness/It's Just a House Without You/The Boll Weevil Song//Think Twice/ Revenge/Walk on the Wild Side	196?	12.00
❑ SR-632-C [PS]	Golden Hits, Vol. 2	196?	12.00

Albums

Number	Title (A Side/B Side)	Yr	NM
ALL PLATINUM			
❑ 3015	This Is Brook Benton	1976	12.00
ALLEGIANCE			
❑ AV-5033	Memories Are Made of This	1986	10.00
COTILLION			
❑ SD 9002	Do Your Own Thing	1969	12.00
❑ SD 9018	Brook Benton Today	1970	12.00
❑ SD 9028	Home Style	1970	12.00
❑ SD 9050	Story Teller	1971	12.00
❑ SD 9058	The Gospel Truth	1972	12.00
EPIC			
❑ LN 3573 [M]	Brook Benton At His Best	1959	50.00
HARMONY			
❑ HL 7346 [M]	The Soul of Brook Benton	196?	12.00
❑ HS 11146 [R]	The Soul of Brook Benton	196?	12.00
HMC			
❑ 830724	Beautiful Memories of Christmas	1983	12.00
MERCURY			
❑ MG-20421 [M]	It's Just a Matter of Time	1959	40.00
❑ MG-20464 [M]	Endlessly	1959	30.00
❑ MG-20565 [M]	So Many Ways I Love You	1960	30.00
❑ MG-20602 [M]	Songs I Love to Sing	1960	30.00
❑ MG-20607 [M]	Golden Hits	1961	20.00
❑ MG-20619 [M]	If You Believe	1961	20.00
❑ MG-20641 [M]	The Boll Weevil Song and 11 Other Great Hits	1961	20.00
❑ MG-20673 [M]	There Goes That Song Again	1962	20.00
❑ MG-20740 [M]	Singing the Blues — Lie to Me	1962	20.00
❑ MG-20774 [M]	Golden Hits, Vol. 2	1963	20.00
❑ MG-20830 [M]	Best Ballads of Broadway	1963	20.00
❑ MG-20886 [M]	Born to Sing the Blues	1964	20.00
❑ MG-20918 [M]	On the Country Side	1964	15.00
❑ MG-20934 [M]	This Bitter Earth	1964	15.00
❑ SR-60077 [S]	It's Just a Matter of Time	1959	50.00
❑ SR-60146 [S]	Endlessly	1959	40.00
❑ SR-60225 [S]	So Many Ways I Love You	1960	40.00
❑ SR-60602 [S]	Songs I Love to Sing	1960	40.00
❑ SR-60607 [S]	Golden Hits	1961	30.00
❑ SR-60619 [S]	If You Believe	1961	30.00
❑ SR-60641 [S]	The Boll Weevil Song and 11 Other Great Hits	1961	30.00
❑ SR-60673 [S]	There Goes That Song Again	1962	30.00
❑ SR-60740 [S]	Singing the Blues — Lie to Me	1962	30.00
❑ SR-60774 [S]	Golden Hits, Vol. 2	1963	30.00
❑ SR-60830 [S]	Best Ballads of Broadway	1963	25.00
❑ SR-60886 [S]	Born to Sing the Blues	1964	25.00
❑ SR-60918 [S]	On the Country Side	1964	20.00
❑ SR-60934 [S]	This Bitter Earth	1964	20.00
❑ 822321-1	It's Just a Matter of Time: His Greatest Hits	1984	10.00
MGM			
❑ SE-4874	Something for Everyone	1973	12.00
MUSICOR			
❑ 4603 [(2)]	The Best of Brook Benton	1977	12.00

Number	Title (A Side/B Side)	Yr	NM
OLDE WORLD			
❑ OWR 7707	Hot and Sensitive	1978	—
—Unreleased?			
PAIR			
❑ PDL2-1100 [(2)]	Brook Benton's Best	1986	12.00
RCA CAMDEN			
❑ CAL-564 [M]	Brook Benton	1960	15.00
❑ CAS-2431	I Wanna Be with You	1970	12.00
RCA VICTOR			
❑ APL1-1044	Book Benton Sings a Love Story	1975	10.00
❑ LPM-3514 [M]	That Old Feeling	1966	15.00
❑ LSP-3514 [S]	That Old Feeling	1966	20.00
❑ LPM-3526 [M]	Mother Nature, Father Time	1965	15.00
❑ LSP-3526 [S]	Mother Nature, Father Time	1965	20.00
❑ LPM-3590 [M]	My Country	1966	15.00
❑ LSP-3590 [S]	My Country	1966	20.00
REPRISE			
❑ R-6268 [M]	Laura (What's He Got That I Ain't Got)	1967	20.00
❑ RS-6268 [S]	Laura (What's He Got That I Ain't Got)	1967	15.00
RHINO			
❑ RNFP 71497 [(2)]	The Brook Benton Anthology (1959-1970)	1986	12.00
WING			
❑ MGW-12314 [M]	Brook Benton	1966	12.00
❑ SRW-16314 [S]	Brook Benton	1966	12.00

BENTON, BROOK, AND DAMITA JO

Also see each artist's individual listings.

45s

Number	Title (A Side/B Side)	Yr	NM
MERCURY			
❑ 72196	Yaba-Taba-Do/ Almost Persuaded	1963	—
—Unreleased			
❑ 72207	Baby, You've Got It Made/ Stop Foolin'	1963	10.00

BERBERIAN, JOHN, WITH THE ROCK EAST ENSEMBLE

Albums

Number	Title (A Side/B Side)	Yr	NM
MAINSTREAM			
❑ S-6123	Impressions East	1969	120.00
VERVE FORECAST			
❑ FTS-3073	Middle Eastern Rock	1969	50.00

BERG, GERTRUDE

Albums

Number	Title (A Side/B Side)	Yr	NM
AMY			
❑ 8007 [M]	How to Be a Jewish Mother	1965	25.00

BERGEN, POLLY

45s

Number	Title (A Side/B Side)	Yr	NM
COLUMBIA			
❑ 41342	He Didn't Call/I Feel Sorry for the Boy	1959	12.00
❑ 41617	It Might As Well Be Spring/ Four Seasons	1960	10.00
❑ 41675	Do It Yourself/The Party's Over	1960	10.00
❑ 41971	Bye Bye Blackbird/The Happiest Girl in the World	1961	10.00
JUBILEE			
❑ 5230	No One Else Will Ever Know/ Let's Make Love	1956	15.00
RCA VICTOR			
❑ 47-3886	Oh Them Dudes/I Got Tookin'	1950	15.00
❑ 47-3958	Just the Way You Are/I Put My Head in the Lion's Mouth	1950	15.00
❑ 47-4022	Out of Sight/Tonda Wanda Hey	1951	15.00

Albums

Number	Title (A Side/B Side)	Yr	NM
COLUMBIA			
❑ CL 994 [M]	Bergen Sings Morgan	1957	30.00
❑ CL 1031 [M]	The Party's Over	1957	30.00
❑ CL 1138 [M]	Polly and Her Pop	1958	25.00
❑ CL 1218 [M]	My Heart Sings	1959	20.00
❑ CL 1300 [M]	All Alone by the Telephone	1959	20.00
❑ CL 1451 [M]	Four Seasons of Love	1960	20.00
❑ CL 1632 [M]	"Do Re Mi" and "Annie Get Your Gun"	1961	20.00
❑ CS 8018 [S]	My Heart Sings	1959	25.00
❑ CS 8100 [S]	All Alone by the Telephone	1959	25.00
❑ CS 8246 [S]	Four Seasons of Love	1960	25.00
❑ CS 8432 [S]	"Do Re Mi" and "Annie Get Your Gun"	1961	25.00
JUBILEE			
❑ JGL-14 [10]	Polly Bergen	1955	50.00
PHILIPS			
❑ PHM 200084 [M]	Act One — Sing, Too	1963	15.00
❑ PHS 600084 [S]	Act One — Sing, Too	1963	20.00

BERLIN

Number	Title (A Side/B Side)	Yr	NM
12-Inch Singles			
COLUMBIA			
❑ CAS 2369 [DJ]	Take My Breath Away (same on both sides)	1986	12.00
GEFFEN			
❑ PRO-A-2004 [DJ]	Sex (I'm A...) (Extended Version 8:10)/(Instrumental 5:06)	1982	20.00
❑ PRO-A-2147 [DJ]	Now It's My Turn (Edit Remix 3:57) (LP Version)	1984	8.00
❑ PRO-A-2572 [DJ]	Like Flames (7" Version) (LP Version)	1986	10.00
❑ PRO-A-2632 [DJ]	Pink and Velvet (same on both sides)	1986	10.00
❑ PRO-A-2686 [DJ]	You Don't Know (Edit)/(LP Version)	1986	10.00
❑ 20195	No More Words (Extended Dance Remix 5:44)/Dancing in Berlin (Extended Dance Remix 5:16)	1984	10.00
IMUSIC			
❑ MUDJ-01136-1 [DJ]	With a Touch (Rafe's Tribal House Remix 8:25) (Georgio Moroder Remxi 6:11) (JohnOTekHousePop Remix 5:17)	2003	20.00
45s			
COLUMBIA			
❑ 38-05903	Take My Breath Away/Radar Radio	1986	3.00
—B-side by Georgio Moroder			
❑ 38-05903 [PS]	Take My Breath Away/Radar Radio	1986	3.00
❑ 38-68719	Take My Breath Away/Top Gun Anthem	1989	3.00
—"Golden Oldies" reissue; B-side by Harold Faltermeyer			
EVATONE			
❑ 13	Masquerade/(B-side blank)	1983	8.00
—Flexi-disc from an issue of Trouser Press			
GEFFEN			
❑ GGEF 0498	No More Words/Now It's My Turn	198?	4.00
—"Back to Back Hits" reissue			
❑ GGEF 0501	Sex (I'm a...)/The Metro	198?	4.00
—"Back to Back Hits" reissue			
❑ 7-28486	You Don't Know/Trash	1987	3.00
❑ 7-28486 [PS]	You Don't Know/Trash	1987	3.00
❑ 7-28563	Like Flames/Hideaway	1986	4.00
❑ 7-28563 [PS]	Like Flames/Hideaway	1986	4.00
❑ 7-29051	No More Words/Crazy for You	1985	3.00
—B-side by Madonna (picture sleeve is under MADONNA as it has no Berlin content)			
❑ 7-29192	Dancing in Berlin/Pictures of You	1984	5.00
❑ 7-29283	Now It's My Turn/Lost in a Crowd	1984	4.00
❑ 7-29283 [PS]	Now It's My Turn/Lost in a Crowd	1984	4.00
❑ 7-29360	No More Words/Rumor of Love	1984	4.00
❑ 7-29360 [PS]	No More Words/Rumor of Love	1984	4.00
❑ 7-29504	Masquerade/Live Sex	1983	5.00
❑ 7-29504 [PS]	Masquerade/Live Sex	1983	5.00
❑ 7-29638	The Metro/World of Smiles	1983	5.00
❑ 7-29638 [PS]	The Metro/World of Smiles	1983	5.00
❑ 7-29747	Sex (I'm a ...)/Tell Me Why	1983	5.00
❑ 7-29747 [PS]	Sex (I'm a ...)/Tell Me Why	1983	8.00
M.A.O.			
❑ F-4	The Metro/Tell Me Why	1981	20.00
❑ F-4 [PS]	The Metro/Tell Me Why	1981	20.00
ZONE H			
❑ ZOH-001	Matter of Time/Overload	1980	25.00
❑ ZOH-001 [PS]	Matter of Time/Overload	1980	25.00
ZONE H/I.R.S.			
❑ 9015	Matter of Time/French Reggae	1980	10.00
—Small hole			
❑ 9015 [PS]	Matter of Time/French Reggae	1980	10.00
Albums			
ENIGMA			
❑ 3 [EP]	Pleasure Victim	1982	25.00
—Original issue			
GEFFEN			
❑ GHS 2036 [EP]	Pleasure Victim	1982	8.00
❑ PRO-A-2121 [EP]	Selections from Love Life	1984	12.00
—Four-song promo sampler (Touch/Now It's My Turn/In My Dreams/No More Words)			
❑ GHS 4025	Love Life	1984	10.00
❑ GHS 24121	Count Three and Pray	1986	8.00
❑ GHS 24187	Best of Berlin 1979-1988	1988	15.00
❑ R 100731	Best of Berlin 1979-1988	1988	20.00
—BMG Direct Marketing edition			
❑ R 153624	Count Three and Pray	1986	10.00
—RCA Music Service edition			

BERLIN PHILHARMONIC

Number	Title (A Side/B Side)	Yr	NM
45s			
POLYDOR			
❑ 15009	"2001" A Space Odyssey/Elvira Madigan Theme	1969	—
—B-side by Geza Anda			

BERLINE, BYRON

Number	Title (A Side/B Side)	Yr	NM
45s			
MCA			
❑ 40673	Best Friends/Lea	1976	—

BERLINE, BYRON & SUNDANCE

Number	Title (A Side/B Side)	Yr	NM
45s			
MCA			
❑ 40633	It Hurts So Much/Storm Over Oklahoma	1976	—

BERLINER, JAY

Number	Title (A Side/B Side)	Yr	NM
Albums			
MAINSTREAM			
❑ 384	Bananas Not Equal	1973	15.00

BERLINER, PAUL, AND KUDU

Number	Title (A Side/B Side)	Yr	NM
Albums			
FLYING FISH			
❑ FF-092	The Sun Rises Later Here	1979	15.00

BERMAN, SHELLEY

Number	Title (A Side/B Side)	Yr	NM
Albums			
METRO			
❑ M-546 [M]	Let Me Tell You a Funny Story	1965	15.00
❑ MS-546 [R]	Let Me Tell You a Funny Story	1965	12.00
VERVE			
❑ MGV-15003 [M]	Inside Shelley Berman	1959	25.00
❑ V-15003 [M]	Inside Shelley Berman	1962	15.00
❑ V6-15003 [R]	Inside Shelley Berman	196?	12.00
❑ MGV-15007 [M]	Outside Shelley Berman	1959	25.00
❑ V-15007 [M]	Outside Shelley Berman	1962	15.00
❑ V6-15007 [R]	Outside Shelley Berman	196?	12.00
❑ MGV-15008-2 [(2)M]	Inside and Outside Shelley Berman	1959	30.00
❑ V-15008-2 [(2)M]	Inside and Outside Shelley Berman	1962	20.00
❑ MGV-15013 [M]	The Edge of Shelley Berman	1960	25.00
❑ V-15013 [M]	The Edge of Shelley Berman	1962	15.00
❑ V6-15013 [R]	The Edge of Shelley Berman	196?	12.00
❑ MGV-15027 [M]	A Personal Appearance	1961	20.00
❑ V-15027 [M]	A Personal Appearance	1962	15.00
❑ V6-15027 [R]	A Personal Appearance	196?	12.00
❑ V-15036 [M]	New Sides	1962	15.00
❑ V6-15036 [R]	New Sides	196?	12.00
❑ V-15043 [M]	The Sex Life of the Primate (And Other Bits of Gossip)	1964	20.00
❑ V6-15043 [R]	The Sex Life of the Primate (And Other Bits of Gossip)	1964	15.00
❑ V-15048 [M]	Great Moments in Comedy	1965	20.00
❑ V6-15048 [R]	Great Moments in Comedy	1965	15.00

BERMUDAS, THE

Number	Title (A Side/B Side)	Yr	NM
45s			
ERA			
❑ 3125	Donnie/Chu Sen Ling	1964	12.00

BERNA-DEAN

Number	Title (A Side/B Side)	Yr	NM
45s			
IMPERIAL			
❑ 5792	I Walk in My Sleep/Little Willie	1961	20.00
❑ 5840	He's Mine/One Gal in Town, Five Men Hagin' Around	1962	20.00
❑ 5877	Morning, Noon and Night/The World Keeps Changing	1962	20.00
❑ 5950	The President Says Walk/I Wonder	1963	20.00
❑ 5978	Hello/Sleepless Nights	1963	20.00

BERNARD, CHRIS

Number	Title (A Side/B Side)	Yr	NM
45s			
REVUE			
❑ 11053	Good Hearted Woman/Mother	1969	30.00

BERNARD, ROD

Number	Title (A Side/B Side)	Yr	NM
45s			
ARBEE			
❑ 101	Recorded in England/Somebody Wrote That Song for My Baby	1965	10.00
❑ 104	Gimme Back My Cadillac/Don't You Think I've Paid Enough	1965	10.00
❑ 105	Those Were Our Songs/Just Another Lie	1966	10.00
ARGO			
❑ 5327	This Should Go On Forever/Pardon Mr. Gordon	1959	20.00
❑ 5338	You're On My Mind/My Life Is a Mystery	1959	20.00
CARL			
❑ (# unknown)	Linda Gail/Little Bitta Mama	1957	25.00
CRAZY CAJUN			
❑ 9020	Papa Thibodeaux/My Little Jollie Blonde	1978	5.00
HALLWAY			
❑ 1806	I Had a Girl/Wedding Bells	1963	15.00
❑ 1902	Who's Gonna Rock My Baby/Colinda	1962	15.00
❑ 1906	New Orleans Jail/Fais Do-Do	1962	15.00
❑ 1915	Forgive/I Want Somebody	1963	15.00
❑ 1917	Diggy Liggy Lo/The Clock	1963	15.00
❑ 1919	Loneliness/Boss Man's Son	1964	15.00
❑ 1922	My Own Mother-in-Law/I Might As Well	1964	15.00
JIN			
❑ 105	This Should Go On Forever/Pardon, Mr. Gordon	1958	40.00
❑ 232	Congratulations to You Darling/You're the Reason I'm in Love	1968	8.00
❑ 237	To Have and Hold/Cajun Honey	1968	8.00
❑ 240	Big Mamou/New Orleans Jail	1969	8.00
❑ 307	Don't You Think I've Paid Enough/Somebody Wrote That Song for Me	1974	5.00
❑ 325	Breaking Up Is Hard to Do/Sometimes I Walk in My Sleep	1975	5.00
❑ 338	This Should Go On Forever/I Spent a Week There Last Night	1975	5.00
❑ 350	A Winner in Love/I Forgot I Had These Memories of You	1975	5.00
❑ 373	Mardi Gras in New Orleans/Oh Mother Dear	1976	5.00
❑ 376	Go On, Go On/I Naver Had the One I Wanted	1976	5.00
MERCURY			
❑ 71507	Shedding Teardrops Over You/One More Chance	1959	20.00
❑ 71592	One of These Days/Let's Get Together Tonight	1960	20.00
❑ 71654	Two Young Fools in Love/Dance Fool Dance	1960	20.00
❑ 71689	Sttrange Kisses/Just a Memory	1960	20.00
❑ 71767	Lonely Hearts Club/Who Knows	1961	16.00
❑ 71842	(Tell Me) Sometime/I'm Not Lonely Anymore	1961	16.00
SCEPTER			
❑ 12195	Those Were Our Songs/Recorded in England	1967	16.00
TEAR DROP			
❑ 3044	Our Teenage Love/Doing the Oo-Wa-Woo	1966	10.00
❑ 3052	You're the Reason I'm in Love/My Jole Blon	1966	10.00
❑ 3060	No Money Down/Little Green Man	1967	10.00
❑ 3117	This Should Go On Forever/Recorded in England	1969	8.00
Albums			
JIN			
❑ LP-4007 [M]	Rod Bernard	196?	60.00

BERNE, TIM

Number	Title (A Side/B Side)	Yr	NM
Albums			
COLUMBIA			
❑ FC 40530	Fulton Street Maul	1987	12.00
❑ FC 44073	Sanctified Dreams	1987	12.00
EMPIRE			
❑ EPC 24K	The Five Year Plan	1979	20.00
❑ EPC 36K	7X	1980	20.00
❑ EPC 48K	Spectres	1981	20.00
❑ EPC 60K-2 [(2)]	Songs and Rituals in Real Time	1982	25.00
JMT			
❑ 834431-1	Fractured Fairy Tales	1989	15.00
SOUL NOTE			
❑ SN-1061	The Ancestors	1983	12.00
❑ SN-1091	Mutant Variations	1984	12.00

BERNE, TIM, AND BILL FRISELL

Number	Title (A Side/B Side)	Yr	NM
Albums			
EMPIRE			
❑ EPC 72K	...Theoretically	1984	20.00

Except when noted otherwise, VG = 25% of NM, and VG+ = 50% of NM. (Example: VG = $2.00, VG+ = $4.00 and NM = $8.00.)

MINOR MUSIC

Number	Title (A Side/B Side)	Yr	NM
❑ 008	...Theoretically	1986	15.00

BERRY, BROOKS, AND SCRAPPER BLACKWELL

Albums

BLUESVILLE

Number	Title (A Side/B Side)	Yr	NM
❑ BVLP-1074 [M]	My Heart Struck Sorrow	1963	80.00
—Blue label, silver print			
❑ BVLP-1074 [M]	My Heart Struck Sorrow	1964	25.00
—Blue label with trident logo			

BERRY, CHUCK

Also see JOE ALEXANDER AND THE CUBANS; BO DIDDLEY/CHUCK BERRY.

45s

ATCO

Number	Title (A Side/B Side)	Yr	NM
❑ 7203	Oh What a Thrill/California	1979	4.00

CHESS

Number	Title (A Side/B Side)	Yr	NM
❑ 1604	Maybellene/Wee Wee Hours	1955	50.00
❑ 1610	Thirty Days (To Come Back Home)/Together	1955	50.00
❑ 1615	No Money Down/ Down Bound Train	1956	50.00
❑ 1626	Roll Over Beethoven/ Drifting Heart	1956	50.00
❑ 1635	Too Much Monkey Business/ Brown Eyed Handsome Man	1956	50.00
❑ 1645	You Can't Catch Me/ Havana Moon	1956	50.00
❑ 1653	School Day (Ring! Ring! Goes the Bell)/Deep Feeling	1957	50.00
❑ 1664	Oh Baby Doll/La Jaunda	1957	50.00
❑ 1671	Rock & Roll Music/Blue Feeling	1957	30.00
❑ 1683	Sweet Little Sixteen/ Reelin' and Rockin'	1958	30.00
❑ 1691	Johnny B. Goode/ Around and Around	1958	30.00
❑ 1697	Beautiful Delilah/Vacation Time	1958	30.00
❑ 1700	Carol/Hey Pedro	1958	30.00
❑ 1709	Sweet Little Rock and Roll/ Joe Joe Gun	1958	30.00
❑ 1714	Run Rudolph Run/ Merry Christmas Baby	1958	40.00
❑ 1716	Anthony Boy/That's My Desire	1959	30.00
❑ 1722	Almost Grown/Little Queenie	1959	30.00
❑ 1729	Back in the U.S.A./ Memphis Tennessee	1959	30.00
❑ 1737	Broken Arrow/Childhood Sweetheart	1959	40.00
❑ 1747	Too Pooped to Pop ("Casey")/ Let It Rock	1960	25.00
❑ 1754	Bye Bye Johnny/ Worried Life Blues	1960	25.00
❑ 1763	I Got to Find My Baby/Mad Lad	1960	25.00
❑ 1767	Our Little Rendezvous/ Jaguar and Thunderbird	1960	25.00
❑ 1779	I'm Talking About You/Little Star	1961	25.00
❑ 1799	Come On/Go-Go-Go	1961	20.00
❑ 1853	I'm Talking About You/ Diploma for Two	1963	20.00
❑ 1866	Memphis/Sweet Little Sixteen	1963	20.00
❑ 1883	Nadine (Is It You?)/O Rangutang	1964	20.00
❑ 1898	No Particular Place to Go/ You Two	1964	20.00
❑ 1898 [PS]	No Particular Place to Go/ You Two	1964	50.00
❑ 1906	You Never Can Tell/Brenda Lee	1964	20.00
❑ 1906 [PS]	You Never Can Tell/Brenda Lee	1964	40.00
❑ 1912	Little Marie/Go Bobby Soxer	1964	15.00
❑ 1912 [PS]	Little Marie/Go Bobby Soxer	1964	40.00
❑ 1916	Promised Land/ Things I Used to Do	1964	15.00
❑ 1916 [PS]	Promised Land/ Things I Used to Do	1964	50.00
❑ 1926	Dear Dad/Lonely School Days	1965	15.00
❑ 1943	It Wasn't Me/Welcome Back Pretty Girl	1965	15.00
❑ 1943 [PS]	It Wasn't Me/Welcome Back Pretty Girl	1965	30.00
❑ 1963	Ramona Say Yes/Havana Moon	1966	15.00
❑ 1963	Ramona Say Yes/ Lonely School Days	1966	15.00
❑ 2090	Tulane/Have Mercy Judge	1970	6.00
❑ 2131	My Ding-a-Ling/ Johnny B. Goode	1972	4.00
—Orange and blue label			
❑ 2131	My Ding-a-Ling/ Johnny B. Goode	1972	6.00
—All-blue label			
❑ 2136	Reelin' & Rockin'/Let's Boogie	1972	4.00
❑ 2140	Roll 'Em Pete/Bio	1973	4.00
❑ 2169	Baby What You Want Me to Do/ Shake, Rattle and Roll	1975	4.00

COLLECTABLES

Number	Title (A Side/B Side)	Yr	NM
❑ 3437	Run Rudolph Run/Merry Christmas Baby	199?	3.00

CROSLEY

Number	Title (A Side/B Side)	Yr	NM
❑ B0001383-21	Johnny B. Goode/Maybellene	2003	5.00
—Record offered with the purchase of a Crosley record player			
❑ B0001383-21 [PS]	Johnny B. Goode/Maybellene	2003	5.00

MERCURY

Number	Title (A Side/B Side)	Yr	NM
❑ 30143	Maybellene/Sweet Little Sixteen	196?	6.00
❑ 30144	Memphis/School Day (Ring, Ring Goes the Bell)	196?	6.00
❑ 30145	Back in the U.S.A./ Roll Over Beethoven	196?	6.00
❑ 30146	Johnny B. Goode/ Rock and Roll Music	196?	6.00
—The Mercury 30000 series are re-recordings of the Chess hits			
❑ 72643	Club Nitty Gritty/Laugh and Cry	1966	10.00
❑ 72680	Back to Memphis/ I Do Really Love You	1967	10.00
❑ 72748	It Hurts Me Too/Feelin' It	1967	10.00
❑ 72840	Louie to Frisco/Ma Dear	1968	10.00
❑ 72963	It's Too Dark in There/ Good Looking Woman	1969	20.00
❑ 72963 [PS]	It's Too Dark in There/ Good Looking Woman	1969	30.00

PHILCO-FORD

Number	Title (A Side/B Side)	Yr	NM
❑ HP-34	Maybellene/Roll Over Beethoven	1969	20.00
—4-inch plastic "Hip Pocket Record" with color sleeve			

7-Inch Extended Plays

CHESS

Number	Title (A Side/B Side)	Yr	NM
❑ CH-5118	School Day (Ring, Ring Goes the Bell)/Wee Wee Hours// Brown Eyed Handsome Man/ Too Much Monkey Business	1957	120.00
❑ CH-5118 [PS]	After School Session	1957	200.00
❑ CH-5119	Rock & Roll Music/Blue Feeling//Oh Baby Doll/ La Jaunda (Espanol)	1957	100.00
❑ CH-5119 [PS]	Rock and Roll Music	1957	200.00
❑ CH-5121	Sweet Little Sixteen/Rockin' at the Philharmonic//Reelin' and Rockin'/Guitar Boogie	1958	100.00
❑ CH-5121 [PS]	Sweet Little Sixteen	1958	200.00
❑ EP-5124	Carol/Hey Pedro//Beautiful Delilah/Vacation Time	1958	100.00
❑ EP-5124 [PS]	Pickin' Berries	1958	200.00
❑ EP-5126	Jo Jo Gun/Sweet Little Rock and Roller//Johnny B. Goode/ Around and Around	1958	100.00
❑ EP-5126 [PS]	Sweet Little Rock and Roller	1958	200.00

Albums

ACCORD

Number	Title (A Side/B Side)	Yr	NM
❑ SN-7171	Toronto Rock 'N' Roll Revival, Vol. 2	1982	10.00
❑ SN-7172	Toronto Rock 'N' Roll Revival, Vol. 3	1982	10.00

ATCO

Number	Title (A Side/B Side)	Yr	NM
❑ SD 38-118	Rockit	1979	12.00

CHESS

Number	Title (A Side/B Side)	Yr	NM
❑ LP-1426 [M]	After School Session	1958	200.00
❑ LPS-1426 [R]	After School Session	196?	12.00
❑ LP-1432 [M]	One Dozen Berrys	1958	200.00
❑ LPS-1432 [R]	One Dozen Berrys	196?	12.00
❑ LP-1435 [M]	Chuck Berry Is On Top	1959	180.00
❑ LPS-1435 [R]	Chuck Berry Is On Top	196?	12.00
❑ LP-1448 [M]	Rockin' at the Hops	1960	180.00
❑ LP-1456 [M]	New Juke Box Hits	1961	180.00
❑ LP-1465 [M]	Chuck Berry Twist	1962	100.00
❑ LP-1465 [M]	More Chuck Berry	1963	120.00
—Retitled version of above			
❑ LPS-1465 [R]	More Chuck Berry	196?	12.00
❑ LP-1480 [M]	Chuck Berry On Stage	1963	120.00
❑ LPS-1480 [R]	Chuck Berry On Stage	196?	12.00
❑ LP-1485 [M]	Chuck Berry's Greatest Hits	1964	120.00
❑ LPS-1485 [R]	Chuck Berry's Greatest Hits	196?	12.00
❑ LP-1488 [M]	St. Louis to Liverpool	1964	60.00
❑ LPS-1488 [S]	St. Louis to Liverpool	1964	80.00
❑ LP-1495 [M]	Chuck Berry in London	1965	30.00
❑ LPS-1495 [S]	Chuck Berry in London	1965	40.00
❑ LP-1498 [M]	Fresh Berry's	1965	30.00
❑ LPS-1498 [S]	Fresh Berry's	1965	40.00
❑ 2CH-1514 [(2)R]	Chuck Berry's Golden Decade	1972	15.00
—New cover has a pink radio			
❑ LP-1514 [(2)M]	Chuck Berry's Golden Decade	1967	40.00
❑ LPS-1514 [(2)R]	Chuck Berry's Golden Decade	1967	20.00
—Old cover does not have a pink radio			
❑ LPS-1550	Back Home	1970	20.00
❑ CH-9171	New Juke Box Hits	1986	10.00
—Reissue of 1456			
❑ CH-9186	St. Louis to Liverpool	1988	10.00
—Reissue of 1488			
❑ CH-9190	More Rock 'n' Roll Rarities	1986	10.00
❑ CH-9256	Chuck Berry Is On Top	1987	10.00
—Reissue of 1435			
❑ CH-9259	Rockin' at the Hop	1987	10.00
—Reissue of 1448			
❑ CH-9284	After School Session	1989	10.00
—Reissue of 1426			
❑ CH-9295	The London Chuck Berry Sessions	1989	10.00
—Reissue of 60020			
❑ CH-9318	Missing Berries: Rarities, Vol. 3	1990	10.00
❑ CH-50008	San Fransisco Dues	1971	20.00
❑ CH-50043	Chuck Berry/Bio	1973	20.00
❑ CH-60020	The London Chuck Berry Sessions	1972	20.00
❑ 2CH-60023 [(2)]	Chuck Berry's Golden Decade, Vol. 2	1973	25.00
❑ 2CH-60028 [(2)]	Chuck Berry's Golden Decade, Vol. 3	1974	25.00
❑ CH6-80001 [(6)]	The Chess Box	1989	50.00
❑ CH2-92500 [(2)]	The Great Twenty-Eight	1983	12.00
❑ CH2-92521 [(2)]	Rock 'n' Roll Rarities	1986	15.00

EVEREST ARCHIVE OF FOLK & JAZZ

Number	Title (A Side/B Side)	Yr	NM
❑ FS-321	Chuck Berry's Greatest Hits	1976	10.00

GUSTO

Number	Title (A Side/B Side)	Yr	NM
❑ 0004	The Best of the Best of Chuck Berry	198?	10.00

MERCURY

Number	Title (A Side/B Side)	Yr	NM
❑ SRM-2-6501 [(2)]	St. Louis to Frisco to Memphis	1972	20.00
❑ MG-21103 [M]	Chuck Berry's Golden Hits	1967	15.00
❑ MG-21123 [M]	Chuck Berry in Memphis	1967	15.00
❑ MG-21138 [M]	Love at the Fillmore Auditorium	1967	20.00
❑ SR-61103 [S]	Chuck Berry's Golden Hits	1967	15.00
❑ SR-61123 [S]	Chuck Berry in Memphis	1967	15.00
❑ SR-61138 [S]	Love at the Fillmore Auditorium	1967	20.00
❑ SR-61176	From St. Louie to Frisco	1968	20.00
❑ SR-61223	Concerto in B Goode	1969	20.00
❑ 826256-1	Chuck Berry's Golden Hits	1985	8.00
—Reissue			

PICKWICK

Number	Title (A Side/B Side)	Yr	NM
❑ PTP-2061 [(2)]	Flashback	1975	12.00
❑ SPC-3327	Johnny B. Goode	1973	10.00
❑ SPC-3345	Sweet Little Rock and Roller	1974	10.00
❑ SPC-3392	Wild Berrys	1974	10.00

QUICKSILVER

Number	Title (A Side/B Side)	Yr	NM
❑ QS-1017	Live Hits	198?	10.00

SSS INTERNATIONAL

Number	Title (A Side/B Side)	Yr	NM
❑ 36	Chuck Berry Live	1981	10.00

BERRY, DAVE

45s

LONDON

Number	Title (A Side/B Side)	Yr	NM
❑ 9666	Memphis Tennessee/ My Baby Left Me	1964	15.00
❑ 9698	The Crying Game/Don't Gimme No Lip Child	1964	16.00
❑ 9781	This Strange Effect/Now	1965	15.00
❑ 20038	Do I Still Figure in Your Life/ Latisha	1968	8.00

PARROT

Number	Title (A Side/B Side)	Yr	NM
❑ 40010	Picture Me Gone/Baby's Gone	1967	10.00

BERRY, JAN

Includes records as "Jan Barry" and "I Jan I." Also see JAN AND DEAN.

45s

A&M

Number	Title (A Side/B Side)	Yr	NM
❑ 1957	Little Queenie/That's the Way It Is	1977	15.00
❑ 2020	Skateboard Surfin' U.S.A. (Sidewalk Surfin' with Me)/ How How I Love You	1978	15.00

LIBERTY

Number	Title (A Side/B Side)	Yr	NM
❑ 55845	The Universal Coward/ I Can't Wait to Love You	1965	20.00
❑ 55845 [PS]	The Universal Coward/ I Can't Wait to Love You	1965	300.00

ODE

Number	Title (A Side/B Side)	Yr	NM
❑ 66023	Mother Earth/Blue Moon Shuffle	1972	20.00
❑ 66034	Don't You Just Know It/ Blue Moon Shuffle	1973	40.00
—With Brian Wilson on co-lead vocals on A-side			
❑ 66050	Tinsel Town/Blow Up Music	1974	20.00
—As "I Jan I"			
❑ 66120	Sing Sang a Song/Sing Sang a Song (Singalong Version)	1976	20.00

RIPPLE

Number	Title (A Side/B Side)	Yr	NM
❑ 6101	Tomorrow's Teardrops/My Midsummer Night's Dream	1961	100.00
—As "Jan Barry"			

BERRY, JOHN

45s

DOT

Number	Title (A Side/B Side)	Yr	NM
❑ 16132	Dance with Me Darlin'/Lucy Lou	1960	12.00

BERRY, KEN

45s

BARNABY

Number	Title (A Side/B Side)	Yr	NM
❑ 2020	Lonely Street/Ain't That a Shame	1970	8.00

B

Number	Title (A Side/B Side)	Yr	NM
❑ 2034	Everyday with You/He'll Have to Go	1971	8.00
Albums			
BARNABY			
❑ Z 30014	R.F.D.	1970	25.00
❑ Z 30094	Ken Berry, R.F.D.	1970	30.00

BERRY, MIKE

Number	Title (A Side/B Side)	Yr	NM
45s			
CORAL			
❑ 62341	A Tribute to Buddy Holly/Every Little Kiss	1962	60.00
❑ 62357	Don't You Think It's Time/Loneliness	1963	30.00
❑ 62483	Gonna Fall in Love/It Comes and Goes	1966	16.00
EPIC			
❑ 50748	I Am a Rocker/Boogaloo Dues	1979	4.00
❑ 50913	Stay Close to Me/One by One	1980	4.00
MCA			
❑ 40432	Don't Be Cruel/It's All Over	1975	5.00
Albums			
EPIC			
❑ JE 36071	I'm a Rocker	1979	10.00
SIRE			
❑ SASD 7524	Rocks in My Head	1976	15.00

BERRY, RICHARD

Number	Title (A Side/B Side)	Yr	NM
45s			
FLAIR			
❑ 1016	I'm Still in Love with You/One Little Prayer	1953	80.00
❑ 1052	Bye Bye/At Last	1954	60.00
—With the Dreamers			
❑ 1055	What You Do to Me/The Big Break	1954	60.00
❑ 1058	Daddy Daddy/Baby Darling	1954	60.00
—With the Dreamers			
❑ 1064	Please Tell Me/Oh Oh Get Out of the Car	1955	50.00
❑ 1068	God Gave Me You/Doncha Go	1955	50.00
❑ 1071	Next Time/Crazy Lover	1955	50.00
❑ 1075	Together/Jelly Roll	1955	50.00
FLIP			
❑ 318	Take the Key/No Kissin' and Huggin'	1956	40.00
❑ 321	Louie, Louie/Rock, Rock, Rock	1957	40.00
❑ 321	Louie, Louie/You Are My Sunshine	1957	60.00
❑ 327	Sweet Sugar You/Rock, Rock, Rock	1957	40.00
❑ 331	You're the Girl/You Look So Good	1958	40.00
❑ 336	Heaven on Wheels/The Mess Around	1958	40.00
❑ 339	Besame Mucho/Do I, Do I	1958	30.00
❑ 349	Have Love, Will Travel/No Room	1960	30.00
❑ 352	I'll Never Ever Love Again/Somewhere There's a Rainbow	1961	30.00
❑ 360	You Look So Good/You Are My Sunshine	1962	30.00
HAPPY TIGER			
❑ 5063	Louie Louie/Rock Rock Rock	1972	8.00
K&G			
❑ 9001	I'm Your Fool/In a Really Big Way	1961	30.00
RPM			
❑ 448	Rockin' Man/Big John	1955	100.00
❑ 452	Pretty Brown Eyes/I Am Bewildered	1956	30.00
❑ 465	Angel of My Life/Yama Yama Pretty Mama	1956	100.00
❑ 477	Wait for Me/Good Love	1956	30.00
SMASH			
❑ 1789	What Good Is a Heart/Everybody's Got a Lover But Me	1963	12.00
❑ 1811	I'm Learning/Empty Chair	1963	12.00
WARNER BROS.			
❑ 5164	Walk Right In/It's All Right	1960	50.00
Albums			
CROWN			
❑ CST-371 [R]	Richard Berry and the Dreamers	1963	30.00
❑ CLP-5371 [M]	Richard Berry and the Dreamers	1963	60.00
PAM			
❑ 1001	Live at the Century Restaurant	1968	40.00
❑ 1002	Wild Berry	196?	40.00

BERRY KIDS, THE

Number	Title (A Side/B Side)	Yr	NM
45s			
MGM			
❑ 12379	Go, Go, Go, Right Into Town/Love Me, Love	1956	80.00
❑ 12496	Rootie Tootie/You're My Teenage Baby	1957	80.00

BEST, BILLY, AND THE DITALIANS

Number	Title (A Side/B Side)	Yr	NM
45s			
MERCURY			
❑ 72923	Baby That Takes the Cake/Time Is Getting Hard Josephine	1969	8.00

BEST, PETER (1)

Former drummer with THE BEATLES.

Number	Title (A Side/B Side)	Yr	NM
45s			
CAMEO			
❑ 391	Boys/Kansas City	1965	80.00
❑ 391 [PS]	Boys/Kansas City	1965	100.00
HAPPENING			
❑ 405	If You Can't Get Her/Don't Play with Me	1964	180.00
❑ 1117/8	If You Can't Get Her/The Way I Feel About You	1966	150.00
—Label credit: "Best of the Beatles (Peter Best)"			
MR. MAESTRO			
❑ 711	I Can't Do Without You Now/Keys to My Heart	1965	150.00
—Label credit: "Best of the Beatles"; blue vinyl			
❑ 711	I Can't Do Without You Now/Keys to My Heart	1965	200.00
—Label credit: "Best of the Beatles"; black vinyl			
❑ 712	Casting My Spell/I'm Blue	1965	150.00
—Black vinyl			
❑ 712	Casting My Spell/I'm Blue	1965	200.00
—Blue vinyl			
ORIGINAL BEATLES DRUMMER			
❑ 800	(I'll Try) Anyway/I Wanna Be There	1964	180.00
Albums			
PHOENIX			
❑ PHX-340	The Beatle That Time Forgot	1982	12.00
SAVAGE			
❑ BM-71	Best of the Beatles	1966	200.00
—Authentic copies have white circle around the word "Savage" and white circle around Pete Best's head on the album cover.			

BEST, PETER (2)

This Peter Best is from Australia.

Number	Title (A Side/B Side)	Yr	NM
45s			
CAPITOL			
❑ 2092	Carousel of Love/Want You	1968	30.00

BEST THINGS, THE

Number	Title (A Side/B Side)	Yr	NM
45s			
UNITED ARTISTS			
❑ 50027	Chicks Are for Kids/You May See Me Cry	1966	10.00

BETH, KAREN

Number	Title (A Side/B Side)	Yr	NM
Albums			
DECCA			
❑ DL 75148	The Joys of Life	1969	15.00
❑ DL 75247	Harvest	1970	15.00

BETTS, DICKEY

Also see THE ALLMAN BROTHERS BAND.

Number	Title (A Side/B Side)	Yr	NM
45s			
ARISTA			
❑ 0255	Nothing You Can Do	1977	4.00
❑ 0269	Bougainvilla/Sweet Virginia	1977	4.00
❑ 0333	Atlanta's Burning Down/Mr. Blues Man	1978	4.00
CAPRICORN			
❑ 0213	Kissimmee Kid/Long Time Gone	1974	5.00
❑ 0221	Highway Call/Rain	1975	5.00
Albums			
ARISTA			
❑ AL 4123	Dickey Betts & Great Southern	1977	10.00
❑ AL 4168	Atlanta's Burning Down	1978	10.00
CAPRICORN			
❑ CP 0123	Highway Call	1974	12.00
—As "Richard Betts"			
EPIC			
❑ FE 44289	Pattern Disruptive	1988	10.00

BEVEL, CHARLES

Number	Title (A Side/B Side)	Yr	NM
45s			
A&M			
❑ 1481	Making a Decision/Meet "Mississippi Charles Bevel"	1973	5.00
❑ 1481	Black Santa Claus/Making A Decision (Bring On Sunshine)	1973	6.00
❑ 1501	Sally B. White/Porcupine Meat	1974	5.00
❑ 1608	Don't Lie to Me/It Ain't Magic	1974	5.00
❑ AM-8725	Black Santa Claus/Sally B. White	199?	3.00
—Reissue			
Albums			
A&M			
❑ SP-4412	Meet "Mississippi Charles"	1973	12.00

BEVERLY, FRANKIE, 'S RAW SOUL

Number	Title (A Side/B Side)	Yr	NM
45s			
GREGAR			
❑ 71-0108	Color Blind/Mother Nature's Been Good to You	1971	200.00
❑ 71-0112	People in the Know/Understanding	1971	200.00
❑ 71-0115	Tomorrow May Not Be Your Day/While I'm Alone	1971	25.00

BEVERLY, FRANKIE, AND THE BUTLERS

Number	Title (A Side/B Side)	Yr	NM
45s			
FAIRMOUNT			
❑ 1012	She Kissed Me/Don't Cry Little Sad Boy	1966	200.00
❑ 1017	Because of My Heart/I Want to Feel I'm Wanted	1966	2000.
—VG 1000; VG+ 1500			
GAMBLE			
❑ 220	If That's What You Wanted/Love (Your Pain Goes Deep)	1968	400.00
SASSY			
❑ 1002	If That's What You Wanted/Love (Your Pain Goes Deep)	196?	250.00

BEVERLY SISTERS, THE

Number	Title (A Side/B Side)	Yr	NM
45s			
LONDON			
❑ 1703	Greensleeves/I'll See You in My Dreams	1956	12.00
❑ 1731	Blow the Wind Southerly/Doodle Doo Doo	1957	12.00
❑ 1757	Old Enough to Know/I Remember Mama	1957	12.00
❑ 1783	Long Black Nylons/Young Cavalier	1958	12.00
❑ 1862	The Little Drummer Boy/Strawberry Fair	1958	12.00
❑ 1891	Little Donkey/Toy Dream	1960	12.00
MERCURY			
❑ 71671	Oh Ricky/Only Me	1960	12.00
ROULETTE			
❑ 4350	Flight 1203/(B-side unknown)	1961	12.00

BI-TONES, THE

Number	Title (A Side/B Side)	Yr	NM
45s			
BLUE JAY			
❑ 1000	Oh How I Love You So/Beatnik Girl	1960	25.00

BIDDU ORCHESTRA

Number	Title (A Side/B Side)	Yr	NM
12-Inch Singles			
EPIC			
❑ AE 348 [DJ]	Funky Tropical (4:09) (same on both sides)	1977	20.00
❑ 28-50397	Funky Tropical (6:17)/Boogiethon (5:45)	1977	20.00
45s			
COLOSSUS			
❑ 125	The Sooner I Get to You/(B-side unknown)	1970	8.00
—As "Biddu"			
EPIC			
❑ 50139	Summer of '42/Northern Dancer	1975	4.00
❑ 50173	I Could Have Danced All Night/Jump for Joy	1975	4.00
❑ 50212	Rainforest/Hot Ice	1976	4.00
❑ 50387	Funky Tropical/Girl You'll Be a Woman Soon	1977	4.00
❑ 50439	Soal Coaxing/Nirvana	1977	4.00
Albums			
EPIC			
❑ PE 33903	Biddu Orchestra	1975	10.00
❑ PE 34230	Rain Forest	1976	10.00
❑ PE 34723	Eastern Man	1977	10.00

Except when noted otherwise, VG = 25% of NM, and VG+ = 50% of NM. (Example: VG = $2.00, VG+ = $4.00 and NM = $8.00.)

Number	Title (A Side/B Side)	Yr	NM

BIG AUDIO DYNAMITE Includes records as "Big Audio Dynamite II" and "Big Audio." Features Mick Jones, formerly of THE CLASH.

12-Inch Singles

COLUMBIA

❑ CAS 01739 [DJ] James Brown (Remix) (LP Version) (Remix Edit)/ If I Were John Carpenter 1989 10.00
❑ CAS 01899 [DJ] Contact (Extended Club Mix) (12" Mix) (7" Version)// Who (Beats)/In Full Effect 1989 8.00
❑ CAS 2252 [DJ] The Bottom Line (Single Version) (LP Version) 1985 8.00
❑ CAS 2302 [DJ] Medicine Show (London Mix) (N.Y. Mix) 1985 8.00
❑ CAS 2361 [DJ] E=MC2 (3 versions) 1985 8.00
❑ CAS 2520 [DJ] C'mon Every Beatbox (LP Version) (Edit) 1986 8.00
❑ CAS 2601 [DJ] V. Thirteen (same on both sides) 1986 8.00
❑ CAS 2647 [DJ] Badrock City (LP Version) (Edit) 1986 8.00
❑ CAS 02697 [DJ] Hollywood Boulevard (Club Mix) (same on both sides) 1987 8.00
❑ CAS 4044 [DJ] Rushdance/Rush (Instrumental) (LP Version)/City Lights 1991 8.00
❑ CAS 4243 [DJ] The Globe (Extended by the Orb) (Dub Version) (Instrumental) (LP Version) (12" Mix 7:42)/ Rush (12" Mix 7:57) 1992 10.00
❑ 44-05324 The Bottom Line/B.A.D. 1985 8.00
❑ 44-05359 Medicine Show (6:10) (8:58)/ This Is Big Audio Dynamite 1986 8.00
❑ 44-05909 E=MC2 (Extended Remix 5:33)/A Party (10:15) 1985 8.00
❑ 44-05963 C'mon Every Beatbox (Extended)/Badrock City/ Beatboxes at Dawn 1986 6.00
❑ CAS 6553 [DJ] Looking for a Song (Zonka/ Shapps Early Mix 6:44) (Zonka/Shapps Remix 7:15) (Zonka's Adventures in Space Mix 4:50) (Extended LP Mix 5:37) 1994 8.00
❑ 44-06780 V. Thirteen/Hollywood Boulevard (Club Mix) (Dub) 1986 6.00
❑ 44-07851 Just Play Music (6:50) (8:57) 1988 8.00
❑ 44-08133 The Other 99 (Extended)/Just Play Music/What Happened to Eddie? 1988 8.00
❑ 44-74134 Rushdance/Rush (Club Instrumental)//Rush (Album Version)/City Lights 1991 8.00
❑ 44-74180 The Globe (Extended by the Orb) (Dub Version) (Instrumental) (LP Version) (12" Mix 7:42)/Rush (12" Mix 7:57) 1992 8.00

DEF JAM

❑ 44-05370 The Bottom Line/B.A.D. 1985 12.00
—Different mixes than on Columbia 05324

WTG

❑ 41-73159 Free (Club Mix 7:17) (Film Mix 3:31)/ The Bottom Line (Film and Club Version 7:20) 1990 8.00

45s

COLUMBIA

❑ 38-05841 Medicine Show/This Is Big Audio Dynamite 1986 3.00
❑ 38-05841 [PS] Medicine Show/This Is Big Audio Dynamite 1986 3.00
❑ 38-05841 [PS] Medicine Show 1986 6.00
—"Demonstration – Not for Sale" on back
❑ 38-06053 E=MC2/A Party 1986 3.00
❑ 38-06053 [PS] E=MC2/A Party 1986 3.00
❑ 38-06364 C'Mon Every Beatbox (Edit)/ Badrock City 1986 3.00
❑ 38-06364 [PS] C'Mon Every Beatbox (Edit)/ Badrock City 1986 3.00
❑ 38-06708 Badrock City/C'mon Every Beatbox 1987 3.00
❑ 38-06708 [PS] Badrock City/C'mon Every Beatbox 1987 3.00
—"Demonstration – Not for Sale" on back
❑ 38-07955 Just Play Music/Much Worse 1988 3.00
❑ 38-07955 [PS] Just Play Music/Much Worse 1988 3.00
❑ 38-08094 The Other 99/What Happened to Eddie 1988 3.00
❑ 38-08094 [PS] The Other 99/What Happened to Eddie 1988 3.00

RADIOACTIVE

❑ RAR7P-3371 [DJ] I Turned Out a Punk/ Suffragette City 1995 10.00
—Promo-only vinyl

Albums

COLUMBIA

❑ BFC 40220 This Is Big Audio Dynamite 1985 10.00
❑ BFC 40445 No. 10 Upping Street 1986 12.00
❑ BFC 40705 No. 10 Upping Street 1986 10.00
—Reissue with extra track, "Badrock City"
❑ FC 44074 Tighten Up Vol. 88 1988 10.00
❑ FC 45212 Megatop Phoenix 1989 10.00
❑ C 46147 The Globe 1991 14.00

RADIOACTIVE

❑ 11280 [(2)] F-Punk 1995 15.00

BIG BEATS, THE Also see TRINI LOPEZ.

45s

COLUMBIA

❑ 41072 Clark's Expedition/Big Boy 1958 25.00
❑ 41179 Rush Me/Sentimental Journey 1958 25.00

Albums

LIBERTY

❑ LRP-3407 [M] The Big Beats Live 1965 30.00
❑ LST-7407 [S] The Big Beats Live 1965 40.00

BIG BLACK No relation to the 1980s punk band of the same name.

45s

HOMESTEAD

❑ HMS 042 Il Duce/Big Money 1985 5.00
❑ HMS 042 [PS] Il Duce/Big Money 1985 5.00

TOUCH & GO

❑ TG 21 Heartbeat/Things to Do/ Today I Can't Believe 1987 6.00
❑ TG 21 [PS] Heartbeat/Things to Do/ Today I Can't Believe 1987 6.00
❑ TG 23 He's a Whore/The Model 1987 15.00
❑ TG 23 [PS] He's a Whore/The Model 1987 15.00
❑ TG 95 Il Duce/Big Money 1992 3.00
—Reissue of Homestead 042
❑ TG 95 [PS] Il Duce/Big Money 1992 3.00

Albums

HOMESTEAD

❑ HMS 007 [EP] Racer X 1983 15.00
❑ HMS 043 Atomizer 1986 15.00
❑ HMS 044 The Hammer Party 1986 15.00

RUTHLESS

❑ (# unknown) [EP] Lungs 1982 50.00
❑ (# unknown) [EP] Bulldozer 1983 50.00

TOUCH & GO

❑ (no #)? [DJ] The Incredibly Corporate Whorish Big Black Interview Album 1987 30.00
❑ TG 20 [EP] Headache 1987 8.00
❑ TG 20 [EP] Headache 1987 100.00
—With "gross" cover (different from regular issue), red vinyl record, bonus 7-inch single, book and poster
❑ TG 24 Songs About Fucking 1987 12.00
❑ TG 81 Pigpile 1992 10.00
❑ TG 89 [EP] Lungs 1992 8.00
—Reissue
❑ TG 90 [EP] Bulldozer 1992 8.00
—Reissue
❑ TG 91 [EP] Racer X 1992 8.00
—Reissue of Homestead 007
❑ TG 93 Atomizer 1992 10.00
—Reissue of Homestead 043
❑ TG 111 Boxes 1992 100.00
—Box set containing the Pigpile LP, video, T-shirt and poster

BIG BOPPER

45s

D

❑ 1008 Chantilly Lace/The Purple People Eater Meets the Witch Doctor 1958 250.00

MERCURY

❑ 71219 Beggar to a King/Crazy Blue 1957 60.00
—As "Jape Richardson"
❑ 71312 A Teenage Mom/Monkey Song 1958 60.00
—As "Jape Richardson"
❑ 71343 Chantilly Lace/The Purple People Eater Meets the Witch Doctor 1958 20.00
❑ 71375 Big Bopper's Wedding/ Little Red Riding Hood 1958 15.00
❑ 71416 Someone's Watching Over You/Walking Through My Dreams 1959 15.00
❑ 71451 It's the Truth, Ruth/That's What I'm Talkin' About 1959 15.00
❑ 71482 Pink Petticoats/Time Clock 1959 15.00

WING

❑ 17000 Chantilly Lace/Someone Watching Over You 196? 10.00
—Reissue

Albums

MERCURY

❑ MG-20402 [M] Chantilly Lace 1959 500.00
—Black label
❑ MG-20402 [M] Chantilly Lace 196? 25.00
—Red label with twelve Mercury logos on label edge
❑ MG-20402 [M] Chantilly Lace 1964 200.00
—Red label with black or black & white Mercury logo at top
❑ MG-20402 [M] Chantilly Lace 1975 15.00
—Chicago skyline label
❑ 832902-1 [M] Chantilly Lace 1988 15.00
—New number, black label

PICKWICK

❑ SPC-3365 Chantilly Lace 1973 15.00

RHINO

❑ R1-70164 Helloooo Baby! The Best of the Big Bopper 1954-1959 1989 12.00

BIG BROTHER

45s

ALL AMERICAN

❑ 5718 E.S.P./Brother, Where Are You 1970 40.00

Albums

ALL-AMERICAN

❑ 5770 Big Brother 1970 250.00

BIG BROTHER AND THE HOLDING COMPANY Also see JANIS JOPLIN.

45s

COLUMBIA

❑ 44626 Piece of My Heart/Turtle Blues 1968 10.00
❑ 45284 Keep On/Home on the Strange 1970 6.00
❑ 45502 Black Widow Spider/ Nu Boogaloo Jam 1971 6.00

MAINSTREAM

❑ 657 All Is Loneliness/Blindman 1967 12.00
❑ 662 Down on Me/Call On Me 1967 12.00
❑ 666 Bye Bye Baby/Intruder 1968 12.00
❑ 675 Women Is Losers/Light Is Faster Than Sound 1968 12.00
❑ 675 Women Is Losers/Caterpillar 1968 80.00
—This is much rarer than the version with the other flip side
❑ 678 Coo Coo/The Last Time 1968 12.00

Albums

COLUMBIA

❑ KCL 2900 [M] Cheap Thrills 1968 300.00
—Red label stock copy has been confirmed
❑ KCS 9700 Cheap Thrills 1970 12.00
—Orange label
❑ KCS 9700 [M] Cheap Thrills 1968 100.00
—White label "Special Mono Radio Station Copy" with stereo number
❑ KCS 9700 [S] Cheap Thrills 1968 25.00
—Red "360 Sound" label
❑ PC 9700 Cheap Thrills 198? 8.00
—Reissue with new prefix
❑ C 30222 Be a Brother 1970 20.00
❑ C 30631 Big Brother and the Holding Company 1971 20.00
—Reissue of Mainstream LP with two extra tracks
❑ C 30738 How Hard It Is 1971 20.00

COLUMBIA SPECIAL PRODUCTS

❑ P 13313 Big Brother and the Holding Company 197? 15.00

MAINSTREAM

❑ S-6099 [S] Big Brother and the Holding Company 1967 50.00
❑ 56099 [M] Big Brother and the Holding Company 1967 100.00

RHINO

❑ RNLP 121 Live 1984 20.00
—Recorded 1966

BIG COUNTRY

12-Inch Singles

MERCURY

❑ PRO 324-1 [DJ] Where the Rose... (same on both sides) 1984 8.00
❑ PRO 221-1 [DJ] In a Big Country (LP Version)/(7" Version) 1983 6.00
❑ PRO239 [DJ] Fields of Fire/Fields of Fire (7" Version) 1984 6.00
❑ PRO 239-1 [DJ] Fields of Fire (LP Version)/ (7" Version) 1984 6.00
❑ PRO 324-1 [DJ] Where the Rose Is Sown (Special AOR Remix) (same on both sides) 1984 8.00

Number	Title (A Side/B Side)	Yr	NM
❑ PRO333 [DJ]	Just a Shadow (Long)/Just a Shadow (Short)	1984	6.00
❑ PRO 333-1 [DJ]	Just a Shadow (Long Version)/(Short Version)	1984	6.00
❑ PRO341 [DJ]	East of Eden (same on both sides)	1984	6.00
❑ PRO 341-1 [DJ]	East of Eden (same on both sides)	1984	7.00
❑ PRO414 [DJ]	Look Away (same on both sides)	1986	6.00
❑ PRO 414-1 [DJ]	Look Away (4:24) (same on both sides)	1986	6.00
❑ PRO442 [DJ]	One Great Thing (same on both sides)	1986	6.00
❑ PRO 442-1 [DJ]	One Great Thing (4:00) (same on both sides)	1986	6.00
❑ 884645-1	Look Away (Outlaw Mix 6:53)/Restless Natives (The Soundtrack Part 1 16:40)	1986	12.00
❑ 884698-1	Look Away (12" Mix 6:32) (7" Mix 4:24)/Restless Natives (4:00)	1986	8.00
❑ 888028-1	One Great Thing (Big Baad Country Mix 6:35)/Look Away (Outlaw Mix 6:53)/Song of the South (7" Version 3:47)	1986	7.00
45s			
COLLECTABLES			
❑ 4856	In a Big Country/Breakout	199?	3.00
—Reissue; B-side by Swing Out Sister			
MERCURY			
❑ 811450-7	Fields of Fire/Angle Park	1983	3.00
❑ 811450-7 [PS]	Fields of Fire/Angle Park	1983	6.00
—Fold-out poster sleeve			
❑ 814467-7	In a Big Country/All of Us	1983	3.00
❑ 814467-7 [PS]	In a Big Country/All of Us	1983	6.00
❑ 818834-7	Wonderland/Lost Patrol (Live)	1984	3.00
❑ 818834-7 [PS]	Wonderland/Lost Patrol (Live)	1984	6.00
❑ 880412-7	Where the Rose Is Sown/Prairie Rose	1984	3.00
❑ 880412-7 [PS]	Where the Rose Is Sown/Prairie Rose	1984	3.00
❑ 880542-7	Just a Shadow/Winter Sky	1985	3.00
❑ 884645-7	Look Away/Restless Natives	1986	3.00
❑ 884645-7 [PS]	Look Away/Restless Natives	1986	4.00
REPRISE			
❑ 27737	King of Emotion/The Travellers	1988	3.00
❑ 27737 [PS]	King of Emotion/The Travellers	1988	3.00
Albums			
MERCURY			
❑ 812870-1	The Crossing	198?	8.00
—No embossed print on front cover			
❑ 812870-1	The Crossing	1983	10.00
—Embossed print on front cover			
❑ 818835-1 [EP]	Wonderland	1984	8.00
❑ 822831-1	Steeltown	1984	10.00
❑ 826844-1	The Seer	1986	10.00
REPRISE			
❑ 25787	Peace in Our Time	1988	10.00

BIG DADDY AND HIS BOYS

Number	Title (A Side/B Side)	Yr	NM
45s			
KING			
❑ 5013	Bacon Fat/Bad Boy	1957	25.00

BIG ED AND HIS COMBO See EDDIE BURNS.

BIG FOOT

Number	Title (A Side/B Side)	Yr	NM
Albums			
WINRO			
❑ 1004	Big Foot	1969	30.00

BIG FRANK AND THE ESSENCES

Number	Title (A Side/B Side)	Yr	NM
45s			
BLUE ROCK			
❑ 4012	Secret/I Won't Let Her See Me Cry	1965	200.00
PHILIPS			
❑ 40283	Secret/I Won't Let Her See Me Cry	1965	100.00

BIG GUYS, THE

Number	Title (A Side/B Side)	Yr	NM
45s			
PALETTE			
❑ 5110	Walkin' the Board/Faith 7	1963	25.00
❑ 5114	Propulsion/(B-side unknown)	1964	25.00
WARNER BROS.			
❑ 7047	Hang My Head and Cry/Mr. Cupid (Don't You Call on Me)	1967	50.00

BIG MAYBELLE

Number	Title (A Side/B Side)	Yr	NM
45s			
BRUNSWICK			
❑ 55234	Candy/Cry	1962	12.00
❑ 55242	Cold, Cold Heart/Why Was I Born	1963	12.00
❑ 55256	Everybody's Got a Home But Me/How Deep Is the Ocean	1963	12.00
CHESS			
❑ 1967	It's a Man's Man's Man's World/Big Maybelle Sings the Blues	1966	10.00
OKEH			
❑ 6931	Gabbin' Blues/Rain Down Rain	1953	40.00
❑ 6955	Way Back Home/Just Want Your Love	1953	40.00
❑ 6998	Send for Me/Jimmy Mule	1953	40.00
❑ 7009	My Country Man/Maybelle's Blues	1953	40.00
❑ 7026	I've Got a Feelin'/You'll Never Know	1954	30.00
❑ 7042	My Big Mistake/I'm Gettin' 'Long Alright	1954	30.00
❑ 7053	Ain't No Use/Don't Leave Poor Me	1955	30.00
❑ 7060	Whole Lotta Shakin' Goin' On/One Monkey Don't Stop No Show	1955	30.00
❑ 7066	Such a Cutie/The Other Night	1956	30.00
❑ 7069	Gabbin' Blues/New Kind of Mambo	1956	30.00
PARAMOUNT			
❑ 0237	Blame It on Your Love/See See Rider	1973	6.00
PORT			
❑ 3002	Let Me Go/No Better for You	1965	12.00
ROJAC			
❑ 112	96 Tears/That's Life	1966	10.00
❑ 115	I Can't Wait Any Longer/Turn the World Around the Other Way	1967	8.00
❑ 116	Mama (He Treats Your Daughter Mean)/Keep That Man	1967	8.00
❑ 118	Quittin' Time/I Can't Wait Any Longer	1967	8.00
❑ 121	Heaven Will Welcome You, Dr. King/Eleanor Rigby	1968	10.00
❑ 124	How It Lies/Old Love Never Dies	1968	8.00
❑ 1003	Careless Love/My Mother's Eyes	196?	8.00
❑ 1969	Don't Pass Me By/It's Been Raining	1966	10.00
SAVOY			
❑ 1195	Candy/That's a Pretty Good Love	1956	20.00
❑ 1500	Mean to Me/Tell Me Who	1956	15.00
❑ 1512	I Don't Want to Cry/All of Me	1957	15.00
❑ 1519	Rock House/Jim	1957	15.00
❑ 1527	So Long/Ring Dang Dilly	1957	15.00
❑ 1536	Blues Early, Early (Part 1)/Blues Early, Early (Part 2)	1958	15.00
❑ 1541	White Christmas/Silent Night	1958	15.00
❑ 1558	Baby Won't You Please Come Home/Say It Isn't Do	1959	15.00
❑ 1572	A Good Man Is Hard to Find/Pitiful	1959	15.00
❑ 1576	Some of These Days/I Understand	1959	15.00
❑ 1583	I Got It Bad and That Ain't Good/Ramblin' Blues	1960	15.00
❑ 1583	I Got It Bad and That Ain't Good/Until the Real Thing Comes Along	1960	15.00
❑ 1595	I Ain't Got Nobody/Going Home Baby	1961	15.00
SCEPTER			
❑ 1288	I Don't Want to Cry/Yesterday's Kisses	1965	12.00
Albums			
BRUNSWICK			
❑ BL 54107 [M]	What More Can a Woman Do	1962	50.00
❑ BL 754107 [S]	What More Can a Woman Do	1962	70.00
❑ BL 754142	The Gospel Soul of Big Maybelle	1968	40.00
EPIC			
❑ EE 22011 [M]	Gabbin' Blues	196?	30.00
—Reissue of Okeh recordings			
PARAMOUNT			
❑ PAS-1011 [(2)]	The Last of Big Maybelle	1973	25.00
ROJAC			
❑ RS 123	Saga of the Good Life and Hard Times	196?	40.00
❑ R 522 [M]	Got a Brand New Bag	1967	40.00
❑ RS 522 [S]	Got a Brand New Bag	1967	40.00
SAVOY			
❑ MG-14005 [M]	Big Maybelle Sings	1957	300.00
❑ MG-14011 [M]	Blues, Candy and Big Maybelle	1958	300.00
SAVOY JAZZ			
❑ SJL-1143	Roots of Rock 'n' Roll Vol. 13: Blues & Early Soul	1985	10.00
❑ SJL-1168	Blues, Candy and Big Maybelle	1986	10.00
—Reissue of 14011			
SCEPTER			
❑ S-522 [M]	The Soul of Big Maybelle	1964	40.00
❑ SS-522 [S]	The Soul of Big Maybelle	1964	50.00

BIG MOUTH

Number	Title (A Side/B Side)	Yr	NM
45s			
SPINDIZZY			
❑ ZS7 4004	Where the Master Lives/Too Busy	1972	6.00

BIG STAR Alex Chilton, formerly of THE BOX TOPS, was lead singer.

Number	Title (A Side/B Side)	Yr	NM
45s			
ARDENT			
❑ 2902	When My Baby's Beside Me/In the Street	1972	25.00
❑ 2904	Watch the Sunrise/Don't Lie to Me	1972	25.00
—With correct song on B-side. Label has the number "AS-01180" on it.			
❑ 2904	Watch the Sunrise/Don't Lie to Me	1972	50.00
—B-side plays the song "Thirteen" in error. Label has the number "AS-01127" on it.			
❑ 2909	O My Soul/Morphatoo—I'm in Love with a Girl	1974	20.00
❑ 2912	September Gurls/(B-side unknown)	1974	20.00
Albums			
ARDENT			
❑ ADS-1501	Radio City	1974	50.00
❑ ADS-2803	#1 Record	1972	75.00
DBK WORKS			
❑ DBK 115	In Space	2005	15.00
4 MEN WITH BEARDS			
❑ 4M-142	3rd	2006	15.00
—Reissue on 180-gram vinyl			
PVC			
❑ 7903	Big Star's Third	1978	40.00
❑ 8933	Sister Lovers	1985	15.00
—Reissue of PVC 7903 with new title			

BIG THREE, THE Also see CASS ELLIOT.

Number	Title (A Side/B Side)	Yr	NM
45s			
FM			
❑ 3003	The Banjo Song/Winkin' Blinkin' and Nod	1964	15.00
—Second issue, distributed by Vee Jay			
❑ 9001	Come Away/Rider	1963	15.00
❑ 9004	The Banjo Song/Winkin' Blinkin' Nod	1963	20.00
—Original issue (possibly promo only), distributed by Roulette			
ROULETTE			
❑ 4689	Nora's Dove (Dink's Song)/Grandfather's Clock	1966	10.00
TOLLIE			
❑ 9006	The Banjo Song/Winkin' Blinkin' and Nod	1964	12.00
—Third issue			
Albums			
FM			
❑ 307 [M]	The Big Three	1963	30.00
❑ S-307 [S]	The Big Three	1963	40.00
❑ 311 [M]	Live at the Recording Studio	1964	30.00
❑ S-311 [S]	Live at the Recording Studio	1964	40.00
ROULETTE			
❑ R-42000 [M]	The Big Three Featuring Cass Elliot	1967	20.00
❑ SR-42000 [S]	The Big Three Featuring Cass Elliot	1967	25.00

BIG WHEELIE AND THE HUB CAPS

Number	Title (A Side/B Side)	Yr	NM
45s			
MCA			
❑ 40951	Sh-Boom (Life Could Be a Dream)/Touch and Go	1978	5.00
SCEPTER			
❑ 12375	Elvis Presley Medley/Chuck Berry Medley	1973	10.00
❑ 12385	Little Richard Medley/Over the Mountain	1973	10.00
❑ 12392	Leader of the Pack/Redneck Rock and Rollers	1974	8.00
Albums			
SCEPTER			
❑ SPS-5109	Solid Grease!	1973	12.00

BIKINIS, THE

Number	Title (A Side/B Side)	Yr	NM
45s			
DOT			
❑ 15808	Fatima the Dreamer/Kitchy Koo	1958	25.00
❑ 15872	Chop Stick Rock/A'Right, A'Ready	1958	40.00

Except when noted otherwise, VG = 25% of NM, and VG+ = 50% of NM. (Example: VG = $2.00, VG+ = $4.00 and NM = $8.00.)

Number	Title (A Side/B Side)	Yr	NM
ROULETTE			
❑ 4073	Bikini/Boogie Rock 'n' Roll	1958	25.00
TOP RANK			
❑ 2032	Crazy Vibrations/Spunky	1959	25.00

BILK, ACKER

Number	Title (A Side/B Side)	Yr	NM
45s			
ATCO			
❑ 6160	Summer Set/Acker's Away	1960	10.00
❑ 6190	Buona Sera/Corinne, Corinna	1961	10.00
❑ 6217	Stranger on the Shore/ Cieleto Lindo	1962	12.00
❑ 6230	Above the Stars/Soft Sands	1962	10.00
❑ 6238	Lonely/Lime Light	1962	10.00
❑ 6247	A Taste of Honey/ Only You (& You Alone)	1963	8.00
❑ 6264	Underneath the Arches/ Lady of the Lake	1963	8.00
❑ 6269	Moonlight Tango/ Never Love a Stranger	1963	8.00
❑ 6282	The Harem/Train Song	1964	8.00
❑ 6311	Dream Ska/Ska Face	1964	8.00
❑ 6323	The Good Life/Theme from Warsaw Concerto	1964	8.00
❑ 6441	La Playa/When You Are There	1966	6.00
❑ 6514	Limehouse Blues/Wot Cher (Knocked 'Em In the Old Kent Road)	1967	6.00
PYE			
❑ 71078	Aria/The Fool on the Hill	1976	4.00
REPRISE			
❑ 20090	Dardenella Part 1/ Dardenella Part 2	1962	15.00
Albums			
ATCO			
❑ 33-129 [M]	Stranger on the Shore	1961	15.00
❑ SD 33-129 [S]	Stranger on the Shore	1961	20.00
❑ 33-144 [M]	Above the Stars	1962	15.00
❑ SD 33-144 [S]	Above the Stars	1962	20.00
❑ 33-150 [M]	Only You	1963	15.00
❑ SD 33-150 [S]	Only You	1963	20.00
❑ 33-158 [M]	Call Me Mister	1963	15.00
❑ SD 33-158 [S]	Call Me Mister	1963	20.00
❑ 33-168 [M]	A Touch of Latin	1964	12.00
❑ SD 33-168 [S]	A Touch of Latin	1964	15.00
❑ 33-170 [M]	Great Themes from Great Foreign Films	1965	12.00
❑ SD 33-170 [S]	Great Themes from Great Foreign Films	1965	15.00
❑ 33-181 [M]	Acker Bilk in Paris	1966	12.00
❑ SD 33-181 [S]	Acker Bilk in Paris	1966	15.00
❑ 33-197 [M]	Mood for Love	1966	12.00
❑ SD 33-197 [S]	Mood for Love	1966	15.00
GNP CRESCENDO			
❑ GNPS-2116	The Best of Acker Bilk: His Clarinet and Strings	198?	10.00
❑ GNPS-2171	The Best of Acker Bilk: His Clarinet and Strings, Vol. 2	198?	10.00
❑ GNPS-2191	Acker Bilk Plays Lennon and McCartney	1988	12.00
REPRISE			
❑ R-6031 [M]	A Stranger No More	1962	20.00
❑ RS-6031 [R]	A Stranger No More	1962	15.00

BILK, ACKER, AND KEN COLYER

Number	Title (A Side/B Side)	Yr	NM
Albums			
STOMP OFF			
❑ SOS-1119	It Looks Like a Big Time Tonight	198?	10.00

BILK, ACKER, AND BENT FABRIC

Also see each artist's individual listings.

Number	Title (A Side/B Side)	Yr	NM
45s			
ATCO			
❑ 6378	Alley Cat/Stranger on the Shore	1965	6.00
Albums			
ATCO			
❑ 33-175 [M]	Together	1965	12.00
❑ SD 33-175 [S]	Together	1965	15.00

BILLARD, DOUG, AND THE SOUL PATROL

Number	Title (A Side/B Side)	Yr	NM
45s			
PARKWAY			
❑ 126	Emily/Genuine Jade	1966	40.00

BILLION DOLLAR BABIES

Members of ALICE COOPER's band.

Number	Title (A Side/B Side)	Yr	NM
45s			
POLYDOR			
❑ 14394	Rock 'N' Roll Radio/ Wasn't I the One	1977	5.00
❑ 14406 [DJ]	Too Young (stereo)/ Too Young (mono)	1977	12.00
Albums			
POLYDOR			
❑ PRO 022 [DJ]	Battle Axe	1977	20.00
—Promo-only sampler			
❑ PD-1-6100	Battle Axe	1977	15.00

BILLY AND LILLIE

Also see LILLIE BRYANT; BILLY FORD.

Number	Title (A Side/B Side)	Yr	NM
45s			
ABC-PARAMOUNT			
❑ 10421	Love Me Sincerely/ Whip It To Me Baby	1963	30.00
❑ 10489	Carry Me Across the Threshold/ Why I Love Billy (Lillie)	1963	30.00
CAMEO			
❑ 412	Nothing Moves (Without a Little Push)/The Two of Us	1966	10.00
❑ 435	You Got Me by the Heart/ Hear You Better Hear	1966	10.00
SWAN			
❑ 4002	La Dee Dah/The Monster	1957	30.00
—"SWAN" in all capital letters; B-side by Billy Ford and the Thunderbirds			
❑ 4002	La Dee Dah/The Monster	1958	20.00
—Only the S in "Swan" is capitalized; B-side by Billy Ford and the Thunderbirds			
❑ 4005	Happiness/Creepin' Crawlin' Cryin'	1958	20.00
❑ 4011	The Greasy Spoon/ Hanging On to You	1958	20.00
❑ 4020	Lucky Ladybug/I Promise You	1958	25.00
❑ 4030	Tumbled Down/A.H. Thomas the Cat	1959	15.00
❑ 4036	Bells, Bells, Bells/Honeymoonin'	1959	15.00
❑ 4042	Terrific Together/Swampy	1959	15.00
❑ 4051	Free for All/The Ins and Outs of Love	1960	15.00
❑ 4058	That's the Way the Cookie Crumbles (Ah-So)/Over the Mountain, Across the Sea	1960	15.00
❑ 4069	Ain't Comin' Back (To You)/ Bananas	1961	15.00

BILLY AND THE BEATERS

See BILLY VERA.

BILLY AND THE ESSENTIALS

Number	Title (A Side/B Side)	Yr	NM
45s			
CAMEO			
❑ 344	Remember Me Baby/The Actor	1965	400.00
JAMIE			
❑ 1229	The Dance Is Over/Steady Girl	1962	30.00
❑ 1239	Over the Weekend/ Maybe You'll Be There	1962	30.00
LANDA			
❑ 691	The Dance Is Over/Steady Girl	1962	50.00
MERCURY			
❑ 72127	Young at Heart/Lonely Weekend	1963	25.00
❑ 72210	Last Dance/Yes Sir, That's My Baby	1963	25.00
SMASH			
❑ 2045	Babalu's Wedding Day/ My Way of Saying	1966	15.00
❑ 2071	Don't Cry (Sing Along with the Music)/Baby Go Away	1966	12.00
SSS INTERNATIONAL			
❑ 706	I Wrote a Song/ Oh What a Feeling	1967	12.00

BILLY BOY

Number	Title (A Side/B Side)	Yr	NM
45s			
COOL			
❑ 103	I Ain't Got No Money/ Hello Stranger	1953	1000.
—As "Billy Boy Arnold"			
VEE JAY			
❑ 146	I Wish You Would/I Was Fooled	1955	80.00
❑ 171	I Ain't Got You/ Don't Stay Out All Night	1956	80.00
—Label lists artist as "Billy Boy Arnold"			
❑ 192	Here's My Picture/ You've Got Me Wrong	1956	40.00
❑ 238	Kissing at Midnight/ My Heart Is Crying	1957	40.00
❑ 260	Rockinitis/Prisoner's Plea	1957	40.00
VIVID			
❑ 109	Prisoner's Plea/ I Wish You Would	1964	25.00
Albums			
PRESTIGE			
❑ PRLP-7389 [M]	Blues on the South Side	1965	30.00
—As "Billy Boy Arnold"			
❑ PRST-7389 [S]	Blues on the South Side	1965	40.00
—As "Billy Boy Arnold"			

BILLY JOE AND THE CHECKMATES

Number	Title (A Side/B Side)	Yr	NM
45s			
DORE			
❑ 620	Percolator (Twist)/Round & Round & Round & Round	1961	15.00
❑ 636	Rocky's Theme/Twist That Thing	1962	12.00
❑ 643	The Chester Drag/ Laughing Machine Gunner	1962	12.00
❑ 652	Chalypso Dancer/ My Friend, the Rain	1962	12.00
❑ 664	Solid Gold Hubcaps/ Laughing Woodpecker	1963	12.00
❑ 668	Bossville/One More Cup	1963	12.00
❑ 680	Shake, Shake, Shake/ Summertime in Venice	1963	12.00
❑ 685	Last Dance/My Friend the Rain	1963	12.00
❑ 694	The Drifter/Nashville West (One More Time)	1963	12.00
❑ 697	Forbidden Planet/ Slauson, Baby, Slauson	1964	12.00
❑ 703	Spotlight Dance/Zip Code	1964	12.00
❑ 720	C'mopn Everybody (Part 1)/ C'mon Everybody (Part 2)	1964	12.00
❑ 728	Bells of Rome/Shadows	1965	10.00
❑ 747	Clair de Looney/Holding Hands	1966	10.00
❑ 756	Voyage to the Bottom of the Sea/Nutty Dance Instructor	1966	10.00
❑ 791	A Man and a Woman/Floatin'	1967	10.00
❑ 857	Ambrosia/Newport Beach Concerto	1971	6.00
❑ 871	Try It, You'll Like It/ Topless Dancer	1972	5.00
❑ 884	Aphrodisiac (Part 1)/ Aphrodisiac (Part 2)	1973	5.00
❑ 892	Flaky (same on both sides)	1974	5.00
❑ 982	Raindrops, Mem'ries, and Tears/ Liuvio, Memorias, y Lagramas	1985	4.00

BILLY THE KID

Number	Title (A Side/B Side)	Yr	NM
45s			
KAPP			
❑ 261	Apron Strings/I Hardly Know You	1959	12.00

BINGHAM, J.B.

Number	Title (A Side/B Side)	Yr	NM
45s			
UNITED ARTISTS			
❑ XW816	All Alone by the Telephone/ Live and You Learn	1976	15.00
❑ XW872	She's Gone/Keep On Walking	1976	15.00
WARNER BROS.			
❑ 7775	Sunshine/Peek-A-Boo	1974	10.00

BINKLEY, CAROLYN

Number	Title (A Side/B Side)	Yr	NM
45s			
COLUMBIA			
❑ 43468	I Want a Baby Brother for Christmas/All I Want for Christmas Is My Two Front Teeth	1965	10.00
❑ 43468 [PS]	I Want a Baby Brother for Christmas/All I Want for Christmas Is My Two Front Teeth	1965	15.00
❑ 4-43918	I Want a Baby Brother for Christmas/Mister Pilot	1966	10.00

BINKLEY, JIMMY

Number	Title (A Side/B Side)	Yr	NM
45s			
ALADDIN			
❑ 3193	Night Life/Hot Smoke	1953	120.00
CHANCE			
❑ 1134	Hey, Hey Sugar Ray/ Midnite Wail	1953	200.00
CHECKER			
❑ 789	Wine, Wine, Wine/ Boogie On the Hour	1954	200.00
❑ 835	Messin' Around/ You Made a Boo-Boo	1956	100.00
NOTE			
❑ 10002	Why Oh Why/Blue Moon	1957	300.00

BIRD WATCHERS, THE

Number	Title (A Side/B Side)	Yr	NM
45s			
LAURIE			
❑ 3399	Turn Around Girl/You Got It	1967	12.00
MALA			
❑ 527	Girl I've Got News for You/ Eddie's Tune	1966	30.00
❑ 536	I'm Gonna Love You Anyway/ A Little Bit of Lovin'	1966	30.00

B

Number	Title (A Side/B Side)	Yr	NM
❑ 548	I'm Gonna Do It to You/I Have No Worried Mind	1966	30.00
❑ 555	Mary Mary (It's to You That I Belong)/Cry a Little Bit	1967	30.00

BIRDSONG, EDWIN

Number	Title (A Side/B Side)	Yr	NM
12-Inch Singles			
PHILADELPHIA INT'L.			
❑ 2Z8 3671	Phiss-Phizz (8:38)/Goldmine (10:43)	1979	15.00
❑ 4Z8 3709 [DJ]	Lollipop (5:59) (2:52)	1979	15.00
SALSOUL			
❑ SG 363 [DJ]	Funtaztik/Win Tonight	1982	10.00
45s			
PHILADELPHIA INT'L			
❑ 3659	Kunta Dance Part 1/Kunta Dance Part 2	1978	4.00
❑ 3670	Phiss-Phizz/Goldmine	1979	4.00
POLYDOR			
❑ 14058	The Old Messiah/Use What You Got	1970	5.00
—With Doug McClure			
❑ 14095	It Ain't No Fun Being a Welfare Recipient/Uncle Tom Game	1971	5.00
❑ 14118	My Father Preaches That God Is the Father of Us All/The Spirit of Do Do	1972	5.00
❑ 14186	Rising Sign/Rising Sign Climax	1973	5.00
❑ 14192	Rising Sign/Grow Some Flowers, You Will Learn to Love the Rain	1973	5.00
❑ 14224	Turn Around Hate (Communicate)/Down on the Beat	1974	5.00
SALSOUL			
❑ 2135	Rapper Dapper Snapper/(Instrumental)	1981	4.00
❑ 7019	Funtaztik/Win Tonight	1982	4.00
❑ 7024	She's Wrapped Too Tight (She's a Button Buster)/(Instrumental)	1982	4.00
Albums			
ABC DUNHILL			
❑ DSX-51036	Can't Stop the Madness	1974	15.00
PHILADELPHIA INT'L.			
❑ JZ 35758	Edwin Birdsong	1978	10.00
POLYDOR			
❑ 24-4071	What It Is	1971	12.00
❑ PD-5057	Super Natural	1973	12.00
SALSOUL			
❑ SA-8550	Funktaztic	1981	10.00

BIRKIN, JANE, AND SERGE GAINSBOURG

Number	Title (A Side/B Side)	Yr	NM
45s			
FONTANA			
❑ 1665	Je T'Aime...Moi Non Plus/Jane B	1969	8.00
❑ 1684	La Decadanse/Les Langues de Chat	1969	5.00
Albums			
FONTANA			
❑ SRF-67610	Je T'aime	1970	20.00

BIRTH CONTROL

Number	Title (A Side/B Side)	Yr	NM
Albums			
PROPHESY			
❑ PRS-1002	Birth Control: A New German Rock Group	1970	40.00

BISCAYNES, THE

Number	Title (A Side/B Side)	Yr	NM
45s			
NORTHRIDGE			
❑ 1001	Church Key/Moment of Truth	1963	60.00
—B-side by the Surfaris			
REPRISE			
❑ 20180	Church Key/Moment of Truth	1963	30.00
—B-side by the Surfaris			

BISHOP, BOB

Number	Title (A Side/B Side)	Yr	NM
45s			
ABC			
❑ 11132	Roses to Reno/It's Gonna Hurt You More Than Me	1968	7.00
❑ 11200	Another Man's World/Somewhere in the Country	1969	7.00
❑ 11243	Man Walks Among Us/If Your Sweet Love Don't Find Me	1969	7.00
GOLDISC			
❑ 3027	Santa Claus (Don't Pass Me By)/Ann Marie	1961	20.00
—As "Bobby Bishop"			
MALA			
❑ 423	Anybody (But You)/That's Where I Belong	1960	20.00
—As "Bobby Bishop"			
WAYSIDE			
❑ 1004	I Hate to Sing and Run/My Crying Chair	1967	8.00
—As "Bobby Bishop"			
Albums			
ABC			
❑ ABCS-667	Somewhere in the Country	1969	15.00

BISHOP, EDDIE

Number	Title (A Side/B Side)	Yr	NM
45s			
ABC			
❑ 10858	Candy Man/What You're Doing to Me	1966	25.00
ABC-PARAMOUNT			
❑ 10799	What Did He Say?/Call Me	1966	60.00

BISHOP, ELVIN

Number	Title (A Side/B Side)	Yr	NM
45s			
CAPRICORN			
❑ 0054	Fooled Around and Fell in Love/Struttin' My Stuff	197?	4.00
—Hall of Fame Series			
❑ 0202	Travelin' Shoes/Fishin'	1974	5.00
❑ 0222	Can't Go Back/Let It Flow	1975	5.00
❑ 0237	Sure Feels Good/Arkansas Line	1975	5.00
❑ 0243	Calling All Cows/Juke Joint Jump	1975	5.00
❑ 0248	Silent Night (Vocal Version)/(Instrumental)	1975	8.00
❑ 0252	Fooled Around and Fell in Love/Slick Titty Boom	1976	5.00
❑ 0252	Fooled Around and Fell in Love/Have a Good Time	1976	6.00
—This is actually the second pressing, bit it's harder to find than the first			
❑ 0256	Struttin' My Stuff/Grab All the Love	1976	5.00
❑ 0266	Spend Some Time/Sugar Dumplin	1976	5.00
❑ 0269	Keep It Cool/Yes Sir	1976	5.00
❑ 0285	Rock My Soul/Yes Sir	1978	4.00
❑ 0296	Fooled Around and Fell in Love/Travelin' Shoes	1978	4.00
❑ 0313	It's a Feeling/Right Now Is the Hour	1979	4.00
EPIC			
❑ 10926	Rock My Soul/Holler and Shout	1973	5.00
❑ 11022	Last Mile/Stealin' Watermelons	1973	5.00
FILLMORE			
❑ 7002	So Fine/(B-side unknown)	1971	6.00
❑ 7003	Don't Fight It, Feel It/(B-side unknown)	1971	6.00
❑ 7004	I Just Can't Go On/(B-side unknown)	1971	6.00
Albums			
ALLIGATOR			
❑ AL-4767	Big Fun	1987	10.00
CAPRICORN			
❑ CP 0134	Let It Flow	1974	12.00
❑ CP 0151	Juke Joint Jump	1975	12.00
❑ CP 0165	Struttin' My Stuff	1975	12.00
❑ CPN-0165	Struttin' My Stuff	1980	10.00
—Reissue with revised prefix and Polygram distribution			
❑ CP 0176	Hometown Boy Makes Good!	1976	12.00
❑ 2CP 0185 [(2)]	Live! Raisin' Hell	1977	15.00
❑ CPN-0215	Hog Heaven	1978	12.00
EPIC			
❑ KE 31563	Rock My Soul	1972	15.00
❑ PE 33693	The Best of Elvin Bishop	1975	12.00
FILLMORE			
❑ F 30001	Elvin Bishop Group	1969	20.00
❑ Z 30239	Feel It	1970	20.00

BISHOP, JOEY

Number	Title (A Side/B Side)	Yr	NM
Albums			
ABC			
❑ ABCS-656	Joey Bishop Sings Country and Western	1968	30.00

BIT 'A SWEET

Number	Title (A Side/B Side)	Yr	NM
45s			
ABC			
❑ 11125	The Second Time/2086	1968	20.00
MGM			
❑ 13695	Out of Sight, Out of Mind/It Is On, It Is Off	1967	25.00
Albums			
ABC			
❑ S-640	Hypnotic 1	1968	40.00

BITTERSWEETS, THE

Number	Title (A Side/B Side)	Yr	NM
45s			
CAMEO			
❑ 368	What a Lonely Way to Start the Summertime/Mark My Words	1965	20.00
ORIGINAL SOUND			
❑ 70	Another Chance/In the Night	1967	20.00
TEMA			
❑ 001	Hurtin' Kind/Summertime	196?	20.00

BJORN AND BENNY Early ABBA.

Number	Title (A Side/B Side)	Yr	NM
45s			
PLAYBOY			
❑ 50014	Merry-Go-Round/People Need Love	1972	30.00
❑ 50018	Another Town, Another Train/I Am Just a Girl	1973	30.00
❑ 50025	Rock 'N Roll Band/Another Town, Another Train	1973	30.00

BLACK, BILL, 'S COMBO

Number	Title (A Side/B Side)	Yr	NM
45s			
COLUMBIA			
❑ 44867	But It's Alright/Slow Action	1969	5.00
❑ 44983	California Dreamin'/Funky Train	1969	5.00
❑ 45092	Heaven Knows/One Five One Eight Chelsea	1970	5.00
❑ 45162	Keep the Customer Satisfied/One Five One Eight Chelsea	1970	5.00
HI			
❑ 2018	Smokie (Part 2)/Smokie (Part 1)	1959	20.00
❑ 2021	White Silver Sands/The Wheel	1960	20.00
❑ 2022	Josephine/Dry Bones	1960	15.00
❑ 2022 [PS]	Josephine/Dry Bones	1960	25.00
❑ 2026	Don't Be Cruel/Rollin'	1960	15.00
❑ 2026 [PS]	Don't Be Cruel/Rollin'	1960	25.00
❑ 2027	Blue Tango/Willie	1960	15.00
❑ 2027 [PS]	Blue Tango/Willie	1960	25.00
❑ 2028	Hearts of Stone/Royal Blue	1961	12.00
❑ 2029	Old Time Religion/He's Got the Whole World in His Hands	1961	40.00
—Stereo single, small hole, plays at 33 1/3 rpm			
❑ 2030	Do Lord/When the Roll Is Called Up Yonder	1961	40.00
—Stereo single, small hole, plays at 33 1/3 rpm			
❑ 2031	Down by the Riverside/It Is No Secret (What God Can Do)	1961	40.00
—Stereo single, small hole, plays at 33 1/3 rpm			
❑ 2032	When the Saints Go Marching In/Nobody Knows the Trouble I've Seen	1961	40.00
—Stereo single, small hole, plays at 33 1/3 rpm			
❑ 2033	Just a Closer Walk with Thee/This Old House	1961	40.00
—Stereo single, small hole, plays at 33 1/3 rpm			
❑ 2036	Ole Buttermilk Sky/Yogi	1961	12.00
❑ 2036 [PS]	Ole Buttermilk Sky/Yogi	1961	25.00
❑ 2038	Movin'/Honky Train	1961	12.00
❑ 2042	Twist-Her/My Girl Josephine	1961	12.00
❑ 2045	Twist-Her/Night Train	1962	40.00
—Stereo single, small hole, plays at 33 1/3 rpm			
❑ 2046	The Hucklebuck/Corrina, Corrina	1962	40.00
—Stereo single, small hole, plays at 33 1/3 rpm			
❑ 2047	Johnny B. Goode/(B-side unknown)	1962	40.00
—Stereo single, small hole, plays at 33 1/3 rpm			
❑ 2048	Josephine/My Girl Josephine	1962	40.00
—Stereo single, small hole, plays at 33 1/3 rpm			
❑ 2049	Slippin' and Slidin'/Twist with Me, Baby	1962	40.00
—Stereo single, small hole, plays at 33 1/3 rpm			
❑ 2052	Twistin' — White Silver Sands/My Babe	1962	12.00
❑ 2052 [PS]	Twistin' — White Silver Sands/My Babe	1962	25.00
❑ 2055	So What/Blues for the Red Boy	1962	12.00
❑ 2059	Joey's Song/Hot Taco	1962	12.00
❑ 2064	Do It — Rat Now/Little Jasper	1963	12.00
❑ 2069	Monkey-Shine/Love Gone	1963	12.00
❑ 2072	Comin' On/Soft Winds	1964	12.00
❑ 2077	Tequila/Raunchy	1964	12.00
❑ 2079	Little Queenie/Boo Ray	1964	12.00
❑ 2085	Come On Home/He'll Have to Go	1964	10.00
❑ 2094	Spootin'/Crazy Feeling	1965	10.00
❑ 2106	Hey, Good Lookin'/Mountain of Love	1966	10.00
❑ 2115	Rambler/You Call Everybody Darling	1966	10.00
❑ 2124	Son of Smokie/Peg Leg	1967	8.00
❑ 2145	Turn On Your Love Life/Ribbon of Darkness	1968	6.00
❑ 2153	Red Light/Bright Lights, Big City	1968	6.00
❑ 2168	Creepin' Around/The Son of Hickory Holler's Tramp	1969	6.00
❑ 2185	No More/Closin' Time	1971	5.00
❑ 2208	Daylite/Four A.M.	1972	5.00

Number	Title (A Side/B Side)	Yr	NM
❑ 2234	Smokey Bourbon Street/ Mighty Fine	1973	5.00
❑ 2277	Soul Serenade/Pickin'	1974	4.00
❑ 2283	Truck Stop/Boilin' Cabbage	1975	4.00
❑ 2291	Almost Persuaded/ Back Up and Push	1975	4.00
❑ 2301	Fire on the Bayou/Memphis Soul	1976	4.00
❑ 2311	I Can Help/Jump Back Joe	1976	4.00
❑ 2317	Redneck Rock/Yakety Sax	1976	4.00
❑ 78508	Cashin' In (A Tribute to Luther Perkins)/L.A. Blues	1978	4.00

MEGA

Number	Title (A Side/B Side)	Yr	NM
❑ 0036	Rings/Cotton Carnival	1971	5.00
❑ 0052	Oh Happy Day/Sugar Cured	1971	5.00
❑ 0070	Harlem Nocturne/Sassy Parts	1972	5.00
❑ 0086	Night Train/Bluff City	1972	5.00
❑ 0113	Listen to the Music/ Memphis Shuffle	1973	5.00
❑ 0117	Satin Sheets/Memphis Shuffle	1973	5.00
❑ 201	Smokie Part 2/Tequila	1973	5.00
❑ 207	Oh Happy Day/ Listen to the Music	1974	4.00

7-Inch Extended Plays

HI

Number	Title (A Side/B Side)	Yr	NM
❑ HSP 2	My Babe/40 Miles of Bad Road/ Ain't That Lovin' You Baby// What'd I Say/The Walk/ Witchcraft	1962	15.00
—33 1/3 rpm jukebox single, small hole			
❑ HSP 2 [PS]	(title unknown)	1962	15.00
❑ SBG-17	White Silver Sands/Josephine/ Hearts of Stone//Blue Tango/ Ole Buttermilk Sky/ Don't Be Cruel	1963	12.00
—Jukebox issue; small hole, plays at 33 1/3 rpm			
❑ SBG-17 [PS]	Bill Black's Greatest Hits	1963	12.00
❑ SBG 26	T.D.'s Boogie Woogie/Tuxedo Junction/Canadian Sunset// Leap Frog/In the Mood/ So Rare	196?	10.00
—33 1/3 rpm jukebox single, small hole			
❑ SBG 26 [PS]	Bill Black's Combo Goes Big Band	196?	10.00
❑ SBG-41	Mr. Beat/It's All in the Game/ Black Beat//Talk Back Trembling Lips/Spootin'/ Oh Lonesome Me	1965	10.00
—Jukebox issue; small hole, plays at 33 1/3 rpm			
❑ SBG-41 [PS]	Mr. Beat	1965	10.00
❑ SBG-48	Hey Good Lookin'/Bouquet of Roses/Anytime//I Walk the Line/Half as Much/ Love's Gonna Live	1965	10.00
—Jukebox issue; small hole, plays at 33 1/3 rpm			
❑ SBG-48 [PS]	All Timers	1965	10.00
❑ SBG-57	The Beat Goes On/Ode to Billy Joe/Let the Good Times Roll// Funky Broadway/The Letter/ A Whiter Shade of Pale	1967	10.00
—Jukebox issue; small hole, plays at 33 1/3 rpm			
❑ SBG-57 [PS]	The Beat Goes On	1967	10.00
❑ SBG-64	Simon Says/Bright Lights Big City/Red Light//Big Boss Man/Shoo-Be-Doo-Be-Doo-Da-Day/The Horse	1968	10.00
—Jukebox issue; small hole, plays at 33 1/3 rpm			
❑ SBG-64 [PS]	Turn On Your Love Light	1968	10.00
❑ SBG-71	Everyday I Have the Blues/ Prowlin'/The Birds and the Bees//Things I Used to Do/ Imperial Tempo/Last Train	1968	10.00
—Jukebox issue; small hole, plays at 33 1/3 rpm			
❑ SBG-71 [PS]	Soulin' the Blues	1968	10.00
❑ HE 22002	Honky Tonk/Cherry Pink// Singing the Blues/ You Win Again	1961	40.00
❑ HE 22002 [PS]	Solid and Raunchy	1961	40.00

LONDON

Number	Title (A Side/B Side)	Yr	NM
❑ SBG-22	School Days/Roll Over Beethoven/Little Queenie// Thirty Days/Brown Eyed Handsome Man/ Memphis, Tennessee	1964	12.00
—Jukebox issue; small hole, plays at 33 1/3 rpm			
❑ SBG-22 [PS]	Bill Black's Combo Plays Tunes By Chuck Berry	1964	12.00
—Cover says label is "Hi," but the record is on London			
❑ SBG-50	You Call Everybody Darling/ Jersey Bounce/Stardust// Stomping at the Savoy/ Moonlight Serenade/Rambler	1965	10.00
—Jukebox issue; small hole, plays at 33 1/3 rpm			
❑ SBG-50 [PS]	Black Lace	1965	10.00
—Cover says label is "Hi," but the record is on London			

Albums

COLUMBIA

Number	Title (A Side/B Side)	Yr	NM
❑ CS 1055	Basic Black	1970	12.00
❑ CS 9848	Black with Sugar	1969	12.00
❑ CS 9957	Raindrops Keep Fallin' on My Head	1970	12.00

HI

Number	Title (A Side/B Side)	Yr	NM
❑ 6005	Award Winners	1978	10.00
❑ 8004	Memphis Tennessee	1977	10.00
❑ HL-12001 [M]	Smokie	1960	40.00
—Orange and white label			
❑ HL-12001 [M]	Smokie	1960	60.00
—Black label with red and silver logo			
❑ HL-12002 [M]	Saxy Jazz	1960	40.00
❑ HL-12003 [M]	Solid and Raunchy	1960	40.00
❑ HL-12004 [M]	That Wonderful Feeling	1961	20.00
❑ HL-12005 [M]	Movin'	1961	20.00
❑ HL-12006 [M]	Let's Twist Her	1961	15.00
—Retitled version of above			
❑ HL-12006 [M]	Bill Black's Record Hop	1961	25.00
❑ HL-12009 [M]	The Untouchable Sound of Bill Black	1962	15.00
❑ HL-12012 [M]	Bill Black's Greatest Hits	1963	15.00
❑ HL-12013 [M]	Bill Black's Combo Goes West	1963	15.00
❑ HL-12015 [M]	Bill Black Plays the Blues	1964	15.00
❑ HL-12017 [M]	Bill Black Plays Tunes by Chuck Berry	1964	15.00
❑ HL-12020 [M]	Bill Black's Combo Goes Big Band	1964	15.00
❑ HL-12023 [M]	More Solid and Raunchy	1965	15.00
❑ HL-12027 [M]	Mr. Beat	1965	15.00
❑ HL-12032 [M]	All Timers	1966	12.00
❑ HL-12033 [M]	Black Lace	1966	12.00
❑ HL-12036 [M]	King of the Road	1966	12.00
❑ HL-12041 [M]	The Beat Goes On	1967	15.00
❑ HL-12044 [M]	Turn Your Lovelight On	1967	15.00
❑ HL-12047 [M]	Soulin' the Blues	1968	15.00
❑ SHL-32001 [R]	Smokie	1964	20.00
❑ SHL-32002 [R]	Saxy Jazz	1964	20.00
❑ SHL-32003 [R]	Solid and Raunchy	1964	20.00
❑ SHL-32004 [S]	That Wonderful Feeling	1961	25.00
❑ SHL-32005 [S]	Movin'	1961	25.00
❑ SHL-32006 [S]	Let's Twist Her	1961	20.00
—Retitled version of above			
❑ SHL-32006 [S]	Bill Black's Record Hop	1961	30.00
❑ SHL-32009 [S]	The Untouchable Sound of Bill Black	1962	20.00
❑ SHL-32012 [S]	Bill Black's Greatest Hits	1963	20.00
❑ SHL-32013 [S]	Bill Black's Combo Goes West	1963	20.00
❑ SHL-32015 [S]	Bill Black Plays the Blues	1964	20.00
❑ SHL-32017 [S]	Bill Black Plays Tunes by Chuck Berry	1964	20.00
❑ SHL-32020 [S]	Bill Black's Combo Goes Big Band	1964	20.00
❑ SHL-32023 [S]	More Solid and Raunchy	1965	20.00
❑ SHL-32027 [S]	Mr. Beat	1965	20.00
❑ SHL-32032 [S]	All Timers	1966	15.00
❑ SHL-32033 [S]	Black Lace	1966	15.00
❑ SHL-32036 [S]	King of the Road	1966	15.00
❑ SHL-32041 [S]	The Beat Goes On	1967	15.00
❑ SHL-32044 [S]	Turn Your Lovelight On	1967	15.00
❑ SHL-32047 [S]	Soulin' the Blues	1968	15.00
❑ SHL-32052	Solid and Raunchy The 3rd	1969	15.00
❑ SHL-32061	More Magic	1971	12.00
❑ XSHL-32078	Bill Black's Greatest Hits, Vol. 2	1973	12.00
❑ XSHL-32088	Solid and Country	1974	12.00
❑ SHL-32093	The World's Greatest Honky Tonk Band	1975	12.00
❑ SHL-32104	It's Honky Tonk Time	1976	12.00

MEGA

Number	Title (A Side/B Side)	Yr	NM
❑ MLPS-600	Bill Black Is Back	1973	12.00
❑ 31-1008	The Memphis Scene	1971	12.00
❑ 31-1014	Juke Box Favorites	1972	12.00
❑ 51-5008	Rock 'n' Roll Forever	1973	12.00

BLACK, CILLA

45s

BELL

Number	Title (A Side/B Side)	Yr	NM
❑ 726	Step Inside Love/I Couldn't Take My Eyes Off You	1968	20.00

CAPITOL

Number	Title (A Side/B Side)	Yr	NM
❑ 5196	You're My World/Suffer Now I Must	1964	15.00
❑ 5258	It's for You/He Won't Ask Me	1964	12.00
❑ 5373	One Little Voice/Is It Love	1965	12.00
❑ 5414	I've Been Wrong Before/ My Love Came Home	1965	12.00
❑ 5595	Love's Just a Broken Heart/ Yesterday	1966	12.00
❑ 5595 [PS]	Love's Just a Broken Heart/ Yesterday	1966	30.00
❑ 5674	Alfie/Night Time Is Here	1966	12.00
❑ 5763	Don't Answer Me/ The Right One Is Left	1966	12.00
❑ 5782	A Fool Am I/For No One	1966	12.00

DJM

Number	Title (A Side/B Side)	Yr	NM
❑ 70007	What the World Needs Now Is Love/Only Forever Will Do	1969	8.00
❑ 70011	Without Him/ It'll Never Happen Again	1969	8.00
❑ 70012	Surround Yourself with Sorrow/ It'll Never Happen Again	1969	8.00
❑ 70014	Conversations/London Bridge	1969	8.00
❑ 70015	If I Thought You'd Ever Change Your Mind/It Feels So Good	1970	8.00
❑ 70016	If I Thought You'd Ever Change Your Mind/Conversations	1970	8.00
❑ 70018 [DJ]	Across the Universe (mono/stereo)	1970	12.00

EMI

Number	Title (A Side/B Side)	Yr	NM
❑ 4003	He Was a Writer/ I'll Never Run Out of You	1974	6.00

PRIVATE STOCK

Number	Title (A Side/B Side)	Yr	NM
❑ 45,040	I'll Take a Tango/To Know Him Is To Love Him	1975	5.00
❑ 45,077	Fantasy/It's Now	1976	5.00

Albums

CAPITOL

Number	Title (A Side/B Side)	Yr	NM
❑ ST 2308 [S]	Is It Love?	1965	40.00
❑ T 2308 [M]	Is It Love?	1965	25.00

BLACK, CODY

45s

CAPITOL

Number	Title (A Side/B Side)	Yr	NM
❑ 2807	Fool in the Wild/I'm Sorry	1970	150.00
❑ 2858	Stop Trying to Do What You See Your Neighbor Do/ Ain't No Love Like Your Love	1970	100.00

D-TOWN

Number	Title (A Side/B Side)	Yr	NM
❑ 1032	Move On/These Chains of Love	196?	200.00
❑ 1057	Mr. Blue/You Must Be in Love	196?	800.00
❑ 1066	Too Many Irons in the Fire/ Would You Let Me Know	196?	200.00

GIG

Number	Title (A Side/B Side)	Yr	NM
❑ 102	It's Our Time to Fall in Love/ You'll Be Sorry	196?	2000.

GROOVE CITY

Number	Title (A Side/B Side)	Yr	NM
❑ 960	Because You First Loved Me/ The Night a Star Was Born	196?	250.00

KING

Number	Title (A Side/B Side)	Yr	NM
❑ 6148	Keep On Hanging On/ I'm Slowly Molding	1968	1200.

PAMELA

Number	Title (A Side/B Side)	Yr	NM
❑ 7453	Come to Me (Girl)/ Stranger Than a Fairy Tale	196?	100.00

RAM-BROCK

Number	Title (A Side/B Side)	Yr	NM
❑ 2002	Going, Going, Gone/ Somebody's Gonna End Up Cryin'	196?	40.00
—Blue label			
❑ 2002	Going, Going, Gone/ Somebody's Gonna End Up Cryin'	196?	30.00
—Red label, silver print			
❑ 2003	Life Goes On/(The Night) A Star Was Born	196?	80.00
❑ 2004	Love Like I Never Had/ Reap What You Sow	196?	100.00

RENAISSANCE

Number	Title (A Side/B Side)	Yr	NM
❑ 0002	Sweet Love/What Goes Around	197?	80.00
❑ 1001	Keep On Tryin'/Steppin' on Toes (You Can't Make It)	197?	60.00

STON-ROC

Number	Title (A Side/B Side)	Yr	NM
❑ 3378	I Still Love You/Ice Cream Song	197?	40.00

WHEELSVILLE

Number	Title (A Side/B Side)	Yr	NM
❑ 107	I Will Give You Love/ I Am Particular	196?	150.00

BLACK, JAY

The second "Jay" of JAY AND THE AMERICANS.

12-Inch Singles

MILLENNIUM

Number	Title (A Side/B Side)	Yr	NM
❑ 20614	Love Is in the Air/Please Stay	1978	15.00

ROULETTE

Number	Title (A Side/B Side)	Yr	NM
❑ 2005	One Night Affair/Fill Me Up	1976	15.00
—B-side by Caress			

45s

ATLANTIC

Number	Title (A Side/B Side)	Yr	NM
❑ 3273	Dolphins/Running Scared	1975	5.00

MIDSONG INT'L

Number	Title (A Side/B Side)	Yr	NM
❑ 72012	The Part of Me That Needs You Most/You Stole the Music	1980	4.00

MILLENNIUM

Number	Title (A Side/B Side)	Yr	NM
❑ 618	Love Is in the Air/Please Stay	1978	5.00

PRIVATE STOCK

Number	Title (A Side/B Side)	Yr	NM
❑ 45,058	Every Time You Walk in the Room/I'd Build a Bridge	1975	5.00

ROULETTE

Number	Title (A Side/B Side)	Yr	NM
❑ 7198	One Night Affair/ Between Two Worlds	1976	6.00

Black Flag, *Six Pack*, SST 005, 1981, $4.

Number	Title (A Side/B Side)	Yr	NM
UNITED ARTISTS			
❑ 50116	What Will My Mary Say/ Return to Me	1967	12.00
❑ 50116 [PS]	What Will My Mary Say/ Return to Me	1967	25.00
BLACK, OSCAR			
45s			
ATLANTIC			
❑ 956	Love, Love, Love/ Troubled Man Blues	1952	150.00
GROOVE			
❑ 0012	I'll Get By/Hold Me Baby	1954	60.00
—With Sue Allen			
❑ 0102	Be My Baby/Ain't Nobody Home But Me	1955	60.00
—With Sue Allen			
❑ 0115	Baby, Please Don't Go/ I'll Live My Life Alone	1955	60.00
—With Sue Allen			
❑ 0130	Think of Tomorrow/ Set a Wedding Day	1955	60.00
—With Sue Allen and the Four Students			
❑ 0168	Into Each Heart (Some Tears Must Fall)/If I Cry Tomorrow	1956	50.00
—With Sue Allen			
SAVOY			
❑ 1600	I Got a Feeling/I'm a Fool to Care	1961	15.00
BLACK, TERRY			
45s			
DUNHILL			
❑ 4005	How Many Guys/Only Sixteen	1965	10.00
❑ 4046	Ordinary Girl/Baby's Gone	1966	10.00
TOLLIE			
❑ 9026	Unless You Care/ Can't We Go Somewhere	1964	12.00
❑ 9041	Say It Again/Everyone Can Tell	1965	12.00
❑ 9041 [PS]	Say It Again/Everyone Can Tell	1965	20.00

Number	Title (A Side/B Side)	Yr	NM
BLACK, TERRY, AND LAUREL WARD			
45s			
KAMA SUTRA			
❑ 540	Goin' Down/Oh Babe	1972	6.00
BLACK, ZELL			
45s			
MOTOWN			
❑ 1281	I'd Hate Myself in the Morning/ Take My Word	1973	5.00
❑ 1290	I Been Had by the Devil/ Confession	1974	5.00
WARNER BROS.			
❑ 8138	Fly Me Part 1/You Make the Sun Keep Shining	1975	4.00
❑ 8202	Fly Me/Ride On Rider	1976	4.00
BLACK CROWES, THE			
45s			
AMERICAN			
❑ 17580-7 [(7)]	Three Snakes and One Charm	1996	50.00
—Entire LP, plus two bonus tracks, in box set; contains 7 45s, 7 picture sleeves, poster and 45 adaptor shaped like snakes			
COLUMBIA			
❑ 38-79142	Only a Fool (Radio Version)/ Peace Anyway	1999	3.00
DEF AMERICAN			
❑ PRO-S-5474 [DJ]	Remedy (same on both sides)	1992	5.00
❑ PRO-S-5474 [PS]	Remedy	1992	5.00
❑ 18803	Thorn in My Pride/Sting Me	1992	3.00
❑ 18877	Remedy/Darling of the Underground Press	1992	4.00
—Non-LP B-side			
❑ 18887	She Talks to Angels/ Hard to Handle	1993	3.00
—Reissue			
❑ 19245	Hard to Handle/Waitin' Guilty	1991	3.00

Number	Title (A Side/B Side)	Yr	NM
❑ 19403	She Talks to Angels/She Talks to Angels (Live Video Version)	1991	3.00
Albums			
AMERICAN			
❑ 43000	Amorica	1994	24.00
—All copies of the vinyl LP retained the cover that was censored on most cassette and CD copies			
DEF AMERICAN			
❑ 24278	Shake Your Money Maker	1990	12.00

BLACK FLAG Note: Most, if not all, the below records on SST remain in print on vinyl. Not all editions are identical, but until we know the differences, we can't differentiate values. (One of the most obvious indicators of a reissue is the presence of a bar code on the back cover.)

Number	Title (A Side/B Side)	Yr	NM
45s			
ALTERNATIVE TENTACLES			
❑ VIRUS 9	Six Pack/I've Heard It Before/ American Waste	1981	10.00
❑ VIRUS 9 [PS]	Six Pack/I've Heard It Before/ American Waste	1981	10.00
—Manufactured in U.S. for export to the U.K. (standard U.S. issue is on SST)			
POSH BOY			
❑ 13	Louie Louie/Damaged 1	1981	10.00
❑ 13 [PS]	Louie Louie/Damaged 1	1981	10.00
SST			
❑ 001	Nervous Breakdown// Fix Me/I've Had It/Wasted	1978	10.00
—First pressing on red labels			
❑ 001	Nervous Breakdown// Fix Me/I've Had It/Wasted	199?	2.00
—Current pressing on blue labels			
❑ 001 [PS]	Nervous Breakdown// Fix Me/I've Had It/Wasted	1978	10.00
—First sleeve: black and white, brick wall background			
❑ 001 [PS]	Nervous Breakdown//Fix Me/ I've Had It/Wasted	198?	5.00
—Second sleeve: Red print			
❑ 001 [PS]	Nervous Breakdown//Fix Me/ I've Had It/Wasted	199?	2.00
—With bar code on back; blue printing			
❑ 005	Six Pack/I've Heard It Before/ American Waste	1981	4.00
❑ 005 [PS]	Six Pack/I've Heard It Before/ American Waste	1981	4.00
❑ 012	TV Party/I've Got to Run/ My Rules	1981	4.00
—Reissue of Unicorn 95006			
❑ 012 [PS]	TV Party/I've Got to Run/ My Rules	1981	4.00
❑ 175	Louie Louie/Damaged 1	198?	4.00
—Reissue of Posh Boy 13			
❑ 175 [PS]	Louie Louie/Damaged 1	198?	4.00
SST/UNICORN			
❑ BOGUS 001	Thirsty and Miserable/ Life of Pain (Live)	1981	30.00
—Promo-only giveaway item for the Liquorice Pizza chain			
❑ 95006	TV Party//I've Got to Run/ My Rules	1981	15.00
Albums			
SST			
❑ 003 [EP]	Jealous Again	1980	8.00
❑ 007	Damaged	198?	10.00
—Reissue of Unicorn 9502			
❑ 015 [(2)]	Everything Went Black	1982	15.00
❑ 021	The First Four Years	1983	12.00
❑ 023	My War	1984	12.00
❑ 026	Family Man	1984	12.00
❑ 029	Slip It In	1984	12.00
❑ 035	Loose Nut	1985	12.00
❑ 037 [EP]	The Process of Weeding Out	1985	8.00
❑ 045	In My Head	1985	12.00
❑ 060	Who's Got the 10 1/2?	1986	12.00
❑ 081 [EP]	Annihilate This Week	1986	8.00
❑ 166	Wasted Again	1987	12.00
❑ 226 [EP]	I Can See You	1989	12.00
❑ 907 [10]	Jealous Again	199?	6.00
—10-inch reissue of 003			
❑ 916 [10]	Nervous Breakdown	199?	6.00
—10-inch reissue of 001 (7-inch EP)			
❑ 924 [10]	The Process of Weeding Out	199?	6.00
—10-inch reissue of 037			
UNICORN/SST			
❑ 9502	Damaged	198?	15.00
—With no stickers on cover			
❑ 9502	Damaged	1981	25.00
—First pressings had stickers on the front and back covers -- the one on the back begins "As a parent..."			
BLACK HEAT			
45s			
ATLANTIC			
❑ 2890	Street of Tears/Chip's Funk	1972	5.00

Except when noted otherwise, VG = 25% of NM, and VG+ = 50% of NM. (Example: VG = $2.00, VG+ = $4.00 and NM = $8.00.)

Number	Title (A Side/B Side)	Yr	NM
❑ 2934	The Jungle Part 1/ The Jungle Part 2	1973	5.00
❑ 2987	No Time to Burn/Supercool	1973	5.00
❑ 3033	Check It All Out/M & M's	1974	5.00
❑ 3258	Drive My Car/ Questions and Conclusions	1975	5.00
Albums			
ATLANTIC			
❑ SD 7237	Black Heat	1972	12.00
❑ SD 7294	No Time to Burn	1974	12.00
❑ SD 18128	Keep On Burnin'	1975	12.00
BLACK IVORY			
45s			
BUDDAH			
❑ 443	Will We Ever Come Together/ Warm Inside	1975	4.00
❑ 489	Feel It/Daily News	1975	4.00
❑ 506	Love Won't You Stay/Daily News	1975	4.00
❑ 561	You Mean Everything to Me/ White Wind	1977	4.00
❑ 610	Mainline/(B-side unknown)	1979	4.00
❑ 616	You Turned My Whole World Around/(B-side unknown)	1979	4.00
KWANZA/WB			
❑ 7800	No One Else Will Do/ What Goes Around	1974	5.00
PANORAMIC			
❑ 200	You Are My Lover/ (B-side unknown)	1984	4.00
PERCEPTION			
❑ 508	You and I/Our Future	1972	6.00
TODAY			
❑ 1501	Don't Turn Around/I Keep Asking You Questions	1971	5.00
❑ 1508	You and I/Our Future	1972	5.00
❑ 1511	I'll Find A Way (Loneliest Man in Town)/Surrender	1972	5.00
❑ 1516	Time Is Love/Got to Be There	1972	5.00
❑ 1520	Spinning Around/Find the One Who Loves You	1973	5.00
❑ 1524	We Made It/Just Leave Me Some	1973	5.00
Albums			
BUDDAH			
❑ BDS-5644	Feel It	1975	10.00
❑ BDS-5658	Black Ivory	1976	10.00
❑ BDS-5722	Hangin' Heavy	1979	10.00
TODAY			
❑ 1005	Don't Turn Around	1972	12.00
❑ 1008	Baby, Won't You Change Your Mind	1972	12.00
BLACK LIGHTNING			
Albums			
TOWER			
❑ ST 5129	Shades of Black Lightning	1968	20.00
BLACK MERDA			
45s			
CHESS			
❑ 2095	Reality/Cynthy-Ruth	1970	12.00
Albums			
CHESS			
❑ LP-1551	Black Merda	1970	50.00
BLACK 'N BLUE Includes Tommy Thayer, now in KISS.			
12-Inch Singles			
GEFFEN			
❑ PRO-A-2534 [DJ]	I Want It All (same on both sides)	1986	6.00
❑ PRO-A-2661 [DJ]	I'll Be There for You (Rock Remix) (same on both sides)	1986	15.00
—Blue vinyl			
45s			
GEFFEN			
❑ PRO-S-2358 [DJ]	Swing Time/Rockin' on Heaven's Door	1985	6.00
❑ PRO-S-2358 [PS]	Swing Time/Rockin' on Heaven's Door	1985	8.00
Albums			
GEFFEN			
❑ GHS 24041	Black 'N Blue	1984	8.00
❑ GHS 24075	Without You	1985	8.00
❑ GHS 24111	Nasty Nasty	1986	8.00
❑ GHS 24180	In Heat	1988	8.00

Number	Title (A Side/B Side)	Yr	NM
BLACK OAK ARKANSAS Includes drummer Tommy Aldridge of PAT TRAVERS and WHITESNAKE fame.			
45s			
ATCO			
❑ 6829	Lord Have Mercy on My Soul/ Uncle Lijah	1971	5.00
❑ 6849	Singing the Blues/Hot and Nasty	1971	5.00
❑ 6878	Keep the Faith/ The Big One's Still Coming	1972	4.00
❑ 6893	Full Moon Ride/ We Help Each Other	1972	4.00
❑ 6925	Hot and Nasty/Hot Rod	1973	4.00
❑ 6948	Jim Dandy/Red Hot Lovin'	1973	5.00
❑ 7003	Hey Y'all/Sting Me	1974	4.00
❑ 7015	Taxman/Dixie	1975	4.00
❑ 7019	Back Door Man/Good Stuff	1975	4.00
CAPRICORN			
❑ 0284	Not Fade Away/Feels So Good	1978	3.00
—As "Black Oak"			
❑ 0305	Ride with Me/Wind in Our Sails	1978	3.00
—As "Black Oak"			
ENTERPRISE			
❑ 9010	King's Row/Older Than Grandpa	1970	10.00
MCA			
❑ 40496	Strong Enough to Be Gentle/ Ace in the Hole	1975	4.00
❑ 40536	Great Balls of Fire/ Highway Pirate	1976	3.00
❑ 40586	A Fistful of Love/Storm of Passion	1976	3.00
❑ 40621	When the Band Was Singin' "Shakin' All Over"/ Bad Boy's Back in School	1976	3.00
Albums			
ATCO			
❑ SD 36-101	Street Party	1974	12.00
❑ SD 36-111	Ain't Life Grand	1975	12.00
❑ SD 36-128	Live! Mutha	1976	12.00
❑ SD 36-150	The Best of Black Oak Arkansas	1976	12.00
❑ SD 33-354	Black Oak Arkansas	1971	15.00
❑ 33-381 [M]	Keep the Faith	1972	30.00
—White label promo, "DJ Copy Monaural" sticker on cover; no stock copies were issued in mono			
❑ SD 33-381 [S]	Keep the Faith	1972	15.00
❑ SD 7008	If An Angel Came to See You, Would You Make Her Feel at Home?	1972	15.00
❑ QD 7019 [Q]	Raunch 'n' Roll/Live	1974	20.00
❑ SD 7019	Raunch 'n' Roll/Live	1973	15.00
❑ SD 7035	High on the Hog	1973	15.00
CAPRICORN			
❑ CP 0191	Race with the Devil	1977	12.00
❑ CP 0207	I'd Rather Be Sailing	1978	12.00
MCA			
❑ 704	X-Rated	198?	8.00
—Budget-line reissue			
❑ 2155	X-Rated	1975	12.00
❑ 2199	Balls of Fire	1976	12.00
❑ 2224	10 Year Overnight Success	1977	12.00
STAX			
❑ STS-5504	Early Times	1974	15.00
BLACK PEARL			
45s			
ATLANTIC			
❑ 2657	White Devil/Mr. Soul Satisfaction	1969	8.00
Albums			
ATLANTIC			
❑ SD 8220	Black Pearl	1969	25.00
PROPHESY			
❑ PRS-1001	Black Pearl — Live!	1970	25.00
BLACK SABBATH Also see OZZY OSBOURNE; DIO; DEEP PURPLE; TRAPEZE.			
12-Inch Singles			
WARNER BROS.			
❑ PRO-A-2430 [DJ]	No Stranger to Love (4:28) (4:02)	1986	15.00
❑ PRO-A-2475 [DJ]	Danger Zone (same on both sides)	1986	12.00
45s			
WARNER BROS.			
❑ PRO 417 [DJ]	Rado Spot for Black Sabbath (same on both sides)	1970	50.00
❑ 7437	Paranoid/Wizard	1970	10.00
❑ 7530	Iron Man/Electric Funeral	1971	8.00
❑ 7625	Laguna Sunrise/ Tomorrow's Dream	1972	8.00
❑ 7764	Sabbath, Bloody Sabbath/ Changes	1973	8.00

Number	Title (A Side/B Side)	Yr	NM
❑ 7802	Iron Man/Electric Funeral	1974	8.00
❑ 8315	Rock 'N' Roll Doctor/It's Alright	1976	6.00
❑ 29434	Stonehenge/Trashed	1983	6.00
❑ 49549	Lady Evil/Children of the Sea	1980	6.00
7-Inch Extended Plays			
WARNER BROS.			
❑ S 2695	Looking for Today/ Sabbath, Bloody Sabbath// Sabbra Cadabra	1973	20.00
—Jukebox issue; small hole, plays at 33 1/3 rpm			
❑ S 2695 [PS]	Sabbath, Bloody Sabbath	1973	25.00
—Part of "Little LP" series (#241)			
Albums			
I.R.S.			
❑ 82002	Headless Cross	1989	10.00
WARNER BROS.			
❑ WS 1871	Black Sabbath	1970	18.00
—Green label			
❑ WS 1871	Black Sabbath	1973	10.00
—"Burbank" palm trees label			
❑ WS 1871	Black Sabbath	1979	8.00
—White or tan label			
❑ WS 1887	Paranoid	1971	15.00
—Green label			
❑ WS 1887	Paranoid	1973	10.00
—"Burbank" palm trees label			
❑ WS4 1887 [Q]	Paranoid	1974	30.00
—All quad copies have "Burbank" palm trees label			
❑ BS 2562	Master of Reality	1971	15.00
—Green label			
❑ BS 2562	Master of Reality Poster	1971	25.00
❑ BS 2562	Master of Reality	1973	10.00
—"Burbank" palm trees label			
❑ BS 2562	Master of Reality	1979	8.00
—White or tan label			
❑ BS 2602	Black Sabbath, Vol. 4	1972	15.00
—Green label			
❑ BS 2602	Black Sabbath, Vol. 4	1973	10.00
—"Burbank" palm trees label			
❑ BS 2602	Black Sabbath, Vol. 4	1979	8.00
—White or tan label			
❑ BS 2695	Sabbath Bloody Sabbath	1974	15.00
—"Burbank" palm trees label			
❑ BS 2695	Sabbath Bloody Sabbath	1979	8.00
—White or tan label			
❑ BS 2822	Sabotage	1975	15.00
—"Burbank" palm trees label			
❑ BS 2822	Sabotage	1979	8.00
—White or tan label			
❑ 2BS 2923 [(2)]	We Sold Our Souls for Rock 'N' Roll	1975	20.00
—"Burbank" palm trees label			
❑ 2BS 2923 [(2)]	We Sold Our Souls for Rock 'N' Roll	1979	10.00
—White or tan label			
❑ BS 2969	Technical Ecstasy	1976	15.00
—"Burbank" palm trees label			
❑ BS 2969	Technical Ecstasy	1979	8.00
—White or tan label			
❑ BSK 3104	Paranoid	1978	10.00
—Reissue; "Burbank" palm trees label			
❑ BSK 3104	Paranoid	1979	8.00
—Reissue; white or tan label			
❑ BSK 3186	Never Say Die!	1978	12.00
❑ BSK 3372	Heaven and Hell	1980	12.00
❑ BSK 3605	Mob Rules	1981	12.00
❑ 23742 [(2)]	Live Evil	1983	15.00
❑ 23978	Born Again	1983	10.00
❑ 25337	Seventh Star	1986	10.00
❑ 25548	The Eternal Idol	1987	10.00
BLACK SATIN See THE FIVE SATINS.			
BLACK SHEEP With Lou Gramm, pre-FOREIGNER.			
45s			
CAPITOL			
❑ 4012	A Little or a Lot/Broken Promises	1974	5.00
CHRYSALIS			
❑ 2038	Stick Around/Cruisin'	1974	5.00
Albums			
CAPITOL			
❑ ST-11369	Black Sheep	1974	20.00
❑ ST-11447	Encouraging Words	1975	20.00
BLACK VELVET			
45s			
EMBER			
❑ 702	Peace and Love Is the Message/ The Clown	1970	10.00
OKEH			
❑ 7330	Come On Heart/Just Came Back	1969	15.00
Albums			
OKEH			
❑ OKS 14130	Love City	1969	25.00

B

BLACKBURN, LOU

45s

IMPERIAL

Number	Title (A Side/B Side)	Yr	NM
❑ 5943	Grand Prix/Jazz-a-Nova	1963	30.00
❑ 5998	Two Note Samba/ 17 Richmond Park	1963	20.00

BLACKBYRDS, THE

Also see DONALD BYRD.

45s

FANTASY

Number	Title (A Side/B Side)	Yr	NM
❑ 729	Do It, Fluid/Summer Love	1974	5.00
❑ 736	Walking in Rhythm/The Baby	1975	4.00
❑ 747	Flyin' High/All I Ask	1975	4.00
❑ 762	Happy Music/Love So Fine	1976	4.00
❑ 771	Rock Creek Park/ Thankful 'Bout Yourself	1976	4.00
❑ 787	Time Is Movin'/Lady	1977	4.00
❑ 794	Party Land/In Life	1977	4.00
❑ 809	Soft and Easy/ Something Special	1977	4.00
❑ 819	Supernatural Feeling/ Looking Ahead	1978	4.00
❑ 819 [PS]	Supernatural Feeling	1978	15.00
—Promo-only sleeve issued with 2:59 promos of the song			
❑ 904	What We Have Is Right/ What's On Your Mind	1980	4.00
❑ 910	Love Don't Strike Twice/ Don't Know What to Say	1981	4.00
❑ 914	Dancin' Dancin'/ Lonelies for Your Love	1981	4.00

Albums

FANTASY

Number	Title (A Side/B Side)	Yr	NM
❑ FPM-4004 [Q]	Flying Start	1975	25.00
❑ F-9444	The Blackbyrds	1974	15.00
❑ F-9472	Flying Start	1974	15.00
❑ F-9490	City Life	1975	15.00
❑ F-9518	Unfinished Business	1976	15.00
❑ F-9535	Action	1977	12.00
❑ F-9570	Night Grooves	1978	12.00
❑ F-9602	Better Days	1980	12.00

BLACKFOOT

Rick Medlocke, both formerly and later of LYNYRD SKYNYRD, was in this group.

12-Inch Singles

ATCO

Number	Title (A Side/B Side)	Yr	NM
❑ PR 347 [DJ]	Train, Train (same on both sides?)	1979	20.00

45s

ATCO

Number	Title (A Side/B Side)	Yr	NM
❑ 7104	Highway Song/Road Fever	1979	5.00
❑ 7207	Train, Train/Baby Blue	1979	5.00
❑ 7303 [DJ]	Spendin' Cabbage (stereo/mono)	1980	6.00
—May be promo only			
❑ 7313	Gimme, Gimme, Gimme/ In the Night	1980	4.00
❑ 7331	Fly Away/Good Morning	1981	4.00
❑ 7338	Searchin'/Payin' For It	1981	4.00
❑ 99690	Morning Dew/Livin' in the City	1984	3.00
❑ 99851	Teenage Idol/Run for Cover	1983	3.00

ATLANTIC

Number	Title (A Side/B Side)	Yr	NM
❑ 89223	Closest Thing to Heaven/ Back on the Streets	1987	3.00
—As "Rick Medlocke and Blackfoot"			

Albums

ANTILLES

Number	Title (A Side/B Side)	Yr	NM
❑ AN 7076	No Reservations	1975	15.00

ATCO

Number	Title (A Side/B Side)	Yr	NM
❑ SD 32-101	Tomcattin'	1980	10.00
❑ SD 32-107	Marauder	1981	10.00
❑ SD 38-112	Strikes	1979	10.00
❑ 90080	Siogo	1983	10.00
❑ 90218	Vertical Smiles	1984	10.00

ATLANTIC

Number	Title (A Side/B Side)	Yr	NM
❑ 81743	Rick Medlocke and Blackfoot	1987	12.00

EPIC

Number	Title (A Side/B Side)	Yr	NM
❑ PE 34378	Flyin' High	1976	15.00
—Orange label			

BLACKFOOT, J.D.

45s

FANTASY

Number	Title (A Side/B Side)	Yr	NM
❑ 741	Twilight/Done on the Ocean	1975	8.00

PHILIPS

Number	Title (A Side/B Side)	Yr	NM
❑ 40625	Epitaph for a Head/ Who's Nuts, Alfred	1969	12.00
❑ 40679	I've Never Seen You/ One Time Woman	1970	12.00

Albums

FANTASY

Number	Title (A Side/B Side)	Yr	NM
❑ F-9468	Song of Crazy Horse	1974	20.00
❑ F-9487	Southbound and Gone	1975	20.00

MERCURY

Number	Title (A Side/B Side)	Yr	NM
❑ SR-61288	The Ultimate Prophecy	1970	150.00

BLACKFOOT SUE

45s

A&M

Number	Title (A Side/B Side)	Yr	NM
❑ 1386	Celestial Plain/ Stranding in the Road	1972	—

BLACKHORSE

Albums

DSDA

Number	Title (A Side/B Side)	Yr	NM
❑ 001	Blackhorse	1979	75.00
—With insert			

BLACKJACK

With Bruce Kulick (later of KISS) and Michael Bolotin (better known as MICHAEL BOLTON). The group on 20th Century is a different band.

45s

POLYDOR

Number	Title (A Side/B Side)	Yr	NM
❑ 2026	For You/Fallin'	1979	7.00
❑ 2046	Without Your Love/ Southern Ballad (If This Means Losing You)	1979	7.00
❑ 2123	My World Is Empty Without You/Airwaves	1980	7.00
❑ 14572	Love Me Tonight/Heart of Mine	1979	7.00

20TH CENTURY

Number	Title (A Side/B Side)	Yr	NM
❑ 2279	Inland Sea/Joyride	1976	8.00

Albums

POLYDOR

Number	Title (A Side/B Side)	Yr	NM
❑ PD-1-6215	Blackjack	1979	12.00
❑ PD-1-6279	Worlds Apart	1980	15.00

BLACKMAN, HONOR

Albums

LONDON

Number	Title (A Side/B Side)	Yr	NM
❑ PS 408 [S]	Everything I've Got	1964	40.00
❑ LL 3408 [M]	Everything I've Got	1964	30.00

BLACKWELL, OTIS

45s

ATLANTIC

Number	Title (A Side/B Side)	Yr	NM
❑ 1165	Make Ready for Love/ When You're Around	1957	40.00
❑ 1178	Turtle Dove/What a Coincidence	1958	40.00

CUB

Number	Title (A Side/B Side)	Yr	NM
❑ 9092	Jeannie's Wedding/I'd Rather Kiss You Than Eat	1961	20.00
❑ 9107	Sister Twister/Ga Ga	1962	20.00

DATE

Number	Title (A Side/B Side)	Yr	NM
❑ 1006	Don't Run Away/ Handle with Care	1958	30.00

EPIC

Number	Title (A Side/B Side)	Yr	NM
❑ 10654	Just Keep It Up/It's All Over Me	1970	25.00

GROOVE

Number	Title (A Side/B Side)	Yr	NM
❑ 0034	Oh, What a Babe/Here I Am	1954	40.00

JAY-DEE

Number	Title (A Side/B Side)	Yr	NM
❑ 784	Daddy Rolling Stone/ Tears! Tears! Tears!	1953	50.00
❑ 787	You're My Love/Bartender Fill It Up Again	1954	50.00
❑ 791	On That Power Line/Don't You Know How I Love You	1954	50.00
❑ 792	I'm Standing at the Doorway/ Nobody Met the Train	1954	50.00
❑ 794	My Josephine/Ain't Got No Time	1954	50.00
❑ 798	Go Away Mr. Blues/ I'm Comin' Back Baby	1955	50.00
❑ 802	You Move Me Baby/ My Poor Broken Heart	1955	50.00
❑ 808	Oh What a Wonderful Time/ Let the Daddy Hold You	1955	50.00

MGM

Number	Title (A Side/B Side)	Yr	NM
❑ 13090	Kiss Away/ Grandaddy of Them All	1962	20.00

RCA VICTOR

Number	Title (A Side/B Side)	Yr	NM
❑ 47-5069	Wake You Fool/ Please Help Me Find	1952	50.00
❑ 47-5225	The Fool That I Be/Number 000	1953	50.00

Albums

DAVIS

Number	Title (A Side/B Side)	Yr	NM
❑ 109 [M]	Singin' the Blues	1956	500.00

INNER CITY

Number	Title (A Side/B Side)	Yr	NM
❑ 1032	These Are My Songs	1977	20.00

BLACKWELL, SCRAPPER

Albums

BLUESVILLE

Number	Title (A Side/B Side)	Yr	NM
❑ BVLP-1047	Mr. Scrapper's Blues	1962	180.00
—Blue label, silver print			
❑ BVLP-1047	Mr. Scrapper's Blues	1964	40.00
—Blue label with trident logo			

BLACKWELLS, THE

45s

GUYDEN

Number	Title (A Side/B Side)	Yr	NM
❑ 2020	Oh My Love/Holey Sombrero	1959	20.00

HICKORY

Number	Title (A Side/B Side)	Yr	NM
❑ 1241	I Won't Be Perfect/ Playin' Heart Strings	1964	10.00
❑ 1261	Ballad of a Young Truck Driver/ She Loves the Love I Give Her	1964	10.00
❑ 1319	Little Bird/I've Been Waiting	1965	10.00

JAMIE

Number	Title (A Side/B Side)	Yr	NM
❑ 1141	You Are Free, I'm Alone/ The Depot	1959	15.00
❑ 1146	The Christmas Holiday/ Little Match Girl	1959	20.00
❑ 1150	Always It's You/Honey, Honey	1960	15.00
❑ 1150 [PS]	Always It's You/Honey, Honey	1960	30.00
❑ 1157	Unchained Melody/ Mansion on the Hill	1960	15.00
❑ 1170	You're a Habit with Me/ Moulin Rouge	1960	15.00
❑ 1173	The Christmas Holiday/ Little Match Girl	1960	15.00
❑ 1179	Love or Money/ Big Daddy and the Cat	1961	12.00
❑ 1199	You Took Advantage of Me/"I"	1961	12.00

LIBERTY

Number	Title (A Side/B Side)	Yr	NM
❑ 55750	Show Me Around/ The Old Coast Road	1964	10.00

BLADES, CAROL

45s

GEE

Number	Title (A Side/B Side)	Yr	NM
❑ 1029	When Will I Know/ What Did I Do Wrong	1957	200.00

BLADES OF GRASS, THE

45s

JUBILEE

Number	Title (A Side/B Side)	Yr	NM
❑ 5582	Happy/That's What a Boy Likes	1967	8.00
❑ 5590	Just Another Face/Baby You're a Real Good Friend of Mine	1967	8.00
❑ 5605	Help/Justah	1967	8.00
❑ 5616	You Won't Find That Girl/ Charlie and Fred	1968	8.00
❑ 5622	The Way You'll Never Be/ You Turned Off the Sun	1968	8.00
❑ 5635	I Love You, Alice B. Toklas/ That's What a Boy Likes	1968	8.00
❑ 5662	Love Her and Cherish Her/ Pageant	1969	8.00

Albums

JUBILEE

Number	Title (A Side/B Side)	Yr	NM
❑ JGS-8007	The Blades of Grass Are Not for Smoking	1968	15.00

BLAINE, HAL

45s

ABC DUNHILL

Number	Title (A Side/B Side)	Yr	NM
❑ 4181	Beverly Drive/Midnight at Fink's	1969	12.00

DUNHILL

Number	Title (A Side/B Side)	Yr	NM
❑ 4006	La Bamba/Topsy '65	1965	15.00
❑ 4021	Secret Agent Man/ Midnight at Pink's	1966	15.00
❑ 4049	Bang Bang Rhythm/ Drums A-Go-Go	1966	15.00
❑ 4074	The Swinger/Drums A-Go-Go	1967	15.00
❑ 4091	Love-In (December)/ Wiggy (November)	1967	15.00
❑ 4102	The Invaders/Secret Agent Man	1967	15.00
❑ 4142	Allegro from "Mac Arthur Park"/ Drums A-Go-Go	1968	15.00

MELODY HOUSE

Number	Title (A Side/B Side)	Yr	NM
❑ 100	Slow Gate/South of Shreveport	1962	40.00

RCA VICTOR

Number	Title (A Side/B Side)	Yr	NM
❑ 47-8147	Hawaii 1963/East Side Story	1963	25.00
❑ 47-8223	Dance with the Surfin' Band/ The Drummer Plays for Me	1963	25.00
❑ 47-8282	Challenger II/Gear Stripper	1963	25.00

ROCK-IT

Number	Title (A Side/B Side)	Yr	NM
❑ 1000	Alamo Rock/Alamo Rock (Part 2)	1959	50.00

Except when noted otherwise, VG = 25% of NM, and VG+ = 50% of NM. (Example: VG = $2.00, VG+ = $4.00 and NM = $8.00.)

Albums

ABC DUNHILL

Number	Title (A Side/B Side)	Yr	NM
❑ DS-50035	Have Fun!!! Play Drums!!!	1968	40.00
—Without instruction booklet			
❑ DS-50035	Have Fun!!! Play Drums!!!	1968	50.00
—With instruction booklet			

DUNHILL

Number	Title (A Side/B Side)	Yr	NM
❑ D-50002 [M]	Drums! Drums! A-Go-Go	1966	30.00
❑ DS-50002 [S]	Drums! Drums! A-Go-Go	1966	40.00
❑ D-50019 [M]	Psychedelic Percussion	1967	40.00
❑ DS-50019 [S]	Psychedelic Percussion	1967	60.00

RCA VICTOR

Number	Title (A Side/B Side)	Yr	NM
❑ LPM-2834 [M]	Deuces, "T's," Roadsters & Drums	1963	100.00
❑ LSP-2834 [S]	Deuces, "T's," Roadsters & Drums	1963	150.00

BLAIR, TOM

45s

DECCA

Number	Title (A Side/B Side)	Yr	NM
❑ 31223	West Coast/With My Hand on My Hearrt	1961	30.00
❑ 31344	Dolar Bills/Since You Are Gone	1961	30.00

DOT

Number	Title (A Side/B Side)	Yr	NM
❑ 16095	Rock It/You Name It	1960	50.00

TEEN TUNES

Number	Title (A Side/B Side)	Yr	NM
❑ 767	Rock It/You Name It	1960	100.00

BLAKE, COREY

45s

CAPITOL

Number	Title (A Side/B Side)	Yr	NM
❑ 4057	How Can I Go On Without You/ Your Love Is Like a Boomerang	1975	1000.

BLAKE, HARRIETTE

45s

LTD

Number	Title (A Side/B Side)	Yr	NM
❑ 403	Two of Us/Turn Around Boy	1966	12.00
❑ 409	Gee You Are/Unspoken Words	1966	12.00

MONUMENT

Number	Title (A Side/B Side)	Yr	NM
❑ 1121	I Laughed Till I Cried/ Tell It Like It Is	1968	8.00

MUSICOR

Number	Title (A Side/B Side)	Yr	NM
❑ 1052	Love Me, Love Me/Wishin'	1965	12.00

PARKWAY

Number	Title (A Side/B Side)	Yr	NM
❑ 961	Dansero/Why Did Our Love Go Wrong	1965	15.00

Albums

HARRIETTE BLAKE

Number	Title (A Side/B Side)	Yr	NM
❑ HBLP-001	This Is My Life	1976	15.00
❑ HBLP-002	My Way	1978	15.00

BLAKE, TOMMY

45s

BUDDY

Number	Title (A Side/B Side)	Yr	NM
❑ 107	I'm a Fool/Kool It	1958	1000.

CHANCELLOR

Number	Title (A Side/B Side)	Yr	NM
❑ 101	I Gotta Be Somewhere/ Three Cheers for the Red, White and Blue	19??	10.00

RCA VICTOR

Number	Title (A Side/B Side)	Yr	NM
❑ 47-6925	Freedom/Mr. Hoody	1957	50.00

SUN

Number	Title (A Side/B Side)	Yr	NM
❑ 278	Flatfoot Sam/Lordy Hoody	1957	100.00
❑ 300	Sweetie Pie/I Dig You	1958	300.00

BLAKE BABIES

Albums

CHEWBUD

Number	Title (A Side/B Side)	Yr	NM
❑ CBTW-001 [EP]	Nicely, Nicely	1987	40.00
—1,000 copies pressed			

MAMMOTH

Number	Title (A Side/B Side)	Yr	NM
❑ MR0016	Earwig	1989	12.00
❑ MR0022	Sunburn	1990	12.00
❑ MR0025 [EP]	Rosy Jack World	1991	10.00
—Red vinyl			

BLAKELY, WELLINGTON

45s

VEE JAY

Number	Title (A Side/B Side)	Yr	NM
❑ 104	Sailor Joe/Gypsy with a Broken Heart	1953	400.00

BLANC, MEL

45s

CAPITOL

Number	Title (A Side/B Side)	Yr	NM
❑ F1330	Woody Woodpecker/Trixie and the Piano Pixie	1950	30.00
❑ F1360	I Tawt I Taw a Puddy Tat/ Yosemite Sam	1951	30.00
❑ F1441	K-K-K-Katy/Flying Saucers	1951	30.00
❑ F1727	10 Little Bottles in the Sink/ OKMNX	1951	30.00
❑ F1853	I Tan't Wait Till Quithmuth/ Christmas Chopsticks	1951	30.00
❑ F1948	That's All Folks!/Wontcha Ever	1952	30.00
❑ F2048	Lord Bless His Soul/Morris	1952	30.00
❑ F2261	The Misses Wouldn't Approve/ I Tell My Troubles to Joe	1952	30.00
❑ F2430	Tia-Juana/Little Red Monkey	1953	25.00
❑ F2470	Somebody Stole My Gal/ I Love Me	1953	25.00
❑ F2619	Ya, Das Ist Ein Christmas Tree/ I Tan't Wait Till Quithmuth	1953	30.00
❑ F2635	I'm in the Mood for Love/ My Kinda Love	1953	25.00
❑ F2718	I Dess I Dotta Doe/ The Lady Bird Song	1954	30.00
❑ F2764	Money/Polly Pretty Polly	1954	25.00
❑ F3902	The Hat I Got for Christmas Is Too Beeg/Pancho's Christmas	1959	25.00

WARNER BROS.

Number	Title (A Side/B Side)	Yr	NM
❑ 5129	Tweety's Twistmas Troubles/ I Keep Hearing Those Bells	1959	25.00
❑ 5156	Blimey/I Can't Fool My Heart	1960	25.00

Albums

CAPITOL

Number	Title (A Side/B Side)	Yr	NM
❑ H-436 [10]	Party Panic	1953	100.00

BLANCHARD, JACK, AND MISTY MORGAN

45s

EPIC

Number	Title (A Side/B Side)	Yr	NM
❑ 11030	Cockroach Stomp/ Carolina Sundown Red	1973	4.00
❑ 11058	Just One More Song/ Why Did I Sleep So Long	1973	4.00
❑ 11097	Something on Your Mind/Here Today and Gone Tomorrow	1974	4.00
❑ 50023	Down to the End of the Wine/ You Can't Say I Didn't Try	1974	4.00
❑ 50082	Chorus/House	1975	4.00
❑ 50122	Because We Love/It's Me	1975	4.00
❑ 50181	I'm High on You/Let's Pretend	1975	4.00
❑ 50205	47 Miles (to the Georgia Line)/ Motel Time	1976	4.00

MEGA

Number	Title (A Side/B Side)	Yr	NM
❑ 0031	There Must Be More to Life/ Fire Hydrant #79	1971	4.00
❑ 0046	Somewhere in Virginia in the Rain/If Eggs Had Legs	1971	4.00
❑ 0063	The Legendary Chicken Fairy/ The Night We Heard the Voice	1972	4.00
❑ 0082	Miami Sidewalks/Washin' Harry Down the Sink	1972	4.00
❑ 0089	Second Tuesday in December/ Don't It Make You Want to Go Home	1972	4.00
❑ 0101	A Handful of Dimes/It Seems Like There Ain't No Going Home	1973	4.00
❑ 0114	Shadows of the Leaves/ Sweet Memories	1973	4.00

UNITED ARTISTS

Number	Title (A Side/B Side)	Yr	NM
❑ XW1004	Tennessee Birdwalk/Living Together	1977	4.00
❑ XW1067	Heartaches/You Come So Easy to Me	1977	4.00

WAYSIDE

Number	Title (A Side/B Side)	Yr	NM
❑ 00	Big Black Bird (Spirit of Our Love)/Autumn Song (On a Yellow Day)	1969	5.00
—Reissue of 1028			
❑ 007	Changin' Times/Poor Jody	1969	5.00
❑ 010	Tennessee Bird Walk/ The Clock of St. James	1970	5.00
❑ 013	Humphrey the Camel/ A Place in My Mind	1970	5.00
❑ 015	You've Got Your Troubles (I've Got Mine)/How I Lost 31 Pounds in 17 Days	1970	5.00
❑ 1024	Bethlehem Steel/ No Sign of Love	1969	6.00
❑ 1028	Big Black Bird (Spirit of Our Love)/Autumn Song (On a Yellow Day)	1969	6.00

Albums

MEGA

Number	Title (A Side/B Side)	Yr	NM
❑ 31-1009	Two Sides	1972	12.00

WAYSIDE

Number	Title (A Side/B Side)	Yr	NM
❑ WWS 33-001	Birds of a Feather	1970	15.00

BLAND, BILLY

45s

OLD TOWN

Number	Title (A Side/B Side)	Yr	NM
❑ 1016	Chicken in the Basket/ The Fat Man	1956	20.00
❑ 1022	Chicken Hop/Oh You for Me	1956	20.00
❑ 1035	If I Could Be Your Man/ I Had a Dream	1957	20.00
❑ 1076	Let the Little Girl Dance/ Sweet Thing	1960	25.00
❑ 1082	You Were Born to Be Loved/ Pardon Me	1960	15.00
❑ 1088	Make Believe Lover/Harmonys	1960	15.00
❑ 1093	Everything That Shines Ain't Gold/Keep Talkin' That Sweet Talk	1960	15.00
❑ 1098	I Cross My Heart/Steady Kind	1961	15.00
❑ 1105	My Heart's On Fire/Can't Stop Her from Dancing	1961	15.00
❑ 1109	Do the Bug with Me/Uncle Bud	1962	15.00
❑ 1114	Busy Little Boy/ All I Want to Do Is Cry	1961	15.00
❑ 1124	Mama Stole the Chicken/ I Spent My Life Loving You	1962	15.00
❑ 1128	Darling Won't You Think of Me/ How Many Hearts	1962	15.00
❑ 1143	Doing the Mule/Farmer in the Dell	1963	15.00
❑ 1151	A Little Touch of Your Love/ Little Boy Blue	1963	15.00

ST. LAWRENCE

Number	Title (A Side/B Side)	Yr	NM
❑ 1005	She's Already Married/ My Divorce	1965	12.00

TIP TOP

Number	Title (A Side/B Side)	Yr	NM
❑ 708	Chicken in the Basket/ Chicken Hop	1958	20.00

BLAND, BOBBY

Includes records by "Bobby 'Blue' Bland."

12-Inch Singles

MCA

Number	Title (A Side/B Side)	Yr	NM
❑ L33-1835 [DJ]	I Feel Good, I Feel Fine/Tit for Tat/Come Fly with Me/ Love to See You Smile	1979	15.00

45s

ABC

Number	Title (A Side/B Side)	Yr	NM
❑ 12105	Yolanda/When You Come to the End of Your Road	1975	4.00
❑ 12134	I Take It On Home/You've Never Been This Far Before	1975	4.00
❑ 12156	Today I Started Loving You Again/Too Far Gone	1976	4.00
❑ 12189	It Ain't the Real Thing/ Who's Foolin' Who	1976	4.00
❑ 12280	The Soul of a Man/ If I Weren't a Gambler	1977	4.00
❑ 12330	Sittin' on a Poor Man's Throne/ I Intend to Take Your Place	1978	4.00
❑ 12360	Love to See You Smile/ I'm Just Your Man	1978	4.00
❑ 12405	Come Fly with Me/ Ain't God Something	1978	4.00

ABC DUNHILL

Number	Title (A Side/B Side)	Yr	NM
❑ 4369	This Time I'm Gone for Good/ Where Baby Went	1973	5.00
❑ 4379	Goin' Down Slow/ Up and Down World	1974	5.00
❑ 15003	Ain't No Love in the Heart of the City/Twenty-Four Hour Blues	1974	5.00
❑ 15015	I Wouldn't Treat a Dog (The Way You Treated Me)/I Ain't Gonna Be the First to Cry	1974	5.00

DUKE

Number	Title (A Side/B Side)	Yr	NM
❑ 3	Turn on Your Love Light/ Jelly, Jelly, Jelly	196?	40.00
—Small hole, plays at 33 1/3 rpm			
❑ 105	Lovin' Blues/I.O.U. Blues	1952	300.00
❑ 115	Army Blues/No Blow, No Show	1953	200.00
❑ 141	Time Out/It's My Life Baby	1955	60.00
❑ 146	You or None/Woke Up Screaming	1955	60.00
❑ 153	I Can't Put You Down/ You've Got Bad Intentions	1956	50.00
❑ 160	I Learned My Lesson/ I Don't Believe	1956	40.00
❑ 160	I Learned My Lesson/ Lead Us On	1956	40.00
❑ 167	Don't Want No Woman/ I Smell Trouble	1957	30.00
❑ 170	Farther Up the Road/ Sometime Tomorrow	1957	30.00
❑ 182	Teach Me/Bobby's Blues	1957	25.00
❑ 185	You Got Me Where You Want Me/Loan a Helping Hand	1958	25.00
❑ 196	Little Boy Blue/Last Night	1958	25.00
❑ 300	You Did Me Wrong/ I Lost Sight of the World	1959	25.00

B

Number	Title (A Side/B Side)	Yr	NM
❑ 303	Wishing Well/I'm Not Ashamed	1959	25.00
❑ 310	Is It Real/Someday	1959	25.00
❑ 314	I'll Take Care of You/That's Why	1959	25.00
❑ 318	Lead Me On/Hold Me Tenderly	1960	25.00
❑ 327	Cry Cry Cry/I've Been Wrong So Long	1960	25.00
❑ 332	I Pity the Fool/Close to You	1961	20.00
❑ 336	Don't Cry No More/How Does a Cheating Woman Feel	1961	20.00
❑ 338	Ain't That Loving You/Jelly, Jelly, Jelly	1961	20.00
❑ 340	Don't Cry No More/Saint James Infirmary	1961	20.00
❑ 344	Turn On Your Love Light/You're the One (That I Need)	1961	20.00
❑ 347	Who Will the Next Fool Be/Blue Moon	1962	20.00
❑ 352	Yield Not to Temptation/How Does a Cheating Woman Feel	1962	20.00
❑ 355	Stormy Monday Blues/Your Friends	1962	20.00
❑ 360	That's the Way Love Is/Call On Me	1962	20.00
❑ 366	Sometimes You Gotta Cry a Little/You're Worth It All	1963	15.00
❑ 369	Ain't It a Good Thing/Queen for a Day	1963	15.00
❑ 370	The Feeling Is Gone/I Can't Stop Singing	1963	15.00
❑ 375	Ain't Nothing You Can Do/Honey Child	1964	15.00
❑ 377	Share Your Love with Me/After It's Too Late	1964	10.00
❑ 383	Ain't Doing Too Bad (Part 1)/Ain't Doing Too Bad (Part 2)	1964	10.00
❑ 385	These Hands (Small But Mighty)/Today	1965	10.00
❑ 386	Blind Man/Black Night	1965	10.00
❑ 390	Dust Got in Daddy's Eyes/Ain't No Telling	1965	10.00
❑ 393	I'm Too Far Gone (To Turn Around)/If You Could Read My Mind	1965	10.00
❑ 402	Good Time Charlie/Good Time Charlie (Part 2)	1966	8.00
❑ 407	Poverty/Building a Fire with Hair	1966	8.00
❑ 412	Back in the Same Old Bag Again/I Ain't Myself Anymore	1966	8.00
❑ 416	You're All I Need/Deep in My Soul	1967	8.00
❑ 421	That Did It/Getting Used to the Blues	1967	8.00
❑ 426	A Touch of the Blues/Shoes	1967	8.00
❑ 432	Driftin' Blues/You Could Read My Mind	1968	8.00
❑ 433	Honey Child/A Piece of Gold	1968	8.00
❑ 435	Save Your Love for Me/Share Your Love with Me	1968	8.00
❑ 440	Rockin' in the Same Old Boat/Wouldn't You Rather Have Me	1968	8.00
❑ 447	Gotta Get to Know You/Baby I'm On My Way	1969	8.00
❑ 449	Chains of Love/Ask Me 'Bout Nothing (But the Blues)	1969	8.00
❑ 458	If You've Got a Heart/Sad Feeling	1970	8.00
❑ 460	Lover with a Reputation/If Love Ruled the World	1970	8.00
❑ 464	Keep On Loving Me (You'll See the Change)/I Just Got to Forget About You	1970	8.00
❑ 466	I'm Sorry/Yum Yum Tree	1971	8.00
❑ 471	Shape Up or Ship Out/The Love That We Share (Is True)	1971	8.00
❑ 472	Do What You Set Out to Do/Ain't Nothing You Can Do	1972	8.00
❑ 477	I'm So Tired/If You Could Read My Mind	1972	8.00
❑ 480	That's All There Is/I Don't Want Another Mountain to Climb	1973	8.00

KENT

Number	Title (A Side/B Side)	Yr	NM
❑ 378	Love You Baby/Drifting	1962	10.00
—With Ike Turner			

MALACO

Number	Title (A Side/B Side)	Yr	NM
❑ 2122	Members Only/I Just Got to Know	1985	3.00
❑ 2126	Can We Make Love Tonight/In the Ghetto	1986	3.00
❑ 2133	Angel/I Hear You Thinkin'	1986	3.00

MCA

Number	Title (A Side/B Side)	Yr	NM
❑ 41140	Tit for Tat/Come Fly with Me	1979	4.00
❑ 41197	Soon as the Weather Breaks/To Be Friends	1980	4.00
❑ 51068	You'd Be a Millionaire/Swat Vibrator	1981	3.00
❑ 51181	What a Difference A Day Makes/Givin' Up the Streets for Love	1982	3.00
❑ 52085	Recess in Heaven/Exactly, Where It's At	1982	3.00
❑ 52136	Here We Go Again/You're About to Win	1982	3.00
❑ 52180	Is This the Blues/You're About to Win	1983	3.00
❑ 52270	If It Ain't One Thing/Tell Mr. Bland	1983	3.00
❑ 52436	Looking Back/You Got Me Loving You	1984	3.00
❑ 52482	Get Real Clean/It's Too Bad	1984	3.00
❑ 52508	You Are My Christmas/New Merry Christmas Baby	1984	3.00

WAND

Number	Title (A Side/B Side)	Yr	NM
❑ 1102	Honey, You've Been On My Mind/You've Got Time	1965	15.00

Albums

ABC

Number	Title	Yr	NM
❑ D-895	Get On Down with Bobby Bland	1975	12.00
❑ AB-1018	Reflections in Blue	1977	10.00
❑ AA-1075	Come Fly with Me	1978	10.00

ABC DUKE

Number	Title	Yr	NM
❑ DLPS-74	Two Steps from the Blues	197?	12.00
❑ DLP-75	Here's the Man!!!	1974	12.00
❑ DLP-77	Call On Me/That's the Way Love Is	1974	12.00
❑ DLP-78	Ain't Nothing You Can Do	1974	12.00
❑ DLP-79	The Soul of the Man	1974	12.00
❑ DLP-84	The Best of Bobby Bland	1974	12.00
❑ DLP-86	The Best of Bobby Bland, Vol. 2	1974	12.00
❑ DLP-88	A Touch of the Blues	1974	12.00
❑ DLP-89	Spotlighting the Man	1974	12.00
❑ DLP 92-2 [(2)]	Introspective of the Early Years	1974	20.00

ABC DUNHILL

Number	Title	Yr	NM
❑ DSX-50163	His California Album	1973	15.00
❑ DSX-50169	Dreamer	1974	15.00

BLUESWAY

Number	Title	Yr	NM
❑ BLS-6065	Call On Me	197?	15.00

DUKE

Number	Title	Yr	NM
❑ DLP-74 [M]	Two Steps from the Blues	1961	250.00
—Purple and yellow label			
❑ DLP-74 [M]	Two Steps from the Blues	1962	100.00
—Orange label, black vinyl			
❑ DLP-74 [M]	Two Steps from the Blues	1962	250.00
—Orange label, red vinyl			
❑ DLPS-74 [R]	Two Steps from the Blues	196?	60.00
❑ DLP-75 [M]	Here's the Man!!!	1962	100.00
—Orange label			
❑ DLP-75 [M]	Here's the Man!!!	1962	200.00
—Purple and yellow label			
❑ DLPS-75 [S]	Here's the Man!!!	196?	100.00
—Without spoken intro to "36-22-36"			
❑ DLPS-75 [S]	Here's the Man!!!	1962	200.00
—With spoken intro to "36-22-36"			
❑ DLP-77 [M]	Call On Me/That's the Way Love Is	1963	100.00
❑ DLPS-77 [S]	Call On Me/That's the Way Love Is	1963	150.00
❑ DLP-78 [M]	Ain't Nothing You Can Do	1964	80.00
❑ DLPS-78 [S]	Ain't Nothing You Can Do	1964	120.00
❑ DLP-79 [M]	The Soul of the Man	1966	80.00
❑ DLPS-79 [S]	The Soul of the Man	1966	120.00
❑ DLP-84 [M]	The Best of Bobby Bland	1967	20.00
❑ DLPS-84 [P]	The Best of Bobby Bland	1967	25.00
❑ DLP-86 [M]	The Best of Bobby Bland, Vol. 2	1968	25.00
❑ DLPS-86 [P]	The Best of Bobby Bland, Vol. 2	1968	20.00
❑ DLP-88 [M]	A Touch of the Blues	1968	25.00
❑ DLPS-88 [S]	A Touch of the Blues	1968	20.00
❑ DLPS-89	Spotlighting the Man	1969	20.00
❑ DLPS-90	If Loving You Is Wrong	1970	20.00

MCA

Number	Title	Yr	NM
❑ 3157	I Feel Good, I Feel Fine	1979	10.00
❑ 4172 [(2)]	Introspective of the Early Years	198?	10.00
—Reissue of Duke 92			
❑ 5145	Sweet Vibrations	1980	10.00
❑ 5233	Try Me, I'm Real	1981	10.00
❑ 5297	Here We Go Again	1982	10.00
❑ 5425	Tell Mr. Bland	1983	10.00
❑ 5503	You've Got Me Loving You	1984	10.00
❑ 27013	The Best of Bobby Bland	198?	8.00
—Reissue of Duke 84			
❑ 27036	Two Steps from the Blues	198?	8.00
—Reissue of Duke 74			
❑ 27038	Here's the Man!!!	198?	8.00
—Reissue of Duke 75			
❑ 27040	Ain't Nothing You Can Do	198?	8.00
—Reissue of Duke 78			
❑ 27041	The Soul of the Man	1984	8.00
—Reissue of Duke 79			
❑ 27042	Call On Me/That's the Way Love Is	1984	8.00
—Reissue of Duke 77			
❑ 27043	Reflections in Blue	1984	8.00
—Reissue of ABC 1018			
❑ 27044	Come Fly with Me	1984	8.00
—Reissue of ABC 1075			
❑ 27045	The Best of Bobby Bland, Vol. 2	1984	8.00
—Reissue of Duke 86			
❑ 27047	A Touch of the Blues	1984	8.00
—Reissue of Duke 88			
❑ 27048	Spotlighting the Man	1984	8.00
—Reissue of Duke 89			
❑ 27073	I Feel Good, I Feel Fine	1985	8.00
—Reissue of MCA 3157			
❑ 27076	Sweet Vibrations	198?	8.00
—Reissue of 5145			

BLAND, BOBBY, AND B.B. KING

Also see each artist's individual listings.

45s

ABC IMPULSE

Number	Title (A Side/B Side)	Yr	NM
❑ 31006	Let the Good Times Roll/Strange Things	1976	4.00
❑ 31009	Everyday I Have the Blues/The Thrill Is Gone	1976	4.00

Albums

ABC DUNHILL

Number	Title	Yr	NM
❑ DSY-50190 [(2)]	Together for the First Time...Live	1974	15.00

ABC IMPULSE!

Number	Title	Yr	NM
❑ 9317	Together Again...Live	1976	12.00

COMMAND

Number	Title	Yr	NM
❑ CQDY-40012 [(2)Q]	Together for the First Time...Live	1974	25.00

MCA

Number	Title	Yr	NM
❑ 4160 [(2)]	Together for the First Time...Live	198?	10.00
—Reissue of ABC Dunhill 50190			
❑ 27012	Together Again...Live	198?	8.00
—Reissue of ABC Impulse! 9317			

BLANDERS, THE

45s

SMASH

Number	Title (A Side/B Side)	Yr	NM
❑ 2005	Jitterbug/Desert Sands	1965	50.00

BLANE, MARCIE

45s

SEVILLE

Number	Title (A Side/B Side)	Yr	NM
❑ 120	Bobby's Girl/Time to Dream	1962	20.00
—Exists with "Seville" logo straight across the top of the label, and with the "Seville" logo curving around the top of the label. No difference in value has yet been noted.			
❑ 123	What Does a Girl Do?/How Can I Tell Him	1963	16.00
❑ 126	Little Miss Fool/Rag Time Sound	1963	16.00
❑ 128	You Gave My Number to Billy/Told You So	1963	16.00
❑ 130	Why Can't I Get a Guy/Who's Going to Take My Daddy's Place	1963	16.00
❑ 133	Bobby Did/After the Laughter	1964	16.00
❑ 137	The Hurtin' Kind/She'll Break the String	1965	16.00

BLASTERS, THE

12-Inch Singles

MCA

Number	Title (A Side/B Side)	Yr	NM
❑ L33-1210 [DJ]	One Bad Stud/Never Be You	1984	6.00
—B-side by Maria McKee			

SLASH

Number	Title (A Side/B Side)	Yr	NM
❑ PRO-A-2017 [DJ]	Barefoot Rock/Fool's Paradise/Long White Cadillac	1983	8.00
❑ PRO-A-2259 [DJ]	Colored Lights/Dark Night	1985	8.00
❑ PRO-A-2346 [DJ]	Trouble Bound (Remix) (Extended)	1985	12.00

45s

MCA

Number	Title (A Side/B Side)	Yr	NM
❑ 52378	Blue Shadows/I Can Dream About You	1984	4.00
—B-side by Dan Hartman			
❑ 52378 [PS]	Blue Shadows/I Can Dream About You	1984	4.00
—Sleeve emphasizes the Dan Hartman hit			

SLASH

Number	Title (A Side/B Side)	Yr	NM
❑ SRS 110	I'm Shakin'/No Other Girl	1981	8.00
❑ SRS 110 [PS]	I'm Shakin'/No Other Girl	1981	8.00
❑ 29055	Colored Lights/Help You Dream	1985	4.00
❑ 29055 [PS]	Colored Lights/Help You Dream	1985	4.00
❑ 29566	Red Rose/Leaving	1983	5.00
❑ 29678	Barefoot Rock/Bus Station	1983	3.00
❑ 29678 [PS]	Barefoot Rock/Bus Station	1983	3.00
❑ 29975	So Long Baby Goodbye/Border Radio	1982	3.00
❑ 29975 [PS]	So Long Baby Goodbye/Border Radio	1982	3.00
❑ 50047	I'm Shakin'/No Other Girl	1982	3.00
❑ 50047 [PS]	I'm Shakin'/No Other Girl	1982	3.00

Albums

CROWN

Number	Title	Yr	NM
❑ CST-392 [S]	Sounds of the Drags	1963	25.00
❑ CLP-5392 [M]	Sounds of the Drags	1963	20.00

Number	Title (A Side/B Side)	Yr	NM
ROLLIN' ROCK			
❑ 021	American Music	1980	75.00
SLASH			
❑ SR 109	The Blasters	1981	15.00
❑ BKS 3680	The Blasters	1982	10.00
—With blue labels; reissue of 109			
❑ 23735 [EP]	Over There: Live at the Venue, London	1982	10.00
❑ 23818	Non Fiction	1983	10.00
❑ 25093	Hard Line	1985	10.00
WARNER BROS.			
❑ WBMS-130 [DJ]	Music and Interviews	1985	40.00
—Part of "The Warner Bros. Music Show" series; one side is The Blasters; the other side is The Smiths, which accounts for this piece's value			

BLAVAT, JERRY

Number	Title (A Side/B Side)	Yr	NM
45s			
CAMEO			
❑ 393	Discophonic Walk/Back to School One More Time	1965	12.00
EPIC			
❑ 10193	Jerry's Theme/Let's Love Again	1967	12.00
FAVOR			
❑ 100	Discophonic Walk/Back to School One More Time	1965	15.00
ROULETTE			
❑ 7085	Tasty (To Me)/Oh Be Joyous	1970	8.00
—With the Geatorettes			

BLAZER BOY

Number	Title (A Side/B Side)	Yr	NM
45s			
IMPERIAL			
❑ 5199	Mornin' Train/Joe's Kid Sister	1952	100.00
❑ 5244	Surprise Blues/Waiting for My Baby	1953	100.00
❑ 5801	New Orleans Twist/That's Where It's At	1962	20.00

BLENDAIRS, THE

Number	Title (A Side/B Side)	Yr	NM
45s			
TIN PAN ALLEY			
❑ 252	My Love Is Just for You/Repetition	1958	150.00

BLENDELLS, THE

Number	Title (A Side/B Side)	Yr	NM
45s			
COTILLION			
❑ 44020	Night After Night/The Love That I Needed	1968	10.00
ERA BACK TO BACK HITS			
❑ 023	Dance with Me/Land of 1000 Dances	197?	5.00
—B-side by Cannibal and the Headhunters			
RAMPART			
❑ 641	La La La La La/Huggies Bunnies	1964	25.00
REPRISE			
❑ 0291	La La La La La/Huggies Bunnies	1964	20.00
❑ 0340	Dance with Me/Get Your Baby	1965	20.00

BLENDERS, THE

Several different groups.

Number	Title (A Side/B Side)	Yr	NM
45s			
AFO			
❑ 305	Graveyard/It Takes Time	1962	300.00
ALADDIN			
❑ 3449	Two Loves/Soda Shop	1959	1500.
CLASS			
❑ 236	My Heart's Desire/Little Rose	1958	40.00
CORTLAND			
❑ 102	Love Is a Treasure/Fisherman	1962	12.00
❑ 103	Everybody's Got a Right/What Have You Got	1962	12.00
DECCA			
❑ 27403	The Masquerade Is Over/Little Small Town Girl	1951	400.00
❑ 27587	All I Gotta Do Is Think of You/The Busiest Corner	1951	300.00
❑ 28092	Just a Little Walk with Me/I'd Be a Fool Again	1952	300.00
❑ 28241	Never in a Million Years/Memories of You	1952	300.00
❑ 48156	Gone/Honeysuckle Rose	1950	300.00
❑ 48158	Count Every Star/Would I Still Be the One in Your Heart	1950	300.00
❑ 48183	I'm So Crazy for Love/What About Tonight	1950	300.00
❑ 48244	My Heart Will Never Forget/You Do the Dreaming	1951	300.00
JAY DEE			
❑ 780	Don't Play Around with You/You'll Never Smile Again	1953	200.00
MAR-V-LUS			
❑ 6010	Your Love Has Got Me Down/Love Is a Good Thing Going	1966	200.00
MGM			
❑ 11488	I Don't Miss You Anymore/If That's the Way You Want It Baby	1953	400.00
❑ 11531	Please Take Me Back/Isn't It a Shame	1953	400.00
RCA VICTOR			
❑ 47-6591	I've Told Every Little Star/Cecilia	1956	60.00
❑ 47-6712	Wake Up to Music/New Sensations in Sound	1956	50.00
❑ 47-7009	I'm Following You/Since I Kissed My Baby Goodbye	1957	50.00
WANGER			
❑ 189	Angel/Old MacDonald	1959	25.00
WITCH			
❑ 114	Daughter/Everybody's Got a Right	1963	16.00
❑ 117	Boys Think/Squat and Squirm	1963	15.00
❑ 123	One Time/(B-side unknown)	1964	15.00

BLENDTONES, THE

Number	Title (A Side/B Side)	Yr	NM
45s			
DON-EL			
❑ 106	She's Gone/Lights Please	1961	100.00
IMPERIAL			
❑ 5758	She's Gone/Lights Please	1961	25.00
SUCCESS			
❑ 101	Lovers/Dear Diary	1963	40.00
❑ 105	Come On Home/The Slide	1963	40.00

BLESSED END

Number	Title (A Side/B Side)	Yr	NM
Albums			
TNS			
❑ 248	Movin' On	1971	250.00

BLESSING, MICHAEL

See MICHAEL NESMITH.

BLEU LIGHTS, THE

Number	Title (A Side/B Side)	Yr	NM
45s			
BAYSOUND			
❑ 67003	Forever/They Don't Know My Heart	1968	40.00
❑ 67007	Bony Moronie/Lonely Man's Prayer	1968	30.00
❑ 67010	Yes I Do/The End of My Dreams	1969	30.00

BLEVINS, CHUCK

Number	Title (A Side/B Side)	Yr	NM
45s			
FOXIE			
❑ 7006	Sleigh Bell Rock/Singing for You	1959	20.00

BLEYER, ARCHIE

Number	Title (A Side/B Side)	Yr	NM
45s			
CADENCE			
❑ 1241	Hernando's Hideaway/S'il Vous Plait	1954	15.00
❑ 1254	The Naughty Lady of Shady Lane/While the Vesper Bells Were Ringing	1954	15.00
❑ 1279	'Cause You're My Lover/Nothing to Do	1955	15.00
—By "Archie and Janet Bleyer"			
❑ 1283	You Tell Me Your Dreams (I'll Tell You Mine)/Bridge of Happiness	1956	12.00
❑ 1293	The Rockin' Ghost/Sleep, Sleep, Daughter	1956	15.00
❑ 1313	Strange One/Jocko's Theme	1957	12.00
❑ 1320	Julie's Jump/Amber	1957	12.00
❑ 1338	Hernando's Hideaway/Steam Heat	1957	12.00
❑ 1383	Mustafa/Jimmie's Blues	1960	10.00
❑ 1426	Moonlight Serenade/Sunrise Serenade	1962	10.00
❑ 1603	Hernando's Hideaway/The Naughty Lady of Shady Lane	196?	8.00
—Reissue			

BLIND FAITH

Also see GINGER BAKER'S AIR FORCE; ERIC CLAPTON; STEVE WINWOOD.

Number	Title (A Side/B Side)	Yr	NM
45s			
POLYDOR			
❑ 871798-7	Presence of the Lord/Can't Find My Way Home	1989	4.00
RSO			
❑ 873	Presence of the Lord/Can't Find My Way Home	1977	8.00
—First single release from 1969 self-titled album			
Albums			
ATCO			
❑ 33-304A [M]	Blind Faith	1969	200.00
—White label promo only			
❑ SD 33-304A [S]	Blind Faith	1969	25.00
—Cover with naked girl on Side 1 and same scene without girl on Side 2			
❑ SD 33-304B [S]	Blind Faith	1969	15.00
—Cover with band photo on Side 1 and song lyrics on Side 2			
MOBILE FIDELITY			
❑ 1-186	Blind Faith	1985	40.00
—Audiophile vinyl			
RSO			
❑ RS-1-3016	Blind Faith	1977	10.00
—Reissue with naked girl on one side and band photo on the other			
❑ 825094-1	Blind Faith	1986	8.00

BLINKY

Number	Title (A Side/B Side)	Yr	NM
45s			
MOTOWN			
❑ 1134	I Wouldn't Change the Man He Is/I'll Always Love You	1968	8.00
❑ 1168	How You Gonna Keep It/This Time Last Summer	1970	100.00
❑ 1233	You Get a Tangle in Your Life Line/This Man of Mine	1973	6.00
MOWEST			
❑ 5019	For Your Precious Love/So Tired	1972	6.00
❑ 5033	T'Ain't Nobody's Bizness If I Do/What More Can I Do	1973	5.00
SOUL			
❑ 35089	How You Gonna Keep It/This Time Last Summer	1971	6.00

BLISTERS, THE

Number	Title (A Side/B Side)	Yr	NM
45s			
LIBERTY			
❑ 55577	Shortnin' Bread/Cookie Rockin' in Her Stockings	1963	12.00
❑ 55647	Rich in My Pocket, Poor in My Heart/Friendly Loans	1963	12.00
TITANIC			
❑ 5005	Fifty Mile Hike/Recitation	1963	20.00

BLOCH, SONNY

Number	Title (A Side/B Side)	Yr	NM
45s			
BEE			
❑ 1000	Beetle Squash/Leapin' Lizards	1964	12.00
—As "Sonny Bloch's Elephants"			
REGAL			
❑ 7503	Ask Me No Questions/Hand of Faith	1958	20.00

BLODWYN PIG

JETHRO TULL related.

Number	Title (A Side/B Side)	Yr	NM
45s			
A&M			
❑ 1158	Dear Jill/Summer Day	1969	8.00
Albums			
A&M			
❑ SP-3180	Ahead Rings Out	1982	10.00
—Budget-line reissue			
❑ SP-4210	Ahead Rings Out	1969	15.00
❑ SP-4243	Getting to This	1970	15.00

BLOND

Number	Title (A Side/B Side)	Yr	NM
45s			
FONTANA			
❑ 1673	Deep Inside My Heart/I Will Bring You Flowers in the Morning	1969	12.00
❑ 1673 [PS]	Deep Inside My Heart/I Will Bring You Flowers in the Morning	1969	16.00
Albums			
FONTANA			
❑ SRF-67067	Blond	1969	20.00

BLONDE ON BLONDE

Number	Title (A Side/B Side)	Yr	NM
Albums			
JANUS			
❑ JLP-3003	Contrasts	1969	25.00

BLONDIE

Number	Title (A Side/B Side)	Yr	NM
12-Inch Singles			
CHRYSALIS			
❑ CHS-10-PDJ [DJ]	One Way or Another (same on both sides)	1979	15.00
❑ CHS-14-PDJ [DJ]	Dreaming (same on both sides)	1979	15.00

B

Blondie, "Island of Lost Souls," Chrysalis 2603, 1980, **$3.**

Number	Title (A Side/B Side)	Yr	NM
❑ CHS-25-PDJ [DJ]	Rapture (Long Version) (Short Version)	1981	15.00
❑ CHS-39-PDJ [DJ]	War Child (same on both sides)	1982	15.00
❑ CHS-40-PDJ [DJ]	Island of Lost Souls (same on both sides)	1982	12.00
❑ CDS-2275	Heart of Glass (Disco Version)/ (Instrumental)	1979	10.00
❑ 58277 [(2)]	Rapture (9 versions)	1994	10.00
❑ 58340 [(2)]	Atomic (9 versions)	1995	15.00
❑ 58387 [(2)]	Heart of Glass (9 versions)	1995	15.00
❑ 58474 [(2)]	Union City Blue (7 versions)	1995	15.00
LOGIC			
❑ 74321-78040-1	Maria (Soul Solution Full Remix 9:27) (Soul Solution Bonus Beats) (Talvin Singh Remix 7:27) (Talvin Singh Rhythmic Remix Edit 4:39) (Album Version 4:51)	1999	10.00
❑ LGSP-78040-1 [DJ]	Maria (Ether Dub) (White Trash Dub)	1999	20.00
LOUD			
❑ 65699 [DJ]	No Exit (The Loud Rock Remix Radio Version 3:58) (AMA Performance Version Radio Version 4:26) (The Loud Rock Remix TV Track 5:12)/ Who's Gonna Cry (No Exit Part 2) (The Infamous Hip Rock Version Radio Version 3:21) (The Infamous Hip Rock Version Instrumental 3:24)/Maria (Talvin Singh Rhythmic Remix Edit 4:39)	1999	15.00
POLYDOR			
❑ PRO-124 [DJ]	Call Me (Remix Extended Version)/Night Drive (instrumental)	1980	20.00

Number	Title (A Side/B Side)	Yr	NM
SALSOUL			
❑ SG 341	Call Me (Spanish)/(Instrumental)	1980	30.00
45s			
CHRYSALIS			
❑ 2220	Denis/I'm On E	1977	5.00
❑ CHE-2242	Picture This/Fade Away and Radiate	1978	10.00
—Small hole; made for export to England; "Picture This" is listed with a time of "2:63"			
❑ 2251	I'm Gonna Love You Too/ Just Go Away	1978	5.00
❑ CHE-2266	Hanging on the Telephone/ Will Anything Happen	1978	10.00
—Large hole; "Made in USA" on label, but exported to England			
❑ 2271	Hanging on the Telephone/ Fade Away and Radiate	1978	5.00
❑ 2271 [PS]	Hanging on the Telephone/ Fade Away and Radiate	1978	5.00
❑ CHE-2275	Heart of Glass/Rifle Range	1979	10.00
—Small hole; "Made in USA" on label, but exported to England; features the original 3:54 LP version complete with "pain in the ass" lyric intact			
❑ 2295	Heart of Glass/11:59	1979	4.00
—Standard issue with 3:22 version			
❑ 2295 [PS]	Heart of Glass/11:59	1979	4.00
❑ 2336	One Way or Another/ Just Go Away	1979	4.00
❑ 2379	Dreaming/Living in the Real World	1979	4.00
❑ 2408	The Hardest Part/Sound Asleep	1980	4.00
❑ 2408 [PS]	The Hardest Part/Sound Asleep	1980	5.00
❑ 2410	Atomic/Die Young Stay Pretty	1980	4.00
❑ 2410 [PS]	Atomic/Die Young Stay Pretty	1980	5.00
❑ 2414	Call Me/(Instrumental)	1980	3.00
❑ 2414 [PS]	Call Me/(Instrumental)	1980	5.00
—Photo of Richard Gere on sleeve.			
❑ 2414 [PS]	Call Me/(Instrumental)	1980	5.00
—Photo of Deborah Harry on sleeve.			
❑ 2465	The Tide Is High/Suzy and Jeffrey	1980	3.00
❑ 2465 [PS]	The Tide Is High/Suzy and Jeffrey	1980	3.00
❑ 2485	Rapture/Walk Like Me	1981	3.00
❑ 2485 [PS]	Rapture/Walk Like Me	1981	3.00
❑ 2603	Island of Lost Souls/Dragonfly	1982	3.00

Number	Title (A Side/B Side)	Yr	NM
❑ 2603 [PS]	Island of Lost Souls/Dragonfly	1982	3.00
❑ S7-18303	Rapture/One Way or Another	1995	3.00
❑ S7-18304	Heart of Glass/Call Me	1995	3.00
❑ S7-18396	Atomic/Atomic (Diddy Remix)	1995	4.00
❑ S7-18848	Union City Blue (Diddy's Remix Edit)/Union City Blue	1995	3.00
❑ 42944	Heart of Glass/ Hanging on the Telephone	1985	3.00
—Silver label reissue; contains a mysterious 4:33 version of "Heart of Glass"			
❑ 42945	One Way or Another/Dreaming	1985	3.00
—Silver label reissue			
❑ 42946	Call Me/Atomic	1985	3.00
—Silver label reissue			
PRIVATE STOCK			
❑ 45,097	X Offender/In the Sun	1976	30.00
❑ 45,097 [DJ]	X Offender (mono)/(stereo)	1976	10.00
❑ 45,141	In the Flesh/Man Overboard	1977	20.00
❑ 45,141 [DJ]	In the Flesh (mono/stereo)	1977	10.00
Albums			
CHRYSALIS			
❑ CHS 24 PDJ [DJ]	At Home with Debbie Harry and Chris Stein	1981	50.00
—Open-end interview with script			
❑ CHR 1165	Blondie	1977	12.00
—Reissue of Private Stock album			
❑ CHR 1166	Plastic Letters	1977	12.00
—Blue and white label			
❑ CHR 1166	Plastic Letters	1977	20.00
—Green label			
❑ CHR 1192	Parallel Lines	1978	15.00
—First pressing, with 3:54 version of "Heart of Glass"			
❑ CHR 1192	Parallel Lines	1979	10.00
—Second pressing, with 5:50 version of "Heart of Glass (Disco Version)"			
❑ CHE 1225	Eat to the Beat	1979	10.00
❑ CHE 1290	Autoamerican	1980	10.00
❑ CHS 1337	The Best of Blondie	1981	10.00
❑ CHR 1384	The Hunter	1982	8.00
❑ CHP 5001 [PD]	Parallel Lines	1979	25.00
—Picture disc			
❑ F1 32748 [(2)]	The Remix Project: Remixed, Remade, Remodeled	1995	15.00
❑ PV 41165	Blondie	1983	8.00
—Reissue			
❑ PV 41166	Plastic Letters	1983	8.00
—Reissue			
❑ FV 41192	Parallel Lines	1983	8.00
—Reissue			
❑ PV 41192	Parallel Lines	1986	8.00
—Reissue			
❑ PV 41225	Eat to the Beat	1983	8.00
—Reissue			
❑ PV 41290	Autoamerican	1983	8.00
—Reissue			
❑ FV 41337	The Best of Blondie	1983	8.00
—Reissue			
❑ PV 41337	The Best of Blondie	1986	8.00
—Reissue			
❑ PV 41384	The Hunter	1983	8.00
—Reissue			
❑ V2X 41658 [(2)]	Once More into the Bleach	1988	15.00
—Remixes of Blondie and Debbie Harry tracks			
❑ R 200816 [(2)]	Once More into the Bleach	1988	18.00
—BMG Music Service edition			
MOBILE FIDELITY			
❑ 1-050	Parallel Lines	1980	30.00
—Audiophile vinyl			
PRIVATE STOCK			
❑ PS-2023	Blondie	1976	25.00

BLOOD, SWEAT AND TEARS

Also see DAVID CLAYTON-THOMAS; AL KOOPER.

Number	Title (A Side/B Side)	Yr	NM
45s			
ABC			
❑ 12310	Blue Street/Somebody I Trusted	1977	4.00
COLUMBIA			
❑ JBQ 501 [Q]	Spinning Wheel/You've Made Me So Very Happy	1973	10.00
—"Special Coin Operator Release" in quadraphonic; contains the full-length versions of the songs (edited versions are on other 45s)			
❑ 10151	Got to Get You Into My Life/ Naked Man	1975	5.00
❑ 10189	No Show/Yesterday's Music	1975	5.00
❑ 10400	You're the One/Heavy Blue	1976	5.00
❑ 44559	I Can't Quit Her/House in the Country	1968	8.00
❑ 44776	You've Made Me So Very Happy/Blues — Part 2	1969	6.00
❑ 44871	Spinning Wheel/More and More	1969	6.00
❑ 45008	And When I Die/ Sometimes in Winter	1969	6.00
❑ 45204	Hi-De-Ho/The Battle	1970	5.00
❑ 45235	Lucretia Mac Evil/ Lucretia's Reprise	1970	5.00

Except when noted otherwise, VG = 25% of NM, and VG+ = 50% of NM. (Example: VG = $2.00, VG+ = $4.00 and NM = $8.00.)

B

Number	Title (A Side/B Side)	Yr	NM
❑ 45427	Go Down Gamblin'/Valentine's Day	1971	5.00
❑ 45427 [PS]	Go Down Gamblin'/Valentine's Day	1971	8.00
❑ 45477	Lisa, Listen to Me/Cowboys and Indians	1971	5.00
❑ 45661	So Long Dixie/Alone	1972	5.00
❑ 45661 [PS]	So Long Dixie/Alone	1972	8.00
❑ 45755	Velvet/I Can't Move No Mountains	1973	5.00
❑ 45937	Roller Coaster/Inner Crisis	1973	5.00
❑ 45965	Save Our Ship/Song for John	1973	5.00
❑ 46059	Tell Me That I'm Wrong/Rock Reprise	1974	5.00
MCA			
❑ 41198	Nuclear Blues/Agitato	1980	4.00
7-Inch Extended Plays			
COLUMBIA			
❑ 7-30590	*Redemption/Lisa, Listen to Me/A Look to My Heart (duet)/A Look to My Heart (inst.)/For My Lady/Mama Gets High	1971	10.00
—Jukebox issue; small hole, plays at 33 1/3 rpm			
❑ 7-30590 [PS]	Blood, Sweat and Tears 4	1971	12.00
Albums			
ABC			
❑ 1015	Brand New Day	1977	10.00
CBS SPECIAL PRODUCTS			
❑ P 16660	Musically Speaking	1982	10.00
COLUMBIA			
❑ CS 9616	Child Is Father to the Man	1970	10.00
—Orange label			
❑ CS 9616 [M]	Child Is Father to the Man	1968	25.00
—White label promo only, "Special Mono Radio Station Copy" sticker on cover, with same number as stereo edition			
❑ CS 9616 [S]	Child Is Father to the Man	1968	15.00
—Red "360 Sound" label			
❑ PC 9619	Child Is Father to the Man	1980	8.00
❑ CS 9720	Blood, Sweat and Tears	1969	15.00
—Red "360 Sound" label			
❑ CS 9720	Blood, Sweat and Tears	1970	10.00
—Orange label			
❑ PC 9720	Blood, Sweat and Tears	1980	8.00
❑ KC 30090	Blood, Sweat and Tears 3	1970	10.00
❑ PC 30090	Blood, Sweat and Tears 3	1986	8.00
❑ KC 30590	BS&T: 4	1971	10.00
❑ CQ 30994 [Q]	Blood, Sweat and Tears	1972	20.00
❑ CQ 31170 [Q]	Blood, Sweat and Tears' Greatest Hits	1972	20.00
❑ KC 31170	Blood, Sweat and Tears' Greatest Hits	1972	10.00
—With the single versions of "You've Made Me So Very Happy," "Spinning Wheel," and "And When I Die" (all in mono)			
❑ PC 31170	Blood, Sweat and Tears' Greatest Hits	1980	8.00
❑ PCQ 31170 [Q]	Blood, Sweat and Tears' Greatest Hits	1976	18.00
—Reissue with new prefix			
❑ KC 31780	New Blood	1972	10.00
❑ KC 32180	No Sweat	1973	10.00
❑ CQ 32929 [Q]	Mirror Image	1974	20.00
❑ PC 32929	Mirror Image	1974	10.00
❑ PC 33484	New City	1975	10.00
❑ PCQ 33484 [Q]	New City	1975	15.00
❑ PC 34233	More Than Ever	1976	10.00
❑ HC 49619	Child Is Father to the Man	1981	50.00
—Half-speed mastered edition			
DIRECT DISK			
❑ SD-16605	Blood, Sweat and Tears	1981	60.00
MCA			
❑ L33-1865 [DJ]	Nuclear Blues	1980	15.00
—Promo only on gold vinyl			
❑ 3061	Nuclear Blues	1980	10.00
❑ 3227	Blood, Sweat and Tears	1981	—
—Canceled?			
MOBILE FIDELITY			
❑ 1-251	Blood, Sweat and Tears	1996	120.00
—Audiophile vinyl; fewer than 2,000 pressed			

BLOODROCK

GRAND FUNK and TERRY KNIGHT related.

Number	Title (A Side/B Side)	Yr	NM
45s			
CAPITOL			
❑ 2736	Fatback/Gotta Find a Way	1970	6.00
❑ 3009	D.O.A./Children's Heritage	1971	8.00
❑ 3089	You Gotta Roll/A Certain Kind	1971	6.00
❑ 3161	Jessica/You Gotta Roll	1971	6.00
❑ 3227	Rock and Roll Candy Man/Don't Eat the Children	1971	6.00
❑ 3320	Erosion/Castle of Thoughts	1972	5.00
❑ 3399	Castle of Thoughts/D.O.A.	1972	5.00
❑ 3451	Help Is On the Way/Thank You Daniel Ellsburg	1972	5.00
❑ 3770	Voices/Thank You Daniel Ellsburg	1973	5.00
❑ PRO-6579/81	[DJ]Help Is On the Way/Bloodrock Interview (By Sol Smaizys/Dennis Gray WXFM-Chicago)	1972	12.00
Albums			
CAPITOL			
❑ ST-435	Bloodrock	1970	15.00
❑ ST-491	Bloodrock 2	1970	15.00
❑ SM-645	Bloodrock U.S.A.	197?	10.00
—Reissue with new prefix			
❑ SMAS-645	Bloodrock U.S.A.	1971	15.00
❑ SM-765	Bloodrock 3	197?	10.00
—Reissue with new prefix			
❑ ST-765	Bloodrock 3	1971	15.00
❑ SVBB-11038 [(2)]	Bloodrock Live	1972	20.00
—Original edition has a lime green label			
❑ SW-11109	Bloodrock Passage	1972	15.00
❑ SMAS-11259	Whirlwind Tongues	1973	15.00
❑ SM-11417	Bloodrock 'N' Roll	1975	12.00

BLOODSTONE

Number	Title (A Side/B Side)	Yr	NM
12-Inch Singles			
MOTOWN			
❑ M00017D1	Just Wanna Get the Feel of It (Vocal) (Instrumental)	1979	8.00
T-NECK			
❑ AS 1888 [DJ]	Instant Love (5:23) (same on both sides)	1984	8.00
❑ 4Z9-02863	We Go a Long Way Back/Nite Time Fun	1982	8.00
❑ 4Z9-03403	My Love Grows Stronger (Part 1 6:16) (Part 2 4:50)	1982	10.00
❑ 4Z9-05085	Bloodstone's Party (5:00) (7:03) (1:30)	1984	8.00
45s			
EPIC			
❑ 50437	Got to Find Myself Another Baby/Weeping Willow Tree	1977	4.00
LONDON			
❑ 1038	Girl/Judy, Judy	1972	5.00
❑ 1042	That's the Way We Make Our Music/This Thing Is Heavy	1972	5.00
❑ 1046	Natural High/Peter's Jones	1973	5.00
❑ 1051	Never Let You Go/You Know We've Learned	1973	5.00
❑ 1052	Outside Woman/Dumb Dude	1974	5.00
❑ 1055	That's Not How It Goes/Everybody Needs Love	1974	5.00
❑ 1059	I Believe You Now/I Need Time	1974	5.00
❑ 1061	My Little Lady/Loving You Is Just a Pastime	1975	5.00
❑ 1062	Give Me Your Heart/Something's Missing	1975	5.00
❑ 1062 [PS]	Give Me Your Heart/Something's Missing	1975	10.00
❑ 1064	Do You Wanna Do a Thing/Save Me	1976	5.00
❑ 1067	Just Like in the Movies/Little Linda	1976	5.00
MOTOWN			
❑ 1458	Just Wanna Get the Feel of It/It's Been a Long Time	1978	4.00
T-NECK			
❑ ZS5-02825	We Go a Long Way Back/Nite Time Fun	1982	4.00
❑ ZS5-03049	Go On and Cry/(Instrumental)	1982	4.00
❑ ZS4-03394	My Love Grows Stronger (Part 1)/(Part 2)	1982	4.00
❑ ZS4-04465	Instant Love/It Feels So Good	1984	4.00
❑ ZS4-04592	Bloodstone's Party/Feel the Heat	1984	4.00
Albums			
LONDON			
❑ XPS 620	Natural High	1973	20.00
❑ XPS 634	Unreal	1973	20.00
❑ APS 647	I Need Time	1974	20.00
❑ PS 654	Riddle of the Sphinx	1975	15.00
❑ PS 671	Do a Thing?	1976	15.00
MOTOWN			
❑ M7-909	Don't Stop!	1978	12.00
T-NECK			
❑ FZ 38115	We Go a Long Way Back	1982	10.00
❑ FZ 39146	Bloodstone's Party	1984	10.00
❑ PZ 40016	Greatest Hits	1985	8.00
❑ PZ 40042	Lullaby of Broadway	1985	8.00

BLOODY MARY

Number	Title (A Side/B Side)	Yr	NM
Albums			
FAMILY PRODUCTIONS			
❑ FPS-2707	Bloody Mary	1972	25.00

BLOOM, BOBBY

Number	Title (A Side/B Side)	Yr	NM
45s			
EARTH			
❑ E-106	Heidi/Sign of the V	1970	8.00
KAMA SUTRA			
❑ 210	Heart of Town/Make the Radio a Little Louder	1966	12.00
—As "Bobby Mann"			
❑ 223	Love, Don't Let Me Down/Where Is the Woman	1967	10.00
❑ 229	Count on Me/Was I Dreamin'	1967	10.00
KAPP			
❑ 710	I Still Remember/Rough and Tough	1965	12.00
L&R			
❑ 157	Montego Bay/Try a Little Harder	1970	6.00
MAP CITY			
❑ 306	Emergency/Again 'N' Again	1970	6.00
MGM			
❑ 14212	Make Me Happy/This Thing I've Gotten Into	1970	5.00
❑ 14246	We're All Goin' Home/Careful Not to Break the Spell	1971	5.00
❑ 14292	We Need Each Other/You Touch Me	1971	5.00
❑ 14343	I Really Got It Bad for You/Until They Say Mercy	1972	5.00
❑ 14437	Stay on Top/Sha La Boom Boom	1972	5.00
❑ 14614	The Island/Oh, I Wish I Knew	1973	5.00
ROULETTE			
❑ 7095	Oh Yesterday/Where Are We Going	1971	5.00
WHITE WHALE			
❑ 285	All I Wanna Do Is Dance/Taggin' Along	1968	8.00
Albums			
BUDDAH			
❑ BDS-5072	Where Are We Going	1971	12.00
L&R			
❑ LR-1035	The Bobby Bloom Album	1970	15.00

BLOOMFIELD, MIKE

Number	Title (A Side/B Side)	Yr	NM
Albums			
COLUMBIA			
❑ CS 9883	It's Not Killing Me	1969	15.00
—Red "360 Sound" label			
❑ C2 37578 [(2)]	Bloomfield	1982	12.00
HARMONY			
❑ KH 30395	It's Not Killing Me	1971	10.00
SUNDAZED			
❑ LP 5105	I'm Cutting Out	2001	12.00
TAKOMA			
❑ C-1059	Analine	1977	10.00
❑ C-1063	Michael Bloomfield	1978	10.00
❑ C-1070	Between a Hard Place and the Ground	1979	10.00
❑ TAK-7059	Analine	198?	8.00
❑ TAK-7063	Michael Bloomfield	198?	8.00
❑ TAK-7070	Between a Hard Place and the Ground	198?	8.00
❑ TAK-7091	Cruisin' for a Bruisin'	198?	8.00
WATERHOUSE			
❑ 11	Living in the Fast Lane	1981	10.00

BLOOMFIELD, MIKE, AND NICK GRAVENITES

Number	Title (A Side/B Side)	Yr	NM
Albums			
COLUMBIA			
❑ CS 9899	My Labors	1969	12.00
—Red "360 Sound" label			
❑ CS 9899	My Labors	1970	10.00
—Orange label			

BLOOMFIELD, MIKE/JOHN PAUL HAMMOND/DR. JOHN

Number	Title (A Side/B Side)	Yr	NM
45s			
COLUMBIA			
❑ 45887	I Yi Yi/Pretty Thing	1973	6.00
Albums			
COLUMBIA			
❑ KC 32172	Triumvirate	1973	12.00

BLOOMFIELD, MIKE, AND AL KOOPER

Also see each artist's individual listings.

Number	Title (A Side/B Side)	Yr	NM
45s			
COLUMBIA			
❑ 44678	The Weight/Mama's Temptation	1968	6.00

Blue Cheer, "Summertime Blues", Philips 40516, 1968, $25.

Number	Title (A Side/B Side)	Yr	NM
Albums			
COLUMBIA			
❑ KGP 6 [(2)]	The Live Adventures of Mike Bloomfield & Al Kooper	1969	25.00
—Red "360 Sound" labels			
❑ PG 6 [(2)]	The Live Adventures of Mike Bloomfield & Al Kooper	197?	12.00
—Reissue with new prefix			

BLOOMFIELD, MIKE/AL KOOPER/STEVE STILLS
Also see each artist's individual listings.

Number	Title (A Side/B Side)	Yr	NM
45s			
COLUMBIA			
❑ 44657	Season of the Witch/Albert's Shuffle	1968	6.00
Albums			
COLUMBIA			
❑ CS 9701	Super Session	1968	20.00
—Red "360 Sound" label			
❑ CS 9701	Super Session	1970	10.00
—Orange label			
❑ PC 9701	Super Session	198?	8.00
—Reissue with new prefix			
❑ CQ 30991 [Q]	Super Session	1971	20.00
MOBILE FIDELITY			
❑ 1-178	Super Session	198?	40.00
—Audiophile vinyl			

BLOSSOMS, THE Probably all the same group.

Number	Title (A Side/B Side)	Yr	NM
45s			
BELL			
❑ 780	You've Lost That Lovin' Feeling/Something So Wrong	1969	8.00
❑ 797	(You're My) Soul and Inspiration/Stand By	1969	8.00
❑ 857	I Ain't Got to Love Nobody Else/Don't Take Your Love	1970	8.00
❑ 937	One Step Away/Break Your Promise	1970	8.00
CAPITOL			
❑ F3822	Move On/He Promised Me	1957	30.00
❑ F3878	Little Louie/Have Faith in Me	1958	25.00
❑ F4072	Baby Daddy-O/No Other Love	1958	25.00
CHALLENGE			
❑ 9109	Son-In-Law/I'll Wait	1961	20.00
—B-side by the Coeds			
❑ 9122	Hard to Get/Write Me a Letter	1961	20.00
❑ 9138	The Search Is Over/Big Talking Jim	1962	20.00
EEOC			
❑ 8172	Things Are Changing (same on both sides)	1965	150.00
❑ 8172 [PS]	Things Are Changing (same on both sides)	1965	150.00
—Promotional item for the Equal Employment Opportunity Commission			
EPIC			
❑ 50434	There's No Greater Love (Than Mine for You My Love)/Walking on Air	1977	5.00
LION			
❑ 108	Touchdown/It's All Up to You	1972	6.00
❑ 125	Grandma's Hands/Cherish What Is Dear to You	1972	6.00
MGM			
❑ 13964	Tweedlee Dee/You Got Me Hummin'	1968	10.00
ODE			
❑ 101	Stoney End/Wonderful	1967	12.00
❑ 106	Cry Like a Baby/Wonderful	1968	12.00
❑ 125	Stoney End/Wonderful	1969	12.00
OKEH			
❑ 7162	I'm in Love/What Makes Love	1963	20.00
REPRISE			
❑ 0436	Good, Good Lovin'/That's When the Tears Start	1965	15.00
❑ 0475	Lover Boy/My Love, Come Home	1966	15.00
❑ 0522	Let Your Love Shine on Me/Deep Into My Heart	1966	15.00
Albums			
LION			
❑ 1007	Shockwave	1972	15.00

BLUE, DAVID

Number	Title (A Side/B Side)	Yr	NM
Albums			
ASYLUM			
❑ 7E-1043	Com'n Back for More	1975	10.00
❑ 7E-1077	Cupid's Arrow	1976	10.00
❑ SD 5052	Stories	1972	12.00
❑ SD 5066	The Nice Baby and the Angel	1973	12.00
ELEKTRA			
❑ EKM-4003 [M]	David Blue	1966	20.00
❑ EKS-74003 [S]	David Blue	1966	20.00
REPRISE			
❑ RS 6296	These 23 Days in September	1968	15.00

BLUE ANGEL

Number	Title (A Side/B Side)	Yr	NM
45s			
POLYDOR			
❑ 2149	I Had a Love/Take a Chance	1980	10.00
Albums			
POLYDOR			
❑ PD-1-6300	Blue Angel	1980	20.00

BLUE BARONS, THE

Number	Title (A Side/B Side)	Yr	NM
Albums			
PHILIPS			
❑ PHM 200017 [M]	Twist to the Great Blues Hits	1962	20.00
❑ PHS 600017 [S]	Twist to the Great Blues Hits	1962	25.00

BLUE BELLES, THE Also see PATTI LaBELLE AND THE BLUE BELLES.

Number	Title (A Side/B Side)	Yr	NM
45s			
ATLANTIC			
❑ 987	The Story of a Fool/Cancel the Call	1953	150.00

BLUE CHEER

Number	Title (A Side/B Side)	Yr	NM
45s			
MERCURY			
❑ 872804-7	Summertime Blues/Just a Little Bit	1989	5.00
—Reissue			
PHILIPS			
❑ 40516	Summertime Blues/Out of Focus	1968	12.00
❑ 40516 [PS]	Summertime Blues/Out of Focus	1968	25.00
❑ 40541	Just a Little Bit/Gypsy Ball	1968	10.00
❑ 40561	Feathers from Your Tree/Sun Cycle	1968	10.00
❑ 40561	Sun Cycle/Albert's Shuffle	1968	10.00
❑ 40561 [PS]	Feathers from Your Tree/Sun Cycle	1968	40.00
❑ 40602	West Coast Child of Sunshine/When It All Gets Old	1969	8.00
❑ 40651	All Night Long/Fortunes	1969	8.00
❑ 40664	Hello L.A., Bye-Bye Birmingham/Natural Man	1970	8.00
❑ 40682	Ain't That the Way/Fool	1970	8.00
❑ 40691	Babji (Twilight Raga)/Pilot	1971	8.00
❑ 40691	Babji (Twilight Raga)/Fool	1971	10.00
Albums			
CAROLINE			
❑ CAROL 1395	The Beast Is Back	1989	12.00
—Reissue			
MEGAFORCE			
❑ MRI 1069	The Beast Is Back	1984	15.00
PHILIPS			
❑ PHM 200264 [M]	Vincebus Eruptum	1968	80.00
❑ PHS 600264 [S]	Vincebus Eruptum	1968	40.00
❑ PHS 600278	Outsideinside	1968	40.00
❑ PHS 600305	New! Improved! Blue Cheer	1969	40.00
❑ PHS 600333	Blue Cheer	1970	40.00
❑ PHS 600347	The Original Human Being	1970	40.00
❑ PHS 600350	Oh! Pleasant Hope	1971	40.00
RHINO			
❑ RNLP 70130	Louder Than God (The Best of Blue Cheer, 1968-1969)	1986	12.00

BLUE DIAMONDS, THE With Ernie Kador (later ERNIE K-DOE)

Number	Title (A Side/B Side)	Yr	NM
45s			
SAVOY			
❑ 1134	Honey Baby/No Money	1954	60.00

B

BLUE EYED SOUL

45s

Number	Title (A Side/B Side)	Yr	NM
CAMEO			
❑ 401	The Shadow of Your Love/ Look Gently at the Rain	1966	20.00
❑ 423	Something New/ Tonight I Am King	1966	20.00
SAND CITY			
❑ 2101	Are You Ready for This/ When Something's Wrong with My Baby	196?	800.00

BLUE HAZE

45s

Number	Title (A Side/B Side)	Yr	NM
A&M			
❑ 1357	Smoke Gets In Your Eyes/ Anna Roseanna	1972	5.00
❑ 1426	You'll Never Walk Alone/ Take Away My Heart Teresa	1973	5.00

BLUE JAYS, THE (1)
Los Angeles-based male vocal group.

45s

Number	Title (A Side/B Side)	Yr	NM
MILESTONE			
❑ 2008 *—Green label*	Lover's Island/You're Gonna Cry	1961	30.00
❑ 2008 *—Light blue and white label*	Lover's Island/You're Gonna Cry	1961	30.00
❑ 2008 *—Dark blue label*	Lover's Island/You're Gonna Cry	1961	40.00
❑ 2009	Tears Are Falling/Tree Tall Men	1961	30.00
❑ 2010	Let's Make Love/ Rock, Rock, Rock	1962	20.00
❑ 2012	The Right to Love/ Rock, Rock, Rock	1962	20.00
❑ 2014	Venus, My Love/Tall Len	1962	60.00

Albums

Number	Title (A Side/B Side)	Yr	NM
MILESTONE			
❑ 1001 [M]	The Blue Jays Meet Little Caesar and the Romans	1962	100.00

BLUE JAYS, THE (2)
Chicago-based (probably) male vocal group.

45s

Number	Title (A Side/B Side)	Yr	NM
CHECKER			
❑ 782 *—VG 1000; VG+ 1500*	White Cliffs of Dover/Hey Poppa	1953	2000.

BLUE JAYS, THE (U)

45s

Number	Title (A Side/B Side)	Yr	NM
LAURIE			
❑ 3037	Sweet Georgia Brown/ J.J.'s Blues	1959	25.00
MAP CITY			
❑ 300	Hang On/Hard Thing to Accept	1969	6.00
❑ 307	Freedom (Where Have You Gone)/(B-side unknown)	1971	6.00
❑ 311	Jackson/Wacka Wacka	1971	6.00
PHILIPS			
❑ 40186	Who (Will I Be Today)?/ Come On Baby	1964	15.00
ROULETTE			
❑ 4169	Practical Joker/Barbara	1959	20.00
❑ 4264	Kum Ba Yah/Cave Man Love	1960	20.00
WARNER BROS.			
❑ 7299	Edgy/I'm Only Dreaming	1969	6.00

BLUE MAGIC

12-Inch Singles

Number	Title (A Side/B Side)	Yr	NM
COLUMBIA			
❑ 44-68789	It's Like Magic/(B-side unknown)	1989	8.00
❑ 44-68849	Secret Lover/There's a Song in My Head	1989	8.00
DEF JAM			
❑ 44-68197	Romeo and Juliet (Vocal) (Instrumental)/Couldn't Get to Sleep Last Night	1989	8.00
MIRAGE			
❑ PR 398 [DJ]	Magic # (5:00) (4:26)	1983	10.00

45s

Number	Title (A Side/B Side)	Yr	NM
ATCO			
❑ 6910	Spell/Guess Who	1972	6.00
❑ 6930	Look Me Up/What's Come Over Me	1973	6.00
❑ 6949	Stop to Start/Where Have You Been	1973	6.00
❑ 6961	Sideshow/Just Don't Want to Be Lonely	1974	6.00
❑ 7004	Three Ring Circus /Welcome to the Club	1974	6.00
❑ 7014	Love Has Found Its Way to Me/ When Ya Coming Home	1975	6.00
❑ 7031	Chasing Rainbows/You Won't Have to Tell Me Goodbye	1975	5.00
❑ 7046	Grateful Part 1/Grateful Part 2	1976	5.00
❑ 7052	Freak-N-Stein/Stop and Get a Hold of Yourself	1976	5.00
❑ 7061	Teach Me (It's Something About Love)/Spark of Love	1976	5.00
❑ 7090	I Waited/Can't Get You Out of My Mind	1978	4.00
CAPITOL			
❑ 4977	Land of Make Believe/ Remember November	1981	6.00
COLUMBIA			
❑ 38-68900	It's Like Magic/Couldn't Get to Sleep Last Night	1989	4.00
❑ 38-69017	Secret Lover/There's a Song in My Head	1989	4.00
DEF JAM			
❑ 38-68566	Romeo and Juliet/Couldn't Get to Sleep Last Night	1989	4.00
LIBERTY			
❑ 56146	Can I Say I Love You/ One, Two, Three	1969	10.00
MIRAGE			
❑ 99843	See Through/(B-side unknown)	1983	4.00
❑ 99869	Since You Been Gone/ If You Move You Lose	1983	4.00
❑ 99914	Magic #/See Through	1983	8.00
WMOT			
❑ 4003	Summer Snow/Spark of Love	1976	5.00

Albums

Number	Title (A Side/B Side)	Yr	NM
ATCO			
❑ SD 36-103	The Magic of the Blue	1974	12.00
❑ SD 38-104	The Message	1977	12.00
❑ SD 36-120	Thirteen Blue Magic Lane	1975	12.00
❑ SD 36-140	Mystic Dragons	1976	12.00
❑ SD 7038	Blue Magic	1974	12.00
CAPITOL			
❑ ST-12143	Welcome Back	1981	10.00
COLLECTABLES			
❑ COL-5031	The Magic of the Blue: Greatest Hits	198?	10.00
COLUMBIA			
❑ C 45092	From Out of the Blue	1989	12.00
MIRAGE			
❑ 90074	Magic #	1983	10.00
OMNI			
❑ 90527	Greatest Hits	1986	10.00

Blue Oyster Cult, *Tyranny and Mutation*, Columbia KC 32017, 1973, **$12.**

BLUE MINK
Also see MADELINE BELL.

45s

Number	Title (A Side/B Side)	Yr	NM
MCA			
❑ 40031	I Can't Find the Answer/ By the Devil I Was Tempted	1973	5.00
❑ 40091	Randy/Another Without You Day	1973	5.00
❑ 40230	Get Up/Loneliness	1974	5.00
PHILIPS			
❑ 40658	Melting Pot/But Not Forever	1969	8.00
❑ 40672	Can You Feel It Baby/ (B-side unknown)	1970	8.00
❑ 40678 *—Canceled*	Good Morning Freedom/ Mary Jane	1970	—
❑ 40686	Our World/Respects to Mrs. Jones	1970	8.00
❑ 40697	Gasoline Alley Bred/ We Have All Been Saved	1971	8.00

Albums

Number	Title (A Side/B Side)	Yr	NM
MCA			
❑ 332	Blue Mink	1973	12.00
PHILIPS			
❑ PHS 600323	Melting Pot	1970	15.00
❑ PHS 600339	Real Mink	1970	15.00

B

BLUE NOTES, THE (1)

This group evolved into HAROLD MELVIN AND THE BLUE NOTES.

Number	Title (A Side/B Side)	Yr	NM
45s			
COLLECTABLES			
❑ 1113	Winter Wonderland/O Holy Night	198?	4.00
—Reissue			
JOSIE			
❑ 800	If You Love Me/There's Something in Your Eyes, Eloise	1956	200.00
❑ 814	Letters/With This Pen	1957	120.00
—As "Todd Randall and the Blue Notes"			
❑ 823	The Retribution Blues/Wagon Wheels	1957	150.00
LOST-NITE			
❑ 317	My Hero/A Good Woman	197?	5.00
—Reissue			
PORT			
❑ 70021	If You Love Me/There's Something in Your Eyes, Eloise	1958	60.00
RED TOP			
❑ 135	My Hero/A Good Woman	1963	30.00
3 SONS			
❑ 103	WPLJ/While I'm Away	1962	30.00
UNI			
❑ 55132	Got Chills and Cold Thrills/Never Gonna Leave You	1969	12.00
❑ 55201	This Time Will Be Different/Lucky Me	1970	12.00
VAL-UE			
❑ 213	My Hero/A Good Woman	1960	80.00
❑ 215	Winter Wonderland/O Holy Night	1960	80.00
Albums			
COLLECTABLES			
❑ COL-5006	The Early Years	1982	12.00

BLUE NOTES, THE (2)

Earlier male vocal group, no relation to (1).

Number	Title (A Side/B Side)	Yr	NM
45s			
RAMA			
❑ 25	If You'll Be Mine/Too Hot to Handle	1953	200.00

BLUE NOTES, THE (U)

None of these appear to be by (1) or (2), but we don't know how many different groups are represented below.

Number	Title (A Side/B Side)	Yr	NM
45s			
DOT			
❑ 15692	My Steady Girl/Mighty Lou	1958	25.00
—B-side by Henry Wilson			
❑ 15720	Darling of Mine/I Love Her So	1958	25.00
TNT			
❑ 150	Darling of Mine/I Love Her So	1958	30.00
20TH CENTURY			
❑ 1213	Blue Star/Pucker Your Lips	1961	15.00

BLUE ORCHIDS, THE

Number	Title (A Side/B Side)	Yr	NM
45s			
LONDON			
❑ 9637	Love Hit Me/Don't Make Me Mad	1964	10.00
❑ 9669	Oo-Chang-a-Lang/I've Got That Feeling	1964	10.00

BLUE OYSTER CULT

Number	Title (A Side/B Side)	Yr	NM
12-Inch Singles			
COLUMBIA			
❑ AS 447 [DJ]	Godzilla (Live) (Studio Version)	1978	15.00
❑ AS 1772 [DJ]	Shooting Shark (Edit) (Album Version)/Take Me Away/Eyes on Fire	1984	12.00
❑ CAS 2430 [DJ]	Dancin' in the Ruins (4:10) (same on both sides)	1986	10.00
45s			
COLUMBIA			
❑ AE7 1156 [DJ]	Godzilla (Live Version)/(Studio Version)	1978	6.00
❑ AE7 1156 [PS]	Godzilla (Live Version)/(Studio Version)	1978	8.00
❑ 18-02415	Burnin' for You/Vengeance (The Pact)	1981	4.00
❑ 18-02415 [DJ]	Burnin' for You (Long Version) (Short Version)	1981	5.00
❑ 18-02415 [PS]	Burnin' for You/Vengeance (The Pact)	1981	8.00
❑ 13-03137	(Don't Fear) The Reaper/Burnin' for You	1982	4.00
—Reissue			
❑ 38-04298	Shooting Shark/Dragon Lady	1984	3.00
❑ 38-04298 [PS]	Shooting Shark/Dragon Lady	1984	6.00
❑ 38-04435	Take Me Away/Let Go	1984	3.00
❑ 38-05845	Dancin' in the Ruins/Shadow Warrior	1986	3.00
❑ 38-06199	Perfect Water/Spy in the House of Night	1986	3.00
❑ 3-10046	Dominance and Submission/Career of Evil	1974	6.00
❑ 3-10169	Born to Be Wild/(B-side unknown)	1975	6.00
❑ 3-10384	(Don't Fear) The Reaper/Tattoo Vampire	1976	5.00
❑ 3-10560	This Ain't the Summer of Love/Debbie Denise	1977	5.00
❑ 3-10659	Goin' Through the Motions/Searchin' for Celine	1977	5.00
❑ 3-10697	Godzilla/Nosferatu	1978	5.00
❑ 3-10725	Godzilla (Live Version)/(Studio Version)	1978	5.00
❑ 3-10841	We Gotta Get Out of This Place/E.T.I. (Extra Terrestrial Intelligence)	1978	5.00
❑ 11055	In Thee/Lonely Teardrops	1979	4.00
❑ 1-11145	You're Not the One (I Was Looking For)/Moon Crazy	1979	4.00
❑ 11-11401	The Marshall Plan/Divine Wind	1980	4.00
❑ 4-45598	Cities on Flame with Rock and Roll/Before the Kiss, A Redcap	1972	10.00
❑ 4-45879	Hot Rails to Hell/Seven Screaming Diz Busters	1973	6.00
❑ 4-45879 [PS]	Hot Rails to Hell/Seven Screaming Diz Busters	1973	15.00
❑ 38-74716	(Don't Fear) The Reaper/Burnin' for You	1992	3.00
—Reissue			
Albums			
COLUMBIA			
❑ KC 31063	Blue Oyster Cult	1972	12.00
❑ PC 31063	Blue Oyster Cult	197?	8.00
—Reissue with new prefix			
❑ CQ 32017 [Q]	Tyranny and Mutation	1973	30.00
❑ KC 32017	Tyranny and Mutation	1973	12.00
❑ PC 32017	Tyranny and Mutation	197?	8.00
—Reissue with new prefix			
❑ CQ 32858 [Q]	Secret Treaties	1974	30.00
❑ KC 32858	Secret Treaties	1974	12.00
❑ PC 32858	Secret Treaties	197?	8.00
—Reissue with new prefix			
❑ KG 33371 [(2)]	On Your Feet or On Your Knees	1975	15.00
❑ PC 34164	Agents of Fortune	1976	10.00
—Original gatefold with no bar code on cover			
❑ PC 34164	Agents of Fortune	198?	8.00
—Budget-line reissue with bar code			
❑ JC 35019	Spectres	1977	10.00
❑ PC 35019	Spectres	198?	8.00
—Budget-line reissue			
❑ JC 35563	Some Enchanted Evening	1978	10.00
❑ PC 35563	Some Enchanted Evening	198?	8.00
—Budget-line reissue			
❑ JC 36009	Mirrors	1979	10.00
❑ PC 36009	Mirrors	198?	8.00
—Budget-line reissue			
❑ JC 36550	Cultosaurus Erectus	1980	10.00
❑ PC 36550	Cultosaurus Erectus	198?	8.00
—Budget-line reissue			
❑ FC 37389	Fire of Unknown Origin	1981	10.00
❑ PC 37389	Fire of Unknown Origin	1984	8.00
—Budget-line reissue			
❑ KG 37946 [(2)]	Extraterrestrial Live	1982	12.00
❑ FC 38947	The Revolution by Night	1983	10.00
❑ PC 38947	The Revolution by Night	1985	8.00
—Budget-line reissue			
❑ FC 39979	Club Ninja	1986	10.00
❑ FC 40618	Imaginos	1988	10.00

BLUE RIDGE RANGERS, THE

See JOHN FOGERTY.

BLUE RONDOS, THE

Number	Title (A Side/B Side)	Yr	NM
45s			
PARKWAY			
❑ 937	Little Baby/Baby I Go for You	1964	12.00

BLUE STARS

Number	Title (A Side/B Side)	Yr	NM
45s			
MERCURY			
❑ 70742	Lullaby of Birdland/That's My Girl	1955	10.00
❑ 70808	Mambo Italiano/Speak Low	1956	10.00
❑ 70877X45	Broadway at Basin Street/The Kissing Dance	1956	10.00
❑ 70924	Jumpin' at the Woodside/Hernando's Hideaway	1956	10.00
Albums			
EMARCY			
❑ MG-36067 [M]	Lullaby of Birdland	1956	40.00

BLUE SWEDE

Number	Title (A Side/B Side)	Yr	NM
45s			
CAPITOL			
❑ 3627	Hooked on a Feeling/Gotta Have Your Love	1973	8.00
EMI			
❑ 3627	Hooked on a Feeling/Gotta Have Your Love	1974	5.00
❑ 3893	Silly Milly/Lonely Sunday Afternoon	1974	4.00
❑ 3938	Never My Love/Pinewood Rally	1974	4.00
❑ 3938 [PS]	Never My Love/Pinewood Rally	1974	6.00
❑ 4029	Hush-I'm Alive/Lonely Summer Afternoon	1975	4.00
❑ 4065	Dr. Rock and Roll/Gotta Have Your Love	1975	4.00
Albums			
EMI			
❑ ST-11266	Hooked on a Feeling	1974	10.00
❑ ST-11346	Out of the Blue	1975	10.00

BLUE THINGS, THE

Number	Title (A Side/B Side)	Yr	NM
45s			
RCA VICTOR			
❑ 47-8692	I Must Be Doing Something Wrong/La Do Da Da	1965	25.00
❑ 47-8860	Doll House/Man on the Street	1966	25.00
❑ 47-8998	Orange Rooftop of Your Mind/One Hour Cleaners	1966	25.00
❑ 47-9203	Twist and Shout/You Can Live in Our Tree	1967	25.00
❑ 47-9308	Yes, My Friend/Somebody Help Me	1967	25.00
RUFF			
❑ 1000	Mary Lou/Your Turn to Cry	1965	40.00
❑ 1002	Pretty Thing/Just Two Days Ago	1965	40.00
Albums			
RCA VICTOR			
❑ LPM-3603 [M]	The Blue Things	1966	250.00
❑ LSP-3603 [S]	The Blue Things	1966	300.00

BLUE TONES, THE

Number	Title (A Side/B Side)	Yr	NM
45s			
BLUE JAY			
❑ 101	I'll Love You Till the End of Time/(Instrumental)	1965	150.00
—Reissued on Swan 4200 by "The Royal Teens"			

BLUE VELVET BAND, THE

Number	Title (A Side/B Side)	Yr	NM
45s			
WARNER BROS.			
❑ 7320	Hitch-Hiker/Sittin' on Top of the World	1969	8.00
Albums			
WARNER BROS.			
❑ WS 1802	Sweet Moments	1969	30.00

BLUENOTES, THE

Probably not related to any of the groups called THE BLUE NOTES, they were a white male vocal group from North Carolina.

Number	Title (A Side/B Side)	Yr	NM
45s			
BROOKE			
❑ 111	I Don't Know What It Is/You Can't Get Away from Love	1959	16.00
❑ 116	Forever on My Mind/I'm Gonna Find Out	1960	15.00
❑ 116 [PS]	Forever on My Mind/I'm Gonna Find Out	1960	30.00
❑ 119	It Had to be You/Summer Love	1960	15.00

BLUES CLIMAX

Number	Title (A Side/B Side)	Yr	NM
Albums			
HORNE			
❑ JC-333	Blues Climax	1969	60.00

BLUES IMAGE

Number	Title (A Side/B Side)	Yr	NM
45s			
ATCO			
❑ 6718	Lay Your Sweet Love on Me/Outside Was Night	1969	4.00
❑ 6746	Ride Captain Ride/Pay My Dues	1970	5.00
❑ 6777	Gas Lamps and Clay/Running the Water	1970	4.00
❑ 6798	Rise Up/Take Me Back	1971	4.00
❑ 6814	Behind Every Man/It's the Truth	1971	4.00
Albums			
ATCO			
❑ SD 33-300	Blues Image	1969	25.00
❑ SD 33-317	Open	1970	20.00
❑ SD 33-346	Red, White and Blues Image	1971	20.00

Except when noted otherwise, VG = 25% of NM, and VG+ = 50% of NM. (Example: VG = $2.00, VG+ = $4.00 and NM = $8.00.)

BLUES MAGOOS

45s

Number	Title (A Side/B Side)	Yr	NM
ABC			
❑ 11226	Heartbreak Hotel/I Can Feel It (Feelin' Time)	1969	8.00
❑ 11250	Never Goin' Back to Georgia/ Feelin' Time	1969	8.00
❑ 11283	Gulf Coast Bound/ Sea Breeze Express	1970	8.00
GANIM			
❑ 1000	Who Do You Love/ Let Your Love Ride	1968	40.00
MERCURY			
❑ 72590	Tobacco Road/Sometimes I Think About You	1966	50.00
❑ 72622	(We Ain't Got) Nothin' Yet/ Gotta Get Away	1966	20.00
❑ 72660	Pipe Dream/There's a Chance We Can Make It	1967	15.00
❑ 72660 [PS]	Pipe Dream/There's a Chance We Can Make It	1967	30.00
❑ 72692	One by One/Dante's Inferno	1967	15.00
❑ 72692 [PS]	One by One/Dante's Inferno	1967	30.00
❑ 72707	I Wanna Be There/ Summer Is the Man	1967	10.00
❑ 72729	Life Is Just a Cher O'Bowlies/ There She Goes	1967	10.00
❑ 72762	Jingle Bells/Santa Claus Is Coming to Town	1967	10.00
❑ 72838	I Can Hear the Grass Grow/ Yellow Rose	1968	10.00
❑ 872806-7	(We Ain't Got) Nothin' Yet/ Pipedream	1989	3.00
—Reissue			
VERVE FOLKWAYS			
❑ 5006	People Had No Faces/So I'm Wrong and You Are Right	1966	15.00
❑ 5006	People Had No Faces/So I'm Wrong and You Are Right	1966	20.00
—As "The Bloos Magoos"			
❑ 5044	People Had No Faces/So I'm Wrong and You Are Right	1967	15.00

Albums

Number	Title (A Side/B Side)	Yr	NM
ABC			
❑ S-697	Never Goin' Back to Georgia	1969	20.00
❑ S-710	Gulf Coast Bound	1970	20.00
MERCURY			
❑ MG-21096 [M]	Psychedelic Lollipop	1966	40.00
—With "21096" in trail-off; this record is mono			
❑ MG-21096 [S]	Psychedelic Lollipop	1966	40.00
—With "2/61096" in trail-off; this record plays stereo, though labeled mono			
❑ 21104/61104	Electric Comic Book Comic Book	1967	15.00
❑ MG-21104 [M]	Electric Comic Book	1967	30.00
❑ SR-61096	Psychedelic Lollipop	197?	12.00
—Reissue on Chicago skyline label			
❑ SR-61096 [S]	Psychedelic Lollipop	1966	50.00
❑ SR-61104 [S]	Electric Comic Book	1967	40.00
❑ SR-61167	Basic Blues Magoos	1968	30.00

BLUES PROJECT, THE

45s

Number	Title (A Side/B Side)	Yr	NM
CAPITOL			
❑ 3374	Crazy Girl/Easy Lady	1972	8.00
MCA			
❑ 40154	Fly Away/Louisiana Blues	1973	5.00
VERVE FOLKWAYS			
❑ 5004	Back Door Man/Violets of Dawn	1966	15.00
❑ 5013	Catch the Wind/I Want to Be Your Driver	1966	15.00
❑ 5019	Where There's Smoke There's Fire/Goin' Down Louisiana	1966	15.00
❑ 5019 [PS]	Where There's Smoke There's Fire/Goin' Down Louisiana	1966	25.00
❑ 5032	I Can't Keep from Crying Sometimes/The Way My Baby Walks	1966	15.00
❑ 5040	No Time Like the Right Time/ Steve's Song	1967	12.00
VERVE FORECAST			
❑ 5063	Gentle Dreams/ Lost in the Shuffle	1967	12.00

Albums

Number	Title (A Side/B Side)	Yr	NM
CAPITOL			
❑ ST-782	Lazarus	1971	12.00
❑ SMAS-11017	The Blues Project	1972	12.00
MCA			
❑ 8003 [(2)]	Reunion in Central Park	1975	15.00
—Reissue of Sounds of the South LP; black rainbow labels			
❑ 25984 [(2)]	Reunion in Central Park	1987	12.00
—Reissue of MCA 8003; blue rainbow labels			
MGM			
❑ GAS-118	The Blues Project	1970	12.00
❑ M3G-4953	Archetypes	1974	12.00
RHINO			
❑ R1-70165	No Time Like the Right Time: The Best of the Blues Project	1989	12.00
SOUNDS OF THE SOUTH			
❑ MCA2-8003 [(2)]	Reunion in Central Park	1973	20.00
—Yellow labels			
VERVE			
❑ 827918-1	Projections	1986	8.00
—Reissue			
VERVE FOLKWAYS			
❑ FT-3000 [M]	Live at the Café a Go Go	1966	20.00
❑ FTS-3000 [S]	Live at the Café a Go Go	1966	25.00
❑ FT-3008 [M]	Projections	1966	20.00
❑ FTS-3008 [S]	Projections	1966	25.00
VERVE FORECAST			
❑ FT-3000 [M]	Live at the Café a Go Go	1967	15.00
—Reissue of Verve Folkways 3000			
❑ FTS-3000 [S]	Live at the Café a Go Go	1967	20.00
—Reissue of Verve Folkways 3000			
❑ FT-3008 [M]	Projections	1967	15.00
—Reissue of Verve Folkways 3008			
❑ FTS-3008 [S]	Projections	1967	20.00
—Reissue of Verve Folkways 3008			
❑ FT-3025 [M]	The Blues Project Live at Town Hall	1967	20.00
❑ FTS-3025 [S]	The Blues Project Live at Town Hall	1967	15.00
❑ FTS-3046	Planned Obsolescence	1968	15.00
❑ FTS-3069	Flanders/Kalb/Katz, Etc.	1969	15.00
❑ FTS-3077	Best of the Blues Project	1969	15.00

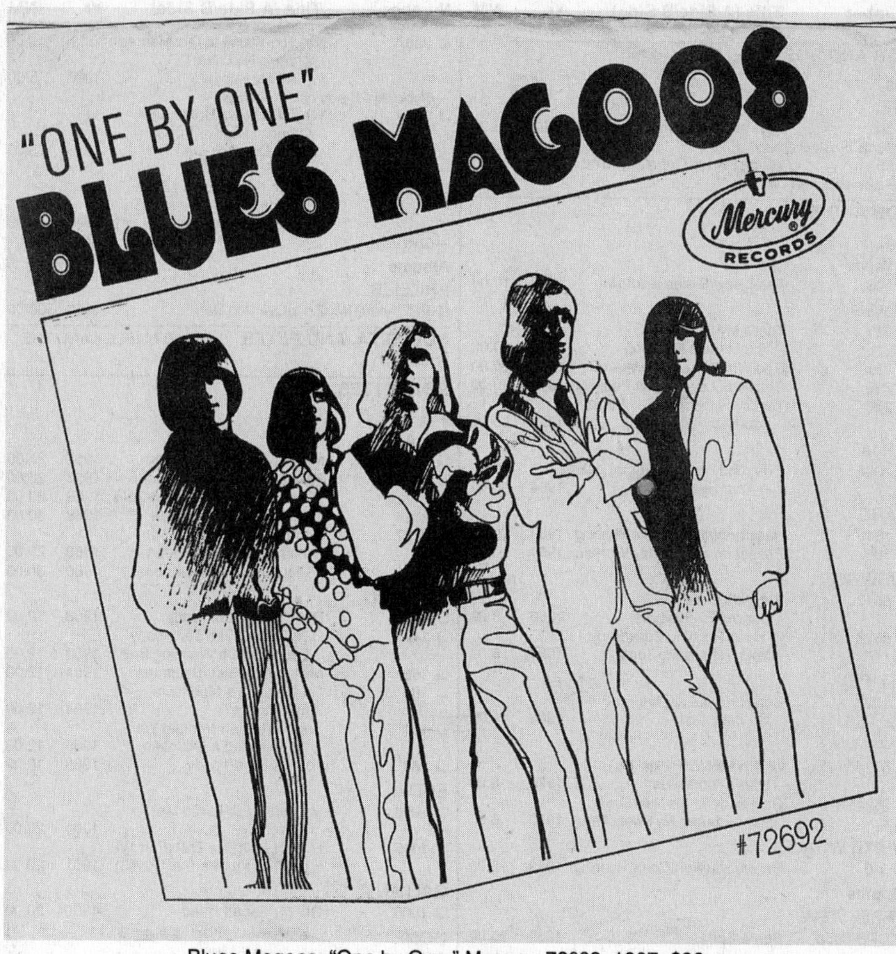

Blues Magoos, "One by One," Mercury 72692, 1967, **$30.**

BLUES TRAVELER

45s

Number	Title (A Side/B Side)	Yr	NM
A&M			
❑ 31458 1174 1	Hook/Run-Around	1995	4.00

Albums

Number	Title (A Side/B Side)	Yr	NM
A&M			
❑ 75021 5308 1	Blues Traveler	1990	15.00

BLUNSTONE, COLIN

Also see THE ZOMBIES.

45s

Number	Title (A Side/B Side)	Yr	NM
EPIC			
❑ 10826	Caroline Goodbye/Misty Roses	1972	5.00
❑ 10868	Say You Don't Mind/ Though You Are Far Away	1972	5.00
❑ 10948	I Don't Believe in Miracles/ I've Always Had You	1973	5.00
❑ 10981	Pay Me Later/I Want Some More	1973	5.00
❑ 11004	Andorra/Carolina Goodbye	1973	5.00
ROCKET			
❑ PB-11356	I'll Never Forget You/ You Are the Way for Me	1978	4.00
❑ PB-11412	Photograph/Touch and Go	1978	4.00

Albums

Number	Title (A Side/B Side)	Yr	NM
EPIC			
❑ E 30974	One Year	1972	12.00
❑ KE 31994	Ennismore	1972	12.00
❑ KE 32962	Journey	1974	12.00
ROCKET			
❑ BXL1-2093	Never Even Thought	1978	10.00

BO GRUMPUS

Albums

Number	Title (A Side/B Side)	Yr	NM
ATCO			
❑ 33-246 [M]	Bo Grumpus	1968	30.00
❑ SD 33-246 [S]	Bo Grumpus	1968	20.00

BO PETE

See NILSSON.

BOA

Albums

Number	Title (A Side/B Side)	Yr	NM
SNAKEFIELD			
❑ SN-001	Wrong Road	1971	500.00

BOB AND BOBBIE

Number	Title (A Side/B Side)	Yr	NM
45s			
HIT			
50	Hey Paula/I Saw Linda Yesterday	1963	8.00
—B-side by Dave Gibson			
58	Young Lovers/Out of My Mind	1963	8.00
—B-side by Jackie Ott			

BOB AND EARL

Number	Title (A Side/B Side)	Yr	NM
45s			
CHENE			
103	The Sissy/(B-side unknown)	1964	10.00
CLASS			
213	That's My Desire/You Made a Boo-Boo	1957	40.00
231	Gee Whiz/When She Walks	1958	30.00
232	Chains of Love/Sweet Pea	1958	30.00
247	That's My Desire/You Made a Boo-Boo	1959	25.00
LOMA			
2004	Everybody Jerk/Just One Look in Your Eyes	1964	10.00
MARC			
104	Harlem Shuffle/I'll Come Running	1963	20.00
105	Puppet on a String/My Woman	1964	20.00
MIRWOOD			
5517	Baby It's Over/Dancin' Everywhere	1966	8.00
5526	I'll Keep Running Back/Baby, Your Time Is My Time	1966	8.00
TEMPE			
102	Don't Ever Leave Me/Oh Baby Doll	1962	15.00
UNI			
55196	Uh Uh No No/(Pickin' Up) Love's Vibrations	1970	6.00
55248	Get Ready for the New Day/Honey, Sugar, My Sweet Thing	1970	6.00
WHITE WHALE			
310	Harlem Shuffle/I'll Come Running	1969	12.00
Albums			
CRESTVIEW			
CRS-3055	Bob & Earl	1969	25.00
TIP			
TLP-1011 [M]	Harlem Shuffle	1964	30.00
TLS-9011 [S]	Harlem Shuffle	1964	50.00

BOB AND LUCILLE

Number	Title (A Side/B Side)	Yr	NM
45s			
DITTO			
121	What's the Password/Demon Lover	1962	80.00
126	Eeny-Meeny-Miney-Moe/The Big Kiss	1962	80.00
DOT			
17327	Dream Baby/Southbound Plane	1969	8.00
—As "Bob Regan and Lucille Starr"			
KING			
5631	Eeny-Meeny-Miney-Moe/The Big Kiss	1962	30.00

BOB AND SHERI

Number	Title (A Side/B Side)	Yr	NM
45s			
SAFARI			
101 [DJ]	The Surfer Moon/Humpty Dumpty	1962	1000.
—White label			
101	The Surfer Moon/Humpty Dumpty	1962	4000.
—Light blue label (other colors and colored vinyl are reproductions or counterfeits). VG 2000; VG+ 3000			

BOB B. SOXX AND THE BLUE JEANS

Number	Title (A Side/B Side)	Yr	NM
45s			
PHILLES			
107	Zip-a-Dee-Doo-Dah/Flip and Nitty	1962	20.00
110	Why Do Lovers Break Each Other's Heart?/Dr. Kaplan's Office	1963	20.00
113	Not Too Young to Get Married/Annette	1963	20.00
PHILLES/COLLECTABLES			
3207	Not Too Young to Get Married/There's No Other (Like My Baby)	1985	6.00
—Gold vinyl; part of box set "Phil Spector Wall of Sound Series Vol. 1"; B-side by the Crystals			
3207	Not Too Young to Get Married/There's No Other (Like My Baby)	1986	5.00
—Black vinyl; B-side by the Crystals			
3209	Why Do Lovers Break Each Other's Heart/Zip-a-Dee Doo-Dah	1985	5.00
—Black vinyl			
3209	Why Do Lovers Break Each Other's Heart/Zip-a-Dee Doo-Dah	1985	6.00
—Gold vinyl			
Albums			
PHILLIES			
PHLP-4002 [M]	Zip-a-Dee Doo-Dah	1963	500.00

BOB, RITA, AND PETER

See BOB MARLEY AND THE WAILERS.

BOBBETTES, THE

Number	Title (A Side/B Side)	Yr	NM
45s			
ATLANTIC			
1144	Mr. Lee/Look at the Stars	1957	25.00
1159	Speedy/Come-a Come-a	1957	20.00
1181	Zoomy/Rock and Ree-Ah-Zole	1958	20.00
1194	The Dream/Um Bow Bow	1958	20.00
2027	Don't Say Goodnight/You Are My Sweetheart	1959	20.00
2069	I Shot Mr. Lee/Untrue Love	1960	30.00
DIAMOND			
133	Row, Row, Row/Teddy	1963	12.00
142	Close Your Eyes/Somebody Bad Stole De Wedding Bell	1963	12.00
156	My Mamma Said/Sandman	1964	12.00
166	I'm Climbing a Mountain/In Paradise	1964	12.00
181	You Ain't Seen Nothing Yet/I'm Climbing a Mountain	1965	12.00
189	Love Is Blind/Teddy	1965	12.00
END			
1093	Mr. Johnny Q/Teach Me Tonight	1961	20.00
1095	I Don't Like It Like That (Part 1)/I Don't Like It Like That (Part 2)	1961	20.00
GALLANT			
1006	Oh, My Papa/I Cried	1960	20.00
GONE			
5112	I Don't Like It Like That (Part 1)/Mr. Johnny Q	1961	15.00
JUBILEE			
5427	Over There/Loneliness	1962	12.00
5442	The Broken Heart/Mama, Papa	1962	12.00
KING			
5490	Oh My Papa/Dance With Me Georgie	1961	15.00
5551	Are You Satisfied/Looking for a Lover	1961	15.00
5623	I'm Stepping Out Tonight/My Dearest	1962	15.00
RCA VICTOR			
47-8832	I've Gotta Face the World/Having Fun	1966	15.00
47-8983	It's All Over/Happy-v-Lucky Me	1966	15.00
TRIPLE-X			
104	I Shot Mr. Lee/Billy	1960	20.00
106	Have Mercy Baby/Dance with Me Georgie	1960	20.00

BOBBIE & BOOBIE

Number	Title (A Side/B Side)	Yr	NM
45s			
DICE			
480	Cool, Cool Christmas/Teenage Party	195?	200.00

BOBBIE JEAN

Number	Title (A Side/B Side)	Yr	NM
45s			
SUN			
342	You Burned the Bridges/Cheaters Never Win	1960	20.00

BOBBY AND BUDDY

Number	Title (A Side/B Side)	Yr	NM
45s			
HIT			
162	Just Give Me Time/or Wrong	1964	8.00
—B-side by Marty Wood			
180	Willow Weep for Me/Bless You Little Girl	1965	8.00
238	Michelle/My Love	1966	10.00
—B-side by Betty York			
246	Woman/Homeward Bound	1966	8.00
—B-side by Sammy and Theodore			

BOBBY AND CONNIE

Number	Title (A Side/B Side)	Yr	NM
45s			
HIT			
281	The Beat Goes On/Sock It To Me Baby	1967	8.00
—B-side by the Jalopy Five			
286	Something Stupid/Dedicated to the One I Love	1967	8.00
—B-side by the Chords (2)			

BOBBY AND HIS ORBITS

Number	Title (A Side/B Side)	Yr	NM
45s			
GONE			
5126	Your Cheatin' Heart/I Don't Stand a Chance	1962	25.00
SEECO			
6005	Felicia/Bandstand Dancing	1959	80.00
6030	Teen Age Love/What Do I Say (When I'm Close to You)	1960	50.00

BOBBY AND THE DUKES

Number	Title (A Side/B Side)	Yr	NM
45s			
PHILIPS			
40293	Ah, Ah, Ah/Come On Along with Me	1965	20.00

BOBBY THE POET

See SENATOR BOBBY.

BOBO, WILLIE

Number	Title (A Side/B Side)	Yr	NM
45s			
BLUE NOTE			
XW977	Kojak Theme/Dreamin'	1977	5.00
CAPITOL			
4253	Funky Sneakers/Funky Sneakers (Part 2)	1976	4.00
COLUMBIA			
10862	Fairytales for Two/Always There	1978	4.00
TICO			
T-433	Diferente/Be's That Way	196?	10.00
VERVE			
CS?-5	Celebrity Scene: Willie Bobo	1967	50.00
—Box set of five singles (10472-10476). Price includes box, all 5 singles, jukebox title strips, bio. Records are sometimes found by themselves, so they are also listed separately.			
10374	Hurt So Bad/It's Not Unusual	1966	8.00
10400	1-2-3 (Uno, Dos, Tres)/Fried Neckbones and Home Fries	1966	8.00
10448	Sockit To Me/Sunshine Superman	1967	8.00
10472	Sunshine Superman/Call Me	1967	8.00
10473	Hurt So Bad/Boogaloo in Room 802	1967	8.00
10474	Blues in the Closet/Spanish Grease	1967	8.00
10475	Sockit To Me/1-2-3 (Uno, Dos, Tres)	1967	8.00
10476	Fried Neckbones and Home Fries/Feelin' So Good	1967	8.00
10482	Shing-a-Ling Baby/Juicy	1967	6.00
10518	Ain't Too Proud to Beg/Knock on Wood	1967	6.00
10550	Evil Ways/Up, Up and Away	1967	6.00
10593	Move It On Over/Tweedlee Dee	1968	6.00
Albums			
BLUE NOTE			
BN-LA711-G	Tomorrow Is Here	1977	40.00
COLUMBIA			
JC 35734	Hell of an Act to Follow	1978	40.00
—Reproductions exist			
JC 36108	Bobo	1979	30.00
—Reproductions exist			
MGM			
LAT-10007	Spanish Grease	197?	40.00
LAT-10011	Uno, Dos, Tres	197?	40.00
LAT-10012	Spanish Blues Band	197?	40.00
ROULETTE			
R-52097 [M]	Bobo's Beat	1962	60.00
SR-52097 [S]	Bobo's Beat	1962	80.00
SUSSEX			
SXBS-7003	Do What You Want to Do	1971	40.00
—Reproductions exist			
TICO			
ST-1108 [S]	Do That Thing	1963	80.00
—Reproductions exist			
T-1108 [M]	Do That Thing	1963	60.00
TRIP			
5013	Latin Beat	1974	10.00
VERVE			
V-8631 [M]	Spanish Grease	1965	30.00
V6-8631 [S]	Spanish Grease	1965	40.00
V-8648 [M]	Uno, Dos, Tres	1966	30.00

Except when noted otherwise, VG = 25% of NM, and VG+ = 50% of NM. (Example: VG = $2.00, VG+ = $4.00 and NM = $8.00.)

Number	Title (A Side/B Side)	Yr	NM
❑ V6-8648 [S]	Uno, Dos, Tres	1966	40.00
❑ V-8669 [M]	Feelin' So Good	1966	40.00
❑ V6-8669 [S]	Feelin' So Good	1966	50.00
❑ V-8685 [M]	Juicy	1967	40.00
❑ V6-8685 [S]	Juicy	1967	40.00
❑ V-8699 [M]	Bobo Motion	1967	40.00
❑ V6-8699 [S]	Bobo Motion	1967	40.00
❑ V-8736 [M]	Spanish Blues Band	1968	60.00
—May be promo only			
❑ V6-8736 [S]	Spanish Blues Band	1968	40.00
❑ V6-8772	A New Dimension	1969	50.00
❑ V6-8781	Evil Ways	1969	40.00

BOCEPHUS See HANK WILLIAMS, JR.

BOCKY AND THE VISIONS

45s

PHILIPS

Number	Title (A Side/B Side)	Yr	NM
❑ 40224	Mojo Hanna/Spirit of '64	1964	25.00
❑ 40242	I'm Pickin' Petals/I'm Not Worth It	1964	25.00

BODACIOUS D.F. MARTY BALIN was in this group.

Albums

RCA VICTOR

Number	Title (A Side/B Side)	Yr	NM
❑ AFL1-0206	Bodacious D.F.	1977	10.00
❑ APL1-0206	Bodacious D.F.	1973	15.00
❑ AYL1-4243	Bodacious D.F.	1982	8.00
—"Best Buy Series reissue			

BOENZEE CRYQUE With Rusty Young, later of POCO.

45s

CHICORY

Number	Title (A Side/B Side)	Yr	NM
❑ 406	Sky Gone Gray/ Still in Love with You Baby	1966	30.00

UNI

Number	Title (A Side/B Side)	Yr	NM
❑ 55012	Sky Gone Gray/Still in Love with You Baby	1967	20.00
❑ 55022	Watch the Time/You Won't Believe It's True	1967	20.00

BOETCHER, CURT

45s

ELEKTRA

Number	Title (A Side/B Side)	Yr	NM
❑ 45834	I Love You More Each Day/ Such a Lady	1973	5.00

Albums

ELEKTRA

Number	Title (A Side/B Side)	Yr	NM
❑ EKS-75037	There's an Innocent Face	1972	20.00

BOFFALONGO

45s

UNITED ARTISTS

Number	Title (A Side/B Side)	Yr	NM
❑ 50607	Tomorrow Not Today/ Mr. Go Away	1969	8.00
❑ 50656	Please Stay/Mr. Go Away	1970	8.00
❑ 50699	Dancing in the Moonlight/ Endless Question	1970	8.00

Albums

UNITED ARTISTS

Number	Title (A Side/B Side)	Yr	NM
❑ UAS-6726	Boffalongo	1969	20.00
❑ UAS-6770	Beyond Your Head	1970	20.00

BOHANNON

12-Inch Singles

COMPLEAT

Number	Title (A Side/B Side)	Yr	NM
❑ CK 101 [DJ]	Rock Your Body (Part 1 and 2)	1983	8.00
❑ CPD 201	Make Your Body Move/ Come Back My Love	1983	7.00
❑ CPD 203	Don't Leave Me (same on both sides?)	1983	10.00
❑ CPD 204	Let's Start the Dance III (2 versions)	1983	8.00
❑ CPD 207	South Africa (2 versions)	1984	8.00

MCA

Number	Title (A Side/B Side)	Yr	NM
❑ L33-17946 [DJ]	House Train (Extended 7:15) (Radio Edit 5:28) (Instrumental 6:48) (Bonus Beats 6:37)	1989	8.00
❑ L33-18106 [DJ]	The Gang's All Here (Vocal) (Dub)/Over the Rainbow	1990	10.00
❑ 23522	Motions (Vocal)/(Instrumental)	1984	10.00
❑ 23967	House Train (2 versions)	1989	6.00
❑ 23997	The Gang's All Here/ Over the Rainbow	1990	10.00

MERCURY

Number	Title (A Side/B Side)	Yr	NM
❑ MK 49 [DJ]	Maybe You Can Dance (12:42)/ I Found My Love	1977	15.00
❑ MK 77 [DJ]	Cut Loose (7:44)/The Beat Part 2 (6:14)	1979	10.00
❑ MK 128 [DJ]	Feel Like Dancin' (7:24)/ The Funk Walk (6:02)	1980	10.00
❑ DS 2001	Bohannon Disco Symphony/ Andrea	1977	15.00
❑ MDS 3002	Cut Loose (7:44)/The Beat Part 2 (6:14)	1979	12.00
❑ 888143-1	Jammin' in the Street (Part 1 6:02) (Part 2 5:12)	1986	8.00

PHASE II

Number	Title (A Side/B Side)	Yr	NM
❑ AS 857 [DJ]	Throw Down the Groove (Part 1 and 2)	1980	12.00
❑ AS 961 [DJ]	Goin' for Another One/ The Happy Dance	1981	12.00
❑ AS 1357 [DJ]	Take the Country to New York City (5:49)/(Instrumental 4:31)	1982	12.00
❑ AS 1497 [DJ]	The Party Train (Parts 1 and 2)	1982	8.00
❑ 4W8-02133	Goin' for Another One/ The Happy Dance	1981	12.00
❑ 4W8-02146	Foot Stompin' in the Summertime/(Instrumental)	1981	12.00
❑ 4Z9-02876	I've Got the Dance Fever (With Rap Intro)/(Without Intro)	1982	10.00

45s

COMPLEAT

Number	Title (A Side/B Side)	Yr	NM
❑ 103	Make Your Body Move/ Come Back My Love	1983	4.00
❑ 107	Don't Leave Me/Funkville	1983	4.00
❑ 114	Wake Up/Enjoy Your Day	1983	4.00
❑ 118	Rock Your Body/(Instrumental)	1983	4.00
❑ 148	South Africa/South Africa (Special Mix)	1984	4.00

DAKAR

Number	Title (A Side/B Side)	Yr	NM
❑ 4518	Save Their Souls/Stop and Go	1973	6.00
❑ 4521	The Pimpwalk/Happiness	1973	6.00
❑ 4525	Run It On Down Mr. DJ (Part 1)/ Run It On Down Mr. DJ (Part 2)	1973	6.00
❑ 4528	Fat Man/Red Bone	1974	6.00
❑ 4534	Happiness/Truck Stop	1974	6.00
❑ 4535	Keep On Dancin' (Part 1)/ Keep On Dancin' (Part 2)	1974	6.00
❑ 4539	South African Music (Pt. 1)/ Have a Good Day	1974	5.00
❑ 4544	Foot Stompin' Music/ Dance with Your Partner	1975	5.00
❑ 4549	Disco Stomp (Part 1)/ Disco Stomp (Part 2)	1975	5.00
❑ 4551	Bohannon's Beat (Pt. 1)/ East Coast Groove	1975	5.00
❑ 4554	Dance Your Ass Off/ Happy Feeling	1976	5.00
❑ 4560	Gittin' Off/Come Winter	1976	5.00

MCA

Number	Title (A Side/B Side)	Yr	NM
❑ 53685	House Train/(Instrumental)	1989	3.00
❑ 53766	The Gang's All Here/ Over the Rainbow	1989	3.00

MERCURY

Number	Title (A Side/B Side)	Yr	NM
❑ 73939	Bohannon Disco Symphony/ Moving Fast	1977	4.00
❑ 73946	Just Doing My Thing/Andrea	1977	4.00
❑ 74015	Let's Start the Dance/ I Wonder Why	1978	4.00
❑ 74035	Me and the Gang/ Summertime Groove	1978	4.00
❑ 74044	Cut Loose/Listen to the Children Play	1979	4.00
❑ 74085	The Groove Machine/ Love Floats	1979	4.00
❑ 76040	Feel Like Dancin'/Funk Walk	1980	4.00
❑ 76054	Baby I'm for Real/ Hurry Mr. Sunshine	1980	4.00
❑ 888143-7	Jammin' in the Street/ (B-side unknown)	1986	3.00

PHASE II

Number	Title (A Side/B Side)	Yr	NM
❑ WS8-02062	Goin' for Another One/ The Happy Dance	1981	4.00
❑ WS8-02145	Foot Stompin' in the Summertime/(Instrumental)	1981	4.00
❑ WS9-02573	Let's Start II Dance Again/ Let's Start the Dance	1981	4.00
❑ ZS5-02682	Take the Country to New York City (Part 1 and 2)	1982	4.00
❑ ZS5-02897	I've Got the Dance Fever (With Rap Intro)/(Without Intro)	1982	4.00
❑ ZS5-02998	The Party Train (Parts I & II)/ Thoughts and Wishes	1982	4.00
❑ 5650	Throw Down the Groove (Part I)/ Throw Down the Groove (Part II)	1980	4.00
❑ 5651	Dance, Dance, Dance All Night/ April My Love (Part 1)	1980	4.00
❑ 5654	Don't Be Ashame to Call My Name/(B-side unknown)	1981	4.00

Albums

COMPLEAT

Number	Title (A Side/B Side)	Yr	NM
❑ CPL-1-1003	Make Your Body Move	1983	10.00
❑ CPL-1-1005	The Bohannon Drive	1984	12.00

DAKAR

Number	Title (A Side/B Side)	Yr	NM
❑ 6910	Keep On Dancing	1973	12.00
❑ 76916	Insides Out	1974	12.00
❑ DK 76917	Bohannon	1975	15.00
❑ DK 76919	Dance Your Ass Off	1976	15.00
❑ DK 76921	Gittin' Off	1976	20.00

MCA

Number	Title (A Side/B Side)	Yr	NM
❑ 42310	Here Comes Bohannon	1989	12.00

MERCURY

Number	Title (A Side/B Side)	Yr	NM
❑ SRM-1-1159	Phase II	1977	10.00
❑ SRM-1-3710	On My Way	1978	10.00
❑ SRM-1-3728	Summertime Groove	1978	10.00
❑ SRM-1-3762	Cut Loose	1979	10.00
❑ SRM-1-3778	Too Hot to Hold	1979	10.00
❑ SRM-1-3813	Music in the Air	1980	10.00

PHASE II

Number	Title (A Side/B Side)	Yr	NM
❑ JW 36867	One Step Ahead	1980	10.00
❑ FZ 37695	Alive	1981	10.00
❑ FZ 38113	Bohannon Fever	1982	10.00

BOHEMIAN VENDETTA

45s

MAINSTREAM

Number	Title (A Side/B Side)	Yr	NM
❑ 681	Riddles and Fairytales/ I Wanna Touch Your Heart	1968	20.00

UNITED ARTISTS

Number	Title (A Side/B Side)	Yr	NM
❑ 50174	Talk the Time/Enough	1967	25.00

Albums

MAINSTREAM

Number	Title (A Side/B Side)	Yr	NM
❑ S-6106 [S]	Bohemian Vendetta	1968	500.00
❑ 56106 [M]	Bohemian Vendetta	1968	500.00

BOLD

45s

CAMEO

Number	Title (A Side/B Side)	Yr	NM
❑ 430	Gotta Get Some/Robin Hood	1966	25.00

DYNOVOICE

Number	Title (A Side/B Side)	Yr	NM
❑ 232	The Train Kept a-Rollin'/Found What I Was Lookin' For	1967	30.00
—As "Steve Walker and the Bold"			

Albums

ABC

Number	Title (A Side/B Side)	Yr	NM
❑ ABCS-705	Bold	1969	75.00

BOLDER DAMN

Albums

HIT

Number	Title (A Side/B Side)	Yr	NM
❑ HRI-5061	Mourning	1971	1000.

BOLIN, TOMMY Also see THE JAMES GANG; ZEPHYR; DEEP PURPLE.

45s

NEMPEROR

Number	Title (A Side/B Side)	Yr	NM
❑ 004	The Grind/Homeward Strut	1976	8.00
❑ 005	Savannah Woman/ Marching Power	1976	8.00

Albums

COLUMBIA

Number	Title (A Side/B Side)	Yr	NM
❑ PC 34329	Private Eyes	1976	12.00
—Original with no bar code on cover			
❑ PC 34329	Private Eyes	198?	8.00
—With bar code on cover			

GEFFEN

Number	Title (A Side/B Side)	Yr	NM
❑ 3GHS 24248 [(3)]	The Ultimate Tommy Bolin	1989	30.00

NEMPEROR

Number	Title (A Side/B Side)	Yr	NM
❑ NE 436	Teaser	1975	12.00
❑ PZ 37534	Teaser	1982	8.00

BOLL WEEVILS, THE

45s

HIT

Number	Title (A Side/B Side)	Yr	NM
❑ 107	Please Please Me/My Bonnie	1964	12.00

BOLTON, MICHAEL Includes records as "Michael Bolotin."

12-Inch Singles

COLUMBIA

Number	Title (A Side/B Side)	Yr	NM
❑ 44-07581	(Sittin' On) The Dock of the Bay (4 versions)	1988	10.00

45s

COLUMBIA

Number	Title (A Side/B Side)	Yr	NM
❑ 38-03800	Fools Game/Fighting for My Life	1983	4.00
❑ 38-04154	I Almost Believed You/ She Did the Same Thing	1983	4.00
❑ 38-04823	Everybody's Crazy/ She Did the Same Thing	1985	3.00
❑ 38-7322	That's What Love Is All About/ Take a Look at My Face	1987	3.00
—U.S. editions are missing the usual "0" after the "38"			
❑ 38-07680	(Sittin' On) The Dock of the Bay/ Call My Name	1988	3.00
❑ 38-07680 [PS]	(Sittin' On) The Dock of the Bay/ Call My Name	1988	3.00

Except when noted otherwise, VG = 25% of NM, and VG+ = 50% of NM. (Example: VG = \$2.00, VG+ = \$4.00 and NM = \$8.00.)

B

Bon Jovi, *New Jersey*, Mercury 836345-1, 1988, $8.

Number	Title (A Side/B Side)	Yr	NM
❑ 38-07680 [PS]	(Sittin' On) The Dock of the Bay/ Call My Name	1988	12.00
—Promo-only sleeve with a message from Mrs. Otis Redding on the back			
❑ 38-07794	Wait on Love/I Almost Believed You	1988	3.00
❑ 38-07794 [PS]	Wait on Love/I Almost Believed You	1988	3.00
❑ 38-07983	Walk Away/The Hunger	1988	3.00
❑ 38-68909	Soul Provider/The Hunger	1989	3.00
❑ 38-73017	How Am I Supposed to Live Without You/Forever Eyes	1989	3.00
❑ 38-73318	How Can We Be Lovers/ That's What Love Is All About	1990	3.00
❑ 38-73342	When I'm Back on My Feet Again/Walk Away	1990	3.00
❑ 38-73490	Georgia on My Mind/ Take a Look at My Face	1990	3.00
❑ 38-73719	Love Is a Wonderful Thing/ Soul Provider	1991	3.00
❑ 38-73889	Time, Love and Tenderness/ That's What Love Is All About	1991	3.00
❑ 38-74020	When a Man Loves a Woman/ Save Me	1991	3.00
❑ 38-74184	Missing You Now/ It's Only My Heart	1992	3.00
❑ 38-74733	To Love Somebody/ Now That I've Found You	1992	3.00
❑ 38-74798	Reach Out I'll Be There/ White Christmas	1992	4.00
❑ 38-77260	Said I Loved You...But I Lied/ Soul Provider	1993	3.00
❑ 38-77376	Completely/That's What Love Is All About	1994	3.00
❑ 38-77991	Can I Touch You...There?/ Ain't Got Nothing If You Ain't Got Love	1995	3.00
RCA			
❑ PB-10650	You Make Me Feel Like Lovin' You/If I Had Your Lovin'	1976	10.00
—As "Michael Bolotin"			
RCA VICTOR			
❑ PB-10283	Your Love/Dream While You Can	1975	10.00
—As "Michael Bolotin"			
Albums			
COLUMBIA			
❑ BFC 38357	Michael Bolton	1983	10.00
❑ PC 38357	Michael Bolton	1985	6.00
—Reissue with new prefix			
❑ BFC 39328	Everybody's Crazy	1985	10.00
❑ FC 40473	The Hunger	1987	8.00
❑ OC 45012	Soul Provider	1989	10.00
❑ C 46771	Time, Love and Tenderness	1991	15.00
RCA VICTOR			
❑ APL1-0992	Michael Bolotin	1975	20.00
—As "Michael Bolotin"			
❑ APL1-1551	Every Day of My Life	1976	20.00
—As "Michael Bolotin"			

BON BONS, THE

Number	Title (A Side/B Side)	Yr	NM
45s			
CORAL			
❑ 62402	What's Wrong with Ringo/ Come On Baby	1964	60.00
❑ 62435	Everybody Wants My Boyfriend/ Each Time	1964	50.00

BON JOVI

Number	Title (A Side/B Side)	Yr	NM
12-Inch Singles			
MERCURY			
❑ PRO 266-1 [DJ]	She Don't Know Me/Breakout	1984	50.00
❑ PRO 347-1 [DJ]	Only Lonely (Edit) (LP Version)	1985	20.00
❑ PRO 381-1 [DJ]	Silent Night (same on both sides)	1986	50.00
—With "The Best Kept Secret in Rock and Roll" gatefold picture cover			
❑ PRO 434-1 [DJ]	You Give Love a Bad Name (same on both sides)	1986	60.00
—With "wet T-shirt" picture cover			
❑ PRO 463-1 [DJ]	Livin' on a Prayer (same on both sides)	1986	20.00
❑ PRO 496-1 [DJ]	Wanted Dead or Alive (Special Rock Radio Edit) (Special Rock Radio Long Version)	1987	20.00
❑ PRO 635-1 [DJ]	Bad Medicine (Edit Version) (same on both sides?)	1988	20.00
❑ 874453-1	Lay Your Hands on Me (Edit)/ Runaway (Live)	1989	8.00
45s			
COLLECTABLES			
❑ 4269	Youy Give Love a Bad Name/ Livin' on a Prayer	199?	3.00
—Reissue			
ISLAND			
❑ 440 063935-7	Everyday (same on both sides)	2002	3.00
❑ 314-562801-7	It's My Life/Next 100 Years	2000	4.00
❑ 314-572770-7	Thank You for Loving Me/ Bed of Roses	2001	4.00
—Red vinyl			
JAMBCO			
❑ 862088-7	In These Arms/Say a Prayer	1993	4.00
❑ 862428-7	I'll Sleep When I'm Dead/ Never Say Goodbye	1993	4.00
❑ 864432-7	Keep the Faith/I Wish Everyday Could Be Like Christmas	1992	5.00
❑ 864852-7	Bed of Roses/Lay Your Hands on Me	1993	4.00
MERCURY			
❑ 818309-7	Runaway/Love Lies	1984	4.00
❑ 818309-7 [PS]	Runaway/Love Lies	1984	5.00
❑ 818958-7	She Don't Know Me/ Burning for Love	1984	10.00
❑ 818958-7 [PS]	She Don't Know Me/ Burning for Love	1984	8.00
❑ 852296-7	Something for the Pain/ Lie to Me	1995	4.00
❑ 856226-7	Always/Living in Sin	1994	4.00
❑ 856824-7	This Ain't a Love Song/Always (Live at A&M Studios)	1995	4.00
❑ 870657-7	Bad Medicine/99 in the Shade	1988	3.00
❑ 870657-7 [PS]	Bad Medicine/99 in the Shade	1988	3.00
❑ 872156-7	Born to Be My Baby/ Love for Sale	1988	3.00
❑ 872156-7 [PS]	Born to Be My Baby/ Love for Sale	1988	3.00
❑ 872564-7	I'll Be There for You/ Homebound Train	1989	3.00
❑ 872564-7 [PS]	I'll Be There for You/ Homebound Train	1989	3.00
❑ 874452-7	Lay Your Hands on Me/ Runaway (Live)	1989	3.00
❑ 874452-7 [PS]	Lay Your Hands on Me/ Runaway (Live)	1989	3.00
❑ 876070-7	Living in Sin/Love Is War	1989	3.00
❑ 876070-7 [PS]	Living in Sin/Love Is War	1989	3.00
❑ 880736-7	Only Lonely/Always Run to You	1985	6.00
❑ 880736-7 [PS]	Only Lonely/Always Run to You	1985	6.00
❑ 880951-7	In and Out of Love/Breakout	1985	6.00
❑ 884299-7	Silent Night/Price of Love	1986	10.00
❑ 884660-7	Runaway/She Don't Know Me	1986	3.00
—Reissue			
❑ 884953-7	You Give Love a Bad Name/ Raise Your Hands	1986	3.00
❑ 884953-7 [PS]	You Give Love a Bad Name/ Raise Your Hands	1986	3.00
❑ 888184-7	Livin' on a Prayer/ Wild in the Streets	1986	3.00
❑ 888184-7 [PS]	Livin' on a Prayer/ Wild in the Streets	1986	3.00
❑ 888396-7	Never Say Goodbye/ Social Disease	1987	—
—Never issued in U.S.			
❑ 888467-7	Wanted Dead or Alive/ I'd Die for You	1987	3.00
❑ 888467-7 [PS]	Wanted Dead or Alive/ I'd Die for You	1987	3.00
Albums			
MERCURY			
❑ 814982-1	Bon Jovi	1984	8.00
❑ 824509-1	7800 Fahrenheit	1985	8.00
❑ 830264-1	Slippery When Wet	1986	8.00
❑ 830822-1	Slippery When Wet	1986	15.00
—Picture disc in plastic cover			
❑ 836345-1	New Jersey	1988	8.00
❑ 836499-1	New Jersey	1988	15.00
—Picture disc in plastic sleeve			

BON JOVI, JON

Number	Title (A Side/B Side)	Yr	NM
45s			
COLLECTABLES			
❑ 4840	Blaze of Glory/Miracle	199?	3.00
—Reissue			
MERCURY			
❑ 875896-7	Blaze of Glory/You Really Got Me Now	1990	3.00
❑ 878392-7	Miracle/Blood Money	1990	3.00
Albums			
MERCURY			
❑ 846473-1	Blaze of Glory (Young Guns II)	1990	15.00

Except when noted otherwise, VG = 25% of NM, and VG+ = 50% of NM. (Example: VG = $2.00, VG+ = $4.00 and NM = $8.00.)

BON-AIRES, THE

45s

RUST

Number	Title (A Side/B Side)	Yr	NM
TR 3	Blue Beat/(B-side unknown)	196?	30.00
5077	My Love My Love/Bye Bye	1964	20.00
5097	The Shrine of St. Ceceia/Jeanie Baby	1965	20.00

BON-AIRS, THE

45s

KING

Number	Title (A Side/B Side)	Yr	NM
4975	Stop the World/Bermuda	1956	30.00

BONADUCE, DANNY

One of the stars of the TV series "The Partridge Family," but he doesn't appear on any of the records.

45s

LION

Number	Title (A Side/B Side)	Yr	NM
145	Blueberry You/Dreamland	1973	10.00
145 [PS]	Blueberry You/Dreamland	1973	25.00

Albums

LION

Number	Title (A Side/B Side)	Yr	NM
LN-1015	Danny Bonaduce	1973	60.00

BONAIRS, THE

45s

DOOTONE

Number	Title (A Side/B Side)	Yr	NM
325	It's Christmas/I'm Alone Tonight	1953	150.00

—B-side by Ernie Tavares Trio

BOND, ANGELO

45s

ABC

Number	Title (A Side/B Side)	Yr	NM
12077	Reach for the Moon (Poor People)/I Never Sang for My Baby	1975	5.00
12135	I Love You for What You Are/Eve	1975	5.00
12153	He Gained the World (But Lost His Soul)/I Love You for What You Are	1976	5.00

Albums

ABC

Number	Title (A Side/B Side)	Yr	NM
D-889	Bondage	1975	10.00

BOND, GRAHAM

45s

ASCOT

Number	Title (A Side/B Side)	Yr	NM
2211	St. James Infirmary/Wade in the Water	1966	10.00

PULSAR

Number	Title (A Side/B Side)	Yr	NM
2405	Love Is the Law/The Naz	1969	8.00
2409	Crossroads of Time/Moving Towards the Light	1969	8.00
2415	Stiffened Chicken/Water, Water	1969	8.00

Albums

MERCURY

Number	Title (A Side/B Side)	Yr	NM
SRM-1-612	We Put Our Magick on You	1971	20.00
SR-61327	Holy Magick	1970	20.00

PULSAR

Number	Title (A Side/B Side)	Yr	NM
10604	Love Is the Law	1969	25.00
10606	Mighty Graham Bond	1969	25.00

WARNER BROS.

Number	Title (A Side/B Side)	Yr	NM
2LS 2555 [(2)]	Solid Bond	1971	20.00

BOND, JOHNNY

45s

COLUMBIA

Number	Title (A Side/B Side)	Yr	NM
2-100 (?)	Take It or Leave It Baby/Till the End of the World	1949	25.00
—Microgroove 7-inch, 33 1/3 rpm single			
2-100 (?)	Tennessee Saturday Night/A Heart Full of Love	1949	25.00
—Microgroove 7-inch, 33 1/3 rpm single			
2-200 (?)	Read It and Weep/Somebody Loves You	1950	25.00
—Microgroove 7-inch, 33 1/3 rpm single			
2-210 (?)	I'm Biting My Fingernails/I Wish I Had a Nickel	1949	25.00
—Microgroove 7-inch, 33 1/3 rpm single			
2-319	Drowning My Sorrows/Women Make a Fool Out of Me	1950	25.00
—Microgroove 7-inch, 33 1/3 rpm single			
2-400 (?)	A Petal from a Faded Rose/Put Me to Bed #2	1950	25.00
—Microgroove 7-inch, 33 1/3 rpm single			
2-532	Love Song in 32 Bars/Tennessee Kentucky & Alabam'	1950	25.00
—Microgroove 7-inch, 33 1/3 rpm single			
2-600 (?)	Cherokee Waltz/Mean Mama Boogie	1950	25.00
—Microgroove 7-inch, 33 1/3 rpm single			
20726	Under the Red, White and Blue/Star Spangled Waltz	1950	20.00
20734	Barrel House Bessie/It Ain't Gonna Happen to Me	1950	20.00
20738	There's a Gold Moon Shining/Cream of Kentucky	1950	20.00
20756	I Wanna Do Something For Santa/Jingle Bell Boogie	1950	20.00
20787	Set 'Em Up Joe/Glad Rags	1951	20.00
20808	Sick, Sober and Sorry/Tennessee Walking Horse	1951	20.00
20844	Ten Trips to the Altar/Keep Your Cotton Pickin' Hands	1951	20.00
20876	Broke, Disgusted and Sad/In Old New Mexico	1952	15.00
20909	I Found You Out/Alabama Boogie Boy	1952	15.00
20948	Louisiana Lucy/The Man Behind the Throttle	1952	15.00
21007	I Went to Your Wedding/Our Love Isn't Legal	1952	15.00
21041	Back Street Affair/Our Love Isn't Legal	1952	15.00
21042	Born to Be Bad/#9 Blues	1952	15.00
21066	Wildcat Boogie/Let Me Go, Devil	1953	15.00
21082	Anybody's Baby/Hills of Kentucky	1953	15.00
21113	Peace Be Still/Ninety & Nine	1953	15.00
21150	Live and Let Live/I Wonder Where You Are Tonight	1953	15.00
21160	Wildcat Boogie/Let Me Go, Devil	1953	15.00
21186	Sweet Mama Tree Top Tall/Put a Little Sweetness in Your Love	1953	15.00
21187	Thanks/I Dreamed I Searched Heaven	1953	15.00
21222	10 Little Bottles/They Got Me	1954	15.00
21243	Firewater/Old Man Blues	1954	15.00
21294	Stealin'/My Darling Lola Lee	1954	15.00
21335	I Lose Again/Everybody Knew the Truth But Me	1954	15.00
21369	Cherokee Waltz/Glad Rags	1955	15.00
21383	Jim, Johnny & Jonas/Louisiana Swing	1955	15.00
21424	Somebody's Pushin'/Carolina Waltz	1955	15.00
21448	Remember the Alamo/Livin' It Up	1955	15.00
21494	Loaded for Bear/Six of One, Half a Dozen of the Other	1956	15.00
21521	Little Rock and Roll/I'll Be Here	1956	50.00
21565	Lonesome Train/Laughing Back the Heartaches	1956	15.00
40080	Santa Got Stuck in the Chimney/I Said a Prayer for Santa Claus	1953	15.00
—With Jimmy Boyd			
40842	Honky Tonk Fever/Lay It on the Line	1957	15.00
40973	All I Can Do Is Cry/Sale of Broken Hearts	1957	15.00
41034	That's Just What I'll Do/Broken Doll	1957	15.00

DITTO

Number	Title (A Side/B Side)	Yr	NM
120	The Tijuana Jail/Fools Paradise	1959	12.00

MGM

Number	Title (A Side/B Side)	Yr	NM
10627	Rag Mop/Music! Music! Music!	1950	40.00
10751	Heart of Gold/Hey Ho Virginia Reel	1950	40.00
14596	Rose of Reynosa/Who Stole the Juke Box	1973	5.00

REPUBLIC

Number	Title (A Side/B Side)	Yr	NM
2005	Hot Rod Lincoln/Five Minute Love Affair	1960	12.00
2008	X-15/The Way a Star Is Born	1960	12.00
2010	Side Car Cycle/Like Nothin' Man	1961	12.00
2022	Sadie Was a Lady/Buck Private's Lament	1961	12.00

SMASH

Number	Title (A Side/B Side)	Yr	NM
1761	I'll Step Aside/Mister Sun	1962	10.00

STARDAY

Number	Title (A Side/B Side)	Yr	NM
618	How to Succeed with Girls (Without Half-Way Trying)/Don't Mention Her Name	1963	8.00
635	True Love (Is Hard to Find)/Cimarron	1963	8.00
649	Three Sheets in the Wind/Let the Tears Begin	1963	8.00
665	Have You Seen My Baby/What Have You Done for Me Lately	1964	8.00
678	Hot Rod Surfin' Hootlebeatnanny/Don't Mama Count Anymore	1964	15.00
690	My Wicked, Wicked Ways/Bachelor Bill	1964	8.00
704	10 Little Bottles/Let It Be Me	1964	8.00
721	Sick, Sober & Sorry/The Man Who Comes Around	1965	8.00
731	The Great Figure Eight Race/Sadie Was a Lady	1965	8.00
749	They Got Me/Silent Walls	1966	8.00
758	Fireball/Over the Hill	1966	8.00
776	Hell's Angels/A Way of Life	1966	8.00
803	Your Old Love Letters/Si Si	1967	8.00
813	I Ain't Gonna Go/Don't Bite the Hand That's Feeding You	1967	8.00
826	Bottom of the Bottle/I'm Gonna Raise Cain (While I'm Able)	1968	8.00
847	Down to Your Last Fool/Invitation to the Blues	1968	8.00
893	It Only Hurts When I Cry/The Girl Who Carried the Torch for Me	1970	6.00
916	Here Come the Elephants/Take Me Back to Tulsa	1970	6.00
931	The Bottle's Empty/The Late and Great Myself	1971	6.00
951	Put the Country Back in Country Music/Fly Me, Try Me	1972	6.00
7021	Hot Rod Lincoln/Barrel House Betsy	197?	5.00
7027	Divorce Me C.O.D./Three Sheets in the Wind	197?	5.00
7033	Tennessee, Kentucky and Alabam'/Glad Rags	197?	5.00

20TH FOX

Number	Title (A Side/B Side)	Yr	NM
156	Gold Rush/The Long Tall Shadow	1959	12.00
231	Jealous Lad/A Kid Named Bell	1960	12.00

7-Inch Extended Plays

COLUMBIA

Number	Title (A Side/B Side)	Yr	NM
B-2820	Sick, Sober and Sorry/Love Song in 32 Bars//Ten Little Bottles/Put Me to Bed	1958	30.00
B-2820 [PS]	Johnny Bond and His Red River Boys (Hall of Fame Series)	1958	30.00

REPUBLIC

Number	Title (A Side/B Side)	Yr	NM
100	(contents unknown)	1960	20.00
100 [PS]	Hot Rod Lincoln	1960	20.00

Albums

CMH

Number	Title (A Side/B Side)	Yr	NM
6212	The Singing Cowboy Again	1981	10.00
6213	The Return of the Singing Cowboy	1981	10.00

HARMONY

Number	Title (A Side/B Side)	Yr	NM
HL 7308 [M]	Johnny Bond's Best	1964	20.00
HL 7353 [M]	Bottled in Bond	1965	20.00

NASHVILLE

Number	Title (A Side/B Side)	Yr	NM
2054	Three Sheets to the Wind	196?	15.00

SHASTA

Number	Title (A Side/B Side)	Yr	NM
LP-516	Johnny Bond Rides Again	197?	15.00

STARDAY

Number	Title (A Side/B Side)	Yr	NM
SLP-147 [M]	That Wild, Wicked But Wonderful Wesy	1961	50.00
SLP-227 [M]	Songs That Made Him Famous	1963	40.00
SLP-298 [M]	Hot Rod Lincoln	1964	50.00
SLP-333 [M]	Ten Little Bottles	1965	30.00
SLP-354 [M]	Famous Hot Rodders I Have Known	1965	40.00
SLP-368 [M]	The Man Who Comes Around	1966	25.00
SLP-378 [M]	Bottles Up	1966	25.00
SLP-388 [M]	The Branded Stock of Johnny Bond	1966	20.00
SLP-402 [M]	Ten Nights in a Barroom	1967	20.00
SLP-416	Drink Up and Go Home	1968	15.00
SLP-444	The Best of Johnny Bond	1969	15.00
SLP-456	Old, New, Patriotic and Blue	1970	15.00
SLP-472	Here Come the Elephants	1971	15.00
954	The Best of Johnny Bond	1976	10.00

BOND, JOHNNY, AND LEFTY FRIZZELL

Also see each artist's individual listings.

45s

COLUMBIA

Number	Title (A Side/B Side)	Yr	NM
40934	Sick, Sober and Sorry/Lover By Appointment	1957	15.00

BOND, JOHNNY, AND RED SOVINE

Also see each artist's individual listings.

45s

STARDAY

Number	Title (A Side/B Side)	Yr	NM
790	The Gearjammer and the Hobo/Sweet Nellie	1966	10.00

BONDS, GARY U.S.

45s

ATCO

Number	Title (A Side/B Side)	Yr	NM
6689	The Star/You Need a Personal Manager	1969	6.00

BLUFF CITY

Number	Title (A Side/B Side)	Yr	NM
221	My Love Song/Blue Grass	1974	5.00

Number	Title (A Side/B Side)	Yr	NM
BOTANIC			
❑ 1002	I'm Glad You're Back/Funky Lies	1968	8.00
EMI AMERICA			
❑ 8079	This Little Girl/Way Back When	1981	4.00
❑ 8079 [PS]	This Little Girl/Way Back When	1981	5.00
❑ 8089	Jole Blon/Just Like a Child	1981	4.00
❑ 8099	Your Love/Just Like a Child	1981	4.00
❑ 8117	Out of Work/Bring Her Back	1982	4.00
❑ 8117 [PS]	Out of Work/Bring Her Back	1982	5.00
❑ 8133	Love's on the Line/ Way Back When	1982	4.00
❑ 8145	Turn the Music Down/ Way Back When	1982	4.00
LEGRAND			
❑ 1003	New Orleans/Please Forgive Me	1960	15.00
—Gold and red label			
❑ 1003	New Orleans/Please Forgive Me	1960	20.00
—Original lists artist as "By-U.S. Bonds"; purple label			
❑ 1005	Not Me/Give Me One More Chance	1961	15.00
—Gold and red label			
❑ 1005	Not Me/Give Me One More Chance	1961	20.00
—Artist listed as "U.S. Bonds"; purple label			
❑ 1008	Quarter to Three/Time Ole Story	1961	15.00
—Artist listed as "U.S. Bonds"; gold and red label			
❑ 1008	Quarter to Three/Time Ole Story	1961	40.00
—Artist listed as "U.S. Bonds"; purple label			
❑ 1008 [PS]	Quarter to Three/Time Ole Story	1961	40.00
❑ 1009	School Is Out/One Million Years	1961	15.00
—Artist listed as "Gary (U.S.) Bonds" as are all later Legrand singles			
❑ 1009	School Is Out/One Million Years	1961	20.00
—Artist listed as "U.S. Bonds"			
❑ 1009 [PS]	School Is Out/One Million Years	1961	40.00
❑ 1012	School Is In/Trip to the Moon	1961	15.00
❑ 1012	School Is In/Trip to the Moon	1971	8.00
—Red label reissue			
❑ 1015	Dear Lady/Havin' So Much Fun	1961	20.00
—Original title of A-side			
❑ 1015	Dear Lady Twist/Havin' So Much Fun	1962	15.00
❑ 1018	Twist, Twist Senora/ Food of Love	1962	15.00
❑ 1019	Seven Day Weekend/ Gettin' a Groove	1962	15.00
❑ 1020	Copy Cat/I'll Change That Too	1962	15.00
❑ 1022	Mixed Up Faculty/ I Dig This Station	1962	15.00
❑ 1025	Do the Limbo with Me/Where Did That Naughty Little Girl Go	1962	15.00
❑ 1027	I Don't Wanta Wait/ What a Dream	1963	12.00
❑ 1029	No More Homework/ She's Alright	1963	12.00
❑ 1030	Perdido Part 1/Perdido Part 2	1963	12.00
❑ 1031	King Kong's Monkey/ My Sweet Ruby Rose	1964	12.00
❑ 1032	The Music Goes Round and Round/Ella Is Yella	1964	12.00
❑ 1034	You Little Angel You/My Little Miss America	1964	12.00
❑ 1035	Oh Yeah, Oh Yeah/Let ❑ Oh Yeah, Oh Yeah/ Let Me Go Lover	1965	10.00
❑ 1039	Beaches U.S.A./Do the Bumpsie	1965	10.00
❑ 1040	Take Me Back to New Orleans/ I'm That Kind of Guy	1966	10.00
❑ 1041	Due to Circumstances Under My Control/Slow Motion	1966	10.00
❑ 1043	Send Her Back to Me/ Workin' for My Baby	1967	10.00
❑ 1045	Call Me for Christmas/ Mixed Up Faculty	1967	12.00
❑ 1046	Sarah Jane/What a Crazy World	1967	10.00
MCA			
❑ 52335	One More Time Around the Block, Ophelia/ Deadline U.S.A.	1984	4.00
—B-side by Shalamar			
❑ 52400	New Orleans/Rhythm of the Rain	1984	4.00
—With Neil Sedaka			
PHOENIX			
❑ 0071	Standing in the Line of Fire/ Wild Nights	1984	5.00
❑ 0071 [PS]	Standing in the Line of Fire/ Wild Nights	1984	5.00
PRODIGAL			
❑ 0612	Grandma's Washboard/ Believing You	1975	5.00
SUE			
❑ 17	One Broken Heart/Can't Use You in My Business	1970	6.00

Number	Title (A Side/B Side)	Yr	NM
Albums			
EMI AMERICA			
❑ SPRO-9666 [EP]	Dedication Sampler	1981	15.00
—Promo-only sampler with limited-edition number on pink sticker			
❑ SO-17051	Dedication	1981	10.00
❑ SO-17068	On the Line	1982	10.00
LEGRAND			
❑ LLP-3001 [M]	Dance 'Til Quarter to Three	1961	100.00
❑ LLP-3002 [M]	Twist Up Calypso	1962	70.00
❑ LLP-3003 [M]	Greatest Hits of Gary U.S. Bonds	1962	70.00
MCA			
❑ 905	The Best of Gary U.S. Bonds	1984	10.00
PHOENIX			
❑ PRT 0072	Standing in the Line of Fire	1984	10.00
RHINO			
❑ RNLP-805	Certified Soul	1981	10.00

BONFIRE, MARS

Real name: Dennis McCrohan. Also see SPARROW; STEPPENWOLF.

Number	Title (A Side/B Side)	Yr	NM
45s			
COLUMBIA			
❑ 44772	Faster Than the Speed of Life/ She	1969	10.00
❑ 44888	In Christina's Arms/ Lady Moon Walker	1969	10.00
Albums			
COLUMBIA			
❑ CS 9834	Faster Than the Speed of Life	1969	30.00
—Reissue of Uni 73027 with slight alterations			
UNI			
❑ 73027	Mars Bonfire	1968	40.00

BONHAM

As in Jason Bonham, John Bonham's son. Jason also drummed with UFO and is currently with FOREIGNER.

Number	Title (A Side/B Side)	Yr	NM
Albums			
WTG			
❑ P 45009	The Disregard of Timekeeping	1989	15.00

BONNEVILLES, THE

More than one group.

Number	Title (A Side/B Side)	Yr	NM
45s			
BARRY			
❑ 104	Lorraine/Zu Zu	1962	50.00
CAPRI			
❑ 102	Give Me Your Love/Until You Say We're Through	1959	50.00
CORAL			
❑ 62273	Johnny/Freeway U.S.A.	1961	20.00
MUNICH			
❑ 103	Lorraine/Zu Zu	1960	100.00
—Black label			
❑ 103	Lorraine/Zu Zu	1960	300.00
—Red label			
WHITEHALL			
❑ 30002	I Do/Make Believe Lovin'	1959	30.00
Albums			
DRUM BOY			
❑ DLM-1001 [M]	Meet the Bonnevilles	1963	100.00
❑ DLS-1001 [S]	Meet the Bonnevilles	1963	150.00
JUSTICE			
❑ JLP-146	Bringing It Home	196?	500.00

BONNEY, GRAHAM

Number	Title (A Side/B Side)	Yr	NM
45s			
CAPITOL			
❑ 2221	I'll Be Your Baby Tonight/ Back from Baltimore	1968	6.00
❑ 5624	Super Girl/Hill of Lovin'	1966	8.00
MIKE			
❑ 4009	Baby's Gone/Later Tonight	1966	8.00

BONNIE AND THE BUTTERFLYS

Number	Title (A Side/B Side)	Yr	NM
45s			
SMASH			
❑ 1878	I Saw Him Standing There/ Dust Storm	1964	20.00

BONNIE AND THE TREASURES

Number	Title (A Side/B Side)	Yr	NM
45s			
PABLO			
❑ 7014	Davey, I'm So Glad It Rained/ The Lonely Surfer	1964	40.00
—B-side by the Mid-Americans			
PHI-DAN			
❑ 5005	Home of the Brave/Our Song	1965	40.00

BONNIE LOU

Number	Title (A Side/B Side)	Yr	NM
45s			
FRATERNITY			
❑ 808	No One Ever Lost More/ Have You Ever Been Lonely	1958	15.00
❑ 812	Friction Heat/I Give My Love to You	1958	15.00
KING			
❑ 1192	Seven Lonely Days/ Just Out of Reach	1953	30.00
❑ 1213	Scrap of Paper/ Dancin' with Someone	1953	30.00
❑ 1237	Tennessee Wig Walk/ Hand Me Down Heart	1953	30.00
❑ 1272	Papaya Mama/ Since You Said Goodbye	1953	30.00
❑ 1279	Texas Polka/No Heart at All	1953	30.00
❑ 1318	Welcome Mat/Don't Stop Kissing Me Goodnight	1954	25.00
❑ 1341	Huckleberry Pie/No One	1954	25.00
❑ 1365	Wait for Me Darling/ Blue Tennessee Rain	1954	25.00
❑ 1373	Two-Step Side Step/Please Don't Laugh When I Cry	1954	25.00
❑ 1384	Tell the World/Darlin' Why	1954	25.00
❑ 1414	Tennessee Mambo/ Train Whistle Blues	1955	25.00
❑ 1436	Tweedle Dee/ Finger of Suspicion	1955	25.00
❑ 1445	Danger, Heartbreak Ahead/ A Rusty Old Halo	1955	25.00
❑ 1476	Drop Me a Line/Old Faithful	1955	25.00
❑ 1506	Barnyard Hop/Miss the Love	1955	25.00
❑ 4835	Daddy-O/Dancing in My Socks	1955	25.00
❑ 4864	Daddy-O/Miss the Love	1956	20.00
❑ 4895	Little Miss Bobby Sox/Beyond the Shadow of a Doubt	1956	20.00
❑ 4900	Bo Weevil/Chaperon	1956	20.00
❑ 4919	I Turn to You/Lonesome Lover	1956	20.00
❑ 4948	No Rock 'N' Roll Tonight/ One Track Love	1956	25.00
❑ 5009	I Want You/Easy Love, Easy Kisses	1957	20.00
❑ 5033	Kit 'N Caboodle/Takes Two	1957	20.00
❑ 5063	Teeange Wedding/Runnin' Away	1957	20.00
❑ 5094	I'm Available/Waiting in Vain	1957	20.00
❑ 5425	Tweedle Dee/Daddy-O	1960	15.00
❑ 5865	Seven Lonely Days/ Tennessee Wig Walk	1964	12.00
Albums			
KING			
❑ 595 [M]	Bonnie Lou Sings	1958	140.00

BONNIE SISTERS, THE

Number	Title (A Side/B Side)	Yr	NM
45s			
RAINBOW			
❑ 45-328	I Saw Mommy Cha Cha Cha with You Know Who?/ Cry Baby	1955	40.00
❑ 45-328	Cry Baby/Broken	1956	30.00
❑ 45-333	Track That Cat/Wandering Heart	1956	30.00
❑ 45-344	Confess/Shuga Duga	1956	30.00

BONNIWELL, T.S.

Sean Bonniwell of THE MUSIC MACHINE.

Number	Title (A Side/B Side)	Yr	NM
45s			
CAPITOL			
❑ 2551	Sleep/Where Am I to Go	1969	10.00
Albums			
CAPITOL			
❑ ST-377	Close	1969	75.00

BONNIWELL'S MUSIC MACHINE

See THE MUSIC MACHINE.

BONO, SONNY

See SONNY; SONNY AND CHER.

BONOFF, KARLA

Number	Title (A Side/B Side)	Yr	NM
45s			
COLUMBIA			
❑ 18-02805	Personally/Dream	1982	4.00
❑ 18-02805 [PS]	Personally/Dream	1982	5.00
❑ 18-03172	Please Be the One/ Just Walk Away	1982	4.00
❑ 38-04472	Somebody's Eyes/ Just Walk Away	1984	4.00
❑ 38-04472 [PS]	Somebody's Eyes/ Just Walk Away	1984	4.00
❑ 3-10618	I Can't Hold On/Falling Star	1977	5.00
❑ 3-10710	Isn't It Always Love/ Rose in the Garden	1978	5.00
❑ 3-10751	Someone to Lay Down Beside Me/Rose in the Garden	1978	5.00
❑ 1-11041	Trouble Again/If He's Even Here	1979	4.00

Except when noted otherwise, VG = 25% of NM, and VG+ = 50% of NM. (Example: VG = $2.00, VG+ = $4.00 and NM = $8.00.)

Number	Title (A Side/B Side)	Yr	NM
❑ 1-11130	When You Walk in the Room/ Never Stop Her Heart	1979	4.00
❑ 1-11206	Baby Don't Go/The Letter	1980	4.00
Albums			
COLUMBIA			
❑ JC 34672	Karla Bonoff	1977	10.00
❑ PC 34672	Karla Bonoff	198?	8.00
—Budget-line reissue			
❑ JC 35799	Restless Nights	1979	10.00
❑ PC 35799	Restless Nights	198?	8.00
—Budget-line reissue			
❑ FC 37444	Wild Heart of the Young	1982	8.00
GOLD CASTLE			
❑ 171014-1	New World	1987	12.00

BONOFF, KARLA, AND THE NITTY GRITTY DIRT BAND

Number	Title (A Side/B Side)	Yr	NM
45s			
MCA			
❑ 55182	You Believed in Me/ Atlanta Reel '96	1996	3.00
—B-side by Michael Omartian			

BONZO DOG BAND, THE Also see VIVIAN STANSHALL.

Number	Title (A Side/B Side)	Yr	NM
45s			
IMPERIAL			
❑ 66345	I'm the Urban Spaceman/ Canyons of Your Mind	1969	15.00
❑ 66373	Mr. Apollo/Ready Made	1969	15.00
—As "The Bonzo Dog Doo-Dah Band"			
UNITED ARTISTS			
❑ 50809	I'm the Urban Spaceman/ Canyons of Your Mind	1971	10.00
❑ 50943	Slush/King of Scurf	1972	15.00
Albums			
IMPERIAL			
❑ LP 9370 [M]	Gorilla	1968	20.00
—Without booklet			
❑ LP 9370 [M]	Gorilla	1968	30.00
—With booklet			
❑ LP 12370 [S]	Gorilla	1968	20.00
—Without booklet			
❑ LP 12370 [S]	Gorilla	1968	30.00
—With booklet			
❑ LP 12432	Urban Spaceman	1968	20.00
—Without booklet			
❑ LP 12432	Urban Spaceman	1968	30.00
—With booklet			
❑ LP 12445	Tadpoles	1969	20.00
❑ LP 12457	Keynsham	1969	20.00
LIBERTY			
❑ LN-10206	Some of the Best of the Bonzo Dog Band	1983	8.00
UNITED ARTISTS			
❑ UA-LA321-H2 [(2)]	The History of the Bonzos	1974	15.00
❑ UAS 5517	The Beast of the Bonzos	1971	15.00
❑ UAS 5584	Let's Make Up and Be Friendly	1972	15.00

BOOGIE KINGS, THE

Number	Title (A Side/B Side)	Yr	NM
45s			
MONTEL			
❑ 939	Crying Man/Two Steps from the Blues	1965	12.00
❑ 984	When She Touches Me/ Philly Walk	196?	10.00
❑ 995	Elaine/Philly Walk	196?	10.00
PAULA			
❑ 260	Tell It Like It Is/Philly Walk	1967	10.00
❑ 272	Bony Maronie/I've Got Your Number	1967	10.00
PIC 1			
❑ 121	The Band Doll/She	196?	15.00
❑ 129	This Is Blue Eyed Soul/ Do 'Em All	196?	15.00
❑ 133	Let It Be Me/That's Really Some Good	196?	15.00
Albums			
MONTEL			
❑ LP-104 [M]	The Boogie Kings	1966	40.00
❑ LP-109 [M]	Blue Eyed Soul	1967	30.00

BOOKENDS, THE

Number	Title (A Side/B Side)	Yr	NM
45s			
CAPITOL			
❑ 4667	Christmas Kisses/Let Me Walk with You	1961	15.00

Karla Bonoff, "Personally," Columbia 18-02805, 1982, **$5.**

BOOKER, JOHN LEE See JOHN LEE HOOKER.

BOOKER T. AND PRISCILLA Also see BOOKER T. AND THE MG'S.

Number	Title (A Side/B Side)	Yr	NM
45s			
A&M			
❑ 1298	The Wedding Song/She	1971	5.00
❑ 1487	Crippled Crow/Wild Fox	1973	5.00
Albums			
A&M			
❑ SP-3504 [(2)]	Booker T. and Priscilla	1971	15.00
❑ SP-4351	Home Grown	1972	10.00
❑ SP-4413	Chronicles	1973	10.00

BOOKER T. AND THE MG'S Also see BOOKER T. AND PRISCILLA; STEVE CROPPER.

Number	Title (A Side/B Side)	Yr	NM
12-Inch Singles			
A&M			
❑ SP-12046 [DJ]	Don't Stop Your Love/ I Came to Love You	1981	15.00
—As "Booker T. Jones"			
❑ SP-17043 [DJ]	Let's Go Dancing (2 versions?)	1978	15.00
—As "Booker T. Jones"			
❑ SP-17188 [DJ]	Don't Stop Your Love (same on both sides?)	1981	15.00
—As "Booker T. Jones"			
❑ SP-20011	Don't Stop Your Love (unknown versions)	1981	12.00
—As "Booker T. Jones"			
45s			
A&M			
❑ 2100	Knockin' on Heaven's Door/ Let's Go Dancin'	1978	4.00
—As "Booker T. Jones"			
❑ 2234	The Best of You/Let's Go Dancin'	1980	4.00
—As "Booker T. Jones"			
❑ 2279	Will You Be the One/Cookie	1980	4.00
—As "Booker T. Jones"			
❑ 2374	I Want You/You're the Best	1981	4.00
❑ 2394	Don't Stop Your Love/ I Came to Love You	1982	4.00
ASYLUM			
❑ 45392	Sticky Stuff/The Stick	1977	4.00
❑ 45424	Grab Bag/Reincarnation	1977	4.00
COLUMBIA			
❑ 38-77526	Cruisin'/Just My Imagination	1994	4.00
EPIC			
❑ 50031	Evergreen/Song for Casey	1974	4.00
❑ 50078	Front Street Rag/Mama Stewart	1975	4.00
❑ 50149	Life Is Funny/Tennessee Voodoo	1975	4.00
STAX			
❑ 0001	Soul-Limbo/Heads Or Tails	1968	8.00
❑ 0013	Hang 'Em High/Over Easy	1968	8.00
❑ 0028	Time Is Tight/Johnny I Love You	1969	8.00
❑ 0037	Mrs. Robinson/Soul Clap '69	1969	8.00
❑ 0049	Slum Baby/Meditation	1969	8.00
❑ 0073	Something/Sunday Sermon	1970	6.00
❑ 0082	Melting Pot/Kinda Easy Like	1970	6.00
❑ 127	Green Onions/Behave Yourself	1962	16.00
—Blue label			
❑ 127	Green Onions/Behave Yourself	1962	20.00
—Gray label			
❑ 131	Jellybread/Aw' Mercy	1963	12.00
❑ 134	Big Train/Burnt Biscuits	1963	12.00
❑ 134	Big Train/Home Grown	1963	12.00
❑ 137	Chinese Checkers/Plum Nellie	1963	12.00
❑ 142	Mo' Onions/Fannie Mae	1963	12.00
❑ 142	Mo' Onions/Tic Tac Toe	1963	12.00
❑ 153	Soul Dressing/MG Party	1964	10.00
❑ 161	Can't Be Still/Terrible Thing	1964	10.00
❑ 169	Boot-Leg/Outrage	1965	10.00
❑ 0169	Sugarcane/Blackride	1973	5.00
—As "The MG's"			
❑ 182	Red Beans and Rice/Be My Lady	1965	10.00
❑ 196	Booker-Loo/My Sweet Potato	1966	10.00
❑ 0200	Breezy/Neckbone	1974	5.00
—As "The MG's"			
❑ 203	Jingle Bells/Winter Wonderland	1966	12.00
❑ 211	Hip-Hug-Her/Summertime	1967	10.00
❑ 224	Groovin'/Slim Jenkin's Place	1967	10.00

B

Number	Title (A Side/B Side)	Yr	NM
❑ 236	Silver Bells/Winter Snow	1967	12.00

VOLT

Number	Title (A Side/B Side)	Yr	NM
❑ 102	Green Onions/Behave Yourself	1962	30.00

Albums

A&M

Number	Title (A Side/B Side)	Yr	NM
❑ SP-4720	Try and Love Again	1978	10.00
—As "Booker T. Jones"			
❑ SP-4798	The Best of You	1979	10.00
—As "Booker T. Jones"			
❑ SP-4874	I Want You	1981	10.00
—As "Booker T. Jones"			

ASYLUM

Number	Title (A Side/B Side)	Yr	NM
❑ 7E-1093	Universal Language	1977	10.00

ATLANTIC

Number	Title (A Side/B Side)	Yr	NM
❑ 8202 [M]	The Best of Booker T. and the MG's	1968	50.00
—Mono is white label promo only			
❑ SD 8202 [S]	The Best of Booker T. and the MG's	1968	20.00
❑ 81285	The Best of Booker T. and the MG's	1985	8.00

EPIC

Number	Title (A Side/B Side)	Yr	NM
❑ KE 33143	Evergreen	1974	12.00

MCA

Number	Title (A Side/B Side)	Yr	NM
❑ 6282	The Runaway	1989	12.00
—As "Booker T. Jones"			

STAX

Number	Title (A Side/B Side)	Yr	NM
❑ ST-701 [M]	Green Onions	1962	70.00
❑ STS-701 [R]	Green Onions	1966	50.00
❑ ST-705 [M]	Soul Dressing	1965	70.00
❑ STS-705 [R]	Soul Dressing	1966	50.00
❑ ST-711 [M]	And Now…Booker T. and the MG's	1966	50.00
❑ STS-711 [S]	And Now…Booker T. and the MG's	1966	80.00
❑ ST-713 [M]	In the Christmas Spirit	1966	400.00
—Fingers and piano keys cover			
❑ ST-713 [M]	In the Christmas Spirit	1967	200.00
—Same as above; Santa Claus cover			
❑ STS-713 [S]	In the Christmas Spirit	1966	400.00
—Fingers and piano keys cover			
❑ STS-713 [S]	In the Christmas Spirit	1967	200.00
—Santa Claus cover			
❑ ST-717 [M]	Hip Hug-Her	1967	40.00
❑ STS-717 [S]	Hip Hug-Her	1967	50.00
❑ ST-724 [M]	Doin' Our Thing	1968	80.00
❑ STS-724 [S]	Doin' Our Thing	1968	50.00
❑ STS-2001	Soul Limbo	1968	25.00
❑ STS-2006	Uptight	1969	25.00
❑ STS-2009	The Booker T. Set	1969	25.00
❑ STS-2027	McLemore Avenue	1970	25.00
❑ STS-2033	Booker T. and the MG's Greatest Hits	1970	15.00
❑ STM-2035 [M]	Melting Pot	1971	40.00
—Mono is white label promo only			
❑ STS-2035 [S]	Melting Pot	1971	15.00
❑ STX-4104	Free Ride	1978	10.00
❑ STX-4113	Soul Limbo	198?	10.00
—Reissue of 2001			
❑ MPS-8505	Booker T. and the MG's Greatest Hits	1981	10.00
❑ MPS-8521	Melting Pot	198?	10.00
—Reissue of 2035			
❑ MPS-8531	The Booker T. Set	1987	10.00
—Reissue of 2009			
❑ MPS-8552	McLemore Avenue	1990	12.00
—Reissue of 2027			

SUNDAZED

Number	Title (A Side/B Side)	Yr	NM
❑ LP 5042	Soul Dressing	2000	15.00
—Reissue on 180-gram vinyl			
❑ LP 5043	And Now! Booker T. and the MG's	2000	15.00
—Reissue on 180-gram vinyl			
❑ LP 5053	In the Christmas Spirit	2000	15.00
—Reissue on 180-gram vinyl			
❑ LP 5079	Green Onions	2002	12.00
—Reissue on 180-gram vinyl			
❑ LP 5080	Hip Hug-Her	2002	12.00
—Reissue on 180-gram vinyl			

BOOMERANG

45s

RCA VICTOR

Number	Title (A Side/B Side)	Yr	NM
❑ 74-0508	Mockingbird/Montreal Jail	1971	8.00
❑ 74-0580	Juke It/Hard Times	1971	8.00

Albums

RCA VICTOR

Number	Title (A Side/B Side)	Yr	NM
❑ LSP-4577	Boomerang	1971	20.00

BOOMTOWN RATS, THE

Includes (Sir!) BOB GELDOF.

12-Inch Singles

COLUMBIA

Number	Title (A Side/B Side)	Yr	NM
❑ AS 544 [DJ]	Rat Trap/Joey's on the Street Again	1979	15.00
❑ AS 920 [DJ]	Up Al Night/Mood Mambo/Banana Republic	1981	8.00
❑ AS 1565 [DJ]	Skin on Skin/Talking in Code	1982	8.00
❑ AS 2170 [DJ]	Drag Me Down (same on both sides)	1984	8.00

45s

COLUMBIA

Number	Title (A Side/B Side)	Yr	NM
❑ 38-03386	Never in a Million Years/Charmed Lives	1982	4.00
❑ 38-04892	Rain/An Icicle in the Sun	1985	4.00
❑ 38-05590	Drag Me Down/Hard Times	1985	4.00
❑ 3-10960	Rat Trap/Do the Rat	1979	6.00
❑ 1-11117	I Don't Like Mondays/It's All the Rage	1979	5.00
❑ 1-11248	Someone's Looking at You/I Don't Like Mondays (Live)	1980	5.00
❑ 11-60512	Up All Night/Another Piece of Bread	1981	5.00

Albums

COLUMBIA

Number	Title (A Side/B Side)	Yr	NM
❑ JC 35750	A Tonic for the Troops	1979	10.00
❑ PC 35750	A Tonic for the Troops	198?	8.00
—Budget-line reissue			
❑ JC 36248	The Fine Art of Surfacing	1979	10.00
❑ PC 36248	The Fine Art of Surfacing	198?	8.00
—Budget-line reissue			
❑ JC 37062	Mondo Bongo	1981	12.00
—With poster			
❑ PC 37062	Mondo Bongo	198?	8.00
—Budget-line reissue			
❑ 5C 38097 [EP]	The Boomtown Rats	1982	8.00
❑ FC 38195	V Deep	1982	10.00
❑ PC 38195	V Deep	198?	8.00
—Budget-line reissue			
❑ 5C 38591 [EP]	Ratrospective	1983	10.00
❑ FC 39335	In the Long Grass	1985	10.00
❑ PC 39335	In the Long Grass	198?	8.00
—Budget-line reissue			

MERCURY

Number	Title (A Side/B Side)	Yr	NM
❑ SRM-1-1188	The Boomtown Rats	1977	15.00

BOONE, DANIEL

45s

EPIC

Number	Title (A Side/B Side)	Yr	NM
❑ 10787	Daddy Don't You Walk So Fast/Tiger Woman	1971	5.00

MERCURY

Number	Title (A Side/B Side)	Yr	NM
❑ 73281	Beautiful Sunday/Truly Julie	1972	5.00
❑ 73339	Annabelle/Sleepyhead	1972	4.00
❑ 73357	Crying/Sunshine Lover	1973	4.00
❑ 73428	Skydiver/Do You Thank the Lord	1973	4.00
❑ 73461	Love Spell/Lilly, I Love You	1974	4.00

PYE

Number	Title (A Side/B Side)	Yr	NM
❑ 71007	A Rock 'N Roll Band/Singing Backing Vocal with a Rock 'N Roll Band	1975	4.00
❑ 71011	Run, Tell the People/Rock 'N' Roll Bum	1975	4.00
❑ 71041	Run, Tell the People/(B-side unknown)	1976	4.00
❑ 71052	I Think of You/(B-side unknown)	1976	4.00

Albums

MERCURY

Number	Title (A Side/B Side)	Yr	NM
❑ SRM-1-649	Beautiful Sunday	1972	10.00

BOONES, THE

45s

MOTOWN

Number	Title (A Side/B Side)	Yr	NM
❑ 1314	Please Mr. Postman/Friend	1974	5.00
—As "The Pat Boone Family"			
❑ 1334	When The Lovelight Starts Shining Through His Eyes/Viva Espana	1975	5.00
❑ 1389	My Guy/When the Lovelight Starts Shining Through His Eyes	1976	5.00

WARNER BROS.

Number	Title (A Side/B Side)	Yr	NM
❑ 8385 [DJ]	Hasta Manana (mono/stereo)	1977	5.00
—Stock copy not known to exist			
❑ 8446	He's a Rebel/You Light Up My Life	1977	6.00
—B-side by Debby Boone			

BOOT

45s

AGAPE

Number	Title (A Side/B Side)	Yr	NM
❑ 9008	Hey Little Girl/Liza Brown	1972	8.00

Albums

AGAPE

Number	Title (A Side/B Side)	Yr	NM
❑ 2601	Boot	1972	25.00

BOOTLES, THE

45s

GNP CRESCENDO

Number	Title (A Side/B Side)	Yr	NM
❑ 311	I'll Let You Hold My Hand/Never Till Now	1964	15.00

BOOTSY'S RUBBER BAND

12-Inch Singles

4TH & B'WAY

Number	Title (A Side/B Side)	Yr	NM
❑ PRO 512-1 [DJ]	Jungle Bass (3 versions)/Disciples of Funk	1990	15.00
❑ 444023-1	Jungle Bass (2 versions)//Disciples of Funk/Interzone	1990	10.00

WARNER BROS.

Number	Title (A Side/B Side)	Yr	NM
❑ 29919	Body Slam/I'd Rather Be With You	1982	15.00

45s

WARNER BROS.

Number	Title (A Side/B Side)	Yr	NM
❑ 8246	I'd Rather Be with You/Vanish in Our Sleep	1976	6.00
❑ 8291	Psychoticbumpschool/Vanish in Our Sleep	1976	6.00
❑ 8328	The Pinocchio Theory/Rubber Duckie	1977	6.00
❑ 8403	Can't Stay Away/Another Point of View	1977	6.00
❑ 8512	Bootzilla/Vanish in Our Sleep	1978	6.00
❑ 8575	Hollywood Squares/What's a Telephone Bill	1978	5.00
❑ 8575 [PS]	Hollywood Squares/What's a Telephone Bill	1978	8.00
❑ 8818	Jam Fan (Hot)/She Jam (Almost Bootsy Show)	1979	5.00
❑ 29889	Body Slam!/I'd Rather Be With You	1982	4.00
❑ 49013	Bootsy Get Live Part 1/Part 2	1979	5.00
❑ 49073	Under the Influence of a Groove/(Disco Version)	1979	5.00
❑ 49599	Mug Push/Scenery	1980	5.00
—As "Bootsy"			
❑ 49599 [PS]	Mug Push/Scenery	1980	6.00
—As "Bootsy"			
❑ 49661	F-Encounter/(Instrumental)	1981	5.00
—As "Bootsy"			
❑ 49708	Is That My Song?/It's a Musical	1981	5.00
—As "Bootsy"			

Albums

WARNER BROS.

Number	Title (A Side/B Side)	Yr	NM
❑ BS 2920	Stretchin' Out in Bootsy's Rubber Band	1976	15.00
❑ BS 2972	Ahh... The Name Is Bootsy, Baby!	1977	15.00
❑ BSK 3093	Bootsy? Player of the Year	1978	10.00
—Without punch-out glasses			
❑ BSK 3093	Bootsy? Player of the Year	1978	15.00
—With perforated punch-out glasses intact			
❑ BSK 3295	This Boot Is Make for Fonk-n	1979	10.00
—Without coloring book			
❑ BSK 3295	This Boot Is Make for Fonk-n	1979	15.00
—With 8-page coloring book			
❑ BSK 3433	Ultra Wave	1980	15.00
—As "Bootsy"			

BOP-A-LOOS, THE

45s

MERCURY

Number	Title (A Side/B Side)	Yr	NM
❑ 70552	Teach Me Tonight/South Parkway Mambo	1955	20.00
❑ 70553	Tweedle Dee/Bongo Mambo	1955	20.00
❑ 70568	Hearts of Stone/Miracle Mambo	1955	20.00
❑ 70569	Sincerely/Cuban Carnival	1955	20.00

BOP-CHORDS, THE

45s

HOLIDAY

Number	Title (A Side/B Side)	Yr	NM
❑ 2601	Castle in the Sky/My Darling to You	1957	200.00
—Black label			
❑ 2601	Castle in the Sky/My Darling to You	196?	25.00
—Red label, single line			
❑ 2601	Castle in the Sky/My Darling to You	196?	50.00
—Red label, double lines			
❑ 2603	When I Woke Up This Morning/I Really Love You	1957	200.00
—Black label			
❑ 2603	When I Woke Up This Morning/I Really Love You	196?	50.00
—Red label			

LOST-NITE

Number	Title (A Side/B Side)	Yr	NM
❑ 175	Castle in the Sky/My Darling to You	196?	6.00
—Reissue			

Except when noted otherwise, VG = 25% of NM, and VG+ = 50% of NM. (Example: VG = $2.00, VG+ = $4.00 and NM = $8.00.)

Number	Title (A Side/B Side)	Yr	NM
❑ 188	When I Woke Up This Morning/ I Really Love You	196?	6.00

—Reissue

BORDERS, TONY

45s

DELTA

Number	Title (A Side/B Side)	Yr	NM
❑ 1902	Counting on You/Can't Stand to See You Cry	196?	40.00

HALL

Number	Title (A Side/B Side)	Yr	NM
❑ 1918	Pass the Word/Soft Wind, Soft Voice	1964	30.00
❑ 1921	Get Yourself Another Man/ Bit by Bit	1964	30.00
❑ 1926	You Are My Treasure/ Can't Stand to See You Cry	1965	30.00

HALLWAY

Number	Title (A Side/B Side)	Yr	NM
❑ 1817	It'll Be My Song/Dreamers Prayer	1963	20.00

QUINVY

Number	Title (A Side/B Side)	Yr	NM
❑ 001/002	For My Woman's Love/Please Don't Break My Heart	196?	50.00

REVUE

Number	Title (A Side/B Side)	Yr	NM
❑ 11025	Cheaters Never Win/ Love and a Friend	1968	20.00
❑ 11040	I Met Her in Church/ What Kind of Spell	1969	30.00
❑ 11054	Polly Wolly/Gentle on My Mind	1970	20.00

SOUTH CAMP

Number	Title (A Side/B Side)	Yr	NM
❑ 7009	You Better Believe It/ What Kind of Spell	196?	40.00

TCF

Number	Title (A Side/B Side)	Yr	NM
❑ 124	Stay By My Side/Love's Been Good to Me	1966	40.00

UNI

Number	Title (A Side/B Side)	Yr	NM
❑ 55180	Lonely Weekend/ You Better Believe	1969	15.00

BORDERSONG

With Ann and Nancy Wilson, later of HEART.

45s

GREAT NORTHWEST

Number	Title (A Side/B Side)	Yr	NM
❑ 704	She's a Good Woman/Morning	1976	25.00

Albums

REAL GOOD

Number	Title (A Side/B Side)	Yr	NM
❑ 1001	Morning	1975	70.00

BOSSTONES, THE

45s

BOSS

Number	Title (A Side/B Side)	Yr	NM
❑ 401	Mope-Itty Mope/ Wings of an Angel	1959	100.00

—As "Boss Tones"

Number	Title (A Side/B Side)	Yr	NM
❑ 501	Mope-Itty Mope/ Wings of an Angel	1959	200.00

—As "Bosstones"

LOST-NITE

Number	Title (A Side/B Side)	Yr	NM
❑ 107	Mope-Itty Mope/ Wings of an Angel	196?	6.00

—Yellow label with "street lamp" logo

V-TONE

Number	Title (A Side/B Side)	Yr	NM
❑ 208	Mope-Itty Mope/ Wings of an Angel	1960	60.00

BOSTIC, EARL

45s

KING

Number	Title (A Side/B Side)	Yr	NM
❑ 4444	Sleep/September Song	1951	30.00
❑ 4454	Always/How Could It Have Been You and I	1951	30.00
❑ 4475	Flamingo/I'm Getting Sentimental Over You	1951	30.00
❑ 4491	I Got Loaded/Chains of Love	1951	40.00
❑ 4511	The Moon Is Low/ Lover Come Back to Me	1952	25.00
❑ 4536	Linger Awhile/Velvet Sunset	1952	25.00
❑ 4550	Moonglow/Ain't Misbehavin'	1952	25.00
❑ 4570	For You/Smoke Gets In Your Eyes	1952	25.00
❑ 4586	You Go to My Head/ Hour of Parting	1953	25.00
❑ 4603	The Sheik of Araby/ Steamwhistle Jump	1953	25.00
❑ 4623	Cherokee/The Song Is Ended	1953	25.00
❑ 4644	Melancholy Serenade/ What, No Pearls?	1953	25.00
❑ 4653	The Very Thought of You/ Memories	1953	25.00
❑ 4674	Deep Purple/Smoke Rings	1953	25.00
❑ 4683	Off Shore/Don't You Do It	1953	25.00
❑ 4699	My Heart at Thy Sweet Voice/ Cracked Ice	1954	20.00
❑ 4708	Jungle Drums/Danube Waves	1954	20.00
❑ 4723	Blue Skies/Mambolino	1954	20.00
❑ 4730	These Foolish Things/ Mambostic	1954	20.00
❑ 4741	Ubangi Stomp/Time on My Hands	1954	20.00
❑ 4754	Song of the Islands/Liebestraum	1954	20.00
❑ 4765	Embraceable You/Night and Day	1955	20.00
❑ 4776	Melody of Love/Sweet Lorraine	1955	20.00
❑ 4790	Cocktails for Two/When Your Lover Has Gone	1955	20.00
❑ 4799	Remember/Cherry Bean	1955	20.00
❑ 4815	East of the Sun/Dream	1955	20.00
❑ 4829	For All We Know/ Beyond the Blue Horizon	1955	20.00
❑ 4845	O Solo Mio/Poeme	1955	20.00
❑ 4883	I Love You Truly/ 'Cause You're My Lover	1956	15.00
❑ 4905	Bugle Call Rag/ I'll String Along with You	1956	15.00
❑ 4943	Roses of Picardy/Where or When	1956	15.00
❑ 4978	Harlem Nocturne/ I Hear a Rhapsody	1956	15.00
❑ 5025	Too Fine for Crying/Avalon	1957	15.00
❑ 5041	Temptation/September Song	1957	15.00
❑ 5056	She's Funny That Way/Exercise	1957	15.00
❑ 5071	Vienna, City of My Dreams/ Just Too Shy	1957	15.00
❑ 5081	A Gay Day/Answer Me	1957	15.00
❑ 5092	Josephine/Jeannie I Dream of Lilac Time	1957	15.00
❑ 5106	Southern Fried/No Name Jive	1958	15.00
❑ 5120	Lester Leaps In/ Pompton Turnpike	1958	15.00
❑ 5127	Honeysuckle Rose/Back Beat	1958	15.00
❑ 5133	Woodchopper's Ball/John's Idea	1958	15.00
❑ 5136	Twilight Time/Over Waves Rock	1958	15.00
❑ 5144	Pinkie/Home Sweet Home Rock	1958	15.00
❑ 5152	Goodnight Sweetheart/ Indian Boogie Woogie	1958	15.00
❑ 5161	Red Skin Cha Cha/ Rockin' with Richard	1958	15.00
❑ 5175	My Reverie Cha Cha/Barcarole	1959	12.00
❑ 5190	Up There in Orbit/Sweet Pea	1959	12.00
❑ 5203	Up There in Orbit (Part 1)/ Up There in Orbit (Part 2)	1959	12.00
❑ 5209	La Cucaracha Cha Cha/ Dancing in the Dark	1959	12.00
❑ 5229	Who Cares/Feeling Cool	1959	12.00
❑ 5252	White Horse/Dark Eyes	1959	12.00
❑ 5263	Gondola/Once in a While	1959	12.00
❑ 5290	Tut-Strut/All the Things You Are	1959	12.00
❑ 5301	Ebb Tide/Hildegarde	1959	12.00
❑ 5309	Let's Move Out/ I Burned Your Letter	1960	12.00
❑ 5314	Off Shore/Hello '60	1960	12.00
❑ 5317	Elegie/Out of Nowhere	1960	12.00
❑ 5345	Make Believe/A Gay Day	1960	12.00
❑ 5362	Tuxedo Junction/Polonaise	1960	12.00
❑ 5402	720 in the Books/Just in Time	1960	12.00
❑ 5454	That Old Black Magic/ Full Moon and Empty Arms	1961	10.00
❑ 5477	Jersey Bounce/Because of You	1961	10.00
❑ 5564	The Thrill Is Gone/ April in Portugal	1961	10.00
❑ 5600	How Deep Is the Ocean/Wrap It	1962	10.00
❑ 5636	Dark Eyes/People Will Say We're in Love	1962	10.00
❑ 5661	More Than You Know/ Don't Blame Me	1962	10.00
❑ 5683	Ducky/Deep in My Heart	1962	10.00
❑ 5699	Autumn Leaves/Anita's Theme	1962	10.00
❑ 5711	El Choclo Bossa Nova/ My Reverie	1963	10.00
❑ 5742	Cherry Pink (And Apple Blossom White)/Your Cheatin' Heart	1963	10.00
❑ 5776	Love Letters in the Sand/Tammy	1963	10.00
❑ 5819	Apple Cake/Don't Do It Please	1963	10.00
❑ 5839	Telstar Drive/Fast Track	1964	8.00
❑ 5861	Let's Dance Little Girl/ Summertime	1964	8.00
❑ 5900	Make Believe/Star Gazer	1964	8.00
❑ 5925	The Pink Panther/ Lawrence of Arabia	1964	8.00
❑ 5944	From Russia with Love/ My Special Dream	1964	8.00
❑ 5955	Theme from The Unforgiven/ Dominique	1964	8.00
❑ 5961	Hello Dolly/Walk on the Wild Side	1964	8.00
❑ 5977	More/Charade	1965	8.00
❑ 6254	September Song/ Harlem Nocturne	1969	5.00

7-Inch Extended Plays

KING

Number	Title (A Side/B Side)	Yr	NM
❑ EP-200	Flamingo/Swing Low Sweet Boogie//I Can't Give You Anything But Love/ The Moon Is Low	195?	25.00
❑ EP-200 [PS]	Earl Bostic and His Alto Sax, Vol. 1	195?	25.00
❑ EP 201	*Sleep/Earl's Imagination/ Lover Come Back to Me/I'm Gettin' Sentimental Over You	1953	25.00
❑ EP 201 [PS]	Earl Bostic and His Alto Sax, Vol. 2	1953	25.00
❑ EP 202	*Always/Linger Awhile/Merry Widow/Earl Blows a Fuse	1953	25.00
❑ EP 202 [PS]	Earl Bostic and His Alto Sax, Vol. 3	1953	25.00
❑ EP 203	*Deep Purple/Velvet Sunset/ Choppin' It Down/ You Go to My Head	1953	25.00
❑ EP 203 [PS]	Earl Bostic and His Alto Sax, Vol. 4	1953	25.00
❑ EP 204	*Cherokee/Seven Steps/No Name Blues/Don't You Do It	1953	25.00
❑ EP 204 [PS]	Earl Bostic and His Alto Sax, Vol. 5	1953	25.00
❑ EP 205	*Moonglow/For You/ Blip Boogie/Wrap It Up	1953	25.00
❑ EP 205 [PS]	Earl Bostic and His Alto Sax, Vol. 6	1953	25.00
❑ EP 206	*Filibuster/The Sheik of Araby/ Smoke Gets in Your Eyes/ The Hour of Parting	1953	25.00
❑ EP 206 [PS]	Earl Bostic and His Alto Sax, Vol. 7	1953	25.00
❑ EP 207	*Serenade/Ain't Misbehavin'/ Smoke Rings/ Steamwhistle Jump	1953	25.00
❑ EP 207 [PS]	Earl Bostic and His Alto Sax, Vol. 8	1953	25.00
❑ EP 245	Melancholy Serenade/ What! No Pearls//The Very Thought of You/Memories	1954	20.00
❑ EP 245 [PS]	Earl Bostic and His Alto Sax, Vol. 9	1954	20.00
❑ EP 284	*Jungle Drums/The Song Is Ended/Off Shore/ Cracked Ice	1954	20.00
❑ EP 284 [PS]	Earl Bostic and His Alto Sax, Vol. 10	1954	20.00
❑ EP 285	*Danube Waves/My Heart at Thy Sweet Voice/Poeme/ O Sole Mio	1954	20.00
❑ EP 285 [PS]	Earl Bostic and His Alto Sax, Vol. 11	1954	20.00
❑ EP 347	*Mambostic/Time on My Hands/Mambolino/Ven-A-Mi	1955	20.00
❑ EP 347 [PS]	Earl Bostic and His Alto Sax, Vol. 12	1955	20.00
❑ KEP 350	Blue Skies/Ubangi Stomp// Song of the Islands/ These Foolish Things	1955	20.00
❑ KEP 350 [PS]	The Artistry of Earl Bostic, Vol. 13	1955	20.00
❑ EP 355	*Cherry Bean/Liebestraum/ Night and Day/ Embraceable You	1955	20.00
❑ EP 355 [PS]	Earl Bostic and His Alto Sax, Vol. 14	1955	20.00
❑ EP 363	*Melody of Love/Cocktails for Two/Blue Moon/Remember	1955	20.00
❑ EP 363 [PS]	Earl Bostic and His Alto Sax, Vol. 15	1955	20.00
❑ EP 375	*Dream/Beyond the Blue Horizon/East of the Sun/ For All We Know	1956	20.00
❑ EP 375 [PS]	Earl Bostic with Strings, Vol. 16	1956	20.00
❑ EP 381	*Bugle Call Rag/I'll String Along with You/I Love You Truly/ 'Cause You're My Lover	1956	20.00
❑ EP 381 [PS]	Bostic Blows, Vol. 17	1956	20.00
❑ KEP 398	Harlem Nocturne/I Hear a Rhapsody//Roses of Picardy/ Where or When	1957	20.00
❑ KEP 398 [PS]	Earl Bostic, Vol. 18	1957	20.00
❑ EP-405	*She's Funny That Way/How Deep Is the Ocean/Avalon/ September Song	1958	20.00
❑ EP-405 [PS]	Earl Bostic Dance Time	1958	20.00
❑ EP-406	*Temptation/Sweet Lorraine/ Away/Exercise	1958	20.00
❑ EP-406 [PS]	Alto-Tude	1958	20.00
❑ EP-409	*Just Too Shy/Laura/ Josephine/A Gay Day	1958	20.00
❑ EP-409 [PS]	Earl Bostic for Listening and Dancing	1958	20.00
❑ EP-410	*Jeannine I Dream of Lilac Time/Answer Me/Vienna, My City of Dreams/Make Believe	1958	20.00
❑ EP-410 [PS]	Bostic Plays	1958	20.00
❑ EP-414	Jumpin' at the Woodside/ Tuxedo Junction//Southern Fried/Jersey Bounce	1958	20.00
❑ EP-414 [PS]	Hits of the Swing Age, Vol. 1	1958	20.00

Except when noted otherwise, VG = 25% of NM, and VG+ = 50% of NM. (Example: VG = $2.00, VG+ = $4.00 and NM = $8.00.)

Number	Title (A Side/B Side)	Yr	NM
❑ EP-415	*720 in the Books/Air Mail Special/Pompton Turnpike/ Woodchopper's Ball	1958	20.00
❑ EP-415 [PS]	Hits of the Swing Age, Vol. 2	1958	20.00
❑ EP-416	*Night Train/Stompin' at the Savoy/Honeysuckle Rose/ No Name Jive	1958	20.00
❑ EP-416 [PS]	Hits of the Swing Age, Vol. 3	1958	20.00
❑ EP-417	(contents unknown)	1958	20.00
❑ EP-417 [PS]	Showcase of Swinging Dance Hits, Vol. 1	1958	20.00
❑ EP-418	Two O'Clock Jump/Back Beat// John's Idea/Royal Garden Blues	1958	20.00
❑ EP-418 [PS]	Showcase of Swinging Dance Hits, Vol. 2	1958	20.00
❑ EP-419	(contents unknown)	1958	20.00
❑ EP-419 [PS]	Showcase of Swinging Dance Hits, Vol. 3	1958	20.00
❑ EP-420	Twilight Time/Stairway to the Stars//Rockin' with Richard/ Be My Love	1958	20.00
❑ EP-420 [PS]	Alto Magic in Hi Fi, Vol. 1	1958	20.00
❑ EP-421	(contents unknown)	1958	20.00
❑ EP-421 [PS]	Alto Magic in Hi Fi, Vol. 2	1958	20.00
❑ EP-422	C Jam Blues/Wee-Gee Board// The Wrecking Rock/ Home Sweet Home Rock	1958	20.00
❑ EP-422 [PS]	Alto Magic in Hi Fi, Vol. 3	1958	20.00

ROYALE

Number	Title (A Side/B Side)	Yr	NM
❑ EP 367	The Man I Love/All On// Hurricane Blues/ The Major and the Minor	195?	15.00
❑ EP 367 [PS]	His Saxophone and Orchestra	195?	15.00

Albums

GRAND PRIX

Number	Title (A Side/B Side)	Yr	NM
❑ K-404 [M]	The Earl of Bostic	196?	15.00
❑ KS-404 [R]	The Earl of Bostic	196?	12.00
❑ K-416 [M]	Wild Man	196?	15.00
❑ KS-416 [R]	Wild Man	196?	12.00

KING

Number	Title (A Side/B Side)	Yr	NM
❑ 295-64 [10]	Earl Bostic and His Alto Sax	1951	200.00
—Black vinyl			
❑ 295-64 [10]	Earl Bostic and His Alto Sax	1951	400.00
—Red vinyl			
❑ 295-65 [10]	Earl Bostic and His Alto Sax	1951	200.00
—Black vinyl			
❑ 295-65 [10]	Earl Bostic and His Alto Sax	1951	400.00
—Red vinyl			
❑ 295-66 [10]	Earl Bostic and His Alto Sax	1951	200.00
—Black vinyl			
❑ 295-66 [10]	Earl Bostic and His Alto Sax	1951	400.00
—Red vinyl			
❑ 295-72 [10]	Earl Bostic and His Alto Sax	1952	200.00
❑ 295-76 [10]	Earl Bostic and His Alto Sax	1952	200.00
❑ 295-77 [10]	Earl Bostic and His Alto Sax	1952	200.00
❑ 295-78 [10]	Earl Bostic and His Alto Sax	1952	200.00
❑ 295-79 [10]	Earl Bostic and His Alto Sax	1952	200.00
❑ 295-95 [10]	Earl Bostic Plays the Old Standards	1954	200.00
❑ 295-103 [10]	Earl Bostic and His Alto Sax	1954	200.00
❑ 395-500 [M]	Dance to the Best of Bostic	195?	80.00
—Second cover with girl in a swimsuit pictured			
❑ 395-500 [M]	Dance to the Best of Bostic	1956	100.00
—Original cover with Earl Bostic pictured			
❑ 395-503 [M]	Bostic for You	1956	100.00
❑ 395-515 [M]	Alto-Tude	1956	100.00
❑ 395-525 [M]	Dance Time	1956	80.00
❑ 395-529 [M]	Let's Dance with Earl Bostic	1956	80.00
❑ 395-547 [M]	Invitation to Dance	1956	80.00
❑ 558 [M]	C'mon and Dance with Earl Bostic	1956	80.00
❑ KS-558 [S]	C'mon and Dance with Earl Bostic	1959	150.00
❑ 571 [M]	Hits of the Swing Age	1957	80.00
❑ 583 [M]	Showcase of Swinging Dance Hits	1958	80.00
❑ 597 [M]	Alto Magic in Hi-Fi	1958	80.00
❑ KS-597 [S]	Alto Magic in Hi-Fi	1959	150.00
❑ 602 [M]	Sweet Tunes of the Fantastic Fifties	1959	50.00
❑ KSD-602 [S]	Sweet Tunes of the Fantastic Fifties	1959	100.00
❑ 613 [M]	Bostic Workshop	1959	50.00
❑ KS-613 [S]	Bostic Workshop	1959	100.00
❑ 620 [M]	Sweet Tunes from the Roaring Twenties	1959	50.00
❑ KS-620 [S]	Sweet Tunes from the Roaring Twenties	1959	100.00
❑ 632 [M]	Sweet Tunes of the Swinging Thirties	1959	50.00
❑ KS-632 [S]	Sweet Tunes of the Swinging Thirties	1959	100.00
❑ 640 [M]	Sweet Tunes of the Sentimental Forties	1960	50.00
❑ KS-640 [S]	Sweet Tunes of the Sentimental Forties	1960	80.00
❑ 662 [M]	Musical Pearls	1960	50.00
❑ KS-662 [S]	Musical Pearls	1960	80.00
❑ 705 [M]	Hit Tunes of Big Broadway Shows	1960	50.00
❑ KS-705 [S]	Hit Tunes of Big Broadway Shows	1960	80.00
❑ 786 [M]	By Popular Demand	1961	50.00
❑ 827 [M]	Earl Bostic Plays Bossa Nova	1963	50.00
❑ 838 [M]	Songs of the Fantastic Fifties, Vol. 2	1963	50.00
❑ 846 [M]	Jazz As I Feel It	1963	50.00
❑ 881 [M]	The Best of Earl Bostic, Vol. 2	1964	50.00
❑ 900 [M]	The New Sound	1964	50.00
❑ 921 [M]	The Great Hits of 1964	1964	50.00
❑ 947 [M]	24 Songs That Earl Loved the Most	1966	40.00
❑ KS-1048 [S]	Harlem Nocturne	1969	25.00
❑ K-5010X	14 Original Greatest Hits	1977	12.00

PHILIPS

Number	Title (A Side/B Side)	Yr	NM
❑ PHM 200262 [M]	The Song Is Not Ended	1967	25.00
❑ PHS 600262 [S]	The Song Is Not Ended	1967	25.00

BOSTIC, EARL, AND BILL DOGGETT

Also see each artist's individual listings.

45s

KING

Number	Title (A Side/B Side)	Yr	NM
❑ 4930	Mean to Me/Bo-Do Rock	1956	15.00
❑ 4954	Indiana/Bubbins Rock	1956	15.00
❑ 5427	Special Delivery Stomp/ Earl's Dog	1960	10.00

7-Inch Extended Plays

KING

Number	Title (A Side/B Side)	Yr	NM
❑ EP-397	*Bubbins Rock/Indiana/ The Bo-Do Rock/Mean to Me	1957	20.00
❑ EP-397 [PS]	Bill Doggett — Earl Bostic	1957	20.00

BOSTIC, EARL/JIMMY LUNCEFORD

Albums

ALLEGRO ELITE

Number	Title (A Side/B Side)	Yr	NM
❑ 4053 [10]	Earl Bostic/Jimmy Lunceford Orchestras	195?	40.00

BOSTICK, CALVIN

45s

CHESS

Number	Title (A Side/B Side)	Yr	NM
❑ 1530	Christmas Won't Be Christmas Without You/Four-Eleven Boogie	1952	150.00

BOSTON

Also see ORION THE HUNTER.

12-Inch Singles

EPIC

Number	Title (A Side/B Side)	Yr	NM
❑ AS 491 [DJ]	Don't Look Back (Special FM Version)//Don't Look Back (Special FM Version)/ The Journey	1978	12.00
❑ EAS 2581 [DJ]	Rock and Roll Band/ More Than a Feeling	1986	50.00

MCA

Number	Title (A Side/B Side)	Yr	NM
❑ L33-17083 [DJ]	Amanda (same on both sides)	1986	12.00
❑ L33-17242 [DJ]	Cool the Engines/The Launch	1987	15.00
❑ L33-17274 [DJ]	Can'tcha Say (You Believe in Me) (same on both sides)	1987	15.00
❑ L33-17333 [DJ]	Hollyann (Short Version 4:22) (Long Version 5:09)	1987	12.00

45s

EPIC

Number	Title (A Side/B Side)	Yr	NM
❑ 15-02355	More Than a Feeling/Long Time	1981	3.00
—"Golden Oldies" reissue			
❑ 15-02365	Peace of Mind/Don't Look Back	1981	3.00
—"Golden Oldies" reissue			
❑ 8-50266	More Than a Feeling/Smokin'	1976	4.00
❑ 8-50329	Long Time/Let Me Take You Home Tonight	1976	4.00
❑ 8-50381	Peace of Mind/Foreplay	1977	4.00
❑ 8-50590	Don't Look Back/The Journey	1978	4.00
❑ 8-50638	A Man I'll Never Be/ Don't Be Afraid	1978	4.00
❑ 8-50677	Feelin' Satisfied/ Used to Bad News	1979	4.00

MCA

Number	Title (A Side/B Side)	Yr	NM
❑ 52756	Amanda/My Destination	1986	3.00
❑ 52756 [PS]	Amanda/My Destination	1986	3.00
❑ 52985	We're Ready/The Launch	1986	3.00
❑ 52985 [PS]	We're Ready/The Launch	1986	3.00
❑ 53029	Can'tcha Say (You Believe in Me)/Still in Love// Cool the Engines	1987	3.00
❑ 53029 [PS]	Can'tcha Say (You Believe in Me)/Still in Love// Cool the Engines	1987	3.00
❑ 53114	Hollyann/To Be a Man	1987	3.00
❑ 53114 [PS]	Hollyann/To Be a Man	1987	4.00
❑ 54803	I Need Your Love/ We Can Make It	1994	3.00
❑ 54917	What's Your Name/ Walk On (Short Walk)	1994	3.00

Albums

EPIC

Number	Title (A Side/B Side)	Yr	NM
❑ E99 34188	Boston	1978	20.00
—Picture disc			
❑ HE 34188	Boston	1981	50.00
—First edition of the half-speed mastered edition			
❑ JE 34188	Boston	1977	8.00
—Second edition; orange label, different prefix			
❑ JE 34188	Boston	1979	6.00
—Third edition; dark blue label			
❑ PE 34188	Boston	1976	10.00
—Original edition; orange label			
❑ FE 35050	Don't Look Back	1978	10.00
—Original edition; orange label			
❑ FE 35050	Don't Look Back	1979	8.00
—Second edition; dark blue label			
❑ HE 44188	Boston	1982	40.00
—Second edition of the half-speed mastered edition			
❑ HE 45050	Don't Look Back	1982	50.00
—Half-speed mastered edition			

MCA

Number	Title (A Side/B Side)	Yr	NM
❑ 6188	Third Stage	1986	8.00
❑ 10973	Walk On	1994	25.00

MOBILE FIDELITY

Number	Title (A Side/B Side)	Yr	NM
❑ 1-249	Boston	1996	50.00
—Audiophile vinyl			

BOSTON CRABS, THE

45s

CAPITOL

Number	Title (A Side/B Side)	Yr	NM
❑ 5493	Down in Mexico/Who?	1965	10.00

TOWER

Number	Title (A Side/B Side)	Yr	NM
❑ 368	Gin House/Leave My Woman Alone	1967	10.00

BOTKIN, PERRY, JR.

45s

A&M

Number	Title (A Side/B Side)	Yr	NM
❑ 1856	Nadia's Theme (The Young and the Restless)/ Down the Line	1976	10.00
—Original issue; Barry DeVorzon's name was added after he threatened legal action			
❑ 1856 [PS]	Nadia's Theme (The Young and the Restless)/ Down the Line	1976	10.00
—Sleeve with only Perry Botkin Jr.'s name on it (see above listing)			
❑ 1967	Looking for Home/Lovers	1977	4.00
❑ 1990	Bridges/Love Theme from Aspen	1977	4.00

DECCA

Number	Title (A Side/B Side)	Yr	NM
❑ 30912	The Execution Theme/ Waltz of the Hunter	1959	12.00

MGM

Number	Title (A Side/B Side)	Yr	NM
❑ 14357	Soley Soley/(B-side unknown)	1972	5.00
—As "Perry Botkin, Inc."			
❑ 14379	Bless the Beasts and Children/ Lost	1972	5.00

PRIDE

Number	Title (A Side/B Side)	Yr	NM
❑ 1005	Journey to Moscow/ Ellie's Theme	1972	5.00

VALIANT

Number	Title (A Side/B Side)	Yr	NM
❑ 719	Where Does Love Go (Instrumental)/Where Does Love Go (Vocal)	1965	8.00
—B-side by Charles Boyer			
❑ 6025	Careless Love/ Wabash Cannonball	1962	10.00

BOUCHER, PEGI

45s

HIBACK

Number	Title (A Side/B Side)	Yr	NM
❑ 101	The Christmas Clock/ Christmas Tree Heaven	1966	8.00
❑ 101 [PS]	The Christmas Clock/ Christmas Tree Heaven	1966	15.00

BOUGALIEU

45s

ROULETTE

Number	Title (A Side/B Side)	Yr	NM
❑ 4767	Let's Do Wrong/When I Was a Child	1967	25.00
❑ 4776	Let's Do Wrong/When I Was a Child	1967	15.00

BOUQUETS

45s

BLUE CAT

Number	Title (A Side/B Side)	Yr	NM
❑ 115	Welcome to My Heart/ Ain't That Love	1965	30.00

Except when noted otherwise, VG = 25% of NM, and VG+ = 50% of NM. (Example: VG = $2.00, VG+ = $4.00 and NM = $8.00.)

Number	Title (A Side/B Side)	Yr	NM
MALA			
❑ 472	I Love Him So/No Love at All	1964	15.00
VEST			
❑ 8000	Yeah Babe/Girls, Girls	1963	15.00

BOW STREET RUNNERS, THE

Albums

Number	Title (A Side/B Side)	Yr	NM
B.T. PUPPY			
❑ BTPS-1026	The Bow Street Runners	1969	1000.
SUNDAZED			
❑ LP 5029	The Bow Street Runners	199?	10.00
—Reissue of B.T. Puppy LP			

BOWEN, JIMMY

45s

Number	Title (A Side/B Side)	Yr	NM
CAPEHART			
❑ 5005	Teenage Dreamworld/ It's Against the Law	1962	20.00
❑ 5005 [PS]	Teenage Dreamworld/ It's Against the Law	1962	50.00
CREST			
❑ 1085	Don't Drop It/Somebody to Love	1961	20.00
REPRISE			
❑ 0264	The Biggest Lover in Town/ The Big Bus	1964	10.00
❑ 0358	The Golden Eagle/ Spanish Cricket	1965	10.00
❑ 0450	Wonder Mother/ Captain Gorgeous	1966	10.00
❑ 0592	Raunchy/It's Such a Pretty World Today	1967	10.00
ROULETTE			
❑ 4001	I'm Stickin' With You/ Ever Lovin' Fingers	1957	20.00
—With the Rhythm Orchids			
❑ 4010	Warm Up to Me Baby/ I Trusted You	1957	20.00
❑ 4017	Ever Since That Night/Don't Tell Me Your Troubles	1957	20.00
❑ 4023	Cross Over/It's Shameful	1957	20.00
❑ 4057	Can She Kiss/Keeping You	1958	20.00
❑ 4083	By the Light of the Silvery Moon/ The Two Step	1958	20.00
❑ 4102	My Kind of Woman/Blue Moon	1958	20.00
❑ 4122	Always Faithful/Wish I Were Tied to You	1958	20.00
❑ 4175	You're Just Wasting Your Time/ Walkin' on Air	1959	20.00
❑ 4224	Oh Yeah! Oh Yeah! Mm Mm/ Your Loving Arms	1960	20.00
TRIPLE D			
❑ 798	I'm Stickin' With You/Party Doll	1956	1000.
—B-side by Buddy Knox			

7-Inch Extended Plays

Number	Title (A Side/B Side)	Yr	NM
ROULETTE			
❑ EPR-1-302	I'm Stickin' with You/Warm Up to Me Baby//Raggedy Anne/ Ever Since That Night	1957	200.00
❑ EPR-1-302 [PS]	Jimmy Bowen	1957	200.00

Albums

Number	Title (A Side/B Side)	Yr	NM
REPRISE			
❑ R-6210 [M]	Sunday Morning with the Comics	1966	30.00
❑ RS-6210 [S]	Sunday Morning with the Comics	1966	40.00
ROULETTE			
❑ R 25004 [M]	Jimmy Bowen	1957	300.00
—Black and silver label			
❑ R 25004 [M]	Jimmy Bowen	1958	150.00
—Red label			
❑ R 25004 [M]	Jimmy Bowen	198?	12.00
—Reissue for Publishers Central Bureau (it says so on the jacket)			

BOWENS, PRIVATE CHARLES

45s

Number	Title (A Side/B Side)	Yr	NM
ROJAC			
❑ 111	Christmas In Viet Nam/ (B-side unknown)	196?	60.00

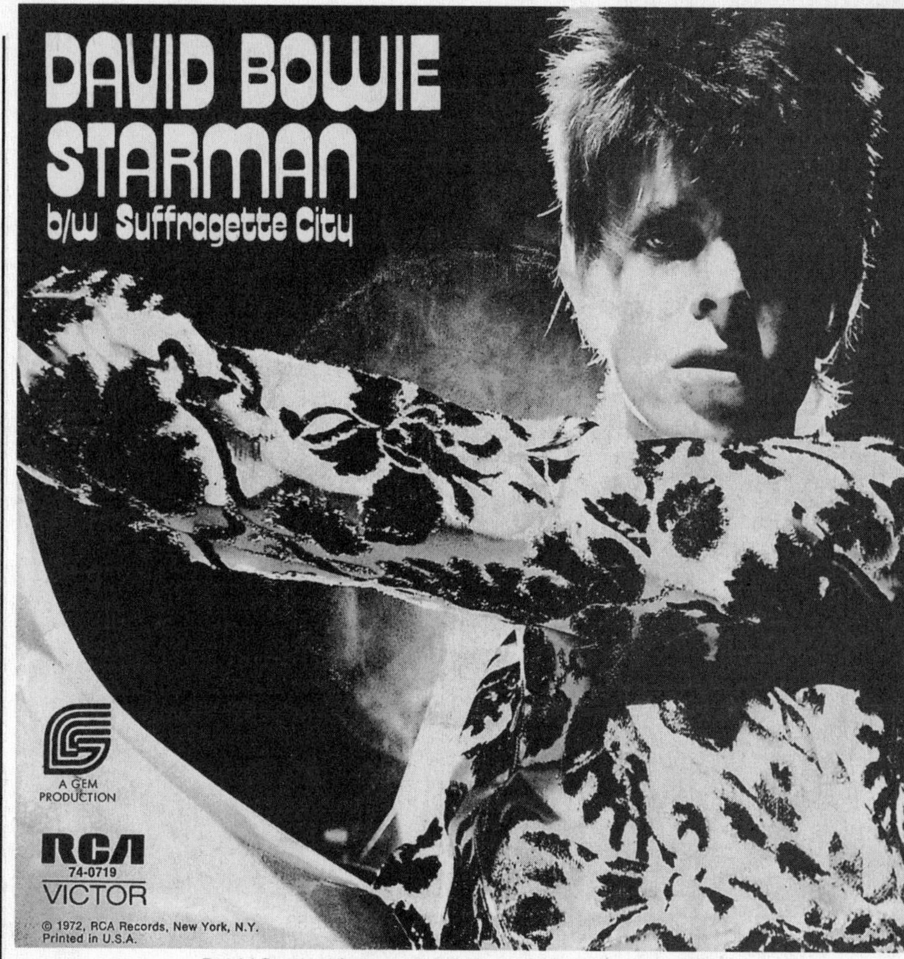

David Bowie, "Starman," RCA Victor 74-0719, 1972, **$30.**

BOWIE, DAVID

12-Inch Singles

Number	Title (A Side/B Side)	Yr	NM
BACKSTREET			
❑ L33-1759 [DJ]	Cat People (Putting Out Fire) (6:41) (4:08)	1982	12.00
EMI			
❑ SPRO-4532 [DJ]	Fame 90 (4 mixes)	1990	15.00
❑ SPRO-04547 [DJ]	Fame 90 (House Mix) (Hip Hop Mix)/(Queen Latifah's Rap Version) (Bonus Beats Instrumental) (Acapulco Rap)	1990	15.00
❑ V-56163	Fame 90 (With Queen Latifah Mix) (House Mix) (Gass Mix)/ (Hip Hop Mix) (Absolutely Nothing Premeditated/ Epic Mix)	1990	8.00
EMI AMERICA			
❑ SPRO-79090 [DJ]	Never Let Me Down (same on both sides)	1987	12.00
❑ SPRO-9996 [DJ]	Day In Day Out (4 versions)	1987	15.00
❑ SPRO-9985 [DJ]	Day In Day Out (same on both sides)	1987	10.00
❑ SPRO-9952 [DJ]	China Girl (Long)/ Shake It (Long)	1983	15.00
❑ SPRO-9904 [DJ]	Let's Dance (same on both sides)	1983	12.00
❑ SPRO-9295 [DJ]	Tonight (same on both sides)	1984	15.00
❑ SPRO-9222 [DJ]	Blue Jean/Dancing with the Big Boys	1984	15.00
❑ V-7805	Let's Dance (Long Version)/Cat People (Putting Out Fire)	1983	8.00
❑ V-7809	China Girl/Shake It	1983	10.00
❑ V-7811	Modern Love/Modern Love (Live)	1983	10.00
❑ V-7838	Blue Jean (Extended Dance Mix)/Dancing with the Big Boys (Extended Dance Mix) (Extended Dub Mix)	1984	8.00
❑ V-7846	Tonight (Vocal Dance Mix 4:29) (Dub 4:18)/Tumble and Twirl (Extended 5:03)	1984	8.00
❑ VG-7858	Loving the Alien (2 versions)/ Don't Look Down	1985	12.00
—With gatefold sleeve and poster			
❑ SEAV-7860	Loving the Alien (Extended Dance Mix) (Extended Dub Mix)/Don't Look Down (Extended Dance Mix)	1985	15.00
—Picture disc			
❑ SPRO-9221/2 [DJ]	Blue Jean/Dancing with the Big Boys	1984	15.00
❑ SPRO-9295 [DJ]	Tonight (same on both sides)	1984	12.00
❑ SPRO 9309/10 [DJ]	This Is Not America (7" Version)/(Instrumental)	z1985	12.00
—With the Pat Metheny Group			
❑ SPRO9670 [DJ]	Underground (Long)/ Underground (Short)	1986	12.00
❑ SPRO 9670/99 [DJ]	Underground (Album Version) (Edited Version)	1986	12.00
❑ SPRO-9904/5 [DJ]	Let's Dance (2 versions)/ Cat People (Putting Out Fire)	1983	12.00
❑ SPRO-9951/2 [DJ]	China Girl (Long)/Shake It (Long)	1983	15.00
❑ SPRO-9985 [DJ]	Day In Day Out (Single Version) (same on both sides)	1987	10.00
❑ SPRO-9996/7 [DJ]	Day In Day Out (7" Dance Edit) (Extended Dance Mix)/ (Edited Dance Mix)	1987	15.00
❑ V-19205	Absolute Beginners (Full Length)/(Dub)	1986	8.00
❑ V-19210	Underground (Extended Dance Mix)/(Dub Mix) (Instrumental Version)	1986	8.00
❑ V-19217	Magic Dance (A Dance Mix)// Magic Dance (Dub)/Within You	1986	8.00
❑ V-19234	Day In Day Out (Extended Dance Mix) (Extended Dub Mix)/Julie	1987	10.00

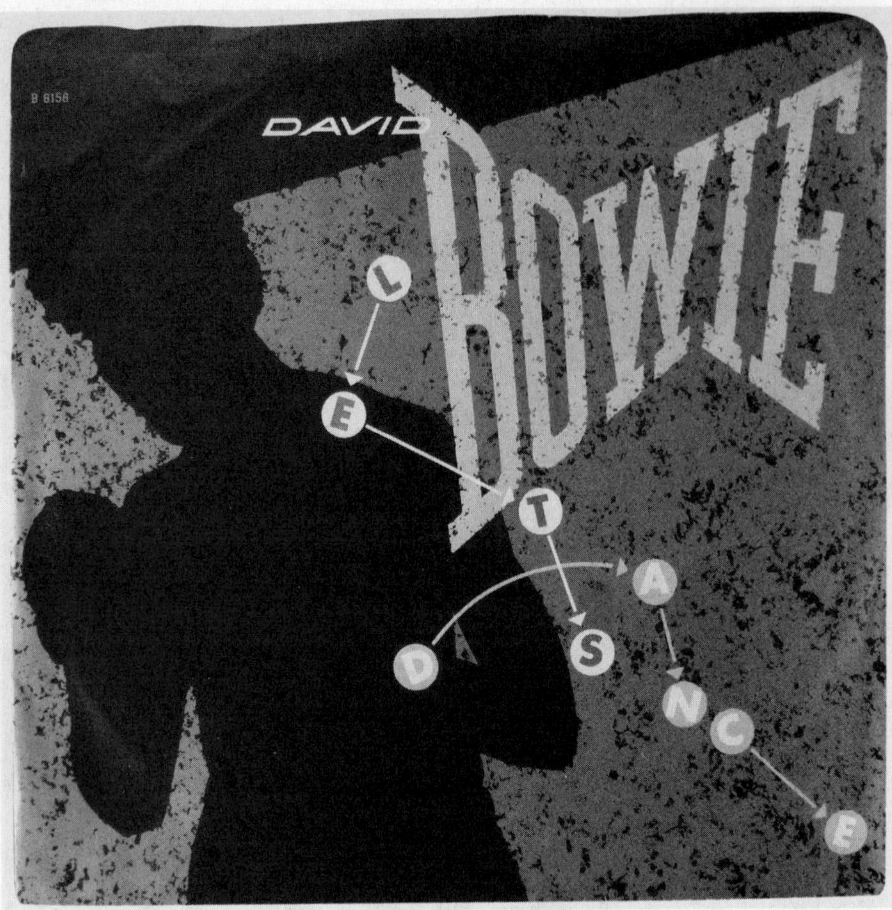

David Bowie, "Let's Dance," EMI 8158, 1983, $3.

Number	Title (A Side/B Side)	Yr	NM
❑ V-19239	Day In Day Out (Groucho Mix) (Extended Dance Mix) (Single Version)	1984	15.00
❑ V-19247	Time Will Crawl (2 versions)/ Girls (2 versions)	1987	10.00
❑ V-19255	Never Let Me Down (Extended Dance Remix) (7" Remix Edit) (Dub) (Acapella) (Instrumental)/ 87 and Cry (Edit)	1987	10.00
❑ SPRO-79090 [DJ]	Never Let Me Down (same on both sides)	1987	10.00
❑ SPRO-79209 [DJ]	Too Dizzy (same on both sides)	1987	20.00
RCA			
❑ JD-12140 [DJ]	Fashion (long)/Fashion (short)	1981	12.00
❑ JD-11306 [DJ]	Peter and the Wolf (Part 1)/ Peter and the Wolf (Part 2)	1978	30.00
❑ PC-11204 [DJ]	Beauty and the Beast/Fame	1978	30.00
❑ DJL1-3795 [DJ]	Space Oddity/Ashes to Ashes (2 versions)	1980	20.00
—Without stamps			
❑ DJL1-3795 [DJ]	Space Oddity/Ashes to Ashes (2 versions)	1980	30.00
—With set of stamps			
❑ DJL1-3255 [DJ]	Star/What in the World/ Breaking Glass	1978	25.00
—White vinyl promo			
❑ DJL1-3255 [DJ]	Star (Live)//What in the World (Live)/Breaking Glass (Live)	1978	25.00
—Promo sampler from the Stage LP; white vinyl (black vinyl versions are counterfeits)			
❑ DJL1-3795 [DJ]	Space Oddity/Ashes to Ashes (Edited) (medley)//Ashes to Ashes (LP Version)	1980	20.00
—Without stamps			
❑ DJL1-3795 [DJ]	Space Oddity/Ashes to Ashes (Edited) (medley)//Ashes to Ashes (LP Version)	1980	30.00
—Also known as "The Continuing Story of Major Tom"; with set of stamps			

Number	Title (A Side/B Side)	Yr	NM
❑ JD-11151 [DJ]	Heroes (Long Version 6:07) (Edited Version 3:31)	1977	25.00
❑ PC-11204 [DJ]	Beauty and the Beast/Fame	1978	30.00
❑ JD-11306 [DJ]	Peter and the Wolf (Part 1 5:52) (Part 2 8:47)/(B-side blank)	1978	30.00
❑ PD-11886	John I'm Only Dancing (Again)/ Golden Years	1980	12.00
❑ JD-12079	Ashes to Ashes/Fashion	1980	—
—Canceled			
❑ JD-12140 [DJ]	Fashion (4:45) (3:23)	1981	12.00
❑ PD-12145	Fashion/Scream Like a Baby	1980	12.00
❑ PD-12249	Up the Hills Backwards/ Crystal Japan	1981	20.00
—Includes sheet of stamps			
❑ PD-13770	1984/TVC 15	1984	8.00
RCA VICTOR			
❑ BOWT 12	Dialogue (Peace On Earth)/ Peace On Earth/Little Drummer Boy// Fantastic Voyage	1982	20.00
—A-side with Bing Crosby; U.K. import			
SAVAGE			
❑ 50039 [DJ]	Jump They Say (5 versions)/ Pallas Athena	1993	12.00
❑ 50039 [DJ]	Jump They Say (5 versions)/ Pallas Athena	1993	15.00
❑ 50042	Jump They Say (5 versions)/ Pallas Athena	1993	10.00
❑ 50045 [DJ]	Black Tie White Noise (7 versions)	1993	15.00
❑ 50045 [DJ]	Black Tie White Noise (Extended Remix) (Club Mix) (Trance Mix)/(Digi Funky's Lush Mix) (Supa Pump Mix) (Funky Crossover Mix) (Extended Urban Mix)	1993	15.00
TOMMY BOY			
❑ TB 510	Sound and Vision (4 versions)	1991	15.00
—As "David Bowie vs. 808 State"			

Number	Title (A Side/B Side)	Yr	NM
VIRGIN			
❑ SPRO-11038 [DJ]	The Hearts Filthy Lesson (Good Karma Mix) (Alt. Mix) (Original Mix)/(Rubber Mix) (Filthy Mix)	1995	12.00
❑ SPRO-11513 [DJ]	Hallo Spaceboy (12" Remix) (7" Remix)/(Lost in Space Mix) (Double Click Mix)	1995	15.00
❑ SPRO-12217 [DJ]	Little Wonder (Junior Vasquez Club Mix) (Album Version)/ (Danny Saber Dance Mix) (Junior Vasquez Club Dub)	1997	12.00
❑ SPRO-12249 [DJ]	Dead Man Walking (Moby Mix 1) (House Mix)/ (Album Version) (Moby Mix 2)	1997	12.00
❑ Y-38618	I'm Afraid of Americans (6 versions)	1997	10.00
WARNER BROS.			
❑ 40575	Real Cool World (4 versions)	1992	10.00
45s			
B&B RECORDS			
❑ 100	Little Drummer Boy/Heroes	197?	50.00
—As "Bing & Bowie"; full-length version with spoken intro; bootleg			
BACKSTREET			
❑ 52024	Cat People (Putting Out Fire)/ Paul's Theme (Jogging Chase)	1982	3.00
—B-side by Georgio Moroder			
❑ 52024 [PS]	Cat People (Putting Out Fire)/ Paul's Theme (Jogging Chase)	1982	3.00
DERAM			
❑ 85009	Rubber Band/There Is a Happy Land	1967	100.00
❑ 85016	Love You Till Tuesday/Did You Ever Have a Dream	1967	100.00
EMI AMERICA			
❑ B-8158	Let's Dance/Cat People (Putting Out Fire)	1983	3.00
❑ B-8158 [PS]	Let's Dance/Cat People (Putting Out Fire)	1983	3.00
❑ B-8165	China Girl/Shake It	1983	3.00
❑ B-8165 [PS]	China Girl/Shake It	1983	6.00
❑ B-8177	Modern Love/ Modern Love (Live)	1983	3.00
❑ B-8177 [PS]	Modern Love/ Modern Love (Live)	1983	3.00
❑ B-8190	Without You/Criminal World	1984	3.00
❑ B-8190 [PS]	Without You/Criminal World	1984	3.00
❑ B-8231	Blue Jean/Dancin' with the Big Boys	1984	3.00
—Second pressing on black vinyl			
❑ B-8231	Blue Jean/Dancin' with the Big Boys	1984	6.00
—First pressing on blue vinyl			
❑ B-8231 [PS]	Blue Jean/Dancin' with the Big Boys	1984	3.00
—Both colors of vinyl have the same picture sleeve			
❑ B-8246	Tonight/Tumble and Twirl	1984	3.00
❑ B-8246 [PS]	Tonight/Tumble and Twirl	1984	6.00
—Fold-out poster sleeve			
❑ B-8251	This Is Not America/ (Instrumental)	1984	3.00
—With the Pat Metheny Group			
❑ B-8251 [PS]	This Is Not America/ (Instrumental)	1984	3.00
❑ BG-8271	Loving the Alien/ Don't Look Down	1985	3.00
❑ BG-8271 [PS]	Loving the Alien/ Don't Look Down	1985	5.00
—Gatefold sleeve			
❑ B-8308	Absolute Beginners/(Dub Mix)	1986	3.00
❑ B-8308 [PS]	Absolute Beginners/(Dub Mix)	1986	4.00
❑ B-8323	Underground/(instrumental)	1986	3.00
❑ B-8323 [PS]	Underground/(instrumental)	1986	4.00
❑ B-8380	Day In Day Out/Julie	1987	3.00
❑ B-8380 [PS]	Day In Day Out/Julie	1987	4.00
❑ B-43020	Time Will Crawl/Girls	1987	3.00
❑ B-43020 [PS]	Time Will Crawl/Girls	1987	15.00
❑ B-43031	Never Let Me Down/'87 and Cry	1987	3.00
❑ B-43031 [PS]	Never Let Me Down/'87 and Cry	1987	4.00
LONDON			
❑ 20079	The Laughing Gnome/ The Gospel According to Tony Day	1973	50.00
MERCURY			
❑ 72949	Space Oddity/Wild-Eyed Boy from Freecloud	1969	50.00
❑ 73075	Memory of a Free Festival Part 1/Part 2	1970	200.00
❑ 73173 [DJ]	All the Madmen (mono/stereo)	1971	100.00
—May be promo only			
❑ 73173 [DJ]	All the Madmen (mono/stereo)	1971	150.00
—May be promo only			

Except when noted otherwise, VG = 25% of NM, and VG+ = 50% of NM. (Example: VG = $2.00, VG+ = $4.00 and NM = $8.00.)

B

Number	Title (A Side/B Side)	Yr	NM

RCA

❑ JE-12087 [DJ] Fashion/It's No Game/ Teenage Wildlife 1980 400.00
❑ PB-10664 TVC 15/We Are the Dead 1976 6.00
❑ PB-10736 Stay/Word on a Wing 1976 6.00
❑ PB-10905 Sound and Vision/A New Career in a New Town 1977 6.00
❑ GB-10938 Fame/Golden Years 1977 3.00
—Gold Standard Series issue
❑ PB-11017 Be My Wife/The Speed of Life 1977 8.00
❑ PB-11121 Heroes/V-2 Schneider 1977 8.00
❑ PB-11190 Beauty and the Beast/ Sense of Doubt 1978 8.00
❑ PB-11585 Boys Keep Swinging/ Fantastic Voyage 1979 6.00
❑ PB-11661 D.J./Fantastic Voyage 1979 8.00
❑ PB-11724 Look Back in Anger/Repetition 1979 6.00
❑ PB-11887 John I'm Only Dancing 1972/ Joe the Lion 1980 6.00
❑ PB-12078 Ashes to Ashes/It's No Game 1980 5.00
❑ PB-12078 [PS] Ashes to Ashes/It's No Game 1980 7.00
—The standard US picture sleeve has David Bowie holding a shoe and looking into it; other variations may exist, but we don't know about them yet
❑ JE-12087 [DJ] Fashion/It's No Game/ Teenage Wildlife 1980 400.00
❑ PB-12134 Fashion/Scream Like a Baby 1980 5.00
❑ PB-12134 [PS] Fashion/Scream Like a Baby 1980 7.00
❑ PH-13400 Peace on Earth-Little Drummer Boy/Fantastic Voyage 1982 5.00
—A-side with Bing Crosby
❑ PH-13400 [PS] Peace on Earth-Little Drummer Boy/Fantastic Voyage 1982 10.00
—A-side with Bing Crosby
❑ PB-13660 White Light-White Heat/ Cracked Actor 1983 5.00
❑ PB-13660 [PS] White Light-White Heat/ Cracked Actor 1983 5.00
❑ PB-13769 1984/TVC 15 1984 5.00
❑ PB-13769 [PS] 1984/TVC 15 1984 6.00

RCA VICTOR

❑ 74-0605 Changes/Andy Warhol 1971 10.00
—Orange label (original)
❑ 74-0605 Changes/Andy Warhol 1974 6.00
—Tan or gray label
❑ 74-0719 Starman/Suffragette City 1972 6.00
❑ 74-0719 [PS] Starman/Suffragette City 1972 30.00
❑ 74-0838 The Jean Genie/ Hang On to Yourself 1972 6.00
❑ 74-0876 Space Oddity/The Man Who Sold the World 1973 6.00
❑ 74-0876 [PS] Space Oddity/The Man Who Sold the World 1973 20.00
❑ APBO-0001 Time/The Prettiest Star 1973 6.00
❑ APBO-0001 [PS] Time/The Prettiest Star 1973 2000.
❑ APBO-0028 Let's Spend the Night Together/ Lady Grinning Soul 1973 6.00
❑ APBO-0160 Sorrow/Amsterdam 1973 6.00
❑ APBO-0287 Rebel Rebel/Lady Grinning Soul 1974 10.00
—All copies contain an alternate mix of "Rebel, Rebel"
❑ APBO-0293 Diamond Dogs/Holy Holy 1974 10.00
—Part of U.S. numbering system, but released only outside the U.S.
❑ PB-10026 1984/Queen Bitch 1974 6.00
❑ PB-10105 Rock and Roll with Me/ Panic in Detroit 1974 6.00
❑ JB-10152 [DJ] Young Americans (3:11) (5:10) 1975 10.00
❑ PB-10152 Young Americans/ Knock on Wood 1975 6.00
—Orange label (West Coast pressing)
❑ PB-10152 Young Americans/ Knock on Wood 1975 6.00
—Tan label (Indianapolis pressing)
❑ JB-10320 [DJ] Fame (Long Version 4:12)/ (Short Version 3:30) 1975 12.00
—Promo-only edition; stock copies contain the 3:30 version
❑ PB-10320 Fame/Right 1975 6.00
—Orange label (West Coast pressing)
❑ PB-10320 Fame/Right 1975 6.00
—Tan label (Indianapolis pressing)
❑ PB-10441 Golden Years/Can You Hear Me 1975 6.00
❑ GB-10468 Changes/Andy Warhol 1975 4.00
—Gold Standard Series issue
❑ GB-10469 Young Americans/ Knock on Wood 1975 4.00
—Gold Standard Series issue
❑ GB-10470 Space Oddity/The Man Who Sold the World 1975 4.00
—Gold Standard Series issue

VIRGIN

❑ S7-19517 Dead Man Walking/Little Wonder 1997 4.00
❑ 58833 Changes/Rebel Rebel 2000 4.00
❑ 58834 Fame/Golden Years 2000 4.00
—Both are full-length versions, not the single edits
❑ 58835 Let's Dance (single edit)/ Modern Love 2000 4.00

WARNER BROS.

❑ 5815 Can't Stop Thinking About Me/ And I Say to Myself 1966 400.00
—As "David Bowie and the Lower Third"

7-Inch Extended Plays

RCA VICTOR

❑ 45-103 [DJ] David Bowie 1972 20.00
❑ 45-103 [DJ] Space Oddity/Moonage Daydream//Life on Mars?/ It Ain't Easy 1972 30.00
❑ 45-103 [PS] David Bowie 1972 30.00

Albums

COLUMBIA

❑ C 86630 Heathen 2002 12.00

DERAM

❑ DE 16003 [M] David Bowie 1967 120.00
❑ DES 18003 [S] David Bowie 1967 150.00

EMI AMERICA

❑ - [DJ] Never Let Me Down: The Interview 1987 25.00
❑ SPRO [(2)DJ] Let's Talk 1983 25.00
—Promo-only interview album
❑ SPRO 9960/1 [(2)DJ] Let's Talk 1983 25.00
—Promo-only interview album
❑ SO-17093 Let's Dance 1983 10.00
❑ SJ-17138 Tonight 1984 10.00
❑ PJ-17267 Never Let Me Down 1987 10.00
❑ SPRO-79112/3 [DJ] Never Let Me Down: The Interview 1987 25.00
❑ R 153730 Let's Dance 1983 12.00
—RCA Music Service edition
❑ R 174212 Never Let Me Down 1987 12.00
—BMG Direct Marketing edition

LONDON

❑ PS 628/9 [(2)] Images 1966-1967 1973 50.00
—Original pressings have dark blue and silver labels. Later pressings, if any, are worth at least 50% less.
❑ LC 50007 Starting Point 1977 12.00

MERCURY

❑ SR 61246 Man of Words, Man of Music 1969 150.00
❑ SR 61325 The Man Who Sold the World 1970 40.00
—An often-counterfeited album; originals have matrix numbers stamped in the trail-off area

MOBILE FIDELITY

❑ 1-064 The Rise and Fall of Ziggy Stardust and the Spiders from Mars 1983 50.00
—Audiophile vinyl
❑ 1-083 Let's Dance 1984 30.00
—Audiophile vinyl

RCA RED SEAL

❑ ARL1-2743 Peter and the Wolf 1978 20.00
—With the Philadelphia Orchestra conducted by Eugene Ormandy; black vinyl
❑ ARL1-2743 Peter and the Wolf 1978 20.00
—With the Philadelphia Orchestra conducted by Eugene Ormandy; green vinyl

RCA VICTOR

❑ [DJ] David Bowie Special 1976 —
—This album has been listed elsewhere, but we can't confirm its existence. The numbering doesn't even make sense.
❑ - [DJ] An Evening with David Bowie 1978 50.00
—Live concert for "Superstars Radio Network"
❑ - [DJ] Bowie Now 1978 75.00
❑ - [DJ] 1980 All Clear 1980 20.00
❑ - [DJ] Scary Monsters Interview 1980 20.00
❑ - [DJ] Special Radio Series, Vol. 1 1980 25.00
❑ - [(2)DJ] Ziggy Stardust, The Motion Picture 1983 50.00
—Promo version on clear vinyl
❑ AFL1-0291 Pin Ups 1978 10.00
—Reissue
❑ APL1-0291 Pin Ups 1973 20.00
❑ CPL1-0576 Diamond Dogs 1974 20.00
—Standard issue, with dog's genitals airbrushed
❑ CPL1-0576 Diamond Dogs 1974 4000.
—Original copies have cover with dog's genitals clearly visible. Almost all were destroyed prior to release.
❑ CPL2-0771 [(2)] David Live 1974 20.00
—At time of release, available with either orange or tan labels
❑ CPL2-0771 [(2)] David Live 1976 12.00
—Reissue with black label, dog near top
❑ APL1-0998 Young Americans 1975 12.00
—At time of release, available with either orange or tan label
❑ APL1-0998 Young Americans 1976 10.00
—Black label
❑ AQK1-0998 Young Americans 1984 10.00
—Reissue
❑ APL1-1327 Station to Station 1976 10.00
—Black label
❑ APL1-1327 Station to Station 1976 12.00
—Originals have a brown label
❑ AQK1-1327 Station to Station 1984 10.00
—Reissue
❑ AFL1-1732 Changesonebowie 1978 10.00
—Reissue
❑ APL1-1732 Changesonebowie 1976 10.00
❑ AQL1-1732 Changesonebowie 1984 10.00
—Reissue
❑ APL1-2030 Low 1977 10.00
❑ AFL1-2522 "Heroes" 1977 10.00
❑ DJL1-2697 [DJ] Bowie Now 1978 60.00
❑ CPL2-2913 [(2)] Stage 1978 20.00
❑ DJL1-3016 [DJ] An Evening with David Bowie 1978 50.00
—Music and interview for "Superstars Radio Network"
❑ AQL1-3254 Lodger 1979 10.00
❑ DJL1-3545 [DJ] 1980 All Clear 1980 25.00
—Promo-only compilation
❑ AQL1-3647 Scary Monsters 1980 10.00
❑ DJL1-3829 [DJ] College Radio Series 1980 25.00
❑ DJL1-3829-A [DJ] Special Radio Series 1980 25.00
—Same material as DJL1-3829
❑ DJL1-3840 [DJ] Scary Monsters Interview 1980 20.00
❑ AYL1-3843 The Rise and Fall of Ziggy Stardust and the Spiders from Mars 1980 8.00
—Reissue
❑ AYL1-3844 Hunky Dory 1980 8.00
—Reissue
❑ AYL1-3856 Low 1980 8.00
—Reissue
❑ AYL1-3857 "Heroes" 1980 8.00
—Reissue
❑ AYL1-3889 Diamond Dogs 1980 8.00
—Reissue
❑ AYL1-3890 Aladdin Sane 1980 8.00
—Reissue
❑ AFL1-4202 Changestwobowie 1981 10.00
❑ AYL1-4234 Lodger 1981 8.00
—Reissue
❑ CPL1-4346 [EP] David Bowie in Berthold Brecht's Baal 1982 10.00
❑ LSP-4623 Hunky Dory 1972 20.00
❑ AYL1-4653 Pin Ups 1982 8.00
—Reissue
❑ AFL1-4702 The Rise and Fall of Ziggy Stardust and the Spiders from Mars 1977 10.00
—Reissue
❑ LSP-4702 The Rise and Fall of Ziggy Stardust and the Spiders from Mars 1972 20.00
—Orange label
❑ LSP-4702 The Rise and Fall of Ziggy Stardust and the Spiders from Mars 1975 12.00
—Tan label
❑ AFL1-4792 Golden Years 1983 10.00
❑ LSP-4813 Space Oddity 1973 20.00
—Reissue of Mercury SR-61246; add 1/3 if bonus poster is enclosed
❑ LSP-4816 The Man Who Sold the World 1973 20.00
—Reissue of Mercury SR-61325; add 1/3 if bonus poster is enclosed
❑ AFL1-4852 Aladdin Sane 1977 10.00
—Reissue
❑ LSP-4852 Aladdin Sane 1973 20.00
—Orange label is original (deduct 50% for tan labels)
❑ CPL2-4862 [(2)] Ziggy Stardust, The Motion Picture 1983 20.00
❑ CPL2-4862 [(2)DJ] Ziggy Stardust, The Motion Picture 1983 50.00
—Promo version on clear vinyl
❑ AFL1-4919 Fame and Fashion 1984 10.00

RYKO ANALOGUE

❑ - [DJ] The Rise and Fall of Ziggy Stardust and the Spiders from Mars 1990 100.00
—Special promo-only package with both the LP and CD versions
❑ RALP 0120/1/2 [(6)] Sound + Vision 1989 80.00
—Six-LP box set on clear vinyl with three gatefold cardboard inner sleeves
❑ RALP 0131 [(2)] Space Oddity 1990 20.00
—Clear vinyl with "Limited Edition" obi
❑ RALP 0132 [(2)] The Man Who Sold the World 1990 20.00
—Clear vinyl with "Limited Edition" obi
❑ RALP 0133 [(2)] Hunky Dory 1990 20.00
—Clear vinyl with "Limited Edition" obi
❑ RALP 0134 [(2)] The Rise and Fall of Ziggy Stardust and the Spiders from Mars 1990 20.00
—Clear vinyl with "Limited Edition" obi
❑ RALP 0135 Aladdin Sane 1990 20.00
—Clear vinyl with "Limited Edition" obi
❑ RALP 0136 Pin Ups 1990 20.00
—Clear vinyl with "Limited Edition" obi
❑ RALP 0137 Diamond Dogs 1990 20.00
—Clear vinyl with "Limited Edition" obi; genitals on dog are restored
❑ RALP 0138/9 [(2)] David Live 1990 20.00
—Clear vinyl with "Limited Edition" obi

B

Number	Title (A Side/B Side)	Yr	NM
❑ RALP 0171 [(2)]	Changesbowie	1990	20.00
—Clear vinyl with "Limited Edition" obi			
❑ LSD-4702 [DJ]	The Rise and Fall of Ziggy Stardust and the Spiders from Mars	1990	100.00
—Special promo-only package with both the LP and CD versions			

BOWIE, DAVID, AND MICK JAGGER

12-Inch Singles

EMI AMERICA

Number	Title (A Side/B Side)	Yr	NM
❑ V-19200	Dancing in the Street (3 versions)	1985	8.00

45s

EMI AMERICA

Number	Title (A Side/B Side)	Yr	NM
❑ B-8288	Dancing in the Street/(Instrumental)	1985	3.00
❑ B-8288 [PS]	Dancing in the Street/(Instrumental)	1985	3.00

BOX OF FROGS Featuring ex-members of THE YARDBIRDS.

12-Inch Singles

EPIC

Number	Title (A Side/B Side)	Yr	NM
❑ AS 1898 [DJ]	Back Where I Started (same on both sides)	1984	10.00
❑ EAS 2384 [DJ]	Get It While You Can (same on both sides)	1986	8.00

45s

EPIC

Number	Title (A Side/B Side)	Yr	NM
❑ 34-04593	Two Steps Ahead/The Edge	1984	5.00

Albums

EPIC

Number	Title (A Side/B Side)	Yr	NM
❑ EAS 1904 [DJ]	Interchords	1984	20.00
—Promo-only interview album			
❑ BFE 39327	Box of Frogs	1984	10.00
❑ BFE 39923	Strange Land	1986	10.00

BOX TOPS, THE Lead singer Alex Chilton was later in BIG STAR.

45s

ARISTA

Number	Title (A Side/B Side)	Yr	NM
❑ 9488	Sweet Cream Ladies/Neon Rainbow	1986	3.00
—"Flashback" oldies series			

BELL

Number	Title (A Side/B Side)	Yr	NM
❑ 865	Come On Honey/You Keep Tightening Up on Me	1970	8.00
❑ 923	Let Me Go/Got to Hold On to You	1970	8.00
❑ 981	King's Highway/Since I've Been Gone	1971	8.00

GUSTO

Number	Title (A Side/B Side)	Yr	NM
❑ 2112	The Letter/Cry Like a Baby	1981	4.00
—Re-recordings			

HI

Number	Title (A Side/B Side)	Yr	NM
❑ 2228	It's All Over/Sugar Creek Woman	1972	6.00
❑ 2242	Hold On Girl/Angel	1973	6.00

MALA

Number	Title (A Side/B Side)	Yr	NM
❑ 565	The Letter/Happy Times	1967	12.00
❑ 580	Neon Rainbow/Everything I Am	1967	10.00
❑ 593	Cry Like a Baby/The Door You Closed to Me	1968	12.00
❑ 12005	Choo Choo Train/Fields of Clover	1968	10.00
❑ 12017	I Met Her in Church/People Gonna Talk	1968	10.00
❑ 12035	Sweet Cream Ladies, Forward March/I See Only Sunshine	1968	10.00
❑ 12038	I Shall Be Released/I Must Be the Devil	1969	10.00
❑ 12040	Soul Deep/The Happy Song	1969	10.00
❑ 12042	Turn On a Dream/Together	1969	10.00

PHILCO-FORD

Number	Title (A Side/B Side)	Yr	NM
❑ HP-27	The Letter/Happy Times	1968	20.00
—4-inch plastic "Hip Pocket Record" with color sleeve			

SPHERE SOUND

Number	Title (A Side/B Side)	Yr	NM
❑ 77001	The Letter/Happy Times	1969	10.00
—Blue label; reissue			
❑ 77001	The Letter/Happy Times	1970	8.00
—Silver label; reissue			
❑ 77002	Cry Like a Baby/The Door You Closed to Me	1970	8.00
—Silver label; reissue			

STAX

Number	Title (A Side/B Side)	Yr	NM
❑ 0199	It's Gonna Be O.K./Willobee and Dale	1974	6.00

Albums

BELL

Number	Title (A Side/B Side)	Yr	NM
❑ 6011 [M]	The Letter/Neon Rainbow	1967	25.00
❑ S-6011 [S]	The Letter/Neon Rainbow	1967	20.00
❑ 6017	Cry Like a Baby	1968	20.00
❑ 6023	Non-Stop	1968	20.00
❑ 6025	The Box Tops Super Hits	1968	20.00
❑ 6032	Dimensions	1969	20.00

RHINO

Number	Title (A Side/B Side)	Yr	NM
❑ RNLP-161	The Greatest Hits	1982	12.00

BOXER, KARL

45s

DOT

Number	Title (A Side/B Side)	Yr	NM
❑ 16853	Hava Nagila/A Piece of the Action	1966	20.00

BOY GEORGE

12-Inch Singles

CENTAUR

Number	Title (A Side/B Side)	Yr	NM
❑ CEN 30011	When Will You Learn (Dado Club Mix) (Main Club Mix)/(Julian Groove Mix) (Santana Dub)	1999	8.00

SBK

Number	Title (A Side/B Side)	Yr	NM
❑ SPRO-04738 [DJ]	The Crying Game (Digifunky String Mix) (Digifunky Diva Dub) (Album Version)/(Third Floor Trance Mix) (Third Floor Trance Dub) (DJ EFX's Tribal as a Mofo Mix)	1993	20.00

VIRGIN

Number	Title (A Side/B Side)	Yr	NM
❑ 1052 [DJ]	Everything I Own (3 versions)/Use Me	1987	7.00
❑ DMD 1052 [DJ]	Everything I Own (3 versions)/Use Me	1987	8.00
❑ 1116 [DJ]	Live My Life (4 versions)	1988	7.00
❑ DMD 1116 [DJ]	Live My Life (4 versions)	1988	10.00
❑ 1292 [DJ]	Don't Take My Mind on a Trip (4 versions)/Girlfriend	1989	8.00
❑ DMD 1292 [DJ]	Don't Take My Mind on a Trip (12" UK Acid Mix) (12" UK Acid Dub) (Boris & Chris 12" Mix) (Main Club Mix)/Girlfriend	1989	12.00
❑ 1353 [DJ]	You've Found Another Guy (3 versions)/I Go Where I Go	1989	6.00
❑ DMD 1353 [DJ]	You Found Another Guy (3 versions)/I Go Where I Go	1989	10.00
❑ 2994 [DJ]	Whisper (Edit)/Whisper (LP version)	1989	6.00
❑ PR 2994 [DJ]	Whisper (Edit) (LP Version)	1989	10.00
❑ SPRO-11052 [DJ]	Same Thing in Reverse (Evolution's Brick in My Handbag Mix) (Evolution's K.Y. Classic Dub) (Country Queen Mix) (Evolution's Kamikaze Full Popswitch Mix) (Clubzone's 303 Is Big Enough for Me Mix)	1995	8.00
❑ SPRO-12815 [DJ]	Funtime (Ramp Alien Spawn Club Mix) (Space Food Dub Mix)	1995	8.00
❑ 96446	Generations of Love (Land of Oz Mix) (Future Dub) (The 70's Club Mix)/(The 80's Mix) (The 70's Edit)	1990	15.00
❑ 96545	You Found Another Guy (3 versions)/I Go Where I Go	1989	8.00
❑ 96577	Don't Take My Mind on a Trip (12" UK Acid Mix) (12" UK Acid Dub)/(Boris & Chris 12" Mix) (Main Club Mix)/Girlfriend	1989	8.00
❑ 96728	Live My Life (12" Klub Mix) (Klub Dub) (12" Soul Remix) (The Quake Dub)	1988	8.00
❑ 96765	Everything I Own (3 versions)/Use Me	1987	6.00

45s

SBK

Number	Title (A Side/B Side)	Yr	NM
❑ S7-56996	The Crying Game/Stand By Your Man	1993	4.00
—Black vinyl; B-side by Lyle Lovett			
❑ S7-56996	The Crying Game/Stand By Your Man	1993	6.00
—Red vinyl; B-side by Lyle Lovett			

VIRGIN

Number	Title (A Side/B Side)	Yr	NM
❑ S7-17709	Everything I Own/Miss Me Blind	1994	4.00
—B-side by "Boy George and Culture Club"			
❑ S7-18735	Funtime/Same Thing in Reverse	1995	4.00
❑ 99159	Whisper/Leave in Love	1989	4.00
❑ 99200	You Found Another Guy/I Go Where I Go	1989	2.00
❑ 99200 [PS]	You Found Another Guy/I Go Where I Go	1989	2.00
❑ 99272	Don't Take My Mind on a Trip/Girlfriend	1988	3.00
❑ 99390	Live My Life (The Mix)/(Soul Remix)	1987	3.00
❑ 99445	Everything I Own/Use Me	1987	4.00
❑ 99445 [PS]	Everything I Own/Use Me	1987	6.00

Albums

VIRGIN

Number	Title (A Side/B Side)	Yr	NM
❑ 90617	Sold	1987	10.00
❑ 91022	High Hat	1989	10.00
❑ R 100843	High Hat	1989	12.00
—BMG Direct Marketing edition			
❑ R 153255	Sold	1987	12.00
—BMG Direct Marketing edition			

BOYCE, TOMMY Also see TOMMY BOYCE AND BOBBY HART.

45s

A&M

Number	Title (A Side/B Side)	Yr	NM
❑ 809	Sunday, The Day Before Monday/The Green Grass (Is Turning Brown)	1966	15.00
❑ 826	In Case the Wind Should Blow/Simon Smith and the Amazing Dancing Bear	1966	25.00

CAPITOL

Number	Title (A Side/B Side)	Yr	NM
❑ 3136	Alice My Sweet/Eve Laurain	1971	5.00

CHELSEA

Number	Title (A Side/B Side)	Yr	NM
❑ BCBO-0101	Thank God for Rock and Roll/Krush on Kris	1973	5.00
—As "Christopher Cloud"			
❑ 78-0118	Zip-a-Dee-Doo-Dah/Interpretation of War	1973	5.00
—As "Christopher Cloud"			

COLPIX

Number	Title (A Side/B Side)	Yr	NM
❑ 794	Let's Go Where the Action Is/(Instrumental)	1966	20.00

DOT

Number	Title (A Side/B Side)	Yr	NM
❑ 16117	The Gypsy Song/Give Me the Clue	1960	20.00

MGM

Number	Title (A Side/B Side)	Yr	NM
❑ 13400	Pretty Thing (You Look Out of Sight Tonight)/I Don't Have to Worry 'Bout You	1965	15.00
❑ 13429	Little Suzy Somethin'/Pee's N' Que's	1965	15.00

R-DELL

Number	Title (A Side/B Side)	Yr	NM
❑ 111	Betty Jean/I'm Not Sure	1960	25.00

RCA VICTOR

Number	Title (A Side/B Side)	Yr	NM
❑ 47-7975	Along Came Linda/You Look So Lonely	1961	20.00
❑ 47-8025	Come Here Joanne/The Way I Used to Do	1962	20.00
❑ 47-8074	I'll Remember Carol/Too Late for Tears	1962	20.00
❑ 47-8126	Have You Had a Change of Heart/Sweet Little Baby, I Care	1963	20.00
❑ 47-8208	Don't Be Afraid/A Million Things to Say	1963	20.00

WOW

Number	Title (A Side/B Side)	Yr	NM
❑ 345	Is It True/Little One	1961	20.00

Albums

RCA CAMDEN

Number	Title (A Side/B Side)	Yr	NM
❑ CAL-2202 [M]	Tommy Boyce	1967	20.00
❑ CAS-2202 [S]	Tommy Boyce	1967	25.00

BOYCE, TOMMY, AND BOBBY HART Also see each artist's individual listings.

45s

A&M

Number	Title (A Side/B Side)	Yr	NM
❑ 858	Out and About/My Little Chickadee	1967	10.00
❑ 858 [PS]	Out and About/My Little Chickadee	1967	20.00
❑ 874	Sometimes She's a Little Girl/Love Every Day	1967	10.00
❑ 874 [PS]	Sometimes She's a Little Girl/Love Every Day	1967	20.00
❑ 893	I Wonder What She's Doing Tonight/The Ambushers	1967	12.00
❑ 893 [PS]	I Wonder What She's Doing Tonight/The Ambushers	1967	20.00
❑ 919	Goodbye Baby (I Don't Want to See You Cry)/Where Angels Go, Trouble Follows	1968	10.00
❑ 919 [PS]	Goodbye Baby (I Don't Want to See You Cry)/Where Angels Go, Trouble Follows	1968	20.00
❑ 948	Alice Long (You're Still My Favorite Girlfriend)/P.O. Box 9847	1968	10.00
❑ 948 [PS]	Alice Long (You're Still My Favorite Girlfriend)/P.O. Box 9847	1968	20.00
❑ 993	We're All Going to the Same Place/6 + 6	1968	10.00
❑ 993 [PS]	We're All Going to the Same Place/6 + 6	1968	10.00
❑ 1017	Maybe Somebody Heard/It's All Happening on the Inside	1969	8.00
❑ 1031	L.U.V. (Let Us Vote)/I Wanna Be Free	1969	8.00

Number	Title (A Side/B Side)	Yr	NM
❑ 1031 [PS]	L.U.V. (Let Us Vote)/I Wanna Be Free	1969	15.00
AQUARIAN			
❑ 380	I'll Blow You a Kiss in the Wind/Smilin'	1970	4.00
❑ 380 [PS]	I'll Blow You a Kiss in the Wind/Smilin'	1970	6.00

Albums

Number	Title (A Side/B Side)	Yr	NM
A&M			
❑ LP-126 [M]	Test Patterns	1967	20.00
❑ LP-143 [M]	I Wonder What She's Doing Tonite?	1968	30.00
❑ SP-4126 [S]	Test Patterns	1967	20.00
❑ SP-4143 [S]	I Wonder What She's Doing Tonite?	1968	20.00
❑ SP-4162	It's All Happening on the Inside	1968	20.00

BOYD, EDDIE

45s

Number	Title (A Side/B Side)	Yr	NM
ART TONE			
❑ 832	I'm Comin' Home/Operator	1962	15.00
BEA & BABY			
❑ 101	I'm Comin' Home/Thank You Baby	1959	15.00
❑ 107	Blue Monday Blues/The Blues Is Here to Stay	1959	15.00
❑ 108	Come Home/You've Got to Reap What You Sow	1959	15.00
CHESS			
❑ 1523	Cool Kind Treatment/Rosa Lee Swing	1952	100.00
❑ 1533	24 Hours/The Tickler	1953	100.00
—Black vinyl			
❑ 1533	24 Hours/The Tickler	1953	400.00
—Red vinyl			
❑ 1541	Third Degree/Back Beat	1953	200.00
—Black vinyl			
❑ 1541	Third Degree/Back Beat	1953	500.00
—Red vinyl			
❑ 1552	That's When I Miss You So/Tortured Soul	1953	80.00
❑ 1561	Nothing But Trouble/Picture in the Frame	1954	60.00
❑ 1573	Hush Baby, Don't You Cry/Came Home This Morning	1954	60.00
❑ 1576	Driftin'/Rattin' and Runnin' Around	1954	60.00
❑ 1582	The Story of Bill/Please Help Me	1954	60.00
❑ 1595	The Nightmare Is Over/Real Good Feeling	1955	50.00
❑ 1606	I'm a Prisoner/I've Been Deceived	1955	50.00
❑ 1621	Don't/Life Gets to Be a Burden	1956	40.00
❑ 1634	Just a Fool/Four Leaf Clover	1956	40.00
❑ 1660	I Got a Woman/Hotel Blues	1957	40.00
❑ 1674	I Got the Blues/She's the One	1957	40.00
HERALD			
❑ 406	Lonesome for My Baby/I'm Goin' Downtown	1953	400.00
J.O.B.			
❑ 1007	Five Long Years/Blue Coat Man	1952	150.00
—Black vinyl			
❑ 1007	Five Long Years/Blue Coat Man	1952	300.00
—Red vinyl			
❑ 1009	It's Miserable to Be Alone/I'm Pleading	1953	300.00
❑ 1114	I Love You/Save Her Doctor	1957	60.00
RCA VICTOR			
❑ 50-0006	What Makes These Things Happen/Chicago Is Just That Way	1950	120.00
—Gray label, orange vinyl			

BOYD, JIMMY

Also see ROSEMARY CLOONEY; FRANKIE LAINE.

45s

Number	Title (A Side/B Side)	Yr	NM
CAPITOL			
❑ 4967	Day Dreamer/I've Got It Made	1963	10.00
COLUMBIA			
❑ 4-152	I Saw Mommy Kissing Santa Claus/Thumbelina	1952	20.00
—Yellow-label Children's Series issue; alternate number is 90174			
❑ 4-152 [PS]	I Saw Mommy Kissing Santa Claus/Thumbelina	1952	25.00
❑ 4-183	Santa Got Stuck in the Chimney/I Said a Prayer for Santa Claus	1953	15.00
—Yellow-label Children's Series issue			
❑ 4-183 [PS]	Santa Got Stuck in the Chimney/I Said a Prayer for Santa Claus	1953	20.00
❑ 21571	Rockin' Down the Mississippi/Crazy Mixed Up Blues	1956	50.00
❑ 39696	God's Little Candles/Owl Lullaby	1952	15.00
❑ 39733	Little Train A-Chuggin'/Needle In, Needle Out	1952	15.00
❑ 39871	I Saw Mommy Kissing Santa Claus/Thumbelina	1952	15.00
❑ 39927	Early Bird/I'll Stay in the House	1953	15.00
❑ 39955	My Bunny and My Sister Sue/Two Easter Sunday Sweethearts	1953	15.00
❑ 40007	Playmates/Shoo Fly Pie and Apple Pan Dowdy	1953	15.00
❑ 40049	Marco, the Polo Pony/God Bless Us All	1953	15.00
❑ 40070	I Saw Mommy Kissing Santa Claus/Santa Claus Is Coming to Town	1953	12.00
❑ 40071	Winter Wonderland/Here Comes Santa Claus	1953	12.00
❑ 40072	Silent Night, Holy Night/Frosty the Snowman	1953	12.00
❑ 40073	The Little Match Girl/Rudolph, the Red-Nosed Reindeer	1953	12.00
❑ 40080	Santa Got Stuck in the Chimney/I Said a Prayer for Santa Claus	1953	15.00
—With Johnny Bond			
❑ 40138	I've Got Those "Wake Up Seven-Thirty, Wash Your Ears They're Dirty, Eat Your Eggs and Oatmeal, Rush to School" Blues/Jelly on My Head	1954	20.00
❑ 40181	Little Bonny Bunny/Jimmy, Roll Me Gently	1954	15.00
❑ 40218	I'm So Glad (I'm a Little Boy and You're a Little Girl)/Kitty in the Basket	1954	15.00
—With Gayla Peevey			
❑ 40253	Ma I Miss Your Apple Pie/Shepherd Boy	1954	15.00
❑ 40304	Little Sir Echo/The Little White Duck	1954	15.00
❑ 40365	I Saw Mommy Do the Mambo (With You Know Who)/Santa Claus Blues	1954	15.00
❑ 40504	I Want a Haircut with a Moon on Top/How Come	1955	12.00
❑ 40601	Reindeer Rock/A Kiss for Christmas	1955	20.00
❑ 40756	Don't Forget to Say Your Prayers/Little Dog	1956	12.00
❑ 40881	I Wanna Go Steady/Gonna Take My Heart on a Hayride	1957	12.00
❑ 41547	Dennis the Menace/Little Josey	1960	20.00
—With Rosemary Clooney			
DOT			
❑ 16126	Dusty/Jambalaya	1960	12.00
IMPERIAL			
❑ 66166	I Would Never Do That/Lazy Me	1966	8.00
❑ 66206	She Chased Me/Will I Cry	1966	8.00
❑ 66233	So Young and So Fine/I Would Never Do That	1967	8.00
JUBILEE			
❑ 5316	Don't Tempt Me/High School Social	1958	12.00
MGM			
❑ 12788	Cream Puff/I Love You So Much	1959	60.00
VEE JAY			
❑ 620	All Alone/In Love In Vain	1964	10.00
❑ 686	That's What I'll Give to You/My Home Town	1965	10.00

7-Inch Extended Plays

Number	Title (A Side/B Side)	Yr	NM
COLUMBIA			
❑ B-1913	I Saw Mommy Kissing Santa Claus/Jingle Bells//I Said A Prayer For Santa Claus/Santa Got Stuck In The Chimney	195?	12.00
❑ B-1913 [PS]	Jimmy Boyd	195?	15.00

Albums

Number	Title (A Side/B Side)	Yr	NM
COLUMBIA			
❑ CL 2543 [10]	I Saw Mommy Kissing Santa Claus	1955	40.00
—"House Party Series" reissue			
❑ CL 6270 [10]	Christmas with Jimmy Boyd	1953	100.00

BOYD, MICKEY, AND THE PLAIN VIEWERS

See THE STRING-A-LONGS.

BOYFRIENDS, THE

Also known as THE FIVE DISCS.

45s

Number	Title (A Side/B Side)	Yr	NM
KAPP			
❑ 569	Let's Fall in Love/Oh Lana	1964	100.00

BOYS NEXT DOOR, THE

45s

Number	Title (A Side/B Side)	Yr	NM
ATCO			
❑ 6443	Mandy/One Face in the Crowd	1966	12.00
❑ 6455	Christmas Kiss/The Wildest Christmas	1966	12.00
❑ 6477	Be Gone Girl/See the Way She's Mine	1967	12.00
CAMEO			
❑ 394	There Is No Greater Sin/I Could See Me Dancing with You	1965	15.00
SOMA			
❑ 1439	Suddenly She Was Gone/Why Be Proud	1965	40.00

BOZ

Boz Burrell, later of KING CRIMSON and BAD COMPANY.

45s

Number	Title (A Side/B Side)	Yr	NM
EPIC			
❑ 10097	Baby Song/Pinocchio	1966	10.00
❑ 10097 [PS]	Baby Song/Pinocchio	1966	15.00

BOZE, CALVIN

45s

Number	Title (A Side/B Side)	Yr	NM
ALADDIN			
❑ 3045	Waiting and Drinking/If You Ever Had the Blues	1950	150.00
❑ 3055	Safronia Blues/Angel City Blues	1950	150.00
❑ 3065	Lizzie Lou/Lizzie Lou (Part 2)	1950	150.00
❑ 3072	Stinkin' from Drinkin'/Look Out for Tomorrow Today	1950	100.00
❑ 3079	Beat Street on Saturday Night/Choo Choo Ch'Boogieing My Baby Back Home	1951	100.00
❑ 3086	Slippin' and Slidin'/Baby, You're Tops with Me	1951	100.00
❑ 3100	I've Got News for You/I Can't Stop Crying	1951	80.00
❑ 3110	I'm Gonna Steam Off the Stamp/Fish Tail	1952	80.00
❑ 3122	Hey, Lawdy Miss Clawdy/My Friend Told Me	1952	80.00
❑ 3132	Good Time Sue/Keep Your Nose Out of My Business	1952	60.00
❑ 3142	The Blue Tango/The Glory of Love	1952	60.00
❑ 3143	Blue Shuffle/Popside	1952	60.00
❑ 3147	Looped/Blow Man Blow	1952	60.00
❑ 3160	Havin' a Time/Shamrock	1953	50.00
❑ 3181	That Other Woman/Shoot De Pistol	1953	50.00
IMPERIAL			
❑ 5844	Shamrock/Safronia B	1962	12.00

BRACELETS, THE

45s

Number	Title (A Side/B Side)	Yr	NM
CONGRESS			
❑ 104	I'll Play Along/Waddle, Waddle	1962	16.00
20TH CENTURY-FOX			
❑ 539	You Better Move On/You're Just Fooling Yourself	1964	12.00

BRADEN, JOHN

45s

Number	Title (A Side/B Side)	Yr	NM
A&M			
❑ 1066	What a Friend We Have in Jesus/Hand Me Down Man	1969	10.00

Albums

Number	Title (A Side/B Side)	Yr	NM
A&M			
❑ SP-4172	John Braden	1969	15.00

BRADLEY, BERRY

45s

Number	Title (A Side/B Side)	Yr	NM
HIT			
❑ 88	That Sunday, That Summer/Don't Think Twice, It's All Right	1963	8.00
—B-side by Jimmy, Wayne and Betty			

BRADLEY, HAROLD

45s

Number	Title (A Side/B Side)	Yr	NM
COLUMBIA			
❑ 4-42694	Devil Woman/Walk On By	1963	10.00
❑ 4-42830	Maria Elena/A La Orilla Del Lago	1963	10.00
❑ 4-43043	Sugarfoot Rag/Wildwood Flower	1964	8.00

Albums

Number	Title (A Side/B Side)	Yr	NM
COLUMBIA			
❑ CL 2014 [M]	Bossa Nova Goes to Nashville	1963	12.00
❑ CL 2073 [M]	Misty Guitar	1963	12.00
❑ CL 2456 [M]	Guitar for Lovers Only	1966	12.00
❑ CS 8814 [S]	Bossa Nova Goes to Nashville	1963	15.00
❑ CS 8873 [S]	Misty Guitar	1963	15.00
❑ CS 9256 [S]	Guitar for Lovers Only	1966	15.00
HARMONY			
❑ H 31324	Guitar for Sentimental Lovers	1971	12.00

BRADLEY, JAN

45s

CHESS

Number	Title (A Side/B Side)	Yr	NM
❑ 1845	Mama Didn't Lie/Lovers Like Me	1962	10.00
❑ 1851	These Tears/Baby What Can I Do	1963	8.00
❑ 1884	Curfew Blues/Pack My Things	1964	8.00
❑ 1897	Please Mr. D.J./Two of a Kind	1964	8.00
❑ 1919	I'm Over You/The Brush-Off	1964	8.00
❑ 1975	Just a Summer Memory/He'll Wait for Me	1966	6.00
❑ 1996	Trust Me/Things a Woman Needs	1967	6.00
❑ 2023	Your Kind of Love/It's Just Your Way	1967	6.00
❑ 2043	You Have Me What's Missing/Nights in New York City	1968	6.00

FORMAL

Number	Title (A Side/B Side)	Yr	NM
❑ 1044	Mama Didn't Lie/Lovers Like Me	1962	200.00
❑ 1048	Dear Sears and Roebuck/(B-side unknown)	1963	12.00

HOOTENANNY

Number	Title (A Side/B Side)	Yr	NM
❑ 1	Christmas Time (Part 1)/Christmas Time (Part 2)	1962	12.00

BRADSHAW, JACK

45s

DECCA

Number	Title (A Side/B Side)	Yr	NM
❑ 29654	My Heart, My Heart/Flirting with You	1955	25.00

GLENN

Number	Title (A Side/B Side)	Yr	NM
❑ 754	No, No/Welcome Heart	1955	60.00
❑ 755	I Got What You Need/You Hurt Me	195?	60.00

MAR-VEL

Number	Title (A Side/B Side)	Yr	NM
❑ 750	Don't Tease Me/Don't Cause Me to Hate You	1954	100.00
❑ 751	Searchin'/My Heart, My Heart	1955	60.00
❑ 752	It Just Ain't Right/Naughty Girls	1955	60.00
❑ 753	Jo Jo/Men Are Weak	1955	100.00
❑ 756	Saturday Night Special/Out of the Picture	195?	60.00

BRADSHAW, TINY

45s

KING

Number	Title (A Side/B Side)	Yr	NM
❑ 4376	After You've Gone/Boogie Green	1950	60.00
❑ 4397	Butterfly/I'm Going to Have Myself a Ball	1950	60.00
❑ 4417	Breaking Up the House/If You Don't Love Me, Tell Me So	1950	60.00
❑ 4427	Walk That Mess/One, Two, Three, Kick Blues	1951	60.00
❑ 4447	Brad's Blues/Two Dry Bones on the Pantry Shelf	1951	60.00
❑ 4457	Bradshaw Boogie/Walkin' the Chalk Line	1951	60.00
❑ 4467	I'm a High Ballin' Daddy/You Came By	1951	60.00
❑ 4487	T-99/Long Time Baby	1951	200.00
❑ 4497	The Train Kept a-Rollin'/Knockin' Blues	1951	200.00
❑ 4537	Mailman's Sack/Newspaper Boy Blues	1952	200.00
❑ 4547	Rippin' and Runnin'/Lay It on the Line	1952	200.00
❑ 4577	Strange/Soft	1952	50.00
❑ 4621	The Blues Came Pouring In/Heavy Juice	1953	50.00
❑ 4664	South of the Orient/Later	1953	50.00
❑ 4687	Powder Puff/Ping Pong	1953	50.00
❑ 4713	Don't Worry 'Bout Me/Overflow	1954	40.00
❑ 4727	Spider Web/The Gypsey	1954	40.00
❑ 4747	A Stack of Dollars/Cat Fruit	1954	40.00
❑ 4757	Light/Choice	1954	40.00
❑ 4777	Cat Nap/Stomping Room Only	1955	40.00
❑ 4787	Phantom Turnpike/Come On	1955	40.00
❑ 5114	Short Shorts/Bushes	1958	25.00

7-Inch Extended Plays

KING

Number	Title (A Side/B Side)	Yr	NM
❑ EP 208	*Soft/Well Oh Well/Heavy Juice/The Train Kept a-Rollin'	195?	40.00
❑ EP 208 [PS]	Tiny Bradshaw	195?	40.00
❑ EP 248	Off and On/Free for All//South of the Orient/Later	195?	40.00
❑ EP 248 [PS]	Tiny Bradshaw, Vol. 2	195?	40.00
❑ EP 307	*Ping Pong/Powder Puff//Spider Web/Overflow	195?	40.00
❑ EP 307 [PS]	Tiny Bradshaw Plays, Vol. 4	195?	40.00

Albums

KING

Number	Title (A Side/B Side)	Yr	NM
❑ 295-74 [10]	Off and On	1955	1000.
❑ 395-501 [M]	Selections	1956	700.00
❑ 653 [M]	Great Composer	1960	300.00
❑ 953 [M]	24 Great Songs	1966	40.00

BRADY, JUNE AND GEORGE

45s

ABC-PARAMOUNT

Number	Title (A Side/B Side)	Yr	NM
❑ 9893	Sweetheart, Sweetheart/You're My Love	1958	20.00

BRADY BUNCH, THE

Also see CHRIS KNIGHT; MIKE LOOKINLAND; MAUREEN McCORMICK; EVE PLUMB; BARRY WILLIAMS.

45s

PARAMOUNT

Number	Title (A Side/B Side)	Yr	NM
❑ 0062	Frosty the Snowman/Silver Bells	1970	12.00
❑ 0062 [PS]	Frosty the Snowman/Silver Bells	1970	30.00
❑ 0141	We Can Make the World a Whole Lot Brighter/Time to Change	1972	12.00
❑ 0167	Time to Change/We'll Always Be Friends	1972	12.00
❑ 0205	Zuckerman's Famous Pig/Charlotte's Web	1973	12.00
❑ 0205 [PS]	Zuckerman's Famous Pig/Charlotte's Web	1973	20.00
❑ 0229	I'd Love You to Want Me/Everything I Do	1973	12.00

—As "The Brady Bunch Kids"

Albums

PARAMOUNT

Number	Title (A Side/B Side)	Yr	NM
❑ PAS-5026	Merry Christmas from the Brady Bunch	1971	80.00
❑ PAS-6032	Meet the Brady Bunch	1972	50.00
❑ PAS-6037	The Kids from the Brady Bunch	1972	40.00
❑ PAS-6058	The Brady Bunch Phonograph Record	1973	80.00

BRAGG, BILLY

12-Inch Singles

ELEKTRA

Number	Title (A Side/B Side)	Yr	NM
❑ ED 5184 [DJ]	Ideology (same on both sides)	1986	10.00
❑ ED 5203 [DJ]	Greetings to the New Brunette (same on both sides)	1986	6.00
❑ ED 5295 [DJ]	Help Save the Youth of America (LP Version) (Live Version)	1988	8.00
❑ ED 5330 [DJ]	Waiting for the Great Leap Forwards (same on both sides)	1988	8.00
❑ ED 5342 [DJ]	She's Got a New Spell (same on both sides)	1988	12.00

Albums

CD PRESENTS

Number	Title (A Side/B Side)	Yr	NM
❑ CD 027	Brewing Up with Billy Bragg	1984	15.00
❑ CD 035	Life's a Riot Etc. (With the Between the Wars EP)	1985	15.00

ELEKTRA

Number	Title (A Side/B Side)	Yr	NM
❑ 60502	Talking to the Taxman About Poetry	1986	12.00
❑ 60726 [(2)]	Back to Basics	1987	12.00
❑ 60787 [EP]	Help Save the Youth of America	1988	8.00
❑ 60824	Workers Playtime	1988	10.00
❑ 61935	William Bloke	1996	12.00

BRAINBOX

With JAN AKKERMAN, later of FOCUS.

45s

CAPITOL

Number	Title (A Side/B Side)	Yr	NM
❑ 2943	Alpha & Omega/Cruel Train	1970	8.00

ELEKTRA

Number	Title (A Side/B Side)	Yr	NM
❑ 45673	Woman's Gone/Down Man	1969	8.00

Albums

CAPITOL

Number	Title (A Side/B Side)	Yr	NM
❑ ST-596	Brainbox	1970	15.00

BRAM TCHAIKOVSKY

12-Inch Singles

ARISTA

Number	Title (A Side/B Side)	Yr	NM
❑ SP-104 [DJ]	Shall We Dance/Miracle Cure	1981	8.00
❑ SP-104 [DJ]	Shall We Dance/Miracle Cure	1981	10.00

POLYDOR

Number	Title (A Side/B Side)	Yr	NM
❑ PRO109 [DJ]	Lady from the USA (same on both sides)	1979	5.00
❑ PRO 109 [DJ]	Lady from the U.S.A. (same on both sides)	1979	7.00

45s

ARISTA

Number	Title (A Side/B Side)	Yr	NM
❑ 0601	Shall We Dance/(B-side unknown)	1981	4.00
❑ 0621	Together My Love/Stand and Deliver	1981	4.00

POLYDOR

Number	Title (A Side/B Side)	Yr	NM
❑ 2016	Lady from the U.S.A./Turn On the Light	1979	5.00
❑ 2101	Let's Dance/Hollywood Nightmare	1980	5.00
❑ 14575	Girl of My Dreams/Sarah Smiles	1979	5.00

Albums

ARISTA

Number	Title (A Side/B Side)	Yr	NM
❑ AB 4292	Funland	1981	10.00

POLYDOR

Number	Title (A Side/B Side)	Yr	NM
❑ PD-1-6211	Strange Man, Changed Man	1979	12.00
❑ PD-1-6273	Pressure	1980	10.00

BRAMLETT, BONNIE

Half of DELANEY AND BONNIE.

45s

CAPRICORN

Number	Title (A Side/B Side)	Yr	NM
❑ 0229	Higher and Higher/It's Time	1975	4.00
❑ 0262	Let's Go, Let's Go, Let's Go/Never Gonna Give You Up	1976	4.00
❑ 0306	Except for Real/I've Just Seen a Face	1978	4.00

COLUMBIA

Number	Title (A Side/B Side)	Yr	NM
❑ 45897	Good Vibrations/How Glad I Am	1973	5.00

Albums

CAPRICORN

Number	Title (A Side/B Side)	Yr	NM
❑ CP 0148	It's Time	1975	12.00
❑ CP 0169	Lady's Choice	1976	12.00
❑ CP 0190	Memories	1978	12.00

COLUMBIA

Number	Title (A Side/B Side)	Yr	NM
❑ KC 31786	Sweet Bonnie Bramlett	1973	15.00

BRAMLETT, DELANEY

Half of DELANEY AND BONNIE.

45s

COLUMBIA

Number	Title (A Side/B Side)	Yr	NM
❑ 45696	I'm Not Your Lover, I'm Your Lover/Over and Over	1972	5.00
❑ 45781	We Can't Be Seen Together/Thank God	1973	5.00
❑ 45950	Are You a Beatle or a Rolling Stone/California Rain	1973	10.00

CREAM

Number	Title (A Side/B Side)	Yr	NM
❑ 8147	What's a Little Love/I Love to Love You	1981	4.00

—By "Delaney and Bekka Bramlett"

GNP CRESCENDO

Number	Title (A Side/B Side)	Yr	NM
❑ 328	Heartbreak Hotel/You Never Looked Sweeter	1964	15.00
❑ 339	Liverpool Lou/You Have No Choice	1965	15.00
❑ 363	Without Your Love/A Better Man Than Me	1965	15.00

INDEPENDENCE

Number	Title (A Side/B Side)	Yr	NM
❑ 76	Guess I Must Be Dreaming/Don't Let It	1967	15.00

Albums

COLUMBIA

Number	Title (A Side/B Side)	Yr	NM
❑ KC 31631	Some Things Coming	1972	12.00
❑ KC 32420	Mobius Strip	1973	12.00

MGM

Number	Title (A Side/B Side)	Yr	NM
❑ M3G-5011	Giving Birth to a Song	1975	10.00

PRODIGAL

Number	Title (A Side/B Side)	Yr	NM
❑ P6-10017S1	Class Reunion	1977	10.00

BRANT, BOBBY

45s

EASTWEST

Number	Title (A Side/B Side)	Yr	NM
❑ 124	Piano Nellie/I Found a New Love	1959	100.00

WHITE ROCK

Number	Title (A Side/B Side)	Yr	NM
❑ 1114	Piano Nellie/I Found a New Love	1959	150.00

BRAUTIGAN, RICHARD

Albums

HARVEST

Number	Title (A Side/B Side)	Yr	NM
❑ ST-424	Listening to Richard Brautigan	1970	30.00

BRAVE BELT

Also see BACHMAN-TURNER OVERDRIVE. Also see RANDY BACHMAN; BACHMAN-TURNER OVERDRIVE.

45s

REPRISE

Number	Title (A Side/B Side)	Yr	NM
❑ 1039	Holy Train/Crazy Arms-Crazy Eyes	1971	5.00
❑ 1061	Never Comin' Home/Can You Feel It	1971	5.00
❑ 1083	Another Way Out/Dunrobin's Gone	1972	5.00

Albums

REPRISE

Number	Title (A Side/B Side)	Yr	NM
❑ MS 2057	Brave Belt II	1972	12.00
❑ MS 2210	Bachman-Turner-Bachman As Brave Belt	1974	10.00
❑ RS 6447	Brave Belt	1971	12.00

Except when noted otherwise, VG = 25% of NM, and VG+ = 50% of NM. (Example: VG = $2.00, VG+ = $4.00 and NM = $8.00.)

BRAVE NEW WORLD

45s

EPIC

Number	Title (A Side/B Side)	Yr	NM
❑ 10123	It's Tomorrow/Cried	1967	20.00

BREAD Also see DAVID GATES; JIMMY GRIFFIN.

45s

ELEKTRA

Number	Title (A Side/B Side)	Yr	NM
❑ 45365	Lost Without Your Love/ Change of Heart	1976	4.00
❑ 45389	Hooked on You/ Our Lady of Sorrow	1977	4.00
❑ 45666	Dismal Day/Anyway You Want Me	1969	8.00
❑ 45668	Could I/You Can't Measure the Cost	1969	6.00
❑ 45686	Make It With You/Why Do You Keep Me Waiting	1970	4.00
—Yellow and black label			
❑ 45686	Make It With You/Why Do You Keep Me Waiting	1970	4.00
—Red, black and white label			
❑ 45701	It Don't Matter to Me/Call on Me	1970	4.00
❑ 45701 [PS]	It Don't Matter to Me/Call on Me	1970	8.00
❑ 45711	Let Your Love Go/ Too Much Love	1971	4.00
❑ 45720	If/Take Comfort	1971	4.00
❑ 45720 [PS]	If/Take Comfort	1971	8.00
❑ 45740	Mother Freedom/ Life in Your Love	1971	4.00
❑ 45751	Baby I'm-a Want You/Truckin'	1971	4.00
❑ 45765	Everything I Own/ I Don't Love You	1972	4.00
❑ 45784	Diary/Down on My Knees	1972	4.00
❑ 45803	The Guitar Man/ Just Like Yesterday	1972	4.00
❑ 45818	Sweet Surrender/ Make It By Yourself	1972	4.00
❑ 45832	Aubrey/Didn't Even Know Her Name	1973	4.00

Albums

ELEKTRA

Number	Title (A Side/B Side)	Yr	NM
❑ BRD-1 [DJ]	Bread	1971	20.00
—In-store sampler; very similar to the future LP "The Best of Bread"			
❑ 6E-108	The Best of Bread	1977	8.00
—Reissue of 75056			
❑ 6E-110	The Best of Bread, Vol. 2	1977	8.00
—Reissue of 7E-1005			
❑ 7E-1005	The Best of Bread, Vol. 2	1974	12.00
❑ 7E-1094	Lost Without Your Love	1976	10.00
❑ EQ-5015 [Q]	Baby I'm-a Want You	1974	20.00
❑ EQ-5056 [Q]	The Best of Bread	1973	20.00
❑ 60414	Anthology of Bread	1985	10.00
❑ EKS-74044	Bread	1969	15.00
—Red label with large stylized "E"			
❑ EKS-74044	Bread	1971	10.00
—Butterfly label			
❑ EKS-74076	On the Waters	1970	15.00
—Red label with large stylized "E"			
❑ EKS-74076	On the Waters	1971	10.00
—Butterfly label			
❑ EKS-74086	Manna	1971	12.00
❑ EKS-75015	Baby I'm-a Want You	197?	10.00
—Front photo is not raised			
❑ EKS-75015	Baby I'm-a Want You	1971	15.00
—Gatefold with raised photo on front			
❑ EKS-75047	Guitar Man	1972	12.00
❑ EKS-75056	The Best of Bread	1973	12.00

BREAD, LOVE AND DREAMS

Albums

LONDON

Number	Title (A Side/B Side)	Yr	NM
❑ PS 566	Bread, Love and Dreams	1969	30.00

BREAKAWAYS, THE

45s

Number	Title (A Side/B Side)	Yr	NM
CAMEO			
❑ 323	That's How It Goes/ He Doesn't Love Me	1964	15.00
LONDON INT'L.			
❑ 10526	That Boy of Mine/ Here She Comes	1963	12.00
MELBOURNE			
❑ 1805	Granada/The Flipper	1964	12.00

BREAKERS, THE

45s

Number	Title (A Side/B Side)	Yr	NM
AMY			
❑ 938	Don't Send Me No Flowers (I Ain't Dead Yet)/ Love of My Life	1965	15.00
BRANA			
❑ 1001/2	Kama-Kaze/Surf Breaker	1963	60.00
DJB			
❑ 116	Jet Stream/Beach Head	1964	50.00
❑ 116	Super Jet Rumble/Beach Head	1964	50.00
—Revised A-side title			
IMPACT			
❑ 14	Surfin' Tragedy/Surf Bird	1963	25.00
—Black vinyl			
❑ 14	Surfin' Tragedy/Surf Bird	1963	80.00
—Gold vinyl			
JERDEN			
❑ 789	All My Nights, All My Days/ Better for the Both of Us	1966	20.00
MARSH			
❑ 206	Balboa Memories/ Long Way Home	1963	50.00
RIVERTON			
❑ 102	All My Nights, All My Days/ Better for the Both of Us	1966	40.00

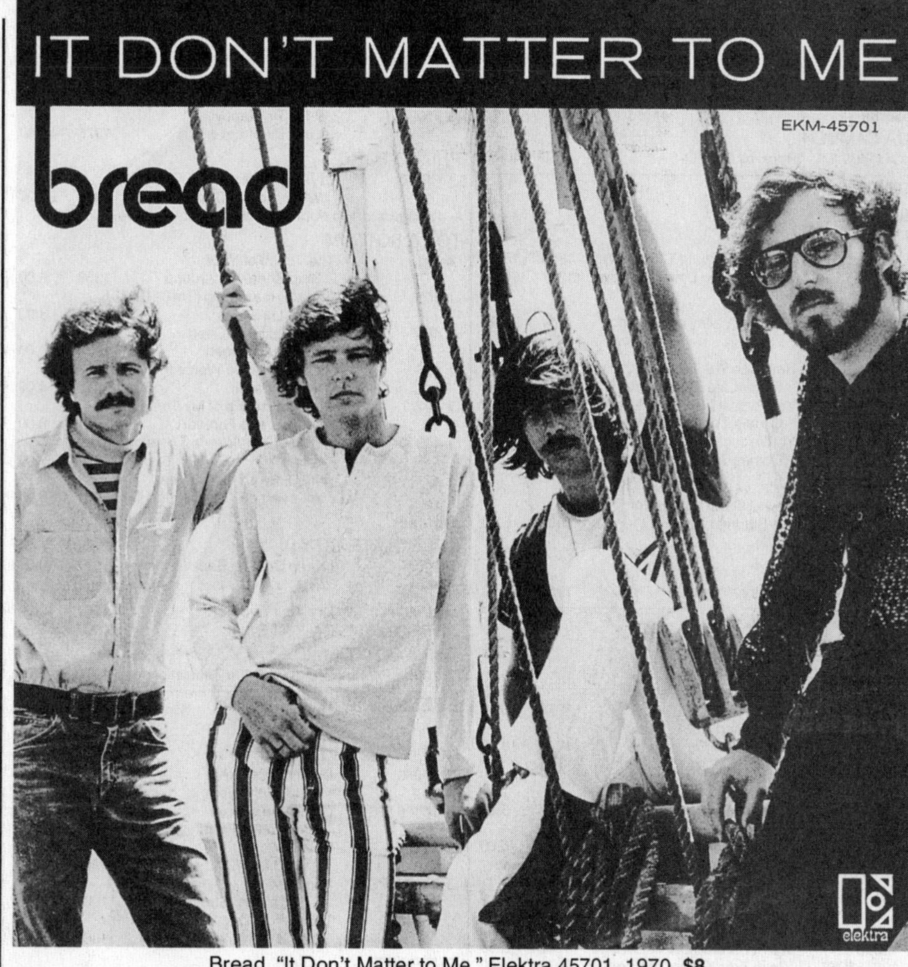

Bread, "It Don't Matter to Me," Elektra 45701, 1970, **$8.**

BRECKER BROTHERS, THE

12-Inch Singles

Number	Title (A Side/B Side)	Yr	NM
ARISTA			
❑ ALD-2 [DJ]	Don't Stop the Music (6:33)/ Finger Lickin' Good (3:58)	1976	40.00
GRP			
❑ GRP8P-4016 [DJ]	Big Idea (unknown versions)	1992	8.00

45s

ARISTA

Number	Title (A Side/B Side)	Yr	NM
❑ 0122	Sneakin' Up Behind You/Sponge	1975	4.00
❑ 0182	If You Wanna Boogie... Forget It/Slick Stuff	1976	4.00
❑ 0253	Don't Stop the Music/ Finger Lickin' Good	1977	4.00
❑ 0365	East River (La-Di-Da)/ Funky Sea, Funky Do	1978	4.00
❑ 0533	You Ga (Ta Give It)/ (B-side unknown)	1980	4.00

Albums

ARISTA

Number	Title (A Side/B Side)	Yr	NM
❑ AL 4037	The Brecker Brothers	1975	12.00
❑ AL 4061	Back to Back	1976	10.00
❑ AQ 4061 [Q]	Back to Back	1976	20.00
❑ AL 4122	Don't Stop the Music	1977	10.00
❑ AB 4185	Heavy Metal Be-Bop	1978	10.00
❑ AB 4272	Détente	1979	10.00
❑ AL 9550	Straphangin'	1981	12.00

BREEDLOVE, JIMMY

45s

Number	Title (A Side/B Side)	Yr	NM
ATCO			
❑ 6094	That's My Baby/Over Somebody Else's Shoulder	1957	25.00
❑ 6105	I Can Still Hear You Say You Love Me/I Wish I Were Twins	1957	25.00
DIAMOND			
❑ 144	Jealous Fool/Lil' Ol' Me	1963	30.00
EPIC			
❑ 9270	Could This Be Love/ This Too Shall Pass Away	1958	20.00
❑ 9283	Love Is All We Need/Lovable	1958	20.00
❑ 9289	Love Is All We Need/Oo-Wee Good Gosh A-Mighty	1958	20.00
❑ 9319	All Is Forgiven/I Say Hello	1959	20.00
❑ 9360	To Belong/Waiting for You	1960	20.00
JUBILEE			
❑ 5551	Jealous Fool/The Greatest Love (Nothing Less, Nothing More)	1966	10.00
OKEH			
❑ 7145	Anytime You Want Me/ My Guardian Angel	1962	12.00
❑ 7152	Don't Let It Happen/Queen Bee	1962	12.00
ROULETTE			
❑ 7010	I Can't Help Lovin' You/ I Saw You	1968	8.00

B

7-Inch Extended Plays

Number	Title (A Side/B Side)	Yr	NM
RCA CAMDEN			
CEP-447	(contents unknown)	1958	25.00
CEP-447 [PS]	Rock 'n' Roll Music	1958	25.00

Albums

Number	Title (A Side/B Side)	Yr	NM
RCA CAMDEN			
CAL-430 [M]	Rock 'N' Roll Hits	1958	40.00

BREEN, BOBBY

45s

Number	Title (A Side/B Side)	Yr	NM
CHIC			
1003	If the Night Could Tell You/Wait	1956	15.00
1013	We Will Make Love/Rainbow	1957	15.00
LYRIC			
105	It's a Sin/Valley of Romance	196?	20.00
MOTOWN			
1053	How Can We Tell Him/Better Late Than Never	1964	25.00
1059	You're Just Like You/Here Comes That Heartache	1964	25.00
1059 [PS]	You're Just Like You/Here Comes That Heartache	1964	40.00
NRC			
055	Hawaii Calls/Theme from A Summer Place	1960	10.00

Albums

Number	Title (A Side/B Side)	Yr	NM
LONDON			
LB 270 [10]	Songs at Yuletide	1953	50.00

BREMERS, BEVERLY

45s

Number	Title (A Side/B Side)	Yr	NM
BRUT			
513	I Just Need Some Music/Let It Play On	197?	6.00
513 [PS]	I Just Need Some Music/Let It Play On	197?	10.00
COLUMBIA			
10180	What I Did for Love/You're Precious to Me	1975	5.00
10451	The Prisoner/Flight 309 to Tennessee	1976	5.00
SCEPTER			
12315	Don't Say You Don't Remember/Get Smart Girl	1971	6.00
12332	When Michael Calls/Toy Girl	1971	5.00
12348	We're Free/Colors of Love	1972	5.00
12348 [PS]	We're Free/Colors of Love	1972	10.00
12363	I'll Make You Music/I Made a Man Out of You, Jimmy	1972	5.00
12370	Heaven Help Us/All That's Left Is the Music	1973	5.00
12378	Run to Her/Baby I Don't Know You	1973	5.00
12380	Daddy's Coming Home/A Little Bit of Love	1973	5.00
12391	Sing a Happy Song/Get Smart Girl	1973	5.00
12399	One Day at a Time/Get Up in the Morning	1975	5.00

Albums

Number	Title (A Side/B Side)	Yr	NM
SCEPTER			
SPS-5102	I'll Make You Music	1972	10.00

BRENDA AND THE TABULATIONS

12-Inch Singles

Number	Title (A Side/B Side)	Yr	NM
CHOCOLATE CITY			
CCD 20006	(I'm a) Superstar (unknown versions)	1977	15.00

45s

Number	Title (A Side/B Side)	Yr	NM
CHOCOLATE CITY			
004	Home to Myself/Leave Me Alone	1976	4.00
009	(I'm a) Superstar/Take It or Leave It	1977	4.00
012	Let's Go All the Way (Down)/I Keep Coming Back for More	1977	4.00
DIONN			
500	Dry Your Eyes/The Wash	1967	10.00
501	Who's Lovin' You/Stay Together Young Lovers	1967	10.00
503	Just Once in a Lifetime/Hey Boy	1967	10.00
504	When You're Gone/Hey Boy	1967	10.00
507	To the One I Love/Baby You're So Right	1968	10.00
509	I Can't Get Over You/That's in the Past	1968	10.00
511	Reason to Live/Hey Boy	1968	10.00
512	That's the Price You Have to Pay/I Wish I Hadn't Done What I Did	1969	10.00
EPIC			
10898	Little Bit of Love/Let Me Be Happy	1972	6.00
10954	One Girl Too Late/The Magic of Your Love	1973	6.00
11000	Key to My Heart/Love Is Just a Carnival	1973	6.00
11059	I'm in Love/Walk On In	1973	6.00
50081	Let Me Be Happy/Little Bit of Love	1975	4.00
PHILCO-FORD			
HP-40	Dry Your Eyes/When You're Gone	1969	20.00
	—4-inch plastic "Hip Pocket Record" with color sleeve		
TOP & BOTTOM			
401	The Touch of You/Stop Sneaking Around	1969	8.00
403	And My Heart Sang (Tra La La)/Lies, Lies, Lies	1970	8.00
404	Don't Make Me Over/You've Changed	1970	8.00
406	A Child No One Wanted/Scuse Us All	1970	8.00
407	Right on the Tip of My Tongue/Always and Forever	1971	8.00
408	A Part of You/Where There's a Will	1971	8.00
411	Why Didn't I Think of That/A Love You Can Depend On	1971	8.00

Albums

Number	Title (A Side/B Side)	Yr	NM
CHOCOLATE CITY			
2002	I Keep Coming Back for More	1977	10.00
DIONN			
LPM-2000 [M]	Dry Your Eyes	1967	40.00
LPS-2000 [S]	Dry Your Eyes	1967	50.00
TOP & BOTTOM			
100	Brenda and the Tabulations	1970	20.00

BRENNAN, WALTER

45s

Number	Title (A Side/B Side)	Yr	NM
DOT			
16066	Dutchman's Gold/Back to the Farm	1960	12.00
16066 [PS]	Dutchman's Gold/Back to the Farm	1960	20.00
16136	Space Mice/The Thievin' Stranger	1960	12.00
16136 [PS]	Space Mice/The Thievin' Stranger	1960	25.00
16348	Tribute to a Dog/Life Gets Tee-Jus Don't It	1962	12.00
EVEREST			
19365	Noah's Ark (Part 1)/Noah's Ark (Part 2)	1960	12.00
KAPP			
2126	Grandad/Man Needs to Know	1971	6.00
LIBERTY			
55436	Old Rivers/The Epic Ride of John B. Glenn	1962	12.00
55477	Houdini/The Old Kelly Place	1962	12.00
55477 [PS]	Houdini/The Old Kelly Place	1962	20.00
55508	Mama Sang a Song/Who Will Take Gramma	1962	12.00
55518	Henry Had A Merry Christmas/White Christmas	1962	12.00
55518 [PS]	Henry Had A Merry Christmas/White Christmas	1962	20.00
55617	Keep a-Movin' Old Man/Waiting for a Train	1963	12.00
LONDON			
141	Yesterday, When I Was Young/Time	1970	6.00
RPC			
502	Knight in Bright Armor/The Soul of Big Jack Dunn	1961	12.00
UNITED ARTISTS			
0055	Old Rivers/Mama Sang a Song	1973	4.00
	—Silver Spotlight Series issue		

Albums

Number	Title (A Side/B Side)	Yr	NM
DOT			
DLP-3309 [M]	Dutchman's Gold	1960	25.00
DLP-25309 [S]	Dutchman's Gold	1960	30.00
EVEREST			
SDBR-1103 [S]	World of Miracles	1960	30.00
SDBR-1123 [S]	The President: A Musical Biography of Our Chief Executive	1960	30.00
LPBR-5103 [M]	World of Miracles	1960	25.00
LPBR-5123 [M]	The President: A Musical Biography of Our Chief Executive	1960	25.00
HAMILTON			
HLP-159 [M]	Dutchman's Gold	1965	12.00
HLP-12159 [S]	Dutchman's Gold	1965	12.00
LIBERTY			
LRP-3233 [M]	Old Rivers	1962	20.00
LRP-3241 [M]	The President: A Musical Biography of Our Chief Executive	1962	15.00
	—Reissue of Everest 5123		
LRP-3244 [M]	World of Miracles	1962	15.00
	—Reissue of Everest 5103		
LRP-3257 [M]	'Twas the Night Before Christmas Back Home	1962	20.00
LRP-3266 [M]	Mama Sang a Song	1963	20.00
LRP-3317 [M]	Talkin' from the Heart	1964	20.00
LRP-3372 [M]	Gunfight at the O.K. Corral	1964	20.00
LST-7233 [S]	Old Rivers	1962	25.00
LST-7241 [S]	The President: A Musical Biography of Our Chief Executive	1962	20.00
	—Reissue of Everest 1123		
LST-7244 [S]	World of Miracles	1962	20.00
	—Reissue of Everest 1103		
LST-7257 [S]	'Twas the Night Before Christmas Back Home	1962	25.00
LST-7266 [S]	Mama Sang a Song	1963	25.00
LST-7317 [S]	Talkin' from the Heart	1964	25.00
LST-7372 [S]	Gunfight at the O.K. Corral	1964	25.00
LONDON			
PS 577	Yesterday, When I Was Young	1970	15.00
R.P.C.			
108 [M]	By the Fireside	1961	30.00
108S [S]	By the Fireside	1961	40.00
SUNSET			
SUM-1100 [M]	Country Heart	1966	12.00
SUS-5100 [S]	Country Heart	1966	12.00
SUS-5269	God and Country	1970	10.00
UNITED ARTISTS			
UA-LA438-E	The Very Best of Walter Brennan	1975	12.00

BRENSTON, JACKIE

45s

Number	Title (A Side/B Side)	Yr	NM
CHESS			
1458	Rocket "88"/Come Back Where You Belong	1951	10000.
	—Early rockabilly classic; obscenely rare, even though the 45s were pressed later. VG 5000; VG+ 7500		
1469	In My Real Gone Rocket/Tuckered Out	1951	1000.
1472	Juiced/Independent Woman	1951	1000.
1496	Leo the Louse/Hi-Ho Baby	1952	500.00
1532	Blues Got Me Again/Starvation	1953	250.00
FEDERAL			
12283	What Can It Be/Gonna Wait for My Chance	1956	50.00
12291	Much Later/The Mistreater	1957	50.00
SUE			
736	Trouble Up the Road/You Ain't the One	1961	20.00

BRENT, CAROLYN

45s

Number	Title (A Side/B Side)	Yr	NM
CONGRESS			
213	My Man (Mon Homme)/Rose of Washington Square	1964	8.00

BRENT, RONNIE

45s

Number	Title (A Side/B Side)	Yr	NM
COLT 45			
101	Crazy Feeling/Shirley Ann	1959	25.00
109	Cowboys and Indians/Flow Gently	1959	25.00
UNITED ARTISTS			
108	My Sweet Verlene/Love	1958	40.00

BRENT, TONY

45s

Number	Title (A Side/B Side)	Yr	NM
ROULETTE			
4113	Girl of My Dreams/Don't Play That Melody	1958	12.00

BREWER AND SHIPLEY

45s

Number	Title (A Side/B Side)	Yr	NM
A&M			
905	The Keeper of the Keys/I Can't See Her	1968	8.00
	—Artist reads "Michael Brewer and Tom Shipley"		
938	Green Bamboo/Truly Right	1968	8.00
	—Artist reads "Michael Brewer and Tom Shipley"		
996	Dreamin' in the Shade/Tame and Changes	1968	8.00
BUDDAH			
154	Rise Up Easy Rider/Boomerang	1970	4.00
CAPITOL			
3933	Fair Play/How Are You	1974	4.00

Number	Title (A Side/B Side)	Yr	NM
❑ 4105	Brain Damage/Rock and Roll Hostage	1975	4.00

KAMA SUTRA

Number	Title (A Side/B Side)	Yr	NM
❑ 512	People Love Each Other/ Witchi-Tai-To	1970	4.00
❑ 516	One Toke Over the Line/ Oh Mommy	1970	5.00
❑ 524	Tarkio Road/Seems Like a Long Time	1971	4.00
❑ 539	Shake Off the Demon/ Indian Summer	1972	4.00
❑ 547	Natural Child/Yankee Lady	1972	4.00
❑ 567	Black Sky/Fly, Fly Fly	1972	4.00

Albums

A&M

Number	Title	Yr	NM
❑ SP-4154	Down in L.A.	1968	15.00

CAPITOL

Number	Title	Yr	NM
❑ ST-11261	ST-11261	1974	10.00
❑ ST-11402	Welcome to Riddle Bridge	1975	10.00

KAMA SUTRA

Number	Title	Yr	NM
❑ KSBS-2016	Weeds	1969	12.00
❑ KSBS-2024	Tarkio	1970	12.00

—LP label calls this "Tarkio Road"

Number	Title	Yr	NM
❑ KSBS-2039	Shake Off the Demon	1971	12.00
❑ KSBS-2058	Rural Space	1972	12.00
❑ KSBS 2613-2 [(2)]	The Best... Brewer & Shipley	1976	15.00

BRIAN, NEIL

45s

JAMIE

Number	Title	Yr	NM
❑ 1216	Lucky Coin/A Fool Was I	1962	20.00

PARKWAY

Number	Title	Yr	NM
❑ 886	My Haunted Heart/ Three Rows Over	1963	20.00
❑ 895	I Made Her Forget/ Lilac and Spanish Moss	1964	20.00

20TH CENTURY FOX

Number	Title	Yr	NM
❑ 6686	Running Scared/Barefoot Girl	1967	12.00

BRICK

12-Inch Singles

BANG

Number	Title	Yr	NM
❑ 4Z9-02253	Sweat (Til You Get Wet)/ Seaside Vibes	1981	12.00
❑ 4Z9-03158	Free Dancer (6:44)/Stick By You	1982	12.00
❑ 4805	Dancin' Man/We'll Love	1979	10.00

MAGIC CITY

Number	Title	Yr	NM
❑ MCR 002	Kum Danz (Vocal 5:30)/ (Instrumental 6:00)	1987	6.00

45s

BANG

Number	Title	Yr	NM
❑ 723	Music Matic/Good High	1976	5.00

—Reissue of Main Street 119

Number	Title	Yr	NM
❑ 727	Dazz/Southern Sunset	1976	5.00
❑ 732	That's What It's All About/ Can't Wait (Tick Tock)	1977	5.00
❑ 734	Dusic/Happy	1977	5.00
❑ 735	Ain't Gonna Hurt Nobody/ Honey Chile	1977	5.00
❑ ZS5-02246	Sweat (Til You Get Wet)/ Seaside Vibes	1981	4.00
❑ ZS5-02599	Wide Open/Seaside Vibes	1981	4.00
❑ ZS5-03157	Free Dancer/Stick By You	1982	4.00
❑ 4802	Raise Your Hands/ Life Is What You Make It	1979	4.00
❑ 4804	Dancin' Man/We'll Love	1979	4.00
❑ 4810	All the Way/Spread Love	1980	4.00

MAIN STREET

Number	Title	Yr	NM
❑ 119	Music Matic/Good High	1975	10.00

Albums

BANG

Number	Title	Yr	NM
❑ BLP-408	Good High	1976	12.00

—Beware of sealed copies — this album has been "reissued" to look exactly like the original

Number	Title	Yr	NM
❑ BLP-409	Brick	1977	12.00
❑ JZ 35969	Stoneheart	1979	10.00
❑ JZ 36262	Waiting on You	1980	10.00
❑ FZ 37471	Summer Heat	1981	10.00
❑ FZ 38170	After 5	1982	10.00

MAGIC CITY

Number	Title	Yr	NM
❑ MCR 1001	Too Tuff	1988	10.00

BRIDES OF FUNKENSTEIN, THE

12-Inch Singles

ATLANTIC

Number	Title	Yr	NM
❑ DSKO 129	Disco to Go (5:06)/ When You're Gone	1978	12.00

45s

ATLANTIC

Number	Title	Yr	NM
❑ 3498	Disco to Go/When You're Gone	1978	5.00
❑ 3556	Amorous/War Ship Touchante	1979	5.00
❑ 3640	Never Buy Texas from a Cowboy (Part 1)/(Part 2)	1979	5.00
❑ 3658	Mother May I/Didn't Mean to Fall in Love	1980	8.00

Albums

ATLANTIC

Number	Title	Yr	NM
❑ SD 19201	Funk or Walk	1978	15.00
❑ SD 19261	Never Buy Texas from a Cowboy	1980	15.00

BRIDGE, THE

See THE BROOKLYN BRIDGE.

BRIGADE, THE

Albums

BAND'N VOCAL

Number	Title	Yr	NM
❑ 1066	Last Laugh	1970	2000.

—VG value 1000; VG+ value 1500

BRIGADIERS, THE

45s

MALA

Number	Title	Yr	NM
❑ 441	The Cry of the Wild Goose/ Dixie Brigade	1961	20.00

BRIGANDS, THE

45s

EPIC

Number	Title	Yr	NM
❑ 10011	(Would I Still Be) Her Big Man/ I'm a Patient Man	1966	20.00

BRIGG

Albums

SUSQUEHANNA

Number	Title	Yr	NM
❑ LP-301	Brigg	1973	200.00

BRIGGS, LILLIAN

45s

ABC-PARAMOUNT

Number	Title	Yr	NM
❑ 10253	I Want You to Be My Baby/ I'm Burning for You	1961	10.00

CORAL

Number	Title	Yr	NM
❑ 62108	Rag Mop/Smile for the People	1959	10.00
❑ 62136	Blues in the Night/Is There a Man in the House	1959	10.00
❑ 62156	Hooray for the Rock/ Diddy Boppers	1959	10.00
❑ 62193	Be Mine/Not a Soul	1960	10.00
❑ 62223	I Care for You/That's What It's Like to Be Lonesome	1960	10.00

EPIC

Number	Title	Yr	NM
❑ 9115	I Want You to Be My Baby/ Don't Stay Away Too Long	1955	30.00
❑ 9120	Give Me a Band and My Baby/ It Could've Been Me	1955	30.00
❑ 9138	Rock and Roll-y Poly Santa Claus/Can't Stop	1955	30.00
❑ 9141	Follow the Leader/That's the Only Way to Live	1956	20.00
❑ 9151	Eddie, My Love/Teens in Jeans from New Orleans	1956	20.00
❑ 9166	The Gypsy Goofed/ Too Close for Comfort	1956	20.00
❑ 9190	I'll Be Gone/Mean Words	1956	20.00
❑ 9214	Sugar Blues/Boogie Blues	1957	15.00
❑ 9249	She Sells Sea Shells/I	1957	15.00

SUNBEAM

Number	Title	Yr	NM
❑ 104	Come Home/Till We Meet Again	1958	12.00
❑ 114	Hey Ba Ba Re Bop/ I've Got Your Heart	1958	12.00

7-Inch Extended Plays

EPIC

Number	Title	Yr	NM
❑ B-7163	(contents unknown)	1956	40.00
❑ B-7163 [PS]	High Priestess of Rock 'n' Roll	1956	40.00

BRIGHTER SIDE OF DARKNESS

45s

MAGIC TOUCH

Number	Title	Yr	NM
❑ 9011	He Made You Mine/Disco Ball	197?	6.00

STAR-VUE

Number	Title	Yr	NM
❑ 1028	Oh Baby/Because I Love You	197?	30.00

20TH CENTURY

Number	Title	Yr	NM
❑ 2002	Love Jones/I'm the Guy	1972	8.00
❑ 2021	Just a Little Bit/Something to Remember You By	1973	15.00
❑ 2034	I Owe You Love/Summer Ride	1973	10.00

Albums

20TH CENTURY

Number	Title	Yr	NM
❑ T-405	Love Jones	1973	30.00

BRIGHTONES, THE

45s

WARNER BROS.

Number	Title	Yr	NM
❑ 5472	Swim, Swim, Swim/Rumors	1964	20.00

BRIGMAN, GEORGE

Albums

SOLID

Number	Title	Yr	NM
❑ SR-001	Jungle Rot	1975	120.00

BRIKS, THE

45s

BISMARK

Number	Title	Yr	NM
❑ 1013	Foolish Baby/Can You See Me	1966	200.00

DOT

Number	Title	Yr	NM
❑ 16876	Foolish Baby/Can You See Me	1966	25.00

BRIMSTONE

Albums

PEPPERMINT

Number	Title	Yr	NM
❑ 1022	Paper Winged Dreams	1973	500.00

BRIMSTONES, THE

45s

MGM

Number	Title	Yr	NM
❑ 13653	It's All Over But the Crying/ What Is This Life	1966	20.00

WORLD PACIFIC

Number	Title	Yr	NM
❑ 77834	Cold Hearted Woman/ I'm in Misery	1966	30.00

BRINSLEY SCHWARZ

Featuring Nick Lowe and Ian Gomm.

45s

CAPITOL

Number	Title	Yr	NM
❑ 3004	Rock and Roll Women/ Hymn to Be	1970	8.00

UNITED ARTISTS

Number	Title	Yr	NM
❑ 50915	Nightingale/Silver Pistol	1972	6.00
❑ 50976	Nervous on the Road/Happy Doing What We're Doing	1972	6.00

Albums

CAPITOL

Number	Title	Yr	NM
❑ ST-589	Brinsley Schwarz	1970	20.00
❑ ST-744	Despite It All	1971	20.00
❑ SWBC-11869 [(2)]	Brinsley Schwarz	1978	15.00

LIBERTY

Number	Title	Yr	NM
❑ LN 10145	Silver Pistol	1980	10.00

—10-track reissue

Number	Title	Yr	NM
❑ LN 10146	Nervous on the Road	1981	10.00

—10-track reissue

UNITED ARTISTS

Number	Title	Yr	NM
❑ UAS-5566	Silver Pistol	1972	15.00
❑ UAS-5647	Nervous on the Road	1972	15.00

BRISTOL, JOHNNY

Also see JOHNNY AND JACKEY.

45s

ATLANTIC

Number	Title	Yr	NM
❑ 3360	Do It to My Mind/Love to Take a Chance to Taste the Wine	1976	4.00
❑ 3391	You Turned Me On to Love/ I Sho Like Groovin' with You	1977	4.00
❑ 3421	Waiting on Love/ She's So Amazing	1977	4.00
❑ 3501	When He Comes (You Will Know)/Strangers in the Dark Corners	1978	4.00
❑ 3526	Why Stop Now/When He Comes (You Will Know)	1978	4.00

HANDSHAKE

Number	Title	Yr	NM
❑ 02594	Take Me Down/Loving and Free	1981	4.00
❑ WS8 5300	My Guy/My Girl//Now	1980	4.00

—A-side with Amii Stewart

Number	Title	Yr	NM
❑ WS8 5304	Love No Longer Has a Hold on Me/Until I See You Again	1981	60.00

MGM

Number	Title	Yr	NM
❑ 14715	Hang On In There Baby/ Take Care of You for Me	1974	5.00
❑ 14762	You and I/It Don't Hurt No More	1974	5.00
❑ 14792	Leave My World/All Goodbyes Aren't Good	1975	5.00
❑ 14814	Love Takes Tears/ Go On and Dream	1975	5.00

POLYDOR

Number	Title	Yr	NM
❑ 813982-7	Hang On In There Baby/ Stand By Me	1983	3.00

—Reissue

Albums

ATLANTIC

Number	Title	Yr	NM
❑ SD 18197	Bristol's Creme	1976	10.00

Except when noted otherwise, VG = 25% of NM, and VG+ = 50% of NM. (Example: VG = $2.00, VG+ = $4.00 and NM = $8.00.)

Number	Title (A Side/B Side)	Yr	NM
❑ SD 19184	Strangers	1978	10.00
HANDSHAKE			
❑ FW 37666	Free to Be Me	1981	10.00
MGM			
❑ M3G-4959	Hang On In There Baby	1974	12.00
❑ M3G-4983	Feeling the Magic	1975	12.00

BRITISH CASUALS, THE See THE CASUALS (3).

BRITISH WALKERS, THE

45s

Number	Title (A Side/B Side)	Yr	NM
CAMEO			
❑ 466	Shake/That Was Yesterday	1967	15.00
CHARGER			
❑ 108	The Girl Can't Help It/ Lonely Lover's Poem	1965	30.00
TRY			
❑ 502	Diddley Daddy/I Found You	1964	30.00

BROADWAY SINGERS, THE

45s

Number	Title (A Side/B Side)	Yr	NM
HIT			
❑ 214	I'll Never Find Another You/ Come Back to Me	1965	8.00

—B-side by William Randolph

BROGUES, THE Two members became part of QUICKSILVER MESSENGER SERVICE.

45s

Number	Title (A Side/B Side)	Yr	NM
CHALLENGE			
❑ 59311	But Now I'm Fine/Someday	1965	30.00
❑ 59316	I Ain't No Miracle Worker/ Don't Shoot Me Down	1965	30.00
TWILIGHT			
❑ 408	But Now I'm Fine/Early Bird	1965	40.00
❑ 408	But Now I'm Fine/Someday	1965	40.00

BROMBERG, DAVID

45s

Number	Title (A Side/B Side)	Yr	NM
COLUMBIA			
❑ 45612	The Holdup/Suffer to Sing the Blues	1972	6.00
❑ 45767	Sharon/Hardworkin' John	1973	8.00
FANTASY			
❑ 785	Such a Night/Bluebirds	1977	4.00
❑ 812	Battle of Bull Run Medley/ I Want to Go Home	1978	4.00
❑ 854	Don't Let Your Deal Go Down/ My Own House	1979	4.00

Albums

Number	Title (A Side/B Side)	Yr	NM
COLUMBIA			
❑ C 31104	David Bromberg	1972	12.00
❑ PC 31104	David Bromberg	198?	8.00
—Budget-line reissue			
❑ KC 31753	Demon in Disguise	1973	12.00
❑ PC 31753	Demon in Disguise	198?	8.00
—Budget-line reissue			
❑ KC 32717	Wanted Dead or Alive	1974	12.00
❑ PC 33397	Midnight on the Water	1975	12.00
—Original with no bar code			
❑ PC 33397	Midnight on the Water	198?	8.00
—Budget-line reissue with bar code			
❑ PC 34467	The Best of David Bromberg: Out of the Blues	1976	12.00
—Original with no bar code			
❑ PC 34467	The Best of David Bromberg: Out of the Blues	198?	8.00
—Budget-line reissue with bar code			
FANTASY			
❑ 9540	Reckless Abandon	1977	12.00
❑ 9555	Bandit in a Bathing Suit	1978	10.00
❑ 9572	My Own House	1979	10.00
❑ 9590	You Should See the Rest of the Band	1980	10.00
❑ 79007 [(2)]	How Late'll Ya Play 'Til?	1976	15.00
ROUNDER			
❑ 3110	Sideman Serenade	1989	12.00

BRONZETTES, THE

45s

Number	Title (A Side/B Side)	Yr	NM
PARKWAY			
❑ 929	Hot Spot/Run, Run, You Little Fool	1964	12.00

BROOKLYN BRIDGE, THE Also see JOHNNY MAESTRO.

45s

Number	Title (A Side/B Side)	Yr	NM
BUDDAH			
❑ 60	Little Red Boat by the River/ From My Window	1968	6.00
❑ 75	Worst That Could Happen/ Your Kite, My Kite	1968	8.00
❑ 95	Welcome Me Love/ Blessed Is the Rain	1969	6.00
❑ 126	Your Husband, My Wife/ Upside Down	1969	6.00
❑ 139	You'll Never Walk Alone/ Minstrel Sunday	1969	6.00
❑ 162	Free as the Wind/ He's Not a Happy Man	1970	6.00
❑ 179	Down by the River/Look Again	1970	6.00
❑ 193	Day Is Done/Easy Way	1970	6.00
❑ 193	Day Is Done/Opposites	1970	6.00
❑ 199	Nights in White Satin/Cynthia	1971	8.00
❑ 230	Wednesday in Your Garden (mono/stereo)	1971	8.00
—Stock copy unknown			
❑ 293	Man in a Band/Bruno's Place	1972	8.00
❑ 317	I Feel Free (mono/stereo)	1972	10.00
—As "The Bridge"; stock copy unknown			
COLLECTABLES			
❑ 3997	Have Yourself a Merry Little Christmas/A Christmas Long Ago (Jingle Jingle)	199?	3.00

—As "Johnny Maestro and the Brooklyn Bridge"; B-side by the Echelons

Albums

Number	Title (A Side/B Side)	Yr	NM
BUDDAH			
❑ BDS-5034	Brooklyn Bridge	1969	20.00
❑ BDS-5042	The Second Brooklyn Bridge	1969	20.00
❑ BDS-5065	The Brooklyn Bridge	1970	20.00
❑ BDS-5107	Bridge in Blue	1972	20.00
COLLECTABLES			
❑ COL-5015	The Greatest Hits	198?	12.00

—As "Johnny Maestro and the Brooklyn Bridge"

BROOKS, BOBBY

45s

Number	Title (A Side/B Side)	Yr	NM
HIT			
❑ 109	See the Funny Little Clown/My Heart Belongs to Only You	1964	8.00
❑ 120	A World Without Love/ Chapel of Love	1964	8.00
—B-side by the Flower Sisters			
❑ 123	Tell Me Why/Be Anything (But Be Mine)	1964	8.00
—B-side by Connie Dee			
❑ 127	Don't Let the Sun Catch You Crying/I'll Touch a Star	1964	8.00
❑ 143	It Hurts to Be in Love/ Do Wah Diddy Diddy	1964	15.00
—B-side by Bobby Cash			
❑ 146	Last Kiss/A Summer Song	1964	8.00
❑ 156	Mountain of Love/Be Yourself	1964	10.00
—B-side by the Jalopy Five			
❑ 176	Wise Like Solomon/ Hold What You've Got	1965	8.00
—B-side by Leroy Jones			
❑ 192	She's Come of Age/ Eight Days a Week	1965	12.00
—B-side by the Jalopy Five			
❑ 199	Hearts Are Funny Things/ Goodnight	1965	8.00
—B-side by Ed Hardin			
❑ 202	I Must Be Seeing Things/Once a Cheater, Always a Cheater	1965	8.00
—B-side by Connie Dee			
❑ 219	What's New Pussycat?/ Down in the Boondocks	1965	8.00
—B-side by Ed Hardin			
❑ 231	England Swings/ A Taste of Honey	1965	8.00
—B-side by the Nashville Five			
❑ 255	Rainy Day Women #12 and 35/ When a Man Loves a Woman	1966	8.00
—B-side by Leroy Jones			
❑ 269	If I Were a Carpenter/ Poor Side of Town	1966	8.00

—B-side by Bobby Sims

BROOKS, CHUCK, AND THE SHARPIES

45s

Number	Title (A Side/B Side)	Yr	NM
DUB			
❑ 2844	Spinning My Wheels/ You Make Me Feel Mean	1958	300.00

BROOKS, DONNIE

45s

Number	Title (A Side/B Side)	Yr	NM
CHALLENGE			
❑ 59331	I Call Your Name/Be Fair	1966	8.00
❑ 59344	Pink Carousel/Mission Man	1966	8.00
ERA			
❑ 3004	Lil' Sweetheart/If You're Lookin'	1959	20.00
❑ 3007	White Orchid/Sway and Move with the Beat	1959	20.00
❑ 3014	The Devil Ain't a Man/How Long	1960	20.00
❑ 3018	Mission Bell/Do It for Me	1960	20.00
❑ 3028	Doll House/Round Robin	1960	15.00
❑ 3028 [PS]	Doll House/Round Robin	1960	25.00
❑ 3042	Memphis/That's Why	1961	15.00
❑ 3042 [PS]	Memphis/That's Why	1961	25.00
❑ 3049	All I Can Give/Wishbone	1961	15.00
❑ 3052	Boomerang/How Long	1961	15.00
❑ 3059	Sweet Lorraine/ Up to My Ears in Tears	1961	15.00
❑ 3063	Goodnight Judy/Your Little Boy's Gone Home	1961	15.00
❑ 3071	My Favorite Kind of Face/ He Stole Flo	1962	15.00
❑ 3077	Oh You Beautiful Doll/ Just a Bystander	1962	15.00
❑ 3095	Cries My Heart/ It's Not That Easy	1962	15.00
❑ 3194	Blue Soldier/Love Is Funny That Way	1968	8.00
HAPPY TIGER			
❑ 526	Abracadabra/I Know You as a Woman	1970	5.00
❑ 544	Hush/I Know You as a Woman	1970	5.00
❑ 551	My God and I/Pink Carousel	1970	5.00
❑ 566	(I Wanna) Have You for Myself/ Rub-a-Dub-Dub	1971	5.00
❑ 579	I'm Gonna Make You Love Me/ Pink Carousel	1971	5.00
MIDSONG INT'L.			
❑ 1007	Big John/Get Fame, Son	1978	4.00
OAK			
❑ 1019	The Song That I Sing Is For You/Country Dude	1971	5.00
REPRISE			
❑ 0261	Gone/Girl Machine	1964	10.00
❑ 0311	Can't Help Lovin' You/ Pickin' Up the Pieces	1964	10.00
❑ 0363	Hey, Little Girl/I Never Get to Love You	1965	10.00
YARDBIRD			
❑ 8006	Sunglasses on the Sand/ Sunshine, Summertime and Love	1968	6.00
❑ 8008	Hush/Sunshine, Summertime and Love	1968	6.00
❑ 8010	Tree Trimming Time/ (Instrumental)	1968	6.00

Albums

Number	Title (A Side/B Side)	Yr	NM
ERA			
❑ EL-105 [M]	The Happiest	1961	150.00

BROOKS, DUSTY, AND HIS TONES WITH JUANITA BROWN

45s

Number	Title (A Side/B Side)	Yr	NM
SUN			
❑ 182	Heaven or Fire/Tears and Wine	1953	3000.

—VG 1500; VG+ 2250

BROOKS, ELKIE

45s

Number	Title (A Side/B Side)	Yr	NM
A&M			
❑ 1781	Where Do We Go from Here (Rich Man's Woman)/ Roll Me Over	1976	5.00
❑ 1935	You Did Something for Me/ Pearl's a Singer	1977	5.00
❑ 1953	Sunshine After the Rain/ You Did Something for Me	1977	5.00
❑ 1968	Love Potion No. 9/Honey, Can I Put On Your Clothes	1977	5.00
❑ 2068	Since You Went Away/ Too Precious	1978	4.00
❑ 2271	Paint Your Pretty Pictures/ Pull On the Rope	1980	4.00
PARROT			
❑ 9699	Nothin' Left to Do But Cry/ Strange Tho It Seems	1964	10.00

Albums

Number	Title (A Side/B Side)	Yr	NM
A&M			
❑ SP-4554	Rich Man's Woman	1975	10.00
❑ SP-4631	Two Days Away	1977	10.00
❑ SP-4695	Shooting Star	1977	10.00

BROOKS, JOHN

45s

Number	Title (A Side/B Side)	Yr	NM
HIT			
❑ 251	Soul and Inspiration/Good Lovin'	1966	12.00

—B-side by the Spartas

BROOKS BROTHERS, THE

45s

Number	Title (A Side/B Side)	Yr	NM
LONDON			
❑ 1987	Warpaint/Sometimes	1961	15.00
❑ 9668	Once in Awhile/Poor Plan	1964	10.00

—As "The Brooks"

Except when noted otherwise, VG = 25% of NM, and VG+ = 50% of NM. (Example: VG = $2.00, VG+ = $4.00 and NM = $8.00.)

Number	Title (A Side/B Side)	Yr	NM
LONDON INT'L.			
❑ 10501	Ain't Gonna Wash for a Week/ One Last Kiss	1962	12.00
❑ 10515	Too Scared/Tell Tale	1962	12.00

BROONZY, BIG BILL

Number	Title (A Side/B Side)	Yr	NM
45s			
CHESS			
❑ 1546	Little City Woman/Lonesome	1953	400.00
MERCURY			
❑ 8160	You've Been Mistreating Me/ I Stay Blue All the Time	1951	30.00
—Released on 78 in 1949			
❑ 8261	Willie Mae Blues/ Hollerin' the Blues	1951	30.00
❑ 8271	Hey Hey/Walkin' the Lonesome Road	1952	30.00
❑ 8284	Mopper's Blues/I Know She Will	1952	30.00
❑ 70039	South Bound Train/Leavin' Day	1953	25.00
❑ 71352	Tomorrow/Hey Hey	1958	20.00
Albums			
BIOGRAPH			
❑ C-15	Big Bill Broonzy 1932-1942	197?	10.00
CHESS			
❑ LP-1468 [M]	Big Bill Broonzy and Washboard Sam	1962	160.00
COLUMBIA			
❑ WL 111 [M]	Big Bill's Blues	1958	100.00
DIAL			
❑ LP-306 [10]	Blues Concert	1952	150.00
EMARCY			
❑ MG-26034 [10]	Folk Blues	1954	120.00
❑ MG-36137 [M]	Blues by Broonzy	1958	100.00
EPIC			
❑ EE 22017 [M]	Big Bill's Blues	196?	20.00
EVEREST ARCHIVE OF FOLK & JAZZ			
❑ 213	Big Bill Broonzy	1967	12.00
FOLKWAYS			
❑ FA-2315 [M]	Big Bill Broonzy	1957	50.00
❑ FA-2326 [M]	Country Blues	1957	50.00
❑ FG-3586 [M]	His Songs and Story	195?	50.00
❑ 31005 [R]	Big Bill Sings Country Blues	196?	15.00
GNP CRESCENDO			
❑ 10004	Feeling Low Down	1974	10.00
❑ 10009	Lonesome Road Blues	1975	10.00
MERCURY			
❑ MG-20822 [M]	Big Bill Broonzy — Memorial	1963	30.00
❑ MG-20905 [M]	Remembering Big Bill Broonzy	1964	30.00
❑ SR-60822 [R]	Big Bill Broonzy — Memorial	1963	20.00
❑ SR-60905 [R]	Remembering Big Bill Broonzy	1964	20.00
PERIOD			
❑ SLP-1114 [M]	Big Bill Broonzy Sings (Blues)	1956	150.00
❑ SLP-1209 [M]	Big Bill Broonzy Sings and Josh White Comes a-Visiting	1958	70.00
PORTRAIT MASTERS			
❑ RJ 44089	Big Bill's Blues	1988	15.00
—Reissue of Columbia 111			
SMITHSONIAN FOLKWAYS			
❑ SF-40023	Big Bill Broonzy Sings Folk Songs	1989	12.00
VERVE			
❑ MGV-3000-5 [(5)M]	The Big Bill Broonzy Story	1959	200.00
❑ MGV-3001 [M]	Last Session, Vol. 1	1959	50.00
❑ MGV-3002 [M]	Last Session, Vol. 2	1959	50.00
❑ MGV-3003 [M]	Last Session, Vol. 3	1959	50.00
YAZOO			
❑ L-1011	The Young Big Bill Broonzy	1969	15.00
❑ L-1035	Do That Guitar Rag	197?	15.00

BROTH

Number	Title (A Side/B Side)	Yr	NM
Albums			
MERCURY			
❑ SR-61298	Broth	1970	20.00

BROTHER FOX AND TAR BABY

Number	Title (A Side/B Side)	Yr	NM
45s			
CAPITOL			
❑ 2940	Electric Chair/Steel Dog Man	1970	10.00
Albums			
CAPITOL			
❑ ST-544	Brother Fox and Tar Baby	1970	30.00
ORACLE			
❑ 1001	Brother Fox and Tar Baby	1969	30.00

BROTHER SISTERS, THE

Number	Title (A Side/B Side)	Yr	NM
45s			
MERCURY			
❑ 71195	Alone (Why Must I Be Alone)/ Pass Me the Mustard	1957	20.00
❑ 71678	Strawberry Shortcake/ Crystal Ball	1960	20.00

BROTHERHOOD OF MAN, THE

Number	Title (A Side/B Side)	Yr	NM
45s			
BELL			
❑ 45456	When Love Catches Up on You/(B-side unknown)	1974	4.00
DERAM			
❑ 85056	Love One Another/ A Little Bit of Heaven	1970	6.00
❑ 85059	United We Stand/Say a Prayer	1970	6.00
❑ 85065	Where Are You Going To My Love/Living in the Land of Love	1970	5.00
❑ 85070	This Boy/You Can Depend on Me	1971	5.00
❑ 85073	Reach Out Your Hand/, A Better Tomorrow	1971	5.00
❑ 85077	Sing in the Sunshine/You and I	1971	5.00
❑ 85078	California Sunday Morning/ Do Your Thing	1972	5.00
❑ 85081	Say a Prayer/Follow Me	1972	5.00
MERCURY			
❑ 882118-7	United We Stand/ My Baby Loves Lovin'	1986	4.00
—Reissue; B-side by White Plains			
PRIVATE STOCK			
❑ 45,148	Oh Boy (The Mood I'm In)/ (B-side unknown)	1977	5.00
❑ 45,165	Angelo/All Night	1977	5.00
PYE			
❑ 71043	Spring of 1912/(B-side unknown)	1976	6.00
❑ 71066	Save Your Kisses for Me/ Let's Love Together	1976	5.00
❑ 71076	Sweet Lady from Georgia/ Sugar Honey Love	1976	5.00
Albums			
DERAM			
❑ DES 18046	United We Stand	1970	15.00

BROTHERS, THE

Number	Title (A Side/B Side)	Yr	NM
45s			
ARGO			
❑ 5318	Lazy Susan/Deep Sleep	1958	20.00
❑ 5329	Sioux City Sue/Deep Sleep	1959	20.00
CHECKER			
❑ 995	My True Love/One Lonely Heart	1961	15.00

BROTHERS AND SISTERS

Number	Title (A Side/B Side)	Yr	NM
45s			
ODE			
❑ 121	The Mighty Quinn/ Chimes of Freedom	1969	8.00
❑ 123	Mr. Tambourine Man/The Times They Are a-Changing	1969	8.00

BROTHERS CAIN, THE

Number	Title (A Side/B Side)	Yr	NM
45s			
ACTA			
❑ 810	Better Times/Pupil Alexander	1967	25.00
❑ 820	It Sure Is Groovy/ Anyway You Like It	1968	25.00
MERCURY			
❑ 72437	In Love with One/Two Wrongs	1965	25.00

BROTHERS GRIMM, THE

Number	Title (A Side/B Side)	Yr	NM
45s			
MERCURY			
❑ 72512	A Man Needs Love/Looky, Looky	1966	10.00

BROTHERS GUIDING LIGHT FEATURING DAVID

Number	Title (A Side/B Side)	Yr	NM
45s			
MERCURY			
❑ 73389	Getting Together/Sweet Stuff	1973	250.00

BROTHERS JOHNSON, THE

Number	Title (A Side/B Side)	Yr	NM
12-Inch Singles			
A&M			
❑ SP-12003	Strawberry Letter 23/ Get the Funk Out Ma Face	1977	20.00
—Red vinyl			
❑ SP-12011	Ain't We Funkin' Now/ (B-side unknown)	1978	15.00
❑ SP-12102	You Keep Me Comin' Back (Remix Version) (Dub Version)	1984	8.00
❑ SP-12262	Kick It to the Curb (5:47) (6:32)/ P.O. Box 2000	1988	8.00
❑ SP-12281	Party Avenue (Dope Dance Mix) (Radio Edit) (Bonus Beats)	1988	8.00
❑ SP-12304	Strawberry Letter 23/Stomp!	1989	10.00
—Reissue of 12-inch mixes			
❑ SP-17046 [DJ]	Ride-O-Rocket/Streetwave	1978	15.00
❑ SP-17111 [DJ]	Stomp! (3:58) (6:22)	1980	15.00
❑ SP-17119 [DJ]	Light Up the Night (Extended Version) (LP Version)	1980	12.00
❑ SP-17160 [DJ]	The Real Thing (unknown versions)	1981	12.00
❑ SP-17170 [DJ]	Dancin' Free (same on both sides)	1981	8.00
❑ SP-17214 [DJ]	Welcome to the Club (2 versions)	1982	8.00
45s			
A&M			
❑ 1229	Party Avenue/Ball of Fire	1988	3.00
❑ 1806	I'll Be Good to You/The Devil	1976	4.00
❑ 1806 [PS]	I'll Be Good to You/The Devil	1976	6.00
❑ 1851	Get the Funk Out Ma Face/ Tomorrow	1976	4.00
❑ 1851 [PS]	Get the Funk Out Ma Face/ Tomorrow	1976	6.00
❑ 1881	Free and Single/Thunder Thumbs and Lightning Licks	1976	4.00
❑ 1949	Strawberry Letter 23/ Dancin' and Prancin'	1977	4.00
❑ 1949 [DJ]	Strawberry Letter 23 (mono/stereo)	1977	15.00
—Promo only on red vinyl			
❑ 1949 [PS]	Strawberry Letter 23/ Dancin' and Prancin'	1977	6.00
❑ 1982	Runnin' for Your Lovin'/Q	1977	4.00
❑ 1982 [PS]	Runnin' for Your Lovin'/Q	1977	6.00
❑ 2015	Love Is/Right On Time	1978	4.00
❑ 2086	Ride-O-Rocket/ Dancin' and Prancin'	1978	4.00
❑ 2098	Ain't We Funkin' Now/ Dancin' and Prancin'	1978	4.00
❑ 2216	Stomp!/Let's Swing	1980	4.00
❑ 2238	Light Up the Night/Street Wave	1980	4.00
❑ 2254	Treasure/Celebrations	1980	4.00
❑ 2280	Smilin' On Ya (mono/stereo)	1980	5.00
—Promo only			
❑ 2343	The Real Thing/I Want You	1981	4.00
❑ 2368	Dancin' Free/Do It for Love	1981	4.00
❑ 2506	Welcome to the Club/ The End of an Era	1982	4.00
❑ 2527	I'm Giving You All My Love/ The Real Thing	1983	4.00
❑ 2654	You Keep Me Coming Back/ Deceiver	1984	4.00
❑ 2689	Lovers Forever/Hot Mama	1984	4.00
❑ 3013	Kick It to the Curb/P.O. Box 2000 (Instrumental)	1988	3.00
❑ 3013 [PS]	Kick It to the Curb/P.O. Box 2000 (Instrumental)	1988	3.00
QWEST			
❑ 28877	Back Against the Wall Part 1/ Part 2	1985	3.00
Albums			
A&M			
❑ SP-3716	Light Up the Night	1980	10.00
❑ SP-3724	Winners	1981	10.00
❑ SP-4567	Look Out for #1	1976	10.00
❑ SP-4644	Right on Time	1977	10.00
❑ PR-4714 [DJ]	Blam!!	1978	20.00
—Promo-only picture disc			
❑ SP-4714	Blam!!	1978	10.00
❑ SP-4927	Blast! (The Latest and the Greatest)	1982	10.00
❑ SP-4965	Out of Control	1984	10.00
❑ SP-5162	Kickin'	1988	10.00
❑ SP-17049 [DJ]	Blam!! Radio Special	1978	20.00
—Promo-only music and interview record			

BROWN, AL

Number	Title (A Side/B Side)	Yr	NM
45s			
AMY			
❑ 804	The Madison/Mo' Madison	1960	25.00
❑ 806	It's True 'Bout Love/ Sweet Little Love	1960	20.00
❑ 811	Take Me Back/Mention Me	1960	20.00
❑ 829	Route 66/Shimmy Swing	1961	20.00
Albums			
AMY			
❑ A-1 [M]	Madison Dance Party	1960	40.00
❑ AS-1 [S]	Madison Dance Party	1960	50.00

BROWN, ARTHUR, THE CRAZY WORLD OF

Number	Title (A Side/B Side)	Yr	NM
45s			
ATLANTIC			
❑ 2556	Fire/Rest Cure	1968	10.00
MERCURY			
❑ 873504-7	Fire/Rest Cure	1990	3.00
—Reissue			

Number	Title (A Side/B Side)	Yr	NM
TRACK			
❑ 2582	I Put a Spell on You/Nightmare	1968	8.00
Albums			
GULL			
❑ GU6-405	Dance	1975	12.00
PASSPORT			
❑ 98003	Journey	1974	12.00
—As Arthur Brown's Kingdom Come			
TRACK			
❑ SD 8198	The Crazy World of Arthur Brown	1968	25.00

BROWN, BILLY (1)

Number	Title (A Side/B Side)	Yr	NM
45s			
CHALLENGE			
❑ 59396	One of the Ten Most Wanted Women/Open Arms	1969	8.00
COLUMBIA			
❑ 4-20766	Jealous Stars/I Never Knew I'd Miss You	1950	50.00
❑ 4-20789	Trusting Heart/I Hope I Don't Live Long Enough to Lose You	1951	50.00
❑ 4-20936	Tight Wad/I'm Sending Back Everything But Memories	1952	50.00
❑ 4-20982	Don't Hold Back/Rich in Love	1952	50.00
❑ 4-41029	Did We Have a Party/It's Love	1957	40.00
❑ 4-41100	Meet Me in the Alley, Sally/I Wanted You	1958	50.00
❑ 4-41297	Flip Out/Echo Mountain	1958	40.00
❑ 4-41380	Run 'Em Off/He'll Have to Go	1959	40.00
DECCA			
❑ 9-29559	Drunk-Drunk Again/High Heels But No Soul	1955	20.00
REPUBLIC			
❑ 2004	The Last Letter/Be Honest with Me	1960	15.00
❑ 2007	Just Out of Reach/Lost Weekend	1960	15.00
❑ 2012	Look Out Heart (Here Comes Love)/It Don't Take Long to Learn	1961	15.00
STARS			
❑ 552	Did We Have a Party/It's Love	1957	100.00

BROWN, BUSTER

Number	Title (A Side/B Side)	Yr	NM
45s			
FIRE			
❑ 507	Sugar Babe/I'm Going — But I'll Be Back	1962	20.00
❑ 516	Raise a Rucks Tonight/Gonna Love My Baby	1962	20.00
❑ 1008	Fannie Mae/Lost in a Dream	1959	25.00
❑ 1020	The Madison Shuffle/John Henry	1960	20.00
❑ 1023	Is You Is or Is You Ain't My Baby/Don't Dog Your Woman	1960	20.00
❑ 1032	Sincerely/Doctor Brown	1960	20.00
❑ 1040	Blues When It Rains/Good News	1961	20.00
❑ 2021	Sugar Babe/Don't Dog Your Woman	1962	15.00
LOST-NITE			
❑ 448	Fannie Mae/Is You Is or Is You Ain't My Baby	197?	6.00
—Reissue			
RCA VICTOR			
❑ PB-10023	Eloise/Fallin' Out of Love	1974	5.00
WHITE WHALE			
❑ 316	The Proud One/I've Got It Made	1969	10.00
Albums			
COLLECTABLES			
❑ COL-5110	Golden Classics: The New King of the Blues	198?	10.00
FIRE			
❑ FLP-102 [M]	The New King of the Blues	1961	300.00
—Red and black label, white cover			
❑ FLP-102 [M]	The New King of the Blues	1961	400.00
—Red and black label, purple cover			
❑ FLP-102 [M]	The New King of the Blues	1961	700.00
—White and red label			
SOUFFLE			
❑ 2014	Get Down	1973	12.00

BROWN, CHARLES

Number	Title (A Side/B Side)	Yr	NM
45s			
ACE			
❑ 561	Educated Fool/I Want to Go Back Home	1959	12.00
—With Amos Milburn			
❑ 599	Love's Like a River/Boys Will Be Boys	1960	12.00
❑ 599	Love's Like a River/Sing My Blues Tonight	1960	12.00
ALADDIN			
❑ 3076	Black Night/Once There Was a Fool	1951	150.00
—Charles Brown records on Aladdin prior to 3076 are unconfirmed on 45 rpm			
❑ 3091	I'll Always Be in Love with You/The Message	1951	80.00
❑ 3092	Seven Long Days/Don't Fool with My Heart	1951	80.00
❑ 3116	Hard Times/Tender Heart	1952	80.00
❑ 3120	Still Water/My Last Affair	1952	80.00
❑ 3138	See/Without Your Love	1952	80.00
❑ 3157	Rollin' Like a Pebble in the Sand/Alley Batting	1952	80.00
❑ 3163	Evening Shadows/Moonrise	1953	60.00
❑ 3176	Take Me/Rising Sun	1953	60.00
❑ 3191	Lonesome Feeling/I Lost Everything	1953	60.00
❑ 3200	All My Life/Don't Leave Me Poor	1953	60.00
❑ 3209	P.S. I Love You/Cryin' and Driftin' Blues	1953	60.00
❑ 3220	Everybody's Got Trouble/I Fool Around with You	1954	40.00
❑ 3235	Let's Walk/Crying Mercy	1954	40.00
❑ 3254	My Silent Love/Foolish	1954	40.00
❑ 3272	By the Bend of the River/Honey Slipper	1955	30.00
❑ 3284	Night After Night/Walk with Me	1955	30.00
❑ 3290	Hot Lips and Seven Kisses/Fools' Paradise	1955	30.00
❑ 3296	My Heart Is Mended/Trees, Trees	1955	30.00
❑ 3316	Please Don't Drive Me Away/One Minute to One	1956	25.00
❑ 3342	Soothe Me/I'll Always Be in Love with You	1956	25.00
❑ 3348	Merry Christmas, Baby/Black Night	1956	25.00
❑ 3366	Please Believe Me/It's a Sin to Tell a Lie	1957	20.00
❑ 3423	Hard Times/Ooh, Ooh Sugar	1958	20.00
BLUES SPECTRUM			
❑ 17	Merry Christmas, Baby/Rockin' Blues	197?	6.00
BLUESWAY			
❑ 61031	Merry Christmas, Baby/Rainy, Rainy Day	1969	6.00
CASH			
❑ 1052	Lost in the Night/I Sold My Heart to the Junkman	1957	30.00
—B-side by the Basin Street Boys			
CHARLENA			
❑ 001	Please Come Home For Christmas/Santa Claus	197?	4.00
❑ 001 [PS]	Please Come Home For Christmas/Santa Claus	197?	5.00
EASTWEST			
❑ 106	When Did You Leave Heaven/We've Got a Lot in Common	1958	20.00
EMI			
❑ S7-18213	Please Come Home for Christmas/Merry Christmas Baby	1994	4.00
—Green vinyl			
GALAXY			
❑ 762	I'm Gonna Push On/Cry No More	1968	10.00
❑ 766	Abraham, Martin, and John/(B-side unknown)	1968	10.00
HOLLYWOOD			
❑ 1006	Pleading for Your Love/The Best I Can Do	1954	40.00
❑ 1021	Merry Christmas Baby/Sleigh Ride	1954	20.00
—Charles Brown's first recording of the A-side, released on 78 on Exclusive 254 (1946); B-side by Lloyd Glenn; maroon label			
❑ 1021	Merry Christmas Baby/Sleigh Ride	196?	8.00
—B-side by Lloyd Glenn; color label			
❑ 1021	Merry Christmas Baby/Sleigh Ride	197?	5.00
—B-side by Lloyd Glenn; black label			
IMPERIAL			
❑ 5830	Fool's Paradise/Lonesome Feeling	1962	10.00
❑ 5902	Merry Christmas Baby/I Lost Everything	1962	10.00
❑ 5905	Black Night/Drifting Blues	1963	10.00
❑ 5961	I'm Savin' My Love for You/Please Don't Drive Me Away	1963	10.00
JEWEL			
❑ 814	Christmas in Heaven/Just a Blessing	1970	6.00
❑ 815	Merry Christmas Baby/Please Come Home for Christmas	1970	6.00
❑ 830	I Don't Know/For You	1972	5.00
❑ 838	I've Got Your Love/I Just Can't Get Over You	1973	5.00
❑ 847	Please Come Home for Christmas/Christmas in Heaven	1974	5.00
KENT			
❑ 501	Merry Christmas Baby/3 O'Clock Blues	1968	10.00
KING			
❑ 5405	Please Come Home for Christmas/Christmas (Comes But Once a Year)	1960	12.00
—B-side by Amos Milburn; original blue label			
❑ 5405	Please Come Home for Christmas/Christmas (Comes But Once a Year)	1970	6.00
—B-side by Amos Milburn; black label			
❑ 5439	Angel Baby/Baby Oh Baby	1961	12.00
❑ 5464	I Wanna Go Back Home/My Little Baby	1961	12.00
—With Amos Milburn			
❑ 5523	Butterfly/This Fool Has Learned	1961	12.00
❑ 5530	Christmas in Heaven/It's Christmas All Year 'Round	1961	12.00
❑ 5570	Without a Friend/If You Play with Cats	1961	12.00
❑ 5722	I'm Just a Drifter/I Don't Want Your Rambling Letters	1963	10.00
❑ 5726	It's Christmas Time/Christmas Finds Me Lonely	1963	10.00
❑ 5731	Christmas Questions/Wrap Yourself in a Christmas Package	1963	10.00
❑ 5802	If You Don't Believe I'm Crying/I Wanna Be Close	1963	10.00
❑ 5825	Lucky Dreamer/Too Fine for Crying	1963	10.00
❑ 5852	Blow Out All the Candles/Come Home	1964	10.00
❑ 5946	Christmas Blues/My Most Miserable Christmas	1964	10.00
❑ 5947	Christmas Comes (But Once a Year)/Bringin' In a Brand New Year	1964	10.00
❑ 6094	Regardless/The Plan	1967	8.00
❑ 6192	Hang On a Little Longer/Black Night	1968	8.00
❑ 6194	Merry Christmas, Baby/Let's Make Every Day Christmas	1968	8.00
❑ 6420	For the Good Times/Lonesome and Driftin'	1973	5.00
LIBERTY			
❑ 1393	Merry Christmas, Baby/Silent Night	1980	5.00
—B-side by Baby Washington			
❑ 5902	Merry Christmas, Baby/I Lost Everything	196?	8.00
—Reissue of Imperial 5902			
LILLY			
❑ 506	Bon Voyage/Bye and Bye	1962	10.00
MAINSTREAM			
❑ 607	Pledging My Love/Tomorrow Night	1965	8.00
NOLA			
❑ 702	Standing on the Outside/I'll Love You (If You Let Me)	1965	8.00
SWING TIME			
❑ 238	Merry Christmas, Baby/Lost In The Night	195?	100.00
—Originally released on 78, but a 45 does exist			
❑ 253	I'll Miss You/New Orleans Blues	1952	120.00
❑ 259	Be Fair with Me/Sunny Road	1952	120.00
TEEM			
❑ 1008	Merry Christmas Baby/Christmas Finds Me Oh So Sad	19??	6.00
UNITED ARTISTS			
❑ 0085	Drifting Blues/Black Night	1973	4.00
—Silver Spotlight Series issue			
❑ 0086	I Lost Everything/Lonesome Feeling	1973	4.00
—Silver Spotlight Series issue			
❑ XW582	Merry Christmas Baby/(B-side unknown)	1974	5.00
UPSIDE			
❑ PRO 002	Santa Claus Boogie (one-sided)	1986	4.00
—Flexidisc			
❑ PRO 002 [PS]	Santa Claus Boogie	1986	4.00

Except when noted otherwise, VG = 25% of NM, and VG+ = 50% of NM. (Example: VG = $2.00, VG+ = $4.00 and NM = $8.00.)

Number	Title (A Side/B Side)	Yr	NM
Albums			
ALADDIN			
❑ LP-702 [10]	Mood Music	1952	4000.
—Black vinyl; VG value 1500; VG+ value 2750			
❑ LP-702 [10]	Mood Music	1952	7500.
—Red vinyl; VG value 3000; VG+ value 5250			
❑ LP-809 [M]	Mood Music	1956	—
—Unreleased?			
ALLIGATOR			
❑ AL-4771	One More for the Road	1989	12.00
BIG TOWN			
❑ 1003	Merry Christmas Baby	1977	12.00
❑ 1005	Music Maestro Please	1978	10.00
BLUESWAY			
❑ BLS-6039	Charles Brown — Legend	1970	25.00
BULLSEYE BLUES			
❑ BB-9501	All My Life	1990	20.00
IMPERIAL			
❑ LP-9178 [M]	Charles Brown Sings Million Sellers	1961	400.00
JEWEL			
❑ 5006	Blues 'N' Brown	1972	12.00
KING			
❑ 775 [M]	Charles Brown Sings Christmas Songs	1961	150.00
❑ KS-775 [S]	Charles Brown Sings Christmas Songs	1963	300.00
—Stereo copies (whether true stereo or rechanneled, we don't know) exist on blue labels with "King" in block letters (no crown)			
❑ 878 [M]	The Great Charles Brown	1963	200.00
MAINSTREAM			
❑ S-6007 [S]	Boss of the Blues	1965	30.00
❑ S-6035 [S]	Ballads My Way	1965	30.00
❑ 56007 [M]	Boss of the Blues	1965	20.00
❑ 56035 [M]	Ballads My Way	1965	20.00
MOSAIC			
❑ MQ7-153 [(7)]	The Complete Aladdin Recordings of Charles Brown	1994	150.00
SCORE			
❑ SLP-4011 [M]	Driftin' Blues	1958	400.00
❑ SLP-4036 [M]	More Blues with Charles Brown	1959	—
—Unreleased			

BROWN, CHARLIE

Number	Title (A Side/B Side)	Yr	NM
45s			
HIT			
❑ 164	Legend of Daniel Boone/Ballad of Daniel Boone	1964	8.00
—B-side by Ricky Dickens			

BROWN, CLARENCE "GATEMOUTH"

Number	Title (A Side/B Side)	Yr	NM
45s			
PEACOCK			
❑ 1600	Baby Take It Easy/Just Got Lucky	1952	400.00
❑ 1607	Dirty Work at the Crossroads/You Got Money	1952	250.00
❑ 1617	Boogie Uproar/Hurry Back Good News	1953	200.00
❑ 1619	Please Tell Me Baby/Gate Walks to Board	1953	200.00
❑ 1633	Midnight Hour/For Now So Long	1954	150.00
❑ 1637	Okie Dokie Stomp/Depression Blues	1954	150.00
❑ 1653	Gate's Salty Blues/Rock My Blues Away	1955	100.00
❑ 1662	Ain't That Dandy/September Song	1956	80.00
❑ 1692	Just Before Dawn/Swinging the Gate	1958	40.00

BROWN, ESTELLE

One of the SWEET INSPIRATIONS.

Number	Title (A Side/B Side)	Yr	NM
45s			
UNITED ARTISTS			
❑ 727	You Got Just What You Asked For/Stick Close	1964	10.00

BROWN, FRED

Number	Title (A Side/B Side)	Yr	NM
45s			
HIT			
❑ 60	Can't Get Used to Losing You/Baby Workout	1963	8.00
—B-side by Leroy Jones			

BROWN, FRED X.

Number	Title (A Side/B Side)	Yr	NM
45s			
HIT			
❑ 16	The Man Who Shot Liberty Valance/It Keeps Right On a-Hurtin'	1962	8.00

BROWN, GENE

Number	Title (A Side/B Side)	Yr	NM
45s			
DOT			
❑ 15709	Playing with My Heart Again/Big Door	1958	60.00

BROWN, GEORGE WASHINGTON

See VAN DYKE PARKS.

BROWN, JAMES

Also see VICKI ANDERSON; BOBBY BYRD; LYN COLLINS; FRED WESLEY AND THE JB'S.

Number	Title (A Side/B Side)	Yr	NM
12-Inch Singles			
POLYDOR			
❑ PRO 040 [DJ]	Eyesight/The Spank	1978	15.00
❑ PRO 059 [DJ]	For Goodness Sake, Look at Those Cakes (11:04) (same on both sides)	1978	25.00
❑ PRO 086 [DJ]	It's Too Funky in Here (6:33) (same on both sides)	1979	20.00
❑ PRO 100 [DJ]	Star Generation (8:07) (4:21)	1979	20.00
❑ PD-510	It's Too Funky in Here (6:33)/Are We Really Dancing	1979	15.00
SCOTTI BROTHERS			
❑ ZAS 2241 [DJ]	Living in America (4:50) (same on both sides)	1985	15.00
❑ 4Z9-05310	Living in America (LP Version) (Dance Mix) (Instrumental)	1985	8.00
❑ 4Z9-05943	Gravity (Extended Dance Mix) (7" Edit) (12" Dub Mix)/The Big G (Dig This Mess)	1986	8.00
❑ 4Z9-05990	How Do You Stop (Special Extended Remix)/Goliath (Special Extended Remix)	1986	10.00
❑ 4Z9-07805	I'm Real/Tribute	1988	8.00
❑ 4Z9-07863	Static (3 versions)/Godfather Runnin' the Joint	1988	10.00
❑ 4Z9-08130	Time to Get Busy (Full Force Remix) (Single Version)/Busy J.B. (Full Force Remix) (Single Version)	1988	8.00
❑ 75286	(So Tired of Standing Still We Got to) Move On (5 versions)	1991	10.00
❑ 75352 [(2)]	Can't Get Any Harder (4 versions)	1993	12.00
❑ 78034	Respect Me (6 versions)	1995	10.00
❑ 78094	Hooked on Brown (Long) (Radio Edit 1) (Radio Edit 2)	1996	15.00
T.K. DISCO			
❑ TKD 452	Rapp Payback (Where Iz Moses) (Part 1 7:00)/(Part 2 3:28)	1980	12.00
45s			
A&M			
❑ 3022	I Got You (I Feel Good)/Nowhere to Run	1988	4.00
—B-side by Martha and the Vandellas			
❑ 3022 [PS]	I Got You (I Feel Good)/Nowhere to Run	1988	4.00
—"Good Morning Vietnam" sleeve			
AUGUSTA SOUND			
❑ 94023	Bring It On ... Bring It On/The Night Time Is the Right Time (To Be With the One That You Love)	1983	4.00
❑ 94023 [PS]	Bring It On ... Bring It On/The Night Time Is the Right Time (To Be With the One That You Love)	1983	4.00
BACKSTREET			
❑ 52215	King of Soul/Theme from Doctor Detroit	1983	3.00
—B-side by Devo			
BETHLEHEM			
❑ 3089	I Loves You Porgy/Yours and Mine	1969	15.00
❑ 3098	A Man Has to Go Back to the Crossroads/The Drunk	1969	15.00
FEDERAL			
❑ 12258	Please, Please, Please/Why Do You Do Me?	1956	40.00
❑ 12264	I Don't Know/I Feel That Old Feeling Coming On	1956	25.00
❑ 12277	No, No, No, No/Hold My Baby's Hand	1956	25.00
❑ 12289	Just Won't Do Right/Let's Make It	1957	25.00
❑ 12290	I Won't Plead No More/Chonnie On Chon	1957	25.00
❑ 12292	Gonna Try/Can't Be the Same	1957	25.00
❑ 12295	Love or a Game/Messing with the Blues	1957	25.00
❑ 12300	I Walked Alone/You're Mine, You're Mine	1957	25.00
❑ 12311	Baby Cries Over the Ocean/That Dood It	1957	25.00
❑ 12316	Begging, Begging/That's When I Lost My Heart	1958	25.00
❑ 12337	Try Me/Tell Me What I Did Wrong	1958	30.00
❑ 12348	I Want You So Bad/There Must Be a Reason	1959	20.00
❑ 12352 [M]	I've Got to Change/It Hurts to Tell You	1959	20.00
❑ S-12352 [S]	I've Got to Change/It Hurts to Tell You	1959	50.00
❑ 12361 [M]	Don't Let It Happen to Me/Good Good Lovin'	1959	20.00
❑ S-12361 [S]	Don't Let It Happen to Me/Good Good Lovin'	1959	50.00
❑ 12364	It Was You/Got to Cry	1959	20.00
❑ 12369	I'll Go Crazy/I Know It's True	1960	20.00
❑ 12370	Think/You've Got the Power	1960	20.00
❑ 12378	This Old Heart/I Wonder When You're Coming Home	1960	20.00
KING			
❑ 5423	The Bells/And I Do Just What I Want	1960	15.00
❑ 5438	The Scratch/Hold It	1961	15.00
❑ 5442	Bewildered/If You Want Me	1961	15.00
❑ 5466	I Don't Mind/Love Don't Love Nobody	1961	15.00
❑ 5485	Sticky/Suds	1961	15.00
❑ 5519	Night Flying/Cross Firing	1961	15.00
❑ 5524	Baby You're Right/I'll Never, Never Let You Go	1961	15.00
❑ 5547	Just You and Me, Darling/I Love You, Yes I Do	1961	15.00
❑ 5573	Lost Someone/Cross Firing	1961	15.00
❑ 5614	Night Train/Why Does Everything Happen to Me	1962	15.00
❑ 5654	Tell Me Why/Say So Long	1962	15.00
—With Yvonne Fair			
❑ 5657	Shout and Shimmy/Come Over Here	1962	15.00
❑ 5672	Mashed Potatoes U.S.A./You Don't Have to Go	1962	15.00
❑ 5687	It Hurts to Be in Love/You Can Make It If You Try	1962	15.00
—With Yvonne Fair			
❑ 5698	(Can You) Feel It Part 1/(Can You) Feel It Part 2	1962	15.00
❑ 5701	Three Hearts in a Tangle/I've Got Money	1962	15.00
❑ 5710	Like a Baby/Every Beat of My Heart	1963	15.00
❑ 5739	Prisoner of Love/Choo Choo	1963	15.00
❑ 5767	These Foolish Things/Can You Feel It — Part 1	1963	15.00
❑ 5803	Signed, Sealed and Delivered/Waiting in Vain	1963	15.00
❑ 5829	The Bells/I've Got to Change	1963	15.00
❑ 5842	Oh Baby Don't You Weep (Part 1)/Oh Baby Don't You Weep (Part 2)	1964	15.00
❑ 5842 [PS]	Oh Baby Don't You Weep (Part 1)/Oh Baby Don't You Weep (Part 2)	1964	25.00
❑ 5853	Please, Please, Please/In the Wee Wee Hours	1964	15.00
❑ 5876	How Long Darling/Again	1964	15.00
❑ 5899	So Long/Dancin' Little Thing	1964	15.00
❑ 5922	Tell Me What You're Gonna Do/I Don't Care	1964	15.00
❑ 5952	Think/Try Me	1964	15.00
❑ 5956	Fine Old Foxy Self/Medley	1964	15.00
❑ 5968	Have Mercy Baby/Just Won't Do Right	1964	15.00
❑ 5995	This Old Heart/It Was You	1965	12.00
❑ 5999	Papa's Got a Brand New Bag Part I/Papa's Got a Brand New Bag Part II	1965	15.00
❑ 6015	I Got You (I Feel Good)/I Can't Help It (I Just Do, Do, Do)	1965	15.00
❑ 6020	I'll Go Crazy/Lost Someone	1966	12.00
❑ 6025	Ain't That a Groove Part I/Ain't That a Groove Part II	1966	12.00
❑ 6029	Prisoner of Love/I've Got to Change	1966	12.00
❑ 6033	Come Over Here/Tell Me What You're Gonna Do	1966	12.00
❑ 6035	It's a Man's Man's Man's World/Is It Yes Or Is It No?	1966	12.00
❑ 6037	I've Got Money/Just Won't Do Right	1966	12.00
❑ 6040	I Don't Care/It Was You	1966	12.00
❑ 6044	This Old Heart/How Long Darling	1966	12.00
❑ 6048	Money Won't Change You Part 1/Money Won't Change You Part 2	1966	12.00
❑ 6056	Don't Be a Drop-Out/Tell Me That You Love Me	1966	12.00
❑ 6064	The Christmas Song (Version 1)/The Christmas Song (Version 2)	1966	15.00

Number	Title (A Side/B Side)	Yr	NM
❑ 6065	Sweet Little Baby Boy (Part 1)/Sweet Little Baby Boy (Part 2)	1966	12.00
❑ 6071	Bring It Up/Nobody Knows	1967	12.00
❑ 6072	Let's Make Christmas Mean Something This Year (Part 1)/Let's Make Christmas Mean Something This Year (Part 2)	1967	12.00
❑ 6086	Kansas City/Stone Fox	1967	12.00
❑ 6091	Think/Nobody Cares	1967	12.00
—A-side: With Vicki Anderson; B-side: Vicki Anderson solo			
❑ 6100	Let Yourself Go/Good Rockin' Tonight	1967	12.00
❑ 6110	Cold Sweat — Part 1/Cold Sweat — Part 2	1967	12.00
❑ 6111	Mona Lisa/It Won't Be Me	1967	60.00
—Evidently not released or pulled shortly after release			
❑ 6112	America Is My Home — Part 1/America Is My Home — Part 2	1967	12.00
❑ 6122	Get It Together (Part 1)/Get It Together (Part 2)	1967	12.00
❑ 6133	The Soul of J.B./Funky Soul #1	1967	12.00
❑ 6141	I Guess I'll Have to Cry, Cry, Cry/Just Plain Funk	1967	12.00
❑ 6144	I Can't Stand Myself (When You Touch Me)/There Was a Time	1967	12.00
❑ 6151	You've Got to Change Your Mind/I'll Lose My Mind	1968	12.00
—A-side: With Bobby Byrd; B-side: Bobby Byrd solo			
❑ 6152	You've Got the Power/What the World Needs Now Is Love	1968	12.00
—A-side: With Vicki Anderson; B-side: Vicki Anderson solo			
❑ 6155	I Got the Feelin'/If I Ruled the World	1968	12.00
❑ 6159	Maybe Good, Maybe Bad (Part 1)/(Part 2)	1968	15.00
❑ 6164	Here I Go/Shhhh	1968	12.00
❑ 6166	Licking Stick — Licking Stick (Part 1)/Licking Stick — Licking Stick (Part 2)	1968	12.00
❑ 6187	Say It Loud — I'm Black and I'm Proud (Part 1)/Say It Loud — I'm Black and I'm Proud (Part 2)	1968	10.00
❑ 6187	Say It Loud — I'm Black But I'm Proud (Part 1)/Say It Loud — I'm Black But I'm Proud (Part 2)	1968	25.00
—Some copies have the above erroneous title on both sides			
❑ 6198	Goodbye My Love/Shades of Brown	1968	10.00
❑ 6203	Santa Claus Go Straight to the Ghetto/You Know It	1968	10.00
❑ 6204	Believers Shall Enjoy/Tit for Tat (Ain't No Turning Back)	1968	10.00
❑ 6205	Let's Unite the World at Christmas/In the Middle (Part 1)	1968	10.00
❑ 6206	In the Middle (Part 2)/Tit for Tat (Ain't No Turning Back)	1969	10.00
—A-side: With Marva Whitney			
❑ 6213	Give It Up or Turnit A Loose/I'll Lose My Mind	1969	10.00
❑ 6216	Shades of Brown (Part 2)/A Talk with the News	1969	10.00
—B-side by Steve Soul			
❑ 6218	You Got to Have a Job/I'm Tired, I'm Tired, I'm Tired	1969	10.00
—A-side with Marva Whitney; B-side: Marva Whitney solo			
❑ 6222	Soul Pride (Part 1)/Soul Pride (Part 2)	1969	10.00
❑ 6223	You've Got to Have a Mother for Me (Part 1)/You've Got to Have a Mother for Me (Part 2)	1969	10.00
❑ 6224	I Don't Want Nobody to Give Me Nothing (Open Up the Door, I'll Get It Myself) Part 1/Part 2	1969	10.00
❑ 6235	Little Groove Maker (Part 1)/Any Day Now	1969	10.00
❑ 6235	Little Groove Maker (Part 1)/I'm Shook	1969	10.00
❑ 6240	The Popcorn/The Chicken	1969	10.00
❑ 6245	Mother Popcorn (You Got to Have a Mother for Me) Part 1/Mother Popcorn (You Got to Have a Mother for Me) Part 2	1969	10.00
❑ 6250	Lowdown Popcorn/Top of the Stack	1969	10.00
❑ 6255	Let a Man Come In and Do the Popcorn Part One/Sometime	1969	10.00
❑ 6258	World (Part 1)/World (Part 2)	1969	10.00
❑ 6273	I'm Not Demanding (Part 1)/I'm Not Demanding (Part 2)	1969	10.00
❑ 6275	Part Two (Let a Man Come In and Do the Popcorn)/Get a Little Hipper	1969	10.00
❑ 6277	It's Christmas Time (Part 1)/It's Christmas Time (Part 2)	1969	10.00
❑ 6280	Ain't It Funky Now (Part 1)/Ain't It Funky Now (Part 2)	1970	8.00
❑ 6290	Funky Drummer (Part 1)/Funky Drummer (Part 2)	1970	8.00
❑ 6292	It's a New Day (Part 1)/It's a New Day (Part 2)	1970	8.00
❑ 6293	Let It Be Me/Baby Don't You Know	1970	8.00
—A-side: With Vicki Anderson; B-side: Vicki Anderson solo			
❑ 6300	Talkin' Loud and Sayin' Nothing (Part 1)/Talkin' Loud and Sayin' Nothing (Part 2)	1970	8.00
❑ 6310	Brother Rapp (Part 1) & (Part 2)/Bewildered	1970	8.00
❑ 6318	Get Up (I Feel Like Being A) Sex Machine (Part 1)/Get Up (I Feel Like Being A) Sex Machine (Part 2)	1970	8.00
❑ 6322	I'm Not Demanding (Part 1)/I'm Not Demanding (Part 2)	1970	8.00
❑ 6329	Super Bad (Part 1 & Part 2)/Super Bad (Part 3)	1970	8.00
❑ 6329	Call Me Super Bad (Part 1 & Part 2)/Call Me Super Bad (Part 3)	1970	20.00
—First pressing: Note longer title			
❑ 6339	Hey America/(Instrumental)	1970	8.00
❑ 6339 [PS]	Hey America/(Instrumental)	1970	15.00
❑ 6340	Santa Claus Is Definitely Here to Stay/(Instrumental)	1970	8.00
❑ 6340 [PS]	Santa Claus Is Definitely Here to Stay/(Instrumental)	1970	30.00
❑ 6347	Get Up, Get Into It, Get Involved Pt. 1/Get Up, Get Into It, Get Involved Pt. 2	1971	8.00
❑ 6359	Talking Loud and Saying Nothing — Part 1/Talking Loud and Saying Nothing — Part 2	1971	8.00
❑ 6363	I Cried/World (Part 2)	1971	8.00
❑ 6366	Spinning Wheel (Part 1)/Spinning Wheel (Part 2)	1971	8.00
❑ 6368	Soul Power Pt. 1/Soul Power Pt 2 & Pt. 3	1971	8.00

MERCURY

Number	Title (A Side/B Side)	Yr	NM
❑ 885190-7	Prisoner of Love/Please, Please, Please	1986	4.00
—Reissue			
❑ 885194-7	Get on the Good Foot/Give It Up or Turnit A Loose	1986	4.00
—Reissue			

PEOPLE

Number	Title (A Side/B Side)	Yr	NM
❑ 664	Everybody Wanna Be Funky One More Time Pt. 1/Everybody Wanna Be Funky One More Time Pt. 2	1976	5.00
❑ 2500	Escape-ism (Part 1)/Escape-ism (Parts 2 & 3)	1971	6.00
❑ 2501	Hot Pants Pt. 1 (She Got to Use What She Got to Get What She Wants)/Hot Pants Pt. 2	1971	6.00

POLYDOR

Number	Title (A Side/B Side)	Yr	NM
❑ 2005	Star Generation/Women Are Something Else	1979	5.00
❑ 2034	The Original Disco Man/Let the Boogie Do the Rest	1979	5.00
❑ 2054	Regrets/Stone Cold Drag	1979	5.00
❑ 2078	Let the Funk Flow/Sometimes That's All There Is	1980	5.00
❑ 2129	Get Up Offa That Thing/It's Too Funky in Here	1980	5.00
❑ 2167	Give the Bass Player Some Part 1/Part 2	1981	5.00
❑ 14088	Make It Funky Part 1/Make It Funky Part 2	1971	6.00
❑ 14098	My Part/Make It Funky, Part 3//Make It Funky, Part 4	1971	6.00
❑ 14100	I'm a Greedy Man Part 1/I'm a Greedy Man Part 2	1971	6.00
❑ 14109	Talking Loud and Saying Nothing Part 1/Part 2	1972	6.00
❑ 14110	Nothing Beats a Try But a Fail/Hot Pants Road	1972	—
—Unreleased			
❑ 14116	King Heroin/Theme from King Heroin	1972	6.00
❑ 14116 [PS]	King Heroin/Theme from King Heroin	1972	10.00
❑ 14125	There It Is Part 1/There It Is Part 2	1972	6.00
❑ 14129	Honky Tonk Part 1/Honky Tonk Part 2	1972	6.00
—Artist credit: "James Brown Soul Train"			
❑ 14139	Get On the Good Foot Part 1/Get On the Good Foot Part 2	1972	6.00
❑ 14153	I Got a Bag of My Own/Public Enemy #1	1972	6.00
❑ 14155	I Got a Bag of My Own/I Know It's True	1972	30.00
—Manufactured in U.S. for export			
❑ 14157	What My Baby Needs Now Is a Little More Lovin'/This Guy-This Girl's in Love	1972	6.00
—With Lyn Collins			
❑ 14161	Santa Claus Goes Straight to the Ghetto/Sweet Little Baby Boy	1972	6.00
❑ 14162	I Got Ants in My Pants (and I want to dance) Part 1/Part 15 and 16	1973	5.00
❑ 14168	Down and Out in New York City/Mama's Dead	1973	5.00
❑ 14169	The Boss/Like It Is, Like It Was	1973	5.00
❑ 14177	Think/Something	1973	5.00
❑ 14185	Think/Something	1973	5.00
❑ 14193	Woman Part 1/Woman Part 2	1973	5.00
❑ 14194	Sexy, Sexy, Sexy/Slaughter Theme	1973	5.00
❑ 14199	Let It Be Me/It's All Right	1973	—
—With Lyn Collins; canceled?			
❑ 14206	I Got a Good Thing Part 1/I Got a Good Thing Part 2	1973	—
—Canceled?			
❑ 14210	Stoned to the Bone Part 1/Stoned to the Bone Part 2	1973	5.00
—Notice corrected title			
❑ 14210	Stone to the Bone Part 1/Stone to the Bone Part 2	1973	10.00
❑ 14223	The Payback Part 1/The Payback Part 2	1974	5.00
❑ 14223 [PS]	The Payback Part 1/The Payback Part 2	1974	10.00
❑ 14244	My Thang/Public Enemy No. 1	1974	5.00
❑ 14255	Papa Don't Take No Mess Part 1/Part 2	1974	5.00
❑ 14258	Funky President (People It's Bad)/Coldblooded	1974	5.00
❑ 14268	Reality/I Need Your Love So Bad	1975	5.00
❑ 14270	Sex Machine Part 1/Sex Machine Part 2	1975	5.00
❑ 14274	Thank You For Letting Me Be Myself And... Part 1/Part 2	1975	5.00
❑ 14279	Dead On It Part 1/Dead On It Part 2	1975	—
—Unreleased			
❑ 14281	Hustle (Dead On It) Part 1/Hustle (Dead On It) Part 2	1975	5.00
❑ 14295	Superbad, Superslick Part 1/Superbad, Superslick Part 2	1975	5.00
❑ 14301	Hot (I Need to Be Loved, Loved, Loved)/Superbad, Superslick	1975	5.00
❑ 14302	Dooley's Junkyard Dogs Part 1/Part 2	1975	5.00
❑ 14304	(I Love You) For Sentimental Reasons/Goodnight My Love	1976	5.00
❑ 14326	Get Up Offa That Thing/Release the Pressure	1976	5.00
❑ 14354	I Refuse to Lose/Home Again	1976	5.00
❑ 14360	Bodyheat Part 1/Bodyheat Part 2	1976	5.00
❑ 14388	Kiss in 77/Woman	1977	5.00
❑ 14409	Give Me Some Skin/People Wake Up and Live	1977	5.00
—With the J.B.'s			
❑ 14433	Take Me Higher and Groove Me/Summertime	1977	5.00
—B-side by Martha and James			
❑ 14438	If You Don't Give a Doggone About It/People Who Criticize	1977	5.00
—With the New J.B.'s			
❑ 14460	Love Me Tender/Have a Happy Day	1978	5.00
—With the New J.B.'s			
❑ 14465	Eyesight/I Never Never Never Will Forget	1978	5.00
❑ 14487	The Spank/Love Me Tender	1978	5.00
❑ 14512	Nature Part 1/Nature Part 2	1978	5.00
❑ 14522	For Goodness Sakes, Look at Those Cakes Part 1/Part 2	1979	5.00
❑ 14540	Someone to Talk To Part 1/Someone to Talk To Part 2	1979	5.00
❑ 14557	It's Too Funky in Here/Are We Really Dancing	1979	5.00
❑ 871804-7	Think/Lost Someone	1989	3.00
—Reissue			
❑ 871808-7	Out of Sight/Maybe the Last Time	1989	3.00
—Reissue			
❑ 871810-7	I Got You (I Feel Good)/Papa's Got a Brand New Bag	1989	3.00
—Reissue			
❑ 887500-7	(Get Up I Feel Like Being a) Sex Machine/Vincent's Theme	1988	3.00
—B-side by Ethan James			
❑ 887500-7 [PS]	(Get Up I Feel Like Being a) Sex Machine/Vincent's Theme	1988	4.00
—B-side by Ethan James			

SCOTTI BROTHERS

Number	Title (A Side/B Side)	Yr	NM
❑ ZS4-05682	Living in America/Farewell	1985	3.00
—B-side by Vince Di Cola			
❑ ZS4-05682 [PS]	Living in America/Farewell	1985	3.00
❑ ZS4-06275	Gravity/Gravity (Dub Mix)	1986	3.00

Number	Title (A Side/B Side)	Yr	NM
❑ ZS4-06275 [PS]	Gravity/Gravity (Dub Mix)	1986	3.00
❑ ZS4-06568	How Do You Stop/House of Rock	1987	3.00
❑ ZS4-06568 [PS]	How Do You Stop/House of Rock	1987	3.00
❑ ZS4-07090	Let's Get Personal/Repeat the Beat	1987	3.00
❑ ZS4-07783	I'm Real/Tribute	1988	3.00
❑ ZS4-07783 [PS]	I'm Real/Tribute	1988	3.00
❑ ZS4-07975	Static/Godfather Runnin' the Joint	1988	3.00
❑ ZS4-08088	Time to Get Busy/Busy J.B.	1988	3.00
❑ ZS4-68559	It's Your Money $/You and Me	1989	3.00
❑ 75286	(So Tired of Standing Still We Got to) Move On/You Are My Everything	1991	4.00

SMASH

Number	Title (A Side/B Side)	Yr	NM
❑ 1898	Caldonia/Evil	1964	12.00
❑ 1898	Caledonia/Evil	1964	12.00
❑ 1898 [PS]	Caledonia/Evil	1964	25.00
❑ 1908	The Things That I Used to Do/Out of the Blue	1964	12.00
❑ 1908 [PS]	The Things That I Used to Do/Out of the Blue	1964	40.00
❑ 1919	Out of Sight/Maybe the Last Time	1964	12.00
❑ 1919 [PS]	Out of Sight/Maybe the Last Time	1964	40.00
❑ 1949	Who's Afraid of Virginia Woolf? Part 1/Part 2	1964	—
—Unreleased			
❑ 1975	Devil's Hideaway/Who's Afraid of Virginia Woolf?	1965	10.00
❑ 1989	I Got You/Only You	1965	50.00
—Withdrawn			
❑ 2008	Try Me/Papa's Got a Brand New Bag	1965	10.00
❑ 2028	New Breed Part 1/New Breed Part 2	1966	10.00
❑ 2042	James Brown's Boo-Ga-Loo/Lost in the Mood of Changes	1966	10.00
❑ 2064	Let's Go Get Stoned/Our Day Will Come	1966	10.00
❑ 2093	Jimmy Mack/What Do You Like	1967	10.00

T.K.

Number	Title (A Side/B Side)	Yr	NM
❑ 1039	Rapp Payback (Where Iz Moses) Part 1/Part 2	1980	4.00
❑ 1042	Stay with Me/Smokin' and Drinkin'	1981	4.00

7-Inch Extended Plays

KING

Number	Title (A Side/B Side)	Yr	NM
❑ EP-430	*Please, Please, Please/That's When I Lost My Heart/Try Me/Tell Me What I Did Wrong	1959	200.00
❑ EP-430 [PS]	Please, Please, Please	1959	400.00
❑ 826	(contents unknown)	1963	80.00
❑ 826 [PS]	Live at the Apollo	1963	120.00

SMASH

Number	Title (A Side/B Side)	Yr	NM
❑ SRS 707-C	New Breed/Lost in the Mood of Changes/Hooks//Jabo/Fat Bag (Part 1)/Fat Bag (Part 2)	196?	50.00
—Jukebox issue; small hole, plays at 33 1/3 rpm			
❑ SRS 707-C [PS]	James Brown Plays New Breed (The Boo-Ga-Loo)	196?	50.00
—Jukebox issue; small hole, plays at 33 1/3 rpm			

Albums

HRB

Number	Title (A Side/B Side)	Yr	NM
❑ 1004 [(2)]	The Fabulous James Brown	1974	25.00

KING

Number	Title (A Side/B Side)	Yr	NM
❑ 610 [M]	Please Please Please	1958	1200.
—"Woman's and man's legs" cover; "King" on label is two inches wide			
❑ 610 [M]	Please Please Please	1961	1000.
—"Woman's and man's legs" cover; "King" on label is three inches wide			
❑ 635 [M]	Try Me!	1959	900.00
—"Woman with cigarette and gun" cover; "King" on label is two inches wide			
❑ 635 [M]	Try Me!	1961	600.00
—"Woman with cigarette and gun" cover; "King" on label is three inches wide			
❑ 683 [M]	Think!	1960	900.00
—"Baby" cover; "King" on label is two inches wide			
❑ 683 [M]	Think!	1961	600.00
—"Baby" cover; "King" on label is three inches wide			
❑ 683 [M]	Think!	1963	100.00
—James Brown photo cover; "crownless" King label			
❑ 683 [M]	Think!	1966	50.00
—James Brown photo cover; "crown" King label			
❑ 743 [M]	The Amazing James Brown	1961	500.00
—"James Brown in suit" cover			
❑ 743 [M]	The Amazing James Brown	1963	150.00
—White title cover; "crownless" King label			
❑ 743 [M]	The Amazing James Brown	1966	500.00
—White title cover with "James Brown" in huge letters; "crown" King label			
❑ 771 [M]	Night Train	1961	300.00
—Original title			
❑ 771 [M]	Twist Around	1962	250.00
—Second title			
❑ 771 [M]	Jump Around	1963	200.00
—Third title			
❑ KS-771 [S]	Jump Around	1963	300.00
—Stereo copies of King 771 only exist with this title			
❑ 780 [M]	Good Good Twistin'	1962	200.00
—"Good Good Twistin'" on either label or cover, or both			
❑ 780 [M]	Shout and Shimmy	1962	250.00
—"Shout and Shimmy" on both cover and label			
❑ 780 [M]	Excitement	1963	150.00
—Third title; "crownless" King label			
❑ 780 [M]	Excitement	1966	50.00
—Third title; "crown" King label			
❑ 804 [M]	James Brown & His Famous Flames Tour the U.S.A.	1962	250.00
—"Crownless" King label			
❑ 804 [M]	James Brown & His Famous Flames Tour the U.S.A.	1966	50.00
—"Crown" King label			
❑ 826 [M]	Live at the Apollo	1963	200.00
—Custom back cover; "crownless" King label			
❑ 826 [M]	Live at the Apollo	1963	800.00
—White label promo, banded for airplay			
❑ 826 [M]	Live at the Apollo	1966	50.00
—"Crown" King label			
❑ 826 [M]	Live at the Apollo	1963	150.00
—Other King albums on back cover; "crownless" King label			
❑ KS-826 [S]	Live at the Apollo	1963	200.00
—Other King albums on back cover; "crownless" King label			
❑ KS-826 [S]	Live at the Apollo	1963	300.00
—Custom back cover; "crownless" King label			
❑ KS-826 [S]	Live at the Apollo	1966	70.00
—"Crown" King label			
❑ 851 [M]	Prisoner of Love	1963	100.00
—Other King albums on back cover; "crownless" King label			
❑ 851 [M]	Prisoner of Love	1963	200.00
—Custom back cover; "crownless" King label			
❑ 851 [M]	Prisoner of Love	1966	50.00
—"Crown" King label			
❑ 883 [M]	Pure Dynamite! Live at the Royal	1964	200.00
—"Crownless" King label			
❑ 883 [M]	Pure Dynamite! Live at the Royal	1964	800.00
—White label promo; banded for airplay			
❑ 883 [M]	Pure Dynamite! Live at the Royal	1966	50.00
—"Crown" King label			
❑ 909 [M]	Please Please Please	1964	100.00
—Reissue of 610; "crownless" King label			
❑ 909 [M]	Please Please Please	1966	50.00
—"Crown" King label			
❑ 919 [M]	The Unbeatable James Brown — 16 Hits	1964	100.00
—Reissue of 635; "crownless" King label			
❑ 919 [M]	The Unbeatable James Brown — 16 Hits	1966	50.00
—"Crown" King label			
❑ 938 [M]	Papa's Got a Brand New Bag	1965	80.00
—Red cover; "crownless" King label			
❑ 938 [M]	Papa's Got a Brand New Bag	1966	40.00
—"Crown" King label			
❑ 938 [M]	Papa's Got a Brand New Bag	1966	50.00
—Green cover; "crownless" King label			
❑ LPS-938 [P]	Papa's Got a Brand New Bag	1965	100.00
—Red cover; "crownless" King label			
❑ LPS-938 [P]	Papa's Got a Brand New Bag	1966	50.00
—"Crown" King label			
❑ LPS-938 [P]	Papa's Got a Brand New Bag	1966	60.00
—Green cover; "crownless" King label			
❑ 946 [M]	I Got You (I Feel Good)	1966	40.00
—"Crown" King label			
❑ 946 [M]	I Got You (I Feel Good)	1966	100.00
—"Crownless" King label			
❑ LPS-946 [S]	I Got You (I Feel Good)	1966	50.00
—"Crown" King label			
❑ LPS-946 [S]	I Got You (I Feel Good)	1966	150.00
—"Crownless" King label			
❑ 961 [M]	Mighty Instrumentals	1966	100.00
❑ LPS-961 [S]	Mighty Instrumentals	1966	150.00
❑ 985 [M]	It's a Man's Man's Man's World	1966	50.00
❑ KS-985 [S]	It's a Man's Man's Man's World	1966	70.00
❑ 1010 [M]	Christmas Songs	1966	100.00
—Wreath on gray wall, no song titles on back			
❑ 1010 [M]	Christmas Songs	1967	80.00
—Wreath on white wall, song titles are on back			
❑ KS-1010 [S]	Christmas Songs	1966	150.00
—Wreath on gray wall, no song titles on back			
❑ KS-1010 [S]	Christmas Songs	1967	100.00
—Wreath on white wall, song titles are on back			
❑ 1016 [M]	Raw Soul	1967	50.00
❑ KS-1016 [P]	Raw Soul	1967	70.00
❑ 1018 [M]	Live at the Garden	1967	80.00
❑ 1018 [M]	Live at the Garden	1967	400.00
—Black label promo; banded for airplay			
❑ KS-1018 [S]	Live at the Garden	1967	100.00
❑ 1020 [M]	Cold Sweat	1967	50.00
❑ KS-1020 [S]	Cold Sweat	1967	70.00
❑ LPS-1022 [(2)]	Live at the Apollo, Vol. II	1968	70.00
❑ LPS-1024	James Brown Presents His Show of Tomorrow	1968	50.00
—Various-artists album			
❑ LPS-1030	I Can't Stand Myself (When You Touch Me)	1968	50.00
❑ LPS-1031	I Got the Feelin'	1968	50.00
❑ LPS-1034	James Brown Plays Nothing But Soul	1968	50.00
❑ LPS-1038	Thinking About Little Willie John and a Few Nice Things	1968	50.00
❑ KS-1040	A Soulful Christmas	1968	80.00
❑ KS-1047	Say It Loud — I'm Black and I'm Proud	1969	50.00
❑ KS-1051	Gettin' Down To It	1969	50.00
❑ KSD-1055	James Brown Plays & Directs The Popcorn	1969	40.00
❑ KSD-1063	It's a Mother	1969	40.00
❑ KSD-1092	Ain't It Funky	1970	40.00
❑ KSD-1095	It's a New Day So Let a Man Come In	1970	40.00
❑ KSD-1100	Soul on Top	1970	40.00
❑ KSD-1110	Sho Is Funky Down Here	1971	40.00
❑ KSD-1115 [(2)]	Sex Machine	1970	50.00
❑ KSD-1124	Hey America!	1970	40.00
❑ KSD-1127	Super Bad	1971	40.00

POLYDOR

Number	Title (A Side/B Side)	Yr	NM
❑ 25-3003 [(2)]	Revolution of the Mind — Live at the Apollo, Vol. III	1971	60.00
❑ PD2-3004 [(2)]	Get On the Good Foot	1972	60.00
❑ PD2-3007 [(2)]	The Payback	1973	50.00
❑ 24-4054	Hot Pants	1971	40.00
❑ PD-5028	There It Is	1972	40.00
❑ SC-5401	James Brown Soul Classics	1972	25.00
❑ SC-5402	Soul Classics, Vol. 2	1973	25.00
❑ PD-6014	Black Caesar	1973	50.00
❑ PD-6015	Slaughter's Big Rip-Off	1973	50.00
❑ PD-1-6039	Reality	1975	40.00
❑ PD-1-6042	Sex Machine Today	1975	40.00
❑ PD-1-6054	Everybody's Doin' the Hustle & Dead On the Double Bump	1975	40.00
❑ PD-1-6059	Hot	1976	40.00
❑ PD-1-6071	Get Up Offa That Thing	1976	40.00
❑ PD-1-6093	Bodyheat	1976	40.00
❑ PD-1-6111	Mutha's Nature	1977	40.00
❑ PD-1-6140	Jam/1980s	1978	40.00
❑ PD-1-6181	Take a Look at Those Cakes	1978	30.00
❑ PD-1-6212	The Original Disco Man	1979	30.00
❑ PD-1-6258	People	1980	30.00
❑ PD-2-6290 [(2)]	James Brown...Live/Hot on the One	1980	50.00
❑ PD-1-6318	Nonstop!	1981	30.00
❑ PD-1-6340	The Best of James Brown	1981	20.00
❑ PD-2-9001 [(2)]	Hell	1974	80.00
❑ PD-2-9004 [(2)]	Sex Machine Live	1976	50.00
❑ 821231-1	Ain't That a Groove: The James Brown Story 1966-1969	1984	15.00
❑ 821232-1	Doing It to Death: The James Brown Story 1970-1973	1984	15.00
❑ 823275-1	The Best of James Brown	1984	12.00
—Reissue of 6340			
❑ 827439-1	Dead on the Heavy Funk: The James Brown Story 1974-1978	1985	15.00
❑ 829254-1 [(2)]	Solid Gold: 30 Golden Hits	1985	20.00
❑ 829417-1	James Brown's Funky People	1986	15.00
—Various-artists LP			
❑ 829624-1	In the Jungle Groove	1986	15.00
❑ 835857-1	James Brown's Funky People 2	1988	15.00
—Various-artists compilation			
❑ 837126-1	Motherlode	1988	15.00
❑ 8434791 [S]	Live at the Apollo	2008	20.00

RHINO

Number	Title (A Side/B Side)	Yr	NM
❑ RNLP-217	Live at the Apollo, Vol. 2, Part 1	1985	15.00
❑ RNLP-218	Live at the Apollo, Vol. 2, Part 2	1985	15.00
❑ RNLP-219	Greatest Hits (1964-1968)	1986	15.00
❑ R1 70194	Santa's Got a Brand New Bag	1986	10.00
—Reissue of King material			
❑ R1-70217	Live at the Apollo, Vol. 2, Part 1	1988	12.00
—Reissue of 217			
❑ R1-70218	Live at the Apollo, Vol. 2, Part 2	1988	12.00
—Reissue of 218			
❑ R1-70219	Greatest Hits (1964-1968)	1988	12.00
—Reissue of 219			

SCOTTI BROTHERS

Number	Title (A Side/B Side)	Yr	NM
❑ FZ 40380	Gravity	1986	12.00
❑ FZ 44241	I'm Real	1988	12.00
❑ FZ 45164	Soul Session Live	1989	15.00
❑ 75225-1	Love Overdue	1991	20.00

SMASH

Number	Title (A Side/B Side)	Yr	NM
❑ MGS-27054 [M]	Showtime	1964	30.00
❑ MGS-27057 [M]	Grits & Soul	1965	30.00
❑ MGS-27058 [M]	Out of Sight	1965	100.00
❑ MGS-27072 [M]	James Brown Plays James Brown — Today & Yesterday	1965	30.00
❑ MGS-27080 [M]	James Brown Plays New Breed	1966	30.00
❑ MGS-27084 [M]	Handful of Soul	1966	30.00
❑ MGS-27087 [M]	The James Brown Show	1967	30.00
—Various-artists LP			
❑ MGS-27093 [M]	James Brown Plays the Real Thing	1967	30.00
❑ SRS-67054 [S]	Showtime	1964	40.00
❑ SRS-67057 [S]	Grits & Soul	1965	40.00
❑ SRS-67058 [S]	Out of Sight	1965	150.00

Number	Title (A Side/B Side)	Yr	NM
❑ SRS-67072 [S]	James Brown Plays James Brown — Today & Yesterday	1965	40.00
❑ SRS-67080 [S]	James Brown Plays New Breed	1966	40.00
❑ SRS-67084 [S]	Handful of Soul	1966	40.00
❑ SRS-67087 [S]	The James Brown Show	1967	40.00
—Various-artists LP			
❑ SRS-67093 [S]	James Brown Plays the Real Thing	1967	40.00
❑ SRS-67109	James Brown Sings Out of Sight	1968	30.00
—Abridged reissue of 67058			

SOLID SMOKE

Number	Title (A Side/B Side)	Yr	NM
❑ SS-8006	Live and Lowdown at the Apollo, Vol. 1	1980	12.00
❑ SS-8013	Can Your Heart Stand It	1981	12.00
❑ SS-8023	The Federal Years, Part 1	198?	12.00
❑ SS-8024	The Federal Years, Part 2	198?	12.00

T.K.

Number	Title (A Side/B Side)	Yr	NM
❑ 615	Soul Syndrome	1980	30.00

BROWN, JAMES (2)

The MGM James Brown is not the same person as the others.

45s

MGM

Number	Title (A Side/B Side)	Yr	NM
❑ K11941	Ballad of Davy Crockett/He's a Rocking Horse Cowboy	1955	15.00
❑ 11987	The Berry Tree/I Lost When I Found You	1955	12.00
❑ 12011	The Kentuckian Song/ The Man from Laramie	1955	12.00
❑ 12080	The White Buffalo/It's Lonesome Out Tonight	1955	12.00
❑ K12211	Blue Harmonica/ Blessed Art Thou	1956	12.00
❑ K12350	Forward Ho/Ghosttown	1956	12.00
❑ K12384	Wagon Train/Goodbye, My Love	1956	12.00

BROWN, JERICHO

45s

DEL-FI

Number	Title (A Side/B Side)	Yr	NM
❑ 4103	I Need You/Lonesome Drifter	1958	25.00

RKO UNIQUE

Number	Title (A Side/B Side)	Yr	NM
❑ 412	Little Neva/Darling I Love Thee	1957	30.00

WARNER BROS.

Number	Title (A Side/B Side)	Yr	NM
❑ 5161	Look for a Star/Don't You Know	1960	12.00
❑ 5213	Rovin' Eye/Someday She'll Come Along	1961	10.00
❑ 5381	Lonely Birthday/Paper Rose and Candy Ring	1963	10.00
❑ 5408	I'll Be Gone/He's Taken My Baby	1964	10.00
❑ 5458	I'm Watching You/ Wisdom of a Fool	1964	10.00

BROWN, JIM ED

Also see THE BROWNS.

45s

RCA

Number	Title (A Side/B Side)	Yr	NM
❑ PB-10619	Let Me Love You Where It Hurts/ I Love You All Over Again	1976	4.00
❑ PB-10786	I've Rode with the Best/ Close the Door	1976	4.00
❑ PB-11134	When I Touch Her There/ Mexican Joe	1977	4.00
❑ PB-11742	You're the Part of Me/Changes	1979	4.00

RCA VICTOR

Number	Title (A Side/B Side)	Yr	NM
❑ 47-8566	I Heard from a Memory Last Night/Just to Satisfy You	1965	8.00
❑ 47-8644	I'm Just a Country Boy/ To Be or Not to Be	1965	8.00
❑ 47-8766	Regular on My Mind/ The Mounties	1966	8.00
❑ 47-8867	A Taste of Heaven/Paint Me the Color of Your Wall	1966	8.00
❑ 47-8997	The Last Laugh/Party Girl	1966	8.00
❑ 47-9077	You Can Have Her/ If You Were Mine, Mary	1967	8.00
❑ 47-9192	Pop a Top/Too Good to Be True	1967	8.00
❑ 47-9329	Bottle, Bottle/It Doesn't Know Any Better	1967	8.00
❑ 47-9434	The Cajun Stripper/ You'll Never Know	1968	8.00
❑ 47-9518	The Enemy/I Just Came from There	1968	8.00
❑ 47-9616	Jack and Jill/Honky Tonkin'	1968	8.00
❑ 47-9677	Longest Beer of the Night/ What's a Girl Like You	1968	6.00
❑ 47-9810	Lift Ring, Pull Open/ Going Up the Country	1970	6.00
❑ 47-9858	Baby, I Tried/The City Cries at Night	1970	6.00
❑ 47-9909	Morning/How to Lose a Good Woman	1970	6.00
❑ 47-9965	Angel's Sunday/ Every Mile of the Way	1971	6.00
❑ 74-0114	Man and Wife Time/ Healing Hands of Time	1969	6.00
❑ 74-0190	The Three Bells/ Beyond the Shadow	1969	6.00
❑ 74-0274	Ginger Is Gentle and Waiting for Me/Drink Boys Drink	1969	6.00
❑ 74-0509	She's Leavin' (Bonnie, Please Don't Go)/Love Is Worth the Tryin'	1971	6.00
❑ 74-0642	Evening/You Keep Right On Loving Me	1972	6.00
❑ 74-0712	How I Love Them Old Songs/ Close	1972	6.00
❑ 74-0785	All I Had to Do/Triangle	1972	6.00
❑ 74-0846	Unbelievable Love/If Her Blue Eyes Don't Get You	1972	6.00
❑ 74-0928	Southern Loving/How Long Does It Take a Memory to Drown	1973	6.00
❑ APBO-0059	Broad-Minded Man/ Helpin' You Get Over Him	1973	5.00
❑ APBO-0180	Sometime Sunshine/ Louisiana Woman	1973	5.00
❑ APBO-0267	It's That Time of Night/ If Wishes Were Horses	1974	5.00
❑ PB-10047	Get Up I Think I Love You/ A Nickel for the Fiddler	1974	5.00
❑ PB-10131	Don Junior/Who's Gonna Love Me	1974	5.00
❑ PB-10233	Barroom Pal, Goodtime Gals/ Nearer My Love to You	1975	5.00
❑ PB-10370	Fine Time to Get the Blues/ Sweet Song	1975	5.00
❑ PB-10531	Another Morning/An Old Flame Never Dies	1975	5.00

Albums

RCA CAMDEN

Number	Title (A Side/B Side)	Yr	NM
❑ ACL1-0197	Hey Good Lookin'	1973	10.00
❑ ACL1-0618	The Three Bells	1974	10.00
❑ CAS-2496	Gentle on My Mind	1971	10.00
❑ CAS-2549	Country Cream	1972	10.00

RCA VICTOR

Number	Title (A Side/B Side)	Yr	NM
❑ APL1-0172	Bar-Rooms & Pop-A-Tops	1973	15.00
❑ APL1-0324	Best of Jim Ed Brown	1973	15.00
❑ APL1-0572	It's That Time of Night	1974	15.00
❑ ANL1-1215	It's That Time of Night	1975	10.00
—Reissue of 0572			
❑ LPM-3569 [M]	Alone with You	1966	20.00
❑ LSP-3569 [S]	Alone with You	1966	25.00
❑ LPM-3744 [M]	Just Jim	1967	25.00
❑ LSP-3744 [S]	Just Jim	1967	20.00
❑ LPM-3853 [M]	Gems by Jim	1967	25.00
❑ LSP-3853 [S]	Gems by Jim	1967	20.00
❑ LPM-3942 [M]	Bottle, Bottle	1968	40.00
❑ LSP-3942 [S]	Bottle, Bottle	1968	20.00
❑ LSP-4011	Country's Best on Record	1968	20.00
❑ LSP-4130	This Is My Best!	1968	20.00
❑ LSP-4175	Jim Ed Sings the Browns	1969	20.00
❑ LSP-4262	Going Up the Country	1970	15.00
❑ LSP-4366	Just for You	1970	15.00
❑ LSP-4461	Morning	1971	15.00
❑ LSP-4525	Angel's Sunday	1971	15.00
❑ LSP-4614	She's Leavin'	1971	15.00
❑ LSP-4713	Evening	1972	15.00
❑ LSP-4755	Brown Is Blue	1972	15.00

BROWN, JOE, AND THE BRUVVERS

45s

BELL

Number	Title (A Side/B Side)	Yr	NM
❑ 45364 [DJ]	Hey Mama (mono/stereo)	1973	6.00
—May be promo only			

CAMEO

Number	Title (A Side/B Side)	Yr	NM
❑ 241	It Only Took a Minute/All Things Bright and Beautiful	1963	12.00

DOT

Number	Title (A Side/B Side)	Yr	NM
❑ 16508	Hava Nagila/That's What Love Will Do	1963	12.00

HICKORY

Number	Title (A Side/B Side)	Yr	NM
❑ 1329	Sally Ann/Little Ukulele	1965	10.00

JAMIE

Number	Title (A Side/B Side)	Yr	NM
❑ 1298	Lonely Circus/Teardrops in the Rain	1965	10.00
❑ 1327	Sea of Heartbreak/ Mrs. O's Theme	1966	10.00

KAPP

Number	Title (A Side/B Side)	Yr	NM
❑ 2068	Adieu, Monsieur Le Professeur/Diamonds of Dew	1969	6.00

LONDON INT'L.

Number	Title (A Side/B Side)	Yr	NM
❑ 10507	What a Crazy World We're Living In/Popcorn	1962	15.00
❑ 10517	A Picture of You/ A Lay-About's Lament	1962	15.00
❑ 10522	Your Tender Look/ The Other Side of Town	1962	15.00

STELLAR

Number	Title (A Side/B Side)	Yr	NM
❑ 1504	Hava Nagila/That's What Love Will Do	1963	15.00

VERTIGO

Number	Title (A Side/B Side)	Yr	NM
❑ 201	I Was Lost/Cincinnati Floor	1974	5.00
—As "Brown's Home Brew"			

WARNER BROS.

Number	Title (A Side/B Side)	Yr	NM
❑ 7055	With a Little Help from My Friends/Won't You Show Me Around	1967	8.00

BROWN, MAXINE (1)

45s

ABC-PARAMOUNT

Number	Title (A Side/B Side)	Yr	NM
❑ 10235	I Don't Need You No More/ Think of Me	1961	12.00
❑ 10255	After All We've Been Through Together/My Life	1961	12.00
❑ 10290	I Got a Funny Kind of Feeling/ What I Don't Know	1962	12.00
❑ 10315	Forget Him/A Man	1962	12.00
❑ 10327	No Time for Cryin'/Wanting You	1962	12.00
❑ 10343	I Kneel at Your Throne/ If I Knew Then	1962	12.00
❑ 10370	Promise Me Anything/ Am I Falling in Love	1962	12.00
❑ 10388	Life Goes On Just the Same/ If You Have No Real Objections	1962	12.00

AVCO

Number	Title (A Side/B Side)	Yr	NM
❑ 4585	Always and Forever/ Make Love to Me	1971	5.00
❑ 4604	Treat Me Like a Lady/I.O.U.	1972	5.00
❑ 4612	Picked Up, Packed and Went Away/(B-side unknown)	1972	5.00

COMMONWEALTH UNITED

Number	Title (A Side/B Side)	Yr	NM
❑ 3001	We'll Cry Together/ Darling Be Home Soon	1969	6.00
❑ 3008	I Can't Get Along Without You/ Reason to Believe	1970	6.00

EPIC

Number	Title (A Side/B Side)	Yr	NM
❑ 10334	Seems You've Forsaken My Love/Plum Outa Sight	1968	10.00
❑ 10424	Love in Them There Hills/ From Loving You	1968	10.00

NOMAR

Number	Title (A Side/B Side)	Yr	NM
❑ 103	All in My Mind/Harry, Let's Marry	1960	15.00
❑ 106	Funny/Now That You've Gone	1961	15.00
❑ 107	Heaven in Your Arms/ Maxine's Place	1961	15.00
—B-side by Frankie and the Flips			

WAND

Number	Title (A Side/B Side)	Yr	NM
❑ 135	Ask Me/Yesterday's Kisses	1963	10.00
❑ 135 [PS]	Ask Me/Yesterday's Kisses	1963	50.00
❑ 142	Coming Back to You/ Since I Found You	1963	10.00
❑ 152	Little Girl Lost/You Upset My Soul	1964	8.00
❑ 158	I Cry Alone/Put Yourself in My Place	1964	8.00
❑ 162	Oh No Not My Baby/ You Upset My Soul	1964	12.00
❑ 173	It's Gonna Be Alright/ You Do Something to Me	1965	8.00
❑ 185	Anything for a Laugh/ One Step at a Time	1965	8.00
❑ 1104	If You Gotta Make a Fool of Somebody/You're in Love	1965	8.00
❑ 1117	One in a Million/Anything You Do Is Alright	1966	8.00
❑ 1128	We Can Work It Out/ Let Me Give You My Lovin'	1966	8.00
❑ 1145	I Don't Need Anything/ The Secret of Livin'	1967	8.00
❑ 1179	Soul Serenade/He's the Only Guy I'll Ever Love	1968	8.00

Albums

COLLECTABLES

Number	Title (A Side/B Side)	Yr	NM
❑ COL-5116	Golden Classics	198?	12.00

COMMONWEALTH UNITED

Number	Title (A Side/B Side)	Yr	NM
❑ CU-6001	We'll Cry Together	1969	20.00

GUEST STAR

Number	Title (A Side/B Side)	Yr	NM
❑ GS-1911 [M]	Maxine Brown	1964	12.00

WAND

Number	Title (A Side/B Side)	Yr	NM
❑ LP-656 [M]	The Fabulous Sound of Maxine Brown	1963	50.00
❑ WDS-656 [S]	The Fabulous Sound of Maxine Brown	1963	60.00
❑ WD-663 [M]	Spotlight on Maxine Brown	1965	30.00
❑ WDS-663 [S]	Spotlight on Maxine Brown	1965	40.00
❑ WD-684 [M]	Maxine Brown's Greatest Hits	1967	20.00
❑ WDS-684 [S]	Maxine Brown's Greatest Hits	1967	25.00
❑ DT-91012 [R]	The Fabulous Sound of Maxine Brown	196?	50.00
—Capitol Record Club edition			

Except when noted otherwise, VG = 25% of NM, and VG+ = 50% of NM. (Example: VG = $2.00, VG+ = $4.00 and NM = $8.00.)

BROWN, NAPPY

45s

ICHIBAN

Number	Title (A Side/B Side)	Yr	NM
❑ 206	Lemon Squeezin' Daddy/Small Red Apples	1989	5.00

SAVOY

Number	Title (A Side/B Side)	Yr	NM
❑ 1129	That Man/I Wonder	1954	30.00
❑ 1135	Is It True, Is It True/Two-Faced Woman	1954	30.00
❑ 1155	Don't Be Angry/It's Really You	1955	25.00
❑ 1162	Piddly Patter Patter/There'll Come a Day	1955	25.00
❑ 1176	Doodle I Love You/Sittin' in the Dark	1955	25.00
❑ 1187	Open Up That Door/Pleasing You	1956	25.00
❑ 1196	Am I/Love Baby	1956	25.00
❑ 1506	Little by Little/I'm Getting Lonesome	1956	20.00
❑ 1511	Pretty Girl (Yea Yea Yea)/I'm Gonna Get You	1957	20.00
❑ 1514	Goody Goody Gum Drops/Bye Bye Baby	1957	20.00
❑ 1525	The Right Time/Oh You Don't Know	1957	20.00
❑ 1530	If You Need Some Lovin'/I'm in the Mood	1958	20.00
❑ 1547	Skidy Wo/I Cried Like a Baby	1958	20.00
❑ 1551	It Don't Hurt No More/My Baby	1958	20.00
❑ 1555	You're Going to Need Someone/Skiddy Woe	1958	20.00
❑ 1562	A Long Time/All Right Now	1959	20.00
❑ 1569	This Is My Confession/For Those Who Love	1959	20.00
❑ 1575	I Cried Like a Baby/So Deep	1959	20.00
❑ 1579	Give Me Your Love/Too Shy	1959	20.00
❑ 1582	Down in the Alley/My Baby Knows	1960	15.00
❑ 1587	Baby, Cry, Cry, Cry, Baby/What's Come Over You	1960	15.00
❑ 1588	Apple of My Eye/Baby I Got News for You	1960	15.00
❑ 1592	The Hole I'm In/Nobody Can Say	1960	15.00
❑ 1594	Coal Miner/Honnie-Bonnie	1961	15.00
❑ 1598	Don't Be Angry/Any Time Is the Right Time	1961	15.00
❑ 1616	Didn't You Know/I've Had My Fun	1962	15.00
❑ 1621	Lock on the Door/So Glad I Don't Have to Cry No More	1963	15.00

Albums

BLACK TOP

Number	Title (A Side/B Side)	Yr	NM
❑ BT-1039	Something Gonna Jump Out the Bushes	1987	15.00

ICHIBAN

Number	Title (A Side/B Side)	Yr	NM
❑ ICH-1056	Apples and Lemons	1990	12.00

KING SNAKE/ICHIBAN

Number	Title (A Side/B Side)	Yr	NM
❑ ICH-9006	Aw! Shucks	1991	15.00

LANDSLIDE

Number	Title (A Side/B Side)	Yr	NM
❑ LD 1008	Tore Up	1984	15.00

MELTONE

Number	Title (A Side/B Side)	Yr	NM
❑ 1502	Deep Sea Diver	1989	15.00

SAVOY

Number	Title (A Side/B Side)	Yr	NM
❑ MG-14002 [M]	Nappy Brown Sings	1958	400.00
❑ MG-14025 [M]	The Right Time	1960	250.00
❑ 14427	Nappy Brown	1977	12.00

SAVOY JAZZ

Number	Title (A Side/B Side)	Yr	NM
❑ SJL-1149	Don't Be Angry	1984	10.00

BROWN, ODELL

45s

CADET

Number	Title (A Side/B Side)	Yr	NM
❑ 5570	Mellow Yellow/Quiet Village	1967	8.00
❑ 5591	The Look of Love/No More Water in the Well	1968	8.00
❑ 5624	The Weight/Think About It	1968	8.00

Albums

CADET

Number	Title (A Side/B Side)	Yr	NM
❑ LP-775 [M]	Raising the Roof	1966	15.00
❑ LPS-775 [S]	Raising the Roof	1966	20.00
❑ LP-788 [M]	Mellow Yellow	1967	20.00
❑ LPS-788 [S]	Mellow Yellow	1967	15.00
❑ LP-800 [M]	Ducky	1967	20.00
❑ LPS-800 [S]	Ducky	1967	15.00
❑ LPS-823	Odell Brown Plays Otis Redding	1969	15.00
❑ LPS-838	Free Delivery	1970	15.00

PAULA

Number	Title (A Side/B Side)	Yr	NM
❑ 4005	Odell Brown	1974	12.00

BROWN, RAY, AND THE WHISPERS

45s

GNP CRESCENDO

Number	Title (A Side/B Side)	Yr	NM
❑ 357	Fool, Fool, Fool/Pride	1965	20.00

PARKWAY

Number	Title (A Side/B Side)	Yr	NM
❑ 951	20 Miles/Devoted to You	1965	30.00

BROWN, RITCHIE

45s

HIT

Number	Title (A Side/B Side)	Yr	NM
❑ 240	Uptight (Everything's Alright)/California Dreamin'	1966	10.00

—B-side by the Jalopy Five

BROWN, ROY

45s

BLUESWAY

Number	Title (A Side/B Side)	Yr	NM
❑ 61002	New Orleans Women/Standing on Broadway (Watching the Girls)	1967	8.00

DELUXE

Number	Title (A Side/B Side)	Yr	NM
❑ 3318	Big Town/Train Time Blues	1951	200.00
—Roy Brown singles on DeLuxe before 3318 are unconfirmed on 45 rpm			
❑ 3318	Big Town/Train Time Blues	1951	400.00
—Blue vinyl			
❑ 3319	Bar Room Blues/Good Rockin' Man	1951	200.00
—Black vinyl			
❑ 3319	Bar Room Blues/Good Rockin' Man	1951	400.00
—Blue vinyl			
❑ 3323	I've Got the Last Laugh Now/Brown Angel	1951	200.00
—Black vinyl			
❑ 3323	I've Got the Last Laugh Now/Brown Angel	1951	400.00
—Blue vinyl			

HOME OF THE BLUES

Number	Title (A Side/B Side)	Yr	NM
❑ 107	Don't Break My Heart/A Man with the Blues	1960	25.00
❑ 110	Tired of Being Alone/Rocking All the Time	1960	25.00
❑ 115	Oh So Wonderful/Sugar Baby	1961	25.00
❑ 122	Rock and Roll Jamboree/I Need a Friend	1961	25.00

IMPERIAL

Number	Title (A Side/B Side)	Yr	NM
❑ 5422	Everybody/Saturday Night	1957	30.00
❑ 5427	Party Doll/I'm Sticking with You	1957	30.00
❑ 5439	Let the Four Winds Blow/Diddy-Y-Diddy-O	1957	30.00
❑ 5455	I'm Convicted of Love/I'm Ready to Play	1957	30.00
❑ 5469	Tick of the Clock/Slow Down Little Eva	1957	30.00
❑ 5489	Ain't Gonna Do It/Sail On Little Girl	1958	30.00
❑ 5510	Hip Shakin' Baby/Be My Love Tonight	1958	30.00
❑ 5969	Let the Four Winds Blow/Diddy-Yi-Diddy-Yo	1963	20.00

KING

Number	Title (A Side/B Side)	Yr	NM
❑ 4602	Travelin' Man/Hurry, Hurry Baby	1953	60.00
❑ 4609	Grandpa Stole My Baby/Money Can't Buy Love	1953	60.00
❑ 4704	Trouble at Midnight/Bootlegging Baby	1954	60.00
❑ 4715	Up Jumped the Devil/This Is My Last Goodbye	1954	60.00
❑ 4722	No Love at All/Don't Let It Rain	1954	60.00
❑ 4731	Ain't It a Shame/Gal from Kokomo	1954	60.00
❑ 4743	Worried Life Blues/Black Diamond	1954	60.00
❑ 4761	Fannie Brown Got Married/Queen of Diamonds	1955	50.00
❑ 4816	Shake 'Em Up Baby/Letter to Baby	1955	50.00
❑ 4834	My Little Angel Child/She's Gone Too Long	1955	50.00
❑ 5178	La-Dee-Dah-Dee/Melinda	1959	20.00
❑ 5207	I Never Had It So Good/Rinky Dinky Doo	1959	20.00
❑ 5218	Hard Luck Blues/Good Looking and Forty	1959	20.00
❑ 5247	School Bell Rock/Ain't No Rocking No More	1959	20.00
❑ 5333	Ain't Got No Blues Today/Adorable One	1960	20.00
❑ 5521	Mighty Mighty Man/Good Man Blues	1961	20.00

MERCURY

Number	Title (A Side/B Side)	Yr	NM
❑ 73166	It's My Fault Darling/Love for Sale	1970	6.00
❑ 73219	Mail Man Blues/Hunky Funky Woman	1971	6.00

Albums

BLUESWAY

Number	Title (A Side/B Side)	Yr	NM
❑ BLS-6019	The Blues Are Brown	1968	25.00
❑ BLS-6056	Hard Times	1973	25.00

EPIC

Number	Title (A Side/B Side)	Yr	NM
❑ E 30473	Live at Monterey	1971	25.00

INTERMEDIA

Number	Title (A Side/B Side)	Yr	NM
❑ QS-5027	Good Rockin' Tonight	198?	10.00

KING

Number	Title (A Side/B Side)	Yr	NM
❑ 956 [M]	Roy Brown Sings 24 Hits	1966	50.00
❑ KS-956 [R]	Roy Brown Sings 24 Hits	1966	50.00
❑ KS-1130	Hard Luck Blues	1971	25.00

BROWN, ROY / WYNONIE HARRIS

Albums

KING

Number	Title (A Side/B Side)	Yr	NM
❑ 607 [M]	Battle of the Blues	1958	600.00
❑ 627 [M]	Battle of the Blues, Vol. 2	1959	800.00

BROWN, ROY / WYNONIE HARRIS / EDDIE VINSON

Albums

KING

Number	Title (A Side/B Side)	Yr	NM
❑ 668 [M]	Battle of the Blues, Vol. 4	1960	2500.

BROWN, RUTH

45s

ATLANTIC

Number	Title (A Side/B Side)	Yr	NM
❑ 893	Happiness Is a Thing Called Joe/Love Me Baby	197?	10.00
—Reissue 45 on glossy yellow label with black "fan" logo (there was no 45 of this in the 1950s)			
❑ 919	Teardrops from My Eyes/Am I Making the Same Mistake	1950	400.00
—This and Atlantic 914 were the label's first two 45s.			
❑ 948	Shine On—Big Bright Moon Shine On/Without My Love	1951	60.00
—Ruth Brown records on Atlantic before 948 (except as listed) are unconfirmed on 45 rpm			
❑ 962	5-10-15 Hours/Be Anything But Be Mine	1952	50.00
❑ 973	Daddy Daddy/Have a Good Time	1952	50.00
❑ 978	Three Letters/Good for Nothing Joe	1952	50.00
❑ 986	(Mama) He Treats Your Daughter Mean/R.B. Blues	1953	60.00
❑ 993	Wild Wild Young Men/Mend Your Ways	1953	40.00
❑ 1005	The Tears Keep Tumblin' Down/I Would If I Could	1953	30.00
❑ 1018	Love Contest/If You Don't Want Me	1954	30.00
❑ 1023	Sentimental Journey/It's All in Your Mind	1954	30.00
❑ 1027	If I Had Any Sense/Hello Little Boy	1954	30.00
❑ 1036	Oh What a Dream/Please Don't Freeze	1954	30.00
❑ 1044	Somebody Touch Me/Mambo Baby	1954	30.00
❑ 1051	Ever Since My Baby's Been Gone/Bye Bye Young Men	1955	30.00
❑ 1059	I Can See Everybody's Baby/As Long As I'm Moving	1955	30.00
❑ 1072	What'd I Say/It's Love Baby (24 Hours of the Day)	1955	30.00
❑ 1077	Love Has Joined Us Together/I Gotta Have You	1955	30.00
—With Clyde McPhatter			
❑ 1082	Old Man River/I Want to Do More	1956	25.00
❑ 1091	Sweet Baby of Mine/I'm Getting Right	1956	25.00
❑ 1102	I Want to Be Loved/Mom, Oh Mom	1956	25.00
❑ 1113	Smooth Operator/I Still Love You	1956	25.00
❑ 1125	Lucky Lips/My Heart Is Breaking Over You	1957	25.00
❑ 1140	When I Get You Baby/One More Time	1957	25.00
❑ 1153	Show Me/I Hope We Meet	1957	25.00
❑ 1166	A New Love/Look Me Up	1957	25.00
❑ 1177	Book of Lies/Just Too Much	1958	25.00
❑ 1197	This Little Girl's Gone Rockin'/Why Me	1958	25.00
❑ 2008	Mama, He Treats Your Daughter Mean/I'll Step Aside	1958	20.00
❑ 2015	5-10-15 Hours/Itty Bitty Girl	1959	20.00
❑ 2026	Jack O'Diamonds/I Can't Hear a Word You Say	1959	20.00
❑ 2035	I Don't Know/Papa Daddy	1959	20.00
❑ 2052	Don't Deceive Me/I Burned Your Letter	1960	20.00

Number	Title (A Side/B Side)	Yr	NM
❑ 2064	The Door Is Still Open/What I Wouldn't Give	1960	20.00
❑ 2075	Taking Care of Business/Honey Boy	1960	20.00
❑ 2088	Sure 'Nuff/Here He Comes	1961	15.00
❑ 2104	It Tears Me All to Pieces/Anyone But You	1961	15.00
DECCA			
❑ 31598	What Happened to You/Yes Sir That's My Baby	1964	10.00
❑ 31640	Come a Little Closer/I Love Him and I Know It	1964	10.00
MAINSTREAM			
❑ 611	On the Good Ship Lollipop/Hurry On Down	1965	10.00
PHILIPS			
❑ 40028	Shake a Hand/Say It Again	1962	12.00
❑ 40056	Mama (He Treats Your Daughter Mean)/Hold My Hand	1962	12.00
❑ 40086	He Tells Me with His Eyes/If You Don't Tell Nobody	1963	12.00
❑ 40119	Satisfied/If You Don't Tell Nobody	1963	12.00
7-Inch Extended Plays			
ATLANTIC			
❑ 505	Teardrops from My Eyes/5-10-15//Mama He Treats Your Daughter Mean/So Long	1953	100.00
❑ 505 [PS]	Ruth Brown Sings	1953	150.00
❑ 585	*Lucky Lips/Mambo Baby/Smooth Operator/Oh What a Dream	1957	60.00
❑ 585 [PS]	Ruth Brown	1957	120.00
Albums			
ATLANTIC			
❑ 1308 [M]	Last Date with Ruth Brown	1959	200.00
—Black label			
❑ 1308 [M]	Last Date with Ruth Brown	1961	50.00
—Red and purple label, "fan" logo in white			
❑ SD 1308 [S]	Last Date with Ruth Brown	1959	300.00
—Green label			
❑ SD 1308 [S]	Last Date with Ruth Brown	1961	60.00
—Blue and green label, "fan" logo in white			
❑ 8004 [M]	Ruth Brown	1957	200.00
—Black label			
❑ 8004 [M]	Ruth Brown	1960	150.00
—White "bullseye" label			
❑ 8004 [M]	Ruth Brown	1961	50.00
—Red and purple label, "fan" logo in white			
❑ 8026 [M]	Miss Rhythm	1959	200.00
—Black label			
❑ 8026 [M]	Miss Rhythm	1960	150.00
—White "bullseye" label			
❑ 8026 [M]	Miss Rhythm	1961	50.00
—Red and purple label, "fan" logo in white			
❑ 8080 [M]	The Best of Ruth Brown	1963	40.00
DOBRE			
❑ 1041	You Don't Know Me	1978	12.00
FANTASY			
❑ F-9661	Have a Good Time	1988	12.00
❑ F-9662	Blues on Broadway	1989	12.00
ICHIBAN			
❑ SPEG-4023	Brown, Black and Beautiful	198?	12.00
MAINSTREAM			
❑ 369	Softly	1972	12.00
❑ S-6034 [S]	Ruth Brown '65	1965	30.00
❑ 56034 [M]	Ruth Brown '65	1965	25.00
PHILIPS			
❑ PHM 200028 [M]	Along Comes Ruth	1962	40.00
❑ PHM 200055 [M]	Gospel Time	1962	30.00
❑ PHS 600028 [S]	Along Comes Ruth	1962	50.00
❑ PHS 600055 [S]	Gospel Time	1962	40.00
SKYE			
❑ SK-13	Black Is Brown and Brown Is Beautiful	1970	15.00

BROWN, SKIPPY

45s

Number	Title (A Side/B Side)	Yr	NM
CHANCE			
❑ 1129	So Many Days/Tale of Woe	1953	250.00

BROWN, TOMMY

45s

Number	Title (A Side/B Side)	Yr	NM
ABC-PARAMOUNT			
❑ 10632	Ain't So/Well, There Goes My Heart	1965	12.00
DOT			
❑ 16130	Tra-La-La/Weepin' and Cryin'	1960	15.00
GROOVE			
❑ 0132	Don't Leave Me/Won't You Forgive Me	1955	30.00
❑ 0143	The Thrill Is Gone/Gambler's Prayer	1956	30.00
IMPERIAL			
❑ 5476	Rock Away My Blues/Someday, Somewhere	1957	50.00
❑ 5533	Just for You/A Heart with No Feeling	1958	30.00
KING			
❑ 4658	How Much Do You Think I Can Stand/Fore Day Train	1953	150.00
❑ 4679	Goodbye, I'm Gone/Since You Left Me Dear	1953	60.00
UNITED			
❑ 183	Remember Me/Southern Woman	1956	150.00

BROWN, WINI

45s

Number	Title (A Side/B Side)	Yr	NM
COLUMBIA			
❑ 1-872	A Good Man Is Hard to Find/This Is the Last Time	1950	40.00
—Microgroove 7-inch, 33 1/3 rpm single			
❑ 6-872	A Good Man Is Hard to Find/This Is the Last Time	1950	30.00
JARO			
❑ 77018	Gone Again/Johnny with the Gentle Hand	1960	20.00
MERCURY			
❑ 5870	Here in My Heart/Your Happiness Is Mine	1952	200.00
❑ 8270	Be Anything — Be Mine/Heaven Knows Why	1952	200.00
❑ 70062	Tear Down the Sky/Can't Stand No More	1953	100.00
RCA VICTOR			
❑ 47-6970	Available Lover/It's All in Your Mind	1957	20.00
Albums			
SAVOY JAZZ			
❑ SJL-1163 [M]	Miss Brown for You	1986	10.00

BROWN SUGAR

45s

Number	Title (A Side/B Side)	Yr	NM
BULLET			
❑ 711	Loneliness (Will Bring Us Together Again)/Don't Hold Back	1972	50.00
CAPITOL			
❑ 4198	The Game Is Over (What's the Matter with You)/I'm Going Through Changes Now	1976	200.00
❑ 4367	Lay Some Lovin' on Me/Don't Tie Me Down	1976	20.00
CHELSEA			
❑ 78-0125	Loneliness (Will Bring Us Together Again)/Don't Hold Back	1973	15.00
❑ BCBO-0149	Didn't I/Moonlight and Taming You	1973	10.00
❑ BCBO-0239	Dance to the Music/Love Can Bring You Down	1974	10.00
DEMAND			
❑ D 45-002	Sweet Symphony/Bye Bye Baby	1978	12.00
Albums			
CHELSEA			
❑ BCL1-0368	Brown Sugar Featuring Clydie King	1973	20.00

BROWN'S HOME BREW

See JOE BROWN AND THE BRUVVERS.

BROWNE, JACKSON

45s

Number	Title (A Side/B Side)	Yr	NM
ASYLUM			
❑ 11004	Doctor My Eyes/Looking Into You	1972	5.00
❑ 11006	Rock Me on the Water/Something Fine	1972	4.00
❑ 11023	Redneck Friend/Those Times You've Come	1973	4.00
❑ 11030	Ready or Not/Take It Easy	1974	4.00
❑ 45227	Walking Slow/Before the Deluge	1975	4.00
❑ 45242	Fountains of Sorrow/The Late Show	1975	4.00
❑ 45379	Here Come Those Tears Again/Linda Paloma	1976	4.00
❑ 45399	The Pretender/Daddy's Tune	1977	4.00
❑ 45460	Running on Empty/Nothing But Time	1978	4.00
❑ 45460 [PS]	Running on Empty/Nothing But Time	1978	5.00
❑ 45485-A/B	Stay/Rosie	1978	5.00
❑ 45485-A/B [PS]	Stay/Rosie	1978	5.00
❑ 45485-A/C	Stay/The Load-Out	1978	4.00
❑ 45543	You Love the Thunder/The Road	1978	4.00
❑ 45543 [PS]	You Love the Thunder/The Road	1978	5.00
❑ 47003	Boulevard/Call It a Loan	1980	4.00
❑ 47003 [PS]	Boulevard/Call It a Loan	1980	5.00
❑ 47036	That Girl Could Sing/Of Missing Persons	1980	4.00
❑ 69543	In the Shape of a Heart/Voice of America	1986	3.00
❑ 69543 [PS]	In the Shape of a Heart/Voice of America	1986	6.00
❑ 69566	For America/Till I Go Down	1986	3.00
❑ 69566 [PS]	For America/Till I Go Down	1986	3.00
❑ 69764	For a Rocker/Downtown	1984	3.00
❑ 69764 [PS]	For a Rocker/Downtown	1984	3.00
❑ 69791	Tender Is the Night/On the Day	1983	3.00
❑ 69791 [PS]	Tender Is the Night/On the Day	1983	3.00
❑ 69826	Lawyers in Love/Say It Isn't True	1983	3.00
❑ 69826 [PS]	Lawyers in Love/Say It Isn't True	1983	3.00
❑ 69982	Somebody's Baby/The Crow on the Cradle [w/Graham Nash & David Lindley]	1982	4.00
❑ 69982 [PS]	Somebody's Baby/The Crow on the Cradle [w/Graham Nash & David Lindley]	1982	4.00
ELEKTRA			
❑ 69262	Chasing You Into the Light/How Long	1989	5.00
❑ 69284	Anything Can Happen/Lights and Virtues	1989	5.00
❑ 69292	World in Motion/My Personal Revenge	1989	4.00
Albums			
ASYLUM			
❑ 6E-107	The Pretender	1977	10.00
—Reissue of 7E-1079			
❑ 6E-113	Running on Empty	1977	10.00
❑ 5E-511	Hold Out	1979	10.00
❑ 7E-1017	Late for the Sky	1974	12.00
❑ EQ-1017 [Q]	Late for the Sky	1974	30.00
❑ 7E-1079	The Pretender	1976	12.00
❑ SD 5051	Jackson Browne (Saturate Before Using)	1972	8.00
—Standard cover			
❑ SD 5051	Jackson Browne (Saturate Before Using)	1972	12.00
—Burlap cover; "clouds" label			
❑ SD 5051	Jackson Browne (Saturate Before Using)	1972	16.00
—Burlap cover, opens at right side; white label with "Asylum Records" logo in a circle at top			
❑ SD 5051	Jackson Browne (Saturate Before Using)	1972	20.00
—Burlap cover, opens at top; white label with "Asylum Records" logo in a circle at top			
❑ SD 5067	For Everyman	1973	12.00
❑ 60268	Lawyers in Love	1983	10.00
❑ 60457	Lives in the Balance	1986	10.00
ELEKTRA			
❑ 60830	World in Motion	1989	10.00
MOBILE FIDELITY			
❑ 1-055	The Pretender	1981	25.00
—Audiophile vinyl			
NINA MUSIC PUBLISHING			
❑ (no #) [(2)]	Songs by Jackson Browne	1967	2000.
—Publisher's demo in plain cardboard jacket; three sides performed by Jackson Browne, one side by Steve Noonan; VG value 1000; VG+ value 1500			

BROWNETTES, THE

45s

Number	Title (A Side/B Side)	Yr	NM
KING			
❑ 6153	Baby, Don't You Know/Never Find a Love Like Mine	1968	20.00

BROWNS, THE

Also see JIM ED BROWN.

45s

Number	Title (A Side/B Side)	Yr	NM
FABOR			
❑ 107	Rio De Janeiro/Lookin' Back to See	1954	25.00
—All on Fabor as "Jim Edward and Maxine Brown"			
❑ 112	Why Am I Falling/Itsy Witsy Bitsy Me	1954	25.00
❑ 118	Here Today and Gone Tomorrow/Draggin' Main Street	1955	25.00
❑ 122	Do Memories Haunt You/Jungle Magic	1955	25.00
❑ 126	You Thought I Thought/Here Today and Gone Tomorrow	1955	25.00

Except when noted otherwise, VG = 25% of NM, and VG+ = 50% of NM. (Example: VG = $2.00, VG+ = $4.00 and NM = $8.00.)

Number	Title (A Side/B Side)	Yr	NM
RCA VICTOR			
❑ 37-7866	Ground Hog/Angel's Dolly	1961	25.00
—"Compact Single 33" (small hole, plays at LP speed)			
❑ 37-7917	Whispering Wine/My Baby's Gone	1961	25.00
—"Compact Single 33" (small hole, plays at LP speed)			
❑ 37-7969	Foolish Pride/Alpha and Omega	1961	25.00
—"Compact Single 33" (small hole, plays at LP speed)			
❑ 47-6480	I Take the Chance /Goo Goo Da Da	1956	20.00
—As "Jim Edward and Maxine Brown"			
❑ 47-6628	Here Today and Gone Tomorrow/ Looking Back to See	1956	20.00
❑ 47-6629	Do Memories Haunt You/ Draggin' Main Street	1956	20.00
❑ 47-6631	Just As Long As You Love Me/ Don't Tell Me Your Troubles	1956	20.00
—As "Jim Edward, Maxine and Bonnie Brown"			
❑ 47-6730	A Man with a Plan/ Just a Lot of Sweet Talk	1956	20.00
—As "Jim, Maxine and Bonnie Brown"			
❑ 47-6823	Money/It Takes a Long Train with a Red Caboose	1957	15.00
❑ 47-6918	I'm in Heaven/Getting Used to Being Lonely	1957	15.00
—As "Jim, Maxine and Bonnie Brown"			
❑ 47-6995	I Heard the Bluebirds Sing/ The Last Thing I Want	1957	15.00
—As "Jim, Maxine and Bonnie Brown"			
❑ 47-7110	The Man in the Moon/ True Love Goes Far Beyond	1957	15.00
❑ 47-7208	Crazy Dreams/ Ain't No Way in the World	1958	15.00
❑ 47-7311	Would You Care?/The Trot	1958	15.00
❑ 47-7427	Beyond the Shadow/ This Time I Would Know	1958	15.00
❑ 47-7555	The Three Bells/ Heaven Fell Last Night	1959	12.00
❑ 47-7614	Scarlet Ribbons (For Her Hair)/ Blue Bells Ring	1959	12.00
❑ 47-7700	The Old Lamplighter/Teen-Ex	1960	12.00
❑ 47-7700 [PS]	The Old Lamplighter/Teen-Ex	1960	25.00
❑ 47-7755	Lonely Little Robin/Margo (The Ninth of May)	1960	12.00
❑ 47-7755 [PS]	Lonely Little Robin/Margo (The Ninth of May)	1960	25.00
❑ 47-7780	The Whiffenpoof Song/ Brighten the Corner Where You Are	1960	12.00
❑ 47-7780 [PS]	The Whiffenpoof Song/ Brighten the Corner Where You Are	1960	25.00
❑ 47-7804	Send Me the Pillow You Dream On/You're So Much a Part of Me	1960	12.00
❑ 47-7820	Blue Christmas/ Greenwillow Christmas	1960	12.00
❑ 47-7866	Ground Hog/Angel's Dolly	1961	10.00
❑ 47-7917	Whispering Wine/ My Baby's Gone	1961	10.00
❑ 47-7969	Foolish Pride/Alpha and Omega	1961	10.00
❑ 47-7997	Buttons and Bows/ Remember Me	1962	10.00
❑ 47-8066	It's Just a Little Heartache/ The Old Master Painter	1962	10.00
❑ 47-8198	The Twelfth Rose/Watching My World Fall Apart	1963	10.00
❑ 47-8242	Oh, No!/Dear Teresa	1963	10.00
❑ 47-8348	Then I'll Stop Loving You/ I Know My Place	1964	8.00
❑ 47-8423	Everybody's Darlin', Plus Mine/ The Outskirts of Town	1964	8.00
❑ 47-8495	I Feel Like Crying/ No Sad Songs for Me	1965	8.00
❑ 47-8603	You Can't Grow Peaches on a Cherry Tree/A Little Too Much to Dream	1965	8.00
❑ 47-8714	Meadowgreen/ One Take Away One	1965	8.00
❑ 47-8838	I'd Just Be Fool Enough/ Springtime	1966	8.00
❑ 47-8942	Coming Back to You/ Gigawachem	1966	8.00
❑ 47-9153	I Hear It Now/He Will Set Your Fields on Fire	1967	8.00
❑ 47-9364	Big Daddy/I Will Bring You Water	1967	8.00
❑ 61-7555 [S]	The Three Bells/ Heaven Fell Last Night	1959	25.00
—"Living Stereo" (large hole, plays at 45 rpm)			
❑ 61-7614 [S]	Scarlet Ribbons (For Her Hair)/ Blue Bells Ring	1959	25.00
—"Living Stereo" (large hole, plays at 45 rpm)			
❑ 61-7700 [S]	The Old Lamplighter/Teen-Ex	1960	25.00
—"Living Stereo" (large hole, plays at 45 rpm)			
❑ 61-7755 [S]	Lonely Little Robin/Margo (The Ninth of May)	1960	25.00
—"Living Stereo" (large hole, plays at 45 rpm)			
❑ 61-7780 [S]	The Whiffenpoof Song/ Brighten the Corner Where You Are	1960	25.00
—"Living Stereo" (large hole, plays at 45 rpm)			
❑ 61-7804 [S]	Send Me the Pillow You Dream On/You're So Much a Part of Me	1960	25.00
—"Living Stereo" (large hole, plays at 45 rpm)			
7-Inch Extended Plays			
RCA VICTOR			
❑ EPA 1-1438	I Heard the Bluebirds Sing/ I'll Hold You in My Heart// The Table Next to Me/ My Isle of Golden Dreams	1957	15.00
❑ EPA 1-1438 [PS]	Jim Edward, Maxine and Bonnie Brown	1957	15.00
❑ EPA-4347	The Three Bells/Be My Love// The Man in the Moon/This Time I Would Know	1959	15.00
❑ EPA-4347 [PS]	The Browns Sing The 3 Bells	1959	15.00
❑ EPA-4352	Scarlet Ribbons/I Still Do// Love Me Tender/We Should Be Together	1959	15.00
❑ EPA-4352 [PS]	Scarlet Ribbons	1959	15.00
❑ EPA-4364	The Old Lamplighter/ Oh! My Pa-Pa//True Love/ The Enchanted Sea	1960	15.00
❑ EPA-4364 [PS]	The Old Lamplighter	1960	15.00
Albums			
RCA CAMDEN			
❑ CAL-885 [M]	I Heard the Bluebirds Sing	1965	12.00
❑ CAS-885 [S]	I Heard the Bluebirds Sing	1965	12.00
❑ CAL-2142 [M]	Big Ones from the Country	1967	12.00
❑ CAS-2142 [S]	Big Ones from the Country	1967	10.00
❑ CAS-2262	The Browns Sing a Harvest of Country Songs	1968	10.00
RCA VICTOR			
❑ ANL1-1083	The Best of the Browns	1975	10.00
❑ LPM-1438 [M]	Jim Edward, Maxine and Bonnie Brown	1957	50.00
❑ LPM-2144 [M]	Sweet Sounds by the Browns	1959	30.00
❑ LSP-2144 [S]	Sweet Sounds by the Browns	1959	40.00
❑ LPM-2174 [M]	Town and Country	1960	20.00
❑ LSP-2174 [S]	Town and Country	1960	25.00
❑ LPM-2260 [M]	The Browns Sing Their Hits	1960	20.00
❑ LSP-2260 [S]	The Browns Sing Their Hits	1960	25.00
❑ LPM-2333 [M]	Our Favorite Folk Songs	1961	20.00
❑ LSP-2333 [S]	Our Favorite Folk Songs	1961	25.00
❑ LPM-2345 [M]	The Little Brown Church Hymnal	1961	20.00
❑ LSP-2345 [S]	The Little Brown Church Hymnal	1961	25.00
❑ LPM-2784 [M]	Grand Ole Opry Favorites	1963	15.00
❑ LSP-2784 [S]	Grand Ole Opry Favorites	1963	20.00
❑ LPM-2860 [M]	This Young Land	1964	15.00
❑ LSP-2860 [S]	This Young Land	1964	20.00
❑ LPM-2987 [M]	Three Shades of Brown	1964	15.00
❑ LSP-2987 [S]	Three Shades of Brown	1964	20.00
❑ LPM-3423 [M]	When Love Is Gone	1965	15.00
❑ LSP-3423 [S]	When Love Is Gone	1965	20.00
❑ LPM-3561 [M]	The Best of the Browns	1966	15.00
❑ LSP-3561 [S]	The Best of the Browns	1966	20.00
❑ LPM-3668 [M]	Our Kind of Country	1966	15.00
❑ LSP-3668 [S]	Our Kind of Country	1966	20.00
❑ LPM-3798 [M]	The Old Country Church	1967	20.00
❑ LSP-3798 [S]	The Old Country Church	1967	15.00

BROWNSVILLE STATION

Number	Title (A Side/B Side)	Yr	NM
45s			
BIG TREE			
❑ 144	Rock with the Music/ (B-side unknown)	1972	5.00
❑ 156	The Red Back Spider/ Rock with the Music	1972	5.00
❑ 161	Let Your Yeah Be Yeah/ Mister Robert	1973	5.00
❑ 15005	I'm the Leader of the Gang/ Fast Phyllis	1974	4.00
❑ 15005	I'm the Leader of the Gang/ Meet Me on the Fourth Floor	1974	4.00
❑ 16001	Kings of the Party/Ostrich	1974	4.00
❑ 16011	Smokin' in the Boy's Room/ Barefootin'	1973	5.00
❑ 16029	I Got It Bad for You/ Mama Don't Allow No Parkin'	1974	4.00
EPIC			
❑ 50695	Love Stealer/Fever	1979	4.00
—As "Brownsville"			
HIDEOUT			
❑ 1957	Rock and Roll Holiday/ Jailhouse Rock	1969	12.00
PALLADIUM			
❑ H-1075	Be-Bop Confidential/City Life	1970	20.00
POLYDOR			
❑ 14017	Rock and Roll Holiday/ Jailhouse Rock	1969	5.00
PRIVATE STOCK			
❑ 45,149	Lady (Put the Light on Me)/ Rockers and Rollers	1977	6.00
❑ 45,167	The Martian Boogie/Mr. Johnson Sez	1977	6.00
WARNER BROS.			
❑ 7441	Be-Bop Confidential/City Life	1970	8.00
❑ 7456	Roadrunner/Do the Bosco	1971	8.00
❑ 7501	That's Fine/Tell Me All About It	1971	8.00
Albums			
BIG TREE			
❑ BTS-2010	A Night on the Town	1972	12.00
❑ BTS-2102	Yeah!	1973	12.00
❑ BT 89500	School Punks	1974	12.00
❑ BT 89510	Motor City Connection	1975	12.00
EPIC			
❑ JE 35606	Air Special	1978	16.00
❑ JE 35606 [DJ]	Air Special	1978	20.00
—Orange vinyl promo			
PALLADIUM			
❑ P-1004	Brownsville Station	1970	30.00
PRIVATE STOCK			
❑ PS-2026	Brownsville Station	1977	10.00
WARNER BROS.			
❑ WS 1888	No B.S.	1970	15.00

BRUBECK, DAVE

Number	Title (A Side/B Side)	Yr	NM
45s			
ATLANTIC			
❑ 3015	Three to Get Ready/ Blue Rondo (A La Turk)	1974	4.00
COLUMBIA			
❑ 30719 [S]	(contents unknown)	1960	12.00
❑ 30720 [S]	(contents unknown)	1960	12.00
❑ 30721 [S]	(contents unknown)	1960	12.00
❑ 30722 [S]	(contents unknown)	1960	12.00
❑ 30723 [S]	(contents unknown)	1960	12.00
❑ 30899 [S]	(contents unknown)	1961	12.00
❑ 30900 [S]	(contents unknown)	1961	12.00
❑ 30901 [S]	(contents unknown)	1961	12.00
❑ 30902 [S]	(contents unknown)	1961	12.00
❑ 30903 [S]	(contents unknown)	1961	12.00
❑ 31312 [S]	(contents unknown)	1962	12.00
❑ 31313 [S]	(contents unknown)	1962	12.00
❑ 31314 [S]	(contents unknown)	1962	12.00
❑ 31315 [S]	(contents unknown)	1962	12.00
❑ 31316 [S]	(contents unknown)	1962	12.00
—Anyone who can fill in these gaps — the above 15 all are Columbia "Stereo 7" singles — please let us know.			
❑ 31443 [S]	Charles Matthew Hallelujah/ Maria	1962	12.00
❑ 31444 [S]	Someday My Prince Will Come/ I'm in a Dancing Mood	1962	12.00
❑ 31445 [S]	Tangerine/The Duke	1962	12.00
❑ 31446 [S]	Far More Blue/ Gone with the Wind	1962	12.00
❑ 31447 [S]	Take the "A" Train/ Camptown Races	1962	12.00
❑ 40776	Lover/I'm in a Dancin' Mood	1956	12.00
❑ 41479	Take Five/Blue Rondo A La Turk	1960	12.00
❑ 41485	Camptown Races/ Shortnin' Bread	1959	12.00
❑ 42068	Paradiddle Joe/Briar Bush	1961	10.00
❑ 42228	Unsquare Dance/ It's a Raggy Waltz	1961	10.00
❑ 42228 [PS]	Unsquare Dance/ It's a Raggy Waltz	1961	15.00
❑ 42404	Countdown/Eleven Four	1962	10.00
❑ 42404 [PS]	Countdown/Eleven Four	1962	15.00
❑ 42651	Bossa Nova U.S.A./ This Can't Be Love	1962	10.00
❑ 42675	Bossa Nova U.S.A./ Camptown Races	1963	8.00
❑ 42804	Summer Song/ Three to Get Ready	1963	8.00
❑ 42920	Cable Car/ Theme from Elementals	1963	8.00
❑ 43091	Unisphere/Toki's Theme	1964	8.00
❑ 43133	Mr. Broadway/Toki's Theme	1964	8.00
❑ 43409	Happy Bandito/Bag O' Heat	1965	8.00
❑ 43663	Three to Get Ready/ Done Her Wrong	1966	8.00
❑ 44345	Raga Theme for Ragu/ Do Not Fold, Staple, Spindle or Mutilate	1968	8.00
❑ 44834	Broke Blues/Blues Roots	1969	6.00
FANTASY			
❑ 501	Lullaby in Rhythm/You Stepped Out of a Dream	1952	15.00
❑ 502	Singing in the Rain/ I'll Remember April	1952	15.00
❑ 503	Body & Soul/Let's Fall in Love	1952	15.00
❑ 504	Indiana/Laura	1952	15.00
—The above four records comprised a box set			
❑ 505	Blue Moon/Tea for Two	1952	15.00

Except when noted otherwise, VG = 25% of NM, and VG+ = 50% of NM. (Example: VG = $2.00, VG+ = $4.00 and NM = $8.00.)

Number	Title (A Side/B Side)	Yr	NM
❑ 506	Undecided/That Old Black Magic	1952	15.00
❑ 507	September Song/ Sweet Georgia Brown	1952	15.00
❑ 508	'S Wonderful/Spring Is Here	1952	15.00
—The above four records comprised a box set			
❑ 509	The Way You Look Tonight/ Love Walked In	1953	15.00
❑ 510	September in the Rain/What Is This Thing Called Love	1953	15.00
❑ 511	Prelude/Fugue on Bob's Theme	1953	15.00
❑ 512	Ipca/Let's Fall in Love	1953	15.00
—The above four records comprised a box set			
❑ 513	Avalon/Perfidia	1953	15.00
❑ 514	Always/I Didn't Know What Time It Was	1953	15.00
❑ 515	Squeeze Me/How High the Moon	1953	15.00
❑ 516	Too Marvelous for Words/ Heart and Soul	1953	15.00
—The above four records comprised a box set			
❑ 517	Somebody Loves Me/ Crazy Chris	1953	15.00
❑ 518	A Foggy Day/Lyons Bust (Theme)	1953	15.00
❑ 519	Mam'selle/Me and My Shadow	1953	15.00
❑ 520	At a Perfume Counter/Frenesi	1953	15.00
—The above four records comprised a box set			
❑ 521	This Can't Be Love/Look for the Silver Lining	1953	15.00
❑ 523	Just One of Those Things/ My Romance	1953	15.00
❑ 524	Stardust/Lulu's Back in Town	1953	15.00
❑ 526	Alice in Wonderland/ All the Things You Are	1953	15.00
❑ 527	On a Little Street in Singapore/ I May Be Wrong	195?	15.00
❑ 530	The Trolley Song/ My Heart Stood Still	195?	15.00
❑ 535	The Trolley Song/ The Trolley Song Rehearsal	195?	20.00
❑ 549	The Piper/Soliloquy	195?	15.00
❑ 558	The Trolley Song/Crazy Chris	1961	12.00

7-Inch Extended Plays

COLUMBIA

Number	Title (A Side/B Side)	Yr	NM
❑ B-435 [PS]	Jazz Goes to College Vol. I	1955	10.00
—Dual-pocket sleeve for 1940 and 1941			
❑ B-436 [PS]	Jazz Goes to College Vol. II	1955	10.00
—Dual-pocket sleeve for 1942 and 1943			
❑ B-465 [PS]	Dave Brubeck at Storyville: 1954 (Vol. 1)	1955	10.00
—Dual-pocket sleeve for 2016 and 2017			
❑ B-473 [PS]	Brubeck Time	1955	10.00
—Dual-pocket sleeve for 2067 and 2068			
❑ B-699 [PS]	Jazz Red Hot and Cool	1956	12.00
—Triple-pocket sleeve for 2280, 2281 and 2282			
❑ 5-1940	Balcony Rock (Beg.)/Le Souk	1955	10.00
—Alternate numbers are "B-435-1" and "B-435-4"			
❑ 5-1941	Balcony Rock (Concl.)/ Out of Nowhere	1955	10.00
—Alternate numbers are "B-435-2" and "B-435-3"			
❑ 5-1942	Take the "A" Train/ The Song Is You	1955	10.00
—Alternate numbers are "B-436-1" and "B-436-4"			
❑ 5-1943	I Want to Be Happy/ Don't Worry 'Bout Me	1955	10.00
—Alternate numbers are "B-436-2" and "B-436-3"			
❑ 5-2016	On the Alamo (Beginning)/Here Lies Love	1955	10.00
—Alternate numbers are "B-465-1" and "B-465-4"			
❑ 5-2017	On the Alamo (Conclusion)/ Don't Worry 'Bout Me	1955	10.00
—Alternate numbers are "B-465-2" and "B-465-3"			
❑ 5-2067	A Fine Romance/Brother, Can You Spare a Dime	1955	10.00
—Alternate numbers are "B-473-1" and "B-473-4"			
❑ 5-2068	Pennies from Heaven/ Why Do I Love You	1955	10.00
—Alternate numbers are "B-473-2" and "B-473-3"			
❑ 5-2280	Lover/Love Walked In	1956	12.00
❑ 5-2281	Little Girl Blue/Indiana	1956	12.00
❑ 5-2282	*The Duke/Fare Thee Well, Annabelle/Sometimes I'm Happy	1956	12.00
❑ B-2552	Laura/Sometimes I'm Happy	195?	10.00
❑ B-2552 [PS]	The Dave Brubeck Quartet (Hall of Fame Series)	195?	10.00

FANTASY

Number	Title (A Side/B Side)	Yr	NM
❑ EP 4002	September Song/Sweet Georgia Brown//Spring Is Here/'S Wonderful	195?	15.00
❑ EP 4002 [PS]	The Dave Brubeck Trio	195?	15.00
❑ EP 4006	How High the Moon/Just Squeeze Me//Too Marvelous for Words/Heart and Soul	195?	15.00
❑ EP 4006 [PS]	The Dave Brubeck Trio	195?	15.00
❑ EP 4014	Blue Moon/Let's Fall in Love	195?	15.00
—Red vinyl			
❑ EP 4014 [PS]	The Brubeck Quartet at Storyville	195?	15.00
—Title not on front cover; it's on the notes on the back			
❑ EP 4019	How High the Moon// Serenades Suite/ Playland-at-the-Beach	195?	15.00
—Green vinyl			
❑ EP 4019 [PS]	Old Sounds from San Francisco, Vol. 1	195?	15.00
❑ EP 4020	The Prisoner's Song/ Schizophrenic Scherzo/ Rondo//You Go to My Head/ Laura/Closing Theme	195?	15.00
—Red vinyl			
❑ EP 4020 [PS]	Old Sounds from San Francisco, Vol. 2	195?	15.00

Albums

ATLANTIC

Number	Title	Yr	NM
❑ SD 2-317 [(2)]	The Art of Dave Brubeck: The Fantasy Years	1975	15.00
❑ SD 1606	Truth Is Fallen	1972	12.00
❑ SD 1607	The Last Set at Newport	1972	12.00
❑ SD 1641	We're All Together Again for the First Time	1973	12.00
❑ SD 1645	Two Generations of Brubeck	1974	12.00
❑ SD 1660	Brother, The Great Spirit Made Us All	1974	12.00
❑ SD 1684	All the Things We Are	1976	12.00

BOOK-OF-THE-MONTH

Number	Title	Yr	NM
❑ 80-5547 [(3)]	Early Fantasies	1980	20.00

COLUMBIA

Number	Title	Yr	NM
❑ C2L 26 [(2)M]	The Dave Brubeck Quartet at Carnegie Hall	1963	25.00
—Red "Guaranteed High Fidelity" label			
❑ C2L 26 [(2)M]	The Dave Brubeck Quartet at Carnegie Hall	1966	15.00
—Red "360 Sound" label			
❑ CL 566 [M]	Jazz Goes to College	1954	80.00
—Dark red label, gold print; released at the same time as 6321 and 6322			
❑ CL 566 [M]	Jazz Goes to College	1955	50.00
—Red/black label with six "eye" logos			
❑ CL 566 [M]	Jazz Goes to College	1962	20.00
—Red "Guaranteed High Fidelity" label			
❑ CL 566 [M]	Jazz Goes to College	1966	12.00
—Red "360 Sound" label			
❑ CL 590 [M]	Dave Brubeck at Storyville: 1954	1954	80.00
—Dark red label, gold print; released at the same time as 6330 and 6331			
❑ CL 590 [M]	Dave Brubeck at Storyville: 1954	1955	50.00
—Red/black label with six "eye" logos			
❑ CL 590 [M]	Dave Brubeck at Storyville: 1954	1962	20.00
—Red "Guaranteed High Fidelity" label			
❑ CL 590 [M]	Dave Brubeck at Storyville: 1954	1966	12.00
—Red "360 Sound" label			
❑ CL 622 [M]	Brubeck Time	1955	60.00
—Red/black label with six "eye" logos			
❑ CL 622 [M]	Brubeck Time	1962	20.00
—Red "Guaranteed High Fidelity" label			
❑ CL 622 [M]	Brubeck Time	1966	12.00
—Red "360 Sound" label			
❑ CL 699 [M]	Jazz: Red Hot and Cool	1955	60.00
—Red/black label with six "eye" logos			
❑ CL 699 [M]	Jazz: Red Hot and Cool	1962	20.00
—Red "Guaranteed High Fidelity" label			
❑ CL 699 [M]	Jazz: Red Hot and Cool	1966	12.00
—Red "360 Sound" label			
❑ C2S 826 [(2)]	The Dave Brubeck Quartet at Carnegie Hall	1971	15.00
—Orange label			
❑ C2S 826 [(2)S]	The Dave Brubeck Quartet at Carnegie Hall	1963	30.00
—Red label, "360 Sound" in black			
❑ C2S 826 [(2)S]	The Dave Brubeck Quartet at Carnegie Hall	1966	20.00
—Red label, "360 Sound" in white			
❑ CL 878 [M]	Brubeck Plays Brubeck	1956	60.00
—Red/black label with six "eye" logos			
❑ CL 878 [M]	Brubeck Plays Brubeck	1962	20.00
—Red "Guaranteed High Fidelity" label			
❑ CL 878 [M]	Brubeck Plays Brubeck	1966	12.00
—Red "360 Sound" label			
❑ CL 932 [M]	American Jazz Festival at Newport '56	1956	50.00
—Red/black label with six "eye" logos			
❑ CL 932 [M]	American Jazz Festival at Newport '56	1962	20.00
—Red "Guaranteed High Fidelity" label			
❑ CL 984 [M]	Jazz Impressions of the U.S.A.	1957	50.00
—Red/black label with six "eye" logos			
❑ CL 984 [M]	Jazz Impressions of the U.S.A.	1962	20.00
—Red "Guaranteed High Fidelity" label			
❑ CL 984 [M]	Jazz Impressions of the U.S.A.	1966	12.00
—Red "360 Sound" label			
❑ CL 1034 [M]	Jazz Goes to Junior College	1957	40.00
—Red/black label with six "eye" logos			
❑ CL 1034 [M]	Jazz Goes to Junior College	1962	20.00
—Red "Guaranteed High Fidelity" label			
❑ CL 1034 [M]	Jazz Goes to Junior College	1966	12.00
—Red "360 Sound" label			
❑ CL 1059 [M]	Dave Digs Disney	1957	40.00
—Red/black label with six "eye" logos			
❑ CL 1059 [M]	Dave Digs Disney	1962	20.00
—Red "Guaranteed High Fidelity" label			
❑ CL 1059 [M]	Dave Digs Disney	1966	12.00
—Red "360 Sound" label			
❑ CL 1168 [M]	The Dave Brubeck Quartet in Europe	1958	40.00
—Red/black label with six "eye" logos			
❑ CL 1168 [M]	The Dave Brubeck Quartet in Europe	1962	20.00
—Red "Guaranteed High Fidelity" label			
❑ CL 1168 [M]	The Dave Brubeck Quartet in Europe	1966	12.00
—Red "360 Sound" label			
❑ CL 1249 [M]	Newport 1958	1958	40.00
—Red/black label with six "eye" logos			
❑ CL 1249 [M]	Newport 1958	1962	20.00
—Red "Guaranteed High Fidelity" label			
❑ CL 1249 [M]	Newport 1958	1966	12.00
—Red "360 Sound" label			
❑ CL 1251 [M]	Jazz Impressions of Eurasia	1958	40.00
—Red/black label with six "eye" logos			
❑ CL 1251 [M]	Jazz Impressions of Eurasia	1962	20.00
—Red "Guaranteed High Fidelity" label			
❑ CL 1251 [M]	Jazz Impressions of Eurasia	1966	12.00
—Red "360 Sound" label			
❑ CL 1347 [M]	Gone with the Wind	1959	40.00
—Red/black label with six "eye" logos			
❑ CL 1347 [M]	Gone with the Wind	1962	20.00
—Red "Guaranteed High Fidelity" label			
❑ CL 1347 [M]	Gone with the Wind	1966	12.00
—Red "360 Sound" label			
❑ CL 1397 [M]	Time Out	1960	25.00
—Red/black label with six "eye" logos			
❑ CL 1397 [M]	Time Out Featuring "Take Five"	1962	15.00
—Red "Guaranteed High Fidelity" label; beginning with this issue, the cover was altered to emphasize the hit			
❑ CL 1397 [M]	Time Out Featuring "Take Five"	1966	12.00
—Red "360 Sound" label			
❑ CL 1439 [M]	Southern Scene	1960	25.00
—Red/black label with six "eye" logos			
❑ CL 1439 [M]	Southern Scene	1962	15.00
—Red "Guaranteed High Fidelity" label			
❑ CL 1439 [M]	Southern Scene	1966	12.00
—Red "360 Sound" label			
❑ CL 1454 [M]	The Riddle	1960	25.00
—Red/black label with six "eye" logos			
❑ CL 1454 [M]	The Riddle	1962	15.00
—Red "Guaranteed High Fidelity" label			
❑ CL 1454 [M]	The Riddle	1966	12.00
—Red "360 Sound" label			
❑ CL 1466 [M]	Bernstein Plays Brubeck Plays Bernstein	1960	25.00
—Red/black label with six "eye" logos			
❑ CL 1466 [M]	Bernstein Plays Brubeck Plays Bernstein	1962	15.00
—Red "Guaranteed High Fidelity" label			
❑ CL 1466 [M]	Bernstein Plays Brubeck Plays Bernstein	1966	12.00
—Red "360 Sound" label			
❑ CL 1553 [M]	Brubeck and Rushing	1961	25.00
—Red/black label with six "eye" logos			
❑ CL 1553 [M]	Brubeck and Rushing	1962	15.00
—Red "Guaranteed High Fidelity" label			
❑ CL 1553 [M]	Brubeck and Rushing	1966	12.00
—Red "360 Sound" label			
❑ CL 1609 [M]	Tonight Only!	1961	25.00
—Red/black label with six "eye" logos			
❑ CL 1609 [M]	Tonight Only!	1962	15.00
—Red "Guaranteed High Fidelity" label			
❑ CL 1609 [M]	Tonight Only!	1966	12.00
—Red "360 Sound" label			
❑ CL 1690 [M]	Time Further Out	1961	25.00
—Red/black label with six "eye" logos			
❑ CL 1690 [M]	Time Further Out	1962	15.00
—Red "Guaranteed High Fidelity" label			
❑ CL 1690 [M]	Time Further Out	1966	12.00
—Red "360 Sound" label			
❑ CL 1775 [M]	Countdown — Time in Outer Space	1962	15.00
—Red "Guaranteed High Fidelity" label			
❑ CL 1775 [M]	Countdown — Time in Outer Space	1962	30.00
—Red/black label with six "eye" logos			
❑ CL 1775 [M]	Countdown — Time in Outer Space	1966	12.00
—Red "360 Sound" label			
❑ CL 1963 [M]	Brandenburg Gate Revisited	1963	20.00
—Red "Guaranteed High Fidelity" label			
❑ CL 1963 [M]	Brandenburg Gate Revisited	1966	12.00
—Red "360 Sound" label			
❑ CL 1998 [M]	Bossa Nova U.S.A.	1963	20.00
—Red "Guaranteed High Fidelity" label			
❑ CL 1998 [M]	Bossa Nova U.S.A.	1966	12.00
—Red "360 Sound" label			
❑ CL 2127 [M]	Time Changes	1964	20.00
—Red "Guaranteed High Fidelity" label			
❑ CL 2127 [M]	Time Changes	1966	12.00
—Red "360 Sound" label			
❑ CL 2212 [M]	Jazz Impressions of Japan	1964	20.00
—Red "Guaranteed High Fidelity" label			
❑ CL 2212 [M]	Jazz Impressions of Japan	1966	12.00
—Red "360 Sound" label			

Except when noted otherwise, VG = 25% of NM, and VG+ = 50% of NM. (Example: VG = $2.00, VG+ = $4.00 and NM = $8.00.)

Number	Title (A Side/B Side)	Yr	NM
❑ CL 2275 [M]	Jazz Impressions of New York	1965	20.00
—Red "Guaranteed High Fidelity" label			
❑ CL 2275 [M]	Jazz Impressions of New York	1966	12.00
—Red "360 Sound" label			
❑ CL 2316 [M]	Take Five	1965	20.00
—Red "Guaranteed High Fidelity" label			
❑ CL 2316 [M]	Take Five	1966	12.00
—Red "360 Sound" label			
❑ CL 2348 [M]	Angel Eyes	1965	20.00
—Red "Guaranteed High Fidelity" label			
❑ CL 2348 [M]	Angel Eyes	1966	12.00
—Red "360 Sound" label			
❑ CL 2437 [M]	My Favorite Things	1966	15.00
❑ CL 2484 [M]	Dave Brubeck's Greatest Hits	1966	15.00
❑ CL 2512 [M]	Time In	1966	15.00
❑ CL 2602 [M]	Anything Goes! Dave Brubeck Quartet Plays Cole Porter	1966	15.00
❑ CL 2695 [M]	Bravo Brubeck!	1967	20.00
❑ CL 2712 [M]	Jackpot	1967	20.00
❑ CL 6321 [10]	Jazz Goes to College, Vol. 1	1954	100.00
❑ CL 6322 [10]	Jazz Goes to College, Vol. 2	1954	100.00
❑ CL 6330 [10]	Dave Brubeck at Storyville: 1954, Vol. 1	1954	80.00
❑ CL 6331 [10]	Dave Brubeck at Storyville: 1954, Vol. 2	1954	80.00
❑ CS 8058 [S]	Jazz Impressions of Eurasia	1959	50.00
—Red/black label with six "eye" logos			
❑ CS 8058 [S]	Jazz Impressions of Eurasia	1962	25.00
—Red label, "360 Sound" in black			
❑ CS 8058 [S]	Jazz Impressions of Eurasia	1966	15.00
—Red label, "360 Sound" in white			
❑ CS 8082 [S]	Newport 1958	1959	50.00
—Red/black label with six "eye" logos			
❑ CS 8082 [S]	Newport 1958	1962	25.00
—Red label, "360 Sound" in black			
❑ CS 8082 [S]	Newport 1958	1966	15.00
—Red label, "360 Sound" in white			
❑ CS 8090 [S]	Dave Digs Disney	1959	50.00
—Red/black label with six "eye" logos			
❑ CS 8090 [S]	Dave Digs Disney	1962	25.00
—Red label, "360 Sound" in black			
❑ CS 8090 [S]	Dave Digs Disney	1966	15.00
—Red label, "360 Sound" in white			
❑ CS 8156	Gone with the Wind	1971	12.00
—Orange label			
❑ CS 8156 [S]	Gone with the Wind	1959	50.00
—Red/black label with six "eye" logos			
❑ CS 8156 [S]	Gone with the Wind	1962	25.00
—Red label, "360 Sound" in black			
❑ CS 8156 [S]	Gone with the Wind	1966	15.00
—Red label, "360 Sound" in white			
❑ CS 8192	Time Out Featuring "Take Five"	1971	12.00
—Orange label			
❑ CS 8192	Time Out	1995	30.00
—Audiophile vinyl, distributed by Classic Records			
❑ CS 8192 [S]	Time Out	1960	30.00
—Red/black label with six "eye" logos			
❑ CS 8192 [S]	Time Out Featuring "Take Five"	1962	20.00
—Red label, "360 Sound" in black; beginning with this issue, the cover was altered to emphasize the hit			
❑ CS 8192 [S]	Time Out Featuring "Take Five"	1966	15.00
—Red label, "360 Sound" in white			
❑ PC 8192	Time Out	1981	8.00
—Reissue with new prefix			
❑ CS 8235 [S]	Southern Scene	1960	30.00
—Red/black label with six "eye" logos			
❑ CS 8235 [S]	Southern Scene	1962	20.00
—Red label, "360 Sound" in black			
❑ CS 8235 [S]	Southern Scene	1966	15.00
—Red label, "360 Sound" in white			
❑ CS 8248 [S]	The Riddle	1960	30.00
—Red/black label with six "eye" logos			
❑ CS 8248 [S]	The Riddle	1962	20.00
—Red label, "360 Sound" in black			
❑ CS 8248 [S]	The Riddle	1966	15.00
—Red label, "360 Sound" in white			
❑ CS 8257	Brubeck Plays Bernstein Plays Brubeck	1971	12.00
—Orange label			
❑ CS 8257 [S]	Brubeck Plays Bernstein Plays Brubeck	1960	30.00
—Red/black label with six "eye" logos			
❑ CS 8257 [S]	Brubeck Plays Bernstein Plays Brubeck	1962	20.00
—Red label, "360 Sound" in black			
❑ CS 8257 [S]	Brubeck Plays Bernstein Plays Brubeck	1966	15.00
—Red label, "360 Sound" in white			
❑ CS 8353 [S]	Brubeck and Rushing	1961	30.00
—Red/black label with six "eye" logos			
❑ CS 8353 [S]	Brubeck and Rushing	1962	20.00
—Red label, "360 Sound" in black			
❑ CS 8353 [S]	Brubeck and Rushing	1966	15.00
—Red label, "360 Sound" in white			
❑ CS 8409 [S]	Tonight Only!	1961	30.00
—Red/black label with six "eye" logos			
❑ CS 8409 [S]	Tonight Only!	1962	20.00
—Red label, "360 Sound" in black			
❑ CS 8409 [S]	Tonight Only!	1966	15.00
—Red label, "360 Sound" in white			
❑ CS 8490	Time Further Out	1971	12.00
—Orange label			
❑ CS 8490 [S]	Time Further Out	1961	30.00
—Red/black label with six "eye" logos			
❑ CS 8490 [S]	Time Further Out	1962	20.00
—Red label, "360 Sound" in black			
❑ CS 8490 [S]	Time Further Out	1966	15.00
—Red label, "360 Sound" in white			
❑ PC 8490	Time Further Out	1981	8.00
—Reissue with new prefix			
❑ CS 8575 [S]	Countdown — Time in Outer Space	1962	20.00
—Red label, "360 Sound" in black			
❑ CS 8575 [S]	Countdown — Time in Outer Space	1962	40.00
—Red/black label with six "eye" logos			
❑ CS 8575 [S]	Countdown — Time in Outer Space	1966	15.00
—Red label, "360 Sound" in white			
❑ CS 8645 [R]	Jazz: Red Hot and Cool	1963	15.00
—Red label, "360 Sound" in black			
❑ CS 8645 [R]	Jazz: Red Hot and Cool	1966	12.00
—Red label, "360 Sound" in white			
❑ CS 8763 [S]	Brandenburg Gate Revisited	1963	25.00
—Red label, "360 Sound" in black			
❑ CS 8763 [S]	Brandenburg Gate Revisited	1966	15.00
—Red label, "360 Sound" in white			
❑ CS 8798 [S]	Bossa Nova U.S.A.	1963	25.00
—Red label, "360 Sound" in black			
❑ CS 8798 [S]	Bossa Nova U.S.A.	1966	15.00
—Red label, "360 Sound" in white			
❑ CS 8927 [S]	Time Changes	1964	25.00
—Red label, "360 Sound" in black			
❑ CS 8927 [S]	Time Changes	1966	15.00
—Red label, "360 Sound" in white			
❑ CS 9012	Jazz Impressions of Japan	1971	12.00
—Orange label			
❑ CS 9012 [S]	Jazz Impressions of Japan	1964	25.00
—Red label, "360 Sound" in black			
❑ CS 9012 [S]	Jazz Impressions of Japan	1966	15.00
—Red label, "360 Sound" in white			
❑ PC 9012	Jazz Impressions of Japan	1981	8.00
—Reissue with new prefix			
❑ CS 9075	Jazz Impressions of New York	1971	12.00
—Orange label			
❑ CS 9075 [S]	Jazz Impressions of New York	1965	25.00
—Red label, "360 Sound" in black			
❑ CS 9075 [S]	Jazz Impressions of New York	1966	15.00
—Red label, "360 Sound" in white			
❑ PC 9075	Jazz Impressions of New York	1981	8.00
—Reissue with new prefix			
❑ CS 9116 [S]	Take Five	1965	25.00
—Red label, "360 Sound" in black			
❑ CS 9116 [S]	Take Five	1966	15.00
—Red label, "360 Sound" in white			
❑ CS 9148 [S]	Angel Eyes	1965	25.00
—Red label, "360 Sound" in black			
❑ CS 9148 [S]	Angel Eyes	1966	15.00
—Red label, "360 Sound" in white			
❑ CS 9237 [S]	My Favorite Things	1966	20.00
—Red "360 Sound" label			
❑ CS 9284	Dave Brubeck's Greatest Hits	1971	12.00
—Orange label			
❑ CS 9284 [S]	Dave Brubeck's Greatest Hits	1966	20.00
—Red "360 Sound" label			
❑ PC 9284	Dave Brubeck's Greatest Hits	1981	8.00
—Reissue with new prefix			
❑ CS 9312	Time In	1971	12.00
—Orange label			
❑ CS 9312 [S]	Time In	1966	20.00
—Red "360 Sound" label			
❑ PC 9312	Time In	1981	8.00
—Reissue with new prefix			
❑ CS 9402	Anything Goes! Dave Brubeck Quartet Plays Cole Porter	1971	12.00
—Orange label			
❑ CS 9402 [S]	Anything Goes! Dave Brubeck Quartet Plays Cole Porter	1966	20.00
—Red "360 Sound" label			
❑ PC 9402	Anything Goes! Dave Brubeck Quartet Plays Cole Porter	1981	8.00
—Reissue with new prefix			
❑ CS 9495	Bravo Brubeck!	1971	12.00
—Orange label			
❑ CS 9495 [S]	Bravo Brubeck!	1967	15.00
—Red "360 Sound" label			
❑ CS 9512 [S]	Jackpot	1967	15.00
—Red "360 Sound" label			
❑ CS 9572	The Last Time We Saw Paris	1971	12.00
—Orange label			
❑ CS 9672	The Last Time We Saw Paris	1968	15.00
—Red "360 Sound" label			
❑ CS 9704	Compadres	1968	15.00
—Red "360 Sound" label			
❑ CS 9704	Compadres	1971	12.00
—Orange label			
❑ CS 9749	Blues Roots	1969	15.00
—Red "360 Sound" label			
❑ CS 9749	Blues Roots	1971	12.00
—Orange label			
❑ CS 9897	Brubeck in Amsterdam	1969	15.00
—Red "360 Sound" label			
❑ CS 9897	Brubeck in Amsterdam	1971	12.00
—Orange label			
❑ C 30522	The Summit Sessions	1971	12.00
❑ G 30625 [(2)]	Adventures in Time	1971	15.00
❑ KG 31298 [(2)]	Brubeck On Campus	1972	15.00
❑ KC 32143	Brubeck at the Berlin Philharmonic	1973	12.00
❑ KG 32761 [(2)]	All-Time Greatest Hits	1974	15.00
❑ CG 33666 [(2)]	Gone with the Wind/Time Out	1975	15.00
❑ PC 37022	A Place in Time	1981	10.00
—Reissue of Odyssey LP			

COLUMBIA JAZZ MASTERPIECES

Number	Title (A Side/B Side)	Yr	NM
❑ CJ 40455	The Dave Brubeck Quartet Plays Music from West Side Story and Other Shows and Films	1987	10.00
❑ CJ 40585	Time Out	1987	10.00
❑ CJ 40627	Gone with the Wind	1987	10.00
❑ CJ 45149	Jazz Goes to College	1989	10.00

COLUMBIA LIMITED EDITION

Number	Title (A Side/B Side)	Yr	NM
❑ LE 10013	Gone with the Wind	197?	10.00

CONCORD JAZZ

Number	Title (A Side/B Side)	Yr	NM
❑ CJ-103	Back Home	1979	10.00
❑ CJ-129	Tritonis	1980	10.00
❑ CJ-178	Paper Moon	1982	10.00
❑ CJ-198	Concord on a Summer Night	1982	10.00
❑ CJ-259	For Iola	1985	10.00
❑ CJ-299	Reflections	1986	10.00
❑ CJ-317	Blue Rondo	1987	10.00
❑ CJ-353	Moscow Night	1988	10.00

CROWN

Number	Title (A Side/B Side)	Yr	NM
❑ CLP-5406 [M]	The Greats	196?	15.00
❑ CLP 5470 [M]	Dave Brubeck and the George Nielson Quartet	196?	15.00

DECCA

Number	Title (A Side/B Side)	Yr	NM
❑ DXSA 7202 [(2)]	The Light in the Wilderness	1968	15.00
—Records are individually numbered "DL 710,155" and "DL 710,156"			
❑ DL 710175	The Gates of Justice	1969	12.00
❑ DL 710181	Brubeck/Mulligan/Cincinnati	1971	12.00

DIRECT DISK

Number	Title (A Side/B Side)	Yr	NM
❑ 106 [(2)]	A Cut Above	1979	25.00

FANTASY

Number	Title (A Side/B Side)	Yr	NM
❑ 3-1 [10]	Dave Brubeck Trio	1951	150.00
❑ 3-2 [10]	Dave Brubeck Trio	1951	150.00
❑ 3-3 [10]	Dave Brubeck Octet	1951	150.00
❑ 3-4 [10]	Dave Brubeck Trio	1952	150.00
❑ 3-5 [10]	Dave Brubeck Quartet with Paul Desmond	1952	150.00
❑ 3-7 [10]	Dave Brubeck Quartet with Paul Desmond	1952	150.00
❑ 3-8 [10]	Jazz at Storyville	1953	150.00
❑ 3-10 [10]	Jazz at the Blackhawk	1953	150.00
❑ 3-11 [10]	Jazz at Oberlin	1953	100.00
—Black vinyl			
❑ 3-11 [10]	Jazz at Oberlin	1953	200.00
—Red vinyl			
❑ 3-13 [10]	Jazz at the College of the Pacific	1954	150.00
❑ 3-16 [10]	Old Sounds from San Francisco	1954	250.00
—Red or purple vinyl			
❑ 3-20 [10]	Paul and Dave's Jazz Interwoven	1955	150.00
❑ OJC-046	Jazz at Oberlin	198?	10.00
—Reissue of 3245			
❑ OJC-047	Jazz at the College of the Pacific	198?	10.00
—Reissue of 3223			
❑ OJC-101	The Dave Brubeck Octet	198?	10.00
—Reissue of Fantasy 3239			
❑ OJC-150	Re-Union	198?	10.00
❑ OJC-200	Brubeck A La Mode	1985	10.00
❑ OJC-236	Near Myth	1986	10.00
—Reissue of Fantasy 3319			
❑ 3204 [M]	Dave Brubeck Trio	195?	60.00
—Black vinyl, red label, non-flexible vinyl			
❑ 3204 [M]	Dave Brubeck Trio	1956	100.00
—Dark red vinyl; reissue of 3-1			
❑ 3204 [M]	Dave Brubeck Trio	196?	40.00
—Black vinyl, red label, flexible vinyl			
❑ 3205 [M]	Dave Brubeck Trio: Distinctive Rhythm Instrumentals	195?	60.00
—Black vinyl, red label, non-flexible vinyl			
❑ 3205 [M]	Dave Brubeck Trio: Distinctive Rhythm Instrumentals	1956	100.00
—Dark red vinyl; reissue of 3-2			
❑ 3205 [M]	Dave Brubeck Trio: Distinctive Rhythm Instrumentals	196?	40.00
—Black vinyl, red label, flexible vinyl			
❑ 3210 [M]	Jazz at the Blackhawk	195?	60.00
—Black vinyl, red label, non-flexible vinyl			
❑ 3210 [M]	Jazz at the Blackhawk	1956	100.00
—Dark red vinyl; reissue of 3-10			
❑ 3210 [M]	Jazz at the Blackhawk	196?	40.00
—Black vinyl, red label, flexible vinyl			
❑ 3223 [M]	Jazz at the College of the Pacific	195?	60.00
—Black vinyl, red label, non-flexible vinyl			
❑ 3223 [M]	Jazz at the College of the Pacific	1956	100.00
—Dark red vinyl; reissue of 3-13			
❑ 3223 [M]	Jazz at the College of the Pacific	196?	40.00
—Black vinyl, red label, flexible vinyl			

Number	Title (A Side/B Side)	Yr	NM
❑ 3229 [M]	Brubeck-Desmond	195?	60.00
—Black vinyl, red label, non-flexible vinyl			
❑ 3229 [M]	Brubeck-Desmond	1956	100.00
—Dark red vinyl; reissue of 3-5			
❑ 3229 [M]	Brubeck-Desmond	196?	40.00
—Black vinyl, red label, flexible vinyl			
❑ 3230 [M]	Dave Brubeck Quartet	195?	60.00
—Black vinyl, red label, non-flexible vinyl			
❑ 3230 [M]	Dave Brubeck Quartet	1956	100.00
—Dark red vinyl; reissue of 3-7			
❑ 3230 [M]	Dave Brubeck Quartet	196?	40.00
—Black vinyl, red label, flexible vinyl			
❑ 3239 [M]	Dave Brubeck Octet	195?	60.00
—Black vinyl, red label, non-flexible vinyl			
❑ 3239 [M]	Dave Brubeck Octet	1956	100.00
—Dark red vinyl; reissue of 3-3			
❑ 3239 [M]	Dave Brubeck Octet	196?	40.00
—Black vinyl, red label, flexible vinyl			
❑ 3240 [M]	Brubeck Desmond: Jazz at Storyville	195?	60.00
—Black vinyl, red label, non-flexible vinyl			
❑ 3240 [M]	Brubeck Desmond: Jazz at Storyville	1957	100.00
—Dark red vinyl; reissue of 3-8			
❑ 3240 [M]	Brubeck Desmond: Jazz at Storyville	196?	40.00
—Black vinyl, red label, flexible vinyl			
❑ 3245 [M]	Jazz at Oberlin	195?	60.00
—Black vinyl, red label, non-flexible vinyl			
❑ 3245 [M]	Jazz at Oberlin	1957	100.00
—Dark red vinyl; reissue of 3-11			
❑ 3245 [M]	Jazz at Oberlin	196?	40.00
—Black vinyl, red label, flexible vinyl			
❑ 3249 [M]	Brubeck & Desmond at Wilshire-Ebell	195?	60.00
—Black vinyl, red label, non-flexible vinyl			
❑ 3249 [M]	Brubeck & Desmond at Wilshire-Ebell	1957	100.00
—Dark red vinyl			
❑ 3249 [M]	Brubeck & Desmond at Wilshire-Ebell	196?	40.00
—Black vinyl, red label, flexible vinyl			
❑ 3259 [M]	Dave Brubeck Plays and Plays and Plays and Plays and...	195?	40.00
—Black vinyl, red label, non-flexible vinyl			
❑ 3259 [M]	Dave Brubeck Plays and Plays and Plays and Plays and...	196?	30.00
—Black vinyl, red label, flexible vinyl			
❑ 3259 [M]	Dave Brubeck Plays and Plays and Plays and Plays and...	1958	60.00
—Red vinyl			
❑ 3268 [M]	Re-Union	195?	40.00
—Black vinyl, red label, non-flexible vinyl			
❑ 3268 [M]	Re-Union	1958	60.00
—Red vinyl			
❑ 3268 [M]	Re-Union	196?	30.00
—Black vinyl, red label, flexible vinyl			
❑ 3298 [M]	Two Knights at the Black Hawk	1959	40.00
—Black vinyl, red label, non-flexible vinyl			
❑ 3298 [M]	Two Knights at the Black Hawk	1959	60.00
—Red vinyl			
❑ 3298 [M]	Two Knights at the Black Hawk	196?	30.00
—Black vinyl, red label, flexible vinyl			
❑ 3301 [M]	Brubeck A La Mode	196?	30.00
—Black vinyl, red label, flexible vinyl			
❑ 3301 [M]	Brubeck A La Mode	1960	40.00
—Black vinyl, red label, non-flexible vinyl			
❑ 3301 [M]	Brubeck A La Mode	1960	60.00
—Red vinyl			
❑ 3319 [M]	Near-Myth	196?	30.00
—Black vinyl, red label, flexible vinyl			
❑ 3319 [M]	Near-Myth	1961	40.00
—Black vinyl, red label, non-flexible vinyl			
❑ 3319 [M]	Near-Myth	1961	60.00
—Red vinyl			
❑ 3331 [M]	Dave Brubeck Trio Featuring Cal Tjader	196?	30.00
—Black vinyl, red label, flexible vinyl			
❑ 3331 [M]	Dave Brubeck Trio Featuring Cal Tjader	1962	40.00
—Black vinyl, red label, non-flexible vinyl			
❑ 3331 [M]	Dave Brubeck Trio Featuring Cal Tjader	1962	60.00
—Red vinyl			
❑ 3332 [M]	Brubeck Tjader	196?	30.00
—Black vinyl, red label, flexible vinyl			
❑ 3332 [M]	Brubeck Tjader	1962	40.00
—Black vinyl, red label, non-flexible vinyl			
❑ 3332 [M]	Brubeck Tjader	1962	60.00
—Red vinyl			
❑ MPF-4528	Greatest Hits from the Fantasy Years	1987	10.00
❑ 8007 [S]	Re-Union	196?	20.00
—Black vinyl, blue label, flexible vinyl			
❑ 8007 [S]	Re-Union	196?	30.00
—Black vinyl, blue label, non-flexible vinyl			
❑ 8007 [S]	Re-Union	1962	50.00
—Blue vinyl			
❑ 8047 [S]	Brubeck A La Mode	196?	20.00
—Black vinyl, blue label, flexible vinyl			

Number	Title (A Side/B Side)	Yr	NM
❑ 8047 [S]	Brubeck A La Mode	196?	30.00
—Black vinyl, blue label, non-flexible vinyl			
❑ 8047 [S]	Brubeck A La Mode	1962	50.00
—Blue vinyl			
❑ 8063 [S]	Near-Myth	196?	20.00
—Black vinyl, blue label, flexible vinyl			
❑ 8063 [S]	Near-Myth	196?	30.00
—Black vinyl, blue label, non-flexible vinyl			
❑ 8063 [S]	Near-Myth	1962	50.00
—Blue vinyl			
❑ 8069 [R]	Jazz at Oberlin	196?	15.00
—Black vinyl, blue label, flexible vinyl			
❑ 8069 [R]	Jazz at Oberlin	196?	20.00
—Black vinyl, blue label, non-flexible vinyl			
❑ 8069 [R]	Jazz at Oberlin	1962	40.00
—Blue vinyl			
❑ 8073 [R]	Dave Brubeck Trio Featuring Cal Tjader	196?	15.00
—Black vinyl, blue label, flexible vinyl			
❑ 8073 [R]	Dave Brubeck Trio Featuring Cal Tjader	1962	20.00
—Black vinyl, blue label, non-flexible vinyl			
❑ 8073 [R]	Dave Brubeck Trio Featuring Cal Tjader	1962	40.00
—Blue vinyl			
❑ 8074 [R]	Brubeck Tjader	196?	15.00
—Black vinyl, blue label, flexible vinyl			
❑ 8074 [R]	Brubeck Tjader	1962	20.00
—Black vinyl, blue label, non-flexible vinyl			
❑ 8074 [R]	Brubeck Tjader	1962	40.00
—Blue vinyl			
❑ 8078 [R]	Jazz at the College of the Pacific	196?	15.00
—Black vinyl, blue label, flexible vinyl			
❑ 8078 [R]	Jazz at the College of the Pacific	196?	20.00
—Black vinyl, blue label, non-flexible vinyl			
❑ 8078 [R]	Jazz at the College of the Pacific	1962	40.00
—Blue vinyl			
❑ 8080 [R]	Jazz at Storyville	196?	15.00
—Black vinyl, blue label, flexible vinyl			
❑ 8080 [R]	Jazz at Storyville	1962	20.00
—Black vinyl, blue label, non-flexible vinyl			
❑ 8080 [R]	Jazz at Storyville	1962	40.00
—Blue vinyl			
❑ 8081 [R]	Two Knights at the Blackhawk	196?	15.00
—Black vinyl, blue label, flexible vinyl			
❑ 8081 [R]	Two Knights at the Blackhawk	1962	20.00
—Black vinyl, blue label, non-flexible vinyl			
❑ 8081 [R]	Two Knights at the Blackhawk	1962	40.00
—Blue vinyl			
❑ 8092 [R]	Brubeck-Desmond	196?	15.00
—Black vinyl, blue label, flexible vinyl			
❑ 8092 [R]	Brubeck-Desmond	1962	20.00
—Black vinyl, blue label, non-flexible vinyl			
❑ 8092 [R]	Brubeck-Desmond	1962	40.00
—Blue vinyl			
❑ 8093 [R]	Dave Brubeck Quartet	196?	15.00
—Black vinyl, blue label, flexible vinyl			
❑ 8093 [R]	Dave Brubeck Quartet	1962	20.00
—Black vinyl, blue label, non-flexible vinyl			
❑ 8093 [R]	Dave Brubeck Quartet	1962	40.00
—Blue vinyl			
❑ 8094 [R]	Dave Brubeck Octet	196?	15.00
—Black vinyl, blue label, flexible vinyl			
❑ 8094 [R]	Dave Brubeck Octet	1962	20.00
—Black vinyl, blue label, non-flexible vinyl			
❑ 8094 [R]	Dave Brubeck Octet	1962	40.00
—Blue vinyl			
❑ 8095 [S]	Brubeck and Desmond at Wilshire-Ebell	196?	20.00
—Black vinyl, blue label, flexible vinyl			
❑ 8095 [S]	Brubeck and Desmond at Wilshire-Ebell	1962	30.00
—Black vinyl, blue label, non-flexible vinyl			
❑ 8095 [S]	Brubeck and Desmond at Wilshire-Ebell	1962	50.00
—Blue vinyl			
❑ 24726 [(2)]	The Dave Brubeck Trio	198?	15.00
❑ 24727 [(2)]	Brubeck-Desmond	1982	15.00
❑ 24728 [(2)]	Stardust	198?	15.00
HARMONY			
❑ HS 11253	Instant Brubeck	1968	12.00
❑ HS 11336	Gone with the Wind	1969	12.00
HORIZON			
❑ SP-703	1975: The Duets	1975	12.00
❑ SP-714	The Dave Brubeck Quartet 25th Anniversary	1976	12.00
JAZZTONE			
❑ J-1272 [M]	Best of Brubeck	195?	40.00
MOBILE FIDELITY			
❑ 1-216	We're All Together Again for the First Time	1994	60.00
—Audiophile vinyl			
MOON			
❑ 028	St. Louis Blues	1992	20.00
ODYSSEY			
❑ 32160248	A Place in Time	1968	12.00

Number	Title (A Side/B Side)	Yr	NM
TOMATO			
❑ 7018	The New Brubeck Quartet at Montreux	1978	12.00

BRUCE, JACK
Ex-member of CREAM.

45s

Number	Title (A Side/B Side)	Yr	NM
RSO			
❑ 507	Keep It Down/Keep On Wondering	1975	6.00

Albums

Number	Title (A Side/B Side)	Yr	NM
ATCO			
❑ SD 33-306	Songs for a Tailor	1969	15.00
❑ SD 33-349	Things We Like	1971	15.00
❑ SD 33-365	Harmony Row	1971	15.00
EPIC			
❑ JE 36827	I've Always Wanted to Do This	1980	10.00
❑ FE 45279	A Question of Time	1989	15.00
POLYDOR			
❑ PD2-3505 [(2)]	Jack Bruce At His Best	1972	15.00
RSO			
❑ RS-1-3021	How's Tricks	1977	10.00
❑ SO 4805	Out of the Storm	1974	10.00

BRUCE, JACK/ROBIN TROWER
Also see each artist's individual listings.

Albums

Number	Title (A Side/B Side)	Yr	NM
CHRYSALIS			
❑ CHR 1352	Truce	1982	10.00
❑ PV 41352	Truce	1983	8.00
—Reissue			

BRUCE, LENNY

Albums

Number	Title (A Side/B Side)	Yr	NM
BIZARRE			
❑ 2XS 6329 [(2)]	The Berkeley Concert	1969	25.00
DOUGLAS			
❑ 2	To Is a Preposition, Come Is a Verb	196?	20.00
❑ 788	The Essential Lenny Bruce Politics	1968	20.00
❑ Z 30872	What I Was Arrested For	1971	15.00
—Reissue of 2			
FANTASY			
❑ FP-1 [DJ]	The Promo Album	196?	200.00
—Promo-only compilation of material from albums 7001, 7003, 7007 and 7011			
❑ 7001 [M]	Interviews of Our Times	1959	40.00
—Non-flexible black vinyl; cover changed to blue tint			
❑ 7001 [M]	Interviews of Our Times	1959	100.00
—Opaque, non-flexible red vinyl; tan cover with Lenny Bruce's name blacked out throughout the back			
❑ 7001 [M]	Interviews of Our Times	1962	20.00
—Flexible black vinyl			
❑ 7001 [M]	Interviews of Our Times	1962	40.00
—Translucent, flexible red vinyl			
❑ 7003 [M]	The Sick Humor of Lenny Bruce	1959	40.00
—Non-flexible black vinyl			
❑ 7003 [M]	The Sick Humor of Lenny Bruce	1959	100.00
—Opaque, non-flexible red vinyl			
❑ 7003 [M]	The Sick Humor of Lenny Bruce	1962	20.00
—Flexible black vinyl			
❑ 7003 [M]	The Sick Humor of Lenny Bruce	1962	40.00
—Translucent, flexible red vinyl			
❑ 7007 [M]	I Am Not a Nut, Elect Me	1960	40.00
—Non-flexible black vinyl			
❑ 7007 [M]	I Am Not a Nut, Elect Me	1960	100.00
—Opaque, non-flexible red vinyl			
❑ 7007 [M]	I Am Not a Nut, Elect Me	1962	20.00
—Flexible black vinyl			
❑ 7007 [M]	I Am Not a Nut, Elect Me	1962	40.00
—Translucent, flexible red vinyl			
❑ 7011 [M]	Lenny Bruce, American	1961	40.00
—Non-flexible black vinyl			
❑ 7011 [M]	Lenny Bruce, American	1961	100.00
—Opaque, non-flexible red vinyl			
❑ 7011 [M]	Lenny Bruce, American	1962	20.00
—Flexible black vinyl			
❑ 7011 [M]	Lenny Bruce, American	1962	40.00
—Translucent, flexible red vinyl			
❑ 7012 [M]	The Best of Lenny Bruce	1962	20.00
—Black vinyl			
❑ 7012 [M]	The Best of Lenny Bruce	1962	50.00
—Red vinyl			
❑ 7017	Thank You Masked Man	1971	15.00
❑ 34201 [(3)]	Lenny Bruce at the Curran Theater	1971	40.00
❑ 79003 [(2)]	The Real Lenny Bruce	1975	20.00
LENNY BRUCE			
❑ LB-3001/2 [M]	Lenny Bruce Is Out Again	196?	300.00
—Privately pressed version with white labels and Lenny's address on cover			
❑ LB-9001/2 [10]	Warning: Sale of This Album...	1962	500.00
—Privately pressed LP with routines used as evidence in Lenny's obscenity trial			

Except when noted otherwise, VG = 25% of NM, and VG+ = 50% of NM. (Example: VG = $2.00, VG+ = $4.00 and NM = $8.00.)

Number	Title (A Side/B Side)	Yr	NM
PHILLIES			
❑ PHLP-4010 [M]	Lenny Bruce Is Out Again	1966	100.00
—Reissue of Lenny Bruce 3001/2			
UNITED ARTISTS			
❑ UAL 3580 [M]	The Midnight Concert	1967	25.00
❑ UAS 6580	The Midnight Concert	1967	20.00
❑ UAS 6794	The Midnight Concert	1972	15.00
—Reissue of 6580			
❑ UAS 9800 [(3)]	Lenny Bruce/Carnegie Hall	1972	25.00
WARNER/SPECTOR			
❑ SP 9101	The Law, the Language and Lenny Bruce	1975	15.00

BRUCE, TOMMY

45s

Number	Title (A Side/B Side)	Yr	NM
CAPITOL			
❑ 4403	Ain't Misbehavin'/ Got the Water Boilin'	1960	12.00
❑ 5354	It's Driving Me Wild/ Over Suzanne	1965	10.00

BRUCE AND TERRY

BRUCE JOHNSTON and TERRY MELCHER.

45s

Number	Title (A Side/B Side)	Yr	NM
COLUMBIA			
❑ 42956	Custom Machine/ Makaha at Midnight	1964	20.00
❑ 43055	Summer Means Fun/Yeah!	1964	20.00
❑ 43238	I Love You Model T/Carmen	1965	20.00
❑ 43378	Raining in My Heart/ Four Strong Winds	1965	16.00
❑ 43479	Thank You Baby/Come Love	1965	16.00
❑ 43582	Don't Run Away/ Girl It's All Right Now	1966	16.00
EQUINOX			
❑ PB-10238	Rebecca/Take It to Mexico	1975	10.00
—As "Bruce Johnston and Terry Melcher"			

BRUFORD, BILL

Albums

Number	Title (A Side/B Side)	Yr	NM
EDITIONS EG			
❑ EGS 48	Earthworks	1987	10.00
❑ EGS 67	Master Strokes 1978-1985	198?	10.00
❑ EGS 106	The Bruford Tapes	1979	10.00
POLYDOR			
❑ PD-1-6149	Feels Good to Me	1977	10.00
❑ PD-1-6205	One of a Kind	1979	10.00
❑ PD-1-6261	Gradually Going Tornado	1980	10.00

BRUINS, THE

45s

Number	Title (A Side/B Side)	Yr	NM
COMET			
❑ 2167	Nobody But You/One More Try	1964	25.00
GENERAL AMERICAN			
❑ 721	Go On and Cry/Can't Believe That You've Grown Up	1965	40.00
ROULETTE			
❑ 4566	Believe Me/The Slide	1964	20.00

BRUNO, BRUCE

45s

Number	Title (A Side/B Side)	Yr	NM
ROULETTE			
❑ 4386	Hey Little One/ Some Time, Some Place	1961	20.00
❑ 4427	Venus in Blue Jeans/ Dear Joanne	1962	20.00

BRUTE FORCE

45s

Number	Title (A Side/B Side)	Yr	NM
B.T. PUPPY			
❑ 561	War/Overture to Hello	1970	8.00
COLUMBIA			
❑ 44091	Cudd'ly/In Jim's Garage	1967	8.00
❑ 44371	Brute's Party/Toys for Tots	1967	8.00
WARNER BROS.			
❑ 7224	Adam & Evening/ The Purpose of a Circus	1968	8.00

Albums

Number	Title (A Side/B Side)	Yr	NM
B.T. PUPPY			
❑ BTPS-1015	Extemporaneous	1971	300.00
COLUMBIA			
❑ CL 2615 [M]	I, Brute Force — Confections of Love	1967	20.00
❑ CS 9415 [S]	I, Brute Force — Confections of Love	1967	20.00
EMBRYO			
❑ 522	Brute Force	1970	20.00
—Different band			

BRYAN, BILLY

See GENE PITNEY.

BRYAN, WES

45s

Number	Title (A Side/B Side)	Yr	NM
CLOCK			
❑ 1013	Honey Baby/So Blue Over You	1959	20.00
ROULETTE			
❑ 4289	I Guess I'll Never Know/ Melodie D'Amour	1960	15.00
UNITED ARTISTS			
❑ 102	Tiny Spacemen/Lonesome Love	1957	30.00
❑ 102 [PS]	Tiny Spacemen/Lonesome Love	1957	60.00
❑ 122	Wait for Me Baby/Freeze!	1958	25.00

BRYANT, J.D.

45s

Number	Title (A Side/B Side)	Yr	NM
SHRINE			
❑ 108	I Won't Be Coming Back/Walk On	1966	4000.
—VG 1500; VG+ 2750			

BRYANT, JAY DEE

45s

Number	Title (A Side/B Side)	Yr	NM
ENJOY			
❑ 2017	You're Hurting Me/Get It	1964	25.00
HERALD			
❑ 570	Come Summer/ I Could Have Cried	1962	30.00
ISLAND			
❑ 008	I Want to Thank You Baby/ Standing Ovation for Love	1975	30.00
JOSIE			
❑ 998	You Don't Know/ Let Me Fix It for You	1968	50.00

BRYANT, LILLIE

Of BILLY AND LILLIE.

45s

Number	Title (A Side/B Side)	Yr	NM
SWAN			
❑ 4029	Smokey Grey Eyes/ I'll Never Be Free	1959	12.00

BRYANT, RAY

45s

Number	Title (A Side/B Side)	Yr	NM
ATLANTIC JAZZ			
❑ 5102	Let It Be/Shake-A-Lady	1971	4.00
CADET			
❑ 5535	Gotta Travel On/ It Was a Very Good Year	1966	6.00
❑ 5558	If You Go Away/Slow Freight	1967	6.00
❑ 5575	Ode to Billie Joe/Ramblin'	1967	6.00
❑ 5580	City Tribal Dance/Little Suzie	1967	6.00
❑ 5587	Pata Pata/Doing My Thing	1968	6.00
❑ 5598	To Sir with Love/ Dinner on the Grounds	1968	5.00
❑ 5615	Mrs. Robinson/Poochie	1968	5.00
❑ 5625	Little Green Apples/ Up Above the Rock	1968	5.00
❑ 5639	After Hours/ Quizas, Quizas, Quizas	1969	5.00
COLUMBIA			
❑ 31339 [S]	(contents unknown)	1961	12.00
❑ 31340 [S]	(contents unknown)	1961	12.00
❑ 31341 [S]	(contents unknown)	1961	12.00
❑ 31342 [S]	(contents unknown)	1961	12.00
❑ 31343 [S]	(contents unknown)	1961	12.00
—Anyone who can fill in these gaps — the above 5 all are Columbia "Stereo 7" singles — please let us know.			
❑ 41553	Little Suzie (Part 1)/ Little Suzie (Part 2)	1960	10.00
❑ 41628	The Madison Time (Part 1)/ The Madison Time (Part 2)	1960	10.00
❑ 41628 [PS]	The Madison Time (Part 1)/ The Madison Time (Part 2)	1960	15.00
❑ 41761	C Jam Blues (Part 1)/ C Jam Blues (Part 2)	1960	10.00
❑ 41940	Sack O' Woe/Walk No More	1961	10.00
❑ 42015	Moonrise/First Lady	1961	10.00
❑ 42390	After Hours/Tonk	1962	10.00
MCA			
❑ 53322	The Madison Time/ Mama Didn't Lie	1988	3.00
—B-side by Jan Bradley			
❑ 53322 [PS]	The Madison Time/ Mama Didn't Lie	1988	3.00
NEW JAZZ			
❑ 505	Joy/Stocking Feet	1959	12.00
SIGNATURE			
❑ 12026	Little Suzie (Part 2)/ Little Suzie (Part 4)	1960	12.00
SUE			
❑ 108	Shake a Lady/Blues March	1964	8.00
❑ 125	Goldfinger/Adalia	1965	8.00
❑ 801	Glissamba/Joey	1963	8.00

Albums

Number	Title (A Side/B Side)	Yr	NM
ATLANTIC			
❑ SD 1564	MCMLXX	1970	15.00
❑ SD 1626	Alone at Montreux	1972	12.00
CADET			
❑ LP-767 [M]	Gotta Travel On	1966	15.00
❑ LPS-767 [S]	Gotta Travel On	1966	20.00
❑ LP-778 [M]	Lonesome Traveler	1966	15.00
❑ LPS-778 [S]	Lonesome Traveler	1966	20.00
❑ LP-781 [M]	Slow Freight	1967	15.00
❑ LPS-781 [S]	Slow Freight	1967	20.00
❑ LP-793 [M]	The Ray Bryant Touch	1967	20.00
❑ LPS-793 [S]	The Ray Bryant Touch	1967	15.00
❑ LP-801 [M]	Take a Bryant Step	1967	20.00
❑ LPS-801 [S]	Take a Bryant Step	1967	15.00
❑ LPS-818	Up Above the Rock	1968	15.00
❑ LPS-830	Sound Ray	1969	15.00
❑ 50038 [(2)]	It Was a Very Good Year	1973	15.00
❑ 50052	In the Cut	1974	12.00
CLASSIC JAZZ			
❑ 130	Hot Turkey	198?	10.00
COLUMBIA			
❑ CL 1449 [M]	Little Susie	1960	20.00
❑ CL 1476 [M]	The Madison Time	1960	25.00
❑ CL 1633 [M]	Con Alma	1961	20.00
❑ CL 1746 [M]	Dancing the Big Twist	1962	20.00
❑ CL 1867 [M]	Hollywood Jazz Beat	1962	20.00
❑ CS 8244 [S]	Little Susie	1960	25.00
❑ CS 8276 [S]	The Madison Time	1960	30.00
❑ CS 8433 [S]	Con Alma	1961	25.00
❑ CS 8546 [S]	Dancing the Big Twist	1962	25.00
❑ CS 8667 [S]	Hollywood Jazz Beat	1962	25.00
COLUMBIA JAZZ MASTERPIECES			
❑ CJ 44058	Con Alma	1988	10.00
EMARCY			
❑ 832235-1	Ray Bryant Plays Basie and Ellington	1987	12.00
❑ 832589-1	The Ray Bryant Trio Today	1988	12.00
❑ 836368-1	Golden Earrings	1989	12.00
EPIC			
❑ LN 3279 [M]	Ray Bryant Trio	1956	70.00
FANTASY			
❑ OJC-213	Alone with the Blues	1987	10.00
—Reissue			
❑ OJC-371	Montreux '77	1989	10.00
—Reissue of Pablo Live 2308 201			
NEW JAZZ			
❑ NJLP-8213 [M]	Alone with the Blues	1959	50.00
—Purple label			
❑ NJLP-8213 [M]	Alone with the Blues	1965	25.00
—Blue label with trident logo			
❑ NJLP-8227 [M]	Ray Bryant Trio	1959	50.00
—Purple label; reissue of Prestige 7098			
❑ NJLP-8227 [M]	Ray Bryant Trio	1965	25.00
—Blue label with trident logo			
PABLO			
❑ 2310764	Here's Ray Bryant	1976	10.00
❑ 2310798	Solo Flight	1977	10.00
❑ 2310820	All Blues	1978	10.00
❑ 2310860	Potpourri	1981	10.00
❑ 2405402	The Best of Ray Bryant	198?	10.00
PABLO LIVE			
❑ 2308201	Montreux '77	1977	10.00
PRESTIGE			
❑ PRLP-7098 [M]	Ray Bryant Trio	1957	70.00
❑ PRLP-7837	Alone with the Blues	1971	15.00
—Reissue of New Jazz 8213			
❑ PRT-7837	Alone with the Blues	1973	12.00
—Reissue; "Distributed by Fantasy Records, Berkeley, California" on label			
❑ 24038 [(2)]	Me and the Blues	1973	15.00
SIGNATURE			
❑ SM-6008 [M]	Ray Bryant Plays	1960	200.00
❑ SS-6008 [S]	Ray Bryant Plays	1960	250.00
SUE			
❑ LP-1016 [M]	Groove House	1963	40.00
❑ LPS-1016 [S]	Groove House	1963	50.00
❑ LP-1019 [M]	Live at Basin Street	1964	40.00
❑ LPS-1019 [S]	Live at Basin Street	1964	50.00
❑ LP-1032 [M]	Cold Turkey	1964	40.00
❑ LPS-1032 [S]	Cold Turkey	1964	50.00
❑ STLP-1036 [M]	Ray Bryant Soul	1965	40.00
❑ STLPS-1036 [S]	Ray Bryant Soul	1965	50.00

BRYDS, THE

45s

Number	Title (A Side/B Side)	Yr	NM
REYNARD			
❑ 10038	Your Lies/Why Did You Have to Break My Heart	1965	400.00

Number	Title (A Side/B Side)	Yr	NM

BRYNDLE Andrew Gold, Karla Bonoff, Wendy Waldman, Kenny Edwards.

45s

A&M

Number	Title (A Side/B Side)	Yr	NM
❑ 1252	Let's Go Home and Start Again/ Woke Up This Morning	1971	10.00

BUBBLE PUPPY, THE Also see DEMIAN.

45s

INTERNATIONAL ARTISTS

Number	Title (A Side/B Side)	Yr	NM
❑ 128	Hot Smoke and Sasafrass/ Lonely	1969	20.00
❑ 133	Beginning/If I Had a Reason	1969	25.00
❑ 136	Days of Our Time/ Thinkin' About Thinkin'	1969	25.00
❑ 138	What Do You See/ Hurry Sundown	1970	25.00
❑ 138 [DJ]	What Do You See/ Hurry Sundown	1970	50.00

—Green vinyl promo

Albums

INTERNATIONAL ARTISTS

Number	Title (A Side/B Side)	Yr	NM
❑ 10	A Gathering of Promises	1969	100.00

—Original does not have "Masterfonics" in the dead wax

Number	Title (A Side/B Side)	Yr	NM
❑ 10	A Gathering of Promises	1979	25.00

—Reissue has "Masterfonics" in the dead wax

BUBI AND BOB

45s

SPHINX

Number	Title (A Side/B Side)	Yr	NM
❑ 1201	The Mummy/Biscayne Beat	1959	30.00

BUCCANEERS, THE

45s

RAINBOW

Number	Title (A Side/B Side)	Yr	NM
❑ 211	Dear Ruth/Fine Brown Flame	1953	800.00

RAMA

Number	Title (A Side/B Side)	Yr	NM
❑ 21	The Stars Will Remember/ Come Back My Love	1954	2000.
❑ 24	In the Mission of St. Augustine/ You Did Me Wrong	1954	2000.

SOUTHERN

Number	Title (A Side/B Side)	Yr	NM
❑ 101	Dear Ruth/Fine Brown Flame	1953	4000.

—All copies are on red vinyl. VG 2000; VG+ 3000

BUCHANAN, BILL Also see BUCHANAN AND ANCELL; BUCHANAN AND CELLA; BUCHANAN AND GOODMAN; BUCHANAN AND GREENFIELD.

45s

GONE

Number	Title (A Side/B Side)	Yr	NM
❑ 5032	The Thing/Happy Day	1958	30.00

UNITED ARTISTS

Number	Title (A Side/B Side)	Yr	NM
❑ 531	The Night Before Halloween/ Beware	1962	15.00

BUCHANAN, ROY

45s

ATLANTIC

Number	Title (A Side/B Side)	Yr	NM
❑ 3342	Keep What You Got/Caruso	1976	4.00
❑ 3414	The Circle/Green Onions	1977	4.00
❑ 3433	The Circle/(B-side unknown)	1977	4.00

POLYDOR

Number	Title (A Side/B Side)	Yr	NM
❑ 14149	Haunted House/Cajun	1972	5.00
❑ 14174	Filthy Teddy/Thank You Lord	1973	5.00
❑ 14178	Sweet Dreams/John's Blues	1973	5.00
❑ 14265	Rescue Me/I'm a Ram	1974	5.00

SWAN

Number	Title (A Side/B Side)	Yr	NM
❑ 4088	Mule Train Stomp/Pretty Please	1961	12.00

Albums

ALLIGATOR

Number	Title (A Side/B Side)	Yr	NM
❑ AL-4741	When a Guitar Plays the Blues	1985	10.00
❑ AL-4747	Dancing on the Edge	1986	10.00
❑ AL-4756	Hot Wires	1988	10.00

ATLANTIC

Number	Title (A Side/B Side)	Yr	NM
❑ SD 18170	A Street Called Straight	1976	12.00
❑ SD 18219	Loading Zone	1977	12.00
❑ SD 19138	Loading Zone	1978	8.00

—Reissue of 18219

Number	Title (A Side/B Side)	Yr	NM
❑ SD 19170	You're Not Alone	1978	12.00

BIOYA

Number	Title (A Side/B Side)	Yr	NM
❑ MM-519	Buch and the Snake Stretchers	1971	300.00

POLYDOR

Number	Title (A Side/B Side)	Yr	NM
❑ PD-5033	Roy Buchanan	1972	15.00
❑ PD-5046	Second Album	1973	15.00
❑ PD-6020	That's What I Am Here For	1974	15.00
❑ PD-6035	In the Beginning	1974	15.00
❑ PD-6048	Live Stock	1975	15.00

WATERHOUSE

Number	Title (A Side/B Side)	Yr	NM
❑ 12	My Babe	1981	10.00

BUCHANAN AND ANCELL Also see BILL BUCHANAN.

45s

FLYING SAUCER

Number	Title (A Side/B Side)	Yr	NM
❑ 501	The Creature/Meet the Creature	1957	40.00

BUCHANAN AND CELLA Also see BILL BUCHANAN.

45s

ABC-PARAMOUNT

Number	Title (A Side/B Side)	Yr	NM
❑ 10033	String Along with Pal-O-Mine/ More and More String Along with Pal-O-Mine	1959	25.00

BUCHANAN AND GOODMAN Also see BILL BUCHANAN; DICKIE GOODMAN.

45s

COMIC

Number	Title (A Side/B Side)	Yr	NM
❑ 500	Flying Saucer the Third/ The Cha Cha Lesson	1959	40.00

LUNIVERSE

Number	Title (A Side/B Side)	Yr	NM
❑ 101	The Flying Saucer Part 1/ The Flying Saucer Part 2	1956	50.00

—Most labels have the entire word "Luniverse" typeset

Number	Title (A Side/B Side)	Yr	NM
❑ 101	The Flying Saucer Part 1/ The Flying Saucer Part 2	1956	100.00

—Original labels have a handwritten "L" at the beginning of the printed word "Universe"

Number	Title (A Side/B Side)	Yr	NM
❑ 101X	Back to Earth Part 1/ Back to Earth Part 2	1956	200.00
❑ 102	Buchanan and Goodman On Trial/Crazy	1956	40.00
❑ 102X	Public Opinion Part 1/ Public Opinion Part 2	1956	—

—Not known to exist

Number	Title (A Side/B Side)	Yr	NM
❑ 103	The Banana Boat Story/ The Mystery (In Slow Motion)	1957	40.00
❑ 105	Flying Saucer The 2nd/ Martian Melody	1957	40.00
❑ 107	Santa and the Satellite Part 1/ Santa and the Satellite Part 2	1957	40.00
❑ 108	The Flying Saucer Goes West/ Saucer Serenade	1958	40.00

NOVELTY

Number	Title (A Side/B Side)	Yr	NM
❑ 301	Frankenstein of '59/ Frankenstein Returns	1959	40.00

BUCHANAN AND GREENFIELD Also see BILL BUCHANAN.

45s

NOVEL

Number	Title (A Side/B Side)	Yr	NM
❑ 711	The Invasion/ What a Lovely Party	1964	30.00

—Originals have all-red labels

Number	Title (A Side/B Side)	Yr	NM
❑ 711	The Invasion/ What a Lovely Party	1972	8.00

—Red and white label reissue

BUCHANAN BROTHERS Early version of CASHMAN, PISTILLI AND WEST.

45s

EVENT

Number	Title (A Side/B Side)	Yr	NM
❑ 201	Get Down with the People/ You Don't Know	1970	6.00
❑ 205	Don't Stop Now/You Don't Know	1971	6.00
❑ 3302	Medicine Man (Part 1)/ Medicine Man (Part 2)	1969	6.00
❑ 3305	Son of a Lovin' Man/ I'll Never Get Enough	1969	6.00
❑ 3307	A Feeling That I Get/ The Last Time	1969	6.00
❑ 3308	Sad Song with a Happy Soul/ Rusianna	1970	6.00

Albums

EVENT

Number	Title (A Side/B Side)	Yr	NM
❑ ES-101	Medicine Man	1969	25.00

BUCHANANS, THE

45s

HIT

Number	Title (A Side/B Side)	Yr	NM
❑ 277	Kind of a Drag/98.6	1967	8.00

—B-side by the Jalopy Five

BUCK, CHARLIE

45s

TAD

Number	Title (A Side/B Side)	Yr	NM
❑ 104	I Wish I Were A Christmas Tree/ We Can't Miss This Christmas	1962	12.00

BUCKACRE

45s

MCA

Number	Title (A Side/B Side)	Yr	NM
❑ 40616	Love Never Lasts Forever/ Bound to Be Blue	1976	4.00
❑ 40702	Just Another Night/ Morning Comes	1977	4.00
❑ 40919	Star That Shines/ Tear Down the Walls	1978	4.00

Albums

MCA

Number	Title (A Side/B Side)	Yr	NM
❑ 2218	Morning Comes	1976	10.00
❑ 2365	Buckacre	1978	10.00

BUCKEYES, THE

45s

DELUXE

Number	Title (A Side/B Side)	Yr	NM
❑ 6110	Since I Fell for You/My Only You	1957	300.00
❑ 6126	Dottie Baby/Begging You Please	1957	400.00

BUCKINGHAM, LINDSEY

12-Inch Singles

ELEKTRA

Number	Title (A Side/B Side)	Yr	NM
❑ ED 4991 [DJ]	Go Insane (same on both sides)	1984	6.00

WARNER BROS.

Number	Title (A Side/B Side)	Yr	NM
❑ PRO-A-2055 [DJ]	Holiday Road (same on both sides)	1983	10.00

45s

ASYLUM

Number	Title (A Side/B Side)	Yr	NM
❑ 47223	Trouble/Mary Lee Jones	1981	4.00
❑ 47223 [PS]	Trouble/Mary Lee Jones	1981	4.00
❑ 47408	It Was I/Love from Here, Love from There	1982	4.00

ELEKTRA

Number	Title (A Side/B Side)	Yr	NM
❑ 69675	Slow Dancing/D.W. Suite	1984	3.00
❑ 69714	Go Insane/Play in the Rain	1984	3.00
❑ 69714 [PS]	Go Insane/Play in the Rain	1984	4.00

WARNER BROS.

Number	Title (A Side/B Side)	Yr	NM
❑ 29570	Holiday Road/The Trip (Theme from Vacation)	1983	4.00

—B-side by Ralph Burns

Albums

ASYLUM

Number	Title (A Side/B Side)	Yr	NM
❑ 5E-561	Law and Order	1981	10.00
❑ 512970	Gift of Screws	2008	22.00

ELEKTRA

Number	Title (A Side/B Side)	Yr	NM
❑ 60363	Go Insane	1984	10.00

BUCKINGHAM NICKS Lindsey Buckingham and Stephanie (later known as Stevie) Nicks. Also see FLEETWOOD MAC.

45s

POLYDOR

Number	Title (A Side/B Side)	Yr	NM
❑ 14209	Don't Let Me Down Again/The Races Are Run	1973	50.00
❑ 14229	Crying in the Night/Without a Leg to Stand On	1974	50.00
❑ 14335	Don't Let Me Down Again/Crystal	1976	30.00
❑ 14428	Crying in the Night/Stephanie	1977	30.00
❑ 14428 [PS]	Crying in the Night/Stephanie	1977	60.00

Albums

POLYDOR

Number	Title (A Side/B Side)	Yr	NM
❑ PD-5058	Buckingham Nicks	1973	40.00

—Gatefold cover

Number	Title (A Side/B Side)	Yr	NM
❑ PD-5058	Buckingham Nicks	1975	12.00

—Regular cover

BUCKINGHAMS, THE (1) Chicago band. Also see THE FALLING PEBBLES. Records on Laurie and Seg-Way are by a different Buckinghams who are outside the scope of this book.

45s

COLUMBIA

Number	Title (A Side/B Side)	Yr	NM
❑ 44053	Don't You Care/ Why Don't You Love Me	1967	8.00
❑ 44053 [PS]	Don't You Care/ Why Don't You Love Me	1967	12.00
❑ 44182	Mercy, Mercy, Mercy/ You Are Gone	1967	8.00
❑ 44182 [PS]	Mercy, Mercy, Mercy/ You Are Gone	1967	12.00
❑ 44254	Hey Baby (They're Playing Our Song)/And Our Love	1967	8.00
❑ 44254 [PS]	Hey Baby (They're Playing Our Song)/And Our Love	1967	12.00
❑ 44378	Susan/Foreign Policy	1967	8.00
❑ 44378 [PS]	Susan/Foreign Policy	1967	12.00
❑ 44533	Back in Love Again/ You Misunderstand Me	1968	8.00
❑ 44533 [PS]	Back in Love Again/ You Misunderstand Me	1968	12.00
❑ 44672	Where Did You Come From/ Song of the Breeze	1968	8.00
❑ 44672 [PS]	Where Did You Come From/ Song of the Breeze	1968	12.00
❑ 44790	This Is How Much I Love You/ Can't You Find the Words	1969	8.00

Except when noted otherwise, VG = 25% of NM, and VG+ = 50% of NM. (Example: VG = $2.00, VG+ = $4.00 and NM = $8.00.)

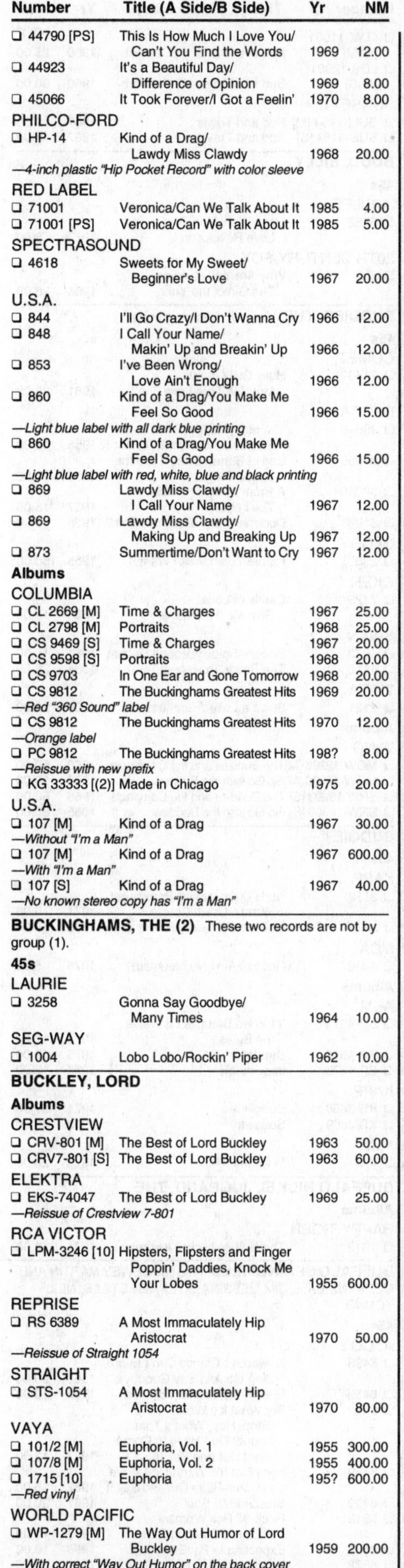

Number	Title (A Side/B Side)	Yr	NM
❑ 44790 [PS]	This Is How Much I Love You/ Can't You Find the Words	1969	12.00
❑ 44923	It's a Beautiful Day/ Difference of Opinion	1969	8.00
❑ 45066	It Took Forever/I Got a Feelin'	1970	8.00

PHILCO-FORD

Number	Title (A Side/B Side)	Yr	NM
❑ HP-14	Kind of a Drag/ Lawdy Miss Clawdy	1968	20.00

—4-inch plastic "Hip Pocket Record" with color sleeve

RED LABEL

Number	Title (A Side/B Side)	Yr	NM
❑ 71001	Veronica/Can We Talk About It	1985	4.00
❑ 71001 [PS]	Veronica/Can We Talk About It	1985	5.00

SPECTRASOUND

Number	Title (A Side/B Side)	Yr	NM
❑ 4618	Sweets for My Sweet/ Beginner's Love	1967	20.00

U.S.A.

Number	Title (A Side/B Side)	Yr	NM
❑ 844	I'll Go Crazy/I Don't Wanna Cry	1966	12.00
❑ 848	I Call Your Name/ Makin' Up and Breakin' Up	1966	12.00
❑ 853	I've Been Wrong/ Love Ain't Enough	1966	12.00
❑ 860	Kind of a Drag/You Make Me Feel So Good	1966	15.00

—Light blue label with all dark blue printing

Number	Title (A Side/B Side)	Yr	NM
❑ 860	Kind of a Drag/You Make Me Feel So Good	1966	15.00

—Light blue label with red, white, blue and black printing

Number	Title (A Side/B Side)	Yr	NM
❑ 869	Lawdy Miss Clawdy/ I Call Your Name	1967	12.00
❑ 869	Lawdy Miss Clawdy/ Making Up and Breaking Up	1967	12.00
❑ 873	Summertime/Don't Want to Cry	1967	12.00

Albums

COLUMBIA

Number	Title (A Side/B Side)	Yr	NM
❑ CL 2669 [M]	Time & Charges	1967	25.00
❑ CL 2798 [M]	Portraits	1968	25.00
❑ CS 9469 [S]	Time & Charges	1967	20.00
❑ CS 9598 [S]	Portraits	1968	20.00
❑ CS 9703	In One Ear and Gone Tomorrow	1968	20.00
❑ CS 9812	The Buckinghams Greatest Hits	1969	20.00

—Red "360 Sound" label

Number	Title (A Side/B Side)	Yr	NM
❑ CS 9812	The Buckinghams Greatest Hits	1970	12.00

—Orange label

Number	Title (A Side/B Side)	Yr	NM
❑ PC 9812	The Buckinghams Greatest Hits	198?	8.00

—Reissue with new prefix

Number	Title (A Side/B Side)	Yr	NM
❑ KG 33333 [(2)]	Made in Chicago	1975	20.00

U.S.A.

Number	Title (A Side/B Side)	Yr	NM
❑ 107 [M]	Kind of a Drag	1967	30.00

—Without "I'm a Man"

Number	Title (A Side/B Side)	Yr	NM
❑ 107 [M]	Kind of a Drag	1967	600.00

—With "I'm a Man"

Number	Title (A Side/B Side)	Yr	NM
❑ 107 [S]	Kind of a Drag	1967	40.00

—No known stereo copy has "I'm a Man"

BUCKINGHAMS, THE (2) These two records are not by group (1).

45s

LAURIE

Number	Title (A Side/B Side)	Yr	NM
❑ 3258	Gonna Say Goodbye/ Many Times	1964	10.00

SEG-WAY

Number	Title (A Side/B Side)	Yr	NM
❑ 1004	Lobo Lobo/Rockin' Piper	1962	10.00

BUCKLEY, LORD

Albums

CRESTVIEW

Number	Title (A Side/B Side)	Yr	NM
❑ CRV-801 [M]	The Best of Lord Buckley	1963	50.00
❑ CRV7-801 [S]	The Best of Lord Buckley	1963	60.00

ELEKTRA

Number	Title (A Side/B Side)	Yr	NM
❑ EKS-74047	The Best of Lord Buckley	1969	25.00

—Reissue of Crestview 7-801

RCA VICTOR

Number	Title (A Side/B Side)	Yr	NM
❑ LPM-3246 [10]	Hipsters, Flipsters and Finger Poppin' Daddies, Knock Me Your Lobes	1955	600.00

REPRISE

Number	Title (A Side/B Side)	Yr	NM
❑ RS 6389	A Most Immaculately Hip Aristocrat	1970	50.00

—Reissue of Straight 1054

STRAIGHT

Number	Title (A Side/B Side)	Yr	NM
❑ STS-1054	A Most Immaculately Hip Aristocrat	1970	80.00

VAYA

Number	Title (A Side/B Side)	Yr	NM
❑ 101/2 [M]	Euphoria, Vol. 1	1955	300.00
❑ 107/8 [M]	Euphoria, Vol. 2	1955	400.00
❑ 1715 [10]	Euphoria	195?	600.00

—Red vinyl

WORLD PACIFIC

Number	Title (A Side/B Side)	Yr	NM
❑ WP-1279 [M]	The Way Out Humor of Lord Buckley	1959	200.00

—With correct "Way Out Humor" on the back cover

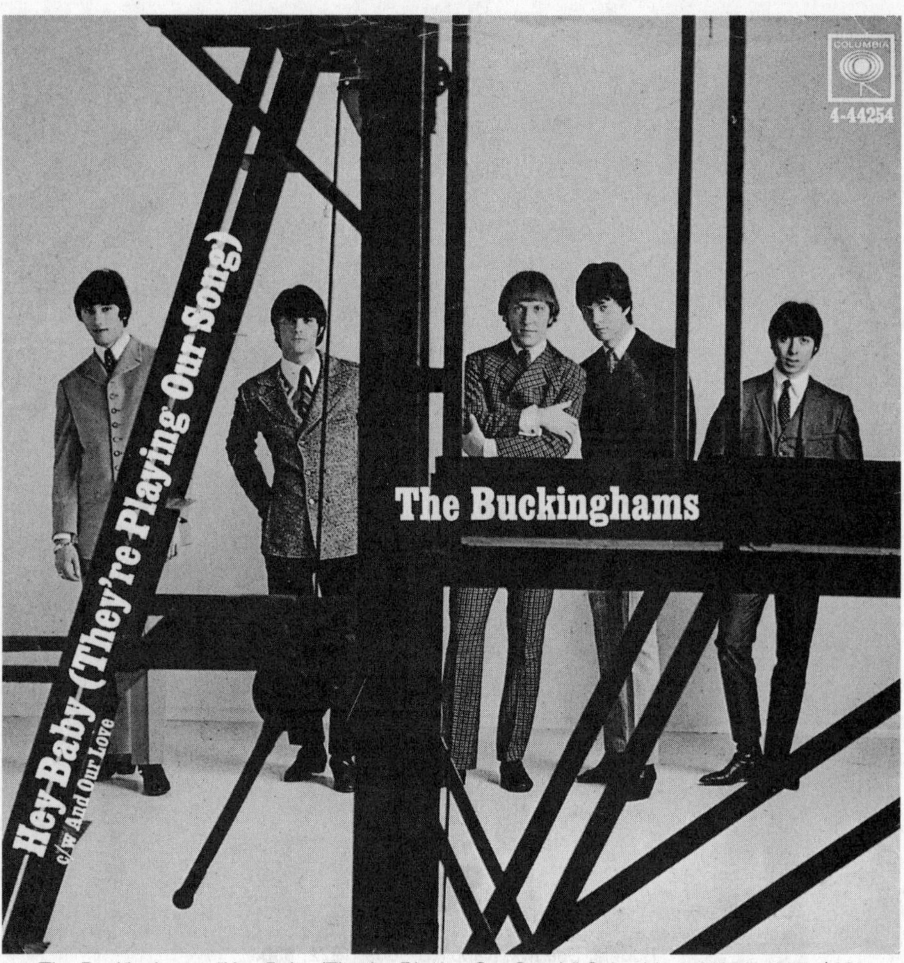

The Buckinghams, "Hey Baby (They're Playing Our Song)," Columbia 4-44254, 1967, **$12.**

Number	Title (A Side/B Side)	Yr	NM
❑ WP-1279 [M]	The Way Out Humor of Lord Buckley	1959	250.00

—With "Far Out Humor" on the back cover

Number	Title (A Side/B Side)	Yr	NM
❑ WP-1815 [M]	Lord Buckley in Concert	1964	50.00

—Reissue of 1279

Number	Title (A Side/B Side)	Yr	NM
❑ WP-1849 [M]	Blowing His Mind (and Yours, Too)	1966	80.00
❑ WPS-21879	Buckley's Best	1968	40.00
❑ WPS-21889	Bad Rapping of the Marquis de Sade	1969	80.00

BUCKLEY, TIM

45s

DISCREET

Number	Title (A Side/B Side)	Yr	NM
❑ 1187	Quicksand/Stone in Love	1973	6.00
❑ 1189	Dolphins/Honey Man	1974	6.00
❑ 1311	Wanda Lu/Who Could Deny You	1974	6.00

ELEKTRA

Number	Title (A Side/B Side)	Yr	NM
❑ 45606	Grief in My Soul/Wings	1966	8.00
❑ 45612	Aren't You the Girl/Strange Street Affair Down Under	1967	8.00
❑ 45618	Once Upon a Time/ Lady Give Me Your Heart	1967	8.00
❑ 45623	Morning Glory/Once I Was	1967	8.00

WARNER BROS.

Number	Title (A Side/B Side)	Yr	NM
❑ 7623	Move with Me/Nighthawkin'	1972	6.00

Albums

DISCREET

Number	Title (A Side/B Side)	Yr	NM
❑ MS 2157	Sefronia	1973	15.00
❑ DS 2201	Look at the Fool	1974	15.00

ELEKTRA

Number	Title (A Side/B Side)	Yr	NM
❑ EKL-318 [M]	Goodbye and Hello	1967	25.00

—Original issue

Number	Title (A Side/B Side)	Yr	NM
❑ EKL-4004 [M]	Tim Buckley	1966	15.00
❑ EKL-4028 [M]	Goodbye and Hello	1968	—

—Reissue of 318; may not exist with this number

Number	Title (A Side/B Side)	Yr	NM
❑ EKS-7318 [S]	Goodbye and Hello	1967	25.00

—Original issue; tan/brown/silvery label

Number	Title (A Side/B Side)	Yr	NM
❑ EKS-74004 [S]	Tim Buckley	1966	20.00
❑ EKS-74028 [S]	Goodbye and Hello	1968	20.00

—Brown labels; reissue of 7318

Number	Title (A Side/B Side)	Yr	NM
❑ EKS-74028 [S]	Goodbye and Hello	1975	10.00

—Butterfly label with Warner Communications logo

Number	Title (A Side/B Side)	Yr	NM
❑ EKS-74045	Happy Sad	1969	20.00
❑ EKS-74074	Lorca	1970	20.00

RHINO

Number	Title (A Side/B Side)	Yr	NM
❑ RNLP-112	The Best of Tim Buckley	1985	10.00

STRAIGHT

Number	Title (A Side/B Side)	Yr	NM
❑ STS-1060	Blue Afternoon	1969	30.00

TPM/RHINO EXCLUSIVE

Number	Title (A Side/B Side)	Yr	NM
❑ 2631	Greetings from L.A.	2008	10.00
❑ 74004	Tim Buckley	2008	10.00

WARNER BROS.

Number	Title (A Side/B Side)	Yr	NM
❑ WS 1842	Blue Afternoon	1970	15.00
❑ WS 1881	Starsailor	1970	15.00
❑ BS 2631	Greetings from L.A.	1972	15.00

BUCKNER, JOE

45s

VEE JAY

Number	Title (A Side/B Side)	Yr	NM
❑ 141	Why Don't Cha/ How Can I Let Her Go	1955	25.00
❑ 172	One More Mile/ Straight and Ready	1956	25.00

—B-side by Tommy Dean

BUCKWHEAT

45s

LONDON

Number	Title (A Side/B Side)	Yr	NM
❑ 156	Carmel Mountain Road/ Long Lonely Road	1971	5.00
❑ 166	Movin' On (Part 1)/ Movin' On (Part 2)	1971	5.00
❑ 176	Simple Song of Freedom/ I Got to Boogie	1972	5.00
❑ 184	Good Book/Hey Little Girl	1972	5.00
❑ 189	I Got to Boogie/I Just Can't Turn My Habit Into Love	1972	5.00
❑ 198	Will the Circle Be Unbroken/ Put Out the Light	1973	5.00

B

Budgie, *Squawk*, Kapp KS-3669, 1972, **$30.**

Number	Title (A Side/B Side)	Yr	NM
Albums			
LONDON			
❑ PS 595	Buckwheat	1971	15.00
❑ PS 609	Movin' On	1972	12.00
❑ XPS 621	Charade	1972	12.00
❑ XPS 635	Hot Tracks	1973	12.00
BUCKWHEAT ZYDECO			
12-Inch Singles			
ISLAND			
❑ PR 2147 [DJ]	My Li'l Girl (Ma 'Tit Fille)/ On a Night Like This	1987	10.00
❑ PR 2425 [DJ]	Why Does Love Got to Be So Sad (same on both sides?)	1988	10.00
45s			
ISLAND			
❑ 99396	My Li'l Girl (Ma 'Tit Fille)/ On a Night Like This	1987	4.00
❑ 875980-7	Hey, Good Lookin'/ Be Good or Be Gone	1990	4.00
MAISON DE SOUL			
❑ 1031	Ya Ya/Walking to New Orleans	1985	6.00
Albums			
BLACK TOP			
❑ 1024	100% Fortified Zydeco	1983	15.00
BLUES UNLIMITED			
❑ 5006	Ils Sont Partis	1981	20.00
❑ 5017	People's Choice	1982	20.00
ISLAND			
❑ 90622	On a Night Like This	1987	10.00
❑ 90968	Taking It Home	1988	10.00
ROUNDER			
❑ 2045	Turning Point	1984	15.00
❑ 2051	Waitin' for My Ya Ya	1985	15.00
BUD AND TRAVIS			
45s			
LIBERTY			
❑ 55202	Truly Do/Bonsoir Dame	1959	10.00
❑ 55221	Poor Boy/Jenny on a Horse	1959	10.00
❑ 55235	Cloudy Summer Afternoon/ E Labas	1959	10.00
❑ 55259	Come to the Dance/ Carmen Carmelia	1960	8.00
❑ 55284	Ballad of the Alamo/The Green Leaves of Summer	1960	8.00
❑ 55612	Tomorrow Is a Long Time/Haiti	1963	6.00
❑ 55681	Maria Cristina/Sabras Que Te Quiero	1964	6.00
❑ 55713	How Long, How Long Blues/ Gimmie Some	1964	6.00
❑ 55764	I Talk to the Trees/ Moment in the Sun	1965	6.00
❑ 55803	Cold Summer/ Girl Sittin' Up in a Tree	1965	6.00
WORLD PACIFIC			
❑ 801	Raspberries Strawberries/ Mexican Wedding Song	1959	12.00
Albums			
LIBERTY			
❑ LRP-3125 [M]	Bud and Travis	1959	30.00
❑ LRP-3138 [M]	Spotlight On Bud and Travis	1960	20.00
❑ LRP-3222 [M]	Bud and Travis In Concert at the Santa Monica Civic Auditorium, Vol. 2	1961	20.00
❑ LRP-3295 [M]	Naturally	1963	20.00
❑ LRP-3341 [M]	Perspective on Bud and Travis	1964	20.00
❑ LRP-3386 [M]	Bud and Travis In Person (At the Cellar Door)	1964	20.00
❑ LRP-3398 [M]	The Latin Album	1965	20.00
❑ LST-7125 [S]	Bud and Travis	1959	40.00
❑ LST-7138 [S]	Spotlight On Bud and Travis	1960	25.00
❑ LST-7222 [S]	Bud and Travis In Concert at the Santa Monica Civic Auditorium, Vol. 2	1961	25.00
❑ LST-7295 [S]	Naturally	1963	25.00
❑ LST-7341 [S]	Perspective on Bud and Travis	1964	25.00
❑ LST-7386 [S]	Bud and Travis In Person (At the Cellar Door)	1964	25.00
❑ LST-7398 [S]	The Latin Album	1965	25.00
❑ LDM-11001 [(2)M]	Bud and Travis...In Concert	1960	25.00
❑ LDS-12001 [(2)S]	Bud and Travis...In Concert	1960	30.00
SUNSET			
❑ SUM-1154 [M]	Bud and Travis	1967	12.00
❑ SUS-5154 [S]	Bud and Travis	1967	12.00
BUDD, BILLY			
45s			
JUBILEE			
❑ 5583	Like I Want You Too/ Love Revolution	1967	8.00
20TH CENTURY-FOX			
❑ 502	Why Are You Running/ The Girl of the Year	1964	8.00
BUDDIES, THE Several different groups.			
45s			
COMET			
❑ 2143	Hully Gully Baby/ Must Be True Love	1961	25.00
DECCA			
❑ 29840	The Most Happy Fella/ Two Skeletons on a Tin Roof	1956	15.00
❑ 29953	Bag of Bones/Every Time the Phone Rings	1956	15.00
❑ 30355	A Prom and a Promise/ The Lottery	1957	15.00
❑ 31920	Duckman Part 1/Duckman Part 2	1966	8.00
GLORY			
❑ 230	I Stole Your Heart/I Waited	1955	150.00
OKEH			
❑ 7123	Castle of Love/ Give Me Your Love	1959	15.00
SWAN			
❑ 4073	Spooky Spider/Lebone Delada	1961	15.00
❑ 4170	The Beatle/Pulsebeat	1964	25.00
TIARA			
❑ 6121	She's a Loser/Heartless	1959	25.00
Albums			
WING			
❑ MGW-12293 [M]	The Buddies and the Compacts	1965	50.00
❑ MGW-12306 [M]	Go Go with the Buddies	1965	50.00
❑ SRW-16293 [S]	The Buddies and the Compacts	1965	80.00
❑ SRW-16306 [S]	Go Go with the Buddies	1965	80.00
BUDGIE			
45s			
KAPP			
❑ 2152	Nude Disintegrating Parachutist Woman/Crash Course	1971	5.00
❑ 2185	Stranded/Whiskey River	1972	5.00
MCA			
❑ 40367	Honey/I Ain't No Mountain	1975	5.00
Albums			
A&M			
❑ SP-4593	If I Were Brittania I'd Waive the Rules	1976	12.00
❑ SP-4618	Bandolier	1975	12.00
❑ SP-4675	Impeckable	1978	12.00
KAPP			
❑ KS-3656	Budgie	1971	30.00
❑ KS-3669	Squawk	1972	30.00
MCA			
❑ 429	In for the Kill	1973	20.00
BUFFALO NICKEL JUGBAND, THE			
Albums			
HAPPY TIGER			
❑ 1018	The Buffalo Nickel Jugband	1971	25.00
BUFFALO SPRINGFIELD Also see DEWEY MARTIN AND MEDICINE BALL; JIM MESSINA; STEPHEN STILLS; NEIL YOUNG.			
45s			
ATCO			
❑ 6428	Nowadays Clancy Can't Even Sing/Go And Say Goodbye	1966	20.00
❑ 6452	Everybody's Wrong/Burned	1966	20.00
❑ 6459	For What It's Worth (Stop, Hey, What's That Sound)/Do I Have to Come Right Out and Say It	1967	12.00
❑ 6459	For What It's Worth/Do I Have to Come Right Out and Say It	1967	15.00
❑ 6499	Bluebird/Mr. Soul	1967	20.00
❑ 6519	Rock 'N' Roll Woman/ A Child's Claim to Fame	1967	10.00
❑ 6545	Expecting to Fly/Everydays	1968	10.00
❑ 6572	Uno Mundo/Merry-Go-Round	1968	10.00

Except when noted otherwise, VG = 25% of NM, and VG+ = 50% of NM. (Example: VG = $2.00, VG+ = $4.00 and NM = $8.00.)

Number	Title (A Side/B Side)	Yr	NM
❑ 6602	Special Care/Kind Woman	1968	10.00
❑ 6615	Four Days Gone/ On the Way Home	1968	10.00

Albums

ATCO

Number	Title (A Side/B Side)	Yr	NM
❑ SD 38-105 [S]	Retrospective/The Best of Buffalo Springfield	197?	8.00
—Reissue of 33-283			
❑ 33-200 [M]	Buffalo Springfield	1967	200.00
—With "Baby Don't Scold Me"			
❑ 33-200A [M]	Buffalo Springfield	1967	25.00
—With "For What It's Worth" replacing "Baby Don't Scold Me"			
❑ SD 33-200 [S]	Buffalo Springfield	1967	200.00
—With "Baby Don't Scold Me"			
❑ SD 33-200A [S]	Buffalo Springfield	1967	25.00
—With "For What It's Worth" replacing "Baby Don't Scold Me"; purple and brown label			
❑ SD 33-200A [S]	Buffalo Springfield	1969	15.00
—Reissue on yellow label			
❑ SD 33-200A [S]	Buffalo Springfield	197?	8.00
—Later white or gray label			
❑ 33-226 [M]	Buffalo Springfield Again	1967	80.00
❑ SD 33-226 [S]	Buffalo Springfield Again	1967	25.00
—Purple and brown label			
❑ SD 33-226 [S]	Buffalo Springfield Again	1969	15.00
—Reissue on yellow label			
❑ SD 33-226 [S]	Buffalo Springfield Again	197?	8.00
—Later white or gray label			
❑ 33-256 [M]	Last Time Around	1968	120.00
—White label promo only			
❑ SD 33-256 [S]	Last Time Around	1968	30.00
—Purple and brown label			
❑ SD 33-256 [S]	Last Time Around	1969	15.00
—Reissue on yellow label			
❑ SD 33-256 [S]	Last Time Around	197?	8.00
—Later white or gray label			
❑ 33-283 [M]	Retrospective/The Best of Buffalo Springfield	1969	100.00
—White label promo only			
❑ SD 33-283 [S]	Retrospective/The Best of Buffalo Springfield	1969	20.00
—Yellow label			
❑ SD 2-806 [(2)]	Buffalo Springfield	197?	12.00
—Later white or gray label			
❑ SD 2-806 [(2)]	Buffalo Springfield	1973	20.00
—Yellow label			

BUFFETT, JIMMY

45s

ABC

Number	Title (A Side/B Side)	Yr	NM
❑ 11399 [DJ]	He Went to Paris (stereo/mono)	1973	12.00
—Number may have been assigned by mistake; double-sided promotional copies are known to exist; regular copies are on ABC Dunhill 4372			
❑ 12113	Door Number Three/Dallas	1975	5.00
❑ 12143	Big Red/Havana Daydreamin'	1975	5.00
❑ 12175	The Captain and the Kid/Cliches	1976	5.00
❑ 12200	Something So Feminine About a Mandolin/Woman Goin' Crazy on Caroline Street	1976	5.00
❑ 12254	Margaritaville/Miss You So Badly	1977	4.00
❑ 12305	Changes in Latitudes, Changes in Attitudes/Landfall	1977	4.00
❑ 12305 [PS]	Changes in Latitudes, Changes in Attitudes/Landfall	1977	6.00
❑ 12358	Cheeseburger in Paradise/ African Friend	1978	4.00
❑ 12391	Livingston Saturday Night/ Cowboy in the Jungle	1978	4.00
❑ 12428	Manana/The Coast of Marsailles	1978	4.00

ABC DUNHILL

Number	Title (A Side/B Side)	Yr	NM
❑ 4348	The Great Filling Station Hold Up/Why Don't We Get Drunk	1973	8.00
❑ 4353	The Great Filling Station Hold Up/They Can't Dance Like Carmen No More	1973	4.00
❑ 4359	Grapefruit-Juicy Fruit/ I Found Me a Home	1973	4.00
❑ 4372	He Went to Paris/ Peanut Butter Conspiracy	1973	4.00
❑ 4378	Ringling, Ringling/Saxophones	1974	4.00
❑ 4385	Come Monday/ The Wino and I Know	1974	5.00
❑ 15008	Come Monday/ The Wino and I Know	1974	4.00
❑ 15011	Brand New Country Star/ Pencil Thin Moustache	1974	4.00
❑ 15029	Presents to Send You/ A Pirate Looks at Forty	1975	4.00

ASYLUM

Number	Title (A Side/B Side)	Yr	NM
❑ 69890	I Don't Know (Spicoli's Theme)/ She's My Baby (And She's Out of Control)	1982	4.00
—B-side by Palmer & Jost			

BARNABY

Number	Title (A Side/B Side)	Yr	NM
❑ 2013	The Christian/Richard Frost	1970	10.00
❑ 2019	He Ain't Free/There Ain't Nothing Soft About Hard Times	1970	10.00
❑ 2023	Captain America/ Truckstop Salvation	1970	10.00

FULL MOON

Number	Title (A Side/B Side)	Yr	NM
❑ 49659	Survive/Send Me Somebody to Love	1981	4.00
—B-side by Kathy Walker			

FULL MOON/ASYLUM

Number	Title (A Side/B Side)	Yr	NM
❑ 47073	Hello Texas/Lyin' Eyes [by the Eagles]	1980	5.00

ISLAND

Number	Title (A Side/B Side)	Yr	NM
❑ 562144-7	Pacing the Cage/ I Will Play for Gumbo	1999	3.00

MCA

Number	Title (A Side/B Side)	Yr	NM
❑ S45-17084 [DJ]	Christmas In The Caribbean (same on both sides)	1985	5.00
❑ 41109	Fins/Dreamsicle	1979	4.00
❑ 41161	Volcano/Stranded on a Sandbar	1979	4.00
❑ 41199	Boat Drinks/Survive	1980	4.00
❑ 51061	It's My Job/Little Miss Magic	1981	4.00
❑ 51105	Stars Fell on Alabama/ Growing Older But Not Up	1981	4.00
❑ 52013	It's Midnight And I'm Not Famous Yet/When Salome Plays the Drum	1982	4.00
❑ 52050	If I Could Just Get It on Paper/ Where's the Party	1982	4.00
❑ 52298	One Particular Harbour/ Distantly in Love	1983	4.00
❑ 52333	Brown Eyed Girl/Twelve Volt Man	1984	4.00
❑ 52438	When the Wild Life Betrays Me/ Ragtop Day	1984	4.00
❑ 52438 [PS]	When the Wild Life Betrays Me/ Ragtop Day	1984	4.00
❑ 52499	Come to the Moon/Bigger Than the Both of Us	1984	4.00
❑ 52550	Who's the Blond Stranger/ She's Going Out of My Mind	1985	3.00
❑ 52607	Gypies in the Palace/ Jolly Mon Sing	1985	3.00
❑ 52664	If the Phone Doesn't Ring, It's Me/Frank and Lola	1985	3.00
❑ 52752	Please Bypass This Heart/ Beyond the End	1986	3.00
❑ 52849	I Love the Now/ No Plane on Sunday	1986	3.00
❑ 52932	Creola/You'll Never Work in Dis Bidness Again	1986	3.00
❑ 52932 [PS]	Creola/You'll Never Work in Dis Bidness Again	1986	4.00
❑ 53035	Take It Back/Floridays	1987	3.00
❑ 53360	Homemade Music/L'air de la Louisiane	1988	3.00
❑ 53360 [PS]	Homemade Music/L'air de la Louisiane	1988	4.00
❑ 53396	Bring Back the Magic/That's What Living Is to Me	1988	3.00
❑ 53396 [PS]	Bring Back the Magic/That's What Living Is to Me	1988	4.00
❑ 53675	Take Another Road/Off to See the Lizard	1989	3.00
❑ 54680	Another Saturday Night/ Souvenirs	1993	3.00

Albums

ABC

Number	Title (A Side/B Side)	Yr	NM
❑ SPDJ-43 [DJ]	Special Jimmy Buffett Sampler	1978	20.00
❑ D-914	Havana Daydreamin'	1976	12.00
❑ AB-990	Changes in Latitudes, Changes in Attitudes	1977	12.00
❑ AK-1008 [(2)]	You Had to Be There	1978	15.00
❑ AA-1046	Son of a Son of a Sailor	1978	12.00

ABC DUNHILL

Number	Title (A Side/B Side)	Yr	NM
❑ DSD-50132	Living and Dying in 3/4 Time	1973	15.00
❑ DSX-50150	A White Sport Coat and a Pink Crustaceon	1974	15.00
❑ DSD-50183	A1A	1975	15.00

BARNABY

Number	Title (A Side/B Side)	Yr	NM
❑ BR-6014	High Cumberland Jubilee	1975	40.00
❑ Z 30093	Down to Earth	1970	100.00

MCA

Number	Title (A Side/B Side)	Yr	NM
❑ 5102	Volcano	1979	10.00
❑ 5169	Coconut Telegraph	1981	10.00
❑ 5285	Somewhere Over China	1982	10.00
❑ 5447	One Particular Harbour	1983	10.00
❑ 5512	Riddles in the Sand	1984	10.00
❑ 5600	Last Mango in Paris	1985	10.00
❑ 5633	Songs You Know By Heart — Jimmy Buffett's Greatest Hit(s)	1985	10.00
❑ 5730	Floridays	1986	10.00
❑ 2-6005 [(2)]	You Had to Be There	1981	10.00
❑ 6314	Off to See the Lizard	1989	10.00
❑ 37023	Havana Daydreamin'	1981	8.00
❑ 37024	Son of a Son of a Sailor	1981	8.00
❑ 37025	Living and Dying in 3/4 Time	1981	8.00
❑ 37026	A White Sport Coat and a Pink Crustaceon	1981	8.00
❑ 37027	A1A	1981	8.00
❑ 37150	Changes in Latitudes, Changes in Attitudes	1982	8.00
❑ 37156	Volcano	1982	8.00
❑ 37246	Somewhere Over China	1984	8.00
❑ 42093	Hot Water	1988	10.00

BUG COLLECTORS, THE

45s

CATCH

Number	Title (A Side/B Side)	Yr	NM
❑ 103	The Beatle Bug/Thief in the Night	1964	20.00

BUG MEN, THE

See THE STRING-A-LONGS.

BUGALOOS, THE

45s

CAPITOL

Number	Title (A Side/B Side)	Yr	NM
❑ 2946	Senses of Our World/For a Friend	1970	12.00

Albums

CAPITOL

Number	Title (A Side/B Side)	Yr	NM
❑ SW-621	The Bugaloos	1970	30.00

BUGGLES, THE

12-Inch Singles

ISLAND

Number	Title (A Side/B Side)	Yr	NM
❑ PRO859 [DJ]	Clean Clean/Living in the Plastic Age	1980	8.00
❑ PRO-A-859 [DJ]	Clean Clean/Living in the Plastic Age	1980	8.00

45s

CARRERE

Number	Title (A Side/B Side)	Yr	NM
❑ ZS5-02759	I Am a Camera/Inner City	1982	5.00

COLLECTABLES

Number	Title (A Side/B Side)	Yr	NM
❑ 2600	Video Killed the Radio Star/ Pilot of the Airwaves	1992	3.00
—Reissue; B-side by Charlie Dore			

ISLAND

Number	Title (A Side/B Side)	Yr	NM
❑ 49114	Video Killed the Radio Star/ Kid Dynamo	1979	7.00
❑ 49209	Clean Clean/Astro Boy (And the Proles on Parade)	1980	5.00
❑ 99871	Video Killed the Radio Star/ Kid Dynamo	1983	8.00
—Purple label stock copy (double A-side promos go for 50% less)			

Albums

CARRERE

Number	Title (A Side/B Side)	Yr	NM
❑ ARZ 37926	Adventures in Modern Recording	1982	15.00

ISLAND

Number	Title (A Side/B Side)	Yr	NM
❑ ILPS 9585	The Age of Plastic	1980	15.00
❑ 90090	The Age of Plastic	1983	10.00
—Reissue			

BUGGS, THE

45s

SOMA

Number	Title (A Side/B Side)	Yr	NM
❑ 1413	The Buggs vs. The Beatles/ She Loves You	1964	25.00

Albums

CORONET

Number	Title (A Side/B Side)	Yr	NM
❑ CX-212 [M]	The Beatle Beat	1964	20.00
❑ CXS-212 [R]	The Beatle Beat	1964	12.00

BUGS, THE

45s

HIT

Number	Title (A Side/B Side)	Yr	NM
❑ 106	She Loves You/Dawn (Go Away)	1964	12.00
—B-side by the Chellows			
❑ 111	Twist and Shout/Stay	1964	12.00
—B-side by the Chellows			
❑ 161	Any Way You Want It/ Sidewalk Surfin'	1964	12.00
—B-side by the Jalopy Five			

BULLDOG

With Gene Cornish and Dino Danelli, ex-members of THE RASCALS.

45s

BUDDAH

Number	Title (A Side/B Side)	Yr	NM
❑ 414	Bad Bad Girl/I Tried to Sleep	1974	4.00

DECCA

Number	Title (A Side/B Side)	Yr	NM
❑ 32996	Good Times Are Comin'/No	1972	4.00

GUYDEN

Number	Title (A Side/B Side)	Yr	NM
❑ 5001	Man of Constant Sorrow/ Inner Spring	1971	5.00

MCA

Number	Title (A Side/B Side)	Yr	NM
❑ 40014	I'm a Madman/Are You Really Happy Together	1973	4.00
❑ 40050	I Tip My Hat/I'm a Madman	1973	4.00

Albums

BUDDAH

Number	Title (A Side/B Side)	Yr	NM
❑ BDS-5600	Smasher	1974	15.00

B

Bulletboys, *Bulletboys*, Warner Bros. 25782, 1988, **$8.**

Number	Title (A Side/B Side)	Yr	NM
DECCA			
❑ DL 75370	Bulldog	1972	20.00

BULLDOGS, THE

45s

Number	Title (A Side/B Side)	Yr	NM
MERCURY			
❑ 72262	John, Paul, George and Ringo/What Do I See	1964	20.00

BULLETBOYS

45s

Number	Title (A Side/B Side)	Yr	NM
WARNER BROS.			
❑ 22876	Smooth Up!/Badlands	1989	3.00
❑ 27554	For the Love of Money/Crank Me Up	1989	3.00
❑ 27554 [PS]	For the Love of Money/Crank Me Up	1989	4.00

Albums

Number	Title (A Side/B Side)	Yr	NM
WARNER BROS.			
❑ 25782	Bulletboys	1988	8.00
❑ R 134757	Freakshow	1991	20.00
—BMG Direct Marketing version; not issued on vinyl to stores			

BUNCH, THE

Albums

Number	Title (A Side/B Side)	Yr	NM
A&M			
❑ SP-4354	The Bunch	1973	25.00

BUNKERS, THE

45s

Number	Title (A Side/B Side)	Yr	NM
RCA VICTOR			
❑ 74-0962	They Can't Take That Away from Me/Oh Babe, What Would You Say	1973	6.00
❑ 74-0962 [PS]	They Can't Take That Away from Me/Oh Babe, What Would You Say	1973	10.00

Albums

Number	Title (A Side/B Side)	Yr	NM
RCA VICTOR			
❑ APL1-0102	Archie and Edith Side by Side	1973	20.00

BUONO, VICTOR

45s

Number	Title (A Side/B Side)	Yr	NM
DORE			
❑ 864	Fat Man's Prayer/Bless Me Doctor	1971	6.00

Albums

Number	Title (A Side/B Side)	Yr	NM
DORE			
❑ 325	Heavy!	1971	15.00

BUOYS, THE

45s

Number	Title (A Side/B Side)	Yr	NM
POLYDOR			
❑ 14201	Liza's Last Ride/Downtown Singer	1973	6.00
SCEPTER			
❑ 12254	These Days/Don't You Know It's Over	1969	8.00
❑ 12275	Timothy/It Feels Good	1970	10.00
❑ 12275 [PS]	Timothy/It Feels Good	1970	20.00
❑ 12318	Give Up Your Guns/Prince of Thieves	1971	8.00
❑ 12331	Tell Me Heaven Is Here/Bloodknot	1971	8.00

Albums

Number	Title (A Side/B Side)	Yr	NM
SCEPTER			
❑ SPS-593	Timothy	1971	25.00

BURDEN, RAY

45s

Number	Title (A Side/B Side)	Yr	NM
CULLMAN			
❑ 6407	Christmas Is Here At Last/Santa, Bring Me A Gal	1958	50.00

BURDETTE, LEW

45s

Number	Title (A Side/B Side)	Yr	NM
DOT			
❑ 15672	Three Strikes and You're Out/Mary Lou	1957	25.00

BURDON, ERIC
Also see THE ANIMALS; ERIC BURDON AND WAR.

45s

Number	Title (A Side/B Side)	Yr	NM
CAPITOL			
❑ 3997	The Real Me/Letter from the County Farm	1974	5.00
❑ 3997 [PS]	The Real Me/Letter from the County Farm	1974	12.00
❑ 4007	Ring of Fire/The Real Me	1974	5.00
MGM			
❑ 14296	Headin' for Home/Soledad	1971	5.00
—With Jimmy Witherspoon			
UNITED ARTISTS			
❑ 50842	Headin' for Home/Soledad	1971	—
—With Jimmy Witherspoon; assigned to MGM			

Albums

Number	Title (A Side/B Side)	Yr	NM
CAPITOL			
❑ ST-11359	Sun Secrets	1974	12.00
❑ S?A?11426	Stop	1975	20.00
—Cover shaped like a hexagon			
❑ ST-11426	Stop	1975	12.00
—Regular square cover			
GNP CRESCENDO			
❑ GNPS-2194	Wicked Man	1988	10.00
LAX			
❑ PW 37110	Sun Secrets	1981	10.00
—Reissue of Capitol 11359			
STRIPED HORSE			
❑ SHL 2006	I Used to Be an Animal	1988	10.00

BURDON, ERIC, AND THE ANIMALS
See THE ANIMALS.

BURDON, ERIC, AND WAR
Also see ERIC BURDON; WAR.

45s

Number	Title (A Side/B Side)	Yr	NM
ABC			
❑ 12244	Magic Mountain/Home Dream	1977	5.00
MGM			
❑ 14118	Spill the Wine/Magic Mountain	1970	6.00
❑ 14118 [PS]	Spill the Wine/Magic Mountain	1970	12.00
❑ 14196	They Can't Take Away Our Music/Home Cookin'	1970	5.00

Albums

Number	Title (A Side/B Side)	Yr	NM
ABC			
❑ D-988	Love Is All Around	1976	12.00
—As "War Featuring Eric Burdon"			
LAX			
❑ PW 37109	Spill the Wine	1981	10.00
—Reissue of MGM 4663 with new title			
MGM			
❑ SE-4663	Eric Burdon Declares "War"	1970	15.00
❑ SE-4710-2 [(2)]	The Black Man's Burdon	1970	20.00
—Add 50% if the package includes an "Official War Bond," entitling the bearer to $1 off any Eric Burdon and War concert before December 31, 1973			

BURGESS, DAVE
Also see THE CHAMPS.

45s

Number	Title (A Side/B Side)	Yr	NM
CHALLENGE			
❑ 1001	Don't Cry. For You I Love/Fire in the Eyes	1957	25.00
—As "Dave Dupree"			
❑ 1002	Flame of Love/Well, It Isn't Fair	1957	25.00
—As "Dave Dupree"			
❑ 1005	A Job Well Done/Our Tomorrow	1957	25.00
—As "Dave Dupree"			
❑ 1008	I'm Available/Who's Gonna Cry	1957	25.00
❑ 1018	Take This Love/Maybelle	1958	20.00
—As "Dave Burgess and the Champs"			
❑ 59032	Lovey Dovey Baby/I Hang My Head and Cry	1958	20.00
❑ 59037	I Don't Want to Know/Lulu	1959	20.00
❑ 59045	Everlovin'/Just for Me	1959	20.00
❑ 59101	Without You/Are You Teasing Me	1961	20.00
OKEH			
❑ 7002	Don't Put a Dent in My Heart/Judalina	1953	25.00
❑ 7044	Gratefully Yours/Too Late for Tears	1954	25.00
TAMPA			
❑ 104	Down, Down/Don't Turn Your Back on Love	1955	25.00
❑ 105	I Love Paris/Five Foot Two, Eyes of Blue	1955	25.00

BURGESS, SONNY

45s

Number	Title (A Side/B Side)	Yr	NM
PHILLIPS INT'L.			
❑ 3551	Sadie's Back in Town/Kiss Goodnight	1960	30.00

Except when noted otherwise, VG = 25% of NM, and VG+ = 50% of NM. (Example: VG = $2.00, VG+ = $4.00 and NM = $8.00.)

B

Number	Title (A Side/B Side)	Yr	NM
SUN			
247	Red Headed Woman/We Wanna Boogie	1956	150.00
263	Ain't Got a Thing/Restless	1957	80.00
285	My Bucket's Got a Hole in It/Sweet Misery	1958	50.00
304	Thunderbird/Itchy	1958	30.00

BURKE, BUDDY

45s

Number	Title (A Side/B Side)	Yr	NM
BULLSEYE			
1002	That Big Old Moon/Street of Sorrows	195?	150.00

BURKE, SOLOMON

12-Inch Singles

Number	Title (A Side/B Side)	Yr	NM
INFINITY			
L33-1023 [DJ]	Sidewalks, Fences and Walls (3:39) (5:15)	1979	12.00

45s

Number	Title (A Side/B Side)	Yr	NM
ABC DUNHILL			
4388	Midnight and You/I Have a Dream	1974	5.00
15009	Midnight and You/I Have a Dream	1974	4.00
AMHERST			
736	Please Don't You Say Goodbye to Me/See That Girl	1978	4.00
APOLLO			
485	Christmas Presents/When I'm All Alone	1955	30.00
487	I'm in Love/Why Do Me That Way	1956	25.00
491	I'm All Alone/To Thee	1956	25.00
500	No Man Walks Alone/Walking in a Dream	1956	25.00
505	A Picture of You/You Can Run But You Can't Hide	1957	25.00
511	I Need You Tonight/This Is It	1957	25.00
512	For You and You Alone/You Are My One Love	1957	25.00
522	They Always Say/Don't Cry	1958	25.00
527	My Heart Is a Chapel/This Is It	1958	25.00
ATLANTIC			
2089	Keep the Magic Working/How Many Times	1961	20.00
2114	Just Out of Reach (Of My Two Open Arms)/Be-Bop Grandma	1961	20.00
2131	Cry to Me/I Almost Lost My Mind	1962	60.00
2147	Down in the Valley/I'm Hanging Up My Heart for You	1962	15.00
2157	I Really Don't Want to Know/Tonight My Heart She Is Crying (Love Is a Bird)	1962	15.00
2170	Go On Back to Him/I Said I Was Sorry	1962	15.00
2180	Words/Home in Your Heart	1963	15.00
2185	If You Need Me/You Can Make It If You Try	1963	15.00
2196	Can't Nobody Love You/Stupidity	1963	15.00
2205	You're Good for Me/Beautiful Brown Eyes	1963	15.00
2218	He'll Have to Go/Rockin' Soul	1964	15.00
2226	Goodbye Baby (Baby Goodbye)/Someone to Love Me	1964	15.00
2241	Everybody Needs Somebody to Love/Looking for My Baby	1964	15.00
2254	Yes I Do/Won't You Give Him (One More Chance)	1964	15.00
2259	The Price/More Rockin' Soul	1964	15.00
2276	Got to Get You Off My Mind/Peepin'	1965	15.00
2288	Tonight's the Night/Maggie's Farm	1965	15.00
2299	Someone Is Watching/Dance, Dance, Dance	1965	12.00
2308	Only Love (Can Save Me Now)/A Little Girl That Loves Me	1965	12.00
2314	Baby Come On Home/(No, No, No) Can't Stop Lovin' You Now	1965	12.00
2327	I Feel a Sin Coming On/Mountain of Pride	1966	10.00
2345	Suddenly/Lawdy Miss Clawdy	1966	10.00
2349	Keep Looking/Don't Want You No More	1966	10.00
2359	When She Touches Me/Woman How Do You Make Me Love You Like I Do	1966	10.00
2369	Presents for Christmas/A Tear Fell	1966	12.00
2378	Keep a Light in the Window Till I Come Home/Time Is a Thief	1967	10.00
2416	Take Me (Just As I Am)/Stayed Away Too Long	1967	10.00
2459	It's Been a Change/Detroit City	1967	10.00
2483	Party People/Need Your Love So Bad	1968	10.00
2507	I Wish I Knew (How It Would Feel to Be Free)/It's Just a Matter of Time Baby	1968	10.00
2527	Save It/Meet Me in Church	1968	10.00
2566	Get Out of My Life Woman/What'd I Say	1968	10.00
BELL			
759	Up Tight Good Woman/I Can't Stop	1969	8.00
783	Proud Mary/What Am I Living For	1969	8.00
806	That Lucky Old Sun/How Big a Fool	1969	8.00
829	I'm Gonna Stay Right Here/Generation of Revelations	1969	8.00
891	God Knows I Love You/In the Ghetto	1970	6.00
CHESS			
ACH-401	I'll Never Stop Loving You (Never Ever Song)/The Do Right Song	1976	6.00
2159	You and Your Baby Blues/I'm Leaving on That Late, Late Train	1975	4.00
2172	Let Me Wrap My Arms Around You/Everlasting Love	1975	4.00
INFINITY			
50046	Sidewalks, Fences and Walls/Boo-Hoo-Hoo (Cra-Cra-Craya)	1979	5.00
MALA			
420	This Little Ring/I'm Not Afraid	1960	20.00
MCI			
712842	You're All I Want for Christmas/No Place Like Home	198?	8.00
—B-side by Rayne			
MGM			
14185	Lookin' Out My Back Door/All for the Love of Sunshine	1970	6.00
14221	The Electronic Magnetism (That's Heavy, Baby)/Bridge of Life	1971	6.00
14279	J.C., I Know Who You Are/The Things Love Will Make You Do	1971	6.00
14302	The Night They Drove Old Dixie Down/PSR 1983	1971	6.00
14353	Love's Street and Fool's Road/I Got to Tell It	1972	6.00
14402	We're Almost Home/Fight Back	1972	6.00
14402 [PS]	We're Almost Home/Fight Back	1972	12.00
14425	Get Up and Do Something for Yourself/We're Almost Home	1972	6.00
14571	Shambala/Love Thy Neighbor	1973	6.00
14651	Georgia Up North/Here Comes the Train	1973	6.00
POINTBLANK			
S7-19520	Ooooooyou/Today Is Your Birthday	1997	4.00
PRIDE			
1017	I Can't Stop Loving You (Part 1)/I Can't Stop Loving You (Part 2)	1972	6.00
1022	All I Want for Christmas/I Can't Stop Loving You (Part 1)	1972	6.00
1028	My Prayer/Ookie Bookie Man	1973	6.00
1038	Sentimental Journey/Vaya Con Dios	1973	6.00
—With Lady Lee			

Albums

Number	Title	Yr	NM
ABC DUNHILL			
DSX-50161	I Have a Dream	1974	12.00
AMHERST			
AMH-1018	Please Don't You Say Goodbye to Me	1978	12.00
APOLLO			
ALP-498 [M]	Solomon Burke	1962	500.00
ATLANTIC			
8067 [M]	Solomon Burke's Greatest Hits	1962	50.00
SD 8067 [S]	Solomon Burke's Greatest Hits	1962	80.00
8085 [M]	If You Need Me	1963	50.00
SD 8085 [S]	If You Need Me	1963	80.00
8096 [M]	Rock N' Soul	1964	50.00
SD 8096 [S]	Rock N' Soul	1964	80.00
8109 [M]	The Best of Solomon Burke	1965	30.00
SD 8109 [S]	The Best of Solomon Burke	1965	40.00
SD 8158	King Solomon	1968	25.00
SD 8185	I Wish I Knew	1968	25.00
BELL			
6033	Proud Mary	1969	20.00
CHESS			
CH-19002	Back to My Roots	1976	12.00
CH-60042	Music to Make Love By	1975	12.00
CLARION			
607 [M]	I Almost Lost My Mind	1966	20.00
SD 607 [S]	I Almost Lost My Mind	1966	25.00
DBK WORKS			
104 [(2)]	Don't Give Up on Me	2003	20.00
INFINITY			
INF-9024	Sidewalks, Fences and Walls	1979	12.00
KENWOOD			
LP-498 [M]	Solomon Burke	1964	200.00
—Reissue of Apollo 498			
MGM			
SE-4767	Electronic Magnetism	1971	15.00
SE-4830	King Heavy	1972	15.00
PRIDE			
0011	The History of Solomon Burke	1972	15.00
ROUNDER			
2042/3 [(2)]	Soul Alive!	1984	12.00
2053	A Change Is Gonna Come	1986	10.00
SAVOY			
14660	Solomon Burke	1981	10.00
14679	Into My Life	1982	10.00
14717	Take Me, Shake Me	1983	10.00

BURLAND, SASCHA & THE SKIPJACK CHOIR

45s

Number	Title (A Side/B Side)	Yr	NM
COLUMBIA			
42009	Gorilla Walk/Hole in My Soul	1960	20.00
RCA VICTOR			
47-8277	Have Yourself a Merry Little Christmas/The Chickens Are in the Chimes	1963	30.00
47-8277 [PS]	Have Yourself a Merry Little Christmas/The Chickens Are in the Chimes	1963	40.00

BURNETT, FRANCES

45s

Number	Title (A Side/B Side)	Yr	NM
CORAL			
62092	Come to Me/So Many Tears	1959	100.00
62127	Please Remember Me/How I Miss You So	1959	100.00
62164	I Love Him So/Too Proud	1960	100.00
62214	She Was Taking My Baby/Sweetie	1960	100.00
DECCA			
30571	Spin the Wheel/A Promise Made a Fool of Me	1958	120.00

BURNETT, T-BONE

12-Inch Singles

Number	Title (A Side/B Side)	Yr	NM
COLUMBIA			
CAS 2772 [DJ]	Killer Moon (same on both sides)	1988	10.00
WARNER BROS.			
PRO-A-2074 [DJ]	Murder Weapon/Fatally Beautiful/Baby Fall Down	1983	15.00

45s

Number	Title (A Side/B Side)	Yr	NM
COLUMBIA			
38-07743	Killer Moon/Gawd	1988	5.00
WARNER BROS.			
29489	Baby Fall Down/Art Movies	1983	5.00
29876	Hold On Tight/Poetry	1982	6.00

Albums

Number	Title	Yr	NM
COLUMBIA			
BFC 40792	Talking Animals	1988	10.00
MCA			
5809	T-Bone Burnett	1986	8.00
TAKOMA			
7080	Truth Decay	1980	10.00
UNI			
73125	The B-52 Band and the Fabulous Skyhawks	1972	30.00
—As "J. Henry Burnett"			
WARNER BROS.			
23691	Trap Door	1982	10.00
23921	Proof Through the Night	1983	10.00

BURNETTE, BILLY

Also see FLEETWOOD MAC. Not to be confused with Billy Joe Burnette.

12-Inch Singles

Number	Title (A Side/B Side)	Yr	NM
MCA CURB			
L33-17065 [DJ]	Roll Over/Guitar Bug	1985	10.00

45s

A&M

Number	Title (A Side/B Side)	Yr	NM
❑ 743	Just Because We're Kids/ Little Girl, Big Love	1964	25.00

—As "Young Billy Bean"; A-side written by Dr. Seuss!

Number	Title (A Side/B Side)	Yr	NM
❑ 1794	Baby/Just Another Love Song	1976	5.00

CAPRICORN

Number	Title (A Side/B Side)	Yr	NM
❑ 18525	I Still Remember (How to Miss You)/I Recovered, I Survived	1993	3.00
❑ 18751	Tangled Up in Texas/ Into the Storm	1992	3.00

COLUMBIA

Number	Title (A Side/B Side)	Yr	NM
❑ 02527	Let the New Love Begin/ I Don't Know Why	1981	4.00
❑ 02699	The Bigger the Love/ I Don't Know Why	1982	4.00
❑ 11380	Don't Say No/Rockin' L.A.	1980	4.00
❑ 11432	Oh Susan/Sittin' On Ready	1981	4.00

ENTRANCE

Number	Title (A Side/B Side)	Yr	NM
❑ 7515	Broken Hearted/ I'm Always Wondering	1972	5.00

MCA CURB

Number	Title (A Side/B Side)	Yr	NM
❑ 52626	Ain't It Just Like Love/Guitar Bug	1985	3.00
❑ 52710	Who's Using Your Heart Tonight/ It Ain't Over	1985	3.00
❑ 52749	It's Not Easy/Try Me	1985	3.00
❑ 52852	Soldier of Love/Guitar Bug	1986	3.00

POLYDOR

Number	Title (A Side/B Side)	Yr	NM
❑ 2024	What's a Little Love Between Friends/Precious Times	1979	4.00
❑ 14530	Dreamin' My Way Back to You/ Shoo-Be-Doo	1979	4.00
❑ 14549	Believe What You Say/ Mississippi Line	1979	4.00

WARNER BROS.

Number	Title (A Side/B Side)	Yr	NM
❑ 7327	Frog Prince/One Extreme to the Other	1969	8.00
❑ 19042	Nothin' to Do (And All Night to Do It)/Can't Get Over You	1992	3.00

Albums

COLUMBIA

Number	Title (A Side/B Side)	Yr	NM
❑ JC 36792	Billy Burnette	1980	10.00
❑ FC 37460	Gimme You	1981	10.00

ENTRANCE

Number	Title (A Side/B Side)	Yr	NM
❑ Z 31228	Billy Burnette	1972	20.00

MCA CURB

Number	Title (A Side/B Side)	Yr	NM
❑ 5604	Try Me	1985	10.00

POLYDOR

Number	Title (A Side/B Side)	Yr	NM
❑ PD-1-6187	Billy Burnette	1979	10.00

BURNETTE, BILLY JOE

45s

BADGER

Number	Title (A Side/B Side)	Yr	NM
❑ 1004	Three Flags/(B-side unknown)	1989	6.00
❑ 2003	Help Me Make It Through the Night/(B-side unknown)	198?	6.00
❑ 2005	Anything to Keep from Going Home/(B-side unknown)	198?	6.00
❑ 2008	Our Last Goodbye/ (B-side unknown)	198?	6.00

GUSTO

Number	Title (A Side/B Side)	Yr	NM
❑ 167	Welcome Home Elvis/ Haven't Seen Mama in Years	1977	8.00
❑ 9009	The Colonel and the King/ Walk Again in the Hills	1978	12.00

—May be promo only

K-ARK

Number	Title (A Side/B Side)	Yr	NM
❑ 961	Blow Smoke on a Kangaroo/ Have I Told You Lately	1970	8.00

MT. VERNON

Number	Title (A Side/B Side)	Yr	NM
❑ 500	Stomp, Shake & Twist/ Don't Let Our Love Go Wrong	1962	800.00

—As "Billy Barnette"

Number	Title (A Side/B Side)	Yr	NM
❑ 501	Billy the Kid/I've Got a Heart	1962	400.00

PARKWAY

Number	Title (A Side/B Side)	Yr	NM
❑ 826	Two Brothers/Marlene	1961	25.00

—As "Billy Barnette"

Albums

GUSTO

Number	Title (A Side/B Side)	Yr	NM
❑ 994	Welcome Home, Elvis	1977	15.00

BURNETTE, DORSEY

Also see DORSEY AND JOHNNY BURNETTE.

45s

ABBOTT

Number	Title (A Side/B Side)	Yr	NM
❑ 188	Let's Fall in Love/ The Devil's Queen	1956	50.00
❑ 190	At a Distance/Jungle Magic	1957	50.00

CALLIOPE

Number	Title (A Side/B Side)	Yr	NM
❑ 8004	Things I Treasure/One Mornin'	1977	6.00
❑ 8012	Soon As I Touched Her/ Dear Hearted Children	1977	6.00

CAPITOL

Number	Title (A Side/B Side)	Yr	NM
❑ 3073	New Orleans Woman/ After the Long Drive Home	1971	5.00
❑ 3190	Shelby County Penal Farm/ Children of the Universe	1971	5.00
❑ 3307	In the Spring (The Roses Always Turn Red)/The Same Old You, The Same Old Me	1972	5.00
❑ 3404	I Just Couldn't Let Her Walk Away/Church Bells	1972	5.00
❑ 3463	Cry Mama/Lonely to Be Alone	1972	5.00
❑ 3529	I Let Another Good One Get Away/Take Your Weapons, Lay 'Em Down	1973	5.00
❑ 3588	Keep Out of My Dreams/ Mama, Mama	1973	5.00
❑ 3678	Darlin' (Don't Come Back)/ Sweet Lovin' Woman	1973	5.00
❑ 3796	It Happens Every Time/ Mr. Jukebox, Sing a Lullaby	1973	5.00
❑ 3829	Bob, All the Playboys, and Me/ The Bootleggers	1974	5.00
❑ 3887	Daddy Loves You Honey/ True Love Means Forgiving	1974	5.00
❑ 3963	What Ladies Can Do (When They Want To)/Tangerine	1974	5.00

CEE-JAM

Number	Title (A Side/B Side)	Yr	NM
❑ 16	Bertha Lou/Til the Law Says Stop	1957	80.00

DOT

Number	Title (A Side/B Side)	Yr	NM
❑ 16230	Rainin' in My Heart/A Full House	1961	16.00
❑ 16230	Rainin'/A Full House	1961	25.00
❑ 16265	The Feminine Touch/Sad Boy	1961	16.00
❑ 16305	A Country Boy in the Army/ A Dying Ember	1961	16.00

ELEKTRA

Number	Title (A Side/B Side)	Yr	NM
❑ 46513	Here I Go Again/What Would It Profit Me	1979	4.00
❑ 46586	B.J. Kick-a-Beaux/What Would It Profit Me	1980	4.00

ERA

Number	Title (A Side/B Side)	Yr	NM
❑ 3012	(There Was a)Tall Oak Tree/ Juarez Town	1960	20.00
❑ 3019	Hey Little One/Big Rock Candy Mountain	1960	16.00
❑ 3025	The Ghost of Billy Malloo/ Red Roses	1960	16.00
❑ 3033	The River and the Mountain/ This Hotel	1960	16.00
❑ 3033 [PS]	The River and the Mountain/ This Hotel	1960	40.00
❑ 3041	Hard Rock Mine/(It's No) Sin	1961	16.00
❑ 3045	Great Shakin' Fever/ That's Me Without You	1961	16.00

HAPPY TIGER

Number	Title (A Side/B Side)	Yr	NM
❑ 546	To Be a Man/Fly Away and Hurry Home	1970	6.00
❑ 563	One Lump Sum/ Call Me Lowdown	1970	6.00

HICKORY

Number	Title (A Side/B Side)	Yr	NM
❑ 1458	The House That Jack Built/ Ain't That Fine	1967	8.00

IMPERIAL

Number	Title (A Side/B Side)	Yr	NM
❑ 5561	Try/You Came as a Miracle	1959	25.00
❑ 5597	Lonely Train/Misery	1959	25.00
❑ 5668	Way in the Middle of the Night/ Your Love	1960	25.00
❑ 5756	House with a Tin Roof Top/ Circle Rock	1961	25.00
❑ 5987	House with a Tin Roof Top/ Circle Rock	1963	15.00

LIBERTY

Number	Title (A Side/B Side)	Yr	NM
❑ 56087	The Greatest Love/Thin Little Simple Little Plain Little Girl	1969	6.00

MEL-O-DY

Number	Title (A Side/B Side)	Yr	NM
❑ 113	Little Acorn/Cold As Usual	1964	15.00
❑ 116	Jimmy Brown/Everybody's Angel	1964	15.00
❑ 118	Long Long Time Ago/ Ever Since the World Began	1964	15.00

MELODYLAND

Number	Title (A Side/B Side)	Yr	NM
❑ 6007	Molly (I Ain't Gettin' Any Younger)/She's Feeling Low	1975	5.00
❑ 6019	Lyin' in Her Arms Again/ Doggone the Dogs	1975	5.00
❑ 6031	Ain't No Heartbreak/ I Dreamed I Saw	1976	5.00

MERCURY

Number	Title (A Side/B Side)	Yr	NM
❑ 72546	To Remember/In the Morning	1966	—

—Unreleased?

MUSIC FACTORY

Number	Title (A Side/B Side)	Yr	NM
❑ 417	I'll Walk Away/Son, You've Got to Make It Alone	1968	8.00

REPRISE

Number	Title (A Side/B Side)	Yr	NM
❑ 0246	Four for Texas/Foolish Pride	1963	15.00
❑ 0246 [PS]	Four for Texas/Foolish Pride	1963	40.00
❑ 20093	Castle in the Sky/Boys Keep Hanging Around	1962	15.00
❑ 20121	Darling Jane/I'm a Waitin' For Ya Baby	1962	15.00
❑ 20177	Invisible Chains/Pebbles	1963	15.00
❑ 20208	One of the Lonely/ Where's the Girl	1963	15.00

SMASH

Number	Title (A Side/B Side)	Yr	NM
❑ 2029	To Remember/In the Morning	1966	10.00
❑ 2039	If You Want to Love Somebody/ Teach Me Little Children	1966	10.00
❑ 2062	Tall Oak Tree/ I Just Can't Be Tamed	1966	10.00

U.S. NAVY

Number	Title (A Side/B Side)	Yr	NM
❑ (# unknown)	Be a Navy Man	196?	40.00
❑ (# unknown) [PS]	Be a Navy Man	196?	20.00

Albums

CALLIOPE

Number	Title (A Side/B Side)	Yr	NM
❑ CAL 7006	Things I Treasure	1977	12.00

CAPITOL

Number	Title (A Side/B Side)	Yr	NM
❑ ST-11094	Here and Now	1972	15.00
❑ ST-11219	Dorsey Burnette	1973	15.00

DOT

Number	Title (A Side/B Side)	Yr	NM
❑ DLP-3456 [M]	Dorsey Burnette Sings	1963	40.00
❑ DLP-25456 [S]	Dorsey Burnette Sings	1963	50.00

ERA

Number	Title (A Side/B Side)	Yr	NM
❑ EL-102 [M]	Tall Oak Tree	1960	150.00
❑ ES-102 [S]	Tall Oak Tree	1960	300.00
❑ ES-800 [M]	Dorsey Burnette's Greatest Hits	1969	25.00

GUSTO

Number	Title (A Side/B Side)	Yr	NM
❑ 0050	The Golden Hits of Dorsey Burnette	197?	12.00

BURNETTE, DORSEY AND JOHNNY

Also see each artist's individual listings.

45s

CORAL

Number	Title (A Side/B Side)	Yr	NM
❑ 62190	Blues Stay Away from Me/ Midnight Train	1960	200.00

—As "Johnny and Dorsey Burnette"

IMPERIAL

Number	Title (A Side/B Side)	Yr	NM
❑ 5509	Warm Love/My Honey	1958	100.00

—As "Burnette Brothers"

REPRISE

Number	Title (A Side/B Side)	Yr	NM
❑ 20153	It Don't Take Much/Hey Sue	1963	20.00

Albums

SOLID SMOKE

Number	Title (A Side/B Side)	Yr	NM
❑ SS-8005	Together Again	1978	15.00

BURNETTE, JOHNNY

Includes the Rock 'N' Roll Trio. Also see DORSEY AND JOHNNY BURNETTE.

45s

CAPITOL

Number	Title (A Side/B Side)	Yr	NM
❑ 5023	All Week Long/It Isn't There	1963	15.00
❑ 5114	You Taught Me the Way to Love You/The Opposite	1964	15.00
❑ 5176	Walkin' Talkin' Doll/Sweet Suzie	1964	15.00

CHANCELLOR

Number	Title (A Side/B Side)	Yr	NM
❑ 1116	I Wanna Thank Your Folks/ The Giant	1962	15.00
❑ 1123	Party Girl/Tag Along	1962	15.00
❑ 1129	Remember Me/ Time Is Not Enough	1962	15.00

CORAL

Number	Title (A Side/B Side)	Yr	NM
❑ 61651	Tear It Up/You're Undecided	1956	300.00
❑ 61675	Midnight Train/Oh Baby Babe	1956	300.00
❑ 61719	The Train Kept a-Rollin'/ Honey Hush	1956	250.00
❑ 61758	Lonesome Train/ I Just Found Out	1956	300.00
❑ 61829	Eager Beaver Baby/Touch Me	1957	300.00
❑ 61869	Drinkin' Wine Spo-Dee-O-Dee/ Butterfingers	1957	300.00
❑ 61918	Rock Billy Boogie/ If You Want It Enough	1957	300.00

FREEDOM

Number	Title (A Side/B Side)	Yr	NM
❑ 44001	I'm Restless/Kiss Me	1958	80.00
❑ 44011	Gumbo/Me and the Bear	1959	80.00
❑ 44017	Sweet Baby Doll/ I'll Never Love Again	1959	80.00

LIBERTY

Number	Title (A Side/B Side)	Yr	NM
❑ 55222	Settin' the Woods on Fire/ Kentucky Waltz	1959	20.00
❑ 55243	Don't Do It/Patrick Henry	1959	20.00
❑ 55258	Dreamin'/Cincinnati Fireball	1960	20.00
❑ 55285	You're Sixteen/ I Beg Your Pardon	1960	20.00

Except when noted otherwise, VG = 25% of NM, and VG+ = 50% of NM. (Example: VG = $2.00, VG+ = $4.00 and NM = $8.00.)

Number	Title (A Side/B Side)	Yr	NM
❑ 55285 [PS]	You're Sixteen/ I Beg Your Pardon	1960	50.00
❑ 55298	Little Boy Sad/ (I Go) Down to the River	1961	15.00
❑ 55298 [PS]	Little Boy Sad/ (I Go) Down to the River	1961	40.00
❑ 55318	Big Big World/Ballad of the One Eyed Jacks	1961	15.00
❑ 55318 [PS]	Big Big World/Ballad of the One Eyed Jacks	1961	40.00
❑ 55345	Girls/I've Got a Lot of Things to Do	1961	15.00
❑ 55377	Honestly I Do/Fools Like Me	1961	15.00
❑ 55379	God, Country and My Baby/ Honestly I Do	1961	15.00
❑ 55416	Clown Shoes/The Way I Am	1962	15.00
❑ 55448	The Fool of the Year/ The Poorest Boy in Town	1962	15.00
❑ 55489	Damn the Defiant/ Lonesome Waters	1962	15.00

MAGIC LAMP

Number	Title (A Side/B Side)	Yr	NM
❑ 515	Bigger Man/Less Than a Heartache	1964	50.00
❑ 515 [PS]	Bigger Man/Less Than a Heartache	1964	300.00

SAHARA

Number	Title (A Side/B Side)	Yr	NM
❑ 512	Fountain of Love/ What a Summer Day	1964	15.00

UNITED ARTISTS

Number	Title (A Side/B Side)	Yr	NM
❑ 0018	Dreamin'/Little Boy Sad	1973	4.00
—Silver Spotlight Series issue			
❑ 0019	You're Sixteen/God, Country and My Baby	1973	4.00
—Silver Spotlight Series issue			

VON

Number	Title (A Side/B Side)	Yr	NM
❑ 1006	You're Undecided/Go, Mule, Go	1954	3000.
—VG 1500; VG+ 2250			

7-Inch Extended Plays

LIBERTY

Number	Title (A Side/B Side)	Yr	NM
❑ LSX-1004	Dreamin'/Love Me// Settin' the Woods on Fire/ Please Help Me, I'm Falling	1960	100.00
❑ LSX-1004 [PS]	Dreamin'	1960	150.00
❑ LSX-1011	Little Boy Sad/Don't Do It// You're Sixteen/ I Go Down to the River	1961	100.00
❑ LSX-1011 [PS]	Johnny Burnette's Hits	1961	150.00

Albums

CORAL

Number	Title (A Side/B Side)	Yr	NM
❑ CRL 57080 [M]	Johnny Burnette & the Rock 'N' Roll Trio	1956	6000.

—Originals have maroon labels, machine-stamped (not engraved) numbers in the dead wax, printing on jacket's spine and "Printed in U.S.A." in lower right of back cover; VG value 2000; VG+ value 4000

LIBERTY

Number	Title (A Side/B Side)	Yr	NM
❑ LRP-3179 [M]	Dreamin'	1960	40.00
❑ LRP-3183 [M]	Johnny Burnette	1961	40.00
❑ LRP-3190 [M]	Johnny Burnette Sings	1961	40.00
❑ LRP-3206 [M]	Johnny Burnette's Hits and Other Favorites	1962	40.00
❑ LRP-3255 [M]	Roses Are Red	1962	40.00
❑ LRP-3389 [M]	The Johnny Burnette Story	1964	40.00
❑ LST-7179 [S]	Dreamin'	1960	60.00
❑ LST-7183 [S]	Johnny Burnette	1961	60.00
❑ LST-7190 [S]	Johnny Burnette Sings	1961	60.00
❑ LST-7206 [S]	Johnny Burnette's Hits and Other Favorites	1962	50.00
❑ LST-7255 [S]	Roses Are Red	1962	50.00
❑ LST-7389 [S]	The Johnny Burnette Story	1964	50.00

MCA

Number	Title (A Side/B Side)	Yr	NM
❑ 1513	Listen to Johnny Burnette and the Rock 'N' Roll Trio	1982	10.00

SOLID SMOKE

Number	Title (A Side/B Side)	Yr	NM
❑ SS-8001	Tear It Up	1978	15.00
—Black viinyl			
❑ SS-8001	Tear It Up	1978	30.00
—Blue vinyl			

SUNSET

Number	Title (A Side/B Side)	Yr	NM
❑ SUM-1179 [M]	Dreamin'	1967	15.00
❑ SUS-5179 [S]	Dreamin'	1967	20.00

UNITED ARTISTS

Number	Title (A Side/B Side)	Yr	NM
❑ UA-LA432-G	The Very Best of Johnny Burnette	1975	10.00

BURNETTE BROTHERS See DORSEY AND JOHNNY BURNETTE.

BURNING BUSH, THE

45s

MERCURY

Number	Title (A Side/B Side)	Yr	NM
❑ 72657	Keep On Burning/Evil Eye	1967	20.00

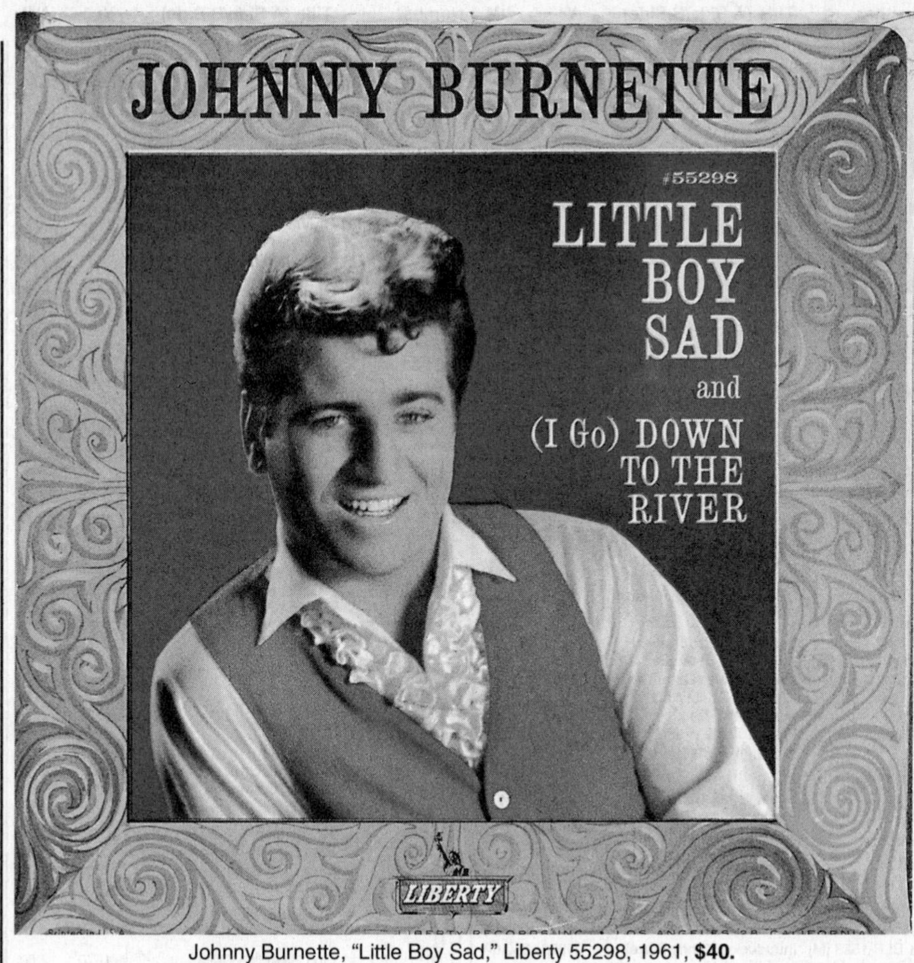

Johnny Burnette, "Little Boy Sad," Liberty 55298, 1961, **$40.**

BURNS, EDDIE

45s

CHECKER

Number	Title (A Side/B Side)	Yr	NM
❑ 790	Biscuit Baking Mama/ Superstition	1954	300.00
—As "Big Ed and His Combo"			

CHESS

Number	Title (A Side/B Side)	Yr	NM
❑ 1672	Treat Me Like I Treat You/ Don't Cha Leave Me Baby	1957	40.00

DELUXE

Number	Title (A Side/B Side)	Yr	NM
❑ 6024	Hello Miss Jessie Lee/ Dealing with the Devil	1953	200.00

HARVEY

Number	Title (A Side/B Side)	Yr	NM
❑ 111	Orange Driver/Hard Hearted Woman	1962	100.00
❑ 115	The Thing to Do/ Mean and Evil (Baby)	1962	30.00
❑ 118	Orange Driver/ Messin' with My Bread	1962	30.00

JVB

Number	Title (A Side/B Side)	Yr	NM
❑ 82	Treat Me Like I Treat You/ Don't Cha Leave Me Baby	1957	100.00

BURNS, RANDY

45s

MERCURY

Number	Title (A Side/B Side)	Yr	NM
❑ 73198	Living in the Country/ 17 Years on the River	1971	6.00

POLYDOR

Number	Title (A Side/B Side)	Yr	NM
❑ 14143	Hold On/Country Rain	1972	6.00

Albums

ESP-DISK'

Number	Title (A Side/B Side)	Yr	NM
❑ 1039	Songs of Love and War	1966	100.00
❑ 1089	Evening of the Magician	1968	75.00
❑ 2007	Song for an Uncertain Lady	1971	50.00

MERCURY

Number	Title (A Side/B Side)	Yr	NM
❑ SR-61329	Randy Burns and the Skydog Band	1971	25.00

POLYDOR

Number	Title (A Side/B Side)	Yr	NM
❑ PD-5030	I'm a Lover, Not a Fool	1972	12.00
❑ PD-5049	Still On Our Feet	1973	12.00

BURNT SUITE

Albums

B.J.W.

Number	Title (A Side/B Side)	Yr	NM
❑ 9	Burnt Suite	1972	200.00

BURRAGE, HAROLD

45s

ALADDIN

Number	Title (A Side/B Side)	Yr	NM
❑ 3194	Sweet Brown Gal/ Way Down Boogie	1953	60.00

COBRA

Number	Title (A Side/B Side)	Yr	NM
❑ 5004	One More Dance/ You Eat Too Much	1956	50.00
❑ 5012	Messed Up/I Don't Care Who Knows	1957	50.00
❑ 5018	Satisfied/Stop for the Red Light	1957	50.00
❑ 5022	She Knocks Me Out/A Heart	1958	50.00
❑ 5026	Betty Jean/I Cry for You	1958	50.00

DECCA

Number	Title (A Side/B Side)	Yr	NM
❑ 48175	Hi Ya/I Need You Baby	1950	100.00

M-PAC!

Number	Title (A Side/B Side)	Yr	NM
❑ 7201	The Master Key/ Faith and Understanding	1963	10.00
❑ 7204	Long Ways Together/ I'll Take One	1963	10.00
❑ 7210	That's a Friend/Everybody's Dancing	1964	10.00
❑ 7211	Baby I'm Alright/Fifty-Fifty	1964	10.00
❑ 7222	Your Friend/Take Me Now	1965	10.00
❑ 7225	Got to Find a Way/ How You Fix Your Mouth	1965	12.00
❑ 7229	More Power to You/ A Long Way Together	1966	10.00
❑ 7234	Take Me Now/You Make Me So Happy	1966	10.00

Number	Title (A Side/B Side)	Yr	NM
STATES			
❑ 144	Feel So Fine/You're Gonna Cry	1955	120.00
—Black vinyl			
❑ 144	Feel So Fine/You're Gonna Cry	1955	250.00
—Red vinyl			
VEE JAY			
❑ 318	What You Don't Know/ Crying for My Baby	1959	25.00
VIVID			
❑ 102	Betty Jean/I Cry for You	1959	40.00

BURRELL, KENNY

45s

Number	Title (A Side/B Side)	Yr	NM
BLUE NOTE			
❑ 1653	Delilah/The Dream's On Me	195?	10.00
❑ 1716	Yes Baby (Part 1)/ Yes Baby (Part 2)	195?	10.00
❑ 1717	Rock Salt (Part 1)/ Rock Salt (Part 2)	195?	10.00
❑ 1884	Good Life/Loie	196?	10.00
❑ 1885	Chittlins Con Carne (Part 1)/ Chittlins Con Carne (Part 2)	196?	10.00
❑ 1886	Wavy Gravy (Part 1)/ Wavy Gravy (Part 2)	196?	10.00
CADET			
❑ 5548	Hot Bossa/Mother-in-Law	1966	6.00
❑ 5555	The Little Drummer Boy/ Silent Night	1966	8.00
❑ 5597	Blues Fuse/Recapitulation	1968	6.00
PRESTIGE			
❑ 110	Don't Cry Baby (Part 1)/ Don't Cry Baby (Part 2)	195?	10.00
❑ 238	Montuno Blues/Out of This World	196?	8.00
❑ 260	I Thought About You/ It's Gettin' Dark	196?	8.00
❑ 281	Freight Trane (Part 1)/ Freight Trane (Part 2)	1963	8.00
VERVE			
❑ 10375	Downstairs/Loie	1966	8.00
❑ 10618	Burning Spear/The Preacher	1968	8.00

Albums

Number	Title	Yr	NM
ARGO			
❑ LP-655 [M]	A Night at the Vanguard	1959	30.00
❑ LPS-655 [S]	A Night at the Vanguard	1959	40.00
BLUE NOTE			
❑ BLP-1523 [M]	Introducing Kenny Burrell	1956	250.00
—Regular version, Lexington Ave. address on label			
❑ BLP-1523 [M]	Introducing Kenny Burrell	1956	400.00
—"Deep groove" version (deep indentation under label on both sides)			
❑ BLP-1523 [M]	Introducing Kenny Burrell	1957	80.00
—W. 63rd St., NYC address on label			
❑ BLP-1523 [M]	Introducing Kenny Burrell	1963	30.00
—New York, USA address on label			
❑ BLP-1543 [M]	Kenny Burrell, Vol. 2	1957	50.00
—W. 63rd St., NYC address on label			
❑ BLP-1543 [M]	Kenny Burrell, Vol. 2	1957	150.00
—Regular version, Lexington Ave. address on label			
❑ BLP-1543 [M]	Kenny Burrell, Vol. 2	1957	200.00
—"Deep groove" version (deep indentation under label on both sides)			
❑ BLP-1543 [M]	Kenny Burrell, Vol. 2	1963	25.00
—New York, USA address on label			
❑ BLP-1596 [M]	Blue Lights, Vol. 1	1958	80.00
—Regular version, W. 63rd St., NYC address on label			
❑ BLP-1596 [M]	Blue Lights, Vol. 1	1958	120.00
—"Deep groove" version (deep indentation under label on both sides)			
❑ BLP-1596 [M]	Blue Lights, Vol. 1	1963	25.00
—New York, USA address on label			
❑ BST-1596 [S]	Blue Lights, Vol. 1	1959	70.00
—Regular version, W. 63rd St., NYC address on label			
❑ BST-1596 [S]	Blue Lights, Vol. 1	1959	100.00
—"Deep groove" version (deep indentation under label on both sides)			
❑ BST-1596 [S]	Blue Lights, Vol. 1	1963	25.00
—New York, USA address on label			
❑ BLP-1597 [M]	Blue Lights, Vol. 2	1958	70.00
—Regular version, W. 63rd St., NYC address on label			
❑ BLP-1597 [M]	Blue Lights, Vol. 2	1958	100.00
—"Deep groove" version (deep indentation under label on both sides)			
❑ BLP-1597 [M]	Blue Lights, Vol. 2	1963	25.00
—New York, USA address on label			
❑ BST-1597 [S]	Blue Lights, Vol. 2	1959	70.00
—Regular version, W. 63rd St., NYC address on label			
❑ BST-1597 [S]	Blue Lights, Vol. 2	1959	100.00
—"Deep groove" version (deep indentation under label on both sides)			
❑ BST-1597 [S]	Blue Lights, Vol. 2	1963	25.00
—New York, USA address on label			
❑ BLP-4021 [M]	On View at the Five Spot Café	1960	70.00
—Regular version, W. 63rd St., NYC address on label			
❑ BLP-4021 [M]	On View at the Five Spot Café	1960	100.00
—"Deep groove" version (deep indentation under label on both sides)			
❑ BLP-4021 [M]	On View at the Five Spot Café	1963	25.00
—New York, USA address on label			
❑ BLP-4123 [M]	Midnight Blue	1963	30.00
—New York, USA address on label			
❑ BST-81523 [R]	Introducing Kenny Burrell	1967	12.00
—"A Division of Liberty Records" on label			
❑ BST-81543 [R]	Kenny Burrell, Vol. 2	1967	12.00
—"A Division of Liberty Records" on label			
❑ BST-81596 [S]	Blue Lights, Vol. 1	1967	15.00
—"A Division of Liberty Records" on label			
❑ BST-81597 [S]	Blue Lights, Vol. 2	1967	15.00
—"A Division of Liberty Records" on label			
❑ BST-84021 [S]	On View at the Five Spot Café	1960	60.00
—W. 63rd St., NYC address on label			
❑ BST-84021 [S]	On View at the Five Spot Café	1963	25.00
—New York, USA address on label			
❑ BST-84021 [S]	On View at the Five Spot Café	1967	15.00
—"A Division of Liberty Records" on label			
❑ BST-84123	Midnight Blue	1985	10.00
—"The Finest in Jazz Since 1939" reissue			
❑ BST-84123 [S]	Midnight Blue	1963	40.00
—New York, USA address on label			
❑ BST-84123 [S]	Midnight Blue	1967	15.00
—"A Division of Liberty Records" on label			
❑ B1-85137	Generation	1987	10.00
❑ B1-90260	Pieces of Blue and the Blues	1988	10.00
CADET			
❑ LP-769 [M]	Men at Work	1965	15.00
—Reissue of Argo 655			
❑ LPS-769 [S]	Men at Work	1965	20.00
—Reissue of Argo 655			
❑ LP-772 [M]	The Tender Gender	1966	15.00
❑ LPS-772 [S]	The Tender Gender	1966	20.00
❑ LP-779 [M]	Have Yourself a Soulful Little Christmas	1966	15.00
❑ LPS-779 [S]	Have Yourself a Soulful Little Christmas	1966	20.00
❑ LP-798 [M]	Ode to 52nd Street	1967	20.00
❑ LPS-798 [S]	Ode to 52nd Street	1967	15.00
CHESS			
❑ CH-9316	A Night at the Vanguard	1990	12.00
—Reissue of Argo 655			
❑ CH-60019 [(2)]	Cool Cookin'	1973	15.00
❑ CH2-92509 [(2)]	Recapitulation	198?	12.00
COLUMBIA			
❑ CL 1703 [M]	Weaver of Dreams	1961	20.00
❑ CS 8503 [S]	Weaver of Dreams	1961	25.00
CONCORD JAZZ			
❑ CJ-45	Tin Tin Deo	1978	10.00
❑ CJ-83	When Lights Are Low	1978	10.00
❑ CJ-121	Moon and Sand	1980	10.00
CONTEMPORARY			
❑ C-14058	Guiding Spirit	1990	12.00
CTI			
❑ 6011	God Bless the Child	1970	12.00
DENON			
❑ 7533	Lush Life	1979	15.00
❑ 7541	'Round Midnight	1979	15.00
FANTASY			
❑ OJC-019	Kenny Burrell	198?	10.00
—Reissue of Prestige 7088			
❑ OJC-216	Two Guitars	198?	10.00
❑ OJC-427	All Night Long	1990	12.00
❑ OJC-456	All Day Long	1990	12.00
❑ MPF-4506	For Duke	1981	10.00
❑ F-9417	'Round Midnight	1972	12.00
❑ F-9427	Both Feet on the Ground	1973	12.00
❑ F-9458	Up the Street	1974	12.00
❑ F-9514	Sky Street	1975	12.00
❑ F-9558	Stormy Monday	1978	12.00
❑ 79005 [(2)]	Ellington Is Forever	1975	15.00
❑ 79008 [(2)]	Ellington Is Forever, Vol. 2	197?	15.00
KAPP			
❑ KL-1326 [M]	Lotta Bossa Nova	1962	20.00
❑ KS-3326 [S]	Lotta Bossa Nova	1962	25.00
MOODSVILLE			
❑ MVLP-29 [M]	Bluesy Burrell	1963	40.00
—Green label			
❑ MVLP-29 [M]	Bluesy Burrell	1965	20.00
—Blue label with trident logo			
❑ MVST-29 [S]	Bluesy Burrell	1963	40.00
—Green label			
❑ MVST-29 [S]	Bluesy Burrell	1965	25.00
—Blue label with trident logo			
MUSE			
❑ 5144	Handcrafted	1979	10.00
❑ 5216	Live at the Village Vanguard	1979	10.00
❑ 5241	Kenny Burrell in New York	1982	10.00
❑ 5264	Listen to the Dawn	1982	10.00
❑ 5281	Groovin' High	1983	10.00
❑ 5317	A La Carte	1984	10.00
PAUSA			
❑ 9000	Midnight	198?	10.00
PRESTIGE			
❑ PRLP-7073 [M]	All Night Long	1957	100.00
—Actually an all-star session; reissued as a Kenny Burrell album, thus it is listed here			
❑ PRLP-7081 [M]	All Day Long	1957	100.00
—Actually an all-star session; reissued as a Kenny Burrell album, thus it is listed here			
❑ PRLP-7088 [M]	Kenny Burrell	1957	80.00
❑ PRLP-7277 [M]	All Day Long	1963	50.00
—Reissue of 7081			
❑ PRST-7277 [R]	All Day Long	1963	20.00
❑ PRLP-7289 [M]	All Night Long	1964	50.00
—Reissue of 7073			
❑ PRST-7289 [R]	All Night Long	1964	20.00
❑ PRLP-7308 [M]	Blue Moods	1964	30.00
—Reissue of 7088			
❑ PRST-7308 [R]	Blue Moods	1964	20.00
❑ PRLP-7315 [M]	Soul Call	1964	25.00
❑ PRST-7315 [S]	Soul Call	1964	30.00
❑ PRLP-7347 [M]	Crash	1964	25.00
❑ PRST-7347 [S]	Crash	1964	30.00
❑ PRLP-7448 [M]	The Best of Kenny Burrell	1967	30.00
❑ PRST-7448 [S]	The Best of Kenny Burrell	1967	20.00
❑ PRST-7578	Out of This World	1968	15.00
—Reissue of Moodsville 29			
❑ 24025 [(2)]	All Day Long & All Night Long	197?	15.00
—Reissue of both albums in one package			
SAVOY JAZZ			
❑ SJL-1120	Monday Stroll	1978	10.00
—Reissue			
VERVE			
❑ UMV-2070	Guitar Forms	198?	10.00
—Reissue of 8612			
❑ V-8553 [M]	Blue Bash!	1963	20.00
❑ V6-8553 [S]	Blue Bash!	1963	25.00
❑ V-8612 [M]	Guitar Forms	1965	15.00
❑ V6-8612 [S]	Guitar Forms	1965	20.00
❑ V-8656 [M]	A Generation Ago Today	1966	15.00
❑ V6-8656 [S]	A Generation Ago Today	1966	20.00
❑ V-8746 [M]	Blues— The Common Ground	1968	20.00
❑ V6-8746 [S]	Blues— The Common Ground	1968	15.00
❑ V6-8751	Night Song	1968	15.00
❑ V6-8773	Asphalt Canyon Suite	1969	15.00
VOSS			
❑ VLP1-42930	Heritage	1988	10.00

BURRELL, KENNY, AND JOHN COLTRANE

Albums

Number	Title	Yr	NM
FANTASY			
❑ OJC-079	The Cats	198?	10.00
—Reissue of New Jazz 8217			
❑ OJC-300	Kenny Burrell and John Coltrane	1987	10.00
NEW JAZZ			
❑ NJLP-8217 [M]	The Cats	1959	80.00
—Purple label			
❑ NJLP-8217 [M]	The Cats	1965	25.00
—Blue label with trident logo			
❑ NJLP-8276 [M]	Kenny Burrell with John Coltrane	1962	60.00
—Purple label			
❑ NJLP-8276 [M]	Kenny Burrell with John Coltrane	1965	25.00
—Blue label with trident logo			
PRESTIGE			
❑ PRLP-7532 [M]	Kenny Burrell Quintet with John Coltrane	1967	30.00
❑ PRST-7532 [S]	Kenny Burrell Quintet with John Coltrane	1967	20.00
❑ 24059 [(2)]	Kenny Burrell & John Coltrane	197?	15.00
—Reissue of New Jazz and Prestige LPs in one package			

BURRELL, KENNY; TINY GRIMES; BILL JENNINGS

Albums

Number	Title	Yr	NM
STATUS			
❑ ST-8318 [M]	Guitar Soul	1965	40.00

BURRELL, KENNY, AND JIMMY RANEY

Albums

Number	Title	Yr	NM
PRESTIGE			
❑ PRLP-7119 [M]	Two Guitars	1957	80.00

BURRELL, KENNY, AND GROVER WASHINGTON. JR.

Albums

Number	Title	Yr	NM
BLUE NOTE			
❑ BT-85106	Togethering	1985	10.00

BURRITO BROTHERS, THE

See THE FLYING BURRITO BROTHERS.

BURROUGHS, WILLIAM

Albums

Number	Title	Yr	NM
ESP-DISK'			
❑ 1050 [M]	Call Me Burroughs	1967	100.00

BURT, TOM

45s

Number	Title (A Side/B Side)	Yr	NM
CAMEO			
❑ 363	OK Girl/All Through the Night	1965	15.00

Except when noted otherwise, VG = 25% of NM, and VG+ = 50% of NM. (Example: VG = $2.00, VG+ = $4.00 and NM = $8.00.)

Number	Title (A Side/B Side)	Yr	NM
BURTON, JAMES			
45s			
PHILIPS			
❑ 40137	Swamp Surfer/Everybody Listen to the Dobro	1963	40.00
—As "Jimmy Dobro"			
BUSH, BILL			
45s			
RONN			
❑ 17	I'm Waiting/A Velvet Touch	1967	1500.
BUSH, DICK			
45s			
ERA			
❑ 1067	Hollywood Party/Exactly	1957	50.00
BUSH, KATE			
12-Inch Singles			
EMI AMERICA			
❑ SPRO [DJ]	Hounds of Love (3:01)/ Hounds of Love (3:44)	1985	25.00
❑ V-7865	Running Up That Hill (Extended)/(Instrumental)/ Under the Ivy	1985	10.00
❑ SPRO 9574/5 [DJ]	Hounds of Love (3:01)/(3:44)	1985	25.00
❑ SPRO 9892 [DJ]	Experiment IV (same on both sides)	1986	15.00
❑ SPRO9892 [DJ]	Experiment IV (same on both sides)	1986	25.00
❑ SPRO9995 [DJ]	Cloudbursting (same on both sides)	1985	12.00
❑ SPRO 9995 [DJ]	Cloudbursting (same on both sides)	1985	12.00
❑ V-19213	The Big Sky (Meterological Mix) (Special Single Mix)/ Not This Time	1986	8.00
❑ V-19228	Experiment IV/Wuthering Heights (New Vocal Version)/ December Will Be Magic Again	1986	10.00
45s			
COLUMBIA			
❑ 73092	Love and Anger/Walk Straight Down the Middle	1990	—
—May be cassette only			
❑ 77280	Rubberband Girl/ This Woman's Work	1993	—
—Cassette only			
EMI			
❑ 5121	December Will Be Magic Again/ Warm And Soothing	1980	10.00
—U.K. import			
❑ 5121 [PS]	December Will Be Magic Again/ Warm And Soothing	1980	15.00
—U.K. import			
EMI AMERICA			
❑ 8003	Wuthering Heights/Kite	1978	10.00
❑ 8003 [PS]	Wuthering Heights/Kite	1978	15.00
❑ 8006	The Man with the Child in His Eyes/Moving	1978	6.00
❑ B-8285	Running Up That Hill/ Under the Ivy	1985	4.00
❑ B-8285 [PS]	Running Up That Hill/ Under the Ivy	1985	5.00
❑ B-8302	Hounds of Love/Burning Bridge	1985	5.00
❑ B-8302 [PS]	Hounds of Love/Burning Bridge	1985	8.00
❑ B-8327	The Big Sky/Not This Time	1986	5.00
❑ B-8327 [PS]	The Big Sky/Not This Time	1986	8.00
❑ B-8363	Experiment IV/Wuthering Heights (New Vocal)	1986	5.00
❑ B-8363 [PS]	Experiment IV/Wuthering Heights (New Vocal)	1986	8.00
❑ B-8386	Cloudbusting/The Man with the Child in His Eyes	1986	5.00
❑ B-8386 [PS]	Cloudbusting/The Man with the Child in His Eyes	1986	8.00
Albums			
COLUMBIA			
❑ OC 44164	The Sensual World	1989	12.00
EMI AMERICA			
❑ SW-17003	The Kick Inside	1978	10.00
—Reissue of Harvest release			
❑ SMAS-17008	Lionheart	1978	15.00
❑ ST-17084	The Dreaming	1982	10.00
❑ ST-17115	Never for Ever	1983	10.00
❑ ST-17171	Hounds of Love	1985	10.00
—Black vinyl			
❑ ST-17171	Hounds of Love	1985	30.00
—Marbled vinyl			
❑ PWAS-17242	The Whole Story	1986	15.00
❑ MLP-19004 [EP]	Kate Bush	1983	15.00
HARVEST			
❑ SW-11761	The Kick Inside	1978	25.00
STEVE STROUT & ASSOC.			
❑ SSA 3021	Kate Bush Radio Special: Self-Portrait	1978	450.00
—Uses The Kick Inside cover with special wrapper band			
BUSTERS, THE			
45s			
ARLEN			
❑ 735	Bust Out/Astronaut's	1963	20.00
❑ 740	All American Surfer/ Pine Tree Hop	1963	20.00
❑ 745	Heartaches/Torrid Zone	1964	20.00
UNITED ARTISTS			
❑ 0145	Bust Out/The Green Mosquito	1973	5.00
—Silver Spotlight Series issue; B-side by the Tune Rockers			
BUTANES, THE			
45s			
ENRICA			
❑ 1007	Don't Forget I Love You/ That My Desire	1961	25.00
BUTLER, CARL Also see CARL BUTLER AND PEARL.			
45s			
CAPITOL			
❑ F1335	Heartbreak Express/White Rose	1950	30.00
❑ F1399	Plastic Man/Country Mile	1951	25.00
❑ F1454	Shake, Rattle & Roll/No Guarantee on My Heart	1951	25.00
❑ F1541	Our Last Rendezvous/ I Live My Life Alone	1951	20.00
❑ F1701	Linda Lou/No Trespassing	1951	20.00
❑ F1813	A String of Empties/You Plus Me	1951	20.00
❑ F1891	Blue Million Tears/River of Love	1951	20.00
❑ F1996	Alone Without You/Vicious Lies	1952	20.00
❑ F2084	Penny for Your Thoughts/ Everything Will Be the Same	1952	20.00
❑ F2158	Stepping on My Heart/ I Need You So	1952	20.00
COLUMBIA			
❑ 4-21353	Angel Band/Hallelujah We Shall Rise	1955	20.00
❑ 4-21407	Wedding Day/If I Could Spend My Heartaches	1955	20.00
❑ 4-21455	It's My Sin/Borrowed Love	1955	20.00
❑ 4-40874	Your Cold Heart Told Me So/ I Know What It Means to Be Lonesome	1957	15.00
❑ 40994	River of Tears/Cry, You Fool, Cry	1957	12.00
❑ 41119	If You've Got the Money (I've Got the Time)/ Nothing I'd Rather Do	1958	10.00
❑ 41205	Jealous Heart/So Close	1958	10.00
❑ 41263	Baby I'm a-Waitin'/ My Cajun Baby	1958	10.00
❑ 41368	I Like to Pretend/ Oh, How I Miss You	1959	10.00
❑ 41475	Remember the Alamo/ Grief in My Heart	1959	10.00
❑ 41560	You Jes' Don't Steal from a Poor Man/Cry, You Fool, Cry	1960	10.00
❑ 41674	The Door/I Know Why I Cry	1960	10.00
❑ 41869	I'm a Prisoner of Love/ For the First Time	1960	10.00
❑ 41997	Honky Tonkitis/ You Were the Orchid	1961	10.00
❑ 42306	Have You Run Out of Lies/ If I Had Only Met You First	1962	10.00
❑ 42593	Don't Let Me Cross Over/ Wonder Drug	1962	10.00
OKEH			
❑ 18003	Just for Fooling Around/ You Can't Insure a House of Dreams	1954	15.00
❑ 18012	Crowded Out/My Heart Tells Me	1954	15.00
❑ 18018	So Close/It's Wrong to Be Jealous	1954	15.00
❑ 18032	A Victim of Lies/I Just Said Goodbye to My Dreams	1955	15.00
❑ 18039	That's All Right/ I'll Go Steppin' Too	1955	20.00
❑ 18052	Kisses Don't Lie/I Wouldn't Change You If I Could	1955	15.00
Albums			
COLUMBIA			
❑ CL 2002 [M]	Don't Let Me Cross Over	1963	20.00
❑ CS 8802 [S]	Don't Let Me Cross Over	1963	25.00
HARMONY			
❑ HL 7385 [M]	The Great Carl Butler Sings	1966	12.00
❑ HS 11185 [S]	The Great Carl Butler Sings	1966	15.00
❑ H 30674	For the First Time	1971	12.00
BUTLER, CARL, AND PEARL Also see CARL BUTLER.			
45s			
CHART			
❑ 5145	Temptation Keeps Twisting Her Arm/I'm So Close to Loving You	1972	4.00
❑ 5160	She Didn't Come Home/ wo of a Kind	1972	4.00
❑ 5191	Heartaches for Lunch/ Fifteen Years Ago	1973	4.00
COLUMBIA			
❑ 42778	Loving Arms/Who'll Be Next	1963	8.00
❑ 42892	Too Late to Try Again/ My Tears Don't Show	1963	8.00
❑ 43030	I'm Hanging Up the Phone/ Just a Message	1964	8.00
❑ 43102	Forbidden Street/When the Door Swings Shut	1964	8.00
❑ 43210	Just Thought I'd Let You Know/ We'd Destroy Each Other	1965	8.00
❑ 43335	Beers and Tears/ Can I Draw the Line	1965	8.00
❑ 43433	Our Ship of Love/ It's Called Cheating	1965	8.00
❑ 43536	Little Mac/Wrong Generation	1966	8.00
❑ 43685	Little Pedro/Cell 29	1966	8.00
❑ 43869	Same Old Me Lovin' Same Old You/Dreaming of a Little Cabin	1966	8.00
❑ 44043	Wild Goose Chase/Lost	1967	6.00
❑ 44252	Guilty of Love/For a Minute	1967	6.00
❑ 44447	If You Should Ever Stop Loving Me/If I'd Only Met You First	1968	6.00
❑ 44587	Punish Me Tomorrow/ Goodbye Tennessee	1968	6.00
❑ 44694	I Never Got Over You/ I Started Loving You Again	1968	6.00
❑ 44862	We'll Sweep Out the Ashes in the Morning/Your Way of Life	1969	6.00
❑ 45112	Used to Own This Train/Caution	1970	5.00
❑ 45228	Bottoms Up/Let the Sun Shine on the People	1970	5.00
Albums			
CHART			
❑ 1051	Temptation Keeps Twistin' Her Arm	1972	15.00
COLUMBIA			
❑ CS 1039	Carl and Pearl Butler's Greatest Hits	1970	15.00
❑ CL 2125 [M]	Loving Arms	1964	20.00
❑ CL 2308 [M]	The Old and the New	1965	15.00
❑ CL 2640 [M]	Avenue of Prayer	1967	20.00
❑ CS 8925 [S]	Loving Arms	1964	25.00
❑ CS 9108 [S]	The Old and the New	1965	20.00
❑ CS 9440 [S]	Avenue of Prayer	1967	15.00
❑ CS 9651	Our Country World	1968	15.00
❑ CS 9769	Honky Tonkin'	1969	15.00
HARMONY			
❑ H 31182	Watch and Pray	1972	12.00
BUTLER, FREDDIE			
45s			
KAPP			
❑ 819	This Thing/There Was a Time	1967	15.00
WHEELSVILLE			
❑ 10001	Save Your Love for Me/ (B-side unknown)	196?	1000.
Albums			
KAPP			
❑ KS-3519	With a Dab of Soul	1968	30.00
BUTLER, JIMMY			
45s			
GEM			
❑ 222	Trim Your Tree/ Cruelty For Kindness	1954	50.00
BUTLER, JOE Also see THE LOVIN' SPOONFUL.			
45s			
KAMA SUTRA			
❑ 264	Revelation, Revolution '69/ War Games	1969	8.00
❑ 264 [PS]	Revelation, Revolution '69/ War Games	1969	20.00
BUTLERS, THE			
45s			
ROUSER			
❑ 1017	Because of My Heart/ (B-side unknown)	196?	3000.

BUTTERFIELD, PAUL

45s

BEARSVILLE

Number	Title (A Side/B Side)	Yr	NM
❑ 49706	Living in Memphis/Footprints on the Windshield (Upside Down)	1981	4.00

ELEKTRA

Number	Title (A Side/B Side)	Yr	NM
❑ 45016	Got My Mojo Working/Mellow Down Easy	1964	10.00
❑ 45609	Come On In/I Got a Mind to Give Up Living	1967	10.00
❑ 45620	Run Out of Time/One More Heartache	1967	10.00
❑ 45620 [PS]	Run Out of Time/One More Heartache	1967	20.00
❑ 45643	In My Own Dream/(B-side unknown)	1968	12.00
❑ 45658	Where Did My Baby Go/In My Own Dream	1969	10.00
❑ 45692	Love March/(B-side unknown)	1970	12.00

Albums

AMHERST

Number	Title (A Side/B Side)	Yr	NM
❑ AMH-3305	The Legendary Paul Butterfield Rides Again	1986	12.00

BEARSVILLE

Number	Title (A Side/B Side)	Yr	NM
❑ BR 2119	Paul Butterfield's Better Days	1973	12.00
❑ BR 2170	It All Comes Back	1973	12.00
❑ BR 6960	Put It In Your Ear	1976	12.00
❑ BRK 6995	North-South	1978	12.00

ELEKTRA

Number	Title (A Side/B Side)	Yr	NM
❑ EKL-294 [M]	The Paul Butterfield Blues Band	1965	20.00
—Gold label with guitar player			
❑ EKL-294 [M]	The Paul Butterfield Blues Band	1966	15.00
—Brown label			
❑ EKL-315 [M]	East-West	1966	20.00
—Gold label with guitar player			
❑ EKL-315 [M]	East-West	1967	15.00
—Brown label			
❑ 7E-2001 [(2)]	The Butterfield Blues Band/Live	1970	25.00
❑ 7E-2005 [(2)]	Golden Butter/The Best of the Paul Butterfield Blues Band	1972	25.00
❑ EKL-4015 [M]	The Resurrection of Pigboy Crabshaw	1967	30.00
❑ EKS-7294 [S]	The Paul Butterfield Blues Band	1965	25.00
—Gold label with guitar player			
❑ EKS-7294 [S]	The Paul Butterfield Blues Band	1966	20.00
—Brown label			
❑ EKS-7294 [S]	The Paul Butterfield Blues Band	1969	15.00
—Red label with large stylized "E"			
❑ EKS-7294 [S]	The Paul Butterfield Blues Band	1971	12.00
—Butterfly label			
❑ EKS-7315 [S]	East-West	1966	25.00
—Gold label with guitar player			
❑ EKS-7315 [S]	East-West	1967	20.00
—Brown label			
❑ EKS-7315 [S]	East-West	1969	15.00
—Red label with large stylized "E"			
❑ EKS-7315 [S]	East-West	1971	12.00
—Butterfly label			
❑ EKS-74015 [S]	The Resurrection of Pigboy Crabshaw	1967	20.00
—Brown label			
❑ EKS-74015 [S]	The Resurrection of Pigboy Crabshaw	1969	15.00
—Red label with large stylized "E"			
❑ EKS-74015 [S]	The Resurrection of Pigboy Crabshaw	1971	12.00
—Butterfly label			
❑ EKS-74025	In My Own Dream	1968	20.00
—Brown label			
❑ EKS-74025	In My Own Dream	1969	15.00
—Red label with large stylized "E"			
❑ EKS-74025	In My Own Dream	1971	12.00
—Butterfly label			
❑ EKS-74053	Keep On Moving	1969	20.00
—Red label with large stylized "E"			
❑ EKS-74053	Keep On Moving	1971	12.00
—Butterfly label			
❑ EKS-75013	Sometimes I Just Feel Like Smilin'	1971	20.00

RHINO

Number	Title (A Side/B Side)	Yr	NM
❑ RNLP-70877	Paul Butterfield's Better Days	1987	8.00
—Reissue of Bearsville 2119			
❑ RNLP-70878	It All Comes Back	1987	8.00
—Reissue of Bearsville 2170			
❑ RNLP-70879	Put It In Your Ear	1987	8.00
—Reissue of Bearsville 6960			
❑ RNLP-70880	North-South	1987	8.00
—Reissue of Bearsville 6995			

SUNDAZED

Number	Title (A Side/B Side)	Yr	NM
❑ LP 5095 [S]	The Paul Butterfield Blues Band	2001	12.00
—Reissue on 180-gram vinyl			
❑ LP 5096	East-West	2001	12.00
—Reissue on 180-gram vinyl			

BUTTERFLYS, THE

45s

RED BIRD

Number	Title (A Side/B Side)	Yr	NM
❑ 10-009	Goodnight Baby/The Swim	1964	25.00
❑ 10-016	I Wonder/Gee, Baby, Gee	1964	25.00

BUTTHOLE SURFERS

10-Inch Singles

CAPITOL

Number	Title (A Side/B Side)	Yr	NM
❑ SPRO [DJ]	Chewin' George Lucas' Chocolate/Goofy's Concern/Beat the Press/Ghandi/Neee Neee	1993	15.00
—Promo-only 10-inch on brown vinyl			
❑ SPRO-11230 [DJ]	Pepper (same on both sides)	1996	6.00
❑ SPRO 79612/3 [DJ]	Chewin' George Lucas' Chocolate/Goofy's Concern/Beat the Press/Ghandi/Neee Neee	1993	20.00
—Promo-only 10-inch on brown vinyl			

12-Inch Singles

CAPITOL

Number	Title (A Side/B Side)	Yr	NM
❑ SPRO-11313 [DJ]	Pepper (3 versions)/Jingle of a Dog's Collar	1996	12.00

45s

CAPITOL

Number	Title (A Side/B Side)	Yr	NM
❑ GAG 94	Good King Wenceslaus/The Lord Is a Monkey	1994	10.00
—Picture disc			
❑ S7-17514	Who Was In My Room Last Night?/Dancing Fool	1993	5.00
❑ S7-19200	Pepper/Birds	1996	4.00
❑ S7-19253	Cough Syrup/Jingle of a Dog's Collar	1996	4.00

ROUGH TRADE

Number	Title (A Side/B Side)	Yr	NM
❑ RUS 97-3	Hurdy Gurdy Man/Barking Dogs	1990	5.00
—Gold vinyl			
❑ RUS 97-3 [PS]	Hurdy Gurdy Man/Barking Dogs	1990	5.00

Albums

ALTERNATIVE TENTACLES

Number	Title (A Side/B Side)	Yr	NM
❑ VIRUS 32 [EP]	Brown Reason to Live	198?	8.00
—Black vinyl			
❑ VIRUS 32 [EP]	Brown Reason to Live	1983	20.00
—Retitled version of debut EP with brown swirl vinyl			
❑ VIRUS 32 [EP]	Butthole Surfers	1983	25.00
—Original pressing of debut EP with no title			
❑ VIRUS 39 [EP]	Live PCPPEP	1984	8.00

CAPITOL

Number	Title (A Side/B Side)	Yr	NM
❑ C1-29842 [(2)]	Electriclarryland	1996	15.00
❑ C1-98798	Independent Worm Saloon	1993	15.00

HOLLYWOOD

Number	Title (A Side/B Side)	Yr	NM
❑ 41447-1	Weird Revolution	2001	15.00
—Pressed in Germany for U.S. release			

LATINO BUGGERVEIL

Number	Title (A Side/B Side)	Yr	NM
❑ LBV 07 [(2)]	Humpty Dumpty LSD	2002	20.00

ROUGH TRADE

Number	Title (A Side/B Side)	Yr	NM
❑ R260	Pioughd	1990	20.00

TOUCH & GO

Number	Title (A Side/B Side)	Yr	NM
❑ 5	Psychic...Powerless...Another Man's Sac	1985	10.00
—Reissue on black vinyl			
❑ 5	Psychic...Powerless...Another Man's Sac	1985	20.00
—Original on clear vinyl			
❑ 8	Rembrandt Pussyhorse	1986	10.00
—Black vinyl			
❑ 8	Rembrandt Pussyhorse	1986	40.00
—Red vinyl; supposedly only 100 were pressed			
❑ 14 [EP]	Cream Corn from the Socket of Davis	1985	10.00
—Black vinyl			
❑ 14 [EP]	Cream Corn from the Socket of Davis	1985	20.00
—Red vinyl			
❑ 14 [EP]	Cream Corn from the Socket of Davis	1985	25.00
—Yellow vinyl in green generic sleeve with sticker			
❑ 19	Locust Abortion Technician	1987	10.00
❑ 29	Hairway to Steven	1988	10.00
❑ 50	Widowermaker!	1989	10.00

BUTTS BAND

With Robbie Krieger and John Densmore of THE DOORS.

12-Inch Singles

RHINO

Number	Title (A Side/B Side)	Yr	NM
❑ RNTI 403	Kinky Reggae/Get Up, Stand Up	1983	25.00
—As "The Krieger-Densmore Reggae Bonanza"			

45s

BLUE THUMB

Number	Title (A Side/B Side)	Yr	NM
❑ 242	Pop a Top/Baja Bus	1973	8.00
❑ 252	I Won't Be Alone Anymore/Kansas City	1974	8.00
❑ 263	Get Up, Stand Up/Mike's Blues	1975	8.00

Albums

BLUE THUMB

Number	Title (A Side/B Side)	Yr	NM
❑ BTS-53	Butts Band	1973	12.00
❑ BTS-6018	Hear and Now	1975	12.00

BUZZCOCKS, THE

MAGAZINE related. Also see PETE SHELLEY. MAGAZINE related. Also see PETE SHELLEY.

45s

I.R.S.

Number	Title (A Side/B Side)	Yr	NM
❑ 9001	Everybody's Happy Nowadays/Why Can't I Touch It	1979	6.00
❑ 9001 [PS]	Everybody's Happy Nowadays/Why Can't I Touch It	1979	6.00
❑ 9010	I Believe/Something's Gone Wrong Again	1980	5.00
❑ 9010 [PS]	I Believe/Something's Gone Wrong Again	1980	5.00
❑ 9017	Are Everything/Why, She's a Girl from the Chain Store	1980	5.00
❑ 9017 [PS]	Are Everything/Why, She's a Girl from the Chain Store	1980	5.00
❑ 9019	Strange Thing/Airwaves Dream	1980	5.00
❑ 9019 [PS]	Strange Thing/Airwaves Dream	1980	5.00
❑ 9020	Running Free/What Do You Know	1981	5.00
❑ 9020 [PS]	Running Free/What Do You Know	1981	5.00

Albums

GO-KART

Number	Title (A Side/B Side)	Yr	NM
❑ GK 058	Modern	1999	10.00

I.R.S.

Number	Title (A Side/B Side)	Yr	NM
❑ - [DJ]	Are Everything/Strange Thing + 4	1980	15.00
—Red vinyl; no cover; some come with numbered sticker			
❑ SP-001	Singles Going Steady	1979	15.00
—Original issue			
❑ SP-009	A Different Kind of Tension	1980	15.00
—Original issue			
❑ SP-70507 [EP]	Parts 1-3	1984	10.00
❑ SP-70955 [DJ]	Parts 1-3	1981	25.00
—Original issue; six-song promo on red vinyl in plastic cover with numbered sticker			
❑ SP-75001	Singles Going Steady	1981	10.00
—Reissue of SP-001			
❑ SP-75009	A Different Kind of Tension	1981	10.00
—Reissue of SP-009			

BYE BYES, THE

45s

MERCURY

Number	Title (A Side/B Side)	Yr	NM
❑ 71530	Blonde Hair, Blue Eyes, Ruby Red Lips/Do You	1959	15.00

BYRD, BOBBY

Two different artists have this name. For records on the Cash, Jamie and Sage & Sand labels, see BOBBY DAY.

45s

ABC

Number	Title (A Side/B Side)	Yr	NM
❑ 11134	Here Is My Everything/Loving You	1968	10.00
—With Vicki Anderson			

BANG

Number	Title (A Side/B Side)	Yr	NM
❑ 562	Whatcha Gonna Do About It/If She's There	1968	6.00

BROWNSTONE

Number	Title (A Side/B Side)	Yr	NM
❑ 4203	Hot Pants - I'm Coming, Coming, I'm Coming	1971	6.00
❑ 4205	Keep On Doin' What You're Doin'/Let Me Know	1971	6.00
❑ 4206	If You Got a Love You Better (Hold On to It)/You Have Got to Change Your Mind	1972	6.00
❑ 4208	Never Get Enough/My Concerto	1972	6.00
❑ 4209	Sayin' It and Doin' It Are Two Different Things/Never Get Enough	1972	6.00
❑ 4210	Signed, Sealed and Delivered/I Need Help (I Can't Do It Alone)	1973	6.00

FEDERAL

Number	Title (A Side/B Side)	Yr	NM
❑ 12486	They Are Sayin'/I Found Out	1963	15.00

INTERNATIONAL BROTHERS

Number	Title (A Side/B Side)	Yr	NM
❑ 901	Back from the Dead/The Way to Get Down	1975	6.00

KING

Number	Title (A Side/B Side)	Yr	NM
❑ 6069	I Found Out/I'll Keep Pressing On	1967	6.00
❑ 6126	Funky Soul #1 (Part 1)/Funky Soul #1 (Part 2)	1967	6.00
❑ 6151	You've Got to Change Your Mind/I'll Lose My Mind	1968	10.00
—A-side with James Brown			
❑ 6165	You Gave My Heart a Brand New Song/Concerto	1968	6.00

Except when noted otherwise, VG = 25% of NM, and VG+ = 50% of NM. (Example: VG = $2.00, VG+ = $4.00 and NM = $8.00.)

Number	Title (A Side/B Side)	Yr	NM
❑ 6289	You Gave My Heart a New Song/ Hang-Ups We Don't Need	1970	6.00
❑ 6308	I'm Not to Blame/It's I Who Loves You (It's Not Him Anymore)	1970	6.00
❑ 6323	I Need Help (Part 1)/ I Need Help (Part 2)	1970	6.00
❑ 6342	You've Got to Change Your Mind/ You Got to Have a Job (If You Don't Work You Can't Eat)	1970	6.00
❑ 6378	I Know You Got Soul/ It's I Who Love You (It's Not Him Anymore)	1971	6.00
KWANZA/WB			
❑ 7703	On the Move/Try It Again	1973	6.00
SMASH			
❑ 1903	Write Me a Letter/I Love You So	1964	8.00
❑ 1928	I'm Lonely/I've Got a Girl	1964	8.00
❑ 1964	No One Like My Baby/ We Are In Love	1965	8.00
❑ 1984	Time Will Make a Change/ The Way I Feel	1965	8.00
❑ 2003	You're Gonna Need My Lovin'/ Let Me Know	1965	8.00
❑ 2018	Lost in the Mood of Changes/ Oh, What a Nite	1966	8.00
❑ 2052	Ain't No Use/Let Me Know	1966	8.00
Albums			
KING			
❑ KS-1118	I Need Help	1970	200.00

BYRD, BOBBY, AND THE IMPALAS See BOBBY DAY.

BYRD, CHARLIE

Number	Title (A Side/B Side)	Yr	NM
45s			
COLUMBIA			
❑ AE 12 [DJ]	Let Go (Canto de Ossanha)/ Here's That Rainy Day	1969	10.00
❑ 43504	Baby Love/Walk Right In	1966	8.00
—With the Lady Byrds			
❑ 43834	The Work Song/ Tomorrow Belongs to Me	1966	8.00
❑ 44214	Zona Sul/Caper of the Golden Bulls	1967	8.00
❑ 44411	Empty Streets/Far Off, Close By	1967	6.00
❑ 44669	Lullaby from Rosemary's Baby/ Happy Together	1969	6.00
❑ 44782	Wichita Lineman/ I Don't Have to Take It	1969	6.00
❑ 45099	I'll Never Fall in Love Again/ I'll Walk with the Rain	1970	5.00
RIVERSIDE			
❑ 4529	The Duck/One Note Samba	1962	10.00
❑ 4544	Meditation (Meditacao)/ Little Boat (O Barquinho)	1962	10.00
❑ 4556	Longing for Bahia/Softly	1963	10.00
Albums			
COLUMBIA			
❑ CS 1053	Let It Be	1970	12.00
❑ CL 2337 [M]	Brazilian Byrd	1965	12.00
—"360 Sound Mono" on label			
❑ CL 2337 [M]	Brazilian Byrd	1965	15.00
—"Guaranteed High Fidelity" on label			
❑ CL 2435 [M]	Travellin' Man Recorded Live	1966	12.00
❑ CL 2504 [M]	A Touch of Gold	1966	12.00
❑ CL 2555 [M]	Christmas Carols for Solo Guitar	1966	15.00
❑ CL 2592 [M]	Byrdland	1967	20.00
❑ CL 2652 [M]	Hollywood Byrd	1967	20.00
❑ CL 2692 [M]	More Brazilian Byrd	1967	20.00
❑ CS 9137	Brazilian Byrd	1971	10.00
—Orange label			
❑ CS 9137 [S]	Brazilian Byrd	1965	15.00
—Red label, "360 Sound" in white			
❑ CS 9137 [S]	Brazilian Byrd	1965	20.00
—Red label, "360 Sound" in black			
❑ PC 9137	Brazilian Byrd	198?	8.00
—Reissue with new prefix			
❑ CS 9235 [S]	Travellin' Man Recorded Live	1966	15.00
❑ CS 9304 [S]	A Touch of Gold	1966	15.00
❑ CS 9355 [S]	Christmas Carols for Solo Guitar	1966	20.00
❑ CS 9392 [S]	Byrdland	1967	15.00
❑ CS 9452 [S]	Hollywood Byrd	1967	15.00
❑ CS 9492 [S]	More Brazilian Byrd	1967	15.00
❑ CS 9582	Sketches of Brazil (Music of Villa Lobos)	1968	15.00
❑ CS 9627 [M]	Hit Trip	1968	25.00
—"Special Mono Radio Station Copy" with white label			
❑ CS 9627 [S]	Hit Trip	1968	15.00
❑ CS 9667	Delicately	1968	15.00
❑ CS 9747	The Great Byrd	1968	15.00
❑ CS 9841	Aquarius	1969	15.00
❑ CS 9869	Let Go	1969	15.00
❑ CS 9970	The Greatest Hits of the 60's	1970	12.00
❑ C 30380	A Stroke of Genius	1971	12.00
❑ G 30622 [(2)]	For All We Know	1971	15.00
❑ C 31025	Onda Nuevo	1972	12.00
❑ CG 31967 [(2)]	The World of Charlie Byrd	1972	15.00
CONCORD JAZZ			
❑ CJ-82	Blue Byrd	1979	10.00
❑ CJ-252	Isn't It Romantic	1984	10.00
❑ CJ-304	Byrd & Brass	1986	10.00
❑ CJ-374	It's a Wonderful World	1989	12.00
CONCORD PICANTE			
❑ P-114	Sugarloaf Suite	1980	10.00
❑ P-173	Brazilville	1981	10.00
CRYSTAL CLEAR			
❑ 8002	Charlie Byrd	1979	30.00
—Direct-to-disc recording; plays at 45 rpm			
FANTASY			
❑ OJC-107	Bossa Nova Pelos Passaros	198?	10.00
—Reissue of Riverside 436			
❑ OJC-262	Byrd at the Gate	1987	10.00
—Reissue of Riverside 9467			
❑ F-9429	Crystal Silence	1973	12.00
❑ F-9466	Byrd by the Sea	1974	12.00
❑ F-9496	Top Hat	1975	12.00
IMPROV			
❑ 7116	Charlie Byrd Swings Downtown	1977	12.00
MILESTONE			
❑ 47005 [(2)]	Latin Byrd	1973	15.00
❑ 47049 [(2)]	Charlie Byrd in Greenwich Village	1978	15.00
MOBILE FIDELITY			
❑ 1-515	Byrd at the Gate	1982	40.00
—Audiophile vinyl			
OFFBEAT			
❑ OJ-3001 [M]	Jazz at the Show Boat, Vol. 1	1959	25.00
❑ OJ-3005 [M]	Jazz at the Show Boat, Vol. 2	1959	25.00
❑ OJ-3006 [M]	Jazz at the Show Boat, Vol. 3	1959	25.00
❑ OJ-3007 [M]	Charlie's Choice	1960	25.00
❑ OLP-3009 [M]	Blues Sonata	1960	25.00
❑ OS-93001 [S]	Jazz at the Show Boat, Vol. 1	1959	30.00
❑ OS-93005 [S]	Jazz at the Show Boat, Vol. 2	1959	30.00
❑ OS-93006 [S]	Jazz at the Show Boat, Vol. 3	1959	30.00
❑ OS-93007 [S]	Charlie's Choice	1960	30.00
❑ OS-93009 [S]	Blues Sonata	1960	30.00
PICKWICK			
❑ SPC-3042	Byrd and the Herd	196?	12.00
RIVERSIDE			
❑ RM-427 [M]	Latin Impressions	1962	20.00
❑ RM-436 [M]	Bossa Nova Pelos Passaros	1962	20.00
❑ RM-448 [M]	Byrd's Word	1963	20.00
❑ RM-449 [M]	Byrd in the Wind	1963	20.00
❑ RM-450 [M]	Mr. Guitar	1963	20.00
❑ RM-451 [M]	The Guitar Artistry of Charlie Byrd	1963	20.00
❑ RM-452 [M]	Charlie Byrd at the Village Vanguard	1963	20.00
❑ RM-453 [M]	Blues Sonata	1963	20.00
❑ RM-454 [M]	Once More! Bossa Nova	1963	20.00
❑ RM-467 [M]	Byrd at the Gate	1964	20.00
❑ RM-481 [M]	Byrd Song	1966	15.00
❑ RM-498 [M]	Solo Flight	1967	20.00
❑ RS-3005	The Guitar Artistry of Charlie Byrd	1968	15.00
❑ RS-3044	Byrd Man with Strings	1969	15.00
❑ 6054	Blues Sonata	197?	10.00
❑ RS-9427 [S]	Latin Impressions	1962	25.00
❑ RS-9436 [S]	Bossa Nova Pelos Passaros	1962	25.00
❑ RS-9448 [S]	Byrd's Word	1963	25.00
❑ RS-9449 [S]	Byrd in the Wind	1963	25.00
❑ RS-9450 [S]	Mr. Guitar	1963	25.00
❑ RS-9451 [S]	The Guitar Artistry of Charlie Byrd	1963	25.00
❑ RS-9452 [S]	Charlie Byrd at the Village Vanguard	1963	25.00
❑ RS-9453 [S]	Blues Sonata	1963	25.00
❑ RS-9454 [S]	Once More! Bossa Nova	1963	25.00
❑ RS-9467 [S]	Byrd at the Gate	1964	25.00
❑ RS-9481 [S]	Byrd Song	1966	20.00
❑ RS-9498 [S]	Solo Flight	1967	15.00
SAVOY			
❑ MG-12099 [M]	Jazz Recital	1957	40.00
❑ MG-12116 [M]	Blues for Night People	1957	40.00
SAVOY JAZZ			
❑ SJL-1121	Midnight Guitar	1980	10.00
❑ SJL-1131	First Flight	1980	10.00

BYRD, CHARLIE, AND FATHER MALCOLM BOYD

Number	Title (A Side/B Side)	Yr	NM
45s			
COLUMBIA			
❑ 43942	It's Christmas Again, Jesus/ It's Morning, Jesus	1966	8.00
Albums			
COLUMBIA			
❑ CL 2548 [M]	Are You Running With Me, Jesus?	1966	15.00
❑ CL 2657 [M]	Happening Prayers for Now	1967	15.00
❑ CS 9348 [S]	Are You Running With Me, Jesus?	1966	20.00
❑ CS 9457 [S]	Happening Prayers for Now	1967	15.00

BYRD, CHARLIE, HERB ELLIS & BARNEY KESSEL

Number	Title (A Side/B Side)	Yr	NM
Albums			
CONCORD JAZZ			
❑ C-4	The Great Guitars	197?	12.00
❑ C-23	The Great Guitars	197?	12.00
❑ CJ-131	The Great Guitars at the Winery	1981	10.00
❑ CJ-209	The Great Guitars at Charlie's Georgetown	1982	10.00
❑ CJD-1002	Straight Tracks	1986	20.00
—Direct-to-disc recording			

BYRD, CURTIS

Number	Title (A Side/B Side)	Yr	NM
45s			
CANDIX			
❑ 340	Pretty Woman/Turn Some More Lights On	1962	25.00

BYRD, DONALD

Number	Title (A Side/B Side)	Yr	NM
12-Inch Singles			
ELEKTRA			
❑ AS 11400 [DJ]	Thank You for Funking Up My Life (4:43)/Loving You (7:20)	1978	15.00
❑ AS 11533 [DJ]	I Feel Like Loving You Today/ I Love Your Love	1981	12.00
❑ 67985	Sexy Dancer/Moonlight	1982	12.00
45s			
BLUE NOTE			
❑ XW212	Black Byrd/Slop Jar Blues	1973	5.00
❑ XW309	Flight Time/Mr. Thomas	1973	5.00
❑ XW445	Witch Hunt/Woman of the World	1974	5.00
❑ XW510	Cristo Redentor/Black Byrd	1974	5.00
❑ XW650	Think Twice/We're Together	1975	5.00
❑ XW726	Change (Makes You Want to Hustle) Part 1/Part 2	1975	5.00
❑ XW783	(Fallin' Like) Dominoes/ Just My Imagination (Runnin' Away with Me)	1976	5.00
❑ XW965	Dancing in the Street/ Onward 'Til Morning	1977	5.00
❑ XW965 [PS]	Dancing in the Street/ Onward 'Til Morning	1977	8.00
❑ 1763	Here Am I (Part 1)/ Here Am I (Part 2)	196?	8.00
❑ 1764	Amen/Fuego	196?	8.00
❑ 1798	Gate City/Little Boy Blue	196?	8.00
❑ 1799	Bo-Blue/Ghana	196?	8.00
❑ 1853	Hush/6 M's	196?	8.00
❑ 1854	Jorgie's (Part 1)/ Jorgie's (Part 2)	196?	8.00
❑ 1916	Brother Isaac/I've Longed and Searched for My Mother	196?	8.00
❑ 1973	The Emperor (Part 1)/ The Emperor (Part 2)	196?	8.00
ELEKTRA			
❑ 45545	Thank You for Funking Up My Life/Loving You	1978	4.00
❑ 46019	Loving You/Cristo Redentor	1979	4.00
❑ 46601	Veronica/Pretty Baby	1980	4.00
❑ 47168	Love Has Come Around/ Love for Sale	1981	4.00
❑ 47241	I Love Your Love/Falling	1981	4.00
❑ 47419	I Feel Like Lovin' You Today/ Butterfly	1982	4.00
❑ 69972	Sexy Dancer/Midnight	1982	4.00
VERVE			
❑ 10344	Blind Man, Blind Man/You've Been Talkin' 'Bout My Baby	1965	8.00
Albums			
AMERICAN RECORDING SOCIETY			
❑ G-437 [M]	Modern Jazz	1957	40.00
BLUE NOTE			
❑ BN-LA047-F	Black Byrd	1973	15.00
❑ LO-047	Black Byrd	1981	8.00
—Reissue of LA047			
❑ BN-LA140-G	Street Lady	1974	15.00
❑ BN-LA368-G	Sleeping Into Tomorrow	1975	15.00
❑ BN-LA549-G	Places and Spaces	1975	15.00
❑ LW-549	Places and Spaces	1981	8.00
—Reissue of LA549			
❑ BN-LA633-G	Caricatures	1976	15.00
❑ BN-LA700-G	Donald Byrd's Best	1976	15.00
❑ LT-991	Chant	1980	12.00
❑ LT-1096	Creeper	1981	12.00
❑ BLP-4007 [M]	Off to the Races	1959	80.00
—W. 63rd St., NYC address on label			
❑ BLP-4007 [M]	Off to the Races	1959	120.00
—"Deep groove" version (deep indentation under label on both sides)			
❑ BLP-4007 [M]	Off to the Races	1963	25.00
—"New York, USA" address on label			
❑ BST-4007 [S]	Off to the Races	1959	60.00
—W. 63rd St., NYC address on label			
❑ BST-4007 [S]	Off to the Races	1959	80.00
—"Deep groove" version (deep indentation under label on both sides)			

Number	Title (A Side/B Side)	Yr	NM
❑ BST-4007 [S]	Off to the Races	1963	25.00
—"New York, USA" address on label			
❑ BLP-4019 [M]	Byrd in Hand	1959	80.00
—W. 63rd St., NYC address on label			
❑ BLP-4019 [M]	Byrd in Hand	1959	120.00
—"Deep groove" version (deep indentation under label on both sides)			
❑ BLP-4019 [M]	Byrd in Hand	1963	25.00
—"New York, USA" address on label			
❑ BLP-4026 [M]	Fuego	1960	80.00
—W. 63rd St., NYC address on label			
❑ BLP-4026 [M]	Fuego	1960	120.00
—"Deep groove" version (deep indentation under label on both sides)			
❑ BLP-4026 [M]	Fuego	1963	25.00
—"New York, USA" address on label			
❑ BLP-4048 [M]	Byrd in Flight	1960	80.00
—W. 63rd St., NYC address on label			
❑ BLP-4048 [M]	Byrd in Flight	1960	120.00
—"Deep groove" version (deep indentation under label on both sides)			
❑ BLP-4048 [M]	Byrd in Flight	1963	25.00
—"New York, USA" address on label			
❑ BLP-4060 [M]	Donald Byrd at the Half Note Café, Vol. 1	1961	80.00
—W. 63rd St., NYC address on label			
❑ BLP-4060 [M]	Donald Byrd at the Half Note Café, Vol. 1	1963	25.00
—"New York, USA" address on label			
❑ BLP-4061 [M]	Donald Byrd at the Half Note Café, Vol. 2	1961	80.00
—W. 63rd St., NYC address on label			
❑ BLP-4061 [M]	Donald Byrd at the Half Note Café, Vol. 2	1963	25.00
—"New York, USA" address on label			
❑ BLP-4075 [M]	The Cat Walk	1961	80.00
—61st St, New York address on label			
❑ BLP-4075 [M]	The Cat Walk	1963	25.00
—"New York, USA" address on label			
❑ BLP-4101 [M]	Royal Flush	1962	20.00
❑ BLP-4118 [M]	Free Form	1963	20.00
❑ BLP-4124 [M]	A New Perspective	1964	20.00
❑ BLP-4188 [M]	I'm Tryin' to Get Home	1965	20.00
❑ BLP-4238 [M]	Mustang!	1966	20.00
❑ BLP-4259 [M]	Blackjack	1967	25.00
❑ LN-10054	Street Lady	1981	8.00
—Budget-line reissue			
❑ B1-31875	Kofi	1995	15.00
❑ B1-36195	Electric Byrd	1996	15.00
❑ BST-84007 [S]	Byrd in Hand	1967	12.00
—"A Division of Liberty Records" on label			
❑ BST-84019	Byrd in Hand	198?	10.00
—"The Finest in Jazz Since 1939" reissue			
❑ BST-84019 [S]	Byrd in Hand	1959	60.00
—W. 63rd St., NYC address on label			
❑ BST-84019 [S]	Byrd in Hand	1963	25.00
—"New York, USA" address on label			
❑ BST-84019 [S]	Byrd in Hand	1967	12.00
—"A Division of Liberty Records" on label			
❑ BST-84026 [S]	Fuego	1959	60.00
—W. 63rd St., NYC address on label			
❑ BST-84026 [S]	Fuego	1963	25.00
—"New York, USA" address on label			
❑ BST-84026 [S]	Fuego	1967	12.00
—"A Division of Liberty Records" on label			
❑ BST-84048 [S]	Byrd in Flight	1960	60.00
—W. 63rd St., NYC address on label			
❑ BST-84048 [S]	Byrd in Flight	1963	25.00
—"New York, USA" address on label			
❑ BST-84048 [S]	Byrd in Flight	1967	12.00
—"A Division of Liberty Records" on label			
❑ BST-84060 [S]	Donald Byrd at the Half Note Café, Vol. 1	1961	60.00
—W. 63rd St., NYC address on label			
❑ BST-84060 [S]	Donald Byrd at the Half Note Café, Vol. 1	1963	25.00
—"New York, USA" address on label			
❑ BST-84060 [S]	Donald Byrd at the Half Note Café, Vol. 1	1967	12.00
—"A Division of Liberty Records" on label			
❑ BST-84061 [S]	Donald Byrd at the Half Note Café, Vol. 2	1961	60.00
—W. 63rd St., NYC address on label			
❑ BST-84061 [S]	Donald Byrd at the Half Note Café, Vol. 2	1963	25.00
—"New York, USA" address on label			
❑ BST-84061 [S]	Donald Byrd at the Half Note Café, Vol. 2	1967	12.00
—"A Division of Liberty Records" on label			
❑ BST-84075 [S]	The Cat Walk	1961	60.00
—61st St, New York address on label			
❑ BST-84075 [S]	The Cat Walk	1963	25.00
—"New York, USA" address on label			
❑ BST-84075 [S]	The Cat Walk	1967	12.00
—"A Division of Liberty Records" on label			
❑ BST-84101 [S]	Royal Flush	1962	25.00
—"New York, USA" address on label			
❑ BST-84101 [S]	Royal Flush	1967	12.00
—"A Division of Liberty Records" on label			
❑ BST-84118	Free Form	1986	10.00
—"The Finest in Jazz Since 1939" reissue			
❑ BST-84118 [S]	Free Form	1963	25.00
—"New York, USA" address on label			

Number	Title (A Side/B Side)	Yr	NM
❑ BST-84118 [S]	Free Form	1967	12.00
—"A Division of Liberty Records" on label			
❑ BST-84124	A New Perspective	198?	10.00
—"The Finest in Jazz Since 1939" reissue			
❑ BST-84124 [S]	A New Perspective	1964	25.00
—"New York, USA" address on label			
❑ BST-84124 [S]	A New Perspective	1967	12.00
—"A Division of Liberty Records" on label			
❑ BST-84124 [S]	A New Perspective	1973	10.00
—"A Division of United Artists Records Inc." on label			
❑ BST-84188	I'm Tryin' to Get Home	1986	10.00
—"The Finest in Jazz Since 1939" reissue			
❑ BST-84188 [S]	I'm Tryin' to Get Home	1965	25.00
—"New York, USA" address on label			
❑ BST-84188 [S]	I'm Tryin' to Get Home	1967	12.00
—"A Division of Liberty Records" on label			
❑ BST-84238 [S]	Mustang!	1966	25.00
—"New York, USA" address on label			
❑ BST-84238 [S]	Mustang!	1967	12.00
—"A Division of Liberty Records" on label			
❑ BST-84259 [S]	Blackjack	1967	20.00
❑ BST-84292	Slow Drag	1968	20.00
❑ BST-84319	Fancy Free	1969	20.00
❑ BST-84349	Electric	1970	20.00
❑ BST-84380	Ethiopian Nights	1972	20.00
❑ B1-89796	Fancy Free	1993	15.00
DELMARK			
❑ DS-407	First Flight	1990	12.00
DISCOVERY			
❑ 869	September Afternoon	198?	10.00
ELEKTRA			
❑ 6E-144	Thank You for F.U.M.L. (Funking Up My Life)	1978	10.00
❑ 6E-247	Donald Byrd and 125th St., N.Y.C.	1980	10.00
❑ 5E-531	Love Byrd	1981	10.00
❑ 60188	Words, Sounds, Colors and Shapes	1982	10.00
LANDMARK			
❑ LLP-1516	Harlem Blues	1988	10.00
❑ LLP-1523	Getting Down to Business	1990	12.00
SAVOY			
❑ MG-12032 [M]	Byrd's Word	1956	100.00
❑ MG-12064 [M]	The Jazz Message of Donald Byrd	1956	120.00
SAVOY JAZZ			
❑ SJL-1101	Long Green	198?	10.00
❑ SJL-1114	Star Eyes	198?	10.00
TRANSITION			
❑ TRLP-4 [M]	Byrd's Eye View	1956	600.00
❑ TRLP-5 [M]	Byrd Jazz	1956	600.00
❑ TRLP-17 [M]	Byrd Blows on Beacon Hill	1956	600.00
TRIP			
❑ 5000 [(2)]	Two Sides of Donald Byrd	1974	15.00
VERVE			
❑ V-8609 [M]	Up with Donald Byrd	1965	20.00
❑ V6-8609 [S]	Up with Donald Byrd	1965	25.00

BYRD, DONALD; HANY MOBLEY; KENNY BURRELL

Albums

Number	Title (A Side/B Side)	Yr	NM
STATUS			
❑ ST-8317 [M]	Donald Byrd, Hank Mobley & Kenny Burrell	1965	40.00

BYRD, ROBERT, AND THE BIRDIES See BOBBY DAY.

BYRDS, THE

Also see SKIP BATTIN; THE BEEFEATERS; GENE CLARK; DAVID CROSBY; ROGER McGUINN; GRAM PARSONS.

45s

Number	Title (A Side/B Side)	Yr	NM
ASYLUM			
❑ 11016	Full Circle/Long Live the King	1973	5.00
❑ 11019	Cowgirl in the Sand/ Long Live the King	1973	5.00
COLUMBIA			
❑ S 160	Chimes of Freedom/ The Bells of Rhymney	2004	2.00
—Part of Sundazed S 7001			
❑ S 160 [PS]	Chimes of Freedom/ The Bells of Rhymney	2004	2.00
—Part of Sundazed S 7001			
❑ S 161	It's All Over Now, Baby Blue/ She Don't Care About Time	2004	2.00
—Part of Sundazed S 7001			
❑ S 161 [PS]	It's All Over Now, Baby Blue/ She Don't Care About Time	2004	2.00
—Part of Sundazed S 7001			
❑ S 162	The Times They Are a-Changin'/ She Has a Way	2004	2.00
—Part of Sundazed S 7001			
❑ S 162 [PS]	The Times They Are a-Changin'/ She Has a Way	2004	2.00
—Part of Sundazed S 7001			
❑ S 163	I Know My Rider/ Psychodrama City	2004	2.00
—Part of Sundazed S 7001			
❑ S 163 [PS]	I Know My Rider/ Psychodrama City	2004	2.00
—Part of Sundazed S 7001			
❑ S 164	My Back Pages/ It Happens Each Day	2004	2.00
—Part of Sundazed S 7001			
❑ S 164 [PS]	My Back Pages/ It Happens Each Day	2004	2.00
—Part of Sundazed S 7001			
❑ 43271	Mr. Tambourine Man/ I Knew I'd Want You	1965	15.00
❑ 43271 [DJ]	Mr. Tambourine Man (same on both sides)	1965	150.00
—Red vinyl promo			
❑ 43271 [PS]	Mr. Tambourine Man	1965	300.00
—Promo-only sleeve promoting the Byrds' appeance on the TV show Hullabaloo			
❑ 43332	All I Really Want to Do/ I'll Feel a Whole Lot Better	1965	15.00
❑ 43332 [DJ]	All I Really Want to Do (same on both sides)	1965	100.00
—Red vinyl promo			
❑ 43332 [DJ]	I'll Feel a Whole Lot Better (same on both sides)	1965	120.00
—Red vinyl promo			
❑ 4-43391	The Times They Are a-Changin'/ She Don't Care About Time	1965	—
—Scheduled but never released			
❑ 4-43391 [PS]	The Times They Are a-Changin'/ She Don't Care About Time	1965	500.00
—Picture sleeve for unreleased single			
❑ 43424	Turn! Turn! Turn! (To Everything There Is a Season)/ She Don't Care About Time	1965	15.00
❑ 43424 [DJ]	Turn! Turn! Turn! (To Everything There Is a Season) (same on both sides)	1965	100.00
—Red vinyl promo			
❑ 43501	It Won't Be Wrong/ Set You Free This Time	1965	12.00
❑ 43578	Eight Miles High/Why	1966	12.00
❑ 43578 [PS]	Eight Miles High/Why	1966	60.00
❑ 43702	5 D (Fifth Dimension)/ Captain Soul	1966	12.00
❑ 43766	Mr. Spaceman/ What's Happening	1966	12.00
❑ 43987	So You Want to Be a Rock 'N' Roll Star/Everybody's Been Burned	1967	12.00
❑ 44054	My Back Pages/ Renaissance Fair	1967	12.00
❑ 44157	Have You Seen Her Face/ Don't Make Waves	1967	10.00
❑ 44157 [PS]	Have You Seen Her Face/ Don't Make Waves	1967	40.00
❑ 44230	Lady Friend/Old John Robertson	1967	10.00
❑ 44362	Goin' Back/Change Is Now	1967	8.00
❑ 44499	Artificial Energy/ You Ain't Going Nowhere	1968	8.00
❑ 44643	Pretty Boy Floyd/I Am a Pilgrim	1968	8.00
❑ 44746	Drug Store Truck Drivin' Man/ Bad Night at the Whiskey	1969	8.00
❑ 44868	Lay Lady Lay/Old Blue	1969	8.00
❑ 44990	Wasn't Born to Follow/ Ballad of Easy Rider	1969	8.00
❑ 44990	Ballad of Easy Rider/ Oil in My Lamp	1969	10.00
❑ 45071	Jesus Is Just Alright/ It's All Over Now, Baby Blue	1970	8.00
❑ 45259	Chestnut Mare/Just a Season	1970	6.00
❑ 45440	Glory Glory/Citizen Kane	1971	6.00
❑ 45514	America's Great National Pastime/Farther Along	1971	6.00
❑ 45761	Jesus Is Just Alright/ Mr. Spaceman	1973	10.00
❑ JZSP 116476 [DJ]	He Was a Friend of Mine (same on both sides)	1966	40.00
SUNDAZED			
❑ S 189	Lazy Days/Reputation	2007	3.00
—Outtake versions from the "Sweetheart of the Rodeo" sessions			
❑ S 189 [PS]	Lazy Days/Reputation	2007	3.00
❑ S 7001 [PS]	Cancelled Flytes	2004	5.00
—Box and insert that goes with the box containing "Columbia" S 160, S 161, S 162, S 163 and S 164 (priced separately)			
SUNDAZED KUSTOM SHOP			
❑ KS7-01	You Movin'/Boston	2002	2.50
—Yellow vinyl			
❑ KS7-01 [PS]	You Movin'/Boston	2002	2.50

Except when noted otherwise, VG = 25% of NM, and VG+ = 50% of NM. (Example: VG = $2.00, VG+ = $4.00 and NM = $8.00.)

Number | Title (A Side/B Side) | Yr | NM

7-Inch Extended Plays

COLUMBIA

❑ ZLP 116003/4 [DJ] A Special Open-End Interview with the Byrds Talking About Their New LP "Fifth Dimension" 1966 120.00

—Promo-only interview; plays at 33 1/3 rpm

❑ ZLP 116003/4 [PS] A Special Open-End Interview with the Byrds Talking About Their New LP "Fifth Dimension" 1966 180.00

COLUMBIA/SCHOLASTIC

❑ CV 10287 Lover of the Bayou/So You Want to Be a Rock and Roll Star//Chimes of Freedom/ Goin' Back 1971 30.00

❑ CV 10287 [PS] The Byrds 1971 30.00

Albums

ASYLUM

❑ 5058 [M] Byrds 1973 40.00

—Mono is white label promo only; "dj copy monaural" sticker on stereo cover

❑ SD 5058 [S] Byrds 1973 12.00

COLUMBIA

❑ CL 2372 [M] Mr. Tambourine Man 1965 40.00

—"Guaranteed High Fidelity" on label

❑ CL 2372 [M] Mr. Tambourine Man 1966 30.00

—"360 Sound Mono" on label

❑ CL 2454 [M] Turn! Turn! Turn! 1965 30.00

❑ CL 2549 [M] Fifth Dimension (5D) 1966 30.00

❑ CL 2642 [M] Younger Than Yesterday 1967 30.00

❑ CL 2716 [M] The Byrds' Greatest Hits 1967 30.00

❑ CL 2775 [M] The Notorious Byrd Brothers 1968 50.00

❑ CS 9172 [S] Mr. Tambourine Man 1965 40.00

—Red label, "360 Sound" in black

❑ CS 9172 [S] Mr. Tambourine Man 1966 25.00

—Red label, "360 Sound" in white

❑ CS 9172 [S] Mr. Tambourine Man 1971 10.00

—Orange label

❑ PC 9172 [S] Mr. Tambourine Man 198? 8.00

—Reissue with new prefix

❑ CS 9254 [S] Turn! Turn! Turn! 1965 25.00

—Red "360 Sound" label

❑ CS 9254 [S] Turn! Turn! Turn! 1971 10.00

—Orange label

❑ PC 9254 [S] Turn! Turn! Turn! 198? 8.00

—Reissue with new prefix

❑ CS 9349 [S] Fifth Dimension (5D) 1966 25.00

—Red "360 Sound" label

❑ CS 9349 [S] Fifth Dimension (5D) 1971 10.00

—Orange label

❑ PC 9349 [S] Fifth Dimension (5D) 198? 8.00

—Reissue with new prefix

❑ CS 9442 [S] Younger Than Yesterday 1967 25.00

—Red "360 Sound" label

❑ CS 9442 [S] Younger Than Yesterday 1971 10.00

—Orange label

❑ PC 9442 [S] Younger Than Yesterday 198? 8.00

—Reissue with new prefix

❑ CS 9516 [S] The Byrds' Greatest Hits 1967 20.00

—Red "360 Sound" label

❑ KCS 9516 [S] The Byrds' Greatest Hits 1971 10.00

—Orange label

❑ PC 9516 [S] The Byrds' Greatest Hits 197? 8.00

—Reissue with another new prefix

❑ CS 9575 [S] The Notorious Byrd Brothers 1968 20.00

—Red "360 Sound" label

❑ CS 9575 [S] The Notorious Byrd Brothers 1971 10.00

—Orange label

❑ PC 9575 [S] The Notorious Byrd Brothers 198? 8.00

—Reissue with new prefix

❑ CS 9670 [M] Sweetheart of the Rodeo 1968 100.00

—"Special Mono Radio Station Copy" with white label

❑ CS 9670 [S] Sweetheart of the Rodeo 1968 20.00

—Red "360 Sound" label

❑ CS 9670 [S] Sweetheart of the Rodeo 1971 10.00

—Orange label

❑ PC 9670 [S] Sweetheart of the Rodeo 198? 8.00

—Reissue with new prefix

❑ CS 9755 [S] Dr. Byrds and Mr. Hyde 1969 20.00

—Red "360 Sound" label

❑ CS 9755 [S] Dr. Byrds and Mr. Hyde 1971 10.00

—Orange label

❑ PC 9755 [S] Dr. Byrds and Mr. Hyde 198? 8.00

—Reissue with new prefix

❑ CS 9942 [S] Ballad of Easy Rider 1969 20.00

—Red "360 Sound" label

❑ CS 9942 [S] Ballad of Easy Rider 1971 10.00

—Orange label

❑ PC 9942 Ballad of Easy Rider 1984 8.00

—Reissue with new prefix

❑ G 30127 [(2)] The Byrds (Untitled) 1970 15.00

—Without "Kathleen" listed on back cover

❑ G 30127 [(2)] The Byrds (Untitled) 1970 20.00

—With "Kathleen" listed on back cover (it is not on the set)

❑ KC 30640 Byrdmaniax 1971 12.00

❑ C 31050 Farther Along 1971 12.00

❑ C 31795 The Best of the Byrds (Greatest Hits, Vol. II) 197? 10.00

—Reissue with new prefix

❑ KC 31795 The Best of the Byrds (Greatest Hits, Vol. II) 1972 12.00

❑ PC 31795 The Best of the Byrds (Greatest Hits, Vol. II) 198? 8.00

—Reissue with another new prefix

❑ C 32183 Preflyte 197? 10.00

—Reissue with new prefix

❑ KC 32183 Preflyte 1973 12.00

—Reissue of Together LP

❑ CG 33645 [(2)] Mr. Tambourine Man Turn! Turn! Turn! 1976 15.00

❑ PC 36293 The Byrds Play Dylan 1980 10.00

❑ FC 37335 The Original Singles Vol. 1 (1965-1967) 1981 10.00

❑ PC 37335 The Original Singles Vol. 1 (1965-1967) 1985 8.00

—Budget-line reissue

COLUMBIA LIMITED EDITION

❑ LE 10215 Farther Along 197? 15.00

—Reissue of 31050

PAIR

❑ PDL2-1040 [(2)] The Very Best of the Byrds 1986 12.00

RE-FLYTE

❑ MH-70318 Never Before 1987 12.00

—Released by Muuray Hill Records via mail order

RHINO

❑ R1-70244 In the Beginning 1988 10.00

SUNDAZED

❑ LP 5057 Mr. Tambourine Man 1999 15.00

—Reissue on 180-gram vinyl

❑ LP 5058 Turn! Turn! Turn! 1999 15.00

—Reissue on 180-gram vinyl

❑ LP 5059 Fifth Dimension 1999 15.00

—Reissue on 180-gram vinyl

❑ LP 5060 Younger Than Yesterday 1999 15.00

—Reissue on 180-gram vinyl

❑ LP 5061 Sanctuary 2000 12.00

❑ LP 5065 Sanctuary II 2000 12.00

❑ LP 5066 Sanctuary III 2001 12.00

❑ LP 5090 Sanctuary IV 2002 12.00

❑ LP 5114 [(2)] The Preflyte Sessions 2001 15.00

❑ LP 5130 [(2)] The Columbia Singles '65-'67 2001 15.00

❑ LP 5197 [M] Mr. Tambourine Man 2006 15.00

—Reissue on 180-gram vinyl

❑ LP 5198 [M] Turn! Turn! Turn! 2006 15.00

—Reissue on 180-gram vinyl

❑ LP 5199 [M] Fifth Dimension 2006 15.00

—Reissue on 180-gram vinyl

❑ LP 5200 [M] Younger Than Yesterday 2006 15.00

—Reissue on 180-gram vinyl

❑ LP 5201 [M] The Notorious Byrd Brothers 2006 15.00

—Reissue on 180-gram vinyl

TOGETHER

❑ ST-T-1001 Preflyte 1969 25.00

BYRNE, DAVID

12-Inch Singles

LUAKA BOP

❑ PRO4989 [DJ] Ava (3 versions)/Nineveh/ Machu Picchu 1991 7.00

❑ PRO-A-3800 [DJ] Make Believe Mambo (12" Remix 6:17) (Video Edit 4:00)/(Acid Mambo 4:56) (Remix Edit 5:15) 1989 8.00

❑ PRO-A-4989 [DJ] Ava (Nu Wage Remix) (Less Space Dance Mix Edit) (Space Dance Mix)/Nineveh (Industrial Mix)/Machu Picchu (Album Version) 1991 10.00

—Also called "Forestry"

❑ 41766 Back in the Box (2 versions)/ Gypsy Woman (Live)/ A Woman's Secret 1994 12.00

SIRE

❑ PRO3800 [DJ] Make Believe Mambo (4 versions) 1989 5.00

❑ PRO-A-953 The Jezebel Spirit/America Is Waiting/Help Me Somebody 1981 15.00

❑ DSRE 50034 Big Blue Plymouth (Eyes Wide Open)// Big Business/My Big Hands (Fall Through the Cracks) 1982 15.00

45s

VIRGIN

❑ 77664 Like Humans Do/U.B. Jesus 2001 4.00

Albums

ECM

❑ 25022 Music for The Knee Plays 1985 15.00

LUAKA BOP

❑ 25990 Rei Momo 1989 12.00

❑ 26799 Uh-Oh 1992 12.00

SIRE

❑ SRK 3645 The Catherine Wheel 1981 10.00

—Songs and music from the Broadway play of the same name

❑ SRK 6093 My Life in the Bush of Ghosts 1981 12.00

—With Brian Eno

VIRGIN

❑ PR 2204 [DJ] The Making of The Last Emperor: An Interview with David Byrne and Ryuichi Sakamoto 1988 25.00

BYRNE, DAVID, AND RYUICHI SAKAMOTO

Albums

VIRGIN

❑ 2204 [DJ] The Making of The Last Emperor: An Interview with... 1988 25.00

BYRNES, EDD

45s

WARNER BROS.

❑ 5047 [M] Kookie, Kookie (Lend Me Your Comb)/You're the Top 1959 20.00

—A-side by Edward Byrnes and Connie Stevens; B-side by Edward Byrnes

❑ 5047 [PS] Kookie, Kookie (Lend Me Your Comb)/You're the Top 1959 40.00

—A-side by Edward Byrnes and Connie Stevens; B-side by Edward Byrnes

❑ S-5047 [S] Kookie, Kookie (Lend Me Your Comb)/You're the Top 1959 50.00

❑ 5087 Like I Love You/ Kookie's Mad Pad 1959 16.00

—Artist credit: "Edd Byrnes and Friend"

❑ 5087 [PS] Like I Love You/ Kookie's Mad Pad 1959 40.00

—Artist credit: "Edd Byrnes and Friend"

❑ 5114 Kookie's Love Song Part 1/ Kookie's Love Song Part 2 1959 16.00

—With the Mary Kay Trio

❑ 5114 [PS] Kookie's Love Song Part 1/ Kookie's Love Song Part 2 1959 40.00

—With the Mary Kay Trio

❑ 5121 Yulesville/Lonely Christmas 1959 16.00

❑ 5121 [PS] Yulesville/Lonely Christmas 1959 40.00

7-Inch Extended Plays

WARNER BROS.

❑ EA 1309 Hot Broad Rock/I Don't Dig You, Kookie//Saturday Night on Sunset Strip/The Kookie Cha-Cha-Cha 1959 50.00

❑ EA 1309 [PS] Kookie 1959 50.00

Albums

WARNER BROS.

❑ W 1309 [M] Kookie 1959 100.00

❑ W/WS 1309 Kookie Bonus Photo 1959 50.00

❑ WS 1309 [S] Kookie 1959 120.00

BYRON, LORD DOUGLAS

45s

DOT

❑ 16685 Surfin' Santa/The Drink That Makes You Shrink 1964 30.00

UNION

❑ 505 Big Bad Ho-Dad/Coffee House 1962 40.00

—B-side by the Continentals

C

C.A. QUINTET, THE

45s

CANDY FLOSS

❑ 102 Smooth as Silk/Dr. of Philosophy 1968 80.00

FALCON

❑ 70 Mickey's Monkey/ I Want You to Love Me Girl 1967 100.00

❑ 71 Blow to My Soul/ She's Got to Be True 1967 100.00

Albums

CANDY FLOSS

❑ 7764 A Trip Through Hell 1969 1500.

—VG value 500; VG+ value 1000

SUNDAZED

❑ LP-5037 [(2)] Trip Thru Hell 1997 15.00

Number	Title (A Side/B Side)	Yr	NM

C.C.S.

45s

Number	Title (A Side/B Side)	Yr	NM
BELL			
❑ 45396	The Band Played the Boogie/Hang It On Me	1973	4.00
RAK			
❑ ZS7 4501	Whole Lotta Love/Boom Boom	1971	6.00
❑ ZS7 4502	Walking/Lookin' for Fun	1971	5.00
❑ ZS7 4507	Save the World/The Tap Turns On the Water	1972	5.00

Albums

Number	Title (A Side/B Side)	Yr	NM
RAK			
❑ Z 30559	Whole Lotta Love	1971	20.00
❑ KZ 31569	C.C.S.	1972	20.00

C.K. STRONG

45s

Number	Title (A Side/B Side)	Yr	NM
EPIC			
❑ 5-10534	Stormbird/Daddy	1969	10.00

Albums

Number	Title (A Side/B Side)	Yr	NM
EPIC			
❑ BN 26473	C.K. Strong	1969	20.00

C.L. AND THE PICTURES

Also see CURTIS LEE.

45s

Number	Title (A Side/B Side)	Yr	NM
DUNES			
❑ 2010	I'm Asking Forgiveness/Let's Take a Ride	1962	25.00
❑ 2017	Afraid/Mary Go 'Round	1962	25.00
❑ 2023	I'm Sorry/That's What's Happening	1963	25.00
JAMIE			
❑ 1398	You Really Slipped One By Me/The Same People (That You Meet Going Up, You Meet Coming Down)	1971	15.00
	—As "C.L. Weldon and the Pictures"		
MONUMENT			
❑ 854	He'll Only Hurt You/Talking About My Baby	1964	20.00
❑ 888	Could This Be Magic/Yolanda	1965	20.00
❑ 958	Baby, Not Now/Jigsaw Puzzle	1966	20.00

C-NOTES, THE

45s

Number	Title (A Side/B Side)	Yr	NM
EVERLAST			
❑ 5005	On Your Mark/From Now On	1957	50.00

C.O.D.'S, THE

45s

Number	Title (A Side/B Side)	Yr	NM
KELLMAC			
❑ 1003	Michael/Cry No More	1965	12.00
❑ 1005	Pretty Baby/I'm a Good Guy	1965	20.00
❑ 1008	I'm Looking Out for Me/I'll Come Running Back to You	1966	20.00
❑ 1010	She's Fire/It Must Be You	1966	1500.
❑ 1012	Coming Back Girl/It Must Be Love	1966	100.00

C-QUENTS, THE

45s

Number	Title (A Side/B Side)	Yr	NM
CAPETOWN			
❑ 4027	All I Want for Christmas Is You/Merry Christmas, Baby	1962	300.00
ESSICA			
❑ 004	Dearest One/It's You and Me	196?	30.00

CABARET VOLTAIRE

12-Inch Singles

Number	Title (A Side/B Side)	Yr	NM
MANHATTAN			
❑ V-56067	Here to Go (Extended Version) (Little Dub) (Big Dub) (7" Version)/Don't Argue (Dance)	1987	10.00
MUTE			
❑ ED 5562 [DJ]	Colours (4 versions)	1991	12.00

45s

Number	Title (A Side/B Side)	Yr	NM
ROUGH TRADE			
❑ RT-US-003	Seconds Too Late/Control Addict	1981	8.00
❑ RT-US-003 [PS]	Seconds Too Late/Control Addict	1981	8.00

Albums

Number	Title (A Side/B Side)	Yr	NM
CAROLINE			
❑ CAROL 1331	The Covenant, the Sword, and the Arm of the Lord	1985	10.00
❑ CAROL 2451 [(2)EP]	Drinking Gasoline	1985	15.00
❑ CAROL 2452 [(2)EP]	The Drain Train	1986	20.00
GIANT			
❑ GR-16009	Eight Crepuscule Tracks	1988	15.00
MANHATTAN			
❑ MLT-46999	Code	1987	15.00
RESTLESS			
❑ 71475	Listen Up with Cabaret Voltaire	1990	10.00
❑ 71476	The Living Legends	1990	10.00
ROUGH TRADE			
❑ ROUGH US-9	The Voice of America	1980	20.00
❑ TRADE US-12 [EP]	Three Crepuscule Tracks	1981	12.00
❑ ROUGH US-15	Red Mecca	1981	20.00
❑ ROUGH US-24	Hai! Live in Japan	1982	20.00

CABINEERS, THE

45s

Number	Title (A Side/B Side)	Yr	NM
PRESTIGE			
❑ 904	Each Time/(B-side unknown)	1952	300.00
❑ 917	Baby Mine/(B-side unknown)	1953	400.00

CABOT, SEBASTIAN

45s

Number	Title (A Side/B Side)	Yr	NM
MGM			
❑ 13650	It Ain't Me Babe/And Mostly They Sing	1966	15.00

Albums

Number	Title (A Side/B Side)	Yr	NM
MGM			
❑ E-4431 [M]	Sebastian Cabot, Actor; Bob Dylan, Poet: A Dramatic Reading with Music	1967	30.00
❑ SE-4431 [S]	Sebastian Cabot, Actor; Bob Dylan, Poet: A Dramatic Reading with Music	1967	40.00

CACTUS

With Tim Bogert and Carmen Appice, ex-VANILLA FUDGE.

45s

Number	Title (A Side/B Side)	Yr	NM
ATCO			
❑ 6782	Brother Bill/You Can't Judge a Book By Its Cover	1971	8.00
❑ 6811	Long Tall Sally/Rock 'n' Roll Christian	1971	8.00
❑ 6842	Token Chokin'/Alaska	1971	8.00
❑ 6872	The Booger Man/Cold Bear	1972	6.00
❑ 6901	Bringing Me Down/Bad Mother Boogie	1972	6.00

Albums

Number	Title (A Side/B Side)	Yr	NM
ATCO			
❑ SD 33-340	Cactus	1970	20.00
❑ SD 33-356	One Way...Or Another	1971	20.00
❑ SD 33-377	Restrictions	1971	20.00
❑ SD 7011	'Ot 'N' Sweaty	1972	20.00

CADETS, THE

Also see THE JACKS.

45s

Number	Title (A Side/B Side)	Yr	NM
JAN-LAR			
❑ 102	Don't/Car Crash	1960	60.00
MODERN			
❑ 956	Don't Be Angry/I Cried	1955	50.00
❑ 960	Rollin' Stone/Fine Lookin' Baby	1955	50.00
❑ 963	I Cried/Fine Lookin' Baby	1955	40.00
❑ 969	Annie Met Henry/So Will I	1955	40.00
❑ 971	Do You Wanna Rock/If It Is Wrong	1956	100.00
❑ 985	Church Bells May Ring/Heartbreak Hotel	1956	40.00
❑ 994	Stranded in the Jungle/I Want You	1956	40.00
❑ 1000	I Got Loaded/Dancin' Dan	1956	40.00
❑ 1006	Fools Rush In/I'll Be Spinning	1956	40.00
❑ 1012	Heaven Help Me/Love Bandit	1957	40.00
❑ 1017	Wiggle Waggle Woo/You Belong to Me	1957	40.00
❑ 1019	Pretty Evey/Rum, Jamaica Rum	1957	50.00
	—As "Aaron Collins and the Cadets"		
❑ 1024	Hands Across the Table/Love Can Do Most Anything	1957	40.00
	—As "Will Jones and the Cadets"		
❑ 1026	Ring Chimes/Baby Ya Know	1957	40.00
SHERWOOD			
❑ 211	One More Chance/I'm Looking for a Job	1960	50.00

Albums

Number	Title (A Side/B Side)	Yr	NM
CROWN			
❑ CST-370 [R]	The Cadets	1963	100.00
❑ CLP-5015 [M]	Rockin' 'n' Reelin'	1957	250.00
	—Black label		
❑ CLP-5370 [M]	The Cadets	1963	150.00
MODERN			
❑ LPM-1215 [M]	Rockin' 'n' Reelin'	1956	—
	—Canceled		
RELIC			
❑ 5025	The Cadets' Greatest Hits	197?	12.00

CADETS, THE (2)

Nashville studio group. Also see ED HARDIN.

45s

Number	Title (A Side/B Side)	Yr	NM
HIT			
❑ 284	Happy Together/There's a Kind of Hush	1967	8.00
	—B-side by the Chellows		

CADILLACS, THE

45s

Number	Title (A Side/B Side)	Yr	NM
ARTIC			
❑ 101	Fool/The Right Kind of Lovin'	1964	100.00
CAPITOL			
❑ 4825	Groovy, Groovy Love/White Gardenia	1962	20.00
❑ 4935	La Bomba/I Saw You	1963	20.00
	—As "Bobby Ray and the Cadillacs"		
JOSIE			
❑ 765	Gloria/I Wonder Why	1954	700.00
	—Original with "joz" logo at top		
❑ 765	Gloria/I Wonder Why	196?	25.00
	—Reissue with 1960s label		
❑ 769	Wishing Well/I Want to Know About Love	1954	500.00
❑ 773	Sympathy/No Chance	1955	100.00
❑ 778	Widow Lady/Down the Road	1955	200.00
❑ 785	Speedoo/Let Me Explain	1955	60.00
❑ 792	Zoom/You Are	1956	50.00
❑ 798	Woe Is Me/Betty My Love	1956	50.00
❑ 805	The Girl I Love/That's All I Need	1956	100.00
❑ 807	Rudolph the Red-Nosed Reindeer/Shack-a Doo	1956	40.00
❑ 812	Sugar Sugar/About That Girl Named Lou	1957	40.00
❑ 820	My Girl Friend/Broken Heart	1957	50.00
❑ 821	Lucy/Hurry Home	1957	40.00
	—As "The Original Cadillacs"		
❑ 829	Buzz-Buzz-Buzz/Yes, Yes Baby	1957	40.00
	—As "The Original Cadillacs"		
❑ 836	Speedo Is Back/A' Looka Here	1958	30.00
❑ 842	Holy Smoke Baby/I Want to Know	1958	30.00
❑ 846	Peek-a-Book/Oh, Oh Lolita	1958	30.00
❑ 857	Copy Cat/Jay Walker	1959	30.00
❑ 861	Cool It Fool/Please Mr. Johnson	1959	30.00
❑ 866 [M]	Romeo/Always My Darling	1959	30.00
❑ 870	Dumbell/Bad Dan McGoon	1959	30.00
❑ 876	Tell Me Today/It's Love	1960	30.00
❑ 883	That's Why/The Boogie Man	1960	30.00
❑ 915	Wayward Wanderer/I'll Never Let You Go	1963	20.00
	—As "The Original Cadillacs"		
JUBILEE			
❑ 8010 [S]	Romeo/Always My Darling	1959	60.00
LANA			
❑ 118	Speedo/Baby It's All Right	196?	6.00
	—Reissue		
❑ 119	Gloria/Hey Bob E Re Bob	196?	6.00
	—Reissue		
MERCURY			
❑ 71738	I'm Willing/Thrill Me So	1961	100.00
POLYDOR			
❑ 14031	Deep in the Heart of the Ghetto (Part 1)/Deep in the Heart of the Ghetto (Part 2)	1969	15.00
	—As "The Original Cadillacs"		
ROULETTE			
❑ 4654	Let's Get Together/She's My Connection	1965	20.00
SMASH			
❑ 1712	You Are to Blame/What to Bet	1961	25.00

Albums

Number	Title (A Side/B Side)	Yr	NM
HARLEM HIT PARADE			
❑ 5009	Cruisin' with the Cadillacs	197?	10.00
JUBILEE			
❑ JGM-1045 [M]	The Fabulous Cadillacs	1957	400.00
	—Blue label		
❑ JGM-1045 [M]	The Fabulous Cadillacs	1959	250.00
	—Flat black label		
❑ JGM-1045 [M]	The Fabulous Cadillacs	1960	100.00
	—Glossy black label		
❑ JGM-1089 [M]	The Crazy Cadillacs	1959	300.00
	—Flat black label		
❑ JGM-1089 [M]	The Crazy Cadillacs	1960	100.00
	—Glossy black label		
❑ JGM-5009 [M]	Twisting with the Cadillacs	1962	200.00
MURRAY HILL			
❑ 1195	The Very Best of the Cadillacs	198?	15.00
❑ 1285 [(5)]	The Cadillacs	198?	40.00
	—Box set		

Except when noted otherwise, VG = 25% of NM, and VG+ = 50% of NM. (Example: VG = $2.00, VG+ = $4.00 and NM = $8.00.)

Number	Title (A Side/B Side)	Yr	NM

CADILLACS, THE/ THE ORIOLES
Also see each artist's individual listings.

Albums

JUBILEE

❑ JGM-1117 [M] The Cadillacs Meet the Orioles 1961 200.00

CAESAR AND CLEO
See SONNY AND CHER.

CAGLE, WADE

45s

SUN

❑ 360 Groovy Train/Highland Rock 1961 25.00

CAHPERONES, THE
See THE CHAPERONES.

CAIN

Albums

A.S.I.

❑ 204 A Pound of Flesh 1974 75.00
❑ 214 Stinger 1975 40.00

CAIROS, THE

45s

SHRINE

❑ 111 Stop Overlooking Me/ Don't Fight It 1966 1200.

CAKE, THE

45s

DECCA

❑ 32179 Mockingbird/Baby That's Me 1967 10.00
❑ 32212 You Can Have Him/I Know 1967 10.00
❑ 32212 [PS] You Can Have Him/I Know 1967 30.00
❑ 32235 Fire Fly/Rainbow Wood 1967 10.00
❑ 32347 PT 280/Have You Heard the News 'Bout Miss Molly 1968 10.00

Albums

DECCA

❑ DL 4927 [M] The Cake 1967 20.00
❑ DL 5039 [M] A Slice of the Cake 1968 50.00
—Mono is white label promo only
❑ DL 74927 [S] The Cake 1967 25.00
❑ DL 75039 [S] A Slice of the Cake 1968 25.00

CALDWELL, LOUISE HARRISON

Albums

RECAR

❑ 2012 [M] All About the Beatles 1965 150.00
—Without insert
❑ 2012 [M] All About the Beatles 1965 200.00
—With insert

CALE, J.J.

45s

LIBERTY

❑ 55840 Dick Tracy/It's a Go-Go Place 1965 15.00
❑ 55881 Outside Lookin' In/In Our Time 1966 15.00
❑ 55931 After Midnight/Slow Motion 1966 15.00

MCA

❑ 51095 Carry On/Deep Dark Dungeon 1981 4.00

MERCURY

❑ 76145 Devil in Disguise/Drifter's Wife 1982 3.00
❑ 814497-7 Losers/Reality 1983 3.00

SHELTER

❑ 7306 Magnolia/Crazy Mama 1971 8.00
❑ 7314 Crazy Mama/Don't Go to Strangers 1971 6.00
❑ 7321 After Midnight/Crying Eyes 1972 6.00
❑ 7326 Lies/Riding Home 1972 6.00
❑ 7332 Going Down/Louisiana Women 1973 6.00
❑ 40238 Cajun Moon/Starbound 1974 5.00
❑ 40290 I'll Be There/Precious Memories 1974 5.00
❑ 40366 I Got the Same Old Blues/ Rock and Roll Records 1975 5.00
❑ 62002 Hey Baby/Cocaine 1976 6.00

Albums

MCA

❑ 5158 Shades 1981 10.00
❑ 37102 5 1981 8.00
—Reissue of Shelter 3163
❑ 37103 Troubadour 1981 8.00
—Reissue of Shelter 52002
❑ 37104 Naturally 1981 8.00
—Reissue of Shelter 52009
❑ 37105 Really 1981 8.00
—Reissue of Shelter 52012
❑ 37106 Okie 1981 8.00
—Reissue of Shelter 52019

MERCURY

❑ SRM-1-4038 Grasshopper 1982 10.00
❑ 810313-1 5 1983 6.00
—Reissue of MCA 37102

Number	Title (A Side/B Side)	Yr	NM

❑ 810314-1 Really 1983 6.00
—Reissue of MCA 37105
❑ 811152-1 #8 1983 10.00
❑ 818633-1 Special Edition 1984 10.00
❑ 822888-1 Grasshopper 1985 6.00
—Reissue of 4038

SHELTER

❑ 2107 Okie 1974 15.00
❑ 2122 Naturally 1974 12.00
—Reissue of SW-8908
❑ 2123 Really 1974 12.00
—Reissue of 8912
❑ 3163 5 1979 12.00
❑ SW-8908 Naturally 1971 15.00
❑ SW-8912 Really 1972 15.00
❑ 52002 Troubadour 1976 15.00
❑ 52009 Naturally 1977 10.00
—Reissue of 2122
❑ 52012 Really 1977 10.00
—Reissue of 2123
❑ 52015 Okie 1977 10.00
—Reissue of 2107

SILVERTONE

❑ 1306-1-J Travel-Log 1990 12.00

CALE, JOHN
Also see THE VELVET UNDERGROUND.

12-Inch Singles

A&M

❑ SP-17154 [DJ] Dead or Alive/Honi Soit 1981 10.00

45s

A&M

❑ 2329 Dead or Alive/Honi Soit 1981 5.00

COLUMBIA

❑ 4-45154 Cleo/Fairweather Friend 1970 10.00
❑ 4-45266 Big White Cloud/Gideon's Bible 1970 10.00

REPRISE

❑ 1108 Legs Larry at Television Center/Days of Steam 1972 10.00

SPY/I.R.S.

❑ 9008 Ready for War/Rosegarden Funeral of Sores 1979 6.00
❑ 9008 [PS] Ready for War/Rosegarden Funeral of Sores 1979 6.00

Albums

A&M

❑ SP-4849 Honi Soit 1981 10.00

ANTILLES

❑ AN-7063 Guts 198? 12.00
—Reissue of Island 9459

COLUMBIA

❑ CS 1037 Vintage Violence 1970 25.00
—Red "360 Sound" label
❑ CS 1037 Vintage Violence 1971 15.00
—Orange label
❑ C 30131 Church of Anthrax 1971 15.00

ISLAND

❑ IXP-2 [DJ] Hear Fear 1975 60.00
—Promo-only interview album
❑ IT-8401 Caribbean Sunset 1984 10.00
❑ IT-8402 John Cale Comes Alive 1984 10.00
❑ ILPS 9301 Fear 1975 20.00
❑ ILPS 9317 Slow Dazzle 1975 15.00
❑ ILPS 9350 Helen of Troy 1975 20.00
❑ ILPS 9459 Guts 1977 20.00

OPAL/WARNER BROS.

❑ 26024 Words for the Dying 1989 12.00

PASSPORT

❑ PB 6019 Music for a New Society 1982 12.00

PVC

❑ 8947 Artificial Intelligence 1985 15.00

REPRISE

❑ MS 2079 The Academy in Peril 1972 75.00
❑ MS 2131 Paris, 1919 1973 35.00

SPY/I.R.S.

❑ SP-004 Sabotage/Live 1980 15.00

CALIFORNIA

45s

LAURIE

❑ 3612 See You in September/Ivy Ivy 1974 4.00
❑ 3639 Song of a Thousand Voices/ Abraham, Martin and John 1976 4.00
❑ 3647 Jeans On/Doo-Wop Music 1976 4.00
❑ 3651 I'm Just Thinking of You/ Doo-Wop Music 1977 4.00
❑ 3695 Summer Fun Medley/Paris 1981 4.00

RCA

❑ PB-11769 Everybody Needs a Little Help/ I'm a Poet 1979 10.00

Number	Title (A Side/B Side)	Yr	NM

RSO

❑ 901 I Can Hear Music/Love's Supposed to Be That Way 1978 10.00

WARNER BROS.

❑ 8253 Happy in Hollywood/ Music, Music, Music 1976 10.00
❑ 8307 (Just to Let You Know) I Love You So/Happy in Hollywood 1977 10.00

CALIFORNIA, RANDY
Also see SPIRIT.

45s

EPIC

❑ 10927 Walkin' the Dog/Live for the Day 1972 8.00

Albums

EPIC

❑ KE 31755 Kapt. Kopter & the Fabulous Twirly Birds 1972 25.00
—Yellow label
❑ KE 31755 Kapt. Kopter & the Fabulous Twirly Birds 1973 12.00
—Orange label

CALIFORNIA MUSIC

45s

EQUINOX

❑ PB-10120 Don't Worry Baby/ Ten Years' Harmony 1974 15.00
❑ PB-10363 Why Do Fools Fall in Love/ Don't Worry Baby 1975 15.00
❑ PB-10572 Jamaica Farewell/ California Music 1976 15.00

CALIFORNIA POPPY PICKERS, THE

Albums

ALSHIRE

❑ S-5153 Blue-Eyed Soul 1969 30.00
❑ S-5163 Today's Chart Busters 1969 20.00
❑ S-5167 Honky Tonk Women 1970 40.00

CALIFORNIANS, THE (1)

45s

CRAZY HORSE

❑ 1318 Nausea Beast/Glass Disguise 1969 10.00

CALIFORNIANS, THE (2)
JESSE BELVIN appears on this record.

45s

FEDERAL

❑ 12231 My Angel/Heavenly Ruby 1955 300.00

CALLENDER, BOBBY

45s

CORAL

❑ 62517 You've Really Got a Hold on Me/I Can't Get Over You 1967 10.00
❑ 62528 Sweet Song of Life/Vicissitude (Or a Day at Jaffry's) 1967 10.00

MGM

❑ 13965 Rainbow/Symphonic Pictures 1968 12.00

ROULETTE

❑ 4471 Little Star/Love and Kisses 1963 16.00

CALVANES, THE

45s

DECK

❑ 579 Dreamworld/5, 7 or 9 1958 100.00
❑ 580 My Love Song/Horror Pictures 1958 100.00

DOOTONE

❑ 371 Crazy Over You/Don't Take Your Love from Me 1956 200.00
❑ 380 One More Kiss/Florabelle 1956 200.00

7-Inch Extended Plays

DOOTONE

❑ 205 *They Call Me Fool/One More Kiss/Don't Take Your Love from Me/Crazy Over You 1956 400.00
❑ 205 [PS] Voices for Lovers 1956 600.00

CAMBRIDGE, GODFREY

Albums

EPIC

❑ FLM 13101 [M] Ready or Not…Here's Godfrey Cambridge 1964 20.00
❑ FLM 13102 [M] Them Cotton Pickin' Days Is Over 1965 20.00
❑ FLM 13108 [M] Godfrey Cambridge Toys with the World 1966 20.00
❑ FLM 13115 [M] The Godfrey Cambridge Show Live at the Aladdin 1968 20.00
❑ FLS 15101 [S] Ready or Not…Here's Godfrey Cambridge 1964 20.00
❑ FLS 15102 [S] Them Cotton Pickin' Days Is Over 1965 20.00

Except when noted otherwise, VG = 25% of NM, and VG+ = 50% of NM. (Example: VG = $2.00, VG+ = $4.00 and NM = $8.00.)

C

Camel, *Moonmadness*, Janus 7024, 1976, **$12.**

Number	Title (A Side/B Side)	Yr	NM
❑ FLS 15108 [S]	Godfrey Cambridge Toys with the World	1966	20.00
❑ FLS 15115 [S]	The Godfrey Cambridge Show Live at the Aladdin	1968	20.00

CAMEL

45s

JANUS

Number	Title (A Side/B Side)	Yr	NM
❑ 262	Another Night/Lunar Sea	1976	6.00

Albums

ARISTA

Number	Title (A Side/B Side)	Yr	NM
❑ AB 4206	Breathless	1979	10.00
❑ AB 4254	I Can See Your House from Here	1980	10.00

JANUS

Number	Title (A Side/B Side)	Yr	NM
❑ 7009	Mirage	1974	12.00
❑ 7016	The Snow Goose	1975	12.00
❑ 7024	Moonmadness	1976	12.00
❑ 7035	Rain Dances	1977	12.00

LONDON

Number	Title (A Side/B Side)	Yr	NM
❑ 820166-1	Pressure Points	1987	10.00

PASSPORT

Number	Title (A Side/B Side)	Yr	NM
❑ PB-6008	Nude	198?	10.00
❑ PB-6013	The Single Factor	198?	10.00
❑ PB-9855	Mirage	198?	8.00
—Reissue of Janus 7009			
❑ PB-9856	The Snow Goose	198?	8.00
—Reissue of Janus 7016			
❑ PB-9857	Moonmadness	198?	8.00
—Reissue of Janus 7024			
❑ PB-9858	Rain Dances	198?	8.00
—Reissue of Janus 7035			

CAMELOTS, THE

45s

AANKO

Number	Title (A Side/B Side)	Yr	NM
❑ 1001	Your Way/Don't Leave Me Baby	1963	80.00
❑ 1004	Sunday Kind of Love/ My Imagination	1963	80.00

CAMEO

Number	Title (A Side/B Side)	Yr	NM
❑ 334	Don't Leave Me Baby/Love Call	1964	30.00
—B-side by the Ebonaires			

COMET

Number	Title (A Side/B Side)	Yr	NM
❑ 930	Scratch/Charge	1962	15.00

CRIMSON

Number	Title (A Side/B Side)	Yr	NM
❑ 1001	Don't Leave Me Baby/The Letter	1963	30.00

DREAM

Number	Title (A Side/B Side)	Yr	NM
❑ 1001	Your Way/I Wonder	1967	8.00

EMBER

Number	Title (A Side/B Side)	Yr	NM
❑ 1108	Pocahontas/Searching for My Baby	1964	20.00

LAURIE

Number	Title (A Side/B Side)	Yr	NM
❑ 3239	Marie/Daddy's Going Away Again	1964	20.00
—As "The Harps"			

LOST-NITE

Number	Title (A Side/B Side)	Yr	NM
❑ 247	Don't Leave Me Baby/The Letter	1963	5.00
—Reissue			

NIX

Number	Title (A Side/B Side)	Yr	NM
❑ 101	Lulu/Never Been in Love Before	1961	20.00

RELIC

Number	Title (A Side/B Side)	Yr	NM
❑ 530	Chain of Broken Hearts/Rat Race	196?	8.00
—B-side by the Bootleggers			
❑ 541	Dance Girl/That's My Baby	1965	8.00
—B-side by the Suns			

TIMES SQUARE

Number	Title (A Side/B Side)	Yr	NM
❑ 32	Dance Girl/That's My Baby	1964	10.00
—B-side by the Suns			

7-Inch Extended Plays

CLIFTON/UGHA

Number	Title (A Side/B Side)	Yr	NM
❑ EP 507/1	Music to My Ears/Daddy's Going Away//Pocahontas/ Don't Leave Me Baby	1981	5.00
❑ EP 507/1 [PS]	(title unknown)	1981	5.00

CAMEO

12-Inch Singles

ATLANTA ARTISTA

Number	Title (A Side/B Side)	Yr	NM
❑ PRO 282-1 [DJ]	Talkin' Out the Side of Your Neck (same on both sides)	1984	20.00

ATLANTA ARTISTS

Number	Title (A Side/B Side)	Yr	NM
❑ PRO 217-1 [DJ]	Slow Movin' (2 versions?)	1983	20.00
❑ PRO 291-1 [DJ]	Hangin' Downtown (same on both sides)	1984	10.00
❑ PRO 543-1 [DJ]	She's Mine (2 versions)	1986	10.00
❑ PRO 839-1 [DJ]	I Want It Now (same on both sides)	1990	15.00
❑ PRO 868-1 [DJ]	Close Quarters (2 versions) (same on both sides)	1990	12.00
❑ 812053-1	Style (5:08) (5:19)	1983	12.00
❑ 818384-1	She's Strange (Club Mix 6:42) (LP Version 7:21)	1984	10.00
❑ 870587-1	You Make Me Work (3 versions)/DKWIG	1988	8.00
❑ 872315-1	Skin I'm In (3 versions)/Honey	1988	10.00
❑ 874051-1	Pretty Girls (12" Remix) (12" Dub) (7" Remix) (7" Dub)	1989	10.00
❑ 875589-1	I Want It Now (12" Edit) (Rough Mix) (Then Dub) (Now Dub)	1990	10.00
❑ 878199-1	Close Quarters (4 versions)/ Honey	1990	8.00
❑ 880038-1	Talkin' Out the Side of Your Neck/She's Strange (Rap Version)	1984	15.00
❑ 880744-1	Attack Me with Your Love (Extended Version 6:31) (7" Dance Remix 4:15)	1985	12.00
❑ 884010-1	Single Life (6:30)/ I've Got Your Image	1985	10.00
❑ 884270-1	A Good-Bye (5:41)/ Little Boys-Dangerous Toys	1985	12.00
❑ 884933-1	Word Up (3 versions)/ Urban Warrior	1986	10.00
❑ 888193-1	Candy/She's Strange	1986	10.00
❑ 888385-1	Back and Forth (12" Club Remix 6:30) (Dub Mix 6:01) (7" Version 3:47)/ You Can Have the World	1987	10.00

CHOCOLATE CITY

Number	Title (A Side/B Side)	Yr	NM
❑ CCD 20005 [DJ]	Rigor Mortis (Disco Mix 6:14)/ (Mono Mix 3:12)	1977	40.00
❑ CCD 20007 [DJ]	Post Mortem/(B-side blank)	1977	25.00
❑ CCD 20013 [DJ]	It's Serious/(B-side blank)	1978	30.00
❑ CCD 20014 [DJ]	Find My Way/Rigor Mortis// (B-side blank)	1978	30.00
❑ CCD 20016 [DJ]	I Just Want to Be/(B-side blank)	1979	30.00
❑ CCD 20020 [DJ]	We're Goin' Out Tonight (4:41)/ (B-side blank)	1980	25.00
❑ CCD 20022	Shake Your Pants (5:59) (4:01)	1980	20.00
❑ CCD 20028	Keep It Hot/Your Love Takes Me Out	1980	20.00
❑ CCD 20034	Don't Be So Cool (4:23)/ I Never Knew (4:34)	1981	20.00
❑ CCD 20035 [DJ]	Just Be Yourself (4:20) (same on both sides)	1982	20.00
❑ CCD 20037	Alligator Woman/(B-side blank?)	1982	15.00
❑ CCD 20038	Flirt (2 versions)	1982	20.00
❑ CCD 20039	Flirt (3 versions)	1982	20.00

REPRISE

Number	Title (A Side/B Side)	Yr	NM
❑ PRO-A-5224 [DJ]	Emotional Violence (Edit) (LP Version)	1992	20.00
❑ PRO-A-5625 [DJ]	Raw But Tasty (Rap Remix) (Funk Mix) (Raw Remix) (Dub) (Ronnie's Mix)	1992	15.00
❑ 40392	Money (Reese Revamp Mix) (Reese Hardcore Instrumental) (Hardsell Mix)/ Front Street	1992	30.00

45s

ATLANTA ARTISTS

Number	Title (A Side/B Side)	Yr	NM
❑ PRO 272-7 [DJ]	She's Strange (Rap)/(Edit)	1984	10.00
❑ 812054-7	Style/Enjoy Your Life	1983	3.00
❑ 812472-7	Can't Help Falling in Love/ For You	1983	3.00
❑ 814077-7	Slow Movin'/For You	1983	3.00
❑ 818384-7	She's Strange/ Tribute to Bob Marley	1984	3.00
❑ 818870-7	Talkin' Out the Side of Your Neck/Leve-Toi	1984	3.00
❑ 870587-7	You Make Me Work/DKWIG	1988	3.00
❑ 870587-7 [PS]	You Make Me Work/DKWIG	1988	3.00
❑ 872314-7	Skin I'm In/Honey	1988	3.00
❑ 872314-7 [PS]	Skin I'm In/Honey	1988	3.00
❑ 872918-7	Single Life/She's Strange	1989	3.00
—Reissue			
❑ 874050-7	Pretty Girls/Pretty Girls (Dub)	1989	3.00
❑ 874050-7 [PS]	Pretty Girls/Pretty Girls (Dub)	1989	3.00
❑ 875588-7	I Want It Now/DKWIG	1990	3.00

Except when noted otherwise, VG = 25% of NM, and VG+ = 50% of NM. (Example: VG = $2.00, VG+ = $4.00 and NM = $8.00.)

Number	Title (A Side/B Side)	Yr	NM
❑ 878198-7	Close Quarters/Honey	1990	3.00
❑ 880169-7	Hangin' Downtown/ Cameo's Dance	1984	3.00
❑ 880744-7	Attack Me With Your Love/ Love You Anyway	1985	3.00
❑ 884010-7	Single Life/I've Got Your Image	1985	3.00
❑ 884270-7	A Good-Bye/Little Boys- Dangerous Toys	1985	3.00
❑ 884933-7	Word Up/Urban Warrior	1986	3.00
❑ 884933-7 [PS]	Word Up/Urban Warrior	1986	3.00
❑ 888193-7	Candy/She's Strange	1986	3.00
❑ 888193-7 [PS]	Candy/She's Strange	1986	3.00
❑ 888385-7	Back and Forth/ You Can Have the World	1987	3.00
❑ 888385-7 [PS]	Back and Forth/ You Can Have the World	1987	3.00
❑ 888711-7	Don't Be Lonely/I've Got Your Image	1987	3.00
❑ 888876-7	She's Mine/I've Got Your Image	1987	3.00

CHOCOLATE CITY

Number	Title (A Side/B Side)	Yr	NM
❑ 001	Find My Way/Good Company	1975	5.00
❑ 005	Rigor Mortis/Stand By My Side	1976	5.00
❑ 008	Find My Way/Rigor Mortis	1977	4.00
❑ 010	Post Mortem/Smile	1977	4.00
❑ 011	Funk Funk/Good Time	1977	4.00
❑ 013	It's Serious/Inflation	1978	4.00
❑ 014	It's Over/Inflation	1978	4.00
❑ 016	Insane/I Want You	1978	4.00
❑ 018	Give Love a Chance/Two of Us	1979	4.00
❑ 019	I Just Want to Be/The Rock	1979	4.00
❑ 3202	Sparkle/Macho	1979	4.00
❑ 3206	We're Goin' Out Tonight/ One the One	1980	4.00
❑ 3210	Shake Your Pants/ I Came for You	1980	4.00
❑ 3219	Keep It Hot/I Came for You	1980	4.00
❑ 3222	Feel Me/Is This the Way	1981	4.00
❑ 3225	Freaky Dancin'/Better Days	1981	4.00
❑ 3227	I Like It/The Sound Table	1981	4.00
❑ 3231	Just Be Yourself/Use It or Lose It	1982	4.00
❑ 3233	Flirt/Owe It All to You	1982	4.00
❑ 3235	Alligator Woman/Soul Away	1982	4.00

Albums

ATLANTA ARTISTS

Number	Title	Yr	NM
❑ 811072-1	Style	1983	10.00
❑ 814984-1	She's Strange	1984	10.00
❑ 824546-1	Single Life	1985	10.00
❑ 830265-1	Word Up!	1986	10.00
❑ 836002-1	Machismo	1988	10.00
❑ 846297-1	Real Men..Wear Black	1990	12.00

CHOCOLATE CITY

Number	Title	Yr	NM
❑ CCLP 2003	Cardiac Arrest	1977	12.00
❑ CCLP 2004	We All Know Who We Are	1978	12.00
❑ CCLP 2006	Ugly Ego	1978	12.00
❑ CCLP 2008	Secret Omen	1979	12.00
❑ CCLP 2011	Cameosis	1980	12.00
❑ CCLP 2016	Feel Me	1980	12.00
❑ CCLP 2019	Knights of the Sound Table	1981	12.00
❑ CCLP 2021	Alligator Woman	1982	12.00

CAMEOS, THE

45s

CAMEO

Number	Title (A Side/B Side)	Yr	NM
❑ 123	Merry Christmas/New Year's Eve	1957	150.00
❑ 123	Merry Christmas/New Year's Eve	197?	10.00

—Reproduction of the original 1957 release

DEAN

Number	Title (A Side/B Side)	Yr	NM
❑ 504	Lost Lover/Wait Up	1961	150.00

JOHNSON

Number	Title (A Side/B Side)	Yr	NM
❑ 108	Lost Lover/Wait Up	1961	80.00

MATADOR

Number	Title (A Side/B Side)	Yr	NM
❑ 1813	Never Before/Canadian Sunset	1963	25.00

CAMERON, JIMMY AND VELLA

45s

REPRISE

Number	Title (A Side/B Side)	Yr	NM
❑ 0483	Lovin' You Is Such a Groove/ I Know a Place	1966	30.00

UNLIMITED GOLD

Number	Title (A Side/B Side)	Yr	NM
❑ 1422	Mornin' Time/ There Is No Other Love	1980	4.00

CAMP, THE

45s

SCEPTER

Number	Title (A Side/B Side)	Yr	NM
❑ 12159	Marching/Long Long Trail	1966	80.00

CAMPANELLA, DAVID, AND THE DELLCHORDS

45s

KANE

Number	Title (A Side/B Side)	Yr	NM
❑ 25593	Over the Rainbow/ Everything's That Way	1959	60.00

CAMPBELL, CHOKER

45s

APT

Number	Title (A Side/B Side)	Yr	NM
❑ 25011	Walk Awhile/Walking on Thin-Soled Shoes	1958	60.00

ATLANTIC

Number	Title (A Side/B Side)	Yr	NM
❑ 1014	Last Call for Whiskey/ How Could You Do This	1953	40.00
❑ 1038	Have You Seen My Baby/ Jackie Mambo	1954	40.00

FORTUNE

Number	Title (A Side/B Side)	Yr	NM
❑ 808	Frankie and Johnny/ Rocking and Jumping	1953	60.00

MOTOWN

Number	Title (A Side/B Side)	Yr	NM
❑ 1072	Come See About Me/ Pride and Joy	1964	25.00

Albums

MOTOWN

Number	Title	Yr	NM
❑ M-620 [M]	Hits of the Sixties	1964	100.00
❑ MS-620 [S]	Hits of the Sixties	1964	150.00

CAMPBELL, EDDIE

Also see EDDIE AND ERNIE.

45s

ARTCO

Number	Title (A Side/B Side)	Yr	NM
❑ 45-103	Contagious Love/Why Do You Treat Me Like You Do	1967	1200.

CAMPBELL, GLEN

Also see THE BEACH BOYS; THE CHAMPS; GEE CEES.

45s

ATLANTIC AMERICA

Number	Title (A Side/B Side)	Yr	NM
❑ 99525	Call Home/Sweet 16	1986	3.00
❑ 99559	Cowpoke/Rag Doll	1986	3.00
❑ 99600	It's Just a Matter of Time/ Gene Autry, My Hero	1985	3.00
❑ 99600 [PS]	It's Just a Matter of Time/ Gene Autry, My Hero	1985	4.00
❑ 99647	(Love Always) Letter to Home/ An American Trilogy	1985	3.00
❑ 99691	A Lady Like You/Tennessee	1984	3.00
❑ 99768	Faithless Love/ Scene of the Crime	1984	3.00
❑ 99893	On the Wings of My Victory/ A Few Good Men	1983	3.00
❑ 99930	I Love How You Love Me/Hang On Baby (Ease My Mind)	1983	3.00
❑ 99967	Old Home Town/Heartache #3	1982	4.00
❑ 99967 [PS]	Old Home Town/Heartache #3	1982	4.00

CAPEHART

Number	Title (A Side/B Side)	Yr	NM
❑ 5008	Death Valley/Nothin' Better Than a Pretty Woman	1961	25.00

CAPITOL

Number	Title (A Side/B Side)	Yr	NM
❑ 2015	By the Time I Get to Phoenix/ You've Still Got a Place in My Heart	1967	7.00
❑ 2076	Hey Little One/My Baby's Gone	1968	7.00
❑ 2076 [PS]	Hey Little One/My Baby's Gone	1968	12.00
❑ 2146	I Wanna Live/ That's All That Matters	1968	7.00
❑ 2224	Dreams of the Everyday Housewife/Kelli Ho-Down	1968	7.00
❑ 2302	Wichita Lineman/Fate of Man	1968	6.00
❑ 2336	Christmas Is for Children/ There's No Place Like Home	1968	8.00
❑ 2428	Galveston/How Come Every Time I Itch I Wind Up Scratchin' You	1969	6.00
❑ 2494	Where's the Playground Susie/ Arkansas	1969	6.00
❑ 2573	True Grit/Hava Nagila	1969	6.00
❑ 2659	Try a Little Kindness/Lonely My Lonely Friend	1969	6.00
❑ 2718	Honey Come Back/Where Do You Go	1970	6.00
❑ 2787	Oh Happy Day/Someone Above	1970	6.00
❑ 2843	Everything a Man Could Ever Need/Norwood (Me and My Guitar)	1970	6.00
❑ 2905	It's Only Make Believe/Pave Your Way Into Tomorrow	1970	6.00
❑ 3062	Dream Baby (How Long Must I Dream)/Here and Now	1971	6.00
❑ 3123	The Last Time I Saw Her/ Bach Talk	1971	6.00
❑ 3254	Oklahoma Sunday Morning/ Everybody's Got to Go There Sometime	1972	6.00
❑ 3305	Manhattan, Kansas/ Wayfaring Stranger	1972	6.00
❑ 3382	We All Pull the Load/ Wherefore and Why	1972	7.00
❑ 3411	I Will Never Pass This Way Again/We All Pull the Load	1972	6.00
❑ 3483	One Last Time/All My Tomorrows	1972	6.00
❑ 3509	I Believe in Christmas/New Snow on the Roof	1972	6.00
❑ 3548	I Knew Jesus (Before He Was a Star)/On This Road	1973	5.00
❑ 3669	Bring Back My Yesterday/ Beautiful Love Song	1973	5.00
❑ 3735	Wherefore and Why/Give Me Back That Old Familiar Feeling	1973	5.00
❑ 3808	Houston (I'm Coming to See You)/Honestly Love	1973	5.00
❑ 3926	Bonaparte's Retreat/ Too Many Mornings	1974	5.00
❑ 3988	It's a Sin When You Love Somebody/If I Were Loving You	1974	5.00
❑ 4095	Rhinestone Cowboy/Lovelight	1975	4.00
❑ 4155	Country Boy (You Got Your Feet in L.A.)/Record Collector's Dream	1975	4.00
❑ 4245	Then You Can Tell Me Goodbye-Don't Pull Your Love/I Miss You Tonight	1976	4.00
❑ 4288	See You on Sunday/Bloodline	1976	4.00
❑ 4376	Southern Nights/ William Tell Overture	1976	4.00
❑ 4445	Sunflower/How High Did We Go	1977	4.00
❑ 4515	God Must Have Blessed America/Amazing Grace	1977	4.00
❑ 4584	Another Fine Mess/Can You Fool	1978	4.00
❑ 4638	Can You Fool/Let's All Sing a Song About It	1978	4.00
❑ 4682	I'm Gonna Love You/ Love Takes You Higher	1979	4.00
❑ 4715	California/Never Tell You No Lies	1979	4.00
❑ 4769	Hound Dog Man/ Tennessee Home	1979	4.00
❑ 4783	Too Late to Worry — Too Blue to Cry/How Do I Tell My Heart Not to Break	1962	15.00
❑ 4799	My Prayer/Don't Lose Me in the Confusion	1979	4.00
❑ 4856	Long Black Limousine/Here I Am	1962	10.00
❑ 4856 [PS]	Long Black Limousine/Here I Am	1962	20.00
❑ 4865	Somethin' 'Bout You Baby I Like/Late Night Confession	1980	4.00

—With Rita Coolidge

Number	Title (A Side/B Side)	Yr	NM
❑ 4867	Kentucky Means Paradise/ Truck Driving Man	1962	15.00

—As "The Green River Boys Featuring Glen Campbell"

Number	Title (A Side/B Side)	Yr	NM
❑ 4909	Hollywood Smiles/ Hooked on Love	1980	4.00
❑ 4925	Oh My Darling/Prima Donna	1963	12.00
❑ 4959	I Don't Want to Know Your Name/Daisy a Day	1981	4.00
❑ 4986	Why Don't We Just Sleep on It Tonight/It's Your World	1981	4.00

—With Tanya Tucker

Number	Title (A Side/B Side)	Yr	NM
❑ 4990	Divorce Me C.O.D./ Dark As a Dungeon	1963	12.00
❑ 5037	As Far As I'm Concerned/ Same Old Places	1963	12.00
❑ 5172	Let Me Tell You About Mary/ Through the Eyes of a Child	1964	12.00
❑ 5279	Summer, Winter, Spring and Fall/Heartaches Can Be Fun	1964	12.00
❑ 5279 [PS]	Summer, Winter, Spring and Fall/Heartaches Can Be Fun	1964	25.00
❑ 5360	It's a Woman's World/ Tomorrow Never Comes	1965	12.00
❑ 5441	Guess I'm Dumb/That's All Right	1965	120.00

—A Brian Wilson "Pet Sounds"-like production

Number	Title (A Side/B Side)	Yr	NM
❑ 5504	The Universal Soldier/ Spanish Shades	1965	10.00
❑ 5545	Less of Me/Private John Q	1965	10.00
❑ 5638	Can't You See I'm Tryin'/ Satisfied Mind	1966	10.00
❑ 5773	Burning Bridges/Only the Lonely	1966	10.00
❑ 5854	I Gotta Have My Baby Back/ Just to Satisfy You	1967	10.00
❑ 5939	Gentle on My Mind/ Just Another Man	1967	8.00

—Orange and yellow swirl, without "A Subsidiary Of"... in perimeter label print

Number	Title (A Side/B Side)	Yr	NM
❑ 5939	Gentle on My Mind/ Just Another Man	1968	6.00

—Orange and yellow swirl label with "A Subsidiary Of" in perimeter print

Number	Title (A Side/B Side)	Yr	NM
❑ 7PRO-79107	On a Good Night (same on both sides)	1990	6.00

—Vinyl is promo only

Number	Title (A Side/B Side)	Yr	NM
❑ 7PRO-79966	Walkin' in the Sun (same on both sides)	1990	6.00

—Vinyl is promo only

CAPITOL CREATIVE PRODUCTS

Number	Title (A Side/B Side)	Yr	NM
❑ 54	Homeward Bound/(Sittin' On) The Dock of the Bay// Mary in the Morning	1969	8.00

Number	Title (A Side/B Side)	Yr	NM
CAPITOL NASHVILLE			
❑ 7PRO-79279	Somebody's Leavin' (same on both sides)	1990	6.00
—Vinyl is promo only			
❑ 7PRO-79494	Unconditional Love (same on both sides)	1991	6.00
—Vinyl is promo only			
CENECO			
❑ 1324	Dreams for Sale/I've Got to Win	1961	25.00
❑ 1356	I Wonder/You, You, You	1961	20.00
COMPLEAT			
❑ 113	Letting Go/(Instrumental)	1983	4.00
CREST			
❑ 1087	Turn Around, Look at Me/Brenda	1961	20.00
—With last name spelled correctly			
❑ 1087	Turn Around, Look at Me/Brenda	1961	30.00
—With last name spelled incorrectly as "Cambpbell"			
❑ 1096	The Miracle of Love/Once More	1962	15.00
EVEREST			
❑ 2500	Delight, Arkansas/Walk Right In	1969	6.00
LIBERTY			
❑ S7-18214	Blue Christmas/Feliz Navidad	1994	5.00
—B-side on EMI Latin by Jose Feliciano; red vinyl			
MCA			
❑ 41323	Dream Lover/Bronco	1980	4.00
—A-side with Tanya Tucker			
❑ 53108	The Hand That Rocks the Cradle/ Arkansas	1987	3.00
—A-side with Steve Wariner			
❑ 53172	Still Within the Sound of My Voice/In My Life	1987	3.00
❑ 53218	I Have You/I'm a One Woman Man	1987	3.00
❑ 53245	I Remember You/For Sure, For Certain, Forever, For Always	1988	3.00
❑ 53426	Heart of the Matter/Light Years	1988	3.00
❑ 53493	More Than Enough/Our Movie	1989	3.00
MIRAGE			
❑ 3845	I Love My Truck/Melody's Melody	1981	4.00
STARDAY			
❑ 853	For the Love of a Woman/ Smokey Blue Eyes	1968	8.00
UNIVERSAL			
❑ UVL-66024	She's Gone, Gone, Gone/ William Tell Overture	1989	4.00
WARNER BROS.			
❑ 49609	Any Which Way You Can/Medley from Any Which Way You Can	1980	4.00
—B-side by Texas Opera Company			
7-Inch Extended Plays			
CAPITOL CREATIVE PRODUCTS			
❑ SU-752	Wichita Lineman/Try a Little Kindness/By the Time I Get to Phoenix//Gentle on My Mind/ I Wanna Live/Galveston	1971	10.00
—Stereo jukebox issue; small hole, plays at 33 1/3 rpm			
❑ SU-752 [PS]	Greatest Hits	1971	10.00
—Part of "Little LP" series (#156)			
Albums			
ATLANTIC AMERICA			
❑ 90016	Old Home Town	1983	8.00
❑ 90164	Letter to Home	1984	8.00
❑ 90483	It's Just a Matter of Time	1985	8.00
CAPITOL			
❑ SM-103	Wichita Lineman	1977	8.00
—Reissue with new prefix			
❑ ST-103	Wichita Lineman	1968	15.00
❑ ST-8-0103	Wichita Lineman	1968	20.00
—Capitol Record Club edition			
❑ ST-210	Galveston	1969	15.00
❑ STBO-268	Glen Campbell — "Live"	1969	20.00
❑ SM-389	Try a Little Kindness	1977	8.00
—Reissue with new prefix			
❑ SW-389	Try a Little Kindness	1970	12.00
❑ SW-443	Oh Happy Day	1970	12.00
❑ SW-493	The Glen Campbell Goodtime Album	1970	12.00
❑ SM-733	The Last Time I Saw Her	1977	8.00
—Reissue with new prefix			
❑ SW-733	The Last Time I Saw Her	1971	12.00
❑ SW-752	Glen Campbell's Greatest Hits	1971	12.00
❑ ST 1810 [S]	Big Bluegrass Special	1962	100.00
—As "The Green River Boys Featuring Glen Campbell"			
❑ T 1810 [M]	Big Bluegrass Special	1962	80.00
—As "The Green River Boys Featuring Glen Campbell"			
❑ ST 1881 [S]	Too Late to Worry, Too Blue to Cry	1963	25.00
❑ T 1881 [M]	Too Late to Worry, Too Blue to Cry	1963	20.00
❑ ST 2023 [S]	The Astounding 12-String Guitar of Glen Campbell	1964	20.00
❑ T 2023 [M]	The Astounding 12-String Guitar of Glen Campbell	1964	15.00

Number	Title (A Side/B Side)	Yr	NM
❑ ST 2392 [S]	The Big Bad Rock Guitar of Glen Campbell	1965	20.00
❑ T 2392 [M]	The Big Bad Rock Guitar of Glen Campbell	1965	15.00
❑ ST 2679 [S]	Burning Bridges	1967	15.00
❑ T 2679 [M]	Burning Bridges	1967	15.00
❑ ST 2809 [S]	Gentle on My Mind	1967	15.00
❑ T 2809 [M]	Gentle on My Mind	1967	15.00
❑ ST 2851 [S]	By the Time I Get to Phoenix	1967	15.00
❑ T 2851 [M]	By the Time I Get to Phoenix	1967	15.00
❑ ST 2878 [S]	Hey, Little One	1968	15.00
❑ T 2878 [M]	Hey, Little One	1968	25.00
❑ ST 2907	A New Place in the Sun	1968	15.00
❑ ST 2978	That Christmas Feeling	1968	15.00
❑ SW-11117	Glen Travis Campbell	1972	10.00
❑ SW-11185	I Knew Jesus (Before He Was a Star)	1973	10.00
❑ SW-11253	I Remember Hank Williams	1973	10.00
❑ SW-11293	Hosuton (I'm Comin' to See You)	1974	10.00
❑ SW-11336	Reunion (The Songs of Jimmy Webb)	1974	10.00
❑ SM-11407	Arkansas	1977	8.00
—Reissue with new prefix			
❑ SW-11407	Arkansas	1975	10.00
❑ SW-11430	Rhinestone Cowboy	1975	10.00
❑ SW-11516	Bloodline	1976	10.00
❑ ST-11577	The Best of Glen Campbell	1976	10.00
❑ SO-11601	Southern Nights	1977	10.00
❑ SWBC-11707 [(2)]	Live at the Royal Festival Hall	1977	12.00
❑ SW-11722	Basic	1978	10.00
❑ SM-11960	Gentle on My Mind	1979	8.00
—Reissue of 2809			
❑ SOO-12008	Highwayman	1979	10.00
❑ SM-12040	By the Time I Get to Phoenix	1979	8.00
—Reissue of 2851			
❑ SOO-12075	Somethin' 'Bout You Baby I Like	1980	10.00
❑ SOO-12124	It's the World Gone Crazy	1981	10.00
❑ SN-16029	Rhinestone Cowboy	1980	6.00
—Budget-line reissue			
❑ SN-16030	Southern Nights	1980	6.00
—Budget-line reissue			
❑ SN-16031	Glen Travis Campbell	1980	6.00
—Budget-line reissue			
❑ SN-16160	Wichita Lineman	1981	6.00
—Budget-line reissue			
❑ SN-16258	Hey Little Girl	1982	6.00
—Budget-line reissue			
❑ SN-16259	Galveston	1982	6.00
—Budget-line reissue			
❑ SN-16297	Glen Campbell's Greatest Hits	1984	6.00
—Budget-line reissue			
❑ SN-16335	The Best of Glen Campbell	1984	6.00
—Budget-line reissue			
❑ SWAK-93157	Limited Collector's Edition	1970	20.00
—Capitol Record Club exclusive; includes tour program			
LONGINES SYMPHONETTE			
❑ LS-218 [(5)]	Glen Campbell's Golden Favorites	1972	25.00
MCA			
❑ 42009	Still Within the Sound of My Voice	1987	8.00
❑ 42210	Light Years	1988	8.00
PAIR			
❑ PDL2-1089 [(2)]	All-Time Favorites	1986	12.00
PICKWICK			
❑ PTP-2048 [(2)]	Only the Lonely	197?	10.00
❑ PC-3052 [M]	The 12 String Guitar of Glen Campbell	196?	12.00
❑ SPC-3052 [S]	The 12 String Guitar of Glen Campbell	196?	10.00
❑ SPC-3134	A Satisfied Mind	197?	8.00
❑ SPC-3274	The Glen Campbell Album	197?	8.00
❑ SPC-3346	I'll Paint You a Song	197?	8.00
STARDAY			
❑ SLP-424	Country Soul	1968	15.00
❑ SLP-437	Country Music Star #1	1969	15.00
SURREY			
❑ S 1007 [M]	Country Shindig	196?	12.00

CAMPBELL, GLEN, AND BOBBIE GENTRY

Also see each artist's individual listings.

Number	Title (A Side/B Side)	Yr	NM
45s			
CAPITOL			
❑ 2314	Less of Me/Morning Glory	1968	6.00
❑ 2387	Let It Be Me/Little Green Apples	1969	6.00
❑ 2745	All I Have to Do Is Dream/ Less of Me	1970	6.00
Albums			
CAPITOL			
❑ ST 2928	Bobbie Gentry & Glen Campbell	1968	15.00
❑ ST 8-2928	Bobbie Gentry & Glen Campbell	1968	20.00
—Capitol Record Club edition			

CAMPBELL, JO ANN

Number	Title (A Side/B Side)	Yr	NM
45s			
ABC-PARAMOUNT			
❑ 10134 [M]	A Kookie Little Paradise/ Bobby, Bobby, Bobby	1960	25.00
❑ S-10134 [S]	A Kookie Little Paradise/ Bobby, Bobby, Bobby	1960	50.00
❑ 10172	But Maybe This Year/ Crazy Daisy	1960	20.00
❑ 10200	Motorcycle Michael/ Puka Puka Pants	1961	20.00
❑ 10224	Eddie My Love/It Wasn't Right	1961	20.00
❑ 10258	Mama Don't Wait/Duane	1961	20.00
❑ 10300	I Changed My Mind Jack/ You Made Me Love You	1962	20.00
❑ 10335	Amateur Night/I Wish It Would Rain All Summer	1962	20.00
CAMEO			
❑ 223	I'm the Girl from Wolverton Mountain/Sloppy Joe	1962	20.00
❑ 237	Let Me Do It My Way/ Mr. Fix-It Man	1962	20.00
❑ 249	Mother Please/Waitin' for Love	1963	20.00
EL DORADO			
❑ 504	Forever Young/Come On Baby	1957	40.00
❑ 509	Funny Thing/I Can't Give You Anything But Love	1957	40.00
GONE			
❑ 5014	Wait a Minute/ I'm in Love with You	1957	30.00
❑ 5014	Wait a Minute/It's True	1957	40.00
❑ 5021	You're Driving Me Mad/ Rock and Roll Love	1958	30.00
❑ 5027	Whassa Matter with You/You-Oo	1958	30.00
❑ 5037	I Really, Really Love You/I'm Nobody's Baby Now	1958	30.00
❑ 5049	Happy New Year Baby/Tall Boy	1958	30.00
❑ 5055	Mama/Nervous	1959	30.00
❑ 5068	Beach Comber/I Ain't Got No Steady Date	1959	30.00
POINT			
❑ 4	I'm Coming Home Late Tonight/ Wherever You Go	1956	40.00
RORI			
❑ 711	Jim Dandy/Five Minutes More	1962	20.00
Albums			
ABC-PARAMOUNT			
❑ 393 [M]	Twistin' and Listenin'	1962	80.00
❑ S-393 [S]	Twistin' and Listenin'	1962	100.00
CAMEO			
❑ C-1026 [M]	All the Hits of Jo Ann Campbell	1962	50.00
❑ SC-1026 [S]	All the Hits of Jo Ann Campbell	1962	100.00
CORONET			
❑ CX-199 [M]	Starring Jo Ann Campbell	196?	20.00
❑ CXS-199 [R]	Starring Jo Ann Campbell	196?	12.00
END			
❑ LP-306 [M]	I'm Nobody's Baby	1959	150.00

CAMPBELL, JOHN

Number	Title (A Side/B Side)	Yr	NM
45s			
HIT			
❑ 64	If You Wanna Be Happy/ Ain't That a Shame	1963	8.00
—B-side by the Chellows			

CAMPER VAN BEETHOVEN CRACKER related.

Number	Title (A Side/B Side)	Yr	NM
12-Inch Singles			
VIRGIN			
❑ PR 2312 [DJ]	Eye of Fatima (Parts 1 and 2)/ Turquoise Jewelry	1988	10.00
❑ PR 2471 [DJ]	Turquoise Jewelry/Waka/Love Is a Weed/Harmony in My Head/Wade in the Water	1988	15.00
❑ PR 2865 [DJ]	Pictures of Matchstick Men (same on both sides)	1989	8.00
Albums			
INDEPENDENT PROJECT			
❑ 016	Telephone Free Landslide Victory	1985	25.00
—"Manufactured and Distributed within the United States of America by Rough Trade" on back cover; non-letterpress edition; several color schemes exist, all of equal value			
❑ 016	Telephone Free Landslide Victory	1985	50.00
—Letterpress cover, "Second Edition: 1175 cp./September 1985" on back (un-numbered promo)			
❑ 016	Telephone Free Landslide Victory	1985	60.00
—Letterpress cover, "Second Edition: 1175 cp./September 1985" on back (numbered edition from 1251-2425)			

Except when noted otherwise, VG = 25% of NM, and VG+ = 50% of NM. (Example: VG = $2.00, VG+ = $4.00 and NM = $8.00.)

C

Number	Title (A Side/B Side)	Yr	NM
❑ 016	Telephone Free Landslide Victory	1985	70.00

—Letterpress cover, "First Edition: June 1985" on back (un-numbered promo); the basic color scheme is red, black and flourescent orange on brown chipboard

Number	Title (A Side/B Side)	Yr	NM
❑ 016	Telephone Free Landslide Victory	1985	80.00

—Letterpress cover, "First Edition: June 1985" on back (numbered edition from 1-1,250); the basic color scheme is white, black and flourescent orange on brown chipboard

PITCH A TENT

Number	Title (A Side/B Side)	Yr	NM
❑ 01	II & III	1985	15.00
❑ 02	Camper Van Beethoven	1986	15.00
❑ 05 [EP]	Vampire Can Mating Oven	1987	15.00

VIRGIN

Number	Title (A Side/B Side)	Yr	NM
❑ 90918	Our Beloved Revolutionary Sweetheart	1988	10.00
❑ 91289	Key Lime Pie	1989	10.00

CAMPERS, THE Includes SONNY CURTIS and THE CRICKETS (1).

45s

PARKWAY

Number	Title (A Side/B Side)	Yr	NM
❑ 974	The Ballad of Batman/ The Batmobile	1966	30.00
❑ 974	The Ballad of Batman/ The Batmobile	1966	35.00

—Original label credit: "The Camps"

CAMPI, RAY

45s

COLPIX

Number	Title (A Side/B Side)	Yr	NM
❑ 166	French Fries/Hear What I Wanna Hear	1960	15.00

D

Number	Title (A Side/B Side)	Yr	NM
❑ 1047	The Ballad of Donna and Peggy Sue/A Man I Met (Tribute to The Big Bopper)	1959	40.00

DOMINO

Number	Title (A Side/B Side)	Yr	NM
❑ 700	My Screamin' Screamin' Meemie/With You	1958	30.00

DOT

Number	Title (A Side/B Side)	Yr	NM
❑ 15617	It Ain't Me/Give That Love to Me	1957	60.00

ROLLIN' ROCK

Number	Title (A Side/B Side)	Yr	NM
❑ 006	Eager Boy/Dobroggie	1978	5.00
❑ 008	Tore Up/If It's All the Same to You	1978	5.00
❑ 014	Sixteen Chicks/ Pan American Boogie	1979	5.00
❑ 019	My Baby Left Me/ A Li'l Bit of Heartache	1979	5.00
❑ 027	Wrong, Wrong, Wrong/Booze It	1980	4.00
❑ 029	Scrumptious Baby/ I Didn't Mean to Be Mean	1980	4.00
❑ 031	Merle's Boogie-Woogie-Missouri/Sweet Temptation Guitar Rag	1980	4.00

—With Merle Travis

Number	Title (A Side/B Side)	Yr	NM
❑ 038	Rockin' at the Ritz/ Quit Your Triplin'	1981	4.00
❑ 044	Rattlin' Daddy/Wild One	1981	4.00
❑ 046	Texas Sands/ How Long Can You Feel	1982	4.00
❑ 047	Sweet Woman Blues/ The Newest Wave	1982	4.00
❑ 052	Rockabilly Man/Hollywood Cats	1983	4.00

TNT

Number	Title (A Side/B Side)	Yr	NM
❑ 145	Caterpillar/Play It Cool	1958	300.00

WINSOR

Number	Title (A Side/B Side)	Yr	NM
❑ 6401	Billie Jean/Shenandoah	1964	30.00

Albums

ROLLIN' ROCK

Number	Title (A Side/B Side)	Yr	NM
❑ 023	Rockabilly Music	1979	12.00

ROUNDER

Number	Title (A Side/B Side)	Yr	NM
❑ 3046	Rockin' at the Ritz	198?	10.00
❑ 3047	Gone, Gone, Gone	198?	10.00

CAMPS, THE See THE CAMPERS.

CANADIAN BEADLES, THE

45s

TIDE

Number	Title (A Side/B Side)	Yr	NM
❑ 2203	I Think I'm Gonna Cry/ I'll Show You the Way	1964	15.00
❑ 2206	I'm Coming Home/ Love Walk Away	1964	15.00

—As "Vic, Paul and Bruce"

Albums

TIDE

Number	Title (A Side/B Side)	Yr	NM
❑ 2005 [M]	Three Faces North	1964	50.00

Camper Van Beethoven, *Key Lime Pie*, Virgin 91289, 1989, **$10.**

CANARIES, THE

45s

B.T. PUPPY

Number	Title (A Side/B Side)	Yr	NM
❑ 557	I'll Cry Again/Baby Don't Surprise Me	1970	8.00

DIMENSION

Number	Title (A Side/B Side)	Yr	NM
❑ 1047	I'm Sorry Baby/ Runaround Ronnie	1965	15.00

Albums

B.T. PUPPY

Number	Title (A Side/B Side)	Yr	NM
❑ BTS-1007	Flying High with the Canaries	1970	100.00

CANDLELIGHTERS, THE

45s

DELTA

Number	Title (A Side/B Side)	Yr	NM
❑ 203	Would You Do the Same for Me/ (B-side unknown)	1958	800.00

CANDY AND THE KISSES

45s

CAMEO

Number	Title (A Side/B Side)	Yr	NM
❑ 336	The 81/Two Happy People	1964	20.00
❑ 355	Soldier Boy (Of Mine)/ Shakin' Time	1964	20.00

DECCA

Number	Title (A Side/B Side)	Yr	NM
❑ 32415	Chains of Love/ Someone Out There	1968	6.00

LOST-NITE

Number	Title (A Side/B Side)	Yr	NM
❑ 229	The 81/Two Happy People	196?	5.00

—Reissue

SCEPTER

Number	Title (A Side/B Side)	Yr	NM
❑ 12106	Keep On Searchin'/Together	1965	15.00
❑ 12125	Sweet and Lovely/ Out in the Streets Again	1965	15.00
❑ 12136	Tonight's the Night/The Last Time	1966	12.00

CANDY STORE, THE

Albums

DECCA

Number	Title (A Side/B Side)	Yr	NM
❑ DL 75147	Turned-On Christmas	1969	25.00

CANDYMEN, THE

45s

ABC

Number	Title (A Side/B Side)	Yr	NM
❑ 10995	Georgia Pines/Movies in My Mind	1967	8.00
❑ 11023	Deep in the Night/ Stone Blues Man	1967	8.00
❑ 11048	Sentimental Lady/Ways	1968	8.00
❑ 11077	Candy Man/Crowded Room	1968	8.00
❑ 11141	Go and Tell the People/It's Gonna Get Good in a Minute	1968	8.00
❑ 11175	I'll Never Forget/Lonely Eyes	1969	8.00

LIBERTY

Number	Title (A Side/B Side)	Yr	NM
❑ 56172	Happy Tonight/Papers	1970	8.00

Albums

ABC

Number	Title (A Side/B Side)	Yr	NM
❑ 616 [M]	The Candymen	1967	25.00
❑ S-616 [S]	The Candymen	1967	20.00
❑ S-633	The Candymen Bring You Candypower	1968	20.00

DIPLOMAT

Number	Title (A Side/B Side)	Yr	NM
❑ FM 100	The Twist	196?	20.00

CANNED HEAT

45s

ALA

Number	Title (A Side/B Side)	Yr	NM
❑ 1996	C.C. Shooter/Harley Davidson Blues	1984	5.00

—As "Heat Brothers '84"

ATLANTIC

Number	Title (A Side/B Side)	Yr	NM
❑ 3010	One More River to Cross/ Highway 401	1974	4.00
❑ 3236	The Harder They Come/ Rock 'N' Roll Show	1975	4.00

Except when noted otherwise, VG = 25% of NM, and VG+ = 50% of NM. (Example: VG = $2.00, VG+ = $4.00 and NM = $8.00.)

Canned Heat, *Canned Heat Cook Book (The Best of Canned Heat)*, Liberty LST-11000, 1969, **$20.**

Number	Title (A Side/B Side)	Yr	NM
CAPITOL			
❑ S7-57890	Christmas Blues/Christmas Is the Time to Say "I Love You"	1992	4.00
—B-side by Billy Squier			
LIBERTY			
❑ 55979	Rolin' and Tumblin'/ Bullfrog Blues	1967	8.00
❑ 55979 [PS]	Rolin' and Tumblin'/ Bullfrog Blues	1967	12.00
❑ 56005	Evil Woman/The World Is a Jug	1967	8.00
❑ 56038	On the Road Again/Boogie Music	1968	6.00
❑ 56077	Going Up the Country/ One Kind Favor	1968	6.00
❑ 56077 [PS]	Going Up the Country/ One Kind Favor	1968	15.00
❑ 56079	Christmas Blues/ The Chipmunk Song	1968	25.00
—B-side with the Chipmunks			
❑ 56097	Time Was/Low Down	1969	6.00
❑ 56127	Sic 'Em Pigs/Poor Man	1969	6.00
❑ 56140	Change My Ways/ Get Off My Back	1969	6.00
❑ 56151	Let's Work Together/I'm Her Man	1970	6.00
❑ 56180	Future Blues/Going Up the Country	1970	6.00
❑ 56217	My TIme Ain't Long/Wooly Bully	1970	6.00
UNITED ARTISTS			
❑ 0058	On the Road Again/This Was	1973	4.00
—"Silver Spotlight Series" reissue			
❑ 0059	Going Up the Country/ Let's Work Together	1973	4.00
—"Silver Spotlight Series" reissue			
❑ XW167	Rock and Roll Music/ Lookin' for My Rainbow	1973	5.00
❑ XW243 [DJ]	Harley Davidson Blues (mono/stereo)	1973	6.00
—Stock copy apparently does not exist			
❑ 50831	Long Way from L.A./Hill's Stomp	1971	5.00
❑ 50892	Rockin' with the King/I Don't Care What You Tell Me	1972	5.00
❑ 50927	Sneakin' Around/ Cherokee Dance	1972	5.00

Number	Title (A Side/B Side)	Yr	NM
Albums			
ACCORD			
❑ SN-7144	Captured Live	1981	10.00
ATLANTIC			
❑ SD 7289	One More River to Cross	1973	15.00
DALI			
❑ DCLP-89022	Reheated	1990	15.00
JANUS			
❑ JLS-3009	Vintage — Canned Heat	1969	15.00
LIBERTY			
❑ LRP-3526 [M]	Canned Heat	1967	25.00
❑ LRP-3541 [M]	Boogie with Canned Heat	1968	40.00
—Stock copy in stereo cover with "Audition Mono LP Not for Sale" sticker			
❑ LST-7526 [S]	Canned Heat	1967	20.00
❑ LST-7541 [S]	Boogie with Canned Heat	1968	20.00
❑ LST-7618	Hallelujah	1969	20.00
❑ LN-10105	Boogie with Canned Heat	1981	8.00
—Budget-line reissue			
❑ LN-10106	Canned Heat Cook Book (The Best of Canned Heat)	1981	8.00
—Budget-line reissue			
❑ LST-11000	Canned Heat Cook Book (The Best of Canned Heat)	1969	20.00
❑ LST-11002	Future Blues	1970	15.00
❑ LST-27200 [(2)]	Living the Blues	1968	25.00
PICKWICK			
❑ SPC-3364	Live at Topanga Canyon	197?	10.00
❑ SPC-3614	Boogie	1978	10.00
SCEPTER CITATION			
❑ CTN-18017	The Best of Canned Heat	1972	10.00
SUNSET			
❑ SUS-5298	Collage	1971	10.00
TAKOMA			
❑ 7066	The Human Condition	1980	12.00
UNITED ARTISTS			
❑ UA-LA049-F	The New Age	1973	15.00
❑ LM-1015	Boogie with Canned Heat	1980	12.00
—Reissue of Liberty 7541			

Number	Title (A Side/B Side)	Yr	NM
❑ UAS-5509	Canned Heat Concert (Recorded Live in Europe)	1971	15.00
❑ UAS-5557	Historical Figures and Ancient Heads	1972	15.00
❑ UAS-9955 [(2)]	Living the Blues	1971	20.00
—Reissue of Liberty 27200			
WAND			
❑ WDS-693	Live at Topanga Canyon	1970	25.00

CANNED HEAT AND JOHN LEE HOOKER See JOHN LEE HOOKER AND CANNED HEAT

CANNIBAL AND THE HEADHUNTERS

Number	Title (A Side/B Side)	Yr	NM
45s			
AIRES			
❑ 1001	Mean So Much/ Dance By the Light	1968	15.00
CAPITOL			
❑ 2393	Get It On Up (Get Up the Courage)/Mean So Much	1969	15.00
DATE			
❑ 1516	La Bamba/Zulu King	1966	15.00
❑ 1525	Land of 1,000 Dances/ Love Bird	1966	15.00
ERA BACK TO BACK HITS			
❑ 023	Land of 1,000 Dances/ Dance with Me	197?	5.00
—B-side by the Blendells			
RAMPART			
❑ 642	Land of 1,000 Dances/I'll Show You How to Love Me	1964	20.00
❑ 644	Here Comes Love/ Nau Ninny Nau	1965	15.00
❑ 646	I Need Your Loving/ Follow the Music	1965	15.00
❑ 654	Out of Sight/Please Baby Please	1965	15.00
Albums			
DATE			
❑ TEM 3001 [M]	Land of 1000 Dances	1966	30.00
❑ TES 4001 [S]	Land of 1000 Dances	1966	40.00
RAMPART			
❑ RM-3302 [M]	Land of 1000 Dances	1965	50.00
❑ RS-3302 [S]	Land of 1000 Dances	1965	70.00

CANNON, FREDDY

Number	Title (A Side/B Side)	Yr	NM
45s			
AMHERST			
❑ 201	Dance to the Bop/(She's a) Mean Rebel Rouser	1983	4.00
❑ 327	Rockin' in My Socks/ Rockin' in My Socks	1988	6.00
BUDDAH			
❑ 242	Rockin' Robin/Red Valley	1971	10.00
CLARIDGE			
❑ 401	Palisades Park/Way Down Yonder in New Orleans	1975	6.00
❑ 416	Sugar/Sugar (Part 2)	1976	6.00
HQ			
❑ (no #) [DJ]	Kennywood Park/ With a Little Love	1987	6.00
❑ (no #) [PS]	Kennywood Park/ With a Little Love	1987	8.00
—Promotional item for KDKA Radio, Pittsburgh, Pa.			
MCA			
❑ 40269	Rock and Roll ABC's/Superman	1974	15.00
METROMEDIA			
❑ 262	If You've Got the Time/ Take Me Back	1972	10.00
MIASOUND			
❑ 1002	Let's Put the Fun Back in Rock and Roll/Your Mama Ain't Always Right	1981	5.00
—With the Belmonts			
RADIO ACTIVE GOLD			
❑ 64	Rockin' Robin/Red Valley	197?	5.00
ROYAL AMERICAN			
❑ 2	Charged-Up, Turned-On Rock-N-Roll Singer/I Ain't Much, But I'm Yours	1970	10.00
❑ 11	Nite Time Lady/I Ain't Much, But I'm Yours	1970	10.00
❑ 288	Strawberry Wine/Blossom Dear	1969	10.00
SIRE			
❑ 4103	Beautiful Downtown Burbank/ If You Give Me a Title	1969	10.00
SWAN			
❑ 4031	Tallahassee Lassie/You Know	1959	20.00
❑ 4038	Okefenokee/Kookie Hat	1959	20.00
❑ 4043	Way Down Yonder in New Orleans/Fractured	1959	20.00

Except when noted otherwise, VG = 25% of NM, and VG+ = 50% of NM. (Example: VG = $2.00, VG+ = $4.00 and NM = $8.00.)

Number	Title (A Side/B Side)	Yr	NM
❑ 4043 [PS]	Way Down Yonder in New Orleans/Fractured	1959	30.00
❑ 4050	Chattanooga Shoe Shine Boy/Boston "My Home Town"	1960	15.00
❑ 4050 [PS]	Chattanooga Shoe Shine Boy/Boston "My Home Town"	1960	30.00
❑ 4053	Jump Over/The Urge	1960	15.00
❑ 4053 [PS]	Jump Over/The Urge	1960	30.00
❑ 4057	Happy Shades of Blue /(Kwa-Na-Va-Ka) Cuernavaca Choo Choo	1960	15.00
❑ 4057 [PS]	Happy Shades of Blue/(Kwa-Na-Va-Ka) Cuernavaca Choo Choo	1960	30.00
❑ 4061	Humdinger/My Blue Heaven	1960	15.00
❑ 4061 [PS]	Humdinger/My Blue Heaven	1960	30.00
❑ 4066	Muskrat Ramble/Two Thousand-88	1961	15.00
❑ 4066 [PS]	Muskrat Ramble/Two Thousand-88	1961	30.00
❑ 4071	Buzz Buzz A-Diddle It/Opportunity	1961	15.00
❑ 4078	Transistor Sister/Walk to the Moon	1961	15.00
❑ 4078 [PS]	Transistor Sister/Walk to the Moon	1961	30.00
❑ 4083	For Me and My Gal/Blue Plate Special	1961	15.00
❑ 4096	Teen Queen of the Week/Wild Guy	1962	15.00
❑ 4106	Palisades Park/June, July and August	1962	16.00
❑ 4117	What's Gonna Happen When Summer's Done/Broadway	1962	15.00
❑ 4122	If You Were a Rock and Roll Record/The Truth, Ruth	1962	15.00
❑ 4132	Come On and Love Me/Four Letter Man	1963	12.00
❑ 4139	Patty Baby/Betty Jean	1963	12.00
❑ 4149	Everybody Monkey/Oh Gloria	1963	25.00
❑ 4155	Do What the Hippies Do/That's the Way Girls Are	1963	12.00
❑ 4168	What a Party/Sweet Georgia Brown	1964	12.00
❑ 4178	The Ups and Downs of Love/It's Been Nice	1964	25.00
WARNER BROS.			
❑ 5409	Abigail Beecher/All American Girl	1964	12.00
❑ 5434	OK Wheeler, The Used Car Dealer/Odie Cologne	1964	12.00
❑ 5448	Summertime U.S.A./Gotta Good Thing Goin'	1964	12.00
❑ 5487	Little Autograph Seeker/Too Much Monkey Business	1964	12.00
❑ 5615	Little Miss A-Go-Go/In the Night	1965	12.00
❑ 5615 [PS]	Little Miss A-Go-Go/In the Night	1965	25.00
❑ 5645	Action/Beachwood City	1965	15.00
❑ 5666	Let Me Show You Where It's At/The Old Rag Man	1965	12.00
❑ 5673	She's Something Else/Little Bitty Corrine	1965	12.00
❑ 5693	The Dedication Song/Come On, Come On	1966	12.00
❑ 5810	The Greatest Show on Earth/Hokie Pokie Girl	1966	12.00
❑ 5832	The Laughing Song/Natalie	1966	12.00
❑ 5859	Run for the Sun/Use Your Imagination	1966	12.00
❑ 5876	A Happy Clown/In My Wildest Dreams	1966	25.00
❑ 7019	Maverick's Flat/Run to the Poet Man	1967	25.00
❑ 7075	20th Century Fox/Cincinnati Woman	1967	25.00
WE MAKE ROCK & ROLL			
❑ 1601	Rock Around the Clock/Sock It to the Judge	1968	6.00
❑ 1604	Sea Cruise/She's a Friday Night Fox	1968	6.00
Albums			
RHINO			
❑ RNLP-210	14 Booming Hits	1982	10.00
SWAN			
❑ LP-502 [M]	The Explosive! Freddy Cannon	1960	120.00
❑ LPS-502 [S]	The Explosive! Freddy Cannon	1960	300.00
❑ LP-504 [M]	Happy Shades of Blue	1960	150.00
❑ LP-505 [M]	Solid Gold Hits	1961	150.00
❑ LP-507 [M]	Freddy Cannon at Palisades Park	1962	150.00
❑ LP-511 [M]	Freddy Cannon Steps Out	1963	150.00
WARNER BROS.			
❑ W 1544 [M]	Freddie Cannon	1964	30.00
❑ WS 1544 [S]	Freddie Cannon	1964	40.00
❑ W 1612 [M]	Action!	1965	30.00
❑ WS 1612 [S]	Action!	1965	40.00
❑ W 1628 [M]	Freddy Cannon's Greatest Hits	1966	30.00
❑ WS 1628 [S]	Freddy Cannon's Greatest Hits	1966	40.00

CANNON, GUS

Number	Title (A Side/B Side)	Yr	NM
Albums			
STAX			
❑ ST-702 [M]	Walk Right In	1962	600.00

CANNON, JACKIE

Number	Title (A Side/B Side)	Yr	NM
45s			
CHAN			
❑ 103	Proof of Your Love/Chill Bumps	1961	40.00
CHESS			
❑ 1807	Proof of Your Love/Chill Bumps	1961	15.00

CANNON, JOHNNY See ACE CANNON.

CANO, EDDIE

Number	Title (A Side/B Side)	Yr	NM
45s			
DUNHILL			
❑ 4072	Monday, Monday/Slip Slip	1967	6.00
❑ 4075	Amy's Theme/La Bamba	1967	6.00
GNP CRESCENDO			
❑ 172	La Casita/Hava Nagilah	1962	8.00
❑ 187	Line for Lyons/Tin Tin Deo	1962	8.00
REPRISE			
❑ PRO 173 [DJ]	Ribbons Down My Back/Theme from The Golden Boy (Night Song)	196?	10.00
❑ 0237	Danke Schoen/Our Day Will Come	1963	8.00
❑ 0254	What Now My Love/Theme from Snow Angel	1963	8.00
❑ 0382	Tortilla Flats (Part 1)/Tortilla Flats (Part 2)	1965	8.00
❑ 20075	A Taste of Honey/Panchita	1962	8.00
❑ 20113	Barsonova Brown/Greenfields	1962	8.00
❑ 20147	Days of Wine and Roses/Our Day Will Come	1963	8.00
Albums			
ATCO			
❑ 33-184 [M]	On Broadway	1966	10.00
❑ SD 33-184 [S]	On Broadway	1966	12.00
DUNHILL			
❑ D-50018 [M]	Brought Back Live from P.J.'s	1967	12.00
❑ DS-50018 [S]	Brought Back Live from P.J.'s	1967	10.00
GNP CRESCENDO			
❑ GNP-77 [M]	A Taste of Cano	1963	12.00
❑ GNPS-77 [S]	A Taste of Cano	1963	15.00
PICKWICK			
❑ SPC-3017	25 Latin Dance Favorites	196?	10.00
RCA VICTOR			
❑ LPM-1672 [M]	Time for Cha Cha Cha	1958	15.00
REPRISE			
❑ R-6030 [M]	Eddie Cano at P.J.'s	1962	12.00
❑ R9-6030 [S]	Eddie Cano at P.J.'s	1962	15.00
❑ R-6055 [M]	Here Is the Fabulous Eddie Cano	1963	12.00
❑ R9-6055 [S]	Here Is the Fabulous Eddie Cano	1963	15.00
❑ R-6068 [M]	Cano Plays Mancini	1963	12.00
❑ R9-6068 [S]	Cano Plays Mancini	1963	15.00
❑ R-6105 [M]	Danke Schoen	1963	12.00
❑ R9-6105 [S]	Danke Schoen	1963	15.00
❑ R-6124 [M]	Broadway — Right Now!	1964	12.00
❑ R9-6124 [S]	Broadway — Right Now!	1964	15.00
❑ R-6145 [M]	The Sound of Music	1965	12.00
❑ RS-6145 [S]	The Sound of Music	1965	15.00

CANTRELL, LANA

Number	Title (A Side/B Side)	Yr	NM
45s			
POLYDOR			
❑ 14261	Like a Sunday Morning/Good Times	1974	4.00
RCA VICTOR			
❑ 47-8978	Breakfast at Tiffany's/Since I Fell for You	1966	6.00
❑ 47-9089	Confession/Theme from The Sand Pebbles	1967	6.00
❑ 47-9205	Sunshine/How Can I Hurt You	1967	6.00
❑ 47-9391	On the Good Ship Lollipop/When You Wish Upon a Star	1967	6.00
❑ 47-9526	The Music Played/Just a Little Lovin'	1968	6.00
❑ 47-9619	The Good Times We Had/Catch the Wind	1968	6.00
❑ 74-0103	Your Mother Should Know/Mr. Bojangles	1969	6.00
❑ 74-0173	All the Things You Are/If I Say No	1969	6.00
❑ 74-0268	I Let the Moment Slip By/Tomorrow Is the First Day of the Rest of My Life	1969	6.00
Albums			
RCA VICTOR			
❑ LPM-3755 [M]	And Then There Was Lana	1967	15.00
❑ LSP-3755 [S]	And Then There Was Lana	1967	12.00
❑ LPM-3862 [M]	Another Shade of Lana	1967	15.00
❑ LSP-3862 [S]	Another Shade of Lana	1967	12.00
❑ LPM-3947 [M]	Act III	1968	15.00
❑ LSP-3947 [S]	Act III	1968	12.00
❑ LSP-4026	Lana!	1968	12.00
❑ LSP-4121	Now or Then	1969	12.00
❑ LSP-4263	The 6th Lana	1970	12.00

CAP-TANS, THE

Number	Title (A Side/B Side)	Yr	NM
45s			
ANNA			
❑ 1122	I'm Afraid/Tight Skirts and Crazy Sweaters	1960	30.00
CORAL			
❑ 65071	Asking/Who Can I Turn To	1951	300.00
DOT			
❑ 15114	I'm So Crazy for Love/With All My Love	1953	100.00
GOTHAM			
❑ 233	My, My, My, Ain't She Pretty/Never Be Lonely	1950	400.00
❑ 268	I Thought I Could Forget You/Waiting at the Station	1951	300.00

CAPALDI, JIM Also see TRAFFIC.

Number	Title (A Side/B Side)	Yr	NM
12-Inch Singles			
ATLANTIC			
❑ PR 545 [DJ]	Tonight You're Mine (same on both sides)	1983	10.00
❑ DMD 786 [DJ]	I'll Keep Holding On/(Instrumental)	1984	8.00
ISLAND			
❑ PR 2491 [DJ]	Something So Strong (same on both sides)	1988	8.00
RSO			
❑ RPO 1014 [DJ]	Shoe Shine (7:39) (same on both sides)	1979	12.00
45s			
ATLANTIC			
❑ 89625	I'll Keep Holding On/Tales of Power	1984	4.00
❑ 89783 [DJ]	Tonight You're Mine (same on both sides)	1983	4.00
—May be promo only			
❑ 89799	Living on the Edge/Gifts of Unknown Things	1983	3.00
❑ 89849	That's Love/Runaway	1983	3.00
❑ 89849 [PS]	That's Love/Runaway	1983	4.00
ISLAND			
❑ 003	It's All Right/Whale Meat Again	1974	5.00
❑ 025	It's All Up to You/I've Got So Much Lovin'	1975	5.00
❑ 045	Love Hurts/Sugar Honey	1976	4.00
❑ 055	Goodbye Love/(B-side unknown)	1976	4.00
❑ 067	Goodnight and Good Morning/Short Cut Draw Blood	1976	4.00
❑ 1204	Eve/Going Down Slow All the Way	1972	6.00
❑ 1205	Oh How We Danced/Open Your Heart	1972	6.00
❑ 1216	Tricky Dicky Rides Again/Love Is All You Can Try	1973	5.00
❑ 99220	Some Came Running/Favela Music	1989	3.00
❑ 99220 [PS]	Some Came Running/Favela Music	1989	3.00
❑ 99266	Something So Strong/Child in the Storm	1988	3.00
❑ 99266 [PS]	Something So Strong/Child in the Storm	1988	3.00
RSO			
❑ 912	Daughter of the Night/I'm Gonna Do It	1978	4.00
Albums			
ANTILLIES			
❑ 7050	Short Cut Draw Blood	198?	8.00
—Reissue of Island 9336			
ATLANTIC			
❑ 80059	Fierce Heart	1983	10.00
❑ 80182	One Man Mission	1984	10.00
ISLAND			
❑ ILPS 9254	Whale Meat Again	1974	10.00
❑ SW-9314	Oh How We Danced	1972	12.00
❑ ILPS 9336	Short Cut Draw Blood	1976	10.00
❑ 91024	Some Came Running	1988	10.00
RSO			
❑ RS-1-3037	Daughter of the Night	1978	10.00
❑ RS-1-3050	Electric Nights	1979	10.00

Number	Title (A Side/B Side)	Yr	NM
CAPEHART, JERRY			
45s			
CASH			
❑ 1021	Walkin' Stick Boogie/Rollin'	1956	200.00
—With Eddie and Hank Cochran			
CREST			
❑ 1101	Song of New Orleans/The Young and Blue (Theme)	1962	50.00
CAPERS, THE			
45s			
DORE			
❑ 587	Rockin' Round the Mountain/What Is This Thing Called Love	1961	12.00
VEE JAY			
❑ 297	Miss You My Dear/Early One Morning	1958	25.00
❑ 315	Candy Store Blues/High School Diploma	1959	25.00
CAPERS & CARSON See HEDGE & DONNA.			
CAPITAL CITY ROCKETS Featuring Eric Moore of THE GODZ.			
45s			
ELEKTRA			
❑ 45855	Breakfast in Bed/Grab Your Honey	1973	10.00
❑ 45872	Little Bit O' Fun/Ten Hole Dollars	1973	10.00
Albums			
ELEKTRA			
❑ EKS-75079	Capital City Rockets	1973	20.00
CAPITOLS, THE (1) Detroit-based R&B vocal group. Records on the Carlton, Cindy, Gateway, Pet and Triumph labels appear to be by different groups with the same name; these are outside the scope of this book.			
45s			
KAREN			
❑ 1524	Cool Jerk/Hello Stranger	1966	15.00
❑ 1525	I Got to Handle It/Zig Zagging	1966	10.00
❑ 1526	We Got a Thing That's In the Groove/Tired Running from You	1966	10.00
❑ 1534	Patty Cake/Take a Chance on Me Baby	1967	10.00
❑ 1536	Cool Pearl/Don't Say Ma ybe Baby	1967	10.00
❑ 1537	Cool Jerk '68/Afro Twist	1968	10.00
❑ 1543	Soul Brother, Soul Sister/Ain't That Terrible	1968	10.00
❑ 1546	Soul Soul/When You're in Trouble	1969	10.00
❑ 1549	I Thought She Loved Me/When You're in Trouble	1969	10.00
Albums			
ATCO			
❑ 33-190 [M]	Dance the Cool Jerk	1966	40.00
❑ SD 33-190 [S]	Dance the Cool Jerk	1966	50.00
❑ 33-201 [M]	We Got a Thing That's In the Groove	1966	40.00
❑ SD 33-201 [S]	We Got a Thing That's In the Groove	1966	50.00
COLLECTABLES			
❑ COL-5105	Golden Classics	1988	10.00
SOLID SMOKE			
❑ 8019	The Capitols: Their Greatest Hits	1983	12.00
CAPITOLS, THE (2) Not group (1).			
45s			
CARLTON			
❑ 461	I Let Her Go/I've Got a Girl	1958	600.00
CAPITOLS, THE (U) None of these is by group (1), though it's possible that one or more is by group (2).			
45s			
CINDY			
❑ 3002	Rosemary/Millie	1957	200.00
GATEWAY			
❑ 721	Day By Day/Little Things	1964	300.00
PET			
❑ 807	Angel of Love/'Cause I Love You	1958	200.00
TRIUMPH			
❑ 601	Three O'Clock Rock/Write Me a Love Letter	1959	30.00

Number	Title (A Side/B Side)	Yr	NM
CAPONE, SUSAN			
45s			
PILGRIM			
❑ 704	I'll Be Dancing/Four or Five Hundred Kisses	1956	25.00
❑ 718	Click-I-Dee, Click-I-Dee/Maybe Someday	1956	25.00
CAPRIS, THE (1) Italian male vocal group from New York.			
45s			
AMBIENT SOUND			
❑ ZS5-02697	There's a Moon Out Again/Morse Code of Love	1982	6.00
CANDLELITE			
❑ 422	Oh, My Darling/Rock Pretty Baby	196?	12.00
LIFETIME			
❑ 1001/2	Oh My Darling/Rock Pretty Baby	1961	100.00
LOST-NITE			
❑ 101	There's a Moon Out Tonight/Indian Girl	196?	8.00
—Yellow label reissue			
❑ 101	There's a Moon Out Tonight/Indian Girl	1961	70.00
—Pink label original; black vinyl			
❑ 101	There's a Moon Out Tonight/Indian Girl	1961	150.00
—Pink label original; red vinyl			
❑ 148	Little Girl/When	196?	8.00
MR. PEEKE			
❑ 118	Limbo/From the Vine Came the Grape	1963	20.00
OLD TOWN			
❑ 1094	There's a Moon Out Tonight/Indian Girl	1961	30.00
—Light blue label			
❑ 1094	There's a Moon Out Tonight/Indian Girl	1962	20.00
—Mostly black label			
❑ 1099	Where I Fell in Love/Some People Think	1961	30.00
❑ 1103	Tears in My Eyes/Why Do I Cry	1961	30.00
❑ 1107	Girl in My Dreams/My Island in the Sun	1961	30.00
PLANET			
❑ 1010	There's a Moon Out Tonight/Indian Girl	1958	1200.
SABRE			
❑ 201/2	My Promise to You/Bop! Bop! Bop!	1959	150.00
TROMMERS			
❑ 101	There's a Moon Out Tonight/Indian Girl	1961	25.00
—Red label			
❑ 101	There's a Moon Out Tonight/Indian Girl	1961	25.00
—White label (not a promo)			
Albums			
AMBIENT SOUND			
❑ FW 37714	There's a Moon Out Again	1982	15.00
COLLECTABLES			
❑ COL-5016	There's a Moon Out Tonight	198?	12.00
CAPRIS, THE (2) Different male vocal group than (1).			
45s			
GOTHAM			
❑ 304	God Only Knows/That's What You're Doing to Me	1954	120.00
—Red label			
❑ 304	God Only Knows/That's What You're Doing to Me	1954	600.00
—Blue label			
❑ 304	God Only Knows/That's What You're Doing to Me	1956	80.00
—Yellow label			
❑ 306	It Was Moonglow/Too Poor to Love	1955	200.00
❑ 308	It's a Miracle/Let's Linger Awhile	1956	120.00
LOST-NITE			
❑ 112	God Only Knows/That's What You're Doing to Me	196?	8.00
20TH CENTURY			
❑ 1201	My Weakness/Yes, My Baby, Please!	1957	60.00
❑ G-7304	God Only Knows/That's What You're Doing to Me	195?	50.00
—White and red label			
Albums			
COLLECTABLES			
❑ COL-5000	Gotham Recording Stars	198?	12.00

Number	Title (A Side/B Side)	Yr	NM
CAPTAIN AND TENNILLE			
45s			
A&M			
❑ 1624	The Way I Want to Touch You/Disney Girls	1974	6.00
❑ 1672	Love Will Keep Us Together/Gentle Stranger	1975	4.00
❑ 1672 [PS]	Love Will Keep Us Together/Gentle Stranger	1975	6.00
❑ 1715	Por Amor Vivremos (Love Will Keep Us Together)/Broddy Bounce	1975	5.00
❑ 1725	The Way I Want to Touch You/Broddy Bounce	1975	4.00
❑ 1725 [PS]	The Way I Want to Touch You/Broddy Bounce	1975	6.00
❑ 1774	Como Yo Quiero Sentorte (The Way I Want to Touch You)/El Rebote de Broddy	1975	8.00
❑ 1782	Lonely Night (Angel Face)/Smile for Me One More Time	1976	4.00
❑ 1782 [PS]	Lonely Night (Angel Face)/Smile for Me One More Time	1976	6.00
❑ 1817	Shop Around/Butterscotch Castle	1976	4.00
❑ 1817 [PS]	Shop Around/Butterscotch Castle	1976	6.00
❑ 1870	Muskrat Love/Honey Come Love Me	1976	4.00
❑ 1870 [PS]	Muskrat Love/Honey Come Love Me	1976	6.00
❑ 1894	Song of Joy/Wedding Song (There Is Love)	1976	—
—Canceled; issued on 8601			
❑ 1912	Can't Stop Dancin'/Mis Canciones (The Good Songs)	1977	4.00
❑ 1912 [PS]	Can't Stop Dancin'/Mis Canciones (The Good Songs)	1977	6.00
❑ 1944	Come In from the Rain/We Never Really Said Goodbye	1977	4.00
❑ 1944 [PS]	Come In from the Rain/We Never Really Said Goodbye	1977	6.00
❑ 1970	Circles/1954 Boogie Blues	1977	4.00
❑ 2027	I'm On My Way/We Never Really Said Goodbye	1978	4.00
❑ 2027 [PS]	I'm On My Way/We Never Really Said Goodbye	1978	6.00
❑ 2063	You Never Done It Like That/"D" Keyboard Blues	1978	4.00
❑ 2063 [PS]	You Never Done It Like That/"D" Keyboard Blues	1978	6.00
❑ 2106	You Need a Woman Tonight/Love Me Like a Baby	1978	4.00
❑ 2106 [PS]	You Need a Woman Tonight/Love Me Like a Baby	1978	6.00
❑ 8600	Lonely Night (Angel Face)/Shop Around	1977	4.00
—"A&M Forget Me Nots" series; green and yellow labels			
❑ 8600	Lonely Night (Angel Face)/Shop Around	198?	3.00
—"A&M Memories" series; white label, pink and black print			
❑ 8600 [PS]	Lonely Night (Angel Face)/Shop Around	1977	6.00
❑ 8601	Song of Joy/Wedding Song (There Is Love)	1977	4.00
—"A&M Forget Me Nots" series; green and yellow labels			
❑ 8601	Song of Joy/Wedding Song (There Is Love)	198?	3.00
—"A&M Memories" series; white label, pink and black print			
❑ 8601 [PS]	Song of Joy/Wedding Song (There Is Love)	1977	6.00
BUTTERSCOTCH CASTLE			
❑ 001	The Way I Want to Touch You/Disney Girls	1974	80.00
CASABLANCA			
❑ 2215	Do That To Me One More Time/Deep in the Dark	1979	4.00
❑ 2243	Love on a Shoestring/How Can You Be So Cold	1980	4.00
❑ 2247	Amame Una Vez Mas (Do That To Me One More Time)/Deep in the Dark	1980	8.00
❑ 2264	Happy Together (A Fantasy)/Baby You Still Got It	1980	4.00
❑ 2320	This Is Not the First Time/Gentle Stranger	1980	4.00
❑ 2328	Don't Forget Me/Keep Our Love Warm	1981	4.00
JOYCE			
❑ 101	The Way I Want to Tocuh You/Disney Girls	1974	40.00
PUREBRED			
❑ 0001	Tahoe Snow/Here Comes Santa Claus	198?	5.00
❑ 0001 [PS]	Tahoe Snow/Here Comes Santa Claus	198?	5.00

Except when noted otherwise, VG = 25% of NM, and VG+ = 50% of NM. (Example: VG = $2.00, VG+ = $4.00 and NM = $8.00.)

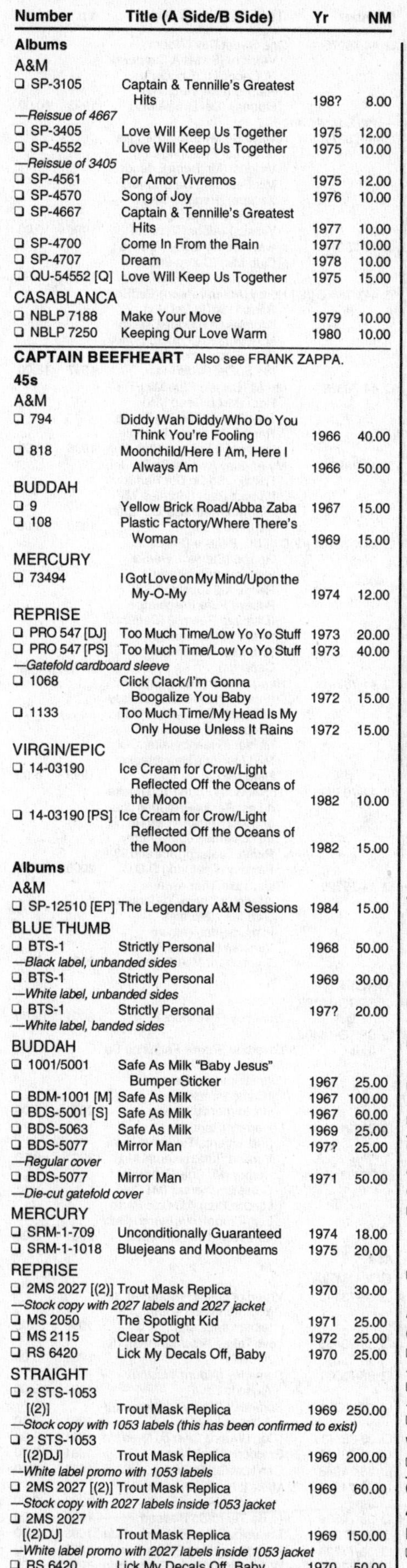

Number	Title (A Side/B Side)	Yr	NM
Albums			
A&M			
❑ SP-3105	Captain & Tennille's Greatest Hits	198?	8.00
—Reissue of 4667			
❑ SP-3405	Love Will Keep Us Together	1975	12.00
❑ SP-4552	Love Will Keep Us Together	1975	10.00
—Reissue of 3405			
❑ SP-4561	Por Amor Vivremos	1975	12.00
❑ SP-4570	Song of Joy	1976	10.00
❑ SP-4667	Captain & Tennille's Greatest Hits	1977	10.00
❑ SP-4700	Come In From the Rain	1977	10.00
❑ SP-4707	Dream	1978	10.00
❑ QU-54552 [Q]	Love Will Keep Us Together	1975	15.00
CASABLANCA			
❑ NBLP 7188	Make Your Move	1979	10.00
❑ NBLP 7250	Keeping Our Love Warm	1980	10.00

CAPTAIN BEEFHEART Also see FRANK ZAPPA.

Number	Title (A Side/B Side)	Yr	NM
45s			
A&M			
❑ 794	Diddy Wah Diddy/Who Do You Think You're Fooling	1966	40.00
❑ 818	Moonchild/Here I Am, Here I Always Am	1966	50.00
BUDDAH			
❑ 9	Yellow Brick Road/Abba Zaba	1967	15.00
❑ 108	Plastic Factory/Where There's Woman	1969	15.00
MERCURY			
❑ 73494	I Got Love on My Mind/Upon the My-O-My	1974	12.00
REPRISE			
❑ PRO 547 [DJ]	Too Much Time/Low Yo Yo Stuff	1973	20.00
❑ PRO 547 [PS]	Too Much Time/Low Yo Yo Stuff	1973	40.00
—Gatefold cardboard sleeve			
❑ 1068	Click Clack/I'm Gonna Boogalize You Baby	1972	15.00
❑ 1133	Too Much Time/My Head Is My Only House Unless It Rains	1972	15.00
VIRGIN/EPIC			
❑ 14-03190	Ice Cream for Crow/Light Reflected Off the Oceans of the Moon	1982	10.00
❑ 14-03190 [PS]	Ice Cream for Crow/Light Reflected Off the Oceans of the Moon	1982	15.00
Albums			
A&M			
❑ SP-12510 [EP]	The Legendary A&M Sessions	1984	15.00
BLUE THUMB			
❑ BTS-1	Strictly Personal	1968	50.00
—Black label, unbanded sides			
❑ BTS-1	Strictly Personal	1969	30.00
—White label, unbanded sides			
❑ BTS-1	Strictly Personal	197?	20.00
—White label, banded sides			
BUDDAH			
❑ 1001/5001	Safe As Milk "Baby Jesus" Bumper Sticker	1967	25.00
❑ BDM-1001 [M]	Safe As Milk	1967	100.00
❑ BDS-5001 [S]	Safe As Milk	1967	60.00
❑ BDS-5063	Safe As Milk	1969	25.00
❑ BDS-5077	Mirror Man	197?	25.00
—Regular cover			
❑ BDS-5077	Mirror Man	1971	50.00
—Die-cut gatefold cover			
MERCURY			
❑ SRM-1-709	Unconditionally Guaranteed	1974	18.00
❑ SRM-1-1018	Bluejeans and Moonbeams	1975	20.00
REPRISE			
❑ 2MS 2027 [(2)]	Trout Mask Replica	1970	30.00
—Stock copy with 2027 labels and 2027 jacket			
❑ MS 2050	The Spotlight Kid	1971	25.00
❑ MS 2115	Clear Spot	1972	25.00
❑ RS 6420	Lick My Decals Off, Baby	1970	25.00
STRAIGHT			
❑ 2 STS-1053 [(2)]	Trout Mask Replica	1969	250.00
—Stock copy with 1053 labels (this has been confirmed to exist)			
❑ 2 STS-1053 [(2)DJ]	Trout Mask Replica	1969	200.00
—White label promo with 1053 labels			
❑ 2MS 2027 [(2)]	Trout Mask Replica	1969	60.00
—Stock copy with 2027 labels inside 1053 jacket			
❑ 2MS 2027 [(2)DJ]	Trout Mask Replica	1969	150.00
—White label promo with 2027 labels inside 1053 jacket			
❑ RS 6420	Lick My Decals Off, Baby	1970	50.00

Caravan, *For Girls Who Go Plump in the Night*, London XPS 637, 1973, **$15.**

Number	Title (A Side/B Side)	Yr	NM
VERVE FORECAST			
❑ FTS-3054	Captain Beefheart and the Magic Band	1968	—
—Canceled			
VIRGIN			
❑ VA 13148	Doc at the Radar Station	1980	12.00
VIRGIN/EPIC			
❑ ARE 38274	Ice Cream for Crow	1982	12.00
WARNER BROS.			
❑ (no #)	Bat Chain Puller	1978	400.00
—Test pressing with different selections than stock version			
❑ BSK 3256	Shiny Beast (Bat Chain Puller)	1978	15.00

CAPTAIN BEYOND

Number	Title (A Side/B Side)	Yr	NM
45s			
CAPRICORN			
❑ 0013	As the Moon Speaks (Return)/A Thousand Days of Yesterdays (Time Since Come & Gone)	1972	6.00
❑ 0029	Drifting in Space/Sufficiently Breathless	1973	6.00
Albums			
CAPRICORN			
❑ CP 0105	Captain Beyond	1972	15.00
—Later covers are normal			
❑ CP 0105	Captain Beyond	1972	30.00
—Original covers are 3-D			
❑ CP 0115	Sufficiently Breathless	1973	15.00
WARNER BROS.			
❑ BS 3047	Dawn Explosion	1977	12.00

CAPTAIN ZAP AND THE MOTORTOWN CUT-UPS

Number	Title (A Side/B Side)	Yr	NM
45s			
MOTOWN			
❑ 1151	The Luney Landing/The Luney Take-Off	1969	20.00

CAPTIVATIONS, THE

Number	Title (A Side/B Side)	Yr	NM
45s			
GARPAX			
❑ 44179	Red Hot Scrambler-Go/Speed Shift	1964	30.00
PENTACLE			
❑ 1635	Red Hot Scramblers-Go/Speed Shift	1964	60.00

CARAVAN

Number	Title (A Side/B Side)	Yr	NM
45s			
LONDON			
❑ 20065	Love to Love You/Golf Girl	1971	6.00
❑ 20080	Headloss/(B-side unknown)	1973	6.00
VERVE FORECAST			
❑ 5102	A Place of My Own/Ride	1969	10.00
Albums			
ARISTA			
❑ AL 4088	Blind Dog at St. Dunstans	1976	10.00
BTM			
❑ 5000	Cunning Stunts	1975	10.00
LONDON			
❑ PS 582	If I Could Do It All Over Again...	1971	15.00
❑ PS 593	In the Land of the Grey & Pink	1971	15.00
❑ XPS 615	Waterloo Lily	1972	15.00
❑ XPS 637	For Girls Who Grow Plump in the Night	1973	15.00
❑ XPS 650	Caravan and the New Symphonia	1974	15.00
❑ LC 50011	The Best of Caravan	1978	10.00
VERVE FORECAST			
❑ FTS-3066	Caravan	1969	40.00

CARAVAN, JIMMY

Number	Title (A Side/B Side)	Yr	NM
Albums			
TOWER			
❑ ST 5103 [S]	Look Into the Flower	1968	20.00
❑ T 5103 [M]	Look Into the Flower	1968	50.00

VAULT

Number	Title (A Side/B Side)	Yr	NM
9007	Hey Jude	1969	20.00

CARAVELLES, THE (1)
British female vocal group.

45s
SMASH

Number	Title (A Side/B Side)	Yr	NM
1852	You Don't Have to Be a Baby to Cry/The Last One to Know	1963	15.00
1869	Have You Ever Been Lonely/Don't Blow Your Cool	1964	12.00
1901	You Are Here/How Can I Be Sure	1964	12.00
1958	I Don't Care If the Sun Don't Shine/I Like a Man	1964	12.00

Albums
SMASH

Number	Title (A Side/B Side)	Yr	NM
MGS-27044 [M]	You Don't Have to Be a Baby to Cry	1963	60.00
SRS-67044 [R]	You Don't Have to Be a Baby to Cry	1963	60.00

CARAVELLES, THE (U)
These may or may not be the same group, but they are definitely not group (1).

45s
JOEY

Number	Title (A Side/B Side)	Yr	NM
301	Falling for You/Shake Baby	1963	150.00
6208	One Little Kiss/Twistin' Marie	1962	100.00

STARMAKER

Number	Title (A Side/B Side)	Yr	NM
1925	Pink Lips/Angry Angel	1961	25.00

CARBO, CHIC

45s
REVUE

Number	Title (A Side/B Side)	Yr	NM
11019	Touch Me/Biggest Fool in Town	1968	20.00

CARBO, CHUCK
Also see THE SPIDERS (1).

45s
ACE

Number	Title (A Side/B Side)	Yr	NM
631	Tears, Tears and More Tears/I Shouldn't, But I Do	1961	12.00
666	Out on a Limb/Getting Out	1962	12.00

IMPERIAL

Number	Title (A Side/B Side)	Yr	NM
5405	That's the Way to Win My Heart/Goodbye	1956	25.00
5423	Honey Bee/That's My Desire	1957	30.00
5452	The Bells Are Ringing/Poor Boy	1957	20.00
5479	I Miss You/The Times	1957	20.00

INSTANT

Number	Title (A Side/B Side)	Yr	NM
3240	In the Night/Run. Henry	1962	12.00
3254	Two Tables Away/What Does It Take	1962	12.00

REX

Number	Title (A Side/B Side)	Yr	NM
1003	Promises/Be My Girl	1959	15.00
1011	Lucy Brown/A Picture of You	1960	15.00
1012	Blue Velvet/It's You	1960	15.00

CARDBOARD ZEPPELIN
Supposedly a pseudonym for THE REGENTS.

45s
LAURIE

Number	Title (A Side/B Side)	Yr	NM
3433	City Lights/Ten Story Building	1968	25.00

CARDINALS, THE (1)
Baltimore-based male vocal group.

45s
ATLANTIC

Number	Title (A Side/B Side)	Yr	NM
952	I'll Always Love You/Pretty Baby Blues	1952	400.00
—Cardinals records on Atlantic before 952 are unconfirmed on 45 rpm			
958	Wheel of Fortune/Kiss Me Baby	1952	600.00
972	The Bump/She Rocks	1952	300.00
995	You Are My Only Love/Lovie Darling	1953	400.00
1025	Please Baby/Under a Blanket of Blue	1954	200.00
1054	The Door Is Still Open/Misirlou	1955	80.00
1067	Come Back My Love/Two Things I Love	1955	100.00
1079	Lovely Girl/There Goes My Heart to You	1955	100.00
1090	Choo Choo/Off Shore	1956	50.00
1103	The End of the Story/I Won't Make You Cry Anymore	1956	50.00
1126	Near You/One Love	1957	40.00

CARDINALS, THE (2)

45s
CHA CHA

Number	Title (A Side/B Side)	Yr	NM
740	I Want You/Tomato Juice	1966	30.00
740 [PS]	I Want You/Tomato Juice	1966	50.00
741	Go Go Baby/Hatchet Face	1966	25.00
742	Saturday Night/I'm Gonna Tell on You	1966	25.00
748	When You're Away/I'm Gonna Tell on You	1966	25.00

CARE PACKAGE

45s
JUBILEE

Number	Title (A Side/B Side)	Yr	NM
5599	To Discover/World of Thursday	1967	10.00

Albums
LIBERTY

Number	Title (A Side/B Side)	Yr	NM
LST-7647	Keep On Keepin' On	1970	25.00

CAREFREES, THE

45s
LONDON INT'L.

Number	Title (A Side/B Side)	Yr	NM
10614	We Love You Beatles/Hot Blooded Lover	1964	20.00
—Gold label			
10614	We Love You Beatles/Hot Blooded Lover	1964	20.00
—Red label			
10614 [PS]	We Love You Beatles/Hot Blooded Lover	1964	40.00
10615	Paddy Whack/Aren't You Glad You're You	1964	15.00

Albums
LONDON

Number	Title (A Side/B Side)	Yr	NM
PS 379 [S]	From England! The Carefrees	1964	100.00
LL 3379 [M]	From England! The Carefrees	1964	80.00

CARETAKERS, THE

45s
ABC

Number	Title (A Side/B Side)	Yr	NM
11110	Get Off My Tulips/Bee Side Blues	1968	12.00

CAREY, MARIAH

12-Inch Singles
COLUMBIA

Number	Title (A Side/B Side)	Yr	NM
CAS 3311 [DJ]	Honey (Def Rascal Anthem) (Def Rascal Dub)	1997	15.00
CAS 4228 [DJ]	Fly Away (Butterfly Reprise) (Fly Away Club Mix) (Def B Fly Mix)/Honey (Def Rascal Dub) (Def Rascal Anthem)	1997	10.00
CAS 6646 [DJ]	Joy to the World (Celebration Mix) (Flava Mix)/(Club Mix) (Crash Dub Crash) (LP Version)	1994	25.00
—Promo only on red vinyl			
CAS 41886 [DJ]	I Still Believe (Stevie J. Remix) (Stevie J. Remix Instrumental) (Stevie J. Remix A Cappella)/I Still Believe-Pure Imagination (Damizza Reemix) (Damizza Reemix Instrumental) (Damizza Reemix A Cappella)	1998	15.00
CAS 41887 [DJ]	I Still Believe (Morales Classic Club Mix) (The Eve of Souls Mix) (The Kings Mix) (The Kings Mix Instrumental)	1998	15.00
CAS 42813 [DJ]	Heartbreaker-If You Should Ever Be Lonely (Junior's Heartbreaker Club Mix) (Junior's Heartbreaker Club Dub) (Junior's Heartbreaker Hard Mix)/Ain't No Fun (Remix)	1999	15.00
44-73560	Someday (New 12" House) (Pianoapercaloopapella) (New 12" Jackswing) (New 7" Straight)/Alone in Love	1991	12.00
44-74037	Emotions (12" Club Mix) (12" Instrumental) (LP Version)/There's Got to Be a Way (12" Mix)	1991	12.00
44-74189	Make It Happen (Extended Version) (Dub Version) (C&C Classic Mix) (LP Version)	1992	20.00
44-77079	Dreamlover (Def Club Mix) (Def Instrumental) (USA Love Dub) (Eclipse Dub) (Def Tribal Mix)	1993	12.00
44-77418	Never Forget You (Extended) (Radio Edit) (Instrumental) (LP Version)/Without You	1994	8.00
44X-77528 [(2)]	Anytime You Need a Friend (All That and More Mix) (Ministry of Sound Mix) (Boriqua Tribe Mix) (C&C Dub) (LP Version)	1994	15.00
44X-78044 [(2)]	Fantasy (Album Version) (Def Club Mix) (MC Mix)/(Puffy's Mix) (Bad Boy with Ol' Dirty Bastard)//(The Boss Mix) (Sweet Dub Mix)/(Puffy's Club Mix) (Bad Boy Mix)	1995	15.00
44-78075	One Sweet Day (Album Version) (Sweet A Cappella) (A Cappella) (Chucky's Remix) (Live Version)/Fantasy (Def Drums Mix)	1995	10.00
—With Boyz II Men			
44-78277	Always Be My Baby (Reggae Soul Dub Featuring Lil' Vicious) (Mr. Dupri Extended Mix Featuring Da Brat and Xscape) (Reggae Soul Acapella Featuring Lil' Vicious) (Album Version)	1996	10.00
44-78313	Always Be My Baby (Always Club Mix) (Dub-a-Baby) (Groove-a-Pella) (St Dub)	1996	8.00
44X-78665 [(2)]	Honey (Album Version) (Bad Boy Remix) (So So Def Mix) (Morales Club Dub) (Classic Mix) (Morales Dub) (Mo' Honey Dub) (Classic Instrumental) (So So Def Radio Mix)	1997	15.00
44-78822	My All (Classic Club Mix)/The Roof (Mobb Deep Mix)/Breakdown (The Mo Thugs Remix) Fly Away (Butterfly Reprise) (Fly Away Club Mix)	1998	8.00
44-78981	My All-Stay Awhile (So So Def Remix) (So So Def Remix Without Rap) (Morales 'My' Club Mix) (Morales 'Def' Club Mix)/The Roof	1998	8.00
44X-79104 [(2)DJ]	I Still Believe (Stevie J. Remix) (Stevie J. Remix Instrumental) (Stevie J. Remix A Cappella)/I Still Believe-Pure Imagination (Damizza Reemix) (Damizza Reemix Instrumental) (Damizza Reemix A Cappella)	1998	12.00
44-79261	Heartbreaker (Featuring Jay-Z) (Featuring Da Brat and Missy Elliott)/Heartbreaker-If You Should Ever Be Lonely (Junior's Heartbreaker Club Mix) (Junior's Heartbreaker Hard Mix)	1999	8.00
44-79339	Thank God I Found You (Make It Last Remix Featuring Joe and Nas) (Make It Last Remix Instrumental) (Celebratory Remix Featuring Joe and 98)/Fantasy (Featuring O.D.B)	2000	8.00
44-79399	Can't Take That Away (Mariah's Theme) (Morales Club Mix) (Morales Instrumental) (Album Version) (Morales Revival Triumphant Mix)/Crybaby	2000	8.00

VIRGIN

Number	Title (A Side/B Side)	Yr	NM
SPRO-16193 [(2)DJ]	Loverboy (7 versions)	2001	15.00
SPRO-16406 [DJ]	Loverboy (Remix Featuring Da Brat and Ludacris) (Instrumental Remix)/(Cameo Version) (Instrumental Mix)	2001	12.00
38791	Loverboy (Remix) (Instrumental Remix) (Album Version) (Instrumental Mix)	2001	6.00
38793 [(2)]	Loverboy (MJ Cole Remix) (MJ Cole Instrumental) (MJ Cole London Dub) (MJ Cole Radio Edit) (Club of Love Remix) (Dub Love Mix) (Drums of Love)	2001	8.00

45s
COLUMBIA

Number	Title (A Side/B Side)	Yr	NM
38-73348	Vision of Love//Prisoner/All In Your Mind/Someday (album snippets)	1990	3.00
38-73455	Love Takes Time/Sent from Up Above	1990	3.00
38-73561	Someday (Album Version)/Alone in Love	1990	5.00
38-73561	Someday (New 7" Jackswing)/Alone in Love	1991	3.00
38-73743	I Don't Wanna Cry/You Need Me	1991	3.00
38-73977	Emotions/Vanishing	1991	3.00
38-74088	Can't Let Go/To Be Around You	1991	3.00
38-74239	Make It Happen/Emotions (Special Motion Edit)	1992	3.00
38-74330	I'll Be There/So Blessed	1992	3.00
38-77080	Dreamlover/Do You Think of Me	1993	3.00
38-77224	Hero/Everything Fades Away	1993	3.00
38-77358	Without You/Never Forget You	1994	3.00

Number	Title (A Side/B Side)	Yr	NM
❑ 38-77499	Anytime You Need a Friend/ Music Box	1994	3.00
❑ 38-77629	Endless Love/(Instrumental)	1994	3.00
—With Luther Vandross			
❑ 38-78043	Fantasy/(Bad Boy with O.D.B.)	1995	3.00
❑ 38-78072	One Sweet Day/I Am Free	1995	8.00
—With Boyz II Men; deleted on day of issue			
❑ 38-78276	Always Be My Baby/Long Ago	1996	3.00
❑ 38-78276 [PS]	Always Be My Baby/Long Ago	1996	3.00
❑ 38-78648	Honey (LP Version)/ (Bad Boy Remix)	1997	3.00
❑ 38-78648 [PS]	Honey (LP Version)/ (Bad Boy Remix)	1997	3.00
❑ 38-78821	My All/Breakdown	1998	3.00
❑ 38-78821 [PS]	My All/Breakdown	1998	3.00
❑ 38-79093	I Still Believe-Pure Imagination/ I Still Believe	1999	3.00
❑ 38-79093 [PS]	I Still Believe-Pure Imagination/ I Still Believe	1999	3.00
❑ 38-79260	Heartbreaker (Featuring Jay-Z)/(Featuring Da Brat and Missy Elliott)	1999	3.00
❑ 38-79338	Thank God I Found You (Album Version)/(Celebratory Mix)	2000	3.00
❑ 38-79348	Can't Take That Away (Mariah's Theme)/Crybaby	2000	3.00
❑ 661070	All I Want for Christmas Is You/ Miss You Most (At Christmas Time)	1994	5.00
❑ 661070 [PS]	All I Want for Christmas Is You/ Miss You Most (At Christmas Time)	1994	6.00
—U.K. import			
MONARC/ISLAND			
❑ 440 063904-7	Through the Rain (same on both sides)	2002	3.00
VIRGIN			
❑ 38808	Loverboy/Never Too Far	2001	3.00
Albums			
COLUMBIA			
❑ C 45202	Mariah Carey	1990	20.00
❑ C 47980	Emotions	1991	15.00
❑ C 53205	Music Box	1993	15.00
❑ C2 63800 [(2)]	Rainbow	1999	15.00
❑ C2 69670 [(2)]	#1's	1998	20.00
ISLAND			
❑ B0003943-01 [(2)]	The Emancipation of Mimi	2005	15.00
❑ 440 063467-1 [(2)]	Charmbracelet	2002	15.00
VIRGIN			
❑ 10797 [(2)]	Glitter	2001	15.00
❑ SPRO-16452 [(2)DJ]	Glitter	2001	20.00
—Promo-only version			

CAREY, MUTT

Number	Title (A Side/B Side)	Yr	NM
Albums			
RIVERSIDE			
❑ RLP-1042 [10]	Mutt Carey Plays the Blues	1954	100.00

CAREY, MUTT, AND PUNCH MILLER

Number	Title (A Side/B Side)	Yr	NM
Albums			
SAVOY			
❑ MG-12038 [M]	Jazz — New Orleans	1955	50.00
❑ MG-12050 [M]	Jazz — New Orleans, Vol. 2	1955	50.00
SAVOY JAZZ			
❑ SJC-415	New Orleans Jazz	1985	10.00

CARGILL, HENSON

Number	Title (A Side/B Side)	Yr	NM
45s			
ARCO			
❑ 6605	Big Town/How Long Is Never	1967	8.00
ATLANTIC			
❑ 4007	Some Old California Memory/ A Writer of Verses and a Singer of Songs	1973	4.00
❑ 4016	She Still Comes to Me (To Pour the Wine)/ But You Know I Love You	1974	4.00
❑ 4021	Stop and Smell the Roses/ Strawberry Wine	1974	4.00
COPPER MOUNTAIN			
❑ 201	Silence on the Line/ Forever in Blue Jeans	1979	4.00
❑ 589	Have a Good Day/ (B-side unknown)	1980	4.00
ELEKTRA			
❑ 45234	Deep in the Heart of Dixie/ It Hurts the Man	1975	4.00
❑ 45273	Something to Hold On To/ Now and Then	1975	4.00
MEGA			
❑ 0030	Pencil Marks on the Wall/ Momma's Waiting	1971	5.00
❑ 0043	Naked and Crying/ Afraid to Rock the Boat	1971	5.00
❑ 0060	I Can't Face the Bed Alone/ Daddy Don't You Walk So Fast	1972	5.00
❑ 0074	Oklahoma Hell/She Likes Warm Summer Days	1972	5.00
❑ 0090	Red Skies Over Georgia/1932	1972	5.00
❑ 0100	Running from the Rain/ My '47 Chevy, My Honky Tonk Guitar, and Me	1973	5.00
MONUMENT			
❑ 1041	Skip a Rope/Very Well Traveled Man	1967	6.00
❑ 1065	Row Row Row/Six White Horses	1968	6.00
❑ 1084	She Thinks I'm On That Train/ It Just Don't Take Me Long to Say Goodbye	1968	6.00
❑ 1106	A Candle for Amy/Wild Flower	1968	6.00
❑ 1122	None of My Business/So Many Ways of Saying She's Gone	1969	6.00
❑ 1142	This Generation Shall Not Pass/ Little Girls and Little Boys	1969	6.00
❑ 1158	Then the Baby Came/Hemphill, Kentucky, Consolidated Coal Mine	1969	6.00
❑ 1178	Silver Bells/The Little Drummer Boy	1969	8.00
❑ 1184	Me & Bobby McGee/ What's My Name	1970	6.00
❑ 1198	The Most Uncomplicated Goodbye I've Ever Heard/ Four Shades of Love	1970	6.00
❑ 1209	Bless 'Em All/How Much Do Mommies Cost?	1970	6.00
TOWER			
❑ 400	Picking White Cotton/ Joe, Jesse and I	1968	8.00
Albums			
ATLANTIC			
❑ SD 7279	This Is Henson Cargill Country	1973	12.00
HARMONY			
❑ KH 31397	Welcome to My World	1972	10.00
MEGA			
❑ 31-1016	On the Road	1972	15.00
MONUMENT			
❑ SLP-18094	Skip a Rope	1968	20.00
❑ SLP-18103	Coming On Strong	1968	20.00
❑ SLP-18117	None of My Business	1969	20.00
❑ SLP-18137	Uncomplicated	1970	20.00

CARIANS, THE

Also see THE CORDIALS.

Number	Title (A Side/B Side)	Yr	NM
45s			
INDIGO			
❑ 136	She's Gone/Snooty Friends	1961	100.00
MAGENTA			
❑ 04	Only a Dream/Girls	1961	50.00

CARLA AND RUFUS

See RUFUS AND CARLA.

CARLE, BOBBY, AND THE BLENDAIRES

Number	Title (A Side/B Side)	Yr	NM
45s			
DECCA			
❑ 30938	I Got It Bad and That Ain't Good/ Guaranteed	1959	30.00

CARLIN, GEORGE

Number	Title (A Side/B Side)	Yr	NM
45s			
LITTLE DAVID			
❑ 720	Eleven O'Clock News (Part 1)/ Eleven O'Clock News (Part 2)	1971	6.00
❑ 731	New News (Part 1)/ New News (Part 2)	1974	6.00
❑ 736	Head Lines (Part 1)/ Head Lines (Part 2)	1977	6.00
RCA VICTOR			
❑ 47-9110	Wonderful WINO/Al Sleet, Your Hippy Dippy Weatherman	1967	10.00
7-Inch Extended Plays			
ATLANTIC			
❑ EP-PR-409 [DJ]	*Have a Nice Day/Rice Krispies/ Second, Third, Fifth, Sixth Announcements/Join the Book Club/Ice Box Man	1981	10.00
❑ EP-PR-409 [PS]	A Place for My Stuff	1981	10.00
Albums			
ATLANTIC			
❑ SD 19326	A Place for My Stuff	1981	10.00
EARDRUM			
❑ 1001	Carlin On Campus	1984	10.00
❑ 90523	Playin' with Your Head	1986	10.00
❑ 90972	What Am I Doing in New Jersey?	1988	10.00
ERA			
❑ EL 103 [M]	George Carlin and Jack Burns At the Playboy Club Tonight	1960	25.00
❑ E 600	The Original George Carlin	1972	12.00
LAFF			
❑ A 219	Killer Carlin	1981	10.00
—Reissue of Era material			
LITTLE DAVID			
❑ LD 1004	Class Clown	1972	10.00
❑ LD 1005	Occupation: Foole	1973	10.00
❑ LD 1008	An Evening with Wally Londo	1975	10.00
❑ LD 1075	On the Road	1977	10.00
❑ LD 1076	Indecent Exposure (Some of the Best of George Carlin)	1978	10.00
❑ LD 3003	Toledo Window Box	1974	10.00
❑ LD 7214	FM & AM	1972	10.00
❑ 90129	Toledo Window Box	1983	8.00
—Reissue of 3003			
❑ 90241	The George Carlin Collection	1984	8.00
RCA CAMDEN			
❑ CAS-2566	Take-Offs and Put-Ons	1972	10.00
RCA VICTOR			
❑ LPM-3772 [M]	Take-Offs and Put-Ons	1967	20.00
❑ LSP-3772 [S]	Take-Offs and Put-Ons	1967	15.00

CARLO

Number	Title (A Side/B Side)	Yr	NM
45s			
LAURIE			
❑ 3063	Happy Time/Rockin' Rocket	1960	20.00
—As "Carlo and Jimmy"			
❑ 3151	Baby Doll/Write Me a Letter	1962	30.00
❑ 3157	Little Orphan Girl/Mairzy Doats	1963	30.00
❑ 3175	Five Minutes More/The Story of Love	1963	30.00
❑ 3227	Ring-a-Ling/Stranger in My Arms	1964	50.00
RAFTIS			
❑ 110	Claudine/Fever	1970	12.00

CARLOS, WALTER

In the early 1980s, he became a she (Wendy Carlos). It's possible that many of the early LPs were reissued with the new name on them, but we have not confirmed this.

Number	Title (A Side/B Side)	Yr	NM
45s			
COLUMBIA			
❑ 8-3322 [PS]	A Second Chance for Bach!	1969	20.00
—Promo-only sleeve that came with JZSP 139195/6			
❑ 44803	Brandenberg Concerto No. 3 in G Major/Two-Part Invention in F Major	1969	10.00
❑ 45033	Third Movement, Brandenburg Concerto No. 4 in D Major/ Scarliotta Sonata	1969	10.00
❑ JZSP 139195/6 [DJ]	Third Movement, Brandenburg Concerto No. 3 (mono/stereo)	1969	12.00
Albums			
CBS MASTERWORKS			
❑ M 39340	Digital Moonscapes	1984	10.00
—As "Wendy Carlos"			
COLUMBIA			
❑ KG 31236 [(2)]	Sonic Seasonings	1972	15.00
❑ KC 31480	Walter Carlos' Clockwork Orange	1972	12.00
COLUMBIA MASTERWORKS			
❑ MS 7194	Switched-On Bach	1968	15.00
—"Standing Bach" cover; gray label with "360 Sound Stereo"			
❑ MS 7194	Switched-On Bach	1968	50.00
—"Sitting Bach" (sometimes called "Constipated Bach") cover that was quickly replaced; gray label with "360 Sound Stereo"			
❑ MS 7194	Switched-On Bach	1970	12.00
—Gray label with orange Columbia logos and no "360 Sound Stereo"			
❑ MS 7194	Switched-On Bach	198?	15.00
—Later reissue under the name "Wendy Carlos"; bar code on back cover			
❑ MS 7286	The Well-Tempered Synthesizer	1969	15.00
—Gray label with "360 Sound Stereo"			
❑ MS 7286	The Well-Tempered Synthesizer	1970	12.00
—Gray label with orange Columbia logos and no "360 Sound Stereo"			
❑ M 32088	Walter Carlos By Request	1973	12.00
❑ KM 32659	More Switched-On Bach	1974	12.00
❑ M2X 35895 [(2)]	Switched-On Brandenburgs	1979	15.00
❑ HM 45950	Switched-On Brandenburgs Vol. 1	1980	100.00
—Half-speed mastered edition			
❑ HM 47194	Switched-On Bach	198?	30.00
—Half-speed mastered edition			

CARLTON, CARL

12-Inch Singles

Number	Title (A Side/B Side)	Yr	NM
CASABLANCA			
❑ 880949-1	Private Property (Club Mix 6:43) (Dub Version 6:23)	1985	10.00
❑ 884274-1	Slipped, Tripped (Fooled Around and Fell in Love) (Special Club Remix) (Dub Version)/Hot	1986	12.00
RCA			
❑ PD-13314	Baby I Need Your Loving (5:56)/Everyone Can Be a Star	1982	10.00
❑ PD-13407	Swing That Sexy Thang/Just One Kiss	1982	10.00
20TH CENTURY			
❑ TCD-129	She's a Bad Mama Jama (She's Built, She's Stacked)/ This Feeling's Rated X-Tra	1981	20.00

45s

Number	Title (A Side/B Side)	Yr	NM
ABC			
❑ 11378	You Can't Stop a Man in Love/ You Times Me Plus Love	1973	5.00
❑ 12059	Smokin' Room/Signed, Sealed, Delivered, I'm Yours	1974	5.00
❑ 12089	Morning, Noon and Nightime/ Our Day Will Come	1975	5.00
❑ 12166	Ain't Gonna Tell Nobody (About You)/Live for Today, Not for Tomorrow	1976	5.00
❑ 12226	Let's Groove/Live for Today, Not for Tomorrow	1976	5.00
BACK BEAT			
❑ 588	Competition Ain't Nothin'/ Three Way Love	1968	30.00
—As "Little Carl Carlton"			
❑ 598	46 Drums — 1 Guitar/Why Don't They Leave Us Alone	1968	6.00
—As "Little Carl Carlton"			
❑ 603	Look at Mary Wonder (How I Got Over)/Bad for Each Other	1969	6.00
—As "Little Carl Carlton"			
❑ 610	Don't Walk Away/ Hold On a Little Longer	1969	6.00
❑ 613	Drop By My Place/Two Timer	1970	6.00
—As "Little Carl Carlton"			
❑ 617	I Can Feel It/You've Got So Much (To Learn About Love)	1970	6.00
❑ 619	Sure Miss Loving You/ Wild Child	1970	6.00
❑ 621	Wild Child/Look at Mary Wonder (How I Got Over)	1971	6.00
❑ 624	The Generation Gap/ Where Have You Been	1972	6.00
❑ 627	I Won't Let That Chump Break Your Heart/Why Don't They Leave Us Alone	1972	6.00
❑ 629	It Ain't Been Easy/I Wanna Be Your Main Squeeze	1973	6.00
❑ 630	Everlasting Love/I Wanna Be Your Main Squeeze	1974	8.00
❑ 27001	Everlasting Love/I Wanna Be Your Main Squeeze	1974	5.00
CASABLANCA			
❑ 880949-7	Private Property/Mama's Boy	1985	3.00
❑ 884274-7	Slipped, Tripped (Fooled Around and Fell in Love)/Hot	1986	3.00
GOLDEN WORLD			
❑ 23	Nothin' No Sweeter Than Love/ I Love True Love	1965	80.00
LANDO			
❑ 8527	So What/(B-side unknown)	1965	50.00
MERCURY			
❑ 73969	Something's Wrong/You, You	1977	4.00
RCA			
❑ PB-13313	Baby I Need Your Loving/ Everyone Can Be a Star	1982	4.00
❑ PB-13406	Swing That Sexy Thang/ Just One Kiss	1982	4.00
20TH CENTURY			
❑ 2459	This Feeling's Rated X-Tra/ Fighting in the Name of Love	1980	4.00
❑ 2488	She's a Bad Mama Jama (She's Built, She's Stacked)/ This Feeling's Rated X-Tra	1981	4.00
❑ 2513	Let Me Love You Till the Morning Comes/Sexy Lady	1982	4.00
❑ 2601	I Think It's Gonna Be Alright/ Let Me Love You Till the Morning Comes	1982	4.00

Albums

Number	Title (A Side/B Side)	Yr	NM
ABC			
❑ D-857	Everlasting Love	1974	12.00
❑ D-910	I Wanna Be with You	1975	12.00
BACK BEAT			
❑ BBLX-71	Can't Stop a Man in Love	1973	15.00
CASABLANCA			
❑ 822705-1	Private Property	1985	10.00
RCA VICTOR			
❑ AFL1-4425	The Bad C.C.	1982	10.00
20TH CENTURY			
❑ T-628	Carl Carlton	1981	10.00

CARLTON, LARRY

12-Inch Singles

Number	Title (A Side/B Side)	Yr	NM
WARNER BROS.			
❑ PRO-A-2043 [DJ]	Tequila (2 versions)	1983	8.00

45s

Number	Title (A Side/B Side)	Yr	NM
BLUE THUMB			
❑ 227	An American Family/ (B-side unknown)	1973	8.00
MCA			
❑ S45-17400 [DJ]	Hello Tomorrow (same on both sides)	1987	6.00
❑ 52844	Smiles and Smiles to Go/ Carrying You	1986	3.00
❑ 52844 [PS]	Smiles and Smiles to Go/ Carrying You	1986	3.00
❑ 53319	Minute by Minute/ Hello Tomorrow	1987	3.00
UNI			
❑ 55080	The Odd Couple/ Monday, Monday	1968	10.00
❑ 55120	Moon People/Son of a Preacher Man	1969	8.00
WARNER BROS.			
❑ 8694	Room 335/Where Did You Come From	1978	4.00
❑ 29590	Tequila/L.A., N.Y.	1983	4.00
❑ 29977	Song for Katie/10:00 P.M.	1982	4.00
❑ 50019	Sleepwalk/Frenchman's Flat	1982	4.00

Albums

Number	Title (A Side/B Side)	Yr	NM
BLUE THUMB			
❑ BTS-46	Singing/Playing	1972	15.00
GRP			
❑ 9611	Collection	1990	12.00
MCA			
❑ 5689	Alone/But Never Alone	1986	8.00
❑ 6237	On Solid Ground	1989	8.00
❑ 6322	Christmas at Our House	1989	10.00
❑ 42003	Discovery	1987	8.00
UNI			
❑ 73036	With a Little Help from My Friends	1968	20.00
WARNER BROS.			
❑ BSK 3221	Larry Carlton	1978	10.00
❑ BSK 3380	Strikes Twice	1980	10.00
❑ BSK 3635	Sleepwalk	1981	10.00
❑ 23834	Friends	1983	8.00

CARMEL SISTERS, THE

Also see CAROL CONNORS.

45s

Number	Title (A Side/B Side)	Yr	NM
COLPIX			
❑ 767	Go, Go, G.T.O./Sunny Winter	1965	300.00
—As "Carol and Cheryl"			
JUBILEE			
❑ 5464	Joey's Comin' Home/The Rumor	1963	20.00

CARMEN, ERIC

Also see CYRUS ERIE; THE QUICK; RASPBERRIES.

12-Inch Singles

Number	Title (A Side/B Side)	Yr	NM
GEFFEN			
❑ 20294	I Wanna Hear It from Your Lips (2 versions)	1984	8.00

45s

Number	Title (A Side/B Side)	Yr	NM
ARISTA			
❑ 0165	All By Myself/Everything	1975	4.00
❑ 0184	Never Gonna Fall in Love Again/No Hard Feelings	1976	4.00
❑ 0200	Sunrise/My Girl	1976	4.00
❑ 0266	She Did It/Someday	1977	4.00
❑ 0266 [PS]	She Did It/Someday	1977	6.00
❑ 0295	Boats Against the Current/ Take It or Leave It	1977	4.00
❑ 0319	Marathon Man/ I Think I Found Myself	1978	4.00
❑ 0354	Change of Heart/Hey Deanie	1978	4.00
❑ 0384	Baby I Need Your Lovin'/ Heaven Can Wait	1979	4.00
❑ 0435	Haven't We Come a Long Way/ End of the World	1979	4.00
❑ 0506	It Hurts Too Much/ You Need Some Lovin'	1980	4.00
❑ 0550	All for Love/Tonight You're Mine	1980	4.00
❑ 9686	Make Me Lose Control/ That's Rock 'N' Roll	1988	3.00
❑ 9686 [PS]	Make Me Lose Control/ That's Rock 'N' Roll	1988	3.00
❑ 9736	Boats Against the Current/ No Hard Feelings	1988	3.00
❑ 9746	Reason to Try/Sunrise	1988	3.00
❑ 9746 [PS]	Reason to Try/Sunrise	1988	3.00
COOL			
❑ 101	The Rock Stops Here (same on both sides)	1988	3.00
❑ 101 [PS]	The Rock Stops Here (same on both sides)	1988	3.00
—Semi-promotional record used to promote Cleveland's candidacy for the site of the Rock and Roll Hall of Fame			
EPIC			
❑ 10669	I'll Hold Out My Hand/It Won't Be the Same Without You	1970	—
—Not known to exist			
GEFFEN			
❑ 29032	I'm Through with Love/ Maybe My Baby	1985	3.00
❑ 29032 [PS]	I'm Through with Love/ Maybe My Baby	1985	3.00
❑ 29118	I Wanna Hear It from Your Lips/ Spotlight	1985	3.00
❑ 29118 [PS]	I Wanna Hear It from Your Lips/ Spotlight	1985	3.00
RCA			
❑ 5315-7-R	Hungry Eyes/Where Are You Tonight	1987	3.00

Albums

Number	Title (A Side/B Side)	Yr	NM
ARISTA			
❑ AL 4057	Eric Carmen	1975	8.00
—Regular non-shiny gold cover			
❑ AL 4057	Eric Carmen	1975	12.00
—Shiny, simulated gold foil cover			
❑ AQ 4057 [Q]	Eric Carmen	1975	18.00
❑ AB 4124	Boats Against the Current	1977	8.00
❑ AB 4184	Change of Heart	1978	8.00
❑ AL 8547	The Best of Eric Carmen	1988	8.00
—Reissues add "Make Me Lose Control"			
❑ AL 8547	The Best of Eric Carmen	1988	15.00
—Original copies do not contain "Make Me Lose Control"			
❑ AL 9513	Tonight You're Mine	1980	8.00
GEFFEN			
❑ GHS 24042	Eric Carmen	1985	8.00

CARMICHAEL, BILL

45s

Number	Title (A Side/B Side)	Yr	NM
HIT			
❑ 38	Limbo Rock/Don't Hang Up	1962	8.00
—B-side by the Dacrons			
❑ 45	It's Up to You/Tell Him	1962	8.00
—B-side by Peggy Gaines			

CARMICHAEL, SANDY

45s

Number	Title (A Side/B Side)	Yr	NM
HIT			
❑ 35	Don't Go Near the Indians/ Return to Sender	1962	8.00
—B-side by Ed Hardin			

CARNATIONS, THE

Several different groups.

45s

Number	Title (A Side/B Side)	Yr	NM
DERBY			
❑ 789	Tree in the Meadow/ Clown of the Masquerade	1952	400.00
ENRICA			
❑ 1001	Gimme, Gimme, Gimme/ Love, Open My Heart	1959	25.00
FRATERNITY			
❑ 863	Red Wing/Casual	1960	25.00
LAURIE			
❑ 3163	Punctuation/Funny Time	1963	25.00
LESCAY			
❑ 3002	Long Tall Girl/Is There Such a World	1961	100.00
LOST-NITE			
❑ 145	Long Tall Girl/Is There Such a World	196?	6.00
—Reissue			

SAVOY

Number	Title (A Side/B Side)	Yr	NM
❑ 1172	Angels Sent You to Me/Night Time Is the Right Time	1955	60.00

TERRY-TONE

Number	Title (A Side/B Side)	Yr	NM
❑ 199	Barbary Coast/Sleepy Hollow	1960	40.00

UNIVERSITY

Number	Title (A Side/B Side)	Yr	NM
❑ 606	Leap Year/A Wing and a Prayer	1960	25.00

CARNE, JUDY

45s

REPRISE

Number	Title (A Side/B Side)	Yr	NM
❑ 0680	Sock It To Me/Right, Said Fred	1968	10.00

CARNES, KIM

Also see GENE COTTON; KENNY ROGERS; BARBRA STREISAND.

12-Inch Singles

EMI AMERICA

Number	Title (A Side/B Side)	Yr	NM
❑ V-7815	Invisible Hands (Dance Mix) (FM Mix)	1983	10.00
❑ V-7819	You Make My Heart Beat Faster (And That's All That Matters) (Dance Mix) (Instrumental)	1983	12.00
❑ V-7829	Hurricane (Extended Vocal Version 5:18) (Instrumental 4:47)	1984	12.00
❑ V-7851	Invitation to Dance (Vocal Dance Mix) (Instrumental Dance Mix)	1985	10.00
❑ V-7857	Crazy in the Night (Barking at Airplanes) (Dance Mix 5:10) (Part II Dub Mix 4:59)	1985	10.00
❑ V-7863	Abadabadango (2 versions)/ He Makes the Sun Rise	1985	10.00
❑ SPRO-9022/3 [DJ]	Invisible Hands (Dance Mix) (FM Mix)	1983	10.00
❑ SPRO 9036/7 [DJ]	It Hurts So Bad/What Am I Gonna Do	1979	12.00
❑ SPRO-9042/3 [DJ]	Invisible Hands (FM Mix)/ You Make My Heart Beat Faster (And That's All That Matters)	1983	12.00
❑ SPRO-9118/9 [DJ]	Hurricane (Extended Vocal Version 5:18) (Instrumental 4:47)	1984	15.00
❑ SPRO 9670/1 [DJ]	Draw of the Cards (Short Version 3:58) (Long Mix 4:54)	1981	20.00
❑ SPRO-9702/3 [DJ]	Divided Hearts (Club Mix 7:29) (Red Mix 4:47) (Dub 6:08) (Instrumental 4:21)	1986	12.00
❑ SPRO 9821 [DJ]	Voyeur (same on both sides)	1982	10.00
❑ SPRO 9845 [DJ]	Voyeur (Extended Version) (same on both sides?)	1982	12.00

45s

A&M

Number	Title (A Side/B Side)	Yr	NM
❑ 1748	Somewhere in the Night/Hang On to Your Airplane (Honeymoon)	1975	5.00
❑ 1767	You're a Part of Me/Hang On to Your Airplane (Honeymoon)	1975	5.00
❑ 1807 [DJ]	Bad Seed (mono/stereo)	1976	8.00
	—No stock copies issued		
❑ 1902	The Last Thing You Ever Wanted to Do/Let Your Love Come Easy	1977	5.00
❑ 1943	Sailin'/He'll Come Home	1977	5.00

AMOS

Number	Title (A Side/B Side)	Yr	NM
❑ 165	I Won't Call You Back/To Love	1971	8.00
❑ 166	To Love Somebody/ Fell in Love with a Poet	1971	8.00
❑ 167	It's Love That Keeps It All Together/Long and Lonely Memories	1971	8.00
	—With Dave Ellingson		

EMI AMERICA

Number	Title (A Side/B Side)	Yr	NM
❑ 8010	Losing Love/Looking for a Big Night	1979	5.00
❑ 8011	It Hurts So Bad/Lookin' for a Big Night	1979	5.00
❑ 8014	What Am I Gonna Do/ Goodnight Moon	1979	5.00
❑ 8045	More Love/Changin'	1980	4.00
❑ 8045 [PS]	More Love/Changin'	1980	6.00
❑ 8058	Cry Like a Baby/In the Chill of the Night	1980	4.00
❑ 8069	Mas Amor/Changin'	1980	8.00
❑ 8077	Bette Davis Eyes/ Miss You Tonight	1981	4.00
❑ 8077 [PS]	Bette Davis Eyes/ Miss You Tonight	1981	4.00
❑ A-8087	Draw of the Cards/Break the Rules Tonite (Out of School)	1981	4.00
❑ A-8087 [PS]	Draw of the Cards/Break the Rules Tonite (Out of School)	1981	4.00
❑ A-8098	Mistaken Identity/Jamaica Sunday Morning	1981	4.00
❑ A-8098 [PS]	Mistaken Identity/Jamaica Sunday Morning	1981	4.00
❑ B-8127	Voyeur/Thrill of the Grill	1982	3.00
❑ B-8127 [PS]	Voyeur/Thrill of the Grill	1982	3.00
❑ B-8147	Does It Make You Remember/ Take It on the Chin	1982	3.00
❑ B-8147 [PS]	Does It Make You Remember/ Take It on the Chin	1982	3.00
❑ B-8154	Say You Don't Know Me/ Breakin' Away from Society	1983	5.00
❑ B-8181	Invisible Hands/I'll Be Here Where the Heart Is	1983	3.00
❑ B-8181 [PS]	Invisible Hands/I'll Be Here Where the Heart Is	1983	3.00
❑ B-8191	You Make My Heart Beat Faster (And That's All That Matters)/ Hangin' On by a Thread	1984	3.00
❑ B-8191 [PS]	You Make My Heart Beat Faster (And That's All That Matters)/ Hangin' On by a Thread	1984	3.00
❑ B-8202	I Pretend/Hurricane	1984	3.00
❑ B-8202 [PS]	I Pretend/Hurricane	1984	3.00
❑ B-8250	Invitation to Dance/Breakthrough	1984	3.00
	—B-side by Haven		
❑ B-8250 [PS]	Invitation to Dance/Breakthrough	1984	3.00
❑ B-8267	Crazy in the Night (Barking at Airplanes)/ Oliver (Voice on the Radio)	1985	3.00
❑ B-8267 [PS]	Crazy in the Night (Barking at Airplanes)/ Oliver (Voice on the Radio)	1985	3.00
❑ B-8281	Abadabadango/He Makes the Sun Rise (Orpheus)	1985	3.00
❑ B-8281 [PS]	Abadabadango/He Makes the Sun Rise (Orpheus)	1985	3.00
❑ B-8290	Rough Edges/Begging for Favors (Learning How Things Work)	1985	4.00
❑ B-8322	Divided Hearts/You Say You Love Me (But I Know You Don't)	1986	3.00
❑ B-8322 [PS]	Divided Hearts/You Say You Love Me (But I Know You Don't)	1986	3.00
❑ B-8335	I'd Lie to You for Your Love/ Black and White	1986	4.00

MCA

Number	Title (A Side/B Side)	Yr	NM
❑ S45-17682 [DJ]	Crazy in Love/(New Version)	1988	5.00
❑ 53387	Speed of the Sound of Loneliness/Blood from the Bandit	1988	3.00
❑ 53433	Crazy in Love/Blood from the Bandit	1988	3.00
❑ 53433 [PS]	Crazy in Love/Blood from the Bandit	1988	4.00
❑ 53494	Fantastic Fire of Love/ Brass and Batons	1989	3.00

Albums

A&M

Number	Title	Yr	NM
❑ SP-3114	Sailin'	198?	8.00
	—Budget-line reissue		
❑ SP-3204	The Best of Kim Carnes	1982	10.00
❑ SP-4548	Kim Carnes	1975	12.00
❑ SP-4606	Sailin'	1976	12.00

AMOS

Number	Title	Yr	NM
❑ AAS 7016	Rest on Me	1971	20.00

EMI AMERICA

Number	Title	Yr	NM
❑ SW-17004	St. Vincent's Court	1978	10.00
❑ SW-17030	Romance Dance	1980	10.00
❑ SO-17052	Mistaken Identity	1981	10.00
❑ SO-17078	Voyeur	1982	10.00
❑ SO-17107	Café Racers	1983	10.00
❑ SO-17159	Barking at Airplanes	1985	10.00
❑ ST-17198	Light House	1986	8.00

MCA

Number	Title	Yr	NM
❑ 914	The Early Years	1984	8.00
❑ 42200	View from the House	1988	8.00

MOBILE FIDELITY

Number	Title	Yr	NM
❑ 1-073	Mistaken Identity	1982	25.00
	—Audiophile vinyl		

CARNIVAL

45s

UNITED ARTISTS

Number	Title (A Side/B Side)	Yr	NM
❑ 50749	Where There's a Heartache (There Must Be a Heart)/ The Truth About It	1971	5.00
❑ 50749 [PS]	Where There's a Heartache (There Must Be a Heart)/ The Truth About It	1971	12.00

WORLD PACIFIC

Number	Title (A Side/B Side)	Yr	NM
❑ 77932	Laia Ladaia/Calito de Carnival	1969	6.00

Albums

WORLD PACIFIC

Number	Title	Yr	NM
❑ ST-21894	The Carnival	1969	12.00

CARO, NYDIA

45s

ROULETTE

Number	Title (A Side/B Side)	Yr	NM
❑ 4588	Ask Me What I Want for Christmas/Hey Johnny What	1964	12.00
❑ 4588 [PS]	Ask Me What I Want for Christmas/Hey Johnny What	1964	20.00

CAROL AND CHERYL

See THE CARMEL SISTERS.

CAROL AND GERRI

45s

MGM

Number	Title (A Side/B Side)	Yr	NM
❑ 13568	How Can I Ever Find the Way/On You, Heartache Looks Good	1966	40.00

CAROL, LINDA AND CATHY

45s

UNITED

Number	Title (A Side/B Side)	Yr	NM
❑ 216	Merry Christmas/I Don't Wanna Be Last On Santa's List	1957	20.00

CAROLINA SLIM

Albums

SHARP

Number	Title	Yr	NM
❑ 2002 [M]	Blues from the Cotton Fields	195?	250.00

CAROLS, THE (1)

Female group.

45s

LAMP

Number	Title (A Side/B Side)	Yr	NM
❑ 2001	My Search Is Over/Keko	1957	50.00

CAROLS, THE (2)

Male group.

45s

SAVOY

Number	Title (A Side/B Side)	Yr	NM
❑ 896	Fifty Million Women/ I Got a Feelin'	1953	150.00

CAROUSEL, THE

45s

ABC

Number	Title (A Side/B Side)	Yr	NM
❑ 10953	One Mistake/Only One for Me	1967	12.00

TEEN TOWN

Number	Title (A Side/B Side)	Yr	NM
❑ 108	I've Been with You/ What Will You Do for Me	1969	15.00
❑ 116	To Say Goodbye/ I Get Along Indefinitely	1969	15.00

CAROUSELS, THE

Possibly more than one group.

45s

ABC-PARAMOUNT

Number	Title (A Side/B Side)	Yr	NM
❑ 10233	Symptoms of Love/ The Hush of Love	1961	25.00

AUTUMN

Number	Title (A Side/B Side)	Yr	NM
❑ 13	Beneath the Willow/Sail Away	1965	10.00

GONE

Number	Title (A Side/B Side)	Yr	NM
❑ 5118	If You Want To/Pretty Little Thing	1961	30.00
❑ 5118	You Can Come If You Want To/ Pretty Little Thing	1961	50.00
❑ 5131	Never Let Him Go/Dirty Tricks	1962	25.00

GUYDEN

Number	Title (A Side/B Side)	Yr	NM
❑ 2102	I Wanna Fly/Something Else	1964	12.00

JAGUAR

Number	Title (A Side/B Side)	Yr	NM
❑ 3029	Drive-In Movie/Rendezvous	1959	60.00

SPRY

Number	Title (A Side/B Side)	Yr	NM
❑ 116	I've Cried Enough/ Did I Cry Enough	1962	150.00

CARP

Actor Gary Busey was in this group.

45s

EPIC

Number	Title (A Side/B Side)	Yr	NM
❑ 10632	Save the Delta Queen/ Mammoth Mountain Blues	1970	8.00
❑ 10647	Pine Creek Bridge/Page 258	1970	8.00

Albums

EPIC

Number	Title	Yr	NM
❑ E 30212	Carp	1970	25.00

CARPENTERS

45s

A&M

Number	Title (A Side/B Side)	Yr	NM
1142	Ticket to Ride/Your Wonderful Parade	1969	10.00
1183	(They Long to Be) Close to You/I Kept On Loving You	1970	5.00
1217	We've Only Just Begun/All of My Life	1970	5.00
1217 [PS]	We've Only Just Begun/All of My Life	1970	6.00
1236	Merry Christmas Darling/Mr. Guder	1970	6.00
—A-side vocal is different than later releases of this song			
1236 [PS]	Merry Christmas Darling/Mr. Guder	1970	8.00
1243	For All We Know/Don't Be Afraid	1971	4.00
1243 [PS]	For All We Know/Don't Be Afraid	1971	6.00
1260	Rainy Days and Mondays/Saturday	1971	4.00
1260 [PS]	Rainy Days and Mondays/Saturday	1971	6.00
1289	Superstar/Bless the Beasts and Children	1971	4.00
1289 [PS]	Superstar/Bless the Beasts and Children	1971	6.00
1322	Hurting Each Other/Maybe It's You	1972	4.00
1322 [PS]	Hurting Each Other/Maybe It's You	1972	6.00
1351	It's Going to Take Some Time/Flat Baroque	1972	4.00
1351 [PS]	It's Going to Take Some Time/Flat Baroque	1972	6.00
1367	Goodbye to Love/Crystal Lullaby	1972	4.00
1367 [PS]	Goodbye to Love/Crystal Lullaby	1972	6.00
1391	Top of the World/Druscilla Penny	1972	—
—Unreleased			
1413	Sing/Druscilla Penny	1973	4.00
1413 [PS]	Sing/Druscilla Penny	1973	6.00
1446	Yesterday Once More/Road Ode	1973	4.00
1446 [PS]	Yesterday Once More/Road Ode	1973	6.00
1468	Top of the World/Heather	1973	3.00
—Second pressings have silvery labels			
1468	Top of the World/Heather	1973	4.00
—Originals have brown labels			
1468 [PS]	Top of the World/Heather	1973	6.00
1521	I Won't Last a Day Without You/One Love	1974	4.00
1521 [PS]	I Won't Last a Day Without You/One Love	1974	6.00
1646	Please Mister Postman/This Masquerade	1974	4.00
1646 [PS]	Please Mister Postman/This Masquerade	1974	6.00
1648	Santa Claus Is Coming to Town/Merry Christmas Darling	1974	5.00
1648 [PS]	Santa Claus Is Coming to Town/Merry Christmas Darling	1974	10.00
1677	Only Yesterday/Happy	1975	4.00
1677 [PS]	Only Yesterday/Happy	1975	6.00
1721	Solitaire/Love Me for What I Am	1975	4.00
1721 [PS]	Solitaire/Love Me for What I Am	1975	6.00
1800	There's a Kind of Hush (All Over the World)/(I'm Caught Between) Goodbye and I Love You	1976	4.00
1800 [PS]	There's a Kind of Hush (All Over the World)/(I'm Caught Between) Goodbye and I Love You	1976	6.00
1828	I Need to Be in Love/Sandy	1976	4.00
1859	Goofus/Boat to Sail	1976	4.00
1940	All You Get from Love Is a Love Song/I Have You	1977	4.00
1978	Calling Occupants of Interplanetary Craft/Can't Smile Without You	1977	4.00
1978 [PS]	Calling Occupants of Interplanetary Craft/Can't Smile Without You	1977	6.00
1991	The Christmas Song/Merry Christmas Darling	1977	5.00
1991 [PS]	The Christmas Song/Merry Christmas Darling	1977	8.00
2008	Sweet, Sweet Smile/I Have You	1978	4.00
2097	I Believe You/B'wana She No Home	1978	4.00
2344	Touch Me When We're Dancing/Because We Are in Love (The Wedding Song)	1981	4.00
2344 [PS]	Touch Me When We're Dancing/Because We Are in Love (The Wedding Song)	1981	4.00
2370	(Want You) Back in My Life Again/Somebody's Been Lyin'	1981	4.00
2386	Those Good Old Dreams/When It's Gone	1981	4.00
2405	Beechwood 4-5789/Two Sides	1982	4.00
2585	Make Believe It's Your First Time/Look to Your Dreams	1983	4.00
2585 [PS]	Make Believe It's Your First Time/Look to Your Dreams	1983	5.00
2620	Sailing on the Tide/Your Baby Doesn't Love You Anymore	1984	4.00
2700	Do You Hear What I Hear/Little Altar Boy	1984	10.00
2735	Yesterday Once More/(They Long to Be) Close to You-We've Only Just Begun	1985	20.00
2735 [PS]	Yesterday Once More/(They Long to Be) Close to You-We've Only Just Begun	1985	20.00
8620	Christmas Song/Merry Christmas Darling	1977	5.00
—"Forget Me Nots" green and gold label			
8620 [PS]	Christmas Song/Merry Christmas Darling	1977	10.00
8629	Calling Occupants of Interplanetary Craft/Don't Cry for Me Argentina	1980	5.00
8629 [PS]	Calling Occupants of Interplanetary Craft/Don't Cry for Me Argentina	1980	15.00
8667	Honolulu City Lights/I Just Fall in Love Again	1986	5.00
8667 [PS]	Honolulu City Lights/I Just Fall in Love Again	1986	10.00
SP-17001	Yesterday Once More/Rainy Days and Mondays	1978	50.00
—This 45 was contained in one of six different "Superstar Teaching Machine" packages. The price includes the record, a poster of the Carpenters, and a book of reading exercises.			

MAGIC LAMP

Number	Title (A Side/B Side)	Yr	NM
704	I'll Be Yours/Looking for Love	1967	2000.
—As "Karen Carpenter", but Richard also was on this record			

7-Inch Extended Plays

A&M

Number	Title (A Side/B Side)	Yr	NM
LLP 3502	Bacharach-David Hit Medley//Superstar/Let Me Be the One/For All We Know	1971	15.00
—Jukebox issue; small hole, plays at 33 1/3 rpm			
LLP 3502 [PS]	Carpenters	1971	15.00
—Part of "Little LP" series (LLP #151)			
LLP 3519	Fun, Fun, Fun/The End of the World/Da Doo Ron Ron (When He Walked Me Home)/Deadman's Curve//Johnyn Angel/The Night Has a Thousand Eyes/Our Day Will Come/One Fine Day	1973	20.00
—Jukebox issue; small hole, plays at 33 1/3 rpm			
LLP 3519 [PS]	Now & Then	1973	20.00
—Part of "Little LP" series (LLP #222)			
LLP 3601	Ticket to Ride/(They Long to Be) Close to You//We've Only Just Begun/Top of the World/Rainy Days and Mondays	1973	20.00
—Jukebox issue; small hole, plays at 33 1/3 rpm			
LLP 3601 [PS]	The Singles 1969-1973	1973	20.00
—Part of "Little LP" series (LLP #238)			
LLP 4271	Help/Baby It's You/I'll Never Fall in Love Again/Love Is Surrender/Maybe It's You/(They Long to Be) Close to You	1970	15.00
—Jukebox issue; small hole, plays at 33 1/3 rpm			
LLP 4271 [PS]	Close to You	1970	15.00
—Part of "Little LP" series (LLP #125)			

Albums

A&M

Number	Title	Yr	NM
SP-3184	Close to You	1982	8.00
—Reissue of 4271			
SP-3197	A Kind of Hush	1982	8.00
—Reissue of 4581			
SP-3199	Passage	1982	8.00
—Reissue of 4703			
SP-3210	Christmas Portrait	198?	8.00
—Reissue of SP-4726			
SP-3270	An Old-Fashioned Christmas	1984	10.00
SP-3502	Carpenters	1971	12.00
SP-3511	A Song for You	1972	12.00
SP-3519	Now & Then	1973	12.00
SP-3601	The Singles 1969-1973	1973	12.00
SP-3723	Made in America	1981	12.00
SP-4205	Offering	1969	80.00
SP-4205	Ticket to Ride	1970	12.00
—Reissue of "Offering" with new title and cover			
SP-4271	Close to You	1970	12.00
SP-4530	Horizon	1975	12.00
SP-4581	A Kind of Hush	1976	12.00
SP-4703	Passage	1977	12.00
SP-4726	Christmas Portrait	1978	15.00
SP-4954	Voice of the Heart	1983	12.00
SP-5172	An Old Fashioned Christmas	1987	8.00
—Reissue of 3270 (record still says 3270 but cover is 5172)			
SP-6601 [(2)]	Yesterday Once More	1985	15.00
QU-53502 [Q]	Carpenters	1974	
—Not released			
QU-53511 [Q]	A Song for You	1974	—
—Not released			
QU-53519 [Q]	Now & Then	1974	20.00
QU-53601 [Q]	The Singles 1969-1973	1974	20.00
QU-54271 [Q]	Close to You	1974	
—Not released			
QU-54530 [Q]	Horizon	1975	20.00
SMAS-94398	A Song for You	1972	20.00
—Capitol Record Club edition; unlike the standard edition, the cover is smooth and not textured			

CARPETS, THE

45s

FEDERAL

Number	Title (A Side/B Side)	Yr	NM
12257	Why Do I/Let Her Go	1956	200.00
12269	Lonely Me/Chicken Backs	1956	200.00

CARR, CATHY

45s

CORAL

Number	Title (A Side/B Side)	Yr	NM
60907	Heartbroken/Half Pink Boogie	1953	12.00
60988	I Just Can't Get That Melody Out of My Mind/Somebody Told You a Lie	1953	12.00
61092	I'll Cry at Your Wedding/Cryin' for the Caroline's	1953	12.00
61646	I'll Cry at Your Wedding/Heartbroken	1956	10.00

FRATERNITY

Number	Title (A Side/B Side)	Yr	NM
718	Morning, Noon and Night/Toward Evening	1955	20.00
734	Ivory Tower/Please Please Believe Me	1956	15.00
743	Heart Hideaway/The Boy on Page 35	1956	15.00
750	Oh Baby/Waltzing to the Blues	1956	15.00
757	It Looks Like Love/Una Momenta	1957	12.00
765	Wild Honey/Speak for Yourself John	1957	12.00
782	House of Heartache/Presents from the Past	1957	12.00
793	Doll Baby/Don't Come to My Party	1958	12.00

LAURIE

Number	Title (A Side/B Side)	Yr	NM
3133	Ivory Tower/Should I Believe Him	1962	10.00
3147	Sailorboy/Next Time a Band Plays a Waltz	1962	10.00
3161	I Waded in the Water/In Place of You	1963	10.00
3206	My Favorite Song/The Ghost of a Broken Heart	1963	10.00
3378	When You Come Home Again/The Ghost of a Broken Heart	1967	6.00

ROULETTE

Number	Title (A Side/B Side)	Yr	NM
4107	To Know Him Is to Love Him/Put Away the Invitation	1958	12.00
4125	First Anniversary/With Love	1959	12.00
4152 [M]	I'm Gonna Change Him/The Little Things You Do	1959	12.00
SSR-4152 [S]	I'm Gonna Change Him/The Little Things You Do	1959	30.00
4187	Shy/Personal Secret	1959	12.00
4219	Little Sister/Dark River	1960	12.00
4248	A Little Time/What Do I Do Now	1960	12.00
4296	I Want to Be Your Pet/Golden Locket	1960	12.00
4323	Johnny's Song/Someone Told You a Lie	1961	12.00
4367	Yearning/Baseball He Loves	1961	12.00
4383	I Can't Begin to Tell You/You're Breaking My Heart	1961	12.00

SMASH

Number	Title (A Side/B Side)	Yr	NM
1726	Footprints in the Snow/Nein, Nein, Fraulein	1961	12.00

Albums

DOT

Number	Title	Yr	NM
DLP-3674 [M]	Ivory Tower	1966	25.00
DLP-25674 [S]	Ivory Tower	1966	25.00

FRATERNITY

Number	Title	Yr	NM
1005 [M]	Ivory Tower	1957	120.00

ROULETTE

Number	Title	Yr	NM
R 25077 [M]	Shy	1959	40.00
SR 25077 [S]	Shy	1959	50.00

CARR, JAMES

45s

ATLANTIC

Number	Title (A Side/B Side)	Yr	NM
2803	Hold On/I'll Put It to You	1971	12.00

GOLDWAX

Number	Title (A Side/B Side)	Yr	NM
108	You Don't Want Me/Only Fools Run Away	1965	30.00

Number	Title (A Side/B Side)	Yr	NM
❑ 112	I Can't Make It/ Lovers' Competition	1965	30.00
❑ 119	He's Better Than You/Talk Talk	1965	30.00
❑ 302	You've Got My Mind Messed Up/ That's What I Want to Know	1966	20.00
❑ 309	Love Attack/Come Back to Me Baby	1966	15.00
❑ 311	Pouring Water on a Drowning Man/Forgetting You	1966	15.00
❑ 317	The Dark End of the Street/ Lovable Girl	1967	16.00
❑ 323	Let It Happen/A Losing Game	1967	15.00
❑ 328	I'm a Fool for You/Gonna Send You Back to Georgia	1967	15.00
❑ 332	A Man Needs a Woman/ Stronger Than Love	1968	15.00
❑ 335	Life Turned Her That Way/ A Message to Young Lovers	1968	15.00
❑ 338	Freedom Train/That's the Way Love Turned Out for Me	1968	15.00
❑ 340	To Love Somebody/ These Ain't Teardrops	1969	15.00
❑ 343	Everybody Needs Somebody/ Row, Row Your Boat	1969	15.00

Albums

GOLDWAX

Number	Title	Yr	NM
❑ 3001S	You Got My Mind Messed Up	1968	150.00
❑ 3002S	A Man Needs a Woman	1968	150.00

CARROLL, ANDREA

45s

BIG TOP

Number	Title	Yr	NM
❑ 515	The Doolang/This Time Tomorrow	1964	40.00
❑ 3156	It Hurts to Be Sixteen/ Why Am I So Shy	1963	20.00

EPIC

Number	Title	Yr	NM
❑ 9438	I've Got a Date with Frankie/ Young and Lonely	1961	100.00
❑ 9450	Please Don't Talk to the Lifeguard/Room of Memories	1961	20.00
❑ 9471	Gee Dad/The Charm on My Arm	1961	20.00
❑ 9471 [PS]	Gee Dad/The Charm on My Arm	1961	40.00
❑ 9523	Miss Happiness/Fifteen Shades of Pink	1962	20.00

RCA VICTOR

Number	Title	Yr	NM
❑ 47-8618	Mr. Music Man/Sally Fool	1965	20.00

UNITED ARTISTS

Number	Title	Yr	NM
❑ 982	The World Isn't Big Enough/She Gets Everything She Wants	1966	20.00
❑ 50039	Hey, Beach Boy/Why Should We Take the Easy Way Out	1966	30.00

CARROLL, ANDREA /BEVERLY WARREN

Also see each artist's individual listings.

Albums

B.T. PUPPY

Number	Title	Yr	NM
❑ BTS-1017	Andrea Carroll and Beverly Warren Side By Side	1971	150.00

CARROLL, BERNADETTE

45s

JULIA

Number	Title	Yr	NM
❑ 1106	My Heart Stood Still/ Sweet Sugar Sweet	1962	15.00

LAURIE

Number	Title	Yr	NM
❑ 3217	Nicky/All the Way Home I Cried	1964	15.00
—The Four Seasons sing backup on this record			
❑ 3238	Party Girl/I Don't Wanna Know	1964	15.00
❑ 3268	Happy Birthday/Ho mecoming Party	1964	15.00
❑ 3278	The Hero/One Little Lie	1964	15.00
❑ 3311	Circus Girl/Don't Hurt Me	1965	15.00
❑ 3320	He's Just a Playboy/ Try Your Luck	1965	15.00

CARROLL, DAVID

45s

MERCURY

Number	Title	Yr	NM
❑ C-30004X45	Melody of Love/La Golondrina	1957	7.00
—"Celebrity Series" reissue			
❑ C-30005X45	Buck Dance/Gadabout	1957	7.00
—"Celebrity Series" reissue			
❑ C-30006X45	Fancy Pants/In a Little Spanish Town	1957	7.00
—"Celebrity Series" reissue			
❑ 70247X45	Gadabout/Caribbean	1953	12.00
❑ 70292X45	Fancy Pants/By Heck	1953	12.00
❑ 70335X45	Buck Dance/Stomp and Whistle	1954	12.00
❑ 70412X45	Grandpa's Rocker/Mine	1954	12.00
❑ 70444X45	In a Little Spanish Town/ Bumpty-Bump	1954	12.00
❑ 70516X45	Melody of Love/La Golondrina	1954	12.00
❑ 70521X45	Melody of Love (With Narration)/(Instrumental)	1955	12.00
❑ 70583X45	Two Timin' Gal/Cecelia	1955	10.00
❑ 70606X45	Till We Meet Again/ The Blue Scarecrow	1955	10.00
❑ 70613X45	The Cuddlin' Song/Scatterbrain	1955	10.00
❑ 70642X45	Alabama Jubilee/Baffi	1955	10.00
❑ 70658X45	The Girl Upstairs/ You're Here My Love	1955	10.00
❑ 70680X45	Red Petticoats/Twin 88 Boogie	1955	10.00
❑ 70717X45	It's Almost Tomorrow/ You Are Mine	1955	10.00
❑ 70822X45	The Little Ballerina/ The Beautiful Girls of Vienna	1956	10.00
❑ 70860X45	Theme from The Swan/ Miss Powder Puff	1956	10.00
❑ 70871X45	Once Upon a Dream/ May in Monaco	1956	10.00
❑ 70896X45	Marimba Charleston/Whispering	1956	10.00
❑ 70907X45	Hell's Bells/Cricket	1956	10.00
❑ 70952X45	Love Theme from "Giant"/ By the Fountains of Rome	1956	10.00
❑ 71000X45	Armen's Theme/Yearning	1956	10.00
❑ 71053X45	Cuddle Up a Little Closer/ Li'l Steel Band	1957	10.00
❑ 71069X45	The Ship That Never Sailed/ I Love You Truly	1957	10.00
—With Franklyn MacCormack as narrator			
❑ 71152X45	Fascination/ Swingin' Sweethearts	1957	10.00
❑ 71226X45	A Beautiful Lady in Blue/ The Ski Song	1957	10.00
❑ 71307X45	Ducky/Do You Ever Think of Me?	1958	8.00
❑ 71335X45	Glow-Worm/Let's Dance	1958	8.00
❑ 71362X45	Live a Little/Have You Ever Been Lonely	1958	8.00
❑ 71459X45	Bouncing Ball/Doodlin' Drummer	1959	8.00
❑ 71535X45	Waltzing Matilda/ Sometimes I'm Happy	1959	8.00
❑ 71620	In a Little Spanish Town Cha Cha/Third Man Theme	1960	8.00
❑ 71703	Midnight Lace/Juke Box Jingle	1960	8.00
❑ 71759	By Heck Cha Cha Cha/ Everything's Coming Up Roses	1961	8.00
❑ 71880	Bonita/Mexican Joe	1961	8.00
❑ 71917	The White Rose of Athens/ Theme from Slaughter on Tenth Avenue	1962	7.00
❑ 71994	Oh Carol/Say Auf Wiederseh'n	1962	7.00
❑ 72046	Jacqueline and Caroline/ Little Pixie	1962	7.00
❑ 72070	Big Girls Don't Cry Limbo/ Linstead Market Limbo	1962	7.00
❑ 72191	The Best Is Yet to Come/ Hallelujah Gathering	1963	7.00
❑ 72218	Dominique/Pamplona	1963	7.00
❑ 72280	For You/Nightmare	1964	7.00
❑ 72353	Gilly Gilly Ossenfeffer Katzenellen Bogen by the Sea/Hey-Ba-Ba-Ree-Bop	1964	7.00

Albums

AMBASSADOR

Number	Title	Yr	NM
❑ S-98051	All Time Great Hits	196?	10.00

MERCURY

Number	Title	Yr	NM
❑ PPS-2000 [M]	Latin Percussion	196?	15.00
❑ PPS-2008 [M]	Percussion Parisienne	196?	15.00
❑ PPS-2022 [M]	All the World Dances	196?	15.00
❑ PPS-6000 [S]	Latin Percussion	196?	20.00
❑ PPS-6008 [S]	Percussion Parisienne	196?	20.00
❑ PPS-6022 [S]	All the World Dances	196?	20.00
❑ MG-20064 [M]	Toe-Tappers	195?	20.00
❑ MG-20086 [M]	Waltzes, Wine and Candlelight	195?	20.00
❑ MG-20109 [M]	Dancer's Delight	195?	20.00
❑ MG-20154 [M]	Shimmering Strings	195?	20.00
❑ MG-20156 [M]	Serenade to a Princess	195?	20.00
❑ MG-20166 [M]	Percussion in Hi-Fi	195?	15.00
❑ MG-20281 [M]	Let's Dance	195?	15.00
❑ MG-20286 [M]	Feathery Feeling	195?	15.00
❑ MG-20301 [M]	Dreams	195?	20.00
❑ MG-20351 [M]	Dance and Stay Young	195?	15.00
❑ MG-20389 [M]	RePercussion	195?	15.00
❑ MG-20411 [M]	Show Stoppers from the Fabulous Fifties	195?	15.00
❑ MG-20470 [M]	Let's Dance Again	195?	15.00
❑ MG-20503 [M]	Solo Encores	195?	15.00
❑ MG-20649 [M]	Let's Dance Dance Dance	196?	15.00
❑ MG-20660 [M]	Mexico and 11 Other Great Hits	196?	15.00
❑ MG-20688 [M]	Let's Dance to the Movie Themes	196?	15.00
❑ MG-20690 [M]	David Carroll Galaxy	196?	15.00
❑ MG-20739 [M]	Let's Dance to America's Waltz Favorites	196?	15.00
❑ MG-20786 [M]	Today's Top Hits	196?	15.00
❑ MG-20846 [M]	Happy Feet	196?	15.00
❑ MG-20867 [M]	Percussion Orientale	196?	15.00
❑ MG-20873 [M]	All the World Dances	196?	15.00
❑ MG-20926 [M]	Music Makes Me Want to Dance!	196?	12.00
❑ MG-20935 [M]	Golden Oldies for Today's Teens	196?	12.00
❑ MG-20955 [M]	Percussion Parisienne	196?	12.00
❑ MG-20962 [M]	House Party Discotheque	196?	12.00
❑ SR-60001 [S]	Let's Dance	1959	20.00
❑ SR-60003 [S]	Percussion in Hi-Fi	1959	20.00
❑ SR-60026 [S]	Feathery Feeling	1959	20.00
❑ SR-60027 [S]	Dance and Stay Young	1959	20.00
❑ SR-60029 [S]	RePercussion	1959	20.00
❑ SR-60060 [S]	Show Stoppers from the Fabulous Fifties	1959	20.00
❑ SR-60152 [S]	Let's Dance Again	1959	20.00
❑ SR-60180 [S]	Solo Encores	195?	20.00
❑ SR-60649 [S]	Let's Dance Dance Dance	196?	20.00
❑ SR-60660 [S]	Mexico and 11 Other Great Hits	196?	20.00
❑ MG-60688 [S]	Let's Dance to the Movie Themes	196?	20.00
❑ SR-60690 [S]	David Carroll Galaxy	196?	20.00
❑ SR-60739 [S]	Let's Dance to America's Waltz Favorites	196?	20.00
❑ SR-60786 [S]	Today's Top Hits	196?	20.00
❑ SR-60846 [S]	Happy Feet	196?	20.00
❑ SR-60867 [S]	Percussion Orientale	196?	20.00
❑ SR-60873 [S]	All the World Dances	196?	20.00
❑ SR-60926 [S]	Music Makes Me Want to Dance!	196?	15.00
❑ SR-60935 [S]	Golden Oldies for Today's Teens	196?	15.00
❑ SR-60955 [S]	Percussion Parisienne	196?	15.00
❑ SR-60962 [S]	House Party Discotheque	196?	15.00

WING

Number	Title	Yr	NM
❑ MGW-12106 [M]	Dance Date	195?	15.00
❑ MGW-12146 [M]	Contrasts	195?	15.00
❑ MGW-12256 [M]	Waltzes	196?	12.00
❑ SRW-12508 [S]	Contrasts	195?	15.00
❑ SRW-16106 [S]	Dance Date	195?	15.00
❑ SRW-16256 [S]	Waltzes	196?	12.00
❑ SRW-16367	Let's Dance	196?	12.00

CARROLL, DELORES, AND THE FOUR TOPS

Also see THE FOUR TOPS.

45s

CHATEAU

Number	Title	Yr	NM
❑ 2002	Everybody Knows/I Just Can't Keep the Tears from Tumblin' Down	1956	300.00

CARROLL, JIM

Not the same Jim Carroll as the Jim Carroll Band ("People Who Died" in 1981).

45s

A&M

Number	Title	Yr	NM
❑ 1329	On and On/I Don't Know	1972	5.00
❑ 1360	Save Me/I Got Plenty	1972	5.00

Albums

A&M

Number	Title	Yr	NM
❑ SP-4323	Jim Carroll	1971	12.00

CARROLL, JIM, BAND

12-Inch Singles

ATLANTIC

Number	Title	Yr	NM
❑ DMD 573 [DJ]	(No More) Luxuries/Voices	1983	12.00
❑ DMD 593 [DJ]	Sweet Jane (same on both sides)	1983	12.00

45s

ATCO

Number	Title	Yr	NM
❑ 7314	People Who Died/ I Want the Angel	1980	8.00
❑ 7323	Day and Night/Wicked Gravity	1981	8.00

ATLANTIC

Number	Title	Yr	NM
❑ 89687 [DJ]	Sweet Jane (same on both sides)	1984	6.00
—Stock copy may not exist			

Albums

ATCO

Number	Title	Yr	NM
❑ SD 38-132	Catholic Boy	1980	20.00
❑ SD 38-145	Dry Dreams	1982	16.00

ATLANTIC

Number	Title	Yr	NM
❑ 80123	I Write Your Name	1984	15.00

CARROLL, JOHNNY

45s

DECCA

Number	Title	Yr	NM
❑ 29940	Rock and Roll Ruby/ Tryin' to Get to You	1956	150.00
❑ 29941	Wild, Wild Women/ Corrine, Corrina	1956	150.00
❑ 30013	Hot Rock/Crazy, Crazy	1956	150.00

PHILLIPS INT'L.

Number	Title	Yr	NM
❑ 3520	That's the Way I Love/I'll Wait	1957	200.00

SARG

Number	Title	Yr	NM
❑ 144	I'll Think of You/ Stars Come Down	1956	80.00

WARNER BROS.

Number	Title	Yr	NM
❑ 5042	Bandstand Doll/The Swing	1959	30.00
❑ 5080	Lost Without You/Sugar	1959	30.00

Albums

HMG/HIGHTONE

Number	Title	Yr	NM
❑ HT 6602	Texabilly	1997	10.00

The Cars, *Panorama*, Elektra 5E-514, 1980, **$10.**

Number	Title (A Side/B Side)	Yr	NM
CARROLL, RONNIE			
45s			
PHILIPS			
❑ 40110	Say Wonderful Things/ Please Tell Me Your Name	1963	12.00
❑ 40388	Tomorrow/Wait for Me	1966	10.00
CARROLL, WAYNE			
45s			
KING			
❑ 5123	Chicken Out/Cindy Lee	1958	50.00
❑ 5134	Rockin' Chair Momma/ There's Been a Change in Me	1958	50.00
❑ 5146	He Cheated/Wall Around Your Heart	1958	50.00
CARROLL BROTHERS, THE			
45s			
CAMEO			
❑ 140	(My Gal Is) Red Hot/ Dearly Beloved	1959	80.00
❑ 213	Don't Knock the Twist/ Bo Diddley	1962	20.00
❑ 221	Sweet Georgia Brown/Boot It	1962	20.00
FELSTED			
❑ 8550	Movin' Day/I Found You	1959	20.00
Albums			
CAMEO			
❑ C-1015 [M]	College Twist Party	1962	25.00
❑ SC-1015 [S]	College Twist Party	1962	40.00
CARS, THE			
12-Inch Singles			
ELEKTRA			
❑ ED 4963 [DJ]	You Might Think (same on both sides)	1984	10.00
❑ ED 5014 [DJ]	Hello Again (Remix) (LP Version) (Dub)	1984	10.00
❑ ED 5102 [DJ]	Tonight She Comes (same on both sides)	1985	8.00
❑ ED 5120 [DJ]	I'm Not the One (Vocal Remix Version 4:07)/ Heartbeat City (4:31)	1986	15.00
❑ ED 5249 [DJ]	You Are the Girl (same on both sides)	1987	8.00
❑ ED 5264 [DJ]	Coming Up You (same on both sides)	1987	8.00
❑ 66929	Hello Again (3 versions)	1984	15.00
45s			
ELEKTRA			
❑ 45118	Let's Go/My Best Friend's Girl	198?	3.00
—"Spun Gold" series			
❑ 45119	Just What I Needed/ Good Times Roll	198?	3.00
—"Spun Gold" series			
❑ 45491	Just What I Needed/I'm in Touch with Your World	1978	5.00
—Black vinyl			
❑ 45491	Just What I Needed/I'm in Touch with Your World	1978	10.00
—Red vinyl			
❑ 45491 [PS]	Just What I Needed/I'm in Touch with Your World	1978	5.00
❑ 45537	My Best Friend's Girl/ Don't Cha Stop	1978	5.00
❑ 46014	Good Times Roll/All Mixed Up	1979	5.00
❑ 46063	Let's Go/That's It	1979	4.00
❑ 46546	It's All I Can Do/Got a Lot on My Head	1979	4.00
❑ 46546 [PS]	It's All I Can Do/Got a Lot on My Head	1979	6.00
❑ 46580	Double Life/Candy-O	1980	5.00
❑ 47039	Touch and Go/Down Boys	1980	4.00
❑ 47080	Don't Tell Me No/ Don't Go to Pieces	1980	5.00
❑ 47101	Gimme Some Slack/ Don't Go to Pieces	1981	5.00
❑ 47250	Shake It Up/Cruiser	1981	3.00
❑ 47250 [PS]	Shake It Up/Cruiser	1981	3.00
❑ 47433	Since You're Gone/Think It Over	1982	3.00
❑ 47433 [PS]	Since You're Gone/Think It Over	1982	4.00
❑ 47479	Victim of Love/ This Could Be Love	1982	5.00
❑ 65983	You Might Think/Magic	198?	3.00
—"Spun Gold" series			
❑ 65984	Drive/Hello Again	198?	3.00
—"Spun Gold" series			
❑ 65996	Shake It Up/Since You're Gone	198?	3.00
—"Spun Gold" series			
❑ 69427	Strap Me In/Door to Door	1988	3.00
❑ 69432	Coming Up You/Double Trouble	1987	2.00
❑ 69432 [PS]	Coming Up You/Double Trouble	1987	2.00
❑ 69446	You Are the Girl/Ta Ta Wayo Wayo	1987	2.00
❑ 69446 [PS]	You Are the Girl/Ta Ta Wayo Wayo	1987	2.00
❑ 69569	I'm Not the One/Heartbeat City	1986	3.00
❑ 69589	Tonight She Comes/ Just What I Needed	1985	3.00
❑ 69657	Why Can't I Have You/ Breakaway	1985	3.00
❑ 69681	Hello Again/Hello Again (Dub)	1984	3.00
❑ 69706	Drive/Stranger Eyes	1984	3.00
❑ 69724	Magic/I Refuse	1984	3.00
❑ 69744	You Might Think/Heartbeat City	1984	2.00
❑ 69744 [PS]	You Might Think/Heartbeat City	1984	2.00
Albums			
DCC COMPACT CLASSICS			
❑ LPZ-2056	The Cars Greatest Hits	1998	25.00
—Audiophile vinyl			
ELEKTRA			
❑ 6E-135	The Cars	1978	10.00
❑ 5E-507	Candy-O	1979	10.00
—No title and artist listed on front cover (information was on a sticker on the shrink wrap)			
❑ 5E-514	Panorama	1980	10.00
❑ 5E-567	Shake It Up	1981	10.00
❑ 5E-567 [PD]	Shake It Up	1981	40.00
—Promo-only picture disc with blank back			
❑ 5E-567 [PD]	Shake It Up	1981	50.00
—Promo-only picture disc with "KMET-FM" imprinted on back			
❑ 60296	Heartbeat City	1984	8.00
❑ 60296 [DJ]	Heartbeat City	1984	15.00
—Promo-only audiophile pressing on Quiex II vinyl			
❑ 60464	Greatest Hits	1985	10.00
❑ 60747	Door to Door	1987	8.00
❑ R 123334	Candy-O	1979	12.00
—RCA Music Service edition has "The Cars Candy-O" printed on upper left front cover			
❑ R 143650	Heartbeat City	1984	10.00
—RCA Music Service edition			
❑ R 144033	The Cars	1978	12.00
—RCA Music Service edition			
❑ R 153702	Greatest Hits	1985	12.00
—RCA Music Service edition			
❑ R 161593	Door to Door	1987	10.00
—BMG Direct Marketing edition			
NAUTILUS			
❑ NR-14	The Cars	1981	30.00
—Audiophile "Super Disc"			
❑ NR-49	Candy-O	1982	30.00
—Audiophile "Super Disc"			
CARSON, MARTHA			
45s			
CAPITOL			
❑ F1900	Satisfied/Hide Me Rock of Ages	1951	15.00
❑ F1982	Weighed the Balance/ You Sure Do Need Him Now	1952	15.00
❑ F2077	I Wanna Rest/ Old Blind Barnabas	1952	15.00
❑ F2145	Beyond the Shadow/I'm Gonna Walk and Talk with the Lord	1952	15.00
❑ F2180	He Will Set Your Fields on Fire/ When God Dips His Love	1952	15.00
❑ F2252	Fear Not/Cryin' Holy Unto the Lord	1952	15.00
❑ F2342	There's a Higher Power/ Inspiration from Above	1953	15.00
❑ F2477	Ask and You Shall Receive /I Feel It in My Soul	1953	15.00
❑ F2634	Singing on the Other Side/ I've Got a Better Place to Go	1953	15.00
❑ F2740	Lazarus/Bye & Bye	1954	15.00
❑ F2825	I Bowed Down/ He'll Part the Water	1954	15.00
❑ F2969	Christmas Time Is Here/Peace On Earth (At Christmas Time)	1954	15.00
❑ F3045	It's Alright/Counting My Blessings	1955	15.00
❑ 4437	Everything's All Right/ High on the Hill	1960	12.00
RCA VICTOR			
❑ 47-6293	Laugh a Little More/ Let the Light Shine on Me	1955	20.00
❑ 47-6413	David and Goliath/I Want to Rest a Little While	1956	20.00

Except when noted otherwise, VG = 25% of NM, and VG+ = 50% of NM. (Example: VG = $2.00, VG+ = $4.00 and NM = $8.00.)

Number	Title (A Side/B Side)	Yr	NM
❑ 47-6510	Dixieland Roll/Music Drives Me Crazy	1956	20.00
❑ 47-6603	All These Things/ Faith Is the Key	1956	20.00
❑ 47-6724	Get That Golden Key/ He Was There	1956	20.00
❑ 47-6861	Satisfied/Let the Light Shine on Me	1957	15.00
❑ 47-6948	Now Stop/Just Whistle or Call	1957	15.00
SIMS			
❑ 144	Everybody Needs Somebody/ It Takes a Lot of Lovin'	1963	10.00
7-Inch Extended Plays			
CAPITOL			
❑ EAP 1-449	*Satisfied/Cryin' Holy Unto the Lord/I Wanna Rest/I'm Gonna Walk and Talk with My Lord	1954	15.00
❑ EAP 1-449 [PS]	Gospel Songs	1954	15.00
Albums			
CAPITOL			
❑ ST 1507 [S]	Satisfied	1960	30.00
❑ T 1507 [M]	Satisfied	1960	25.00
❑ ST 1607 [S]	A Talk with the Lord	1961	30.00
❑ T 1607 [M]	A Talk with the Lord	1961	25.00
RCA VICTOR			
❑ LPM-1145 [M]	Journey to the Sky	1955	40.00
❑ LPM-1490 [M]	Rock-a My Soul	1957	50.00
SIMS			
❑ LP-100 [M]	Martha Carson	196?	25.00
CARSON, MINDY			
45s			
COLUMBIA			
❑ 4-39879	('Cause I Love You) That's-a Why/Train of Love	1952	15.00
—With Guy Mitchell			
❑ 4-39889	All the Time and Everywhere/ Barrels 'n Barrels of Roses	1952	15.00
❑ 4-39914	Tell Me You're Mine (Per Un Bacio D'amour)/The Chop Boy Song	1953	12.00
❑ 4-39989	Three Red Roses/ I Cry Your Name	1953	12.00
❑ 4-39992	Tell Us Where the Good Times Are/There's Nothing As Sweet As My Baby	1953	12.00
—With Guy Mitchell			
❑ 4-40033	Free Home Demonstration/ Honey-Darlin'	1953	12.00
❑ 4-40057	I Never Let You Cross My Mind/ Darlin', Darlin'	1953	12.00
❑ 4-40129	Music Box/Crazy, Madly, Wildly in Love	1953	12.00
❑ 4-40206	This Above All/Speedy Gonzales	1954	12.00
❑ 4-40276	You Could'a Knocked Me Over/ Only a Bridesmaid	1954	12.00
❑ 4-40347	I Didn't Mean to Hear You/ What Am I Gonna Do	1954	12.00
❑ 4-40438	The Fish/Bring Me Your Love	1955	12.00
❑ 4-40537	Wake the Town and Tell the People/Hold Me Tight	1955	12.00
❑ 4-40573	Memories Are Made of This/ Cryin' for Your Kisses	1955	12.00
❑ 4-40641	You Can't Be True to Two/ My Sweet Watusi	1956	10.00
❑ 4-40728	I Don't Want to Know/ I Took a Stroll in the Park	1956	10.00
❑ 4-40789	Since I Met You Baby/ Goodnight, My Love	1956	10.00
❑ 4-40857	Time's Runnin' Out on Me/Please Take Back Your Introduction	1957	10.00
❑ 4-40923	Sugaree/Time and Tears	1957	10.00
❑ 4-41021	Sweet Georgia Brown/ Water Wheel	1957	10.00
❑ 4-41091	Just My Luck/Hidden in My Heart	1958	10.00
❑ 4-41153	I Was Born/Sentimental Touch	1958	10.00
❑ 4-41221	My Foolish Heart/ Knock on Wood	1958	10.00
JOY			
❑ 236	Wake the Town and Tell the People/When I Fall in Love	1960	15.00
❑ 242	A Little Love (Will Go a Long, Long Way)/You're the End	1960	15.00
RCA VICTOR			
❑ 47-2950	One More Time/Twelve O'Clock and All Is Well	1949	20.00
❑ 47-2980	Song of Surrender/Blame My Absent Minded Heart	1949	20.00
❑ 47-3017	Lonely Girl/You're Different	1949	20.00
❑ 47-3108	Too-Whit! Too-Whoo! (Bring My Loved One to Me)/All the Bees Are Buzzin' 'Round My Honey	1949	20.00
❑ 47-3204	Candy and Cake/ My Foolish Heart	1950	15.00

Number	Title (A Side/B Side)	Yr	NM
❑ 47-3718	Go to Sleep, Go to Sleep, Go to Sleep/Ask Me No Questions	1950	15.00
—With Don Cornell			
❑ 47-3725	Be Mine/Little Darlin', Little Angel	1950	15.00
❑ 47-3801	I Wish, I Wish/I'm Bashful	1950	15.00
❑ 47-3878	You're Not in My Arms Tonight/ The Touch of Your Lips	1950	15.00
❑ 47-3921	A Rainy Day Refrain/Looks Like a Cold, Cold Winter	1950	15.00
❑ 47-3944	If I Were a Bell/Just For a While	1950	15.00
❑ 47-4018	When You Return/Boutenniere	1951	15.00
❑ 47-4039	Button Up Your Overcoat/ Together	1951	15.00
❑ 47-4040	Just a Memory/ Thank Your Father	1951	15.00
❑ 47-4041	You're the Cream in My Coffee/ The Best Things in Life Are Free	1951	15.00
❑ 47-4088	I'm Late/'Twas Brillig	1951	30.00
❑ 47-4119	Got to Find Somebody to Love/ When You and I Were Young Maggie Blues	1951	15.00
❑ 47-4151	Lonely Little Robin/ You Only Want Me When You're Lonesome	1951	15.00
❑ 47-4259	Hangin' Around with You/ Out in the Cold Again	1951	15.00
❑ 47-4454	Be My Life's Companion/ Tuh Pocket	1952	15.00
❑ 47-4457	Dance Me Loose/ Allegheny Fiddler	1952	15.00
❑ 47-4681	Come Out, Come Out, Wherever You Are/Ho Ho	1952	15.00
CARTER, BRENDA			
45s			
MUSICOR			
❑ 1353	Everything's Found a Home with Me But You/ Mama and the Teacher	1969	7.00
❑ 1386	Miss Nosy Brown/ Shadow from Her Eyes	1969	7.00
❑ 1399	Life of Riley's/While You're Forgetting Me	1970	7.00
CARTER, CALVIN			
45s			
VEE JAY			
❑ 419	The Roach/What'd I Say	1962	15.00
❑ 436	Twisting Bones/Crazy Little Mama Twist	1962	15.00
—As "The Cal Carter Singers"			
❑ 439	Mashed Potatoes/Wimoweh	1962	15.00
Albums			
VEE JAY			
❑ LP-1041 [M]	Twist with Calvin Carter	1962	100.00
❑ SR-1041 [S]	Twist with Calvin Carter	1962	150.00
CARTER, CARLENE			
45s			
EPIC			
❑ 38-03952	Heart to Heart/One Way Ticket	1983	4.00
GIANT			
❑ 7-17853	Love Like This/One Tender Night	1995	3.00
❑ 7-17962	Hurricane/One Tender Night	1995	3.00
❑ 7-18006	Rockin' Little Christmas/ The Working Elf Blues	1994	4.00
—B-side by Daron Norwood			
❑ 7-18265	I Love You 'Cause I Want To/ Nowhere Train	1994	4.00
❑ 7-18373	Unbreakable Heart/ Wastin' Time with You	1993	3.00
❑ 7-18527	Every Little Thing/ Long Hard Fall	1993	5.00
REPRISE			
❑ 7-19255	One Love/Easy from Now On	1991	4.00
❑ 7-19398	The Sweetest Thing/ Goodnight Dallas	1991	4.00
❑ 7-19564	Come On Back/The Leavin' Side	1990	4.00
❑ 7-19915	I Fell in Love/Guardian Angel	1990	4.00
WARNER BROS.			
❑ 8576	Never Together But Close Sometimes/Who Needs Words	1978	5.00
❑ 8658	Love Is Gone/Smoke Dreams	1978	5.00
❑ 49083	Do It in a Heartbeat/ Swap-Meet Rag	1979	4.00
❑ 49155	Old Photographs/Two Sides to Every Woman	1980	4.00
Albums			
EPIC			
❑ BFE 38663	C'est C Bon	1983	10.00
WARNER BROS.			
❑ BSK 3204	Carlene Carter	1979	10.00
❑ BSK 3616	Blue Nun	1981	10.00

Number	Title (A Side/B Side)	Yr	NM
CARTER, CARLENE, AND DAVE EDMUNDS			
45s			
WARNER BROS.			
❑ 49572	Baby Ride Easy/ Too Bad About Sandy	1980	4.00
CARTER, CLARENCE			
45s			
ABC			
❑ 12058	Warning/On Your Way Down	1974	4.00
❑ 12094	Everything Comes Up Roses/ A Very Special Love Song	1975	4.00
❑ 12130	I Got Caught/Take It All Off	1975	4.00
❑ 12162	Dear Abby/Love Ain't Here No More	1976	4.00
❑ 12224	Heart Full of Song/All Messed Up	1976	4.00
ATLANTIC			
❑ 2461	I Can't See Myself/ Looking for a Fox	1967	6.00
❑ 2508	Slip Away/Funky Fever	1968	8.00
❑ 2569	Too Weak to Fight/ Let Me Comfort You	1968	6.00
❑ 2576	Back Door Santa/ That Old Time Feeling	1968	8.00
❑ 2605	Snatching It Back/Making Love	1969	6.00
❑ 2642	The Feeling Is Right/You Can't Miss What You Can't Measure	1969	6.00
❑ 2660	Doin' Our Thing/I Smell a Rat	1969	6.00
❑ 2702	Take It Off Him and Put It On Me/A Few Troubles I've Had	1970	6.00
❑ 2726	I Can't Leave Your Love Alone/ Devil Woman	1970	6.00
❑ 2748	Patches/Say It One More Time	1970	6.00
❑ 2774	It's All in Your Mind/Till I Can't Take It Anymore	1970	6.00
❑ 2801	The Court Room/ Getting the Bills	1971	6.00
❑ 2818	Slipped, Tripped, and Fell in Love/I Hate to Love and Run	1971	6.00
❑ 2842	I'm the One/Scratch My Back	1971	6.00
❑ 2875	If You Can't Beat 'Em/ Lonesomest Lonesome	1972	6.00
—With Candi Carter			
FAME			
❑ XW179	Put On Your Shoes and Walk/ I Found Somebody New	1973	5.00
❑ XW250	Sixty Minute Man/Mother-in-Law	1973	5.00
❑ XW330	I'm the Midnight Special/ I Got Another Woman	1973	5.00
❑ XW415	Love's Trying to Come to You/ Heartbreak Woman	1974	5.00
❑ 1010	Tell Daddy/I Stayed Away Too Long	1966	12.00
❑ 1013	Thread the Needle/ Don't Make My Baby Cry	1967	12.00
❑ 1016	Road of Love/She Ain't Gonna Do Right	1967	12.00
❑ 91006	Back in Your Arms/Holdin' Out	1972	5.00
ICHIBAN			
❑ 101	Messin' with My Mind/ I Was in the Neighborhood	1986	3.00
❑ 106	If You Let Me Take You Home/ So You're Leaving Me	1986	3.00
❑ 108	Strokin'/Love Me with Feelin'	1987	8.00
❑ 116	Doctor C.C./I Stayed Away Too Long	1987	3.00
❑ 131	Grandpa Can't Find His Kate/ What'd I Say	1988	3.00
❑ 135	Trying to Sleep Tonight/ (B-side unknown)	1988	3.00
❑ 158	I'm Just Not Good/I'm the Best	1989	3.00
❑ 164	Why Do I Stay Here and Take This Shit fro You/It's a Man Down There	1989	3.00
❑ 213	In Between a Rock and a Hard Place/Dance to the Blues	1990	3.00
❑ 222	Things Ain't Like They Used to Be/Pickin' 'Em Up, Layin' 'Em Down	1990	3.00
❑ 238	I Ain't Leaving, Girl/ If You See My Lady	1991	3.00
❑ 262	"G" Spot/Hot Dog	1992	3.00
❑ 275	Hand Me Down Love/ Let's Get a Quickie	1992	3.00
RONN			
❑ 90	I Couldn't Refuse Your Love/ What Was I Supposed to Do?	1977	5.00
VENTURE			
❑ 130	Jimmy's Disco/Searching	1980	4.00
❑ 141	Let's Burn/If I Stay	1980	4.00
❑ 145	It's a Monster Thang/ If I Were Yours	1981	4.00
❑ 147	Can We Slip Away Again/ If I Were Yours	1981	4.00

Except when noted otherwise, VG = 25% of NM, and VG+ = 50% of NM. (Example: VG = $2.00, VG+ = $4.00 and NM = $8.00.)

7-Inch Extended Plays

ATLANTIC

Number	Title (A Side/B Side)	Yr	NM
❑ EP-1020 [DJ]	Look What I Got/I'd Rather Go Blind//Road of Love/Steal Away	1969	15.00
—Promo only; white label, large hole			
❑ EP-1020 [PS]	The Dynamic Clarence Carter	1969	20.00
❑ EP 1021 [DJ]	Bad News/Soul Deep//I Can't Do Without You/I Smell a Rat	1969	15.00
—Promo only; white label, large hole			
❑ EP 1021 [PS]	Testifyin'	1969	20.00

Albums

ABC

Number	Title (A Side/B Side)	Yr	NM
❑ X-833	Real	1974	15.00
❑ X-896	Loneliness & Temptation	1975	15.00
❑ X-943	A Heart Full of Song	1976	15.00

ATLANTIC

Number	Title (A Side/B Side)	Yr	NM
❑ SD 8192	This Is Clarence Carter	1968	30.00
❑ SD 8199	The Dynamic Clarence Carter	1969	30.00
❑ SD 8238	Testifyin'	1969	30.00
❑ 8267 [M]	Patches	1970	60.00
—Mono is white label promo only; "d/j copy monaural" sticker on stereo cover			
❑ SD 8267 [S]	Patches	1970	30.00
❑ SD 8282	The Best of Clarence Carter	1971	20.00

FAME

Number	Title (A Side/B Side)	Yr	NM
❑ FM-LA186-F	Sixty Minutes	1973	15.00

ICHIBAN

Number	Title (A Side/B Side)	Yr	NM
❑ ICH-1001	Messin' with My Mind	1986	12.00
❑ ICH-1003	Dr. C.C.	1986	12.00
❑ ICH-1016	Hooked on Love	1987	12.00
❑ ICH-1032	Touch of Blues	1988	12.00
❑ ICH-1068	Between a Rock and a Hard Place	1989	12.00
❑ ICH-1116	The Best of Clarence Carter: The Dr.'s Greatest Presciptions	1991	12.00

VENTURE

Number	Title (A Side/B Side)	Yr	NM
❑ VL 1005	Let's Burn	1980	10.00
❑ VL 1009	Mr. Clarence Carter In Person	1981	10.00

CARTER, LYNDA

45s

EPIC

Number	Title (A Side/B Side)	Yr	NM
❑ 8-50569	Toto (Don't It Feel Like Paradise)/Put On a Show	1978	6.00
❑ 8-50624	All Night Long/Put On a Show	1978	6.00

Albums

EPIC

Number	Title (A Side/B Side)	Yr	NM
❑ 35308 [PD]	Portrait	1978	60.00
—Picture disc version			
❑ JE 35308	Portrait	1978	15.00

CARTER, MEL

45s

AMOS

Number	Title (A Side/B Side)	Yr	NM
❑ 132	Everything Stops for a Little While/This Is My Life	1970	6.00
❑ 139	Kiss Tomorrow Goodbye/This Is My Life	1970	6.00

ARWIN

Number	Title (A Side/B Side)	Yr	NM
❑ 123	Sugar/I'm Coming Home	1960	15.00

BELL

Number	Title (A Side/B Side)	Yr	NM
❑ 743	Didn't We/I Pretend	1968	6.00
❑ 775	Another Saturday Night/Coming From You	1969	6.00

CREAM

Number	Title (A Side/B Side)	Yr	NM
❑ 8041	You Changed My Life Again/(B-side unknown)	1980	4.00
❑ 8143	Who's Right, Who's Wrong/I Don't Wanna Get Over You	1981	4.00

DERBY

Number	Title (A Side/B Side)	Yr	NM
❑ 1003	When a Boy Falls in Love/So Wonderful	1963	12.00
❑ 1005	Time of Young Love/Wonderful Love	1963	12.00
❑ 1008	Why I Call Her Mine/After the Party, the Meeting Is Sweeter	1964	12.00

IMPERIAL

Number	Title (A Side/B Side)	Yr	NM
❑ 66052	'Deed I Do/What's On Your Mind	1964	8.00
❑ 66078	I'll Never Be Free/The Richest Man Alive	1964	8.00
❑ 66101	High Noon/I Just Can't Imagine	1965	8.00
❑ 66113	Hold Me, Thrill Me, Kiss Me/Sweet Little Girl	1965	10.00
❑ 66138	(All of a Sudden) My Heart Sings/When I Hold the Hand of the One I Love	1965	8.00
❑ 66148	Love Is All We Need/I Wish I Didn't Love You So	1965	8.00
❑ 66165	Band of Gold/Detour	1966	8.00
❑ 66183	You You You/If You Lose Her	1966	8.00
❑ 66208	Take Good Care of Her/Tar and Cement	1966	8.00
❑ 66228	As Time Goes By/Look to the Rainbow	1966	8.00

LIBERTY

Number	Title (A Side/B Side)	Yr	NM
❑ MLC-1 [DJ]	The Star Spangled Banner (same on both sides)	196?	12.00
—Promo only; "This record is issued by Liberty Records as a Public Service" on label			
❑ 55970	Edelweiss/For Once in My Life	1968	6.00
❑ 55987	Star Dust/Enter Laughing	1967	6.00
❑ 56000	Be My Love/Look Into My Love	1967	6.00
❑ 56015	Excuse Me/The Other Woman	1968	6.00

PRIVATE STOCK

Number	Title (A Side/B Side)	Yr	NM
❑ 45,057	Put a Little Love Away/Dancing for Dimes	1975	4.00
❑ 45,087	My Coloring Book	1976	4.00

ROMAR

Number	Title (A Side/B Side)	Yr	NM
❑ 711	She Is Me/Do Me Wrong, But Do Me	1973	4.00
❑ 714	Treasure of Love/Do Me Wrong, But Do Me	1973	4.00
❑ 716	I Only Have Eyes for You/Treasure of Love	1974	4.00

Albums

AMOS

Number	Title (A Side/B Side)	Yr	NM
❑ 7010	This Is My Life	1971	12.00

DERBY

Number	Title (A Side/B Side)	Yr	NM
❑ LPM-702 [M]	When a Boy Falls in Love	1963	300.00

IMPERIAL

Number	Title (A Side/B Side)	Yr	NM
❑ LP-9289 [M]	Hold Me, Thrill Me, Kiss Me	1965	15.00
❑ LP-9300 [M]	All of a Sudden My Heart Sings	1966	15.00
❑ LP-9319 [M]	Easy Listening	1966	15.00
❑ LP-12289 [S]	Hold Me, Thrill Me, Kiss Me	1965	20.00
❑ LP-12300 [S]	All of a Sudden My Heart Sings	1966	20.00
❑ LP-12319 [S]	Easy Listening	1966	20.00

SUNSET

Number	Title (A Side/B Side)	Yr	NM
❑ SUS-5227	Mel Carter	1968	10.00
❑ SUS-5295	Easy Goin'	1970	10.00

CARTER, SONNY

45s

CARLTON

Number	Title (A Side/B Side)	Yr	NM
❑ 481	Crying Over You/My Lonely Life	1959	—
—Unreleased?			

DOT

Number	Title (A Side/B Side)	Yr	NM
❑ 15921	Crying Over You/My Lonely Life	1959	30.00

KING

Number	Title (A Side/B Side)	Yr	NM
❑ 4739	There Is No Greater Love/Oh Baby	1954	50.00
❑ 4756	It's Strange but True/I Solemnly Swear	1954	50.00

CARTER, WILF See MONTANA SLIM.

CARTER FAMILY, THE

45s

COLUMBIA

Number	Title (A Side/B Side)	Yr	NM
❑ 3-10387	Papa's Sugar/In the Pines (The Longest Train I Ever Saw)	1976	5.00
❑ 3-10502	My Father's Fiddle/My Ship Will Sail	1977	5.00
❑ 4-20920	Fair and Tender Ladies/Foggy Mountain Top	1952	25.00
❑ 4-20974	I Never Will Marry/The Sun's Gonna Shine in My Back Door	1952	25.00
❑ 4-20986	Amazing Grace/Softly and Tenderly	1952	25.00
❑ 4-21184	You Are My Flower/I Ain't Gonna Work Tomorrow	1953	25.00
❑ 4-21233	Love, Oh Crazy Love/Time's a Wastin'	1954	25.00
❑ 4-21316	Are You Afraid to Remember Me/He Went Slippin' Around	1954	25.00
❑ 4-43004	Keep on the Sunny Side/Fair and Tender Ladies	1964	10.00
❑ 4-43235	Farewell/You Win Again	1965	10.00
❑ 4-43579	I Walk the Line/For Lovin' Me	1966	8.00
❑ 4-44136	Once Around the Briar Patch/Bye Bye	1967	8.00
❑ 4-44982	If I Live Long Enough/Break My Mind	1969	8.00
❑ 4-45428	A Song to Mama/One More Summer in Virginia	1971	8.00
❑ 4-45581	Travelin' Minstrel Band/2001 (Ballad to the Future)	1972	7.00
❑ 4-45679	The World Needs a Melody/A Bird with Broken Wings Can't Fly	1972	7.00
—As "The Carter Family with Johnny Cash"			

LIBERTY

Number	Title (A Side/B Side)	Yr	NM
❑ 55501	Fourteen Carat Nothing/Get Up Early in the Morning	1962	12.00

MERCURY

Number	Title (A Side/B Side)	Yr	NM
❑ 870397-7	Dixie Darlin'/Ain't Gonna Work Tomorrow	1988	4.00

Albums

ACME

Number	Title (A Side/B Side)	Yr	NM
❑ LP-1 [M]	All Time Favorites	1960	200.00
❑ LP-2 [M]	In Memory of A.P. Carter	1960	200.00

COLUMBIA

Number	Title (A Side/B Side)	Yr	NM
❑ CL 2319 [M]	The Best of the Carter Family	1965	15.00
❑ CL 2617 [M]	Country Album	1967	25.00
❑ CS 9119 [S]	The Best of the Carter Family	1965	20.00
❑ CS 9417 [S]	Country Album	1967	20.00
❑ KC 31454	Travelin' Minstrel Band	1972	20.00
❑ KC 33084	Three Generations	1974	20.00
❑ KC 34266	Country's First Family	1976	20.00

DECCA

Number	Title (A Side/B Side)	Yr	NM
❑ DL 4404 [M]	A Collection of Favorites by the Carter Family	1963	30.00
❑ DL 4557 [M]	More Favorites by the Carter Family	1964	30.00

LIBERTY

Number	Title (A Side/B Side)	Yr	NM
❑ LRP-3230 [M]	The Carter Family Album	1962	30.00
❑ LST-7230 [S]	The Carter Family Album	1962	40.00

RCA CAMDEN

Number	Title (A Side/B Side)	Yr	NM
❑ ACL1-0047 [R]	My Old Cottage Home	1973	10.00
❑ CAL-586 [M]	The Original and Great Carter Family	1960	15.00
—Two-tone blue label with "RCA Camden" at top			
❑ CAL-586 [M]	The Original and Great Carter Family	1969	10.00
—All-blue label with "RCA" on its side at left and "Camden" straight at right (reissue)			
❑ CAL-2473 [M]	Lonesome Pine Special	1971	12.00
❑ CAS-2554(e) [R]	More Golden Gems from the Original Carter Family	1972	10.00

RCA VICTOR

Number	Title (A Side/B Side)	Yr	NM
❑ LPM-2772 [M]	'Mid the Green Fields of Virginia	1963	40.00
❑ LSP-2772 [R]	'Mid the Green Fields of Virginia	1963	20.00

STARDAY

Number	Title (A Side/B Side)	Yr	NM
❑ SLP-248 [M]	Echoes of the Carter Family	1963	40.00

CARTEY, RIC

45s

ABC-PARAMOUNT

Number	Title (A Side/B Side)	Yr	NM
❑ 10415	Poor Me/Something in My Eye	1963	12.00

NRC

Number	Title (A Side/B Side)	Yr	NM
❑ 503	My Heart Belongs to You/Scratching on the Screen	1959	50.00

RCA VICTOR

Number	Title (A Side/B Side)	Yr	NM
❑ 47-6751	Young Love/Oooh-Eee	1956	80.00
❑ 47-6828	Heart Throb/I Wancha to Know	1957	80.00
❑ 47-6920	Let Me Tell You About Love/Born to Love One Woman	1957	120.00
❑ 47-7011	My Babe/Hello Down Easy	1957	120.00

STARS

Number	Title (A Side/B Side)	Yr	NM
❑ 539	Young Love/Oooh-Eee	1956	150.00

CARTOONE

45s

ATLANTIC

Number	Title (A Side/B Side)	Yr	NM
❑ 2598	Mr. Poor Man/Knik Knak Man	1969	8.00
❑ 2630	Reflections on a Common Theme/Penny for the Sun	1969	6.00

Albums

ATLANTIC

Number	Title (A Side/B Side)	Yr	NM
❑ SD 8219	Cartoone	1969	20.00

CARVETTES, THE

45s

COPA

Number	Title (A Side/B Side)	Yr	NM
❑ 200-1/2	A Lover's Prayer/Never Gonna Leave Me	1959	800.00

CASANOVAS, THE

45s

APOLLO

Number	Title (A Side/B Side)	Yr	NM
❑ 471	That's All/Are You for Real	1955	100.00
❑ 474	It's Been a Long Time/Hush-a-Mecca	1955	150.00
❑ 477	I Don't Want You to Go/Please Be My Love	1955	150.00
❑ 483	My Baby's Love/Sleepy Head Mama	1956	150.00
❑ 519	Please Be Mine/For You and You Alone	1957	100.00
❑ 523	(I Got a) Good Lookin' Baby/You Are My Queen	1957	100.00

Except when noted otherwise, VG = 25% of NM, and VG+ = 50% of NM. (Example: VG = $2.00, VG+ = $4.00 and NM = $8.00.)

C

CASCADES, THE
Probably all the same group.

45s

Number	Title (A Side/B Side)	Yr	NM
ARWIN			
❑ 132	Cheryl's Going Home/Truly Julie's Blues	1966	8.00
❑ 134	Midnight Lace/All's Fair in Love and War	1966	8.00
CANBASE			
❑ 714	I Started a Joke/Sweet America	1972	5.00
CHARTER			
❑ 1018	She Was Never Mine (To Really Lose)/My Best Girl	1964	15.00
❑ 1018	She Was Never Really Mine (To Lose)/My Best Girl	1964	20.00
ERA BACK TO BACK HITS			
❑ 027	Rhythm of the Rain/Harlem Shuffle	197?	5.00
—A-side is a re-recording; B-side by Bob and Earl			
LIBERTY			
❑ 55822	She'll Love Again/I Bet You Won't Stay	1965	10.00
LONDON			
❑ 177	Two-Sided Man/The Woman's A Girl	1972	5.00
PROBE			
❑ 453	Two-Sided Man/Everyone Is Blossoming	1968	8.00
❑ 453 [PS]	Two-Sided Man/Everyone Is Blossoming	1968	15.00
RCA VICTOR			
❑ 47-8206	Cinderella/A Little Like Lovin'	1963	15.00
❑ 47-8268	For Your Sweet Love/Jeannie	1963	12.00
❑ 47-8321	Little Betty Falling Star/Those Were the Good Old Days	1964	15.00
❑ 47-8402	I Dare You to Cry/Awake	1964	12.00
❑ 47-8206 [PS]	Cinderella/A Little Like Lovin'	1963	20.00
RENEE			
❑ 105	Pains in My Heart/One That I Can Spare	19??	20.00
SMASH			
❑ 2083	Hey Little Girl of Mine/Blue Hours	1967	8.00
❑ 2101	Flying on the Ground/Main Street	1967	8.00
UNI			
❑ 55152	Maybe the Rain Will Fall/Naggin' Cries	1969	8.00
❑ 55169	Indian River/Big City Country Boy	1969	8.00
❑ 55200	But For Love/Hazel Autumn Cocoa Brown	1970	8.00
❑ 55231	April, May, June and July/Big Ugly Sky	1970	8.00
VALIANT			
❑ 6021	There's a Reason/Second Chance	1962	25.00
❑ 6026	Rhythm of the Rain/Let Me Be	1962	20.00
❑ 6028	Shy Girl/The Last Leaf	1963	15.00
❑ 6032	I Wanna Be Your Lover/My First Day Alone	1963	15.00
WARNER BROS.			
❑ 7114	Rhythm of the Rain/The Last Leaf	1968	5.00
—"Back to Back Hits" series; originals on green "W7" label			

Albums

Number	Title	Yr	NM
UNI			
❑ 73069	Maybe the Rain Will Fall	1969	25.00
VALIANT			
❑ W 405 [M]	Rhythm of the Rain	1963	150.00
❑ WS 405 [S]	Rhythm of the Rain	1963	300.00

CASEY, AL
Also see DUANE EDDY.

45s

Number	Title (A Side/B Side)	Yr	NM
BLUE HORIZON			
❑ 925	Cookin'/Hot Foot	1962	25.00
DOT			
❑ 15524	A Fool's Blues/Juice	1956	30.00
❑ 15563	Guitar Man/Come What May	1957	40.00
HIGHLAND			
❑ 1002	Got the Teenage Blues/(B-side unknown)	1959	40.00
❑ 1004	Night Beat/The Stinger	1960	25.00
LIBERTY			
❑ 55117	Willa Mae/She Gotta Shake	1957	20.00
MCI			
❑ 1005	Pink Panther/If I Told You	1965	15.00
STACY			
❑ 925	Cookin'/Hot Foot	1962	15.00
❑ 936	Jivin' Around/Doin' the Shotish	1962	15.00
❑ 950	Laughin'/Chicken Feathers	1962	15.00
❑ 956	Doin' It/Monte Carlo	1963	15.00
❑ 961	Full House/Indian Love Call	1963	15.00
❑ 962	Surfin' Hootenanny/Easy Pickin'	1963	20.00
—Black vinyl			
❑ 962	Surfin' Hootenanny/Easy Pickin'	1963	40.00
—Red vinyl			
❑ 964	Surfin' Blues/Guitars, Guitars, Guitars	1963	15.00
❑ 971	Cookin'/What Are We Gonna Do in '64	1964	15.00
UNITED ARTISTS			
❑ 158	The Stinger/Keep Talking	1959	25.00
❑ 494	Jivin' Around/Doin' the Shotish	1962	25.00

Albums

Number	Title	Yr	NM
STACY			
❑ STM-100 [M]	Surfin' Hootenanny	1963	300.00
❑ STS-100 [S]	Surfin' Hootenanny	1963	400.00
SUNDAZED			
❑ LP-5026	Surfin' Hootenanny	1996	10.00

CASEY, AL (2)

Albums

Number	Title	Yr	NM
MOODSVILLE			
❑ MVLP-12 [M]	The Al Casey Quartet	1960	50.00
—Green label			
❑ MVLP-12 [M]	The Al Casey Quartet	1965	25.00
—Blue label, trident logo at right			
SWINGVILLE			
❑ SVLP-2007 [M]	Buck Jumpin'	1960	50.00
—Purple label			
❑ SVLP-2007 [M]	Buck Jumpin'	1965	25.00
—Blue label, trident logo at right			

CASH, ALVIN

45s

Number	Title (A Side/B Side)	Yr	NM
CHESS			
❑ 2098	Getaway/Saddle Up	1970	8.00
DAKAR			
❑ 4559	Doin' the Ali Shuffle/The Feeling	1976	5.00
MAR-V-LUS			
❑ 6002	Twine Time/The Bump	1964	15.00
❑ 6005	The Barracuda/Do It One More Time	1965	10.00
❑ 6006	Un-Wind the Twine/The Penguin	1965	10.00
❑ 6009	Boston Monkey/Unwind the Twine	1965	10.00
❑ 6012	The Philly Freeze/No Deposit No Return	1966	10.00
❑ 6014	Alvin's Boo-Ga-Loo/Let's Do Some Good Timing	1966	10.00
❑ 6015	Doin' the Ali Shuffle/Feel So Good	1967	10.00
❑ 6019	Different Strokes for Different Folks/The Change	1967	10.00
SEVENTY-7			
❑ 112	Alvin's Doing His Thing/It's a Party	1972	6.00
❑ 118	Doin' the Creep/Party Time	1972	6.00
SOUND STAGE 7			
❑ 1509	Funky Washing Machine/I Don't Want It	1973	6.00
TODDLIN' TOWN			
❑ 104	Alvin's Bag/Whip It On Me	1968	8.00
❑ 111	Keep On Dancing/(Instrumental)	1968	8.00
❑ 119	Funky '69/Moaning and Groaning	1969	8.00
❑ 124	Poppin' Popcorn/(Instrumental)	1969	8.00
WESTBOUND			
❑ 159	Stone Thing (Part 1)/Stone Thing (Part 2)	1970	8.00

Albums

Number	Title	Yr	NM
MAR-V-LUS			
❑ 1827 [M]	Twine Time	1965	30.00

CASH, BOBBY

45s

Number	Title (A Side/B Side)	Yr	NM
HIT			
❑ 143	Do Wah Diddy Diddy/It Hurts to Be in Love	1964	15.00
—B-side by Bobby Brooks			
KING			
❑ 5844	Mona Lisa/Teen Love	1964	30.00
❑ 5864	Only Make Believe/Run, Fool, Run	1964	30.00
❑ 5894	The Answer to My Dreams/I Don't Need Your Love and Kisses	1964	30.00

CASH, EDDIE

45s

Number	Title (A Side/B Side)	Yr	NM
PEAK			
❑ 1001	Doing All Right/Land of Promises	1958	120.00
❑ 1010	Come On Home/(B-side unknown)	1960	15.00
ROULETTE			
❑ 4380	Stormy Weather/Lonely Island	1961	12.00
TODD			
❑ 1057	Thinkin' Man/Livin' Lovin' Temptation	1960	12.00

CASH, JOE

45s

Number	Title (A Side/B Side)	Yr	NM
HIT			
❑ 17	A Steel Guitar and a Glass of Wine/Playboy	1962	8.00
—B-side by Peggy Gaines			
❑ 47	The Night Has a Thousand Eyes/Loop-De-Loop	1963	8.00
—B-side by Herbert Hunter			

CASH, JOHNNY

12-Inch Singles

Number	Title (A Side/B Side)	Yr	NM
COLUMBIA			
❑ AS 921 [DJ]	Without Love (one-sided)	1980	15.00
—Black B-side has etched autographs of Johnny Cash and Nick Lowe			

45s

Number	Title (A Side/B Side)	Yr	NM
A&M			
❑ 2291	The Death of Me/One More Shot	1980	4.00
—With Levon Helm			
AMERICAN			
❑ 18091	Drive On/Delia's Gone	1994	4.00
CACHET			
❑ 4504	Wings in the Morning/What on Earth	1980	5.00
❑ 4504 [PS]	Wings in the Morning/What on Earth	1980	5.00
COLUMBIA			
❑ 02189	Mobile Bay/The Hard Way	1981	4.00
❑ 02669	The Reverend Mr. Black/Chattanooga City Limit Sign	1982	4.00
❑ 03058	Georgia on a Fast Train/Sing a Song	1982	4.00
❑ 03317	Fair Weather Friends/Ain't Gonna Hobo No More	1982	4.00
❑ 03524	I'll Cross Over Jordan Some Day/We Must Believe in Magic	1983	4.00
❑ 04060	I'm Ragged, But I'm Right/Brand New Dance	1983	4.00
❑ 04227	Johnny 99/New Cut Road	1983	3.00
❑ 04428	That's the Truth/Joshua Gone Barbados	1984	3.00
❑ 04513	The Chicken in Black/The Battle of Nashville	1984	3.00
❑ 04740	They Killed Him/The Three Bells	1985	3.00
—With the Carter Family			
❑ 04860	Crazy Old Soldier/It Ain't Gonna Worry My Mind	1985	3.00
—A-side: Ray Charles and Johnny Cash; B-side: Ray Charles and Mickey Gilley			
❑ 04881	Highwayman/The Human Condition	1985	3.00
—A-side: Willie Nelson/Waylon Jennings/Johnny Cash/Kris Kristofferson; B-side: Nelson, Cash			
❑ 04881 [PS]	Highwayman/The Human Condition	1985	5.00
—A-side: Willie Nelson/Waylon Jennings/Johnny Cash/Kris Kristofferson; B-side: Nelson, Cash			
❑ 05594	Desperadoes Waiting for a Train/The Twentieth Century Is Almost Over	1985	3.00
—A-side: Willie Nelson/Waylon Jennings/Johnny Cash/Kris Kristofferson; B-side: Nelson, Cash			
❑ 05672	I'm Leaving Now/Easy Street	1985	3.00
❑ 08406	Highwayman/Desperadoes Waiting for a Train	1988	3.00
—Waylon Jennings/Willie Nelson/Johnny Cash/Kris Kristofferson; reissue			
❑ 10011	The Junkie and the Juicehead/Crystal Chandeliers and Burgundy	1974	5.00
❑ 10048	Father and Daughter, Father and Son/Don't Take Your Love to Town	1974	5.00
—With Rosey Nix			
❑ 10066	The Lady Came from Baltimore/Lonesome to the Bone	1974	5.00
❑ 10116	My Old Kentucky Home (Turpentine and Dandelion Wine)/Hard Times Comin'	1975	5.00
❑ 10177	Look at Them Beans/All Around Cowboy	1975	5.00
❑ 10237	Texas — 1947/I Hardly Ever Sing Beer Drinking Songs	1975	5.00
❑ 10279	Strawberry Cake/I Got Stripes	1975	5.00
❑ 10321	One Piece at a Time/Go On Blues	1976	5.00
❑ 10381	Sold Out of Flagpoles/Mountain Lady	1976	5.00

Number	Title (A Side/B Side)	Yr	NM
❑ 10424	It's All Over/Ridin' on the Cotton Belt	1976	5.00
❑ 10483	The Last Gunfighter Ballad/ City Jail	1977	5.00
❑ 10587	Lady/Hit the Road and Go	1977	5.00
❑ 10623	After the Ball/Calilou	1977	5.00
❑ 10681	I Would Like to See You Again/ Lately	1978	5.00
❑ 10817	Gone Girl/I'm Alright Now	1978	5.00
❑ 10855	It'll Be Her/It Comes and Goes	1978	5.00
❑ 10888	I Will Rock and Roll with You/ A Song for the Life	1979	5.00
❑ 10961	(Ghost) Riders in the Sky/ I'm Gonna Sit on the Porch and Pick on My Guitar	1979	5.00
❑ 10961 [PS]	(Ghost) Riders in the Sky/ I'm Gonna Sit on the Porch and Pick on My Guitar	1979	6.00
❑ 11103	I'll Say It's True/Cocaine Blues	1979	5.00
❑ 11237	Bull Rider/Lonesome to the Bone	1980	4.00
❑ 11283	Song of a Patriot/She's a Go-er	1980	4.00
❑ 11340	Cold Lonesome Morning/ The Cowboy Who Started the Fight	1980	4.00
❑ 11399	The Last Time/Rockabilly Blues (Texas 1965)	1980	4.00
❑ 11424	Without Love/It Ain't Nothing New Babe	1981	4.00
❑ S7 30427 [S]	I Got Stripes/Five Feet High and Rising	1959	30.00
—"Stereo Seven" single; small hole, plays at 33 1/3 rpm			
❑ S7 30843 [S]	Loading Coal/Slow Rider	1960	30.00
❑ S7 30844 [S]	Lumberjack/Dorrance of Ponchartrain	1960	30.00
❑ S7 30845 [S]	When Papa Played the Dobro/ Going to Memphis	1960	30.00
❑ S7 30846 [S]	Old Doc Brown/Boss Jack	1960	30.00
—The above four are "Stereo Seven" 33 1/3 rpm jukebox singles from set "JS 7-12" and the album "Ride This Train"			
❑ S7 30847 [S]	One More Ride/Run Softly, Blue River	1960	30.00
—"Stereo Seven" 33 1/3 rpm jukebox single from "JS 7-12," but from the album "The Fabulous Johnny Cash"			
❑ 31109 [S]	Seasons of My Heart/ I Couldn't Keep from Crying	1961	30.00
❑ 31110 [S]	My Shoes Keep Walking Back to You/Time Changes Everything	1961	30.00
❑ 31111 [S]	Transfusion Blues/I'd Just Be Fool Enough (To Fall)	1961	30.00
❑ 31112 [S]	I'm So Lonesome I Could Cry/ I Will Miss You When You Go	1961	30.00
❑ S7 31113 [S]	Just One More/Honky Tonk Girl	1961	30.00
—The above five are "Stereo Seven" 33 1/3 rpm jukebox singles from set "JS 7-29" entitled "Now There Was a Song"			
❑ 3-38990	Hey Porter/Big River	1964	30.00
—Jukebox single, small hole, plays at 33 1/3 rpm; rather than the usual rainbow "target" label of Columbia "Stereo Seven" singles, this one has green labels			
❑ 41251	All Over Again/What Do I Care	1958	15.00
❑ 41251 [PS]	All Over Again/What Do I Care	1958	40.00
❑ 41313	Don't Take Your Guns to Town/ I Still Miss Someone	1959	15.00
❑ 41313 [PS]	Don't Take Your Guns to Town/ I Still Miss Someone	1959	40.00
❑ 41371	Frankie's Man, Johnny/ You, Dreamer, You	1959	15.00
❑ 41427	I Got Stripes/Five Feet High and Rising	1959	15.00
❑ 41481	The Little Drummer Boy/ I'll Remember You	1959	15.00
❑ 41481 [PS]	The Little Drummer Boy/ I'll Remember You	1959	40.00
❑ 41618	Seasons of My Heart/ Smiling Bill McCall	1960	15.00
❑ 41707	Second Honemoon/ Honky Tonk Girl	1960	15.00
❑ 41804	Going to Memphis/ Loading Coal	1960	15.00
❑ 41920	Girl in Saskatoon/ Locomotive Man	1960	15.00
❑ 41995	The Rebel-Johnny Yuma/ Forty Shades of Green	1961	12.00
❑ 41995 [PS]	The Rebel-Johnny Yuma/ Forty Shades of Green	1961	25.00
❑ 42147	Tennessee Flat Top Box/ Tall Men	1961	12.00
❑ 42147 [PS]	Tennessee Flat Top Box/ Tall Men	1961	25.00
❑ 42301	The Big Battle/What I've Learned	1962	12.00
❑ 42301 [PS]	The Big Battle/What I've Learned	1962	25.00
❑ 42425	In the Jailhouse Now/ A Little at a Time	1962	12.00
❑ 42425 [PS]	In the Jailhouse Now/ A Little at a Time	1962	25.00
❑ 42512	Bonanza!/Pick a Bale o' Cotton	1962	12.00
❑ 42615	Peace in the Valley/ Were You There	1962	12.00
—With the Carter Family			
❑ 42665	Busted/Send a Picture of Mother	1963	10.00
❑ 42665 [PS]	Busted/Send a Picture of Mother	1963	25.00
❑ 42788	Ring of Fire/I'd Still Be There	1963	10.00
❑ 42788 [DJ]	Ring of Fire (same on both sides)	1963	40.00
—Red vinyl promo			
❑ 42788 [PS]	Ring of Fire/I'd Still Be There	1963	30.00
❑ 42880	The Matador/Still in Town	1963	10.00
❑ 42880 [PS]	The Matador/Still in Town	1963	20.00
❑ 4-42964	Understand Your Man/ Dark as a Dungeon	1964	10.00
❑ 4-42964 [DJ]	Understand Your Man (same on both sides)	1964	40.00
—Red vinyl, white label promo			
❑ 43058	The Ballad of Ira Hayes/ Bad News	1964	10.00
❑ 4-43145	It Ain't Me, Babe/ Time and Time Again	1964	10.00
❑ 4-43145 [DJ]	It Ain't Me, Babe (same on both sides)	1964	40.00
—Red vinyl, white label promo			
❑ 43206	Orange Blossom Special/All of God's Children Ain't Free	1965	8.00
❑ 43313	Mister Garfield/Streets or Laredo	1965	8.00
❑ 43342	The Sons of Katie Elder/ A Certain Kinda Hurtin'	1965	8.00
❑ 43420	Happy to Be with You/ Pickin' Time	1965	8.00
❑ 43496	The One on the Right Is On the Left/Cotton Pickin' Hands	1965	8.00
❑ 43673	Everybody Loves a Nut/ Austin Prison	1966	6.00
❑ 43763	Boa Constrictor/ Bottom of a Mountain	1966	6.00
❑ 43921	You Beat All I Ever Saw/ Put the Sugar to Bed	1966	6.00
❑ 44288	The Wind Changes/Red Velvet	1967	6.00
❑ 44373	Rosanna's Going Wild/Roll Call	1967	6.00
❑ 44373 [PS]	Rosanna's Going Wild/Roll Call	1967	10.00
❑ 44513	Folsom Prison Blues/ The Folk Singer	1968	6.00
❑ 44513 [PS]	Folsom Prison Blues/ The Folk Singer	1968	10.00
❑ 44689	Daddy Sang Bass/He Turned the Water Into Wine	1968	6.00
❑ 44944	A Boy Named Sue/San Quentin	1969	6.00
❑ 45020	Blistered/See Ruby Fall	1969	6.00
❑ 45134	What Is Truth/Sing a Traveling Song	1970	5.00
❑ 45211	Sonday Morning Coming Down/I'm Gonna Try to Be That Way	1970	5.00
❑ 45269	Flesh and Blood/ This Side of the Law	1970	5.00
❑ 45339	Man in Black/Little Bit of Yesterday	1971	5.00
❑ 45393	Singing in Viet Nam Talking Blues/You've Got a New Light Shining	1971	5.00
❑ 45460	Papa Was a Good Man/ I Promise You	1971	5.00
❑ 45534	A Thing Called Love/Daddy	1972	5.00
❑ 45590	Kate/Miracle Man	1972	5.00
❑ 45660	Oney/Country Trash	1972	5.00
❑ 45740	Any Old Wind That Blows/ Kentucky Straight	1972	5.00
❑ 45786	Children/Last Summer	1973	5.00
❑ 45938	Pick the Wildwood Flower/ Diamonds in the Rough	1973	5.00
—With Mother Maybelle and the Carter Family			
❑ 45979	Christmas As I Knew It/ That Christmasy Feeling	1973	5.00
—With Tommy Cash			
❑ 45997	Orleans Parish Prison/ Jacob Green	1974	5.00
❑ 46028	Ragged Old Flag/Don't Go Near the Water	1974	5.00
❑ CS7 56799 [DJ]	Folsom Prison Blues (Live)/ I'll Remember You	2002	6.00
—Promo-only 70th birthday tribute; both tracks previously unreleased; label is a replica of the 1957-58 yellow and black 45 label			
❑ CS7 56799 [PS]	Folsom Prison Blues (Live)/ I'll Remember You	2002	6.00
—Cardboard sleeve			
❑ 60516	The Baron/I Will Dance with You	1981	4.00
❑ 69067	Ragged Old Flag/ I'm Leaving Now	1989	3.00
❑ 73233	America Remains/Silver Stallion	1990	3.00
—Waylon Jennings/Willie Nelson/Johnny Cash/Kris Kristofferson			
❑ 73381	Born and Raised in Black and White/Texas	1990	3.00
—The Highwaymen (Waylon Jennings/Willie Nelson/Johnny Cash/ Kris Kristofferson)			
❑ 73572	American Remains/Texas	1990	3.00
—The Highwaymen (Waylon Jennings/Willie Nelson/Johnny Cash/ Kris Kristofferson)			
EPIC			
❑ 50778	There Ain't No Good Chain Gang/ I Wish I Was Crazy Again	1979	5.00
—Johnny Cash/Waylon Jennings			
LIBERTY			
❑ S7-18486	It Is What It Is/The Devil's Right Hand	1995	3.00
—By The Highwaymen			
MERCURY			
❑ 870010-7	W. Lee O'Daniel (And the Light Crust Dough Boys)/ Letters from Homes	1987	3.00
❑ 870237-7	Cry, Cry, Cry/Get Rhythm	1988	3.00
❑ 870688-7	Tennessee Flat Top Box/That Old Wheel	1988	3.00
—A-side with Hank Williams, Jr.			
❑ 872420-7	Ballad of a Teenage Queen/Get Rhythm	1988	3.00
—With Roseanne Cash and the Everly Brothers			
❑ 874562-7	The Last of the Drifters/Water from the Wells of Home	1989	3.00
—A-side with Tom T. Hall			
❑ 875626-7	Cat's in the Cradle/ I Love You, Love You	1990	3.00
❑ 878292-7	Goin' By the Book/ Beans for Breakfast	1990	3.00
❑ 878710-7	The Greatest Cowboy of Them All/Hey Porter	1990	3.00
❑ 878968-7	The Mystery of Life/ I'm an Easy Rider	1990	3.00
❑ 888459-7	The Night Hank Williams Came to Town/I'd Rather Have You	1987	3.00
❑ 888719-7	Sixteen Tons/The Ballad of Barbara	1987	3.00
❑ 888838-7	Let Him Roll/My Ship Will Sail	1987	3.00
SCOTTI BROS.			
❑ 02803	The General Lee/Duelin' Dukes	1982	4.00
—Narration on B-side: Sorrell Booke			
SMASH			
❑ 884934-7	Sixteen Candles/Rock & Roll (Fais-Do-Do)	1986	4.00
—With Jerry Lee Lewis, Roy Orbison and Carl Perkins			
❑ 888142-7	We Remember the King/ Class of '55	1987	4.00
—With Jerry Lee Lewis, Roy Orbison and Carl Perkins; B-side by Carl Perkins solo			
SUN			
❑ 7-36/39	Folsom Prison Blues/ I Walk the Line	1969	20.00
—"Premium" on label; possibly a giveaway with specially marked packages of Dr Pepper soda			
❑ 221	Hey Porter/Cry, Cry, Cry	1955	40.00
❑ 232	Folsom Prison Blues/ So Doggone Lonesome	1956	30.00
❑ 241	I Walk the Line/Get Rhythm	1956	40.00
❑ 258	Train of Love/There You Go	1956	30.00
❑ 266	Next in Line/Don't Make Me Go	1957	30.00
❑ 279	Home of the Blues/ Give My Love to Rose	1957	30.00
❑ 283	Ballad of a Teenage Queen/ Big River	1958	25.00
❑ 295	Guess Things Happen That Way/Come In Stranger	1958	25.00
❑ 295 [PS]	Guess Things Happen That Way/Come In Stranger	1958	40.00
❑ 302	The Ways of a Woman in Love/ You're the Nearest Thing to Heaven	1958	25.00
❑ 309	It's Just About Time/Just Thought You'd Like to Know	1958	25.00
❑ 316	Luther Played the Boogie/ Thanks a Lot	1959	20.00
❑ 321	Katy Too/I Forgot to Remember to Forget	1959	20.00
❑ 331	Goodbye Little Darlin'/ You Tell Me	1959	20.00
❑ 334	Straight A's in Love/ I Love You Because	1960	20.00
❑ 343	The Story of a Broken Heart/ Down the Street to 301	1960	20.00
❑ 347	Mean Eyed Cat/Port of Lonely Hearts	1960	20.00
❑ 355	Oh Lonesome Me/Life Goes On	1961	20.00
❑ 363	Sugartime/My Treasurer	1961	20.00
❑ 376	Born to Lose/Blue Train	1962	20.00
❑ 392	Wide Open Road/Belshazar	1964	20.00
❑ 1103	Get Rhythm/Hey Porter	1969	6.00
❑ 1111	Rock Island Line/Next in Line	1970	6.00
❑ 1121	Big River/Come In Stranger	1971	5.00

7-Inch Extended Plays

Number	Title (A Side/B Side)	Yr	NM
COLUMBIA			
❑ B-2155	The Rebel — Johnny Yuma/ Remember the Alamo//The Ballad of Boot Hill/Lorena	1961	15.00
❑ B-2155 [PS]	The Rebel — Johnny Yuma	1961	15.00
❑ 7-9639	Folsom Prison Blues/The Long Black Veil/I Got Stripes// Cocaine Blues/Jackson/ Dirty Old Egg-Sucking Dog	1968	12.00
—Jukebox issue; small hole, plays at 33 1/3 rpm			
❑ 7-9639 [PS]	Johnny Cash at Folsom Prison	1968	12.00

Except when noted otherwise, VG = 25% of NM, and VG+ = 50% of NM. (Example: VG = $2.00, VG+ = $4.00 and NM = $8.00.)

Number	Title (A Side/B Side)	Yr	NM
❑ 7-9943	I've Got a Thing About Trains/Wrinkled, Crinkled Wadded Dollar Bill/Southwind//To Beat the Devil/Sing a Traveling Song	1970	12.00
—Jukebox issue; small hole, plays at 33 1/3 rpm			
❑ 7-9943 [PS]	Hello, I'm Johnny Cash	1970	12.00
❑ B-12531	Run Softly, Blue River/That's All Over//I Still Miss Someone/Supper-Time	1958	12.00
❑ B-12531 [PS]	The Fabulous Johnny Cash, Vol. I	1958	12.00
❑ B-12532	Frankie's Man, Johnny/The Troubadour//Don't Take Your Guns to Town/That's Enough	1958	12.00
❑ B-12532 [PS]	The Fabulous Johnny Cash, Vol. II	1958	12.00
❑ B-12533	I'd Rather Die Young/One More Ride//Pickin' Time/Shepherd of My Heart	1958	12.00
❑ B-12533 [PS]	The Fabulous Johnny Cash, Vol. III	1958	12.00
❑ B-12841	It Was Jesus/I Saw a Man//Are All the Children In?/The Old Account	1959	12.00
❑ B-12841 [PS]	Hymns by Johnny Cash, Vol. I	1959	12.00
❑ B-12842	Lead Me Gently Home/Swing Low, Sweet Chariot//Snow in His Hair/Lead Me Father	1959	12.00
❑ B-12842 [PS]	Hymns by Johnny Cash, Vol. II	1959	12.00
❑ B-12843	I Call Him/These Things Shall Pass//He'll Be a Friend/God Will	1959	12.00
❑ B-12843 [PS]	Hymns by Johnny Cash, Vol. III	1959	12.00
❑ B-13391	*Drink to Me/Five Feet High and Rising/The Man on the Hill/Hank and Joe and Me	1959	12.00
❑ B-13391 [PS]	Songs of Our Soil, Vol. I	1959	12.00
❑ B-13392	*Grandfather's Clock/It Could Be You (Instead of Him)/Old Apache Squaw/Don't Step on Mother's Roses	1959	12.00
❑ B-13392 [PS]	Songs of Our Soil, Vol. II	1959	12.00
❑ B-13393	Old Apache Squaw/Don't Step on Mother's Roses//My Grandfather's Clock/It Could Be You	1959	12.00
❑ B-13393 [PS]	Songs of Our Soil, Vol. III	1959	12.00
❑ B-14631	Seasons of My Heart/I Feel Better All Over//I Couldn't Keep from Crying/Time Changes Everything	1960	12.00
❑ B-14631 [PS]	Now, There Was a Song, Vol. I	1960	12.00
❑ B-14632	My Shoes Just Keep Walking Back to You/I'd Just Be Fool Enough (To Fall)//Transfusion Blues/Why Do You Punish Me	1960	12.00
❑ B-14632 [PS]	Now, There Was a Song, Vol. II	1960	12.00
❑ B-14633	I Will Miss You When You Go/I'm So Lonesome I Could Cry//Just One More/Honky Tonk Girl	1960	12.00
❑ B-14633 [PS]	Now, There Was a Song, Vol. III	1960	12.00
❑ OBS-81221	Don't Take Your Guns to Town/That's Enough//Frankie's Man Johnny/The Troubadour	1959	40.00
—Stereo EP with large hole			
❑ OBS-81221 [PS]	The Fabulous Johnny Cash	1959	40.00

SUN

Number	Title (A Side/B Side)	Yr	NM
❑ EPA-111	I Can't Help It/You Win Again//Hey Good Lookin'/I Could Never Be Ashamed	1956	40.00
❑ EPA-111 [PS]	Johnny Cash Sings Hank Williams	1956	60.00
❑ EPA-112	Rock Island Line/I Heard That Lonesome Whistle//Country Boy/If the Good Lord's Willin'	1956	30.00
❑ EPA-112 [PS]	Country Boy	1956	50.00
❑ EPA-113	I Walk the Line/The Wreck of the Old '97//Folsom Prison Blues/Doin' My Time	1958	30.00
❑ EPA-113 [PS]	I Walk the Line	1958	50.00
❑ EPA-114	The Ways of a Woman in Love/Next in Line//Guess Things Happen That Way/Train of Love	1958	30.00
❑ EPA-114 [PS]	His Top Hits	1958	50.00
❑ SEP-116	You're the Nearest Thing to Heaven/I Can't Help It//Home of the Blues/Big River	1959	30.00
❑ SEP-116 [PS]	Home of the Blues	1959	50.00
❑ SEP-117	So Doggone Lonesome/I Was There When It Happened//Cry, Cry, Cry/Remember Me	1958	30.00
❑ SEP-117 [PS]	Johnny Cash	1958	50.00

Albums

ACCORD

Number	Title (A Side/B Side)	Yr	NM
❑ SN-7134	I Walk the Line	1983	10.00
❑ SN-7208	Years Gone By	1983	10.00

ALLEGIANCE

Number	Title (A Side/B Side)	Yr	NM
❑ AV-5017	The First Years	1986	10.00

AMERICAN

Number	Title (A Side/B Side)	Yr	NM
❑ B0002769-01	American V: A Hundred Highways	2006	12.00
❑ 43097	Unchained	1996	120.00
❑ 45520	American Recordings	1994	80.00
❑ 440-063336-1 [(2)]	American IV: The Man Comes Around	2002	20.00

ARCHIVE OF FOLK MUSIC

Number	Title (A Side/B Side)	Yr	NM
❑ 278	Johnny Cash	198?	12.00

CACHET

Number	Title (A Side/B Side)	Yr	NM
❑ 9001	A Believer Sings the Truth	1979	15.00

COLUMBIA

Number	Title (A Side/B Side)	Yr	NM
❑ GP 29 [(2)]	The World of Johnny Cash	1970	15.00
❑ C2L 38 [(2)M]	Ballads of the True West	1965	25.00
❑ C2S 838 [(2)S]	Ballads of the True West	1965	25.00
❑ CL 1253 [M]	The Fabulous Johnny Cash	1958	20.00
❑ CL 1284 [M]	Hymns by Johnny Cash	1959	25.00
❑ CL 1339 [M]	Songs of Our Soil	1959	25.00
❑ CL 1463 [M]	Now, There Was a Song!	1960	25.00
❑ CL 1464 [M]	Ride This Train	1960	25.00
❑ CL 1622 [M]	The Lure of the Grand Canyon	1961	40.00
—Cash narrates; with Andre Kostelanetz and His Orchestra			
❑ CL 1722 [M]	Hymns from the Heart	1962	20.00
❑ CL 1802 [M]	The Sound of Johnny Cash	1962	20.00
❑ CL 1930 [M]	Blood, Sweat & Tears	1963	20.00
❑ STS 2004 [(2)]	The Heart of Johnny Cash	196?	20.00
—"Columbia Star Series" release; has "360 Sound" labels			
❑ CL 2052 [M]	Ring of Fire (The Best of Johnny Cash)	1963	20.00
❑ CL 2117 [M]	The Christmas Spirit	1963	25.00
❑ CL 2190 [M]	I Walk the Line	1964	15.00
❑ CL 2248 [M]	Bitter Tears (Ballads of the American Indian)	1964	15.00
❑ CL 2309 [M]	Orange Blossom Special	1965	15.00
❑ CL 2446 [M]	Mean as Hell	1965	15.00
❑ CL 2492 [M]	Everybody Loves a Nut	1966	15.00
❑ CL 2537 [M]	That's What You Get for Lovin' Me	1966	15.00
❑ CL 2647 [M]	From Sea to Shining Sea	1967	20.00
❑ CL 2678 [M]	Johnny Cash's Greatest Hits, Vol. 1	1967	20.00
❑ CL 2839 [M]	Johnny Cash at Folsom Prison	1968	150.00
—Red label with "Mono" at bottom; this is a stock copy			
❑ CS 8122 [S]	The Fabulous Johnny Cash	1959	40.00
❑ CS 8125 [S]	Hymns by Johnny Cash	1959	40.00
❑ CS 8148 [S]	Songs of Our Soil	1959	40.00
❑ CS 8254 [S]	Now, There Was a Song!	1960	40.00
❑ CS 8255 [S]	Ride This Train	1960	40.00
❑ CS 8255 [S]	Ride This Train	197?	10.00
—Reissue on orange label			
❑ CS 8422 [S]	The Lure of the Grand Canyon	1961	50.00
—Cash narrates; with Andre Kostelanetz and His Orchestra			
❑ CS 8522 [S]	Hymns from the Heart	1962	30.00
❑ CS 8602 [S]	The Sound of Johnny Cash	1962	30.00
❑ CS 8730 [S]	Blood, Sweat & Tears	1963	25.00
❑ CS 8852 [S]	Ring of Fire (The Best of Johnny Cash)	1963	25.00
❑ CS 8917 [S]	The Christmas Spirit	1963	30.00
❑ CS 8990 [S]	I Walk the Line	1964	20.00
❑ CS 9048 [S]	Bitter Tears (Ballads of the American Indian)	1964	20.00
❑ CS 9109 [S]	Orange Blossom Special	1965	20.00
❑ CS 9246 [S]	Mean as Hell	1965	20.00
❑ CS 9292 [S]	Everybody Loves a Nut	1966	20.00
❑ CS 9337 [S]	That's What You Get for Lovin' Me	1966	20.00
❑ CS 9447 [S]	From Sea to Shining Sea	1967	20.00
❑ CS 9478 [S]	Johnny Cash's Greatest Hits, Vol. 1	1967	20.00
❑ CS 9639 [M]	Johnny Cash at Folsom Prison	1968	50.00
—White label promo with stereo number; "Special Mono Radio Station Copy" sticker on cover			
❑ CS 9639 [S]	Johnny Cash at Folsom Prison	1968	20.00
—Red label with "360 Sound Stereo" at bottom			
❑ KCS 9726	The Holy Land	1969	15.00
❑ CS 9827	Johnny Cash at San Quentin	1969	12.00
❑ KCS 9943	Hello, I'm Johnny Cash	1970	12.00
❑ C 30100	The Johnny Cash Show	1970	12.00
❑ S 30397	I Walk the Line	1970	12.00
—Soundtrack from movie			
❑ KC 30550	Man in Black	1971	12.00
❑ KC 30887	The Johnny Cash Collection (His Greatest Hits, Vol. II)	1971	12.00
❑ CQ 30961 [Q]	Johnny Cash at San Quentin	1971	20.00
❑ KC 31256	Give My Love to Rose	1972	12.00
❑ KC 31332	A Thing Called Love	1972	12.00
❑ KC 31645	Johnny Cash: America (A 200-Year Salute in Story and Song)	1972	12.00
❑ KC 32091	Any Old Wind That Blows	1973	12.00
❑ C 32240	Sunday Morning Coming Down	1973	12.00
❑ C 32253	The Gospel Road	1973	12.00
❑ CG 32253 [(2)]	The Gospel Road	1973	25.00
❑ KC 32898	Children's Album	1974	12.00
❑ C 32917	The Ragged Old Flag	1974	12.00
❑ C 32951	Five Feet High and Rising	1974	12.00
❑ KC 33086	The Junkie and the Juicehead	1974	12.00
❑ C 33087	Johnny Cash Sings Precious Memories	1974	12.00
❑ KC 33370	John R. Cash	1975	12.00
❑ CG 33639 [(2)]	Johnny Cash at Folsom Prison/Johnny Cash at San Quentin	1974	15.00
❑ KC 33814	Look at Them Beans	1975	12.00
❑ KC 34088	Strawberry Cake	1976	12.00
❑ KC 34193	One Piece at a Time	1976	12.00
❑ JC 34314	The Last Gunfighter Ballad	1977	12.00
❑ JC 34833	The Rambler	1977	12.00
❑ KC 35313	I Would Like to See You Again	1978	10.00
❑ JC 35637	Johnny Cash's Greatest Hits, Vol. 3	1978	12.00
❑ KC 35646	Gone Girl	1978	12.00
❑ JC 36086	Silver	1979	12.00
❑ JC 36779	Rockabilly Blues	1980	10.00
❑ JC 36866	Classic Christmas	1980	12.00
❑ FC 37179	The Baron	1981	10.00
❑ FC 37355	Encore	1981	10.00
❑ PC 38074	A Believer Sings the Truth	1985	8.00
—Reissue of Priority 38074			
❑ FC 38094	The Adventures of Johnny Cash	1982	10.00
❑ FC 38317	Johnny Cash's Biggest Hits	1982	10.00
❑ FC 38696	Johnny 99	1983	10.00
❑ PC 38696	Johnny 99	1986	8.00
—Budget-line reissue			
❑ FC 39951	Rainbow	1985	10.00
❑ FC 40056	Highwayman	1985	10.00
—Waylon Jennings/Willie Nelson/Johnny Cash/Kris Kristofferson			
❑ C 45240	Highwayman 2	1990	15.00
—Waylon Jennings/Willie Nelson/Johnny Cash/Kris Kristofferson			

COLUMBIA LIMITED EDITION

Number	Title (A Side/B Side)	Yr	NM
❑ LE 10063 [S]	The Fabulous Johnny Cash	197?	15.00
—Reissue of 8122			

COLUMBIA SPECIAL PRODUCTS

Number	Title (A Side/B Side)	Yr	NM
❑ 363	Legends and Love Songs	196?	20.00
❑ P 13043	Destination Victoria Station	1977	40.00
—Alternate number is "VS 150"			
❑ P 13832	Hello, I'm Johnny Cash	1977	12.00

DORAL/CSP

Number	Title (A Side/B Side)	Yr	NM
❑ (# unknown)	Doral Presents Johnny Cash	1972	40.00
—Mail-order offer from Doral cigarettes			

EVEREST

Number	Title (A Side/B Side)	Yr	NM
❑ 276	Johnny Cash	19??	12.00

HARMONY

Number	Title (A Side/B Side)	Yr	NM
❑ HS 11249	Golden Sounds of Country Music	1968	12.00
❑ HS 11342	Johnny Cash	1969	12.00
❑ KH 30138	The Walls of a Prison	1970	12.00
❑ KH 30916	Understand Your Man	1971	12.00
❑ KH 31602	The Johnny Cash Songbook	1972	12.00
❑ KH 32388	Ballads of the American Indian	1973	12.00

MERCURY

Number	Title (A Side/B Side)	Yr	NM
❑ 832031-1	Johnny Cash Is Coming to Town	1987	10.00
❑ 834778-1	Water from the Wells of Home	1988	10.00

MUSIC WORLD ENTERTAINMENT

Number	Title (A Side/B Side)	Yr	NM
❑ CR 9295121 [(2)]	Johnny Cash Remixed	2008	30.00

PAIR

Number	Title (A Side/B Side)	Yr	NM
❑ PDL2-1107 [(2)]	Classic Cash	1986	15.00

POWER PAK

Number	Title (A Side/B Side)	Yr	NM
❑ 246	Country Gold	198?	10.00

PRIORITY

Number	Title (A Side/B Side)	Yr	NM
❑ UG 32253 [(2)]	The Gospel Road	1981	15.00
—Reissue of Columbia album of the same name			
❑ PU 33087	Johnny Cash Sings Precious Memories	1982	12.00
—Reissue of Columbia album of the same name			
❑ PU 38074	A Believer Sings the Truth	1982	12.00
—Reissue of Cachet album			

RHINO

Number	Title (A Side/B Side)	Yr	NM
❑ RNLP 70229	The Vintage Years	1987	12.00

SHARE

Number	Title (A Side/B Side)	Yr	NM
❑ 5000	I Walk the Line	197?	12.00
❑ 5001	Folsom Prison Blues	197?	12.00
❑ 5002	The Blue Train	197?	12.00
❑ 5003	Johnny Cash Sings the Greatest Hits	197?	12.00

SUN

Number	Title (A Side/B Side)	Yr	NM
❑ LP-100	Original Golden Hits, Vol. I	1969	12.00
❑ LP-101	Original Golden Hits, Vol. II	1969	12.00
❑ LP-104	Story Songs of the Trains and Rivers	1969	12.00
❑ LP-105	Get Rhythm	1969	12.00
❑ LP-106	Showtime	1969	12.00
❑ LP-115	The Singing Story Teller	1970	12.00
❑ LP-118 [(2)]	Johnny Cash — The Legend	1970	20.00

Number	Title (A Side/B Side)	Yr	NM
❑ LP-122	The Rough Cut King of Country Music	1971	12.00
❑ LP-126 [(2)]	Johnny Cash: The Man, The World, His Music	1971	20.00
❑ LP-127	Original Golden Hits, Vol. III	1972	12.00
❑ LP-139	I Walk the Line	1979	10.00
❑ LP-140	Folsom Prison Blues	1979	10.00
❑ LP-141	The Blue Train	1979	10.00
❑ LP-142	Johnny Cash Sings the Greatest Hits	1979	10.00
❑ 1002	Superbilly (1955-58)	198?	10.00
❑ 1006	The Original Johnny Cash	1980	10.00
❑ SLP-1220 [M]	Johnny Cash with His Hot and Blue Guitar	1956	100.00
❑ SLP-1220 [R]	Johnny Cash with His Hot and Blue Guitar	196?	20.00
—Reissue in rechanneled stereo; front cover says "STEREO"			
❑ SLP-1235 [M]	The Songs That Made Him Famous	1958	100.00
❑ SLP-1235 [R]	The Songs That Made Him Famous	196?	20.00
—Reissue in rechanneled stereo; front cover says "STEREO"			
❑ SLP-1240 [M]	Johnny Cash's Greatest!	1959	50.00
❑ SLP-1245 [M]	Johnny Cash Sings Hank Williams	1960	50.00
❑ SLP-1245 [R]	Johnny Cash Sings Hank Williams	196?	20.00
—Reissue in rechanneled stereo; front cover says "STEREO"			
❑ SLP-1255 [M]	Now Here's Johnny Cash	1961	50.00
❑ SLP-1255 [R]	Now Here's Johnny Cash	196?	20.00
—Reissue in rechanneled stereo; front cover says "STEREO"			
❑ SLP-1270 [M]	All Aboard the Blue Train	1963	50.00
❑ SLP-1275 [M]	The Original Sun Sound of Johnny Cash	1965	50.00
❑ DT-90668 [R]	The Songs That Made Him Famous	1966	25.00
—Capitol Record Club edition			
❑ T-90668 [M]	The Songs That Made Him Famous	1966	40.00
—Capitol Record Club edition			
❑ DT-90678 [R]	Now Here's Johnny Cash	1966	20.00
—Capitol Record Club edition			
❑ DT-91284 [R]	Johnny Cash Sings Hank Williams	196?	25.00
—Capitol Record Club edition			
❑ T-91284 [M]	Johnny Cash Sings Hank Williams	196?	40.00
—Capitol Record Club edition			
❑ DT-91458 [R]	All Aboard the Blue Train	196?	25.00
—Capitol Record Club edition			
❑ ST-92085	Original Golden Hits, Vol. I	1969	20.00
—Capitol Record Club edition; uses older Sun label			
❑ ST-92086	Original Golden Hits, Vol. II	1969	20.00
—Capitol Record Club edition; uses older Sun label			
❑ SQBO-93213 [(2)]	The Greatness of Johnny Cash	197?	20.00
—Capitol Record Club exclusive			
SUNDAZED			
❑ LP-5170	Town Hall Party Live! 1958	2003	15.00
—Reissue on 180-gram vinyl			
❑ LP-5171	Town Hall Party Live! 1959	2003	15.00
—Reissue on 180-gram vinyl			
❑ LP-5176	Blood, Sweat & Tears	2003	15.00
—Reissue on 180-gram vinyl			
TIME-LIFE			
❑ TLCS-3 [(3)]	Country & Western Classics	1982	20.00
❑ STW-108	Country Music	1981	12.00
WORD			
❑ WR-8333	Believe in Him	1986	12.00

CASH, JOHNNY, AND JUNE CARTER

45s

COLUMBIA

Number	Title (A Side/B Side)	Yr	NM
❑ 10436	Old Time Feeling/Far Side Banks of Jordan	1976	5.00
❑ 44011	Jackson/Pack Up Your Sorrows	1967	6.00
❑ 44158	Long-Legged Guitar Pickin' Man/You'll Be All Right	1967	6.00
❑ 45064	If I Were a Carpenter/ 'Cause I Love You	1970	5.00
❑ 45431	No Need to Worry/ I'll Be Loving You	1971	5.00
❑ 45631	If I Had a Hammer/I Gotta Go	1972	5.00
❑ 45758	The Loving Gift/Help Me Make It Through the Night	1973	5.00
❑ 45890	Praise the Lord and Pass the Soup/The Ballad of Barbara	1973	5.00
❑ 45929	Allegheny/We're for Love	1973	5.00

Albums

COLUMBIA

Number	Title (A Side/B Side)	Yr	NM
❑ CL 2728 [M]	Carryin' On with Johnny Cash and June Carter	1967	20.00
❑ CS 9528 [S]	Carryin' On with Johnny Cash and June Carter	1967	20.00
❑ KC 32443	Johnny Cash and His Woman	1973	15.00

CASH, JOHNNY, AND WAYLON JENNINGS

Also see each artist's individual listings.

45s

COLUMBIA

Number	Title (A Side/B Side)	Yr	NM
❑ 05896	Even Cowgirls Get the Blues/ American by Birth	1986	3.00
❑ 06287	The Ballad of $40/ Field of Diamonds	1986	3.00
❑ 10742	There Ain't No Good Chain Gang/ I Wish I Was Crazy Again	1978	5.00

CASH, JOHNNY/TAMMY WYNETTE

Albums

COLUMBIA MUSICAL TREASURIES

Number	Title (A Side/B Side)	Yr	NM
❑ DS 608 [(2)]	The King/The Queen	1969	15.00
—One record by Johnny Cash, the other by Tammy Wynette			
❑ P4S 5376 [(4)]	The King/The Queen	1969	25.00
—Box set; two records by Johnny Cash, two records by Tammy Wynette; records are individually numbered from DS 562 through DS 565			

CASHMAN, TERRY

Also see BUCHANAN BROTHERS; CASHMAN AND WEST; CASHMAN, PISTILLI AND WEST.

45s

BOOM

Number	Title (A Side/B Side)	Yr	NM
❑ 60005	Try Me/Pretty Face	1966	15.00
LIFESONG			
❑ 45015	Baby, Baby I Love You/ We'll Be Together	1976	4.00
❑ 45021	The Dreamer/Football U.S.A.	1977	4.00
❑ 45086	Willie, Mickey and "The Duke" (Talkin' Baseball)/It's So Easy to Sing a Love Song	1980	5.00
❑ 45086 [PS]	Willie, Mickey and "The Duke" (Talkin' Baseball)/It's So Easy to Sing a Love Song	1980	10.00
❑ 45087	Baseball (America's National Pastime)/Willie, Mickey and "The Duke" (Talkin' Baseball)	1981	5.00
❑ 45087 [PS]	Baseball (America's National Pastime)/Willie, Mickey and "The Duke" (Talkin' Baseball)	1981	10.00
❑ 45096	Talkin' Baseball (Philadelphia Phillies Version)/Baby, Baby I Love You	1982	4.00
❑ 45096 [PS]	Talkin' Baseball (Philadelphia Phillies Version)/Baby, Baby I Love You	1982	4.00
—Green "Talkin' Baseball" sleeve with custom sticker			
❑ 45097	Talkin' Baseball (New York Yankees Version)/ Baby, Baby I Love You	1982	4.00
❑ 45097 [PS]	Talkin' Baseball (New York Yankees Version)/ Baby, Baby I Love You	1982	4.00
—Green "Talkin' Baseball" sleeve with custom sticker			
❑ 45098	Talkin' Baseball (Los Angeles Dodgers Version)/ Baby, Baby I Love You	1982	4.00
❑ 45098 [PS]	Talkin' Baseball (Los Angeles Dodgers Version)/ Baby, Baby I Love You	1982	4.00
—Green "Talkin' Baseball" sleeve with custom sticker			
❑ 45099	Talkin' Baseball (Cleveland Indians Version)/ Baby, Baby I Love You	1982	4.00
❑ 45099 [PS]	Talkin' Baseball (Cleveland Indians Version)/ Baby, Baby I Love You	1982	4.00
—Green "Talkin' Baseball" sleeve with custom sticker			
❑ 45100	Talkin' Baseball (Texas Rangers Version)/ Baby, Baby I Love You	1982	4.00
❑ 45100 [PS]	Talkin' Baseball (Texas Rangers Version)/ Baby, Baby I Love You	1982	4.00
—Green "Talkin' Baseball" sleeve with custom sticker			
❑ 45101	Talkin' Baseball (Cincinnati Reds Version)/Baby, Baby I Love You	1982	4.00
❑ 45101 [PS]	Talkin' Baseball (Cincinnati Reds Version)/Baby, Baby I Love You	1982	4.00
—Green "Talkin' Baseball" sleeve with custom sticker			
❑ 45102	Talkin' Baseball (San Francisco Giants Version)/ Baby, Baby I Love You	1982	4.00
❑ 45102 [PS]	Talkin' Baseball (San Francisco Giants Version)/ Baby, Baby I Love You	1982	4.00
—Green "Talkin' Baseball" sleeve with custom sticker			
❑ 45103	Talkin' Baseball (Detroit Tigers Version)/Baby, Baby I Love You	1982	4.00
❑ 45103 [PS]	Talkin' Baseball (Detroit Tigers Version)/Baby, Baby I Love You	1982	4.00
—Green "Talkin' Baseball" sleeve with custom sticker			
❑ 45104CC	Talkin' Baseball (Baseball and the Cubs)/Baby, Baby I Love You	1982	4.00
❑ 45104CC [PS]	Talkin' Baseball (Special Cubs Version)/Baby, Baby I Love You	1982	6.00
—Green "Talkin' Baseball" sleeve with square Chicago Cubs sticker			
❑ 45105	Talkin' Baseball (Baltimore Orioles Version)/Baby, Baby I Love You	1982	4.00
❑ 45105 [PS]	Talkin' Baseball/Baby, Baby I Love You	1982	4.00
—Green "Talkin' Baseball" sleeve with "For Orioles Fans" custom sticker			
❑ 45105 [PS]	Talkin' Baseball (Baltimore Orioles Version)/Baby, Baby I Love You	1982	5.00
—Orange sleeve with photo of Cal Ripken Jr.			
❑ 45106	Talkin' Baseball (Boston Red Sox Version)/Baby, Baby I Love You	1982	4.00
❑ 45106 [PS]	Talkin' Baseball (Boston Red Sox Version)/Baby, Baby I Love You	1982	4.00
—Green "Talkin' Baseball" sleeve with custom sticker			
❑ 45107	Talkin' Baseball (St. Louis Cardinals Version)/ Baby, Baby I Love You	1982	4.00
❑ 45107 [PS]	Talkin' Baseball (St. Louis Cardinals Version)/ Baby, Baby I Love You	1982	4.00
—Green "Talkin' Baseball" sleeve with custom sticker			
❑ 45108	Talkin' Baseball (New York Mets Version)/Baby, Baby I Love You	1982	4.00
❑ 45108 [PS]	Talkin' Baseball (New York Mets Version)/Baby, Baby I Love You	1982	4.00
—Green "Talkin' Baseball" sleeve with custom sticker			
❑ 45109	Talkin' Baseball (Pittsburgh Pirates Version)/Baby, Baby I Love You	1982	4.00
❑ 45109 [PS]	Talkin' Baseball (Pittsburgh Pirates Version)/Baby, Baby I Love You	1982	4.00
—Green "Talkin' Baseball" sleeve with custom sticker			
❑ 45110	Talkin' Baseball (Atlanta Braves Version)/Baby, Baby I Love You	1982	4.00
❑ 45110 [PS]	Talkin' Baseball (Atlanta Braves Version)/Baby, Baby I Love You	1982	4.00
—Green "Talkin' Baseball" sleeve with custom sticker			
❑ 45111	Talkin' Baseball (Kansas City Royals Version)/ Baby, Baby I Love You	1982	4.00
❑ 45111 [PS]	Talkin' Baseball (Kansas City Royals Version)/Baby, Baby I Love You	1982	4.00
—Green "Talkin' Baseball" sleeve with custom sticker			
❑ 45112	Talkin' Baseball (Houston Astros Version)/Baby, Baby I Love You	1982	4.00
❑ 45112 [PS]	Talkin' Baseball (Houston Astros Version)/ Baby, Baby I Love You	1982	4.00
—Green "Talkin' Baseball" sleeve with custom sticker			
❑ 45113	Talkin' Baseball (Milwaukee Brewers Version)/ Baby, Baby I Love You	1982	4.00
❑ 45113 [PS]	Talkin' Baseball (Milwaukee Brewers Version)/ Baby, Baby I Love You	1982	4.00
—Green "Talkin' Baseball" sleeve with custom sticker			
❑ 45114	Talkin' Baseball (Minnesota Twins Version)/ Baby, Baby I Love You	1982	4.00
❑ 45114 [PS]	Talkin' Baseball (Minnesota Twins Version)/ Baby, Baby I Love You	1982	4.00
—Green "Talkin' Baseball" sleeve with custom sticker			
❑ 45115	Talkin' Baseball (Montreal Expos Version)/ Baby, Baby I Love You	1982	4.00
❑ 45115 [PS]	Talkin' Baseball (Montreal Expos Version)/ Baby, Baby I Love You	1982	4.00
—Green "Talkin' Baseball" sleeve with custom sticker			
❑ 45117	Cooperstown (The Town Where Baseball Lives)/ Baseball Ballet	1983	5.00
❑ 45119	The Earl of Baltimore/ Baseball Ballet	1983	4.00
❑ 45121 [DJ]	Football U.S.A. (same on both sides)	1983	4.00
—May be promo only			

Except when noted otherwise, VG = 25% of NM, and VG+ = 50% of NM. (Example: VG = $2.00, VG+ = $4.00 and NM = $8.00.)

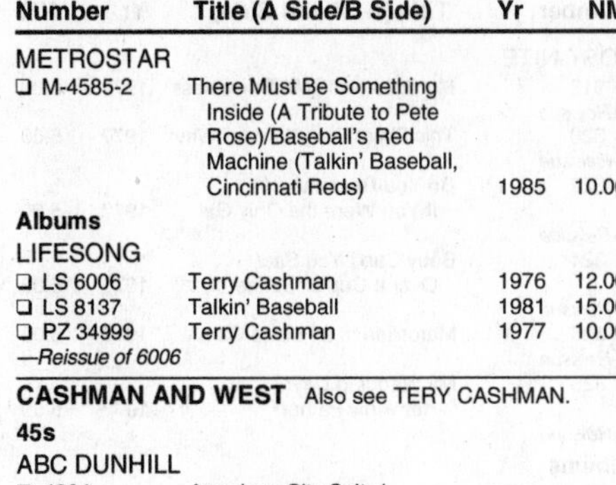

Number	Title (A Side/B Side)	Yr	NM
METROSTAR			
❑ M-4585-2	There Must Be Something Inside (A Tribute to Pete Rose)/Baseball's Red Machine (Talkin' Baseball, Cincinnati Reds)	1985	10.00
Albums			
LIFESONG			
❑ LS 6006	Terry Cashman	1976	12.00
❑ LS 8137	Talkin' Baseball	1981	15.00
❑ PZ 34999	Terry Cashman	1977	10.00
—Reissue of 6006			

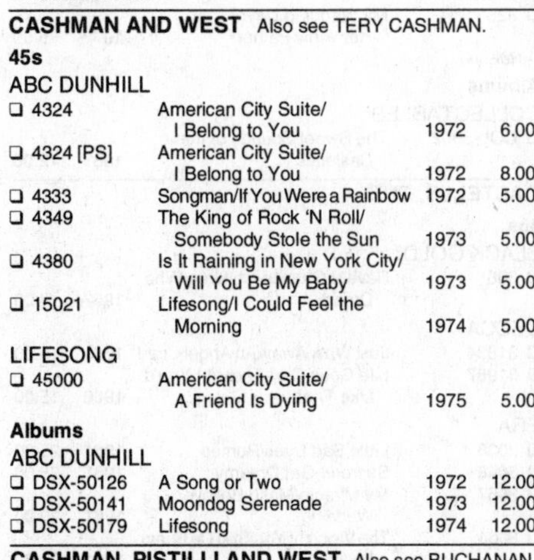

CASHMAN AND WEST Also see TERY CASHMAN.

Number	Title (A Side/B Side)	Yr	NM
45s			
ABC DUNHILL			
❑ 4324	American City Suite/ I Belong to You	1972	6.00
❑ 4324 [PS]	American City Suite/ I Belong to You	1972	8.00
❑ 4333	Songman/If You Were a Rainbow	1972	5.00
❑ 4349	The King of Rock 'N Roll/ Somebody Stole the Sun	1973	5.00
❑ 4380	Is It Raining in New York City/ Will You Be My Baby	1973	5.00
❑ 15021	Lifesong/I Could Feel the Morning	1974	5.00
LIFESONG			
❑ 45000	American City Suite/ A Friend Is Dying	1975	5.00
Albums			
ABC DUNHILL			
❑ DSX-50126	A Song or Two	1972	12.00
❑ DSX-50141	Moondog Serenade	1973	12.00
❑ DSX-50179	Lifesong	1974	12.00

CASHMAN, PISTILLI AND WEST Also see BUCHANAN BROTHERS; TERRY CASHMAN; CASHMAN AND WEST; GENE PISTILLI.

Number	Title (A Side/B Side)	Yr	NM
45s			
ABC			
❑ 11047	But for Love/Song That Never Comes	1968	8.00
❑ 11079	Spring Has a Tear in Her Eye/ Little Girl	1968	8.00
❑ 11111	My Side of the Sky/ You Can Write a Song	1968	8.00
CAPITOL			
❑ 2462	Some of My Best Friends Are People/Sausalito	1969	6.00
❑ 2582	Proud Mary-Dock of the Bay/ Sister John	1969	6.00
❑ 2671	Signs/Dolphins	1969	6.00
❑ 2747	She Never Looked Better/ Goodbye Jo	1970	6.00
❑ 2863	Midnight Man/Automatic Pilot	1970	6.00
Albums			
ABC			
❑ ABCS-629	Bound to Happen	1968	20.00
CAPITOL			
❑ ST-211	Cashman, Pistilli, and West	1969	15.00

CASHMERES, THE Possibly more than one group.

Number	Title (A Side/B Side)	Yr	NM
45s			
HEM			
❑ 1000	Show Stopper/Don't Let the Door Hit Your Back	1965	5000.
—VG 2500; VG+ 3750			
HERALD			
❑ 474	Little Dream Girl/Do I Upset You	1956	80.00
JOSIE			
❑ 894	Life Line/Where Have You Been	1961	12.00
LAKE			
❑ 703	Everything's Gonna Be Alright/ Four Lonely Nights	1960	30.00
❑ 705	Satisfied/Satisfied (Part 2)	1961	25.00
LAURIE			
❑ 3078	I Believe in St. Nick/A Very Special Birthday	1960	40.00
❑ 3088	I Gotta Go/Singing Waters	1961	25.00
❑ 3105	Poppa Said/Bobby Come On Home	1961	25.00
MERCURY			
❑ 70501	My Sentimental Heart/ Yes, Yes, Yes	1954	80.00
❑ 70617	Don't Let It Happen Again/ Boom Mag-Azeno-Vip Vay	1955	80.00
❑ 70679	There's a Rumor/ Second Hand Heart	1955	80.00
RELIC			
❑ 1005	Satisfied/Satisfied (Part 2)	1970	6.00

Shaun Cassidy, "Midnight Sun," Warner Bros. WBS 8698, 1978, $5.

CASINOS, THE (1) Male vocal group from Cincinnati. Records by the Casinos on Airtown, Alto, Casino, Certron, Itzy, Name, Olimpic, Sims and Terry may all be by a different group, thus are outside the scope of this book.

Number	Title (A Side/B Side)	Yr	NM
45s			
BUCCANEER			
❑ 3000	Then You Can Tell Me Goodbye/I Still Love You	196?	8.00
—Reissue of Fraternity release			
FRATERNITY			
❑ 944	She's Out of Sight/The Gallop	1965	10.00
❑ 949	Right There Beside You/ The Gallop	1965	10.00
❑ 977	Then You Can Tell Me Goodbye/I Still Love You	1967	12.00
❑ 985	It's All Over Now/Tailor Made	1967	10.00
❑ 987	Forever and a Night/ How Long Has It Been	1967	10.00
❑ 995	When I Stop Dreaming/ Please Love	1967	10.00
❑ 997	Bye Bye Love/Walk Through This World with Me	1967	10.00
❑ 1020	These Are the Things We'll Share/Casinos Having Fun	1969	10.00
❑ 1028	I Wish I Were Anyone But Me/ I Just Want to Stay Here	1969	10.00
❑ 1200	Father John/The Old Saloon	1970	10.00
❑ 1201	Wisdom of Love/My House	1970	10.00
❑ 1250	Loving Her Was Easier/ A Restless Wind	1971	10.00
MILLION			
❑ 13	I'm Walking Behind You/Angels Were All Asleep	1972	10.00
—As "Gene Hughes and the Casinos"			
UNITED ARTISTS			
❑ 50255	Here I Am/Peggy	1968	10.00
—As "Gene Hughes and the Casinos"			
❑ 50313	Nobody's Child/Leaving Makes the Rain Come Down	1968	10.00
—As "Gene Hughes and the Casinos"			
Albums			
FRATERNITY			
❑ LP-1019 [M]	Then You Can Tell Me Goodbye	1967	40.00
❑ LPS-1019 [S]	Then You Can Tell Me Goodbye	1967	60.00

CASINOS, THE (U) Some of these no doubt are group (1), but not all of them are, and we're not sure which is which.

Number	Title (A Side/B Side)	Yr	NM
45s			
AIRTOWN			
❑ 002	That's the Way/Too Good to Be True	1967	15.00
ALTO			
❑ 2002	I Like It Like That/Baby Don't Do It	1961	30.00
CASINO			
❑ 111	My Love for You/Why Am I a Fool	1960	40.00
CERTRON			
❑ 10015	Coal River/(B-side unknown)	1970	6.00
ITZY			
❑ 2	Do You Recall?/The Swim	1964	50.00
NAME			
❑ 7739	Do You Recall?/The Swim	1962	250.00
OLIMPIC			
❑ 251	Do You Recall?/The Swim	1963	150.00
SIMS			
❑ 306	Moon River/Soul Serenade	1966	12.00
TERRY			
❑ 115	Gee Whiz/Lovely One	1964	60.00
❑ 116	That's the Way/Too Good to Be True	1964	50.00

CASSIDY, DAVID Also see THE PARTRIDGE FAMILY.

Number	Title (A Side/B Side)	Yr	NM
45s			
BELL			
❑ 45150	Cherish/All I Want to Do Is Touch You	1971	5.00

Number	Title (A Side/B Side)	Yr	NM
❑ 45150 [PS]	Cherish/All I Want to Do Is Touch You	1971	6.00
❑ 45187	Could It Be Forever/Blind Hope	1972	4.00
❑ 45187 [PS]	Could It Be Forever/Blind Hope	1972	6.00
❑ 45220	How Can I Be Sure/Ricky's Tune	1972	4.00
❑ 45260	Rock Me Baby/Two Time Loser	1972	4.00
❑ 45386	Daydream/Can't Go Home Again	1973	4.00
❑ 45413	Daydreamer/The Puppy Song	1973	4.00
❑ 45605	Breaking Up Is Hard to Do/ Please Please Me	1974	4.00
MCA			
❑ 41101	Hurt So Bad/Once a Fool	1979	4.00
❑ 41101 [PS]	Hurt So Bad/Once a Fool	1979	5.00
RCA			
❑ PB-10788	I'll Have to Go Away (Saying Goodbye)/ Gettin' It in the Streets	1976	8.00
❑ PB-10921	Saying Goodbye Ain't Easy (We'll Have to Go Away)/ Rosa's Cantina	1977	8.00
RCA VICTOR			
❑ PB-10321	Get It Up for Love/Love In Bloom	1975	10.00
❑ PB-10405	This Could Be the Night/ Darlin'	1975	10.00
❑ PB-10585	Tomorrow/Bedtime	1976	10.00
❑ PB-10647	Breakin' Down Again/On Fire	1976	10.00
Albums			
BELL			
❑ 1109	Rock Me Baby	1972	20.00
❑ 1132	Dreams Are Nothing More Than Wishes	1973	20.00
❑ 1312	Cassidy Live	1974	25.00
❑ 1321	David Cassidy's Greatest Hits	1974	15.00
❑ 6070	Cherish	1972	20.00
RCA VICTOR			
❑ APL1-1066	The Higher They Climb...	1975	15.00
—Black vinyl			
❑ APL1-1066	The Higher They Climb...	1975	100.00
—Blue vinyl			
❑ APL1-1309	Home Is Where the Heart Is	1976	15.00
❑ APL1-1852	Gettin' It in the Street	1976	40.00

CASSIDY, SHAUN

Number	Title (A Side/B Side)	Yr	NM
45s			
WARNER BROS.			
❑ 8365	Da Doo Ron Ron/Holiday	1977	4.00
❑ 8365 [PS]	Da Doo Ron Ron/Holiday	1977	6.00
❑ 8423	That's Rock 'N' Roll/ I Wanna Be with You	1977	4.00
❑ 8423 [PS]	That's Rock 'N' Roll/ I Wanna Be with You	1977	5.00
❑ 8488	Hey Deanie/Strange Sensation	1977	4.00
❑ 8488 [PS]	Hey Deanie/Strange Sensation	1977	4.00
❑ 8533	Do You Believe in Magic/ Teen Dream	1978	4.00
❑ 8533 [PS]	Do You Believe in Magic/ Teen Dream	1978	4.00
❑ 8634	Our Night/Right Before Your Eyes	1978	4.00
❑ 8634 [PS]	Our Night/Right Before Your Eyes	1978	4.00
❑ 8698	Midnight Sun/She's Right	1978	5.00
❑ 8698 [PS]	Midnight Sun/She's Right	1978	5.00
❑ 8859	You're Usin' Me/ You Still Surprise Me	1979	5.00
❑ 8859 [PS]	You're Usin' Me/ You Still Surprise Me	1979	5.00
❑ 49039	Are You Afraid of Me?/ You're Usin' Me	1979	4.00
❑ 49154	Heaven in Your Eyes/Star Trek	1980	4.00
❑ 49568	Rebel, Rebel/Cool Fire	1980	5.00
❑ 49629	So Sad About Us/Cool Fire	1980	—
—Canceled?			
❑ 49640	So Sad About Us/Cool Fire	1980	5.00
—A-side with Todd Rundgren's Utopia			
Albums			
WARNER BROS.			
❑ BS 3067	Shaun Cassidy	1977	8.00
❑ BSK 3126	Born Late	1977	8.00
❑ BSK 3222	Under Wraps	1978	8.00
❑ HS 3265	Live/That's Rock and Roll	1979	10.00
❑ BSK 3351	Room Service	1979	10.00
❑ BSK 3451	Wasp	1980	15.00

CASSIDY, TED

Number	Title (A Side/B Side)	Yr	NM
45s			
CAPITOL			
❑ 5503	The Lurch/Wesley	1965	20.00
❑ 5503 [PS]	The Lurch/Wesley	1965	120.00

CASTALEERS, THE

Number	Title (A Side/B Side)	Yr	NM
45s			
DONNA			
❑ 1349	That's Why I Cry/My Baby's All Right	1961	25.00
FELSTED			
❑ 8504	Come Back/Hi-Fi Baby	1958	50.00
❑ 8512	Lonely Boy/My Bull Fightin' Baby	1958	40.00
❑ 8585	You're My Dream/I'll Be Around	1959	60.00
PLANET			
❑ 44	That's Why I Cry/My Baby's All Right	1961	40.00

CASTANETS, THE

Number	Title (A Side/B Side)	Yr	NM
45s			
TCF			
❑ 1	I Love Him/Funky Wunky Piano	1963	10.00

CASTAWAYS, THE (1)

Garage rock band from Minnesota.

Number	Title (A Side/B Side)	Yr	NM
45s			
BEAR			
❑ 2000	I Feel So Fine/Hit the Road Jack	1967	40.00
ERA BACK TO BACK HITS			
❑ 016	Liar, Liar/Surfin' Bird	197?	5.00
—B-side by the Trashmen			
ERIC			
❑ 247	Liar, Liar/Surfin' Bird	197?	5.00
—B-side by the Trashmen; reissue			
FONTANA			
❑ 1615	Walking in Different Circles/ Just On High	1968	15.00
❑ 1626	Lavender Popcorn/ What Kind of Face	1968	15.00
LANA			
❑ 151	Liar, Liar/Sam	196?	8.00
—Oldies reissue			
SOMA			
❑ 1433	Liar, Liar/Sam	1965	15.00
❑ 1442	Goodbye Babe/A Man's Gotta Be a Man	1965	12.00
❑ 1461	Girl in Love/Should Happen to Me	1966	12.00
❑ 1469	Liar, Liar/Surfin' Bird	1966	12.00
—B-side by the Trashmen			
TAUNAH			
❑ 7745	(I) Feel So Fine/Hit the Road Jack	1967	12.00

CASTAWAYS, THE (2)

Not sure who they are, but they are not (1), (3) or (4).

Number	Title (A Side/B Side)	Yr	NM
45s			
CAPITOL			
❑ 4340	The Twitch/Vibrations	1960	12.00

CASTAWAYS, THE (3)

Not sure who they are, but they are not (1), (2) or (4).

Number	Title (A Side/B Side)	Yr	NM
45s			
EXCELLO			
❑ 2038	I Wish/Teasin'	1954	40.00

CASTAWAYS, THE (4)

Different group, probably from California.

Number	Title (A Side/B Side)	Yr	NM
45s			
GNP CRESCENDO			
❑ 302	Tarzan/Wild Boy	1963	10.00
❑ 310	Moritat/Pass It Around	1964	10.00

CASTAWAYS, THE (U)

May go with (4) above, or possibly not.

Number	Title (A Side/B Side)	Yr	NM
45s			
WITCH			
❑ 124	Don't You Just Know It/I Go Ape	1964	30.00

CASTELLES, THE

Number	Title (A Side/B Side)	Yr	NM
45s			
ATCO			
❑ 6069	Happy and Gay/Hey Baby Baby	1956	100.00
CLASSIC ARTISTS			
❑ 114	At Christmas Time/ One Little Teardrop	1989	4.00
GRAND			
❑ 101	My Girl Awaits Me/Sweetness	1954	2000.
—Blue label original			
❑ 103	This Silver Ring/Wonder Why	1954	2000.
—Glossy yellow label original			
❑ 105	Do You Remember/ If You Were the Only Girl	1954	1500.
—Glossy yellow label original			
❑ 109	Baby Can't You See/ Over a Cup of Coffee	1954	2000.
—Blue label original			
❑ 114	Marcella/I'm a Fool to Care	1955	1200.
—Cream label original			
❑ 122	My Wedding Day/ Heavenly Father	1955	7000.
—Cream label original			
LOST-NITE			
❑ 318	My Girl Awaits Me/Sweetness	197?	5.00
—Reissue			
❑ 320	This Silver Ring/Wonder Why	197?	5.00
—Reissue			
❑ 322	Do You Remember/ If You Were the Only Girl	197?	5.00
—Reissue			
❑ 324	Baby Can't You See/ Over a Cup of Coffee	197?	5.00
—Reissue			
❑ 326	Marcella/I'm a Fool to Care	197?	5.00
—Reissue			
❑ 328	My Wedding Day/ Heavenly Father	197?	5.00
—Reissue			
Albums			
COLLECTABLES			
❑ COL-5002	The Sweet Sounds of the Castelles	198?	12.00

CASTELLS, THE

Number	Title (A Side/B Side)	Yr	NM
45s			
BLACK GOLD			
❑ 306	Save a Chance/Children Who Dream	196?	8.00
DECCA			
❑ 31834	Just Walk Away/An Angel Cried	1965	15.00
❑ 31967	Life Goes On/I Thought You'd Like That	1966	15.00
ERA			
❑ 3038	Little Sad Eyes/Romeo	1961	25.00
❑ 3048	Sacred/I Get Dreamy	1961	25.00
❑ 3057	My Miracle/Make Believe Wedding	1961	20.00
❑ 3064	The Vision of You/Stiki De Boom Boom	1961	20.00
❑ 3073	So This Is Love/On the Street of Tears	1962	20.00
❑ 3083	Oh, What It Seemed to Be/ Stand There, Mountain	1962	20.00
❑ 3089	Echoes in the Night/ The Only One	1962	20.00
❑ 3098	Clown Prince/Eternal Spring, Eternal Love	1962	20.00
❑ 3102	Little Sad Eyes/Initials	1963	20.00
❑ 3107	Some Enchanted Evening/ What Do Little Girls Dream Of	1963	20.00
LAURIE			
❑ 3444	I'd Like to Know/Rocky Ridges	1968	10.00
UNITED ARTISTS			
❑ 50324	Two Lovers/Jerusalem	1968	10.00
WARNER BROS.			
❑ 5421	I Do/Teardrops	1964	80.00
—A-side written and produced by Brian Wilson			
❑ 5445	Could This Be Magic/ Shinny Up Your Own Side	1964	30.00
❑ 5486	Love Finds a Way/ Tell Her If I Could	1964	20.00
Albums			
ERA			
❑ EL-109 [M]	So This Is Love	1962	120.00
❑ ES-109 [S]	So This Is Love	1962	400.00

CASTLE, JOEY

Number	Title (A Side/B Side)	Yr	NM
45s			
HEADLINE			
❑ 1008	Rock and Roll Daddy-O/ Wild Love	1959	400.00
RCA VICTOR			
❑ 47-7283	That Ain't Nothin' But Right/ Come A Little Closer Baby	1958	60.00

CASTLE, TONY

Number	Title (A Side/B Side)	Yr	NM
45s			
EASTWEST			
❑ 107	Terry/Young and In Love	1958	30.00
GONE			
❑ 5099	Salty/Salty, Part 2	1961	20.00
❑ 5099	Salty/Hi Lili, Hi Lo	1961	25.00
❑ 5105	Sincerely/Tara's Themes	1961	20.00
❑ 5107	Seems Like Old Times/The Loneliest Girl in the World	1961	20.00
TREY			
❑ 3002	Kiss Me Goodnight/The Fool	1960	25.00

CASTLE KINGS, THE

Number	Title (A Side/B Side)	Yr	NM
45s			
ATLANTIC			
❑ 2107	You Can Get Him Frankenstein/ Loch Lomond	1961	30.00
—Produced by Phil Spector			

Except when noted otherwise, VG = 25% of NM, and VG+ = 50% of NM. (Example: VG = $2.00, VG+ = $4.00 and NM = $8.00.)

Number	Title (A Side/B Side)	Yr	NM
❑ 2158	Jeanette/The Caissons Go Rolling Along	1962	15.00

CASTLEMAN, BOOMER

Number	Title (A Side/B Side)	Yr	NM
45s			
BNA			
❑ 006	Summertime Blues/ (B-side unknown)	198?	6.00
❑ 007	Hot Day in the South/ Losin' My Touch	198?	6.00
GRT			
❑ 069	That House Up On the Hill/ Chihuahua	1976	6.00
❑ 082	Mississippi Mud/ (B-side unknown)	1976	6.00
MUMS			
❑ ZS8 6038	Judy Mae/Three Feet High and Growing	1975	6.00

CASTON, BOBBY

Number	Title (A Side/B Side)	Yr	NM
45s			
ATLAS			
❑ 1103	Call Me Darling/ Why Wasn't I Told	1958	100.00

CASTOR, JIMMY, BUNCH Also see THE CLINTONIAN CUBS.

Number	Title (A Side/B Side)	Yr	NM
12-Inch Singles			
CATAWBA			
❑ 4Z9-05299	Godzilla (Vocal 4:28) (Instrumental)	1985	8.00
COTILLION			
❑ DSKO 183 [DJ]	Don't Do That! (7:08) (same on both sides)	1979	15.00
❑ DSKO 206 [DJ]	Party People (6:30) (same on both sides)	1979	20.00
❑ DK 4731	Don't Do That! (7:08)/ Psych-Out (6:55)	1979	20.00
DREAM			
❑ DG 707	Amazon (Long Version 5:45) (Short Version 3:45) (Dub 7:30) (Bonus Acapella 1:45)	1984	20.00
❑ DG 708	It Gets to Me (Vocal 6:33) (Short Version 3:45) (Dub 6:30) (Bonus Beats Acapella 2:15)	1984	15.00
SALSOUL			
❑ SG 361	E-Man Boogie/Any Way, Any Where, Any Time	1982	15.00
45s			
ATLANTIC			
❑ 3011	Maggie (Part 1)/Maggie (Part 2)	1974	5.00
❑ 3045	Everything Man (E-Man)/ Heaven Kissed	1974	5.00
❑ 3232	The Bertha Butt Boogie (Part 1)/The Bertha Butt Boogie (Part 2)	1975	5.00
❑ 3270	Potential/Daniel	1975	5.00
❑ 3295	King Kong (Part 1)/ King Kong (Part 2)	1975	5.00
❑ 3302	The Christmas Song (Chestnuts Roasting on an Open Fire)/Merry Christmas	1975	7.00
❑ 3316	Supersound/Drifting	1976	4.00
❑ 3331	Bom Bom/What's Best	1976	4.00
❑ 3362	Everything Is Beautiful to Me/ The Magic Is in the Music	1976	4.00
❑ 3369 [DJ]	I Don't Wanna Lose You (mono/ stereo)	1976	5.00
—May be promo-only			
❑ 3375	Space Age/Dracula	1976	4.00
❑ 3396	I Love a Mellow Groove/ I Don't Want to Lose You	1977	4.00
❑ 3424	The Return of Leroy (Part 1)/ The Return of Leroy (Part 2)	1977	4.00
❑ 3451	Magnolia/TR-7	1978	4.00
❑ 3455	Maximum Stimulation/It Was You	1978	4.00
ATOMIC			
❑ 100	Somebody Mentioned Your Name/This Girl of Mine	1957	500.00
CAPITOL			
❑ 2358	Hey Shorty (Part 1)/ Hey Shorty (Part 2)	1968	8.00
❑ 2487	Psycho Man/The Real McCoy	1969	8.00
❑ 2634	Helpless/Make Me	1969	8.00
CATAWBA			
❑ ZS4-05676	Godzilla/(Instrumental)	1985	4.00
COMPASS			
❑ 7019	Soul Sister/Rattlesnake	1968	8.00
COTILLION			
❑ 44253	Don't Do That!/Don't Do That! (Part 2)	1979	4.00
❑ 45004	Party People/I Just Wanna Stop	1979	4.00
DECCA			
❑ 31963	In a Boogaloo Bag (Part 1)/ In a Boogaloo Bag (Part 2)	1966	10.00
DREAM			
❑ D7-0359	Don't Cry Out Loud/ (Instrumental)	1983	5.00
❑ D7-0360	Amazon/She's an Amazon	1984	5.00
❑ D 70361	It Gets to Me/(Instrumental)	1984	5.00
DRIVE			
❑ 6271	Bertha Butt Encounters Vadar/ Mystery of Me	1978	4.00
❑ 6276	You Light Up My Life/Let It Out	1978	4.00
HULL			
❑ 758	Poor Loser/Oh Suzzana	1963	20.00
LONG DISTANCE			
❑ 701/2	Stay with Me (Spend the Night)/ Can't Help Falling in Love with You	1980	5.00
RCA VICTOR			
❑ 48-1024	Say Leroy (The Creature from the Black Lagoon Is Your Father) (Parts 1 & 2)	1972	5.00
❑ 48-1029	Troglodyte (Cave Man)/ I Promise to Remember	1972	6.00
❑ 74-0583	My Brightest Day/ You Better Be Good	1971	5.00
❑ 74-0763	Luther the Anthropod/Party Life	1972	5.00
❑ 74-0836	Paradise/The First Time Ever I Saw Your Face	1972	5.00
❑ 74-0953	Soul Serenade/ Purple Haze-Foxey Lady (Tribute to Jimi Hendrix)	1973	5.00
❑ APBO-0047	How Beautiful You Are/ I'm Not a Child Anymore	1973	5.00
❑ AMBO-0120	Troglodyte (Cave Man)/ Luther the Anthropod	1973	4.00
—Gold Standard Series			
SALSOUL			
❑ 7018	E-Man Boogie/Any Way, Any Where, Any Time	1982	4.00
❑ 7058	E-Man Boogie '83/It's Just Begun	1983	4.00
SMASH			
❑ 2069	Hey, Leroy, Your Mama's Calling You/Ham Hocks Espanol	1966	8.00
❑ 2085	Just You Girl/Magic Saxophone	1967	8.00
❑ 2099	Leroy Is In the Army/Dry	1967	8.00
❑ 2120	Jamaica Farewell/Mini-Sonata	1967	8.00
WING			
❑ 90078	I Promise/I Know the Meaning of Love	1956	120.00
Albums			
ATLANTIC			
❑ SD 7305	The Everything Man	1974	10.00
❑ SD 18124	Butt Of Course	1975	10.00
❑ SD 18150	Supersound	1975	10.00
❑ SD 18186	E-Man Groovin'	1976	10.00
❑ SD 19111	Maximum Stimulation	1977	10.00
COTILLION			
❑ SD 5215	The Jimmy Castor Bunch	1979	12.00
DRIVE			
❑ 407	Let It Out	1978	12.00
LONG DISTANCE			
❑ 1201	C	1980	12.00
RCA VICTOR			
❑ APD1-0103 [Q]	Dimension III	1973	20.00
—All copies are quadraphonic			
❑ APL1-0313	The Everything Man	1974	15.00
❑ LSP-4640	It's Just Begun	1972	15.00
❑ LSP-4783	Phase Two	1972	15.00
SMASH			
❑ MGS-27091 [M]	Hey Leroy!	1967	40.00
❑ SRS-67091 [S]	Hey Leroy!	1967	40.00

CASTROES, THE

Number	Title (A Side/B Side)	Yr	NM
45s			
GRAND			
❑ 2002	Dearest Darling/Dance with Me	1959	150.00

CASUAL ASSOCIATION, THE

Number	Title (A Side/B Side)	Yr	NM
45s			
PARKWAY			
❑ 158	Georgy Girl/Nickels and Dimes	1967	12.00

CASUALAIRS, THE

Number	Title (A Side/B Side)	Yr	NM
45s			
AUTUMN			
❑ 21	Just For You/This Is a Mean World	1965	25.00
CRAIG			
❑ 5001	Bossa Nova Twist/Cruising	1962	40.00
MONA-LEE			
❑ 136	At the Dance/Satsfied	1959	40.00

CASUALS, THE (1) See THE ORIGINAL CASUALS.

CASUALS, THE (2)

Number	Title (A Side/B Side)	Yr	NM
45s			
DOT			
❑ 15557	Somebody Help Me/ My Love Song for You	1957	25.00
❑ 15671	Hello Love/Till You Come Back to Me	1957	25.00

CASUALS, THE (3) British group.

Number	Title (A Side/B Side)	Yr	NM
45s			
MAINSTREAM			
❑ 692	I've Got Something Too/ Jesamine (A Butterfly Child)	1968	10.00
❑ 697	Touched/Toy	1968	10.00
—As "The British Casuals"			

CASUALS, THE (4)

Number	Title (A Side/B Side)	Yr	NM
45s			
MINARET			
❑ 109	Money/Big Hammer	1963	15.00
MONUMENT			
❑ 905	Promise Her Anything (But Give Her Love)/Walk	1965	12.00
❑ 937	Walk Away/If You Don't	1966	12.00
SOUND STAGE 7			
❑ 2534	Mustang 2 + 2/Play Me a Sad Song	1964	15.00

CAT MOTHER AND THE ALL NIGHT NEWS BOYS

Number	Title (A Side/B Side)	Yr	NM
45s			
POLYDOR			
❑ 14002	Good Old Rock 'N Roll/ Bad News	1969	8.00
❑ 14007	Can You Dance to It/Marie	1969	6.00
—Both of the above were produced by Jimi Hendrix			
❑ 14029	Last Go-Round/I Must Be Dreaming	1970	6.00
❑ 14126	Letter to the President/ Ode to Oregon	1972	6.00
❑ 14138	She Came from a Different World/Three and Me	1972	6.00
Albums			
POLYDOR			
❑ 24-4001	The Street Giveth…And the Street Taketh Away	1969	25.00
—Produced by Jimi Hendrix			
❑ 24-4023	Albion Doo-Wah	1970	15.00
❑ PD-5017	Cat Mother	1972	15.00
❑ PD-5042	Last Chance Dance	1972	15.00

CATALINAS, THE (1) Studio band of Los Angeles session pros.

Number	Title (A Side/B Side)	Yr	NM
45s			
RIC			
❑ 113	Banzai Wipeout/Beach Walkin'	1964	25.00
❑ 164	Boss Barracuda/Surfer Boy	1965	25.00
SIMS			
❑ 134	Bail Out/Bulletin	1963	15.00
Albums			
RIC			
❑ M-1006 [M]	Fun, Fun, Fun	1964	100.00
❑ S-1006 [S]	Fun, Fun, Fun	1964	150.00

CATALINAS, THE (2) Five-man vocal group.

Number	Title (A Side/B Side)	Yr	NM
45s			
LITTLE			
❑ 811/2	Give Me Your Love/ Castle of Love	1957	200.00

CATALINAS, THE (U)

Number	Title (A Side/B Side)	Yr	NM
45s			
BACK BEAT			
❑ 513	Speechless/Flying Formation with You	1958	30.00
DEE JAY			
❑ 1010	Bail Out/Bulletin	1963	40.00
DIAL			
❑ 3008	Cha Cha Joe/Echo One	1963	12.00
GLORY			
❑ 285	Marlene/With Your Girl — Yeah!	1958	20.00
ORIGINAL SOUND			
❑ 48	Your Tender Lips/Gonna Tell	1964	12.00
RITA			
❑ 1006	Ring of Stars/Wooly Wooly Willie	1960	20.00

C

Cat Mother and the All Night News Boys, *Cat Mother*, Polydor PD-5017, 1972, **$15.**

Number	Title (A Side/B Side)	Yr	NM
SCEPTER			
❑ 12188	Tick Tock/You Haven't the Right	1967	15.00
20TH FOX			
❑ 286	Sweetheart/Unchained Melody	1962	30.00
❑ 299	Safari/Pretty Little Nashville Girl	1962	30.00

CATANOOGA CATS, THE

Number	Title (A Side/B Side)	Yr	NM
Albums			
FORWARD			
❑ ST-F-1018	The Catanooga Cats	1969	40.00

CATAPILLA

Number	Title (A Side/B Side)	Yr	NM
Albums			
VERTIGO			
❑ 1006	Catapilla	1971	36.00

CATES, GEORGE

Number	Title (A Side/B Side)	Yr	NM
45s			
CORAL			
❑ 9-60215	Chug-a-Lug/She's Shimmyin' on the Beach Again	1950	15.00
❑ 9-60249	Baseball Polka/On the Beach	1950	15.00
❑ 9-60262	Tzena, Tzena, Tzena/They Put the Light Out	1950	15.00
❑ 9-60291	Beloved, Be Faithful/Honestly, I Love You	1950	15.00
❑ 9-60302	Sleigh Ride/Tubby the Tuba Song	1950	15.00
❑ 9-60326	Silver Bells/Jing-a-Ling, Jing-a-Ling	1950	15.00
❑ 9-60328	Remember Me in Your Dreams/Winter Waltz	1950	15.00
❑ 9-60365	Down by the Old Zuyder River/There's More Pretty Girls Than One	1951	15.00
❑ 9-60436	The Syncopated Clock/On Top of Old Smokey	1951	15.00
❑ 9-60479	No More/Riverderci (We Will Meet Again)	1951	15.00
❑ 9-60546	Hi-Diddle-Diddle/Looking for You	1951	15.00
❑ 9-60556	Jingle Bells Around the World/The Winter Song	1951	15.00
❑ 9-60627	Snowflakes/River in the Moonlight	1952	12.00
❑ 9-60810	Carmen's Boogie/Babalu	1952	12.00
❑ 9-61007	When Someone Wonderful Thinks You're Wonderful/Lost	1953	12.00
❑ 9-61226	Double-Gated/Athena	1954	12.00
❑ 9-61432	If I Had Three Wishes/If We Never Had Said Alone	1955	12.00
❑ 9-61512	Royal Blue/Rememb'ring	1955	12.00
❑ 9-61618	Moonglow and Theme from "Picnic"/Rio Batucada	1956	12.00
❑ 9-61655	Away All Boats/The Proud and Profane (To Love Ya)	1956	12.00
❑ 9-61683	Where There's Life/One Night in Monte Carlo	1956	12.00
❑ 9-61702	Friendly Persuasion/There's Never Been Anyone Else But You	1956	12.00
❑ 9-61750	A New-Fangled Tango/Much Better, Thanks	1956	12.00
❑ 9-61774	Last Night/The Poodle Walk	1957	10.00
❑ 9-61810	Boy on a Dolphin/Your Kiss	1957	10.00
❑ 9-61825	Remember When/I'll See You in Oklahoma	1957	10.00
❑ 9-61872	Valley of the Redwoods/You Can Say That Again	1957	10.00
❑ 9-61965	Champagne Time/Madame Zajj	1958	10.00
❑ 9-62011	Acapulco/Caracas	1958	10.00
❑ 9-62032	Neat Beat/Exciting	1958	10.00
DOT			
❑ 16271	Ka-Lu-A/Take Five	1961	8.00
❑ 16330	In a Little Spanish Town (Twist)/Star Dust	1962	8.00
❑ 16376	Third Man Theme/Quiet Village	1962	8.00
❑ 16409	Woodchopper's Ball/Poinciana	1962	8.00
❑ 16461	Diamond Head/How the West Was Won	1963	8.00
❑ 16481	Canadian Sunset/The Flip	1963	8.00
❑ 16581	Ghost Guitar/Peanut Vendor	1964	8.00
HAMILTON			
❑ 50041	Flowers on the Wall/Cristo Redentor	1966	8.00
❑ 50042	The Sidewinder/(B-side unknown)	1966	8.00
SIGNATURE			
❑ 12005	Give Me All Your Love/So Tired	1959	10.00
❑ 12016	My Darling Laura Lee/Waltzing Matilda	1959	10.00
❑ 12034	The Dipsy Doodle/Weary Blues	1960	10.00
7-Inch Extended Plays			
CORAL			
❑ EC 81076	Sleigh Ride/Jingle Bells Around The World//Silver Bells/Jing-A-Ling Jing-A-Ling	195?	12.00
❑ EC 81076 [PS]	Sleigh Ride	195?	12.00
Albums			
CORAL			
❑ CRL 57126 [M]	Under European Skies	1957	40.00
❑ CRL 57220 [M]	Exciting	1958	30.00
DOT			
❑ DLP-3355 [M]	Polynesian Percussion	1961	12.00
❑ DLP-3400 [M]	Take Five	1961	12.00
❑ DLP-3422 [M]	Twistin' 12 Great Hits	1962	15.00
❑ DLP-3464 [M]	Third Man Theme	1962	12.00
❑ DLP-3564 [M]	Hit Songs — Hit Sounds	1964	12.00
❑ DLP-25355 [S]	Polynesian Percussion	1961	20.00
❑ DLP-25400 [S]	Take Five	1961	20.00
❑ DLP-25422 [S]	Twistin' 12 Great Hits	1962	20.00
❑ DLP-25464 [S]	Third Man Theme	1962	15.00
❑ DLP-25564 [S]	Hit Songs — Hit Sounds	1964	15.00
HAMILTON			
❑ HLP-127 [M]	The Great Hit Sounds of George Cates	1964	10.00
❑ HLP-161 [M]	1965's Great Hits	1966	15.00
❑ HLP-12127 [S]	The Great Hit Sounds of George Cates	1964	12.00
❑ HLP-12161 [S]	1965's Great Hits	1966	20.00
RANWOOD			
❑ 8039	Hawaii	1969	12.00

CATES SISTERS, THE

Number	Title (A Side/B Side)	Yr	NM
45s			
CAPRICE			
❑ 2024	Mr. Guitar/Love Is a Beautiful Thing	1976	5.00
❑ 2030	Out of My Mind/Run Your Sweet Love By Me	1976	5.00
—As "The Cates"			
❑ 2032	Can't Help It/(B-side unknown)	1977	5.00
❑ 2036	I'll Always Love You/Second Chance	1977	5.00
❑ 2038	Throw Out Your Loveline/West Virginia Smile	1977	5.00
❑ 2041	I've Been Loved/Faded Love	1977	5.00
❑ 2047	Long Gone Blues/San Antonio Rose	1978	5.00
❑ 2051	Lovin' You Off My Mind/Amazing Grace	1978	5.00
MCA			
❑ 40032	He Fiddled His Way Into My Heart/Crazy Dreams	1973	8.00
—As "Marcy and Margie"			
❑ 40211	Uncle Pen/Double Your Pleasure	1974	6.00
OVATION			
❑ 1123	Going Down Slow/Can I See You Tonight	1979	5.00
—All on Ovation as "The Cates"			
❑ 1126	Make Love to Me/Day After Day	1979	5.00
❑ 1126 [PS]	Make Love to Me/Day After Day	1979	8.00
❑ 1134	Let's Go Through the Motions/Don't Say Love	1979	5.00
❑ 1144	Gonna Get Along Without You Now/I've Been Lovin' You Too Long	1980	5.00
❑ 1155	Lightnin' Strikin'/Touch and Go	1980	5.00
Albums			
OVATION			
❑ 1740	Steppin' Out	1979	12.00
—As "The Cates"			

CATHY JEAN AND THE ROOMATES Also see THE ROOMATES.

Number	Title (A Side/B Side)	Yr	NM
45s			
PHILIPS			
❑ 40106	My Heart Belongs to Only You/I Only Want You	1963	20.00
—As "Cathy Jean"			
❑ 40143	Double Trouble/Believe Me	1963	20.00
—As "Cathy Jean"			

Except when noted otherwise, VG = 25% of NM, and VG+ = 50% of NM. (Example: VG = $2.00, VG+ = $4.00 and NM = $8.00.)

Number | Title (A Side/B Side) | Yr | NM

VALMOR

❑ 007 Please Love Me Forever/Canadian Sunset 1961 15.00

—Black label

❑ 007 Please Love Me Forever/Canadian Sunset 1961 25.00

—Red label

❑ 007 [PS] Please Love Me Forever/Canadian Sunset 1961 70.00

—Sleeve is promo only

❑ 009 Make Me Smile Again/Sugar Cake 1961 25.00

❑ 011 I Only Want You/One Love 1961 20.00

❑ 016 Please Tell Me/Sugar Cake 1962 20.00

Albums

VALMOR

❑ 78 [M] Great Oldies 1962 800.00

—Reissue of 789 with titles on cover and no group shot

❑ 789 [M] At the Hop! 1961 900.00

CAUTIONS, THE

45s

SHRINE

❑ 104 Watch Your Step/Is It Right 1965 700.00

❑ 115 No Other Way/Poor Loser 1966 800.00

CAVALIERE, FELIX

Also see FELIX AND THE ESCORTS; THE RASCALS.

45s

BEARSVILLE

❑ 0300 High Price to Pay/Mountain Men 1974 5.00

❑ 0302 Everlasting Love/Future Train 1975 6.00

❑ 0305 Never Felt Love Before/Love Came 1975 6.00

EPIC

❑ 9-50785 Castles in the Air/Outside Your Window 1979 4.00

❑ 9-50829 Only a Lonely Heart Sees/You Turned Me Around 1980 4.00

❑ 9-50880 Good to Have Love Back/Dancin' the Night Away 1980 4.00

Albums

BEARSVILLE

❑ BR 6955 Felix Cavaliere 1974 12.00

❑ BR 6958 Destiny 1975 12.00

EPIC

❑ JE 35990 Castles in the Air 1979 10.00

CAVALIERS, THE (1)

Washington, D.C. group renowned in "Northern Soul" circles.

45s

RCA VICTOR

❑ 47-9054 Dance Little Girl/Hold On to My Baby 1966 100.00

❑ 47-9321 I Really Love You/I've Gotta Find Her 1967 80.00

SHRINE

❑ 119 Do What I Need/Tighten Up 1966 1200.

CAVALIERS, THE (U)

None of these are by group (1).

45s

APT

❑ 25004 Dance, Dance, Dance/Play By the Rules of Love 1958 40.00

CORAL

❑ 62245 Teen Fever/Funky 1961 12.00

DECCA

❑ 29556 Somewhere, Sometime, Someday/Honor Bright 1955 15.00

GALENA

❑ 1277 Blowin' Smoke/Ten More Miles 1962 20.00

MUSIC WORLD

❑ 101 The Magic Age of Sixteen/So Young, So Warm, So Beautiful 1963 30.00

NRC

❑ 028 Dreamy Bikini/Charm Bracelet 1959 15.00

CAVE, NICK, AND THE BAD SEEDS

Albums

ANTI

❑ 86668 Nocturama 2003 15.00

—Actually contains two records, but the second record is a single-sided disc with one song

ENIGMA

❑ 7 75401-1 Tender Prey 1988 30.00

HOMESTEAD

❑ HMS 026 The Firstborn is Dead 1985 30.00

❑ HMS 065 Kicking Against the Pricks 1986 30.00

❑ HMS 073 Your Funeral, My Trial 1986 40.00

CAVE DWELLERS, THE

45s

ABC-PARAMOUNT

❑ 10735 Sinking Feeling/Sling My Rock 1965 20.00

CELEBRITYS, THE

45s

CAROLINE

❑ 2301 Juanita/(B-side unknown) 1956 600.00

❑ 2302 Absent Minded/We Made Romance 1956 600.00

CELLOS, THE

45s

APOLLO

❑ 510 Rang Tang Ding Dong (I Am the Japanese Sandman)/You Took My Love 1957 25.00

❑ 510 Rang Tang Ding Dong/You Took My Love 1957 80.00

❑ 515 Under Your Spell/The Juicy Crocodile 1957 50.00

❑ 516 The Be-Bop Mouse/Girlie That I Love 1957 50.00

❑ 524 I Beg for Your Love/What's the Matter with You 1958 60.00

CELTICS, THE

45s

AL-JACK'S

❑ 0002 Can You Remember/Send Me Someone to Love 1958 5000.

—VG 2500; VG+ 3750

WAR CONN

❑ 2216 Darline, Darling/Only the Lonely 1962 400.00

CENTAURUS

Albums

AZRA

❑ 61549 Centaurus 1978 50.00

—Issued on clear vinyl

CENTIPEDE

Albums

RCA VICTOR

❑ CPL2-5042 [(2)] Septober Energy 1974 40.00

CENTRAL NERVOUS SYSTEM

45s

LAURIE

❑ 3421 It Takes All Kinds/I'm Still Hung Up on You 1968 10.00

❑ 3446 Alice in Wonderland/Something Happened to Me 1968 10.00

Albums

MUSIC FACTORY

❑ MF-12003 [M] I Could Have Danced All Night 1968 30.00

—White label promo only (no stock copies were issued in mono)

❑ MFS-12003 [S] I Could Have Danced All Night 1968 20.00

CENTURIES, THE

45s

CLEOPATRA

❑ 2 The Outer Limits/Polynesian Paradise 1963 30.00

❑ 3 Jack 23/4th Dimension 1964 30.00

CENTURIONS, THE

Albums

DEL-FI

❑ DFLP-1228 [M] Surfer's Pajama Party 1963 100.00

❑ DFST-1228 [S] Surfer's Pajama Party 1963 200.00

—Above has the same title and number, and almost the same cover, as the album of the same name by Bruce Johnston, but the contents are different

CESANA

Albums

MODERN

❑ M-100 [M] Tender Emotions 1964 20.00

CEYLEIB PEOPLE, THE

45s

VAULT

❑ 940 Changes/Ceyladd Seyta 1968 20.00

Albums

VAULT

❑ LP-117 Tanyet 1968 200.00

—With Ry Cooder; both mono and stereo, same price

CHACKSFIELD, FRANK

45s

CORAL

❑ 9-60966 Little Red Monkey/Roundabouts and Swings 1953 20.00

LONDON

❑ 1342 Terry's Theme from "Limelight"/Limelight 1953 12.00

❑ 1358 Ebb Tide/Waltzing Bugle Boy 1953 12.00

❑ 1368 A Girl Called Linda/Golden Violins 1953 12.00

❑ 1381 Dancing Princess/Golden Tango 1954 12.00

❑ 1406 Prelude to a Memory/Flirtation Waltz 1954 12.00

❑ 1439 Fiddler's Boogie/Picnic for Strings 1954 12.00

❑ 1484 Black Velvet/Misty Valley 1954 12.00

❑ 1487 Smile/Piper in the Heather 1954 12.00

❑ 1530 Glorious/Pavements of Paris 1955 10.00

❑ 1535 Blue Mirage/Mademoiselle de Paris 1955 10.00

❑ 1636 Lights of Vienna/Cockleshell Heroes 1956 10.00

❑ 1671 Donkey Cart/Banks of the Seine 1956 10.00

❑ 1694 Sahara/Fanagalo 1956 10.00

❑ 1722 Breath of Spring/Your Love Is My Love 1957 10.00

❑ 1725 Temptation/Lullaby of the Leaves 1957 10.00

❑ 1749 Voyage of the Mayflower/Catalan Sunshine 1957 10.00

❑ 1772 Costa Brava/Katsumi Love Theme 1958 10.00

❑ 1797 Arrividerci Roma/Blue Hawaii 1958 10.00

❑ 1841 My Heart's in Portugal/Rodeo 1958 10.00

❑ 1876 Java Boogie/Smile 1959 10.00

❑ 1901 On the Beach/A Paris Valentine 1959 10.00

❑ 1945 Theme from "The Dark at the Top of the Stairs"/Caroline 1960 8.00

❑ 1964 Conscious/Madeleine 1960 8.00

❑ 1990 Theme from "Carnival"/Lullaby in Blue 1961 8.00

❑ 9502 Theme from "King of Kings"/Theme from "Francis of Assisi" 1961 8.00

❑ 9519 Ebb Tide/Face to Face 1962 8.00

❑ 9580 Parakeets of Paraguay/Theme from "Lawrence of Arabia" 1963 8.00

❑ 9611 She Loves Me/Will He Like Me 1963 8.00

❑ 9617 Theme from "A New Kind of Love"/Street of Goodbye 1963 8.00

❑ 9788 Jipijapa/Here I Am 1965 8.00

❑ 9803 The Phoenix Love Theme/Marriage Lines 1965 8.00

❑ 11013 Ebb Tide/Waltzing Bugle Boy 196? 6.00

—"Demand Performance" reissue

❑ 11014 Terry's Theme from "Limelight"/Limelight 196? 6.00

—"Demand Performance" reissue

❑ 20022 My Star/Caves of Manacor 1966 7.00

❑ 20029 Summer Samba/I'll See You in Montreal 1967 7.00

❑ 20036 Along About Now/Sabor Flamenco 1968 7.00

❑ 20043 Blue Lace/Sunshine 1969 7.00

7-Inch Extended Plays

LONDON

❑ BEP.6128 (contents unknown) 195? 10.00

❑ BEP.6128 [PS] Frank Chacksfield 195? 10.00

❑ BEP.6172 (contents unknown) 195? 10.00

❑ BEP.6172 [PS] Evening in Paris 195? 10.00

❑ BEP.6174 *Vous Que Passez Sans Me Voir/J'Attendrai/Mademoiselle de Paris/Boom 195? 10.00

❑ BEP.6174 [PS] (title unknown) 195? 10.00

❑ BEP.6197 (contents unknown) 195? 10.00

❑ BEP.6197 [PS] Music of Noel Coward 195? 10.00

❑ BEP.6258 (contents unknown) 195? 10.00

❑ BEP.6258 [PS] Vieni Sul Mar 195? 10.00

❑ BEP.6276 (contents unknown) 195? 10.00

❑ BEP.6276 [PS] Love Walked In 195? 10.00

Albums

COMPLEAT

❑ 671020-1 TV's Golden Hits 198? 12.00

EXCELSIOR

❑ XRP-7001 Great Film Music 1980 10.00

❑ XRP-7004 In the Country 1980 12.00

❑ XRP-7005 After the Lovin' 1980 12.00

❑ XRP-7006 Sunflower 1980 12.00

❑ XRP-7007 Weekend in New England 1980 12.00

❑ XRP-7008 Dust in the Wind 1980 12.00

❑ XRP-7009 Love Is in the Air 1980 12.00

LONDON

❑ CHA-S-1 [(2)] Academy Award Hit Songs 1934-1967 1969 12.00

❑ PS 120 [S] Music of George Gershwin 195? 15.00

C

Chad and Jeremy, "If I Loved You," World Artists 1041, 1965, **$20.**

Number	Title (A Side/B Side)	Yr	NM
❑ PS 122 [S]	Immortal Serenades	195?	15.00
❑ PS 126 [S]	Evening in Rome, Evening in Paris	195?	15.00
❑ PS 135 [S]	Evening in London	195?	15.00
❑ PS 145 [S]	Love Letters in the Sand	195?	15.00
❑ PS 203 [S]	On the Beach	1960	15.00
❑ PS 246 [S]	King of Kings and Other Film Spectaculars	196?	12.00
❑ PS 298 [S]	Lawrence of Arabia and Other Themes	196?	12.00
❑ PS 304 [S]	Magic Strings	196?	12.00
❑ PS 316 [S]	Music from "She Loves Me"	196?	12.00
❑ PS 320/1 [(2)S]	Hollywood Almanac — Award Winners 1934-1957	195?	20.00
❑ PS 322 [S]	Ebb Tide	196?	12.00
❑ PS 330 [S]	Here's Love	196?	12.00
❑ PS 347 [S]	Best of the New Film Themes	196?	12.00
❑ PS 416 [S]	The First Hits of 1965	1965	12.00
❑ PS 436 [S]	Great Country and Western Hits	1965	12.00
❑ LL 997 [M]	Evening in Paris	195?	15.00
❑ LL 1041 [M]	Frank Chacksfield and His Orchestra, Vol. 1	195?	15.00
❑ LL 1062 [M]	Music of Noel Coward	195?	15.00
❑ LL 1203 [M]	Music of George Gershwin	195?	15.00
❑ LL 1205 [M]	Evening in Rome	195?	15.00
❑ LL 1355 [M]	You	195?	15.00
❑ LL 1440 [M]	Mean to Me	195?	15.00
❑ LL 1440 [M]	Velvet	195?	15.00
❑ LL 1509 [M]	Broadway Melodies	195?	12.00
❑ LL 1538 [M]	South Sea Island Magic	195?	12.00
❑ LL 1588 [M]	Mediterranean Moonlight	195?	12.00
❑ LL 1603 [M]	Waltzes to Remember	195?	12.00
❑ LL 1614 [M]	Lovely Lady — The Music of Jimmy McHugh	195?	12.00
❑ LL 3027 [M]	Love Letters in the Sand	195?	12.00
❑ LL 3038 [M]	Evening in London	195?	12.00
❑ LL 3061 [M]	Immortal Serenades	195?	12.00
❑ LL 3102/3 [(2)M]	Hollywood Almanac — Award Winners 1934-1957	195?	15.00
❑ LL 3158 [M]	On the Beach	1960	12.00
❑ LL 3257 [M]	King of Kings and Other Film Spectaculars	196?	10.00

Number	Title (A Side/B Side)	Yr	NM
❑ LL 3298 [M]	Lawrence of Arabia and Other Themes	196?	10.00
❑ LL 3304 [M]	Magic Strings	196?	10.00
❑ LL 3316 [M]	Music from "She Loves Me"	196?	10.00
❑ LL 3322 [M]	Ebb Tide	196?	10.00
❑ LL 3330 [M]	Here's Love	196?	10.00
❑ LL 3347 [M]	Best of the New Film Themes	196?	10.00
❑ LL 3416 [M]	The First Hits of 1965	1965	10.00
❑ LL 3431 [M]	The New Limelight	1965	10.00
❑ LL 3436 [M]	Great Country and Western Hits	1965	10.00
❑ SPC 21092	Opera's Golden Moments	197?	10.00
LONDON PHASE 4			
❑ SP-44053	The New Ebb Tide	1964	15.00
❑ SP-44059	Globetrotting	196?	15.00
❑ SP-44066 [S]	The New Limelight	1965	15.00
❑ SP-44077	The Great TV Themes	196?	15.00
❑ SP-44087	Hawaii	196?	15.00
❑ SP-44090	France	196?	15.00
❑ SP-44102	Music from Doctor Dolittle	196?	15.00
❑ SP-44112	Foreign Film Festival	196?	15.00
❑ SP-44141	New York	196?	15.00
❑ SP-44142	Chacksfield Plays the Beatles' Songbook	1970	15.00
❑ SP-44151	Chacksfield Plays Simon and Garfunkel and Jim Webb	1970	15.00
❑ SP-44158	Chacksfield Plays Bacharach	197?	15.00
❑ SP-44185	The Music of Cole Porter	1972	15.00
❑ SP-44194	The Glory That Was ... Gershwin	1973	12.00
❑ SP-44213	The Incomparable Jerome Kern	1974	15.00
❑ SP-44223	Frank Chacksfield Plays Rodgers and Hart	1975	15.00
❑ SP-44249	Frank Chacksfield Plays Lerner and Loewe	197?	15.00
❑ SP-44254	Frank Chacksfield Plays Irving Berlin	197?	15.00
❑ SP-44275	Frank Chacksfield Plays Hoagy Carmichael	197?	15.00
❑ SP-44289	Vintage '52	1977	15.00
❑ SW-95146	The Glory That Was ... Gershwin	1973	15.00

—Longines Symphonette Record Club edition

Number	Title (A Side/B Side)	Yr	NM
MCA			
❑ 5239	Love Songs	1981	12.00
PHOENIX 20			
❑ P20-604	How Deep Is Your Love	1980	8.00
PICKWICK			
❑ SPC-3231	Ebb Tide	197?	8.00
RICHMOND			
❑ B 20045 [M]	Million Sellers	195?	10.00
❑ B 20046 [M]	South Pacific	195?	10.00
❑ B 20056 [M]	Music for a Merry Christmas	1959	10.00
❑ B 20059 [M]	Porgy and Bess/Show Boat	1960	10.00
❑ B 20073 [M]	Great Strauss Waltzes	1960	10.00
❑ B 20078 [M]	Ebb Tide	1960	10.00
❑ B 20080 [M]	Songs of Sunny Italy	196?	10.00
❑ B 20086 [M]	The Best of Herbert and Romberg	196?	10.00
❑ B 20087 [M]	Love Themes from Great Operas	196?	10.00
❑ B 20093 [M]	My Gypsy Love	196?	10.00
❑ B 20095 [M]	Movie Themes	196?	10.00
❑ S 30045 [S]	Million Sellers	195?	12.00
❑ S 30046 [S]	South Pacific	195?	12.00
❑ S 30056 [S]	Music for a Merry Christmas	1959	12.00
❑ S 30059 [S]	Porgy and Bess/Show Boat	1960	12.00
❑ S 30073 [S]	Great Strauss Waltzes	1960	12.00
❑ S 30078 [S]	Ebb Tide	1960	12.00
❑ S 30080 [S]	Songs of Sunny Italy	196?	12.00
❑ S 30086 [S]	The Best of Herbert and Romberg	196?	12.00
❑ S 30087 [S]	Love Themes from Great Operas	196?	12.00
❑ S 30093 [S]	My Gypsy Love	196?	12.00
❑ S 30095 [S]	Movie Themes	196?	12.00
STARBORNE			
❑ SB-9002	Mirrors	1980	25.00
❑ SB-9003	People in Love	1980	25.00

CHAD AND JEREMY Also see CHAD AND JILL STUART.

45s

Number	Title (A Side/B Side)	Yr	NM
CAPITOL STARLINE			
❑ 6087	A Summer Song/ Willow Weep for Me	1966	8.00
—Green and white swirl label			
COLUMBIA			
❑ 43277	Before and After/Fare Thee Well	1965	10.00
❑ 43277 [DJ]	Before and After (same on both sides)	1965	40.00
—Promo only on red vinyl			
❑ 43277 [PS]	Before and After/Fare Thee Well	1965	50.00
—Basically identical to the more common "I Don't Want to Lose You Baby," except that on this sleeve, the blurbs on the front and back begin "Columbia Records Proudly Introduces..."			
❑ 43339	I Don't Wanna Lose You Baby/ Pennies	1965	8.00
❑ 43339 [PS]	I Don't Wanna Lose You Baby/ Pennies	1965	20.00
—Basically identical to the "Before and After" sleeve, except that this one has the words "Columbia Records Proudly Presents..." on front and back			
❑ 43414	I Have Dreamed/Should I?	1966	8.00
❑ 43490	Teenage Failure/ Early Morning Rain	1965	8.00
❑ 43490 [PS]	Teenage Failure/ Early Morning Rain	1965	20.00
❑ 43682	Distant Shores/Last Night	1966	8.00
❑ 43682 [PS]	Distant Shores/Last Night	1966	20.00
❑ 43807	You Are She/I Won't Cry	1966	8.00
❑ 43807 [PS]	You Are She/I Won't Cry	1966	20.00
❑ 44131	Rest in Peace/Family Way	1967	8.00
❑ 44379	Painted Dayglow Smile/Editorial	1967	8.00
❑ 44525	Sister Marie/Rest in Peace	1968	8.00
❑ 44660	Paxton Quigley's Had the Course/You Need Feet	1968	8.00
❑ 44660 [PS]	Paxton Quigley's Had the Course/You Need Feet	1968	16.00
—Promo-only sleeve of a Nazi military rally			
LANA			
❑ 145	Yesterday's Gone/Lemon Tree	196?	6.00
—Oldies reissue			
❑ 146	A Summer Song/ No Tears for Johnny	196?	6.00
ROCSHIRE			
❑ 95046	Bite the Bullet/How Many Trains	1983	4.00
❑ 95050 [DJ]	Bite the Bullet/Interview	1983	12.00
❑ 95061	Dreams/Zanzibar Sunset	1983	4.00
WORLD ARTISTS			
❑ 1021	Yesterday's Gone/Lemon Tree	1964	10.00
—As "Chad Stuart and Jeremy Clyde"			
❑ 1027	A Summer Song/ No Tears for Johnny	1964	10.00
—As "Chad Stuart and Jeremy Clyde"			
❑ 1034	Willow Weep for Me/ If She Was Mine	1964	10.00
❑ 1034 [PS]	Willow Weep for Me/ If She Was Mine	1964	20.00
❑ 1041	If I Loved You/Donna, Donna	1965	10.00
❑ 1041 [PS]	If I Loved You/Donna, Donna	1965	20.00

Except when noted otherwise, VG = 25% of NM, and VG+ = 50% of NM. (Example: VG = $2.00, VG+ = $4.00 and NM = $8.00.)

Number	Title (A Side/B Side)	Yr	NM
❑ 1052	What Do You Want with Me/A Very Good Year	1965	10.00
—As "Chad Stuart and Jeremy Clyde"			
❑ 1052 [PS]	What Do You Want with Me/A Very Good Year	1965	50.00
—As "Chad Stuart and Jeremy Clyde"			
❑ 1056	From a Window/My Coloring Book	1965	10.00
❑ 1060	September in the Rain/Only for the Young	1965	10.00

Albums

CAPITOL

Number	Title (A Side/B Side)	Yr	NM
❑ ST 2470 [P]	The Best of Chad and Jeremy	1966	12.00
—Black label with colorband			
❑ ST 2470 [P]	The Best of Chad and Jeremy	1967	10.00
—"Starline" label			
❑ T 2470 [M]	The Best of Chad and Jeremy	1966	10.00
—Black label with colorband			
❑ T 2470 [M]	The Best of Chad and Jeremy	1967	8.00
—"Starline" label			
❑ STT 2546 [P]	More Chad and Jeremy	1966	12.00
❑ TT 2546 [M]	More Chad and Jeremy	1966	10.00
❑ SN-16135 [P]	The Best of Chad and Jeremy	1980	8.00
—Budget-line reissue			

COLUMBIA

Number	Title (A Side/B Side)	Yr	NM
❑ CL 2374 [M]	Before and After	1965	20.00
❑ CL 2398 [M]	I Don't Want to Lose You Baby	1966	25.00
❑ CL 2564 [M]	Distant Shores	1966	20.00
❑ CL 2671 [M]	Of Cabbages and Kings	1967	20.00
❑ CL 2899 [M]	The Ark	1968	25.00
❑ CS 9174 [S]	Before and After	1965	30.00
❑ CS 9198 [S]	I Don't Want to Lose You Baby	1966	40.00
❑ CS 9364 [P]	Distant Shores	1966	25.00
—"Distant Shores" is rechanneled			
❑ CS 9471 [S]	Of Cabbages and Kings	1967	25.00
❑ CS 9699 [S]	The Arc	1968	25.00
—Some copies spell the LP title this way on the cover			
❑ CS 9699 [S]	The Ark	1968	25.00
—Correct spelling of LP title on cover			

FIDU

Number	Title (A Side/B Side)	Yr	NM
❑ FM-101 [M]	5 + 10 = 15 Fabulous Hits	1966	10.00
❑ FS-101 [P]	5 + 10 = 15 Fabulous Hits	1966	12.00

HARMONY

Number	Title (A Side/B Side)	Yr	NM
❑ HS 11357 [S]	Chad and Jeremy	1973	8.00

ROCSHIRE

Number	Title (A Side/B Side)	Yr	NM
❑ XR-22018	Chad Stuart and Jeremy Clyde	1983	10.00

WORLD ARTISTS

Number	Title (A Side/B Side)	Yr	NM
❑ WAM-2002 [M]	Yesterday's Gone	1964	12.00
❑ WAM-2005 [M]	Chad and Jeremy Sing for You	1965	12.00
❑ WAS-3002 [P]	Yesterday's Gone	1964	15.00
—"Yesterday's Gone" is rechanneled.			
❑ WAS-3005 [S]	Chad and Jeremy Sing for You	1965	15.00

CHAFFIN, ERNIE

45s

SUN

Number	Title (A Side/B Side)	Yr	NM
❑ 262	Feelin' Low/Lonesome for My Baby	1957	30.00
❑ 275	Laughin' and Jokin'/I'm Lonesome	1957	30.00
❑ 307	Nothing Can Change My Love for You/Born to Lose	1958	25.00
❑ 320	Don't Ever Leave Me/Miracle of You	1959	25.00

CHAIN REACTION

This Chain Reaction includes Steve Tallarico, later known as Steve Tyler of AEROSMITH.

45s

DATE

Number	Title (A Side/B Side)	Yr	NM
❑ 1538	When I Needed You/The Sun	1966	30.00

CHAIRMEN OF THE BOARD

45s

INVICTUS

Number	Title (A Side/B Side)	Yr	NM
❑ 1251	Finder's Keepers/Finder's Keepers (Part 2)	1973	5.00
❑ 1263	Life & Death/Love with Me, Love with Me	1974	5.00
❑ 1268	Everybody Party All Night/Morning Glory	1974	5.00
❑ 1271	Let's Have Some Fun/Love at First Sight	1974	5.00
❑ 1276	The Skin I'm In/Love at First Sight	1975	5.00
❑ 1278	You've Got Extra Added Power in Your Love/Someone Just Like You	1975	5.00
❑ 9074	Give Me Just a Little More Time/Since the Days of Pigtails	1970	6.00
❑ 9078	(You've Got Me) Dangling on a String/I'll Come Crawling	1970	5.00
❑ 9079	Everything's Tuesday/Patches	1970	5.00
❑ 9081	Pay to the Piper/Bless You	1970	5.00
❑ 9081 [PS]	Pay to the Piper/Bless You	1970	10.00
❑ 9086	Chairman of the Board/When Will She Tell Me She Needs Me	1971	5.00
❑ 9089	Hanging On (To) A Memory/Tracked and Trapped	1971	5.00
❑ 9099	Try On My Love for Size/Working on a Building of Love	1971	5.00
❑ 9103	Men Are Getting Scarce/Bravo! Hurray!	1971	5.00
❑ 9106	Bittersweet/Elmo James	1972	5.00
❑ 9122	Everybody's Got a Song to Sing/Working on a Building of Love	1972	5.00
❑ 9126	Let Me Down Easy/I Can't Find Myself	1972	5.00

Albums

INVICTUS

Number	Title (A Side/B Side)	Yr	NM
❑ ST-7300	Chairmen of the Board (Featuring "Give Me Just a Little More Time")	1970	40.00
❑ SKAO-7304	In Session	1970	40.00
❑ ST-9801	Bittersweet	1972	40.00
❑ KZ 32526	The Skin I'm In	1974	40.00

CHAKACHAS, THE

45s

AVCO

Number	Title (A Side/B Side)	Yr	NM
❑ 4596	Judas Kiss/Stories	1972	5.00

JANUS

Number	Title (A Side/B Side)	Yr	NM
❑ 237	Africa Yama (Part 1)/Africa Yama (Part 2)	1974	5.00

POLYDOR

Number	Title (A Side/B Side)	Yr	NM
❑ 15030	Jungle Fever/Cha Ka Cha	1972	6.00
❑ 15102	Jungle Fever '75/Liza (And Brook)	1975	4.00

Albums

POLYDOR

Number	Title (A Side/B Side)	Yr	NM
❑ PD-5504	Jungle Fever	1972	15.00

CHAKIRIS, GEORGE

45s

CAPITOL

Number	Title (A Side/B Side)	Yr	NM
❑ 4844	Maria/Once Upon a Time	1962	8.00
❑ 4892	My Coloring Book/I've Got Your Number	1962	8.00
❑ 5113	My Place/Love Being Here with You	1964	8.00
❑ 5209	Invisible Tears/Not for Me	1964	8.00
❑ 5426	Days of the Waltz/Finding Words for Spring	1965	8.00
❑ 5458	Blue Summer/Ship of Fools	1965	8.00

HORIZON

Number	Title (A Side/B Side)	Yr	NM
❑ 356	But Not for Me/Embraceable You	1962	12.00
❑ 363	Cool/Embraceable You	1962	12.00

Albums

CAPITOL

Number	Title (A Side/B Side)	Yr	NM
❑ ST 1750 [S]	George Chakiris	1962	20.00
❑ T 1750 [M]	George Chakiris	1962	15.00
❑ ST 1813 [S]	Memories Are Made of These	1963	20.00
❑ T 1813 [M]	Memories Are Made of These	1963	15.00
❑ ST 2391 [S]	It's Been a Swingin' Summer	1965	15.00
❑ T 2391 [M]	It's Been a Swingin' Summer	1965	12.00

HORIZON

Number	Title (A Side/B Side)	Yr	NM
❑ ST-1610 [S]	The Gershwin Songbook	1962	20.00
❑ WP-1610 [M]	The Gershwin Songbook	1962	15.00

CHAKRAS, THE

45s

REPRISE

Number	Title (A Side/B Side)	Yr	NM
❑ 0838	Things We Said Today/Just with You	1969	15.00
❑ 0859	Agnes Vandalism/City Boy	1969	15.00

CHALETS, THE

45s

DART

Number	Title (A Side/B Side)	Yr	NM
❑ 1026	Who's Laughing-Who's Crying/Fat Fat Fat! Mom-Mi-O	1961	25.00

LAURIE

Number	Title (A Side/B Side)	Yr	NM
❑ 3348	She's Not the Marrying Type/(Theme from) She's Not the Marrying Type	1966	12.00

MUSICNOTE

Number	Title (A Side/B Side)	Yr	NM
❑ 1001	Who's Laughing-Who's Crying/Fat Fat Fat! Mom-Mi-O	1962	20.00

TRU-LITE

Number	Title (A Side/B Side)	Yr	NM
❑ 1001	Who's Laughing-Who's Crying/Mom-Mia	1961	50.00

CHALLENGERS, THE (1)

California surf and instrumental group.

45s

GNP CRESCENDO

Number	Title (A Side/B Side)	Yr	NM
❑ 362	The Man from U.N.C.L.E./Summer Nights	1965	10.00
❑ 362	The Man from U.N.C.L.E./The Streets of London	1965	10.00
❑ 368	Walk with Me/How Could It	1966	10.00
❑ 376	Wipe Out/North Beach	1966	10.00
❑ 380	Milord/What If It Should Rain	1966	10.00
❑ 396	The Water Country/Everything to Me	1967	10.00
❑ 400	Color Me In/Before You	1968	10.00
❑ 412	Chitty Chitty Bang Bang/Lonely Little Girl	1968	10.00

TRIUMPH

Number	Title (A Side/B Side)	Yr	NM
❑ 112	Pipeline/Asphalt Spinner	1966	30.00

VAULT

Number	Title (A Side/B Side)	Yr	NM
❑ 900	Bull Dog/Torquay	1963	20.00
❑ 902	Moondawg/Tidal Wave	1963	20.00
❑ 904	Foot Tapper/On the Move	1963	20.00
❑ 910	Hot Rod Hootenanny/Maybellene	1964	30.00
❑ 913	Hot Rod Show/K-39	1964	30.00
❑ 918	Channel Nine/Can't Seem to Make You Mine	1965	20.00

Albums

FANTASY

Number	Title (A Side/B Side)	Yr	NM
❑ F-9443	Where Were You in the Summer of '62	1973	12.00

GNP CRESCENDO

Number	Title (A Side/B Side)	Yr	NM
❑ GNP-609 [(2)M]	25 Great Instrumental Hits	1967	25.00
❑ GNPS-609 [(2)S]	25 Great Instrumental Hits	1967	20.00
❑ GNP-2010 [M]	The Challengers at the Teenage Fair	1965	20.00
❑ GNPS-2010 [S]	The Challengers at the Teenage Fair	1965	25.00
❑ GNP-2018 [M]	The Man from U.N.C.L.E.	1965	20.00
❑ GNPS-2018 [S]	The Man from U.N.C.L.E.	1965	25.00
❑ GNP-2025 [M]	California Kicks	1966	20.00
❑ GNPS-2025 [S]	California Kicks	1966	25.00
❑ GNP-2030 [M]	Billy Strange and the Challengers	1966	20.00
❑ GNPS-2030 [S]	Billy Strange and the Challengers	1966	25.00
❑ GNP-2031 [M]	Wipe Out	1966	20.00
❑ GNPS-2031 [S]	Wipe Out	1966	25.00
❑ GNPS-2045	Light My Fire with Classical Gas	1968	20.00
❑ GNPS-2056	Vanilla Funk	1970	20.00
❑ GNPS-2093	Sidewalk Surfing	1975	12.00

RHINO

Number	Title (A Side/B Side)	Yr	NM
❑ RNLP-053	Best of the Challengers	1982	10.00

TRIUMPH

Number	Title (A Side/B Side)	Yr	NM
❑ TR-100 [M]	The Challengers Go Sidewalk Surfing	1965	20.00
❑ TRS-100 [S]	The Challengers Go Sidewalk Surfing	1965	25.00

VAULT

Number	Title (A Side/B Side)	Yr	NM
❑ LP-100 [M]	Surfbeat	1963	50.00
❑ VS-100 [S]	Surfbeat	1963	80.00
—Black vinyl			
❑ VS-100 [S]	Surfbeat	1963	250.00
—Orange vinyl			
❑ VS-100 [S]	Surfbeat	1963	250.00
—Red vinyl			
❑ VS-100 [S]	Surfbeat	1963	250.00
—Yellow vinyl			
❑ LP-101 [M]	Surfin' with the Challengers	1963	50.00
—Altered title			
❑ LP-101 [M]	Lloyd Thaxton Goes Surfin' with the Challengers	1963	60.00
—Original title			
❑ VS-101 [S]	Surfin' with the Challengers	1963	80.00
—Altered title; black vinyl			
❑ VS-101 [S]	Lloyd Thaxton Goes Surfin' with the Challengers	1963	100.00
—Original title; black vinyl			
❑ VS-101 [S]	(Lloyd Thaxton Goes) Surfin' with the Challengers	1963	250.00
—Either title; blue vinyl			
❑ VS-101 [S]	(Lloyd Thaxton Goes) Surfin' with the Challengers	1963	250.00
—Either title; orange vinyl			
❑ VS-101 [S]	(Lloyd Thaxton Goes) Surfin' with the Challengers	1963	250.00
—Either title; red vinyl			
❑ VS-101 [S]	(Lloyd Thaxton Goes) Surfin' with the Challengers	1963	250.00
—Either title; yellow vinyl			
❑ LP-102 [M]	The Challengers On The Move	1963	40.00
❑ VS-102 [S]	The Challengers On The Move	1963	60.00
❑ LP-107 [M]	K-39	1964	80.00
❑ LP-109 [M]	The Surf's Up	1965	40.00
❑ VS-109 [S]	The Surf's Up	1965	60.00
❑ LP-110 [M]	The Challengers A-Go-Go	1966	30.00

The Chambers Brothers, "I Can't Turn You Loose," Columbia 4-44679, 1968, **$10.**

Number	Title (A Side/B Side)	Yr	NM
❑ VS-110 [S]	The Challengers A-Go-Go	1966	40.00
❑ LP-111 [M]	The Challengers' Greatest Hits	1967	25.00
❑ VS-111 [S]	The Challengers' Greatest Hits	1967	25.00

CHALLENGERS, THE (2) Mid-1960s R&B group.

45s

CHESS

Number	Title (A Side/B Side)	Yr	NM
❑ 1957	Tossin' and Turnin'/ Don;t You Know It	1966	10.00

CHALLENGERS, THE (3) Members of this group later recorded as THE OLYMPICS.

45s

MELATONE

Number	Title (A Side/B Side)	Yr	NM
❑ 1002	I Can Tell/The Mambo Beat	1956	300.00

CHALLENGERS, THE (4) Members of this group later recorded as UNDERGROUND SUNSHINE.

45s

NIGHT OWL

Number	Title (A Side/B Side)	Yr	NM
❑ 6794	I Wanna Hold You/The Challengers Take a Ride on the Jefferson Airplane	1967	30.00

CHALLENGERS, THE (5) British group.

45s

TRIODEX

Number	Title (A Side/B Side)	Yr	NM
❑ 102	Goofus/Lazy Twist	1960	20.00
❑ 107	Deadline/Cry of the Wild Goose	1961	20.00

CHALLENGERS, THE (U) May be another record by group (2), but we're not sure.

45s

CUCA

Number	Title (A Side/B Side)	Yr	NM
❑ 1500	Hear My Message/ I Wanna Hold You	1968	8.00

CHALLENGERS III, THE

45s

TRI-PHI

Number	Title (A Side/B Side)	Yr	NM
❑ 1012	Stay/Honey, Honey, Honey	1962	30.00
—As "The Challengers"			
❑ 1012	Stay/Honey, Honey, Honey	1962	50.00
—As "The Challengers III"			
❑ 1020	Every Day/I Hear an Echo	1963	50.00

CHAMAELEON CHURCH Chevy Chase was in this group.

45s

MGM

Number	Title (A Side/B Side)	Yr	NM
❑ 13929	Your Golden Love/ Camillia I Changing	1968	12.00

Albums

MGM

Number	Title (A Side/B Side)	Yr	NM
❑ SE-4574	Chamaeleon Church	1968	20.00

CHAMBERLAIN, RICHARD

45s

MCA

Number	Title (A Side/B Side)	Yr	NM
❑ 40691	Secret Kingdom/The Slipper and the Rose Waltz	1977	4.00

MGM

Number	Title (A Side/B Side)	Yr	NM
❑ K13075	Theme from Dr. Kildare (Three Stars Will Shine Tonight)/ A Kiss to Build a Dream On	1962	10.00
❑ K13075 [PS]	Theme from Dr. Kildare (Three Stars Will Shine Tonight)/ A Kiss to Build a Dream On	1962	20.00
❑ K13097	Love Me Tender/All I Do Is Dream of You	1962	10.00
❑ K13097 [PS]	Love Me Tender/All I Do Is Dream of You	1962	20.00
❑ K13121	All I Have to Do Is Dream/ Hi-Lili, Hi-Lo	1963	10.00
❑ K13121 [PS]	All I Have to Do Is Dream/ Hi-Lili, Hi-Lo	1963	20.00
❑ K13148	I Will Love You/True Love	1963	10.00
❑ K13148 [PS]	I Will Love You/True Love	1963	20.00
❑ K13170	Blue Guitar/They Long to Be Close to You	1963	10.00
❑ K13170 [PS]	Blue Guitar/They Long to Be Close to You	1963	20.00
❑ K13205	Stella By Starlight/ Georgia on My Mind	1964	8.00
❑ K13205 [PS]	Stella By Starlight/ Georgia on My Mind	1964	20.00
❑ K13285	Rome Will Never Leave You/ You Always Hurt the One You Love	1964	8.00
❑ K13285 [PS]	Rome Will Never Leave You/You Always Hurt the One You Love	1964	15.00
❑ K13340	Joy in the Morning/April Love	1965	8.00
❑ K13340 [PS]	Joy in the Morning/April Love	1965	20.00

Albums

METRO

Number	Title (A Side/B Side)	Yr	NM
❑ M-564 [M]	Richard Chamberlain Sings	1966	12.00
❑ MS-564 [S]	Richard Chamberlain Sings	1966	12.00

MGM

Number	Title (A Side/B Side)	Yr	NM
❑ E-4088 [M]	Richard Chamberlain Sings	1962	15.00
❑ SE-4088 [S]	Richard Chamberlain Sings	1962	20.00
❑ E-4185 [M]	Twilight of Honor	1963	15.00
❑ SE-4185 [S]	Twilight of Honor	1963	20.00
❑ E-4287 [M]	Joy in the Morning	1965	15.00
❑ SE-4287 [S]	Joy in the Morning	1965	20.00
❑ ST 90512 [S]	Richard Chamberlain Sings	1965	30.00
—Capitol Record Club edition			
❑ T 90512 [M]	Richard Chamberlain Sings	1965	25.00
—Capitol Record Club edition			

CHAMBERLAIN, WILT "THE STILT"

45s

END

Number	Title (A Side/B Side)	Yr	NM
❑ 1066	By the River/That's Easy to Say	1960	25.00

CHAMBERS BROTHERS, THE

45s

AVCO

Number	Title (A Side/B Side)	Yr	NM
❑ 4632	Let's Go, Let's Go, Let's Go/ Do You Believe in Magic	1974	4.00
❑ 4638	1-2-3/Looking Back	1974	4.00
❑ 4657	Miss Lady Brown/ Stealin' Watermelons	1975	4.00

COLUMBIA

Number	Title (A Side/B Side)	Yr	NM
❑ 4-43816	Time Has Come Today (2:37)/ Dinah	1966	12.00
—A-side is a different recording than the later hit, both vocally and instrumentally			
❑ 43957	All Strung Out Over You/ Falling in Love	1967	6.00
❑ 44080	Please Don't Leave Me/ I Can't Stand It	1967	6.00
❑ 44296	Uptown/Love Me Like the Rain	1967	6.00
❑ 4-44414	Time Has Come Today (4:45)/ People Get Ready	1968	8.00
—Hit version; label refers to the album "The Time Has Come"			
❑ 4-44414	Time Has Come Today (3:05)/ People Get Ready	1968	10.00
—No reference to the album "The Time Has Come"; despite the listed time, this plays the 4:45 hit version (master number in trail-off ends in "3B"); we're not sure if stock copies list 3:05 and play 3:05, too			
❑ 4-44414 [DJ]	Time Has Come Today (3:05) (same on both sides)	1968	15.00
—"Special Rush Reservice" on label; this plays a 3:05 edit of the long LP version (master numbers in trail-off end in "1B" on one side and "1F" on the other)			
❑ 4-44679	I Can't Turn You Loose/ Do Your Thing	1968	6.00
❑ 4-44679 [PS]	I Can't Turn You Loose/ Do Your Thing	1968	10.00
❑ 44779	Are You Ready/You Got the Power to Turn Me On	1969	6.00
❑ 44890	Wake Up/Everybody Needs Someone	1969	6.00
❑ 44986	Have a Little Faith/Baby Takes Care of Business	1969	5.00
❑ 4-45055	Merry Christmas, Happy New Year/Did You Stop to Pray This Morning	1969	6.00
❑ 45088	Love, Peace and Happiness/ If You Want Me To	1970	5.00
❑ 45146	To Love Somebody/Let's Do It	1970	5.00
❑ 45277	Love, Peace and Happiness/ Funky	1970	5.00
❑ 45394	When the Evening Comes/ New Generation	1971	5.00
❑ 45488	Heaven/(By the Hair on) My Chinny Chin Chin	1971	6.00
❑ 45518	Merry Christmas, Happy New Year/Did You Stop to Pray This Morning	1971	6.00
❑ 45837	Boogie Children/You Make the Magic	1973	6.00

ROXBURY

Number	Title (A Side/B Side)	Yr	NM
❑ 2034	Bring It On Down Front Pretty Mama/Midnight Blue	1976	5.00

Except when noted otherwise, VG = 25% of NM, and VG+ = 50% of NM. (Example: VG = $2.00, VG+ = $4.00 and NM = $8.00.)

Number	Title (A Side/B Side)	Yr	NM
VAULT			
❑ 920	Call Me/Seventeen	1965	15.00
❑ 923	Pretty Girls Everywhere/ Love Me Like the Rain	1966	12.00
❑ 945	Shout Part 1/Shout Part 2	1968	8.00
❑ 955	Just a Closer Walk with Thee/ Girls We Love You	1969	6.00
❑ 967	House of the Rising Sun/ Blues Get Off My Shoulder	1970	6.00
Albums			
AVCO			
❑ 11013	Unbonded	1974	12.00
❑ 69003	Night Move	1975	20.00
COLUMBIA			
❑ KGP 20 [(2)]	Love, Peace and Happiness	1969	25.00
❑ CL 2722 [M]	The Time Has Come	1967	30.00
❑ CS 9522	The Time Has Come	1971	12.00
—Orange label			
❑ CS 9522 [S]	The Time Has Come	1967	20.00
—Red "360 Sound" label			
❑ PC 9522	The Time Has Come	198?	8.00
—Reissue with new prefix			
❑ CS 9671	A New Time — A New Day	1968	20.00
❑ C 30032	New Generation	1970	15.00
❑ C 30871	The Chambers Brothers' Greatest Hits	1971	15.00
❑ PC 30871	The Chambers Brothers' Greatest Hits	198?	8.00
—Reissue with new prefix			
❑ KC 31158	Oh My God	1972	—
—Canceled			
❑ CG 33642 [(2)]	The Time Has Come/A New Time — A New Day	1975	15.00
FANTASY			
❑ 24718 [(2)]	The Best of the Chambers Brothers	1973	15.00
FOLKWAYS			
❑ 31008	Groovin' Time	1968	15.00
ROXBURY			
❑ RLX-106	Live In Concert on Mars	1976	30.00
VAULT			
❑ LP-115 [M]	The Chambers Brothers Now	1967	15.00
❑ VS-115 [S]	The Chambers Brothers Now	1967	15.00
❑ VS-120	The Chambers Brothers Shout	1968	15.00
❑ VS-128	Feelin' the Blues	1969	15.00
❑ VS-135 [(2)]	The Chambers Brothers Greatest Hits	1970	20.00
❑ LP-9003 [M]	People Get Ready	1966	20.00
❑ LPS-9003 [S]	People Get Ready	1966	25.00

CHAMP, BILLY

Number	Title (A Side/B Side)	Yr	NM
45s			
ABC-PARAMOUNT			
❑ 10518	Believe Me/Hush-A-Bye	1964	30.00

CHAMPLAINS, THE

FRED PARRIS of THE FIVE SATINS is the lead voice.

Number	Title (A Side/B Side)	Yr	NM
45s			
UNITED ARTISTS			
❑ 346	Ding Dong/Have You Changed Your Mind	1961	40.00

CHAMPS, THE

Also see DAVE BURGESS; GLEN CAMPBELL; CHUCK RIO; SEALS AND CROFTS.

Number	Title (A Side/B Side)	Yr	NM
45s			
CHALLENGE			
❑ 1016	Tequila/Train to Nowhere	1958	25.00
❑ 1016	Tequila/Train to Nowhere	1958	600.00
—Blue vinyl (one known to exist)			
❑ 9113	The Shoddy Shoddy/Sombrero	1961	20.00
❑ 9116	Cantina/Panic Button	1961	20.00
❑ 9131	Tequila Twist/Limbo Rock	1961	20.00
❑ 9140	Experiment in Terror/ La Cucaracha	1962	15.00
❑ 9143	What a Country/ I've Just Seen Her	1962	15.00
❑ 9162	Limbo Dance/Latin Limbo	1962	15.00
❑ 9174	Varsity Rock/That Did It	1962	15.00
❑ 9180	Mr. Cool//3/4 Mash	1963	15.00
❑ 9189	Nik Nak/Shades	1963	15.00
❑ 9199	Cactus Juice/Roots	1963	15.00
❑ 59007	El Rancho Rock/Midnighter	1958	20.00
❑ 59018	Chariot Rock/Subway	1958	20.00
❑ 59026	Turnpike/Rockin' Mary	1958	20.00
❑ 59035	Gone Train/Beatnik	1958	20.00
❑ 59043	Moonlight Bay/Caramba	1959	20.00
❑ 59049	Night Train/The Rattler	1959	20.00
❑ 59053	Sky High/Double Eagle Rock	1959	20.00
❑ 59063	Too Much Tequila/Twenty Thousand Leagues	1960	20.00
❑ 59076	Red Eye/The Little Matador	1960	20.00
❑ 59086	Alley Cat/Coconut Grove	1960	20.00
❑ 59097	The Face/Tough Train	1960	20.00
❑ 59103	Hokey Pokey/Jumping Bean	1961	20.00
❑ 59219	San Juan/Jalisco	1963	15.00
❑ 59236	Switzerland/Only the Young	1964	15.00
❑ 59263	Fraternity Waltz/Kahlua	1964	15.00
❑ 59276	French 75/Bright Lights, Big City	1965	15.00
❑ 59314	The Man from Durango/ Red Pepper	1965	15.00
❑ 59322	Anna/Buckaroo	1965	15.00
LANA			
❑ 155	Tequila/Sky High	196?	8.00
—Possibly re-recorded version of A-side			
REPUBLIC			
❑ 246	Tequila '76 (Long)/Tequila '76 (Short)	1976	8.00
❑ 246 [PS]	Tequila '76 (Long)/Tequila '76 (Short)	1976	8.00
WE'RE BACK			
❑ 1	Tequila '77/From Me to You	1977	8.00
7-Inch Extended Plays			
CHALLENGE			
❑ EP-7100	Tequila/I'll Be There//Train to Nowhere/Lollipop	1958	150.00
❑ EP-7100 [PS]	Tequila	1958	150.00
Albums			
CHALLENGE			
❑ CHL-601 [M]	Go Champs Go	1958	250.00
❑ CHL-601 [M]	Go Champs Go	1958	2400.
—Blue vinyl; VG value 800; VG+ value 1600			
❑ CHL-605 [M]	Everybody's Rockin' with the Champs	1959	200.00
❑ CHL-613 [M]	Great Dance Hits	1962	120.00
❑ CHL-614 [M]	All American Music from the Champs	1962	120.00
❑ CHS-2500 [S]	Everybody's Rockin' with the Champs	1959	300.00
❑ CHS-2513 [S]	Great Dance Hits	1962	200.00
❑ CHS-2514 [S]	All American Music from the Champs	1962	200.00

CHANCE, NOLAN

Number	Title (A Side/B Side)	Yr	NM
45s			
BUNKY			
❑ 161	Just Like the Weather/ (B-side unknown)	1965	1200.
CONSTELLATION			
❑ 144	She's Gone/If He Makes You	1965	25.00
❑ 161	Don't Use Me/Just Like the Weather	1965	120.00

CHANCERS, THE

Number	Title (A Side/B Side)	Yr	NM
45s			
DOT			
❑ 15870	Shirley Ann/My One	1958	30.00

CHANDELLES, THE

Number	Title (A Side/B Side)	Yr	NM
45s			
DOT			
❑ 16553	El Gato/Jetster	1963	25.00

CHANDLER, BARBARA

Number	Title (A Side/B Side)	Yr	NM
45s			
ABC-PARAMOUNT			
❑ 10369	Clinging Vine/The Boy You Used to Go With	1962	20.00
❑ 10429	Girl Talk/Broken Hearted	1963	30.00
CAMEO			
❑ 458	I Go/(You Forgot) In the Still of the Night	1967	10.00
KAPP			
❑ 542	It Hurts to Be Sixteen/ Running, Running Johnny	1963	30.00
❑ 555	I Live to Love You/Fool's Errand	1963	30.00
❑ 575	A Lonely New Year/I'm Going Out With The Girls	1964	12.00
MUSICOR			
❑ 1321	How Can I Say No to You/ Pretty Shade of Blue	1968	10.00

CHANDLER, DENIECE (DENISE)

See DENIECE WILLIAMS.

CHANDLER, GENE

Includes records as "The Duke of Earl." Also see THE DUKAYS.

Number	Title (A Side/B Side)	Yr	NM
12-Inch Singles			
CHI-SOUND			
❑ TCD 68	Get Down (8:14) (same on both sides)	1978	15.00
❑ TCD 73	Get Down/Contact	1979	15.00
—B-side by Edwin Starr			
❑ TCD 110	Does She Have a Friend?/ Let Me Make Love to You	1980	10.00
❑ CH-2001	I'll Make the Living If You Make the Loving Worthwhile (Disco Version 6:10)/Time Is a Thief	1982	15.00
20TH CENTURY			
❑ TCD 80	When You're #1 (8:59)/ I'll Remember You	1979	20.00
❑ TCD 98	Do What Comes So Natural (5:00)/That Funky Disco Rhythm (5:39)	1979	15.00
45s			
BRUNSWICK			
❑ 55312	Girl Don't Care/My Love	1967	8.00
❑ 55339	There Goes the Lover/ Tell Me What I Can Do	1967	8.00
❑ 55383	There Was a Time/Those Were the Good Old Days	1968	8.00
❑ 55394	Teacher, Teacher/ Pit of Loneliness	1968	8.00
❑ 55413	Eleanor Rigby/ Familiar Footsteps	1969	8.00
❑ 55425	This Bitter Earth/Suicide	1969	8.00
CHECKER			
❑ 1155	I Fooled You This Time/ Such a Pretty Thing	1966	8.00
❑ 1165	To Be a Lover/After the Laughter	1967	8.00
❑ 1190	I Won't Need You/ No Peace, No Satisfaction	1967	8.00
❑ 1199	River of Tears/It's Time to Settle Down	1968	8.00
❑ 1220	Go Back Home/In My Baby's House	1969	8.00
CHI-SOUND			
❑ 1001	I'll Make the Living If You Make the Loving Worthwhile/ (B-side unknown)	1982	5.00
❑ 1168	Give Me the Cue/Tomorrow We May Not Feel the Same	1978	4.00
❑ 2386	Get Down/I'm the Traveling Kind	1978	4.00
❑ 2404	Please Sunrise/Greatest Love Ever Known	1979	4.00
❑ 2411	When You're #1/ I'll Remember You	1979	5.00
❑ 2451	Does She Have a Friend?/ Let Me Make Love to You	1980	4.00
❑ 2468	Lay Me Gently/You've Been So Good to Me	1980	4.00
❑ 2480	Rainbow '80/I'll Be There	1980	4.00
❑ 2494	I'm Attracted to You/ I've Got to Meet You	1981	4.00
❑ 2507	Love Is the Answer/Godsend	1981	4.00
CONSTELLATION			
❑ 104	From Day to Day/It's No Good for Me	1963	10.00
❑ 110	Pretty Little Girl/A Little Like Lovin'	1963	10.00
❑ 112	Think Nothing About It/ Wish You Were Here	1964	10.00
❑ 114	Soul Hootenanny (Part 1)/ Soul Hootenanny (Part 2)	1964	10.00
❑ 124	A Song Called Soul/You Left Me	1964	10.00
❑ 130	Just Be True/A Song Called Soul	1964	10.00
❑ 136	Bless Our Love/London Town	1964	10.00
❑ 141	What Now/If You Can't Be True	1964	10.00
❑ 146	You Can't Hurt Me No More/ Everybody Let's Dance	1965	8.00
❑ 149	Nothing Can Stop Me/ The Big Lie	1965	8.00
❑ 158	Rainbow '65 (Part 1)/ Rainbow '65 (Part 2)	1965	8.00
❑ 160	Good Times/No One Can Love You	1965	8.00
❑ 164	Here Come the Tears/ Soul Hootenanny (Part 2)	1965	8.00
❑ 166	Baby That's Love/ Bet You Never Thought	1966	8.00
❑ 167	(I'm Just a) Fool for You/ Buddy Ain't It a Shame	1966	8.00
❑ 169	I Can Take Care of Myself/If I Can't Save It	1966	8.00
❑ 172	Mr. Big Shot/I Hate to Be the One to Say	1966	8.00
CURTOM			
❑ 1979	Don't Have to Be Lyin' Babe (Part 1)/Don't Have to Be Lyin' Babe (Part 2)	1973	5.00
❑ 1986	Baby I Still Love You/ I Understand	1973	5.00
❑ 1992	Without You Here/Just Be There	1973	5.00
FASTFIRE			
❑ 7003	Haven't I Heard That Line Before/ You'll Never Be Free of Me	1985	5.00
❑ 7005	Lucy/Please You Tonight	1986	5.00
LOST-NITE			
❑ 310	Duke of Earl/Rainbow	197?	5.00
MERCURY			
❑ 73083	Groovy Situation/Not the Marrying Kind	1970	6.00
❑ 73121	Simply Call It Love/ Give Me a Chance	1970	6.00

Except when noted otherwise, VG = 25% of NM, and VG+ = 50% of NM. (Example: VG = $2.00, VG+ = $4.00 and NM = $8.00.)

Number	Title (A Side/B Side)	Yr	NM
❑ 73206	You're a Lady/Stone Cold Feeling	1971	6.00
❑ 73258	Yes I'm Ready (If I Don't Get to Go)/Pillars of Glass	1971	6.00

SALSOUL

Number	Title (A Side/B Side)	Yr	NM
❑ 7051	You're the One/I Keep Comin' Back for More	1983	4.00

—With Jaime Lynn

20TH CENTURY

Number	Title (A Side/B Side)	Yr	NM
❑ 2411	When You're #1/ I'll Remember You	1979	4.00
❑ 2428	Do What Comes So Natural/ That Funky Disco Rhythm	1979	4.00

VEE JAY

Number	Title (A Side/B Side)	Yr	NM
❑ 416	Duke of Earl/Kissin' in the Kitchen	1961	25.00
❑ 416	Duke of Earl/Kissin' in the Kitchen	1962	20.00
—Some later pressings as "The Duke of Earl"			
❑ 440	Walk On with the Duke/ London Town	1962	15.00
—As "The Duke of Earl"			
❑ 450	Daddy's Home/The Big Lie	1962	15.00
—As "The Duke of Earl"			
❑ 455	I'll Follow You/You Left Me	1962	15.00
—As "The Duke of Earl"			
❑ 461	Tear for Tear/Miracle After Miracle	1962	15.00
❑ 468	You Threw a Lucky Punch/ Rainbow	1962	15.00
❑ 511	Check Yourself/Forgive Me	1963	15.00
❑ 536	Baby, That's Love/ Man's Temptation	1963	15.00

Albums

BRUNSWICK

Number	Title (A Side/B Side)	Yr	NM
❑ BL 54124 [M]	The Girl Don't Care	1967	25.00
❑ BL 754124 [S]	The Girl Don't Care	1967	20.00
❑ BL 754131	There Was a Time	1968	20.00
❑ BL 754149	The Two Sides of Gene Chandler	1969	20.00

CHECKER

Number	Title (A Side/B Side)	Yr	NM
❑ LP-3003 [M]	The Duke of Soul	1967	50.00
❑ LPS-3003 [R]	The Duke of Soul	1967	30.00

CHI-SOUND

Number	Title (A Side/B Side)	Yr	NM
❑ T-578	Get Down	1978	10.00

CONSTELLATION

Number	Title (A Side/B Side)	Yr	NM
❑ LP 1421 [M]	Greatest Hits by Gene Chandler	1964	50.00
❑ LP 1423 [M]	Just Be True	1964	50.00
❑ LP 1425 [M]	Gene Chandler — Live On Stage in '65	1965	50.00

MERCURY

Number	Title (A Side/B Side)	Yr	NM
❑ SR-61304	The Gene Chandler Situation	1970	15.00

SOLID SMOKE

Number	Title (A Side/B Side)	Yr	NM
❑ SS-8027	Stroll On with the Duke	198?	10.00

20TH CENTURY

Number	Title (A Side/B Side)	Yr	NM
❑ T-605	Gene Chandler '80	1980	10.00
❑ T-625	Ear Candy	1980	10.00
❑ T-629	Here's to Love	1981	10.00

UPFRONT

Number	Title (A Side/B Side)	Yr	NM
❑ UPF 105	Duke of Earl	197?	10.00

VEE JAY

Number	Title (A Side/B Side)	Yr	NM
❑ LP-1040 [M]	The Duke of Earl	1962	120.00
❑ SR-1040 [M]	The Duke of Earl	196?	50.00
—"Stereophonic" on front; no "Important Notice..." on back; record plays mono. Most labels are all-black with "VJ" in brackets. This was a semi-authorized reissue after ex-Vee Jay executives bought the company's remnants in bankruptcy court in 1966.			
❑ SR-1040 [S]	The Duke of Earl	1962	250.00
—"Stereo" sticker on mono cover; "Stereo" on record labels			
❑ SR-1040 [S]	The Duke of Earl	1962	800.00
—"Stereophonic" on front cover; top back cover contains note that begins: "Important Notice...This Is a Stereophonic Record"; "Stereo" on record labels			
❑ VJLP-1040	The Duke of Earl	198?	10.00
—Mid-1980s authorized reissue			

CHANDLER, GENE, AND BARBARA ACKLIN

Also see each artist's individual listings.

45s

BRUNSWICK

Number	Title (A Side/B Side)	Yr	NM
❑ 55366	Love Won't Start/Show Me the Way to Go	1968	8.00
❑ 55387	From the Teacher to the Preacher/Anywhere But Nowhere	1968	8.00
❑ 55405	Little Green Apples/ Will I Find You	1969	8.00

CHANDLER, GENE, AND JERRY BUTLER

Also see each artist's individual listings.

45s

MERCURY

Number	Title (A Side/B Side)	Yr	NM
❑ 73163	You Just Can't Win (By Making the Same Mistake)/The Show Is Grooving	1971	6.00
❑ 73195	Two and Two (Take This Woman Off the Corner)/ Everybody Is Waiting	1971	6.00

Albums

MERCURY

Number	Title (A Side/B Side)	Yr	NM
❑ SR-61330	Gene & Jerry — One & One	1971	15.00

CHANDLER, JEFF

45s

DECCA

Number	Title (A Side/B Side)	Yr	NM
❑ 9-29004	I Should Care/More Than Anyone	1954	15.00
❑ 9-29175	Lamplight/That's All She's Waiting to Hear	1954	12.00
❑ 9-29345	Always/Everything Happens to Me	1955	12.00
❑ 9-29405	My Prayer/When Spring Comes	1955	12.00
❑ 9-29532	Shaner Maidel/Foxfire	1955	12.00
❑ 9-29600	Only the Very Young/A Little Love Can Go a Long, Long Way	1955	12.00

LIBERTY

Number	Title (A Side/B Side)	Yr	NM
❑ 55092	Half of My Heart/Hold Me	1957	10.00

Albums

LIBERTY

Number	Title (A Side/B Side)	Yr	NM
❑ LRP-3067 [M]	Jeff Chandler Sings to You	1957	40.00
❑ LRP-3074 [M]	Warm and Easy	1958	40.00

SUNSET

Number	Title (A Side/B Side)	Yr	NM
❑ SUS-5127	Sincerely Yours	1969	12.00

CHANDLER, KENNY

45s

AMY

Number	Title (A Side/B Side)	Yr	NM
❑ 890	I Don't Know Why/Happy to Be Unhappy	1963	10.00

CORAL

Number	Title (A Side/B Side)	Yr	NM
❑ 62309	It Might Have Been/ Yours and Yours Alone	1962	10.00

EPIC

Number	Title (A Side/B Side)	Yr	NM
❑ 9758	Come Softly to Me/ S.O.S. (Sweet On Susie)	1965	8.00
❑ 10009	I'll Be Coming Back/ Sunshine Sweetheart	1966	8.00

LAURIE

Number	Title (A Side/B Side)	Yr	NM
❑ 3140	Man on the Run/Leave Me If You Want To	1962	10.00
❑ 3158	Heart/Wait for Me	1963	10.00
❑ 3181	I Tell Myself/I Can't Stand Tears at a Party	1963	10.00

TOWER

Number	Title (A Side/B Side)	Yr	NM
❑ 354	Sleep/Nickles and Dimes	1967	8.00
❑ 405	Beyond Love/Charity	1968	8.00

UNITED ARTISTS

Number	Title (A Side/B Side)	Yr	NM
❑ 342	The Magic Ring/Drums	1961	12.00
❑ 384	Please Mr. Mountain/What Kind of Love Is Yours	1961	12.00

CHANDLER, LORRAINE

45s

GIANT

Number	Title (A Side/B Side)	Yr	NM
❑ 703	What Can I Do/ Tell Me You're Mine	1966	60.00

RCA VICTOR

Number	Title (A Side/B Side)	Yr	NM
❑ 47-8810	What Can I Do/ Tell Me You're Mine	1966	30.00
❑ 47-8980	I Can't Hold On/ She Don't Want You	1966	30.00
❑ 47-9349	I Can't Change/Oh How I Need Your Love	1967	50.00

CHANELS, THE

See THE FIVE CHANELS.

CHANGIN' TIMES, THE

45s

BELL

Number	Title (A Side/B Side)	Yr	NM
❑ 675	Free Spirit/You Just Seem to Know	1967	20.00
❑ 711	Show Me the Way to Go Home/ When the Good Sun Shines	1968	20.00

PHILIPS

Number	Title (A Side/B Side)	Yr	NM
❑ 40320	Pied Piper/Thank You Babe	1965	20.00
❑ 40341	How Is the Air Up There/Young and Innocent Girl	1965	20.00
❑ 40368	Goin' Lovin' with You/I Should Have Brought Her Home	1966	15.00
❑ 40401	Aladdin/All in the Mind of a Young Girl	1966	15.00

CHANGING SCENE, THE

45s

FONTANA

Number	Title (A Side/B Side)	Yr	NM
❑ 1669	Is It Really Worth It/Sing Me Something Pretty	1969	12.00

CHANNEL, BRUCE

45s

ELEKTRA

Number	Title (A Side/B Side)	Yr	NM
❑ 46587	One More Last Chance/ That's the Truth, Ruth	1980	4.00

KING

Number	Title (A Side/B Side)	Yr	NM
❑ 5294	Will I Ever Love Again/Blow Down Baby	1959	30.00
❑ 5331	Now or Never/Boy, This Stuff Kills Me	1960	30.00
❑ 5620	Now or Never/Will I Ever Love Again	1962	20.00

LE CAM

Number	Title (A Side/B Side)	Yr	NM
❑ 122	Going Back to Louisiana/ Forget Me Not	1964	10.00
❑ 125	My Baby/Blue Monday	1964	10.00
❑ 953	Hey! Baby/Dream Girl	1961	40.00
❑ 1117	A Presley Medley/A Man Without a Woman	1977	5.00
❑ 7277	The King Is Free (Love Me)/ Funky Dude	1977	5.00
—B-side by Andy and the Dude			

MALA

Number	Title (A Side/B Side)	Yr	NM
❑ 579	Mr. Bus Driver/It's Me	1967	10.00
❑ 592	Keep On/Barbara Allen	1968	10.00
❑ 12011	California/Water the Family Tree	1968	10.00
❑ 12027	Try Me/Nobody	1968	10.00
❑ 12041	The Web/Mrs. P	1969	10.00

MANCO

Number	Title (A Side/B Side)	Yr	NM
❑ 1035	Run Romance, Run/ Don't Leave Me	1962	20.00

MEL-O-DY

Number	Title (A Side/B Side)	Yr	NM
❑ 112	That's What's Happenin'/ Satisfied Mind	1964	15.00
❑ 114	You Make Me Happy/ You Never Looked Better	1964	15.00

SMASH

Number	Title (A Side/B Side)	Yr	NM
❑ 1731	Hey! Baby/Dream Girl	1962	20.00
❑ 1752	Number One Man/ If Only I Had Known	1962	15.00
❑ 1769	Come On Baby/Mine Exclusively	1962	15.00
❑ 1780	Stand Tough/Somewhere in This Town	1962	15.00
❑ 1780 [PS]	Stand Tough/Somewhere in This Town	1962	30.00
❑ 1792	Oh Baby/Let's Hurt Together	1962	15.00
❑ 1826	No Other Baby/Night People	1963	15.00
❑ 1826 [PS]	No Other Baby/Night People	1963	30.00
❑ 1838	The Dipsy Doodle/ Send Her Home	1963	15.00
❑ 1838 [PS]	The Dipsy Doodle/ Send Her Home	1963	30.00

TEENAGER

Number	Title (A Side/B Side)	Yr	NM
❑ 601	Run Romance, Run/ Don't Leave Me	1960	30.00

Albums

SMASH

Number	Title (A Side/B Side)	Yr	NM
❑ MGS-27008 [M]	Hey! Baby (And 11 Other Songs About Your Baby)	1962	100.00
❑ SRS-67008 [R]	Hey! Baby (And 11 Other Songs About Your Baby)	1962	60.00

CHANNELLS, THE

See THE CHANNELS (2).

CHANNELS, THE (1)

Group led by Earl Lewis.

45s

CHANNEL

Number	Title (A Side/B Side)	Yr	NM
❑ 1000	Gloria/You Said You Loved Me	1971	10.00
—Black vinyl			
❑ 1000	Gloria/You Said You Loved Me	1971	20.00
—Red vinyl			
❑ 1001	We Belong Together/Hey Girl, I'm in Love with You	1972	10.00
❑ 1002	You Got What It Takes/ Crazy Mixed-Up World	1972	10.00
❑ 1003	Close Your Eyes/Work with Me Annie	1973	10.00
❑ 1004	Over Again/In My Arms to Stay	1973	10.00
❑ 1006	A Thousand Miles Away/Don't Let the Green Grass Fool You	1974	10.00

FIRE

Number	Title (A Side/B Side)	Yr	NM
❑ 1001	My Heart Is Sad/ The Girl Next Door	1959	50.00
—As "Earl Lewis and the Channels"			

Except when noted otherwise, VG = 25% of NM, and VG+ = 50% of NM. (Example: VG = $2.00, VG+ = $4.00 and NM = $8.00.)

Number | Title (A Side/B Side) | Yr | NM

FURY
❑ 1021 Bye Bye Baby/My Love Will Never Die 1959 50.00
❑ 1071 Bye Bye Baby/My Love Will Never Die 1963 40.00

GONE
❑ 5012 That's My Desire/ Stay As You Are 1957 60.00
❑ 5019 Altar of Love/All Alone 1957 60.00

LANA
❑ 122 The Closer You Are/Sad Song 196? 10.00
❑ 123 That's My Desire/My Love Will Never Die 196? 10.00

LOST-NITE
❑ 348 The Closer You Are/ Now You Know 197? 5.00
—Reissue
❑ 350 The Gleam in Your Eyes/ Stars in the Sky 197? 5.00
—Reissue
❑ 352 I Really Love You/ What Do You Do 197? 5.00
—Reissue
❑ 354 Flames in My Heart/ My Lovin' Baby 197? 5.00
—Reissue
❑ 356 Bye Bye Baby/My Love Will Never Die 197? 5.00
—Reissue
❑ 359 My Heart Is Sad/ The Girl Next Door 197? 5.00
—Reissue

PORT
❑ 70014 The Closer You Are/ Now You Know 1960 25.00
—Reissue of Whirlin' Disc 100
❑ 70017 The Gleam in Your Eyes/ Stars in the Sky 1960 25.00
—Reissue of Whirlin' Disc 102
❑ 70022 Flames in My Heart/ My Lovin' Baby 1961 25.00
—Reissue of Whirlin' Disc 109
❑ 70023 I Really Love You/ What Do You Do 1961 25.00
—Reissue of Whirlin' Disc 107

RARE BIRD
❑ 5017 She Blew My Mind/Breaking Up Is Hard to Do 1971 10.00

WHIRLIN' DISC
❑ 100 The Closer You Are/ Now You Know 1956 100.00
—Label name is all caps, but not in block letters
❑ 100 The Closer You Are/ Now You Know 1956 200.00
—Block-letter label name; publisher listed as "Spinning Wheel Music"
❑ 100 The Closer You Are/ Now You Know 1956 250.00
—Block-letter label name; publisher listed as "Bob-Dan Music"
❑ 102 The Gleam in Your Eyes/ Stars in the Sky 1956 200.00
❑ 107 I Really Love You/ What Do You Do 1957 200.00
❑ 109 Flames in My Heart/ My Lovin' Baby 1957 200.00

Albums

COLLECTABLES
❑ COL-5012 New York's Finest: The Best of Earl Lewis and the Channels 198? 12.00

LOST-NITE
❑ LLP-15 [10] The Channels 1981 12.00
—Red vinyl
❑ LLP-16 [10] The Channels 1981 12.00
—Red vinyl

CHANNELS, THE (2) Group led by Tony and Gene Williams.

45s

ENJOY
❑ 2001 Sad Song/My Love 1963 25.00

GROOVE
❑ 58-0046 Anything You Do/I've Got My Eyes on You 1964 25.00
❑ 58-0061 Old Chinatown/You Can Count on Me 1965 25.00

HIT RECORD
❑ 700 In My Arms to Stay/You Hurt Me 1963 40.00
—As "The Channells"

CHANNELS, THE (3) Neither of the above.

45s

MERCURY
❑ 71501 Earthquake/Jungle Lights 1959 12.00

CHANTAY'S

45s

DOT
❑ 145 Pipeline/Move It 1966 8.00
—Reissue; black label
❑ 145 Pipeline/Move It 1969 6.00
—Reissue; orange-red label
❑ 16440 Pipeline/Move It 1963 25.00
❑ 16492 Monsoon/Scotch Highs 1963 20.00

DOWNEY
❑ 104 Pipeline/Move It 1963 60.00
❑ 108 Monsoon/Scotch Highs 1963 30.00
❑ 116 Space Probe/Continental Missile 1964 20.00
❑ 120 Only If You Care/Love Can Be Cruel 1964 20.00
❑ 126 Beyond/I'll Be Back Someday 1964 20.00
❑ 130 Three Coins in the Fountain/ Greens 1965 20.00

Albums

DOT
❑ DLP 3516 [M] Pipeline 1963 50.00
❑ DLP 3771 [M] Two Sides of the Chantays 1966 50.00
❑ DLP 25516 [S] Pipeline 1963 80.00
❑ DLP 25771 [S] Two Sides of the Chantays 1966 80.00

DOWNEY
❑ DLP-1002 [M] Pipeline 1963 220.00
❑ DLPS-1002 [S] Pipeline 1963 350.00

CHANTECLAIRS, THE

45s

DOT
❑ 1227 Baby Please/Someday Love Will Come My Way 1954 75.00
❑ 15404 Believe Me, Beloved/I've Never Been There 1955 60.00

CHANTELS, THE Also see ARLENE SMITH; THE VENEERS.

45s

CARLTON
❑ 555 Look in My Eyes/Glad to Be Back 1961 20.00
❑ 564 Still/Well, I Told You 1961 20.00
❑ 569 Summertime/ Here It Comes Again 1962 20.00

END
❑ 1001 He's Gone/The Plea 1957 80.00
—Black label
❑ 1001 He's Gone/The Plea 1959 20.00
—Multi-color label
❑ 1005 Maybe/Come My Little Baby 1957 80.00
—Black label
❑ 1005 Maybe/Come My Little Baby 1958 40.00
—Gray (white) label
❑ 1005 Maybe/Come My Little Baby 1959 20.00
—Multi-color label
❑ 1015 Every Night/Whoever You Are 1958 30.00
—Gray (white) label
❑ 1015 Every Night/Whoever You Are 1959 20.00
—Multi-color label
❑ 1020 I Love You So/How Could You Call It Off 1958 40.00
❑ 1026 Prayer/Sure of Love 1958 25.00
❑ 1030 If You Try/Congratulations 1958 25.00
❑ 1037 Never Let Go/I Can't Take It 1959 25.00
❑ 1048 I'm Confessin'/Goodbye to Love 1959 25.00
❑ 1069 Whoever You Are/How Could You Call It Off 1960 25.00
❑ 1103 Believe Me (My Angel)/I 1961 60.00
—Originally released on Princeton 102 as "The Veneers"
❑ 1105 There's Our Song Again/ I'm the Girl 1961 25.00

LANA
❑ 100 Look in My Eyes/Glad to Be Back 196? 8.00
—Oldies reissue

LUDIX
❑ 101 Eternally/Swamp Water 1963 20.00
❑ 106 That's Why I'm Happy/ Some Tears Fall Dry 1963 20.00

RCA VICTOR
❑ 74-0347 I'm Gonna Win Him Back/ Love Makes All the Difference in the World 1970 10.00

ROULETTE
❑ 7064 Maybe/He's Gone 1969 10.00

TCF HALL
❑ 123 Take Me As I Am/There's No Forgetting Me 1965 15.00

VERVE
❑ 10387 You're Welcome to My Heart/ Soul of a Soldier 1966 15.00
❑ 10435 Indian Giver/It's Just Me 1966 15.00

7-Inch Extended Plays

END
❑ 201 Sure of Love/Prayee//I Love You So/How Could You Call It Off 1958 150.00
❑ 201 [PS] I Love You So 1958 250.00
❑ 202 (contents unknown) 1958 100.00
❑ 202 [PS] C'est Si Bon 1958 200.00

Albums

CARLTON
❑ LP-144 [M] The Chantels On Tour/Look in My Eyes 1962 200.00
❑ STLP-144 [P] The Chantels On Tour/ Look in My Eyes 1962 400.00
—Eight tracks are true stereo, two are mono, two are rechanneled

END
❑ END-301 [R] We Are the Chantels 197? 25.00
—Reissue in rechanneled stereo; orange bar through center hole and "END" on both sides of center hole
❑ LP-301 [M] We Are the Chantels 1958 1500.
—Group photo on front cover; gray label with "11-17-58" in trail-off wax; VG value 500; VG+ value 1000
❑ LP-301 [M] We Are the Chantels 1959 400.00
—Jukebox on front cover; gray label, "11-17-58" in trail-off wax
❑ LP-301 [M] We Are the Chantels 1962 200.00
—Jukebox on front cover; gray label, "1962" in trail-off wax
❑ LP-301 [M] We Are the Chantels 1965 80.00
—Jukebox on front cover; multicolor label, "8-65" in trail-off wax
❑ LP-301 [M] We Are the Chantels 1965 100.00
—Jukebox on front cover; gray label, "8-65" in trail-off wax
❑ LP-312 [M] There's Our Song Again 1962 120.00

FORUM
❑ F-9104 [M] The Chantels Sing Their Favorites 1964 50.00
❑ FS-9104 [R] The Chantels Sing Their Favorites 1964 25.00

CHANTERS, THE (1)

45s

COMBO
❑ 78 Why/Watts 1954 500.00
❑ 92 I Love You/Hot Mamma 1955 400.00

DELUXE
❑ 6162 My My Darling/I Need Your Tenderness (I Love You Darling) 1958 50.00
❑ 6166 Row Your Boat/Stars in the Skies 1958 20.00
—Yellow label
❑ 6166 Row Your Boat/Stars in the Skies 1958 40.00
—Black label
❑ 6172 Angel Darling/Five Little Kisses 1958 50.00
❑ 6177 No, No, No/Over the Rainbow 1958 40.00
❑ 6191 No, No, No/I Make This Pledge (To You) 1961 30.00
❑ 6194 My My Darling/At My Door 1961 40.00
❑ 6200 Row Your Boat/No, No, No 1963 30.00

KEM
❑ 2740 Lonesome Me/Golden Apple 1955 300.00

RPM
❑ 415 Tell Me, Thrill Me/ She Wants to Mambo 1954 300.00

CHANTERS, THE (2)

45s

MGM
❑ 13750 Free As A Bird/Bongo, Bongo 1967 6.00

CHANTEURS, THE With Eugene Record, later of THE CHI-LITES.

45s

VEE JAY
❑ 519 You've Got a Great Love/ The Grizzly Bear 1963 20.00

CHANTONES, THE

45s

CAPITOL
❑ 4661 Stormy Weather/Sweet Georgia Brown 1961 25.00

CARLTON
❑ 485 Five Little Numbers/It's Just a Summer Love 1958 30.00

TOP RANK
❑ 2066 Don't Open That Door/ Tangerock 1960 25.00

CHANTS, THE (1) British soul group.

45s

CAMEO
❑ 277 I Don't Care/Come Go with Me 1963 20.00
❑ 297 I Could Write a Book/ A Thousand Stars 1964 20.00

INTERPHON
❑ 7703 She's Mine/Then I'll Be Home 1964 15.00

Except when noted otherwise, VG = 25% of NM, and VG+ = 50% of NM. (Example: VG = $2.00, VG+ = $4.00 and NM = $8.00.)

CHANTS, THE (U) None of these are by group (1), but we doubt all of them are by the same group.

45s

Number	Title (A Side/B Side)	Yr	NM
CAPITOL			
❑ F3949	Lost and Found/Close Friends	1958	20.00
CHECKER			
❑ 1209	Surfside/Chicken 'N' Gravy	1968	8.00
EKO			
❑ 3567/77	Respectable/Kiss Me Goodbye	1961	30.00
MGM			
❑ 13008	Respectable/Kiss Me Goodbye	1961	20.00
NITE OWL			
❑ 40	Heaven and Paradise/ When I'm With You	196?	20.00
—Blue vinyl			
❑ 40	Heaven and Paradise/ When I'm With You	196?	20.00
—Red vinyl			
❑ 40	Heaven and Paradise/ When I'm With You	196?	20.00
—Yellow vinyl			
❑ 40	Heaven and Paradise/ When I'm With You	1960	40.00
—Black label, black vinyl			
❑ 40	Heaven and Paradise/ When I'm With You	1960	300.00
—Maroon label original			
U.W.R.			
❑ 4243	Rockin' Santa/Respectable	1962	25.00
VERVE			
❑ 10244	Dick Tracy/Choo Choo	1961	20.00

CHAPEL, JEAN

45s

Number	Title (A Side/B Side)	Yr	NM
CHALLENGE			
❑ 59350	Tell It Like It Is/I'm Your Woman	1966	8.00
❑ 59362	You Can Take Me/Stamp Out Loneliness	1967	8.00
❑ 59370	In the Reach of Your Arms/ This Waltz Is Mine	1967	8.00
❑ 59376	Hungry Eyes/Green Paper	1967	8.00
❑ 59381	Dino's TV Door/If I Never Get You	1967	8.00
❑ 59386	See and Ye Shall Find/ I Really Go for You	1968	8.00
KAPP			
❑ 2034	Bluebird Ridge/I Started Loving You Again	1969	6.00
❑ 2082	I'm Your Woman/The Roll Call	1970	6.00
RCA VICTOR			
❑ 47-6681	I Won't Be Rockin' Tonight/ Welcome to the Club	1956	40.00
❑ 47-6892	Oo-Ba La Baby/I Had a Dream	1957	25.00
SMASH			
❑ 1829	Don't Let Go/Your Tender Love	1963	12.00
SUN			
❑ 244	I Won't Be Rockin' Tonight/ Welcome to the Club	1956	50.00

CHAPERONES, THE

45s

Number	Title (A Side/B Side)	Yr	NM
JOSIE			
❑ 880	Dance with Me/ Cruise to the Moon	1960	25.00
—With correct group name on label			
❑ 880	Dance with Me/ Cruise to the Moon	1960	150.00
—With typographical error listing group as "The Cahperones"			
❑ 885	Shining Star/My Shadow and Me	1960	25.00
❑ 891	Man from the Moon/ Blueberry Sweet	1961	50.00

CHAPIN, HARRY Also see THE CHAPINS.

45s

Number	Title (A Side/B Side)	Yr	NM
BOARDWALK			
❑ NB7-11-119	Story of a Love/Salt and Pepper	1981	4.00
❑ 5700	Sequel/I Finally Found It Sandy	1980	4.00
❑ 5705	Remember When the Music/ Northwest 222	1981	4.00
ELEKTRA			
❑ 45203	Cat's in the Cradle/Vacancy	1974	4.00
❑ 45236	I Wanna Learn a Love Song/She Sings Songs Without Words	1975	4.00
❑ 45264	Dreams Go By/Sandy	1975	4.00
❑ 45285	Tangled-Up Puppet/Dirt Get Under the Fingernails	1975	4.00
❑ 45304	Star Tripper/The Rock	1976	4.00
❑ 45327	Better Place to Be (Part 1)/ Better Place to Be (Part 2)	1976	4.00
❑ 45368	Corey's Coming/If My Mary Were Here	1976	4.00
❑ 45426	Dance Band on the Titanic/ I Wonder What Happened to Him	1977	4.00
❑ 45445	My Old Lady/I'd Do It for You, Jane	1977	4.00
❑ 45497	I Wonder What Would Happen to This World/If You Want to Feel	1978	4.00
❑ 45524	Flowers Are Red/Jenny	1978	4.00
❑ 45770	Taxi/Empty	1972	5.00
❑ 45792	Could You Put Your Light On, Please?/Any Old Kind of Day	1972	4.00
❑ 45811	Sunday Morning Sunshine/ Burning Herself	1972	4.00
❑ 45828	Better Place to Be/Winter Song	1973	4.00
❑ 45874	WOLD/Short Stories	1973	4.00
❑ 45893	What Made America Famous/ Old College Avenue	1974	4.00

Albums

Number	Title (A Side/B Side)	Yr	NM
BOARDWALK			
❑ FW 36872	Sequel	1980	10.00
ELEKTRA			
❑ 6E-142	Living Room Suite	1978	10.00
❑ 9E-301 [(2)]	Dance Band on the Titanic	1977	12.00
❑ BB-703 [(2)]	Legends of the Lost and Found — New Greatest Stories Live	1979	12.00
❑ 7E-1012	Verities & Balderdash	1974	10.00
❑ 7E-1041	Portrait Gallery	1975	10.00
❑ 7E-1082	On the Road to Kingdom Come	1976	10.00
❑ 7E-2009 [(2)]	Greatest Stories Live	1976	12.00
❑ 8E-6003 [(2)]	Greatest Stories Live	1978	10.00
—Reissue of 7E-2009			
❑ 60413	Anthology of Harry Chapin	1985	10.00
❑ EKS-75023	Heads and Tales	1972	10.00
❑ EKS-75042	Sniper and Other Love Songs	1972	10.00
❑ EKS-75065	Short Stories	1973	10.00

CHAPINS, THE HARRY CHAPIN; Steve Chapin; Tom Chapin.

45s

Number	Title (A Side/B Side)	Yr	NM
EPIC			
❑ 10761	Workin' On My Life/The Only Thing (You Ever Really Have to Do Is Die)	1971	12.00
ROCK-LAND			
❑ 664	Old Time Movies/Not Your Kind	1966	15.00
❑ 664 [PS]	Old Time Movies/Not Your Kind	1966	25.00

Albums

Number	Title (A Side/B Side)	Yr	NM
ROCK-LAND			
❑ RR-66 [M]	Chapin Music	1966	75.00
—As "The Chapin Brothers"; both mono and stereo, same price			

CHAPMAN, BETH NIELSEN

45s

Number	Title (A Side/B Side)	Yr	NM
CAPITOL			
❑ 4843	Hazel's Song (Every Time You Leave Me)/If Only I'd Known	1980	6.00
REPRISE			
❑ 7-17269	Sand and Water/Beyond the Blue	1997	3.00

Albums

Number	Title (A Side/B Side)	Yr	NM
CAPITOL			
❑ ST-12050	Hearing It First	1980	50.00

CHAPMAN, CEE CEE

45s

Number	Title (A Side/B Side)	Yr	NM
CURB			
❑ 10518	Gone But Not Forgotten/ Love Is a Liar	1988	3.00
❑ 10529	Frontier Justice/Love Is a Liar	1989	3.00
❑ 10547	Twist of Fate/Back to Santa Fe	1989	3.00
CURB/CAPITOL			
❑ 7PRO-79277	Everything (same on both sides)	1990	5.00
—Vinyl is promo only			
❑ 7PRO-79479	Exit 99 (same on both sides)	1990	5.00
—Vinyl is promo only			

CHAPMAN, GARY

45s

Number	Title (A Side/B Side)	Yr	NM
RCA			
❑ 5285-7-R	When We're Together/ Your Love Stays with Me	1987	4.00
❑ 7601-7-R	Everyday Man/Cecil (Love Goes On)	1987	4.00

Albums

Number	Title (A Side/B Side)	Yr	NM
RCA			
❑ 6375-1-R	Everyday Man	1988	10.00

CHAPMAN, GRADY

45s

Number	Title (A Side/B Side)	Yr	NM
IMPERIAL			
❑ 5591	Garden of Memories/ Tell Me That You Care	1959	12.00
❑ 5611	Come Away/Let's Talk About Us	1959	12.00
KNIGHT			
❑ 2003	Say You Will Be Mine/ Starlight, Starbright	1958	30.00
MERCURY			
❑ 71632	Sweet Thing/I Know What I Want	1960	12.00
❑ 71698	Ambush/My Life Would Be Worth Living	1960	50.00
❑ 71771	I'll Never Question Your Love/ This, That, 'N the Other	1961	12.00
MONEY			
❑ 204	I Need You So/Don't Blooper	1955	300.00
ZEPHYR			
❑ 016	My Love Will Never Change/ Smiling	1957	30.00

CHAPMAN, MARSHALL

45s

Number	Title (A Side/B Side)	Yr	NM
EPIC			
❑ 8-50307	Somewhere South of Macon/ Sweet Carolina and Texas	1976	5.00
❑ 8-50376	Know My Needs/Next Time	1977	5.00
❑ 9-50799	Rock and Roll Clothes/ Don't Make Me Pregnant	1979	5.00

Albums

Number	Title (A Side/B Side)	Yr	NM
EPIC			
❑ PE 34422	Me, I'm Feelin' Free	1977	10.00
❑ JE 35341	Jaded Virgin	1978	10.00
❑ JE 36192	Marshall	1979	10.00
ROUNDER			
❑ 3069	Take It On Home	1982	12.00

CHAPMAN, TRACY

12-Inch Singles

Number	Title (A Side/B Side)	Yr	NM
ELEKTRA			
❑ ED 5286 [DJ]	Fast Car (Edit 4:26) (same on both sides?)	1988	12.00
❑ ED 5315 [DJ]	Talkin' 'Bout a Revolution (same on both sides)	1988	10.00
❑ ED 5340 [DJ]	Baby Can I Hold You (same on both sides)	1988	10.00
❑ ED 5403 [DJ]	Crossroads (same on both sides)	1989	10.00
❑ ED 5424 [DJ]	All That You Have Is Your Soul (Edit) (LP Version)	1989	10.00
❑ ED 5441 [DJ]	Born to Fight (same on both sides)	1989	8.00
❑ ED 5455 [DJ]	This Time (Edit) (LP Version)	1990	10.00

45s

Number	Title (A Side/B Side)	Yr	NM
ELEKTRA			
❑ 7-64346	Give Me One Reason/ Rape of the World	1996	5.00
—Most copies have A-side label on both sides (no difference in value)			
❑ 65938	Fast Car/Talkin' 'Bout a Revolution	1989	3.00
—"Spun Gold" series			
❑ 7-69242	All That You Have Is Your Soul/ Material World	1990	6.00
❑ 7-69273	Crossroads/Born to Fight	1989	3.00
❑ 7-69273 [PS]	Crossroads/Born to Fight	1989	3.00
❑ 7-69356	Baby Can I Hold You/If Not Now	1988	3.00
❑ 7-69356 [PS]	Baby Can I Hold You/If Not Now	1988	4.00
❑ 7-69383	Talkin' 'Bout a Revolution/ Behind the Wall	1988	3.00
❑ 7-69383 [PS]	Talkin' 'Bout a Revolution/ Behind the Wall	1988	4.00
❑ 7-69412	Fast Car/For You	1988	5.00

Albums

Number	Title (A Side/B Side)	Yr	NM
ELEKTRA			
❑ 60774	Tracy Chapman	1988	10.00
❑ 60888	Crossroads	1989	12.00
❑ R 142496	Crossroads	1989	12.00
—BMG Direct Marketing edition			
❑ R 153582	Tracy Chapman	1988	12.00
—BMG Direct Marketing edition			

CHARGERS, THE Also see JESSE BELVIN.

45s

Number	Title (A Side/B Side)	Yr	NM
RCA VICTOR			
❑ 47-7301	Old MacDonald/Dandelion	1958	30.00

CHARIOT

Albums

Number	Title (A Side/B Side)	Yr	NM
NATIONAL GENERAL			
❑ NG-2003	Chariot	1971	75.00

CHARIOTEERS, THE Also see BILLY WILLIAMS.

45s

Number	Title (A Side/B Side)	Yr	NM
COLUMBIA			
❑ 1-168	A Kiss and a Rose/A Cottage in Old Donegal	1949	600.00
—Microgroove 7-inch, 33 1/3 rpm single			
❑ 1-363	This Side of Heaven/ Hawaiian Sunset	1949	600.00
—Microgroove 7-inch, 33 1/3 rpm single			

Except when noted otherwise, VG = 25% of NM, and VG+ = 50% of NM. (Example: VG = $2.00, VG+ = $4.00 and NM = $8.00.)

Number	Title (A Side/B Side)	Yr	NM
JOSIE			
❑ 787	I've Got My Heart on My Sleeve/ Don't Play No Mambo	1955	80.00
MGM			
❑ 12569	The Candles/I Didn't Mean to Be Mean to You	1957	80.00
RCA VICTOR			
❑ 47-6098	Easy Does It/Tremble, Tremble, Tremble	1955	80.00
Albums			
COLUMBIA			
❑ CL 6014 [10]	Sweet and Low	1949	300.00
HARMONY			
❑ HL 7089 [M]	The Charioteers with Billy Williams	1957	100.00

CHARIOTS, THE

Number	Title (A Side/B Side)	Yr	NM
45s			
TIME			
❑ 1006	Gloria/A Sunday Morning Love	1959	40.00

CHARISMA

Number	Title (A Side/B Side)	Yr	NM
45s			
ROULETTE			
❑ 7075	What's It Like/(B-side unknown)	1970	8.00
❑ 7096	Bizwambi/(B-side unknown)	1971	8.00
Albums			
ROULETTE			
❑ SR-42037	Charisma	1970	20.00

CHARITY

Number	Title (A Side/B Side)	Yr	NM
45s			
PHILIPS			
❑ 40614	Never Change Your Mind/ Windy City Woman	1969	10.00
UNI			
❑ 55159	Never Change Your Mind/ I Still Love You	1969	8.00
Albums			
UNI			
❑ 73061	Charity Now	1969	25.00

CHARLATANS, THE

Number	Title (A Side/B Side)	Yr	NM
45s			
KAPP			
❑ 779	The Shadow Knows/32-20	1967	50.00
❑ 779 [PS]	The Shadow Knows/32-20	1967	80.00
PHILIPS			
❑ 40610	High Coin/When I Go Sailin' By	1969	40.00
❑ 40610 [PS]	High Coin/When I Go Sailin' By	1969	80.00
—Sleeve is promo only			
❑ 44824 [DJ]	Date: May 19, 1969	1969	60.00
—One-sided, promo only			
Albums			
PHILIPS			
❑ PHS 600309	The Charlatans	1969	100.00

CHARLENE

Number	Title (A Side/B Side)	Yr	NM
45s			
ARIOLA AMERICA			
❑ 7696	Are You Free/We Know	1977	5.00
MOTOWN			
❑ 1262	Give It One More Try/Relove	1973	8.00
❑ 1285	All That Love Went to Waste/ Give It One More Try	1973	8.00
❑ 1492	Hungry/I Won't Remember Ever Loving You	1980	4.00
❑ 1611	I've Never Been to Me/ Somewhere in My Life	1982	3.00
❑ 1621	Nunca He Ido A Mi/ If I Could See Myself	1982	4.00
❑ 1650	Used to Be/I Want to Come Back As A Song	1982	3.00
—A-side with Stevie Wonder			
❑ 1650 [PS]	Used to Be/I Want to Come Back As A Song	1982	3.00
❑ 1663	I Want to Go Back There Again/ Richie's Song	1983	3.00
❑ 1734	We're Both in Love with You/ I Want the World to Know He's Mine	1984	3.00
❑ 1761	Hit and Run Lover/Last Song	1984	3.00
PRODIGAL			
❑ 0632	It Ain't Easy Coming Down/ On My Way to You	1977	5.00
❑ 0633	Freddie/(B-side unknown)	1977	5.00
❑ 0633 [PS]	Freddie/(B-side unknown)	1977	10.00
❑ 0636	I've Never Been to Me/ It's Really Nice to Be in Love Again	1977	20.00
Albums			
MOTOWN			
❑ 6007 ML	Charlene	1981	10.00
❑ 6027 ML	Used to Be	1982	10.00
❑ 6090 ML	Hit and Run Lover	1985	10.00
PRODIGAL			
❑ P6-10015	Charlene	1976	20.00
❑ P6-10018	Songs of Love	1977	20.00

CHARLES, BOBBY

Number	Title (A Side/B Side)	Yr	NM
45s			
BEARSVILLE			
❑ 0010	Small Town Talk/Save Me Jesus	1973	4.00
CHESS			
❑ 1609	Later Alligator/On Bended Knee	1955	50.00
❑ 1617	Why Did You Leave/ Don't You Know I Love You	1956	50.00
❑ 1628	Only Time Will Tell/ Take It Easy. Greasy	1956	50.00
❑ 1638	Laura Lee/No Use Knocking	1956	50.00
❑ 1647	Put Your Arms Around Me/ Why Can't You, Honey	1957	40.00
❑ 1658	No More/You Can Suit Yourself	1957	40.00
❑ 1670	One Eyed Jack/Yea Yea Baby	1957	40.00
IMPERIAL			
❑ 5542	Since She's Gone/ At the Jamboree	1958	20.00
❑ 5557	Oh Yeah/Since I Lost You	1958	20.00
❑ 5579	The Town Is Talking/ What Can I Do	1959	20.00
❑ 5642	Bye Bye Baby/Those Eyes	1960	20.00
❑ 5681	What a Party/I Just Want You	1960	20.00
❑ 5691	Four Winds/Nothing Sweet As You	1960	20.00
JEWEL			
❑ 728	Everybody's Laughing/ Everybody Knows	1964	10.00
❑ 729	Goodnight Irene/I Hope	1964	10.00
❑ 735	Ain't Misbehavin'/ Preacher's Daughter	1964	10.00
❑ 740	Oh Lonesome Me/ One More Glass of Wine	1964	10.00
PAULA			
❑ 226	The Walk/Worrying Over You	1965	10.00
Albums			
CHESS			
❑ CH 9175	Chess Masters	1984	15.00

CHARLES, DON

Number	Title (A Side/B Side)	Yr	NM
45s			
WORLD ARTISTS			
❑ 1031	She's Mine/Big Talk from a Little Man	1964	10.00

CHARLES, JIMMY

Number	Title (A Side/B Side)	Yr	NM
45s			
PROMO			
❑ 1002	A Million to One/Hop Scotch Hop	1960	15.00
❑ 1002	A Million to One/ Hop Scotch Polka	1960	20.00
❑ 1003	The Age for Love/ Follow the Swallow	1960	15.00
❑ 1003 [PS]	The Age for Love/ Follow the Swallow	1960	20.00
❑ 1004	Santa Won't Be Blue This Christmas/I Saw Mommy Kissing Santa Claus	1960	15.00
❑ 1004 [PS]	Santa Won't Be Blue This Christmas/I Saw Mommy Kissing Santa Claus	1960	20.00
❑ 1005	Christmasville U.S.A./A Little White Mouse Called Steve	1960	15.00
❑ 1005 [PS]	Christmasville U.S.A./A Little White Mouse Called Steve	1960	20.00
❑ 1006	I Wonder How It Feels to Fall in Love/Just Whistle for Me	1961	15.00

CHARLES, LEE

Number	Title (A Side/B Side)	Yr	NM
45s			
BAMBOO			
❑ 110	Girl You Turned Your Back on Me/I Never Want to Lose My Sweet Thing	1970	20.00
❑ 111	Why Do You Have to Go/ I Never Want to Lose My Sweet Thing	1970	15.00
❑ 117	You Can't Get Away/Girl You Turned Your Back on Me	1970	15.00
❑ 119	You Got to Get It for Yourself/ Get High on My Baby's Love	1971	80.00
BRUNSWICK			
❑ 55401	I'll Never Love Again/ Wrong Number	1969	20.00
DAKAR			
❑ 601	Then Would You Love Me/ It's All Over Between Us	1969	20.00
HOT WAX			
❑ 7303	I Just Want to Be Loved/ Somebody's Gonna Hurt You Like You Hurt Me	1973	8.00
INVICTUS			
❑ 1260	Get Your House in Order/ Sittin' on a Time Bomb	1974	8.00
REVUE			
❑ 11007	Standing on the Outside/ If That Ain't Lovin' You	1968	15.00
❑ 11022	Someone, Somewhere/ Wrong Number	1968	15.00

CHARLES, RAY
Also see BILLY JOEL.

Number	Title (A Side/B Side)	Yr	NM
12-Inch Singles			
COLUMBIA			
❑ CAS 1421 [DJ]	I Wish I'd Never Loved You at All (same on both sides?)	1988	12.00
WARNER BROS.			
❑ PRO-A-4425 [DJ]	I'll Take Care of You (same on both sides)	1990	15.00
❑ PRO-A-4696 [DJ]	Living Without You (same on both sides)	1990	12.00
❑ PRO-A-5977 [DJ]	A Song for You (same on both sides)	1993	10.00
45s			
ABC			
❑ 10808	Let's Go Get Stoned/At the Train	1966	8.00
❑ 10840	I Chose to Sing the Blues/ Hopelessly	1966	8.00
❑ 10865	Please Say You're Fooling/I Don't Need No Doctor	1966	8.00
❑ 10901	I Want to Talk About You/ Something Inside Me	1967	8.00
❑ 10938	Here We Go Again/Somebody Ought to Write a Book About It	1967	8.00
❑ 10970	In the Heat of the Night/ Somebody's Got to Change	1967	8.00
❑ 11009	Yesterday/Never Had Enough of Nothing Yet	1967	8.00
❑ 11045	That's a Lie/Go On Home	1968	8.00
❑ 11045 [PS]	That's a Lie/Go On Home	1968	15.00
❑ 11090	Eleanor Rigby/Understanding	1968	8.00
❑ 11133	Sweet Young Thing Like You/ Listen, They're Playing Our Song	1968	8.00
❑ 11170	If It Wasn't for Bad Luck/ When I Stop Dreaming	1969	8.00
—With Jimmy Lewis			
❑ 11193	I'll Be Your Servant/I Don't Know What Time It Was	1969	8.00
❑ 11213	Let Me Love You/I'm Satisfied	1969	8.00
❑ 11239	We Can Make It/I Can't Stop Loving You Baby	1969	8.00
❑ 11251	Someone to Watch Over Me/ Claudie Mae	1969	8.00
❑ 11259	Laughin' and Clownin'/ That Thing Called Love	1970	8.00
❑ 11271	If You Were Mine/Till I Can't Take It Anymore	1970	8.00
❑ 11291	Don't Change on Me/ Sweet Memories	1971	8.00
❑ 11308	Feel So Bad/Your Love Is So Doggone Good	1971	6.00
❑ 11317	What Am I Living For/ Tired of My Tears	1971	6.00
❑ 11329	Look What They've Done to My Song, Ma/America the Beautiful	1972	10.00
❑ 11337	Hey Mister/There'll Be No Peace Without All Men as One	1972	6.00
❑ 11344	Every Saturday Night/Take Me Home, Country Roads	1973	6.00
❑ 11351	I Can Make It Through the Days (But Oh Those Lonely Nights)/Ring of Fire	1973	6.00
ABC-PARAMOUNT			
❑ 410-1 [S]	You Don't Know Me/ Bye, Bye Love	1962	20.00
❑ 410-2 [S]	Half As Much/I Love You So Much It Hurts	1962	20.00
❑ 410-3 [S]	Born to Lose/Just a Little Lovin'	1962	20.00
❑ 410-4 [S]	Worried Mind/It Makes No Difference Now	1962	20.00
❑ 410-5 [S]	You Win Again/Careless Love	1962	20.00
—The above five are 33 1/3 rpm, small hole jukebox singles excerpted from the LP "Modern Sounds in Country and Western Music"			
❑ 435-1 [S]	(titles unknown)	1962	20.00
❑ 435-2 [S]	(titles unknown)	1962	20.00
❑ 435-3 [S]	Someday (You'll Want Me to Want You)/I'll Never Stand in Your Way	1962	20.00

C

Number	Title (A Side/B Side)	Yr	NM
❑ 435-4 [S]	Making Believe/Don't Tell Me Your Troubles	1962	20.00
❑ 435-5 [S]	Oh, Lonesome Me/ Hang Your Head in Shame	1962	20.00

—The above five are 33 1/3 rpm, small hole jukebox singles excerpted from the LP "Modern Sounds in Country and Western Music, Vol. Two"

Number	Title (A Side/B Side)	Yr	NM
❑ 465-1 [S]	Busted/(B-side unknown)	1963	20.00
❑ 465-2 [S]	That Lucky Old Sun/ (B-side unknown)	1963	20.00
❑ 465-3 [S]	Ol' Man River/(B-side unknown)	1963	20.00
❑ 465-4 [S]	Ol' Man Time/(B-side unknown)	1963	20.00

—The above four are 33 1/3 rpm, 7-inch jukebox singles with small holes, excerpted from the LP "Ingredients in a Recipe for Soul"

Number	Title (A Side/B Side)	Yr	NM
❑ 480-1 [S]	Don't Cry Baby/Teardrops from My Eyes	1964	20.00
❑ 480-2 [S]	Baby, Don't You Cry/ Cry Me a River	1964	20.00
❑ 480-3 [S]	I Cried for You/Cry	1964	20.00
❑ 480-4 [S]	A Tear Fell/No One to Cry To	1964	20.00
❑ 480-5 [S]	You've Got Me Crying Again/ After My Laughter Came Tears	1964	20.00

—The above five are 33 1/3 rpm, small hole jukebox singles excerpted from the LP "Sweet and Sour Tears"

Number	Title (A Side/B Side)	Yr	NM
❑ 10081	My Baby/Who You Gonna Love	1960	15.00
❑ 10118	Sticks and Stones/ Worried Life Blues	1960	12.00
❑ 10135	Georgia on My Mind/Carry Me Back to Old Virginny	1960	15.00
❑ 10141	Them That Got/I Wonder	1960	12.00
❑ 10164	Ruby/Heard Hearted Woman	1960	12.00
❑ 10244	Hit the Road Jack/ The Danger Zone	1961	15.00
❑ 10266	Unchain My Heart/But on the Other Hand, Baby	1961	15.00
❑ 10314	Hide 'Nor Hair/At the Club	1962	12.00
❑ 10330	I Can't Stop Loving You/ Born to Lose	1962	15.00
❑ 10345	You Don't Know Me/ Careless Love	1962	15.00
❑ 10375	You Are My Sunshine/ Your Cheating Heart	1962	12.00
❑ 10405	Don't Set Me Free/ The Brightest Smile in Town	1963	12.00
❑ 10435	Take These Chains from My Heart/No Letter Today	1963	15.00
❑ 10453	No One/Without Love (There Is Nothing)	1963	12.00
❑ 10481	Busted/Making Believe	1963	15.00
❑ 10509	That Lucky Old Sun/ Ol' Man Time	1963	12.00
❑ 10530	Baby Don't You Cry/My Heart Cries for You	1964	12.00
❑ 10557	My Baby Don't Dig Me/ Something's Wrong	1964	12.00
❑ 10571	No One to Cry To/A Tear Fell	1964	12.00
❑ 10588	Smack Dab in the Middle/ I Wake Up Crying	1964	12.00
❑ 10609	Makin' Whoopee/(Instrumental)	1964	12.00
❑ 10615	Cry/Teardrops from My Eyes	1965	12.00
❑ 10649	I Gotta Woman (Part 1)/ I Gotta Woman (Part 2)	1965	12.00
❑ 10663	Without a Song (Part 1)/ Without a Song (Part 2)	1965	12.00
❑ 10700	I'm a Fool to Care/ Love's Gonna Live Here	1965	12.00
❑ 10720	The Cincinnati Kid/ That's All I Am to You	1965	12.00
❑ 10739	Crying Time/When My Dreamboat Comes Home	1965	15.00
❑ 10785	Together Again/You're Just About to Lose Your Clown	1966	12.00

ATLANTIC

Number	Title (A Side/B Side)	Yr	NM
❑ 976	Roll with Me Baby/ The Midnight Hour	1952	500.00
❑ 984	The Sun's Gonna Shine Again/ Jumpin' in the Morning	1953	400.00
❑ 999	Mess Around/Funny (But I Still Love You)	1953	200.00
❑ 1008	Feelin' Sad/Heartbreaker	1953	100.00
❑ 1021	It Should've Been Me/ Sinner's Prayer	1954	50.00
❑ 1037	Don't You Know/Losing Hand	1954	30.00
❑ 1050	I've Got a Woman/Come Back	1954	50.00
❑ 1063	This Little Girl of Mine/ A Fool for You	1955	30.00
❑ 1076	Blackjack/Greenbacks	1955	30.00
❑ 1085	Drown in My Own Tears/ Mary Ann	1956	25.00
❑ 1096	Hallelujah, I Love Her So/ What Would I Do Without You	1956	20.00
❑ 1108	Lonely Avenue/Leave My Woman Alone	1956	20.00
❑ 1124	I Want to Know/Ain't That Love	1957	20.00
❑ 1143	It's All Right/Get On the Right Track Baby	1957	20.00
❑ 1154	Swanee River Rock (Talkin' 'Bout That River)/ I Want a Little Girl	1957	20.00
❑ 1172	Talkin' 'Bout You/What Kind of a Man Are You	1958	15.00
❑ 1180	Yes Indeed/I Had a Dream	1958	15.00

—With the Cookies

Number	Title (A Side/B Side)	Yr	NM
❑ 1196	My Bonnie/You Be My Baby	1958	15.00
❑ 2006	Rockhouse (Part 1)/ Rockhouse (Part 2)	1958	15.00
❑ 2010	(Night Time Is) The Right Time/ Tell All the World About You	1959	15.00
❑ 2022	Tell Me How Do You Feel/ That's Enough	1959	15.00
❑ 2031	What'd I Say (Part I)/ What'd I Say (Part II)	1959	20.00
❑ 2043	I'm Movin' On/I Believe to My Soul	1959	12.00
❑ 2047	Let the Good Times Roll/Don't Let the Sun Catch You Cryin'	1960	12.00
❑ 2055	Heartbreaker/Just for a Thrill	1960	12.00
❑ 2068	Tell the Truth/Sweet Sixteen Bars	1960	12.00
❑ 2084	Come Rain or Come Shine/ Tell Me You'll Wait for Me	1960	12.00
❑ 2094	Early in the Morning/A Bit of Soul	1961	12.00
❑ 2106	Am I Blue/It Should've Been Me	1961	12.00
❑ 2118	I Wonder Who/Hard Times (No One Knows Better Than I)	1961	12.00
❑ 2174	Carryin' That Load/Feelin' Sad	1963	10.00
❑ 2239	Talkin' 'Bout You/In a Little Spanish Town	1964	10.00
❑ 2470	Come Rain or Come Shine/ Tell Me You'll Wait for Me	1968	10.00
❑ 3443	I Can See Clearly Now/ Anonymous Love	1977	5.00
❑ 3473	A Peace That We Never Could Enjoy/Game Number Nine	1978	5.00
❑ 3527	Riding Thumb/You Forgot Your Memories	1978	5.00
❑ 3549 [DJ]	Christmas Time (same on both sides)	1978	6.00

—May be promo-only

Number	Title (A Side/B Side)	Yr	NM
❑ 3611	Some Enchanted Evening/ 20th Century Fox	1979	5.00
❑ 3634	Just Because/Love Me or Set Me Free	1979	5.00
❑ 3762	Compared To What/Now That We've Found Each Other	1980	5.00
❑ 5005	Doodlin' (Part 1)/Doodlin' (Part 2)	1960	15.00

BARONET

Number	Title (A Side/B Side)	Yr	NM
❑ 7111	See See Rider/I Used to be So Happy	1960	12.00
❑ 7111 [PS]	See See Rider/I Used to be So Happy	1960	25.00

COLUMBIA

Number	Title (A Side/B Side)	Yr	NM
❑ 38-03429	String Bean/Born to Love Me	1982	4.00
❑ 38-03810	You Feel Good All Over/ 3/4 Time	1983	3.00
❑ 38-04083	Ain't Your Memory Got No Pride at All/I Don't Want No Strangers Sleeping in My Bed	1983	3.00
❑ 38-04297	We Didn't See a Thing/I Wish You Were Here Tonight	1983	3.00

—A-side with George Jones and Chet Atkins

Number	Title (A Side/B Side)	Yr	NM
❑ 38-04420	Do I Ever Cross Your Mind/ They Call It Love	1984	3.00
❑ 38-04500	Woman (Sensuous Woman)/ I Was On Georgia Time	1984	3.00
❑ 38-04531	Rock and Roll Shoes/ Then I'll Be Over You	1984	3.00

—Ray Charles and B.J. Thomas

Number	Title (A Side/B Side)	Yr	NM
❑ 38-04715	Seven Spanish Angels/ Who Cares	1984	3.00

—A-side with Willie Nelson; B-side with Janie Frickie

Number	Title (A Side/B Side)	Yr	NM
❑ 38-04860	It Ain't Gonna Worry My Mind/ Crazy Old Soldier	1985	3.00

—A-side with Mickey Gilley; B-side with Johnny Cash

Number	Title (A Side/B Side)	Yr	NM
❑ 38-05575	Two Old Cats Like Us/ Little Hotel Room	1985	3.00

—A-side with Hank Williams, Jr.; B-side with Merle Haggard

Number	Title (A Side/B Side)	Yr	NM
❑ 38-06172	Pages of My Mind/Slip Away	1986	3.00
❑ 38-06370	Dixie Moon/A Little Bit of Heaven	1986	3.00
❑ 38-08393	Seven Spanish Angels/It Ain't Gonna Worry My Mind	1988	3.00

—Reissue; A-side with Willie Nelson, B-side with Mickey Gilley

CROSSOVER

Number	Title (A Side/B Side)	Yr	NM
❑ 973	Come Live with Me/ Everybody Sing	1973	5.00
❑ 974	Louise/Somebody	1974	5.00
❑ 981	Living for the City/Then We'll Be Home	1975	5.00
❑ 985	America the Beautiful/Sunshine	1976	6.00

—A-side is a different recording than that on the B-side of ABC 11329

IMPULSE!

Number	Title (A Side/B Side)	Yr	NM
❑ 200	One Mint Julep/Let's Go	1961	10.00
❑ 202	I've Got News for You/ I'm Gonna Move to the Outskirts of Town	1961	10.00

RCA

Number	Title (A Side/B Side)	Yr	NM
❑ PB-10800	Oh Lawd, I'm On My Way/ Oh Bess, Where's My Bess	1976	5.00

ROCKIN'

Number	Title (A Side/B Side)	Yr	NM
❑ 504	Walkin' and Talkin' (To Myself)/ I'm Wonderin' and Wonderin'	1952	300.00

SITTIN' IN WITH

Number	Title (A Side/B Side)	Yr	NM
❑ 641	Baby Let Me Hear You Call My Name/Guitar Blues	1952	300.00

SWING TIME

Number	Title (A Side/B Side)	Yr	NM
❑ 250	Baby, Let Me Hold Your Hand/ Lonely Boy	1951	500.00

—Ray Charles records on Swing Time before 250 are unconfirmed on 45 rpm

Number	Title (A Side/B Side)	Yr	NM
❑ 274	Kissa Me Baby/I'm Glad for Your Sake	1952	500.00
❑ 300	Baby Let Me Hear You Call My Name/Guitar Blues	1952	500.00
❑ 326	The Snow Is Falling/ Misery in My Heart	1953	500.00

TANGERINE

Number	Title (A Side/B Side)	Yr	NM
❑ 1015	Booty Butt/Sidewinder	1971	6.00

TIME

Number	Title (A Side/B Side)	Yr	NM
❑ 1026	I Found My Baby/Guitar Blues	1960	15.00
❑ 1054	Why Did You Go/Back Home	1962	12.00

WARNER BROS.

Number	Title (A Side/B Side)	Yr	NM
❑ 18611	A Song for You/I Can't Get Enough	1993	3.00
❑ 49608	Beers to You/Cotton-Eyed Clint	1980	5.00

—A-side with Clint Eastwood; B-side by Texas Opera Company

7-Inch Extended Plays

ABC

Number	Title (A Side/B Side)	Yr	NM
❑ EP-ABCS 595	Yesterday/People//Here We Go Again/I'll Be Seeing You	1967	20.00

—Jukebox issue; small hole, plays at 33 1/3 rpm

Number	Title (A Side/B Side)	Yr	NM
❑ EP-ABCS 595 [PS]	Ray Charles Invites You to Listen	1967	20.00
❑ EP-ABCS 625	Eleanor Rigby/Understanding a Sweet Young Thing Like You// The Sun Died/I Won't Leave	1968	25.00

—Jukebox issue; small hole, plays at 33 1/3 rpm

Number	Title (A Side/B Side)	Yr	NM
❑ EP-ABCS 625 [PS]	A Portrait of Ray	1968	25.00

ABC-PARAMOUNT

Number	Title (A Side/B Side)	Yr	NM
❑ EP 410	Half As Much/I Love You So Much It Hurts//You Win Again/ It Makes No Difference Now	196?	30.00

—Jukebox issue; small hole, plays at 33 1/3 rpm

Number	Title (A Side/B Side)	Yr	NM
❑ EP 410 [PS]	Modern Sounds in Country and Western Music	196?	30.00
❑ EP A-410	I Can't Stop Loving You/Born to Lose//You Don't Know Me/ Careless Love	1962	25.00
❑ EP A-410 [PS]	Modern Sounds in Country and Western Music	1962	25.00
❑ EP 415	Them That Got/Unchain My Heart/Hit the Road Jack// Sticks and Stones/I Wonder/ The Danger Zone	1962	30.00

—Jukebox issue; small hole, plays at 33 1/3 rpm

Number	Title (A Side/B Side)	Yr	NM
❑ EP 415 [PS]	Ray Charles' Greatest Hits	1962	30.00
❑ EP-ABCS 480-2	Guess I'll Hang My Tears Out to Dry/Teardrops from My Eyes// No One to Cry To/Don't Cry Baby/After My Laughter Came Tears	1964	25.00

—Jukebox issue; small hole, plays at 33 1/3 rpm

Number	Title (A Side/B Side)	Yr	NM
❑ EP-ABCS 480-2 [PS]	Sweet and Sour Tears	1964	25.00
❑ EP-ABCS 500	I Gotta Woman Pt. 1/I Gotta Woman Pt. 2/Margie//Baby Don't You Cry/Hide Nor Hair/ Hallelujah I Love Her So	1965	25.00

—Jukebox issue; small hole, plays at 33 1/3 rpm

Number	Title (A Side/B Side)	Yr	NM
❑ EP-ABCS 500 [PS]	Ray Charles Live in Concert	1965	25.00
❑ EP-ABCS 520	Together Again/I've Got a Tiger by the Tail/Next Door to the Blues//I Don't Care/Blue Moon of Kentucky/Light Out of Darkness	1965	25.00

—Jukebox issue; small hole, plays at 33 1/3 rpm

Number	Title (A Side/B Side)	Yr	NM
❑ EP-ABCS 520 [PS]	Country and Western Meets Rhythm and Blues	1965	25.00

ATLANTIC

Number	Title (A Side/B Side)	Yr	NM
❑ EP 587	*Ain't That Love/Greenbacks/ Drown in My Own Tears/ Hallelujah I Love Her So	1956	100.00
❑ EP 587 [PS]	Ray Charles	1956	100.00
❑ EP 597	Doodlin'/Sweet Sixteen Bars	1957	100.00
❑ EP 597 [PS]	The Great Ray Charles	1957	100.00
❑ EP 607	*A Fool for You/Mary Ann/ Blackjack/Lonely Avenue	1958	100.00
❑ EP 607 [PS]	Rock with Ray Charles	1958	100.00

Except when noted otherwise, VG = 25% of NM, and VG+ = 50% of NM. (Example: VG = $2.00, VG+ = $4.00 and NM = $8.00.)

Number	Title (A Side/B Side)	Yr	NM
❑ EP 619	*Let the Good Times Roll/Come Rain or Come Shine/Don't Let the Sun Catch You Cryin'/ Alexander's Ragtime Band	1959	100.00
❑ EP 619 [PS]	The Genius of Ray Charles	1959	100.00

Albums

ABC

Number	Title (A Side/B Side)	Yr	NM
❑ S-335 [S]	The Genius Hits the Road	1967	12.00
❑ S-355 [S]	Dedicated to You	1967	12.00
❑ S-410 [S]	Modern Sounds in Country and Western Music	1967	12.00
❑ S-415 [S]	Ray Charles' Greatest Hits	1967	12.00
❑ S-435 [S]	Modern Sounds in Country and Western Music (Vol. Two)	1967	12.00
❑ S-465 [S]	Ingredients in a Recipe for Soul	1967	12.00
❑ S-480 [S]	Sweet & Sour Tears	1967	12.00
❑ S-495 [S]	Have a Smile with Me	1967	12.00
❑ S-500 [S]	Ray Charles Live in Concert	1967	12.00
❑ S-520 [S]	Together Again	1967	12.00
❑ S-544 [S]	Crying Time	1967	12.00
❑ S-550 [S]	Ray's Moods	1967	12.00
❑ 590X [(2)M]	A Man and His Soul	1967	15.00
❑ S-590X [(2)S]	A Man and His Soul	1967	20.00
❑ 595 [M]	Ray Charles Invites You to Listen	1967	20.00
❑ S-595 [S]	Ray Charles Invites You to Listen	1967	15.00
❑ S-625	A Portrait of Ray	1968	12.00
❑ S-675	I'm All Yours — Baby!	1969	12.00
❑ S-695	Doing His Thing	1969	12.00
❑ S-707	Love Country Style	1971	12.00
❑ S-726	Volcanic Action of My Soul	1971	12.00
❑ H-731 [(2)]	A 25th Anniversary in Show Business Salute to Ray Charles	1971	15.00
❑ X-755	A Message from the People	1972	12.00
❑ X-765	Through the Eyes of Love	1972	12.00
❑ X-781/2 [(2)]	All-Time Great Country & Western Hits	1973	15.00
❑ QBO-91036 [(2)M]	The Ray Charles Story	1967	30.00
—Capitol Record Club exclusive			
❑ SQBO-91036 [(2)S]	The Ray Charles Story	1967	25.00
—Capitol Record Club exclusive			
❑ ST-91233 [S]	Ray Charles Invites You to Listen	1967	15.00
—Capitol Record Club edition			

ABC IMPULSE!

Number	Title (A Side/B Side)	Yr	NM
❑ AS-2 [S]	Genius + Soul = Jazz	1968	12.00

ABC-PARAMOUNT

Number	Title (A Side/B Side)	Yr	NM
❑ 335 [M]	The Genius Hits the Road	1960	20.00
❑ S-335 [S]	The Genius Hits the Road	1960	30.00
❑ 355 [M]	Dedicated to You	1961	20.00
❑ S-355 [S]	Dedicated to You	1961	30.00
❑ 410 [M]	Modern Sounds in Country and Western Music	1962	25.00
❑ S-410 [S]	Modern Sounds in Country and Western Music	1962	30.00
❑ 415 [M]	Ray Charles' Greatest Hits	1962	20.00
❑ S-415 [S]	Ray Charles' Greatest Hits	1962	25.00
❑ 435 [M]	Modern Sounds in Country and Western Music (Vol. Two)	1962	20.00
❑ S-435 [S]	Modern Sounds in Country and Western Music (Vol. Two)	1962	25.00
❑ 465 [M]	Ingredients in a Recipe for Soul	1963	20.00
❑ S-465 [S]	Ingredients in a Recipe for Soul	1963	25.00
❑ 480 [M]	Sweet & Sour Tears	1964	20.00
❑ S-480 [S]	Sweet & Sour Tears	1964	25.00
❑ 495 [M]	Have a Smile with Me	1964	20.00
❑ S-495 [S]	Have a Smile with Me	1964	25.00
❑ 500 [M]	Ray Charles Live in Concert	1965	15.00
❑ S-500 [S]	Ray Charles Live in Concert	1965	20.00
❑ 520 [M]	Together Again	196?	15.00
—Retitled version of "Country and Western Meets Rhythm and Blues"			
❑ 520 [M]	Country & Western Meets Rhythm & Blues	1965	15.00
❑ S-520 [S]	Together Again	196?	20.00
—Retitled version of "Country and Western Meets Rhythm and Blues"			
❑ S-520 [S]	Country & Western Meets Rhythm & Blues	1965	20.00
❑ 544 [M]	Crying Time	1966	15.00
❑ S-544 [S]	Crying Time	1966	20.00
❑ 550 [M]	Ray's Moods	1966	15.00
❑ S-550 [S]	Ray's Moods	1966	20.00
❑ ST-90144 [S]	Ray Charles Live in Concert	1965	20.00
—Capitol Record Club edition			
❑ T-90144 [M]	Ray Charles Live in Concert	1965	20.00
—Capitol Record Club edition			
❑ ST-90625 [S]	Crying Time	1966	20.00
—Capitol Record Club edition			
❑ T-90625 [M]	Crying Time	1966	20.00
—Capitol Record Club edition			
❑ ST-90847 [S]	Together Again	1966	25.00
—Capitol Record Club edition			
❑ ST-90929 [S]	Ray's Moods	1966	25.00
—Capitol Record Club edition			

ATLANTIC

Number	Title (A Side/B Side)	Yr	NM
❑ SD 2-503 [(2)]	Ray Charles Live	1973	15.00
❑ 2-900 [(2)M]	The Ray Charles Story	1962	40.00
❑ 1259 [M]	The Great Ray Charles	1957	50.00
—Black label			
❑ 1259 [M]	The Great Ray Charles	1960	25.00
—Red and white label, white fan logo on right			
❑ 1259 [M]	The Great Ray Charles	1962	20.00
—Red and white label, black fan logo on right			
❑ SD 1259 [S]	The Great Ray Charles	1959	50.00
—Green label			
❑ SD 1259 [S]	The Great Ray Charles	1960	25.00
—Blue and green label, white fan logo on right			
❑ SD 1259 [S]	The Great Ray Charles	1962	20.00
—Blue and green label, black fan logo on right			
❑ 1289 [M]	Ray Charles at Newport	1958	50.00
—Black label			
❑ 1289 [M]	Ray Charles at Newport	1960	25.00
—Red and white label, white fan logo on right			
❑ 1289 [M]	Ray Charles at Newport	1962	20.00
—Red and white label, black fan logo on right			
❑ SD 1289 [S]	Ray Charles at Newport	1959	50.00
—Green label			
❑ SD 1289 [S]	Ray Charles at Newport	1960	25.00
—Blue and green label, white fan logo on right			
❑ SD 1289 [S]	Ray Charles at Newport	1962	20.00
—Blue and green label, black fan logo on right			
❑ 1312 [M]	The Genius of Ray Charles	1960	25.00
—Red and white label, white fan logo on right			
❑ 1312 [M]	The Genius of Ray Charles	1960	40.00
—Black label			
❑ 1312 [M]	The Genius of Ray Charles	1960	40.00
—White "bullseye" label			
❑ 1312 [M]	The Genius of Ray Charles	1962	20.00
—Red and white label, black fan logo on right			
❑ SD 1312 [S]	The Genius of Ray Charles	1960	25.00
—Blue and green label, white fan logo on right			
❑ SD 1312 [S]	The Genius of Ray Charles	1960	50.00
—Green label			
❑ SD 1312 [S]	The Genius of Ray Charles	1960	50.00
—White "bullseye" label			
❑ SD 1312 [S]	The Genius of Ray Charles	1962	20.00
—Blue and green label, black fan logo on right			
❑ SD 1312 [S]	The Genius of Ray Charles	1968	20.00
—Brown and purple label			
❑ 1369 [M]	The Genius After Hours	1961	25.00
—Red and white label, white fan logo on right			
❑ 1369 [M]	The Genius After Hours	1962	20.00
—Red and white label, black fan logo on right			
❑ SD 1369 [S]	The Genius After Hours	1961	30.00
—Blue and green label, white fan logo on right			
❑ SD 1369 [S]	The Genius After Hours	1962	25.00
—Blue and green label, black fan logo on right			
❑ SD 1543	The Best of Ray Charles	1970	12.00
❑ 3700 [(6)]	Ray Charles: A Life in Music	198?	50.00
❑ SD 7101 [S]	The Great Hits of Ray Charles Recorded on 8-Track Stereo	1966	25.00
❑ 8006 [M]	Ray Charles (Rock and Roll)	1957	90.00
—Black label			
❑ 8006 [M]	Ray Charles (Rock and Roll)	1960	25.00
—Red and white label, white fan logo on right			
❑ 8006 [M]	Hallelujah! I Love Her So	1962	20.00
—Red and white label, black fan logo on right; retitled version			
❑ 8025 [M]	Yes, Indeed!	1958	50.00
—Black label; cover has screaming girls			
❑ 8025 [M]	Yes, Indeed!	1960	25.00
—Red and white label, white fan logo on right; cover has screaming girls			
❑ 8025 [M]	Yes, Indeed!	1962	20.00
—Red and white label, black fan logo on right; cover has Ray on it			
❑ 8029 [M]	What'd I Say	1959	50.00
—Black label			
❑ 8029 [M]	What'd I Say	1960	25.00
—Red and white label, white fan logo on right			
❑ 8029 [M]	What'd I Say	1960	40.00
—White "bullseye" label			
❑ 8029 [M]	What'd I Say	1962	20.00
—Red and white label, black fan logo on right			
❑ 8039 [M]	Ray Charles In Person	1960	25.00
—Red and white label, white fan logo on right			
❑ 8039 [M]	Ray Charles In Person	1960	40.00
—Black label			
❑ 8039 [M]	Ray Charles In Person	1962	20.00
—Red and white label, black fan logo on right			
❑ 8052 [M]	The Genius Sings the Blues	1961	25.00
—Red and white label, white fan logo on right			
❑ 8052 [M]	The Genius Sings the Blues	1962	20.00
—Red and white label, black fan logo on right			
❑ 8054 [M]	Do the Twist!	1961	25.00
—Red and white label, white fan logo on right			
❑ 8054 [M]	Do the Twist!	1962	20.00
—Red and white label, black fan logo on right			
❑ 8063 [M]	The Ray Charles Story, Vol. 1	1962	20.00
❑ 8064 [M]	The Ray Charles Story, Vol. 2	1962	20.00
❑ 8083 [M]	The Ray Charles Story, Vol. 3	1963	20.00
❑ 8094 [M]	The Ray Charles Story, Vol. 4	1964	20.00
❑ SD 8094 [S]	The Ray Charles Story, Vol. 4	1964	25.00
❑ SD 19142	True to Life	1977	12.00
❑ SD 19199	Love and Peace	1978	12.00
❑ SD 19251	Ain't It So	1979	12.00
❑ SD 19281	Brother Ray Is At It Again	1980	12.00
❑ 90464	The Genius After Hours	1986	10.00
—Reissue			

BARONET

Number	Title (A Side/B Side)	Yr	NM
❑ B-111 [M]	The Artistry of Ray Charles	196?	12.00
❑ BS-111 [R]	The Artistry of Ray Charles	196?	10.00
❑ B-117 [M]	The Great Ray Charles	196?	12.00
❑ BS-117 [R]	The Great Ray Charles	196?	10.00

BLUESWAY

Number	Title (A Side/B Side)	Yr	NM
❑ 6053	The Genius Live	1973	12.00

COLUMBIA

Number	Title (A Side/B Side)	Yr	NM
❑ AS 1920 [DJ]	Friendship Radio Show	1984	20.00
❑ FC 38293	Wish You Were Here Tonight	1983	10.00
❑ PC 38293	Wish You Were Here Tonight	1985	8.00
—Budget-line reissue			
❑ FC 38990	Do I Ever Cross Your Mind	1984	10.00
❑ FC 39415	Friendship	1985	10.00
❑ FC 40125	The Spirit of Christmas	1985	10.00
❑ FC 40338	From the Pages of My Mind	1986	10.00
❑ FC 45062	Seven Spanish Angels and Other Hits (1982-1986)	1989	12.00

CORONET

Number	Title (A Side/B Side)	Yr	NM
❑ CX-173 [M]	Ray Charles	196?	12.00
❑ CXS-173 [R]	Ray Charles	196?	10.00

CROSSOVER

Number	Title (A Side/B Side)	Yr	NM
❑ 9000	Come Live with Me	1974	12.00
❑ 9005	Renaissance	1975	12.00
❑ 9007	My Kind of Jazz, Part 3	1976	12.00

DCC COMPACT CLASSICS

Number	Title (A Side/B Side)	Yr	NM
❑ LPZ-2012	Greatest Country and Western Hits	1995	100.00
—Audiophile vinyl			

DUNHILL COMPACT CLASSICS

Number	Title (A Side/B Side)	Yr	NM
❑ DZL-038	Genius + Soul = Jazz	1988	15.00
—Clear vinyl reissue			

EVEREST ARCHIVE OF FOLK & JAZZ

Number	Title (A Side/B Side)	Yr	NM
❑ 244	Ray Charles	1970	12.00
❑ 292	Ray Charles, Vol. 2	197?	10.00
❑ 358	Rockin' with Ray	1979	10.00

HOLLYWOOD

Number	Title (A Side/B Side)	Yr	NM
❑ 504 [M]	The Original Ray Charles	1959	150.00
❑ 505 [M]	The Fabulous Ray Charles	1959	150.00

IMPULSE!

Number	Title (A Side/B Side)	Yr	NM
❑ A-2 [M]	Genius + Soul = Jazz	1961	25.00
❑ AS-2 [S]	Genius + Soul = Jazz	1961	30.00

INTERMEDIA

Number	Title (A Side/B Side)	Yr	NM
❑ QS-5013	Goin' Down Slow	198?	10.00

LONGINES SYMPHONETTE

Number	Title (A Side/B Side)	Yr	NM
❑ 95647 [(5)]	The Greatest Hits of Ray Charles	1974	40.00

PAIR

Number	Title (A Side/B Side)	Yr	NM
❑ PDL2-1139 [(2)]	The Real Ray Charles	1986	12.00

PREMIER

Number	Title (A Side/B Side)	Yr	NM
❑ PM 2004 [M]	The Great Ray Charles	196?	12.00
❑ PS 2004 [R]	The Great Ray Charles	196?	10.00
❑ PS-6001 [R]	Fantastic Ray Charles	196?	10.00

RHINO

Number	Title (A Side/B Side)	Yr	NM
❑ R1-70097	Greatest Hits, Vol. 1	1988	10.00
❑ R1-70098	Greatest Hits, Vol. 2	1988	10.00
❑ R1-70099	Modern Sounds in Country and Western Music	1988	10.00

TANGERINE

Number	Title (A Side/B Side)	Yr	NM
❑ 1512	My Kind of Jazz	1970	12.00
❑ 1516	My Kind of Jazz No. II	1973	12.00

WARNER BROS.

Number	Title (A Side/B Side)	Yr	NM
❑ 26343	Would You Believe?	1990	15.00

CHARLES, RAY / HARRY BELAFONTE

Also see each artist's individual listings.

Albums

CORONET

Number	Title (A Side/B Side)	Yr	NM
❑ CX-203 [M]	The Greatest Ever	196?	12.00
❑ CXS-203 [R]	The Greatest Ever	196?	10.00

CHARLES, RAY, AND BETTY CARTER

45s

ABC-PARAMOUNT

Number	Title (A Side/B Side)	Yr	NM
❑ 10298	Baby It's Cold Outside/ We'll Be Together Again	1962	10.00

Albums

ABC

Number	Title (A Side/B Side)	Yr	NM
❑ S-385 [S]	Ray Charles and Betty Carter	1967	20.00
—Reissue of ABC-Paramount ABCS-385			

ABC-PARAMOUNT

Number	Title (A Side/B Side)	Yr	NM
❑ ABC-385 [M]	Ray Charles and Betty Carter	1961	60.00
❑ ABCS-385 [S]	Ray Charles and Betty Carter	1961	80.00

DCC COMPACT CLASSICS

Number	Title (A Side/B Side)	Yr	NM
❑ LPZ-2005	Ray Charles and Betty Carter	1995	150.00
—Audiophile vinyl			

DUNHILL COMPACT CLASSICS

Number	Title (A Side/B Side)	Yr	NM
❑ DZL-039	Ray Charles and Betty Carter	1988	15.00
—Clear vinyl reissue			

CHARLES, RAY/IVORY JOE HUNTER/JIMMY RUSHING

Also see RAY CHARLES; IVORY JOE HUNTER.

Number	Title (A Side/B Side)	Yr	NM
Albums			
DESIGN			
❑ DLP-909 [M]	Three of a Kind	196?	12.00
❑ DLS-909 [R]	Three of a Kind	196?	10.00

CHARLES, RAY, AND MILT JACKSON

Number	Title (A Side/B Side)	Yr	NM
7-Inch Extended Plays			
ATLANTIC			
❑ 614	Blue Funk/Cosmic Ray	1958	70.00
❑ 614 [PS]	Soul Brothers	1958	70.00
Albums			
ATLANTIC			
❑ 1279 [M]	Soul Brothers	1958	50.00
—Black label			
❑ 1279 [M]	Soul Brothers	1960	25.00
—Red and white label, white fan logo on right			
❑ 1279 [M]	Soul Brothers	1962	20.00
—Red and white label, black fan logo on right			
❑ SD 1279 [S]	Soul Brothers	1959	50.00
—Green label			
❑ SD 1279 [S]	Soul Brothers	1960	25.00
—Blue and green label, white fan logo on right			
❑ SD 1279 [S]	Soul Brothers	1962	20.00
—Blue and green label, black fan logo on right			
❑ 1360 [M]	Soul Meeting	1961	25.00
—Red and white label, white fan logo on right			
❑ 1360 [M]	Soul Meeting	1962	20.00
—Red and white label, black fan logo on right			
❑ SD 1360 [S]	Soul Meeting	1961	30.00
—Blue and green label, white fan logo on right			
❑ SD 1360 [S]	Soul Meeting	1962	25.00
—Blue and green label, black fan logo on right			

CHARLES, RAY, AND CLEO LAINE

Number	Title (A Side/B Side)	Yr	NM
Albums			
RCA VICTOR			
❑ CPL2-1831 [(2)]	Porgy & Bess	1976	15.00
❑ DJL1-2163	Porgy & Bess	1976	20.00
—Promo-only excerpts from 2-record set			

CHARLES, RAY, SINGERS

No relation to the above Ray Charles.

Number	Title (A Side/B Side)	Yr	NM
45s			
COMMAND			
❑ SE# 41SD [S]	Misty/East of the Sun	196?	8.00
—Jukebox issue; small hole, plays at 33 1/3 rpm			
❑ 4046	Love Me with All Your Heart/Sweet Little Mountain Bird	1964	6.00
—With the Ray Charles Singers receiving a more "apt" credit			
❑ 4046	Love Me with All Your Heart/Sweet Little Mountain Bird	1964	10.00
—The LP title "Something Special for Young Lovers" is in bold, with "The Ray Charles Singers" in tiny print at bottom			
❑ 4049	Al Di La/Till the End of Time	1964	6.00
❑ 4057	One More Time/Bluesette	1964	6.00
❑ 4059	This Is My Prayer/A Toy for a Boy	1965	6.00
❑ 4070	Hey, Pretty Pussycat/The Nut Song	1965	6.00
❑ 4073	My Love, Forgive Me/My Guitar and My Song	1965	6.00
❑ 4074	Christmas Is a Birthday/A Toy for a Boy	1965	10.00
❑ 4079	One of Those Songs/To You	1966	5.00
❑ 4082	Blue Roses/My World (Il Mondo)	1966	5.00
❑ 4085	It's Time to Sing/Promises	1966	5.00
❑ 4086	Minneapolis/The Bells	1966	5.00
❑ 4090	Don't Cry/There's No Place Like Home	1967	5.00
❑ 4092	Birds of a Feather/Step By Step	1967	5.00
❑ 4096	Bless Your Heart/Little By Little and Step By Step	1967	5.00
❑ 4103	Then You Can Tell Me Goodbye/Blame It on Me	1968	5.00
❑ 4105	Take Me Along/Walkin' Lonely	1968	5.00
❑ 4115	I Can See It Now/Quiz Me	1968	5.00
❑ 4123	I Wish I Knew How It Would Feel to Be Free/Let Go	1969	4.00
❑ 4130	Holly/Summer Warning	1969	4.00
❑ 4135	Move Me, O Wondrous Music/I'll Fly Away	1969	4.00
DECCA			
❑ 30834	Hip Hop/A Touch of Pink	1959	10.00
MGM			
❑ 12068	Autumn Leaves/Early Autumn	1955	10.00
❑ 12108	Autumn in New York/Autumn in Rome	1955	10.00
❑ 12217	Spring Is Here/Spring! Spring! Spring!	1956	10.00
❑ 12274	June Night/When the Red, Red Robin Comes Bob, Bob, Bobbin' Along	1956	10.00
❑ 12333	September in the Rain/'Tis Autumn	1956	10.00
❑ 12363	Moonlight in Vermont/Button Up Your Overcoat	1956	10.00
❑ 12413	I've Got My Love to Keep Me Warm/When Winter Comes	1957	10.00
❑ 12445	Mam'selle/Madamoiselle de Paris	1957	10.00
❑ 12470	When It's Springtime in the Rockies/Lovelier Than Ever	1957	10.00
❑ 12507	Around the World/Take a Trip to Memory Lane	1957	10.00
❑ 12524	Lazy Afternoon/Mountain Greenery	1957	10.00
❑ 12563	The Things We Did Last Summer/Shine On Harvest Moon	1957	10.00
❑ 12606	Let It Snow, Let It Snow, Let It Snow/You're My Girl	1957	12.00
7-Inch Extended Plays			
MGM			
❑ X-1503	Here's to My Lady/You Must Have Been a Beautiful Baby//The Very Thought of You/You're Getting to Be a Habit with Me	1957	10.00
❑ X-1503 [PS]	Here's to My Lady, Vol. 1	1957	10.00
Albums			
ABC			
❑ X-772	Moods of Love	1973	10.00
ATCO			
❑ SD 33-263	Memories of a Middle-Aged Movie Fan	1970	10.00
COMMAND			
❑ 33-827 [M]	Something Wonderful	1961	10.00
❑ SD 827 [S]	Something Wonderful	1961	12.00
❑ 33-839 [M]	Rome Revisited	1962	10.00
❑ SD 839 [S]	Rome Revisited	1962	12.00
❑ 33-845 [M]	Paradise Islands	1962	10.00
❑ SD 845 [S]	Paradise Islands	1962	12.00
❑ 33-866 [M]	Something Special for Young Lovers	1964	10.00
❑ SD 866 [S]	Something Special for Young Lovers	1964	12.00
❑ 33-870 [M]	Al-Di-La and Other Extra Special Songs for Young Lovers	1964	10.00
❑ SD 870 [S]	Al-Di-La and Other Extra Special Songs for Young Lovers	1964	12.00
❑ 33-874 [M]	Songs for Lonesome Lovers	1964	10.00
❑ SD 874 [S]	Songs for Lonesome Lovers	1964	12.00
❑ 33-876 [M]	Command Performances	1965	10.00
❑ SD 876 [S]	Command Performances	1965	12.00
❑ 33-886 [M]	Songs for Latin Lovers	1965	10.00
❑ SD 886 [S]	Songs for Latin Lovers	1965	12.00
❑ 33-890 [M]	Young Lovers on Broadway	1965	10.00
❑ SD 890 [S]	Young Lovers on Broadway	1965	12.00
❑ 33-896 [M]	Command Performances Vol. 2	1966	10.00
❑ SD 896 [S]	Command Performances Vol. 2	1966	12.00
❑ 33-898 [M]	One of Those Songs	1966	10.00
❑ SD 898 [S]	One of Those Songs	1966	12.00
❑ 33-903 [M]	What the World Needs Now Is Love	1966	10.00
❑ SD 903 [S]	What the World Needs Now Is Love	1966	12.00
❑ 33-914 [M]	Special Something	1967	12.00
❑ SD 914 [S]	Special Something	1967	10.00
❑ SD 923	At the Movies	1968	10.00
❑ SD 926	Take Me Along	1968	10.00
❑ SD 936	MacArthur Park	1969	10.00
❑ SD 949	Move Me, O Wondrous Music	1969	10.00
❑ CQ-40005 [Q]	Love Me with All of Your Heart	1972	15.00
DECCA			
❑ DL 8787 [M]	Highest Fidelity — Love and Marriage	1958	12.00
❑ DL 8838 [M]	Sunrise Serenade	1958	12.00
❑ DL 8874 [M]	In the Evening by the Moonlight	1959	12.00
❑ DL 8940 [M]	We Gather Together — Beloved Hymns	1959	12.00
❑ DL 8988 [M]	Deep Night	1960	12.00
❑ DL 78787 [S]	Highest Fidelity — Love and Marriage	1958	15.00
❑ DL 78838 [S]	Sunrise Serenade	1958	15.00
❑ DL 78874 [S]	In the Evening by the Moonlight	1959	15.00
❑ DL 78940 [S]	We Gather Together — Beloved Hymns	1959	15.00
❑ DL 78988 [S]	Deep Night	1960	15.00
MCA			
❑ 4162 [(2)]	The Best of the Ray Charles Singers	1980	10.00
METRO			
❑ M-507 [M]	Spring, Spring, Spring	1965	10.00
❑ MS-507 [S]	Spring, Spring, Spring	1965	10.00
MGM			
❑ E-3387 [M]	Winter Wonderland	1956	15.00
—Yellow label			
❑ E-3387 [M]	Winter Wonderland	1960	12.00
—Black label			
❑ E-3568 [M]	Here's to My Lady	1957	15.00
—Yellow label			
❑ E-3568 [M]	Here's to My Lady	1960	12.00
—Black label			
❑ E-4163 [M]	Autumn Moods	1963	12.00
❑ SE-4163 [S]	Autumn Moods	1963	12.00
❑ E-4164 [M]	Songs for a Lazy Summer Afternoon	1963	12.00
❑ SE-4164 [S]	Songs for a Lazy Summer Afternoon	1963	12.00
❑ E-4165 [M]	We Love Paris	1963	12.00
❑ SE-4165 [S]	We Love Paris	1963	12.00
❑ E-4166 [M]	Christmas at Home	1963	12.00
❑ SE-4166 [S]	Christmas at Home	1963	12.00
❑ E-4257 [M]	The Very Best of the Ray Charles Singers	1964	12.00
❑ SE-4257 [S]	The Very Best of the Ray Charles Singers	1964	12.00
SOMERSET			
❑ P-21400 [M]	Quiet Moments for Young Lovers	196?	10.00
❑ SF-21400 [S]	Quiet Moments for Young Lovers	196?	10.00
❑ P-21500 [M]	Young Lovers in Far Away Places	196?	10.00
❑ SF-21500 [S]	Young Lovers in Far Away Places	196?	10.00
VOCALION			
❑ VL 3784 [M]	Love Is a Many-Splendored Thing	196?	10.00
❑ VL 73784 [S]	Love Is a Many-Splendored Thing	196?	10.00

CHARLES, SONNY

Also see THE CHECKMATES LTD.

Number	Title (A Side/B Side)	Yr	NM
45s			
FRATERNITY			
❑ 935	Speechless/These Two Feet	1964	12.00
HIGHRISE			
❑ 2001	Put It in a Magazine/The Week-End Father Song	1982	5.00
❑ 2006	Always on My Mind/One-Eyed Jacks	1983	5.00
RCA VICTOR			
❑ 74-0645	It's Alright in the City/Nicasio	1972	6.00
Albums			
HIGHRISE			
❑ HR-102	The Sun Still Shines	1982	12.00

CHARLES AND CARL

Number	Title (A Side/B Side)	Yr	NM
45s			
RED ROBIN			
❑ 137	Lucky Star/One More Chance	1955	100.00

CHARLES RIVER VALLEY BOYS, THE

Number	Title (A Side/B Side)	Yr	NM
Albums			
ELEKTRA			
❑ EKL-4006 [M]	Beatle Country	1967	20.00
❑ EKS-74006 [S]	Beatle Country	1967	25.00

CHARLETTES, THE

Number	Title (A Side/B Side)	Yr	NM
45s			
ANGIE			
❑ 1002	The Fight's Not Over/Whatever Happened to Our Love	1963	25.00

CHARMAINES, THE

Number	Title (A Side/B Side)	Yr	NM
45s			
DOT			
❑ 16351	Where Is the Boy Tonight/On the Wagon	1961	20.00

CHARMERS, THE (1)

Female group.

Number	Title (A Side/B Side)	Yr	NM
45s			
ALADDIN			
❑ 3337	All Alone/Johnny My Dear	1956	60.00
❑ 3341	He's Gone/Oh! Yes	1956	60.00
IMPERIAL			
❑ 5957	All Alone/Johnny My Dear	1963	12.00
—Reissue of Aladdin 3337			

CHARMERS, THE (2)

Another female group, not the same as group (1).

Number	Title (A Side/B Side)	Yr	NM
45s			
CENTRAL			
❑ 1002	The Beating of My Heart/Why Does It Have to Be Me	1954	800.00
❑ 1006	Tony, My Darling/In the Rain	1954	1000.
LOST-NITE			
❑ 141	Tony, My Darling/In the Rain	196?	8.00
—Reissue			
❑ 142	The Beating of My Heart/Why Does It Have to Be Me	1954	8.00
—Reissue			

Except when noted otherwise, VG = 25% of NM, and VG+ = 50% of NM. (Example: VG = $2.00, VG+ = $4.00 and NM = $8.00.)

Number	Title (A Side/B Side)	Yr	NM
TIMELY			
❑ 1009	I Was Wrong/The Mambo	1955	1000.
❑ 1011	The Church on the Hill/Battle Axe	1955	1000.

CHARMERS, THE (U) Probably none of these are group (1) or (2), but which ones go together, we don't yet know.

45s

Number	Title (A Side/B Side)	Yr	NM
CO-REC			
❑ 101	The Letter/Watch What You Do	1963	20.00
JAF			
❑ 2021	Little Fool/Hard to Get	1961	25.00
LAURIE			
❑ 3142	My Kind of Love/Johnny	1962	20.00
❑ 3173	Shy Guy/I Cried	1963	20.00
❑ 3203	Work It Out/Sweet Talk	1963	20.00
LOUIS			
❑ 6806	It's a Funny Way We Met/ Where's the Boy	1965	12.00
PIP			
❑ 8000	Looking for Trouble/ After You Walk Me Home	1964	12.00
SILHOUETTE			
❑ 522	Rock, Rhythm and Blues/ Letters Don't Have Arms	1957	60.00
SURE SHOT			
❑ 104	Lessons from the Stars/My Love	1963	300.00
TERRACE			
❑ 7512	Visiting Day/Whatever Happened to Baby Jane	1962	25.00

CHARMETTES, THE

45s

Number	Title (A Side/B Side)	Yr	NM
FEDERAL			
❑ 12345	Johnny, Johnny/School Letter	1959	40.00
HI			
❑ 2003	My Love with All My Heart/ Skating in Blue Light	1958	20.00
KAPP			
❑ 547	Please Don't Kiss Me Again/ What Is a Tear	1963	30.00
❑ 570	Oozi-Oozi-Ooh/He's a Wise Guy	1964	25.00
MALA			
❑ 491	My Lover Is a Boy Scout/Mailbox	1964	12.00
TRI-DISC			
❑ 103	Why Oh Why/On a Night Like Tonight	1962	25.00
WORLD ARTISTS			
❑ 1053	Stop the Wedding (Preacher Man)/Sugar Boy	1965	25.00

CHARMS, THE Also see OTIS WILLIAMS AND THE CHARMS.

45s

Number	Title (A Side/B Side)	Yr	NM
CHART			
❑ 608	Love's Our Inspiration/ Love, Love Stick Stov	1956	40.00
❑ 613	Heart of a Rose/I Offer You	1956	40.00
❑ 623	I'll Be True/Boom Diddy Boom Boom	1956	40.00
DELUXE			
❑ 6000	Heaven Only Knows/ Loving Baby	1953	500.00
❑ 6014	Happy Are We/What Do You Know About That	1953	400.00
❑ 6034	Bye Bye Baby/Please Believe in Me	1954	400.00
❑ 6050	Quiet Please/55 Seconds	1954	400.00
❑ 6056	Come to Me Baby/My Baby, Dearest Darling	1954	200.00
❑ 6062	Hearts of Stone/Who Knows	1954	50.00
❑ 6065	Two Hearts/The First Time We Met	1954	50.00
❑ 6072	Crazy, Crazy Love/ Mambo Sh-Mambo	1955	50.00
❑ 6076	Ling, Ting, Tong/Bazoom (I Need Your Lovin')	1955	50.00
❑ 6080	Ko Ko Mo (I Love You So)/ Whadya Want?	1955	50.00
❑ 6082	Whadya Want?/ Crazy, Crazy Love	1955	40.00
❑ 6087	When We Get Married/Let the Happenings Happen	1955	40.00
❑ 6089	One Fine Day/It's You, You, You	1955	40.00
ROCKIN'			
❑ 516	Heaven Only Knows/ Loving Baby	1953	800.00

7-Inch Extended Plays

Number	Title (A Side/B Side)	Yr	NM
DELUXE			
❑ EP-357	*Hearts of Stone/Bazoom (I Need Your Lovin')/Ling Ting Tong/Crazy, Crazy Love	1955	400.00
❑ EP-357 [PS]	Hits by the Charms	1955	400.00

CHARTERS, THE May all be the same group.

45s

Number	Title (A Side/B Side)	Yr	NM
ALVA			
❑ 1001	I Lost You/My Little Girl	1963	300.00
MEL-O-DY			
❑ 104	Trouble Lover/Show Me Some Sign	1962	2000.
MERRY-GO-ROUND			
❑ 103	Lost in a Dream/This Makes Me Mad	1963	60.00
TARX			
❑ 1003	My Rose/El Merengue	1962	100.00

CHARTS, THE

45s

Number	Title (A Side/B Side)	Yr	NM
EVERLAST			
❑ 5001	Deserie/Zoop	1957	80.00
❑ 5002	Dance Girl/Why Do You Cry	1957	80.00
❑ 5006	You're the Reason (I'm in Love)/I've Been Wondering	1958	60.00
❑ 5008	I Told You So/All Because of Love	1958	60.00
❑ 5010	My Diane/All Because of You	1958	70.00
❑ 5026	Deserie/Zoop	1963	25.00
GUYDEN			
❑ 2021	For the Birds/Ooba-Gooba	1959	20.00
LANA			
❑ 117	Deserie/I Wanna Take You Home	196?	8.00
LOST-NITE			
❑ 173	Deserie/Zoop	196?	6.00
—Reissue			
❑ 180	Dance Girl/Why Do You Cry	196?	6.00
—Reissue			
❑ 186	You're the Reason (I'm in Love)/I've Been Wondering	196?	6.00
—Reissue			
❑ 377	My Diane/Baby Be Mine	197?	5.00
—Reissue			
❑ 381	I Told You So/All Because of Love	197?	5.00
—Reissue			
WAND			
❑ 1112	Deserie/Fell in Love with Your Baby	1966	25.00
❑ 1124	Livin' the Night Life/Nobody Made You Love Me	1966	60.00

Albums

Number	Title (A Side/B Side)	Yr	NM
COLLECTABLES			
❑ COL-5029	Greatest Hits	1986	12.00
LOST-NITE			
❑ LLP-10 [10]	The Charts	1981	12.00
—Red vinyl			

CHAVELLES, THE

45s

Number	Title (A Side/B Side)	Yr	NM
VITA			
❑ 127	Valley of Love/Red Tape	1956	150.00

CHAVIS BROTHERS, THE

45s

Number	Title (A Side/B Side)	Yr	NM
ASCOT			
❑ 2177	Torture Me/Humpty Dumpty Time	1965	12.00
CLOCK			
❑ 1025	I Love You/So Tired	1960	25.00
CORAL			
❑ 62270	Old Time Rock and Roll/ Baby, Don't Leave Me	1961	30.00
—As "The Five Chavis Brothers"			
PARKWAY			
❑ 851	Slippin' and Slidin'/ Good Old Mountain Dew	1962	15.00

CHEAP TRICK

10-Inch Singles

Number	Title (A Side/B Side)	Yr	NM
EPIC			
❑ AS 790 [DJ]	Everything Works If You Let It (3:06) (3:26)	1980	10.00

12-Inch Singles

Number	Title (A Side/B Side)	Yr	NM
COLUMBIA			
❑ CAS 2379 [DJ]	Mighty Wings (same on both sides)	1986	10.00
EPIC			
❑ EAS 2121 [DJ]	Tonight It's You (same on both sides)	1985	12.00
❑ EAS 2186 [DJ]	Little Sister (same on both sides)	1985	12.00
❑ EAS 2237 [DJ]	How About You (same on both sides)	1985	12.00
❑ EAS 2566 [DJ]	It's Only Love (LP Version) (7" Version)	1986	12.00
❑ 49-03402	Saturday at Midnight (Super New Dance Remix) (Super Dub Mix)	1982	15.00
PASHA			
❑ AS 1827 [DJ]	Up the Creek (Original) (A Cappella)	1984	12.00

45s

Number	Title (A Side/B Side)	Yr	NM
ASYLUM			
❑ 47187	Reach Out/I Must Be Dreamin'	1981	4.00
❑ 47187 [PS]	Reach Out/I Must Be Dreamin'	1981	6.00
COLUMBIA			
❑ 38-06137	Mighty Wings/Dog Fight #3	1986	3.00
—B-side by Harold Faltermeyer			
❑ 38-06137 [PS]	Mighty Wings/Dog Fight #3	1986	3.00
EPIC			
❑ AE7 1206 [DJ]	Everything Works If You Let It (same on both sides)	1980	5.00
—Included as an "extra" in the 10-inch version of the EP "Found All the Parts"; sometimes found separately, though it was never sold separately with this number			
❑ 14-02968	If You Want My Love/ Four Letter Word	1982	5.00
❑ 34-03233	She's Tight/All I Really Want to Do	1982	4.00
❑ 34-03233 [PS]	She's Tight/All I Really Want to Do	1982	5.00
❑ 34-03741	Saturday at Midnight/One on One	1983	4.00
❑ 15-03845	If You Want My Love/She's Tight	1983	4.00
—Reissue			
❑ 34-04078	Dancing the Night Away/ Don't Make Our Love a Crime	1983	4.00
❑ 34-04078 [PS]	Dancing the Night Away/ Don't Make Our Love a Crime	1983	5.00
❑ 34-04216	I Can't Take It/You Talk Too Much	1983	4.00
❑ 34-05431	Tonight It's You/ Wild, Wild Women	1985	4.00
❑ 34-05431 [PS]	Tonight It's You/ Wild, Wild Women	1985	5.00
—With B-side listed on back cover			
❑ 34-05431 [PS]	Tonight It's You/ Wild, Wild Women	1985	5.00
—With no B-side listed on back cover			
❑ 34-06540	It's Only Love/Name of the Game	1987	4.00
❑ 34-06540 [PS]	It's Only Love/Name of the Game	1987	5.00
❑ 34-07745	The Flame/Through the Night	1988	3.00
—Custom label			
❑ 34-07745 [PS]	The Flame/Through the Night	1988	3.00
❑ 34-07965	Don't Be Cruel/I Know What I Want	1988	3.00
❑ 34-07965 [PS]	Don't Be Cruel/I Know What I Want	1988	3.00
❑ 34-08097	Ghost Town/Wrong Side of Love	1988	3.00
❑ 34-08097 [PS]	Ghost Town/Wrong Side of Love	1988	3.00
❑ 8-50375	Oh, Candy/Daddy Should Have Stayed in High School	1977	10.00
❑ 8-50435	I Want You to Want Me/Oh Boy	1977	10.00
❑ 8-50485	Southern Girls/You're All Talk	1977	10.00
❑ 8-50570	Surrender/Auf Wiedersehn	1978	10.00
❑ 8-50625	California Man/I Want You to Want Me	1978	10.00
—B-side was first American issue of version that became a hit on Epic 50680			
❑ 8-50680	I Want You to Want Me/ Clock Strikes Ten	1979	4.00
❑ 8-50680 [PS]	I Want You to Want Me/ Clock Strikes Ten	1979	10.00
❑ 9-50743	Ain't That a Shame/Elo Kiddies	1979	5.00
❑ 9-50774	Dream Police/Heaven Tonight	1979	5.00
❑ 9-50774 [PS]	Dream Police/Heaven Tonight	1979	10.00
❑ 9-50814	Voices/The House Is Rockin' (With Domestic Problems)	1979	4.00
❑ 9-50814 [PS]	Voices/The House Is Rockin' (With Domestic Problems)	1979	10.00
❑ 9-50887	Everything Works If You Let It/ Way of the World	1980	5.00
❑ 19-50942	Stop This Game/Who D'King	1980	5.00
❑ 19-50970	The World's Greatest Lover/ High Priest of Rhythmic Noise	1981	5.00
❑ 34-68563	Never Had a Lot to Lose/ All We Need Is a Dream	1989	3.00
❑ 34-73444	Can't Stop Fallin' Into Love/ You Drive, I'll Steer	1990	3.00
❑ 34-73580	Wherever Would I Be/Busted	1990	3.00
❑ 34-73792	The Flame/Through the Night	1991	3.00
—Reissue			

Cheap Trick, *The Doctor*, Epic FE 40405, 1987, **$10.**

Number	Title (A Side/B Side)	Yr	NM
EPIC LEGACY			
❑ ES7 8290 [DJ]	I Want You to Want Me (Alternate Version)/Waitin' for the Man/Heroin (Live)	1996	5.00
❑ ES7 8290 [PS]	I Want You to Want Me (Alternate Version)/Waitin' for the Man/Heroin (Live)	1996	5.00
❑ ES7 58323 [DJ]	Oh Boy (Vocal Version) (Demo)/If You Want My Love (Demo)	2004	5.00
❑ ES7 58323 [PS]	Oh Boy (Vocal Version) (Demo)/If You Want My Love (Demo)	2004	5.00
PASHA			
❑ ZS4-04392	Up the Creek/Passion in the Dark (One Track Heart)	1984	4.00
—B-side by Danny Spanos			
SUB POP			
❑ 393	Baby Talk/Brontosaurus	1997	2.50
❑ 393 [PS]	Baby Talk/Brontosaurus	1997	2.50
WARNER BROS.			
❑ 29723	Spring Break/Get Ready	1983	6.00

Albums

Number	Title (A Side/B Side)	Yr	NM
EPIC			
❑ AS 518 [DJ]	From Tokyo to You	1979	30.00
—Promo-only sampler from Cheap Trick at Budokan			
❑ PE 34400	Cheap Trick	1976	12.00
—Originals have orange labels			
❑ PE 34400	Cheap Trick	1979	8.00
—Later editions have dark blue labels; may or may not have bar code on back			
❑ JE 34884	In Color	1977	12.00
—Originals have orange labels			
❑ PE 34884	In Color	1979	8.00
—Later editions have dark blue labels; may or may not have bar code on back			
❑ JE 35312	Heaven Tonight	1978	12.00
—Originals have orange labels			
❑ PE 35312	Heaven Tonight	1979	8.00
—Later editions have dark blue labels; may or may not have bar code on back			
❑ FE 35773	Dream Police	1979	10.00
—Despite lower number, this came out after Epic 35795			
❑ PE 35773	Dream Police	1984	8.00
❑ FE 35795	Cheap Trick at Budokan	1979	10.00
—Dark blue label; some copies came with gold-colored obi (add 100% if there) and all came with booklet (deduct 20% if missing)			
❑ FE 35795	Cheap Trick at Budokan	1979	12.00
—Orange label; came with gold-colored obi (add 5/6 if there) and booklet (deduct 1/6 if missing)			
❑ FE 35795 [DJ]	Cheap Trick at Budokan	1979	20.00
—White label promo			
❑ PE 35795	Cheap Trick at Budokan	1984	8.00
❑ FE 36498	All Shook Up	1980	10.00
❑ PE 36498	All Shook Up	1984	8.00
❑ FE 38021	One on One	1982	10.00
❑ PE 38021	One on One	1984	8.00
❑ PE 38541 [EP]	Found All the Parts	1983	8.00
—Six-song reissue of Epic/Nu-Disk release on 12-inch LP			
❑ FE 38794	Next Position Please	1983	10.00
❑ PE 38794	Next Position Please	1985	8.00
❑ FE 39592	Standing on the Edge	1985	10.00
❑ PE 39592	Standing on the Edge	1987	8.00
❑ FE 40405	The Doctor	1986	10.00
❑ PE 40405	The Doctor	1987	8.00
—Reissue with new prefix on cover			
❑ OE 40922	Lap of Luxury	1988	10.00
❑ E 46013	Busted	1990	12.00
EPIC/NU-DISK			
❑ 4E 36453 [10]	Found All the Parts	1980	15.00
—10-inch, four-track EP with bonus 45, "Everything Works If You Let It" (AE7 1206)			

CHECKER, CHUBBY
Also see BOBBY RYDELL; DEE DEE SHARP.

12-Inch Singles

Number	Title (A Side/B Side)	Yr	NM
AMHERST			
❑ AMH-D-4	The Rub (5:02)/Move It (4:45)	1976	20.00
SEA BRIGHT			
❑ 7128	Read You Like a Book (Extended Version) (Radio Version)	1986	8.00

45s

Number	Title (A Side/B Side)	Yr	NM
ABKCO			
❑ 4001	The Twist/Loddy Lo	1972	5.00
❑ 4002	The Hucklebuck/Pony Time	1972	5.00
❑ 4003	Limbo Rock/Let's Twist Again	1972	5.00
❑ 4004	Hey Bobba Needle/Hooka Tooka	1972	5.00
❑ 4027	Slow Twistin'/Birdland	1973	5.00
AMHERST			
❑ 716	The Rub/Move It	1976	4.00
BUDDAH			
❑ 100	Back in the U.S.S.R./Windy Cream	1969	12.00
COLLECTABLES			
❑ 3857	The Twist/Let's Twist Again	199?	3.00
—Re-recordings			
❑ 3857 [PS]	The Twist/Let's Twist Again	1996	5.00
—Special issue for the VHS release of the movie "Twister," available only as a giveaway at Sam Goody and Musicland stores			
❑ 3858	Limbo Rock/Pony Time	199?	3.00
—Re-recordings			
MCA			
❑ 51233	Running/Is Tonight the Night	1982	5.00
❑ 52015	Running/Is Tonight the Night	1982	4.00
❑ 52043	Harder Than Diamond/Your Love	1982	4.00
PARKWAY			
❑ 003 [DJ]	Never on Sunday/Alouette	1962	40.00
—Yellow label, black print, promo only			
❑ 004 [DJ]	Love Is Like a Twist/Peppermint Twist	1962	40.00
—Yellow label, black print, promo only			
❑ 005 [DJ]	Your Lips and Mine/Dear Lady Twist	1962	40.00
—Yellow label, black print, promo only			
❑ 006 [DJ]	The Jet/The Ray Charles-ton	1962	30.00
❑ 105	You Got the Power/Looking at Tomorrow	1966	15.00
❑ 112	Karate Monkey/Her Heart	1966	15.00
❑ 804	The Class/Schooldays, Oh Schooldays	1959	30.00
❑ 808	Samson and Delilah/Whole Lotta Laughin'	1959	25.00
❑ 810	Dancing Dinosaur/Those Private Eyes (Keep Watchin' Me)	1960	25.00
—The existence of both 808 and 810 has been confirmed			
❑ 811	The Twist/Toot	1960	20.00
—Second pressings have orange label with black print			
❑ 811	The Twist/Toot	1960	30.00
—First pressings have white label with blue print			
❑ 811	The Twist/Twistin' U.S.A.	1961	15.00
❑ 811 [DJ]	The Twist/Twistin' U.S.A.	1961	150.00
—Promo copy on yellow vinyl			
❑ 811 [DJ]	The Twist/Twistin' U.S.A.	1961	200.00
—Promo copy on red vinyl			
❑ 811 [PS]	The Twist/Twistin' U.S.A.	1961	25.00
❑ 813	The Hucklebuck/Whole Lotta Shakin' Goin' On	1960	15.00
❑ 818	Pony Time/Oh, Susannah	1960	15.00
❑ 822	Dance the Mess Around/Good, Good Lovin'	1961	15.00
❑ 824	Let's Twist Again/Everything's Gonna Be Alright	1961	15.00
❑ 824	Let's Twist Again/Everything's Gonna Be Alright	1961	200.00
—Orange vinyl			
❑ 824 [PS]	Let's Twist Again/Everything's Gonna Be Alright	1961	25.00
❑ 830	The Fly/That's the Way It Goes	1961	15.00
❑ 830 [PS]	The Fly/That's the Way It Goes	1961	25.00
❑ 835	Slow Twistin'/La Paloma Twist	1962	15.00
—Features female vocal by Dee Dee Sharp			
❑ 835 [PS]	Slow Twistin'/La Paloma Twist	1962	25.00
❑ 842	Dancin' Party/Gotta Get Myself Together	1962	15.00
❑ 842 [PS]	Dancin' Party/Gotta Get Myself Together	1962	25.00
❑ 849	Limbo Rock/Popeye The Hitch-Hiker	1962	15.00
❑ 849 [PS]	Limbo Rock/Popeye The Hitch-Hiker	1962	25.00
❑ 862	Twenty Miles/Let's Limbo Some More	1963	15.00
❑ 862 [PS]	Twenty Miles/Let's Limbo Some More	1963	25.00
❑ 873	Birdland/Black Cloud	1963	15.00
❑ 873 [PS]	Birdland/Black Cloud	1963	25.00
❑ 879	Surf Party/Twist It Up	1963	15.00
❑ 879 [PS]	Surf Party/Twist It Up	1963	25.00
❑ 890	Loddy Lo/Hooka Tooka	1963	15.00
❑ 890	Loddy Lo/Everything's Gonna Be Alright	1963	16.00
❑ 890 [PS]	Loddy Lo/Hooka Tooka	1963	25.00
❑ 890 [PS]	Loddy Lo/Everything's Gonna Be Alright	1963	28.00
❑ 907	Hey Bobba Needle/Spread Joy	1964	15.00
❑ 907 [PS]	Hey Bobba Needle/Spread Joy	1964	25.00
❑ 920	Lazy Elsie Molly/Rosie	1964	15.00
❑ 920 [PS]	Lazy Elsie Molly/Rosie	1964	25.00
❑ 922	She Wants T'Swim/You Better Believe It, Baby	1964	12.00
❑ 922 [PS]	She Wants T'Swim/You Better Believe It, Baby	1964	25.00

Except when noted otherwise, VG = 25% of NM, and VG+ = 50% of NM. (Example: VG = $2.00, VG+ = $4.00 and NM = $8.00.)

Number	Title (A Side/B Side)	Yr	NM
❑ 936	Lovely, Lovely (Loverly, Loverly)/The Weekend's Here	1964	12.00
❑ 936 [PS]	Lovely, Lovely (Loverly, Loverly)/ The Weekend's Here	1964	25.00
❑ 949	Let's Do the Freddie/ (At the) Discotheque	1965	12.00

—Original A-side title (number is P-949-A) and probably correct B-side title

Number	Title (A Side/B Side)	Yr	NM
❑ 949	Do the Freddie/(Do the) Discotheque	1965	20.00

—Reissue with new A-side title (number is P-949-C) and probably incorrect B-side title

Number	Title (A Side/B Side)	Yr	NM
❑ 959	Everything's Wrong/ Cu Me La Be-Stay	1965	50.00
❑ 965	You Just Don't Know/Two Hearts Make One Love	1965	1500.
❑ 989	Hey You! Little Boo-Ga-Loo/ Pussy Cat	1966	12.00

SEA BRIGHT

Number	Title (A Side/B Side)	Yr	NM
❑ 5128	Read You Like a Book/ (B-side unknown)	1986	4.00

TIN PAN APPLE

Number	Title (A Side/B Side)	Yr	NM
❑ 887571-7 [PS]	The Twist (Yo, Twist!)/ (Buffapella)	1988	3.00
❑ 887571-7 [PS]	The Twist (Yo, Twist!)/ (Buffapella)	1988	3.00

—"Stupid def vocals" on a Fat Boys record

20TH CENTURY

Number	Title (A Side/B Side)	Yr	NM
❑ 2040	Reggae My Way/Gypsy	1973	5.00
❑ 2075	She's a Bad Woman/ Happiness Is a Girl Like You	1974	5.00

7-Inch Extended Plays

PARKWAY

Number	Title (A Side/B Side)	Yr	NM
❑ 5001	The Ray Charles-ton/The Mess Around//The Jet/The Continental Walk	1961	60.00

—Small hole, plays at 33 1/3 rpm

Number	Title (A Side/B Side)	Yr	NM
❑ 5001 [PS]	Chubby Checker	1961	60.00

—Paper die-cut sleeve

Albums

ABKCO

Number	Title (A Side/B Side)	Yr	NM
❑ 4219 [(2)]	Chubby Checker's Greatest Hits	1972	20.00

EVEREST

Number	Title (A Side/B Side)	Yr	NM
❑ 4111	Chubby Checker's Greatest Hits	1981	12.00

MCA

Number	Title (A Side/B Side)	Yr	NM
❑ 5291	The Change Has Come	1982	10.00

PARKWAY

Number	Title (A Side/B Side)	Yr	NM
❑ P 7001 [M]	Twist with Chubby Checker	1960	40.00

—All-orange label

Number	Title (A Side/B Side)	Yr	NM
❑ P 7001 [M]	Twist with Chubby Checker	1962	30.00

—Orange and yellow label

Number	Title (A Side/B Side)	Yr	NM
❑ P 7002 [M]	For Twisters Only	1960	40.00

—All-orange label

Number	Title (A Side/B Side)	Yr	NM
❑ P 7002 [M]	For Twisters Only	1962	30.00

—Orange and yellow label

Number	Title (A Side/B Side)	Yr	NM
❑ P 7003 [M]	It's Pony Time	1961	40.00

—All-orange label

Number	Title (A Side/B Side)	Yr	NM
❑ P 7003 [M]	It's Pony Time	1962	30.00

—Orange and yellow label

Number	Title (A Side/B Side)	Yr	NM
❑ P 7004 [M]	Let's Twist Again	1961	40.00

—All-orange label

Number	Title (A Side/B Side)	Yr	NM
❑ P 7004 [M]	Let's Twist Again	1962	30.00

—Orange and yellow label

Number	Title (A Side/B Side)	Yr	NM
❑ P 7007 [M]	Your Twist Party	1961	40.00

—All-orange label

Number	Title (A Side/B Side)	Yr	NM
❑ P 7007 [M]	Your Twist Party	1962	30.00

—Orange and yellow label

Number	Title (A Side/B Side)	Yr	NM
❑ P 7008 [M]	Twistin' Round the World	1962	30.00
❑ SP 7008 [B]	Twistin' Round the World	1962	40.00
❑ P 7009 [M]	For Teen Twisters Only	1962	30.00
❑ SP 7009 [S]	For Teen Twisters Only	1962	40.00
❑ P 7014 [M]	All the Hits (For Your Dancin' Party)	1962	30.00
❑ P 7020 [M]	Limbo Party	1962	30.00
❑ SP 7020 [S]	Limbo Party	1962	40.00
❑ P 7022 [M]	Chubby Checker's Biggest Hits	1962	30.00
❑ SP 7022 [R]	Chubby Checker's Biggest Hits	1962	30.00
❑ P 7026 [M]	Chubby Checker In Person	1963	30.00
❑ SP 7026 [S]	Chubby Checker In Person	1963	40.00

—The above record is labeled "Twist It Up"

Number	Title (A Side/B Side)	Yr	NM
❑ P 7027 [M]	Let's Limbo Some More	1963	30.00
❑ SP 7027 [S]	Let's Limbo Some More	1963	40.00
❑ P 7030 [M]	Beach Party	1963	30.00
❑ SP 7030 [S]	Beach Party	1963	40.00
❑ P 7036 [M]	Chubby Checker With Sy Oliver and His Orchestra	1964	30.00
❑ SP 7036 [S]	Chubby Checker With Sy Oliver and His Orchestra	1964	40.00
❑ P 7040 [M]	Folk Album	1964	30.00
❑ SP 7040 [S]	Folk Album	1964	40.00
❑ P 7045 [M]	Discotheque	1965	30.00
❑ SP 7045 [S]	Discotheque	1965	40.00
❑ P 7048 [M]	Chubby Checker's Eighteen Golden Hits	1966	30.00

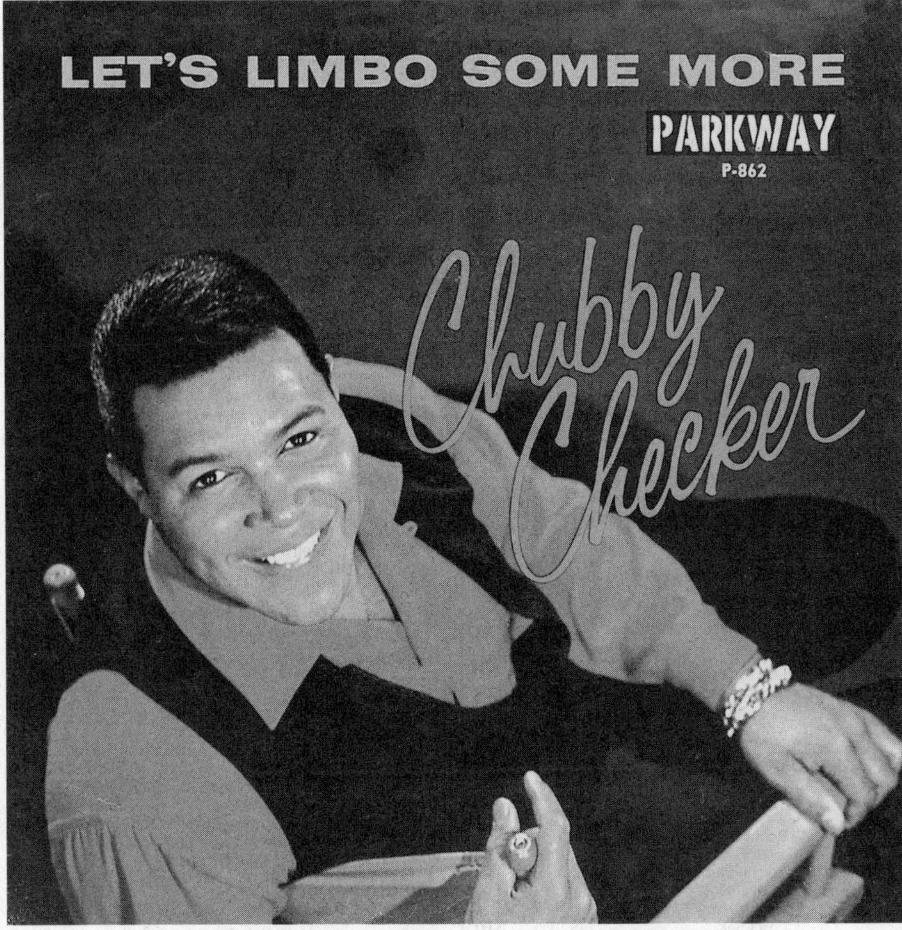

Chubby Checker, "Let's Limbo Some More," Parkway 862, 1963, **$25.**

Number	Title (A Side/B Side)	Yr	NM
❑ SP 7048 [P]	Chubby Checker's Eighteen Golden Hits	1966	40.00

CHECKERLADS, THE

45s

RCA VICTOR

Number	Title (A Side/B Side)	Yr	NM
❑ 47-8986	Shake Yourself Down/ Baby Send for Me	1966	25.00

CHECKERS, THE (1)

45s

FEDERAL

Number	Title (A Side/B Side)	Yr	NM
❑ 12355	So Fine/Sentimental Heart	1959	50.00
❑ 12375	White Cliffs of Dover/ Let Me Come Back	1960	50.00

KING

Number	Title (A Side/B Side)	Yr	NM
❑ 4558	Flame in My Heart/ Oh, Oh, Oh Baby	1952	1000.
❑ 4581	Night's Curtains/ Let Me Come Back	1952	1000.
❑ 4596	My Prayer Tonight/ Love Wasn't There	1953	1000.
❑ 4626	Ghost of My Baby/I Wanna Know	1953	800.00
❑ 4673	I Promise You/You Never Had It So Good	1953	500.00
❑ 4675	White Cliffs of Dover/ Without a Song	1953	500.00
❑ 4710	House with No Windows/ Don't Stop Dan	1954	500.00
❑ 4719	Over the Rainbow/You've Been Fooling Around	1954	400.00
❑ 4751	I Wasn't Thinking, I Was Drinking/Mama's Daughter	1954	500.00
❑ 4764	Trying to Hold My Girl/ Can't Find My Sadie	1955	500.00
❑ 5156	Heaven Only Knows/ Nine More Miles	1958	400.00
❑ 5592	Over the Rainbow/ Love Wasn't There	1962	20.00

—As "The Original Checkers"

CHECKERS, THE (2) Different group than (1).

45s

ARVEE

Number	Title (A Side/B Side)	Yr	NM
❑ 5035	Skooby Doo (Part 1)/ Skooby Doo (Part 2)	1961	20.00
❑ 5037	Swingin' Summer/Skooby Doo	1961	20.00

CHECKERS, THE (3) Not the same group as (1) though on the same label. Also see THE FIVE WINGS.

45s

KING

Number	Title (A Side/B Side)	Yr	NM
❑ 5199	Teardrops Are Falling/ Rock-A-Locka	1959	60.00

—Originally released as King 4781 by The Five Wings

CHECKERS, THE (U) Some of these may be the same group as (2), but not all of them.

45s

DOTTIE

Number	Title (A Side/B Side)	Yr	NM
❑ 1001	Big Car/Buzz	196?	20.00

JERDEN

Number	Title (A Side/B Side)	Yr	NM
❑ 710	Black Cat/Soft Blue	1963	20.00

MERCURY

Number	Title (A Side/B Side)	Yr	NM
❑ 72354	Red Ball Express/ Come Back Home	1964	12.00

SKYLA

Number	Title (A Side/B Side)	Yr	NM
❑ 1120	Blue Saturday/Cascade	1961	20.00

CHECKMATES, THE

Albums

JUSTICE

Number	Title (A Side/B Side)	Yr	NM
❑ JLP-149	The Checkmates	1966	400.00

CHECKMATES LTD., THE Also see SONNY CHARLES.

45s

A&M

Number	Title (A Side/B Side)	Yr	NM
❑ 1006	Spanish Harlem/Baby Don't You Get Crazy	1968	8.00

Number | Title (A Side/B Side) | Yr | NM

❑ 1040 Love Is All I Have to Give/Never Should Have Lied 1969 8.00
❑ 1053 Black Pearl/Lazy Susan 1969 10.00
—As "Sonny Charles and the Checkmates Ltd."
❑ 1127 Spanish Harlem/Proud Mary 1969 8.00
—As "Sonny Charles and the Checkmates Ltd."
❑ 1130 Proud Mary/Do You Love Your Baby 1969 8.00
—As "Sonny Charles and the Checkmates Ltd."

CAPITOL
❑ 5603 Do the Walk/Glad for You 1966 20.00
❑ 5753 I Can Hear the Rain/Kissin' Her and Cryin' for You 1966 30.00
❑ 5814 Please Don't Take My World Away/Mastered the Art of Love 1966 20.00
❑ 5922 Walk in the Sunlight/A & I 1967 20.00

FANTASY
❑ 800 Let's Do It/Take All the Time You Need 1977 5.00
❑ 823 Greedy for Your Love/That's How It Feels (When Two People Fall in Love) 1978 5.00

GREEDY
❑ 111 I'm Laying My Heart on the Line/Make Love to Your Mind 1977 5.00

POLYDOR
❑ 14313 All Alone by the Telephone/Body Language 1976 5.00

Albums

A&M
❑ SP-4183 Love Is All I Have to Give 1969 25.00

CAPITOL
❑ ST 2840 [S] Live at Caesar's Palace 1968 20.00
❑ T 2840 [M] Live at Caesar's Palace 1968 30.00

FANTASY
❑ 9541 We Got the Moves 1978 15.00

CHEECH AND CHONG

45s

MCA
❑ 52655 Born in East L.A./I'm a (Modern) Man 1985 3.00
❑ 52655 [PS] Born in East L.A./I'm a (Modern) Man 1985 4.00
❑ 52732 I'm Not Home Right Now/Hot Saki 1985 3.00
❑ 52732 [PS] I'm Not Home Right Now/Hot Saki 1985 4.00

ODE
❑ 50471 Bloat On (Featuring the Bloaters)/Just Say "Right On" 1977 4.00
❑ 50471 [PS] Bloat On (Featuring the Bloaters)/Just Say "Right On" 1977 6.00
❑ 50499 Santa Claus and His Old Lady/Rudolph the Red-Nosed Reindeer 1977 10.00
❑ 66021 Santa Claus and His Old Lady/Dave 1971 8.00
❑ 66021 [PS] Santa Claus and His Old Lady/Dave 1971 12.00
❑ 66038 Basketball Jones/Don't Bug Me 1973 5.00
❑ 66038 [PS] Basketball Jones/Don't Bug Me 1973 6.00
❑ 66041 Sister Mary Elephant/Wink Dinkerson 1974 5.00
❑ 66041 [PS] Sister Mary Elephant/Wink Dinkerson 1974 6.00
❑ 66049 Earache My Eye (Featuring Alice Bowie)/Turn That Thing Down 1974 —
—Unreleased?
❑ 66102 Earache My Eye (Featuring Alice Bowie)/Turn That Thing Down 1974 4.00
❑ 66102 [PS] Earache My Eye (Featuring Alice Bowie)/Turn That Thing Down 1974 6.00
❑ 66104 Black Lassie (Featuring Johnny Stash)/Coming Attractions 1974 4.00
❑ 66104 [PS] Black Lassie (Featuring Johnny Stash)/Coming Attractions 1974 6.00
❑ 66115 How I Spent My Summer Vacation, Or A Day at the Beach with Pedro and Man (Part 1/Part 2) 1975 4.00
❑ 66124 Framed/Pedro's Request 1976 4.00

WARNER BROS.
❑ 8666 Up in Smoke/Rock Fight 1978 5.00
❑ 8666 [PS] Up in Smoke/Rock Fight 1978 10.00

Albums

MCA
❑ 5640 Get Out of My Room 1985 8.00

ODE
❑ PE 34947 Cheech and Chong 1977 10.00
—Reissue of 77010
❑ PE 34951 Los Cochinos 1977 10.00
—Reissue of 77019
❑ PE 34954 Cheech and Chong's Wedding Album 1977 10.00
—Reissue of 77025
❑ PE 34960 Sleeping Beauty 1977 10.00
—Reissue of 77040
❑ SP-77010 Cheech and Chong 1971 12.00
❑ SP-77014 Big Bambu 1972 12.00
—Add 50% if rolling paper is still enclosed
❑ SP-77019 Los Cochinos 1973 12.00
❑ SP-77025 Cheech and Chong's Wedding Album 1974 12.00
❑ SP-77040 Sleeping Beauty 1976 12.00

WARNER BROS.
❑ BSK 3249 Up in Smoke 1978 10.00
❑ BSK 3250 Cheech and Chong 1978 8.00
❑ BSK 3251 Big Bambu 1978 8.00
❑ BSK 3252 Los Cochinos 1978 8.00
❑ BSK 3253 Cheech and Chong's Wedding Album 1978 8.00
❑ BSK 3254 Sleeping Beauty 1978 8.00
❑ HS 3391 Let's Make a New Dope Deal 1980 10.00
❑ BSK 3614 Cheech and Chong's Greatest Hit 1982 8.00

CHEERIOS, THE

45s

GOLDEN OLDIES
❑ 1 Ding Dong Honeymoon/Where Are You Tonight 196? 20.00

INFINITY
❑ 011 Ding Dong Honeymoon/Where Are You Tonight 1961 400.00

CHEERS, THE

1970s game-show host Bert Convy was a member.

45s

CAPITOL
❑ F2921 Bazoom (I Need Your Lovin')/Arrivederci 1954 25.00
❑ F2921 I Need Your Lovin' (Bazoom)/Arrivederci 1954 40.00
❑ F3019 Whadaya Want/Bernie's Tune 1955 25.00
❑ F3075 Can't We Be More Than Friends/Blueberries 1955 25.00
❑ F3146 I Must Be Dreaming/Fancy Meeting You Here 1955 25.00
❑ F3219 Black Denim Trousers and Motorcycle Boots/Some Night in Alaska 1955 25.00
❑ F3219 Black Denim Trousers/Some Night in Alaska 1955 25.00
—Shorter A-side title; we're not sure which came first
❑ F3353 The Chicken/Don't Do Anything 1956 20.00
❑ F3409 Heaven on Earth/Que Pasa Muchacha 1956 20.00

MERCURY
❑ 71083 Chug Chug Toot Toot/Big Feet 1957 15.00
❑ 71100 Two Hearts/You Never Have the Time 1957 15.00
—As "Bert Convy and the Cheers"

NRC
❑ 5003 Hold That Line/Blue Serenade 1958 15.00

CHEETAHS, THE

45s

PHILIPS
❑ 40239 Mecca/That Goodnight Kiss 1964 10.00

CHELLOWS, THE

45s

HIT
❑ 30 Sherry/Teenage Idol 1962 8.00
—As "The Four Chellows"; B-side by Barney Fox
❑ 37 Big Girls Don't Cry/Mama Sang a Song 1962 8.00
—B-side by Sandy Atkinson
❑ 51 Walk Like a Man/Send Me Some Lovin' 1963 8.00
—B-side by Leroy Jones
❑ 64 Ain't That a Shame/If You Wanna Be Happy 1963 8.00
—B-side by John Campbell
❑ 77 Candy Girl/Hello Muddah, Hello Faddah 1963 8.00
—B-side by Dick Martin
❑ 106 Dawn (Go Away)/She Loves You 1964 12.00
—B-side by the Bugs
❑ 111 Stay/Twist and Shout 1964 12.00
—B-side by the Bugs
❑ 115 Ronnie/Dead Man's Curve 1964 8.00
—B-side by the Roamers
❑ 134 Rag Doll/A Hard Day's Night 1964 8.00
—B-side by the Jalopy Five
❑ 160 Big Man in Town/We Build a 409 1964 12.00
—B-side by the Roamers
❑ 187 Bye Bye Baby/This Diamond Ring 1965 8.00
❑ 203 The Sun Will Still Shine/Don't Let Me Be Misunderstood 1965 10.00
—B-side by the Chords (2)
❑ 220 California Girls/Help! 1965 12.00
—B-side by the Jalopy Five
❑ 237 Barbara Ann/No Matter What Shape (Your Stomach's In) 1966 8.00
—B-side by the Upsetters
❑ 241 Working My Way Back to You/These Boots Are Made for Walking 1966 8.00
—B-side by Betty Richards
❑ 247 The Cheater/Sure Gonna Miss Her 1966 8.00
—B-side by Ed Hardin
❑ 248 Time Won't Let Me/Secret Agent Man 1966 8.00
—B-side by Marty Woods
❑ 252 Gloria/Monday, Monday 1966 12.00
—B-side by the Jalopy Five
❑ 262 Little Red Riding Hood/Wild Thing 1966 8.00
—B-side by the Jalopy Five
❑ 264 Bus Stop/Cherish 1966 8.00
❑ 270 Reach Out I'll Be There/Satisfied Mind 1966 8.00
—B-side by Leroy Jones
❑ 278 Nashville Cats/Georgy Girl 1967 8.00
—B-side by the Chords (2)
❑ 283 Ruby Tuesday/Then You Can Tell Me Goodbye 1967 8.00
—B-side by the Jalopy Five
❑ 284 There's a Kind of Hush/Happy Together 1967 8.00
—B-side by the Cadets (2)
❑ 288 Western Union/Get Me to the World on Time 1967 8.00
❑ 292 Him or Me — What's It Gonna Be?/Creeque Alley 1967 8.00
—B-side by the Chords (2)
❑ 295 Somebody to Love/Groovin' 1967 8.00
—B-side by the Jalopy Five
❑ 298 Little Bit o' Soul/I'll Take It Back 1967 8.00
—B-side by Kathy Shannon
❑ 305 Never My Love/Gimme Little Sign 1967 8.00
—B-side by Bergen Justice
❑ 308 Holiday/Incense and Peppermints 1967 8.00
—B-side by the Chords (2)

CHELSEA

Future Kiss member Peter Criss (as "Peter Cris") played drums on this LP.

Albums

DECCA
❑ DL 75262 The Chelsea Album 1972 100.00

CHER

Also see ALLMAN AND WOMAN; SONNY AND CHER.

12-Inch Singles

CASABLANCA
❑ NBD 20150 [DJ] Take Me Home (7:30)/(B-side blank) 1979 25.00
❑ NBD 20168 Take Me Home (7:30)/Wasn't It Good (7:03) 1979 15.00
❑ NBD 20189 [DJ] Hell on Wheels (Disco Remix 7:13)/Git Down (Guitar Groupie) (Disco Remix 7:14) 1979 25.00

GEFFEN
❑ PRO-A-3154 [DJ] Skin Deep (Extended Dance Mix) (Dub) (Bonus Beats) (Percapella) 1987 10.00
❑ PRO-A-4295 [DJ] Love and Understanding (unknown versions) 1991 8.00
❑ 20937 Skin Deep (Extended Dance Mix 7:48) (Dub 5:40) (Bonus Beats 3:40)/Perfection 1988 12.00
❑ 21657 Love and Understanding (5 versions)/Trail of Broken Hearts 1991 8.00
❑ 22230 The Shoop Shoop Song (It's In His Kiss) (4 versions) 1990 15.00

REPRISE
❑ PRO-A-8015 [DJ] One by One (5 versions) 1995 12.00
❑ PRO-A-8375 [DJ] Paradise Is Here (Sunrise Mix 6:50) (Padapella 8:20)/(Glow Stick Dub 8:30) (Tribal Beats 5:54) 1995 12.00
❑ PRO-A-8428 [DJ] One by One (Junior's Pride Mix) (Bonus Beats) (Piano Dub)/

Except when noted otherwise, VG = 25% of NM, and VG+ = 50% of NM. (Example: VG = $2.00, VG+ = $4.00 and NM = $8.00.)

Number	Title (A Side/B Side)	Yr	NM
	Walking in Memphis (Shut Up and Dance Mix) (Rated PG Mix)	1996	10.00
❑ 43643	One by One (4 versions)/I Wouldn't Treat a Dog (The Way You Treated Me)	1996	10.00
❑ 43759 [(2)]	Paradise Is Here (Junior's Arena Anthem) (Glow Stick Mix) (Runway Mix) (Give Me the Night Dub)//(Padapella) (Glow Stick Dub) (Tribal Beats) (Sunrise Mix)	1996	15.00
❑ 43759-A [DJ]	Paradise Is Here (Junior's Arena Anthem 10:45) (Glow Stick Mix 8:33) (Runway Mix 8:32) (Give Me the Night Dub 8:35)	1996	12.00

—Promo version is only one record

WARNER BROS.

Number	Title (A Side/B Side)	Yr	NM
❑ PRO-A-4208 [(2)DJ]	All or Nothing (Danny Tenaglia Cherbot Vocadub)/(Danny Tenaglia International Mix)//(Danny Tenaglia Inchermental)/(Metro Radio Mix) (Cherbots)	1999	15.00
❑ PRO-A-9719 [(2)DJ]	Strong Enough (8 versions)	1999	15.00
❑ PRO-A-9926-A [(2)DJ]	All or Nothing (5 versions)	1999	15.00
❑ 44576 [(2)]	Believe (8 versions)	1998	12.00
❑ 44644 [(2)]	Strong Enough (8 versions)	1999	10.00
❑ 44774 [(2)]	All or Nothing (8 versions)	1999	10.00

45s

ANNETTE

Number	Title (A Side/B Side)	Yr	NM
❑ 1000	Ringo I Love You/Beatles Blues	1964	700.00

—As "Bonnie Jo Mason"; a Phil Spector production

ATCO

Number	Title (A Side/B Side)	Yr	NM
❑ 6658	Yours Until Tomorrow/Thought of Loving You	1969	6.00
❑ 6684	I Walk on Gilded Splinters/Chastity's Song	1969	6.00
❑ 6704	For What It's Worth/Hangin' On	1969	6.00
❑ 6713	You've Made Me So Very Happy/First Time	1969	6.00
❑ 6793	Superstar/First Time	1971	6.00
❑ 6868	Lay Baby Lay/(Just Enough to Keep Me) Hangin' On	1972	5.00

CASABLANCA

Number	Title (A Side/B Side)	Yr	NM
❑ 965	Take Me Home/My Song (Too Far Gone)	1979	4.00
❑ 987	Wasn't It Good/It's Too Late to Love Me Now	1979	4.00
❑ 2208	Hell on Wheels/Git Down (Guitar Groupie)	1979	4.00
❑ 2228	Holdin' Out for Love/Boys and Girls	1979	4.00

COLUMBIA

Number	Title (A Side/B Side)	Yr	NM
❑ 18-02850	Rudy/Do I Ever Cross Your Mind	1982	4.00
❑ 18-02850 [PS]	Rudy/Do I Ever Cross Your Mind	1982	5.00
❑ 18-03150	I Paralyze/Walk With Me	1982	4.00

GEFFEN

Number	Title (A Side/B Side)	Yr	NM
❑ 19023	Love and Understanding/Trail of Broken Hearts	1991	4.00
❑ 19105	Save Up All Your Tears/A World Without Heroes	1991	3.00
❑ 19659	The Shoop Shoop Song (It's In His Kiss)/Love on a Rooftop	1990	3.00
❑ 19953	Heart of Stone/All Because of You	1990	3.00
❑ 22844	Just Like Jesse James/Starting Over	1989	3.00
❑ 22886	If I Could Turn Back Time/Some Guys	1989	3.00
❑ 22886 [PS]	If I Could Turn Back Time/Some Guys	1989	5.00
❑ 27529	After All (Love Theme from "Chances Are")/Dangerous Times	1989	3.00

—A-side with Peter Cetera

Number	Title (A Side/B Side)	Yr	NM
❑ 27529 [PS]	After All (Love Theme from "Chances Are")/Dangerous Times	1989	5.00
❑ 27742	Main Man/(It's Been Hard Enough) Gettin' Over You	1988	3.00
❑ 27742 [PS]	Main Man/(It's Been Hard Enough) Gettin' Over You	1988	3.00
❑ 27894	Skin Deep/Perfection	1988	3.00
❑ 27894 [PS]	Skin Deep/Perfection	1988	3.00
❑ 27986	We All Sleep Alone/Working Girl	1988	3.00
❑ 27986 [PS]	We All Sleep Alone/Working Girl	1988	3.00
❑ 28191	I Found Someone/Dangerous Times	1987	3.00
❑ 28191 [PS]	I Found Someone/Dangerous Times	1987	3.00

IMPERIAL

Number	Title (A Side/B Side)	Yr	NM
❑ 66081	Dream Baby/Stan Quetzal	1964	40.00

—By "Cherilyn"

Number	Title (A Side/B Side)	Yr	NM
❑ 66114	All I Really Want to Do/I'm Gonna Love You	1965	12.00
❑ 66136	Where Do You Go/See See Blues	1965	12.00
❑ 66160	Bang Bang (My Baby Shot Me Down)/Needles and Pins	1966	12.00
❑ 66160	Bang Bang (My Baby Shot Me Down)/Our Day Will Come	1966	12.00
❑ 66192	Alfie/She's No Better Than Me	1966	10.00
❑ 66217	Behind the Door/Magic in the Air	1966	10.00
❑ 66223	Dream Baby/Mama (When My Dollies Have Babies)	1966	10.00
❑ 66252	Hey Joe/Our Day Will Come	1967	10.00
❑ 66261	You Better Sit Down Kids/Mama (When My Dollies Have Babies)	1967	10.00
❑ 66261	You Better Sit Down Kids/Elusive Butterfly	1967	12.00
❑ 66282	Click Song Number One/But I Can't Love You More	1968	8.00
❑ 66307	Take Me for a Little While/A Song Called Children	1968	8.00

KAPP

Number	Title (A Side/B Side)	Yr	NM
❑ 2134	Classified 1-A/Don't Put It on Me	1971	6.00
❑ 2146	Gypsys, Tramps and Thieves/He'll Never Know	1971	4.00

—Multi-color label; black Kapp logo stands alone

Number	Title (A Side/B Side)	Yr	NM
❑ 2146	Gypsys, Tramps and Thieves/He'll Never Know	1971	5.00

—Multi-color label; white Kapp logo in black box

Number	Title (A Side/B Side)	Yr	NM
❑ 2146	Gypsys, Tramps and Thieves/He'll Never Know	1971	6.00

—Black label

Number	Title (A Side/B Side)	Yr	NM
❑ 2158	The Way of Love/Don't Put It on Me	1972	4.00
❑ 2171	Living in a House Divided/One Honest Man	1972	4.00
❑ 2184	Don't Hide Your Love/First Time	1972	4.00

MCA

Number	Title (A Side/B Side)	Yr	NM
❑ 40039	Am I Blue/How Long Has This Been Going On	1973	4.00
❑ 40102	Half-Breed/Melody	1973	4.00
❑ 40161	Dark Lady/Two People Clinging to a Thread	1973	4.00
❑ 40245	Train of Thought/Dixie Girl	1974	4.00
❑ 40273	I Saw a Man and He Danced With His Wife/I Hate to Sleep Alone	1974	4.00
❑ 40324	Carousel Man/When You Find Out Where You're Going Let Me Know	1974	4.00
❑ 40375	Rescue Me/Dixie Girl	1975	4.00

REPRISE

Number	Title (A Side/B Side)	Yr	NM
❑ 17695	One by One/I Wouldn't Treat a Dog (The Way You Treated Me)	1996	3.00

UNITED ARTISTS

Number	Title (A Side/B Side)	Yr	NM
❑ 0106	All I Really Want to Do/Where Do You Go	1973	4.00

—"Silver Spotlight Series" reissue

Number	Title (A Side/B Side)	Yr	NM
❑ 0107	Bang Bang (My Baby Shot Me Down)/You Better Sit Down Kids	1973	4.00

—"Silver Spotlight Series" reissue

Number	Title (A Side/B Side)	Yr	NM
❑ XW511	Sunny/Alfie	1974	4.00
❑ 50864	Reason to Believe/Will You Still Love Me Tomorrow	1971	4.00
❑ 50974	Old Man River/Our Day Will Come	1972	4.00

WARNER BROS.

Number	Title (A Side/B Side)	Yr	NM
❑ 8096	Geronimo's Cadillac/These Days	1975	4.00
❑ 8263	Borrowed Time/Long Distance Love Affair	1976	4.00
❑ 8311	Pirate/Send the Man Over	1976	4.00
❑ 8366	War Paint and Soft Feathers/Sand the Man Over	1977	4.00
❑ 17119	Believe (Album Version)/(Xenomania Mix)	1998	3.00

WARNER/SPECTOR

Number	Title (A Side/B Side)	Yr	NM
❑ 0400	Baby, I Love You/A Woman's Story	1974	10.00
❑ 0402	A Love Like Yours/Just Enough to Keep Me Hangin' On	1975	10.00

—With Nilsson

Albums

ATCO

Number	Title (A Side/B Side)	Yr	NM
❑ 33-298 [M]	3614 Jackson Highway	1969	30.00

—White label promo only (no stock copies issued in mono)

Number	Title (A Side/B Side)	Yr	NM
❑ SD 33-298 [S]	3614 Jackson Highway	1969	20.00

CASABLANCA

Number	Title (A Side/B Side)	Yr	NM
❑ NBLP-7133	Take Me Home	1979	10.00
❑ NBPIX-7133 [PD]	Take Me Home	1979	50.00
❑ NBLP-7184	Prisoner	1980	10.00

COLUMBIA

Number	Title (A Side/B Side)	Yr	NM
❑ FC 38096	I Paralyze	1982	10.00

GEFFEN

Number	Title (A Side/B Side)	Yr	NM
❑ GHS 24164	Cher	1987	10.00
❑ GHS 24239	Heart of Stone	1989	10.00

—Later cover with larger picture of Cher and no rock

Number	Title (A Side/B Side)	Yr	NM
❑ GHS 24239	Heart of Stone	1989	15.00

—Original cover with Cher in heart-shaped pose next to "skeleton rock"

IMPERIAL

Number	Title (A Side/B Side)	Yr	NM
❑ LP-9292 [M]	All I Really Want to Do	1965	20.00
❑ LP-9301 [M]	The Sonny Side of Cher	1966	20.00
❑ LP-9320 [M]	Cher	1966	15.00
❑ LP-9358 [M]	With Love — Cher	1967	15.00
❑ LP-12292 [S]	All I Really Want to Do	1965	25.00
❑ LP-12301 [S]	The Sonny Side of Cher	1966	25.00
❑ LP-12320 [S]	Cher	1966	20.00
❑ LP-12358 [S]	With Love — Cher	1967	20.00
❑ LP-12373 [M]	Backstage	1968	40.00

—Stereo cover with designate mono sticker attached; label is stock

Number	Title (A Side/B Side)	Yr	NM
❑ LP-12373 [S]	Backstage	1968	20.00
❑ LP-12406	Cher's Golden Greats	1968	20.00

KAPP

Number	Title (A Side/B Side)	Yr	NM
❑ KS-3649	Gypsys, Tramps & Thieves	1971	15.00

—Retitled version of above LP; red and orange swirl label

Number	Title (A Side/B Side)	Yr	NM
❑ KS-3649	Cher	1971	20.00

—Original title of LP (without "Gypsys, Tramps & Thieves" title on front cover)

Number	Title (A Side/B Side)	Yr	NM
❑ KRS-5514	Foxy Lady	1972	15.00
❑ KRS-5549	Gypsys, Tramps & Thieves	1972	15.00

—Reissue of 3649; black label

Number	Title (A Side/B Side)	Yr	NM
❑ SW-94485	Foxy Lady	1972	20.00

—Capitol Record Club edition

LIBERTY

Number	Title (A Side/B Side)	Yr	NM
❑ LN-10110	The Very Best of Cher, Vol. 1	1981	8.00
❑ LN-10111	The Very Best of Cher, Vol. 2	1981	8.00

MCA

Number	Title (A Side/B Side)	Yr	NM
❑ 624	Cher	197?	10.00
❑ 2101	Bittersweet White Light	1973	12.00
❑ 2104	Half-Breed	1973	12.00
❑ 2113	Dark Lady	1974	12.00
❑ 2127	Greatest Hits	1974	12.00
❑ 37028	Greatest Hits	1981	8.00

—Reissue of MCA 2127

PICKWICK

Number	Title (A Side/B Side)	Yr	NM
❑ SPC-3619	This Is Cher	1978	10.00

SPRINGBOARD

Number	Title (A Side/B Side)	Yr	NM
❑ SPB-4028	Cher's Greatest Hits	197?	10.00
❑ SPB-4029	Cher Sings the Hits	197?	10.00

SUNSET

Number	Title (A Side/B Side)	Yr	NM
❑ SUS-5276	This Is Cher	1970	15.00

UNITED ARTISTS

Number	Title (A Side/B Side)	Yr	NM
❑ UXS-88 [(2)]	Cher Superpak	1971	20.00
❑ UXS-89 [(2)]	Cher Superpak, Vol. II	1972	20.00

—The above are reissues of Imperial recordings

Number	Title (A Side/B Side)	Yr	NM
❑ UA-LA237-G	The Very Best of Cher	1974	12.00
❑ UA-LA377-E	The Very Best of Cher	1975	10.00
❑ UA-LA435-E	The Very Best of Cher, Vol. 2	1975	12.00

WARNER BROS.

Number	Title (A Side/B Side)	Yr	NM
❑ BS 2850	Stars	1975	12.00
❑ BS 2898	I'd Rather Believe in You	1976	12.00
❑ BS 3046	Cherished	1977	12.00

CHEROKEE

45s

ABC

Number	Title (A Side/B Side)	Yr	NM
❑ 11295	Rosiana/All the Way Home	1971	8.00
❑ 11295 [PS]	Rosiana/All the Way Home	1971	12.00
❑ 11304	Girl, I've Got News for You/All the Way Home	1971	8.00

Albums

ABC

Number	Title (A Side/B Side)	Yr	NM
❑ ABCS-719	Cherokee	1970	20.00

CHEROKEES, THE (1)

45s

CHALLENGE

Number	Title (A Side/B Side)	Yr	NM
❑ 9135	Cherokee Stomp/Uprisin'	1961	20.00

CHEROKEES, THE (2) Male vocal group.

45s

GRAND

Number	Title (A Side/B Side)	Yr	NM
❑ 106	Rainbow of Love/I Had a Thrill	1954	1000.
❑ 110	Please Tell Me So/Remember When	1954	1000.

LOST-NITE

Number	Title (A Side/B Side)	Yr	NM
❑ 321	Rainbow of Love/I Had a Thrill	197?	5.00

—Reissue

Number	Title (A Side/B Side)	Yr	NM
❑ 325	Please Tell Me So/Remember When	197?	5.00
—Reissue			
PEACOCK			
❑ 1656	Drip Drip/Is She Real	1955	200.00

CHEROKEES, THE (3)

Number	Title (A Side/B Side)	Yr	NM
45s			
GUYDEN			
❑ 2044	Cherokee/Harlem Nocturne	1960	15.00
❑ 2044 [PS]	Cherokee/Harlem Nocturne	1960	30.00

CHEROKEES, THE (4) British band.

Number	Title (A Side/B Side)	Yr	NM
45s			
MGM			
❑ 13334	Seven Daffodils/Wondrous Place	1964	15.00
❑ 13433	Dig a Little Deeper/I Will Never Turn My Back on You	1965	20.00

CHEROKEES, THE (5) FRED PARRIS of THE FIVE SATINS was a member.

Number	Title (A Side/B Side)	Yr	NM
45s			
UNITED ARTISTS			
❑ 367	My Heavenly Angel/Bed Bug	1961	100.00

CHERRY, DON (2)

Number	Title (A Side/B Side)	Yr	NM
Albums			
A&M			
❑ SP-5258	Art Deco	1989	20.00
ANTILLES			
❑ AN 7034	The Eternal Now	197?	50.00
ATLANTIC			
❑ SD 18217	Hear and Now	1977	50.00
BASF			
❑ 20680	Eternal Rhythm	1972	30.00
BLUE NOTE			
❑ BLP-4226 [M]	Complete Communion	1966	50.00
—"New York, USA" address on label			
❑ BLP-4247 [M]	Symphony for Improvisers	1966	50.00
—"New York, USA" address on label			
❑ BST-84226 [S]	Complete Communion	1966	60.00
—"New York, USA" address on label			
❑ BST-84226 [S]	Complete Communion	1968	40.00
—"A Division of Liberty Records" on label			
❑ BST-84247 [S]	Symphony for Improvisers	1966	60.00
—"New York, USA" address on label			
❑ BST-84247 [S]	Symphony for Improvisers	1968	40.00
—"A Division of Liberty Records" on label			
❑ BST-84311	Where Is Brooklyn?	1969	60.00
—"A Division of Liberty Records" on label			
ECM			
❑ ECM1-1230	El Corazon	1982	15.00
—With Ed Blackwell; distributed by Warner Bros.			
HORIZON			
❑ SP-717	Don Cherry	1976	30.00
INNER CITY			
❑ IC 1009	Togetherness	197?	20.00
JCOA			
❑ 1006	Relativity Suite	1974	50.00
MOSAIC			
❑ MQ3-145 [(3)]	The Complete Blue Note Recordings of Don Cherry	199?	60.00
PICCADILLY			
❑ PIC-3515	Tibet	1981	30.00

CHERRY PEOPLE, THE

Number	Title (A Side/B Side)	Yr	NM
45s			
HERITAGE			
❑ 801	And Suddenly/Imagination	1968	8.00
❑ 801 [PS]	And Suddenly/Imagination	1968	15.00
❑ 807	Gotta Get Back to the Good Life/I'm the One Who Loves You	1968	8.00
❑ 807 [PS]	Gotta Get Back to the Good Life/I'm the One Who Loves You	1968	15.00
❑ 810	Feelings/Mr. Hyde	1969	8.00
❑ 810 [PS]	Feelings/Mr. Hyde	1969	15.00
❑ 815	Light of Love/On to Something New	1969	8.00
Albums			
HERITAGE			
❑ HT 35000 [M]	The Cherry People	1968	40.00
—Stereo cover with "Mono" and "DJ" stickers attached; all records appear to be white label promos			
❑ HTS 35000 [S]	The Cherry People	1968	20.00

CHERRY SLUSH

Number	Title (A Side/B Side)	Yr	NM
45s			
U.S.A.			
❑ 895	I Cannot Stop You/Don't Walk Away	1968	20.00

Number	Title (A Side/B Side)	Yr	NM
❑ 904	Gotta Take It Easy/Day Don't Come	1968	20.00

CHESS, TUBBY, AND HIS CANDY STRIPE TWISTERS

Number	Title (A Side/B Side)	Yr	NM
Albums			
GRAND PRIX			
❑ K-187 [M]	Do the Twist	1962	15.00
❑ KS-187 [S]	Do the Twist	1962	20.00

CHESTER, GARY

Number	Title (A Side/B Side)	Yr	NM
Albums			
DCP			
❑ DCL 3803 [M]	Yeah, Yeah, Yeah	1964	20.00
❑ DCS 6803 [S]	Yeah, Yeah, Yeah	1964	25.00

CHESTERFIELDS, THE (1)

Number	Title (A Side/B Side)	Yr	NM
45s			
A&M			
❑ 2041	That Is Rock and Roll/Why Do Fools Fall in Love	1978	5.00

CHESTERFIELDS, THE (2)

Number	Title (A Side/B Side)	Yr	NM
45s			
CHESS			
❑ 1559	I'm in Heaven/All Messed Up	1954	400.00

CHESTERFIELDS, THE (3)

Number	Title (A Side/B Side)	Yr	NM
45s			
CUB			
❑ 9008	I Got Fired/Meet Me at the Candy Store	1958	25.00

CHESTERFIELDS, THE (4)

Number	Title (A Side/B Side)	Yr	NM
45s			
PHILIPS			
❑ 40060	A Dream Is But a Dream/You Walked Away	1962	200.00

CHESTERS, THE See LITTLE ANTHONY AND THE IMPERIALS.

CHESTNUT, MORRIS

Number	Title (A Side/B Side)	Yr	NM
45s			
AMY			
❑ 981	Too Darned Soulful/You Don't Love Me Anymore	1967	250.00

CHEVRONS, THE

Number	Title (A Side/B Side)	Yr	NM
45s			
BRENT			
❑ 7000	That Comes With Love/Don't Be Heartless	1959	50.00
❑ 7007	Lullabye/The Day After Forever	1959	50.00
❑ 7015	Little Darlin'/Little Star	1960	50.00
TIME			
❑ 1	Come Go with Me/I'm in Love Again	1960	40.00
Albums			
TIME			
❑ T-10008 [M]	Sing-a-Long Rock & Roll	1961	80.00

CHI-LITES, THE

Number	Title (A Side/B Side)	Yr	NM
12-Inch Singles			
CHI-SOUND			
❑ TCD 121 [DJ]	Have You Seen Her (Long Version 5:28) (Short Version 3:39)	1981	15.00
❑ TCD 122	Have You Seen Her/Super Mad (About You Baby)	1981	12.00
❑ TCD 132 [DJ]	Me and You (stereo/mono)	1981	10.00
❑ TCD 136	Hot on a Thing (Called Love) (6:16)/Whole Lot of Good, Good Lovin'	1981	12.00
❑ TCD 138	Try My Side (Of Love)/Get Down with Me	1982	12.00
ICHIBAN			
❑ 12 PO 46	There's a Change (same on both sides)	1990	7.00
❑ 12 PO 55	Eternity (3 versions)	199?	7.00
❑ 12 PO 61	Solid Love Affair/Happy Music	199?	7.00
NUANCE			
❑ NU 1252	Hard Act to Follow (Vocal 5:24) (House Mix 6:57) (Vocal Edit 4:04)	1985	7.00
PRIVATE I			
❑ 4Z9-04962	Stop What You're Doin' (Club Version 6:17) (Instrumental 3:32)	1984	10.00
❑ 4Z9-05016	Gimme Whatcha Got (Club Version 6:20) (Dub Mix)	1984	10.00

Number	Title (A Side/B Side)	Yr	NM
T.K. DISCO			
❑ TKD-414	Higher (8:14)/Stay a Little Longer	1979	12.00
45s			
BLUE ROCK			
❑ 4007	I'm So Jealous/The Mix-Mix Song	1965	25.00
❑ 4020	Doing the Snatch/Bassology	1965	25.00
❑ 4037	Never No More/She's Mine	1965	50.00
BRUNSWICK			
❑ 55398	Give It Away/What Do I Wish For	1969	8.00
❑ 55414	Let Me Be the Man My Daddy Was/The Twelfth of Never	1969	8.00
❑ 55422	I'm Gonna Make You Love Me/To Change My Love	1969	8.00
❑ 55426	24 Hours of Sadness/You're No Longer Part of My Heart	1970	8.00
❑ 55438	I Like Your Lovin' (Do You Like Mine)/You're No Longer Part of My Heart	1970	8.00
❑ 55442	Are You My Woman (Tell Me So)/Troubles A-Comin'	1970	8.00
❑ 55450	(For God's Sake) Give More Power to the People/Troubles A-Comin'	1971	8.00
❑ 55455	We Are Neighbors/What Do I Wish For	1971	8.00
❑ 55458	I Want to Pay You back (For Loving Me)/Love Uprising	1971	8.00
❑ 55462	Have You Seen Her/Yes I'm Ready	1971	6.00
❑ 55471	Oh Girl/Being in Love	1972	6.00
❑ 55478	The Coldest Days of My Life (Part 1)/The Coldest Days of My Life (Part 2)	1972	6.00
❑ 55483	A Lonely Man/The Man and the Woman (The Boy and the Girl)	1972	6.00
❑ 55489	We Need Order/Living in the Footsteps of Another Man	1972	6.00
❑ 55491	A Letter to Myself/Sally	1973	6.00
❑ 55496	My Heart Just Keeps On Breakin'/Just Two Teenage Kids	1973	6.00
❑ 55500	Stoned Out of My Mind/Someone Else's Arms	1973	6.00
❑ 55502	I Found Someone/Marriage License	1973	6.00
❑ 55505	Homely Girl/Never Had It So Good and Felt So Bad	1974	6.00
❑ 55512	There Will Never Be Any Peace (Until God Is Seated at the Conference Table)/Too Good to Be Forgotten	1974	6.00
❑ 55514	You Got to Be the One/Happiness Is Your Middle Name	1974	6.00
❑ 55515	Toby/That's How Long	1974	6.00
❑ 55520	It's Time for Love/Here I Am	1975	6.00
❑ 55522	Don't Burn No Bridges/(Instrumental)	1975	6.00
—With Jackie Wilson			
❑ 55525	The Devil Is Doing His Work/I'm Not a Gambler	1976	6.00
❑ 55528	You Don't Have to Go/(Instrumental)	1976	6.00
❑ 55546	First Time/Marriage License	1978	5.00
CHI-SOUND			
❑ 2472	Heavenly Body/Strung Out	1980	4.00
❑ 2481	Have You Seen Her/Super Mad (About You Baby)	1981	4.00
❑ 2495	All I Wanna Do Is Make Love to You/Round and Round	1981	4.00
❑ 2503	Me and You/Tell Me Where It Hurts	1981	4.00
❑ 2600	Hot on a Thing (Called Love)/Whole Lot of Good Lovin'	1982	4.00
❑ 2604	Try My Side (Of Love)/Get Down with Me	1982	4.00
DAKAR			
❑ 600	Baby It's Time/Price of Love	1968	12.00
—As "Marshall and the Chi-Lites"			
DARAN			
❑ 011	One by One/You Did That to Me	1964	100.00
—As "The Hi-Lites"			
❑ 0111	Pretty Girl/Love Bandit	1966	50.00
—As "Marshall and the Chi-Lites"			
❑ 222	I'm So Jealous/The Mix-Mix Song	1964	100.00
—As "The Hi-Lites"			
ICHIBAN			
❑ 90-205	There's a Change/Happy Music	1990	4.00
INPHASION			
❑ 7205	Higher/Stay a Little Longer	1979	5.00
❑ 7208	The Only One for Me (One in a Million)/You Won't Be Lonely Too Long	1979	5.00

Except when noted otherwise, VG = 25% of NM, and VG+ = 50% of NM. (Example: VG = $2.00, VG+ = $4.00 and NM = $8.00.)

Number	Title (A Side/B Side)	Yr	NM
JA-WES			
❑ 0888	You Did That to Me/ I Won't Care About You	1966	15.00
LARC			
❑ 81015	Bottom's Up/Bottom's Up Groove	1983	4.00
❑ 81023	Bad Motor Scooter/ I Just Wanna Hold You	1983	4.00
MERCURY			
❑ 73844	Happy Being Lonely/ Love Can Be Dangerous	1976	5.00
❑ 73886	Vanishing Love/I Turn Away	1977	5.00
❑ 73934	My First Mistake/Stop Still	1977	5.00
❑ 73954	If I Had a Girl/I've Got Love on My Mind	1977	5.00
NUANCE			
❑ 752	Hard Act to Follow/(Instrumental)	1985	4.00
PRIVATE I			
❑ ZS4-04365	Stop What You're Doin'/Little Girl	1984	3.00
❑ ZS4-04484	Gimme Whatcha Got/Let Today Come Back Tomorrow	1984	3.00
REVUE			
❑ 11005	Love Is Gone/Love Me	1967	12.00
❑ 11018	(Um, Um) My Baby Loves Me/ That's My Baby for You	1968	12.00
Albums			
BRUNSWICK			
❑ BL 754152	Give It Away	1969	25.00
❑ BL 754165	I Like Your Lovin', Do You Like Mine?	1970	25.00
❑ BL 754170	(For God's Sake) Give More Power to the People	1971	25.00
❑ BL 754179	A Lonely Man	1972	25.00
❑ BL 754184	The Chi-Lites Greatest Hits	1972	25.00
❑ BL 754188	A Letter to Myself	1973	25.00
❑ BL 754197	Chi-Lites	1973	25.00
❑ BL 754200	Toby	1974	25.00
❑ BL 754204	Half a Love	1975	25.00
❑ BL 754208	The Chi-Lites Greatest Hits, Vol. 2	1976	25.00
CHI-SOUND			
❑ T-619	Heavenly Body	1980	15.00
❑ T-635	Me and You	1982	15.00
EPIC			
❑ PE 38627	Greatest Hits	1983	10.00
ICHIBAN			
❑ ICH-1057	Just Say You Love Me	198?	10.00
LARC			
❑ 8103	Bottom's Up	1983	12.00
MERCURY			
❑ SRM-1-1118	Happy Being Lonely	1976	15.00
❑ SRM-1-1147	Fantastic	1977	15.00
PRIVATE I			
❑ FZ 39316	Steppin' Out	1984	10.00
❑ PZ 39316	Steppin' Out	1985	8.00
—Budget-line reissue			

CHIC

Number	Title (A Side/B Side)	Yr	NM
12-Inch Singles			
ATLANTIC			
❑ DSKO 101 [DJ]	Dance, Dance, Dance (Yowsah, Yowsah, Yowsah) (8:21) (3:45)	1977	20.00
❑ DSKO 109 [DJ]	Everybody Dance (8:25)/ You Can Get By (5:20)	1978	15.00
❑ DSKO 131 [DJ]	Le Freak (5:30)/Savoir Faire (5:02)	1978	40.00
—Promo-only picture disc			
❑ DSKO 146 [DJ]	I Want Your Love/(Funny) Bone	1979	12.00
❑ DSKO 178 [DJ]	Le Freak (5:24)/You Can Get By (5:20)	1979	12.00
—Disco oldies reissue			
❑ DSKO 179 [DJ]	Dance, Dance, Dance (Yowsah, Yowsah, Yowsah) (8:21)/ Everybody Dance (8:25)	1979	12.00
—Disco oldies reissue			
❑ DSKO 192 [DJ]	Good Times (8:13) (3:42)	1979	30.00
❑ DSKO 207 [DJ]	My Forbidden Lover (6:29)/ What About Me (4:10)	1979	20.00
❑ DSKO 220 [DJ]	My Feet Keep Dancing (Disco Mix 6:44) (same on both sides)	1979	15.00
❑ DMD 241 [DJ]	Rebels Are We (4:55) (same on both sides)	1980	15.00
❑ DMD 247 [DJ]	Real People (5:28) (same on both sides)	1980	15.00
❑ DMD 306 [DJ]	Stage Fright (3:55)/ So Fine (4:10)	1981	10.00
❑ DMD 371 [DJ]	Hangin' (unknown versions)	1982	10.00
❑ DMD 693 [DJ]	Give Me the Lovin' (Long Version) (Short Version)	1983	12.00
❑ DMD 1115 [DJ]	Jack Le Freak (Vocal Long Version 8:22) (same on both sides)	1987	12.00
❑ DK 4600	Dance, Dance, Dance (Yowsah, Yowsah, Yowsah) (8:21)/Sao Paulo (4:45)	1977	15.00
❑ DK 4621	Dance, Dance, Dance (Yowsah, Yowsah, Yowsah) (8:21)/ Everybody Dance (8:25)	1979	12.00
—Disco oldies reissue			
❑ DK 4700	Le Freak (5:24)/Savoir Faire (4:53)	1978	20.00
❑ DK 4712	I Want Your Love (6:53)/ (Funny) Bone	1979	40.00
—Pink vinyl			
❑ DK 4801	Good Times (8:13)/A Warm Summer Night	1979	30.00
❑ 86606	Dance, Dance, Dance (Yowsah, Yowsah, Yowsah)/Only in My Dreams (2 versions)	1988	10.00
—B-side by Debbie Gibson; "Twin Winners" reissue			
❑ 86634	Jack Le Freak (Vocal Long Version 8:22)/Savoir Faire	1987	12.00
❑ 86919	Chic Cheer (unknown versions)	1984	12.00
BUDDAH			
❑ DSC 121	Dance, Dance, Dance (Yowsah, Yowsah, Yowsah) (8:30)/Sao Paulo (4:58)	1977	40.00
MIRAGE			
❑ DM 4827	Soup for One (7:58)/ Bum Hard (5:12)	1982	15.00
WARNER BROS.			
❑ PRO-A-5069 [DJ]	Chic Mystique (6 versions)	1992	12.00
❑ PRO-A-5457 [DJ]	Your Love (Hank's Mix) (LP Edit)	1992	10.00
❑ 40225	Chic Mystique (7 versions)	1992	7.00
❑ 40393	Your Love (5 versions)/ M.M.F.T.C.F.	1992	7.00
45s			
ATLANTIC			
❑ 3435	Dance, Dance, Dance (Yowsah, Yowsah, Yowsah)/Sao Paulo	1977	4.00
❑ 3469	Everybody Dance/ You Can Get By	1978	4.00
❑ 3519	Le Freak/Savoir Faire	1978	4.00
❑ 3519 [PS]	Le Freak/Savoir Faire	1978	5.00
❑ 3557	I Want Your Love/(Funny) Bone	1979	4.00
❑ 3557 [PS]	I Want Your Love/(Funny) Bone	1979	5.00
❑ 3584	Good Times/A Warm Summer Night	1979	4.00
❑ 3584 [PS]	Good Times/A Warm Summer Night	1979	5.00
❑ 3620	My Forbidden Lover/ What About Me	1979	4.00
❑ 3638	My Feet Keep Dancing/ Will You Cry (When You Hear This Song)	1979	4.00
❑ 3665	Rebels Are We/Open Up	1980	4.00
❑ 3768	Real People/Chip Off the Old Block	1980	4.00
❑ 3887	Stage Fright/So Fine	1982	4.00
❑ 89725	Give Me the Lovin'/You Got Some Love for Me	1983	3.00
❑ 89954	Hangin'/Chic (Everybody Say)	1982	3.00
ATLANTIC OLDIES SERIES			
❑ OS 13211	Dance, Dance, Dance (Yowsah, Yowsah, Yowsah)/ Everybody Dance	1979	3.00
—Reissue			
❑ OS 13215	Le Freak/I Want Your Love	1980	3.00
—Reissue			
❑ OS 13216	Good Times/My Forbidden Lover	1980	3.00
—Reissue			
BUDDAH			
❑ 583	Dance, Dance, Dance (Yowsah, Yowsah, Yowsah)/Sao Paulo	1977	20.00
MIRAGE			
❑ 4032	Soup for One/Burn Hard	1982	4.00
❑ 4051	Why/Why	1982	4.00
—B-side by Carly Simon			
Albums			
ATLANTIC			
❑ SD 16003	Risque	1979	8.00
❑ SD 16011	Les Plus Grands Succes de Chic — Chic's Greatest Hits	1979	8.00
❑ SD 16016	Real People	1980	8.00
❑ SD 19153	Chic	1977	8.00
❑ SD 19209	C'est Chic	1978	8.00
❑ SD 19323	Take It Off	1981	8.00
❑ 80031	Tongue in Chic	1982	8.00
❑ 80107	Believer	1983	8.00

CHIC-LETS, THE

Number	Title (A Side/B Side)	Yr	NM
45s			
JOSIE			
❑ 919	I Want You to Be My Boyfriend/ Don't Goof on Me	1964	15.00

CHICAGO

Number	Title (A Side/B Side)	Yr	NM
12-Inch Singles			
COLUMBIA			
❑ AS 539 [DJ]	No Tell Lover (3:49) (4:15)	1979	20.00
WARNER BROS.			
❑ PRO-A-2134 [DJ]	Stay the Night (same on both sides)	1984	15.00
❑ PRO-A-2183 [DJ]	Hard Habit to Break (Edit) (LP Version)	1984	12.00
❑ PRO-A-2256 [DJ]	Along Comes a Woman (Remix) (same on both sides)	1985	12.00
❑ PRO-A-2293 [DJ]	Along Comes a Woman (Dance Mix 6:12) (same on both sides)	1985	10.00
❑ PRO-A-2560 [DJ]	25 or 6 to 4 (same on both sides)	1986	12.00
45s			
COLUMBIA			
❑ 10049	Wishing You Were Here/ Life Saver	1974	5.00
❑ 10092	Harry Truman/Till We Meet Again	1975	5.00
❑ 10092 [PS]	Harry Truman/Till We Meet Again	1975	6.00
❑ 10131	Old Days/Hideaway	1975	5.00
❑ 10200	Brand New Love Affair/Hideaway	1975	5.00
❑ 3-10360	Another Rainy Day in New York City/Hope for Love	1976	5.00
❑ 3-10390	If You Leave Me Now/ Together Again	1976	5.00
❑ 3-10523	You Are On My Mind/ Gently I'll Wake You	1977	5.00
❑ 3-10620	Baby, What a Big Surprise/ Takin' It On Uptown	1977	5.00
❑ 3-10620 [PS]	Baby, What a Big Surprise/ Takin' It On Uptown	1977	15.00
—Sleeve appears to be promo only			
❑ 3-10683	Little One/Till the End of Time	1978	5.00
❑ 3-10737	Take Me Back to Chicago/ Policeman	1978	5.00
❑ 3-10845	Alive Again/Love Was New	1978	5.00
❑ 3-10879	No Tell Lover/Take a Chance	1979	5.00
❑ 3-10935	Gone Long Gone/The Greatest Love on Earth	1979	4.00
❑ 1-11061	Must Have Been Crazy/ Closer to You	1979	4.00
❑ 1-11124	Street Player/Window Dreamin'	1979	4.00
❑ 1-11341	Song for You/I'd Rather Be Rich	1980	—
—Canceled?			
❑ 1-11345	Thunder and Lightning/ I'd Rather Be Rich	1980	4.00
❑ 11-11376	Song for You/The American Dream	1980	4.00
❑ 4-44909	Questions 67 and 68/Listen	1969	8.00
❑ 4-44909 [DJ]	Questions 67 and 68 (3:07)/ (4:45)	1969	12.00
—Both versions mono; A-side "Edited Version" has a master number of "JZSP 151568"; B-side's master number is "JZSP 151534"			
❑ 4-44909 [PS]	Questions 67 and 68/Listen	1969	12.00
❑ 45011	Beginnings/Poem 58	1969	6.00
❑ 45127	Make Me Smile/Colour My World	1970	5.00
❑ 45127 [PS]	Make Me Smile/Colour My World	1970	8.00
❑ 45194	25 or 6 to 4/Where Do We Go from Here	1970	5.00
❑ 4-45264	Does Anybody Really Know What Time It Is?/Listen	1970	5.00
❑ 4-45264 [DJ]	Does Anybody Really Know What Time It Is? (3:17)/(2:53)	1970	10.00
—A-side master number is "JZSP 154094"; B-side master number is "JZSP 154096"			
❑ 4-45264 [PS]	Does Anybody Really Know What Time It Is?/Listen	1970	10.00
❑ 45331	Free/Free Country	1971	5.00
❑ 45331 [PS]	Free/Free Country	1971	8.00
❑ 45370	Lowdown/Loneliness Is Just a Word	1971	5.00
❑ 45370 [PS]	Lowdown/Loneliness Is Just a Word	1971	8.00
❑ 45417	Beginnings/Colour My World	1971	5.00
❑ 45417 [PS]	Beginnings/Colour My World	1971	8.00
❑ 45467	Questions 67 and 68/I'm a Man	1971	5.00
❑ 45657	Saturday in the Park/Alma Mater	1972	5.00
❑ 45717	Dialogue (Parts 1 and 2)/ Now That You've Gone	1972	5.00
❑ 45717 [PS]	Dialogue (Parts 1 and 2)/ Now That You've Gone	1972	6.00
❑ 45880	Feelin' Stronger Every Day/ Jenny	1973	5.00
❑ 45933	Just You 'N' Me/Critic's Choice	1973	5.00
❑ 46020	(I've Been) Searchin' So Long/ Byblos	1974	5.00
❑ 46062	Call On Me/Prelude to Aire	1974	5.00

C

Number	Title (A Side/B Side)	Yr	NM
FULL MOON			
❑ 29798	What You're Missing/Rescue You	1983	4.00
❑ 29911	Love Me Tomorrow/Bad Advice	1982	4.00
❑ 29979	Hard to Say I'm Sorry/Sonny Think Twice	1982	4.00
REPRISE			
❑ 19466	Chasin' the Wind/Only Time Can Heal the Wounded	1991	3.00
❑ 22741	What Kind of Man Would I Be?/25 or 6 to 4	1990	3.00
❑ 22741 [PS]	What Kind of Man Would I Be?/25 or 6 to 4	1990	5.00
❑ 22985	We Can Last Forever/One More Day	1989	3.00
❑ 27757	You're Not Alone/It's Alright	1988	3.00
❑ 27757 [PS]	You're Not Alone/It's Alright	1988	3.00
❑ 27766	Look Away/Come In from the Night	1988	3.00
❑ 27766 [PS]	Look Away/Come In from the Night	1988	3.00
❑ 27855	I Don't Wanna Live Without Your Love/I Stand Up	1988	3.00
❑ 27855 [PS]	I Don't Wanna Live Without Your Love/I Stand Up	1988	3.00
WARNER BROS.			
❑ 28283	Niagara Falls/I Believe	1987	3.00
❑ 28283 [PS]	Niagara Falls/I Believe	1987	5.00
❑ 28424	If She Would Have Been Faithful.../Forever	1987	3.00
❑ 28424 [PS]	If She Would Have Been Faithful.../Forever	1987	3.00
❑ 28512	Will You Still Love Me/25 or 6 to 4	1986	3.00
❑ 28628	25 or 6 to 4/One More Day	1986	3.00
❑ 28628 [PS]	25 or 6 to 4/One More Day	1986	3.00
❑ 29082	Along Comes a Woman/We Can't Stop the Hurtin'	1985	3.00
❑ 29126	You're the Inspiration/Once in a Lifetime	1984	3.00
❑ 29214	Hard Habit to Break/Remember the Feeling	1984	3.00
❑ 29214 [PS]	Hard Habit to Break/Remember the Feeling	1984	3.00
❑ 29306	Stay the Night/Only You	1984	3.00
❑ 29306 [PS]	Stay the Night/Only You	1984	3.00
7-Inch Extended Plays			
COLUMBIA			
❑ 7-KGP 24	Movin' In/Wake Up Sunshine/To Be Free//West Virginia Fantasies/Colour My World/It Better End Soon, 2nd Movement	1970	10.00
—Jukebox issue; small hole, plays at 33 1/3 rpm			
❑ 7-KGP 24 [PS]	Chicago	1970	10.00
❑ 7-30110	Canon/Once Upon a Time/Mother//Loneliness Is Just a Word/What Else Can I Say/At the Sunrise	1971	10.00
—Jukebox issue; small hole, plays at 33 1/3 rpm			
❑ 7-30110 [PS]	Chicago III	1971	10.00
❑ 7-32400	What's This World Comin' To/Darlin' Bear//Discovery/In Terms of Two	1973	10.00
—Jukebox issue; small hole, plays at 33 1/3 rpm			
❑ 7-32400 [PS]	Chicago VI	1973	10.00
Albums			
ACCORD			
❑ SN-7140	Toronto Rock 'n Roll Revival, Part I	1982	12.00
—Reissue of Magnum LP			
COLUMBIA			
❑ (no #) [(17)]	Chicago	1976	250.00
—Promo-only set: The first 10 Chicago LPs with gold stamps on covers, box, side panel and wraparound			
❑ GP 8 [(2)]	Chicago Transit Authority	1969	25.00
—Red labels with "360 Sound" at bottom			
❑ GP 8 [(2)]	Chicago Transit Authority	1970	15.00
—Orange labels; most copies add a Roman numeral "I" to the title on spine			
❑ KGP 24 [(2)]	Chicago II	1970	15.00
—Orange labels			
❑ KGP 24 [(2)]	Chicago II	1970	25.00
—Red labels with "360 Sound" at bottom; label and spine call the album "Chicago II"			
❑ KGP 24 [(2)]	Chicago	1970	40.00
—Red labels with "360 Sound" at bottom; label and spine call the album "Chicago"			
❑ C2 30110 [(2)]	Chicago III	1971	15.00
❑ C2Q 30110 [(2)Q]	Chicago III	1974	30.00
❑ KG 30863 [(2)]	Chicago at Carnegie Hall, Vol. 1 & 2	1971	15.00
—First half of the 4-LP box, possibly for Columbia Record Club only			
❑ KG 30864 [(2)]	Chicago at Carnegie Hall, Vol. 3 & 4	1971	15.00
—Second half of the 4-LP box, possibly for Columbia Record Club only			

Number	Title (A Side/B Side)	Yr	NM
❑ C4Q 30865 [(4)Q]	Chicago at Carnegie Hall	1971	—
—Scheduled but never released			
❑ C4X 30865 [(4)]	Chicago at Carnegie Hall	1971	30.00
—With box, 4 posters and program; deduct for missing items			
❑ CQ 31102 [Q]	Chicago V	1974	25.00
❑ KC 31102	Chicago V	1972	15.00
❑ CQ 32400 [Q]	Chicago VI	1974	25.00
❑ KC 32400	Chicago VI	1973	12.00
❑ C2 32810 [(2)]	Chicago VII	1974	15.00
❑ C2Q 32810 [(2)Q]	Chicago VII	1974	30.00
❑ PC 33100	Chicago VIII	1975	12.00
❑ PCQ 33100 [Q]	Chicago VIII	1975	25.00
❑ GQ 33255 [(2)Q]	Chicago Transit Authority	1975	25.00
❑ GQ 33258 [(2)Q]	Chicago II	1975	25.00
❑ PC 33900	Chicago IX — Chicago's Greatest Hits	1975	10.00
❑ PCQ 33900 [Q]	Chicago IX — Chicago's Greatest Hits	1975	25.00
❑ PC 34200	Chicago X	1976	10.00
❑ PCQ 34200 [Q]	Chicago X	1976	25.00
❑ JC 34860	Chicago XI	1977	10.00
❑ FC 35512	Hot Streets	1978	10.00
❑ FC 36105	Chicago 13	1979	12.00
❑ FC 36517	Chicago XIV	1980	12.00
❑ FC 37682	Chicago — Greatest Hits, Vol. II	1981	12.00
❑ PC 38590	If You Leave Me Now	1982	12.00
❑ PC 39579	Take Me Back to Chicago	1983	12.00
❑ HC 43900	Chicago IX — Chicago's Greatest Hits	1982	30.00
—Half-speed mastered edition			
❑ HC 44200	Chicago X	1982	40.00
—Half-speed mastered edition			
FULL MOON			
❑ 23689	Chicago 16	1982	8.00
MAGNUM			
❑ MR 604	Chicago Transit Authority Live in Concert	1978	20.00
—Taken from their 1969 Toronto Rock 'n Roll Revival performance			
MOBILE FIDELITY			
❑ 2-128 [(2)]	Chicago Transit Authority	1983	80.00
—Audiophile vinyl			
REPRISE			
❑ 25714	Chicago 19	1988	8.00
❑ 26080	Greatest Hits 1982-1989	1989	10.00
❑ R 110533	Twenty 1	1991	20.00
—BMG Direct Marketing version			
WARNER BROS.			
❑ 25060 [DJ]	Chicago 17	1984	20.00
—Promo pressing on Quiex II vinyl			
❑ 25060	Chicago 17	1984	8.00
❑ 25509	Chicago 18	1986	8.00

CHICAGO CUBS, THE

Number	Title (A Side/B Side)	Yr	NM
45s			
CHESS			
❑ 2075	Pennant Fever/Slide	1969	12.00
❑ 2075 [PS]	Pennant Fever/Slide	1969	30.00

CHICKEN SHACK

Also see CHRISTINE McVIE; features Stan Webb.

Number	Title (A Side/B Side)	Yr	NM
45s			
BLUE HORIZON			
❑ 100	Tears in the Wind/The Things You Put Me Through	1970	6.00
❑ 302	Maudie/Diary of Your Life	1972	6.00
DERAM			
❑ 7537	As Time Goes Passing By/(B-side unknown)	1972	5.00
EPIC			
❑ 10414	Six Nights in Seven/Worried About My Woman	1968	10.00
Albums			
BLUE HORIZON			
❑ BH 4809	Accept Chicken Shack	1970	25.00
❑ BH 7705	O.K. Ken?	1969	25.00
❑ BH 7706	100-Ton Chicken	1969	25.00
DERAM			
❑ DES 18063	Imagination Lady	1972	20.00
EPIC			
❑ LN 24414 [M]	Forty Blue Fingers, Freshly Packed and Ready to Serve	1968	100.00
❑ BN 26414 [S]	Forty Blue Fingers, Freshly Packed and Ready to Serve	1968	30.00
LONDON			
❑ XPS 632	Unlucky Boy	1973	20.00

CHIEFTAINS, THE

Number	Title (A Side/B Side)	Yr	NM
45s			
ISLAND			
❑ 048	Love Theme from "Barry Lyndon"/Timpan Reel	1976	6.00
SHANACHIE			
❑ 702	Cotton Eyed Joe/The Gold Ring	1981	10.00
Albums			
COLUMBIA			
❑ JC 35612	The Chieftains 7	1979	12.00
❑ PC 35612	The Chieftains 7	198?	8.00
—Budget-line reissue			
❑ JC 35726	The Chieftains 8	1980	12.00
❑ JC 36401	Boil the Breakfast Early	1981	12.00
❑ PC 36401	Boil the Breakfast Early	198?	8.00
—Budget-line reissue			
ISLAND			
❑ ILPS 9334	The Chieftains 5	1975	12.00
—Black label original			
❑ ILPS 9364	The Chieftains 1	1976	12.00
—Black label original; first US issue			
❑ ILPS 9365	The Chieftains 2	1976	12.00
—Black label original; first US issue			
❑ ILPS 9379	The Chieftains 3	1976	12.00
—Black label original; first US issue			
❑ ILPS 9380	The Chieftains 4	1976	12.00
—Black label original; first US issue			
❑ ILPS 9432	Bonaparte's Retreat	1977	12.00
❑ ILPS 9501	The Chieftains Live	1978	12.00
RCA			
❑ 6358-1-R	Celtic Wedding	1987	10.00
❑ 7858-1-R	A Chieftains Celebration	1989	12.00
SHANACHIE			
❑ 79019	Cotton-Eyed Joe	198?	10.00
❑ 79021	The Chieftains 1	1982	10.00
—Reissue of Island 9364			
❑ 79022	The Chieftains 2	198?	10.00
—Reissue of Island 9365			
❑ 79023	The Chieftains 3	198?	10.00
—Reissue of Island 9379			
❑ 79024	The Chieftains 4	198?	10.00
—Reissue of Island 9380			
❑ 79025	The Chieftains 5	198?	10.00
—Reissue of Island 9334			
❑ 79026	Bonaparte's Retreat	198?	10.00
—Reissue of Island 9432			
❑ 79036	Year of the French	1983	10.00
❑ 79050	The Chieftains in China	198?	10.00
❑ 79051	The Ballad of Iron Horse	198?	10.00

CHIFFONS, THE

Number	Title (A Side/B Side)	Yr	NM
45s			
B.T. PUPPY			
❑ 558	Secret Love/Strange, Strange Feeling	1970	10.00
BIG DEAL			
❑ 6003	Tonight's the Night/Do You Know	1960	80.00
BUDDAH			
❑ 171	So Much in Love/Strange, Strange Feeling	1970	10.00
LAURIE			
❑ 3152	He's So Fine/Oh My Love	1963	20.00
❑ 3152	He's So Fine/Oh My Lover	1963	20.00
—Both B-side titles have been confirmed; we're not sure which came first			
❑ 3166	Lucky Me/Why Am I So Shy?	1963	15.00
❑ 3179	One Fine Day/Why Am I So Shy	1963	20.00
❑ 3195	A Love So Fine/Only My Friend	1963	12.00
❑ 3212	I Have a Boyfriend/I'm Gonna Dry My Eyes	1963	12.00
❑ 3224	Tonight I Met an Angel/Easy to Love	1964	12.00
❑ 3262	Sailor Boy/When Summer's Through	1964	12.00
❑ 3275	What Am I Gonna Do with You/Strange, Strange Feeling	1964	12.00
❑ 3301	Nobody Knows What's Going On (In My Mind But Me)/Did You Ever Go Steady	1965	12.00
❑ 3301	Nobody Knows What's Going On (In My Mind But Me)/The Real Thing	1965	12.00
❑ 3318	Tonight I'm Gonna Dream/Heavenly Place	1965	12.00
❑ 3340	Sweet Talkin' Guy/Did You Ever Go Steady	1966	15.00
❑ 3350	Out of This World/Just a Boy	1966	10.00
❑ 3357	Stop, Look, Listen/March	1966	10.00
❑ 3364	My Boyfriend's Back/I Got Plenty of Nuttin'	1966	10.00
❑ 3377	If I Knew Then/Keep the Boy Happy	1967	10.00
❑ 3423	Just for Tonight/Keep the Boy Happy	1968	10.00

Except when noted otherwise, VG = 25% of NM, and VG+ = 50% of NM. (Example: VG = $2.00, VG+ = $4.00 and NM = $8.00.)

Number	Title (A Side/B Side)	Yr	NM
❑ 3423	Just for Tonight/Teach Me How	1968	10.00
❑ 3460	Up on the Bridge/March	1968	10.00
❑ 3497	Love Me Like You're Gonna Lose Me/Three Dips of Ice Cream	1969	10.00
❑ 3630	My Sweet Lord/Main Nerve	1975	10.00
❑ 3648	Dream, Dream, Dream/ Oh My Lover	1976	10.00

REPRISE

❑ 20103	After Last Night/Doctor of Hearts	1962	20.00

RUST

❑ 5070	When the Boy's Happy (The Girl's Happy Too)/ Hockaday, Part 1	1963	25.00

—As "The Four Pennies"

❑ 5071	Dry Your Eyes/My Block	1963	25.00

—As "The Four Pennies"

WILDCAT

❑ 601	Never Never/No More Tomorrows	1961	25.00

Albums

B.T. PUPPY

❑ S-1011	My Secret Love	1970	400.00

COLLECTABLES

❑ COL-5042	Golden Classics	198?	12.00

LAURIE

❑ LLP-2018 [M]	He's So Fine	1963	120.00
❑ LLP-2020 [M]	One Fine Day	1963	200.00
❑ LLP-2036 [M]	Sweet Talkin' Guy	1966	100.00
❑ SLP-2036 [S]	Sweet Talkin' Guy	1966	150.00
❑ 4001	Everything You Always Wanted to Hear by the Chiffons	1975	20.00
❑ DT-90075 [R]	He's So Fine	1965	200.00

—Capitol Record Club edition

❑ ST-90779 [S]	Sweet Talkin' Guy	1966	200.00

—Capitol Record Club edition

CHILDREN, THE

45s

ATCO

❑ 6633	Maypole/I'll Be Your Sunshine	1968	20.00

CINEMA

❑ 025	Pills/(B-side unknown)	1968	30.00

LARAMIE

❑ 666	Picture Me/(B-side unknown)	1967	40.00

MAP CITY

❑ 304	What If I/Evil Woman	1970	12.00

ODE

❑ 66005	From the Very Start/ Such a Fine Night	1970	20.00
❑ 66013	Fire King/Hand of a Lady	1971	20.00

Albums

ATCO

❑ SD 33-271	Rebirth	1968	25.00

CINEMA

❑ CLP-1	Rebirth	1968	200.00

CHILLIWACK Also see THE COLLECTORS.

12-Inch Singles

MILLENNIUM

❑ JD-11821 [DJ]	Tell It to the Telephone/ (B-side blank)	1981	8.00
❑ JD-13116 [DJ]	Whatcha Gonna Do (Extended Dance Mix 6:06) (LP Version 3:50)	1982	10.00
❑ YD-13118	Secret Information/ Really Don't Mind	1982	8.00

45s

A&M

❑ 1310	Lonesome Mary/Ridin'	1971	8.00
❑ 1395	Ground Hog/Nothin' to Do	1972	8.00

MILLENNIUM

❑ YB-11813	My Girl (Gone, Gone, Gone)/ Sign Here	1981	4.00
❑ YB-13102	I Believe/Living in Stereo	1981	4.00
❑ YB-13110	Whatcha Gonna Do/ Really Don't Mind	1982	4.00
❑ YB-13117	Secret Information/ Really Don't Mind	1982	4.00
❑ YB-13123	Lean On Me/Night Time	1983	—

—Canceled

MUSHROOM

❑ 7022	California Girl/Reach	1976	4.00
❑ 7024	Fly By Night/Mary Lou and Me	1977	4.00
❑ 7025	Something Better/Rain-O	1977	4.00
❑ 7028	Baby Blue/Something Better	1977	4.00
❑ 7033	Arms of Mary/I Wanna Be the One	1978	4.00
❑ 7038	Never Be the Same/ I Wanna Be the One	1978	4.00
❑ 7046	Communication Breakdown/ Are You With Me	1980	4.00

Chilliwack, *All Over You*, A&M SP-4375, 1972, **$15.**

Number	Title (A Side/B Side)	Yr	NM

PARROT

❑ 350	I Must Have Been Blind/ Chain Train	1970	8.00
❑ 357	Everyday/Sundown	1970	8.00

SIRE

❑ 716	Crazy Talk/In and Out	1974	5.00
❑ 718	Come On Over/Time Don't Mean a Thing to You	1975	5.00
❑ 720	If You Want My Love/ Train's a-Comin' Back	1975	5.00
❑ 723	Last Day in December/Magnolia	1976	5.00

Albums

A&M

❑ SP-3509 [(2)]	Chilliwack	1971	25.00
❑ SP-4375	All Over You	1972	15.00

MILLENNIUM

❑ BXL1-7759	Wanna Be a Star	1981	10.00
❑ BXL1-7766	Opus X	1982	10.00

MUSHROOM

❑ MRS-5006	Dreams, Dreams, Dreams	1977	12.00
❑ MRS-5011	Lights from the Valley	1978	12.00
❑ MRS-5015	Breakdown in Paradise	1980	12.00

PARROT

❑ PAS 71040	Chilliwack	1970	30.00

SIRE

❑ SASD-7506	Chilliwack	1975	15.00
❑ SASD-7511	Rockerbox	1976	15.00

CHIMES, THE (1)

45s

LAURIE

❑ 3211	Whose Heart Are You Breaking Now/Baby's Coming Home	1963	15.00

LOST-NITE

❑ 208	Once in Awhile/Summer Night	196?	5.00

—Reissue

METRO

❑ 1	Whose Heart Are You Breaking Now/Baby's Coming Home	1963	40.00

Number	Title (A Side/B Side)	Yr	NM

TAG

❑ 444	Once in Awhile/Summer Night	1960	40.00

—Light blue label

❑ 444	Once in Awhile/Summer Night	1960	40.00

—Maroon label

❑ 444	Once in Awhile/Oh, How I Love You So	1960	50.00

—B-side is actually by a group called the Bi-Tones, though credited to the Chimes

❑ 445	I'm in the Mood for Love/ Only Love	1961	30.00
❑ 447	Let's Fall in Love/Dream Girl	1961	25.00
❑ 450	Paradise/My Love	1961	30.00

CHIMES, THE (2) On the Arrow label, see FREDDIE SCOTT.

CHIMES, THE (3) On the Flair label, see THE FLAIRS.

CHIMES, THE (U) Some of these may be group (1).

45s

HOUSE OF BEAUTY

❑ 3	Tears from An Angel's Eyes/ (B-side unknown)	1959	80.00

LIMELIGHT

❑ 3000	Cry, Baby, Cry/Angel Child	1963	25.00
❑ 3002	Du Wap/Stop, Look and Listen	1963	25.00

RESERVE

❑ 120	When School Starts Again/ Nervous Heart	1957	40.00

ROYAL ROOST

❑ 577	Dearest Darling/A Fool Was I	1955	700.00

SPECIALTY

❑ 555	Tears on My Pillow/Cindy Lou	1955	60.00
❑ 574	Chop Chop/Pretty Little Girl	1956	60.00

Number	Title (A Side/B Side)	Yr	NM

CHIPMUNKS, THE, DAVID SEVILLE AND Listings only include the "original" group, which made recordings from 1958-68. Also see ROSS BAGDASARIAN; DAVID SEVILLE.

45s

Number	Title (A Side/B Side)	Yr	NM
DOT			
❑ 16997	Apple Picker/Sorry About That, Herb	1967	12.00
EMI			
❑ S7-17645	The Chipmunk Song/ Frosty the Snowman	1993	4.00
—Green vinyl			
LIBERTY			
❑ 55168	The Chipmunk Song/ Almost Good	1958	25.00
—Blue-green label			
❑ 55168	The Chipmunk Song/ Almost Good	1958	30.00
—Black label			
❑ 55168	The Chipmunk Song/ Almost Good	1958	30.00
—Dark blue label			
❑ 55179	Alvin's Harmonica/Mediocre	1959	20.00
❑ 55200 [M]	Ragtime Cowboy Joe/Flip Side	1959	20.00
❑ 55200 [PS]	Ragtime Cowboy Joe/Flip Side	1959	40.00
❑ 55233	Alvin's Orchestra/Copyright 1960	1960	15.00
❑ 55233 [PS]	Alvin's Orchestra/Copyright 1960	1960	40.00
❑ 55246	Coming 'Round the Mountain/ Sing a Goofy Song	1960	15.00
❑ 55246 [PS]	Coming 'Round the Mountain/ Sing a Goofy Song	1960	40.00
❑ 55250	The Chipmunk Song/ Alvin's Harmonica	1959	15.00
—Blue-green label, no horizontal lines			
❑ 55250	The Chipmunk Song/ Alvin's Harmonica	1961	12.00
—Blue-green label with horizontal lines			
❑ 55250 [PS]	The Chipmunk Song/ Alvin's Harmonica	1959	40.00
—Sleeve has Chipmunks depicted somewhat like real chipmunks			
❑ 55250 [PS]	The Chipmunk Song/ Alvin's Harmonica	1961	30.00
—Sleeve has Chipmunks depicted as the familiar cartoon characters			
❑ 55277	Alvin for President/Sack Time	1960	15.00
❑ 55277 [PS]	Alvin for President/Sack Time	1960	40.00
❑ 55289	Rudolph, the Red-Nosed Reindeer/Spain	1960	15.00
❑ 55289 [PS]	Rudolph, the Red-Nosed Reindeer/Spain	1960	40.00
❑ 55424	The Alvin Twist/I Wish I Could Speak French	1962	15.00
❑ 55452	America the Beautiful/ My Wild Irish Rose	1962	15.00
❑ 55544	Alvin's All Star Chipmunk Band/ Old MacDonald Cha Cha Cha	1963	15.00
❑ 55544 [PS]	Alvin's All Star Chipmunk Band/ Old MacDonald Cha Cha Cha	1963	40.00
❑ 55632	Eefin' Alvin/Flip Side	1963	15.00
❑ 55635	The Night Before Christmas/ Wonderful Day	1963	15.00
❑ 55635 [PS]	The Night Before Christmas/ Wonderful Day	1963	30.00
❑ 55734	All My Lovin'/Do You Want to Know a Secret	1964	15.00
❑ 55773	Do-Re-Mi/Supercali- fragilisticexpialidocious	1965	12.00
❑ 55832	I'm Henry VIII, I Am/ What's New Pussycat	1965	12.00
❑ 56079	The Chipmunk Song/ Christmas Blues	1968	16.00
—With Canned Heat			
❑ 77200 [S]	Ragtime Cowboy Joe/Flip Side	1959	40.00
SUNSET			
❑ 61002	Talk to the Animals/ My Friend the Doctor	1968	10.00
❑ 61002 [PS]	Talk to the Animals/ My Friend the Doctor	1968	15.00
❑ 61003	Chitty Chitty Bang Bang/ Hushabye Mountain	1968	10.00
❑ 61003 [PS]	Chitty Chitty Bang Bang/ Hushabye Mountain	1968	15.00
UNITED ARTISTS			
❑ 0056	The Chipmunk Song/ Ragtime Cowboy Joe	1973	8.00
—"Silver Spotlight Series" reissue			
❑ 0057	Alvin's Harmonica/Rudolph, the Red-Nosed Reindeer	1973	8.00
—"Silver Spotlight Series" reissue			
❑ XW576	The Chipmunk Song/Rudolph, the Red-Nosed Reindeer	1974	6.00

7-Inch Extended Plays

Number	Title (A Side/B Side)	Yr	NM
LIBERTY			
❑ LSX-1007	The Chipmunk Song/Ragtime Cowboy Joe//Alvin's Harmonica/If You Love Me	1960	30.00
❑ LSX-1007 [PS]	Let's All Sing with the Chipmunks	1960	50.00
❑ LSX-1008	"Alvin's Orchestra/Swanee River/Sing a Goofy Song/ Witch Doctor	1960	30.00
❑ LSX-1008 [PS]	Sing Again with the Chipmunks	1960	50.00
❑ LSX-1016	Rudolph the Red-Nosed Reindeer/Jingle Bells// Frosty the Snowman/Santa Claus Is Comin' to Town	1962	20.00
❑ LSX-1016 [PS]	Christmas with the Chipmunks	1962	50.00
❑ LSX-1017	Wonderful Day/Christmas Time//Deck The Halls/ The Night Before Christmas	1963	20.00
❑ LSX-1017 [PS]	Christmas with the Chipmunks, Vol. 2	1963	50.00

Albums

Number	Title (A Side/B Side)	Yr	NM
LIBERTY			
❑ LM-1070	Christmas with the Chipmunks	1980	8.00
—Reissue with two tracks omitted			
❑ LRP-3132 [M]	Let's All Sing with the Chipmunks	1959	30.00
—Black vinyl; original cover features "realistic" chipmunks and no reference to "The Alvin Show"			
❑ LRP-3132 [M]	Let's All Sing with the Chipmunks	1959	60.00
—Red vinyl			
❑ LRP-3132 [M]	Let's All Sing with the Chipmunks	1961	20.00
—Second cover features the "cartoon" Chipmunks and a reference to "The Alvin Show"			
❑ LRP-3159 [M]	Sing Again with the Chipmunks	1960	40.00
—Original cover features "realistic" chipmunks			
❑ LRP-3159 [M]	Sing Again with the Chipmunks	1961	20.00
—Second cover features the "cartoon" Chipmunks			
❑ LRP-3170 [M]	Around the World with the Chipmunks	1960	40.00
—Original cover features "realistic" chipmunks on and near a plane			
❑ LRP-3170 [M]	Around the World with the Chipmunks	1961	20.00
—Second cover features the "cartoon" Chipmunks on and near a camel			
❑ LRP-3209 [M]	The Alvin Show	1961	25.00
❑ LRP-3229 [M]	The Chipmunks Songbook	1962	25.00
❑ LRP-3256 [M]	Christmas with the Chipmunks	1962	25.00
❑ LRP-3334 [M]	Christmas with the Chipmunks, Vol. 2	1963	25.00
❑ LRP-3388 [M]	The Chipmunks Sing the Beatles Hits	1964	30.00
❑ LRP-3405 [M]	The Chipmunks Sing with Children	1965	20.00
❑ LRP-3424 [M]	The Chipmunks A-Go-Go	1965	20.00
❑ LST-7132 [S]	Let's All Sing with the Chipmunks	1959	40.00
—Black vinyl; original cover features "realistic" chipmunks and no reference to "The Alvin Show"			
❑ LST-7132 [S]	Let's All Sing with the Chipmunks	1959	80.00
—Red vinyl			
❑ LST-7132 [S]	Let's All Sing with the Chipmunks	1961	25.00
—Second cover features the "cartoon" Chipmunks and a reference to "The Alvin Show"			
❑ LST-7159 [S]	Sing Again with the Chipmunks	1960	50.00
—Original cover features "realistic" chipmunks			
❑ LST-7159 [S]	Sing Again with the Chipmunks	1961	25.00
—Second cover features the "cartoon" Chipmunks			
❑ LST-7170 [S]	Around the World with the Chipmunks	1960	25.00
—Second cover features the "cartoon" Chipmunks on and near a camel			
❑ LST-7170 [S]	Around the World with the Chipmunks	1960	50.00
—Original covers have "realistic" chipmunks on and near a plane.			
❑ LST-7209 [S]	The Alvin Show	1961	30.00
❑ LST-7229 [S]	The Chipmunks Songbook	1962	30.00
❑ LST-7256 [S]	Christmas with the Chipmunks	1962	30.00
❑ LST-7334 [S]	Christmas with the Chipmunks, Vol. 2	1963	30.00
❑ LST-7388 [S]	The Chipmunks Sing the Beatles Hits	1964	40.00
❑ LST-7405 [S]	The Chipmunks Sing with Children	1965	25.00
❑ LST-7424 [S]	The Chipmunks A-Go-Go	1965	25.00
MISTLETOE			
❑ MLP-1216	Christmas with the Chipmunks	197?	8.00
—Reissue of Liberty LST-7256			
❑ MLP-1217	Christmas with the Chipmunks, Vol. 2	197?	8.00
—Reissue of Liberty LST-7334			
PICKWICK			
❑ SPC-1034	Christmas with the Chipmunks	1980	10.00
❑ SPC-1035	The Twelve Days of Christmas with The Chipmunks	1980	10.00
—Reissue of "Christmas with the Chipmunks, Vol. 2"			
SUNSET			
❑ LST-7334 [S]	Christmas with the Chipmunks, Vol. 2	1968	20.00
—Budget-line reissue of Liberty LST-7334			
❑ LST-7424 [S]	The Chipmunks A-Go-Go	196?	15.00
—Same cover as Liberty 7424, but with "SUNSET" sticker at upper right			
UNITED ARTISTS			
❑ UA-LA352-E2 [(2)]	Christmas with the Chipmunks	1974	20.00
—Entire contents of both original Liberty LPs			

CHIPS, THE (1) Male vocal group.

45s

Number	Title (A Side/B Side)	Yr	NM
JOSIE			
❑ 803	Rubber Biscuit/Oh My Darlin'	1956	100.00

CHIPS, THE (2)

45s

Number	Title (A Side/B Side)	Yr	NM
PHILIPS			
❑ 40520	Mixed Up Shook Up Girl/ Break It Gently	1968	10.00
❑ 40520 [PS]	Mixed Up Shook Up Girl/ Break It Gently	1968	40.00

CHIPS, THE (3) Memphis group.

45s

Number	Title (A Side/B Side)	Yr	NM
SATELLITE			
❑ 105	As You can See/You Make Me Feel So Good	1961	120.00

CHIPS, THE (4)

45s

Number	Title (A Side/B Side)	Yr	NM
STRAND			
❑ 25027	Darling (I Need Your Love)/ You're On My Side	1961	40.00
VENICE			
❑ 101	Darling (I Need Your Love)/ You're On My Side	1961	120.00

CHIPS, THE (5) Lead singer: JOE SOUTH.

45s

Number	Title (A Side/B Side)	Yr	NM
TOLLIE			
❑ 9042	Party People/Long Lonely Winter	1965	10.00

CHIPS, THE (U)

45s

Number	Title (A Side/B Side)	Yr	NM
EMBER			
❑ 1077	What a Lie/Bye, Bye, My Love	1961	20.00

CHOCO AND HIS MALIMBA DRUM RHYTHMS

Albums

Number	Title (A Side/B Side)	Yr	NM
AUDIO FIDELITY			
❑ AFLP-2102 [M]	African Latin Voodoo Drums	1962	20.00
❑ AFSD-6102 [S]	African Latin Voodoo Drums	1962	30.00

CHOCOLATE WATCH BAND, THE

45s

Number	Title (A Side/B Side)	Yr	NM
TOWER			
❑ 373	Are You Gonna Be There (At the Love-In)/No Way Out	1967	50.00
UPTOWN			
❑ 740	Baby Blue/Sweet Young Thing	1967	300.00
❑ 749	Misty Lane/She Weaves a Tender Trap	1967	50.00

Albums

Number	Title (A Side/B Side)	Yr	NM
RHINO			
❑ RNLP-108	The Best of the Chocolate Watch Band	1983	12.00
TOWER			
❑ ST 5096 [S]	No Way Out	1967	500.00
❑ T 5096 [M]	No Way Out	1967	500.00
❑ ST 5106 [S]	The Inner Mystique	1968	500.00
❑ T 5106 [M]	The Inner Mystique	1968	500.00
❑ ST 5153	One Step Beyond	1969	250.00

CHOIR, THE Two members went on to form the RASPBERRIES.

45s

Number	Title (A Side/B Side)	Yr	NM
CANADIAN AMERICAN			
❑ 203	It's Cold Outside/I'm Goin' Home	1967	40.00
INTREPID			
❑ 75020	Gonna Have a Good Time Tonight/So Much Love	1970	20.00
ROULETTE			
❑ 4738	It's Cold Outside/I'm Goin' Home	1967	15.00
❑ 4760	No One Here to Play With/Don't You Feel a Little Sorry for Me	1967	15.00
❑ 7005	Changin' My Mind/When You Were With Me	1968	15.00

Albums

Number	Title (A Side/B Side)	Yr	NM
SUNDAZED			
❑ LP 5009	Choir Practice	1992	10.00

C

CHORDCATS, THE See THE CHORDS.

CHORDETTES, THE

45s

ATLANTIC

Number	Title (A Side/B Side)	Yr	NM
❑ 89310	Lollipop/Never on Sunday	1986	3.00
❑ 89310 [PS]	Lollipop/Never on Sunday	1986	3.00

CADENCE

Number	Title (A Side/B Side)	Yr	NM
❑ 1239	It's You, It's You I Love/True Love Goes On and On	1954	15.00
❑ 1247	Mr. Sandman/I Don't Wanna See You Cryin'	1954	15.00
❑ 1259	Lonely Lips/The Dudelsack Song	1955	12.00
❑ 1267	Hummingbird/I Told a Lie	1955	12.00
❑ 1273	The Wedding/I Don't Know, I Don't Care	1955	12.00
❑ 1284	Eddie My Love/Whispering Willie	1956	12.00
❑ 1291	Born to Be with You/Love Never Changes	1956	12.00
❑ 1299	Lay Down Your Arms/Teen Age Goodnight	1956	12.00
❑ 1307	Come Home to My Arms/(Fifi's) Walking the Poodle	1957	12.00
❑ 1319	Echo of Love/Like a Baby	1957	12.00
❑ 1330	Just Between You and Me/Soft Sands	1957	12.00
❑ 1341	Photographs/Baby of Mine	1957	12.00
❑ 1345	Lollipop/Baby Come-a Back-a	1958	15.00
❑ 1349	Zorro/Love Is a Two-Way Street	1958	12.00
❑ 1349 [PS]	Zorro/Love Is a Two-Way Street	1958	25.00
❑ 1361	No Other Arms, No Other Lips/We Should Be Together	1959	10.00
❑ 1366	A Girl's Work Is Never Done/No Wheels	1959	10.00
❑ 1366 [PS]	A Girl's Work Is Never Done/No Wheels	1959	25.00
❑ 1367	Forever/Ho Hum	1959	10.00
❑ 1382	All My Sorrows/A Broken Vow	1960	10.00
❑ 1402	Never on Sunday/A Faraway Star	1961	10.00
❑ 1412	The Exodus Song/Theme from Goodbye Again (Say No More-It's Goodbye)	1961	10.00
❑ 1417	Adios/White Rose of Athens	1962	10.00
❑ 1425	In the Deep Blue Sea/All My Sorrows	1962	10.00
❑ 1442	True Love Goes On and On/All My Sorrows	1963	10.00

COLUMBIA

Number	Title (A Side/B Side)	Yr	NM
❑ 38756	When You Were Sweet Sixteen/Moonlight Bay	1950	15.00
❑ 38757	Carry Me Back to Old Virginny/Ballin' the Jack	1950	15.00
❑ 38758	Tell Me Why/Shine On Harvest Moon	1950	15.00
❑ 38759	I'd Love to Live in Loveland (With a Love Like You)/When Day Is Done	1950	15.00
—The above four comprise box set B-201			
❑ 39251	Runnin' Wild/Alice Blue Gown	1951	15.00
❑ 39252	Love Me and the World Is Mine/Lonesome That's All	1951	15.00
❑ 39253	Moonlight on the Ganges/Let the Rest of the World Go By	1951	15.00
❑ 39254	The World Is Waiting for the Sunrise/Love's Old Sweet Song	1951	15.00
❑ 39793	Carolina Moon//The Anniversary Waltz/Sentimental Journey	1952	15.00
❑ 39794	A Little Street Where Old Friends Meet//Basin Street Blues + 1	1952	15.00
❑ 39795	Drifting and Dreaming + 1//I'm Drifting Back to Dreamland/Angry	1952	15.00
❑ 39796	S'posin'/The Sweetheart of Sigma Chi//Kentucky Babe/In the Sweet Long Ago	1952	15.00

7-Inch Extended Plays

CADENCE

Number	Title (A Side/B Side)	Yr	NM
❑ CEP 101	Mr. Sandman/Hummingbird//Born to Be with You/Soft Sands	1956	15.00
❑ CEP 101 [PS]	The Chordettes	1956	15.00
❑ CEP 102	Just Between You and Me/Eddie My Love//Lay Down Your Arms/Teen Age Goodnight	1957	15.00
❑ CEP 102 [PS]	The Chordettes	1957	15.00

COLUMBIA

Number	Title (A Side/B Side)	Yr	NM
❑ B-241 [PS]	Harmony Time, Vol. II	195?	12.00
—Double-pocket sleeve for 1145 and 1146			
❑ B-401 [PS]	The Chordettes Sing Your Requests	195?	12.00
—Double-pocket sleeve for 1878 and 1879			
❑ 5-1145	Runnin' Wild/Love Me and the World Is Mine//Lonesome, That's All/Alice Blue Gown	195?	12.00
—Alternate numbers are "B-241-1" and "B-241-4"			
❑ 5-1146	Moonlight on the Ganges/The World Is Waiting for the Sunrise//Love's Old Sweet Song/Let the Rest of the World Go By	195?	12.00
—Alternate numbers are "B-241-2" and "B-241-3"			
❑ 5-1878	Wait Till the Sun Shines Nellie/They Say It's Wonderful//Wonderful One/Darkness on the Delta	195?	12.00
❑ 5-1879	I Wonder Who's Kissing Her Now?/For Me and My Gal//I Believe/Down Among the Sheltering Pines	195?	12.00

Albums

BARNABY

Number	Title (A Side/B Side)	Yr	NM
❑ BR-4003	All the Very Best of the Chordettes	1976	12.00

CADENCE

Number	Title (A Side/B Side)	Yr	NM
❑ CLP-1002 [10]	Close Harmony	1955	50.00
❑ CLP-3001 [M]	The Chordettes	1957	40.00
❑ CLP-3020 [M]	Barbershop Harmony	1958	40.00
❑ CLP-3056 [M]	Never on Sunday	1962	20.00
❑ CLP-25056 [S]	Never on Sunday	1962	30.00

COLUMBIA

Number	Title (A Side/B Side)	Yr	NM
❑ CL 956 [M]	Listen	1955	50.00
❑ CL 2519 [10]	The Chordettes	1955	40.00
❑ CL 6111 [10]	Harmony Time	1950	50.00
❑ CL 6170 [10]	Harmony Time, Vol. 2	1951	50.00
❑ CL 6218 [10]	Harmony Encores	1952	50.00
❑ CL 6285 [10]	Your Requests	1953	50.00

HARMONY

Number	Title (A Side/B Side)	Yr	NM
❑ HL 7164 [M]	The Chordettes	196?	15.00

RHINO

Number	Title (A Side/B Side)	Yr	NM
❑ R1-70849	The Best of the Chordettes	1989	12.00

CHORDS, THE

45s

ATCO

Number	Title (A Side/B Side)	Yr	NM
❑ 6213	Sh-Boom/Little Maiden	1961	15.00
—As "The Sh-Booms"			

ATLANTIC

Number	Title (A Side/B Side)	Yr	NM
❑ 2074	Blue Moon/Short Skirts	1960	20.00
—As "The Sh-Booms"			

CASINO

Number	Title (A Side/B Side)	Yr	NM
❑ 451	Tears in Your Eyes/Don't Be a Jumpin' Jack	1958	30.00

CAT

Number	Title (A Side/B Side)	Yr	NM
❑ 104	Sh-Boom/Little Maiden	1954	60.00
❑ 104	Sh-Boom/Cross Over the Bridge	1954	120.00
❑ 109	Zippety Zum (I'm in Love)/Bless You (For Being an Angel)	1954	40.00
❑ 112	A Girl to Love/Hold Me Baby	1955	40.00
—As "The Chordcats"			
❑ 117	Could It Be/Pretty Wild	1955	40.00
—As "The Sh-Booms"			

METRO

Number	Title (A Side/B Side)	Yr	NM
❑ 20015	Elephant Walk/Pretty Face	1959	20.00

VIK

Number	Title (A Side/B Side)	Yr	NM
❑ 0295	I Don't Want to Set the World on Fire/Lu Lu	1957	30.00
—As "The Sh-Booms"			

CHORDS, THE (2) Nashville studio group.

45s

HIT

Number	Title (A Side/B Side)	Yr	NM
❑ 163	Two Plus Two/Mr. Lonely	1964	8.00
—B-side by Fred York			
❑ 174	Have You Been There/Downtown	1965	8.00
—B-side by Betty York			
❑ 186	The Jolly Green Giant/Ring Telephone	1965	8.00
—B-side by Connie Dee			
❑ 203	Don't Let Me Be Misunderstood/The Sun Will Still Shine	1965	10.00
—B-side by the Chellows			
❑ 212	Mrs. Brown You've Got a Lovely Daughter/Where Were You	1965	10.00
❑ 216	I'm Henry VIII, I Am/One Dyin' and a-Buryin'	1965	10.00
—B-side by Marty Anderson			
❑ 232	Over and Over/We Can Work It Out	1965	12.00
—B-side by the Jalopy Five			
❑ 233	Fever/Make the World Go Away	1965	8.00
—B-side by Johnny Singer			
❑ 236	As Tears Go By/Five O'Clock World	1966	12.00
—B-side by the McCalls			
❑ 242	Listen People/Ballad of the Green Berets	1966	8.00
—B-side by Herb Eaton			
❑ 254	Leaning on the Lamp Post/How Does That Grab You Darlin'	1966	8.00
—B-side by Betty Richards			
❑ 256	A Groovy Kind of Love/Green Grass	1966	8.00
—B-side by Ed Hardin			
❑ 263	This Door Swings Both Ways/Mother's Little Helper	1966	10.00
—B-side by the Jalopy Five			
❑ 265	Dandy/Sunshine Superman	1966	8.00
—B-side by Joe King			
❑ 271	Have You Seen Your Mother, Baby/The Hair on My Chinny Chin Chin	1966	10.00
—B-side by the Jalopy Five			
❑ 272	Snoopy vs. the Red Baron/That's Life	1966	8.00
—B-side by Bobby Sims			
❑ 278	Georgy Girl/Nashville Cats	1967	8.00
—B-side by the Chellows			
❑ 282	Pretty Ballerina/Baby I Need Your Lovin'	1967	8.00
—B-side by Ed Hardin			
❑ 286	Dedicated to the One I Love/Something Stupid	1967	8.00
—B-side by Bobby and Connie			
❑ 291	Don't You Care/You Got What It Takes	1967	8.00
❑ 292	Creeque Alley/Him or Me — What's It Gonna Be?	1967	8.00
—B-side by the Chellows			
❑ 294	Mirage/Release Me	1967	8.00
—B-side by Ed Hardin			
❑ 299	Up, Up and Away/Windy	1967	8.00
—B-side by the Jalopy Five			
❑ 300	Carrie-Anne/Pleasant Valley Sunday	1967	8.00
—B-side by the Jalopy Five			
❑ 302	Mercy, Mercy, Mercy/Light My Fire	1967	8.00
—B-side by the Fantastics			
❑ 303	White Rabbit/Ode to Billie Joe	1967	8.00
—B-side by Kathy Shannon			
❑ 307	The Letter/Dandelion	1967	10.00
—B-side by the Jalopy Five			
❑ 308	Incense and Peppermints/Holiday	1967	8.00
—B-side by the Chellows			
❑ 314	Massachusetts/Pata Pata	1967	8.00
—B-side by the Fantastics			
❑ 319	I Can Take or Leave Your Loving/Love Is Blue	1968	8.00
—B-side by the New Society Group			
❑ 325	The Unicorn/Young Girl	1968	8.00
—B-side by the Jalopy Five			
❑ 326	Lady Madonna/A Beautiful Morning	1968	8.00
—B-side by the Classmates			
❑ 332	Reach Out of the Darkness/D.W. Washburn	1968	8.00
—B-side by the Jalopy Five			
❑ 335	Turn Around, Look at Me/The Look of Love	1968	8.00
—B-side by the Classmates			
❑ 337	Sunshine of Your Love/You Keep Me Hangin' On	1968	8.00
—B-side by Leroy Jones			
❑ 339	Hello, I Love You/Dreams of the Everyday Housewife	1968	8.00
—B-side by Bobby Sims			
❑ 342	Born to Be Wild/Revolution	1968	10.00
—B-side by the Jalopy Five			
❑ 344	My Special Angel/Over You	1968	8.00
—B-side by the Fantastics			
❑ 346	Girl Watcher/Those Were the Days	1968	8.00
—B-side by Kathy Shannon			
❑ 353	Worst That Could Happen/Son-of-a-Preacher-Man	1969	8.00
—B-side by Kathy Shannon			

CHOSEN FEW, THE Many different groups.

45s

AUTUMN

Number	Title (A Side/B Side)	Yr	NM
❑ 17	Nobody But Me/I Think It's Time	1965	10.00

CANADIAN AMERICAN

Number	Title (A Side/B Side)	Yr	NM
❑ 202	Cute Thing/One of Those Songs	1967	12.00

CANUSA

Number	Title (A Side/B Side)	Yr	NM
❑ 504	Summer's Love/Hey Joe	1967	15.00

CANYON

Number	Title (A Side/B Side)	Yr	NM
❑ 1000	Talking All the Love I Can/Birth of a Playboy	196?	10.00

CO-OP

Number	Title (A Side/B Side)	Yr	NM
❑ 510	Why Can't I Love You/La La La La La	1966	12.00

C

Number	Title (A Side/B Side)	Yr	NM
❑ 511	Summer's Love/(Instrumental)	1967	12.00
CRYSTAL			
❑ 1107	You're a Big Girl Now/(B-side unknown)	196?	10.00
DART			
❑ 1080	Foolin' Around with Me/We Walk Together	1967	8.00
DENIM			
❑ 1092	Pink Clouds and Lemonade/Stop in the Name of Love	196?	8.00
LIBERTY			
❑ 55919	Synthetic Man/The Last Man Alive	1966	10.00
❑ 55962	Asian Chrome/Earth Above, Sky Below	1967	10.00
NORTH BEACH			
❑ 1003	Nobody But Me/I Think It's Time	1965	15.00
PLAYBOY			
❑ 106	I've Had It/Ask Me Baby	196?	10.00
POWER INTERNATIONAL			
❑ 872	Another Goodbye/Forget About the Past	1966	40.00
RCA VICTOR			
❑ 74-0217	Maybe the Rain Will Fall/Deeper In	1969	8.00
❑ 74-0254	I'll Never Change You/Talk with Me	1969	8.00
ROULETTE			
❑ 7015	Footsee/You Can Never Be Wrong	1968	8.00
Albums			
MAPLE			
❑ 6000	Takin' All the Love I Can	196?	20.00
RCA VICTOR			
❑ LSP-4242	The Chosen Few	1969	20.00

CHRISTIAN, DIANE

Number	Title (A Side/B Side)	Yr	NM
45s			
BELL			
❑ 610	It Happened One Night/Wonderful Guy	1965	10.00
❑ 617	Little Boy/Why Don't the Boy Leave Me Alone	1965	10.00
SMASH			
❑ 1862	Has Anybody Seen My Boyfriend/There's So Much About My Baby	1963	10.00

CHRISTIAN, NEIL

Number	Title (A Side/B Side)	Yr	NM
45s			
MORNING STAR			
❑ 517	That's Nice/She's Got the Action	19??	8.00
RCA VICTOR			
❑ 47-8828	That's Nice/She's Got the Action	1966	8.00

CHRISTIAN, ROGER

Number	Title (A Side/B Side)	Yr	NM
45s			
RENDEZVOUS			
❑ 195	The Meaning of Merry Christmas/Little Mary Christmas	1962	25.00

CHRISTIE

Number	Title (A Side/B Side)	Yr	NM
45s			
EPIC			
❑ 10626	Yellow River/Down the Mississippi Line	1970	5.00
❑ 10695	San Bernadino/Here I Am	1971	4.00
❑ 10732	Man of Many Faces/Country Sam	1971	4.00
Albums			
EPIC			
❑ E 30403	Yellow River	1970	15.00

CHRISTIE, LOU

Also see THE CLASSICS (2); THE CLAMS; THE CRITTERS.

Number	Title (A Side/B Side)	Yr	NM
45s			
ALCAR			
❑ 207	Close Your Eyes/Funny Thing	1963	25.00
❑ 208	You're With It/Tomorrow Will Come	1963	25.00
AMERICAN MUSIC MAKERS			
❑ 006	The Jury/Little Did I Know	1963	30.00
BUDDAH			
❑ 65	Genesis and the Third Verse/Rake Up the Leaves	1968	8.00
❑ 76	Canterbury Road/Saints of Aquarius	1969	8.00
❑ 116	I'm Gonna Make You Mine/I'm Gonna Get Married	1969	6.00
❑ 149	Are You Getting Any Sunshine/It'll Take Time	1970	5.00
❑ 163	Love Is Over/She Sold Me Magic	1970	5.00
❑ 192	Indian Lady/Glory River	1970	5.00
❑ 231	Waco/Chucky Wagon	1971	20.00
—This has been proven to exist			
❑ 231 [DJ]	Waco (same on both sides)	1971	6.00
❑ 235	Waco/Lighthouse	1971	5.00
❑ 257	Mickey's Monkey/She Sold Me Magic	1971	25.00
❑ 285	Sing Me, Sing Me/Paper Song	1972	5.00
❑ 285 [PS]	Sing Me, Sing Me/Paper Song	1972	10.00
—Sleeve appears to be promo only			
❑ 312	Shuffle On Down to Pittsburgh/I'm Gonna Get Married	1972	20.00
C&C			
❑ 102	The Gypsy Cried/Red Sails in the Sunset	1962	200.00
CO & CE			
❑ 235	Outside the Gates of Heaven/All That Glitters Isn't Gold	1966	10.00
COLPIX			
❑ 735	Merry-Go-Round/Guitars and Bongos	1964	12.00
❑ 753	Pot of Gold/Have I Sinned	1964	12.00
❑ 770	Make Summer Last Forever/Why Did You Do It Baby	1965	12.00
❑ 778	A Teenager in Love/Back Track	1965	12.00
❑ 799	Cryin' on My Knees/Big Time	1966	12.00
❑ 799 [PS]	Cryin' on My Knees/Big Time	1966	25.00
COLUMBIA			
❑ 44062	Shake Hands and Walk Away Cryin'/Escape	1967	15.00
❑ 44177	Self Expression/Back to the Days of the Romans	1967	15.00
❑ 44240	(I Remember) Gina/Escape	1967	15.00
❑ 44338	Back to the Days of the Romans/Don't Stop Me	1967	15.00
EPIC			
❑ 8-50244	Summer in Malibu/Ridin' in My Van	1976	15.00
LIFESONG			
❑ 1775	Theme from "People" (Part 1)/Theme from "People" (Part 2)	1978	50.00
—As "Sacco"			
MGM			
❑ 13412	Lightnin' Strikes/Cryin' in the Streets	1965	15.00
❑ 13473	Rhapsody in the Rain/Trapeze	1966	15.00
—Revised A-side has altered lyrics: "We fell in love in the rain/And in this car, love came like a falling star." Matrix number in dead wax is "66-XY-308 D.J."			
❑ 13473	Rhapsody in the Rain/Trapeze	1966	20.00
—Original version of A-side had racy (by 1966 standards) lyrics: "We were makin' out in the rain/And in this car, our love went much too far." Matrix number in dead wax is "66-XY-308"			
❑ 13473 [PS]	Rhapsody in the Rain/Trapeze	1966	20.00
❑ 13533	Painter/Du Ronda	1966	10.00
❑ 13533 [PS]	Painter/Du Ronda	1966	20.00
❑ 13576	If My Car Could Only Talk/Song of Lita	1966	10.00
❑ 13576 [PS]	If My Car Could Only Talk/Song of Lita	1966	25.00
❑ 13623	Since I Don't Have You/Wild Life's in Season	1966	10.00
MIDLAND INT'L.			
❑ MB-10848	You're Gonna Make Love to Me/Fantasies	1976	15.00
❑ MB-10959	Spanish Wine/Dancing in the Sand	1977	15.00
MIDSONG INT'L.			
❑ 72013	Don't Knock My Love (Short)/Don't Knock My Love (Long)	1980	10.00
—With Pia Zadora			
PLATEAU			
❑ 4551	Guardian Angels/(B-side unknown)	1981	40.00
RHINO			
❑ 90105	O Holy Night (same on both sides)	1991	6.00
—With the University of Pittsburgh Men's Glee Club			
ROULETTE			
❑ 4457	The Gypsy Cried/Red Sails in the Sunset	1963	15.00
—Pink label			
❑ 4457	The Gypsy Cried/Red Sails in the Sunset	1963	20.00
—White label with spokes			
❑ 4457	The Gypsy Cried/Red Sails in the Sunset	1964	10.00
—Orange and yellow label			
❑ 4481	Two Faces Have I/All That Glitters Isn't Gold	1963	15.00
❑ 4504	How Many Teardrops/You and I (Have a Right to Cry)	1963	12.00
❑ 4527	Shy Boy/It Can Happen	1963	12.00
❑ 4545	Stay/There They Go	1964	15.00
❑ 4554	Maybe You'll Be There/When You Dance	1964	25.00
SLIPPED DISC			
❑ 45270	Summer Days/The One and Only Original Sunshine Kid	1976	15.00
THREE BROTHERS			
❑ 400	Blue Canadian Rocky Dream/Wilma Lee and Stoney	1973	8.00
❑ 402	Beyond the Blue Horizon/Saddle the Wind	1974	5.00
❑ 403	You Were the One/Good Morning	1974	8.00
❑ 405	Hey You Cajun/Sunbeam	1974	10.00
WORLD			
❑ 1002	The Jury/Little Did I Know	1963	30.00
Albums			
BUDDAH			
❑ BDS-5052	I'm Gonna Make You Mine	1969	15.00
❑ BDS-5073	Paint America Love	1971	15.00
CO & CE			
❑ LP-1231 [M]	Lou Christie Strikes Back	1966	40.00
—The front cover and spine use this title, but the back cover and label use "Lou Christie Strikes Again"			
COLPIX			
❑ CP-4001 [M]	Lou Christie Strikes Again	1966	30.00
❑ SCP-4001 [S]	Lou Christie Strikes Again	1966	50.00
51 WEST			
❑ P 18260	Lou Christie Does Detroit	1983	15.00
MGM			
❑ E-4360 [M]	Lightnin' Strikes	1966	15.00
❑ SE-4360 [S]	Lightnin' Strikes	1966	20.00
❑ E-4394 [M]	Painter of Hits	1966	15.00
❑ SE-4394 [S]	Painter of Hits	1966	20.00
RHINO			
❑ R1-70246	EnLightnin'Ment: The Best of Lou Christie	1988	12.00
ROULETTE			
❑ R 25208 [M]	Lou Christie	1963	40.00
—White wall in background on front cover			
❑ R 25208 [M]	Lou Christie	1963	50.00
—Blue background on front cover			
❑ SR 25208 [S]	Lou Christie	1963	60.00
—White wall in background on front cover			
❑ SR 25208 [S]	Lou Christie	1963	80.00
—Blue background on front cover			
❑ R 25332 [M]	Lou Christie Strikes Again	1966	25.00
❑ SR 25332 [S]	Lou Christie Strikes Again	1966	30.00
SPIN-O-RAMA			
❑ M-173 [M]	Starring Lou Christie and the Classics	1966	20.00
❑ S-173 [R]	Starring Lou Christie and the Classics	1966	12.00
—The above LP also includes other artists			
THREE BROTHERS			
❑ THB-2000	Lou Christie	1973	20.00

CHRISTIE, SUSAN

Number	Title (A Side/B Side)	Yr	NM
45s			
COLUMBIA			
❑ 43595	I Love Onions/Take Me As You Find Me	1966	10.00
❑ 43595 [PS]	I Love Onions/Take Me As You Find Me	1966	50.00
❑ 44117	Tonight You Belong to Me/Toy Balloon	1967	6.00
❑ 44327	All I Have to Do Is Dream/Anywhere You Are	1967	6.00

CHRISTMAS SPIRIT, THE (1)

William B. Williams, narrator.

Number	Title (A Side/B Side)	Yr	NM
45s			
DUEL			
❑ 503	It's Christmas/A World to Grow Up In	1961	12.00

CHRISTMAS SPIRIT, THE (2)

Members of THE TURTLES with LINDA RONSTADT.

Number	Title (A Side/B Side)	Yr	NM
45s			
WHITE WHALE			
❑ 290	Christmas Is My Time of Year/Will You Still Believe	1968	80.00

CHRISTOPHER, JORDAN

Number	Title (A Side/B Side)	Yr	NM
45s			
JUBILEE			
❑ 5440	Goodbye My Love/Broken Hearted Boy	1962	10.00

Except when noted otherwise, VG = 25% of NM, and VG+ = 50% of NM. (Example: VG = $2.00, VG+ = $4.00 and NM = $8.00.)

Number	Title (A Side/B Side)	Yr	NM
❑ 5440 [PS]	Goodbye My Love Broken Hearted Boy	1962	25.00
UNITED ARTISTS			
❑ 954	The Knack/Big Time	1965	8.00
❑ 954 [PS]	The Knack/Big Time	1965	25.00
❑ 993	Hello Lover/Taste of Honey	1966	8.00
❑ 50049	Put Your Tears Away/World Down on Your Knees	1966	8.00
❑ 50072	When That I Was (A Little Tiny Boy)/(B-side unknown)	1966	8.00
❑ 50131	To Live a Lie/Angelica	1967	8.00
Albums			
UNITED ARTISTS			
❑ UAL 3479 [M]	Jordan Christopher Has the Knack	1966	20.00
❑ UAS 6479 [S]	Jordan Christopher Has the Knack	1966	25.00

CHRISTOPHER, TONY

Number	Title (A Side/B Side)	Yr	NM
45s			
HIT			
❑ 56	What Will My Mary Say/ South Street	1963	8.00
—B-side by the Dacrons			

CHRISTOPHER (1)

Number	Title (A Side/B Side)	Yr	NM
45s			
BELL			
❑ 679	Hey Girl/Every Boy in the World	1967	15.00
DATE			
❑ 1664	Spring/Santa Ana Winds	1970	12.00
Albums			
BELL			
❑ 1203	R.P.M.	1970	20.00

CHRISTOPHER (2)
Band from North Carolina.

Number	Title (A Side/B Side)	Yr	NM
Albums			
CHRIS-TEE			
❑ 12411	What'cha Gonna Do	1969	3000.
—100 copies were pressed; VG value 1500; VG+ value 2250			

CHRISTOPHER (3)
Band fron Texas.

Number	Title (A Side/B Side)	Yr	NM
Albums			
METROMEDIA			
❑ 1024	Christopher	1970	400.00

CHRISTOPHER (U)

Number	Title (A Side/B Side)	Yr	NM
45s			
DOT			
❑ 17133	Valerie/Sunday Life	1968	15.00
WOODEN NICKEL			
❑ BWBO-0207	Get Me Goin' the Right Direction/ Henry's Highway Fillin' Station	1974	6.00

CHRISTY, DON
See SONNY.

CHRISTY, JUNE

Number	Title (A Side/B Side)	Yr	NM
45s			
CAPITOL			
❑ F1207	He Can Come Back Any Time He Wants To/A Mile Down the Highway	1950	20.00
❑ F1647	Get Happy/I'll Remember April	1951	12.00
—Reissue			
❑ F2163	Live Oak Tree/The Man I Love	1952	15.00
❑ F2199	Bei Mir Bist Du Schoen/ Some Folks Do	1952	15.00
❑ F2308	My Heart Belongs to Only You/ I Was a Fool	1952	15.00
❑ F2384	I've Got a Letter/Let Me Share Your Name	1953	15.00
❑ F2432	Great Scot/I Lived When I Met You	1953	15.00
❑ F2590	Not I/Whee Baby	1953	15.00
❑ F2765	First Thing You Know/ Magazines Are Magic	1954	15.00
❑ F3213	Pete Kelly's Blues/Kicks	1955	12.00
❑ F3375	I Never Wanna Look Into Those Eyes Again/Look Out Up There	1956	12.00
❑ F3471	Intrigue/You Took Advantage of Me	1956	12.00
❑ 4864	One Note Samba/Bossa Nova	1963	8.00
7-Inch Extended Plays			
CAPITOL			
❑ EAP 1-448	My Heart Belongs to Only You/ Get Happy//The Man I Love/ I Lived When I Met You	195?	20.00
❑ EAP 1-448 [PS]	Get Happy with June Christy	195?	20.00
Albums			
CAPITOL			
❑ H 516 [10]	Something Cool	1954	80.00
❑ SM-516 [S]	Something Cool	197?	10.00
❑ ST 516 [S]	Something Cool	1960	15.00
—Re-recording of the original mono LP; issued with different cover than original mono LP, in color with June's eyes open; black label, Capitol logo at left			
❑ T 516 [M]	Something Cool	1955	50.00
—Turquoise label; blue-green cover with June's eyes closed			
❑ T 516 [M]	Something Cool	1959	25.00
—Black label with colorband, logo at left; with original blue-green cover with June's eyes closed			
❑ T 516 [M]	Something Cool	1962	15.00
—Black label with colorband, logo at top; issued with different cover than original mono LP, in color with June's eyes open			
❑ T 656 [M]	Duets	1955	40.00
—Turquoise label			
❑ T 725 [M]	The Misty Miss Christy	1956	40.00
—Turquoise label			
❑ T 833 [M]	June — Fair and Warmer!	1957	40.00
—Turquoise label			
❑ T 902 [M]	Gone for the Day	1957	40.00
—Turquoise label			
❑ T 1006 [M]	This Is June Christy!	1958	40.00
—Turquoise label			
❑ ST 1076 [S]	June's Got Rhythm	1958	40.00
—Black label with colorband, Capitol logo at left			
❑ T 1076 [M]	June's Got Rhythm	1958	30.00
—Black label with colorband, Capitol logo at left			
❑ ST 1114 [S]	The Song Is June!	1959	40.00
—Black label with colorband, Capitol logo at left			
❑ T 1114 [M]	The Song Is June!	1959	30.00
—Black label with colorband, Capitol logo at left			
❑ ST 1202 [S]	June Christy Recalls Those Kenton Days	1959	40.00
—Black label with colorband, Capitol logo at left			
❑ T 1202 [M]	June Christy Recalls Those Kenton Days	1959	30.00
—Black label with colorband, Capitol logo at left			
❑ ST 1308 [S]	Ballads for Night People	1959	40.00
—Black label with colorband, Capitol logo at left			
❑ T 1308 [M]	Ballads for Night People	1959	30.00
—Black label with colorband, Capitol logo at left			
❑ STBO 1327 [(2)S]	Road Show	1960	40.00
—Black label with colorband, Capitol logo at left			
❑ TBO 1327 [(2)M]	Road Show	1960	30.00
—Black label with colorband, Capitol logo at left			
❑ ST 1398 [S]	The Cool School	1960	40.00
—Black label with colorband, Capitol logo at left			
❑ T 1398 [M]	The Cool School	1960	30.00
—Black label with colorband, Capitol logo at left			
❑ ST 1498 [S]	Off Beat	1961	50.00
—Black label with colorband, Capitol logo at left			
❑ T 1498 [M]	Off Beat	1961	40.00
—Black label with colorband, Capitol logo at left			
❑ ST 1586 [S]	Do-Re-Mi	1961	50.00
—Black label with colorband, Capitol logo at left			
❑ T 1586 [M]	Do-Re-Mi	1961	40.00
—Black label with colorband, Capitol logo at left			
❑ ST 1605 [S]	That Time of Year	1961	50.00
—Black label with colorband, Capitol logo at left			
❑ T 1605 [M]	That Time of Year	1961	40.00
❑ ST 1693 [S]	The Best of June Christy	1962	30.00
—Black logo with colorband			
❑ T 1693 [M]	The Best of June Christy	1962	25.00
—Black label with colorband			
❑ ST 1845 [S]	Big Band Specials	1962	25.00
❑ T 1845 [M]	Big Band Specials	1962	20.00
❑ ST 1953 [S]	The Intimate June Christy	1963	25.00
❑ T 1953 [M]	The Intimate June Christy	1963	20.00
❑ ST 2410 [S]	Something Broadway, Something Latin	1965	30.00
❑ T 2410 [M]	Something Broadway, Something Latin	1965	25.00
❑ SM-11961	The Best of June Christy	1979	10.00
DISCOVERY			
❑ DS-836	Impromptu	1982	12.00
❑ DS-911	Interlude	1986	10.00
❑ DS-919	The Misty Miss Christy	1986	10.00
HINDSIGHT			
❑ HSR-219	June Christy, Vol. 1	1986	10.00
❑ HSR-235	June Christy, Vol. 2	1988	10.00
PAUSA			
❑ 9039	Big Band Specials	198?	10.00

CHRYSALIS

Number	Title (A Side/B Side)	Yr	NM
Albums			
MGM			
❑ SE-4547	Definition	1968	30.00
❑ SE-4547 [Mono]	Definition	1968	75.00

CHUBBY AND THE TURNPIKES
Some members later were in TAVARES.

Number	Title (A Side/B Side)	Yr	NM
45s			
CAPITOL			
❑ 5840	I Didn't Try/I Know the Inside Story	1967	30.00

CHUCK-A-LUCKS, THE

Number	Title (A Side/B Side)	Yr	NM
45s			
BOW			
❑ 305	Heaven Knows/Chuck-a-Luck	1957	50.00
CANDLELITE			
❑ 424	Heaven Knows/Chuck-a-Luck	196?	12.00
JUBILEE			
❑ 5415	Tarzan's Date/Unconditional Surrender	1961	20.00
LIN			
❑ 5010	Who Am I?/The Devil's Train	1958	25.00
❑ 5014	The Magic of First Love/ Disc Jockey Fever	1958	50.00
MEL-O-DY			
❑ 106	Sugar Cane Curtain/ Dingbat Diller	1963	25.00
WARNER BROS.			
❑ 5198	Long John/Pick Up and Deliver	1961	20.00
❑ 5234	Cotton Pickin' Love/I'm Hospitalized Over You	1961	20.00

CHUCKLES, THE
Also see THE THREE CHUCKLES.

Number	Title (A Side/B Side)	Yr	NM
45s			
ABC-PARAMOUNT			
❑ 10276	Runaround/Lonely Traveler	1961	15.00

CHURCH, EUGENE
Also see THE CLIQUES.

Number	Title (A Side/B Side)	Yr	NM
45s			
CLASS			
❑ 235	Pretty Girls Everywhere/ For the Rest of My Life	1958	25.00
❑ 254	Miami/I Ain't Goin' for That	1959	12.00
❑ 261	Jack of All Trades/Without Soul	1959	12.00
❑ 266	The Struttin' Kind/ That's What's Happenin'	1960	12.00
KING			
❑ 5545	Mind Your Own Business/ You Got the Right Idea	1961	12.00
❑ 5589	That's All I Need/Geneva	1962	10.00
❑ 5610	Light of the Moon/I'm Your Taboo Man	1962	10.00
❑ 5659	The Right Girl, the Right Time/ Pretty Baby Won't You Come On Home	1962	10.00
❑ 5715	Sixteen Tons/Time Has Brought About a Change	1963	10.00
RENDEZVOUS			
❑ 132	Good News/Polly	1960	12.00
SPECIALTY			
❑ 604	How Long/Open Up Your Heart	1957	20.00
WORLD PACIFIC			
❑ 77866	Dollar Bill/U Maka Hanna	1967	15.00

CHURCH, THE
Features Steven Kilbey and Marty Willson-Piper. Features Steven Kilbey and Marty Willson-Piper.

Number	Title (A Side/B Side)	Yr	NM
12-Inch Singles			
ARISTA			
❑ ADP 2036 [DJ]	Terra Nova Cain/Take It Back// Grind (Acoustic Version)	1990	15.00
❑ ADP 2436 [DJ]	Feel (Extended Urban Mix) (Techno Dub) (Ragga Mix)/ Under the Milky Way	1992	10.00
❑ ADP 9669 [DJ]	Under the Milky Way/Musk	1988	10.00
—Add 50% if poster is included			
❑ ADP 9718 [DJ]	Reptile (Rock Radio Remix 4:44) (same on both sides)	1988	10.00
❑ 9750 [DJ]	Destination/Destination (Edit)	1988	10.00
❑ ADP 9750 [DJ]	Destination (Edit) (Album Version)	1988	10.00
WARNER BROS.			
❑ PRO2197 [DJ]	Constant in Opal/Shadow Cabinet	1984	15.00
❑ PRO2428 [DJ]	Tantalized (4:57)/Tantalized (3:58)	1985	15.00
❑ PRO2484 [DJ]	Columbus (2 versions)/ Happy Hunting Ground	1986	12.00
❑ PRO-A-2197 [DJ]	Constant in Opal/ Shadow Cabinet	1984	15.00
❑ PRO-A-2428 [DJ]	Tantalized (Extended Version 4:57) (3:58)	1985	15.00
❑ PRO-A-2484 [DJ]	Columbus (LP Version 3:48)// (Edit 3:23)/Happy Hunting Ground	1986	12.00
45s			
ARISTA			
❑ 2027 [DJ]	Metropolis (same on both sides)	1990	6.00
—Vinyl 45 is promo only			
❑ 9673	Under the Milky Way/Musk	1988	4.00

C

The Church, *Gold Afternoon Fix*, Arista AL 8579, 1990, **$10.**

Number	Title (A Side/B Side)	Yr	NM
❑ 9673 [DJ]	Under the Milky Way/Musk	1988	6.00
—Promo-only (?) version with small center hole			
❑ 9673 [PS]	Under the Milky Way/Musk	1988	4.00
❑ 9733	Reptile//Under the Milky Way (Acoustic)/Tantalized	1988	4.00
❑ 9733 [PS]	Reptile//Under the Milky Way (Acoustic)/Tantalized	1988	5.00
CAPITOL			
❑ B-5087	The Unguarded Moment/ Busdriver	1982	8.00
WARNER BROS.			
❑ 28700	Columbus/As You Will	1986	4.00
❑ 28700 [PS]	Columbus/As You Will	1986	6.00
Albums			
ARISTA			
❑ AL 8521	Starfish	1988	10.00
❑ AL 8563	Of Skins and Heart	1988	10.00
—First U.S. issue of first Australian album			
❑ AL 8564	The Blurred Crusade	1988	10.00
—First U.S. issue of second Australian album			
❑ AL 8565	Seance	1988	10.00
—First U.S. issue of third Australian album			
❑ AL 8566	Remote Luxury	1988	10.00
—Reissue of Warner Bros. 25152			
❑ AL 8567	Heyday	1988	10.00
—Reissue of Warner Bros. 25370			
❑ AL 8579	Gold Afternoon Fix	1990	10.00
❑ ADP 9713 [DJ]	Sum of the Parts	1988	40.00
—Interviews and live acoustic tracks			
❑ ADP9713 [DJ]	Sum of the Parts	1988	40.00
—Interviews and live acoustic tracks			
❑ 18727-1 [(2)]	Sometime Anywhere	1994	15.00
❑ R 171667	Gold Afternoon Fix	1990	12.00
—BMG Direct Marketing edition			
❑ R 173703	Starfish	1988	12.00
—BMG Direct Marketing edition			
CAPITOL			
❑ ST-12193	The Church	1982	15.00
WARNER BROS.			
❑ 25152	Remote Luxury	1984	15.00
❑ 25370	Heyday	1985	15.00

Number	Title (A Side/B Side)	Yr	NM
CHURCH STREET FIVE, THE			
45s			
LEGRAND			
❑ 1004	A Nite with Daddy "G" Part 1/ Part 2	1961	15.00
—Red, gold and white "shield" label			
❑ 1004	A Nite with Daddy "G" Part 1/ Part 2	1961	25.00
—Purple label original			
❑ 1010	Fallen Arches/Everybody's Happy	1961	20.00
❑ 1014	Church Street Walk/I'm Gonna Sue	1961	20.00
❑ 1021	Daddy G Rides Again/Hey Now	1962	20.00
❑ 1026	Moonlight in Vermont/ Sing a Song Children	1963	20.00
CINDERELLA			
12-Inch Singles			
MERCURY			
❑ PRO 426-1 [DJ]	Shake Me (same on both sides)	1986	12.00
❑ PRO 445-1 [DJ]	Nobody's Fool (same on both sides?)	1986	12.00
❑ PRO 587-1 [DJ]	Gypsy Road (same on both sides)	1988	10.00
❑ PRO 664-1 [DJ]	The Last Mile (same on both sides)	1989	10.00
❑ PRO 723-1 [DJ]	Coming Home (LP Version 4:55) (Edit Version 3:48)	1989	12.00
45s			
MERCURY			
❑ 870644-7	Don't Know What You Got (Till It's Gone)/Fire and Ice	1988	3.00
❑ 870644-7 [PS]	Don't Know What You Got (Till It's Gone)/Fire and Ice	1988	3.00
❑ 872148-7	The Last Mile/Long Cold Winter	1988	3.00
❑ 872148-7 [PS]	The Last Mile/Long Cold Winter	1988	3.00
❑ 872982-7	Coming Home/Take Me Back	1989	3.00
❑ 872982-7 [PS]	Coming Home/Take Me Back	1989	3.00
❑ 874578-7	Gypsy Road/Jumpin' Jack Flash	1989	4.00
❑ 878700-7	Shelter Me/Electric Love	1990	4.00

Number	Title (A Side/B Side)	Yr	NM
❑ 884851-7	Nobody's Fool/Push, Push	1986	3.00
❑ 884851-7 [PS]	Nobody's Fool/Push, Push	1986	3.00
❑ 884869-7	Shake Me/Night Songs	1986	5.00
❑ 888483-7	Somebody Save Me/ Hell on Wheels	1987	3.00
❑ 888483-7 [PS]	Somebody Save Me/ Hell on Wheels	1987	3.00
Albums			
MERCURY			
❑ 522947-1	Still Climbing	1995	12.00
—Numbered limited edition on clear vinyl; CD version issued in late 1994			
❑ 830076-1	Night Songs	1986	8.00
❑ 832255-1 [PD]	Night Songs	1987	20.00
—Picture disc in plastic sleeve with sticker			
❑ 834612-1	Long Cold Winter	1988	8.00
❑ 848018-1	Heartbreak Station	1990	12.00
CINDERELLAS, THE (1) Female vocal group.			
45s			
COLUMBIA			
❑ 41540	The Trouble with Boys/ Puppy Dog	1959	15.00
DECCA			
❑ 30830	Mr. Dee Jay/Yum Yum Yum	1959	25.00
❑ 30925	I Was Only 15/You Never Shoulda Gone Away	1959	25.00
CINDERELLAS, THE (2) Another female vocal group.			
45s			
DIMENSION			
❑ 1026	Baby, Baby, I Still Love You/ Please Don't Wake Me	1964	40.00
MERCURY			
❑ 72394	Fairy Tale/Mr. Happy Love	1965	10.00
CINDERS, THE			
45s			
ORIGINAL SOUND			
❑ 43	I'll Follow You/The Story	1964	10.00
WARNER BROS.			
❑ 5326	The Cinnamon Cinder/ C'mon Wobble	1962	12.00
CINDY AND LINDY			
45s			
ABC-PARAMOUNT			
❑ 9847	The Language of Love/ Brigette's Song	1957	25.00
❑ 9886	Shakin'/Sittin' It Out	1958	25.00
CORAL			
❑ 62008	The Wonder That Is You/ I'll String Along with You	1958	20.00
❑ 62072	Saturday Night in Tia-Juana/ You Can't Mail an Elephant	1959	20.00
❑ 62119	Before and After/Big Bells and Bongo Drummers	1959	20.00
❑ 62165	Let's Go Steady/There Are Such Things	1960	20.00
PILGRIM			
❑ 702	Let's Go Steady/ The Wedding Is Over	1956	15.00
❑ 705	Hungry Heart/Livin' and Bein' Loved	1956	15.00
CINNAMON ANGELS May be the same group as THE CINNAMONS.			
45s			
B.T. PUPPY			
❑ 559	Calypso Girl/ Let's Be Sweethearts	1970	8.00
CINNAMONS, THE			
45s			
B.T. PUPPY			
❑ 503	I'm Not Gonna Worry Strange, Strange Feeling	1964	8.00
❑ 508	Mr. Cupid '65/Dance to the Music	1965	8.00
CIRCUS			
45s			
METROMEDIA			
❑ 68-0112	Feel So Right/Jonah's Fable	1973	5.00
❑ 265	Stop, Wait and Listen/ I Need Your Love	1972	6.00
Albums			
METROMEDIA			
❑ 7401	Circus	1973	75.00

Except when noted otherwise, VG = 25% of NM, and VG+ = 50% of NM. (Example: VG = $2.00, VG+ = $4.00 and NM = $8.00.)

Number	Title (A Side/B Side)	Yr	NM

CIRCUS MAXIMUS Group features JERRY JEFF WALKER.

45s

VANGUARD

Number	Title (A Side/B Side)	Yr	NM
❑ 35063	Lonely Man/ Negative Dreamer Girl	1968	20.00

Albums

VANGUARD

Number	Title (A Side/B Side)	Yr	NM
❑ VRS-9260 [M]	Circus Maximus	1967	20.00
❑ VSD-79260 [S]	Circus Maximus	1967	25.00
❑ VSD-79274	Neverland Revisited	1968	25.00

CITATIONS, THE More than one group.

45s

BALLAD

Number	Title (A Side/B Side)	Yr	NM
❑ 101	I Will Stand By You/ To Win the Race	1967	100.00

CANADIAN AMERICAN

Number	Title (A Side/B Side)	Yr	NM
❑ 136	Mystery of Love/Magic Eyes	1962	30.00

—As "Nicki North and the Citations"

DON-EL

Number	Title (A Side/B Side)	Yr	NM
❑ 113	It Hurts Me/Kiss in the Night	1961	40.00

EPIC

Number	Title (A Side/B Side)	Yr	NM
❑ 9603	Moon Race/Slippin' and Slidin'	1963	25.00

FRATERNITY

Number	Title (A Side/B Side)	Yr	NM
❑ 910	The Girl Next Door/ Ten Miles from Nowhere	1963	20.00
❑ 992	The Girl Next Door/Ten Miles from Nowhere	1967	12.00

MERCURY

Number	Title (A Side/B Side)	Yr	NM
❑ 72286	Chicago/The Stomp	1964	15.00

MGM

Number	Title (A Side/B Side)	Yr	NM
❑ 13373	That Girl of Mine/Down Went the Curtain	1965	20.00

PRINCESS

Number	Title (A Side/B Side)	Yr	NM
❑ 54	Carmen P./Everybody Philly	1965	30.00

ROULETTE

Number	Title (A Side/B Side)	Yr	NM
❑ 4623	Carmen P./Everybody Philly	1965	15.00

SARA

Number	Title (A Side/B Side)	Yr	NM
❑ 3301	Moon Race/Slippin' and Slidin'	1963	50.00

SWAN

Number	Title (A Side/B Side)	Yr	NM
❑ 4062	Fiddlin' Around/Fire Ritual	1960	40.00

VANGEE

Number	Title (A Side/B Side)	Yr	NM
❑ 301	The Girl Next Door/Ten Miles from Nowhere	1963	40.00

CITY, THE CAROLE KING was a member.

45s

ODE

Number	Title (A Side/B Side)	Yr	NM
❑ 113	Snow Queen/Paradise Alley	1968	12.00
❑ 117	That Old Sweet Rule/Why Are You Leaving	1968	12.00
❑ 119	(Hi-De-Ho) That Old Sweet Roll/Why Are You Leaving	1969	12.00

Albums

ODE

Number	Title (A Side/B Side)	Yr	NM
❑ Z12 44012	Now That Everything's Been Said	1968	80.00

—Color front cover

Number	Title (A Side/B Side)	Yr	NM
❑ Z12 44012	Now That Everything's Been Said	1971	12.00

—Black & white front cover

CITY BOY

12-Inch Singles

MERCURY

Number	Title (A Side/B Side)	Yr	NM
❑ MK 55 [DJ]	5.7.0.5. (same on both sides)	1978	20.00

45s

ATLANTIC

Number	Title (A Side/B Side)	Yr	NM
❑ 3612	The Day the Earth Caught Fire/ Ambition	1979	4.00
❑ 3789 [DJ]	You're Leaving Me (same on both sides)	1981	4.00

—May be promo only

Number	Title (A Side/B Side)	Yr	NM
❑ 3789 [DJ]	You're Leaving Me (same on both sides)	1981	6.00

—May be promo only

MERCURY

Number	Title (A Side/B Side)	Yr	NM
❑ 73835	Haymaking Time/The Greatest Story Ever Told	1976	6.00
❑ 73858	Hap-Ki-Do Kid/Surgery Hours (Doctor Doctor)	1976	6.00
❑ 73900	The Violin/Narcissus	1977	6.00
❑ 73953	I've Been Spun/ Goodbye Blue Monday	1977	6.00
❑ 73968	Runaround/She's Got Style	1977	6.00
❑ 73999	5.7.0.5/Bad for Business	1978	5.00
❑ 73999 [PS]	5.7.0.5/Bad for Business	1978	10.00
❑ 74032	What a Night/Goodbye Laurelie	1978	5.00

Cinderella, "The Last Mile," Mercury 872148-7, 1988, $3.

Albums

ATLANTIC

Number	Title (A Side/B Side)	Yr	NM
❑ SD 19249	The Day the Earth Caught Fire	1979	10.00
❑ SD 19285	Heads Are Rolling	1980	10.00

MERCURY

Number	Title (A Side/B Side)	Yr	NM
❑ SRM-1-1098	City Boy	1976	12.00
❑ SRM-1-1121	Dinner at the Ritz	1977	12.00
❑ SRM-1-1182	Young Men Gone West	1977	12.00
❑ SRM-1-3737	Book Early	1978	10.00

CITY SURFERS, THE

45s

CAPITOL

Number	Title (A Side/B Side)	Yr	NM
❑ 5002	Beach Ball/Sun Tan Baby	1963	25.00
❑ 5052	Powder Puff/Fifty Miles to Go	1963	25.00

CLAMS, THE

45s

THREE BROTHERS

Number	Title (A Side/B Side)	Yr	NM
❑ 404	Close to You/First Time Ever I Saw Your Face	1974	10.00

—LOU CHRISTIE appears on this record

CLANTON, JIMMY

45s

ACE

Number	Title (A Side/B Side)	Yr	NM
❑ 537	I Trusted You/That's You Baby	1958	20.00
❑ 546	Just a Dream/You Aim to Please	1958	20.00
❑ 551	A Letter to An Angel/A Part of Me	1958	20.00
❑ 560	My Love Is Strong/ Ship on a Stormy Sea	1959	15.00
❑ 567 [M]	My Own True Love/ Little Boy in Love	1959	15.00
❑ 567 [PS]	My Own True Love/ Little Boy in Love	1959	30.00
❑ 567 [S]	My Own True Love/ Little Boy in Love	1959	30.00
❑ 575	Go, Jimmy, Go/I Trusted You	1959	20.00

—Normal white label

Number	Title (A Side/B Side)	Yr	NM
❑ 575	Go, Jimmy, Go/I Trusted You	1959	25.00

—Purple label

Number	Title (A Side/B Side)	Yr	NM
❑ 575 [PS]	Go, Jimmy, Go/I Trusted You	1959	30.00
❑ 585	Another Sleepless Night/ I'm Gonna Try	1960	15.00
❑ 585 [PS]	Another Sleepless Night/ I'm Gonna Try	1960	30.00
❑ 600	Come Back/Wait	1960	15.00
❑ 600 [PS]	Come Back/Wait	1960	30.00
❑ 607	What Am I Gonna Do/If I	1961	15.00
❑ 607 [PS]	What Am I Gonna Do/If I	1961	30.00
❑ 616	Down the Aisle/No Longer Blue	1961	15.00
❑ 616 [PS]	Down the Aisle/No Longer Blue	1961	30.00

—With Mary Ann Mobley

Number	Title (A Side/B Side)	Yr	NM
❑ 622	I Just Wanna Make Love/ Don't Look at Me	1961	15.00
❑ 622 [PS]	I Just Wanna Make Love/ Don't Look at Me	1961	30.00
❑ 634	Lucky in Love with You/ Not Like a Brother	1961	15.00
❑ 634 [PS]	Lucky in Love with You/ Not Like a Brother	1961	30.00
❑ 641	Twist On Little Girl/ Wayward Love	1962	15.00
❑ 641 [PS]	Twist On Little Girl/ Wayward Love	1962	30.00
❑ 642	Twist On Little Girl/Wayward Love//Green Light/ Happy Times	1962	50.00
❑ 642 [PS]	Teenage Millionaire	1962	50.00
❑ 655	Just a Moment/Because I Do	1962	15.00
❑ 655 [PS]	Just a Moment/Because I Do	1962	30.00
❑ 664 [DJ]	Venus in Blue Jeans/ Highway Bound	1962	25.00

—No stock copies exist with this catalog number

Number	Title (A Side/B Side)	Yr	NM
❑ 668	Heart Hotel/Many Dreams	1963	12.00
❑ 8001	Venus in Blue Jeans/ Highway Bound	1962	15.00
❑ 8005	Darkest Street in Town/ Dreams of a Fool	1962	10.00
❑ 8006	Endless Nights/Another Day, Another Heartache	1963	10.00

Number	Title (A Side/B Side)	Yr	NM
❑ 8006 [PS]	Endless Nights/Another Day, Another Heartache	1963	20.00
❑ 8007	Cindy/I Care Enough (To Give the Very Best)	1963	10.00
IMPERIAL			
❑ 66242	Absence of Lisa/C'mon Jim	1967	8.00
❑ 66274	Calico Junction/I'll Be Loving You	1968	8.00
LAURIE			
❑ 3508	Curly/The Girl Who Cried Love (Once Too Often)	1969	8.00
❑ 3508	Curly/I'll Never Forget Your Love	1969	10.00
❑ 3534	Tell Me/I'll Never Forget Your Love	1969	8.00
MALA			
❑ 500	Hurting Each Other/Don't Keep Your Friends Away	1965	10.00
❑ 516	Everything I Touch Turns to Tears/That Special Way	1965	10.00
PHILIPS			
❑ 40161	Red Don't Go with Blue/All the Words in the World	1963	10.00
❑ 40181	I'll Step Aside/I Won't Cry Anymore	1964	10.00
❑ 40208	If I'm a Fool for Loving You/A Million Drums	1964	10.00
❑ 40219	Follow the Sun/Lock the Windows	1964	10.00
SPIRAL			
❑ 3406	The Coolest Hot Pants/(Instrumental)	1971	5.00
STARCREST			
❑ 078 [DJ]	Old Rock 'N Roller (mono/stereo)	1978	5.00
—May be promo only			
STARFIRE			
❑ 104	I Wanna Go Home/You Kissed a Fool Goodbye	1976	5.00
UNITED ARTISTS			
❑ (no #) [S]	Teenage Millionaire	1961	30.00
—Cardboard record; B-side promotes the movie of the same name			
VIN			
❑ 1028	What Am I Living For/Wedding Blues	1962	10.00

7-Inch Extended Plays

Number	Title	Yr	NM
ACE			
❑ 101	(contents unknown)	1959	100.00
❑ 101 [PS]	Jimmy Clanton	1959	100.00
❑ 102	(contents unknown)	1959	150.00
❑ 102 [PS]	Thinking of You	1959	150.00

Albums

Number	Title	Yr	NM
ACE			
❑ DLP-100	Jimmy's Happy/Jimmy's Blue Poster	1960	80.00
❑ DLP-100 [M]	Jimmy's Happy/Jimmy's Blue	1960	150.00
—Black vinyl; also released as two separate albums, 1007 and 1008			
❑ DLP-100 [M]	Jimmy's Happy/Jimmy's Blue	1960	400.00
—The "Happy" album is red vinyl, the "Blue" album is blue			
❑ 1001 [M]	Just a Dream	1959	120.00
❑ 1007 [M]	Jimmy's Happy	1960	40.00
❑ 1008 [M]	Jimmy's Blue	1960	40.00
❑ 1011 [M]	My Best to You	1960	100.00
❑ 1014 [M]	Teenage Millionaire	1961	100.00
❑ 1026 [M]	Venus in Blue Jeans	1962	100.00
PHILIPS			
❑ PHM 200154 [M]	The Best of Jimmy Clanton	1964	25.00
❑ PHS 600154 [S]	The Best of Jimmy Clanton	1964	30.00

CLANTON, JIMMY/BRISTOW HOOPER

Albums

Number	Title	Yr	NM
DESIGN			
❑ DLP-176 [M]	Jimmy Clanton and Bristow Hooper	196?	15.00
❑ DLS-176 [R]	Jimmy Clanton and Bristow Hooper	196?	10.00

CLAP

Albums

Number	Title	Yr	NM
NOVA SOL			
❑ 1001	Have You Reached Yet?	1972	1000.

CLAPTON, ERIC

Also see BLIND FAITH; CREAM; DEREK AND THE DOMINOS; GEORGE HARRISON AND FRIENDS; B.B. KING; JOHN MAYALL; THE YARDBIRDS.

12-Inch Singles

Number	Title (A Side/B Side)	Yr	NM
DUCK			
❑ PRO-A-2000 [DJ]	I've Got a Rock n' Roll Heart (same on both sides)	1983	20.00
❑ PRO-A-2248 [DJ]	Forever Man (same on both sides)	1985	10.00
❑ PRO-A-2306 [DJ]	See What Love Can Do (same on both sides)	1985	15.00
❑ PRO-A-2578 [DJ]	Tearing Us Apart (same on both sides)	1986	20.00
—With Tina Turner			
❑ PRO-A-2616 [DJ]	It's In the Way That You Use It (same on both sides)	1986	15.00
❑ PRO-A-2683 [DJ]	Miss You (same on both sides)	1986	20.00
❑ PRO-A-2700 [DJ]	Run (same on both sides)	1986	15.00
REPRISE			
❑ PRO-A-4200 [(2)DJ]	(I) Get Lost (David Morales Club Mix 8:11) (David Morales Club Mix with Guitar Intro 8:27) (Stereo Dub 7:31) (Stereo Beats 7:40) (Yost Nothing Without U Mix 7:36) (Yost Nothing Without U Radio Edit 4:01) (Yost Lost & Found Dub 8:03) (Yost Acoustic Tears Mix 7:54)	1999	25.00
❑ PRO-A-4203 [DJ]	(I) Get Lost (Lost & Found Dub 8:03) (Stereo Dub 7:31)	1999	15.00
❑ PRO-A-9350 [DJ]	Pilgrim (Organized Noize Mix) (Organized Noize Instrumental) (Acappella) (Keith Crouch Mix) (Keith Crouch Instrumental) (Background Acappella) (Remix Edit)	1998	20.00
❑ 43855	Rip Stop (4 versions)/Seven (Blackmarket Roll Out Mix)	1997	10.00
RSO			
❑ RPO 1005 [DJ]	Promises/Watch Out for Lucy	1978	30.00

45s

Number	Title (A Side/B Side)	Yr	NM
ATCO			
❑ 6784	After Midnight/Easy Now	1970	6.00
DUCK			
❑ 28279	Tearing Us Apart/Hold On	1987	3.00
—A-side with Tina Turner			
❑ 28279 [PS]	Tearing Us Apart/Hold On	1987	3.00
❑ 28391	Behind the Sun/Grand Illusion	1987	3.00
❑ 28514	It's in the Way That You Use It/Grand Illusion	1986	3.00
❑ 28514 [PS]	It's in the Way That You Use It/Grand Illusion	1986	3.00
❑ 28986	See What Love Can Do/She's Waiting	1985	3.00
❑ 29081	Forever Man/Too Bad	1985	3.00
❑ 29081 [PS]	Forever Man/Too Bad	1985	3.00
❑ 29647	Pretty Girl/The Shape You're In	1983	4.00
❑ 29780	I've Got a Rock n' Roll Heart/Man in Love	1983	4.00
—Silver label with Duck logo			
POLYDOR			
❑ 15049	Let It Rain/Easy Now	1972	6.00
❑ 15056	Bell Bottom Blues/Little Wing	1973	5.00
—Reissue of Derek and the Dominos recordings, but under Clapton's name			
❑ 887403-7	After Midnight/I Can't Stand It	1988	3.00
❑ 887403-7 [PS]	After Midnight/I Can't Stand It	1988	3.00
REPRISE			
❑ 17621	Change the World/Danny Boy	1996	4.00
❑ 18044	Motherless Child/Driftin'	1994	4.00
❑ 18787	Layla/Signe	1992	4.00
❑ 19038	Tears in Heaven/Tracks and Lines	1992	5.00
❑ 22732	Pretending/Before You Accuse Me	1989	3.00
❑ 22732 [PS]	Pretending/Before You Accuse Me	1989	3.00
RSO			
❑ 409	I Shot the Sheriff/Give Me Strength	1974	5.00
❑ 500	I Shot the Sheriff/Give Me Strength	1974	4.00
❑ 503	Willie and the Hand Jive/Main Line Florida	1975	4.00
❑ 509	Swing Low Sweet Chariot/Pretty Blue Eyes	1975	4.00
❑ 513	Knockin' on Heaven's Door/Someone Like You	1975	4.00
❑ 861	Hello Old Friend/All Our Pastimes	1976	4.00
❑ 868	Carnival/Hungry	1976	4.00
❑ 886	Lay Down Sally/Next Time You See Her	1978	4.00
❑ 895	Wonderful Tonight/Peaches and Diesel	1978	4.00
❑ 910	Promises/Watch Out for Lucy	1978	4.00
❑ 928	Tulsa Time/Cocaine	1979	5.00
—Studio versions of the two songs			
❑ 1039	Tulsa Time/Cocaine	1980	4.00
—Live versions of the two songs			
❑ 1051	Blues Power/Early in the Morning	1980	4.00
❑ 1060	I Can't Stand It/Black Rose	1981	4.00
❑ 1064	Another Ticket/Rita Mae	1981	4.00
❑ 1064 [PS]	Another Ticket/Rita Mae	1981	5.00
WARNER BROS.			
❑ 29780	I've Got a Rock n' Roll Heart/Man in Love	1983	5.00
—Original pressing on white WB label			

Albums

Number	Title	Yr	NM
ATCO			
❑ 33-329 [DJ]	Eric Clapton	1970	100.00
—Mono pressing is promo only			
❑ SD 33-329	Eric Clapton	1970	20.00
❑ SD 33-329	Eric Clapton	1970	200.00
—Odd pressing with alternate takes of "After Midnight" and "Blues Power" plus remixes of other tracks. Look for "CTH" in trail-off area.			
❑ SD 2-803 [(2)]	History of Eric Clapton	1972	20.00
—Contains tracks from the Yardbirds, John Mayall's Bluesbreakers, Cream, Blind Faith, and solo records			
DUCK			
❑ 23773	Money and Cigarettes	1983	10.00
❑ 25166	Behind the Sun	1985	10.00
❑ 25476	August	1986	10.00
MOBILE FIDELITY			
❑ 1-220	Eric Clapton	1995	25.00
—Audiophile vinyl			
NAUTILUS			
❑ NR-32 [(2)]	Just One Night	1981	150.00
—Audiophile vinyl			
POLYDOR			
❑ PD 3503 [(2)]	Eric Clapton at His Best	1972	20.00
—Compiles tracks from his first solo album plus Derek and the Dominos			
❑ 24-5526	Clapton	1973	15.00
—Compiles tracks from his first solo album plus Derek and the Dominos			
❑ SKBO-94837 [(2)]	Eric Clapton at His Best	1972	30.00
—Capitol Record Club edition			
❑ 835261-1 [(6)]	Crossroads	1988	50.00
—Box set; contains material from all phases of his career			
❑ 1775318	461 Ocean Boulevard	2008	20.00
❑ 8171881	Slowhand	2008	20.00
—Audiophile vinyl			
REPRISE			
❑ 26074	Journeyman	1989	12.00
❑ W1-26420 [(2)]	24 Nights	1991	25.00
—Vinyl copies released only through Columbia House			
❑ 48423-1	Me and Mr. Johnson	2004	20.00
—Regular edition on 140-gram vinyl; distributed by Classic Records			
❑ 48423-1 SV	Me and Mr. Johnson	2004	30.00
—200-gram vinyl edition, distributed by Classic Records			
RSO			
❑ PRO 035 [DJ]	Slowhand	1977	40.00
—White vinyl promo sampler			
❑ SO 877	Eric Clapton's Rainbow Concert	1973	15.00
❑ RPO-1009 [DJ]	Limited Backless	1978	50.00
—White vinyl promo			
❑ RS-1-3004	No Reason to Cry	1976	12.00
❑ RS-1-3008	Eric Clapton	1977	12.00
—Reissue of Atco LP of the same name			
❑ RS-1-3023	461 Ocean Boulevard	1977	12.00
—Reissue of RSO 4801			
❑ RS-1-3030	Slowhand	1977	12.00
❑ RS-1-3039	Backless	1978	12.00
❑ RX-1-3095	Another Ticket	1981	10.00
❑ RS-1-3099	Time Pieces/The Best of Eric Clapton	1982	10.00
❑ RS-2-4202 [(2)]	Just One Night	1980	15.00
❑ QD 4801 [Q]	461 Ocean Boulevard	1974	25.00
❑ SO 4801	461 Ocean Boulevard	1974	12.00
—With "Better Make It Through the Day"			
❑ SO 4801	461 Ocean Boulevard	1974	15.00
—With "Give Me Strength"			
❑ QD 4806 [Q]	There's One in Every Crowd	1975	25.00
❑ SO 4806	There's One in Every Crowd	1975	12.00
❑ SO 4809	E.C. Was Here	1975	12.00
❑ 811697-1	461 Ocean Boulevard	198?	8.00
—Reissue of RSO 3023			
❑ 823276-1	Slowhand	1983	8.00
—Reissue of RSO 3030			
❑ 825093-1	Eric Clapton	1984	8.00
—Reissue of RSO 3008			
❑ 825382-1	Time Pieces/The Best of Eric Clapton	1984	8.00
—Reissue of RSO 3099			
❑ 825391-1 [(2)]	Just One Night	1984	10.00
—Reissue of RSO 4202			
❑ 827579-1	Another Ticket	1985	8.00
—Reissue of RSO 3095			

Number	Title (A Side/B Side)	Yr	NM

CLARA AND THE CLEFTONES See CLARA WILSON AND THE CLEFTONES.

CLAREMONTS, THE

45s

APOLLO

Number	Title (A Side/B Side)	Yr	NM
❑ 517	Why Keep Me Dreaming/ Angel of Romance	1957	60.00
❑ 751	Why Keep Me Dreaming/ Angel of Romance	1963	25.00

CLARK, CHRIS

45s

MOTOWN

Number	Title (A Side/B Side)	Yr	NM
❑ 1114	From Head to Toe/The Beginning of the End	1967	15.00
❑ 1121	Whisper You Love Me Boy/ The Beginning of the End	1968	15.00

V.I.P.

Number	Title (A Side/B Side)	Yr	NM
❑ 25031	Do Right, Baby, Do Right/ Don't Be Too Long	1965	15.00
❑ 25038	Love's Gone Bad/Put Yourself in My Place	1965	20.00
—Same song as above A-side, but with corrected title			
❑ 25038	Love's Gone Mad/Put Yourself in My Place	1965	60.00
❑ 25041	I Love You/I Want to Go Back There Again	1966	15.00

Albums

MOTOWN

Number	Title (A Side/B Side)	Yr	NM
❑ M-664 [M]	Soul Sounds	1967	50.00
❑ MS-664 [S]	Soul Sounds	1967	60.00

WEED

Number	Title (A Side/B Side)	Yr	NM
❑ 801	C.C. Rides Again	1969	80.00

CLARK, CLAUDINE

45s

CHANCELLOR

Number	Title (A Side/B Side)	Yr	NM
❑ 1113	Party Lights/Disappointed	1962	20.00
—exists on two different labels			
❑ 1124	Telephone Game/Walkin' Through a Cemetery	1962	12.00
❑ 1130	Walk Me Home/Who Will You Hurt	1963	12.00

HERALD

Number	Title (A Side/B Side)	Yr	NM
❑ 523	Teenage Blues/ Angel of Happiness	1958	40.00

JAMIE

Number	Title (A Side/B Side)	Yr	NM
❑ 1279	Moon Madness/(The Strength) To Be Strong	1964	10.00
❑ 1291	Buttered Popcorn/ A Sometimes Thing	1964	10.00

TCF HALL

Number	Title (A Side/B Side)	Yr	NM
❑ 18	Foxy/Standin' on Tip Toes	196?	10.00

Albums

CHANCELLOR

Number	Title (A Side/B Side)	Yr	NM
❑ CHL-5029 [M]	Party Lights	1962	250.00

CLARK, DAVE, FIVE

45s

CONGRESS

Number	Title (A Side/B Side)	Yr	NM
❑ 212	I Knew It All the Time/ That's What I Said	1964	20.00
❑ 212 [PS]	I Knew It All the Time/ That's What I Said	1964	40.00

EPIC

Number	Title (A Side/B Side)	Yr	NM
❑ 9656	Glad All Over/I Know You	1964	15.00
❑ 9656 [PS]	Glad All Over/I Know You	1964	20.00
❑ 9671	Bits and Pieces/All of the Time	1964	12.00
❑ 9678	Do You Love Me/Chaquita	1964	12.00
❑ 9692	Can't You See That She's Mine/ No TIme to Lose	1964	12.00
❑ 9692 [PS]	Can't You See That She's Mine/ No TIme to Lose	1964	20.00
❑ 9704	Because/Theme Without a Name	1964	12.00
❑ 9704 [PS]	Because/Theme Without a Name	1964	20.00
❑ 9722	Everybody Knows (I Still Love You)/Ol' Sol	1964	12.00
❑ 9722 [PS]	Everybody Knows (I Still Love You)/Ol' Sol	1964	20.00
❑ 9739	Any Way You Want It/ Crying Over You	1964	12.00
❑ 9763	Come Home/Your Turn to Cry	1965	12.00
❑ 9763 [PS]	Come Home/Your Turn to Cry	1965	20.00
❑ 9786	Reelin' and Rockin'/I'm Thinking	1965	12.00
❑ 9811	I Like It Like That/Hurting Inside	1965	12.00
❑ 9811 [PS]	I Like It Like That/Hurting Inside	1965	20.00
❑ 9833	Catch Us If You Can/On the Move	1965	12.00
❑ 9833 [PS]	Catch Us If You Can/On the Move	1965	20.00

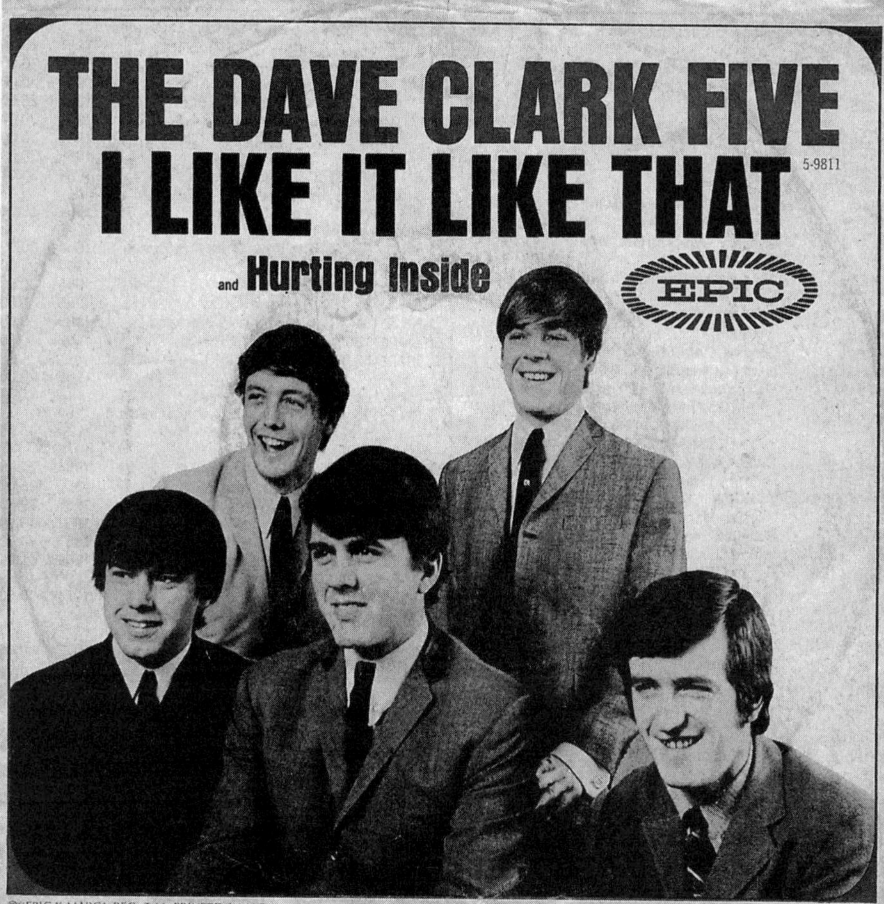

The Dave Clark Five, "I Like It Like That," Epic 5-9811, 1965, **$20.**

Number	Title (A Side/B Side)	Yr	NM
❑ 9863	Over and Over/I'll Be Yours (My Love)	1965	12.00
❑ 9863 [DJ]	Over and Over (same on both sides)	1965	40.00
—Promo only on red vinyl			
❑ 9863 [PS]	Over and Over/I'll Be Yours (My Love)	1965	20.00
❑ 9863 [PS]	Over and Over	1965	400.00
—Promo-only black and white sleeve			
❑ 9882	At the Scene/I Miss You	1966	12.00
❑ 9882 [PS]	At the Scene/I Miss You	1966	20.00
❑ 10004	Try Too Hard/All Night Long	1966	12.00
❑ 10004 [PS]	Try Too Hard/All Night Long	1966	20.00
❑ 10031	Please Tell Me Why/ Look Before You Leap	1966	12.00
❑ 10031 [PS]	Please Tell Me Why/ Look Before You Leap	1966	20.00
❑ 10053	Satisfied with You/ Don't Let Me Down	1966	12.00
❑ 10053 [PS]	Satisfied with You/ Don't Let Me Down	1966	20.00
❑ 10076	Nineteen Days/Sitting Here Baby	1966	12.00
❑ 10076 [DJ]	Nineteen Days (same on both sides)	1966	40.00
—Promo only on red vinyl			
❑ 10076 [PS]	Nineteen Days/Sitting Here Baby	1966	20.00
❑ 10114	I've Got to Have a Reason/ Good Time Woman	1966	12.00
❑ 10114 [PS]	I've Got to Have a Reason/ Good Time Woman	1966	20.00
❑ 10144	You Got What It Takes/ Doctor Rhythm	1967	12.00
❑ 10144 [PS]	You Got What It Takes/ Doctor Rhythm	1967	20.00
❑ 10179	You Must Have Been a Beautiful Baby/Man in the Pin Stripe Suit	1967	12.00
❑ 10179 [PS]	You Must Have Been a Beautiful Baby/Man in the Pin Stripe Suit	1967	25.00
❑ 10209	A Little Bit Now/You Don't Play Me Around	1967	15.00
❑ 10209 [PS]	A Little Bit Now/You Don't Play Me Around	1967	20.00
❑ 10244	Red and Blue/Concentration Baby	1967	15.00
❑ 10265	Everybody Knows/Inside and Out	1967	15.00
❑ 10265 [PS]	Everybody Knows/Inside and Out	1967	30.00
❑ 10265/60 [DJ]	Everybody Knows/Best of Both Worlds	1968	25.00
—B-side by Lulu; odd promo			
❑ 10325	Please Stay/Forget	1968	15.00
❑ 10375	Red Balloon/Maze of Love	1968	15.00
❑ 10375 [PS]	Red Balloon/Maze of Love	1968	25.00
❑ 10476	Paradise (Is Half As Nice)/ 34-06	1969	15.00
❑ 10476 [PS]	Paradise (Is Half As Nice)/ 34-06	1969	30.00
❑ 10509	If Somebody Loves You/ Best Day's Work	1969	15.00
❑ 10547	Bring It On Home to Me/ Darling, I Love You	1969	15.00
❑ 10547 [PS]	Bring It On Home to Me/ Darling, I Love You	1969	20.00
❑ 10635	Here Comes Summer/ Five by Five	1970	15.00
❑ 10684	Good Old Rock and Roll (Medley)/One Night	1970	20.00
❑ 10684 [PS]	Good Old Rock and Roll (Medley)/One Night	1970	30.00
❑ 10704	Southern Man/If You Wanna See Me Cry	1971	40.00
❑ 10768	Won't You Be My Lady/ Into Your Life	1971	20.00
❑ 10894	Rub It In/I'm Sorry Baby	1972	20.00

EPIC MEMORY LANE

Number	Title (A Side/B Side)	Yr	NM
❑ 2225	Glad All Over/Bits and Pieces	1972	4.00
❑ 2230	Because/Do You Love Me	1972	4.00
❑ 2234	Any Way You Want It/Can't You See That She's Mine	1972	4.00
❑ 2239	I Like It Like That/Everybody Knows (I Still Love You)	1972	4.00

Number	Title (A Side/B Side)	Yr	NM
❑ 2248	Over and Over/Catch Us If You Can	1972	4.00
❑ 2294	Bring It On Home to Me/ If Somebody Loves You	1972	4.00
❑ 2313	I Like It Like That/Can't You See That She's Mine	1972	4.00
❑ 2316	Come Home/You Got What It Takes	1972	4.00

HOLLYWOOD

Number	Title (A Side/B Side)	Yr	NM
❑ 65909	Over and Over/You Got What It Takes	1993	4.00
❑ 65909 [PS]	Over and Over/You Got What It Takes	1993	6.00
❑ 65910	I Like It Like That/Reelin' and Rockin'	1993	4.00
❑ 65910 [PS]	I Like It Like That/Reelin' and Rockin'	1993	6.00
❑ 65911	Glad All Over/Bits and Pieces	1993	4.00
❑ 65911 [PS]	Glad All Over/Bits and Pieces	1993	6.00
❑ 65912	Do You Love Me/Can't You See That She's Mine	1993	4.00
❑ 65912 [PS]	Do You Love Me/Can't You See That She's Mine	1993	6.00
❑ 65913	Catch Us If You Can/ Try Too Hard	1993	4.00
❑ 65913 [PS]	Catch Us If You Can/T ry Too Hard	1993	6.00
❑ 65914	Because/Everybody Knows (I Still Love You)	1993	4.00
❑ 65914 [PS]	Because/Everybody Knows (I Still Love You)	1993	6.00
❑ 65915	Any Way You Want It/ Come Home	1993	4.00
❑ 65915 [PS]	Any Way You Want It/ Come Home	1993	6.00

JUBILEE

Number	Title (A Side/B Side)	Yr	NM
❑ 5476	Chaquita/In Your Heart	1964	30.00

LAURIE

Number	Title (A Side/B Side)	Yr	NM
❑ 3188	I Walk the Line/First Love	1963	—

—Not known to exist

RUST

Number	Title (A Side/B Side)	Yr	NM
❑ 5078	I Walk the Line/First Love	1964	40.00

7-Inch Extended Plays

EPIC

Number	Title (A Side/B Side)	Yr	NM
❑ E 26185	Over and Over/Can't You See That She's Mine/I Like It Like That//Catch Us If You Can/ Because/Glad All Over	1966	70.00
—33 1/3 rpm, small hole, jukebox edition			
❑ E 26185 [PS]	The Dave Clark Five's Greatest Hits	1966	70.00
❑ E 26221	Try Too Hard/Please Tell Me Why/Reelin' and Rockin'// Satisfied with You/At the Scene/All Night Long	1966	70.00
—33 1/3 rpm, small hole, jukebox edition			
❑ E 26221 [PS]	More Greatest Hits	1966	70.00

Albums

CORTLEIGH

Number	Title (A Side/B Side)	Yr	NM
❑ C-1073 [M]	The Dave Clark Five with Ricky Astor	1964	30.00
—With two early DC5 tracks and assorted other stuff by other artists			
❑ CS-1073 [R]	The Dave Clark Five with Ricky Astor	1964	15.00
—With two early DC5 tracks and assorted other stuff by other artists			

CROWN

Number	Title (A Side/B Side)	Yr	NM
❑ CST-400 [R]	The Dave Clark Five with the Playbacks	1964	15.00
—With two early DC5 tracks and assorted other stuff by other artists			
❑ CST-473 [R]	Chaquita/In Your Heart	1964	15.00
—With two early DC5 tracks and assorted other stuff by other artists			
❑ CST-644 [R]	The Dave Clark Five with the Playbacks	196?	12.00
—Reissue			
❑ CLP-5400 [M]	The Dave Clark Five with the Playbacks	1964	30.00
—With two early DC5 tracks and assorted other stuff by other artists			
❑ CLP-5473 [M]	Chaquita/In Your Heart	1964	30.00
—With two early DC5 tracks and assorted other stuff by other artists			

CUSTOM

Number	Title (A Side/B Side)	Yr	NM
❑ CS 1098 [R]	The Dave Clark Five with the Playbacks	196?	12.00
—Reissue			

EPIC

Number	Title (A Side/B Side)	Yr	NM
❑ LN 24093 [M]	Glad All Over	1964	40.00
—Group photo with instruments			
❑ LN 24093 [M]	Glad All Over	1964	80.00
—Group photo, no instruments			
❑ LN 24104 [M]	The Dave Clark Five Return	1964	40.00
❑ LN 24117 [M]	American Tour	1964	40.00
❑ LN 24128 [M]	Coast to Coast	1965	40.00
❑ LN 24139 [M]	Weekend in London	1965	40.00
❑ LN 24162 [M]	Having a Wild Weekend	1965	40.00
❑ LN 24178 [M]	I Like It Like That	1965	40.00
❑ LN 24185 [M]	The Dave Clark Five's Greatest Hits	1966	25.00
❑ LN 24198 [M]	Try Too Hard	1966	30.00
❑ LN 24212 [M]	Satisfied with You	1966	30.00
❑ LN 24221 [M]	More Greatest Hits	1966	25.00
❑ LN 24236 [M]	5 by 5	1967	30.00
❑ LN 24312 [M]	You Got What It Takes	1967	30.00
❑ LN 24354 [M]	Everybody Knows	1968	30.00
❑ BN 26093 [R]	Glad All Over	1964	30.00
—Group photo with instruments			
❑ BN 26093 [R]	Glad All Over	1964	50.00
—Group photo, no instruments			
❑ BN 26104 [R]	The Dave Clark Five Return	1964	30.00
❑ BN 26117 [R]	American Tour	1964	30.00
❑ BN 26128 [R]	Coast to Coast	1965	30.00
❑ BN 26139 [R]	Weekend in London	1965	30.00
❑ BN 26162 [R]	Having a Wild Weekend	1965	30.00
❑ BN 26178 [R]	I Like It Like That	1965	30.00
❑ BN 26185 [R]	The Dave Clark Five's Greatest Hits	1966	20.00
—Yellow label			
❑ BN 26185 [R]	The Dave Clark Five's Greatest Hits	1973	40.00
—Orange label			
❑ BN 26198 [R]	Try Too Hard	1966	25.00
❑ BN 26212 [R]	Satisfied with You	1966	25.00
❑ BN 26221 [R]	More Greatest Hits	1966	20.00
❑ BN 26236 [S]	5 by 5	1967	40.00
❑ BN 26312 [S]	You Got What It Takes	1967	40.00
❑ BN 26354 [S]	Everybody Knows	1968	40.00
❑ EG 30434 [(2)S]	The Dave Clark Five	1971	100.00
—Twenty hits and near-hits, all in true stereo! Yellow label.			
❑ EG 30434 [(2)S]	The Dave Clark Five	1973	80.00
—Twenty hits and near-hits, all in true stereo! Orange label.			
❑ KEG 33459 [(2)M]	Glad All Over Again	1975	50.00
❑ XEM 77238/9 [DJ]	The Dave Clark Five Interview	1964	600.00

CLARK, DEE

Also see THE DELEGATES (3); KOOL GENTS.

45s

ABNER

Number	Title (A Side/B Side)	Yr	NM
❑ (no #) [DJ]	Blues Get Off My Shoulder (B-side blank)	1959	100.00
—White label; noted as "Special D.J. Release from Latest E.P."			
❑ 1019	Nobody But You/When I Call on You	1958	25.00
❑ 1026	Just Keep It Up/ Whispering Grass	1959	25.00
—The stereo version has a gray label with black print.			
❑ 1029	Hey Little Girl/If It Wasn't for Love	1959	25.00
❑ 1029 [PS]	Hey Little Girl/If It Wasn't for Love	1959	40.00
❑ 1032	How About That/Blues Get Off My Shoulder	1959	25.00
❑ 1037	At My Front Door/Cling-a-Ling	1960	25.00

CHELSEA

Number	Title (A Side/B Side)	Yr	NM
❑ 3025	Ride a Wild Horse/(Instrumental)	1975	5.00

COLUMBIA

Number	Title (A Side/B Side)	Yr	NM
❑ 44200	In These Very Tender Moments/ Lost Girl	1967	8.00

CONSTELLATION

Number	Title (A Side/B Side)	Yr	NM
❑ 108	Crossfire Time/I'm Going Home	1963	12.00
❑ 113	It's Raining/That's My Girl	1964	200.00
❑ 120	Come Closer/That's My Girl	1964	150.00
❑ 132	Warm Summer Breeze/ Heartbreak	1964	12.00
❑ 142	Ain't Gonna Be Your Fool/ In My Apartment	1964	12.00
❑ 147	T.C.B./It's Impossible	1965	12.00
❑ 155	I Can't Run Away/She's My Baby	1965	12.00
❑ 165	I Don't Need (Nobody Like You)/Hot Potatoe	1966	12.00
❑ 173	Old Fashion Love/ I'm Goin' Home	1966	12.00

FALCON

Number	Title (A Side/B Side)	Yr	NM
❑ 1002	Gloria/Kangaroo Hop	1957	30.00
❑ 1005	Seven Nights/24 Boy Friends	1957	40.00
❑ 1009	Oh Little Girl/Wondering	1958	40.00

LIBERTY

Number	Title (A Side/B Side)	Yr	NM
❑ 56152	24 Hours of Loneliness/Where Did All the Good Times Go	1970	5.00

LOST-NITE

Number	Title (A Side/B Side)	Yr	NM
❑ 303	Raindrops/I Want to Love You	197?	5.00
—Reissue			

UNITED ARTISTS

Number	Title (A Side/B Side)	Yr	NM
❑ 50759	You Can Make Me Feel So Good/Old Time Religion	1971	5.00

VEE JAY

Number	Title (A Side/B Side)	Yr	NM
❑ 355	You're Looking Good/Gloria	1960	15.00
❑ 372	Your Friends/Because I Love You	1961	15.00
❑ 383	Raindrops/I Want to Love You	1961	20.00
❑ 394	Gotos Delluvia (Raindrops)/ Livin' with Vivian	1961	15.00
—B-side by Al Smith			
❑ 409	Don't Walk Away from Me/ You're Telling Our Secrets	1961	15.00
❑ 428	You Are Like the Wind/ Drums in My Heart	1962	15.00
❑ 443	Dance On Little Girl/Fever	1962	15.00
❑ 462	I'm Going Back to School/ Nobody But You	1962	15.00
❑ 487	I'm a Soldier Boy/Shook Up Over You	1963	15.00
❑ 532	How Is He Treating You/ The Jones Boy	1963	15.00
❑ 548	Walking My Dog/Nobody But Me	1963	15.00

WAND

Number	Title (A Side/B Side)	Yr	NM
❑ 1177	Nobody But You (Part 1)/ Nobody But You (Part 2)	1968	8.00

WARNER BROS.

Number	Title (A Side/B Side)	Yr	NM
❑ 7720	Raindrops '73/I'm a Happy Man	1973	5.00

7-Inch Extended Plays

ABNER

Number	Title (A Side/B Side)	Yr	NM
❑ 900	(contents unknown)	1959	120.00
❑ 900 [PS]	Dee Clark	1959	120.00

Albums

ABNER

Number	Title (A Side/B Side)	Yr	NM
❑ LP-2000 [M]	Dee Clark	1959	120.00
❑ SR-2000 [S]	Dee Clark	1959	350.00
❑ LP-2002 [M]	How About That	1960	80.00
❑ SR-2002 [S]	How About That	1960	120.00

SOLID SMOKE

Number	Title (A Side/B Side)	Yr	NM
❑ 8026	His Best Recordings	1983	10.00

SUNSET

Number	Title (A Side/B Side)	Yr	NM
❑ SUS-5217	Wondering	1968	12.00

VEE JAY

Number	Title (A Side/B Side)	Yr	NM
❑ LP-1019 [M]	You're Looking Good	1960	50.00
❑ LP-1037 [M]	Hold On, It's Dee Clark	1961	50.00
❑ SR-1037 [S]	Hold On, It's Dee Clark	1961	100.00
❑ LP-1047 [M]	The Best of Dee Clark	1964	50.00
❑ SR-1047 [S]	The Best of Dee Clark	1964	100.00
❑ VJLP-1047	The Best of Dee Clark	1986	12.00
—Authorized reissue			

CLARK, DICK

See VARIOUS ARTISTS COLLECTIONS.

CLARK, DOUG, AND THE HOT NUTS

45s

JUBILEE

Number	Title (A Side/B Side)	Yr	NM
❑ 5536	Baby Let Me Bang Your Box Part 1/Baby Let Me Bang Your Box Part 2	1966	20.00
❑ 5546	Milk the Cow/Go, Doug, Go	1966	15.00

Albums

GROSS

Number	Title (A Side/B Side)	Yr	NM
❑ 101	Nuts to You	196?	30.00
❑ 102	On Campus	196?	30.00
❑ 103	Homecoming	196?	30.00
❑ 104	Rush Week	1967	30.00
❑ 105	Panty Raid	196?	30.00
❑ 106	Summer Session	196?	30.00
❑ 107	Hell Night	196?	30.00
❑ 108	Freak Out	196?	30.00
❑ 109	With a Hat On	196?	30.00

CLARK, FRANK

45s

HIT

Number	Title (A Side/B Side)	Yr	NM
❑ 29	Ramblin' Rose/Send Me the Pillow You Dream On	1962	8.00
—B-side by Fred York			
❑ 69	Those Lazy-Hazy-Crazy Days of Summer/Blue on Blue	1963	8.00
—B-side by John Preston			

CLARK, GENE

Also see THE BYRDS.

45s

ASYLUM

Number	Title (A Side/B Side)	Yr	NM
❑ 45222	Life's Greatest Fool/ From a Silver Petal	1974	5.00

COLUMBIA

Number	Title (A Side/B Side)	Yr	NM
❑ 43903	Echoes/I Found You	1966	15.00
❑ 43903 [PS]	Echoes/I Found You	1966	300.00
❑ 44088	Is Yours Mine/So You Say You Lost Your Baby	1967	15.00

RSO

Number	Title (A Side/B Side)	Yr	NM
❑ 876	Home Run King/Lonely Saturday	1977	5.00

Albums

A&M

Number	Title (A Side/B Side)	Yr	NM
❑ SP-4292	White Light	1971	15.00

ASYLUM

Number	Title (A Side/B Side)	Yr	NM
❑ 7E-1016	No Other	1974	40.00

Except when noted otherwise, VG = 25% of NM, and VG+ = 50% of NM. (Example: VG = $2.00, VG+ = $4.00 and NM = $8.00.)

Number	Title (A Side/B Side)	Yr	NM
COLUMBIA			
❑ CL 2618 [M]	Gene Clark with the Gosdin Brothers	1967	30.00
❑ CS 9418 [S]	Gene Clark with the Gosdin Brothers	1967	50.00
❑ KC 31123	Early L.A. Sessions	1972	15.00
RSO			
❑ RS-1-3011	Two Sides to Every Story	1976	20.00
SUNDAZED			
❑ LP 5062	Gene Clark with the Gosdin Brothers	2000	15.00
—Reissue of Columbia LP			
TAKOMA			
❑ TAK-7112	Firebyrd	1984	10.00

CLARK, PETULA

45s

Number	Title (A Side/B Side)	Yr	NM
ABC DUNHILL			
❑ 15007	Never Been a Horse That Couldn't Be Rode/I'm the Woman You Need	1974	5.00
❑ 15019	Loving Arms/I'm the Woman You Need	1974	5.00
CORAL			
❑ 60971	Song of the Mermaid/ Tell Me Truly	1953	25.00
❑ 61077	Where Did My Snowman Go/ Three Little Kittens	1953	25.00
ESSEX			
❑ (# unknown)	Majorca/Fascinating Rhythm	1955	—
—We have not been able to confirm this record's existence. Readers?			
IMPERIAL			
❑ 5582	The Little Blue Man/Baby Lover	1959	20.00
❑ 5600	Where Do I Go from Here/ Mama's Talkin' Soft	1959	20.00
❑ 5655	Now That I Need You/ I Love a Violin	1960	20.00
KING			
❑ 1371	The Little Shoemaker/Helpless	1954	25.00
LAURIE			
❑ 3143	Jumble Sale/The Road	1962	15.00
❑ 3156	I Will Follow Him/Darling Cheri	1963	15.00
❑ 3236	Elle Est Finie/J'ai Tout Oublie	1964	15.00
❑ 3259	In Love/The Road	1964	15.00
❑ 3316	In Love/Darling Cheri	1965	12.00
❑ 3573	Jumble Sale/The Road	1971	6.00
LONDON INT'L.			
❑ 10504	My Friend the Sea/ With All My Love	1962	15.00
❑ 10510	I'm Counting on You/ Some Other World	1962	15.00
❑ 10516	Tender Love/Whistlin' for the Moon	1962	15.00
MGM			
❑ 12049	The Pendulum Song/ Romance in Rome	1955	25.00
❑ 14392	My Guy/Little Bit of Lovin'	1972	5.00
❑ 14431	Wedding Song (There Is Love)/ Song Without End	1972	5.00
❑ 14511	Serenade of Love/I Can't Remember	1973	5.00
❑ 14577	Gratification/I Can't Remember	1973	5.00
❑ 14673	Silver Spoon/Fixing to Live	1973	5.00
❑ 14708	Come On Home/The Old Fashioned Way	1974	5.00
SCOTTI BROS.			
❑ 02676	Natural Love/Because I Love Him	1982	4.00
❑ 02979	Blue Eyes Crying in the Rain/ Love Won't Always Pass You By	1982	4.00
❑ 03171	Dreamin' with My Eyes Wide Open/Afterglow	1982	4.00
WARNER BROS.			
❑ 5494	Downtown/You'd Better Love Me	1964	10.00
—Later pressings have orange labels			
❑ 5494	Downtown/You'd Better Love Me	1964	15.00
—Originals have red labels with arrows			
❑ 5612	I Know a Place/Jack and John	1965	10.00
❑ 5643	You'd Better Come Home/Heart	1965	10.00
❑ 5661	Round Every Corner/Two Rivers	1965	10.00
❑ 5684	My Love/Where Am I Going	1965	10.00
❑ 5802	A Sign of the Times/ Time for Love	1966	10.00
❑ 5835	I Couldn't Live Without Your Love/Your Way of Life	1966	10.00
❑ 5863	Who Am I/Love Is a Long Journey	1966	10.00
❑ 5882	Color My World/Take Me Home Again	1966	10.00
❑ 7002	This Is My Song/High	1967	10.00
❑ 7049	Don't Sleep in the Subway/ Here Comes the Morning	1967	10.00
❑ 7073	The Cat in the Window (The Bird in the Sky)/Fancy Dancin' Man	1967	10.00
❑ 7097	The Other Man's Grass Is Always Greener/At the Crossroads	1967	10.00
❑ 7170	Kiss Me Goodbye/I've Got Love Going for Me	1968	8.00
—Later pressings have green labels with "W7" logo			
❑ 7170	Kiss Me Goodbye/I've Got Love Going for Me	1968	10.00
—Originals have orange labels			
❑ 7216	Don't Give Up/Every Time I See a Rainbow	1968	8.00
❑ 7244	American Boys/Look to the Sky	1968	8.00
❑ 7275	Happy Heart/Love Is the Only Thing	1969	8.00
❑ 7310	Look at Mine/If Somebody Loves You	1969	8.00
❑ 7343	No One Better Than You/ Things Bringht and Beautiful	1969	8.00
❑ 7422	Beautiful Sounds/The Song Is Love	1970	8.00
❑ 7467	The Song of My Life/ Couldn't Sleep	1971	8.00
❑ 7484	I Don't Know How to Love Him (Superstar)/Maybe	1971	8.00
WARWICK			
❑ 652	Romeo/Isn't It a Lovely Day	1961	20.00

7-Inch Extended Plays

Number	Title (A Side/B Side)	Yr	NM
WARNER BROS.			
❑ S 1743	Have Another Dream on Me/ Your Love Is Everywhere/ One in a Million//The Sun Shines Out of Your Shoes/ Days/Why Can't I Cry?	1968	12.00
—Jukebox issue; small hole, plays at 33 1/3 rpm			
❑ S 1743 [PS]	Petula	1968	12.00

Albums

Number	Title	Yr	NM
COCA-COLA			
❑ 103 [DJ]	Petula Clark Swings the Jingle	1966	150.00
GNP CRESCENDO			
❑ 2069	Live at the Royal Albert Hall	1972	10.00
❑ 2170	The Greatest Hits of Petula Clark	1984	8.00
IMPERIAL			
❑ LP-9079 [M]	Pet Clark	1959	50.00
❑ LP-9281 [M]	Uptown with Petula Clark	1965	20.00
—Reissue of Imperial 9079			
❑ LP-12027 [S]	Pet Clark	1959	80.00
❑ LP-12281 [S]	Uptown with Petula Clark	1965	25.00
—Reissue of Imperial 12079			
JANGO			
❑ 779	Give It a Try	1986	10.00
LAURIE			
❑ LLP-2032 [M]	In Love!	1965	15.00
❑ SLP-2032 [S]	In Love!	1965	15.00
❑ ST-90497 [S]	In Love!	1965	20.00
—Capitol Record Club edition			
❑ T-90497 [M]	In Love!	1965	20.00
—Capitol Record Club edition			
MGM			
❑ SE-4859	Pet Clark Now	1972	10.00
PREMIER			
❑ PM-9016 [M]	The English Sound Starring Petula Clark	1965	12.00
❑ PS-9016 [S]	The English Sound Starring Petula Clark	1965	15.00
ROULETTE			
❑ 1 [(3)]	Petula	1975	20.00
SUNSET			
❑ SUM-1101 [M]	This Is Petula Clark	1965	12.00
❑ SUS-5101 [S]	This Is Petula Clark	1965	15.00
WARNER BROS.			
❑ W 1590 [M]	Downtown	1965	15.00
—Originals have gray labels			
❑ W 1590 [M]	Downtown	1966	12.00
—Reissues have gold labels			
❑ WS 1590 [S]	Downtown	1965	20.00
—Originals have gold labels			
❑ W 1598 [M]	I Know a Place	1965	15.00
—Originals have gray labels			
❑ W 1598 [M]	I Know a Place	1966	12.00
—Reissues have gold labels			
❑ WS 1598 [S]	I Know a Place	1965	20.00
—Originals have gold labels			
❑ WS 1598 [S]	I Know a Place	1968	12.00
—Green label with "W7" logo in box at top			
❑ W 1608 [M]	The World's Greatest International Hits	1965	12.00
—Reissues have gold labels			
❑ W 1608 [M]	The World's Greatest International Hits	1965	15.00
—Originals have gray labels			
❑ WS 1608 [S]	The World's Greatest International Hits	1965	20.00
—Originals have gold labels			
❑ W 1630 [M]	My Love	1966	10.00
❑ WS 1630 [S]	My Love	1966	12.00
❑ W 1645 [M]	I Couldn't Live Without Your Love	1966	10.00
❑ WS 1645 [S]	I Couldn't Live Without Your Love	1966	12.00
❑ W 1673 [M]	Color My World/Who Am I	1967	10.00
❑ WS 1673 [S]	Color My World/Who Am I	1967	12.00
❑ W 1698 [M]	These Are My Songs	1967	10.00
❑ WS 1698 [S]	These Are My Songs	1967	12.00
❑ W 1719 [M]	The Other Man's Grass Is Always Greener	1968	12.00
❑ WS 1719 [P]	The Other Man's Grass Is Always Greener	1968	12.00
—"The Other Man's Grass Is Always Greener" is rechanneled.			
❑ W 1743 [M]	Petula	1968	12.00
❑ WS 1743 [S]	Petula	1968	12.00
❑ WS 1765	Greatest Hits, Vol. I	1968	10.00
❑ WS 1789	Portrait of Petula	1969	10.00
❑ WS 1823	Just Pet	1969	10.00
❑ WS 1862	Memphis	1970	10.00
❑ WS 1865	Warm and Tender (The Song of My Life)	1971	10.00
❑ ST-91348 [S]	These Are My Songs	1967	15.00
—Capitol Record Club edition			
❑ ST-91598	Greatest Hits, Vol. I	1968	15.00
—Capitol Record Club edition			
❑ SQBO-93215 [(2)P]	Hits...My Way	1969	25.00
—Capitol Record Club exclusive; "The Other Man's Grass Is Always Greener" is rechanneled.			

CLARK, SANFORD

45s

Number	Title (A Side/B Side)	Yr	NM
DOT			
❑ 15481	The Fool/Lonesome for a Letter	1956	25.00
—Second pressings have black labels			
❑ 15481	The Fool/Lonesome for a Letter	1956	50.00
—Originals have maroon labels			
❑ 15516	A Cheat/Usta Be My Baby	1956	25.00
❑ 15534	Oooo Baby/9 Lb. Hammer	1957	25.00
❑ 15556	The Glory of Love/Darling Dear	1957	25.00
❑ 15585	Love Charms/Loo-Be-Doo	1957	25.00
❑ 15646	Swanee River Rock/The Man Who Made an Angel Cry	1957	25.00
❑ 15738	Modern Romance/Travelin' Man	1958	150.00
JAMIE			
❑ 1107	Sing 'Em Some Blues/ Still as the Night	1958	20.00
❑ 1120	Bad Luck/My Jealousy	1959	20.00
❑ 1129	Run Boy Run/New Kind of Fool	1959	20.00
❑ 1139	I Can't Help It/Son-of-a-Gun	1959	20.00
❑ 1153	Go On Home/Pledging My Love	1960	20.00
LHI			
❑ 1203	The Son of Hickory Holler's Tramp/Black Widow Spider	1968	8.00
❑ 1213	Love Me Till Then/Farm Labor Camp No. 2	1968	8.00
MCI			
❑ 1003	The Fool/Lonesome for a Letter	1956	200.00
RAMCO			
❑ 1972	The Fool '66/Step Aside	1966	15.00
❑ 1976	Shades/Once Upon a Time	1966	12.00
❑ 1979	They Call Me Country/ Climbin' the Walls	1967	12.00
❑ 1987	It's Nothing to Me/ Calling All Hearts	1967	12.00
❑ 1992	The Big Lie/Where's the Floor	1967	12.00
TREY			
❑ 3016	It Hurts Me Too/Guess It's Love	1961	20.00
WARNER BROS.			
❑ 5473	She Taught Me/Just Blessin'	1964	15.00
❑ 5624	Houston/Hard Feelings	1965	15.00

Albums

Number	Title	Yr	NM
LHI			
❑ 12003	Return of the Fool	1968	60.00

CLARKE, ALLAN Also see THE HOLLIES.

45s

Number	Title (A Side/B Side)	Yr	NM
ASYLUM			
❑ 45313	Light a Light/If You Think You Know How to Love Me	1976	4.00
ATLANTIC			
❑ 3459	(I Will Be Your) Shadow in the Street/The Passenger	1978	4.00
❑ 3497	I Wasn't Born Yesterday/ The Man Who Manufactured Daydreams	1978	4.00
❑ 3522	I'm Betting My Life on You/ Who's Goin' Out the Back Door	1978	4.00
ELEKTRA			
❑ 46617	Slipstream/Imagination's Child	1979	4.00
❑ 47019	The Only Ones/Driving the Doomsday Cars	1980	4.00

C

The Clash, *Cut The Crap*, Epic FE 40017, 1985, **$10.**

Number	Title (A Side/B Side)	Yr	NM
EPIC			
❑ 5-10914	Baby It's Alright with Me/Ruby	1972	4.00
Albums			
ASYLUM			
❑ 7E-1056	I've Got Time	1976	10.00
ATLANTIC			
❑ SD 19175	I Wasn't Born Yesterday	1978	10.00
ELEKTRA			
❑ 6E-267	Legendary Heroes	1980	10.00
EPIC			
❑ KE 31757	My Real Name Is 'Arold	1972	15.00

CLARKE, STANLEY

Number	Title (A Side/B Side)	Yr	NM
12-Inch Singles			
EPIC			
❑ AS 779 [DJ]	You-Me Together/We Supply	1980	10.00
❑ EAS 2528 [DJ]	I'm Here to Stay (Edit) (LP Version)	1986	8.00
❑ 49-04792 [DJ]	Are You Ready (same on both sides)	1984	8.00
❑ 49-05015	Heaven Sent You (5:57) (6:00)	1984	8.00
❑ 49-05120	Spacerunner/Future	1984	8.00
❑ 49-05210	Born in the U.S.A. (5:10) (3:48)/ Campo Americano	1985	8.00
❑ 49-05993	Listen to the Beat of Your Heart (3 versions)/Where Do We Go	1986	8.00
—With Angela Bofill			
NEMPEROR			
❑ ASD 450 [DJ]	More Hot Fun/Slow Dance	1978	15.00
❑ ASD 456 [DJ]	Rock 'n' Roll Jelly (same on both sides?)	1978	10.00
❑ 4Z8-7522	Just a Feeling (Special Disco Version)/The Streets of Philadelphia	1979	15.00
PORTRAIT			
❑ RAS 1226 [DJ]	Funny How Time Flies (When You're Having Fun) (same on both sides)	1988	10.00

Number	Title (A Side/B Side)	Yr	NM
45s			
EPIC			
❑ 14-03038	Straight to the Top/ The Force of Love	1982	3.00
❑ 34-03388	You Are the One for Me/ Play the Bass	1982	3.00
❑ 34-04485	Heaven Sent You/Speedball	1984	3.00
❑ 34-04914	Born in the U.S.A./Camp Americano	1985	3.00
❑ 34-05584	What If I Should Fall in Love/ Stereotypica	1985	3.00
❑ 34-06388	I'm Here to Stay/The Boys of Johnson Street	1986	3.00
❑ 34-06591	Listen to the Beat of Your Heart/ Where Do We Go	1986	3.00
—With Angela Bofill			
❑ 9-50890	We Supply/Underestimation	1980	3.00
❑ 9-50924	You-Me Together/Rocks, Pebbles and Sand	1980	3.00
NEMPEROR			
❑ 001	Lopsy Lu/Vulcan Princess	1974	4.00
❑ 002	Silly Putty/Hello Jeff	1975	4.00
❑ 009	Hot Fun/Life Is Just a Game	1976	4.00
❑ 7518	Slow Dance/Rock 'n' Roll Jelly	1978	4.00
❑ 7521	Jamaican Boy/Rock 'n' Roll Jelly	1979	4.00
❑ 7523	Together Again (Part 1)/ Together Again (Part 2)	1980	4.00
PORTRAIT			
❑ 37-08051	Funny How Time Flies (When You're Having Fun)/If This Bass Could Only Talk	1988	4.00
Albums			
EPIC			
❑ JE 36506	Rocks, Pebbles and Sand	1980	10.00
❑ PE 36973	Stanley Clarke	1981	8.00
—Reissue of Nemperor 431			
❑ PE 36974	Journey to Love	1981	8.00
—Reissue of Nemperor 433			
❑ PE 36975	School Days	1981	8.00
—Reissue of Nemperor 900			
❑ FE 38086	Let Me Know You	1982	12.00

Number	Title (A Side/B Side)	Yr	NM
❑ FE 38688	Time Exposure	1984	10.00
❑ FE 40040	Find Out!	1985	10.00
❑ FE 40275	Hideaway	1986	10.00
NEMPEROR			
❑ NE 431	Stanley Clarke	1974	12.00
❑ NE 433	Journey to Love	1975	12.00
❑ NE 439	School Days	1976	12.00
❑ SD 900	School Days	1978	10.00
—Reissue of 439			
❑ JZ 35303	Modern Man	1978	10.00
—Original issue			
❑ PZ 35303	Modern Man	1985	8.00
—Reissue with new prefix and bar code			
❑ KZ2 35680 [(2)]	I Wanna Play for You	1979	15.00
POLYDOR			
❑ PD-5531	Children of Forever	1973	15.00
❑ 827559-1	Children of Forever	1985	8.00
—Reissue			
PORTRAIT			
❑ FR 40923	If This Bass Could Only Talk	1988	10.00

CLARKE, STANLEY, AND GEORGE DUKE

Number	Title (A Side/B Side)	Yr	NM
12-Inch Singles			
EPIC			
❑ AS 1808 [DJ]	Trip You in Love/The Good Times	1983	10.00
❑ 49-04156	Heroes (Vocal) (Instrumental)	1983	10.00
❑ 49-73553	Mothership Connection (4 versions)	1990	8.00
45s			
EPIC			
❑ 19-01052	Sweet Baby/Never Judge a Cover By Its Book	1981	3.00
❑ 14-02397	I Just Want to Love You/ Finding My Way	1981	3.00
❑ 14-02568	Touch and Go/Wild Dog	1981	3.00
❑ 34-04155	Heroes/Atlanta	1983	3.00
❑ 34-04322	Good Times/Great Danes	1984	3.00
❑ 34-73422	Lady/Find Out Who You Are	1990	4.00
Albums			
EPIC			
❑ FE 36918	The Clarke/Duke Project	1981	12.00
❑ PE 36918	The Clarke/Duke Project	198?	8.00
—Budget-line reissue			
❑ FE 38934	The Clarke/Duke Project II	1983	10.00

CLASH, THE

Also see JOE STRUMMER; BIG AUDIO DYNAMITE. Also see JOE STRUMMER; BIG AUDIO DYNAMITE.

Number	Title (A Side/B Side)	Yr	NM
10-Inch Singles			
EPIC			
❑ AS749 [DJ]	Train in Vain (Stand By Me) (same on both sides)	1980	25.00
❑ AS 749 [DJ]	Train in Vain (Stand By Me) (same on both sides)	1980	40.00
❑ AS 788 [DJ]	Clampdown/Brand New Cadillac/Spanish Bombs	1980	25.00
❑ AS788 [DJ]	Clampdown/Brand New Cadillac/Spanish Bombs	1980	25.00
12-Inch Singles			
EPIC			
❑ AS 617 [DJ]	Gates of the West/Groovy Times/I Fought the Law	1979	20.00
❑ AS 723 [DJ]	Clampdown/Lost in the Supermarket/The Card Cheat/London Calling	1979	20.00
❑ AS723 [DJ]	Clampdown/Lost in the Supermarket/The Card Cheat/London Calling	1979	20.00
❑ AS905 [DJ]	The Magnificent Seven/ Lightning Strikes/One More Time/One More Dub	1980	15.00
❑ AS 905 [DJ]	The Magnificent Seven/ Lightning Strikes (Not Once But Twice)/One More Time/ One More Dub	1980	30.00
—The Clash's name is not on the label			
❑ AS1464 [DJ]	Rock the Casbah/ Overpowered by Funk/ Should I Stay or Should I Go/ Death Is a Star	1982	15.00
❑ AS 1464 [DJ]	Rock the Casbah/ Overpowered by Funk/ Should I Stay or Should I Go/ Death Is a Star	1982	20.00
❑ 49-02036	The Magnificent Dance/The Magnificent Seven// The Call Up/The Cool Out	1981	15.00
❑ EAS2230 [DJ]	This Is England (same on both sides)	1985	6.00
❑ EAS 2230 [DJ]	This Is England (same on both sides)	1985	10.00
❑ EAS2277 [DJ]	Fingerpoppin' (AOR Remix) (same on both sides)	1985	6.00
❑ EAS 2277 [DJ]	Fingerpoppin' (AOR Remix) (same on both sides)	1985	10.00

Except when noted otherwise, VG = 25% of NM, and VG+ = 50% of NM. (Example: VG = $2.00, VG+ = $4.00 and NM = $8.00.)

Number	Title (A Side/B Side)	Yr	NM
❑ 49-02662	This Is Radio Clash/Radio Clash//Outside Broadcast/Radio 5	1981	10.00
❑ 49-03144	Rock the Casbah/Mustapha Dance	1982	15.00
❑ 49H-06899	This Is Radio Clash/The Magnificent Seven	1985	12.00
—"Mixed Masters" reissue			
❑ 49H-07829	Rock the Casbah/Mustapha Dance	1988	12.00
—"Mixed Masters" reissue			

45s

EPIC

Number	Title (A Side/B Side)	Yr	NM
❑ AE7 1178 [DJ]	Gates of the West/Groovy Times	1979	8.00
—Single included with original pressings of the LP "The Clash"			
❑ AE71178 [DJ]	Gates of the West/Groovy Times	1979	8.00
—Single included with original pressings of the LP "The Clash"			
❑ 19-02055	The Magnificent Seven/The Magnificent Dance	1981	10.00
❑ 14-03006	Should I Stay or Should I Go/Inoculated City	1982	8.00
❑ 14-03034	Should I Stay or Should I Go/First Night Back in London	1982	8.00
❑ 14-03061	Should I Stay or Should I Go/First Night Back in London	1982	6.00
❑ 14-03061 [PS]	Should I Stay or Should I Go/First Night Back in London	1982	6.00
❑ 15-03088	Train in Vain (Stand By Me)/London Calling	1982	4.00
—Reissue; originals have "Memory Lane" flower petals label (gray label $3 NM)			
❑ 34-03245	Rock the Casbah/Long Time Jerk	1982	4.00
❑ 34-03547	Should I Stay Or Should I Go?/Cool Confusion	1983	4.00
❑ 34-03547 [PS]	Should I Stay Or Should I Go?/Cool Confusion	1983	4.00
❑ ENR-03571	Should I Stay Or Should I Go?/(B-side blank)	1983	6.00
—One-sided budget release			
❑ 15-05540	Rock the Casbah/Long Time Jerk	1984	3.00
—Gray label reissue			
❑ 15-08470	Rock the Casbah/Should I Stay Or Should I Go	1988	3.00
—Reissue			
❑ 9-50738	I Fought the Law/White Man in Hammersmith Palais	1979	10.00
❑ 9-50851	Train in Vain (Stand By Me)/London Calling	1980	5.00
❑ 19-51013	Hitsville U.K./Police on My Back	1981	10.00

Albums

EPIC

Number	Title (A Side/B Side)	Yr	NM
❑ - [DJ]	Combat Rock	1982	30.00
—Camouflage green vinyl promo			
❑ AS913 [DJ]	Sandinista Now!	1981	20.00
—Promo-only sampler			
❑ AS 913 [DJ]	Sandinista Now!	1981	45.00
—Promo-only sampler			
❑ AS952 [DJ]	If Music Could Talk (Interchords)	1981	30.00
—Promo-only interview record			
❑ AS 952 [DJ]	If Music Could Talk (Interchords)	1981	40.00
—Promo-only interview record			
❑ AS 99-1592 [PD]	Combat Rock	1982	40.00
—Promo-only picture disc			
❑ AS 1594 [DJ]	The World According to the Clash	1982	40.00
—Promo-only sampler			
❑ AS1594 [DJ]	The World According to the Clash	1982	40.00
—Promo-only sampler			
❑ AS 99-1595 [DJ]	Combat Rock	1982	30.00
—Camouflage green vinyl promo			
❑ JE 35543	Give 'Em Enough Rope	1978	15.00
—Block letters on cover; orange label			
❑ JE 35543	Give 'Em Enough Rope	1978	15.00
—Script cover; orange label			
❑ JE 35543 [DJ]	Give 'Em Enough Rope	1978	30.00
—White label promo; timing strip; back cover has one incorrect song title			
❑ JE35543 [DJ]	Give 'Em Enough Rope	1978	30.00
—White label promo; timing strip; back cover has one incorrect song title			
❑ JE 36060	The Clash	1979	15.00
❑ PE 36060	The Clash	1979	8.00
—Budget-line reissue; no bonus single			
❑ E2 36238 [DJ]	London Calling	1980	25.00
—White label promo			
❑ E236238 [DJ]	London Calling	1980	25.00
—White label promo			
❑ E2 36329 [(2)]	London Calling	1979	15.00
❑ E3X 37037 [(3)]	Sandinista!	1981	25.00
❑ FE 37689	Combat Rock	1982	10.00
—Second and later pressings (with standard dark blue labels) delete commercial during "Inoculated City"			
❑ FE 37689	Combat Rock	1982	15.00
—First pressings (with custom labels) contain a commercial in the middle of the song "Inoculated City"			
❑ PE 38540	Black Market Clash	1982	10.00
—12-inch version of 10-inch record			
❑ FE 40017	Cut the Crap	1985	10.00
❑ E2 44025 [(2)]	The Story of the Clash, Vol. 1	1988	15.00

The Clash, *Give 'Em Enough Rope*, Epic JE 35543, 1978, **$15.**

Number	Title (A Side/B Side)	Yr	NM
EPIC LEGACY			
❑ E3 53191 [(3)10]	Super Black Market Clash	1993	30.00
EPIC NU-DISK			
❑ 4E 36846 [10]	Black Market Clash	1980	15.00

CLASS-AIRES, THE

45s

HONEY BEE

Number	Title (A Side/B Side)	Yr	NM
❑ (# unknown)	Too Old to Cry/My Tears Start to Fall	195?	2000.

Albums

HONEY BEE

Number	Title (A Side/B Side)	Yr	NM
❑ (# unknown)	Tears Start to Fall	195?	300.00

CLASS-NOTES, THE

45s

Number	Title (A Side/B Side)	Yr	NM
DOT			
❑ 15786	You Inspire Me/Goodness Gracious	1958	30.00
HAMILTON			
❑ 50011	Take It Back/Bessie's House	1959	60.00

CLASSIC IV, THE

45s

Number	Title (A Side/B Side)	Yr	NM
ALGONQUIN			
❑ 1650	Limbo Under The Christmas Tree/Early Christmas	1962	30.00
TWIST			
❑ 1001	Island of Paradise/Heavenly Bliss	1962	100.00

CLASSIC SULLIVANS, THE

45s

Number	Title (A Side/B Side)	Yr	NM
CHURCH KEY			
❑ 03	Shame, Shame, Shame/We Can Make It	197?	400.00
KWANZA			
❑ 7678	I Don't Want to Lose You/Paint Yourself Into a Corner	1973	25.00
❑ 7715	A Ring Don't Mean a Thing Without Love/Right Before My Eyes	1973	30.00

CLASSICS, THE (1)

Brooklyn vocal group led by Emil Stucchio.

45s

Number	Title (A Side/B Side)	Yr	NM
BED-STUY			
❑ 222	Again/The Way You Look Tonight	196?	10.00
DART			
❑ 1015	So in Love/Cinderella	1960	30.00
❑ 1024	Life Is But a Dream, Sweetheart/That's the Way	1961	200.00
❑ 1032	Angel Angela/Eenie Minie Mo	1961	50.00
LOST-NITE			
❑ 200	Till Then/Eenie Minie Mo	196?	5.00
—Reissue			
MERCURY			
❑ 71829	Life Is But a Dream, Sweetheart/That's the Way	1961	25.00
MUSICNOTE			
❑ 118	P.S. I Love You/Wrap Your Troubles in Dreams	1963	25.00
❑ 1116	Till Then/Eenie Minie Mo	1963	25.00
—Black vinyl, blue label			
❑ 1116	Till Then/Eenie Minie Mo	1963	30.00
—Black vinyl, yellow label			
❑ 1116	Till Then/Eenie Minie Mo	1963	100.00
—Gold vinyl			
❑ 1116	Till Then/Eenie Minie Mo	1963	150.00
—Multi-color vinyl			
MUSICTONE			
❑ 1114	So in Love/Cinderella	1963	20.00
❑ 6131	Too Young/Who's Laughing, Who's Crying	1964	20.00
PICCOLO			
❑ 500	I Apologize/Love for Today	1965	25.00

Number	Title (A Side/B Side)	Yr	NM
STORK			
❑ STK-2	You'll Never Know/Dancing with You	1964	25.00
STREAM LINE			
❑ 1028	Life Is But a Dream, Sweetheart/Nuttin' in the Noggin	1961	25.00

CLASSICS, THE (2) With LOU CHRISTIE.

Number	Title (A Side/B Side)	Yr	NM
45s			
STARR			
❑ 508	Close Your Eyes/Funny Things	1960	200.00
—Reissued on Alcar with Lou Christie's name prominently mentioned			

CLASSICS, THE (3) Canadian group.

Number	Title (A Side/B Side)	Yr	NM
45s			
JERDEN			
❑ 742	Till I Met You/It Didn't Take Much	1964	30.00

CLASSICS, THE (U) Some of these could be group (1); none of them are group (2); probably none of these are group (3).

Number	Title (A Side/B Side)	Yr	NM
45s			
CLASS			
❑ 219	If Only the Sky Was a Mirror/Gosh, But This Is Love	1958	70.00
CREST			
❑ 1063	Let Me Dream/You're the Prettiest One	1959	80.00
MV			
❑ 1000	Christmas Is Here/(B-side unknown)	19??	10.00
PROMO			
❑ 1010	Blue Moon/Little Boy Lost	1961	30.00
—As "Herb Lance and the Classics"			
RO-ANN			
❑ 1002	Je Vous Aime/Burning Desire	1959	1000.
SHELTER			
❑ 7318	Mr. Fire Coal-Man/Flashing My Whip	1972	5.00
—B-side by Hugh Roy			
TOP RANK			
❑ 2061	You're Everything/Burning Love	1960	25.00
YAN-G			
❑ 4665	So Glad That I Found You/(B-side unknown)	196?	2000.

CLASSICS IV

Number	Title (A Side/B Side)	Yr	NM
45s			
ARLEN			
❑ 746	Don't Make Me Wait/It's Too Late	1964	20.00
CAPITOL			
❑ 5710	Cry Baby/Pollyanna	1966	15.00
—As "The Classics"			
❑ 5816	Little Darlin'/Nothing to Lose	1966	15.00
IMPERIAL			
❑ 66259	Spooky/Poor People	1967	8.00
❑ 66293	Soul Train/Strange Changes	1968	8.00
❑ 66304	Mama's and Papa's/Waves	1968	8.00
❑ 66328	Stormy/24 Hours of Loneliness	1968	8.00
❑ 66328	Stormy/Ladies' Man	1968	20.00
❑ 66352	Traces/Mary, Mary Row Your Boat	1969	8.00
❑ 66378	Everyday With You Girl/Sentimental Lady	1969	8.00
❑ 66393	Change of Heart/Rainy Day	1969	6.00
—Starting here, "Dennis Yost and the Classics IV"			
❑ 66424	Midnight/The Comic	1969	6.00
❑ 66439	The Funniest Thing/Nobody Loves You But Me	1970	6.00
LIBERTY			
❑ 56182	God Knows I Loved Her/We Miss You	1970	6.00
❑ 56200	Where Did All the Good Times Go/Ain't It the Truth	1970	6.00
MGM			
❑ 14785	My First Day Without You/Lovin' Each Other	1975	4.00
MGM SOUTH			
❑ 7002	What Am I Crying For/All in Your Mind	1972	5.00
❑ 7012	Rosanna/One Man Show	1973	5.00
❑ 7016	Save the Sunlight/Make Me Believe It	1973	5.00
❑ 7020	I Knew It Would Happen/Love Me or Leave Me Alone	1973	5.00
❑ 7027	It's Now Winter's Day/Losing My Mind	1974	5.00
UNITED ARTISTS			
❑ 0125	Stormy/Spooky	1973	4.00
—"Silver Spotlight Series" reissue			
❑ 0126	Traces/Everyday with You Girl	1973	4.00
—"Silver Spotlight Series" reissue			
❑ 50777	Most of All/It's Time for Love	1971	5.00
❑ 50805	Cherry Hill Park/Pick Up the Pieces	1971	5.00
Albums			
ACCORD			
❑ SN-7107	Stormy	1981	10.00
IMPERIAL			
❑ LP-9371 [M]	Spooky	1968	40.00
—Mono has stock copy label inside stereo cover with white "Monaural" sticker			
❑ LP-12371 [S]	Spooky	1968	20.00
❑ LP-12407	Mamas and Papas/Soul Train	1969	20.00
❑ LP-12429	Traces	1969	20.00
❑ LP-16000	Dennis Yost & the Classics IV/Golden Greats - Vol. I	1969	20.00
LIBERTY			
❑ LN-10109	The Very Best of the Classics IV	198?	8.00
❑ LST-11003	Song	1970	15.00
MGM SOUTH			
❑ 702	Dennis Yost and the Classics IV	1973	15.00
UNITED ARTISTS			
❑ UA-LA446-E	The Very Best of the Classics IV	1975	12.00

CLASSMATES, THE

Number	Title (A Side/B Side)	Yr	NM
45s			
HIT			
❑ 324	Tighten Up/Cowboys to Girls	1968	8.00
—B-side by the Fantastics			
❑ 326	A Beautiful Morning/Lady Madonna	1968	8.00
—B-side by the Chords (2)			
❑ 335	The Look of Love/Turn Around, Look at Me	1968	8.00
—B-side by the Chords (2)			
❑ 338	Classical Gas/People Got to Be Free	1968	8.00
❑ 345	Suzie-Q/Midnight Confessions	1968	8.00
—B-side by the Jalopy Five			

CLAY, CASSIUS

Number	Title (A Side/B Side)	Yr	NM
45s			
COLUMBIA			
❑ 43007	Stand By Me/I Am the Greatest	1964	25.00
❑ 43007 [PS]	Stand By Me/I Am the Greatest	1964	50.00
❑ ZSP 75717/77185 [DJ]	The Prediction/Will the Real Sonny Liston Please Fall Down	1964	40.00
❑ ZSP 75717/77185 [PS]	The Prediction/Will the Real Sonny Liston Please Fall Down	1964	80.00
Albums			
COLUMBIA			
❑ CL 2093 [M]	I Am the Greatest!	1963	40.00
❑ CS 8893 [S]	I Am the Greatest!	1963	50.00

CLAY, CHRIS

Number	Title (A Side/B Side)	Yr	NM
45s			
VELTONE			
❑ 111	Santa Under Analysis Part 1/Santa Under Analysis Part 2	1960	25.00

CLAY, JOE

Number	Title (A Side/B Side)	Yr	NM
45s			
VIK			
❑ 0211	Duck Tail/Sixteen Chicks	1956	100.00
❑ 0218	Get On the Right Track Cracker Jack	1956	100.00

CLAY, JUDY Also see WILLIAM BELL, BILLY VERA.

Number	Title (A Side/B Side)	Yr	NM
45s			
ATLANTIC			
❑ 2669	Get Together/Sister Pitiful	1969	6.00
❑ 2697	Greatest Love/Saving All for You	1969	6.00
EMBER			
❑ 1080	More Than You Know/I Thought I'd Gotten Over You	1961	12.00
❑ 1085	Stormy Weather/Do You Think That's Right	1962	12.00
SCEPTER			
❑ 1273	My Arms Aren't Strong Enough/That's All	1964	8.00
❑ 1281	Lonely People Do Foolish Things/I'm Comin' Home	1964	8.00
❑ 12135	The Way You Look Tonight/Haven't You Got What It Takes	1966	8.00
❑ 12157	He's the Kind of Guy/You Busted My Mind	1966	8.00
❑ 12218	I Want You/He's the Kind of Guy	1968	8.00
STAX			
❑ 0006	Bed of Roses/Remove the Clouds	1968	6.00
❑ 0026	It Ain't Long Enough/Give Love to Save Love	1969	6.00
❑ 230	You Can't Run Away from Your Heart/It Takes a Lot of Good Love	1967	8.00

CLAY, OTIS

Number	Title (A Side/B Side)	Yr	NM
45s			
COTILLION			
❑ 44001	She's About a Mover/You Don't Miss Your Water	1968	8.00
❑ 44009	Do Right Woman, Do Right Man/That Kind of Lovin'	1968	7.00
❑ 44068	Pouring Water on a Drowning Man/Hard Working Women	1970	7.00
❑ 44101	Is It Over/I'm Qualified	1970	7.00
DAKAR			
❑ 610	Baby Jane/You Hurt Me for the Last Time	1969	7.00
ECHO			
❑ 2002	Check It Out/Messing with My Mind	1975	10.00
❑ 2003	The Only Way Is Up/Special Kind of Love	1980	120.00
ELKA			
❑ 301	Turn Back the Hands of Time/Good Lovin'	197?	8.00
GLADES			
❑ 1736	All I Need Is You/Special Kind of Soul	1976	10.00
HI			
❑ 2206	Home Is Where the Heart Is/Brand New Thing	1972	6.00
❑ 2214	Precious Precious/Too Many Hands	1972	6.00
❑ 2226	Trying to Live My Life Without You/Let Me Be the One	1972	7.00
❑ 2239	I Can't Make It Alone/I Didn't Know the Meaning of Pain	1973	6.00
❑ 2252	If I Could Reach Out/I Die a Little Bit Each Day	1973	6.00
❑ 2266	Woman Don't Live Here No More/You Can't Escape the Hands of Love	1974	6.00
❑ 2270	You Did Something to Me/I Was Jealous	1974	6.00
KAYVETTE			
❑ 5130	All Because of Your Love/Today My World Fell	1977	5.00
❑ 5133	Let Me In/Sweet Woman's Love	1977	5.00
ONE-DERFUL!			
❑ 4834	Three Is a Crowd/Flame in Your Heart	1965	10.00
❑ 4837	I Paid the Price/Tired of Falling In (And Out of) Love	1966	10.00
❑ 4841	I Testify/I'm Satisfied	1966	10.00
❑ 4846	Flame in Your Heart/It's Easier Said, Than Done	1967	8.00
❑ 4848	That's How It Is (When You're in Love)/Show Place	1967	8.00
❑ 4850	A Lasting Love/Got to Find a Way	1967	8.00
❑ 4852	Don't Pass Me By/That'll Get You What You Want	1968	8.00
Albums			
HI			
❑ HLP 6003	I Can't Take It	1977	15.00
❑ SHL 32075	Trying to Live My Life Without You	1972	20.00
ROOSTER BLUES			
❑ R-7609 [(2)]	Soul Man: Live in Japan	1985	15.00

CLAY, TOM

Number	Title (A Side/B Side)	Yr	NM
45s			
BIG TOP			
❑ 3055	The Little Boy/That's All	1960	20.00
CHANT			
❑ 103	Marry Me/(B-side unknown)	1959	100.00
IBBB			
❑ ZTSC 97436/7	Remember, We Don't Like Them, We Love Them: Official IBBB Interview	1964	150.00
—Interviews with the Beatles			
MOWEST			
❑ 5002	What the World Needs Now Is Love/Abraham, Martin and John//The Victors	1971	5.00
—Blue and yellow label			
❑ 5002	What the World Needs Now Is Love/Abraham, Martin and John//The Victors	1971	6.00
—Mostly orange label			

Except when noted otherwise, VG = 25% of NM, and VG+ = 50% of NM. (Example: VG = $2.00, VG+ = $4.00 and NM = $8.00.)

Number | Title (A Side/B Side) | Yr | NM

❑ 5007 Whatever Happened to Love/Baby I Need Your Loving 1971 4.00

Albums

MOWEST

❑ 103 What the World Needs Now Is Love 1971 15.00

CLAYTON, MERRY

45s

CAPITOL

❑ 4984 It's In His Kiss/The Magic of Romance 1963 10.00
❑ 5100 Usher Boy/Nothing Left to Do But Cry 1963 10.00
❑ 5164 Beg Me/La La Jace Song 1964 10.00
❑ 5243 This Is My Dream/The Knocks on the Door 1964 10.00

MCA

❑ 41195 Emotion/Let Me Make You Cry a Little Longer 1980 4.00
❑ 41266 You're Always There When I Need You/When the World Turns Blue 1980 4.00

ODE

❑ 66003 Gimme Shelter/Good Girls 1970 5.00
❑ 66007 Country Road/Forget It, I Got It 1970 5.00
❑ 66011 Lift Every Voice and Sing/I Ain't Gonna Worry My Life Away 1970 5.00
❑ 66016 The Times They Are a-Changing/Wouldn't It Be Nice 1971 30.00
—B-side by the Beach Boys
❑ 66018 After All This Time/Whatever 1971 4.00
❑ 66020 Steamroller/After All This Time 1971 4.00
❑ 66024 Southern Man/Oh No, Not My Baby 1972 4.00
❑ 66030 Oh No, Not My Baby/Suspicious Minds 1972 4.00
❑ 66108 The Acid Queen/Eyesight to the Blind 1975 4.00
—B-side by Richie Havens
❑ 66110 Keep Your Eye on the Sparrow/Love Grows Up Slow 1975 4.00
❑ 66116 One More Ride/If I Lose 1976 4.00

RCA

❑ 6989-7-R Yes/In the Still of the Night 1988 3.00
—B-side by the Five Satins
❑ 8917-7-R Almost Paradise/Hungry Eyes 1989 3.00
—B-side with Eric Carmen

Albums

MCA

❑ 3200 Emotion 1980 10.00

ODE

❑ PE 34948 Merry Clayton 1977 8.00
❑ PE 34957 Keep Your Eye on the Sparrow 1977 8.00
❑ SP-77001 Gimme Shelter 1970 15.00
❑ SP-77012 Merry Clayton 1971 12.00
❑ SP-77030 Keep Your Eye on the Sparrow 1975 12.00

CLAYTON-THOMAS, DAVID

Also see BLOOD, SWEAT AND TEARS.

45s

ATCO

❑ 6347 Hey Hey Hey Hey/Walk That Walk 1965 15.00

COLUMBIA

❑ 45569 Sing a Song/We're All Meat from the Same Bone 1972 5.00
❑ 45603 North Beach Racetrack/Magnificent Sanctuary Band 1972 5.00
❑ 45675 Yesterday's Music/Falling by Degrees 1972 5.00

DECCA

❑ 32556 Say Boss Man/Done Somebody Wrong 1969 10.00

EPIC

❑ 34-03792 I Can't Blame a Broken Heart/Some Hearts Get All the Breaks 1983 4.00

RCA VICTOR

❑ 74-0966 Hernando's Hideaway/Harmony Junction 1973 4.00
❑ APBO-0078 Workin' on the Railroad/Prof. Longhair 1973 4.00
❑ APBO-0216 Yolanda/Workin' on the Railroad 1974 4.00
❑ APBO-0296 Take the Money and Run/Anytime... Babe 1974 4.00

ROULETTE

❑ 7048 No, No, No/Monopoly 1969 10.00

TOWER

❑ 206 Take Me Back/Out of the Sunshine 1966 12.00
❑ 263 Born with the Blues/Brainwashed 1966 12.00

Albums

ABC

❑ AA-1104 Clayton 1978 10.00

COLUMBIA

❑ KC 31000 David Clayton-Thomas 1972 15.00
❑ KC 31700 Tequila Sunrise 1972 15.00

DECCA

❑ DL 75146 David Clayton-Thomas! 1969 20.00

RCA VICTOR

❑ APD1-0173 [Q] David Clayton-Thomas 1973 20.00
❑ APL1-0173 David Clayton-Thomas 1973 12.00

CLEAN LIVING

45s

VANGUARD

❑ 35162 In Heaven There Is No Beer/Backwoods Girl 1972 5.00
❑ 35170 Old Time Music/Jenny Regardless 1973 4.00
❑ 35171 Far North Again/Me and You 1973 4.00

Albums

VANGUARD

❑ VSD-79318 Clean Living 1972 10.00
❑ VSD-79334 Meadow Muffin 1973 10.00

CLEANLINESS AND GODLINESS SKIFFLE BAND, THE

Also see THE MASKED MARAUDERS.

Albums

VANGUARD

❑ VSD-79285 Greatest Hits 1968 25.00

CLEAR LIGHT

Also see CLIFF DeYOUNG.

45s

ELEKTRA

❑ 45622 She's Ready to Be Free/Black Roses 1967 12.00
❑ 45626 They Who Have Nothing/Ballad of Freddie and Larry 1968 12.00

Albums

ELEKTRA

❑ EKL-4011 [M] Clear Light 1967 40.00
❑ EKS-74011 [S] Clear Light 1967 35.00

SUNDAZED

❑ LP 5125 Clear Light 2002 12.00
—Reissue on 180-gram vinyl

CLEARY, DON

Albums

PALOMINO

❑ 302 [M] Don Cleary Sings Traditional Cowboy Songs 1966 50.00

CLEAVER, ELDRIDGE

Albums

MORE

❑ 4000 [M] Soul On Wax 1968 25.00

CLEE-SHAYS, THE

45s

TRIUMPH

❑ 65 The Man from U.N.C.L.E./Dynamite 1966 20.00

CLEFS OF LAVENDER HILL, THE

45s

DATE

❑ 1510 Stop! — Get a Ticket/First Tell Me Why 1966 20.00
❑ 1530 One More Time/So I'll Try 1966 20.00
❑ 1533 Play with Fire/It Won't Be Long 1966 20.00
❑ 1567 Gimme One Good Reason/Oh, Say My Love 1967 20.00

THAMES

❑ 100 Stop! — Get a Ticket/First Tell Me Why 1966 40.00

CLEFTONES, THE

45s

CLASSIC ARTISTS

❑ 121 She's So Fine/Trudy 1990 4.00

GEE

❑ 1000 You Baby You/I Was Dreaming 1955 60.00
❑ 1011 Little Girl of Mine/You're Driving Me Mad 1956 40.00
❑ 1016 Can't We Be Sweethearts/Niki-Hoeky 1956 40.00
❑ 1025 String Around My Heart/Happy Memories 1956 40.00
❑ 1031 Why You Do Me Like You Do/I Like Your Style of Making Love 1957 40.00
❑ 1038 See You Next Year/Ten Pairs of Shoes 1957 40.00
❑ 1041 Hey Babe/What Did I Do That Was Wrong 1957 40.00
❑ 1048 Lover Boy/Beginners in Love 1958 30.00
❑ 1064 Heart and Soul/How Do You Feel 1961 25.00
❑ 1067 (I Love You) For Sentimental Reasons/'Deed I Do 1961 20.00
❑ 1074 Earth Angel/Blues in the Night 1961 20.00
❑ 1077 Again/Do You 1961 20.00
❑ 1079 Lover Come Back to Me/There She Goes 1962 20.00
❑ 1080 How Deep Is the Ocean/Some Kinda Blue 1962 20.00

OLD TOWN

❑ 1011 The Masquerade Is Over/My Dearest Darling 1955 500.00

ROULETTE

❑ 4094 Trudy/She's So Fine 1958 25.00
❑ 4161 Mish Mash Baby/Cuzin Casanova 1959 25.00
❑ 4302 She's Gone/Shadows on the Very Last Row 1960 25.00

WARE

❑ 6001 She's Forgotten You/Right from the Git Go 1964 15.00

Albums

GEE

❑ GLP-705 [M] Heart and Soul 1961 200.00
❑ SGLP-705 [S] Heart and Soul 1961 500.00
❑ GLP-707 [M] For Sentimental Reasons 1961 250.00
❑ SGLP-707 [S] For Sentimental Reasons 1961 1200.

CLEMENT, JACK

45s

ELEKTRA

❑ 45397 Just Because You Ask Me To/When I Dream 1977 4.00
❑ 45474 We Must Believe in Magic/When I Dream 1978 4.00
❑ 45518 All I Want to Do in Life/It'll Be Her 1978 4.00
❑ 45547 Gone Girl/There She Goes 1978 4.00

HALLWAY

❑ 1796 Time After Time After Time/My Voice Is Changing 1963 15.00

JMI

❑ 10 The One on the Right Is the One on the Left/The Child That's in the Manger 1972 6.00
❑ 14 She Thinks I Still Care/Never Give a Heartache a Place to Go 1973 6.00
❑ 20 Steal Away/(B-side unknown) 1973 6.00
❑ 43 The One on the Right Is on the Left/Feet 1974 6.00

RCA VICTOR

❑ 47-7602 Whole Lotta Lookin'/Edge of Town 1959 15.00

SUN

❑ 291 Ten Years/Your Lover Boy 1958 25.00
❑ 311 The Black Haired Man/Wrong 1958 25.00

Albums

ELEKTRA

❑ 6E-122 All I Want to Do in Life 1978 12.00

CLEMENTINO, CLAIRETTE

45s

CAPITOL

❑ 5003 Everywhere/See Me 1963 10.00
❑ 5003 [PS] Everywhere/See Me 1963 15.00
❑ 5081 Adonis/Bless My Soul 1963 10.00
❑ 5177 Since I Fell in Love with You/It's Happening to Me 1964 10.00
❑ 5276 He Don't Want Your Love Anymore/Never Love a Wandering Boy 1964 10.00

CLEVELAND, JAMES (REV.)

The below discography, though comprehensive, is incomplete; we'd appreciate any revisions and filling in gaps.

45s

HOB

❑ 115 Good Enough for Me/Jesus Will 197? 6.00
—With the Original Chimes
❑ 116 Look Up and Live/He's Got His Eyes on You 197? 6.00
—With the Original Chimes
❑ 120 One More Time/Deep River 197? 6.00
—With the Original Chimes

Number	Title (A Side/B Side)	Yr	NM
❑ 139	Something's Got a Hold on Me/ Greater Day	197?	6.00
—With the Voices of Tabernacle			
❑ 166	Lord Do It/Meetin' Tonight	197?	6.00
—With the Voices of Tabernacle			
SAVOY			
❑ 4141	He's Alright with Me/Just Like He Said He Would	1960	15.00
❑ 4146	Just to Behold His Face/ He Laid His Hands on Me	1960	15.00
❑ 4154	Oh Lord, I'm Satisfied/There's a Brighter Day Somewhere	1961	15.00
❑ 4157	I Need Jesus on My Journey/ Love of God	1961	15.00
❑ 4166	Deep Down in My Heart/ What a Mighty God	1962	15.00
❑ 4176	Sit Down Servant/There Is No Failure in God	1962	12.00
—With the Gospel Chimes			
❑ 4182	Jesus Will Bring Things Out/ Trust Him	1962	15.00
❑ 4188	Redeemed/Leave It There	1963	15.00
❑ 4192	The Sun Will Shine After Awhile/No Need to Worry	1963	12.00
❑ 4211	He's Always Doing Something Good for Me/I've Come a Long Ways	1964	12.00
❑ 4217	Peace Be Still Pt. 1/Pt. 2	1964	12.00
—With the Angelic Choir			
❑ 4230	Two Wings/That Will Be Good Enough for Me	1965	12.00
❑ 4252	It's Real/Down by the River	1965	12.00
❑ 4256	I Stood on the Banks of Jordan Pt. 1/Pt. 2	1965	12.00
❑ 4269	Without a Song/ (B-side unknown)	1966	10.00
❑ 4276	Beautiful Garden of Prayer Pt. 1/Pt. 2	1967	10.00
❑ 4285	God Is Not Dead Pt. 1/Pt. 2	1968	10.00
❑ 4290	Martin Luther King Memorial Pt. 1/Pt. 2	1968	15.00
—With Rev. Lawrence Roberts			
❑ 4302	Free at Last/Somebody Knows	1969	10.00
❑ 4315	It All Belongs to My Father/It's In My Heart	1969	10.00
❑ 4316	I Don't Need Nobody Else/That's What I Like About Jesus	1969	10.00
—With the Cleveland Singers			
❑ 4317	Old Ship of Zion/Sweet Hour of Prayer	1969	10.00
❑ 4318	God Is Enough/No Cross	1969	10.00
—With the Angelic Choir			
❑ 4319	If I Had a Hammer/ Look Up and Live	1969	10.00
—With the Cleveland Singers			
❑ 4320	I Can't Make It Without You/ No Night There	1969	10.00
—With Hular Gene Hurley			
❑ 4321	He's a Miracle Worker (Part 1)/ (Part 2)	1969	10.00
❑ 4322	Abide with Me/My Faith Looks Up to Thee	1969	10.00
❑ 4323	How Tedious and Tasteless (Part 1)/(Part 2)	1969	10.00
—With the Cleveland Singers			
❑ 4324	Grace of God/Trouble Don't Last Always	1969	10.00
—With the Angelic Choir			
❑ 4327	Father I Stretch My Hand to Thee/(B-side unknown)	1970	10.00
❑ 4334	Amazing Grace/Try Love	197?	6.00
—With the Southern California Community Choir			
❑ 4346	In the Ghetto/When the Saints Go Marching In	197?	6.00
—With the Southern California Community Choir			
❑ 4364	As Long As There's God/Say You Love Him	197?	6.00
—With the Charles Fold Singers			
❑ 4372	Prayer (Part 1)/(Part 2)	1979	10.00
Albums			
APOLLO			
❑ LP-509	In the Beginning	197?	15.00
HOB			
❑ 233	Love of God	197?	15.00
—With the Voices of Tabernacle			
❑ 239	Give Glory to God	197?	15.00
❑ 253	The Best of James Cleveland	197?	15.00
KENWOOD			
❑ LP-509	In the Beginning	197?	15.00
SAVOY			
❑ DBL-7014 [(2)]	Live at Carnegie Hall	1977	15.00
❑ DBL-7020 [(2)]	Vol. 3/Recorded Live in Cincinnati, Ohio/(Is There Any Hope for) Tomorrow	1978	15.00
—With the Charles Fold Singers			
❑ SGL-7035 [(2)]	It's a New Day	1979	15.00
—With the Southern California Community Choir			
❑ SGL-7038 [(2)]	Lord Let Me Be an Instrument	1979	15.00
—With the Charles Fold Singers			
❑ SGL-7046 [(2)]	James Cleveland and the Voices of Cornerstone	1979	15.00
❑ SGL-7059 [(2)]	James Cleveland Sings with the World's Greatest Choirs	1980	15.00
❑ SGL-7066 [(2)]	Where Is Your Faith	1981	15.00
—With the Southern California Community Choir			
❑ SGL-7071 [(2)]	I Want to Be Ready When You Come	1981	20.00
—With the Los Angeles Chapter of the GMWA			
❑ SGL-7072 [(2)]	This, Too, Will Pass	1981	20.00
—With the Charles Fold Singers			
❑ SGL-7103 [(2)]	The Last Live Recording of the King of Gospel Music	1991	15.00
—With the L.A. Gospel Messengers			
❑ MG-14068	The Soul of James Cleveland	196?	30.00
❑ MG-14076	Peace Be Still	1964	30.00
—With the Angelic Choir			
❑ MG-14085	The Sun Will Shine After Awhile	196?	30.00
❑ MG-14096	Vol. 4	196?	30.00
❑ MG-14131	He Leadeth Me	196?	30.00
❑ MG-14159	Jame Cleveland in Hollywood	196?	30.00
❑ MG-14176	Songs My Mother Taught Me	196?	30.00
❑ MG-14195	Merry Christmas from James Cleveland and the Angelic Choir	196?	25.00
❑ MG-14205	Vol. 8 — Part 1	196?	25.00
—With the Angelic Choir			
❑ MG-14211	James Cleveland and the Cleveland Singers	196?	20.00
❑ MG-14226	James Cleveland and the Voices of Tabernacle	196?	20.00
❑ MG-14252	The One and Only	197?	20.00
❑ MG-14260	Amazing Grace	197?	20.00
—With the Southern California Community Choir			
❑ MG-14265	James Cleveland and the Cleveland Singers	197?	20.00
❑ MG-14269	Somehow I Can Sing	197?	15.00
❑ MG-14282	I'll Do His Will	197?	15.00
—With the Southern California Community Choir			
❑ MG-14311	Down Memory Lane	197?	15.00
❑ MG-14352	God Has Smiled on Me	1975	12.00
❑ MG-14360	To the Glory of God	1975	12.00
—With the Southern California Community Choir			
❑ SL 14412	Give It To Me	197?	12.00
❑ SL 14425	The Lord Is My Life	197?	12.00
❑ SL 14438	Think of His Goodness to You	197?	12.00
❑ SL 14541	Victory Shall Be Mine	197?	12.00
—With the Salem Inspirational Choir			
UPFRONT			
❑ UPF-163	I Walk with God	197?	12.00
❑ UPF-190	Rev. James Cleveland	197?	12.00

CLIBURN, VAN

Number	Title (A Side/B Side)	Yr	NM
45s			
RCA VICTOR			
❑ SP-45-102 [DJ]	Romantic Theme (from MacDowell Piano Concerto No. 2 in D Minor, Op. 23) (same on both sides)	1960	10.00
—Promo-only single release			
❑ SP-45-102 [PS]	Romantic Theme (from MacDowell Piano Concerto No. 2 in D Minor, Op. 23)	1960	20.00
Albums			
RCA VICTOR RED SEAL			
❑ LM-2252 [M]	Tchaikovsky: Piano Concerto No. 1	1958	20.00
❑ LSC-2252 [S]	Tchaikovsky: Piano Concerto No. 1	1958	25.00
—"Shaded dog" pressing ("Living Stereo" on label)			
❑ LSC-2252 [S]	Tchaikovsky: Piano Concerto No. 1	1965	15.00
—"White dog" pressing ("Stereo" on label)			
❑ LSC-2252 [S]	Tchaikovsky: Piano Concerto No. 1	1969	12.00
—"No dog" pressing ("RCA" sideways at left)			
❑ LSC-2252 [S]	Tchaikovsky: Piano Concerto No. 1	1976	8.00
—"Late dog" pressing (dog near top)			
❑ LM-2355 [M]	Rachmaninoff: Piano Concerto No. 3	1959	20.00
❑ LSC-2355 [S]	Rachmaninoff: Piano Concerto No. 3	1959	25.00
—"Shaded dog" pressing ("Living Stereo" on label)			
❑ LSC-2355 [S]	Rachmaninoff: Piano Concerto No. 3	1965	15.00
—"White dog" pressing ("Stereo" on label)			
❑ LSC-2355 [S]	Rachmaninoff: Piano Concerto No. 3	1969	12.00
—"No dog" pressing ("RCA" sideways at left)			
❑ LM-2455 [M]	Schumann: Piano Concerto in A Minor	1960	15.00
❑ LSC-2455 [S]	Schumann: Piano Concerto in A Minor	1960	20.00
—"Shaded dog" pressing ("Living Stereo" on label)			
❑ LSC-2455 [S]	Schumann: Piano Concerto in A Minor	1965	15.00
—"White dog" pressing ("Stereo" on label)			
❑ LSC-2455 [S]	Schumann: Piano Concerto in A Minor	1969	12.00
—"No dog" pressing ("RCA" sideways at left)			
❑ LM-2507 [M]	Prokofiev: Piano Concerto No. 3; MacDowell: Piano Concerto No. 2	1961	15.00
❑ LSC-2507 [S]	Prokofiev: Piano Concerto No. 3; MacDowell: Piano Concerto No. 2	1961	30.00
—"Shaded dog" pressing ("Living Stereo" on label)			
❑ LSC-2507 [S]	Prokofiev: Piano Concerto No. 3; MacDowell: Piano Concerto No. 2	1965	30.00
—"White dog" pressing ("Stereo" on label)			
❑ LSC-2507 [S]	Prokofiev: Piano Concerto No. 3; MacDowell: Piano Concerto No. 2	1969	12.00
—"No dog" pressing ("RCA" sideways at left)			
❑ LM-2562 [M]	Beethoven: Piano Concerto No. 5 (Emperor Concerto)	1961	15.00
❑ LSC-2562 [S]	Beethoven: Piano Concerto No. 5 (Emperor Concerto)	1961	20.00
—"Shaded dog" pressing ("Living Stereo" on label)			
❑ LSC-2562 [S]	Beethoven: Piano Concerto No. 5 (Emperor Concerto)	1964	20.00
—"White dog" pressing ("Stereo" on label)			
❑ LSC-2562 [S]	Beethoven: Piano Concerto No. 5 (Emperor Concerto)	1969	12.00
—"No dog" pressing ("RCA" sideways at left)			
❑ LM-2576 [M]	My Favorite Chopin	1962	15.00
❑ LSC-2576 [S]	My Favorite Chopin	1962	20.00
—"Shaded dog" pressing ("Living Stereo" on label)			
❑ LSC-2576 [S]	My Favorite Chopin	1965	15.00
—"White dog" pressing ("Stereo" on label)			
❑ LSC-2576 [S]	My Favorite Chopin	1969	12.00
—"No dog" pressing ("RCA" sideways at left)			
❑ LSC-2576 [S]	My Favorite Chopin	1976	8.00
—"Late dog" pressing (dog near top)			
❑ LM-2581 [M]	Brahms: Piano Concerto No. 2	1962	15.00
❑ LSC-2581 [S]	Brahms: Piano Concerto No. 2	1962	20.00
—"Shaded dog" pressing ("Living Stereo" on label)			
❑ LSC-2581 [S]	Brahms: Piano Concerto No. 2	1965	15.00
—"White dog" pressing ("Stereo" on label)			
❑ LSC-2581 [S]	Brahms: Piano Concerto No. 2	1969	12.00
—"No dog" pressing ("RCA" sideways at left)			
❑ LSC-2581 [S]	Brahms: Piano Concerto No. 2	1976	8.00
—"Late dog" pressing (dog near top)			
❑ LM-2601 [M]	Rachmaninoff: Piano Concerto No. 2	1962	15.00
❑ LSC-2601 [S]	Rachmaninoff: Piano Concerto No. 2	1962	15.00
—"White dog" pressing ("Stereo" on label)			
❑ LSC-2601 [S]	Rachmaninoff: Piano Concerto No. 2	1962	20.00
—"Shaded dog" pressing ("Living Stereo" on label)			
❑ LSC-2601 [S]	Rachmaninoff: Piano Concerto No. 2	1969	12.00
—"No dog" pressing ("RCA" sideways at left)			
❑ LM-2680 [M]	Beethoven: Piano Concerto No. 4	1963	12.00
❑ LSC-2680 [S]	Beethoven: Piano Concerto No. 4	1963	15.00
—"Shaded dog" pressing ("Living Stereo" on label)			
❑ LSC-2680 [S]	Beethoven: Piano Concerto No. 4	1965	12.00
—"White dog" pressing ("Stereo" on label)			
❑ LSC-2680 [S]	Beethoven: Piano Concerto No. 4	1969	10.00
—"No dog" pressing ("RCA" sideways at left)			
❑ LSC-3323	The World's Favorite Piano Music	196?	12.00
❑ ARP1-4441	Tchaikovsky: Piano Concerto No. 1	198?	10.00
—Half-speed mastered reissue			
❑ ARP1-4688	Rachmaninoff: Piano Concerto No. 3	198?	10.00
—Half-speed mastered reissue			

CLICKETTES, THE

Number	Title (A Side/B Side)	Yr	NM
45s			
CHECKER			
❑ 1060	I Just Can't Help It/(Instrumental)	1963	20.00
DICE			
❑ 83/84	Jive Time Turkey/A Teenager's First Love	1959	150.00
❑ 92/93	To Be a Part of You/ Because of My Best Friend	1959	120.00
❑ 94/95	Warm, Soft and Lovely/ Why Oh Why	1959	120.00
❑ 96/97	Lover's Prayer/Grateful	1959	70.00
❑ 96/97	Lover's Prayer/Grateful	1959	150.00
—With distribution by Memo Record Corp.			
❑ 100	But Not for Me/I Love You I Swear	1960	120.00
GUYDEN			
❑ 2043	Where Is He/The Lone Lover	1960	30.00

Except when noted otherwise, VG = 25% of NM, and VG+ = 50% of NM. (Example: VG = $2.00, VG+ = $4.00 and NM = $8.00.)

Number	Title (A Side/B Side)	Yr	NM
LOST-NITE			
138	Lover's Prayer/Grateful	196?	8.00
—Reissue			
139	Because of My Best Friend/Grateful	196?	8.00
140	To Be a Part of You/Grateful	196?	8.00
TUFF			
373	I Just Can't Help It/(Instrumental)	1964	20.00

CLICKS, THE

45s

Number	Title (A Side/B Side)	Yr	NM
JOSIE			
780	Come Back to Me/Peace and Commitment	1955	300.00

CLIFF, BENNY

45s

Number	Title (A Side/B Side)	Yr	NM
DRIFT			
1441	Shake Um Um Rock/The Breaking Point	1959	3000.
—VG 1000; VG+ 2000			

CLIFF, JIMMY

12-Inch Singles

Number	Title (A Side/B Side)	Yr	NM
COLUMBIA			
CAS 1185 [DJ]	Hanging Fire (Edit) (12" Mix) (Dub)	1987	8.00
CAS 1351 [DJ]	Soar Like an Eagle (same on both sides)	198?	10.00
AS 1809 [DJ]	We All Are One (same on both sides)	1983	10.00
CAS 2380 [DJ]	Seven Day Weekend (same on both sides)	1986	10.00
—With Elvis Costello			
44-03045	Special/Peace Officer (Dub Version)	1982	12.00
44-03507	Treat the Youths Right (6:49)/Roots Radical (6:51)	1983	10.00
44-04126	Reggae Night (Remix 6:17) (Dub Mix 6:12)	1983	10.00
44-04966	We All Are One (2 versions)	1983	10.00
44-05029	Reggae Night (Remix) (Dub)	1984	10.00
44-05235	Hot Shot (Extended) (Instrumental) (7" Version)	1985	7.00
44-07565	Love Me, Love Me (Popstand Remix) (Jimmy Love Dub) (Perc-apella) (Chant-apella)	1988	8.00

45s

Number	Title (A Side/B Side)	Yr	NM
A&M			
1146	Wonderful World, Beautiful People/Waterfall	1969	8.00
1146 [PS]	Wonderful World, Beautiful People/Waterfall	1969	12.00
1167	Come Into My Life/Viet Nam	1970	8.00
1167 [PS]	Come Into My Life/Viet Nam	1970	12.00
1201	You Can Get It If You Really Want/Be Aware	1970	8.00
1270	Goodbye Yesterday/Let's Seize the Time	1971	8.00
COLUMBIA			
38-03216	Special/Peace Officer	1982	4.00
38-04141	Reggae Night/Love Heights	1983	4.00
38-04335	We All Are One/Roots Woman	1984	4.00
38-05396	Hot Shot/Modern World	1985	4.00
38-05716	American Sweet/Reggae Movement	1985	4.00
38-06135	Seven Day Weekend/Brightest Star	1986	4.00
—A-side with Elvis Costello			
38-06235	Club Paradise/Third World People	1986	3.00
38-06235 [PS]	Club Paradise/Third World People	1986	4.00
38-07692	Love Me, Love Me/Sunshine in the Music	1988	4.00
MANGO			
7500	The Harder They Come/You Can Get It If You Really Want	1973	8.00
MCA			
51043	I Am the Living/Love Again	1981	5.00
51094	Another Summer/It's the Beginning of the End	1981	5.00
51211	My Philosophy/Shelter of Your Love	1981	4.00
REPRISE			
1177	Black Queen/Born to Win	1973	6.00
1315	You Can't Be Wrong and Get Right/Music Maker	1974	6.00
1383	The Harder They Come/Viet Nam	1977	10.00
VEEP			
1265	Aim and Ambition/Give and Take	1967	15.00
1276	That's the Way Life Goes/Thank You	1968	15.00

Albums

Number	Title (A Side/B Side)	Yr	NM
A&M			
SP-3189	Wonderful World, Beautiful People	198?	8.00
—Reissue of 4251			
SP-4251	Wonderful World, Beautiful People	1970	25.00
COLUMBIA			
FC 38099	Special	1982	10.00
PC 38099	Special	198?	8.00
—Budget-line reissue			
FC 38986	The Power and the Glory	1983	10.00
PC 38996	The Power and the Glory	1985	8.00
—Budget-line reissue			
FC 40002	Cliff Hanger	1985	10.00
FC 40845	Hanging Fire	1988	10.00
ISLAND			
SW-9343	Struggling Man	1973	20.00
MANGO			
ILPS 9235	Struggling Man	197?	12.00
—Reissue of Island SW-9343			
MCA			
813	I Am the Living	198?	8.00
—Reissue of 5153			
820	Give the People What They Want	198?	8.00
—Reissue of 5217			
5153	I Am the Living	1980	12.00
5217	Give the People What They Want	1981	12.00
REPRISE			
MS 2147	Unlimited	1973	15.00
MS 2188	Music Maker	1974	15.00
MS 2218	Follow My Mind	1975	15.00
MS 2256	In Concert: The Best of Jimmy Cliff	1976	15.00
VEEP			
VPS-16536	Can't Get Enough of It	1969	40.00
WARNER BROS.			
BSK 3240	Give Thankx	1978	12.00

CLIFFORD, BUZZ

45s

Number	Title (A Side/B Side)	Yr	NM
A&M			
878	Just Can't Wait/On My Way	1967	10.00
CAPITOL			
5880	Bored to Tears/Swing in My Back Yard	1967	10.00
COLUMBIA			
41774	Blue Lagoon/Hello, Mr. Moonlight	1960	20.00
41774 [PS]	Blue Lagoon/Mr. Moonlight	1960	100.00
—Sleeve calls B-side "Mr. Moonlight"; may be promo only			
41876	Baby Sittin' Boogie/Driftwood	1960	20.00
41876	Baby Sitter Boogie/Driftwood	1960	25.00
41876 [PS]	Baby Sittin' Boogie/Driftwood	1960	50.00
41876	Baby Sittin' Boogie/Driftwood	1972	10.00
—Gray label			
41979	Three Little Fishes/Just Because	1961	20.00
41979 [PS]	Three Little Fishes/Just Because	1961	50.00
42019	I'll Never Forget/The Awakening	1961	50.00
42019 [PS]	I'll Never Forget/The Awakening	1961	80.00
42177	Moving Day/Loneliness	1961	20.00
42177 [PS]	Moving Day/Loneliness	1961	50.00
42290	Forever/Magic Circle	1962	25.00
42290 [PS]	Forever/Magic Circle	1962	50.00
DOT			
17329	(Baby I Could Be) So Good At Loving You/Children Are Crying Aloud	1970	6.00
17344	Procter and Gunther/I Am the River	1971	6.00
RCA VICTOR			
47-8935	Until Then/Let Her Go (It's All Right)	1966	12.00
ROULETTE			
4451	No One Loves Me Like You Do/More Dead Than Alive	1962	15.00

Albums

Number	Title (A Side/B Side)	Yr	NM
COLUMBIA			
CL 1616 [M]	Baby Sittin' with Buzz	1961	100.00
CS 8416 [S]	Baby Sittin' with Buzz	1961	150.00
DOT			
DLP-25965	See Your Way Clear	1969	30.00

CLIFFORD, DOUG

Of CREEDENCE CLEARWATER REVIVAL.

45s

Number	Title (A Side/B Side)	Yr	NM
FANTASY			
686	Latin Music/Take a Train	1972	5.00
686 [PS]	Latin Music/Take a Train	1972	6.00

Albums

Number	Title (A Side/B Side)	Yr	NM
FANTASY			
9411	Cosmo	1972	15.00

CLIFFORD, MIKE

45s

Number	Title (A Side/B Side)	Yr	NM
AMERICAN INT'L.			
138	Broken Hearted Man/When Cindy When	1970	5.00
158	Do Your Own Thing/You Better Start Singing Soon	1971	5.00
171	You Say Love/It's a Dream Way	1970	4.00
CAMEO			
381	Before I Loved Her/Shirl Girl	1965	10.00
395	Out in the Country/Courtin'	1966	10.00
COLUMBIA			
41862	Stranger/Poor Little Girl	1960	12.00
41862 [PS]	Stranger/Poor Little Girl	1960	30.00
41964	Look in Any Window/Uh Huh	1961	12.00
42029	Pretty Little Girl in the Yellow Dress/At Last	1961	12.00
42226	When We Marry/Bombay	1961	12.00
42226 [PS]	When We Marry/Bombay	1961	25.00
42335	Joanna/Mary, Mary	1962	12.00
LIBERTY			
55207	Should I/Whisper Whisper	1959	15.00
—With Patience and Prudence			
55219	I Don't Know Why/I'm Afraid to Say I Love You	1959	12.00
SIDEWALK			
917	Send Her Flowers/This Time, Time May Be Wrong	1967	8.00
939	Gas Hassle/Mary Jane	1968	8.00
UNITED ARTISTS			
489	Close to Cathy/She's Just Another Girl	1962	12.00
557	What to Do with Laurie/That's What They Said	1963	10.00
588	Danny's Dream/One Boy Too Late	1963	10.00
614	Gee, I Don't Remember/Cotton Dresses	1963	10.00
713	It Had Better Be Tonight/All the Colors of the Rainbow	1964	10.00
763	See You in September/One By One, The Roses Died	1964	10.00
794	Don't Make Her Cry/Barbara's Theme	1964	10.00
823	How to Murder Your Wife/Here's To My Lover	1965	10.00

Albums

Number	Title (A Side/B Side)	Yr	NM
UNITED ARTISTS			
UAL-3409 [M]	For the Love of Mike	1965	20.00
UAS-6409 [S]	For the Love of Mike	1965	25.00

CLIMATES, THE

45s

Number	Title (A Side/B Side)	Yr	NM
HOLIDAY INN			
2206	Don't Be Cruel/Tell Him Tonite	1967	12.00
SUN			
404	No You for Me/Breaking Up Again	1967	25.00

CLIMAX

With Sonny Geraci, formerly of THE OUTSIDERS.

45s

Number	Title (A Side/B Side)	Yr	NM
CAROUSEL			
30050	Hard Rock Group/(B-side unknown)	1971	5.00
30055	Precious and Few/Park Preserve	1971	5.00
PARAMOUNT			
0023	You've Gotta Try/Friendship	1970	6.00
ROCKY ROAD			
30055	Precious and Few/Park Preserve	1972	4.00
—Reissue of Carousel 30055			
30061	Life and Breath/If It Feels Good, Do It	1972	4.00
30064	Caroline This Time/Rainbow Rides Are Free	1972	4.00
30072	Rock and Roll Heaven/Face the Music	1973	5.00
30074	Walking in the Georgia Rain/(B-side unknown)	1973	4.00
30077	It's Gonna Get Better/(B-side unknown)	1974	4.00

Albums

Number	Title (A Side/B Side)	Yr	NM
ROCKY ROAD			
3506	Climax	1972	15.00

CLIMAX BLUES BAND

Includes records as "Climax Chicago Blues Band."

12-Inch Singles

Number	Title (A Side/B Side)	Yr	NM
WARNER BROS.			
PRO-A-807 [DJ]	Fat City/Summer Rain/Children of the Nightime	1979	10.00

45s

SIRE

Number	Title (A Side/B Side)	Yr	NM
❑ 351	Reap What I've Sowed/ (B-side unknown)	1971	8.00
❑ 358	Hey Mama/That's All	1972	8.00
❑ 705	Shake Your Love/ Mule on the Dole	1973	8.00
❑ 712	Goin' to New York/I Am Constant	1974	6.00
❑ 713	Sense of Direction/ Losin' the Humbles	1974	6.00
❑ 715	Reaching Out/Milwaukee Truckin' Blues	1974	6.00
❑ 721	Using the Power/Running Out of Time	1975	6.00
❑ 736	Couldn't Get It Right/ Sav'ry Gravy	1977	5.00
❑ 747	Together and Free/Berlin Blues	1977	4.00
❑ 1026	Makin' Love/Gospel Singer	1978	4.00
❑ 1031	Mistress Moonshine/Teardrops	1978	4.00
❑ 49012	Children of the Nightime/ Long Distance Love	1979	4.00
❑ 49098	Summer Rain/Money in Your Pocket	1979	4.00

WARNER BROS.

Number	Title (A Side/B Side)	Yr	NM
❑ 49605	Gotta Have More Love/ One for Me and You	1980	4.00
❑ 49669	I Love You/Horizontalized	1981	5.00
❑ 49850	Darlin'/This Time You're the Singer	1981	4.00
❑ 50018	Breakdown/Shake It Lucy	1982	4.00

Albums

SIRE

Number	Title	Yr	NM
❑ SRK 3334	Real to Reel	1979	10.00
❑ SES-4901	#3	1971	15.00
❑ SES-5903	Tightly Knit	1972	15.00
❑ SR 6003	The Climax Chicago Blues Band	1978	10.00
❑ SR 6004	Lot of Bottle	1977	10.00
❑ SR 6008	Tightly Knit	1977	10.00
❑ 2XS 6013 [(2)]	FM/Live	1977	12.00
❑ SR 6016	Stamp Album	1977	10.00
❑ SR 6033	The Climax Chicago Blues Band Plays On	1978	10.00
❑ SRK 6056	Shine On	1978	10.00
❑ SES-7402	Rich Man	1972	15.00
❑ SAS-2-7411 [(2)]	FM/Live	1973	15.00
❑ SAS-7501	Sense of Direction	1974	12.00
❑ SASD-7507	Stamp Album	1975	12.00
❑ SASD-7523	Gold Plated	1976	12.00
❑ SES-97013	The Climax Chicago Blues Band	1969	15.00
❑ SES-97023	The Climax Chicago Blues Band Plays On	1970	15.00

VIRGIN/EPIC

Number	Title	Yr	NM
❑ FE 38631	Sample and Hold	1983	10.00

WARNER BROS.

Number	Title	Yr	NM
❑ BSK 3493	Flying the Flag	1981	12.00
❑ BSK 3623	Lucky for Some	1982	10.00

CLIMBERS, THE

45s

J&S

Number	Title (A Side/B Side)	Yr	NM
❑ 1652/3	My Darlin' Dear/Angels in Heaven Know I Love You	1957	100.00
❑ 1658	I Love You/Train, Car, Boat or Plane	1957	800.00

CLINE, PATSY

45s

CORAL

Number	Title (A Side/B Side)	Yr	NM
❑ 61464	A Church, a Courtroom, Then Goodbye/Honky Tonk Merry-Go-Round	1955	30.00
❑ 61523	Turn the Cards Slowly/Hidin' Out	1955	30.00
❑ 61583	I Love You Honey/Come Right In	1956	25.00

DECCA

Number	Title (A Side/B Side)	Yr	NM
❑ 25673	South of the Border/San Antonio Rose	1965	12.00
❑ 25686	I Love You So Much It Hurts/ Seven Lonely Days	1966	12.00
❑ 25694	Shoes/Half As Much	1966	12.00
❑ 25699	Lonely Street/You Were Only Fooling (While I Was Falling in Love)	1966	12.00
❑ 25707	That's My Desire/Foolin' 'Round	1967	12.00
❑ 25712	You Took Him Off My Hands/ Does Your Heart Beat for Me	196?	12.00
❑ 25718	Have You Ever Been Lonely/ Hidin' Out	196?	12.00
❑ 25724	True Love/Love, Love, Love Me Honey Do	196?	12.00
❑ 25732	Always/Pick Me Up on Your Way Down	196?	12.00
❑ 25738	Too Many Secrets/You Made Me Love You	196?	12.00
❑ 25744	Anytime/In Care of the Blues	196?	12.00
❑ 25747	Crazy Arms/The Wayward Wind	196?	12.00
❑ 29963	Stop, Look and Listen/I've Loved and Lost Again	1956	20.00
❑ 9-30221	Walkin' After Midnight/A Poor Man's Roses (Or a Rich Man's Gold)	1957	20.00
—Black label, star under "Decca"			
❑ 9-30221	Walkin' After Midnight/A Poor Man's Roses (Or a Rich Man's Gold)	1957	30.00
—Black label, lines on either side of "Decca"			
❑ 9-30221 [PS]	Walkin' After Midnight/A Poor Man's Roses (Or a Rich Man's Gold)	1957	80.00
❑ 30339	Try Again/Today, Tomorrow and Forever	1957	15.00
❑ 30406	Three Cigarettes in an Ashtray/ A Stranger in My Arms	1957	15.00
❑ 30504	I Don't Wanta/Then You'll Know	1957	15.00
❑ 30542	Stop the World/Walking Dream	1958	15.00
❑ 30659	Come On In/Let the Teardrops Fall	1958	15.00
❑ 30706	Never No More/I Can See an Angel	1958	15.00
❑ 30746	Just Out of Reach (Of My Two Open Arms)/If I Could See The World	1958	15.00
❑ 30794	Dear God/He Will Do for You	1958	15.00
❑ 30846	Yes, I Understand/Cry Not for Me	1959	15.00
❑ 30929	Got a Lot of Rhythm in My Soul/ I'm Blue Again	1959	20.00
❑ 31061	Lovesick Blues/How Can I Face Tomorrow	1960	12.00
❑ 31128	There He Goes/Crazy Dream	1960	12.00
❑ 31205	I Fall to Pieces/Lovin' in Vain	1961	12.00
❑ 31317	Crazy/Who Can I Count On	1961	12.00
❑ 31354	She's Got You/Strange	1962	12.00
❑ 31377	When I Get Thru with You (You'll Love Me Too)/Imagine That	1962	12.00
❑ 31377 [PS]	When I Get Thru with You (You'll Love Me Too)/Imagine That	1962	25.00
❑ 31406	So Wrong/You're Stronger Than Me	1962	12.00
❑ 31429	Heartaches/Why Can't He Be You	1962	12.00
❑ 31455	Leavin' On Your Mind/Tra Le La Le La Triangle	1963	10.00
❑ 31455 [PS]	Leavin' On Your Mind/Tra Le La Le La Triangle	1963	25.00
❑ 31483	Sweet Dreams (Of You)/ Back in Baby's Arms	1963	10.00
❑ 31522	Faded Love/Blue Moon of Kentucky	1963	10.00
❑ 31552	When You Need a Laugh/ I'll Sail My Ship Alone	1963	10.00
❑ 31588	Your Kinda Love/Someday You'll Want Me to Love You	1964	10.00
❑ 31616	Love Letters in the Sand/That's How a Heartache Begins	1964	10.00
❑ 31671	He Called Me Baby/Bill Bailey Won't You Please Come Home	1964	10.00
❑ 31754	Your Cheatin' Heart/I Can't Help It (If I'm Still in Love with You)	1965	10.00
❑ 7-34130 [S]	Foolin' 'Round/The Wayward Wind	1962	20.00
❑ 7-34131 [S]	South of the Border (Down Mexico Way)/I Love You So Much It Hurts	1962	20.00
❑ 7-34132 [S]	Crazy/Seven Lonely Days	1962	25.00
❑ 7-34133 [S]	San Antonio Rose/True Love	1962	20.00
—The above four are 33 1/3, small hole jukebox singles			

EVEREST

Number	Title (A Side/B Side)	Yr	NM
❑ 2011	Then You'll Know/Hungry for Love	1963	12.00
❑ 2020	Walking After Midnight/ That Wonderful Someone	1963	12.00
❑ 2031	I Can See an Angel/Just Out of Reach	1963	12.00
❑ 2039	I've Loved and Lost Again/ I Love You Honey	1964	10.00
❑ 2045	In Care of the Blues/If I Could See the World (Through the Eyes of a Child)	1964	10.00
❑ 2052	Got a Lot of Rhythm (In My Soul)/ Love Me, Love Me, Honey Do	1964	10.00
❑ 2060	Crazy Dream/There He Goes	1965	10.00
❑ 20005	I Don't Wanta/I Can't Forget	1962	15.00

4 STAR

Number	Title (A Side/B Side)	Yr	NM
❑ AP-39 [DJ]	Dear God/He Will Do for You	195?	30.00
—4 Star promo-only item			
❑ 1033	Life's Railway to Heaven/ If I Could See the World	1978	5.00

KAPP

Number	Title (A Side/B Side)	Yr	NM
❑ 659	Just a Closer Walk with Thee	1965	15.00
—One-sided release, possibly promo only			

MCA

Number	Title (A Side/B Side)	Yr	NM
❑ 41303	Always/I Sail My Ship Alone	1980	4.00
❑ 51038	I Fall to Pieces/True Love	1980	4.00
❑ 52052	So Wrong/I Fall to Pieces	1982	3.00
—A-side: With Jim Reeves (electronically created duet)			
❑ 52684	Sweet Dreams/Blue Moon of Kentucky	1985	3.00
❑ 60061	Walkin' After Midnight/South of the Border (Down Mexico Way)	1973	5.00
—Reissue; black label with rainbow			
❑ 60062	I Fall to Pieces/He Called Me Baby	1973	5.00
—Reissue; black label with rainbow			
❑ 60063	Crazy/Your Cheatin' Heart	1973	5.00
—Reissue; black label with rainbow			
❑ 60063	Crazy/Your Cheatin' Heart	1980	3.00
—Reissue; blue label with rainbow			
❑ 60102	Pick Me Up on Your Way Down/ Crazy Arms	1973	5.00
—Reissue; black label with rainbow			

RCA

Number	Title (A Side/B Side)	Yr	NM
❑ PB-12346	Have You Ever Been Lonely (Have You Ever Been Blue)/ Welcome to My World	1981	3.00
—With Jim Reeves (electronically created duet)			

STARDAY

Number	Title (A Side/B Side)	Yr	NM
❑ 7030	Walking After Midnight/ Lovesick Blues	1965	10.00
❑ 8024	Walking After Midnight/ Lovesick Blues	1971	6.00

7-Inch Extended Plays

CORAL

Number	Title	Yr	NM
❑ EC 81159	*Honky Tonk Merry-Go-Round/A Church, a Courtroom, and Then Goodbye/Turn the Cards Slowly/Hidin' Out	1958	25.00
❑ EC 81159 [PS]	Songs by Patsy Cline	1958	30.00

DECCA

Number	Title	Yr	NM
❑ ED 2542	That Wonderful Someone/Three Cigarettes (In an Ashtray)// Hungry for Love/Fingerprints	1958	20.00
❑ ED 2542 [PS]	Patsy Cline	1958	20.00
❑ ED 2703	*I Fall to Pieces/Lovin' in Vain/ Lovesick Blues/There He Goes	1961	15.00
❑ ED 2703 [PS]	Patsy Cline	1961	15.00
❑ ED 2707	Crazy/Foolin' Around//Who Can I Count On/South of the Border	1961	15.00
❑ ED 2707 [PS]	Patsy Cline	1961	15.00
❑ ED 2719	*She's Got You/Strange/The Wayward Wind/I Love You So Much It Hurts	1962	15.00
❑ ED 2719 [PS]	She's Got You	1962	15.00
❑ ED 2729	So Wrong/You're Stronger Than Me//Heartaches/Your Cheatin' Heart	1962	15.00
❑ ED 2729 [PS]	Patsy Cline	1962	15.00
❑ ED 2757	*Leavin' on Your Mind/Tra Le La Le La Triangle/Half As Much/Lonely Street	1963	15.00
❑ ED 2757 [PS]	Leavin' on Your Mind	1963	15.00
❑ ED 2759	Just a Closer Walk with Thee/ Life's Railroad to Heaven// Dear God/He Will Do for You	1963	15.00
❑ ED 2759 [PS]	Dear God	1963	15.00
❑ ED 2768	I'm Blue Again/How Can I Face Tomorrow//I'm Moving Along/ Love Love Love Me Honey Do	1964	15.00
❑ ED 2768 [PS]	How Can I Face Tomorrow	1964	15.00
❑ ED 2770	Someday You'll Want Me to Want You/Faded Love// When You Need a Laugh/ I'll Sail My Ship Alone	1964	15.00
❑ ED 2770 [PS]	Someday You'll Want Me to Want You	1964	15.00
❑ ED 2794	(contents unknown)	1965	15.00
❑ ED 2794 [PS]	Portrait of Patsy Cline	1965	15.00
❑ ED 2802	(contents unknown)	1965	15.00
❑ ED 2802 [PS]	Love Letters in the Sand	1965	15.00
❑ 7-34180	Strange/South of the Border/ Sweet Dreams (Of You)// I Fall to Pieces/I Love You So Much It Hurts/A Poor Man's Roses (Or a Rich Man's Gold)	196?	20.00
—Jukebox issue; small hole, plays at 33 1/3 rpm			
❑ 7-34180 [PS]	The Patsy Cline Story	196?	20.00
—Number on cover is "DXSB 7176"			
❑ 7-34285	That's How a Heartache Begins/Lovesick Blues/Bill Bailey, Won't You Please Come Home//There He Goes/I'm Blue Again/Shoes	196?	20.00
—Jukebox issue; small hole, plays at 33 1/3 rpm			
❑ 7-34285 [PS]	That's How a Heartache Begins	196?	20.00

Except when noted otherwise, VG = 25% of NM, and VG+ = 50% of NM. (Example: VG = $2.00, VG+ = $4.00 and NM = $8.00.)

Number	Title (A Side/B Side)	Yr	NM
❑ DL 34822	She's Got You/Crazy/South of the Border//I Fall to Pieces/Sweet Dreams/Walking After Midnight	197?	15.00

—Jukebox issue; small hole, plays at 33 1/3 rpm

Number	Title (A Side/B Side)	Yr	NM
❑ DL 34822 [PS]	The Patsy Cline Story	197?	15.00

—Part of "Little LP" series (LLP # 131)

4 STAR

❑ EPF-12 [DJ] Walking After Midnight/I've Loved and Lost Again//I Love You Honey/Honky Tonk Merry Go Round 195? 50.00
—Sometimes said to be on the "Patsy Cline" label, but it is a 4 Star promo-only item; not issued with cover?

❑ EPF-16 [DJ] Try Again/Turn the Cards Slowly//Come On In/Stop Look and Listen 195? 50.00
—Sometimes said to be on the "Patsy Cline" label, but it is a 4 Star promo-only item; not issued with cover?

❑ EP-21 [DJ] Three Cigarettes (In an Ashtray)/Hungry for Love//Fingerprints/That Wonderful Someone 195? 50.00
—Sometimes said to be on the "Patsy Cline" label, but it is a 4 Star promo-only item; not issued with cover?

❑ EP-31 [DJ] Just Out of Reach/Come On In//Let the Tear Drops Fall/Don't Ever Leave Me Again 195? 50.00
—Sometimes said to be on the "Patsy Cline" label, but it is a 4 Star promo-only item; not issued with cover?

❑ EP-38 [DJ] Just Out of Reach/I Can See an Angel//If I Could See the World (Through the Eyes of a Child)/Never No More 195? 50.00
—4 Star promo-only item; not issued with cover?

❑ EP-41 [DJ] Cry Not for Me/Yes, I Understand//Am I That Easy to Forget/Such Is Life 1959 40.00
—B-side by Carl Belew; sometimes said to be on the "Patsy Cline" label, but it is a 4 Star promo-only item; not issued with cover?

❑ EP-43 [DJ] How Can I Face Tomorrow/A Church, a Courtroom, Then Goodbye//That's What I Get for Loving You/My Baby's Not Here (In Town Tonight) 1959 40.00
—B-side by Carl Belew; sometimes said to be on the "Patsy Cline" label, but it is a 4 Star promo-only item; not issued with cover?

Albums

ACCORD

❑ SN-7153 Let the Teardrops Fall 1981 10.00

ALLEGIANCE

❑ AV-5021 Stop, Look and Listen 198? 10.00

DECCA

❑ DXB 176 [(2)M] The Patsy Cline Story 1963 40.00
❑ DL 4202 [M] Patsy Cline Showcase 1961 40.00
❑ DL 4282 [M] Sentimentally Yours 1962 30.00
❑ DL 4508 [M] A Portrait of Patsy Cline 1964 30.00
❑ DL 4586 [M] That's How a Heartache Begins 1964 30.00
❑ DL 4854 [M] Patsy Cline's Greatest Hits 1967 20.00
❑ DXSB 7176 [(2)S] The Patsy Cline Story 1963 50.00
❑ DL 8611 [M] Patsy Cline 1957 100.00
—Black label with silver print
❑ DL 8611 [M] Patsy Cline 1960 50.00
—Black label with color bars
❑ DL 74202 [S] Patsy Cline Showcase 1961 50.00
❑ DL 74282 [S] Sentimentally Yours 1962 40.00
❑ DL 74508 [S] A Portrait of Patsy Cline 1964 40.00
❑ DL 74586 [S] That's How a Heartache Begins 1964 40.00
❑ DL 74854 [S] Patsy Cline's Greatest Hits 1967 25.00

EVEREST

❑ 1200 [R] Golden Hits 1962 12.00
❑ 1204 [R] Encores 1962 12.00
❑ 1217 [R] In Memoriam 1963 12.00
❑ 1229 [R] Reflections 1964 12.00
❑ 5200 [M] Golden Hits 1962 20.00
❑ 5204 [M] Encores 1962 20.00
❑ 5217 [M] In Memoriam 1963 20.00
❑ 5223 [M] Legend 1963 20.00
❑ 5229 [M] Reflections 1964 20.00
❑ ST-90070 [R] Golden Hits 1962 15.00
—Capitol Record Club edition

HILLTOP

❑ 6001 [M] Today, Tomorrow, Forever 1965 12.00
❑ S-6001 [R] Today, Tomorrow, Forever 1965 10.00
❑ 6016 [M] I Can't Forget You 1966 12.00
❑ S-6016 [R] I Can't Forget You 1966 10.00
❑ S-6039 Stop the World 1968 10.00
❑ JS-6072 In Care of the Blues 1969 10.00
❑ 6148 Country Music Hall of Fame 197? 10.00

MCA

❑ 12 Patsy Cline's Greatest Hits 1973 12.00
—Reissue of Decca 74854; black label with rainbow
❑ 12 Patsy Cline's Greatest Hits 1977 10.00
—Tan label
❑ 12 Patsy Cline's Greatest Hits 1980 8.00
—Blue label with rainbow
❑ 87 Patsy Cline Showcase 1973 12.00
—Reissue of Decca 74202; black label with rainbow
❑ 90 Sentimentally Yours 1973 12.00
—Reissue of Decca 74282; black label with rainbow
❑ 224 A Portrait of Patsy Cline 1973 12.00
—Reissue of Decca 74508; black label with rainbow
❑ 736 The Great Patsy Cline 198? 10.00
—Reissue of Vocalion 73872
❑ 738 Here's Patsy Cline 198? 10.00
—Reissue of Vocalion 73753
❑ 1440 Stop, Look and Listen 198? 8.00
❑ 1463 Today, Tomorrow and Forever 198? 8.00
❑ 3263 Always 1980 15.00
❑ 4038 [(2)] The Patsy Cline Story 1974 15.00
—Reissue of Decca 7176; black labels with rainbow
❑ 6149 Sweet Dreams — The Life and Times of Patsy Cline 1985 10.00
❑ 27069 Always 198? 8.00
❑ 42142 Live at the Opry 1988 10.00
❑ 42284 Live Vol. 2 1989 12.00

METRO

❑ M-540 [M] Gotta Lot of Rhythm in My Soul 1965 12.00
❑ MS-540 [R] Gotta Lot of Rhythm in My Soul 1965 10.00

RHINO

❑ R1-70048 Her First Recordings, Vol. 1: Walkin' Dreams 1989 12.00
❑ R1-70049 Her First Recordings, Vol. 2: Hungry for Love 1989 12.00
❑ R1-70050 Her First Recordings, Vol. 3: The Rockin' Side 1989 12.00

SEARS

❑ SP-102 [M] Walkin' After Midnight 196? 30.00
❑ SPS-102 [R] Walkin' After Midnight 196? 20.00
❑ SPS-112 I Can't Forget You 1968 25.00
❑ SPS-127 In Care of the Blues 1968 25.00

VOCALION

❑ VL 3753 [M] Here's Patsy Cline 1965 12.00
❑ VL 73753 [R] Here's Patsy Cline 1965 10.00
❑ VL 73872 Country Great! 1969 10.00

CLINTON, GEORGE

Also see FUNKADELIC; PARLIAMENT; THE PARLIAMENTS.

12-Inch Singles

CAPITOL

❑ V-8538 Loopzilla (5:58) (8:48) 1982 15.00
❑ V-8544 Atomic Dog (Album Version) (Single Version) 1982 25.00
❑ V-8572 Nubian Nut (LP Version 5:59)/Free Alterations 1983 10.00
❑ V-8580 Quickie/Last Dance 1984 12.00
❑ V-8581 Last Dance/Get Dressed 1984 10.00
❑ V-8603 Atomic Dog (Atomic Mix Long Version) (Instrumental) 1984 15.00
❑ V-8642 Double Oh-Oh (For Your Ears Only Mashed Mix) (LP Version) (Mixing Parts) 1985 10.00
❑ V-8653 Bullet Proof (Extended)/Silly Millameter 1985 12.00
❑ SPRO-9038/9 [DJ] Nubian Nut (LP Version) (Single Version) 1983 10.00
❑ SPRO-9065/70 [DJ] Last Dance (LP Version) (Single Version) 1984 12.00
❑ SPRO-9136 [DJ] Quickie (same on both sides?) 1984 15.00
❑ SPRO-9628 [DJ] Do Fries Go with That Shake (Thick Mix) (same on both sides) 1986 15.00
❑ SPRO-9728/9 [DJ] Hey Good Lookin' (Rush This Mix 7:52) (Mirror Mix 4:33) (Marvelous Mix 5:35) 1986 10.00
❑ SPRO-9825/6 [DJ] Loopzilla (Single Mix 4:13) (Broadcast Version 6:36) 1982 30.00
❑ V-15219 Do Fries Go with That Shake (10:15)/Scratch Medley: Do Fries Go with That Shake-Pleasures of Exhaustion (12:36) 1986 12.00
❑ V-15241 Hey Good Lookin' (Rush This Mix) (Mirror Mix) (Marvelous Mix) 1986 12.00
❑ V-15263 R&B Skeletons (In the Closet)/Nubian Nut 1986 10.00
❑ V-15562 Atomic Dog (Special Atomic Mix) (LP Version) (Instrumental) 1990 10.00
❑ 53576 Atomic Dog (2 versions)/Knee Deep/Hey Good Lookin'/Do Fries Go with That Shake 2000 8.00
—Red vinyl
❑ SPRO-79901 [DJ] Atomic Dog (Special Atomic Mix) (same on both sides) 1990 12.00

550 MUSIC

❑ BAS 7697 [DJ] If Anybody Gets Funked Up (It's Gonna Be You) (4 versions) 1996 15.00
❑ BAS 7906 [DJ] If Anybody Gets Funked Up (It's Gonna Be You) (6 versions) 1996 10.00
❑ BAS 8309 [DJ] Summer Swim (LP Version) (Edit Version) (Instrumental) (Acappella) 1996 15.00
❑ 46-78391 Summer Swim (6 versions) 1996 10.00

FOX

❑ 10013 Erotic City (Extended Sweat Mix) (Groovestramental)/Stomp (LP Version) (Sir Nose Goes On) 1994 12.00

INTERSOUND

❑ 9284 Ain't Nuthin' But a Jam Y'All (4:02) (Instrumental) 1997 12.00
—With the Dazz Band

PAISLEY PARK

❑ PRO-A-3717 [DJ] Tweakin' (Edit) (LP Version) 1989 8.00
❑ PRO-A-5995 [DJ] Martial Law (Hey Man... Smell My Finger) (Single Version 4:14) (LP Version 7:13) 1993 10.00
❑ PRO-A-5998 [(2)DJ] Martial Law (Hey Man... Smell My Finger) (Scratch & Sniff Mix 7:37) (Where's Your Finger Been Mix 7:28) (Smell My Finger Mix 9:05) (Stank Finger Mix) (2 Phunky Finger Mix) (Middle Finger Instrumental Mix) (Somethin' Stinks and I Want Some Bonus Beats Mix) (Single Version Edit) 1993 15.00
—One record is red vinyl, the other is green
❑ 21157 Why Should I Dog U Out? (4 versions) 1989 10.00
❑ 21337 Tweakin' (A-Mix) (Dub Mix) (C-Mixapella) (Radio Remix) (Hysterical Remix) 1989 10.00
❑ 41057 Paint the White House Black (3 versions)/Picture This/Booty 1993 10.00

45s

ABC

❑ 12040 Hold On to Your Lady/Nothing in This Whole World 1974 7.00

CAPITOL

❑ B-5160 Loopzilla/Pot Sharing Tots 1982 4.00
❑ B-5201 Atomic Dog/(Instrumental) 1983 4.00
❑ B-5201 [PS] Atomic Dog/(Instrumental) 1983 6.00
❑ B-5222 Get Dressed/Free Alterations 1983 4.00
❑ B-5222 [PS] Get Dressed/Free Alterations 1983 4.00
❑ B-5296 Nubian Nut/Free Alterations 1983 4.00
❑ B-5296 [PS] Nubian Nut/Free Alterations 1983 4.00
❑ B-5324 Quickie/Last Dance 1984 4.00
❑ B-5324 [PS] Quickie/Last Dance 1984 4.00
❑ B-5332 Last Dance/Get Dressed 1984 4.00
❑ B-5332 [PS] Last Dance/Get Dressed 1984 4.00
❑ B-5473 Double Oh-Oh/Bangladesh 1985 4.00
❑ B-5473 [PS] Double Oh-Oh/Bangladesh 1985 4.00
❑ B-5504 Bullet Proof/Silly Millimeter 1985 4.00
❑ B-5558 Do Fries Go With That Shake/Pleasure of Exhaustion (Do It Till I Drop) 1986 4.00
❑ B-5602 Hey Good Lookin' (Remix)/Hey Good Lookin' (Mirror Mix) 1986 4.00
❑ B-5642 R&B Skeletons (In the Closet)/Nubian Nut 1986 4.00

FOX

❑ 10012 Stomp/Pump It Up 1994 5.00
—B-side by Mudhoney
❑ 10012 [PS] Stomp/Pump It Up 1994 5.00

PAISLEY PARK

❑ PRO-S-3438 [DJ] Why Should I Dog U Out? (same on both sides?) 1989 6.00
❑ 22790 Tweakin'/French Kiss 1989 4.00
❑ 27557 Why Should I Dog U Out?/(Instrumental) 1989 3.00
❑ 27557 [PS] Why Should I Dog U Out?/(Instrumental) 1989 3.00

Albums

ABC

❑ D-831 The George Clinton Band Arrives 1974 15.00

CAPITOL

❑ ST-12246 Computer Games 1982 10.00
❑ ST-12308 You Shouldn't-Nuf Bit Fish 1984 10.00
❑ ST-12417 Some of My Best Jokes Are Friends 1985 10.00
❑ ST-12481 R&B Skeletons in the Closet 1986 10.00
❑ MLP-15021 [EP] The Mothership Connection Live from Houston, Texas 1986 15.00
❑ C1-33911 [(2)] Greatest Funkin' Hits 1996 12.00
—Red vinyl

Except when noted otherwise, VG = 25% of NM, and VG+ = 50% of NM. (Example: VG = $2.00, VG+ = $4.00 and NM = $8.00.)

Number	Title (A Side/B Side)	Yr	NM
❑ CJ-48424	The Best of George Clinton	1987	10.00
550 MUSIC			
❑ B2 67144 [(2)]	T.A.P.O.A.F.O.M. — The Awesome Power of a Fully Operational Mothership	1996	15.00
—Red vinyl			
INVICTUS			
❑ ST-9815	Black Vampire	1973	20.00
PAISLEY PARK			
❑ PRO-A-6537 [(2)DJ]	Hey Man... Smell My Finger	1993	25.00
—Promo-only vinyl issue			
❑ 25994	The Cinderella Theory	1989	12.00
WARNER BROS.			
❑ 25887	George Clinton Presents Our Gang Funky	1988	10.00
❑ 25991	Under a Nouveau Groove	1989	10.00

CLINTONIAN CUBS, THE JIMMY CASTOR was a member.

45s

Number	Title (A Side/B Side)	Yr	NM
MY BROTHERS			
❑ 508	She's Just My Size/Confusion	1960	300.00

CLIQUE, THE (1) Texas band.

45s

Number	Title (A Side/B Side)	Yr	NM
CINEMA			
❑ 001	Stay By Me/Splash One	1967	30.00
SCEPTER			
❑ 12202	Stay By Me/Splash One	1967	20.00
❑ 12212	Gotta Get Away/Love Ain't Easy	1967	20.00
WHITE WHALE			
❑ 312	Superman/Shadow of Your Love	1969	12.00
❑ 323	Sugar on Sunday/Superman	1969	15.00
❑ 333	Soul Mate/I'll Hold Out My Hand	1969	10.00
❑ 338	I'm Alive/Sparkle and Shine	1970	10.00
❑ 361	Memphis/Southbound Wind	1970	10.00
❑ 367 [DJ]	Judy, Judy, Judy (same on both sides)	1970	12.00
—May be promo only			

Albums

Number	Title (A Side/B Side)	Yr	NM
WHITE WHALE			
❑ WWS-7126	The Clique	1969	20.00

CLIQUE, THE (2) British band.

45s

Number	Title (A Side/B Side)	Yr	NM
ABC-PARAMOUNT			
❑ 10655	She Ain't No Good/Time, Time, Time	1965	10.00

CLIQUE, THE (U) This could be an early record by group (1) or a later record by group (2).

45s

Number	Title (A Side/B Side)	Yr	NM
LAURIE			
❑ 3365	Sun Come Up/Drifter's Melody	1966	10.00

CLIQUES, THE Also see JESSE BELVIN; EUGENE CHURCH.

45s

Number	Title (A Side/B Side)	Yr	NM
MODERN			
❑ 987	Girl in My Dreams/I Wanna Know Why	1956	30.00
—Black label			
❑ 987	Girl in My Dreams/I Wanna Know Why	1956	50.00
—Blue label			
❑ 995	My Desire/I'm in Love with a Gal	1956	30.00

CLOUD, CHRISTOPHER See TOMMY BOYCE.

CLOVER, TIMOTHY

Albums

Number	Title (A Side/B Side)	Yr	NM
TOWER			
❑ ST 5114	A Harvard Square Affair	1968	20.00

CLOVERS, THE

45s

Number	Title (A Side/B Side)	Yr	NM
ATLANTIC			
❑ 934	Don't You Know I Love You/Skylark	1951	1000.
❑ 944	Fool, Fool, Fool/Needless	1951	250.00
❑ 963	One Mint Julep/Middle of the Night	1952	100.00
—Yellow label, no "fan" logo			
❑ 963	One Mint Julep/Middle of the Night	1961	25.00
—Red label, no "fan" logo			
❑ 969	Ting-A-Ling/Wonder Where My Baby's Gone	1952	100.00
❑ 977	I Played the Fool/Hey, Miss Fannie	1952	250.00
❑ 989	Yes, It's You/Crawlin'	1953	60.00
❑ 1000	Good Lovin'/Here Goes a Fool	1953	80.00
❑ 1010	Comin' On/The Feeling Is So Good	1953	150.00
❑ 1022	Lovey Dovey/Little Mama	1954	50.00
❑ 1035	Your Cash Ain't Nothin' But Trash/I've Got My Eyes on You	1954	50.00
❑ 1046	I Confess/Alrighty, Oh Sweetie	1954	50.00
❑ 1052	Blue Velvet/If You Love Me (Why Don't You Tell Me So)	1955	60.00
❑ 1060	Love Bug/In the Morning Time	1955	50.00
❑ 1073	Nip Sip/If I Could Be Loved By You	1955	50.00
❑ 1083	Devil or Angel/Hey, Doll Baby	1956	40.00
—Red label, no "fan" logo			
❑ 1083	Devil or Angel/Hey, Doll Baby	1956	200.00
—Yellow label, no "fan" logo			
❑ 1083	Devil or Angel/Hey, Doll Baby	1956	4000.
—Red label, no "fan" logo; red vinyl; value is conjecture. VG 2000; VG+ 3000			
❑ 1094	Love, Love, Love/Your Tender Lips	1956	40.00
❑ 1107	From the Bottom of My Heart/Bring Me Love	1956	30.00
❑ 1118	A Lonely Fool/Baby, Baby, Oh My Darling	1956	30.00
❑ 1129	Here Comes Romance/You Good-Looking Woman	1957	30.00
❑ 1139	I-I-I Love You/So Young	1957	30.00
❑ 1152	There's No Tomorrow/Down in the Alley	1957	30.00
❑ 1175	Wishing for Your Love/All About You	1958	30.00
❑ 2129	Drive It Home/The Bootie Green	1961	20.00
BRUNSWICK			
❑ 55249	Love! Love! Love!/The Kickapoo	1963	12.00
JOSIE			
❑ 992	For Days/Too Long Without Some Loving	1968	10.00
❑ 997	Try My Lovin' On You/Sweet Side of a Soulful Woman	1968	10.00
LANA			
❑ 113	Love Potion No. 9/Hey Little Girl	196?	8.00
—B-side by the Deltones			
❑ 114	Devil or Angel/Since I Met You	196?	8.00
—B-side by the Deltones			
POPLAR			
❑ 110	The Gossip Wheel/Please Come On to Me	1958	25.00
❑ 111	The Good Old Summertime/Idaho	1958	25.00
PORT			
❑ 3004	Poor Baby/He Sure Could Hypnotize	1965	10.00
PORWIN			
❑ 1001/2	Stop Pretending/One More Time	1963	15.00
—As "Buddy Baliey and the Clovers"			
❑ 1004	It's All in the Game/That's What I Will Be	1963	15.00
—As "Buddy Baliey and the Clovers"			
STENTON			
❑ 7001	Please Mr. Sun/Gimme, Gimme, Gimme	1961	80.00
—As "Tippie and the Clovermen"			
TIGER			
❑ 201	Bossa Nova Baby/The Bossa Nova (My Heart Said)	1962	15.00
—As "Tippie and the Clovers"			
UNITED ARTISTS			
❑ 0133	Love Potion #9/Stay Awhile	1973	4.00
—"Silver Spotlight Series" reissue			
❑ 174	Rock and Roll Tango/That Old Black Magic	1959	25.00
❑ 180	Love Potion #9/Stay Awhile	1959	25.00
❑ 209	One Mint Julep/Lovey	1960	25.00
❑ 227	Easy Lovin'/I'm Confessin' That I Love You	1960	25.00
❑ 263	Yes It's You/Burning Fire	1960	25.00
❑ 307	The Honeydripper/Have Gun	1961	25.00
WINLEY			
❑ 255	Let Me Hold You/Wrapped Up in a Dream	1961	15.00
❑ 265	I Need You Now/Gotta Quit You	1962	15.00
❑ 265	They're Rockin' Down the Street/Be My Baby	1962	15.00
—As "The Fabulous Clovers"			

7-Inch Extended Plays

Number	Title (A Side/B Side)	Yr	NM
ATLANTIC			
❑ 504	One Mint Julep/Fool, Fool, Fool//Hey, Miss Fannie/I Played the Fool	1953	200.00
❑ 504 [PS]	The Clovers Sing	1953	200.00
❑ 537	(contents unknown)	1954	150.00
❑ 537 [PS]	The Clovers Sing	1954	200.00
❑ 590	*Love, Love, Love/Devil or Angel/Blue Velvet/From the Bottom of My Heart	1955	150.00
❑ 590 [PS]	The Clovers	1955	200.00

Albums

Number	Title (A Side/B Side)	Yr	NM
ATCO			
❑ SD 33-374	Their Greatest Recordings/The Early Years	1971	12.00
ATLANTIC			
❑ 1248 [M]	The Clovers	1956	600.00
❑ 8009 [M]	The Clovers	1957	400.00
—Reissue of 1248 on the "pop" series; black label			
❑ 8009 [M]	The Clovers	1960	300.00
—White "bullseye" label			
❑ 8009 [M]	The Clovers	1961	200.00
—Red and white label			
❑ 8034 [M]	Dance Party	1959	400.00
—Black label			
❑ 8034 [M]	Dance Party	1960	300.00
—White "bullseye" label			
❑ 8034 [M]	Dance Party	1961	200.00
—Red and white label			
GRAND PRIX			
❑ K-428 [M]	The Original Love Potion Number Nine	1964	30.00
❑ KS-428 [R]	The Original Love Potion Number Nine	1964	12.00
POPLAR			
❑ 1001 [M]	The Clovers In Clover	1958	400.00
UNITED ARTISTS			
❑ UAL-3033 [M]	The Clovers In Clover	1959	300.00
❑ UAL-3099 [M]	Love Potion Number Nine	1959	250.00
❑ UAS-6033 [R]	The Clovers In Clover	196?	200.00
❑ UAS-6099 [S]	Love Potion Number Nine	1959	500.00

CLOWNEY, DAVID See DAVE "BABY" CORTEZ.

CLUSTERS, THE

45s

Number	Title (A Side/B Side)	Yr	NM
END			
❑ 1115	Pardon My Heart/Darling Can't You Tell	1962	40.00
EPIC			
❑ 9330	Forecast of Our Love/Long Legged Maggie	1959	80.00
TEE GEE			
❑ 102	Pardon My Heart/Darling Can't You Tell	1958	120.00
—With Gone distribution mentioned; publishing by Real Gone Music			
❑ 102	Pardon My Heart/Darling Can't You Tell	1958	300.00
—No mention of Gone distribution			
❑ 102	Pardon My Heart/Darling Can't You Tell	1958	300.00
—With Gone distribution mentioned; publishing by Emkay Music			

COASTERS, THE Also see THE ROBINS.

45s

Number	Title (A Side/B Side)	Yr	NM
AMERICAN INT'L.			
❑ 1122	If I Had a Hammer/If I Had a Hammer (Disco Version)	1976	5.00
—As "The World Famous Coasters"			
ATCO			
❑ 6064	Down in Mexico/Turtle Dovin'	1956	80.00
❑ 6073	One Kiss Led to Another/Brazil	1956	60.00
❑ 6087	Searchin'/Young Blood	1957	25.00
—White and yellow label			
❑ 6087	Searchin'/Young Blood	1957	70.00
—Maroon label (first pressing)			
❑ 6098	Idol with the Golden Head/(When She Wants Good Lovin') My Baby Comes to Me	1957	40.00
❑ 6104	Sweet Georgia Brown/What Is the Secret of Your Success	1957	40.00
❑ 6111	Dance!/Gee, Golly	1958	40.00
❑ 6116	Yakety Yak/Zing Went the Strings of My Heart	1958	25.00
❑ 6126	The Shadow Knows/Sorry But I'm Gonna Have to Pass	1958	25.00
❑ 6132 [M]	Charlie Brown/Three Cool Cats	1959	25.00
❑ SD-45-6132 [S]	Charlie Brown/Three Cool Cats	1959	60.00
—Blue label, silver print, "Stereo" under the "O" of "Atco"			
❑ 6141	Along Came Jones/That Is Rock and Roll	1959	20.00
❑ 6146	Poison Ivy/I'm a Hog for You	1959	20.00
❑ 6153	Run Red Run/What About Us	1959	20.00
❑ 6163	Besame Mucho (Part 1)/Besame Mucho (Part 2)	1960	25.00
❑ 6168	Wake Me, Shake Me/Stewball	1960	25.00
❑ 6178	Shoppin' for Clothes/The Snake and the Book Worm	1960	25.00
❑ 6186	Thumbin' a Ride/Wait a Minute	1961	20.00
❑ 6192	Little Egypt (Ying-Yang)/Keep On Rolling	1961	20.00

Except when noted otherwise, VG = 25% of NM, and VG+ = 50% of NM. (Example: VG = $2.00, VG+ = $4.00 and NM = $8.00.)

Number	Title (A Side/B Side)	Yr	NM
❑ 6204	Girls, Girls, Girls (Part 1)/Girls, Girls, Girls (Part 2)	1961	20.00
❑ 6210	Bad Blood/(Ain't That) Just Like Me	1961	20.00
❑ 6219	Teach Me How to Shimmy/Ridin' Hood	1962	20.00
❑ 6234	The Climb/(Instrumental)	1962	20.00
❑ 6251	The P.T.A./Bull Tick Waltz	1962	20.00
❑ 6287	Speedo's Back in Town/T'Ain't Nothin' to Me	1964	15.00
❑ 6300	Lovey Dovey/Bad Detective	1964	15.00
❑ 6321	Wild One/I Must Be Dreaming	1964	15.00
❑ 6341	Hungry/Lady Like	1965	15.00
❑ 6356	Money Honey/Let's Go Get Stoned	1965	15.00
❑ 6379	Bell Bottom Slacks and a Chinese Kimono (She's My Little Spodee-O)/Crazy Baby	1965	25.00
❑ 6407	Saturday Night Fish Fry/She's a Yum Yum	1966	15.00
ATLANTIC			
❑ 89361	Yakety Yak/Stand By Me	1986	3.00
❑ 89361 [PS]	Yakety Yak/Stand By Me	1986	3.00
—B-side by Ben E. King. See listing of this record under "King, Ben E." for more information.			
CHELAN			
❑ 2000	Searchin' '75/Young BLood	1975	5.00
—As "The Coasters 2+2"			
DATE			
❑ 1552	Soul Pad/Down Home Girl	1967	20.00
❑ 1607	Everybody's Woman/She Can	1968	20.00
❑ 1617	D.W. Washburn/Everybody's Woman	1968	20.00
KING			
❑ 6385	Love Potion #9/D.W. Washburn	1972	6.00
❑ 6389	Cool Jerk/Talkin' 'Bout a Woman	1972	6.00
❑ 6404	Soul Pad/D.W. Washburn	1972	6.00
SAL WA			
❑ 1001	Take It Easy, Greasy/You Move Me	1975	5.00
TURNTABLE			
❑ 504	Act Right/The World Is Changing	1969	10.00
7-Inch Extended Plays			
ATCO			
❑ 4501	Searchin'/Young Blood//(When She Wants Good Lovin') My Baby Comes to Me/Idol with the Golden Head	1958	150.00
❑ 4501 [PS]	Rock and Roll with the Coasters	1958	200.00
❑ 4503	Yakety Yak/Framed//Loop De Loop Mambo/Riot in Cell Block Number Nine	1959	200.00
❑ 4503 [PS]	Keep Rockin' with the Coasters	1959	200.00
❑ 4506	Charlie Brown/Three Cool Cats/The Shadow Knows/Sorry But I'm Gonna Have to Pass	1959	150.00
❑ 4506 [PS]	The Coasters	1959	150.00
❑ 4507	Along Came Jones/That Is Rock & Roll//Dance!/Gee, Golly	1959	150.00
❑ 4507 [PS]	The Coasters' Top Hits	1959	150.00
Albums			
ATCO			
❑ 33-101 [M]	The Coasters	1958	300.00
—Yellow "harp" label			
❑ 33-101 [M]	The Coasters	196?	60.00
—Gold and dark blue label			
❑ 33-111 [M]	The Coasters' Greatest Hits	1959	150.00
—Yellow "harp" label			
❑ 33-111 [M]	The Coasters' Greatest Hits	196?	60.00
—Gold and gray label			
❑ 33-123 [M]	One By One	196?	60.00
—Gold and gray label			
❑ 33-123 [M]	One By One	1960	150.00
—Yellow "harp" label			
❑ SD 33-123 [S]	One By One	196?	150.00
—Purple and brown label			
❑ SD 33-123 [S]	One By One	1960	400.00
—Yellow "harp" label			
❑ 33-135 [M]	Coast Along with the Coasters	1962	100.00
—Gold and gray label			
❑ SD 33-135 [P]	Coast Along with the Coasters	1962	150.00
—Purple and brown label; "Wait a Minute" is rechanneled			
❑ SD 33-371	Their Greatest Recordings/The Early Years	1971	20.00
CLARION			
❑ 605 [M]	That Is Rock and Roll	1965	40.00
❑ SD 605 [S]	That Is Rock and Roll	1965	50.00
KING			
❑ KS-1146	The Coasters On Broadway	1971	25.00
POWER PAK			
❑ 310	Greatest Hits	198?	10.00
TRIP			
❑ 8028	It Ain't Sanitary	197?	12.00

COBHAM, BILLY

Number	Title (A Side/B Side)	Yr	NM
45s			
ATLANTIC			
❑ 2998	Stratus (Part 1)/Stratus (Part 2)	1973	4.00
❑ 3014	Crosswinds/Le Lis	1974	4.00
❑ 3250	Bandit/Moon Germs	1975	4.00
COLUMBIA			
❑ 10858	Bolinas/Indigo	1978	4.00
❑ 11076	What Is Your Fantasy/Dana	1979	4.00
❑ 11142	Bring Up the House Lights/What Is Your Fantasy	1979	4.00
Albums			
ATLANTIC			
❑ SD 7268	Spectrum	1973	15.00
—Original pressings have "1841 Broadway" address on label			
❑ SD 7300	Crosswinds	1974	15.00
—Original pressings have "1841 Broadway" address on label			
❑ SD 18121	Total Eclipse	1974	15.00
❑ SD 18139	Shabazz (Recorded Live in Europe)	1975	15.00
❑ SD 18149	A Funky Thide of Sings	1975	12.00
❑ SD 18166	Life & Times	1976	12.00
❑ SD 19174	Inner Conflicts	1978	12.00
❑ SD 19238	The Best of Billy Cobham	1979	12.00
COLUMBIA			
❑ JC 34939	Magic	1977	12.00
❑ JC 35457	Simplicity of Expression — Depth of Thought	1978	12.00
❑ JC 35993	B.C.	1979	12.00
❑ JC 36400	The Best of Billy Cobham	1980	12.00
ELEKTRA/MUSICIAN			
❑ 60123	Observations &	1982	15.00
❑ 60233	Smokin'	1983	15.00
GRP			
❑ GR-1020	Warning	1986	12.00
❑ GR-1027	Power Play	1986	10.00
❑ GR-1040	Picture This	1987	10.00
❑ GR-9575	Billy's Best Hits	1988	10.00

COBHAM, BILLY, AND GEORGE DUKE

Number	Title (A Side/B Side)	Yr	NM
Albums			
ATLANTIC			
❑ SD 18194	Live On Tour in Europe	1976	10.00

COBRAS, THE (1)

Stevie Ray Vaughan was a member of this Cobras.

Number	Title (A Side/B Side)	Yr	NM
45s			
ARMADILLO			
❑ 79-1	Blow Joe Blow (Crazy 'Bout a Saxophone)/Sugaree	1980	100.00

COBRAS, THE (2)

Number	Title (A Side/B Side)	Yr	NM
45s			
CASINO			
❑ 1309	La La/Goodbye Molly	1963	80.00
LOST-NITE			
❑ 230	La La/Goodbye Molly	196?	5.00
—Reissue			
SWAN			
❑ 4176	La La/Goodbye Molly	1964	25.00

COBRAS, THE (3)

Number	Title (A Side/B Side)	Yr	NM
45s			
MODERN			
❑ 964	Cindy/I Will Return	1955	150.00
—Revised spelling of A-side			
❑ 964	Sindy/I Will Return	1955	300.00
—Original spelling of A-side			

COBRAS, THE (U)

These may be by group (2), but we're not sure.

Number	Title (A Side/B Side)	Yr	NM
45s			
MONOGRAM			
❑ 519	Thumpin'/Don't Even Know Your Name	1964	12.00
STAX			
❑ 148	Shake Up/Restless	1964	15.00

COCHRAN, EDDIE

Also see COCHRAN BROTHERS; JEWEL AND EDDIE.

Number	Title (A Side/B Side)	Yr	NM
45s			
CREST			
❑ 1026	Skinny Jim/Half Loved	1956	300.00
LIBERTY			
❑ 55056	Sittin' in the Balcony/Dark Lonely Street	1957	30.00
❑ 55070	Mean When I'm Mad/One Kiss	1957	30.00
❑ 55070 [PS]	Mean When I'm Mad/One Kiss	1957	1500.
❑ 55087	Drive In Show/Am I Blue	1957	30.00
❑ 55112	Twenty Flight Rock/Cradle Baby	1957	150.00
❑ 55123	Jeannie, Jeannie, Jeannie/Pocketful of Hearts	1958	30.00
❑ 55138	Pretty Girl/Theresa	1958	35.00
❑ 55144	Summertime Blues/Live Again	1958	30.00
❑ 55166	C'mon Everybody/Don't Ever Let Me Go	1958	30.00
❑ 55177	Teen Age Heaven/I Remember	1959	30.00
❑ 55177	Teenage Heaven/I Remember	1959	40.00
—Note difference in title			
❑ 55203	The Boll Weevil Song/Somethin' Else	1959	30.00
❑ 55217	Hallelujah I Love Her So/Little Angel	1959	30.00
❑ 55242	Three Steps to Heaven/Cut Across Shorty	1960	40.00
❑ 55278	Lonely/Sweetie Pie	1960	25.00
❑ 55389	Weekend/Lonely	1961	30.00
UNITED ARTISTS			
❑ 0014	Summertime Blues/Cut Across Shorty	1973	4.00
❑ 0015	C'mon Everybody/Twenty Flight Rock	1973	4.00
❑ 0016	Sittin' in the Balcony/Somethin' Else	1973	4.00
—0014, 0015, 0016 are "Silver Spotlight Series" reissues			
7-Inch Extended Plays			
LIBERTY			
❑ LEP 1-3061	Sittin' in the Balcony/Proud of You//Stockings and Shoes/Have I Told You Lately That I Love You	1958	200.00
❑ LEP 1-3061 [PS]	Singin' to My Baby (Part One)	1958	200.00
❑ LEP 2-3061	(contents unknown)	1958	200.00
❑ LEP 2-3061 [PS]	Singin' to My Baby (Part Two)	1958	200.00
❑ LEP 3-3061	(contents unknown)	1958	200.00
❑ LEP 3-3061 [PS]	Singin' to My Baby (Part Three)	1958	200.00
Albums			
EMI AMERICA			
❑ SQ 17245	On the Air	1987	15.00
LIBERTY			
❑ LRP-3061 [M]	Singin' to My Baby	1957	800.00
—Green label			
❑ LRP-3061 [M]	Singin' to My Baby	1960	300.00
—Black label			
❑ LRP-3172 [M]	Eddie Cochran (12 of His Biggest Hits)	1960	120.00
❑ LRP-3220 [M]	Never to Be Forgotten	1962	100.00
❑ LN-10137	Singin' to My Baby	198?	12.00
—Budget-line reissue			
❑ LN-10204	Great Hits	198?	8.00
SUNSET			
❑ SUM-1123 [M]	Summertime Blues	1966	40.00
❑ SUS-5123 [R]	Summertime Blues	1966	25.00
UNITED ARTISTS			
❑ UA-LA428-E	The Very Best of Eddie Cochran	1975	12.00
❑ UAS-9959 [(2)]	Legendary Masters Series #4	1972	25.00

COCHRAN, HANK

Also see COCHRAN BROTHERS.

Number	Title (A Side/B Side)	Yr	NM
45s			
CAPITOL			
❑ 4585	Willie/Uphill All the Way	1978	4.00
—A-side with Merle Haggard			
❑ 4635	Ain't Life Hell/I'm Going With You This Time	1978	5.00
—With Willie Nelson			
DOT			
❑ 17361	One Night for Willie/Back to His	1970	6.00
ELEKTRA			
❑ 46596	Make the World Go Away/I Don't Do Windows	1980	4.00
❑ 47062	A Little Bitty Tear/He's Got You	1980	4.00
GAYLORD			
❑ 6426	Yesterday's Memories/When You Gotta Go (You Gotta Go)	1963	12.00
❑ 6431	A Good Country Song/Same Old Hurt	1963	12.00
❑ 6432	Just for the Record/If She Could See Me Now	1963	12.00
LIBERTY			
❑ 55402	Lonely Little Mansion/Has Anybody Seen Me Lately	1962	12.00
❑ 55461	Sally Was a Good Old Girl/The Picture Behind the Picture	1962	12.00
❑ 55498	I'd Fight the World/Lucy, Let Your Lovelight Shine	1962	12.00
❑ 55520	I Remember/Private John Q	1963	10.00
❑ 55644	Tootsie's Orchid Lounge/Go On Home	1963	10.00

Number	Title (A Side/B Side)	Yr	NM
MONUMENT			
❑ 994	All of Me Belongs to You/ I Just Burned a Dream	1967	6.00
❑ 1012	It Couldn't Happen to a Nicer Guy/Tootsie's Orchid Lounge	1967	6.00
❑ 1033	A Happy Goodbye/Speak Well of Me to the Kids	1967	6.00
❑ 1051	Has Anybody Seen Me Lately/ I Woke Up	1968	6.00
RCA VICTOR			
❑ 47-8329	My Baby's His Baby Now/ What Kind of Bird Is That	1964	10.00
❑ 47-8457	I Want to Go with You/Sad Songs and Waltzes	1964	10.00
❑ 47-8528	Somewhere in My Dreams/ Going in Training	1965	10.00
❑ 47-8616	Who's Gonna/Let's Be Different	1965	10.00
❑ 47-8694	Hank Today and Him Tomorrow/I'm Alone	1965	10.00
❑ 47-8827	The Crying Section/Only You Can Make Me Well	1966	8.00
❑ 47-8955	That's What I'll Say/I Lie a Lot	1966	8.00
Albums			
CAPITOL			
❑ ST-11807	With a Little Help from His Friends	1978	12.00
ELEKTRA			
❑ 6E-277	Make the World Go Away	1980	10.00
MONUMENT			
❑ SLP-18089	The Heart of Hank	1968	20.00
RCA VICTOR			
❑ LPM-3303 [M]	Hits from the Heart	1965	20.00
❑ LSP-3303 [S]	Hits from the Heart	1965	25.00
❑ LPM-3431 [M]	Going in Training	1965	20.00
❑ LSP-3431 [S]	Going in Training	1965	25.00

COCHRAN, JACKIE LEE

Number	Title (A Side/B Side)	Yr	NM
45s			
ABC-PARAMOUNT			
❑ 9930	Buy a Car/I Want You	1958	80.00
DECCA			
❑ 30206	Ruby Pearl/Mama Don't You Think I Know	1957	120.00
JAGUAR			
❑ 3031	Georgia Lee Brown/ I Wanna See You	1959	120.00
SIMS			
❑ 107	Hip Shakin' Mama/ Riverside Jump	1956	200.00
SPRY			
❑ 120	Pity Me/Endless Love	1959	250.00
VIV			
❑ 988	I Want You/Buy a Car	1958	150.00

COCHRAN, WAYNE

Number	Title (A Side/B Side)	Yr	NM
45s			
BETHLEHEM			
❑ 3097	Hey Jude/Eleanor Rigby	1970	6.00
CHESS			
❑ 2020	When My Baby Cries/ Some-a Your Sweet Lovin'	1967	8.00
❑ 2029	Get Ready/Hootchie Cootchie Man	1967	8.00
❑ 2054	You Can't Judge a Book By Its Cover/Up in My Mind	1968	8.00
EPIC			
❑ 10859	Do You Like the Sound of Music/Everybody's Been Cuttin' In on My Groove	1972	5.00
❑ 10893	Long, Long Day/Sleepless Nights	1972	5.00
KING			
❑ 5832	Little Orphan Annie/ Monkey, Monkey	1963	12.00
❑ 5856	Last Kiss/I Dreamed, I Gambled, I Lost	1964	12.00
❑ 5874	Cindy Marie/The Coo	1964	12.00
❑ 5950	Mr. Lonely/Wrong Number, Wrong Gal	1964	12.00
❑ 5994	You Left the Water Running/ Think	1965	12.00
❑ 6358	Let Me Come with You (Part 1)/ Let Me Come with You (Part 2)	1971	6.00
MERCURY			
❑ 72507	Harlem Shuffle/ Somebody Please	1965	10.00
❑ 72552	Got Down with It/No Rest for the Wicked	1966	10.00
❑ 72623	Goin' Back to Miami/ I'm in Trouble	1966	10.00
SCOTTIE			
❑ 1303	My Little Girl/The Coo	1959	20.00
Albums			
BETHLEHEM			
❑ 10002	High and Ridin'	1970	15.00
CHESS			
❑ LPS-1519	Wayne Cochran!	1968	40.00
EPIC			
❑ KE 30889	Cochran	1972	15.00
KING			
❑ KS-1116	Alive and Well	1970	20.00

COCHRAN BROTHERS

EDDIE COCHRAN and HANK COCHRAN, who are not brothers.

Number	Title (A Side/B Side)	Yr	NM
45s			
EKKO			
❑ 1003	Mr. Fiddle/Two Blue Singing Stars	1955	250.00
❑ 1005	Guilty Conscience/Your Tomorrow Never Comes	1955	250.00
❑ 3001	Tired and Sleepy/Fool's Paradise	1956	300.00

COCKBURN, BRUCE

Number	Title (A Side/B Side)	Yr	NM
12-Inch Singles			
GOLD MOUNTAIN			
❑ GG-81209 [DJ]	Lovers in a Dangerous Time/ Nicaragua	1984	12.00
❑ GG-81210 [DJ]	Lovers in a Dangerous Time (LP Version) (Live)	1984	12.00
MCA			
❑ L33-17139 [DJ]	Call It Democracy (Edit) (same on both sides)	1986	12.00
❑ L33-17182 [DJ]	See How I Miss You (same on both sides)	1986	10.00
❑ L33-17203 [DJ]	People See Through You (same on both sides)	1986	10.00
MILLENNIUM			
❑ JD-11822 [DJ]	Radio Shoes/(B-side blank)	1981	20.00
—With custom picture cover			
45s			
GOLD MOUNTAIN			
❑ 82009	Lovers in a Dangerous Time/ Sahara Gold	1984	6.00
❑ 82013	If I Had a Rocket Launcher/ Nicaragua	1984	6.00
MILLENNIUM			
❑ YB-11786	Wondering Where the Lions Are/After the Rain	1979	4.00
❑ YB-11795	Rumours of Glory/You Get Bigger As You Go	1980	5.00
❑ YB-11798	Tokyo/Guerrilla Betrayed	1980	6.00
❑ YB-11806	The Coldest Night of the Year/ Lord of the Starfields	1981	6.00
❑ YB-11820	Radio Shoes/(B-side unknown)	1981	6.00
Albums			
EPIC			
❑ E 30812	True North	1971	20.00
❑ KE 31768	Sunwheel Dance	1972	20.00
GOLD CASTLE			
❑ D1-71320	Big Circumstance	1988	8.00
❑ 171005-1 [(2)]	Waiting for a Miracle	1987	12.00
❑ 171008-1	The Trouble with Normal	1987	8.00
—Reissue of Gold Mountain GM-3283			
❑ 171009-1	Dancing in the Dragon's Jaws	1987	8.00
—Reissue of Gold Mountain GM-3276			
❑ 171010-1	Stealing Fire	1987	8.00
—Reissue of Gold Mountain GM-80012			
GOLD MOUNTAIN			
❑ GM-3276	Dancing in the Dragon's Jaws	1985	8.00
—Reissue of Millennium BXL1-7747			
❑ GM-3283	The Trouble with Normal	1985	8.00
❑ GM-80012	Stealing Fire	1984	8.00
ISLAND			
❑ ILTN 9463	In the Falling Dark	1976	12.00
❑ ILTA 9475 [(2)]	Circles in the Stream	1977	15.00
❑ ILSP 9528	Furhter Adventures of	1978	12.00
MCA			
❑ 5772	World of Wonders	1986	8.00
MILLENNIUM			
❑ DJL1-(# unknown) [DJ]	Selected Cuts from 1980 U.S. Tour	1980	50.00
—Promo-only four-song live EP			
❑ DJL1-3583 [DJ]	RCA Special Radio Series	1980	20.00
—Promo-only music and interview			
❑ DJL1-3830 [DJ]	RCA College Radio Series, Vol. II	1980	20.00
—Promo-only music and interview			
❑ BXL1-7747	Dancing in the Dragon's Jaws	1979	10.00
❑ BXL1-7752	Humans	1980	10.00
❑ BXL1-7757	Resume	1981	10.00
❑ BXL1-7761	Inner City Front	1981	10.00

COCKER, JOE

Number	Title (A Side/B Side)	Yr	NM
12-Inch Singles			
CAPITOL			
❑ SPRO-9144/5 [DJ]	Civilized Man/Tempted	1984	8.00
❑ SPRO 9660 [DJ]	You Can Leave Your Hat On (LP Version 4:14) (same on both sides)	1986	8.00
❑ V-15237	You Can Leave Your Hat On (Extended Dressed Mix 6:22) (Acacussion Mix 4:01) (LP Version 4:14)	1986	15.00
❑ SPRO 79246 [DJ]	Two Wrongs (same on both sides)	1988	10.00
45s			
A&M			
❑ 928	Marjorine/New Age of the Lily	1968	10.00
❑ 991	With a Little Help from My Friends/Something's Coming On	1968	10.00
❑ 1063	Feeling Alright/ Sandpaper Cadillac	1969	6.00
—Reissued in 1971 with the same number			
❑ 1112	Delta Lady/She's So Good to Me	1969	5.00
❑ 1147	She Came In Through the Bathroom Window/ Change in Louise	1969	5.00
❑ 1147 [PS]	She Came In Through the Bathroom Window/ Change in Louise	1969	6.00
❑ 1174	The Letter/Space Captain	1970	5.00
❑ 1174 [PS]	The Letter/Space Captain	1970	6.00
❑ 1200	Cry Me a River/Give Peace a Chance	1970	5.00
❑ 1200	Cry Me a River/Please Give Peace a Chance	1970	5.00
❑ 1200 [PS]	Cry Me a River/Give Peace a Chance	1970	6.00
❑ 1258	High Time We Went/ Black-Eyed Blues	1971	4.00
❑ 1258 [PS]	High Time We Went/ Black-Eyed Blues	1971	6.00
❑ 1370	Midnight Rider/Woman to Woman	1972	4.00
❑ 1370 [PS]	Midnight Rider/Woman to Woman	1972	6.00
❑ 1407	Pardon Me Sir/St. James Infirmary Blues	1973	4.00
❑ 1407 [PS]	Pardon Me Sir/St. James Infirmary Blues	1973	6.00
❑ 1539	Put Out the Light/If I Love You	1974	4.00
❑ 1539 [PS]	Put Out the Light/If I Love You	1974	6.00
❑ 1626	I Can Stand a Little Rain/ I Get Mad	1974	4.00
❑ 1641	You Are So Beautiful/It's a Sin When You Love Somebody	1974	4.00
❑ 1749	I Think It's Going to Rain Today/ Oh Mama	1975	4.00
❑ 1758	Jamaica Say You Will/It's All Over But the Shoutin'	1975	4.00
❑ 1805	The Man in Me (Part 1)/ The Man in Me (Part 2)	1976	4.00
❑ 1830	Jealous Kind/You Came Along	1976	4.00
❑ 1855	I Broke Down/You Came Along	1976	4.00
❑ 2019	Feeling Alright/Cry Me a River	1978	4.00
ASYLUM			
❑ 45540	Fun Time/Watching the River Flow	1978	4.00
❑ 46001	Lady Put the Light Out/ Wasted Years	1978	4.00
CAPITOL			
❑ B-5338	Civilized Man/A Girl Like You	1984	3.00
❑ B-5338 [PS]	Civilized Man/A Girl Like You	1984	4.00
❑ B-5390	Crazy in Love/Come On In	1984	3.00
❑ B-5412	Edge of a Dream/Tempted	1984	3.00
❑ B-5412 [PS]	Edge of a Dream/Tempted	1984	4.00
❑ B-5557	Shelter Me/Tell Me There's a Way	1986	3.00
❑ B-5589	You Can Leave Your Hat On/ Long Drag of the Cigarette	1986	5.00
❑ B-5589 [PS]	You Can Leave Your Hat On/ Long Drag of the Cigarette	1986	6.00
❑ B-5626	Don't Drink the Water/Don't You Love Me Anymore	1986	3.00
❑ S7-18124	The Simple Things/Unchain My Heart (90's Version)	1994	3.00
—White vinyl			
❑ B-44072	Unchain My Heart/Satisfied	1987	3.00
❑ B-44072 [PS]	Unchain My Heart/Satisfied	1987	3.00
❑ B-44101	Two Wrongs (Don't Make a Right)/Isolation	1987	3.00
❑ B-44182	A Woman Loves a Man/ La Vie En Rose	1988	3.00
—B-side by Edith Piaf			

Except when noted otherwise, VG = 25% of NM, and VG+ = 50% of NM. (Example: VG = $2.00, VG+ = $4.00 and NM = $8.00.)

Number	Title (A Side/B Side)	Yr	NM
❑ B-44182 [PS]	A Woman Loves a Man/La Vie En Rose	1988	3.00
❑ NR-44590	Living in the Promiseland/She Came In Through the Bathroom Window (Live)	1990	4.00
❑ S7-57988	Feels Like Forever/When the Night Comes	1992	3.00
❑ 7PRO-79025 [DJ]	What Are You Doing with a Fool Like Me (same on both sides)	1990	5.00
—Vinyl is promo only			
❑ 7PRO-79711 [DJ]	When the Night Comes (same on both sides)	1989	5.00
—Vinyl is promo only			

ISLAND

Number	Title (A Side/B Side)	Yr	NM
❑ 99875	Throw It Away/Easy Rider	1983	4.00

MCA

Number	Title (A Side/B Side)	Yr	NM
❑ 51177	I'm So Glad I'm Standing Here Today/Standing Tall	1981	4.00
—With the Crusaders			
❑ 51222	This Old World's Too Funky for Me/Standing Tall	1981	4.00
—With the Crusaders			
❑ 53077	Love Lives On/On My Way to You	1987	4.00
❑ 53077 [PS]	Love Lives On/On My Way to You	1987	4.00

PHILIPS

Number	Title (A Side/B Side)	Yr	NM
❑ 40255	I'll Cry Instead/Precious Words	1965	40.00
—Artist listed as "Joe Cocker"			
❑ 40255	I'll Cry Instead/Precious Words	1965	40.00
—Originally by "Vance Arnold and the Avengers"			

THE RIGHT STUFF

Number	Title (A Side/B Side)	Yr	NM
❑ S7-19857	Human Touch/One Step Up	1998	3.00
—B-side by Paul Cebar			

Albums

A&M

Number	Title	Yr	NM
❑ SP-3106	With a Little Help from My Friends	1980	8.00
❑ SP-3175	I Can Stand a Little Rain	1980	8.00
❑ SP-3257	Joe Cocker's Greatest Hits	1982	8.00
❑ SP-3633	I Can Stand a Little Rain	1974	10.00
❑ SP-4182	With a Little Help from My Friends	1969	12.00
—Brown label			
❑ SP-4182	With a Little Help from My Friends	1974	10.00
—Silver label			
❑ SP-4224	Joe Cocker!	1969	12.00
—Brown label			
❑ SP-4224	Joe Cocker!	1974	10.00
—Silver label			
❑ SP-4368	Joe Cocker	1972	12.00
—Brown label			
❑ SP-4368	Joe Cocker	1974	10.00
—Silver label			
❑ SP-4529	Jamaica Say You Will	1975	10.00
❑ SP-4574	Stingray	1976	10.00
❑ SP-4670	Joe Cocker's Greatest Hits	1977	10.00
❑ SP-6002 [(2)]	Mad Dogs and Englishmen	1970	15.00
—Brown labels			
❑ SP-6002 [(2)]	Mad Dogs and Englishmen	1974	12.00
—Silver labels			
❑ QU-54182 [Q]	With a Little Help from My Friends	1974	—
—Not released			
❑ QU-54224 [Q]	Joe Cocker!	1974	—
—Not released			

ASYLUM

Number	Title	Yr	NM
❑ 6E-145	Luxury You Can Afford	1978	10.00
❑ DP-400 [PD]	Luxury You Can Afford	1978	15.00

CAPITOL

Number	Title	Yr	NM
❑ ST-12335	Civilized Man	1984	10.00
❑ ST-12394	Cocker	1986	10.00
❑ CLT-48285	Unchain My Heart	1988	10.00
❑ C1-92861	One Night of Sin	1989	12.00

ISLAND

Number	Title	Yr	NM
❑ IL 9750	Sheffield Steel	1982	10.00
❑ 90096	One More Time	1983	10.00

MOBILE FIDELITY

Number	Title	Yr	NM
❑ 1-223	Sheffield Steel	1995	40.00
—Audiophile vinyl			

COCKER, JOE, AND JENNIFER WARNES

Also see each artist's individual listings.

45s

ISLAND

Number	Title (A Side/B Side)	Yr	NM
❑ 99996	Up Where We Belong/Sweet Li'l Woman	1982	4.00
❑ 99996 [PS]	Up Where We Belong/Sweet Li'l Woman	1982	4.00

COE, DAVID ALLAN

45s

COLUMBIA

Number	Title (A Side/B Side)	Yr	NM
❑ 11-02118	Tennessee Whiskey/The Bottle (In My Hand)	1981	4.00
❑ 18-02492	(Sittin' On) The Dock of the Bay/I Love Robbin's Trains	1981	4.00
❑ 18-02612	Juanita/I'll Always Be a Fool for You	1981	4.00
❑ 18-02678	Now I Lay Me Down to Cheat If I Knew	1981	4.00
❑ 18-02815	Take Time to Know Her/London Homesick Blues	1982	4.00
❑ 18-03022	What Made You Change Your Mind/Pouring Water on a Drowning Man	1982	4.00
❑ 13-03129	Jack Daniel's, If You Please/Tennessee Whiskey	1982	3.00
—Hall of Fame Series reissue			
❑ 38-03343	Whiskey, Whiskey (Take My Mind)/Those Low Down Blues	1982	4.00
❑ 38-03778	The Ride/Son of a Rebel Son	1983	4.00
❑ 38-03997	Cheap Thrills/You Never Even Call Me by My Name	1983	4.00
❑ 38-03997 [PS]	Cheap Thrills/You Never Even Call Me by My Name	1983	6.00
❑ 38-04136	Crazy Old Soldier/Drinkin' to Forget	1983	4.00
❑ 38-04396	Mona Lisa Lost Her Smile/Someone Special	1984	4.00
❑ 38-04553	It's Great to Be Single Again/Sweet Angeline	1984	4.00
❑ 38-04688	She Used to Love Me a Lot/For Lovers Only (Part IV)	1984	4.00
❑ 38-04846	Don't Cry Darlin'/You're the Only Song I Sing Today	1985	4.00
❑ 38-05451	My Elusive Dreams/Call Me the Breeze	1985	4.00
❑ 38-05631	I'm Gonna Hurt Her on the Radio/He Has to Pay (For What I Get for Free)	1985	4.00
❑ 38-05876	A Country Boy (Who Rolled the Rock Away)/Take My Advice	1986	4.00
❑ 38-06227	I've Already Cheated on You/Take My Advice	1986	4.00
—A-side with Willie Nelson			
❑ 38-06394	Son of the South/Gemini Girl	1986	4.00
❑ 38-06661	Need a Little Time Off for Bad Behavior/It's a Matter of Life and Death	1987	4.00
❑ 38-07129	Tanya Montana/The Ten Commandments of Love	1987	4.00
❑ 38-08527	Love Is a Never Ending War/Action Speaks Louder Than Words	1989	4.00
❑ 3-10024	(If I Could Climb) The Walls of the Bottle/Another Pretty Country Song	1974	5.00
❑ 3-10093	Would You Be My Lady/Rock and Roll Holiday	1975	5.00
❑ 3-10159	You Never Even Called Me By My Name/Would You Lay with Me (In a Field of Stone)	1975	6.00
❑ 3-10254	Longhaired Redneck/Family Reunion	1975	5.00
❑ 3-10323	When She's Got Me (Where She Wants Me)/Living on the Run	1976	5.00
❑ 3-10395	Willie, Waylon and Me/Please Come to Boston	1976	5.00
❑ 3-10475	Lately I've Been Thinking Too Much Lately/Under Rachel's Wings	1977	5.00
❑ 3-10583	Just to Prove My Love for You/Play Me a Sad Song	1977	5.00
❑ 3-10621	Face to Face/Play Me a Sad Song	1977	5.00
❑ 3-10701	Divers Do It Deeper/Million Dollar Memories	1978	5.00
❑ 3-10753	You Can Count on Me/Bad Impressions	1978	5.00
❑ 3-10816	If This Is Just a Game/Tomorrow's Another Day	1978	5.00
❑ 3-10860	Bright Morning Light/Suicide	1978	5.00
❑ 3-10911	Jack Daniel's, If You Please/Human Emotions	1979	5.00
❑ 1-11098	X's and O's (Kisses and Hugs)/Gone (Like)	1979	5.00
❑ 1-11167	Loving You Comes So Natural/Lost	1979	5.00
—With Johnny Rodriguez			
❑ 1-11230	The Great Nashville Railroad Disaster (True Story)/Take It Easy Rider	1980	5.00
❑ 1-11277	Get a Little Dirt on Your Hands/What Can I Do	1980	5.00
—A-side with Bill Anderson			
❑ 1-11352	Hank Williams Jr., Jr./I've Got Something to Say	1980	5.00
❑ 4-46012	Sad Country Song/Atlantic Song	1974	6.00
❑ 11-60501	Stand By Your Man/Take This Job and Shove It	1981	4.00

KAT FAMILY

Number	Title (A Side/B Side)	Yr	NM
❑ ZS4-04258	Ride 'Em Cowboy/Yesterday's Wine	1983	4.00

PLANTATION

Number	Title (A Side/B Side)	Yr	NM
❑ 99	How High's the Watergate, Martha/Tricky Dicky, The Only Son of King Fu	1973	8.00
❑ 104	Keep Those Big Wheels Rolling/Memphis in My Blood	1973	8.00

SSS INTERNATIONAL

Number	Title (A Side/B Side)	Yr	NM
❑ 804	Penitentiary Blues/Monkey David Wine	1971	—
—Canceled			
❑ 825	Tobacco Road/Death Row	1971	10.00
❑ 864	Two-Tone Brown/Funeral Parlor Blues	1972	10.00

Albums

COLUMBIA

Number	Title	Yr	NM
❑ KC 32942	Mysterious Rhinestone Cowboy	1974	12.00
❑ PC 32942	Mysterious Rhinestone Cowboy	197?	10.00
—Early reissue with new prefix and no bar code			
❑ KC 33085	Once Upon a Rhyme	1975	12.00
❑ PC 33085	Once Upon a Rhyme	197?	10.00
—Early reissue with new prefix and no bar code			
❑ PC 33916	Longhaired Redneck	1976	10.00
❑ PC 34310	David Allan Coe Rides Again	1977	10.00
❑ PC 34780	Tattoo	1977	10.00
❑ KC 35306	Family Album	1978	10.00
❑ KC 35535	Human Emotions — Happy Side/Su-I-Side	1978	10.00
❑ KC 35627	Greatest Hits	1978	10.00
❑ PC 35627	Greatest Hits	198?	8.00
—Budget-line reissue			
❑ KC 35789	Spectrum, VII	1979	10.00
❑ JC 36277	Compass Point	1980	10.00
❑ PC 36277	Compass Point	198?	8.00
—Budget-line reissue with new prefix			
❑ JC 36489	I've Got Something to Say	1980	10.00
❑ PC 36489	I've Got Something to Say	198?	8.00
—Budget-line reissue with new prefix			
❑ JC 36970	Invictus (Means) Unconquered	1981	10.00
❑ PC 36970	Invictus (Means) Unconquered	198?	8.00
—Budget-line reissue with new prefix			
❑ FC 37352	Encore	1981	10.00
❑ PC 37352	Encore	198?	8.00
—Budget-line reissue with new prefix			
❑ FC 37454	Tennessee Whiskey	1981	10.00
❑ PC 37454	Tennessee Whiskey	198?	8.00
—Budget-line reissue with new prefix			
❑ FC 37736	Rough Rider	1982	10.00
❑ PC 37736	Rough Rider	198?	8.00
—Budget-line reissue with new prefix			
❑ FC 38093	D.A.C.	1982	10.00
❑ FC 38318	Biggest Hits	1982	10.00
❑ FC 38535	Castles in the Sand	1983	10.00
❑ PC 38535	Castles in the Sand	1985	8.00
—Budget-line reissue with new prefix			
❑ FC 38926	Hello In There	1983	10.00
❑ FC 39269	Just Divorced	1984	10.00
❑ PC 39269	Just Divorced	1986	8.00
—Budget-line reissue with new prefix			
❑ KC2 39585 [(2)]	For the Record — The First 10 Years	1984	12.00
❑ FC 39617	Darlin', Darlin'	1985	10.00
❑ FC 40195	Unchained	1985	10.00
❑ FC 40346	Son of the South	1986	10.00
❑ FC 40571	A Matter of Life... And Death	1987	10.00
❑ FC 45057	Crazy Daddy	1989	10.00

PAIR

Number	Title	Yr	NM
❑ PDL2-1075 [(2)]	Best of David Allan Coe	1986	12.00

PLANTATION

Number	Title	Yr	NM
❑ 507	Texas Moon	197?	15.00

SSS INTERNATIONAL

Number	Title	Yr	NM
❑ 9	Penitentiary Blues	1968	75.00
❑ SSS 31	Requiem for a Harlequin	1973	320.00

COE, JAMIE

45s

ABC-PARAMOUNT

Number	Title (A Side/B Side)	Yr	NM
❑ 10120	Goodbye, My Love, Goodbye/There's Never Been a Night	1960	20.00
❑ 10149	The Story of Jesse James/Say You	1960	20.00
❑ 10203	I'm Gettin' Married/Two Dozen and a Half	1961	20.00
❑ 10267	How Low Is Low/Little Darling, Little Darling	1961	20.00

ADDISON

Number	Title (A Side/B Side)	Yr	NM
❑ 15001	Summertime Symphony/There's Gonna Be a Day	1959	20.00
❑ 15003	I'll Go On Loving You/School Day Blues	1959	20.00

BIG TOP

Number	Title (A Side/B Side)	Yr	NM
❑ 3107	Cleopatra/But Yesterday	1962	20.00

Except when noted otherwise, VG = 25% of NM, and VG+ = 50% of NM. (Example: VG = $2.00, VG+ = $4.00 and NM = $8.00.)

Number	Title (A Side/B Side)	Yr	NM
❑ 3139	The Fool/I've Got That Feeling Again	1963	20.00
CAMEO			
❑ 424	Greenback Dollar/But Yesterday	1966	15.00
ENTERPRISE			
❑ 5005	The Dealer/Close Your Eyes	1964	12.00
❑ 5050	My Girl/I Cried on My Pillow	1964	12.00
❑ 5055	Good Enough for a King/I Was the One	1965	12.00
❑ 5070	The One Who Really Loves You/A Long Time Ago	1965	12.00
❑ 5080	Greenback Dollar/But Yesterday	1965	20.00
❑ 5095	First Girl/Very Few	1966	15.00
REPRISE			
❑ 0295	Close Your Eyes/The Dealer	1964	12.00

COEFIELD, BRICE

Number	Title (A Side/B Side)	Yr	NM
45s			
A&M			
❑ 774	Ain't That Right/Work for My Baby	1965	600.00
MADISON			
❑ 137	Cha Cha Twist/Tempted	1960	50.00
OMEN			
❑ 10	Ain't That Right/Just One More Night	1965	600.00

COFFEE, RED

Number	Title (A Side/B Side)	Yr	NM
45s			
WARNER BROS.			
❑ 5128	Ducky Christmas/Jolly Jingle Bells	1959	15.00

COFFEY, DENNIS

Number	Title (A Side/B Side)	Yr	NM
12-Inch Singles			
WESTBOUND			
❑ DSKO 117 [DJ]	Calling Planet Earth (5:06) (same on both sides)	1978	12.00
45s			
SUSSEX			
❑ 208	Getting It On/Summertime Girl	1970	5.00
❑ 226	Scorpio/Sad Angel	1971	5.00
❑ 233	Taurus/Can You Feel It	1972	5.00
❑ 237	Ride, Sally, Ride/Getting It On	1972	5.00
❑ 251	Capricorn's Thing/Lonely Moon Child	1973	5.00
❑ 511	Theme from "Enter the Dragon"/Junction Flats	1973	5.00
❑ 631	Getting It On '75/Chicano	1974	5.00
WARNER BROS.			
❑ 7769	Theme from "Black Belt Jones"/Love Theme from "Black Belt Jones"	1974	5.00
WESTBOUND			
❑ 5020	Finger Lickin' Good/Wild Child	1975	4.00
❑ 5028	Honky Tonk/El Tigre	1976	4.00
❑ 55402	Our Love Goes On Forever/Back Home	1977	4.00
❑ 55414	Calling Planet Earth/A Sweet Taste of Sin	1978	4.00
Albums			
ORPHEUS			
❑ D1-75617	Under the Moonlight	1989	12.00
SUSSEX			
❑ SUX-7004	Evolution	1971	12.00
❑ SUX-7010	Goin' for Myself	1972	12.00
❑ SUX-7021	Electric Coffey	1972	12.00
❑ SUX-8031	Instant Coffey	1974	12.00
WESTBOUND			
❑ W-212	Finger Lickin' Good	1975	10.00
❑ WD 300	Home	1977	10.00
❑ 6105	The Sweet Taste of Sin	1978	10.00

COGAN, ALMA

Number	Title (A Side/B Side)	Yr	NM
45s			
AMERICAN ARTS			
❑ 4	I Love You Much Too Much/Tennessee Waltz	1964	10.00
CAPITOL			
❑ F4170	Mama Says/Last Night on the Back Porch	1959	12.00
❑ 4547	Cowboy Jimmy Joe/Just Couldn't Resist Her with Her Pocket Transistor	1961	12.00
LAURIE			
❑ TL 18	Snakes Snails and Puppy Dog Tails/How Many Days How Many Nights	1965	10.00
RCA VICTOR			
❑ 47-6063	Blue Again/Paper Kisses	1955	15.00
❑ 47-6236	Got N' Idea/Give a Fool a Chance	1955	15.00
❑ 47-6405	Twenty Tiny Fingers/Never Do a Tango with an Eskimo	1956	12.00
❑ 47-6573	Willie Can/Pickin' a Chicken	1956	12.00

COHEN, LEONARD

Number	Title (A Side/B Side)	Yr	NM
45s			
COLUMBIA			
❑ 44439	Suzanne/Hey, That's No Way to Say Goodbye	1968	6.00
❑ 44827	Bird on the Wire/Seems So Long Ago (Nancy)	1969	6.00
❑ 45852	Nancy/Passing Thru	1973	5.00
Albums			
COLUMBIA			
❑ CL 2733 [M]	Leonard Cohen	1967	25.00
❑ CS 9533 [S]	Leonard Cohen	1967	12.00
—Red "360 Sound" label			
❑ CS 9533 [S]	Leonard Cohen	1970	10.00
—Orange label			
❑ PC 9533	Leonard Cohen	198?	8.00
—Reissue with new prefix			
❑ CS 9767	Songs From a Room	1969	12.00
—Red "360 Sound" label			
❑ CS 9767	Songs From a Room	1970	10.00
—Orange label			
❑ PC 9767	Songs From a Room	198?	8.00
—Reissue with new prefix			
❑ C 30103	Songs of Love and Hate	1971	12.00
❑ PC 30103	Songs of Love and Hate	198?	8.00
—Budget-line reissue			
❑ KC 31724	Leonard Cohen: Live Songs	1973	12.00
❑ KC 33167	New Skin for the Old Ceremony	1974	12.00
❑ PC 34077	The Best of Leonard Cohen	1975	10.00
—No bar code			
❑ PC 34077	The Best of Leonard Cohen	198?	8.00
—Reissue with bar code			
❑ JC 36264	Recent Songs	1979	10.00
❑ PC 36264	Recent Songs	198?	8.00
—Budget-line reissue			
❑ FC 44191	I'm Your Man	1988	10.00
❑ C 85953	Ten New Songs	2001	20.00
PASSPORT			
❑ PB-6045	Various Positions	1985	10.00
WARNER BROS.			
❑ BSK 3125	Death of a Ladies' Man	1977	10.00

COHEN, MYRON

Number	Title (A Side/B Side)	Yr	NM
45s			
CORAL			
❑ 61280	Mr. and Mrs./Soup and Fish	1954	12.00
Albums			
AUDIO FIDELITY			
❑ 701 [M]	Myron Cohen	196?	20.00
RCA VICTOR			
❑ LPM-3534 [M]	Everybody Gotta Be Someplace	1966	12.00
❑ LSP-3534 [S]	Everybody Gotta Be Someplace	1966	15.00
❑ LPM-3791 [M]	It's Not a Question	1967	12.00
❑ LSP-3791 [S]	It's Not a Question	1967	15.00
❑ VPS-6052 [(2)]	This Is Myron Cohen	1972	15.00

COINS, THE

Number	Title (A Side/B Side)	Yr	NM
45s			
GEE			
❑ 10	Cheatin' Baby/Blue, Can't Get No Place with You	1954	2000.
❑ 11	Look at Me Girl/S.R. Blues	1954	2000.
❑ 1007	Look at Me Girl/Two Loves Have I	1956	600.00
—B-side by the Colonials			
MODEL			
❑ 2001	Loretta/Please	1955	2000.

COLBERT, GODOY

Number	Title (A Side/B Side)	Yr	NM
45s			
REVUE			
❑ 11037	Baby I Like It/I Wanna Thank You	1969	150.00

COLD BLOOD

Number	Title (A Side/B Side)	Yr	NM
45s			
ABC			
❑ 12173	I Get Off on You/We Came Down Here	1976	4.00
—As "Lydia Pense and Cold Blood"			
REPRISE			
❑ 1092	Down to the Bone/Valdes in the Country	1972	5.00
❑ 1157	Baby I Love You/Livin' Your Dream	1973	5.00
SAN FRANCISCO			
❑ 60	You Got Me Hummin'/If You Will	1970	6.00
❑ 61	I Wish I Knew How It Would Feel to Be Free/I'm a Good Woman	1970	6.00
❑ 62	Too Many People/I Can't Stay	1970	6.00
❑ 66	Understanding/Shop Talk	1971	6.00
Albums			
ABC			
❑ D-917	Lydia Pense and Cold Blood	1976	10.00
REPRISE			
❑ MS 2074	First Taste of Sin	1972	12.00
❑ MS 2130	Thriller!	1973	12.00
SAN FRANCISCO			
❑ SD 200	Cold Blood	1969	20.00
❑ SD 205	Sisyphus	1970	20.00
WARNER BROS.			
❑ BS 2806	Lydia	1974	10.00

COLDER, BEN

See SHEB WOOLEY.

COLE, ANN

Number	Title (A Side/B Side)	Yr	NM
45s			
BATON			
❑ 218	Are You Satisfied?/Darling Don't Hurt Me	1955	20.00
❑ 224	Easy Easy Baby/New Love	1956	20.00
❑ 229	I'm Waiting for You/My Tearful Heart	1956	20.00
❑ 232	In the Chapel/Each Day	1956	25.00
❑ 237	Got My Mo-Jo Working/I've Got a Little Boy	1957	40.00
❑ 243	You're Mine/No Star Is Lost	1957	20.00
❑ 247	Give Me Love or Nothing/I've Got Nothing Working Now	1957	20.00
❑ 258	Love in My Heart/Summer Nights	1958	20.00
MGM			
❑ 12954	In the Chapel/Plain As the Nose on Your Face	1960	15.00
ROULETTE			
❑ 4452	Don't Stop the Wedding/Have Fun	1962	15.00
SIR			
❑ 272	Nobody But Me/That's Enough	1959	15.00
❑ 275	A Love of My Own/Brand New House	1960	15.00
TIMELY			
❑ 1006	Danny Boy/Smilin' Through	1954	25.00
❑ 1007	I'll Find a Way/Oh Love of Mine	1954	25.00
❑ 1010	So Proud of You/Down in the Valley	1955	25.00

COLE, COZY

Number	Title (A Side/B Side)	Yr	NM
45s			
BETHLEHEM			
❑ 3067	Big Boss/Cozy and Bossa	1963	8.00
COLUMBIA			
❑ 43657	Whole Lotta Shakin' Goin' On/Watch It	1966	8.00
CORAL			
❑ 62339	Big Noise from Winnetka (Part 1)/Big Noise from Winnetka (Part 2)	1962	8.00
❑ 62379	Rockin' Drummer/Sing, Sing, Sing (With a Swing)	1963	8.00
—With Gary Chester			
❑ 62395	Ol' Man Moses/Christopher Columbus	1964	8.00
❑ 62417	Cozy Beat/Night Beach	1964	8.00
FELSTED			
❑ 8546	Caravan Part 1/Caravan Part 2	1959	10.00
GRAND AWARD			
❑ 1023	Caravan Part 1/Caravan Part 2	1959	12.00
KING			
❑ 5222	Blow-Up/Flop-Down	1959	10.00
❑ 5242	Strange/D Natural Rock	1959	10.00
❑ 5254	Melody of a Dreamer/Soft	1959	10.00
❑ 5265	Boy Meets Girl/Playtime Blues	1959	10.00
—With Lee Parker			
❑ 5287	Stain Glass/D'Mitri	1959	10.00
❑ 5303	Play, Cozy, Play/Cozy's Mambo	1960	10.00
❑ 5316	Blockhead/Teen-Age Ideas	1960	10.00
❑ 5337	Drum Fever/Bag of Tricks	1960	10.00
❑ 5363	Cozy's Corner/Red Ball	1960	10.00
❑ 5390	Ha Ha Cha-Cha/The Pogo Hop	1960	10.00
LOVE			
❑ 5003/4	Topsy I/Topsy II	1958	15.00
❑ 5014	Turvy I/Turvy II	1958	12.00
❑ 16-5016	Topsy-Turvy (Everything Is)/Bad	1958	12.00
MERCURY			
❑ 71385	St. Louis Blues/Father Cooperates	1958	12.00

Except when noted otherwise, VG = 25% of NM, and VG+ = 50% of NM. (Example: VG = $2.00, VG+ = $4.00 and NM = $8.00.)

Number	Title (A Side/B Side)	Yr	NM
MGM			
❑ 11794	Hound Dog Special/ Terrible Sight	1954	12.00
Albums			
AUDITION			
❑ 33-5943 [M]	Cozy Cole	1955	50.00
BETHLEHEM			
❑ BCP-21 [M]	Jazz at the Metropole Café	1955	50.00
CHARLIE PARKER			
❑ PLP-403 [M]	A Cozy Conaption of Carmen	1962	20.00
❑ PLP-403S [S]	A Cozy Conaption of Carmen	1962	25.00
COLUMBIA			
❑ CL 2553 [M]	It's a Rockin' Thing	1965	15.00
❑ CS 9353 [S]	It's a Rockin' Thing	1965	20.00
CORAL			
❑ CRL 57423 [M]	Drum Beat Dancing Feet	1962	15.00
❑ CRL 57457 [M]	It's a Cozy World	1964	15.00
❑ CRL 757423 [S]	Drum Beat Dancing Feet	1962	20.00
❑ CRL 757457 [S]	It's a Cozy World	1964	20.00
FELSTED			
❑ 2002 [S]	Cozy's Caravan/Earl's Backroom	1958	40.00
❑ 7002 [M]	Cozy's Caravan/Earl's Backroom	1958	50.00
GRAND AWARD			
❑ GA 33-334 [M]	After Hours	1956	40.00
KING			
❑ 673 [M]	Cozy Cole	1959	60.00
❑ KS-673 [S]	Cozy Cole	1959	150.00
LOVE			
❑ 500M [M]	Topsy	1959	100.00
❑ 500S [S]	Topsy	1959	200.00
PARIS			
❑ 122 [M]	Cozy Cole and His All-Stars	1958	50.00
PLYMOUTH			
❑ P 12-155 [M]	Cozy Cole and His All Stars	195?	30.00
SAVOY			
❑ MG-12197 [M]	Concerto for Cozy	196?	20.00
WHO'S WHO IN JAZZ			
❑ 21003	Lionel Hampton Presents Cozy Cole & Marty Napoleon	1977	10.00

COLE, COZY/JIMMY MCPARTLAND

Number	Title (A Side/B Side)	Yr	NM
Albums			
WALDORF MUSIC HALL			
❑ MH 33-162 [10]	After Hours	195?	50.00

COLE, DON

Number	Title (A Side/B Side)	Yr	NM
45s			
COED			
❑ 548	Free Flight/Squad Car	1961	20.00
GUYDEN			
❑ 2059	Lie Detector Machine/Born to Be with You	1961	100.00
KENT			
❑ 305	Saturday Night Party Time/ Sweet Lovin' Honey	1958	80.00
RPM			
❑ 502	Snake Eyed Mama/Kiss of Love	1957	200.00
—With Al Casey			

COLE, JERRY

Number	Title (A Side/B Side)	Yr	NM
45s			
CAPITOL			
❑ 5056	Midnight Mary/Land of Dreams	1963	12.00
❑ 5106	Pokey/One Color Blues	1964	10.00
❑ 5141	Night Rumble/Boss Dance	1964	10.00
❑ 5265	Meet Me on the Corner/ Life Will Go On	1964	10.00
❑ 5394	Every Window in the City/ Come On Over to My Place	1965	10.00
Albums			
BEAT ROCKET			
❑ BR 117	Guitars A-Go-Go!	2000	12.00
❑ BR 118	Wild Strings!	2001	12.00
CAPITOL			
❑ ST 2044 [S]	Outer Limits	1963	80.00
❑ T 2044 [M]	Outer Limits	1963	50.00
❑ (S)T 2061	Hot Rod Dance Party Bonus Photo	1964	25.00
❑ ST 2061 [S]	Hot Rod Dance Party	1964	100.00
❑ T 2061 [M]	Hot Rod Dance Party	1964	80.00
❑ ST 2112 [S]	Surf Age	1964	100.00
—With bonus single missing			
❑ ST 2112 [S]	Surf Age	1964	120.00
—With bonus single by Dick Dale, "Thunder Wave"/"Spanish Kiss"			
❑ T 2112 [M]	Surf Age	1964	80.00
—With bonus single missing			
❑ T 2112 [M]	Surf Age	1964	100.00
—With bonus single by Dick Dale, "Thunder Wave"/"Spanish Kiss"			

Nat King Cole, "Dear Lonely Hearts," Capitol 4870, 1962, **$20.**

Number	Title (A Side/B Side)	Yr	NM
LIBERTY			
❑ LRP-3362 [M]	Sounds of the Big Irons	1964	50.00
❑ LST-7362 [S]	Sounds of the Big Irons	1964	60.00

COLE, KEYSHIA

Number	Title (A Side/B Side)	Yr	NM
45s			
A&M			
❑ B0003683-21	I Changed My Mind (same on both sides)	2004	3.00

COLE, NAT KING

Includes reissues of material by the King Cole Trio.

Number	Title (A Side/B Side)	Yr	NM
45s			
AMERICAN PIE			
❑ 9067	The Christmas Song/ Ramblin' Rose	198?	5.00
—Reissue			
CAPITOL			
❑ 54-529	These Foolish Things/ Cole Capers	1949	20.00
—Part of "CCF-156"			
❑ F529	These Foolish Things/ Cole Capers	1950	15.00
—Part of "CCF-156"; reissue of 54-529			
❑ 54-530	Three Little Words/I'll Never Be the Same	1949	20.00
—Part of "CCF-156"			
❑ F530	Three Little Words/I'll Never Be the Same	1950	15.00
—Part of "CCF-156"; reissue of 54-530			
❑ 54-531	Blues in My Shower/How High the Moon	1949	20.00
—Part of "CCF-156"			
❑ F531	Blues in My Shower/How High the Moon	1950	15.00
—Part of "CCF-156"; reissue of 54-531			
❑ F606	Lillian/Lush Life	1949	15.00
—Add 1/3 if "O.C." (optional center) is still in the center of the record			
❑ 54-680	(It's Easy to See) The Trouble with Me Is You/Who Do You Know in Heaven	1949	20.00
❑ 54-716	Land of Love/Yes Sir, That's My Baby	1949	20.00
❑ F883	It's Only a Paper Moon/ Embraceable You	1950	20.00
—As "The King Cole Trio"			
❑ F889	I Almost Lost My Mind/Baby Won't You Say You Love Me	1950	15.00
—Nat King Cole records on Capitol before F889 are unconfirmed on 45 rpm, except as listed			
❑ F1010	Mona Lisa/The Greatest Inventor (Of Them All)	1950	15.00
❑ F1030	I Don't Know Why/You're the Cream in My Coffee	1950	15.00
❑ F1032	I'm in the Mood for Love/ Don't Blame Me	1950	15.00
❑ F1033	(I Love You) For Sentimental Reasons/I Can't See for Lookin'	1950	15.00
❑ F1034	Little Girl/What Can I Say	1950	15.00
❑ F1035	Portrait of Jenny/Lost April	1950	15.00
❑ F1036	Exactly Like You/That's What	1950	15.00
❑ F1037	Sweet Georgia Brown/ I Know That You Know	1950	15.00
❑ F1038	This Way Out/Rex Rhumba	1950	15.00
❑ F1068	I'll Never Say "Never Again" Again/A Little Bit Independent	1950	20.00
❑ F1133	Home (When Shadows Fall)/ Tunnel of Love	1950	15.00
❑ F1176	Get Out and Get Under/ Hey, Not Now	1950	15.00
❑ F1184	Orange Colored Sky/Jambo	1950	15.00
❑ F1203	Frosty the Snow Man/ A Little Christmas Tree	1950	30.00
❑ F1270	Time Out for Tears/Get to Gettin'	1951	12.00
❑ F1365	Jet/Magic Tree	1951	12.00
❑ F1401	Always You/Destination Moon	1951	12.00
❑ F1449	Too Young/That's My Girl	1951	12.00
❑ F1468	Red Sails in the Sunset/ Little Child	1951	12.00
❑ F1501	Because of Rain/Song of Delilah	1951	12.00
❑ F1565	Early American/My Brother	1951	12.00
❑ F1613	Sweet Lorraine/Kee-Mo Ky-Mo	1951	12.00
❑ F1627	Lost April/Calypso Blues	1951	12.00

C

Number	Title (A Side/B Side)	Yr	NM
❑ F1650	Embraceable You/It's Only a Paper Moon	1951	10.00
—As "The King Cole Trio"			
❑ F1663	Nature Boy/For All We Know	1951	10.00
❑ F1669	Makin' Whoopee/This Is My Night to Dream	1951	10.00
❑ F1672	Lush Life/I Miss You So	1951	10.00
❑ F1673	Mona Lisa/No Moon at All	1951	10.00
❑ F1674	Too Young/(I Love You) For Sentimental Reasons	1952	10.00
❑ F1689	Pretend/Unforgettable	1954	10.00
—Most of the Capitol 1600 series were reissues, some of material from 78s			
❑ F1747	Make Believe Land/I'll Always Remember You	1951	12.00
❑ F1808	Unforgettable/My First, My Last Love	1951	12.00
❑ F1815	I Still See Elisa/You're OK for TV	1951	12.00
❑ F1863	Walkin'/I'm Hurtin'	1951	12.00
❑ F1893	Here's to My Lady/Miss Me	1951	12.00
❑ F1925	Wine, Women and Song/A Weaver of My Dreams	1952	12.00
❑ F1968	You Weren't There/You Will Never Grow Old	1952	10.00
❑ F1994	Easter Sunday Morning/Summer Is a Comin' On	1952	10.00
❑ SXE-2-2008 [S]	When My Sugar Walks Down the Street/Warm and Willing	196?	10.00
—"Capitol Compact 33," small hole, plays at 33 1/3 rpm			
❑ F2069	Somewhere Along the Way/What Does It Take to Make You Take Me	1952	10.00
❑ 2088	Thank You, Pretty Baby/Brazilian Love Song	1968	6.00
❑ F2130	Walking My Baby Back Home/Funny (Not Much)	1952	10.00
❑ F2212	Because You're Mine/I'm Never Satisfied	1952	10.00
❑ F2230	Faith Can Move Mountains/The Ruby and the Pearl	1952	10.00
❑ F2309	Strange/How (Do I Go About It)	1952	10.00
❑ F2346	Pretend/Don't Let Your Eyes Go Shopping	1953	10.00
❑ F2389	Can't I/Blue Gardenia	1953	10.00
❑ 2451	I'm Gonna Laugh You Right Out of My Life/People	1969	6.00
❑ F2459	I Am in Love/My Flaming Heart	1953	10.00
❑ F2498	Return to Paradise/Angel Eyes	1953	10.00
❑ F2540	A Fool Was I/If Love Is Good to Me	1953	10.00
❑ F2610	Lover Come Back to Me/That's All	1953	10.00
❑ F2616	Mrs. Santa Claus/The Little Boy That Santa Claus Forgot	1953	20.00
❑ F2687	Answer Me, My Love/Why	1953	10.00
❑ F2754	It Happens to Be Me/Alone Too Long	1954	10.00
❑ F2803	Make Her Mine/I Envy	1954	10.00
❑ F2897	Smile/It's Crazy	1954	10.00
❑ F2949	Hajji Baba (Persian Lament)/Unbelievable	1954	10.00
❑ F2955	The Christmas Song (Merry Christmas to You)/My Two Front Teeth (All I Want for Christmas)	1954	20.00
❑ F2985	Open Up the Doghouse/Long, Long Ago	1954	15.00
—With Dean Martin			
❑ F3027	Darling Je Vous Aime Beaucoup/The Sand and the Sea	1955	10.00
❑ F3095	A Blossom Fell/If I May	1955	15.00
—B-side with the Four Knights			
❑ F3136	My One Sin/Blues from Kiss Me Deadly	1955	10.00
❑ F3234	Forgive My Heart/Someone You Love	1955	10.00
❑ F3305	Take Me Back to Toyland/I'm Gonna Laugh You Right Out of My Life	1955	20.00
—With A-side title as shown			
❑ F3305	Toyland/I'm Gonna Laugh You Right Out of My Life	1955	30.00
—With A-side title incorrect as shown			
❑ F3328	Ask Me/Nothing Ever Changes My Love for You	1956	10.00
❑ F3390	Too Young to Go Steady/Never Let Me Go	1956	10.00
❑ F3456	That's All There Is to That/My Dream Sonata	1956	10.00
❑ F3551	Night Lights/To the Ends of the Earth	1956	10.00
❑ F3560	Mrs. Santa Claus/Take Me Back to Toyland	1956	15.00
❑ 3561	The Christmas Song (Merry Christmas to You)/The Little Boy That Santa Claus Forgot	1960	8.00
—Purple label, Capitol logo on side			
❑ 3561	The Christmas Song (Merry Christmas to You)/The Little Boy That Santa Claus Forgot	1962	6.00
—Orange and yellow swirl label			
❑ 3561	The Christmas Song (Merry Christmas to You)/The Little Boy That Santa Claus Forgot	1973	4.00
—Orange label with "Capitol" at bottom			
❑ F3561	The Christmas Song (Merry Christmas to You)/The Little Boy That Santa Claus Forgot	1956	15.00
—Original with "F" prefix, Capitol logo on top			
❑ F3619	Ballerina/You Are My First Love	1957	10.00
❑ F3702	When Rock and Roll Come to Trinidad/China Gate	1957	15.00
❑ F3737	Send for Me/My Personal Possession	1957	15.00
—B-side with the Four Knights			
❑ F3782	With You on My Mind/The Song of Raintree County	1957	10.00
❑ F3860	Angel Smile/Back in My Arms	1957	10.00
❑ F3939	Looking Back/Do I Like It	1958	10.00
❑ F4004	Come Closer to Me/Nothing in the World	1958	10.00
❑ F4056	Non Dimenticar (Don't Forget)/Bend a Little My Way	1958	10.00
❑ F4125	Madrid/Give Me Your Love	1959	10.00
❑ F4184	You Made Me Love You/I Must Be Dreaming	1959	10.00
❑ F4248	Sweet Bird of Youth/Midnight Flyer	1959	10.00
❑ F4248 [PS]	Sweet Bird of Youth/Midnight Flyer	1959	30.00
❑ 4301	The Happiest Christmas Tree/Buon Natale	1959	12.00
❑ 4301 [PS]	The Happiest Christmas Tree/Buon Natale	1959	25.00
❑ 4325	What'cha Gonna Do/Time and the River	1960	8.00
❑ 4369	Is It Better to Have Loved and Lost/That's You	1960	8.00
❑ 4393	My Love/Steady	1960	8.00
❑ 4481	If I Knew/World in My Arms	1960	8.00
❑ 4519	Illusion/When It's Summer	1961	8.00
❑ 4555	Goodnight, Little Leaguer/The First Baseball Game	1961	8.00
❑ 4555 [PS]	Goodnight, Little Leaguer/The First Baseball Game	1961	20.00
❑ 4582	Take a Fool's Advice/Make It Last	1961	8.00
❑ 4623	Let True Love Begin/Cappuccina	1961	8.00
❑ 4672	Magic Moment/Step Right Up	1961	8.00
❑ 4714	Look No Further/The Right Thing to Say	1962	8.00
❑ 4804	Ramblin' Rose/Good Times	1962	12.00
❑ 4804 [PS]	Ramblin' Rose/Good Times	1962	20.00
❑ 4870	Dear Lonely Hearts/Who's Next in Line	1962	12.00
❑ 4870 [PS]	Dear Lonely Hearts/Who's Next in Line	1962	20.00
❑ 4919	All Over the World/Nothing Goes Up (Without Coming Down)	1963	8.00
❑ 4965	Those Lazy-Hazy-Crazy Days of Summer/In the Cool of Day	1963	12.00
❑ 4965 [PS]	Those Lazy-Hazy-Crazy Days of Summer/In the Cool of Day	1963	20.00
❑ 5027	That Sunday, That Summer/Mr. Wishing Well	1963	12.00
❑ 5125	My True Carrie, Love/A Rag a Bone, A Hank of Hair	1964	8.00
❑ 5155	I Don't Want to Be Hurt Anymore/People	1964	8.00
❑ 5219	Marnie/More and More of the Amore	1964	8.00
❑ 5261	L-O-V-E/I Don't Want to See Tomorrow	1964	8.00
❑ 5412	The Ballad of Cat Ballou/They Can't Make Her Cry	1965	8.00
—With Stubby Kay			
❑ 5412 [PS]	The Ballad of Cat Ballou/They Can't Make Her Cry	1965	15.00
❑ 5486	Wanderlust/You'll See	1965	8.00
❑ 5549	One Sun/Looking Back	1965	8.00
❑ 5683	Let Me Tell You, Babe/For the Want of a Kiss	1966	8.00
❑ F15509	Straighten Up and Fly Right/Nature Boy	1950	15.00
—All the Capitol 15000 series on 45s are from multi-disc box sets			
❑ F15510	You Call It Madness/The Frim Fram Sauce	1950	15.00
❑ F15511	(Get Your Kicks on) Route 66/Gee Baby Ain't I Been Good to You	1950	15.00
❑ F15552	Yes Sir That's My Baby/I Used to Love You	1950	15.00
❑ F15553	For All We Know/'Tis Autumn	1950	15.00
❑ F15554	Bop Kick/Laugh Cool Clown	1950	15.00
❑ F15564	Sweet Lorraine/It's Only a Paper Moon	1950	15.00
❑ F15565	The Man I Love/Body and Soul	1950	15.00
❑ F15566	Embraceable You/What Is This Thing Called Love	1950	15.00
❑ F15643	Jumpin' at Capitol/Love for Sale	1950	15.00
—B-side by Benny Carter Orchestra			
❑ F15728	Makin' Whoopee/Honeysuckle Rose	1951	12.00
❑ F15729	I'll String Along with You/Too Marvelous for Words	1951	12.00
❑ F15730	This Is My Night to Dream/Rhumba Azul	1951	12.00
❑ F15843	Return Trip/St. Louis Blues	1952	12.00
—B-side by Freddie Slack			
❑ F15868	Penthouse Serenade/If I Should Lose You	1952	12.00
❑ F15869	Somebody Loves Me/Down by the Old Mill Stream	1952	12.00
❑ F15870	Laura/Polka Dots and Moonbeams	1952	12.00
❑ F15922	Walkin' My Baby Back Home/Kay's Lament	1952	12.00
—B-side by Kay Starr			
❑ S7-19764	Mrs. Santa Claus/Take Me Back to Toyland	1997	3.00
❑ S7-57887	The Christmas Song/O Holy Night	1992	4.00
—Originals on black vinyl			
❑ S7-57887	The Christmas Song/O Holy Night	1993	4.00
—Second pressing on red vinyl			
❑ F90036	(All I Want for Christmas Is) My Two Front Teeth/The Christmas Song (Merry Christmas To You)	1949	20.00
—B-side is the original King Cole Trio hit version, possibly its only U.S. release on 45			

TAMPA

Number	Title (A Side/B Side)	Yr	NM
❑ 134	Vom-Vim-Veedle/All for You	1957	12.00
❑ 134 [PS]	Vom-Vim-Veedle/All for You	1957	25.00

7-Inch Extended Plays

CAPITOL

Number	Title (A Side/B Side)	Yr	NM
❑ EAP 1-332	(contents unknown)	195?	12.00
❑ EAP 1-332 [PS]	Penthouse Serenade, Part 1	195?	12.00
❑ EAP 2-332	(contents unknown)	195?	12.00
❑ EAP 2-332 [PS]	Penthouse Serenade, Part 2	195?	12.00
❑ EBF-332 [PS]	Penthouse Serenade	195?	15.00
—Gatefold sleeve for some copies of 1-332 and 2-332			
❑ EAP 1-357	Unforgettable/Portrait of Jennie//(I Love You) For Sentimental Reasons/Red Sails in the Sunset	195?	12.00
❑ EAP 1-357 [PS]	Unforgettable Songs by Nat King Cole, Part 1	195?	12.00
❑ EAP 2-357	What'll I Do/Lost April//Too Young/Mona Lisa	195?	12.00
❑ EAP 2-357 [PS]	Unforgettable Songs by Nat King Cole, Part 2	195?	12.00
❑ EAP 3-357	Answer Me, My Love/Hajji Baba//Pretend/Make Her Mine	195?	12.00
❑ EAP 3-357 [PS]	Unforgettable Songs by Nat King Cole, Part 3	195?	12.00
❑ EBF-357 [PS]	Unforgettable	195?	15.00
—Gatefold sleeve for some copies of 1-357 and 2-357			
❑ EAP 1-420	*Love Is Here to Stay/A Handful of Stars/Almost Like Being in Love/Tenderly	1954	12.00
❑ EAP 1-420 [PS]	Two in Love, Part 1	1954	12.00
❑ EAP 2-420	*A Little Street Where Old Friends Meet/This Can't Be Love/Dinner for One Please, James/There Goes My Heart	1954	12.00
❑ EAP 2-420 [PS]	Two in Love, Part 2	1954	12.00
❑ EPA 1-500	*Lover Come Back/Pretend/A Fool Was I/I'm Hurtin'	1954	12.00
❑ EPA 1-500 [PS]	Songs by Nat King Cole	1954	12.00
❑ EAP 1-514	Dream a Little Dream of Me/There I've Said It Again//Too Soon/Rough Ridin'	1954	12.00
❑ EAP 1-514 [PS]	Tenth Anniversary Album, Part 1	1954	12.00
❑ EAP 2-514	(contents unknown)	1954	12.00
❑ EAP 2-514 [PS]	Tenth Anniversary Album, Part 2	1954	12.00
❑ EAP 3-514	The Love Nest/But All I've Got Is Me//Lovelight/Where Were You	1954	12.00
❑ EAP 3-514 [PS]	Tenth Anniversary Album, Part 3	1954	12.00
❑ EAP 4-514	Peaches/I Can't Be Bothered//Mother Nature and Father Time/Wish I Were Somebody Else	1954	12.00
❑ EAP 4-514 [PS]	Tenth Anniversary Album, Part 4	1954	12.00
❑ EBF 1-514 [PS]	Tenth Anniversary Album, Parts 1 and 2	1954	20.00
—Gatefold sleeve for some editions of EAP 1-514 and 2-514			
❑ EBF 2-514 [PS]	Tenth Anniversary Album, Parts 3 and 4	1954	20.00
—Gatefold sleeve for some editions of EAP 3-514 and 4-514			

Except when noted otherwise, VG = 25% of NM, and VG+ = 50% of NM. (Example: VG = $2.00, VG+ = $4.00 and NM = $8.00.)

Number	Title (A Side/B Side)	Yr	NM
❑ EAP 1-633	Darling, Je Vous Aime Beaucoup/If I May//A Blossom Fell/The Sand and the Sea	1955	12.00
❑ EAP 1-633 [PS]	Moods in Song	1955	12.00
❑ EAP 1-782	Sometimes I'm Happy//Just You, Just Me/When I Grow Too Old to Dream	1956	10.00
❑ EAP 1-782 [PS]	After Midnight, Part 1	1956	10.00
❑ EAP 2-782	Lonely One/I Know That You Know//Sweet Lorraine	1956	10.00
❑ EAP 2-782 [PS]	After Midnight, Part 2	1956	10.00
❑ EAP 3-782	You're Looking at Me//Caravan/(Get Your Kicks on) Route 66	1956	10.00
❑ EAP 3-782 [PS]	After Midnight, Part 3	1956	10.00
❑ EAP 4-782	It's Only a Paper Moon/Don't Let It Go to Your Head//Blame It On My Youth	1956	10.00
❑ EAP 4-782 [PS]	After Midnight, Part 4	1956	10.00
❑ EBF 1-782 [PS]	After Midnight, Parts 1 & 2	1956	20.00
—Gatefold sleeve for some editions of EAP 1-782 and 2-782			
❑ EAP 1-801	Night Lights/Nothing Ever Changes My Love for You//To the Ends of the Earth/My Dream Sonata	1957	12.00
❑ EAP 1-801 [PS]	Night Lights	1957	12.00
❑ EAP 1-813	Around the World/Fascination//An Affair to Remember (Our Love Affair)/There's a Gold Mine in the Sky	1957	12.00
❑ EAP 1-813 [PS]	Around the World	1957	12.00
❑ EAP 1-824	Love Is the Thing/Stay as Sweet as You Are//When I Fall in Love/Where Can I Go Without You?	1957	12.00
❑ EAP 1-824 [PS]	Love Is the Thing, Part 1	1957	12.00
❑ EAP 2-824	Maybe It's Because I Love You Too Much/It's All in the Game//Stardust/When Sunny Gets Blue	1957	12.00
❑ EAP 2-824 [PS]	Love Is the Thing, Part 2	1957	12.00
❑ EAP 3-824	(contents unknown)	1957	12.00
❑ EAP 3-824 [PS]	Love Is the Thing, Part 3	1957	12.00
❑ EAP 1-903	(contents unknown)	195?	12.00
❑ EAP 1-903 [PS]	Just One of Those Things, Part 1	195?	12.00
❑ EAP 2-903	Don't Get Around Much Anymore/The Party's Over//Once in a While/Just for the Fun of It	195?	12.00
❑ EAP 2-903 [PS]	Just One of Those Things, Part 2	195?	12.00
❑ EAP 3-903	(contents unknown)	195?	12.00
❑ EAP 3-903 [PS]	Just One of Those Things, Part 3	195?	12.00
❑ EAP 1-960	Looking Back/Send for Me//Do I Like It/Angel Smile	1958	10.00
❑ EAP 1-960 [PS]	Looking Back	1958	10.00
❑ EAP 1-993	*Overture (Introducing "Love Theme" and "Hesitating Blues")/Harlem Blues/Yellow Dog Blues/St. Louis Blues	1958	12.00
❑ EAP 1-993 [PS]	St. Louis Blues, Part 1	1958	12.00
❑ EAP 2-993	Morning Star/Memphis Blues//Chantez Les Bas/Friendless Blues	1958	12.00
❑ EAP 2-993 [PS]	St. Louis Blues, Part 2	1958	12.00
❑ EAP 3-993	Stay/Joe Turner's Blues//Beale Street Blues/Careless Love	1958	12.00
❑ EAP 3-993 [PS]	St. Louis Blues, Part 3	1958	12.00
❑ EAP 1-1031	*Cachito/Maria Elena/Las Mananitas/Quizas, Quizas, Quizas	1958	12.00
❑ EAP 1-1031 [PS]	Cole Espanol, Part 1	1958	12.00
❑ EAP 2-1031	(contents unknown)	1958	12.00
❑ EAP 2-1031 [PS]	Cole Espanol, Part 2	1958	12.00
❑ EAP 3-1031	(contents unknown)	1958	12.00
❑ EAP 3-1031 [PS]	Cole Espanol, Part 3	1958	12.00
❑ EAP 1-1084	Paradise/Cherchez La Femme//Impossible/Found A Million Dollar Baby (In A Five And Ten Cent Store)	195?	10.00
❑ EAP 1-1084 [PS]	The Very Thought of You, Part 1	195?	10.00
❑ EAP 2-1084	(contents unknown)	195?	10.00
❑ EAP 2-1084 [PS]	The Very Thought of You, Part 2	195?	10.00
❑ EAP-1138	(contents unknown)	195?	10.00
❑ EAP-1138 [PS]	Non Dimenticar	195?	10.00
❑ EAP 1346	(contents unknown)	195?	10.00
❑ EAP 1346 [PS]	The Happiest Christmas Tree	195?	10.00
❑ EAP-1500	(contents unknown)	196?	10.00
❑ EAP-1500 [PS]	Songs by Nat King Cole	196?	10.00
❑ EAP-1535	(contents unknown)	195?	10.00
❑ EAP-1535 [PS]	By the Beautiful Sea	195?	10.00
❑ EAP-1696	(contents unknown)	196?	10.00
❑ EAP-1696 [PS]	Love Songs by Nat King Cole	196?	10.00
❑ EAP-1709	(contents unknown)	196?	10.00
❑ EAP-1709 [PS]	Strip for Action	196?	10.00

Number	Title (A Side/B Side)	Yr	NM
❑ SXA-2195	Your Love/My Kind of Girl/Three Little Words//L-O-V-E/Coquette/More	1965	10.00
—33 1/3 rpm, small hole			
❑ SXA-2195 [PS]	L-O-V-E	1965	10.00
❑ SU-2944	Sweet Lorraine/Too Young//L-O-V-E/Answer Me, My Love/Ramblin' Rose	197?	12.00
—Stereo jukebox issue; small hole, plays at 33 1/3 rpm			
❑ SU-2944 [PS]	The Best of Nat King Cole	197?	12.00
—Part of "Little LP" series (#177)			
❑ EAP 1-9026	The Christmas Song/Mrs. Santa Claus//Frosty The Snowman/The Little Christmas Tree	195?	12.00
❑ EAP 1-9026 [PS]	The Christmas Song	195?	12.00
❑ EAP 1-9110	*Somewhere Along the Way/Funny (Not Much)/Walkin' My Baby Back Home/Faith Can Move Mountains	195?	15.00
❑ EAP 1-9110 [PS]	Nat King Cole's Top Pops, Part I	195?	15.00
❑ EAP 2-9110	*Because You're Mine/I'm Never Satisfied/The Ruby and the Pearl/A Weaver of Dreams	195?	15.00
❑ EAP 2-9110 [PS]	Nat King Cole's Top Pops, Part II	195?	15.00
❑ EAP 1-9120	If I Give My Heart To You/Hold My Hand//Pappa Loves Mambo/Teach Me Tonight	1954	12.00
❑ EAP 1-9120 [PS]	Nat King Cole Sings	1954	12.00
❑ EAP 1-9128	Love Is a Many-Splendored Thing/Breezin' Along with the Breeze//Autumn Leaves/You Are My Sunshine	1955	12.00
❑ EAP 1-9128 [PS]	Nat King Cole	1955	12.00

Albums

CAMAY

Number	Title	Yr	NM
❑ CA-3004	Nat King Cole	196?	12.00

CAPITOL

Number	Title	Yr	NM
❑ H 8 [10]	The King Cole Trio	1950	100.00
❑ H 29 [10]	The King Cole Trio, Vol. 2	1950	100.00
❑ H 59 [10]	The King Cole Trio, Vol. 3	1950	100.00
❑ H 156 [10]	Nat King Cole at the Piano	1950	100.00
❑ H 177 [10]	The King Cole Trio, Vol. 4	1950	70.00
❑ H 213 [10]	Harvest of Hits	1950	70.00
—Original; purple label			
❑ L 213 [10]	Harvest of Hits	195?	60.00
—Reissue; maroon label, "H""H" mechanically crossed out on back cover with "L" stamped next to it			
❑ H 220 [10]	The Nat King Cole Trio	1950	60.00
❑ DWBB-252 [(2)]	Close-Up	1969	15.00
—Reissue of 680 and 1891			
❑ ST-310	There! I've Said It Again	1969	12.00
❑ H 332 [10]	Penthouse Serenade	1951	60.00
—Original; purple label			
❑ L 332 [10]	Penthouse Serenade	195?	50.00
—Reissue; maroon label, "H" mechanically crossed out on back cover with "L" stamped next to it			
❑ T 332 [M]	Penthouse Serenade	1955	40.00
❑ DT 357 [R]	Unforgettable	1965	12.00
❑ H 357 [10]	Unforgettable	1952	60.00
❑ SM-357	Unforgettable	197?	8.00
—Reissue with new prefix			
❑ T 357 [M]	Unforgettable	1955	40.00
—Turquoise label			
❑ T 357 [M]	Unforgettable	1958	30.00
—Black label with colorband, "Capitol" at left			
❑ T 357 [M]	Unforgettable	1962	20.00
—Black label with colorband, "Capitol" at top			
❑ SKAO-373	Nat King Cole's Greatest	1969	12.00
❑ DT 420 [R]	Nat King Cole Sings for Two in Love	1963	15.00
❑ H 420 [10]	Nat King Cole Sings for Two in Love	1953	50.00
—Original; purple label			
❑ L 420 [10]	Nat King Cole Sings for Two in Love	195?	50.00
—Reissue; maroon label, back cover probably has "H" mechanically crossed out with "L" stamped next to it			
❑ T 420 [M]	Nat King Cole Sings for Two in Love	1955	40.00
—Turquoise label			
❑ T 420 [M]	Nat King Cole Sings for Two in Love	1958	30.00
—Black label with colorband, "Capitol" at left			
❑ T 420 [M]	Nat King Cole Sings for Two in Love	1962	20.00
—Black label with colorband, "Capitol" at top			
❑ STBB-503 [(2)]	Walkin' My Baby Back Home/A Blossom Fell	1970	15.00
❑ H1-514 [10]	Tenth Anniversary Album, Part 1	1954	50.00
—Contains Side 1 of W 514			

Number	Title	Yr	NM
❑ H2-514 [10]	Tenth Anniversary Album, Part 2	1954	50.00
—Contains Side 2 of W 514			
❑ W 514 [M]	Tenth Anniversary Album	1955	40.00
—Gray label; released simultaneously with H1-514 and H2-514			
❑ T 591 [M]	Vocal Classics	1955	40.00
❑ T 592 [M]	Instrumental Classics	1955	40.00
❑ DT 680 [R]	Ballads of the Day	1963	15.00
—Black label with colorband			
❑ T 680 [M]	Ballads of the Day	1956	40.00
—Turquoise label			
❑ T 680 [M]	Ballads of the Day	1958	30.00
—Black label with colorband, "Capitol" at left			
❑ T 680 [M]	Ballads of the Day	1962	20.00
—Black label with colorband, "Capitol" at top			
❑ W 689 [M]	The Piano Style of Nat King Cole	1956	40.00
—Turquoise label			
❑ W 689 [M]	The Piano Style of Nat King Cole	1958	30.00
—Black label with colorband, "Capitol" at left			
❑ W 689 [M]	The Piano Style of Nat King Cole	1962	20.00
—Black label with colorband, "Capitol" at top			
❑ W 782 [M]	After Midnight	1956	40.00
—Turquoise label			
❑ W 782 [M]	After Midnight	1958	30.00
—Black label with colorband, "Capitol" at left			
❑ W 782 [M]	After Midnight	1962	20.00
—Black label with colorband, "Capitol" at top			
❑ SM-824	Love Is the Thing	197?	8.00
—Reissue with new prefix			
❑ SW 824 [S]	Love Is the Thing	1959	30.00
—Black label with colorband, "Capitol" at left			
❑ SW 824 [S]	Love Is the Thing	1962	20.00
—Black label with colorband, "Capitol" at top			
❑ SW 824 [S]	Love Is the Thing	1969	12.00
—Lime green label			
❑ W 824 [M]	Love Is the Thing	1957	40.00
—Turquoise or gray label			
❑ W 824 [M]	Love Is the Thing	1958	30.00
—Black label with colorband, "Capitol" at left			
❑ W 824 [M]	Love Is the Thing	1962	20.00
—Black label with colorband, "Capitol" at top			
❑ DT 870 [R]	This Is Nat "King" Cole	1963	15.00
—Black label with colorband			
❑ T 870 [M]	This Is Nat "King" Cole	1957	40.00
—Turquoise or gray label			
❑ T 870 [M]	This Is Nat "King" Cole	1958	30.00
—Black label with colorband, "Capitol" at left			
❑ T 870 [M]	This Is Nat "King" Cole	1962	20.00
—Black label with colorband, "Capitol" at top			
❑ SW 903 [S]	Just One of Those Things	1959	30.00
—Black label with colorband, "Capitol" at left			
❑ SW 903 [S]	Just One of Those Things	1962	20.00
—Black label with colorband, "Capitol" at top			
❑ W 903 [M]	Just One of Those Things	1957	40.00
—Turquoise or gray label			
❑ W 903 [M]	Just One of Those Things	1958	30.00
—Black label with colorband, "Capitol" at left			
❑ W 903 [M]	Just One of Those Things	1962	20.00
—Black label with colorband, "Capitol" at top			
❑ SW 993 [S]	St. Louis Blues	1959	50.00
—Black label with colorband, "Capitol" at left			
❑ W 993 [M]	St. Louis Blues	1958	50.00
—Turquoise or gray label			
❑ W 993 [M]	St. Louis Blues	1962	40.00
—Black label with colorband, "Capitol" at left			
❑ DW 1031 [R]	Cole Espanol	196?	15.00
—Black label with colorband			
❑ SM-1031	Cole Espanol	197?	8.00
—Reissue with new prefix			
❑ W 1031 [M]	Cole Espanol	1958	30.00
—Black label with colorband, "Capitol" at left			
❑ W 1031 [M]	Cole Espanol	1962	20.00
—Black label with colorband, "Capitol" at top			
❑ SW 1084 [S]	The Very Thought of You	1959	30.00
—Black label with colorband, "Capitol" at left			
❑ SW 1084 [S]	The Very Thought of You	1962	20.00
—Black label with colorband, "Capitol" at top			
❑ W 1084 [M]	The Very Thought of You	1958	30.00
—Black label with colorband, "Capitol" at left			
❑ W 1084 [M]	The Very Thought of You	1962	20.00
—Black label with colorband, "Capitol" at top			
❑ SW 1120 [S]	Welcome to the Club	1959	40.00
—Black label with colorband, "Capitol" at left			
❑ W 1120 [M]	Welcome to the Club	1959	30.00
—Black label with colorband, "Capitol" at left			
❑ SW 1190 [S]	To Whom It May Concern	1959	40.00
—Black label with colorband, "Capitol" at left			
❑ W 1190 [M]	To Whom It May Concern	1959	30.00
—Black label with colorband, "Capitol" at left			
❑ SW 1220 [S]	A Mis Amigos	1959	40.00
—Black label with colorband, "Capitol" at left			
❑ SW 1220 [S]	A Mis Amigos	1962	25.00
—Black label with colorband, "Capitol" at top			
❑ W 1220 [M]	A Mis Amigos	1959	30.00
—Black label with colorband, "Capitol" at left			
❑ W 1220 [M]	A Mis Amigos	1962	20.00
—Black label with colorband, "Capitol" at top			
❑ SW 1249 [S]	Every Time I Feel the Spirit	1960	30.00
—Black label with colorband, "Capitol" at left			
❑ W 1249 [M]	Every Time I Feel the Spirit	1960	25.00
—Black label with colorband, "Capitol" at left			
❑ SW 1331 [S]	Tell Me About Yourself	1960	30.00
—Black label with colorband, "Capitol" at left			

Number	Title (A Side/B Side)	Yr	NM
❑ W 1331 [M]	Tell Me About Yourself	1960	25.00
—Black label with colorband, "Capitol" at left			
❑ SWAK 1392 [S]	Wild Is Love	1960	30.00
—Black label with colorband, "Capitol" at left			
❑ WAK 1392 [M]	Wild Is Love	1960	25.00
—Black label with colorband, "Capitol" at left			
❑ SW 1444 [S]	The Magic of Christmas	1960	20.00
❑ W 1444 [M]	The Magic of Christmas	1960	20.00
❑ SW 1574 [S]	The Touch of Your Lips	1961	25.00
—Black label with colorband, "Capitol" at left			
❑ SW 1574 [S]	The Touch of Your Lips	1962	20.00
—Black label with colorband, "Capitol" at top			
❑ W 1574 [M]	The Touch of Your Lips	1961	20.00
—Black label with colorband, "Capitol" at left			
❑ W 1574 [M]	The Touch of Your Lips	1962	15.00
—Black label with colorband, "Capitol" at top			
❑ SWCL 1613 [(3)S]	The Nat King Cole Story	1961	30.00
❑ WCL 1613 [(3)M]	The Nat King Cole Story	1961	25.00
❑ SM-1675	Nat King Cole Sings/ George Shearing Plays	197?	8.00
—Reissue with new prefix			
❑ SW 1675 [S]	Nat King Cole Sings/ George Shearing Plays	1962	30.00
—Black label with colorband, "Capitol" at left			
❑ SW 1675 [S]	Nat King Cole Sings/ George Shearing Plays	1963	20.00
—Black label with colorband, "Capitol" at top			
❑ W 1675 [M]	Nat King Cole Sings/ George Shearing Plays	1962	25.00
—Black label with colorband, "Capitol" at left			
❑ W 1675 [M]	Nat King Cole Sings/ George Shearing Plays	1963	15.00
—Black label with colorband, "Capitol" at top			
❑ SW 1713 [S]	Nat King Cole Sings the Blues	1962	25.00
—Black label with colorband, "Capitol" at left			
❑ W 1713 [M]	Nat King Cole Sings the Blues	1962	20.00
—Black label with colorband, "Capitol" at left			
❑ SM-1749	More Cole Espanol	197?	8.00
—Reissue with new prefix			
❑ SW 1749 [S]	More Cole Espanol	1962	30.00
—Black label with colorband, "Capitol" at left			
❑ SW 1749 [S]	More Cole Espanol	1963	20.00
—Black label with colorband, "Capitol" at top			
❑ W 1749 [M]	More Cole Espanol	1962	25.00
—Black label with colorband, "Capitol" at left			
❑ W 1749 [M]	More Cole Espanol	1963	15.00
—Black label with colorband, "Capitol" at top			
❑ ST 1793 [S]	Ramblin' Rose	1962	20.00
❑ T 1793 [M]	Ramblin' Rose	1962	15.00
❑ ST 1838 [S]	Dear Lonely Hearts	1962	20.00
❑ T 1838 [M]	Dear Lonely Hearts	1962	15.00
❑ SW 1859 [S]	Where Did Everyone Go?	1963	20.00
❑ W 1859 [M]	Where Did Everyone Go?	1963	15.00
❑ DT 1891 [R]	Nat King Cole's Top Pops	1963	12.00
❑ T 1891 [M]	Nat King Cole's Top Pops	1963	15.00
❑ SW 1926 [S]	The Nat King Cole Story, Vol. 1	1962	15.00
❑ W 1926 [M]	The Nat King Cole Story, Vol. 1	1962	12.00
❑ SW 1927 [S]	The Nat King Cole Story, Vol. 2	1963	15.00
❑ W 1927 [M]	The Nat King Cole Story, Vol. 2	1963	12.00
❑ SW 1928 [S]	The Nat King Cole Story, Vol. 3	1963	15.00
❑ W 1928 [M]	The Nat King Cole Story, Vol. 3	1963	12.00
❑ SW 1929 [S]	Nat King Cole Sings the Blues, Vol. 2	1963	20.00
❑ W 1929 [M]	Nat King Cole Sings the Blues, Vol. 2	1963	15.00
❑ ST 1932 [S]	Those Lazy-Hazy-Crazy Days of Summer	1963	20.00
❑ T 1932 [M]	Those Lazy-Hazy-Crazy Days of Summer	1963	15.00
❑ SM-1967 [S]	The Christmas Song	197?	8.00
—Budget-line reissue			
❑ SW 1967 [S]	The Christmas Song	1962	15.00
—Black label with colorband			
❑ SW 1967 [S]	The Christmas Song	1969	12.00
—Lime-green label			
❑ SW 1967 [S]	The Christmas Song	1971	12.00
—Red label			
❑ SW 1967 [S]	The Christmas Song	1973	10.00
—Orange label, "Capitol" at bottom			
❑ W 1967 [M]	The Christmas Song	1962	15.00
—Reissue of W 1444 with title song added and another deleted			
❑ SW 2008 [S]	Let's Face the Music	1963	20.00
❑ W 2008 [M]	Let's Face the Music	1963	15.00
❑ SM-2117	My Fair Lady	197?	8.00
—Reissue with new prefix			
❑ SW 2117 [S]	My Fair Lady	1964	20.00
—Black label with colorband			
❑ SW 2117 [S]	My Fair Lady	1969	12.00
—Lime green label			
❑ W 2117 [M]	My Fair Lady	1964	15.00
❑ ST 2118 [S]	I Don't Want to Be Hurt Anymore	1964	20.00
❑ T 2118 [M]	I Don't Want to Be Hurt Anymore	1964	15.00
❑ ST 2195 [S]	L-O-V-E	1965	20.00
❑ T 2195 [M]	L-O-V-E	1965	15.00
❑ T 2311 [M]	The Nat King Cole Trio	1965	12.00
❑ ST 2340 [S]	Songs from "Cat Ballou" and Other Motion Pictures	1965	15.00
❑ T 2340 [M]	Songs from "Cat Ballou" and Other Motion Pictures	1965	12.00
❑ DT 2348 [R]	Nature Boy	1965	12.00
❑ T 2348 [M]	Nature Boy	1965	15.00
❑ ST 2361 [S]	Looking Back	1965	15.00
❑ T 2361 [M]	Looking Back	1965	12.00
❑ MAS 2434 [M]	Nat King Cole at the Sands	1966	12.00
❑ SM-2434	Nat King Cole at the Sands	197?	8.00
—Reissue with new prefix			
❑ SMAS 2434 [S]	Nat King Cole at the Sands	1966	15.00
❑ ST 2454 [S]	Hymns and Spirituals	1966	15.00
❑ T 2454 [M]	Hymns and Spirituals	1966	12.00
❑ T 2529 [M]	The Vintage Years	1966	12.00
❑ ST 2558 [S]	The Great Songs!	1966	15.00
❑ T 2558 [M]	The Great Songs!	1966	12.00
❑ ST 2680 [S]	Sincerely, Nat King Cole	1967	12.00
❑ T 2680 [M]	Sincerely, Nat King Cole	1967	15.00
❑ ST 2759 [S]	Thank You Pretty Baby	1967	12.00
❑ T 2759 [M]	Thank You Pretty Baby	1967	15.00
❑ ST 2820 [S]	Beautiful Ballads	1967	12.00
❑ T 2820 [M]	Beautiful Ballads	1967	15.00
❑ STCL 2873 [(3)P]	The Nat King Cole Deluxe Set	1968	25.00
❑ TCL 2873 [(3)M]	The Nat King Cole Deluxe Set	1968	30.00
❑ SKAO 2944	The Best of Nat King Cole	1968	12.00
❑ H 9110 [10]	Eight Top Pops	1954	50.00
❑ M-11033 [M]	Trio Days	1972	15.00
❑ SWAK-11355	Love Is Here to Stay	1974	12.00
❑ SM-11796	After Midnight	1978	10.00
❑ SM-11804	Songs from "Cat Ballou" and Other Motion Pictures	1978	10.00
❑ SM-11882	Looking Back	1979	10.00
❑ ST-12219	16 Grandes Exitos	1982	10.00
❑ SN-16032	Ramblin' Rose	1980	8.00
❑ SN-16033	The Nat King Cole Story, Vol. 1	1980	8.00
❑ SN-16034	The Nat King Cole Story, Vol. 2	1980	8.00
❑ SN-16035	The Nat King Cole Story, Vol. 3	1980	8.00
❑ SN-16036	The Best of Nat King Cole	1980	8.00
❑ SN-16037	Wild Is Love	1980	8.00
❑ SN-16136	A Mis Amigos	1980	8.00
❑ SN-16137	St. Louis Blues	1980	8.00
❑ SN-16162	Unforgettable	1981	8.00
❑ SN-16163	Love Is the Thing	1981	8.00
❑ DN-16164	Walkin' My Baby Back Home	1981	8.00
❑ DN-16165	A Blossom Fell	1981	8.00
❑ N-16166	Cole Espanol	1981	8.00
❑ SN-16167	More Cole Espanol	1981	8.00
❑ N-16260	The Best of the King Cole Trio — Vol. 1	1982	8.00
❑ N-16281	The Best of the King Cole Trio — Vol. 2	1982	8.00
❑ SQBO 90938 [(2)]	The Velvet Moods of Nat King Cole	1967	25.00
—Capitol Record Club exclusive			
❑ SQBO 91278 [(2)]	The Swingin' Moods of Nat King Cole	1967	25.00
—Capitol Record Club exclusive			
❑ SQBO-93741 [(2)]	The Man and His Music	197?	20.00
—Capitol Record Club exclusive; with booklet			

DCC COMPACT CLASSICS

Number	Title (A Side/B Side)	Yr	NM
❑ LPZ-2029	Love Is the Thing	1997	120.00
—Audiophile vinyl			
❑ LPZ-2047	The Very Thought of You	1998	100.00
—Audiophile vinyl			
❑ LPZ-2061 [(2)]	The Greatest Hits	1998	120.00
—Audiophile vinyl			

DECCA

Number	Title (A Side/B Side)	Yr	NM
❑ DL 8260 [M]	In the Beginning	1956	40.00
—Black label, silver print			
❑ DL 8260 [M]	In the Beginning	1960	25.00
—Black label with color bars			

EVEREST ARCHIVE OF FOLK & JAZZ

Number	Title (A Side/B Side)	Yr	NM
❑ 290	Nature Boy	197?	10.00

MARK 56

Number	Title (A Side/B Side)	Yr	NM
❑ 739 [(2)]	Early 1940s	197?	15.00

MCA

Number	Title (A Side/B Side)	Yr	NM
❑ 4020 [(2)]	From the Very Beginning	1973	12.00

MOBILE FIDELITY

Number	Title (A Side/B Side)	Yr	NM
❑ 1-081	Nat King Cole Sings/ George Shearing Plays	1981	40.00
—Audiophile vinyl			

MOSAIC

Number	Title (A Side/B Side)	Yr	NM
❑ MR27-138 [(27)]	The Complete Capitol Recordings of the Nat King Cole Trio	1991	800.00

PAIR

Number	Title (A Side/B Side)	Yr	NM
❑ PDL2-1025 [(2)]	Weaver of Dreams	1986	12.00
❑ PDL2-1026 [(2)]	Love Moods	1986	12.00
❑ PDL2-1128 [(2)]	Tenderly	1986	12.00

PICKWICK

Number	Title (A Side/B Side)	Yr	NM
❑ PTP-2058 [(2)]	Nature Boy	1973	12.00
❑ SPC-3046	Love Is a Many Splendored Thing	196?	10.00
❑ SPC-3071	When You're Smiling	196?	10.00
❑ SPC-3105	Stay As Sweet As You Are	196?	10.00
❑ SPC-3154	You're My Everything	197?	10.00
❑ SPC-3249	Nature Boy	197?	10.00

SAVOY JAZZ

Number	Title (A Side/B Side)	Yr	NM
❑ SJL-1205	Nat King Cole & The King Cole Trio	1989	12.00

SCORE

Number	Title (A Side/B Side)	Yr	NM
❑ SLP-4019 [M]	The King Cole Trio and Lester Young	1957	80.00

TIME-LIFE

Number	Title (A Side/B Side)	Yr	NM
❑ SLGD-01 [(2)]	Legendary Singers: Nat King Cole	1985	15.00
❑ SLGD-15 [(2)]	Legendary Singers: Nat King Cole: Take Two	1986	15.00

TRIP

Number	Title (A Side/B Side)	Yr	NM
❑ 7	The Nat "King" Cole Trio	197?	12.00

VERVE

Number	Title (A Side/B Side)	Yr	NM
❑ VSP-14 [M]	Nat Cole at JATP	1966	15.00
❑ VSPS-14 [R]	Nat Cole at JATP	1966	12.00
❑ VSP-25 [M]	Nat Cole at JATP 2	1966	15.00
❑ VSPS-25 [R]	Nat Cole at JATP 2	1966	12.00

COLE, NATALIE

12-Inch Singles

CAPITOL

Number	Title (A Side/B Side)	Yr	NM
❑ SPRO-8990/1 [DJ]	I'm Catching Hell (Living Here Alone) (7:28) (stereo/mono)	1978	15.00

ELEKTRA

Number	Title (A Side/B Side)	Yr	NM
❑ ED 6256 [(2)DJ]	Livin' for Love (unknown versions)	2000	12.00
❑ 67153 [(2)]	Livin' for Love (Hex HQ2 Club Mix) (Acappella) (Frankie Knuckles Classic Club Mix) (Album Version) (Hex HQ2 Instrumental) (Hex HQ2 Radio Mix) (Frankie Knuckles Classic Instrumental) (Frankie Knuckles Dubbin' 4 Love)	2000	10.00

EMI

Number	Title (A Side/B Side)	Yr	NM
❑ SPRO 04265 [DJ]	Miss You Like Crazy (same on both sides?)	1989	10.00
❑ SPRO 04441/2 [DJ]	As a Matter of Fact (4 versions)	1989	10.00
❑ SPRO 04449 [DJ]	Starting Over Again (same on both sides?)	1989	15.00
❑ V-56161	Wild Women Do (7 versions)	1990	8.00

EMI MANHATTAN

Number	Title (A Side/B Side)	Yr	NM
❑ V-56084	Pink Cadillac (Radio Version) (Club Vocal) (Bass It Dub)/ I Wanna Be That Woman	1988	10.00

EPIC

Number	Title (A Side/B Side)	Yr	NM
❑ AS 1748 [DJ]	Keep It on the Outside/ I Won't Deny You	1983	8.00
❑ 49-04001	Too Much Mister/ Where's Your Angel	1983	8.00

MANHATTAN

Number	Title (A Side/B Side)	Yr	NM
❑ V-56053	Jump Start (Extended Remix) (Dub Version) (Radio Edit)/ More Than Stars	1987	8.00
❑ SPRO-79136/7 [DJ]	Jump Start (Extended Version) (Car Mix) (Deluxe Dub Mix)	1987	12.00
❑ SPRO-79154 [DJ]	I Live for Your Love (same on both sides)	1987	10.00

MODERN

Number	Title (A Side/B Side)	Yr	NM
❑ DMD 903 [DJ]	Secrets (Extended) (LP Version)	1985	10.00
❑ 96841	Secrets (Extended) (Instrumental)	1985	8.00
❑ 96885	Dangerous (Extended Dance Mix) (Dub Mix) (Acappella)	1985	10.00

45s

CAPITOL

Number	Title (A Side/B Side)	Yr	NM
❑ 4109	This Will Be/Joey	1975	5.00
❑ 4193	Inseparable/How Come You Won't Stay Here	1975	4.00
❑ 4259	Sophisticated Lady (She's a Different Lady)/Good Morning Heartache	1976	4.00
❑ 4328	Mr. Melody/Not Like Mine	1976	4.00
❑ 4360	I've Got Love on My Mind/ Unpredictable You	1976	4.00
❑ 4439	Party Lights/Peaceful Living	1977	4.00
❑ 4509	Our Love/La Costa	1977	4.00
❑ 4572	Annie Mae/Just Can't Stay Away	1978	4.00
❑ 4623	Lucy in the Sky with Diamonds/ Lovers	1978	4.00
❑ 4690	Stand By/Who Will Carry On	1979	4.00
❑ 4722	Sorry/You're So Good	1979	4.00

Number	Title (A Side/B Side)	Yr	NM
❑ 4767	Your Lonely Heart/The Winner	1979	4.00
❑ 4869	Someone That I Used to Love/ Don't Look Back	1980	4.00
❑ 4924	Hold On/Paradise	1980	4.00
❑ A-5021	You Were Right Girl/ Across the Nation	1981	4.00
❑ A-5045	Nothin' But a Fool/ The Joke Is On You	1981	4.00
ELEKTRA			
❑ 64816	The Christmas Song (Chestnuts Roasting on an Open Fire)/Nature Boy	1991	4.00
❑ 64875	Unforgettable/Cottage for Sale	1991	4.00
EMI			
❑ B-50185	Miss You Like Crazy/ Good to Be Back	1989	3.00
❑ B-50185 [PS]	Miss You Like Crazy/ Good to Be Back	1989	5.00
❑ B-50213	I Do/Miss You Like Crazy	1989	3.00
❑ B-50231	As a Matter of Fact/ (B-side unknown)	1989	5.00
EMI MANHATTAN			
❑ B-50117	Pink Cadillac/I Wanna Be That Woman	1988	3.00
❑ B-50138	When I Fall in Love/Pink Cadillac	1988	3.00
❑ B-50138 [PS]	When I Fall in Love/Pink Cadillac	1988	4.00
EPIC			
❑ 34-04000	Too Much Mister/ Where's Your Angel	1983	4.00
❑ 34-04147	Keep 'Em on the Outside/ I Won't Deny You	1983	4.00
GEFFEN			
❑ 28152	Over You/After Midnite	1987	3.00
—With Ray Parker Jr.			
MANHATTAN			
❑ B-50073	Jump Start/More Than the Stars	1987	3.00
❑ B-50073 [PS]	Jump Start/More Than the Stars	1987	4.00
❑ B-50094	I Live for Your Love/ More Than the Stars	1987	3.00
❑ B-50094 [PS]	I Live for Your Love/ More Than the Stars	1987	4.00
MODERN			
❑ 99589	Secrets/Nobody's Soldier	1985	3.00
❑ 99630	A Little Bit of Heaven/When I Need It Bad, You Got It Good	1985	3.00
❑ 99648	Dangerous/Love Is On the Way	1985	3.00
❑ 99648 [PS]	Dangerous/Love Is On the Way	1985	3.00
Albums			
CAPITOL			
❑ ST-11429	Inseparable	1975	10.00
❑ ST-11517	Natalie	1976	10.00
❑ SO-11600	Unpredictable	1977	10.00
❑ SW-11708	Thankful	1978	10.00
❑ SKBL-11709 [(2)]	Natalie..Live!	1978	12.00
❑ SO-11928	I Love You So	1979	10.00
❑ ST-12079	Don't Look Back	1980	10.00
❑ ST-12165	Happy Love	1981	10.00
❑ ST-12242	A Collection	1982	10.00
❑ SN-16038	Inseparable	198?	8.00
—Budget-line reissue			
❑ SN-16310	A Collection	1985	8.00
—Budget-line reissue			
ELEKTRA			
❑ 61049 [(2)]	Unforgettable	1991	20.00
EMI			
❑ E1-48902	Good to Be Back	1989	10.00
EPIC			
❑ FE 38280	I'm Ready	1983	10.00
MANHATTAN			
❑ 53051	Everlasting	1987	10.00
MOBILE FIDELITY			
❑ 1-032	Thankful	1980	20.00
—Audiophile vinyl			
MODERN			
❑ 90270	Dangerous	1985	10.00
COLE, NATALIE, AND PEABO BRYSON			
45s			
CAPITOL			
❑ 4804	Gimme Some Time/ Love Will Find You	1979	4.00
❑ 4826	What You Won't Do for Love/ Your Lonely Heart	1980	4.00
Albums			
CAPITOL			
❑ SOO-12025	We're the Best of Friends	1979	10.00
COLE, TONY			
45s			
20TH CENTURY			
❑ 2001	Suite: Man and Woman/ All I Meant to Do	1972	10.00
❑ 2011	The King Is Dead/Ruby	1973	10.00
❑ 2055	Scorpio/Mermaid	1973	10.00
Albums			
20TH CENTURY			
❑ T-403	If the Music Stops	1972	12.00
❑ T-416	Magnificently Mad	1973	12.00
COLEMAN, JIMMY			
45s			
REVUE			
❑ 11002	Cloudy Days/Don't Seem Like You Love Me	1967	20.00
COLEMAN, RAY			
45s			
ARCADE			
❑ 147	Jukebox Rock and Roll/ Rock, Chicken Rock	1957	200.00
COLESON, BETTY			
45s			
HIT			
❑ 93	Dominique/Since I Fell for You	1963	8.00
—B-side by Tom Tripp			
❑ 131	The Girl from Ipanema/Dang Me	1964	8.00
—B-side by Harvey Frolic			
❑ 144	We'll Sing in the Sunshine/ Tottle-Dee Doodle, Dee Doo	1964	8.00
—B-side by Jackie Preston			
❑ 173	The Wedding/Song of Love	1965	8.00
—B-side by William Randolph			
❑ 201	I Know a Place/I'm in a Very Romantic Mood	1965	8.00
—B-side by William Randolph			
COLLAGE, THE			
45s			
SMASH			
❑ 2135	Any Day's a Sunday Afternoon/ Lookin' at a Baby	1967	8.00
❑ 2135 [PS]	Any Day's a Sunday Afternoon/ Lookin' at a Baby	1967	15.00
❑ 2150	Driftin'/Any Day's a Sunday Afternoon	1968	8.00
❑ 2170	The Story of Rock & Roll/Virginia Day's Ragtime Stories	1968	8.00
COLLECTORS, THE Early incarnation of CHILLIWACK.			
45s			
VALIANT			
❑ 760	Old Man/Looking at a Baby	1967	30.00
WARNER BROS.			
❑ 7059	Listen to the Words/ Fisherwoman	1967	20.00
❑ 7159	Make It Easy/Fat Bird	1968	20.00
❑ 7194	Lydia Purple/I Ain't No Rich Man	1968	12.00
❑ 7194	Lydia Purple/She (Will O' the Wind)	1968	15.00
❑ 7300	Early Morning/My Love Delights Me	1969	12.00
Albums			
WARNER BROS.			
❑ W 1746 [M]	The Collectors	1968	50.00
—May be white label promo only			
❑ WS 1746 [S]	The Collectors	1968	25.00
❑ WS 1774	Grass and Wild Strawberries	1969	25.00
COLLEGIANS, THE (1)			
45s			
LOST-NITE			
❑ 123	Zoom, Zoom, Zoom/ On Your Merry Way	196?	8.00
—Reissue			
❑ 158	Let's Go for a Ride/ Heavenly Night	196?	6.00
—Reissue			
WINLEY			
❑ 224	Zoom, Zoom, Zoom/ On Your Merry Way	1958	50.00
❑ 261	Oh I Need Your Love/ Tonite, Oh Tonite	1962	30.00
❑ 263	Right Around the Corner/ Teenie Weenie Little Bit	1962	30.00
X-TRA			
❑ 108	Let's Go for a Ride/ Heavenly Night	1958	300.00
—Small print label (title and artist about 1/8-inch high)			
❑ 108	Let's Go for a Ride/ Heavenly Night	1961	60.00
—Large print label (title and artist about 1/4-inch high)			
Albums			
LOST-NITE			
❑ LLP-5 [10]	The Best of the Collegians	1981	10.00
—Red vinyl			
WINLEY			
❑ LP-6004 [M]	Sing Along with the Collegians	195?	400.00
COLLEGIANS, THE (U) Some of these may be by group (1), but others are not.			
45s			
CAT			
❑ 110	Rickety Tickety Melody/ The Sackbut, the Psaltery and the Dulcimer	1954	25.00
GROOVE			
❑ 0163	Blue Solitude/Please Let Me Be the One	1956	40.00
HILLTOP			
❑ 1866	Nomad/Fred's Boogie	1960	20.00
❑ 1867	The Saints (Part 1)/ The Saints (Part 2)	1960	20.00
❑ 1868	Cookin'/Happy Parakeet	1961	20.00
HUDCO			
❑ STAR-1/2	Ooh Poo Pah Doo/Silver Dollar	196?	12.00
POST			
❑ 10002	I'm Ready/Grandma Told Me So	1962	20.00
COLLIER, MITTY			
45s			
CHESS			
❑ 1791	I've Got Love/Got to Get Away from It All	1961	15.00
❑ 1856	Miss Loneliness/My Babe	1963	20.00
❑ 1871	I'm Your Part Time Love/ Don't You Forget It	1963	15.00
❑ 1889	Pain/Let Them Talk	196?	100.00
❑ 1907	I Had a Talk with My Man/ Free Girl (In the Morning)	1964	20.00
❑ 1918	No Faith, No Love/Together	1964	15.00
❑ 1934	Ain't That Love/Come Back Baby	1965	12.00
❑ 1942	Help Me/For My Man	1965	25.00
❑ 1953	Sharing You/Walk Away	1966	20.00
❑ 1964	My Party/I'm Satisfied	1966	40.00
❑ 1987	Like Only Yesterday/ Watching and Waiting	1967	20.00
❑ 2015	You're the Only One/ Do It with Confidence	1967	20.00
❑ 2035	Git Out/That'll Be Good Enough for Me	1967	15.00
❑ 2050	Everybody Makes a Mistake Sometimes/Gotta Get Away from It All	1968	15.00
ENTRANCE			
❑ ZS7 7512	I'd Like to Change Places/ If This Is Our Last Time	1972	10.00
PEACHTREE			
❑ 121	I Can't Lose/You Hurt So Good	1969	15.00
❑ 122	I'd Like to Change Places/ Share What You Got	1969	50.00
❑ 123	True Love Never Comes Easy/ Fly Me to the Moon	1969	20.00
❑ 125	Lovin' on Borrowed Time/ One Heck of a Lover	1970	30.00
❑ 128	Your Sign Is a Good Sign/ Mama, He Treats Your Daughter Mean	1970	20.00
Albums			
CHESS			
❑ LP-1492 [M]	Shades of a Genius	1965	80.00
❑ LPS-1492 [S]	Shades of a Genius	1965	120.00
COLLINS, ALBERT			
45s			
GREAT SCOTT			
❑ 007	Albert's Alley/Defrost	1963	30.00
HALLWAY			
❑ 1913	Albert's Alley/Defrost	1963	20.00
❑ 1920	Frosty/Tremble	1964	30.00
❑ 1925	Backstroke/Thaw Out	1964	20.00
IMPERIAL			
❑ 66351	Ain't Got Time/Got a Good Thing Goin'	1969	8.00
❑ 66391	Do the Sissy/Turnin' On	1969	8.00
❑ 66412	Conversation for Collins/ And Then It Started Raining	1969	8.00
KANGAROO			
❑ 103	Freeze/(B-side unknown)	1958	60.00
❑ 104	Collins Shuffle/(B-side unknown)	1958	60.00

C

Number	Title (A Side/B Side)	Yr	NM
LIBERTY			
❑ 56184	Coon 'n Collards/Do What You Want to Do	1970	8.00
TCF HALL			
❑ 104	Sno Cone (Part 1)/Sno Cone (Part 2)	1965	10.00
❑ 116	Dyin' Flu/Hot 'N' Cold	1966	10.00
❑ 127	Frost Bite/Don't Lose Your Cool	1966	10.00
TUMBLEWEED			
❑ 1007	Eight Days on the Road/(B-side unknown)	1972	8.00
20TH FOX			
❑ 6708	Cookin' Catfish/Taking My Time	1968	8.00
Albums			
ALLIGATOR			
❑ AL-4713	Ice Pickin'	1978	10.00
❑ AL-4719	Frostbite	1980	10.00
❑ AL-4725	Frozen Alive!	1981	10.00
❑ AL-4730	Don't Lose Your Cool	1983	10.00
❑ AL-4733	Live in Japan	1984	10.00
❑ AL-4743	Showdown!	1985	10.00
—With Robert Cray and Johnny Copeland			
❑ AL-4752	Cold Snap	1986	10.00
BLUE THUMB			
❑ BTS 8	Truckin' with Albert Collins	1969	25.00
—Reissue of TCF Hall LP			
IMPERIAL			
❑ LP-12428	Love Can Be Found Anywhere	1968	30.00
❑ LP-12438	Trash Talkin'	1969	30.00
❑ LP-12449	The Compleat Albert Collins	1970	30.00
MOBILE FIDELITY			
❑ 1-217	Showdown!	1995	30.00
—With Robert Cray and Johnny Copeland; audiophile vinyl			
❑ 1-226	Cold Snap	1995	20.00
—Audiophile vinyl			
TCF HALL			
❑ 8002 [M]	The Cool Sound of Albert Collins	1965	300.00
TUMBLEWEED			
❑ TWS-103	There's Gotta Be a Change	1971	15.00

COLLINS, BIG TOM

Number	Title (A Side/B Side)	Yr	NM
45s			
KING			
❑ 4483	Heartache Blues/Real Good Feeling	1951	100.00
❑ 4568	Heart Breaking Woman/Watchin' My Stuff	1952	100.00

COLLINS, BOOTSY

Number	Title (A Side/B Side)	Yr	NM
12-Inch Singles			
COLUMBIA			
❑ 44-07878	Party on Plastic (What's Bootsy Doin'?) (3 versions)/A Creative Nuisance	1988	10.00
❑ 44-08173	1st One 2 the Egg Wins (Screwin' Up) (Street Legal) (Human Race) (Street Legal Instrumental)	1988	10.00
45s			
COLUMBIA			
❑ 38-07991	Party on Plastic (What's Bootsy Doin'?)/Save What's Mine for Me	1988	3.00
❑ 38-07991 [PS]	Party on Plastic (What's Bootsy Doin'?)/Save What's Mine for Me	1988	3.00
❑ 38-08496	1st One 2 the Egg Wins (Human Race)/1st One 2 the Egg Wins (Street Legal)	1988	3.00
WARNER BROS.			
❑ 8215	Stretchin' Out (In a Rubber Band)/Physical Love	1976	6.00
❑ 29965	Shine-O-Myte (Rag Popping)/So Nice You Name Him Twice	1982	4.00
❑ 50044	Take a Lickin' and Keep On Kickin'/Shine-O-Myte (Rag Poppin')	1982	4.00
Albums			
COLUMBIA			
❑ FC 44107	What's Bootsy Doin'?	1988	10.00
WARNER BROS.			
❑ BSK 3667	The One Giveth, The Count Taketh Away	1982	10.00

COLLINS, BRIAN

Number	Title (A Side/B Side)	Yr	NM
45s			
ABC DOT			
❑ 17527	That's the Way Love Should Be/Come a Little Bit Closer	1974	5.00
❑ 17546	I'd Still Be in Love with You/Sweet Memories	1975	5.00
❑ 17564	Faithless Love/You Won't Get Away with Mine	1975	5.00
❑ 17593	Queen of Temptation/Before You Close the Door	1975	5.00
❑ 17613	To Show You That I Love You/My Heart Would Know	1976	5.00
❑ 17694	If You Love Me (Let Me Know)/Round and Round	1977	5.00
DOT			
❑ 17466	I Wish (You Had Stayed)/Hand in Hand with Love	1973	5.00
❑ 17483	I Don't Plan on Losing You/Lonely Too Long	1973	5.00
❑ 17499	Statue of a Fool/How Can I Tell Her	1974	5.00
MEGA			
❑ 0012	Walkin'/Your Kind of Man	1970	6.00
❑ 0022	New Way to Live/What Are You Gonna Do	1971	6.00
❑ 0038	All I Want to Do Is Say I Love You/Time to Try My Wings	1971	6.00
❑ 0058	There's a Kind of Hush (All Over the World)/Ain't Gonna Be Your Fool No More	1972	6.00
❑ 0078	Spread It Around/Let's Give It a Try	1972	6.00
PRIMERO			
❑ 1001	Before I Got to Know Her/Something Very Special	1982	5.00
❑ 1010	I'll Be Around/(B-side unknown)	1983	5.00
❑ 1018	Nickel's Worth of Heaven/Something Very Special	1983	5.00
RCA			
❑ PB-11277	Old Flames (Can't Hold a Candle to You)/Falsely Accused	1978	5.00
❑ PB-11350	Moonlight and Magnolias/Crazy You, Crazy Me	1978	5.00
❑ PB-11478	Hello Texas/Barefoot Angels	1979	5.00
Albums			
ABC			
❑ AC-1029	The ABC Collection	1977	15.00
ABC DOT			
❑ DOSD-2008	That's the Way Love Should Be	1974	15.00
DOT			
❑ DLP-26017	This Is Brian Collins	1973	15.00

COLLINS, EDDIE

Number	Title (A Side/B Side)	Yr	NM
45s			
FERNWOOD			
❑ 104	Patience Baby/Can't Face Life Alone	1958	100.00

COLLINS, GLENDA

Number	Title (A Side/B Side)	Yr	NM
45s			
LAWN			
❑ 250	Lollipop/Everybody's Gotta Fall in Love	1965	10.00

COLLINS, JUDY

Number	Title (A Side/B Side)	Yr	NM
45s			
ELEKTRA			
❑ 45008	Turn, Turn, Turn/Farewell	1963	10.00
❑ 45253	Send In the Clowns/Houses	1975	5.00
—Large print label (original)			
❑ 45253	Send In the Clowns/Houses	1977	4.00
—Small print label (reissue)			
❑ 45289	Angel, Spread Your Wings/The Moon Is a Harsh Mistress	1975	4.00
❑ 45355	Bread and Roses/Out of Control	1976	4.00
❑ 45355 [PS]	Bread and Roses/Out of Control	1976	6.00
❑ 45372	Everything Must Change/Special Delivery	1976	4.00
❑ 45415	Born to the Breed/Special Delivery	1977	4.00
❑ 45601	I'll Keep It With Mine/Thirsty Boots	1965	8.00
❑ 45610	I Think It's Going to Rain Today/Hard Lovin' Losers	1966	8.00
❑ 45639	Both Sides Now/Who Knows Where the Time Goes	1968	6.00
—Yellow and black label			
❑ 45639	Both Sides Now/Who Knows Where the Time Goes	1968	8.00
—Red, white and black label			
❑ 45649	Someday Soon/My Father	1969	6.00
❑ 45657	Chelsea Morning/Pretty Polly	1969	6.00
❑ 45657 [PS]	Chelsea Morning/Pretty Polly	1969	15.00
❑ 45680	Pack Up Your Sorrows/Turn, Turn, Turn	1970	5.00
❑ 45709	Amazing Grace/Nightingale II	1971	5.00
❑ 45755	Open the Door/Innisfree	1971	5.00
❑ 45813	In My Life/Sunny Goodge Street	1972	4.00
❑ 45831	Cook with Honey/So Begins the Task	1973	4.00
❑ 45849	The Hostage/Secret Gardens	1973	4.00
❑ 46020	Hard Times for Lovers/Happy End	1979	4.00
❑ 46020 [PS]	Hard Times for Lovers/Happy End	1979	6.00
❑ 46050	Where or When/Dorothy	1979	4.00
❑ 46623	Bright Morning Star/Almost Free	1980	4.00
❑ 46651	The Rainbow Connection/Running for My Life	1980	4.00
❑ 47243	Memory/The Life You Dream	1981	4.00
❑ 47434	It's Gonna Be One of Those Nights/Mama Mama	1982	4.00
❑ 47437 [DJ]	Drink a Round to Ireland (stereo)/(mono)	1982	10.00
—Promo only on green vinyl			
❑ 69662	Only You/Dream On	1985	3.00
❑ 69697	Home Again/Dream On	1984	4.00
—A-side with T.G. Sheppard			
Albums			
DCC COMPACT CLASSICS			
❑ LPZ-2067	Colors of the Day/The Best of Judy Collins	1998	25.00
—Audiophile vinyl			
DIRECT DISK			
❑ SD-16607	Judith	1980	40.00
—Audiophile vinyl			
ELEKTRA			
❑ JC-1 [DJ]	Judy Collins	1967	15.00
—Promo-only compilation of six songs, each in mono on one side, stereo on the other			
❑ 6E-111	Judith	1977	8.00
—Reissue of 7E-1032			
❑ 6E-171	Hard Times for Lovers	1979	10.00
❑ EKL-209 [M]	Maid of Constant Sorrow	1961	40.00
—"Guitar player" label			
❑ EKL-209 [M]	Maid of Constant Sorrow	1966	20.00
—Gold/tan label			
❑ EKL-222 [M]	Golden Apples of the Sun	1962	30.00
—"Guitar player" label			
❑ EKL-222 [M]	Golden Apples of the Sun	1966	20.00
—Gold/tan label			
❑ EKL-243 [M]	Judy Collins #3	1963	30.00
—"Guitar player" label			
❑ EKL-243 [M]	Judy Collins #3	1966	20.00
—Gold/tan label			
❑ 6E-253	Running for My Life	1980	10.00
❑ EKL-280 [M]	Judy Collins' Concert	1964	30.00
—"Guitar player" label			
❑ EKL-280 [M]	Judy Collins' Concert	1966	20.00
—Gold/tan label			
❑ EKL-300 [M]	Judy Collins' Fifth Album	1965	30.00
—"Guitar player" label			
❑ EKL-300 [M]	Judy Collins' Fifth Album	1966	20.00
—Gold/tan label			
❑ EKL-320 [M]	In My Life	1966	20.00
❑ DS 500	Judy	1969	15.00
—Columbia Record Club exclusive; red label with large stylized "E"			
❑ 7E-1032	Judith	1975	12.00
❑ EQ-1032 [Q]	Judith	1975	20.00
❑ 7E-1076	Bread and Roses	1976	10.00
❑ EKL-4012 [M]	Wildflowers	1967	25.00
❑ EQ-5030 [Q]	Colors of the Day/The Best of Judy Collins	1973	20.00
❑ 8E-6002 [(2)]	So Early in the Spring: The First 15 Years	1977	12.00
❑ EKS-7209 [R]	Maid of Constant Sorrow	1964	20.00
—"Guitar player" label (first edition)			
❑ EKS-7209 [R]	Maid of Constant Sorrow	1966	12.00
—Gold/tan label or red label with large stylized "E"			
❑ EKS-7209 [R]	Maid of Constant Sorrow	1971	10.00
—Butterfly label, no Warner Communications logo			
❑ EKS-7209 [R]	Maid of Constant Sorrow	1975	8.00
—Any label with Warner Communications logo			
❑ EKS-7222 [R]	Golden Apples of the Sun	196?	12.00
—Gold/tan label or red label with large stylized "E"			
❑ EKS-7222 [R]	Golden Apples of the Sun	1971	10.00
—Butterfly label, no Warner Communications logo			
❑ EKS-7222 [R]	Golden Apples of the Sun	1975	8.00
—Any label with Warner Communications logo			
❑ EKS-7243 [S]	Judy Collins #3	1963	40.00
—"Guitar player" label			
❑ EKS-7243 [S]	Judy Collins #3	1966	25.00
—Gold/tan label			
❑ EKS-7243 [S]	Judy Collins #3	1969	15.00
—Red label with large stylized "E"			
❑ EKS-7243 [S]	Judy Collins #3	1971	10.00
—Butterfly label, no Warner Communications logo			
❑ EKS-7243 [S]	Judy Collins #3	1975	8.00
—Any label with Warner Communications logo			
❑ EKS-7280 [S]	Judy Collins' Concert	1964	40.00
—"Guitar player" label			
❑ EKS-7280 [S]	Judy Collins' Concert	1966	25.00
—Gold/tan label			
❑ EKS-7280 [S]	Judy Collins' Concert	1969	15.00
—Red label with large stylized "E"			
❑ EKS-7280 [S]	Judy Collins' Concert	1971	12.00
—Butterfly label, no Warner Communications logo			
❑ EKS-7280 [S]	Judy Collins' Concert	1975	8.00
—Any label with Warner Communications logo			

Except when noted otherwise, VG = 25% of NM, and VG+ = 50% of NM. (Example: VG = $2.00, VG+ = $4.00 and NM = $8.00.)

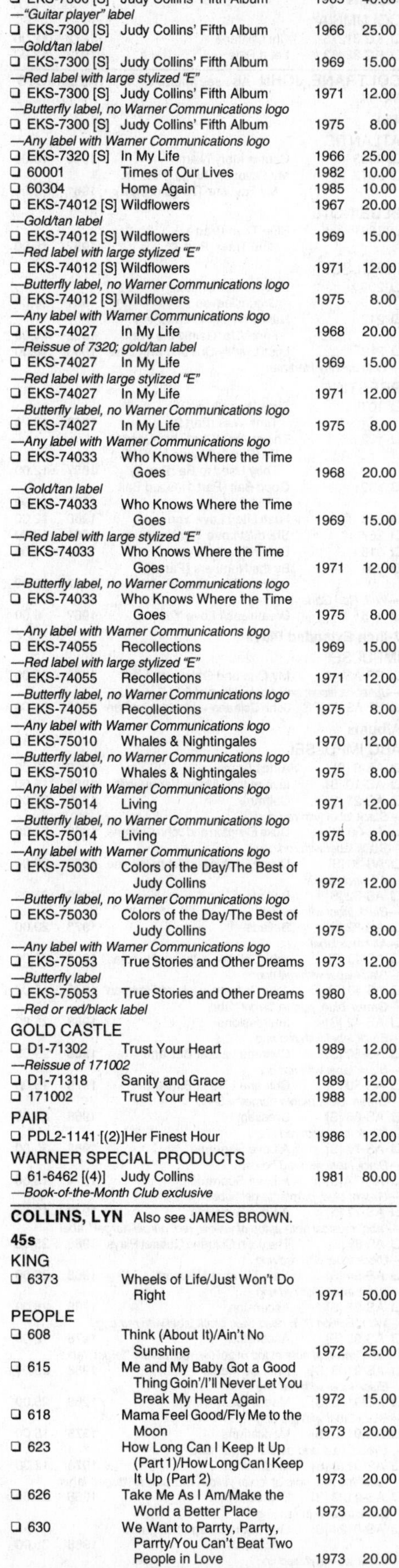

Number	Title (A Side/B Side)	Yr	NM
❑ EKS-7300 [S]	Judy Collins' Fifth Album	1965	40.00
—"Guitar player" label			
❑ EKS-7300 [S]	Judy Collins' Fifth Album	1966	25.00
—Gold/tan label			
❑ EKS-7300 [S]	Judy Collins' Fifth Album	1969	15.00
—Red label with large stylized "E"			
❑ EKS-7300 [S]	Judy Collins' Fifth Album	1971	12.00
—Butterfly label, no Warner Communications logo			
❑ EKS-7300 [S]	Judy Collins' Fifth Album	1975	8.00
—Any label with Warner Communications logo			
❑ EKS-7320 [S]	In My Life	1966	25.00
❑ 60001	Times of Our Lives	1982	10.00
❑ 60304	Home Again	1985	10.00
❑ EKS-74012 [S]	Wildflowers	1967	20.00
—Gold/tan label			
❑ EKS-74012 [S]	Wildflowers	1969	15.00
—Red label with large stylized "E"			
❑ EKS-74012 [S]	Wildflowers	1971	12.00
—Butterfly label, no Warner Communications logo			
❑ EKS-74012 [S]	Wildflowers	1975	8.00
—Any label with Warner Communications logo			
❑ EKS-74027	In My Life	1968	20.00
—Reissue of 7320; gold/tan label			
❑ EKS-74027	In My Life	1969	15.00
—Red label with large stylized "E"			
❑ EKS-74027	In My Life	1971	12.00
—Butterfly label, no Warner Communications logo			
❑ EKS-74027	In My Life	1975	8.00
—Any label with Warner Communications logo			
❑ EKS-74033	Who Knows Where the Time Goes	1968	20.00
—Gold/tan label			
❑ EKS-74033	Who Knows Where the Time Goes	1969	15.00
—Red label with large stylized "E"			
❑ EKS-74033	Who Knows Where the Time Goes	1971	12.00
—Butterfly label, no Warner Communications logo			
❑ EKS-74033	Who Knows Where the Time Goes	1975	8.00
—Any label with Warner Communications logo			
❑ EKS-74055	Recollections	1969	15.00
—Red label with large stylized "E"			
❑ EKS-74055	Recollections	1971	12.00
—Butterfly label, no Warner Communications logo			
❑ EKS-74055	Recollections	1975	8.00
—Any label with Warner Communications logo			
❑ EKS-75010	Whales & Nightingales	1970	12.00
—Butterfly label, no Warner Communications logo			
❑ EKS-75010	Whales & Nightingales	1975	8.00
—Any label with Warner Communications logo			
❑ EKS-75014	Living	1971	12.00
—Butterfly label, no Warner Communications logo			
❑ EKS-75014	Living	1975	8.00
—Any label with Warner Communications logo			
❑ EKS-75030	Colors of the Day/The Best of Judy Collins	1972	12.00
—Butterfly label, no Warner Communications logo			
❑ EKS-75030	Colors of the Day/The Best of Judy Collins	1975	8.00
—Any label with Warner Communications logo			
❑ EKS-75053	True Stories and Other Dreams	1973	12.00
—Butterfly label			
❑ EKS-75053	True Stories and Other Dreams	1980	8.00
—Red or red/black label			
GOLD CASTLE			
❑ D1-71302	Trust Your Heart	1989	12.00
—Reissue of 171002			
❑ D1-71318	Sanity and Grace	1989	12.00
❑ 171002	Trust Your Heart	1988	12.00
PAIR			
❑ PDL2-1141 [(2)]	Her Finest Hour	1986	12.00
WARNER SPECIAL PRODUCTS			
❑ 61-6462 [(4)]	Judy Collins	1981	80.00
—Book-of-the-Month Club exclusive			

COLLINS, LYN Also see JAMES BROWN.

45s

Number	Title (A Side/B Side)	Yr	NM
KING			
❑ 6373	Wheels of Life/Just Won't Do Right	1971	50.00
PEOPLE			
❑ 608	Think (About It)/Ain't No Sunshine	1972	25.00
❑ 615	Me and My Baby Got a Good Thing Goin'/I'll Never Let You Break My Heart Again	1972	15.00
❑ 618	Mama Feel Good/Fly Me to the Moon	1973	20.00
❑ 623	How Long Can I Keep It Up (Part 1)/How Long Can I Keep It Up (Part 2)	1973	20.00
❑ 626	Take Me As I Am/Make the World a Better Place	1973	20.00
❑ 630	We Want to Parrty, Parrty, Parrty/You Can't Beat Two People in Love	1973	20.00
❑ 633	Take Me Just As I Am/Don't Make Me Over	1973	12.00
❑ 636	Give It Up or Turnit A Loose/What the World Needs Now Is Love	1974	30.00
❑ 641	Wide Awake in a Dream/Rock Me Again & Again & Again & Again & Again & Again	1974	30.00
❑ 650	Rock Me Again & Again & Again & Again & Again/You Can't Love Me If You Don't Respect Me	1974	30.00
❑ 657	Baby Don't Do It/How Long Can I Keep It Up	1975	20.00
❑ 659	If You Don't Know Me By Now/Baby Don't Do It	1975	20.00
❑ 662	Mr. Big Stuff/Rock Me Again & Again & Again & Again & Again	1975	25.00
POLYDOR			
❑ 14107	Wheels of Life/Just Won't Do Right	1971	20.00
—Reissue of King 6373			

Albums

Number	Title	Yr	NM
PEOPLE			
❑ PE-5602	Think (About It)	1972	150.00
—This album has been "reissued"; be careful of sealed copies			
❑ PE-6605	Check Me Out	1975	100.00
—This album has been "reissued"; be careful of sealed copies			

Phil Collins, "One More Night," Atlantic 89588, 1985, $3.

COLLINS, PHIL Also see GENESIS; BRAND X; BRIAN ENO. Phil also drummed in ROBERT PLANT's solo band.

12-Inch Singles

Number	Title (A Side/B Side)	Yr	NM
ATLANTIC			
❑ PR 470 [DJ]	You Can't Hurry Love (same on both sides)	1982	15.00
❑ PR 483 [DJ]	I Cannot Believe It's True (same on both sides)	1983	10.00
❑ PR 483 [DJ]	Like China/I Cannot Believe It's True	1983	12.00
—With sticker on sleeve: "Like China AOL Top Track"			
❑ PR 496 [DJ]	I Cannot Believe It's True (Special Live Version) (LP Version)	1982	15.00
❑ PR 700 [DJ]	One More Night (same on both sides)	1985	15.00
❑ PR 717 [DJ]	Sussudio (Extended Remix 6:53) (LP Version 4:23)	1985	15.00
❑ PR 724 [DJ]	Don't Lose My Number (same on both sides)	1985	10.00
❑ PR 783 [DJ]	Don't Lose My Number (Remix) (LP Version)	1985	12.00
❑ PR 787 [DJ]	Separate Lives (same on both sides)	1985	12.00
—With Marilyn Martin			
❑ PR 808 [DJ]	Take Me Home (5:51) (8:03)	1985	10.00
❑ DMD 831 [DJ]	Sussudio (Extended Mix) (LP Version)/The Man with the Horn	1985	10.00
❑ DMD 872 [DJ]	Don't Lose My Number (Extended Mix 6:32) (LP Version)/We Said Hello Goodbye	1985	15.00
❑ DMD 1534 [DJ]	Something Happened on the Way to Heaven (One World Mix 5:38) (same on both sides)	1990	10.00
❑ DMD 1568 [DJ]	Hang In Long Enough (Club Mix) (Dub 1) (Dub 2)	1990	10.00
❑ DMD 2418 [DJ]	In the Air Tonight (2 versions)	1997	10.00
❑ PR 2445 [DJ]	Groovy Kind of Love (same on both sides)	1988	12.00
❑ PR 2554 [DJ]	Two Hearts (same on both sides)	1988	10.00
❑ 85417	In the Air Tonight (2 versions)	1997	8.00
❑ 86111	Hang In Long Enough (3 versions)	1990	8.00
❑ 86821	Take Me Home (Extended Mix 8:03) (LP Mix)/Only You Know and I Know	1986	8.00
❑ 86863	Don't Lose My Number (Remix) (LP Version)/We Said Hello Goodbye	1985	6.00
❑ 86895	Sussudio (2 versions)/The Man with the Horn	1985	8.00

45s

ATLANTIC

Number	Title (A Side/B Side)	Yr	NM
❑ PR 655 [DJ]	In the Air Tonight (same on both sides?)	1984	8.00

—Promo-only radio reservice after the song was successfully used in the TV series "Miami Vice"

Number	Title (A Side/B Side)	Yr	NM
❑ 3790	I Missed Again/I'm Not Moving	1981	3.00
❑ 3790 [PS]	I Missed Again/I'm Not Moving	1981	6.00
❑ 3824	In the Air Tonight/ The Roof Is Leaking	1981	3.00
❑ 3824 [PS]	In the Air Tonight/ The Roof Is Leaking	1981	6.00
❑ 87800	Hang In Long Enough/ Separate Lives	1990	3.00
❑ 87885	Something Happened on the Way to Heaven/Lionel	1990	3.00
❑ 87955	Do You Remember?/I Wish It Would Rain Down (Live)	1990	3.00
❑ 88738	I Wish It Would Rain Down/ You've Been in Love (That Little Bit)	1989	3.00
❑ 88738 [PS]	I Wish It Would Rain Down/ You've Been in Love (That Little Bit)	1989	3.00
❑ 88774	Another Day in Paradise/ Heat on the Street	1989	3.00
❑ 88774 [PS]	Another Day in Paradise/ Heat on the Street	1989	3.00
❑ 88980	Two Hearts/The Robbery	1989	3.00
❑ 88980 [PS]	Two Hearts/The Robbery	1989	4.00
❑ 89017	Groovy Kind of Love/Big Noise	1988	3.00
❑ 89017 [PS]	Groovy Kind of Love/Big Noise	1988	4.00
❑ 89472	Take Me Home/Only You Know and I Know	1985	3.00
❑ 89472 [PS]	Take Me Home/Only You Know and I Know	1985	4.00
❑ 89498	Separate Lives (Love Theme from White Nights)/ I Don't Wanna Know	1985	3.00

—A-side with Marilyn Martin

Number	Title (A Side/B Side)	Yr	NM
❑ 89498 [PS]	Separate Lives (Love Theme from White Nights)/ I Don't Wanna Know	1985	4.00

—With photo of Phil and Marilyn on front of sleeve

Number	Title (A Side/B Side)	Yr	NM
❑ 89498 [PS]	Separate Lives (Love Theme from White Nights)/ I Don't Wanna Know	1985	5.00

—With promo shot from the movie on front of sleeve

Number	Title (A Side/B Side)	Yr	NM
❑ 89536	Don't Lose My Number/ We Said Hello Goodbye	1985	3.00
❑ 89536 [PS]	Don't Lose My Number/ We Said Hello Goodbye	1985	3.00
❑ 89560	Sussudio/I Like the Way	1985	3.00
❑ 89560 [PS]	Sussudio/I Like the Way	1985	3.00
❑ 89588	One More Night/The Man with the Horn	1985	3.00
❑ 89588 [PS]	One More Night/The Man with the Horn	1985	3.00
❑ 89700	Against All Odds (Take a Look at Me Now)/The Search	1984	3.00

—B-side by Larry Carlton

Number	Title (A Side/B Side)	Yr	NM
❑ 89700 [PS]	Against All Odds (Take a Look at Me Now)/The Search	1984	3.00
❑ 89864	I Cannot Believe It's True/ Thru These Walls	1983	3.00
❑ 89877	I Don't Care Anymore/ The West Side	1983	3.00
❑ 89877 [PS]	I Don't Care Anymore/ The West Side	1983	3.00
❑ 89933	You Can't Hurry Love/ Do You Know	1982	3.00
❑ 89933 [PS]	You Can't Hurry Love/ Do You Know	1982	3.00

ATLANTIC OLDIES SERIES

Number	Title (A Side/B Side)	Yr	NM
❑ OS 13231	In the Air Tonight/I Missed Again	1984	3.00

—Reissue

Albums

ATLANTIC

Number	Title (A Side/B Side)	Yr	NM
❑ PR 759 [DJ]	Collins on Collins: Exclusive Candid Interview	1985	30.00

—Promo-only interview album with cue sheets

Number	Title (A Side/B Side)	Yr	NM
❑ SD 16029	Face Value	1981	8.00
❑ 80035	Hello, I Must Be Going!	1982	8.00
❑ 81240	No Jacket Required	1985	8.00
❑ 82050	... But Seriously	1989	12.00
❑ 82157 [(2)]	Serious Hits... Live!	1990	20.00

COLOGNES, THE

45s

LUMMTONE

Number	Title (A Side/B Side)	Yr	NM
❑ 102	A River Flows/A Bird and a Bee	1960	150.00

COLORADO

With members of THE FIREBALLS.

45s

UNI

Number	Title (A Side/B Side)	Yr	NM
❑ 55280	My Babe/Country Comfort	1971	6.00
❑ 55302	Dogwood/Moonshine	1971	6.00

COLOSSEUM

Gary Moore and Don Airey are Colosseum alumni.

45s

ABC DUNHILL

Number	Title (A Side/B Side)	Yr	NM
❑ 4200	Those Who Are About to Die Salute You/Walking in the Park	1969	8.00
❑ 4211	Kettle/Plenty Hard Luck	1969	8.00

Albums

ABC DUNHILL

Number	Title (A Side/B Side)	Yr	NM
❑ DS-50062	Those Who Are About to Die Salute You	1969	20.00
❑ DS-50079	The Grass Is Green	1970	20.00
❑ DSX-50101	Daughter of Time	1971	15.00

WARNER BROS.

Number	Title (A Side/B Side)	Yr	NM
❑ PRO 500 [DJ]	Colosseum Live	1972	15.00

—Highlights for radio

Number	Title (A Side/B Side)	Yr	NM
❑ 2WS 1942 [(2)]	Colosseum Live	1972	15.00

COLOURS

45s

DOT

Number	Title (A Side/B Side)	Yr	NM
❑ 17181	Hyannis Port Soul/ Run Away from Here	1968	8.00

Albums

DOT

Number	Title (A Side/B Side)	Yr	NM
❑ DLP-3854 [M]	Colours	1968	50.00

—Record has a black label, resembling a stock copy, but it is in a stereo cover with "Monaural" and "Promotional Copy Not for Sale" stickers on front

Number	Title (A Side/B Side)	Yr	NM
❑ DLP-25854 [S]	Colours	1968	25.00
❑ DLP-25935	Atmosphere	1969	25.00

COLTON, TONY

45s

ABC-PARAMOUNT

Number	Title (A Side/B Side)	Yr	NM
❑ 10705	I Stand Accused/Further On Down the Track	1965	15.00
❑ 10792	You're Wrong Baby/Have You Lost Your Mind	1966	15.00

ROULETTE

Number	Title (A Side/B Side)	Yr	NM
❑ 4475	Tell the World/Goodbye Cindy, Goodbye	1963	15.00

COLTRANE, ALICE

Widow of JOHN COLTRANE. She played in his group for a time.

45s

ABC IMPULSE!

Number	Title (A Side/B Side)	Yr	NM
❑ 279	Journey in Satchidananda (Part 1)/Journey in Satchidananda (Part 2)	1970	6.00

Albums

ABC IMPULSE!

Number	Title (A Side/B Side)	Yr	NM
❑ AS-9156	A Monastic Trio	1968	80.00
❑ AS-9185	Huntington Ashram Monastery	1969	60.00
❑ AS-9196	Ptah the El Daoud	1969	50.00
❑ AS-9203	Journey in Satchidananda	1970	50.00
❑ AS-9210	Universal Consciousness	1971	60.00
❑ AS-9218	World Galaxy	1972	40.00
❑ AS-9224	Lord of Lords	1972	40.00
❑ AS-9232 [(2)]	Reflection On Creation and Space	1973	30.00

GRP/IMPULSE!

Number	Title (A Side/B Side)	Yr	NM
❑ IMP-228	Journey in Satchidanada	1997	15.00

—180-gram reissue

WARNER BROS.

Number	Title (A Side/B Side)	Yr	NM
❑ BS 2916	Eternity	1975	20.00
❑ BS 2986	Radha-Krsna Nama Sankirtana	1976	25.00
❑ BS 3077	Transcendence	1977	20.00
❑ 2WB 3218 [(2)]	Transfiguration	1978	40.00

COLTRANE, ALICE, AND CARLOS SANTANA

Albums

COLUMBIA

Number	Title (A Side/B Side)	Yr	NM
❑ PC 32900	Illuminations	1974	20.00

—No bar code on cover

COLTRANE, CHI

45s

CLOUDS

Number	Title (A Side/B Side)	Yr	NM
❑ 10	What's Happening to Me (It's a Spell)/Changes	1978	4.00

COLUMBIA

Number	Title (A Side/B Side)	Yr	NM
❑ 45640	Thunder and Lightning/ Time to Come In	1972	5.00
❑ 45749	It's Really Come to This/ Go Like Elijah	1972	5.00
❑ 45802	Turn Me Around/ You Are My Friend	1973	5.00
❑ 45960	Myself to You/Who Every Told You	1973	4.00

Albums

COLUMBIA

Number	Title (A Side/B Side)	Yr	NM
❑ KC 31275	Chi Coltrane	1972	12.00
❑ KC 32463	Let It Ride	1973	12.00

COLTRANE, JOHN

Also see MILES DAVIS; THELONIOUS MONK.

45s

ATLANTIC

Number	Title (A Side/B Side)	Yr	NM
❑ 5003	Cousin Mary/Naimi	1960	10.00
❑ 5012	My Favorite Things (Part 1)/ My Favorite Things (Part 2)	1961	12.00

BLUE NOTE

Number	Title (A Side/B Side)	Yr	NM
❑ 1691	Blue Train (Part 1)/ Blue Train (Part 2)	1957	15.00

IMPULSE!

Number	Title (A Side/B Side)	Yr	NM
❑ 203	Easy to Remember/ Greensleeves	1961	10.00
❑ 212	Nancy (With the Laughing Face)/Up 'Gainst the Wall	1962	10.00
❑ 218	Lush Life/My One and Only Love	1963	10.00

—With Johnny Hartman

PRESTIGE

Number	Title (A Side/B Side)	Yr	NM
❑ 107	Time Was (Part 1)/ Time Was (Part 2)	195?	12.00
❑ 122	Things Ain't What They Used to Be (Part 1)/Things Ain't What They Used to Be (Part 2)	195?	12.00
❑ 139	Good Bait (Part 1)/Good Bait (Part 2)	195?	12.00
❑ 249	Lush Life/I Love You	1960	12.00
❑ 267	Stardust/Love Thy Neighbor	1961	12.00
❑ 315	Dakar/The Believer	1963	10.00
❑ 394	By the Numbers (Part 1)/ By the Numbers (Part 2)	196?	8.00

—With Red Garland

Number	Title (A Side/B Side)	Yr	NM
❑ 415	Breathless/I Love You	196?	8.00

7-Inch Extended Plays

IMPULSE!

Number	Title (A Side/B Side)	Yr	NM
❑ EP AS-40	My One and Only/Lush Life	1963	20.00

—Jukebox issue; small hole, plays at 33 1/3 rpm

Number	Title (A Side/B Side)	Yr	NM
❑ EP AS-40 [PS]	John Coltrane + Johnny Hartman	1963	20.00

Albums

ABC IMPULSE!

Number	Title (A Side/B Side)	Yr	NM
❑ AS-6 [S]	Africa/Brass	1968	30.00
❑ AS-10 [S]	Live at the Village Vanguard	1968	15.00
❑ AS-21 [S]	Coltrane	1968	25.00

—Black label with red ring

Number	Title (A Side/B Side)	Yr	NM
❑ AS-30 [S]	Duke Ellington and John Coltrane	1968	50.00

—Black label with red ring

Number	Title (A Side/B Side)	Yr	NM
❑ AS-30 [S]	Duke Ellington and John Coltrane	1973	25.00

—All-black label

Number	Title (A Side/B Side)	Yr	NM
❑ AS-32 [S]	Ballads	1968	25.00

—Black label with red ring

Number	Title (A Side/B Side)	Yr	NM
❑ AS-32 [S]	Ballads	1973	20.00

—All-black label

Number	Title (A Side/B Side)	Yr	NM
❑ AS-40 [S]	John Coltrane + Johnny Hartman	1968	25.00

—Black label with red ring

Number	Title (A Side/B Side)	Yr	NM
❑ AS-40 [S]	John Coltrane + Johnny Hartman	1975	15.00

—Green blue, purple "target" label

Number	Title (A Side/B Side)	Yr	NM
❑ AS-42 [S]	Impressions	1968	25.00

—Black label with red ring

Number	Title (A Side/B Side)	Yr	NM
❑ AS-50 [S]	Coltrane Live at Birdland	1968	25.00

—Black label with red ring

Number	Title (A Side/B Side)	Yr	NM
❑ AS-50 [S]	Coltrane Live at Birdland	1975	15.00

—Green blue, purple "target" label

Number	Title (A Side/B Side)	Yr	NM
❑ AS-66 [S]	Crescent	1968	25.00

—Black label with red ring

Number	Title (A Side/B Side)	Yr	NM
❑ AS-77 [S]	A Love Supreme	1968	30.00

—Black label with red border

Number	Title (A Side/B Side)	Yr	NM
❑ AS-77 [S]	A Love Supreme	1974	15.00

—Green, blue, purple "target" label

Number	Title (A Side/B Side)	Yr	NM
❑ AS-77 [S]	A Love Supreme	1978	12.00

—"abc" musical note at top of yellow, red, purple "target" label

Number	Title (A Side/B Side)	Yr	NM
❑ AS-85 [S]	The John Coltrane Quartet Plays	1968	25.00

—Black label with red ring

Number	Title (A Side/B Side)	Yr	NM
❑ AS-94 [S]	New Thing at Newport	1968	25.00

—Black label with red ring

Number	Title (A Side/B Side)	Yr	NM
❑ AS-95 [S]	Ascension	1968	25.00

—With "Edition II" in dead wax; black label with red ring

Number	Title (A Side/B Side)	Yr	NM
❑ AS-95 [S]	Ascension	1978	12.00

—"abc" musical note at top of yellow, red, purple "target" label

Number	Title (A Side/B Side)	Yr	NM
❑ AS-9106 [S]	Kulu Se Mama	1968	25.00

—Black label with red ring

Number	Title (A Side/B Side)	Yr	NM
❑ AS-9110 [S]	Meditations	1968	25.00

—Black label with red ring

Number	Title (A Side/B Side)	Yr	NM
❑ AS-9110 [S]	Meditations	1975	15.00

—Green, blue and purple "target" label

Number	Title (A Side/B Side)	Yr	NM
❑ AS-9110 [S]	Meditations	1978	12.00

—"abc" musical note at top of yellow, red, purple "target" label

Number	Title (A Side/B Side)	Yr	NM
❑ AS-9120 [S]	Expression	1968	25.00

—Black label with red ring

Number	Title (A Side/B Side)	Yr	NM
❑ AS-9124 [S]	Live at the Village Vanguard Again!	1968	25.00

—Black label with red ring

Except when noted otherwise, VG = 25% of NM, and VG+ = 50% of NM. (Example: VG = $2.00, VG+ = $4.00 and NM = $8.00.)

Number	Title (A Side/B Side)	Yr	NM
❑ AS-9124 [S]	Live at the Village Vanguard Again!	1975	15.00
—Green, blue and purple "target" label			
❑ AS-9140 [S]	Om	1968	25.00
—Black label with red ring			
❑ AS-9148	Cosmic Music	1969	20.00
—Credited to "Alice and John Coltrane"; reissue of Coltrane LP			
❑ AS-9161	Selflessness	1969	20.00
❑ AS-9195	Transition	1969	20.00
❑ AS-9200 [(2)]	Greatest Years	1971	20.00
❑ AS-9202 [(2)]	Live in Seattle	1971	20.00
❑ AS-9211	Sun Ship	1971	20.00
❑ AS-9223 [(2)]	Greatest Years, Vol. 2	1973	15.00
❑ AS-9225	Infinity	1973	12.00
❑ IA-9246 [(2)]	Concert Japan	1973	15.00
❑ AS-9273	Africa/Brass, Vol. 2	1974	40.00
❑ IA-9277	Interstellar Space	1974	12.00
❑ IA-9278 [(2)]	Greatest Years, Vol. 3	1974	15.00
❑ IA-9306 [(2)]	The Gentle Side of John Coltrane	1976	15.00
❑ IA-9325 [(2)]	The Other Village Vanguard Tapes	1977	15.00
❑ IA-9332	First Meditations	1978	12.00
❑ IZ-9345 [(2)]	The Mastery of John Coltrane Vol. 1: Feelin' Good	1978	12.00
❑ IZ-9346 [(2)]	The Mastery of John Coltrane Vol. 2: Different Drum	1978	12.00
❑ IA-9360	The Mastery of John Coltrane Vol. 3: Jupiter Variation	1978	12.00
❑ IZ-9361 [(2)]	The Mastery of John Coltrane Vol. 4: Trane's Moods	1978	12.00

ATLANTIC

Number	Title (A Side/B Side)	Yr	NM
❑ SD 2-313 [(2)]	The Art of John Coltrane	1973	15.00
❑ 1311 [M]	Giant Steps	1959	50.00
—Black label			
❑ 1311 [M]	Giant Steps	1960	25.00
—Orange and purple label, white fan logo			
❑ 1311 [M]	Giant Steps	1962	15.00
—Orange and purple label, black fan logo			
❑ SD 1311 [S]	Giant Steps	1959	60.00
—Green label			
❑ SD 1311 [S]	Giant Steps	1959	70.00
—"Bullseye" label			
❑ SD 1311 [S]	Giant Steps	1960	25.00
—Green and blue label, white fan logo			
❑ SD 1311 [S]	Giant Steps	1962	15.00
—Green and blue label, black fan logo			
❑ SD 1311 [S]	Giant Steps	1969	12.00
—Red and green label			
❑ 1354 [M]	Coltrane Jazz	1960	30.00
—Orange and purple label, white fan logo			
❑ 1354 [M]	Coltrane Jazz	1962	15.00
—Orange and purple label, black fan logo			
❑ SD 1354 [S]	Coltrane Jazz	1960	30.00
—Green and blue label, white fan logo			
❑ SD 1354 [S]	Coltrane Jazz	1962	15.00
—Green and blue label, black fan logo			
❑ SD 1354 [S]	Coltrane Jazz	1969	12.00
—Red and green label			
❑ 1361 [M]	My Favorite Things	1961	30.00
—Orange and purple label, white fan logo			
❑ 1361 [M]	My Favorite Things	1962	15.00
—Orange and purple label, black fan logo			
❑ SD 1361 [S]	My Favorite Things	1961	30.00
—Green and blue label, white fan logo			
❑ SD 1361 [S]	My Favorite Things	1962	15.00
—Green and blue label, black fan logo			
❑ SD 1361 [S]	My Favorite Things	1969	12.00
—Red and green label			
❑ 1373 [M]	Ole' Coltrane	1961	30.00
—Orange and purple label, white fan logo			
❑ 1373 [M]	Ole' Coltrane	1962	15.00
—Orange and purple label, black fan logo			
❑ SD 1373 [S]	Ole' Coltrane	1961	30.00
—Green and blue label, white fan logo			
❑ SD 1373 [S]	Ole' Coltrane	1962	15.00
—Green and blue label, black fan logo			
❑ SD 1373 [S]	Ole' Coltrane	1969	12.00
—Red and green label			
❑ 1382 [M]	Coltrane Plays the Blues	1962	30.00
❑ SD 1382 [S]	Coltrane Plays the Blues	1962	30.00
—Green and blue label, black fan logo			
❑ SD 1382 [S]	Coltrane Plays the Blues	1969	12.00
—Red and green label			
❑ 1419 [M]	Coltrane's Sound	1964	25.00
❑ SD 1419 [S]	Coltrane's Sound	1964	25.00
—Green and blue label, black fan logo			
❑ SD 1419 [S]	Coltrane's Sound	1969	12.00
—Red and green label			
❑ 1451 [M]	The Avant Garde	1966	25.00
❑ SD 1451 [S]	The Avant Garde	1966	25.00
—Green and blue label, black fan logo			
❑ SD 1451 [S]	The Avant Garde	1969	12.00
—Red and green label			
❑ SD 1541	The Best of John Coltrane	1970	12.00
❑ SD 1553	The Coltrane Legacy	1971	12.00
❑ 90041	The Avant-Garde	1983	10.00
❑ 90462	Countdown	1986	10.00

ATLANTIC/RHINO

Number	Title (A Side/B Side)	Yr	NM
❑ R1-71984 [(12)]	The Heavyweight Champion: The Complete Atlantic Recordings	1995	250.00
—Box set with liner notes; albums pressed on 150-gram vinyl			

ATLANTIC/RHINO HANDMADE

Number	Title (A Side/B Side)	Yr	NM
❑ RHM1-7784 [(12)]	The Heavyweight Champion: The Complete Atlantic Recordings (Year 2000 Second Edition)	2000	200.00
—"Year 2000 Second Edition" at lower right back cover; limited, numbered edition of 1,500 copies on 180-gram vinyl			
❑ RHM1-7784 [(12)]	The Heavyweight Champion: The Complete Atlantic Recordings (Year 2000 Second Edition)	2000	200.00
—"Year 2000 Second Edition" on lower left back cover; limited edition of 1,500, un-numbered, on 180-gram vinyl; pressed in the U.S. for export			

BLUE NOTE

Number	Title (A Side/B Side)	Yr	NM
❑ BLP-1577 [M]	Blue Train	1957	250.00
—Regular version, W. 63rd St., NYC address on label			
❑ BLP-1577 [M]	Blue Train	1957	500.00
—"Deep groove" version; W. 63rd St., NYC address on label			
❑ BLP-1577 [M]	Blue Train	1965	60.00
—"New York, USA" address on label			
❑ BST-1577 [S]	Blue Train	1959	200.00
—Regular version, W. 63rd St., NYC address on label			
❑ BST-1577 [S]	Blue Train	1959	300.00
—"Deep groove" version; W. 63rd St., NYC address on label			
❑ BST-1577 [S]	Blue Train	1965	50.00
—"New York, USA" address on label			
❑ B1-46095	Blue Train	1997	15.00
—180-gram reissue			
❑ B1-81577	Blue Train	1988	12.00
—Reissue with new prefix			
❑ BST-81577	Blue Train	1967	25.00
—"A Division of Liberty Records" on label			
❑ BST-81577	Blue Train	198?	12.00
—"The Finest in Jazz Since 1939" reissue			

COLTRANE

Number	Title (A Side/B Side)	Yr	NM
❑ AU-4950	Cosmic Music	1966	300.00
❑ AU-5000	Cosmic Music	1966	200.00

DCC COMPACT CLASSICS

Number	Title (A Side/B Side)	Yr	NM
❑ LPZ-2032	Lush Life	1997	60.00
—Audiophile vinyl			

FANTASY

Number	Title (A Side/B Side)	Yr	NM
❑ OJC-020	Coltrane	198?	10.00
❑ OJC-021	Soultrane	198?	10.00
❑ OJC-078	Settin' the Pace	198?	10.00
❑ OJC-127	Tenor Conclave	1991	12.00
❑ OJC-131	Lush Life	198?	10.00
❑ OJC-189	Traneing In	1986	10.00
❑ OJC-246	Standard Coltrane	1987	10.00
❑ OJC-352	Black Pearls	1989	10.00
❑ OJC-393	Dakar	1989	10.00
❑ OJC-394	Last Trane	1989	10.00
❑ OJC-415	Bahia	1990	12.00
❑ OJC-460	Cattin' with Coltrane and Quinichette	1990	12.00

GRP/IMPULSE!

Number	Title (A Side/B Side)	Yr	NM
❑ GR-155	A Love Supreme	1995	15.00
❑ GR-156	Ballads	1995	15.00
❑ GR-157	John Coltrane + Johnny Hartman	1995	15.00
❑ IMP-166	Duke Ellington and John Coltrane	1997	15.00
❑ IMP-167	Sun Ship	1997	15.00
❑ IMP-169	Stellar Regions	1995	15.00
❑ IMP-198	Coltrane Live at Birdland	1997	15.00
❑ IMP-200	Crescent	1997	15.00
❑ IMP-213	Live at the Village Vanguard Again!	1997	15.00
❑ IMP-214	The John Coltrane Quartet Plays	1997	15.00
❑ IMP-215	Coltrane	1997	15.00

IMPULSE!

Number	Title (A Side/B Side)	Yr	NM
❑ A-6 [M]	Africa/Brass	1961	80.00
❑ AS-6 [S]	Africa/Brass	1961	100.00
❑ A-10 [M]	Live at the Village Vanguard	1962	60.00
❑ AS-10 [S]	Live at the Village Vanguard	1962	80.00
❑ A-21 [M]	Coltrane	1962	80.00
❑ AS-21 [S]	Coltrane	1962	100.00
❑ A-30 [M]	Duke Ellington and John Coltrane	1963	100.00
❑ AS-30 [S]	Duke Ellington and John Coltrane	1963	150.00
❑ A-32 [M]	Ballads	1963	80.00
❑ AS-32 [S]	Ballads	1963	100.00
❑ A-40 [M]	John Coltrane + Johnny Hartman	1963	100.00
❑ AS-40 [S]	John Coltrane + Johnny Hartman	1963	120.00
❑ A-42 [M]	Impressions	1963	60.00
❑ AS-42 [S]	Impressions	1963	80.00
❑ A-50 [M]	Coltrane Live at Birdland	1963	80.00
❑ AS-50 [S]	Coltrane Live at Birdland	1963	100.00
❑ A-66 [M]	Crescent	1964	80.00
❑ AS-66 [S]	Crescent	1964	100.00
❑ A-77 [M]	A Love Supreme	1965	120.00
❑ AS-77 [S]	A Love Supreme	1965	150.00
❑ A-85 [M]	The John Coltrane Quartet Plays	1965	60.00
❑ AS-85 [S]	The John Coltrane Quartet Plays	1965	80.00
❑ A-94 [M]	New Thing at Newport	1965	60.00
❑ AS-94 [S]	New Thing at Newport	1965	80.00
❑ A-95 [M]	Ascension	1965	150.00
—Without "Edition II" in dead wax			
❑ A-95 [M]	Ascension	1966	100.00
—With "Edition II" in dead wax			
❑ AS-95 [S]	Ascension	1965	180.00
—Without "Edition II" in dead wax			
❑ AS-95 [S]	Ascension	1966	120.00
—With "Edition II" in dead wax			
❑ A-9106 [M]	Kulu Se Mama	1966	100.00
❑ AS-9106 [S]	Kulu Se Mama	1966	120.00
❑ A-9110 [M]	Meditations	1966	80.00
❑ AS-9110 [S]	Meditations	1966	100.00
❑ A-9120 [M]	Expression	1967	100.00
❑ AS-9120 [S]	Expression	1967	80.00
❑ A-9124 [M]	Live at the Village Vanguard Again!	1967	100.00
❑ AS-9124 [S]	Live at the Village Vanguard Again!	1967	80.00
❑ A-9140 [M]	Om	1967	150.00
❑ AS-9140 [S]	Om	1967	80.00
❑ SMAS-90232 [S]	Coltrane Live at Birdland	1964	80.00
—Capitol Record Club edition			
❑ SMAS-91288 [S]	Expression	1967	60.00
—Capitol Record Club edition			

MCA

Number	Title (A Side/B Side)	Yr	NM
❑ 4131 [(2)]	Greatest Years	1981	10.00
❑ 4132 [(2)]	Greatest Years, Vol. 2	1981	10.00
❑ 4133 [(2)]	Greatest Years, Vol. 3	1981	10.00
❑ 4134 [(2)]	Live in Seattle	1981	10.00
❑ 4135 [(2)]	Concert Japan	1981	10.00
❑ 4136 [(2)]	The Gentle Side of John Coltrane	1981	10.00
❑ 4137 [(2)]	The Other Village Vanguard Tapes	1981	10.00
❑ 4138 [(2)]	The Mastery of John Coltrane Vol. 1: Feelin' Good	1981	10.00
❑ 4139 [(2)]	The Mastery of John Coltrane Vol. 2: Different Drum	1981	10.00
❑ 4140 [(2)]	The Mastery of John Coltrane Vol. 4: Trane's Moods	1981	10.00
❑ 29007	Africa/Brass	1981	8.00
❑ 29008	Africa/Brass, Vol. 2	1981	8.00
❑ 29009	Live at the Village Vanguard	1981	8.00
❑ 29010	Live at the Village Vanguard Again!	1981	8.00
❑ 29011	Coltrane	1981	8.00
❑ 29012	Ballads	1981	8.00
❑ 29013	John Coltrane + Johnny Hartman	1981	8.00
❑ 29014	Impressions	1981	8.00
❑ 29015	Coltrane Live at Birdland	1981	8.00
❑ 29016	Crescent	1981	8.00
❑ 29017	A Love Supreme	1981	8.00
❑ 29018	The John Coltrane Quartet Plays	1981	8.00
❑ 29019	New Thing at Newport	1981	8.00
❑ 29020	Ascension	1981	8.00
❑ 29021	Kulu Se Mama	1981	8.00
❑ 29022	Meditations	1981	8.00
❑ 29023	Expression	1981	8.00
❑ 29024	Om	1981	8.00
❑ 29025	Cosmic Music	1981	8.00
❑ 29026	Selflessness	1981	8.00
❑ 29027	Transition	1981	8.00
❑ 29028	Sun Ship	1981	8.00
❑ 29029	Interstellar Space	1981	8.00
❑ 29030	First Meditations	1981	8.00
❑ 29031	The Mastery of John Coltrane Vol. 3: Jupiter Variation	1981	8.00
❑ 29032	Duke Ellington and John Coltrane	1981	8.00

MCA/IMPULSE!

Number	Title (A Side/B Side)	Yr	NM
❑ 5660	A Love Supreme	1986	10.00
❑ 5661	John Coltrane + Johnny Hartman	1986	10.00
❑ 5883	Coltrane	1987	10.00
❑ 5885	Ballads	1987	10.00
❑ 5887	Impressions	1987	10.00
❑ 5889	Crescent	1987	10.00
❑ 33109	Coltrane Live at Birdland	198?	10.00
❑ 33110	The John Coltrane Quartet Plays	198?	10.00
❑ 39103	Duke Ellington and John Coltrane	1988	10.00
❑ 39118	Om	1988	10.00
❑ 39136	Live at the Village Vanguard	1988	10.00
❑ 42231	Africa/Brass	1988	10.00
❑ 42232	Africa/Brass, Vol. 2	1988	10.00

PABLO

Number	Title (A Side/B Side)	Yr	NM
❑ 2405417	The Best of John Coltrane	198?	10.00

PABLO LIVE

Number	Title (A Side/B Side)	Yr	NM
❑ 2308217	The Paris Concert	1980	12.00
❑ 2308222	European Tour	1981	12.00
❑ 2308227	Bye Bye Blackbird	1981	12.00
❑ 2620101 [(2)]	Afro Blue Impressions	198?	12.00

PRESTIGE

Number	Title (A Side/B Side)	Yr	NM
❑ PRLP-7105 [M]	Coltrane	1957	100.00
—Yellow label			

Number	Title (A Side/B Side)	Yr	NM
❑ PRLP-7105 [M]	Coltrane	1964	30.00
—Blue label with trident logo			
❑ PRLP-7123 [M]	John Coltrane and the Red Garland Trio	1957	100.00
—Yellow label			
❑ PRLP-7123 [M]	Traneing In	1964	30.00
—Blue label with trident logo; reissue with new title			
❑ PRLP-7142 [M]	Soultrane	1958	80.00
—Yellow label			
❑ PRLP-7142 [M]	Soultrane	1964	25.00
—Blue label with trident logo			
❑ PRLP-7158 [M]	Cattin' with Coltrane and Quinichette	1959	80.00
—Yellow label			
❑ PRLP-7158 [M]	Cattin' with Coltrane and Quinichette	1964	25.00
—Blue label with trident logo			
❑ PRLP-7188 [M]	Lush Life	1960	80.00
—Yellow label			
❑ PRLP-7188 [M]	Lush Life	1964	25.00
—Blue label with trident logo			
❑ PRLP-7213 [M]	Settin' the Pace	1961	80.00
—Yellow label			
❑ PRLP-7213 [M]	Settin' the Pace	1964	25.00
—Blue label with trident logo			
❑ PRLP-7243 [M]	Standard Coltrane	1962	40.00
—Yellow label			
❑ PRLP-7243 [M]	Standard Coltrane	1964	25.00
—Blue label with trident logo			
❑ PRST-7243 [S]	Standard Coltrane	1962	50.00
—Silver label			
❑ PRST-7243 [S]	Standard Coltrane	1964	25.00
—Blue label with trident logo			
❑ PRLP-7247 [M]	Mating Call	1962	40.00
—Yellow label			
❑ PRLP-7247 [M]	Mating Call	1964	25.00
—Blue label with trident logo			
❑ PRST-7247 [R]	Mating Call	196?	25.00
—Silver label			
❑ PRST-7247 [R]	Mating Call	1964	20.00
—Blue label with trident logo			
❑ PRLP-7249 [M]	Tenor Conclave	1962	40.00
—Yellow label			
❑ PRLP-7249 [M]	Tenor Conclave	1964	25.00
—Blue label with trident logo			
❑ PRST-7249 [R]	Tenor Conclave	196?	25.00
—Silver label			
❑ PRST-7249 [R]	Tenor Conclave	1964	20.00
—Blue label with trident logo			
❑ PRLP-7268 [M]	Stardust	1963	40.00
—Yellow label			
❑ PRLP-7268 [M]	Stardust	1964	25.00
—Blue label with trident logo			
❑ PRST-7268 [S]	Stardust	1963	40.00
—Silver label			
❑ PRST-7268 [S]	Stardust	1964	25.00
—Blue label with trident logo			
❑ PRLP-7280 [M]	Dakar	1963	40.00
—Yellow label			
❑ PRLP-7280 [M]	Dakar	1964	25.00
—Blue label with trident logo			
❑ PRST-7280 [S]	Dakar	1963	40.00
—Silver label			
❑ PRST-7280 [S]	Dakar	1964	25.00
—Blue label with trident logo			
❑ PRLP-7292 [M]	The Believer	1964	25.00
—Blue label with trident logo			
❑ PRLP-7292 [M]	The Believer	1964	40.00
—Yellow label			
❑ PRST-7292 [S]	The Believer	1964	25.00
—Blue label with trident logo			
❑ PRST-7292 [S]	The Believer	1964	40.00
—Silver label			
❑ PRLP-7316 [M]	Black Pearls	1964	25.00
—Blue label with trident logo			
❑ PRLP-7316 [M]	Black Pearls	1964	40.00
—Yellow label			
❑ PRST-7316 [S]	Black Pearls	1964	25.00
—Blue label with trident logo			
❑ PRST-7316 [S]	Black Pearls	1964	40.00
—Silver label			
❑ PRLP-7353 [M]	Bahia	1965	25.00
❑ PRST-7353 [S]	Bahia	1965	25.00
❑ PRLP-7378 [M]	The Last Trane	1965	30.00
❑ PRST-7378 [S]	The Last Trane	1965	25.00
❑ PRLP-7426 [M]	John Coltrane Plays for Lovers	1966	25.00
❑ PRST-7426 [S]	John Coltrane Plays for Lovers	1966	25.00
❑ PRLP-7531 [M]	Soultrane	1967	25.00
❑ PRST-7531 [R]	Soultrane	1967	12.00
❑ PRST-7581 [R]	Lush Life	1968	12.00
❑ PRST-7609 [R]	The First Trane	1969	12.00
❑ PRST-7651 [R]	Traneing In	1969	12.00
❑ PRST-7670 [R]	Two Tenors	1969	12.00
❑ PRST-7725	Mating Call	1970	12.00
❑ PRST-7746	Trane's Reign	1970	12.00
❑ PRST-7825	The Master	1971	12.00
❑ 24003 [(2)]	John Coltrane	1972	15.00
❑ 24014 [(2)]	More Lasting Than Bronze	1973	15.00
❑ 24037 [(2)]	Black Pearls	1974	15.00
❑ 24056 [(2)]	The Stardust Session	197?	15.00
❑ 24069 [(2)]	Wheelin'	197?	12.00
❑ 24084 [(2)]	On a Misty Night	198?	12.00
❑ 24094 [(2)]	Rain or Shine	198?	12.00
❑ 24104 [(2)]	Dakar	198?	12.00
❑ 24110 [(2)]	Bahia	198?	12.00
RHINO			
❑ R1-75203	Giant Steps	2003	15.00
—Reissue on 180-gram vinyl			
SOLID STATE			
❑ SM-17025 [M]	Coltrane Time	1968	25.00
❑ SS-18025 [S]	Coltrane Time	1968	15.00
TRIP			
❑ 5001 [(2)]	Trane Tracks	1974	15.00
UNITED ARTISTS			
❑ UAS-5638	Coltrane Time	1972	12.00
—Reissue of 15001			
❑ UAJ-14001 [M]	Coltrane Time	1962	40.00
❑ UAJS-15001 [S]	Coltrane Time	1962	50.00

COLTS, THE

45s

Number	Title (A Side/B Side)	Yr	NM
ANTLER			
❑ 4003	Never No More/ The Shiek of Araby	1959	40.00
❑ 4007	Guiding Angel/ The Shiek of Araby	1959	40.00
MAMBO			
❑ 112	Adorable/Lips Red as Wine	1955	400.00
PLAZA			
❑ 505	Hey, Pretty Baby/Sweet Sixteen	1962	20.00
VITA			
❑ 112	Adorable/Lips Red as Wine	1955	150.00
❑ 121	Honey Bun/Sweet Sixteen	1955	120.00
❑ 130	Never No More/Hey You Shoo-Bee-Ooh-Bee	1956	120.00

COLUMBUS PHARAOHS, THE

45s

Number	Title (A Side/B Side)	Yr	NM
ESTA			
❑ 290	Give Me Your Love/China Girl	1958	1000.

COLWELL-WINFIELD BLUES BAND, THE

45s

Number	Title (A Side/B Side)	Yr	NM
VERVE FORECAST			
❑ 5098	Cold Wind Blues/ Free Will Fantasy	1968	10.00

Albums

Number	Title (A Side/B Side)	Yr	NM
VERVE FORECAST			
❑ FTS-3056	Cold Wind Blues	1968	20.00
ZA-ZOO			
❑ 1	Live Bust	1971	200.00

COLYER, KEN

45s

Number	Title (A Side/B Side)	Yr	NM
LONDON			
❑ 1655	Down by the Riverside/ Take This Hammer	1956	12.00
❑ 1674	Casey Jones/Streamline Train	1956	12.00

Albums

Number	Title (A Side/B Side)	Yr	NM
GHB			
❑ 161	Live at the 100 Club	198?	10.00
LONDON			
❑ PB 904 [10]	New Orleans to London	1954	50.00
❑ LL 1340 [M]	Back to the Delta	1956	40.00
❑ LL 1618 [M]	Club Session with Colyer	1957	40.00
STORYVILLE			
❑ SLP-144	Ken's Early Days	197?	12.00

COMBINATIONS, THE

45s

Number	Title (A Side/B Side)	Yr	NM
KELLMAC			
❑ 1007	Why/Come Back	1966	30.00
❑ 1011	What'cha Gonna Do/ Like I Never Did Before	1966	1500.

COMFORTABLE CHAIR, THE

45s

Number	Title (A Side/B Side)	Yr	NM
ODE			
❑ 109	Be Me/Some Soon, Some Day	1968	10.00
❑ 112	I'll See You/Now	1968	10.00

Albums

Number	Title (A Side/B Side)	Yr	NM
ODE			
❑ Z12 44005	The Comfortable Chair	1968	20.00

COMMANDER CODY AND HIS LOST PLANET AIRMEN

Includes records as "Commander Cody Band" and "Commander Cody."

45s

Number	Title (A Side/B Side)	Yr	NM
ARISTA			
❑ 0271	Seven-Eleven/You Snooze You Lose	1977	4.00
❑ 0344	Thank You Lone Ranger/ My Day	1978	4.00
DOT			
❑ 17487	Daddy's Drinking Up Our Christmas/Honeysuckle Honey	1973	6.00
❑ 17500	Diggy Liggy Lo/Outgoing Person	1974	5.00
PARAMOUNT			
❑ 0130	Lost in the Ozone/Midnight Shift	1971	6.00
❑ 0130 [PS]	Lost in the Ozone/Midnight Shift	1971	10.00
❑ 0146	Hot Rod Lincoln/My Home in My Hand	1972	6.00
❑ 0169	Beat Me Daddy, Eight to the Bar/Daddy's Gonna Treat You Right	1972	6.00
❑ 0169 [PS]	Beat Me Daddy, Eight to the Bar/Daddy's Gonna Treat You Right	1972	10.00
❑ 0178	Truck Stop Rock/Mama Hated Diesels	1972	6.00
❑ 0178 [PS]	Truck Stop Rock/Mama Hated Diesels	1972	10.00
❑ 0193	Semi-Truck/Watch My .38	1973	6.00
❑ 0216	Smoke! Smoke! Smoke! (That Cigarette)/Rock That Boogie	1973	6.00
❑ 0216 [PS]	Smoke! Smoke! Smoke! (That Cigarette)/Rock That Boogie	1973	10.00
❑ 0278	Riot in Cell Block No. 9/ Oh, Momma Momma	1974	6.00
WARNER BROS.			
❑ 8073	Don't Let Go/Keep On Lovin' Her	1975	4.00
❑ 8164	It's Gonna Be One of Those Nights/Roll Your Own	1975	4.00

Albums

Number	Title (A Side/B Side)	Yr	NM
ARISTA			
❑ AL 4125	Rock 'N' Roll Again	1977	10.00
❑ AB 4183	Flying Dreams	1978	15.00
BLIND PIG			
❑ BP-2086	Let's Rock	1986	10.00
MCA			
❑ 659	Live from Deep in the Heart of Texas	1980	8.00
—Reissue of Paramount 1017			
❑ 660	Country Casanova	1980	8.00
—Reissue of Paramount 6054			
❑ 661	Hot Licks, Cold Steel & Truckers Favorites	1980	8.00
—Reissue of Paramount 6031			
❑ 37101	Lost in the Ozone	1980	8.00
—Reissue of Paramount 6017			
PARAMOUNT			
❑ PAS-1017	Live from Deep in the Heart of Texas	1974	12.00
❑ PAS-6017	Lost in the Ozone	1971	15.00
❑ PAS-6031	Hot Licks, Cold Steel & Truckers Favorites	1972	12.00
❑ PAS-6054	Country Casanova	1973	12.00
WARNER BROS.			
❑ BS 2847	Commander Cody and His Lost Planet Airmen	1975	10.00
❑ BS 2883	Tales from the Ozone	1975	10.00
❑ 2LS 2939 [(2)]	We've Got a Live One Here!	1976	12.00

COMMERCIALS, THE

45s

Number	Title (A Side/B Side)	Yr	NM
DAYHILL			
❑ 2012	Power in Your Love/I Guess, I Guess, I Guess	196?	30.00

COMMODORES

Popular 1970s and 1980s soul group. Few, if any, of their records use the word "The" before "Commodores."

12-Inch Singles

Number	Title (A Side/B Side)	Yr	NM
MOTOWN			
❑ M 00007D1	Brick House (6:11) (same on both sides)	1977	15.00
❑ PR-56 [DJ]	Still (5:51)/Sail On (5:35)	1979	20.00
❑ PR-70 [DJ]	Jesus Is Love (Short Version 4:26) (Long Version 6:04)	1980	20.00
❑ PR-87 [DJ]	Keep On Taking Me Higher (5:18)/Why You Wanna Try Me (4:36)	1981	12.00
❑ PR-166 [DJ]	Nightshift (Radio Edit of Club Mix 4:48) (Club Mix 7:02) (Dub Mix 7:12)	1985	12.00

Except when noted otherwise, VG = 25% of NM, and VG+ = 50% of NM. (Example: VG = $2.00, VG+ = $4.00 and NM = $8.00.)

Number	Title (A Side/B Side)	Yr	NM
❑ 4533MG	Nightshift (Edit of Club Mix 4:48) (Club Mix 7:02) (Instrumentakl Mix 7:12)	1985	8.00
❑ 4535MG	Animal Instinct (Club Mix 9:46)/ Lightin' Up the Night	1985	8.00
POLYDOR			
❑ PRO 467-1 [DJ]	Goin' to the Bank (Club Mix) (Dub)	1986	12.00
❑ PRO 501-1 [DJ]	United in Love (Edit) (LP Version)	1986	8.00
❑ PRO 641-1 [DJ]	Solitaire (same on both sides)	1988	10.00
❑ PRO 684-1 [DJ]	Homeless (same on both sides)	1988	8.00
❑ 871371-1	Grrip (6 versions)	1989	8.00
❑ 885358-1	Goin' to the Bank (7:17) (4:19)	1986	8.00
❑ 885538-1	Take It from Me (4 versions)/ I Wanna Rock You	1987	8.00
45s			
MOTOWN			
❑ 1268	Are You Happy/There's a Song in My Heart	1973	6.00
❑ 1307	Machine Gun/There's a Song in My Heart	1974	5.00
❑ 1307 [DJ]	Machine Gun (stereo/mono)	1974	15.00
—Promo only on red vinyl			
❑ 1319	I Feel Sanctified/It Is As Good As You Make It	1974	5.00
❑ 1338	Slippery When Wet/The Bump	1975	5.00
❑ 1361	This Is Your Life/Look What You've Done to Me	1975	5.00
❑ 1366	Wide Open/(B-side unassigned)	1975	—
—Unreleased			
❑ 1381	Sweet Love/Better Never Than Forever	1976	4.00
❑ 1381 [DJ]	Sweet Love (stereo/mono)	1976	15.00
—Promo only on yellow vinyl			
❑ 1394	Come Inside/Time	1976	—
—Unreleased			
❑ 1399	High on Sunshine/ Thumpin' Music	1976	—
—Unreleased			
❑ 1402	Just to Be Close to You/ Thumpin' Music	1976	4.00
❑ 1408	Fancy Dancer/Cebu	1977	4.00
❑ 1418	Easy/Can't Let You Tease Me	1977	4.00
❑ 1425	Brick House/Captain Quickdraw	1977	4.00
❑ 1432	Too Hot Ta Trot/Funky Situation	1977	4.00
❑ 1443	Three Times a Lady/Look What You've Done to Me	1978	4.00
❑ 1452	Flying High/X-Rated Movie	1978	4.00
❑ 1457	Say Yeah/(B-side unassigned)	1978	—
—Unreleased			
❑ 1466	Sail On/Thumpin' Music	1979	4.00
❑ 1474	Still/Such a Woman	1979	4.00
❑ 1479	Wonderland/Lovin' You	1979	4.00
❑ 1489	Old Fashion Love/Sexy Lady	1980	4.00
❑ 1495	Heroes/Funky Situation	1980	4.00
❑ 1502	Jesus Is Love/Mighty Spirit	1980	6.00
❑ 1514	Lady (You Bring Me Up)/Gettin' It	1981	4.00
❑ 1527	Oh No/Lovin' You	1981	4.00
❑ 1604	Why You Wanna Try Me/ X-Rated Movie	1982	4.00
❑ 1651	Painted Pictures/Reach High	1982	3.00
❑ 1661	Sexy Lady/Reach High	1983	3.00
❑ 1694	Only You/Cebu	1983	3.00
❑ 1719	Been Lovin' You/ Turn Off the Lights	1984	3.00
❑ 1773	Nightshift/I Keep Running	1985	3.00
❑ 1773 [PS]	Nightshift/I Keep Running	1985	6.00
❑ 1788	Animal Instinct/Lightin' Up the Sky	1985	3.00
❑ 1802	Janet/I'm in Love	1985	3.00
MOWEST			
❑ 5009	I'm Looking for Love/At the Zoo	1972	8.00
❑ 5038	Determination/ Don't You Be Worried	1973	8.00
POLYDOR			
❑ 871370-7	Grrip/Ain't Giving Up	1989	3.00
❑ 885358-7	Goin' to the Bank/Serious Love	1986	3.00
❑ 885358-7 [PS]	Goin' to the Bank/Serious Love	1986	3.00
❑ 885538-7	Take It from Me/ I Wanna Rock You	1987	3.00
❑ 885538-7 [PS]	Take It from Me/ I Wanna Rock You	1987	3.00
❑ 885760-7	United in Love/Talk to Me	1987	3.00
❑ 885760-7 [PS]	United in Love/Talk to Me	1987	3.00
❑ 887939-7	Solitaire/Stretchhh	1988	3.00
❑ 887939-7 [PS]	Solitaire/Stretchhh	1988	3.00
Albums			
MOTOWN			
❑ PR 39 [DJ]	1978 Platinum Tour	1978	20.00
—Promo-only compilation			
❑ M5-121V1	Machine Gun	1981	10.00
—Reissue			
❑ M5-179V1	Movin' On	1981	8.00
❑ M5-222V1	Commodores	1982	8.00
❑ M5-240V1	Caught in the Act	1982	8.00
❑ M6-798	Machine Gun	1974	15.00
❑ M6-820	Caught in the Act	1975	10.00
❑ M6-848	Movin' On	1975	10.00
❑ M6-867	Hot on the Tracks	1976	10.00
❑ M7-884	Commodores	1977	10.00
❑ M9-894 [(2)]	Commodores Live!	1977	12.00
❑ M7-902	Natural High	1978	10.00
❑ M7-912	Commodores' Greatest Hits	1978	10.00
❑ M8-926	Midnight Magic	1979	10.00
❑ M8-939	Heroes	1980	10.00
❑ M8-955	In the Pocket	1981	10.00
❑ 5257 ML	Hot on the Tracks	1983	8.00
❑ 5293 ML	Natural High	1983	8.00
❑ 6028 ML	All the Great Hits	1982	10.00
❑ 6044 ML2 [(2)]	Anthology	1983	12.00
❑ 6054 ML	Commodores 13	1983	10.00
❑ 6124 ML	Nightshift	1985	10.00
POLYDOR			
❑ 831194-1	United	1986	10.00
❑ 835369-1	Rock Solid	1988	10.00

COMMODORES, THE None of the below are the popular 1970s-1980s group, but they aren't all the same group, either.

Number	Title (A Side/B Side)	Yr	NM
45s			
ATLANTIC			
❑ 2633	Keep On Dancing/Rise Up	1969	8.00
BRUNSWICK			
❑ 55126	Laughing with Tears/Who Dat	1959	20.00
CHALLENGE			
❑ 1004	Sweet Angel/Not a Day Goes By	1957	20.00
❑ 1007	Faith/I'll Be There	1957	20.00
DOT			
❑ 15372	Uranium/Riding on a Train	1955	25.00
❑ 15425	Cream Puff/Close to My Heart	1955	25.00
❑ 15439	Speedoo/Whole Lotta Shakin' Goin' On	1956	25.00
❑ 15461	Two Loves Have I/Who Said I Said That	1956	25.00

COMMON PEOPLE, THE

Number	Title (A Side/B Side)	Yr	NM
Albums			
CAPITOL			
❑ ST-266	Of the People/By the People/ For the People/From the Common People	1969	200.00

COMPANIONS, THE More than one group.

Number	Title (A Side/B Side)	Yr	NM
45s			
AMY			
❑ 852	No Fool Am I/How Could You	1962	100.00
ARLEN			
❑ 722	These Foolish Things/ It's Too Late	1963	80.00
BROOK'S			
❑ 100	Why, Oh Why Baby/I Didn't Know (You Got Married)	1959	60.00
COLUMBIA			
❑ 42279	I'll Always Love You/ A Little Bit of Blue	1962	30.00
DOVE			
❑ 240	Falling/Oh, What a Feeling!	1958	120.00
FEDERAL			
❑ 12397	Why, Oh Why Baby/I Didn't Know (You Got Married)	1960	30.00
GENERAL AMERICAN			
❑ 711	Be Yourself/Help a Lonely Guy	1962	20.00
GINA			
❑ 722	These Foolish Things/ It's Too Late	1963	50.00

COMPETITORS, THE

Number	Title (A Side/B Side)	Yr	NM
45s			
DOT			
❑ 16560	Power Shift/Little Stick Nomad	1963	40.00
Albums			
DOT			
❑ DLP-3542 [M]	Hits of the Street and Strip	1963	150.00
❑ DLP-25542 [S]	Hits of the Street and Strip	1963	200.00

COMPLIMENTS, THE

Number	Title (A Side/B Side)	Yr	NM
45s			
CONGRESS			
❑ 243	Shake It Up, Shake It Down/ You Are My Sunshine	1965	50.00
❑ 252	The Time of Her Life/Everybody Loves a Lover	1965	50.00
MIDAS			
❑ 304	Borrow 'Til Morning/ Beware, Beware	1968	30.00

COMPOSERS, THE

Number	Title (A Side/B Side)	Yr	NM
45s			
AMPEN			
❑ 221	Woe Is Me/Elephant Drag	196?	300.00
ERA			
❑ 3118	I Had a Dream/You and Yours	1963	20.00

COMSTOCK, BOBBY

Number	Title (A Side/B Side)	Yr	NM
45s			
ASCOT			
❑ 2164	Right Hand Man/Always	1964	15.00
❑ 2175	I'm a Man/I'll Make You Glad	1965	12.00
❑ 2193	This Magic Moment/ Shotgun Sally	1965	12.00
❑ 2216	Can't Judge a Book/Out of Sight	1966	12.00
ATLANTIC			
❑ 2051	Jambalaya/Let's Talk It Over	1960	20.00
BLAZE			
❑ 349	Tennessee Waltz/Sweet Talk	1959	25.00
FESTIVAL			
❑ 25000	Garden of Eden/Piece of Paper	1961	20.00
JUBILEE			
❑ 5392	Bony Maronie/Do That Little Thing	1960	20.00
❑ 5396	Jezebel/Your Big Brown Eyes	1961	20.00
LAWN			
❑ 202	Let's Stomp/I Want to Do It	1963	15.00
❑ 210	Susie Baby/Take a Walk	1963	15.00
❑ 217	The Chicken Back/Sunny	1963	15.00
❑ 219	Your Boyfriend's Back/This Little Love of Mine	1963	20.00
❑ 224	I Can't Help Myself/ Run My Heart	1963	15.00
❑ 229	The Beatle Bounce/ Since You Been Gone	1964	20.00
❑ 232	Can It Be True/Ain't That Just Like Me	1964	15.00
❑ 255	I Wanna Do It/This Little Love of Mine	1965	12.00
LOST-NITE			
❑ 227	Let's Stomp/I Want to Do It	196?	5.00
—Reissue			
MOHAWK			
❑ 124	The Wayward Wind/ Everyday Blues	1960	20.00
TRIUMPH			
❑ 602	Jealous Fool/Zig Zag	1959	25.00
Albums			
ASCOT			
❑ AM-13026 [M]	Out of Sight	1966	25.00
❑ AS-16026 [S]	Out of Sight	1966	30.00

CONCORDS, THE (1)

Number	Title (A Side/B Side)	Yr	NM
45s			
BOOM			
❑ 60021	Down the Aisle of Love/ I Feel Love Comin'	1966	40.00
EPIC			
❑ 9697	Should I Cry/It's Our Wedding Day	1964	60.00
GRAMERCY			
❑ 304	Cross My Heart/ Our Last Goodbye	1961	50.00
—No candy canes on label			
❑ 304	Cross My Heart/ Our Last Goodbye	1961	200.00
—With candy canes on label			
❑ 305	My Dreams/Scarlet Ribbons	1961	40.00
HERALD			
❑ 576	Marlene/Our Love Wasn't Meant to Be	1962	25.00
❑ 578	Cold and Frosty Morning/ Don't Go Now	1963	30.00
POLYDOR			
❑ 14036	Down the Aisle of Love/I Feel a Love Comin' On	1970	12.00
RCA VICTOR			
❑ 47-7911	Again/The Boy Most Likely	1961	30.00
RUST			
❑ 5048	One Step from Heaven/Away	1962	30.00

CONCORDS, THE (2)

Number	Title (A Side/B Side)	Yr	NM
45s			
EMBER			
❑ 1007	I'm Satisfied with Rock 'N' Roll/ I'll Always Say Please	1956	60.00
HARLEM			
❑ 2328	Candlelight/Monticello	1954	600.00

CONCORDS, THE (U)
Probably a Nashville studio group and no relation to the others, but we're not sure.

45s

HIT

Number	Title (A Side/B Side)	Yr	NM
❑ 121	Diane/Walk On By	1964	8.00
—B-side by Mary Jones			

CONCRETE BLONDE

10-Inch Singles

CAPITOL

Number	Title (A Side/B Side)	Yr	NM
❑ SPRO-79245/6 [DJ]	Jonestown (LP Version) (Jim Jones Edit)/ Simple Twist of Fate	1993	20.00

12-Inch Singles

I.R.S.

Number	Title (A Side/B Side)	Yr	NM
❑ I33-17231 [DJ]	Still in Hollywood (Censored Version) (Uncensored Version)/I'll Chew You Up and Spit You Out	1986	12.00
❑ L33-17268 [DJ]	True (same on both sides?)	1986	8.00
❑ L33-17310 [DJ]	Dance Along the Edge (Edit) (LP Version)	1988	10.00
❑ SPRO 67099 [DJ]	I Wanna Be Your Friend Again (Stone Cold Extended Mix) (Fluttering Dub) (Stone Cold Bonus)	1992	15.00
❑ 74001	God Is a Bullet//Free/Little Wing	1989	15.00

45s

I.R.S.

Number	Title (A Side/B Side)	Yr	NM
❑ 52982	Still in Hollywood/ Cold Part of Town	1986	5.00
❑ 53053	True/True II (Instrumental)	1987	5.00
❑ 53053 [PS]	True/True II (Instrumental)	1987	5.00
❑ 53113	Dance Along the Edge/Only One Can Make Me Cry	1987	5.00
❑ 53113 [PS]	Dance Along the Edge/Only You Can Make Me Cry	1987	5.00

Albums

I.R.S.

Number	Title (A Side/B Side)	Yr	NM
❑ 5835	Concrete Blonde	1987	12.00
❑ X1-13037	Bloodletting	1990	40.00
—Stock copy; red vinyl			
❑ 82001	Free	1989	12.00
❑ 82037 [DJ]	Bloodletting	1990	30.00
—Promo only, sticker on generic cover, black vinyl			

CONCRETE COWBOY BAND

45s

EXCELSIOR

Number	Title (A Side/B Side)	Yr	NM
❑ 1006	Concrete Cowboys/ (B-side unknown)	1981	6.00
❑ 1011	Country Is the Closest Thing to Heaven (You Can Hear)/ San Antonio Rose	1981	5.00

Albums

EXCELSIOR

Number	Title (A Side/B Side)	Yr	NM
❑ 88007	Concrete Cowboys	1981	12.00

CONDELLO

45s

SCEPTER

Number	Title (A Side/B Side)	Yr	NM
❑ 12233	Crystal Clear/See What Tomorrow Brings	1968	12.00

Albums

SCEPTER

Number	Title (A Side/B Side)	Yr	NM
❑ SPS-542	Phase 1	1968	75.00
—Avaliable in mono and stereo; both same price			

CONDORS, THE

45s

HUNTER

Number	Title (A Side/B Side)	Yr	NM
❑ 2503/4	Swetest Angel/Little Curly Top	1960	1000.

CONEY ISLAND KIDS, THE

45s

JOSIE

Number	Title (A Side/B Side)	Yr	NM
❑ 791	I Love It/Red Light, Green Light	1956	30.00
❑ 802	We Want a Rock & Roll President/Thwistle Rock and Thwistle Roll	1956	30.00
❑ 809	Popcorn and Candy/Not You, Pie Face	1957	30.00

JUBILEE

Number	Title (A Side/B Side)	Yr	NM
❑ 5215	Moonlight Beach/Baby Baby You	1955	40.00

CONFESSIONS, THE

45s

EPIC

Number	Title (A Side/B Side)	Yr	NM
❑ 9474	Be-Bop Baby/Before You Change Your Mind	1961	25.00

CONLEY, ARTHUR

45s

ATCO

Number	Title (A Side/B Side)	Yr	NM
❑ 6463	Sweet Soul Music/ Let's Go Steady	1967	10.00
❑ 6494	Shake, Rattle and Roll/ You Don't Have to See Me	1967	8.00
❑ 6529	Whole Lot of Woman/ Love Comes and Goes	1967	8.00
❑ 6563	Funky Street/Put Our Love Together	1968	8.00
❑ 6588	People Sure Act Funny/ Burning Fire	1968	8.00
❑ 6622	Is That You Love/Aunt Dora's Love Soul Shack	1968	8.00
❑ 6640	Ob-La-Di, Ob-La-Da/ Otis Sleep On	1968	8.00
❑ 6661	Speak Her Name/Run On	1969	6.00
❑ 6706	Star Review/Love Sure Is a Powerful Thing	1969	6.00
❑ 6733	Hurt/They Call the Wind Maria	1970	6.00
❑ 6747	God Bless/(Your Love Has Brought Me A) Mighty Long Way	1970	6.00
❑ 6790	Nobody's Fault But Mine/Day-O	1970	6.00

CAPRICORN

Number	Title (A Side/B Side)	Yr	NM
❑ 0001	More Sweet Soul Music/ Walking on Eggs	1972	10.00
❑ 0006	Rita/More Sweet Soul Music	1972	8.00
❑ 0047	Bless You/It's So Nice	1973	8.00
❑ 8017	I'm Living Good/I'm So Glad You're Here	1971	10.00

FAME

Number	Title (A Side/B Side)	Yr	NM
❑ 1007	I Can't Stop/In the Same Old Way	1966	15.00
❑ 1009	Take Me (Just As I Am)/I'm Gonna Forget About You	1966	15.00

JOTIS

Number	Title (A Side/B Side)	Yr	NM
❑ 470	I'm a Lonely Stranger/Where Lead Me	1965	20.00
❑ 472	Who's Fooling Who/There's a Place for Us	1966	20.00

PHILCO-FORD

Number	Title (A Side/B Side)	Yr	NM
❑ HP-15	Sweet Soul Music/You Don't Have to See Me	1968	15.00
—4-inch plastic "Hip Pocket Record" with color sleeve			

Albums

ATCO

Number	Title (A Side/B Side)	Yr	NM
❑ 33-215 [M]	Sweet Soul Music	1967	40.00
❑ SD 33-215 [S]	Sweet Soul Music	1967	30.00
❑ 33-220 [M]	Shake, Rattle & Roll	1967	40.00
❑ SD 33-220 [S]	Shake, Rattle & Roll	1967	30.00
❑ 33-243 [M]	Soul Directions	1968	60.00
—Mono is white label promo only; "Mono" sticker over the word "Stereo" on front cover			
❑ SD 33-243 [S]	Soul Directions	1968	30.00
❑ 33-276 [M]	More Sweet Soul	1969	70.00
—Mono is white label promo only; "d/j copy monaural" sticker on stereo cover			
❑ SD 33-276 [S]	More Sweet Soul	1969	30.00

CONNIE AND CLARA

45s

HIT

Number	Title (A Side/B Side)	Yr	NM
❑ 61	I Will Follow Him/Take These Chains from My Heart	1963	8.00
—B-side by Herbert Hunter			

CONNORS, CAROL
Also see THE CARMEL SISTERS; THE TEDDY BEARS.

45s

CAPITOL

Number	Title (A Side/B Side)	Yr	NM
❑ 5152	Never/Angel, My Angel	1964	25.00

COLUMBIA

Number	Title (A Side/B Side)	Yr	NM
❑ 41976	You Are My Answer/My Diary	1961	25.00
❑ 42155	Listen to the Beat/My Special Boy	1961	25.00
❑ 42337	That's All It Takes/What Do You See in Him	1962	25.00

ERA

Number	Title (A Side/B Side)	Yr	NM
❑ 3084	Two Rivers/Big, Big Love	1962	30.00
❑ 3096	Tommy Go Away/I Wanna Know	1962	30.00

MIRA

Number	Title (A Side/B Side)	Yr	NM
❑ 219	Lonely Little Beach Girl/My Baby Looks, But He Don't Touch	1965	25.00
❑ 219 [PS]	Lonely Little Beach Girl/My Baby Looks, But He Don't Touch	1965	50.00

N.T.C.

Number	Title (A Side/B Side)	Yr	NM
❑ 3131	Yum Yum Yamaha	1964	50.00
—One-sided single			
❑ 3131 [PS]	Yum Yum Yamaha	1964	100.00

CONNORS, NORMAN

12-Inch Singles

ARISTA

Number	Title (A Side/B Side)	Yr	NM
❑ SP-99 [DJ]	Take It to the Limit (same on both sides?)	1980	15.00

CAPITOL

Number	Title (A Side/B Side)	Yr	NM
❑ V-15376	You're My One and Only Love (5 versions)	1988	10.00

45s

ARISTA

Number	Title (A Side/B Side)	Yr	NM
❑ 0343	This Is Your Life/ Captain Connors	1978	4.00
❑ 0377	Wouldn't You Like to See/Listen	1978	4.00
❑ 0443	Your Love/Disco Land	1979	4.00
❑ 0460	Hand Me Gently/ Be There In the Morning	1979	4.00
❑ 0548	Take It to the Limit/ You Bring Me Joy	1980	4.00
❑ 0581	Melancholy Fire/You've Been On My Mind	1980	4.00
❑ 0632	She's Gone/Mr. C.	1981	4.00

BUDDAH

Number	Title (A Side/B Side)	Yr	NM
❑ 499	Valentine Love/Aria	1975	5.00
❑ 534	We Both Need Each Other/ You Are My Starship	1976	6.00
❑ 542	You Are My Starship/Bubbles	1976	5.00
❑ 554	Betcha By Golly Wow/Kwasi	1976	5.00
❑ 570	Once I've Been There/ Romantic Journey	1977	5.00
❑ 580	For You Everything/ Give the Drummer Some	1977	5.00

CAPITOL

Number	Title (A Side/B Side)	Yr	NM
❑ B-44110	I Am Your Melody/ Samba for Maria	1988	3.00
❑ B-44159	You're My One and Only Love/ I Am Your Melody	1988	3.00

THE RIGHT STUFF

Number	Title (A Side/B Side)	Yr	NM
❑ 58849	Didn't I (Blow Your Mind This Time)/River of Love	2000	3.00

Albums

ACCORD

Number	Title (A Side/B Side)	Yr	NM
❑ SN-7210	Just Imagine	1982	8.00

ARISTA

Number	Title (A Side/B Side)	Yr	NM
❑ AB 4177	This Is Your Life	1978	10.00
❑ AB 4216	Invitation	1979	10.00
❑ AL 9534	Take It to the Limit	1980	10.00
❑ AL 9575	Mr. C.	1981	10.00

BUDDAH

Number	Title (A Side/B Side)	Yr	NM
❑ BDS-5142	Love from the Sun	1973	12.00
❑ BDS-5611	Slewfoot	1974	12.00
❑ BDS-5643	Saturday Night Special	1975	10.00
❑ BDS-5655	You Are My Starship	1976	10.00
❑ BDS-5674	Dance of Magic	1977	20.00
—Reissue of Cobblestone 9024			
❑ BDS-5675	Dark of Light	1977	20.00
—Reissue of Cobblestone 9035			
❑ BDS-5682	Romantic Journey	1977	10.00
❑ BDS-5716	The Best of Norman Connors & Friends	1978	10.00

CAPITOL

Number	Title (A Side/B Side)	Yr	NM
❑ C1-48515	Passion	1988	10.00

COBBLESTONE

Number	Title (A Side/B Side)	Yr	NM
❑ 9024	Dance of Magic	1972	25.00
❑ 9035	Dark of Light	1973	25.00

CONNY

45s

CAPITOL

Number	Title (A Side/B Side)	Yr	NM
❑ 4526	Midi Midnette/Little Girl	1961	12.00

Albums

CAPITOL

Number	Title (A Side/B Side)	Yr	NM
❑ T 10253 [M]	Germany's Greatest Record Star	1960	30.00

CONRAD, BOB

45s

WARNER BROS.

Number	Title (A Side/B Side)	Yr	NM
❑ 5211	I Want You (Pretty Baby)/ Ballin' the Jack	1961	10.00
❑ 5211 [PS]	I Want You (Pretty Baby)/ Ballin' the Jack	1961	25.00
❑ 5242	Bye, Bye Baby/Love You	1961	10.00
❑ 5242 [PS]	Bye, Bye Baby/Love You	1961	25.00
❑ 5267	Keep It Up/Noah's Ark	1962	10.00
❑ 5306	Crazy Magician/I Just Gotta Have You	1962	10.00
❑ 5317	Cindy Is Gone/Again	1962	10.00

Number	Title (A Side/B Side)	Yr	NM

CONRAD, JESS

45s

LONDON

Number	Title (A Side/B Side)	Yr	NM
❑ 1967	Mystery Girl/Just the Two of Us	1961	12.00
❑ 2005	Little Ship/Walk Away	1961	12.00

CONSORTS, THE

45s

APT

Number	Title (A Side/B Side)	Yr	NM
❑ 25066	Please Be Mine/Time After Time	1962	120.00

COUSINS

Number	Title (A Side/B Side)	Yr	NM
❑ 1004	Please Be Mine/Time After Time	1961	400.00

CONTENDERS, THE More than one group.

45s

BETH

Number	Title (A Side/B Side)	Yr	NM
❑ 1001	I'll Show You How to Love/ (B-side unknown)	195?	20.00

BLUE SKY

Number	Title (A Side/B Side)	Yr	NM
❑ 105	Mr. Dee Jay/Yes I Do	1959	600.00

CHATTAHOOCHIE

Number	Title (A Side/B Side)	Yr	NM
❑ 644	The Dune Bugy/Go Ahead	1964	25.00
❑ 656	Johnny B. Goode/Rise 'N' Shine	1964	25.00

JACKPOT

Number	Title (A Side/B Side)	Yr	NM
❑ 48002	Tequila Song/Wild Man	1959	40.00

JAVA

Number	Title (A Side/B Side)	Yr	NM
❑ 101	The Clock/Look at Me	196?	25.00
—Red label			
❑ 101	The Clock/Look at Me	196?	100.00
—Gold label			

CONTINENTAL GEMS, THE

45s

GUYDEN

Number	Title (A Side/B Side)	Yr	NM
❑ 2091	My Love Will Follow You/ Everywhere	1963	400.00

CONTINENTALS, THE (1)

45s

ERA

Number	Title (A Side/B Side)	Yr	NM
❑ 3003	Cool Penguin/Soap Sudz	1959	20.00

PENGUIN

Number	Title (A Side/B Side)	Yr	NM
❑ 1002	Cool Penguin/Soap Sudz	1959	40.00

CONTINENTALS, THE (2)

45s

LOST-NITE

Number	Title (A Side/B Side)	Yr	NM
❑ 349	Dear Lord/Fine Fine Frame	197?	5.00
—Reissue			
❑ 351	Picture of Love/Soft and Sweet	197?	5.00
—Reissue			

PORT

Number	Title (A Side/B Side)	Yr	NM
❑ 70018	Dear Lord/Fine Fine Frame	1960	30.00
❑ 70024	Picture of Love/Soft and Sweet	1961	30.00

WHIRLIN' DISC

Number	Title (A Side/B Side)	Yr	NM
❑ 101	Dear Lord/Fine Fine Frame	1956	200.00
❑ 105	Picture of Love/Soft and Sweet	1957	200.00

CONTINENTALS, THE (3)

45s

RAMA

Number	Title (A Side/B Side)	Yr	NM
❑ 190	You Are An Angel/Giddy Up a Ding Dong	1956	150.00
—Red label			
❑ 190	You Are An Angel/Giddy Up a Ding Dong	1956	1500.
—Blue label			

CONTINENTALS, THE (U) Some of these may be groups (1), (2) or (3); many are not.

45s

AOK

Number	Title (A Side/B Side)	Yr	NM
❑ 1025	Take Me/She Wants You	1966	25.00

BOLO

Number	Title (A Side/B Side)	Yr	NM
❑ 720	I'm Coming Home/ The Turnaround	1960	30.00

CUCA

Number	Title (A Side/B Side)	Yr	NM
❑ 1063	Tic-Toc/Sue	1961	30.00

DAVIS

Number	Title (A Side/B Side)	Yr	NM
❑ 466	Don't Do It, Baby/Tongue Twister	1959	40.00

HUNTER

Number	Title (A Side/B Side)	Yr	NM
❑ 3503	It Doesn't Matter/Whisper It	1960	1200.

KEY

Number	Title (A Side/B Side)	Yr	NM
❑ 517	Take a Gamble on Me/ Meanwhile Back at the Ranch	1956	100.00

LIFETIME

Number	Title (A Side/B Side)	Yr	NM
❑ 1019	Cathy's Clown/Maybe Baby	1966	10.00

VANDAN

Number	Title (A Side/B Side)	Yr	NM
❑ 8067	No Money No Luck Blues/ Pink Champagne	196?	20.00

CONTOURS, THE

12-Inch Singles

MOTOWN

Number	Title (A Side/B Side)	Yr	NM
❑ 4611MG	Do You Love Me (6:26) (Edited Version 2:37) (Original Version 2:53)	1988	15.00

45s

GORDY

Number	Title (A Side/B Side)	Yr	NM
❑ 7005	Do You Love Me/Move Mr. Man	1962	20.00
❑ 7012	Shake Sherry/You Better Get in Line	1963	15.00
❑ 7016	Don't Let Her Be Your Baby/ It Must Be Love	1963	12.00
❑ 7019	Pa I Need a Car/You Get Ugly	1963	12.00
❑ 7029	Can You Do It/I'll Stand By You	1964	12.00
❑ 7037	Can You Jerk Like Me/That Day When She Needed Me	1964	12.00
❑ 7044	First I Look at the Purse/ Searching for a Girl	1965	12.00
❑ 7052	Just a Little Misunderstanding/ Determination	1966	12.00
❑ 7059	It's So Hard Being a Loser/ Your Love Grows More Precious Every Day	1967	12.00

HOB

Number	Title (A Side/B Side)	Yr	NM
❑ 116	I'm So Glad/Yours Is My Heart Alone	1961	120.00

MOTOWN

Number	Title (A Side/B Side)	Yr	NM
❑ 1008	Whole Lotta Woman/Come On and Be Mine	1961	500.00
❑ 1012	The Stretch/Funny	1962	800.00

MOTOWN YESTERYEAR

Number	Title (A Side/B Side)	Yr	NM
❑ 448	Do You Love Me/Shake Sherry	1972	4.00
❑ 448 [PS]	Do You Love Me/Shake Sherry	1988	5.00
—"Dirty Dancing" sleeve; without cut-out hole			

ROCKET

Number	Title (A Side/B Side)	Yr	NM
❑ 41192	I'm a Winner/Makes Me Wanna Come Back	1980	4.00

TAMLA

Number	Title (A Side/B Side)	Yr	NM
❑ 7012	Shake Sherry/You Better Get in Line	1963	150.00
—Tamla label used in error for a Gordy release			

Albums

GORDY

Number	Title (A Side/B Side)	Yr	NM
❑ G 901 [M]	Do You Love Me?	1962	500.00

MOTOWN

Number	Title (A Side/B Side)	Yr	NM
❑ M5-188V1	Do You Love Me?	1981	10.00

CONVINCERS, THE

45s

MOVIN'

Number	Title (A Side/B Side)	Yr	NM
❑ 100	Rejected Love/Go Back Baby	1962	400.00

CONWAY, JULIE

Albums

HARMONY

Number	Title (A Side/B Side)	Yr	NM
❑ HL 7143 [M]	Good Housekeeping's Plan for Reducing Off-the-Record	1960	20.00

COODER, RY Also see THE ROLLING STONES.

12-Inch Singles

WARNER BROS.

Number	Title (A Side/B Side)	Yr	NM
❑ PRO-A-943 [DJ]	Crazy 'Bout an Automobile/ If Walls Could Talk/The Very Thing That Makes You Rich/ Look at Granny Run	1981	20.00

45s

MUSICOR

Number	Title (A Side/B Side)	Yr	NM
❑ 1148	Life Game/1983	1966	10.00

REPRISE

Number	Title (A Side/B Side)	Yr	NM
❑ 0910	Goin' to Brownsville/ Available Space	1970	6.00
❑ 0940	Alimony/Pigmeat	1970	6.00
❑ 1009	Dark Is the Night/On a Monday	1971	6.00
❑ 1071	Billy the Kid/Money Honey	1972	6.00
❑ 1167	Billy the Kid/Boomer's Story	1973	6.00

WARNER BROS.

Number	Title (A Side/B Side)	Yr	NM
❑ 8384	School Is Out/Jesus on the Mainline	1977	5.00
❑ 27945	Get Rhythm/Get Back to Okinawa	1988	4.00
❑ 28158	All Shook Up/Get Your Lies Straight	1987	4.00
❑ 28158 [PS]	All Shook Up/Get Your Lies Straight	1987	4.00
❑ 28723	Crossroads/Feel It (Bad Blues)	1986	4.00
❑ 28725	Tell Me Something Slick/ Billy and Annie	1986	4.00
❑ 49055	Down in Hollywood/Little Sister	1979	5.00
❑ 49081	The Very Thing That Makes You Rich/Little Sister	1979	5.00
❑ 49677	Girls from Texas/Borderline	1981	4.00
❑ 49704	Crazy 'Bout an Automobile/ Borderline	1981	4.00

Albums

MOBILE FIDELITY

Number	Title (A Side/B Side)	Yr	NM
❑ 1-085	Jazz	198?	400.00
—Audiophile vinyl			

REPRISE

Number	Title (A Side/B Side)	Yr	NM
❑ PRO 588 [DJ]	The Ry Cooder Radio Show	1976	100.00
❑ MS 2052	Into the Purple Valley	1972	12.00
❑ MS 2117	Boomer's Story	1973	12.00
❑ MS 2179	Paradise and Lunch	1974	12.00
❑ MS 2254	Chicken Skin Music	1976	12.00
❑ RS-6402	Ry Cooder	1969	15.00
—Two-tone orange label with "r:" and "W7" logos			
❑ RS-6402	Ry Cooder	1970	12.00
—No "W7" on label; one-tone orange (almost tan) label			

WARNER BROS.

Number	Title (A Side/B Side)	Yr	NM
❑ BS 3059	Show Time	1977	10.00
❑ BSK 3197	Jazz	1978	10.00
❑ BSK 3358	Bop Till You Drop	1979	10.00
❑ HS 3448	The Long Riders	1980	10.00
❑ BSK 3489	Borderline	1980	10.00
❑ BSK 3651	The Slide Area	1982	10.00
❑ 25270	Paris, Texas	1984	10.00
❑ 25399	Crossroads	1986	10.00
❑ 25639	Get Rhythm	1987	10.00
❑ 25996	Johnny Handsome	1989	10.00

COOK, KEN

45s

PHILLIPS INT'L.

Number	Title (A Side/B Side)	Yr	NM
❑ 3534	I Was a Fool/Crazy Baby	1959	50.00
—Roy Orbison appears on this record (uncredited)			

COOK, PETER, AND DUDLEY MOORE

45s

PARROT

Number	Title (A Side/B Side)	Yr	NM
❑ 3016	Bedazzled/Love Me	1967	8.00

COOKE, SAM

45s

CHERIE

Number	Title (A Side/B Side)	Yr	NM
❑ 4501	Darling I Need You Now/ Win Your Love for Me	1971	8.00

KEEN

Number	Title (A Side/B Side)	Yr	NM
❑ 8-1001	You Send Me/Love You Most of All	1960	15.00
—Gold label; early reissue series			
❑ 3-2005	Stealing Kisses/All of My Life	1958	25.00
❑ 3-2006 [M]	Win Your Love for Me/Love Song from "Houseboat" (Almost in Your Arms)	1958	25.00
❑ 5-2006 [S]	Win Your Love for Me/Love Song from "Houseboat" (Almost in Your Arms)	1959	100.00
—Blue vinyl			
❑ 3-2008	Love You Most of All/Blue Moon	1958	25.00
❑ 3-2018 [M]	Everybody Likes to Cha Cha Cha/Little Things You Do	1959	25.00
❑ 5-2018 [S]	Everybody Likes to Cha Cha Cha/Little Things You Do	1959	40.00
❑ 2022 [M]	Only Sixteen/Let's Go Steady Again	1959	25.00
❑ 5-2022 [S]	Only Sixteen/Let's Go Steady Again	1959	50.00
❑ 2101	Summertime/Summertime (Part 2)	1959	25.00
❑ 8-2105	There! I've Said It Again/One Hour Ahead of the Posse	1959	25.00
❑ 2118	Steal Away/So Glamorous	1960	20.00
❑ 2122	Mary, Mary Lou/Eee-Yi-Ee-Yi-Oh	1960	20.00
❑ 4009	You Were Made for Me/ Lonely Island	1958	25.00
❑ 3-4013	You Send Me/Summertime	195?	20.00
—Multicolor label; note slightly different number than original (34013)			
❑ 34002	(I Love You) For Sentimental Reasons/Desire Me	1958	25.00
—Black label			
❑ 34013	You Send Me/Summertime	1957	25.00
—Black label (original)			
❑ 82111	'T'ain't Nobody's Bizness (If I Do)/No One	1960	25.00
❑ 82112	Wonderful World/Along the Navajo Trail	1960	20.00
❑ 82117	With You/I Thank God	1960	20.00

RCA

Number	Title (A Side/B Side)	Yr	NM
❑ PB-14146	Bring It On Home to Me/Nothing Can Change This Love	1985	8.00

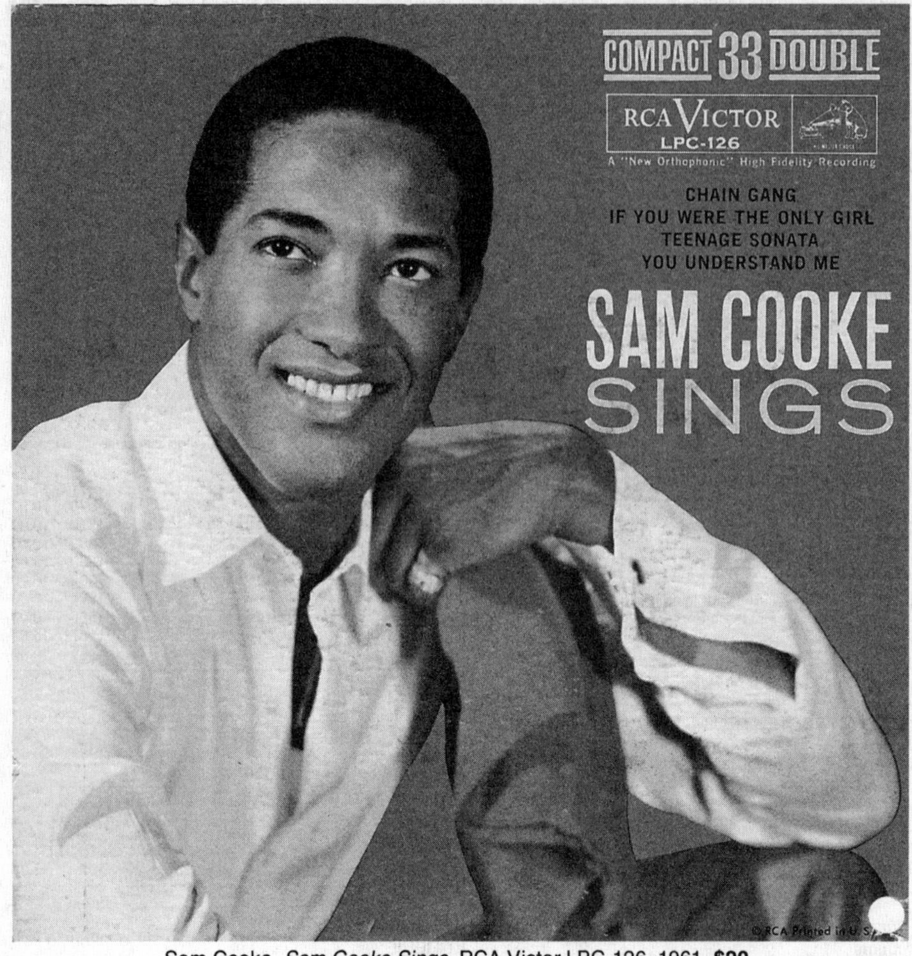

Sam Cooke, *Sam Cooke Sings*, RCA Victor LPC-126, 1961, **$20.**

Number	Title (A Side/B Side)	Yr	NM
RCA VICTOR			
❑ 37-7853	That's It-I Quit-I'm Movin' On/ What Do You Say	1961	60.00
—"Compact Single 33" (small hole, plays at LP speed)			
❑ 47-7701	Teenage Sonata/If You Were the Only Girl	1960	20.00
❑ 47-7730	You Understand Me/ I Belong to Your Heart	1960	15.00
❑ 47-7730 [PS]	You Understand Me /I Belong to Your Heart	1960	25.00
❑ 47-7783	Chain Gang/I Fall in Love Every Day	1960	15.00
❑ 47-7783 [PS]	Chain Gang/I Fall in Love Every Day	1960	25.00
❑ 47-7816	Sad Mood/Love Me	1960	15.00
❑ 47-7853	That's It-I Quit-I'm Movin' On/ What Do You Say	1961	15.00
❑ 47-7883	Cupid/Farewell, My Darling	1961	15.00
❑ 47-7883 [PS]	Cupid/Farewell, My Darling	1961	25.00
❑ 47-7927	Feel It/It's All Right	1961	15.00
❑ 47-7927 [PS]	Feel It/It's All Right	1961	25.00
❑ 47-7983	Twistin' the Night Away/ One More Time	1962	15.00
❑ 47-8036	Bring It On Home to Me/ Having a Party	1962	15.00
❑ 47-8088	Nothing Can Change This Love/Somebody Have Mercy	1962	15.00
❑ 47-8088 [PS]	Nothing Can Change This Love/Somebody Have Mercy	1962	25.00
❑ 47-8129	Send Me Some Lovin'/ Baby, Baby, Baby	1963	15.00
❑ 47-8129 [PS]	Send Me Some Lovin'/ Baby, Baby, Baby	1963	25.00
❑ 47-8164	Another Saturday Night/ Love Will Find a Way	1963	15.00
❑ 47-8164 [PS]	Another Saturday Night/ Love Will Find a Way	1963	25.00
❑ 47-8215	Frankie and Johnny/Cool Train	1963	12.00
❑ 47-8215 [PS]	Frankie and Johnny/Cool Train	1963	25.00
❑ 47-8247	Little Red Rooster/ You Gotta Move	1963	12.00
❑ 47-8247 [PS]	Little Red Rooster/ You Gotta Move	1963	25.00
❑ 47-8299	Good News/Basin Street Blues	1963	12.00
❑ 47-8299	Ain't That Good News/ Basin Street Blues	1963	20.00
—Original A-side title (or a scarce reissue)			
❑ 47-8368	Good Times/Tennessee Waltz	1964	12.00
❑ 47-8426	Cousin of Mine/That's Where It's At	1964	12.00
❑ 47-8486	Shake/A Change Is Gonna Come	1964	12.00
❑ 47-8539	It's Got the Whole World Shakin'/ Ease My Troublin' Mind	1965	10.00
❑ 47-8586	When a Boy Falls in Love/ The Piper	1965	10.00
❑ 47-8631	Sugar Dumpling/Bridge of Tears	1965	10.00
❑ 47-8631 [PS]	Sugar Dumpling/Bridge of Tears	1965	25.00
❑ 47-8751	Feel It/That's All	1965	10.00
❑ 47-8803	Let's Go Steady Again/ Trouble Blues	1966	10.00
❑ 47-8934	Meet Me at Mary's Place/ If I Had a Hammer	1966	10.00
❑ SP-45-173 [DJ]	A Change Is Gonna Come (same on both sides)	1968	50.00
—Promo-only number; this appears to be a radio reissue in the wake of events going on in 1968			
❑ VP-2-2555 [S]	Twistin' in the Kitchen with Dinah/A Whole Lotta Woman	1962	25.00
—Small hole, plays at 33 1/3 rpm			
❑ VP-3-2555 [S]	The Twist/Movin' & Groovin'	1962	25.00
—Small hole, plays at 33 1/3 rpm			
❑ VP-4-2555 [S]	Somebody Have Mercy/ Camptown Girl	1962	25.00
—Small hole, plays at 33 1/3 rpm			
SAR			
❑ 122 [DJ]	Just for You/Made for Me	1961	100.00
—Promo only (some copies have "Audition" on label, some do not); possibly made as leverage during contract renegotiation at RCA Victor			
SPECIALTY			
❑ 596	Forever/Lovable	1957	30.00
—As "Dale Cook"			
❑ 619	I'll Come Running Back to You/ Forever	1957	30.00
❑ 627	That's All I Need to Know/ I Don't Want to Cry	1958	30.00
❑ 667	Happy in Love/I Need You Now	1959	30.00
❑ 921	Must Jesus Bear the Cross Alone/The Last Mile of the Way	1970	10.00
—With the Soul Stirrers			
❑ 928	Just Another Day/Christ Is All	1973	10.00
—With the Soul Stirrers			
❑ 930	That's Heaven to Me/ Lord, Remember Me	1974	10.00
—With the Soul Stirrers			
7-Inch Extended Plays			
KEEN			
❑ B-2001	The Bells of Saint Mary's/ Tammy//Moonlight in Vermont/So Long	1958	80.00
❑ B-2001 [PS]	Songs by Sam Cooke, Vol. 1	1958	80.00
❑ B-2002	*You Send Me/The Lonesome Road/That Lucky Old Sun/ Canadian Sunset	1958	80.00
❑ B-2002 [PS]	Songs by Sam Cooke, Vol. 2	1958	80.00
❑ B-2003	Summertime/Danny Boy// Around the World/ Ol' Man River	1958	80.00
❑ B-2003 [PS]	Songs by Sam Cooke, Vol. 3	1958	80.00
❑ B-2006	*Mary, Mary Lou/The Gypsy/Oh, Look at Me Now/Someday	1958	80.00
❑ B-2006 [PS]	Encore, Vol. 1	1958	80.00
❑ B-2007	*When I Fall in Love/I Cover the Waterfront/Running Wild/ Today I Sing the Blues	1958	80.00
❑ B-2007 [PS]	Encore, Vol. 2	1958	80.00
❑ B-2008	It's the Talk of the Town/Along the Navajo Trail//My Foolish Heart/ Accentuate the Positive	1958	80.00
❑ B-2008 [PS]	Encore, Vol. 3	1958	80.00
❑ B-2010	Love Song from Houseboat/ Lonely Island//Win Your Love for Me/All of My Life	1959	80.00
❑ B-2010 [PS]	Sam Cooke Sings His Hits	1959	80.00
❑ B-2012	Let's Call the Whole Thing Off/ God Bless the Child//Comes Love/Lover Girl	1959	80.00
❑ B-2012 [PS]	Tribute to the Lady, Vol. 1	1959	80.00
❑ B-2013	(contents unknown)	1959	80.00
❑ B-2013 [PS]	Tribute to the Lady, Vol. 2	1959	80.00
❑ B-2014	Solitude/Lover Come Back to Me/ /T'Aint Nobody's Bizness (If I Do)/She's Funny That Way	1959	80.00
❑ B-2014 [PS]	Tribute to the Lady, Vol. 3	1959	80.00
RCA VICTOR			
❑ LPC-126	Chain Gang/If You Were the Only Girl//Teenage Sonata/ You Understand Me	1961	20.00
❑ LPC-126 [PS]	Sam Cooke Sings	1961	20.00
❑ EPA-4375	Another Saturday Night/ You Send Me//Only Sixteen/ Bring It On Home to Me	1963	20.00
❑ EPA-4375 [PS]	Another Saturday Night	1963	20.00
Albums			
ABKCO			
❑ 1124-1	Sam Cooke's Night Beat	1995	12.00
—Reissue			
❑ 2970-1	Sam Cooke at the Copa	1988	12.00
—Reissue			
FAMOUS			
❑ 502	Sam's Songs	1969	40.00
❑ 505	Only Sixteen	1969	40.00
❑ 508	So Wonderful	1969	40.00
❑ 509	You Send Me	1969	40.00
❑ 512	Cha-Cha-Cha	1969	40.00
51 WEST			
❑ Q 16032	My Foolish Heart	198?	12.00
KEEN			
❑ A-2001 [M]	Sam Cooke	1958	200.00
❑ A-2003 [M]	Encore	1958	200.00
❑ A-2004 [M]	Tribute to the Lady	1959	150.00
❑ AS-2004 [S]	Tribute to the Lady	1959	200.00
❑ 86101 [M]	Hit Kit	1959	250.00
❑ 86103 [M]	I Thank God	1960	400.00
❑ 86106 [M]	The Wonderful World of Sam Cooke	1960	350.00
PAIR			
❑ PDL2-1006 [(2)]	You Send Me	1986	15.00
RCA CAMDEN			
❑ ACS1-0445	You Send Me	1974	12.00
❑ CAL-2264 [M]	The One and Only Sam Cooke	1967	20.00
❑ CAS-2264 [R]	The One and Only Sam Cooke	1967	12.00
❑ CAS-2433	Sam Cooke	1970	12.00
❑ CAS-2610	The Unforgettable Sam Cooke	1972	12.00
RCA VICTOR			
❑ LPM-2221 [M]	Cooke's Tour	1960	40.00
❑ LSP-2221 [S]	Cooke's Tour	1960	50.00
❑ LPM-2236 [M]	Hits of the 50's	1960	40.00
❑ LSP-2236 [S]	Hits of the 50's	1960	50.00
❑ LPM-2293 [M]	Swing Low	1960	40.00

Except when noted otherwise, VG = 25% of NM, and VG+ = 50% of NM. (Example: VG = $2.00, VG+ = $4.00 and NM = $8.00.)

Number	Title (A Side/B Side)	Yr	NM
❑ LSP-2293 [S]	Swing Low	1960	50.00
❑ LPM-2392 [M]	My Kind of Blues	1961	40.00
❑ LSP-2392 [S]	My Kind of Blues	1961	50.00
❑ LPM-2555 [M]	Twistin' the Night Away	1962	40.00
❑ LSP-2555 [S]	Twistin' the Night Away	1962	50.00
❑ AFL1-2625	The Best of Sam Cooke	1977	12.00
—Reissue with new prefix			
❑ LPM-2625 [M]	The Best of Sam Cooke	1962	30.00
❑ LSP-2625 [R]	The Best of Sam Cooke	1962	20.00
❑ ANL1-2658	Sam Cooke at the Copa	1977	12.00
—Reissue of LSP-2970			
❑ LPM-2673 [M]	Mr. Soul	1963	30.00
❑ LSP-2673 [S]	Mr. Soul	1963	40.00
❑ LPM-2709 [M]	Night Beat	1963	30.00
❑ LSP-2709 [S]	Night Beat	1963	40.00
❑ LPM-2899 [M]	Ain't That Good News	1964	30.00
❑ LSP-2899 [S]	Ain't That Good News	1964	40.00
❑ LPM-2970 [M]	Sam Cooke at the Copa	1964	30.00
❑ LSP-2970 [S]	Sam Cooke at the Copa	1964	40.00
❑ LPM-3367 [M]	Shake	1965	25.00
❑ LSP-3367 [S]	Shake	1965	30.00
❑ LPM-3373 [M]	The Best of Sam Cooke, Vol. 2	1965	25.00
❑ LSP-3373 [S]	The Best of Sam Cooke, Vol. 2	1965	30.00
❑ LPM-3435 [M]	Try a Little Love	1965	25.00
❑ LSP-3435 [S]	Try a Little Love	1965	30.00
❑ LPM-3517 [M]	The Unforgettable Sam Cooke	1966	20.00
❑ LSP-3517 [S]	The Unforgettable Sam Cooke	1966	25.00
❑ AYL1-3863	The Best of Sam Cooke	1981	8.00
—Budget-line reissue			
❑ LPM-3991 [M]	The Man Who Invented Soul	1968	50.00
❑ LSP-3991 [S]	The Man Who Invented Soul	1968	25.00
❑ AFL1-5181	Live at the Harlem Square Club, 1963	1985	12.00
❑ VPS-6027 [(2)]	This Is Sam Cooke	1970	20.00
❑ CPL2-7127 [(2)]	The Man and His Music	1986	15.00

SPECIALTY

Number	Title (A Side/B Side)	Yr	NM
❑ SPS-2106	Sam Cooke and the Soul Stirrers	1970	15.00
❑ SPS-2116	The Gospel Soul of Sam Cooke, Vol. 1	1970	15.00
❑ SPS-2119	Two Sides of Sam Cooke	1970	15.00
❑ SPS-2128	The Gospel Soul of Sam Cooke, Vol. 2	197?	15.00
❑ SPS-2146	That's Heaven to Me	197?	15.00

TRIP

Number	Title (A Side/B Side)	Yr	NM
❑ 8030 [(2)]	The Golden Sound of Sam Cooke	1972	15.00

UPFRONT

Number	Title (A Side/B Side)	Yr	NM
❑ 160	The Billie Holiday Story	1973	15.00

COOKER, JOHN LEE See JOHN LEE HOOKER.

COOKIE AND HIS CUPCAKES

45s

CHESS

Number	Title (A Side/B Side)	Yr	NM
❑ 1848	Got You On My Mind/I've Been So Lonely	1963	15.00

JUDD

Number	Title (A Side/B Side)	Yr	NM
❑ 1002	Matilda/Married Life	1958	30.00
—Without "H" in A-side title			
❑ 1002	Mathilda/Married Life	1958	50.00
—With "H" in A-side title			
❑ 1015	Until Then/Close Up the Back Door	1959	40.00

KHOURY'S

Number	Title (A Side/B Side)	Yr	NM
❑ 703	Mathilda/Married Life	1958	60.00

LYRIC

Number	Title (A Side/B Side)	Yr	NM
❑ 1003	Mathilda/I'm Twisted	1963	20.00
❑ 1004	Got You On My Mind/I've Been So Lonely	1963	20.00
❑ 1008	All My Lovin' Baby/I Heard That Story Before	196?	20.00
❑ 1009	Breaking Up Is Hard to Do/I Cried	196?	20.00
❑ 1012	Until Then/Close Up the Back Door	196?	15.00
❑ 1015	Hey Little School Girl/Charged with Cheating	196?	15.00
❑ 1016	Walking Down the Aisle/Even Though	196?	15.00
❑ 1017	Long Time Ago/Kissing Someone Else	196?	15.00
❑ 1020	Belinda/Trouble in My Life	196?	15.00

MERCURY

Number	Title (A Side/B Side)	Yr	NM
❑ 71748	Matilda Has Finally Come Back/As Part of Everything	1961	20.00

PAULA

Number	Title (A Side/B Side)	Yr	NM
❑ 221	Mathilda/I'm Twisted	1965	12.00
❑ 230	Belinda/Trouble in My Life	1965	10.00

COOKIES, THE

45s

ATLANTIC

Number	Title (A Side/B Side)	Yr	NM
❑ 1061	Precious Love/Later, Later	1955	30.00
❑ 1084	In Paradise/Passing Time	1956	30.00
❑ 1110	Down By the River/My Lover	1956	25.00
❑ 2079	Passing Time/In Paradise	1960	20.00

DIMENSION

Number	Title (A Side/B Side)	Yr	NM
❑ 1002	Chains/Stranger in My Arms	1962	20.00
❑ 1008	Don't Say Nothin' Bad (About My Baby)/Softly in the Night	1963	15.00
❑ 1008	Don't Say Nothin' Bad/Softly in the Night	1963	20.00
❑ 1012	I Want a Boy for My Birthday/Will Power	1963	15.00
❑ 1020	Girls Grow Up Faster Than Boys/Only to Other People	1963	15.00
❑ 1032	I Never Dreamed/The Old Crowd	1964	15.00

JOSIE

Number	Title (A Side/B Side)	Yr	NM
❑ 822	King of Hearts/Hippy-Dippy-Daddy	1957	30.00

LAMP

Number	Title (A Side/B Side)	Yr	NM
❑ 8008	Don't Let Go/All Night Mambo	1954	40.00

WARNER BROS.

Number	Title (A Side/B Side)	Yr	NM
❑ 7025	All My Trials/Wounded	1967	10.00
❑ 7047	Mr. Cupid (Don't You Call on Me)/Hang My Head and Cry	1967	10.00
—B-side by the Big Guys			

COOKIES, THE/LITTLE EVA/CAROLE KING

Albums

DIMENSION

Number	Title (A Side/B Side)	Yr	NM
❑ DLP-6001 [M]	The Dimension Dolls, Vol. 1	1964	250.00

COOL, CALVIN, AND THE SURF KNOBS

45s

CHARTER

Number	Title (A Side/B Side)	Yr	NM
❑ 7	Beach Bash/El Tocolote	1963	40.00

Albums

CHARTER

Number	Title (A Side/B Side)	Yr	NM
❑ CLP-103 [M]	The Surfer's Beat	1963	40.00
❑ CLS-103 [S]	The Surfer's Beat	1963	50.00

COOL HEAT See WIND.

COOL SOUNDS, THE

45s

PULSAR

Number	Title (A Side/B Side)	Yr	NM
❑ 2421	Comin' Home (Free)/Rag Doll	1969	50.00

WARNER BROS.

Number	Title (A Side/B Side)	Yr	NM
❑ 7538	I'll Take You Back/Where Do We Go from Here	1971	30.00
❑ 7575	A Love Like Ours Could Last a Million Years or More/Who Can I Turn To	1972	30.00
❑ 7615	Boy Wonder/Free	1972	30.00

COOLBREEZERS, THE

45s

ABC-PARAMOUNT

Number	Title (A Side/B Side)	Yr	NM
❑ 9865	You Know I Go for You/My Brother	1957	100.00

BALE

Number	Title (A Side/B Side)	Yr	NM
❑ 100/101	The Greatest Love of All/Eda Weda Bug	1958	60.00
❑ 102/103	Let Christmas Ring/Hello, Mister New Year	1958	200.00

EBONY

Number	Title (A Side/B Side)	Yr	NM
❑ 1015	Won't You Come In/Pack Your Bags and Go	1956	500.00
—As "The Little Coolbreezers"			

COOPER, ALICE Also see NAZZ (2); THE SPIDERS (2).

12-Inch Singles

EPIC

Number	Title (A Side/B Side)	Yr	NM
❑ EAS 1347 [DJ]	I Got a Line on You (same on both sides)	1988	10.00
❑ EAS 1663 [DJ]	Poison (same on both sides)	1989	10.00
❑ EAS 1686 [DJ]	Trash (same on both sides)	1989	10.00

MCA

Number	Title (A Side/B Side)	Yr	NM
❑ L33-17177 [DJ]	He's Back (The Man Behind the Mask) (same on both sides)	1986	10.00
❑ L33-17205 [DJ]	Give It Up (same on both sides)	1986	10.00
❑ L33-17416 [DJ]	Freedom (same on both sides)	1987	10.00

WARNER BROS.

Number	Title (A Side/B Side)	Yr	NM
❑ PRO-A-864 [DJ]	Clones (We're All)/Model Citizen	1980	20.00
❑ PRO-A-1059 [DJ]	I Like Girls (same on both sides)	1981	20.00

45s

ATLANTIC

Number	Title (A Side/B Side)	Yr	NM
❑ 3254	Only Women/Cold Ethyl	1975	5.00
❑ 3280	Department of Youth/Some Folks	1975	5.00
❑ 3298	Welcome to My Nightmare/Cold Ethyl	1975	5.00

EPIC

Number	Title (A Side/B Side)	Yr	NM
❑ 34-08114	I Got a Line on You/Livin' on the Edge	1988	3.00
—B-side by Britney Fox			
❑ 34-68958	Poison/Trash	1989	3.00
❑ 34-73085	House of Fire/Ballad of Dwight Fry	1989	3.00
❑ 34-73845	Hey Stoopid/It Rained All Night	1991	3.00
❑ 34-73983	Love's a Loaded Gun/Fire	1991	3.00

MCA

Number	Title (A Side/B Side)	Yr	NM
❑ 52904	He's Back (The Man Behind the Mask)/Billion Dollar Baby	1986	3.00
❑ 52904 [PS]	He's Back (The Man Behind the Mask)/Billion Dollar Baby	1986	4.00
❑ 53212	Freedom/Time to Kill	1987	3.00
❑ 53212 [PS]	Freedom/Time to Kill	1987	4.00

STRAIGHT

Number	Title (A Side/B Side)	Yr	NM
❑ 101	Reflected/Living	1969	300.00
—Promos worth about 10% of this value			

WARNER BROS.

Number	Title (A Side/B Side)	Yr	NM
❑ GWB 7141	Eighteen/Caught in a Dream	1972	4.00
—"Back to Back Hits" series; green label			
❑ GWB 7141	Eighteen/Caught in a Dream	1973	3.00
—"Back to Back Hits" series; "Burbank" palm trees label			
❑ 7398	Shoe Salesman/Return of the Spiders	1970	20.00
❑ 7449	Eighteen/Body	1971	5.00
❑ 7490	Caught in a Dream/Hallowed Be My Name	1971	5.00
❑ 7529	Under My Wheels/Desperado	1971	5.00
❑ 7568	Be My Lover/Yeah, Yeah, Yeah	1972	5.00
❑ 7596	School's Out/Gutter Cat	1972	5.00
❑ 7596 [PS]	School's Out/Gutter Cat	1972	15.00
❑ 7631	Elected/Luney Tune	1972	5.00
❑ 7631 [PS]	Elected/Luney Tune	1972	15.00
❑ 7673	Hello Hurray/Generation Landslide	1972	5.00
❑ 7691	No More Mr. Nice Guy/Raped and Freezin'	1973	5.00
❑ 7724	Billion Dollar Babies/Mary Ann	1973	5.00
❑ 7762	Teenage Lament '74/Hard Hearted Alice	1973	5.00
❑ 7783	Muscle of Love/Crazy Little Child	1974	5.00
❑ 8023	I'm Eighteen/Muscle of Love	1974	5.00
❑ 8228	I Never Cry/Go to Hell	1976	4.00
❑ 8349	You and Me/It's Hot Tonight	1977	4.00
❑ 8349 [PS]	You and Me/It's Hot Tonight	1977	8.00
❑ 8448	(No More) Love at Your Convenience/I Never Wrote Those Songs	1977	5.00
❑ 8607	School's Out/Eighteen	1978	8.00
❑ 8695	How You Gonna See Me Now/No Tricks	1978	5.00
❑ 8760	From the Inside/Nurse Rosetta	1979	4.00
❑ 29828	I Am the Future/Tag, You're It	1982	4.00
❑ 29928	I Like Girls/Zorro's Ascent	1982	4.00
❑ 49204	Clones (We're All)/Model Citizen	1980	4.00
❑ 49204 [PS]	Clones (We're All)/Model Citizen	1980	5.00
❑ 49526	Dance Yourself to Death/Talk Talk	1980	4.00
❑ 49780	You Want It, You Got It/Who Do You Think We Are	1981	4.00
❑ 49848	Generation Landslide '81/Seven and Seven Is	1981	4.00

7-Inch Extended Plays

WARNER BROS.

Number	Title (A Side/B Side)	Yr	NM
❑ S 2748	Working Up a Sweat/Never Been Sold Before//Muscle of Love/Teenage Lament	1973	20.00
—Jukebox issue; small hole, plays at 33 1/3 rpm			
❑ S 2748 [PS]	Muscle of Love	1973	20.00
—Part of "Little LP" series (LLP #235)			

Albums

ACCORD

Number	Title (A Side/B Side)	Yr	NM
❑ SN-7162	Toronto Rock 'n' Roll Revival 1969	1981	12.00

ATLANTIC

Number	Title (A Side/B Side)	Yr	NM
❑ SD 18130	Welcome to My Nightmare	1975	10.00
❑ SD 19157	Welcome to My Nightmare	1978	8.00
—Reissue of 18130			

EPIC

Number	Title (A Side/B Side)	Yr	NM
❑ OE 45137	Trash	1989	12.00
❑ E 46786	Hey Stoopid	1991	15.00

MCA

Number	Title (A Side/B Side)	Yr	NM
❑ 5761	Constrictor	1986	8.00
❑ 42091	Raise Your Fist and Yell	1987	8.00

MOBILE FIDELITY

Number	Title (A Side/B Side)	Yr	NM
❑ 1-063	Welcome to My Nightmare	1980	50.00
—Audiophile vinyl			

PAIR

Number	Title (A Side/B Side)	Yr	NM
❑ PDL2-1163 [(2)]	A Man Called Alice	1987	15.00

STRAIGHT

Number	Title (A Side/B Side)	Yr	NM
❑ STS-1051	Pretties for You	1969	150.00
—Yellow label stock copy			

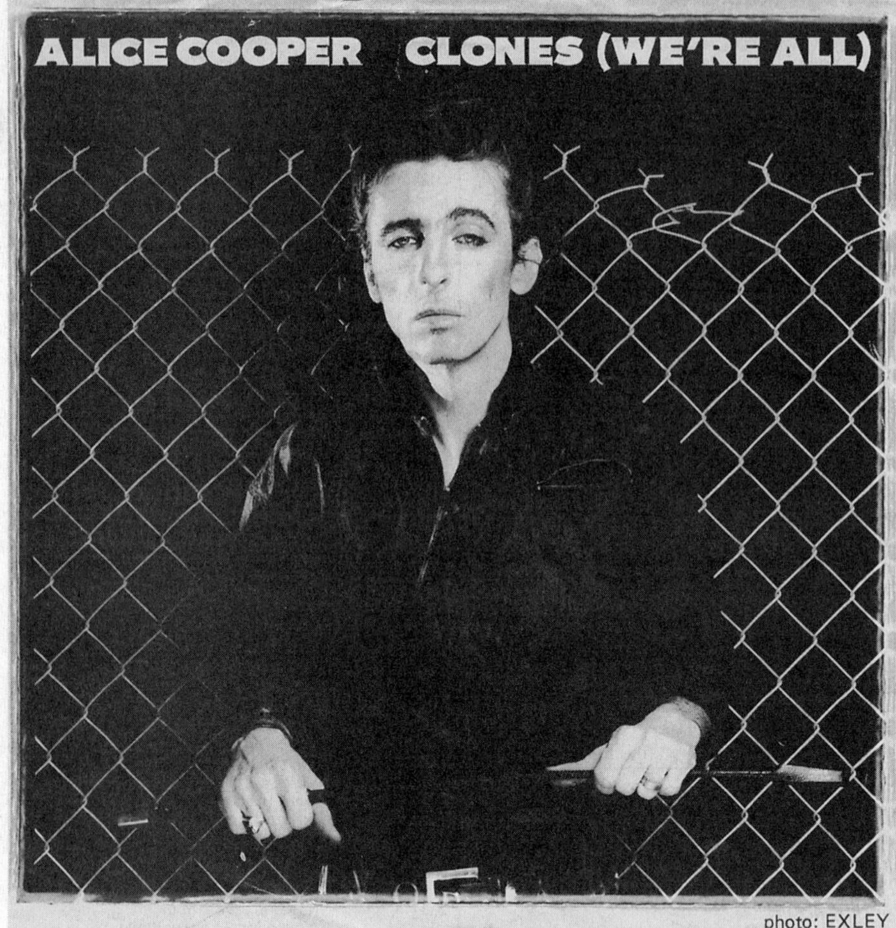

Alice Cooper, "Clones (We're All)," Warner Bros. 48204, 1980, **$5.**

Number	Title (A Side/B Side)	Yr	NM
❑ STS-1051 [DJ]	Pretties for You	1969	200.00
—White label promo			
❑ WS 1840	Pretties for You	1970	60.00
—Pink label stock copy			
❑ WS 1845	Easy Action	1970	30.00
—Pink label stock copy; "Alice Cooper" in white on cover			
❑ WS 1845	Easy Action	1970	50.00
—Pink label stock copy; "Alice Cooper" in black on cover			
❑ WS 1845 [DJ]	Easy Action	1970	100.00
—White label promo			
❑ WS 1883	Love It to Death	1971	50.00
—Pink label stock copy			
❑ WS 1883 [DJ]	Love It to Death	1971	100.00
—White label promo			
TPM/RHINO EXCLUSIVE			
❑ 1840	Pretties for You	2008	10.00
❑ 1845	Easy Action	2008	10.00
❑ 1883	Love It to Death	2008	10.00
WARNER BROS.			
❑ PRO 789 [DJ]	The Alice Cooper Radio Show	1978	25.00
❑ WS 1840	Pretties for You	1971	25.00
—Green label; comes in "Straight" cover			
❑ WS 1840	Pretties for You	1973	20.00
—"Burbank" palm trees label; comes in Straight cover			
❑ WS 1883	Love It to Death	1971	12.00
—Version 4: Green "WB" label; with "I'm Eighteen" box and Alice's protruding thumb airbrushed off the cover			
❑ WS 1883	Love It to Death	1971	20.00
—Version 2: Green "WB" label; same as above, but has a white box reading "Contains the Hit 'I'm Eighteen' "			
❑ WS 1883	Love It to Death	1971	20.00
—Version 3: Green "WB" label; cover has large white areas at top and bottom with lower half of the photo cropped out			
❑ WS 1883	Love It to Death	1971	30.00
—Version 1: Green "WB" label; cover has Alice's thumb sticking out in such a way that it appears to be another part of the body			
❑ BS 2567	Killer	1971	30.00
—Early copies have an attached 1972 calendar/poster			
❑ BS 2567	Killer	1972	12.00
—Later copies no longer have the calendar/poster			
❑ BS 2623	School's Out	1972	12.00
—No panties, with song titles listed			
❑ BS 2623	School's Out	1972	20.00
—Back cover does not list song titles, but panties are missing			
❑ BS 2623	School's Out	1972	30.00
—With paper panties intact; back cover lists song titles			
❑ BS 2623	School's Out	1972	40.00
—With paper panties intact; back cover does not list song titles			
❑ BS 2685	Billion Dollar Babies	1973	12.00
—Green "WB" label			
❑ BS4 2685 [Q]	Billion Dollar Babies	1974	25.00
❑ BS 2748	Muscle of Love	1973	10.00
❑ BS4 2748 [Q]	Muscle of Love	1974	25.00
❑ BS4 2803 [Q]	Alice Cooper's Greatest Hits	1974	—
—Not released			
❑ W 2803	Alice Cooper's Greatest Hits	1974	10.00
❑ BS 2896	Alice Cooper Goes to Hell	1976	10.00
❑ BSK 3027	Lace and Whiskey	1977	10.00
❑ BSK 3107	Alice Cooper's Greatest Hits	1977	8.00
—Reissue of BS 2803			
❑ BSK 3138	The Alice Cooper Show	1977	10.00
❑ BSK 3263	From the Inside	1978	10.00
❑ BSK 3436	Flush the Fashion	1980	10.00
❑ BSK 3581	Special Forces	1981	10.00
❑ 23719	Zipper Catches Skin	1982	10.00
❑ 23969	Da Da	1983	10.00

COOPER, BO See RON DANTE.

COOPER, CHRISTINE

Number	Title (A Side/B Side)	Yr	NM
45s			
PARKWAY			
❑ 122	I Must Have You (Or No One)/ Good Looks (They Don't Count)	1966	15.00
❑ 971	S.O.S./Say What You Feel	1966	25.00
❑ 983	(They Call Him) A Bad Boy/ Heartaches Away My Boy	1966	40.00

COOPER, DOLLY

Number	Title (A Side/B Side)	Yr	NM
45s			
DOT			
❑ 15495	Big Rock Inn/I'm Looking Through Your Window	1956	12.00
❑ 15535	The Confession of a Fool/ Tell Me, Tell Me	1957	12.00
EBB			
❑ 109	Wild Love/Time Brings About a Change	1957	12.00
MODERN			
❑ 965	My Man/Ay La Bas	1955	40.00
❑ 977	Teenage Prayer/Down So Long	1956	50.00
❑ 986	Teenage Wedding Bells/ Every Day and Every Night	1956	50.00
SAVOY			
❑ 1121	You Gotta Be Good to Yourself/ Love Can't Be Blind	1954	20.00

COOPER, LES, AND THE SOUL ROCKERS Also see THE EMPIRES (1).

Number	Title (A Side/B Side)	Yr	NM
45s			
ARRAWAK			
❑ 1008	I Can Do the Soul Jerk/ At the World's Fair	1965	12.00
ATCO			
❑ 6644	Gonna Have a Lotta Fun/ Thank God for You	1969	8.00
DIMENSION			
❑ 1023	Motor City/Swobblin'	1963	20.00
ENJOY			
❑ 2024	Owee Baby/Let's Do the Boston Monkey	1965	10.00
EVERLAST			
❑ 5016	Twistin'/Dig Yourself	1963	12.00
❑ 5019	Wiggle Wobble/Dig Yourself	1963	15.00
❑ 5023	Garbage Can/Bossa Nova Dance	1963	12.00
LOST-NITE			
❑ 388	Wiggle Wobble/Dig Yourself	197?	5.00
—Reissue			
Albums			
EVERLAST			
❑ ELP-202 [M]	Wiggle Wobble	1963	50.00

COOPER, PAT

Number	Title (A Side/B Side)	Yr	NM
45s			
UNITED ARTISTS			
❑ 922	Everyone Is Equal/Mama's Moo-Len-Yenna (The Eggplant Song)	1965	7.00
❑ 938	Mama's Moo-Len-Yenna (The Eggplant Song)/The More You Make, The More You Spend	1965	7.00
❑ 50113	The Pepperoni Kid/Little Red Scooter	1967	7.00
❑ 50294	You Don't Have to Be Italian/ Conchetta	1968	6.00
❑ 50641	It's the Italian in Me/ I Don't Wanna Go Home	1970	6.00
Albums			
UNITED ARTISTS			
❑ UAL 3446 [M]	Our Hero...Pat Cooper	1966	12.00
❑ UAL 3548 [M]	Spaghetti Sauce & Other Delights	1966	12.00
❑ UAS 6446 [S]	Our Hero...Pat Cooper	1966	15.00
❑ UAS 6548 [S]	Spaghetti Sauce & Other Delights	1966	15.00
❑ UAS 6600	You Don't Have to Be Italian To Like Pat Cooper	1968	12.00
❑ UAS 6690	More Saucy Stories from... Pat Cooper	1969	12.00

COOPERETTES, THE

Number	Title (A Side/B Side)	Yr	NM
45s			
ABC			
❑ 11156	Peace Maker/Trouble	1968	12.00
❑ 11197	Spiral Road/Trouble	1969	12.00
BRUNSWICK			
❑ 55296	Goodbye School/Goodbye School (Part 2)	1966	15.00
❑ 55307	Don't Trust Him/Everything's Wrong	1966	15.00
❑ 55329	(Life Has) No Meaning Now/ Shing-a-Ling	1967	25.00

COPAS, COWBOY

Number	Title (A Side/B Side)	Yr	NM
45s			
DOT			
❑ 15668	Blue Kimono/Breeze	1957	20.00
❑ 15735	Circle Rock/My Little Red Wagon	1958	60.00
❑ 15847	A World That's Real/Looking for an Angel	1958	20.00
KING			
❑ 951	The Strange Little Girl/ You'll Never See Me Cry	1951	40.00
❑ 964	Tennessee Flat Guitar/ I Love You	1951	30.00

Except when noted otherwise, VG = 25% of NM, and VG+ = 50% of NM. (Example: VG = $2.00, VG+ = $4.00 and NM = $8.00.)

Number	Title (A Side/B Side)	Yr	NM
❑ 980	I'm Glad I'm On the Inside/ Four Books in the Bible	1951	30.00
❑ 1000	'Tis Sweet to Be Remembered/ Because of You	1951	30.00
❑ 1003	O Little Town of Bethlehem/ It Came Upon the Midnight Clear	1951	30.00
❑ 1004	White Christmas/Jingle Bells	1951	30.00
❑ 1034	Copy Cat/Those Gone and Left Me Blues	1952	30.00
❑ 1040	I'll Pay the Price/'Tis Sweet to Be Remembered	1951	30.00
❑ 1046	Four Bare Walls and a Ceiling/ I Can't Stop Loving You	1952	30.00
❑ 1064	Boomerang/It's Enough to Make Anyone Cry	1952	30.00
❑ 1080	Golden Moon/I Can't Remember to Forget	1952	30.00
❑ 1136	I've Grown So Used to You/ It's No Sin to Love You	1952	30.00
❑ 1139	Purple Rose/Some Fine Morning	1952	30.00
❑ 1151	Feelin' Low/Love Me Now	1952	30.00
❑ 1166	Doll of Clay/If Wishes Were Horses	1953	25.00
❑ 1200	I Can't Go On/A Wreath at the Door of My Heart	1953	25.00
❑ 1234	Tennessee Senorita/If You Will Let Me Be Your Love	1953	25.00
❑ 1253	Look What I Got/Will You Forget	1953	25.00
❑ 1274	Blue Waltz/A Heartache Ago	1953	25.00
❑ 1306	He Stands By His Window/ The Man Upstairs	1954	25.00
❑ 1313	Unwanted Alone/Sorry	1954	25.00
❑ 1329	I'll Be There/I'm a Stranger in My Home	1954	25.00
❑ 1359	Return to Sender/I'll Waltz with You	1954	25.00
❑ 1386	Carbon Copy/I'm Glad for Your Sake	1954	25.00
❑ 1407	When I Lost You/Why Should I Want Her	1954	25.00
❑ 1424	Hello Darling/The Talking Mule	1955	25.00
❑ 1444	The Stone Was Rolled Away/ The Silver That Nailed Him to the Cross	1955	25.00
❑ 1456	Pledging My Love/Shamed of Myself	1955	25.00
❑ 1464	The Party's Over/ Summer Kisses	1955	25.00
❑ 1486	Tragic Romance/ Listen to My Heart	1955	25.00
❑ 1507	Blue Yesterday/Tell Me More	1955	25.00
❑ 4865	Any Old Time/Don't Shake Hands with the Devil	1956	20.00
❑ 5270	Tennessee Waltz/Signed, Sealed and Delivered	1959	15.00
—As "Lloyd Copas"			
❑ 5392	Carolina Sunshine Girl/ Rose of Tennessee	1960	15.00
❑ 5437	A Stranger in My Home/ Old Faithful and True Love	1960	15.00
❑ 5479	It's a Shame/You Walked Right Out of My Dreams	1961	15.00
❑ 5544	It's a Lonely World/Don't Let Them Change Your Mind	1961	15.00
❑ 5571	Sweet Thing/Signed, Sealed, Then Forgotten	1961	15.00
❑ 5638	I Built a Fence Around My Heart/My Blues Are Gone	1962	15.00
❑ 5676	When Jesus Beckons Me Home/I Saw the Light	1962	15.00
❑ 5733	Signed, Sealed and Delivered/ The Hopes of a Broken Heart	1963	12.00
❑ 5734	Breeze/The Road of Broken Hearts	1963	12.00

STARDAY

Number	Title (A Side/B Side)	Yr	NM
❑ 476	Mom and Dad's Affair/ Black Cloud Risin'	1959	15.00
❑ 493	South Pacific Shore/That's All I Can Remember	1960	15.00
❑ 501	Alabam/I Can	1960	20.00
❑ 524	I Have a Friend/The Hem of His Garment	1960	15.00
❑ 528	Sittin' Flat on Ready/ Midnight in Heaven	1960	15.00
❑ 542	Flat Top/True Love (Is the Greatest Thing)	1961	15.00
❑ 552	Sunny Tennessee/Dreaming	1961	15.00
❑ 559	Signed, Sealed and Delivered/ New Filipino Baby	1961	15.00
❑ 573	Sal/A Thousand Miles of Ocean	1961	15.00
❑ 585	There'll Come a Time Someday/ Seven Seas from You	1962	15.00
❑ 595	Sold the Farm/Table in the Corner	1962	15.00
❑ 606	Bury Me Face Down/ Heart on the Run	1962	15.00
❑ 612	Family Reunion/ Smoke on the Water	1962	15.00
❑ 621	Goodbye Kisses/ The Gypsy Girl	1963	12.00
❑ 641	Louisian/Break Away, Break Away	1963	12.00
❑ 658	Autobiography/The Rainbow and the Rose	1963	12.00
❑ 685	Old Man's Story/ Pretty Diamonds	1964	12.00
❑ 708	Ride in My Little Red Wagon/ Black Eyed Susie	1965	10.00
❑ 729	Waltzing with Sin/Blue Kimono	1965	10.00
❑ 750	Cowboy's Deck of Cards/ Beyond the Sunset	1966	10.00
❑ 7000	Alabam/Goodbye Kisses	197?	5.00
❑ 7001	Signed, Sealed and Delivered/ New Filipino Baby	197?	5.00
❑ 7015	I Dreamed of a Hillbilly Heaven/ Tragic Romance	197?	5.00
❑ 8006	Signed, Sealed and Delivered/ Hillbilly Heaven	197?	5.00
❑ 8029	Alabam/Filipino Baby	197?	5.00

Albums

KING

Number	Title	Yr	NM
❑ 553 [M]	Cowboy Copas Sings His All-Time Hits	1957	100.00
❑ 556 [M]	Favorite Sacred Songs	1957	80.00
❑ 619 [M]	Sacred Songs by Cowboy Copas	1959	80.00
❑ 714 [M]	Tragic Tales of Love and Life	1960	80.00
❑ 720 [M]	Broken Hearted Melodies	1960	80.00
❑ 817 [M]	Country Gentleman of Song	1963	40.00
❑ 824 [M]	As You Remember Cowboy Copas	1963	40.00
❑ 894 [M]	Cowboy Copas Hymns	1964	40.00

STARDAY

Number	Title	Yr	NM
❑ SLP-118 [M]	All Time Country Music Great	1960	40.00
❑ SLP-133 [M]	Inspirational Songs	1961	40.00
❑ SLP-144 [M]	Cowboy Copas	1961	40.00
❑ SLP-157 [M]	Opry Star Spotlight on Cowboy Copas	1962	40.00
❑ SLP-175 [M]	Mister Country Music	1962	40.00
❑ SLP-184 [M]	Songs That Made Him Famous	1962	40.00
❑ SLP-208 [M]	Country Music Entertainer #1	1963	40.00
❑ SLP-212 [M]	Beyond the Sunset	1963	40.00
❑ SLP-234 [M]	The Unforgettable Cowboy Copas	1963	40.00
❑ SLP-247 [M]	Star of the Grand Ole Opry	1963	40.00
❑ SLP-268 [M]	Cowboy Copas and His Friends	1964	40.00
❑ SLP-317 [M]	The Legend Lives On	1965	30.00
❑ SLP (9)-347 [(2)R]	The Cowboy Copas Story	1965	25.00
❑ SLP-347 [(2)M]	The Cowboy Copas Story	1965	30.00
❑ SLP-458	The Best of Cowboy Copas	1970	15.00

COPAS, COWBOY, AND HAWKSHAW HAWKINS

Also see each artist's individual listings.

Albums

KING

Number	Title	Yr	NM
❑ 835 [M]	In Memory	1963	40.00
❑ 850 [M]	The Legend of Cowboy Copas and Hawkshaw Hawkins	1964	40.00
❑ 984 [M]	24 Great Hits	1968	25.00

COPAS, COWBOY/HAWKSHAW HAWKINS/PATSY CLINE

Also see each artist's individual listings.

Albums

STARDAY

Number	Title	Yr	NM
❑ SLP-346 [M]	Gone But Not Forgotten	1965	30.00

COPASETICS, THE

45s

PREMIUM

Number	Title (A Side/B Side)	Yr	NM
❑ 409	Believe in Me/Collegian	1956	200.00

COPE, JULIAN

Also see THE TEARDROP EXPLODES.

12-Inch Singles

ISLAND

Number	Title	Yr	NM
❑ PR 988 [DJ]	World Shut Your Mouth (same on both sides)	1987	8.00
❑ DMD 1288 [DJ]	5 O'Clock World/S.P.Q.R.	1988	10.00
❑ PR 2000 [DJ]	Trampolene (same on both sides)	1987	8.00
❑ PR 2523 [DJ]	Charlotte Anne (Edit) (LP Version)	1988	10.00
❑ 868909-1	Head (3:34) (6:07)//Love (6:51)/Early Risin' (8:18)	1991	10.00

45s

ISLAND

Number	Title (A Side/B Side)	Yr	NM
❑ 99241	Five O'Clock World/S.P.Q.R.	1989	4.00
❑ 99241 [PS]	Five O'Clock World/S.P.Q.R.	1989	4.00
❑ 99448	Eve's Volcano/Almost Beautiful Child	1987	4.00
❑ 99479	World Shut Your Mouth/ Umpteenth Unnatural Blues	1987	3.00
❑ 99479 [PS]	World Shut Your Mouth/ Umpteenth Unnatural Blues	1987	3.00

Albums

ISLAND

Number	Title	Yr	NM
❑ PR12 6667 [EP]	Peggy Suicide (Sampler)	1991	12.00
—Promo only; 6 tracks			
❑ 90560 [EP]	World Shut Your Mouth (Julian Cope)	1987	8.00
❑ 90571	Saint Julian	1987	10.00
❑ 91025	My Nation Underground	1988	10.00

COPELAND, KEN

45s

DOT

Number	Title (A Side/B Side)	Yr	NM
❑ 15686	Where the Rio Rosa Flows/ Locked in the Arms of Love	1958	15.00

IMPERIAL

Number	Title (A Side/B Side)	Yr	NM
❑ 5432	Pledge of Love/Night Air	1957	20.00
—B-side by The Mints			
❑ 5453	Teenage/Bed of Lies	1957	20.00
❑ 5466	I Want to Go Steady/ I Would Give My Heart	1957	20.00

LIN

Number	Title (A Side/B Side)	Yr	NM
❑ 5007	Pledge of Love/Night Air	1957	40.00
—B-side by The Mints			
❑ 5017	Fanny Brown/Chaser of Hearts	1957	40.00

COPELAND, STEWART

Also see KLART KENT; THE POLICE.

12-Inch Singles

A&M

Number	Title	Yr	NM
❑ SP-12159	Gong Rock (Remix) (Dub Version)	1985	12.00

Albums

A&M

Number	Title	Yr	NM
❑ SP-6-4983	Rumble Fish	1983	12.00
❑ SP-5084	The Rhythmatist	1985	10.00

I.R.S.

Number	Title	Yr	NM
❑ 42099	The Equalizer and Other Cliffhangers	1988	10.00

COPELAND, STEWART/ADAM ANT

12-Inch Singles

I.R.S.

Number	Title	Yr	NM
❑ L33-17166 [DJ]	Out of Bounds (Extended) (LP Version)	1986	10.00

45s

I.R.S.

Number	Title (A Side/B Side)	Yr	NM
❑ 52885	Out of Bounds/(B-side unknown)	1986	5.00

COPELAND, STEWART/STANARD RIDGWAY

12-Inch Singles

A&M

Number	Title	Yr	NM
❑ SP-17260 [DJ]	Don't Box Me In (same on both sides)	1983	10.00

45s

A&M

Number	Title (A Side/B Side)	Yr	NM
❑ 2604	Don't Box Me In/Drama at Home	1983	5.00

COPPER PLATED INTEGRATED CIRCUIT, THE

Albums

COMMAND

Number	Title	Yr	NM
❑ RS-945 SD	Plugged In Pop	1969	25.00

COPS 'N ROBBERS

45s

CORAL

Number	Title (A Side/B Side)	Yr	NM
❑ 62466	I Could Have Danced All Night/ Just Keep Right On	1965	10.00
❑ 62473	It's All Over Now, Baby Blue/ I Found Out	1965	10.00

PARROT

Number	Title (A Side/B Side)	Yr	NM
❑ 9716	St. James Infirmary/There's Got to Be a Reason	1964	10.00

CORDEL, PAT

Also see THE ELEGANTS.

45s

CLUB

Number	Title (A Side/B Side)	Yr	NM
❑ 1011	Darling, Come Back/ My My Tears	1956	1500.
—And the Crescents			

MICHELLE

Number	Title (A Side/B Side)	Yr	NM
❑ 503	Darling, Come Back/ My My Tears	1959	150.00
—And the Elegants			

VICTORY

Number	Title (A Side/B Side)	Yr	NM
❑ 1001	Darling, Come Back/ My My Tears	1963	80.00
—And the Elegants			

CORDELLS, THE

Number	Title (A Side/B Side)	Yr	NM
45s			
BARGAIN			
❑ 5004	The Beat of My Heart/Laid Off	1962	50.00
BULLSEYE			
❑ 1017	Believe in Me/Please Don't Go	1958	100.00

CORDET, LOUISE

Number	Title (A Side/B Side)	Yr	NM
45s			
LONDON			
❑ 9560	I'm Just a Baby/In a Matter of Moments	1963	12.00

CORDIALS, THE Several different groups.

Number	Title (A Side/B Side)	Yr	NM
45s			
BETHLEHEM			
❑ 3019	What's the Matter with Me/I'm Not Crying Anymore	1961	25.00
CORDIAL			
❑ 1001	I'm Ashamed/Sentimental Jorney	1960	100.00
FELSTED			
❑ 8653	Once in a Lifetime/What Kind of Fool Am I	1962	30.00
LIBERTY			
❑ 55784	Oh, How I Love Her/You Can't Believe in Love	1965	25.00
REVEILLE			
❑ 106	Eternal Love/The International Twist	1962	300.00
7 ARTS			
❑ 707	Dawn Is Almost Here/Keep An Eye	1961	100.00
WHIP			
❑ 276	Listen My Heart/My Heart's Desire	1961	250.00
Albums			
CATAMOUNT			
❑ 902	Blue Eyed Soul	1967	25.00

CORDOVANS, THE

Number	Title (A Side/B Side)	Yr	NM
45s			
JOHNSON			
❑ 731	Come On Baby/My Heart	1960	25.00

COREA, CHICK

Number	Title (A Side/B Side)	Yr	NM
45s			
POLYDOR			
❑ 14538	Bagatelle #4/Central Park	1979	4.00
Albums			
ATLANTIC			
❑ SD 2-305 [(2)]	Inner Space	1973	15.00
BLUE NOTE			
❑ BN-LA395-H2 [(2)]	Chick Corea	1975	15.00
—"The Blue Note Reissue Series" labels			
❑ LWB-395 [(2)]	Chick Corea	1981	10.00
—Reissue with new prefix			
❑ BN-LA472-H2 [(2)]	Circling In	1976	20.00
—"The Blue Note Reissue Series" labels			
❑ BN-LA882-J2 [(2)]	Circulus	1978	20.00
❑ BST-84353	Song of Singing	1970	40.00
—"A Division of Liberty Records" on label			
❑ BST-84353	Song of Singing	1984	20.00
—Reissue, "The Finest in Jazz Since 1939" on label			
❑ B1-90055	Now He Sings, Now He Sobs	1988	12.00
—Reissue; "The Finest in Jazz Since 1939" on label			
ECM			
❑ 1009 ST	A.R.C.	197?	15.00
—Original issue, made in Germany?			
❑ ECM1-1009	A.R.C.	1977	12.00
—Distributed by Polydor			
❑ 1014 ST	Piano Improvisations, Vol. 1	1974	15.00
—Original edition; made in Germany?			
❑ ECM-1-1014	Piano Improvisations, Vol. 1	1977	12.00
—Distributed by Polydor			
❑ 1020 ST	Piano Improvisations, Vol. 2	197?	15.00
—Original edition; made in Germany?			
❑ ECM1-1020	Piano Improvisations, Vol. 2	1977	12.00
—Distributed by Polydor			
❑ 1232 [(2)]	Trio Music	198?	12.00
❑ 1267	Children's Songs	1984	12.00
—Made in Germany			
❑ 1282	Voyage	1985	12.00
—Made in Germany			
❑ 1297	Septet	1985	12.00
—Made in Germany			
❑ 25005	Children's Songs	1984	10.00
—Distributed by Warner Bros.			
❑ 25013	Voyage	1985	10.00
—Distributed by Warner Bros.			
❑ 25035	Septet	1985	10.00
—Distributed by Warner Bros.			
ELEKTRA/MUSICIAN			
❑ 60167	Again & Again	1984	10.00
51 WEST			
❑ Q 16078	Jazzman	1979	15.00
GROOVE MERCHANT			
❑ GM 530	Sundance	1974	15.00
—Reissue of 2202			
❑ 2202	Sundance	1972	30.00
❑ 4406 [(2)]	Piano Giants	197?	20.00
GRP			
❑ GRP-A-1026	The Chick Corea Elektric Band	1987	10.00
❑ GR-1036	Light Years	1987	10.00
❑ GR-1053	Eye of the Beholder	1988	10.00
❑ GR-9582	The Chick Corea Akoustic Band	1989	12.00
❑ GR-9601	Inside Out	1991	15.00
MUSE			
❑ MR 5011	Bliss!	1973	20.00
PACIFIC JAZZ			
❑ LN-10057	Now He Sings, Now He Sobs	1981	10.00
—Reissue of Solid State 18039			
POLYDOR			
❑ PD-6062	The Leprechaun	1976	10.00
❑ PD-1-6130	The Mad Hatter	1978	10.00
❑ PD-1-6160	Friends	1978	10.00
❑ PD-1-6176	Secret Agent	1979	10.00
❑ PD-1-6208	Delphi I	1979	10.00
❑ PD-2-6334 [(2)]	Delphi II & III	1982	15.00
❑ PD-2-9003 [(2)]	My Spanish Heart	1976	15.00
QUINTESSENCE			
❑ QJ-25011	Before Forever	1978	12.00
SOLID STATE			
❑ SS-18039	Now He Sings, Now He Sobs	1969	20.00
❑ SS-18055	Chick Corea "Is"	1969	20.00
VORTEX			
❑ 2004	Tones for Joan's Bones	1971	30.00
WARNER BROS.			
❑ BSK 3425	Tap Step	1980	10.00
❑ BSK 3552	Three Quartets	1981	10.00
❑ 23699	Touchstone	1983	10.00

COREA, CHICK, AND LIONEL HAMPTON

Number	Title (A Side/B Side)	Yr	NM
Albums			
WHO'S WHO IN JAZZ			
❑ WWLP 21016	Live at Midem	1980	15.00

COREA, CHICK; HERBIE HANCOCK; KEITH JARRETT; MCCOY TYNER

Number	Title (A Side/B Side)	Yr	NM
Albums			
ATLANTIC			
❑ SD 1696	Corea/Hancock/Jarrett/Tyner	1976	12.00

COREY, JILL

Number	Title (A Side/B Side)	Yr	NM
45s			
COLUMBIA			
❑ 4-40123	Rose of Calvary/Minneapolis	1953	15.00
❑ 4-40177	Cleo and Meo/Do You Know What Lips Are For	1954	12.00
—With the Four Lads			
❑ 4-40188	Should I Tell/A Good Night's Work	1954	12.00
❑ 4-40268	One God/He Is a Man (I Am a Woman)	1954	12.00
❑ 4-40327	Where Are You/Number One Boy	1954	12.00
❑ 4-40410	Edward/I'm Not at All in Love	1955	12.00
❑ 4-40502	That's All I Need/Come to Me for Everything	1955	12.00
❑ 4-40566	Look! Look!/Ching-a-Ling	1955	12.00
❑ 4-40627	First Love/Wait for Tomorrow	1955	12.00
❑ 4-40687	Your Prayers Are Always Answered/Summer Nights	1956	12.00
❑ 4-40743	What Am I to Do/Let Him Know	1956	12.00
❑ 4-40794	I Love My Baby (My Baby Loves Me)/Egghead	1956	12.00
❑ 4-40878	Let It Be Me/Make Like a Bunny, Honey	1957	15.00
—With Jimmy Carroll; A-side is the first English-language recording of the song, which later was a hit for several other artists			
❑ 4-40955	Love Me to Pieces/Love	1957	12.00
❑ 4-41023	I Feel Pretty/How Can I Tell	1957	12.00
❑ 4-41068	I Told a Lie to My Darlin'/Exactly Like You	1957	12.00
❑ 4-41108	Give It All You've Got/Uh Huh, Oh Yeah	1958	12.00
❑ 4-41164	Loveable/Sweet Sugar Lips	1958	12.00
❑ 4-41202	Big Daddy/Wherefore Art Thou, Romeo	1958	12.00
❑ 4-41300	I Found a New Baby/My Reverie	1958	12.00
❑ 4-41360	Dream Boy/Love Will Find Out the Way	1959	10.00
❑ 4-41435	The President Song/Have I Told You Lately That I Love You	1959	10.00
❑ 4-41498	I Can't Hide a Mountain/Seems Like Old Times	1959	10.00
❑ 4-41621	Have You Ever Been Lonely/I Gotta Have My Baby Back	1960	10.00
❑ 4-41772	Stick 'Em Up Stuck Up/Ten Gallon Hat	1960	10.00
MERCURY			
❑ 71913	I Miss You Already/It's Only Me	1962	10.00
Albums			
COLUMBIA			
❑ CL 1095 [M]	Sometimes I'm Happy, Sometimes I'm Blue	1957	30.00

COREY, JOHN

Number	Title (A Side/B Side)	Yr	NM
45s			
VEE JAY			
❑ 466	Pollyanna/I'll Forget	1962	30.00
—Backing group: The Four Seasons			
❑ 514	Hey Little Runaround/The Prettiest Girl I've Kissed Today	1963	10.00

CORNELIUS BROTHERS AND SISTER ROSE

Number	Title (A Side/B Side)	Yr	NM
45s			
PLATINUM			
❑ 105/6	Treat Her Like a Lady/Over at My Place	1970	12.00
UNITED ARTISTS			
❑ 0131	Treat Her Like a Lady/Over at My Place	1973	4.00
—"Silver Spotlight Series" reissue			
❑ XW208	Let Me Down Easy/Gonna Be Sweet for You	1973	5.00
❑ XW313	I Just Can't Stop Loving You/These Lonely Nights	1973	5.00
❑ XW377	Big Time Lover/Wonderful Tune	1974	5.00
❑ XW512	Too Late to Turn Back Now/Don't Ever Be Lonely (A Poor Little Fool Like Me)	1974	4.00
—Reissue			
❑ XW533	Trouble Child/Got to Testify	1974	5.00
❑ XW534	Since I Found My Baby/I Love Music	1974	5.00
❑ 50721	Treat Her Like a Lady/Over at My Place	1970	5.00
❑ 50910	Too Late to Turn Back Now/Lift Your Love Higher	1972	5.00
❑ 50954	Don't Ever Be Lonely (A Poor Little Fool Like Me)/I'm So Glad to Be Loved by You	1972	5.00
❑ 50996	I'm Never Gonna Be Alone Anymore/Let's Stay Together	1972	5.00
Albums			
UNITED ARTISTS			
❑ UA-LA593-G	Greatest Hits	1976	12.00
❑ UAS-5568	Cornelius Brothers and Sister Rose	1972	15.00

CORNELL, DON Also see TERESA BREWER.

Number	Title (A Side/B Side)	Yr	NM
45s			
ABC-PARAMOUNT			
❑ 10687	Italian Wedding Song/Please Lie to Me	1965	6.00
❑ 10740	Dingle Ling, Dingle Ling/Careless Hands	1965	6.00
CORAL			
❑ 60659	I'll Walk Alone/That's the Chance You Take	1952	12.00
❑ 60690	I'm Yours/My Mother's Pearls	1952	12.00
❑ 60748	This Is the Beginning of the End/I Can't Cry Anymore	1952	12.00
❑ 60859	Let's Have an Old Fashioned Christmas/I've Got the Christmas Spirit	1952	15.00
❑ 60860	I/Be Fair	1952	12.00
❑ 60900	For You/I Was Lucky	1953	10.00
❑ 60901	Stay As Sweet As You Are/We Three (My Echo, My Shadow and Me)	1953	10.00
❑ 60902	It Isn't Fair/Something to Remember You By	1953	10.00
❑ 60903	S'posin/If You Were Only Mine	1953	10.00
❑ 60968	There's No Escape/Many Are the Times	1953	12.00
❑ 61011	Who Loves Me/When the Hands of the Clock Pray at Midnight	1953	12.00
❑ 61030	Please Play Our Song (Mister Record Man)/If I Should Love Again	1953	12.00
❑ 61068	I'm Yearning/You're On Trial	1953	12.00
❑ 61125	Hold Me/Size 12	1954	12.00

Except when noted otherwise, VG = 25% of NM, and VG+ = 50% of NM. (Example: VG = $2.00, VG+ = $4.00 and NM = $8.00.)

Number	Title (A Side/B Side)	Yr	NM
❑ 61171	Believe in Me/Little Lucy	1954	12.00
❑ 61206	Hold My Hand/I'm Blessed	1954	12.00
❑ 61253	No Man Is an Island/All at Once	1954	12.00
❑ 61333	Athena/No Man Is an Island	1955	10.00
❑ 61367	When You Are in Love/Give Me Your Love	1955	10.00
❑ 61393	Most of All/The Door Is Still Open to My Heart	1955	10.00
❑ 61407	Unchained Melody/All of You	1955	10.00
❑ 61467	The Bible Tells Me So/Love Is a Many-Splendored Thing	1955	10.00
❑ 61521	Young Abe Lincoln/Dream World	1955	10.00
❑ 61549	Make a Wish/There Once Was a Beautiful...	1955	10.00
❑ 61584	Teenage Meeting (Gonna Rock It Up Right)/I Still Have a Prayer	1956	15.00
❑ 61613	Rock Island Line/Na-Ne-Na-Na	1956	10.00
❑ 61631	But Love Me/Fort Knox	1956	10.00
❑ 61659	Grazie/Could You	1956	10.00
❑ 61687	Heaven Only Knows/Life Is a Song	1956	10.00
❑ 61721	See-Saw/From the Bottom of My Heart	1956	10.00
❑ 61757	Let's Be Friends/Ma-Ma Pa-Pa Cha-Cha	1956	10.00
❑ 61790	Afternoon in Madrid/Let's Get Lost	1957	10.00
❑ 61811	Sittin' in the Balcony/My Faith, My Hope, My Love	1957	10.00
❑ 61817	Mama Guitar/A Face in the Crowd	1957	10.00
❑ 61854	Mailman, Bring Me No More Blues/No Matter What	1957	10.00
❑ 61905	Non Dimenticar/Before It's Time to Say Goodnight	1957	10.00
❑ 61993	You Go to My Head/Village in Capri	1958	10.00
❑ 62019	But Not Your Heart/Once More	1958	10.00
DOT			
❑ 15938	Heart of My Heart/This Earth Is Mine	1959	8.00
❑ 16044	I/Size 12	1960	8.00
JUBILEE			
❑ 5423	Night Train to Memphis/Bring Down the Curtain	1962	8.00
RCA VICTOR			
❑ 47-2914	Baby It's Cold Outside/Whispering Waters	1949	15.00
—With Laura Leslie			
❑ 47-3239	Come Back to Me/My Baby Is Blue	1949	15.00
❑ 47-3776	You Dreamer You/I Surrender Dear	1950	15.00
❑ 47-3839	You Wonderful You/Hawaii	1950	15.00
❑ 47-3884	I Need You So/It Couldn't Happen to a Sweeter Girl	1950	15.00
❑ 47-3909	Au Revoir Again/A Whistle and a Prayer	1950	15.00
❑ 47-3950	Take Me in Your Arms/The Breeze	1950	15.00
❑ 47-3991	Sue Me/Velvet Lips	1950	15.00
❑ 47-4042	Wedding Bells/Let a Smile Be Your Umbrella	1951	12.00
❑ 47-4043	Was That the Human Thing to Do/That Old Feeling	1951	12.00
❑ 47-4044	I'll Be Seeing You/When I Take My Sugar to Tea	1951	12.00
❑ 47-4083	My Inspiration/You Can't Tell a Lie to Your Heart	1951	15.00
❑ 47-4149	Why Don't You Tell Me So/If I Had Another Chance	1951	15.00
ROULETTE			
❑ 4355	The Flying Trapeze/Wish I Was	1961	8.00
SIGNATURE			
❑ 12002	Forever Couldn't Be Long Enough/Sempre Amore	1959	8.00
❑ 12020	Forever/There's Still Time Brother	1959	8.00
❑ 12027	Grateful/Only Time Will Tell	1960	8.00
❑ 12032	Your Kiss/I Have But One Heart	1960	8.00
20TH CENTURY FOX			
❑ 464	Forget About Me/Lost Dreams & Lonely Tears	1964	8.00
❑ 515	If You Love Her Tell Her So/You Know You Don't Want Me	1964	8.00
7-Inch Extended Plays			
CORAL			
❑ EC 81002	I'm Yours/This Is the Beginning of the End//I'll Walk Alone/(I've Cried Until) I Can't Cry Anymore	1953	12.00
❑ EC 81002 [PS]	I'm Yours	1953	12.00
❑ EC 81118	Most of All/All of You//Unchained Melody/Danger Heartbreak Ahead	1955	10.00
❑ EC 81118 [PS]	Your Date with Don ...	1955	10.00
❑ EC 81501	Hold My Hand/I'm Yours//It Isn't Fair/I'll Walk Alone	195?	12.00
❑ EC 81501 [PS]	Don Cornell	195?	12.00
❑ 83010 [DJ]	Let's Have an Old Fashioned Christmas/I've Got the Christmas Spirit//Sing a Song Of Santa Claus/Winter's Here Again	195?	15.00
—B-side by the Ames Brothers			
RCA CAMDEN			
❑ CAE-239	The Breeze (Bringin' My Honey Back to Me)/Are You Lonesome Tonight//Wedding Bells Are Breaking Up That Old Gang of Mine/Have You Ever Been Lonely	195?	10.00
❑ CAE-239 [PS]	Don Cornell	195?	10.00
RCA VICTOR			
❑ 547-0242	It Isn't Fair/Take Me in Your Arms//I Surrender Dear/I Need You So	1952	12.00
—One record of 2-EP set EPB-3116; Side 1, track 1 credited to "Swing and Sway with Sammy Kaye, vocal refrain by Don Cornell"			
❑ 547-0243	Come Back to Me/Why Don't You Tell Me So//Au Revoir Again/(The Breeze) Bringin' My Honey Back to Me	1952	12.00
—One record of 2-EP set EPB-3116			
❑ EPB 3116 [PS]	Don Cornell Sings	1952	15.00
—Fold-open cover for 2-EP set (547-0242, 547-0243)			
Albums			
ABC-PARAMOUNT			
❑ ABC-537 [M]	Incomparable	1966	12.00
❑ ABCS-537 [S]	Incomparable	1966	15.00
CORAL			
❑ CRL 57055 [M]	Don	1955	30.00
❑ CRL 57133 [M]	For Teenagers Only	1957	30.00
DOT			
❑ DLP-3160 [M]	Don Cornell's Great Hits	1959	25.00
❑ DLP-25160 [S]	Don Cornell's Great Hits	1959	30.00
MOVIETONE			
❑ 71013 [M]	I Wish You Love	1966	12.00
❑ S-72013 [S]	I Wish You Love	1966	15.00
SIGNATURE			
❑ SM-1001 [M]	Don Cornell Sings Love Songs	1960	20.00
❑ SS-1001 [S]	Don Cornell Sings Love Songs	1960	25.00
VOCALION			
❑ VL 3657 [M]	Don Cornell	196?	12.00

CORNELL, DON; JOHNNY DESMOND; ALAN DALE

Number	Title (A Side/B Side)	Yr	NM
45s			
CORAL			
❑ 61076	The Gang That Sang "Heart of My Heart"/I Think I'll Fall in Love Today	1953	12.00

CORNELLS, THE

Number	Title (A Side/B Side)	Yr	NM
45s			
GAREX			
❑ 100	Mama's Little Baby/Wak-A-Cha	1962	30.00
❑ 102	Malibu Surf/Agua Caliente	1963	30.00
❑ 201	Beach Bound/Lone Star Stomp	1963	30.00
❑ 206	Surf Fever/Do the Slauson	1963	30.00
Albums			
GAREX			
❑ LPGA-100 [M]	Beach Bound	1963	500.00
SUNDAZED			
❑ LP-5013	Surf Fever!	199?	10.00

CORNISH, GENE Also see THE RASCALS.

Number	Title (A Side/B Side)	Yr	NM
45s			
DAWN			
❑ 550	Let's Do the Capri/Lonely I Will Say	1964	30.00
❑ 551	I Wanna Be a Beatle/Oh Misery	1964	40.00
VASSAR			
❑ 319	Since I Lost You/Winner Take All	1962	20.00
❑ 321	My Baby Ran Away from Me/Now the Story Can Be Told	1962	25.00

CORONETS, THE

Number	Title (A Side/B Side)	Yr	NM
45s			
CHESS			
❑ 1549	Nadine/I'm All Alone	1953	200.00
—Silver top label			
❑ 1549	Nadine/I'm All Alone	1958	12.00
—All-blue label			
❑ 1553	It Would Be Heavenly/Baby's Coming Home	1953	400.00
—Black vinyl			
❑ 1553	It Would Be Heavenly/Baby's Coming Home	1953	800.00
—Red vinyl			
GROOVE			
❑ 0114	I Love You More/Crime Doesn't Pay	1955	100.00
❑ 0116	The Bible Tells Me So/Hush	1955	150.00
STERLING			
❑ 903	Don't Deprive Me/Little Boy	1955	250.00

CORPORATION, THE

Number	Title (A Side/B Side)	Yr	NM
45s			
CAPITOL			
❑ 2467	Highway/I Want to Get Out of My Grave	1969	15.00
CUCA			
❑ 1496	You Make Me Feel Good/Sitting by the Sea	1968	15.00
Albums			
AGE OF AQUARIUS			
❑ 4150	Get On Our Swing	1968	30.00
❑ 4250	Hassles in My Mind	1969	30.00
CAPITOL			
❑ ST-175	The Corporation	1969	50.00

CORPUS

Number	Title (A Side/B Side)	Yr	NM
Albums			
ACORN			
❑ 1001	Creation: A Child	1971	200.00
—Second pressing, green/pink label, unbanded			
❑ 1001	Creation: A Child	1971	500.00
—Banded tracks			

CORSAIRS, THE

Number	Title (A Side/B Side)	Yr	NM
45s			
HY-TONE			
❑ 110	Goodbye Darling/Rock Lilly Rock	1957	1500.
SMASH			
❑ 1715	Time Waits/It Won't Be a Sin	1961	15.00
TUFF			
❑ 375	Save a Little Monkey/(Instrumental)	1963	10.00
❑ 402	On the Spanish Side/The Change in You	1964	10.00
TUFF/CHESS			
❑ 1808	Smoky Places/Thinkin'	1961	25.00
❑ 1818	I'll Take You HJome/Sittin' on Your Doorstep	1962	12.00
❑ 1830	Dancing Shadows/While	1962	12.00
❑ 1840	At the Stroke of Midnight/Listen to My Little Heart	1962	12.00
❑ 1847	Stormy/It's Almost Sunday Morning	1963	12.00

CORT, BOB

Number	Title (A Side/B Side)	Yr	NM
45s			
LONDON			
❑ 1713	Don't You Rock Me Daddy-O/It Takes a Worried Man to Sing a Worried Blues	1957	15.00
❑ 1742	Freight Train/Roll Jen Jenkins	1957	12.00
❑ 1748	Maggie Mae/Jessamine	1957	12.00
—With Liz Winters			

CORTEZ, DAVE "BABY"

Number	Title (A Side/B Side)	Yr	NM
45s			
ALL PLATINUM			
❑ 2339	Funky Robot (Part 1)/Funky Robot (Part 2)	1972	5.00
❑ 2342	Unaddressed Letter/Funky Robot (Part 1)	1972	5.00
❑ 2343	Someone Has Taken Your Place/Born Funky	1973	5.00
❑ 2345	Hell Street Junction/(Instrumental)	1973	5.00
❑ 2347	Soul Walkin'/(B-side unknown)	1974	5.00
ARGO			
❑ 5462	Let It Be You/I'm Gonna Stay	1964	10.00
CHESS			
❑ 1829	Rinky Dink/Getting Right	1962	10.00
❑ 1834	Happy Weekend/Fiddle Sticks	1962	10.00
❑ 1842	Tweedle Dee/Gift of Love	1962	10.00
❑ 1850	Hot Cakes! 1st Serving/Hot Cakes! 2nd Serving	1963	8.00
❑ 1861	Organ Shout/Precious You	1963	8.00
❑ 1874	Happy Feet/Gettin' to the Point	1963	8.00
CLOCK			
❑ 1006	You're the Girl/Eeny Meeny Minie Mo	1958	20.00
❑ 1009	The Happy Organ/Love Me As I Love You	1959	20.00
❑ 1012	The Whistling Organ/I'm Happy	1959	12.00

Number	Title (A Side/B Side)	Yr	NM
❑ 1014	Piano Shuffle/It's a Sin to Tell a Lie	1959	12.00
❑ 1016	Dave's Special/Whispers	1959	12.00
❑ 1020	You're Just Right/Deep in the Heart of Texas	1960	12.00
❑ 1021	You're the Girl/I'm Happy	1960	12.00
❑ 1024	Cat Nip/Talk Is Cheap	1960	12.00
❑ 1031	Hurricane/The Shift	1960	12.00
❑ 1034	Summertime/Walking with You	1961	12.00
❑ 1036	Tootsie/Second Chance	1961	12.00
❑ 71824	Tootsie/Second Chance	1961	10.00
❑ 71851	The Happy Organ/Piano Shuffle	1961	10.00
❑ 71875	C'mon and Stomp/Calypso Love Song	1961	10.00
EMBER			
❑ 1011	Soft Lights/Movin' and Groovin'	1956	40.00
—As "David Clowney"			
EMIT			
❑ 301	Fiesta/Hey-Hey-Hey	1962	10.00
EPIC			
❑ 9732	Poppin' Popcorn/The Question	1964	10.00
JULIA			
❑ 1829	Rinky Dink/Getting Right	1962	25.00
OKEH			
❑ 7102	You Give Me Heebie Jeebies/Honey Baby	1958	20.00
❑ 7208	Popping Popcorn/The Question (Do You Love Me)	1964	8.00
PARIS			
❑ 513	Shakin'/Hoot Owl	1958	30.00
—As "Dave Clowney"			
ROULETTE			
❑ 4628	Tweetie Pie/Things Ain't What They Used to Be	1965	8.00
❑ 4679	Count Down/Summertime	1966	8.00
❑ 4693	Sticks and Stones/Do Any Dance	1966	8.00
❑ 4717	Belly Rub (Part 1)/Belly Rub (Part 2)	1967	8.00
❑ 4759	Hula Hoop/Come Back	1967	8.00
❑ 4783	Hot Chocolate/Soul Groovin'	1967	8.00
T-NECK			
❑ 907	I Turned You On/I Know Who You Been Socking It To	1969	6.00
❑ 913	Save Me/My Little Girl	1969	6.00
WINLEY			
❑ 259	Jamin' (Part 1)/Jamin' (Part 2)	1961	10.00
❑ 262	Skins and Sounds/Little Paris Melody	1962	10.00
❑ 267	Scotty (Part 1)/Scotty (Part 2)	1962	10.00
7-Inch Extended Plays			
CLOCK			
❑ EP 1-4039-C	The Happy Organ/The Whistling Organ//Catnip/Deep in the Heart of Texas	1959	25.00
❑ EP 1-4039-C [PS]	Dave "Baby" Cortez and His Happy Organ	1959	25.00
RCA VICTOR			
❑ EPA-4342 [M]	*The Happy Organ/Love Me As I Love You/Dave's Special/You're the Girl	1959	12.00
❑ EPA-4342 [PS]	The Happy Organ	1959	12.00
❑ ESP-4342 [PS]	The Happy Organ	1959	20.00
❑ ESP-4342 [S]	*The Happy Organ/Love Me As I Love You/Dave's Special/You're the Girl	1959	20.00
Albums			
CHESS			
❑ LP-1473 [M]	Rinky Dink	1962	50.00
CLOCK			
❑ C-331 [M]	Dave "Baby" Cortez	1960	40.00
❑ CS-331 [S]	Dave "Baby" Cortez	1960	50.00
❑ MGC-20647 [M]	Dave "Baby" Cortez	1961	30.00
❑ SRC-60647 [S]	Dave "Baby" Cortez	1961	40.00
CORONET			
❑ CX-201 [M]	The Whistling Organ	196?	15.00
DESIGN			
❑ DLP-163 [R]	The Happy Organ	1962	12.00
METRO			
❑ M-550 [M]	The Fabulous Organ of Dave "Baby" Cortez	1965	15.00
❑ MS-550 [R]	The Fabulous Organ of Dave "Baby" Cortez	1965	12.00
RCA VICTOR			
❑ LPM-2099 [M]	The Happy Organ	1959	80.00
❑ LSP-2099 [S]	The Happy Organ	1959	100.00
ROULETTE			
❑ R-25298 [M]	Organ Shindig	1965	20.00
❑ SR-25298 [S]	Organ Shindig	1965	25.00
❑ R-25315 [M]	Tweety Pie	1966	20.00
❑ SR-25315 [S]	Tweety Pie	1966	25.00
❑ R-25328 [M]	In Orbit with Dave "Baby" Cortez	1966	20.00
❑ SR-25328 [S]	In Orbit with Dave "Baby" Cortez	1966	25.00
T-NECK			
❑ TNS-3005	The Isley Brothers Way	1970	20.00

CORVELLS, THE

45s

Number	Title (A Side/B Side)	Yr	NM
ABC-PARAMOUNT			
❑ 10324	Take My Love/Daisy	1962	200.00
BLAST			
❑ 203	The Bells/Don't Forget	1961	150.00
CUB			
❑ 9122	One (Is Such a Lonely Number)/The Joke's On Me	1963	20.00
LIDO			
❑ 509	We Made a Vow/Miss Jones	1957	200.00
LUPINE			
❑ 104	He's So Fine/Baby Sitting	1962	25.00
TIP TOP			
❑ 509	We Made a Vow/Miss Jones	1957	300.00

COSBY, BILL

45s

Number	Title (A Side/B Side)	Yr	NM
CAPITOL			
❑ 4258	Yes, Yes, Yes/Ben	1976	4.00
❑ 4299	I Luv Myself Better Than I Luv Myself/Do It To Me	1976	4.00
❑ 4501	Boogie on Your Face/What's in a Slang	1977	4.00
❑ 4523	Merry Christmas Mama (Vocal)/(Instrumental)	1977	20.00
TETRAGRAMMATON			
❑ 1539	Football/Golf	1969	6.00
UNI			
❑ 55184	Hikky Burr/Hikky Burr	1969	6.00
—A-side with the Bunions; B-side by the Bradford Band			
❑ 55223	Grover Henson Feels Forgotten/(Instrumental)	1970	6.00
❑ 55247	Hybish Skybish/Martin's Funeral	1970	5.00
—With Bad Foot Brown			
WARNER BROS.			
❑ 5499	Stand Still for My Lovin'/When I Marry	1965	10.00
❑ 7072	Little Ole Man (Uptight-Everything's Alright)/Hush Hush	1967	8.00
❑ 7096	Hooray for the Salvation Army Band/Ursalena	1968	8.00
❑ 7126	Little Ole Man (Uptight-Everything's Alright)/Funky North Philly	1969	6.00
—Hall of Fame Hits (originals have green labels with "W7" logo)			
❑ 7171	Funky North Philly/Stop, Look and Listen	1968	8.00

Albums

Number	Title (A Side/B Side)	Yr	NM
CAPITOL			
❑ ST-11530	Bill Cosby Is Not Himself These Days, Rat Own, Rat Own, Rat Own	1976	10.00
❑ ST-11590	My Father Confused Me…What Must I Do? What Must I Do?	1977	10.00
❑ ST-11683	Let's Boogie (Disco Bill)	1977	10.00
❑ ST-11731	Bill's Best Friend	1978	10.00
GEFFEN			
❑ GHS 24104	Those of You With or Without Children, You'll Understand	1986	10.00
MCA			
❑ 169	When I Was a Kid	197?	8.00
—Reissue of Uni 73100			
❑ 333	Fat Albert	1973	10.00
❑ 553	For Adults Only	197?	8.00
—Reissue of Uni 73112			
❑ 554	Inside the Mind of Bill Cosby	197?	8.00
—Reissue of Uni 73139			
❑ 8005 [(2)]	Bill	197?	12.00
MOTOWN			
❑ 5364 ML	Bill Cosby "Himself"	198?	10.00
—Reissue of 6026 with new cover			
❑ 6026 ML	Bill Cosby "Himself"	1982	10.00
TETRAGRAMMATON			
❑ TD-5100 [(2)]	8:15 12:15	1969	20.00
UNI			
❑ 73066	Bill Cosby	1969	10.00
❑ 73082	"Live" Madison Square Garden Center	1970	10.00
❑ 73100	When I Was a Kid	1971	10.00
❑ 73101	Bill Cosby Talks to Kids About Drugs	1971	15.00
❑ 73112	For Adults Only	1971	10.00
❑ 73139	Inside the Mind of Bill Cosby	1972	10.00
WARNER BROS.			
❑ PRO 249 [DJ]	Radio Sampler Album — The Best of Bill Cosby	1969	20.00
—Promo LP with edits of 12 tracks for radio use			
❑ W 1518 [M]	Bill Cosby Is a Very Funny Fellow Right!	1964	15.00
❑ W 1567 [M]	I Started Out as a Child	1964	15.00
❑ WS 1567 [S]	I Started Out as a Child	1964	20.00
—Gold label			
❑ W 1606 [M]	Why Is There Air?	1965	15.00
❑ WS 1606 [S]	Why Is There Air?	1965	20.00
—Gold label			
❑ W 1634 [M]	Wonderfulness	1966	15.00
❑ WS 1634 [S]	Wonderfulness	1966	15.00
—Gold label			
❑ W 1691 [M]	Revenge	1967	15.00
❑ W 1709 [M]	Bill Cosby Sings/Silver Throat	1967	15.00
❑ WS 1709 [S]	Bill Cosby Sings/Silver Throat	1967	12.00
❑ W 1728 [M]	Bill Cosby Sings/Hooray for the Salvation Army Band	1968	15.00
❑ WS 1728 [S]	Bill Cosby Sings/Hooray for the Salvation Army Band	1968	12.00
❑ W 1734 [M]	To Russell, My Brother, Whom I Slept With	1968	15.00
❑ WS 1734 [S]	To Russell, My Brother, Whom I Slept With	1968	12.00
❑ WS 1757	200 M.P.H.	1968	12.00
❑ WS 1770	It's True! It's True!	1969	12.00
❑ WS 1798	The Best of Bill Cosby	1969	12.00
❑ WS 1836	More of the Best of Bill Cosby	1970	12.00

COSMIC RAYS, THE

45s

Number	Title (A Side/B Side)	Yr	NM
SATURN			
❑ 222	Bye Bye/Someone's in Love	1960	3000.
❑ 401	Daddy's Gonna Tell You No Lies/Dreaming	1960	2000.

COSMO, TONY

45s

Number	Title (A Side/B Side)	Yr	NM
FLING			
❑ 716	Wise to You/Ponytail Annie and Crewcut Joe	1960	12.00
❑ 716 [PS]	Wise to You/Ponytail Annie and Crewcut Joe	1960	25.00
ROULETTE			
❑ 4265	A Teenager for President/Give Me Some	1960	10.00
VANN			
❑ 100	Big Party/Tiny Hands and Funny Dimples	1961	15.00

COSTA, DON

45s

Number	Title (A Side/B Side)	Yr	NM
ABC-PARAMOUNT			
❑ 9693	Flamenco Love/Heart of Paris	1956	15.00
❑ 9717	Magic Melody/Lullaby to an Angel	1956	15.00
❑ 9729	For Me and My Gal/Beer Barrel Polka	1956	15.00
❑ 9770	Around the World/Everybody Loves Pierre	1956	15.00
❑ 9783	By the Fireside/C'est Ca!	1957	15.00
❑ 9835	Bella Nunziata/Tennessee Tulip	1957	15.00
❑ 9943	Bing Bang Bong/Almost in Your Arms	1958	15.00
COLUMBIA			
❑ 4-42307	Flamenco Guitar/Sugar Blues	1962	10.00
❑ 4-42442	Theme from The Miracle Worker/Hully Gully	1962	10.00
❑ 4-42494	Theme from The Wonderful World of the Brothers Grimm/Above the Stars	1962	10.00
❑ 4-42705	Diamonds/The Harem	1963	8.00
❑ 4-42785	Losing You/Tamoure	1963	8.00
DCP			
❑ 1100	Theme from "Golden Boy"/Main Street	1964	8.00
❑ 1121	If I Had a Hammer/Put Your Head on My Shoulder	1964	8.00
❑ 1124	I Will Wait for You/Pretty Blue Eyes	1965	8.00
❑ 1132	How to Murder Your Wife/Elise	1965	8.00
DCP INTERNATIONAL			
❑ 1002	Love Theme from "Tom Jones"/Off Broadway	1964	8.00
ESSEX			
❑ 405	Under the Linden Tree/Safe in the Harbor	1955	15.00
JAMIE			
❑ 1123	I'm in Heaven/The Main One	1959	12.00
MERCURY			
❑ 72841	Mrs. Robinson/Sound of Silence	1968	7.00

Number	Title (A Side/B Side)	Yr	NM
❑ 72932	Love So Fine/On the South Side of Chicago	1969	8.00

MGM

Number	Title (A Side/B Side)	Yr	NM
❑ K13520	Theme from "A Study in Terror"/Titoli	1966	7.00
❑ K14201	Gemini Trip/Rosy's Theme (From Ryan's Daughter)	1970	6.00
❑ K14467	Gone/Song for Anna	1972	6.00

UNITED ARTISTS

Number	Title (A Side/B Side)	Yr	NM
❑ 035	Never on Sunday/Theme from The Unforgiven	1973	5.00
—"Silver Spotlight Series"			
❑ 190	I'll Walk the Line/Cat Walk	1959	12.00
❑ 221	Theme from "The Unforgiven"/Streets of Paris	1960	10.00
❑ 221 [PS]	Theme from "The Unforgiven"/Streets of Paris	1960	50.00
—Promo-only sleeve with photos of Audrey Hepburn and Burt Lancaster			
❑ 234	Never on Sunday/The Sound of Love	1960	10.00
❑ 234 [PS]	Never on Sunday/The Sound of Love	1960	25.00
❑ 286	The Misfits/Chi-Chi	1961	12.00
❑ 286 [PS]	The Misfits/Chi-Chi	1961	40.00
—With photos of Clark Gable, Marilyn Monroe and Montgomery Clift			
❑ 318	How in the World/That's the Way with Love	1961	10.00
❑ 349	La La La/These Things Remain	1961	10.00
❑ 1500	Never on Sunday/Exodus	196?	6.00
—B-side by Ferrante and Teicher; "Silver Series" reissue			
❑ 1523	The Song from Moulin Rouge/Laura	196?	6.00
—"Silver Series" issue			
❑ 1524	An Affair to Remember/Invitation	196?	6.00
—"Silver Series" issue			
❑ 1525	The Third Man Theme/From Here to Eternity	196?	6.00
—"Silver Series" issue			
❑ 1526	Stella by Starlight/Picnic	196?	6.00
—"Silver Series" issue			
❑ 1602	Never on Sunday/Theme from The Unforgiven	196?	6.00
—"Silver Series" issue			

VERVE

Number	Title (A Side/B Side)	Yr	NM
❑ 10511	Illya Darling/Trini's Tune	1967	8.00
❑ 10511 [PS]	Illya Darling/Trini's Tune	1967	15.00
❑ 10558	Theme from Valley of the Dolls/Up, Up and Away	1967	7.00
❑ 10559	Can't Take My Eyes Off You/Society's Child	1967	7.00

Albums

ABC-PARAMOUNT

Number	Title	Yr	NM
❑ ABC-107 [M]	Music to Break a Lease	1956	25.00
❑ ABC-212 [M]	Music to Break a Sub-Lease	1958	25.00
❑ ABC-362 [M]	Don Costa Conducts His 15 Hits	1961	25.00

COLUMBIA

Number	Title	Yr	NM
❑ CL 1880 [M]	Hollywood Premiere	1962	15.00
❑ CL 2041 [M]	Hits! Hits! Hits!	1963	15.00
❑ CS 8680 [S]	Hollywood Premiere	1962	25.00
❑ CS 8841 [S]	Hits! Hits! Hits!	1963	25.00

DCP INTERNATIONAL

Number	Title	Yr	NM
❑ DCL 3802 [M]	The Golden Touch	1964	12.00
❑ DCL 3806 [M]	Don Costa Plays Music from Umbrellas of Cherbourg and Other Film Music	1965	12.00
❑ DCS 6802 [S]	The Golden Touch	1964	15.00
❑ DCS 6806 [S]	Don Costa Plays Music from Umbrellas of Cherbourg and Other Film Music	1965	15.00

HARMONY

Number	Title	Yr	NM
❑ HL 7347 [M]	Days of Wine and Roses and Other Great Hits	1965	12.00
❑ HS 11147 [S]	Days of Wine and Roses and Other Great Hits	1965	15.00

MERCURY

Number	Title	Yr	NM
❑ SR 61177	Instrumental Versions of Simon and Garfunkel	1968	20.00
❑ SR 61216	The Don Costa Concept	1969	20.00

UNITED ARTISTS

Number	Title	Yr	NM
❑ UAL 3119 [M]	The Unforgiven	1960	20.00
❑ UAL 3134 [M]	Magnificent Motion Picture Music	1960	15.00
❑ WW 3513 [M]	The Sound of the Million Sellers	1960	15.00
❑ UAS 6134 [S]	Magnificent Motion Picture Music	1960	20.00
❑ WW 7501 [M]	Echoing Voices and Trombones	1960	20.00
❑ WWS 8501 [S]	Echoing Voices and Trombones	1960	30.00
❑ WWS 8513 [S]	The Sound of the Million Sellers	1960	25.00

VERVE

Number	Title	Yr	NM
❑ V-8702 [M]	Modern Delights	1967	20.00
❑ V6-8702 [S]	Modern Delights	1967	15.00

COSTELLO, ELVIS

12-Inch Singles

COLUMBIA

Number	Title (A Side/B Side)	Yr	NM
❑ AS 1510 [DJ]	Man Out of Time/Beyond Belief	1982	12.00
❑ AS1510 [DJ]	Man Out of Time/Beyond Belief	1982	12.00
❑ CAS 2310 [DJ]	Don't Let Me Be Misunderstood (live) (same on both sides)	1986	15.00
❑ CAS2310 [DJ]	Don't Let Me Be Misunderstood (live) (same on both sides)	1986	15.00
❑ CAS2371 [DJ]	Loveable (same on both sides)	1986	7.00
❑ CAS 2371 [DJ]	Lovable (same on both sides)	1986	8.00
❑ CAS2380 [DJ]	Seven Day Weekend (same on both sides)	1986	8.00
❑ CAS2500 [DJ]	Tokyo Storm Warning/Tokyo Storm Warning {Part 1)	1986	6.00
❑ CAS 2500 [DJ]	Tokyo Storm Warning (Part 1) (Part 2)	1986	8.00
❑ 44-04115	Everyday I Write the Book (2 versions)//Heathen Town/Night Time	1983	12.00
❑ 44-05081	The Only Flame in Town (Special Mix)//Pump It Up (Monster Mix)/Baby It's You	1984	12.00

WARNER BROS.

Number	Title (A Side/B Side)	Yr	NM
❑ PRO3424 [DJ]	Veronica (same on both sides)	1989	15.00
❑ PRO-A-3424 [DJ]	Veronica (same on both sides)	1989	15.00

45s

COLUMBIA

Number	Title (A Side/B Side)	Yr	NM
❑ AE7 1171 [DJ]	Accidents Will Happen/Alison/Watching the Detectives	1979	3.00
—Small hole; extra record included in first editions of LP "Armed Forces"			
❑ AE71171 [DJ]	Accidents Will Happen/Alison/Watching the Detectives	1979	3.00
—Extra record included in first editions of LP "Armed Forces"			
❑ AE7 1171 [PS]	Live at Hollywood High	1979	5.00
❑ AE7 1172 [DJ]	My Funny Valentine/(What's So Funny 'Bout) Peace, Love and Undestanding	1980	12.00
—Promo only on red vinyl			
❑ AE71172 [DJ]	My Funny Valentine/(What's So Funny 'Bout) Peace, Love and Undestanding	1980	12.00
—Promo only on red vinyl			
❑ 18-02629	A Good Year for the Roses/The Angel Steps Out of Heaven	1981	5.00
❑ 18-03202	Man Out of Time/Town Cryer	1982	5.00
❑ CNR-03269	Man Out of Time/(B-side blank)	1982	8.00
—One-sided budget release			
❑ 38-04045	Everyday I Write the Book/Heathen Town	1983	5.00
❑ 38-04045 [PS]	Everyday I Write the Book/Heathen Town	1983	5.00
❑ 38-04266	Let Them All Talk/Shipbiulding	1983	5.00
❑ 38-04502	The Only Flame in Town/Turning the Town Red	1984	5.00
❑ 38-04502 [PS]	The Only Flame in Town/Turning the Town Red	1984	5.00
❑ 38-04625	I Wanna Be Loved/Love Field	1984	5.00
❑ 38-05809	Don't Let Me Be Misunderstood/Brand New Hairdo	1986	4.00
—By "The Costello Show Featuring Elvis Costello"			
❑ 38-06059	Lovable/Get Yourself Another Fool	1986	4.00
—By "The Costello Show Featuring Elvis Costello"			
❑ 38-06326	Tokyo Storm Warning (Part 1)/(Part 2)	1986	5.00
❑ 3-10641	Alison/Miracle Man	1977	10.00
—Contains a remix of "Alison" otherwise unavailable on U.S. vinyl			
❑ 3-10696	Watching the Detectives//Blame It on Cain/Mystery Dance	1978	10.00
❑ 3-10705	Alison/Watching the Detectives	1978	10.00
—Contains the same remix of "Alison" as on 10641			
❑ 3-10762	This Year's Girl/Big Tears	1978	6.00
❑ 3-10919	Accidents Will Happen/Sunday's Best	1979	8.00
❑ 1-11194	I Can't Stand Up for Falling Down/Girls Talk	1980	7.00
❑ 1-11284	New Amsterdam/Wednesday Week	1980	5.00
❑ 1-11389	Getting Mighty Crowded/Radio Sweetheart	1980	5.00
❑ 3-33401	Accidents Will Happen/Alison	198?	3.00
—"Hall of Fame" reissue; gray label			
❑ 3-33401	Accidents Will Happen/Alison	1980	5.00
—"Hall of Fame" reissue; red and black label			
❑ 11-60519	Watch Your Step/Luxembourg	1981	5.00
❑ 11-60519 [PS]	Watch Your Step/Luxembourg	1981	5.00

DECCA

Number	Title (A Side/B Side)	Yr	NM
❑ DECUVI 001 [DJ]	I Still Have That Other Girl/The Sweetest Punch	1998	10.00
❑ DECUVI 001 [PS]	I Still Have That Other Girl/The Sweetest Punch	1998	10.00
—Promo-only issue; available at Tower Records to purchasers of the CD "Painted from Memory"			

WARNER BROS.

Number	Title (A Side/B Side)	Yr	NM
❑ 22981	Veronica/You're No Good	1989	3.00
❑ 22981 [PS]	Veronica/You're No Good	1989	3.00

7-Inch Extended Plays

COLUMBIA

Number	Title	Yr	NM
❑ 1-11251	I Can't Stand Up for Falling Down/Girls Talk//Secondary Modern/King Horse	1980	6.00
❑ 1-11251 [PS]	I Can't Stand Up for Falling Down/Girls Talk//Secondary Modern/King Horse	1980	6.00

Albums

COLUMBIA

Number	Title	Yr	NM
❑ (no #) [PD]	My Aim Is True/This Year's Model	1978	80.00
—Promo-only picture disc; contains six songs from one album and six from the other			
❑ AS 529 [EP]	Live at Hollywood High	1978	20.00
—Promo-only 12-inch version of 7-inch single			
❑ AS 958 [DJ]	The Elvis Costello Interview with Tom Snyder	1981	20.00
❑ AS958 [DJ]	Tom Snyder Interview	1981	20.00
❑ AS1318 [DJ]	Almost Blue	1981	40.00
—Radio sampler with introductions by Elvis before each track			
❑ AS 1318 [DJ]	Almost Blue: Elvis Introduces His Favorite Country Songs	1981	50.00
—Radio sampler with introductions by Elvis before each track			
❑ JC 35037	My Aim Is True	1977	15.00
—First pressings have yellow back covers			
❑ JC 35037	My Aim Is True	1978	10.00
—Second pressings have a white back cover and no bar code			
❑ PC 35037	My Aim Is True	1984	8.00
—Budget-line reissue with new prefix			
❑ JC 35331	This Year's Model	1978	10.00
—With standard Columbia label			
❑ JC 35331	This Year's Model	1978	12.00
—With "Costello" replacing "Columbia" on labels			
❑ PC 35331	This Year's Model	1984	8.00
—Budget-line reissue with new prefix			
❑ JC 35709	Armed Forces	1979	10.00
—Stock copy; add 30 percent if bonus 7-inch single is there; add another 50 percent if the 7-inch's picture sleeve is there			
❑ JC 35709 [DJ]	Armed Forces	1979	15.00
—White label promo; add 20 percent if bonus 7-inch single is there; add another 33 percent if the 7-inch's picture sleeve is there			
❑ JC35709 [DJ]	Armed Forces	1979	15.00
—White label promo, includes bonus 7" single			
❑ PC 35709	Armed Forces	1984	8.00
—Budget-line reissue with new prefix; not issued with bonus single			
❑ JC 36347	Get Happy!!	1980	10.00
❑ PC 36347	Get Happy!!	1984	8.00
—Budget-line reissue with new prefix			
❑ JC 36839	Taking Liberties	1980	8.00
❑ JC 36839	Taking Liberties	1980	10.00
—With custom old-style Columbia label			
❑ PC 36839	Taking Liberties	1984	8.00
—Budget-line reissue with new prefix			
❑ JC 37051	Trust	1981	10.00
❑ PC 37051	Trust	1984	8.00
—Budget-line reissue with new prefix			
❑ FC 37562	Almost Blue	1981	10.00
❑ PC 37562	Almost Blue	1984	8.00
—Budget-line reissue with new prefix			
❑ FC 38157	Imperial Bedroom	1982	10.00
❑ PC 38157	Imperial Bedroom	1984	8.00
—Budget-line reissue with new prefix			
❑ FC 38897	Punch the Clock	1983	10.00
❑ FC 39429	Goodbye Cruel World	1984	10.00
❑ PC 39429	Goodbye Cruel World	198?	8.00
—Budget-line reissue with new prefix			
❑ FC 40101	The Best of Elvis Costello	1985	12.00
❑ FC 40173	King of America	1986	10.00
—By "The Costello Show Featuring Elvis Costello"			
❑ PC 40173	King of America	198?	8.00
—By "The Costello Show Featuring Elvis Costello"; budget-line reissue with new prefix			
❑ FC 40518	Blood & Chocolate	1986	10.00
❑ HC 48157	Imperial Bedroom	1982	50.00
—Half-speed mastered edition			

COSTELLO

Number	Title	Yr	NM
❑ AS 847 [EP]	Taking Liberties	1980	15.00
—Promo-only four-song sampler "Costello" is where "Columbia" would normally be on the 78-rpm-style label			

LOST HIGHWAY

Number	Title	Yr	NM
❑ B0002593-01 [(2)]	The Delivery Man	2004	20.00
❑ B0003905-01 [10]	Delta-Verite: The Clarksdale Sessions	2005	10.00
❑ B0003905-01 [10]	Delta-Verite: The Clarksdale Sessions	2005	10.00
—Black vinyl; this album has been counterfeited; originals have a white border around all four sides of the front cover and the words "The			

Number	Title (A Side/B Side)	Yr	NM

Round-Up Factor" at the bottom of the back cover, and counterfeits do not; also, counterfeits use the catalog number "CN-005" and have white labels

RHINO

❑ R1-74285	My Aim Is True	2003	15.00

—180-gram vinyl; first U.S. issue of British track lineup

WARNER BROS.

❑ - 3488 [(2)DJ]	Spike — The Elvis Costello Hour	1989	30.00

—Music and conversation; generic gatefold sleeve with sticker on cover

❑ PRO-A-3488 [(2)DJ]	The Elvis Costello Hour	1989	40.00

—Music and interview; generic gatefold sleeve with sticker on cover

❑ 25848	Spike	1989	10.00
❑ 46198	All This Useless Beauty	1996	100.00
❑ R 100841	Spike	1989	12.00

—BMG Direct Marketing edition

COTTON, GENE

45s

(NO LABEL)

❑ NR-16361 [DJ]	Child Of Peace (same on both sides)	1981	8.00

ABC

❑ 12087	Country Spirit/Damn It All	1975	5.00
❑ 12137	Let Your Love Flow/ Keepin' It on the Road	1975	5.00
❑ 12227	You've Got Me Runnin'/It's Over, Goodbye	1976	5.00
❑ 12250	Rain On/A Song for You	1977	5.00
❑ 12282	My Love Comes Alive/ Sweet Destiny	1977	5.00

ARIOLA AMERICA

❑ 7675	Before My Heart Finds Out/ Like a Sunday in Salem	1977	5.00
❑ 7723	Like a Sunday in Salem (The Amos and Andy Song)/Shine On (You Got to Shine On)	1978	4.00
❑ 7778	Michael/Ocean of Love	1979	4.00

KNOLL

❑ 5002	If I Could Get You (Into My Life)/ Rained On Before	1982	5.00

MYRRH

❑ 116	American Indian Blues/ Lessons of History	1973	6.00
❑ 117	Lean On One Another/ (B-side unknown)	1973	6.00
❑ 123	Great American Noel/Mrs. Oliver	1973	6.00
❑ 137	Sunshine Roses/Mrs. Oliver	1974	6.00

Albums

ABC

❑ D-933	For All the Young Writers	1975	10.00
❑ D-983	Rain On	1977	10.00

ARIOLA AMERICA

❑ SW-50031	Save the Dancer	1978	10.00
❑ SW-50070	No Strings Attached	1979	10.00

KNOLL

❑ 1001	Eclipse of the Blue Moon	1981	10.00

MYRRH

❑ MSB-6517	In the Gray of the Morning	1973	12.00
❑ MSB-6524	Liberty	1974	12.00

COTTON, GENE, AND KIM CARNES

Also see each artist's individual listings.

45s

ARIOLA AMERICA

❑ 7704	You're a Part of Me/Shine On (You Got to Shine On)	1978	5.00

COTTON, JAMES

45s

BUDDAH

❑ 461	Boogie Thing/Fever	1975	5.00
❑ 468	Rocket 88/One More Mile	1975	5.00

LOMA

❑ 2042	Laying in the Weeds/ Complete This Order	1966	12.00

SUN

❑ 199	My Baby/Straighten Up, Baby	1954	1500.
❑ 206	Cotton Crop Blues/Hold Me in Your Arms	1954	1800.

VERVE FORECAST

❑ 5053	Good Time Charlie/Off the Wall	1967	10.00
❑ 5066	Feelin' Good/Don't Start Me Talkin'	1967	10.00
❑ 5107	The Coach's Better Days/ (B-side unknown)	1969	8.00

Albums

ALLIGATOR

❑ AL-4737	High Compression	1984	10.00
❑ AL-4746	Live from Chicago	1986	10.00

ANTONE'S

❑ ANT-0007	James Cotton Live	1988	12.00

BLIND PIG

❑ BP-2587	Take Me Back	1987	10.00

BUDDAH

❑ BDS-5620	100% Cotton	1974	12.00
❑ BDS-5650	High Energy	1975	12.00
❑ BDS-5661 [(2)]	Live & On the Move!	1976	15.00

CAPITOL

❑ SM-814	Taking Care of Business	197?	10.00

—Reissue with new prefix

❑ ST-814	Taking Care of Business	1971	15.00

INTERMEDIA

❑ QS-5006	Dealing with the Devil	198?	10.00
❑ QS-5011	Two Sides of the Blues	198?	10.00

VANGUARD

❑ VSD-79283	Cut You Loose!	1969	15.00

VERVE FORECAST

❑ FT-3023 [M]	The James Cotton Blues Band	1967	25.00
❑ FTS-3023 [S]	The James Cotton Blues Band	1967	20.00
❑ FTS-3038	Pure Cotton	1968	20.00

COTTON PICKERS, THE

Albums

PHILIPS

❑ PHM 200025 [M]	Country Guitar	1962	20.00
❑ PHS 600025 [S]	Country Guitar	1962	25.00

COUCH, ORVILLE

45s

CUSTOM

❑ 101	Hello Trouble/Anywhere There's a Crowd	1962	30.00

MERCURY

❑ 71718	Downtown/Big Jim Sandy	1960	20.00

MONUMENT

❑ 915	Down Here Where the Hurt Begins/Permanent Wave	1966	12.00
❑ 949	The Best Things in Life/ Farmington, New Mexico	1966	12.00

STARDAY

❑ 305	You're Dreamin'/King for a Day	1957	30.00
❑ 326	Five Cent Candy/I Will If You Will	1957	30.00

VEE JAY

❑ 470	Hello Trouble/Anywhere There's a Crowd	1962	20.00
❑ 528	Did I Miss You?/The Lonesomes	1963	20.00
❑ 589	Strike a Match/Dance Her By Me	1964	20.00
❑ 631	Hello Doll/Uncle Red	1964	20.00
❑ 693	Greenville Diner/Big Daddy of the Bayou	1965	20.00
❑ 706	Color Me Gone/You're a Little Heartache	1965	20.00

Albums

VEE JAY

❑ VJLP-1087 [M]	Hello Trouble	1964	20.00
❑ VJS-1087 [S]	Hello Trouble	1964	40.00

COULSON, DEAN, MCGUINNESS, FLINT

Also see McGUINNESS FLINT.

Albums

SIRE

❑ SAS-7405	Lo and Behold	1972	20.00

COUNT FIVE, THE

45s

DOUBLE SHOT

❑ 104	Psychotic Reaction/ They're Gonna Get You	1966	12.00

—Later pressings, with label logo at side

❑ 104	Psychotic Reaction/ They're Gonna Get You	1966	15.00

—First pressing, with label logo at top

❑ 106	Peace of Mind/The Morning After	1966	12.00
❑ 110	You Must Believe Me/Teeny Bopper, Teeny Bopper	1967	12.00
❑ 115	Merry-Go-Round/Contrast	1967	12.00
❑ 125	Declaration of Independence/ Revelation in Slow Motion	1968	12.00
❑ 141	Mailman/Pretty Big Mouth	1969	12.00

Albums

DOUBLE SHOT

❑ DSM-1001 [M]	Psychotic Reaction	1966	40.00
❑ DSS-5001 [R]	Psychotic Reaction	1966	25.00

COUNT ROCKIN' SIDNEY

See ROCKIN' SIDNEY.

COUNT STEPHEN

See STEVE ALAIMO.

COUNTRY BOYS, THE

Also see DAVID GATES.

45s

DEL-FI

❑ 4245	The Okie Surfer/Blue Surf	1964	40.00

COUNTRY HAMS, THE

See PAUL McCARTNEY.

COUNTRY JOE AND THE FISH

Includes releases by "Country Joe McDonald."

45s

FANTASY

❑ 758	Breakfast for Two/ Lost My Connection	1976	4.00
❑ 765	Save the Whales/Oh Jamaica	1976	4.00
❑ 780	Love Is a Fire/I Need You	1976	4.00
❑ 814	Southern Cross/Coyote	1978	4.00
❑ 822	Bring Back the Sixties, Man/ Sunshine Through My Window	1978	4.00
❑ 876	Private Parts/Take Time Out	1979	4.00

PHILCO-FORD

❑ HP-35	Not So Sweet Martha Lorraine/ Masked Marauder	1969	25.00

—4-inch plastic "Hip Pocket Record" with color sleeve

VANGUARD

❑ 35052	Not So Sweet Martha Lorraine/ The Masked Marauder	1967	10.00
❑ 35059	Janis (Part 1)/Janis (Part 2)	1967	10.00
❑ 35061	Who Am I/Thursday	1968	10.00
❑ 35061 [PS]	Who Am I/Thursday	1968	20.00
❑ 35068	Rock and Soul (Part 1)/ Rock and Soul (Part 2)	1968	10.00
❑ 35090	Here I Go Again/Baby, You're Driving Me Crazy	1969	8.00
❑ 35112	I-Feel-Like-I'm-Fixin'-to-Die Rag/ Janis	1970	8.00
❑ 35133	Hold On, It's Coming/ Playing with Fire	1971	5.00

—Starting here, as "Country Joe McDonald"

❑ 35150	Hang On/Hand of Man	1972	5.00
❑ 35161	Fantasy/I Seen a Rocket	1972	5.00
❑ 35181	Doctor Hip/Satisfactorily	1973	4.00
❑ 35184	Chloe/Jesse James	1974	4.00

7-Inch Extended Plays

RAG BABY

❑ 1001	(contents unknown)	1966	100.00
❑ 1001 [PS]	Rag Baby	1966	200.00

—Actually an envelope in which the record came

Albums

CUSTOM FIDELITY

❑ CFS-2348	Joe McDonald	1968	1000.

—Recorded in 1964, 200 copies were pressed for Joe McDonald; VG value 500; VG+ value 750

FANTASY

❑ 9495	Paradise with an Ocean View	1975	10.00
❑ 9511	Love Is a Fire	1976	10.00
❑ 9525	Goodbye Blues	1977	10.00
❑ 9530	Reunion	1977	12.00
❑ 9544	Rock and Roll Music From the Planet Earth	1978	10.00
❑ 9586	Leisure Suite	1980	10.00

FIRST AMERICAN

❑ PIC-3309	The Early Years	1979	10.00

MOBLIE FIDELITY

❑ 1-056	Paradise with an Ocean View	1981	30.00

—Audiophile vinyl

VANGUARD

❑ VSD-27/28 [(2)]	The Life and Times of Country Joe & the Fish From Haight-Ashbury to Woodstock	1971	20.00
❑ VSD-85/86 [(2)]	The Essential Country Joe	1977	12.00
❑ VSD-6545	Country Joe & The Fish/ Greatest Hits	1969	20.00
❑ VSD-6546	Thinking of Woody	1969	15.00
❑ VSD-6555	C.J. Fish	1970	20.00
❑ VSD-6557	Tonight I'm Singing Just for You	1970	15.00
❑ VRS-9244 [M]	Electric Music for the Mind and Body	1967	80.00

—Gold label

❑ VRS-9244 [M]	Electric Music for the Mind and Body	1967	100.00

—Black label (unverified)

❑ 9266/79266	I-Feel-Like-I'm-Fixin'-to-Die "Fish Game" Poster	1967	10.00
❑ VRS-9266 [M]	I-Feel-Like-I'm-Fixin'-to-Die	1967	20.00
❑ VSQ-40004/5 [(2)Q]	The Life and Times of Country Joe & the Fish From Haight-Ashbury to Woodstock	197?	40.00

Except when noted otherwise, VG = 25% of NM, and VG+ = 50% of NM. (Example: VG = $2.00, VG+ = $4.00 and NM = $8.00.)

Number	Title (A Side/B Side)	Yr	NM
❑ VSD-79244 [S]	Electric Music for the Mind and Body	1967	40.00
—Gold label			
❑ VSD-79244 [S]	Electric Music for the Mind and Body	1967	50.00
—Black label (unverified)			
❑ VSD-79266 [S]	I-Feel-Like-I'm-Fixin'-to-Die	1967	20.00
❑ VSD-79277	Together	1968	20.00
❑ VSD-79299	Here We Are Again	1969	20.00
❑ VSD-79304	Hold On It's Coming	1971	15.00
❑ VSD-79315	War, War, War	1971	15.00
❑ VSD-79316	Incredible! Live!	1972	12.00
❑ VSD-79328	Paris Sessions	1973	12.00
❑ VSD-79348	Country Joe	1974	12.00

COUNTRY STORE, THE

45s

Number	Title (A Side/B Side)	Yr	NM
T-A			
❑ 189	To Love You/Heartache	1969	25.00
❑ 196	Your Love (Is the Only Love)/Caught with My Heart Down	1970	40.00
❑ 203	Days of Icy Fingers/(B-side unknown)	1970	10.00

COUNTS, THE (1)

Male vocal group from Indianapolis.

45s

Number	Title (A Side/B Side)	Yr	NM
DOT			
❑ 1188	Darling Dear/I Need You Always	1954	60.00
❑ 1199	Hot Tamales/Baby Don't You Know	1954	50.00
❑ 1210	My Dear, My Darling/She Won't Say Yes	1954	40.00
❑ 1226	Baby I Want You/Waitin' Around for You	1954	40.00
❑ 1235	Wailin' Little Mama/Let Me Go	1955	30.00
❑ 1243	From This Day On/Love and Understanding	1955	30.00
❑ 1265	I Need You Tonight/Sally Walker	1955	30.00
❑ 1275	To Our Love/Heartbreaker	1956	25.00
❑ 16105	Darling Dear/I Need You Always	1960	20.00
NOTE			
❑ 20000	Sweet Names/I Guess I Brought It All on Myself	1956	200.00

COUNTS, THE (2)

Detroit-based funk group.

45s

Number	Title (A Side/B Side)	Yr	NM
AWARE			
❑ 038	Funk/Too Bad	1974	5.00
❑ 046	Sacrifice/Funk Pump	1974	5.00
❑ 049	At the Fair/I'm the Music	1975	5.00
❑ 054	Magic Ride/Short Cut	1975	5.00
WESTBOUND			
❑ 191	Thinking Single/Why Not Start All Over Again	1972	5.00

Albums

Number	Title (A Side/B Side)	Yr	NM
AWARE			
❑ 2002	Love Sign	1973	25.00
❑ 2006	Funk Pump	1975	20.00
WESTBOUND			
❑ 2011	What's Up Front That Counts	1972	30.00

COUNTS, THE (U)

It appears as if none of these are by group (1) or (2), and they aren't all by the same group.

45s

Number	Title (A Side/B Side)	Yr	NM
COUNT			
❑ 5	The Beat/After Beat	196?	20.00
MANCO			
❑ 1060	Surfer's Paradise/Chug-a-Lug	1964	40.00
MERCURY			
❑ 71318	Shake the Town/Teenage Guy and Girl	1958	15.00
PANORAMA			
❑ 9	Chitlins, Etc./Clyde, Clyde, The Cow's Outside	1965	10.00
❑ 33	Come Now/Since I Fell for You	1966	10.00
SEA CREST			
❑ 6003	Turn On Song/Enchanted Sea	1964	20.00
❑ 6004	Doggin'/And Then I Cried	1964	15.00
SHRINE			
❑ 117	Peaches Baby/My Only Love	1966	3000.
—VG 1000; VG+ 2000			
SMASH			
❑ 1821	Stormy Weather/True Love's Gone	1963	10.00
YES			
❑ 102	Stronger Than Ever/Gospel Truth	196?	400.00
❑ 103	Ask the Lonely/If You Don't Love Me	196?	400.00

COURCY, JOANNE

45s

Number	Title (A Side/B Side)	Yr	NM
TWIRL			
❑ 2020	Silly Girl/My Poor Broken Heart	1966	30.00
❑ 2026	I Got the Power/I'm Gonna Keep You	1966	700.00

COURTLAND, JEROME

Albums

Number	Title (A Side/B Side)	Yr	NM
JUBILEE			
❑ LP 22 [10]	Through a Long and Sleepless Night	1955	40.00

COURTNEY, LOU

45s

Number	Title (A Side/B Side)	Yr	NM
BUDDAH			
❑ 121	Let Me Turn You On/Tryin' to Find My Woman	1969	8.00
EPIC			
❑ 11062	What Do You Want Me to Do/Beware	1973	5.00
❑ 11088	I Don't Need Nobody Else/Why	1974	5.00
❑ 50046	The Best Thing a Man Can Do for His Woman/I'm Serious About Lovin' You	1974	5.00
❑ 50070	Just to Let Him Break Your Heart/Somebody New Is Lovin' You	1975	5.00
IMPERIAL			
❑ 66006	Come On Home/The Man with the Cigar	1963	12.00
❑ 66043	Little Old Love Maker/Professional Lover	1964	12.00
PHILIPS			
❑ 40287	I Watched You Slowly Slip Away/I'll Cry If I Want To	1965	100.00
POP-SIDE			
❑ 4594	Hey Joyce/I'm Mad About You	1967	10.00
❑ 4596	If the Shoe Fits/It's Love Now	1968	10.00
RIVERSIDE			
❑ 4588	Skate Now/I Can Always Tell	1966	10.00
❑ 4589	Do the Thing/Man Is Lonely	1967	10.00
❑ 4591	You Ain't Ready/I've Got Just the Thing	1967	10.00
VERVE			
❑ 10602	Do the Horse/Rubber Neckin'	1968	8.00
❑ 10631	Please Stay/You Can Give Your Love to Me	1968	8.00

Albums

Number	Title (A Side/B Side)	Yr	NM
EPIC			
❑ KE 33011	I'm in Need of Love	1974	12.00
RCA VICTOR			
❑ APL1-1969	Buffalo Smoke	1976	12.00
RIVERSIDE			
❑ 92000	Skate Now (Shing-a-Ling)	1967	25.00

COURTSHIP, THE

45s

Number	Title (A Side/B Side)	Yr	NM
TAMLA			
❑ 54217	It's the Same Old Love/Last Row, First Balcony	1972	5.00
❑ 54227	Oops, It Just Slipped Out/Love Ain't Love	1973	5.00

COURVALE, KEITH

45s

Number	Title (A Side/B Side)	Yr	NM
DOT			
❑ 15844	Trapped Love/Steelworker Blues	1958	100.00

COUSINS, THE (1)

45s

Number	Title (A Side/B Side)	Yr	NM
DECCA			
❑ 30609	I'm in Love with You/Be Nice to Me	1958	20.00
FIDELITY			
❑ 3010	Love Is Blind/How We'll Love	1959	30.00

COUSINS, THE (2)

45s

Number	Title (A Side/B Side)	Yr	NM
PARKWAY			
❑ 823	St. Louis Blues/No One Knows	1961	15.00
❑ 848	When My Baby Smiles at Me/Some of These Days	1962	12.00
❑ 870	Sweet Georgia Brown/Outside the Wall	1963	12.00

Albums

Number	Title (A Side/B Side)	Yr	NM
PARKWAY			
❑ P-7005 [M]	Music of the Strip	1961	20.00
❑ SP-7005 [S]	Music of the Strip	1961	25.00

COUSINS, THE (U)

Neither group (1) nor group (2).

45s

Number	Title (A Side/B Side)	Yr	NM
VERSATILE			
❑ 105	Down That Lonely Road/(B-side unknown)	1960	80.00
WYNNE			
❑ 132	Guilty/(B-side unknown)	1959	500.00

COVAY, DON

Also see THE SOLDIER BOYS.

45s

Number	Title (A Side/B Side)	Yr	NM
ARNOLD			
❑ 1002	Pony Time/Love Boat	1961	12.00
—As "Don Covay and the Goodtimers"			
❑ 1002	Pony Time/Love Boat	1961	25.00
—As "The Goodtimers"			
ATLANTIC			
❑ 1147	Bip Bop Bip/Silver Dollar	1957	80.00
—As "Pretty Boy"			
❑ 2280	The Boomerang/Daddy Loves Baby	1965	10.00
❑ 2286	Please Do Something/A Woman's Love	1965	10.00
❑ 2301	See Saw/I Never Get Enough of Your Love	1965	10.00
❑ 2323	Sookie Sookie/Watching the Late Late Show	1966	10.00
❑ 2340	You Put Something On Me/Iron Out the Rough Spots	1966	10.00
❑ 2357	Somebody's Got to Love You/Temptation Was Too Strong	1966	10.00
❑ 2375	Shing-Aling '67/I Was There	1967	10.00
❑ 2407	40 Days — 40 Nights/The Usual Place	1967	10.00
❑ 2440	You've Got Me on the Critical List/Never Had No Love	1967	10.00
❑ 2481	Chain of Fools/Prove It	1968	10.00
❑ 2494	Don't Let Go/It's In the Wind	1968	10.00
❑ 2521	Gonna Send You Back to Your Mama/House on the Corner	1968	10.00
❑ 2565	I Stole Some Love/Snake in the Grass	1968	10.00
❑ 2609	Sweet Pea/C.C. Rider Blues	1969	10.00
❑ 2666	Ice Cream Man (The Gimmie Game)/Black Woman	1969	10.00
❑ 2725	Everything I Do Goin' Be Funky/Key to the Kighway	1970	8.00
❑ 2742	Soul Stirrer/Sookie Sookie	1970	8.00
BIG			
❑ 617	Switchin' in the Kitchen/Rockin' the Mule	1958	80.00
—As "Pretty Boy"			
BIG TOP			
❑ 3060	Hey There/I'm Coming Down with the Blues	1960	15.00
BLAZE			
❑ 350	Standing in the Doorway/(B-side unknown)	1958	30.00
CAMEO			
❑ 239	The Popeye Waddle/One Little Bot Had Money	1962	12.00
❑ 251	Wiggle Wobble/Do the Bug	1963	12.00
COLUMBIA			
❑ 41981	Shake Wid the Snake/Every Which-a Way	1961	20.00
❑ 42058	Hand Jive Workout/See About Me	1961	20.00
❑ 42197	Now That I Need You/Teen Life Swag	1961	100.00
EPIC			
❑ 9484	It's Twistin' Time/Twistin' Train	1961	15.00
—As "The Goodtimers"			
JANUS			
❑ 164	Sweet Thang/Standing in the Grits Line	1971	6.00
❑ 181	Daddy Please Don't Go Out/Shoes Under My Bed	1972	6.00
LANDA			
❑ 704	You're Good for Me/Truth of the Lite	1965	10.00
MERCURY			
❑ 71385	I Was Checkin' Out She Was Checkin' In/Money	1973	6.00
❑ 71430	Somebody's Been Enjoying My Home/Bad Mouthing	1973	6.00
❑ 71469	It's Better to Have (And Don't Need)/Leave Him (Part 1)	1974	6.00
❑ 73311	Overtime Man/Dungeon #3	1972	6.00
❑ 73648	Rumble in the Jungle/We Can't Make It No More	1975	6.00
NEWMAN			
❑ 500	Badd Boy/(Instrumental)	1980	5.00

C

Number	Title (A Side/B Side)	Yr	NM
PARKWAY			
❑ 894	Ain't That Silly/Turn It On	1964	12.00
❑ 910	The Froog/One Little Boy Had Money	1964	12.00
PHILADELPHIA INT'L.			
❑ 3594	Right Time for Love/No Tell Motel	1976	5.00
❑ 3602	Travelin' in Heavy Traffic/Once You Have It	1976	5.00
ROSEMART			
❑ 801	Mercy Mercy/Can't Stay Away	1964	15.00
❑ 802	Take This Hurt Off Me/Please Don't Let Me Know	1964	12.00
SUE			
❑ 709	Betty Jean/Believe It or Not	1958	30.00
U-VON			
❑ 102	Back to the Roots (Part 1)/Back to the Roots (Part 2)	1977	5.00
Albums			
ATLANTIC			
❑ 8104 [M]	Mercy	1965	40.00
❑ SD 8104 [S]	Mercy	1965	50.00
❑ 8120 [M]	See Saw	1966	40.00
❑ SD 8120 [S]	See Saw	1966	50.00
❑ SD 8237	The House of Blue Lights	1969	25.00
JANUS			
❑ 3038	Different Strokes for Different Folks	1972	15.00
MERCURY			
❑ SRM-1-653	Super Dude I	1973	12.00
❑ SRM-1-1020	Hot Blood	1974	12.00
❑ 835030-1	Checkin' In with Don Covay	1988	10.00
PHILADELPHIA INT'L.			
❑ PZ 33958	Travelin' In Heavy Traffic	1977	10.00

COVEN Features Jinx Dawson.

Number	Title (A Side/B Side)	Yr	NM
45s			
ABC			
❑ 11377	One Tin Soldier (The Legend of Billy Jack)/I Think You Always Knew	1973	6.00
BUDDAH			
❑ 440	I Need a Hundred of You/(B-side unknown)	1974	4.00
LION			
❑ 192	Nightingale/Jailhouse Rock	1972	4.00
MERCURY			
❑ 72973	Wicked Woman/White Witch of Rose Hall	1969	6.00
❑ 72973 [PS]	Wicked Woman/White Witch of Rose Hall	1969	10.00
MGM			
❑ 14308	One Tin Soldier/I Guess It's a Beautiful Day Today	1971	5.00
❑ 14348	Nightingale/Jailhouse Rock	1972	4.00
SGC			
❑ 003	I Shall Be Released/I've Come Too Far	1968	6.00
WARNER BROS.			
❑ BJS 0101	One Tin Soldier, The Legend of Billy Jack/Johnnie	1973	4.00
—B-side by Teresa Kelly			
❑ 7509	One Tin Soldier, The Legend of Billy Jack/Say Goodbye, 'Cause You're Leavin'	1971	5.00
Albums			
BUDDAH			
❑ BDS-5614	Blood on the Snow	1974	25.00
MERCURY			
❑ SR 61239	Witchcraft Destroys Minds and Reaps Souls	1969	45.00
MGM			
❑ SE-4801	Coven	1971	40.00

COWBOY CHURCH SUNDAY SCHOOL, THE

Number	Title (A Side/B Side)	Yr	NM
45s			
DECCA			
❑ 9-29367	Open Up Your Heart (And Let the Sun Shine In)/The Lord Is Counting on You	1954	12.00
—Black label, star under "Decca"			
❑ 9-29367	Open Up Your Heart (And Let the Sun Shine In)/The Lord Is Counting on You	1954	20.00
—Black label, lines on either side of "Decca"			
❑ 9-29530	The Little Black Sheep/Go On By	1955	12.00
❑ 9-29757	Those Bad, Bad Kids/A Handful of Sunshine	1955	12.00
❑ 9-29958	It Is No Secret (What God Can Do)/Don't Send Those Kids to Sunday School	1956	12.00

COWBOY JUNKIES

Number	Title (A Side/B Side)	Yr	NM
12-Inch Singles			
RCA			
❑ 8759 [DJ]	Sweet Jane (same on both sides)	1988	12.00
❑ 8759-1-RDAB [DJ]	Sweet Jane (same on both sides)	1988	12.00
❑ 8958-1-R	Misguided Angel/Misguided Angel (Live), Sweet Jane (Live) + 2 more live at the Roxy	1989	30.00
45s			
RCA			
❑ 8879-7-R	Sweet Jane/200 More Miles	1989	5.00
❑ 8879-7-R [PS]	Sweet Jane/200 More Miles	1989	5.00
❑ 8997-7-R	Misguided Angel/Postcard Blues	1989	8.00
Albums			
LATENT RECORDINGS			
❑ LATEX 4	Whites Off Earth Now!!	1986	30.00
—Canada-only release			
RCA			
❑ 8568-1-R	The Trinity Session	1988	15.00
❑ 8568-1-R	The Trinity Session	1997	40.00
—Classic Records reissue on audiophile vinyl			

COWSILL, BILL Also see THE COWSILLS.

Number	Title (A Side/B Side)	Yr	NM
45s			
MGM			
❑ 14166	When Everybody's Here/I Wish I Could Say the Same About You	1970	6.00
Albums			
MGM			
❑ SE-4706	Nervous Breakthrough	1970	15.00

COWSILL, JOHN Also see THE COWSILLS.

Number	Title (A Side/B Side)	Yr	NM
45s			
MGM			
❑ 14003	Path of Love/Captain Sad and His Ship of Fools	1968	8.00

COWSILL, SUSAN Also see THE COWSILLS.

Number	Title (A Side/B Side)	Yr	NM
45s			
WARNER BROS.			
❑ 8232	It Might As Well Rain Until September/Mohammad's Radio	1976	5.00
❑ 8333	The Next Time That I See You/I Think of You	1977	5.00

COWSILLS, THE Also see BILL COWSILL; JOHN COWSILL; SUSAN COWSILL.

Number	Title (A Side/B Side)	Yr	NM
45s			
GASATANKA/ROCKVILLE			
❑ 6139	Christmastime (Song for Marissa)/Some Good Years	1993	3.00
—Green vinyl			
❑ 6139	Christmastime (Song For Marisa)/Some Good Years	1993	4.00
—Clear vinyl			
❑ 6139 [PS]	Christmastime (Song for Marissa)/Some Good Years	1993	3.00
JODA			
❑ 103	All I Really Wanta Be Is Me/And the Next Day, Too	1965	30.00
LONDON			
❑ 149	On My Side/There Is No Child	1971	8.00
❑ 153	You/Crystal Claps	1971	8.00
❑ 170	Blue Road/Covered Wagon	1972	8.00
MGM			
❑ 13810	The Rain, the Park and Other Things/River Blue	1967	10.00
❑ 13810 [PS]	The Rain, the Park and Other Things/River Blue	1967	12.00
❑ 13886	We Can Fly/A Time for Remembrance	1967	8.00
❑ 13886 [PS]	We Can Fly/A Time for Remembrance	1967	12.00
❑ 13909	In Need of a Friend/Mister Flynn	1968	8.00
❑ 13909 [PS]	In Need of a Friend/Mister Flynn	1968	12.00
❑ 13944	Indian Lake/Newspaper Blanket	1968	8.00
—Second pressings have blue and gold labels			
❑ 13944	Indian Lake/Newspaper Blanket	1968	10.00
—First pressings have black labels			
❑ 13944 [PS]	Indian Lake/Newspaper Blanket	1968	12.00
❑ 13981	Poor Baby/Meet Me at the Wishing Well	1968	8.00
❑ 14011	The Impossible Years/Candy Kid	1968	8.00
❑ 14026	Hair/What Is Happy	1969	12.00
❑ 14063	The Prophecy of Daniel and John the Divine (Six-Six-Six)/Gotta Get Away from It All	1969	8.00
❑ 14063 [PS]	The Prophecy of Daniel and John the Divine (Six-Six-Six)/Gotta Get Away from It All	1969	15.00
❑ 14084	Silver Threads and Golden Needles/Love, American Style	1969	10.00
❑ 14084 [PS]	Silver Threads and Golden Needles/Love, American Style	1969	12.00
❑ 14106	Start to Love/Two by Two	1970	8.00
PHILIPS			
❑ 40382	Most of All/Siamese Cat	1966	10.00
❑ 40382 [PS]	Most of All/Siamese Cat	1966	15.00
❑ 40406	Party Girl/What's It Gonna Be Like	1966	10.00
❑ 40437	A Most Peculiar Man/Could It Be, Let Me Know	1967	10.00
7-Inch Extended Plays			
MGM			
❑ PEP-1	The Milk Song/All My Days//Nothing to Do/The Fun Song	1969	10.00
—American Dairy Association promotional item			
❑ PEP-1 [PS]	The Cowsills Collector's Record	1969	25.00
—American Dairy Association promotional item			
Albums			
LONDON			
❑ PS 587	On My Side	1971	30.00
MGM			
❑ GAS-103	The Cowsills (Golden Archive Series)	1970	15.00
❑ E-4498 [M]	The Cowsills	1967	20.00
❑ SE-4498 [S]	The Cowsills	1967	15.00
❑ E-4534 [M]	We Can Fly	1968	30.00
—Appears to exist only as a yellow label promo			
❑ SE-4534 [S]	We Can Fly	1968	15.00
❑ E-4554 [M]	Captain Sad and His Ship of Fools	1968	40.00
—Mono appears to be yellow label promo only			
❑ SE-4554 [S]	Captain Sad and His Ship of Fools	1968	15.00
❑ SE-4597	The Best of the Cowsills	1968	15.00
❑ SE-4619	The Cowsills in Concert	1969	15.00
❑ SE-4639	II X II	1969	20.00
WING			
❑ SRW-16354	The Cowsills Plus the Lincoln Park Zoo	1968	12.00

COXON'S ARMY Pat Benatar was in this group.

Number	Title (A Side/B Side)	Yr	NM
Albums			
SAM MILLER EXCHANGE			
❑ (no cat #)	Live from Sam Miller's Exchange Cafe	1974	250.00
—Original is on Sam Miller Exchange purple label			
TRACE			
❑ (no cat #)	Live from Sam Miller's Exchange Cafe	1975	250.00
—Reprint is on black Trace label			

CRABBY APPLETON

Number	Title (A Side/B Side)	Yr	NM
45s			
ELEKTRA			
❑ 45687	Go Back/Try	1970	6.00
❑ 45702	Lucy/Some Madness	1970	5.00
❑ 45716	Grab On/Can't Live My Life	1971	5.00
❑ 45754	It's So Hard/Tomorrow Is a New Day	1971	5.00
❑ 45781	Love Can Change Everything/Smokin' in the Mornin'	1972	5.00
Albums			
ELEKTRA			
❑ EKS-74067	Crabby Appleton	1970	15.00
❑ EKS-74106	Rotten to the Core!	1971	15.00

CRACK THE SKY

Number	Title (A Side/B Side)	Yr	NM
45s			
LIFESONG			
❑ 1763	Give Myself to You/A Night on the Town (With Snow White)	1978	4.00
❑ 1764	Long Nights/Give Myself to You	1978	4.00
❑ 1782	I Am the Walrus/Lighten Up McGraw	1979	4.00
❑ 45003	She's a Dancer/Robots for Ronnie	1976	4.00
❑ 45016	We Want Mine (We Don't Want Your Money)/Invaders from Mars	1976	4.00
❑ 45081	Techni-Generation/Suspicion	1980	4.00
Albums			
GRUDGE			
❑ 4500-1-F	From the Greenhouse	1989	10.00
LIFESONG			
❑ LS 6000	Crack the Sky	1975	15.00
❑ LS 6005	Animal Notes	1976	15.00
❑ LS 6015	Safety in Numbers	1978	15.00

Number	Title (A Side/B Side)	Yr	NM
❑ LS 8133	Photoflamingo	1981	10.00
❑ PZ 34994	Crack the Sky	1977	10.00
—Reissue of 6000			
❑ PZ 34998	Animal Notes	1977	10.00
—Reissue of 6004			
❑ PZ 35041	Safety in Numbers	1978	10.00
—Reissue of 6015			
❑ PZ 35620	Live Sky	1978	12.00

CRADDOCK, BILLY "CRASH" Also recorded as "Bill Craddock" and "Crash Craddock," both included below.

45s

ABC

Number	Title (A Side/B Side)	Yr	NM
❑ 11342	Afraid I'll Want to Love Her One More Time/Treat Her Right	1972	6.00
❑ 11349	Don't Be Angry/I'm a White Boy	1973	6.00
❑ 11364	Slippin' and Slidin'/ Living Example	1973	6.00
❑ 11379	'Till the Water Stops Runnin'/ What Does a Loser Say	1973	6.00
❑ 11412	Sweet Magnolia Blossom/ Home Is Such a Lonely Place to Go	1973	6.00
❑ 11437	Rub It In/It's Hard to Love a Hungry, Worried Man	1974	6.00
❑ 12013	Rub It In/It's Hard to Love a Hungry, Worried Man	1974	4.00
❑ 12036	Ruby, Baby/Walk When Love Walks	1974	5.00
❑ 12068	Still Thinkin' 'Bout You/Stay a Little Longer in Your Bed	1975	5.00
❑ 12104	I Love the Blues and the Boogie Woogie/No Deposit, No Return	1975	5.00
❑ 12335	Another Woman/The Words Still Rhyme	1978	4.00
❑ 12357	Think I'll Go Somewhere (And Cry Myself to Sleep)/ It All Came Back	1978	4.00
❑ 12384	Don Juan/Things Are Mostly Fine	1978	4.00

ABC DOT

Number	Title (A Side/B Side)	Yr	NM
❑ 17584	Easy As Pie/She's Mine	1975	5.00
❑ 17619	Walk Softly/She's About a Mover	1976	5.00
❑ 17635	You Rubbed It In All Wrong/ I Need Somebody to Love Me	1976	5.00
❑ 17659	Broken Down in Tiny Pieces/ Shake It Easy	1976	5.00
❑ 17682	Just a Little Thing/The First Time	1977	5.00
❑ 17701	A Tear Fell/A Piece of the Rock	1977	5.00
❑ 17723	The First Time/Walk When Love Walks	1977	5.00

ATLANTIC

Number	Title (A Side/B Side)	Yr	NM
❑ 88851	Just Another Miserable Day (Here in Paradise)/Softly Diana	1989	3.00
❑ 88851 [PS]	Just Another Miserable Day (Here in Paradise)/Softly Diana	1989	4.00

CAPITOL

Number	Title (A Side/B Side)	Yr	NM
❑ 4545	I Cheated on a Good Woman's Love/Not a Day Goes By	1978	4.00
❑ 4575	I've Been Too Long Lonely Baby/Jailhouse Rock	1978	4.00
❑ 4624	Hubba Hubba/Let's Go Back to the Beginning	1978	4.00
❑ 4672	If I Could Write a Song As Beautiful As You/Never Ending	1978	4.00
❑ 4707	My Mama Never Heard Me Sing/As Long As I Live	1979	4.00
❑ 4753	Robinhood/We Never Made It to Chicago	1979	4.00
❑ 4792	Till I Stop Shaking/Sneak Out of Love with You	1979	4.00
❑ 4838	I Just Had You on My Mind/ You Just Wanta Be Mine	1980	4.00
❑ 4875	Sea Cruise/She's Got Legs	1980	4.00
❑ 4935	A Real Cowboy (You Say You're)/One Dream Coming, One Dream Going	1980	4.00
❑ 4972	It Was You/Betty Ruth	1981	4.00
❑ 5011	I Just Need You For Tonight/ Leave Your Love A-Smokin'	1981	4.00
❑ 5051	Now That the Feeling's Gone/ She's Good to Me	1981	4.00
❑ 5139	Love Busted/Darlin' Take Care of Yourself	1982	4.00
❑ 5170	The New Will Never Wear Off on You/Hold Me Tight	1982	4.00

CARTWHEEL

Number	Title (A Side/B Side)	Yr	NM
❑ 193	Knock Three Times/ The Best I Ever Had	1971	7.00
❑ 196	Dream Lover/I Ran Out of Time	1971	7.00
❑ 201	You Better Move On/Confidence and Common Sense	1971	7.00
❑ 210	Ain't Nothin' Shakin' (But the Leaves on the Trees)/ She's My Angel	1972	7.00
❑ 216	I'm Gonna Knock on Your Door/ What He Don't Know	1972	7.00
❑ 222	Afraid I'll Want to Love Her One More Time/Treat Her Right	1972	12.00

CEE CEE

Number	Title (A Side/B Side)	Yr	NM
❑ 5400	Tell Me When I'm Hot/When the Feeling Is Right	1983	5.00

CHART

Number	Title (A Side/B Side)	Yr	NM
❑ 1004	Go On Home Girl/Learning to Live Without You	1967	8.00
❑ 1025	Your Love Is What Is/Anything That's Part of You	1968	8.00
❑ 1415	There Ought to Be a Law/ Two Arms Full of Lonely	1966	10.00
❑ 1450	Whipping Boy/The Love We Live Without	1967	10.00
❑ 5126	Go On Home Girl/Whipping Boy	1971	8.00
❑ 5154	Your Love Is What Is/ Whipping Boy	1972	8.00

COLONIAL

Number	Title (A Side/B Side)	Yr	NM
❑ 721	Bird Doggin'/Millionaire	1958	40.00

COLUMBIA

Number	Title (A Side/B Side)	Yr	NM
❑ 41316	Am I to Be the One/ I Miss You So Much	1959	25.00
❑ 41367	Sweetie Pie/Blabbermouth	1959	30.00
❑ 41470	Don't Destroy Me/ Boom Boom Baby	1959	25.00
❑ 41470 [PS]	Don't Destroy Me/ Boom Boom Baby	1959	50.00
❑ 41536	I Want That/Since She Turned Seventeen	1960	30.00
❑ 41619	All I Want Is You/Letter of Love	1960	25.00
❑ 41619 [PS]	All I Want Is You/Letter of Love	1960	50.00
❑ 41677	One Last Kiss/Is It True or False	1960	20.00
❑ 41822	Heavenly Love/Good Time Billy	1961	20.00

DATE

Number	Title (A Side/B Side)	Yr	NM
❑ 1007	Lulu Lee/Ah, Poor Little Baby	1958	40.00

KING

Number	Title (A Side/B Side)	Yr	NM
❑ 5912	Betty, Betty/Right Around the Corner	1964	25.00
❑ 5924	My Baby's Got Flat Feet/ One Heartache Too Many	1964	25.00
❑ 5964	Teardrops on Your Letter/ Love You More Everyday	1964	20.00

MERCURY

Number	Title (A Side/B Side)	Yr	NM
❑ 71811	Truly True/How Lonely He Must Be	1961	20.00
❑ 71862	A Diamond Is Forever/ Old King Cole	1962	25.00

Albums

ABC

Number	Title (A Side/B Side)	Yr	NM
❑ X-777	Two Sides of "Crash"	1973	15.00
—Retitled version of above			
❑ X-777	Afraid I'll Want to Love Her One More Time	1973	25.00
❑ X-788	Mr. Country Rock	1973	15.00
❑ X-817	Rub It In	1974	12.00
—Multicolor label			
❑ X-817	Rub It In	1974	15.00
—Black label			
❑ X-850	Greatest Hits — Vol. One	1975	12.00
❑ ABCD-875	Still Thinkin' Bout You	1975	12.00
❑ AB-1078	Billy "Crash" Craddock Sings His Greatest Hits	1978	10.00

ABC DOT

Number	Title (A Side/B Side)	Yr	NM
❑ DOSD-2040	Easy As Pie	1976	12.00
❑ 2063	Crash	1976	12.00
❑ 2082	Live!	1977	12.00

ATLANTIC

Number	Title (A Side/B Side)	Yr	NM
❑ 82012	Back on Track	1989	12.00

CAPITOL

Number	Title (A Side/B Side)	Yr	NM
❑ ST-11758	Billy "Crash" Craddock	1978	10.00
❑ SW-11853	Turning Up and Turning On	1978	10.00
❑ ST-11946	Laughing and Crying, Living and Dying	1979	10.00
❑ ST-12054	Changes	1980	10.00
❑ ST-12249	The New Will Never Wear Off	1981	10.00
❑ ST-12304	Greatest Hits	1983	10.00

CARTWHEEL

Number	Title (A Side/B Side)	Yr	NM
❑ 193	Knock Three Times	1971	20.00
❑ 05001	You Better Move On	1972	20.00

CHART

Number	Title (A Side/B Side)	Yr	NM
❑ 1053	The Best of Billy Crash Craddock	1973	15.00

HARMONY

Number	Title (A Side/B Side)	Yr	NM
❑ KH 32186	Billy "Crash" Craddock	1973	12.00

KING

Number	Title (A Side/B Side)	Yr	NM
❑ 912 [M]	I'm Tore Up	1964	100.00

MCA

Number	Title (A Side/B Side)	Yr	NM
❑ 662	Greatest Hits — Vol. One	1981	8.00
—Reissue of ABC 850			
❑ 663	Billy "Crash" Craddock Sings His Greatest Hits	1981	8.00
—Reissue of ABC 1078			
❑ 664	Easy As Pie	1981	8.00
—Reissue of ABC Dot 2040			
❑ 665	Live!	1981	8.00
—Reissue of ABC Dot 2082			
❑ 666	The First Time	1981	8.00
❑ 4165 [(2)]	The Best of Billy "Crash" Craddock	198?	12.00

MCA DOT

Number	Title (A Side/B Side)	Yr	NM
❑ 39054	Crash Craddock	1986	10.00

STARDAY

Number	Title (A Side/B Side)	Yr	NM
❑ 3005	16 Favorite Hits	1978	10.00

CRAIG, JIMMY

45s

BRILL

Number	Title (A Side/B Side)	Yr	NM
❑ 1	All for You/Gonna Love My Baby	1959	80.00

IMPERIAL

Number	Title (A Side/B Side)	Yr	NM
❑ 5592	Walking in Darkness/Oh Little Girl	1959	15.00

WARWICK

Number	Title (A Side/B Side)	Yr	NM
❑ 542	Drifter/Let Me Stay	1960	15.00

CRAIG, THE

45s

FONTANA

Number	Title (A Side/B Side)	Yr	NM
❑ 1579	I Must Be Mad/Suspense	1967	25.00

CRAMPS, THE

12-Inch Singles

ENIGMA

Number	Title (A Side/B Side)	Yr	NM
❑ EPRO253 [DJ]	Bikini Girls with Machine Guns (same on both sides)	1989	10.00
❑ EPRO 253 [DJ]	Bikini Girls with Machine Guns (same on both sides)	1989	12.00

45s

I.R.S.

Number	Title (A Side/B Side)	Yr	NM
❑ 9014	Garbage Man/Drug Train	1980	20.00
❑ 9014 [PS]	Garbage Man/Drug Train	1980	20.00
❑ 9021	Goo Goo Muck/She Said	1981	15.00
❑ 9021 [PS]	Goo Goo Muck/She Said	1981	15.00

MEDICINE LABEL

Number	Title (A Side/B Side)	Yr	NM
❑ 17932	Naked Girl Falling Down the Stairs/Confessions of a Psycho Cat	1995	7.00
❑ 17976	Ultra Twist/No Club Low Wolf	1995	7.00
❑ 18045	Let's Get F*cked Up/How Come You Do Me	1994	5.00

VENGEANCE

Number	Title (A Side/B Side)	Yr	NM
❑ 666	Surfin' Bird/The Way I Walk	1978	50.00
❑ 666 [PS]	Surfin' Bird/The Way I Walk	1978	60.00
❑ 668	Human Fly/Domino	1978	50.00
❑ 668 [PS]	Human Fly/Domino	1978	60.00
❑ 676	Big Black Witchcraft Rock/ Butcher Pete	2003	7.00
—Red vinyl			
❑ 676 [PS]	Big Black Witchcraft Rock/ Butcher Pete	2003	7.00

Albums

ENIGMA

Number	Title (A Side/B Side)	Yr	NM
❑ 21	Smell of Female	1983	15.00
❑ 268 [DJ]	Stay Sick!	1990	20.00
—Promo-only version			
❑ EPRO 268 [DJ]	Stay Sick!	1990	25.00
—Promo-only version			
❑ 73543	Stay Sick!	1990	15.00

EPITAPH

Number	Title (A Side/B Side)	Yr	NM
❑ 86449	Flamejob	199?	12.00
—Reissue of Medicine Label 24592			
❑ 86516	Big Beat from Badsville	1997	12.00

I.R.S.

Number	Title (A Side/B Side)	Yr	NM
❑ SP-007	Songs the Lord Taught Us	1980	20.00
❑ SP-501 [EP]	Gravest Hits	1979	25.00
❑ SP-70007	Songs the Lord Taught Us	198?	12.00
—Reissue of 007			
❑ SP-70016	Psychedelic Jungle	1981	20.00
❑ SP-70042	Bad Music for Bad People	1984	15.00
❑ SP-70501 [EP]	Gravest Hits	198?	10.00
—Reissue of 501			

MEDICINE LABEL

Number	Title (A Side/B Side)	Yr	NM
❑ 24592	Flamejob	1994	15.00

CRANE, BOB

45s

EPIC

Number	Title (A Side/B Side)	Yr	NM
❑ 10038	Theme from Get Smart/ Happy Feet	1966	12.00
❑ 10038 [PS]	Theme from Get Smart/ Happy Feet	1966	30.00
❑ 10108	Theme from Hogan's Heroes/ Theme from "F" Troop	1966	12.00

Number	Title (A Side/B Side)	Yr	NM

Albums

EPIC

Number	Title (A Side/B Side)	Yr	NM
❑ LN 24224 [M]	The Funny Side of TV	1966	25.00
❑ BN 26224 [S]	The Funny Side of TV	1966	30.00

CRANE, LES

45s

WARNER BROS.

Number	Title (A Side/B Side)	Yr	NM
❑ 7520	Desiderata/A Different Drummer	1971	5.00
❑ 7520 [PS]	Desiderata/A Different Drummer	1971	6.00
❑ 7548	Desiderata (Spanish)/ Desiderata (English)	1972	6.00
❑ 7582	Children Learn What They Live/ The Wilderness	1972	4.00

Albums

WARNER BROS.

Number	Title (A Side/B Side)	Yr	NM
❑ BS 2570	Desiderata	1971	10.00
❑ SW-94266	Desiderata	1972	12.00
—Capitol Record Club edition			

CRANE, SHERRY

45s

SUN

Number	Title (A Side/B Side)	Yr	NM
❑ 328	Willie Willie/Winnie the Parakeet	1959	25.00

CRAWFORD, BOBBY

Also see THE CRAWFORD BROTHERS.

45s

DEL-FI

Number	Title (A Side/B Side)	Yr	NM
❑ 4211	Mrs. Smith, Please Wake Up/ That Little Old Lovemaker Me	1963	15.00
❑ 4236	I Want to Be a Good Guy/ (B-side unknown)	1964	15.00

CRAWFORD, CAROLYN

45s

MERCURY

Number	Title (A Side/B Side)	Yr	NM
❑ 74036	Coming On Strong/ Love Song for You	1978	5.00
—Mercury titles as "Caroline Crawford"			
❑ 74054	You'll Wait/Breakdown	1979	5.00
❑ 76013	The Strut/I'll Be Here for You	1979	5.00

MOTOWN

Number	Title (A Side/B Side)	Yr	NM
❑ 1050	Forget About Me/ Devil in His Heart	1963	40.00
❑ 1064	My Smile Is Just a Frown (Turned Upside Down)/I'll Come Running	1964	20.00
—Revised version of A-side title			
❑ 1064	My Smile Is Just a Frown Turned Upside Down/ I'll Come Running	1964	50.00
—Original version of A-side title			
❑ 1070	My Heart/When Someone's Good to You	1964	40.00

PHILADELPHIA INT'L.

Number	Title (A Side/B Side)	Yr	NM
❑ 3553	Just Got to Be More Careful/ Saving All the Love I Got for You	1974	5.00
❑ 3570	It Takes Two to Make One/ No Matter How Bad Things Are, I Still Love You	1975	5.00
❑ 3580	Good & Plenty/If You Move, You Lose	1975	5.00

CRAWFORD, HANK

45s

ATLANTIC

Number	Title (A Side/B Side)	Yr	NM
❑ 5013	Misty (Part 1)/Misty (Part 2)	1961	10.00
❑ 5016	Easy Living/Playmates	1961	10.00
❑ 5022	Don't Cry Baby/The Peeper	1962	10.00
❑ 5030	Blueberry Hill/Any Time	1963	10.00
❑ 5033	Skunky Green/Whispering Grass	1963	10.00
❑ 5039	Shake a-Plenty/Mellow Down	1964	10.00
❑ 5042	Merry Christmas Baby/ Read 'Em and Weep	1964	10.00
❑ 5049	Don't Get Around Much Anymore/Bluff City Blues	1966	8.00
❑ 5066	Soul Shoutin'/Who Can I Turn To When Nobody Needs Me	1968	8.00
❑ 5079	Smoky City/Hush Puppies	1969	8.00

KUDU

Number	Title (A Side/B Side)	Yr	NM
❑ 905	Brian's Song/In the Wee Small Hours of the Morning	1972	5.00
❑ 908	Help Me Make It Through the Night/Uncle Funky	1972	5.00
❑ 911	The Christmas Song/ Winter Wonderland	1974	5.00
❑ 923	Sho Is Funky/(B-side unknown)	1975	5.00
❑ 944	Daytime Friends/I Don't Want No Happy Songs	1978	5.00

Albums

ATLANTIC

Number	Title (A Side/B Side)	Yr	NM
❑ SD 2-315 [(2)]	The Art of Hank Crawford	1973	15.00
❑ 1356 [M]	More Soul	1960	20.00
—Purple and red label, white fan logo			
❑ 1356 [M]	More Soul	1962	12.00
—Purple and red label, black fan logo			
❑ SD 1356 [S]	More Soul	1960	25.00
—Green and blue label, white fan logo			
❑ SD 1356 [S]	More Soul	1962	15.00
—Green and blue label, black fan logo			
❑ 1372 [M]	The Soul Clinic	1961	20.00
—Purple and red label, white fan logo			
❑ 1372 [M]	The Soul Clinic	1962	12.00
—Purple and red label, black fan logo			
❑ SD 1372 [S]	The Soul Clinic	1961	25.00
—Green and blue label, white fan logo			
❑ SD 1372 [S]	The Soul Clinic	1962	15.00
—Green and blue label, black fan logo			
❑ 1387 [M]	From the Heart	1962	15.00
❑ SD 1387 [S]	From the Heart	1962	20.00
❑ 1405 [M]	Soul of the Ballad	1963	15.00
❑ SD 1405 [S]	Soul of the Ballad	1963	20.00
❑ 1423 [M]	True Blue	1964	15.00
❑ SD 1423 [S]	True Blue	1964	20.00
❑ 1436 [M]	Dig These Blues	1965	15.00
❑ SD 1436 [S]	Dig These Blues	1965	20.00
❑ 1455 [M]	After Hours	1966	15.00
❑ SD 1455 [S]	After Hours	1966	20.00
❑ 1470 [M]	Mr. Blues	1967	20.00
❑ SD 1470 [S]	Mr. Blues	1967	15.00
❑ SD 1503	Double Cross	1968	25.00
❑ SD 1523	Mr. Blues Plays Lady Soul	1969	15.00
❑ SD 1557	The Best of Hank Crawford	1970	15.00

COTILLION

Number	Title (A Side/B Side)	Yr	NM
❑ SD 18003	It's a Funky Thing to Do	1971	20.00

KUDU

Number	Title (A Side/B Side)	Yr	NM
❑ KU-06	Help Me Make It Through the Night	1972	20.00
❑ KU-08	We've Got a Good Thing	1973	20.00
❑ KU-15	Wildflower	1974	20.00
❑ KU-19	Don't You Worry 'Bout a Thing	1975	20.00
❑ KU-26	I Hear a Symphony	1976	20.00
❑ KU-33	Hank Crawford's Back	1977	15.00
❑ KU-35	Tico Rico	1977	15.00
❑ KU-39	Cajun Sunrise	1979	15.00

MILESTONE

Number	Title (A Side/B Side)	Yr	NM
❑ M-9112	Midnight Ramble	1983	10.00
❑ M-9119	Indigo Blue	1984	10.00
❑ M-9129	Down on the Deuce	1985	10.00
❑ M-9140	Roadhouse Symphony	1986	10.00
❑ M-9149	Mr. Chips	1987	10.00
❑ M-9168	Night Beat	1988	10.00
❑ M-9182	Groove Master	1990	12.00

MOBILE FIDELITY

Number	Title (A Side/B Side)	Yr	NM
❑ 1-224	Soul of the Ballad	1995	25.00
—Audiophile vinyl			

CRAWFORD, HANK, AND JIMMY MCGRIFF

Also see each artist's individual listings.

Albums

MILESTONE

Number	Title (A Side/B Side)	Yr	NM
❑ M-9142	Soul Survivors	1986	10.00
❑ M-9153	Steppin' Up	1988	10.00
❑ M-9177	On the Blue Side	1990	12.00

CRAWFORD, JOHNNY

Also see THE CRAWFORD BROTHERS.

45s

DEL-FI

Number	Title (A Side/B Side)	Yr	NM
❑ 4162	Daydreams/So Goes the Story	1961	15.00
❑ 4162 [PS]	Daydreams/So Goes the Story	1961	25.00
❑ 4165	Your Love Is Growing Cold/ Treasure	1961	15.00
❑ 4165 [PS]	Your Love Is Growing Cold/ Treasure	1961	25.00
❑ 4172	Patti Ann/Donna	1962	15.00
❑ 4178	Cindy's Birthday/ Something Special	1962	15.00
❑ 4178 [PS]	Cindy's Birthday/ Something Special	1962	25.00
❑ 4181	Your Nose Is Gonna Grow/ Mr. Blue	1962	15.00
❑ 4181 [PS]	Your Nose Is Gonna Grow/ Mr. Blue	1962	25.00
❑ 4188	Rumors/No One Really Loves a Clown	1962	15.00
❑ 4188 [PS]	Rumors/No One Really Loves a Clown	1962	25.00
❑ 4193	Proud/Lonesome Town	1963	15.00
❑ 4203	Cry on My Shoulder/ When I Fall in Love	1963	15.00
❑ 4215	What Happened to Janie/ Petite Chanson	1963	15.00
❑ 4221	Cindy's Gonna Cry/Debbie	1963	15.00
❑ 4229	Sandy/Ol' Shorty	1963	15.00
❑ 4231	Judy Loves Me/Living in the Past	1963	15.00
❑ 4242	The Girl Next Door (Once Upon a Time)/Sittin' and Watchin'	1964	15.00
❑ 4305	Am I Too Young/Janie Please Believe It	1965	15.00

SIDEWALK

Number	Title (A Side/B Side)	Yr	NM
❑ 932	Angelica/Everybody Has Their Day	1968	12.00
❑ 941	Good Guys Finish Last/Everyone Should Own a Dream	1968	12.00

WYNNE

Number	Title (A Side/B Side)	Yr	NM
❑ 124	Dance with the Dolly (With the Hole in Her Stocking)/Ask	1958	20.00

Albums

DEL-FI

Number	Title (A Side/B Side)	Yr	NM
❑ DFLP-1220 [M]	The Captivating Johnny Crawford	1962	40.00
❑ DFLP-1223 [M]	A Young Man's Fancy	1962	30.00
❑ DFST-1223 [S]	A Young Man's Fancy	1962	40.00
❑ DFLP-1224 [M]	Rumors	1963	30.00
❑ DFST-1224 [S]	Rumors	1963	40.00
❑ DFLP-1229 [M]	His Greatest Hits	1963	30.00
❑ DFST-1229 [S]	His Greatest Hits	1963	40.00
❑ DFLP-1248 [M]	Greatest Hits, Vol. 2	1964	20.00
❑ DFST-1248 [S]	Greatest Hits, Vol. 2	1964	25.00

GUEST STAR

Number	Title (A Side/B Side)	Yr	NM
❑ GS-1470 [M]	Johnny Crawford	196?	20.00
❑ GSS-1470 [S]	Johnny Crawford	196?	25.00

RHINO

Number	Title (A Side/B Side)	Yr	NM
❑ RNDF-202	The Best of Johnny Crawford	1982	12.00

SUPREME

Number	Title (A Side/B Side)	Yr	NM
❑ M-110 [M]	Songs from "The Restless Ones"	1965	20.00
❑ MS-210 [S]	Songs from "The Restless Ones"	1965	25.00

CRAWFORD, ODESSA

45s

HIT

Number	Title (A Side/B Side)	Yr	NM
❑ 289	I Never Loved a Man the Way I Love You/Bernadette	1967	8.00
—B-side by the Fantastics			

CRAWFORD BROTHERS, THE

Also see BOBBY CRAWFORD; JOHNNY CRAWFORD.

45s

DEL-FI

Number	Title (A Side/B Side)	Yr	NM
❑ 4191	Good Buddies/You Gotta Wear Shoes	1963	15.00
❑ 4191 [PS]	Good Buddies/You Gotta Wear Shoes	1963	25.00

CRAWLER

See BACK STREET CRAWLER.

CRAYNE, LESLIE 'UGGAMS'

See LESLIE UGGAMS.

CRAYONS, THE

45s

COUNSEL

Number	Title (A Side/B Side)	Yr	NM
❑ 122	Love at First Sight/I Saw You	1963	30.00

CRAYTON, PEE WEE

45s

ALADDIN

Number	Title (A Side/B Side)	Yr	NM
❑ 3112	When It Rains It Pours/Daybreak	1952	100.00
❑ 3112	When It Rains It Pours/Daybreak	1952	1500.
—Green vinyl			

EDCO

Number	Title (A Side/B Side)	Yr	NM
❑ 1009	Ev'ry Night About This Time/ (B-side unknown)	196?	25.00
❑ 1010	Money Tree/When Darkness Falls	196?	25.00

FOX

Number	Title (A Side/B Side)	Yr	NM
❑ 10069	Give Me One More Chance/ (B-side unknown)	196?	30.00

GUYDEN

Number	Title (A Side/B Side)	Yr	NM
❑ 2048	I'm Still in Love with You/ Time on My Hands	1961	15.00

IMPERIAL

Number	Title (A Side/B Side)	Yr	NM
❑ 5288	Do Unto Others/Every Dog Has a Day	1954	200.00
❑ 5297	Wine-O/Hurry Hurry	1954	500.00
❑ 5321	I Need Your Love/ You Know — Yeah	1955	50.00
❑ 5338	My Idea About You/ I Got News for You	1955	50.00
❑ 5345	Eyes Full of Tears/Runnin' Wild	1955	50.00
❑ 5353	Yours Truly/Be Faithful	1955	50.00

JAMIE

Number	Title (A Side/B Side)	Yr	NM
❑ 1190	'Tain't Nobody's Business If I Do/Little Bitty Things	1961	15.00

MODERN

Number	Title (A Side/B Side)	Yr	NM
❑ 892	Cool Evening/Have You Lost Your Love for Me	1951	100.00

POST

Number	Title (A Side/B Side)	Yr	NM
❑ 2007	Don't Go/I Must Go On	1955	40.00

Except when noted otherwise, VG = 25% of NM, and VG+ = 50% of NM. (Example: VG = $2.00, VG+ = $4.00 and NM = $8.00.)

Number	Title (A Side/B Side)	Yr	NM
RECORDED IN HOLLYWOOD			
❑ 408	Pappy's Blues/Crying and Walking	1954	100.00
❑ 426	Baby Pat the Floor/ I'm Your Prisoner	1954	100.00
SMASH			
❑ 1774	Sabre Twist/Hillbilly Blues	1962	12.00
VEE JAY			
❑ 214	A Frosty Night/The Telephone Is Ringing	1956	40.00
❑ 252	I Don't Care/I Found My Peace of Mind	1957	40.00
❑ 266	Fiddle Dee Dee/Is This the Price I Pay	1957	40.00
Albums			
CROWN			
❑ CLP-5175 [M]	Pee Wee Crayton	1959	100.00
—Black label			
❑ CLP-5175 [M]	Pee Wee Crayton	196?	20.00
—Gray label			
VANGUARD			
❑ VSD-6566	The Things I Used to Do	1971	15.00

CRAZY ELEPHANT

Number	Title (A Side/B Side)	Yr	NM
45s			
BELL			
❑ 763	Gimme Gimme Good Lovin'/ Dark Part of My Mind	1969	8.00
❑ 804	Pam/Sunshine, Red Wine	1969	6.00
❑ 817	Gimme Some More/ My Babe (Honey Pie)	1969	6.00
❑ 846	There's a Better Day a-Comin' (Na, Na, Na, Na)/Space Buggy	1969	6.00
❑ 875	Land Rover/There Ain't No Umbopo	1970	6.00
Albums			
BELL			
❑ 6034	Crazy Elephant	1969	20.00

CRAZY HORSE Also see NEIL YOUNG.

Number	Title (A Side/B Side)	Yr	NM
45s			
EPIC			
❑ 10925	Rock and Roll Band/ Outside Lookin' In	1972	5.00
M.O.C.			
❑ 671	Love/High on Lovin'	1967	12.00
REPRISE			
❑ 1007	Downtown/Crow Jane Lady	1971	5.00
❑ 1025	Dance, Dance, Dance/Carolay	1971	5.00
❑ 1046	Beggars Day/Dirty, Dirty	1971	5.00
❑ 1075	All Alone Now/One Thing I Love	1972	5.00
Albums			
EPIC			
❑ KE 31710	Crazy Horse at Crooked Lake	1972	15.00
—Yellow label			
❑ KE 31710	Crazy Horse at Crooked Lake	1973	12.00
—Orange label			
RCA VICTOR			
❑ AFL1-3054	Crazy Moon	1978	12.00
REPRISE			
❑ MS 2059	Loose	1972	15.00
❑ RS 6438	Crazy Horse	1971	15.00

CREACH, PAPA JOHN Also see HOT TUNA; JEFFERSON AIRPLANE; JEFFERSON STARSHIP.

Number	Title (A Side/B Side)	Yr	NM
45s			
BUDDAH			
❑ 509	I'm the Fiddle Man/Joyce	1975	4.00
DJM			
❑ 1102	All the World Loves a Winner/ Southern Strut	1979	4.00
GRUNT			
❑ 65-0501	Over the Rainbow/The Janitor Drives a Cadillac	1971	5.00
❑ 65-0505	Papa John's Down Home Blues/String Jet Rock	1971	5.00
❑ 65-0508	Filthy Funky (Part 1)/ Filthy Funky (Part 2)	1972	5.00
Albums			
BUDDAH			
❑ BDS-5649	I'm the Fiddle Man	1975	12.00
❑ BDS-5660	Rock Father	1977	12.00
DJM			
❑ 11	Cat & Fiddle	1977	12.00
❑ 18	Inphasion	1978	12.00
GRUNT			
❑ BFL1-0418	Playing My Fiddle for You	1974	15.00
❑ BXL1-1003	Papa John Creach	197?	12.00
—Reissue with new prefix			
❑ FTR-1003	Papa John Creach	1971	15.00
❑ BXL1-1009	Filthy!	197?	12.00
—Reissue with new prefix			
❑ FTR-1009	Filthy!	1972	15.00

CREAM Also see GINGER BAKER'S AIR FORCE; JACK BRUCE; ERIC CLAPTON.

Number	Title (A Side/B Side)	Yr	NM
45s			
ATCO			
❑ 6462	I Feel Free/N.S.U.	1967	15.00
❑ 6488	Strange Brew/Tales of Brave Ulysses	1967	15.00
❑ 6522	Spoonful/Spoonful (Part 2)	1967	15.00
❑ 6544	Sunshine of Your Love/ SWLABR	1968	8.00
❑ 6575	Anyone for Tennis/Pressed Rat and Warthog	1968	8.00
❑ 6617	White Room/Those Were the Days	1968	8.00
❑ 6646	Crossroads/Passing the Time	1969	8.00
❑ 6668	Badge/What a Bringdown	1969	8.00
❑ 6708	Sweet Wine/Lawdy Mama	1969	10.00
Albums			
ATCO			
❑ 33-206 [M]	Fresh Cream	1967	50.00
❑ SD 33-206 [S]	Fresh Cream	1967	30.00
—Purple and brown labels			
❑ SD 33-206 [S]	Fresh Cream	1969	15.00
—Yellow labels			
❑ 33-232 [M]	Disraeli Gears	1967	50.00
❑ SD 33-232 [S]	Disraeli Gears	1967	30.00
—Purple and brown labels			
❑ SD 33-232 [S]	Disraeli Gears	1969	15.00
—Yellow labels			
❑ SD 33-291	Best of Cream	1969	25.00
❑ SD 33-328	Live Cream	1970	25.00
❑ 2-700 [(2)M]	Wheels of Fire	1968	200.00
—White label promo; no stock copies are mono			
❑ SD 2-700 [(2)S]	Wheels of Fire	1968	50.00
—Purple and brown labels; foil-like cover			
❑ SD 2-700 [(2)S]	Wheels of Fire	1969	20.00
—Yellow labels; dull gray cover			
❑ SD 7001	Goodbye	1969	15.00
—Yellow labels			
❑ SD 7001	Goodbye	1969	30.00
—Purple and brown labels; deduct 33% if poster is missing			
❑ SD 7005	Live Cream — Vol. II	1972	25.00
DCC COMPACT CLASSICS			
❑ LPZ-2015	Fresh Cream	1996	100.00
—Audiophile vinyl			
MOBILE FIDELITY			
❑ 2-066 [(2)]	Wheels of Fire	1980	90.00
—Audiophile vinyl			
❑ 1-264	Goodbye	1996	—
—Audiophile vinyl; canceled			
POLYDOR			
❑ 24-3502 [(2)]	Heavy Cream	1972	15.00
❑ 24-5529	Off the Top	1973	15.00
❑ 1775315 [S]	Disraeli Gears	2008	20.00
❑ 8275781 [(2)S]	Wheels of Fire	2009	30.00
REPRISE			
❑ 49416-1 [(3)]	Royal Albert Hall London May 2-3-5-6 2005	2005	50.00
—Box set; contains three 180-gram LPs, each in its own cardboard cover, plus a 12x12 cardboard poster and bubble padding			
RSO			
❑ 015 [(2)DJ]	Classic Cuts	1978	40.00
—Promo-only compilation			
❑ RS-1-3009	Fresh Cream	1977	12.00
❑ RS-1-3010	Disraeli Gears	1977	12.00
❑ RS-1-3012	Best of Cream	1977	12.00
❑ RS-1-3013	Goodbye	1977	12.00
❑ RS-1-3014	Live Cream	1977	12.00
❑ RS-1-3015	Live Cream — Vol. 2	1977	12.00
❑ RS-2-3802 [(2)]	Wheels of Fire	1977	15.00
SPRINGBOARD			
❑ SPB 4037	Early Cream	1972	15.00

CREATION, THE

Number	Title (A Side/B Side)	Yr	NM
45s			
DECCA			
❑ 32155	If I Stay Too Long/Nightmares	1967	12.00
❑ 32227	How Does It Feel to Feel/ Life Is Just Beginning	1967	12.00
PLANET			
❑ 116	Making Time/Try and Stop Me	1966	15.00
❑ 119	Painter Man/Biff Bang Pow	1966	15.00

CREATION OF SUNLIGHT

Number	Title (A Side/B Side)	Yr	NM
Albums			
WINDI			
❑ 1001	Creation of Sunlight	1968	600.00

CREATIONS, THE Many different groups.

Number	Title (A Side/B Side)	Yr	NM
45s			
GLOBE			
❑ 102	Just Remember Me/ Times Are Changing	1967	20.00
❑ 103	I've Got to Find Her/ Times Are Changing	1967	20.00
❑ 1000	Oh Baby/Plenty of Love	1967	20.00
JAMIE			
❑ 1197	The Bells/Shang Shang	1961	25.00
LIDO			
❑ 501	You Are My Darling/There Goes the Girl I Love	1956	300.00
MEL-O-DY			
❑ 101	This Is Our Night/You're My Inspiration	1962	—
MERIDIAN			
❑ 7550	The Wedding/I've Got a Feeling	1962	100.00
PATTI-JO			
❑ 1703	Seventeen/You'll Always Be Mine	1962	200.00
PENNY			
❑ 9022	Lady Luck/We're in Love	1962	60.00
PINE CREST			
❑ 101	Woke Up in the Morning/ Strolling Through the Park	1961	400.00
RADIANT			
❑ 103	Don't Listen to What Others Say/Don't Listen to What Others Say, Part 2	1964	25.00
TAKE TEN			
❑ 1501	Lady Luck/We're in Love	1963	30.00
TIP TOP			
❑ 400	Every Night I Pray/Mommy and Daddy	1956	200.00
❑ 501	You Are My Darling/There Goes the Girl I Love	1956	200.00
—At least one source claims this is a bootleg.			
TOP HAT			
❑ 1003	Crash/Chickie Darling	1964	40.00
❑ 1003 [PS]	Crash/Chickie Darling	1964	80.00
❑ 1004	Don't Be Mean/41 Willies	1965	50.00
❑ 1004 [PS]	Don't Be Mean/41 Willies	1965	100.00
VIRTUE			
❑ 2517	I'm So in Love with You/Save the People	1971	6.00
❑ 2518	Don't Let Me Down/ The Price I Have to Pay	1971	6.00
❑ 2520	Nothing Too Good for You/ You Mean So Much	1972	6.00
❑ 2521	You Make Me Feel So Good/ That's How Strong My Love Is	1972	6.00
❑ 2522	How Sweetly Simple/ Lovin' Simple	1973	6.00
ZODIAC			
❑ 1005	A Dream/Foot Steps	1967	8.00

CREATIVE SOURCE

Number	Title (A Side/B Side)	Yr	NM
45s			
POLYDOR			
❑ 14291	Pass the Feelin' On/Turn On to Music	1975	5.00
❑ 14334	I'll Find You Anywhere/ Singin' Funky Music	1976	—
—Canceled			
SUSSEX			
❑ 501	You Can't Hide Love/Lovesville	1973	5.00
❑ 508	You're Too Good to Be True/ Oh Love	1973	5.00
❑ 509	Who Is He and What Is He to You (Part 1)/Who Is He and What Is He to You (Part 2)	1974	5.00
❑ 622	Keep On Movin'/I Just Can't See Myself Without You	1974	5.00
❑ 632	Migration/I Just Can't See Myself Without You	1974	5.00
Albums			
POLYDOR			
❑ PD-1-6052	Pass the Feelin' On	1975	12.00
❑ PD-1-6065	Consider the Source	1976	12.00
SUSSEX			
❑ SUS-8027	Creative Source	1973	15.00
❑ SUS-8035	Migration	1974	15.00

CREATORS, THE (1)

Number	Title (A Side/B Side)	Yr	NM
45s			
DOOTO			
❑ 463	I've Had You/Drafted, Volunteered, Enlisted	1961	25.00

Creedence Clearwater Revival, "Travelin' Band," Fantasy 637, 1970, **$12.**

Number	Title (A Side/B Side)	Yr	NM
DORE			
❑ 635	Too Far to Turn Around/Hello There, Mister Grave Digger	1962	60.00

CREATORS, THE (2)

45s

Number	Title (A Side/B Side)	Yr	NM
EPIC			
❑ 9605	Crazy Love/Cross Fire	1963	15.00
HI-Q			
❑ 5021	Wear My Ring/Booga Bear	1961	25.00
—Bold print label			
❑ 5021	Wear My Ring/Booga Bear	1961	80.00
—Normal print label			
TIME			
❑ 1038	Do You Remember/There's Going to Be an Angel	1961	25.00

CREATORS, THE (3)

45s

Number	Title (A Side/B Side)	Yr	NM
PHILIPS			
❑ 40058	Boy, He's Got It/Yeah, He's Got It	1962	25.00
❑ 40083	I'll Stay Home (New Year's Eve)/Shoom Ba Boom	1962	300.00
T-KAY			
❑ 110	I'll Never, Never Do It Again/Boy, He's Got It!	1962	80.00

CREATURES, THE

45s

Number	Title (A Side/B Side)	Yr	NM
COLUMBIA			
❑ 43689	Night Is Warm/String Along	1966	10.00
❑ 43894	Looking at Tomorrow/Someone Needs You	1967	8.00

CREEDENCE CLEARWATER REVIVAL

Also see DOUG CLIFFORD; JOHN FOGERTY; TOM FOGERTY; TOMMY FOGERTY AND THE BLUE VELVETS; THE GOLLIWOGS.

12-Inch Singles

Number	Title (A Side/B Side)	Yr	NM
FANTASY			
❑ 759-D-LP [DJ]	I Heard It Through the Grapevine (11:05) (same on both sides)	1976	20.00

45s

Number	Title (A Side/B Side)	Yr	NM
FANTASY			
❑ 616	Suzie Q (Part One)/Suzie Q (Part Two)	1968	6.00
❑ 617	I Put a Spell on You/Walk on the Water	1968	8.00
❑ 619	Proud Mary/Born on the Bayou	1969	6.00
❑ 622	Bad Moon Rising/Lodi	1969	6.00
❑ 625	Green River/Commotion	1969	6.00
❑ 634	Down on the Corner/Fortunate Son	1969	6.00
❑ 634 [PS]	Down on the Corner/Fortunate Son	1969	12.00
❑ 637	Travelin' Band/Who'll Stop the Rain	1970	6.00
❑ 637 [PS]	Travelin' Band/Who'll Stop the Rain	1970	12.00
❑ 641	Up Around the Bend/Run Through the Jungle	1970	6.00
❑ 641 [PS]	Up Around the Bend/Run Through the Jungle	1970	12.00
❑ 645	Lookin' Out My Back Door/Long As I Can See the Light	1970	6.00
❑ 645 [PS]	Lookin' Out My Back Door/Long As I Can See the Light	1970	12.00
❑ 655	Have You Ever Seen the Rain/Hey Tonight	1971	6.00
❑ 665	Sweet Hitch-Hiker/Door to Door	1971	6.00
❑ 665 [PS]	Sweet Hitch-Hiker/Door to Door	1971	12.00
❑ 676	Someday Never Comes/Tearin' Up the Country	1972	6.00
❑ 759	I Heard It Through the Grapevine/Good Golly Miss Molly	1976	4.00
❑ 759 [PS]	I Heard It Through the Grapevine/Good Golly Miss Molly	1976	5.00
❑ 908	Tombstone Shadow/Commotion	1981	4.00
❑ 917	Medley U.S.A./Bad Moon Rising	1981	4.00
❑ 920	Cotton Fields/Lodi	1981	4.00
❑ 957	Medley (from "I Heard It Through the Grapevine" to "Up Around the Bend")/Medley (from "Proud Mary" to "Lodi")	1985	10.00
❑ 2832/3 [DJ]	45 Revolutions Per Minute (Part 1)/45 Revolutions Per Minute (Part 2)	1970	40.00
❑ 2832/3 [PS]	45 Revolutions Per Minute (Part 1)/45 Revolutions Per Minute (Part 2)	1970	60.00
SCORPIO			
❑ 412	Porterville/Call It Pretending	1968	80.00

Albums

Number	Title	Yr	NM
ANALOGUE PRODUCTIONS			
❑ AAPP-8382	Creedence Clearwater Revival	2002	25.00
—Audiophile edition on heavy vinyl			
❑ AAPP-8387	Bayou Country	2002	25.00
—Audiophile edition on heavy vinyl			
❑ AAPP-8393	Green River	2002	25.00
—Audiophile edition on heavy vinyl			
❑ AAPP-8397	Willie and the Poor Boys	2002	25.00
—Audiophile edition on heavy vinyl			
❑ AAPP-8402	Cosmo's Factory	2002	25.00
—Audiophile edition on heavy vinyl			
❑ AAPP-9404	Mardi Gras	2002	25.00
—Audiophile edition on heavy vinyl			
DCC COMPACT CLASSICS			
❑ LPZ-2019	Willie and the Poor Boys	1996	50.00
—Audiophile vinyl			
FANTASY			
❑ CCR-1 [(2)]	Live in Europe	1973	12.00
❑ CCR-2 [(2)]	Chronicle (The 20 Greatest Hits)	1976	15.00
—Brown labels			
❑ CCR-2 [(2)]	Chronicle (The 20 Greatest Hits)	1979	12.00
—Whitish or light blue labels			
❑ CCR-3 [(2)]	Chronicle, Vol. 2	1987	15.00
❑ CCR-68 [(2)]	Creedence Clearwater Revival 1968/69	1981	12.00
—Compilation of 8382 and 8387			
❑ CCR-69 [(2)]	Creedence Clearwater Revival 1969	1981	12.00
—Compilation of 8393 and 8397			
❑ CCR-70 [(2)]	Creedence Clearwater Revival 1970	1981	12.00
—Compilation of 8402 and 8410			
❑ FPM-4001 [Q]	Creedence Gold	1975	50.00
❑ MPF-4501	The Royal Albert Hall Concert	1980	15.00
—Album withdrawn and changed when it was discovered this didn't come from the Royal Albert Hall			
❑ MPF-4501	The Concert	1981	10.00
—Retitled version			
❑ MPF-4509	Creedence Country	1981	10.00
❑ ORC-4512	Creedence Clearwater Revival	1981	8.00
—Reissue of 8382			
❑ ORC-4513	Bayou Country	1981	8.00
—Reissue of 8387			
❑ ORC-4514	Green River	1981	8.00
—Reissue of 8393			
❑ ORC-4515	Willy and the Poor Boys	1981	8.00
—Reissue of 8397			
❑ ORC-4516	Cosmo's Factory	1981	8.00
—Reissue of 8402			
❑ ORC-4517	Pendulum	1981	8.00
—Reissue of 8410			
❑ ORC-4518	Mardi Gras	1981	8.00
—Reissue of 9404			
❑ MPF-4522	The Movie Album	1985	8.00
❑ ORC-4526 [(2)]	Live in Europe	1986	10.00
❑ F-8382	Creedence Clearwater Revival	1968	15.00
—With "Susie Q" mentioned on the front cover; dark blue label			
❑ F-8382	Creedence Clearwater Revival	1968	25.00
—With no reference to "Susie Q" on the front cover			
❑ F-8382	Creedence Clearwater Revival	1973	10.00
—Brown label			
❑ F-8382 [DJ]	Creedence Clearwater Revival	1968	80.00
—White label promo			
❑ F-8387	Bayou Country	1969	15.00
—Dark blue label			
❑ F-8387	Bayou Country	1973	10.00
—Brown label			
❑ F-8387 [DJ]	Bayou Country	1969	80.00
—White label promo			
❑ F-8393	Green River	1969	15.00
—Dark blue label			
❑ F-8393	Green River	1973	10.00
—Brown label			
❑ F-8393 [DJ]	Green River	1969	80.00
—White label promo			
❑ F-8397	Willy and the Poor Boys	1969	15.00
—Dark blue label			
❑ F-8397	Willy and the Poor Boys	1973	10.00
—Brown label			
❑ F-8397 [DJ]	Willy and the Poor Boys	1969	80.00
—White label promo			

Except when noted otherwise, VG = 25% of NM, and VG+ = 50% of NM. (Example: VG = $2.00, VG+ = $4.00 and NM = $8.00.)

Number	Title (A Side/B Side)	Yr	NM
❑ F-8402	Cosmo's Factory	1970	15.00
—Dark blue label			
❑ F-8402	Cosmo's Factory	1973	10.00
—Brown label			
❑ F-8402 [DJ]	Cosmo's Factory	1970	80.00
—White label promo			
❑ F-8410	Pendulum	1970	15.00
—Dark blue label			
❑ F-8410	Pendulum	1973	10.00
—Brown label			
❑ F-9404	Mardi Gras	1972	15.00
—Dark blue label			
❑ F-9404	Mardi Gras	1973	10.00
—Brown label			
❑ F-9418	Creedence Gold	1972	10.00
❑ F-9430	More Creedence Gold	1973	10.00
❑ F-9621	Chooglin'	1982	8.00
HEARTLAND			
❑ HR 2039 [(3)]	Creedence Clearwater Revival	1990	15.00
K-TEL			
❑ NU 9360	The Best of Creedence Clearwater Revival — 20 Super Hits	1978	15.00
MOBILE FIDELITY			
❑ 1-037	Cosmo's Factory	1979	70.00
—Audiophile vinyl			
TIME-LIFE			
❑ SCLR-18 [(2)]	Classic Rock: Creedence Clearwater Revival	1989	15.00

CRESCENDOS, THE (1) Nashville-based vocal group.

Number	Title (A Side/B Side)	Yr	NM
45s			
NASCO			
❑ 6005	Oh Julie/My Little Girl	1957	25.00
❑ 6009	School Girl/Crazy Hop	1958	25.00
❑ 6009 [PS]	School Girl/Crazy Hop	1958	50.00
❑ 6021	Rainy Sunday/Young and In Love	1958	25.00
❑ 6021 [PS]	Rainy Sunday/Young and n Love	1958	50.00
NASHBORO			
❑ (no #) [PS]	The Crescendos	1957	50.00
—Large-hole omnibus sleeve, often found with "Oh Julie," but may have been used on other Nasco singles			
TAP			
❑ 7027	Oh Julie/Angel Face	1962	15.00
❑ 7027 [PS]	Oh Julie/Angel Face	1962	25.00
Albums			
GUEST STAR			
❑ G-1453 [M]	Oh Julie	1962	50.00
❑ GS-1453 [R]	Oh Julie	1962	20.00

CRESCENDOS, THE (2)

Number	Title (A Side/B Side)	Yr	NM
45s			
ATLANTIC			
❑ 1109	Sweet Dreams/Finders Keepers	1956	30.00
❑ 2014	I'll Be Seeing You/Sweet Dreams	1959	15.00

CRESCENDOS, THE (U) Some of these may be group (1); it's unlikely that any are group (2).

Number	Title (A Side/B Side)	Yr	NM
45s			
DOMAIN			
❑ 1025	A Fellow Needs a Girl/Black Cat	1964	15.00
IMPRO			
❑ 5006	Tidal Wave/Crescendo Special	1962	40.00
NU SOUND			
❑ 1007	Count Down/Hawk Walk	1961	30.00
❑ 1014	Sweet Talk/Movin' Wild	1961	30.00
SCARLET			
❑ 4007	Strange Love/Let's Take a Walk	1960	30.00
❑ 4009	Angel Face/I'm So Ashamed	1961	50.00

CRESCHENDOS, THE

Number	Title (A Side/B Side)	Yr	NM
45s			
GONE			
❑ 5100	My Heart's Desire/Take My Heart	1961	30.00
MUSIC CITY			
❑ 831	My Heart's Desire/Take My Heart	1960	200.00
—Maroon label			
❑ 831	My Heart's Desire/Take My Heart	1960	400.00
—Green label			
❑ 831	My Heart's Desire/Take My Heart	1961	50.00
—Black label			
❑ 839	Teenage Prayer/I Don't Mind	1961	250.00
SATURN			
❑ 404	Surfing Strip/Hanging Ten	1963	50.00

CRESENTS, THE

Number	Title (A Side/B Side)	Yr	NM
45s			
JOYCE			
❑ 102	Everybody Knew But Me/Rosemarie	1957	250.00

CRESTONES, THE

Number	Title (A Side/B Side)	Yr	NM
45s			
MARKIE			
❑ 117	She's a Bad Motorcycle/Grasshopper Dance	1963	50.00
U.S.A.			
❑ 835	My Girl/The Chopper	1965	12.00

CRESTS, THE Also see JOHNNY MAESTRO.

Number	Title (A Side/B Side)	Yr	NM
45s			
COED			
❑ 501	Pretty Little Angel/I Thank the Moon	1958	40.00
—"Coed" in red and black print			
❑ 501	Pretty Little Angel/I Thank the Moon	1958	150.00
—"Coed" in red print			
❑ 506	16 Candles/Beside You	1958	30.00
❑ 509	Six Nights a Week/I Do	1959	25.00
❑ 511	Flower of Love/Molly Mae	1959	25.00
❑ 515	The Angels Listened In/I Thank the Moon	1959	30.00
❑ 521	A Year Ago Tonight/Paper Clown	1959	25.00
❑ 525	Step by Step/Gee (But I'd Give the World)	1960	25.00
❑ 531	Trouble in Paradise/Always You	1960	25.00
❑ 535	Journey of Love/If My Heart Could Write a Letter	1960	20.00
❑ 537	Isn't It Amazing/Molly Mae	1960	20.00
❑ 543	I Remember (In the Still of the Night)/Good Golly Miss Molly	1961	25.00
❑ 561	Little Miracles/Baby I Gotta Know	1962	30.00
CORAL			
❑ 62403	You Blew Out the Candles/A Love to Last a Lifetime	1964	30.00
HARVEY			
❑ 5002	Sixteen Candles/My Juanita	1981	10.00
—Red vinyl			
JOYCE			
❑ 103	My Juanita/Sweetest One	1957	300.00
—Label name: "JoYce"			
❑ 103	My Juanita/Sweetest One	1959	50.00
—Label name: "Joyce"			
❑ 105	No One to Love/Wish She Was Mine	1957	300.00
KING TUT			
❑ 172	Earth Angel/Tweedlee Dee	197?	8.00
LANA			
❑ 101	16 Candles/Besides You	196?	8.00
—Oldies reissue			
❑ 102	Trouble in Paradise/I Thank the Moon	196?	8.00
—Oldies reissue			
❑ 103	Step by Step/Gee (But I'd Give the World)	196?	8.00
—Oldies reissue			
LOST-NITE			
❑ 156	No One to Love/Wish She Was Mine	196?	6.00
—Reissue			
❑ 163	Six Nights a Week/I Do	196?	6.00
—Reissue			
❑ 166	Step by Step/Gee (But I'd Give the World)	196?	6.00
—Reissue			
❑ 168	16 Candles/Beside You	196?	6.00
—Reissue			
❑ 171	The Angels Listened In/I Thank the Moon	196?	6.00
—Reissue			
❑ 209	My Juanita/Sweetest One	196?	6.00
—Reissue			
❑ 211	Flower of Love/Molly Mae	196?	6.00
—Reissue			
❑ 229	Pretty Little Angel/I Thank the Moon	196?	5.00
—Reissue			
MUSICTONE			
❑ 1106	My Juanita/Sweetest One	1961	20.00
SCEPTER			
❑ 12112	I'm Stepping Out of the Picture/Afraid of Love	1965	15.00
SELMA			
❑ 311	Guilty/Number One with Me	1962	25.00
—A-side does not have spoken intro			
❑ 311	Guilty/Number One with Me	1962	75.00
—A-side has spoken intro			
❑ 4000	Did I Remember/Tears Will Fall	1963	30.00
TIMES SQUARE			
❑ 2	No One to Love/Wish She Was Mine	1962	20.00
—Red vinyl			
❑ 6	Baby/I Love You So	1964	15.00
❑ 97	Baby/I Love You So	1964	12.00
TRANS ATLAS			
❑ 696	The Actor/Three Tears in a Bucket	1962	30.00
7-Inch Extended Plays			
COED			
❑ EPC-101	The Angels Listened In/Flower of Love//16 Candles/Six Nights a Week	1959	400.00
❑ EPC-101 [PS]	The Angels Listened In	1959	400.00
Albums			
COED			
❑ LPC-901 [M]	The Crests Sing All Biggies	1960	200.00
—Red label			
❑ LPC-901 [M]	The Crests Sing All Biggies	1960	400.00
—Yellow label, black print			
❑ LPC-904 [M]	The Best of the Crests/16 Fabulous Hits	1961	400.00
—Label simply calls this "16 Fabulous Hits"			
COLLECTABLES			
❑ COL-5009	Greatest Hits	1982	12.00
POST			
❑ 3000	The Crests Sing	196?	40.00
RHINO			
❑ R1-70948	The Best of the Crests	1989	12.00

CRESTS, THE (2) Nashville studio group.

Number	Title (A Side/B Side)	Yr	NM
45s			
HIT			
❑ 227	You're the One/Treat Her Right	1965	8.00
—B-side by Cal York and the Roamers			

CREW CUTS, THE

Number	Title (A Side/B Side)	Yr	NM
45s			
ABC-PARAMOUNT			
❑ 10450	Hip-Huggers/You're a Star, Donna, Donna	1963	12.00
CHESS			
❑ 1892	Ain't That Nice/Yeah, Yeah, She Wants Me	1964	10.00
FIREBIRD			
❑ 1805	My Heart Belongs to Only You/You've Been In	1970	5.00
4 CORNERS OF THE WORLD			
❑ 120	Don't Be Angry/Earth Angel	1962	10.00
MERCURY			
❑ 70341	Crazy 'Bout You Baby/Angela Mia	1954	20.00
❑ 70404	Sh-Boom/I Spoke Too Soon	1954	25.00
❑ 70404	Sh-Boom/I Spoke Too Soon	1954	50.00
—7-inch 78 rpm on vinyl			
❑ 70404 [PS]	Sh-Boom/I Spoke Too Soon	1954	100.00
—Sleeve accompanying the 78: "PopSi Hit Record of the Month"			
❑ 70443	Oop-Shoop/Do Me Good Baby	1954	15.00
❑ 70490	All I Wanna Do/The Barking Dog	1954	15.00
❑ 70491	Dance, Mr. Snowman, Dance/Twinkle Toes	1954	15.00
❑ 70494	The Whippenpoof Song/Varsity Drag	1954	15.00
❑ 70529	Ko Ko Mo (I Love You So)/Earth Angel	1955	15.00
❑ 70597	Don't Be Angry/Chop Chop Boom	1955	15.00
❑ 70598	Unchained Melody/Two Hearts, Two Kisses	1955	15.00
❑ 70634	A Story Untold/Carmen's Boogie	1955	15.00
❑ 70668	Gum Drop/Song of the Fool	1955	15.00
❑ 70710	Slam! Bam!/Are You Having Any Fun	1955	15.00
❑ 70741	Angels in the Sky/Mostly Martha	1955	15.00
❑ 70782	Seven Days/That's Your Mistake	1956	15.00
❑ 70840	Out of the Picture/Honey Hair, Sugar Lips, Eyes of Blue	1956	15.00
❑ 70890	Tell Me Why/Rebel in Town	1956	15.00
❑ 70922	Bei Mir Bist Du Schoen/Thirteen Going on Fourteen	1956	15.00
❑ 70977	Love in a Home/Keeper of the Flame	1956	15.00
❑ 70988	The Varsity Drag/Halls of Ivy	1956	15.00
❑ 71022	Young Love/Little by Little	1956	15.00
❑ 71076	The Angelus/Whatever, Whenever, Whoever	1957	15.00
❑ 71125	Suzie Q/Such a Shame	1957	15.00
❑ 71168	I Sit in My Window/Hey, You Face	1957	15.00
❑ 71223	I Like It Like That/Be My Only Love	1957	15.00
RCA VICTOR			
❑ 47-7320	Forever My Darling/Hey Stella	1958	12.00
❑ 47-7359	That's My Desire/Baby Be Mine	1958	12.00
❑ 47-7446	Fraternity Pin/Can You Hear Me	1959	12.00
❑ 47-7509	Gone, Gone, Gone/Someone in Heaven	1959	12.00

Number	Title (A Side/B Side)	Yr	NM
❑ 47-7577	Bermuda/Kin-Ni-Ki-Nic	1959	12.00
❑ 47-7667	It Is No Secret/ No, No, Nevermore	1960	12.00
❑ 47-7734	American Beauty Rose/ The Shrine on Top of the Hill	1960	12.00
❑ 47-7759	Aura Lee/Going to Church on Sunday	1960	12.00
VEE JAY			
❑ 569	The Three Bells/Spanish Is the Loving Tongue	1963	12.00
WARWICK			
❑ 558	Over the Mountain/Searchin'	1960	12.00
❑ 585	You and the Angels/ I Care for You	1960	12.00
❑ 595	Malaguena/Why Not	1960	12.00
❑ 623	The Legend of Gunga Din/ Number One with Me	1961	12.00
WHALE			
❑ 507	Twistin' All the World/ Electric Chair	1962	12.00
❑ 508	Laura Love/Little Donkey	1962	12.00
❑ 509	Hush Little Baby/Ti-Pi-Tum	1962	12.00
7-Inch Extended Plays			
MERCURY			
❑ EP-1-3274	Down the Old Ox Road/The Whiffenpoof Song//We're Working Our Way Through College/Varsity Drag	1956	12.00
❑ EP-1-3274 [PS]	The Crew Cuts On Campus	1956	12.00
❑ EP-1-3275	Buckle Down, Winsocki/Betty Co-Ed//You Gotta Be a Football Hero/Collegiate	195?	12.00
❑ EP-1-3275 [PS]	3 Cheers for the Crew Cuts	195?	12.00
❑ EP-1-3325	Carmen's Boogie/Here//Red Hot Serenade/When, When, When	195?	12.00
❑ EP-1-3325 [PS]	Crew Cuts Go Long Hair	195?	12.00
❑ EP-1-3326	Full Set of Everything/Till the End of Time//The Urge/ Mostly Martha	195?	12.00
❑ EP-1-3326 [PS]	The Crew-Cuts	195?	12.00
Albums			
CAMAY			
❑ CA-1002 [M]	The Great New Sound of the Crew Cuts	196?	20.00
❑ CA-3002 [S]	The Great New Sound of the Crew Cuts	196?	25.00
MERCURY			
❑ MG-20067 [M]	The Crew Cuts Go Longhair	1955	50.00
❑ MG-20140 [M]	The Crew Cuts On Campus	1956	50.00
❑ MG-20143 [M]	Crew Cut Capers	1956	50.00
❑ MG-20144 [M]	Rock and Roll Bash	1956	80.00
❑ MG-20199 [M]	Music A La Carte	1957	50.00
❑ MG-25200 [10]	The Crew Cuts On Campus	1956	80.00
PICADILLY			
❑ PIC-3560	The Wonderful Happy Crazy Innocent World	1980	10.00
RCA VICTOR			
❑ PR-102 [M]	The Crew Cuts Sing Out!	1960	25.00
❑ PR-129 [M]	The Crew Cuts Have a Ball	1960	25.00
—Produced for Ebonite bowling balls; Side 2 has "Bowling Tips by Top Stars"			
❑ LPM-1933 [M]	Surprise Package	1958	30.00
❑ LSP-1933 [S]	Surprise Package	1959	40.00
❑ LPM-2037 [M]	The Crew Cuts Sing	1959	30.00
❑ LSP-2037 [S]	The Crew Cuts Sing	1959	40.00
❑ LPM-2067 [M]	You Must Have Been a Beautiful Baby	1960	30.00
❑ LSP-2067 [S]	You Must Have Been a Beautiful Baby	1960	40.00
WING			
❑ MGW-12125 [M]	Rock and Roll Bash	196?	25.00
❑ MGW-12145 [M]	The Crew Cuts On Campus	196?	20.00
❑ MGW-12177 [M]	The Crew Cuts	196?	20.00
❑ MGW-12180 [M]	High School Favorites	196?	20.00
❑ MGW-12195 [M]	The Crew Cuts Sing the Masters	196?	20.00

CREWE, BOB

Includes records as "The Bob Crewe Generation" and similar names.

Number	Title (A Side/B Side)	Yr	NM
45s			
ABC-PARAMOUNT			
❑ 10204	Swingin' Family Tree/ La La Loretta	1961	12.00
❑ 10246	One More Lie/I'm Goin' Home (On My Way)	1961	12.00
❑ 10273	Another Day/Come to Me	1961	12.00
BRUNSWICK			
❑ 55021	I Can't Shake the Blues/ Torn and Tattered Heart	1957	15.00
CORAL			
❑ 61688	Melody for Lovers/ Can't Get Away from It	1956	15.00
CREWE			
❑ 605	Dandylion/Day By Day & Prepare Ye	1971	5.00
DYNO VOICE			
❑ 229	Music to Watch Girls By/ Girls on the Rocks	1966	8.00
❑ 231	After the Ball/One More Year	1967	6.00
❑ 233	Mini Skirts in Moscow, or ... / Theme for a Lazy Girl	1967	6.00
❑ 233 [PS]	Mini Skirts in Moscow, or ... / Theme for a Lazy Girl	1967	10.00
❑ 237	A Lover's Concerto/Y ou Only Live Twice	1967	6.00
❑ 902	Birds of Britain/I Will Wait for You	1968	6.00
❑ 906	Winter Warm/Song from Moulin Rouge	1968	6.00
❑ 915	To Give (The Reason I Live)/ Battle Hymn of the Republic	1968	6.00
❑ 928	Angel Is Love/ Black Queen's Beads	1968	6.00
ELEKTRA			
❑ 45346	Time for You and Me/ Free (Medley)	1976	4.00
❑ 45380	Menage a Trois/I Am Free-Keep Walkin'	1976	4.00
❑ 45404	It Took a Long Time (For the First Time in My Life)/ In Another Life	1977	4.00
❑ 45425	Marriage Made in Heaven/ In Another Life	1977	4.00
JUBILEE			
❑ 5148	Cash Register Heart/ Change of Heart	1954	20.00
❑ 5164	Punch/It's All Over	1954	20.00
MELBA			
❑ 119	Guessin' Games/ Don't Call Me Chicken	1957	15.00
METROMEDIA			
❑ 229	Mammy Blue/Better Be Gone	1972	5.00
❑ 243	Takin' Care of Each Other/ (B-side unknown)	1972	5.00
PHILIPS			
❑ 40241	Rag Doll/Ronnie	1964	8.00
❑ 40241 [PS]	Rag Doll/Ronnie	1964	15.00
—Has photo of the Four Seasons on it; the sleeve even looks as if it belongs to a Four Seasons record until you read a bit more closely!			
SPOTLIGHT			
❑ 387	The Rhythm and the Blues/ The Bumblebee	1955	25.00
❑ 393	Penny Nickel Dime Quarter (On a Teenage Date)/How Long	1956	20.00
20TH CENTURY			
❑ 2271	Street Talk/Street Talk (Part 2)	1976	4.00
VIK			
❑ 0307	Charm Bracelet/Do Be Do Be Do	1957	25.00
❑ 0333	Of Sun, the Sea and the Sand/ Sweet Talk	1958	20.00
WARWICK			
❑ 519	The Whippenpoof Song/ Let's Pretend	1959	12.00
❑ 534	Cool Time/Quite a Picture	1960	12.00
❑ 553	Silhouettes/Let's Get Serious	1960	12.00
❑ 579	Little Girl of Mine/To Ev'ry Girl, To Ev'ry Boy	1960	12.00
❑ 601	Oh, How I Miss You Tonight/ Ev'rytime	1960	12.00
❑ 616	She's Only Wonderful/On the Street Where You Live	1961	12.00
Albums			
CGC			
❑ 1000	Let Me Touch You	1970	12.00
DYNO VOICE			
❑ DV-1902 [M]	Music to Watch Birds By	1967	15.00
❑ DV-1906 [M]	The Bob Crewe Generation In Classic Form	1968	15.00
❑ DV-9003 [M]	Music to Watch Girls By	1967	15.00
❑ DVS-9003 [S]	Music to Watch Girls By	1967	12.00
❑ DV-31902 [S]	Music to Watch Birds By	1967	12.00
❑ DV-31906 [S]	The Bob Crewe Generation In Classic Form	1968	12.00
ELEKTRA			
❑ 7E-1083	Street Talk	1976	12.00
❑ 7E-1103	Motivation	1977	12.00
PHILIPS			
❑ PHM 200150 [M]	All the Song Hits of the Four Seasons	1964	25.00
❑ PHM 200238 [M]	Bob Crewe Plays the Four Seasons' Hits	1967	20.00
❑ PHS 600150 [S]	All the Song Hits of the Four Seasons	1964	30.00
❑ PHS 600238 [S]	Bob Crewe Plays the Four Seasons' Hits	1967	15.00
WARWICK			
❑ W-2009 [M]	Kicks	1960	25.00
❑ WST-2009 [S]	Kicks	1960	50.00
❑ W-2034 [M]	Crazy in the Heart	1961	25.00
❑ WST-2034 [S]	Crazy in the Heart	1961	50.00

CRIBBINS, BERNARD

Number	Title (A Side/B Side)	Yr	NM
45s			
CAPITOL			
❑ 5933	When I'm Sixty-Four/ Oh My Word	1967	10.00
UNITED ARTISTS			
❑ 907	Right Said Fred/Quietly Bonkers	1965	10.00

CRICKETS, THE (1)

BUDDY HOLLY'S group. Includes records credited to "The Crickets" both during and after Holly's life. Also see SONNY CURTIS; IVAN; NIKI SULLIVAN. Includes records with and without BUDDY HOLLY. There also was a Crickets black vocal group who made records on Davis, Jay Dee and MGM; these are outside the scope of this book.

Number	Title (A Side/B Side)	Yr	NM
45s			
BARNABY			
❑ 2061	Rockin' 50's Rock 'N' Roll/ True Love Ways	1972	20.00
BRUNSWICK			
❑ 55009	That'll Be the Day/I'm Lookin' for Someone to Love	1957	50.00
❑ 55035	Oh, Boy!/Not Fade Away	1957	50.00
—Note: Picture sleeves for this record are bootlegs			
❑ 55053	Maybe Baby/Tell Me How	1958	50.00
❑ 55072	Think It Over/Fool's Paradise	1958	50.00
❑ 55094	It's So Easy/Lonesome Tears	1958	50.00
❑ 55124	Love's Made a Fool of You/ Someone, Someone	1959	40.00
❑ 55153	When You Ask About Love/ Deborah	1959	40.00
CORAL			
❑ 62198	More Than I Can Say/ Baby, My Heart	1960	40.00
❑ 62238	Peggy Sue Got Married/ Don't Cha Know	1960	40.00
❑ 62407	Maybe Baby/Not Fade Away	1964	30.00
EPIC			
❑ 34-08028	T-Shirt/Hollywould	1988	5.00
❑ 34-08028 [PS]	T-Shirt/Hollywould	1988	5.00
LIBERTY			
❑ 55392	He's Old Enough to Know Better/I'm Feeling Better	1961	25.00
❑ 55441	Don't Ever Change/ I'm Not a Bad Boy	1962	25.00
❑ 55492	I Believe in You/Parisian Girl	1962	25.00
❑ 55495	Little Hollywood Girl/Parisian Girl	1962	25.00
❑ 55540	My Little Girl/Teardrops Fall Like Rain	1963	25.00
❑ 55603	Don't Say You Love Me/ April Avenue	1963	25.00
❑ 55660	Lonely Avenue/You Can't Be In-Between	1964	25.00
❑ 55668	Please, Please Me/ From Me to You	1964	50.00
❑ 55696	(They Call Her) La Bomba/ All Over You	1964	25.00
❑ 55742	We Gotta Get Together/I Think I've Caught the Blues	1964	25.00
❑ 55767	Everybody's Got a Little Problem/Now Hear This	1965	25.00
MGM			
❑ 14541	Hayride/Wasn't It Nice	1973	15.00
MUSIC FACTORY			
❑ 415	Million Dollar Movie/ A Million Miles Apart	1968	20.00
7-Inch Extended Plays			
BRUNSWICK			
❑ EB 71036	*I'm Looking for Someone to Love/That'll Be the Day/Not Fade Away/Oh! Boy	1957	300.00
❑ EB 71036 [PS]	The Chirping Crickets	1957	300.00
❑ EB 71038	*Maybe Baby/Rock Me My Baby/Send Me Some Lovin'/ Tell Me How	1958	250.00
❑ EB 71038 [PS]	The Sound of the Crickets	1958	250.00
Albums			
BARNABY			
❑ Z 30268	Rockin' 50's Rock 'N' Roll	1970	25.00

Except when noted otherwise, VG = 25% of NM, and VG+ = 50% of NM. (Example: VG = $2.00, VG+ = $4.00 and NM = $8.00.)

Number	Title (A Side/B Side)	Yr	NM
BRUNSWICK			
❑ BL 54038 [M]	The "Chirping" Crickets	1957	800.00
—Textured cover			
❑ BL 54038 [M]	The "Chirping" Crickets	1958	600.00
—Regular cover			
CORAL			
❑ CRL 57320 [M]	In Style with the Crickets	1960	200.00
❑ CRL 757320 [S]	In Style with the Crickets	1960	400.00
EPIC			
❑ FE 44446	T-Shirt	1988	15.00
LIBERTY			
❑ LRP-3272 [M]	Something Old, Something New, Something Blue, Somethin' Else	1962	150.00
❑ LRP-3351 [M]	California Sun/She Loves You	1964	100.00
❑ LST-7272 [S]	Something Old, Something New, Something Blue, Somethin' Else	1962	200.00
❑ LST-7351 [S]	California Sun/She Loves You	1964	150.00
VERTIGO			
❑ VEL-1020	Remnants	1973	20.00

CRICKETS, THE (2) Black vocal group featuring Dean Barlow.

Number	Title (A Side/B Side)	Yr	NM
45s			
DAVIS			
❑ 459	I'm Going to Live My Life Alone/Man from the Moon	1958	60.00
JAY DEE			
❑ 777	Dreams and Wishes/When I Met You	1953	200.00
❑ 781	Fine As Wine/I'm Not the Same One You Love	1953	200.00
❑ 785	Changing Partners/Your Love	1954	150.00
❑ 786	Just You/My Little Baby's Shoes	1954	150.00
❑ 789	Are You Looking for a Sweetheart/Never Give Up Hope	1954	150.00
❑ 795	I'm Going to Live My Life Alone/Man from the Moon	1954	150.00
MGM			
❑ 11428	You're Mine/Milk and Gin	1953	250.00
❑ 11507	I'll Cry No More/For You I Have Eyes	1953	200.00
Albums			
RELIC			
❑ LP-5040	The Crickets Featuring Dean Barlow	1987	10.00

CRISS, GARY

Number	Title (A Side/B Side)	Yr	NM
12-Inch Singles			
SALSOUL			
❑ 2059	Rio De Janeiro/My Rio Lady	1978	10.00
❑ 2074	Brazilian Nights (6:14)/Amazon Queen (7:08)	1978	20.00
45s			
DIAMOND			
❑ 114	Welcome Home to My Heart/Our Favorite Melodies	1962	12.00
❑ 122	My Heavenly Angel/The Girl I Told You About	1962	12.00
❑ 127	Long Lonely Nights/I Still Miss You So	1963	10.00
❑ 145	Little Joe/Sweet, Warm and Soft	1963	10.00
❑ 182	Hands of My Baby/If This Is Goodbye	1965	8.00
❑ 190	My Baby Left Me/This Love of Mine	1965	8.00
❑ 228	Welcome Home to My Heart/Hands Off Buddy	1967	20.00
SALSOUL			
❑ 2082	Brazilian Nights/Amazon Queen	1979	6.00
STRAND			
❑ 25044	Good Golly Miss Molly/I'll Love Only You	1961	30.00

CRISS, PETER Also see CHELSEA; KISS.

Number	Title (A Side/B Side)	Yr	NM
45s			
CASABLANCA			
❑ 952	Don't You Let Me Down/Hooked on Rock and Roll	1978	7.00
❑ 961	You Still Matter to Me/Hooked on Rock and Roll	1979	7.00
❑ 2311	I Found Love/By Myself	1980	7.00
Albums			
CASABLANCA			
❑ NBLP-7122	Peter Criss	1978	20.00
❑ NBPIX-7122 [PD]	Peter Criss	1978	50.00
❑ NBLP-7240	Out of Control	1980	25.00

CRITTERS, THE

Number	Title (A Side/B Side)	Yr	NM
45s			
KAPP			
❑ 727	He'll Make You Cry/Children & Flowers	1965	10.00
❑ 752	Younger Girl/Gone for a While	1966	12.00
❑ 769	Mr. Dieingly Sad/It Just Won't Be That Way	1966	12.00
❑ 769 [PS]	Mr. Dieingly Sad/It Just Won't Be That Way	1966	20.00
❑ 793	Bad Misunderstanding/Forever or No More	1966	10.00
❑ 805	Marryin' Kind of Love/New York Bound	1967	10.00
❑ 838	Don't Let the Rain Fall Down on Me/Walk Like a Man Again	1967	10.00
❑ 858	Little Girl/Dancing in the Streets	1967	10.00
MUSICOR			
❑ 1044	I'm Gonna Give/Georgianna	1964	20.00
PRANCER			
❑ 6001	No One But You/I'm Telling Everyone	1969	8.00
PROJECT 3			
❑ 1326	Good Morning Sunshine/A Moment of Being with You	1968	8.00
❑ 1332	Touch 'N' Go/Younger Generation	1968	8.00
❑ 1349	Cool Sunday Morning/Lisa, But Not the Same	1969	8.00
❑ 1363	She Said She Loved Him/I Just Want to Sit Right Here and Look at You	1969	8.00
Albums			
KAPP			
❑ KL-1485 [M]	Younger Girl	1966	30.00
❑ KS-3485 [S]	Younger Girl	1966	40.00
PROJECT 3			
❑ PR 4001SD	Touch 'n Go with the Critters	1968	30.00
❑ PR 4002SD	The Critters	1969	30.00

CRITTERS, THE /THE YOUNG RASCALS/LOU CHRISTIE

Number	Title (A Side/B Side)	Yr	NM
Albums			
BOUTIQUE			
❑ CA-1079 [M]	A Taste of the Critters & The Young Rascals & Lou Christie	1966	40.00

CROCE, JIM

Number	Title (A Side/B Side)	Yr	NM
45s			
ABC			
❑ 11328	You Don't Mess Around with Jim/Photographs and Memories	1972	4.00
❑ 11335	Operator (That's Not the Way It Feels)/Rapid Roy (The Stock Car Boy)	1972	4.00
❑ 11346	One Less Set of Footsteps/It Doesn't Have to Be That Way	1973	4.00
❑ 11359	Bad, Bad Leroy Brown/A Good Time Man Like Me Ain't Got No Business (Singin' the Blues)	1973	4.00
—Regular ABC logo			
❑ 11359	Bad, Bad Leroy Brown/A Good Time Man Like Me Ain't Got No Business (Singin' the Blues)	1973	5.00
—ABC logo in children's building blocks			
❑ 11389	I Got a Name/Alabama Rain	1973	4.00
❑ 11405	Time in a Bottle/Hard Time Losin' Man	1973	4.00
❑ 11413	It Doesn't Have to Be That Way/Roller Derby Queen	1973	4.00
❑ 11413 [PS]	It Doesn't Have to Be That Way/Roller Derby Queen	1973	5.00
❑ 11424	I'll Have to Say I Love You in a Song/Salon and Saloon	1974	4.00
❑ 11447	Workin' at the Car Wash Blues/Thursday	1974	4.00
❑ 12015	Workin' at the Car Wash Blues/Thursday	1974	5.00
LIFESONG			
❑ 45001	Chain Gang Medley/Stone Walls	1975	4.00
❑ 45005	Maybe Tomorrow/Mississippi Lady	1976	4.00
❑ 45018 [DJ]	It Doesn't Have to Be That Way (mono/stereo)	1976	5.00
—Promo-only release; Lifesong sleeve has custom sticker (add $4)			
21 RECORDS			
❑ 94969	Workin' at the Car Wash Blues/Rapid Roy (The Stock Car Boy)	1987	3.00
❑ 94970	It Doesn't Have to Be That Way/Time in a Bottle	1987	3.00
❑ 94971	I'll Have to Say I Love You in a Song/I Got a Name	1987	3.00
❑ 94972	You Don't Mess Around with Jim/Photographs and Memories	1987	3.00
❑ 94973	Bad, Bad Leroy Brown/Operator (That's Not the Way It Feels)	1987	3.00
7-Inch Extended Plays			
ABC			
❑ PRO-769	Dreamin' Again/One Less Set of Footsteps/Next Time, This Time//Roller Derby Queen/A Good Time Man Like Me Ain't Got No Business (Singin' the Blues)/Bad, Bad Leroy Brown	1973	10.00
—Jukebox issue; small hole, plays at 33 1/3 rpm			
❑ PRO-769 [PS]	Life and Times	1973	10.00
—Part of "Little LP" series (LLP #232)			
❑ PRO-40008	I Got a Name/Lover's Cross/I'll Have to Say I Love You in a Song//Top Hat Bar and Grille/Thursday/Workin' at the Car Wash Blues	1973	20.00
—Quadraphonic jukebox single; small hole, plays at 33 1/3 rpm			
❑ PRO-40008 [PS]	I Got a Name	1973	20.00
Albums			
ABC			
❑ ABCX-756	You Don't Mess Around with Jim	1972	20.00
—Original covers have no green box advertising "Time in a Bottle"			
❑ ABCX-756	You Don't Mess Around with Jim	1973	15.00
—Posthumous covers have a green box advertising "Time in a Bottle"			
❑ ABCX-769	Life and Times	1973	15.00
❑ ABCX-797	I Got a Name	1973	15.00
❑ ABCD-835	Photographs & Memories/His Greatest Hits	1974	15.00
CAPITOL			
❑ SMAS-315	Jim and Ingrid Croce	1970	30.00
COMMAND			
❑ QD-40006 [Q]	You Don't Mess Around with Jim	1974	30.00
—With wide border around the outside of front cover			
❑ QD-40006 [Q]	You Don't Mess Around with Jim	1974	25.00
—Without border around outside of front cover			
❑ QD-40007 [Q]	Life and Times	1974	25.00
❑ QD-40008 [Q]	I Got a Name	1974	25.00
❑ QD-40020 [Q]	Photographs & Memories/His Greatest Hits	1974	25.00
CROCE			
❑ 101	Facets	1966	300.00
DCC COMPACT CLASSICS			
❑ LPZ-2054	His Greatest Recordings	1998	40.00
—Audiophile vinyl			
LIFESONG			
❑ LS 900 [(2)]	The Faces I've Been	1975	15.00
❑ LS 6007	Time in a Bottle — Jim Croce's Greatest Love Songs	1976	12.00
❑ JZ 34993	You Don't Mess Around with Jim	1978	10.00
❑ JZ 35000	Time in a Bottle — Jim Croce's Greatest Love Songs	1978	10.00
❑ JZ 35008	Life and Times	1978	10.00
❑ JZ 35009	I Got a Name	1978	10.00
❑ JZ 35010	Photographs & Memories/His Greatest Hits	1978	10.00
❑ JZ 35571	Bad, Bad Leroy Brown: Jim Croce's Greatest Character Songs	1978	10.00
MOBILE FIDELITY			
❑ 1-079	You Don't Mess Around with Jim	1981	40.00
—Audiophile vinyl			
PICKWICK			
❑ SPC-3332	Another Day, Another Town	1973	10.00
—Reissue of Capitol LP			
21 RECORDS			
❑ 90467	Photographs & Memories/His Greatest Hits	1985	8.00
❑ 90468	Time in a Bottle — Jim Croce's Greatest Love Songs	1985	8.00
❑ 90469	Down the Highway	1985	10.00

CROCKETT, HOWARD

Number	Title (A Side/B Side)	Yr	NM
45s			
DOT			
❑ 15593	If You'll Let Me/You've Got Me Lyin'	1957	50.00
❑ 15701	The Night Rider/Branded	1958	40.00
❑ 17457	The House Where Momma Lived/Last Will and Testament (Of a Drinking Man)	1973	6.00
❑ 17482	I Feel More Like Myself Than I Did a While Ago/I'd Like to Be Everybody for Just One Day	1973	6.00
❑ 17509	The Calling/Pictures and Memories	1974	6.00

Number	Title (A Side/B Side)	Yr	NM
MANCO			
❑ 1002	Sluefoot the Bear/Polly Ann	1960	50.00
❑ 1012	That Old Juke Box/Steamboat Bill	1961	30.00
❑ 1023	Just a Poor Man/I've Got You Worried Too	1961	30.00
MEL-O-DY			
❑ 109	The Big Wheel/That Silver-Haired Daddy of Mine	1963	25.00
❑ 111	Bringing In the Gold/I've Been a Long Time Leaving	1963	25.00
❑ 115	My Lil's Run Off/Spanish Lace and Memories	1964	25.00
❑ 119	Put Me in Your Pocket/The Miles	1964	25.00
❑ 121	All the Good Times Are Gone/The Great Titanic	1965	25.00
SMASH			
❑ 1721	Deep Elm Dave/Going Down to Soldiers	1961	40.00
❑ 1750	Break Away Billy Boy/Out of Bounds Again	1962	40.00
❑ 1782	Jessie and the Glendale Train/Trail of Tears	1962	80.00
STOP			
❑ 136	The Big Cat/You're Messin' Up My Mind	1968	8.00
❑ 172	The Big Day/You Can't Get to All of 'Em Jack	1968	8.00
❑ 210	Soap and Water/A Man with No Face	1969	8.00
❑ 238	Where Were You/The Story of Bango	1969	8.00
❑ 250	The Law Says/Ask Little Brother	1969	8.00

CROME SYRCUS, THE

45s

Number	Title (A Side/B Side)	Yr	NM
COMMAND			
❑ 4111	Cover Up/Take It Like a Man	1968	10.00
JERDEN			
❑ 921	Elevator Operator/Lord in Black	196?	12.00
PICCADILLY			
❑ 256	Lord in Black/Long Hard Road	196?	12.00

Albums

Number	Title (A Side/B Side)	Yr	NM
COMMAND			
❑ RS 925 SD	The Love Cycle	1968	75.00

CROMER, SIR HAROLD J.

45s

Number	Title (A Side/B Side)	Yr	NM
CAMEO			
❑ 369	The Thing/Nick & Joe Callin'	1965	12.00

CROPPER, STEVE

Also see BOOKER T. AND THE MG's; MAR-KEYS.

45s

Number	Title (A Side/B Side)	Yr	NM
MCA			
❑ 51078	Playin' My Thang/Why Do You Say You Love Me	1981	4.00
❑ 51115	Sandy Beaches/Fly	1981	4.00
❑ 52103	Night After Night/634-5789	1982	4.00

Albums

Number	Title (A Side/B Side)	Yr	NM
MCA			
❑ 5171	Playin' My Thang	1980	10.00
❑ 5340	Night After Night	1982	10.00
VOLT			
❑ VOS-6006	With a Little Help from My Friends	1970	15.00

CROSBY, BING

Includes most of his duets with other performers. Crosby was past his peak of popularity when 45s and LPs were introduced; while much of his material showed up on these formats, many of his 1930s and 1940s releases did not. The list below is exhaustive as to the availability of Bing's music on vinyl, but probably not complete; it's likely that other singles in the 23000, 24000 and 25000 series exist on 45s, as well as other EPs. Also see DAVID BOWIE; FRANK SINATRA.

45s

Number	Title (A Side/B Side)	Yr	NM
AMOS			
❑ 111	Hey Jude/Lonely Street	1969	6.00
❑ 116	It's All in the Game/More and More	1969	5.00
BING CROSBY			
❑ (no #) [DJ]	How Lovely Is Christmas/Never Be Afraid	195?	20.00
—Crowley's Milk promotional item			
CAPITOL			
❑ F3507	True Love/Well, Did You Evah?	1956	15.00
—A-side with Grace Kelly; B-side with Frank Sinatra			
❑ F3695	Man on Fire/Seven Nights a Week	1957	12.00
❑ 4548	Simple Love Affair/That's How I Met Your Mother	1978	4.00
❑ 5088	Do You Hear What I Hear/Christmas Dinner Country Style	1963	8.00
❑ S7-19766	Do You Hear What I Hear?/I Wish You a Merry Christmas	1997	3.00
COLUMBIA			
❑ 41104	Straight Down the Middle/Tomorrow's My Lucky Day	1958	12.00
❑ 41387	Say One for Me/I Couldn't Care Less	1959	12.00
❑ 41496	The Secret of Christmas/Just What I Wanted for Christmas	1959	15.00
DAYBREAK			
❑ 1001	A Time to Be Jolly/And the Bells Rang	1971	5.00
—Yellow label			
❑ 1001	A Time to Be Jolly/And the Bells Rang	1971	6.00
—Black label			
❑ 1001 [PS]	A Time to Be Jolly/And the Bells Rang	1971	5.00
DECCA			
❑ 9-65 [(4)]	Merry Christmas	1950	50.00
—Includes records 23281, 23777, 23778 and 23779 (also priced separately) and box			
❑ 9-66 [(4)]	Christmas Greetings	1950	50.00
—Includes records and box			
❑ 1-256 [PS]	Jingle Bells/Santa's Coming	19??	15.00
—With the Andrews Sisters; alternate number is 23281			
❑ 23281	Jingle Bells/Santa Claus Is Comin' to Town	1950	12.00
—With the Andrews Sisters; lines label; Sides 1 and 2 of "Album No. 9-65"			
❑ 9-23484	Pistol Packin' Mama/Don't Fence Me In	1950	12.00
—With the Andrews Sisters; "lines" label			
❑ 9-23484	Pistol Packin' Mama/Don't Fence Me In	1955	10.00
—With the Andrews Sisters; star under "Decca"			
❑ 23495	McNamara's Band/Dear Old Donegal	1950	12.00
—Reissue of 78; part of "Album No. 9-31"			
❑ 23777	Silent Night/Adeste Fideles (O Come All Ye Faithful)	1950	12.00
—Lines label; Sides 3 and 4 of "Album No. 9-65"			
❑ 23777	Silent Night/Adeste Fideles (O Come All Ye Faithful)	1955	10.00
—Star on label			
❑ 23777	Silent Night/Adeste Fideles (O Come All Ye Faithful)	1960	8.00
—Color bars on label			
❑ 23777 [PS]	Silent Night/Adeste Fideles (O Come All Ye Faithful)	1960	15.00
—Sleeve came with early 1960s pressings			
❑ 23778	White Christmas/God Rest Ye Merry Gentlemen	1960	8.00
—Color bars on label			
❑ 23778 [PS]	White Christmas/God Rest Ye Merry Gentlemen	1960	15.00
—Sleeve came with early 1960s pressings			
❑ 9-23778	White Christmas/God Rest Ye Merry Gentlemen	1950	12.00
—Lines label; Sides 5 and 6 of "Album No. 9-65"			
❑ 9-23778	White Christmas/God Rest Ye Merry Gentlemen	1955	10.00
—Star on label			
❑ 23779	I'll Be Home for Christmas (If Only in My Dreams)/Faith of Our Fathers	1950	12.00
—Lines label; Sides 7 and 8 of "Album No. 9-65"			
❑ 23786	Who Threw the Overalls in Mrs. Murphy's Chowder?/It's the Same Old Overalls	1950	12.00
—Reissue of 78; part of "Album No. 9-31"			
❑ 23787	Did Your Mother Come from Ireland?/Where the River Shannon Flows	1950	12.00
—Reissue of 78; part of "Album No. 9-31"			
❑ 23789	Too-Ra-Loo-Ra-Loo-Ral/I'll Take You Home Again Kathleen	1950	12.00
—Reissue of 78; part of "Album No. 9-31"			
❑ 24659	You're All I Want for Christmas/The First Noel	1950	15.00
—78 rpm issued in 1949; lines label			
❑ 25003	Take Me Back to My Boots and Saddle/My Little Buckaroo	1950	12.00
—Reissue of 78; part of "Album No. 9-145"			
❑ 25020	Clementine/The Old Oaken Bucket	1950	12.00
—Reissue of 78; part of "Album No. 9-145"			
❑ 25497	Sierra Sue/Along the Santa Fe Trail	1950	12.00
—Reissue of 78; part of "Album No. 9-145"			
❑ 25520	Memories Are Made of This/My Blue Heaven	1961	6.00
❑ 25540	Moments to Remember/Vaya Con Dios	1961	6.00
❑ 25643	Avalon/On the Alamo	1964	6.00
❑ 25661	Chinatown, My Chinatown/I'm Confessin' (That I Love You)	1965	6.00
❑ 25665	Between the Devil and the Deep Blue Sea/Georgia on My Mind	1965	6.00
❑ 27013	Jamboree Jones/Dixieland Band	1950	12.00
❑ 27018	I Didn't Slip, I Wasn't Pushed, I Fell/So Tall a Tree	1950	12.00
❑ 27019	Home Cookin'/When the Sun Goes Down	1950	12.00
❑ 27111	La Vie En Rose/I Cross My Fingers	1950	12.00
❑ 27112	Play a Simple Melody/Sam's Song	1950	12.00
—By "Gary Crosby and Friend" (guess who the friend is)			
❑ 27117	All My Love/The Friendly Islands	1950	12.00
❑ 27143	This Could Be Forever/Helpless	1950	12.00
—With Louanne Hogan			
❑ 27158	Ave Maria/Home Sweet Home	1950	12.00
❑ 27159	Rudolph, the Red-Nosed Reindeer/The Teddy Bear's Picnic	1950	12.00
❑ 27159/30126 [DJ]	Rudolph The Red-Nosed Reindeer/I Heard The Bells On Christmas Day	1956	20.00
—Green label promo with two different numbers on the record!			
❑ 27173	Life Is So Peculiar/High on the List	1950	12.00
—With the Andrews Sisters			
❑ 27219	Harbor Lights/Beyond the Reef	1950	12.00
❑ 27228	Mele Kalikimaka/Poppa Santa Claus	1950	12.00
—With the Andrews Sisters			
❑ 27229	Silver Bells/That Christmas Feeling	1950	12.00
—A-side with Carol Richards			
❑ 27230	A Marshmallow World/Looks Like a Cold, Cold Winter	1950	12.00
❑ 27231	Autumn Leaves/This Is the Time	1950	12.00
❑ 27232	If I Were a Bell/I've Never Been in Love Before	1950	12.00
—A-side with Patti Andrews			
❑ 27241	And You'll Be Mine/Accidents Will Happen	1950	12.00
❑ 27249	A Crosby Christmas (Part 1)/A Crosby Christmas (Part 2)	1950	—
—As "Gary, Phillip, Dennis, Lindsay and Bing Crosby"; unreleased on this number?			
❑ 27250	The Best Thing for You/Marrying for Love	1950	12.00
❑ 27263	Wouldn't It Be Funny/One More for the Blue and White	1950	12.00
❑ 27264	Accidents Will Happen/Milady	1950	12.00
—With Dorothy Kirsten			
❑ 27275	Oh! What a Beautiful Morning/People Will Say We're in Love	1950	10.00
❑ 27276	If I Loved You/Close As Pages in a Book	1950	10.00
❑ 27277	They Say It's Wonderful/I Love You	1950	10.00
❑ 27278	Evalina/The Eagle and Me	1950	10.00
❑ 27404	May the Good Lord Bless and Keep You/A Perfect Day	1951	10.00
❑ 27441	An Early American/My Own Bit of Land	1951	10.00
❑ 27443	The Meadows of Heaven/The Last Mile Home	1951	10.00
❑ 27461	Then You've Never Been Blue/You Gotta Show Me	1951	10.00
❑ 27477	Sparrow in the Tree Top/Forsaking All Others	1951	10.00
—With the Andrews Sisters			
❑ 27478	St. Patrick's Day Parade/With My Shillelagh Under My Arm	1951	10.00
❑ 27483	Sentimental Music/Any Town Is Paris When You're Young	1951	10.00
❑ 27500	Feudin' and Fightin'/Goodbye, My Lovers, Goodbye	1951	10.00
❑ 27505	When My Dreamboat Comes Home/Walking the Floor Over You	1951	10.00
❑ 27508	Silver Moon/More I Cannot Wish You	1951	10.00
❑ 27536	Maria Bonita/Quizas, Quizas, Quizas	1951	10.00
❑ 27549	Yours Is My Heart Alone/Beautiful Love	1951	10.00
❑ 27550	I Kiss Your Hand, Madame/The Kiss in Your Eyes	1951	10.00
❑ 27551	Girl of My Dreams/I'll Remember April	1951	10.00
❑ 27553	Country Style/Home Cookin'	1951	10.00
❑ 27554	I Only Want a Buddy — Not a Sweetheart/When the White Azaleas Start Blooming	1951	10.00
❑ 27555	Weddin' Day/(B-side unknown)	1951	10.00
—With the Andrews Sisters			
❑ 27577	Moonlight Bay/When You and I Were Young Maggie Blues	1951	10.00
—As "Gary and Bing Crosby"			

Except when noted otherwise, VG = 25% of NM, and VG+ = 50% of NM. (Example: VG = \$2.00, VG+ = \$4.00 and NM = \$8.00.)

Number	Title (A Side/B Side)	Yr	NM
❑ 27588	Hello Young Lovers/ Something Wonderful	1951	10.00
❑ 27589	Getting to Know You/ I Whistle a Happy Tune	1951	10.00
❑ 27595	With This Ring I Thee Wed/ Here Ends the Rainbow	1951	10.00
❑ 27605	Going My Way/ Swinging on a Star	1951	10.00
❑ 27606	Old Soldiers Never Die/ My Own Bit of Land	1951	10.00
❑ 27631	Black Ball Ferry Line/ The Yodeling Ghost	1951	10.00
—With the Andrews Sisters			
❑ 27643	I Might Be Your Once in a While/ Indian Summer	1951	10.00
❑ 27653	(Why Did I Twll You I Was Going to) Shanghai/I've Got to Fall in Love Again	1951	10.00
❑ 27667	Row, Row, Row/ Love Me or Leave Me	1951	10.00
❑ 27678	In the Cool, Cool, Cool of the Evening/Misto Christophe Columbo	1951	10.00
—With Jane Wyman			
❑ 27679	Your Own Little House/ Bonne Nuit	1951	10.00
❑ 27768	I Will Remember You/ The Loneliness of Evening	1951	10.00
❑ 27830	Domino/When the World Was Young	1951	10.00
❑ 9-27831	Christmas in Killarney/ It's Beginning to Look Like Christmas	1951	15.00
❑ 27852	A Weaver of Dreams/ I Still See Alisa	1951	10.00
❑ 27934	At Last, At Last!/ The Isle of Innisfree	1952	10.00
❑ 27951	Copacabana/Granada	1952	10.00
❑ 28048	2 Shillelagh O'Sullivan/That Tumbledown Shack in Athlone	1952	10.00
❑ 28061	Don't Ever Be Afraid to Go Home/ Rosaleen	1952	10.00
❑ 28195	Galway Bay/The Isle of Innisfree	1952	10.00
❑ 28210	Mine/You've Got Me Where You Want Me	1952	12.00
—With Judy Garland			
❑ 28217	Just for You/A Flight of Fancy	1952	10.00
❑ 28254	On the 10:10 from Ten-Ten-Tennessee/Just for You	1952	10.00
❑ 28255	Zing a Little Zong/The Maiden of Guadaloupe	1952	10.00
—With Jane Wyman			
❑ 28256	The Live Oak Tree/ I'll Si-Si You in Bahia	1952	10.00
—With the Andrews Sisters			
❑ 28261	The Bells of St. Mary's/Kathleen	1952	10.00
❑ 28265	Till the End of the World/ Just a Little Lovin'	1952	10.00
—With Grady Martin			
❑ 28303	Poinciana/Symphony	1952	10.00
❑ 28319	Deep in the Heart of Texas/ Do You Care	1952	10.00
❑ 28419	Cool Water/South Rampart Street Parade	1952	10.00
—With the Andrews Sisters			
❑ 28463	Sleigh Ride/Little Jack Frost Get Lost	1952	15.00
❑ 28470	Open Up Your Heart/You Don't Know What Lonesome Is	1952	10.00
❑ 28511	Sleigh Bell Serenade/ Keep It a Secret	1952	15.00
❑ 28513	The Road to Bali/Chicago Style	1952	10.00
—With Bob Hope			
❑ 28514	Merry Go Run Around/Hoot Mon	1952	10.00
—With Peggy Lee and Bob Hope			
❑ 28515	To See You/Moonflowers	1952	10.00
—B-side by Peggy Lee			
❑ 28581	Hush-a-Bye/Mother Darlin'	1953	10.00
❑ 28610	A Quiet Girl/Ohio	1953	10.00
❑ 28683	I Love My Baby (My Baby Loves Me)/There's Music in You	1953	10.00
❑ 28733	Tenderfoot/Walk Me By the River	1953	10.00
❑ 28743	It Had to Be You/Granada	1953	10.00
❑ 28805	Magic Window/Cela Mi Est Egal	1953	10.00
❑ 28814	Mademoiselle de Paris/ Embrasse — Moi Bien	1953	10.00
❑ 28955	Down By the Riverside/What a Little Moonlight Can Do	1953	10.00
—As "Bing and Gary Crosby"			
❑ 28963	Ida! Sweet as Apple Cider/I Can't Believe ThatYou're in Love	1953	10.00
❑ 28969	Y'All Come/Changing Partners	1954	10.00
❑ 29024	Secret Love/My Love, My Love	1954	10.00
❑ 29054	Young at Heart/I Get So Lonely	1954	10.00
❑ 29144	If You Love Me (Really Love Me)/ Liebchen	1954	10.00
❑ 29147	Call of the South/ Cornbelt Symphony	1954	10.00
—As "Bing and Gary Crosby"			

Number	Title (A Side/B Side)	Yr	NM
❑ 29212	In the Good Old Summertime/ Oh Tell Me Why (The Stars Do Shine)	1954	10.00
❑ 29251	Count Your Blessings Instead of Sheep/What Can You Do with a General	1954	10.00
❑ 29341	Old Man-Mandy/Gee, I Wish I Was Back in the Army	1954	10.00
❑ 29342	White Christmas/Snow	1954	15.00
—A-side with Danny Kaye; B-side by Peggy Lee and Trudi Stevens			
❑ 29357	The Song from Desiree/ Who Gave You the Roses	1954	10.00
❑ 29376	River/Tobermory Bay	1954	10.00
❑ 29409	Dissertation on State of Bliss/ It's Mine, It's Yours	1955	10.00
❑ 29410	The Land Around Us/ The Search Is Through	1955	10.00
❑ 29483	Farewell/Jim, Johnny & Jonah	1955	10.00
❑ 29493	Silver Moon/Nobody	1955	10.00
❑ 29568	She Is the Sunshine of Virginia/ (All She'd Say Was) Uh-Huh	1955	10.00
❑ 29634	You Are My Sunshine/ Nobody's Darling But Mine	1955	10.00
❑ 29636	Angel Bells/Let's Harmonize	1955	10.00
❑ 29777	The First Snowfall/The Next Time It Happens	1956	8.00
❑ 29790	Christmas Is A-Comin'/ Is Christmas Only a Tree	1955	12.00
❑ 29817	John Barleycorn/When You're in Love	1956	8.00
❑ 29850	In a Little Spanish Town ('Twas On a Night Like This)/ Ol' Man River	1956	8.00
❑ 29981	Honeysucle Rose/Swanee	1956	8.00
❑ 30023	When My Baby Smiles at Me/ April Showers	1956	8.00
❑ 30082	Now Is the Hour/Tumbling Tumbleweeds	1956	8.00
❑ 30120	Around the World/ Love in a Home	1956	10.00
❑ 30126	I Heard the Bells on Christmas Day/Christmas Is a-Comin'	1956	12.00
❑ 30126 [DJ]	I Heard the Bells on Christmas Day/Christmas Is a-Comin'	1956	12.00
—Pink label, black type			
❑ 30262	Around the World/ Around the World	1957	8.00
—B-side by Victor Young			
❑ 30262 [PS]	Around the World/ Around the World	1957	15.00
❑ 30488	Chinatown My Chinatown/ Alabamy Bound	1957	8.00
❑ 30555	Gigi/Trust Your Destiny to Your Star	1958	8.00
❑ 30828	Rain/Church Bells	1959	8.00
❑ 38031 [DJ]	Around the World/ Mississippi Mud	1957	10.00
—Green label			
❑ 38031 [PS]	Around the World/ Mississippi Mud	1957	20.00
❑ 40181	A Crosby Christmas (Part 1)/ A Crosby Christmas (Part 2)	1950	30.00
—As "Gary, Phillip, Dennis, Lindsay and Bing Crosby"			
KAPP			
❑ 196	How Lovely Is Christmas/ My Own Individual Star	1957	12.00
❑ 196 [PS]	How Lovely Is Christmas/ My Own Individual Star	1957	20.00
LITTLE GOLDEN			
❑ EP407	Boy At A Window/How Lovely Is Christmas	195?	10.00
❑ EP407 [PS]	Boy At A Window/How Lovely Is Christmas	195?	12.00
LONDON			
❑ 20095	There's Nothing I Haven't Sung About/The Way We Were	1977	4.00
MCA			
❑ 38056	Rudolph The Red-Nosed Reindeer/I Heard The Bells On Christmas Day	198?	4.00
❑ 40830	White Christmas/When the Blue of the Night Meets the Gold of the Day	1977	5.00
❑ 40830 [PS]	White Christmas/When the Blue of the Night Meets the Gold of the Day	1977	5.00
❑ 65019	Jingle Bells/Santa Claus Is Comin' to Town	1973	4.00
—With the Andrews Sisters; black label with rainbow			
❑ 65019	Jingle Bells/Santa Claus Is Comin' to Town	1980	3.00
—With the Andrews Sisters; blue label with rainbow			
❑ 65021	Silent Night/Adeste Fideles (O Come All Ye Faithful)	1973	4.00
—Black label with rainbow			
❑ 65021	Silent Night/Adeste Fideles (O Come All Ye Faithful)	1980	3.00
—Blue label with rainbow			

Number	Title (A Side/B Side)	Yr	NM
❑ 65022	White Christmas/God Rest Ye Merry Gentlemen	1973	4.00
—Black label with rainbow			
❑ 65022	White Christmas/God Rest Ye Merry Gentlemen	1980	3.00
—Blue label with rainbow			
MGM			
❑ 12946	The Second Time Around/ Incurably Romantic	1960	8.00
P.I.P.			
❑ 8903	Where the Rainbow Ends/ What's More American	197?	5.00
POLYDOR			
❑ 14452	Yesterday, When I Was Young/ June in January	1978	4.00
RCA VICTOR			
❑ 47-7695	It's a Good Day/ The Music of Home	1960	8.00
REPRISE			
❑ 0283	Don't Be a Do-Badder/ The Hukilau Song	1964	6.00
❑ 0315	It's Christmas Time Again/ Christmas Candles	1964	12.00
—With Fred Waring and the Pennsylvanians			
❑ 0315 [PS]	It's Christmas Time Again/ Christmas Candles	1964	15.00
❑ 0424	The White World of Winter/ The Secret of Christmas	1965	8.00
❑ 0478	How Green Was My Valley/ Far from Home	1966	5.00
❑ 0645	Step to the Rear/What Do We Do with the World	1967	5.00
UNITED ARTISTS			
❑ XW700	Send In the Clowns/ That's What Life Is All About	1975	4.00
VERVE			
❑ 2025	I've Got Five Dollars/ Mountain Greenery	1956	10.00
❑ 10089	Heat Wave/September in the Rain	1957	10.00
WARNER BROS.			
❑ PRO 146 [DJ]	I Wish You a Merry Christmas/ Winter Wonderland// The Littlest Angel	1962	20.00
7-Inch Extended Plays			
DECCA			
❑ ED 547 [PS]	Merry Christmas	195?	25.00
—Cover for 2-EP set			
❑ ED 561 [PS]	Christmas Greetings	195?	25.00
—Cover for 2-EP set (91129 and 91130)			
❑ ED 581 [PS]	Stardust	195?	20.00
—Cover for 2-EP set			
❑ ED 662 [PS]	Down Memory Lane	195?	20.00
—Cover for 2-EP set			
❑ ED 850 [PS]	A Christmas Sing with Bing Around the World	195?	20.00
—Gatefold cover for 91835, 91836 and 91837			
❑ ED 1800 [PS]	Old Masters	195?	20.00
—Box for records 91611 through 91619			
❑ ED 2000	Red Sails in the Sunset/Far Away Places//Harbor Lights/ On Treasure Island	195?	12.00
❑ ED 2000 [PS]	Bing Crosby, Vol. 1	195?	12.00
❑ ED 2036	*Going My Way/Swinging on a Star/Too-Ra-Loo-Ra-Loo-Ral/The Day After Forever	195?	12.00
❑ ED 2036 [PS]	Going My Way	195?	12.00
❑ ED 2107	Do You Ever Think of Me/I Never Knew//Somebody Loves Me/After You've Gone	195?	12.00
❑ ED 2107 [PS]	Some Fine Old Chestnuts, Vol. 1	195?	12.00
❑ ED 2108	Sleepy Time Gal/Dinah//I Never Knew/I Can't Give You Anything But Love	1954	12.00
❑ ED 2108 [PS]	Some Fine Old Chestnuts, Vol. 2	1954	12.00
❑ ED 2426	April Showers/When My Baby Smiles at Me//My Blue Heaven/ A Little Kiss Each Morning (A Little Kiss Each Night)	195?	15.00
❑ ED 2426 [PS]	Song I Wish I Had Sung the First Time Around... Part 1	195?	15.00
❑ ED 2427	Prisoner of Love/Ain't Misbehavin'//Paper Doll/ This Love of Mine	1956	15.00
❑ ED 2427 [PS]	Song I Wish I Had Sung the First Time Around... Part 2	1956	15.00
❑ ED 2535	When I Take My Sugar to Tea/On the Alamo//I'm Confessin' (That I Love You)/Between the Devil and the Deep Blue Sea	195?	12.00
❑ ED 2535 [PS]	New Tricks...	195?	12.00
❑ ED 2547	Silent Night, Holy Night/Adeste Fideles//White Christmas/ Jingle Bells	195?	12.00
❑ ED 2547 [PS]	Christmas Time	195?	12.00

C

Number	Title (A Side/B Side)	Yr	NM
❑ ED 2659	Silver Bells/The Christmas Song//Christmas Carols/God Rest Ye Merry Gentlemen	195?	12.00
❑ ED 2659 [PS]	Christmas Songs	195?	12.00
❑ 7-34184	White Christmas/Santa Claus Is Comin' to Town/Silver Bells//I'll Be Home for Christmas/It's Beginning to Look a Lot Like Christmas/Silent Night	196?	12.00
—Rechanneled stereo jukebox issue; small hole, plays at 33 1/3 rpm			
❑ 7-34184 [PS]	Merry Christmas	196?	12.00
❑ 7-38274	The First Nowell/Medley: Deck The Hall-Away In A Manger-I Saw Three Ships//God Rest Ye Merry, Gentlemen/Jingle Bells	196?	12.00
—Small hole, plays at 33 1/3 rpm; Side 1 is mono and has the number ED 38274, Side 2 is "stereo" (rechanneled) and has the number ED 738274			
❑ 7-38274 [PS]	General Electric Wishes You a Merry Christmas	196?	12.00
❑ 91123	Silent Night/Adeste Fideles//White Christmas/God Rest Ye Merry Gentlemen	195?	12.00
—Part of 2-EP set ED 547			
❑ 91124	I'll Be Home for Christmas/Faith of Our Fathers//Jingle Bells/Santa Claus Is Comin' to Town	195?	12.00
—Part of 2-EP set ED 547			
❑ 91129	Here Comes Santa Claus/Twelve Days of Christmas//You're All I Want for Christmas/The First Nowell	195?	12.00
—Part of 2-EP set ED 561			
❑ 91130	Christmas Carols, Part 1/Christmas Carols, Part 2//The Christmas Song/O, Fir Tree Dark	195?	12.00
—Part of 2-EP set ED 561			
❑ 91168	I Cried for You/My Melancholy Baby//Star Dust/Deep Purple	195?	12.00
—Part of 2-EP set ED 581			
❑ 91169	The One Rose/Moonlight and Shadows//A Blue Serenade/S'posin'	195?	12.00
—Part of 2-EP set ED 581			
❑ 91289	Please/I Found a Million Dollar Baby//I Wonder What's Become of Sally/Mary's a Grand Old Name	195?	12.00
—Part of 2-EP set ED 662			
❑ 91290	I'm Waiting for Ships That Never Come In/When Day Is Done//I Don't Want to Walk Without You/Moonlight Cocktail	195?	12.00
—Part of 2-EP set ED 662			
❑ 91611	Someday, Sweetheart/Would You//How Soon/I'll See You in My Dreams	195?	8.00
—Side 1 and Side 18 of ED 1800			
❑ 91612	(contents unknown)	195?	8.00
—Side 2 and Side 17 of ED 1800			
❑ 91613	Dear Old Girl/You Must Have Been a Beautiful Baby//Sweet Lorraine/The One I Love (Belongs to Somebody Else)	195?	8.00
—Side 3 and Side 16 of ED 1800			
❑ 91614	It's the Dreamer in Me/My Reverie//I Want My Mama/So in Love	195?	8.00
—Side 4 and Side 15 of ED 1800			
❑ 91615	Old Folks/Don't Be That Way//On Behalf of the Visiting Firemen/One Sweet Letter from You	195?	8.00
—Side 5 and Side 14 of ED 1800			
❑ 91616	Mr. Crosby and Mr. Mercer/The Moon of Manakoora//Pretending/These Foolish Things (Remind Me of You)	195?	8.00
—Side 6 and Side 13 of ED 1800			
❑ 91617	Lazy/It's the Talk of the Town//And the Angels Sing/On the Atchison, Topeka and the Santa Fe	195?	8.00
—Side 7 and Side 12 of ED 1800			
❑ 91618	What's New/If I Knew Then (What I Know Now)//A Gal in Calico/Bue Beautiful	195?	8.00
—Side 8 and Side 11 of ED 1800			
❑ 91619	My Buddy/I Ain't Got Nobody (And Nobody Cares for Me)//Mister Meadowlark/Imagination	195?	8.00
—Side 9 and Side 10 of ED 1800			
❑ 91836	Happy Holiday/Joy to the World/Hark! The Herald Angels Sing//God Rest Ye Merry Gentlemen/O Little Town of Bethlehem/Silent Night	195?	8.00
—Side 1 and Side 6 of ED 850; titles not listed on labels			
❑ 91837	White Christmas/Adeste Fideles/We Three Kings of Orient Are//Away in a Manger/Thou Descendeth from the Stars (Descendi de la Stelli)/Deck the Hall	195?	8.00
—Side 2 and Side 5 of ED 850; titles not listed on labels			
❑ 91838	The First Noel/Carol of the Bells/What Christmas Means to Me//Good King Wenceslas/Jesus, Sweet Savior (Jesus, Sauveur Adorable)/Angels We Have Heard on High	195?	8.00
—Side 3 and Side 4 of ED 850; song titles not listed on labels			
RCA VICTOR			
❑ EPA 3-1473	Mack the Knife/Tell Me//Down Among the Sheltering Palms/Mama Loved Papa	1957	8.00
❑ EPA 3-1473 [PS]	Bing with a Beat	1957	10.00
Albums			
AMOS			
❑ AAS-7001	Hey Jude/Hey Bing!	1969	12.00
BIOGRAPH			
❑ M-1	When the Blue of the Night Meets the Gold of the Day	197?	10.00
❑ C-13	Bing Crosby 1929-33	1973	12.00
BRUNSWICK			
❑ BL 54005 [M]	The Voice of Bing in the 1930s	1957	25.00
❑ BL 58000 [10]	Bing Crosby, Vol. 1	1950	50.00
❑ BL 58001 [10]	Bing Crosby, Vol. 2	1950	50.00
CAPITOL			
❑ ST 2300 [S]	That Travelin' Two-Beat	1965	20.00
❑ T 2300 [M]	That Travelin' Two-Beat	1965	15.00
❑ ST 2346 [S]	Great Country Hits	1965	20.00
❑ T 2346 [M]	Great Country Hits	1965	15.00
❑ SM-11732	Bing Crosby's Christmas Classics	1977	10.00
—"A Capitol Re-Issue"; same recordings as on Warner Bros. 1484			
❑ SM-11736	That Travelin' Two-Beat	1977	10.00
❑ SM-11737	Great Country Hits	1977	10.00
❑ SM-11738	Bing Crosby Classics, Vol. 1	1977	10.00
❑ SM-11739	Bing Crosby Classics, Vol. 2	1977	10.00
❑ SM-11740	Bing Crosby Classics, Vol. 3	1977	10.00
COLUMBIA			
❑ C2L 43 [(2)]	Bing in Hollywood 1930-1934	196?	15.00
—Red "360 Sound" labels			
❑ C2L 43 [(2)]	Bing in Hollywood 1930-1934	1971	12.00
—Orange labels			
❑ CL 2502 [10]	Der Bingle	1955	40.00
❑ CL 6027 [10]	Crosby Classics	1949	50.00
❑ CL 6105 [10]	Crosby Classics, Vol. 2	1950	50.00
❑ C 35093	Bing Crosby Collection, Vol. 1	1977	10.00
❑ C 35094	Bing Crosby Collection, Vol. 2	1977	10.00
❑ C4X 44229 [(4)]	The Crooner: The Columbia Years	1988	40.00
COLUMBIA SPECIAL PRODUCTS			
❑ CE2E-201 [(2)]	The Bing Crosby Story, Vol. 1	1974	12.00
—Reissue of Encore E2E-201			
❑ P 14369	Bing	197?	10.00
DAYBREAK			
❑ 2006	A Time to Be Jolly	1971	12.00
❑ 2014	Bing and Basie	1972	12.00
DECCA			
❑ DX 151 [(5)M]	Bing: A Musical Autobiography	195?	150.00
❑ DX 152 [(3)M]	Old Masters	195?	150.00
❑ DXB 184 [(2)M]	The Best of Bing	1965	25.00
❑ DL 4086 [M]	My Golden Favorites	1961	25.00
❑ DL 4250 [M]	Bing's Hollywood: Easy to Remember	1962	25.00
❑ DL 4251 [M]	Bing's Hollywood: Pennies from Heaven	1962	25.00
❑ DL 4252 [M]	Bing's Hollywood: Pocket Full of Dreams	1962	25.00
❑ DL 4253 [M]	Bing's Hollywood: East Side of Heaven	1962	25.00
❑ DL 4254 [M]	Bing's Hollywood: The Road Begins	1962	25.00
❑ DL 4255 [M]	Bing's Hollywood: Only Forever	1962	25.00
❑ DL 4256 [M]	Bing's Hollywood: Holiday Inn	1962	25.00
❑ DL 4257 [M]	Bing's Hollywood: Swinging on a Star	1962	25.00
❑ DL 4258 [M]	Bing's Hollywood: Accentuate the Positive	1962	25.00
❑ DL 4259 [M]	Bing's Hollywood: Blue Skies	1962	25.00
❑ DL 4260 [M]	Bing's Hollywood: But Beautiful	1962	25.00
❑ DL 4261 [M]	Bing's Hollywood: Sunshine Cake	1962	25.00
❑ DL 4262 [M]	Bing's Hollywood: Cool of the Evening	1962	25.00
❑ DL 4263 [M]	Bing's Hollywood: Zing a Little Zong	1962	25.00
❑ DL 4264 [M]	Bing's Hollywood: Anything Goes	1962	25.00
❑ DL 4281 [M]	Holiday in Europe	1962	25.00
❑ DL 4283	Two Favorite Stories by Bing Crosby	1962	25.00
❑ DL 4415 [M]	Songs Everybody Knows	1964	25.00
❑ DLP 5000 [10]	Hits from Musical Comedies	1949	50.00
❑ DLP 5001 [10]	Jerome Kern Songs	1949	50.00
❑ DLP 5010 [10]	Stephen Foster Songs	1949	50.00
❑ DLP 5011 [10]	El Bingo	1949	50.00
❑ DL 5019 [10]	Merry Christmas	1950	50.00
—Second editions have a blue-green cover, but a "DL" prefix on the record, though not necessarily on the cover			
❑ DL 5019 [10]	Merry Christmas	1951	40.00
—Third editions have a brand-new red and green cover			
❑ DLP 5019 [10]	Merry Christmas	1949	60.00
—Original editions have a light blue-green cover and "DLP" prefix			
❑ DLP 5020 [10]	Christmas Greetings	1949	60.00
❑ DL 5028 [10]	Auld Lang Syne	1950	50.00
❑ DL 5037 [10]	St. Patrick's Day	1950	50.00
❑ DL 5039 [10]	St. Valentine's Day	1950	50.00
❑ DL 5042 [10]	Blue Skies	1950	50.00
❑ DL 5052 [10]	Going My Way/The Bells of St. Mary's	1950	60.00
❑ DL 5063 [10]	Don't Fence Me In	1950	50.00
❑ DL 5064 [10]	Cole Porter Songs	1950	50.00
❑ DL 5081 [10]	Songs by Gershwin	1950	50.00
❑ DL 5102 [10]	Blue of the Night	1950	50.00
❑ DL 5107 [10]	Cowboy Songs	1950	50.00
❑ DL 5119 [10]	Drifting and Dreaming	1950	50.00
❑ DL 5122 [10]	Hawaiian Songs	1950	50.00
❑ DL 5126 [10]	Stardust	1950	50.00
❑ DL 5129 [10]	Cowboy Songs, Vol. 2	1950	50.00
❑ DL 5220 [10]	Bing Sings Hits	1950	50.00
❑ DL 5272 [10]	Top o' the Morning/The Emperor Waltz	1950	50.00
❑ DL 5284 [10]	Mr. Music	1950	50.00
❑ DL 5298 [10]	Hits from Broadway Shows	1951	50.00
❑ DL 5299 [10]	Favorite Hawaiian Songs	1951	50.00
❑ DL 5302 [10]	Go West, Young Man	1951	50.00
❑ DL 5310 [10]	Way Back Home	1951	50.00
❑ DL 5323 [10]	Bing and the Dixieland Bands	1951	50.00
❑ DL 5326 [10]	Yours Is My Heart Alone	1951	50.00
❑ DL 5331 [10]	Country Style	1951	50.00
❑ DL 5340 [10]	Down Memory Lane	1951	50.00
❑ DL 5343 [10]	Down Memory Lane, Vol. 2	1951	50.00
❑ DL 5351 [10]	Beloved Hymns	1951	50.00
❑ DL 5355 [10]	Bing Sings Victor Herbert	1951	50.00
❑ DL 5390 [10]	Bing and Connee	1953	50.00
—With Connee Boswell			
❑ DL 5403 [10]	When Irish Eyes Are Smiling	1952	50.00
❑ DL 5417 [10]	Just for You	1952	50.00
❑ DL 5444 [10]	The Road to Bali	1952	60.00
❑ DL 5499 [10]	Song Hits of Paris/Le Bing	1953	50.00
❑ DL 5508 [10]	Some Fine Old Chestnuts	1953	50.00
❑ DL 5520 [10]	Bing Sings the Hits	1954	50.00
❑ DL 5556 [10]	Country Girl/Little Boy Lost/Anything Goes	1954	50.00
❑ DL 6000 [10]	Two Favorite Stories by Bing Crosby	1950	60.00
❑ DL 6001 [10]	Ichabod/Rip Van Winkle	1950	50.00
❑ DL 6008 [10]	Collector's Classics: Mississippi/Here Is My Heart	1951	60.00
❑ DL 6009 [10]	Collector's Classics: Anything Goes/Two for Tonight	1951	60.00
❑ DL 6010 [10]	Collector's Classics: Rhythm on the Range/Pennies from Heaven	1951	60.00
❑ DL 6011 [10]	Collector's Classics: Waikiki Wedding	1951	60.00
❑ DL 6012 [10]	Collector's Classics: Paris Honeymoon	1951	60.00
❑ DL 6013 [10]	Collector's Classics: The Star Maker/Doctor Rhythm	1951	60.00
❑ DL 6014 [10]	Collector's Classics: Big Broadcast of 1936	1951	60.00
❑ DL 6015 [10]	Collector's Classics: The Road to Singapore/If I Had My Way	1951	60.00
❑ DXSB 7184 [(2)R]	The Best of Bing	1965	15.00
❑ DL 8020 [M]	The Man Without a Country/What So Proudly We Hail	1950	40.00
❑ DL 8110 [M]	Lullaby Time	1955	40.00
❑ DL 8128 [M]	Merry Christmas	1955	40.00
—Expanded version of 10-inch LP; all-black label			
❑ DL 8128 [M]	Merry Christmas	1960	25.00
—Reissue on black label with color bars			
❑ DL 8178 [M]	Merry Christmas	196?	60.00
—Black label with color bars; at least one copy is known to exist on red vinyl			
❑ DL 8207 [M]	Shillelaghs and Shamrocks	1956	40.00
❑ DL 8210 [M]	Home on the Range	1956	40.00
❑ DL 8262 [M]	When Irish Eyes Are Smiling	1956	40.00
❑ DL 8268 [M]	Drifting and Dreaming	1956	40.00
❑ DL 8269 [M]	Blue Hawaii	1956	40.00
❑ DL 8272 [M]	High Tor	1956	400.00
❑ DL 8318 [M]	Anything Goes	1956	50.00
❑ DL 8352 [M]	Song I Wish I Had Sung… The First Time Around	1956	40.00
❑ DL 8365 [M]	Twilight on the Trail	1957	40.00
❑ DL 8374 [M]	Some Fine Old Chestnuts	1957	40.00
❑ DL 8419 [M]	A Christmas Sing with Bing Around the World	1957	40.00
❑ DL 8493 [M]	Bing and the Dixieland Bands	1957	40.00
❑ DL 8575 [M]	New Tricks	1957	40.00

Number | Title (A Side/B Side) | Yr | NM

❑ DL 8687 [M] Around the World 1958 40.00
❑ DL 8780 [M] Bing in Paris 1958 40.00
❑ DL 8781 [M] That Christmas Feeling 1958 30.00
—Expanded version of DL 5020; all-black label, textured cover
❑ DL 8781 [M] That Christmas Feeling 1960 20.00
—Reissue on black label with color bars, smooth cover
❑ DL 8846 [M] In a Little Spanish Town 1959 30.00
❑ DL 9054 [M] Bing: A Musical Autobiography 1927-1934 1961 40.00
❑ DL 9064 [M] Bing: A Musical Autobiography 1934-1941 1961 40.00
❑ DL 9067 [M] Bing: A Musical Autobiography 1941-44 1961 40.00
❑ DL 9077 [M] Bing: A Musical Autobiography 1944-47 1961 40.00
❑ DL 9078 [M] Bing: A Musical Autobiography 1947-1953 1961 40.00
❑ DL 9106 [M] Ichabod/Rip Van Winkle 1962 25.00
❑ DL 34522 Favorite Songs of Christmas 1968 15.00
—Decca Records Custom Division pressing
❑ DL 74281 [R] Holiday in Europe 1962 15.00
❑ DL 74283 [R] The Small One 1962 10.00
❑ DL 74415 [R] Songs Everybody Knows 1964 15.00
❑ DL 78128 [R] Merry Christmas 196? 10.00
❑ DL 78207 [R] Shillelaghs and Shamrocks 196? 10.00
❑ DL 78262 [R] When Irish Eyes Are Smiling 196? 10.00
❑ DL 78352 [R] Songs I Wish I Had Sung… The First Time Around 196? 10.00
❑ DL 78419 [R] A Christmas Sing with Bing Around the World 196? 10.00
❑ DL 78781 [R] That Christmas Feeling 196? 10.00
❑ DL 79106 [R] Ichabod/Rip Van Winkle 1962 10.00

ENCORE
❑ E2E-201 [(2)] The Bing Crosby Story, Vol. 1 1968 15.00
❑ E2E-202 [(2)] The Bing Crosby Story, Vol. 2 1968 15.00

FOX AMERICAN
❑ SMF 210 Bing Crosby Sings Christmas 1978 10.00
—Side 1 from radio show Dec. 19, 1951; Side 2 from radio show Dec. 14, 1949

GNP CRESCENDO
❑ GNP-9044 The Radio Years, Vol. 1 1985 8.00
❑ GNP-9046 The Radio Years, Vol. 2 1986 8.00
❑ GNP-9047 The Radio Years, Vol. 3 1986 8.00
❑ GNP-9048 The Radio Years, Vol. 4 1986 8.00

GOLDEN
❑ A298:20 [M] Ali Baba and the 40 Thieves 1957 25.00
❑ A298:21 [M] How Lovely Is Christmas/A Christmas Story 195? 25.00

HARMONY
❑ HL 7094 [M] Crosby Classics 1958 15.00
❑ HS 11313 [R] Crosby Classics 196? 10.00

LONDON
❑ PS 679 Feels Good 1977 12.00

MARK 56
❑ 762 Original Radio Broadcasts 197? 10.00

MCA
❑ 177 Shillelaghs and Shamrocks 1973 10.00
❑ 519 When Irish Eyes Are Smiling 197? 10.00
❑ 915 Hey Bing! 198? 10.00
❑ 1502 Rare 1930-31 Brunswick Recordings 198? 10.00
❑ 3031 Bing Crosby's Greatest Hits 1977 10.00
❑ 2-4045 [(2)] The Best of Bing 197? 10.00
—Blue labels with rainbow; regular cover
❑ 2-4045 [(2)] The Best of Bing 197? 12.00
—Black labels with rainbow; gatefold cover
❑ 15017 Two Favorite Stories by Bing Crosby 197? 10.00
—Reissue of Decca DL 4283
❑ 15018 [R] A Christmas Sing with Bing Around the World 197? 8.00
—Reissue of Decca DL7-8419
❑ 15019 [R] That Christmas Feeling 1973 8.00
—Reissue of Decca DL7-8781
❑ 15024 [R] Merry Christmas 197? 8.00
—Reissue of Decca DL7-8128
❑ 37076 Bing Crosby's Greatest Hits 198? 8.00

METRO
❑ M-523 [M] Bing Crosby 1965 12.00
❑ MS-523 [S] Bing Crosby 1965 15.00

MGM
❑ E-3890 [M] Senor Bing 1961 15.00
❑ SE-3890 [S] Senor Bing 1961 20.00
❑ E-4129 [M] The Great Standards 1963 15.00
❑ SE-4129 [S] The Great Standards 1963 20.00
❑ E-4203 [M] The Very Best of Bing Crosby 1964 15.00
❑ SE-4203 [S] The Very Best of Bing Crosby 1964 20.00

MOBILE FIDELITY
❑ 1-260 Bing Sings Whilst Bregman Swings 1996 20.00
—Audiophile vinyl

MURRAY HILL
❑ 894637 [(4)] Bing Crosby and His Friends 197? 25.00

P.I.P.
❑ 6802 Thoroughly Modern Bing 1971 12.00

PHILCO
❑ LP 436 [10] Crosby Classics 195? 40.00
—Custom item for Philco (front cover has "Philco: Famous for Quality the World Over")

PICKWICK
❑ SPC-3583 Thoroughly Modern Bing 1978 8.00

POLYDOR
❑ PD-1-6128 Seasons: The Closing Chapter 1978 12.00

RCA VICTOR
❑ LPM-1473 [M] Bing with a Beat 1957 25.00
❑ AFL1-1854 Fancy Meeting You Here 1977 10.00
❑ LPM-1854 [M] Fancy Meeting You Here 1958 20.00
❑ LSP-1854 [S] Fancy Meeting You Here 1958 30.00
❑ LPM-2071 [M] Young Bing Crosby 1959 20.00
❑ CPL1-2086(e) A Legendary Performer 1976 10.00

READER'S DIGEST
❑ RDA-175 Christmas with Bing 1980 10.00
—Repackage of Warner Bros.and Capitol recordings

REPRISE
❑ R-6106 [M] Return to Paradise Islands 1964 15.00
❑ R9-6106 [S] Return to Paradise Islands 1964 20.00

SPOKANE
❑ 1 Bing Crosby On the Air, 1934 and 1938 197? 10.00
❑ 5 Der Bingle, Vol. 1 197? 10.00
❑ 10 Der Bingle, Vol. 2 197? 10.00
❑ 12 Bing in the 30's 197? 10.00
❑ 14 Bing in the 30s, Vol. 2 197? 10.00
❑ 15 Holiday Inn/The Bells of St. Mary's 197? 10.00
❑ 16 Kraft Music Hall Highlights 197? 10.00
❑ 19 Kraft Music Hall Highlights, Vol. 2 197? 10.00
❑ 20 Der Bingle, Vol. 3 197? 10.00
❑ 21 Bing Crosby & the Music Maids 197? 10.00
❑ 24 Bing in the 30s, Vol. 3 1986 8.00
❑ 25 Bing in the 30s, Vol. 4 1986 8.00
❑ 26 Bing in the 30s, Vol. 5 1986 8.00
❑ 27 Bing in the 30s, Vol. 6 1986 8.00

SUNBEAM
❑ 502 Distinctively Bing, Vol. 1 197? 10.00
❑ 504 Distinctively Bing, Vol. 2 197? 10.00

TIME-LIFE
❑ SLGD-06 [(2)] Legendary Singers: Bing Crosby 1985 15.00

20TH CENTURY
❑ T-551 A Holiday Toast 1977 12.00

UNITED ARTISTS
❑ UA-LA554-G That's What Life Is All About 1976 12.00

VERVE
❑ MGV 2020 [M] Bing Sings Whilst Bregman Swings 1956 50.00
❑ V-2020 [M] Bing Sings Whilst Bregman Swings 1961 25.00

VOCALION
❑ VL 3603 [M] Bing Crosby Sings 195? 15.00
❑ VL 73603 [R] Bing Crosby Sings 196? 10.00

WARNER BROS.
❑ W 1363 [M] Join with Bing and Sing Along 1960 15.00
❑ WS 1363 [S] Join with Bing and Sing Along 1960 20.00
❑ 2W 1401 [(2)M] 101 Gang Songs 1961 20.00
❑ 2WS 1401 [(2)S] 101 Gang Songs 1961 25.00
❑ W 1422 [M] Join Bing in a Gang Song Sing-Along 1961 15.00
❑ WS 1422 [S] Join Bing in a Gang Song Sing-Along 1961 20.00
❑ W 1435 [M] Join Bing and Sing Along 1962 15.00
❑ WS 1435 [S] Join Bing and Sing Along 1962 20.00
❑ W 1482 [M] On the Happy Side 1962 15.00
❑ WS 1482 [S] On the Happy Side 1962 20.00
❑ W 1484 [M] I Wish You a Merry Christmas 1962 15.00
❑ WS 1484 [S] I Wish You a Merry Christmas 1962 20.00

"X"
❑ XLVA-4250 [M] Young Bing Crosby 1955 50.00

CROSBY, BING, AND LOUIS ARMSTRONG

Also see each artist's individual listings.

45s

DECCA
❑ 27623 Gone Fishin'/We All Have a Song in My Heart 1951 15.00

MGM
❑ SB 26 [S] Muskrat Ramble/Way Down in New Orleans 1960 15.00
❑ SB 27 [S] Dardanella/Brother Bill 1960 15.00
❑ SB 28 [S] Preacher/Little Ol' Tune 1960 15.00
❑ SB 29 [S] Let's Sing Like a Dixieland Band/At the Jazz Band Ball 1960 15.00
❑ SB 30 [S] Rocky Mountain Moon/Bye Bye Blues 1960 15.00
—The above five are 33 1/3 rpm jukebox singles
❑ 12961 Dardanella/Muskrat Ramble 1960 10.00

Albums

CAPITOL
❑ SM-11735 Bing Crosby and Louis Armstrong 1977 10.00

MGM
❑ E-3882 [M] Bing and Satchmo 1960 15.00
❑ SE-3882 [S] Bing and Satchmo 1960 20.00

CROSBY, BING, AND FRED ASTAIRE

Albums

UNITED ARTISTS
❑ UA-LA588-G A Couple of Song and Dance Men 1976 12.00

CROSBY, BING, AND PEGGY LEE

Also see each artist's individual listings.

45s

DECCA
❑ 28238 Watermelon Weather/The Moon Came Up with a Great Idea Last Night 1952 12.00

CROSBY, DAVID

Also see THE BYRDS; CROSBY, STILLS AND NASH; CROSBY, STILLS, NASH AND YOUNG; GRAHAM NASH AND DAVID CROSBY.

45s

ATLANTIC
❑ 2792 Laughing/Music Is Love 1971 5.00
❑ 2809 Orleans/Traction in the Rain 1971 5.00
❑ 87360 Hero/Coverage 1993 3.00
—A-side with Phil Collins

Albums

A&M
❑ SP-5232 Oh Yes I Can 1989 10.00

ATLANTIC
❑ SD 7203 If I Could Only Remember My Name… 1971 15.00
❑ SD 7203 If I Could Only Remember My Name… 2000 25.00
—Classic Records reissue on audiophile vinyl

CROSBY, DAVID, AND GRAHAM NASH

See GRAHAM NASH AND DAVID CROSBY.

CROSBY, GARY

45s

DECCA
❑ 9-27112 Play a Simple Melody/Sam's Song 1950 12.00
—By "Gary Crosby and Friend" (guess who the friend is)
❑ 9-27577 Moonlight Bay/When You and I Were Young Maggie Blues 1951 10.00
—As "Gary and Bing Crosby"
❑ 9-28955 Down By the Riverside/What a Little Moonlight Can Do 1953 10.00
—As "Bing and Gary Crosby"
❑ 9-29147 Call of the South/Cornbelt Symphony 1954 10.00
—As "Bing and Gary Crosby"
❑ 9-29272 Mambo in the Moonlight/Got My Eyes on You 1954 12.00
❑ 9-29291 Ready, Willing and Able/There's a Small Hotel 1954 12.00
❑ 9-29378 Loop-de-Loop Mambo/Palsy Walsy 1954 12.00
❑ 9-29420 Ko Ko Mo/Struttin' with Some Barbecue 1955 12.00
❑ 9-29527 His and Hers/Truly Do 1955 25.00
—With the Paris Sisters
❑ 9-29538 Mississippi Pecan Pie/Ayuh, Ayuh 1955 12.00
❑ 9-29692 Give Me a Band and My Baby/Yaller Yaller Gold 1955 12.00
❑ 9-29779 Get a Load o' Me/Noah Found Grace in the Eyes of the Lord 1956 10.00
❑ 9-29921 Lazy Bones/Easy Street 1956 12.00
—With Lous Armstrong
❑ 9-40181 A Crosby Christmas (Part 1)/A Crosby Christmas (Part 2) 1950 30.00
—As "Gary, Phillip, Dennis, Lindsay and Bing Crosby"

GREGMARK
❑ 11 That's Alright Baby/Who 1962 30.00

HICKORY
❑ 1448 I'm Gonna Call My Baby/Town Girl 1967 10.00

VERVE
❑ 10153 Judy, Judy/Cheatin' on Me 1958 15.00
❑ 10163 Sentimental Journey/After the Lights Go Down Low 1959 15.00
❑ 10173 The Happy Bachelor/This Little Girl of Mine 1959 15.00

C

Christopher Cross, "All Right," Warner Bros. 92 98437, 1983, $4.

Number	Title (A Side/B Side)	Yr	NM
WARNER BROS.			
❑ 5208	Baby Won't You Please Come Home/You're Nobody 'Till Somebody Loves You	1961	12.00

Albums

Number	Title (A Side/B Side)	Yr	NM
VERVE			
❑ MGV-2112 [M]	Gary Crosby Belts the Blues	1959	100.00

CROSBY, STILLS, NASH & YOUNG

Also see DAVID CROSBY; GRAHAM NASH; STEPHEN STILLS; NEIL YOUNG.

Albums

Number	Title (A Side/B Side)	Yr	NM
ATLANTIC			
❑ - [(2)DJ]	4 Way Street	1971	50.00
—White label stereo promo			
❑ PR165 [M]	Celebration/CSNY Month	1974	100.00
—Promo-only LP in mono			
❑ PR165 [n/a]	Celebration/CSNY Month	1974	50.00
—Promo-only LP in stereo			
❑ SD7200 [DJ]	Deja Vu	1970	60.00
—White label stereo promo			
❑ PR18102 [DJ]	A Rap with C, S, N & Y	1974	50.00
—Promo-only interview album			

CROSBY, STILLS AND NASH

Also see DAVID CROSBY; GRAHAM NASH; STEPHEN STILLS.

12-Inch Singles

Number	Title (A Side/B Side)	Yr	NM
ATLANTIC			
❑ PR (# unk) [DJ]	Southern Cross (LP Version)/Too Much Love to Hide	1982	15.00
❑ PR 445 [DJ]	Wasted on the Way/Daylight Again	1982	8.00
❑ PR 508 [DJ]	War Games/For What It's Worth/Turn Your Back on Love	1983	8.00
❑ PR 3377 [DJ]	Live It Up (2 versions)	1990	10.00

45s

Number	Title (A Side/B Side)	Yr	NM
ATLANTIC			
❑ 2652	Marrakesh Express/Helplessly Hoping	1969	6.00
❑ 2676	Suite: Judy Blue Eyes/Long Time Gone	1969	6.00
❑ 3401	Just a Song Before I Go/Dark Star	1977	4.00
❑ 3401 [PS]	Just a Song Before I Go/Dark Star	1977	5.00
❑ 3432	Fair Game/Anything at All	1977	4.00
❑ 3453	I Give You Give Blind/Carried Away	1978	4.00
❑ 3784	Carry On/Shadow Captain	1980	5.00
❑ 4058	Wasted on the Way/Delta	1982	3.00
❑ 4058 [PS]	Wasted on the Way/Delta	1982	4.00
❑ 87909	Live It Up/Chuck's Lament	1990	4.00
❑ 89775	Raise a Voice/For What It's Worth	1983	3.00
❑ 89812	War Games/Shadow Captain	1983	3.00
❑ 89812 [PS]	War Games/Shadow Captain	1983	4.00
❑ 89888	Too Much Love to Hide/Song for Susan	1983	3.00
❑ 89969	Southern Cross/Into the Darkness	1982	3.00
❑ 89969 [PS]	Southern Cross/Into the Darkness	1982	4.00

Albums

Number	Title (A Side/B Side)	Yr	NM
ATLANTIC			
❑ SD 8229	Crosby, Stills & Nash	1969	20.00
❑ SD 8229	Crosby, Stills & Nash	2000	25.00
—Classic Records reissue on 180-gram vinyl			
❑ SD 16026	Replay	1980	12.00
—Also has solo cuts by Stephen Stills			
❑ SD 19104	CSN	1977	12.00
❑ SD 19117	Crosby, Stills & Nash	1977	10.00
—Reissue of 8229			
❑ SD 19360	Daylight Again	1982	12.00
❑ 80075	Allies	1983	12.00
❑ 82107	Live It Up	1990	15.00
NAUTILUS			
❑ NR-48	Crosby, Stills and Nash	1982	150.00
—Audiophile vinyl			

CROSBY, STILLS, NASH & YOUNG

Also see DAVID CROSBY; GRAHAM NASH; STEPHEN STILLS; NEIL YOUNG.

12-Inch Singles

Number	Title (A Side/B Side)	Yr	NM
ATLANTIC			
❑ PR 2496 [DJ]	American Dream (same on both sides)	1988	15.00

45s

Number	Title (A Side/B Side)	Yr	NM
ATLANTIC			
❑ 2723	Woodstock/Helpless	1970	6.00
❑ 2735	Teach Your Children/Carry On	1970	6.00
❑ 2740	Ohio/Find the Cost of Freedom	1970	6.00
❑ 2740 [PS]	Ohio/Find the Cost of Freedom	1970	12.00
❑ 2760	Our House/Deja Vu	1970	6.00
❑ 88966	Got It Made/This Old House	1989	3.00
❑ 88966 [PS]	Got It Made/This Old House	1989	3.00
❑ 89003	American Dream/Compass	1988	3.00
❑ 89003 [PS]	American Dream/Compass	1988	3.00

Albums

Number	Title (A Side/B Side)	Yr	NM
ATLANTIC			
❑ PR 165 [M]	Celebration/CSNY Month	1974	100.00
—Promo-only LP in mono			
❑ PR 165 [S]	Celebration/CSNY Month	1974	50.00
—Promo-only LP in stereo			
❑ 2-902 [(2)M]	4 Way Street	1971	100.00
—White label promo; no stock copies are mono			
❑ SD 2-902 [(2)]	4 Way Street	1971	20.00
❑ SD 2-902 [(2)DJ]	4 Way Street	1971	50.00
—White label stereo promo			
❑ 7200 [M]	Deja Vu	1970	150.00
—White label promo; no stock copies are mono			
❑ SD 7200	Deja Vu	1970	15.00
—Pasted-on front cover photo must still be intact			
❑ SD 7200 [DJ]	Deja Vu	1970	60.00
—White label stereo promo			
❑ SD 18100	So Far	1974	12.00
❑ PR 18102 [DJ]	A Rap with C, S, N & Y	1974	50.00
—Promo-only interview album			
❑ SD 19118	Deja Vu	1977	10.00
—Reissue of 7200, this time with photo as part of the cover rather than as a paste-on			
❑ SD 19119	So Far	1977	10.00
—Reissue of 18100			
❑ 81888	American Dream	1988	10.00
MOBILE FIDELITY			
❑ 1-088	Deja Vu	198?	200.00
—Audiophile vinyl			

CROSS, CHRISTOPHER

12-Inch Singles

Number	Title (A Side/B Side)	Yr	NM
WARNER BROS.			
❑ PRO-A-1094 [DJ]	All Right (same on both sides)	1983	12.00
❑ PRO-A-2379 [DJ]	Charm the Snake (same on both sides)	1985	6.00
❑ PRO-A-2415 [DJ]	Every Turn of the World (Edit Version 3:41) (LP Version 4:02)	1985	6.00

45s

Number	Title (A Side/B Side)	Yr	NM
ARISTA			
❑ 9530	Loving Strangers/Seven Summers	1986	3.00
—B-side by Cruzados			
❑ 9530 [PS]	Loving Strangers/Seven Summers	1986	3.00
COLUMBIA			
❑ 38-04492	A Chance for Heaven/Talking in My Sleep	1984	3.00
❑ 38-04492 [PS]	A Chance for Heaven/Talking in My Sleep	1984	4.00
REPRISE			
❑ 7-27673	Swept Away ("Growing Pains" Aloha Show Theme)/(B-side unknown)	1989	3.00
❑ 7-27673 [PS]	Swept Away ("Growing Pains" Aloha Show Theme)/(B-side unknown)	1989	4.00
❑ 7-27795	I Will (Take You Forever)/Just One Look	1988	3.00
—With Frances Ruffelle			
❑ 7-27795 [PS]	I Will (Take You Forever)/Just One Look	1988	3.00
WARNER BROS.			
❑ 28761	Love Is Love (In Any Language)/Love Found a Home	1986	3.00
❑ 28804	Every Turn of the World/Open Your Heart	1986	3.00
❑ 28864	Charm the Snake/Open Your Heart	1985	3.00
❑ 28864 [PS]	Charm the Snake/Open Your Heart	1985	3.00
❑ 29658	Think of Laura/Words of Wisdom	1983	4.00

Except when noted otherwise, VG = 25% of NM, and VG+ = 50% of NM. (Example: VG = $2.00, VG+ = $4.00 and NM = $8.00.)

Number	Title (A Side/B Side)	Yr	NM
❑ 29662	No Time for Talk/ Words of Wisdom	1983	4.00
❑ 29843	All Right/Long World	1983	4.00
❑ 29843 [PS]	All Right/Long World	1983	4.00
❑ 49184	Ride Like the Wind/ Minstrel Gigolo	1980	4.00
❑ 49507	Sailing/Poor Shirley	1980	4.00
❑ 49580	Never Be the Same/ The Light Is On	1980	4.00
❑ 49705	Say You'll Be Mine/Spinning	1981	4.00
❑ 49787	Arthur's Theme (Best That You Can Do)/Minstrel Gigolo	1981	4.00
❑ 49787 [PS]	Arthur's Theme (Best That You Can Do)/Minstrel Gigolo	1981	5.00

Albums

REPRISE

Number	Title	Yr	NM
❑ 25685	Back of My Mind	1988	10.00

WARNER BROS.

Number	Title	Yr	NM
❑ BSK 3383	Christopher Cross	1979	8.00
❑ 23757	Another Page	1983	8.00
❑ 25341	Every Turn of the World	1985	8.00

CROSS, JIMMY

45s

CHICKEN

Number	Title	Yr	NM
❑ 101	Hey Little Girl/Hey Little Girl (Part 2)	1966	12.00

RECORDO

Number	Title	Yr	NM
❑ 502	Pretty Girls Everywhere/ Suntan Sally	1961	15.00

RED BIRD

Number	Title	Yr	NM
❑ 10-042	Hey Little Girl/Super Duper Man	1965	15.00

TOLLIE

Number	Title	Yr	NM
❑ 9039	I Want My Baby Back/ Play the Other Side	1965	20.00
❑ 9044	The Ballad of James Bong/ Play the Other Side Again	1965	15.00

CROSS COUNTRY

Includes three members of THE TOKENS.

45s

ATCO

Number	Title	Yr	NM
❑ 6932	Rock and Roll Music/ Just a Thought	1973	8.00
❑ 6934	In the Midnight Hour/ The Smile Song	1973	8.00
❑ 6947	Tastes So Good to Me/ A Ball Song	1973	8.00

Albums

ATCO

Number	Title	Yr	NM
❑ 7024 [M]	Cross Country	1973	40.00
—Mono is white label promo only; "d/j copy monaural" sticker on cover			
❑ SD 7024 [S]	Cross Country	1973	15.00

CROSSFIRES, THE (1)

Group evolved into THE TURTLES.

45s

CAPCO

Number	Title	Yr	NM
❑ 104	Fiberglass Jungle/ Dr. Jekyll and Mr. Hyde	1963	80.00

LUCKY TOKEN

Number	Title	Yr	NM
❑ 112	One Potato, Two Potato/ That'll Be the Day	1965	50.00

Albums

RHINO

Number	Title	Yr	NM
❑ RNLP-019	Out of Control	1981	10.00

CROSSFIRES, THE (2)

45s

CUCA

Number	Title	Yr	NM
❑ 1027	Young Love/When My Blue Moon Turns to Gold Again	1961	12.00

CROSSFIRES, THE (3)

Albums

STRAND

Number	Title	Yr	NM
❑ SL-1083 [M]	Limbo Rock	1963	20.00
❑ SLS-1083 [S]	Limbo Rock	1963	25.00

CROSSFIRES, THE (4)

45s

TOWER

Number	Title	Yr	NM
❑ 278	Who'll Be the Next One/ Making Love Is Fun	1966	20.00

CROW

BLACK SABBATH's first single was a cover of this band's "Evil Woman."

45s

AMARET

Number	Title (A Side/B Side)	Yr	NM
❑ 106	Busy Day/Time to Make a Turn	1969	6.00
❑ 112	Evil Woman Don't Play Your Games with Me/ Gonna Leave a Mark	1969	8.00
❑ 119	Cottage Cheese/Busy Day	1970	6.00
❑ 119	Cottage Cheese/Slow Down	1970	6.00
❑ 125	Don't Try to Lay No Boogie-Woogie on the "King of Rock 'n' Roll"/Satisfied	1970	6.00
❑ 129	Watching Can Waste Up the Time/Yellow Dawg	1971	5.00
❑ 133	Something in Your Blood/ Yellow Dawg	1971	5.00
❑ 145	Everything Has Got to Be Free/ Mobile Blues	1972	5.00
❑ 148	If It Feels Good, Do It/ Cado Queen	1972	5.00

Albums

AMARET

Number	Title	Yr	NM
❑ ST-5002	Crow Music	1969	20.00
❑ ST-5006	Crow By Crow	1970	20.00
❑ ST-5009	Mosaic	1971	20.00
❑ AST-5012	Best of Crow	1972	15.00
❑ ST-5013	David Crow d/b/a Crow	1973	15.00

CROWDED HOUSE

12-Inch Singles

CAPITOL

Number	Title	Yr	NM
❑ SPRO-79774 [DJ]	Chocolate Cake (same on both sides)	1991	10.00
❑ SPRO-79169 [DJ]	Now We're Getting Somewhere (same on both sides)	1987	10.00
❑ SPRO [DJ]	World Where You Live/Mean to Me/Something So Strong	1986	15.00
❑ SPRO-9693/4 [DJ]	World Where You Live/Mean to Me/Something So Strong	1986	15.00
❑ SPRO-9775 [DJ]	Don't Dream It's Over (same on both sides)	1986	10.00
❑ SPRO-9991 [DJ]	Something So Strong (same on both sides)	1987	12.00
❑ V-15240	World Where You Live/Mean to Me/Something So Strong	1986	10.00
❑ V-15292	Something So Strong/Can't Carry On/I Walk Away	1987	10.00
❑ SPRO-79169 [DJ]	Now We're Getting Somewhere (same on both sides)	1987	12.00
❑ SPRO-79774 [DJ]	Chocolate Cake (same on both sides)	1991	15.00

45s

AMERICAN PIE

Number	Title	Yr	NM
❑ 9047	Don't Dream It's Over/ Something So Strong	1990	3.00
—Reissue			

CAPITOL

Number	Title	Yr	NM
❑ 7PRO-79653 [DJ]	I Feel Possessed (same on both sides)	1989	6.00
—Vinyl version appears to be promo-only			
❑ B-5614	Don't Dream It's Over/ That's What I Call Love	1986	3.00
❑ B-5614 [PS]	Don't Dream It's Over/ That's What I Call Love	1986	5.00
❑ B-5634	Mean to Me/Love You 'Til I Die	1986	—
—Unreleased?			
❑ B-5695	Something So Strong/ I Walk Away	1987	3.00
❑ B-5695 [PS]	Something So Strong/ I Walk Away	1987	3.00
❑ S7-17706	Nails in My Feet/You Can Touch	1994	4.00
❑ S7-17905	Locked Out/My Sharona	1994	5.00
—B-side by The Knack			
❑ S7-17966	Distant Sun/Walking on the Spot	1994	4.00
❑ S7-18041	Private Universe/ Black and White Boy	1994	5.00
—Gold/orange vinyl			
❑ B-44033	World Where You Live/ Hole in the River	1987	3.00
❑ B-44033 [PS]	World Where You Live/ Hole in the River	1987	3.00
❑ B-44083	Now We're Getting Somewhere/ Tombstone	1987	3.00
❑ B-44083 [PS]	Now We're Getting Somewhere/Tombstone	1987	3.00
❑ B-44164	Better Be Home Soon/Kill Eye	1988	3.00
❑ B-44164 [PS]	Better Be Home Soon/Kill Eye	1988	3.00
❑ B-44226	Into Temptation/ Better Be Home Soon	1988	3.00
❑ B-44226 [PS]	Into Temptation/ Better Be Home Soon	1988	3.00
❑ S7-57699	It's Only Natural/Fame Is	1992	4.00
❑ 7PRO-79440	Into Temptation (Fade)/ (LP Version)	1988	6.00
—Promo only number			
❑ 7PRO-79653	I Feel Possessed (same on both sides)	1989	6.00
—7-inch vinyl is promo only			

Albums

CAPITOL

Number	Title	Yr	NM
❑ ST-12485	Crowded House	1987	10.00
❑ C1-48763	Temple of Low Men	1988	12.00
❑ C1-93559	Woodface	1991	15.00
❑ R 114827	Temple of Low Men	1988	12.00
—BMG Direct Marketing edition			
❑ R 133277	Crowded House	1987	12.00
—BMG Direct Marketing edition			

CROWELL, RODNEY

12-Inch Singles

COLUMBIA

Number	Title	Yr	NM
❑ CAS 2383 [DJ]	Let Freedom Ring (same on both sides)	1986	8.00

45s

COLUMBIA

Number	Title	Yr	NM
❑ 38-06102	Let Freedom Ring/The Best I Can	1986	3.00
❑ 38-06415	When I'm Free Again/ The Best I Can	1986	3.00
❑ 38-06584	She Loves the Jerk/ Passed Like a Mask	1987	3.00
❑ 38-07137	Looking for You/ Stay (Don't Be Cruel)	1987	3.00
❑ 38-07693	It's Such a Small World/ Crazy Baby	1988	3.00
—A-side: With Roseanne Cash			
❑ 38-07918	I Couldn't Leave You If I Tried/ The Blue Hour Comes	1988	3.00
❑ 38-08080	She's Crazy for Leavin'/ Brand New Rag	1988	3.00
❑ 38-68585	After All This Time/ Oh King Richard	1989	4.00
—Originals were pressed on styrene (record appears translucent dark red when held to a light)			
❑ 38-68585	After All This Time/ Oh King Richard	199?	3.00
—Reissues were pressed on vinyl			
❑ 38-68948	Above and Beyond/ She Loves the Jerk	1989	3.00
❑ 38-73042	Many a Long & Lonesome Highway/I Know You're Married	1989	3.00
❑ 38-73254	If Looks Could Kill/I Didn't Know I Could Lose You	1990	3.00
❑ 38-73423	My Past Is Present/ You Been On My Mind	1990	3.00
❑ 38-73569	Now That We're Alone/I Guess We've Been Together for Too Long	1990	3.00
❑ 38-73760	Things I Wish I'd Said/Soul Searchin'	1991	3.00
❑ 38-74250	Lovin' All Night/I Didn't Know I Could Lose You	1992	3.00
❑ 38-74360	What Kind of Love/Nobody's Gonna Tear My Playhouse Down	1992	3.00
❑ 38-77240	Even Cowgirls Get the Blues/ Standing on a Rock	1993	3.00

MCA

Number	Title	Yr	NM
❑ 54821	Let the Picture Paint Itself/ The Rose of Memphis	1994	3.00
❑ 54880	Big Heart/The Best Years of Our Lives	1994	3.00
❑ 54946	I Don't Fall in Love So Easy/ That Ol' Door	1994	3.00
❑ 55024	Please Remember Me/ Give My Heart a Rest	1995	3.00

REPRISE

Number	Title	Yr	NM
❑ 7-17149	I Walk the Line Revisited/ Stars on the Water	1998	3.00
—A-side with Johnny Cash			

WARNER BROS.

Number	Title	Yr	NM
❑ 8637	Elvira/Ashes By Now	1978	5.00
❑ 8693	Song for the Life/Baby, Better Start Turnin' 'Em Down	1978	5.00
❑ 8794	(Now and Then There's) A Fool Such As I/Voila, An American Dream	1979	5.00
❑ 49224	Ashes By Now/Blues in the Daytime	1980	5.00
❑ 49535	Ain't No Money/ One About England	1980	4.00
❑ 49591	Heartbroke/Here Come the 80's	1980	4.00
❑ 49810	Stars on the Water/Don't Need No Other Now	1981	4.00
❑ 50008	Victim or a Fool/Only Two Hearts	1982	4.00

Number	Title (A Side/B Side)	Yr	NM

Albums

COLUMBIA

Number	Title (A Side/B Side)	Yr	NM
❑ CAS 2001 [DJ]	Dialog with T-Bone Burnett	1989	30.00
—Promo-only interview record			
❑ CAS 2456 [DJ]	Street Language Interchords	1986	30.00
—Promo-only interview record			
❑ FC 40116	Street Language	1986	8.00
❑ FC 44076	Diamonds and Dirt	1988	10.00
❑ FC 45242	Keys to the Highway	1989	12.00

WARNER BROS.

Number	Title (A Side/B Side)	Yr	NM
❑ BSK 3228	Ain't Living Long Like This	1978	15.00
❑ BSK 3407	But What Will the Neighbors Think	1980	10.00
❑ BSK 3587	Rodney Crowell	1981	10.00

CROWN, BOBBY

45s

FELCO

Number	Title (A Side/B Side)	Yr	NM
❑ 102	One Way Ticket/ Your Conscience	1960	800.00

MANCO

Number	Title (A Side/B Side)	Yr	NM
❑ 1005	I've Never Had a Broken Heart/ Wait a Minute	1960	40.00

CROWN HEIGHTS AFFAIR

12-Inch Singles

DE-LITE

Number	Title (A Side/B Side)	Yr	NM
❑ MK 79 [DJ]	Dance Lady Dance (6:25)/ The Rock Is Hot (7:14)	1979	20.00
❑ MK 142 [DJ]	Sure Shot (6:20) (same on both sides)	1980	20.00
❑ PRO 225-1 [DJ]	Let Me Ride on the Wave of Your Love (5:44) (same on both sides)	1982	20.00
❑ DDS 582	Do It the French Way/Sexy Ways	1977	40.00
❑ DDS 588	Dancin' (6:13)/Love Me (6:01)	1977	40.00

SBK

Number	Title (A Side/B Side)	Yr	NM
❑ V-19703	I'll Do Anything (Radio Edit 3:54) (Nineties Club Mix 6:53) (Red Zone Mix 6:04) (Marsha Mix 9:14)	1989	10.00

45s

DE-LITE

Number	Title (A Side/B Side)	Yr	NM
❑ 803	You Gave Me Love/ Tell Me You Love Me	1980	4.00
❑ 805	Sure Shot/I See the Light	1980	4.00
❑ 821	Somebody Tell Me What to Do/ You Gave Me Love	1982	4.00
❑ 823	Let Me Ride on the Wave of Your Love/Wine and Dine You	1982	4.00
❑ 908	Say a Prayer for Two/ Galaxy of Love	1978	4.00
❑ 911	I Love You/Dream World	1978	4.00
❑ 912	Dance Lady Dance/Come Fly with Me	1979	4.00
❑ 915	Empty Soul of Mine/Rock Is Hot	1979	4.00
❑ 1570	Dreaming a Dream/Dreaming a Dream (Part 2)	1975	4.00
❑ 1575	Every Beat of My Heart/ Every Beat of My Heart (Disco Version)	1975	4.00
❑ 1581	Foxy Lady/Picture Show	1976	4.00
❑ 1588	Dancin'/Love Me	1976	4.00
❑ 1592	Do It the French Way/Sexy Ways	1977	4.00
❑ 1592 [PS]	Do It the French Way/Sexy Ways	1977	6.00

RCA VICTOR

Number	Title (A Side/B Side)	Yr	NM
❑ APBO-0023	Super Rod (Part 1)/ Super Rod (Part 2)	1973	5.00
❑ APBO-0243	Leave the Kids Alone/Rip-Off	1974	5.00
❑ PB-10018	Special Kind of Woman/ Streaking	1974	5.00

Albums

DE-LITE

Number	Title (A Side/B Side)	Yr	NM
❑ 2017	Dreaming a Dream	1975	10.00
❑ 2021	Foxy Lady	1976	10.00
❑ 2022	Do It	1977	10.00
❑ 8504	Think Positive	1982	10.00
❑ 9506	Dream World	1978	10.00
❑ 9512	Dance Lady Dance	1979	10.00
❑ 9517	Sure Shot	1980	10.00

RCA VICTOR

Number	Title (A Side/B Side)	Yr	NM
❑ APL1-0492	Crown Heights Affair	1974	12.00
❑ ANL1-2660	Crown Heights Affair	1977	8.00
—Reissue of above LP			

CROWNS, THE (1)

45s

CHORDETTE

Number	Title (A Side/B Side)	Yr	NM
❑ 1001	Party Time/Amazon Basin Pop	1962	20.00

CROWNS, THE (2)

45s

OLD TOWN

Number	Title (A Side/B Side)	Yr	NM
❑ 1171	Possibility/Watch Out	1964	15.00
—Black label with moon			
❑ 1171	Possibility/Watch Out	1964	40.00
—Old light blue Old Town label			

CROWNS, THE (3)

Four members of THE FIVE CROWNS plus Benjamin Nelson (BEN E. KING). Also see THE DRIFTERS.

45s

R&B

Number	Title (A Side/B Side)	Yr	NM
❑ 6901	Kiss and Make Up/I'll Forget About You	1958	80.00

CROWNS, THE (4)

45s

VEE JAY

Number	Title (A Side/B Side)	Yr	NM
❑ 546	Better Luck Next Time/ You Make Me Blue	1963	15.00

CROWS, THE

45s

RAMA

Number	Title (A Side/B Side)	Yr	NM
❑ 3	Seven Lonely Days/ No Help Wanted	1953	500.00
❑ 5	Gee/I Love You So	1953	70.00
—Blue label, black vinyl			
❑ 5	Gee/I Love You So	1953	400.00
—Blue label, red vinyl			
❑ 5	Gee/I Love You So	1955	30.00
—Red label, black vinyl			
❑ GG 8	Gee/Baby, Baby	196?	12.00
—"Golden Goodies Hits Series"; B-side is mistitled (the song is actually "Baby") and mis-credited to "The Teenagers"			
❑ 10	Heartbreaker/Call a Doctor	1953	400.00
—Black vinyl			
❑ 10	Heartbreaker/Call a Doctor	1953	600.00
—Black vinyl, label says "The Jewels"			
❑ 10	Heartbreaker/Call a Doctor	1953	600.00
—Black vinyl, label says "The Jewels" on one side, "The Crows" on the other			
❑ 10	Heartbreaker/Call a Doctor	1953	800.00
—Red vinyl			
❑ 10	Heartbreaker/Call a Doctor	1953	1200.
—Red vinyl; label says "The Jewels"			
❑ 29	Baby/Untrue	1954	200.00
❑ 30	Miss You/I Really, Really Love You So	1954	400.00
—Black vinyl			
❑ 30	Miss You/I Really, Really Love You So	1954	1000.
—Red vinyl			
❑ 50	Baby Doll/Sweet Sue (It's You)	1954	400.00

TICO

Number	Title (A Side/B Side)	Yr	NM
❑ 1082	Mambo Shevitz/Mambo #5	1955	200.00
—B-side by Melino and Orchestra; black vinyl			
❑ 1082	Mambo Shevitz/Mambo #5	1955	300.00
—B-side by Melino and Orchestra; red vinyl			

CROWS, THE / THE HARPTONES

Albums

ROULETTE

Number	Title (A Side/B Side)	Yr	NM
❑ RE-114 [(2)]	Echoes of a Rock Era: The Groups	1973	20.00

CRUDUP, ARTHUR

45s

ACE

Number	Title (A Side/B Side)	Yr	NM
❑ 503	I Wonder/My Baby Boogies All the Time	1955	200.00

FIRE

Number	Title (A Side/B Side)	Yr	NM
❑ 1501	Rock Me Mama/Mean Ole Frisco	1962	15.00
❑ 1502	Katie Mae/Dig Myself a Hole	1962	15.00

GROOVE

Number	Title (A Side/B Side)	Yr	NM
❑ 0011	I Love My Baby/Fall on Your Knees and Pray	1954	40.00
❑ 0026	She's Got No Hair/If You Ever Been to Georgia	1954	40.00

RCA VICTOR

Number	Title (A Side/B Side)	Yr	NM
❑ 47-4367	Love Me Mama/Where Did You Stay Last Night	1951	100.00
❑ 47-4572	Goin' Back to Georgia/ Mr. So and So	1952	80.00
❑ 47-4753	Worried 'Bout You Baby/ Late in the Evening	1952	80.00
❑ 47-4933	Second Man Blues/ Do It If You Want	1952	80.00
❑ 47-5070	Lookin' for My Baby/Pearly Lee	1952	80.00
❑ 47-5167	Keep On Drinkin'/Nelvina	1953	80.00
❑ 47-5563	War Is Over/My Wife and Woman	1953	80.00
❑ 50-0000	That's All Right/ Crudup's After Hours	1949	400.00
—Gray label, orange vinyl; the first R&B 45 rpm record!			
❑ 50-0001	Boy Friend Blues/Katie May	1949	100.00
—Gray label, orange vinyl			
❑ 50-0013	Shout Sister Shout/Crudup's Vicksburg Blues	1949	100.00
—Gray label, orange vinyl			
❑ 50-0032	Hoodoo Lady Blues/ Tired of Worry	1949	100.00
—Gray label, orange vinyl			
❑ 50-0046	Come Back Baby/Mercy Blues	1949	100.00
—Gray label, orange vinyl			
❑ 50-0074	Dust My Broom/You Know That I Love You	1950	100.00
—Gray label, orange vinyl			
❑ 50-0092	Mean Old Santa Fe/ Oo Wee Baby	1950	100.00
—Gray label, orange vinyl			
❑ 50-0100	Lonesome World to Me/Hand Me Down My Walking Cane	1950	100.00
—Gray label, orange vinyl			
❑ 50-0105	She's Just Like Caldonia/ (B-side unknown)	1951	100.00
—Gray label, orange vinyl			
❑ 50-0109	My Baby Left Me/Anytime Is the Right Time	1951	150.00
—Gray label, orange vinyl			
❑ 50-0117	Nobody Wants Me/ Star Bootlegger	1951	100.00
—Gray label, black vinyl			
❑ 50-0126	Roberta Blues/Behind Closed Doors	1951	100.00
—Gray label, black vinyl			
❑ 50-0141	I'm Gonna Dig Myself a Hole/ Too Much Competition	1951	100.00
—Gray label, black vinyl			

Albums

COLLECTABLES

Number	Title (A Side/B Side)	Yr	NM
❑ COL-5130	Mean Ol' Frisco	1988	10.00

DELMARK

Number	Title (A Side/B Side)	Yr	NM
❑ DS-614	Look on Yonder's Wall	1969	40.00
❑ DS-621	Crudup's Mood	1969	40.00

FIRE

Number	Title (A Side/B Side)	Yr	NM
❑ 103 [M]	Mean Ol' Frisco	1960	900.00

RCA VICTOR

Number	Title (A Side/B Side)	Yr	NM
❑ LVP-573	Father of Rock and Roll	1971	20.00

TRIP

Number	Title (A Side/B Side)	Yr	NM
❑ 7501	Mean Ol' Frisco	1975	15.00

CRUM, SIMON

See FERLIN HUSKY.

CRUSADERS, THE (1)

Jazz and soul band. Originally recorded as "The Jazz Crusaders"; all releases on Pacific Jazz and World Pacific use that name.

12-Inch Singles

MCA

Number	Title (A Side/B Side)	Yr	NM
❑ L33-1190 [DJ]	Dead End/Night Ladies	1984	10.00
❑ L33-1748 [DJ]	This Old World's Too Funky for Me/Standing Tall	1981	15.00
—A-side with Joe Cocker			
❑ L33-1833 [DJ]	Street Life (6:02) (same on both sides)	1979	20.00
❑ 13991	New Moves (Remixed Version 5:35) (Dub Version 6:26) (Single Mix 3:45)	1984	8.00

45s

ABC BLUE THUMB

Number	Title (A Side/B Side)	Yr	NM
❑ 261	Stomp and Buck Dance/ A Ballad for Joe (Louis)	1975	5.00
❑ 267	Creole/I Feel the Love	1975	5.00
❑ 269	Keep That Same Old Feeling/ 'Til the Sun Shines	1976	5.00
❑ 270	And Then There Was the Blues/ Feeling Funky	1976	5.00
❑ 272	Feel It/The Way We Was	1977	5.00
❑ 273	Free as the Wind/The Way We Was	1977	5.00
❑ 278	Bayou Bottoms/Covert Action	1978	5.00

BLUE THUMB

Number	Title (A Side/B Side)	Yr	NM
❑ 208	Put It Where You Want It/Mosadi	1972	5.00
❑ 217	So Far Away/That's How I Feel	1972	5.00
❑ 225	Don't Let It Get You Down/ Journey from Within	1973	5.00
❑ 232	Take It or Leave It/ That's How I Feel	1973	5.00
❑ 245	Lay It On the Line/Let's Boogie	1974	5.00
❑ 249	Scratch/Way Back Home	1974	5.00

CHISA

Number	Title (A Side/B Side)	Yr	NM
❑ 8010	Way Back Home/Jackson	1970	6.00
—As "Jazz Crusaders"			
❑ 8013	Pass the Plate/Greasy Spoon	1971	6.00

MCA

Number	Title (A Side/B Side)	Yr	NM
❑ 41054	Street Life/Hustler	1979	4.00
❑ 41295	Sweet Gentle Love/ Soul Shadows	1980	4.00
❑ 51029	Last Call/Honky Tonk Struttin'	1980	4.00

Except when noted otherwise, VG = 25% of NM, and VG+ = 50% of NM. (Example: VG = $2.00, VG+ = $4.00 and NM = $8.00.)

Number	Title (A Side/B Side)	Yr	NM
❑ 51177	I'm So Glad I'm Standing Here Today/Standing Tall	1981	4.00

—A-side with Joe Cocker

Number	Title (A Side/B Side)	Yr	NM
❑ 51222	This Old World's Too Funky for Me/Standing Tall	1981	4.00

—A-side with Joe Cocker

Number	Title (A Side/B Side)	Yr	NM
❑ 51222 [PS]	This Old World's Too Funky for Me/Standing Tall	1981	10.00

—Promo-only sleeve with only the record number (neither title) and the following: "Happy Thanksgiving. If you're expecting a turkey ... this isn't it. We have a lot to be thankful for thanks to you. The Crusaders"

Number	Title (A Side/B Side)	Yr	NM
❑ 52098	Street Life/Overture	1982	4.00

—With B.B. King and the London Symphony Orchestra

Number	Title (A Side/B Side)	Yr	NM
❑ 52365	New Move/Mr. Cool	1984	4.00
❑ 52398	Dream Street/Dead End	1984	4.00
❑ 52454	Gotta Lotta Shakalada/ Zalal 'E Mini	1984	4.00
❑ 52966	The Way It Goes/Good Times	1986	4.00
❑ 53330	A.C. (Alternating Currents)/ Mulholland Nights	1988	3.00

MOWEST

Number	Title (A Side/B Side)	Yr	NM
❑ 5028	Spanish Harlem/Papa Hooper's Barrelhouse Groove	1972	6.00

PACIFIC JAZZ

Number	Title (A Side/B Side)	Yr	NM
❑ 340	Sinnin' Sam/Tonight	1962	12.00
❑ 342	Young Rabbits/(B-side unknown)	1962	12.00
❑ 371	No Name Samba/Tough Talk	1963	10.00
❑ 88125	Uptight (Everything's Alright)/ Scratch	1966	8.00
❑ 88144	Eleanor Rigby/Ooga Boogaloo	1968	6.00
❑ 88146	Hey Jude/Love and Peace	1969	6.00
❑ 88153	Get Back/Willie and Laura Mae Jones	1969	6.00

WORLD PACIFIC

Number	Title (A Side/B Side)	Yr	NM
❑ 388	Boopie/Turkish Black	1963	10.00

—As "Jazz Crusaders"

Number	Title (A Side/B Side)	Yr	NM
❑ 401	Heat Wave/On Broadway	1964	10.00
❑ 412	I Remember Tomorrow/ Long John	1964	10.00
❑ 77800	The Thing/Tough Talk	1965	8.00
❑ 77806	Aqua Dulce/Soul Bourgeoise	1966	8.00

Albums

ABC BLUE THUMB

Number	Title (A Side/B Side)	Yr	NM
❑ SPMK-42 [DJ]	Crusaders In-Store Sampler Album	1978	20.00

—Promo-only issue

Number	Title (A Side/B Side)	Yr	NM
❑ BT-6001 [(2)]	Crusaders 1	1975	12.00
❑ BT-6010	Scratch	1975	10.00

—Reissue

Number	Title (A Side/B Side)	Yr	NM
❑ 6022	Chain Reaction	1975	10.00
❑ 6024	Those Southern Knights	1976	10.00
❑ 6027 [(2)]	The Best of the Crusaders	1976	12.00
❑ 6029	Free As the Wind	1977	10.00
❑ BA-6030	Images	1978	10.00
❑ BTSY-9002 [(2)]	Southern Comfort	1974	12.00

APPLAUSE

Number	Title (A Side/B Side)	Yr	NM
❑ APBL-2313	Powerhouse	197?	12.00

—Reissue of Pacific Jazz 20136

BLUE NOTE

Number	Title (A Side/B Side)	Yr	NM
❑ BN-LA170-G [(2)]	Tough Talk	1974	12.00
❑ BN-LA530-H2 [(2)]	Young Rabbits	1977	12.00
❑ LWB-530 [(2)]	Young Rabbits	1981	10.00

—Reissue of BN-LA530-H2

Number	Title (A Side/B Side)	Yr	NM
❑ LT-1046	Live Sides	1980	10.00

BLUE THUMB

Number	Title (A Side/B Side)	Yr	NM
❑ BTSA 1 [DJ]	The Crusaders Promotional Album	1973	20.00

—Promo-only album contains one side of material from "Crusaders 1" and one side from "The 2nd Crusade"

Number	Title (A Side/B Side)	Yr	NM
❑ BT-6001 [(2)]	Crusaders 1	1972	15.00
❑ BT-6007	Unsung Heroes	1973	12.00
❑ BT-6010	Scratch	1974	12.00
❑ BT-7000 [(2)]	The 2nd Crusade	1973	15.00

CHISA

Number	Title (A Side/B Side)	Yr	NM
❑ 804	Old Socks, New Shoes... New Socks, Old Shoes	1970	12.00

—As "Jazz Crusaders"

Number	Title (A Side/B Side)	Yr	NM
❑ 807	Pass the Plate	1971	12.00

CRUSADERS

Number	Title (A Side/B Side)	Yr	NM
❑ 16000	Street Life	1982	25.00

—Audiophile vinyl

Number	Title (A Side/B Side)	Yr	NM
❑ 16002	Ongaku-Kai: Live in Japan	1982	25.00

—Audiophile vinyl

LIBERTY

Number	Title (A Side/B Side)	Yr	NM
❑ LST-11005	Give Peace a Chance	1970	15.00

—As "Jazz Crusaders"

MCA

Number	Title (A Side/B Side)	Yr	NM
❑ 3094	Street Life	1979	10.00
❑ 5124	Rhapsody and Blues	1980	10.00
❑ 5254	Standing Tall	1981	10.00
❑ 5429	Ghetto Blaster	1984	10.00
❑ 5781	The Good and Bad Times	1987	10.00
❑ 6006 [(2)]	The Best of the Crusaders	1980	10.00

—Reissue of Blue Thumb 6027

Number	Title (A Side/B Side)	Yr	NM
❑ 6014 [(2)]	Crusaders 1	198?	10.00

—Reissue of Blue Thumb 6001

Number	Title (A Side/B Side)	Yr	NM
❑ 6015 [(2)]	2nd Crusade	198?	10.00

—Reissue of Blue Thumb 7000

Number	Title (A Side/B Side)	Yr	NM
❑ 6016 [(2)]	Southern Comfort	198?	10.00

—Reissue of Blue Thumb 9002

Number	Title (A Side/B Side)	Yr	NM
❑ 8017 [(2)]	Royal Jam	1982	12.00
❑ 37072	Scratch	198?	8.00

—Reissue of Blue Thumb 6010

Number	Title (A Side/B Side)	Yr	NM
❑ 37073	Free As the Wind	198?	8.00

—Reissue of Blue Thumb 6029

Number	Title (A Side/B Side)	Yr	NM
❑ 37074	Images	198?	8.00

—Reissue of Blue Thumb 6030

Number	Title (A Side/B Side)	Yr	NM
❑ 37146	Chain Reaction	198?	8.00

—Reissue of Blue Thumb 6022

Number	Title (A Side/B Side)	Yr	NM
❑ 37147	Those Southern Knights	198?	8.00

—Reissue of Blue Thumb 6024

Number	Title (A Side/B Side)	Yr	NM
❑ 37174	Rhapsody and Blues	198?	8.00

—Reissue of 5124

Number	Title (A Side/B Side)	Yr	NM
❑ 37240	Standing Tall	1985	8.00

—Reissue of 5254

Number	Title (A Side/B Side)	Yr	NM
❑ 42087	The Vocal Album	1988	10.00
❑ 42168	Life in the Modern World	1988	10.00

MOBILE FIDELITY

Number	Title (A Side/B Side)	Yr	NM
❑ 1-010	Chain Reaction	1979	20.00

—Audiophile vinyl

MOTOWN

Number	Title (A Side/B Side)	Yr	NM
❑ M5-195V1	The Crusaders At Their Best	1981	10.00
❑ M 796	The Crusaders At Their Best	1973	12.00

MOWEST

Number	Title (A Side/B Side)	Yr	NM
❑ 118	Hollywood	1972	12.00

PACIFIC JAZZ

Number	Title (A Side/B Side)	Yr	NM
❑ PJ-27 [M]	Freedom Sound	1961	25.00
❑ ST-27 [S]	Freedom Sound	1961	30.00
❑ PJ-43 [M]	Lookin' Ahead	1962	25.00
❑ ST-43 [S]	Lookin' Ahead	1962	30.00

—Black vinyl

Number	Title (A Side/B Side)	Yr	NM
❑ ST-43 [S]	Lookin' Ahead	1962	60.00

—Yellow vinyl

Number	Title (A Side/B Side)	Yr	NM
❑ PJ-57 [M]	The Jazz Crusaders at the Lighthouse	1962	25.00
❑ ST-57 [S]	The Jazz Crusaders at the Lighthouse	1962	30.00
❑ PJ-68 [M]	Tough Talk	1963	25.00
❑ ST-68 [S]	Tough Talk	1963	30.00
❑ PJ-76 [M]	Heat Wave	1963	25.00
❑ ST-76 [S]	Heat Wave	1963	30.00
❑ PJ-83 [M]	Stretchin' Out	1964	25.00
❑ ST-83 [S]	Stretchin' Out	1964	30.00
❑ PJ-87 [M]	The Thing	1964	25.00
❑ ST-87 [S]	The Thing	1964	30.00
❑ PJ-10092 [M]	Chili Con Soul	1965	20.00
❑ PJ-10098 [M]	Live at the Lighthouse '66	1966	20.00
❑ PJ-10106 [M]	Talk That Talk	1966	20.00
❑ PJ-10115 [M]	The Festival Album	1967	25.00
❑ PJ-10124	Uh Huh	1967	25.00
❑ ST-20092 [S]	Chili Con Soul	1965	25.00
❑ ST-20098 [S]	Live at the Lighthouse '66	1966	25.00
❑ ST-20106 [S]	Talk That Talk	1966	25.00
❑ ST-20115 [S]	The Festival Album	1967	20.00
❑ ST-20124	Uh Huh	1967	20.00
❑ ST-20131	Lighthouse '68	1968	20.00
❑ ST-20136	Powerhouse	1968	20.00
❑ ST-20165	The Jazz Crusaders at the Lighthouse '69	1969	20.00
❑ ST-20175	The Best of the Jazz Crusaders	1969	20.00
❑ ST-90481 [S]	The Jazz Crusaders at the Lighthouse	1965	30.00

—Capitol Record Club edition

Number	Title (A Side/B Side)	Yr	NM
❑ T-90598 [M]	Chili Con Soul	1965	25.00

—Capitol Record Club edition

PAUSA

Number	Title (A Side/B Side)	Yr	NM
❑ 9005	The Best of the Jazz Crusaders	1979	10.00

—As "Jazz Crusaders"

WORLD PACIFIC JAZZ

Number	Title (A Side/B Side)	Yr	NM
❑ ST-20098 [S]	Live at the Lighthouse '66	1970	15.00

—Reissue with "Liberty/UA" on label

CRUSADERS, THE (U)

None of these are by group (1).

45s

CAMEO

Number	Title (A Side/B Side)	Yr	NM
❑ 285	Boogie Woogie/At the Club	1963	12.00

DKR

Number	Title (A Side/B Side)	Yr	NM
❑ (no #)	Seminole/Busted Surfboard	1962	40.00

DOOTO

Number	Title (A Side/B Side)	Yr	NM
❑ 472	Swinging Week-End/ I Found Someone	1963	15.00

TOWER

Number	Title (A Side/B Side)	Yr	NM
❑ 286	The Little Drummer Boy/ Battle Hymn of the Republic	1966	10.00
❑ 328	Make a Joyful Noise/ Praise We the Lord	1967	10.00

CRYAN' SHAMES, THE

45s

COLUMBIA

Number	Title (A Side/B Side)	Yr	NM
❑ 43836	I Wanna Meet You/ We Could Be Happy	1966	10.00
❑ 44037	Mr. Unreliable/Georgia	1967	10.00
❑ 44191	It Could Be We're in Love/ I Was Lonely When	1967	10.00
❑ 44191 [PS]	It Could Be We're in Love/ I Was Lonely When	1967	20.00
❑ 44457	Up On the Roof/The Sailing Ship	1968	10.00
❑ 44545	Young Birds Fly/Sunshine Psalm	1968	8.00
❑ 44638	Greenburg, Blickstein, Charles, David Smith & Jones The Warm	1968	8.00
❑ 44759	First Train to California/ A Master's Fool	1969	8.00
❑ 45027	Rainmaker/Bits and Pieces	1969	8.00

DESTINATION

Number	Title (A Side/B Side)	Yr	NM
❑ 624	Sugar and Spice/Ben Franklin's Almanac	1966	15.00

Albums

COLUMBIA

Number	Title (A Side/B Side)	Yr	NM
❑ CL 2589 [M]	Sugar & Spice	1967	35.00
❑ CL 2786 [M]	A Scratch in the Sky	1967	25.00
❑ CS 9389 [S]	Sugar & Spice	1967	20.00
❑ CS 9586 [S]	A Scratch in the Sky	1967	20.00
❑ CS 9719	Synthesis	1969	20.00

CRYIN' SHAMES, THE

Not the same group as THE CRYAN' SHAMES.

45s

LONDON

Number	Title (A Side/B Side)	Yr	NM
❑ 1001	What's New Pussycat/ Please Stay (Don't Go)	1966	10.00

CRYSTALS, THE (1)

Records on the Aladdin, Brent, Cub, DeLuxe, Felsted, Indigo, Luna, Mercury, Metro, Regalia, Rockin', and Specialty are by different groups outside the scope of this book. Well-known girl group.

45s

GUSTO

Number	Title (A Side/B Side)	Yr	NM
❑ 2090	Da Doo Ron Ron/ Then He Kissed Me	1979	4.00

—Re-recordings

MICHELLE

Number	Title (A Side/B Side)	Yr	NM
❑ 4113	Ring-a-Ting-a-Ling/Should I Keep On Waiting	1967	10.00

PAVILLION

Number	Title (A Side/B Side)	Yr	NM
❑ 03333	Rudolph the Red-Nosed Reindeer/I Saw Mommy Kissing Santa Claus	1982	5.00

—B-side by The Ronettes

PHILLES

Number	Title (A Side/B Side)	Yr	NM
❑ 100	There's No Other (Like My Baby)/Oh Yeah, Maybe Baby	1961	40.00
❑ 102	Uptown/What a Nice Way to Turn Seventeen	1962	40.00
❑ 105	He Hit Me (And It Felt Like a Kiss)/No One Ever Tells You	1962	100.00
❑ 106	He's a Rebel/I Love You Eddie	1962	40.00

—Light blue label

Number	Title (A Side/B Side)	Yr	NM
❑ 106	He's a Rebel/I Love You Eddie	1962	60.00

—Orange label

Number	Title (A Side/B Side)	Yr	NM
❑ 106	He's a Rebel/I Love You Eddie	1964	25.00

—Yellow and red label

Number	Title (A Side/B Side)	Yr	NM
❑ 109	He's Sure the Boy I Love/ Walkin' Along (La-La-La)	1962	30.00
❑ 111	(Let's Dance) The Screw — Part 1/(Let's Dance) The Screw — Part 2	1963	6000.

—Light blue label; no "D.J. Only Not for Sale" on label; "Audio Matrix" stamped in dead wax (counterfeits do not have this). VG 3000; VG+ 4500

Number	Title (A Side/B Side)	Yr	NM
❑ 111 [DJ]	(Let's Dance) The Screw — Part 1/(Let's Dance) The Screw — Part 2	1963	4000.

—White label; copies exist with the title as "Let's Dance The Screw" (no parentheses) also, with the same value as above. VG 2000; VG+ 3000

Number	Title (A Side/B Side)	Yr	NM
❑ 112	Da Doo Ron Ron (When He Walked Me Home)/Git' It	1963	30.00
❑ 115	Then He Kissed Me/ Brother Julius	1963	25.00

—Yellow and red label

Number	Title (A Side/B Side)	Yr	NM
❑ 115	Then He Kissed Me/ Brother Julius	1963	40.00

—Light blue label

Number	Title (A Side/B Side)	Yr	NM
❑ 119	Little Boy/Harry (From West Virginia) and Milt	1964	25.00
❑ 119X	Little Boy/Harry (From West Virginia) and Milt	1964	20.00
❑ 122	All Grown Up/Irving (Jaggered Sixteenths)	1964	25.00

—Possible Rolling Stones involvement on instrumental B-side; "Jaggered" refers to Mick

C

Number	Title (A Side/B Side)	Yr	NM
PHILLES/COLLECTABLES			
❑ 3200	He's a Rebel/He Hit Me (And It Felt Like a Kiss)	1985	6.00
—Red vinyl; part of box set "Phil Spector Wall of Sound Series Vol. 2"			
❑ 3200	He's a Rebel/He Hit Me (And It Felt Like a Kiss)	1986	5.00
—Black vinyl			
❑ 3201	Then He Kissed Me/Puddin' and Tain	1985	6.00
—Red vinyl; part of box set "Phil Spector Wall of Sound Series Vol. 2"; B-side by the Alley Cats			
❑ 3201	Then He Kissed Me/Puddin' and Tain	1986	5.00
—Black vinyl			
❑ 3202	Uptown/He's Sure the Boy I Love	1985	6.00
—Red vinyl; part of box set "Phil Spector Wall of Sound Series Vol. 2"			
❑ 3202	Uptown/He's Sure the Boy I Love	1986	5.00
—Black vinyl			
❑ 3204	There's No Other (Like My Baby)/Not Too Young to Get Married	1985	6.00
—Gold vinyl; part of box set "Phil Spector Wall of Sound Series Vol. 1"; B-side by Bob B. Soxx and the Blue Jeans			
❑ 3204	There's No Other (Like My Baby)/Not Too Young to Get Married	1986	5.00
—Black vinyl; B-side by Bob B. Soxx and the Blue Jeans			
❑ 3206	Da Doo Ron Ron/All Grown Up	1985	6.00
—Gold vinyl; part of box set "Phil Spector Wall of Sound Series Vol. 1"			
❑ 3206	Da Doo Ron Ron/All Grown Up	1986	5.00
—Black vinyl			
UNITED ARTISTS			
❑ 927	You Can't Tie a Good Girl Down/My Place	1965	15.00
❑ 994	I Got a Man/Are You Trying to Get Rid of Me, Baby	1966	15.00
Albums			
PHILLES			
❑ PHLP-4000 [M]	Twist Uptown	1962	600.00
❑ PHLP-4001 [M]	He's a Rebel	1963	600.00
❑ PHLP-4003 [M]	The Crystals Sing the Greatest Hits, Vol. 1	1963	600.00
❑ DT-90722 [R]	Twist Uptown	1965	1200.
—Capitol Record Club edition			
❑ T-90722 [M]	Twist Uptown	1965	600.00
—Capitol Record Club edition			

CRYSTALS, THE (2)

Number	Title (A Side/B Side)	Yr	NM
45s			
ALADDIN			
❑ 3355	I Love My Baby/I Do Believe	1957	60.00

CRYSTALS, THE (3)

Number	Title (A Side/B Side)	Yr	NM
45s			
BRENT			
❑ 7011	Malaguena/Gypsy Ribbon	1960	15.00
CUB			
❑ 9064	Oh My You/Watching You	1960	15.00
INDIGO			
❑ 114	Dreams and Wishes/Mr. Brush	1961	20.00
METRO			
❑ 20026	Better Come Back to Me/That's Where I Belong	1960	15.00
REGALIA			
❑ 17	Pony in Dixie/Espresso	1961	15.00

CRYSTALS, THE (4)

Number	Title (A Side/B Side)	Yr	NM
45s			
DELUXE			
❑ 6013	Four Women/My Dear	1953	2000.
❑ 6037	Have Faith in Me/My Love	1954	2000.
❑ 6077	God Only Knows/My Girl	1955	200.00
LUNA			
❑ 100	Squeeze Me Baby/Come to Me, Darling	1954	400.00
❑ 5001	Squeeze Me Baby/Come to Me, Darling	1954	200.00
ROCKIN'			
❑ 518	My Girl/Don't You Go	1953	250.00

CRYSTALS, THE (5)

Number	Title (A Side/B Side)	Yr	NM
45s			
FELSTED			
❑ 8566	Mary Ellen/Blind Date	1959	20.00
MERCURY			
❑ 71381	Vampire/Tropical Illusion	1958	15.00
SPECIALTY			
❑ 657	In the Deep/Love You So	1959	15.00

CUBY AND THE BLIZZARDS

Number	Title (A Side/B Side)	Yr	NM
45s			
PHILIPS			
❑ 40685	Thursday Night/Going Home	1970	8.00
Albums			
PHILIPS			
❑ PHS 600307	Cuby and the Blizzards Live	1969	20.00
❑ PHS 600331	King of the World	1970	20.00

CUES, THE

Number	Title (A Side/B Side)	Yr	NM
45s			
CAPITOL			
❑ F3245	Burn That Candle/Oh My Darling	1955	20.00
❑ F3310	Charlie Brown/You're On My Mind	1956	20.00
❑ F3400	Destination 2100 and 65/Don't Make Believe	1956	20.00
❑ F3483	The Girl I Love/Crackerjack	1956	20.00
❑ F3582	Why/Prince or Pauper	1956	20.00
JUBILEE			
❑ 5201	Only You/I Feel for Your Loving	1955	20.00
LAMP			
❑ 8007	Forty 'Leven Dozen Ways/Scoochie Scoochie	1954	20.00
PREP			
❑ 104	I Pretend/Crazy, Crazy Party	1957	20.00

CUFF LINKS, THE (1)

Records on the Dooto/Dootone label are by a different group outside the scope of this book. Studio band with RON DANTE as lead singer.

Number	Title (A Side/B Side)	Yr	NM
45s			
ATCO			
❑ 6867	Sandi/The Oke-Fen-Okee Electric Harmonica Band	1972	5.00
DECCA			
❑ 32533	Tracy/Where Do You Go	1969	6.00
❑ 32533 [PS]	Tracy/Where Do You Go	1969	25.00
—Three-piece gatefold sleeve			
❑ 32592	When Julie Comes Around/Sally Ann	1969	5.00
❑ 32639	Run, Sally, Run/I Remember	1970	5.00
❑ 32687	Lay a Little Love on Me/Robin's World	1970	5.00
❑ 32732	Thank You Pretty Baby/Kiss	1970	5.00
❑ 32791	All Because of You/Wake Up Judy	1971	5.00
Albums			
DECCA			
❑ DL 75160	Tracy	1969	20.00
❑ DL 75235	The Cuff Links	1970	20.00

CUFF LINKS, THE (2)

Black vocal group.

Number	Title (A Side/B Side)	Yr	NM
45s			
DOOTO			
❑ 409	Guided Missiles/My Heart	1957	80.00
❑ 413	How You Lied/The Winner	1957	40.00
❑ 414	Twinkle/One Day Blues	1957	40.00
❑ 422	It's Too Late Now/Saxophone Rag	1957	50.00
❑ 474	Changing My Love/I Don't Want Nobody	1963	25.00
DOOTONE			
❑ 409	Guided Missiles/My Heart	1956	200.00

CULLEY, FRANK "FLOORSHOW"

Number	Title (A Side/B Side)	Yr	NM
45s			
BATON			
❑ 226	After Hours Express (Part 1)/(Part 2)	1956	40.00
Albums			
BATON			
❑ BL 1201 [M]	Rock 'n Roll: Instrumentals for Dancing the Lindy Hop	1955	600.00
—B-side tracks by Buddy Tate Orchestra			

CULMER, LITTLE IRIS, AND THE MAJESTICS

Also see THE MAJESTICS.

Number	Title (A Side/B Side)	Yr	NM
45s			
MARLIN			
❑ 803	Frankie, My Eyes Are On You/(B-side unknown)	1957	2500.
—VG 1000; VG+ 1500			

CULT, THE

Features Billy Duffy and Ian Astbury. Features Billy Duffy and Ian Astbury.

Number	Title (A Side/B Side)	Yr	NM
12-Inch Singles			
REPRISE			
❑ PRO-A-5599 [DJ]	The Witch (LP Version) (Edit)	1992	8.00
—Regular black vinyl promo			
❑ PRO-A-5599 [DJ]	The Witch (LP Version) (Edit)	1992	20.00
—Purple vinyl promo			
SIRE			
❑ PRO2394 [DJ]	She Sells Sanctuary (same on both sides)	1985	12.00
❑ PRO2427 [DJ]	Rain (same on both sides)	1985	15.00
❑ PRO2691 [DJ]	Love Removal Machine (7" Edit) (same on both sides)	1987	7.00
❑ PRO2726 [DJ]	Li'l Devil (same on both sides)	1987	6.00
❑ PRO2775 [DJ]	Wildflower/Wildflower (Remix)	1987	12.00
❑ PRO3435 [DJ]	Fire Woman (same on both sides)	1989	8.00
❑ PRO-A-2394 [DJ]	She Sells Sanctuary (same on both sides)	1985	12.00
❑ PRO-A-2427 [DJ]	Rain (same on both sides)	1985	15.00
❑ PRO-A-2691 [DJ]	Love Removal Machine (7" Edit) (same on both sides)	1987	7.00
❑ PRO-A-2726 [DJ]	Lil' Devil (same on both sides)	1987	8.00
❑ PRO-A-2775 [DJ]	Wildflower (Remix) (7" Version)	1987	10.00
❑ PRO-A-3435 [DJ]	Fire Woman (same on both sides)	1989	8.00
❑ 20407	She Sells Sanctuary (12" Mix) (Howling Mix)/Little Face	1985	10.00
❑ 20641	Love Removal Machine (2 versions)/Wolf Child's Blues	1987	8.00
❑ 20743	Wildflower (3 versions)	1987	10.00
❑ 21195	Fire Woman (Extended)//Automatic Blues/Messin' Up the Blues	1989	8.00
45s			
SIRE			
❑ 21945	She Sells Sanctuary/Love Removal Machine	198?	4.00
—Reissue			
❑ 22873	Edie (Ciao Baby)/Love Removal Machine	1989	3.00
❑ 27543	Fire Woman/Automatic Blues	1989	3.00
❑ 27543 [PS]	Fire Woman/Automatic Blues	1989	3.00
❑ 28213	Wildflower/Love Trooper	1987	4.00
❑ 28213 [PS]	Wildflower/Love Trooper	1987	12.00
—Fold-open poster sleeve			
❑ 28290	Lil' Devil/Memphis Hip Shake	1987	4.00
❑ 28290 [PS]	Lil' Devil/Memphis Hip Shake	1987	4.00
❑ 28820	She Sells Sanctuary/Little Face	1986	5.00
Albums			
SIRE			
❑ 25259	Love	1985	10.00
❑ 25555	Electric	1987	10.00
❑ 25871	Sonic Temple	1989	10.00
❑ R 101015	Sonic Temple	1989	12.00
—BMG Direct Marketing edition			
❑ R 134608	Love	1985	12.00
—RCA Music Service edition			
❑ R 184083	Electric	1987	12.00
—RCA Music Service edition			
WARNER BROS.			
❑ - [DJ]	Electric Interview	1987	40.00
❑ WBMS-147 [DJ]	Electric Interview	1987	50.00
—Part of "The Warner Bros. Music Show" series			

CULTURE CLUB

Number	Title (A Side/B Side)	Yr	NM
12-Inch Singles			
EPIC			
❑ AS 1642 [DJ]	Time (Clock of the Heart)/Romance Beyond the Alphabet	1983	10.00
❑ AS1642 [DJ]	Time/Romance Beyond the Alphabet	1983	10.00
❑ AS 1752 [DJ]	Church of the Poison Mind (same on both sides)	1983	10.00
❑ AS1752 [DJ]	Church of the Poison Mind (same on both sides)	1983	10.00
❑ 49-03307	I'm Afraid of Me (Extended Dance Mix 7:20)/Murder Rap Trap	1982	15.00
❑ 49-03393	Do You Really Want to Hurt Me/Love Is Cold (You Were Never So Good)	1982	10.00
❑ 49-03913	I'll Tumble 4 Ya (Extended Remix)/Man Shake	1983	10.00
❑ 49-04145	Church of the Poison Mind/Mystery Boy	1983	10.00
VIRGIN/EPIC			
❑ EAS2296 [DJ]	Move Away (same on both sides)	1986	7.00
❑ EAS 2296 [DJ]	Move Away (same on both sides)	1986	10.00
❑ 49-04977	Miss Me Blind/It's a Miracle (Extended Dance Remix)//Colour By Numbers	1984	8.00
❑ 49-05107	The War Song (Ultimate Mix 6:51) (Shriek Mix 6:16)/La Cancion de Guerra	1984	8.00
❑ 49-05360	Move Away (Extended Version 7:24)/Sexuality (Tango Dub Remix 10:34)	1986	8.00
❑ 49-05916	Gusto Blusto (Extended Dance Mix) (Rock Mix)	1986	15.00

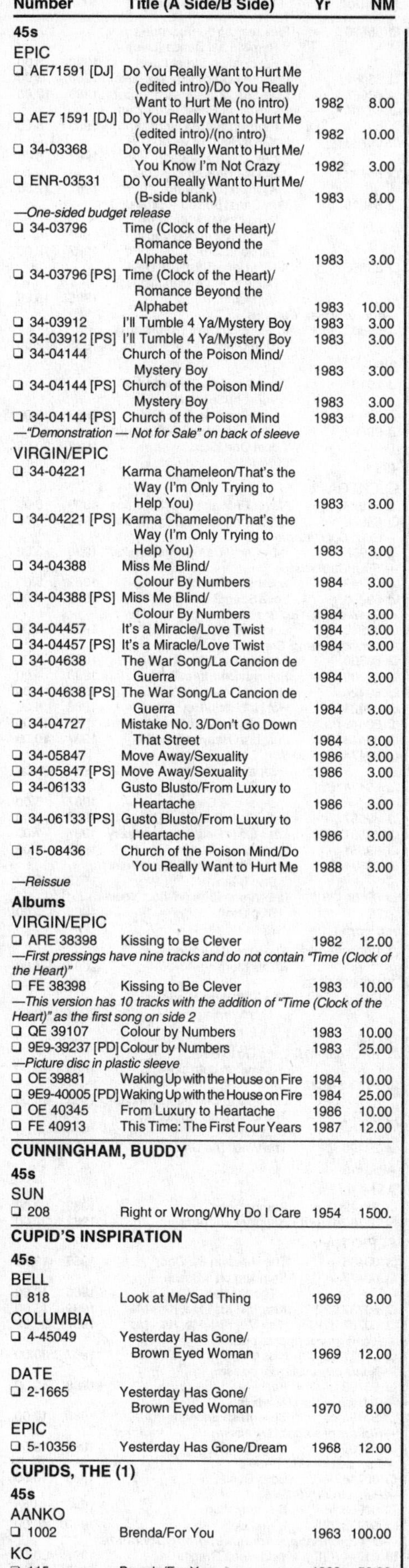

Number	Title (A Side/B Side)	Yr	NM
45s			
EPIC			
❑ AE71591 [DJ]	Do You Really Want to Hurt Me (edited intro)/Do You Really Want to Hurt Me (no intro)	1982	8.00
❑ AE7 1591 [DJ]	Do You Really Want to Hurt Me (edited intro)/(no intro)	1982	10.00
❑ 34-03368	Do You Really Want to Hurt Me/ You Know I'm Not Crazy	1982	3.00
❑ ENR-03531	Do You Really Want to Hurt Me/ (B-side blank)	1983	8.00
—One-sided budget release			
❑ 34-03796	Time (Clock of the Heart)/ Romance Beyond the Alphabet	1983	3.00
❑ 34-03796 [PS]	Time (Clock of the Heart)/ Romance Beyond the Alphabet	1983	10.00
❑ 34-03912	I'll Tumble 4 Ya/Mystery Boy	1983	3.00
❑ 34-03912 [PS]	I'll Tumble 4 Ya/Mystery Boy	1983	3.00
❑ 34-04144	Church of the Poison Mind/ Mystery Boy	1983	3.00
❑ 34-04144 [PS]	Church of the Poison Mind/ Mystery Boy	1983	3.00
❑ 34-04144 [PS]	Church of the Poison Mind	1983	8.00
—"Demonstration — Not for Sale" on back of sleeve			
VIRGIN/EPIC			
❑ 34-04221	Karma Chameleon/That's the Way (I'm Only Trying to Help You)	1983	3.00
❑ 34-04221 [PS]	Karma Chameleon/That's the Way (I'm Only Trying to Help You)	1983	3.00
❑ 34-04388	Miss Me Blind/ Colour By Numbers	1984	3.00
❑ 34-04388 [PS]	Miss Me Blind/ Colour By Numbers	1984	3.00
❑ 34-04457	It's a Miracle/Love Twist	1984	3.00
❑ 34-04457 [PS]	It's a Miracle/Love Twist	1984	3.00
❑ 34-04638	The War Song/La Cancion de Guerra	1984	3.00
❑ 34-04638 [PS]	The War Song/La Cancion de Guerra	1984	3.00
❑ 34-04727	Mistake No. 3/Don't Go Down That Street	1984	3.00
❑ 34-05847	Move Away/Sexuality	1986	3.00
❑ 34-05847 [PS]	Move Away/Sexuality	1986	3.00
❑ 34-06133	Gusto Blusto/From Luxury to Heartache	1986	3.00
❑ 34-06133 [PS]	Gusto Blusto/From Luxury to Heartache	1986	3.00
❑ 15-08436	Church of the Poison Mind/Do You Really Want to Hurt Me	1988	3.00
—Reissue			
Albums			
VIRGIN/EPIC			
❑ ARE 38398	Kissing to Be Clever	1982	12.00
—First pressings have nine tracks and do not contain "Time (Clock of the Heart)"			
❑ FE 38398	Kissing to Be Clever	1983	10.00
—This version has 10 tracks with the addition of "Time (Clock of the Heart)" as the first song on side 2			
❑ QE 39107	Colour by Numbers	1983	10.00
❑ 9E9-39237 [PD]	Colour by Numbers	1983	25.00
—Picture disc in plastic sleeve			
❑ OE 39881	Waking Up with the House on Fire	1984	10.00
❑ 9E9-40005 [PD]	Waking Up with the House on Fire	1984	25.00
❑ OE 40345	From Luxury to Heartache	1986	10.00
❑ FE 40913	This Time: The First Four Years	1987	12.00

CUNNINGHAM, BUDDY

Number	Title (A Side/B Side)	Yr	NM
45s			
SUN			
❑ 208	Right or Wrong/Why Do I Care	1954	1500.

CUPID'S INSPIRATION

Number	Title (A Side/B Side)	Yr	NM
45s			
BELL			
❑ 818	Look at Me/Sad Thing	1969	8.00
COLUMBIA			
❑ 4-45049	Yesterday Has Gone/ Brown Eyed Woman	1969	12.00
DATE			
❑ 2-1665	Yesterday Has Gone/ Brown Eyed Woman	1970	8.00
EPIC			
❑ 5-10356	Yesterday Has Gone/Dream	1968	12.00

CUPIDS, THE (1)

Number	Title (A Side/B Side)	Yr	NM
45s			
AANKO			
❑ 1002	Brenda/For You	1963	100.00
KC			
❑ 115	Brenda/For You	1963	50.00

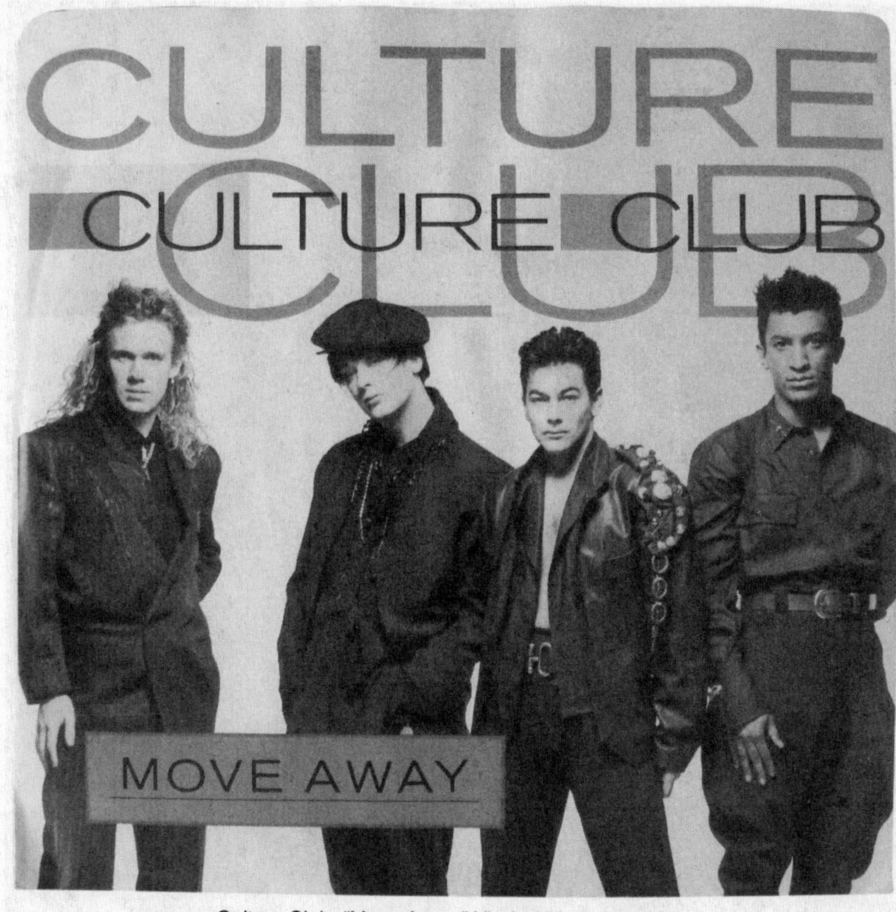

Culture Club, "Move Away," Virgin 05847, 1986, **$3.**

CUPIDS, THE (2)

Number	Title (A Side/B Side)	Yr	NM
45s			
ALADDIN			
❑ 3404	Now You Tell Me/Lillie Mae	1957	60.00
—Maroon label			
❑ 3404	Now You Tell Me/Lillie Mae	1958	25.00
—Black label			

CUPIDS, THE (3)

Number	Title (A Side/B Side)	Yr	NM
45s			
DECCA			
❑ 30279	The Answer to Your Prayer/ My Dog Likes Your Dog	1957	40.00

CUPIDS, THE (U)

Some of these may be groups (1), (2) or (3), but more likely they aren't. It's also likely they aren't all the same.

Number	Title (A Side/B Side)	Yr	NM
45s			
CHAN			
❑ 107	I Don't Know/Troubles Not At End	1956	80.00
MUSICNOTE			
❑ 119	Lorraine/Little Girl of Mine	1963	15.00
TIMES SQUARE			
❑ 1	Pretty Baby/Let's Rock	1964	15.00
UWR			
❑ 4241/2	True Love, True Love/Let's Twist	1962	40.00

CURB, MIKE

Includes the Mike Curb Congregation.

Number	Title (A Side/B Side)	Yr	NM
45s			
BUENA VISTA			
❑ 492	Robin Hood March/Oo-De-Lally	1973	5.00
❑ 494	Winnie the Pooh/ Zip-a-Dee-Doo-Dah	1973	5.00
❑ 499	Mickey Mouse March/Mickey Mouse Alma Mater	1974	5.00
—B-side by Jimmy Dodd and the Mouseketeers			
❑ 499 [PS]	Mickey Mouse March/Mickey Mouse Alma Mater	1974	8.00
CAPITOL			
❑ 4054	Po'r Folk/You Were On My Mind	1975	4.00
❑ 4102	Mickey Mouse March/ You Were On My Mind	1975	4.00
❑ 4166	Fools Rush In (Where Angels Fear to Tread)/Do You Wanna Dance	1975	4.00
FORWARD			
❑ 124	Bandstand Theme/Oh, Calcutta	1970	5.00
❑ 124 [PS]	Bandstand Theme/Oh, Calcutta	1970	10.00
—Called "The New Bandstand Theme" on sleeve			
MGM			
❑ 14110	Long Haired Lover from Liverpool/Sweet Gingerbread Man	1970	4.00
❑ 14151	Burning Bridges/We'll Sing in the Sunshine	1970	4.00
❑ 14243	I Was Born in Love with You/ Sweet Gingerbread Man	1971	4.00
❑ 14265	Sweet Gingerbread Man/Fly Me a Place for the Summer	1971	4.00
❑ 14336	Softly Whispering I Love You/ Forty Days and Forty Nights	1971	4.00
❑ 14366	I Saw the Light/Take Up the Hammer of Hope	1972	4.00
❑ 14391	The Very Same Time Next Year/See You in September	1972	4.00
❑ 14442	This Land Is Your Land/ I Understand	1972	4.00
❑ 14494	It's a Small, Small World/ Shinin' on Me	1973	4.00
REPRISE			
❑ 0287	Hot Dawg/Velocita	1964	20.00
SMASH			
❑ 1938	The Rebel (Without a Cause)/ Carole's Rebel	1964	12.00
TOWER			
❑ 202	Sunshine/Suzie Darling	1966	10.00
❑ 480	Let's Go/Eight Young Me (The Devil's Theme)	1969	8.00

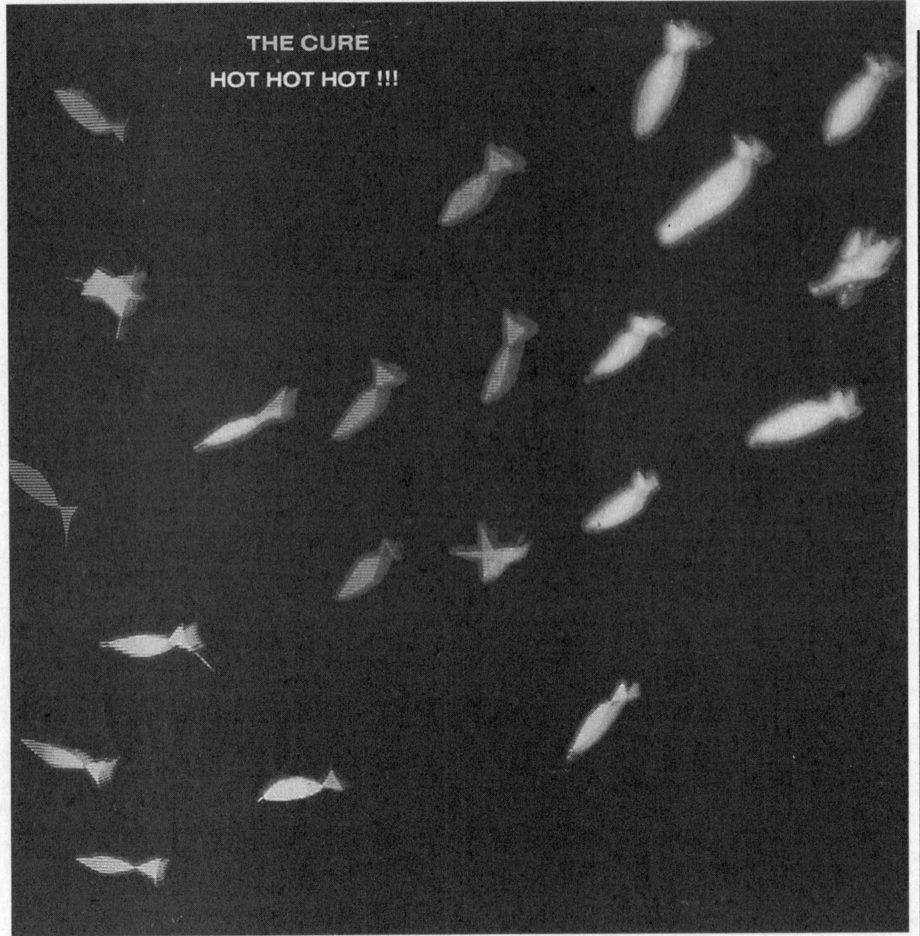

The Cure, "Hot Hot Hot !!!," Elektra 7-69424, 1988, **$4.**

Number	Title (A Side/B Side)	Yr	NM
WARNER BROS.			
❑ 8463	Cotton Fields/Dance On, Maria	1977	4.00
Albums			
COBURT			
❑ CO 1002	Come Together	1970	10.00
❑ CO 1003	Sweet Gingerbread Man	1970	10.00
MGM			
❑ SE-4761	Burning Bridges and Other Great Motion Picture Themes	1971	10.00
❑ SE-4785	Put Your Hand in the Hand	1971	10.00
❑ SE-4804	The Mike Curb Congregation Sing Their Hits from the Glen Campbell Show	1971	10.00
❑ SE-4821	Softly Whispering I Love You	1972	10.00
❑ SE-4844	Song for a Young Love	1972	10.00
WARNER BROS.			
❑ BS 3129	The Mike Curb Congregation	1977	10.00

CURE, THE

12-Inch Singles

Number	Title (A Side/B Side)	Yr	NM
ELEKTRA			
❑ ED 5085 [DJ]	In Between Days (LP Version) (Extended Version)/Stop Dead	1985	12.00
❑ ED5118 [DJ]	Close to Me (Extended)/ Close to Me (Edit Remix)	1985	15.00
❑ ED 5118 [DJ]	Close to Me (Extended Remix 6:31)/(Edit of Remix 3:38)	1985	20.00
❑ ED 5130 [DJ]	A Night Like This (same on both sides)	1986	15.00
❑ ED 5146 [DJ]	Let's Go to Bed (same on both sides)	1986	12.00
❑ ED5146 [DJ]	Let's Go to Bed (same on both sides)	1986	12.00
❑ ED5175 [DJ]	Boys Don't Cry (2:36)/ Boys Don't Cry (5:29)	1986	15.00
❑ ED 5175 [DJ]	Boys Don't Cry (English Mix 2:36) (Extended Mix 5:29)	1986	15.00
❑ ED 5252 [DJ]	Just Like Heaven (Remix)/ (LP Version)	1987	15.00
❑ ED5252 [DJ]	Just Like Heaven (Remix)/Just Like Heaven (LP Version)	1987	18.00
❑ ED5273 [DJ]	Hot Hot Hot (3 versions)	1987	8.00
❑ ED 5273 [DJ]	Hot Hot Hot!!! (Extended Vocal Remix) (Remix) (LP Version)	1987	12.00
❑ ED5374 [DJ]	Fascination Street (Extended)/ Fascination Street (Remix)	1989	7.00
❑ ED 5374 [DJ]	Fascination Street (Extended Remix 8:48)/(Remix 4:17)	1989	12.00
❑ ED5390 [DJ]	Love Song (same on both sides)	1989	8.00
❑ ED 5390 [DJ]	Love Song (LP Version) (same on both sides)	1989	10.00
❑ ED 5398 [DJ]	Love Song (Remix)/ (Extended Remix)	1989	10.00
❑ ED5398 [DJ]	Love Song (Remix)/Love Song (Extended Remix)	1989	12.00
❑ ED5418 [DJ]	Lullaby (3 versions)	1989	12.00
❑ ED 5418 [DJ]	Lullaby (Extended Remix) (LP Version) (Remix)	1989	12.00
❑ ED5452 [DJ]	Pictures of You (4:44)/ Pictures of You (8:05)	1990	12.00
❑ ED 5452 [DJ]	Pictures of You (Remix 4:44)/ (Extended Remix 8:05)	1990	12.00
❑ ED 5489 [DJ]	Never Enough (2 versions)/ Harold and Joe/Let's Go to Bed (Milk Mix)	1990	15.00
❑ ED5489 [DJ]	Never Enough (2 versions)/ Harold and Joe/Let's Go to Bed (Milk Mix)	1990	15.00
❑ ED 5513 [DJ]	Close to Me (closer mix)/Just Like Heaven (dizzy mix)/ Primary (red mix)	1990	10.00
❑ ED5513 [DJ]	Close to Me (closer mix)/Just Like Heaven (dizzy mix)/ Primary (red mix)	1990	15.00
❑ ED 5527 [DJ]	In Between Days (Shiver Remix) (LP Version)	1991	15.00
❑ 66595	Close to Me (closer mix)/Just Like Heaven (dizzy mix)/ Primary (red mix)	1990	8.00
❑ 66604	Never Enough (Big Mix)/ Harold and Joe/Let's Go to Bed (Milk Mix)	1990	10.00
❑ 66639	Pictures of You (Extended Remix)/Last Dance (Live)/ Fascination Street (Live)	1990	8.00
❑ 66664	Lullaby/Untitled/Homesick (Live)	1989	8.00
❑ 66687	Love Song/2 Late/Fear of Ghosts	1989	12.00
❑ 66704	Fascination Street (Extended Remix)/Babble/Out of Mind	1989	8.00
❑ 66783	Hot Hot Hot!!! (2 versions)/ Hey You (Extended)	1987	8.00
❑ 66793	Just Like Heaven/Breathe/ A Chain of Flowers	1987	12.00
❑ 66810	Why Can't I Be You? (Extended Remix 8:04)/A Japanese Dream (Extended Vocal Version 5:50)	1987	12.00
❑ 66856	A Night Like This/New Day/ Close to Me/A Man Inside My Mouth	1985	15.00
—Also known as "Quadpus"			
❑ 66882	In Between Days (2 versions)/ Stop Dead	1985	12.00
SIRE			
❑ 20161	The Love Cats (Extended Version)/Speak My Language/Mr. Pink Eyes	1983	15.00
❑ 29689	Let's Go to Bed (2 versions)/ Just One Kiss	1983	20.00

45s

Number	Title (A Side/B Side)	Yr	NM
ELEKTRA			
❑ 64928	Never Enough/Harold and Joe	1990	5.00
❑ 65936	Love Song/Fascination Street	1990	3.00
—"Spun Gold" reissue			
❑ 65967	Why Can't I Be You/Hot Hot Hot!!	1990	3.00
—"Spun Gold" reissue			
❑ 69249	Lullaby/Homesick	1989	5.00
❑ 69280	Love Song/2 Late	1989	3.00
—First pressing: Red and black label			
❑ 69280	Love Song/2 Late	1989	5.00
—Second pressing: Gray label			
❑ 69300	Fascination Street/Babble	1989	4.00
❑ 69300 [PS]	Fascination Street/Babble	1989	4.00
❑ 69424	Hot Hot Hot!!!/Hey You!!!	1988	4.00
❑ 69424 [PS]	Hot Hot Hot!!!/Hey You!!!	1988	5.00
❑ 69443	Just Like Heaven/Breathe	1987	10.00
❑ 69443 [PS]	Just Like Heaven/Breathe	1987	10.00
❑ 69474	Why Can't I Be You?/ Japanese Dream	1987	5.00
❑ 69474 [PS]	Why Can't I Be You?/ Japanese Dream	1987	5.00
❑ 69537	Let's Go to Bed/Boys Don't Cry	1986	6.00
❑ 69537 [PS]	Let's Go to Bed/Boys Don't Cry	1986	7.00
❑ 69551	Close to Me/Sinking	1986	8.00
❑ 69604	In Between Days (Without You)/ Stop Dead	1985	5.00
❑ 69604 [PS]	In Between Days (Without You)/ Stop Dead	1985	6.00
GEFFEN			
❑ B0002970-21	The End of the World/ This Morning	2004	4.00
❑ B0002970-21 [PS]	The End of the World/ This Morning	2004	6.00
SIRE			
❑ PRO2022 [DJ]	Let's Go to Bed (same on both sides)	1983	20.00
❑ PRO-S-2022 [DJ]	Let's Go to Bed (stereo/mono)	1983	20.00
❑ 29376	The Love Cats/Speak My Language	1984	10.00
❑ 29490	The Walk/The Dream	1983	10.00

Albums

Number	Title (A Side/B Side)	Yr	NM
A&M			
❑ SP-4902	Pornography	1982	20.00
❑ SP-6020 [(2)]	Happily Ever After	1981	30.00
ELEKTRA			
❑ 60435	The Head on the Door	1985	12.00
❑ 60477	Standing on a Beach — The Singles	1986	10.00
❑ 60737 [(2)]	Kiss Me, Kiss Me, Kiss Me	1987	15.00
❑ 60737 [(2)DJ]	Kiss Me, Kiss Me, Kiss Me	1987	30.00
—Promo-only audiophile pressing			
❑ 60737 [(2)DJ]	Kiss Me, Kiss Me, Kiss Me	1987	30.00
—Promo-only audiophile pressing			
❑ 60783	Faith	1988	10.00
—Reissue of first U.K. album			
❑ 60784	Seventeen Seconds	1988	10.00
—Reissue of second U.K. album			
❑ 60785	Pornography	1988	10.00
—Reissue of A&M SP-4902			
❑ 60786	Boys Don't Cry	1988	10.00
—Reissue of PVC 7916			
❑ 60855	Disintegration	1989	10.00
❑ 60978 [(2)]	Mixed Up	1990	40.00
—LP version has one extra track not on CD or cassette			
❑ 61744 [(2)]	Wild Mood Swings	1996	30.00
❑ 62117 [(2)]	Galore: The Singles 1987-1997	1997	80.00

Except when noted otherwise, VG = 25% of NM, and VG+ = 50% of NM. (Example: VG = $2.00, VG+ = $4.00 and NM = $8.00.)

Number	Title (A Side/B Side)	Yr	NM
❑ 62236 [(2)]	Bloodflowers	2000	40.00
❑ R 101109	Disintegration	1989	12.00
—BMG Direct Marketing edition			
❑ R 150024	Standing on a Beach — The Singles	1986	12.00
—BMG Direct Marketing edition			
❑ R 242404	Kiss Me, Kiss Me, Kiss Me	1987	18.00
—BMG Direct Marketing edition			
❑ R 274190	Mixed Up	1990	25.00
—BMG Direct Marketing edition			
GEFFEN			
❑ B0002870-01 [(2)]	The Cure	2004	15.00
PVC			
❑ 7916	Boys Don't Cry	1980	15.00
SIRE			
❑ 23928 [EP]	The Walk	1983	12.00
❑ 25076	Japanese Whispers	1983	15.00
❑ 25086	The Top	1984	15.00

CURLEY AND THE JADES

45s

Number	Title (A Side/B Side)	Yr	NM
MUSIC MAKERS			
❑ 109	Bullfighter/Boom Stix	1962	60.00
REPRISE			
❑ 20046	Bullfighter/Boom Stix	1962	30.00

CURRENTS, THE

45s

Number	Title (A Side/B Side)	Yr	NM
LAURIE			
❑ 3205	Night Run/Riff Raff	1963	30.00

CURRIE, CHERIE AND MARIE

Lead singer of the RUNAWAYS plus her sister.

45s

Number	Title (A Side/B Side)	Yr	NM
CAPITOL			
❑ 4754	Since You've Been Gone/Longer Than Forever	1979	5.00
❑ 4754 [PS]	Since You've Been Gone/Longer Than Forever	1979	10.00
❑ 4841	Secrets/This Time	1980	5.00
❑ 4861	All I Want/Messin' with the Boys	1980	5.00

Albums

Number	Title (A Side/B Side)	Yr	NM
CAPITOL			
❑ ST-12022	Messin' with the Boys	1979	20.00

CURTIS, EDDIE

45s

Number	Title (A Side/B Side)	Yr	NM
GEE			
❑ 7	Candy Man/The Girl I Left Behind	1954	40.00
—As "Eddie 'Tex' Curtis"			
❑ 9	Prayer to the Moon/Shake, Pretty Baby, Shake	1954	40.00
—As "Eddie 'Tex' Curtis"			
JOSIE			
❑ 957	Those Foxes and Pussycats (Part 1)/(Part 2)	1966	10.00
OKEH			
❑ 7063	Sweet Stuff/I Didn't Wanna Love You	1955	30.00
—As "Eddie 'Tex' Curtis"			

CURTIS, MAC

45s

Number	Title (A Side/B Side)	Yr	NM
DOT			
❑ 16315	You're the One/Dance Her By Me (One More Time)	1962	10.00
EPIC			
❑ 10257	Too Close to Home/Too Good to Be True	1967	6.00
❑ 10324	The Quiet Kind/Love's Been Good to Me	1968	6.00
❑ 10385	The Sunshine Man/It's My Way	1968	6.00
❑ 10438	Almost Persuaded/The Friendly City	1969	6.00
❑ 10468	Happiness Lives in This House/Little Ole Wine Drinker Me	1969	6.00
❑ 10530	Don't Make Love/Us	1969	6.00
❑ 10574	Honey Don't/Today's Teardrops	1970	6.00
FELSTED			
❑ 8592	Come Back Baby/No, Never Alone	1959	20.00
GRT			
❑ 26	Early in the Morning/When the Hurt Moves In	1970	5.00
❑ 41	Gulf Stream Line/I'd Run a Mile	1971	5.00
KING			
❑ 4927	If I Had Me a Woman/Just So You Call Me	1956	150.00
❑ 4949	Grandaddy's Rockin'/Half Hearted Love	1956	150.00
❑ 4965	You Ain't Treatin' Me Right/The Low Road	1956	150.00
❑ 4995	That Ain't Nothin' But Right/Don't You Love Me	1956	150.00
❑ 5007	What You Want/To Protect the Innocent	1957	100.00
❑ 5059	Say So/I'll Be Gentle	1957	40.00
❑ 5107	What You Want/You Are My Special Baby	1958	60.00
❑ 5121	Missy Ann/Little Miss Linda	1958	60.00
RANWOOD			
❑ 1017	Pistol Packin' Mama/Asphalt Cowboy, Parking Lot Lover	1975	5.00
❑ 1033	Keep Doin' What You're Doin' Now/She Knows All the Good Ways to Be Bad	1975	5.00
❑ 1041	More Like I Do Now/Nine Times Out of Ten	1975	5.00
❑ 1050	We Made It All the Way/West Texas Women	1976	5.00
TOWER			
❑ 319	Ties That Bind/Stepping Out on You	1967	6.00

Albums

Number	Title (A Side/B Side)	Yr	NM
EPIC			
❑ BN 26419	The Sunshine Man	1969	20.00
HMG/HIGHTONE			
❑ HT 6601	Rockabilly Uprising: The Best of Mac Curtis	1997	10.00
ROLLIN' ROCK			
❑ LP-002	Ruffabilly	1975	40.00
❑ LP-002	Ruffabilly	1977	20.00
—Reissue			
❑ LP-007	Good Rockin' Tomorrow	1975	40.00

CURTIS, SONNY

Also see THE CRICKETS (1).

45s

Number	Title (A Side/B Side)	Yr	NM
A&M			
❑ 1359	Lights of L.A./Sunny Mornin'	1972	30.00
❑ 1408	Love Is All Around/Last Days of Childhood	1973	—
—Unreleased?			
CAPITOL			
❑ 4158	Lovesick Blues/It's Only a Question of Time	1975	12.00
❑ 4227	It's Only a Question of Time/When It's Just You and Me	1976	12.00
❑ 4240	Where's Patricia Now/When It's Just You and Me	1976	12.00
CORAL			
❑ 60954	Someday You're Gonna Be Sorry/Forever Yours	1953	25.00
❑ 61023	No More Tears/The Best Way to Hold a Girl	1953	25.00
❑ 62207	Red Headed Stranger/Talk About My Baby	1960	40.00
DIMENSION			
❑ 1017	So Used to Loving You/The Last Song I'm Ever Gonna Sing	1963	20.00
❑ 1024	A Beatle I Want to Be/So Used to Loving You	1964	25.00
DOT			
❑ 15754	Wrong Again/Laughing Stock	1958	40.00
❑ 15799	A Pretty Girl/Willa May Jones	1958	30.00
ELEKTRA			
❑ 46526	The Cowboy Singer/Cheatin' Clouds	1979	5.00
❑ 46568	Do You Remember Roll Over Beethoven/Walk Right Back	1979	5.00
❑ 46616	The Real Buddy Holly Story/Ain't Nobody Honest	1980	6.00
❑ 46643	Love Is All Around/The Clone Song	1980	5.00
❑ 47048	You Made My Life a Song/50 Ways to Leave Your Lover	1980	5.00
❑ 47129	Good Ol' Girls/So Used to Loving You	1981	5.00
❑ 47176	Married Woman/I Live Your Music	1981	5.00
❑ 47231 [DJ]	The Christmas Song/Little Drummer Boy	1981	8.00
—B-side by Hank Williams, Jr.			
❑ 69942	Together Alone/Dream Well All of You Children	1982	5.00
LIBERTY			
❑ 55710	Bo Diddley Bach/I Pledge My Love to You	1964	20.00
MERCURY			
❑ 73438	Rock and Rol (I Gave You the Best Years of My Life)/My Mama Sure Left Me Some Good Old Days	1973	15.00
OVATION			
❑ 1006	Love Is All Around/Here, There and Everywhere	1970	20.00
❑ 1023	Unsaintly Judy/You Don't Belong in This Place	1970	15.00
'STEEM			
❑ 110185	Now I've Got a Heart of Gold/(B-side unknown)	1985	6.00
VIVA			
❑ 602	My Way of Life/Last Call	1966	15.00
❑ 607	The Collection/Destiny's Child	1966	15.00
❑ 617	I'm a Gypsy Man/I Wanna Go Bummin' Around	1967	15.00
❑ 626	Day Drinker/Atlanta, Georgia Stray	1968	15.00
❑ 630	The Straight Life/How Little Men Care	1968	15.00
❑ 634	Holiday for Clowns/Day Gig	1969	15.00
❑ 636	Girl of the North/Hung Up in Your Eyes	1969	15.00

Albums

Number	Title (A Side/B Side)	Yr	NM
ELEKTRA			
❑ 6E-227	Sonny Curtis	1979	10.00
❑ 6E-283	Love Is All Around	1980	10.00
❑ 6E-349	Rollin'	1981	10.00
IMPERIAL			
❑ LP-9276 [M]	Beatle Hits Flamenco Style	1964	40.00
❑ LP-12276 [S]	Beatle Hits Flamenco Style	1964	50.00
VIVA			
❑ V-36012	The First of Sonny Curtis	1968	25.00
❑ V-36021	The Sonny Curtis Style	1969	25.00

CUSTER AND THE SURVIVORS

45s

Number	Title (A Side/B Side)	Yr	NM
ASCOT			
❑ 2207	I Saw Her Walking/Flapjacks	1965	16.00
GOLDEN STATE			
❑ 1657	I Saw Her Walking/Flapjacks	1965	12.00
VARDAN			
❑ 202	I Saw Her Walking/Flapjacks	1965	20.00

CUTE-TEENS, THE

45s

Number	Title (A Side/B Side)	Yr	NM
ALADDIN			
❑ 3458	When My Teenage Days Are Over/From This Day Forward	1959	250.00

CYCLONE III

45s

Number	Title (A Side/B Side)	Yr	NM
PHILIPS			
❑ 40258	You've Got a Bomb/Surfnanny	1965	40.00

CYKLE, THE

45s

Number	Title (A Side/B Side)	Yr	NM
LABEL			
❑ 101	If You Can/(B-side unknown)	1969	30.00
❑ 101 [PS]	If You Can/(B-side unknown)	1969	60.00

Albums

Number	Title (A Side/B Side)	Yr	NM
LABEL			
❑ 9-261	The Cykle	1969	500.00

CYMANDE

45s

Number	Title (A Side/B Side)	Yr	NM
JANUS			
❑ 203	The Message/Zion I	1972	5.00
❑ 215	Bra/Ras Tafarian Folk Song	1973	5.00
❑ 225	Anthracite/Fug	1973	5.00

Albums

Number	Title (A Side/B Side)	Yr	NM
JANUS			
❑ 3044	Cymande	1972	10.00
❑ 3054	Second Time Round	1973	10.00

CYMARRON

45s

Number	Title (A Side/B Side)	Yr	NM
ENTRANCE			
❑ 7500	Rings/Like Children	1971	5.00
❑ 7502	Valerie/Across the Kansas Sky	1971	4.00
❑ 7506	Right Can Be Wrong/What's a Little Dirt	1972	4.00
❑ 7514	Keep Me Warm/Start Again	1972	4.00

Albums

Number	Title (A Side/B Side)	Yr	NM
ENTRANCE			
❑ Z 30962	Rings	1971	12.00

CYMBAL, JOHNNY

Includes releases as "Derek" on the Bang label. Also see CYMBAL AND CLINGER.

45s

Number	Title (A Side/B Side)	Yr	NM
AMARET			
❑ 110	Big River/Girl from Willow County	1969	8.00

The Cyrkle, "Camaro," Columbia Special Products CSM-466, 1967, $50.

Number	Title (A Side/B Side)	Yr	NM
❑ 111	Ode to Bubblegum/Save All Your Lovin' (Hold It for Me)	1969	8.00
BANG			
❑ 558	Cinnamon/This Is My Story	1968	8.00
❑ 566	Back Door Man/Tell Your Soul	1969	6.00
❑ 571	Inside Out-Outside In/ Sell Your Soul	1969	6.00
COLUMBIA			
❑ 43842	Good Morning Blues/Jessica	1966	8.00
DCP			
❑ 1135	Go, VW, Go/Sorrow and Pain	1965	30.00
❑ 1146	My Last Day/Summertime's Here at Last	1965	15.00
KAPP			
❑ 503	Mr. Bass Man/Sacred Lovers' Vow	1963	20.00
❑ 524	Teenage Heaven/ Cinderella Baby	1963	15.00
❑ 539	(Surfin' at) Tia Juana/ Dum Dum Dee Dum	1963	15.00
❑ 556	Marshmallow/Hurdy Gurdy Man	1963	15.00
❑ 576	There Goes a Bad Girl/ Refreshment Time	1964	15.00
❑ 594	Robinson Crusoe on Mars/Mitsu	1964	15.00
❑ 614	Connie/Little Miss Lonely	1964	15.00
❑ 634	Cheat, Cheat/16 Shades of Blue	1964	15.00
KEDLEN			
❑ 2001	Bachelor Man/Growing Up with You	1962	20.00
MGM			
❑ 12935	It'll Be Me/Always, Always	1960	20.00
❑ 12978	The Water Was Red/The Bunny	1961	20.00
MUSICOR			
❑ 1261	It Looks Like Love/May I Get to Know You	1967	12.00
❑ 1272	Breaking Your Balloon/The Marriage of Charlotte Brown	1967	12.00
VEE JAY			
❑ 495	Bachelor Man/Growing Up with You	1963	15.00
Albums			
KAPP			
❑ KL-1324 [M]	Mr. Bass Man	1963	50.00
❑ KS-3324 [S]	Mr. Bass Man	1963	70.00

CYMBAL & CLINGER Also see JOHNNY CYMBAL.

Number	Title (A Side/B Side)	Yr	NM
45s			
CHELSEA			
❑ 78-0106	God Bless You Rock & Roll/ Forever and Forever	1972	5.00
❑ 78-0112	Dying River/Little Bit No, Little Bit Yes	1973	5.00
MARINA			
❑ 502	Pool Shooter/ Mookie Mookie Man	1971	6.00
MGM			
❑ 14256	Pool Shooter/ Mookie Mookie Man	1971	5.00
Albums			
CHELSEA			
❑ 1002	Cymbal & Clinger	1972	12.00

CYPRESS, BUDDY

Number	Title (A Side/B Side)	Yr	NM
45s			
FLASH			
❑ 118	I'm in Love with You/ Don't Forsake Me	1957	50.00

CYRKLE, THE

Number	Title (A Side/B Side)	Yr	NM
45s			
COLUMBIA			
❑ CSM-466	Camaro/SS 396	1967	25.00
—B-side by Paul Revere and the Raiders			
❑ CSM-466 [PS]	Camaro/SS 396	1967	50.00
—B-side by Paul Revere and the Raiders			
❑ 43589	Red Rubber Ball/How Can I Leave Her	1966	12.00
❑ 43589 [DJ]	Red Rubber Ball (same on both sides)	1966	40.00
—Promo only on red vinyl			
❑ 43589 [PS]	Red Rubber Ball/How Can I Leave Her	1966	400.00
❑ 43729	Turn-Down Day/ Big, Little Woman	1966	10.00
❑ 43729 [DJ]	Turn-Down Day (same on both sides)	1966	40.00
—Promo only on red vinyl			
❑ 43729 [PS]	Turn-Down Day/ Big, Little Woman	1966	15.00
❑ 43871	Please Don't Ever Leave Me/ Money to Burn	1966	8.00
❑ 43965	I Wish You Could Be Here/ The Visit (She Was Here)	1967	8.00
❑ 43965 [PS]	I Wish You Could Be Here/ The Visit (She Was Here)	1967	12.00
❑ 44108	We Had a Good Thing Goin'/ Two Rooms	1967	8.00
❑ 44224	Penny Arcade/The Words	1967	8.00
❑ 44366	Turn of the Century/Don't Cry, No Fears, No Tears Comin'	1967	8.00
❑ 44426	Friends/Reading Her Papers	1968	8.00
❑ 44491	Red Chair Fade Away/ Where Are You Going	1968	8.00
7-Inch Extended Plays			
SUNDAZED KUSTOM SHOP			
❑ KS7-03	7 Up The Uncola/Their Hearts Were Full of Spring//Sigma Stomp/Waiting in the Rain	2002	2.50
❑ KS7-03 [PS]	The Cyrkle	2002	2.50
Albums			
COLUMBIA			
❑ CL 2544 [M]	Red Rubber Ball	1966	20.00
❑ CL 2632 [M]	Neon	1967	15.00
❑ CS 9344 [S]	Red Rubber Ball	1966	30.00
❑ CS 9432 [S]	Neon	1967	20.00

CYRUS ERIE Early ERIC CARMEN.

Number	Title (A Side/B Side)	Yr	NM
45s			
EPIC			
❑ 10451	Sparrow/Get the Message	1969	12.00

D

D-MEN, THE Early incarnation of THE FIFTH ESTATE.

Number	Title (A Side/B Side)	Yr	NM
45s			
KAPP			
❑ 691	So Little Time/Every Moment of Every Day	1965	12.00
VEEP			
❑ 1206	Don't You Know/No Hope for Me	1965	15.00
❑ 1209	Just Don't Care/Mousin' Around	1965	15.00

D'ABO, MIKE Lead singer of MANFRED MANN in the "Mighty Quinn" era.

Number	Title (A Side/B Side)	Yr	NM
45s			
A&M			
❑ 1374	Little Miss Understood/Belinda	1972	5.00
❑ 1628	Fuel to Burn/Hold On Sweet Darling	1974	4.00
BELL			
❑ 956	Miss Me in the Morning/ Arabella Cinderella	1971	6.00
Albums			
A&M			
❑ SP-3634	Broken Rainbows	1974	12.00
❑ SP-4346	Down at Rachel's Place	1972	12.00

D'RONE, FRANK

Number	Title (A Side/B Side)	Yr	NM
45s			
CADET			
❑ 5585	The Copla Song/I Wouldn't Know Where to Begin	1967	10.00
❑ 5595	Think I Will/Make Me Rainbows	1968	10.00
❑ 5619	Brand New Morning/Bluesette	1968	10.00
CAMEO			
❑ 282	Mr. Blue/Have a Good Time	1963	15.00
COLUMBIA			
❑ 4-43460	Falling in Love in the Fall/ Names in a Heart	1965	10.00
❑ 4-43733	Too Good to Be Forgotten/ Who's Afraid	1966	10.00
MERCURY			
❑ 71193	My Special Angel/Once in a Million Years	1957	15.00
❑ 71329	Our Summer Love/Little Pixie	1958	15.00
❑ 71429	Fascinating Rhythm/Yesterdays	1959	15.00
❑ 71544	I Love You/Serenade in Blue	1959	12.00
❑ 71589	Joey, Joey, Joey/The House and the Old Wisteria Tree	1960	12.00
❑ 71626	After the Ball/Warm All Over	1960	12.00

Except when noted otherwise, VG = 25% of NM, and VG+ = 50% of NM. (Example: VG = $2.00, VG+ = $4.00 and NM = $8.00.)

Number	Title (A Side/B Side)	Yr	NM
❑ 71720	Strawberry Blonde/Time Hurries By	1960	12.00
❑ 71775	(When You're Young and) Only Seventeen/Yea, Yea, Baby	1961	12.00
❑ 71846	Again/If You Were the Only Girl in the World	1961	12.00
❑ 71939	Twist Li'l Liza/What's In It for Me	1962	12.00
❑ 71980	I'm in Love/Show Me the Way to Go Home	1962	12.00

Albums

CADET

Number	Title	Yr	NM
❑ LPS-806	Brand New Morning	1968	15.00

MERCURY

Number	Title	Yr	NM
❑ MG-20418 [M]	Frank D'Rone Sings	1959	30.00
❑ MG-20586 [M]	After the Ball	1960	30.00
❑ MG-20721 [M]	Frank D'Rone In Person	196?	25.00
❑ SR-60246 [S]	After the Ball	1960	40.00
❑ SR-60721 [S]	Frank D'Rone In Person	196?	30.00
❑ SR-90064 [S]	Frank D'Rone Sings	1959	40.00

D.C. BLOSSOMS, THE

45s

SHRINE

Number	Title	Yr	NM
❑ 107	I Know About Her/Hey Boy	1966	800.00

DA-PREES, THE

45s

TWIST

Number	Title	Yr	NM
❑ 70913	Pay Day/Sometimes	1963	150.00

DACHE, BERTELL

TONY ORLANDO with CAROLE KING on backing vocals.

45s

DIAMOND

Number	Title	Yr	NM
❑ 201	Don't Stop the World for Me/Anchors Awaeigh Girl	1966	15.00

UNITED ARTISTS

Number	Title	Yr	NM
❑ 260	All the World Loves a Lover/You Gotta Have Chicks	1960	25.00
❑ 290	Not Just Tomorrow, But Today/Love Eyes	1961	25.00

DACRONS, THE

45s

HIT

Number	Title	Yr	NM
❑ 38	Don't Hang Up/Limbo Rock	1962	8.00
—B-side by Bill Carmichael			
❑ 56	South Street/What Will My Mary Say	1963	8.00
—B-side by Tony Christopher			
❑ 57	He's So Fine/Follow the Boys	1963	8.00
—B-side by Connie Landers			
❑ 81	Then He Kissed Me/Surfer Girl	1963	8.00
—B-side by the Jalopy Five			

DADDY COOL

45s

REPRISE

Number	Title	Yr	NM
❑ 1038	Eagle Rock/Bom Bom	1971	6.00
❑ 1064	Hi Honey Ho/Come Back Again	1972	6.00
❑ 1087	Teenage Blues/Donna Forgive Me	1972	6.00
❑ 1090	I'll Never Smile Again/Daddy Rocks Off	1972	6.00

Albums

REPRISE

Number	Title	Yr	NM
❑ MS 2088	Teenage Heaven	1972	20.00
❑ RS 6471	Daddy Who? Daddy Cool!	1971	15.00

DADDY DEWDROP

12-Inch Singles

T.K. DISCO

Number	Title	Yr	NM
❑ TKD 118	Nanu, Nanu (I Wanna Funky with You)/The Real Thing	1978	15.00
❑ TKD 153	The Real Thing (Vocal 7:40)/(Instrumental 6:13)	1979	15.00

45s

CAPITOL

Number	Title	Yr	NM
❑ 4066	Dynamite Dyna/Goddaughter	1975	4.00

INPHASION

Number	Title	Yr	NM
❑ 7201	Nanu, Nanu (I Wanna Funky with You)/The Real Thing	1978	4.00
❑ 7203	The Real Thing/(Instrumental)	1978	4.00
❑ 7206	If You Wanna Wanna/Turn On the Motion	1979	4.00

SUNFLOWER

Number	Title	Yr	NM
❑ 105	Chick-a-Boom (Don't Ya Jes' Love It)/John Jacob Jingleheimer Smith	1971	5.00
❑ 111	Fox Huntin' (On a Weekend)/March of the White Corpuscles	1971	4.00
❑ 119	Chantilly Lace/Migraine Headaches	1972	4.00

Albums

SUNFLOWER

Number	Title	Yr	NM
❑ SNF-5006	Daddy Dewdrop	1971	20.00

DAILEY, DON

Albums

CROWN

Number	Title	Yr	NM
❑ CST-314 [R]	Surf Stompin'	1963	15.00
❑ CLP-5314 [M]	Surf Stompin'	1963	30.00

DAILY FLASH, THE

45s

PARROT

Number	Title	Yr	NM
❑ 308	Jack of Diamonds/Queen Jane Approximately	1966	12.00

UNI

Number	Title	Yr	NM
❑ 55001	French Girl/Green Rocky Road	1967	12.00

DAISIES, THE

45s

CAPITOL

Number	Title	Yr	NM
❑ 5667	Cold Wave/Put Your Arms Around Me	1966	25.00

ROULETTE

Number	Title	Yr	NM
❑ 4571	I Wanna Swim with Him/You Just Said You Loved Me	1964	12.00

DAKIL, FLOYD

45s

EARTH

Number	Title	Yr	NM
❑ 402	Bad Boy/Stoppin' Traffic	1965	40.00
❑ 403	Kitty Kitty/It Takes a Lot to Hurt	1965	30.00
❑ 404	Stronger Than Dirt/You're the Kind of Girl	1965	30.00

GUYDEN

Number	Title	Yr	NM
❑ 2111	Dance, Franny, Dance/Look What You've Gone and Done	1964	30.00

JETSTAR

Number	Title	Yr	NM
❑ 103	Dance, Franny, Dance/Look What You've Gone and Done	1964	100.00

POMPEII

Number	Title	Yr	NM
❑ 66687	Merry Christmas, Baby/One Girl	1968	25.00

DAKOTAS, THE

Also see BILLY J. KRAMER AND THE DAKOTAS.

45s

LIBERTY

Number	Title	Yr	NM
❑ 55618	The Cruel Surf/The Millionaire	1963	40.00

DAKUS, WES

45s

KAPP

Number	Title	Yr	NM
❑ 806	Sad Souvenirs/Armful of Teddy Bears	1967	10.00
—As "Barry Allen with Wes Dakus' Rebels"			
❑ 815	Peggy Sue/See Saw	1967	10.00
—As "Dennis Paul with Wes Dakus' Rebels"			

DALE, DICK, AND THE DEL-TONES

45s

ACCENT

Number	Title	Yr	NM
❑ 1243	Eyes of a Child/Just a-Waitin'	1968	8.00

CAPITOL

Number	Title	Yr	NM
❑ 4963	King of the Surf Guitar/Havah Nagilah	1963	20.00
❑ 4963 [PS]	King of the Surf Guitar/Havah Nagilah	1963	80.00
❑ 5010	Secret Surfin' Spot/Surfin' and a-Swingin'	1963	20.00
❑ 5048	Wild Ideas/Scavenger	1963	20.00
❑ 5098	The Wedge/Night Rider	1963	20.00
❑ 5140	The Victor/Mr. Eliminator	1964	15.00
❑ 5187	Wild, Wild Mustang/Grunge Run	1964	15.00
❑ 5225	Never on Sunday/Glory Wave	1964	15.00
❑ 5290	Oh Marie/Who Can It Be	1964	15.00
❑ 5389	Let's Go Trippin' '65/Watusi Jo	1965	15.00

COLUMBIA

Number	Title	Yr	NM
❑ 38-07340	Pipeline/Love Struck Baby	1987	4.00
—B-side by Stevie Ray Vaughan			
❑ 38-07340 [PS]	Pipeline/Love Struck Baby	1987	6.00

CONCERT ROOM

Number	Title	Yr	NM
❑ 371	We'll Never Hear the End of It/Fairest of Them All	1963	25.00

COUGAR

Number	Title	Yr	NM
❑ 711	Ramblin' Man/You're Hurtin' Now	1967	15.00
❑ 712	Taco Wagon/Spanish Kiss	1967	15.00

CUPID

Number	Title	Yr	NM
❑ 106	We'll Never Hear the End of It/Fairest of Them All	1960	30.00
—Black vinyl			
❑ 106	We'll Never Hear the End of It/Fairest of Them All	1960	80.00
—Gold vinyl			

DELTONE

Number	Title	Yr	NM
❑ 4939	Misirlou/Eight Till Midnight	1963	20.00
❑ 4940	Surf Beat/Peppermint Man	1963	20.00
—Deltone 4939 and 4940 were part of the Capitol numbering system			
❑ 5012	Oh Whee Marie/Breaking Heart	1959	60.00
❑ 5013	Stop Teasin'/Without Your Love	1959	60.00
❑ 5014	Jessie Pearl/St. Louis Blues	1960	100.00
❑ 5017	Let's Go Trippin'/Del-Tone Rock	1961	30.00
❑ 5018	Shake and Stomp/Jungle Fever	1962	40.00
❑ 5019	Misirlou/Eight Till Midnight	1962	25.00
❑ 5020	Peppermint Man/Surf Beat	1962	25.00
❑ 5028	Run for Your Life/Lovin' on My Brain	1963	30.00

GNP CRESCENDO

Number	Title	Yr	NM
❑ 804	Let's Go Trippin'/Those Memories of You	1975	6.00

RENDEZVOUS

Number	Title	Yr	NM
❑ 204	Reincarnation (Part 1)/Reincarnation (Part 2)	1963	20.00

SATURN

Number	Title	Yr	NM
❑ 401	We'll Never Hear the End of It/Fairest of Them All	1963	30.00

U.S. ARMY

Number	Title	Yr	NM
❑ 1301 [DJ]	The Enlistment Twist/Dream Girl Waltz	1962	30.00
—B-side by Craig Adams and His Country Cousins; blue vinyl			
❑ 1301 [PS]	The Enlistment Twist/Dream Girl Waltz	1962	30.00

YES

Number	Title	Yr	NM
❑ 7014	We'll Never Hear the End of It/Fairest of Them All	1963	30.00
❑ 7014 [PS]	We'll Never Hear the End of It/Fairest of Them All	1963	40.00

Albums

CAPITOL

Number	Title	Yr	NM
❑ ST 1930 [S]	King of the Surf Guitar	1963	100.00
❑ T 1930 [M]	King of the Surf Guitar	1963	60.00
❑ ST 2002 [S]	Checkered Flag	1963	80.00
❑ T 2002 [M]	Checkered Flag	1963	50.00
❑ ST 2053 [S]	Mr. Eliminator	1964	80.00
❑ T 2053 [M]	Mr. Eliminator	1964	50.00
❑ ST 2111 [S]	Summer Surf	1964	70.00
—Without bonus single			
❑ ST 2111 [S]	Summer Surf	1964	120.00
—With bonus single by Jerry Cole, "Racing Waves"/"Movin' Surf," in front cover pocket			
❑ T 2111 [M]	Summer Surf	1964	50.00
—Without bonus single			
❑ T 2111 [M]	Summer Surf	1964	100.00
—With bonus single by Jerry Cole, "Racing Waves"/"Movin' Surf," in front cover pocket			
❑ ST 2293 [S]	Rock Out — Live at Ciro's	1965	150.00
❑ T 2293 [M]	Rock Out — Live at Ciro's	1965	100.00

CLOISTER

Number	Title	Yr	NM
❑ CLP-6301 [M]	Silver Sounds of the Surf	1963	200.00
—With tracks by the Stompers			

DELTONE

Number	Title	Yr	NM
❑ LPM-1001 [M]	Surfer's Choice	1962	150.00
❑ DT 1886 [R]	Surfer's Choice	1962	40.00
❑ T 1886 [M]	Surfer's Choice	1962	60.00

DUB TONE

Number	Title	Yr	NM
❑ LP-1246 [M]	The Surf Family	1964	30.00
—With tracks by the Hollywood Surfers			

GNP CRESCENDO

Number	Title	Yr	NM
❑ GNPS-2095	Greatest Hits	1975	12.00

RHINO

Number	Title	Yr	NM
❑ RNLP-70074	King of the Surf Guitar: The Best of Dick Dale and the Del-Tones, 1961-1964	1986	12.00

DALE AND GRACE

45s

GUYDEN

Number	Title	Yr	NM
❑ 6002	What's Happening to Me/Darling It's Wonderful	1972	5.00

HANNA-BARBERA

Number	Title	Yr	NM
❑ 472	Let Them Talk/I'd Rather Be Free	1966	8.00

MICHELLE

Number	Title	Yr	NM
❑ 921	I'm Leaving It Up to You/That's What I Like	1963	25.00
❑ 923	Stop and Think It Over/Bad Luck	1963	15.00
❑ 928	The Loneliest Night/I'm Not Free	1964	15.00
❑ 930	Darling It's Wonderful/What's Happening to Me	1964	15.00
❑ 936	Cool Water/Rules of Love	1964	15.00

Roger Daltrey, "Free Me," Polydor 2105, 1980, $4.

Number	Title (A Side/B Side)	Yr	NM
MONTEL			
❑ 921	I'm Leaving It Up to You/That's What I Like About You	1963	12.00
❑ 922	Stop and Think It Over/Bad Luck	1963	12.00
❑ 928	The Loneliest Night/I'm Not Free	1964	12.00
❑ 930	Darling It's Wonderful/ What's Happening to Me	1964	12.00
❑ 936	Cool Water/Rules of Love	1964	12.00
❑ 958	Make the World Go Away/ Stranger	1965	12.00
❑ 989	It Keeps Right On a-Hurtin'/ So Fine	1967	12.00
MONTEL/MICHELLE			
❑ 942	Something Special/What Am I Living For	1964	12.00
Albums			
MICHELLE			
❑ 100 [M]	I'm Leaving It Up to You	1964	150.00
MONTEL			
❑ 100 [M]	I'm Leaving It Up to You	1964	150.00

DALEY, JIMMY, AND THE DING-A-LINGS

Number	Title (A Side/B Side)	Yr	NM
45s			
DECCA			
❑ 30163	Rock, Pretty Baby/Can I Steal a Little Love	1956	40.00
❑ 30358	Red Lips and Green Eyes/ How's About a Little Kiss?	1957	40.00
❑ 30532	Hole in the Wall/Bongo Rock	1957	40.00
7-Inch Extended Plays			
DECCA			
❑ ED 2480	Rock Pretty Baby/Dark Blue/ Free & Easy//What's It Gonna Be/Rockin' the Boogie	1957	50.00
❑ ED 2480 [PS]	Rock Pretty Baby, Part 1	1957	50.00
❑ ED 2481	Rockabye Lullaby Blues/Teen Age Bop/The Most//Can I Steal a Little Love/Juke Box/ The Saints Rock 'n' Roll	1957	50.00
❑ ED 2481 [PS]	Rock Pretty Baby, Part 2	1957	50.00
❑ ED 2482	Picnic by the Sea/Young Love// Happy Is a Boy Named Me/Hot Rod/Big Band Rock and Roll	1957	50.00
❑ ED 2482 [PS]	Rock Pretty Baby, Part 3	1957	50.00

DALLAS, MARIA

Number	Title (A Side/B Side)	Yr	NM
45s			
RCA VICTOR			
❑ 47-9279	Ambush/Lonely for You	1967	10.00
❑ 47-9386	Don't Love Me Too Much/It's Such a Pretty World Today	1967	10.00
❑ 47-9552	Everybody/Two Ships Passing in the Night	1968	10.00

DALTON, KATHY

Number	Title (A Side/B Side)	Yr	NM
45s			
DISCREET			
❑ 1191	At the Tropicana/Long Gone Charlie Hit & Run	1974	5.00
❑ 1210	Boogie Bands and One Night Stands/Pour Your Wine All Over Me	1974	5.00
❑ 1313	Midnight Creeper/Justine	1974	5.00
Albums			
DISCREET			
❑ MS 2168	Amazing	1973	18.00
❑ DS 2208	Boogie Bands and One Night Stands	1974	12.00

DALTON, LACY J.

Number	Title (A Side/B Side)	Yr	NM
45s			
CAPITOL			
❑ NR-44519	Black Coffee/I'm Right Here	1990	4.00
❑ 7PRO-79962	Black Coffee (same on both sides)	1990	5.00
—Promo version; stock copy is on 44519			
CAPITOL NASHVILLE			
❑ 7PRO-79126	Where Did We Go Right (same on both sides)	1990	6.00
—Vinyl is promo only			
❑ 7PRO-79370	Lonesome (same on both sides)	1990	6.00
—Vinyl is promo only			
❑ 7PRO-79616	Forever in My Heart (same on both sides)	1991	6.00
—Vinyl is promo only			
COLUMBIA			
❑ 11-01036	Whisper/China Doll	1981	3.00
❑ 18-02188	Takin' It Easy/Golden Memories	1981	3.00
❑ 18-02637	Everybody Makes Mistakes/ Wild Turkey	1981	3.00
❑ 18-02847	Slow Down/One of the Unsatisfied	1982	3.00
❑ 18-03184	16th Avenue/You Can't Take the Texas Out of Me	1982	3.00
❑ 38-03926	Dream Baby (How Long Must I Dream)/Hold Me Again	1983	3.00
❑ 38-04133	Windin' Down/Dixie Devil	1983	3.00
❑ 38-04696	If That Ain't Love/Too Many Miles	1984	3.00
❑ 38-04884	You Can't Run Away from Your Heart/The Night Has a Heart of Its Own	1985	3.00
❑ 38-05644	The Night Has a Heart of Its Own/Adios and Run	1985	3.00
❑ 38-05759	Don't Fall in Love with Me/ Over You	1985	3.00
❑ 38-06098	Working Class Man/Can't See Me Without You	1986	3.00
❑ 38-06360	This Ol' Town/Up with the Wind	1986	3.00
❑ 11107	Crazy Blue Eyes/Late Night Kind of Lonesome	1979	4.00
❑ 11190	Tennessee Waltz/ Beer Drinkin' Song	1980	4.00
❑ 11253	Losing Kind of Love/Carolina Come-On	1980	4.00
❑ 11343	Hard Times/Old Soldier	1980	4.00
❑ 11410	Hillbilly Girl with the Blues/ Me 'n' You	1980	4.00
UNIVERSAL			
❑ 53487	The Heart/Hard Luck Ace	1989	3.00
❑ UVL-66007	I'm a Survivor/Walkin' Wounded	1989	3.00
❑ UVL-66015	Hard Luck Ace/Turn to the One	1989	3.00
Albums			
COLUMBIA			
❑ JC 36322	Lacy J. Dalton	1980	10.00
❑ PC 36322	Lacy J. Dalton	198?	6.00
—Budget-line reissue with new prefix			
❑ JC 36763	Hard Times	1980	10.00
❑ PC 36763	Hard Times	1985	6.00
—Budget-line reissue with new prefix			
❑ FC 37327	Takin' It Easy	1981	8.00
❑ PC 37327	Takin' It Easy	1985	6.00
—Budget-line reissue with new prefix			
❑ FC 37975	16th Avenue	1982	8.00
❑ FC 38604	Dream Baby	1983	8.00
❑ FC 38883	Greatest Hits	1984	8.00
❑ FC 40028	Can't Run Away from Your Heart	1985	8.00
❑ FC 40393	Highway Diner	1986	8.00
❑ FC 40780	Blue Eyed Blues	1987	8.00
HARBOR			
❑ 001	Jill Croston	1978	25.00
—As "Jill Croston"			
UNIVERSAL			
❑ 42294	Survivor	1989	10.00

DALTON, LARRY, AND THE DALTON GANG

Number	Title (A Side/B Side)	Yr	NM
45s			
SOUNDWAVES			
❑ 4645	Cowboy/Too Many Nights	1981	5.00
❑ 4672	Tomorrow/Ain't It Funny	1982	5.00

DALTON BOYS, THE

Number	Title (A Side/B Side)	Yr	NM
45s			
SKYLA			
❑ 1124	I'm Thinkin'/It's Much More Stronger	1962	30.00
TEEN			
❑ 505	Who's Gonna Hold Your Hand/ Walkin'	1959	50.00
V.I.P.			
❑ 25025	I've Been Cheated/ Something's Bothering You	1965	50.00
❑ 25025	I've Been Cheated/ Take My Hand	1965	200.00

DALTREY, ROGER Also see THE WHO.

Number	Title (A Side/B Side)	Yr	NM
12-Inch Singles			
ATLANTIC			
❑ PR 572 [DJ]	Walking in My Sleep (3:20) (same on both sides)	1984	7.00
—Label spells his last name "Daltry"			
❑ PR 832 [DJ]	Quicksilver Lightning (LP Version 4:46) (same on both sides)	1986	7.00
❑ PR 982 [DJ]	Move Better in the Night (LP Version 4:01) (same on both sides)	1986	8.00

Except when noted otherwise, VG = 25% of NM, and VG+ = 50% of NM. (Example: VG = $2.00, VG+ = $4.00 and NM = $8.00.)

Number	Title (A Side/B Side)	Yr	NM
MCA			
❑ L33-1962 [DJ]	One of the Boys/Please Don't Say Goodbye	1977	15.00
—B-side by Steve Gibbons			
45s			
A&M			
❑ 1779	Love's Dream/Orpheus Song	1975	5.00
—With Rick Wakeman			
ATLANTIC			
❑ 89419	Under a Raging Moon/The Pride You Hide	1986	3.00
❑ 89457	Quicksilver Lightning/Love Me Like You Do	1986	3.00
❑ 89457 [PS]	Quicksilver Lightning/Love Me Like You Do	1986	5.00
❑ 89471	Let Me Down Easy/Fallen Angel	1985	3.00
❑ 89471 [PS]	Let Me Down Easy/Fallen Angel	1985	3.00
❑ 89491	After the Fire/Don't Satisfy Me	1985	3.00
❑ 89491 [PS]	After the Fire/Don't Satisfy Me	1985	3.00
❑ 89667	Parting Would Be Painless/Is There Anyone Out There?	1984	3.00
❑ 89704	Walking in My Sleep/Somebody Told Me	1984	3.00
❑ 89704 [PS]	Walking in My Sleep/Somebody Told Me	1984	3.00
MCA			
❑ 40453	Come and Get Your Love/Heart's Right	1975	5.00
❑ 40512	Oceans Away/Feeling	1976	5.00
❑ 40761	One of the Boys/Doing It All Again	1977	5.00
❑ 40765	Satin and Lace/Say It Ain't So, Joe	1977	4.00
❑ 40800	Avenging Annie/The Prisoner	1977	4.00
❑ 40862	Leon/The Prisoner	1978	4.00
❑ 52051	Martyrs and Madmen/Avenging Annie	1982	4.00
ODE			
❑ 66040	I'm Free/Underture	1973	5.00
POLYDOR			
❑ 2105	Free Me/McVicar	1980	4.00
❑ 2105 [PS]	Free Me/McVicar	1980	3.00
❑ 2121	Without Your Love/Escape (Part 1)	1980	4.00
❑ 2153	Waiting for a Friend/Bitter and Twisted	1981	4.00
❑ 2153 [DJ]	Waiting for a Friend (same on both sides)	1981	6.00
—One label has name misspelled as "Rodger Daltrey"			
❑ 15098	See Me, Feel Me-Listening to You/Overture from Tommy	1975	5.00
—B-side by Pete Townshend			
❑ 15098 [PS]	See Me, Feel Me-Listening to You/Overture from Tommy	1975	7.00
TRACK			
❑ 40053	Giving It All Away/Way of the World	1973	6.00
—B-side by Bryan Daly & the London Festival Orchestra			
❑ 40084	Thinking/There Is Love	1973	8.00
Albums			
ATLANTIC			
❑ 80128	Parting Should Be Painless	1984	10.00
❑ 81269	Under a Raging Moon	1985	10.00
❑ 81759	Can't Wait to See the Movie	1987	10.00
MCA			
❑ 2147	Ride a Rock Horse	1975	12.00
❑ 2271	One of the Boys	1977	12.00
❑ 2349	Daltrey	1977	10.00
—Reissue of Track 328			
❑ 5301	Best Bits	1982	10.00
❑ 37030	Ride a Rock Horse	1980	8.00
—Budget-line reissue			
❑ 37031	One of the Boys	1980	8.00
—Budget-line reissue			
❑ 37032	Daltrey	1980	8.00
—Budget-line reissue			
POLYDOR			
❑ PD-1-6284	McVicar	1980	10.00
TRACK			
❑ 328	Daltrey	1973	12.00

DAMIN EIH, A.L.K. AND BROTHER CLARK

Number	Title (A Side/B Side)	Yr	NM
Albums			
DEMELOT			
❑ 7310	Never Mind	1973	150.00

DAMITA JO Also see BROOK BENTON AND DAMITA JO.

Number	Title (A Side/B Side)	Yr	NM
45s			
ABC-PARAMOUNT			
❑ 9822	How Will I Know/I'll Never Cry	1957	15.00
❑ 9849	My Heart Is Home/Disillusioned Lovers	1957	15.00
❑ 10176	How Will I Know/Disillusioned Lovers	1961	10.00
BANG BANG			
❑ 4105	Why Love a Stranger/Whoa Now Boy	196?	12.00
EPIC			
❑ 9766	Tomorrow Night/Silver Dollar	1965	8.00
❑ 9797	Gotta Travel On/Something You Got	1965	8.00
❑ 9821	Nobody Knows You When You're Down and Out/Whispering Grass (Don't Tell the Trees)	1965	8.00
❑ 9860	Sweet Pussycat/Who Could Ask for More	1965	8.00
❑ 9887	That Special Way/Tossin' and Turnin'	1966	8.00
❑ 10061	If You Go Away/When the Fog Rolls In to San Francisco	1966	8.00
❑ 10061 [DJ]	If You Go Away (same on both sides)	1966	20.00
—Promo only on yellow vinyl			
❑ 10176	No Guilty Feelings/Yellow Days	1967	8.00
❑ 10235	Dinner For One/Please, James	1967	8.00
MERCURY			
❑ 71493	The Dance Was Over/Look at Yourself	1959	12.00
❑ 71568	What Would You Do/Widow Talk	1960	12.00
❑ 71608	Little Things Mean a Lot/I Burned Your Letter	1960	12.00
❑ 71690	I'll Save the Last Dance for You/Forgive	1960	15.00
❑ 71760	Keep Your Hands Off of Him/Hush, Somebody's Calling My Name	1961	12.00
❑ 71793	Sweet Georgia Brown/Do What You Want	1961	12.00
❑ 71840	I'll Be There/Love Laid Its Hands on Me	1962	15.00
❑ 71840 [PS]	I'll Be There/Love Laid Its Hands on Me	1962	25.00
❑ 71871	Dance with a Dolly (With a Hole in Her Stocking)/You're Nobody 'Til Somebody Loves You	1962	12.00
❑ 71929	I Didn't Know I Was Crying/I Built My World Around a Dream	1962	12.00
❑ 71946	You're Nobody 'Til Somebody Loves You/Joey	1962	12.00
❑ 71946 [PS]	You're Nobody 'Til Somebody Loves You/Joey	1962	20.00
❑ 71984	Another Dancing Partner/Please Send Me Someone to Love	1962	12.00
❑ 72019	The Window Up Above/Tennessee Waltz	1962	12.00
❑ 72019 [PS]	The Window Up Above/Tennessee Waltz	1962	20.00
❑ 72056	Dance Him By Me/Las Vegas	1962	12.00
❑ 72056 [PS]	Dance Him By Me/Las Vegas	1962	20.00
❑ 72086	Little Things/Mr. Blues (Found a Home with Me)	1963	10.00
❑ 72086 [PS]	Little Things/Mr. Blues (Found a Home with Me)	1963	20.00
❑ 72121	Drama of Love/Hobo Flats	1963	10.00
❑ 72121 [PS]	Drama of Love/Hobo Flats	1963	25.00
❑ 72162	In the Dark/Melancholy Baby	1963	10.00
RANWOOD			
❑ 820	Loving You/Reason to Believe	1968	6.00
❑ 826	Grown-Up Games/Lonely Letters	1968	6.00
❑ 844	Brother Love's Traveling Salvation Show/I'll Save the Last Dance for You	1969	6.00
❑ 857	Lonely Teardrops/Ain't Misbehavin'	1969	6.00
❑ 869	Paint Me Loving You/Tomorrow Is the First Day of the Rest of My Life	1970	6.00
❑ 884	Mrs. Robinson/Two Worlds	1970	5.00
❑ 894	Hallelujah Baby/Two Worlds	1971	5.00
RCA VICTOR			
❑ 47-4685	Lonesome and Blue/I Need You	1952	15.00
—By John Greer, vocals by Damita Jo			
❑ 47-5022	I'd Do It Again/I Don't Care	1952	15.00
❑ 47-5120	Go 'Way From My Window/Let Me Share Your Name	1953	15.00
❑ 47-5253	Missing/The Widow Walk	1953	15.00
❑ 47-5328	Do Me a Favor/Don't You Care	1953	15.00
❑ 47-5570	Face to Face/Sadie Thompson's Song	1953	15.00
❑ 47-5987	Win or Lose/My Tzatskele	1955	15.00
❑ 47-6096	Feelin' Kinda Happy/Nuff of That Stuff	1955	15.00
—B-side by Steve Gibson and His Red Caps			
❑ 47-6185	In My Heart/Abracadabra	1955	15.00
❑ 47-6281	Always/Freehearted	1955	15.00
VEE JAY			
❑ 661	I'm Waiting for Ships That Never Come In/Hurt a Fool	1965	8.00
Albums			
ABC-PARAMOUNT			
❑ 378 [M]	The Big Fifteen	1961	80.00
❑ S-378 [S]	The Big Fifteen	1961	100.00
EPIC			
❑ LN 24131 [M]	This Is Damita Jo	1965	15.00
❑ LN 24164 [M]	One More Time with Feeling	1965	15.00
❑ LN 24202 [M]	Midnight Session	1966	15.00
❑ LN 24244 [M]	If You Go Away	1967	20.00
❑ BN 26131 [S]	This Is Damita Jo	1965	20.00
❑ BN 26164 [S]	One More Time with Feeling	1965	20.00
❑ BN 26202 [S]	Midnight Session	1966	20.00
❑ BN 26244 [S]	If You Go Away	1967	15.00
MERCURY			
❑ MG-20642 [M]	I'll Save the Last Dance for You	1961	30.00
❑ MG-20703 [M]	Damita Jo Live at the Diplomat	1962	25.00
❑ MG-20734 [M]	Sing a Country Song	1962	25.00
❑ MG-20818 [M]	This One's for Me	1963	20.00
❑ SR-60642 [S]	I'll Save the Last Dance for You	1961	40.00
❑ SR-60703 [S]	Damita Jo Live at the Diplomat	1962	30.00
❑ SR-60734 [S]	Sing a Country Song	1962	30.00
❑ SR-60818 [S]	This One's for Me	1963	25.00
RANWOOD			
❑ RLP.8037	Miss Damita Jo	1968	15.00
RCA CAMDEN			
❑ CAL-900 [M]	Go Go with Damita Jo	196?	15.00
❑ CAS-900(e) [R]	Go Go with Damita Jo	196?	12.00
SUNSET			
❑ SUS-5198	The Irresistible Damita Jo	1968	12.00
VEE JAY			
❑ LP-1137 [M]	Damita Jo Sings	1965	25.00
❑ LPS-1137 [S]	Damita Jo Sings	1965	50.00
WING			
❑ WC-16333	This One's for Me	196?	12.00

DAMNATION OF ADAM BLESSING, THE

Number	Title (A Side/B Side)	Yr	NM
45s			
UNITED ARTISTS			
❑ 50609	Morning Dew/Cookbook	1969	8.00
❑ 50666	Last Train to Clarksville/Lonely	1970	8.00
❑ 50726	Back to the River/The Driver	1970	8.00
❑ 50819	Fingers on a Windmill/Leaving It Up to You	1971	6.00
❑ 50912	Cookbook/Leaving It Up to You	1972	6.00
Albums			
UNITED ARTISTS			
❑ UAS-5533	Which Is the Justice, Which Is the Thief	1971	20.00
❑ UAS-6738	The Damnation of Adam Blessing	1970	20.00
❑ UAS-6773	The Second Damnation	1970	20.00

DAMNED, THE

Number	Title (A Side/B Side)	Yr	NM
12-Inch Singles			
MCA			
❑ 17235 [DJ]	In Dulce Decorum (same on both sides)	1986	8.00
❑ 23625	Eloise/Beat Girl/Temptation	1986	8.00
❑ 23721	Anything/Year of the Jackal/Thanks for the Night	1986	8.00
45s			
BIG BEAT			
❑ NS 92	There Ain't No Sanity Clause (Remix)/Looking At You (Live)	1982	6.00
—U.K. import; reissue of Chiswick 139			
❑ NS 92 [PS]	There Ain't No Sanity Clause (Remix)/Looking At You (Live)	1982	6.00
—U.K. import; reissue of Chiswick 139			
CHISWICK			
❑ 139	There Ain't No Sanity Clause//Hit Or Miss/Looking At You (Live)	1981	6.00
—U.K. import			
❑ 139 [PS]	There Ain't No Sanity Clause//Hit Or Miss/Looking At You (Live)	1981	12.00
—U.K. import			
I.R.S.			
❑ 9022	Dr. Jeckyl and Mr. Hyde/Looking at You (Live)	1981	8.00
MCA			
❑ 53051	Alone Again Or/In Dulce Decorum	1987	3.00
❑ 53051 [PS]	Alone Again Or/In Dulce Decorum	1987	3.00
Albums			
FRONTIER			
❑ 1003	Damned Damned Damned	1987	15.00
—Reissue of 1976-77 material			

Number	Title (A Side/B Side)	Yr	NM
I.R.S.			
❑ SP-70012	The Black Album	1980	12.00
MCA			
❑ 5966	Anything	1987	10.00
❑ 2-8024 [(2)]	Light at the End of the Tunnel	1988	15.00
❑ 39039	Phantasmagoria	1986	10.00

DAMON

Albums

Number	Title (A Side/B Side)	Yr	NM
ANKH			
❑ 968	Song of a Gypsy	1969	1500.
—Gatefold cover			
❑ 968	Song of a Gypsy	1969	1500.
—Regular cover			

DAMON, LIZ, 'S ORIENT EXPRESS

45s

Number	Title (A Side/B Side)	Yr	NM
ANTHEM			
❑ 51005	Loneliness Remembers/Quiet Sound	1971	10.00
❑ 51006	All in All/Walking Backwards Down the Road	1971	10.00
MAKAHA			
❑ 503	1900 Yesterday/You're Falling in Love	1970	12.00
WHITE WHALE			
❑ 368	1900 Yesterday/You're Falling in Love	1970	6.00
❑ 370	But For Love/You Make Me Feel Like Someone	1970	6.00

Albums

Number	Title (A Side/B Side)	Yr	NM
MAKAHA			
❑ MS-5003	Liz Damon's Orient Express	1970	20.00
WHITE WHALE			
❑ WWS 5003	Liz Damon's Orient Express	1971	12.00

DAN AND DALE

45s

Number	Title (A Side/B Side)	Yr	NM
TIFTON			
❑ 125	Batman Theme/Robin's Theme	1966	10.00
❑ 125 [PS]	Batman Theme/Robin's Theme	1966	20.00

Albums

Number	Title (A Side/B Side)	Yr	NM
DIPLOMAT			
❑ D-2340 [M]	Dear Heart, Willow Weep for Me and Other Love Songs	196?	10.00
❑ DS-2340 [S]	Dear Heart, Willow Weep for Me and Other Love Songs	196?	12.00
❑ D-2343 [M]	Themes from Goldfinger and Zorba the Greek	196?	10.00
❑ DS-2343 [S]	Themes from Goldfinger and Zorba the Greek	196?	12.00
❑ D-2361 [M]	Country and Western Waltzes	196?	10.00
❑ DS-2361 [S]	Country and Western Waltzes	196?	12.00
❑ D-2364 [M]	Country & Western Hits	196?	10.00
❑ DS-2364 [S]	Country & Western Hits	196?	12.00
❑ D-2390 [M]	The Nearness of You	196?	10.00
❑ DS-2390 [S]	The Nearness of You	196?	12.00
TIFTON			
❑ M-8002 [M]	Batman and Robin	1966	30.00
❑ S-78002 [S]	Batman and Robin	1966	40.00

DANA, BILL See JOSE JIMENEZ.

DANCER, PRANCER, AND NERVOUS

45s

Number	Title (A Side/B Side)	Yr	NM
CAPITOL			
❑ 4300	The Happy Reindeer/Dancer's Waltz	1959	12.00
❑ 4300 [PS]	The Happy Reindeer/Dancer's Waltz	1959	25.00
❑ 4353	I Wanta Be an Easter Bunny/The Happy Birthday Song	1960	12.00
—As "The Singing Reindeer"			

DANDERLIERS, THE

45s

Number	Title (A Side/B Side)	Yr	NM
B&F			
❑ 150	Shu-Wop/My Loving Partner	1960	25.00
❑ 160	My Love/She's Mine	1960	25.00
❑ 1344	Chop Chop Boom/My Autumn Love	1961	20.00
MIDAS			
❑ 9004	All the Way/Walk On with Your Nose Up	196?	20.00
STATES			
❑ 147	Chop Chop Boom/My Autumn Love	1955	400.00
—Black vinyl			
❑ 147	Chop Chop Boom/My Autumn Love	1955	1200.
—Red vinyl			
❑ 150	Shu-Wop/My Loving Partner	1955	200.00
❑ 152	May God Be With You/Little Man	1956	200.00
❑ 160	My Love/She's Mine	1956	250.00

DANDLEERS, THE See THE DANLEERS.

DANDY DAN

45s

Number	Title (A Side/B Side)	Yr	NM
CAMEO			
❑ 484	(I Don't Stand a) Ghost of a Chance/If Love Is	1967	10.00

DANE, BARBARA

12-Inch Singles

Number	Title (A Side/B Side)	Yr	NM
ARHOOLIE			
❑ 1600	Gipper Gate Blues (3:27) (9:17)/Boulevard of Broken Dreams	1986	12.00

45s

Number	Title (A Side/B Side)	Yr	NM
TREY			
❑ 3012	I'm On My Way/Go 'Way from My Window	1960	100.00

Albums

Number	Title (A Side/B Side)	Yr	NM
BARBARY COAST			
❑ 33014 [M]	Trouble in Mind	1959	40.00
—Reissue of San Francisco LP			
CAPITOL			
❑ ST 1758 [S]	On My Way	1962	40.00
❑ T 1758 [M]	On My Way	1962	30.00
DOT			
❑ DLP-3177 [M]	Living with the Blues	1959	30.00
❑ DLP-25177 [S]	Living with the Blues	1959	40.00
FOLKWAYS			
❑ FA-2468	Barbara Dane and the Chambers Brothers	1966	50.00
❑ FA-2471	Folk Songs	1966	30.00
HORIZON			
❑ WP-1602 [M]	When I Was a Young Girl	1962	30.00
❑ WPS-1602 [S]	When I Was a Young Girl	1962	40.00
—Black vinyl			
❑ WPS-1602 [S]	When I Was a Young Girl	1962	60.00
—Gold vinyl			
PAREDON			
❑ 1003	FTA! Songs of the GI Resistance	1970	15.00
❑ 1014	I Hate the Capitalist System	1973	15.00
❑ 1046	When We Make It Through	1982	15.00
SAN FRANCISCO			
❑ 33014 [M]	Trouble in Mind	1957	60.00

DANETTA AND THE STARLETS

45s

Number	Title (A Side/B Side)	Yr	NM
OKEH			
❑ 7155	You Belong to Me (We're Going Steady)/Impression	1962	100.00

DANIELS, CHARLIE, BAND

45s

Number	Title (A Side/B Side)	Yr	NM
A&M			
❑ 2290	Riding with Jesse James/Wish We Were Back in Missouri	1980	4.00
—B-side by Emmylou Harris			
EPIC			
❑ 02154	In America/The Legend of Wooley Swamp	1981	3.00
—Reissue			
❑ 02185	Sweet Home Alabama/Falling in Love for the Night	1981	4.00
❑ 02828	Still in Saigon/Blowing Along with the Wind	1982	4.00
❑ 02995	Ragin' Cajun/Universal Hand	1982	4.00
❑ 03251	We Had It All One Time/Makes You Want to Go Home	1982	4.00
❑ 03918	Stroker's Theme/(B-side unknown)	1983	4.00
❑ 34-05638	American Farmer/Runnin' with That Crowd	1985	3.00
❑ 34-05638 [PS]	American Farmer/Runnin' with That Crowd	1985	3.00
❑ 38-05699	Still Hurtin' Me/American Rock and Roll	1985	3.00
❑ 38-05699 [PS]	Still Hurtin' Me/American Rock and Roll	1985	3.00
❑ 05835	Drinkin' My Baby Goodbye/Ever Changing Lady	1986	3.00
❑ 08002	Boogie Woogie Fiddle Country Blues/Working Man You Got It All	1988	3.00
❑ 08519	Uneasy Rider '88/Boogie Woogie Fiddle	1988	4.00
❑ 50243	Wichita Jail/It's My Life	1976	4.00
❑ 50278	Sweet Louisiana/Sweetwater, Texas	1976	4.00
❑ 50322	Billy the Kid/Slow Song	1976	4.00
❑ 50456	Heaven Can Be Anywhere (Twin Pines Theme)/Good Ole Boy	1977	4.00
❑ 50516	Sugar Hill Saturday Night/Maria Teresa	1977	4.00
❑ 50637	Sweet Lousiana/Trudy	1978	4.00
❑ 50700	The Devil Went Down to Georgia/Rainbow Ride	1979	4.00
❑ 50768	Mississippi/Passing Lane	1979	4.00
❑ 50806	Behind Your Eyes/Blue Star	1979	4.00
❑ 50845	Long Haired Country Boy/Sweet Lousiana	1980	4.00
❑ 50888	In America/Blue Star	1980	4.00
❑ 50921	The Legend of Wooley Swamp/Money	1980	4.00
❑ 50955	Carolina (I Remember You)/South Sea Song	1980	4.00
❑ 19-50955 [DJ]	Carolina (I Remember You) (Long Version)/(Short Version)	1980	5.00
❑ 19-50955 [PS]	Carolina (I Remember You)	1980	5.00
—Sleeve may have been promo only			
❑ 68542	Cowboy Hat in Dallas/Easy Rider	1988	3.00
❑ 68738	Midnight Train/Back to Dixie	1989	3.00
❑ 73030	Simple Man/Ill Wind	1989	3.00
❑ 73236	Mister DJ/It's My Life	1990	3.00
❑ 73426	(What This World Needs Is) A Few More Rednecks/It's My Life	1990	3.00
❑ 73577	Oh Atlanta/What Is 26	1990	3.00
❑ 73768	Honky Tonk Life/Willie Jones	1991	3.00
❑ 74061	Little Folks/Let Freedom Ring	1991	3.00
❑ 74866	The Twang Factor/Old Rock 'n Roll	1991	4.00
HANOVER			
❑ 4541	Robot Bomp/Rover Had a Party	1959	30.00
KAMA SUTRA			
❑ 553	Great Big Bunches of Love/(B-side unknown)	1972	6.00
❑ 576	Uneasy Rider/Funky Junky	1973	6.00
❑ 590	Whiskey/(B-side unknown)	1974	5.00
❑ 593	Way Down Yonder/I've Been Down	1974	5.00
❑ 595	Land of Opportunity/(B-side unknown)	1974	5.00
❑ 598	The South's Gonna Do It/King Size Rosewood Bed	1974	5.00
❑ 601	Long Haired Country Boy/I've Been Down	1975	5.00
❑ 606	Birmingham Blues/Damn Good Cowboy	1975	5.00
❑ 607	Texas/Everything Is Kinda Alright	1975	5.00
LIBERTY			
❑ S7-17398	All Night Long/America, I Believe in You	1993	5.00
PAULA			
❑ 246	The Middle of a Heartache/Skip It	1966	15.00
❑ 418	The Middle of a Heartache/Skip It	1976	4.00

7-Inch Extended Plays

Number	Title (A Side/B Side)	Yr	NM
KAMA SUTRA			
❑ KSBS EP-10	Volunteer Jam Part (1)//Volunteer Jam Part (2)/Volunteer Jam Part (3)	1974	3.00
—Small hole, plays at 33 1/3 rpm; not issued separately; only released as bonus with Fire on the Mountain LP			
❑ KSBS EP-10 [PS]	Volunteer Jam	1974	3.00
—Picture sleeve with above bonus disc			

Albums

Number	Title (A Side/B Side)	Yr	NM
CAPITOL			
❑ ST-790	Charlie Daniels	1971	25.00
❑ ST-11414	Charlie Daniels	1975	12.00
—Reissue of ST-790			
❑ SN-16039	Charlie Daniels	1979	8.00
—Budget-line reissue			
EPIC			
❑ AS 586 [DJ]	Interchords	1979	15.00
—Music and interviews; promo only			
❑ EAS 1780 [DJ]	The Charlie Daniels Story	1990	15.00
—Promo-only interview/radio show			
❑ PE 34150	Saddle Tramp	1976	10.00
—Orange label, no bar code on cover			
❑ PE 34150	Saddle Tramp	198?	8.00
—With bar code on cover			
❑ JE 34365	Fire on the Mountain	1976	10.00
—Reissue of Kama Sutra 2603 without bonus EP; orange label, no bar code on cover			
❑ PE 34365	Fire on the Mountain	198?	8.00
—Budget-line reissue			
❑ JE 34369	Uneasy Rider	1976	10.00
—Reissue of Kama Sutra 2071 with new name; orange label, no bar code on cover			
❑ PE 34369	Uneasy Rider	198?	8.00
—Budget-line reissue			
❑ JE 34377	High Lonesome	1976	10.00
—Orange label, no bar code on cover			
❑ PE 34377	High Lonesome	198?	8.00
—Budget-line reissue			
❑ JE 34402	Nightrider	1977	10.00
—Reissue of Kama Sutra 2607; orange label, no bar code on cover			

Number	Title (A Side/B Side)	Yr	NM
❑ PE 34402	Nightrider	198?	8.00
—Budget-line reissue			
❑ JE 34664	Whiskey	1977	10.00
—Reissue of Kama Sutra 2076 with new name; orange label, no bar code on cover			
❑ PE 34664	Whiskey	198?	8.00
—Budget-line reissue			
❑ JE 34665	Te John, Grease and Wolfman	1977	10.00
—Reissue of Kama Sutra 2060; orange label, no bar code on cover			
❑ PE 34665	Te John, Grease and Wolfman	198?	8.00
—Budget-line reissue			
❑ JE 34970	Midnight Wind	1977	10.00
—Orange label, no bar code on cover			
❑ PE 34970	Midnight Wind	198?	8.00
—Budget-line reissue			
❑ JE 35751	Million Mile Reflections	1979	10.00
❑ PE 35751	Million Mile Reflections	198?	8.00
—Budget-line reissue			
❑ FE 36571	Full Moon	1980	10.00
❑ PE 36571	Full Moon	198?	8.00
—Budget-line reissue			
❑ FE 37694	Windows	1982	10.00
❑ PE 37694	Windows	198?	8.00
—Budget-line reissue			
❑ FE 38795	A Decade of Hits	1983	10.00
❑ FE 39878	Me and the Boys	1985	10.00
❑ PE 39878	Me and the Boys	198?	8.00
—Budget-line reissue			
❑ FE 40760	Powder Keg	1987	8.00
❑ FE 44324	Homesick Man	1988	8.00
❑ HE 44365	Fire on the Mountain	1982	40.00
—Half-speed mastered edition			
❑ FE 45316	Simple Man	1989	12.00
❑ HE 45751	Million Mile Reflections	1982	40.00
—Half-speed mastered edition			
KAMA SUTRA			
❑ KSBS 2060	Te John, Grease and Wolfman	1972	15.00
❑ KSBS 2071	Honey in the Rock	1973	15.00
❑ KSBS 2076	Way Down Yonder	1974	15.00
❑ KSBS 2603	Fire on the Mountain	1974	15.00
—Includes bonus EP, "Volunteer Jam" (deduct 20% if missing)			
❑ KSBS 2607	Nightrider	1975	15.00
MOBILE FIDELITY			
❑ 1-176	Million Mile Reflections	1984	30.00
—Audiophile vinyl			

DANIELS, DAN, AND THE SQUIRRELS

45s

Number	Title (A Side/B Side)	Yr	NM
CAMEO			
❑ 432	Just Me and My Mom and Dad/The Theme from Just Me and My Mom and Dad	1966	15.00
❑ 447	The First Christmas Carol/Grandma's House	1966	15.00

DANIELS, JEFF

45s

Number	Title (A Side/B Side)	Yr	NM
ASTRO			
❑ 108	Foxy Dan/Someday You'll Remember	1960	100.00
BIG HOWDY			
❑ 777	Switch Blade Sam/You're Still on My Mind	1959	100.00
❑ 8120	Uh-Huh/Table for Two	196?	100.00
❑ 8121	Foxy Dan/Someday You'll Remember	1961	100.00
MELADEE			
❑ 117	Daddy-O Rock/Hey Woman	1958	400.00

DANIELS, ROLY

45s

Number	Title (A Side/B Side)	Yr	NM
COLUMBIA			
❑ 4-44793	Love Is a Symphony/Another Teardrop	1969	10.00

DANKO, RICK

45s

Number	Title (A Side/B Side)	Yr	NM
ARISTA			
❑ 0306	What a Town/Shake It	1978	4.00
❑ 0320	Java Blues/Shake It	1978	4.00

Albums

Number	Title (A Side/B Side)	Yr	NM
ARISTA			
❑ AB 4141	Rick Danko	1977	12.00

DANLEERS, THE

45s

Number	Title (A Side/B Side)	Yr	NM
AMP 3			
❑ 2115	One Summer Night/Wheelin' and Dealin'	1958	40.00
—Corrected group name on label			
❑ 2115	One Summer Night/Wheelin' and Dealin'	1958	200.00
—By "Dandleers"			
EPIC			
❑ 9367	I Live Half a Block from an Angel/If You Don't Care	1960	30.00
❑ 9421	I'll Always Be in Love with You/Little Lover	1960	30.00
EVEREST			
❑ 19412	Foolish/I'm Looking Around	1961	30.00
LEMANS			
❑ 004	The Truth Hurts/Baby You've Got It	1963	10.00
❑ 008	I'm Sorry/This Thing Called Love	1963	10.00
MERCURY			
❑ 71322	One Summer Night/Wheelin' and a-Dealin'	1958	20.00
❑ 71356	I Really Love You/My Flaming Heart	1958	20.00
❑ 71401	A Picture of You/Prelude to Love	1959	20.00
❑ 71441	I Can't Sleep/Your Love	1959	20.00
SMASH			
❑ 1872	Were You There/If	1964	12.00
❑ 1895	Where Is Love/The Angels Sent You	1964	12.00

DANNY AND DEANIE

45s

Number	Title (A Side/B Side)	Yr	NM
HIT			
❑ 137	Bread and Butter/House of the Rising Sun	1964	15.00
—B-side by the Spartas			

DANNY AND JERRY "Danny" is Danny Rapp of DANNY AND THE JUNIORS.

45s

Number	Title (A Side/B Side)	Yr	NM
RONN			
❑ 5	We've Got a Groovy Thing Goin'/You Must Be Fooling	1966	12.00
❑ 12	I've Got Pride/Connection	1967	12.00
❑ 24	I Can't See Nobody/Mo'Reen	1967	12.00

DANNY AND THE JUNIORS

45s

Number	Title (A Side/B Side)	Yr	NM
ABC-PARAMOUNT			
❑ 9871	At the Hop/Sometimes (When I'm All Alone)	1957	30.00
❑ 9888	Rock and Roll Is Here to Stay/School Boy Romance	1958	30.00
❑ 9926	Dottie/In the Meantime	1958	25.00
❑ 9953	A Thief/Crazy Cave	1958	25.00
❑ 9978	Sassy Fran/I Feel So Lonely	1958	50.00
❑ 10004	Do You Love Me/Somehow I Can't Forget	1959	25.00
❑ 10052	Playing Hard to Get/Of Love	1959	25.00
CRUNCH			
❑ 018001	At the Hop/Let the Good Times Roll	1973	5.00
GUYDEN			
❑ 2076	Oo-La-La-Limbo/Now and Then	1962	20.00
LUV			
❑ 252	Rock and Roll Is Here to Stay/Sometimes (When I'm All Alone)	1968	10.00
MCA			
❑ D-2411	At the Hop/Rock and Roll Is Here to Stay	1980	4.00
—Reissue			
MERCURY			
❑ 72240	Sad Girl/Let's Go Ski-ing	1964	20.00
ROULETTE			
❑ GG-121	At the Hop/Rock and Roll Is Here to Stay	1973	4.00
—"Golden Goodies Hit Series" issue			
SINGULAR			
❑ 711	At the Hop/Sometimes	1957	1000.
—Blue label, machine-stamped in dead wax, no mention of Artie Singer on label			
❑ 711	At the Hop/Sometimes	1957	1000.
—Blue label, machine-stamped in dead wax, with "Orchestra Directed by Artie Singer" credit. Both versions have a "count-in" before the song starts. Singular records on black labels or without the count-in are probably reproductions.			
SWAN			
❑ 4060	Twistin' U.S.A./A Thousand Miles Away	1960	20.00
❑ 4064	Candy Cane. Sugary Plum/Oh Holy Night	1960	25.00
❑ 4064 [PS]	Candy Cane. Sugary Plum/Oh Holy Night	1960	250.00
❑ 4068	Daydreamer/Pony Express	1961	20.00
❑ 4072	Cha Cha Go Go (Chicago Cha-Cha)/Mister Whisper	1961	20.00
❑ 4082	Back to the Hop/The Charleston Fish	1961	20.00
❑ 4082 [PS]	Back to the Hop/The Charleston Fish	1961	100.00
❑ 4084	Just Because/You Hair's Too Long	1961	—
—Unreleased?			
❑ 4092	Twistin' All Night Long/Some Kind of Nut	1962	20.00
❑ 4100	(Do the) Mashed Potatoes/Doin' the Continental Walk	1962	20.00
❑ 4113	We Got Soul/Funny	1962	20.00

7-Inch Extended Plays

Number	Title (A Side/B Side)	Yr	NM
ABC-PARAMOUNT			
❑ EP-11	At The Hop/School Boy Romance//Rock And Roll Is Here To Stay/Sometimes (When I'm All Alone)	1958	600.00
❑ EP-11 [PS]	At the Hop	1958	900.00

Albums

Number	Title (A Side/B Side)	Yr	NM
MCA			
❑ 1555	Rockin' with Danny and the Juniors	1987	10.00

DANNY AND THE MEMORIES "Danny" is Danny Whitten, later of CRAZY HORSE.

45s

Number	Title (A Side/B Side)	Yr	NM
VALIANT			
❑ 705	Can't Help Lovin' That Girl of Mine/Don't Go	1965	25.00
❑ 6049	Can't Help Lovin' That Girl of Mine/Don't Go	1964	25.00

DANNY AND THE OTHER GUYS

45s

Number	Title (A Side/B Side)	Yr	NM
CP			
❑ (# unknown)	Hard Times/(B-side unknown)	196?	800.00

DANTE

45s

Number	Title (A Side/B Side)	Yr	NM
A&M			
❑ 788	Speedoo/Sweet Lover	1966	10.00
DARROW			
❑ 515	How Much I Care/Baby Baby	1960	40.00
DECCA			
❑ 31178	If You Don't Know/Leave Your Tears Behind You	1960	15.00
❑ 31268	Bye Bye Baby/That's Why	1961	15.00
❑ 31319	Ring or Write or Call/Say It to Me	1961	15.00
IMPERIAL			
❑ 5798	Something Happens/Are You Just My Friend	1961	15.00
❑ 5827	Miss America/Now I've Got You	1962	15.00
❑ 5867	Magic Ring/Am I the One	1962	15.00
—Imperial titles as "Dante and His Friends"			
MADISON			
❑ 130	Alley Oop/The Right Time	1960	20.00
—As "Dante and the Evergreens"			
❑ 135	Time Machine/Dream Land	1960	15.00
❑ 143	What Are You Doing New Year's Eve/Yeah Baby	1960	15.00
—As "Dante and the Evergreens"			
❑ 154	Think Sweet Thoughts/Da Doo	1961	15.00
MERCURY			
❑ 71621	How Much I Care/Baby Baby	1960	20.00
TIDE			
❑ 003	My Lament/Aching Heart	1960	20.00

Albums

Number	Title (A Side/B Side)	Yr	NM
MADISON			
❑ MA-LP 1002 [M]	Dante and the Evergreens	1961	500.00

DANTE, RON Also see THE ARCHIES; THE CUFF LINKS (1); THE DETERGENTS.

45s

Number	Title (A Side/B Side)	Yr	NM
ALMONT			
❑ 307	Little Lollypop/Funny	1963	15.00
BELL			
❑ 45460	Christine/Don't Call It Love	1974	5.00
—As "Bo Cooper"			
❑ 45610	Charmer/Yesterday Dreamin'	1974	4.00
❑ 45619	Midnight Show/The Christian	1974	4.00
COLUMBIA			
❑ 43720	Think/221 East Maple	1966	10.00
❑ 43862	I Give You Things/Janie, Janie	1966	10.00
DOT			
❑ 17023	Absence of Lisa/Gypsy Be Mine	1967	10.00
HANDSHAKE			
❑ 02107	Show and Tell/God Bless Rock and Roll	1981	4.00
❑ 02552	Letter from Zowie/God Bless Rock and Roll	1981	4.00

Bobby Darin, "Mack the Knife," Atco 6147, 1959, **$40.**

Number	Title (A Side/B Side)	Yr	NM
INFINITY			
❑ 50008	Ain't Misbehavin' (One Never Knows, Do One?)/'Round About Midnight	1979	5.00
❑ 50018	Fire Island/They're Playing Our Song	1979	5.00
❑ 50038	Brand New Key/They're Playing Our Song	1979	5.00
—Infinity sides as "Dante's Inferno"			
KIRSHNER			
❑ 63-1010	How Do You Know/ Let Me Bring You Up	1970	6.00
❑ 63-1010 [PS]	How Do You Know/ Let Me Bring You Up	1970	10.00
❑ 63-5007	Sweet Taste of Love/C'mon Girl	1970	6.00
MERCURY			
❑ 72812	Follow a Dream/He's Raining in My Sunshine	1968	10.00
MUSIC VOICE			
❑ 503	If You Love Me, Laurie/ Don't Stand Up in a Canoe	1964	15.00
MUSICOR			
❑ 1058	Look at Me/There's Love	1965	12.00
❑ 1090	In the Rain/Poor Boys	1965	12.00
❑ 1105	If You Love Me, Laurie/ Don't Stand Up in a Canoe	1965	12.00
❑ 1134	Hey Mom, Hey Pop/(Heart) Stop Calling Her Name	1965	12.00
RCA			
❑ PB-10898	How Am I to Know/Sky Rider	1977	4.00
RCA VICTOR			
❑ PB-10340	Sugar, Sugar/Sugar, Sugar (Disco)	1975	5.00
SCEPTER			
❑ 12333 [DJ]	That's What Life Is All About (mono/stereo)	1971	6.00
—Stock copy may not exist			

Number	Title (A Side/B Side)	Yr	NM
Albums			
HANDSHAKE			
❑ JW 37341	Street Angel	1981	12.00
KIRSHNER			
❑ KES-106	Ron Dante Brings You Up	1970	20.00

DANTES, THE (1) Band from Columbus, Ohio.

Number	Title (A Side/B Side)	Yr	NM
45s			
CAMEO			
❑ 431	Under My Thumb/Can I Get a Witness	1966	30.00
JAMIE			
❑ 1314	Can't Get Enough of You Love/ 80-96	1966	30.00
MAIN LINE			
❑ 1366	Connection/Satisfied	1967	25.00

DANTES, THE (2) Pittsburgh band including Bob Palombi.

Number	Title (A Side/B Side)	Yr	NM
45s			
ROTATE			
❑ 5008	Top Down Time/ How Many Times	1965	100.00

DANZIG Glenn Danzig was also in MISFITS and SAMHAIN.

Number	Title (A Side/B Side)	Yr	NM
12-Inch Singles			
DEF AMERICAN			
❑ PRO-A-4121 [DJ]	Her Black Wings (same on both sides)	1990	8.00
Albums			
AMERICAN			
❑ 45647	4	1994	20.00
DEF AMERICAN			
❑ DEF 24208	Danzig	1988	12.00
❑ DEF 24281	Lucifuge	1990	18.00

DANZIG, GLENN Also see DANZIG; THE MISFITS. This is Glenn's classical album.

Number	Title (A Side/B Side)	Yr	NM
45s			
PLAN 9			
❑ PL 1015	Who Killed Marilyn?/ Spook City USA	1981	65.00
—Black vinyl (5,000 made)			
❑ PL 1015	Who Killed Marilyn?/ Spook City USA	1981	135.00
—Purple vinyl (500 made)			
❑ PL 1015	Who Killed Marilyn?/ Spook City USA	1981	500.00
—Black and purple swirl vinyl (25 made); value is conjecture			
❑ PL 1015 [PS]	Who Killed Marilyn?/ Spook City USA	1981	65.00
Albums			
PLAN 9			
❑ PL9-11	Black Aria	1992	28.00

DAPPERS, THE

Number	Title (A Side/B Side)	Yr	NM
45s			
EPIC			
❑ 9423	My Love Is Real/Baby You Know You're Wrong	1960	25.00
FOXIE			
❑ 7005	Chicken Twist/Lonely Street	1961	40.00
GROOVE			
❑ 0156	Unwanted Love/That's All, That's All, That's All	1956	200.00
PEACOCK			
❑ 1651	Come Back to Me/ Mambo Oongh	1955	150.00
RAINBOW			
❑ 373	Bop Bop Bu/How I Need You Baby	1956	40.00
STAR-X			
❑ 505	We're in Love/Spellbound	1958	250.00

DAPPERS QUINTET, THE

Number	Title (A Side/B Side)	Yr	NM
45s			
FLAYR			
❑ 500	Look What I've Found/ (B-side unknown)	1955	1500.

DAPS, THE

Number	Title (A Side/B Side)	Yr	NM
45s			
MARTERRY			
❑ 5429	When You're Alone/ Down and Out	1956	60.00

DARBISHIRE, STEVE

Number	Title (A Side/B Side)	Yr	NM
45s			
LONDON			
❑ 1011	Trains Trains/Yum Yum	1966	8.00

DARCEL, DENISE

Number	Title (A Side/B Side)	Yr	NM
Albums			
CAMEO			
❑ C-1002 [M]	Banned in Boston	1958	40.00

DARIN, BOBBY

Number	Title (A Side/B Side)	Yr	NM
45s			
ATCO			
❑ (no #) [DJ]	She's Tanfastic!/ Moments of Love	1960	40.00
—Ferrion Inc. "Special Premium Record"			
❑ 6092	Million Dollar Baby/Talk to Me	1957	30.00
❑ 6103	Don't Call My Name/Pretty Betty	1957	30.00
❑ 6109	Just in Case You Change Your Mind/So Mean	1958	30.00
❑ 6117	Splish Splash/Judy, Don't Be Moody	1958	20.00
❑ 6121	Early in the Morning/ Now We're One	1958	20.00
❑ 6121	Early in the Morning/ Now We're One	1958	40.00
—As "The Rinky Dinks"			
❑ 6127	Queen of the Hop/Lost Love	1958	20.00
❑ 6128	Mighty Mighty Man/You're Gone	1958	20.00
❑ 6128	Mighty Mighty Man/You're Gone	1958	40.00
—As "The Rinky Dinks"			
❑ 6133 [M]	Plain Jane/While I'm Gone	1959	20.00
❑ 6133 [PS]	Plain Jane/While I'm Gone	1959	50.00
❑ SD-45-6133 [S]	Plain Jane/While I'm Gone	1959	40.00
❑ 6140	Dream Lover/Bullmoose	1959	20.00
❑ 6140 [PS]	Dream Lover/Bullmoose	1959	50.00
❑ 6147	Mack the Knife/Was There a Call for Me	1959	20.00
❑ 6147 [PS]	Mack the Knife/Was There a Call for Me	1959	40.00
❑ 6158	Beyond the Sea/That's the Way Love Is	1960	20.00

Except when noted otherwise, VG = 25% of NM, and VG+ = 50% of NM. (Example: VG = $2.00, VG+ = $4.00 and NM = $8.00.)

Number	Title (A Side/B Side)	Yr	NM
❑ 6158 [PS]	Beyond the Sea/That's the Way Love Is	1960	40.00
❑ 6161	Clementine/Tall Story	1960	20.00
❑ 6161 [PS]	Clementine/Tall Story	1960	40.00
❑ 6167	Won't You Come Home Bill Bailey/I'll Be There	1960	20.00
❑ 6167 [PS]	Won't You Come Home Bill Bailey/I'll Be There	1960	30.00
❑ 6173	Beachcomber/Autumn Blues	1960	20.00
❑ 6173 [PS]	Beachcomber/Autumn Blues	1960	30.00
❑ 6179	Artificial Flowers/ Somebody to Love	1960	20.00
❑ 6179 [PS]	Artificial Flowers/ Somebody to Love	1960	30.00
❑ 6183	Christmas Auld Lang Syne/ Child of God	1960	25.00
❑ 6183 [PS]	Christmas Auld Lang Syne/ Child of God	1960	40.00
❑ 6188	Lazy River/Oo-Ee Train	1961	12.00
❑ 6188 [PS]	Lazy River/Oo-Ee Train	1961	20.00
❑ 6196	Nature Boy/Look for My True Love	1961	12.00
❑ 6196 [PS]	Nature Boy/Look for My True Love	1961	20.00
❑ 6200	Come September/ Walk Back to Me	1961	15.00
❑ 6200 [PS]	Come September/ Walk Back to Me	1961	50.00
❑ 6206	You Must Have Been a Beautiful Baby/Sorrow Tomorrow	1961	12.00
❑ 6206 [PS]	You Must Have Been a Beautiful Baby/Sorrow Tomorrow	1961	20.00
❑ 6211	Ave Maria/O Come All Ye Faithful	1961	12.00
❑ 6211 [PS]	Ave Maria/O Come All Ye Faithful	1961	160.00
❑ 6214	Irresistible You/Multiplication	1961	12.00
❑ 6214 [PS]	Irresistible You/Multiplication	1961	20.00
❑ 6221	What'd I Say (Part 1)/ What'd I Say (Part 2)	1962	12.00
❑ 6221 [PS]	What'd I Say (Part 1)/ What'd I Say (Part 2)	1962	20.00
❑ 6229	Things/Jalier Bring Me Water	1962	12.00
❑ 6236	Baby Face/You Know How	1962	12.00
❑ 6244	I Found a New Baby/ Keep a-Walkin'	1962	12.00
❑ 6297	Milord/Golden Earrings	1964	10.00
❑ 6316	Swing Low Sweet Chariot/ Similau	1964	10.00
❑ 6334	Minnie the Moocher/ Hard Hearted Hannah	1965	10.00
ATLANTIC			
❑ 2305	Funny What Love Can Do/We Didn't Ask to Be Brought Here	1965	8.00
❑ 2317	Silver Dollar/The Breaking Point	1966	8.00
❑ 2329	Mame/Walking in the Shadow of Love	1966	8.00
❑ 2341	Who's Afraid of Virginia Woolf?/ Merci, Cheri	1966	8.00
❑ 2350	If I Were a Carpenter/Rainin'	1966	10.00
❑ 2367	The Girl That Stood Beside Me/ Reason to Believe	1966	8.00
❑ 2376	Lovin' You/Amy	1967	8.00
❑ 2395	The Lady Came from Baltimore/I Am	1967	8.00
❑ 2420	Darlin' Be Home Soon/ Hello, Sunshine	1967	8.00
❑ 2433	Talk to the Animals/After Today	1967	8.00
❑ 2433	Talk to the Animals/She Knows	1967	8.00
❑ 89166	Beyond the Sea/Mack the Knife	1987	3.00
❑ 89166 [PS]	Beyond the Sea/Mack the Knife	1987	3.00
—From the movie "Big Town"			
BRUNSWICK			
❑ 55073	Early in the Morning/ Now We're One	1958	80.00
—As "The Ding Dongs"; also see Atco 6121			
CAPITOL			
❑ 4837	If a Man Answers/ True, True Love	1962	10.00
❑ 4837 [PS]	If a Man Answers/ True, True Love	1962	15.00
❑ 4897	You're the Reason I'm Living/ Now You're Gone	1962	10.00
❑ 4897 [PS]	You're the Reason I'm Living/ Now You're Gone	1962	15.00
❑ 4970	18 Yellow Roses/Not for Me	1963	10.00
❑ 4970 [PS]	18 Yellow Roses/Not for Me	1963	15.00
❑ 5019	Treat My Baby Good/ Down So Long	1963	10.00
❑ 5079	Be Mad Little Girl/Since You've Been Gone	1963	10.00
❑ 5126	I Wonder Who's Kissing Her Now/As Long As I'm Singing	1964	10.00
❑ 5257	The Things in This House/ Wait by the Water	1964	10.00
❑ 5359	Hello, Dolly!/Golden Earrings	1965	10.00
❑ 5399	A World Without You/Venice Blue	1965	10.00
❑ 5443	When I Get Home/Lonely Road	1965	10.00
❑ 5443 [PS]	When I Get Home/Lonely Road	1965	25.00
❑ 5481	Gyp the Cat/That Funny Feeling	1965	10.00

Number	Title (A Side/B Side)	Yr	NM
DECCA			
❑ 29883	Rock Island Line/Timber	1956	40.00
❑ 29922	Silly Willy/Blue Eyed Mermaid	1956	50.00
❑ 30031	The Greatest Builder (Of Them All)/Hear Them Bells	1956	40.00
❑ 30225	Dealer in Dreams/Help Me	1957	40.00
❑ 30737	Silly Willy/Dealer in Dreams	1958	30.00
DIRECTION			
❑ 350	Long Line Rider/Change	1968	8.00
❑ 351	Song for a Dollar/ Mr. and Mrs. Hohner	1969	8.00
❑ 352	Distractions (Part 1)/Jive	1969	8.00
❑ 4000	Sugar Man/(9 to 5) Jive's Alive	1970	8.00
❑ 4001	Baby May/Sweet Reason	1970	8.00
❑ 4002	Maybe We Can Get It Together/ Rx Pyro (Prescription: Fire)	1970	8.00
MOTOWN			
❑ 1183	Melodie/Someday We'll Be Together	1971	6.00
❑ 1193	Simple Song of Freedom/ I'll Be Your Baby Tonight	1971	6.00
❑ 1203	Sail Away/Something in Her Love	1972	6.00
❑ 1212	Average People/Something in Her Love	1972	6.00
❑ 1217	Happy/Something in Her Love	1973	6.00
7-Inch Extended Plays			
ATCO			
❑ 4502	*Splish Splash/Judy, Don't Be Moody/I Found a Million Dollar Baby/(Since You're Gone) I Can't Go On	1959	50.00
❑ 4502 [PS]	Bobby Darin	1959	50.00
❑ 4504	Mack the Knife/That's the Way Love Is//Beyond the Sea/ That's All	1959	50.00
❑ 4504 [PS]	That's All	1959	50.00
❑ 4505	Queen of the Hop/Lost Love// Plain Jane/While I'm Gone	1960	50.00
❑ 4505 [PS]	Bobby Darin	1960	50.00
❑ 4508	Clementine/My Gal Sal//Guys and Dolls/Down with Love	1960	50.00
❑ 4508 [PS]	This Is Darin	1960	50.00
❑ 4512	I Got A Woman/You'd Be So Nice To Come Home To// Medley: By Myself-When Your Lover Has Gone/ Love For Sale	1960	50.00
❑ 4512 [PS]	Darin at the Copa	1960	50.00
❑ EP 4513-D	I Want You With Me/You Know How//Hush, Somebody's Calling My Name/ Keep a-Walkin'	1960	70.00
❑ EP 4513-D [PS]	For Teenagers Only	1960	70.00
—Special promotional sleeve; has photo of LP 1001			
CAPITOL CUSTOM			
❑ TB-2262/3	18 Yellow Roses/Not for Me/ The Things in This House// You're the Reason I'm Living/ Treat My Baby Good/Wait by the Water, Lillian	1963	30.00
—Small hole, plays at 33 1/3 rpm			
❑ TB-2262/3 [PS]	Bobby Darin Presents	1963	40.00
—"Manufactured by Capitol Records, Inc., Custom Services Department for Artistic Records"			
❑ MB-2849/50	If a Man Answers/True, True Love//Sermon of Samson/ All By Myself	1962	20.00
❑ MB-2849/50 [PS]	Scripto Inc. Presents Bobby Darin	1962	30.00
—Value is for sleeve alone; the pen that came with the package is very rare			
DECCA			
❑ ED 2676	(contents unknown)	1957	100.00
❑ ED 2676 [PS]	Hear Them Bells	1957	100.00
MOTOWN			
❑ PR-4 [DJ]	If I Were a Carpenter/Moritat (Mack the Knife)// Blue Monday/Happy	1973	15.00
❑ PR-4 [PS]	(title unknown)	1973	20.00
Albums			
ATCO			
❑ 33-102 [M]	Bobby Darin	1958	100.00
—Yellow "harp" label			
❑ 33-102 [M]	Bobby Darin	1962	30.00
—Gold and dark blue label			
❑ 33-104 [M]	That's All	1959	40.00
—Yellow "harp" label			
❑ 33-104 [M]	That's All	1962	20.00
—Gold and dark blue label			
❑ SD 33-104 [S]	That's All	1959	100.00
—Yellow "harp" label			
❑ SD 33-104 [S]	That's All	1962	25.00
—Purple and brown label			
❑ 33-115 [M]	This Is Darin	1960	40.00
—Yellow "harp" label			

Number	Title (A Side/B Side)	Yr	NM
❑ 33-115 [M]	This Is Darin	1962	20.00
—Gold and dark blue label			
❑ SD 33-115 [S]	This Is Darin	1960	25.00
—Purple and brown label			
❑ SD 33-115 [S]	This Is Darin	1960	80.00
—Yellow "harp" label			
❑ 33-122 [M]	Darin at the Copa	1960	40.00
—Yellow "harp" label			
❑ 33-122 [M]	Darin at the Copa	1962	20.00
—Gold and dark blue label			
❑ SD 33-122 [S]	Darin at the Copa	1960	80.00
—Yellow "harp" label			
❑ SD 33-122 [S]	Darin at the Copa	1962	25.00
—Purple and brown label			
❑ 33-124 [M]	It's You or No One	1960	40.00
—Yellow "harp" label			
❑ 33-124 [M]	It's You or No One	1962	20.00
—Gold and dark blue label			
❑ SD 33-124 [S]	It's You or No One	1960	80.00
—Yellow "harp" label			
❑ SD 33-124 [S]	It's You or No One	1962	25.00
—Purple and brown label			
❑ 33-125 [M]	The 25th Day of December	1960	50.00
—Yellow "harp" label			
❑ 33-125 [M]	The 25th Day of December	1962	20.00
—Gold and dark blue label			
❑ SD 33-125 [S]	The 25th Day of December	1960	60.00
—Yellow "harp" label			
❑ SD 33-125 [S]	The 25th Day of December	1962	25.00
—Gold and dark blue label			
❑ 33-126 [M]	Two of a Kind	1961	40.00
—Yellow "harp" label			
❑ 33-126 [M]	Two of a Kind	1962	20.00
—Gold and dark blue label			
❑ SD 33-126 [S]	Two of a Kind	1961	50.00
—Yellow "harp" label			
❑ SD 33-126 [S]	Two of a Kind	1962	25.00
—Purple and brown label			
❑ 33-131 [M]	The Bobby Darin Story	1961	40.00
—Yellow "harp" label; white cover			
❑ 33-131 [M]	The Bobby Darin Story	1962	20.00
—Gold and dark blue label; black cover			
❑ SD 33-131	The Bobby Darin Story	1969	12.00
—Yellow label, "Atco" on left			
❑ SD 33-131	The Bobby Darin Story	1978	8.00
—Any later Atco label			
❑ SD 33-131 [S]	The Bobby Darin Story	1961	50.00
—Yellow "harp" label; white cover			
❑ SD 33-131 [S]	The Bobby Darin Story	1962	25.00
—Purple and brown label; black cover			
❑ 33-134 [M]	Love Swings	1961	40.00
—Yellow "harp" label			
❑ 33-134 [M]	Love Swings	1962	20.00
—Gold and dark blue label			
❑ SD 33-134 [S]	Love Swings	1961	50.00
—Yellow "harp" label			
❑ SD 33-134 [S]	Love Swings	1962	25.00
—Purple and brown label			
❑ 33-138 [M]	Twist with Bobby Darin	1961	40.00
—Yellow "harp" label			
❑ 33-138 [M]	Twist with Bobby Darin	1962	20.00
—Gold and dark blue label			
❑ SD 33-138 [S]	Twist with Bobby Darin	1961	50.00
—Yellow "harp" label			
❑ SD 33-138 [S]	Twist with Bobby Darin	1962	25.00
—Purple and brown label			
❑ 33-140 [M]	Bobby Darin Sings Ray Charles	1962	25.00
❑ SD 33-140 [S]	Bobby Darin Sings Ray Charles	1962	30.00
❑ 33-146 [M]	Things & Other Things	1962	25.00
❑ SD 33-146 [S]	Things & Other Things	1962	30.00
❑ 33-167 [M]	Winners	1964	25.00
❑ SD 33-167 [S]	Winners	1964	30.00
❑ SP 1001 [M]	For Teenagers Only	1960	75.00
—With extras missing			
❑ SP 1001 [M]	For Teenagers Only	1960	150.00
—Gatefold with fold-open poster and paper insert			
❑ 90484	Two of a Kind	1986	10.00
ATLANTIC			
❑ 8121 [M]	The Shadow of Your Smile	1966	15.00
❑ SD 8121 [S]	The Shadow of Your Smile	1966	20.00
❑ 8126 [M]	In a Broadway Bag	1966	15.00
❑ SD 8126 [S]	In a Broadway Bag	1966	20.00
❑ 8135 [M]	If I Were a Carpenter	1967	15.00
❑ SD 8135 [S]	If I Were a Carpenter	1967	50.00
—Inexplicably rare in stereo			
❑ 8142 [M]	Inside Out	1967	15.00
❑ SD 8142 [S]	Inside Out	1967	30.00
❑ 8154 [M]	Bobby Darin Sings Doctor Dolittle	1967	15.00
❑ SD 8154 [S]	Bobby Darin Sings Doctor Dolittle	1967	15.00
BAINBRIDGE			
❑ 6220	Bobby Darin at the Copa	1981	10.00
CAPITOL			
❑ ST 1791 [S]	Oh! Look at Me Now	1962	20.00
❑ SW 1791 [S]	Oh! Look at Me Now	1962	25.00
❑ T 1791 [M]	Oh! Look at Me Now	1962	15.00
❑ W 1791 [M]	Oh! Look at Me Now	1962	20.00
❑ ST 1826 [S]	Earthy	1963	20.00
❑ T 1826 [M]	Earthy	1963	15.00
❑ ST 1866 [S]	You're the Reason I'm Living	1963	20.00
❑ T 1866 [M]	You're the Reason I'm Living	1963	15.00

Number	Title (A Side/B Side)	Yr	NM
❑ ST 1942 [S]	18 Yellow Roses	1963	20.00
❑ T 1942 [M]	18 Yellow Roses	1963	15.00
❑ ST 2007 [S]	Golden Folk Hits	1963	20.00
❑ T 2007 [M]	Golden Folk Hits	1963	15.00
❑ ST 2084 [S]	As Long As I'm Singing	1964	200.00

—Canceled; price is for an acetate, which is known to exist

Number	Title (A Side/B Side)	Yr	NM
❑ T 2084 [M]	As Long As I'm Singing	1964	—

—Canceled

Number	Title (A Side/B Side)	Yr	NM
❑ ST 2194 [S]	From Hello Dolly to Goodbye Charlie	1964	20.00
❑ T 2194 [M]	From Hello Dolly to Goodbye Charlie	1964	15.00
❑ ST 2322 [S]	Venice Blue	1965	20.00
❑ T 2322 [M]	Venice Blue	1965	15.00
❑ ST 2571 [S]	The Best of Bobby Darin	1966	15.00
❑ T 2571 [M]	The Best of Bobby Darin	1966	15.00

CLARION

Number	Title (A Side/B Side)	Yr	NM
❑ 603 [M]	Clementine	1966	20.00
❑ SD 603 [S]	Clementine	1966	25.00

DIRECTION

Number	Title (A Side/B Side)	Yr	NM
❑ 1936	Born Walden Robert Cassotto	1968	25.00
❑ 1937	Commitment	1969	25.00

MOTOWN

Number	Title (A Side/B Side)	Yr	NM
❑ M5-185V1	Darin 1936-1973	1981	12.00

—Reissue

Number	Title (A Side/B Side)	Yr	NM
❑ MS-739	Finally	1972	500.00

—Unreleased; value is for RCA test pressing

Number	Title (A Side/B Side)	Yr	NM
❑ M 753L	Bobby Darin	1972	20.00
❑ M6-813L	Darin 1936-1973	1974	15.00

DARIUS

Albums

CHARTMAKER

Number	Title (A Side/B Side)	Yr	NM
❑ 1102	Darius	1968	500.00

DARLING, JOHNNY

45s

DELUXE

Number	Title (A Side/B Side)	Yr	NM
❑ 6167	I Don't Want to Wind Up in Love/ Baseball Baby	1956	150.00

DARNELL, LARRY

45s

ANNA

Number	Title (A Side/B Side)	Yr	NM
❑ 1109	With Tears in My Eyes/ I'll Get Along Somehow	1960	400.00

ARGO

Number	Title (A Side/B Side)	Yr	NM
❑ 5372	With Tears in My Eyes/ I'll Get Along Somehow	1960	25.00

DELUXE

Number	Title (A Side/B Side)	Yr	NM
❑ 6123	Ramblin' Man/I Care	1957	30.00
❑ 6136	If You Go/Fing Fang Foy	1957	30.00
❑ 6141	Just Tell Me When/ It Must Be Love	1957	30.00

OKEH

Number	Title (A Side/B Side)	Yr	NM
❑ 6848	Work Baby Work/Left My Baby	1952	25.00
❑ 6869	Darlin'/Boogie-Oogie	1952	25.00
❑ 6902	What's On Your Mind/Better Be on My Way	1952	25.00
❑ 6916	No Time at All/Singin' My Blues	1952	25.00
❑ 6919	I'll Get Along Somehow (Part 1)/ I'll Get Along Somehow (Part 2)	1952	25.00
❑ 6926	Christmas Blues/ I Am the Sparrow	1952	25.00
❑ 6954	I'll Be Sittin', I'll Be Rockin'/ Crazy She Calls Me	1953	25.00
❑ 7024	I'll Carry On/What More Do You Want Me to Do	1954	20.00
❑ 7039	I'm Gonna Change/ Thank You, Darlin'	1954	20.00
❑ 7056	My Love for You/Feelin' Mighty Sad and Low	1955	20.00

REGAL

Number	Title (A Side/B Side)	Yr	NM
❑ 3328	Do You Love Me Baby/ Sad and Lonesome	1951	25.00

—Larry Darnell records on Regal before 3328 are unconfirmed on 45 rpm

SAVOY

Number	Title (A Side/B Side)	Yr	NM
❑ 1151	That's All I Want from You/ Who Showed My Baby How to Love Me	1955	30.00

WARWICK

Number	Title (A Side/B Side)	Yr	NM
❑ 506	If I Had You/Thankful	1959	20.00

7-Inch Extended Plays

EPIC

Number	Title (A Side/B Side)	Yr	NM
❑ 7072	(contents unknown)	1961	20.00
❑ 7072 [PS]	For You My Love	1961	20.00

DARNELLS, THE

See THE MARVELETTES.

DARRELL, JOHNNY

45s

CAPRICORN

Number	Title (A Side/B Side)	Yr	NM
❑ 0207	Orange Blossom Special/ Glendale, Arizona	1974	4.00
❑ 0223	Pieces of My Life/Glendale, Arizona	1975	4.00
❑ 0234	Rose Colored Gin/ Glendale, Arizona	1975	4.00

CARTWHEEL

Number	Title (A Side/B Side)	Yr	NM
❑ 203	Don't It Seem to Rain a Lot/ I'll Never Get Up This Slow	1971	5.00
❑ 209	Mr. Tambourine Man/ Let Me Stay Awhile	1972	5.00

GUSTO

Number	Title (A Side/B Side)	Yr	NM
❑ 9001	Hard to Be Friends/These Days	1978	4.00
❑ 9011	Was Yesterday That Long Ago/ Spanish Song	1978	4.00

MONUMENT

Number	Title (A Side/B Side)	Yr	NM
❑ 8570	Crazy Daddy/Uncle Veneer	1973	5.00
❑ 8579	Dakota the Dancing Bear/ Just a Memory	1973	5.00

UNITED ARTISTS

Number	Title (A Side/B Side)	Yr	NM
❑ 869	Green, Green Grass of Home/ Deepening Snow	1965	8.00
❑ 943	As Long As the Wind Blows/ Beggars Can't Be Choosers	1965	8.00
❑ 50008	Johnny Lose It All/For Old Times' Sake	1966	8.00
❑ 50047	She's Mighty Gone/Baby Sitter	1966	8.00
❑ 50126	Ruby, Don't Take Your Love to Town/Little Things I Love	1967	8.00
❑ 50183	My Elusive Dreams/ Pickin' with Gold	1967	8.00
❑ 50207	Come See What's Left of Your Man/Passin' Through	1967	8.00
❑ 50235	The Son of Hickory Holler's Tramp/But That's Alright	1967	8.00
❑ 50235 [PS]	The Son of Hickory Holler's Tramp/But That's Alright	1967	15.00
❑ 50292	With Pen in Hand/Poetry of Love	1968	6.00
❑ 50442	I Ain't Buying/Little Things	1968	6.00
❑ 50481	Woman Without Love/ I Fought the Law	1968	6.00
❑ 50503	The Coming of the Roads/ The Other Side of the Coin	1969	6.00

—With Anita Carter

Number	Title (A Side/B Side)	Yr	NM
❑ 50518	Why You Been Gone So Long/ You're Always the One	1969	6.00
❑ 50572	River Bottom/Ain't That Living	1969	6.00
❑ 50610	She's Headed for the Country/ Trouble Maker	1969	6.00
❑ 50629	Mama Come'n Get Your Baby Boy/These Days	1970	6.00
❑ 50675	Brother River/Bed of Roses	1970	6.00
❑ 50716	They'll Never Take Her Love from Me/One Love, Two Hearts, Three Lives	1970	6.00
❑ 50739	Look Out Cleveland/ Winter's Comin' On	1971	6.00

Albums

CAPRICORN

Number	Title (A Side/B Side)	Yr	NM
❑ CP 0154	Water Glass Full of Whiskey	1975	10.00

SUNSET

Number	Title (A Side/B Side)	Yr	NM
❑ SUS-5232	The Johnny Darrell Sound	1969	10.00

UNITED ARTISTS

Number	Title (A Side/B Side)	Yr	NM
❑ UAL 3594 [M]	Ruby, Don't Take Your Love to Town	1967	25.00
❑ UAS 6594 [S]	Ruby, Don't Take Your Love to Town	1967	20.00
❑ UAS 6634	The Son of Hickory Holler's Tramp	1968	20.00
❑ UAS 6660	With Pen in Hand	1968	20.00
❑ UAS 6707	Why You Been Gone So Long	1969	20.00
❑ UAS 6752	California Stop-Over	1970	20.00
❑ UAS 6759	The Best of Johnny Darrell, Vol. 1	1970	15.00

DARRELL AND THE OXFORDS

See THE TOKENS.

DARREN, JAMES

45s

BUDDAH

Number	Title (A Side/B Side)	Yr	NM
❑ 177	That's My World/Wheeling, West Virginia	1970	5.00

COLPIX

Number	Title (A Side/B Side)	Yr	NM
❑ 102	There's No Such Thing/ Mighty Pretty Territory	1959	15.00
❑ 102 [PS]	There's No Such Thing/ Mighty Pretty Territory	1959	30.00
❑ 113	Gidget/You	1959	15.00
❑ 119 [M]	Angel Face/I Don't Wanna Lose Ya	1959	15.00
❑ 119 [PS]	Angel Face/I Don't Wanna Lose Ya	1959	30.00
❑ SCP-119 [S]	Angel Face/I Don't Wanna Lose Ya	1959	40.00
❑ 128	I Ain't Sharin' Sharon/ Love Among the Young	1959	15.00
❑ 130	Teenage Tears/ Let There Be Love	1959	15.00
❑ 138	You Are My Dream/Your Smile	1960	15.00
❑ 142	Because They're Young/ Tears in My Eyes	1960	15.00
❑ 142 [PS]	Because They're Young/ Tears in My Eyes	1960	30.00
❑ 145	P.S. I Love You/Traveling Down a Lonesome Road	1960	15.00
❑ 155	How Sweet You Are/ All the Young Men	1960	15.00
❑ 168	Man About Town/ Come On My Love	1960	15.00
❑ 181	Walking My Baby Back Home/ Goodbye My Lady	1960	15.00

—Colpix 102-181 by "Jimmy Darren"

Number	Title (A Side/B Side)	Yr	NM
❑ 185	Fool's Paradise/Gotta Have Love	1961	15.00
❑ 189	Gidget Goes Hawaiian/ Wild About the Girl	1961	15.00
❑ 194	Hand in Hand/You Are My Dream	1961	15.00
❑ 609	Goodbye Cruel World/Valerie	1961	15.00
❑ 609 [PS]	Goodbye Cruel World/Valerie	1961	25.00
❑ 622	Her Royal Majesty/If I Could Only Tell You	1962	12.00
❑ 630	Conscience/Dream Big	1962	12.00
❑ 644	Mary's Little Lamb/The Life of the Party	1962	12.00
❑ 655	Hail to the Conquering Hero/ Too Young to Go Steady	1962	12.00
❑ 664	Hear What I Want to Hear/ I'll Be Loving You	1962	12.00
❑ 672	Pin a Medal on Joey/ Diamond Head	1963	12.00
❑ 685	They Should Have Given You the Oscar/Blame It on My Youth	1963	12.00
❑ 696	Gegetta/Grande Luna, Italiana	1963	12.00
❑ 708	Under the Yum Yum Tree/ Backstage	1963	12.00
❑ 758	Punch and Judy/Just Think of Tonight	1964	20.00
❑ 765	A Married Man/Baby, Talk to Me	1964	10.00

KIRSHNER

Number	Title (A Side/B Side)	Yr	NM
❑ 63-1012	I Think Somebody Loves Me/Ain't Been Home in a Long Time	1970	5.00
❑ 63-5013	Bring Me Down Slow/ More and More	1971	5.00
❑ 63-5015	Mammy Blue/As Long As You Love Me	1971	5.00
❑ 63-5025	Brian's Song/Thnak Heaven for Little Girls	1973	5.00

MGM

Number	Title (A Side/B Side)	Yr	NM
❑ 14558	Let the Heartaches Begin/Sad Song	1973	4.00
❑ 14667	Sad-Eyed Romany Woman/Stay	1973	4.00

PRIVATE STOCK

Number	Title (A Side/B Side)	Yr	NM
❑ 45,050	Love on the Screen/Losing You	1975	4.00
❑ 45,064	One Has My Name, The Other Has My Heart/Sleepin' in a Bed of Lies	1975	4.00
❑ 45,136	You Take My Heart Away/You Take My Heart Away (Disco)	1977	4.00
❑ 45,152 [DJ]	Only a Dream Away (mono/stereo)	1977	5.00

—Stock copies may not exist

RCA

Number	Title (A Side/B Side)	Yr	NM
❑ PB-11316	Let Me Take You in My Arms Again/California	1978	4.00
❑ PB-11419	Next Time/Something Like Nothing Before	1978	4.00

WARNER BROS.

Number	Title (A Side/B Side)	Yr	NM
❑ 5648	Because You're Mine/ Millions of Roses	1965	8.00
❑ 5689	I Want to Be Lonely/Tom Hawk	1966	8.00
❑ 5812	Where Did We Go Wrong/ Counting the Cracks	1966	8.00
❑ 5838	Crazy Me/They Don't Know	1966	8.00
❑ 5856	Love Is Where You Find It/ (Let's Worry About) Tomorrow Tomorrow	1966	8.00
❑ 5874	All/Misty Morning Eyes	1966	8.00
❑ 7013	I Miss You So/Since I Don't Have You	1967	8.00
❑ 7053	Didn't We/Counting the Cracks	1967	8.00
❑ 7071	The House Song/ They Don't Know	1967	8.00
❑ 7152	Cherie/Wait Until Dark	1967	8.00
❑ 7206	A Little Bit of Heaven/Each and Every Part of Me	1968	8.00

Except when noted otherwise, VG = 25% of NM, and VG+ = 50% of NM. (Example: VG = $2.00, VG+ = $4.00 and NM = $8.00.)

Albums

COLPIX

Number	Title (A Side/B Side)	Yr	NM
❑ CP-406 [M]	James Darren (Album No. 1)	1960	40.00
—Black vinyl			
❑ CP-406 [M]	James Darren (Album No. 1)	1960	150.00
—Green vinyl			
❑ CP-418 [M]	Gidget Goes Hawaiian (James Darren Sings the Movies)	1961	30.00
❑ SCP-418 [S]	Gidget Goes Hawaiian (James Darren Sings the Movies)	1961	40.00
❑ CP-424 [M]	James Darren Sings for All Sizes	1962	30.00
❑ SCP-424 [S]	James Darren Sings for All Sizes	1962	40.00
❑ CP-428 [M]	Love Among the Young	1962	30.00
❑ SCP-428 [S]	Love Among the Young	1962	40.00

KIRSHNER

Number	Title (A Side/B Side)	Yr	NM
❑ KES-115	Mammy Blue	1971	15.00
❑ KES-116	Love Songs from the Movies	1972	15.00

WARNER BROS.

Number	Title (A Side/B Side)	Yr	NM
❑ W 1668 [M]	James Darren/All	1967	15.00
❑ WS 1668 [S]	James Darren/All	1967	20.00

DARREN, JAMES/ SHELLEY FABARES/PAUL PETERSEN

Albums

COLPIX

Number	Title (A Side/B Side)	Yr	NM
❑ CP-444 [M]	Teenage Triangle	1963	40.00
❑ SCP-444 [R]	Teenage Triangle	1963	40.00
❑ CP-468 [M]	More Teenage Triangle	1964	40.00
❑ SCP-468 [P]	More Teenage Triangle	1964	60.00

DARTELLS, THE

45s

ARLEN

Number	Title (A Side/B Side)	Yr	NM
❑ 509	Hot Pastrami/Dartell Stomp	1963	25.00
❑ 513	Dance, Everybody, Dance/ The Scoobie Song	1963	25.00

DOT

Number	Title (A Side/B Side)	Yr	NM
❑ 16453	Hot Pastrami/Dartell Stomp	1963	20.00
❑ 16502	Dance, Everybody, Dance/ The Scoobie Song	1963	20.00
❑ 16551	Convicted/Sweet Pea	1963	15.00
❑ 16646	Swiss Cheese/Dartell Stomp	1964	15.00

HANNA-BARBERA

Number	Title (A Side/B Side)	Yr	NM
❑ 457	Clap Your Hands/Where Do We Stand	1965	15.00

SANDE

Number	Title (A Side/B Side)	Yr	NM
❑ 103	The Girl Can't Help It/ Stranger on the Shore	1964	30.00

Albums

DOT

Number	Title (A Side/B Side)	Yr	NM
❑ DLP-3522 [M]	Hot Pastrami	1963	30.00
❑ DLP-25522 [S]	Hot Pastrami	1963	40.00

DARTS, THE

Albums

DEL-FI

Number	Title (A Side/B Side)	Yr	NM
❑ DFLP-1244 [M]	Hollywood Drag	1963	40.00
❑ DFST-1244 [S]	Hollywood Drag	1963	50.00

DARVELL, BARRY

45s

ATLANTIC

Number	Title (A Side/B Side)	Yr	NM
❑ 2128	Lost Love/Silver Dollar	1961	20.00
❑ 2138	Adam and Eve/A King for Tonight	1962	20.00

COLT 45

Number	Title (A Side/B Side)	Yr	NM
❑ 104	Teenage Love/(B-side unknown)	1959	20.00
❑ 107	Geronimo Stomp/How Will It End	1959	60.00
❑ 110	Butterfly Baby/Send Me Some Loving	1960	25.00
❑ 301	Run Little Billy/All I Need Is You	1961	20.00

COLUMBIA

Number	Title (A Side/B Side)	Yr	NM
❑ 44197	My World of Make Believe/ Beggar's Paradise	1967	8.00

CUB

Number	Title (A Side/B Side)	Yr	NM
❑ 9088	Little Angel Lost/Fountain of Love	1961	20.00

PROVIDENCE

Number	Title (A Side/B Side)	Yr	NM
❑ 404	When You're Alone/ It's Rainin', It's Pourin'	1964	12.00

WORLD ARTISTS

Number	Title (A Side/B Side)	Yr	NM
❑ 1042	I'll Remember/Where Is the Love for Me	1965	12.00
❑ 1058	I Found a Daisy (in the City)/ Kissable Lips	1965	12.00

DASH, JULIAN

45s

VEE JAY

Number	Title (A Side/B Side)	Yr	NM
❑ 144	Zero/Rhythm Punch	1955	50.00

DASHIEL, BUD, AND THE KINSMEN

45s

WARNER BROS.

Number	Title (A Side/B Side)	Yr	NM
❑ 5231	Pom Pa Lum/I Talk to the Trees	1961	10.00
❑ 5276	In Tarrytown/Big Manuel	1962	10.00

Albums

WARNER BROS.

Number	Title (A Side/B Side)	Yr	NM
❑ W 1429 [M]	Folk Music in a Contemporary Manner	1961	25.00
❑ WS 1429 [S]	Folk Music in a Contemporary Manner	1961	30.00
❑ W 1432 [M]	Live Concert Extraordinaire — Bud Dashiel and the Kinsmen Sing Everybody's Hits	1961	25.00
❑ WS 1432 [S]	Live Concert Extraordinaire — Bud Dashiel and the Kinsmen Sing Everybody's Hits	1961	30.00

DATE WITH SOUL, A

See HALE AND THE HUSHABYES.

DAUGHTERS OF ALBION, THE

45s

FONTANA

Number	Title (A Side/B Side)	Yr	NM
❑ 1619	Well Wired/The Story of Sad	1968	10.00

Albums

FONTANA

Number	Title (A Side/B Side)	Yr	NM
❑ SRF-67586	The Daughters of Albion	1968	40.00

DAVE AND THE CARDIGANS

45s

BAY

Number	Title (A Side/B Side)	Yr	NM
❑ 216	My Falling Star/Cha Cha Baby	1963	200.00

DAVE AND THE MARKSMEN

With Dave Marks, former member of THE BEACH BOYS.

45s

A&M

Number	Title (A Side/B Side)	Yr	NM
❑ 730	Cruisin'/Kustom Kar Show	1964	50.00

WARNER BROS.

Number	Title (A Side/B Side)	Yr	NM
❑ 5485	I Wanna Cry/I Could Make You Mine	1964	30.00

WESTCO

Number	Title (A Side/B Side)	Yr	NM
❑ 10	Down the Tubes/ Ooh Poo Pa Doo	1963	50.00
—Black vinyl			
❑ 10	Down the Tubes/ Ooh Poo Pa Doo	1963	100.00
—Yellow vinyl			

DAVE DEE, DOZY, BEAKY, MICK & TICH

45s

ATLANTIC

Number	Title (A Side/B Side)	Yr	NM
❑ 89757 [DJ]	Staying With It same on both sides)	1983	5.00
—May be promo only			

BELL

Number	Title (A Side/B Side)	Yr	NM
❑ 905	Kelly/Annabella	1970	6.00
—As "Dave Dee"			
❑ 942	Frisco Annie/Hey! Mr. President	1970	6.00
—As "D.B.M. & T."			

COTILLION

Number	Title (A Side/B Side)	Yr	NM
❑ 44061	Bad News/Tonight-Today	1970	6.00
—As "Dozy, Beaky, Mick & Tich"			
❑ 44061 [PS]	Bad News/Tonight-Today	1970	10.00
—As "Dozy, Beaky, Mick & Tich"			

FONTANA

Number	Title (A Side/B Side)	Yr	NM
❑ 1537	You Make It Move/No Time	1965	10.00
❑ 1545	Hold Tight/You Know What I Want	1966	10.00
❑ 1553	Hideaway/Here's a Heart	1966	10.00
❑ 1559	Bend It/She's So Good	1966	12.00
—With "clean" lyrics that refer to a dance (starts "Bend it, bend it, show me you can move and do the dance that's really in the groove"); matrix number of "Bend It" is YW1-38890			
❑ 1559	Bend It/She's So Good	1966	20.00
—With "dirty" lyrics that don't mention a dance (starts "Bend it, bend it, just a little bit and take it easy, show you're likin' it"); matrix number of "Bend It" is YW1-39024			
❑ 1569	Save Me/Shame	1967	10.00
❑ 1591	Okay/Master Llewellyn	1967	10.00

IMPERIAL

Number	Title (A Side/B Side)	Yr	NM
❑ 66270	Zabadak/The Sun Goes Down	1968	10.00
❑ 66287	Legend of Xanadu/Please	1968	8.00
❑ 66309	Break Out/Mrs. Thursday	1968	8.00
❑ 66325	Break Out/Mrs. Thursday	1968	8.00
❑ 66339	Wreck of the Antoinette/ Margarita Linman	1968	8.00

Albums

FONTANA

Number	Title (A Side/B Side)	Yr	NM
❑ MGF-27567 [M]	Greatest Hits	1967	30.00
❑ SRF-67567 [P]	Greatest Hits	1967	40.00
—"Bend It" and "Hold Tight" are rechanneled.			

IMPERIAL

Number	Title (A Side/B Side)	Yr	NM
❑ LP-12402 [P]	Time to Take Off	1968	40.00
—"Zabadak" is rechanneled.			

DAVENPORT SISTERS, THE

45s

TRI-PHI

Number	Title (A Side/B Side)	Yr	NM
❑ 1008	You've Got Me Crying Again/ Hoy Hoy	1962	60.00

DAVEY AND THE BADMEN

Albums

GOTHIC

Number	Title (A Side/B Side)	Yr	NM
❑ KRW-054	Wanted	1963	200.00

DAVI

45s

SPARK

Number	Title (A Side/B Side)	Yr	NM
❑ 110	Reason for Love/Go, Charley, Go	1962	300.00

DAVID, KAL, AND THE EXCEPTIONS

See THE EXCEPTIONS.

45s

Number	Title (A Side/B Side)	Yr	NM
❑			—

DAVID, THE

45s

20TH CENTURY FOX

Number	Title (A Side/B Side)	Yr	NM
❑ 6663	40 Miles/Bus Token	1966	30.00

V.M.C.

Number	Title (A Side/B Side)	Yr	NM
❑ 716	I'm Not Alone/(B-side unknown)	1968	25.00

Albums

V.M.C.

Number	Title (A Side/B Side)	Yr	NM
❑ 124	Another Day, Another Lifetime	1968	200.00
—Mono and stereo versions same price			

DAVID AND JONATHAN

45s

AMY

Number	Title (A Side/B Side)	Yr	NM
❑ 11012	Softly Whispering I Love You/ Something's Gotten Hold of My Heart	1968	6.00

CAPITOL

Number	Title (A Side/B Side)	Yr	NM
❑ 5563	Michelle/How Bitter the Taste of Love	1965	10.00
❑ 5625	I Know/Speak Her Name	1966	8.00
❑ 5625 [PS]	I Know/Speak Her Name	1966	12.00
❑ 5700	On My Word/Lovers of the World, Unite	1966	8.00
❑ 5777	The Magic Book/Time	1966	8.00
❑ 5870	Ten Stories High/Looking for My Life	1967	8.00
❑ 5934	She's Leaving Home/ One Born Every Minute	1967	8.00

20TH FOX

Number	Title (A Side/B Side)	Yr	NM
❑ 6641	Modesty/Willie Waltz	1966	8.00

Albums

CAPITOL

Number	Title (A Side/B Side)	Yr	NM
❑ ST 2473 [S]	Michelle	1966	20.00
❑ T 2473 [M]	Michelle	1966	15.00

DAVID AND RUBEN

45s

WARNER BROS.

Number	Title (A Side/B Side)	Yr	NM
❑ 7316	(I Love Her So Much) It Hurts Me/The Girl in My Dreams	1969	400.00

DAVIDSON, JOHN

45s

COLUMBIA

Number	Title (A Side/B Side)	Yr	NM
❑ 43531	I Can't Help This Feeling I Feel/ I Still Send Her Flowers	1966	6.00
❑ 43635	Summer Love/I'll Try Lovin' You Less	1966	6.00
❑ 44005	Daydream/I'll Always Remember	1967	6.00
❑ 44005 [PS]	Daydream/I'll Always Remember	1967	8.00
❑ 44210	In the Sunshine Days/If You Can Put That in a Bottle	1967	6.00
❑ 44334	What Is a Woman/How Come You Love Me Like You Do	1967	6.00
❑ 44478	Visions of Sugarplums/Flame	1968	6.00
❑ 44770	Words/The Wonder of You	1969	6.00
❑ 44896	California Blood Lines/I Am Now	1969	6.00
❑ 45034	It's Such a Lovely Time of Year/ What Makes a Woman Run	1969	6.00
❑ 45155	Five O'Clock Shadow/ A Promise and a Lie	1970	5.00
❑ 45196	I Got Love/Politician	1970	5.00
❑ 45254	Let's Get Lost In Now/What You're Doing to Me	1970	5.00

Number	Title (A Side/B Side)	Yr	NM
45423	Say It Again/Just Magic	1971	5.00
45486	Good Times/A Clown Never Cries	1971	5.00

MERCURY

Number	Title (A Side/B Side)	Yr	NM
73362	As Lonely As You/What She Left of Me	1973	5.00

20TH CENTURY

Number	Title (A Side/B Side)	Yr	NM
2063	We Had It All/I Want to Spend My Life with You	1973	4.00
2121	Have a Nice Day/Less Than the Sun	1974	4.00
2175	The Other Woman/What Will I Tell the Kids	1975	4.00
2293	Everytime I Sing a Love Song/Love in the Shadows	1976	4.00
2313	I Let You Walk Away/Steal Her Away	1976	4.00
2326	Patch It Up/Save the Last Dance for Me	1976	4.00

Albums

ACCORD

Number	Title (A Side/B Side)	Yr	NM
SN-7202	Closeup	1981	8.00

COLPIX

Number	Title (A Side/B Side)	Yr	NM
CP-485 [M]	The Young Warm Sound of John Davidson	1964	15.00
SCP-485 [S]	The Young Warm Sound of John Davidson	1964	20.00

COLUMBIA

Number	Title (A Side/B Side)	Yr	NM
CL 2580 [M]	The Time of My Life	1966	10.00
CL 2648 [M]	My Best to You	1967	10.00
CL 2734 [M]	A Kind of Hush	1967	10.00
CS 9380 [S]	The Time of My Life	1966	12.00
CS 9448 [S]	My Best to You	1967	12.00
CS 9534 [S]	A Kind of Hush	1967	12.00
CS 9654	Goin' Places	1968	10.00
CS 9795	John Davidson	1969	10.00
CS 9859	My Cherie Amour	1969	10.00
CS 9864	My Christmas Favorites	1969	12.00
C 30098	Everything Is Beautiful	1970	10.00
PC 36956	Incredible	1981	8.00

MERCURY

Number	Title (A Side/B Side)	Yr	NM
SRM-1-658	Well, Here I Am	1973	10.00

20TH CENTURY

Number	Title (A Side/B Side)	Yr	NM
T-429	Touch Me	1974	10.00
T-512	Every Time I Sing	1976	10.00

DAVIE, HUTCH

45s

ATCO

Number	Title (A Side/B Side)	Yr	NM
6110	Woodchopper's Ball/Honky Tonk Train	1958	12.00
6123	In the Mood/Gwendolyn and the Werewolf	1958	12.00
6136	Begin the Beguine/The Dipsy Doodle	1959	12.00
6149	Sweet Georgia Brown/Heartaches	1959	12.00

CANADIAN AMERICAN

Number	Title (A Side/B Side)	Yr	NM
126	The Glow Worm/Down Home	1961	10.00

CLARIDGE

Number	Title (A Side/B Side)	Yr	NM
311	East Is East (Part 1)/East Is East (Part 2)	1966	8.00

CONGRESS

Number	Title (A Side/B Side)	Yr	NM
102	But I Do/Time Was	1962	10.00

DYNO VOICE

Number	Title (A Side/B Side)	Yr	NM
904	Never My Love/A Lover's Concerto	1968	6.00

NEW VOICE

Number	Title (A Side/B Side)	Yr	NM
823	Swingin' Shepherd Blues/Salty	1967	6.00

Albums

ATCO

Number	Title (A Side/B Side)	Yr	NM
33-105 [M]	Much Hutch	1958	50.00

DAVIE, ROBERT

45s

CONGRESS

Number	Title (A Side/B Side)	Yr	NM
224	As Time Goes By/The Gypsy	1964	8.00
231	Oh! What It Seemed to Be/Because of You	1964	8.00

DAVIES, CYRIL

45s

DOT

Number	Title (A Side/B Side)	Yr	NM
16515	Chicago Calling/Country Line Special	1963	12.00

DAVIES, DAVE Also see THE KINKS.

45s

RCA

Number	Title (A Side/B Side)	Yr	NM
PB-12089	Imagination's Real/Wild Man	1980	5.00
PB-12089 [PS]	Imagination's Real/Wild Man	1980	8.00
PB-12147	Doing the Best for You/Got No More to Lose	1981	5.00

REPRISE

Number	Title (A Side/B Side)	Yr	NM
0614	Death of a Clown/Love Me Till the Sun Shines	1967	40.00
0660	Suzannah's Still Alive/Funny Face	1968	40.00

WARNER BROS.

Number	Title (A Side/B Side)	Yr	NM
29425	Mean Disposition/Cold Winter	1983	25.00
29425 [DJ]	Mean Disposition (same on both sides)	1983	8.00
29509	Love Gets You/One Night with You	1983	25.00
29509 [DJ]	Love Gets You (same on both sides)	1983	8.00

Albums

RCA VICTOR

Number	Title (A Side/B Side)	Yr	NM
AFL1-3603	AFL1-3603	1980	10.00
AFL1-4036	Glamour	1981	10.00

WARNER BROS.

Number	Title (A Side/B Side)	Yr	NM
23917	Chosen People	1983	10.00

DAVIS, ANDREA See MINNIE RIPERTON.

DAVIS, BILLIE

45s

JERDEN

Number	Title (A Side/B Side)	Yr	NM
758	Last One to Be Loved/You Don't Know	1965	10.00
772	No Other Baby/Hands Off	1965	10.00

LONDON

Number	Title (A Side/B Side)	Yr	NM
20041	I Want You to Be My Baby/Suffer	1968	6.00
20049	I Can Remember/I'll Come Home	1968	6.00
20062	There Must Be a Reason/Love	1971	5.00

DAVIS, BILLY

45s

COBBLESTONE

Number	Title (A Side/B Side)	Yr	NM
731	Stanky (Get Funky)/I've Tried	1969	6.00

HI

Number	Title (A Side/B Side)	Yr	NM
2146	It's All Over/Once in a Lifetime	1968	6.00

DAVIS, BILLY, JR. Also see THE FIFTH DIMENSION.

45s

ABC

Number	Title (A Side/B Side)	Yr	NM
12106	Three Steps from True Love/Light a Candle	1975	5.00

DAVIS, BO

45s

CREST

Number	Title (A Side/B Side)	Yr	NM
1027	Let's Coast Awhile/Drownin' All My Sorrows	1956	150.00

—Eddie Cochran plays guitar on this record.

DAVIS, DANNY, AND THE NASHVILLE BRASS Also includes Danny Davis credited alone. Also see HANK LOCKLIN.

45s

HICKORY

Number	Title (A Side/B Side)	Yr	NM
1005	Can't You Feel It in Your Heart/Second Hand Dreams for Sale	1954	12.00

JAROCO

Number	Title (A Side/B Side)	Yr	NM
8742	Green Eyes (Cryin' Those Blue Tears)/Little Pink Cloud	1987	5.00

LIBERTY

Number	Title (A Side/B Side)	Yr	NM
55213	Beauty and the Beast/Glory Bugle	1959	10.00

MGM

Number	Title (A Side/B Side)	Yr	NM
11103	Crazy Heart/I'm Not Alone	1951	15.00
11175	Please Bring Back the Sunshine/Deep Water	1952	15.00
11244	Always/Do You Ever Think of Me	1952	15.00
11286	Forget/Love Came Out of the Night	1952	15.00
11443	I Don't Want Your Kisses/Come to the Wedding	1953	15.00
13077	Pots 'N' Pans/Travelin' Trumpets	1962	8.00
13106	Little Bandits of Juarez/Theme from "Kill Or Cure"	1962	8.00
13270	Circus World/There Goes My Heart	1964	6.00
13295	Night Train from Jamaica/Ska Dee Wah	1964	6.00

—With Byron Lee

Number	Title (A Side/B Side)	Yr	NM
13368	Ballad of Cat Ballou/Theme from "The Saint"	1965	6.00
13374	I'm Henry VIII, I Am/The End of the World	1965	6.00

RCA

Number	Title (A Side/B Side)	Yr	NM
PB-10871	Country Disco/Disco Dante	1977	4.00
PB-11073	How I Love Them Old Songs/Tara Jeanne	1977	4.00
PB-11278	Old Fashioned Love Song/Falsely Accused	1978	4.00
PB-11466	Sugarfoot Rag/Let Your Lovelight Shine	1979	4.00
PB-11612	Ain't Misbehavin'/I'm Gonna Sit Right Down and Write Myself a Letter	1979	4.00
PB-12070	Cotton Eyed Joe/Colinda	1980	4.00

RCA VICTOR

Number	Title (A Side/B Side)	Yr	NM
47-9785	Wabash Cannon Ball/Sweet Dreams	1969	4.00
47-9847	Columbus Stockade Blues/Wings of a Dove	1970	4.00
47-9905	Down Yonder/May the Circle Be Unbroken	1970	4.00
47-9936	Jingling Brass/Silent Night	1970	6.00
47-9936 [DJ]	Jingling Brass/Silent Night	1970	6.00

—Promos available on either yellow or green labels

Number	Title (A Side/B Side)	Yr	NM
74-0439	I Can't Stop Loving You/Rose Garden	1971	4.00
74-0506	Highland Brass/Ruby, Don't Take Your Love to Town	1971	4.00
74-0560	Wait for the Light to Shine/Blue Bayou	1971	4.00
74-0649	Java/Flowers on the Wall	1972	4.00
74-0760	From Dixie with Love/Under the Double Eagle	1972	4.00
74-0847	I'll Fly Away/Woman	1972	4.00
74-0858	White Christmas/Winter Wonderland	1972	5.00
APBO-0019	Superstar/Come See Us	1973	4.00
APBO-0301	Ruby, Are You Mad at Your Man/Rollin' in My Sweet Baby's Arms	1974	4.00
PB-10232	Singing the Blues/Stay a Little Longer	1975	4.00
PB-10255	Branigan/Peppy Time Tune	1975	4.00
PB-10375	Running Bear/Nashville Brass Hoedown	1975	4.00
PB-10570	Paloma Blanca/Nashville Express	1976	4.00
PB-10814	Why Don't You Love Me/He'll Have to Go	1976	4.00

VERVE

Number	Title (A Side/B Side)	Yr	NM
10233	Theme from "Carnival"/Stardust	1961	10.00

WARTRACE

Number	Title (A Side/B Side)	Yr	NM
730	I Dropped Your Name/(B-side unknown)	1985	4.00

Albums

PICKWICK

Number	Title (A Side/B Side)	Yr	NM
ACL-7034	Down Yonder	197?	8.00
ACL-7048	Super Country	1977	8.00

RCA SPECIAL PRODUCTS

Number	Title (A Side/B Side)	Yr	NM
DPL1-0176	America 200 Years Young	1976	15.00

—Available only at Amana dealers

RCA VICTOR

Number	Title (A Side/B Side)	Yr	NM
APD1-0034 [Q]	Travelin'	1973	12.00
APD1-0232 [Q]	Cairbbean Cruise	1973	15.00
APL1-0232	Cairbbean Cruise	1973	10.00
APL1-0425	The Best of Danny Davis and the Nashville Brass	1973	10.00
APD1-0565 [Q]	Bluegrass Country	1974	15.00
APL1-0565	Bluegrass Country	1974	10.00
APD1-0774 [Q]	The Latest and Greatest	1974	15.00
APL1-0774	The Latest and Greatest	1974	10.00
ANL1-0902	Orange Blossom Special	1974	10.00
APD1-1043 [Q]	Dream Country	1975	12.00
APL1-1043	Dream Country	1975	10.00
APD1-1240 [Q]	Gold	1975	12.00
APL1-1240	Gold	1975	10.00
APD1-1578 [Q]	Texas	1976	12.00
APL1-1578	Texas	1976	10.00
ANL1-1930	Christmas with Danny Davis and the Nashville Brass	1976	8.00

—Reissue of LSP-4377

Number	Title (A Side/B Side)	Yr	NM
APL1-1986	Super	1976	10.00
APL1-2310	Live Vegas	1977	10.00
APL1-2721	How I Love Them Ol' Songs	1977	10.00
APL1-2980	Cookin' Country	1978	10.00
AHL1-3415	Great Songs of the Big Band Era	1979	10.00
AHL1-4022	Cotton Eyed Joe	1981	10.00
LSP-4059	The Nashville Sound	1969	10.00
LSP-4176	More Nashville Sounds	1969	10.00
LSP-4232	Movin' On	1969	10.00
LSP-4334	You Ain't Heard Nothin' Yet	1970	10.00
LSP-4377	Christmas with Danny Davis and the Nashville Brass	1970	10.00
LSP-4424	Down Homers	1970	10.00
LSP-4475	Somethin' Else	1971	10.00
LSP-4571	Super Country	1971	10.00
LSP-4627	Turns to Gold	1972	10.00
LSP-4720	Live — In Person	1972	10.00
LSP-4803	Turn On Some Happy!	1972	10.00

Except when noted otherwise, VG = 25% of NM, and VG+ = 50% of NM. (Example: VG = $2.00, VG+ = $4.00 and NM = $8.00.)

DAVIS, DANNY, AND WILLIE NELSON

Also see each artist's individual listings.

45s

Number	Title (A Side/B Side)	Yr	NM
RCA			
❑ PB-11893	Night Life/December Day	1980	4.00
❑ PB-11999	Funny How Time Slips Away/The Local Memory	1980	4.00

DAVIS, EUNICE

45s

Number	Title (A Side/B Side)	Yr	NM
ATLANTIC			
❑ 992	Go to Work Pretty Daddy/My Beat Is 125th Street	1953	60.00
CORAL			
❑ 65075	Work Daddy Work/What Do You Want	1952	20.00
DELUXE			
❑ 6068	Get Your Enjoys/24 Hours a Day	1954	30.00
DERBY			
❑ 760	Evening Train/I'm a Wild West Woman	1951	30.00
❑ 768	Good News for You Baby/Tell Me I'm the Baby	1951	30.00
GRAND			
❑ 130	Let's Have a Party/Every Time Your Lips Meet Mine	1955	20.00

DAVIS, HAL

45s

Number	Title (A Side/B Side)	Yr	NM
ALDEN			
❑ 1301	My Young Heart/(B-side unknown)	1959	40.00
❑ 1303	King of Lovers/(B-side unknown)	1959	40.00
DEL-FI			
❑ 4146	You're Playing with Me/Read the Book of Love	1960	30.00
DYNAMITE			
❑ 1010	I Don't Want Nobody/(B-side unknown)	195?	200.00
FEDERAL			
❑ 12429	My Only Flower/You're the Girl	1961	12.00
GARDENA			
❑ 125	One More Chance/Show Me	1962	30.00
GSP			
❑ 2	I Don't Know/Lover's Plan	1963	30.00
KELLEY			
❑ 105	Way to My Heart/(B-side unknown)	196?	100.00
—Red vinyl			
MINASA			
❑ 6714	It's You/(B-side unknown)	196?	30.00
MJC			
❑ 104	You'll Find Love/(B-side unknown)	196?	30.00
VEE JAY			
❑ 387	Merchant of Love/What Do You Mean to Me	1961	20.00
WIZARD			
❑ 101	Merchant of Love/What Do You Mean to Me	1961	70.00
❑ 102	I Need Someone/(B-side unknown)	1961	30.00

DAVIS, JAN

45s

Number	Title (A Side/B Side)	Yr	NM
A&M			
❑ 733	Boss Machine/The Fugitive	1964	15.00
❑ 744	Guitar Star/The Unwanted	1964	15.00
ALJO			
❑ 104	The Surfin' Matador/Scramble	1964	30.00
BEAR			
❑ 1000	Hornet's Nest/Flamenco Funk (Mosaic)	1969	6.00
BIG BIRD			
❑ 128	International Love Process (Part 1)/International Love Process (Part 2)	1967	15.00
COLUMBIA			
❑ 43224	More (Theme from Mondo Cane)/Mystique	1965	15.00
DIRECT HIT			
❑ 1002	Raunchy 1970/Dark Blue	1970	6.00
HOLIDAY			
❑ 1213	Pooky/Watusi Zombie	1964	15.00
QUAD-ETT			
❑ 10039	Hot Sauce/Soul Mate	1974	5.00
RANWOOD			
❑ 1015	Hot Sauce/Soulmate	1974	5.00
❑ 1023	Gypsy Fox/Child of June (Danny's Theme)	1974	5.00
❑ 1035	El Lobo/Maiden Spain	1975	5.00
RCA VICTOR			
❑ 47-9018	Time Tunnel/Walkin' Back	1966	12.00
❑ 47-9923	Raunchy 1970/Dark Blue	1970	5.00
RENDEZVOUS			
❑ 131	Sleepless/Damascus	1960	20.00
—With the Ricco-Shays			
❑ 149	Sabre Dance/Hop, Skip and Jump	1961	20.00
❑ 205	Malaguena/Hop, Skip and Jump	1963	20.00
❑ 214	You're Not Welcome (Anymore)/Don't Walk Away	1963	30.00
❑ 218	Delicado/Sahara	1963	20.00
SHAMLEY			
❑ 44016	Hornet's Nest/Flamenco Funk (Mosaic)	1969	5.00
SMASH			
❑ 1863	The Snow Surfin' Matador/Scramble	1963	25.00
UNI			
❑ 55029	International Love Process (Part 1)/International Love Process (Part 2)	1967	8.00
❑ 55197	Walk Don't Run/Flamenco Funk	1970	5.00
WHITE WHALE			
❑ 226	Lost in Space/Run for Your Life	1966	12.00

DAVIS, JESSE

45s

Number	Title (A Side/B Side)	Yr	NM
ERA			
❑ 3189	Gonna Hang On In There Girl/Albuquerque	1967	600.00
❑ 3192	You Don't Need a Crown/Something to Think About	1967	250.00
JABOTH			
❑ 1	There's Room for Me/It's Too Late to Be Sorry	196?	2000.
❑ 4001	So Full of Love/This Is the Meaning of Love	196?	1000.
MULBERRY SQUARE			
❑ 3935	Benji's Theme — I Feel Love/Benji's Theme — Part II	1975	20.00
❑ 3935 [PS]	Benji's Theme — I Feel Love/Benji's Theme — Part II	1975	30.00
REVERE			
❑ 101	There's Room for Me/It's Too Late to Be Sorry	196?	1000.
—As "Jessie Davis"			
❑ 101 [PS]	There's Room for Me/It's Too Late to Be Sorry	196?	1500.

DAVIS, JESSE ED

45s

Number	Title (A Side/B Side)	Yr	NM
ATCO			
❑ 6807	Every Night Is Saturday Night/Golden Sun Goddess	1971	5.00
❑ 6825	Reno Street Incident/Washita Love Child	1971	5.00
❑ 6873	Sue Me, Sue You Blues/My Captain	1972	8.00
❑ 6889	Ululu/Alcatraz	1972	5.00
EPIC			
❑ 11021	She's a Pain/Natural Anthem	1973	4.00

Albums

Number	Title (A Side/B Side)	Yr	NM
ATCO			
❑ SD 33-346	Jesse Ed Davis	1970	15.00
❑ SD 33-382	Ululu	1972	15.00
EPIC			
❑ KE 32133	Keep On Comin'	1973	12.00

DAVIS, LEE

45s

Number	Title (A Side/B Side)	Yr	NM
CUB			
❑ 9026	Three Young Men/The Flower Song	1959	15.00
—B-side by the Naturals			

DAVIS, MAC

45s

Number	Title (A Side/B Side)	Yr	NM
CAPITOL			
❑ 5554	Bad Scene/I Protest	1965	8.00
CASABLANCA			
❑ 2244	It's Hard to Be Humble/Greatest Gift of All	1980	4.00
❑ 2286	Let's Keep It That Way/I Know You're Out There Somewhere	1980	3.00
❑ 2305	Texas in My Rear View Mirror/Sad Songs	1980	3.00
❑ 2327	Hooked On Music/Me and Fat Boy	1981	3.00
❑ 2336	Secrets/Remember When Beverly	1981	3.00
❑ 2341	You're My Bestest Friend/You Are So Lovely	1981	3.00
❑ 2346	Midnight Crazy/I Got the Hots for You	1981	3.00
❑ 2350	Rodeo Clown/Dammit Girl	1982	3.00
❑ 2355	The Beer Drinkin' Song/You Are So Lovely	1982	3.00
❑ 2363	Lying Here Lying/Quiet Times	1982	3.00
❑ 818168-7	Most of All/Springtime Down in Dixie	1984	3.00
❑ 818929-7	Caroline's Still in Georgia/I've Got a Dream	1984	3.00
COLUMBIA			
❑ 10018	Stop and Smell the Roses/Poor Boy Boogie	1974	4.00
❑ 10070	Rock 'n' Roll (I Gave You the Best Years of My Life)/Emily Suzanne	1974	4.00
❑ 10111	(If You Add) All the Love in the World/Smiley	1975	4.00
❑ 10148	Burnin' Thing/A Special Place in Heaven	1975	4.00
❑ 10187	I Still Love You (You Still Love Me)/The Hits Just Keep On Comin'	1975	4.00
❑ 10304	Forever Lovers/The Love Lamp	1976	4.00
❑ 10418	Every Now and Then/'m Just in Love	1976	4.00
❑ 10535	Picking Up the Pieces of My Life/Do It (With Someone You Love)	1977	4.00
❑ 10745	Music in My Life/You Are	1978	4.00
❑ 45117	Whoever Finds This, I Love You/Half and Half	1970	5.00
❑ 45117 [PS]	Whoever Finds This, I Love You/Half and Half	1970	8.00
❑ 45192	I'll Paint You a Song/The Closest I Ever Came	1970	5.00
❑ 45245	I Believe in Music/Poor Man's Gold	1970	5.00
❑ 45302	Beginning to Feel the Pain/Butterfly Girl	1971	5.00
❑ 45355	Lucas Was a Red-Neck/Fall in Love with Your Wife	1971	5.00
❑ 45404	Sweet Dreams and Sarah/Poem for My Little Lady	1971	5.00
❑ 45456	I Believe in Music/Hollywood Humpty Dumpty	1971	5.00
❑ 45576	Beginning to Feel the Pain/Butterfly Girl	1972	4.00
❑ 45618	Baby Don't Get Hooked on Me/Poem for My Little Lady	1972	4.00
❑ 45727	Everybody Loves a Love Song/Friend, Lover, Woman, Wife	1972	4.00
❑ 45773	Dream Me Home/Spread Your Love on Me	1973	4.00
❑ 45839	Your Side of the Bed/(Hope You Didn't) Chop No Wood	1973	4.00
❑ 45911	Kiss It and Make It Better/Sunshine	1973	4.00
❑ 46004	One Hell of a Woman/A Poor Man's Gold	1974	4.00
JAMIE			
❑ 1227	I'm a Poor Loser/Let Him Try	1962	10.00
MCA			
❑ 52573	I Never Made Love (Till I Made Love to You)/I Think I'm Gonna Rain	1985	3.00
❑ 52669	I Feel the Country Callin' Me/Rainy Day Lovin'	1985	3.00
❑ 52765	Sexy Young Girl/Special Place in Heaven	1986	3.00
❑ 52826	Somewhere in America/I Need a Hug	1986	3.00
VEE JAY			
❑ 492	A Little Dutch Town/Looking at Linda	1963	10.00

Albums

Number	Title (A Side/B Side)	Yr	NM
ACCORD			
❑ SN-7165	Little Touch of Love	1981	8.00
❑ SN-7189	With Love	1981	8.00
ALLEGIANCE			
❑ AV-5019	Vol. XC	198?	8.00
❑ AV-5031	Losers	198?	8.00
CASABLANCA			
❑ NBLP 7207	It's Hard to Be Humble	1980	8.00
❑ NBLP 7239	Texas in My Rear View Mirror	1980	8.00
❑ NBLP 7257	Midnight Crazy	1981	8.00
❑ 822638-1	The Very Best and More	1984	8.00

D

Number	Title (A Side/B Side)	Yr	NM
COLUMBIA			
❑ CS 9969	Song Painter	1970	15.00
—Red "360 Sound" label			
❑ CS 9969	Song Painter	1974	10.00
—Orange label			
❑ C 30926	I Believe in Music	1971	10.00
❑ CQ 31770 [Q]	Baby Don't Get Hooked on Me	1972	15.00
❑ KC 31770	Baby Don't Get Hooked on Me	1972	10.00
❑ KC 32206	Mac Davis	1973	10.00
❑ CQ 32582 [Q]	Stop and Smell the Roses	1974	15.00
❑ KC 32582	Stop and Smell the Roses	1974	10.00
❑ PC 32582	Stop and Smell the Roses	1986	6.00
—Budget-line reissue			
❑ PC 32927	All the Love in the World	1975	10.00
❑ PCQ 32927 [Q]	All the Love in the World	1975	15.00
❑ PC 33551	Burnin' Thing	1975	10.00
❑ PC 34105	Forever Lovers	1976	10.00
❑ PCQ 34105 [Q]	Forever Lovers	1976	—
—Not released			
❑ PC 34313	Thunder in the Afternoon	1976	10.00
❑ PCQ 34313 [Q]	Thunder in the Afternoon	1976	15.00
❑ JC 35284	Fantasy	1978	10.00
❑ JC 36317	Greatest Hits	1979	10.00
❑ PC 36317	Greatest Hits	198?	6.00
—Budget-line reissue			
❑ FC 38950	Who's Lovin' You	1983	8.00
❑ PC 38950	Who's Lovin' You	198?	6.00
—Budget-line reissue			
MCA			
❑ 5590	Till I Made It with You	1985	8.00
❑ 5718	Somewhere in America	1986	8.00
SPRINGBOARD			
❑ SPB-4024	Mac Davis	197?	8.00
TRIP			
❑ 9502	Mac Davis	1973	8.00

DAVIS, MAXWELL

Albums

Number	Title (A Side/B Side)	Yr	NM
ALADDIN			
❑ LP-709 [10]	Maxwell Davis	1955	400.00
❑ LP-804 [M]	Maxwell Davis	1956	200.00
SCORE			
❑ SLP-4106 [M]	Blue Tango	1957	200.00

DAVIS, MELVIN

45s

Number	Title (A Side/B Side)	Yr	NM
FORTUNE			
❑ 551	I Won't Be Your Fool/Playboy (Don't You Play in School)	196?	60.00
GROOVESVILLE			
❑ 1003	I Must Love You/Still in My Heart	1966	500.00
INVICTUS			
❑ ZS7 1259	You Made Me Over/I'm Worried	1973	200.00
❑ 9115	I'm Worried/Just As Long	1972	50.00
JACK POT			
❑ 3800	I Don't Want You/About Love	1963	400.00
KE-KE			
❑ 1815	Wedding Bells/It's No News	1964	600.00
MALA			
❑ 590	Save It (Never Too Late)/ This Love Was Meant to Be	1968	60.00
❑ 12009	Faith/Love Bug Got a Bear Hug	1968	50.00
ROCK MILL			
❑ 5238	Let Love in Your Life/ Wacky World	1991	20.00
—As "Mel Davis"			
❑ 32484	Double or Nothing/ You Can't Run Away	198?	20.00
—As "Mel Davis"			
❑ 32485	Saving Myself for You/ Wacky World	198?	30.00
—As "Mel Davis"			
WHEEL CITY			
❑ 1003	Find a Quiet Place (And Be Lonely)/This Ain't the Way	196?	1000.

DAVIS, MILES

12-Inch Singles

Number	Title (A Side/B Side)	Yr	NM
COLUMBIA/LEGACY			
❑ CAS 42193 [DJ]	Bitches Brew (Edit 11:32)/ Spanish Key (Edit 11:50)	1999	15.00
—Red vinyl; entitled "Bitches Brew — Singles"			

45s

Number	Title (A Side/B Side)	Yr	NM
BLUE NOTE			
❑ 1595	Dear Old Stockholm/ Wouldn't You	195?	15.00
❑ 1596	Chance It/Yesterdays	195?	15.00
❑ 1597	Donna/The Squirrel 2nd Master	195?	15.00
❑ 1618	Enigma/Tempus Fugit	195?	15.00
❑ 1619	Ray's Idea/I Waited for You	195?	15.00
❑ 1620	Kelo/C.T.A.	195?	15.00
❑ 1633	Donna/Well You Needn't	195?	15.00
❑ 1649	Lazy Susan/Tempus Fugit	195?	15.00
❑ 1650	The Leap/Weirdo	195?	15.00
CAPITOL			
❑ F1221	Venus de Milo/Darn That Dream	1950	25.00
COLUMBIA			
❑ 38-02467	Shout/Fat Time	1981	5.00
❑ 38-04564	Code M.D./Decoy	1984	5.00
❑ 10110	Red China Blues/Maiysha	1975	6.00
❑ 30735 [S]	(contents unknown)	1960	15.00
❑ 30736 [S]	(contents unknown)	1960	15.00
❑ 30737 [S]	(contents unknown)	1960	15.00
❑ 30738 [S]	(contents unknown)	1960	15.00
❑ 30739 [S]	(contents unknown)	1960	15.00
❑ S7 31094 [S]	De Buzzard Song/Gone	1961	15.00
❑ S7 31095 [S]	Gone, Gone, Gone/Summertime	1961	15.00
❑ S7 31096 [S]	Bess, Oh Where's My Bess/ Fishermen, Strawberries and Devil Crab	1961	15.00
❑ S7 31097 [S]	It Ain't Necessarily So/Here Comes De Honey Man	1961	15.00
❑ S7 31098 [S]	I Loves You Porgy/There's a Boat That's Leaving Soon for New York	1961	15.00
—The above five are "Stereo Seven" 33 1/3 rpm jukebox singles from set "JS 7-26" entitled "Porgy and Bess"			
❑ 31377 [S]	(contents unknown)	1962	15.00
❑ 31378 [S]	(contents unknown)	1962	15.00
❑ 31379 [S]	(contents unknown)	1962	15.00
❑ 31380 [S]	(contents unknown)	1962	15.00
❑ 31381 [S]	(contents unknown)	1962	15.00
—Anyone who can fill in these gaps — the above 15 all are Columbia "Stereo 7" singles — please let us know.			
❑ 42057	It Ain't Necessarily So/All Blues	1961	12.00
❑ 42069	I Loves You, Porgy/It Ain't Necessarily So	1961	12.00
❑ 42583	Slow Samba/New Rhumba	1962	12.00
❑ 42853	Seven Steps to Heaven/ Devil May Care	1963	12.00
❑ 44652	Girls of Kilimanjaro/ (B-side unknown)	1969	8.00
❑ 45090	Great Expectations/ Little Blue Frog	1970	8.00
❑ 4-45171	Miles Runs the Voodoo Down/ Spanish Key	1970	8.00
❑ 45327	Friday Miles/Saturday Miles	1971	8.00
❑ 45709	Molester/(B-side unknown)	1972	8.00
❑ 45822	Vote for Miles (Part 1)/ Vote for Miles (Part 2)	1973	8.00
❑ 45946	Big Fun/Holly-Wood	1973	8.00
❑ 46074	Great Expectations/ Go Ahead John	1974	8.00
PRESTIGE			
❑ 103	Green Haze (Part 1)/ Green Haze (Part 2)	195?	15.00
❑ 114	A Night in Tunisia (Part 1)/ A Night in Tunisia (Part 2)	195?	15.00
❑ 123	If I Were a Bell (Part 1)/ If I Were a Bell (Part 2)	195?	15.00
❑ 157	Walkin' (Part 1)/Walkin' (Part 2)	1957	15.00
❑ 165	It Never Entered My Mind (Part 1)/It Never Entered My Mind (Part 2)	1957	15.00
❑ 195	When I Fall in Love (Part 1)/ When I Fall in Love (Part 2)	195?	15.00
❑ 248	Surrey with the Fringe on Top/ Diane	196?	15.00
❑ 268	S'posin'/Just Squeeze Me	196?	12.00
❑ 321	It's Only a Paper Moon/Dig	1964	12.00
❑ 353	Smooch/Valentine	196?	12.00
❑ 376	You Don't Know/That Old Devil Moon	196?	12.00
❑ 413	'Round Midnight/Airegin	196?	12.00
❑ 734	Morpheus/Blue Room	1952	20.00
❑ 742	Down/Whispering	195?	20.00
❑ 766	My Old Flame (Part 1)/ My Old Flame (Part 2)	195?	20.00
❑ 777	Dig (Part 1)/Dig (Part 2)	1956	20.00
❑ 817	It's Only a Paper Moon (Part 1)/ It's Only a Paper Moon (Part 2)	195?	20.00
❑ 846	Bluing (Part 1)/Bluing (Part 2)	195?	20.00
❑ 868	Conception/Bluing 3	195?	20.00
❑ 876	Out of the Blue (Part 1)/ Out of the Blue (Part 2)	195?	20.00
❑ 884	Tasty Pudding (Part 1)/ Tasty Pudding (Part 2)	195?	20.00
❑ 893	Blue Haze (Part 1)/ Blue Haze (Part 2)	1956	20.00
❑ 898	That Old Devil Moon/Four	195?	20.00
❑ 902	Miles Ahead/When Lights Are Low	195?	20.00
❑ 915	But Not for Me (Part 1)/ But Not for Me (Part 2)	195?	20.00

7-Inch Extended Plays

Number	Title (A Side/B Side)	Yr	NM
CAPITOL			
❑ EAP 1-459	*Jeru/Deception/Moon Dreams/Venus De Milo	1954	40.00
❑ EAP 1-459 [PS]	Classics in Jazz, Part 1	1954	40.00
❑ EAP 2-459	*Rocker/Israel/Godchild/Rouge	1954	40.00
❑ EAP 2-459 [PS]	Classics in Jazz, Part 2	1954	40.00

Albums

Number	Title (A Side/B Side)	Yr	NM
ALA			
❑ AJ-503	Archives of Jazz, Vol. 3	198?	12.00
BLUE NOTE			
❑ BLP-1501 [M]	Miles Davis, Vol. 1	1955	500.00
—"Deep groove" version; Lexington Ave. address on label			
❑ BLP-1501 [M]	Miles Davis, Vol. 1	1958	100.00
—Regular version, W. 63rd St. address on label			
❑ BLP-1501 [M]	Miles Davis, Vol. 1	1958	250.00
—"Deep groove" version, W. 63rd St. address on label			
❑ BLP-1501 [M]	Miles Davis, Vol. 1	1963	40.00
—"New York, USA" address on label			
❑ BLP-1501 [M]	Miles Davis, Vol. 1	1966	20.00
—With "A Division of Liberty Records" on label			
❑ BLP-1502 [M]	Miles Davis, Vol. 2	1955	250.00
—"Deep groove" version; W. 63rd St. address on label			
❑ BLP-1502 [M]	Miles Davis, Vol. 2	1955	500.00
—"Deep groove" version; Lexington Ave. address on label			
❑ BLP-1502 [M]	Miles Davis, Vol. 2	1958	100.00
—Regular version, W. 63rd St. address on label			
❑ BLP-1502 [M]	Miles Davis, Vol. 2	1963	40.00
—With New York, USA address on label			
❑ BLP-1502 [M]	Miles Davis, Vol. 2	1966	25.00
—With "A Division of Liberty Records" on label			
❑ BLP-5013 [10]	Miles Davis (Young Man with a Horn)	1952	1000.
❑ BLP-5022 [10]	Miles Davis, Vol. 2	1953	1000.
❑ BLP-5040 [10]	Miles Davis, Vol. 3	1954	1000.
❑ BLP-81501	Miles Davis, Vol. 1	1968	15.00
—Rechanneled stereo version of 1501			
❑ BST-81501	Miles Davis, Vol. 1	1985	12.00
—"The Finest in Jazz Since 1939" reissue label			
❑ BLP-81502	Miles Davis, Vol. 2	1968	15.00
—Rechanneled stereo version of 1502			
❑ BST-81502	Miles Davis, Vol. 2	1985	12.00
—"The Finest in Jazz Since 1939" reissue label			
BOOK-OF-THE-MONTH CLUB			
❑ 91-7725 [(3)]	Master of Styles	198?	40.00
CAPITOL			
❑ H 459 [10]	Classics in Jazz	1954	250.00
—First 33 1/3 rpm issue of some of the "Birth of the Cool" sessions			
❑ T 762 [M]	Birth of the Cool	1956	200.00
—Turquoise label			
❑ T 762 [M]	Birth of the Cool	1958	100.00
—Black label wirh rainbow ring, Capitol logo at left			
❑ T 762 [M]	Birth of the Cool	2003	40.00
—Classic Records reissue on 200-gram vinyl			
❑ DT 1974 [R]	Birth of the Cool	1963	15.00
❑ T 1974 [M]	Birth of the Cool	1963	40.00
—Reissue of 762; black label with rainbow ring, Capitol logo at top			
❑ M-11026 [M]	The Complete Birth of the Cool	1972	20.00
❑ N-16168 [M]	The Complete Birth of the Cool	198?	10.00
—Budget-line reissue			
CHARLIE PARKER			
❑ PLP-824	Many Miles of Davis	196?	50.00
COLUMBIA			
❑ J 1	Facets	1973	12.00
❑ J 17	Miles Davis at Newport	1973	12.00
❑ C2L 20 [(2)M]	Miles Davis in Person (Friday & Saturday Nights at the Blackhawk, San Francisco)	1961	50.00
—Six "eye" logos on label			
❑ C2L 20 [(2)M]	Miles Davis in Person (Friday & Saturday Nights at the Blackhawk, San Francisco)	1963	30.00
—"Guaranteed High Fidelity" on label			
❑ C2L 20 [(2)M]	Miles Davis in Person (Friday & Saturday Nights at the Blackhawk, San Francisco)	1965	25.00
—"Mono" on label			
❑ GP 26 [(2)]	Bitches Brew	1970	25.00
—Orange labels; no bar code on cover			
❑ GP 26 [(2)]	Bitches Brew	1970	60.00
—"360 Sound Stereo" on red labels			
❑ PG 26 [(2)]	Bitches Brew	1977	15.00
—Orange labels, new prefix; some have bar code on cover			
❑ C2S 820 [(2)]	Miles Davis in Person (Friday & Saturday Nights at the Blackhawk, San Francisco)	1971	15.00
—Orange labels			
❑ C2S 820 [(2)S]	Miles Davis in Person (Friday & Saturday Nights at the Blackhawk, San Francisco)	1961	60.00
—Red and black label with six "eye" logos			
❑ C2S 820 [(2)S]	Miles Davis in Person (Friday & Saturday Nights at the Blackhawk, San Francisco)	1963	30.00
—"360 Sound Stereo" in black on label			
❑ C2S 820 [(2)S]	Miles Davis in Person (Friday & Saturday Nights at the Blackhawk, San Francisco)	1965	25.00
—"360 Sound Stereo" in white on label			
❑ CL 949 [M]	'Round About Midnight	1957	50.00
—Six "eye" logos on label			

Number	Title (A Side/B Side)	Yr	NM
❑ CL 949 [M]	'Round About Midnight	1963	25.00
—"Guaranteed High Fidelity" on label			
❑ CL 949 [M]	'Round About Midnight	1965	20.00
—"Mono" on label			
❑ CL 1041 [M]	Miles Ahead	1957	100.00
—Red and black label with six "eye" logos; cover has Miles Davis blowing his trumpet			
❑ CL 1041 [M]	Miles Ahead	1957	200.00
—Red and black label with six "eye" logos; cover has a while woman and her child on a sailboat			
❑ CL 1041 [M]	Miles Ahead	1963	40.00
—"Guaranteed High Fidelity" on label			
❑ CL 1041 [M]	Miles Ahead	1965	30.00
—"360 Sound Mono" on label			
❑ CL 1193 [M]	Milestones	1958	80.00
—Red and black label with six "eye" logos			
❑ CL 1193 [M]	Milestones	1963	40.00
—"Guaranteed High Fidelity" on label			
❑ CL 1193 [M]	Milestones	1965	25.00
—"360 Sound Mono" on label			
❑ CL 1268 [M]	Jazz Track	1958	70.00
—Red and black label with six "eye" logos; with Miles and a woman on cover			
❑ CL 1268 [M]	Jazz Track	1958	100.00
—Red and black label with six "eye" logos; with abstract drawing on cover			
❑ CL 1274 [M]	Porgy and Bess	1958	50.00
—Six "eye" logos on label			
❑ CL 1274 [M]	Porgy and Bess	1963	25.00
—"Guaranteed High Fidelity" on label			
❑ CL 1274 [M]	Porgy and Bess	1965	20.00
—"Mono" on label			
❑ CL 1355 [M]	Kind of Blue	1959	100.00
—Red and black label with six "eye" logos			
❑ CL 1355 [M]	Kind of Blue	1963	50.00
—"Guaranteed High Fidelity" on label			
❑ CL 1355 [M]	Kind of Blue	1965	30.00
—"360 Sound Mono" on label			
❑ A2S 1374 [(2)DJ]	Miles to Go	1982	40.00
—Promo-only compilation			
❑ CL 1480 [M]	Sketches of Spain	1960	50.00
—Six "eye" logos on label			
❑ CL 1480 [M]	Sketches of Spain	1963	25.00
—"Guaranteed High Fidelity" on label			
❑ CL 1480 [M]	Sketches of Spain	1965	20.00
—"Mono" on label			
❑ CL 1656 [M]	Someday My Prince Will Come	1961	40.00
—Six "eye" logos on label			
❑ CL 1656 [M]	Someday My Prince Will Come	1963	25.00
—"Guaranteed High Fidelity" on label			
❑ CL 1656 [M]	Someday My Prince Will Come	1965	20.00
—"Mono" on label			
❑ CL 1669 [M]	Miles Davis in Person, Vol. 1 (Friday Nights at the Blackhawk, San Francisco)	1961	30.00
—Red and black label with six "eye" logos; later pressings may exist			
❑ CL 1670 [M]	Miles Davis in Person, Vol. 2 (Saturday Nights at the Blackhawk, San Francisco)	1961	30.00
—Six "eye" logos on label; later pressings may exist			
❑ CL 1812 [M]	Miles Davis at Carnegie Hall	1962	50.00
—Red and black label with six "eye" logos			
❑ CL 1812 [M]	Miles Davis at Carnegie Hall	1963	25.00
—"Guaranteed High Fidelity" on label			
❑ CL 1812 [M]	Miles Davis at Carnegie Hall	1965	20.00
—"Mono" on label			
❑ CL 2051 [M]	Seven Steps to Heaven	1963	25.00
—"Guaranteed High Fidelity" on label			
❑ CL 2051 [M]	Seven Steps to Heaven	1965	20.00
—"Mono" on label			
❑ CL 2106 [M]	Quiet Nights	1964	25.00
—"Guaranteed High Fidelity" on label			
❑ CL 2106 [M]	Quiet Nights	1965	20.00
—"Mono" on label			
❑ CL 2183 [M]	Miles Davis in Europe	1964	40.00
—"Guaranteed High Fidelity" on label			
❑ CL 2183 [M]	Miles Davis in Europe	1965	25.00
—"360 Sound Mono" on label			
❑ CL 2306 [M]	My Funny Valentine	1965	20.00
—"Mono" on label			
❑ CL 2306 [M]	My Funny Valentine	1965	25.00
—"Guaranteed High Fidelity" on label			
❑ CL 2350 [M]	E.S.P.	1965	20.00
—"360 Sound Mono" on label			
❑ CL 2350 [M]	E.S.P.	1965	25.00
—"Guaranteed High Fidelity" on label			
❑ CL 2453 [M]	"Four" & More — Recorded Live in Concert	1966	30.00
❑ CL 2601 [M]	Miles Smiles	1966	40.00
❑ CL 2628 [M]	Milestones	1967	30.00
—Reissue of 1193?			
❑ CL 2732 [M]	Sorcerer	1967	30.00
❑ CL 2794 [M]	Nefertiti	1968	50.00
❑ CL 2828 [M]	Miles in the Sky	1968	150.00
❑ CS 8021 [S]	Milestones	1959	200.00
—Red and black label with six "eye" logos			
❑ CS 8021 [S]	Milestones	1963	100.00
—"360 Sound Stereo" in black on label			
❑ CS 8021 [S]	Milestones	1965	60.00
—"360 Sound Stereo" in white on label			
❑ CS 8085	Porgy and Bess	1971	12.00
—Orange label			
❑ CS 8085 [S]	Porgy and Bess	1959	50.00
—Six "eye" logos on label			
❑ CS 8085 [S]	Porgy and Bess	1963	25.00
—"360 Sound Stereo" in black on label			
❑ CS 8085 [S]	Porgy and Bess	1965	20.00
—"360 Sound Stereo" in white on label			
❑ KCS 8085	Porgy and Bess	1974	10.00
—Orange label, new prefix			
❑ PC 8085	Porgy and Bess	1977	8.00
—Orange label, new prefix			
❑ CS 8163	Kind of Blue	1971	20.00
—Orange label			
❑ CS 8163 [(2)]	Kind of Blue	1997	150.00
—Contains both the original Side 1, which was mastered slightly fast, and the "correct" Side 1 (as Side 3), with an alternate take of "Flamenco Sketches" on Side 4 (at 45 rpm); distributed by Classic Records			
❑ CS 8163	Kind of Blue	2001	30.00
—200-gram pressing; distributed by Classic Records; contains Side 1 at its "correct" speed			
❑ CS 8163	Kind of Blue	2002	200.00
—Blue vinyl; 180-gram edition; distributed by Classic Records; 500 copies were pressed			
❑ CS 8163	Kind of Blue	2002	300.00
—Blue vinyl; 200-gram edition; distributed by Classic Records; approximately 100 copies were pressed			
❑ CS 8163 [S]	Kind of Blue	1959	250.00
—Black and red label with "Stereo Fidelity" at top and "Columbia" in white at bottom; six white "eye" logos on label			
❑ CS 8163 [S]	Kind of Blue	1963	60.00
—"360 Sound Stereo" in black on label			
❑ CS 8163 [S]	Kind of Blue	1965	40.00
—"360 Sound Stereo" in white on label			
❑ CS 8163-45 [(4)]	Kind of Blue	1999	100.00
—Distributed by Classic Records; pressed on four single-sided 12-inch 45 rpm records			
❑ KCS 8163	Kind of Blue	1974	12.00
—Orange label, new prefix			
❑ PC 8163	Kind of Blue	1977	8.00
—Orange label, new prefix; some have bar codes			
❑ CS 8271	Sketches of Spain	1971	12.00
—Orange label			
❑ CS 8271 [S]	Sketches of Spain	1960	80.00
—Red and black label with six "eye" logos			
❑ CS 8271 [S]	Sketches of Spain	1963	25.00
—"360 Sound Stereo" in black on label			
❑ CS 8271 [S]	Sketches of Spain	1965	20.00
—"360 Sound Stereo" in white on label			
❑ CS 8271 [S]	Sketces of Spain	1999	25.00
—Audiophile reissue; distributed by Classic Records			
❑ KCS 8271	Sketches of Spain	1974	10.00
—Orange label, new prefix			
❑ PC 8271	Sketches of Spain	1977	8.00
—Orange label, new prefix			
❑ CS 8456	Someday My Prince Will Come	1971	12.00
—Orange label			
❑ CS 8456 [S]	Someday My Prince Will Come	1961	40.00
—Six "eye" logos on label			
❑ CS 8456 [S]	Someday My Prince Will Come	1963	25.00
—"360 Sound Stereo" in black on label			
❑ CS 8456 [S]	Someday My Prince Will Come	1965	20.00
—"360 Sound Stereo" in white on label			
❑ KCS 8456	Someday My Prince Will Come	1974	10.00
—Orange label, new prefix			
❑ PC 8456	Someday My Prince Will Come	1977	8.00
—Orange label, new prefix			
❑ CS 8469 [S]	Miles Davis in Person, Vol. 1 (Friday Nights at the Blackhawk, San Francisco)	1961	30.00
—Red and black label with six "eye" logos; later pressings may exist			
❑ CS 8470 [S]	Miles Davis in Person, Vol. 2 (Saturday Nights at the Blackhawk, San Francisco)	1961	30.00
—Six "eye" logos on label; later pressings may exist			
❑ CS 8612	Miles Davis at Carnegie Hall	1971	15.00
—Orange label			
❑ CS 8612 [S]	Miles Davis at Carnegie Hall	1962	30.00
—"360 Sound Stereo" in black on label			
❑ CS 8612 [S]	Miles Davis at Carnegie Hall	1962	60.00
—Red and black label with six "eye" logos			
❑ CS 8612 [S]	Miles Davis at Carnegie Hall	1965	25.00
—"360 Sound Stereo" in white on label			
❑ KCS 8612	Miles Davis at Carnegie Hall	1974	12.00
—Orange label, new prefix			
❑ PC 8612	Miles Davis at Carnegie Hall	1977	8.00
—Orange label, new prefix; may have bar code on back cover			
❑ PC 8612	Miles Davis at Carnegie Hall	199?	12.00
—180-gram vinyl reissue			
❑ CS 8633	Miles Ahead	1971	12.00
—Orange label			
❑ CS 8633 [R]	Miles Ahead	1963	15.00
—"360 Sound Stereo" in white on label			
❑ CS 8633 [R]	Miles Ahead	1963	20.00
—Rechanneled stereo version of 1041; "360 Sound Stereo" in black on label			
❑ KCS 8633	Miles Ahead	1974	10.00
—Orange label, new prefix			
❑ PC 8633	Miles Ahead	1977	8.00
—Orange label, new prefix; some have bar codes			
❑ CS 8649	'Round About Midnight	1971	12.00
—Orange label			
❑ CS 8649 [R]	'Round About Midnight	1963	12.00
—Rechanneled stereo version of 949			
❑ KCS 8649	'Round About Midnight	1974	10.00
—Orange label, new prefix			
❑ PC 8649	'Round About Midnight	1977	8.00
—Orange label, new prefix			
❑ CS 8851	Seven Steps to Heaven	1971	12.00
—Orange label			
❑ CS 8851 [S]	Seven Steps to Heaven	1963	25.00
—"360 Sound Stereo" in black on label			
❑ CS 8851 [S]	Seven Steps to Heaven	1965	20.00
—"360 Sound Stereo" in white on label			
❑ KCS 8851	Seven Steps to Heaven	1974	10.00
—Orange label, new prefix			
❑ PC 8851	Seven Steps to Heaven	1977	8.00
—Orange label, new prefix			
❑ CS 8906	Quiet Nights	1971	12.00
—Orange label			
❑ CS 8906 [S]	Quiet Nights	1964	25.00
—"360 Sound Stereo" in black on label			
❑ CS 8906 [S]	Quiet Nights	1965	20.00
—"360 Sound Stereo" in white on label			
❑ KCS 8906	Quiet Nights	1974	10.00
—Orange label, new prefix			
❑ PC 8906	Quiet Nights	1977	8.00
—Orange label, new prefix			
❑ CS 8983	Miles Davis in Europe	1971	15.00
—Orange label			
❑ CS 8983 [S]	Miles Davis in Europe	1964	40.00
—"360 Sound Stereo" in black on label			
❑ CS 8983 [S]	Miles Davis in Europe	1965	25.00
—"360 Sound Stereo" in white on label			
❑ KCS 8983	Miles Davis in Europe	1974	12.00
—Orange label, new prefix			
❑ PC 8983	Miles Davis in Europe	1977	8.00
—Orange label, new prefix; some have bar codes			
❑ PC 8983	Miles Davis in Europe	199?	12.00
—180-gram reissue			
❑ CS 9106	My Funny Valentine	1971	12.00
—Orange label			
❑ CS 9106 [S]	My Funny Valentine	1965	20.00
—"360 Sound Stereo" in white on label			
❑ CS 9106 [S]	My Funny Valentine	1965	25.00
—"360 Sound Stereo" in black on label			
❑ KCS 9106	My Funny Valentine	1974	10.00
—Orange label, new prefix			
❑ PC 9106	My Funny Valentine	1977	8.00
—Orange label, new prefix			
❑ CS 9150	E.S.P.	1971	20.00
—Orange label			
❑ CS 9150 [S]	E.S.P.	1965	50.00
—"360 Sound Stereo" in white on label			
❑ CS 9150 [S]	E.S.P.	1965	60.00
—"360 Sound Stereo" in black on label			
❑ KCS 9150	E.S.P.	1974	15.00
—Orange label, new prefix			
❑ PC 9150	E.S.P.	1977	8.00
—Orange label, new prefix; some have bar code on back			
❑ PC 9150	E.S.P.	199?	12.00
—180-gram reissue			
❑ CS 9253	"Four" & More — Recorded Live in Concert	1971	15.00
—Orange label			
❑ CS 9253 [S]	"Four" & More — Recorded Live in Concert	1966	30.00
—"360 Sound Stereo" on red label			
❑ KCS 9253	"Four" & More — Recorded Live in Concert	1974	12.00
—Orange label, new prefix			
❑ PC 9253	"Four" & More — Recorded Live in Concert	1977	8.00
—Orange label, new prefix; some have bar codes			
❑ PC 9253	"Four" & More — Recorded Live in Concert	199?	12.00
—180-gram reissue			
❑ CS 9401	Miles Smiles	1971	15.00
—Orange label			
❑ CS 9401 [S]	Miles Smiles	1966	30.00
—"360 Sound Stereo" on red label			
❑ KCS 9401	Miles Smiles	1974	12.00
—Orange label, new prefix			
❑ PC 9401	Miles Smiles	1977	8.00
—Orange label, new prefix; some have bar codes			
❑ PC 9401	Miles Smiles	199?	12.00
—180-gram reissue			
❑ CS 9428	Milestones	1971	15.00
—Orange label			
❑ CS 9428 [R]	Milestones	1967	25.00
—"360 Sound Stereo" on red label; reissue of 8021			
❑ KCS 9428	Milestones	1974	12.00
—Orange label, new prefix			
❑ PC 9428	Milestones	1977	8.00
—Orange label, new prefix; some have bar codes			
❑ CS 9532	Sorcerer	1971	12.00
—Orange label			
❑ CS 9532 [S]	Sorcerer	1967	20.00
—"360 Sound Stereo" on red label			
❑ KCS 9532	Sorcerer	1974	10.00
—Orange label, new prefix			
❑ PC 9532	Sorcerer	1977	8.00
—Orange label, new prefix			

D

Number	Title (A Side/B Side)	Yr	NM
❑ CS 9594	Nefertiti	1971	12.00
—Orange label			
❑ CS 9594 [S]	Nefertiti	1968	20.00
—"360 Sound Stereo" on red label			
❑ KCS 9594	Nefertiti	1974	10.00
—Orange label, new prefix			
❑ PC 9594	Nefertiti	1977	8.00
—Orange label, new prefix			
❑ CS 9628	Miles in the Sky	1971	15.00
—Orange label			
❑ CS 9628 [S]	Miles in the Sky	1968	25.00
—"360 Sound Stereo" on red label			
❑ KCS 9628	Miles in the Sky	1974	12.00
—Orange label, new prefix			
❑ PC 9628	Miles in the Sky	1977	8.00
—Orange label, new prefix; some have bar codes			
❑ PC 9628	Miles in the Sky	199?	12.00
—180-gram reissue			
❑ CS 9750	Filles de Kilimanjaro	1969	20.00
—"360 Sound Stereo" on red label			
❑ CS 9750	Filles de Kilimanjaro	1971	12.00
—Orange label			
❑ KCS 9750	Filles de Kilimanjaro	1974	10.00
—Orange label, new prefix			
❑ PC 9750	Filles de Kilimanjaro	1977	8.00
—Orange label, new prefix; some have bar codes			
❑ PC 9750	Filles de Kilimanjaro	199?	12.00
—180-gram reissue			
❑ CS 9808	Miles Davis' Greatest Hits	1969	20.00
—"360 Sound Stereo" on red label			
❑ CS 9808	Miles Davis' Greatest Hits	1971	12.00
—Orange label			
❑ KCS 9808	Miles Davis' Greatest Hits	1974	10.00
—Orange label, new prefix			
❑ PC 9808	Miles Davis' Greatest Hits	1977	8.00
—Orange label, new prefix; some have bar codes			
❑ PC 9808	Miles Davis' Greatest Hits	199?	12.00
—180-gram reissue			
❑ CS 9875	In a Silent Way	1969	40.00
—"360 Sound Stereo" on red label			
❑ CS 9875	In a Silent Way	1971	20.00
—Orange label			
❑ KCS 9875	In a Silent Way	1974	12.00
—Orange label, new prefix			
❑ PC 9875	In a Silent Way	1977	8.00
—Orange label, new prefix; some have bar codes			
❑ CG 30038 [(2)]	Miles Davis at Fillmore	197?	15.00
—Later prefix			
❑ G 30038 [(2)]	Miles Davis at Fillmore	1970	25.00
—Original prefix			
❑ KC 30455	A Tribute to Jack Johnson	1971	20.00
—Original issue			
❑ PC 30455	A Tribute to Jack Johnson	1977	8.00
—Orange label, new prefix; some with bar codes			
❑ PC 30455	A Tribute to Jack Johnson	199?	12.00
—180-gram reissue			
❑ S 30455	Jack Johnson	1971	50.00
—Original issue on gray "Masterworks" label			
❑ G 30954 [(2)]	Live-Evil	1971	25.00
—Original edition			
❑ GQ 30954 [(2)Q]	Live-Evil	1973	60.00
❑ GQ 30997 [(2)Q]	Bitches Brew	1972	60.00
❑ KC 31906	On the Corner	1972	12.00
❑ PC 31906	On the Corner	1977	8.00
—Orange label, new prefix			
❑ C 32025	Basic Miles — The Classic Performances of Miles Davis	1973	20.00
—Original prefix			
❑ PC 32025	Basic Miles — The Classic Performances of Miles Davis	198?	8.00
—Budget-line reissue; bar code on cover			
❑ PC 32025	Basic Miles — The Classic Performances of Miles Davis	199?	12.00
—180-gram reissue			
❑ KG 32092 [(2)]	In Concert	1973	25.00
❑ PG 32092 [(2)]	In Concert	1977	15.00
—Orange labels, new prefix			
❑ C 32470	Jazz at the Plaza, Vol. 1	1973	20.00
—Original prefix			
❑ PC 32470	Jazz at the Plaza, Vol. 1	1977	8.00
—Reissue with new prefix; some have bar codes			
❑ PC 32470	Jazz at the Plaza, Vol. 1	199?	12.00
—180-gram reissue			
❑ CG 32866 [(2)]	Big Fun	1974	25.00
—Original prefix			
❑ PG 32866 [(2)]	Big Fun	1977	15.00
—Orange labels, new prefix			
❑ KG 33236 [(2)]	Get Up With It	1974	30.00
—Original prefix			
❑ PG 33236 [(2)]	Get Up With It	1977	20.00
—Orange labels, new prefix			
❑ PG 33967 [(2)]	Agharta	1976	40.00
❑ PC 34396	Water Babies	1977	12.00
—Original has no bar code			
❑ PC 34396	Water Babies	198?	8.00
—Reissue with bar code			
❑ KC2 36278 [(2)]	Circle in the Round	1980	20.00
❑ KC2 36472 [(2)]	Directions	1981	20.00
❑ FC 36790	The Man with the Horn	1981	12.00
—Original edition			
❑ PC 36790	The Man with the Horn	198?	8.00
—Budget-line reissue with new prefix			
❑ PC 36790	The Man with the Horn	199?	12.00
—180-gram reissue			
❑ C6X 36976 [(6)]	The Miles Davis Collection Vol. 1: 12 Sides of Miles	1980	100.00
❑ C2 38005 [(2)]	We Want Miles	1982	12.00
❑ C2 38266 [(2)]	Live at the Plugged Nickel	1982	20.00
❑ C2 38506 [(2)]	Heard 'Round the World	1983	20.00
❑ FC 38657	Star People	1983	10.00
❑ FC 38991	Decoy	1984	12.00
—Original issue			
❑ FC 38991	Decoy	199?	12.00
—180-gram reissue			
❑ FC 40023	You're Under Arrest	1985	10.00
❑ C5X 45000 [(5)]	The Columbia Years 1955-1985	1988	60.00
❑ C2X 45332	Aura	1989	25.00
❑ HC 46790	The Man with the Horn	1982	50.00
—"Half-Speed Mastered" on cover			

COLUMBIA JAZZ MASTERPIECES

Number	Title (A Side/B Side)	Yr	NM
❑ C2J 40577 [(2)]	Bitches Brew	1987	15.00
❑ CJ 40578	Sketches of Spain	1987	10.00
❑ CJ 40579	Kind of Blue	1987	15.00
—Reissue; when this version of the album was prepared, Columbia discovered that all of Side 1 on the original LP was mastered at the wrong speed; this album was the first time it was mastered "correctly"			
❑ CJ 40580	In a Silent Way	1987	10.00
❑ CJ 40580	In a Silent Way	199?	12.00
—180-gram reissue			
❑ CJ 40609	Live Miles: More Music from the Legendary Carnegie Hall Concert	1987	10.00
❑ CJ 40609	Live Miles: More Music from the Legendary Carnegie Hall Concert	199?	12.00
—180-gram reissue			
❑ CJ 40610	'Round About Midnight	1987	10.00
❑ CJ 40645	Cookin' at the Plugged Nickel	1987	15.00
❑ CJ 40647	Porgy and Bess	1987	10.00
❑ CJ 40784	Miles Ahead	1987	10.00
❑ CJ 40784	Miles Ahead	199?	12.00
—180-gram reissue			
❑ CJ 40837	Milestones	1987	10.00
❑ CJ 40837	Milestones	199?	12.00
—180-gram reissue			
❑ CJ 40947	Someday My Prince Will Come	1987	10.00
❑ CJ 44052	Miles and Coltrane	1988	10.00
❑ CJ 44052	Miles and Coltrane	199?	12.00
—180-gram reissue			
❑ CJ 44151	Ballads	1988	10.00
❑ CJ 44151	Ballads	199?	12.00
—180-gram reissue			
❑ CJ 44257	Miles Davis in Person, Vol. 1 (Friday Nights at the Blackhawk, San Francisco)	1988	10.00
❑ CJ 44257	Miles Davis in Person, Vol. 1 (Friday Nights at the Blackhawk, San Francisco)	199?	12.00
—180-gram reissue			
❑ CJ 44425	Miles Davis in Person, Vol. 2 (Saturday Nights at the Blackhawk, San Francisco)	1989	10.00

COLUMBIA LIMITED EDITION

Number	Title (A Side/B Side)	Yr	NM
❑ LE 10018	Miles Davis in Person, Vol. 1 (Friday Nights at the Blackhawk, San Francisco)	197?	15.00
❑ LE 10076	Miles Davis in Person, Vol. 2 (Saturday Nights at the Blackhawk, San Francisco)	197?	15.00

COLUMBIA SPECIAL PRODUCTS

Number	Title (A Side/B Side)	Yr	NM
❑ P 13811	Facets	1977	12.00

CONTEMPORARY

Number	Title (A Side/B Side)	Yr	NM
❑ C-7645	Miles Davis and the Lighthouse All-Stars At Last!	1985	15.00

DEBUT

Number	Title (A Side/B Side)	Yr	NM
❑ DEB 120 [M]	Blue Moods	1955	400.00

EVEREST ARCHIVE OF FOLK & JAZZ

Number	Title (A Side/B Side)	Yr	NM
❑ FS-283	Miles Davis	197?	10.00

FANTASY

Number	Title (A Side/B Side)	Yr	NM
❑ OJC-004	The Musings of Miles	198?	12.00
—Reissue of Prestige 7007			
❑ OJC-005	Dig Miles Davis/Sonny Rollins	198?	12.00
—Reissue of Prestige 7012			
❑ OJC-006	Miles — The New Miles Davis Quintet	198?	12.00
—Reissue of Prestige 7014			
❑ OJC-012	Miles Davis and the Milt Jackson Quintet/Sextet	198?	10.00
—Reissue of Prestige 7034			
❑ OJC-043	Blue Moods	198?	12.00
—Reissue of Fantasy 6001			
❑ OJC-053	Miles Davis and Horns	198?	12.00
—Reissue of Prestige 7025			
❑ OJC-071	Collectors' Item	198?	12.00
—Reissue of Prestige 7044			
❑ OJC-093	Blue Haze	198?	12.00
—Reissue of Prestige 7054			
❑ OJC-128	Cookin' with the Miles Davis Quintet	198?	12.00
—Reissue of Prestige 7094			
❑ OJC-190	Relaxin' with the Miles Davis Quintet	1985	10.00
—Reissue of Prestige 7129			
❑ OJC-213	Walkin'	1987	10.00
—Reissue of Prestige 7076			
❑ OJC-245	Bags Groove	1987	12.00
—Reissue of Prestige 7109			
❑ OJC-296	Workin' with the Miles Davis Quintet	1987	10.00
—Reissue of Prestige 7166			
❑ OJC-347	Miles Davis and the Modern Jazz Giants	198?	12.00
—Reissue of Prestige 7150			
❑ OJC-391	Steamin' with the Miles Davis Quintet	1989	10.00
—Reissue of Prestige 7200			
❑ OJC-480	Miles Davis and the Lighthouse All-Stars At Last!	1991	12.00
—Reissue of Contemporary 7645			
❑ 6001 [M]	Blue Moods	1962	150.00
—Reissue of Debut album; red vinyl			
❑ 6001 [M]	Blue Moods	1963	70.00
—Black vinyl, red label			
❑ 86001 [R]	Blue Moods	1962	60.00
—Blue vinyl			
❑ 86001 [R]	Blue Moods	1963	30.00
—Black vinyl, blue label			

FONTANA

Number	Title (A Side/B Side)	Yr	NM
❑ MGF-27532 [M]	Jazz on the Screen	1965	40.00
—With Art Blakey and the Jazz Messengers			
❑ SRF-67532 [S]	Jazz on the Screen	1965	40.00

JAZZ HERITAGE

Number	Title (A Side/B Side)	Yr	NM
❑ 913427F [M]	Dig Miles Davis/Sonny Rollins	198?	15.00
—Mail-order reissue			

MOBILE FIDELITY

Number	Title (A Side/B Side)	Yr	NM
❑ 1-177	Someday My Prince Will Come	1985	80.00
—Audiophile vinyl			

MOSAIC

Number	Title (A Side/B Side)	Yr	NM
❑ MQ10-158 [(10)]	The Complete Plugged Nickel Sessions	1995	300.00
❑ MQ11-164 [(11)]	Miles Davis & Gil Evans: The Complete Columbia Studio Recordings	1996	400.00
❑ MQ10-177 [(10)]	The Complete Studio Recordings of the Miles Davis Quintet 1965-June 1968	1998	150.00
❑ MQ6-183 [(6)]	The Complete Bitches Brew Sessions	1999	100.00
❑ MQ9-191 [(9)]	The Complete Columbia Recordings of Miles Davis with John Coltrane	2000	170.00
❑ MQ5-209 [(5)]	The Complete In a Silent Way Sessions (September 1968-February 1969)	2002	80.00
❑ MQ6-220 [(6)]	The Complete Blackhawk Sessions	2003	100.00

PAIR

Number	Title (A Side/B Side)	Yr	NM
❑ PDL2-1095 [(2)]	Best of Miles Davis	1986	12.00

PHILIPS

Number	Title (A Side/B Side)	Yr	NM
❑ 836305-1	Elevator to the Scaffold (L'Ancenseur Pour L'Echafaud)	198?	12.00
—Reissue of Columbia 1268			

PRESTIGE

Number	Title (A Side/B Side)	Yr	NM
❑ 16-3 [M]	Miles Davis and the Modern Jazz Giants	1957	1000.
—This album plays at 16 2/3 rpm and is marked as such; white label			
❑ P-12 [(12)]	Chronicle: The Complete Prestige Recordings	1980	150.00
❑ PRLP-124 [10]	The New Sounds of Miles Davis	1952	250.00
❑ PRLP-140 [10]	Blue Period	1953	250.00
❑ PRLP-154 [10]	Miles Davis Plays Al Cohn Compositions	1953	250.00
❑ PRLP-161 [10]	Miles Davis Featuring Sonny Rollins	1953	250.00
❑ PRLP-182 [10]	Miles Davis Sextet	1954	250.00
❑ PRLP-185 [10]	Miles Davis Quintet	1954	250.00
❑ PRLP-187 [10]	Miles Davis Quintet Featuring Sonny Rollins	1954	250.00
❑ PRLP-196 [10]	Miles Davis All Stars, Vol. 1	1955	250.00
❑ PRLP-200 [10]	Miles Davis All Stars, Vol. 2	1955	250.00
❑ PRLP-7007 [M]	The Musings of Miles	1955	400.00
—Yellow label with W. 50th St. address			
❑ PRLP-7012 [M]	Dig Miles Davis/Sonny Rollins	1956	250.00
—Gray cover			
❑ PRLP-7012 [M]	Dig Miles Davis/Sonny Rollins	1957	200.00
—Color cover; yellow label with W. 50th St. address			
❑ PRLP-7014 [M]	Miles — The New Miles Davis Quintet	1956	300.00
—Yellow label with W. 50th St. address			
❑ PRLP-7025 [M]	Miles Davis and Horns	1956	400.00
—Yellow label with W. 50th St. address			

Except when noted otherwise, VG = 25% of NM, and VG+ = 50% of NM. (Example: VG = $2.00, VG+ = $4.00 and NM = $8.00.)

Number	Title (A Side/B Side)	Yr	NM
❑ PRLP-7025 [M]	Miles Davis and Horns	1958	250.00
—Yellow label, Bergenfield, N.J. address			
❑ PRLP-7034 [M]	Miles Davis and the Milt Jackson Quintet/Sextet	1956	400.00
—With W. 50th St. address on yellow label			
❑ PRLP-7034 [M]	Miles Davis and the Milt Jackson Quintet/Sextet	1958	250.00
—Yellow label with Bergenfield, N.J. address			
❑ PRLP-7034 [M]	Miles Davis and the Milt Jackson Quintet/Sextet	196?	40.00
—With trident on blue label			
❑ PRLP-7044 [M]	Collectors' Item	1956	200.00
—With W. 50th St. address on yellow label			
❑ PRLP-7044 [M]	Collectors' Item	196?	40.00
—With trident on blue label			
❑ PRLP-7054 [M]	Blue Haze	1956	200.00
—With W. 50th St. address on yellow label			
❑ PRLP-7054 [M]	Blue Haze	196?	40.00
—With trident on blue label			
❑ PRLP-7076 [M]	All Stars	1957	200.00
—With W. 50th St. address on yellow label			
❑ PRLP-7076 [M]	All Stars	1958	100.00
—With Bergenfield, N.J. address on yellow label			
❑ PRLP-7076 [M]	All Stars	196?	40.00
—With trident on blue label			
❑ PRLP-7094 [M]	Cookin' with the Miles Davis Quintet	1957	300.00
—With W. 50th St. address on yellow label			
❑ PRLP-7094 [M]	Cookin' with the Miles Davis Quintet	1958	120.00
—With Bergenfield, N.J. address on yellow label			
❑ PRLP-7094 [M]	Cookin' with the Miles Davis Quintet	196?	40.00
—With trident on blue label			
❑ PRLP-7109 [M]	Bags Groove	1957	200.00
—With W. 50th St. address on yellow label			
❑ PRLP-7109 [M]	Bags Groove	1958	100.00
—With Bergenfield, N.J. address on yellow label			
❑ PRLP-7109 [M]	Bags Groove	196?	40.00
—With trident on blue label			
❑ PRLP-7129 [M]	Relaxin' with the Miles Davis Quintet	1957	120.00
—With Bergenfield, NJ address on yellow label			
❑ PRLP-7129 [M]	Relaxin' with the Miles Davis Quintet	1957	300.00
—With W. 50th St. address on yellow label			
❑ PRLP-7129 [M]	Relaxin' with the Miles Davis Quintet	196?	40.00
—With trident on blue label			
❑ PRLP-7150 [M]	Miles Davis and the Modern Jazz Giants	1958	250.00
—With Bergenfield, NJ address on yellow label			
❑ PRLP-7150 [M]	Miles Davis and the Modern Jazz Giants	196?	40.00
—With trident on blue label			
❑ PRLP-7166 [M]	Workin' with the Miles Davis Quintet	1959	80.00
—With Bergenfield, NJ address on yellow label			
❑ PRLP-7166 [M]	Workin' with the Miles Davis Quintet	196?	30.00
—With trident on blue label			
❑ PRLP-7168 [M]	Early Miles	1959	150.00
—Reissue of 7025; with Bergenfield, NJ address on yellow label			
❑ PRLP-7168 [M]	Early Miles	196?	40.00
—With trident on blue label			
❑ PRLP-7200 [M]	Steamin' with the Miles Davis Quintet	196?	30.00
—With trident on blue label			
❑ PRLP-7200 [M]	Steamin' with the Miles Davis Quintet	1961	80.00
—With Bergenfield, NJ address on yellow label			
❑ PRLP-7221 [M]	The Beginning	196?	30.00
—With trident on blue label			
❑ PRLP-7221 [M]	The Beginning	1962	50.00
—Reissue of 7007; with Bergenfield, NJ address on yellow label			
❑ PRLP-7254 [M]	The Original Quintet	196?	30.00
—With trident on blue label			
❑ PRLP-7254 [M]	The Original Quintet	1963	50.00
—Reissue of 7014; with Bergenfield, NJ address on yellow label			
❑ PRST-7254 [R]	The Original Quintet	1963	20.00
❑ PRLP-7281 [M]	Diggin'	196?	40.00
—With trident on blue label			
❑ PRLP-7281 [M]	Diggin'	1963	100.00
—Reissue of 7012; with Bergenfield, NJ address on yellow label			
❑ PRST-7281 [R]	Diggin'	1963	25.00
❑ PRLP-7322 [M]	Miles Davis Plays Richard Rodgers	1964	30.00
❑ PRST-7322 [R]	Miles Davis Plays Richard Rodgers	1964	20.00
❑ PRLP-7352 [M]	Miles Davis Plays for Lovers	1965	30.00
❑ PRST-7352 [R]	Miles Davis Plays for Lovers	1965	20.00
❑ PRLP-7373 [M]	Jazz Classics	1965	30.00
❑ PRST-7373 [R]	Jazz Classics	1965	20.00
❑ PRLP-7457 [M]	Miles Davis' Greatest Hits	1967	30.00
❑ PRST-7457 [R]	Miles Davis' Greatest Hits	1967	15.00
❑ PRST-7540 [R]	Odyssey	1968	12.00
—Reissue of 7034			
❑ PRST-7580 [R]	Steamin'	1968	12.00
—Reissue of 7200			
❑ PRST-7608 [R]	Walkin'	1969	12.00
—Reissue of 7076			
❑ PRST-7650 [R]	Miles Davis and the Modern Jazz Giants	1969	20.00
—Reissue of 7150			
❑ PRST-7674 [R]	Early Miles	1969	15.00
—Reissue of 7168			
❑ PRST-7744 [R]	Conception	1970	20.00
❑ PRST-7822 [R]	Miles Ahead!	1971	15.00
❑ PRST-7847	Oleo	1972	12.00
❑ PR-24001 [(2)]	Miles Davis	1972	20.00
❑ 24012 [(2)]	The Tallest Trees	1972	15.00
❑ P-24022 [(2)]	Collector's Items	1973	20.00
❑ 24034 [(2)]	Workin' and Steamin'	1973	15.00
❑ P-24054 [(2)]	Dig	197?	15.00
❑ P-24064 [(2)]	Green Haze	1976	20.00
❑ 24077 [(2)]	Tune Up	197?	12.00

SAVOY JAZZ

Number	Title (A Side/B Side)	Yr	NM
❑ SJL-1196	First Miles	1989	12.00

TRIP

Number	Title (A Side/B Side)	Yr	NM
❑ 5015	Miles of Jazz	1974	10.00

UNITED ARTISTS

Number	Title (A Side/B Side)	Yr	NM
❑ UAS-9952 [(2)]	Miles Davis	1972	20.00
—Reissue of Blue Note material			

WARNER BROS.

Number	Title (A Side/B Side)	Yr	NM
❑ 25490	Tutu	1986	10.00
❑ 25873	Amandla	1989	20.00
❑ 26938	Doo-Bop	1992	15.00

DAVIS, MILES, AND JOHN COLTRANE

Also see each artist's individual listings.

Albums

MOODSVILLE

Number	Title (A Side/B Side)	Yr	NM
❑ MVLP-32 [M]	Miles Davis and John Coltrane Play Richard Rodgers	1963	50.00
—Green label			
❑ MVLP-32 [M]	Miles Davis and John Coltrane Play Richard Rodgers	1965	25.00
—Blue label, trident logo at right			

PRESTIGE

Number	Title (A Side/B Side)	Yr	NM
❑ PRLP-7322 [M]	Miles Davis and John Coltrane Play Rodgers and Hart	1964	40.00
❑ PRST-7322 [R]	Miles Davis and John Coltrane Play Rodgers and Hart	1964	20.00

DAVIS, MILES, AND TADD DAMERON

Albums

COLUMBIA

Number	Title (A Side/B Side)	Yr	NM
❑ JC 34804	Paris Festival International, May 1949	1978	20.00

DAVIS, MILES, AND THELONIOUS MONK

Also see each artist's individual listings.

Albums

COLUMBIA

Number	Title (A Side/B Side)	Yr	NM
❑ CL 2178 [M]	Miles and Monk at Newport	1964	40.00
—"Guaranteed High Fidelity" on label			
❑ CL 2178 [M]	Miles and Monk at Newport	1965	25.00
—"360 Sound Mono" on label			
❑ CS 8978 [S]	Miles and Monk at Newport	1964	60.00
—"360 Sound Stereo" in black on label			
❑ CS 8978 [S]	Miles and Monk at Newport	1965	30.00
—"360 Sound Stereo" in white on label			
❑ KCS 8978	Miles and Monk at Newport	1974	10.00
—Orange label, new prefix			
❑ PC 8978	Miles and Monk at Newport	1977	8.00
—Orange label, new prefix; some have bar codes			
❑ PC 8978	Miles and Monk at Newport	199?	12.00
—180-gram reissue			

DAVIS, SAMMY, JR.

45s

APPLAUSE

Number	Title (A Side/B Side)	Yr	NM
❑ 100	Smoke, Smoke, Smoke (That Cigarette)/We Could Have Been the Closest of Friends	1982	5.00

CAPITOL

Number	Title (A Side/B Side)	Yr	NM
❑ F943	Inka Dinka Doo/Laura	1950	20.00
❑ F1050	I'm Sorry Dear/Dedicated to You	1950	15.00

DDR

Number	Title (A Side/B Side)	Yr	NM
❑ 101/2	Who Needs Spring/ (B-side unknown)	197?	8.00
—Red vinyl			

DECCA

Number	Title (A Side/B Side)	Yr	NM
❑ 29199	Hey There/And This Is My Beloved	1954	12.00
❑ 29200	Because of You (Part 1)/ Because of You (Part 2)	1954	12.00
❑ 29310	Glad to Be Unhappy/Red Grapes	1954	12.00
❑ 29393	The Birth of the Blues/Love	1954	12.00
❑ 29402	All of You/Six Bridges to Cross	1955	12.00
❑ 29484	Love Me or Leave Me/ Something's Gotta Give	1955	12.00
❑ 29541	That Old Black Magic A Man with a Dream	1955	12.00
❑ 29620	I Go for You/A Fine Romance	1955	12.00
—With Carmen McRae			
❑ 29649	Back Track/It's Bigger Than You and Me	1955	12.00
❑ 29672	I'll Know/Adelaide	1955	12.00
❑ 29737	Ac-Cent-Tchu-Ate the Positive/ Beat Me, Daddy, Eight to the Bar	1955	12.00
—With Gary Crosby			
❑ 29759	The Man with the Golden Arm/ In a Persian Blanket	1955	12.00
❑ 29795	Frankie and Johnny/Circus	1956	12.00
❑ 29861	Too Close for Comfort/Jacques d'Iraque	1956	12.00
❑ 29929	Without You I'm Nothing/Get Out of the Car	1956	12.00
❑ 29976	Five/You're Sensational	1956	12.00
❑ 30035	Earthbound/Just One of Those Things	1956	12.00
❑ 30111	New York's My Home/Never Like This	1956	12.00
❑ 30158	All About Love/Dangerous	1956	12.00
❑ 30189	The Golden Key/Long Before I Knew You	1957	10.00
❑ 30300	Good Bye, So Long, I'm Gone/ French Friend Potatoes and Ketchup	1957	10.00
❑ 30371	Doncha Go 'Way Mad/ 'Specially for Little Girls	1957	10.00
❑ 30400	Baby It's Cold Outside/Happy to Make Your Acquaintance	1957	10.00
❑ 30441	Mad Ball/Cool Credo	1957	10.00
❑ 30479	All Dressed Up and No Place to Go/Moment of Madness	1957	10.00
❑ 30536	Hallelujah I Love Her So/I'm Comin' Home	1958	10.00
❑ 30611	No Fool Like an Old Fool/ Unspoken	1958	10.00
❑ 30679	Song and Dance Man/I Ain't Gonna Change	1958	10.00
❑ 30769	That's Anna/I Never Got Out of Paris	1958	10.00
❑ 30898	Fair Warning/You'll Never Get Away from Me	1959	10.00
❑ 30915	I Got Plenty of Nothin'/There's a Boat Dat's Leaving Soon for New York	1959	10.00
❑ 31136	I Got a Woman/Mess Around	1960	10.00
❑ 31177	This Little Girl of Mine/ Face to Face	1960	10.00
❑ 32470	Rhythm of Life/(B-side unknown)	1969	6.00

MGM

Number	Title (A Side/B Side)	Yr	NM
❑ 14320	The Candy Man/I Want to Be Happy	1971	6.00
❑ 14426	Mr. Bojangles/The People Tree	1972	5.00
❑ 14513	(I'd Be) A Legend in My Time/ I'm Not Anyone	1973	5.00
❑ 14685	Singin' in the Rain/ Chattanooga Choo Choo	1973	5.00
❑ 14736	That's Entertainment/ Singin' in the Rain	1974	4.00
❑ 14759	Sing/This Is the House of the People	1974	4.00

MOTOWN

Number	Title (A Side/B Side)	Yr	NM
❑ 1738	Hello Detroit (Part 1)/ Hello Detroit (Part 2)	1984	4.00

REPRISE

Number	Title (A Side/B Side)	Yr	NM
❑ (no #) [DJ]	Here's A Kiss For Christmas (The Christmas Seal Song)/ What Kind Of Fool Am I	1963	15.00
❑ OE-DJ-2 [DJ]	Open End Disc Jockey Interview	196?	40.00
—Small hole, plays at 33 1/3 rpm			
❑ 0248	What Kind of Fool Am I/Gonna Build a Mountain	1963	8.00
❑ 0278	Choose/Bee Bom	1964	8.00
❑ 0289	Not for Me/Night Song	1964	8.00
❑ 0321	Hello, Dolly!/Take the Moment	1964	15.00
—Possibly released only outside the U.S.			
❑ 0322	Don't Shut Me Out/Disorderly Orderly	1964	8.00
❑ 0345	If I Ruled the World/Flash, Bang, Wallop	1965	8.00
❑ 0361	Hello, Dolly!/Take the Moment	1965	8.00
❑ 0370	Unforgettable/No One Can Live Forever	1965	8.00
❑ 0399	Love, At Last You Have Found Me/Courage	1965	8.00
❑ 0416	Yes I Can/Courage	1965	8.00
❑ 0425	If You Want This Love of Mine/ Second-Best Secret Agent in the Whole Wide World	1965	8.00
❑ 0437	Lonely Weekends/More Than One Way	1965	8.00
❑ 0502	All That Jazz/Ev'ry Time We Say Goodbye	1966	6.00
❑ 0521	The Good Life/We'll Be Together Again	1966	6.00

Number	Title (A Side/B Side)	Yr	NM
❑ 0549	The Birth of the Blues/With a Song in My Heart	1967	6.00
❑ 0566	Don't Blame the Children/She Believes in Me	1967	6.00
❑ 0621	Talk to the Animals/Something in Your Smile	1967	6.00
❑ 0673	Lonely Is the Name/Flash, Bang, Wallop	1968	6.00
❑ 0720	What Kind of Fool Am I/Gonna Build a Mountain	1968	4.00
—"Back to Back Hits" series			
❑ 0733	I've Gotta Be Me/Lonely Is the Name	1970	4.00
—"Back to Back Hits" series			
❑ 0757	Break My Mind/Children, Children	1968	6.00
❑ 0779	I've Gotta Be Me/Bein' Natural Bein' Me	1968	8.00
❑ 0827	I Have But One Life to Live/The Goin's Great	1969	6.00
❑ 0989	She Is Today/Runaround	1971	5.00
❑ 20003	I'm a Fool to Want You/Back in Your Own Back Yard	1961	10.00
❑ 20018	One More Time (A Tribute to Ray Charles)/There Was a Tavern in the Town	1961	10.00
❑ 20048	What Kind of Fool Am I/Gonna Build a Mountain	1962	10.00
❑ 20079	The Fool I Used to Be/Everybody Calls Me Joe	1962	10.00
❑ 20087	Once in a Lifetime/Someone Nice Like You	1962	10.00
❑ 20128	Me and My Shadow/Sam's Song	1962	15.00
—A-side: With Frank Sinatra; B-side: With Dean Martin			
❑ 20128 [PS]	Me and My Shadow/Sam's Song	1962	30.00
❑ 20138	As Long As She Needs Me/Two for the Seesaw	1963	10.00
❑ 20212	We Kiss in a Shadow/Bye, Bye Blackbird	1963	10.00
❑ 20216	The Shelter of Your Arms/This Was My Love	1963	10.00
❑ 20227	The Shelter of Your Arms/Falling in Love with Love	1963	20.00
—Released only in England			
20TH CENTURY			
❑ 2236	Snap Your Fingers/Song and Dance Man	1975	4.00
❑ 2282	Chico and the Man (Main Theme)/(I'd Be) A Legend in My Time	1976	5.00
—May be promo only			
❑ 2292	Baretta's Theme (Keep Your Eye on the Sparrow)/I Heard a Song	1976	4.00
UNITED ARTISTS			
❑ 50334	Salt and Pepper/I Like the Way You Dance	1968	6.00
VERVE			
❑ 10219	Ain't That a Kick in the Head/Eee-O Eleven	1960	8.00
WARNER BROS.			
❑ 49047	Showtime/That Old Black Magic	1979	4.00

7-Inch Extended Plays

Number	Title (A Side/B Side)	Yr	NM
DECCA			
❑ ED 2214	Hey There/Glad to Be Unhappy//And This Is My Beloved/Easy to Love	195?	12.00
❑ ED 2214 [PS]	Starring Sammy Davis, Jr., Part 1	195?	12.00
❑ ED 2215	(contents unknown)	195?	12.00
❑ ED 2215 [PS]	Starring Sammy Davis, Jr., Part 2	195?	12.00
❑ ED 2216	*Birth of the Blues (Remake)/Lonesome Road/Because of You (Part 1 and Part 2)	195?	12.00
❑ ED 2216 [PS]	Starring Sammy Davis, Jr., Part 3	195?	12.00
❑ ED 2508	*Begin the Beguine/By Myself/That Old Black Magic/Oo-Shoo-Be-Doo-Be	195?	12.00
❑ ED 2508 [PS]	(title unknown)	195?	12.00
REPRISE			
❑ SR 6214	Come Back to Me/What Now My Love/What The World Needs Now Is Love//What Kind of Fool Am I/I Know a Place/Please Don't Talk About Me When I'm Gone	197?	10.00
—Jukebox issue; small hole, plays at 33 1/3 rpm			
❑ SR 6214 [PS]	The Sounds of '66	197?	10.00
—Part of "Little LP" series (LLP #211); paper envelope; this may also have been issued as a jukebox EP in 1966 with a cardboard cover, but we have no evidence of that at this time			

Albums

Number	Title (A Side/B Side)	Yr	NM
DECCA			
❑ DXB 192 [(2)M]	The Best of Sammy Davis, Jr.	1966	15.00
❑ DL 4153 [M]	Mr. Entertainment	1961	15.00
❑ DL 4381 [M]	Forget-Me-Nots for First Nighters	1963	15.00
❑ DL 4582 [M]	Try a Little Tenderness	1965	12.00
❑ DXSB 7192 [(2)S]	The Best of Sammy Davis, Jr.	1966	20.00
❑ DL 8118 [M]	Starring Sammy Davis, Jr.	1955	30.00
❑ DL 8170 [M]	Just for Lovers	1955	30.00
❑ DL 8351 [M]	Here's Looking at You	1956	25.00
❑ DL 8486 [M]	Sammy Swings	1957	25.00
❑ DL 8641 [M]	It's All Over But the Swingin'	1957	25.00
❑ DL 8676 [M]	Mood to Be Wooed	1958	25.00
❑ DL 8779 [M]	All the Way And Then Some	1958	25.00
❑ DL 8841 [M]	Sammy Davis, Jr., at Town Hall	1959	20.00
❑ DL 8854 [M]	Porgy and Bess	1959	20.00
❑ DL 8921 [M]	The Sammy Awards	1960	20.00
❑ DL 8981 [M]	I Got a Right to Swing	1960	20.00
❑ DL 74153 [S]	Mr. Entertainment	1961	20.00
❑ DL 74381 [S]	Forget-Me-Nots for First Nighters	1963	20.00
❑ DL 74582 [S]	Try a Little Tenderness	1965	15.00
❑ DL 78841 [S]	Sammy Davis, Jr., at Town Hall	1959	25.00
❑ DL 78854 [S]	Porgy and Bess	1959	25.00
❑ DL 78921 [S]	The Sammy Awards	1960	25.00
❑ DL 78981 [S]	I Got a Right to Swing	1960	25.00
HARMONY			
❑ HS 11299	The Great Sammy Davis, Jr.	196?	12.00
❑ HS 11365	Let There Be Love	1970	10.00
❑ H 30568	What Kind of Fool Am I	1971	10.00
MCA			
❑ 4109 [(2)]	Sammy Davis Jr. At His Greatest	1975	12.00
MGM			
❑ SE-4832	Sammy Davis Jr. Now	1972	10.00
❑ SE-4852	Portrait of Sammy Davis, Jr.	1972	10.00
❑ M3G-4965	That's Entertainment!	1974	10.00
MOTOWN			
❑ MS 710	Something for Everyone	1970	12.00
❑ 4519 ML	Hello Detroit!	1984	10.00
PICKWICK			
❑ SPC-3002	The Many Faces of Sammy Davis, Jr.	196?	10.00
REPRISE			
❑ R-2003 [M]	The Wham of Sam	1961	15.00
❑ R9-2003 [S]	The Wham of Sam	1961	20.00
❑ R-2010 [M]	Sammy Davis, Jr., Belts the Best of Broadway	1962	15.00
❑ R9-2010 [S]	Sammy Davis, Jr., Belts the Best of Broadway	1962	20.00
❑ R-6033 [M]	All Star Spectacular	1962	15.00
❑ R9-6033 [S]	All Star Spectacular	1962	20.00
❑ R-6051 [M]	What Kind of Fool Am I and Other Show-Stoppers	1962	15.00
❑ R9-6051 [S]	What Kind of Fool Am I and Other Show-Stoppers	1962	20.00
❑ R-6063 [(2)M]	Sammy Davis Jr. at the Cocoanut Grove	1963	20.00
❑ R9-6063 [(2)S]	Sammy Davis Jr. at the Cocoanut Grove	1963	25.00
❑ R-6082 [M]	As Long As She Needs Me	1963	15.00
❑ R9-6082 [S]	As Long As She Needs Me	1963	20.00
❑ R-6095 [M]	Sammy Davis Jr. Salutes the Stars of the London Palladium	1964	15.00
❑ RS-6095 [S]	Sammy Davis Jr. Salutes the Stars of the London Palladium	1964	20.00
❑ R-6096 [M]	Treasury of Golden Hits	1964	15.00
❑ RS-6096 [S]	Treasury of Golden Hits	1964	20.00
❑ R-6114 [M]	The Shelter of Your Arms	1964	15.00
❑ RS-6114 [S]	The Shelter of Your Arms	1964	20.00
❑ R-6126 [M]	California Suite	1964	15.00
❑ RS-6126 [S]	California Suite	1964	20.00
❑ R-6131 [M]	Sammy Davis Jr. Sings the Big Ones for Young Lovers	1964	12.00
❑ RS-6131 [S]	Sammy Davis Jr. Sings the Big Ones for Young Lovers	1964	15.00
❑ R-6144 [M]	When the Feeling Hits You	1965	12.00
❑ RS-6144 [S]	When the Feeling Hits You	1965	15.00
❑ R-6159 [M]	If I Ruled the World	1965	12.00
❑ RS-6159 [S]	If I Ruled the World	1965	15.00
❑ R-6164 [M]	The Nat Cole Song Book	1965	12.00
❑ RS-6164 [S]	The Nat Cole Song Book	1965	15.00
❑ R-6169 [M]	Sammy's Back on Broadway	1965	12.00
❑ RS-6169 [S]	Sammy's Back on Broadway	1965	15.00
❑ R-6188 [M]	The Sammy Davis, Jr., Show	1965	12.00
❑ RS-6188 [S]	The Sammy Davis, Jr., Show	1965	15.00
❑ R-6214 [M]	The Sounds of '66	1966	12.00
❑ RS-6214 [S]	The Sounds of '66	1966	15.00
❑ R-6236 [M]	Sammy Davis. Jr., Sings/Laurindo Almeida Plays	1966	12.00
❑ RS-6236 [S]	Sammy Davis. Jr., Sings/Laurindo Almeida Plays	1966	15.00
❑ R-6237 [(2)M]	That's All	1967	15.00
❑ RS-6237 [(2)S]	That's All	1967	20.00
❑ R-6264 [M]	Sammy Davis Jr. Sings the Complete Dr. Dolittle	1967	20.00
❑ RS-6264 [S]	Sammy Davis Jr. Sings the Complete Dr. Dolittle	1967	12.00
❑ RS-6291	Sammy Davis, Jr.'s Greatest Hits	1968	12.00
❑ RS-6308	Lonely Is the Name	1968	12.00
❑ RS-6324	I've Gotta Be Me	1969	12.00
❑ RS-6339	The Goin's Great	1969	12.00
❑ RS-6410	Sammy Davis, Jr., Steps Out	1970	12.00
WARNER BROS.			
❑ BSK 3128	Live Performance	1977	10.00
WARNER SPECIAL PRODUCTS			
❑ OP-1501	The Sound of Sammy	1978	10.00
—Special item for Alka-Seltzer			

DAVIS, SAMMY, JR., AND COUNT BASIE

Also see each artist's individual listings.

Albums

Number	Title (A Side/B Side)	Yr	NM
MGM			
❑ SE-4825	Sammy Davis Jr. and Count Basie	1972	10.00
—Reissue of Verve LP?			
VERVE			
❑ V-8605 [M]	Our Shining Hour	1965	12.00
❑ V6-8605 [S]	Our Shining Hour	1965	15.00

DAVIS, SAMMY, JR., AND CARMEN MCRAE

Albums

Number	Title (A Side/B Side)	Yr	NM
DECCA			
❑ DL 8490 [M]	Boy Meets Girl	1957	30.00

DAVIS, SPENCER, GROUP

Includes Spencer Davis solo. Also see STEVE WINWOOD.

45s

Number	Title (A Side/B Side)	Yr	NM
ATCO			
❑ 6400	Keep On Running/High Time Baby	1966	15.00
❑ 6416	Somebody Help Me/Stevie's Blues	1966	15.00
FONTANA			
❑ 1960	I Can't Stand It/Midnight Train	1964	15.00
UNITED ARTISTS			
❑ SP 78 [DJ]	Voter Registration Promo Spot (:60 with music)/(:30 without music)	1972	15.00
❑ 0115	Gimme Some Lovin'/Keep On Running	1973	4.00
—"Silver Spotlight Series" reissue			
❑ 0116	I'm a Man/Somebody Help Me	1973	4.00
—"Silver Spotlight Series" reissue			
❑ 1668	I'm a Man/I Can't Get Enough of It	196?	5.00
—Silver Spotlight Series			
❑ 50108	Gimme Some Lovin'/Blues in F	1966	12.00
❑ 50144	I'm a Man/Can't Get Enough of It	1967	12.00
❑ 50162	Somebody Help Me/On the Green Light	1967	10.00
❑ 50202	Time Seller/Don't Want You No More	1967	10.00
❑ 50202 [PS]	Time Seller/Don't Want You No More	1967	20.00
❑ 50286	Looking Back/After Tea	1968	10.00
❑ 50922	Listen to the Rhythm/Sunday Walk in the Rain	1972	6.00
—Spencer Davis solo			
❑ 50993	Rainy Season/Tumble-Down Tenement Row	1972	6.00
—Spencer Davis solo			
VERTIGO			
❑ 110	Don't You Let It Bring You Down/Today Gluggo, Tomorrow the World	1973	5.00
❑ 112	Living in a Back Street/Need a Helping Hand	1974	5.00

Albums

Number	Title (A Side/B Side)	Yr	NM
ALLEGIANCE			
❑ AV-442	Crossfire	1983	10.00
DATE			
❑ TES-4021	Funky	1971	150.00
—Deleted almost immediately upon release			
MEDIARTS			
❑ 41-11	It's Been So Long	1971	12.00
RHINO			
❑ RNLP 117	The Best of the Spencer Davis Group	1983	8.00
❑ RNLP 70172	The Best of the Spencer Davis Group (Golden Archive Series)	1987	12.00
UNITED ARTISTS			
❑ UA-LA433-E	The Very Best of the Spencer Davis Group	1975	10.00
❑ UAL 3578 [M]	Gimme Some Lovin'	1967	50.00
❑ UAL 3589 [M]	I'm a Man	1967	40.00
❑ UAS 6578 [R]	Gimme Some Lovin'	1967	40.00
❑ UAS 6589 [P]	I'm a Man	1967	50.00

Number	Title (A Side/B Side)	Yr	NM
❑ UAS 6641 [P]	The Spencer Davis Group's Greatest Hits	1968	25.00
❑ UAS 6652	With Their New Face On	1968	20.00
❑ UAS 6691	Heavies	1969	20.00
❑ ST-91127 [R]	Gimme Some Lovin'	1967	50.00
—Capitol Record Club edition			
VERTIGO			
❑ VEL-1015	Gluggo	1973	12.00
❑ VEL-1021	Living in a Back Street	1974	12.00

DAVIS, TYRONE

45s

Number	Title (A Side/B Side)	Yr	NM
ABC			
❑ 11030	Bet You Win/What If a Man	1967	12.00
COLUMBIA			
❑ 02269	Just My Luck/Let's Be Closer Together	1981	4.00
❑ 02634	Leave Well Enough Alone/ I Won't Let Go	1981	4.00
❑ 10388	Give It Up (Turn It Loose)/ You're Too Much	1976	5.00
❑ 10457	Close to You/Wrong Doers	1976	5.00
❑ 10528	This I Swear/Givin' Myself to You	1977	5.00
❑ 10604	All You Got/I Got Carried Away	1977	5.00
❑ 10684	Get It Up (Disco)/It's You, It's You	1978	5.00
❑ 10773	Can't Help But Say/Bunky	1978	4.00
❑ 10904	In the Mood/I Can't Wait	1979	4.00
❑ 11035	Ain't Nothing I Can Do/ The Love I Need	1979	4.00
❑ 11128	Be With Me/Love You Forever	1979	4.00
❑ 11199	Can't You Tell It's Me/I Don't Think You Heard Me	1980	4.00
❑ 11246	Keep On Dancin'/Heart Failure	1980	4.00
❑ 11344	How Sweet It Is (To Be Loved By You)/I Can't Wait	1980	4.00
❑ 11415	I Just Can't Keep On Going/ We Don't Need No Music	1980	4.00
DAKAR			
❑ 602	Can I Change My Mind/A Woman Needs to Be Loved	1968	10.00
❑ 605	Is It Something You've Got/ Undying Love	1969	8.00
❑ 609	All the Waiting Is Not in Vain/ Need Your Lovin' Everybody	1969	8.00
❑ 611	If It's Love That You're After/ When I'm Not Around	1969	8.00
❑ 615	If I Didn't Love You/You Can't Keep a Good Man Down	1969	8.00
❑ 616	Turn Back the Hands of Time/ I Keep Coming Back	1970	8.00
❑ 618	I'll Be Right Here/ Just Because of You	1970	6.00
❑ 621	Let Me Back In/Love Bones	1970	6.00
❑ 623	Could I Forget You/Just My Way of Loving You	1971	6.00
❑ 624	One-Way Ticket/We Got a Love	1971	6.00
❑ 626	You Keep Me Holding On/We Got a Love No One Can Deny	1971	6.00
❑ 1452	Can I Change My Mind/A Woman Needs to Be Loved	1968	12.00
❑ 4501	I Had It All the Time/You Wouldn't Believe	1972	5.00
❑ 4507	Was I Just a Fool/After All This Time	1972	5.00
❑ 4510	Come and Get This Ring/After All This Time	1972	5.00
❑ 4513	If You Had a Change in Mind/ Was It Just a Feelin'	1972	5.00
❑ 4519	Without You in My Life/ How Could I Forget You	1973	5.00
❑ 4523	There It Is/You Wouldn't Believe	1973	5.00
❑ 4526	Wrapped Up in Your Warm and Tender Love/True Love Is Hard to Find	1973	5.00
❑ 4529	I Wish It Was Me/You Don't Have to Beg Me to Stay	1974	5.00
❑ 4532	What Goes Up (Must Come Down)/There's Got to Be an Answer	1974	5.00
❑ 4536	Happiness Is Being with You/ Where Lovers Meet	1974	5.00
❑ 4538	I Can't Make It Without You/You Wouldn't Believe	1974	5.00
❑ 4541	Homewreckers/This Time	1975	5.00
❑ 4545	A Woman Needs to Be Loved/ Just Because of You (I Can See My Way Through)	1975	5.00
❑ 4550	Turning Point/Don't Let It Be Too Late	1975	5.00
❑ 4553	So Good (To Be Home with You)/I Can't Bump	1976	5.00
❑ 4558	I Can't Bump, Part 2/ Saving My Love for You	1976	5.00
❑ 4561	Ever Lovin' Girl/Forever	1976	5.00
❑ 4563	Where Lovers Meet (At the Dark End of the Street)/ It's All in the Game	1977	5.00
FUTURE			
❑ 101	Sexy Thing/Save Me	1987	5.00
❑ 102	I'm in Love Again/Serious Love	1987	4.00
❑ 103	Do You Feel It/(Instrumental)	1988	4.00
❑ 104	It's a Miracle/Wrong Doers	1988	4.00
❑ 204	Flashin' Back/Flashin' Back (LP Version)	1988	4.00
HIGHRISE			
❑ 2005	Are You Serious/Overdrive	1982	4.00
❑ 2009	A Little Bit of Loving (Goes a Long Way)/Where Did We Lose	1983	4.00
ICHIBAN			
❑ 139	Can I Change My Mind/Hey There Lonely Girl	1989	4.00
—B-side by Eddie Holman			
❑ 226	I'll Always Love You/Can I Change My Mind	1991	3.00
❑ 237	Mom's Apple Pie/Do U Still Love Me	1991	3.00
❑ 255	Something's Mighty Wrong/ Let Me Love You	1992	3.00
❑ 261	Running In and Out of My Life/ I've Gotta Get Over You	1992	3.00
❑ 273	Don't Make Me Choose/ Ain't Gonna Get It	1992	3.00
❑ 285	It's a Miracle/Do You Feel It	1993	3.00
❑ 292	I Found Myself When I Lost You/ Something About a Woman	1993	3.00
OCEAN-FRONT			
❑ 2001	I Found Myself When I Lost You/(Instrumental)	1983	4.00
❑ 2004	Let Me Be Your Pacifier/ Turning Point	1984	4.00

Albums

Number	Title (A Side/B Side)	Yr	NM
COLUMBIA			
❑ PC 34268	Love and Touch	1976	12.00
❑ PC 34654	Let's Be Closer Together	1977	12.00
❑ JC 35305	I Can't Go On This Way	1978	12.00
❑ JC 35723	In the Mood with Tyrone Davis	1979	12.00
❑ JC 36230	Can't You Tell It's Me	1979	12.00
❑ JC 36598	I Just Can't Keep On Going	1980	12.00
❑ FC 37366	Everything in Place	1981	12.00
❑ PC 37979	The Best of Tyrone Davis	1982	10.00
DAKAR			
❑ DK-9005	Can I Change My Mind	1969	30.00
❑ DK-9027	Turn Back the Hands of Time	1970	30.00
❑ DK-76901	I Had It All the Time	1972	30.00
❑ DK-76902	Tyrone Davis' Greatest Hits	1972	25.00
❑ DK-76904	Without You in My Life	1973	25.00
❑ DK-76909	It's All in the Game	1974	20.00
❑ DK-76915	Homewrecker	1975	20.00
❑ DK-76918	Turning Point	1976	20.00
EPIC			
❑ PE 38626	Tyrone Davis' Greatest Hits	1983	8.00
HIGHRISE			
❑ 103	Tyrone Davis	1982	10.00
ICHIBAN			
❑ ICH 1103	I'll Always Love You	1991	12.00

DAVIS SISTERS, THE

SKEETER DAVIS and Betty Davis (replaced by Georgia Davis).

45s

Number	Title (A Side/B Side)	Yr	NM
FORTUNE			
❑ 170	Jealous Love/Going Down the Road	1952	40.00
—B-side by Roy Hall			
❑ 174	Kaw-Liga/Sorrow and Pain	1952	25.00
❑ 175	Heartbreak Ahead/Steelwood	1952	25.00
RCA VICTOR			
❑ 47-5345	I Forgot More Than You'll Ever Know/Rock-a-Bye Boogie	1953	25.00
❑ 47-5460	You're Gone/Sorrow and Pain	1953	15.00
❑ 47-5607	Takin' Time Out for Tears/ Gotta Get a-Goin'	1954	15.00
❑ 47-5701	You Weren't Ashamed to Kiss Me Last Night/Foggy Mountain Top	1954	15.00
❑ 47-5843	Show Me/Just Like Me	1954	15.00
❑ 47-5906	The Christmas Boogie/ Tomorrow I'll Cry	1954	15.00
❑ 47-5966	Everlovin'/Tomorrow's Just Another Day to Cry	1954	15.00
❑ 47-6086	Fiddle Diddle Diddle/ Come Back to Me	1955	15.00
❑ 47-6187	I'll Get Him Back/I've Closed the Door	1955	15.00
❑ 47-6291	Baby Be Mine/It's the Girl Who Gets the Blame	1955	15.00
❑ 47-6409	Don't Take HIm for Granted/ Blues for Company	1956	15.00
❑ 47-6490	Lonely and Blue/ Lying Brown Eyes	1956	15.00

Selected 78s

Number	Title (A Side/B Side)	Yr	NM
RCA VICTOR			
❑ 20-5906	The Christmas Boogie/ Tomorrow I'll Cry	1954	12.00

DAWE, TIM

Also see IRON BUTTERFLY.

Albums

Number	Title (A Side/B Side)	Yr	NM
STRAIGHT			
❑ STS-1058	Penrod	1969	75.00
WARNER BROS.			
❑ WS 1841	Penrod	1970	15.00

DAWN (1)

Includes "Dawn featuring Tony Orlando" and "Tony Orlando and Dawn." Records on Apt, Cadet, Laurie, Rust and United Artists are by different perfomers who are outside the scope of this book. Also see TONY ORLANDO. One-man, two-woman vocal group featuring TONY ORLANDO. Includes records issued as "Dawn Featuring Tony Orlando" and "Tony Orlando and Dawn."

45s

Number	Title (A Side/B Side)	Yr	NM
ARISTA			
❑ 0105	Gimme a Good Old Mammy Song/Little Heads in Bunk Beds	1975	4.00
❑ 0156	Skybird/That's the Way a Wallflower Grows	1975	4.00
❑ 0301	Tie a Yellow Ribbon Round the Ole Oak Tree/Say, Has Anybody Seen My Sweet Gypsy Rose	1978	4.00
BELL			
❑ 903	Candida/Look At...	1970	6.00
❑ 938	Knock Three Times/Home	1970	6.00
❑ 970	I Play and Sing/Get Out from Where We Are	1971	5.00
❑ 45107	Summer Sand/The Sweet Soft Sounds of Love	1971	5.00
❑ 45141	What Are You Doing Sunday/The Sweet Soft Sounds of Love	1971	5.00
❑ 45175	Runaway-Happy Together/ Don't Act Like a Baby	1972	5.00
❑ 45225	Vaya Con Dios/I Can't Believe How Much I Love You	1972	5.00
❑ 45285	You're a Lady/In the Park	1972	4.00
❑ 45318	Tie a Yellow Ribbon Round the Ole Oak Tree/I Can't Believe How Much I Love You	1973	5.00
❑ 45374	Say, Has Anybody Seen My Sweet Gypsy Rose/The Spark of Love Is Kindlin'	1973	4.00
❑ 45424	Who's in the Strawberry Patch with Sally/Ukulele Man	1973	4.00
❑ 45450	It Only Hurts When I Try to Smile/ Sweet Summer Days of My Life	1974	4.00
❑ 45601	Steppin' Out (Gonna Boogie Tonight)/She Can't Hold a Candle to You	1974	4.00
—As "Tony Orlando and Dawn"			
❑ 45620	Look in My Eyes Pretty Woman/ My Love Has No Pride	1974	4.00
ELEKTRA			
❑ 45240	He Don't Love You (Like I Love You)/Pick It Up	1975	4.00
❑ 45260	Mornin' Beautiful/Dance, Rosalie, Dance	1975	4.00
❑ 45275	You're All I Need to Get By/ Know You Like a Book	1975	4.00
❑ 45302	Cupid/You're Growin' on Me	1976	4.00
❑ 45319	Midnight Love Affair/ The Selfish Ones	1976	4.00
❑ 45387	Sing/Sweet on Candy	1977	4.00
❑ 45432	Growin' on Me/You're All I Need to Get By	1977	4.00
❑ 45501	Bring It On Home to Me/ Don't Let Go	1978	4.00
❑ 45542	I Count the Tears/ A Lover's Question	1978	4.00
❑ 45542	I Count the Tears/This Is Rock and Roll	1978	4.00

Albums

Number	Title (A Side/B Side)	Yr	NM
ARISTA			
❑ AL 4045	Greatest Hits	1975	10.00
❑ AQ 4045 [Q]	Greatest Hits	1975	15.00
❑ AL 4059	Skybird	1975	10.00
❑ A2L 9006 [(2)]	The World of Tony Orlando and Dawn	1977	12.00
BELL			
❑ 1112	Tuneweaving	1973	10.00
❑ 1130	Dawn's New Ragtime Follies	1973	10.00
❑ 1317	Prime Time	1974	10.00
❑ 1320	Candida & Knock Three Times	1974	10.00
—Reissue of 6052			
❑ 1322	Tony Orlando & Dawn II	1974	10.00
—Reissue of 6069			
❑ 6052	Candida	1970	12.00
❑ 6069	Dawn Featuring Tony Orlando	1971	12.00

Number	Title (A Side/B Side)	Yr	NM
ELEKTRA			
❑ 7E-1034	He Don't Love You (Like I Love You)	1975	10.00
❑ EQ-1034 [Q]	He Don't Love You (Like I Love You)	1975	15.00
❑ 7E-1049	To Be with You	1976	10.00
❑ EQ-1049 [Q]	To Be with You	1976	15.00

DAWN (2)
Girl group.

Number	Title (A Side/B Side)	Yr	NM
45s			
ABC-PARAMOUNT			
❑ 10791	Baby's Gone Away/Gotta Get Away	1966	8.00
APT			
❑ 25088	Can't Get Him Off My Mind/Two of a Kind	1965	15.00

DAWN (3)
Said to be THE FIVE DISCS in disguise.

Number	Title (A Side/B Side)	Yr	NM
45s			
LAURIE			
❑ 3388	I'm Afraid They're All Talking About Me/Lovers' Melody	1967	12.00
❑ 3417	Sandy/For the Love of Money	1968	12.00
RUST			
❑ 5128	Baby I Love You/Bring It On Home	1968	12.00

DAWN (U)
Definitely not groups (1) or (3), these may be by group (2), but we're not sure.

Number	Title (A Side/B Side)	Yr	NM
45s			
CADET			
❑ 5644	The Fifth Day of June/Ballad of Gene	1969	6.00
GAMBLE			
❑ 4002	Ba Ba Ba De Ba (On the Way Through My Mind)/In Love Again	1969	6.00
❑ 4002 [PS]	Ba Ba Ba De Ba (On the Way Through My Mind)/In Love Again	1969	12.00
UNITED ARTISTS			
❑ 50096	Love Is a Magic Word/How Can I Get Off This Merry-Go-Round	1966	12.00

DAWSON, RON

Number	Title (A Side/B Side)	Yr	NM
45s			
COLUMBIA			
❑ 4-44757	If Baby's Still on My Mind/The Dark Side of Lovin' You	1969	8.00
❑ 4-44978	She Cried/Steel Rail Blues	1969	8.00

DAWSON, RONNIE

Number	Title (A Side/B Side)	Yr	NM
45s			
BACK BEAT			
❑ 522	Action Packed/I Make the Love	1958	100.00
—As "Ronnie Dee"			
MAVERICK			
❑ 101	My Big Desire/How Can We Tell Her	1961	200.00
ROCKIN'			
❑ 1	Rockin' Bones/Congratulations to Me	1959	400.00
—Reproductions of this record exist			
SWAN			
❑ 4047	Ain't That a Kick in the Head/Hazel	1960	20.00
❑ 4054	Summer's Comin'/Decided by the Angels	1960	20.00

DAY, BING

Number	Title (A Side/B Side)	Yr	NM
45s			
FEDERAL			
❑ 12320	Pony Tail Partner/Since You Left Me	1958	70.00
MERCURY			
❑ 71446	I Can't Help It/Mama's Place	1959	60.00
❑ 71494	How Do I Do It/Mary's Place	1959	20.00

DAY, BOBBY

Number	Title (A Side/B Side)	Yr	NM
45s			
CASH			
❑ 1031	The Truth Hurts/Let's Live Together As One	1956	100.00
—As "Bobby Byrd and the Birds"			
CLASS			
❑ 207	Come Seven/So Long Baby	1957	20.00
❑ 211	Little Bitty Pretty One/When the Swallows Come Back to Capistrano	1957	25.00
❑ 215	Beep-Beep-Beep/Darling, If I Had You	1957	20.00
❑ 225	Little Turtle Dove/Saving My Life for You	1958	20.00
❑ 229	Rock-N Robin/Over and Over	1958	30.00
❑ 241	The Bluebird, the Buzzard, and the Oriole/Alone Too Long	1959	20.00
❑ 245	That's All I Want/Say Yes	1959	15.00
❑ 252	Mr. and Mrs. Rock & Roll/Gotta New Girl	1959	15.00
❑ 255	Ain't Gonna Cry No More/Love Is a One-Time Affair	1959	15.00
❑ 257	Unchained Melody/Three Young Rebs from Georgia	1959	15.00
❑ 263	My Blue Heaven/I Don't Want To	1960	15.00
❑ 705	Don't Leave Me Hangin' on a String/When I Started Dancin'	1965	12.00
CORVET			
❑ 1017	Why/Gotta Girl	1958	60.00
—As "Bobby Byrd and the Impalas"			
JAMIE			
❑ 1039	Bippin' and Boppin' Over You/Strawberry Stomp	1957	30.00
—As "Robert Byrd and His Birdies"			
RCA VICTOR			
❑ 47-8133	Another Country, Another World/Know-It-All	1963	10.00
❑ 47-8196	Buzz Buzz Buzz/Pretty Little Girl Next Door	1963	10.00
❑ 47-8230	Down on My Knees/Jole Blon, Little Darling	1963	10.00
❑ 47-8316	When I See My Baby Smile/On the Street Where You Live	1964	10.00
RENDEZVOUS			
❑ 130	Teenage Philosopher/Undecided	1960	12.00
❑ 133	Rockin' Robin/Over and Over	1960	12.00
❑ 136	Gee Whiz/Over and Over	1960	12.00
❑ 146	I Need Help/Life Can Be Beautiful	1961	12.00
❑ 158	King's Highway/What Fools We Mortals Be	1961	12.00
❑ 167	Don't Worry 'Bout Me/Oop-E-Du-Pers Ball	1962	12.00
❑ 175	Undecided/Slow Pokey Joe	1962	12.00
SAGE AND SAND			
❑ 203	Please Don't Hurt Me/Delicious Are Your Kisses	1955	40.00
—As "Bobby Byrd"			
SPARK			
❑ 501	Bippin' and Boppin' Over You/Strawberry Stomp	1957	50.00
—As "Robert Byrd and His Birdies"			
SURE SHOT			
❑ 5036	So Lonely/Spicks and Specks	1967	8.00
ZEPHYR			
❑ 70-018	If We Should Meet Again/Looby Loo	1957	30.00
—As "Bobby Byrd"			
Albums			
CLASS			
❑ LP-5002 [M]	Rockin' with Robin	1959	400.00
COLLECTABLES			
❑ COL-5074	Golden Classics	198?	10.00
RENDEZVOUS			
❑ M-1312 [M]	Rockin' with Robin	196?	80.00
RHINO			
❑ RNDF-208	The Best of Bobby Day	1984	12.00

DAY, DARLENE

Number	Title (A Side/B Side)	Yr	NM
45s			
MUSIC MAKERS			
❑ 106	I Love You So/Will	1961	100.00

DAY, DAVE DIDDLE

Number	Title (A Side/B Side)	Yr	NM
45s			
FEE BEE			
❑ 212	Blue Moon Baby/Suzanne My Love	1958	25.00
❑ 215	Jelly Belly/Deep in My Heart	1958	25.00
❑ 219	Motorcycle Mike/Tired of Waiting	1958	15.00
MERCURY			
❑ 71114	Blue Moon Baby/Suzanne My Love	1957	150.00

DAY, JOHNNY
May or may not be the same singer as JOHNNY DAYE.

Number	Title (A Side/B Side)	Yr	NM
45s			
CAMEO			
❑ 371	I've Made Up My Mind/Something Little	1965	20.00

DAY, LITTLE SUNNY, AND THE CLOUDS

Number	Title (A Side/B Side)	Yr	NM
45s			
TANDEM			
❑ 7001	Lou Ann/Baby Doll	1961	400.00

DAY, TERRY
See TERRY MELCHER.

DAY BLINDNESS

Number	Title (A Side/B Side)	Yr	NM
Albums			
STUDIO 10			
❑ DBX-101	Day Blindness	1969	60.00

DAYBREAKERS, THE (1)

Number	Title (A Side/B Side)	Yr	NM
45s			
ALADDIN			
❑ 3434	I Wonder Why/Up, Up and Away	1958	40.00
LAMP			
❑ 2016	I Wonder Why/Up, Up and Away	1958	60.00

DAYBREAKERS, THE (2)

Number	Title (A Side/B Side)	Yr	NM
45s			
DIAL			
❑ 4066	Psychedelic Siren/Afterthoughts	1967	30.00

DAYE, EDDIE, AND 4 BARS

Number	Title (A Side/B Side)	Yr	NM
45s			
SHRINE			
❑ 112	Guess Who Loves You/What Am I Gonna Do	1966	1000.

DAYE, JOHNNY
May or may not be the same as JOHNNY DAY.

Number	Title (A Side/B Side)	Yr	NM
45s			
BLUE STAR			
❑ 230	I'll Keep On Loving You/One of These Days	196?	150.00
JOMADA			
❑ 600	Marry Me/Give Me Back My Ring	1965	10.00
❑ 603	Good Time/I've Got Soul	1966	15.00
PARKWAY			
❑ 119	A Lot of Progress/You're on Top	1966	20.00
STAX			
❑ 0004	Stay Baby Stay/I Love Love	1968	40.00
❑ 238	I Need Somebody/What'll I Do for Satisfaction	1968	40.00

DAYTONAS, THE
Also see RONNY AND THE DATYONAS.

Number	Title (A Side/B Side)	Yr	NM
45s			
AMY			
❑ 961	Hey Little Girl/Please Go Away	1966	20.00

DAYTONES, THE

Number	Title (A Side/B Side)	Yr	NM
45s			
JUBILEE			
❑ 5452	Krambuli/Bless My Love	1963	20.00

DAYTONS, THE

Number	Title (A Side/B Side)	Yr	NM
45s			
NORGOLDE			
❑ 101	King of Broken Hearts/Friday Better Come	1959	200.00

DB'S, THE

Number	Title (A Side/B Side)	Yr	NM
45s			
BEARSVILLE			
❑ 29188	Love Is for Lovers/Darby Hall	1984	4.00
CAR			
❑ (# unknown)	If and When/I Thought (You Wanted to Know)	1978	7.50
❑ (# unknown) [PS]	If and When/I Thought (You Wanted to Know)	1978	7.50
I.R.S.			
❑ 53198	I Lie (Edited)/Sharon	1987	3.00
❑ 53198 [PS]	I Lie (Edited)/Sharon	1987	3.00
MCA			
❑ 53468	The Changing Times/21 Jump Street	1988	3.00
—B-side by Holly Robinson			
SHAKE			
❑ 100	Black and White/Soul Kiss Part 1 & 2	1980	4.00
❑ 100 [PS]	Black and White/Soul Kiss art 1 & 2	1980	4.00
Albums			
BEARSVILLE			
❑ 25146	Like This	1984	15.00
I.R.S.			
❑ 42055	The Sound of Music	1987	12.00

Except when noted otherwise, VG = 25% of NM, and VG+ = 50% of NM. (Example: VG = $2.00, VG+ = $4.00 and NM = $8.00.)

Number	Title (A Side/B Side)	Yr	NM
RHINO			
R1-70891	Like This	1988	10.00
—Reissue of Bearsville LP			

DE BONAIRS

Number	Title (A Side/B Side)	Yr	NM
45s			
PING			
1000	Lanky Linda/Mother's Son	1956	300.00
1001	Say a Prayer for Me/racker-Jack Daddy	1956	400.00

DE-FENDERS, THE

Number	Title (A Side/B Side)	Yr	NM
45s			
DEL-FI			
4226	Little Deuce Coupe/Hayburner	1963	30.00
—B-side by the Deuce Coupes			
WORLD PACIFIC			
382	(Dance to the) Yakety Sax/Wild One	1963	40.00
Albums			
DEL-FI			
DFLP-1242 [M]	Drag Beat	1963	50.00
DFST-1242 [S]	Drag Beat	1963	60.00
WORLD PACIFIC			
ST-1810 [S]	The De-Fenders Play the Big Ones	1963	70.00
—Black vinyl			
ST-1810 [S]	The De-Fenders Play the Big Ones	1963	150.00
—Green vinyl			
ST-1810 [S]	The De-Fenders Play the Big Ones	1963	150.00
—Red vinyl			
WP-1810 [M]	The De-Fenders Play the Big Ones	1963	50.00

DE VONS, THE

Number	Title (A Side/B Side)	Yr	NM
45s			
KING			
6226	Someone to Treat Me (The Way You Used To)/Soul Party	1969	10.00
MR. G			
825	Groovin' with My Thing/Wise Up	1968	12.00
PARKWAY			
976	Put Me Down/Freddie	1966	30.00

DEACON AND THE ROCK 'N' ROLLERS

Number	Title (A Side/B Side)	Yr	NM
45s			
NAU-VOO			
804	Rockin' on the Moon/I Don't Wanna Leave	1959	1500.

DEAD BOYS

Number	Title (A Side/B Side)	Yr	NM
45s			
SIRE			
1004	Sonic Reducer/Down in Flames	1977	12.00
1004 [PS]	Sonic Reducer/Down in Flames	1977	12.00
1029	Tell Me/Not Anymore/Ain't Nothin' to Do	1978	15.00
1029 [PS]	Tell Me/Not Anymore/Ain't Nothin' to Do	1978	15.00
Albums			
BOMP!			
4017	Night of the Living Dead Boys	1981	15.00
SIRE			
SR-6038	Young, Loud & Snotty	1977	25.00
SRK-6054	We Have Come for Your Children	1978	30.00
SRK-6054	We Have Come for Your Children	1978	50.00
—With original title Down To Kill on label			

DEAD KENNEDYS Featuring Jello Biafra.

Number	Title (A Side/B Side)	Yr	NM
12-Inch Singles			
ALTERNATIVE TENTACLES			
VIRUS 23	Bleed for Me/Life Sentence	1982	8.00
VIRUS 28	Halloween/Saturday Night Holocaust	1982	8.00
45s			
ALTERNATIVE TENTACLES			
VIRUS 2	Too Drunk to Fuck/The Prey	1981	8.00
VIRUS 2 [PS]	Too Drunk to Fuck/The Prey	1981	8.00
—Picture sleeve and lyric insert			
VIRUS 6	Nazi Punks Fuck Off/Moral Majority	1981	7.50
VIRUS 6 [PS]	Nazi Punks Fuck Off/Moral Majority	1981	7.50
—Lyric sheet and armband in plastic bag, not actually a picture sleeve			
VIRUS 23	Bleed for Me/Life Sentence	1982	5.00
VIRUS 23 [PS]	Bleed for Me/Life Sentence	1982	5.00
VIRUS 28	Halloween/Saturday Night Holocaust	1982	5.00
VIRUS 28 [PS]	Halloween/Saturday Night Holocaust	1982	5.00
AT-95-41	California Uber Alles/The Man with the Dogs	1979	20.00
AT-95-41 [PS]	California Uber Alles/The Man with the Dogs	1979	20.00
—Picture sleeve and lyric insert			
I.R.S./FAULTY PRODUCTS			
9016	Holiday in Cambodia/Policetruck	1980	10.00
9016 [PS]	Holiday in Cambodia/Policetruck	1980	10.00
OPTIONAL MUSIC			
OPT-2	California Uber Alles/The Man with the Dogs	1979	12.00
OPT-2 [PS]	California Uber Alles/The Man with the Dogs	1979	12.00
OPT-4	Holiday in Cambodia/Policetruck	1980	10.00
OPT-4 [PS]	Holiday in Cambodia/Policetruck	1980	10.00
—Picture sleeve and lyric insert			
SUBTERRANEAN			
SUB 24	Nazi Punks Fuck Off/Moral Majority	1981	10.00
SUB 24 [PS]	Nazi Punks Fuck Off/Moral Majority	1981	10.00
—Lyric sheet and armband in plastic bag, not actually a picture sleeve			
Albums			
ALTERNATIVE TENTACLES			
VIRUS 1	Fresh Fruit for Rotting Vegetables	1988	18.00
—Reissue of I.R.S. album			
VIRUS 5 [EP]	In God We Trust, Inc.	1981	15.00
VIRUS 27	Plastic Surgery Disasters	1982	15.00
VIRUS 45	Frankenchrist	1985	15.00
—Originals have a poster of H.R. Giger's painting Landscape #20, which was involved in an obscenity trial. The poster is still available, but only by mailing in a coupon inside the LP.			
VIRUS 50	Bedtime for Democracy	1986	15.00
—Originals have a newspaper insert			
VIRUS 57	Give Me Convenience or Give Me Death	1987	15.00
FAULTY			
70014	Fresh Fruit for Rotting Vegetables	1982	40.00
—With nursing home photo on back cover, no reference to I.R.S. on label or cover			
I.R.S./FAULTY PRODUCTS			
SP-70014	Fresh Fruit for Rotting Vegetables	1980	20.00
—Originals have an orange cover "to distinguish it from imports"			
SP-70014	Fresh Fruit for Rotting Vegetables	1980	22.00
—Reissues have a black front cover, same as imports; it was changed at the insistence of band member Jello Biafra			

DEAD OR ALIVE

Number	Title (A Side/B Side)	Yr	NM
12-Inch Singles			
EPIC			
AS 1793 [DJ]	What I Want (Short Version 3:42) (Album Version 5:28)	1983	12.00
49-04202	What I Want (Dance Mix 4:52)/The Stranger	1983	12.00
49-04979	I'd Do Anything (Megamix)/Give It to Me	1983	20.00
49-04979 [DJ]	I'd Do Anything (Megamix) (same on both sides)	1983	10.00
49-05012	That's the Way (I Like It) (Dance Version)/Keep That Body Strong (That's the Way I Like It)	1983	10.00
49-05208	You Spin Me Round (Like a Record) (Murder Mix 8:00)/Misty Circles (Extended Version 9:10)	1985	10.00
49-05278	Lover Come Back to Me (2 versions)/Far Too Hard	1985	10.00
49-05327	My Heart Goes Bang (Get Me to the Doctor) (American Wipe-Out Mix 6:15) (7:20)	1985	10.00
49-05965	Brand New Lover (The Dust Monkey's Love Bubble Mix 9:00) (Instrumental 4:15) (Up Ducky Mix 6:35)/In Too Deep (Live 4:34)	1986	10.00
49-06750	Something in My House (Mortevicar Mix) (Flamenco Mix) (US Wipe Out Mix Part 2) (Instrumental)	1987	8.00
49-07482	I'll Save You All My Kisses (The Sonia Mezumbda Memorial Mix 5:18) (The Long Wet Sloppy Kiss Mix 7:10)/I Wanna Be a Toy (3:58)	1987	10.00
49-68777	Come Home with Me Baby (6:20) (Deadhouse Dub)	1989	8.00
49H-69181	You Spin Me Round (Like a Record) (Murder Mix 8:00)/Misty Circles (Extended Version 9:10)	1989	10.00
—"Mixed Masters" reissue			
49-73101	Baby Don't Say Goodbye (Club Mix 8:32) (Instrumental 4:51) (Cheer's Vocal 7:09) (Danny's Dub 3:29) (Radio Edit 4:29)	1989	10.00
49-78588	You Spin Me Round (Like a Record) (Murder Mix 8:00)/Brand New Lover (9:00)	1997	15.00
—"Mixed Masters" reissue			
45s			
EPIC			
34-04309	What I Want/The Stranger	1984	8.00
34-04573	That's the Way (I Like It)/Do It	1984	8.00
34-04894	You Spin Me Round (Like a Record)/Misty Circles	1985	4.00
34-05607	Lover Come Back to Me/Far Too Hard	1985	3.00
34-05607 [PS]	Lover Come Back to Me/Far Too Hard	1985	3.00
34-05832	My Heart Goes Bang (Get Me to the Doctor)/My Cake And Eat It	1986	4.00
34-06374	Brand New Lover/In Too Deep	1986	3.00
34-06374 [PS]	Brand New Lover/In Too Deep	1986	3.00
34-07022	Something in My House/D.J. Hit That Button	1987	3.00
34-07022 [PS]	Something in My House/D.J. Hit That Button	1987	8.00
15-08468	You Spin Me Round (Like a Record)/Lover Come Back to Me	1988	3.00
—Reissue			
15-08469	That's the Way (I Like It)/My Heart Goes Bang (Get Me to the Doctor)	1988	3.00
—Reissue			
34-68885	Come Home With Me Baby/(Deadhouse Dub 7" Edit)	1989	3.00
Albums			
EPIC			
EAS 2668 [DJ]	Radio Special with Pete Burns	1986	70.00
—Promo-only music and interviews			
BFE 39274	Sophisticated Boom Boom	1984	12.00
FE 39274	Sophisticated Boom Boom	1985	8.00
—Reissue with new prefix			
BFE 40119	Youthquake	1985	10.00
FE 40119	Youthquake	1985	8.00
—Reissue with new prefix			
FE 40572	Mad, Bad and Dangerous to Know	1986	12.00
OE 44255	Rip It Up	1988	12.00
OE 45224	Nude	1989	12.00

DEADLY ONES, THE

Number	Title (A Side/B Side)	Yr	NM
Albums			
VEE JAY			
LP-1090 [M]	It's Monster Surfing Time	1964	100.00
LPS-1090 [S]	It's Monster Surfing Time	1964	120.00

DEAL, BILL, AND THE RHONDELS

Number	Title (A Side/B Side)	Yr	NM
45s			
BUDDAH			
318	It's Too Late/So What If It Rains	1972	6.00
330	Everybody's Got Something to Hide/I Live in the Night	1972	6.00
GIG/WAY			
902006	Freak 'N' Freeze/(Instrumental)	1978	5.00
HERITAGE			
803	May I/Day By Day My Love Grows	1968	8.00
812	I've Been Hurt/I've Got My Seeds	1969	8.00
812 [PS]	I've Been Hurt/I've Got My Needs	1969	15.00
817	What Kind of Fool Do You Think I Am/Are You Ready for This	1969	8.00
818	Swingin' Tight/Tuck's Theme	1969	8.00
818 [PS]	Swingin' Tight/Tuck's Theme	1969	15.00
821	Nothing Succeeds Like Success/Swingin' Tight	1969	8.00
824	I'm Gonna Make You Love Me/Hey Bulldog	1970	6.00
MALA			
502	Big Toe in the Wind/Don't Put Me Down	1965	30.00
—As "Bill Deal and the Big Deals"			
POLYDOR			
14042	Do I Love You/Won't You Set Me Free	1970	6.00
14061	19 Years (Everything I Do Is Wrong)/Sea of Life	1971	6.00
14103	Sea of Life/You Can Make It	1971	6.00
Albums			
HERITAGE			
HTS 35003	Vintage Rock	1969	30.00
HTS 35006	The Best of Bill Deal and the Rhondels	1970	30.00

Number	Title (A Side/B Side)	Yr	NM
RHINO			
❑ RNLP-70129	The Best of Bill Deal and the Rhondels (1969-1970)	1986	10.00

DEAL, DON

Number	Title (A Side/B Side)	Yr	NM
45s			
CAPITOL			
❑ 4901	How Do You Lie to a Heart/Ain't Gonna Try No More	1963	10.00
❑ 5028	You'll Get Used to Being Lonely/A-11	1963	10.00
CASH			
❑ 1028	Cryin' in One Eye/Broken Hearted Fellow	1956	50.00
—Eddie Cochran plays guitar on this record			
CHALLENGE			
❑ 59389	Love Touched Me/Piece at a Time	1968	8.00
DONJIM			
❑ 1007	I Don't Change My Mind Overnight/My Good Thing's Gone	1979	7.00
ERA			
❑ 1039	Unfaithful Diane/Devil of Deceit	1957	15.00
❑ 1051	My Blind Date/Even Then	1957	15.00
❑ 1060	She Was Here But She's Gone/You'd Look Good with a Tear in Your Eye	1957	15.00
❑ 1070	Sweet Love/The First Teenager	1958	15.00
❑ 1077	Just Thought I'd Call/A Chance Is All I Ask	1958	15.00
MGM			
❑ K13235	Lyin' Again/After the Boy Gets the Girl	1964	10.00
SAND			
❑ 432	You Make It Summer All Winter Long/A Drop at a Time	1969	8.00
❑ 438	Our Last Night/So What	1970	8.00

DEAN, ALAN

Number	Title (A Side/B Side)	Yr	NM
45s			
LONDON			
❑ 45-1002	Really and Truly/Yodelling Ghost	1951	20.00
MGM			
❑ K11156	Since My Love Has Gone/If You Go (Si Tu Partais)	1952	15.00
❑ K11187	Be Anything/All My Life	1952	15.00
❑ K11226	You'll Never Be Mine/Do You Care	1952	15.00
❑ K11269	Luna Rossa (Blushing Moon)/I'll Forget You	1952	15.00
❑ K11327	Raggle Taggle Gypsies/Let's Call It a Day	1952	15.00
❑ K11365	Half a Heart/Give Me Your Lips	1952	15.00
❑ K11393	Say You Love Me/High on a Windy Hill	1953	12.00
❑ K11454	Serenade of the Mandolins/The Moon Was Yellow	1953	12.00
❑ K11513	Love Me, Love Me/Make Me Your Slave	1953	12.00
❑ K11578	Why Do You Pretend/Don't Make Me Love	1953	12.00
❑ K11658	What Are You Waiting For/Call Me Any Time at All	1954	12.00
❑ K11683	Hold Me Close/Positively No Dancing	1954	12.00
❑ K11747	Who's Afraid/I'm a Man	1954	12.00
❑ K11801	Lover's Quarrel/I'm Looking for Someone	1954	12.00
❑ K11844	Tonight, My Love/The Song from Desiree	1954	12.00
❑ K11920	Too Much in Love to Care/Ladder of Love	1955	12.00
❑ K12012	Remember Me Wherever You Go/Love Is All That Matters	1955	12.00
❑ K12088	So Long/You Made Me Care (When I Wasn't in Love)	1955	12.00
❑ K12189	Take a Bow/Without You	1956	12.00
❑ K12311	I'll Share Your Tears, Your Laughter and Your Dreams/A Kiss Is Forever	1956	12.00
RAMA			
❑ 211	Rock and Roll Tarantella/Life Is But a Dream	1956	12.00
❑ 218	The Memory Followed Me Home/The Letter That I Never Mailed	1956	12.00
ROULETTE			
❑ 4028	How Far Can Any Man Go?/The Heart of a Fool	1957	12.00
Albums			
DESIGN			
❑ DLP-102 [M]	Songs of Faith	1959	12.00
❑ SDLP-300 [S]	The Lord's Prayer	1969	10.00
GRAND PRIX			
❑ K-184 [M]	Songs of Faith	196?	10.00
❑ KS-184 [S]	Songs of Faith	196?	12.00
INTERNATIONAL AWARD SERIES			
❑ AK-184 [M]	Songs of Faith	196?	10.00
❑ AKS-184 [S]	Songs of Faith	196?	12.00
MGM			
❑ E-3461 [M]	Heart and Soul	1956	25.00
STEREO-SPECTRUM			
❑ SS-45 [S]	Songs of Faith	1959	15.00

DEAN, BOBBY

Number	Title (A Side/B Side)	Yr	NM
45s			
CHESS			
❑ 1673	Just Go Wild Over Rock and Roll/Dime Store Pony Tail	1958	30.00
❑ 1710	I'm Ready/Go Mr. Dillon	1959	30.00
PROFILE			
❑ 4006	Just Between Tears/It's a Fad	1959	40.00

DEAN, CHARLES

Number	Title (A Side/B Side)	Yr	NM
45s			
BENTON			
❑ 103	Itchy/(B-side unknown)	1958	250.00

DEAN, DEBBIE

Number	Title (A Side/B Side)	Yr	NM
45s			
MOTOWN			
❑ 1007	Don't Let Him Shop Around/A New Girl	1961	40.00
❑ 1014	Itty, Bitty, Pity Love/But I'm Afraid	1961	30.00
❑ 1025	Everybody's Talking About My Baby/I Cried All Night	1962	40.00
❑ 1025 [PS]	Everybody's Talking About My Baby/I Cried All Night	1962	80.00
V.I.P.			
❑ 25044	Why Am I Lovin' You/Stay My Love	1967	300.00

DEAN, LENNY See THE ROCKIN' CHAIRS.

DEAN, RITCHIE

Number	Title (A Side/B Side)	Yr	NM
45s			
AMCAN			
❑ 400	Now You Tell Me/Schagone! (She's Gone)	196?	40.00
SWIRL			
❑ 105	Rose Marie/One Girl	1961	20.00
TOWER			
❑ 102	Goodbye Girl/I'd Do Anything	1964	20.00
❑ 183	Farewell Angelica/Time (Can't Heal This Pain of Mine)	1965	15.00
❑ 228	It's Rainin', It's Pourin'/The Old Cathedral	1966	15.00

DEAN, TERRI

Number	Title (A Side/B Side)	Yr	NM
45s			
LAUREL			
❑ 1003	I'm Confessin' (That I Love You)/I Blew Out the Flame	1959	15.00
LAURIE			
❑ 3032	Adonis/You Treat Me Like a Boy	1959	15.00
❑ 3049	Friendship Ring/Oh My Papa	1960	15.00
MADISON			
❑ 167	Your Heart's Not Made of Wood/Lover Boy	1961	20.00
POPLAR			
❑ 102	Dream Boy (Oh, Oh, Oh)/It's Just Your Kiss	1958	40.00
—As "Terry Dean"			

DEAN AND JEAN

Number	Title (A Side/B Side)	Yr	NM
45s			
EMBER			
❑ 1048	We're Gonna Get Married/Too Young to Know	1958	12.00
❑ 1054	Turn It Off/Never Let Your Love Fade Away	1959	12.00
RUST			
❑ TR 1	Seven Day Wonder/The Man Who Will Never Grow Old	196?	12.00
❑ 5044	Come Take a Walk with Me/Dance the Roach	1962	10.00
❑ 5046	Mack the Knife/You Can't Be Happy by Yourself	1962	10.00
❑ 5067	Tra La La La Suzy/I Love the Summertime	1963	10.00
❑ 5075	Hey Jean, Hey Dean/Please Don't Tell Me Now	1964	15.00
❑ 5081	I Wanna Be Loved/Thread Your Needle	1964	10.00
❑ 5085	Goddess of Love/The Man Who Will Never Grow Old	1964	10.00
❑ 5089	Sticks and Stones/In My Way	1964	10.00
❑ 5100	Lovingly Yours/Goddess of Love	1965	10.00
❑ 5107	She's Too Respectable/I Love the Summertime	1965	10.00

DEAN AND MARC Also see THE NEWBEATS.

Number	Title (A Side/B Side)	Yr	NM
45s			
BULLSEYE			
❑ 1025	Tell Him No/Change of Heart	1959	50.00
❑ 1026	Cry/The Beginning of Love	1959	25.00
CHECKMATE			
❑ 1008	Boogie Woogie Twist (Parts 1 & 2)	1962	15.00
HICKORY			
❑ 1227	With Tears in My Eyes/Kissin' Game	1963	10.00
—Hickory titles as "Dean and Mark" unless noted			
❑ 1249	When I Stop Dreaming/There Oughta Be a Law	1964	10.00
❑ 1294	Just a Step Away/A Falling Star	1965	10.00
❑ 1353	In the Middle of the Night/You'll Never Really Know	1965	10.00
❑ 1414	When I Stop Dreaming/With Tears in My Eyes	1966	10.00
—As "The Mathis Brothers"			
MAY			
❑ 135	Somebody's Smiling (While I'm Crying)/Pins and Needles (In My Heart)	1963	12.00
—As "Dean and Mark"			

DEANS, THE

Number	Title (A Side/B Side)	Yr	NM
45s			
LAURIE			
❑ 3114	I Don't Want to Wait/Little White Gardenia	1961	20.00
MOHAWK			
❑ 114	My Heart Is Low/I'll Love You Forever	1960	25.00
❑ 119	Humpty Dumpty/La Chiam	1960	25.00
❑ 126	It's You/I Don't Wanna Wait	1960	40.00
STAR MAKER			
❑ 1928	Oh Little Star/You Got Me Baby	1961	100.00
❑ 1931	Chills, Chills, Chills/(Lady of the) Caravan	1962	60.00

DEAUVILLE, RONNIE

Number	Title (A Side/B Side)	Yr	NM
45s			
DOT			
❑ 16025	Heaven in Hawaii/Honey Hill	1959	15.00
ERA			
❑ 1055	I Concentrate on You/As Children Do	1957	20.00
❑ 1055 [PS]	I Concentrate on You/As Children Do	1957	40.00
❑ 1056	Laura/It Wasn't Much of a Town	1957	20.00
❑ 1056 [PS]	Laura/It Wasn't Much of a Town	1957	60.00
❑ 1066	Hong Kong Affair/Crazy, Wonderful	1957	20.00
IMPERIAL			
❑ 5559	King of Fools/Blame Your Eyes	1959	15.00
Albums			
ERA			
❑ 20002 [M]	Smoke Dreams	1957	40.00
IMPERIAL			
❑ LP-9060 [M]	Romance	1959	25.00
❑ LP-12009 [S]	Romance	1959	30.00

DEBBIE AND THE TEEN DREAMS

Number	Title (A Side/B Side)	Yr	NM
45s			
VERNON			
❑ 101	Santa, Teach Me How To Dance/The Time	1962	25.00

DEBERRY, JIMMY

Number	Title (A Side/B Side)	Yr	NM
45s			
SUN			
❑ 185	Take a Little Chance/Time Has Made a Change	1953	3000.

DEBONAIRES, THE (1)

Number	Title (A Side/B Side)	Yr	NM
45s			
DORE			
❑ 526	Every Once in a While/Mama Don't Care	1959	80.00
—As "The Debonairs"			
❑ 592	Every Once in a While/Gert's Skirt	1961	30.00

Number	Title (A Side/B Side)	Yr	NM
❑ 654	Hold Back the Dawn/ Mama Don't Care	1962	25.00
❑ 702	Every Once in a While/ Gert's Skirt	1964	20.00
❑ 712	Everybody's Movin'/ Mama Don't Care	1964	20.00
GEE			
❑ 1008	Won't You Tell Me/I'm Gone	1956	80.00
❑ 1054	We'll Wait/Make Believe Lover	1960	25.00
HERALD			
❑ 509	Darlin'/Whispering Blues	1957	60.00
❑ 509	Darlin'/Whispering Blues	1957	200.00
—As "The Five Debonaires"			
LOST-NITE			
❑ 419	Darlin'/Whispering Blues	197?	5.00
—Reissue			

DEBONAIRES, THE (2)

45s

Number	Title (A Side/B Side)	Yr	NM
ELMONT			
❑ 1004	This Must Be Paradise/ I Need You Darling	1958	200.00

DEBONAIRES, THE (3)

45s

Number	Title (A Side/B Side)	Yr	NM
GOLDEN WORLD			
❑ 17	A Little Too Long/Please Don't Say We're Through	1964	30.00
❑ 26	Eenie Meenie Gypsaleenie/ Please Don't Say We're Through	1965	20.00
❑ 38	Big Time Fun/How's Your New Love Treating You	1966	50.00
❑ 44	C.O.D./How's Your New Love Treating You	1966	30.00
SOLID HIT			
❑ 102	Loving You Takes All of My Time/Headache in My Heart	1967	2000.
—VG 1000; VG+ 1500			
❑ 104	I'm in Love Again/Headache in My Heart	1967	200.00

DEBONAIRES, THE (U)

This may be one of groups (1), (2) or (3), or it may be a completely different group.

45s

Number	Title (A Side/B Side)	Yr	NM
GALAXY			
❑ 774	Woman, Why?/Stop, Let's Be United	1971	40.00
❑ 787	I Want to Talk About It/ (B-side unknown)	1972	50.00
MASKE			
❑ 804	Every Other Day/Jivin' Guy	1959	40.00

DEBS, THE

More than one group.

45s

Number	Title (A Side/B Side)	Yr	NM
BRUCE			
❑ 129	Shoo-Doo-De-Doo/ Whadaya Want	1955	60.00
CROWN			
❑ 153	If You Were Here Tonight/Look What You're Doin' to Me	1955	40.00
DOUBLE L			
❑ 727	Danger Ahead/Just Another Fool	1964	12.00
KEEN			
❑ 34003	Johnny Darling/Doom-a-Roca	1957	25.00
MERCURY			
❑ 72458	Give Him My Love/Goodbye Boy	1965	20.00
❑ 72566	My Best Friend/The Life and Soul of the Party	1966	15.00

DEBUTANTES, THE (1)

45s

Number	Title (A Side/B Side)	Yr	NM
KAYO			
❑ 928	Going Steady/Memories	1958	250.00

DEBUTANTES, THE (2)

45s

Number	Title (A Side/B Side)	Yr	NM
LUCKY ELEVEN			
❑ 237	Love Is Strange/ A New Love Today	196?	15.00

DEBUTANTES, THE (3)

45s

Number	Title (A Side/B Side)	Yr	NM
SAVOY			
❑ 1191	Just Leave It to Me/Is It Too Soon	1956	30.00

DECARLO, YVONNE

45s

Number	Title (A Side/B Side)	Yr	NM
IMPERIAL			
❑ 5484	The Secret of Love/That's Love	1956	80.00
❑ 5532	Rockin' in Orbit/I Would Give My Heart	1958	80.00

Albums

Number	Title (A Side/B Side)	Yr	NM
MASTERSEAL			
❑ MS33-1869/70 [M]	Yvonne DeCarlo Sings	1957	80.00

DECARO, NICK

45s

Number	Title (A Side/B Side)	Yr	NM
A&M			
❑ 838	Amy's Theme/Spanish Flea	1967	6.00
❑ 1037	Happy Heart/Love Is All	1969	6.00
❑ 1109	I'm Gonna Make You Love Me/ Amy's Theme	1969	6.00

Albums

Number	Title (A Side/B Side)	Yr	NM
A&M			
❑ SP-4176	Happy Heart	1969	10.00

DECASTRO SISTERS, THE

45s

Number	Title (A Side/B Side)	Yr	NM
ABBOTT			
❑ 3001	Teach Me Tonight/It's Love	1954	15.00
❑ 3002	I'm Bewildered/To Say You're Mine	1955	12.00
❑ 3003	Boom Boom Boomerang/ Let Your Love Walk In	1955	12.00
❑ 3004	Cuckoo in the Clock/ If I Ever Fall in Love	1955	12.00
❑ 3007	Cuban Love Song/I Can't Escape from You	1955	12.00
❑ 3008	Wedding Song/I'm Bewildered	1955	12.00
❑ 3011	Too Late Now/Give Me Time	1955	12.00
❑ 3012	Snowbound for Christmas/ Christmas Is a-Comin'	1955	15.00
❑ 3014	Rockin' and Rollin' in Hawaii/ Cry Baby Blues	1956	12.00
❑ 3019	No One to Blame But You/ Cowboys Don't Cry	1956	12.00
ABC-PARAMOUNT			
❑ 9932	Who Are They to Say/When You Look at Me	1958	10.00
❑ 9988	Teach Me Tonight Cha Cha/ The Things I Tell My Pillow	1958	10.00
❑ 10007	Close to You/With My Eyes Wide Open	1959	10.00
BOHA			
❑ 1001	Feliz Navidad/Santa Claus Is Coming To Town	197?	4.00
CAPITOL			
❑ 4537	The Bells/Red Sails in the Sunset	1961	8.00
RCA VICTOR			
❑ 47-6661	Don't Call Me Sweetie/It's Yours	1956	10.00
❑ 47-6774	I Never Meant to Hurt You/I Hear a Melody	1956	10.00
❑ 47-6862	Flowers on a Hillside/ I Know Plenty	1957	10.00
❑ 47-7028	Where Have You Been All My Life/That Little Word Called Love	1957	10.00
❑ 47-7108	Old Timers' Tune/Blue and Broken Hearted	1957	10.00
❑ 47-7177	You Take Care of Me/ What a Relief	1958	10.00
ZODIAC			
❑ 1016	Before the Next Teardrop Falls/ Teach Me Tonight	1977	4.00

Albums

Number	Title (A Side/B Side)	Yr	NM
ABBOTT			
❑ 5002 [M]	The DeCastro Sisters	1956	60.00
CAPITOL			
❑ ST 1402 [S]	The DeCastros Sing	1960	30.00
❑ T 1402 [M]	The DeCastros Sing	1960	25.00
❑ ST 1501 [S]	The Rockin' Beat	1961	30.00
❑ T 1501 [M]	The Rockin' Beat	1961	25.00

DECEMBER'S CHILDREN

45s

Number	Title (A Side/B Side)	Yr	NM
CAPITOL			
❑ 5883	A Girl Like You/Makin' Music	1967	12.00
LIBERTY			
❑ 56195	You're My Girl/Dirty City	1970	10.00
MAINSTREAM			
❑ 728	Sweet Talking Woman/ (B-side unknown)	1970	15.00
WORLD PACIFIC			
❑ 77887	Backwards and Forwards/ Kissin' Time	1968	10.00
❑ 77895	Lovin' Things/Extraordinary Man	1968	10.00
❑ 77910	I've Been Hurt/Good Time Boy	1969	10.00

Albums

Number	Title (A Side/B Side)	Yr	NM
MAINSTREAM			
❑ S-6128	December's Children	1970	150.00

DEE, CONNIE

45s

Number	Title (A Side/B Side)	Yr	NM
HIT			
❑ 12	Everybody Loves Me But You/ Old Rivers	1962	8.00
—B-side by Charlie Jarrett			
❑ 14	Second Hand Love/I Can't Stop Loving You	1962	8.00
—B-side by Herbert Hunter			
❑ 85	Hello Heartache, Goodbye Love/Sugar Shack	1963	8.00
—B-side by Ricky Dickens			
❑ 90	She's a Fool/It's All Right	1963	8.00
—B-side by Leroy Jones			
❑ 108	Navy Blue/Stop and Think It Over	1964	8.00
—B-side by Dotty and Dan			
❑ 114	That's the Way Boys Are/ The Shoop Shoop Song	1964	8.00
—B-side by Denny Dugan			
❑ 123	Be Anything (But Be Mine)/ Tell Me Why	1964	8.00
—B-side by Bobby Brooks			
❑ 128	My Boy Lollipop/Tears and Roses	1964	8.00
—B-side by Marty Wood			
❑ 186	Ring Telephone/The Jolly Green Giant	1965	8.00
—B-side by the Chords (2)			
❑ 189	Look of Love/King of the Road	1965	8.00
—B-side by Charlie Bare			
❑ 197	Whisper Tell Me Sweetly/ I've Got a Tiger by the Tail	1965	8.00
—B-side by Jack White			
❑ 202	Once a Cheater, Always a Cheater/I Must Be Seeing Things	1965	8.00
—B-side by Bobby Brooks			
❑ 274	Sugar Town/Single Girl	1966	8.00
—B-side by Sherry Young			

DEE, DONNA

45s

Number	Title (A Side/B Side)	Yr	NM
ABC-PARAMOUNT			
❑ 10296	Television/Nobody's Gonna Hurt You	1962	20.00

DEE, FRANKIE

45s

Number	Title (A Side/B Side)	Yr	NM
ABCO			
❑ 1002	Walking in the Rain/ Everybody's Doin' It	195?	20.00
RCA VICTOR			
❑ 47-7276	Shake It Up Baby/ After Graduation	1958	60.00
20TH FOX			
❑ 146	Swingin' in a Hammock/ I Had the Craziest Dream	1959	30.00

DEE, JACKIE

See JACKIE DeSHANNON.

DEE, JIMMY

45s

Number	Title (A Side/B Side)	Yr	NM
DOT			
❑ 15664	Henrietta/Don't Cry No More	1957	40.00
❑ 15721	Here I Come/You're Late, Miss Kate	1958	40.00
TNT			
❑ 148	Henrietta/Don't Cry No More	1957	80.00
❑ 152	Here I Come/You're Late, Miss Kate	1958	80.00
❑ 161	Feel Like Rockin'/ Rock-Tick-Rock	1958	60.00

DEE, JOEY, AND THE STARLITERS

45s

Number	Title (A Side/B Side)	Yr	NM
BONUS			
❑ 7009	Lorraine/The Girl I Walk to School	1963	50.00
❑ 7009 [PS]	Lorraine/The Girl I Walk to School	1963	80.00
JUBILEE			
❑ 5532	Feel Good About It Part 1/ Feel Good About It Part 2	1966	15.00
❑ 5539	Dancing on the Beach/ Good Little You	1966	15.00
❑ 5554	She's So Exceptional/ It's Got You	1966	15.00
❑ 5566	Can't Sit Down/Put Your Heart In It	1967	15.00
—Stock copy may not exist			
LITTLE			
❑ 813/4	Lorraine/The Girl I Walk to School	1958	400.00
MONUMENT			
❑ (# unknown) [DJ]	Ya Ya Twist/Runaround Sue	1962	25.00
—B-side by Dion			

Joey Dee and the Starlighters (sic), *The Peppermint Twisters*, Scepter 503, 1962, mono, **$25.**

Number	Title (A Side/B Side)	Yr	NM
ROULETTE			
❑ 4401	Peppermint Twist — Part 1/Peppermint Twist — Part 2	1961	16.00
❑ 4408	Hey, Let's Twist/Roly Poly	1962	15.00
❑ 4408 [PS]	Hey, Let's Twist/Roly Poly	1962	25.00
❑ 4416	Shout — Part 1/Shout — Part 2	1962	15.00
❑ 4416 [PS]	Shout — Part 1/Shout — Part 2	1962	25.00
❑ 4431	Every Time (I Think About You) Part 1/Every Time (I Think About You) Part 2	1962	12.00
❑ 4438	What Kind of Love Is This/Wing Ding	1962	10.00
—Pink label			
❑ 4438	What Kind of Love Is This/Wing Ding	1962	12.00
—White label with colored "spokes"			
❑ 4438 [PS]	What Kind of Love Is This/Wing Ding	1962	25.00
❑ 4456	I Lost My Baby/Keep Your Mind on What You're Doing	1962	12.00
❑ 4456 [PS]	I Lost My Baby/Keep Your Mind on What You're Doing	1962	25.00
❑ 4467	Baby You're Driving Me Crazy/Help Me Pick Up the Pieces	1963	12.00
❑ 4488	Hot Pastrami with Mashed Potatoes — Part 1/Hot Pastrami with Mashed Potatoes — Part 2	1963	12.00
❑ 4503	Dance, Dance, Dance/Let's Have a Party	1963	12.00
❑ 4523	Ya Ya/Fanny Mae	1963	12.00
❑ 4539	Down by the Riverside/Getting Nearer	1963	20.00
❑ 4617	Cry a Little Sometime/Wing Ding	1965	12.00
SCEPTER			
❑ 1210	Face of An Angel/Shimmy Baby	1960	30.00
—Originals have "Scepter" at top of label and are credited as "Joey Dee and the Starlights"			
❑ 1210	Face of An Angel/Shimmy Baby	1961	20.00
—Reissues have "Scepter Records" at side of label and are credited as listed			
❑ 1225	Three Memories/(Bad) Bulldog	1961	30.00

Number	Title (A Side/B Side)	Yr	NM
VASELINE HAIR TONIC			
❑ (no #)	Learn to Dance the Authentic Peppermint Twist (Parts 1 & 2)	1962	15.00
❑ (no #) [PS]	Learn to Dance the Authentic Peppermint Twist (Parts 1 & 2)	1962	15.00
Albums			
FORUM			
❑ FC 9099 [M]	Joey Dee and the Starliters	1963	12.00
❑ FCS 9099 [S]	Joey Dee and the Starliters	1963	12.00
JUBILEE			
❑ JGM-8000 [M]	Hitsville	1966	20.00
❑ JGS-8000 [S]	Hitsville	1966	25.00
ROULETTE			
❑ R-25166 [M]	Doin' the Twist at the Peppermint Lounge	1961	40.00
❑ SR-25166 [S]	Doin' the Twist at the Peppermint Lounge	1961	50.00
❑ R-25171 [M]	All the World Is Twistin'	1962	30.00
❑ SR-25171 [S]	All the World Is Twistin'	1962	40.00
❑ R-25173 [M]	Back at the Peppermint Lounge — Twistin'	1962	30.00
❑ SR-25173 [S]	Back at the Peppermint Lounge — Twistin'	1962	40.00
❑ R-25197 [M]	Joey Dee	1963	25.00
❑ SR-25197 [S]	Joey Dee	1963	30.00
❑ R-25221 [M]	Dance, Dance, Dance	1963	25.00
❑ SR-25221 [S]	Dance, Dance, Dance	1963	30.00
SCEPTER			
❑ S 503 [M]	The Peppermint Twisters	1962	25.00
❑ SS 503 [S]	The Peppermint Twisters	1962	30.00

DEE, JOHNNY See JOHN D. LOUDERMILK.

DEE, KIKI Also see ELTON JOHN AND KIKI DEE.

Number	Title (A Side/B Side)	Yr	NM
45s			
FONTANA			
❑ 1649	On a Magic Carpet Ride/Now the Flowers Die	1969	5.00
LIBERTY			
❑ 55994	Stop and Think/I	1967	6.00
❑ 56030	I'm Going Out/Patterns	1968	6.00
❑ 56089	On a Magic Carpet Ride/Now the Flowers Die	1969	6.00
POSSE			
❑ 5008	Nothing Can Stop Us Now/(B-side unknown)	1981	4.00
RARE EARTH			
❑ 5025	Love Makes the World Go Round/Jimmy	1970	5.00
RCA			
❑ PB-12347	Star/There's a Need	1981	4.00
❑ PB-13043	Loving You Is Sweeter Than Ever/Twenty-Four Hours	1982	—
—Unreleased			
ROCKET			
❑ YB-11413	One Step/Dark Side of Your Soul	1978	4.00
❑ YB-11490	Don't Stop Loving Me/One Step Ahead of the Storm	1979	4.00
❑ 40095	The Last Good Man in My Life/Lonnie and Josie	1973	4.00
❑ 40157	Amoureuse/Rest My Head	1973	4.00
❑ 40256	Super Cool/Loving and Free	1974	4.00
❑ 40293	I've Got the Music in Me/Simple Melody	1974	5.00
❑ 40355	Step by Step/Amoureuse	1975	4.00
❑ 40401	How Glad I Am/Peter	1975	4.00
❑ 40506	Once a Fool/Someone to Me	1976	4.00
❑ 40730	Chicago/Bad Day Child	1977	4.00
TAMLA			
❑ 54193	The Day Will Come Between Sunday and Monday/My Whole World Ended (The Moment You Left Me)	1970	5.00
❑ 54193 [PS]	The Day Will Come Between Sunday and Monday/My Whole World Ended (The Moment You Left Me)	1970	15.00
WORLD PACIFIC			
❑ 77820	I Dig You Baby/Small Town	1966	8.00
Albums			
LIBERTY			
❑ LST-7613	Patterns	1969	15.00
❑ LN-10148	Patterns	1981	8.00
—Budget-line reissue			
RCA VICTOR			
❑ AFL1-4180	Perfect Timing	1981	10.00
ROCKET			
❑ PIG-395	Loving and Free	1973	10.00
❑ PIG-458	I've Got the Music In Me	1974	12.00
❑ BXL1-2257	Kiki Dee	1977	10.00
❑ BXL1-3011	Stay with Me	1979	10.00
TAMLA			
❑ TS 303	Great Expectations	1970	15.00

DEE, LENNY

Number	Title (A Side/B Side)	Yr	NM
45s			
DECCA			
❑ 25531	Parade of the Wooden Soldiers/Twilight Time	1961	6.00
❑ 25563	Ain't She Sweet/Alabamy Bound	1962	6.00
❑ 25578	Baubles, Bangles and Beads/Blues in the Night	1962	6.00
❑ 25592	Moon Over Miami/Atlanta G.A.	1963	6.00
❑ 25613	Wagon Wheels/Hominy Grits	1963	6.00
❑ 25633	Devil Woman/San Antonio Rose	1964	6.00
❑ 25678	The Gang That Sang Heart of My Heart/Down by the Old Mill Stream	1965	6.00
❑ 25696	Yakety Organ/A Walk in the Black Forest	1966	6.00
❑ 25702	Kerry Dancers/One of Those Songs	1966	6.00
❑ 25717	Cute/Daydream	1967	5.00
❑ 25725	There's a Kind of Hush/Exodus	1967	5.00
❑ 25735	Gentle on My Mind/Rossana's Theme	1968	5.00
❑ 25745	Folsom Prison Blues/Turn Around, Look at Me	1969	5.00
❑ 25750	Help Yourself/Try a Little Tenderness	1969	5.00
❑ 25755	Yesterday, When I Was Young/Ruby, Don't Take Your Love to Town	1970	5.00
❑ 27891	Have You Ever Been Lonely/Cotton Walk	1951	12.00
❑ 28109	Carolina in the Morning/Viennese Waltz Medley	1952	12.00
❑ 28413	Begin the Beguine/Peanut Vendor	1952	12.00
❑ 28500	Midnight/Bye Bye Blues	1952	10.00
❑ 28639	Oh Johnny Oh/Them There Eyes	1953	10.00
❑ 29360	Plantation Boogie/The Birth of the Blues	1954	10.00

Number	Title (A Side/B Side)	Yr	NM
❑ 29579	Crazy Organ Rag/ Punxsutawney Boogie	1955	10.00
❑ 29596	Little Brown Jug/The World Is Waiting for the Sunrise	1955	10.00
❑ 29689	Honeydripper/Flea Hop Boogie	1955	10.00
❑ 30032	Honky Tonk Train Blues/ Yodelin' Organ	1956	8.00
❑ 30201	Stormy Weather/ Goodnight Sweet Love	1957	8.00
❑ 30296	High Tide Boogie/Tara Lara	1957	8.00
❑ 30429	Big Boogie Dee/Cecelia	1957	8.00
❑ 30718	June Night/After You've Gone	1958	8.00
❑ 30801	Night Train/Chicken in the Rough	1959	8.00
❑ 31332	Mr. Santa/Auld Lang Syne	1961	10.00
❑ 32691	Rock Me Back to Little Rock/ Sweet and Sassy	1970	5.00
❑ 32804	Help Me Make It Through the Night/Remember Me	1971	4.00
❑ 33026	All I Ever Need Is You/ Vaya Con Dios	1972	4.00

7-Inch Extended Plays

DECCA

Number	Title (A Side/B Side)	Yr	NM
❑ ED 2266	(contents unknown)	195?	10.00
❑ ED 2266 [PS]	Dee-Lirious, Part 1	195?	10.00
❑ ED 2267	Five Foot Two, Eyes of Blue/ Out of Nowhere//Caravan/ That's My Weakness Now	195?	10.00
❑ ED 2267 [PS]	Dee-Lirious, Part 2	195?	10.00
❑ ED 2345	Delicious/Fan Tango//Stompin' at the Savoy//(I'm in Heaven When I See You Smile) Diane	195?	10.00
❑ ED 2345 [PS]	(title unknown)	195?	10.00
❑ ED 2552	(contents unknown)	195?	10.00
❑ ED 2552 [PS]	Mr. Dee Goes to Town	195?	10.00
❑ ED 2613	(contents unknown)	195?	10.00
❑ ED 2613 [PS]	Dee-Day	195?	10.00
❑ ED 2628 [M]	(contents unknown)	1959	10.00
❑ ED 2628 [PS]	Mellow-Dee	1959	10.00
❑ ED 7-2628 [PS]	Mellow-Dee	1959	15.00
❑ ED 7-2628 [S]	(contents unknown)	1959	15.00
❑ ED 2645	(contents unknown)	195?	10.00
❑ ED 2645 [PS]	Lenny Dee Plays the Hits	195?	10.00
❑ 7-34111	Mississippi Mud/Georgia on My Mind/Carolina in the Morning// When It's Sleepy Time Down South/Way Down Yonder in New Orleans/Beautiful Cypress Gardens	196?	10.00
—Jukebox issue; small hole, plays at 33 1/3 rpm			
❑ 7-34111 [PS]	Lenny Dee Down South	196?	10.00

Albums

DECCA

Number	Title (A Side/B Side)	Yr	NM
❑ DL 4112 [M]	Golden Organ Favorites	1961	10.00
❑ DL 4146 [M]	Happy Holi-Dee	1961	10.00
❑ DL 4315 [M]	Lenny Dee In Hollywood	1962	10.00
❑ DL 4365 [M]	Lenny Dee Down South	1963	10.00
❑ DL 4429 [M]	By Popular Dee-Mand	1963	10.00
❑ DL 4498 [M]	Something Special	1964	10.00
❑ DL 4572 [M]	Most Requested	1964	10.00
❑ DL 4632 [M]	Sweethearts on Parade	1965	10.00
❑ DL 4654 [M]	The Lenny Dee Tour	1965	10.00
❑ DL 4706 [M]	My Favorite Things	1966	10.00
❑ DL 4818 [M]	In the Mood	1967	10.00
❑ DL 4880 [M]	Moving On	1967	12.00
❑ DL 4946 [M]	Relaxin'	1968	12.00
❑ DL 4994 [M]	Gentle on My Mind	1968	12.00
❑ DXS 7199 [(2)]	The Best of Lenny Dee	1968	12.00
❑ DL 8114 [M]	Dee-Lightful	1955	15.00
❑ DL 8165 [M]	Dee-Lirious	1956	12.00
❑ DL 8275 [M]	Dee-Licious	1956	12.00
❑ DL 8308 [M]	Dee-Most	1956	12.00
❑ DL 8406 [M]	Hi-Dee-Fi	1957	12.00
❑ DL 8497 [M]	Mr. Dee Goes to Town	1957	12.00
❑ DL 8628 [M]	Dee-Day	1957	12.00
❑ DL 8718 [M]	Dee-Latin Hi-Fi Organ	1958	12.00
❑ DL 8796 [M]	Mellow-Dee	1959	12.00
❑ DL 8857 [M]	Lenny Dee Plays the Hits	1959	12.00
❑ DL 8913 [M]	The Lenny Dee Show	1960	10.00
❑ DL 8978 [M]	Songs Everybody Knows	1960	10.00
❑ DL 74112 [S]	Golden Organ Favorites	1961	12.00
❑ DL 74146 [S]	Happy Holi-Dee	1961	12.00
❑ DL 74315 [S]	Lenny Dee In Hollywood	1962	12.00
❑ DL 74365 [S]	Lenny Dee Down South	1963	12.00
❑ DL 74429 [S]	By Popular Dee-Mand	1963	12.00
❑ DL 74498 [S]	Something Special	1964	12.00
❑ DL 74572 [S]	Most Requested	1964	12.00
❑ DL 74632 [S]	Sweethearts on Parade	1965	12.00
❑ DL 74654 [S]	The Lenny Dee Tour	1965	12.00
❑ DL 74706 [S]	My Favorite Things	1966	12.00
❑ DL 74818 [S]	In the Mood	1967	12.00
❑ DL 74946 [S]	Relaxin'	1968	10.00
❑ DL 74994 [S]	Gentle on My Mind	1968	10.00
❑ DL 75073	Turn Around, Look at Me	1969	10.00
❑ DL 75112	Little Green Apples	1969	10.00
❑ DL 75152	Spinning Wheel	1969	10.00
❑ DL 75196	Easy Come, Easy Go	1970	10.00
❑ DL 75255	Remember Me	1971	10.00
❑ DL 75320	Easy Lovin'	1972	10.00

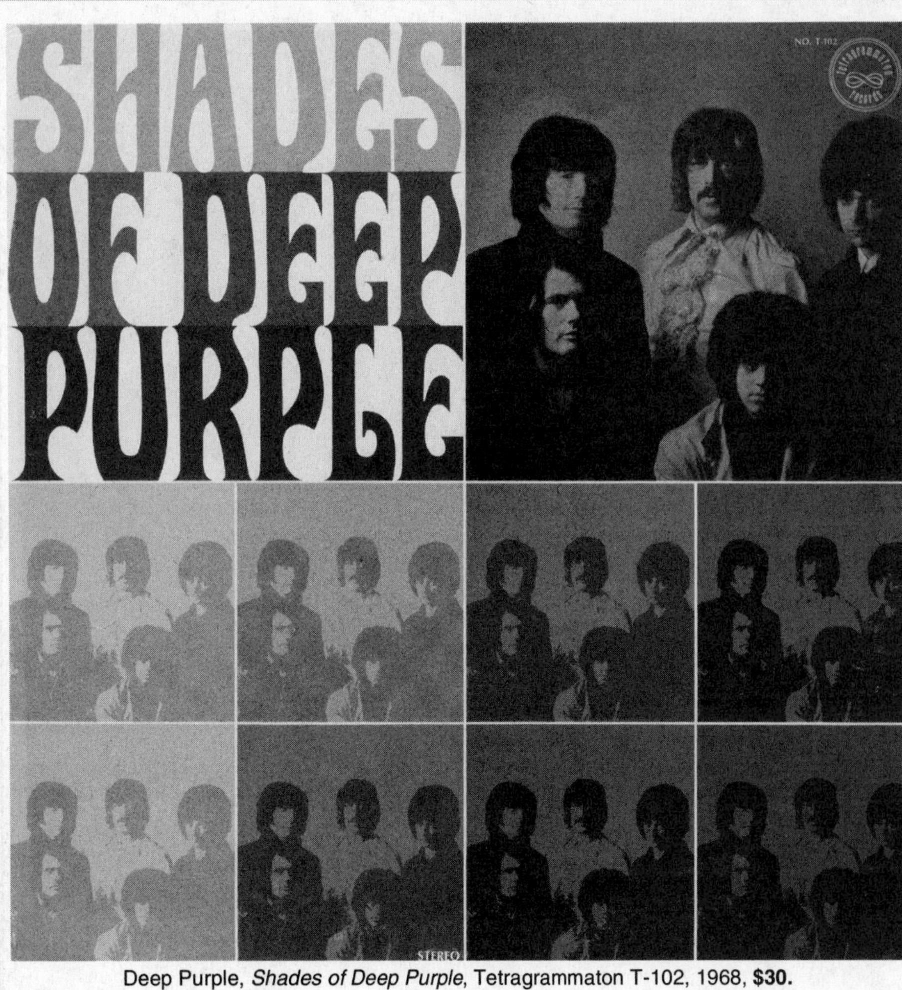

Deep Purple, *Shades of Deep Purple*, Tetragrammaton T-102, 1968, **$30.**

Number	Title (A Side/B Side)	Yr	NM
❑ DL 75366	Where Is the Love	1972	10.00
❑ DL 78796 [S]	Mellow-Dee	1959	15.00
❑ DL 78857 [S]	Lenny Dee Plays the Hits	1959	15.00
❑ DL 78880 [S]	Moving On	1967	10.00
❑ DL 78913 [S]	The Lenny Dee Show	1960	12.00
❑ DL 78978 [S]	Songs Everybody Knows	1960	12.00

MCA

Number	Title (A Side/B Side)	Yr	NM
❑ 26	Remember Me	1971	8.00
—Reissue of Decca 75255			
❑ 172	In the Mood	1973	8.00
—Reissue of Decca 74818			
❑ 182	Golden Organ Favorites	1973	8.00
—Reissue of Decca 74112			
❑ 221	Something Special	1973	8.00
—Reissue of Decca 74498			
❑ 231	Most Requested	1973	8.00
—Reissue of Decca 74572			
❑ 241	My Favorite Things	1973	8.00
—Reissue of Decca 74706			
❑ 271	Gentle on My Mind	1973	8.00
—Reissue of Decca 74994			
❑ 279	Little Green Apples	1973	8.00
—Reissue of Decca 75112			
❑ 290	Easy Come, Easy Go	1973	8.00
—Reissue of Decca 75196			
❑ 297	Easy Lovin'	1973	8.00
—Reissue of Decca 75320			
❑ 334	"Sing" and Others	1973	8.00
❑ 334	Lenny Dee	1973	8.00
❑ 379	"Lenny"	1973	8.00
❑ 455	Steppin' Out with Lenny Dee	1974	8.00
❑ 476	City Lights	1974	8.00
❑ 504	Where Is the Love	1974	8.00
—Reissue of Decca 75366			
❑ 533	Songs Everybody Knows	1975	8.00
—Reissue of Decca 78978			
❑ 2162	I'll Play for You	1975	8.00
❑ 2200	Take It to the Limit	1976	8.00
❑ 2236	Misty Blue	1976	8.00
❑ 2301	Organ Magic	1977	8.00
❑ 2370	Organ Celebration	1978	8.00
❑ 4042 [(2)]	The Best of Lenny Dee	197?	10.00
—Reissue of Decca 7179			
❑ 4084 [(2)]	The Best of Lenny Dee, Vol. II	1977	10.00

VOCALION

Number	Title (A Side/B Side)	Yr	NM
❑ VL 3782 [M]	Here's Lenny Dee at the Organ	1967	10.00
❑ VL 73782 [S]	Here's Lenny Dee at the Organ	1967	10.00
❑ VL 73817	Organ Special	1968	10.00
❑ VL 73819	Varieties	1969	10.00

DEE, RONNIE See RONNIE DAWSON.

DEE, TOMMY

45s

CHALLENGE

Number	Title (A Side/B Side)	Yr	NM
❑ 59083	The Hobo and the Puppy/ There's a Star Spangled Banner Waving Somewhere	1960	20.00
❑ 59087	Ballad of a Drag Race/ The Story of Susie	1960	20.00

CREST

Number	Title (A Side/B Side)	Yr	NM
❑ 1057 [M]	Three Stars/I'll Never Change	1959	25.00
—With backing group and B-side credited to "Carol Kay and the Teen-Aires"			
❑ 1057 [M]	Three Stars/I'll Never Change	1959	30.00
—With backing group and B-side credited to "The Teen Tones and Orchestra"			
❑ 1057 [S]	Three Stars/I'll Never Change	1959	50.00
—With backing group and B-side credited to "Carol Kay and the Teen-Aires"			
❑ 1061	The Chair/Hello Lonesome	1959	20.00
❑ 1067	Merry Christmas, Mary/ Angel of Love	1959	25.00
—With Carol Kay			

PIKE

Number	Title (A Side/B Side)	Yr	NM
❑ 5906	Loving You (On Someone Else's Time)/Halfway to Hell	1961	20.00
❑ 5909	A Little Dog Cried/Look Homeward, Dear Angel	1961	20.00
❑ 5917	Missing on a Mountain/Look Homeward, Dear Angel	1962	20.00

SIMS

Number	Title (A Side/B Side)	Yr	NM
❑ 260	Missing While Surfing/ Goodbye High School	1966	20.00

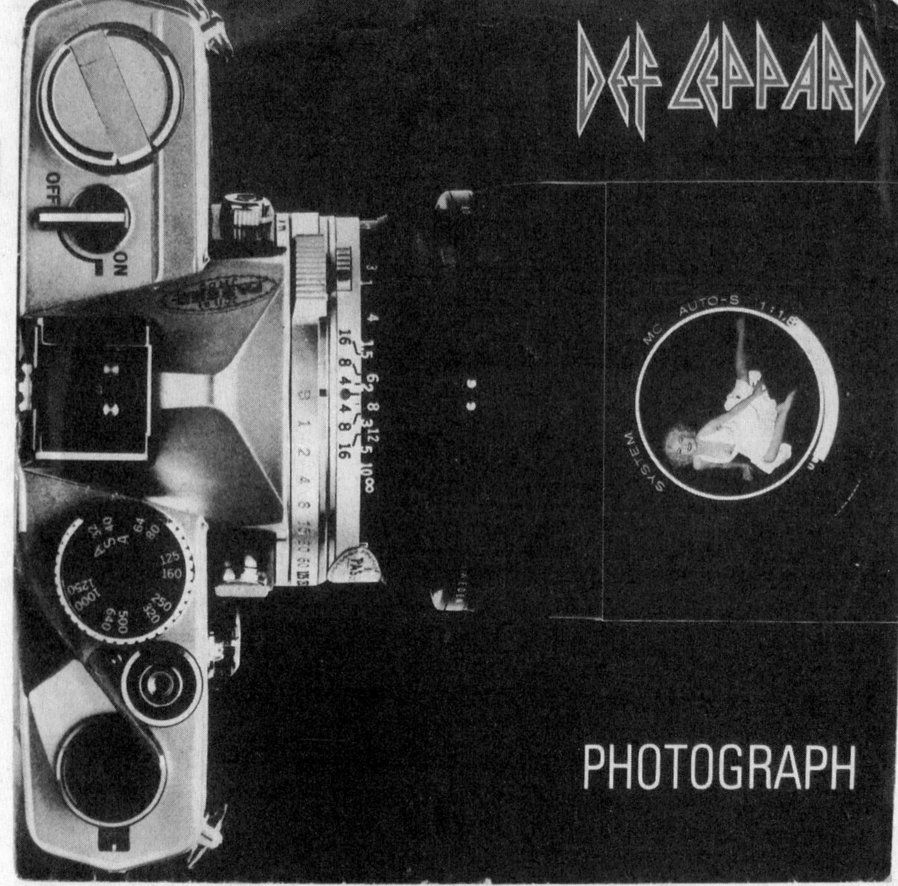

Def Leppard, "Photograph," Mercury 811215-7, 1983, **$12.**

Number	Title (A Side/B Side)	Yr	NM
❑ 308	How's Your Mama Em/ Goodbye High School	1966	15.00
STARDAY			
❑ 802	Roger, Ed and Gus (America's Astronaut Heroes)/ School for Fools	1967	8.00
DEE, WILLIE			
45s			
TUMBLEWEED			
❑ 100	Tear Filled Eyes/My Daddy's Not a Young Man Anymore	1968	20.00
DEEP, THE			
Albums			
PARKWAY			
❑ P 7051 [M]	Psychedelic Moods	1966	300.00
❑ SP 7051 [S]	Psychedelic Moods	1966	500.00
DEEP PURPLE Also see BLACK SABBATH; TOMMY BOLIN; CAPTAIN BEYOND; GILLAN; IAN GILLAN BAND; RAINBOW; TRAPEZE; WHITESNAKE.			
12-Inch Singles			
MERCURY			
❑ PRO 332-1 [DJ]	Knocking at Your Back Door (AOR Edit Version) (Album Version)	1984	15.00
❑ PRO 334-1 [DJ]	Nobody's Home/Under the Gun	1984	30.00
❑ PRO 473-1 [DJ]	Bad Attitude (same on both sides)	1987	15.00
❑ PRO 485-1 [DJ]	Call of the Wild (same on both sides)	1987	10.00
45s			
MERCURY			
❑ 880477-7	Knocking at Your Back Door/ Wasted Sunset	1984	4.00
❑ 880477-7 [PS]	Knocking at Your Back Door/ Wasted Sunset	1984	5.00
❑ 885617-7	Call of the Wild/Dead or Alive	1987	3.00
❑ 885617-7 [PS]	Call of the Wild/Dead or Alive	1987	4.00
❑ 885820-7	Bad Attitude/Black and White	1987	3.00

Number	Title (A Side/B Side)	Yr	NM
TETRAGRAMMATON			
❑ 1503	Hush/One More Rainy Day	1968	15.00
❑ 1503 [PS]	Hush/One More Rainy Day	1968	600.00
❑ 1508	Kentucky Woman/Hard Road	1968	15.00
❑ 1508 [PS]	Kentucky Woman/Hard Road	1968	30.00
❑ 1514	River Deep, Mountain High/ Listen, Learn, Read On	1969	10.00
❑ 1519	The Bird Has Flown/Emmaretta	1969	10.00
❑ 1537	Hallelujah (I Am the Preacher)/ April Part 1	1969	10.00
WARNER BROS.			
❑ PRO 402 [DJ]	Radio Spot for Concerto	1970	150.00
❑ 7405	Black Night/Into the Fire	1970	8.00
❑ 7493	Strange Kind of Woman/ I'm Alone	1971	8.00
❑ 7528	Fire Ball/I'm Alone	1971	8.00
❑ 7572	Never Before/When a Blind Man Cries	1972	6.00
❑ 7595	Lazy/When a Blind Man Cries	1972	6.00
❑ 7634	Highway Star (Part 1)/ Highway Star (Part 2)	1972	6.00
❑ 7654	Hush/Kentucky Woman	1972	6.00
❑ 7672	Woman from Tokyo/Super Trouper	1972	6.00
❑ 7710	Smoke on the Water (Edited Version) Studio/ Smoke on the Water (Edited Version) Live	1973	5.00
❑ 7737	Woman from Tokyo/ Super Trouper	1973	5.00
❑ 7784	Might Just Take Your Life/ Coronorias Regid	1974	5.00
❑ 7784 [DJ]	Might Just Take Your Life (Mono 3:35/Stereo 4:36)	1974	8.00
❑ 7809	Burn/Coronarias Regid	1974	5.00
❑ 8049	High Ball Shooter/ You Can't Do It Right	1974	5.00
❑ 8069	Stormbringer/Love Don't Mean a Thing	1975	5.00
❑ 8182	Gettin' Tighter/Love Child	1976	6.00

Number	Title (A Side/B Side)	Yr	NM
7-Inch Extended Plays			
WARNER BROS.			
❑ S 2701	Smoke on the Water/ Highway Star	1973	15.00
—Full-length versions; jukebox issue; small hole, plays at 33 1/3 rpm			
❑ S 2701 [PS]	Made in Japan	1973	15.00
—Part of "Little LP" series (LLP #214)			
❑ S 2766	Burn//Lay Down Stay Down/ You Fool No One	1974	15.00
—Full-length versions; jukebox issue, small hole, plays at 33 1/3 rpm			
❑ S 2766 [PS]	Burn	1974	15.00
—Part of "Little LP" series (LLP #250)			
Albums			
DCC COMPACT CLASSICS			
❑ LPZ-2052 [(2)]	Made in Japan	1998	40.00
—Audiophile vinyl			
EAGLE ROCK			
❑ ER 20083-1 [(2)]	Rapture of the Deep	2005	20.00
MERCURY			
❑ 824003-1	Perfect Strangers	1984	10.00
❑ 831318-1	The House of Blue Light	1987	8.00
❑ 835897-1	Nobody's Perfect	1988	10.00
RCA			
❑ 2421-1-R	Slaves and Masters	1990	15.00
RHINO			
❑ R1-75622	Machine Head	2003	15.00
—180-gram reissue			
SCEPTER CITATION			
❑ CTN-18010	The Best of Deep Purple	1972	20.00
TETRAGRAMMATON			
❑ T-102	Shades of Deep Purple	1968	30.00
❑ T-107	The Book of Taliesyn	1968	30.00
❑ T-119	Deep Purple	1969	30.00
❑ T-131	Concerto for Group and Orchestra	1970	200.00
WARNER BROS.			
❑ WS 1860	Concerto for Group and Orchestra	1970	12.00
❑ WS 1877	Deep Purple in Rock	1970	12.00
❑ BS 2564	Fireball	1971	12.00
❑ BS 2607	Machine Head	1972	12.00
—Original copies have green "WB" labels			
❑ BS 2607	Machine Head	1973	10.00
—"Burbank" labels			
❑ BS4 2607 [Q]	Machine Head	1974	25.00
❑ 2LS 2644 [(2)]	(Purple Passages)	1972	15.00
❑ BS 2678	Who Do We Think We Are!	1973	10.00
—"Burbank" labels			
❑ BS 2678	Who Do We Think We Are!	1973	12.00
—Original copies have green "WB" labels			
❑ 2WS 2701 [(2)]	Made in Japan	1973	15.00
❑ 2WS 2701 [(2)]	Made in Japan	1979	12.00
—White labels			
❑ W 2766	Burn	1974	10.00
❑ BSK 3100	Machine Head	1976	8.00
WARNER BROS./PURPLE			
❑ PR 2832	Stormbringer	1974	10.00
❑ PR4 2832 [Q]	Stormbringer	1974	25.00
❑ PR 2895	Come Taste the Band	1975	10.00
❑ PR 2995	Made in Europe	1976	10.00
❑ PRK 3223	When We Rock, We Rock, and When We Roll, We Roll	1978	10.00
❑ PRK 3486	Deepest Purple: The Best of Deep Purple	1980	10.00
DEEP SIX, THE			
45s			
LIBERTY			
❑ 55838	Rising Sun/Strolling Blues	1965	8.00
❑ 55858	I Wanna Shout/Things We Say	1966	8.00
❑ 55882	When Morning Breaks/ Counting	1966	8.00
❑ 55901	Why Say Goodbye/What Would You Wish from the Golden Fish	1966	8.00
❑ 55926	Image of a Girl/C'mon Baby	1966	8.00
Albums			
LIBERTY			
❑ LRP-3475 [M]	The Deep Six	1966	15.00
❑ LST-7475 [S]	The Deep Six	1966	20.00
DEERFIELD			
Albums			
FLAT ROCK			
❑ FRS-1	Nil Desperandum	1971	200.00
DEES, SAM			
45s			
ATLANTIC			
❑ 2991	So Tied Up/Signed Miss Heroin	1973	20.00
❑ 3205	Worn Out Broken Heart/ Come Back Strong	1974	20.00

Except when noted otherwise, VG = 25% of NM, and VG+ = 50% of NM. (Example: VG = $2.00, VG+ = $4.00 and NM = $8.00.)

Number	Title (A Side/B Side)	Yr	NM
❑ 3243	The Show Must Go On/ Child of the Streets	1975	20.00
❑ 3287	Fragile, Handle with Care/ Save the Love at Any Cost	1975	300.00
BIG TREE			
❑ 16054	Storybook Children/Just As Sure	1976	100.00
—With Bettye Swann			
CHESS			
❑ 2109	Can You Be a One Man Woman/ Put You Back in Your Place	1971	150.00
❑ 2122	Love Starvation/Maryanna	1972	60.00
CLINTONE			
❑ 010	Claim Jumping/I'm So Very Glad	1972	25.00
LOLO			
❑ 2306	Easier to Say Than Do/ Soul Sister	1969	50.00
POLYDOR			
❑ 14455	Say Yeah/My World	1978	50.00
SSS INTERNATIONAL			
❑ 732	Lonely for You Baby/ I Need You Girl	1968	400.00
Albums			
ATLANTIC			
❑ SD 18134	The Show Must Go On	1975	150.00

DEF LEPPARD Also see DIO.

Number	Title (A Side/B Side)	Yr	NM
12-Inch Singles			
MERCURY			
❑ MK 144 [DJ]	Rock Brigade (same on both sides)	1980	150.00
❑ MK 182 [DJ]	Bringin' On the Heartbreak/ Me and My Wine	1981	50.00
❑ MK 234 [DJ]	Rock of Ages/Too Late for Love	1983	25.00
❑ PRO 273-1 [DJ]	Bringin' On the Heartbreak (Remix)/Me and My Wine (Remix)	1984	40.00
❑ PRO 523-1 [DJ]	Women (same on both sides)	1987	20.00
❑ PRO 623-1 [DJ]	Love Bites (same on both sides)	1988	30.00
❑ PRO 705-1 [DJ]	Rocket (same on both sides)	1989	30.00
45s			
MERCURY			
❑ 76064	Rock Brigade/When the Walls Came Tumbling Down	1980	25.00
❑ 76120 [DJ]	Let It Go (same on both sides)	1981	20.00
—May be promo only			
❑ 562151-7	Promises/Pour Some Sugar on Me	1999	5.00
❑ 811215-7	Photograph/Action, Not Words	1983	4.00
—Black label			
❑ 811215-7	Photograph/Action, Not Words	1983	5.00
—Chicago skyline label			
❑ 811215-7 [PS]	Photograph/Action, Not Words	1983	10.00
❑ 812604-7	Rock of Ages/Billy's Got a Gun	1983	4.00
❑ 814178-7	Foolin'/Comin' Under Fire	1983	4.00
❑ 818779-7	Bringin' On the Heartbreak/ Me and My Wine	1984	4.00
❑ 818779-7 [PS]	Bringin' On the Heartbreak/ Me and My Wine	1984	6.00
❑ 852424-7	When Love & Hate Collide/Can't Keep Away from the Flame	1995	5.00
❑ 858080-7	Miss You in a Heartbeat/ Let's Get Rocked (Live)	1993	5.00
❑ 862016-7	Tonight/She's Too Tough	1993	5.00
❑ 864038-7	Make Love Like a Man/ Miss You in a Heartbeat	1992	5.00
❑ 864136-7	Have You Ever Needed Someone So Bad/Elected	1992	4.00
❑ 864604-7	Stand Up (Kick Love Into Motion)/From the Inside	1993	5.00
❑ 866568-7	Let's Get Rocked/Only After Dark	1992	5.00
❑ 870004-7	Hysteria/Ride Into the Sun	1988	3.00
❑ 870004-7 [PS]	Hysteria/Ride Into the Sun	1988	3.00
❑ 870298-7	Pour Some Sugar on Me/ Ring of Fire	1988	3.00
❑ 870298-7 [PS]	Pour Some Sugar on Me/ Ring of Fire	1988	3.00
❑ 870402-7	Love Bites/Billy's Got a Gun	1988	3.00
❑ 870402-7 [PS]	Love Bites/Billy's Got a Gun	1988	3.00
❑ 870692-7	Armageddon It/Release Me	1988	3.00
—B-side by "Stumpus Maximus and the Good Ol' Boys" (Def Leppard in disguise)			
❑ 870692-7 [PS]	Armageddon It/Release Me	1988	3.00
❑ 872614-7	Rocket/Women	1989	3.00
❑ 872614-7 [PS]	Rocket/Women	1989	3.00
❑ 874444-7	Foolin'/Bringin' On the Heartbreak	1989	4.00
—"Timepieces" reissue			
❑ 888757-7	Women/Tear It Down	1987	3.00
❑ 888757-7 [PS]	Women/Tear It Down	1987	3.00
❑ 888832-7	Animal/I Wanna Be Your Hero	1987	3.00
❑ 888832-7 [PS]	Animal/I Wanna Be Your Hero	1987	3.00
Albums			
MERCURY			
❑ SRM-1-3828	On Through the Night	1980	12.00
—Chicago skyline label			
❑ SRM-1-4021	High 'n' Dry	1981	12.00
—Chicago skyline label			
❑ 810308-1	Pyromania	1983	8.00
❑ 810308-1	Pyromania	2008	20.00
❑ 818836-1	High 'n' Dry	1984	8.00
—Altered version of 4021; "Bringin' on the Heartbreak" is remixed, and "Me & My Wine" is added			
❑ 822533-1	On Through the Night	198?	8.00
—Reissue of 3828			
❑ 830675-1	Hysteria	1987	8.00
❑ 832962-1 [PD]	Hysteria	1987	30.00
—Limited-edition picture disc in plastic sleeve			
❑ 1775319	Hysteria	2008	20.00

DEFENDERS, THE

Number	Title (A Side/B Side)	Yr	NM
45s			
PARKWAY			
❑ 926	Island of Love/I Laughed So Hard	1964	10.00

DEFRANCO FAMILY, THE

Number	Title (A Side/B Side)	Yr	NM
45s			
20TH CENTURY			
❑ 2030	Heartbeat — It's a Lovebeat/ Sweet, Sweet Loretta	1973	4.00
❑ 2030 [PS]	Heartbeat — It's a Lovebeat/ Sweet, Sweet Loretta	1973	6.00
❑ 2070	Abra-Ca-Dabra/Some Kind a' Love	1973	4.00
❑ 2070 [PS]	Abra-Ca-Dabra/Some Kind a' Love	1973	6.00
❑ 2088	Save the Last Dance for Me/ Because We Both Are Young	1974	4.00
❑ 2088 [PS]	Save the Last Dance for Me/ Because We Both Are Young	1974	6.00
❑ 2128	Baby Blue/Write Me a Letter	1974	4.00
❑ 2128 [PS]	Baby Blue/Write Me a Letter	1974	6.00
❑ 2214	We Belong Together/ Time Enough for Love	1975	8.00
❑ 2214 [PS]	We Belong Together/ Time Enough for Love	1975	10.00
Albums			
20TH CENTURY			
❑ T-422	Heartbeat, It's a Lovebeat	1973	10.00
❑ T-441	Save the Last Dance for Me	1974	10.00

DEJOHN SISTERS, THE

Number	Title (A Side/B Side)	Yr	NM
45s			
COLUMBIA			
❑ 40799	Mah Little Baby/Mu-Cha-Cha	1956	15.00
❑ 40843	Don't Promise Me (The Can Can Song)/He's Got Time	1957	12.00
EPIC			
❑ 9009	Should I Run/All Present But One	1953	15.00
❑ 9031	I Took Him from You/ Juke-Box Polka	1954	15.00
❑ 9055	A Kiss and a Rose/ Crazy Song of India	1954	15.00
❑ 9080	Lover's Slang/Mandolino	1954	15.00
❑ 9085	(My Baby Don't Love Me) No More/Theresa	1954	15.00
❑ 9097	D'Ja Hear What I Say/ A Present for Bob	1955	12.00
❑ 9108	He Loves Me/Pass the Plate of Happiness Around	1955	12.00
❑ 9124	(Love Is) The Tender Trap/ I'm Learning the Charleston	1955	—
—Canceled			
❑ 9131	C'est La Vie/Uninvited Love	1955	12.00
❑ 9133	The Only Thing I Want for Christmas/That's How Santa Claus Will Look This Year	1955	15.00
❑ 9145	Hotta Chocolotta/The Man with the Blue Guitar	1956	12.00
❑ 9172	Big D/In My Innocence	1956	12.00
MERCURY			
❑ 71131	Where Would I Be/Who Am I	1957	10.00
❑ 71203	Absence Makes the Heart Grow Fonder/That's My Weakness Now	1957	10.00
OKEH			
❑ 6989	The Angel Passed By/ Never Since Then	1953	20.00
SUNBEAM			
❑ 106	Straighten Up and Fly Right/ Wrong Guy	1958	10.00
❑ 116	Do-Die/Wedding Postponed	1958	10.00
❑ 124	Watermelon Heart/Sorry for Myself	1959	10.00
❑ 126	Hoppity Moe Joe/Don't Forget to Remember	1959	10.00
UNITED ARTISTS			
❑ 213	Be Anything (But Be Mine)/ Yes Indeed	1960	8.00
Albums			
EPIC			
❑ LN 1116 [M]	The DeJohn Sisters	195?	30.00
UNITED ARTISTS			
❑ UAL-3103 [M]	Yes Indeed	1960	20.00
❑ UAS-6103 [S]	Yes Indeed	1960	25.00

DEKKER, DESMOND, AND THE ACES

Number	Title (A Side/B Side)	Yr	NM
45s			
UNI			
❑ 55129	Israelites/My Precious World	1969	6.00
❑ 55150	It Mek/Problems	1969	6.00
❑ 55261	You Can Get It If You Really Want It/Perseverance	1970	6.00
Albums			
BULLDOG			
❑ 1037	The Israelites	198?	10.00
UNI			
❑ 73059	Israelites	1969	30.00

DEL-AIRES, THE

Number	Title (A Side/B Side)	Yr	NM
45s			
CORAL			
❑ 62370	Elaine/Just Wigglin' and a-Wobblin'	1963	40.00
❑ 62404	The Drag/My Funny Valentine	1964	40.00
—As "Ronnie and the Del-Aires"			
❑ 62419	Arlene/I'm Yours Baby	1964	70.00

DEL AND THE ESCORTS

Number	Title (A Side/B Side)	Yr	NM
45s			
ROME			
❑ 103	Baby Doll/Someone to Watch Over Me	1961	50.00
SYMBOL			
❑ 913	You Don't Love Me/Skokiian	1960	—
—Unreleased?			
TAURUS			
❑ 350/1	Happy/You're for Me (And I'm for You)	1961	30.00

DEL LORDS, THE Also see THE DICTATORS.

Number	Title (A Side/B Side)	Yr	NM
12-Inch Singles			
ENIGMA			
❑ 097 [DJ]	A Lover's Prayer (same on both sides)	1988	6.00
45s			
ENIGMA			
❑ EPRO 090 [DJ]	Judas Kiss (Radio Edit)/Judas Kiss (Vocal Edit)	1988	6.00
Albums			
EMI AMERICA			
❑ ST-17183	Johnny Comes Marching Home	1986	12.00
ENIGMA			
❑ D1-73326	Based on a True Story	1988	10.00

DEL-PHIS, THE Early incarnation of MARTHA AND THE VANDELLAS.

Number	Title (A Side/B Side)	Yr	NM
45s			
CHECKMATE			
❑ 1005	I'll Let You Know/It Takes Two	1961	200.00

DEL RAYS, THE

Number	Title (A Side/B Side)	Yr	NM
45s			
CORD			
❑ 1001	Our Love Is True/One Kiss, One Smile and a Dream	1958	4000.
MOON			
❑ 110	Have a Heart/Around the Corner	1959	300.00
WARNER BROS.			
❑ 5022	My Darling/The One I Adore	1958	80.00

DEL-RHYTHMETTES

Number	Title (A Side/B Side)	Yr	NM
45s			
JVB			
❑ 5000	Chic-a-Boomer/ I Need Your Love	1959	60.00

DEL RIO SISTERS, THE

Number	Title (A Side/B Side)	Yr	NM
45s			
TONE-CRAFT			
❑ 201	The Wallflower (Dance with Me, Henry)/Baby Be Sweet to Me	1955	20.00
❑ 203	Beautiful Eyes/Beginning to Miss You	1955	20.00

Number	Title (A Side/B Side)	Yr	NM

DEL RIOS, THE Probably more than one group.

45s

BET-T
- ❑ 7001 Heavenly Angel/Dangerous Lover 1962 1200.

METEOR
- ❑ 5038 Lizzie/Alone on a Rainy Night 1956 800.00

NEPTUNE
- ❑ 108 Wait Wait Wait/I'm Crying 1959 60.00

RUST
- ❑ 5066 Valerie/Mystery 1963 60.00

STAX
- ❑ 125 There's a Love/Just Across the Street 1962 50.00

DEL SATINS

45s

B.T. PUPPY
- ❑ 506 Hang Around/Candy Apple 'Vette 1965 15.00
- ❑ 509 Sweets for My Sweet/A Girl Named Arlene 1965 30.00
- ❑ 514 Relief/Throwaway Song 1966 15.00
- ❑ 563 I'll Do My Crying Tomorrow/A Girl Named Arlene 1970 12.00

COLUMBIA
- ❑ 42802 Feelin' No Pain/Who Cares 1963 25.00
- ❑ 42802 [PS] Feelin' No Pain/Who Cares 1963 100.00

DIAMOND
- ❑ 216 A Little Rain Must Fall/Love, Hate, Revenge (If I Want You to Cry) 1967 15.00

END
- ❑ 1096 I'll Pray for You/I Remember the Night 1961 200.00

LAURIE
- ❑ 3132 Teardrops Follow Me/Best Wishes, Good Luck, Goodbye 1962 25.00
- ❑ 3149 Ballad of a Deejay/Does My Love Stand a Chance 1962 25.00

MALA
- ❑ 475 Believe in Me/Two Broken Hearts 1964 20.00

WIN
- ❑ 702 Counting Teardrops/Remember 1961 60.00

—Orange label
- ❑ 702 Counting Teardrops/Remember 1961 120.00

—Black label

Albums

B.T. PUPPY
- ❑ BTS-1019 Out to Lunch 1972 300.00

DEL-VETTS, THE

45s

DUNWICH
- ❑ 125 Last Time Around/Everytime 1966 20.00
- ❑ 142 I Call My Baby STP/That's the Way It Is 1966 20.00
- ❑ 142 [PS] I Call My Baby STP/That's the Way It Is 1966 30.00

—Some sleeves contain an STP decal.

SEEBERG
- ❑ 3018 [M] Ram Charger/Little Latin Lupe Lu 1965 30.00
- ❑ 3018 [S] Little Latin Lupe Lu/Ram Charger 1965 40.00

—With "Stereo" on label

7-Inch Extended Plays

SUNDAZED
- ❑ SEP 124 Last Time Around/Everytime//I Call My Baby STP/That's the Way It Is 1997 3.00

—Gold vinyl
- ❑ SEP 124 [PS] The Del-Vetts 1997 3.00

DEL VIKINGS, THE Usually considered to be one group, but actually three: Two of them splintered from the original group, one featuring Kripp Johnson, the other featuring Gus Backus. For convenience's sake, all are listed together.

45s

ABC-PARAMOUNT
- ❑ 10208 I'll Never Stop Crying/Bring Back Your Heart 1961 25.00
- ❑ 10248 I Hear Bells (Wedding Bells)/Don't Get Slick on Me 1961 50.00
- ❑ 10278 Kiss Me/Face the Music 1961 25.00
- ❑ 10304 Big Silence/One More River to Cross 1962 25.00
- ❑ 10341 Confession of Love/Kilimanjaro 1962 25.00
- ❑ 10385 An Angel Up in Heaven/Fishing Chant 1962 50.00
- ❑ 10425 Too Many Miles/Sorcerer's Apprentice 1963 25.00

ALPINE
- ❑ 66 Pistol Packin' Mama/The Sun 1960 80.00
- ❑ 66 [PS] Pistol Packin' Mama/The Sun 1960 100.00

BIM BAM BOOM
- ❑ 111 Cold Feet/A Little Man Cried 1972 5.00
- ❑ 113 Watching the Moon/You Say You Love Me 1972 5.00
- ❑ 115 I'm Spinning/Girl Girl 1972 5.00

DOT
- ❑ 15538 Come Go with Me/How Can I Find True Love 1957 30.00
- ❑ 15571 What Made Maggie Run/Little Billy Boy 1957 30.00
- ❑ 15592 Whispering Bells/Don't Be a Fool 1957 30.00
- ❑ 15636 I'm Spinning/When I Come Home 1957 30.00

—As "Kripp Johnson with the Dell-Vikings"
- ❑ 16092 Come Go with Me/How Can I Find True Love 1960 20.00
- ❑ 16236 Come Go with Me/Whispering Bells 1961 20.00
- ❑ 16248 I Hear Bells (Wedding Bells)/Don't Get Slick on Me 1961 20.00

DRC
- ❑ 101 Can't You See/Oh I 196? 40.00

FEE BEE
- ❑ 173 Welfare Blues/Hollywood and Vine 1977 5.00
- ❑ 205 Come Go with Me/How Can I Find True Love 1957 250.00

—Orange label, one side has bee, the other side doesn't
- ❑ 205 Come Go with Me/How Can I Find True Love 1957 500.00

—Orange label, bee on top
- ❑ 205 Come Go with Me/How Can I Find True Love 1961 30.00

—Orange label, no bee
- ❑ 205 Come Go with Me/Whispering Bells 1964 20.00
- ❑ 206 Down in Bermuda/Maggie 1964 80.00
- ❑ 210 What Made Maggie Run/Uh Uh Baby 1957 80.00
- ❑ 210 What Made Maggie Run/When I Come Home 1957 120.00
- ❑ 210 What Made Maggie Run/Down by the Stream 1964 30.00
- ❑ 214 Whispering Bells/Don't Be a Fool 1957 400.00
- ❑ 218 I'm Spinning/You Say You Love Me 1957 120.00

—Bee on label
- ❑ 218 I'm Spinning/You Say You Love Me 1964 30.00

—No bee on label
- ❑ 221 Willette/I Want to Marry You 1958 80.00
- ❑ 221 Willette/Woke Up This Morning 1958 100.00
- ❑ 227 Tell Me/Finger Poppin' Woman 1959 80.00
- ❑ 902 True Love/Baby, Let Me Know 1964 30.00

—As "The Original Dell Vikings"

GATEWAY
- ❑ 743 We Three/I've Got to Know 1964 30.00

JOJO
- ❑ 108 Keep On Walkin'/My Body, Your Shadow 1976 5.00

LUNIVERSE
- ❑ 106 Somewhere Over the Rainbow/Hey, Senorita 1957 100.00
- ❑ 110 Yours/Heaven and Paradise 1958 20.00
- ❑ 113 In the Still of the Night/The White Cliffs of Dover 1958 20.00
- ❑ 114 There I Go/Girl Girl 1958 20.00

—The above three Luniverse 45s are bootlegs, but they perversely do have collector's value!

MERCURY
- ❑ 71132 Cool Shake/Jitterbug Mary 1957 30.00
- ❑ 71180 Come Along with Me/Whatcha Gonna Lose 1957 30.00
- ❑ 71198 I'm Spinning/When I Come Home 1957 30.00
- ❑ 71241 Snowbound/Your Book of Life 1957 30.00
- ❑ 71266 The Voodoo Man/Can't Wait 1958 30.00
- ❑ 71345 You Cheated/Pretty Little Things Called Girls 1958 30.00

—Black label
- ❑ 71345 You Cheated/Pretty Little Things Called Girls 1958 40.00

—Blue label
- ❑ 71390 How Could You/Flat Tire 1958 30.00

SCEPTER
- ❑ 12367 Come Go with Me/When You're Asleep 1973 5.00

SHIP
- ❑ 214 Sunday Kind of Love/Over the Rainbow 197? 4.00

7-Inch Extended Plays

DOT
- ❑ DEP-1058 Come Go with Me/Don't Be a Fool//Whispering Bells/What Made Maggie Run 1957 100.00
- ❑ DEP-1058 [PS] Come Go with Us 1957 200.00

MERCURY
- ❑ EP 1-3359 Come Along with Me/A Sunday Kind of Love//(There'll Be Blue Birds Over) The White Cliffs of Dover/Now Is the Hour 1957 100.00
- ❑ EP 1-3359 [PS] They Sing — They Swing, Vol. 1 1957 150.00
- ❑ EP 1-3362 Heart and Soul/My Foolish Heart//Down in Bermuda/I'm Sitting on Top of the World 1957 100.00
- ❑ EP 1-3362 [PS] They Sing — They Swing, Vol. 2 1957 150.00
- ❑ EP 1-3363 Somewhere Over the Rainbow/Is It Any Wonder//Yours/Summertime 1957 100.00
- ❑ EP 1-3363 [PS] They Sing — They Swing, Vol. 3 1957 150.00

Albums

COLLECTABLES
- ❑ COL-5010 The Best of the Dell-Vikings 198? 12.00

DOT
- ❑ DLP-3685 [M] Come Go with Me 1966 200.00
- ❑ DLP-25685 [R] Come Go with Me 1966 150.00

LUNIVERSE
- ❑ LP-1000 [M] Come Go with the Del Vikings 1957 500.00

—Eight tracks, cover is composed of slicks. Counterfeits have more tracks and a preprinted cover (not slicks)

MERCURY
- ❑ MG-20314 [M] They Sing — They Swing 1957 300.00
- ❑ MG-20353 [M] A Swinging, Singing Record Session 1958 200.00

DEL VIKINGS, THE / THE SONNETS

Albums

CROWN
- ❑ CLP-5368 [M] The Del Vikings and the Sonnets 1963 40.00

DEL-VUES, THE

45s

U-TOWN
- ❑ 8008 After New Year's/My Confession 195? 600.00

DELACARDOS, THE (1)

45s

ELGEY
- ❑ 1001 A Letter to a School Girl/I'll Never Let You Down 1959 50.00

SHELL
- ❑ 308 Dream Girl/I Just Want to Know 1961 20.00
- ❑ 311 Love Is the Greatest Thing/Girl-Girl 1962 20.00

UNITED ARTISTS
- ❑ 276 I Got It/Thing-A-Ma-Jig 1960 15.00
- ❑ 310 Hold Back the Tears/Mr. Dillon 1961 20.00

DELACARDOS, THE (2)

45s

ATLANTIC
- ❑ 2368 Got No One/She's the One I Love 1966 10.00
- ❑ 2389 I Know I'm Not Much/You Don't Have to See Me 1967 10.00
- ❑ 2419 They Put a Spell on You/A Fool for You 1967 10.00

DELACARDOS, THE (U) These may be group (1) or (2), or they may be a completely different group or groups.

45s

DIMENSION
- ❑ 1040 Forget About the Guy/Dance, Gypsy, Dance 1964 20.00

IMPERIAL
- ❑ 5992 On the Beach/Everybody's Rockin' 1963 15.00

DELANCEYS, THE

45s

ABC-PARAMOUNT
- ❑ 10353 High Voltage/The Scratch 1962 25.00

DELANEY AND BONNIE Also see BONNIE BRAMLETT; DELANEY BRAMLETT.

45s

ATCO
- ❑ 6725 Groupie (Superstar)/Comin' Home 1969 8.00
- ❑ 6756 Soul Shake/Free the People 1970 8.00
- ❑ 6788 Miss Ann/They Call It Rock and Roll Music 1970 8.00

Except when noted otherwise, VG = 25% of NM, and VG+ = 50% of NM. (Example: VG = $2.00, VG+ = $4.00 and NM = $8.00.)

Number	Title (A Side/B Side)	Yr	NM
❑ 6804	Never Ending Song of Love/ Don't Deceive Me	1971	8.00
❑ 6838	Only You Know and I Know/ God Knows I Love You	1971	6.00
❑ 6866	Sing My Way Home/ Move 'Em Out	1972	5.00
❑ 6883	Where There's a Will There's a Way/Lonesome and a Long Way from Home	1972	5.00
❑ 6904	Sing My Way Home/Will the Circle Be Unbroken	1972	5.00
COLUMBIA			
❑ 45608	Country Life/Walk in the River Jordan	1972	5.00
ELEKTRA			
❑ 45660	Soldiers of the Cross/ Get Ourselves Together	1969	10.00
❑ 45662	When the Battle Is Over/ Get Ourselves Together	1969	10.00
GARPAX			
❑ 44184	Cherry Pie/Hey Mr. Weatherman	1964	15.00
—As "Lani & Boni"			
INDEPENDENCE			
❑ 78	You've Lost That Lovin' Feelin'/ Don't Let It (Be the Last Time)	1967	12.00
STAX			
❑ 0003	It's Been a Long Time Coming/ We've Just Been Feeling Bad	1968	10.00
❑ 0057	Hard to Say Goodbye/ Just Plain Beautiful	1969	10.00

Albums

Number	Title	Yr	NM
ATCO			
❑ SD 33-326	Delaney & Bonnie & Friends On Tour with Eric Clapton	197?	10.00
—Later pressings on other labels			
❑ SD 33-326	Delaney & Bonnie & Friends On Tour with Eric Clapton	1970	25.00
—Yellow label original			
❑ 33-341 [M]	To Bonnie from Delaney	1970	40.00
—White label promo; no stock copies were issued in mono			
❑ SD 33-341 [S]	To Bonnie from Delaney	1970	25.00
❑ SD 33-358	Motel Shot	1971	25.00
❑ SD 33-383	Country Life	1972	20.00
❑ SD 7014	The Best of Delaney and Bonnie	1972	20.00
COLUMBIA			
❑ KC 31377	D&B Together	1972	20.00
ELEKTRA			
❑ EKS-74039	Accept No Substitute — The Original Delaney & Bonnie & Friends	1969	30.00
GNP CRESCENDO			
❑ GNPS-2054	Genesis	1970	20.00
STAX			
❑ STS-2026	Home	1969	30.00

DELEGATES, THE (1)
Novelty group.

45s

Number	Title	Yr	NM
MAINSTREAM			
❑ 5525	Convention '72 (same on both sides)	1972	8.00
—Stock copy; "Funky Butt" deleted because of retailers' protests to the title			
❑ 5525	Convention '72/Funky Butt	1972	10.00
❑ 5530	Richard M. Nixon Faces the Issues (same on both sides)	1972	8.00
❑ 5530	Richard M. Nixon Faces the Issues/Touzie's Blues	1972	10.00

Albums

Number	Title	Yr	NM
MAINSTREAM			
❑ 100	The Delegates	1973	20.00

DELEGATES, THE (2)
See BILLY LARKIN.

DELEGATES, THE (3)
DEE CLARK was a member.

45s

Number	Title	Yr	NM
VEE JAY			
❑ 212	The Convention/Jay's Rock	1956	60.00
—B-side by Big Jay McNeely			
❑ 243	Mother's Son/I'm Gonna Be Glad	1957	60.00

DELFONICS, THE
Also see MAJOR HARRIS.

45s

Number	Title	Yr	NM
ARISTA			
❑ 0308	Don't Throw It All Away/I Don't Care What People Say	1978	4.00
CAMEO			
❑ 472	You've Been Untrue/I Was There	1967	15.00
MOON SHOT			
❑ 6703	He Don't Really Love You/ Without You	1967	15.00
PHILLY GROOVE			
❑ 150	La-La Means I Love You/ Can't Get Over Losing You	1968	10.00
❑ 151	I'm Sorry/You're Gone	1968	10.00
❑ 152	Break Your Promise/Alfie	1968	10.00
❑ 154	Ready Or Not Here I Come (Can't Hide from Love)/ Somebody Loves You	1968	10.00
❑ 156	Funny Feeling/My New Love	1969	10.00
❑ 157	You Got Yours and I'll Get Mine/ Loving Him	1969	10.00
❑ 161	Didn't I (Blow Your Mind This Time)/Down Is Up, Up Is Down	1970	10.00
❑ 162	Trying to Make a Fool of Me/ Baby I Love You	1970	10.00
❑ 163	When You Get Right Down To It/I Gave to You	1970	10.00
❑ 166	Over and Over/Hey! Love	1971	8.00
❑ 169	Walk Right Up to the Sun/ Round and Round	1971	8.00
❑ 172	Tell Me This Is a Dream/ I'm a Man	1972	8.00
❑ 174	Think It Over/I'm a Man	1972	8.00
❑ 176	I Don't Want to Make You Wait/ Baby I Miss You	1973	8.00
❑ 177	Alfie/Start All Over Again	1973	8.00
❑ 182	I Told You So/Seventeen and In Love	1973	8.00
❑ 184	Lying to Myself/Hey Baby	1974	8.00
❑ NS-1001/2	La-La Means I Love You/ Can't Get Over Losing You	1968	20.00
—Light blue label with no regular catalog number			

Albums

Number	Title	Yr	NM
ARISTA			
❑ AL 8333	The Best of the Delfonics	198?	10.00
COLLECTABLES			
❑ COL-5109	Golden Classics	198?	10.00
KORY			
❑ 1002	The Best of the Delfonics	1977	12.00
PHILLY GROOVE			
❑ 1150	La La Means I Love You	1968	80.00
❑ 1151	The Sexy Sound of Soul	1969	80.00
❑ 1152	The Delfonics Super Hits	1969	50.00
❑ 1153	The Delfonics	1970	50.00
❑ 1154	Tell Me This Is a Dream	1972	50.00
❑ 1501	Alive & Kicking	1974	50.00
POOGIE			
❑ 121680	The Delfonics Return	1981	12.00

DELICATES, THE
More than one group?

45s

Number	Title	Yr	NM
CELESTE			
❑ 676	My Pillow/I Played 1,2,3,4	1961	30.00
CHALLENGE			
❑ 59232	I've Been Hurt/Come On Everybody	1964	15.00
❑ 59267	I Want to Get Married/ Home from Camp	1965	15.00
❑ 59304	Stop Shovin' Me Around/ Comin' Down with Love	1965	15.00
DEE DEE			
❑ 677	My Pillow/I Played 1,2,3,4	1961	30.00
ROULETTE			
❑ 4321	Little Ship/Not Tomorrow	1961	20.00
❑ 4360	Little Boy of Mine/ Dickie Went and Did It	1961	20.00
❑ 4387	I Don't Know Why (I Just Do)/ Strange Love	1961	20.00
UNART			
❑ 2017	Black and White Thunderbird/ Ronnie Is My Lover	1959	25.00
❑ 2024	Ringa Ding/Meusurry	1959	25.00
UNITED ARTISTS			
❑ 210	Flip Flip/Your Happiest Years	1960	20.00
❑ 228	The Kiss/Too Young to Date	1960	20.00

DELL, DICKEY, AND THE BING BONGS

45s

Number	Title	Yr	NM
DRAGON			
❑ 10205	Ding-a-Ling-a-Ling-Ding-Dong/ The Cling	1958	150.00

DELL, EVELYN, AND THE VIBRATIONS

45s

Number	Title	Yr	NM
ABC-PARAMOUNT			
❑ 10218	Sincerely/Please Tell Me Why	1961	25.00

DELL, LENNY, AND THE DEMENSIONS
See THE DEMENSIONS.

DELL, RICHIE

45s

Number	Title	Yr	NM
KING			
❑ 5888	Come On Let's Sing/King Lover	1964	20.00

DELL, TONY

45s

Number	Title	Yr	NM
KING			
❑ 5766	My Girl/Magic Wand	1963	50.00

DELL-COEDS, THE

45s

Number	Title	Yr	NM
DOT			
❑ 16314	Hey Mr. Banjo/Love in Return	1962	12.00

DELL VIKINGS, THE
See THE DEL-VIKINGS.

DELLS, THE

45s

Number	Title	Yr	NM
ABC			
❑ 12386	Super Woman/My Life Is So Wonderful	1978	5.00
❑ 12422	(I Wanna) Testify/Don't Save Me	1978	5.00
❑ 12422	(I Wanna) Testify/Drowning for Your Love	1978	5.00
❑ 12440	(You Bring Out) The Best in Me/ Wrapped Up Tight	1978	5.00
ARGO			
❑ 5415	God Bless the Child/ I'm Going Home	1962	12.00
❑ 5428	The (Bossa Nova) Bird/ Eternally	1962	12.00
❑ 5442	Hi Diddle Dee Dum Dum (It's a Good Feelin')/If It Ain't One Thing, It's Another	1963	12.00
❑ 5456	After You/Goodbye Mary Ann	1963	12.00
CADET			
❑ 5538	Thinkin' About You/The Change We Go Thru (For Love)	1966	6.00
❑ 5551	Over Again/Run for Cover	1967	6.00
❑ 5563	You Belong to Someone Else/ Inspiration	1967	6.00
❑ 5574	O-O, I Love You/There Is	1967	6.00
❑ 5590	There Is/Show Me	1968	8.00
❑ 5599	Wear it On Our Face/Please Don't Change Me Now	1968	6.00
❑ 5612	Stay in My Corner/ Love Is So Simple	1969	6.00
❑ 5621	Always Together/ I Want My Mama	1968	6.00
❑ 5631	Does Anybody Know I'm Here/ Make Sure (You Have Somebody to Love You)	1968	6.00
❑ 5636	I Can't Do Enough/ Hallways of My Mind	1969	6.00
❑ 5641	I Can Sing a Rainbow-Love Is Blue/Hallelujah Baby	1969	6.00
❑ 5649	Oh What a Night/Believe Me	1969	6.00
❑ 5658	On the Dock of the Bay/ When I'm in Your Arms	1969	6.00
❑ 5663	Oh What a Day/The Change We Go Thru (For Love)	1970	6.00
❑ 5667	Open Up My Heart/Nadine	1970	6.00
❑ 5672	Long Lonely Nights/A Little Understanding	1970	6.00
❑ 5679	The Glory of Love/A Whiter Shade of Pale	1970	6.00
❑ 5683	The Love We Had (Stays on My Mind)/Freedom Means	1971	6.00
❑ 5689	It's All Up to You/Oh, My Dear	1972	6.00
❑ 5691	Walk On By/This Guy's in Love with You	1972	6.00
❑ 5694	Just As Long As We're in Love/ I'd Rather Be with You	1972	6.00
❑ 5696	Give Your Baby a Standing Ovation/Closer	1973	6.00
❑ 5698	My Pretending Days Are Over/ Let's Make It Last	1973	6.00
❑ 5700	I Miss You/Don't Make Me a Storyteller	1973	6.00
❑ 5702	I Wish It Was Me You Loved/ Two Together Is Better Than One	1974	6.00
❑ 5703	Bring Back the Love of Yesterday/Learning to Love You Was Easy (It's So Hard Trying to Get Over You)	1974	6.00
❑ 5703	Sweeter as the Days Go By/ Learning to Love You Was Easy (It's So Hard Trying to Get Over You)	1974	6.00
—A-side is the same song with a new title			

Number	Title (A Side/B Side)	Yr	NM
❑ 5707	The Glory of Love/You're the Greatest	1975	6.00
❑ 5711	We Got to Get Our Thing Together/The Power of Love	1975	8.00
CHECKER			
❑ 794	Darling I Know/Christine	1954	1200.
—As "The El Rays"			
LOST-NITE			
❑ 264	Tell the World/Blues at Three	197?	5.00
—Reissue			
❑ 272	Dreams of Contentment/Zing, Zing, Zing	197?	5.00
—Reissue			
❑ 281	Why Do You Have to Go/Dance, Dance, Dance	197?	5.00
—Reissue			
❑ 290	Stay in My Corner/A Distant Love	197?	5.00
❑ 297	Pain in My Heart/Time Makes You Change	197?	5.00
—Reissue			
❑ 305	Oh What a Nite/Jo-Jo	197?	5.00
—Reissue			
MCA			
❑ 41051	Plastic People/What I Could	1979	5.00
MERCURY			
❑ 73723	We Got to Get Our Thing Together/Reminiscing	1975	5.00
❑ 73759	The Power of Love/Gotta Get Home to My Baby	1976	5.00
❑ 73807	Slow Motion/Ain't No Black and White in Music	1976	5.00
❑ 73842	No Way Back/Too Late for Love	1976	5.00
❑ 73901	Betcha Never Been Loved (Like This Before)/Get On Down	1977	5.00
❑ 73909	Our Love/Could It Be	1977	5.00
❑ 73977	Private Property/Teaser	1977	5.00
PHILCO-FORD			
❑ HP-32	There Is/Show Me	1968	20.00
—4-inch plastic "Hip Pocket Record" with color sleeve			
PRIVATE I			
❑ 04343	Don't Want Nobody/You Can't Just Walk Away	1984	4.00
❑ 04448	One Step Closer/Come On Back to Me	1984	4.00
❑ 04540	Love On/Don't Want Nobody	1984	4.00
SKYLARK			
❑ 558	I Can't Help Myself/She's Just an Angel	198?	4.00
❑ 581	Someone to Call Me Darling/Now I Pray	198?	4.00
20TH CENTURY			
❑ 2463	I Touched a Dream/All About the Paper	1980	4.00
❑ 2475	Passionate Breezes/Your Song	1980	4.00
❑ 2504	Happy Song/Look at Us Now	1981	4.00
❑ 2602	Ain't It a Shame/Stay in My Corner	1982	4.00
VEE JAY			
❑ 134	Tell the World/Blues at Three	1955	2000.
❑ 134	Tell the World/Blues at Three	1955	5000.
—Red vinyl. VG 2500; VG+ 3750			
❑ 166	Dreams of Contentment/Zing, Zing, Zing	1955	200.00
❑ 204	Oh What a Nite/Jo-Jo	1956	120.00
❑ 230	Movin' On/I Wanna Go Home	1956	40.00
❑ 236	Why Do You Have to Go/Dance, Dance, Dance	1957	40.00
❑ 251	A Distant Love/O-Bop She-Bop	1957	40.00
❑ 258	Pain in My Heart/Time Makes You Change	1957	40.00
❑ 274	The Springer/What You Say Baby	1958	30.00
❑ 292	I'm Calling/Jeepers Creepers	1958	30.00
❑ 300	Wedding Day/My Best Girl	1958	100.00
❑ 324	Dry Your Eyes/Baby Open Up Your Heart	1959	40.00
❑ 338	Oh What a Nite/I Wanna Go Home	1960	20.00
❑ 376	Hold On to What You've Got/Swingin' Teens	1961	20.00
❑ 595	Shy Girl/What Do We Prove	1964	12.00
❑ 595 [PS]	Shy Girl/What Do We Prove	1964	50.00
—Promo-only sleeve			
❑ 615	Wait Till Tomorrow/Oh What a Good Night	1964	12.00
❑ 674	Stay in My Corner/It's Not Unusual	1965	12.00
❑ 712	Poor Little Boy/Hey Sugar (Don't Get Serious)	1966	12.00
VETERAN			
❑ 7-101	Thought of You Just a Little Too Much/(B-side unknown)	1989	5.00

Number	Title (A Side/B Side)	Yr	NM
Albums			
ABC			
❑ AA-1100	New Beginnings	1978	12.00
❑ AA-1113	Face to Face	1978	12.00
BUDDAH			
❑ BDS-5053	The Dells	1969	15.00
CADET			
❑ LPS-804	There Is	1968	50.00
❑ LPS-822	The Dells Musical Menu/Always Together	1969	50.00
❑ LPS-824	The Dells Greatest Hits	1969	50.00
❑ LPS-829	Love Is Blue	1969	50.00
❑ LPS-837	Like It Is, Like It Was	1970	50.00
❑ 50004	Freedom Means	1971	25.00
❑ 50017	The Dells Sing Dionne Warwicke's Greatest Hits	1972	25.00
❑ 50021	Sweet As Funk Can Be	1972	25.00
❑ 50037	Give Your Baby a Standing Ovation	1973	25.00
❑ 50046	The Dells	1973	25.00
❑ 60030	The Mighty Mighty Dells	1974	25.00
❑ 60036	The Dells' Greatest Hits, Vol. 2	1975	20.00
CHESS			
❑ CH-9103	The Dells	198?	10.00
—Reissue			
❑ CH-9288	There Is	1989	10.00
—Reissue of Cadet 804			
LOST-NITE			
❑ LLP-21 [10]	The Dells	1981	15.00
—Red vinyl, generic red cover			
MERCURY			
❑ SRM-1-1059	We Got to Get Our Thing Together	1975	15.00
❑ SRM-1-1084	No Way Back	1976	15.00
❑ SRM-1-1145	They Said It Couldn't Be Done	1977	15.00
❑ SRM-1-3711	Love Connection	1977	15.00
PRIVATE I			
❑ BFZ 39309	One Step Closer	1984	10.00
SOLID SMOKE			
❑ 8029	Breezy Ballads and Tender Tunes: The Best of the Early Years (1955-65)	1984	10.00
20TH CENTURY			
❑ T-618	I Touched a Dream	1980	12.00
❑ T-633	Whatever Turns You On	1981	12.00
UPFRONT			
❑ UPF-105	Stay In My Corner	1968	15.00
URGENT			
❑ URG-4108	The Second Time	1991	12.00
VEE JAY			
❑ LP 1010 [M]	Oh What a Nite	1959	800.00
—Maroon label			
❑ LP 1010 [M]	Oh What a Nite	1961	300.00
—Black label with colorband			
❑ VJLP-1010	Oh What a Nite	198?	10.00
—Late-80s reissue on reactivated Vee Jay label. "Trade Mark Reg." on label.			
❑ LP 1141 [M]	It's Not Unusual	1965	100.00
❑ LPS 1141 [S]	It's Not Unusual	1965	150.00
VJ INTERNATIONAL			
❑ 7305	The Dells In Concert	197?	12.00
ZOO			
❑ 11023	I Salute You	1992	15.00

DELLS, THE, AND THE DRAMATICS Also see each artist's individual listings.

Number	Title (A Side/B Side)	Yr	NM
45s			
CADET			
❑ 5710	Love Is Missing from Our Lives/I'm in Love	1975	6.00
Albums			
CADET			
❑ 60027	The Dells Vs. the Dramatics	1974	25.00

DELLTONES, THE

Number	Title (A Side/B Side)	Yr	NM
45s			
BATON			
❑ 212	Don't Be Long/Baby Say You Love Me	1955	30.00
❑ 223	My Special Love/Believe It	1956	30.00
BRUNSWICK			
❑ 84015	My Heart's on Fire/Yours Alone	1953	200.00
RAINBOW			
❑ 244	I'm Not in Love with You/Little Short Daddy	1954	100.00

DELMIRAS, THE

Number	Title (A Side/B Side)	Yr	NM
45s			
DADE			
❑ 1821	Dry Your Eyes/The Big Sound	1961	300.00

DELMONICOS, THE

Number	Title (A Side/B Side)	Yr	NM
45s			
MUSICTONE			
❑ 6122	World's Biggest Fool/Until You	1963	30.00

DELPHS, JIMMY

Number	Title (A Side/B Side)	Yr	NM
45s			
CARLA			
❑ 1904	Dancing a Hole in the World/(B-side unknown)	1968	1200.
❑ 2535	Almost/I've Been Fooled Before	1967	25.00
KAREN			
❑ 1538	Don't Sign the Paper Baby (I Want You Back)/Almost	1968	12.00
❑ 1541	Feels Like Summer's Coming On/Mrs. Percy Please Have Mercy	1968	12.00
❑ 1550	Am I Losing You/Love, I Want You Back	1968	12.00

DELRONS, THE See REPARATA AND THE DELRONS.

DELROYS, THE

Number	Title (A Side/B Side)	Yr	NM
45s			
APOLLO			
❑ 514	Bermuda Shorts/Time	1957	25.00

DELTAIRS, THE

Number	Title (A Side/B Side)	Yr	NM
45s			
FELSTED			
❑ 8525	Who Would Have Thought It/You Won't Be Satisfied	1959	30.00
IVY			
❑ 101	Lullaby of the Bells/It's Only You Dear	1957	150.00
—Yellow label			
❑ 101	Lullaby of the Bells/It's Only You Dear	1958	30.00
❑ 105	Standing at the Altar/I Might Like It	1958	30.00

DELTAS, THE More than one group?

Number	Title (A Side/B Side)	Yr	NM
45s			
CAMBRIDGE			
❑ 124	Goodnight My Love/Give My Love a Chance	1962	40.00
GONE			
❑ 5010	Let Me Share Your Dream/Lamplight	1957	80.00
—Multi-color label			
❑ 5010	Let Me Share Your Dream/Lamplight	1957	3000.
—Black label			
PHILIPS			
❑ 40023	My Own True Love/Hold Me, Thrill Me, Kiss Me	1962	15.00
❑ 40023	My Own True Love/Work Song	1962	20.00

DELTONES, THE

Number	Title (A Side/B Side)	Yr	NM
45s			
JUBILEE			
❑ 5374	La La La/Bow-Legged Annie	1959	25.00
LANA			
❑ 113	Hey Little Girl/Love Potion No. 9	196?	8.00
—B-side by the Clovers			
❑ 114	Since I Met You/Devil or Angel	196?	8.00
—B-side by the Clovers			
VEE JAY			
❑ 288	I'm Coming Home/Early Morning Rock	1958	40.00
❑ 303	A Lover's Prayer/First Man to the Moon	1958	40.00

DELTOURS, THE

Number	Title (A Side/B Side)	Yr	NM
45s			
STARVILLE			
❑ 1206	Sweet and Lovely/(B-side unknown)	196?	1500.

DELVETTS, THE

Number	Title (A Side/B Side)	Yr	NM
45s			
END			
❑ 1106	I Want a Boy for Christmas/Repeat After Me	1961	30.00
❑ 1107	Will You Love Me in Heaven/Repeat After Me	1962	20.00

DEMARCO, RALPH

Number	Title (A Side/B Side)	Yr	NM
45s			
GUARANTEED			
❑ 202	More Than Riches/Old Shep	1959	20.00
❑ 202 [PS]	More Than Riches/Old Shep	1959	40.00

Number	Title (A Side/B Side)	Yr	NM
SHELLEY			
❑ 1011	Donna/For All We Know	1960	40.00
20TH FOX			
❑ 309	Keep On Walkin'/ Lonely for a Girl	1962	20.00

DEMATTEO, NICKY

Number	Title (A Side/B Side)	Yr	NM
45s			
ABC-PARAMOUNT			
❑ 10186	Right Now/Mirror, Mirror On the Wall	1961	15.00
CAMEO			
❑ 407	I Wanna Be Lonely/ Little Red Kitten	1966	25.00
—With the Sorrows			
DIAMOND			
❑ 138	The Story of My Life/ Baby, That's All	1963	15.00
GUYDEN			
❑ 2024	Suddenly/I Couldn't Sleep a Wink Last Night	1960	15.00
❑ 2042	Close to You Forever/As Big As My Love for You	1960	15.00
PARIS			
❑ 529	Secret of Love/Story of Love	1959	15.00
TORE			
❑ 1007	Young Love Is an Old, Old Story/Make Her Mine	1959	25.00

DEMENS, THE

Number	Title (A Side/B Side)	Yr	NM
45s			
TEENAGE			
❑ 1006	Take Me As I Am/You Broke My Heart	1958	200.00
❑ 1007	I'm Not in Love with You/ Short Daddy	1958	200.00
❑ 1008	The Greatest of Them All/ Hey Young Girl	1958	200.00

DEMENSIONS, THE

Number	Title (A Side/B Side)	Yr	NM
45s			
CORAL			
❑ 62277	Again/Count Your Blessings Instead of Sheep	1961	25.00
❑ 62293	As Time Goes By/ Seven Days a Week	1961	25.00
❑ 62323	Young at Heart/ Your Cheatin' Heart	1962	20.00
❑ 62344	My Foolish Heart/Just One More Chance	1963	30.00
❑ 62344 [PS]	My Foolish Heart/Just One More Chance	1963	100.00
❑ 62359	Fly Me to the Moon/You'll Never Know	1963	25.00
❑ 62382	Just a Shoulder to Cry On/ Don't Worry About Bobby	1963	25.00
❑ 62392	A Little White Gardenia/ Don't Cry Pretty Baby	1964	20.00
❑ 62432	This Time Next Year/ My Old Girlfriend	1964	20.00
—As "Lenny Dell and the Demensions"			
❑ 62444	Once a Day/Ting Along Ting Toy	1965	20.00
—As "Lenny Dell and the Demensions"			
❑ 65559	Over the Rainbow/Zing Went the Strings of My Heart	1962	20.00
❑ 65611	As Time Goes By/ My Foolish Heart	1967	15.00
MOHAWK			
❑ 116	Over the Rainbow/ Nursery Rhyme Rock	1960	25.00
—Red label			
❑ 116	Over the Rainbow/ Nursery Rhyme Rock	1960	30.00
—Brown label			
❑ 116	Over the Rainbow/ Nursery Rhyme Rock	1960	50.00
—Maroon label			
❑ 120	Zing Went the Strings of My Heart/Don't Take Your Love from Me	1960	25.00
—As "The Dimensions"			
❑ 121	God's Christmas/Ave Maria	1960	60.00
❑ 123	A Tear Fell/Theresa	1961	60.00
Albums			
CORAL			
❑ CRL 57430 [M]	My Foolish Heart	1963	150.00
❑ CRL 757430 [S]	My Foolish Heart	1963	300.00

DEMIAN Includes members of BUBBLE PUPPY.

Number	Title (A Side/B Side)	Yr	NM
45s			
ABC			
❑ 11297	Face the Crowd/Love People	1970	20.00
Albums			
ABC			
❑ ABCS-718	Demian	1970	100.00

DEMILLES, THE

Number	Title (A Side/B Side)	Yr	NM
45s			
LAURIE			
❑ 3230	Donna Lee/Um Ba Pa	1964	30.00
❑ 3247	Lazy Love/Cry and Be On Your Way	1964	50.00

DEMOLYRS, THE

Number	Title (A Side/B Side)	Yr	NM
45s			
JASON SCOTT			
❑ 7	Rain/Hey Little Rosie	1978	6.00
U.W.R.			
❑ 900	Rain/Hey Little Rosie	1964	500.00

DEMOTRONS, THE

Number	Title (A Side/B Side)	Yr	NM
45s			
ATLANTIC			
❑ 2589	I Want a Home in the Country/ I Don't Want to Play No More	1969	10.00
CAMEO			
❑ 456	Beg, Borrow and Steal/ Midnight in New York	1967	10.00
DORSET			
❑ 5010	Frisky/Steel Driving Man	196?	20.00
ENRICA			
❑ 1003	Rock-A-Way Special/Bugle Boy	1959	30.00
RADAR			
❑ 2615	Hombre/Swinging Soiree	1962	20.00
❑ 2616	Pretzel Twist/Meet Mister Callaghan	1962	20.00
❑ 2621	Sticks and Stones/Theme from "Adventures in Paradise"	1962	20.00
RUST			
❑ 5025	Rockin' with Mother Goose/ Home on the Pad	1960	20.00
SCEPTER			
❑ 12148	Take This Love I Have/ Sleep, Sleep, Sleep	1966	12.00
❑ 12174	Brother Where Are You/ Take This Love I Have	1966	12.00

DEMURES, THE

Number	Title (A Side/B Side)	Yr	NM
45s			
BRUNSWICK			
❑ 55284	Raining Teardrops/He's Got Your Number	1965	100.00

DENBY, JUNIOR

Number	Title (A Side/B Side)	Yr	NM
45s			
KING			
❑ 4717	With This Ring/I'm Still Lonesome	1954	60.00
❑ 4725	This Fool Has Learned/If You Only Have Faith in Me	1954	60.00
❑ 5217	With This Ring/I'm Still Lonesome	1959	30.00

DENE, TERRY

Number	Title (A Side/B Side)	Yr	NM
45s			
LONDON			
❑ 1802	Stairway of Love/Lover, Lover	1958	12.00

DENNIS, BILL

Number	Title (A Side/B Side)	Yr	NM
45s			
SHRINE			
❑ 113	I'll Never Let You Get Away/ Poor Little Fool	1966	1000.

DENNIS, RICHIE

Number	Title (A Side/B Side)	Yr	NM
45s			
CAMEO			
❑ 417	Dear Judy (The Summer's Gone)/Forever and a Day	1966	25.00
JULIA			
❑ 1101	I Am Alone/I'll Cry	196?	30.00
❑ 1102	Kissin' Crazy/Without Your Tender Love	196?	30.00
❑ 1103	Cotton Heart/I'm the One	196?	30.00
❑ 1104	Moonlight in Vermont/ Everything Will Turn Out	196?	30.00

DENNIS AND THE EXPLORERS See THE EXPLORERS.

DENNY, SANDY Also see FAIRPORT CONVENTION.

Number	Title (A Side/B Side)	Yr	NM
45s			
A&M			
❑ 1331	Crazy Lady Blues/Let's Jump the Broomstick	1972	6.00
❑ 1410	Tomorrow Is a Long Time/ Listen Listen	1973	6.00
Albums			
A&M			
❑ SP-4317	The Northstar Grassman and the Ravens	1971	15.00
❑ SP-4371	Sandy	1972	15.00
CARTHAGE			
❑ CGLP-4423	Rendezvous	1985	10.00
—Reissue of Island 9433			
❑ CGLP-4425	Like an Old Fashioned Waltz	1985	10.00
—Reissue of Island 9340			
❑ CGLP-4429	The Northstar Grassman and the Ravens	1985	10.00
—Reissue of A&M 4317			
HANNIBAL			
❑ HNBX-5301 [(3)]	Who Knows Where the Time Goes	198?	20.00
ISLAND			
❑ SW-9340	Like an Old Fashioned Waltz	1974	15.00
❑ ILPS 9433	Rendezvous	1977	15.00

DENOBLE, TOMMY

Number	Title (A Side/B Side)	Yr	NM
45s			
DOT			
❑ 45-16168	Count Every Star/ Anyone But You	1960	10.00
SHERYL			
❑ 333	Count Every Star/ Anyone But You	1960	20.00
❑ 336	Teenage Dream/Young Love (Can Be a True Love)	1961	20.00
STAR SATELLITE			
❑ 1003	I Wanta Go with You/Don't Procrastinate with Me Baby	1959	15.00
❑ 1006	Tell Me That You Care/Deborah	1959	15.00

DENSON, LEE

Number	Title (A Side/B Side)	Yr	NM
45s			
ENTERPRISE			
❑ 9086	A Mom and Dad for Christmas/ The Miracle of the Rosary	1973	5.00
KENT			
❑ 306	High School Hop/Devil Doll	1958	60.00
VIK			
❑ 0251	Heart of a Fool/The Pied Piper	1957	40.00
❑ 0281	New Shoes/Climb Love Mountain	1957	80.00
—With Eddie Cochran on guitar			

DENTON, BOB

Number	Title (A Side/B Side)	Yr	NM
45s			
CHANCELLOR			
❑ 1112	I Guess I'm Still in Love with You/Wrong Side of the Door	1962	12.00
DOT			
❑ 15622	Love Me, So I'll Know/I'm Sending You This Record	1957	20.00
❑ 15833	Playboy/Twenty-Four Hour Night	1958	20.00
JUDD			
❑ 1001	Sweet and Innocent/ Back to School Again	1958	15.00
❑ 1013	I'll Always Be Yours/ A Lover's Prayer	1959	15.00

DENTON, MICKEY

Number	Title (A Side/B Side)	Yr	NM
45s			
AMY			
❑ 902	Top Ten/Now I'm Mr. Blue	1964	12.00
BIG TOP			
❑ 3078	Steady Kind/Now You Can't Give Them Away	1961	25.00
❑ 3094	Nature Boy/Ain't Nobody	1962	20.00
❑ 3114	Tell Her/How Mighty Hath Fallen	1962	20.00
❑ 3142	Dance With Me Mary/ The Other Side of Betty	1963	20.00
IMPACT			
❑ 1002	Ain't Love Grand/Mi Amore	1965	20.00
❑ 1011	Heartache Is My Name/ King Lonely the Blue	1966	20.00
WORLD ARTISTS			
❑ 1043	One More Time/Don't Throw My Toys Away	1965	12.00

DENVER, JOHN Also see DENVER, BOISE & JOHNSON; THE MITCHELL TRIO.

Number	Title (A Side/B Side)	Yr	NM
12-Inch Singles			
RCA			
❑ JD-11189 [DJ]	Bet On the Blues (same on both sides)	1977	12.00

D

Number	Title (A Side/B Side)	Yr	NM
45s			
CHERRY MOUNTAIN			
❑ 01/02	Let Us Begin (What Are We Making Weapons For)/Flying for Me	1986	4.00
COLUMBIA			
❑ 02679	Perhaps Love/Annie's Song	1982	4.00
—With Placido Domingo			
❑ 03148	Perhaps Love/Annie's Song	1982	3.00
—With Placido Domingo; reissue			
LEGACY			
❑ 77993	For You/Rocky Mountain High (Live)	1995	2.00
❑ 77993 [PS]	For You/Rocky Mountain High (Live)	1995	3.00
RCA			
❑ 5086-7-R	Love Again/Let Us Begin (What Are We Making Weapons For)	1987	3.00
❑ PB-10774	Like a Sad Song/Pegasus	1976	4.00
❑ PB-10854	Baby, You Look Good to Me Tonight/Wrangle Mountain Song	1976	4.00
❑ PB-10911	My Sweet Lady/Welcome to My Morning	1977	4.00
❑ GB-10940	I'm Sorry/Fly Away	1977	3.00
—Gold Standard Series			
❑ PB-11036	How Can I Leave You Again/To the Wild Country	1977	4.00
❑ PB-11214	It Amazes Me/Druthers	1978	4.00
❑ PB-11267	I Want to Live/Tradewinds	1978	4.00
❑ GB-11327	My Sweet Lady/Like a Sad Song	1978	3.00
—Gold Standard Series			
❑ PB-11479	Downhill Stuff/Life Is So Good	1979	4.00
❑ PB-11535	Sweet Melinda/What's On Your Mind	1979	4.00
❑ PB-11637	Garden Song/Berkeley Woman	1979	4.00
❑ PB-11915	Autograph/The Mountain Song	1980	4.00
❑ PB-11915 [PS]	Autograph/The Mountain Song	1980	4.00
❑ PB-12017	Dancing with the Mountains/American Child	1980	4.00
❑ PB-12246	Some Days Are Diamonds (Some Days Are Stone)/Country Love	1981	4.00
❑ PB-12345	The Cowboy and the Lady/Till You Opened My Eyes	1981	4.00
❑ PB-13071	Shanghai Breezes/What One Man Can Do	1982	4.00
❑ PB-13270	Seasons of the Heart/Islands	1982	4.00
❑ PB-13371	Opposite Tables/Relatively Speaking	1982	4.00
❑ PB-13562	Wild Montana Skies/I Remember Romance	1983	4.00
—A-side with Emmylou Harris			
❑ PB-13642	Flight (The Higher We Fly)/Hold On Tightly	1983	4.00
❑ PB-13740	World Games/It's About Time	1984	3.00
❑ PB-13782	The Way I Am/The Gold and Beyond	1984	3.00
❑ PB-13931	Love Again/It's About Time	1984	3.00
—A-side: With Sylvie Vartan			
❑ GB-14075	Calypso/Some Days Are Diamonds (Some Days Are Stone)	1985	3.00
—Gold Standard Series			
❑ PB-14115	Don't Close Your Eyes Tonight/A Wild Heart Looking for Home	1985	3.00
❑ PB-14227	Dreamland Express/African Sunrise	1985	3.00
❑ PB-14227 [PS]	Dreamland Express/African Sunrise	1985	4.00
❑ PB-14366 [DJ]	Flying for Me (same on both sides)	1986	4.00
—No stock copies were issued			
❑ PB-14406	Along for the Ride ('56 T-Bird)/Let Us Begin (What Are We Making Weapons For)	1986	3.00
RCA VICTOR			
❑ 74-0275	Daydream/I Wish I Knew How It Would Feel to Be Free	1969	10.00
❑ 74-0305	Anthem (Revelation)/Sticky Summer Weather	1970	10.00
❑ 74-0332	Follow Me/Isabel	1970	10.00
❑ 74-0376	Sail Away Home/I Wish I Could Have Been There	1970	10.00
❑ 74-0391	Whose Garden Is This/Mr. Bojangles	1970	10.00
❑ 74-0445	Take Me Home, Country Roads/Poems, Prayers and Promises	1971	8.00
—With Fat City			
❑ 74-0567	Friends with You/Starwood in Aspen	1971	6.00
❑ 74-0647	Everyday/City of New Orleans	1972	6.00
❑ 74-0737	Goodbye Again/The Eagle and the Hawk	1972	6.00
❑ 74-0801	Late Winter, Early Spring/Hard Life Hard Times	1972	6.00

Number	Title (A Side/B Side)	Yr	NM
❑ 74-0829	Rocky Mountain High/Spring	1972	5.00
❑ 74-0955	I'd Rather Be a Cowboy/Sunshine on My Shoulders	1973	4.00
❑ APBO-0067	Farewell Andromeda (Welcome to My Morning)/Whiskey Basin Blues	1973	4.00
❑ APBO-0182	Please, Daddy (Don't Get Drunk This Christmas)/Rocky Mountain High	1973	5.00
❑ APBO-0213	Sunshine on My Shoulders/Around and Around	1974	4.00
❑ APBO-0295	Annie's Song/Cool An' Green An' Shady	1974	4.00
❑ PB-10065	Back Home Again/It's Up to You	1974	4.00
❑ PB-10148	Sweet Surrender/Summer	1974	4.00
❑ PB-10239	Thank God I'm a Country Boy/My Sweet Lady	1975	4.00
❑ PB-10353	I'm Sorry/Calypso	1975	4.00
❑ PB-10464	Christmas for Cowboys/Silent Night, Holy Night	1975	4.00
❑ GB-10472	Annie's Song/Cool An' Green An' Shady	1975	3.00
—Gold Standard Series			
❑ GB-10473	Back Home Again/It's Up to You	1975	3.00
—Gold Standard Series			
❑ GB-10474	Sunshine on My Shoulders/Around and Around	1975	3.00
—Gold Standard Series			
❑ GB-10475	Farewell Andromeda (Welcome to My Morning)/Whiskey Basin Blues	1975	3.00
—Gold Standard Series			
❑ GB-10476	Thank God I'm a Country Boy/My Sweet Lady	1975	3.00
—Gold Standard Series			
❑ GB-10477	Rocky Mountain High/Spring	1975	3.00
—Gold Standard Series			
❑ GB-10478	Sweet Surrender/Summer	1975	3.00
—Gold Standard Series			
❑ PB-10517	Fly Away/Two Shots	1975	4.00
❑ PB-10586	Looking for Space/Windsong	1976	4.00
❑ PB-10687	It Makes Me Giggle/Spirit	1976	4.00
WINDSTAR			
❑ 75720	Country Girl in Paris/Bread and Roses	1988	5.00
❑ 75720 [PS]	Country Girl in Paris/Bread and Roses	1988	6.00
7-Inch Extended Plays			
RCA			
❑ DTF0-2008 [PS]	Rocky Mountain High	1973	25.00
❑ DTF0-2008 [S]	Season Suite/Summer/Fall Goodbye Again//Mother Nature's Son/For Baby (For Bobbie)/Paradise	1973	25.00
—Jukebox issue; small hole, plays at 33 1/3 rpm			
Albums			
HJD			
❑ 66	John Denver Sings	1966	500.00
—Private issue of 300 or so, made by JD as Christmas gifts to friends.			
MERCURY			
❑ SRM-1-704	Beginnings	1972	20.00
—With illustration on cover			
❑ SRM-1-704	Beginnings	1974	12.00
—With mountain scene on cover			
RCA			
❑ 7624-1-R	Back Home Again	1988	10.00
—Last vinyl reissue			
❑ 7631-1-R	Poems, Prayers and Promises	1988	10.00
—Last vinyl reissue			
❑ 7632-1-R	Rocky Mountain High	1988	10.00
—Last vinyl reissue			
RCA VICTOR			
❑ DJL1-0075 [DJ]	The John Denver Radio Show	1973	30.00
❑ APL1-0101	Farewell Andromeda	1973	12.00
—Orange label			
❑ APL1-0101	Farewell Andromeda	1975	10.00
—Tan label or black label, dog near top			
❑ APL1-0374	John Denver's Greatest Hits	197?	8.00
—Reissue			
❑ AQL1-0374	John Denver's Greatest Hits	197?	8.00
—Later reissue			
❑ CPL1-0374	John Denver's Greatest Hits	1974	10.00
—Orange label			
❑ CPL1-0374	John Denver's Greatest Hits	1975	8.00
—Tan label or black label, dog near top			
❑ AFL1-0548	Back Home Again	197?	8.00
—Reissue			
❑ AQL1-0548	Back Home Again	197?	8.00
—Later reissue			
❑ CPL1-0548	Back Home Again	1974	10.00
—Orange or tan label			
❑ CPL1-0548	Back Home Again	1976	8.00
—Black label, dog near top			
❑ DJL1-0683 [DJ]	The Second John Denver Radio Show	1974	30.00

Number	Title (A Side/B Side)	Yr	NM
❑ CPL2-0764 [(2)]	An Evening with John Denver	1975	12.00
—Orange or tan labels			
❑ CPL2-0764 [(2)]	An Evening with John Denver	1976	10.00
—Black label, dog near top			
❑ AFL1-1183	Windsong	197?	8.00
—Reissue			
❑ APL1-1183	Windsong	1975	10.00
—Tan label			
❑ APL1-1183	Windsong	1976	8.00
—Black label, dog near top			
❑ AQL1-1183	Windsong	197?	8.00
—Later reissue			
❑ AFL1-1201	Rocky Mountain Christmas	197?	8.00
—Reissue			
❑ APL1-1201	Rocky Mountain Christmas	1975	10.00
—Tan label			
❑ APL1-1201	Rocky Mountain Christmas	1976	8.00
—Black label, dog near top			
❑ APL2-1263 [(2)]	The John Denver Gift Pak	1974	30.00
—Contains "Rocky Mountain Christmas" and "Windsong" in a special Christmas sleeve.			
❑ AFL1-1694	Spirit	197?	8.00
—Reissue			
❑ APL1-1694	Spirit	1976	10.00
—Originals are black label, dog near top			
❑ AQL1-2195	John Denver's Greatest Hits, Vol. 2	197?	8.00
—Reissue			
❑ CPL1-2195	John Denver's Greatest Hits, Vol. 2	1977	10.00
❑ AFL1-2521	I Want to Live	1977	8.00
❑ AQL1-3075	John Denver	1979	8.00
❑ AQL1-3449	Autograph	1980	8.00
❑ AFL1-4055	Some Days Are Diamonds	1981	8.00
❑ LSP-4207	Rhymes & Reasons	1969	15.00
—Orange label, non-flexible vinyl			
❑ AFL1-4256	Seasons of the Heart	1982	8.00
❑ LSP-4278	Take Me to Tomorrow	1970	15.00
—Orange label, non-flexible vinyl			
❑ LSP-4414	Whose Garden Was This?	1970	15.00
—Orange label, non-flexible vinyl			
❑ AFL1-4499	Poems, Prayers and Promises	197?	8.00
—Reissue			
❑ LSP-4499	Poems, Prayers and Promises	1971	12.00
—Orange label			
❑ LSP-4499	Poems, Prayers and Promises	1975	10.00
—Tan label or black label, dog near top			
❑ AFL1-4607	Aerie	197?	8.00
—Reissue			
❑ LSP-4607	Aerie	1971	12.00
—Orange label			
❑ LSP-4607	Aerie	1975	10.00
—Tan label or black label, dog near top			
❑ AFL1-4683	It's About Time	1983	8.00
❑ AFL1-4731	Rocky Mountain High	197?	8.00
—Reissue			
❑ AQL1-4731	Rocky Mountain High	197?	8.00
—Later reissue			
❑ LSP-4731	Rocky Mountain High	1972	12.00
—Orange label			
❑ LSP-4731	Rocky Mountain High	1975	10.00
—Tan label or black label, dog near top			
❑ AYL1-5189	Poems, Prayers and Promises	198?	6.00
—"Best Buy Series" reissue			
❑ AYL1-5190	Rocky Mountain High	198?	6.00
—"Best Buy Series" reissue			
❑ AYL1-5191	Windsong	198?	6.00
—"Best Buy Series" reissue			
❑ AYL1-5192	I Want to Live	198?	6.00
—"Best Buy Series" reissue			
❑ AYL1-5193	Back Home Again	198?	6.00
—"Best Buy Series" reissue			
❑ AYL1-5194	Spirit	198?	6.00
—"Best Buy Series" reissue			
❑ AYL1-5195	Farewell Andromeda	198?	6.00
—"Best Buy Series" reissue			
❑ AJL1-5313	John Denver's Greatest Hits, Vol. 3	1984	8.00
❑ DJL1-5398 [DJ]	The John Denver Holiday Radio Show	1984	20.00
❑ AFL1-5458	Dreamland Express	1985	8.00
❑ AFL1-5811	One World	1986	8.00

DENVER, JOHN, AND THE MUPPETS

Number	Title (A Side/B Side)	Yr	NM
45s			
RCA			
❑ PB-11767	Have Yourself a Merry Little Christmas//We Wish You a Merry Christmas/A Baby Just Like You	1979	5.00
❑ PB-11767 [PS]	Have Yourself a Merry Little Christmas//We Wish You a Merry Christmas/A Baby Just Like You	1979	5.00
Albums			
RCA VICTOR			
❑ AFL1-3451	A Christmas Together	1979	12.00

Number	Title (A Side/B Side)	Yr	NM

DENVER, JOHN, AND THE NITTY GRITTY DIRT BAND Also see each artist's individual listings.

45s

UNIVERSAL

Number	Title (A Side/B Side)	Yr	NM
❑ UVL-66008	And So It Goes/Amazing Grace	1989	4.00

DENVER, KARL

45s

LONDON

Number	Title (A Side/B Side)	Yr	NM
❑ 2020	Marcheta/Joe Sweeney	1961	15.00
❑ 9521	Wimoweh/Sleepy Lagoon	1962	12.00
❑ 9534	Zimba/Uska Dara	1962	12.00
❑ 9576	Blue Weekend/ Pastures of Plenty	1963	12.00

DENVER, BOISE, & JOHNSON Also see JOHN DENVER.

45s

REPRISE

Number	Title (A Side/B Side)	Yr	NM
❑ 0695	Take Me to Tomorrow/'68 Nixon (This Year's Model)	1968	12.00

DEODATO

45s

CTI

Number	Title (A Side/B Side)	Yr	NM
❑ 12	Also Sprach Zarathustra (2001)/Spirit of Summer	1972	5.00
❑ 16	Rhapsody in Blue/Superstrut	1973	4.00
❑ 16 [PS]	Rhapsody in Blue/Superstrut	1973	6.00
❑ 42	Also Sprach Zarathustra (2001)/Spirit of Summer	1977	4.00

MCA

Number	Title (A Side/B Side)	Yr	NM
❑ 40252	Havana Strut/Moonlight Serenade	1974	4.00
❑ 40469	Caravan/Watusi Street	1975	4.00
❑ 40631	Peter Gunn/Amani	1976	4.00

WARNER BROS.

Number	Title (A Side/B Side)	Yr	NM
❑ 8588	Pina Colada/Love Island	1978	4.00
❑ 8606	Whistle Bump/Love Island	1978	4.00
❑ 29984	Happy Hour/Sweet Magic	1982	3.00

Albums

ATLANTIC

Number	Title (A Side/B Side)	Yr	NM
❑ 82048	Somewhere Out There	1989	12.00

CTI

Number	Title (A Side/B Side)	Yr	NM
❑ CTS-6021	Prelude	1972	12.00
❑ CTSQ-6021 [Q]	Prelude	1973	18.00
❑ CTS-6029	Deodato 2	1973	12.00
❑ CTSQ-6029 [Q]	Deodato 2	1973	18.00
❑ 7081	2001	1977	10.00
❑ 8021	Prelude	198?	8.00

—Reissue of 6021

MCA

Number	Title (A Side/B Side)	Yr	NM
❑ 410	Whirlwinds	1974	10.00
❑ 457	Artistry	1974	10.00
❑ 491	First Cuckoo	1975	10.00
❑ 697	Very Together	198?	8.00

—Reissue of 2219

Number	Title (A Side/B Side)	Yr	NM
❑ 2219	Very Together	1976	10.00

WARNER BROS.

Number	Title (A Side/B Side)	Yr	NM
❑ BSK 3132	Love Island	1978	10.00
❑ BSK 3321	Knights of Fantasy	1979	10.00
❑ BSK 3467	Night Cruiser	1980	12.00
❑ BSK 3649	Happy Hour	1981	10.00
❑ 25175	Motion	1984	10.00

DEODATO/AIRTO

45s

CTI

Number	Title (A Side/B Side)	Yr	NM
❑ 18	Do It Again/Branches (O Galho Da Roseira)	1974	4.00

Albums

CTI

Number	Title (A Side/B Side)	Yr	NM
❑ CTS-6041	In Concert	1974	12.00
❑ CTSQ-6041 [Q]	In Concert	1974	20.00

DEPECHE MODE

12-Inch Singles

REPRISE

Number	Title (A Side/B Side)	Yr	NM
❑ PRO-A-8600 [(2)DJ]	Barrel of a Gun (Underworld Hard Mix 9:36) (United Mix 6:34) (Underworld Hard Instrumental 9:11) (One Inch Punch Mix V2 5:28) (3 Phase Mix 5:23) (Album Version 5:29)/Painkiller (Plastikman Mix 8:39) (Single Version 7:28)	1997	20.00
❑ PRO-A-8662-A [DJ]	It's No Good (Speedy J Mix 5:04) (Hardfloor Mix 6:44) (Club 69 Future Mix 8:35) (Club 69 Future Dub 7:06) (Club 69 Funk Dub 5:26)	1997	100.00

—2,000 made; highly collectible because the Club 69 mixes are unavailable on any other legitimate release in any format anywhere else in the world

Number	Title (A Side/B Side)	Yr	NM
❑ PRO-A-9362 [(2)DJ]	Only When I Lose Myself (Dan the Automator Remix 4:55)/ Painkiller (Kill the Pain Mix - DJ Shadow vs Depeche Mode 6:32)/Headstar (Luke Slater Remix 5:47)/ Surrender (Catalan FC Out of Reach Mix 7:00)/Only When I Lose Myself (Gus Gus Long Play Mix 11:20)/Headstar (The Single Version 4:25)/ Only When I Lose Myself (Subsonic Legacy Remix 7:03)/Surrender (Single Version 6:17)	1998	25.00
❑ 42398 [(2)]	I Feel Loved (Danny Tenaglia's Labor of Love Edit) (Thomas Brinkmann Mix) (Chamber's Remix) (Danny Tenaglia's Labor of Love Instrumental) (Extended Instrumental)/Dirt (Single Version)	2001	10.00

—

Number	Title (A Side/B Side)	Yr	NM
❑ 43828	Barrel of a Gun (Album Version 5:29) (Underworld Hard Mix 9:37) (3 Phase Mix 5:23) (One Inch Punch Mix V2 5:28) (Underworld Soft Mix 6:29)	1997	10.00
❑ 43845	It's No Good (Hardfloor Mix 6:44) (Bass Bounce Mix 7:14) (Speedy J Mix 5:01)/Slowblow (Darren Price Mix 6:29)	1997	10.00
❑ 43906	Home (The Noodles & The Damage Done Edit 6:22) (LFO Meant to Be 4:26)/ Useless (CJ Bolland Ultrasonar Mix 6:00) (CJ Bolland Funky Sub Mix 5:38)	1997	8.00
❑ 44562 [(2)]	Only When I Lose Myself (Dan the Automator Remix 4:55)/ Painkiller (Kill the Pain Mix - DJ Shadow vs Depeche Mode 6:32)/Headstar (Luke Slater Remix 5:47)/Surrender (Catalan FC Out of Reach Mix 7:00)/Only When I Lose Myself (Gus Gus Long Play Mix 11:20)/Headstar (The Single Version 4:25)/Only When I Lose Myself (Subsonic Legacy Remix 7:03)/Surrender (Single Version 6:17)	1998	10.00
❑ 44982 [(2)]	Dream On (Bushwacka Tough Guy Mix 6:08) (Dave Clarke Acoustic Version 4:24) (Dave Clarke Club Mix 5:13) (Kid 606 Mix 4:45) (Bushwacka Blunt Mix 6:48) (Octagon Man Mix 5:30) (Bushwacka Tough Guy Dub 6:08)/Easy Tiger (Bertrand Burgalat & A.S Dragon Version 4:52)	2001	10.00

—

Number	Title (A Side/B Side)	Yr	NM
❑ PRO-A-100562 [(2)DJ]	Dream On (Morel's Pink Noise Club Mix 7:38) (Dave Clark Club Mix 5:13) (Bushwacka Tough Guy Vocal Mix 6:08) (Dave Clarke Acoustic Version 4:24) (Morel's Pink Noise Dub 6:59) (Bushwacka Tough Guy Dub 6:08) (Bushwacka Blunt Mix 6:48) (Kid 606 Mix 4:45)	2001	50.00

—Red labels

Number	Title (A Side/B Side)	Yr	NM
❑ PRO-A-100562-A [(2)DJ]	Dream On (Morel's Pink Noise Club Mix 7:38) (Dave Clark Club Mix 5:13) (Bushwacka Tough Guy Vocal Mix 6:08) (Dave Clarke Acoustic Version 4:24) (Morel's Pink Noise Dub 6:59) (Bushwacka Tough Guy Dub 6:08) (Bushwacka Blunt Mix 6:48) (Kid 606 Mix 4:45)	2001	50.00

—White labels with "Advance Only." below center holes

Number	Title (A Side/B Side)	Yr	NM
❑ PRO-A-100670-A [DJ]	Dream On (The BRAT Mix 8:28) (Morel's Pain Is Waiting Mix)	2001	40.00
❑ PRO-A-100714-A [DJ]	I Feel Loved (Danny Tenaglia's Labor of Love Mix 14:02) (Thomas Brinkmann Mix 5:27) (Extended Instrumental 8:27)	2001	40.00
❑ PRO-A-100720-A [DJ]	I Feel Loved (Danny Tenaglia's Labor of Love Dub 12:10) (Danny Tenaglia's Labor of Love Edit 7:57) (Danny Tenaglia's Labor of Love Radio Edit 3:17)	2001	30.00
❑ PRO-A-100794 [(2)DJ]	Freelove (Deep Dish Freedom Remix 11:43) (Josh Wink Vocal Interpretation 8:49)// (Deep Dish Freedom Dub 11:13) (Powder Productions Remix 7:57)	2001	30.00

SIRE

Number	Title (A Side/B Side)	Yr	NM
❑ PRO-A-999 [DJ]	Just Can't Get Enough (Schizomix 6:41)/ New Life (Edit)	1981	80.00
❑ PRO-A-1025 [DJ]	Big Muff/Photographic// Nodisco/Boys Say Go!	1981	70.00

—Four-song sampler from album "Speak & Spell"; plays at 45 rpm

Number	Title (A Side/B Side)	Yr	NM
❑ PRO-A-1084 [DJ]	Leave in Silence/A Photograph of You//My Secret Garden/ (Further Excerpts from) My Secret Garden	1982	30.00

—Four-song sampler from "A Broken Frame"; plays at 45 rpm

Number	Title (A Side/B Side)	Yr	NM
❑ PRO-A-2097 [DJ]	Everything Counts (In Larger Amounts)/(Edit)	1983	25.00
❑ PRO-A-2221 [DJ]	Master and Servant (LP Version) (US Black and Blue Version)	1984	30.00
❑ PRO-A-2271 [DJ]	Blasphemous Rumours (Edit)/ Something to Do/(Set Me Free) Remotivate Me (Edit)	1985	50.00
❑ PRO-A-2504 [DJ]	A Question of Lust (Remix Edit) (LP Version)	1986	30.00
❑ PRO-A-2780 [DJ]	Strangelove (Pain Mix 7:18) (7" Version 3:44)/ Agent Orange (5:04)	1987	20.00
❑ PRO-A-2847 [DJ]	Never Let Me Down Again (same on both sides)	1987	30.00
❑ PRO-A-2952 [DJ]	Behind the Wheel (Extended Remix 5:50) (Dub 6:00) (Beatmasters Mix 8:00) (7" DJ Remix 3:48)	1987	20.00
❑ PRO-A-3213 [DJ]	Strangelove (Remix Edit 3:46) (7" Version 3:44) (7" Blind Edit 3:57) (Highjack Mix 6:29)	1988	30.00
❑ PRO-A-3696 [DJ]	Personal Jesus (Acoustic Version) (same on both sides)	1989	40.00
❑ PRO-A-4507 [DJ]	World in My Eyes (Oil Tank Mix 7:29) (Single Edit 3:57)	1990	25.00
❑ PRO-A-6022 [DJ]	I Feel You (Helmet at the Helm Mix 6:41) (Afghan Surgery Mix 4:58) (Throb Mix 6:47) (Babylon Mix 7:53) (Life's Too Short Mix 8:33)	1993	25.00
❑ 20165	Everything Counts (7:23)/ Work Hard (6:58)	1983	15.00
❑ 20214	People Are People (Different Mix 7:12) (On-U Sound Remix 7:30)/In Your Memory (Slik Mix Edit 4:00)	1984	10.00
❑ 20283	Master and Servant (US Black and Blue Version)/(Set Me Free) Remotivate Me/ Are People People?	1984	10.00
❑ 20402	It's Called a Heart (Emotion Remix) (Emotion Dub) (Album Version)/ Flexible (Deportation Mix)	1985	15.00
❑ 20530	A Question of Time/Something to Do (Live)/A Question of Lust/Black Celebration (Live)	1986	20.00

Number	Title (A Side/B Side)	Yr	NM
❑ 20578	But Not Tonight (Extended Mix 6:17)/Breathing In Fumes (6:04)/Stripped (Highland Mix 6:41)/Black Day (2:35)	1986	12.00
❑ 20696	Strangelove (Maxi-Mix 6:32) (Midi-Mix 1:38) (Blind Mix 6:10)/FPMIP (5:19)	1987	10.00
❑ 20769	Strangelove (Pain Mix 7:18) (7" Version 3:44)/Agent Orange (5:04)	1987	10.00
❑ 20783	Never Let Me Down Again (Split Mix 9:35) (Aggro Mix 4:56) (Tsangerides Mix 4:23)/ Pleasure Little Treasure (Glitter Mix 5:36) (Join Mix 5:04)	1987	10.00
❑ 20858	Behind the Wheel/Route 66 (Megamix 7:50) (Megadub 6:14)/Behind the Wheel (Extended Remix 5:50) (Beatmasters Mix 8:00)	1987	15.00
❑ 21022	Strangelove (Highjack Remix) (Remix Edit)/Nothing (Zip-Hop Mix) (Dub)	1988	10.00
❑ 21183	Everything Counts (Absolut Mix 6:04) (Tim Simenon/Mark Saunders Mix 5:32) (Live 5:47)/Nothing (Live 4:15)/ Sacred (Live 4:42)/A Question of Lust (Live 5:14)	1989	10.00
❑ 21328	Personal Jesus (Holier Than Thou Approach 5:43) (7" Version 3:43) (Pump Mix 7:19)/Dangerous (Hazchemix 5:35) (7" Version 4:19)	1989	10.00
❑ 21490	Enjoy the Silence (The Quad: Final Mix 15:27) (Ecstatic Dub 5:54) (Bass Line 7:40) (Hands and Feet Mix 7:20)/ Memphisto (Single Version 4:05)	1990	10.00
❑ 21534	Policy of Truth (Capitol Mix 8:00) (Pavlov's Dub 6:02) (Beat Box Mix 7:13)/Kaleid (When Worlds Mix 5:22)	1990	10.00
❑ 21735	World in My Eyes (Oil Tank Mix 7:29) (Dub in My Eyes 6:54) (Mode to Joy 6:32)/Sea of Sin (Sensoria 6:07)/Happiest Girl (Jack Mix 4:58)	1990	10.00
❑ 29704	Get the Balance Right (Combination Mix 8:56) (7" Mix 3:12)/The Great Outdoors (5:02)/Tora, Tora, Tora (Live 4:09)	1983	15.00
❑ 29957	See You (4:50) (3:55)/ The Meaning of Love/ Now This Is Fun	1982	20.00
❑ 40767	I Feel You (Babylon Mix 7:53) (Helmet at the Helm Mix 6:41) (Afghan Surgery Mix 4:58) (Life's Too Short Mix 8:33) (Swamp Mix 7:26) (Throb Mix 6:47)/One Caress (Album Version 3:31)	1993	12.00
❑ 40852	Walking in My Shoes (Extended 12" Mix 6:54) (Random Carpet Mix 6:35) (Grungy Gonads Mix 6:24) (Anandamidic Mix 6:11) (Ambient Whale Mix 4:54)/ My Joy (Slow Slide Mix 5:11)	1993	10.00
❑ 41058	Condemnation (Live) (Paris Mix)/Enjoy the Silence (Live)/ Halo (Live)/Death's Door (Jazz Mix)/Rush (Spiritual Guidance Mix) (Nitrate Mix) (Wild Planet Mix)	1993	10.00
❑ 41362	In Your Room (Extended Zephyr Mix 6:43) (Apex Mix 6:43) (The Jeep Rock Mix 6:19)/Higher Love (Adrenaline Mix 7:49)	1994	10.00

45s

REPRISE

Number	Title (A Side/B Side)	Yr	NM
❑ 16732	Dream On/I Feel Loved	2001	4.00
❑ 17314	Home/Useless	1997	3.00
❑ 17390	It's No Good/Slowblow	1997	6.00
❑ 17409	Barrel of a Gun/Painkiller	1997	4.00

SIRE

Number	Title (A Side/B Side)	Yr	NM
❑ 18506	Walking in My Shoes/My Joy	1993	4.00
❑ 18600	I Feel You/One Caress	1993	4.00
❑ 18889	Personal Jesus/Policy of Truth	1992	5.00
—"Back to Back Hits" series; first U.S. 45 release of "Personal Jesus"			
❑ 18890	World in My Eyes/Enjoy the Silence	1992	5.00
—"Back to Back Hits" series; first U.S. 45 release of "World in My Eyes"			
❑ 19842	Policy of Truth/Kaleid	1990	5.00
❑ 19885	Enjoy the Silence/Memphisto	1990	5.00
❑ 21886	Strangelove/Behind the Wheel	198?	3.00
—"Back to Back Hits" reissue			
❑ 21994	People Are People/ A Question of Lust	198?	3.00
—"Back to Back Hits" reissue			
❑ 22993	Everything Counts (Live)/ Nothing (Live)	1989	3.00
❑ 22993 [PS]	Everything Counts (Live)/ Nothing (Live)	1989	4.00
❑ 27777	Strangelove/Nothing	1988	3.00
❑ 27777 [PS]	Strangelove/Nothing	1988	3.00
❑ 27991	Behind the Wheel//Route 66/ Behind the Wheel	1988	3.00
❑ 27991 [PS]	Behind the Wheel//Route 66/ Behind the Wheel	1988	4.00
❑ 28189	Never Let Me Down Again/ Pleasure Little Treasure	1987	4.00
❑ 28189 [PS]	Never Let Me Down Again/ Pleasure Little Treasure	1987	4.00
❑ 28366	Strangelove/FPMIP	1987	4.00
❑ 28366 [PS]	Strangelove/FPMIP	1987	4.00
❑ 28564	But Not Tonight/Stripped	1986	5.00
❑ 28564 [PS]	But Not Tonight/Stripped	1986	20.00
❑ 28697	A Question of Lust/ Christmas Island	1986	4.00
❑ 28697 [PS]	A Question of Lust/ Christmas Island	1986	4.00
❑ 28697DJ [DJ]	A Question of Lust (Edit)/(Remix)	1986	10.00
❑ 28835	Shake the Disease/Flexible	1985	5.00
❑ 28835 [PS]	Shake the Disease/Flexible	1985	12.00
❑ 28918	Master and Servant/ (Set Me Free) Remotivate Me	1985	3.00
❑ 28918 [PS]	Master and Servant/ (Set Me Free) Remotivate Me	1985	4.00
❑ 29221	People Are People/ In Your Memory	1984	3.00
❑ 29221 [PS]	People Are People/ In Your Memory	1984	4.00
❑ 29482	Everything Counts/Work Hard	1983	6.00
❑ 29482 [PS]	Everything Counts/Work Hard	1983	—
—The existence of this picture sleeve has been questioned			
❑ 50029	Just Can't Get Enough/ Tora, Tora, Tora	1982	15.00

Albums

MUTE

Number	Title	Yr	NM
❑ MUTEL 5 [(3)]	The Singles 86-98	1998	30.00
—Numbered, limited box set pressed in England with U.S. bar code sticker			

SIRE

Number	Title	Yr	NM
❑ SRK 3642	Speak & Spell	1981	15.00
❑ PRO-A-5192 [(2)DJ]	Selections from the Commercially Available Limited Edition Box Sets One and Two	1991	40.00
—Promo-only sampler			
❑ PRO-A-5242 [(2)DJ]	Selections from the Commercially Available Limited Edition Box Set Three	1991	40.00
❑ 23751	A Broken Frame	1982	12.00
❑ 23900	Construction Time Again	1983	12.00
❑ 25124	People Are People	1984	10.00
❑ 25194	Some Great Reward	1984	12.00
❑ 25346	Catching Up with Depeche Mode	1985	10.00
❑ 25429	Black Celebration	1986	10.00
❑ 25614	Music for the Masses	1987	10.00
❑ 25853 [(2)]	101	1989	15.00
❑ 26081	Violator	1990	15.00
❑ R 100560	Catching Up with Depeche Mode	1990	12.00
—BMG Direct Marketing edition; reissue			
❑ R 100598	Music for the Masses	1988	12.00
—BMG Direct Marketing edition			
❑ R 143674	Catching Up with Depeche Mode	1985	12.00
—RCA Music Service edition			
❑ R 173408	Violator	1990	15.00
—BMG Direct Marketing edition			

DEPENDABLES, THE

Albums

UNITED ARTISTS

Number	Title	Yr	NM
❑ UAS-6799	Klaatu Berrada Niktu	1971	20.00

DEPOLIS, CHRIS

45s

CAMEO

Number	Title (A Side/B Side)	Yr	NM
❑ 310	Miss Daisy DeLite/ View from My Window	1964	12.00

DERBY-HATVILLE

45s

SEA ELL

Number	Title (A Side/B Side)	Yr	NM
❑ 102	You'll Forget Me/ (B-side unknown)	1967	40.00
❑ 104	Instant Replay/ (B-side unknown)	1967	40.00

DEREK See JOHNNY CYMBAL.

DEREK AND THE DOMINOS Also see ERIC CLAPTON.

45s

ATCO

Number	Title (A Side/B Side)	Yr	NM
❑ 6780	Tell the Truth/Roll It Over	1970	50.00
—Yellow and white label stock copy; withdrawn shortly after release, this is much rarer than promos			
❑ 6780 [DJ]	Tell the Truth/Roll It Over	1970	25.00
—Produced by Phil Spector; all-white label			
❑ 6803	Bell Bottom Blues/ Keep On Growing	1971	10.00
❑ 6809	Layla (2:43)/I Am Yours	1971	10.00
❑ 6809	Layla (7:10)/I Am Yours	1972	6.00

POLYDOR

Number	Title (A Side/B Side)	Yr	NM
❑ 15040	Layla/I Am Yours	1972	—
—Unreleased?			

RSO

Number	Title (A Side/B Side)	Yr	NM
❑ 400	Presence of the Lord/Why Does Love Got to Be So Sad	1973	6.00

Albums

ATCO

Number	Title	Yr	NM
❑ 2-704 [(2)M]	Layla and Other Assorted Love Songs	1970	300.00
—White label promo only			
❑ SD 2-704 [(2)DJ]	Layla and Other Assorted Love Songs	1970	200.00
—White label promo			
❑ SD 2-704 [(2)S]	Layla and Other Assorted Love Songs	1970	30.00

DIRECT DISK

Number	Title	Yr	NM
❑ SD-16629 [(2)]	Layla and Other Assorted Love Songs	1981	150.00
—Audiophile vinyl			

MOBILE FIDELITY

Number	Title	Yr	NM
❑ 2-239 [(2)]	Derek and the Dominos in Concert	1996	50.00
—Audiophile vinyl			

MOTOWN

Number	Title	Yr	NM
❑ 5310373 [(2)]	Layla and Other Assorted Love Songs	2008	30.00

POLYDOR

Number	Title	Yr	NM
❑ PD2-3501 [(2)]	Layla and Other Assorted Love Songs	1972	20.00

RSO

Number	Title	Yr	NM
❑ RS-2-3801 [(2)]	Layla and Other Assorted Love Songs	1977	15.00
❑ SO 2-8800 [(2)]	Derek and the Dominos in Concert	1973	20.00

DERRINGER, RICK Also see THE McCOYS; DIO, BLACK SABBATH; DUST; ALCATRAZZ; PAT BENATAR; includes records as DERRINGER ('76 to '78).

45s

BLUE SKY

Number	Title (A Side/B Side)	Yr	NM
❑ 2751	Rock and Roll Hoochie Koo/ Time Warp	1974	5.00
❑ 2752	Teenage Love Affair/ Slide Over Slinky	1974	4.00
❑ 2753	It's Raining/Cheqap Tequila	1974	4.00
❑ 2755	Hang On Sloopy/ Skyscraper Blues	1975	4.00
❑ 2757	Don't Ever Say Goodbye/ Gimme More	1975	4.00
❑ 2765	Let Me In/You Can Have Me	1976	4.00
—As "Derringer"			
❑ 2767	Don't Stop Loving Me/ Let's Make It	1977	4.00
—As "Derringer"			
❑ 2770	Lawyers, Guns and Money/ Sleepless	1977	4.00
—As "Derringer"			
❑ 2774	Midnight Road/Rocka-Rolla	1978	4.00
—As "Derringer"			
❑ 2783	Need a Little Girl (Just Like You)/Something Warm	1979	4.00
❑ 2788	Don't Ever Say Godbye/Timeless	1980	4.00
❑ 2793	Runaway/Teenage Love Affair	1980	4.00
❑ 2794	Let the Music Play/ You'll Get Yours	1980	4.00

EPIC

Number	Title (A Side/B Side)	Yr	NM
❑ 05830	The Real America/ Grab Them Cakes	1986	3.00

Albums

BLUE SKY

Number	Title	Yr	NM
❑ PRO 265	Live in Cleveland	1977	24.00
—Promo			
❑ KZ 32481	All American Boy	1973	15.00
❑ PZ 32481	All American Boy	197?	8.00
—Reissue with new prefix			
❑ ZQ 32481 [Q]	All American Boy	1974	20.00
❑ PZ 33423	Spring Fever	1975	12.00

 Except when noted otherwise, VG = 25% of NM, and VG+ = 50% of NM. (Example: VG = $2.00, VG+ = $4.00 and NM = $8.00.)

Number	Title (A Side/B Side)	Yr	NM
❑ PZQ 33423 [Q]	Spring Fever	1975	20.00
❑ PZ 34181	Derringer	1976	12.00
❑ PZ 34470	Sweet Evil	1977	15.00
❑ PZ 34848	Derringer Live	1977	12.00
—Without bar code			
❑ PZ 34848	Derringer Live	198?	8.00
—Reissue with bar code			
❑ JZ 35075	If I Weren't So Romantic I'd Shoot You	1978	10.00
❑ JZ 36092	Guitars and Women	1979	10.00
❑ JZ 36551	Face to Face	1980	10.00
PASSPORT			
❑ PB-6025	Good Dirty Fun	1983	10.00
DESCENDENTS			
45s			
ORCA			
❑ 1056	Ride the Wild/It's a Hectic World	1978	50.00
❑ 1056 [PS]	Ride the Wild/It's a Hectic World	1978	50.00
PINSICATO			
❑ 001	Ride the Wild/It's a Hectic World	1978	50.00
❑ 001 [PS]	Ride the Wild/It's a Hectic World	1978	50.00
7-Inch Extended Plays			
FAT WRECK CHORDS			
❑ FAT 671	Nothing with You/'Merican//Here with Me/I Quit	2004	2.00
❑ FAT 671 [PS]	'Merican	2004	2.00
NEW ALLIANCE			
❑ NAR-005	My Dad Sucks/Mr. Bass//I Like Food/Hey Hey/Der Wienerschnitzel	1981	40.00
❑ NAR-005 [PS]	Fat	1981	40.00
Albums			
EPITAPH			
❑ 86481	Everything Sucks	1996	12.00
FAT WRECK CHORDS			
❑ FAT 673	Cool to Be You	2004	12.00
NEW ALLIANCE			
❑ NAR-012	Milo Goes to College	1982	15.00
❑ NAR-025	Bonus Fat	1985	15.00
❑ NAR-026	I Don't Want to Grow Up	1985	15.00
❑ NAR-029	Enjoy!	1986	15.00
SST			
❑ 112	All	1987	12.00
❑ 142	Milo Goes to College	198?	12.00
❑ 143	I Don't Want to Grow Up	198?	12.00
❑ 144	Bonus Fat	198?	12.00
❑ 163	Liveage!	1988	12.00
❑ 205	Hallraker Live!	1988	12.00
❑ 242	Enjoy!	1989	12.00
❑ 259 [(2)]	Somery	1991	15.00
DESHANNON, JACKIE			
45s			
AMHERST			
❑ 725	I Don't Think I Can Wait/Don't Let the Flame Burn Out	1978	12.00
❑ 728	To Love Somebody/Just to Feel This Love from You	1978	12.00
❑ 733	You're the Only Dancer/Tonight You're Doin' It Right	1979	12.00
❑ 737	Things We Said Today/Way Above the Angels	1979	12.00
ATLANTIC			
❑ 2871	Only Love Can Break Your Heart/Vanilla Olay	1972	10.00
❑ 2895	I Wanna Roo You/Paradise	1972	10.00
❑ 2919	Sweet Sixteen/Speak Out to Me	1972	10.00
❑ 2924	Chains on My Soul/Peaceful in My Soul	1972	10.00
❑ 2994	Your Baby Is a Lady/(If You Never Have a Big Hit Record) You're Still Gonna Be My Star	1973	10.00
❑ 3041	You've Changed/Jimmie, Just Sing Me One More Song	1974	10.00
CAPITOL			
❑ 3130	Salinas/Keep Me Warm	1971	10.00
❑ 3185	Stone Cold Soul/West Virginia Mine	1971	10.00
COLUMBIA			
❑ 10221	Boat to Sail/Let the Sailors Dance	1975	15.00
—With Brian Wilson on backing vocal			
❑ 10340	Fire in the City/All Night Desire	1976	10.00
DOT			
❑ 15928	Cajun Blues/Just Another Lie	1959	25.00
—As "Jackie Shannon"			
❑ 15980	Trouble/Lies	1959	25.00
—As "Jackie Shannon"			
EDISON INTERNATIONAL			
❑ 416	I Wanna Go Home/So Warm	1960	100.00
❑ 418	Put My Baby Down/The Foolish One	1960	100.00

Number	Title (A Side/B Side)	Yr	NM
GONE			
❑ 5008	How Wrong I Was/I'll Be True	1957	30.00
—As "Jackie Dee"			
IMPERIAL			
❑ 66110	What the World Needs Now Is Love/I Remember the Boy	1965	8.00
❑ 66132	A Lifetime of Loneliness/Don't Turn Your Back on Me	1965	6.00
❑ 66171	Come and Get Me/Splendor in the Grass	1966	6.00
❑ 66194	Will You Love Me Tomorrow/Are You Ready for This	1966	6.00
❑ 66196	So Long Johnny/Windows and Doors	1966	6.00
❑ 66202	I Can Make It with You/To Be Myself	1966	6.00
❑ 66224	Come On Down/Find Me Love	1967	6.00
❑ 66236	Where Does the Sun Go/Wishing Doll	1967	6.00
❑ 66251	It's All in the Game/Changin' My Mind	1967	6.00
❑ 66281	Me About You/I Keep Wanting You	1968	6.00
❑ 66301	Nobody's Home to Go Home To/Nicole	1968	6.00
❑ 66312	Didn't Want to Have to Do It/Splendor in the Grass	1968	6.00
❑ 66313	The Weight/Splendor in the Grass	1968	6.00
❑ 66342	Holly Would/My Heart's Been Marching	1968	6.00
❑ 66370	What Is This/Trust Me	1969	5.00
❑ 66385	Put a Little Love in Your Heart/Always Together	1969	6.00
❑ 66419	Love Will Find a Way/I Let Go Completely	1969	5.00
❑ 66430	One Christmas/Do You Know How Christmas Trees Are Grown	1969	6.00
❑ 66438	Brighton Hill/You Can Come to Me	1970	5.00
❑ 66452	You Keep Me Hangin' On-Hurt So Bad/What Was Your Day Like	1970	5.00
LIBERTY			
❑ 55148	Buddy/Strolypso Dance	1958	25.00
—As "Jackie Dee"			
❑ 55288	Lonely Girl/Teach Me	1960	15.00
❑ 55342	Think About You/Heaven Is Being with You	1961	15.00
❑ 55358	I Won't Turn You Down/Wish I Could Find a Boy	1961	15.00
❑ 55387	Baby (When You Kiss Me)/Ain't That Love	1961	15.00
❑ 55425	The Prince/I'll Drown in My Own Tears	1962	15.00
❑ 55425	The Prince/That's What Boys Are Made Of	1962	15.00
❑ 55484	Guess Who/Just Like in the Movies	1962	15.00
❑ 55497	You Won't Forget Me/I Don't Think So Much of Myself	1962	15.00
❑ 55526	Faded Love/Dancing Silhouettes	1962	15.00
❑ 55526 [PS]	Faded Love/Dancing Silhouettes	1962	40.00
❑ 55563	Needles and Pins/Did He Call Today, Mama?	1963	15.00
❑ 55602	Little Yellow Roses/500 Miles	1963	15.00
❑ 55602	Little Yellow Roses/Oh Sweet Chariot	1963	15.00
❑ 55602 [DJ]	Little Yellow Roses	1963	80.00
—Yellow vinyl promo			
❑ 55645	When You Walk in the Room/Til You Say You're Mine	1963	15.00
❑ 55673	I'm Gonna Be Strong/Should I Cry	1964	15.00
❑ 55678	Oh Boy/I'm Looking for Someone to Love	1964	15.00
❑ 55705	Hold Your Head High/She Don't Understand Him Like I Do	1964	15.00
❑ 55730	He's Got the Whole World in His Hands/It's Love Baby	1964	15.00
❑ 55735	When You Walk in the Room/Over You	1964	12.00
❑ 55787	What the World Needs Now Is Love/A Lifetime of Loneliness	1965	—
—Unreleased			
❑ 56187	Mediterranean Sky/It's So Nice	1970	6.00
PJ			
❑ 101	Trouble/Lies	1959	40.00
—As "Jackie Shannon"			
RCA			
❑ PB-11902	I Don't Need You Anymore/Find Love	1980	5.00
SAGE AND SAND			
❑ 290	Just Another Lie/Cajun Blues	1960	25.00
❑ 330	Trouble/Lies	1960	25.00

Number	Title (A Side/B Side)	Yr	NM
UNITED ARTISTS			
❑ 0033	What the World Needs Now Is Love/Needles and Pins	1973	6.00
—"Silver Spotlight Series" reissue			
❑ 0034	Put a Little Love in Your Heart/When You Walk in the Room	1973	6.00
—"Silver Spotlight Series" reissue			
Albums			
AMHERST			
❑ AMX 1010	You're the Only Dancer	1977	12.00
❑ AMH 1016	Quick Touches	1978	12.00
ATLANTIC			
❑ SD 7231	Jackie	1972	12.00
❑ SD 7303	Your Baby Is a Lady	1974	12.00
CAPITOL			
❑ ST-772	Songs	1971	12.00
COLUMBIA			
❑ PC 33500	New Arrangement	1975	12.00
IMPERIAL			
❑ LP-9286 [M]	This Is Jackie DeShannon	1965	20.00
—Black and pink label			
❑ LP-9286 [M]	This Is Jackie DeShannon	1966	15.00
—Black and green label			
❑ LP-9294 [M]	You Won't Forget Me	1965	20.00
—Black and pink label			
❑ LP-9294 [M]	You Won't Forget Me	1966	15.00
—Black and green label			
❑ LP-9296 [M]	In the Wind	1965	20.00
—Black and pink label			
❑ LP-9296 [M]	In the Wind	1966	15.00
—Black and green label			
❑ LP-9328 [M]	Are You Ready for This?	1966	15.00
❑ LP-9344 [M]	New Image	1967	15.00
❑ LP-9352 [M]	For You	1967	15.00
❑ LP-12286 [S]	This Is Jackie DeShannon	1965	25.00
—Black and pink label			
❑ LP-12286 [S]	This Is Jackie DeShannon	1966	20.00
—Black and green label			
❑ LP-12294 [S]	You Won't Forget Me	1965	25.00
—Black and pink label			
❑ LP-12294 [S]	You Won't Forget Me	1966	20.00
—Black and green label			
❑ LP-12296 [S]	In the Wind	1965	25.00
—Black and pink label			
❑ LP-12296 [S]	In the Wind	1966	20.00
—Black and green label			
❑ LP-12328 [S]	Are You Ready for This?	1966	20.00
❑ LP-12344 [S]	New Image	1967	20.00
❑ LP-12352 [S]	For You	1967	20.00
❑ LP-12386	Me About You	1968	15.00
❑ LP-12404	What the World Needs Now Is Love	1968	15.00
❑ LP-12415	Laurel Canyon	1969	15.00
❑ LP-12442	Put a Little Love in Your Heart	1969	15.00
❑ LP-12453	To Be Free	1970	15.00
LIBERTY			
❑ LRP-3320 [M]	Jackie DeShannon	1963	40.00
❑ LRP-3390 [M]	Breakin' It Up on the Beatles Tour!	1964	40.00
❑ LST-7320 [S]	Jackie DeShannon	1963	50.00
❑ LST-7390 [S]	Breakin' It Up on the Beatles Tour!	1964	50.00
❑ LN-10179	The Very Best of Jackie DeShannon	1983	8.00
—Reissue of United Artists 434			
❑ LN-10265	Jackie DeShannon	1985	8.00
SUNSET			
❑ SUS-5225	Lonely Girl	1968	12.00
❑ SUS-5322	Jackie DeShannon	1970	12.00
UNITED ARTISTS			
❑ UA-LA434-E	The Very Best of Jackie DeShannon	1975	12.00
DESIRES, THE More than one group.			
45s			
DASA			
❑ 102	Phyllis Beloved/The Girl for Me	1962	30.00
HERALD			
❑ 532	Bobby You/Cold Lonely Heart	1958	25.00
HULL			
❑ 730	Hey Lena/Let It Please Be You	1959	80.00
❑ 733	Set Me Free/Rendezvous with You	1960	80.00
SEVILLE			
❑ 118	The Story of Love/I Ask You	1962	30.00
SMASH			
❑ 1763	There I Go Again/I Never Loved Like This	1962	25.00
20TH FOX			
❑ 195	I Don't Know Why/Longing	1960	25.00

DESMOND, JOHNNY

Also see DON CORNELL/JOHNNY DESMOND/ALAN DALE.

45s

Number	Title (A Side/B Side)	Yr	NM
ARTISTS OF AMERICA			
❑ 119	Moonlight Serenade/ (Instrumental)	1976	4.00
ATCO			
❑ 6404	My Melancholy Baby/ Common Touch	1966	6.00
❑ 6425	The Last of the Big Time Losers/I Wanna Believe You	1966	6.00
COLUMBIA			
❑ 41302	Willingly/The Apple	1958	10.00
❑ 41343	Goodbye, My Love, Goodbye/ Bye-Bye Barbara	1959	8.00
❑ 41414	Dancin' Man/Hey Little Dolly	1959	8.00
❑ 41525	Maria/Please	1959	8.00
❑ 41631	Eighth Wonder of the World/ Never Meant to Fall in Love	1960	8.00
❑ 41661	Hawk/Playing the Field	1960	8.00
❑ 41788	Lover Come Back to Me/I Got a Right to Sing the Blues	1960	—
—Canceled			
❑ 41803	Lover Come Back to Me/ No One Ever Tells You	1960	8.00
CORAL			
❑ 60629	Oh My Darlin'/Until	1952	12.00
❑ 60670	Festival/Confetti, I Stood and Threw	1952	12.00
❑ 60736	Battle Hymn of the Republic/ How Much Will I Miss You	1952	12.00
❑ 60798	One Way Heart/It's Meant to Be That Way	1952	12.00
❑ 60823	Trying/Wild Guitars	1952	12.00
❑ 60848	Nina Never Knew/Stay Where You Are	1952	12.00
❑ 60862	Christmas in the Air/ Christmas Is a Time	1952	15.00
❑ 60929	The Gay Caballero/Thanks for Letting Me Know	1953	12.00
❑ 60978	The Japanese Sandman/ Danger	1953	12.00
❑ 61031	It's So Nice to Be Your Neighbor/I'm a Love You	1953	12.00
❑ 61069	Woman/By the River Seine	1953	12.00
❑ 61153	Would You Let Me Hold Your Heart/The Zoo	1954	12.00
❑ 61198	Backward, Turn Backward/ Forever Love	1954	15.00
—With Jane Russell			
❑ 61204	The High and the Mighty/ In God We Trust	1954	12.00
❑ 61227	A Husband/A Wife	1954	12.00
—B-side by Eileen Barton			
❑ 61232	The High and the Mighty/ Got No Time	1954	12.00
❑ 61255	Here I Go Walkin' Down the Road/Brooklyn Bridge	1954	12.00
❑ 61301	My Own True Love/The Song from Desiree	1954	12.00
❑ 61379	Play Me Hearts and Flowers (I Wanna Cry)/I'm So Ashamed	1955	10.00
❑ 61410	Togetherness/A Straw Hat and a Cane	1955	10.00
❑ 61436	It's a Sin to Tell a Lie/ Learnin' the Blues	1955	10.00
❑ 61447	Land of the Pharaohs/ This Too Shall Pass	1955	10.00
❑ 61476	The Yellow Rose of Texas/ You're in Love with Someone	1955	10.00
❑ 61505	Miss America/Gentlemen Marry Brunettes	1955	10.00
❑ 61529	Sixteen Tons/Ballo Italiano	1955	10.00
❑ 61543	Santo Natale/Happy Holidays to You	1955	12.00
❑ 61569	In My Diary/I'll Cry Tomorrow	1956	10.00
❑ 61570	Now Is the Time/Never Again	1956	10.00
❑ 61608	The Most Happy Fella/ Without You	1956	10.00
❑ 61632	A Little Love Can Go a Long, Long Way/Please Don't Forget Me Dear	1956	10.00
❑ 61663	The Proud Ones/I Only Know I Love You	1956	10.00
❑ 61729	A Girl Named Mary/Bueno	1956	10.00
❑ 61747	Old Fashioned Christmas/ Birthday Party of the King	1956	12.00
❑ 61768	Down Where the River Meets the Sea/18th Century Music Box	1957	8.00
❑ 61797	I Just Want You to Want Me/ That's Where I Shine	1957	8.00
❑ 61835	A White Sport Coat (And a Pink Carnation)/Just Lookin'	1957	8.00
❑ 61846	Shenandoah Rose/ Consideration	1957	8.00
❑ 61880	Be Patient with Me/Missing	1957	8.00
❑ 61896	Rich Man, Poor Man/ I Would Love You Still	1957	8.00
❑ 61910	Keep Me in Mind/Lonely Lament	1957	8.00
❑ 61934	Farewell to Naples/ Temperamental You	1958	8.00
❑ 61952	The Sands of Time/The Jealous Boyfriend	1958	8.00
❑ 61968	Anniversary Song/ First, Last and Always	1958	8.00
DIAMOND			
❑ 108	Twistin' Rose of Texas/ Hello Honey	1962	8.00
MGM			
❑ 10703	The Picnic Song/I've Got a Heart	1950	15.00
—Earlier Johnny Desmond singles on MGM are unconfirmed on 45 rpm			
❑ 10736	Pagalle/Stars	1950	15.00
❑ 10758	Just Say I Love Her/ If Anyone Desires	1950	15.00
❑ 10800	A Bushel and a Peck/ So Long Sally	1950	15.00
❑ 10827	Sleigh Ride/Marshmallow World	1950	15.00
❑ 10850	C'est La Vie/You're for Me	1950	15.00
❑ 10920	Too Young/I Fell	1951	15.00
❑ 10930	The Chapel of the Roses/ Forever and Always	1951	15.00
❑ 10939	Mama/My Yiddishe Momme	1951	15.00
❑ 10947	Because of You/Andiano	1951	15.00
❑ 10974	Mister and Mississippi/ I Fall in Love	1951	15.00
❑ 10992	Out o' Breath/I'm Glad I Gave It Up for You	1951	15.00
❑ 11005	America's Prayer/I See God	1951	15.00
❑ 11027	I Want to Be Near You/ I Will Never Change	1951	15.00
❑ 11049	So/More Love	1951	15.00
❑ 11078	True Love/Simple, Simple, Simple	1951	15.00
❑ 11122	My Lost Love/Hands Across the Table	1951	15.00
❑ K11955	Darling Je Vous Aime Beaucoup/I'll Be Yours	1955	12.00
RCA VICTOR			
❑ 47-8233	I Can't Help Falling in Love/ I Still Look at You That Way	1963	6.00
20TH CENTURY FOX			
❑ 546	Fate Is the Hunter/Rio Conchos	1964	8.00
VIGOR			
❑ 710	Untouchable/Red Lips	1973	4.00

7-Inch Extended Plays

Number	Title (A Side/B Side)	Yr	NM
CORAL			
❑ 83011	Christmas in the Air/Christmas Is a Time//The Little Match Girl/ The Night Before Christmas	195?	15.00
—B-side by Eileen Barton			
PRI			
❑ SPL 11	All of You/The Last Time I Saw Paris/I Can't Get Started/ You'd Be So Nice to Come Home To//Tenderly/This Can't Be Love/That Old Devil Moon/There's a Small Hotel	196?	10.00
—Small hole, plays at 33 1/3 rpm			
❑ SPL 11 [PS]	So Nice!	196?	10.00
RCA CAMDEN			
❑ CAE-260	Guilty/I'll Close My Eyes// Just Plain Love/If It's True	1955	12.00
❑ CAE-260 [PS]	Johnny Desmond Sings	1955	12.00

Albums

Number	Title (A Side/B Side)	Yr	NM
COLUMBIA			
❑ CL 1399 [M]	Once Upon a Time	1959	20.00
❑ CL 1477 [M]	Blue Smoke	1960	15.00
❑ CS 8194 [S]	Once Upon a Time	1959	25.00
❑ CS 8268 [S]	Blue Smoke	1960	20.00
CORAL			
❑ CRL 56124 [10]	Hearts and Flowers	1955	60.00
❑ CRL 57073 [M]	Desmo Sings Desmond	195?	50.00
❑ CRL 57079 [M]	Souvenir d'Italie	195?	40.00
❑ CRL 57130 [M]	Easy Come Easy Go	195?	40.00
CORONET			
❑ CXS-236 [S]	Johnny Desmond In Las Vegas!	196?	10.00
CRAFTSMEN			
❑ C-8019 [M]	Hymns	196?	10.00
❑ C-8030 [M]	Johnny Desmond Sings for Dancing	196?	10.00
EVON			
❑ 343 [M]	Johnny Desmond Sings Hymns for You	196?	10.00
GOLDEN TONE			
❑ C-4031 [M]	Hymns	196?	10.00
❑ C-4045 [M]	Dance Party Featuring Johnny Desmond	196?	10.00
❑ 9628 S [S]	Hymns	196?	12.00
❑ 14045 [S]	Dance Party Featuring Johnny Desmond	196?	12.00
LION			
❑ L-70061 [M]	Dreams of Paris	1958	15.00
MAYFAIR			
❑ 9628 S [S]	Hymns	1958	15.00
—Yellow vinyl			
❑ 9635 S [S]	Johnny Desmond Swings	1958	15.00
—Yellow vinyl			
MGM			
❑ E-186 [10]	Hands Across the Table	1952	40.00
❑ E-3561 [M]	Hands Across the Table	1957	25.00
MOVIETONE			
❑ 71011 [M]	Johnny Desmond On Location	1966	12.00
❑ S-72011 [S]	Johnny Desmond On Location	1966	15.00
PICKWICK			
❑ SPC-3558	Hymns for the Family	197?	10.00
RONDO			
❑ 1762 [M]	Dance Party Featuring Johnny Desmond	196?	10.00
❑ 9762 [S]	Dance Party Featuring Johnny Desmond	196?	12.00
TOPS			
❑ L1628 [M]	Hymns	1958	10.00
❑ L1635 [M]	Johnny Desmond Swings	1958	12.00
❑ 1762 [M]	Dance Party Featuring Johnny Desmond	196?	10.00
❑ 9762 [S]	Dance Party Featuring Johnny Desmond	196?	12.00
VENISE			
❑ 7013 [M]	So Nice!	196?	10.00
❑ 10013 [S]	So Nice!	196?	15.00
—Yellow vinyl			
VOCALION			
❑ VL 3773 [M]	Johnny Desmond	1966	12.00
❑ VL 73773 [R]	Johnny Desmond	1966	10.00

DESMOND, JOHNNY/JOHNNY KAY

Albums

Number	Title (A Side/B Side)	Yr	NM
CORONET			
❑ CX-193 [M]	Johnny Desmond Sings	196?	12.00
❑ CXS-193 [R]	Johnny Desmond Sings	196?	10.00

DESMOND, PAUL

Also see DAVE BRUBECK (Desmond was the saxophone player on many of his LPs).

45s

Number	Title (A Side/B Side)	Yr	NM
RCA VICTOR			
❑ 47-8035	Advise and Consent/ Desmond Blue	1962	10.00
❑ 47-8264	Take Ten/Embarcadero	1963	10.00

Albums

Number	Title (A Side/B Side)	Yr	NM
A&M			
❑ SP-3015	Summertime	1969	15.00
❑ SP-3024	From the Hot Afternoon	1969	15.00
❑ SP9-3024	From the Hot Afternoon	198?	20.00
—"Audio Master Plus" reissue			
❑ SP-3032	Bridge Over Troubled Water	1970	20.00
ARTISTS HOUSE			
❑ AH 2	Paul Desmond	1978	10.00
CTI			
❑ CTS-6039	Skylark	1974	10.00
❑ CTS-6059	Pure Desmond	1975	10.00
CTI/CBS ASSOCIATED			
❑ FZ 40806	Pure Desmond	1987	10.00
—Reissue of CTI 6059			
❑ FZ 44170	Skylark	1988	10.00
—Reissue of CTI 6039			
DISCOVERY			
❑ 840	East of the Sun	198?	10.00
FANTASY			
❑ 3-21 [10]	Paul Desmond	1955	100.00
❑ OJC-119	Paul Desmond Quartet Featuring Don Elliott	198?	10.00
—Reissue of Fantasy 3235			
❑ 3235 [M]	Paul Desmond Quartet Featuring Don Elliott	1956	80.00
—Red vinyl			
❑ 3235 [M]	Paul Desmond Quartet Featuring Don Elliott	1957	40.00
—Black vinyl, red label, non-flexible vinyl			
❑ 3235 [M]	Paul Desmond Quartet Featuring Don Elliott	1962	20.00
—Black vinyl, red label, flexible vinyl			
FINESSE			
❑ FW 37487	Paul Desmond and the Modern Jazz Quartet	1981	10.00

Except when noted otherwise, VG = 25% of NM, and VG+ = 50% of NM. (Example: VG = $2.00, VG+ = $4.00 and NM = $8.00.)

Number	Title (A Side/B Side)	Yr	NM
HORIZON			
❑ 850 [(2)]	Paul Desmond Live	1976	15.00
MOSAIC			
❑ MR6-120 [(6)]	The Complete Recordings of the Paul Desmond Quartet with Jim Hall	199?	300.00
RCA CAMDEN			
❑ ACL1-0201	Samba de Orfeo	1973	10.00
RCA VICTOR			
❑ LPM-2438 [M]	Desmond Blue	1961	30.00
❑ LSP-2438 [S]	Desmond Blue	1961	30.00
❑ LPM-2569 [M]	Take Ten	1962	25.00
❑ LSP-2569 [S]	Take Ten	1962	30.00
❑ LPM-2654 [M]	Two of a Mind	1963	25.00
❑ LSP-2654 [S]	Two of a Mind	1963	30.00
❑ ANL1-2807	Pure Gold	1978	10.00
❑ LPM-3320 [M]	Boss Antigua	1965	20.00
❑ LSP-3320 [S]	Boss Antigua	1965	25.00
❑ LPM-3407 [M]	Glad to Be Unhappy	1965	20.00
❑ LSP-3407 [S]	Glad to Be Unhappy	1965	25.00
❑ LPM-3480 [M]	Easy Living	1965	20.00
❑ LSP-3480 [S]	Easy Living	1965	25.00
WARNER BROS.			
❑ W 1356 [M]	First Place Again	1960	30.00
❑ WS 1356 [S]	First Place Again	1960	30.00

DETERGENTS, THE Also see RON DANTE.

Number	Title (A Side/B Side)	Yr	NM
45s			
KAPP			
❑ 735	I Can Never Eat Home Anymore/Igor's Cellar	1966	15.00
❑ 753	Pushin' the Panic Button/ Some Sunday Morning	1966	15.00
ROULETTE			
❑ 4590	Leader of the Laundromat/Ulcers	1964	20.00
❑ 4590 [PS]	Leader of the Laundromat/Ulcers	1964	40.00
❑ 4603	Double-O-Seven/ The Blue Kangaroo	1965	15.00
❑ 4616	Tea and Trumpets/ Mrs. Jones (How "Bout It)	1965	15.00
❑ 4626	Little Dum-Dum/Soldier Girl	1965	15.00
❑ 4642	Bad Girl/Here She Comes	1965	15.00
Albums			
ROULETTE			
❑ R 25308 [M]	The Many Faces of the Detergents	1965	120.00
❑ SR 25308 [R]	The Many Faces of the Detergents	1965	100.00

DETOURS, THE

Number	Title (A Side/B Side)	Yr	NM
45s			
ATCO			
❑ 6448	Who Do You Love/Peace of Mind	1966	25.00
MCSHERRY			
❑ 1285	Bring Back My Beatles to Me/ Money	1964	25.00
❑ 1285	Bring Back My Beatles/Money	1964	25.00

DETROIT Mitch Ryder's post-Detroit Wheels band.

Number	Title (A Side/B Side)	Yr	NM
45s			
PARAMOUNT			
❑ 0094	It Ain't Easy/Long Neck Goose	1971	6.00
❑ 0133	Rock 'N Roll/Box of Old Roses	1971	6.00
❑ 0158	Gimmie Shelter/Oh Oh La La La Dee Da Doo	1972	6.00
Albums			
PARAMOUNT			
❑ PAS-6010	Detroit	1971	15.00

DETROIT CITY LIMITS, THE

Number	Title (A Side/B Side)	Yr	NM
45s			
OKEH			
❑ 7308	98c + Tax/Honey Chile	1968	8.00
Albums			
OKEH			
❑ OKS 14127	98c + Tax	1968	30.00

DETROIT EMERALDS

Number	Title (A Side/B Side)	Yr	NM
45s			
RIC TIC			
❑ 135	Show Time/(Instrumental)	1968	12.00
❑ 138	Shades Down/Ode to Billie Joe	1968	12.00
❑ 141	Take Me the Way I Am/ I'll Keep On Coming Back	1968	12.00
WESTBOUND			
❑ 147	Holding On/Things Are Looking Up	1969	8.00
❑ 156	If I Lose Your Love/I Bet You Get the One	1969	8.00
❑ 161	I Can't See Myself Doing Without You/Just Now and Then	1970	8.00
❑ 172	Do Me Right/Just Now and Then	1970	8.00
❑ 181	Wear This Ring (With Love)/ Bet You Got the One Who Loves You	1971	6.00
❑ 192	You Want It, You Got It/Till You Decide to Come Home	1971	6.00
❑ 203	Baby Let Me Take You (In My Arms)/I'll Never Sail the Sea Again	1972	6.00
❑ 209	Feel the Need in Me/There's a Love for Me Somewhere	1972	6.00
❑ 213	You're Gettin' a Little Too Smart/ Heaven Couldn't Be Like This	1973	6.00
❑ 220	Lee/Whatcha Gonna Wear Tomorrow	1973	6.00
❑ 226	I'm Qualified/Set It Out	1974	6.00
❑ 5005	Yes I Know I'm in Love/ Rosetta Stone	1974	6.00
❑ 55401	Feel the Need/Love Has Come to Me	1977	5.00
❑ 55404	Set It Out (Part 1)/ Set It Out (Part 2)	1977	5.00
❑ 55410	Turn On Lady/Just Don't Know About This Girl of Mine	1977	5.00
Albums			
WESTBOUND			
❑ 302	Feel the Need	1977	15.00
❑ 2006	Do Me Right	1971	40.00
❑ 2013	You Want It, You Got It	1972	40.00
❑ 2018	I'm in Love with You	1973	40.00
❑ 6101	Let's Get Together	1978	15.00

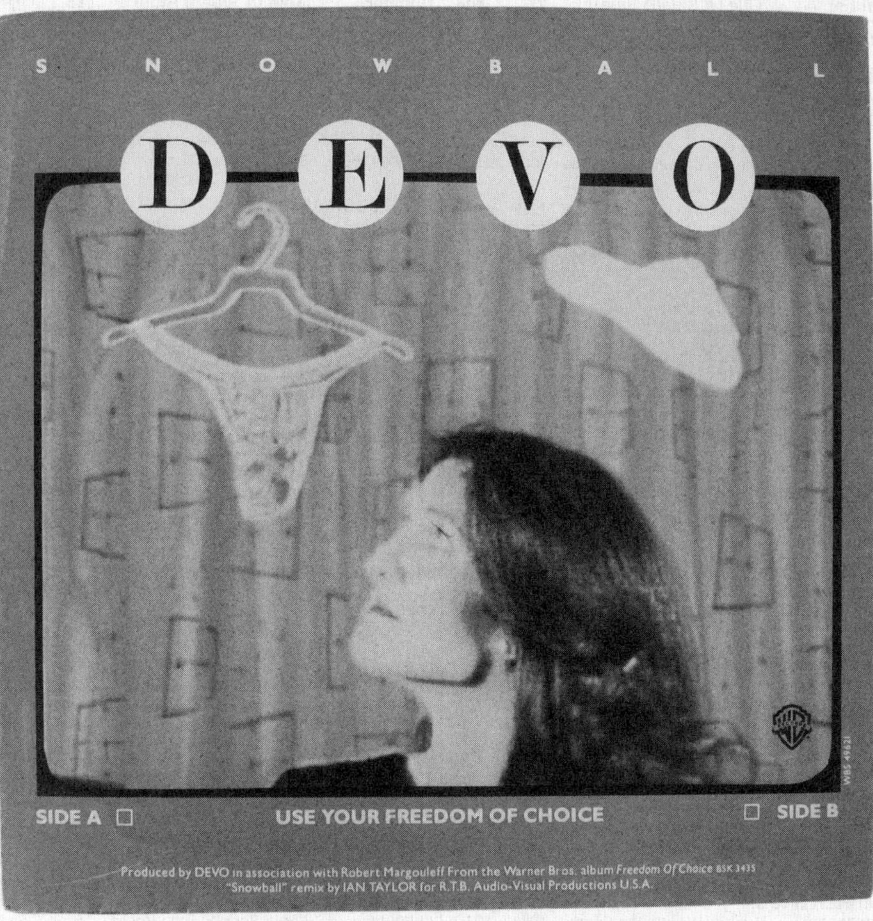

Devo, "Snowball," Warner Bros. 49621, 1980, **$3.**

DETROIT WHEELS, THE Mitch Ryder's band after he went solo.

Number	Title (A Side/B Side)	Yr	NM
45s			
INFERNO			
❑ 5002	Linda Sue Dixon/Tally Ho	1968	20.00
❑ 5003	Think (Part 1)/Think (Part 2)	1968	20.00

DEUCE COUPES, THE May be two different groups.

Number	Title (A Side/B Side)	Yr	NM
Albums			
CROWN			
❑ CST-393 [S]	The Shut Downs	1963	25.00
❑ CLP-5393 [M]	The Shut Downs	1963	20.00
DEL-FI			
❑ DFLP-1243 [M]	Hotrodder's Choice	1963	50.00
❑ DFST-1243 [S]	Hotrodder's Choice	1963	60.00

DEUCES OF RHYTHM AND THE TEMPO TOPPERS, THE Also see LITTLE RICHARD.

Number	Title (A Side/B Side)	Yr	NM
45s			
PEACOCK			
❑ 1616	Ain't That Good News/ A Fool at the Wheel	1953	80.00
❑ 1628	Always/Rice, Red Beans and Turnip Greens	1954	80.00

DEVAUGHN, WILLIAM

Number	Title (A Side/B Side)	Yr	NM
45s			
ROXBURY			
❑ BRBO-0236	Be Thankful for What You Got-Pt. 1/Be Thankful for What You Got-Pt. 2	1974	5.00
❑ 2001	Blood Is Thicker Than Water/ Blood Is Thicker Than Water (Part 2)	1974	5.00
❑ 2005	Give the Little Man a Great Big Hand/Something Being Done	1974	5.00
❑ 2018	Kiss and Make Up/ (B-side unknown)	1975	5.00
TEC			
❑ 767	Figures Can't Calculate/ (B-side unknown)	1980	4.00
Albums			
ROXBURY			
❑ RLX-100	Be Thankful For What You Got	1974	12.00

Number	Title (A Side/B Side)	Yr	NM

DEVAURS, THE

45s

D-TONE

❑ 3 Baby Doll/Teenager 1958 250.00

MOON

❑ 105 Where Are You/Boy in Mexico 1959 200.00

RED FOX

❑ 104 Where Are You/Boy in Mexico 1965 40.00

DEVIANTS, THE

Albums

SIRE

❑ SES-97001 Ptoof! 1968 60.00
❑ SES-97005 Disposable 1969 60.00
❑ SES-97016 No. 3 1969 60.00

DEVIL'S ANVIL, THE

Albums

COLUMBIA

❑ CL 2664 [M] Hard Rock from the Middle East 1967 75.00
❑ CS 9464 [S] Hard Rock from the Middle East 1967 75.00

DEVILED HAM

Albums

SUPER K

❑ SKS-6003 I Had Too Much to Dream Last Night 1968 25.00

DEVILS, THE

More than one group.

45s

MAINSTREAM

❑ 644 Trouble with Angels/ Rachel Says Goodbye 1966 15.00

PEOPLE

❑ 637 The X-Sorcist/Hip Hug-Her 1974 40.00

SARA

❑ 1449 Tell Me/Love and Understanding 1967 25.00
❑ 1450 I'll Say Yes/I'm Leaving You 1967 25.00

DEVO

10-Inch Singles

WARNER BROS.

❑ 49826 [PD] Beautiful World/Nu'tra Speaks 1981 10.00
—Shaped picture disc

12-Inch Singles

BACKSTREET

❑ L33-1106 [DJ] Theme from Doctor Detroit (same on both sides) 1983 8.00
❑ L33-1113 [DJ] Theme from Doctor Detroit (2 versions)/Luv Luv 1983 8.00
❑ 13968 Theme from Doctor Detroit (2 versions)/Luv Luv 1983 8.00

ENIGMA

❑ EPRO 148 [DJ] Baby Doll (5 versions) 1988 8.00
❑ EPRO 298 [DJ] Post Post-Modern Man (7 versions) 1990 12.00
❑ 75511 Disco Dancer (3 versions) 1988 8.00
❑ 75515 Baby Doll (5 mixes)/Agitated 1988 8.00
❑ 75551 Post Post-Modern Man (7 versions) 1990 8.00

FULL MOON/ASYLUM

❑ 11523 [DJ] Working in a Coal Mine (same on both sides) 1981 8.00

WARNER BROS.

❑ PRO-A-199 [DJ] Selections from "Oh No! It's Devo" 1983 15.00
❑ PRO-A-881 [DJ] Gates of Steel/Mr's B's Ballroom/ Whip It 1980 8.00
❑ PRO-A-993 [DJ] Jerkin' Back 'n' Forth//Going Under/Through Being Cool 1981 8.00
❑ PRO-1-2006 [DJ] That's Good/Speed Racer 1983 25.00
—Promo-only picture disc
❑ PRO-A-2217 [DJ] Are You Experienced?/ Please Please 1984 10.00
❑ 20316 Here to Go (2 versions)/ Shout (2 versions) 1985 10.00
❑ 29906 Peek-A-Boo//Peek-A-Boo/ Find Out 1982 8.00

45s

BACKSTREET

❑ 52215 Theme from Doctor Detroit/ King of Soul 1983 3.00
—B-side by James Brown

BOOJI BOY

❑ 7033-14 Jocko Homo/Mongoloid 1977 10.00
❑ 7033-14 [PS] Jocko Homo/Mongoloid 1977 12.00
❑ 72843/75677 Satisfaction/Sloppy 1978 5.00
❑ 72843/75677 [PS] Satisfaction/Sloppy 1978 12.00

ENIGMA

❑ 75023 Disco Dancer/Disco Dancer 1989 3.00
❑ 75029 Baby Doll (Ivan Ivan Mix)/ Baby Doll (Devo Mix) 1988 3.00
❑ 75029 [PS] Baby Doll (Ivan Ivan Mix)/ Baby Doll (Devo Mix) 1988 6.00

FULL MOON/ASYLUM

❑ 47204 Working in the Coal Mine/ Planet Earth 1981 3.00
❑ 47204 [PS] Working in the Coal Mine/ Planet Earth 1981 6.00

REFLEX

❑ 5 Bush Whacked 1988 3.00
—One-sided flexi-disc given away with Reflex magazine

WARNER BROS.

❑ GWB 0400 Whip It/Girl U Want 198? 3.00
—Back to Back Hits series
❑ EP 3595 Working in the Coal Mine (same on both sides) 1981 3.00
—Issued with the New Traditionalists LP
❑ 8675 (I Can't Get No) Satisfaction/ Uncontrollable Urge 1978 5.00
❑ 8745 Come Back Jonee/ Praying Hands 1979 5.00
❑ 29133 Are You Experienced/ Growing Pains 1984 3.00
❑ 29133 [PS] Are You Experienced/ Growing Pains 1984 3.00
❑ 29811 That's Good/What I Must Do 1983 3.00
❑ 29931 Peek-A-Boo/Find Out 1982 3.00
❑ 29931 [PS] Peek-A-Boo/Find Out 1982 4.00
❑ 49028 Secret Agent Man/Red Eye 1979 3.00
❑ 49524 Girl U Want/Mr. B's Ballroom 1980 4.00
❑ 49550 Whip It/Turn Around 1980 4.00
❑ 49621 [PS] Freedom of Choice/ Snowball (Remix) 1980 3.00
❑ 49621 Freedom of Choice/ Snowball (Remix) 1980 4.00
❑ 49715 Gates of Steel (Live)/ Be Still (Live) 1981 4.00
❑ 49834 Beautiful World/Enough Said 1981 4.00
❑ 49834 [PS] Beautiful World/Enough Said 1981 6.00
❑ 50010 Jerkin' Back 'N' Forth/Mecha Mania Boy 1982 4.00
❑ 50048 Through Being Cool/ Going Under 1982 4.00

Albums

DUTCH EAST INDIA

❑ DE-112008-1 Smooth Noodle Maps 1991 30.00
—Red vinyl, 1,000 copies pressed

ENIGMA

❑ EPRO 326 [DJ] Smooth Noodle Maps 1990 20.00
—Promo only, no picture cover
❑ 73303 Total Devo 1988 12.00
❑ 73514 Now It Can Be Told! 1989 12.00

WARNER BROS.

❑ PRO-A-928 [EP] Freedom of Choice/Whip It/ Be Still/Gates of Steel 1980 16.00
—Promo version of "Dev-O Live"
❑ BSK 3239 Q: Are We Not Men? A: We Are Devo! 1978 15.00
❑ BSK 3337 Duty Now for the Future 1979 12.00
❑ BSK 3435 Freedom of Choice 1980 10.00
❑ MINI 3548 [EP] Dev-O Live 1981 10.00
—All copies came in plastic sleeve
❑ BSK 3595 New Traditionalists 1981 18.00
—First pressings include bonus 45 (EP 3595) and poster; deduct 1/3 if missing
❑ 23741 Oh No! It's Devo 1982 10.00
❑ W1-23741 Oh No! It's Devo 1982 12.00
—Columbia House version, no easel cutout on back cover
❑ 25097 Shout 1984 12.00

DEVONS, THE (1)

45s

DECCA

❑ 31777 Honda Bike/Free Fall 1965 80.00
❑ 31822 Are You Really Real/It's All Over Now, Baby Blue 1965 40.00
❑ 31899 Come On/A Little Extra Effort 1966 40.00

DEVONS, THE (2)

Also recorded as SIR DOUGLAS QUINTET.

45s

PIC ONE

❑ 111 Wine, Wine, Wine/Joey's Guitar 1965 80.00

DEVORZON, BARRY

Also see BARRY AND THE TAMERLANES; BARRY DeVORZON AND PERRY BOTKIN, JR.

45s

A&M

❑ 2129 Theme from "The Warriors"/ Baseball Furies' Chase 1979 4.00

COLUMBIA

❑ 41464 Betty, Betty/Across the Street from Your House 1959 30.00
❑ 41612 Hey Little Darlin'/Rosemary 1960 25.00
❑ 41663 Love You Baby/Can-Can Ladies 1960 25.00
❑ 42031 Penny Moved Away/Lindy Lou 1961 25.00
❑ 3-42031 Penny Moved Away/Lindy Lou 1961 40.00
—"Compact 33" single with small hole

RCA VICTOR

❑ 47-7124 Barbara Jean/Baby Doll 1957 30.00
❑ 47-7226 False Love/Raindrops at My Window 1958 30.00
❑ 47-7406 Honey Bunny/Too Soon 1958 30.00
❑ 47-7510 Cora Lee/Blue, Green and Gold 1959 30.00

Albums

ARISTA

❑ AL 4104 Nadia's Theme 1976 10.00

DEVORZON, BARRY, AND PERRY BOTKIN, JR.

Also see each artist's individual listings.

45s

A&M

❑ 1856 Nadia's Theme (The Young and the Restless)/Down the Line 1976 4.00
—Reissue; the original is listed under PERRY BOTKIN, JR.
❑ 1856 [PS] Nadia's Theme (The Young and the Restless)/Down the Line 1976 4.00
—Green sleeve
❑ 1856 [PS] Nadia's Theme (The Young and the Restless)/Down the Line 1976 6.00
—Black sleeve
❑ 1856 [PS] Nadia's Theme (The Young and the Restless)/Down the Line 1976 6.00
—Blue sleeve
❑ 1890 Bless the Beasts and Children/ Down the Line 1976 4.00

DEVOTIONS, THE

45s

DELTA

❑ 1001 Rip Van Winkle/I Love You for Sentimental Reasons 1961 150.00

KAPE

❑ 701 (How Do You Speak) To An Angel/Teardrops Follow Me 1966 12.00

ROULETTE

❑ 4406 Rip Van Winkle/I Love You for Sentimental Reasons 1962 40.00
❑ 4541 Rip Van Winkle/I Love You for Sentimental Reasons 1964 20.00
❑ 4556 A Sunday Kind of Love/Tears from a Broken Heart 1964 30.00
❑ 4580 Snow White/Zindy Lou 1964 30.00

DEWEY, GEORGE AND JACK

45s

RAVEN

❑ 700 The Flying Saucers Have Landed/The Flying Saucers Have Landed (Part 2) 195? 30.00

DEWITT, GEORGE

Albums

EPIC

❑ BN 531 [S] George DeWitt Sings That Tune 1959 30.00
❑ LN 3562 [M] George DeWitt Sings That Tune 1959 20.00

DEXTER, LARRY

45s

HIT

❑ 52 Ruby Baby/You're the Reason I'm Living 1963 8.00
—B-side by Rett Hardin

DEY, TRACEY

Also see DEY AND KNIGHT.

45s

AMY

❑ 894 Teddy's the Boy I Love/Here Comes the Boy 1963 15.00
❑ 901 Gonna Get Along Without You Now/Go Away 1964 15.00
❑ 908 Hangin' On to My Baby/ Ska-Doo-Dee-Yah 1964 15.00
❑ 912 I Won't Tell/Any Kind of Love 1964 15.00
❑ 917 Blue Turns to Grey/Didn't Ya 1964 20.00
❑ 928 Hanky Panky/Shakin' the Blues Away 1965 15.00

Except when noted otherwise, VG = 25% of NM, and VG+ = 50% of NM. (Example: VG = $2.00, VG+ = $4.00 and NM = $8.00.)

Number	Title (A Side/B Side)	Yr	NM
LIBERTY			
❑ 55604	Teenage Cleopatra/Who's That	1963	15.00
VEE JAY			
❑ 467	Jerry (I'm Your Sherry)/ Once in a Blue Moon	1962	25.00
❑ 506	Jealous Eyes/Long Time, No See	1963	20.00

DEY AND KNIGHT
Also see TRACEY DEY.

45s

Number	Title (A Side/B Side)	Yr	NM
COLUMBIA			
❑ 43466	Young Love/I'm Gonna Love You Tomorrow	1965	12.00
❑ 43693	Sayin' Somethin'/ Ooh Da La Da Lay	1966	12.00

DEYOUNG, CLIFF
Also see CLEAR LIGHT.

45s

Number	Title (A Side/B Side)	Yr	NM
MCA			
❑ 40156	My Sweet Lady/Sunshine on My Shoulders	1973	4.00
❑ 40156 [PS]	My Sweet Lady/Sunshine on My Shoulders	1973	5.00
❑ 40239	Escaping Reality/She Bent Me Straight Again	1974	4.00
❑ 40294	It Hurts a Little Even Now/Lives	1974	4.00
❑ 40388	If I Could Put You in My Song/ You Will Never Know	1975	4.00

Albums

Number	Title (A Side/B Side)	Yr	NM
MCA			
❑ 387	Sunshine	1973	15.00
❑ 432	Cliff DeYoung	1974	10.00

DIABLITO

45s

Number	Title (A Side/B Side)	Yr	NM
PARKWAY			
❑ 850	The Jungle/Merengue Potatoes	1962	12.00

DIABLOS, THE (1)
See NOLAN STRONG AND THE DIABLOS.

DIABLOS, THE (2)

45s

Number	Title (A Side/B Side)	Yr	NM
JUBILEE			
❑ 5553	Hombre/El Bandito	1966	20.00

DIABLOS, THE (3)

45s

Number	Title (A Side/B Side)	Yr	NM
PYRAMID			
❑ 159	White Christmas/Danny Boy	19??	20.00

DIALOGUE

Albums

Number	Title (A Side/B Side)	Yr	NM
COLD			
❑ (no #)	Dialogue	1972	150.00
—Orange cover with insert			
❑ (no #)	Dialogue	1974	150.00
—White cover with insert			

DIALS, THE

45s

Number	Title (A Side/B Side)	Yr	NM
HILLTOP			
❑ 219	No Hard Feelings/Win Yourself a Lover	1961	50.00
❑ 2009	Wondering About Your Love/ Sorrento	1960	150.00
❑ 2010	School Bells Are Ringing/ Ring Ting-a-Ling	1960	300.00
NORGOLDE			
❑ 105	Ring Ting-a Ling/ All Kinds of Twistin'	1961	80.00
PHILIPS			
❑ 40040	These Foolish Things/At the Start of a New Romance	1962	40.00
TIME			
❑ 1068	Monkey Dance/Monkey Walk	1963	20.00

Albums

Number	Title (A Side/B Side)	Yr	NM
TIME			
❑ S-2100 [S]	It's Monkey Time	1964	30.00
❑ 52100 [M]	It's Monkey Time	1964	25.00

DIALTONES, THE (1)

45s

Number	Title (A Side/B Side)	Yr	NM
DIAL			
❑ 4054	Don't Let the Sun Shine on Me/ You Don't Know, You Just Don't Know	1967	20.00

DIALTONES, THE (2)

45s

Number	Title (A Side/B Side)	Yr	NM
GOLDISC			
❑ 3005	Till I Heard It from You/Johnny	1960	30.00
❑ 3020	Till I Heard It from You/Johnny	1961	20.00

DIALTONES, THE (U)
Probably neither (1) nor (2), but we're not sure.

45s

Number	Title (A Side/B Side)	Yr	NM
LAWN			
❑ 203	So Young/Chicago Bird	1963	25.00

DIAMOND, BRIAN, AND THE CUTTERS

45s

Number	Title (A Side/B Side)	Yr	NM
HICKORY			
❑ 1321	Big Bad Wolf/See If I Care	1965	10.00

DIAMOND, LARRY

45s

Number	Title (A Side/B Side)	Yr	NM
ARGO			
❑ 5330	Bye Bye Doll/True Love, Come My Way	1959	12.00

DIAMOND, NEIL
Also see BARBRA AND NEIL; NEIL AND JACK; TEN BROKEN HEARTS.

12-Inch Singles

Number	Title (A Side/B Side)	Yr	NM
CONTINUUM II			
❑ 001	We Wrote a Song Together/ Beautiful Noise	1976	2000.
—Private pressing done for the grade school class of Jesse Diamond, Neil's son. All were autographed by Neil; the version of "Beautiful Noise" is an alternate take. Supposedly, between 30 and 40 copies were made.			

45s

Number	Title (A Side/B Side)	Yr	NM
BANG			
❑ 105	Cherry, Cherry/Girl, You'll Be a Woman Soon	1973	4.00
—Reissue			
❑ 108	Solitary Man/I'm a Believer	1973	4.00
—Reissue			
❑ 519	Solitary Man/Do It	1966	15.00
❑ 528	Cherry, Cherry/I'll Come Running	1966	12.00
❑ 536	I Got the Feelin' (Oh No No)/ The Boat That I Row	1966	12.00
❑ 540	You Got to Me/Someday Baby	1967	12.00
❑ 542	Girl, You'll Be a Woman Soon/ You'll Forget	1967	12.00
❑ 547	Thank the Lord for the Night Time/The Long Way Home	1967	10.00
—Title altered on second pressing			
❑ 547	I Thank the Lord for the Night Time/The Long Way Home	1967	15.00
❑ 551	Kentucky Woman/ The Time Is Now	1967	10.00
❑ 554	New Orleans/Hanky Panky	1968	10.00
❑ 556	Red Red Wine/Red Rubber Ball	1968	8.00
❑ 561	Shilo/La Bamba	1968	8.00
❑ 575	Shilo/La Bamba	1970	6.00
❑ 578	Solitary Man/The Time Is Now	1970	6.00
❑ 580	Do It/Hanky Panky	1970	6.00
❑ 586	I'm a Believer/Crooked Street	1971	6.00
❑ 586	I'm a Believer/Crooked Street	1971	15.00
—Rare pressing with both sides in stereo			
❑ 703	The Long Way Home/ Monday, Monday	1973	5.00
CAPITOL			
❑ 4939	Love on the Rocks/Acapulco	1980	4.00
❑ 4939 [PS]	Love on the Rocks/Acapulco	1980	4.00
❑ 4960	Hello Again/Amazed and Confused	1981	4.00
❑ 4960 [PS]	Hello Again/Amazed and Confused	1981	4.00
❑ 4994	America/Songs of Life	1981	4.00
❑ 4994 [PS]	America/Songs of Life	1981	4.00
COLUMBIA			
❑ AE7 1115 [DJ]	Song Sung Blue (mono/stereo)	1977	10.00
—Live version from "Love at the Greek"			
❑ 18-02604	Yesterday's Songs/ Guitar Heaven	1981	3.00
❑ 18-02604 [PS]	Yesterday's Songs/ Guitar Heaven	1981	3.00
❑ 18-02712	On the Way to the Sky/Save Me	1982	3.00
❑ 18-02712 [PS]	On the Way to the Sky/Save Me	1982	3.00
❑ 18-02928	Be Mine Tonight/Right By You	1982	3.00
❑ 38-03219	Heartlight/You Don't Know Me	1982	3.00
❑ 38-03219 [PS]	Heartlight/You Don't Know Me	1982	4.00
❑ CNR-03345	Heartlight/(B-side blank)	1982	6.00
—One-sided budget release			
❑ 38-03503	I'm Alive/Lost Among the Stars	1983	3.00
❑ CNR-03572	I'm Alive/(B-side blank)	1983	6.00
—One-sided budget release			
❑ 38-03801	Front Page Story/I'm Guilty	1983	3.00
❑ 38-03801 [PS]	Front Page Story/I'm Guilty	1983	3.00
❑ 38-04541	Turn Around/Brooklyn on a Saturday Night	1984	3.00
❑ 38-04541 [PS]	Turn Around/Brooklyn on a Saturday Night	1984	3.00
❑ 38-04646	Sleep with Me Tonight/ One by One	1984	4.00
❑ 38-04719	You Make It Feel Like Christmas/Crazy	1984	6.00
❑ 38-05889	Headed for the Future/Angel	1986	3.00
❑ 38-05889 [PS]	Headed for the Future/Angel	1986	3.00
❑ 38-06136	The Story of My Life/Love Doesn't Live Here Anymore	1986	3.00
❑ 38-06136 [PS]	The Story of My Life/Love Doesn't Live Here Anymore	1986	3.00
❑ 38-07614	I Dreamed a Dream/ Sweet Caroline	1987	3.00
❑ 38-07614 [PS]	I Dreamed a Dream/ Sweet Caroline	1987	3.00
❑ 38-07751	Cherry, Cherry/America	1988	4.00
❑ 38-08514	This Time/If I Couldn't See You Again	1988	4.00
❑ 10043	Longfellow Serenade/ Rosemary's Wine	1974	5.00
❑ 10084	I've Been This Way Before/ Reggae Strut	1975	5.00
❑ 10138	The Last Picasso/ The Gift of Song	1975	5.00
❑ 3-10366	If You Know What I Mean/ Street Life	1976	5.00
❑ 3-10405	Don't Think...Feel/Home Is a Wounded Heart	1976	5.00
❑ 3-10452	Beautiful Noise/Signs	1976	5.00
❑ 3-10657	Desiree/Once in a While	1977	5.00
❑ 3-10897	Forever in Blue Jeans/ Remember Me	1979	4.00
❑ 3-10945	Say Maybe/Diamond Girls	1979	4.00
❑ 1-11175	September Morn/I'm a Believer	1980	4.00
❑ 1-11232	The Good Lord Loves You/ Jazz Time	1980	4.00
❑ 42809	Clown Town/At Night	1963	500.00
❑ 42809 [DJ]	Clown Town/At Night	1963	250.00
❑ 45942	Be/Flight of the Gull	1973	5.00
❑ 45998	Skybird/Lonely Looking Sky	1974	5.00
❑ 38-68741	The Best Years of Our Lives/ Carmelita's Eyes	1989	4.00
❑ 38-78242	One Good Love/Kentucky Woman	1996	3.00
—A-side with Waylon Jennings			
MCA			
❑ 40017	Cherry, Cherry from Hot August Night/Morningside	1973	5.00
❑ 40092	The Last Thing on My Mind/ Canta Libra	1973	5.00
PHILCO-FORD			
❑ HP-5	Girl, You'll Be a Woman Soon/ Cherry, Cherry	1967	15.00
—4-inch plastic "Hip Pocket Record" with color sleeve			
❑ HP-17	Solitary Man/You Got to Me	1967	15.00
—4-inch plastic "Hip Pocket Record" with color sleeve			
UNI			
❑ 55065	Brooklyn Roads/ Holiday Inn Blues	1968	8.00
❑ 55075	Two-Bit Manchild/ Broad Old Woman	1968	8.00
❑ 55075 [DJ]	Two-Bit Manchild (same on both sides)	1968	80.00
—Red vinyl			
❑ 55075 [PS]	Two-Bit Manchild/ Broad Old Woman	1968	25.00
❑ 55084	Sunday Sun/Honey-Drippin' Times	1968	8.00
❑ 55109	Brother Love's Travelling Salvation Show/A Modern-Day Version of Love	1969	6.00
❑ 55136	Sweet Caroline (Good Times Never Seemed So Good)/ Dig In	1969	6.00
❑ 55175	Holly Holy/Hurtin' You Don't Come Easy	1969	6.00
❑ 55204	Until It's Time for You to Go/And the Singer Sings His Song	1970	6.00
❑ 55224	Soolaimon (African Trilogy II)/ And the Grass Won't Pay No Mind	1970	6.00
❑ 55224 [PS]	Soolaimon (African Trilogy II)/ And the Grass Won't Pay No Mind	1970	15.00
❑ 55250	Cracklin' Rosie/Lordy	1970	6.00
❑ 55264	He Ain't Heavy...He's My Brother/Free Life	1970	6.00
❑ 55278	I Am...I Said/Done Too Soon	1971	5.00
❑ 55310	Stones/Crunchy Granola Suite	1971	5.00
❑ 55326	Song Sung Blue/Gitchy Goomy	1972	5.00
❑ 55346	Play Me/Porcupine Pie	1972	5.00
❑ 55352	Walk on Water/High Rolling Man	1972	5.00

7-Inch Extended Plays

Number	Title (A Side/B Side)	Yr	NM
UNI			
❑ 34818	Kentucky Woman/Solitary Man/Thank the Lord for the Night Time//Brother Love's Travelling Salvation Show/ Sweet Caroline	1970	15.00
—Jukebox issue; small hole, plays at 33 1/3 rpm			
❑ 34818 [PS]	Gold	1970	15.00
—Part of "Little LP" series (LLP #127)			

Except when noted otherwise, VG = 25% of NM, and VG+ = 50% of NM. (Example: VG = $2.00, VG+ = $4.00 and NM = $8.00.)

Number	Title (A Side/B Side)	Yr	NM
❑ 34871	Suzanne/Husbands and Wives// I Am... I Said/Stones/ Chelsea Morning	1971	15.00
—Jukebox issue; small hole, plays at 33 1/3 rpm			
❑ 34871 [PS]	Stones	1971	15.00
—Part of "Little LP" series (LLP #172)			

Albums

BANG

Number	Title (A Side/B Side)	Yr	NM
❑ BLP 214 [M]	The Feel of Neil Diamond	1966	60.00
—All tracks play mono			
❑ BLP 214 [P]	The Feel of Neil Diamond	1966	80.00
—Album is labeled mono, but plays in stereo			
❑ BLPS 214	The Feel of Neil Diamond	1974	12.00
—Later pressing on blue "clouds" label			
❑ BLPS 214 [P]	The Feel of Neil Diamond	1966	100.00
—Album is labeled stereo and plays in stereo (except "Solitary Man," "Do It," "I'll Come Running" are rechanneled)			
❑ BLP 217 [M]	Just for You	1967	40.00
—With blurb for "Thank the Lord for the Night Time" on cover			
❑ BLPS 217	Just for You	1974	12.00
—Later pressing on blue "clouds" label			
❑ BLPS 217 [P]	Just for You	1967	50.00
—With blurb for "Thank the Lord for the Night Time" on cover			
❑ BLPS 217 [P]	Just for You	1968	40.00
—With blurb for "Shilo" pasted over "Thank the Lord for the Night Time" blurb			
❑ BLPS 217 [P]	Just for You	1970	20.00
—With blurb for "Shilo" imprinted on cover			
❑ BLPS 219	Neil Diamond's Greatest Hits	1974	12.00
—Later pressing on blue "clouds" label			
❑ BLPS 219 [P]	Neil Diamond's Greatest Hits	196?	20.00
—Later editions have an alternate take of "Solitary Man" in true stereo			
❑ BLPS 219 [P]	Neil Diamond's Greatest Hits	1968	40.00
—First editions have the single version of "Solitary Man" in rechanneled stereo			
❑ BLPS 221	Shilo	1974	12.00
—Later pressing on blue "clouds" label			
❑ BLPS 221 [S]	Shilo	1970	40.00
❑ BLPS 224	Do It!	1974	12.00
—Later pressing on blue "clouds" label			
❑ BLPS 224 [P]	Do It!	1971	30.00
❑ BLPS 227 [(2)]	Double Gold	1974	15.00
—Later pressing on blue "clouds" label			
❑ BLPS-227 [(2)S]	Double Gold	1973	40.00

CAPITOL

Number	Title (A Side/B Side)	Yr	NM
❑ SWAV-12120	The Jazz Singer	1980	10.00

COLUMBIA

Number	Title (A Side/B Side)	Yr	NM
❑ AS 99-1586 [DJ]	Heartlight	1982	25.00
—Promo-only picture disc			
❑ KS 32550	Jonathan Livingston Seagull	1973	12.00
—With booklet			
❑ PC 32919	Serenade	1974	12.00
❑ PCQ 32919 [Q]	Serenade	1974	25.00
❑ PC 33965	Beautiful Noise	1976	12.00
—Originals have no bar code			
❑ KC2 34404 [(2)]	Love at the Greek	1977	15.00
❑ JC 34990	I'm Glad You're Here with Me Tonight	1977	12.00
❑ FC 35625	You Don't Bring Me Flowers	1978	12.00
❑ FC 36121	September Morn	1979	12.00
❑ TC 37628	On the Way to the Sky	1981	10.00
❑ TC 38068	12 Greatest Hits, Vol. II	1982	10.00
❑ TC 38359	Heartlight	1982	10.00
❑ PC 38792	Classics — The Early Years	1983	10.00
—Possibly a reissue of Frog King 1			
❑ QC 39199	Primitive	1984	10.00
❑ 9C9 39915 [PD]	Primitive	1984	20.00
❑ OC 40368	Headed for the Future	1986	8.00
❑ CG2 40990 [(2)]	Hot August Night II	1987	12.00
❑ HC 42550	Jonathan Livingston Seagull	1982	50.00
—Half-speed mastered edition			
❑ OC 45025	The Best Years of Our Lives	1988	8.00
❑ HC 45625	You Don't Bring Me Flowers	1982	40.00
—Half-speed mastered edition			
❑ HC 47628	On the Way to the Sky	1982	30.00
—Half-speed mastered edition			
❑ HC 48068	12 Greatest Hits, Vol. II	1982	100.00
—Half-speed mastered edition			
❑ HC 48359	Heartlight	1982	40.00
—Half-speed mastered edition			
❑ C 48610	Lovescape	1991	25.00
❑ 8-2876-77507-1 [(2)]	12 Songs	2006	20.00

DIRECT DISK

Number	Title (A Side/B Side)	Yr	NM
❑ SD 16612	His 12 Greatest Hits	1982	50.00
—Audiophile vinyl			

FROG KING

Number	Title (A Side/B Side)	Yr	NM
❑ AAR-1	Early Classics	1972	40.00
—Compilation of Bang material for Columbia Record Club; includes songbook (deduct 25% if missing)			

MCA

Number	Title (A Side/B Side)	Yr	NM
❑ 1489	Neil Diamond/ His 12 Greatest Hits	1987	8.00
—Reissue of MCA 5219			
❑ 2005	Moods	1973	10.00
❑ 2006	Touching You Touching Me	1973	10.00
❑ 2007	Neil Diamond/Gold	1973	10.00
❑ 2008	Stones	1973	10.00
❑ 2011	Sweet Caroline (Brother Love's Travelling Salvation Show)	1973	10.00
❑ 2013	Tap Root Manuscript	1973	10.00
❑ 2103	Rainbow	1973	15.00
—Compilation of Uni tracks			
❑ 2106	Neil Diamond/ His 12 Greatest Hits	1974	15.00
❑ 2227	And the Singer Sings His Song	1976	15.00
❑ 5219	Neil Diamond/ His 12 Greatest Hits	1981	10.00
—Reissue of MCA 2106			
❑ 5239	Love Songs	1981	10.00
❑ 6896 [(2)]	Hot August Night	1980	12.00
—Reissue of MCA 2-8000			
❑ 8000 [(2)]	Hot August Night	1972	20.00
❑ 37056	Velvet Gloves and Spit	1980	8.00
❑ 37057	Sweet Caroline/Brother Love's Travelling Salvation Show	1980	8.00
❑ 37058	Touching You Touching Me	1980	8.00
❑ 37059	Rainbow	1980	8.00
❑ 37060	And the Singer Sings His Song	1980	8.00
❑ 37194	Moods	1981	8.00
❑ 37195	Stones	1981	8.00
❑ 37196	Tap Root Manuscript	1981	8.00
❑ 37209	Gold	1981	8.00
❑ 37252	Neil Diamond/ His 12 Greatest Hits	198?	8.00
—Reissue of MCA 5219			

MOBILE FIDELITY

Number	Title (A Side/B Side)	Yr	NM
❑ 2-024 [(2)]	Hot August Night	1979	40.00
—Audiophile vinyl			
❑ 1-071	The Jazz Singer	1981	30.00
—Audiophile vinyl			

SILVER EAGLE

Number	Title (A Side/B Side)	Yr	NM
❑ MSM-35151 [(3)]	The Neil Diamond Collection	1988	25.00
—Mail-order offer; contains material from his Uni period			

UNI

Number	Title (A Side/B Side)	Yr	NM
❑ ND-11 [DJ]	Neil Diamond DJ Sampler	1970	200.00
❑ 1913 [DJ]	Open-End Interview with Neil Diamond	1971	300.00
❑ 73030	Velvet Gloves and Spit	1968	30.00
—First editions do not include "Shilo"			
❑ 73030-N	Velvet Gloves and Spit	1970	20.00
—Later editions add a new recording of "Shilo"			
❑ 73047	Brother Love's Travelling Salvation Show	1969	20.00
—Later editions add "Sweet Caroline"			
❑ 73047.	Brother Love's Travelling Salvation Show	1969	30.00
—First editions do not include "Sweet Caroline"			
❑ 73071	Touching You Touching Me	1969	20.00
❑ 73084	Neil Diamond/Gold	1970	20.00
❑ 73092	Tap Root Manuscript	1970	20.00
❑ 93030-N	Velvet Gloves and Spit	1971	15.00
—Reissue of the version with "Shilo" added, with new number			
❑ 93047	Brother Love's Travelling Salvation Show	1971	15.00
—Reissue of the version with "Sweet Caroline," with new number			
❑ 93071	Touching You Touching Me	1971	15.00
—Reissue of 73071			
❑ 93106	Stones	1971	20.00
❑ 93136	Moods	1972	20.00
❑ ST-93501	Tap Root Manuscript	1970	25.00
—Capitol Record Club issue			

DIAMONDS, THE (1)

The group on Atlantic is a different group than those below, and are outside the scope of this book.

45s

CORAL

Number	Title (A Side/B Side)	Yr	NM
❑ 61502	Black Denim Trousers and Motorcycle Boots/Nip Sip	1955	20.00
❑ 61577	Be My Lovin' Baby/Smooch Me	1956	20.00

GUSTO

Number	Title (A Side/B Side)	Yr	NM
❑ 2019	Little Darlin'/The Stroll	1979	4.00
—Re-recordings			

MERCURY

Number	Title (A Side/B Side)	Yr	NM
❑ 70790	Why Do Fools Fall in Love/ You Baby You	1956	20.00
❑ 70835	The Church Bells May Ring/ Little Girl of Mine	1956	20.00
❑ 70889	Love, Love, Love/Every Night About This Time	1956	20.00
❑ 70934	Ka-Ding-Dong/Soft Summer Breeze	1956	20.00
❑ 70983	My Judge and My Jury/ Put Your House in Order	1956	20.00
❑ 71021	A Thousand Miles Away/ Ev'ry Minute of the Day	1956	20.00
❑ 71060	Little Darlin'/Faithful and True	1957	25.00
—Black label, "Mercury" and logo in double oval at top			
❑ 71060	Little Darlin'/Faithful and True	1957	30.00
—Maroon Label, "Mercury" and logo in double oval at top			
❑ 71060	Little Darlin'/Faithful and True	1957	40.00
—Maroon label, "Mercury" and logo by themselves at top			
❑ 71128	Words of Love/ Don't Say Goodbye	1957	20.00
❑ 71165	Zip Zip/Oh How I Wish	1957	20.00
❑ 71197	Silhouettes/Daddy Cool	1957	20.00
❑ 71242	The Stroll/Land of Beauty	1957	30.00
❑ 71291	High Sign/Chick-Lets (Don't Let Me Down)	1958	15.00
❑ 71291 [PS]	High Sign/Chick-Lets (Don't Let Me Down)	1958	100.00
❑ 71330	Kathy-O/Happy Years	1958	15.00
❑ 71366	Walking Along/Eternal Lovers	1958	15.00
❑ 71404	She Say (Oom Dooby Doom)/ From the Bottom of My Heart	1959	20.00
❑ 71449	A Mother's Love/Gretchen	1959	15.00
❑ 71468	Sneaky Alligator/ Holding Your Hand	1959	15.00
❑ 71505	Young in Years/ The Twenty-Second Day	1959	15.00
❑ 71534	Walking the Stroll/Batman, Wolfman, Frankenstein or Dracula	1959	20.00
❑ 71586	Real True Love/Tell the Truth	1960	15.00
❑ 71633	The Pencil Song/Slave Girl	1960	15.00
❑ 71734	The Crumble/You'd Be Mine	1960	15.00
❑ 71782	You Sure Changed Me/ I Sure Lawd Will	1961	15.00
❑ 71818	The Munch/Woomai Ling	1961	15.00
❑ 71831	One Summer Night/It's a Doggone Shame	1961	15.00
❑ 71956	The Vanishing American/ The Horizontal Lieutenant	1962	15.00

7-Inch Extended Plays

BRUNSWICK

Number	Title (A Side/B Side)	Yr	NM
❑ EB 71031	(contents unknown)	1957	150.00
❑ EB 71031 [PS]	The Diamonds	1957	150.00

MERCURY

Number	Title (A Side/B Side)	Yr	NM
❑ EP 1-3356	Shoo Ya Blues/You Are the Limit//My Dog Likes Your Dog/Oh, How I Wish	1957	40.00
❑ EP 1-3356 [PS]	The Diamonds	1957	40.00
❑ EP 1-3357	Honey Bird/For You Alone// Zip Zip/Cool, Cool Baby	1957	40.00
❑ EP 1-3357 [PS]	The Diamonds	1957	40.00
❑ EP 1-3358	Till My Baby Comes Home/Girl of Mine//One and Only/Honey	1957	40.00
❑ EP 1-3358 [PS]	The Diamonds: America's Number One Singing Stylists	1957	40.00
❑ EP 1-3367	Silhouettes/Daddy Cool// Passion Flower/ Sweet Wild Honey	1957	40.00
❑ EP 1-3367 [PS]	The Diamonds	1957	40.00
❑ EP 1-3390	(contents unknown)	1958	40.00
❑ EP 1-3390 [PS]	The Stroll	1958	40.00

Albums

MERCURY

Number	Title (A Side/B Side)	Yr	NM
❑ MG-20213 [M]	Collection of Golden Hits	1956	120.00
❑ MG-20309 [M]	The Diamonds	1957	120.00
❑ MG-20368 [M]	The Diamonds Meet Pete Rugolo	1958	80.00
❑ MG-20480 [M]	Songs from the Old West	1959	80.00
❑ SR-60076 [S]	The Diamonds Meet Pete Rugolo	1959	120.00
❑ SR-60159 [S]	Songs from the Old West	1959	120.00

RHINO

Number	Title (A Side/B Side)	Yr	NM
❑ RNDF-209	The Best of the Diamonds	1984	12.00

WING

Number	Title (A Side/B Side)	Yr	NM
❑ MGW-12114 [M]	The Diamonds: America's Famous Song Stylists	1959	30.00
❑ MGW-12178 [M]	Pop Hits by the Diamonds	1962	30.00

DIAMONDS, THE (2)

Black vocal group. Also see SONNY WRIGHT (1).

45s

ATLANTIC

Number	Title (A Side/B Side)	Yr	NM
❑ 981	A Beggar for Your Kisses/ Call, Baby, Call	1952	1500.
❑ 1003	I'll Live Again/Two Loves Have I	1953	600.00
❑ 1017	Romance in the Dark/Cherry	1954	600.00

DIANE AND THE DARLETTES

45s

DUNES

Number	Title (A Side/B Side)	Yr	NM
❑ 2016	Just You/The Wobble	1962	25.00
❑ 2026	Here She Comes/Just You	1963	15.00
—As "The Darlettes"			

DIBANGO, MANU

12-Inch Singles

CELLULOID

Number	Title (A Side/B Side)	Yr	NM
❑ CEL 171	Abele Dance/Abele Dance Dub	1984	8.00
❑ CEL 182	Makossa Rock (2 versions)/ Gammatron	1985	8.00

ISLAND

Number	Title (A Side/B Side)	Yr	NM
❑ 8680 [DJ]	Big Blow/Aloko Party	1976	8.00

45s

ATLANTIC

Number	Title (A Side/B Side)	Yr	NM
❑ 2971	Soul Makossa/Lily	1973	5.00
❑ 2983	Dangwa/Obaso	1973	5.00

Except when noted otherwise, VG = 25% of NM, and VG+ = 50% of NM. (Example: VG = \$2.00, VG+ = \$4.00 and NM = \$8.00.)

Number	Title (A Side/B Side)	Yr	NM
❑ 3000	Weya/Moni	1974	4.00
❑ 3263	Super Kimba/Wasa N'Doto	1975	4.00
WARNER BROS.			
❑ 8680	Aloko Party/Big Blow	1978	4.00
Albums			
ATLANTIC			
❑ SD 7267	Soul Makossa	1973	10.00
❑ SD 7276	Makossa Man	1974	10.00
ISLAND			
❑ ILPS 9526	Afrovision	1976	12.00

DICK AND DEEDEE

Also see DICK ST. JOHN.

Number	Title (A Side/B Side)	Yr	NM
45s			
DOT			
❑ 17145	Escape Suite/I'm Not Gonna Get Hung-Up About It	1968	15.00
❑ 17261	We'll Sing in the Sunshine/ In the Season of Our Love	1969	10.00
❑ 17305	Do I Love You/You Came Back to Haunt Me	1970	10.00
LAMA			
❑ 7778	The Mountain's High/ I Want Someone	1961	20.00
❑ 7780	Goodbye to Love/Swing Low	1961	16.00
❑ 7783	Tell Me/Will You Always Love Me	1961	16.00
LIBERTY			
❑ 55350	The Mountain's High/ I Want Someone	1961	15.00
❑ 55382	Goodbye to Love/Swing Low	1961	12.00
❑ 55412	Tell Me/Will You Always Love Me	1962	12.00
❑ 55478	All I Want/Life's Just a Play	1962	12.00
UNITED ARTISTS			
❑ 0036	The Mountain's High/Tell Me	1973	5.00
—"Silver Spotlight Series" reissue			
WARNER BROS.			
❑ 5320	The River Took My Baby/ My Lonely Self	1962	10.00
❑ 5320 [PS]	The River Took My Baby/ My Lonely Self	1962	25.00
❑ 5342	Young and In Love/Say to Me	1963	12.00
❑ 5364	Love Is a Once in a Lifetime Thing/Chug-a Chug-a Choo Choo	1963	10.00
❑ 5383	Where Did the Good Times Go/ Guess Our Love Must Show	1963	10.00
❑ 5396	Turn Around/Don't Leave Me	1963	10.00
❑ 5411	All My Trials/Don't Think Twice, It's All Right	1964	10.00
❑ 5426	Not Fade Away/The Gift	1964	10.00
❑ 5451	You Were Mine/Remember Then	1964	10.00
❑ 5470	The Riddle Song/ Without Your Love	1964	10.00
❑ 5482	Thou Shalt Not Steal/Just 'Round the River Bend	1964	10.00
—Orange label			
❑ 5482	Thou Shalt Not Steal/Just 'Round the River Bend	1964	15.00
—Red label with arrows			
❑ 5482 [PS]	Thou Shalt Not Steal/Just 'Round the River Bend	1964	25.00
❑ 5608	Be My Baby/Room 404	1965	10.00
❑ 5627	Blue Turns to Grey/Some Things Just Stick in Your Mind	1965	20.00
—Both sides are Mick Jagger-Keith Richards songs produced by Andrew Loog Oldham			
❑ 5652	The World Is Waiting/Vini, Vini	1965	10.00
❑ 5671	P.S. 1402 (Your Local Charm School)/Use What You've Got	1965	10.00
❑ 5680	New Orleans/Use What You've Got	1965	10.00
❑ 5699	Till/Sha-Ta	1966	10.00
❑ 5830	She Didn't Even Say Goodbye/ So Many Things We Didn't Know	1966	10.00
❑ 5860	Make Up Before We Break Up/ Can't Get Enough of Your Love	1966	10.00
❑ 7017	Long Lonely Nights/ I'll Always Be Around	1967	10.00
❑ 7069	One in a Million/Baby, I Need You	1967	10.00
❑ 7109	Young and In Love/ Thou Shalt Not Steal	1968	8.00
—"Back to Back Hits" series; originals have green labels with "W7" logo			
Albums			
LIBERTY			
❑ LRP-3236 [M]	Tell Me/The Mountain's High	1962	50.00
❑ LST-7236 [R]	Tell Me/The Mountain's High	1962	40.00
WARNER BROS.			
❑ W 1500 [M]	Young and In Love	1963	25.00
❑ WS 1500 [S]	Young and In Love	1963	30.00
❑ W 1538 [M]	Turn Around	1964	25.00
❑ WS 1538 [S]	Turn Around	1964	30.00
❑ W 1586 [M]	Thou Shalt Not Steal	1965	25.00
❑ WS 1586 [S]	Thou Shalt Not Steal	1965	30.00
❑ W 1623 [M]	Song We've Sung on "Shindig"	1966	25.00
❑ WS 1623 [S]	Song We've Sung on "Shindig"	1966	30.00

DICKENS, THE

See NRBQ.

DICKENS, RICKY

Number	Title (A Side/B Side)	Yr	NM
45s			
HIT			
❑ 79	If I Had a Hammer/Hey Girl	1963	8.00
—B-side by Leroy Jones			
❑ 85	Sugar Shack/Hello Heartache, Goodbye Love	1963	8.00
—B-side by Connie Dee			
❑ 98	Midnight Mary/Drip Drop	1963	8.00
—B-side by Ed Hardin			
❑ 102	Daisy Petal Pickin'/ Hey Little Cobra	1964	8.00
—B-side by the Roamers			
❑ 164	Ballad of Daniel Boone/ Legend of Daniel Boone	1964	8.00
—B-side by Charlie Brown			

DICKIE G. AND THE DON'TS

See DICKIE GOODMAN.

DICKIES, THE

Famously covered BLACK SABBATH'S "Paranoid."

Number	Title (A Side/B Side)	Yr	NM
45s			
A&M			
❑ 2092	Silent Night/Sounds Of Silence	1978	10.00
—All copies on white vinyl			
❑ 2092 [DJ]	Silent Night/Sounds Of Silence	1978	8.00
—All copies on white vinyl			
❑ 2092 [PS]	Silent Night/Sounds Of Silence	1978	10.00
❑ 2225	Nights in White Satin/Manny, Moe and Jack	1980	10.00
❑ 2225 [PS]	Nights in White Satin/Manny, Moe and Jack	1980	50.00
—Withdrawn; shows Dickies in KKK robes			
❑ 2241	Banana Splits (The Tra La La Song)/Sounds of Silence	1980	10.00
❑ 2241 [PS]	Banana Splits (The Tra La La Song)/Sounds of Silence	1980	10.00
Albums			
A&M			
❑ SP-4742	The Incredible Shrinking Dickies	1979	15.00
❑ SP-4742	The Incredible Shrinking Dickies	1979	20.00
—First pressing on yellow vinyl			
❑ SP-4796	Dawn of the Dickies	1979	15.00
ENIGMA			
❑ D1-73289	Second Coming	1989	8.00
❑ D1-73322 [EP]	Killer Klowns (From Outer Space)	1988	8.00
PVC			
❑ 6903	Stukas Over Disneyland	1983	12.00
TAANG!			
❑ 56	Locked and Loaded	1991	15.00
TRIPLE X			
❑ 51168	Idjit Savant	1994	15.00

DICKY DOO AND THE DON'TS

Number	Title (A Side/B Side)	Yr	NM
45s			
ASCOT			
❑ 2178	Click Clack '65/Don't Count Me Out	1965	10.00
CASINO			
❑ 106	Click Clack/Lonely Hours Lady	196?	12.00
❑ 107	Flip Top Box/That's Life (That's Tough)	196?	12.00
DANNA			
❑ 4001	The Judge/Doo Plus Two	1967	10.00
SWAN			
❑ 4001	Click Clack/Did You Cry	1958	20.00
❑ 4006	Ne Ne Na Na Na Na Nu Nu/ Flip Top Box	1959	25.00
❑ 4014	Leave Me Alone (Let Me Cry)/ Wild Party	1959	20.00
❑ 4025	Teardrops Will Fall/ Come with Us	1959	20.00
❑ 4033	Ballad of a Train/ Dear Heart, Don't Cry	1959	20.00
❑ 4046	Wabash Cannonball/The Drums of Richard A. Doo	1960	20.00
UNITED ARTISTS			
❑ 238	Teen Scene/Pity, Pity	1960	20.00
❑ 362	The Judge/The Little Dog Cried	1961	20.00
Albums			
UNITED ARTISTS			
❑ UAL-3094 [M]	The Madison and Other Dances	1959	40.00
❑ UAL-3097 [M]	Teen Scene	1959	40.00
❑ UAS-6094 [S]	The Madison and Other Dances	1959	50.00
❑ UAS-6097 [S]	Teen Scene	1959	50.00

DICTATORS, THE

Number	Title (A Side/B Side)	Yr	NM
45s			
ASYLUM			
❑ 45420	Disease/Hey Boys	1977	10.00
❑ 45470	Science Has Gone Too Far/ Sleepin' with the T.V. On	1978	10.00
❑ 45523	I Stand Tall/Two Much Fun	1978	10.00
Albums			
ASYLUM			
❑ 6E-147	Bloodbrothers	1978	15.00
❑ 7E-1109	Manifest Destiny	1977	16.00
EPIC			
❑ KE 33348	The Dictators Go Girl Crazy	1975	22.00

DIDDLEY, BO

Number	Title (A Side/B Side)	Yr	NM
45s			
CHECKER			
❑ 814	Bo Diddley/I'm a Man	1955	50.00
❑ 819	Diddley Daddy/She's Fine, She's Mine	1955	60.00
—A-side backing vocals: The Moonglows			
❑ 827	Pretty Thing/Bring It to Jerome	1955	50.00
❑ 832	Diddy Wah Diddy/I Am Looking for a Woman	1956	50.00
❑ 842	Who Do You Love?/I'm Bad	1956	40.00
—Note altered B-side title			
❑ 842	Who Do You Love?/In Bad	1956	60.00
❑ 850	Cops and Robbers/ Down Home Special	1956	40.00
❑ 860	Hey! Bo Diddley/Mona	1957	50.00
—Originals of Checker 816-860 have "Checker" over a checkerboard on top of label			
❑ 878	Say! Boss Man/ Before You Accuse Me	1957	25.00
❑ 896	Dearest Darling/ Hush Your Mouth	1958	25.00
❑ 907	Bo Meets the Monster/ Willie and Lillie	1958	30.00
❑ 914	I'm Sorry/Oh Yeah	1959	25.00
❑ 924	Crackin' Up/The Great Grandfather	1959	25.00
❑ 931	Say Man/Clock Strikes Twelve	1959	30.00
❑ 931 [PS]	Say Man/Clock Strikes Twelve	1959	400.00
❑ 936	Say Man, Back Again/ She's Alright	1959	25.00
❑ 942	Road Runner/My Story	1960	20.00
❑ 951	Walkin' and Talkin'/Crawdad	1960	20.00
❑ 965	Gun Slinger/Signifying	1960	20.00
❑ 976	No Guilty/Aztec	1961	20.00
❑ 985	Pills/Call Me	1961	30.00
❑ 997	Bo Diddley/I'm a Man	1961	20.00
❑ 1019	You Can't Judge a Book By Its Cover/I Can Tell	1962	25.00
❑ 1045	Surfers' Love Call/Greatest Lover in the World	1963	20.00
❑ 1058	Memphis/Monkey Diddle	1963	20.00
❑ 1083	Jo Ann/Mama, Keep Your Big Mouth Shut	1964	20.00
❑ 1089	Bo's Beat/Chuck's Beat	1964	20.00
—B-side by Chuck Berry			
❑ 1098	Hey, Good Lookin'/You Ain't Bad	1965	15.00
❑ 1123	500% More Man/ Let the Kids Dance	1965	15.00
❑ 1142	We're Gonna Get Married/ Do the Frog	1966	15.00
❑ 1158	Ooh Baby/Back to School	1966	15.00
❑ 1168	Bo-Ga-Loo Before You Go/ Wrecking My Love Life	1967	15.00
❑ 1200	Another Sugardaddy/ I'm High Again	1968	15.00
❑ 1213	Bo Diddley 1969/Soul Train	1969	12.00
❑ 1238	The Shape I'm In/Pollution	1970	12.00
CHESS			
❑ 2117	I Love You More Than You'll Ever Know/I Said Shut Up Woman	1971	10.00
❑ 2129	Bo Diddley-Itis/Infatuation	1972	10.00
❑ 2134	Bo-Jam/Husband-in-Law	1972	10.00
❑ 2142	I Don't Want No Lyin' Woman/ Make a Hit Record	1973	10.00
PHILCO-FORD			
❑ HP-33	I'm a Man/Song of Bo Diddley	1968	30.00
—4-inch plastic "Hip Pocket Record" with color sleeve			
RCA VICTOR			
❑ PB-10618	Not Fade Away/Drag On	1976	10.00
7-Inch Extended Plays			
CHESS			
❑ 5125	Bo Diddley/I'm a Man// Willie and Lillie/Bo Meets the Monster	1958	120.00
❑ 5125 [PS]	Bo Diddley	1958	180.00

Except when noted otherwise, VG = 25% of NM, and VG+ = 50% of NM. (Example: VG = $2.00, VG+ = $4.00 and NM = $8.00.)

Albums

ACCORD

Number	Title (A Side/B Side)	Yr	NM
❑ SN-7182	Toronto Rock and Roll Revival, Vol. 5	1982	20.00

CHECKER

Number	Title (A Side/B Side)	Yr	NM
❑ LP 1431 [M]	Bo Diddley	1958	150.00
❑ LP 1436 [M]	Go Bo Diddley	1959	150.00
❑ LP 2974 [M]	Have Guitar, Will Travel	1960	150.00
❑ LP 2976 [M]	Spotlight on Bo Diddley	1960	150.00
❑ LP 2977 [M]	Bo Diddley Is a Gunslinger	1961	150.00
❑ LP 2980 [M]	Bo Diddley Is a Lover	1961	150.00
❑ LP 2982 [M]	Bo Diddley's a Twister	1962	100.00
❑ LP 2982 [M]	Road Runner	1967	80.00
—Reissue of "Bo Diddley's a Twister"			
❑ LPS- 2982 [R]	Road Runner	1967	50.00
❑ LP 2984 [M]	Bo Diddley	1962	100.00
❑ LP 2985 [M]	Bo Diddley and Company	1963	120.00
❑ LP 2987 [M]	Surfin' with Bo Diddley	1964	120.00
❑ LPS 2987 [R]	Surfin' with Bo Diddley	1964	30.00
❑ LP 2988 [M]	Bo Diddley's Beach Party	1963	100.00
❑ LP 2989 [M]	16 All Time Greatest Hits	1964	50.00
❑ LPS 2989 [R]	16 All Time Greatest Hits	1964	30.00
❑ LP 2992 [M]	Hey! Good Lookin'	1965	60.00
❑ LPS 2992 [R]	Hey! Good Lookin'	1965	30.00
❑ LP 2996 [M]	500% More Man	1965	60.00
❑ LPS 2996 [R]	500% More Man	1965	30.00
❑ LP 3001 [M]	The Originator	1966	30.00
❑ LPS 3001 [S]	The Originator	1966	40.00
❑ LP 3006 [M]	Go Bo Diddley	1967	50.00
—Reissue of 1436			
❑ LPS 3006 [R]	Go Bo Diddley	1967	40.00
❑ LP 3007 [M]	Boss Man	1967	80.00
—Reissue of Chess 1431			
❑ LPS 3007 [R]	Boss Man	1967	50.00
❑ LPS 3013	The Black Gladiator	1968	30.00

CHESS

Number	Title (A Side/B Side)	Yr	NM
❑ LP 1431 [M]	Bo Diddley	1958	200.00
❑ CH-9106	His Greatest Sides, Vol. 1	1984	10.00
❑ CH-9187	Have Guitar, Will Travel	1985	10.00
—Reissue of Checker 2974			
❑ CH-9194	Bo Diddley	1986	10.00
—Reissue of 1431			
❑ CH-9196	Go Bo Diddley	1986	10.00
—Reissue of Checker 1436			
❑ CH-9264	Spotlight on Bo Diddley	1987	10.00
—Reissue of Checker 2976			
❑ CH-9285	Bo Diddley Is a Gunslinger	1989	10.00
—Reissue of Checker 2977			
❑ CH-9296	The London Bo Diddley Sessions	1989	10.00
—Reissue of 50029			
❑ CH3-19502 [(3)]	The Chess Box	1990	40.00
❑ CH 50001	Another Dimension	1971	40.00
❑ CH 50016	Where It All Began	1972	40.00
❑ CH 50029	The London Bo Diddley Sessions	1973	25.00
❑ CH 50047	Big Bad Bo	1974	25.00
❑ 2CH 60005 [(2)]	Got My Own Bag of Tricks	1972	25.00

RCA VICTOR

Number	Title (A Side/B Side)	Yr	NM
❑ APL1-1229	The 20th Anniversary of Rock and Roll	1976	20.00

DIDDLEY, BO/CHUCK BERRY

Also see each artist's individual listings.

Albums

CHECKER

Number	Title (A Side/B Side)	Yr	NM
❑ LP 2991 [M]	Two Great Guitars	1964	60.00
❑ LPS 2991 [R]	Two Great Guitars	1964	40.00

CHESS

Number	Title (A Side/B Side)	Yr	NM
❑ CH-9170	Two Great Guitars	1985	10.00
—Reissue of Checker 2991			

DIDDLEY, BO/MUDDY WATERS/HOWLIN' WOLF

Also see each artist's individual listings.

Albums

CHECKER

Number	Title (A Side/B Side)	Yr	NM
❑ LP 3010 [M]	Super, Super Blues Band	1968	50.00
❑ LPS 3010 [S]	Super, Super Blues Band	1968	40.00

CHESS

Number	Title (A Side/B Side)	Yr	NM
❑ CH-9169	Super, Super Blues Band	1985	10.00
—Reissue of Checker 3010			

DIDDLEY, BO/MUDDY WATERS/LITTLE WALTER

Also see each artist's individual listings.

Albums

CHECKER

Number	Title (A Side/B Side)	Yr	NM
❑ LP 3008 [M]	Super Blues Band	1968	50.00
❑ LPS 3008 [S]	Super Blues Band	1968	40.00

CHESS

Number	Title (A Side/B Side)	Yr	NM
❑ CH-9168	Super Blues Band	1985	10.00
—Reissue of Checker 3008			

DIFFERENT SHADES OF BROWN

45s

TAMLA

Number	Title (A Side/B Side)	Yr	NM
❑ 54219	Label Me Love/Life's a Ball	1972	5.00

DILEO, BOB

45s

COLUMBIA

Number	Title (A Side/B Side)	Yr	NM
❑ 4-44858	Just Can't Help Believin'/Mind Excursion	1969	8.00
❑ 4-44958	Jessica/Sing to Me	1969	8.00

DILL, DANNY

45s

ABC-PARAMOUNT

Number	Title (A Side/B Side)	Yr	NM
❑ 9681	My Girl and His Girl/Geisha Sweetheart	1956	30.00
❑ 9734	I'm Hungry for Your Lovin'/The Stranger of Abilene	1956	50.00

CUB

Number	Title (A Side/B Side)	Yr	NM
❑ 9045	He's Biding His Time/He Ain't Gonna Study War	1959	20.00

DILLARD, DOUG

Albums

TOGETHER

Number	Title (A Side/B Side)	Yr	NM
❑ STT-1003	The Banjo Album	1970	80.00

DILLARD, VARETTA

45s

CUB

Number	Title (A Side/B Side)	Yr	NM
❑ 9073	Teaser/I Know I'm Good for You	1960	12.00
❑ 9083	Little Bitty Tear/Mercy Mr. Percy	1961	12.00
❑ 9091	You Better Come Home/I Don't Know What It Is, But I Like It	1961	12.00

GROOVE

Number	Title (A Side/B Side)	Yr	NM
❑ 0139	Darling, Listen to the Words of This Song/Mama Don't Want (What Poppa Don't Want)	1956	40.00
❑ 0152	Gonna Tell My Daddy/Cherry Blossom	1956	25.00
❑ 0159	Got You On My Mind/Skinny Jimmy	1956	25.00
❑ 0167	I Miss You Jimmy/If You Want to Be My Baby	1956	25.00
❑ 0177	One More Time/I Can't Help Myself	1956	25.00

RCA VICTOR

Number	Title (A Side/B Side)	Yr	NM
❑ 47-6869	Pray for Me Mother/Leave a Happy Fool Alone	1957	20.00
❑ 47-6936	Time Was/I Got a Lot of Love	1957	20.00
❑ 47-7057	Undecided/That's Why I Cry	1957	20.00
❑ 47-7144	Star of Fortune/The Blues of Love	1958	20.00
❑ 47-7285	What'll I Do/Just Multiply	1958	20.00

SAVOY

Number	Title (A Side/B Side)	Yr	NM
❑ 822	Love and Wine/Please Come Back to Me	1951	50.00
❑ 839	Hurry Up/Please Tell Me Why	1952	40.00
❑ 847	Easy, Easy Baby/A Letter in Blue	1952	40.00
❑ 851	I'm Yours/Here in My Heart	1952	40.00
❑ 871	I Cried and Cried/Double Crossing Daddy	1952	40.00
❑ 884	Three Lies/Getting Ready for My Daddy	1953	40.00
❑ 897	Mercy, Mr. Percy/No Kinda Good No How	1953	40.00
❑ 1118	I Ain't Gonna Tell/(That's the Way) My Mind Is Working	1953	30.00
❑ 1137	Send Me Some Money/Love	1954	30.00
❑ 1153	Johnny Has Gone/So Many Ways	1955	30.00
❑ 1160	You're the Answer to My Prayer/Promise Mr. Thomas	1955	30.00
❑ 1166	I'll Never Forget You/I Can't Stop Now	1955	30.00

TRIUMPH

Number	Title (A Side/B Side)	Yr	NM
❑ 608	Good Gravy Baby/Scorched	1959	15.00

Albums

SAVOY JAZZ

Number	Title (A Side/B Side)	Yr	NM
❑ SJL-1203	Mercy, Mr. Percy, Vol. 1	1989	12.00

DILLARD AND CLARK

Albums

A&M

Number	Title (A Side/B Side)	Yr	NM
❑ SP-4158	The Fantastic Expedition of Dillard and Clark	1968	20.00
—Brown label			

DILLARDS, THE

45s

ANTHEM

Number	Title (A Side/B Side)	Yr	NM
❑ 101	It's About Time/One A.M.	1971	5.00
❑ 51014	Billy Jack/America	1971	5.00

CAPITOL

Number	Title (A Side/B Side)	Yr	NM
❑ 5494	Nobody Knows/Ebo Walker	1965	8.00
❑ 5524	Lemon Chimes/The Last Thing on My Mind	1965	8.00

ELEKTRA

Number	Title (A Side/B Side)	Yr	NM
❑ 45003	Dooley/Dong's Love	1964	10.00
❑ 45006	Hootin' Banjo/Polly Vaughn	1964	10.00
❑ 45641	Reason to Believe/Nobody Knows	1968	8.00
❑ 45661	Listen to the Sound/The Biggest Whatever	1969	8.00
❑ 45679	Rain Maker/West Montana Hanna	1970	8.00
❑ 45681	Close the Door Lightly/Touch Her If You Can	1970	8.00

K-ARK

Number	Title (A Side/B Side)	Yr	NM
❑ 619	My Only True Love/Doug's Breakdown	196?	20.00
—As "The Dillard Brothers"; recorded in 1958, but probably not issued until the Dillards were recording for Elektra			

UNITED ARTISTS

Number	Title (A Side/B Side)	Yr	NM
❑ XW382	Hot Rod Banjo/Love Has Gone Away	1974	5.00

WHITE WHALE

Number	Title (A Side/B Side)	Yr	NM
❑ 351	One Too Many Mornings/Turn It Around	1970	6.00
❑ 359	Comin' Home Again	1970	6.00

Albums

ANTHEM

Number	Title (A Side/B Side)	Yr	NM
❑ ANS-5901	Roots and Branches	1972	15.00

CRYSTAL CLEAR

Number	Title (A Side/B Side)	Yr	NM
❑ CCS-5007	Mountain Rock	1979	25.00
—Direct-to-disc recording			

ELEKTRA

Number	Title (A Side/B Side)	Yr	NM
❑ EKL-232 [M]	Back Porch Bluegrass	1963	25.00
❑ EKL-265 [M]	The Dillards, Live!!! Almost!!!	1964	20.00
❑ EKL-285 [M]	Pickin' and Fiddlin'	1965	20.00
❑ EKS-7232 [S]	Back Porch Bluegrass	1963	30.00
—Mandolin-player label			
❑ EKS-7265 [S]	The Dillards, Live!!! Almost!!!	1964	25.00
—Mandolin-player label			
❑ EKS-7285 [S]	Pickin' and Fiddlin'	1965	25.00
—Mandolin-player label			
❑ EKS-74035	Wheatstraw Suite	1968	20.00
—Tan label with large stylized "E" on top			
❑ EKS-74035	Wheatstraw Suite	1969	15.00
—Red label with large stylized "E" on top			
❑ EKS-74054	Copperfields	1969	20.00
—Red label with large stylized "E" on top			

FLYING FISH

Number	Title (A Side/B Side)	Yr	NM
❑ FF 040	The Dillards Vs. the Incredible L.A. Time Machine	1977	12.00
❑ FF 082	Decade Waltz	1979	12.00
❑ FF 215	Homecoming and Family Reunion	1979	12.00

POPPY

Number	Title (A Side/B Side)	Yr	NM
❑ PP-LA175-F	Tribute to the American Duck	1973	15.00

DIMPLES, THE

Probably more than one group.

45s

CAMEO

Number	Title (A Side/B Side)	Yr	NM
❑ 325	Dreaming of You/Please Don't Be Angry with Me	1964	15.00

DORE

Number	Title (A Side/B Side)	Yr	NM
❑ 517	An Invitation to a Party/My Sister's Beau	1959	20.00

ERA

Number	Title (A Side/B Side)	Yr	NM
❑ 1079	Gimme Jimmy/Toy Telephone	1958	20.00

DING DONGS, THE

See BOBBY DARIN.

DINNING, MARK

45s

CAMEO

Number	Title (A Side/B Side)	Yr	NM
❑ 299	January/Joey	1964	10.00
❑ 313	Should We Do It/Call Her Your Sweetheart	1964	10.00

HICKORY

Number	Title (A Side/B Side)	Yr	NM
❑ 1293	Dial AL1-4883/I'm Glad We Fell in Love	1965	8.00
❑ 1368	Last Rose/There Stands a Lady	1966	8.00
❑ 1404	Run, Opie, Run/He Reminds Me of Me	1966	8.00

MGM

Number	Title (A Side/B Side)	Yr	NM
❑ 12447	A Million Years Ago/Shameful Ways	1957	25.00
❑ 12553	School Fool/When You're Tired of Breaking Hearts	1957	25.00
❑ 12691	You Thrill Me/Do You Know	1958	25.00
❑ 12732	Blackeyed Gypsy/Secretly in Love with You	1958	25.00
❑ 12775	Cutie, Cutie/A Life of Love	1959	25.00
❑ 12845	Teen Angel/Bye Now Baby	1959	25.00
❑ 12888	A Star Is Born (A Love Has Died)/You Win Again	1960	20.00
❑ 12888 [PS]	A Star Is Born (A Love Has Died)/You Win Again	1960	25.00

Except when noted otherwise, VG = 25% of NM, and VG+ = 50% of NM. (Example: VG = $2.00, VG+ = $4.00 and NM = $8.00.)

Number	Title (A Side/B Side)	Yr	NM
❑ 12929	The Lovin' Touch/Come Back to Me (My Love)	1960	20.00
❑ 12929 [PS]	The Lovin' Touch/Come Back to Me (My Love)	1960	25.00
❑ 12958	She Cried On My Shoulder (When She Talked About You)/(Where Can You Hide Away) The World Is Getting Smaller	1960	20.00
❑ 12980	Top Forty, News, Weather and Sports/Suddenly (There's Only You)	1961	15.00
❑ 13007	Another Lonely Girl/Can't Forget	1961	15.00
❑ 13024	Lonely Island/Turn Me On	1961	15.00
❑ 13048	What Will My Mary Say/In a Matter of Moments	1961	15.00
❑ 13061	The Pickup/All of This for Sally	1962	15.00
❑ 13091	She's Changed/I Catch Myself Crying	1962	12.00
❑ 13150	The Twelfth of Never/Somebody Catch Me Kissin' Mary	1963	12.00

UNITED ARTISTS

Number	Title (A Side/B Side)	Yr	NM
❑ 50169	It's Such a Pretty World Today/Atlanta, Georgia Stray	1967	8.00
❑ 50225	Hangin' On/Maggie (I Wish We'd Never Met)	1967	8.00
❑ 50305	Throw a Little Love My Way/Dissatisfied Man	1968	8.00
❑ 50540	How Little Men Care/Lemon Yellow	1969	8.00

Albums

MGM

Number	Title (A Side/B Side)	Yr	NM
❑ E-3828 [M]	Teen Angel	1960	80.00
❑ SE-3828 [S]	Teen Angel	1960	150.00
❑ E-3855 [M]	Wanderin'	1960	80.00
❑ SE-3855 [S]	Wanderin'	1960	120.00

DINO, KENNY

45s

COLUMBIA

Number	Title (A Side/B Side)	Yr	NM
❑ 43062	Betty Jean/Show Me	1964	20.00

DOT

Number	Title (A Side/B Side)	Yr	NM
❑ 16207	Just Wait and See/A Little Bit	1961	12.00

MUSICOR

Number	Title (A Side/B Side)	Yr	NM
❑ 1013	You Ma Said You Cried in Your Sleep Last Night/Dream a Girl	1962	20.00
❑ 1015	Rosie, Why Do You Wear My Ring/What Did I Do	1962	15.00
❑ 1021	What Good Are Dreams/What Did I Do	1962	15.00
❑ 1027	Remembering Helps Me to Forget/Heartless Moon	1962	15.00

SMASH

Number	Title (A Side/B Side)	Yr	NM
❑ 1827	Time Will Tell/I Wanna Know	1963	12.00
❑ 1861	You Had Your Chance/Danhoff's Theme	1963	12.00

DINO, PAUL

45s

ENTRE

Number	Title (A Side/B Side)	Yr	NM
❑ 101	I Like Your Style/Your Candy Kisses	1963	15.00

PROMO

Number	Title (A Side/B Side)	Yr	NM
❑ 2180	Ginnie Bell/Bye-Bye	1961	10.00

UNITED ARTISTS

Number	Title (A Side/B Side)	Yr	NM
❑ 481	That's How I Miss You/Tonight's the Night	1962	80.00

DINO AND SEMBELLO

45s

DATE

Number	Title (A Side/B Side)	Yr	NM
❑ 2-1667	Imogene and Me/See the Light	1970	8.00

DINO AND THE DIPLOMATS

45s

LAURIE

Number	Title (A Side/B Side)	Yr	NM
❑ 3103	I Can't Believe/My Dream	1961	30.00

VIDA

Number	Title (A Side/B Side)	Yr	NM
❑ 100/101	Hushabye My Love/Homework	1961	30.00
❑ 102/103	Soft Wind/Such a Fool for You	1961	30.00

DINO, DESI AND BILLY

45s

COLUMBIA

Number	Title (A Side/B Side)	Yr	NM
❑ 4-44975	Hawley/Let's Talk It Over	1969	12.00

REPRISE

Number	Title (A Side/B Side)	Yr	NM
❑ 0324	We Know/Since You Broke My Heart	1964	15.00
❑ 0367	I'm a Fool/So Many Ways	1965	12.00
❑ 0367 [PS]	I'm a Fool/So Many Ways	1965	20.00
❑ 0401	Not the Lovin' Kind/Chimes of Freedom	1965	10.00
❑ 0401 [PS]	Not the Lovin' Kind/Chimes of Freedom	1965	20.00
❑ 0426	Please Don't Fight It/The Rebel Kind	1965	10.00
❑ 0426 [PS]	Please Don't Fight It/The Rebel Kind	1965	20.00
❑ 0444	Superman/I Can't Get Her Out of My Mind	1966	8.00
❑ 0462	It's Just the Way You Are/Tie Me Down	1966	8.00
❑ 0496	Look Out Girls/She's So Far Out She's In	1966	8.00
❑ 0529	I Hope She's There Tonight/Josephine	1966	8.00
❑ 0544	If You're Thinkin' What I'm Thinkin'/Pretty Flamingo	1966	8.00
❑ 0579	Two in the Afternoon/Good Luck, Best Wishes to You	1967	10.00
❑ 0619	Kitty Doyle/Without Hurtin' Some	1967	10.00
❑ 0653	My What a Shame/The Inside Outside Caspar Milquetoast Eskimo Flash	1967	12.00
❑ 0653 [PS]	My What a Shame/The Inside Outside Caspar Milquetoast Eskimo Flash	1967	20.00
❑ 0698	Tell Someone You Love Them/General Outline	1968	12.00
❑ 0716	I'm a Fool/Not the Lovin' Kind	1968	8.00
—"Back to Back Hits" series; originals have both "W7" and "r:" logos			
❑ 0965	Lady Love/A Certain Sound	1970	30.00
—A-side is a Brian Wilson composition			

UNI

Number	Title (A Side/B Side)	Yr	NM
❑ 55127	Someday/Thru Spray Colored Glasses	1969	12.00

Albums

REPRISE

Number	Title (A Side/B Side)	Yr	NM
❑ R 6176 [M]	I'm a Fool	1965	20.00
❑ RS 6176 [S]	I'm a Fool	1965	25.00
❑ R 6194 [M]	Our Time's Coming	1966	20.00
❑ RS 6194 [S]	Our Time's Coming	1966	25.00
❑ R 6198 [M]	Memories Are Made of This	1966	20.00
❑ RS 6198 [S]	Memories Are Made of This	1966	25.00
❑ R 6224 [M]	Souvenir	1966	20.00
❑ R/RS 6224	Souvenir Bonus Photo Sheet	1966	5.00
❑ RS 6224 [S]	Souvenir	1966	25.00

DINOSAUR JR

45s

HOMESTEAD

Number	Title (A Side/B Side)	Yr	NM
❑ 032	Repulsion/Bulbs of Passion	1985	10.00
❑ 032 [PS]	Repulsion/Bulbs of Passion	1985	10.00
—By "Dinosaur"			

SST

Number	Title (A Side/B Side)	Yr	NM
❑ 220	Freak Scene/Keep the Glove	1988	5.00
—Small hole, black vinyl			
❑ 220	Freak Scene/Keep the Glove	1988	10.00
—Large hole, clear vinyl			
❑ 220 [PS]	Freak Scene/Keep the Glove	1988	5.00
❑ 244	Just Like Heaven/Throw Down-Chunks	1989	3.00
❑ 244	Just Like Heaven/Throw Down-Chunks	1989	12.00
—Green vinyl			
❑ 244 [PS]	Just Like Heaven/Throw Down-Chunks	1989	3.00

SUB POP

Number	Title (A Side/B Side)	Yr	NM
❑ 68	The Wagon/Better Than Gone	1990	12.50
—9,800 on white vinyl			
❑ 68	The Wagon/Better Than Gone	1990	62.50
—200 on purple vinyl			
❑ 68 [PS]	The Wagon/Better Than Gone	1990	12.50

Albums

HOMESTEAD

Number	Title (A Side/B Side)	Yr	NM
❑ 015-2	Dinosaur	1985	50.00
—Released under the name "Dinosaur"			

RHINO VINYL

Number	Title (A Side/B Side)	Yr	NM
❑ 77630	Green Mind	2006	15.00
—Reissue on 180-gram vinyl			
❑ 77631	Where You Been	2006	15.00
—Reissue of Sire 45108 on 180-gram vinyl			

SIRE

Number	Title (A Side/B Side)	Yr	NM
❑ 26479	Green Mind	1991	40.00
❑ 45108	Where You Been	1993	15.00
❑ 45719	Without a Sound	1994	10.00

SST

Number	Title (A Side/B Side)	Yr	NM
❑ 130	You're Living All Over Me	1987	10.00
—As "Dinosaur Jr"; black vinyl			
❑ 130	You're Living All Over Me	1987	15.00
—As "Dinosaur Jr"; purple swirl vinyl			
❑ 130	You're Living All Over Me	1987	20.00
—First released under the name "Dinosaur"			
❑ 152 [EP]	Dinosaur Jr	1987	12.00
—Originals on purple swirl vinyl			
❑ 216	Bug	1988	10.00
❑ 244 [EP]	Just Like Heaven	1989	8.00
❑ 275 [EP]	Fossils	1991	8.00
❑ 910 [10]	Dinosaur Jr	1987	8.00
❑ 914 [10]	Just Like Heaven	1989	8.00
❑ 925 [10]	Fossils	1991	8.00

DIO

Also see RONNIE DIO; ELF; RAINBOW; BLACK SABBATH.

Albums

WARNER BROS.

Number	Title (A Side/B Side)	Yr	NM
❑ WB 23836	Holy Diver	1983	10.00
❑ WB 25100	The Last in Line	1984	10.00
❑ WB 25292	Sacred Heart	1985	8.00
❑ WB 25443	Intermission	1986	8.00
❑ WB 25612	Dream Evil	1987	8.00
❑ W 1262121	Lock Up The Wolves	1990	14.00

DIO, ANDY

45s

CRUSADE

Number	Title (A Side/B Side)	Yr	NM
❑ 1023	Bonnie Jean/Rough and Bold	1961	40.00

GONE

Number	Title (A Side/B Side)	Yr	NM
❑ 5038	Daisy Belle/Hey Little Bluebird	1958	50.00

JOHNSON

Number	Title (A Side/B Side)	Yr	NM
❑ 114	You Are My Sunshine/Satellite	1962	20.00

JOY

Number	Title (A Side/B Side)	Yr	NM
❑ 283	Daisy Belle/Some of These Days	1964	40.00

MUSICOR

Number	Title (A Side/B Side)	Yr	NM
❑ 1118	Sass-Afrass/Shout	1965	10.00
❑ 1162	Dancing Bull/Sorrento	1966	10.00

DIO, RONNIE

Also see THE ELECTRIC ELVES; ELF; THE ELVES.

45s

ATLANTIC

Number	Title (A Side/B Side)	Yr	NM
❑ 2145	The Ooh-Poo-Pah-Doo/Love Pains	1962	100.00

KAPP

Number	Title (A Side/B Side)	Yr	NM
❑ 697	Say You're Mine Again/Where You Gonna Run To, Girl	1965	50.00
❑ 725	Smiling by Day (Crying by Night)/Dear Darlin' (I Won't Be Comin' Home)	1965	50.00
❑ 770	The Way of Love/Walking Alone	1966	50.00

LAWN

Number	Title (A Side/B Side)	Yr	NM
❑ 218	Swingin' Street/Gonna Make It Alone	1963	150.00

PARKWAY

Number	Title (A Side/B Side)	Yr	NM
❑ 143	Walking in Different Circles/Ten Days with Brenda	1967	40.00

SENECA

Number	Title (A Side/B Side)	Yr	NM
❑ S 178-102	An Angel Is Missing/What'd I Say?	1959	200.00
—As "Ronnie Dio and the Red Caps"			

SWAN

Number	Title (A Side/B Side)	Yr	NM
❑ 4165	Mr. Misery/Our Year	1963	80.00

VALEX

Number	Title (A Side/B Side)	Yr	NM
❑ 001	Love Potion No. 9 (same on both sides)	1964	200.00

Albums

JOVE

Number	Title (A Side/B Side)	Yr	NM
❑ J-108	Dio at Domino's	1963	200.00

DION

Also see DION AND THE BELMONTS; DION AND THE TIMBERLANES.

45s

ARISTA

Number	Title (A Side/B Side)	Yr	NM
❑ 9797	And the Night Stood Still/Tower of Love	1989	4.00
❑ 9797 [PS]	And the Night Stood Still/Tower of Love	1989	4.00

BIG TREE/SPECTOR

Number	Title (A Side/B Side)	Yr	NM
❑ 16063	Born to Be with You/Running Close Behind You	1976	15.00
—Produced by Phil Spector			

COLUMBIA

Number	Title (A Side/B Side)	Yr	NM
❑ (no #) [PS]	"Dion Is Now on Columbia Records"	1962	50.00
—Promo-only sleeve issued with promos of Columbia 42662			
❑ 42662	Ruby Baby/He'll Only Hurt You	1962	20.00
❑ 42662 [PS]	Ruby Baby/He'll Only Hurt You	1962	40.00
❑ 42776	This Little Girl/The Loneliest Man in the World	1963	15.00
❑ 42810	Be Careful of Stones That You Throw/I Can't Believe (That You Don't Love Me Anymore)	1963	15.00
❑ 42810 [DJ]	Be Careful of Stones That You Throw (same on both sides)	1963	100.00
—Colored vinyl (some sources say blue, others red)			
❑ 42852	Donna the Prima Donna/You're Mine	1963	20.00

Number	Title (A Side/B Side)	Yr	NM
❑ 42852 [DJ]	Donna the Prima Donna (same on both sides)	1963	80.00
—Promo only on red vinyl			
❑ 42917	Drip Drop/No One's Waiting for Me	1963	15.00
❑ 42977	I'm the Hoochie Coochie Man/ The Road I'm On	1964	15.00
❑ 42977 [PS]	I'm the Hoochie Coochie Man/ The Road I'm On	1964	40.00
❑ 43096	Johnny B. Goode/Chicago Blues	1964	15.00
❑ 43213	Sweet Sweet Baby/ Unloved, Unwanted Me	1965	15.00
❑ 43293	Spoonful/Kickin' Child	1965	15.00
❑ 43423	Tomorrow Won't Bring the Rain/You Move Me Babe	1965	15.00
❑ 43423 [PS]	Tomorrow Won't Bring the Rain/You Move Me Babe	1965	150.00
❑ 43483	Time in My Heart for You/ Wake Up Baby	1965	15.00
❑ 43692	So Much Younger/ Two-Ton Feather	1966	15.00
❑ 44719	I Can't Help But Wonder Where I'm Bound/Southern Train	1968	10.00

DAYSPRING

Number	Title (A Side/B Side)	Yr	NM
❑ 622 [DJ]	The Best (mono/stereo)	197?	5.00

LAURIE

Number	Title (A Side/B Side)	Yr	NM
❑ 3070	Lonely Teenager/Little Miss Blue	1960	20.00
❑ 3070 [PS]	Lonely Teenager/Little Miss Blue	1960	50.00
❑ 3081	Havin' Fun/Northeast End of the Corner	1961	20.00
❑ 3081 [PS]	Havin' Fun/Northeast End of the Corner	1961	50.00
❑ 3090	Kissin Game/Heaven Help Me	1961	20.00
❑ 3090 [PS]	Kissin Game/Heaven Help Me	1961	50.00
❑ 3101	Somebody Nobody Wants/ Could Somebody Take My Place Tonight	1961	20.00
❑ 3110 [M]	Runaround Sue/Runaway Girl	1961	25.00
❑ 3110 [PS]	Runaround Sue/Runaway Girl	1961	40.00
❑ 3110 [S]	Runaround Sue/Runaway Girl	1961	50.00
—"Stereo" in white area at right of label			
❑ 3115 [M]	The Wanderer/The Majestic	1961	25.00
❑ 3115 [M]	The Wanderer/The Majestic	1979	10.00
—Reissue on regular Laurie label with "From the Orion Motion Picture 'The Wanderers'" on label			
❑ 3115 [PS]	The Wanderer/The Majestic	1961	40.00
❑ 3115 [S]	The Wanderer/The Majestic	1961	50.00
—"Stereo" in white area at right of label			
❑ 3123	Lovers Who Wander/ (I Was) Born to Cry	1962	20.00
❑ 3123 [PS]	Lovers Who Wander/ (I Was) Born to Cry	1962	40.00
❑ 3134	Little Diane/Lost for Sure	1962	20.00
❑ 3134 [PS]	Little Diane/Lost for Sure	1962	40.00
❑ 3145	Love Came to Me/Little Girl	1962	20.00
❑ 3153	Sandy/Faith	1963	20.00
❑ 3171	Come Go with Me/ King Without a Queen	1963	20.00
❑ 3187	Lonely World/Tag Along	1963	20.00
❑ 3225	After the Dance/ Then I'll Be Tired of You	1964	20.00
❑ 3240	Shout/Little Girl	1964	20.00
❑ 3303	I Got the Blues/ (I Was) Born to Cry	1965	20.00
❑ 3464	Abraham, Martin, and John/ Daddy Rollin' (In Your Arms)	1968	12.00
❑ 3478	Purple Haze/The Dolphins	1969	12.00
❑ 3495	From Both Sides Now/ Sun Fun Song	1969	12.00
❑ 3504	Loving You Is Sweeter Than Ever/He Looks a Lot Like Me	1969	12.00

LAURIE DOUBLE GOLD

Number	Title (A Side/B Side)	Yr	NM
❑ 100	Runaround Sue/I Wonder Why	197?	4.00
—B-side by Dion and the Belmonts			
❑ 101	The Wanderer/No One Knows	197?	4.00
—B-side by Dion and the Belmonts			
❑ 103	Lonely Teenager/Little Diane	197?	4.00
❑ 104	Lovers Who Wander/ Where or When	197?	4.00
—B-side by Dion and the Belmonts			
❑ 105	Love Came to Me/Sandy	197?	4.00
❑ 118	Abraham, Martin and John/ From Both Sides Now	197?	4.00

LIFESONG

Number	Title (A Side/B Side)	Yr	NM
❑ 1765	Heart of Saturday Night/You've Awakened Something in Me	1978	6.00
❑ 1770	Midtown American Main Street Gang/Guitar Queen	1978	6.00
❑ 1785	(I Used to Be a) Brooklyn Dodger/Streetheart Theme	1979	6.00
❑ 45082	Fire in the Night/Street Mama	1980	25.00

MONUMENT

Number	Title (A Side/B Side)	Yr	NM
❑ (# unknown) [DJ]	Runaround Sue/Ya Ya Twist	1962	25.00
—B-side by Joey Dee and the Starliters			

THE RIGHT STUFF

Number	Title (A Side/B Side)	Yr	NM
❑ S7-17651	Christmas (Baby Please Come Home)/Jingle Bell Rock	1993	5.00
—Red vinyl			
❑ S7-19769	Please Come Home for Christmas/Wintertime	1997	4.00
—B-side by the Belmonts on United Artists			

WARNER BROS.

Number	Title (A Side/B Side)	Yr	NM
❑ PRO-537 [DJ]	Seagull/Soft Parade	1972	15.00
❑ PRO-814 [DJ]	The Wanderer (same on both sides)	1979	15.00
❑ 7356	Natural Man/If We Only Have Love	1969	10.00
❑ 7401	Your Own Back Yard/ Sit Down Old Friend	1970	10.00
❑ 7469	Let It Be/Close to It All	1970	10.00
❑ 7491	Josie/Sunniland	1970	10.00
❑ 7537	Sanctuary/Brand New Morning	1971	10.00
❑ 7537 [PS]	Sanctuary/Brand New Morning	1971	20.00
❑ 7663	Seagull/Running Close Behind You	1972	10.00
❑ 7704	Doctor Rock and Roll/ Sunshine Lady	1973	10.00
❑ 7793	New York City Song/ Richer Than a Rich Man	1974	10.00
❑ 8234	Hey My Love/ Lover Boy Supreme	1976	6.00
❑ 8258	The Way You Do the Things You Do/Lover Boy Supreme	1976	6.00
❑ 8293	Oh the Night/Queen of '59	1976	6.00
❑ 8406	Young Virgin Eyes (I'm All Wrapped Up)/Oh the Night	1977	6.00

WARNER/SPECTOR

Number	Title (A Side/B Side)	Yr	NM
❑ 0403	Make the Woman Love Me/ Running Close Behind You	1975	15.00
—Produced by Phil Spector			

Albums

ARISTA

Number	Title (A Side/B Side)	Yr	NM
❑ AL 8549	Yo Frankie	1989	10.00

COLLECTABLES

Number	Title (A Side/B Side)	Yr	NM
❑ 5027	Runaround Sue	198?	10.00

COLUMBIA

Number	Title (A Side/B Side)	Yr	NM
❑ CL 2010 [M]	Ruby Baby	1963	30.00
❑ CL 2107 [M]	Donna the Prima Donna	1963	30.00
❑ CS 8810 [S]	Ruby Baby	1963	40.00
❑ CS 8907 [S]	Donna the Prima Donna	1963	40.00
❑ CS 9773	Wonder Where I'm Bound	1969	20.00
❑ KC 31942	Dion's Greatest Hits	1973	20.00
❑ PC 31942	Dion's Greatest Hits	198?	8.00
—Budget-line reissue			

DAYSPRING

Number	Title (A Side/B Side)	Yr	NM
❑ DST-4022	Inside Job	1980	12.00
❑ DST-4027	Only Jesus	198?	12.00
❑ WR-8111	I Put Away My Idols	198?	12.00
❑ WR-8112	Seasons (The Best of Dion)	198?	12.00
❑ 7-01-412901-5	Seasons	1984	12.00

LAURIE

Number	Title (A Side/B Side)	Yr	NM
❑ LLP 2004 [M]	Alone with Dion	1960	200.00
—With three wallet-size photos on inside strip (deduct 50% if missing)			
❑ LLP 2009 [M]	Runaround Sue	1961	100.00
—Black vinyl			
❑ LLP 2009 [M]	Runaround Sue	1961	800.00
—Colored vinyl (gold, green or blue)			
❑ LLP 2009 [M]	Runaround Sue	1962	80.00
—Black vinyl; with sticker on front cover: "Includes the Hit Singles 'The Majestic'/'The Wanderer'"			
❑ LLP 2012 [M]	Lovers Who Wander	1962	70.00
❑ LLP 2013 [M]	Dion Sings His Greatest Hits	1962	70.00
❑ SLP 2013 [R]	Dion Sings His Greatest Hits	196?	50.00
❑ LLP 2015 [M]	Love Came to Me	1963	70.00
❑ LLP 2017 [M]	Dion Sings to Sandy (And All His Other Girls)	1963	50.00
❑ LLP 2019 [M]	Dion Sings the 15 Million Sellers	1963	50.00
❑ SLP 2019 [R]	Dion Sings the 15 Million Sellers	196?	30.00
❑ LLP 2022 [M]	More of Dion's Greatest Hits	1964	50.00
❑ SLP 2022 [R]	More of Dion's Greatest Hits	196?	30.00
❑ SLP 2047	Dion	1968	20.00
❑ LES-4004	Abraham, Martin and John	197?	12.00
—Reissue of SLP-2047			
❑ LES-4013	Dion Sings the Hits of the 50's and 60's	1978	12.00
❑ DT-90366 [R]	Dion Sings His Greatest Hits	1965	120.00
—Capitol Record Club edition			
❑ T-90366 [M]	Dion Sings His Greatest Hits	1965	120.00
—Capitol Record Club edition			
❑ DT-91027 [R]	Runaround Sue	196?	120.00
—Capitol Record Club edition			
❑ T-91027 [M]	Runaround Sue	196?	120.00
—Capitol Record Club edition			
❑ DT-91128 [R]	More of Dion's Greatest Hits	196?	120.00
—Capitol Record Club edition			
❑ T-91128 [M]	More of Dion's Greatest Hits	196?	120.00
—Capitol Record Club edition			
❑ ST-91577	Dion	1968	25.00
—Capitol Record Club edition			

LIFESONG

Number	Title (A Side/B Side)	Yr	NM
❑ JZ 35356	Return of the Wanderer	1978	12.00

WARNER BROS.

Number	Title (A Side/B Side)	Yr	NM
❑ WS 1826	Sit Down, Old Friend	1969	20.00
❑ WS 1872	You're Not Alone	1971	15.00
❑ WS 1945	Sanctuary	1971	15.00
❑ BS 2642	Suite for Late Summer	1972	15.00
❑ BS 2954	Streetheart	1976	15.00

WORD

Number	Title (A Side/B Side)	Yr	NM
❑ WR-8285	Kingdom in the Streets	1985	12.00

DION AND THE BELMONTS

Also see THE BELMONTS; CARLO; DION.

45s

ABC

Number	Title (A Side/B Side)	Yr	NM
❑ 10868	My Girl the Month of May/ Berimbau	1966	12.00
❑ 10896	For Bobbie/Movin' Man	1967	12.00

LAURIE

Number	Title (A Side/B Side)	Yr	NM
❑ ST-607 [S]	In the Still of the Night/ All the Things You Are	196?	80.00
—Small hole, plays at 33 1/3 rpm			
❑ ST-608 [S]	Swinging on a Star/ In Other Words	196?	80.00
—Small hole, plays at 33 1/3 rpm			
❑ ST-610 [S]	I've Cried Before/ September Song	196?	80.00
—Small hole, plays at 33 1/3 rpm			
❑ 3013	I Wonder Why/Teen Angel	1958	20.00
—Black, red and white label			
❑ 3013	I Wonder Why/Teen Angel	1958	30.00
—Light blue label			
❑ 3013	I Wonder Why/Teen Angel	1958	60.00
—Gray label			
❑ 3015	No One Knows/I Can't Go On (Rosalie)	1958	20.00
—Black, red and white label			
❑ 3015	No One Knows/I Can't Go On (Rosalie)	1958	30.00
—Light blue label			
❑ 3015	No One Knows/I Can't Go On (Rosalie)	1958	50.00
—Gray label			
❑ 3021	Don't Pity Me/Just You	1958	25.00
❑ 3027 [M]	A Teenager in Love/ I've Cried Before	1959	25.00
❑ S-3027 [S]	A Teenager in Love/ I've Cried Before	1959	50.00
❑ 3035	Every Little Thing I Do/ A Lover's Prayer	1959	25.00
❑ 3035 [PS]	Every Little Thing I Do/ A Lover's Prayer	1959	50.00
❑ 3044	Where or When/That's My Desire	1959	25.00
❑ 3044 [PS]	Where or When/That's My Desire	1959	50.00
❑ 3052	When You Wish Upon a Star/ Wonderful Girl	1960	25.00
❑ 3052 [PS]	When You Wish Upon a Star/ Wonderful Girl	1960	50.00
❑ 3059	In the Still of the Night/A Funny Feeling	1960	25.00
❑ 3059 [PS]	In the Still of the Night/A Funny Feeling	1960	50.00

LAURIE DOUBLE GOLD

Number	Title (A Side/B Side)	Yr	NM
❑ 100	I Wonder Why/Runaround Sue	197?	4.00
—B-side by Dion			
❑ 101	No One Knows/The Wanderer	197?	4.00
—B-side by Dion			
❑ 102	A Teenager in Love/ A Lover's Prayer	197?	4.00
❑ 104	Where or When/ Lovers Who Wander	197?	4.00
—B-side by Dion			

MOHAWK

Number	Title (A Side/B Side)	Yr	NM
❑ 106	Teenage Clementine/ Santa Margarita	1957	60.00
—May be listed as "The Belmonts"			
❑ 107	Tag Along/We Went Away	1957	60.00

7-Inch Extended Plays

LAURIE

Number	Title (A Side/B Side)	Yr	NM
❑ EP-301	I Wonder Why/No One Knows// Don't Pity Me/A Teenager in Love	1959	120.00
❑ EP-301 [PS]	Dion and the Belmonts: Their Hits	1959	180.00
❑ 302	Where or When/You Better Not Do That//Wonderful Girl/ That's My Desire	1959	100.00
❑ 302 [PS]	Where or When	1959	150.00

Albums

ABC

Number	Title (A Side/B Side)	Yr	NM
❑ 599 [M]	Together Again	1967	30.00
❑ S-599 [S]	Together Again	1967	40.00

ARISTA

Number	Title (A Side/B Side)	Yr	NM
❑ A2L 8206 [(2)]	24 Original Classics	1984	12.00

Except when noted otherwise, VG = 25% of NM, and VG+ = 50% of NM. (Example: VG = \$2.00, VG+ = \$4.00 and NM = \$8.00.)

Number	Title (A Side/B Side)	Yr	NM
COLLECTABLES			
❑ 5025	Presenting Dion & The Belmonts	198?	10.00
❑ 5026	Wish Upon a Star	198?	10.00
❑ 5041	20 Golden Classics	198?	10.00
LAURIE			
❑ LLP 1002 [M]	Presenting Dion & The Belmonts	1959	250.00
❑ LLP 2002 [M]	Presenting Dion & The Belmonts	1960	150.00
❑ SLP 2002 [R]	Presenting Dion & The Belmonts	196?	900.00
—Despite its rechanneled stereo sound, this record is collectible because of its utter rarity			
❑ LLP 2006 [M]	Wish Upon a Star	1960	150.00
❑ LLP 2016 [M]	"Together" On Records — By Special Request	1963	50.00
❑ LES 4002	Everything You Always Wanted to Hear by Dion and the Belmonts	197?	15.00
❑ SLP 6000 [(3)]	60 Greatest Hits	197?	20.00
—In regular cover			
❑ SLP 6000 [(3)]	60 Greatest Hits	197?	30.00
—In box			
PAIR			
❑ PDL2-1142 [(2)]	The Best of Dion and the Belmonts	1986	12.00
PICKWICK			
❑ SPC-3521	Doo Wop	1975	10.00
—Reissue of ABC tracks			
RHINO			
❑ RNLP 70228	Reunion — Live at Madison Square Garden — 1972	1987	10.00
—Reissue of ABC tracks			
WARNER BROS.			
❑ BS 2664	Reunion — Live at Madison Square Garden — 1972	1973	15.00

DION AND THE TIMBERLANES
Early version of DION AND THE BELMONTS.

45s

Number	Title (A Side/B Side)	Yr	NM
JUBILEE			
❑ 5294	The Chosen Few/Out in Colorado	1957	30.00
MOHAWK			
❑ 105	The Chosen Few/Out in Colorado	1957	60.00

DIPPERS QUINTET, THE

45s

Number	Title (A Side/B Side)	Yr	NM
FLAYR			
❑ 500	It's Almost Christmas/Look What I've Found	1955	4000.
—VG 2000; VG+ 3000			

DIRE STRAITS
Also see MARK KNOPFLER.

12-Inch Singles

Number	Title (A Side/B Side)	Yr	NM
WARNER BROS.			
❑ PRO-A-783 [DJ]	Sultans of Swing (6:00)//Sultans of Swing (4:40)/Eastbound Train	1979	10.00
—These appear to be the original (non-LP) versions of "Sultans of Swing"			
❑ PRO-A-926 [DJ]	Skateaway (Edit 4:52)//Tunnel of Love (Part 1 4:59) (Part 2 3:15)	1980	20.00
❑ PRO-A-2286 [DJ]	Walk of Life (4:07)/So Far Away (3:59)	1985	20.00
❑ PRO-A-2328 [DJ]	Money for Nothing (Long Edit 4:38) (Edit 4:05) (LP Version 7:04)	1985	25.00
❑ PRO-A-2384 [DJ]	Walk of Life (4:07) (same on both sides)	1985	12.00
❑ PRO-A-2413 [DJ]	Ride Across the River (6:57) (same on both sides)	1985	20.00
❑ PRO-A-2464 [DJ]	So Far Away (Extended Version 5:06) (7" Single Version 3:59)	1985	20.00

45s

Number	Title (A Side/B Side)	Yr	NM
WARNER BROS.			
❑ GWB 0385	Sultans of Swing/Down to the Waterline	198?	4.00
—B-side makes its first U.S. 45 appearance here			
❑ 8736	Sultans of Swing/Southbound Again	1979	6.00
—"Burbank" palm trees label; labels we've seen don't have the "RE-1" though the disc plays the 5:49 LP version (master number is "WAA 8382 S"); erroneous "Produced by Dire Straits" credit on A-side			
❑ 8736 RE-1	Sultans of Swing/Southbound Again	1979	4.00
—With white label; contains 5:49 LP version (master number on A-side is "WAA 8382 S"); "Produced by Muff Winwood" on A-side label			
❑ 8736 RE-1	Sultans of Swing/Southbound Again	1979	5.00
—White label; contains 5:49 LP version (master number on A-side is "WAA 8382 S"); "Produced by Dire Straits" on A-side label in error			
❑ 8736 [DJ]	Sultans of Swing (Long Version 5:52)/(Edit 4:38)	1979	10.00
—Contains demo version (master number "WAA 8510 S") and edit of demo version (master number is "WAA 8510 V1S"); this was quickly changed to the LP version; we know of no stock copies with the "WAA 8510 S" master number			
❑ 8736 RE-1 [DJ]	Sultans of Swing (Long Version 5:49)/(Edit 4:44)	1979	8.00
—Contains LP version (master number "WAA 8382 S") and edit of LP version (master number "WAA 8382 V1S DJ")			
❑ 7-19094	Heavy Fuel/Kingdom Come	1992	4.00
❑ 7-19199	Calling Elvis/Millionaire Blues	1992	5.00
❑ 7-21995	Walk of Life/So Far Away	198?	3.00
—"Back to Back Hits" reissue			
❑ 7-21996	Money for Nothing/Twisting by the Pool	198?	3.00
—"Back to Back Hits" reissue			
❑ 7-28789	So Far Away/If I Had You	1986	3.00
❑ 7-28789 [PS]	So Far Away/If I Had You	1986	3.00
❑ 7-28878	Walk of Life/One World	1985	3.00
❑ 7-28878 [PS]	Walk of Life/One World	1985	3.00
❑ 7-28950	Money for Nothing/Love Over Gold (Live)	1985	4.00
❑ 7-28950 [DJ]	Money for Nothing (Edit 4:05)/(Long Edit 4:38)	1985	8.00
❑ 7-28950 [PS]	Money for Nothing/Love Over Gold (Live)	1985	5.00
❑ 7-29013	Walk of Life/One World	1985	10.00
❑ 7-29706	Twisting by the Pool/Badges, Posters, Stickers, T-Shirts	1983	8.00
❑ 7-29880	Industrial Disease/Badges, Posters, Stickers, T-Shirts	1982	8.00
❑ 49006	Lady Writer/Where Do You Think You're Going	1979	6.00
❑ 49006 [PS]	Lady Writer/Where Do You Think You're Going	1979	6.00
❑ 49082	Once Upon a Time in the West/News	1979	20.00
❑ 49082 [DJ]	Once Upon a Time in the West (Edit 3:00)/(Long Version 5:24)	1979	8.00
❑ 49632	Skateaway/Solid Rock	1980	5.00
❑ 49632 [PS]	Skateaway/Solid Rock	1980	5.00
❑ 49688	Romeo and Juliet/Solid Rock	1981	12.00
❑ 49688 [DJ]	Romeo and Juliet (Edit)/(Long Version)	1981	5.00

Albums

Number	Title (A Side/B Side)	Yr	NM
WARNER BROS.			
❑ WBMS-109 [DJ]	Dire Straits Live	1980	80.00
—"The Warner Bros. Music Show" promo			
❑ PRO-A-2149 [EP]	Selectins from Dire Straits Live — Alchemy	1984	15.00
—Three-song promo-only sampler			
❑ BSK 3266	Dire Straits	1979	10.00
❑ HS 3330	Communique	1979	10.00
❑ BSK 3480	Making Movies	1980	10.00
❑ 23728	Love Over Gold	1982	10.00
—On U.S. stock copies, the times of the songs as listed on the labels are rounded to the nearest 0 or 5			
❑ 23728 [DJ]	Love Over Gold	1982	50.00
—Promo on Quiex II vinyl; the times of the songs are listed differently than on stock copies, for they are not rounded to the nearest 0 or 5			
❑ 25085 [(2)]	Dire Straits Live — Alchemy	1984	12.00
❑ 25085 [(2)DJ]	Dire Straits Live — Alchemy	1984	60.00
—Promo on Quiex II vinyl			
❑ 25264	Brothers in Arms	1985	10.00
❑ 25264 [DJ]	Brothers in Arms	1985	50.00
—Promo on Quiex II vinyl			
❑ 25794	Money for Nothing	1989	15.00
❑ 26680	On Every Street	1991	25.00
❑ 29800 [EP]	Twisting by the Pool	1983	6.00
—Also known as "ExtendeDancEPlay"			
❑ 49377-1 [(2)]	Brothers in Arms	2006	30.00
—Remastered reissue; contains the full-length version of the album as it appears on the CD version, with longer versions of five songs			

DIRECT FLIGHT

Albums

Number	Title (A Side/B Side)	Yr	NM
DIRECT DISC			
❑ DD-104	Spectrum	1980	25.00
—Direct-to-disc recording			

DIRKSEN, SENATOR EVERETT MCKINLEY

45s

Number	Title (A Side/B Side)	Yr	NM
CAPITOL			
❑ 2034	The First Time the Christmas Story Was Told/I Heard the Bells on Christmas Day	1967	8.00
❑ 5805	Gallant Men/The New Colossus	1966	6.00
❑ 5805 [PS]	Gallant Men/The New Colossus	1966	8.00
❑ 5912	Man Is Not Alone/The Shepherd and His Flock	1967	5.00

Albums

Number	Title (A Side/B Side)	Yr	NM
CAPITOL			
❑ ST 2643 [S]	Gallant Men	1966	15.00
❑ T 2643 [M]	Gallant Men	1966	15.00
❑ ST 2754 [S]	Man Is Not Alone	1967	15.00
❑ T 2754 [M]	Man Is Not Alone	1967	20.00
❑ ST 2792 [S]	Everett McKinley Dirksen at Christmas Time	1967	20.00
❑ T 2792 [M]	Everett McKinley Dirksen at Christmas Time	1967	30.00

DIRT BAND, THE
See NITTY GRITTY DIRT BAND.

DIRTY BLUES BAND, THE

45s

Number	Title (A Side/B Side)	Yr	NM
BLUESWAY			
❑ 61016	Hound Dog/New Orleans Woman	1968	8.00

Albums

Number	Title (A Side/B Side)	Yr	NM
BLUESWAY			
❑ BLS-6010	The Dirty Blues Band	1968	20.00
❑ BLS-6020	Stone Dirt	1968	20.00

DISCO-TEX AND THE SEX-O-LETTES

45s

Number	Title (A Side/B Side)	Yr	NM
CHELSEA			
❑ 3004	Get Dancin' (Part I)/Get Dancin' (Part II)	1974	4.00
❑ 3015	I Wanna Dance Wit'choo (Part I)/I Wanna Dance Wit'choo (Part II)	1975	4.00
❑ 3026	Jam Band/Jam Band Reprise	1975	4.00
❑ 3040	Hot Lava/Hot Lava 2	1976	4.00
❑ 3045	Dancin' Kid (Part I)/Dancin' Kid (Part II)	1976	4.00
❑ 3054	Strollin'/We're Havin' a Party (It's Gonna Be Alright)	1976	4.00
❑ 3070	Wooly Bully/On Broadway	1977	4.00

Albums

Number	Title (A Side/B Side)	Yr	NM
CHELSEA			
❑ CHL 505	Disco-Tex and His Sex-O-Lettes	1975	10.00
❑ CHL 516	Manhattan Millionaire	1976	10.00
❑ CHL 555	A Piece of the Rock	1977	10.00

DISENTRI, TURNER
Actually Bob Gaudio of THE ROYAL TEENS and THE FOUR SEASONS.

45s

Number	Title (A Side/B Side)	Yr	NM
TOPIX			
❑ 6001	10,000,000 Tears/Spanish Lace	1961	100.00

DISTANTS, THE

45s

Number	Title (A Side/B Side)	Yr	NM
NORTHERN			
❑ 3732	Come On/Always	1960	600.00
WARWICK			
❑ 546	Come On/Always	1960	100.00
❑ 577	Always/Open Up Your Heart	1960	100.00

DIXIE CUPS, THE

45s

Number	Title (A Side/B Side)	Yr	NM
ABC			
❑ 10855	Love Ain't So Bad (After All)/Daddy Said No	1966	12.00
ABC-PARAMOUNT			
❑ 10692	That's Where It's At/Two-Way-Poc-A-Way	1965	12.00
❑ 10715	I'm Not the Kind of Girl (To Marry)/What Goes Up Must Go Down	1965	12.00
❑ 10755	A-B-C Song/That's What the Kids Said	1965	12.00
ANTILLES			
❑ 707	Iko Iko/Hey Hey (Indian's Coming)	1987	4.00
—B-side by The Wild Tchoupitoulas			
❑ 707 [PS]	Iko Iko/Hey Hey (Indian's Coming)	1987	4.00
LANA			
❑ 144	Chapel of Love/Ain't That Nice	196?	8.00
—Oldies reissue			
RED BIRD			
❑ 10-001	Chapel of Love/Ain't That Nice	1964	30.00
❑ 10-006	People Say/Girls Can Tell	1964	20.00
❑ 10-012	You Should Have Seen the Way He Looked at Me/No True Love	1964	20.00
❑ 10-017	Little Bell/Another Boy Like Me	1964	20.00
❑ 10-024	Iko Iko/Gee, Baby, Gee	1965	20.00
❑ 10-024	Iko Iko/I'm Gonna Get You Yet	1965	20.00
❑ 10-032	Gee, the Moon Is Shining Bright/I'm Gonna Get You Yet	1965	20.00

Albums

Number	Title (A Side/B Side)	Yr	NM
ABC-PARAMOUNT			
❑ 525 [M]	Riding High	1965	60.00
❑ S-525 [S]	Riding High	1965	80.00
RED BIRD			
❑ RB 20-100 [M]	Chapel of Love	1964	60.00
❑ RBS 20-100 [S]	Chapel of Love	1964	80.00
❑ RB 20-103 [M]	Iko Iko	1965	150.00

Number	Title (A Side/B Side)	Yr	NM
DIXIEBELLES, THE			
45s			
SOUND STAGE 7			
❑ 2507	(Down at) Papa Joe's/ Rock, Rock, Rock	1963	10.00
❑ 2517	Southtown U.S.A./Why Don't You Set Me Free	1964	10.00
❑ 2521	New York Town/ The Beale Street Dog	1964	10.00
Albums			
SOUND STAGE 7			
❑ SSM-5000 [M]	Down at Papa Joe's	1963	40.00
❑ SSS-15000 [R]	Down at Papa Joe's	1963	30.00
DIXIES, THE			
45s			
AUTUMN			
❑ 12	He's Got You/Geisha Girl	1965	15.00
DIXON, BILLY, AND THE TOPICS See THE FOUR SEASONS.			
DIXON, FLOYD			
45s			
ALADDIN			
❑ 3101	Do I Love You/Time and Place	1951	200.00
—Earlier Floyd Dixon 45s on Aladdin may exist			
❑ 3111	Too Much Jelly Roll/ Baby, Let's Go to the Woods	1952	200.00
❑ 3121	Blues for Cuba/ Bad Neighborhood	1952	200.00
❑ 3135	Wine, Wine, Wine/ Call Operator 210	1952	200.00
❑ 3144	Red Cherries/The River	1952	300.00
—Black vinyl			
❑ 3144	Red Cherries/The River	1952	700.00
—Red vinyl			
❑ 3151	Tired, Broke and Busted/ Come Back Baby	1952	150.00
❑ 3166	You Played Me for a Fool/ Broken Hearted Traveler	1953	150.00
❑ 3196	Lovin'/Married Woman	1953	150.00
❑ 3230	You Need Me Now/ A Long Time Ago	1954	100.00
CASH			
❑ 1057	Oh Baby/Never Can Tell	1957	50.00
CAT			
❑ 106	Moonshine/Roll Baby Roll	1954	60.00
❑ 114	Hey Bartender/It Is True	1955	60.00
CHATTAHOOCHIE			
❑ 652	Tell Me, Tell Me/There Goes My Heart	1964	10.00
CHECKER			
❑ 857	Alarm Clock Blues/ I'm Ashamed of Myself	1957	30.00
DODGE			
❑ 807	Opportunity Blues/Daisy	1961	15.00
EBB			
❑ 105	What Is Life Without a Home/ Oh-Ee Little Girl	1957	30.00
IMPERIAL			
❑ 5849	Tired, Broke and Busted/ Call Operator 210	1962	12.00
KENT			
❑ 311	Change Your Mind/ Dance the Thing	1958	20.00
SPECIALTY			
❑ 468	Hard Living Alone/ Please Don't Go	1953	80.00
—Black vinyl			
❑ 468	Hard Living Alone/ Please Don't Go	1953	200.00
—Red vinyl			
❑ 477	Hole in the Wall/Old Memories	1953	80.00
❑ 486	Ooh-Eee Ooh-Eee/Nose Job	1954	80.00
SWINGIN'			
❑ 626	Tight Skirts/Wake Up and Live	1960	20.00
DMZ Features Jeff "Mono Man" Conolly, later of THE LYRES.			
Albums			
BOMP			
❑ VXS 200004	Relics	1981	25.00
SIRE			
❑ SRK 6051	DMZ	1978	35.00
DOBKINS, CARL, JR.			
45s			
ATCO			
❑ 6283	If Teardrops Were Diamonds/ I'm So Sorry Little Girl	1964	12.00
CHALET			
❑ 1053	Days of Sand and Shovel/ Linda the Motel Maid	1969	10.00
❑ 1056	My Heart Is an Open Book/ Pictures	1969	10.00
COLPIX			
❑ 762	His Loss Is My Gain/A Little Bit Later On Down the Line	1965	12.00
DECCA			
❑ 30656	Love Is Everything/If You Don't Want My Lovin'	1958	20.00
❑ 30803	My Heart Is an Open Book/ My Pledge to You	1959	25.00
❑ 31020	Lucky Devil/In My Heart	1959	20.00
❑ 31020 [PS]	Lucky Devil/In My Heart	1959	30.00
❑ 31088	Exclusively Yours/One Little Girl	1960	15.00
❑ 31088 [PS]	Exclusively Yours/One Little Girl	1960	30.00
❑ 31143	Different Kind of Love/Genie	1960	15.00
❑ 31182	Lovelight/Take Time Out	1960	15.00
❑ 31260	Pretty Little Girl in the Yellow Dress/That's What I Call True Love	1961	15.00
❑ 31301	Sawdust Dolly/A Chance to Belong	1961	15.00
❑ 31353	Ask Me No Questions/ Promise Me	1962	15.00
FRATERNITY			
❑ 794	That's Why I'm Asking/ Take Hold of My Hand	1958	30.00
7-Inch Extended Plays			
DECCA			
❑ ED 2664	My Heart Is An Open Book/ My Pledge to You//Love Is Everything/If You Don't Want My Lovin'	1959	40.00
❑ ED 2664 [PS]	My Heart Is An Open Book	1959	40.00
DOBRO, JIMMY See JAMES BURTON.			
DOBRO, LON			
45s			
4 STAR			
❑ 1754	I Just Like You/All the Time	1961	60.00
TROY			
❑ 1003	Undercurrent/Mid-Night Surf	1963	50.00
DOC HOLLIDAY			
45s			
METROMEDIA			
❑ 68-0114	Whiskey Lady/Magga Blue	1973	8.00
Albums			
METROMEDIA			
❑ 1017	Doc Holliday	1973	20.00
DR. FEELGOOD AND THE INTERNS Also see PIANO RED.			
45s			
COLUMBIA			
❑ 43372	Doctor of Love/Let the House Rock On	1965	8.00
❑ 43615	Where Did You Go/ Don't Tell Me No Dirty	1966	8.00
OKEH			
❑ 7144	Mr. Moonlight/Dr. Feel-Good	1962	12.00
❑ 7153	Bald Headed Lena/ What's Up Doc	1962	12.00
❑ 7156	The Right String But the Wrong Yo-Yo/What's Up Doc	1962	12.00
❑ 7161	Let's Have a Good Time Tonight/The Same Old Things Keep Happening	1962	12.00
❑ 7167	My Gal Jo/Bald Headed Lena	1963	12.00
❑ 7185	The Doctor's Boogie/Blang Dong	1963	12.00
Albums			
OKEH			
❑ OKM 12101 [M]	Dr. Feelgood and the Interns	1962	100.00
❑ OKS 14101 [S]	Dr. Feelgood and the Interns	1962	200.00
DR. HOOK Includes records as "Dr. Hook and the Medicine Show." Also see RAY SAWYER.			
45s			
CAPITOL			
❑ 4081	Levitate/Cooky and Lila	1975	4.00
❑ 4104	The Millionaire/Cooky and Lila	1975	4.00
❑ 4171	Only Sixteen/Let Me Be Your Lover	1975	5.00
❑ 4280	A Little Bit More/A Couple More Years	1976	5.00
❑ 4364	If Not You/Bad Eye Bill	1976	4.00
❑ 4423	Walk Right In/Sexy Energy	1977	4.00
❑ 4534	Making Love and Music/Who Dat	1978	4.00
❑ 4615	I Don't Want to Be Alone Tonight/You Make My Pants Want to Get Up and Dance	1978	4.00
❑ 4621	Sharing the Night Together/ You Make My Pants Want to Get Up and Dance	1978	4.00
❑ 4677	All the Time in the World/ Dooley Jones	1979	4.00
❑ 4705	When You're in Love with a Beautiful Woman/ Knowing She's There	1979	4.00
❑ 4785	Better Love Next Time/ Mountain Mary	1979	4.00
❑ 4831	Sexy Eyes/Help Me Mama	1980	4.00
❑ 4885	Years from Now/I Don't Feel Much Like Smilin'	1980	4.00
❑ 4885 [PS]	Years from Now/I Don't Feel Much Like Smilin'	1980	5.00
❑ SPRO-8220/1 [DJ]	Interview Record for Use in Promoting the Album Release of "Bankrupt"	1975	8.00
❑ SPRO-8220/1 [PS]	The Stimu Dr. Hook	1975	12.00
CASABLANCA			
❑ 2314	Girls Can Get It/Doin' It	1980	4.00
❑ 2325	S.O.S. For Love/99 and Me	1981	4.00
❑ 2347	Baby Makes Her Blue Jeans Talk/The Turn On	1981	4.00
❑ 2347 [PS]	Baby Makes Her Blue Jeans Talk/The Turn On	1981	5.00
❑ 2351	Loveline/Pity the Fool	1981	4.00
COLUMBIA			
❑ 3-10032	Make It Easy/Ballad of Lucy Jordan	1974	6.00
—All as "Dr. Hook and the Medicine Show"			
❑ 4-45392	Last Morning/One More Ride (Lucille and Bunky)	1971	6.00
❑ 4-45562	Sylvia's Mother/Makin' It Natural	1972	5.00
—Gray label			
❑ 4-45562	Sylvia's Mother/Makin' It Natural	1972	6.00
—Orange label with "Columbia" background print			
❑ 4-45667	Carry Me, Carrie/ Call That True Love	1972	5.00
❑ 4-45667 [PS]	Carry Me, Carrie/ Call That True Love	1972	6.00
❑ 4-45732	The Cover of "Rolling Stone"/ Queen of the Silver Dollar	1972	5.00
—Orange label			
❑ 4-45732	The Cover of "Rolling Stone"/ Queen of the Silver Dollar	1972	6.00
—Gray label			
❑ 4-45878	Roland the Roadie and Gertrude the Groupie/ Put a Little Bit on Me	1973	5.00
❑ 4-45925	Life Ain't Easy/Wonderful Stone Soup	1973	5.00
❑ 4-46026	Monterey Jzack/ Cops and Robbers	1974	5.00
Albums			
CAPITOL			
❑ ST-11397	Bankrupt	1975	10.00
❑ ST-11522	A Little Bit More	1976	10.00
❑ ST-11632	Makin' Love and Music	1977	10.00
❑ SW-11859	Pleasure and Pain	1978	10.00
❑ ST-12018	Sometimes You Win...	1979	10.00
❑ SOO-12023	Sometimes You Win...	1979	10.00
—Other than the prefix and the number, we don't know if there are any differences between this and 12018, but both do exist			
❑ ST-12114	Live	1981	10.00
❑ SOO-12122	Dr. Hook/Greatest Hits	1980	10.00
❑ ST-12325	The Rest of Dr. Hook	1984	8.00
❑ SN-16179	Bankrupt	198?	8.00
—Budget-line reissue			
❑ SN-16180	A Little Bit More	198?	8.00
—Budget-line reissue			
❑ SN-16181	Pleasure and Pain	198?	8.00
—Budget-line reissue			
❑ SN-16228	Makin' Love and Music	198?	8.00
—Budget-line reissue			
❑ SN-16229	Sometimes You Win...	198?	8.00
—Budget-line reissue			
❑ SN-16325	Dr. Hook/Greatest Hits	198?	8.00
—Budget-line reissue			
CASABLANCA			
❑ NBLP-7251	Rising	1980	10.00
❑ NBLP-7264	Players in the Dark	1982	10.00
COLUMBIA			
❑ KC 30898	Dr. Hook & The Medicine Show	1972	15.00
❑ PC 30898	Dr. Hook & The Medicine Show	198?	8.00
—Budget-line reissue			
❑ KC 31622	Sloppy Seconds	1972	15.00
❑ PC 31622	Sloppy Seconds	198?	8.00
—Budget-line reissue			
❑ KC 32270	Belly Up!	1973	15.00
❑ C 34147	Dr. Hook and the Medicine Show Revisited	1976	10.00

Except when noted otherwise, VG = 25% of NM, and VG+ = 50% of NM. (Example: VG = $2.00, VG+ = $4.00 and NM = $8.00.)

Number	Title (A Side/B Side)	Yr	NM
❑ PC 34147	Dr. Hook and the Medicine Show Revisited	198?	8.00
—Budget-line reissue			
MERCURY			
❑ 800054-1	Players in the Dark	1983	8.00
—Reissue of Casablanca 7264			

DR. HOOK AND THE MEDICINE SHOW
See DR. HOOK.

DR. JOHN
Also see MIKE BLOOMFIELD/JOHN PAUL HAMMOND/DR. JOHN; HUEY "PIANO" SMITH.

45s

Number	Title (A Side/B Side)	Yr	NM
A.F.O.			
❑ 309	The Point/One Naughty Flat	1962	25.00
—As "Mac Rebenack"			
ACE			
❑ 611	Good Times/Sahara	1961	25.00
—As "Mac Rebennack"			
ATCO			
❑ 6607	I Walk on Gilded Splinters (Part 1)/I Walk on Gilded Splinters (Part 2)	1968	12.00
❑ 6635	Jump Sturdy/Mama Roox	1968	12.00
❑ 6697	Patriotic Flag Waver (Long)/Patriotic Flag Waver (Short)	1969	8.00
❑ 6755	Wash, Mama, Wash/Loup Gardo	1970	12.00
❑ 6882	Iko Iko/The Huey Smith Medley	1972	10.00
❑ 6898	Wang Dang Doodle/Big Chief	1972	6.00
❑ 6900	Let the Good Times Roll/Stack-A-Lee	1972	6.00
❑ 6914	Right Place Wrong Time/I Been Hoodood	1973	6.00
❑ 6937	Such a Night/Cold, Cold, Cold	1973	6.00
❑ 6957	(Everybody Wanna Get Rich) Rite Away/Mos'Scocious	1974	6.00
❑ 6971	Let's Make a Better World/Me Minus You Equals Loneliness	1974	6.00
HORIZON			
❑ 117	Wild Honey/Dance the Night Away with You	1979	4.00
❑ 125	Keep That Music Simple/I Thought I Heard New Orleans	1979	4.00
RCA			
❑ PB-11285	Take Me Higher/Sweet Rider	1978	4.00
REX			
❑ 1008	Storm Warning/Foolish Little Girl	1959	50.00
—As "Mac Rebennack"			
SCEPTER			
❑ 12393	One Night Late/She's Just a Square	1974	5.00
WARNER BROS.			
❑ 22976	Makin' Whoopee!/More Than You Know	1989	3.00
❑ 22976 [PS]	Makin' Whoopee!/More Than You Know	1989	3.00
❑ 49703	The Sailor and the Mermaid/One Good Turn	1981	4.00
—A-side with Libby Titus; B-side by Al Jarreau			

Albums

Number	Title (A Side/B Side)	Yr	NM
ACCORD			
❑ SN-7118	Love Potion	1982	10.00
ALLIGATOR			
❑ AL-3901	Dr. John's Gumbo	1986	10.00
—Reissue of Atco 7006			
❑ AL-3904	Gris-Gris	1987	10.00
—Reissue of Atco 33-234			
ATCO			
❑ SD 33-234	Gris-Gris	1968	15.00
—Yellow label			
❑ SD 33-234	Gris-Gris	1968	30.00
—Purple and brown label			
❑ SD 33-270	Babylon	1969	15.00
❑ SD 33-316	Remedies	1970	15.00
❑ SD 33-362	Dr. John, The Night Tripper (The Sun, Moon & Herbs)	1971	15.00
❑ SD 7006	Dr. John's Gumbo	1972	12.00
❑ SD 7018	In the Right Place	1973	12.00
❑ SD 7043	Desitively Bonaroo	1974	12.00
CLEAN CUTS			
❑ 705	Dr. John Plays Mac Rebennack	1982	10.00
❑ 707	The Brightest Smile in Town	1984	10.00
HORIZON			
❑ SP-732	City Lights	1978	10.00
❑ SP-740	Tango Palace	1979	10.00
KARATE			
❑ 5404	One Night Late	1978	10.00
TRIP			
❑ TLX-350 [(2)]	Superpak	1975	12.00
UNITED ARTISTS			
❑ UA-LA552-G	Hollywood Be Thy Name	1975	12.00
WARNER BROS.			
❑ 25889	In a Sentimental Mood	1989	12.00

DR. JOHN AND CHRIS BARBER
Also see each artist's individual listings.

Albums

Number	Title (A Side/B Side)	Yr	NM
GREAT SOUTHERN			
❑ GS-11024	On a Mardi Gras Day	1991	12.00

DOCTOR ROSS

45s

Number	Title (A Side/B Side)	Yr	NM
HI-Q			
❑ 5027	Cannonball/Numbers Blues	1963	20.00
❑ 5033	Call the Doctor/New York Breakdown	1963	20.00
SUN			
❑ 193	Chicago Breakdown/Come Back Baby	1954	600.00
❑ 212	The Boogie Disease/Juke Box Boogie	1954	2000.

Albums

Number	Title (A Side/B Side)	Yr	NM
FORTUNE			
❑ F-3011 [M]	Doctor Ross, The Harmonica Boss	1962	50.00
❑ FS-3011 [S]	Doctor Ross, The Harmonica Boss	1962	100.00
TESTAMENT			
❑ 2206 [M]	Doctor Ross	196?	20.00

DR. WEST'S MEDICINE SHOW AND JUG BAND
Also see NORMAN GREENBAUM.

45s

Number	Title (A Side/B Side)	Yr	NM
GO GO			
❑ 100	The Eggplant That Ate Chicago/You Can't Fight City Hall Blues	1966	12.00
❑ 102	Gondoliers, Shakespeares, Overseers, Playboys and Bums/Daddy, I Know	1967	10.00
❑ 102 [PS]	Gondoliers, Shakespeares, Overseers, Playboys and Bums/Daddy, I Know	1967	20.00
❑ 104	You Can Fly/The Circus Left Town Today	1967	10.00
GREGAR			
❑ 71-0100	Gondoliers, Shakespeares, Overseers, Playboys and Bums/Daddy, I Know	1969	10.00
❑ 106	Bullets Laverne/Jigsaw	1968	10.00

Albums

Number	Title (A Side/B Side)	Yr	NM
GO GO			
❑ 22-17-001 [M]	The Eggplant That Ate Chicago	1967	50.00
❑ 22-17-002 [S]	The Eggplant That Ate Chicago	1967	25.00
GREGAR			
❑ GG-101	Norman Greenbaum with Dr. West's Medicine Show and Jug Band	1970	20.00

DODD, DICK
Also see THE STANDELLS.

45s

Number	Title (A Side/B Side)	Yr	NM
ATTARACK			
❑ 102	Guilty/Requiem 820	1970	10.00
TOWER			
❑ 447	Lonely Weekends/Little Sister	1968	12.00
❑ 447 [PS]	Lonely Weekends/Little Sister	1968	30.00
❑ 490	Fanny/Don't Be Ashamed to Call My Name	1969	12.00

DODD, JIMMIE

45s

Number	Title (A Side/B Side)	Yr	NM
ABC-PARAMOUNT			
❑ 9665	Mouseketeer Theme/Hi to You	1956	20.00
❑ 9680	Mickey Mouse Mambo/Humphrey Hop-Pussy Cat	1956	20.00
❑ 9691	Zip-A-Dee-Doo-Dah/Song of the South	1956	20.00
—B-side by Jeanne Gayle			

7-Inch Extended Plays

Number	Title (A Side/B Side)	Yr	NM
OFFICIAL MICKEY MOUSE CLUB			
❑ DBR 69	Annette/Hey! Cubby Boy!//Banjo Joe/Karen	195?	25.00
❑ DBR 69 [PS]	Walt Disney's Annette	195?	25.00

Albums

Number	Title (A Side/B Side)	Yr	NM
DISNEYLAND			
❑ WDL-1014 [M]	Jimmie Dodd Sings His Favorite Hymns	1959	25.00
—Reissue of 3014 with new number			
❑ DQ-1235 [M]	Sing Along with Jimmie Dodd	1963	30.00
❑ DQ-1302 [M]	Favorite Hymns for Family Singing	1967	15.00
—Reissue of 1014			
❑ WDL-3014 [M]	Jimmie Dodd Sings His Favorite Hymns	1958	25.00
IMPERIAL			
❑ LP-9089 [M]	Lonely Guitar	1959	40.00
❑ LP-9121 [M]	Swing-A-Spell	1960	40.00
❑ LP-12058 [S]	Swing-A-Spell	1960	50.00

DODD, KEN

45s

Number	Title (A Side/B Side)	Yr	NM
LIBERTY			
❑ 55733	All of My Life/Happiness	1964	12.00
❑ 55835	Tears (For Souvenirs)/You and I	1965	10.00
❑ 55859	The River/My Thanks to You	1966	10.00
❑ 55893	Promises/Thank You for Being You	1966	10.00
LONDON			
❑ 1942	Love Is Like a Violin/Treasure in My Heart	1960	12.00

Albums

Number	Title (A Side/B Side)	Yr	NM
LIBERTY			
❑ LRP-3442 [M]	Tears and The River	1966	15.00
❑ LST-7442 [S]	Tears and The River	1966	20.00

DODDS, MALCOLM

45s

Number	Title (A Side/B Side)	Yr	NM
AMY			
❑ 861	A Rendezvous with a Broken Heart/All My Wildest Dreams	1962	8.00
AURORA			
❑ 3250	Ich Bin Verry Happy (Merry, Merry Christmas)/Perfect Strangers	1962	10.00
DECCA			
❑ 30653	The Swingin' Platoon/Your Voice	1958	12.00
❑ 30766	I'll Always Be with You/This Is Real (This Is Love)	1958	12.00
❑ 30857	Deep Inside/Tremble	1959	12.00
❑ 30922	I've Waited So Long/Somehow	1959	12.00
❑ 30970	I Feel Peculiar/Only for You	1959	12.00
END			
❑ 1000	It Took a Long Time/Beauty and the Beast	1957	60.00
❑ 1004	Fools Rush In/Can't See You	1957	80.00
❑ 1010	Tonight/Unspoken Love	1958	60.00
MGM			
❑ 12975	All for the Love of a Woman/Come, Oh Come	1961	10.00
❑ 13029	Without a Song/Laugh My Heart	1961	10.00
PROJECT 3			
❑ 1319	Hey World/I Don't Want to Cry	196?	6.00
❑ 1338	I Love, I Live, I Love/Mr. Broadloom	196?	6.00

Albums

Number	Title (A Side/B Side)	Yr	NM
RCA CAMDEN			
❑ CAL-873 [M]	Happiness Is a Thing Called Love	196?	15.00
❑ CAS-873 [S]	Happiness Is a Thing Called Love	196?	12.00

DODDS, NELLA

45s

Number	Title (A Side/B Side)	Yr	NM
WAND			
❑ 167	Come See About Me/You Don't Love Me Anymore	1964	15.00
❑ 171	Finders Keepers Losers Weepers/A Girl's Life	1964	12.00
❑ 178	Your Love Back/P's and Q's	1965	12.00
❑ 187	Come Back Baby/Dream Boy	1965	12.00
❑ 1111	Gee Whiz/Maybe Baby	1966	15.00
❑ 1136	Honey Boy/I Just Gotta Have You	1966	80.00

DODO, JOE, AND THE GROOVERS

45s

Number	Title (A Side/B Side)	Yr	NM
RCA VICTOR			
❑ 47-7207	Groovy/Goin' Steady	1958	25.00

DOGGETT, BILL
Also see EARL BOSTIC.

45s

Number	Title (A Side/B Side)	Yr	NM
ABC-PARAMOUNT			
❑ 10611	Mudcat/The Kicker	1965	6.00
CHUMLEY			
❑ 90001	Blue Point of View/Funky Feet	1974	4.00
COLUMBIA			
❑ 42384	Buster/Ladies Choice	1962	10.00
❑ 42531	Oops/Choo Choo	1962	10.00
❑ 42689	Soda Pop/Ham Fat	1963	10.00
❑ 42792	The Worm/Hot Fudge	1963	10.00
CORAL			
❑ 61739	A Pretty Girl Is Like a Melody/If I Should Lose You	1956	12.00
KING			
❑ S-7 1609 [S]	The Madison/After Hours	196?	25.00
—33 1/3 rpm jukebox single, small hole			
❑ S-7 1611 [S]	Mr. Ballard/The Eagle Speaks	196?	25.00
—33 1/3 rpm jukebox single, small hole			

D

Bill Doggett, *Dame Dreaming*, King 532, 1958, **$60.**

Number	Title (A Side/B Side)	Yr	NM
❑ 4548	Please Don't Ever Let Me Go/ Glo' Glug	1952	20.00
❑ 4702	It's a Dream/The Song Is Ended	1954	20.00
❑ 4711	There's No You/Easy	1954	20.00
❑ 4720	Sweet Lorraine/Tailor Made	1954	20.00
❑ 4732	Sweet Slumber/High Heels	1954	20.00
❑ 4738	The Nearness of You/Honey	1954	20.00
❑ 4742	The Christmas Song/ Winter Wonderland	1954	20.00
❑ 4759	Tara's Theme/Gumbo	1955	15.00
❑ 4769	My Reverie/King Bee	1955	15.00
❑ 4784	Wild Oats/I'll Be Around	1955	15.00
❑ 4795	Oof/Street Scene	1955	15.00
❑ 4808	Quaker City/True Blue	1955	15.00
❑ 4825	You Don't Know What Love Is/ Shove Off	1955	15.00
❑ 4838	Honey Boy/Misty Moon	1955	15.00
❑ 4888	In a Sentimental Mood/ Who's Who	1956	15.00
❑ 4917	Squashy/We Found Love	1956	15.00
❑ 4936	What a Difference a Day Makes/Stella by Starlight	1956	15.00
❑ 4950	Honky Tonk (Part 1)/ Honky Tonk (Part 2)	1956	20.00
❑ 5000	Slow Walk/Hand in Hand	1956	15.00
❑ 5001	Honky Tonk (Vocal)/ Peacock Alley	1956	15.00
—Vocal by Tommy Brown			
❑ 5020	Ram-Bunk-Shush/Blue Largo	1957	12.00
❑ 5044	Chloe/Number Three	1957	12.00
❑ 5058	Ding Dong/Cling to Me	1957	12.00
❑ 5070	Hammer Head/Shindig	1957	12.00
❑ 5080	Hot Ginger/Soft	1957	12.00
❑ 5096	Hippy Dippy/Flying Home	1957	12.00
❑ 5101	Leaps and Bounds (Part 1)/ Leaps and Bounds (Part 2)	1958	12.00
❑ 5125	Boo Da Ba/Pimento	1958	12.00
❑ 5130	How Could You/Blues for Handy	1958	12.00
❑ 5138	Tanya/Blip Bop	1958	12.00
❑ 5149	Birdie/Hold It	1958	12.00
❑ 5159	Rainbow Riot (Part 1)/ Rainbow Riot (Part 2)	1958	12.00
❑ 5176	Monster Party/Scott's Bluff	1959	12.00

Number	Title (A Side/B Side)	Yr	NM
❑ 5204	The Madison/Ocean Liner	1959	12.00
❑ 5227	After Hours/Big City Drag	1959	12.00
❑ 5256	Yucky Dock (Part 1)/Yucky Dock (Part 2)	1959	12.00
❑ 5281	The Goofy Organ/Zee	1959	12.00
❑ 5310	Smokie Part 2/Evening Dreams	1960	10.00
❑ 5319	Back Woods/Raw Turkey	1960	10.00
❑ 5339	Big Boy/Smoochie	1960	10.00
❑ 5364	Buttered Popcorn/The Slush	1960	10.00
❑ 5387	A Lover's Dream/Trav'lin' Light	1960	10.00
❑ 5419	Slidin'/Afternoon Jump	1960	10.00
❑ 5444	Honky Tonk (Part 2)/ Floyd's Guitar Blues	1961	10.00
❑ 5482	Bugle Nose/The Doodle	1961	10.00
❑ 5561	High and Wide/In the Wee Hours	1961	10.00
❑ 5599	The Doodle Twist/Gene's Dream	1962	8.00
❑ 5642	George Washington Twist/ Eleven O'Clock Twist	1962	8.00
❑ 5665	Teardrops/Moon Dust	1962	8.00
❑ 5684	Hometown Shout/ For All We Know	1962	8.00
❑ 5718	Honky Tonk Bossa Nova (Part 2)/ Ocean Liner Bossa Nova	1963	8.00
❑ 5740	Down Home Bossa Nova/ Si Si Nova	1963	8.00
❑ 5788	The Fog/Groovy Movie	1963	8.00
❑ 5873	The Rail/Hey Big Boy, Hey Hey	1964	8.00
❑ 5878	Night Train (Part 1)/ Night Train (Part 2)	1964	8.00
❑ 5948	Crackers/That's Enough, Lock 'Em Up	1964	8.00
❑ 5957	Snuff Box/Blood Pressure	1964	8.00
❑ 6019	Teardrops/Slidin'	1966	6.00
❑ 6217	Take Your Shot/Mad	1969	5.00
❑ 6225	Twenty-Five Miles/For Once in My Life	1969	5.00
❑ 6239	Honky Tonk Popcorn/ Honky Tonk	1969	5.00
❑ 6312	The Nearness of You/Moon Dust	1970	4.00
❑ 6350	High Heels/Soft	1971	4.00
❑ 6356	In a Sentimental Mood/Eventide	1971	4.00
ROULETTE			
❑ 4732	Sapphire/Ko-Ko	1967	6.00

Number	Title (A Side/B Side)	Yr	NM
❑ 4749	Lovin' Mood/The Funky Wrestler	1967	6.00
SUE			
❑ 10-002	Fat Back/Si Si Cisco	1968	5.00
WARNER BROS.			
❑ 5181	Jack Rabbit/Let's Do the Hully Gully Twist	1960	12.00
❑ 5209	Let's Do the Continental/ Pony Walk	1961	12.00
❑ 5223	You Can't Sit Down (Part 1)/ You Can't Sit Down (Part 2)	1961	12.00
7-Inch Extended Plays			
KING			
❑ EP-259	*Early Bird/Percy Speaks/ Ready Mix/Moon Dust	1954	25.00
❑ EP-259 [PS]	Bill Doggett	1954	25.00
❑ EP-325	*The Song Is Ended/Eventide/ And the Angels Sing/ Tailor Made	1955	25.00
❑ EP-325 [PS]	Bill Doggett, Vol. 2	1955	25.00
❑ EP-334	*Honey/It's a Dream/High Heels/Real Gone Mambo	1955	25.00
❑ EP-334 [PS]	Bill Doggett, His Organ and Combo, Vol. 4	1955	25.00
❑ EP-346	White Christmas/Silent Ninght/ /Jingle Bells/I Saw Mommy Kissing Santa Claus	195?	25.00
—The label of the copy we examined has the listed typo on the song "Silent Night"			
❑ EP-346 [PS]	All-Time Christmas Favorites	195?	25.00
—The label of the copy we examined has the listed typo on the song "Silent Night"			
❑ EP-352	*Sweet Slumber/The Nearness of You/Gumbo/Tara's Theme	1955	25.00
❑ EP-352 [PS]	Bill Doggett, His Organ and Combo, Vol. 5	1955	25.00
❑ EP-382	*I'll Be Around/Street Scene/ You Don't Know What Love Is/Misty Moon	1956	25.00
❑ EP-382 [PS]	Doggett Dreams	1956	25.00
❑ EP-388	*Quaker City/Oof!/Wild Oats/ Shove Off	1956	25.00
❑ EP-388 [PS]	Doggett Jumps	1956	25.00
❑ EP-390	Honky Tonk (Part 1)/Honky Tonk (Part 2)//Squashy/ Who's Who	1956	30.00
❑ EP-390 [PS]	Honky Tonk	1956	30.00
❑ EP-391	*Leaps and Bounds/On the Sunny Side of the Street/ True Blue	1956	20.00
❑ EP-391 [PS]	Bill Doggett, Vol. 1	1956	20.00
❑ EP-392	*Honky Tonk Number Three/ When Your Lover Has Gone/ Big Boy/Nothin' Yet	1956	20.00
❑ EP-392 [PS]	Bill Doggett, Vol. 2	1956	20.00
❑ EP-393	*Slow Walk/Afternoon Jump/ Peacock Alley/Honey Boy	1956	20.00
❑ EP-393 [PS]	Bill Doggett, Vol. 3	1956	20.00
❑ EP-394	*I Hadn't Anyone Till You/ Yesterdays/A Cottage for Sale/As You Desire Me	1957	20.00
❑ EP-394 [PS]	As You Desire Me, Vol. 1	1957	20.00
❑ EP-395	*Alone/As Time Goes By/ Dedicated to You/ Sweet and Lovely	1957	20.00
❑ EP-395 [PS]	As You Desire Me, Vol. 2	1957	20.00
❑ EP-396	*Dream/Don't Blame Me/This Love of Mine/Fools Rush In	1957	20.00
❑ EP-396 [PS]	As You Desire Me, Vol. 3	1957	20.00
❑ EP-399	*Caravan/Solitude/I'm Just a Lucky So and So/Prelude to a Kiss	1958	15.00
❑ EP-399 [PS]	A Salute to Ellington, Vol. 1	1958	15.00
❑ EP-400	*I Let a Song Go Out of My Heart/Don't Get Around Much Anymore/I Got It Bad and That Ain't Good	1958	15.00
❑ EP-400 [PS]	A Salute to Ellington, Vol. 2	1958	15.00
❑ EP-401	*C Jam Blues/Sophisticated Lady/Perdido/Satin Doll	1958	15.00
❑ EP-401 [PS]	A Salute to Ellington, Vol. 3	1958	15.00
❑ EP-402	*Sweet Lorraine/Diane/Dinah/ Cherry	1958	15.00
❑ EP-402 [PS]	Dame Dreaming, Vol. 1	1958	15.00
❑ EP-403	*Ramona/Cynthia/Tangerine/ Nancy	1958	15.00
❑ EP-403 [PS]	Dame Dreaming, Vol. 2	1958	15.00
❑ EP-404	*Marcheta/Laura/Jeannine/ Estrellita	1958	15.00
❑ EP-404 [PS]	Dame Dreaming, Vol. 3	1958	15.00
❑ EP-407	*Ram-Bunk-Shus/Cling to Me/ Ding Dong/Chloe	1958	15.00
❑ EP-407 [PS]	Hot Doggett	1958	15.00
❑ EP-408	*Soft/Hammer Head/Shindig/ Hot Ginger	1958	15.00
❑ EP-408 [PS]	Soft	1958	15.00

Except when noted otherwise, VG = 25% of NM, and VG+ = 50% of NM. (Example: VG = $2.00, VG+ = $4.00 and NM = $8.00.)

Number	Title (A Side/B Side)	Yr	NM
❑ KSS-7-723	Smokie/The Slush/Night Train - Part 1//Night Train - Part 2/ Buttered Popcorn/Bugle Nose	196?	30.00

—Stereo jukebox issue; small hole, plays at 33 1/3 rpm

Number	Title (A Side/B Side)	Yr	NM
❑ KSS-7-723 [PS]	Back Again with More	196?	30.00

Albums

ABC-PARAMOUNT

Number	Title (A Side/B Side)	Yr	NM
❑ 507 [M]	Wow!	1965	20.00
❑ S-507 [S]	Wow!	1965	25.00

AFTER HOURS

Number	Title (A Side/B Side)	Yr	NM
❑ AFT-4112	The Right Choice	1991	15.00

COLUMBIA

Number	Title (A Side/B Side)	Yr	NM
❑ CL 1814 [M]	Oops!	1962	20.00
❑ CL 1942 [M]	Prelude to the Blues	1963	20.00
❑ CL 2082 [M]	Fingertips	1963	20.00
❑ CS 8614 [S]	Oops!	1962	25.00
❑ CS 8742 [S]	Prelude to the Blues	1963	25.00
❑ CS 8882 [S]	Fingertips	1963	25.00

KING

Number	Title (A Side/B Side)	Yr	NM
❑ 295-82 [10]	Bill Doggett — His Organ and Combo	1955	150.00
❑ 295-83 [10]	Bill Doggett — His Organ and Combo, Vol. 2	1955	150.00
❑ 295-89 [10]	All-Time Christmas Favorites	1955	200.00
❑ 295-102 [10]	Sentimentally Yours	1956	150.00
❑ 395-502 [M]	Moondust	1957	60.00
❑ 395-514 [M]	Hot Doggett	1957	60.00
❑ 395-523 [M]	As You Desire	1957	60.00
❑ KLP-523 [M]	As You Desire	1987	10.00

—Reissue with "Highland Records" on label

Number	Title (A Side/B Side)	Yr	NM
❑ 395-531 [M]	Everybody Dance to the Honky Tonk	1958	60.00
❑ 395-532 [M]	Dame Dreaming	1958	60.00
❑ KLP-532 [M]	Dame Dreaming	1987	10.00

—Reissue with "Highland Records" on label

Number	Title (A Side/B Side)	Yr	NM
❑ 395-533 [M]	A Salute to Ellington	1958	60.00
❑ 395-557 [M]	The Doggett Beat for Dancing Feet	1958	60.00
❑ KLP-557 [M]	The Doggett Beat for Dancing Feet	1987	10.00

—Reissue with "Highland Records" on label

Number	Title (A Side/B Side)	Yr	NM
❑ 395-563 [M]	Candle Glow	1958	60.00
❑ 395-582 [M]	Swingin' Easy	1959	60.00
❑ 395-585 [M]	Dance Awhile	1959	60.00
❑ KLP-585 [M]	Dance Awhile	1987	10.00

—Reissue with "Highland Records" on label

Number	Title (A Side/B Side)	Yr	NM
❑ 395-600 [M]	A Bill Doggett Christmas	1959	40.00
❑ 395-609 [M]	Hold It	1959	60.00
❑ 633 [M]	High and Wide	1959	50.00
❑ 641 [M]	Big City Dance Party	1959	50.00
❑ 667 [M]	Bill Doggett On Tour	1959	50.00
❑ 706 [M]	For Reminiscent Lovers, Romantic Songs	1960	50.00
❑ 723 [M]	Back Again with More	1960	50.00
❑ 759 [M]	Bonanza of 24 Songs	1960	50.00
❑ 778 [M]	The Many Moods of Bill Doggett	1960	50.00
❑ KLP-778 [M]	The Many Moods of Bill Doggett	1987	10.00

—Reissue with "Highland Records" on label

Number	Title (A Side/B Side)	Yr	NM
❑ 830 [M]	American Songs in the Bossa Nova Style	1963	40.00
❑ 868 [M]	Impressions	1964	40.00
❑ 908 [M]	The Best of Bill Doggett	1964	40.00
❑ 959 [M]	Bonanza of 24 Hit Songs	1966	30.00
❑ KS-1078	Honky Tonk Popcorn	1969	50.00
❑ KS-1097	The Nearness of You	1970	25.00
❑ KS-1101	Ram-Bunk-Shush	1970	25.00
❑ KS-1104	Sentimental Journey	1970	25.00
❑ KS-1108	Soft	1970	25.00
❑ K-5009	14 Original Greatest Hits	1977	10.00

POWER PAK

Number	Title (A Side/B Side)	Yr	NM
❑ 269	Hold It!	197?	10.00

ROULETTE

Number	Title (A Side/B Side)	Yr	NM
❑ R 25330 [M]	Honky Tonk A La Mod	1966	20.00
❑ SR 25330 [S]	Honky Tonk A La Mod	1966	25.00

STARDAY

Number	Title (A Side/B Side)	Yr	NM
❑ 3023	16 Bandstand Favorites	197?	10.00

WARNER BROS.

Number	Title (A Side/B Side)	Yr	NM
❑ W 1404 [M]	3,046 People Danced 'Til 4 AM	1960	20.00
❑ WS 1404 [S]	3,046 People Danced 'Til 4 AM	1960	25.00
❑ W 1421 [M]	The Band with the Beat	1961	20.00
❑ WS 1421 [S]	The Band with the Beat	1961	25.00
❑ W 1452 [M]	Bill Doggett Swings	1962	20.00
❑ WS 1452 [S]	Bill Doggett Swings	1962	25.00

WHO'S WHO IN JAZZ

Number	Title (A Side/B Side)	Yr	NM
❑ 21002	Lionel Hampton Presents Bill Doggett	1977	12.00

DOHENY, NED

45s

ASYLUM

Number	Title (A Side/B Side)	Yr	NM
❑ 11024	On & On/I Know Sorrow	1973	6.00

COLUMBIA

Number	Title (A Side/B Side)	Yr	NM
❑ 3-10438	A Love of Your Own/Valentine	1976	6.00
❑ 3-10476	If You Should Fall/I've Got Your Number	1977	6.00

Albums

ASYLUM

Number	Title (A Side/B Side)	Yr	NM
❑ SD 5059	Ned Doheny	1973	20.00

COLUMBIA

Number	Title (A Side/B Side)	Yr	NM
❑ PC 34259	Hard Candy	1976	15.00

DOHERLY, SID

45s

CAMEO

Number	Title (A Side/B Side)	Yr	NM
❑ 497	Lonely Sounds/When the Lights Go Out Tonight	1967	20.00

DOHERTY, DENNY

Also see THE MAMAS AND THE PAPAS; THE MUGWUMPS.

45s

ABC

Number	Title (A Side/B Side)	Yr	NM
❑ 11318	To Claudia on Thursday/ Tuesday Morning	1972	6.00

COLUMBIA

Number	Title (A Side/B Side)	Yr	NM
❑ 45779	Indian Girl/Baby Catch the Moon	1973	5.00
❑ 45779 [PS]	Indian Girl/Baby Catch the Moon	1973	15.00
❑ 45866	My Song/Indian Girl	1973	5.00

PARAMOUNT

Number	Title (A Side/B Side)	Yr	NM
❑ 0286	Good Night and Good Morning/ You'll Never Know	1974	5.00

PLAYBOY

Number	Title (A Side/B Side)	Yr	NM
❑ 6066	Simone (mono/stereo)	1976	5.00

—May be promo only

Albums

ABC DUNHILL

Number	Title (A Side/B Side)	Yr	NM
❑ DS-50096	Watcha' Gonna Do?	1970	15.00

EMBER

Number	Title (A Side/B Side)	Yr	NM
❑ EMS-1036	Waiting for a Song	1975	12.00

DOJO

Albums

ECLIPSE

Number	Title (A Side/B Side)	Yr	NM
❑ ES-7309	Down for the Last Time	1971	25.00

DOLBY, THOMAS

12-Inch Singles

CAPITOL

Number	Title (A Side/B Side)	Yr	NM
❑ 8561	Get Out of My Mix (2 mixes)	1983	6.00
❑ 8576	Hyperactive/Get Out of My Mix	1984	8.00
❑ 8594	Dissidents: The Search for the Truth Pts. 1 and 2	1984	8.00
❑ SPRO 9067/8 [DJ]	Hyperactive! (5:00)/ Hyperactive (4:12)	1984	10.00
❑ SPRO 9975 [DJ]	Get Out of My Mix (2 mixes)	1983	8.00
❑ SPRO 9980 [DJ]	Airwaves (same on both sides)	1983	6.00

EMI MANHATTAN

Number	Title (A Side/B Side)	Yr	NM
❑ 56086	Airhead (3 mixes)/ Budapest by Blimp	1988	6.00
❑ 56104	Airheads' Revenge/Revenge Rap/Airhead (2 new mixes)	1988	6.00
❑ 56114	Hot Sauce (3 mixes)/Salsa Picante/Get Out of My Mix	1988	6.00

MCA

Number	Title (A Side/B Side)	Yr	NM
❑ 17165 [DJ]	Hunger City (same on both sides)	1986	5.00

—As "Dolby's Cube"

Number	Title (A Side/B Side)	Yr	NM
❑ 23645	Howard the Duck (2 versions)/ Don't Turn Away	1986	8.00

—As "Dolby's Cube"

45s

CAPITOL

Number	Title (A Side/B Side)	Yr	NM
❑ 5204	She Blinded Me with Science/ Flying North	1983	4.00

—Not issued with picture sleeve in U.S.

Number	Title (A Side/B Side)	Yr	NM
❑ 5238	Europa and the Pirate Twins/ Radio Silence	1983	3.00
❑ 5238 [PS]	Europa and the Pirate Twins/ Radio Silence	1983	3.00
❑ 5321	Hyperactive/Get Out of My Mix	1984	3.00
❑ 5321 [PS]	Hyperactive/Get Out of My Mix	1984	3.00
❑ 5355	Dissidents/I Scare Myself	1984	3.00
❑ 5374	Dissidents/Dissidents (Dub)	1984	3.00
❑ 5374 [PS]	Dissidents/Dissidents (Dub)	1984	3.00
❑ S7-18904	She Blinded Me with Science/ The Politics of Dancing	1996	3.00

—A-side is different mix than original 45; B-side by Re-Flex

EMI MANHATTAN

Number	Title (A Side/B Side)	Yr	NM
❑ 50125	Airhead/Budapest by Blimp	1988	3.00
❑ 50125 [PS]	Airhead/Budapest by Blimp	1988	3.00
❑ 50148	Hot Sauce/Salsa Picante	1988	3.00
❑ 50148 [PS]	Hot Sauce/Salsa Picante	1988	3.00

HARVEST

Number	Title (A Side/B Side)	Yr	NM
❑ 5155	Europa and the Pirate Twins/ Radio Silence	1982	10.00
❑ 5204	She Blinded Me with Science/ Flying North	1983	10.00

MCA

Number	Title (A Side/B Side)	Yr	NM
❑ 52868	Howard the Duck/ Don't Turn Away	1986	3.00

—Credited to "Dolby's Cube"

Number	Title (A Side/B Side)	Yr	NM
❑ 52868 [PS]	Howard the Duck/ Don't Turn Away	1986	3.00

—Credited to "Dolby's Cube"

Albums

CAPITOL

Number	Title (A Side/B Side)	Yr	NM
❑ ST 12271	The Golden Age of Wireless	1983	10.00
❑ ST-12309	The Flat Earth	1984	10.00

EMI MANHATTAN

Number	Title (A Side/B Side)	Yr	NM
❑ E1-48075	Aliens Ate My Buick	1988	10.00

HARVEST

Number	Title (A Side/B Side)	Yr	NM
❑ ST 12271	The Golden Age of Wireless	1982	12.00
❑ MLP 15007 [EP]	Blinded by Science	1983	12.00

DOLENZ, MICKEY

Also see DOLENZ, JONES & TORK; DOLENZ, JONES, BOYCE & HART; THE MONKEES.

45s

BELL

Number	Title (A Side/B Side)	Yr	NM
❑ 986	Do It in the Name of Love/Lady Jane	1971	50.00

—With Davy Jones; value is for stock copy (promos worth about 50% of this)

CHALLENGE

Number	Title (A Side/B Side)	Yr	NM
❑ 59353	Don't Do It/Plastic Symphony III	1967	20.00
❑ 59353 [PS]	Don't Do It/Plastic Symphony III	1967	40.00
❑ 59372	Huff Puff/(The Obvious) Fate	1967	20.00
❑ 59372 [PS]	Huff Puff/(The Obvious) Fate	1967	60.00

CHRYSALIS

Number	Title (A Side/B Side)	Yr	NM
❑ 2297	Alicia/Love Light	1979	6.00

MGM

Number	Title (A Side/B Side)	Yr	NM
❑ 14309	Easy on You/Oh Someone	1971	20.00
❑ 14395	A Lover's Prayer/Unattended in the Dungeon	1972	20.00

ROMAR

Number	Title (A Side/B Side)	Yr	NM
❑ 710	Daybreak/Love War	1973	20.00
❑ 715	Buddy Holly Tribute/ Ooh, Se's So Young	1974	20.00

DOLENZ, MICKEY, AND PETER TORK (OF THE MONKEES)

See THE MONKEES.

DOLENZ, JONES & TORK

Also see MICKEY DOLENZ; DAVY JONES; THE MONKEES.

45s

CHRISTMAS

Number	Title (A Side/B Side)	Yr	NM
❑ 700	Christmas Is My Time of Year/ White Christmas	1976	20.00

—B-side by Davy Jones; green label

Number	Title (A Side/B Side)	Yr	NM
❑ 700 [PS]	Christmas Is My Time of Year/ White Christmas	1976	40.00

—Actually an insert with the lyrics that came with the first edition

Number	Title (A Side/B Side)	Yr	NM
❑ 702/3	Christmas Is My Time of Year/ White Christmas	1986	20.00

—Reissue on gold label credited on both sides to "We Three Monkees"

Number	Title (A Side/B Side)	Yr	NM
❑ 702/3 [PS]	Christmas Is My Time of Year/ White Christmas	1986	40.00

—Actual picture sleeve rather than an insert; the order as listed on the sleeve is "Davy Jones, Micky Dolenz and Peter Tork"

DOLENZ, JONES, BOYCE & HART

Also see TOMMY BOYCE; TOMMY BOYCE AND BOBBY HART; MICKEY DOLENZ; BOBBY HART; DAVY JONES; THE MONKEES.

45s

CAPITOL

Number	Title (A Side/B Side)	Yr	NM
❑ 4180	You and I/I Remember the Feeling	1975	10.00
❑ 4271	Savin' My Love for You/I Love You (And I'm Glad I Said It)	1976	10.00

Albums

CAPITOL

Number	Title (A Side/B Side)	Yr	NM
❑ ST-11513	Dolenz, Jones, Boyce & Hart	1976	15.00

DOLLS, THE

45s

LOMA

Number	Title (A Side/B Side)	Yr	NM
❑ 2036	The Reason Why/And That Reminds Me	1966	15.00

MALTESE

Number	Title (A Side/B Side)	Yr	NM
❑ 100	This Is Our Day/What Next	1965	60.00
❑ 107	The Aeroplane Song/ A Lover's Stand	1965	1200.

—As "Norma Jenkins and the Dolls"

OKEH

Number	Title (A Side/B Side)	Yr	NM
❑ 7122	In Love/Please Come Home	1959	12.00

Number	Title (A Side/B Side)	Yr	NM
TEENAGE			
❑ 1010	Just Before You Leave/I Love	1958	1000.

DOLLY AND THE FASHIONS

Number	Title (A Side/B Side)	Yr	NM
45s			
TRI DISC			
❑ 111	Absence Made My Heart Grow Fonder/Waiting for My Man	1963	12.00

DOMINO, FATS

Number	Title (A Side/B Side)	Yr	NM
45s			
ABC			
❑ 10902	I Don't Want to Set the World on Fire/I'm Living Right	1967	10.00
ABC-PARAMOUNT			
❑ ABCS 455-1 [S]	I Got a Right to Cry/When I'm Walking (Let Me Walk)	1963	20.00
—Small hole, plays at 33 1/3 rpm			
❑ 10444	There Goes (My Heart Again)/Can't Go On Without You	1963	10.00
❑ 10475	When I'm Walking (Let Me Walk)/I've Got a Right to Cry	1963	10.00
❑ 10484	Red Sails in the Sunset/Song for Rosemary	1963	12.00
❑ 10512	Who Cares/Just a Lonely Man	1963	10.00
❑ 10531	Lazy Lady/I Don't Want to Set the World on Fire	1964	10.00
❑ 10545	If You Don't Know What Love Is/Something You Got, Baby	1964	10.00
❑ 10567	Mary, Oh Mary/Packin' Up	1964	10.00
❑ 10584	Sally Was a Good Old Girl/For You	1964	10.00
❑ 10596	Heartbreak Hill/Kansas City	1964	10.00
❑ 10631	Why Don't You Do Right/Wigs	1965	10.00
❑ 10644	Let Me Call You Sweetheart/Goodnight Sweetheart	1965	10.00
BROADMOOR			
❑ 104	The Lady in Black/Work My Way Up Steady	1967	15.00
❑ 105	Big Mouth/Wait 'Til It Happens to You	1968	20.00
IMPERIAL			
❑ 45-5058	The Fat Man/Detroit City Blues	1950	2000.
—Blue-label "script" logo; pressed in 1952 or so; counterfeits exist			
❑ 45-5099	Korea Blues/Every Night About This Time	1950	800.00
—Blue-label "script" logo; pressed in 1952 or so			
❑ 45-5167	You Know I Miss You/I'll Be Gone	1952	500.00
—Fats Domino records on Imperial before 5167 are unconfirmed on 45 rpm, except those listed above.			
❑ 45-5180	Goin' Home/Reeling and Rocking	1952	300.00
❑ 45-5197	Poor Poor Me/Trust in Me	1952	200.00
❑ 45-5209	How Long/Dreaming	1952	80.00
—Black vinyl			
❑ 45-5209	How Long/Dreaming	1952	300.00
—Red vinyl			
❑ 45-5220	Nobody Loves Me/Cheatin'	1953	80.00
—Black vinyl			
❑ 45-5220	Nobody Loves Me/Cheatin'	1953	300.00
—Red vinyl			
❑ 45-5231	Going to the River/Mardi Gras in New Orleans	1953	100.00
—Black vinyl			
❑ 45-5231	Going to the River/Mardi Gras in New Orleans	1953	500.00
—Red vinyl			
❑ 45-5240	Please Don't Leave Me/The Girl I Love	1953	60.00
—Black vinyl			
❑ 45-5240	Please Don't Leave Me/The Girl I Love	1953	300.00
—Red vinyl			
❑ 45-5251	You Said You Loved Me/Rose Mary	1953	60.00
❑ X5262	Something's Wrong/Don't Leave Me This Way	1954	50.00
—Black vinyl			
❑ X5262	Something's Wrong/Don't Leave Me This Way	1954	250.00
—Red vinyl			
❑ X5272	Little School Girl/You Done Me Wrong	1954	60.00
❑ X5283	Baby, Please/Where Did You Stay	1954	60.00
❑ X5301	You Can Pack Your Suitcase/I Lived My Life	1954	40.00
❑ X5313	Love Me/Don't You Hear Me Calling You	1954	40.00
❑ X5323	I Know/Thinking of You	1955	50.00
—Black vinyl			
❑ X5323	I Know/Thinking of You	1955	500.00
—Red vinyl			
❑ X5340	Don't You Know/Helping Hand	1955	40.00
❑ X5348	Ain't It a Shame/La La	1955	40.00
❑ X5357	All By Myself/Troubles of My Own	1955	25.00
—Red or maroon label, block logo			
❑ X5357	All By Myself/Troubles of My Own	1955	80.00
—Red label, script logo			
❑ X5369	Poor Me/I Can't Go On	1955	25.00
❑ X5375	Bo Weevil/Don't Blame It on Me	1956	25.00
❑ X5386	I'm in Love Again/My Blue Heaven	1956	25.00
❑ X5396	When My Dreamboat Comes Home/So-Long	1956	25.00
❑ X5407	Blueberry Hill/Honey Chile	1956	25.00
—Black vinyl, red label			
❑ X5407	Blueberry Hill/Honey Chile	1956	150.00
—Red vinyl			
❑ X5407	Blueberry Hill/Honey Chile	1957	15.00
—Black vinyl, black label			
❑ X5417	Blue Monday/What's the Reason I'm Not Pleasing You	1957	25.00
❑ X5428	I'm Walkin'/I'm in the Mood for Love	1957	25.00
—Maroon or red label			
❑ X5428 [PS]	I'm Walkin'/I'm in the Mood for Love	1957	50.00
❑ X5442	Valley of Tears/It's You I Love	1957	25.00
❑ X5454	When I See You/What Will I Tell My Heart	1957	25.00
❑ X5467	Wait and See/I Still Love You	1957	25.00
❑ X5477	The Big Beat/I Want You to Know	1957	25.00
❑ X5477 [PS]	The Big Beat/I Want You to Know	1957	60.00
❑ X5492	Yes, My Darling/Don't You Know I Love You	1958	25.00
—Black vinyl			
❑ X5492	Yes, My Darling/Don't You Know I Love You	1958	150.00
—Red vinyl			
❑ X5515	Sick and Tired/No, No	1958	25.00
❑ X5526	Little Mary/The Prisoner's Song	1958	25.00
❑ X5537	Young School Girl/It Must Be Love	1958	25.00
❑ X5553	Whole Lotta Loving/Coquette	1958	25.00
—Black label			
❑ X5553	Whole Lotta Loving/Coquette	1958	30.00
—Red label			
❑ X5553	Whole Lotta Loving/Coquette	1958	150.00
—Red vinyl (translucent)			
❑ X5569	Telling Lies/When the Saints Go Marching In	1959	15.00
❑ X5585	I'm Ready/Margie	1959	15.00
❑ X5606	I Want to Walk You Home/I'm Gonna Be a Wheel Some Day	1959	20.00
❑ X5606 [PS]	I Want to Walk You Home/I'm Gonna Be a Wheel Some Day	1959	—
—Rumored to exist, but without conclusive evidence, we will delete this from future editions			
❑ X5629	Be My Guest/I've Been Around	1959	15.00
❑ X5629 [PS]	Be My Guest/I've Been Around	1959	50.00
❑ X5645	Country Boy/If You Need Me	1960	15.00
❑ X5660	Tell Me That You Love Me/Before I Grow Too Old	1960	15.00
❑ X5675	Walking to New Orleans/Don't Come Knockin'	1960	20.00
❑ X5687	Three Nights a Week/Put Your Arms Around Me Honey	1960	15.00
❑ X5704	My Girl Josephine/Natural Born Lover	1960	20.00
❑ X5723	What a Price/Ain't That Just Like a Woman	1961	15.00
❑ 5734	Shu Rah/Fell in Love on Monday	1961	15.00
❑ 5753	It Keeps Rainin'/I Just Cry	1961	15.00
❑ 5764	Let the Four Winds Blow/Good Hearted Man	1961	15.00
❑ 5779	What a Party/Rockin' Bicycle	1961	15.00
❑ 5796	Jambalaya (On the Bayou)/I Hear You Knocking	1961	15.00
❑ 5816	You Win Again/Ida Jane	1962	15.00
❑ 5833	My Real Name/My Heart Is Bleeding	1962	15.00
❑ 5863	Nothing New (Same Old Thing)/Dance with Mr. Domino	1962	15.00
❑ 5875	Did You Ever See a Dream Walking/Stop the Clock	1962	15.00
❑ 5895	Won't You Come On Back/Hands Across the Table	1962	15.00
❑ 5895	Won't You Come On Back/Your Cheatin' Heart	1962	15.00
❑ 5909	Hum Diddy Doo/Those Eyes	1963	15.00
❑ 5937	You Always Hurt the One You Love/Trouble Blues	1963	15.00
❑ 5959	Isle of Capri/True Confession	1963	15.00
❑ 5980	One Night/I Can't Go On This Way	1963	15.00
❑ 5999	Your Cheatin' Heart/Goin' Home	1963	15.00
❑ 66005	I Can't Give You Anything But Love/Goin' Home	1963	12.00
❑ 66016	When I Was Young/Your Cheatin' Heart	1964	12.00
MERCURY			
❑ 72463	I Left My Heart in San Francisco/I Done Got Over You	1965	10.00
❑ 72485	It's Never Too Late/What's That You Got	1965	10.00
❑ 72485 [PS]	It's Never Too Late/What's That You Got	1965	20.00
REPRISE			
❑ 0696	One for the Highway/Honest Papas Love Their Mamas Better	1968	15.00
❑ 0763	Lady Madonna/One for the Highway	1968	15.00
❑ 0775	Lovely Rita/Wait Till It Happens to You	1968	15.00
❑ 0810	Everybody's Got Someting to Hide (Except Me and My Monkey)/So Swell When You're Well	1969	15.00
❑ 0891	Have You Seen My Baby?/Make Me Belong to You	1970	15.00
❑ 0944	New Orleans Ain't the Same/Sweet Patootie	1970	15.00
THE RIGHT STUFF			
❑ S7-18216	Christmas Is a Special Day/Please Come Home for Christmas (Christmas Once Again)	1994	4.00
—Red vinyl			
❑ S7-19768	Frosty the Snowman/Every Heart Is Home at Christmas	1997	5.00
—B-side by the Five Keys on Aladdin			
TOOT TOOT			
❑ 001	My Toot Toot/My Toot Toot (Rock)	1985	5.00
—With Doug Kershaw			
❑ 002	Don't Mess with My Popeye's/My Toot Toot	1985	5.00
—With Doug Kershaw			
UNITED ARTISTS			
❑ 0001	Ain't That a Shame/Goin' Home	1973	4.00
❑ 0002	Blue Monday/I'm Gonna Be a Wheel Someday	1973	4.00
❑ 0003	I'm in Love Again/Whole Lotta Lovin'	1973	4.00
❑ 0004	Blueberry Hill/Bo Weevil	1973	4.00
❑ 0005	I'm Walkin'/One Night	1973	4.00
❑ 0006	I Hear You Knockin'/My Blue Heaven	1973	4.00
❑ 0007	Walkin' to New Orleans/Country Boy	1973	4.00
❑ 0008	I Want to Walk You Home/It's You I Love	1973	4.00
❑ 0009	I'm Ready/Wait and See	1973	4.00
❑ 0010	My Girl Josephine/When My Dreamboat Comes Home	1973	4.00
❑ 0011	Three Nights a Week/Let the Four Winds Blow	1973	4.00
—0001 through 0011 are "Silver Spotlight Series" reissues			
❑ XW 514	The Fat Man/Valley of Tears	1974	5.00
—Reissue			
WARNER BROS.			
❑ 49610	Whiskey Heaven/Beers to You	1980	4.00
—B-side by Texas Opera Company			
7-Inch Extended Plays			
ABC-PARAMOUNT			
❑ EP-ABCS 479	I Don't Want to Set the World on Fire/Old Man Trouble/Love Me//You Know I Miss You/The Fat Man/Valley of Tears	1964	25.00
—Stereo jukebox issue; small hole, plays at 33 1/3 rpm			
❑ EP-ABCS 479 [PS]	Fats on Fire	1964	25.00
IMPERIAL			
❑ IMP 127	Going to the River/Every Night About This Time//Going Home/Please Don't Leave Me	1955	100.00
—Maroon label, block-letter logo			
❑ IMP 127	Going to the River/Every Night About This Time//Going Home/Please Don't Leave Me	1955	150.00
—"Script" label			
❑ IMP 127	Going to the River/Every Night About This Time//Going Home/Please Don't Leave Me	1958	25.00
—Black label			
❑ IMP 127 [PS]	Fats Domino	1955	50.00
❑ IMP 138	Domino Stomp/The Girl I Love//Don't You Know/The Fat Man	1956	100.00
—Maroon label, block-letter logo			
❑ IMP 138	Domino Stomp/The Girl I Love//Don't You Know/The Fat Man	1958	25.00
—Black label			
❑ IMP 138 [PS]	Rock and Rollin' with Fats Domino	1956	50.00
❑ IMP 139	Rosemary/All By Myself//Tired of Crying/You Said You Loved Me	1956	100.00
—Maroon label, block-letter logo			

Except when noted otherwise, VG = 25% of NM, and VG+ = 50% of NM. (Example: VG = $2.00, VG+ = $4.00 and NM = $8.00.)

Number	Title (A Side/B Side)	Yr	NM
❑ IMP 139	Rosemary/All By Myself//Tired of Crying/You Said You Loved Me	1958	25.00
—Black label			
❑ IMP 139 [PS]	Rock and Rollin' with Fats Domino	1956	50.00
❑ IMP 140	Ain't It a Shame/Poor Me//Bo Weevil/Don't Blame It on Me	1956	100.00
—Maroon label, block-letter logo			
❑ IMP 140	Ain't It a Shame/Poor Me//Bo Weevil/Don't Blame It on Me	1958	25.00
—Black label			
❑ IMP 140 [PS]	Rock and Rollin' with Fats Domino	1956	50.00
❑ IMP 141	My Blue Heaven/Swanee River Hop//Second Line Jump/Goodbye	1956	100.00
—Maroon label, block-letter logo			
❑ IMP 141	My Blue Heaven/Swanee River Hop//Second Line Jump/Goodbye	1958	25.00
—Black label			
❑ IMP 141 [PS]	Rock and Rollin'	1956	50.00
❑ IMP 142	Careless Love/I Love Her//I'm in Love Again/When My Dreamboat Comes Home	1956	100.00
—Maroon label, block-letter logo			
❑ IMP 142	Careless Love/I Love Her//I'm in Love Again/When My Dreamboat Comes Home	1958	25.00
—Black label			
❑ IMP 142 [PS]	Rock and Rollin'	1956	50.00
❑ IMP 143	Are Your Going My Way/If You Need Me//My Heart Is In Your Hands/Fats Frenzy	1956	100.00
—Maroon label, block-letter logo			
❑ IMP 143	Are Your Going My Way/If You Need Me//My Heart Is In Your Hands/Fats Frenzy	1958	25.00
—Black label			
❑ IMP 143 [PS]	Rock and Rollin'	1956	50.00
❑ IMP 144	Blueberry Hill/Honey Chile//Troubles of My Own/You Done Me Wrong	1956	100.00
—Maroon label, block-letter logo			
❑ IMP 144	Blueberry Hill/Honey Chile//Troubles of My Own/You Done Me Wrong	1958	25.00
—Black label			
❑ IMP 144 [PS]	This Is Fats Domino	1956	50.00
❑ IMP 145	What's the Reason I'm Not Pleasing You/Blue Monday//Reeling and Rocking/The Fat Man's Hop	1956	100.00
—Maroon label, block-letter logo			
❑ IMP 145	What's the Reason I'm Not Pleasing You/Blue Monday//Reeling and Rocking/The Fat Man's Hop	1958	25.00
—Black label			
❑ IMP 145 [PS]	This Is Fats Domino	1956	50.00
❑ IMP 146	So Long/La La//Poor, Poor Me/Trust in Me	1956	100.00
—Maroon label, block-letter logo			
❑ IMP 146	So Long/La La//Poor, Poor Me/Trust in Me	1958	25.00
—Black label			
❑ IMP 146 [PS]	This Is Fats Domino	1956	50.00
❑ IMP 147	The Rooster Song/My Happiness//As Time Goes By/Hey La Bas	1956	100.00
—Maroon label, block-letter logo			
❑ IMP 147	The Rooster Song/My Happiness//As Time Goes By/Hey La Bas	1958	25.00
—Black label			
❑ IMP 147 [PS]	Here Comes Fats	1956	50.00
❑ IMP 148	Detroit City Blues/Hide Away Blues//She's My Baby/New Baby	1957	100.00
—Maroon label, block-letter logo			
❑ IMP 148	Detroit City Blues/Hide Away Blues//She's My Baby/New Baby	1958	25.00
—Black label			
❑ IMP 148 [PS]	Here Stands Fats Domino	1957	50.00
❑ IMP 149	Little Bee/Every Night About This Time//I'm Walkin'/Cheatin'	1957	100.00
—Maroon label, block-letter logo			
❑ IMP 149	Little Bee/Every Night About This Time//I'm Walkin'/Cheatin'	1958	25.00
—Black label			
❑ IMP 149 [PS]	Here Stands Fats Domino	1957	50.00
❑ IMP 150	I'm in the Mood for Love/You Can Pack Your Suitcase//Hey! Fat Man/I'll Be Gone	1957	100.00
—Maroon label, block-letter logo			
❑ IMP 150	I'm in the Mood for Love/You Can Pack Your Suitcase//Hey! Fat Man/I'll Be Gone	1958	25.00
—Black label			
❑ IMP 150 [PS]	Here Stands Fats Domino	1957	50.00
❑ IMP 151	Love Me/Don't You Hear Me Calling You//It's You I Love/Valley of Tears	1957	100.00
—Maroon label, block-letter logo			
❑ IMP 151	Love Me/Don't You Hear Me Calling You//It's You I Love/Valley of Tears	1958	25.00
—Black label			
❑ IMP 151 [PS]	Cookin' with Fats	1957	50.00
❑ IMP 152	Thinking of You/You Know I Miss You//Where Did You Stay/Baby Please	1957	100.00
—Maroon label, block-letter logo			
❑ IMP 152	Thinking of You/You Know I Miss You//Where Did You Stay/Baby Please	1958	25.00
—Black label			
❑ IMP 152 [PS]	Rockin' with Fats	1957	50.00

MERCURY

Number	Title (A Side/B Side)	Yr	NM
❑ SR-659-C	Introduction/Blueberry Hill/Oh, What a Price/Let the Four Winds Blow//I'm Gonna Be a Wheel Some Day/So Long/Ain't That a Shame	1965	20.00
—Stereo jukebox issue; small hole, plays at 33 1/3 rpm			
❑ SR-659-C [PS]	Fats Domino '65	1965	20.00

Albums

ABC

Number	Title	Yr	NM
❑ S-455 [S]	Here Comes... Fats Domino	1967	15.00
❑ S-479 [S]	Fats on Fire	1967	15.00
❑ S-510 [S]	Get Away with Fats Domino	1967	15.00
❑ ST-90167 [S]	Get Away with Fats Domino	1969	25.00
—Capitol Record Club edition; reissue			

ABC-PARAMOUNT

Number	Title	Yr	NM
❑ 455 [M]	Here Comes... Fats Domino	1963	20.00
❑ S-455 [S]	Here Comes... Fats Domino	1963	25.00
❑ 479 [M]	Fats on Fire	1964	20.00
❑ S-479 [S]	Fats on Fire	1964	25.00
❑ 510 [M]	Get Away with Fats Domino	1965	20.00
❑ S-510 [S]	Get Away with Fats Domino	1965	25.00
❑ ST-90167 [S]	Get Away with Fats Domino	1965	30.00
—Capitol Record Club edition			
❑ T-90167 [M]	Get Away with Fats Domino	1965	25.00
—Capitol Record Club edition			

ATLANTIC

Number	Title	Yr	NM
❑ 81751	Live in Montreux	1987	12.00

COLUMBIA

Number	Title	Yr	NM
❑ C 35996	When I'm Walking	1979	10.00
—Reissue of Harmony LP			
❑ PC 35996	When I'm Walking	1986	8.00
—Budget-line reissue			

COLUMBIA SPECIAL PRODUCTS

Number	Title	Yr	NM
❑ P2 13197 [(2)]	The Legendary Music Man	1976	15.00
—Candelite Music TV offer			

EVEREST ARCHIVE OF FOLK & JAZZ

Number	Title	Yr	NM
❑ 280	Fats Domino	1974	10.00
❑ 330	Fats Domino, Vol. II	1975	10.00

GRAND AWARD

Number	Title	Yr	NM
❑ 267 [M]	Fats Domino	196?	20.00
❑ S-267 [R]	Fats Domino	196?	10.00

HARLEM HIT PARADE

Number	Title	Yr	NM
❑ 5005	Fats' Hits	197?	10.00

HARMONY

Number	Title	Yr	NM
❑ HS 11343	When I'm Walking	1969	12.00

IMPERIAL

Number	Title	Yr	NM
❑ LP-9004 [M]	Rock and Rollin' with Fats Domino	1956	150.00
—Maroon label			
❑ LP-9004 [M]	Rock and Rollin' with Fats Domino	1958	80.00
—Black label with stars on top			
❑ LP-9004 [M]	Rock and Rollin' with Fats Domino	1964	25.00
—Black and pink label			
❑ LP-9004 [M]	Rock and Rollin' with Fats Domino	1967	20.00
—Black and green label			
❑ LP-9009 [M]	Fats Domino Rock and Rollin'	1956	150.00
—Maroon label			
❑ LP-9009 [M]	Fats Domino Rock and Rollin'	1958	80.00
—Black label with stars on top			
❑ LP-9009 [M]	Fats Domino Rock and Rollin'	1964	25.00
—Black and pink label			
❑ LP-9009 [M]	Fats Domino Rock and Rollin'	1967	20.00
—Black and green label			
❑ LP-9028 [M]	This Is Fats Domino!	1957	150.00
—Maroon label			
❑ LP-9028 [M]	This Is Fats Domino!	1958	80.00
—Black label with stars on top			
❑ LP-9028 [M]	This Is Fats Domino!	1964	25.00
—Black and pink label			
❑ LP-9028 [M]	This Is Fats Domino!	1967	20.00
—Black and green label			
❑ LP-9038 [M]	Here Stands Fats Domino	1957	150.00
—Maroon label			
❑ LP-9038 [M]	Here Stands Fats Domino	1958	80.00
—Black label with stars on top			
❑ LP-9038 [M]	Here Stands Fats Domino	1964	25.00
—Black and pink label			
❑ LP-9038 [M]	Here Stands Fats Domino	1967	20.00
—Black and green label			
❑ LP-9040 [M]	This Is Fats	1957	150.00
—Maroon label			
❑ LP-9040 [M]	This Is Fats	1958	80.00
—Black label with stars on top			
❑ LP-9040 [M]	This Is Fats	1964	25.00
—Black and pink label			
❑ LP-9040 [M]	This Is Fats	1967	20.00
—Black and green label			
❑ LP-9055 [M]	The Fabulous Mr. D.	1958	100.00
—Black label with stars on top			
❑ LP-9055 [M]	The Fabulous Mr. D.	1964	30.00
—Black and pink label			
❑ LP-9055 [M]	The Fabulous Mr. D.	1967	20.00
—Black and green label			
❑ LP-9062 [M]	Fats Domino Swings	1959	100.00
—Black label with stars on top			
❑ LP-9062 [M]	Fats Domino Swings	1964	30.00
—Black and pink label			
❑ LP-9062 [M]	Fats Domino Swings	1967	20.00
—Black and green label			
❑ LP-9065 [M]	Let's Play Fats Domino	1959	100.00
—Black label with stars on top			
❑ LP-9065 [M]	Let's Play Fats Domino	1964	30.00
—Black and pink label			
❑ LP-9065 [M]	Let's Play Fats Domino	1967	20.00
—Black and green label			
❑ LP-9103 [M]	Million Record Hits	1960	100.00
—Black label with stars on top			
❑ LP-9103 [M]	Million Record Hits	1964	30.00
—Black and pink label			
❑ LP-9103 [M]	Million Record Hits	1967	20.00
—Black and green label			
❑ LP-9127 [M]	A Lot of Dominos	1960	100.00
—Black label with stars on top			
❑ LP-9127 [M]	A Lot of Dominos	1964	30.00
—Black and pink label			
❑ LP-9127 [M]	A Lot of Dominos	1967	20.00
—Black and green label			
❑ LP-9138 [M]	I Miss You So	1961	100.00
—Black label with stars on top			
❑ LP-9138 [M]	I Miss You So	1964	30.00
—Black and pink label			
❑ LP-9138 [M]	I Miss You So	1967	20.00
—Black and green label			
❑ LP-9153 [M]	Let the Four Winds Blow	1961	100.00
—Black label with stars on top			
❑ LP-9153 [M]	Let the Four Winds Blow	1964	30.00
—Black and pink label			
❑ LP-9153 [M]	Let the Four Winds Blow	1967	20.00
—Black and green label			
❑ LP-9164 [M]	What a Party	1962	60.00
—Black label with stars on top			
❑ LP-9164 [M]	What a Party	1964	30.00
—Black and pink label			
❑ LP-9164 [M]	What a Party	1967	20.00
—Black and green label			
❑ LP-9170 [M]	Twistin' the Stomp	1962	60.00
—Black label with stars on top			
❑ LP-9170 [M]	Twistin' the Stomp	1964	30.00
—Black and pink label			
❑ LP-9170 [M]	Twistin' the Stomp	1967	20.00
—Black and green label			
❑ LP-9195 [M]	Million Sellers by Fats	1962	50.00
—Black label with stars on top			
❑ LP-9195 [M]	Million Sellers by Fats	1964	30.00
—Black and pink label			
❑ LP-9195 [M]	Million Sellers by Fats	1967	20.00
—Black and green label			
❑ LP-9208 [M]	Just Domino	1962	50.00
—Black label with stars on top			
❑ LP-9208 [M]	Just Domino	1964	30.00
—Black and pink label			
❑ LP-9208 [M]	Just Domino	1967	20.00
—Black and green label			
❑ LP-9227 [M]	Walking to New Orleans	1963	50.00
—Black label with stars on top			
❑ LP-9227 [M]	Walking to New Orleans	1964	30.00
—Black and pink label			
❑ LP-9227 [M]	Walking to New Orleans	1967	20.00
—Black and green label			
❑ LP-9239 [M]	Let's Dance with Domino	1963	50.00
—Black label with stars on top			
❑ LP-9239 [M]	Let's Dance with Domino	1964	30.00
—Black and pink label			
❑ LP-9239 [M]	Let's Dance with Domino	1967	20.00
—Black and green label			
❑ LP-9248 [M]	Here He Comes Again	1963	50.00
—Black label with stars on top			
❑ LP-9248 [M]	Here He Comes Again	1964	30.00
—Black and pink label			
❑ LP-9248 [M]	Here He Comes Again	1967	20.00
—Black and green label			
❑ LP-12066 [S]	A Lot of Dominos	1961	150.00
—Black label with silver top			

D

Number	Title (A Side/B Side)	Yr	NM
❑ LP-12066 [S]	A Lot of Dominos	1964	40.00
—Black and pink label			
❑ LP-12066 [S]	A Lot of Dominos	1967	25.00
—Black and green label			
❑ LP-12073 [S]	Let the Four Winds Blow	1961	150.00
—Black label with silver top			
❑ LP-12073 [S]	Let the Four Winds Blow	1964	40.00
—Black and pink label			
❑ LP-12073 [S]	Let the Four Winds Blow	1967	25.00
—Black and green label			
❑ LP-12091 [R]	Fats Domino Swings	1964	20.00
—Black and pink label			
❑ LP-12091 [R]	Fats Domino Swings	1967	15.00
—Black and green label			
❑ LP-12103 [R]	Million Record Hits	1964	20.00
—Black and pink label			
❑ LP-12103 [R]	Million Record Hits	1967	15.00
—Black and green label			
❑ LP-12195 [R]	Million Sellers by Fats	1964	20.00
—Black and pink label			
❑ LP-12195 [R]	Million Sellers by Fats	1967	15.00
—Black and green label			
❑ LP-12227 [R]	Walking to New Orleans	1964	20.00
—Black and pink label			
❑ LP-12227 [R]	Walking to New Orleans	1967	15.00
—Black and green label			
❑ LP-12248 [R]	Here He Comes Again	1964	20.00
—Black and pink label			
❑ LP-12248 [R]	Here He Comes Again	1967	15.00
—Black and green label			
❑ LP-12387 [R]	Rock and Rollin' with Fats Domino	1968	12.00
—Rechanneled reissue of 9004			
❑ LP-12388 [R]	Fats Domino Rock and Rollin'	1968	12.00
—Rechanneled reissue of 9009			
❑ LP-12389 [R]	This Is Fats Domino!	1968	12.00
—Rechanneled reissue of 9028			
❑ LP-12390 [R]	Here Stands Fats Domino	1968	12.00
—Rechanneled reissue of 9038			
❑ LP-12391 [R]	This Is Fats	1968	12.00
—Rechanneled reissue of 9040			
❑ LP-12394 [R]	The Fabulous Mr. D.	1968	12.00
—Rechanneled reissue of 9055			
❑ LP-12395 [R]	Let's Play Fats Domino	1968	12.00
—Rechanneled reissue of 9065			
❑ LP-12398 [R]	I Miss You So	1968	12.00
—Rechanneled reissue of 9138			
LIBERTY			
❑ LWB-122 [(2)]	Cookin' with Fats (Superpak)	1981	12.00
—Budget-line reissue of UA 122			
❑ LM-1027	Million Sellers by Fats	1981	8.00
—Budget-line reissue of UA 1027			
❑ LWB-9958 [(2)]	Legendary Masters	1981	10.00
—Budget-line reissue of UA 9958			
❑ LN-10135	Let's Play Fats Domino	1981	8.00
—Budget-line reissue			
❑ LN-10136	The Fabulous Mr. D.	1981	8.00
—Budget-line reissue			
MCA/SILVER EAGLE			
❑ 6170	Greatest Hits	198?	10.00
MERCURY			
❑ MG-21039 [M]	Fats Domino '65	1965	25.00
❑ 21065/61065	Southland U.S.A.	1966	
—Canceled			
❑ SR-61039 [S]	Fats Domino '65	1965	40.00
PICKWICK			
❑ SPC-3111	Blueberry Hill	197?	10.00
❑ SPC-3165	When My Dreamboat Comes Home	197?	10.00
❑ SPC-3295	My Blue Heaven	1971	10.00
QUICKSILVER			
❑ QS-1016	Live Hits	198?	10.00
REPRISE			
❑ RS 6304	Fats Is Back	1968	30.00
❑ RS 6439	Fats	1970	500.00
—Officially unreleased, test pressings and coverless stock copies are known to exist			
SEARS			
❑ SPS-473	Blueberry Hill!	1970	25.00
SUNSET			
❑ SUM-1103 [M]	Fats Domino	1966	12.00
❑ SUM-1158 [M]	Stompin' Fats Domino	1967	12.00
❑ SUS-5103 [R]	Fats Domino	1966	12.00
❑ SUS-5158 [R]	Stompin' Fats Domino	1967	12.00
❑ SUS-5200 [P]	Trouble in Mind	1968	20.00
❑ SUS-5299 [R]	Ain't That a Shame	1970	12.00
UNITED ARTISTS			
❑ UAMG-104 [DJ]	The Fats Domino Sound	1973	40.00
—Promo compilation of 30 excerpts of Fats hits			
❑ UA-LA122-F2 [(2)]	Cookin' with Fats (Superpak)	1974	30.00
❑ UA-LA122-F2 [(2)DJ]	Cookin' with Fats (Superpak)	1974	300.00
—Promo with one black vinyl record and one colored vinyl record			
❑ UA-LA233-G	The Very Best of Fats Domino	1974	12.00
❑ LM-1027	Million Sellers by Fats	1980	10.00
❑ UAS-9958 [(2)]	Legendary Masters	1972	15.00

DOMINOES, THE See BILLY WARD AND THE DOMINOES.

❑

DON AND DEWEY

Number	Title (A Side/B Side)	Yr	NM
45s			
FIDELITY			
❑ 3017	Jump Awhile/H.B. Boogie	1960	15.00
❑ 3018	Kill Me/Little Sally Walker	1960	15.00
RUSH			
❑ 1003	Don't Ever Leave Me (Don't Make Me Cry)/Heart Attack	196?	20.00
SHADE			
❑ 100	Miss Sue/My Heart Is Aching	195?	150.00
SPECIALTY			
❑ 599	Jungle Hop/A Little Love	1957	25.00
❑ 610	Leavin' It All Up to You/Jelly Bean	1957	30.00
❑ 617	Just a Little Lovin'/When the Sun Has Begun to Shine	1957	25.00
❑ 631	Justine/Bim Bam	1958	25.00
❑ 639	The Letter/Koko Joe	1958	25.00
❑ 659	Farmer John/Big Boy Pete	1959	25.00
❑ 691	Annie Lee/Get Your Hat	196?	12.00
Albums			
SPECIALTY			
❑ SPS-2131	They're Rockin' Til Midnight, Rollin' Til Dawn	1970	30.00
—Original labels are black and gold			

DON AND HIS ROSES

Number	Title (A Side/B Side)	Yr	NM
45s			
DOT			
❑ 15755	Since You Went Away to School/Right Now	1958	50.00
❑ 15874	Leave Those Cats Alone/Don't Try to Change Me	1958	150.00

DON AND JUAN

Number	Title (A Side/B Side)	Yr	NM
45s			
BIG TOP			
❑ 3079	What's Your Name/Chicken Necks	1961	25.00
❑ 3106	Two Fools Are We/Pot Luck	1962	20.00
❑ 3121	Magic Wand/What I Really Meant to Say	1962	40.00
❑ 3145	True Love Never Runs Smooth/Is It All Right If I Love You	1963	50.00
LANA			
❑ 150	What's Your Name/Chicken Necks	196?	8.00
—Oldies reissue			
LOST-NITE			
❑ 219	What's Your Name/Chicken Necks	196?	5.00
—Reissue			
MALA			
❑ 469	Lonely Man/Could This Be Love	1963	12.00
❑ 479	Pledging My Love/Molinda	1964	12.00
❑ 484	Sincerely/Maryana Cherie	1964	12.00
❑ 494	I Can't Help Myself/All That's Missing Is You	1964	12.00
❑ 509	The Heartbreaking Truth/Thank Goodness	1965	30.00
TWIRL			
❑ 2021	Because I Love You/Are You Putting Me on the Shelf	1966	30.00

DON AND THE CHEVELLS

"Don" is Don Ciccone, later of THE CRITTERS and THE FOUR SEASONS.

Number	Title (A Side/B Side)	Yr	NM
45s			
SPEEDWAY			
❑ 1000	Inner Limits/The Only Girl	1964	80.00

DON AND THE GOODTIMES

Number	Title (A Side/B Side)	Yr	NM
45s			
BURDETTE			
❑ 3	Colors of Life/You Did It Before	196?	20.00
DUNHILL			
❑ 4008	Little Green Thing/Little Sally Tease	1965	10.00
❑ 4015	I'll Be Down Forever/Big Big Knight (On a Big White Horse)	1965	10.00
❑ 4022	Sweets for My Sweet/Hey There Mary Mae	1966	10.00
EPIC			
❑ 10145	I Could Be So Good to You/And It's So Good	1967	10.00
❑ 10145 [PS]	I Could Be So Good to You/And It's So Good	1967	15.00
❑ 10199	If You Love Her, Cherish Her and Such/Happy and Me	1967	10.00
❑ 10241	Bambi/Sally (Studio A at 6 O'Clock in the Morning)	1967	10.00
❑ 10280	Ball of Fire/May My Heart Be Cast Into Stone	1968	10.00
JERDEN			
❑ 762	You'll Never Walk Away/Little Sally Tease	1965	12.00
WAND			
❑ 165	Turn On/Make It	1964	10.00
❑ 184	Straight Scepter/There's Something on Your Mind	1965	10.00
Albums			
BEAT ROCKET			
❑ BR-130	The Original Northwest Sound of Don and the Goodtimes	2000	12.00
BURDETTE			
❑ 300 [M]	Don and the Goodtimes' Greatest Hits	1966	150.00
❑ 300S [R]	Don and the Goodtimes' Greatest Hits	1966	100.00
—LP plays rechanneled stereo			
❑ 300S [S]	Don and the Goodtimes' Greatest Hits	1966	300.00
—LP plays true stereo			
EPIC			
❑ LN 24311 [M]	So Good	1967	30.00
❑ BN 26311 [S]	So Good	1967	40.00
PICCADILLY			
❑ 3394	Goodtime Rock 'n' Roll	1980	25.00
WAND			
❑ WDS-679	Where the Action Is	1969	30.00

DON, DICK & JIMMY

Number	Title (A Side/B Side)	Yr	NM
45s			
CROWN			
❑ 113	The Old Gray Mare/It Shall Come to Pass	195?	15.00
❑ 116	Ol' Man River/Hawaiian War Chant	1954	15.00
❑ 125	That's What I Like/You Can't Have Your Cake and Eat It, Too	1954	15.00
❑ 131	The Touch of Your Lips/I Go to You	1954	15.00
❑ 138	Make Yourself Comfortable/Songs from Desiree	1955	15.00
❑ 147	Baby, You!/Nobody Likes to Cry	1955	15.00
❑ 152	This Little Piggie/Make Me a Present	1955	15.00
❑ 158	Love Is a Many-Splendored Thing/In Madrid	1955	15.00
❑ 162	Stolen Love/Adios My Madonna	1956	15.00
DOT			
❑ 15768	Too Young to Bop/This Was My Sin	1958	12.00
VERVE			
❑ 2020	That's the Way I Feel/Two Voices in the Night	1956	12.00
❑ 10043	A Man's Gotta Do/My Faith, My Hope, My Love	1957	12.00
❑ 10062	Be Sweet to Me/Building a Paradise	1957	12.00
Albums			
CROWN			
❑ CLP-5005 [M]	Spring Fever	1958	40.00
DOT			
❑ DLP-3152 [M]	Don, Dick & Jimmy	1959	30.00
MODERN			
❑ MLP-1205 [M]	Spring Fever	1957	120.00
VERVE			
❑ MGV-2084 [M]	Medium Rare	1958	40.00
❑ MGV-2107 [M]	Songs for the Hearth	1959	40.00

DON JUANS, THE

Number	Title (A Side/B Side)	Yr	NM
45s			
ONEZY			
❑ 101	The Girl of My Dreams/Dolores	1959	2000.

DONALDSON, BO, AND THE HEYWOODS

Number	Title (A Side/B Side)	Yr	NM
45s			
ABC			
❑ 11402	Deeper and Deeper/Drive Me Crazy	1973	4.00
❑ 11402 [PS]	Deeper and Deeper/Drive Me Crazy	1973	8.00
❑ 11435	Billy, Don't Be a Hero/Don't Ever Look Back	1974	4.00
❑ 12006	Who Do You Think You Are/Fool's Way of Lovin'	1974	4.00
❑ 12011	Billy, Don't Be a Hero/Don't Ever Look Back	1974	5.00
❑ 12039	The Heartbreak Kid/Girl Don't Make Me Wait	1974	4.00

Except when noted otherwise, VG = 25% of NM, and VG+ = 50% of NM. (Example: VG = $2.00, VG+ = $4.00 and NM = $8.00.)

Number	Title (A Side/B Side)	Yr	NM
❑ 12039 [PS]	The Heartbreak Kid/Girl Don't Make Me Wait	1974	8.00
❑ 12072	Make the Most of This World/House on Telegraph Hill	1975	4.00
❑ 12108	Our Last Song Together/Make the Most of This World	1975	4.00

CAPITOL

Number	Title (A Side/B Side)	Yr	NM
❑ 4237	Oh Boy/Tie Me Down	1976	4.00
❑ 4282	Teenage Rampage/Tie Me Down	1976	4.00

FAMILY PRODUCTIONS

Number	Title (A Side/B Side)	Yr	NM
❑ 0917	Thank You Girl/You Don't Own Me	1972	5.00
❑ 0918	All Over the World/Just for You	1972	5.00
❑ 0918 [PS]	All Over the World/Just for You	1972	15.00
—Sleeve may be promo only			
❑ 0923	Da Doo Ron Ron/Just Because	1973	5.00

PLAYBOY

Number	Title (A Side/B Side)	Yr	NM
❑ 5820	Are You Cuckoo/Gimmie Some Time	1977	4.00

Albums

ABC

Number	Title (A Side/B Side)	Yr	NM
❑ D-824	Bo Donaldson and the Heywoods	1974	10.00

CAPITOL

Number	Title (A Side/B Side)	Yr	NM
❑ ST-11501	Farther On	1976	15.00

FAMILY PRODUCTIONS

Number	Title (A Side/B Side)	Yr	NM
❑ FPS-2711	Special Someone	1972	15.00

DONALDSON, LOU

45s

ARGO

Number	Title (A Side/B Side)	Yr	NM
❑ 5449	Signifyin'/Time After Time	1963	8.00
❑ 5478	Possum Head/Laura	1964	8.00
❑ 5494	Soul Gumbo/Cole Slaw	1965	8.00

BLUE NOTE

Number	Title (A Side/B Side)	Yr	NM
❑ XW189	You Are the Sunshine of My Life/Long Goodbye	1973	5.00
❑ XW287	Pillow Talk/Sassy Soul Strut	1973	5.00
❑ XW381	Sanford and Son/Good Morning Heartache	1974	5.00
❑ 1598	Roccus/Cheek to Cheek	195?	15.00
❑ 1599	The Things We Did Last Summer/Lou's Blues	195?	15.00
❑ 1609	The Best Things in Life/Sweet Juice	195?	15.00
❑ 1610	If I Love Again/Down Home	195?	15.00
❑ 1622	You Go to My Head/Brownie Speak	1954	20.00
—With Clifford Brown			
❑ 1623	Cookin'/Bellarosa	1954	15.00
❑ 1624	Dedah/Carving the Rock	1954	15.00
❑ 1662	Caravan/Old Folks	1955	15.00
❑ 1663	That Good Old Feeling/L.D. Blues	1955	15.00
❑ 1680	Dorothy/Peck Time	195?	15.00
❑ 1681	Grits and Gravy/Herman's Mambo	195?	15.00
❑ 1713	Sputnik (Part 1)/Sputnik (Part 2)	1957	15.00
❑ 1720	The Masquerade Is Over/Blue Walk	195?	15.00
❑ 1721	Autumn Nocturne/Play Ray	195?	15.00
❑ 1752	Mack the Knife/The Nearness of You	1959	15.00
❑ 1753	Be My Love/Lou's Blues	1959	15.00
❑ 1772	Blue Moon/Smooth Groove	196?	12.00
❑ 1773	Goose Grease/The Truth	196?	12.00
❑ 1774	Politely/Blues for J.P.	196?	12.00
❑ 1806	Hog Maw/Day Dreams	196?	12.00
❑ 1807	Here 'Tis (Part 1)/Here 'Tis (Part 2)	196?	12.00
❑ 1808	Watusi Jump (Part 1)/Watusi Jump (Part 2)	196?	12.00
❑ 1830	Gravy Train (Part 1)/Gravy Train (Part 2)	196?	10.00
❑ 1831	Polka Dots and Moonbeams/South of the Border	196?	10.00
❑ 1832	Glory of Love/Avalon	196?	10.00
❑ 1868	Funky Mama (Part 1)/Funky Mama (Part 2)	196?	10.00
❑ 1869	That's All (Part 1)/That's All (Part 2)	196?	10.00
❑ 1934	Alligator Boogaloo/Reverend Moses	1967	8.00
❑ 1936	Say It Loud/Snake Bone	1968	8.00
❑ 1949	Hot Dog/Who's Making Love	1969	8.00
❑ 1956	Everything I Do Gohn Be Funky/Minor Bash	1970	6.00
❑ 1970	Caterpillar/Make It with You	1971	6.00

CADET

Number	Title (A Side/B Side)	Yr	NM
❑ 5521	Musty Rusty (Part 1)/Musty Rusty (Part 2)	1966	6.00

Albums

ARGO

Number	Title (A Side/B Side)	Yr	NM
❑ LP-724 [M]	Signifyin'	1963	25.00
❑ LPS-724 [S]	Signifyin'	1963	25.00
❑ LP-734 [M]	Possum Head	1964	25.00
❑ LPS-734 [S]	Possum Head	1964	25.00
❑ LP-747 [M]	Cole Slaw	1965	25.00
❑ LPS-747 [S]	Cole Slaw	1965	25.00

BLUE NOTE

Number	Title (A Side/B Side)	Yr	NM
❑ BN-LA024-F	Sophisticated Lou	1972	25.00
❑ BN-LA109-F	Sassy Soul Strut	1973	30.00
❑ BN-LA259-G	Sweet Lou	1974	25.00
❑ LT-1028	Midnight Sun	1980	30.00
❑ BLP-1537 [M]	Lou Donaldson Quartet/Quintet/Sextet	1957	400.00
—"Deep groove" version; Lexington Ave. address on label			
❑ BLP-1537 [M]	Lou Donaldson Quartet/Quintet/Sextet	1958	100.00
—Regular version with W. 63rd St. address on label			
❑ BLP-1537 [M]	Lou Donaldson Quartet/Quintet/Sextet	1958	300.00
—"Deep groove" version; W. 63rd St. address on label			
❑ BLP-1537 [M]	Lou Donaldson Quartet/Quintet/Sextet	1963	40.00
—With New York, USA address on label			
❑ BLP-1545 [M]	Wailing with Lou	1957	150.00
—Regular version with W. 63rd St. address on label			
❑ BLP-1545 [M]	Wailing with Lou	1957	250.00
—"Deep groove" version; W. 63rd St. address on label			
❑ BLP-1545 [M]	Wailing with Lou	1963	40.00
—With New York, USA address on label			
❑ BLP-1566 [M]	Swing and Soul	1957	150.00
—Regular version with W. 63rd St. address on label			
❑ BLP-1566 [M]	Swing and Soul	1957	250.00
—"Deep groove" version; W. 63rd St. address on label			
❑ BLP-1566 [M]	Swing and Soul	1963	40.00
—With New York, USA address on label			
❑ BST-1566 [S]	Swing and Soul	1959	100.00
—Regular version with W. 63rd St. address on label			
❑ BST-1566 [S]	Swing and Soul	1959	150.00
—"Deep groove" version; W. 63rd St. address on label			
❑ BST-1566 [S]	Swing and Soul	1963	30.00
—With New York, USA address on label			
❑ BLP-1591 [M]	Lou Takes Off	1958	150.00
—Regular version with W. 63rd St. address on label			
❑ BLP-1591 [M]	Lou Takes Off	1958	250.00
—"Deep groove" version; W. 63rd St. address on label			
❑ BLP-1591 [M]	Lou Takes Off	1963	40.00
—With New York, USA address on label			
❑ BST-1591 [S]	Lou Takes Off	1959	100.00
—Regular version with W. 63rd St. address on label			
❑ BST-1591 [S]	Lou Takes Off	1959	150.00
—"Deep groove" version; W. 63rd St. address on label			
❑ BST-1591 [S]	Lou Takes Off	1963	30.00
—With New York, USA address on label			
❑ BLP-1593 [M]	Blues Walk	1958	150.00
—Regular version with W. 63rd St. address on label			
❑ BLP-1593 [M]	Blues Walk	1958	250.00
—"Deep groove" version; W. 63rd St. address on label			
❑ BLP-1593 [M]	Blues Walk	1963	40.00
—With New York, USA address on label			
❑ BST-1593 [S]	Blues Walk	1959	50.00
—Regular version with W. 63rd St. address on label			
❑ BST-1593 [S]	Blues Walk	1959	80.00
—"Deep groove" version (deep indentation under label on both sides)			
❑ BST-1593 [S]	Blues Walk	1963	20.00
—With New York, USA address on label			
❑ BLP-4012 [M]	LD + 3	1959	120.00
—Regular version with W. 63rd St. address on label			
❑ BLP-4012 [M]	LD + 3	1959	200.00
—"Deep groove" version; W. 63rd St. address on label			
❑ BLP-4012 [M]	LD + 3	1963	40.00
—With New York, USA address on label			
❑ BST-4012 [S]	LD + 3	1960	80.00
—Regular version with W. 63rd St. address on label			
❑ BST-4012 [S]	LD + 3	1960	150.00
—"Deep groove" version; W. 63rd St. address on label			
❑ BST-4012 [S]	LD + 3	1963	30.00
—With New York, USA address on label			
❑ BLP-4025 [M]	The Time Is Right	1960	80.00
—Regular version with W. 63rd St. address on label			
❑ BLP-4025 [M]	The Time Is Right	1960	120.00
—"Deep groove" version (deep indentation under label on both sides)			
❑ BLP-4025 [M]	The Time Is Right	1963	25.00
—With New York, USA address on label			
❑ BLP-4036 [M]	Sunny Side Up	1960	120.00
—Regular version with W. 63rd St. address on label			
❑ BLP-4036 [M]	Sunny Side Up	1960	200.00
—"Deep groove" version; W. 63rd St. address on label			
❑ BLP-4036 [M]	Sunny Side Up	1963	40.00
—With New York, USA address on label			
❑ BLP-4053 [M]	Light Foot	1960	120.00
—With W. 63rd St. address on label			
❑ BLP-4053 [M]	Light Foot	1963	50.00
—With New York, USA address on label			
❑ BLP-4066 [M]	Here 'Tis	1961	200.00
—With W. 63rd St. address on label			
❑ BLP-4066 [M]	Here 'Tis	1963	80.00
—With New York, USA address on label			
❑ BLP-4079 [M]	Gravy Train	1962	200.00
—With W. 63rd St. address on label			
❑ BLP-4079 [M]	Gravy Train	1963	100.00
—With New York, USA address on label			
❑ BLP-4108 [M]	The Natural Soul	1963	150.00
❑ BLP-4125 [M]	Good Gracious	1963	80.00
❑ 4254/84254	Sweet Slumber	1967	—
—Canceled			
❑ BLP-4263 [M]	Alligator Boogaloo	1967	80.00
❑ BLP-4271 [M]	Mr. Shing-a-Ling	1968	120.00
❑ BLP-5021 [10]	Lou Donaldson Quintet/Quartet	1953	500.00
❑ BLP-5030 [10]	Lou Donaldson-Clifford Brown	1954	500.00
❑ BLP-5055 [10]	Lou Donaldson Sextet, Vol. 2	1955	500.00
❑ B1-28267	Hot Dog	1994	15.00
—Reissue of 84318			
❑ B1-31248	Everything I Play Is Funky	1995	15.00
—Reissue of 84337			
❑ B1-31876	The Scorpion: Live at the Cadillac Club	1995	15.00
❑ B1-32095	Sunny Side Up	1995	15.00
—Reissue of 84036			
❑ B1-81537	Lou Donaldson Quartet/Quintet/Sextet	1989	12.00
—Reissue of 1537			
❑ BST-81591 [S]	Lou Takes Off	1966	20.00
—With "A Division of Liberty Records" on label			
❑ BST-81593	Blues Walk	1985	12.00
—"The Finest in Jazz Since 1939" reissue			
❑ BST-81593 [S]	Blues Walk	1967	12.00
—With "A Division of Liberty Records" on label			
❑ BST-84025 [S]	The Time Is Right	1960	100.00
—With W. 63rd St. address on label			
❑ BST-84025 [S]	The Time Is Right	1963	50.00
—With New York, USA address on label			
❑ BST-84036 [S]	Sunny Side Up	1960	100.00
—With W. 63rd St. address on label			
❑ BST-84036 [S]	Sunny Side Up	1963	50.00
—With New York, USA address on label			
❑ BST-84053 [S]	Light Foot	1960	100.00
—With W. 63rd St. address on label			
❑ BST-84053 [S]	Light Foot	1963	50.00
—With New York, USA address on label			
❑ BST-84066 [S]	Here 'Tis	1961	100.00
—With W. 63rd St. address on label			
❑ BST-84066 [S]	Here 'Tis	1963	50.00
—With New York, USA address on label			
❑ BST-84066 [S]	Here 'Tis	1967	20.00
—With "A Division of Liberty Records" on label			
❑ BST-84079 [S]	Gravy Train	1962	100.00
—With W. 63rd St. address on label			
❑ BST-84079 [S]	Gravy Train	1963	50.00
—With New York, USA address on label			
❑ BST-84079 [S]	Gravy Train	1967	25.00
—With "A Division of Liberty Records" on label			
❑ BST-84108	The Natural Soul	1987	12.00
—"The Finest in Jazz Since 1939" reissue			
❑ BST-84108 [S]	The Natural Soul	1963	60.00
—With "New York, USA" on label			
❑ BST-84108 [S]	The Natural Soul	1967	20.00
—With "A Division of Liberty Records" on label			
❑ BST-84125 [S]	Good Gracious	1963	50.00
—With "New York, USA" on label			
❑ BST-84125 [S]	Good Gracious	1967	20.00
—With "A Division of Liberty Records" on label			
❑ BST-84254	Lush Life	1986	15.00
—"The Finest in Jazz Since 1939" label; first issue of this LP			
❑ BST-84263 [S]	Alligator Boogaloo	1967	50.00
—With "A Division of Liberty Records" on label			
❑ BST-84271 [S]	Mr. Shing-a-Ling	1968	50.00
—With "A Division of Liberty Records" on label			
❑ BST-84280	Midnight Creeper	1968	60.00
—"A Division of Liberty Records" on label			
❑ BST-84299	Say It Loud!	1969	50.00
—With "A Division of Liberty Records" on label			
❑ BST-84318	Hot Dog	1969	50.00
—With "A Division of Liberty Records" on label			
❑ BST-84337	Everything I Play Is Funky	1970	50.00
—With "A Division of Liberty Records" on label			
❑ BST-84359	Pretty Things	1970	15.00
❑ BST-84370	Cosmos	1971	15.00
❑ B1-89794	Pretty Thing	1993	15.00
—Reissue of 84359			

CADET

Number	Title (A Side/B Side)	Yr	NM
❑ LP-724 [M]	Signifyin'	1966	20.00
—Reissue of Argo 724			
❑ LPS-724 [S]	Signifyin'	1966	15.00
—Reissue of Argo 724			
❑ LP-734 [M]	Possum Head	1966	20.00
—Reissue of Argo 734			
❑ LPS-734 [S]	Possum Head	1966	15.00
—Reissue of Argo 734			
❑ LP-747 [M]	Cole Slaw	1966	20.00
—Reissue of Argo 747			
❑ LPS-747 [S]	Cole Slaw	1966	15.00
—Reissue of Argo 747			
❑ LP-759 [M]	Musty Rusty	1966	25.00
❑ LPS-759 [S]	Musty Rusty	1966	25.00
❑ LP-768 [M]	Rough House Blues	1966	25.00
❑ LPS-768 [S]	Rough House Blues	1966	25.00
❑ LP-789 [M]	Blowin' in the Wind	1967	25.00
❑ LPS-789 [S]	Blowin' in the Wind	1967	20.00
❑ LPS-815	Lou Donaldson At His Best	1969	20.00
❑ LPS-842	Fried Buzzard — Lou Donaldson Live	1970	20.00

Number	Title (A Side/B Side)	Yr	NM
CHESS			
❑ 2CA 60007	Ha' Mercy	1972	12.00
COTILLION			
❑ SD 9905	A Different Scene	1976	15.00
❑ SD 9915	Color As a Way of Life	1977	15.00
MUSE			
❑ MR-5247	Sweet Poppa Lou	1982	12.00
❑ MR-5292	Back Street	1983	12.00
SUNSET			
❑ SUS-5258	Down Home	1969	12.00
❑ SUS-5318	I Won't Cry Anymore	1970	12.00
TIMELESS			
❑ SJP-153	Forgotten Man	198?	10.00

DONAYS, THE

45s

Number	Title (A Side/B Side)	Yr	NM
BRENT			
❑ 7033	Devil in His Heart/Bad Boy	1962	40.00

DONEGAN, LONNIE

UK skiffle king.

45s

Number	Title (A Side/B Side)	Yr	NM
APT			
❑ 25067	Pick a Bale of Cotton/Ramblin' Round	1962	10.00
ATLANTIC			
❑ 2058	My Old Man's a Dustman/The Golden Vanity	1960	12.00
❑ 2063	Take This Hammer/Nobody Understands Me	1960	12.00
❑ 2081	Lorelei/Junco Partner	1960	12.00
❑ 2108	Have a Drink On Me/Beyond the Sunset	1961	12.00
❑ 2123	Wreck of the John B/Sorry, But I'm Gonna Have to Pass	1961	12.00
DOT			
❑ 15792	The Grand Coulee Dam/Nobody Loves Like an Irishman	1958	20.00
❑ 15873	Sally Don't You Grieve/Times Are Getting Hard, Boys	1958	20.00
❑ 15911	Does Your Chewing Gum Lose Its Flavor (On the Bedpost Overnight)/Aunt Rhody	1959	20.00
—Reissued in 1961 with the same number			
❑ 15953	Fort Worth Jail/Whoa, Back, Back	1959	20.00
❑ 16263	Whoa, Back, Back/Light from the Lighthouse	1961	15.00
FELSTED			
❑ 8630	Rock Island Line/John Henry	1961	12.00
HICKORY			
❑ 1247	Lemon Tree/A Very Good Year	1964	10.00
❑ 1267	Fisherman's Luck/There's a Big Wheel	1964	10.00
❑ 1274	Bad News/Interstate 40	1964	10.00
❑ 1299	Louisiana Man/Lovey Told Me Goodbye	1965	10.00
❑ 1345	Cajun Jo (Bully of the Bayou)/Nothing to Gain	1965	10.00
LONDON			
❑ 1650	Rock Island Line/John Henry	1956	30.00
❑ 20055	Juanita/Who Knows Where the Time Goes	1969	6.00
MERCURY			
❑ 70872	Lost John/Stewball	1956	25.00
❑ 70949	Bring a Little Water, Sylvie/Dead or Alive	1956	25.00
❑ 71026	Don't You Rock Me Daddy-O/How Long, How Long Blues	1957	25.00
❑ 71094	Cumberland Gap/Wabash Cannonball	1957	25.00
❑ 71181	Puttin' On the Style/Gamblin' Man	1957	25.00
❑ 71248	My Dixie Darling/I'm Just a Rolling Stone	1957	25.00

Albums

Number	Title (A Side/B Side)	Yr	NM
ABC-PARAMOUNT			
❑ 433 [M]	Sing Hallelujah	1963	20.00
❑ S-433 [S]	Sing Hallelujah	1963	25.00
ATLANTIC			
❑ 8038 [M]	Skiffle Folk Songs	1960	40.00
❑ SD 8038 [S]	Skiffle Folk Songs	1960	50.00
DOT			
❑ DLP-3159 [M]	Lonnie Donegan	1959	40.00
MERCURY			
❑ MG-20229 [M]	An Englishman Sings American Folk Songs	1957	50.00
UNITED ARTISTS			
❑ UA-LA827-?	Puttin' On the Style	1977	10.00

DONLEY, JIMMY

45s

Number	Title (A Side/B Side)	Yr	NM
CHESS			
❑ 1843	Santa, Don't Pass Me By/Think It Over	1962	12.00
CRAZY CAJUN			
❑ 9001	Santa, Don't Pass Me By/Think It Over	197?	5.00
❑ 9002	Forever Lillie Mae/I Still Care	197?	6.00
❑ 9003	Love Bug/I Still Care	197?	6.00
❑ 9004	I Really Got the Blues/Just a Game	197?	6.00
❑ 9005	You're Why I'm So Lonely/Let Me Hold You	197?	6.00
❑ 9006	Baby, Heaven Sent Me You/Door to My Heart	197?	6.00
❑ 9007	A Woman's Gotta Have Her Way/Hello, Remember Me	197?	6.00
❑ 9008	Please Mr. Sandman/Honey Stop	197?	6.00
❑ 9009	Lovin' Cajun Style/(B-side unknown)	197?	6.00
❑ 9010	Born to Be a Loser/Now I Know	197?	6.00
DECCA			
❑ 30308	Kickin' My Hound Around/Come Along	1957	80.00
❑ 30392	South of the Border/The Trail of the Lonesome Pine	1957	25.00
❑ 30519	Baby How Long/I Gotta Go	1957	25.00
❑ 30574	Please Baby Come Home/Born to Be a Loser	1958	25.00
❑ 30738	Radio, Jukebox and TV/I'm Alone	1958	25.00
❑ 30887	What Must I Do/The Shape You Left Me In	1959	25.00
❑ 31005	Now I Know/I Can't Love You	1959	25.00
❑ 31116	My Baby's Gone/Our Love	1960	40.00
TEARDROP			
❑ 3005	Honey Stop Twistin'/Hello, Remember Me	1962	15.00
❑ 3007	Santa, Don't Pass Me By/Forever Lillie Mae	1962	12.00
❑ 3007	Think It Over/Forever Lillie Mae	1962	12.00
❑ 3009	Baby, Heaven Sent Me You/Loving Cajun Style	1963	12.00
❑ 3017	You're Why I'm So Lonely/Let Me Hold You	1963	12.00
❑ 3021	Santa, Don't Pass Me By/Santa's Alley	1963	12.00
❑ 3026	I Really Got the Blues/Just a Game	1964	10.00
❑ 3034	I'm So Lonesome Without the Blues/Forget the Past	1964	10.00
❑ 3051	Love Bug/I'm to Blame	196?	10.00
❑ 3119	My Forbidden Love/Strange, Strange Feeling	196?	8.00

DONNER, RAL

45s

Number	Title (A Side/B Side)	Yr	NM
CHICAGO FIRE			
❑ 7402	The Wedding Song/Godfather Per Me	1974	8.00
END			
❑ GG-19	You Don't Know What You've Got (Until You Lose It)/She's Everything (I Wanted You to Be)	1963	30.00
—An early, and sought-after, reissue			
FONTANA			
❑ 1502	Poison Ivy League/A Tear in My Eye	1965	25.00
❑ 1502	Poison Ivy League/You Finally Said Something Good	1965	25.00
❑ 1515	Good Lovin'/The Other Side of Me	1965	25.00
GONE			
❑ 5102	Girl of My Best Friend/It's Been a Long, Long Time	1961	25.00
—Multi-color label			
❑ 5102	Girl of My Best Friend/It's Been a Long, Long Time	1961	40.00
—Black label			
❑ 5108	You Don't Know What You've Got (Until You Lose It)/So Close to Heaven	1961	30.00
❑ 5108	To Love/And Then	1961	40.00
—Deleted shortly after release			
❑ 5114	Please Don't Go/I Didn't Figure on Him	1961	25.00
❑ 5119	School of Heartbreakers/Because We're Young	1961	40.00
❑ 5121	She's Everything (I Wanted You to Be)/Because We're Young	1961	25.00
❑ 5121	She's Everything (I Wanted You to Be)/Will You Love Me in Heaven	1961	30.00
—B-side sung by a girl group, not Ral Donner.			
❑ 5125	To Love Someone/Will You Love Me in Heaven	1962	25.00
—B-side sung by Ral Donner as advertised			
❑ 5129	Loveless Life/Bells of Love	1962	25.00
❑ 5133	To Love/Sweetheart	1962	25.00
MID-EAGLE			
❑ 101	(If I Had My) Life to Live Over/Lost	1968	10.00
❑ 275	The Wedding Song/So Much Lovin'	1976	6.00
MJ			
❑ 222	(All of a Sudden) My Heart Sings/Lovin' Place	1970	6.00
❑ 222 [PS]	(All of a Sudden) My Heart Sings/Lovin' Place	1970	6.00
RED BIRD			
❑ 10-057	Love Isn't Like That/It Will Only Make You Love	1966	150.00
REPRISE			
❑ 20135	(These Are the Things That Make Up) Christmas Day/Second Miracle (Of Christmas)	1962	40.00
❑ 20141	I Got Burned/A Tear in My Eye	1963	40.00
❑ 20141 [PS]	I Got Burned/A Tear in My Eye	1963	180.00
❑ 20176	I Wish This Night Would Never End/Don't Put Your Heart in His Hand	1963	50.00
❑ 20192	Beyond the Heartbreak/Run Little Linda	1963	60.00
RISING SONS			
❑ 714	Just a Little Sunshine (In the Rain)/If I Promise	1968	10.00
SCOTTIE			
❑ 1310	Tell Me Why/That's All Right with Me	1959	250.00
SMASH			
❑ 34774/5 [DJ]	Good Lovin'/The Other Side of Me	1964	40.00
—A Fontana promo using Smash labels in error and omitting the Fontana number?			
STARFIRE			
❑ 100	Don't Let It Slip Away/Wait a Minute Now	1978	10.00
—White vinyl			
❑ 100	Don't Let It Slip Away/Wait a Minute Now	1978	10.00
—Black vinyl			
❑ 100 [PS]	Don't Let It Slip Away/Wait a Minute Now	1978	10.00
❑ 103	(Things That Make Up) Christmas Day/Second Miracle (Of Christmas)	1978	10.00
—Green vinyl			
❑ 103 [PS]	(Things That Make Up) Christmas Day/Second Miracle (Of Christmas)	1978	10.00
❑ 114	Rip It Up/Don't Leave Me Now	1979	10.00
❑ 114	Rip It Up/Don't Leave Me Now	1979	25.00
—Picture disc			
❑ 114 [PS]	Rip It Up/Don't Leave Me Now	1979	10.00
SUNLIGHT			
❑ 1006	Don't Let It Slip Away/Wait a Minute Now	1972	12.00
TAU			
❑ 105	Loneliness of a Star/And Then	1963	30.00
—Yellow label			
❑ 105	Loneliness of a Star/And Then	1963	50.00
—Blue label			
THUNDER			
❑ 7801	The Day the Beat Stopped/Rock on Me	1978	6.00

Albums

Number	Title (A Side/B Side)	Yr	NM
GONE			
❑ LP-5012 [M]	Takin' Care of Business	1961	300.00
STARFIRE			
❑ 1004	An Evening with Ral Donner	1982	15.00
—All copies on multi-color vinyl			

DONNER, RAL/RAY SMITH/BOBBY DALE

Albums

Number	Title (A Side/B Side)	Yr	NM
CROWN			
❑ CST-335 [R]	Ral Donner, Ray Smith and Bobby Dale	1963	20.00
❑ CLP-5335 [M]	Ral Donner, Ray Smith and Bobby Dale	1963	40.00

Except when noted otherwise, VG = 25% of NM, and VG+ = 50% of NM. (Example: VG = $2.00, VG+ = $4.00 and NM = $8.00.)

DONNIE AND THE DARLINGTONS

45s

ABC-PARAMOUNT

Number	Title (A Side/B Side)	Yr	NM
❑ 10633	Poppin' My Clutch/Since Grandpa Got a Rail Job	1965	25.00

DONNIE AND THE DELCHORDS

45s

EPIC

Number	Title (A Side/B Side)	Yr	NM
❑ 9495	So Lonely/When You're Alone	1962	25.00

TAURUS

Number	Title (A Side/B Side)	Yr	NM
❑ 352	So Lonely/When You're Alone	1962	40.00
❑ 357	I Don't Care/I'll Be With You in Apple Blossom Time	1963	25.00
❑ 361	Transylvania Mist/ That Old Feeling	1963	25.00
❑ 363	Be with You/I Found Heaven	1963	25.00
❑ 364	I'm in the Mood for Love/I've Got a Woman	1964	25.00

Albums

TAURUS

Number	Title (A Side/B Side)	Yr	NM
❑ 1000	Sing with Triple Stereo	1967	300.00

DONNIE AND THE DREAMERS

45s

DECCA

Number	Title (A Side/B Side)	Yr	NM
❑ 31312	Carole/Ruby My Love	1961	50.00

WHALE

Number	Title (A Side/B Side)	Yr	NM
❑ 500	Dorothy/Count Every Star	1961	25.00
❑ 505	Teenage Love/My Memories of You	1961	40.00

DONNO, EDDIE

45s

CAPEHART

Number	Title (A Side/B Side)	Yr	NM
❑ 5003	Rough Stuff/Our Love	1960	25.00
❑ 5003 [PS]	Rough Stuff/Our Love	1960	200.00

DONNYBROOKS, THE

45s

CALICO

Number	Title (A Side/B Side)	Yr	NM
❑ 108	Every Time We Kiss/ Break the Glass	1959	20.00
❑ 112	Coming Home from School/ Mandolins of Love	1959	20.00

DONOVAN

45s

ALLEGIANCE

Number	Title (A Side/B Side)	Yr	NM
❑ 3910	Lady of the Stars/ (B-side unknown)	1983	4.00

ARISTA

Number	Title (A Side/B Side)	Yr	NM
❑ 0280	Dare to Be Different/ International Man	1977	4.00

EPIC

Number	Title (A Side/B Side)	Yr	NM
❑ 10045	Sunshine Superman/The Trip	1966	10.00
❑ 10045 [DJ]	Sunshine Superman/The Trip	1966	40.00
—Promo only on red vinyl			
❑ 10045 [PS]	Sunshine Superman/The Trip	1966	15.00
❑ 10098	Mellow Yellow/Sunny South Kensington	1966	10.00
❑ 10098 [PS]	Mellow Yellow/Sunny South Kensington	1966	15.00
❑ 10127	Epistle to Dippy/Preachin' Love	1967	8.00
❑ 10127 [PS]	Epistle to Dippy/Preachin' Love	1967	12.00
❑ 10212	There Is a Mountain/ Sand and Foam	1967	8.00
❑ 10253	Wear Your Love Like Heaven/ Oh Gosh	1967	8.00
❑ 10253 [PS]	Wear Your Love Like Heaven/ Oh Gosh	1967	12.00
❑ 10300	Jennifer Juniper/Poor Cow	1968	8.00
❑ 10300 [PS]	Jennifer Juniper/Poor Cow	1968	12.00
❑ 10345	Hurdy Gurdy Man/Teen Angel	1968	8.00
—Features John Paul Jones, Jimmy Page, and possibly John Bonham, all later of Led Zeppelin			
❑ 10345 [PS]	Hurdy Gurdy Man/Teen Angel	1968	12.00
❑ 10393	Lalena/Aye My Love	1968	8.00
❑ 10393 [PS]	Lalena/Aye My Love	1968	12.00
❑ 10434	Atlantis/To Susan on the West Coast Waiting	1969	8.00
❑ 10434 [PS]	Atlantis/To Susan on the West Coast Waiting	1969	12.00
❑ 10510	Goo Goo Barabajagal (Love Is Hot)/Trust	1969	8.00
❑ 10510 [PS]	Goo Goo Barabajagal (Love Is Hot)/Trust	1969	12.00
—With the Jeff Beck Group			
❑ 10649	Riki Tiki Tavi/Roots of Oak	1970	8.00
❑ 10649 [PS]	Riki Tiki Tavi/Roots of Oak	1970	12.00
❑ 10694	Celia of the Seals/Song of the Wandering Aengus	1971	8.00

Donovan, "Mellow Yellow," Epic 5-10098, 1966, **$15.**

Number	Title (A Side/B Side)	Yr	NM
❑ 10694 [PS]	Celia of the Seals/Song of the Wandering Aengus	1971	12.00
❑ 10983	I Like You/Earth Sign Man	1973	5.00
❑ 11023	Maria Magenta/Intergalactic Laxative	1973	5.00
❑ 11108	Yellow Star/Sailing Homeward	1974	5.00
❑ 50016	Rock and Roll with Me/Divine Daze of Deathless Delight	1974	5.00
❑ 50077	Rock and Roll Souljer/How Silly	1975	5.00
❑ 50237	Dark Eyed Blue Jean Angel/ Well Known Has-Been	1976	5.00

HICKORY

Number	Title (A Side/B Side)	Yr	NM
❑ 1309	Catch the Wind/Why Do You Treat Me Like You Do	1965	15.00
❑ 1324	Colours/Josie	1965	12.00
❑ 1338	Universal Soldier/Do You Hear Me Now	1965	12.00
❑ 1375	You're Gonna Need Somebody on Your Mind/Little Tin Soldier	1966	12.00
❑ 1402	Turquoise/To Try for the Sun	1966	12.00
❑ 1417	Hey Gyp/The War Drags On	1966	12.00
❑ 1470	Sunny Goodge Street/Summer Day Reflection Song	1967	10.00
❑ 1492	Do You Hear Me Now/Why Do You Treat Me Like You Do	1968	10.00

JANUS

Number	Title (A Side/B Side)	Yr	NM
❑ 138	Keep On Truckin'/Hey Gyp	1971	8.00

Albums

ALLEGIANCE

Number	Title (A Side/B Side)	Yr	NM
❑ AV-437	Lady of the Stars	1983	10.00

ARISTA

Number	Title (A Side/B Side)	Yr	NM
❑ AB 4143	Donovan	1980	10.00

BELL

Number	Title (A Side/B Side)	Yr	NM
❑ 1135	Early Treasures	1973	10.00

COLUMBIA LIMITED EDITION

Number	Title (A Side/B Side)	Yr	NM
❑ LE 10184	Mellow Yellow	197?	10.00

EPIC

Number	Title (A Side/B Side)	Yr	NM
❑ B2N 171 [(2)S]	A Gift from a Flower to a Garden	1967	25.00
—Boxed set of two LPs with portfolio of lyrics and drawings. The two records also were issued separately as Epic 26349 and 26350.			
❑ E2 171 [(2)]	A Gift from a Flower to a Garden	1979	15.00
—Blue label			
❑ L2N 6071 [(2)M]	A Gift from a Flower to a Garden	1967	50.00
—Boxed set of two LPs with portfolio of lyrics and drawings. The two records also were issued separately as Epic 24349 and 24350.			
❑ LN 24217 [M]	Sunshine Superman	1966	30.00
—Contains the single version of "Sunshine Superman"			
❑ LN 24239 [M]	Mellow Yellow	1967	30.00
❑ LN 24349 [M]	Wear Your Love Like Heaven	1967	12.00
—Part of Epic 6071, issued simultaneously			
❑ LN 24350 [M]	For Little Ones	1967	12.00
—Part of Epic 6071, issued simultaneously			
❑ BN 26217 [R]	Sunshine Superman	1966	15.00
—Contains the single version of "Sunshine Superman" (rechanneled)			
❑ BN 26239 [R]	Mellow Yellow	1967	15.00
❑ BN 26349 [S]	Wear Your Love Like Heaven	1967	15.00
—Part of Epic 171, issued simultaneously			
❑ BN 26350 [S]	For Little Ones	1967	15.00
—Part of Epic 171, issued simultaneously			
❑ BN 26386	Donovan in Concert	1968	12.00
❑ BN 26420 [M]	Hurdy Gurdy Man	1968	70.00
—Mono is white label promo only; "Mono" sticker on stereo front cover			
❑ BN 26420 [S]	Hurdy Gurdy Man	1968	12.00
❑ PE 26420	Hurdy Gurdy Man	1986	8.00
—Blue label, new prefix			
❑ BXN 26439 [P]	Donovan's Greatest Hits	1969	12.00
—Yellow label; "Mellow Yellow" is rechanneled; "Sunshine Superman" is the full-length version in stereo; "Catch the Wind" and "Colours" were re-recorded			
❑ BXN 26439 [P]	Donovan's Greatest Hits	1973	10.00
—Orange label			
❑ PE 26439	Donovan's Greatest Hits	1979	8.00
—Blue label			
❑ BN 26481	Barabajagal	1969	12.00
❑ PE 26481	Barabajagal	1987	8.00
—Blue label, new prefix			
❑ E 30125	Open Road	1970	12.00
❑ KEG 31210 [(2)]	The World of Donovan	1972	12.00
❑ KE 32156	Cosmic Wheels	1973	15.00
—With enclosed poster			

Number	Title (A Side/B Side)	Yr	NM
❑ KE 32800	Essence to Essence	1974	12.00
❑ PE 33245	7-Tease	1974	12.00
❑ EG 33731 [(2)]	Hurdy Gurdy Man/Barabajagal	1975	15.00
❑ EG 33734 [(2)]	Donovan in Concert/Sunshine Superman	1975	15.00
❑ PE 33945	Slow Down World	1976	12.00

HICKORY

Number	Title (A Side/B Side)	Yr	NM
❑ LPM-123 [M]	Catch the Wind	1965	25.00
—Most pressings have Donovan facing left, so he is correctly strumming his guitar with his right hand			
❑ LPM-123 [M]	Catch the Wind	1965	40.00
—First pressings have Donovan facing right, so it appears as if he's strumming his guitar with his left hand			
❑ LPS-123 [R]	Catch the Wind	1965	25.00
❑ LPM-127 [M]	Fairy Tale	1965	20.00
❑ LPS-127 [P]	Fairy Tale	1965	25.00
—"Colours" is rechanneled			
❑ LPM-135 [M]	The Real Donovan	1966	20.00
❑ LPS-135 [P]	The Real Donovan	1966	25.00
—Half stereo, including "Colours," the rest rechanneled.			
❑ LPS-143 [P]	Like It Is, Was and Evermore Shall Be	1968	20.00
❑ LPS-149 [P]	The Best of Donovan	1969	20.00

JANUS

Number	Title (A Side/B Side)	Yr	NM
❑ 3022	Donovan P. Leitch	1970	10.00
❑ 3025	Hear Me Now	1971	10.00

KORY

Number	Title (A Side/B Side)	Yr	NM
❑ 3012	Early Treasures	1977	8.00

PYE

Number	Title (A Side/B Side)	Yr	NM
❑ 502	Donovan	1975	10.00

DONTELS, THE

45s

BELTONE

Number	Title (A Side/B Side)	Yr	NM
❑ 2040	Lover's Reunion/Make a Chance	1963	250.00

DOOBIE BROTHERS, THE

Also see MICHAEL McDONALD; PATRICK SIMMONS.

12-Inch Singles

WARNER BROS.

Number	Title (A Side/B Side)	Yr	NM
❑ PRO-A-894 [DJ]	Real Love (4:16) (same on both sides)	1980	10.00
❑ WBSD 8778	What a Fool Believes/Don't Stop to Watch the Wheels	1979	10.00

45s

ASYLUM

Number	Title (A Side/B Side)	Yr	NM
❑ 46630	Power/Cape Fear River	1980	5.00
—A-side: With John Hall and James Taylor; B-side by Sweet Honey in the Rock			

CAPITOL

Number	Title (A Side/B Side)	Yr	NM
❑ B-44376	The Doctor/Too High a Price	1989	3.00
❑ B-44376 [PS]	The Doctor/Too High a Price	1989	3.00
❑ 7PRO-79723 [DJ]	Need a Little Taste of Love (same on both sides)	1989	6.00
—Vinyl is promo only			

SESAME STREET

Number	Title (A Side/B Side)	Yr	NM
❑ 49642	Wynken, Blynken and Nod/In Harmony	1980	5.00
—B-side by Kate Taylor and the Simon-Taylor Family			
❑ 49642 [PS]	Wynken, Blynken and Nod/In Harmony	1980	5.00

WARNER BROS.

Number	Title (A Side/B Side)	Yr	NM
❑ 7495	Nobody/Slippery St. Paul	1971	6.00
❑ 7527	Travelin' Man/Feelin' Down Partner	1971	6.00
❑ 7544	Beehive State/Closer Every Day	1971	6.00
❑ 7619	Listen to the Music/Toulouse Street	1972	5.00
❑ 7661	Jesus Is Just Alright/Rockin' Down the Highway	1972	5.00
❑ 7698	Long Train Runnin'/Without You	1973	4.00
❑ 7728	China Grove/Evil Woman	1973	4.00
❑ 7795	Another Park, Another Sunday/Black Water	1974	5.00
❑ 7832	Eyes of Silver/You Just Can't Stop It	1974	5.00
❑ 8011	Eyes of Silver/You Just Can't Stop It	1974	4.00
❑ 8041	Nobody/Flying Cloud	1974	4.00
❑ 8062	Black Water/Song to See You Through	1974	4.00
❑ 8092	Take Me in Your Arms (Rock Me)/Slat Key Soquel Rag	1975	4.00
❑ 8126	Sweet Maxine/Double Dealin' Four Flusher	1975	4.00
❑ 8161	I Cheat the Hangman/Music Man	1975	4.00
❑ 8196	Takin' It to the Streets/For Someone Special	1976	4.00
❑ 8233	Wheels of Fortune/Slat Key Soquel Rag	1976	4.00
❑ 8282	It Keeps You Runnin'/Turn It Loose	1976	4.00
❑ 8408	Little Darling (I Need You)/Losin' End	1977	4.00
❑ 8471	Echoes of Love/There's a Light	1977	4.00
❑ 8500	Livin' on the Fault Line/Nothin' but a Heartache	1977	4.00
❑ 8725	What a Fool Believes/Don't Stop to Watch the Wheels	1978	4.00
❑ 8725 [PS]	What a Fool Believes/Don't Stop to Watch the Wheels	1978	5.00
❑ 8828	Minute by Minute/Sweet Feelin'	1979	4.00
❑ 29552	You Belong to Me/South City Midnight Lady	1983	4.00
❑ 29552 [PS]	You Belong to Me/South City Midnight Lady	1983	5.00
❑ 49029	Dependin' on You/How Do the Fools Survive	1979	4.00
❑ 49503	Real Love/Thank You Love	1980	4.00
❑ 49503 [PS]	Real Love/Thank You Love	1980	5.00
❑ 49622	One Step Closer/South Bay Street	1980	4.00
❑ 49670	Keep This Train A-Rollin'/Just in Time	1981	4.00
❑ 50001	Here to Love You/Wynken, Bliinken and Nod	1982	4.00

7-Inch Extended Plays

WARNER BROS.

Number	Title (A Side/B Side)	Yr	NM
❑ S 2694	China Grove/Busted Down Around O'Connelly Corners/Long Train Runnin'//Without You/Natural Thing	1973	8.00
—Jukebox issue, small hole, plays at 33 1/3 rpm			
❑ S 2694 [PS]	The Captain and Me	1973	8.00
—Part of "Little LP" series (LLP #221)			
❑ S 2750	Eyes of Silver/Pursuit on 53rd St./Spirit//Road Angel/Tell Me What You Want	1974	8.00
—Jukebox issue, small hole, plays at 33 1/3 rpm			
❑ S 2750 [PS]	What Were Once Vices Are Now Habits	1974	10.00
—Part of Little LP series (LLP #247)			

Albums

CAPITOL

Number	Title (A Side/B Side)	Yr	NM
❑ C1-90371	Cycles	1989	12.00
❑ C1-594623	Brotherhood	1991	20.00
—U.S. vinyl version available only through Columbia House			

DCC COMPACT CLASSICS

Number	Title (A Side/B Side)	Yr	NM
❑ LPZ-2053	Best of the Doobies	1998	40.00
—Audiophile vinyl			

MOBILE FIDELITY

Number	Title (A Side/B Side)	Yr	NM
❑ 1-122	Takin' It to the Streets	1983	40.00
—Audiophile vinyl			

NAUTILUS

Number	Title (A Side/B Side)	Yr	NM
❑ NR-5	The Captain and Me	1980	40.00
—Audiophile vinyl			
❑ NR-18	Minute by Minute	1981	30.00
—Audiophile vinyl			

PICKWICK

Number	Title (A Side/B Side)	Yr	NM
❑ SPC-3721	Introducing the Doobie Brothers	1980	40.00
—Pre-Warner Bros. recordings; withdrawn shortly after release			

TPM/RHINO EXCLUSIVE

Number	Title (A Side/B Side)	Yr	NM
❑ 9000	Minute by Minute	2008	20.00

WARNER BROS.

Number	Title (A Side/B Side)	Yr	NM
❑ WS 1919	The Doobie Brothers	1971	15.00
—Green label original			
❑ WS 1919	The Doobie Brothers	1973	10.00
—"Burbank" label			
❑ BS 2634	Toulouse Street	1972	15.00
—Green label original			
❑ BS 2634	Toulouse Street	1973	10.00
—"Burbank" label			
❑ BS4 2634 [Q]	Toulouse Street	1975	25.00
❑ BS 2694	The Captain and Me	1973	12.00
—"Burbank" label			
❑ BS 2694	The Captain and Me	1973	20.00
—Green label			
❑ BS 2694	The Captain and Me	1979	8.00
—Cream label			
❑ BS4 2694 [Q]	The Captain and Me	1974	20.00
❑ W 2750	What Were Once Vices Are Now Habits	1974	10.00
—"Burbank" label			
❑ W 2750	What Were Once Vices Are Now Habits	1979	8.00
—Cream label			
❑ W4 2750 [Q]	What Were Once Vices Are Now Habits	1974	20.00
❑ BS 2835	Stampede	1975	10.00
—"Burbank" label			
❑ BS 2835	Stampede	1979	8.00
—Cream label			
❑ BS4 2835 [Q]	Stampede	1975	20.00
❑ BS 2899	Takin' It to the Streets	1976	10.00
—"Burbank" label			
❑ BS 2899	Takin' It to the Streets	1979	8.00
—Cream label			
❑ BS 2978	Best of the Doobies	1976	12.00
❑ BSK 3045	Livin' on the Fault Line	1977	8.00
—Cream label			
❑ BSK 3045	Livin' on the Fault Line	1977	10.00
—"Burbank" label			
❑ BSK 3112	Best of the Doobies	1978	10.00
—"Burbank" label			
❑ BSK 3112	Best of the Doobies	1979	8.00
—Cream label			
❑ BSK 3193	Minute by Minute	1978	10.00
❑ HS 3452	One Step Closer	1980	10.00
❑ BSK 3612	Best of the Doobies, Vol. 2	1981	10.00
❑ 23772 [(2)]	Farewell Tour	1983	15.00

DOODLES, THE

45s

HIT

Number	Title (A Side/B Side)	Yr	NM
❑ 104	I Want to Hold Your Hand/A Fool Never Learns	1964	12.00
—B-side by Fred York			

DOONE, LORNA

45s

RCA VICTOR

Number	Title (A Side/B Side)	Yr	NM
❑ 47-8532	Dangerous Town/Who Knows It?	1965	50.00

DOONICAN, VAL

45s

DECCA

Number	Title (A Side/B Side)	Yr	NM
❑ 32252	I'd Rather Think of You/If the Whole World Stopped Lovin'	1968	5.00
❑ 32337	The Sun Always Shines When You're Young/Now	1968	5.00

LONDON

Number	Title (A Side/B Side)	Yr	NM
❑ 1014	Two Streets/It Must Be You	1967	6.00
❑ 9717	Walk Tall/Only the Heartaches	1964	10.00
❑ 9735	The Special Years/Traveling Home	1965	10.00
❑ 9753	I'm Gonna Get There Somehow/How Can I Find Her	1965	10.00

PRESS

Number	Title (A Side/B Side)	Yr	NM
❑ 5008	Gentle Mary/What Would I Be	1967	6.00

Albums

DECCA

Number	Title (A Side/B Side)	Yr	NM
❑ DL 4962 [M]	If the Whole World Stopped Lovin'	1968	15.00
❑ DL 74962 [S]	If the Whole World Stopped Lovin'	1968	12.00

LONDON

Number	Title (A Side/B Side)	Yr	NM
❑ PS 515 [S]	The Many Shades of Val Doonican	1967	15.00
❑ LL 3515 [M]	The Many Shades of Val Doonican	1967	12.00

DOORS, THE

Also see BUTTS BAND; RAY MANZAREK.

12-Inch Singles

ELEKTRA

Number	Title (A Side/B Side)	Yr	NM
❑ ED 4942 [DJ]	Gloria (clean edit)/Gloria (dirty LP)	1983	20.00
❑ ED 4955 [DJ]	Love Me Two Times/Moonlight Drive	1983	15.00
❑ ED 5245 [DJ]	Light My Fire (edit)/Light My Fire (live edit)	1987	15.00

45s

ELEKTRA

Number	Title (A Side/B Side)	Yr	NM
❑ 45051	Light My Fire/Love Me Two Times	1972	6.00
—"Spun Gold" series; originals have a very dark gold label			
❑ 45051	Light My Fire/Love Me Two Times	1975	4.00
—"Spun Gold" series; reissues have a lighter gold label			
❑ 45052	Touch Me/Hello, I Love You	1972	6.00
—"Spun Gold" series; originals have a very dark gold label			
❑ 45052	Touch Me/Hello, I Love You	1975	4.00
—"Spun Gold" series; reissues have a lighter gold label			
❑ 45059	Riders on the Storm/Love Her Madly	1973	6.00
—"Spun Gold" series; originals have a very dark gold label			
❑ 45059	Riders on the Storm/Love Her Madly	1975	4.00
—"Spun Gold" series; reissues have a lighter gold label			
❑ 45122	L.A. Woman/Roadhouse Blues	1983	4.00
—"Spun Gold" series; lighter gold label			
❑ 45123	People Are Strange/Break On Through	1983	4.00
—"Spun Gold" series; lighter gold label			
❑ 45611	Break On Through (To the Other Side)/End of the Night	1966	30.00
—Originals have a yellow and black label with "ELEKTRA" in all capital letters and a woman's head above a white line at the top of the label			
❑ 45611	Break On Through (To the Other Side)/End of the Night	1967	20.00
—Red, black and pink label			
❑ 45611	Break On Through (To the Other Side)/End of the Night	1967	20.00
—Red, black and white label			

Except when noted otherwise, VG = 25% of NM, and VG+ = 50% of NM. (Example: VG = $2.00, VG+ = $4.00 and NM = $8.00.)

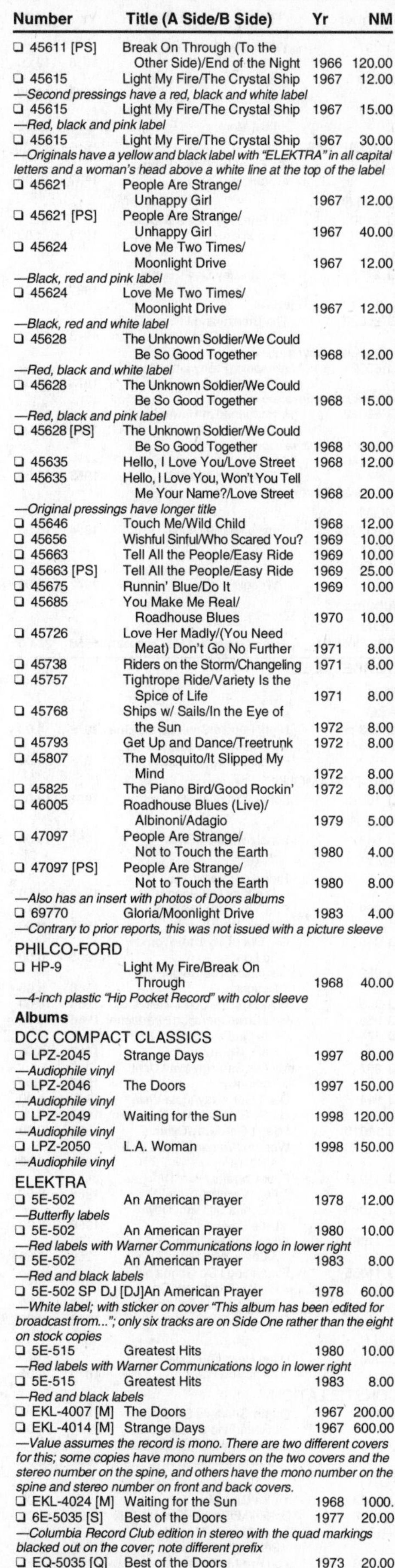

Number	Title (A Side/B Side)	Yr	NM
❑ 45611 [PS]	Break On Through (To the Other Side)/End of the Night	1966	120.00
❑ 45615	Light My Fire/The Crystal Ship	1967	12.00
—Second pressings have a red, black and white label			
❑ 45615	Light My Fire/The Crystal Ship	1967	15.00
—Red, black and pink label			
❑ 45615	Light My Fire/The Crystal Ship	1967	30.00
—Originals have a yellow and black label with "ELEKTRA" in all capital letters and a woman's head above a white line at the top of the label			
❑ 45621	People Are Strange/ Unhappy Girl	1967	12.00
❑ 45621 [PS]	People Are Strange/ Unhappy Girl	1967	40.00
❑ 45624	Love Me Two Times/ Moonlight Drive	1967	12.00
—Black, red and pink label			
❑ 45624	Love Me Two Times/ Moonlight Drive	1967	12.00
—Black, red and white label			
❑ 45628	The Unknown Soldier/We Could Be So Good Together	1968	12.00
—Red, black and white label			
❑ 45628	The Unknown Soldier/We Could Be So Good Together	1968	15.00
—Red, black and pink label			
❑ 45628 [PS]	The Unknown Soldier/We Could Be So Good Together	1968	30.00
❑ 45635	Hello, I Love You/Love Street	1968	12.00
❑ 45635	Hello, I Love You, Won't You Tell Me Your Name?/Love Street	1968	20.00
—Original pressings have longer title			
❑ 45646	Touch Me/Wild Child	1968	12.00
❑ 45656	Wishful Sinful/Who Scared You?	1969	10.00
❑ 45663	Tell All the People/Easy Ride	1969	10.00
❑ 45663 [PS]	Tell All the People/Easy Ride	1969	25.00
❑ 45675	Runnin' Blue/Do It	1969	10.00
❑ 45685	You Make Me Real/ Roadhouse Blues	1970	10.00
❑ 45726	Love Her Madly/(You Need Meat) Don't Go No Further	1971	8.00
❑ 45738	Riders on the Storm/Changeling	1971	8.00
❑ 45757	Tightrope Ride/Variety Is the Spice of Life	1971	8.00
❑ 45768	Ships w/ Sails/In the Eye of the Sun	1972	8.00
❑ 45793	Get Up and Dance/Treetrunk	1972	8.00
❑ 45807	The Mosquito/It Slipped My Mind	1972	8.00
❑ 45825	The Piano Bird/Good Rockin'	1972	8.00
❑ 46005	Roadhouse Blues (Live)/ Albinoni/Adagio	1979	5.00
❑ 47097	People Are Strange/ Not to Touch the Earth	1980	4.00
❑ 47097 [PS]	People Are Strange/ Not to Touch the Earth	1980	8.00
—Also has an insert with photos of Doors albums			
❑ 69770	Gloria/Moonlight Drive	1983	4.00
—Contrary to prior reports, this was not issued with a picture sleeve			
PHILCO-FORD			
❑ HP-9	Light My Fire/Break On Through	1968	40.00
—4-inch plastic "Hip Pocket Record" with color sleeve			
Albums			
DCC COMPACT CLASSICS			
❑ LPZ-2045	Strange Days	1997	80.00
—Audiophile vinyl			
❑ LPZ-2046	The Doors	1997	150.00
—Audiophile vinyl			
❑ LPZ-2049	Waiting for the Sun	1998	120.00
—Audiophile vinyl			
❑ LPZ-2050	L.A. Woman	1998	150.00
—Audiophile vinyl			
ELEKTRA			
❑ 5E-502	An American Prayer	1978	12.00
—Butterfly labels			
❑ 5E-502	An American Prayer	1980	10.00
—Red labels with Warner Communications logo in lower right			
❑ 5E-502	An American Prayer	1983	8.00
—Red and black labels			
❑ 5E-502 SP DJ [DJ]	An American Prayer	1978	60.00
—White label; with sticker on cover "This album has been edited for broadcast from..."; only six tracks are on Side One rather than the eight on stock copies			
❑ 5E-515	Greatest Hits	1980	10.00
—Red labels with Warner Communications logo in lower right			
❑ 5E-515	Greatest Hits	1983	8.00
—Red and black labels			
❑ EKL-4007 [M]	The Doors	1967	200.00
❑ EKL-4014 [M]	Strange Days	1967	600.00
—Value assumes the record is mono. There are two different covers for this; some copies have mono numbers on the two covers and the stereo number on the spine, and others have the mono number on the spine and stereo number on front and back covers.			
❑ EKL-4024 [M]	Waiting for the Sun	1968	1000.
❑ 6E-5035 [S]	Best of the Doors	1977	20.00
—Columbia Record Club edition in stereo with the quad markings blacked out on the cover; note different prefix			
❑ EQ-5035 [Q]	Best of the Doors	1973	20.00
—Butterfly labels			

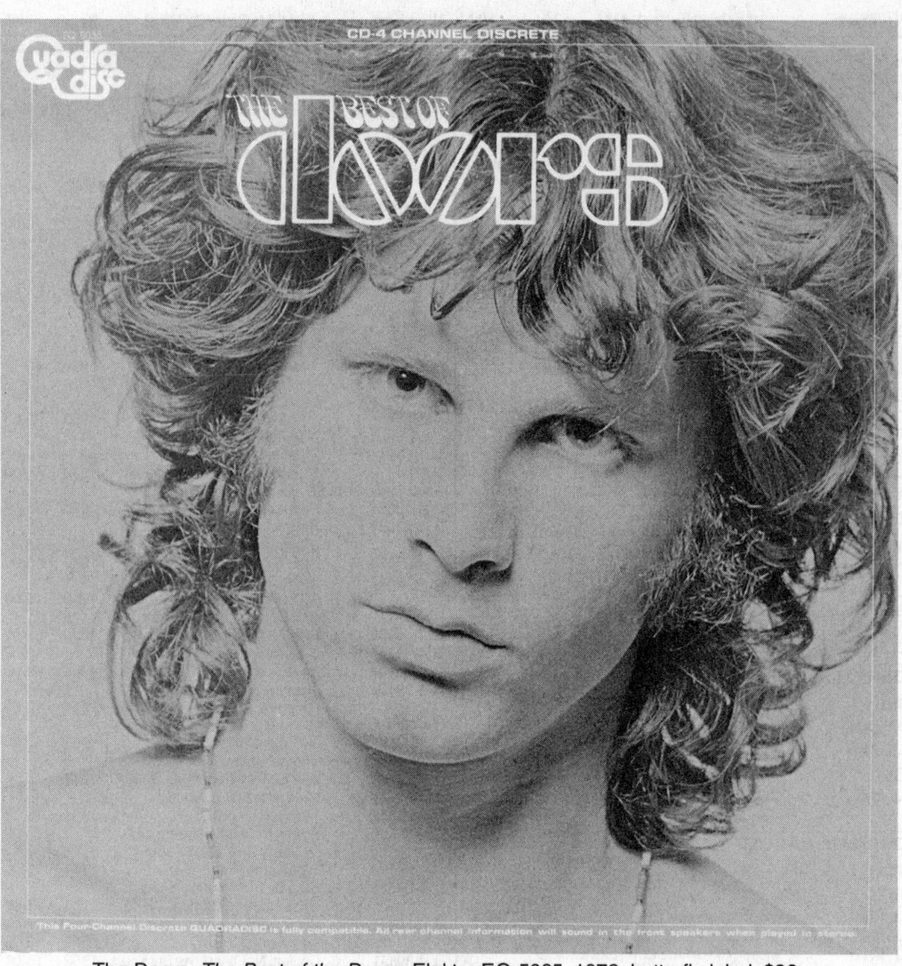

The Doors, *The Best of the Doors*, Elektra EQ-5035, 1973, butterfly label, **$20.**

Number	Title (A Side/B Side)	Yr	NM
❑ EQ-5035 [Q]	Best of the Doors	1980	12.00
—Red labels with Warner Communications logo in lower right			
❑ EQ-5035 [Q]	Best of the Doors	1983	10.00
—Red and black labels			
❑ 8E-6001 [(2)]	Weird Scenes Inside the Gold Mine	1972	20.00
—Butterfly labels			
❑ 8E-6001 [(2)]	Weird Scenes Inside the Gold Mine	1980	12.00
—Red labels with Warner Communications logo in lower right			
❑ 8E-6001 [(2)]	Weird Scenes Inside the Gold Mine	1983	10.00
—Red and black labels			
❑ EKS-9002 [(2)]	Absolutely Live	1970	25.00
—Butterfly labels			
❑ EKS-9002 [(2)]	Absolutely Live	1980	15.00
—Red labels with Warner Communications logo in lower right			
❑ EKS-9002 [(2)]	Absolutely Live	1983	12.00
—Red and black labels			
❑ EKS-9002 [(2)DJ]	Absolutely Live	1970	80.00
—White label promo			
❑ 60269	Alive, She Cried	1984	12.00
❑ 60345 [(2)]	The Best of the Doors	1985	15.00
❑ 60345 [(2)]	The Best of the Doors	1985	40.00
—White label promo on audiophile vinyl			
❑ 60417	Classics	1986	12.00
❑ 60741 [EP]	Live at the Hollywood Bowl	1988	12.00
❑ E1-61047	The Doors	1991	100.00
—Soundtrack from the movie; only available on US vinyl from Columbia House			
❑ 61812	An American Prayer	1995	15.00
—Remastered and lengthened version of 5E-502			
❑ EKS-74007 [S]	The Doors	1967	50.00
—Brown labels			
❑ EKS-74007 [S]	The Doors	1969	15.00
—Red labels with large stylized "E"			
❑ EKS-74007 [S]	The Doors	1971	12.00
—Butterfly labels			
❑ EKS-74007 [S]	The Doors	1980	10.00
—Red labels with Warner Communications logo in lower right			
❑ EKS-74007 [S]	The Doors	1983	8.00
—Red and black labels			

Number	Title (A Side/B Side)	Yr	NM
❑ EKS-74014 [S]	Strange Days	1967	40.00
—Brown labels			
❑ EKS-74014 [S]	Strange Days	1969	15.00
—Red labels with large stylized "E"			
❑ EKS-74014 [S]	Strange Days	1971	12.00
—Butterfly labels			
❑ EKS-74014 [S]	Strange Days	1980	10.00
—Red labels with Warner Communications logo in lower right			
❑ EKS-74014 [S]	Strange Days	1983	8.00
—Red and black labels			
❑ EKS-74024 [S]	Waiting for the Sun	1968	30.00
—Brown labels			
❑ EKS-74024 [S]	Waiting for the Sun	1968	150.00
—White label promo			
❑ EKS-74024 [S]	Waiting for the Sun	1969	15.00
—Red labels with large stylized "E"			
❑ EKS-74024 [S]	Waiting for the Sun	1971	12.00
—Butterfly labels			
❑ EKS-74024 [S]	Waiting for the Sun	1980	10.00
—Red labels with Warner Communications logo in lower right			
❑ EKS-74024 [S]	Waiting for the Sun	1983	8.00
—Red and black labels			
❑ EKS-74079	13	1970	15.00
—Butterfly labels			
❑ EKS-74079	13	1980	10.00
—Red labels with Warner Communications logo in lower right			
❑ EKS-74079	13	1983	8.00
—Red and black labels			
❑ EKS-74079 [DJ]	13	1970	40.00
—White label promo			
❑ EKS-75005	The Soft Parade	1969	20.00
—Red labels with large stylized "E"			
❑ EKS-75005	The Soft Parade	1969	50.00
—Brown or tan labels			
❑ EKS-75005	The Soft Parade	1971	12.00
—Butterfly labels			
❑ EKS-75005	The Soft Parade	1980	10.00
—Red labels with Warner Communications logo in lower right			
❑ EKS-75005	The Soft Parade	1983	8.00
—Red and black labels			
❑ EKS-75007	Morrison Hotel	1970	25.00
—Red labels with large stylized "E"			
❑ EKS-75007	Morrison Hotel	1970	60.00
—Brown or tan labels			

Number	Title (A Side/B Side)	Yr	NM
❑ EKS-75007	Morrison Hotel	1971	12.00
—Butterfly labels			
❑ EKS-75007	Morrison Hotel	1980	10.00
—Red labels with Warner Communications logo in lower right			
❑ EKS-75007	Morrison Hotel	1983	8.00
—Red and black labels			
❑ EKS-75007 [DJ]	Morrison Hotel	1970	100.00
—White label promo			
❑ EKS-75011	L.A. Woman	197?	12.00
—Butterfly label, standard cover			
❑ EKS-75011	L.A. Woman	1971	50.00
—With see-through window on cover and yellow innersleeve with photo of Jim Morrison on a cross			
❑ EKS-75011	L.A. Woman	1980	10.00
—Red labels with Warner Communications logo in lower right			
❑ EKS-75011	L.A. Woman	1983	8.00
—Red and black labels			
❑ EKS-75011 [DJ]	L.A. Woman	1971	100.00
—White label promo			
❑ EKS-75017	Other Voices	1971	15.00
❑ EKS-75038	Full Circle	1972	15.00

MOBILE FIDELITY

Number	Title (A Side/B Side)	Yr	NM
❑ 1-051	The Doors	1980	80.00
—Audiophile vinyl			

DOOTONES, THE

45s

DOOTONE

Number	Title (A Side/B Side)	Yr	NM
❑ 366	Teller of Fortune/Ay Si Si	1955	200.00
❑ 470	Strange Love Affair/The Day You Said Goodbye	1962	30.00
❑ 471	Sailor Boy/Down the Road	1962	30.00

DORELLS, THE

45s

ATLANTIC

Number	Title (A Side/B Side)	Yr	NM
❑ 2244	Beating of My Heart/Maybe Baby	1964	15.00

GEI

Number	Title (A Side/B Side)	Yr	NM
❑ 4401	Beating of My Heart/Maybe Baby	1963	30.00

DORMAN, HAROLD

45s

RITA

Number	Title (A Side/B Side)	Yr	NM
❑ 1003	Mountain of Love/To Be with You	1960	25.00
❑ 1008	I'll Come Running/River of Tears	1960	20.00
❑ 1012	Moved to Kansas City/Take a Chance on Me	1960	20.00

SANTO

Number	Title (A Side/B Side)	Yr	NM
❑ 9005	In an Instant/There on Yonder Hill	1962	15.00
❑ 9051	Ain't Gonna Change/What Comes Next	1962	15.00

SUN

Number	Title (A Side/B Side)	Yr	NM
❑ 362	I'll Stick By You/There They Go	1961	20.00
❑ 370	Just One Step/Uncle Jonah's Place	1961	20.00
❑ 377	Wait 'Til Saturday Night/In the Beginning	1962	20.00

DORN, JERRY

45s

ARWIN

Number	Title (A Side/B Side)	Yr	NM
❑ 122	Brother, Can You Spare a Dime/Disappointed Lover	1959	12.00

FLING

Number	Title (A Side/B Side)	Yr	NM
❑ 711	Rocking Chair Rock/Prayer of Love	1959	50.00

KING

Number	Title (A Side/B Side)	Yr	NM
❑ 4932	Wishing Well/Sentimental Heaven	1956	80.00
❑ 4968	I'm So in Love with You/Nightmare	1956	15.00
❑ 5029	Quicksand/The Key	1957	15.00

DORRELLES, THE

45s

RSVP

Number	Title (A Side/B Side)	Yr	NM
❑ 1108	You Are/Good Luck to the Lucky Girl	1965	12.00

DORSAM, TOM

45s

LOREN

Number	Title (A Side/B Side)	Yr	NM
❑ 5001	Baby of Mine/(B-side unknown)	1964	500.00

DORSEY, GERRY See ENGELBERT HUMPERDINCK.

DORSEY, JACK

45s

PARKWAY

Number	Title (A Side/B Side)	Yr	NM
❑ 938	Ringo's Dog/March of the Gonks	1965	12.00

DORSEY, JIMMY

45s

COLUMBIA

Number	Title (A Side/B Side)	Yr	NM
❑ 1-426	Johnson Rag/Charlie, My Boy	1949	40.00
—Microgroove 33 1/3 rpm single, small hole			
❑ 1-449	I'll Hold You in My Arms Once More/Lost in a Dream	1950	40.00
—Microgroove 33 1/3 rpm single, small hole			
❑ 1-499	Rag Mop/That's a Plenty	1950	40.00
—Microgroove 33 1/3 rpm single, small hole			
❑ 1-554	Clap Hands (Here Comes Charlie)/When You Were a Tulip	1950	40.00
—Microgroove 33 1/3 rpm single, small hole			
❑ 1-700 (?)	It's a Long, Long Way to Tipperary/You Don't Have to Be a Baby to Cry	1950	40.00
—Microgroove 33 1/3 rpm single, small hole			
❑ 1-790 (?)	Let a Smile Be Your Umbrella/In a Little Spanish Town	1950	40.00
—Microgroove 33 1/3 rpm single, small hole			
❑ 1-865 (?)	Dixieland Band from Santa Claus Land/It's The Dreamer In Me	1950	40.00
—Microgroove 33 1/3 rpm single, small hole			
❑ 4-38654	Panama/Jazz Me Blues	1950	15.00
❑ 4-38655	Struttin' with Some Barbecue/Chimes Blues	1950	15.00
❑ 4-38656	High Society/Muskrat Ramble	1950	15.00
❑ 4-38657	South Rampart Street Parade/Tin Roof Blues	1950	15.00
—The above four comprise a box set			
❑ 4-39138	Lily of the Valley/By Heck	1950	20.00
❑ 4-39161	Clarinet Polka/Julida Polka	1951	12.00
❑ 4-39162	Acapulco Polka/Laugh Polka	1951	12.00
❑ 4-39163	Licorice Stick Polka/Helena Polka	1951	12.00
❑ 4-39164	We're Gonna Have Some Fun Tonight/Barbara Polka	1951	12.00
—The above four comprise a box set			
❑ 4-39258	Just for Tonight/Baby-O, Baby-O	1951	15.00
❑ 4-39477	Mine Alone/The World Your Balloon	1951	15.00
❑ 4-39526	A Kiss to Build a Dream On/Cherry Pink (And Apple Blossom White)	1951	15.00
❑ 4-39558	Step by Step/Young Folks Should Get Married	1951	15.00
❑ 4-39651	Wimoweh/I'll Always Be Following You	1952	15.00
❑ 4-39691	Confetti/No Other Love But Yours	1952	15.00
❑ 4-39728	Tell me True/The Night Is Filled with Echoes	1952	15.00
❑ 4-39896	Love Came Out of the Night/Hump Back Honey	1952	15.00

CORAL

Number	Title (A Side/B Side)	Yr	NM
❑ 9-60448	I Got Rhythm/Love Walked In	1951	15.00
❑ 9-60449	Love Is Here to Stay/Let's Call the Whole Thing Off	1951	15.00
❑ 9-60450	I Was Doing Alright/They Can't Take That Away from Me	1951	15.00
❑ 9-60451	Slap That Bass/They All Laughed	1951	15.00

DECCA

Number	Title (A Side/B Side)	Yr	NM
❑ 9-25119	The Breeze and I/Green Eyes (Aquellos Ojos Verdes)	1950	15.00
—Black label, lines on either side of "Decca"			
❑ 9-25120	Amapola (Pretty Little Poppy)/Maria Elena	1950	15.00
—Black label, lines on either side of "Decca"			
❑ 25121	Always in My Heart/Yours (Quiereme Mucho)	1961	7.00
—Black label with color bars			
❑ 9-25121	Always in My Heart/Yours (Quiereme Mucho)	1950	15.00
—Black label, lines on either side of "Decca"			
❑ 9-25121	Always in My Heart/Yours (Quiereme Mucho)	1955	12.00
—Black label, star under "Decca"			
❑ 9-25122	Brazil (Aquarela do Brasil)/At the Cross-Roads	1950	15.00
—Black label, lines on either side of "Decca"			
❑ 9-25255	It Happened in Hawaii/Tangerine	1950	15.00
—Black label, lines on either side of "Decca"			
❑ 9-28457	Always in My Heart/Yours (Quiereme Mucho)	1952	15.00
—Black label with lines on either side of "Decca"; reissue of two of his early 1940s hits on a 45			
❑ 32108	Arkansas Traveler/What's the Reason (I'm Not Pleasing You)	1967	8.00

DOT

Number	Title (A Side/B Side)	Yr	NM
❑ 128	So Rare/Jay Dee's Boogie Woogie	196?	8.00
—Black label with multicolor "Dot" logo			

FRATERNITY

Number	Title (A Side/B Side)	Yr	NM
❑ 755	So Rare/Sophisticated Swing	1957	15.00
❑ 777	June Night/Jay-Dee's Boogie Woogie	1957	12.00
❑ 797	When You Took Your Love/No One Ever Lost More	1958	12.00
❑ 816	Love on the Rocks/Under a Texas Moon	1958	12.00
❑ 868	Mambo en Sax/No One Ever Lost More	1960	10.00

GOLDIES 45

Number	Title (A Side/B Side)	Yr	NM
❑ 2716	So Rare/Jay Dee's Boogie Woogie	197?	5.00

GUSTO

Number	Title (A Side/B Side)	Yr	NM
❑ 2100	So Rare/Jay Dee's Boogie Woogie	197?	4.00

MCA

Number	Title (A Side/B Side)	Yr	NM
❑ 2716	So Rare/Jay Dee's Boogie Woogie	198?	3.00
—Blue label with rainbow			
❑ 60020	The Breeze and I/Green Eyes (Aquellos Ojos Verdes)	1973	5.00
—Black label with rainbow			
❑ 60021	Amapola (Pretty Little Poppy)/Maria Elena	1973	5.00
—Black label with rainbow			
❑ 60022	It Happened in Hawaii/Tangerine	1973	5.00
—Black label with rainbow			
❑ 60148	Always in My Heart/Yours (Quiereme Mucho)	1973	5.00
—Black label with rainbow			

MGM

Number	Title (A Side/B Side)	Yr	NM
❑ K11739	Angela Mia/Ballerina	1954	15.00

TRIP

Number	Title (A Side/B Side)	Yr	NM
❑ 176	So Rare/Jay Dee's Boogie Woogie	197?	5.00

Albums

LION

Number	Title (A Side/B Side)	Yr	NM
❑ L-70063 [M]	Jimmy Dorsey and His Orchestra	1958	20.00

DORSEY, LEE

45s

ABC

Number	Title (A Side/B Side)	Yr	NM
❑ 12326	Night People/Can I Be the One	1978	4.00
❑ 12361	God Must Have Blessed America/Say It Again	1978	4.00

ABC-PARAMOUNT

Number	Title (A Side/B Side)	Yr	NM
❑ 10192	Lottie Mo/Lover of Love	1961	15.00

ACE

Number	Title (A Side/B Side)	Yr	NM
❑ 640	Lonely Evening/Rock	1961	15.00

AMY

Number	Title (A Side/B Side)	Yr	NM
❑ 927	Ride Your Pony/The Kitty Cat Song	1965	8.00
❑ 939	Can You Hear Me/Work, Work, Work	1965	8.00
❑ 945	Get Out of My Life, Woman/So Long	1965	8.00
❑ 952	Confusion/The Neighbors' Daughter	1966	8.00
❑ 958	Working in the Coal Mine/Mexico	1966	10.00
❑ 965	Holy Cow/Operation Heartache	1966	8.00
❑ 974	Gotta Find a Job/Rain, Rain, Rain, Go Away	1967	6.00
❑ 987	My Old Car/Why Wait Until Tomorrow	1967	6.00
❑ 994	Can't Get Away/Vista Vista	1967	6.00
❑ 998	Go-Go Girl/I Can Hear You Callin'	1967	6.00
❑ 11010	I Can't Get Away/Cynthia	1968	6.00
❑ 11020	Wonder Woman/A Little Dab A Do Ya	1968	6.00
❑ 11031	Four Corners (Part 1)/Four Corners (Part 2)	1968	6.00
❑ 11048	I'm Gonna Sit Right Down/Little Ba-By	1968	6.00
❑ 11052	What Now My Love/A Lover Was Born	1969	6.00
❑ 11055	Everything I Do Gonna be Funky (From Now On)/There Should Be a Book	1969	6.00
❑ 11057	Give It Up/Candy Man	1969	6.00

BELL

Number	Title (A Side/B Side)	Yr	NM
❑ 908	I Can Hear You Callin'/What You Want	1970	5.00

CONSTELLATION

Number	Title (A Side/B Side)	Yr	NM
❑ 115	Organ Grinder's Swing/I Gotta Find a New Love	1964	20.00
❑ 135	You're Breaking Me Up/Messed Around and Fell in Love	1964	20.00

FURY

Number	Title (A Side/B Side)	Yr	NM
❑ 1053	Ya Ya/Give Me You	1961	15.00
❑ 1056	Do-Re-Mi/People Gonna' Talk	1961	12.00
❑ 1061	Eenie Meenie Miny Moe/Behind the 8-Ball	1962	12.00
❑ 1066	You Are My Sunshine/Give Me Your Love	1962	12.00

Except when noted otherwise, VG = 25% of NM, and VG+ = 50% of NM. (Example: VG = $2.00, VG+ = $4.00 and NM = $8.00.)

Number	Title (A Side/B Side)	Yr	NM
❑ 1074	Hoodlum Joe/When I Met My Baby	1963	12.00
LOST-NITE			
❑ 385	Ya Ya/Give Me You	197?	5.00
—Reissue			
POLYDOR			
❑ 14038	Yes We Can — Part 1/ O Me O, My O	1970	5.00
❑ 14055	Sneakin' Sally Through the Alley/ Tears, Tears and More Tears	1971	5.00
❑ 14106	Freedom for the Stallion/ If She Won't (Find Someone Who Will)	1971	5.00
❑ 14147	When Can I Come Home/ Gator Tail	1972	5.00
❑ 14181	On Your Way Down/ Freedom for the Stallion	1973	5.00
REX			
❑ 1005	Rock/Lonely Evening	1959	25.00
SANSU			
❑ 474	Love Lots of Lovin'/ Take Care of Our Love	1967	12.00
—With Betty Harris			
SMASH			
❑ 1842	Hello Good Looking/Someday	1963	10.00
SPRING			
❑ 114	Occapella/Tears, Tears and More Tears	1971	5.00
VALIANT			
❑ 1001	Lottie Mo/Lover of Love	1958	40.00
Albums			
AMY			
❑ 8010 [M]	Ride Your Pony	1966	30.00
❑ 8010-S [S]	Ride Your Pony	1966	40.00
❑ 8011 [M]	The New Lee Dorsey/Working in the Coal Mine-Holy Cow	1966	25.00
❑ 8011-S [S]	The New Lee Dorsey/Working in the Coal Mine-Holy Cow	1966	30.00
ARISTA			
❑ AL 8387	Holy Cow! The Best of Lee Dorsey	1985	10.00
FURY			
❑ 1002 [M]	Ya Ya	1962	300.00
POLYDOR			
❑ 24-4024	Yes We Can	1970	12.00
SPHERE SOUND			
❑ SR-7003 [M]	Ya Ya	196?	100.00
—Reissue of Fury 1002			
❑ SSR-7003 [R]	Ya Ya	196?	50.00
—Rechanneled reissue of Fury 1002			

DOTS, THE

Number	Title (A Side/B Side)	Yr	NM
45s			
CADDY			
❑ 101	I Confess/I Wish I Could Meet You	1956	80.00
❑ 107	I Lost You/Johnny	1957	80.00
❑ 111	Good Luck to You/Heartsick and Lonely	1957	80.00
REV			
❑ 3512	Ring Chimes/Wolf Call	1958	1500.

DOTTIE AND MILLIE

Number	Title (A Side/B Side)	Yr	NM
45s			
TOPPER			
❑ 1014	Talkin' About My Baby/ Nothing in This World	196?	300.00

DOTTY AND DAN

Number	Title (A Side/B Side)	Yr	NM
45s			
HIT			
❑ 89	I'm Leaving It Up to You/ Down at Papa Joe's	1963	8.00
—B-side by the Tennessee Six and Four More			
❑ 108	Stop and Think It Over/Navy Blue	1964	8.00
—B-side by Connie Dee			

DOUBLE SIX OF PARIS, THE

Number	Title (A Side/B Side)	Yr	NM
45s			
CAPITOL			
❑ 4394	French Rat Race/ Meet Benny Bailey	1960	15.00
PHILIPS			
❑ 40192	One Mint Julep/Hallelujah I Love Her So	1964	25.00
❑ 40220	Lonely Avenue/Sherri	1964	25.00
Albums			
CAPITOL			
❑ ST 10259 [S]	The Double Six of Paris	1961	100.00
❑ T 10259 [M]	The Double Six of Paris	1961	80.00
PHILIPS			
❑ PHM 200026 [M]	Swingin' Singin'	1962	40.00
❑ PHM 200141 [M]	The Double Six of Paris Sings Ray Charles	1964	100.00
❑ PHS 600026 [S]	Swingin' Singin'	1962	60.00
❑ PHS 600141 [S]	The Double Six of Paris Sings Ray Charles	1964	150.00

DOUGLAS, CARL

Number	Title (A Side/B Side)	Yr	NM
45s			
OKEH			
❑ 7268	Crazy Feeling/Keep It to Myself	1966	12.00
❑ 7287	Let the Birds Sing/ Something for Nothing	1967	12.00
20TH CENTURY			
❑ 2140	Kung Fu Fighting/Gamblin' Man	1974	4.00
❑ 2168	Dance the Kung Fu/ Changing Times	1975	4.00
❑ 2179	Blue Eyed Soul (Part 1)/ Blue Eyed Soul (Part 2)	1975	4.00
❑ 2192	Witchfinder General/Never Had This Dream Before	1975	4.00
Albums			
20TH CENTURY			
❑ T-464	Kung Fu Fighting and Other Great Love Songs	1974	12.00

DOUGLAS, CAROL

Number	Title (A Side/B Side)	Yr	NM
12-Inch Singles			
MIDSONG INT'L.			
❑ L33-1975 [DJ]	Night Fever (6:20) (same on both sides)	1978	10.00
❑ 13905	Night Fever/Let You Come Into My Life	1978	12.00
45s			
MIDLAND INT'L.			
❑ MB-10113	Doctor's Orders/Baby, Don't Let This Good Love Die	1974	4.00
❑ MB-10229	Hurricane Is Coming Tonight/ I Fell in Love with You	1975	4.00
❑ MB-10304	Will We Make It Tonight/Take Me (Make Me Lose Control)	1975	4.00
❑ MB-10372	Headline News/Boy, YouKnow Just What I'm After	1975	4.00
❑ MB-10753	Midnight Love Affair/Midnight Love Affair (Long Version)	1976	4.00
❑ MB-10870	Dancing Queen/In the Morning	1976	4.00
❑ MB-10979	We Do It/Lie to Me	1977	4.00
MIDSONG INT'L.			
❑ 1008	I Got the Answer/ We're Gonna Make It	1979	4.00
❑ 40860	Night Fever/Let You Come Into My Life	1978	4.00
—A-side appeared in the movie Saturday Night Fever, but not on the soundtrack LP			
❑ 40912	So You Win Again/Let You Come Into My Life	1978	4.00
❑ 40945	Let's Get Down to Doin' It Tonight/Burnin'	1978	4.00
RCA VICTOR			
❑ GB-10479	Doctor's Orders/Baby, Don't Let This Good Love Die	1975	3.00
—Gold Standard Series			
20TH CENTURY			
❑ 2484	Slip Into Something Comfortable/ My Simple Heart	1981	3.00
Albums			
MIDLAND INT'L.			
❑ BKL1-0931	The Carol Douglas Album	1975	10.00
❑ BKL1-1798	Midnight Love Affair	1976	10.00
❑ BKL1-2222	Full Bloom	1977	10.00
MIDSONG INT'L.			
❑ 3048	Burnin'	1978	10.00
❑ W 36852	The Best of Carol Douglas	1980	10.00

DOUGLAS, CRAIG

Number	Title (A Side/B Side)	Yr	NM
45s			
BETHLEHEM			
❑ 3057	When My Little Girl Is Smiling/ Ring-a-Ding	1963	12.00
EMBASSY			
❑ 202	No Greater Love/We'll Have a Lot to Tell	1962	12.00
JARO			
❑ 77016	My First Love Affair/ What Do You Want	1960	12.00
❑ 77030	Heart of a Teenage Girl/New Boy	1960	12.00
LONDON			
❑ 9611	Danke Schoen/Love Her While She's Young	1963	12.00
TCF HALL			
❑ 107	Around the Corner/Find the Girl	1965	10.00

DOUGLAS, KELLIE

Number	Title (A Side/B Side)	Yr	NM
45s			
RCA VICTOR			
❑ 47-8005	My Mama Don't Like Him/ Big Hunky Baby	1962	12.00

DOUGLAS, KIRK

Number	Title (A Side/B Side)	Yr	NM
45s			
DECCA			
❑ 29355	A Whale of a Tale/The Moon Grew Brighter and Brighter	1954	25.00

DOUGLAS, LEW

Number	Title (A Side/B Side)	Yr	NM
45s			
CARLTON			
❑ 533	Theme from "The Angel Wore Red"/"From the Terrace" Love Theme	1960	10.00
Albums			
CARLTON			
❑ LP 12-126 [M]	Themes from Motion Pictures and TV	1960	25.00

DOUGLAS, MIKE

Number	Title (A Side/B Side)	Yr	NM
45s			
ATLANTIC			
❑ 3328	Philadelphia/Smile, Smile, Smile	1976	4.00
❑ 3344	Loneliness/Dancin' Again	1976	4.00
BLUE RIVER			
❑ 220	Tonight/High on a Hill	196?	8.00
DECCA			
❑ 32495	The Day After Forever/ Someday You'll Be Sorry	1969	5.00
❑ 32567	Jean/Rainbow of Love	1969	5.00
❑ 32618	That's a Woman/Tell Me Why, Why Don't You Cry	1970	5.00
EPIC			
❑ 9876	The Men in My Little Girl's Life/ Stranger on the Shore	1965	6.00
❑ 10002	Here's to My Jenny/While We're Young	1966	6.00
❑ 10041	The Parents of the Kids in Love/ Real Love	1966	6.00
❑ 10041 [PS]	The Parents of the Kids in Love/ Real Love	1966	8.00
❑ 10078	Cabaret/House of Love	1966	6.00
❑ 10089	Touch Hands on Christmas Morning/(The Story Of) The First Christmas Carol	1966	12.00
❑ 10126	What Is a Square/That's How Love Goes	1967	6.00
❑ 10132	Galway/A Little Town in Old County Down	1967	6.00
❑ 10170	Here Comes My Baby Back Again/Someone Took the Sweetness Out of Sweetheart	1967	6.00
❑ 10223	Father of the Bride/Hold Me	1967	6.00
❑ JZSP 135100/1 [DJ]	Silver Bells (mono/stereo)	1967	10.00
MGM			
❑ 14337	For a Little While/ Heaven Everyday	1971	4.00
❑ 14453	Ole Buttermilk Sky/ Wonderful World	1972	4.00
❑ 14508	High Hopes/Song for Erik	1973	4.00
PROJECT 3			
❑ 1335	Do Unto Others/Young at Heart	1968	6.00
—With Pearl Bailey			
STAX			
❑ 0211	Birthday Song/Mother's Day	1974	4.00
Albums			
ATLANTIC			
❑ SD 18168	Mike Douglas Sings It All	1976	10.00
EPIC			
❑ LN 24169 [M]	It's Time for Mike Douglas	1965	12.00
❑ LN 24179 [M]	You Don't Have to Be Irish	1965	12.00
❑ LN 24186 [M]	The Men in My Little Girl's Life	1966	12.00
❑ LN 24205 [M]	Dear Mike, Please Sing	1966	12.00
❑ LN 24322 [M]	My Kind of Christmas	1967	12.00
❑ BN 26169 [S]	It's Time for Mike Douglas	1965	15.00
❑ BN 26179 [S]	You Don't Have to Be Irish	1965	15.00
❑ BN 26186 [S]	The Men in My Little Girl's Life	1966	15.00
❑ BN 26205 [S]	Dear Mike, Please Sing	1966	15.00
❑ BN 26322 [S]	My Kind of Christmas	1967	12.00
HARMONY			
❑ HS 11263	Young at Heart	1968	12.00
WORD			
❑ WR-8791	I'll Sing This Song for You	197?	10.00
❑ 8815	Christmas Album	198?	10.00

DOUGLAS, SCOTT, AND THE VENTURE QUINTET
See THE VENTURES.

DOUGLAS, STEVE

45s

Number	Title (A Side/B Side)	Yr	NM
CAPITOL			
❑ 5527	Yesterday (Part 1)/ Yesterday (Part 2)	1965	12.00
GRAPEVINE			
❑ 601	Rockin' Green Sleeves/ (B-side unknown)	1961	20.00
MGM			
❑ 13218	Snowplows Schussing (Part 1)/ Snowplows Schussing (Part 2)	1964	12.00
PHILLES			
❑ 104	Yes Sir, That's My Baby/ Lt. Col. Bogey's Parade	1962	25.00
TANDEM			
❑ 7000	Magic Sound/There You Go	1961	20.00

Albums

Number	Title (A Side/B Side)	Yr	NM
CROWN			
❑ CLP-5251 [M]	Twist with Steve Douglas and the Rebel Rousers	1962	20.00
MERCURY			
❑ SR-61217	Reflections in a Golden Horn	1969	25.00

DOUGLAS, STEVE

45s

Number	Title (A Side/B Side)	Yr	NM
TEXAS OPRY			
❑ 588	Tyke (The Christmas Elf)/ (Instrumental)	198?	8.00

DOUGLAS, WAYNE
See DOUG SAHM.

DOVAL, JIM, AND THE GAUCHOS

45s

Number	Title (A Side/B Side)	Yr	NM
ABC-PARAMOUNT			
❑ 10621	Annie Ya Ya/Out of Sight	1965	10.00
❑ 10637	I Know You're Fooling Around/ Uptown Caballero	1965	10.00
DIPLOMACY			
❑ 3	Donna/The Scrub	1964	20.00
❑ 5	Stranded in the Pool/Right Now	1964	20.00
❑ 6	Beatles Rule/Pink Elephant	1964	25.00
❑ 7	She's a Very Nice Girl/ Bony Moronie	1964	100.00
❑ 8	The Good and the Bad/ Fireballed	1965	20.00
❑ 17	She's So Fine/Mama, Keep Your Big Mouth Shut	1965	20.00
❑ 1000	Love Me One More Time (Part 1)/ Love Me One More Time (Part 2)	1963	20.00
—As "Jim SanDoval and the Gauchos"			
DOT			
❑ 16468	Fire Ball/Good and Bad	1963	15.00
❑ 16548	Love Me One More Time (Part 1)/ Love Me One More Time (Part 2)	1963	15.00
❑ 16571	Barracuda/The Scrub	1964	15.00

Albums

Number	Title (A Side/B Side)	Yr	NM
ABC-PARAMOUNT			
❑ ABC-506 [M]	The Gauchos Featuring Jim Doval	1965	30.00
❑ ABCS-506 [S]	The Gauchos Featuring Jim Doval	1965	40.00

DOVE, RONNIE

45s

Number	Title (A Side/B Side)	Yr	NM
DECCA			
❑ 31288	Party Doll/Yes Darling, I'll Be Around	1961	200.00
—Price is for stock copy; promos go for 20 to 25 percent of this value			
❑ 32853	Just the Other Side of Nowhere/ If I Cried	1971	6.00
❑ 32919	Kiss the Hurt Away/He Cries Like a Baby	1972	6.00
❑ 32997	It's No Sin/My World of Memories	1972	6.00
❑ 33038	Lilacs in Winter/Is It Wrong	1972	6.00
DIAMOND			
❑ 163	Sweeter Than Sugar/I Believed in You	1964	10.00
❑ 167	Say You/Let Me Stay Today	1964	10.00
❑ 173	Right or Wrong/Baby Put Your Arms Around Me	1964	8.00
❑ 176	Hello Pretty Girl/Keep It a Secret	1965	8.00
❑ 179	One Kiss for Old Times' Sake/ Bluebird	1965	8.00
❑ 179	One Kiss for Old Times' Sake/ No Greater Love	1965	8.00
❑ 184	A Little Bit of Heaven/ If I Live to Be a Hundred	1965	8.00
❑ 188	I'll Make All Your Dreams Come True/I Had to Lose You	1965	8.00
❑ 191	Kiss Away/Where in the World	1965	8.00
❑ 195	When Liking Turns to Loving/ I'm Learning How to Smile Again	1965	8.00
❑ 198	Let's Start All Over Again/ That Empty Feeling	1966	8.00
❑ 205	Happy Summer Days/Long After	1966	8.00
❑ 205 [PS]	Happy Summer Days/Long After	1966	15.00
❑ 208	I Really Don't Want to Know/ Years of Tears	1966	8.00
❑ 214	Cry/Autumn Rhapsody	1966	8.00
❑ 217	One More Mountain to Climb/All	1967	8.00
❑ 221	My Babe/Put My Mind at Ease	1967	10.00
—A-side written and produced by Neil Diamond			
❑ 227	I Want to Love You for What You Are/I Thank You for Your Love	1967	8.00
❑ 233	Dancin' Out of My Heart/ Back from Baltimore	1967	20.00
—B-side written and produced by Neil Diamond, who also supplies backing vocals			
❑ 240	In Some Time/ Livin' for Your Lovin'	1968	8.00
❑ 244	Mountain of Love/ Never Gonna Cry	1968	8.00
❑ 249	Tomboy/Tell Me Tomorrow	1968	8.00
❑ 256	What's Wrong with My World/ That Empty Feeling	1969	6.00
❑ 260	I Need You Now/Bluebird	1969	6.00
❑ 271	Chains of Love/If I Live to Be a Hundred	1970	15.00
—Promos, with "Chains of Love" on both sides, go for about half this amount			
❑ 378	Heart (same on both sides)	1987	10.00
❑ 378	Heart/Old Time Rock and Roll	1987	20.00
—The version with a B-side is much harder to find than the version with the same song on both sides; also, this version was not issued with a picture sleeve			
❑ 378 [PS]	Heart (same on both sides)	1987	20.00
❑ 379	Rise and Shine/ (B-side unknown)	1987	5.00
DOVE			
❑ 1021	Lover Boy/I'll Be Around	1959	4000.
—As "Ronnie Dove and the Bell-Tones". VG 1500; VG+ 2750			
HITSVILLE			
❑ 6038	Tragedy/Songs We Sang As Children	1976	5.00
❑ 6045	The Morning After the Night Before/Why Daddy	1976	5.00
JALO			
❑ 1406	No Greater Love/Saddest Hour	1962	25.00
M.C.			
❑ 5013	The Angel in Your Eyes (Brings Out the Devil in Me)/ Songs We Sang As Children	1978	6.00
MCA			
❑ 40106	So Long Dixie/Take My Love	1973	5.00
MELODYLAND			
❑ 6004	Please Come to Nashville/ Pictures on Paper	1975	5.00
❑ 6011	Things/Here We Go Again	1975	5.00
❑ 6021	Drina (Take Your Lady Off for Me)/Your Sweet Love	1975	5.00
❑ 6030	Right or Wrong/Guns	1976	5.00

Albums

Number	Title (A Side/B Side)	Yr	NM
DIAMOND			
❑ D 5002 [M]	Right or Wrong	1964	20.00
❑ DS 5002 [S]	Right or Wrong	1964	25.00
❑ D 5003 [M]	One Kiss for Old Times' Sake	1965	20.00
❑ DS 5003 [S]	One Kiss for Old Times' Sake	1965	25.00
❑ D 5004 [M]	I'll Make All Your Dreams Come True	1965	20.00
❑ DS 5004 [S]	I'll Make All Your Dreams Come True	1965	25.00
❑ D 5005 [M]	The Best of Ronnie Dove	1966	15.00
❑ DS 5005 [S]	The Best of Ronnie Dove	1966	20.00
❑ D 5006 [M]	Ronnie Dove Sings the Hits for You	1966	15.00
❑ DS 5006 [S]	Ronnie Dove Sings the Hits for You	1966	20.00
❑ D 5007 [M]	Cry	1967	15.00
❑ DS 5007 [S]	Cry	1967	20.00
❑ D-5008 [M]	The Best of Ronnie Dove — Vol. 2	1968	30.00
❑ SD-5008 [S]	The Best of Ronnie Dove — Vol. 2	1968	15.00
POWER PAK			
❑ 286	Greatest Hits	1975	12.00

DOVELLS, THE
Also see LEN BARRY.

45s

Number	Title (A Side/B Side)	Yr	NM
ABKCO			
❑ 4011	Bristol Stomp/You Can't Sit Down	1972	4.00
❑ 4029	Baby Workout/Hully Gully Baby	1973	10.00
❑ 4032	Bristol Twistin' Annie/ Betty in Bermudas	1973	4.00
EVENT			
❑ 216	Dancing in the Street/ Back on the Road Again	1974	5.00
❑ 3310	Roll Over Beethoven/ Something About You Boy	1970	5.00
JAMIE			
❑ 1369	Our Winter Love/Blue	1969	10.00
MGM			
❑ 13628	There's a Girl/Love Is Everywhere	1966	10.00
❑ 14568	Don't Vote for Luke McCabe/ Mary's Magic Show	1973	5.00
PARAMOUNT			
❑ 0134	L-O-V-E Love/We're All In This Together	1971	5.00
PARKWAY			
❑ 819	No, No, No/Letters of Love	1961	20.00
❑ 827	Bristol Stomp/Letters of Love	1961	15.00
❑ 827	Bristol Stomp/Out in the Cold Again	1961	30.00
❑ 833	Do the New Continental/ Mope-Itty Mope Stomp	1962	15.00
❑ 833 [PS]	Do the New Continental/ Mope-Itty Mope Stomp	1962	30.00
❑ 838	Bristol Twistin' Annie/The Actor	1962	15.00
❑ 838 [PS]	Bristol Twistin' Annie/The Actor	1962	30.00
❑ 845	Hully Gully Baby/ Your Last Chance	1962	15.00
❑ 845 [PS]	Hully Gully Baby/ Your Last Chance	1962	30.00
❑ 855	The Jitterbug/Kissin' in the Kitchen	1962	15.00
❑ 855 [PS]	The Jitterbug/Kissin' in the Kitchen	1962	30.00
❑ 861	Save Me Baby/You Can't Run Away from Yourself	1963	20.00
❑ 861 [PS]	Save Me Baby/You Can't Run Away from Yourself	1963	30.00
❑ 867	You Can't Sit Down/Stompin' Everywhere	1963	12.00
❑ 867	You Can't Sit Down/ Wildwood Days	1963	15.00
❑ 867 [PS]	You Can't Sit Down/ Stompin' Everywhere	1963	40.00
❑ 867 [PS]	You Can't Sit Down/ Wildwood Days	1963	40.00
❑ 882	Betty in Bermudas/ Dance the Froog	1963	12.00
❑ 882 [PS]	Betty in Bermudas/ Dance the Froog	1963	30.00
❑ 889	Stop Monkeyin' Aroun'/ No, No, No	1963	12.00
❑ 889 [PS]	Stop Monkeyin' Aroun'/ No, No, No	1963	30.00
❑ 901	Be My Girl/Dragster on the Prowl	1964	20.00
❑ 911	One Potato/Happy Birthday Just the Same	1964	15.00
❑ 925	Watusi with Lucy/What in the World's Come Over You	1964	12.00
❑ 925 [PS]	Watusi with Lucy/What in the World's Come Over You	1964	30.00
SWAN			
❑ 4231	Happy/(Hey, Hey, Hey) Alright	1965	20.00
VERVE			
❑ 10701	Far Away/Sometimes	1973	5.00

Albums

Number	Title (A Side/B Side)	Yr	NM
CAMEO			
❑ C-1082 [M]	Len Barry Sings with the Dovells	1965	30.00
❑ SC-1082 [S]	Len Barry Sings with the Dovells	1965	50.00
PARKWAY			
❑ P 7006 [M]	The Bristol Stomp	1961	80.00
—Light orange label			
❑ P 7006 [M]	The Bristol Stomp	1962	50.00
—Dark orange and yellow label			
❑ P 7010 [M]	All the Hits of the Teen Groups	1962	50.00
❑ P 7021 [M]	For Your Hully Gully Party	1962	50.00
❑ P 7025 [M]	You Can't Sit Down	1963	50.00
WYNCOTE			
❑ SW 9052 [R]	Discotheque	1965	15.00
❑ W 9052 [M]	Discotheque	1965	20.00
❑ SW 9114 [R]	The Dovells' Biggest Hits	1965	15.00
❑ W 9114 [M]	The Dovells' Biggest Hits	1965	20.00

Except when noted otherwise, VG = 25% of NM, and VG+ = 50% of NM. (Example: VG = $2.00, VG+ = $4.00 and NM = $8.00.)

DOVER, NEAL

45s

Number	Title (A Side/B Side)	Yr	NM
DIAMOND			
❑ 270	Mr. Bus Driver/Paper Man	1970	25.00

DOWD, LARRY

45s

Number	Title (A Side/B Side)	Yr	NM
SPINNING			
❑ 6004	Why, Oh Why/Forbidden Love	1958	25.00
❑ 6009	Blue Swinging Mama/ Pink Cadillac	1959	150.00

DOWELL, JOE

45s

Number	Title (A Side/B Side)	Yr	NM
JOURNEY			
❑ 1238 [DJ]	Homeward on the Wind (mono/stereo)	1973	6.00
—Stock copy not known to exist			
❑ 1238 [PS]	Homeward on the Wind (mono/stereo)	1973	6.00
MONUMENT			
❑ 952	If I Could Find Out What Is Wrong/Indian Summer Days	1966	8.00
SMASH			
❑ 1708	Wooden Heart/Little Bo Peep	1961	15.00
❑ 1708 [PS]	Wooden Heart/Little Bo Peep	1961	25.00
❑ 1717	The Bridge of Love/Just Love Me	1961	12.00
❑ 1717 [PS]	The Bridge of Love/Just Love Me	1961	16.00
❑ 1728	(I Wonder) Who's Spending Christmas with You/ A Kiss for Christmas	1961	15.00
❑ 1730	The Sound of Sadness/ The Thorn on the Rose	1962	12.00
❑ 1759	Little Red Rented Rowboat/ The One I Left for You	1962	12.00
❑ 1759 [PS]	Little Red Rented Rowboat/ The One I Left for You	1962	12.00
❑ 1786	Poor Little Cupid/No Secrets	1962	12.00
❑ 1786 [PS]	Poor Little Cupid/No Secrets	1962	16.00
❑ 1799	Our School Days/ Bringa-Branga-Brought	1963	12.00
❑ 1799 [PS]	Our School Days/ Bringa-Branga-Brought	1963	16.00
❑ 1816	Bobby Blue Loves Linda Lou/My Darling Wears White Today	1963	12.00
❑ 1816 [PS]	Bobby Blue Loves Linda Lou/My Darling Wears White Today	1963	16.00

Albums

Number	Title (A Side/B Side)	Yr	NM
SMASH			
❑ MGS-27000 [M]	Wooden Heart	1961	40.00
❑ MGS-27011 [M]	German American Hits	1962	25.00
❑ SRS-67000 [S]	Wooden Heart	1961	50.00
❑ SRS-67011 [S]	German American Hits	1962	30.00
WING			
❑ MGW-12328 [M]	Wooden Heart	196?	20.00
❑ SRW-16328 [S]	Wooden Heart	196?	20.00

DOWLANDS, THE

45s

Number	Title (A Side/B Side)	Yr	NM
TOLLIE			
❑ 9002	All My Loving/Hey Sally	1964	15.00

DOWNBEATS, THE (1)

45s

Number	Title (A Side/B Side)	Yr	NM
GEE			
❑ 1019	My Girl/China Girl	1956	800.00
—Red label			
❑ 1019	My Girl/China Girl	1958	30.00
—Gray label			
PEACOCK			
❑ 1689	You're So Fine/Someday She'll Come Along	1958	25.00

DOWNBEATS, THE (2)

45s

Number	Title (A Side/B Side)	Yr	NM
SARG			
❑ 168	Darling of Mine/Come On Over	1959	40.00
❑ 173	Run to Me Baby/ I Need Your Love	1959	40.00
❑ 197	Falling Stars/I Just Can't Understand	1960	40.00
—As "O.S. Grant and the Downbeats"			
❑ 200	You Did Me Wrong/This Woman I Love	1960	40.00
❑ 223	Greyhound (Part 1)/ Greyhound (Part 2)	196?	20.00
❑ 228	Grant's Soul Blues/ Sock It Uptight	196?	20.00
❑ 233	Soul Bag/Dardling Dear	196?	20.00
—As "O.S. Grant and the Downbeats"			

DOWNBEATS, THE (3)

If the record in question is on the TAMLA or V.I.P. label, see THE ELGINS.

DOWNBEATS, THE (4)

45s

Number	Title (A Side/B Side)	Yr	NM
WILCO			
❑ 9	Alfalfa/Red X	1960	20.00
❑ 16	Playin' Possum/One at a Time	1960	20.00

DOWNEY, MORTON, JR.

45s

Number	Title (A Side/B Side)	Yr	NM
ARTISTS OF AMERICA			
❑ 109	He Played a Yo-Yo in Nashville/ You'll Never Have to Ask Me If I Love You	1976	5.00
—As "Sean Morton Downey"			
❑ 123	He Played a Yo-Yo in Nashville/ You'll Never Have to Ask Me If I Love You	1976	4.00
—As "Sean Morton Downey"			
❑ 124	You Made Me Love You/As Time Goes By	1976	4.00
—As "Sean Morton Downey"			
BULLDOG			
❑ 105	A Tear Fell in the Chapel/ Tender Years	1959	15.00
—As "Sean Downey"			
CADENCE			
❑ 1407	The Ballad of Billy Brown/ Flattery	1961	10.00
CONTENDER			
❑ 1317	Love Bug/Rags to Riches	1959	15.00
CUB			
❑ 9004	You Let Go/Hearts Are Wild	1958	12.00
—As "Sean Downey"			
ESO			
❑ 932	Green Eyed Girl/ (B-side unknown)	1981	8.00
—As "Sean Morton Downey"			
IMPERIAL			
❑ 5556	Boulevard of Broken Dreams/ Proud Possession	1958	10.00
LAKE ERIE			
❑ (# unknown)	Cleveland's Coming Back Again/(B-side unknown)	197?	8.00
MAGIC LAMP			
❑ 517	The Ballad of Billy Brown/Flattery	1964	8.00
NRLC			
❑ 1977	Got a Right to Live/ Theme for Life	197?	6.00
PERSONALITY			
❑ 3506	Little Miss U.S.A./Football Freddy	1959	12.00
PRIVATE STOCK			
❑ 45,168	Family Tree/Spanish Harlem	1977	4.00
SCEPTER			
❑ 12316	Love Theme from Christine/ Christine's a Lady	1971	6.00
—As "Sean Morton Downey, Jr."			
❑ 12360	Break the Habit of Hate/ Second Chance Lord	1972	6.00
—As "Sean Downey"			
STAX			
❑ 0195	I Believe in America/ My Last Day on Earth	1974	4.00
—As "Sean Downey"			
WYE			
❑ 1010	I Beg Your Pardon/Three Steps to the Phone	1961	12.00

Albums

Number	Title (A Side/B Side)	Yr	NM
ARTISTS OF AMERICA			
❑ AOA-5005	You'll Never Ask Me If I Love You	1976	12.00
COMPOSE			
❑ 9901	Morton Downey Jr. Sings!	1989	15.00

DOWNEY, PAUL

45s

Number	Title (A Side/B Side)	Yr	NM
HICKORY			
❑ 1632	Camp Meeting, U.S.A./Love	1972	7.00

DOWNEY, SEAN; DOWNEY, SEAN MORTON

See MORTON DOWNEY, JR.

DOWNING, BIG AL

45s

Number	Title (A Side/B Side)	Yr	NM
CARLTON			
❑ 489	Miss Lucy/Just Around the Corner	1959	50.00
❑ 507	It Must Be Love/When My Blue Moon Turns to Gold Again	1959	40.00
CHALLENGE			
❑ 59006	Down on the Farm/Oh Babe	1958	50.00
CHESS			
❑ 1817	The Story of My Life/ I'd Love to Be Loved	1962	12.00
❑ 2158	I'll Be Holding On/ Baby Let's Talk It Over	1974	5.00
COLUMBIA			
❑ 43028	I'm Just Nobody/All I Want Is You	1964	10.00
❑ 43185	I Feel Good/Georgia Slop	1964	10.00
DOOR KNOB			
❑ 328	I Guess By Now/ (B-side unknown)	1989	5.00
❑ 340	Bound for Baltimore/ (B-side unknown)	1989	5.00
❑ 345	Father #1/(B-side unknown)	1989	5.00
JANUS			
❑ 211	Thank You Baby/ (B-side unknown)	1974	6.00
❑ 234	I'll Be Holding On/Hands	1974	6.00
LENOX			
❑ 5565	You Never Miss Your Water (Till the Well Runs Dry)/ If You Want It (I Got It)	1963	12.00
—As "Little Esther Phillips and Big Al Downing"			
❑ 5572	Mr. Hurt Walked In/If I Had Our Love to Live Over	1963	12.00
POLYDOR			
❑ 14311	I Love to Love/I'm Just Nobody	1976	5.00
SILVER FOX			
❑ 3	Cornbreak Row/The Saints	1969	8.00
❑ 11	Medley of Soul/These Arms You Push Away	1969	8.00
TEAM			
❑ 1001	I'll Be Loving You/Don't Mess with an Angel	1982	5.00
❑ 1002	Darlene/(B-side unknown)	1982	5.00
❑ 1003	Let's Sing About Love/We Can Only Say Goodbye	1983	5.00
❑ 1004	It Takes Love/If You're Leaving	1983	5.00
❑ 1007	The Best of Families/ Fool of the Year	1983	5.00
❑ 1008	There'll Never Be a Better Night for Bein' Wrong/ (B-side unknown)	1984	5.00
V-TONE			
❑ 215	Yes, I'm Loving You/ Please Come Home	1960	12.00
❑ 220	If I Had Our Love to Live Over/ Words of Love	1961	12.00
❑ 230	So Many Memories/ There'll Come a Time	1961	12.00
VINE ST.			
❑ 103	How Beautiful You Are (To Me)/ The Only Thing Missing Is You	1986	6.00
❑ 105	Just One Night Won't Do/How Beautiful You Are (To Me)	1987	6.00
❑ 106	How Ya Gonna Do It/The Only Thing Missing Is You	1987	6.00
WARNER BROS.			
❑ 8716	Mr. Jones/I Don't Cry (The Onion Song)	1978	5.00
❑ 8787	Touch Me (I'll Be Your Fool Once More)/I Ain't No Fool	1979	5.00
❑ 49034	Midnight Lace/Counting Highway Signs	1979	4.00
❑ 49141	I Ain't No Fool/Mr, Jones	1979	4.00
❑ 49161	The Story Behind the Story/ Daddy Played the Banjo	1980	4.00
❑ 49270	Bring It On Home/ Beer Drinking People	1980	4.00
WHITE ROCK			
❑ 1111	Down on the Farm/Oh Babe	1958	150.00
❑ 1113	Miss Lucy/Just Around the Corner	1958	150.00

Albums

Number	Title (A Side/B Side)	Yr	NM
TEAM			
❑ 2001	Big Al Downing	1982	12.00

DOWNLINERS SECT, THE

45s

Number	Title (A Side/B Side)	Yr	NM
SMASH			
❑ 1954	Little Egypt/I Feel Good	1965	12.00

DOWNS, HUGH

Albums

Number	Title (A Side/B Side)	Yr	NM
EPIC			
❑ BN 541 [S]	An Evening with Hugh Downs	1961	30.00
❑ LN 3597 [M]	An Evening with Hugh Downs	1961	25.00

DOYLE, BOBBY, THREE
KENNY ROGERS was in this group.

Number	Title (A Side/B Side)	Yr	NM
Albums			
COLUMBIA			
❑ CL 1858 [M]	In a Most Unusual Way	1962	40.00
❑ CS 8658 [S]	In a Most Unusual Way	1962	50.00

DOYLE, MIKE

Number	Title (A Side/B Side)	Yr	NM
Albums			
FLEETWOOD			
❑ FLP-3018 [M]	The Secrets of Surfing	1963	120.00

DOZIER, GENE, AND THE BROTHERHOOD

Number	Title (A Side/B Side)	Yr	NM
45s			
MINIT			
❑ 32026	House of Funk/One for Bess	1967	10.00
❑ 32031	I Wanna Testify/Mustang Sally	1967	10.00
❑ 32041	Funky Broadway/Soul Stroll	1968	10.00
Albums			
MINIT			
❑ 24010 [S]	Blues Power	1967	25.00
❑ 40010 [M]	Blues Power	1967	25.00

DOZIER, LAMONT
Also see HOLLAND-DOZIER; THE VOICE MASTERS.

Number	Title (A Side/B Side)	Yr	NM
12-Inch Singles			
WARNER BROS.			
❑ 8802	Boogie Business/True Love Is Bittersweet	1979	10.00
45s			
ABC			
❑ 11407	Trying to Hold On to My Woman/We Don't Want Nobody to Come Between Us	1973	4.00
—Also see "Holland-Dozier"			
❑ 11438	Fish Ain't Bitin'/Breaking Out All Over	1974	4.00
❑ 12012	Fish Ain't Bitin'/Breaking Out All Over	1974	4.00
❑ 12044	Let Me Start Tonite/I Wanna Be with You	1974	4.00
❑ 12076	All Cried Out/Rose	1975	4.00
❑ 12234	Out Here on My Own/Take Off Your Make-Up	1976	4.00
ANNA			
❑ 1125	Let's Talk It Over/Benny the Skinny Man	1960	25.00
—As "Lamont Anthony"			
❑ 1125	Let's Talk It Over/Popeye	1960	250.00
—As "Lamont Anthony"			
CHECKMATE			
❑ 1001	Just to Be Loved/I Didn't Know	1961	250.00
—As "Lamont Anthony"			
COLUMBIA			
❑ 02035	Cool Me Out/Starting Over (We've Made the Necessary Changes)	1981	4.00
❑ 02238	Too Little Too Long/Chained (To Your Love)	1981	4.00
M&M			
❑ 502	Shout About It/(Instrumental)	1982	5.00
MEL-O-DY			
❑ 102	Dearest One/Fortune Teller Please Tell Me	1962	100.00
WARNER BROS.			
❑ 8432	Sight for Sore Eyes/Tear Down the Walls	1977	4.00
❑ 8792	Boogie Business/True Love Is Bittersweet	1979	4.00
Albums			
ABC			
❑ D-804	Out Here on My Own	1973	10.00
❑ D-839	Black Bach	1974	10.00
INVICTUS			
❑ KZ 33134	Love and Beauty	1974	12.00
WARNER BROS.			
❑ BS 2929	Right There	1976	10.00
❑ BS 3039	Peddlin'	1977	10.00
❑ BSK 3282	Bittersweet	1979	10.00

DOZY, BEAKY, MICK & TICH
See DAVE DEE, DOZY, BEAKY, MICK & TICH.

DRAFI

Number	Title (A Side/B Side)	Yr	NM
45s			
LONDON			
❑ 105	Trouble/I Wanna Take You Home	1967	8.00
❑ 10039	Shake Hands/Come On, Let's Go	196?	10.00
—As "Drafi Deutscher"			
❑ 10825	Marble Breaks and Iron Bends/Amanda	1966	8.00

DRAG KINGS, THE

Number	Title (A Side/B Side)	Yr	NM
45s			
UNITED ARTISTS			
❑ 676	Bearing Burners/Nitro	1963	30.00

DRAGONFLY

Number	Title (A Side/B Side)	Yr	NM
Albums			
MEGAPHONE			
❑ MS-1202	Dragonfly	1970	300.00

DRAGONS, THE
With Daryl Dragon, later of THE CAPTAIN AND TENNILLE.

Number	Title (A Side/B Side)	Yr	NM
45s			
CAPITOL			
❑ 5278	Elephant Stomp/Troll	1964	20.00

DRAGSTERS, THE

Number	Title (A Side/B Side)	Yr	NM
Albums			
WING			
❑ MGW-12269 [M]	Hey Little Cobra/Drag City	1964	80.00
❑ SRW-16269 [S]	Hey Little Cobra/Drag City	1964	100.00

DRAKE, CHARLIE

Number	Title (A Side/B Side)	Yr	NM
45s			
UNITED ARTISTS			
❑ 398	My Boomerang Won't Come Back/She's My Girl	1961	15.00
—With A-side lyric "Practiced 'til I was blue in the face."			
❑ 398	My Boomerang Won't Come Back/She's My Girl	1961	30.00
—With A-side lyric "Practiced 'til I was black in the face."			
❑ 437	Tanglefoot/Drake's Progress	1962	12.00
❑ 477	Sweet Freddie Green/Zulu Drake	1962	12.00

DRAKE, GUY

Number	Title (A Side/B Side)	Yr	NM
45s			
ROYAL AMERICAN			
❑ 1	Welfare Cadillac/Keep Off My Grass	1970	7.00
❑ 15	Politickin' Pete/Born to Be an Opry Star	1970	7.00
Albums			
ROYAL AMERICAN			
❑ 1001	Welfare Cadillac	1970	25.00

DRAKE, NICK

Number	Title (A Side/B Side)	Yr	NM
Albums			
ANTILLES			
❑ AN-7010	Five Leaves Left	1976	85.00
—Released in England in 1969			
❑ AN-7028	Bryter Layter	1977	80.00
—Released in England in 1970			
HANNIBAL			
❑ HNBL-1318	Time of No Reply	1987	55.00
❑ HNBX-5302 [(4)]	Fruit Tree	1986	170.00
ISLAND			
❑ SMAS-9307	Nick Drake	1971	80.00
—U.S.-only compilation of selected songs from his first two British LPs			
❑ SMAS-9318	Pink Moon	1972	125.00

DRAKES, THE

Number	Title (A Side/B Side)	Yr	NM
45s			
CONQUEST			
❑ 1001	Oo Wee So Good/Kitty	1958	600.00
OLIMPIC			
❑ 252	I Made a Wish/Ole King Cole	1965	120.00

DRAMATICS, THE
Probably all the same group. Also see THE DELLS AND THE DRAMATICS.

Number	Title (A Side/B Side)	Yr	NM
45s			
ABC			
❑ 12090	Mr. and Mrs. Jones/I Cried All the Way Home	1975	5.00
❑ 12125	(I'm Going By) The Stars in Your Eyes/Trying to Get Over You	1975	5.00
❑ 12150	You're Fooling You/I'll Make It So Good	1975	5.00
❑ 12180	Treat Me Like a Man/I Was the Life of the Party	1976	5.00
❑ 12220	Finger Fever/Say the Word	1976	5.00
❑ 12235	Be My Girl/The Nicest Man Alive	1976	5.00
❑ 12258	I Can't Get Over You/Sundown Is Coming (Hold Back the Night)	1977	5.00
❑ 12299	Shake It Well/That Heaven Kind of Feeling	1977	5.00
❑ 12331	Ocean of Thoughts and Dreams/Come Inside	1978	5.00
❑ 12372	Stop Your Weeping/California Sunrise	1978	5.00
❑ 12400	Do What You Want to Do/Jane	1978	5.00
❑ 12429	Why Do You Wanna Do Me Wrong/Yo' Love (Can Only Bring Me Happiness)	1978	5.00
❑ 12460	I Just Wanna Dance with You/I've Got a Schoolboy Crush on You	1979	5.00
CADET			
❑ 5704	Door to Your Heart/Choosing Up on You	1974	6.00
❑ 5706	Don't Make Me No Promises/Tune Up	1974	6.00
❑ 5710	Love Is Missing from Our Lives/I'm in Love	1975	6.00
—With the Dells			
CAPITOL			
❑ B-5103	Live It Up/She's My Kind of Girl	1982	4.00
❑ B-5140	Treat Me Right/Night Life	1982	4.00
CRACKERJACK			
❑ 4015	Toy Soldier/Hello Summer	1968	60.00
FANTASY			
❑ 966	Luv's Calling/Dream Lady	1985	3.00
❑ 967	One Love Ago/Dream Lady	1986	3.00
MAINSTREAM			
❑ 5571	No Rebate on Love/Feel It	1976	5.00
MCA			
❑ 12460	I Just Wanna Dance with You/I've Got a Schoolboy Crush on You	1979	4.00
❑ 41017	I Just Wanta Dance With You/I've Got a Schoolboy Crush on You	1979	4.00
❑ 41056	That's My Favorite Song/Bottom Line Woman	1979	4.00
❑ 41178	Welcome Back Home/Marriage on Paper Only	1980	4.00
❑ 41241	Be With the One You Love/If You Feel Like You Wanna Dance, Dance	1980	4.00
❑ 51004	Share Your Love with Me/Get It	1980	4.00
❑ 51041	(We Need More) Lovin' Time/You're the Best Thing in My Life	1980	4.00
SPORT			
❑ 101	All Because of You/If You Haven't Got Love	1967	60.00
VOLT			
❑ 302	Bridge Over Troubled Water/(B-side unknown)	1989	4.00
❑ 4029	Since I've Been in Love/Your Love Was Strange	1969	8.00
❑ 4058	Whatcha See Is Whatcha Get/Thankful for Your Love	1971	8.00
❑ 4071	Get Up and Get Down/Fall in Love, Lady Love	1971	8.00
❑ 4075	In the Rain/Good Soul Music	1972	8.00
❑ 4082	Toast to the Fool/Your Love Was Strange	1972	8.00
❑ 4090	Hey You! Get Off My Mountain/The Devil Is Dope	1973	8.00
❑ 4099	Fell for You/Now You Got Me Loving You	1973	8.00
❑ 4105	And I Panicked/Beware of the Man	1974	8.00
❑ 4108	I Made Myself Lonely/Highway to Heaven	1974	8.00
WINGATE			
❑ 18	Somewhere/Bingo!	1966	50.00
—As "The Dynamics"			
❑ 22	Baby I Need You/Inky Dinky Wang Dang Doo	1966	50.00
—As "The Dynamics"			
Albums			
ABC			
❑ D-867	The Dramatic Jackpot	1975	15.00
❑ D-916	Drama V	1975	15.00
❑ D-955	Joy Ride	1976	15.00
❑ AB-1010	Shake It Well	1977	15.00
❑ AA-1072	Do What You Wanna Do	1978	15.00
❑ AA-1125	Anytime, Anyplace	1979	15.00
CAPITOL			
❑ ST-12205	New Dimension	1982	10.00
FANTASY			
❑ 9642	Somewhere in Time: A Dramatic Reunion	1986	12.00
MCA			
❑ 761	Dramatic Way	198?	8.00
—Reissue of 5149			
❑ 762	10 1/2	198?	8.00
—Reissue of 3196			
❑ AA-1125	Anytime, Anyplace	1979	12.00
—Reissue of ABC 1125			
❑ 3196	10 1/2	1980	10.00

Number	Title (A Side/B Side)	Yr	NM
❑ 5149	Dramatic Way	1981	10.00
STAX			
❑ STX-4111	Whatcha See Is Whatcha Get	1978	12.00
—Reissue of Volt 6018			
❑ STX-4131	A Dramatic Experience	1979	12.00
—Reissue of Volt 6019			
❑ MPS-8523	Dramatically Yours	198?	8.00
—Reissue of Volt 9501			
❑ MPS-8526	The Best of the Dramatics	198?	10.00
❑ MPS-8545	The Dramatics Live	1988	10.00
VOLT			
❑ V-3402	Positive State of Mind	1989	10.00
❑ V-3407	Stone Cold	1990	10.00
❑ VOS-6018	Whatcha See Is Whatcha Get	1972	25.00
❑ VOS-6019	A Dramatic Experience	1973	25.00
❑ VOS-9501	Dramatically Yours	1974	25.00
DREAD ZEPPELIN LED ZEPPELIN tribute band with a reggae beat.			
45s			
BIRDCAGE			
❑ 45-2690	Whole Lotta Love/Tour-Telvis: A Bad Trip	1989	10.00
—Pink vinyl			
❑ 45-2690 [PS]	Whole Lotta Love/Tour-Telvis: A Bad Trip	1989	10.00
I.R.S.			
❑ S7-19353	All I Want for Christmas Is My Two Front Teeth/Happy Xmas (War Is Over)	1996	3.00
—B-side by the Alarm			
Albums			
I.R.S.			
❑ X1-13048	Un-Led-Ed	1990	20.00
—All copies on gold vinyl			
DREAM 6			
Albums			
HAPPY HERMIT			
❑ 1983 [EP]	Dream 6	1983	40.00
DREAM GIRLS, THE			
45s			
BIG TOP			
❑ 3059	Don't Break My Heart/I Could Write a Book	1960	20.00
❑ 3085	Wanted/Mr. Fine	1961	20.00
—The rest of the Big Top singles as "Bobbie Smith and the Dream Girls"			
❑ 3100	Duchess of Earl/Mine All Mine	1962	20.00
❑ 3111	Here Comes Baby/I Got a Feeling My Love	1962	20.00
❑ 3129	Your Lovey Dovey Ways/Now He's Gone	1962	20.00
CAMEO			
❑ 165	Don't Break My Heart/Oh This Is Why	1959	25.00
METRO			
❑ 20029	I'm in Love with You/Cryin' in the Night	1960	30.00
❑ 20034	Heartaches/Love Hen	1961	25.00
TWIRL			
❑ 1002	Don't Break My Heart/Oh This Is Why	1959	50.00
DREAM KINGS, THE			
45s			
CHECKER			
❑ 858	M.T.Y.L.T.T./Oh What a Baby	1957	150.00
DREAM SYNDICATE, THE			
12-Inch Singles			
BIG TIME			
❑ 6014	Out of the Grey/Out of the Grey (Edit)	1986	5.00
❑ 6029	50 in a 25 Zone (2 versions)/Drinking Problem/Blood Money + 1	1987	8.00
45s			
FORCED EXPOSURE			
❑ 004	Ballad of Dwight Frye/Low Rider	1986	30.00
❑ 004 [PS]	Ballad of Dwight Frye/Low Rider	1986	30.00
Albums			
A&M			
❑ SP-12511	This Is Not the New Dream Syndicate Album...Live	1984	12.00
BIG TIME			
❑ 10022	Out of the Grey	1985	10.00
DOWN THERE			
❑ 2 [EP]	Sure Thing + 3	1982	20.00

Number	Title (A Side/B Side)	Yr	NM
ENIGMA			
❑ 73341	Ghost Stories	1988	8.00
RUBY			
❑ 807	The Days of Wine and Roses	1982	20.00
SLASH			
❑ 23844	The Days of Wine and Roses	1982	15.00
DREAM TEAM, THE			
45s			
EPIC			
❑ 9701	I'm Not Afraid/Inka Dinka Doo	1964	12.00
DREAM WEAVERS, THE			
45s			
DECCA			
❑ 29683	It's Almost Tomorrow/You've Got Me Wondering	1955	15.00
❑ 29818	You're Mine/Into the Night	1956	12.00
❑ 29905	A Little Love Can Go a Long, Long Way/Is There Somebody Else	1956	12.00
❑ 29990	Give Us This Day/Why I Chose You	1956	12.00
❑ 30156	Till We Meet Again/All This Is Home	1956	12.00
❑ 30276	Fool's Gold/I'll Try, I'll Try	1957	12.00
DREAMERS, THE Several different groups.			
45s			
ABC-PARAMOUNT			
❑ 9746	The Girl Down the Street/The Right Time for Love	1956	20.00
ALADDIN			
❑ 3303	My Plea/Charles My Darling	1955	150.00
APT			
❑ 25053	Mary's Little Lamb/I Sing This Song	1960	25.00
BLUE STAR			
❑ 8001	I Really Love You/You Made Me Darling	1960	25.00
COUSINS			
❑ 1005	Because of You/Little Girl	1961	100.00
EVENT			
❑ 4270	Rock 'N Roll Baby/Ding Dong	1958	30.00
FAIRMOUNT			
❑ 612	Daydreamin' of You/The Promise	1963	20.00
FLIP			
❑ 319	Since You've Been Gone/Do Not Forget	1956	40.00
❑ 354	Since You've Been Gone/Do Not Forget	1961	20.00
GOLDISC			
❑ 3015	Teenage Vows of Love/Natalie	1961	30.00
GRAND			
❑ 131	Tears in My Eyes/535	1955	300.00
GUARANTEED			
❑ 219	Mary, Mary/Canadian Sunset	1961	15.00
JUBILEE			
❑ 5053	These Things I Miss/Can't Get You Off My Mind	1951	300.00
LOST-NITE			
❑ 329	Tears in My Eyes/535	197?	5.00
—Reissue of Grand 131			
MANHATTAN			
❑ 503	Lips Were Meant for Kissing/No Obligation	1956	100.00
MAY			
❑ 133	Because of You/Little Girl	1963	40.00
MERCURY			
❑ 5843	I'm Gonna Hate Myself in the Morning/Ain't Gonna Worry No More	1952	150.00
❑ 70019	Please Don't Leave Me/Walkin' My Blues	1953	150.00
NUGGET			
❑ 1000	Don't Cry/It's Gonna Be Alright	1959	30.00
ROLLIN'			
❑ 1001	No Man Is an Island/Melba	1954	800.00
UNITED ARTISTS			
❑ 841	Henry, Henry, Henry/Love, Love, Love	1965	12.00
DREAMETTES, THE			
45s			
UNITED ARTISTS			
❑ 921	Gonna Make That Little Boy Mine/Run, Steven, Run	1965	20.00

Number	Title (A Side/B Side)	Yr	NM
DREAMLOVERS, THE			
45s			
CAMEO			
❑ 326	These Will Be the Good Old Days/Oh Baby Mine (I Get So Lonely)	1964	15.00
CASINO			
❑ 1308	Amazons and Coyotes/Together	1963	15.00
COLUMBIA			
❑ 42698	Sad, Sad Boy/If I Were a Magician	1963	20.00
❑ 42752	Sad, Sad Boy/Black Bottom	1963	12.00
❑ 42842	Pretty Little Girl/I'm Through with You	1963	50.00
END			
❑ 1114	If I Should Lose You/I Miss You	1962	20.00
HERITAGE			
❑ 102	When We Get Married/Just Because	1961	20.00
❑ 104	Welcome Home/Let Them Love (And Be Loved)	1961	15.00
❑ 107	Zoom, Zoom, Zoom/While We Were Dancing	1962	15.00
LEN			
❑ 1006	Take It from a Fool/For the First Time	1958	200.00
LOST-NITE			
❑ 213	You Gave Me Someone to Love/Doin' Things Together with You	196?	5.00
—Reissue			
❑ 214	When We Get Married/Just Because	196?	5.00
—Reissue			
❑ 240	Amazons and Coyotes/Together	196?	5.00
—Reissue			
MERCURY			
❑ 72595	Bless Your Soul/Bad Time Make the Good Times	1966	10.00
❑ 72630	Calling Jo-Ann/You Gave Me Someone to Love	1966	10.00
SWAN			
❑ 4167	Amazons and Coyotes/Together	1963	12.00
—Black label			
❑ 4167	Amazons and Coyotes/Together	1963	20.00
—White label			
V-TONE			
❑ 211	Annabelle Lee/Home Is Where the Heart Is	1960	20.00
❑ 229	May I Kiss the Bride/Time	1961	20.00
WARNER BROS.			
❑ 5619	You Gave Me Someone to Love/Doin' Things Together with You	1965	25.00
Albums			
COLLECTABLES			
❑ COL-5004	The Best of the Dreamlovers	198?	12.00
❑ COL-5005	The Best of the Dreamlovers, Vol. Two	198?	12.00
COLUMBIA			
❑ CL 2020 [M]	The Bird and Other Golden Dancing Grooves	1963	40.00
❑ CS 8820 [S]	The Bird and Other Golden Dancing Grooves	1963	50.00
DREAMS			
45s			
COLUMBIA			
❑ 45300	Devil Lady/Maryanne	1971	5.00
❑ 45369	Try Me/15 Miles to Provo	1971	5.00
❑ 45524	Medicated Goo/New York	1972	5.00
Albums			
COLUMBIA			
❑ C 30225	Dreams	1970	15.00
❑ C 30960	Imagine My Surprise	1971	15.00
DREAMS, THE			
45s			
SAVOY			
❑ 1130	Darlene/A Letter to My Girl	1954	200.00
❑ 1140	Under the Willow/I'm Losing My Mind	1954	120.00
—A copy on gold vinyl with a blue Savoy label has shown up; its authenticity is unknown			
❑ 1157	I'll Be Faithful/My Little Honeybun	1955	100.00
DREAMS AND ILLUSIONS			
Albums			
VERVE FORECAST			
❑ FTS-3040	Dreams and Illusions	1968	20.00

D

DREW, PATTI

Also see THE DREW-VELS.

45s

CAPITOL

Number	Title (A Side/B Side)	Yr	NM
❑ 2042	Where Is Daddy/Sufferer	1967	8.00
❑ 2121	Keep On Movin'/There'll Never Be Another	1968	8.00
❑ 2197	Workin' on a Groovy Thing/Without a Doubt	1968	8.00
❑ 2339	Hard to Handle/Just Can't Forget About You	1968	8.00
❑ 2389	I've Been Here All the Time/Welcome Back	1969	8.00
❑ 2473	The Love That a Woman Should Give to a Man/Save the Last Dance for Me	1969	8.00
❑ 2575	He's the One/Which One Should I Choose	1969	8.00
❑ 2712	Wild Is Love/World of No Return	1969	8.00
—B-side by John Stewart			
❑ 2713	The Pick-Up/Hundreds and Thousands of Guys	1970	8.00
❑ 2989	I'm Calling/It's Just a Dream	1970	8.00
❑ 5861	Tell Him/Turn Away from Me	1967	8.00
❑ 5969	Stop and Listen/Tired of Falling In and Out of Love	1967	8.00

QUILL

Number	Title (A Side/B Side)	Yr	NM
❑ 101	Where Is Daddy/Sufferer	1966	10.00

Albums

CAPITOL

Number	Title (A Side/B Side)	Yr	NM
❑ ST-156	I've Been Here All the Time	1969	20.00
❑ ST-408	Wild Is Love	1970	20.00
❑ ST 2804 [S]	Tell Him	1968	30.00
❑ T 2804 [M]	Tell Him	1968	30.00

DREW-VELS, THE

Also see PATTI DREW.

45s

CAPITOL

Number	Title (A Side/B Side)	Yr	NM
❑ 5055	Tell Him/Just Because	1963	12.00
❑ 5145	It's My Time/Everybody Knows	1964	10.00
❑ 5244	Creepin'/I've Known	1964	10.00

QUILL

Number	Title (A Side/B Side)	Yr	NM
❑ 100	True Enough/Chilly Kisses	1966	10.00

DRIFTERS, THE

Several different groups with a common heritage, thus we list them together. Also see BEN E. KING; RUDY LEWIS; CLYDE McPHATTER; BILL PINKNEY. Several different groups with a common heritage, thus we list them together. Records on Capitol, Coral, Rama and Steeltown are unrelated to these Drifters and are oustide the scope of this book. Also see BEN E. KING; CLYDE McPHATTER.

45s

ATLANTIC

Number	Title (A Side/B Side)	Yr	NM
❑ 1006	Money Honey/The Way I Feel	1953	80.00
❑ 1019	Such a Night/Lucille	1954	70.00
❑ 1029	Honey Love/Warm Your Heart	1954	50.00
❑ 1043	Bip Bam/Someday You'll Want Me to Want You	1954	40.00
❑ 1048	White Christmas/The Bells of St. Mary's	1954	60.00
—Yellow label, no spinner (original)			
❑ 1048	White Christmas/The Bells of St. Mary's	1956	25.00
—Red label, no "fan" logo at lower left			
❑ 1048	White Christmas/The Bells of St. Mary's	1962	8.00
—Red label with "fan" logo at lower left			
❑ 1048	White Christmas/The Bells of St. Mary's	197?	5.00
—Glossy yellow label with "fan" logo			
❑ 1048 [DJ]	White Christmas/The Bells of St. Mary's	196?	25.00
—White/red label promo, no "fan" logo, with holly leaves encircling "45 R.P.M."			
❑ 1055	What'Cha Gonna Do/Gone	1955	50.00
❑ 1078	Adorable/Steamboat	1955	40.00
❑ 1089	Ruby Baby/Your Promise to Be Mine	1956	30.00
❑ 1101	Soldier of Fortune/I Got to Get Myself a Woman	1956	30.00
❑ 1123	Fools Fall in Love/It Was a Tear	1957	30.00
❑ 1141	Hypnotized/Drifting Away from You	1957	30.00
❑ 1161	I Know/Yodee Yakee	1957	30.00
❑ 1187	Drip Drop/Moonlight Bay	1958	30.00
—Last record by the "old" Drifters. The below Atlantic 45s are by a completely different group, although personnel changes resulted in at least one "old" Drifter (Johnny Moore) spending time with the "new" Drifters.			
❑ 2025	There Goes My Baby/Oh My Love	1959	25.00
❑ 2040	Dance with Me/(If You Cry) True Love, True Love	1959	20.00
❑ 2050	This Magic Moment/Baltimore	1960	20.00
❑ 2062	Lonely Winds/Hey Senorita	1960	20.00
❑ 2071	Save the Last Dance for Me/Nobody But Me	1960	20.00
❑ 2087	I Count the Tears/Suddenly There's a Valley	1960	15.00
❑ 2096	Some Kind of Wonderful/Honey Bee	1961	15.00
❑ 2105	Please Stay/No Sweet Lovin'	1961	15.00
❑ 2117	Sweets for My Sweet/Loneliness or Happiness	1961	15.00
❑ 2127	Room Full of Tears/Somebody New Dancin' with You	1961	15.00
❑ 2134	When My Little Girl Is Smiling/Mexican Divorce	1962	15.00
❑ 2143	Stranger on the Shore/What to Do	1962	15.00
❑ 2151	Sometimes I Wonder/Jackpot	1962	15.00
❑ 2162	Up On the Roof/Another Night with the Boys	1962	20.00
❑ 2182	On Broadway/Let the Music Play	1963	15.00
❑ 2191	Rat Race/If You Don't Come Back	1963	15.00
❑ 2201	I'll Take You Home/I Feel Good All Over	1963	15.00
❑ 2216	Vaya Con Dios/In the Land of Make Believe	1964	15.00
❑ 2225	One Way Love/Didn't It	1964	15.00
❑ 2237	Under the Boardwalk/I Don't Want to Go On Without You	1964	15.00
❑ 2253	I've Got Sand in My Shoes/He's Just a Playboy	1964	12.00
❑ 2260	Saturday Night at the Movies/Spanish Lace	1964	12.00
❑ 2260 [PS]	Saturday Night at the Movies/Spanish Lace	1964	40.00
❑ 2261	The Christmas Song/I Remember Christmas	1964	12.00
❑ 2261 [PS]	The Christmas Song/I Remember Christmas	1964	30.00
❑ 2268	At the Club/Answer the Phone	1965	10.00
❑ 2285	Come On Over to My Place/Chains of Love	1965	10.00
❑ 2292	Follow Me/The Outside World	1965	10.00
❑ 2298	I'll Take You Where the Music's Playing/Far from the Maddening Crowd	1965	10.00
❑ 2310	Nylon Stockings/We Gotta Sing	1965	10.00
❑ 2325	Memories Are Made of This/My Islands in the Sun	1966	8.00
❑ 2336	Up in the Streets of Harlem/You Can't Love Them All	1966	8.00
❑ 2366	Aretha/Baby What I Mean	1966	8.00
❑ 2426	Up Jumped the Devil/Ain't It the Truth	1967	8.00
❑ 2471	I Need You Now/Still Burning in My Heart	1968	8.00
❑ 2624	Your Best Friend/Steal Away	1969	8.00
❑ 2746	You Got to Pay Your Dues/Black Silk	1970	10.00
❑ 2786	A Rose By Any Other Name/Be My Lady	1971	10.00
❑ 89189	Ruby Baby/Fever	1987	4.00
—B-side by Little Willie John			
❑ 89189 [PS]	Ruby Baby/Fever	1987	4.00
—From the movie "Big Town"			

BELL

Number	Title (A Side/B Side)	Yr	NM
❑ 45320	You've Got Your Troubles/I'm Feelin' Sad	1973	5.00
❑ 45387	The Songs We Used to Sing/Like Sister and Brother	1973	5.00
❑ 45600	Kissin' in the Back Row of the Movies/I'm Feelin' Sad	1974	5.00

CROWN

Number	Title (A Side/B Side)	Yr	NM
❑ 108	The World Is Changing/Sacroiliac Swing	1954	200.00

EMI-CAPITOL MUSIC

Number	Title (A Side/B Side)	Yr	NM
❑ S7-19351	Christmas Time Is Here/I'll Be Home for Christmas	1996	3.00
—As "The Drifters Featuring Rick Sheppard"			

MUSICOR

Number	Title (A Side/B Side)	Yr	NM
❑ 1498	Midsummer Night in Harlem/Lonely Drifter, Don't Cry	1974	5.00
—As "Charlie Thomas and the Drifters"			

S&J

Number	Title (A Side/B Side)	Yr	NM
❑ 800826	(More Than a Number in My) Little Red Book/I Count the Tears	196?	10.00
—As "Bill Pinkney and the Original Drifters"			

7-Inch Extended Plays

ATLANTIC

Number	Title (A Side/B Side)	Yr	NM
❑ 534	(contents unknown)	1954	200.00
❑ 534 [PS]	Clyde McPhatter and the Drifters	1954	300.00
❑ 592	Fools Fall in Love/Adorable//Steamboat/Ruby Baby	1957	100.00
❑ 592 [PS]	The Drifters	1957	200.00

Albums

ARISTA

Number	Title (A Side/B Side)	Yr	NM
❑ AB 4140	Every Night Is Saturday Night	1976	12.00

ATCO

Number	Title (A Side/B Side)	Yr	NM
❑ SD 33-375 [R]	Their Greatest Recordings — The Early Years	1971	12.00

ATLANTIC

Number	Title (A Side/B Side)	Yr	NM
❑ 8003 [M]	Clyde McPhatter and the Drifters	1956	500.00
—Black label			
❑ 8003 [M]	Clyde McPhatter and the Drifters	1959	60.00
—Red and purple label, white "fan" logo at right			
❑ 8003 [M]	Clyde McPhatter and the Drifters	1963	40.00
—Red and purple label, black "fan" logo at right			
❑ 8022 [M]	Rockin' and Driftin'	1958	500.00
—White "bullseye" label			
❑ 8022 [M]	Rockin' and Driftin'	1958	600.00
—Black label			
❑ 8022 [M]	Rockin' and Driftin'	1959	60.00
—Red and purple label, white "fan" logo at right			
❑ 8022 [M]	Rockin' and Driftin'	1963	40.00
—Red and purple label, black "fan" logo at right			
❑ 8041 [M]	The Drifters' Greatest Hits	1960	100.00
—Red and purple label, white "fan" logo at right			
❑ 8041 [M]	The Drifters' Greatest Hits	1960	600.00
—Black label			
❑ 8041 [M]	The Drifters' Greatest Hits	1963	50.00
—Red and purple label, black "fan" logo at right			
❑ 8059 [M]	Save the Last Dance for Me	1962	120.00
—Red and purple label, white "fan" logo at right			
❑ 8059 [M]	Save the Last Dance for Me	1963	60.00
—Red and purple label, black "fan" logo at right			
❑ SD 8059 [S]	Save the Last Dance for Me	1962	200.00
—Green and blue label, white "fan" logo at right			
❑ SD 8059 [S]	Save the Last Dance for Me	1963	100.00
—Green and blue label, black "fan" logo at right			
❑ SD 8059 [S]	Save the Last Dance for Me	1969	25.00
—Red and green label, white horizontal stripe through center hole			
❑ 8073 [M]	Up on the Roof — The Best of the Drifters	1963	100.00
—Red and purple label, black "fan" logo at right			
❑ SD 8073 [S]	Up on the Roof — The Best of the Drifters	1963	150.00
—Green and blue label, black "fan" logo at right			
❑ 8093 [M]	Our Biggest Hits	1964	60.00
—Red and purple label, white "fan" logo at right			
❑ SD 8093 [S]	Our Biggest Hits	1964	80.00
—Mostly red label, black "fan" logo			
❑ 8099 [M]	Under the Boardwalk	1964	50.00
—Color photo of group on cover			
❑ 8099 [M]	Under the Boardwalk	1964	80.00
—Black and white photo of group on cover			
❑ SD 8099 [S]	Under the Boardwalk	1964	60.00
—Color photo of group on cover			
❑ SD 8099 [S]	Under the Boardwalk	1964	120.00
—Black and white photo of group on cover			
❑ 8103 [M]	The Good Life with the Drifters	1965	40.00
❑ SD 8103 [S]	The Good Life with the Drifters	1965	50.00
❑ 8113 [M]	I'll Take You Where the Music's Playing	1965	40.00
❑ SD 8113 [S]	I'll Take You Where the Music's Playing	1965	50.00
❑ 8153 [M]	The Drifters' Golden Hits	1968	30.00
❑ SD 8153 [P]	The Drifters' Golden Hits	1968	30.00
—Green and blue label			
❑ SD 8153 [P]	The Drifters' Golden Hits	1969	15.00
—Red and green label			
❑ 81927 [(2)]	Let the Boogie-Woogie Roll: Greatest Hits 1953-1958	1989	15.00
❑ 81931 [(2)]	All-Time Greatest Hits and More: 1959-1965	1989	15.00

CLARION

Number	Title (A Side/B Side)	Yr	NM
❑ 608 [M]	The Drifters	1964	20.00
❑ SD 608 [P]	The Drifters	1964	30.00

GUSTO

Number	Title (A Side/B Side)	Yr	NM
❑ 0063	Greatest Hits — The Drifters	1980	10.00

TRIP

Number	Title (A Side/B Side)	Yr	NM
❑ TOP-16-6	16 Greatest Hits — The Drifters	1976	10.00

DRIFTERS, THE (2)

Instrumental group from England, and backing band for CLIFF RICHARD. They had one record in the US on Capitol; see THE SHADOWS, the name they adopted after the R&B Drifters became popular.

DRIFTERS, THE (3)

45s

CORAL

Number	Title (A Side/B Side)	Yr	NM
❑ 65037	Wine Head Woman/I'm the Caring Kind	1950	300.00
❑ 65040	And I Shook/I Had to Find Out for Myself	1951	300.00

DRIFTERS, THE (4)

45s

RAMA

Number	Title (A Side/B Side)	Yr	NM
❑ 22	Besame Mucho/Summertime	1953	200.00

DRIFTERS, THE (U)
Definitely not group (2), (3) or (4), though it could be one of the many variants of group (1).

45s

STEELTOWN

Number	Title (A Side/B Side)	Yr	NM
❑ 671	Peace of Mind/The Struggler	1973	5.00

DRIFTIN' SLIM

Albums

MILESTONE

Number	Title (A Side/B Side)	Yr	NM
❑ MLS-93004 [(2)]	Driftin' Slim and His Blues Band	1968	25.00

DRIVERS, THE
More than one group.

45s

Number	Title (A Side/B Side)	Yr	NM
COMET			
❑ 2142	High Gear/Low Gear	1961	25.00
DELUXE			
❑ 6094	Women/Smooth, Slow and Easy	1956	100.00
❑ 6104	My Lonely Prayer/Midnight Hours	1957	200.00
❑ 6117	Dangerous Lips/Oh Miss Nellie	1957	80.00
KING			
❑ 5645	Mr. Astronaut/Dry Bones Twist	1962	12.00
LIN			
❑ 1002	A Man's Glory/Teeter Totter	1954	400.00
RCA VICTOR			
❑ 47-7023	Blue Moon/I Get Weak	1957	60.00

DRONGOS, THE

45s

WHITE WHALE

Number	Title (A Side/B Side)	Yr	NM
❑ 235	Under My Thumb/If You Wanna Know	1966	20.00

DRUIDS OF STONEHENGE, THE

45s

UNI

Number	Title (A Side/B Side)	Yr	NM
❑ 55021	A Garden Where Nothing Grows/Painted Woman	1967	20.00

Albums

UNI

Number	Title (A Side/B Side)	Yr	NM
❑ 3004 [M]	Creation	1967	100.00
❑ 73004 [S]	Creation	1967	150.00

DRUSKY, ROY

45s

Number	Title (A Side/B Side)	Yr	NM
CAPITOL			
❑ 3859	Close to Home/One Day at a Time	1974	6.00
❑ 3942	Dixie Lily/If I Could Paint the World	1974	6.00
❑ 4028	I'm Knee Deep in Loving You/The Baptism of Jesse Taylor	1975	6.00
❑ 4132	Sunrise/Warm, Warm Bed	1975	6.00
❑ 4232	When My Room Gets Dark Again/This Life of Mine	1976	6.00
❑ 4281	Battle for Daddy's Soul/Never Before	1976	6.00
COLUMBIA			
❑ 4-21478	Come On Back and Love Me/What Am I Worth	1955	20.00
❑ 4-21516	I Just Can't Help Me Lovin' You/So in Love Again	1956	20.00
❑ 4-21537	Three Blind Mice/I'll Make Amends	1956	20.00
❑ 4-40830	That's When My Heartaches Began/God Planned It That Way	1957	20.00
❑ 4-40964	Walkin'/I Walk to Heaven	1957	20.00
DECCA			
❑ 30793	Wait and See/Just About That Time	1958	15.00
❑ 30943	Such a Fool/Our Church — Your Wedding	1959	15.00
❑ 31024	Another/The Same Corner	1959	15.00
❑ 31109	Anymore/I'm So Helpless	1960	15.00
❑ 31193	Three Hearts in a Tangle/I'd Rather Loan You Out	1961	12.00
❑ 31297	I Went Out of My Way (To Make You Happy)/I've Got Some	1961	12.00
❑ 31366	There's Always One (Who Loves a Lot)/Marking Time	1962	12.00
❑ 31411	After You Turn Out Your Light/I'm Not Getting Over You	1962	12.00
❑ 31443	Second Hand Rose/It Worries Me	1962	12.00
❑ 31486	Divided Love/She Never Cried When She Was Mine	1963	10.00
❑ 31717	Summer, Winter, Spring and Fall/Almost Can't	1964	10.00
MERCURY			
❑ 72204	Peel Me a Nanner/The Room Across the Hall	1963	10.00
❑ 72204 [PS]	Peel Me a Nanner/The Room Across the Hall	1963	20.00
❑ 72265	Pick of the Week/Yesterday	1964	10.00
❑ 72325	All for the Love of a Girl/So Much Got Lost	1964	10.00
❑ 72376	(From Now On All My Friends Are Gonna Be) Strangers/Birmingham Jail	1964	10.00
❑ 72471	White Lightnin' Express/Lonely Thing Called Me	1965	8.00
❑ 72532	Rainbows and Roses/A Thing Called Sadness	1966	8.00
❑ 72561	Rainbows and Roses/Too Many Dollars	1966	8.00
❑ 72586	The World Is Round/Unless You Make Him Set You Free	1966	8.00
❑ 72627	If the Whole World Stopped Lovin'/Too Many Fingerprints	1966	8.00
❑ 72689	New Lips/Now	1967	8.00
❑ 72742	Weakness in a Man/I've Got a Right to the Blues	1967	8.00
❑ 72784	You Better Sit Down Kids/Let's Put Our World Back Together	1968	8.00
❑ 72823	Jody and the Kid/Your Little Deeds of Kindness	1968	8.00
❑ 72865	I Wouldn't Be Alone/Memphis Morning	1968	8.00
❑ 72886	Where the Blue and Lonely Go/I'm Gonna Get You Off My Mind	1969	8.00
❑ 72928	My Grass Is Green/Alone with You	1969	8.00
❑ 72964	Such a Fool/All Over My Mind	1969	8.00
❑ 73007	I'll Make Amends/Our Everlasting Love Has Died	1970	7.00
❑ 73056	Long Long Texas Road/Emotion — Devotion	1970	7.00
❑ 73111	All My Hard Times/At Times Everybody's Blind	1970	7.00
❑ 73178	I Love the Way That You've Been Lovin' Me/On and On and On	1971	7.00
❑ 73212	I Can't Go On Loving You/You're Shaking the Hand	1971	7.00
❑ 73252	Red Red Wine/Without You Baby	1971	7.00
❑ 73293	Sunshine and Rainbows/The Night's Not Over Yet	1972	7.00
❑ 73314	The Last Time I Called Somebody Darlin'/Long Way Back to Love	1972	7.00
❑ 73356	I Must Be Doin' Something Right/Always You, Always Me	1972	7.00
❑ 73376	That Rain Makin' Baby of Mine/This Time of the Year	1973	7.00
❑ 73405	Satisfied Mind/I'll Take Care of You	1973	7.00
PLANTATION			
❑ 183	Beautiful Sunday/You've Got Your Troubles	1979	5.00
❑ 187	The Last Farewell/Welcome Home	1979	5.00
❑ 194	What a Difference a Day Makes/(B-side unknown)	1980	5.00
SCORPION			
❑ 154	I Used to Be a Cowboy/Don't Touch Me	1978	4.00
❑ 0515	Deep in the Heart of Dixie/Last Call for Alcohol	1976	5.00
❑ 0521	Night Flying/Lifetime in a Week	1976	5.00
❑ 0527	Lovers, Friends and Strangers/Five String Hero	1977	5.00
❑ 0540	Betty's Song/Naked Truth	1977	5.00
STARDAY			
❑ 185	Such a Fool/Mumbling to Myself	1955	40.00

Albums

Number	Title (A Side/B Side)	Yr	NM
DECCA			
❑ DL 4160 [M]	Anymore with Roy Drusky	1961	25.00
❑ DL 4340 [M]	It's My Way	1962	20.00
❑ DL 74160 [S]	Anymore with Roy Drusky	1961	30.00
❑ DL 74340 [S]	It's My Way	1962	25.00
MERCURY			
❑ MG-20883 [M]	Songs of the Cities	1963	20.00
❑ MG-20919 [M]	Yesterday's Gone	1964	20.00
❑ MG-20973 [M]	The Pick of the Country	1964	20.00
❑ MG-21006 [M]	Country Music All Around the World	1965	20.00
❑ MG-21052 [M]	Roy Drusky's Greatest Hits	1965	20.00
❑ MG-21083 [M]	In a New Dimension	1966	20.00
❑ MG-21097 [M]	If the Whole World Stopped Lovin'	1966	20.00
❑ MG-21118 [M]	Now Is a Lonely Time	1967	25.00
❑ MG-21145 [M]	Roy Drusky's Greatest Hits Vol. 2	1968	40.00
—Mono is white label promo only			
❑ SR-60883 [S]	Songs of the Cities	1963	25.00
❑ SR-60919 [S]	Yesterday's Gone	1964	25.00
❑ SR-60973 [S]	The Pick of the Country	1964	25.00
❑ SR-61006 [S]	Country Music All Around the World	1965	25.00
❑ SR-61052 [S]	Roy Drusky's Greatest Hits	1965	25.00
❑ SR-61083 [S]	In a New Dimension	1966	25.00
❑ SR-61097 [S]	If the Whole World Stopped Lovin'	1966	25.00
❑ SR-61118 [S]	Now Is a Lonely Time	1967	20.00
❑ SR-61145 [S]	Roy Drusky's Greatest Hits Vol. 2	1968	20.00
❑ SR-61173	Jody and the Kid	1968	20.00
❑ SR-61206	Portrait of Roy Drusky	1969	20.00
❑ SR-61233	My Grass Is Green	1969	20.00
❑ SR-61260	I'll Make Amends	1970	20.00
❑ SR-61266	The Best of Roy Drusky	1970	20.00
❑ SR-61306	All My Hard Times	1970	20.00
❑ SR-61336	I Love the Way That You've Been Lovin' Me	1971	20.00

DRY CITY SCAT BAND, THE

Albums

ELEKTRA

Number	Title (A Side/B Side)	Yr	NM
❑ EKL-292 [M]	The Dry City Scat Band	1965	25.00
❑ EKS-7292 [S]	The Dry City Scat Band	1965	30.00

DRYSDALE, DON

45s

REPRISE

Number	Title (A Side/B Side)	Yr	NM
❑ 20162	Give Her Love/One Love	1963	10.00
❑ 20162 [PS]	Give Her Love/One Love	1963	20.00

DU DROPPERS, THE

45s

Number	Title (A Side/B Side)	Yr	NM
GROOVE			
❑ 0001	Speed King/Dead Broke	1954	80.00
❑ 0013	Just Whisper/How Much Longer	1954	100.00
❑ 0036	Boot 'Em Up/Let Nature Take Its Course	1955	50.00
❑ 0104	Talk That Talk/Give Me Some Consideration	1955	50.00
❑ 0120	I Wanna Love You/You're Mine Already	1955	50.00
RCA VICTOR			
❑ 47-5229	I Wanna Know/Laughing Blues	1953	40.00
❑ 47-5321	I Found Out/Little Girl, Little Girl	1953	40.00
❑ 47-5425	Whatever You're Doin'/Somebody Work on My Baby's Mind	1953	40.00
❑ 47-5504	Don't Pass Me By/Get Lost	1953	40.00
❑ 47-5543	The Note in the Bottle/Mama's Gone Goodbye	1953	40.00
—With Sunny Gale			
RED ROBIN			
❑ 108	Can't Do Sixty No More/Chain Me Baby (Blues of Desire)	1952	200.00
❑ 108	Can't Do Sixty No More/Chain Me Baby (Blues of Desire)	1952	500.00
—Red vinyl			
❑ 116	Come On and Love Me Baby/Go Back	1953	150.00

7-Inch Extended Plays

GROOVE

Number	Title (A Side/B Side)	Yr	NM
❑ 2	(contents unknown)	1955	200.00
❑ 2 [PS]	Talk That Talk	1955	200.00
❑ 5	(contents unknown)	1955	200.00
❑ 5 [PS]	Tops in Rhythm and Blues	1955	200.00

DUALS, THE

45s

Number	Title (A Side/B Side)	Yr	NM
ARC			
❑ 4446	Nearest to My Heart/Bye Bye	1959	20.00
FURY			
❑ 1013	Wait Up Baby/Forever and Ever	1958	40.00
INFINITY			
❑ 032	Oozy Groove/The Big Race	1964	25.00
JUGGY			
❑ 321	Oozy Groove/The Big Race	1964	50.00
STAR REVUE			
❑ 1031	Stick Shift/Cruising	1961	800.00
SUE			
❑ 745	Stick Shift/Cruising	1961	30.00
❑ 758	Travelin' Guitar/Cha Cha Guitar	1962	25.00
UNITED ARTISTS			
❑ 0128	Stick Shift/Keem-O-Sabe	1973	4.00
—"Silver Spotlight Series" reissue; B-side by The Electric Indian			

Number	Title (A Side/B Side)	Yr	NM

Albums

SUE

Number	Title (A Side/B Side)	Yr	NM
❑ LP-2002 [M]	Stick Shift	1961	400.00
—Cartoon cover			
❑ LP-2002 [M]	Stick Shift	1964	200.00
—Photo cover			

DU'AMBRA, JOEY

45s

ABC-PARAMOUNT

Number	Title (A Side/B Side)	Yr	NM
❑ 9917	Baby Sue/Come Back-A Little Mama	1958	30.00

DUANE, DICK

45s

ABC-PARAMOUNT

Number	Title (A Side/B Side)	Yr	NM
❑ 9656	Sobony/Now	1955	30.00
❑ 9677	To Make a Mistake/Blue Prelude	1956	30.00
❑ 9709	Fame and Fortune/ Mean Don't Cry	1956	30.00

GNP

Number	Title (A Side/B Side)	Yr	NM
❑ 127	What Good Does It Do/Savannah	1957	20.00
❑ 130	Eternally/I'll Never Make You Cry Again	1957	20.00

DUBS, THE

45s

ABC-PARAMOUNT

Number	Title (A Side/B Side)	Yr	NM
❑ 10056	No One/Early in the Evening	1959	25.00
❑ 10100	Don't Laugh at Me/ You Never Belong to Me	1960	50.00
❑ 10150	For the First Time/Ain't That So	1960	25.00
❑ 10198	If I Only Had Magic/ Joogie Boogie	1961	30.00
❑ 10269	Lullaby/Down, Down, Down I Go	1961	30.00

CLIFTON

Number	Title (A Side/B Side)	Yr	NM
❑ 2	Where Do We Go from Here/ I Only Have Eyes for You	1973	6.00

END

Number	Title (A Side/B Side)	Yr	NM
❑ 1108	Now That We Broke Up/ This to Me Is Love	1962	50.00

GONE

Number	Title (A Side/B Side)	Yr	NM
❑ 5002	Don't Ask Me (To Be Lonely)/ Darling	1957	25.00
—Multi-color label			
❑ 5002	Don't Ask Me (To Be Lonely)/ Darling	1957	60.00
—Black label, clown-face logo			
❑ 5002	Don't Ask Me (To Be Lonely)/ Darling	1957	100.00
—Black label, "shadow" logo			
❑ 5011	Could This Be Magic/Such Lovin'	1957	25.00
—Multi-color label			
❑ 5011	Could This Be Magic/Such Lovin'	1957	50.00
—Black label			
❑ 5020	Beside My Love/Gonna Make a Change	1957	60.00
❑ 5034	Song in My Heart/Be Sure (My Love)	1958	60.00
❑ 5046	Chapel of Dreams/Is There a Love for Me	1958	60.00
❑ 5069	Chapel of Dreams/Is There a Love for Me	1959	50.00
❑ 5138	You're Free to Go/Is There a Love for Me	1962	50.00

JOHNSON

Number	Title (A Side/B Side)	Yr	NM
❑ 097	Connie/Home Under My Hat	1973	6.00
❑ 098	Somebody Goofed/I Won't Have You Breaking My Heart	1973	6.00
❑ 102	Don't Ask Me (To Be Lonely)/ Darling	1957	1500.

JOSIE

Number	Title (A Side/B Side)	Yr	NM
❑ 911	Wisdom of a Fool/This I Swear	1963	20.00

LANA

Number	Title (A Side/B Side)	Yr	NM
❑ 115	Could This Be Magic/Blue Velvet	1964	8.00
—A-side is an alternate take of the hit version			
❑ 116	Don't Ask Me (To Be Lonely)/ Your Very First Love	1964	8.00
—A-side is an alternate take of the hit version			

MARK-X

Number	Title (A Side/B Side)	Yr	NM
❑ 8008	Be Sure My Love/Song in My Heart	1960	20.00

VICKIE

Number	Title (A Side/B Side)	Yr	NM
❑ 229	I'm Downtown/Lost in the Wilderness	1971	10.00
—As "Richard Blandon and the Dubs"			

WILSHIRE

Number	Title (A Side/B Side)	Yr	NM
❑ 201	Just You/Your Very First Love	1963	40.00

Albums

CANDELITE

Number	Title (A Side/B Side)	Yr	NM
❑ 1003	You've Got to Be Good to Make It in New York City	197?	12.00
❑ 1004	The Best of the Dubs	197?	12.00

DUBS, THE / THE SHELLS

Also see each artist's individual listings.

Albums

JOSIE

Number	Title (A Side/B Side)	Yr	NM
❑ JM-4001 [M]	The Dubs Meet the Shells	1962	300.00
❑ JSS-4001 [S]	The Dubs Meet the Shells	1962	600.00

DUCKS DELUXE

45s

RCA VICTOR

Number	Title (A Side/B Side)	Yr	NM
❑ APBO-0297	Daddy Put the Bomp/Please, Please, Please	1974	8.00

Albums

RCA VICTOR

Number	Title (A Side/B Side)	Yr	NM
❑ AFL1-3025	Don't Mind Rockin' Tonight	1978	10.00
❑ LPL1-5008	Ducks Deluxe	1973	15.00

DUDLEY, DAVE

45s

GOLDEN RING

Number	Title (A Side/B Side)	Yr	NM
❑ 3030	Cowboy Boots/I Think I'll Cheat (A Little Tonight)	1963	12.00
—"Golden Ring" on two lines, curved at top of label			
❑ 3030	Cowboy Boots/I Think I'll Cheat (A Little Tonight)	1963	15.00
—"Golden Ring" straight across top of label			

GOLDEN WING

Number	Title (A Side/B Side)	Yr	NM
❑ 3020	Six Days on the Road/ I Feel a Cry Coming On	1963	12.00
—Black vinyl			
❑ 3020	Six Days on the Road/ I Feel a Cry Coming On	1963	30.00
—Blue vinyl			

JUBILEE

Number	Title (A Side/B Side)	Yr	NM
❑ 5436	Under Cover of the Night/ Please Let Me Prove (My Love for You)	1962	20.00

KING

Number	Title (A Side/B Side)	Yr	NM
❑ 1508	Cry Baby Cry/This Is the Last Time	1955	40.00
❑ 4866	Ink Dries Quicker Than Tears/ I'll Be Waiting for You	1956	40.00
❑ 4933	Rock and Roll Nursery/I Guess You Know You're Right	1956	40.00
❑ 5792	Ink Dries Quicker Than Tears/ I'll Be Waiting for You	1963	20.00

MERCURY

Number	Title (A Side/B Side)	Yr	NM
❑ 72212	Last Day in the Mines/ Last Year's Heartaches	1963	10.00
❑ 72254	Big Ole House/If I Had One	1964	10.00
❑ 72308	Mad/Don't Be Surprised	1964	10.00
❑ 72384	Two Six Packs Away/ Hiding Behind the Curtain	1965	10.00
❑ 72442	Truck Drivin' Son-of-a-Gun/ I Got Lost	1965	10.00
❑ 72500	What We're Fighting For/ Coffee, Coffee, Coffee	1965	10.00
❑ 72550	Viet Nam Blues/Then I'll Come Home Again	1966	8.00
❑ 72585	Lonelyville/Time and Place	1966	8.00
❑ 72618	Long Time Gone/I Feel a Cry Comin' On	1966	8.00
❑ 72655	My Kind of Love/ Subject to Change	1967	8.00
❑ 72697	Trucker's Prayer/Don't Come Cryin' to Me	1967	8.00
❑ 72741	Anything Leaving Town Today/ I'd Rather Be Forgotten	1967	8.00
❑ 72779	There Ain't No Easy Run/ Why I Can't Be With You (Is a Shame)	1968	8.00
❑ 72818	I Keep Coming Back for More/ Where Does a Little Boy Go	1968	8.00
❑ 72856	Please Let Me Prove (My Love for You)/I'll Be Moving Along	1968	8.00
❑ 72902	One More Mile/Angel	1969	8.00
❑ 72952	George (And the North Woods)/ It's Not a Very Pleasant Day Today	1969	8.00
❑ 73029	The Pool Shark/The Bigger They Come, The Harder They Fall	1970	8.00
❑ 73089	This Night (Ain't Fit for Nothing But Drinking)/I'm Not So Easy Anymore	1970	7.00
❑ 73138	Listen Betty (I'm Singing Your Song)/I Hope My Kind of Love	1970	7.00
❑ 73142	Six Tons of Toys/Old Time Merry Christmas	1970	8.00
❑ 73193	Comin' Down/Six-O-One	1971	7.00
❑ 73225	Fly Away Again/There You Are Again	1971	7.00
❑ 73274	If It Feels Good Do It/Sometime in the Future	1972	7.00
❑ 73309	You've Gotta Cry Girl/Arms of a Satisfied Woman	1972	7.00
❑ 73367	Keep On Truckin'/It Won't Hurt As Much Tomorrow	1973	7.00
❑ 73404	It Takes Time/I Almost Didn't Make It Through the Door	1973	7.00

NEW STAR

Number	Title (A Side/B Side)	Yr	NM
❑ 6420	Under Cover of the Night/Please Let Me Prove (My Love for You)	1962	30.00

NRC

Number	Title (A Side/B Side)	Yr	NM
❑ 024	Where There's a Will There's a Way/I Won't Be Just Your Friend	1959	25.00

RICE

Number	Title (A Side/B Side)	Yr	NM
❑ 5064	Rollin' Rig/Six Days on the Road	1973	8.00
❑ 5067	Have It Your Way/ Blue Bedroom Eyes	1974	8.00
❑ 5069	Counterfeit Cowboy/ That's How Cold	1974	8.00
❑ 5070	Devils in Heaven Bound Machines/Farewell to Arms	1974	8.00
❑ 5074	Rollin' On, We Gone/ Farewell Two Arms	197?	7.00
❑ 5077	One A.M. Alone/If Seeing Is Believing	1978	7.00
—B-side by Billy D. Smith			
❑ 5078	Fly Away Again/ Tavern Telephone	1978	7.00
—B-side by Paul Click			
❑ 5083	I Do/Farewell, Two Arms	1981	7.00
❑ 5084	I Was Country Before Barbara Mandrell/(B-side unknown)	1981	7.00

STARDAY

Number	Title (A Side/B Side)	Yr	NM
❑ 364	Cry Baby/Careless Fool	1958	40.00
❑ 499	It's Gotta Be That Way/ Where Do I Go from Here	1960	20.00

SUN

Number	Title (A Side/B Side)	Yr	NM
❑ 1140	Moonlight in Vermont/Moritat	1979	6.00
❑ 1150	White Line Fever/The Last Run	1980	6.00
❑ 1154	Rolaids, Doan's Pills and Preparation H/Maybe I Can	1980	6.00
❑ 1155	Big Fanny/Where's the Truck	1980	6.00
—With Charlie Douglas			
❑ 1158	Cowboy, You're America/ The Driver	1980	6.00
❑ 1166 [DJ]	The Eagle (same on both sides)	1981	7.00
—Unknown on stock copy			
❑ 1180	I Wish I Had a Nickel/ Fools Rush In	1982	6.00

UNITED ARTISTS

Number	Title (A Side/B Side)	Yr	NM
❑ XW585	How Come It Took So Long (To Say Goodbye)/I've Lived Like a Piece of Grass	1974	6.00
❑ 613	Six Days on the Road/ I Feel a Cry Coming On	1963	—
—Canceled			
❑ XW630	Fireball Rolled a Seven/ Blue Bedroom Eyes	1975	6.00
❑ XW693	Where Did All the Cowboys Go/ Wave At 'Em Billy Boy	1975	6.00
❑ XW722	Me and Ole C.B./I Can't Remember You	1975	6.00
❑ XW766	Sentimental Journey/The Night You Broke the News	1976	6.00
❑ XW773	Seventeen Seventy-Six (1776)/ I Don't See the Rain	1976	6.00
❑ XW836	38 and Lonely/Texas Ruby	1976	6.00
❑ XW882	Where Does a Little Boy Go/ Rooster Hill	1977	6.00

VEE

Number	Title (A Side/B Side)	Yr	NM
❑ 7003	Maybe I Do/Your Only One	1961	30.00

Albums

GOLDEN RING

Number	Title (A Side/B Side)	Yr	NM
❑ GR 110 [M]	Dave Dudley Sings Six Days on the Road	1963	80.00

MERCURY

Number	Title (A Side/B Side)	Yr	NM
❑ SRM-1-669	Keep On Truckin'	1973	15.00
❑ MG-20899 [M]	Songs About the Working Man	1964	20.00
❑ MG-20927 [M]	Travelin' with Dave Dudley	1964	20.00
❑ MG-20970 [M]	Talk of the Town	1964	20.00
❑ MG-20999 [M]	Rural Route #1	1965	20.00
❑ MG-21028 [M]	Truck Drivin' Son-of-a-Gun	1965	20.00
❑ MG-21046 [M]	Dave Dudley's Greatest Hits	1965	20.00
❑ MG-21057 [M]	There's a Star Spangled Banner Waving Somewhere	1966	20.00
❑ MG-21074 [M]	Lonelyville	1966	20.00
❑ MG-21098 [M]	Free and Easy	1966	20.00
❑ MG-21133 [M]	Dave Dudley Country	1967	25.00
❑ MG-21144 [M]	Greatest Hits Vol. 2	1968	30.00
❑ SR-60899 [S]	Songs About the Working Man	1964	25.00
❑ SR-60927 [S]	Travelin' with Dave Dudley	1964	25.00
❑ SR-60970 [S]	Talk of the Town	1964	25.00
❑ SR-60999 [S]	Rural Route #1	1965	25.00
❑ SR-61028 [S]	Truck Drivin' Son-of-a-Gun	1965	25.00
❑ SR-61046 [S]	Dave Dudley's Greatest Hits	1965	25.00

Except when noted otherwise, VG = 25% of NM, and VG+ = 50% of NM. (Example: VG = $2.00, VG+ = $4.00 and NM = $8.00.)

Number	Title (A Side/B Side)	Yr	NM
❑ SR-61057 [S]	There's a Star Spangled Banner Waving Somewhere	1966	25.00
❑ SR-61074 [S]	Lonelyville	1966	25.00
❑ SR-61098 [S]	Free and Easy	1966	20.00
❑ SR-61133 [S]	Dave Dudley Country	1967	20.00
❑ SR-61144 [S]	Greatest Hits Vol. 2	1968	20.00
❑ SR-61172	Thanks for All the Miles	1968	20.00
❑ SR-61215	One More Mile	1969	20.00
❑ SR-61268	The Best of Dave Dudley	1970	15.00
❑ SR-61276	The Pool Shark	1970	15.00
❑ SR-61315	Dave Dudley Sings "Listen Betty, I'm Singing Your Song"	1971	15.00
❑ SR-61351	Will the Real Dave Dudley Please Sing	1971	15.00
❑ SR-61365	The Original Traveling Man	1972	15.00

UNITED ARTISTS

Number	Title (A Side/B Side)	Yr	NM
❑ UA-LA512-G	Uncommonly Good Country	1975	12.00

DUDLEY, DAVE, AND TOM T. HALL

45s

MERCURY

Number	Title (A Side/B Side)	Yr	NM
❑ 73139	Day Drinkin'/Get On with the Show	1970	7.00

DUDLEY, DAVE, AND KAREN O'DONNAL

45s

MERCURY

Number	Title (A Side/B Side)	Yr	NM
❑ 73345	We Know It's Over/Gettin' Back Together	1972	7.00

DUFFILL, TAM

45s

GROOVE

Number	Title (A Side/B Side)	Yr	NM
❑ 58-0004	Cooly Dooly/You Put the Hurt on Me	1963	60.00

DUGAN, DENNY

45s

HIT

Number	Title (A Side/B Side)	Yr	NM
❑ 114	The Shoop Shoop Song/That's the Way Boys Are	1964	8.00
—B-side by Connie Dee			

DUKAYS, THE

Also see GENE CHANDLER.

45s

NAT

Number	Title (A Side/B Side)	Yr	NM
❑ 4001	The Big Lie/The Girl's a Devil	1961	20.00
❑ 4002	Nite Owl/Festival of Love	1961	20.00

VEE JAY

Number	Title (A Side/B Side)	Yr	NM
❑ 430	Nite Owl/Festival of Love	1962	15.00
❑ 442	I'm Gonna Love You So/Please Help	1962	15.00
❑ 460	I Feel Good All Over/I Never Knew	1962	15.00
❑ 491	Combination/Every Step	1963	15.00

DUKE, BILLY

45s

ABC-PARAMOUNT

Number	Title (A Side/B Side)	Yr	NM
❑ 9816	Chalypso/Fork in the Road	1957	20.00
❑ 9826	Ready to Go Steady/Let Me Know	1957	20.00

CAPITOL

Number	Title (A Side/B Side)	Yr	NM
❑ 4784	New Orleans/Show Me the Way to Go Home	1962	12.00
❑ 4831	Summer at the Shore/Good Old Days	1962	12.00
❑ 4907	Goodbye Stranger/Millionaire	1963	12.00
❑ 5012	Echoes/The Best Man	1963	12.00

CASINO

Number	Title (A Side/B Side)	Yr	NM
❑ 138	Flip, Flop and Fly/Fun Lovin' Mama	1956	60.00

CORAL

Number	Title (A Side/B Side)	Yr	NM
❑ 9-61203	I Cried/Love Ya, Love Ya, Love Ya	1954	25.00

DATE

Number	Title (A Side/B Side)	Yr	NM
❑ 1005	Roland/What You Told Me	1958	20.00

PEAK

Number	Title (A Side/B Side)	Yr	NM
❑ 104	Chalypso/Fork in the Road	1957	30.00

SEVILLE

Number	Title (A Side/B Side)	Yr	NM
❑ 132	I'm the Lonesomest Guy in Town/While the Bloom Is on the Roses	1964	12.00
❑ 134	Six-O-Nine/Ciumachella (Tender Flower)	1964	12.00
❑ 136	Prisoner of Love/Sugar and Spice	1965	12.00

TEEN

Number	Title (A Side/B Side)	Yr	NM
❑ 110	Paradise Princess/I Know I Was Wrong	1955	40.00
❑ 112	Rocky Piano/Daddy Rock & Roll	1955	40.00

20TH FOX

Number	Title (A Side/B Side)	Yr	NM
❑ 242	The River Flows On/This Is What I Ask	1961	12.00
❑ 276	Be a Dreamer/Where Is That Feeling	1961	12.00
❑ 296	Amen/Walking Cane	1962	12.00
❑ 301	(Oooh Looka There) Ain't She Pretty/Timbuctu	1962	12.00
❑ 301 [PS]	(Oooh Looka There) Ain't She Pretty/Timbuctu	1962	50.00

DUKE, DENVER, AND JEFFERY NULL

45s

BLUE HEN

Number	Title (A Side/B Side)	Yr	NM
❑ 127	A Babe, A Star, A Manger/Christ, Who Came To Bethlehem	19??	12.00

MERCURY

Number	Title (A Side/B Side)	Yr	NM
❑ 70970	Hank Williams Isn't Dead/Rock and Roll Blues	1956	60.00

DUKE, GEORGE

12-Inch Singles

ELEKTRA

Number	Title (A Side/B Side)	Yr	NM
❑ ED 5162 [DJ]	Broken Glass (4 versions)	1986	8.00

EPIC

Number	Title (A Side/B Side)	Yr	NM
❑ AE 595 [DJ]	Straight from the Heart/Pluck	1979	10.00
—Red vinyl			
❑ 05052	Celebrate (Extended)/(Instrumental)	1983	8.00

WARNER BROS.

Number	Title (A Side/B Side)	Yr	NM
❑ PRO-A-6463 [DJ]	6 O'Clock (4 versions)	1993	8.00

45s

ELEKTRA

Number	Title (A Side/B Side)	Yr	NM
❑ 69296	Love Ballad/560SL	1989	3.00
❑ 69315	Guilty/(Instrumental)	1989	3.00
❑ 69504	Good Friend/African Violet	1986	3.00
❑ 69504 [PS]	Good Friend/African Violet	1986	3.00
❑ 69524	Broken Glass/Island Girl	1986	3.00
❑ 69649	Thief in the Night/La La	1985	3.00

EPIC

Number	Title (A Side/B Side)	Yr	NM
❑ 02701	Shine On/Positive Energy	1982	4.00
❑ 02932	Ride On Love/Let Your Love Shine	1982	4.00
❑ 03760	Reach Out (Part 1)/Reach Out (Part 2)	1983	4.00
❑ 50463	Reach For It/Just for You	1977	4.00
❑ 50531	Dukey Stick (Part One)/Dukey Stick(Part Two)	1978	4.00
❑ 50593	Movin' On/The Way I Feel	1978	4.00
❑ 50660	Say That You Will/I Am for Real (May the Funk Be With You)	1979	4.00
❑ 50719	Straight from the Heart/Pluck	1979	4.00
❑ 50792	I Want You for Myself/Party Down	1979	4.00
❑ 50853	Every Little Step I Take/Games	1980	4.00

Albums

ELEKTRA

Number	Title (A Side/B Side)	Yr	NM
❑ 60398	Thief in the Night	1985	15.00
❑ 60480	George Duke	1986	12.00
❑ 60778	Night After Night	1989	12.00

EPIC

Number	Title (A Side/B Side)	Yr	NM
❑ PE 34469	From Me to You	1977	12.00
—Orange label, no bar code on cover			
❑ PE 34469	From Me to You	198?	8.00
—Budget-line reissue; dark blue label, bar code on cover			
❑ JE 34883	Reach For It	1977	15.00
—Orange label; no bar code on cover			
❑ PE 34883	Reach For It	198?	8.00
—Budget-line reissue; dark blue label, bar code on back			
❑ JE 35366	Don't Let Go	1978	12.00
❑ PE 35366	Don't Let Go	198?	8.00
—Budget-line reissue with new prefix and bar code			
❑ JE 35701	Follow the Rainbow	1979	15.00
❑ JE 36263	Master of the Game	1979	15.00
❑ PE 36263	Master of the Game	198?	10.00
—Budget-line reissue with new prefix			
❑ FE 36483	A Brazilian Love Affair	1980	15.00
❑ FE 37532	Dream On	1982	12.00
❑ FE 38208	1976 Solo Keyboard Album	1983	20.00
❑ FE 38513	Guardian of the Light	1983	12.00
❑ FE 39262	Rendezvous	1984	15.00

LIBERTY

Number	Title (A Side/B Side)	Yr	NM
❑ ST-11004	Save the Country	1970	30.00
—Original issue			

MPS/BASF

Number	Title (A Side/B Side)	Yr	NM
❑ 22018	Faces in Reflection	1974	15.00
❑ 22835	Liberated Fantasies	1976	15.00
❑ 25355	Feel	1974	20.00
❑ 25613	The Aura Will Prevail	1975	20.00
❑ 25671	I Love the Blues, She Heard My Cry	1975	20.00

PACIFIC JAZZ

Number	Title (A Side/B Side)	Yr	NM
❑ PJ-LA891-H	George Duke	1978	15.00
❑ LN-10127	Save the Country	198?	12.00
—Reissue			

PAUSA

Number	Title (A Side/B Side)	Yr	NM
❑ PR 7042	The Aura Will Prevail	198?	10.00
—Reissue of MPS/BASF 25613			
❑ PR7070	I Love the Blues	1980	10.00

PICKWICK

Number	Title (A Side/B Side)	Yr	NM
❑ SPC-3588	Save the Country	1978	15.00
—Reissue of Liberty 11004			

VERVE/MPS

Number	Title (A Side/B Side)	Yr	NM
❑ 821665-1	Feel	1984	10.00
—Reissue of MPS/BASF 25355			
❑ 821837-1	The Aura Will Prevail	1984	10.00
—Reissue of Pausa 7042			

DUKE, PATTY

45s

UNITED ARTISTS

Number	Title (A Side/B Side)	Yr	NM
❑ 0127	Don't Just Stand There/Say Something Funny	1973	4.00
—"Silver Spotlight Series" reissue			
❑ 875	Don't Just Stand There/Everything But Love	1965	10.00
❑ 875 [PS]	Don't Just Stand There/Everything But Love	1965	20.00
❑ 915	Funny Little Butterflies/Say Something Funny	1965	8.00
❑ 915 [PS]	Funny Little Butterflies/Say Something Funny	1965	20.00
❑ 958	Why Don't They Understand/Ribbons and Roses	1965	—
—Unreleased			
❑ 978	Whenever She Holds You/Nothing But Me	1966	8.00
❑ 50034	Little Things Mean a Lot/The World Is Watching Us	1966	8.00
❑ 50034 [PS]	Little Things Mean a Lot/The World Is Watching Us	1966	25.00
❑ 50057	The Wall Came Tumbling Down/What Makes You Special	1966	8.00
❑ 50073	Why Don't They Understand/Danke Schoen	1966	8.00
❑ 50216	Come Live with Me/My Own Little Place	1967	6.00
❑ 50299	Dona, Dona/And We Were Strangers	1968	6.00

Albums

UNART

Number	Title (A Side/B Side)	Yr	NM
❑ 20005 [M]	TV's Teen Star	1967	12.00
❑ S 20005 [S]	TV's Teen Star	1967	15.00

UNITED ARTISTS

Number	Title (A Side/B Side)	Yr	NM
❑ UAL-3452 [M]	Don't Just Stand There	1965	20.00
❑ UAL-3492 [M]	Patty	1966	20.00
❑ UAL-3535 [M]	Patty Duke's Greatest Hits	1966	15.00
❑ UAS-6452 [S]	Don't Just Stand There	1965	30.00
❑ UAS-6492 [S]	Patty	1966	30.00
❑ UAS-6535 [S]	Patty Duke's Greatest Hits	1966	25.00
❑ UAS-6623	Songs from the Valley of the Dolls	1968	25.00

DUKE, PATTY, WITH NORMAN VINCENT PEALE

Albums

GUIDEPOSTS

Number	Title (A Side/B Side)	Yr	NM
❑ GP-101 [M]	Guideposts for Christmas	1963	80.00

DUKE OF EARL, THE

See GENE CHANDLER.

DUKES, THE

Possibly more than one group.

45s

FLIP

Number	Title (A Side/B Side)	Yr	NM
❑ 343	Looking for You/Groceries Sir	1959	30.00
❑ 345	I Love You/Leap Year Cha Cha	1959	40.00

IMPERIAL

Number	Title (A Side/B Side)	Yr	NM
❑ 5401	Teardrop Eyes/Shimmies and Shakes	1956	250.00
❑ 5415	Wini Brown/Cotton Pickin' Hands	1956	120.00

SPECIALTY

Number	Title (A Side/B Side)	Yr	NM
❑ 543	Ooh Bop She Bop/Oh-Kay	1954	75.00

DUKES OF DIXIELAND, THE

45s

COLUMBIA

Number	Title (A Side/B Side)	Yr	NM
❑ OP 50 [DJ]	If I Were a Bell/(B-side unknown)	195?	12.00
—"Special Coin-Operator Release"			
❑ 31356 [S]	(contents unknown)	1962	8.00
❑ 31357 [S]	(contents unknown)	1962	8.00
❑ 31358 [S]	(contents unknown)	1962	8.00
❑ 31359 [S]	(contents unknown)	1962	8.00
❑ 31360 [S]	(contents unknown)	1962	8.00
❑ 31575 [S]	(contents unknown)	1962	8.00
❑ 31576 [S]	(contents unknown)	1962	8.00
❑ 31577 [S]	(contents unknown)	1962	8.00

Number	Title (A Side/B Side)	Yr	NM
❑ 31578 [S]	(contents unknown)	1962	8.00
❑ 31579 [S]	(contents unknown)	1962	8.00

—Anyone who can fill in these gaps — the above 10 all are Columbia "Stereo 7" singles — please let us know.

Number	Title (A Side/B Side)	Yr	NM
❑ 42416	What's the Time?/Too Bad	1962	8.00
❑ 42599	Bye and Bye/Deep River	1962	8.00
❑ 43013	Fair Is Fair/Big Parade	1964	8.00

DECCA

Number	Title (A Side/B Side)	Yr	NM
❑ 25693	Everybody Loves My Baby/ Yvette	1966	5.00
❑ 25715	Baby Face/Rose of Washington Square	1967	5.00
❑ 25729	Smile/More and More	1968	5.00
❑ 31798	I Will Wait for You/ Exactly Like You	1966	6.00

Albums

AUDIO FIDELITY

Number	Title (A Side/B Side)	Yr	NM
❑ AFLP-1823 [M]	You Have to Hear It to Believe It — The Dukes of Dixieland, Vol. 1	1956	15.00
❑ AFLP-1840 [M]	You Have to Hear It to Believe It — The Dukes of Dixieland, Vol. 2	1957	15.00
❑ AFLP-1851 [M]	Marching Along with the Dukes of Dixieland, Vol. 3	1957	15.00
❑ AFLP-1860 [M]	The Dukes of Dixieland On Bourbon Street, Vol. 4	1958	15.00
❑ AFLP-1861 [M]	Minstrel Time with the Phenomenal Dukes of Dixieland, Vol. 5	1957	15.00
❑ AFLP-1862 [M]	Mardi Gras Time	1958	15.00
❑ AFLP-1891 [M]	The Dukes of Dixieland On Campus	1959	15.00
❑ AFLP-1892 [M]	Up the Mississippi	1959	15.00
❑ AFLP-1918 [M]	Carnegie Hall Concert	1959	15.00
❑ AFLP-1924 [M]	Louie and the Dukes of Dixieland	1960	15.00
❑ AFLP-1928 [M]	Piano Ragtime (Vol. 11)	1960	15.00
❑ AFLP-1956 [M]	The Best of the Dukes of Dixieland	1961	15.00
❑ AFLP-1976 [M]	More of the Best of the Dukes of Dixieland	1962	15.00
❑ AFSD-5823 [S]	You Have to Hear It to Believe It — The Dukes of Dixieland, Vol. 1	196?	20.00
❑ AFSD-5840 [S]	You Have to Hear It to Believe It — The Dukes of Dixieland, Vol. 2	196?	20.00
❑ AFSD-5851 [S]	Marching Along with the Dukes of Dixieland, Vol. 3	1958	20.00
❑ AFSD-5860 [S]	The Dukes of Dixieland On Bourbon Street, Vol. 4	1958	20.00
❑ AFSD-5861 [S]	Minstrel Time with the Phenomenal Dukes of Dixieland, Vol. 5	1958	20.00
❑ AFSD-5862 [S]	Mardi Gras Time	1958	20.00
❑ AFSD-5891 [S]	The Dukes of Dixieland On Campus	1959	20.00
❑ AFSD-5892 [S]	Up the Mississippi	1959	20.00
❑ AFSD-5918 [S]	Carnegie Hall Concert	1959	15.00
❑ AFSD-5924 [S]	Louie and the Dukes of Dixieland	1960	15.00
❑ AFSD-5928 [S]	Piano Ragtime (Vol. 11)	1960	15.00
❑ AFSD-5956 [S]	The Best of the Dukes of Dixieland	1961	15.00
❑ AFSD-5976 [S]	More of the Best of the Dukes of Dixieland	1962	15.00
❑ AFSD-6172	Tailgating	1967	12.00
❑ AFSD-6174	The Dukes of Dixieland On Parade	1967	12.00

COLUMBIA

Number	Title (A Side/B Side)	Yr	NM
❑ CL 1728 [M]	Breakin' It Up on Broadway	1962	12.00
❑ CL 1871 [M]	Dixieland Hootenanny!	1963	12.00
❑ CL 1966 [M]	The Dukes at Disneyland, Vol. 1	1963	12.00
❑ CL 2194 [M]	Struttin' at the World's Fair	1964	12.00
❑ CS 8528 [S]	Breakin' It Up on Broadway	1962	15.00
❑ CS 8671 [S]	Dixieland Hootenanny!	1963	15.00
❑ CS 8766 [S]	The Dukes at Disneyland, Vol. 1	1963	15.00
❑ CS 8994 [S]	Struttin' at the World's Fair	1964	15.00

DECCA

Number	Title (A Side/B Side)	Yr	NM
❑ DL 4653 [M]	"Live" At Bourbon Street, Chicago	1965	12.00
❑ DL 4708 [M]	Come On and Hear	1966	12.00
❑ DL 4807 [M]	Sunrise, Sunset	1966	12.00
❑ DL 4863 [M]	Come to the Cabaret	1967	15.00
❑ DL 4864 [M]	Thoroughly Modern Millie	1967	15.00
❑ DL 74653 [S]	"Live" At Bourbon Street, Chicago	1965	15.00
❑ DL 74708 [S]	Come On and Hear	1966	15.00
❑ DL 74807 [S]	Sunrise, Sunset	1966	15.00
❑ DL 74863 [S]	Come to the Cabaret	1967	12.00
❑ DL 74864 [S]	Thoroughly Modern Millie	1967	12.00
❑ DL 74975	Dixieland's Greatest Hits	1968	12.00

HARMONY

Number	Title (A Side/B Side)	Yr	NM
❑ HL 7349 [M]	Best of the Dukes of Dixieland	1965	12.00
❑ HS 11149 [S]	Best of the Dukes of Dixieland	1965	12.00

MCA

Number	Title (A Side/B Side)	Yr	NM
❑ 268	Dixieland's Greatest Hits	1973	10.00

—Reissue of Decca 74975

RCA VICTOR

Number	Title (A Side/B Side)	Yr	NM
❑ LPM-2097 [M]	The Dukes of Dixieland at the Jazz Band Ball	1960	12.00
❑ LSP-2097(e) [R]	The Dukes of Dixieland at the Jazz Band Ball	1960	15.00

ROULETTE

Number	Title (A Side/B Side)	Yr	NM
❑ R-25029 [M]	Curtain Going Up	1958	20.00

VIK

Number	Title (A Side/B Side)	Yr	NM
❑ LX-1025 [M]	The Dukes of Dixieland at the Jazz Band Ball	1956	30.00

VOCALION

Number	Title (A Side/B Side)	Yr	NM
❑ VL 73846	Hello, Dolly!	1968	10.00

DUMAURIERS, THE

45s

FURY

Number	Title (A Side/B Side)	Yr	NM
❑ 1011	Baby I Love You/All Night Long	1957	100.00

LOST-NITE

Number	Title (A Side/B Side)	Yr	NM
❑ 363	Baby I Love You/All Night Long	197?	5.00

—Reissue

DUNAVAN, TERRY

45s

FANFARE

Number	Title (A Side/B Side)	Yr	NM
❑ 727	Rock It on Mars/ Earthquake Boogie	195?	400.00

DUNBAR, AYNSLEY

Also see JEFFERSON AIRPLANE; JOURNEY; JOHN MAYALL.

Albums

BLUE THUMB

Number	Title (A Side/B Side)	Yr	NM
❑ BTS-4	The Aynsley Dunbar Retaliation	1968	30.00
❑ BTS-6	Doctor Dunbar's Prescription	1969	25.00
❑ BTS-16	To Mum From Aynsley and the Boys	1970	25.00

DUNBAR, TED

Albums

XANADU

Number	Title (A Side/B Side)	Yr	NM
❑ 155	Opening Remarks	1978	15.00
❑ 181	Secundum Artem	1980	12.00
❑ 196	Jazz Guitarist	1982	12.00

DUNCAN, HERBIE

45s

GLENN

Number	Title (A Side/B Side)	Yr	NM
❑ 1400	Hot Lips Baby/Little Angel	1961	400.00
❑ 1401	Roll Along/Escape	1961	120.00
❑ 1402	That's All/End of the Rainbow	1961	80.00

MAR-VEL

Number	Title (A Side/B Side)	Yr	NM
❑ 1400	Hot Lips Baby/Little Angel	1960	100.00

DUNDEE, CARLYLE, AND THE DUNDEES

45s

SPACE

Number	Title (A Side/B Side)	Yr	NM
❑ 201	Never/Evil One	1954	400.00

DUNGAREE DARLINGS, THE

45s

KAREN

Number	Title (A Side/B Side)	Yr	NM
❑ 1005	Boy of My Dreams/ Little Wallflower	1959	100.00

REGO

Number	Title (A Side/B Side)	Yr	NM
❑ 1003	Boy of My Dreams/ Little Wallflower	1958	250.00

—As "The Dungaree Dolls"

DUNGAREE DOLLS, THE

See THE DUNGAREE DARLINGS.

DUNN, JOHN

45s

HIT

Number	Title (A Side/B Side)	Yr	NM
❑ 22	Ahab the Arab/Dancin' Party	1962	8.00

—B-side by Herbert Hunter

DUPONTS, THE

Little Anthony's group before joining the Imperials. They are NOT the same group as the Imperials.

45s

ROULETTE

Number	Title (A Side/B Side)	Yr	NM
❑ 4060	Half Past Nothing/A Screamin' Ball (At Dracula Hall)	1958	25.00

ROYAL ROOST

Number	Title (A Side/B Side)	Yr	NM
❑ 627	Somebody/Prove It Tonight	1957	50.00

SAVOY

Number	Title (A Side/B Side)	Yr	NM
❑ 1552	Must Be Falling in Love/You	1958	25.00

—As "Little Anthony Guardine and the Dupонts"

WINLEY

Number	Title (A Side/B Side)	Yr	NM
❑ 212	Must Be Falling in Love/You	1957	80.00

DUPREE, CHAMPION JACK

45s

ATLANTIC

Number	Title (A Side/B Side)	Yr	NM
❑ 2032	Frankie and Johnny/Strollin'	1959	12.00

—As "Champion Jack"

Number	Title (A Side/B Side)	Yr	NM
❑ 2095	My Mother-in-Law/Evil Woman	1961	10.00

EVERLAST

Number	Title (A Side/B Side)	Yr	NM
❑ 5025	Shake Baby Shake/Walking Down the Highway	1963	10.00
❑ 5032	Highway Blues/ Shake Baby Shake	1964	8.00

FEDERAL

Number	Title (A Side/B Side)	Yr	NM
❑ 12408	Two Below Zero/Sharp Harp	1961	12.00

GROOVE

Number	Title (A Side/B Side)	Yr	NM
❑ 0171	Lonely Road Blues/When I Get Married	1956	40.00

—With Mr. Bear

KING

Number	Title (A Side/B Side)	Yr	NM
❑ 4695	Hard Feeling/Walking Upside Your Head	1954	30.00
❑ 4706	Camille/Rub a Little Boogie	1954	30.00
❑ 4779	Blues for Everybody/ Two Below Zero	1955	30.00
❑ 4797	Let the Doorbell Ring/ Harelip Blues	1955	30.00
❑ 4812	Walking the Blues/ Daybreak Rock	1955	30.00

—B-side by Mr. Bear and the Bearcats

Number	Title (A Side/B Side)	Yr	NM
❑ 4827	That's My Pa/Stumbling Block	1955	30.00
❑ 4859	Silent Partner/ She Cooks Me Cabbage	1955	30.00
❑ 4876	Me and My Mule/ Failing Health Blues	1956	30.00
❑ 4906	So Sorry, So Sorry/Overhead	1956	30.00
❑ 4938	Big Leg Woman/ Mail Order Woman	1956	30.00
❑ 6299	Blues for Everybody/ Tongue-Tied Blues	1970	6.00

RED ROBIN

Number	Title (A Side/B Side)	Yr	NM
❑ 109	Stumblin' Block Blues/ Number Nine Blues	1952	400.00
❑ 112	Shake Baby Shake/ Highway Blues	1952	200.00
❑ 130	Drunk Again/Shim Sham Shimmy	1954	200.00

VIK

Number	Title (A Side/B Side)	Yr	NM
❑ 0260	Just Like a Woman/Dirty Woman	1957	40.00
❑ 0279	Old Time Rock and Roll/ Rocky Mountain	1957	40.00
❑ 0304	Shake Baby Shake/ Lollipop Baby	1957	40.00

Albums

ATLANTIC

Number	Title (A Side/B Side)	Yr	NM
❑ 8019 [M]	Blues from the Gutter	1959	150.00
—Black label			
❑ 8019 [M]	Blues from the Gutter	1960	50.00
—White "fan" logo at right of label			
❑ 8019 [M]	Blues from the Gutter	1963	20.00
—Black "fan" logo at right of label			
❑ SD 8019 [S]	Blues from the Gutter	1959	200.00
—Green label			
❑ SD 8019 [S]	Blues from the Gutter	1960	60.00
—Green and blue label, white "fan" logo at right of label			
❑ SD 8019 [S]	Blues from the Gutter	1963	25.00
—Green and blue label, black "fan" logo at right of label			
❑ 8045 [M]	Natural and Soulful Blues	1961	50.00
—White "fan" logo at right of label			
❑ 8045 [M]	Natural and Soulful Blues	1963	20.00
—Black "fan" logo at right of label			
❑ SD 8045 [S]	Natural and Soulful Blues	1961	60.00
—Green and blue label, white "fan" logo at right of label			
❑ SD 8045 [S]	Natural and Soulful Blues	1963	25.00
—Green and blue label, black "fan" logo at right of label			
❑ 8056 [M]	Champion of the Blues	1961	50.00
—White "fan" logo at right of label			
❑ 8056 [M]	Champion of the Blues	1963	20.00
—Black "fan" logo at right of label			
❑ SD 8056 [R]	Champion of the Blues	196?	15.00
❑ SD 8255	Blues from the Gutter	1970	15.00

BLUE HORIZON

Number	Title (A Side/B Side)	Yr	NM
❑ 7702	When You Feel the Feeling	1969	25.00

BULLSEYE

Number	Title (A Side/B Side)	Yr	NM
❑ BB-9502	Back Home In New Orleans	1990	12.00

CONTINENTAL

Number	Title (A Side/B Side)	Yr	NM
❑ CLP-16002 [M]	Low Down Blues	1961	250.00

EVEREST ARCHIVE OF FOLK & JAZZ

Number	Title (A Side/B Side)	Yr	NM
❑ 217	Champion Jack Dupree	197?	10.00

FOLKWAYS

Number	Title (A Side/B Side)	Yr	NM
❑ FS-3825 [M]	Women Blues of Champion Jack Dupree	1961	25.00

Except when noted otherwise, VG = 25% of NM, and VG+ = 50% of NM. (Example: VG = $2.00, VG+ = $4.00 and NM = $8.00.)

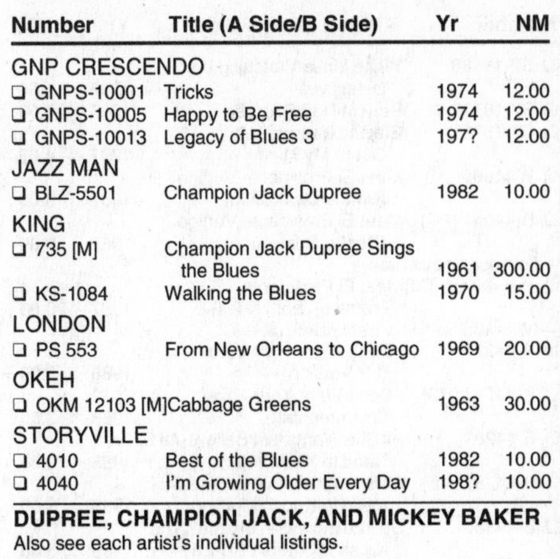

Number	Title (A Side/B Side)	Yr	NM
GNP CRESCENDO			
❑ GNPS-10001	Tricks	1974	12.00
❑ GNPS-10005	Happy to Be Free	1974	12.00
❑ GNPS-10013	Legacy of Blues 3	197?	12.00
JAZZ MAN			
❑ BLZ-5501	Champion Jack Dupree	1982	10.00
KING			
❑ 735 [M]	Champion Jack Dupree Sings the Blues	1961	300.00
❑ KS-1084	Walking the Blues	1970	15.00
LONDON			
❑ PS 553	From New Orleans to Chicago	1969	20.00
OKEH			
❑ OKM 12103 [M]	Cabbage Greens	1963	30.00
STORYVILLE			
❑ 4010	Best of the Blues	1982	10.00
❑ 4040	I'm Growing Older Every Day	198?	10.00

DUPREE, CHAMPION JACK, AND MICKEY BAKER

Also see each artist's individual listings.

Albums

Number	Title (A Side/B Side)	Yr	NM
SIRE			
❑ SES-97010	In Heavy Blues	1969	30.00

DUPREE, CHAMPION JACK, AND JIMMY RUSHING

Albums

Number	Title (A Side/B Side)	Yr	NM
AUDIO LAB			
❑ AL-1512 [M]	Two Shades of Blue	1958	200.00

DUPREE, DAVE See DAVE BURGESS.

DUPREE, SIMON, AND THE BIG SOUND

45s

Number	Title (A Side/B Side)	Yr	NM
TOWER			
❑ 427	Daytime, Night Time/I've Seen It All Before	1968	8.00

Albums

Number	Title (A Side/B Side)	Yr	NM
TOWER			
❑ ST-5097 [S]	Without Reservations	1968	40.00
❑ T-5097 [M]	Without Reservations	1968	100.00

DUPREES, THE

45s

Number	Title (A Side/B Side)	Yr	NM
COED			
❑ 569	You Belong to Me/Take Me As I Am	1962	20.00
❑ 571	My Own True Love/Ginny	1962	20.00
❑ 574	I'd Rather Be Here in Your Arms/I Wish I Could Believe You	1963	15.00
❑ 576	Gone with the Wind/Let's Make Love Again	1963	15.00
❑ 580	I Gotta Tell Her Now/Take Me As I Am	1963	15.00
❑ 584	Why Don't You Believe Me/My Dearest One	1963	15.00
❑ 584	Why Don't You Believe Me/The Things I Love	1963	30.00
❑ 585	Have You Heard/Love Eyes	1963	15.00
❑ 587	(It's No) Sin/The Sand and the Sea	1964	15.00
❑ 591	Please Let Her Know/Where Are You	1964	15.00
❑ 593	Unbelievable/So Many Have Told Me	1964	15.00
❑ 595	So Little Time/It Isn't Fair	1964	15.00
❑ 596	I'm Yours/Wishing Ring	1964	15.00
COLOSSUS			
❑ 110	Check Yourself/The Sky's the Limit	1970	6.00
—As "The Italian Asphalt and Pavement Company" or "The I.A.P. Co." for short			
❑ 110 [PS]	Check Yourself/The Sky's the Limit	1970	6.00
—As "The Italian Asphalt and Pavement Company" or "The I.A.P. Co." for short			
COLUMBIA			
❑ 43336	Around the Corner/They Said It Couldn't Be Done	1965	12.00
❑ 43464	Norma Jean/She Waits for Him	1965	12.00
❑ 43577	The Exodus Song/Let Them Talk	1966	12.00
❑ 43802	It's Not Time Now/Don't Want to Have to Do It	1966	10.00
❑ 44078	Be My Love/I Understand	1967	10.00
HERITAGE			
❑ 804	My Special Angel/Ring of Love	1968	10.00
❑ 805	Goodnight My Love/Ring of Love	1968	10.00
❑ 805 [PS]	Goodnight My Love/Ring of Love	1968	20.00
❑ 808	My Love, My Love/The Sky's the Limit	1968	10.00
❑ 808 [PS]	My Love, My Love/The Sky's the Limit	1968	20.00
❑ 811	Two Different Worlds/Hope	1969	10.00
❑ 811 [PS]	Two Different Worlds/Hope	1969	20.00
❑ 826	Have You Heard/My Love, My Love	1970	10.00
LOST-NITE			
❑ 165	You Belong to Me/Take Me As I Am	196?	6.00
—Reissue			
❑ 225	Why Don't You Believe Me/My Dearest One	196?	5.00
—Reissue			
❑ 228	Have You Heard/It Isn't Fair	196?	5.00
—Reissue			
❑ 232	Gone with the Wind/Let's Make Love Again	196?	5.00
—Reissue			
❑ 236	My Own True Love/Ginny	196?	5.00
—Reissue			
RCA VICTOR			
❑ PB-10407	The Sky's the Limit/Delicious	1975	10.00

Albums

Number	Title (A Side/B Side)	Yr	NM
COED			
❑ LPC-905 [M]	You Belong to Me	1962	300.00
❑ LPC-906 [M]	Have You Heard	1963	200.00
COLLECTABLES			
❑ COL-5008	The Best of the Duprees	198?	12.00
COLOSSUS			
❑ 5000	Duprees Gold	1970	30.00
—As "The Italian Asphalt & Pavement Co."			
HERITAGE			
❑ HT-35002 [M]	Total Recall	1968	80.00
—Mono is promo only; in stereo cover with "DJ Monaural" sticker on front			
❑ HTS-35002 [S]	Total Recall	1968	30.00
POST			
❑ 1000	The Duprees Sing	196?	30.00

Duran Duran, *Carnival*, Harvest DLP-15006, 1982, **$20.**

DURAN DURAN

12-Inch Singles

Number	Title (A Side/B Side)	Yr	NM
CAPITOL			
❑ 8551	Is There Something I Should Know? (Monster Mix 6:40)/Faith in This Colour (4:05)	1983	8.00
❑ 8567	Union of the Snake (12" Version 6:22)//(Single Version 4:20)/Secret Oktober (2:44)	1983	8.00
❑ V-8587	The Reflex (Dance Mix 6:35)(Dance Mix Edit 4:25)	1984	10.00
❑ V-8617	The Wild Boys (Wilder Than the Wild Boys Extended Mix 8:00)(4:14)/(I'm Looking for) Cracks in the Pavement (4:00)	1984	10.00
❑ SPRO-9060 [DJ]	New Moon on Monday (4:18) (same on both sides)	1983	10.00
❑ SPRO-9080 [DJ]	New Moon on Monday (Dance Mix 5:59) (same on both sides)	1983	15.00
❑ SPRO-9093/4 [DJ]	The Reflex (LP Version 5:28) (Single Version 4:25) (Live 5:52)/New Religion (Live 4:52)	1984	20.00
❑ SPRO-9266/7 [DJ]	The Wild Boys (4:14) (Wilder Than the Wild Boys Extended Mix 8:00)	1984	15.00
❑ SPRO-9314/5 [DJ]	Save a Prayer (Single Edit 3:45) (Album Version 5:33) (Live Edit 3:35) (Live Album Version 6:12)	1984	20.00
❑ SPRO-9391 [DJ]	A View to a Kill (same on both sides)	1985	25.00

Except when noted otherwise, VG = 25% of NM, and VG+ = 50% of NM. (Example: VG = $2.00, VG+ = $4.00 and NM = $8.00.)

Number	Title (A Side/B Side)	Yr	NM
❑ SPRO-9875/6 [DJ]	Notorious (Extended Mix 5:14) (45 Mix 3:58)	1986	30.00

—Promo only on clear vinyl

Number	Title (A Side/B Side)	Yr	NM
❑ SPRO-9939 [DJ]	Is There Something I Should Know? (4:05) (same on both sides)	1983	15.00
❑ SPRO-12085 [DJ]	Electric Barbarella (The Electric Sex Remix 5:02) (The Electric Sex Instrumental Remix 5:04) (The Americruiser Remix 6:08) (The Yo Shorty Americruiser Remix 5:01)	1997	12.00
❑ SPRO-12097 [DJ]	Electric Barbarella (All Fired Up Mix 7:09) (Barbarella Bonus Beats 4:45) (Album Version 5:15) (Edit 4:16)	1997	12.00
❑ SPRO-12098 [DJ]	Electric Barbarella (Tee's Club Mix 5:41) (Tee's Speed Dub 6:15) (Tee's Dance Mix 5:12) (TNT In-House Mix 5:12) (Tee's Capella 2:11)	1997	12.00
❑ SEAX-12352	The Reflex (Dance Mix 6:35) (Dance Mix Edit 4:25)	1984	30.00

—Picture disc with embossed outer sleeve; deduct 25% if cover is missing

Number	Title (A Side/B Side)	Yr	NM
❑ V-15264	Notorious (Extended Mix 5:14) (45 Mix 3:58)/ Winter Marches On	1986	10.00
❑ V-15266	Notorious (Latin Rascals Mix 6:16) (45 Mix 3:58)/ Winter Marches On	1986	15.00
❑ V-15274	Skin Trade (Stretch Mix 7:36) (Album Cut 5:58)/ We Need You	1986	10.00
❑ V-15294	The Presidential Suite: Meet El Presidente (7:12)/Meet El Beat (5:30)/Meet El Presidente (3:38)/Vertigo (Do the Demolition) (4:43)	1987	10.00
❑ VB-15320-1/2 [(2)]	Master Mixes: American Science (Chemical Reaction Mix 7:51)/Vertigo (Do the Demolition) (Mantronix Mix 6:35)/Skin Trade (Parisian Mix 8:10)//American Science (Meltdown Dub 7:33)/Vertigo (Do the Demolition) (B-Boy Mix 6:07)/Master Mix (Notoriousaurus Rex 7:20)	1986	40.00

—Two one-sided 12-inch records

Number	Title (A Side/B Side)	Yr	NM
❑ V-15417	I Don't Want Your Love (7" Mix 3:46) (Album Version 4:06) (Big Mix 7:25)	1988	8.00
❑ V-15434	All She Wants Is (US Mastermix 7:17) (Eurohouse Mix 7:32) (45 Mix 4:34)//I Believe/All I Need to Know (medley)	1988	8.00
❑ V-15456	Do You Believe in Shame/Krush Brothers LSD Edit/Notorious (Live)/Drug (It's Just a State of Mind) (Original Version)	1989	10.00
❑ V-15546	Burning the Ground/Decadance (Extended Mix 7:57) (3:29)	1989	8.00
❑ V-15612	Violence of Summer (Love's Taking Over) (Power Mix 4:56) (Dub Mix 4:47) (Rock Mix 4:23) (The Story Mix 3:14)/Throb (Instrumental 4:25)	1990	8.00
❑ Y-15995	Drowning Man (12" A 6:29) (Instrumental 6:29) (Dub 6:28) (Ambient Mix 6:45) (Album Version 5:15)	1993	20.00
❑ Y-58044 [DJ]	Too Much Information (Trance Mix 12" 6:00) (Trance Instrumental 12" 6:58) (Deptford Dub 6:26) (Club 2 Mix 4:15)	1993	20.00

—Blue vinyl

Number	Title (A Side/B Side)	Yr	NM
❑ Y 58674	Electric Barbarella (Tee's Club Mix 5:54) (Tee's Dance Mix 6:16) (All Fired Up Mix 7:12) (Barbarella Bonus Beats 4:49)	1997	10.00
❑ SPRO-79008/9 [DJ]	The Presidential Suite: Meet El Presidente (7:12)/Meet El Beat (5:30)/Meet El Presidente (Radio 3:38)// Skin Trade (Parisian Mix 8:10) (S.O.S. Dub 7:16)	1987	20.00
❑ SPRO-79269/70 [DJ]	Too Much Information (Trance Mix 12" 6:00) (Trance Instrumental 12" 6:58) (Deptford Dub 6:26) (Club 2 Mix 4:15)	1993	15.00
❑ SPRO-79482/3 [DJ]	All She Wants Is (US Mastermix 7:17) (US Masterdub 6:43) (Eurohouse Mix 7:32) (Eurohouse Dub I 7:07) (Eurohouse Dub II 5:43)	1988	30.00
❑ SPRO-79529 [DJ]	Do You Believe in Shame (same on both sides)	1989	20.00
❑ SPRO-79542/3/4/5 [(2)DJ]	White Lines (Junior's House Mix 5:37) (Sound Factory Dub 6:30) (70s Club Mix 7:54) (Oakland Funk Mix 5:29) (Freestyle Mix 5:41) (Sound Factory Dub 2 6:20) (Global Groove Mix 5:25) (Rif Raf Mix 5:35)	1994	25.00

HARVEST

Number	Title (A Side/B Side)	Yr	NM
❑ SPRO-9636/7 [DJ]	Planet Earth (Club Version 6:20) (Radio Version 3:59)	1981	80.00
❑ SPRO-9662 [DJ]	Careless Memories//Is There Anyone Out There/ Girls on Film	1981	30.00
❑ SPRO-9680/1 [DJ]	Girls On Film (Club Version 5:27) (Radio Version 3:30)	1981	20.00
❑ SPRO-9786/7 [DJ]	Hungry Like the Wolf (3:35)/ Lonely in Your Nightmare (3:52)/Rio (5:32)	1982	20.00

45s

CAPITOL

Number	Title (A Side/B Side)	Yr	NM
❑ B-5195	Hungry Like the Wolf (4:11)/ Hungry Like the Wolf (5:14)	1983	5.00

—Reissue of Harvest 5195 on purple label; much scarcer than the Harvest edition

Number	Title (A Side/B Side)	Yr	NM
❑ B-5215	Rio (3:57)/Hold Back the Rain (6:26)	1983	3.00
❑ B-5215 [PS]	Rio (3:57)/Hold Back the Rain (6:26)	1983	6.00
❑ B-5233	Is There Something I Should Know?/Careless Memories	1983	3.00
❑ B-5233 [PS]	Is There Something I Should Know?/Careless Memories	1983	4.00
❑ B-5290	Union of the Snake/ Secret Oktober	1983	3.00

—Custom label

Number	Title (A Side/B Side)	Yr	NM
❑ B-5290 [PS]	Union of the Snake/ Secret Oktober	1983	3.00
❑ B-5309	New Moon on Monday/ Tiger Tiger	1984	3.00
❑ B-5309 [PS]	New Moon on Monday/ Tiger Tiger	1984	3.00
❑ B-5345	The Reflex/New Religion	1984	4.00
❑ B-5345 [PS]	The Reflex/New Religion	1984	5.00

—Fold-open poster sleeve

Number	Title (A Side/B Side)	Yr	NM
❑ B-5345 [PS]	The Reflex/New Religion	1984	10.00

—Regular picture sleeve; released late in this single's chart run, this is much scarcer than the poster sleeve

Number	Title (A Side/B Side)	Yr	NM
❑ B-5417	The Wild Boys/(I'm Looking for) Cracks in the Pavement	1984	3.00
❑ B-5417 [PS]	The Wild Boys/(I'm Looking for) Cracks in the Pavement	1984	3.00
❑ B-5438	Save a Prayer/Save a Prayer (From the Arena)	1985	3.00
❑ B-5438 [PS]	Save a Prayer/Save a Prayer (From the Arena)	1985	3.00
❑ B-5475	A View to a Kill/A View to a Kill (That Fatal Kiss)	1985	3.00

—B-side by John Barry

Number	Title (A Side/B Side)	Yr	NM
❑ B-5475 [PS]	A View to a Kill/A View to a Kill (That Fatal Kiss)	1985	4.00
❑ B-5648	Notorious/Winter Marches On	1986	3.00
❑ B-5648 [PS]	Notorious/Winter Marches On	1986	3.00
❑ PB-5648 [DJ]	Notorious (same on both sides)	1986	20.00

—Clear vinyl in heavy clear plastic sleeve

Number	Title (A Side/B Side)	Yr	NM
❑ B-5670	Skin Trade/We Need You	1987	3.00
❑ B-5670 [PS]	Skin Trade/We Need You	1987	3.00

—American all-red sleeve

Number	Title (A Side/B Side)	Yr	NM
❑ B-5670 [PS]	Skin Trade/We Need You	1987	25.00

—Canada-only nude butt sleeve

Number	Title (A Side/B Side)	Yr	NM
❑ PB-5670 [DJ]	Skin Trade (same on both sides)	1987	20.00

—Red vinyl in heavy clear plastic sleeve

Number	Title (A Side/B Side)	Yr	NM
❑ 7-PRO-9330 [DJ]	Save a Prayer (Rio Edit)/ (Arena Edit)	1985	8.00
❑ 7-PRO-9330 [PS]	Save a Prayer (Rio Edit)/ (Arena Edit)	1985	12.00
❑ S7-17316	Come Undone/Skin Trade	1993	10.00
❑ S7-17438	Too Much Information/ Drowning Man	1993	5.00
❑ S7-18488	White Lines/Watching the Detectives	1995	4.00
❑ S7-18577	Perfect Day/Success	1995	4.00
❑ S7-19721	Electric Barbarella/ Out of My Mind	1997	4.00
❑ B-44001	Meet El Presidente/Vertigo (Do the Demolition)	1987	3.00
❑ B-44001 [PS]	Meet El Presidente/Vertigo (Do the Demolition)	1987	6.00

—Fold-open poster sleeve

Number	Title (A Side/B Side)	Yr	NM
❑ P-B-44001 [DJ]	Meet El Presidente (same on both sides)	1987	20.00

—White vinyl in heavy clear plastic sleeve

Number	Title (A Side/B Side)	Yr	NM
❑ B-44237	I Don't Want Your Love/ (LP Version)	1988	3.00
❑ B-44237 [PS]	I Don't Want Your Love/ (instrumental)	1988	3.00
❑ B-44287	All She Wants Is//I Believe-All I Need to Know (Medley)	1988	3.00
❑ B-44287 [PS]	All She Wants Is//I Believe-All I Need to Know (Medley)	1988	3.00
❑ B-44337	Do You Believe in Shame?/The Krush Brothers LSD Edit	1989	3.00
❑ B-44337 [PS]	Do You Believe in Shame?/The Krush Brothers LSD Edit	1989	3.00
❑ S7-56945	Ordinary World/Save a Prayer	1993	6.00

HARVEST

Number	Title (A Side/B Side)	Yr	NM
❑ A-5017	Planet Earth/To the Shore	1981	30.00
❑ P-A-5017 [DJ]	Planet Earth (same on both sides)	1981	15.00
❑ A-5070	Girls on Film/Faster Than Light	1981	25.00
❑ P-A-5070 [DJ]	Girls on Film (same on both sides)	1981	12.00
❑ B-5134	Hungry Like the Wolf (3:23)/ Careless Memories	1982	25.00
❑ P-B-5134 [DJ]	Hungry Like the Wolf (3:23 (same on both sides)	1982	15.00
❑ B-5175	Rio (4:34)/Hold Back the Rain (3:59)	1982	25.00

—Custom label; different mixes than on Capitol B-5215

Number	Title (A Side/B Side)	Yr	NM
❑ PB-5175 [DJ]	Rio (4:34) (same on both sides)	1982	15.00
❑ B-5195	Hungry Like the Wolf (4:11)/ Hungry Like the Wolf (5:14)	1982	3.00
❑ B-5195 [PS]	Hungry Like the Wolf (4:11)/ Hungry Like the Wolf (5:14)	1982	10.00

Albums

CAPITOL

Number	Title (A Side/B Side)	Yr	NM
❑ ST-12158	Duran Duran	1983	10.00

—Reissue of Harvest 12158 with new cover and 9 tracks, adding "Is There Something I Should Know"

Number	Title (A Side/B Side)	Yr	NM
❑ ST-12211	Rio	1983	8.00

—Version 4: Capitol logo replaces Harvest logo on back cover, otherwise it's the same as Harvest Version 3, with the same trail-off markings

Number	Title (A Side/B Side)	Yr	NM
❑ ST-12310	Seven and the Ragged Tiger	1983	8.00
❑ SWAV-12374	Arena	1984	10.00

—With booklet (deduct 25% if cut out or if booklet is missing)

Number	Title (A Side/B Side)	Yr	NM
❑ PJ-12540	Notorious	1986	8.00
❑ SPRO-79097/8 [EP]	Duran Goes Dutch	1987	80.00

—Promo-only five-song EP recorded live in Rotterdam

Number	Title (A Side/B Side)	Yr	NM
❑ C1-90958	Big Thing	1988	10.00

—Deduct 25% for cut-outs

Number	Title (A Side/B Side)	Yr	NM
❑ C1-93178	Decade	1989	12.00
❑ C1-94292	Liberty	1990	15.00
❑ R 100682	Big Thing	1988	12.00

—BMG Direct Marketing edition

Number	Title (A Side/B Side)	Yr	NM
❑ R 114794	Notorious	1987	12.00

—RCA Music Service edition

Number	Title (A Side/B Side)	Yr	NM
❑ R 134452	Duran Duran	1983	12.00

—RCA Music Service edition; with "Is There Something I Should Know?"

Number	Title (A Side/B Side)	Yr	NM
❑ R 140395	Arena	1984	12.00

—RCA Music Service edition

Number	Title (A Side/B Side)	Yr	NM
❑ R 163452	Rio	1983	15.00

—RCA Music Service edition; contains Harvest Version 1 of the album

Number	Title (A Side/B Side)	Yr	NM
❑ R 163458	Liberty	1990	15.00

—BMG Direct Marketing edition

Number	Title (A Side/B Side)	Yr	NM
❑ R 173573	Decade	1989	12.00

—BMG Direct Marketing edition

Number	Title (A Side/B Side)	Yr	NM
❑ ST-512211	Rio	1983	10.00

—Columbia House edition; otherwise the same as Version 4

EPIC

Number	Title (A Side/B Side)	Yr	NM
❑ E2 92900 [(2)]	Astronaut	2004	15.00

HARVEST

Number	Title (A Side/B Side)	Yr	NM
❑ ST-12158	Duran Duran	1981	15.00

—Original US issue with yellow label and 8 songs

Number	Title (A Side/B Side)	Yr	NM
❑ ST-12211	Rio	1982	12.00

—Version 3: Harvest logo on lower back cover, with five songs remixed by David Kershenbaum, but with a different mix of "Hungry Like the Wolf" than Version 2; Side 1 trail-off wax number is "ST-1-12211-Z18"

Number	Title (A Side/B Side)	Yr	NM
❑ ST-12211	Rio	1982	15.00

—Version 2: Harvest logo on lower back cover, with five songs remixed by David Kershenbaum; Side 1 trail-off wax number is "ST-1-12211-Z13-RE1 #1"

Number	Title (A Side/B Side)	Yr	NM
❑ ST-12211	Rio	1982	20.00

—Version 1: Harvest logo on lower back cover, contains the same versions of the songs as the original UK release; trail-off wax number on Side 1 is "ST-1-12211 Z1"

Number	Title (A Side/B Side)	Yr	NM
❑ MLP-15006 [EP]	Carnival	1982	20.00

MOBILE FIDELITY

Number	Title (A Side/B Side)	Yr	NM
❑ 1-182	Seven and the Ragged Tiger	1985	20.00
—Audiophile vinyl			

DURANTE, JIMMY

45s

DECCA

Number	Title (A Side/B Side)	Yr	NM
❑ 9-11046	Start Off Each Day with a Song/Inka Dinka Doo	195?	12.00
—"Collector's Classics" reissue; A-side with Eddie Jackson			
❑ 9-11046 [PS]	Start Off Each Day with a Song/Inka Dinka Doo	195?	15.00

MGM

Number	Title (A Side/B Side)	Yr	NM
❑ 30257	Frosty The Snowman/Christmas Comes But Once A Year	1950	15.00

WARNER BROS.

Number	Title (A Side/B Side)	Yr	NM
❑ 5382	September Song/Young at Heart	1963	8.00
❑ 5410	Hello Young Lovers/This Is All I Ask	1964	8.00
❑ 5456	This Train/When Love Flies Out the Window	1964	8.00
❑ 5483	Old Man Time/I Came Here to Swim	1964	8.00
❑ 5686	(I Wonder) What Became of Life/One of Those Songs	1965	8.00
❑ 5823	Mame/We're Going UFO'ing	1966	12.00
❑ 5843	Bill Bailey (Won't You Please Come Home)/Margie	1966	8.00
❑ 7024	Hellzapoppin'/M.F. O'Brien	1967	6.00
❑ 7253	He Touched Me/Amen	1968	6.00
❑ 7367	He Ain't Heavy, He's My Brother/Look Ahead Little Girl	1970	6.00

Albums

DECCA

Number	Title (A Side/B Side)	Yr	NM
❑ DL 5116 [10]	Jimmy Durante	195?	50.00
❑ DL 8884 [M]	Jimmy Durante at the Piano	1959	15.00
❑ DL 9049 [M]	Club Durant	195?	25.00
❑ DL 78884 [S]	Jimmy Durante at the Piano	1959	20.00

LION

Number	Title (A Side/B Side)	Yr	NM
❑ L-70053 [M]	Jimmy Durante in Person	195?	30.00

MGM

Number	Title (A Side/B Side)	Yr	NM
❑ E-3242 [M]	Jimmy Durante in Person	1955	30.00
❑ E-4207 [M]	The Very Best of Jimmy Durante	1964	12.00
❑ SE-4207 [S]	The Very Best of Jimmy Durante	1964	15.00

ROULETTE

Number	Title (A Side/B Side)	Yr	NM
❑ R-25123 [M]	Jimmy Durante at the Copacabana	1961	20.00
❑ SR-25123 [S]	Jimmy Durante at the Copacabana	1961	25.00

WARNER BROS.

Number	Title (A Side/B Side)	Yr	NM
❑ W 1506 [M]	September Song	1963	15.00
❑ WS 1506 [S]	September Song	1963	20.00
❑ W 1531 [M]	Hello Young Lovers	1964	15.00
❑ WS 1531 [S]	Hello Young Lovers	1964	20.00
❑ W 1577 [M]	Jimmy Durante's Way of Life	1965	15.00
❑ WS 1577 [S]	Jimmy Durante's Way of Life	1965	20.00
❑ W 1655 [M]	One of Those Songs	1966	15.00
❑ WS 1655 [S]	One of Those Songs	1966	20.00
❑ W 1713 [M]	Songs for Sunday	1967	15.00
❑ WS 1713 [S]	Songs for Sunday	1967	20.00

DURY, IAN, AND THE BLOCKHEADS

12-Inch Singles

STIFF

Number	Title (A Side/B Side)	Yr	NM
❑ SP 19 [DJ]	Wake Up and Make Love to Me/Billericay Dickie	1978	12.00

STIFF/EPIC

Number	Title (A Side/B Side)	Yr	NM
❑ AE 819 [DJ]	Hit Me with Your Rhythm Stick/Clever Bastards	1978	12.00
❑ 50779	Hit Me With Your Rhythm Stick/Reasons to Be Cheerful Pt. 3	1979	15.00

45s

STIFF

Number	Title (A Side/B Side)	Yr	NM
❑ SS 1000	Wake Up and Make Love to Me/Billericay Dickie	1978	4.00

STIFF/EPIC

Number	Title (A Side/B Side)	Yr	NM
❑ AE7 1190 [DJ]	Reasons for Promotion Pt. 3	1979	10.00
—With Tom Couch and Eddie Gorodetsky			
❑ 50726	Hit Me With Your Rhythm Stick/There Ain't Half Been Some Clever Bastards	1979	4.00
❑ 50726 [PS]	Hit Me With Your Rhythm Stick/There Ain't Half Been Some Clever Bastards	1979	4.00
❑ 50800	Reasons to Be Cheerful Pt. 3/Hit Me With Your Rhythm Stick (Dance Version)	1979	4.00

Albums

POLYDOR

Number	Title (A Side/B Side)	Yr	NM
❑ PD1-6337	Lord Upminster	1981	14.00

STIFF

Number	Title (A Side/B Side)	Yr	NM
❑ STF 0002	New Boots and Panties	1978	10.00

STIFF AMERICA

Number	Title (A Side/B Side)	Yr	NM
❑ USE 02	New Boots and Panties	1980	10.00
—Reissue of Stiff 0002			
❑ USE 17	Juke Box Dury	1981	12.00

STIFF/EPIC

Number	Title (A Side/B Side)	Yr	NM
❑ JE 36104	Do It Yourself	1979	12.00
❑ JE 36998	Laughter	1980	12.00

DUSK With Peggy Santaglia of THE ANGELS.

45s

BELL

Number	Title (A Side/B Side)	Yr	NM
❑ 961	Angel Baby/If We Just Leave Today	1971	6.00
❑ 961	Angel Baby/Reach Out and Speak My Name	1971	6.00
❑ 990	I Hear Those Church Bells Ringing/I Cannot See to See You	1971	6.00
❑ 45148	Suburbia U.S.A./Treat Me Like a Good Piece of Candy	1971	6.00
❑ 45207	Point of No Return/(B-side unknown)	1972	6.00

DUST

45s

KAMA SUTRA

Number	Title (A Side/B Side)	Yr	NM
❑ 534	Stone Woman/(B-side unknown)	1971	6.00
❑ 541	Love Me Hard/(B-side unknown)	1972	6.00

Albums

KAMA SUTRA

Number	Title (A Side/B Side)	Yr	NM
❑ KSBS-2041	Dust	1971	25.00
—Pink label			
❑ KSBS-2059	Hard Attack	1972	25.00
—Pink label			

DUSTERS, THE (1)

45s

ABC-PARAMOUNT

Number	Title (A Side/B Side)	Yr	NM
❑ 9887	Pretty Girl/Coolation	1958	30.00

CUPID

Number	Title (A Side/B Side)	Yr	NM
❑ 5003	Rock at the Hop/She's Mine	1958	70.00

GLORY

Number	Title (A Side/B Side)	Yr	NM
❑ 287	Darling Love/Teen-Age Jamboree	1958	50.00

DUSTERS, THE (2) TOMMY TUCKER was a member of this group.

45s

ARC

Number	Title (A Side/B Side)	Yr	NM
❑ 3000	Give Me Time/Sallie Mae	1956	300.00

DUVALL, HUELYN

45s

CHALLENGE

Number	Title (A Side/B Side)	Yr	NM
❑ 1012	Teen Queen/Comin' or Goin'	1957	30.00
—Maroon label			
❑ 1012	Teen Queen/Comin' or Goin'	1957	100.00
—Blue label			
❑ 59002	Hum-Dinger/You Knock Me Out	1958	30.00
❑ 59014	Little Boy Blue/Three Months to Kill	1958	40.00
❑ 59025	Friday Night on a Dollar Bill/Juliette	1958	30.00
❑ 59069	Pucker Paint/Boom Boom Baby	1960	30.00

DWARVES

45s

SUB POP

Number	Title (A Side/B Side)	Yr	NM
❑ 50	She's Dead/Fuckhead	1990	7.50
—Black vinyl pressing of 1,500			
❑ 50	She's Dead/Fuckhead	1990	22.50
—White vinyl pressing of 1,500			
❑ 50 [PS]	She's Dead/Fuckhead	1990	7.50
—#16 in Sub Pop Singles Club series			
❑ 113	Lucky Tonight	1991	5.00
—All copies on orange vinyl			
❑ 113 [PS]	Lucky Tonight	1991	5.00
❑ 183	Underworld/Lies	1993	5.00
❑ 183 [PS]	Underworld/Lies	1993	5.00
❑ 183-5	Underworld/Lies	1993	12.50
—Special 5-inch single pressing on orange vinyl			
❑ 183-5 [PS]	Underworld/Lies	1993	12.50
—Picture sleeve for the above			
❑ 195	Anybody Out There	1993	5.00
❑ 195 [PS]	Anybody Out There	1993	5.00

7-Inch Extended Plays

SUB POP

Number	Title (A Side/B Side)	Yr	NM
❑ 81	Drugstore	1990	5.00
❑ 81	Drugstore	1990	10.00
—Purple vinyl			
❑ 81 [PS]	Drugstore	1990	5.00
—Without pin			
❑ 81 [PS]	Drugstore	1990	10.00
—With "Fuck you up and get high" pin			

Albums

SUB POP

Number	Title (A Side/B Side)	Yr	NM
❑ 67	Blood, Guts and Pussy	1990	15.00
❑ 67	Blood, Guts and Pussy	1990	20.00
—First 1,000 on red vinyl			
❑ 126	Thank Heaven for Little Girls	1991	15.00
❑ 197	Sugar Fix	1993	15.00

DYKE AND THE BLAZERS

45s

ARTCO

Number	Title (A Side/B Side)	Yr	NM
❑ 45-101	Funky Broadway — Part 1/Funky Broadway — Part 2	1966	100.00

ORIGINAL SOUND

Number	Title (A Side/B Side)	Yr	NM
❑ 64	Funky Broadway — Part 1/Funky Broadway — Part 2	1966	10.00
❑ 69	So Sharp/Don't Bug Me	1967	8.00
❑ 79	Funky Walk Part 1 — East/Funky Walk Part 2 — West	1967	8.00
❑ 83	Funky Bull — Part 1/Funky Bull — Part 2	1968	8.00
❑ 86	We Got More Soul/Shotgun Slim	1969	8.00
❑ 89	Let a Woman Be a Woman — Let a Man Be a Man/Uhh	1969	8.00
❑ 90	You Are My Sunshine/City Dump	1969	8.00
❑ 91	Uhh/My Sister's and My Brother's Day Is Coming	1970	8.00
❑ 96	Runaway People/I'm So All Alone	1970	8.00

Albums

ORIGINAL SOUND

Number	Title (A Side/B Side)	Yr	NM
❑ LP 8876 [M]	The Funky Broadway	1967	50.00
❑ LPS 8876 [S]	The Funky Broadway	1967	75.00
❑ LPS 8877	Dyke's Greatest Hits	1968	75.00

DYLAN, BOB Also see HARRY BELAFONTE; GEORGE HARRISON AND FRIENDS; CAROLYN HESTER.

12-Inch Singles

COLUMBIA

Number	Title (A Side/B Side)	Yr	NM
❑ CAS 2169 [DJ]	When the Night Comes Falling from the Sky (Edit) (same on both sides)	1985	10.00

45s

ASYLUM

Number	Title (A Side/B Side)	Yr	NM
❑ 11033	On a Night Like This/You Angel You	1974	6.00
❑ 11035	Something There Is About You/Going, Going, Gone	1974	6.00
❑ 11043	Most Likely You Go Your Way (And I'll Go Mine)/Stage Fright	1974	6.00
—With The Band			
❑ 45212	All Along the Watchtower/It Ain't Me Babe	1974	12.00

COLUMBIA

Number	Title (A Side/B Side)	Yr	NM
❑ AE 25 [DJ]	All the Tired Horses (mono/stereo)	1970	40.00
❑ AE7 1039 [DJ]	If Not for You/Tomorrow Is a Long Time	1971	40.00
❑ 02510	Heart of Mine/The Groom's Still Waiting at the Altar	1981	4.00
❑ 02510 [PS]	Heart of Mine/The Groom's Still Waiting at the Altar	1981	5.00
❑ 04301	Sweetheart Like You/Union Sundown	1983	4.00
❑ 04301 [PS]	Sweetheart Like You/Union Sundown	1983	5.00
❑ 04425	Jokerman/Isis	1984	5.00
❑ 04933	Tight Connection to My Heart (Has Anybody Seen My Love)/We Better Talk This Over	1985	4.00
❑ 04933 [PS]	Tight Connection to My Heart (Has Anybody Seen My Love)/We Better Talk This Over	1985	4.00
❑ 05697	Emotionaly Yours/When the Night Comes Falling from the Sky	1985	4.00
❑ 07970	Silvio/Too Far from Home	1988	5.00
❑ 10106	Tangled Up in Blue/If You See Her Say Hello	1975	6.00
❑ 10217	Million Dollar Bash/Tears of Rage	1975	10.00
❑ 10245	Hurricane (Part 1)/Hurricane (Part 2)	1975	6.00
❑ 10245 [DJ]	Hurricane (mono/stereo)	1975	15.00
—Plays at 33 1/3 rpm; has "Special Rush Reservice" on label			
❑ 10245 [DJ]	Hurricane (mono/stereo)	1975	20.00
—Plays at 33 1/3 rpm; does not have "Special Rush Reservice" on label			
❑ 10245 [PS]	Hurricane (Part 1)/Hurricane (Part 2)	1975	12.00
❑ 10245 [PS]	Hurricane (mono/stereo)	1975	15.00
—Special sleeve for above record			
❑ 10298	Mozambique/Oh, Sister	1976	6.00

D

Bob Dylan, *Highway 61 Revisited*, Columbia CL 2389, 1965, mono, **$80.**

Number	Title (A Side/B Side)	Yr	NM
❑ 10454	Stuck Inside of Mobile with the Memphis Blues Again/ Rita Mae	1976	5.00
❑ 10454 [PS]	Stuck Inside of Mobile with the Memphis Blues Again/ Rita Mae	1976	6.00
❑ 10805	Baby Stop Crying/New Pony	1978	5.00
❑ 10851	Changing of the Guards/Senor (Tales of Yankee Power)	1978	4.00
❑ 10851 [DJ]	Changing of the Guards (Short 3:39)/(Long 6:36)	1978	8.00
❑ 11072	Gotta Serve Somebody/ Trouble in Mind	1979	4.00
❑ 11168	Man Gave Names to All the Animals/When You Gonna Wake Up	1979	4.00
❑ 11235	Slow Train/Do Right to Me Baby (Do Unto Others)	1980	4.00
❑ 11235 [PS]	Slow Train/Do Right to Me Baby (Do Unto Others)	1980	5.00
❑ 11318	Solid Rock/Covenant Woman	1980	4.00
❑ 11370	Saved/Are You Ready	1980	25.00
—Scarce on stock copy (promos worth about 20%)			
❑ 88697-16378-1 [DJ]	Most Likely You'll Go Your Way (And I'll Go Mine) (Mark Ronson Re-Version)/Most Likely You'll Go Your Way (And I'll Go Mine) (Original Version)	2007	10.00
—Small hole; given out at select record stores with the purchase of the CD "Dylan: His Greatest Songs"			
❑ 88697-16378-1 [PS]	Most Likely You'll Go Your Way (And I'll Go Mine) (Mark Ronson Re-Version)/Most Likely You'll Go Your Way (And I'll Go Mine) (Original Version)	2007	10.00
—Cardboard sleeve			
❑ CS7 32660 [DJ]	Tweedle Dee & Tweedle Dum/ Bye & Bye	2001	10.00
—Promo only on red label with black cardboard sleeve			

Number	Title (A Side/B Side)	Yr	NM
❑ 4-33100	Like a Rolling Stone/Rainy Day Women #12 and 35	196?	5.00
—"Hall of Fame" reissue; red and black label			
❑ 4-33178	Lay Lady Lay/I Threw It All Away	1970	5.00
—"Hall of Fame" reissue; red and black label			
❑ 13-33221	Positively 4th Street/ Subterranean Home Sick Blues	198?	5.00
—Gray label; "Home Sick" is two words on label			
❑ 4-33221	Positively 4th Street/ Subterranean Home Sick Blues	197?	6.00
—"Hall of Fame" reissue; red and black label			
❑ 42656	Mixed-Up Confusion/ Corrina, Corrina	1962	1500.
—Orange label			
❑ 42656 [DJ]	Mixed-Up Confusion/ Corrina, Corrina	1962	500.00
—White label			
❑ 42856	Blowin' in the Wind/Don't Think Twice, It's All Right	1963	500.00
❑ 42856 [DJ]	Blowin' in the Wind/Don't Think Twice, It's All Right	1963	300.00
—Regular promo			
❑ 42856 [PS]	Blowin' in the Wind/Don't Think Twice, It's All Right	1963	800.00
—"Rebel with a Cause" promotional flyer			
❑ 43242	Subterranean Homesick Blues/ She Belongs to Me	1965	20.00
❑ 43242	Subterranean Homesick Blues/ She Belongs to Me	1972	30.00
—Briefly issued on gray label, which was used for about six months in 1972			
❑ 43242 [DJ]	Subterranean Homesick Blues (same on both sides)	1965	250.00
—Promo only on red vinyl			
❑ 43242 [PS]	Subterranean Homesick Blues/ She Belongs to Me	1965	1500.
—Only issued with some promos			
❑ 43346	Like a Rolling Stone/ Gates of Eden	1965	20.00

Number	Title (A Side/B Side)	Yr	NM
❑ 43346 [DJ]	Like a Rolling Stone (same on both sides)	1965	200.00
—Promo only on red vinyl			
❑ 43389	Positively 4th Street/ From a Buick 6	1965	20.00
—Standard version			
❑ 43389	Positively 4th Street/ From a Buick 6	1965	30.00
—Odd version, possibly pressed for export, that plays at 45 but has a small center hole			
❑ 43389	Positively 4th Street/ From a Buick 6	1965	150.00
—A-side contains alternate version of "Can You Please Crawl Out Your Window." Evidently must be heard to identify.			
❑ 43389	Positively 4th Street/ From a Buick 6	1972	25.00
—Briefly issued on gray label, which was used for about six months in 1972			
❑ 43389 [DJ]	Positively 4th Street/ From a Buick 6	1965	120.00
—A-side contains alternate version of "Can You Please Crawl Out Your Window." Evidently must be heard to identify.			
❑ 43389 [DJ]	Positively 4th Street (same on both sides)	1965	150.00
—Promo only on red vinyl			
❑ 43389 [PS]	Positively 4th Street/ From a Buick 6	1965	70.00
❑ 43477	Can You Please Crawl Out Your Window?/Highway 61 Revisited	1965	20.00
❑ 43541	One of Us Must Know (Sooner or Later)/ Queen Jane Approximately	1966	20.00
❑ 43592	Rainy Day Women #12 and 35/ Pledging My Time	1966	15.00
❑ 43592 [DJ]	Rainy Day Women #12 and 35 (same on both sides)	1966	150.00
—Promo only on red vinyl			
❑ 43683	I Want You/Just Like Tom Thumb's Blues (Live)	1966	15.00
❑ 43683 [DJ]	I Want You (same on both sides)	1966	150.00
—Promo only on red vinyl			
❑ 43683 [PS]	I Want You/Just Like Tom Thumb's Blues (Live)	1966	80.00
❑ 43792	Just Like a Woman/ Obviously 5 Believers	1966	15.00
❑ 44069	Leopard-Skin Pill-Box Hat/ Most Likely You'll Go Your Way and I'll Go Mine	1967	20.00
❑ 44826	I Threw It All Away/ Drifter's Escape	1969	8.00
❑ 44926	Lay Lady Lay/Peggy Day	1969	8.00
❑ 45004	Tonight I'll Be Staying Here with You/Country Pie	1969	10.00
❑ 45199	Wigwam/Copper Kettle (The Pale Moonlight)	1970	6.00
—Orange label with "Columbia" background print			
❑ 45199	Wigwam/Copper Kettle (The Pale Moonlight)	1970	6.00
—Red label, "Columbia" repeated around outside of label			
❑ 45199	Wigwam/Copper Kettle (The Pale Moonlight)	1970	6.00
—Red label, black print			
❑ 45409	Watching the River Flow/ Spanish Is the Loving Tongue	1971	6.00
❑ 45516	George Jackson (Acoustic Version)/George Jackson (Big Band Version)	1971	10.00
❑ 45913	Knockin' on Heaven's Door/ Turkey Chase	1973	5.00
❑ 45982	A Fool Such As I/Lily of the West	1973	6.00
❑ 73042	Everything Is Broken/ Dead Man, Dead Man	1989	8.00
❑ JZSP 75606/7 [DJ]	Blowin' in the Wind/Don't Think Twice, It's All Right	1963	300.00
—"Special Album Excerpt" promo			
❑ JZSP 110939/40 [DJ]	Like a Rolling Stone (Part 1)/ Like a Rolling Stone (Part 2)	1965	60.00
❑ JZSP 113096/147 [DJ]	One Of Us Must Know (Sooner or Later) (4:49)/ (3:07)	1966	100.00
—Promo only, long and short versions			

MCA

Number	Title (A Side/B Side)	Yr	NM
❑ 52811	Band of the Hand/Theme from Joe's Death	1986	3.00
—By "Bob Dylan and the Heartbreakers"			
❑ 52811 [PS]	Band of the Hand/Theme from Joe's Death	1986	3.00

Albums

ASYLUM

Number	Title	Yr	NM
❑ AB-201 [(2)]	Before the Flood	1974	20.00
❑ AB-201 [(2)DJ]	Before the Flood	1974	50.00
—White label promo			
❑ 7E-1003	Planet Waves	1974	15.00
—Without wraparound (olive green) second cover			

Except when noted otherwise, VG = 25% of NM, and VG+ = 50% of NM. (Example: VG = $2.00, VG+ = $4.00 and NM = $8.00.)

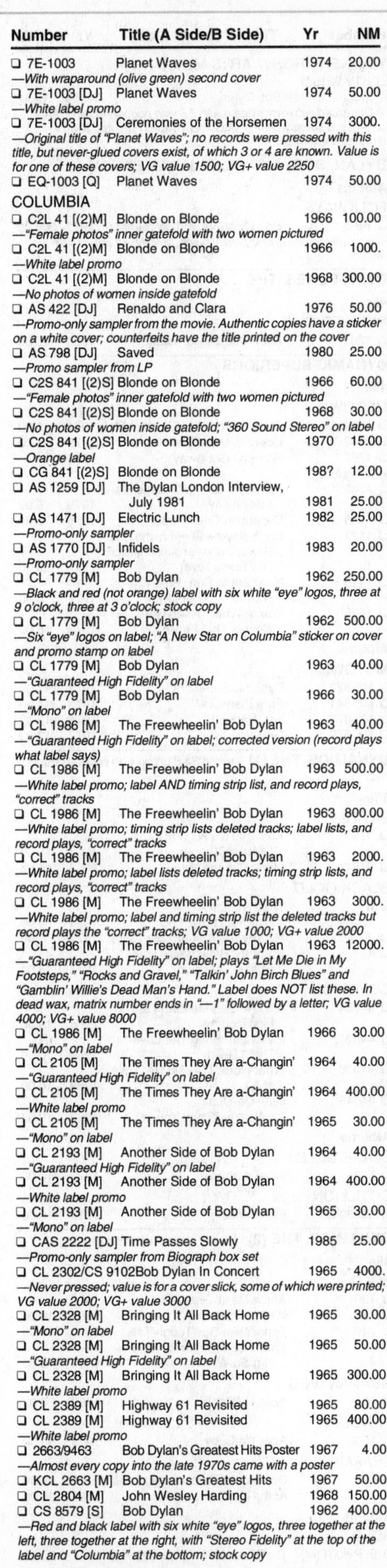

Number	Title (A Side/B Side)	Yr	NM
❑ 7E-1003	Planet Waves	1974	20.00
—With wraparound (olive green) second cover			
❑ 7E-1003 [DJ]	Planet Waves	1974	50.00
—White label promo			
❑ 7E-1003 [DJ]	Ceremonies of the Horsemen	1974	3000.
—Original title of "Planet Waves"; no records were pressed with this title, but never-glued covers exist, of which 3 or 4 are known. Value is for one of these covers; VG value 1500; VG+ value 2250			
❑ EQ-1003 [Q]	Planet Waves	1974	50.00
COLUMBIA			
❑ C2L 41 [(2)M]	Blonde on Blonde	1966	100.00
—"Female photos" inner gatefold with two women pictured			
❑ C2L 41 [(2)M]	Blonde on Blonde	1966	1000.
—White label promo			
❑ C2L 41 [(2)M]	Blonde on Blonde	1968	300.00
—No photos of women inside gatefold			
❑ AS 422 [DJ]	Renaldo and Clara	1976	50.00
—Promo-only sampler from the movie. Authentic copies have a sticker on a white cover; counterfeits have the title printed on the cover			
❑ AS 798 [DJ]	Saved	1980	25.00
—Promo sampler from LP			
❑ C2S 841 [(2)S]	Blonde on Blonde	1966	60.00
—"Female photos" inner gatefold with two women pictured			
❑ C2S 841 [(2)S]	Blonde on Blonde	1968	30.00
—No photos of women inside gatefold; "360 Sound Stereo" on label			
❑ C2S 841 [(2)S]	Blonde on Blonde	1970	15.00
—Orange label			
❑ CG 841 [(2)S]	Blonde on Blonde	198?	12.00
❑ AS 1259 [DJ]	The Dylan London Interview, July 1981	1981	25.00
❑ AS 1471 [DJ]	Electric Lunch	1982	25.00
—Promo-only sampler			
❑ AS 1770 [DJ]	Infidels	1983	20.00
—Promo-only sampler			
❑ CL 1779 [M]	Bob Dylan	1962	250.00
—Black and red (not orange) label with six white "eye" logos, three at 9 o'clock, three at 3 o'clock; stock copy			
❑ CL 1779 [M]	Bob Dylan	1962	500.00
—Six "eye" logos on label; "A New Star on Columbia" sticker on cover and promo stamp on label			
❑ CL 1779 [M]	Bob Dylan	1963	40.00
—"Guaranteed High Fidelity" on label			
❑ CL 1779 [M]	Bob Dylan	1966	30.00
—"Mono" on label			
❑ CL 1986 [M]	The Freewheelin' Bob Dylan	1963	40.00
—"Guaranteed High Fidelity" on label; corrected version (record plays what label says)			
❑ CL 1986 [M]	The Freewheelin' Bob Dylan	1963	500.00
—White label promo; label AND timing strip list, and record plays, "correct" tracks			
❑ CL 1986 [M]	The Freewheelin' Bob Dylan	1963	800.00
—White label promo; timing strip lists deleted tracks; label lists, and record plays, "correct" tracks			
❑ CL 1986 [M]	The Freewheelin' Bob Dylan	1963	2000.
—White label promo; label lists deleted tracks; timing strip lists, and record plays, "correct" tracks			
❑ CL 1986 [M]	The Freewheelin' Bob Dylan	1963	3000.
—White label promo; label and timing strip list the deleted tracks but record plays the "correct" tracks; VG value 1000; VG+ value 2000			
❑ CL 1986 [M]	The Freewheelin' Bob Dylan	1963	12000.
—"Guaranteed High Fidelity" on label; plays "Let Me Die in My Footsteps," "Rocks and Gravel," "Talkin' John Birch Blues" and "Gamblin' Willie's Dead Man's Hand." Label does NOT list these. In dead wax, matrix number ends in "—1" followed by a letter; VG value 4000; VG+ value 8000			
❑ CL 1986 [M]	The Freewheelin' Bob Dylan	1966	30.00
—"Mono" on label			
❑ CL 2105 [M]	The Times They Are a-Changin'	1964	40.00
—"Guaranteed High Fidelity" on label			
❑ CL 2105 [M]	The Times They Are a-Changin'	1964	400.00
—White label promo			
❑ CL 2105 [M]	The Times They Are a-Changin'	1965	30.00
—"Mono" on label			
❑ CL 2193 [M]	Another Side of Bob Dylan	1964	40.00
—"Guaranteed High Fidelity" on label			
❑ CL 2193 [M]	Another Side of Bob Dylan	1964	400.00
—White label promo			
❑ CL 2193 [M]	Another Side of Bob Dylan	1965	30.00
—"Mono" on label			
❑ CAS 2222 [DJ]	Time Passes Slowly	1985	25.00
—Promo-only sampler from Biograph box set			
❑ CL 2302/CS 9102	Bob Dylan In Concert	1965	4000.
—Never pressed; value is for a cover slick, some of which were printed; VG value 2000; VG+ value 3000			
❑ CL 2328 [M]	Bringing It All Back Home	1965	30.00
—"Mono" on label			
❑ CL 2328 [M]	Bringing It All Back Home	1965	50.00
—"Guaranteed High Fidelity" on label			
❑ CL 2328 [M]	Bringing It All Back Home	1965	300.00
—White label promo			
❑ CL 2389 [M]	Highway 61 Revisited	1965	80.00
❑ CL 2389 [M]	Highway 61 Revisited	1965	400.00
—White label promo			
❑ 2663/9463	Bob Dylan's Greatest Hits Poster	1967	4.00
—Almost every copy into the late 1970s came with a poster			
❑ KCL 2663 [M]	Bob Dylan's Greatest Hits	1967	50.00
❑ CL 2804 [M]	John Wesley Harding	1968	150.00
❑ CS 8579 [S]	Bob Dylan	1962	400.00
—Red and black label with six white "eye" logos, three together at the left, three together at the right, with "Stereo Fidelity" at the top of the label and "Columbia" at the bottom; stock copy			

Bob Dylan, *Blood on the Tracks*, Columbia PC 33235, 1975, black print on back, **$12.**

Number	Title (A Side/B Side)	Yr	NM
❑ CS 8579 [S]	Bob Dylan	1962	600.00
—Six "eye" logos on label; "A New Star on Columbia" sticker on cover and promo stamp on label			
❑ CS 8579 [S]	Bob Dylan	1963	40.00
—"360 Sound Stereo" in black on label			
❑ CS 8579 [S]	Bob Dylan	1965	25.00
—"360 Sound Stereo" in white on label			
❑ CS 8579 [S]	Bob Dylan	1970	12.00
—Orange label			
❑ JC 8579 [S]	Bob Dylan	197?	8.00
—Some copies of this pressing of the above album may have the song "You're No Good" listed on the label as "She's No Good." No extra premium has been attached to this error as yet.			
❑ KCS 8579 [S]	Bob Dylan	197?	10.00
❑ PC 8579 [S]	Bob Dylan	198?	8.00
—Budget-line reissue			
❑ PC 8579 [S]	Bob Dylan	2001	12.00
—Reissue on 180-gram vinyl (sealed copies have a sticker indicating this)			
❑ CS 8786 [S]	The Freewheelin' Bob Dylan	1963	50.00
—"360 Sound Stereo" in black on label (no arrows)			
❑ CS 8786 [S]	The Freewheelin' Bob Dylan	1963	400.00
—Canadian pressing with the deleted tracks listed on the front cover. The label lists, and the record plays, the "correct" tracks.			
❑ CS 8786 [S]	The Freewheelin' Bob Dylan	1963	30000.
—"360 Sound Stereo" in black on label (no arrows); record plays, and label lists, "Let Me Die in My Footsteps," "Rocks and Gravel," "Talkin' John Birch Blues" and "Gamblin' Willie's Dead Man's Hand." No known stereo copies play these without listing them, but just in case, check the trail-off for the numbers "XSM-58719-1A" and "XSM-58720-1A." If the number after the dash is "2" or higher, it's the standard version; VG value 15000; VG+ value 22500			
❑ CS 8786 [S]	The Freewheelin' Bob Dylan	1964	40.00
—"360 Sound Stereo" in black on label (with arrows)			
❑ CS 8786 [S]	The Freewheelin' Bob Dylan	1965	25.00
—"360 Sound Stereo" in white on label			
❑ CS 8786 [S]	The Freewheelin' Bob Dylan	197?	1000.
—Orange label; unauthorized red vinyl pressing			
❑ CS 8786 [S]	The Freewheelin' Bob Dylan	1970	12.00
—Orange label			
❑ KCS 8786 [S]	The Freewheelin' Bob Dylan	197?	10.00
❑ PC 8786 [S]	The Freewheelin' Bob Dylan	198?	8.00
—Budget-line reissue			

Number	Title (A Side/B Side)	Yr	NM
❑ PC 8786 [S]	The Freewheelin' Bob Dylan	2001	12.00
—Reissue on 180-gram vinyl (sealed copies have a sticker indicating this)			
❑ CS 8905 [S]	The Times They Are a-Changin'	1964	40.00
—"360 Sound Stereo" in black on label			
❑ CS 8905 [S]	The Times They Are a-Changin'	1965	25.00
—"360 Sound Stereo" in white on label			
❑ CS 8905 [S]	The Times They Are a-Changin'	1970	12.00
—Orange label			
❑ KCS 8905 [S]	The Times They Are a-Changin'	197?	10.00
❑ PC 8905 [S]	The Times They Are a-Changin'	198?	8.00
—Budget-line reissue			
❑ PC 8905 [S]	The Times They Are a-Changin'	2001	12.00
—Reissue on 180-gram vinyl (sealed copies have a sticker indicating this)			
❑ CS 8993 [S]	Another Side of Bob Dylan	1964	40.00
—"360 Sound Stereo" in black on label			
❑ CS 8993 [S]	Another Side of Bob Dylan	1965	25.00
—"360 Sound Stereo" in white on label			
❑ CS 8993 [S]	Another Side of Bob Dylan	1970	12.00
—Orange label			
❑ KCS 8993 [S]	Another Side of Bob Dylan	197?	10.00
❑ PC 8993 [S]	Another Side of Bob Dylan	198?	8.00
—Budget-line reissue			
❑ PC 8993 [S]	Another Side of Bob Dylan	2001	12.00
—Reissue on 180-gram vinyl (sealed copies have a sticker indicating this)			
❑ CS 9128 [S]	Bringing It All Back Home	1965	25.00
—"360 Sound Stereo" in white on label			
❑ CS 9128 [S]	Bringing It All Back Home	1965	40.00
—"360 Sound Stereo" in black on label			
❑ CS 9128 [S]	Bringing It All Back Home	1970	12.00
—Orange label			
❑ JC 9128 [S]	Bringing It All Back Home	197?	10.00
❑ KCS 9128 [S]	Bringing It All Back Home	197?	10.00
❑ PC 9128 [S]	Bringing It All Back Home	198?	8.00
—Budget-line reissue			
❑ PC 9128 [S]	Bringing It All Back Home	2001	12.00
—Reissue on 180-gram vinyl (sealed copies have a sticker indicating this)			
❑ CS 9189 [S]	Highway 61 Revisited	1965	30.00
—With "regular" take of "From a Buick 6." Matrix number on Side 1 will end in "—2" or higher, plus a letter; "360 Sound Stereo" on label			

Number	Title (A Side/B Side)	Yr	NM
❑ CS 9189 [S]	Highway 61 Revisited	1965	250.00

—With alternate take of "From a Buick 6." Matrix number on Side 1 will end in "—1" plus a letter

Number	Title (A Side/B Side)	Yr	NM
❑ CS 9189 [S]	Highway 61 Revisited	1970	12.00
—Orange label			
❑ JC 9189 [S]	Highway 61 Revisited	197?	10.00
❑ KCS 9189 [S]	Highway 61 Revisited	197?	10.00
❑ PC 9189 [S]	Highway 61 Revisited	198?	8.00
—Budget-line reissue			
❑ PC 9189 [S]	Highway 61 Revisited	2001	12.00
—Reissue on 180-gram vinyl (sealed copies have a sticker indicating this)			
❑ JC 9463 [S]	Bob Dylan's Greatest Hits	197?	10.00
❑ JC 9463 [S]	Bob Dylan's Greatest Hits	2001	12.00
—Reissue on 180-gram vinyl (sealed copies have a sticker indicating this)			
❑ KCS 9463 [S]	Bob Dylan's Greatest Hits	1967	15.00
—"360 Sound Stereo" label			
❑ KCS 9463 [S]	Bob Dylan's Greatest Hits	1970	12.00
—Orange label			
❑ CS 9604 [S]	John Wesley Harding	1968	20.00
—"360 Sound Stereo" label			
❑ CS 9604 [S]	John Wesley Harding	1970	12.00
—Orange label			
❑ JC 9604 [S]	John Wesley Harding	197?	10.00
❑ KCS 9604 [S]	John Wesley Harding	197?	10.00
❑ PC 9604 [S]	John Wesley Harding	198?	8.00
—Budget-line reissue			
❑ PC 9604 [S]	John Wesley Harding	2001	12.00
—Reissue on 180-gram vinyl (sealed copies have a sticker indicating this)			
❑ JC 9825	Nashville Skyline	197?	10.00
❑ KCS 9825	Nashville Skyline	1969	30.00
—"360 Sound Stereo" label			
❑ KCS 9825	Nashville Skyline	1970	12.00
—Orange label			
❑ PC 9825	Nashville Skyline	198?	8.00
—Budget-line reissue			
❑ C2X 30050 [(2)]	Self Portrait	1970	20.00
—Orange labels			
❑ C2X 30050 [(2)]	Self Portrait	1970	150.00
—"360 Sound Stereo" labels			
❑ CG 30050 [(2)]	Self Portrait	198?	12.00
❑ P2X 30050 [(2)]	Self Portrait	197?	15.00
❑ KC 30290	New Morning	1970	15.00
❑ PC 30290	New Morning	197?	8.00
❑ PC 30290	New Morning	2001	12.00
—Reissue on 180-gram vinyl (sealed copies have a sticker indicating this)			
❑ CG 31120 [(2)]	Bob Dylan's Greatest Hits, Vol. II	198?	10.00
❑ KG 31120 [(2)]	Bob Dylan's Greatest Hits, Vol. II	1971	15.00
❑ PG 31120 [(2)]	Bob Dylan's Greatest Hits, Vol. II	197?	12.00
❑ KC 32460	Pat Garrett and Billy the Kid	1973	15.00
❑ PC 32460	Pat Garrett and Billy the Kid	197?	8.00
❑ PC 32747	Dylan	1973	15.00
—No bar code on cover			
❑ PC 32747	Dylan	1979	8.00
—With bar code on back cover			
❑ KCQ 32825 [Q]	Nashville Skyline	1973	30.00
❑ PC 33235	Blood on the Tracks	1975	10.00
—Third editions have liner notes restored (after they won a Grammy), but in white print			
❑ PC 33235	Blood on the Tracks	1975	12.00
—First editions have liner notes on the back cover in black print			
❑ PC 33235	Blood on the Tracks	1975	15.00
—With drawing on back cover and no liner notes. Actually a second pressing, but available only for a short time			
❑ PC 33235	Blood on the Tracks	1975	2000.
—First edition cover; with the original rejected version of Side 2, though Side 1 is the standard version; the master number in the trail-off wax on Side 2 is "-1A"; one copy known, but others may exist			
❑ PC 33235	Blood on the Tracks	1979	8.00
—With bar code on back cover			
❑ PC 33235	Blood on the Tracks	2001	12.00
—Reissue on 180-gram vinyl (sealed copies have a sticker indicating this)			
❑ PC 33235 [DJ]	Blood on the Tracks	1975	30.00
—Regular white label promo			
❑ PC 33235 [DJ]	Blood on the Tracks	1975	5000.
—Test pressing with radically different versions of five songs including "Idiot Wind" and "Tangled Up in Blue"; VG value 2500; VG+ value 3750			
❑ CG 33682 [(2)]	The Basement Tapes	198?	12.00
❑ PC2 33682 [(2)]	The Basement Tapes	1975	20.00
❑ PC2 33682 [(2)DJ]	The Basement Tapes	1975	40.00
—White label promo			
❑ JC 33893	Desire	1977	10.00
—No bar code on back cover			
❑ JC 33893	Desire	1979	8.00
—With bar code on back cover			
❑ PC 33893	Desire	1976	12.00
❑ PC 33893 [DJ]	Desire	1976	30.00
—White label promo			
❑ PCQ 33893 [Q]	Desire	1976	30.00
❑ JC 34349	Hard Rain	1977	10.00
❑ PC 34349	Hard Rain	1976	12.00
—No bar code on back cover			
❑ PC 34349	Hard Rain	198?	8.00
—With bar code on back cover			
❑ PC 34349 [DJ]	Hard Rain	1976	30.00
—White label promo			
❑ JC 35453	Street Legal	1978	12.00
❑ JC 35453 [DJ]	Street Legal	1978	25.00
—White label promo			
❑ PC 35453	Street Legal	198?	8.00
❑ CG 36067 [(2)]	Bob Dylan at Budokan	198?	12.00
❑ PC2 36067 [(2)]	Bob Dylan at Budokan	1979	15.00
❑ PC2 36067 [(2)DJ]	Bob Dylan at Budokan	1979	30.00
—White label promo			
❑ FC 36120	Slow Train Coming	1979	10.00
❑ FC 36120 [DJ]	Slow Train Coming	1979	25.00
—White label promo			
❑ PC 36120	Slow Train Coming	198?	8.00
—Budget-line reissue			
❑ FC 36553	Saved	1980	10.00
❑ PC 36553	Saved	198?	8.00
—Budget-line reissue with new cover			
❑ PC 37496	Shot of Love	198?	8.00
—Budget-line reissue			
❑ TC 37496	Shot of Love	1981	10.00
❑ PC 37637	Planet Waves	1981	10.00
—Reissue of Asylum 7E-1003			
❑ CG 37661 [(2)]	Before the Flood	1983	12.00
—Reissue of Asylum AB-201			
❑ PC 38819	Infidels	1986	8.00
—Budget-line reissue			
❑ QC 38819	Infidels	1983	10.00
❑ C5X 38830 [(5)]	Biograph	1985	30.00
❑ FC 39944	Real Live	1984	10.00
❑ FC 40110	Empire Burlesque	1985	10.00
❑ OC 40439	Knocked Out Loaded	1986	10.00
❑ OC 40957	Down in the Groove	1988	10.00
❑ HC 43235	Blood on the Tracks	198?	50.00
—Half-speed mastered edition			
❑ OC 45056	Dylan and the Dead	1989	12.00
—With backing by The Grateful Dead			
❑ OC 45281	Oh Mercy	1989	12.00
❑ C 46794	Under the Red Sky	1990	12.00
❑ HC 49825	Nashville Skyline	198?	60.00
—Half-speed mastered edition			
❑ C 53200	Good As I Been to You	1992	60.00
❑ CK2-65759-1 [(2)]	The Bootleg Series Vol. 4: Bob Dylan Live 1966, The "Royal Albert Hall" Concert	1999	100.00
—Classic Records box set with 12x12 booklet and two records individually packaged in cardboard jackets and sleeves			
❑ C2 67000 [(2)]	MTV Unplugged	1995	15.00
❑ C2 68556 [(2)]	Time Out of Mind	1998	15.00
❑ C2 85975 [(2)]	Love and Theft	2001	15.00
❑ C2K-87047-1 [(3)]	The Bootleg Series Vol. 5: Rolling Thunder Revue Starring Bob Dylan	2003	50.00
—Similar to the other package, but records are pressed on 140-gram vinyl and come in plain paper (rather than lined) sleeves			
❑ C2K-87047-1 [(3)]	The Bootleg Series Vol. 5: Rolling Thunder Revue Starring Bob Dylan	2003	100.00
—Classic Records box set with 12x12 booklet, three 200-gram 12-inch records individually packaged in cardboard jackets and sleeves, a blue vinyl 7-inch single in a picture sleeve, a poster, a souvenir handbill and facsimile tickets to the show			
❑ 82876-87606-1 [(2)]	Modern Times	2006	15.00
❑ 474000 [(3)]	Bob Dylan — The 30th Anniversary Concert Celebration	1993	30.00
—Albums pressed in US for export to Europe; some stayed here			
ISLAND			
❑ AB-201 [(2)]	Before the Flood	1974	40.00
—Error pressing with wrong labels (should be Asylum)			
MOBILE FIDELITY			
❑ 1-114	The Times They Are a-Changin'	1982	75.00
—Audiophile vinyl			
SUNDAZED			
❑ LP 5070 [M]	Bringing It All Back Home	2001	15.00
—180-gram reissue of the original mono mix			
❑ LP 5071 [M]	Highway 61 Revisited	2001	15.00
—180-gram reissue of the original mono mix			
❑ LP 5108 [M]	The Times They Are a-Changin'	2001	15.00
—180-gram reissue of the original mono mix			
❑ LP 5110 [(2)M]	Blonde on Blonde	2002	25.00
—180-gram reissue of the original mono mix			
❑ LP 5115 [M]	The Freewheelin' Bob Dylan	2001	15.00
—180-gram reissue of the original mono mix			
❑ LP 5120 [M]	Bob Dylan	2004	15.00
—180-gram reissue of the original mono mix			
❑ LP 5121 [M]	Another Side of Bob Dylan	2002	15.00
—180-gram reissue of the original mono mix			
❑ LP 5123 [M]	John Wesley Harding	2003	15.00
—180-gram reissue of the original mono mix			
❑ LP 5156 [M]	Bob Dylan's Greatest Hits	2003	15.00
—180-gram reissue of the original mono mix			
WARNER BROS./7 ARTS MUSIC			
❑ XTV 221567 [DJ]	Bob Dylan	1969	1500.
—One-sided publisher's demo with 8 Dylan performances of then-unreleased songs from the "Basement Tapes" era; add $500 if includes sheet music.			

DYLAN, BOB, AND ALAN J. WEBERMAN

Albums

FOLKWAYS

Number	Title (A Side/B Side)	Yr	NM
❑ FB-5322 [M]	Bob Dylan Vs. A.J. Weberman	1977	300.00

—A tape-recorded phone conversation; quickly withdrawn from the market

DYNA-SORES, THE

45s

RENDEZVOUS

Number	Title (A Side/B Side)	Yr	NM
❑ 120	Alley-Oop/Jungle Walk	1960	25.00

DYNAMIC SUPERIORS

45s

MOTOWN

Number	Title (A Side/B Side)	Yr	NM
❑ 1324	Shoe Shoe Shine/Release Me	1974	6.00
❑ 1342	Leave It Alone/One-Nighter	1975	6.00
❑ 1357	Romeo/I Got Away	1975	—
—Canceled?			
❑ 1359	Nobody's Gonna Change Me/I Got Away	1975	6.00
❑ 1365	Deception/One Nighter	1975	6.00
❑ 1413	Can't Stay Away (From the One I Love)/Supersensuosensation (Try Some Love)	1977	6.00
❑ 1419	Nowhere to Run, Pt. 1/Nowhere to Run, Pt. 2	1977	6.00
❑ 1428	You're What I Need/Here Comes That Feeling	1977	6.00

Albums

MOTOWN

Number	Title (A Side/B Side)	Yr	NM
❑ M6-822	Dynamic Superiors	1974	12.00
❑ M6-841	Pure Pleasure	1975	12.00
❑ M6-875	You Name It	1976	12.00
❑ M6-879	Give and Take	1977	12.00

DYNAMICS, THE (1)

Detroit R&B group with several charted hits.

45s

Number	Title (A Side/B Side)	Yr	NM
BIG TOP			
❑ 516	And That's a Natural Fact/I Wanna Know	1964	15.00
❑ 3161	Misery/I'm the Man	1963	15.00
BLACK GOLD			
❑ 8	What a Shame/Shucks, I Love You	1973	6.00
❑ 9	Funkey Key/Count Your Chips	1973	6.00
❑ 11	She's for Real (Bless You)/(B-side unknown)	1974	6.00
COTILLION			
❑ 44004	Ain't No Sun/Murder in the First Degree	1968	10.00
❑ 44021	Ice Cream Song/The Love That I Need	1969	10.00
❑ 44038	What Would I Do/Ain't No Love at All	1969	10.00
❑ 44045	Dum-De-Dum/I Want to Thank You	1969	10.00

Albums

Number	Title (A Side/B Side)	Yr	NM
BLACK GOLD			
❑ 5001	What a Shame	1973	12.00
COTILLION			
❑ SD 9009	First Landing	1969	15.00

DYNAMICS, THE (2)

Mostly an instrumental group.

45s

Number	Title (A Side/B Side)	Yr	NM
BOLO			
❑ 730	At the Mardi Gras/J.A.J.	1962	10.00
❑ 735	Wild Child/Spongy	1962	10.00
❑ 740	Tennessee Boy/Tough Talk	1963	10.00
❑ 751	Knee Poppin'/Who's Afraid of Virginia Woolf?	1964	10.00
GUARANTEED			
❑ 201	Aces Up/Baby	1959	20.00
PENGUIN			
❑ 1006	Aces Up/Baby	1959	50.00
SEAFAIR			
❑ 100	Onion Salad/Lonesome Llama	1960	20.00
❑ 107	At the Mardi Gras/J.A.J.	1961	20.00

Albums

BOLO

Number	Title (A Side/B Side)	Yr	NM
❑ BLP-8001 [M]	The Dynamics with Jimmy Hanna	1964	50.00

Except when noted otherwise, VG = 25% of NM, and VG+ = 50% of NM. (Example: VG = $2.00, VG+ = $4.00 and NM = $8.00.)

DYNAMICS, THE (3) Early version of ANTHONY AND THE SOPHOMORES.

Number	Title (A Side/B Side)	Yr	NM
45s			
HERALD			
❑ 569	Forever Love/Betty My Own	1962	500.00

DYNAMICS, THE (4) Band from Chicago (probably).

Number	Title (A Side/B Side)	Yr	NM
45s			
U.S.A.			
❑ 769	Summertime in the U.S.A./ Coast to Coast	1964	25.00

DYNAMICS, THE (5) For records on Wingate, see THE DRAMATICS.

DYNAMICS, THE (6) Vocal group from Pittsburgh, Pa.

Number	Title (A Side/B Side)	Yr	NM
45s			
CINDY			
❑ 3005	When the Saints Come Marching In/Gone Is My Love	1957	80.00
IMPALA			
❑ 501	Moonlight/Someone	1959	120.00
SEECO			
❑ 6008	Moonlight/Someone	1959	40.00

DYNAMICS, THE (U) Some of these may be groups (1) or (2). We're pretty sure that none of these are groups (3), (4), (5) or (6). It's possible that five more groups, if not more, are represented below. Any help in grouping these correctly will be appreciated.

Number	Title (A Side/B Side)	Yr	NM
45s			
ARC			
❑ 4450	Enchanted Love/ Happiness and Love	1959	40.00
CAPRI			
❑ 104	No One but You/Always, I Have Loved You	1959	400.00
COLUMBIA			
❑ 3-10666	We Found Love/You Can Make It If You Try	1978	5.00
DECCA			
❑ 31046	How Should I Feel/Seems Like Only Yesterday	1960	30.00
❑ 31129	At the End of Each Day/ Girl by the Gate	1960	30.00
❑ 31450	How Should I Feel/Seems Like Only Yesterday	1962	15.00
DELTA			
❑ 1002	Blue Moon/Pigeon-Toed	1959	30.00
DO-KAY-LO			
❑ 101	I Guess You Don't Love Me (No More)/Oh Night of Nights	1963	30.00
DOUGLAS			
❑ 200	I Love to Be Loved/You Don't Seem to Realize	1961	30.00
DYNAMIC			
❑ 109	Don't Be Late/Eenie Meenie	1959	40.00
❑ 504	The Girl I Met Last Night/ Nobody's Going Out with Me	1959	40.00
❑ 578/9	Christmas Plea/Dream Girl	1962	70.00
❑ 1001	Don't Leave Me/Wasted	1959	50.00
❑ 1002	So Fine/Delsinia	1963	40.00
❑ 1008	If She Should Call/Dream Girl	1961	40.00
FARRALL			
❑ 964	Later On/Departure	196?	30.00
JERDEN			
❑ 800	I'll Be Standing There/ All She Said	1966	10.00
LAVERE			
❑ 186	Wrap Your Troubles in Dreams/ I Can't Give You Anything But Love	1961	25.00
LIBAN			
❑ 1006	If I Give My Heart to You/ Blind Date	1962	80.00
LIBERTY			
❑ 55628	Chapel on a Hill/Conquistador	1963	40.00
PANORAMA			
❑ 51	Stop and Take a Look Around/ (B-side unknown)	1967	10.00
RCA VICTOR			
❑ 47-9084	Love Me/I Need Your Love	1967	40.00
❑ 47-9278	Lights Out/You Make Me Feel So Good	1967	60.00
—As "Zerben R. Hicks and the Dynamics"			
REPRISE			
❑ 20183	So Fine/Delsinia	1963	15.00
TOP TEN			
❑ 100	Yes I Love You Baby/Soul Sloopy	1965	80.00
❑ 927	Love to a Guy/Whenever I'm Without You	196?	60.00
WARNER			
❑ 1016	A Hundred Million Les/Ka Joom	1957	80.00

DYNAMO, SKINNY

Number	Title (A Side/B Side)	Yr	NM
45s			
EXCELLO			
❑ 2097	So Long, So Long/Jingle Bell	1956	30.00

DYNATONES, THE (1)

Number	Title (A Side/B Side)	Yr	NM
45s			
HANNA-BARBERA			
❑ 494	The Fife Piper/And I Always Will	1966	10.00
ST. CLAIR			
❑ 117	The Fife Piper/And I Always Will	1966	30.00
Albums			
HANNA-BARBERA			
❑ HLP-8509 [M]	The Fife Piper	1966	20.00
❑ HST-8509 [S]	The Fife Piper	1966	25.00

DYNELLS, THE

Number	Title (A Side/B Side)	Yr	NM
45s			
ATCO			
❑ 6638	Call On Me/Let Me Prove That I Love You	1968	800.00

DYSON, RONNIE

Number	Title (A Side/B Side)	Yr	NM
45s			
COLUMBIA			
❑ 10071	Captain of Your Soul/ Life and Breath	1974	5.00
❑ 10211	Lady in Red/Cup (Runneth Over)	1975	5.00
❑ 10356	The More You Do It (The More I Like It Done to Me)/You and Me	1976	5.00
❑ 10441	(I Like Being) Close to You/ Lovin' Feelin'	1976	5.00
❑ 10599	Don't Be Afraid/I Just Want to Be There	1977	5.00
❑ 10667	Ain't Nothing Wrong/ Just As You Are	1978	5.00
❑ 10716	Sara Smile/No Way	1978	4.00
❑ 4-45025	Are We Ready for Love/God Bless the Children	1969	6.00
❑ 4-45110	(If You Let Me Make Love to You Then) Why Can't I Touch You?/Girl Don't Care	1970	5.00
❑ 4-45240	I Don't Wanna Cry/She's Gone	1970	5.00
❑ 4-45387	When You Get Right Down To It…/Sleeping Sun	1971	5.00
❑ 4-45599	Jesus Is Just Alright/ Love Is Slipping Away	1972	6.00
❑ 4-45776	One Man Band (Plays All Alone)/I Think I'll Tell Her	1973	5.00
❑ 4-45776 [PS]	One Man Band (Plays All Alone)/I Think I'll Tell Her	1973	8.00
❑ 4-45867	Just Don't Want to Be Lonely/ Point of No Return	1973	5.00
❑ 4-45974	Wednesday in Your Garden/ I Think I'll Tell Her	1973	6.00
❑ 4-46021	We Can Make It Last Forever/ Just a Little Love from Me	1974	5.00
COTILLION			
❑ 47005	Heart to Heart/Bring It On Home	1982	3.00
❑ 99811	You Better Be Fierce/ (B-side unknown)	1983	4.00
❑ 99841	All Over Your Face/ Don't Need You Now	1983	3.00
RCA VICTOR			
❑ 74-0128	Aquarius/Hair	1969	10.00
—By "Ronald Dyson & Co."			
❑ GB-10658	Aquarius/Hair	1976	5.00
—"Gold Standard Series" reissue			
Albums			
COLUMBIA			
❑ C 30223	(If You Let Me Make Love to You Then) Why Can't I Touch You?	1970	12.00
❑ KC 31305	Back Home	1972	12.00
❑ KC 32211	One Man Band	1973	12.00
❑ PC 34350	The More You Do	1976	10.00
❑ PC 34866	Love in All Flavors	1977	10.00
COTILLION			
❑ 90119	Brand New Day	1982	10.00

E

E-TYPES, THE

Number	Title (A Side/B Side)	Yr	NM
45s			
DOT			
❑ 16864	I Can't Do It/Long Before	1966	12.00
LINK			
❑ 1	I Can't Do It/Long Before	1966	30.00
❑ 1 [PS]	I Can't Do It/Long Before	1966	30.00
SUNBURST			
❑ 001	Love of the Loved/She Moves Me	1966	25.00
SUNDAZED			
❑ 133	I Can't Do It/Long Before	199?	2.00
❑ 133 [PS]	I Can't Do It/Long Before	199?	2.00
TOWER			
❑ 325	Put the Clock Back On the Wall/ 14th Street	1967	25.00
UPTOWN			
❑ 754	Big City/Back to Me	1967	25.00

EADY, ERNESTINE

Number	Title (A Side/B Side)	Yr	NM
45s			
JUNIOR			
❑ 1007	The Change/That's the Way It Goes	1963	30.00
SCEPTER			
❑ 12102	The Change/That's the Way It Goes	1965	12.00

EAGER, BRENDA LEE Also see JERRY BUTLER.

Number	Title (A Side/B Side)	Yr	NM
12-Inch Singles			
PRIVATE I			
❑ 4Z9 05092	Watch My Body Talk (6:03) (Dub 5:45)	1984	10.00
45s			
MERCURY			
❑ 73292	I'm a Lonely Woman/ In My World	1972	6.00
❑ 73450	Let Me Be/When I'm With You	1974	5.00
❑ 73607	Ah, Sweet Mystery of Life/ There Ain't No Way	1974	5.00
❑ 73627	You Gave Me Everything/ When I'm With You	1974	5.00
PLAYBOY			
❑ 6047	Good Old Fashioned Lovin'/ I'll Get By	1975	5.00
PRIVATE I			
❑ ZS4 04621	Watch My Body Talk/ (Instrumental)	1984	4.00

EAGER, JIMMY

Number	Title (A Side/B Side)	Yr	NM
45s			
SABRE			
❑ 100	Please Mr. Doctor/I Should Have Loved Her More	1953	200.00

EAGER, VINCE

Number	Title (A Side/B Side)	Yr	NM
45s			
LONDON INT'L.			
❑ 10527	It's Only Make Believe/ I Shall Not Be Moved	1964	12.00

EAGLE Also see THE BEACON STREET UNION.

Number	Title (A Side/B Side)	Yr	NM
45s			
JANUS			
❑ 113	Kickin' It Back to You/ Come In, It's All for Free	1970	8.00
❑ 135	Brown Hair/Working Man	1970	8.00
Albums			
JANUS			
❑ JLS-3011	Come Under Nancy's Tent	1970	60.00

EAGLES Also see DON FELDER; GLENN FREY; DON HENLEY; RANDY MEISNER; TIMOTHY B. SCHMIT; JOE WALSH.

Number	Title (A Side/B Side)	Yr	NM
12-Inch Singles			
ASYLUM			
❑ AS 11402 [DJ]	Please Come Home for Christmas/Funky New Year (both stereo)// same (both mono)	1978	20.00
45s			
ASYLUM			
❑ 11005	Take It Easy/Get You in the Mood	1972	5.00
❑ 11008	Witchy Woman/Early Bird	1972	4.00
❑ 11013	Peaceful Easy Feeling/Trying	1973	4.00
❑ 11017	Tequila Sunrise/21	1973	4.00
❑ 11025	Outlaw Man/Certain Kind of Fool	1973	4.00
❑ 11036	Already Gone/Is It True	1974	4.00
❑ 45202	James Dean/Good Day in Hell	1974	4.00
❑ 45218	Best of My Love/Ol' 55	1974	4.00
❑ 45257	One of These Nights/Visions	1975	4.00
❑ 45279	Lyin' Eyes/Too Many Hands	1975	4.00
❑ 45293	Take It to the Limit/ After the Thrill Is Gone	1975	4.00

Eagles, "Please Come Home for Christmas," Asylum 45555, 1978, $4.

Number	Title (A Side/B Side)	Yr	NM
❑ 45373	New Kid in Town/Victim of Love	1976	4.00
❑ 45386	Hotel California/Pretty Maids All in a Row	1977	4.00
❑ 45403	Life in the Fast Lane/ The Last Resort	1977	4.00
❑ 45555	Please Come Home for Christmas/Funky New Year	1978	4.00
—Original with "clouds" label			
❑ 45555	Please Come Home for Christmas/Funky New Year	1984	3.00
—Reissue with black and yellow label			
❑ 45555 [PS]	Please Come Home for Christmas/Funky New Year	1978	4.00
—Sleeve was available with both original and reissue			
❑ 46545	Heartache Tonight/Teenage Jail	1979	4.00
❑ 46569	The Long Run/ The Disco Strangler	1979	4.00
❑ 46608	I Can't Tell You Why/The Greeks Don't Want No Freaks	1980	4.00
❑ 47100	Seven Bridges Road/ The Long Run	1980	4.00
FULL MOON			
❑ 49654	I Can't Tell You Why/Outside	1981	5.00
—B-side by Ambrosia			
FULL MOON/ASYLUM			
❑ 47004	Lyin' Eyes/Looking for Love	1980	4.00
—B-side by Johnny Lee; contains the full-length version of "Lyin' Eyes"			
❑ 47004 [PS]	Lyin' Eyes/Looking for Love	1980	5.00
❑ 47073	Lyin' Eyes/Hello Texas	1980	5.00
—B-side by Jimmy Buffett			
GEFFEN			
❑ 19376	Get Over It/Get Over It (Live)	1994	5.00
Albums			
ASYLUM			
❑ 6E-103	Hotel California	1977	8.00
❑ 6E-105	Eagles — Their Greatest Hits 1971-1975	1977	8.00
❑ 5E-508	The Long Run	1979	8.00
❑ BB-705 [(2)]	Eagles Live	1980	12.00
❑ 7E-1004	On the Border	1974	12.00
—Clouds label			
❑ EQ 1004 [Q]	On the Border	1974	20.00
❑ 7E-1039	One of These Nights	1975	10.00
—Clouds label			
❑ EQ 1039 [Q]	One of These Nights	1975	20.00
❑ 7E-1052	Eagles — Their Greatest Hits 1971-1975	1976	10.00
❑ 7E-1084	Hotel California	1976	10.00
❑ 5054 [M]	Eagles	1972	40.00
—Promo only; white label with "d/j copy monaural" sticker on cover			
❑ SD 5054	Eagles	1972	15.00
—Gatefold cover; white label with door-in-a-circle logo at top			
❑ SD 5054	Eagles	1973	12.00
—Regular cover; clouds label			
❑ SD 5068	Desperado	1973	12.00
—Clouds label			
❑ 60205	Eagles Greatest Hits, Vol. 2	1982	10.00
DCC COMPACT CLASSICS			
❑ LPZ-2043	Hotel California	1997	120.00
—Audiophile vinyl			
❑ LPZ-2051	Eagles — Their Greatest Hits 1971-1975	1998	100.00
—Audiophile vinyl			
ELEKTRA			
❑ 60422	Anthology of the Eagles	1985	—
—Canceled			
MOBILE FIDELITY			
❑ 1-126	Hotel California	1984	100.00
—Audiophile vinyl			

EAGLES, THE (2)

Number	Title (A Side/B Side)	Yr	NM
45s			
MERCURY			
❑ 70391	Tryin' to Get to You/ Please, Please	1954	30.00
❑ 70464	Such a Fool/Don't You Wanna Be Mine	1954	30.00
❑ 70524	I Told Myself/What a Crazy Feeling	1955	30.00

EAGLES, THE (3) British group.

Number	Title (A Side/B Side)	Yr	NM
45s			
SMASH			
❑ 1837	Christine/Stalactite	1963	12.00

EAGLES, THE (U) The record on Prep may be group (2); the record on Warner Bros. may be group (3). Then again, maybe not.

Number	Title (A Side/B Side)	Yr	NM
45s			
PREP			
❑ 18	Kiss Them for Me/ Ladies in the Sky	1957	20.00
WARNER BROS.			
❑ 5654	Ballad to a Lady/Eagle	1965	12.00

EAGLES OF DEATH METAL

Number	Title (A Side/B Side)	Yr	NM
Albums			
IPECAC			
❑ IPC 111	Heart On	2009	20.00

EAGLIN, SNOOKS

Number	Title (A Side/B Side)	Yr	NM
Albums			
ARHOOLIE			
❑ 2014	Possum Up a Simmon Tree	198?	10.00
BLACK TOP			
❑ BT-1037	Baby, You Can Get Your Gun	1987	10.00
❑ BT-1046	Out of Nowhere	198?	10.00
BLUESVILLE			
❑ BVLP-1046 [M]	That's All Right	1962	60.00
—Blue label, silver print			
❑ BVLP-1046 [M]	That's All Right	1964	25.00
—Blue label, trident logo at right			
FOLKWAYS			
❑ FA-2476 [M]	New Orleans Street Singer	1959	40.00
GNP CRECENDO			
❑ 10023	Down Yonder	1979	10.00

EANES, JIM

Number	Title (A Side/B Side)	Yr	NM
45s			
BLUE RIDGE			
❑ 510	Long Journey Home/ Lady of Spain	1960	15.00
DECCA			
❑ 9-28140	I Cried Again/Between the Lines	1952	20.00
❑ 9-28387	Prisoner of War/Tomorrow May Be Different	1952	25.00
❑ 9-28522	Kiss Me! Kiss Me!/ Little Brown Hand	1952	20.00
❑ 9-28609	When the One That You Love Is in Love with You/ Gloomy Tomorrow	1953	20.00
❑ 9-28825	I'd Love to Be Your Darling/ The Beginning of the End	1953	20.00
❑ 9-28938	Rose Garden Waltz/ Take This Broken Heart	1953	20.00
❑ 9-28949	Plunkin' Rag/Riding the Waves	1953	20.00
—Credited to "Shenandoah Valley Boys"			
❑ 9-29112	Wiggle Worm Wiggle/In a Spanish Restaurant	1954	30.00
❑ 9-29201	Shopworn Heart/Just Suppose	1954	20.00
❑ 9-29446	Possum Hollow/The Things I Love About You	1955	20.00
❑ 9-29536	Cotton Pickers Stomp/ There's No Place Like Home	1955	20.00
❑ 9-29841	Don't Go Lookin' for Trouble/ It's a Shame	1956	15.00
❑ 9-46403	I Cried Again/They Locked God Outside the Iron Curtain	1952	25.00
FOLLY			
❑ 001	It's the Good Times/Who's Gonna Feed Them Hogs	196?	10.00
❑ 004	Heavyfoot Harry Curtis/ Unwanted and Alone	196?	10.00
MERCURY			
❑ 71229x45	Settle Down/Two Hearts Are Better Than One	1957	15.00
SALEM			
❑ 503	Tears the World Can't See/ Riding the Roads	1964	12.00
❑ 512	Wide, Wide Road/ Throw Me Together	1964	12.00
❑ 545	These Memories/She Took the Bus (And Left the Crying to Me)	1965	15.00
STARDAY			
❑ 297	Your Old Standby/ Don't Stop Now	1957	30.00
❑ 312	No Need to Be So Lonely/ Walk Slowly	1957	30.00
❑ 407	Don't Make Me Ashamed/ Blue Sunday	1958	20.00
❑ 414	Christmas Doll/It Won't Seem Like Christmas	1958	20.00
❑ 426	Orchids of Love/Road Walked by Fools	1959	20.00
❑ 456	Budded Roses/Log Cabin in the Lane	1959	20.00
❑ 482	Celebration/Road of No Return	1960	15.00

Except when noted otherwise, VG = 25% of NM, and VG+ = 50% of NM. (Example: VG = $2.00, VG+ = $4.00 and NM = $8.00.)

Number	Title (A Side/B Side)	Yr	NM
❑ 504	I Gotta Know/There'll Come a Time	1960	150.00
❑ 535	Borderline/Mark of Cain	1961	15.00
❑ 554	You Made Me What I Am/Mary Was a Little Lamb	1961	15.00
TOWER			
❑ 129	These Memories/She Took the Bus (And Left the Crying to Me)	1965	8.00

Albums

Number	Title (A Side/B Side)	Yr	NM
JESSUP			
❑ 152	Statesman of Bluegrass Music	1977	15.00
LEATHER			
❑ 7703	Where the Cool Waters Flow	1978	20.00
REBEL			
❑ 1643	Bluegrass Ballads	198?	15.00
❑ 1653	Reminiscing	1987	15.00
❑ 1673	Let Him Lead You	1989	15.00
ROUNDER			
❑ 1016	The Early Days of Bluegrass. Vol. 4	1978	15.00
RURAL RHYTHM			
❑ 197	Jim Eanes with Red Smiley and the Bluegrass Cutups	1968	15.00
❑ 221	Jim Eanes	1969	15.00
WEBCO			
❑ WLPS 0110	Shenandoah Grass, Yesterday and Today	1983	15.00

EARL-JEAN

45s

Number	Title (A Side/B Side)	Yr	NM
COLPIX			
❑ 729	I'm Into Somethin' Good/We Love and Learn	1964	12.00
❑ 748	Randy/They're Jealous of Me	1964	10.00

EARLAND, CHARLES

45s

Number	Title (A Side/B Side)	Yr	NM
COLUMBIA			
❑ 02710	The Only One/Never Knew Love Like This Before	1982	3.00
❑ 02881	Animal/Guilty	1982	3.00
❑ 11427	Coming to You (Live)/(B-side unknown)	1981	3.00
MERCURY			
❑ 73793	From My Heart to Yours/Intergalactic Love Song	1976	4.00
❑ 73869	Ahead of Your Time/Driftin'	1976	4.00
PRESTIGE			
❑ 731	Black Talk (Part 1)/Black Talk (Part 2)	1970	5.00
❑ 732	More Today Than Yesterday/Mighty Burner	197?	5.00
❑ 736	Raindrops Keep Falling on My Head/Sing a Simple Song	197?	5.00
❑ 741	Westbound No. 9 (Part 1)/Westbound No. 9 (Part 2)	197?	5.00
❑ 746	One for Scotty/I Was Made to Love Her	197?	5.00
❑ 755	Will You Still Love Me Tomorrow/'Cause I Love Her	197?	5.00
❑ 761	Charles III/Girl You Need a Change of Mind	197?	5.00
❑ 763	Brown Eyes/Leaving This Planet	197?	5.00

Albums

Number	Title (A Side/B Side)	Yr	NM
COLUMBIA			
❑ JC 36449	Coming to You Live	1980	10.00
❑ FC 37573	Earland's Jam	1982	10.00
❑ FC 38547	Earland's Street Themes	1983	10.00
FANTASY			
❑ OJC-335	Black Talk!	1988	10.00
—Reissue of Prestige 7758			
MERCURY			
❑ SRM-1-1049	Odyssey	1976	10.00
❑ SRM-1-1139	The Great Pyramid	1976	10.00
❑ SRM-1-1149	Revelation	1977	10.00
❑ SRM-1-3720	Perception	1978	10.00
MILESTONE			
❑ M-9165	Front Burner	1988	10.00
❑ M-9175	Third Degree Burn	1989	10.00
MUSE			
❑ MR-5126	Smokin'	1978	10.00
❑ MR-5156	Mama Roots	1979	10.00
❑ MR-5181	Infant Eyes	1980	10.00
❑ MR-5201	Pleasant Afternoon	1981	10.00
❑ MR-5240	In the Pocket	1984	10.00
PRESTIGE			
❑ 2501	Burners	1982	10.00
❑ PRST-7758	Black Talk!	1970	20.00
❑ PRST-7815	Black Drops	1970	15.00
❑ 10009	Living Black!	1971	12.00
❑ 10018	Soul Story	1971	12.00
❑ 10024	Black Talk!	1971	10.00
—Reissue of 7758			
❑ 10029	Black Drops	1971	10.00
—Reissue of 7815			
❑ 10041	Intensity	1972	12.00
❑ 10051	Live at the Lighthouse	1972	12.00
❑ 10061	Charles III	1973	12.00
❑ 10095	Kharma	1975	12.00
❑ 66002 [(2)]	Leaving This Planet	1974	15.00
TRIP			
❑ 5004	Charles Earland	1974	10.00

EARLE, STEVE

12-Inch Singles

Number	Title (A Side/B Side)	Yr	NM
MCA			
❑ 17129 [DJ]	Someday/Fearless Heart/Good Ol' Boy	1986	6.00
❑ 17327 [DJ]	I Ain't Ever Satisfied (same on both sides)	1987	6.00
❑ 23693	Someday/State Trooper (Live)/Good Ol' Boy (Live)	1986	8.00

45s

Number	Title (A Side/B Side)	Yr	NM
EPIC			
❑ 34-04070	Nothin' But You/Continental Trailways Blues	1983	5.00
❑ 34-04307	Squeeze Me In/The Devil's Right Hand	1984	5.00
❑ 34-04666	What'll You Do About Me/Cry Myself to Sleep	1984	5.00
❑ 34-04784	A Little Bit in Love/The Crush	1985	4.00
❑ 34-04784 [PS]	A Little Bit in Love/The Crush	1985	4.00
❑ 34-04784 [PS]	A Little Bit in Love	1985	8.00
—"Demonstration — Not for Sale" on back			
MCA			
❑ 52785	Hillbilly Highway/Down the Road	1986	3.00
❑ 52856	Guitar Town/Little Rock 'N' Roller	1986	3.00
❑ 52920	Someday/Hillbilly Highway	1986	3.00
❑ 53011	Goodbye's All We Got Left/Good Ol' Boy (Gettin' Tough)	1987	3.00
❑ 53103	Nowhere Road/I Ain't Ever Satisfied	1987	3.00
❑ 53182	Sweet Little '66/Angry Young Man	1987	3.00
❑ 53249	Six Days on the Road/The Week of Living Dangerously	1988	3.00
❑ 53532	Guitar Town/Hillbilly Highway	1988	3.00
—"Double Hit" reissue			
❑ 53608	Someday/Goodbye's All We Got Left to Say	1988	3.00
—"Double Hit" reissue			
UNI			
❑ 55018	Back to the Wall/Little Sister (Live)	1988	4.00

7-Inch Extended Plays

Number	Title (A Side/B Side)	Yr	NM
LSI			
❑ 8209	*Nothin' But You/Continental Trailways Blues/Squeeze Me In/My Baby Worships Me	1982	25.00
❑ 8209 [PS]	Pink and Black	1982	25.00

Albums

Number	Title (A Side/B Side)	Yr	NM
EPIC			
❑ FE 39226	Early Tracks	1987	14.00
MCA			
❑ 5713	Guitar Town	1986	10.00
❑ 5998	Exit 0	1987	10.00
❑ R 143506	Exit 0	1987	12.00
—BMG Direct Marketing edition			
❑ R 154072	Guitar Town	1986	12.00
—RCA Music Service edition			
UNI			
❑ 7	Copperhead Road	1988	10.00
❑ R 100679	Copperhead Road	1988	12.00
—BMG Direct Marketing edition			

EARLS, JACK, AND THE JIMBOS

45s

Number	Title (A Side/B Side)	Yr	NM
SUN			
❑ 240	Slow Down/A Fool for Loving You	1956	60.00

EARLS, THE (1)

All of the below are by the same group or closely related.

45s

Number	Title (A Side/B Side)	Yr	NM
ABC			
❑ 11109	It's Been a Long Time Coming/My Lonely, Lonely Room	1968	15.00
BARRY			
❑ 1021	I Believe/Don't Forget	1963	40.00
CLIFTON			
❑ 39	Lookin' for My Baby/Cross My Heart	1974	5.00
❑ 43	Lost Love/My Heart's Desire	1974	5.00
❑ 47	Dreams Come True/My Heart's Desire	1974	5.00
COLUMBIA			
❑ 3-10225	Goin' Uptown/Mrs. Woman	1975	8.00
GONE			
❑ 5117	I'll Never Cry/My Heart's Desire	1961	60.00
HARVEY			
❑ 100	A Sunday Kind of Love/Teenage Dreams	1975	8.00
MR. G			
❑ 801	If I Could Do It Over Again/Papa	1967	15.00
OLD TOWN			
❑ 1130	Remember Then/Let's Waddle	1963	25.00
—Mostly black label with moon			
❑ 1130	Remember Then/Let's Waddle	1963	50.00
—Blue label			
❑ 1133	Never/I Keep a-Telling You	1963	20.00
—Mostly black label with moon			
❑ 1133	Never/I Keep a-Telling You	1963	40.00
—Blue label			
❑ 1141	Eyes/Look My Way	1963	20.00
❑ 1145	Cry, Cry, Cry/Kissin'	1963	20.00
❑ 1149	I Believe/Don't Forget	1963	20.00
—Mostly black label with moon			
❑ 1149	I Believe/Don't Forget	1963	40.00
—Blue label			
❑ 1169	Oh What a Time/Ask Anybody	1964	30.00
❑ 1181 [DJ]	Remember Me Baby/Amor	1965	50.00
—Assigned 1181 in error, as another record had been released with the number			
❑ 1182	Remember Me Baby/Amor	1965	20.00
—Error was corrected on stock copies			
POWER MARTIN			
❑ 1005	Stormy Weather/Could This Be Magic	1975	5.00
—B-side by the Pretenders			
ROME			
❑ 101	Life Is But a Dream/Without You	1961	40.00
❑ 101	Life Is But a Dream/It's You	1961	120.00
❑ 102	Lookin' for My Baby/Cross My Heart	1961	40.00
❑ 111	Stormy Weather/Could This Be Magic	1976	5.00
—B-side by the Pretenders			
❑ 112/3	Little Boy and Girl/Lost Love	1976	4.00
❑ 114/5	All Through Our Teens/Whoever You Are	1976	8.00
—Black vinyl			
❑ 114/5	All Through Our Teens/Whoever You Are	1976	12.00
—Colored vinyl			
WOODBURY			
❑ 101	Tonight (Could Be the Night)/Meditation	1977	8.00

Albums

Number	Title (A Side/B Side)	Yr	NM
CHANCE			
❑ 1001	The Earls Today	1983	12.00
OLD TOWN			
❑ LP-104 [M]	Remember Me Baby	1963	500.00
—Counterfeit identification: Counterfeits have more than 1-inch trailoffs or as little as 1/2 inch trailoffs; legitimate copies have 5/8- to 3/4-inch trailoff			
WOODBURY			
❑ 104	Remember Me Baby	1976	15.00

EARLS, THE (2)

45s

Number	Title (A Side/B Side)	Yr	NM
GEM			
❑ 221	Believe Me My Love/Spinnin'	1954	400.00
❑ 227	My Marie/Out of This World	197?	8.00
—There are differences of opinion on this record. Some claim that it was released in 1954 not long after Gem 221; others claim that it's a 1970s reproduction on a number that Gem never used. As no 78s are known to exist of this title, we lean toward the latter, but would appreciate positive evidence one way or the other.			

EARLY, SAM

45s

Number	Title (A Side/B Side)	Yr	NM
APT			
❑ 25041	Do You Love Me/You Are the Greatest of Them All	1960	25.00

EARTH AND FIRE

Produced by members of GOLDEN EARRING.

45s

Number	Title (A Side/B Side)	Yr	NM
ATCO			
❑ 6744	Seasons/Hazy Paradise	1970	10.00

Albums

Number	Title (A Side/B Side)	Yr	NM
RED BULLET			
❑ RBLP-3000	Earth and Fire	197?	15.00

EARTH ISLAND

45s

PHILIPS

Number	Title (A Side/B Side)	Yr	NM
❑ 40673	Doomsday Afternoon/Tuesday Afternoon	1970	8.00

Albums

PHILIPS

Number	Title (A Side/B Side)	Yr	NM
❑ PHS 600340	We Must Survive	1970	25.00

EARTH OPERA

45s

ELEKTRA

Number	Title (A Side/B Side)	Yr	NM
❑ 45636	American Eagle Tragedy/When You Were Full of Wonder	1968	8.00
❑ 45650	Home to You/Alfie Finney	1969	8.00

Albums

ELEKTRA

Number	Title (A Side/B Side)	Yr	NM
❑ EKS-74016	Earth Opera	1968	20.00
❑ EKS-74038	The Great American Eagle Tragedy	1969	20.00

EARTH QUAKE

45s

A&M

Number	Title (A Side/B Side)	Yr	NM
❑ 1301	Tickler/Guarding You	1971	8.00
❑ 1338	I Get the Sweetest Feeling/Live and Let Live	1972	8.00
❑ 1338 [PS]	I Get the Sweetest Feeling/Live and Let Live	1972	15.00
❑ 1365	Bright Lights/Live and Let Live	1972	8.00

BESERKLEY

Number	Title (A Side/B Side)	Yr	NM
❑ 5701	Friday on My Mind/Roadrunner	1975	10.00
—B-side by Jonathan Richman and the Modern Lovers			
❑ 5701 [PS]	Friday on My Mind/Roadrunner	1975	10.00
❑ 5734/5	Mr. Security/Madness	1975	5.00
❑ 5736/7	Friday on My Mind/Tall Order for a Short Guy	1975	5.00
❑ 5742	Hit the Floor/Don't Want to Go Back	1976	5.00
❑ 5747	Kicks/Trainride	1977	5.00

Albums

A&M

Number	Title (A Side/B Side)	Yr	NM
❑ SP-4308	Earth Quake	1971	15.00
❑ SP-4337	Why Don't You Try Me?	1972	15.00

BESERKLEY

Number	Title (A Side/B Side)	Yr	NM
❑ 0045	Rockin' the World	1975	12.00
❑ 0047	8.5	1976	12.00
❑ 0054	Leveled	1977	12.00
❑ BZ-10065	Two Years in a Padded Cell	1979	10.00
❑ PZ 34752	Rockin' the World	1977	10.00
—Reissue of 0045			
❑ PZ 34754	8.5	1977	10.00
—Reissue of 0047			
❑ PZ 34801	Leveled	1977	10.00
—Reissue of 0054			

EARTH, WIND, AND FIRE Also see WADE FLEMONS.

12-Inch Singles

ARC

Number	Title (A Side/B Side)	Yr	NM
❑ AS 853 [DJ]	Let Me Talk (Remix)/(Instrumental)	1980	10.00
❑ AS 924 [DJ]	And Love Goes On (Single Version)/(LP Version)	1980	10.00

COLUMBIA

Number	Title (A Side/B Side)	Yr	NM
❑ AS 1648 [DJ]	Side by Side/Something Special	1983	8.00
❑ AS 1842 [DJ]	Moonwalk/We're Living in Our Own Time	1983	8.00
❑ 44-04008	Spread Your Love/Freedom of Choice	1983	6.00
❑ 44-04211	Magnetic (Extended Dance Remix)/(Album Version)	1983	6.00
❑ 44-04211	Magnetic (Extended Dance Remix)/(Instrumental)	1983	6.00
❑ 44-07475	System of Survival (4 versions)	1987	6.00
❑ 44-07562	Evil Roy (4 versions)	1987	6.00
❑ 44-08140	Turn On (The Beat Box) (4 versions)	1988	6.00
❑ 23-10512	Saturday Nite/On Your Face	1977	15.00
❑ 23-10786	Got to Get You Into My Life/I'll Write a Song for You	1978	10.00
❑ 73157	Heritage (Extended)/Heritage (Edit)	1990	6.00
❑ 73193	For the Love of You (6 versions)	1990	8.00

45s

ARC

Number	Title (A Side/B Side)	Yr	NM
❑ 02536	Let's Groove/(Instrumental)	1981	4.00
❑ 02688	Wanna Be with You/Kalimba Tree	1982	4.00
❑ 10854	September/Love's Holiday	1978	5.00
❑ 11033	After the Love Has Gone/Rock That!	1979	5.00
❑ 11093	In the Stone/You and I	1979	4.00
❑ 11165	Star/You and I	1979	4.00
❑ 11366	Let Me Talk/(Instrumental)	1980	4.00
❑ 11366 [PS]	Let Me Talk/(Instrumental)	1980	5.00
❑ 11407	You/Share Your Love	1980	4.00
❑ 11434	And Love Goes On/Win or Lose	1981	4.00

COLUMBIA

Number	Title (A Side/B Side)	Yr	NM
❑ 13-03136	Let's Groove/Sing a Song	1982	3.00
—Reissue			
❑ 38-03375	Fall in Love with Me/(Instrumental)	1982	4.00
❑ 38-03375 [PS]	Fall in Love with Me/(Instrumental)	1982	4.00
❑ CNR-03566	Fall in Love with Me	1983	6.00
—One-sided budget release			
❑ 38-03814	Side by Side/Something Special	1983	4.00
❑ 38-04002	Spread Your Love/Freedom of Choice	1983	4.00
❑ 38-04210	Magnetic/Speed of Love	1983	4.00
❑ 38-04210 [PS]	Magnetic/Speed of Love	1983	4.00
❑ 38-04329	Touch/Sweet Sassy Lady	1984	4.00
❑ 38-04329 [PS]	Touch/Sweet Sassy Lady	1984	4.00
❑ 38-04427	Moonwalk/We're Living in Our Own Time	1984	4.00
❑ 38-07608	System of Survival/Writing on the Wall	1987	3.00
❑ 38-07608 [PS]	System of Survival/Writing on the Wall	1987	3.00
❑ 38-07678	You and I/Musical Interlude: New Horizons	1988	3.00
❑ 38-07687	Evil Roy/(Instrumental)	1988	3.00
❑ 38-07687 [PS]	Evil Roy/(Instrumental)	1988	4.00
❑ 38-07695	Thinking of You/Money Tight	1988	3.00
❑ 38-07695 [PS]	Thinking of You/Money Tight	1988	3.00
❑ 38-08107	Turn On (The Beat Box)/(Instrumental)	1988	3.00
❑ 3-10026	Devotion/Fair But So Uncool	1974	6.00
❑ 3-10056	Hot Dawgit/R.L. Tambura	1974	5.00
—With Ramsey Lewis			
❑ 3-10090	Shining Star/Yearnin', Learnin'	1975	5.00
❑ 3-10090 [PS]	Shining Star/Yearnin', Learnin'	1975	10.00
❑ 3-10103	Sun Goddess/Jungle Strut	1975	5.00
—With Ramsey Lewis			
❑ 3-10172	That's the Way of the World/Africano	1975	5.00
❑ 3-10251	Sing a Song/(Instrumental)	1975	5.00
—Later pressings have title as three words			
❑ 3-10251	Singasong/(Instrumental)	1975	6.00
—Original pressings have title as one word			
❑ 3-10309	Can't Hide Love/Gratitude	1976	5.00
❑ 3-10373	Getaway/(Instrumental)	1976	5.00
❑ 3-10373 [PS]	Getaway/(Instrumental)	1976	10.00
❑ 3-10439	Saturday Nite/Departure	1976	5.00
❑ 3-10492	On Your Face/Biyo	1977	5.00
❑ 3-10625	Serpentine Fire/(Instrumental)	1977	5.00
❑ 3-10688	Fantasy/Runnin'	1978	5.00
❑ 3-10796	Got to Get You Into My Life/I'll Write a Song for You	1978	5.00
❑ 4-45747	Power/M-O-M	1972	6.00
❑ 4-45800	Tims Is On Your Side/Where Have All the Flowers Gone	1973	6.00
❑ 4-45888	Evil/Clover	1973	5.00
❑ 4-45888 [PS]	Evil/Clover	1973	10.00
❑ 4-45953	Keep Your Head to the Sky/Build Your Nest	1973	5.00
❑ 4-46007	Mighty Mighty/Drum Song	1974	5.00
❑ 4-46007 [PS]	Mighty Mighty/Drum Song	1974	10.00
❑ 4-46070	Kalimba Story/Tee Nine Chee Bit	1974	5.00
❑ 73205	Heritage/Gotta Find Out	1990	5.00

WARNER BROS.

Number	Title (A Side/B Side)	Yr	NM
❑ 7480	Fan the Fire/This World Today	1971	6.00
❑ 7492	Love Is Life/This World Today	1971	6.00
❑ 7549	I Think About Lovin' You/C'mon Children	1972	6.00

Albums

ARC

Number	Title (A Side/B Side)	Yr	NM
❑ FC 35647	The Best of Earth, Wind & Fire, Vol. 1	1978	10.00
❑ FC 35730	I Am	1979	10.00
❑ PC 35730	I Am	1984	8.00
—Budget-line reissue			
❑ KC2 36795 [(2)]	Faces	1980	12.00
❑ PC 37548	Raise!	1984	8.00
—Budget-line reissue			
❑ TC 37548	Raise!	1981	10.00
❑ HC 45647	The Best of Earth, Wind & Fire, Vol. 1	1981	30.00
—Half-speed mastered edition			
❑ HC 45730	I Am	1981	30.00
—Half-speed mastered edition			
❑ HC 47548	Raise!	1982	30.00
—Half-speed mastered edition			

COLUMBIA

Number	Title (A Side/B Side)	Yr	NM
❑ KC 31702	Last Days and Time	1972	15.00
❑ PC 31702	Last Days and Time	197?	8.00
—Reissue			
❑ CQ 32194 [Q]	Head to the Sky	1973	20.00
❑ KC 32194	Head to the Sky	1973	12.00
❑ PC 32194	Head to the Sky	197?	8.00
—Reissue			
❑ CQ 32712 [Q]	Open Our Eyes	1974	20.00
❑ KC 32712	Open Our Eyes	1974	12.00
❑ PC 32712	Open Our Eyes	197?	8.00
—Reissue			
❑ PC 33280	That's the Way of the World	1975	12.00
—No bar code			
❑ PC 33280	That's the Way of the World	198?	8.00
—Budget-line reissue with bar code			
❑ PCQ33280 [Q]	That's the Way of the World	1975	20.00
❑ PG 33694 [(2)]	Gratitude	1975	15.00
—No bar code			
❑ PG 33694 [(2)]	Gratitude	198?	10.00
—Budget-line reissue with bar code			
❑ PC 34241	Spirit	1976	12.00
—No bar code			
❑ PC 34241	Spirit	198?	8.00
—Budget-line reissue with bar code			
❑ PCQ 34241 [Q]	Spirit	1976	25.00
❑ JC 34905	All 'N All	1977	12.00
❑ PC 34905	All 'N All	198?	8.00
—Budget-line reissue			
❑ PC 38367	Powerlight	1984	8.00
—Budget-line reissue			
❑ TC 38367	Powerlight	1983	10.00
❑ QC 38980	Electric Universe	1983	10.00
❑ FC 40596	Touch the World	1987	10.00
❑ OC 45013	The Best of Earth, Wind & Fire, Vol. II	1988	10.00
❑ C 45268	Heritage	1990	15.00
❑ HC 48367	Powerlight	1983	40.00
—Half-speed mastered edition			

MOBILE FIDELITY

Number	Title (A Side/B Side)	Yr	NM
❑ 1-159	That's the Way of the World	198?	30.00
—Audiophile vinyl			

PAIR

Number	Title (A Side/B Side)	Yr	NM
❑ PDL2-1064 [(2)]	Beat It to Life	1986	12.00

WARNER BROS.

Number	Title (A Side/B Side)	Yr	NM
❑ WS 1905	Earth, Wind, and Fire	1971	20.00
—Green label			
❑ WS 1958	The Need of Love	1971	20.00
—Green label			
❑ 2WS 2798 [(2)]	Another Time	1974	20.00
—"Burbank" palm trees labels			

EARTH, WIND, AND FIRE WITH THE EMOTIONS

12-Inch Singles

ARC

Number	Title (A Side/B Side)	Yr	NM
❑ 10950	Boogie Wonderland/(Instrumental)	1979	8.00

45s

ARC

Number	Title (A Side/B Side)	Yr	NM
❑ 10956	Boogie Wonderland/(Instrumental)	1979	5.00

EAST

45s

CAPITOL

Number	Title (A Side/B Side)	Yr	NM
❑ 3321	Some Sweet Day/Chanson D'Amour	1972	6.00
❑ 3400	Beautiful Morning/Black Hearted Woman	1972	6.00

Albums

CAPITOL

Number	Title (A Side/B Side)	Yr	NM
❑ ST-11083	East	1972	25.00

EAST L.A. CAR POOL

45s

GRC

Number	Title (A Side/B Side)	Yr	NM
❑ 2064	Like They Say in L.A./Linda Chicana	1975	8.00

EAST OF EDEN

45s

DERAM

Number	Title (A Side/B Side)	Yr	NM
❑ 85042	Southern Hemisphere/Communion	1969	8.00
❑ 85075	Jig-a-Jig/Marcus Junior	1971	8.00

Albums

DERAM

Number	Title (A Side/B Side)	Yr	NM
❑ DES 18023	Mercator Projected	1969	20.00
❑ DES 18043	Snafu	1970	20.00

HARVEST

Number	Title (A Side/B Side)	Yr	NM
❑ SW-806	East of Eden	1971	20.00

EASTWOOD, CLINT

45s

CAMEO

Number	Title (A Side/B Side)	Yr	NM
❑ 240	Rowdy/Cowboy Wedding Song	1963	20.00
❑ 240 [PS]	Rowdy/Cowboy Wedding Song	1963	50.00

Except when noted otherwise, VG = 25% of NM, and VG+ = 50% of NM. (Example: VG = $2.00, VG+ = $4.00 and NM = $8.00.)

Number	Title (A Side/B Side)	Yr	NM
CERTRON			
❑ 10010	Burning Bridges/When I Loved Her	1970	10.00
❑ 10010 [PS]	Burning Bridges/When I Loved Her	1970	25.00
GNP CRESCENDO			
❑ 177	Get Yourself Another Fool/For You, For Me, Forevermore	1962	40.00
❑ 177 [PS]	Get Yourself Another Fool/For You, For Me, Forevermore	1962	100.00
GOTHIC			
❑ 005	Unknown Girl of My Dreams/For All We Know	1961	25.00
❑ 005 [PS]	Unknown Girl of My Dreams/For All We Know	1961	60.00
PARAMOUNT			
❑ 0010	Best Things/Wand'rin' Star	1969	12.00
—B-side by Lee Marvin			
WARNER BROS.			
❑ 49760	Cowboy in a Three-Piece Business Suit/Dark Blue Feeling	1981	5.00
Albums			
CAMEO			
❑ SC-1056 [S]	Clint Eastwood Sings Cowboy Favorites	1963	150.00

EASY RIDERS, THE See TERRY GILKYSON.

EASYBEATS, THE

Number	Title (A Side/B Side)	Yr	NM
45s			
ASCOT			
❑ 2214	In My Book/Make You Feel Alright (Women)	1966	15.00
❑ 2214 [PS]	In My Book/Make You Feel Alright (Women)	1966	40.00
RARE EARTH			
❑ 5009	St. Louis/Can't Find Love	1969	15.00
UNITED ARTISTS			
❑ 0114	Friday on My Mind/Gonna Have a Good Time	1973	4.00
—"Silver Spotlight Series" reissue			
❑ 50106	Friday on My Mind/Made My Bed; Gonna Lie in It	1966	15.00
❑ 50187	Pretty Girl/Heaven and Hell	1967	10.00
❑ 50206	Falling Off the Edge of the World/Remember Sam	1967	10.00
❑ 50289	Come In, You'll Get Pneumonia/Hello, How Are You	1968	10.00
❑ 50488	Gonna Have a Good Time/Lay Me Down and Die	1969	10.00
Albums			
RARE EARTH			
❑ 517	Easy Ridin'	1970	—
—Canceled			
RHINO			
❑ RNLP-124	The Best of the Easybeats	1985	8.00
UNITED ARTISTS			
❑ UAL 3588 [M]	Friday on My Mind	1967	40.00
❑ UAS 6588 [P]	Friday on My Mind	1967	50.00
—"Make You Feel Alright" is rechanneled.			
❑ UAS 6667 [P]	Falling Off the Edge of the World	1968	40.00
—"Women" is rechanneled.			

EATON, CONNIE

Number	Title (A Side/B Side)	Yr	NM
45s			
ABC			
❑ 12098	If I Knew Enough to Come Out of the Rain/Magic Mystery	1975	5.00
ABC DOT			
❑ 17571	It Was the Thing to Do/Who's Gonna Love Me Now	1975	5.00
ABC DUNHILL			
❑ 15022	Lonely Men, Lonely Women/Midnight Train to Georgia	1974	5.00
CHART			
❑ 1048	Too Many Dollars, Not Enough Sense/Bonnie	1968	8.00
❑ 1067	He's a Night Owl/Something's Wrong in California	1969	8.00
❑ 5009	And Say Good-Bye/Raining Blue	1969	7.00
❑ 5027	I've Got Life to Live/A Million Shades of Blue	1969	7.00
❑ 5048	Angel of the Morning/One Time Too Many	1969	7.00
❑ 5056	Tennessee Bird Walk/If You Can't Bring It Home	1970	7.00
—With Tony Martin			
❑ 5084	Memories/Tomorrow My Babies Are Coming Home	1970	7.00
❑ 5094	These Hills/The Best of Everything	1970	7.00
❑ 5110	Sing a Happy Song/Glad to Be Your Woman	1971	6.00
❑ 5120	And Say Goodbye/Leave Me	1971	6.00
❑ 5138	Don't Hang No Halos on Me/These Hills	1971	6.00
❑ 5148	Let Me Be the One/You May Wonder	1972	6.00
❑ 5162	Tar and Cement/Angel of the Morning	1972	6.00
❑ 5182	Love Is So Elusive/These Hills	1973	6.00
❑ 5196	The Other Side of Town/God Paints Pictures	1973	6.00
ENTERPRISE			
❑ 9096	Love Is So Elusive/It's You	1974	6.00
❑ 9105	I Wanna Be Wrong Right Now/Let's Get Together	1974	6.00
MUSICTOWN			
❑ 002	Davy Jones' Locker/A Million Shades of Blue	197?	6.00

EATON, HERB

Number	Title (A Side/B Side)	Yr	NM
45s			
HIT			
❑ 242	Ballad of the Green Berets/Listen People	1966	8.00
—B-side by the Chords (2)			

EBB TIDES, THE See NINO AND THE EBB TIDES.

EBBTIDES, THE May be four different groups!

Number	Title (A Side/B Side)	Yr	NM
45s			
DUANE			
❑ 1022	Star of Love/First Love	1964	4000.
—VG 2000; VG+ 3000			
JAN-LAR			
❑ 101	Love Doctor/Lonesome	1959	300.00
MONUMENTAL			
❑ 520	Come On and Cry/Straightaway	1960	40.00
TEEN			
❑ 121	What Is Your Name Dear/Only Be Mine	1957	4000.
—VG 2000; VG+ 3000			

EBBTONES, THE

Number	Title (A Side/B Side)	Yr	NM
45s			
EBB			
❑ 100	I've Got a Feeling/Danny's Blues	1957	150.00
PORT			
❑ 70026	Rockin' on the Range/Ram Induction	1961	25.00

EBON-KNIGHTS, THE

Number	Title (A Side/B Side)	Yr	NM
45s			
STEPHENY			
❑ 1817	Poor Butterfly/The Way the Ball Bounces	1958	25.00
❑ 1822	First Date/Only Only You	1958	25.00
Albums			
STEPHENY			
❑ 4001 [M]	First Date	1959	1500.

EBONAIRES, THE

Number	Title (A Side/B Side)	Yr	NM
45s			
ALADDIN			
❑ 3211	3 O'Clock in the Morning/Baby, You're the One	1953	500.00
❑ 3212	You're Nobody 'Til Somebody Loves You/Lawd, Lawd, Lawd	1954	500.00
COLONIAL			
❑ 117	We're in Love/Thinkin' and Thinkin'	1959	120.00
HOLLYWOOD			
❑ 1046	Love For Christmas/Jingle Bell Hop	1955	400.00
❑ 1062	Let's Kiss and Say Hello Again/Jivarama Hop	1956	400.00
LENA			
❑ 101	Love Call/Somewhere in My Heart	1959	200.00
LOST-NITE			
❑ 118	Love Call/Somewhere in My Heart	196?	8.00
—Reissue			
MONEY			
❑ 220	The Very Best Luck in the World/Hey Baby Stop	1956	80.00
STARFIRE			
❑ 116	Ooh Baby Baby/Most of the Pretty Young Girls	1979	5.00
❑ 116 [PS]	Ooh Baby Baby/Most of the Pretty Young Girls	1979	5.00

EBONY JAM

Number	Title (A Side/B Side)	Yr	NM
45s			
AMOS			
❑ 122	Ride On/(Instrumental)	1969	15.00

EBONYS, THE

Number	Title (A Side/B Side)	Yr	NM
45s			
BUDDAH			
❑ 537	Makin' Love Ain't No Fun (Without the One You Love) Part 1/Part 2	1976	6.00
PHILADELPHIA INT'L.			
❑ 3503	You're the Reason Why/Sexy Ways	1971	8.00
❑ 3510	Determination/Do It	1971	8.00
❑ 3513 [DJ]	(Christmas Ain't Christmas, New Year's Ain't New Year's) Without The One You Love (mono/stereo)	1971	8.00
❑ 3514	Do You Like the Way I Love/I'm So Glad I'm Me	1972	8.00
❑ 3529	It's Forever/Sexy Ways	1973	7.00
❑ 3541	I Believe/Nation Time	1974	7.00
❑ 3548	Life in the Country/Hook Up and Get Down	1974	7.00
SOUL CLOCK			
❑ 108	Don't Knock Me/Can't Get Enough	1969	15.00
Albums			
BUDDAH			
❑ BDS 5679	Sing About Life	1976	40.00
PHILADELPHIA INT'L.			
❑ KZ 32419	The Ebonys	1973	12.00

EBSEN, BUDDY Also see FESS PARKER.

Number	Title (A Side/B Side)	Yr	NM
45s			
MGM			
❑ K13210	Mail Order Bride/Ballad of Jed Clampett	1964	20.00
REPRISE			
❑ 0389	Howdy/Bonaparte's Retreat	1965	15.00
Albums			
REPRISE			
❑ R-6174 [M]	Buddy Ebsen Sings Howdy!	1965	30.00
❑ RS-6174 [S]	Buddy Ebsen Sings Howdy!	1965	40.00

ECHO AND THE BUNNYMEN

Number	Title (A Side/B Side)	Yr	NM
12-Inch Singles			
SIRE			
❑ PRO-A-2164 [DJ]	Seven Seas/Silver	1984	12.00
❑ PRO-A-2398 [DJ]	Bring On the Dancing Horses/Bring On the Dancing Horses (7")	1985	10.00
❑ PRO-A-2774 [DJ]	New Direction (same on both sides)	1987	6.00
❑ PRO-A-2977 [DJ]	Bedbugs and Ballyhoo (2 versions)	1987	6.00
❑ 20203	Killing Moon (all night version)/Killing Moon (Live)/Do It Clean (Live)	1983	12.00
❑ 20784	Lips Like Sugar (3 versions)/Rollercoaster	1987	6.00
❑ 20838	Bedbugs and Ballyhoo (2 versions)/Run Run Run/Paint It Black/Friction	1988	6.00
45s			
SIRE			
❑ 28113	Bed Bugs and Ballyhoo/Run, Run, Run (Live)	1988	2.50
❑ 28113 [PS]	Bed Bugs and Ballyhoo/Run, Run, Run (Live)	1988	2.50
❑ 28260	Lips Like Sugar/Rollercoaster	1987	3.00
❑ 28260 [PS]	Lips Like Sugar/Rollercoaster	1987	3.00
❑ 28791	Bring On the Dancing Horses/Read It in Books	1986	2.50
❑ 28791 [PS]	Bring On the Dancing Horses/Read It in Books	1986	2.50
❑ 29288	Seven Seas/Angels and Devils	1984	3.00
❑ 29664	The Cutter/Gods Will Be Gods	1983	3.00
Albums			
SIRE			
❑ SRK 3569	Heaven Up Here	1981	10.00
❑ SRK 6096	Crocodiles	1980	10.00
❑ 23770	Porcupine	1983	10.00
❑ 23987 [EP]	The Echo	1983	10.00
❑ 25084	Ocean Rain	1984	12.00
❑ 25360	Songs to Learn and Sing	1986	12.00

Number	Title (A Side/B Side)	Yr	NM
❑ 25597	Echo and the Bunnymen	1987	10.00

ECHO VALLEY BOYS, THE

45s

ISLAND

Number	Title (A Side/B Side)	Yr	NM
❑ 1/2	Ramblin' Man/Wash Machine Boogie	195?	300.00

ECHOES, THE (1)

45s

SEG-WAY

Number	Title (A Side/B Side)	Yr	NM
❑ 103	Baby Blue/Boomerang	1961	25.00
❑ 106	Sad Eyes (Don't You Cry)/ It's Raining	1961	25.00
❑ 1002	Angel of My Heart/Gee Oh Gee	1962	40.00

SMASH

Number	Title (A Side/B Side)	Yr	NM
❑ 1766	Bluebirds Over the Mountain/ A Chicken Ain't Nothin' But a Bird	1962	15.00
❑ 1807	Keep an Eye on Her/A Million Miles from Nowhere	1963	15.00
❑ 1850	Annabelle Lee/If Love Is	1963	15.00

SRG

Number	Title (A Side/B Side)	Yr	NM
❑ 101	Baby Blue/Boomerang	1960	200.00

ECHOES, THE (2) Early version of THE INNOCENTS.

45s

ANDEX

Number	Title (A Side/B Side)	Yr	NM
❑ 22102	Time/Dee Dee Di Oh	1958	30.00

ECHOES, THE (3) Eddie Sulik was the singer of this group, which used Nashville professionals as backing musicians.

45s

COLUMBIA

Number	Title (A Side/B Side)	Yr	NM
❑ 4-41549	Bye-Bye My Baby/ Do I Love You?	1960	15.00
❑ 4-41709	Loving and Losing/Ecstasy	1960	15.00

HARD ROCK HATTIE

Number	Title (A Side/B Side)	Yr	NM
❑ LS 1000-05	Bye-Bye My Baby/Do I Love You? ('Deed I Do)	2000	3.00

—Red vinyl; credited to "The Echoes - Eddie Sulik"; came as part of a 7x7 package called "Sweet Memories," which includes a CD, gatefold sleeve and poster

Number	Title (A Side/B Side)	Yr	NM
❑ LS 1000-06	Loving and Losing/Ecstasy	2000	3.00

—Blue vinyl

ECHOES, THE (4)

45s

COMBO

Number	Title (A Side/B Side)	Yr	NM
❑ 128	My Little Honey/Aye Senorita	1957	40.00

ECHOES, THE (5) BONNIE GUITAR was in this group.

45s

DOLTON

Number	Title (A Side/B Side)	Yr	NM
❑ 18	Born to Be With You/ My Guiding Light	1960	20.00

ECHOES, THE (6)

45s

ROCKIN'

Number	Title (A Side/B Side)	Yr	NM
❑ 523	All That Wine Is Gone/ Please Say You're Mine	1953	400.00

ECHOES, THE (U) Some of these may belong with the above groups. The record on Felsted is a reissue of the Hi Tide release.

45s

ASCOT

Number	Title (A Side/B Side)	Yr	NM
❑ 2188	I Love Candy/Paper Roses	1965	50.00

FELSTED

Number	Title (A Side/B Side)	Yr	NM
❑ 8614	Angel of Love/Twistin' Town	1961	50.00

GEE

Number	Title (A Side/B Side)	Yr	NM
❑ 1028	Ding Dong/My Heart Beats for You	1957	60.00

HI TIDE

Number	Title (A Side/B Side)	Yr	NM
❑ 106	Angel of Love/Twistin' Town	1961	200.00

—Black vinyl

Number	Title (A Side/B Side)	Yr	NM
❑ 106	Angel of Love/Twistin' Town	1961	400.00

—Colored vinyl

SPECIALTY

Number	Title (A Side/B Side)	Yr	NM
❑ 601	Over the Rainbow/Someone	1957	30.00

SWAN

Number	Title (A Side/B Side)	Yr	NM
❑ 4013	Scratch My Back/ The Little Green Man	1959	12.00

ECKSTINE, BILLY Also see SARAH VAUGHAN.

45s

A&M

Number	Title (A Side/B Side)	Yr	NM
❑ 1858	The Best Thing/Love Theme from "The Getaway"	1976	4.00
❑ 1858 [PS]	The Best Thing/Love Theme from "The Getaway"	1976	6.00

ENTERPRISE

Number	Title (A Side/B Side)	Yr	NM
❑ 9009	Stormy/When You Look in the Mirror	1970	6.00
❑ 9025	I Wanna Be Your Baby/ The Name of My Sorrow	1970	6.00
❑ 9046	When Something Is Wrong with My Baby/Today Was Tomorrow Yesterday	1972	6.00
❑ 9076	I Didn't Mean to Love You/ I Wanna Be Your Man	1973	5.00
❑ 9093	If She Walked Into My Life/ Remembering	1974	5.00

MERCURY

Number	Title (A Side/B Side)	Yr	NM
❑ 71161	All of My Life/Poor Little Heart	1957	10.00
❑ 71217	Boulevard of Broken Dreams/ If I Can Help Somebody	1957	10.00
❑ 71250	Gigi/Trust in Me	1957	10.00
❑ 71325	Vertigo/In the Rain	1958	10.00
❑ 71372	Prisoner of Love/Funny	1958	10.00
❑ 71861	Theme from Exodus/It Isn't Fair	1961	8.00
❑ 71907	Jeannie/Alright, Okay, You Win	1961	8.00
❑ 71967	Guilty/I Want to Talk About You	1962	8.00
❑ 72022	What Kind of Fool Am I/ Till There Was You	1962	8.00
❑ 72050	You've Changed/The Beauty of True Love	1962	8.00
❑ 72128	Everything I Have Is Yours/ Darling, Why Did You	1963	8.00
❑ 72264	People/Sweet Georgia Brown	1963	8.00
❑ 72302	Wanted/What Are You Afraid Of	1964	8.00

MGM

Number	Title (A Side/B Side)	Yr	NM
❑ K10525	O Come, All Ye Faithful/ O, Holy Night	1949	15.00
❑ K10623	My Foolish Heart/Sure Thing	1950	20.00
❑ K10643	Free/Baby Won't You Say You Love Me	1950	20.00
❑ K10684	My Destiny/Roses	1950	20.00
❑ K10690	You're All I Need/ Dedicated to You	1950	20.00
❑ K10716	I Wanna Be Loved/Stardust	1950	20.00
❑ K10778	The Show Must Go On/You've Got Me Cryin' Again	1950	20.00
❑ K10796	Blue Christmas/ The Lonely Shepherd	1950	20.00
❑ K10799	Be My Love/Only a Moment Ago	1950	20.00
❑ K10825	I'll Know/I've Never Been in Love Before	1951	15.00
❑ K10856	I'm So Crazy for Love/ Guess I'll Have to Dream	1951	15.00
❑ K10896	If/When You Return	1951	15.00
❑ K10903	I Apologize/Bring Back the Thrill	1951	15.00
❑ K10916	I Left My Hat/Here Come the Blues	1951	15.00
❑ K10944	I'm Yours to Command/What Will I Tell My Heart	1951	15.00
❑ K10982	I'm a Fool/Lose Me	1951	15.00
❑ K10996	Pandora/Wonder Why	1951	15.00
❑ K11028	Enchanted Land/I've Got My Mind on You	1951	15.00
❑ K11073	Once/Out in the Cold	1951	15.00
❑ K11101	Taking a Chance/You're Driving Me Crazy	1951	15.00
❑ K11111	Jalousie/Strange Interlude	1951	15.00
❑ K11125	Take Me Back/Weaver of Dreams	1952	15.00
❑ K11144	Every Day/I Love You	1952	15.00
❑ K11177	Carnival/Room with a View	1952	15.00
❑ K11217	If They Ask Me/Hold Me Close to You	1952	15.00
❑ K11225	Kiss of Fire/Never Like This	1952	15.00
❑ K11291	Have a Good Time/ Strange Sensation	1952	15.00
❑ K11301	Early Autumn/ Because You're Mine	1952	15.00
❑ K11351	Be Fair/Come to the Mardi Gras	1952	15.00
❑ K11396	Until Eternity/Everything Depends on You	1953	15.00
❑ K11439	A Fool in Love/Until Today	1953	15.00
❑ K11511	Send My Baby Back to Me/ Laugh to Keep From Crying	1953	15.00
❑ K11550	It Can't Be Wrong/I Can Read Between the Lines	1953	15.00
❑ K11573	St. Louis Blues (Part 1)/ St. Louis Blues (Part 2)	1953	15.00
❑ K11587	I'm Saving Dreams/Fortune Telling Cards	1953	15.00
❑ K11623	What Are You Doing New Year's Eve/Christmas Eve	1953	20.00
❑ K11655	Rendezvous/I'm In a Mood	1954	15.00
❑ K11694	Don't Get Around Much Anymore/Lost in Loveliness	1954	15.00
❑ K11712	No One But You/Seabreeze	1954	15.00
❑ K11744	Beloved/Temporarily Blue	1954	15.00
❑ K11803	Olay, Olay/You Leave Me Breathless	1954	15.00
❑ K11845	Mood Indigo/Do Nothing 'Till You Hear from Me	1954	15.00
❑ K11855	Love Me/One Sweet Kiss	1954	15.00
❑ K11915	What More Is There to Say/ Touching Shoulders	1955	12.00
❑ K11948	Give Me Another Chance/ More Than You'll Ever Know	1955	12.00
❑ K11984	Love Me or Leave Me/Only You	1955	12.00
❑ K11998	Careless Lips/A Man Doesn't Know	1955	12.00
❑ K12055	September Song/Pass the Word Around	1955	12.00
❑ K12105	La De Do De Do (The Honey Bug Song)/Farewell to Romance	1955	12.00
❑ K12160	You'll Get Yours/Lonely Avenue	1955	12.00
❑ K12180	Good-Bye/The Show Must Go On	1956	12.00
❑ K12237	Out of My Mind/My Fickle Heart	1956	12.00
❑ K12400	I Thought I'd Seen Everything/ I Let a Song Go to My Heart	1956	12.00
❑ K12617	Bali Ha'i/Younger Than Springtime	1958	10.00

MOTOWN

Number	Title (A Side/B Side)	Yr	NM
❑ 1077	Had You Been Around/ Down to Earth	1965	12.00
❑ 1091	Wish You Were Here/ Slender Thread	1966	12.00
❑ 1100	A Warmer World/And There You Were	1966	12.00
❑ 1105	I Wonder Why (Nobody Loves Me)/I've Been Blessed	1967	12.00
❑ 1120	Is Anyone Here Going My Way/ Thank You Love	1968	10.00
❑ 1131	For Love of Ivy/A Woman	1968	10.00
❑ 1143	My Cup Runneth Over/ Ask the Lonely	1969	10.00

RCA VICTOR

Number	Title (A Side/B Side)	Yr	NM
❑ 47-6436	The Bitter with the Sweet/ Grapevine	1956	12.00
❑ 47-6488	My Heart Says No/ Joey, Joey, Joey	1956	12.00
❑ 47-6524	Tennessee Rock 'n' Roll/ Condemned for Life	1956	20.00
❑ 47-6691	The Chosen Few/ Just Call Me Crazy	1956	12.00
❑ 47-6827	Blue Illusion/Oh My Pretty Pretty	1957	12.00

ROULETTE

Number	Title (A Side/B Side)	Yr	NM
❑ 4199	Anything You Wanna Do/ Like Wow	1959	12.00
❑ 4239	I Love You/I Apologize	1960	12.00

Selected 78s

MGM

Number	Title (A Side/B Side)	Yr	NM
❑ 10916	I Left My Hat/Here Come the Blues	1951	8.00

7-Inch Extended Plays

EMARCY

Number	Title (A Side/B Side)	Yr	NM
❑ 16041	(contents unknown)	195?	20.00
❑ 16041 [PS]	Billy's Blues	195?	20.00

MGM

Number	Title (A Side/B Side)	Yr	NM
❑ X1011	(contents unknown)	195?	20.00
❑ X1011 [PS]	My Foolish Heart	195?	20.00
❑ X1015	(contents unknown)	195?	15.00
❑ X1015 [PS]	I Apologize	195?	15.00
❑ X1041	(contents unknown)	195?	20.00
❑ X1041 [PS]	Songs by Billy Eckstine	195?	20.00
❑ X1052	Tenderly/If You Could See Me Now//Laura/One for My Baby (And One More for the Road)	1953	15.00
❑ X1052 [PS]	Billy Eckstine Sings "Tenderly"	1953	15.00
❑ X-1053	(contents unknown)	195?	15.00
❑ X-1053 [PS]	Smoke Gets In Your Eyes	195?	15.00
❑ X1078	St. Louis Blues — Parts 1 and 2/ How High the Moon — Parts 1 and 2	195?	15.00
❑ X1078 [PS]	Billy Eckstine and the Metronome All-Stars	195?	15.00
❑ X-1084	(contents unknown)	195?	15.00
❑ X-1084 [PS]	A Fool in Love	195?	15.00
❑ X-1099	(contents unknown)	195?	15.00
❑ X-1099 [PS]	Love Songs, Vol. 1	195?	15.00
❑ X-1100	(contents unknown)	195?	15.00
❑ X-1100 [PS]	Love Songs, Vol. 2	195?	15.00
❑ X-1103	(contents unknown)	195?	15.00
❑ X-1103 [PS]	Billy Eckstine Favorites, Vol. 1	195?	15.00
❑ X-1104	"Bewildered/My Foolish Heart/ Everything I Have Is Yours/ Fool That I Am	195?	15.00
❑ X-1104 [PS]	Billy Eckstine Favorites, Vol. 2	195?	15.00
❑ X-1110	(contents unknown)	1955	15.00
❑ X-1110 [PS]	I Let a Song Go Out of My Heart, Vol. 1	1955	15.00
❑ X-1111	(contents unknown)	1955	15.00
❑ X-1111 [PS]	I Let a Song Go Out of My Heart, Vol. 2	1955	15.00
❑ X-1152	Early Autumn/September Song//Blue Moon/ Oh! You Crazy Moon	1955	12.00
❑ X-1152 [PS]	Early Autumn	1955	12.00

Number	Title (A Side/B Side)	Yr	NM
Albums			
AUDIO LAB			
❑ AL-1549 [M]	Mr. B	1960	120.00
DELUXE			
❑ FA-2010 [M]	Billy Eckstine and His Orchestra	195?	80.00
EMARCY			
❑ MG-26025 [10]	Blues for Sale	1954	120.00
❑ MG-26027 [10]	The Love Songs of Mr. B	1954	120.00
❑ MG-36010 [M]	I Surrender, Dear	1955	80.00
❑ MG-36029 [M]	Blues for Sale	1955	80.00
❑ MG-36030 [M]	The Love Songs of Mr. B	1955	80.00
❑ MG-36129 [M]	Billy Eckstine's Imagination	1958	60.00
ENTERPRISE			
❑ ENS-1013	Stormy	1971	15.00
❑ ENS-1017	Feel the Warm	1971	15.00
❑ ENS-5004	Senior Soul	1972	15.00
FORUM			
❑ F-9027 [M]	Once More with Feeling	196?	15.00
❑ SF-9027 [S]	Once More with Feeling	196?	15.00
KING			
❑ 295-12 [10]	The Great Mr. B	1953	300.00
LION			
❑ L-70057 [M]	The Best of Billy Eckstine	1958	25.00
MERCURY			
❑ MG-20333 [M]	Billy's Best	1958	40.00
❑ MG-20637 [M]	Broadway, Bongos and Mr. B	1961	25.00
❑ MG-20674 [M]	Billy Eckstine and Quincy Jones at Basin St. East	1962	25.00
❑ MG-20736 [M]	Don't Worry 'Bout Me	1962	25.00
❑ MG-20796 [M]	The Golden Hits of Billy Eckstine	1963	15.00
❑ SR-60086 [S]	Billy's Best	1958	50.00
❑ SR-60637 [S]	Broadway, Bongos and Mr. B	1961	30.00
❑ SR-60674 [S]	Billy Eckstine and Quincy Jones at Basin St. East	1962	30.00
❑ SR-60736 [S]	Don't Worry 'Bout Me	1962	30.00
❑ SR-60796 [S]	The Golden Hits of Billy Eckstine	1963	20.00
METRO			
❑ M-537 [M]	Everything I Have Is Yours	1965	15.00
❑ MS-537 [R]	Everything I Have Is Yours	1965	12.00
MGM			
❑ E-153 [10]	Billy Eckstine Sings Rodgers & Hammerstein	1952	150.00
❑ E-219 [10]	Tenderly	1953	150.00
❑ E-257 [10]	I Let a Song Go Out of My Heart	1954	150.00
❑ E-523 [10]	Songs by Billy Eckstine	1951	160.00
❑ E-548 [10]	Favorites	1951	160.00
❑ E-3176 [M]	Mr. B with a Beat	1955	50.00
❑ E-3209 [M]	Rendezvous	1955	50.00
❑ E-3275 [M]	That Old Feeling	1956	50.00
MOTOWN			
❑ M 632 [M]	Prime of My Life	1965	20.00
❑ MS 632 [S]	Prime of My Life	1965	25.00
❑ M 646 [M]	My Way	1966	20.00
❑ MS 646 [S]	My Way	1966	25.00
❑ MS 677	For Love of Ivy	1969	25.00
NATIONAL			
❑ NLP-2001 [10]	Billy Eckstine Sings	1949	200.00
REGENT			
❑ MG-6052 [M]	Prisoner of Love	1957	50.00
❑ MG-6053 [M]	The Duke, the Blues and Me	1957	50.00
❑ MG-6054 [M]	My Deep Blue Dream	1957	50.00
❑ MG-6058 [M]	You Call It Madness	1957	50.00
ROULETTE			
❑ R-25052 [M]	No Cover, No Minimum	1961	25.00
❑ SR-25052 [S]	No Cover, No Minimum	1961	30.00
❑ R-25104 [M]	Once More with Feeling	1962	25.00
❑ SR-25104 [S]	Once More with Feeling	1962	30.00
SAVOY			
❑ 1127	Billy Eckstine Sings	1979	12.00
❑ SJL-2214 [(2)]	Mr. B and the Band/The Savoy Sessions	1976	15.00
TRIP			
❑ 5567	The Modern Sound of Mr. B	197?	10.00
VERVE			
❑ 819442-1 [(2)]	Everything I Have Is Yours: The MGM Years	1986	15.00
XANADU			
❑ 207	I Want to Talk About You	1987	10.00

ECKSTINE, BILLY, AND SARAH VAUGHAN

See SARAH VAUGHAN AND BILLY ECKSTINE.

ECLECTION

Number	Title (A Side/B Side)	Yr	NM
Albums			
ELEKTRA			
❑ EKS-74023	Eclection	1968	15.00

ECSTASIES, THE

Number	Title (A Side/B Side)	Yr	NM
45s			
AMY			
❑ 853	That Lucky Old Sun/Time for Love	1962	50.00
CLIFTON			
❑ 40	White Christmas/Silent Night	19??	15.00

ECSTASY, PASSION AND PAIN

Number	Title (A Side/B Side)	Yr	NM
45s			
ROULETTE			
❑ 7151	I Wouldn't Give You Up/Don't Burn Your Bridges Behind You	1973	8.00
❑ 7156	Good Things Don't Last Forever/Born to Lose You	1974	8.00
❑ 7159	Ask Me/I'll Take the Blame	1974	8.00
❑ 7163	One Beautiful Day/Try to Believe Me	1975	8.00
❑ 7178	There's So Much Love All Around Me/(Long Version)	1975	8.00
❑ 7182	Touch and Go/I'll Do Anything for You	1976	6.00
—As "Ecstasy, Passion and Pain Featuring Barbara Roy"			
❑ 7203	Passion/There's So Much Love All Around Me	1976	8.00
❑ 7209	Dance the Night Away/There's So Much Love All Around Me	1977	8.00
Albums			
ROULETTE			
❑ SR-3013	Ecstasy, Passion and Pain	1974	15.00

EDDIE AND BETTY

Number	Title (A Side/B Side)	Yr	NM
45s			
LARK			
❑ 4512	Sweet Someone/Saturday Night Fish Fry	1959	20.00
SIX THOUSAND			
❑ 601	Sweet Someone/Saturday Night Fish Fry	1957	25.00
WARNER BROS.			
❑ 5054	Sweet Someone/Saturday Night Fish Fry	1959	15.00
❑ 5079	Embarcadeno Boogie/Give Up Your Twin Pipe Mother	1959	15.00

EDDIE AND DUTCH

Number	Title (A Side/B Side)	Yr	NM
45s			
IVANHOE			
❑ 502	My Wife, the Dancer/Can't Help Lovin' That Girl	1970	6.00
❑ 505	My Mother-in-Law Came Out of Retirement/Bambino	1970	6.00
❑ 507	Ah-Choo, Gesundheit/Rignt in My Own Back Yard	1970	10.00

EDDIE AND ERNIE

Also see EDDIE CAMPBELL; ERNIE JOHNSON.

Number	Title (A Side/B Side)	Yr	NM
45s			
BUDDAH			
❑ 250	Hiding in the Shadows/Standing at the Crossroads	1971	30.00
CHECKER			
❑ 1057	Who's That Knocking at My Door/It's a Weak Man That Cries	1963	25.00
—As "Ernie and Eddie"			
❑ 1086	Time Waits for No One/That's the Way It Is	1964	25.00
CHESS			
❑ 1984	We Try Harder/I Believe She Will	1967	20.00
COLUMBIA			
❑ 4-44276	Doggone It/Falling Tears (Indian Drums)	1967	20.00
EASTERN			
❑ 45-602	Time Waits for No One/That's the Way It Is	1965	15.00
❑ 45-603	Turn Here/I'm a Young Man	1965	15.00
❑ 45-606	I'm Goin' for Myself/The Cat	1965	15.00
❑ E 608	Outcast/I'm Gonna Always Love You	1966	20.00
❑ E 609	I Can't Do It (I Just Can't Leave You)/Lost Friends	1966	20.00
REVUE			
❑ R 11049	Thanks for Yesterday/Woman, What Do You Be Doing	1969	15.00
❑ R 11063	You Give Me Love to Go On/Tell It Like It Is	1969	15.00
SHAZAM			
❑ 1004	We Try Harder/I Believe She Will	1967	150.00

EDDIE AND THE EVERGREENS

See SHA NA NA.

EDDIE AND THE SHOWMEN

Number	Title (A Side/B Side)	Yr	NM
45s			
LIBERTY			
❑ 55566	Toes on the Nose/Border Town	1963	30.00
❑ 55608	Squad Car/Scratch	1963	30.00
❑ 55659	Movin'/Mr. Rebel	1963	30.00
❑ 55695	Faw Away Places/Lanky Bones	1964	30.00
❑ 55720	We Are the Young/Young and Lonely	1964	30.00

EDDIE AND THE STARLITES

Number	Title (A Side/B Side)	Yr	NM
45s			
ALJON			
❑ 1260	Come On Home/(B-side unknown)	1963	30.00
SCEPTER			
❑ 1202	To Make a Long Story Short/Pretty Little Girl	1958	30.00
—Red label			
❑ 1202	To Make a Long Story Short/Pretty Little Girl	1958	60.00
—White label			

EDDY, DUANE

Also see AL CASEY; DUANE AND MIRRIAM EDDY.

Number	Title (A Side/B Side)	Yr	NM
45s			
BIG TREE			
❑ 157	Renegade/Nightly News	1972	8.00
CAPITOL			
❑ B-44018	Spies/Rockabilly Holiday	1987	5.00
❑ B-44018 [PS]	Spies/Rockabilly Holiday	1987	5.00
CHINA			
❑ 42986	Peter Gunn/Something Always Happens	1986	3.00
—With Art of Noise; B-side does not feature Eddy			
❑ 42986 [PS]	Peter Gunn/Something Always Happens	1986	3.00
COLPIX			
❑ 779	Trash/South Phoenix	1965	15.00
❑ 788	Don't Think Twice, It's All Right/House of the Rising Sun	1965	15.00
❑ 788 [PS]	Don't Think Twice, It's All Right/House of the Rising Sun	1965	50.00
❑ 795	El Rancho Grande/Poppa's Movin' On	1966	15.00
CONGRESS			
❑ 6010	Freight Train/Put a Little Love in Your Heart	1970	15.00
ELEKTRA			
❑ 45359	You Are My Sunshine/From 8 to 7	1977	5.00
FORD			
❑ 500	Ramrod/Caravan	1957	1500.
—As "Duane Eddy and His Rock-A-Billies"			
GREGMARK			
❑ 5	Caravan (Part 1)/Caravan (Part 2)	1961	15.00
—Credited to Duane Eddy, but is actually Al Casey			
GUSTO			
❑ 2047	Rebel Rouser/40 Miles of Bad Road	1979	4.00
—Re-recordings			
JAMIE			
❑ JLP-71 [S]	Lonesome Road/I Almost Lost My Mind	1960	25.00
❑ JLP-72 [S]	Loving You/Anything	1960	25.00
❑ JLP-73 [S]	Peter Gunn/Along the Navaho Trail	1960	25.00
❑ JLP-74 [S]	Hard Times/Along Came Linda	1960	25.00
❑ JLP-75 [S]	The Battle/You Are My Sunshine	1960	25.00
—The above five are 33 1/3 rpm singles with small holes			
❑ 1101	Moovin N' Groovin'/Up and Down	1958	25.00
—All-yellow label, "Jamie" at top			
❑ 1101	Moovin N' Groovin'/Up and Down	1958	50.00
—Originals have pink labels			
❑ 1104	Rebel-'Rouser/Stalkin'	1958	25.00
❑ 1109	Ramrod/The Walker	1958	25.00
❑ 1111	Cannonball/Mason Dixon Lion	1958	20.00
❑ 1117 [M]	The Lonely One/Detour	1959	20.00
❑ 1117 [S]	The Lonely One/Detour	1959	50.00
❑ 1122	Yep!/Three-30-Blues	1959	20.00
❑ 1122 [PS]	Yep!/Three-30-Blues	1959	50.00
❑ 1126 [M]	Forty Miles of Bad Road/The Quiet Three	1959	20.00
❑ 1126 [PS]	Forty Miles of Bad Road/The Quiet Three	1959	50.00
❑ 1126 [S]	Forty Miles of Bad Road/The Quiet Three	1959	50.00
❑ 1130 [M]	Some Kind-a Earthquake/First Love, First Tears	1959	20.00

Number	Title (A Side/B Side)	Yr	NM
❑ 1130 [PS]	Some Kind-a Earthquake/ First Love, First Tears	1959	40.00
❑ 1130 [S]	Some Kind-a Earthquake/ First Love, First Tears	1959	50.00
❑ 1144	Bonnie Came Back/Lost Island	1959	20.00
❑ 1144 [PS]	Bonnie Came Back/Lost Island	1959	40.00
❑ 1151	Shazam!/The Secret Seven	1960	15.00
❑ 1151 [PS]	Shazam!/The Secret Seven	1960	30.00
❑ 1156	Because They're Young/ Rebel Walk	1960	15.00
❑ 1156 [PS]	Because They're Young/ Rebel Walk	1960	30.00
❑ 1163	Kommotion/Theme for Moon Children	1960	15.00
❑ 1163 [PS]	Kommotion/Theme for Moon Children	1960	30.00
❑ 1168	Peter Gunn/Along the Navaho Trail	1960	15.00
❑ 1168 [PS]	Peter Gunn/Along the Navaho Trail	1960	30.00
❑ 1175	"Pepe"/Lost Friend	1960	15.00
❑ 1175 [PS]	"Pepe"/Lost Friend	1960	30.00
—Yellow sleeve			
❑ 1175 [PS]	"Pepe"/Lost Friend	1960	40.00
—Red sleeve			
❑ 1183	Theme from Dixie/Gidget Goes Hawaiian	1961	15.00
❑ 1183 [PS]	Theme from Dixie/Gidget Goes Hawaiian	1961	30.00
❑ 1187	Ring of Fire/Bobbie	1961	15.00
❑ 1187 [PS]	Ring of Fire/Bobbie	1961	30.00
❑ 1195	Drivin' Home/Tammy	1961	15.00
❑ 1195 [PS]	Drivin' Home/Tammy	1961	30.00
❑ 1200	My Blue Heaven/ Along Came Linda	1961	15.00
❑ 1200 [PS]	My Blue Heaven/ Along Came Linda	1961	30.00
❑ 1206	The Avenger/Londonderry Air	1961	15.00
❑ 1209	The Battle/Trambone	1962	15.00
❑ 1224	Runaway Pony/Just Because	1962	15.00
❑ 1303	Rebel Rouser/Movin' N' Groovin'	1965	12.00
RCA VICTOR			
❑ 47-7999	Deep in the Heart of Texas/ Saints and Sinners	1962	12.00
❑ 47-7999 [PS]	Deep in the Heart of Texas/ Saints and Sinners	1962	25.00
❑ 47-8047	The Ballad of Paladin/ The WIld Westerner	1962	12.00
❑ 47-8047 [PS]	The Ballad of Paladin/ The WIld Westerner	1962	25.00
❑ 47-8087	(Dance with the) Guitar Man/ Stretchin' Out	1962	15.00
❑ 47-8087 [PS]	(Dance with the) Guitar Man/ Stretchin' Out	1962	30.00
❑ 47-8131	Boss Guitar/Desert Rat	1963	12.00
❑ 47-8131 [PS]	Boss Guitar/Desert Rat	1963	25.00
❑ 47-8180	Lonely Boy, Lonely Guitar/ Joshin'	1963	12.00
❑ 47-8180 [PS]	Lonely Boy, Lonely Guitar/ Joshin'	1963	25.00
❑ 47-8214	Your Baby's Gone Surfin'/ Shuckin'	1963	15.00
❑ 47-8214 [PS]	Your Baby's Gone Surfin'/ Shuckin'	1963	30.00
❑ 47-8276	The Son of Rebel Rouser/ The Story of Three Loves	1963	12.00
❑ 47-8276 [PS]	The Son of Rebel Rouser/ The Story of Three Loves	1963	25.00
❑ 47-8335	Guitar Child/Jerky Jalopy	1964	12.00
❑ 47-8376	Water Skiing/Theme from A Summer Place	1964	12.00
❑ 47-8442	Guitar Star/The Iguana	1964	12.00
❑ 47-8442 [PS]	Guitar Star/The Iguana	1964	30.00
❑ 47-8507	Moonshot/Roughneck	1965	12.00
❑ 47-8507 [PS]	Moonshot/Roughneck	1965	120.00
❑ 47-8335 [PS]	Guitar Child/Jerky Jalopy	1964	30.00
❑ 47-8376 [PS]	Water Skiing/Theme from A Summer Place	1964	60.00
REPRISE			
❑ 0504	Daydream/This Guitar Was Made for Twangin'	1966	10.00
❑ 0557	Roarin'/Monsoon	1967	10.00
❑ 0662	There Is a Mountain/This Town	1968	10.00
❑ 0690	Niki-Hoeky/Velvet Nights	1968	10.00
UNI			
❑ 55237	The Five-Seventeen/ Something	1970	15.00
7-Inch Extended Plays			
JAMIE			
❑ JEP-100	Cannonball/Moovin' N' Groovin'//Mason-Dixon Lion/ The Lonely One	1958	50.00
❑ JEP-100 [PS]	Duane Eddy	1958	50.00
❑ JEP-301	Lonesome Road/I Almost Lost My Mind//Detour/Loving You	1959	50.00
❑ JEP-301 [PS]	Detour	1959	50.00

Number	Title (A Side/B Side)	Yr	NM
❑ JEP-302	Yep/Three-30 Blues//Anytime/ Stalkin'	1959	50.00
❑ JEP-302 [PS]	Yep!	1959	50.00
❑ JEP-303	Shazam/Tiger Love//My Blue Heaven/Night Train To Memphis	1960	50.00
❑ JEP-303 [PS]	Shazam!	1960	50.00
❑ JEP-304	Because They're Young/Easy/ /Rebel Walk/The Battle	1960	50.00
❑ JEP-304 [PS]	Because They're Young	1960	50.00
Albums			
CAPITOL			
❑ ST-12567	Duane Eddy	1987	12.00
COLPIX			
❑ CP-490 [M]	Duane A-Go-Go	1965	30.00
❑ CPS-490 [S]	Duane A-Go-Go	1965	40.00
❑ CPL-494 [M]	Duane Eddy Does Bob Dylan	1965	30.00
❑ SCP-494 [S]	Duane Eddy Does Bob Dylan	1965	40.00
JAMIE			
❑ JLP-3000 [M]	Have "Twangy" Guitar — Will Travel	1958	120.00
—Duane sitting with guitar case, title on cover in white (1st)			
❑ JLP-3000 [M]	Have "Twangy" Guitar — Will Travel	1959	50.00
—Duane standing with guitar (3rd)			
❑ JLP-3000 [M]	Have "Twangy" Guitar — Will Travel	1959	100.00
—Duane sitting with guitar case, title on cover in green and red (2nd)			
❑ JLPS-3000 [R]	Have "Twangy" Guitar — Will Travel	196?	50.00
—Duane standing with guitar (3rd), album plays fake stereo			
❑ JLPS-3000 [S]	Have "Twangy" Guitar — Will Travel	1958	400.00
—Duane sitting with guitar case, title on cover in white (1st)			
❑ JLPS-3000 [S]	Have "Twangy" Guitar — Will Travel	1959	100.00
—Duane standing with guitar (3rd), album plays true stereo			
❑ JLPS-3000 [S]	Have "Twangy" Guitar — Will Travel	1959	300.00
—Duane sitting with guitar case, title on cover in green and red (2nd)			
❑ JLPM-3006 [M]	Especially for You…	1959	40.00
❑ JLPS-3006 [S]	Especially for You…	1959	60.00
❑ JLPM-3009 [M]	The "Twangs" The "Thang"	1959	40.00
❑ JLPS-3009 [S]	The "Twangs" The "Thang"	1959	60.00
❑ JLPM-3011 [M]	Songs of Our Heritage	196?	30.00
—Regular cover			
❑ JLPM-3011 [M]	Songs of Our Heritage	1960	80.00
—Gatefold cover			
❑ JLPS-3011 [S]	Songs of Our Heritage	196?	40.00
—Regular cover			
❑ JLPS-3011 [S]	Songs of Our Heritage	1960	100.00
—Gatefold cover			
❑ JLPS-3011 [S]	Songs of Our Heritage	1960	500.00
—Gatefold cover, blue vinyl			
❑ JLPS-3011 [S]	Songs of Our Heritage	1960	500.00
—Gatefold cover, red vinyl			
❑ JLPM-3014 [M]	$1,000,000.00 Worth of Twang	1960	40.00
❑ JLPS-3014 [S]	$1,000,000.00 Worth of Twang	1960	70.00
—All but one song — "Up and Down" — is in true stereo			
❑ JLPM-3019 [M]	Girls! Girls! Girls!	1961	40.00
❑ JLPS-3019 [R]	Girls! Girls! Girls!	1961	30.00
❑ JLPM-3021 [M]	$1,000,000.00 Worth of Twang, Vol. 2	1962	40.00
❑ JLPS-3021 [R]	$1,000,000.00 Worth of Twang, Vol. 2	1962	30.00
❑ JLPM-3022 [M]	Twistin' with Duane Eddy	1962	40.00
❑ JLPS-3022 [P]	Twistin' with Duane Eddy	1962	40.00
❑ JLPM-3024 [M]	Surfin'	1963	50.00
❑ JLPS-3024 [S]	Surfin'	1963	80.00
❑ JLPM-3025 [M]	Duane Eddy & The Rebels — In Person	1963	30.00
❑ JLPS-3025 [S]	Duane Eddy & The Rebels — In Person	1963	40.00
❑ JLPM-3026 [M]	16 Greatest Hits	1964	40.00
❑ JLPS-3026 [R]	16 Greatest Hits	1964	30.00
❑ ST-90663 [S]	Duane Eddy & The Rebels — In Person	1965	50.00
—Capitol Record Club edition			
❑ T-90663 [M]	Duane Eddy & The Rebels — In Person	1965	40.00
—Capitol Record Club edition			
❑ ST-90682 [S]	Have "Twangy" Guitar — Will Travel	1965	80.00
—Capitol Record Club edition			
❑ T-90682 [M]	Have "Twangy" Guitar — Will Travel	1965	60.00
—Capitol Record Club edition			
❑ ST-91301 [S]	The "Twangs" The "Thang"	1966	60.00
—Capitol Record Club edition			
❑ T-91301 [M]	The "Twangs" The "Thang"	1966	60.00
—Capitol Record Club edition			
RCA VICTOR			
❑ LPM-2525 [M]	Twistin' 'N' Twangin'	1962	25.00
❑ LSP-2525 [S]	Twistin' 'N' Twangin'	1962	40.00
❑ LPM-2576 [M]	Twangy Guitar — Silky Strings	1962	25.00
❑ LSP-2576 [S]	Twangy Guitar — Silky Strings	1962	40.00
❑ LPM-2648 [M]	Dance with the Guitar Man	1962	25.00
❑ LSP-2648 [S]	Dance with the Guitar Man	1962	40.00

Number	Title (A Side/B Side)	Yr	NM
❑ ANL1-2671	Pure Gold	1978	10.00
❑ LPM-2681 [M]	Twang a Country Song	1963	25.00
❑ LSP-2681 [S]	Twang a Country Song	1963	40.00
❑ LPM-2700 [M]	"Twangin'" Up a Storm!	1963	25.00
❑ LSP-2700 [S]	"Twangin'" Up a Storm!	1963	40.00
❑ LPM-2798 [M]	Lonely Guitar	1964	20.00
❑ LSP-2798 [S]	Lonely Guitar	1964	30.00
❑ LPM-2918 [M]	Water Skiing	1964	20.00
❑ LSP-2918 [S]	Water Skiing	1964	30.00
❑ LPM-2993 [M]	Twangin' the Golden Hits	1965	20.00
❑ LSP-2993 [S]	Twangin' the Golden Hits	1965	30.00
❑ LPM-3432 [M]	Twangsville	1965	20.00
❑ LSP-3432 [S]	Twangsville	1965	30.00
❑ LPM-3477 [M]	The Best of Duane Eddy	1965	20.00
❑ LSP-3477 [P]	The Best of Duane Eddy	1965	25.00
—Black "Stereo" label			
❑ LSP-3477 [P]	The Best of Duane Eddy	1969	15.00
—Orange label			
REPRISE			
❑ R-6218 [M]	The Biggest Twang of Them All	1966	30.00
❑ RS-6218 [S]	The Biggest Twang of Them All	1966	40.00
❑ R-6240 [M]	The Roaring Twangies	1967	30.00
❑ RS-6240 [S]	The Roaring Twangies	1967	40.00
SIRE			
❑ SASH-3707-2 [(2)]	The Vintage Years	1975	25.00

EDDY, DUANE AND MIRRIAM Also see JESSI COLTER, DUANE EDDY.

Number	Title (A Side/B Side)	Yr	NM
45s			
REPRISE			
❑ 0622	Guitar on My Mind/Wicked Women from Wickenborg	1967	10.00

EDELMAN, RANDY

Number	Title (A Side/B Side)	Yr	NM
45s			
ARISTA			
❑ 0268	Can't It All Be Love/ Sentimental Fools	1977	6.00
❑ 0309	Take My Hand/ Today (June Song)	1978	6.00
❑ 0347	Autumn Days with You/ (B-side unknown)	1978	6.00
❑ 0434	You're the One/Don't Let Go of Me	1979	6.00
LION			
❑ 144	Mexico/(B-side unknown)	1972	8.00
❑ 153	The Laughter and the Tears/Lost	1973	8.00
MGM			
❑ 14599	Everybody Wants to Call You Sweetheart/Ball-Buster Circus	1973	8.00
SUNFLOWER			
❑ 108	Give a Little Laughter/ Just Somebody	1971	8.00
❑ 121	My Cabin/T-Shirt 'n' Jeans	1972	8.00
20TH CENTURY			
❑ 2134	What Are You Going to Do When the Plumbing Goes/ Pistol Packin' Melody	1974	6.00
❑ 2155	Everybody Wants to Find a Bluebird/Pistol Packin' Melody	1974	6.00
❑ 2196	Isn't It a Shame/Everybody Wants to Call You Sweetheart	1975	6.00
❑ 2245	Fresh Out'a Love/Bring the Baby In with the Bacon	1975	8.00
❑ 2274	Concrete and Clay/Weekend in New England	1976	8.00
Albums			
ARISTA			
❑ AB 4139	If Love Is Real	1977	12.00
❑ AB 4210	You're the One	1979	12.00
LION			
❑ LN-1013	The Laughter and the Tears	1972	15.00
SUNFLOWER			
❑ SNF-5005	Randy Edelman	1971	15.00
20TH CENTURY			
❑ T-443	Prime Cuts	1974	15.00
❑ T-494	Farewell Fairbanks	1975	12.00

EDEN, BARBARA

Number	Title (A Side/B Side)	Yr	NM
45s			
DOT			
❑ 16999	Bend It/I Wouldn't Be a Fool	1967	8.00
❑ 17022	Rebel/Heartaches	1967	8.00
❑ 17032	Pledge of Love/I'm a Fool to Care	1967	8.00
PLANTATION			
❑ 178	Widow Jones/We Tried	1978	5.00
Albums			
DOT			
❑ DLP-3795 [M]	Miss Barbara Eden	1967	40.00
❑ DLP-25795 [S]	Miss Barbara Eden	1967	50.00

Except when noted otherwise, VG = 25% of NM, and VG+ = 50% of NM. (Example: VG = $2.00, VG+ = $4.00 and NM = $8.00.)

EDEN, CHANCE

45s

BIG TREE

Number	Title (A Side/B Side)	Yr	NM
❑ 107	Your Ma Said You Cried/Cry	1970	15.00

BIRTHSTONE

Number	Title (A Side/B Side)	Yr	NM
❑ 1037	First Love Affair/ Maybe I'll Love Again	196?	20.00

ROULETTE

Number	Title (A Side/B Side)	Yr	NM
❑ 4592	Things I Love/You'd Better Go	1965	15.00
❑ 4602	Here I Am Broken Hearted/ String Along	1965	15.00
❑ 4664	I'm Looking Through You/ Another Love	1966	20.00
❑ 4698	Barefoot Through the Grass/I Could Have Loved You So Well	1966	15.00

EDEN'S CHILDREN

45s

ABC

Number	Title (A Side/B Side)	Yr	NM
❑ 11053	Goodbye Girl/Just Let Go	1968	12.00

Albums

ABC

Number	Title (A Side/B Side)	Yr	NM
❑ 624 [M]	Eden's Children	1968	40.00
❑ S-624 [S]	Eden's Children	1968	25.00
❑ S-652	Sure Looks Real	1968	20.00

EDGE, GRAEME Of THE MOODY BLUES.

45s

LONDON

Number	Title (A Side/B Side)	Yr	NM
❑ 1071	Everybody Needs Somebody/ Be My Eyes	1977	5.00

—With Adrian Gurvitz

THRESHOLD

Number	Title (A Side/B Side)	Yr	NM
❑ 67018	We Like to Do It/Shotgun	1974	5.00
❑ 67022	The Tunnel/Bareback Rider	1975	5.00

Albums

LONDON

Number	Title (A Side/B Side)	Yr	NM
❑ PS 686	Paradise Ballroom	1977	12.00

THRESHOLD

Number	Title (A Side/B Side)	Yr	NM
❑ THS 15	Kick Off Your Muddy Boots	1975	15.00

EDGE, THE

Albums

NOSE

Number	Title (A Side/B Side)	Yr	NM
❑ NRS-48003	The Edge	1970	40.00

EDGEWOOD

45s

TMI

Number	Title (A Side/B Side)	Yr	NM
❑ ZS7 9011	Ain't Had No Lovin'/Silent	1972	7.00

EDISON ELECTRIC BAND, THE

45s

CAMEO

Number	Title (A Side/B Side)	Yr	NM
❑ 490	The Name of the Game/ Mary Ethel	1967	25.00

—As "The Thomas A. Edison Electric Band"

COTILLION

Number	Title (A Side/B Side)	Yr	NM
❑ 44071	Ship of the Future/West Wind	1970	10.00

Albums

COTILLION

Number	Title (A Side/B Side)	Yr	NM
❑ SD 9022	Bless You, Dr. Woodward	1970	20.00

EDISON LIGHTHOUSE

45s

BELL

Number	Title (A Side/B Side)	Yr	NM
❑ 858	Love Grows (Where My Rosemary Goes)/ Every Lonely Day	1970	6.00
❑ 907	She Works in a Woman's Way/ It's Gonna Be a Lonely Summer	1970	5.00
❑ 960	It's Up to You Petula/ Let's Make It Up	1971	5.00
❑ 989	Take a Little Time/ What's Happening	1971	5.00

EDMUNDS, DAVE Also see LOVE SCULPTURE; ROCKPILE.

12-Inch Singles

COLUMBIA

Number	Title (A Side/B Side)	Yr	NM
❑ AS 1660 [DJ]	Slipping Away (same on both sides)	1982	8.00
❑ AS99-1725 [DJ]	Information	1983	25.00

—Promo-only picture disc

Number	Title (A Side/B Side)	Yr	NM
❑ AS 1911 [DJ]	Something About You (same on both sides)	1984	6.00
❑ CAS 2077 [DJ]	Do You Want to Dance (same on both sides)	1985	6.00
❑ CAS 02598 [DJ]	The Wanderer/Dave Edmunds Mega-Mix	1986	6.00

45s

CAPITOL

Number	Title (A Side/B Side)	Yr	NM
❑ 7PRO-79973 [DJ]	Closer to the Flame (same on both sides)	1990	10.00

COLUMBIA

Number	Title (A Side/B Side)	Yr	NM
❑ 02960	From Small Things (Big Things One Day Come)/Warmed Over Kisses (Left Over Love)	1982	4.00

—A-side is a Bruce Springsteen composition.

Number	Title (A Side/B Side)	Yr	NM
❑ 03428	Run Rudolph Run/Deep in the Heart of Texas	1982	4.00
❑ 03428 [PS]	Run Rudolph Run/Deep in the Heart of Texas	1982	8.00
❑ 03877	Slipping Away/Don't Call Me Tonight	1983	3.00
❑ 04080	Information/What Have I Got to Do to Win	1983	3.00
❑ 04585	Something About You/ Can't Get Enough	1984	3.00
❑ 04700	Breaking Out/How Could I Be So Wrong	1984	3.00
❑ 04762	High School Nights /Porky's Revenge	1985	2.50
❑ 04762 [PS]	High School Nights/ Porky's Revenge	1985	2.50
❑ 04887	Queen of the Hop/I Don't Want to Do It	1985	20.00

—B-side by George Harrison, thus accounting for this 45's value

Number	Title (A Side/B Side)	Yr	NM
❑ 04923	Do You Want to Dance/ Don't Call Me Tonight	1985	3.00
❑ 05487	Run Rudolph Run/From Small Things (Big Things One Day Come)	198?	3.00

—"Golden Oldies" reissue

Number	Title (A Side/B Side)	Yr	NM
❑ 06599	The Wanderer/Here Comes the Weekend	1987	3.00
❑ 06599	The Wanderer/Information	1987	3.00
❑ 07040	Paralyzed/Here Comes the Weekend	1987	3.00

MAM

Number	Title (A Side/B Side)	Yr	NM
❑ 3601	I Hear You Knocking/Black Bill	1970	8.00
❑ 3608	I'm Coming Home/Country Roll	1971	6.00
❑ 3611	Blue Monday/I'll Get Along	1971	6.00

MCA

Number	Title (A Side/B Side)	Yr	NM
❑ 53256	Gonna Move/Red River Rock	1988	2.50

—B-side by Silicon Teens

Number	Title (A Side/B Side)	Yr	NM
❑ 53256 [PS]	Gonna Move/Red River Rock	1988	2.50

—B-side by Silicon Teens

RCA VICTOR

Number	Title (A Side/B Side)	Yr	NM
❑ 74-0882	Baby I Love You/Maybe	1973	6.00
❑ LPBO-5000	Born to Be with You/ Pick Axe Rag	1973	6.00
❑ PB-10118	Let It Be Me/Need a Shot of Rhythm and Blues	1974	5.00

SWAN SONG

Number	Title (A Side/B Side)	Yr	NM
❑ 70113	I Knew the Bride/Little Darlin'	1978	4.00
❑ 70116	Get Out of Denver/ Work Out Suits	1978	4.00
❑ 70118	Trouble Boys/What Looks Best on You	1978	4.00
❑ 71001	Girls Talk/Creature from the Black Lagoon	1979	5.00
❑ 71002	Crawling from the Wreckage/ Queen of Hearts	1979	5.00
❑ 72000	Almost Saturday Night/ You'll Never Get Me Up	1981	3.00
❑ 72000 [PS]	Almost Saturday Night/ You'll Never Get Me Up	1981	3.00
❑ 72003	The Race Is On/Singin' the Blues	1981	5.00

—Backing group: Stray Cats

Albums

ATLANTIC

Number	Title (A Side/B Side)	Yr	NM
❑ PR 320 [DJ]	College Network	1978	50.00

—Promo-only interview album

CAPITOL

Number	Title (A Side/B Side)	Yr	NM
❑ C1-90372	Closer to the Flame	1990	15.00

COLUMBIA

Number	Title (A Side/B Side)	Yr	NM
❑ FC 37930	D.E. 7th	1982	12.00
❑ PC 37930	D.E. 7th	198?	8.00

—Budget-line reissue ("02" added to bar code on back cover)

Number	Title (A Side/B Side)	Yr	NM
❑ FC 38651	Information	1983	12.00
❑ PC 38651	Information	198?	8.00

—Budget-line reissue ("02" added to bar code on back cover)

Number	Title (A Side/B Side)	Yr	NM
❑ FC 39273	Riff Raff	1984	10.00
❑ FC 40603	I Hear You Rockin'	1987	10.00
❑ PC 40603	I Hear You Rockin'	198?	8.00

—Budget-line reissue ("02" added to bar code on back cover)

MAM

Number	Title (A Side/B Side)	Yr	NM
❑ 3	Rockpile	1972	40.00

RCA VICTOR

Number	Title (A Side/B Side)	Yr	NM
❑ AYL1-4238	Subtle as a Flying Mallet	1982	10.00

—Reissue (black label, dog near top)

Number	Title (A Side/B Side)	Yr	NM
❑ LPL1-5003	Subtle as a Flying Mallet	1975	12.00

SWAN SONG

Number	Title (A Side/B Side)	Yr	NM
❑ SS 8418	Get It	1977	15.00
❑ SS 8505	Trax on Wax 4	1978	15.00
❑ SS 8507	Repeat When Necessary	1979	15.00
❑ SS 8510	The Best of Dave Edmunds	1981	12.00
❑ SD 16034	Twangin'	1981	12.00

EDMUNDS, DAVE, AND NICK LOWE

45s

COLUMBIA

Number	Title (A Side/B Side)	Yr	NM
❑ AE7-1219	Take a Message to Mary/ Crying in the Rain//Poor Jenny/When Will I Be Loved	1980	6.00

—Bonus EP included in the Rockpile LP "Seconds of Pleasure"

Number	Title (A Side/B Side)	Yr	NM
❑ AE7-1219 [PS]	Nick Lowe and Dave Edmunds Sing The Everly Brothers	1980	6.00

EDSELS, THE

45s

CAPITOL

Number	Title (A Side/B Side)	Yr	NM
❑ 4588	Bone Shaker Joe/ My Jealous One	1961	20.00
❑ 4675	If Your Pillow Could Talk/ Shake Shake Sherry	1961	20.00
❑ 4836	Shaddy Daddy Dip Dip/ Don't You Feel	1962	20.00

DOT

Number	Title (A Side/B Side)	Yr	NM
❑ 16311	My Whispering Heart/Could It Be	1962	25.00

DUB

Number	Title (A Side/B Side)	Yr	NM
❑ 2843	Rama Lama Ding Dong/Bells	1958	50.00

—Repress with corrected title and the same recording as on Twin 700

Number	Title (A Side/B Side)	Yr	NM
❑ 2843	Lama Rama Ding Dong/Bells	1958	70.00

—Originals have the wrong title and the same recording as on Twin 700

Number	Title (A Side/B Side)	Yr	NM
❑ 2843	Rama Lama Ding Dong/Bells	197?	5.00

—Reproduction with an alternate take of the A-side; this has confused many who believe that the original Dub and Twin records are different.

EMBER

Number	Title (A Side/B Side)	Yr	NM
❑ 1078	Three Precious Words/Let's Go	1961	25.00

LOST-NITE

Number	Title (A Side/B Side)	Yr	NM
❑ 206	Rama Lama Ding Dong/Bells	196?	8.00

—Reissue

MUSICTONE

Number	Title (A Side/B Side)	Yr	NM
❑ 1144	Rama Lama Ding Dong/Bells	1961	12.00

ROULETTE

Number	Title (A Side/B Side)	Yr	NM
❑ 4151	Do You Love Me/ Rink-a-Dink-a-Doo	1959	25.00

TAMMY

Number	Title (A Side/B Side)	Yr	NM
❑ 1010	What Brought Us Together/ Don't Know What to Do	1960	50.00
❑ 1014	Three Precious Words/Let's Go	1960	50.00
❑ 1023	The Girl I Love/Got to FInd Out About Love	1961	40.00
❑ 1027	Count the Tears/Twenty-Four Hours	1961	40.00

TWIN

Number	Title (A Side/B Side)	Yr	NM
❑ 700	Rama Lama Ding Dong/Bells	1961	25.00

EDWARD BEAR

45s

CAPITOL

Number	Title (A Side/B Side)	Yr	NM
❑ 2801	You, Me and Mexico/ Sinking Ship	1970	6.00
❑ 2955	You Can't Deny It/Toe Jam	1970	6.00
❑ 3351	Masquerade/The Pirate King	1972	4.00
❑ 3452	Last Song/Best Friend	1972	5.00
❑ 3452 [PS]	Last Song/Best Friend	1972	8.00
❑ 3581	Close Your Eyes/Cachet County	1973	4.00
❑ 3581 [PS]	Close Your Eyes/Cachet County	1973	10.00
❑ 3683	I Love Her (You Love Me)/ Walking On Back	1973	4.00
❑ 3683 [PS]	I Love Her (You Love Me)/ Walking On Back	1973	10.00
❑ 3780	Coming Home Christmas/ Does Your Mother Know	1973	8.00
❑ 3804	Same Old Feeling/Fool	1973	4.00
❑ 3869	I Had Dreams/You, Me and Mexico	1974	4.00
❑ 3978	Freedom for the Stallion/ Why Don't You Marry Me	1974	4.00

Albums

CAPITOL

Number	Title (A Side/B Side)	Yr	NM
❑ SKAO-426	Bearings	1970	15.00
❑ ST-580	Eclipse	1971	15.00
❑ ST-11157	Edward Bear	1972	10.00
❑ ST-11192	Close Your Eyes	1973	10.00

E

EDWARDS, BOBBY

45s

CAPITOL

Number	Title (A Side/B Side)	Yr	NM
❑ 4674	What's the Reason/ Walk Away Slowly	1961	8.00
❑ 4726	Singing the Blues/What'll I Do Without You	1962	8.00
❑ 4789	Someone New/Here's My Heart	1962	8.00
❑ 4874	Remember Who Brought You Here/The Way I Am	1962	8.00
❑ 5006	Don't Pretend/Help Me	1963	8.00

CHART

Number	Title (A Side/B Side)	Yr	NM
❑ 1020	I'm Sorry to See You Go/ Once a Fool (Always a Fool)	1968	5.00
❑ 1045	Each Time You Cross My Mind/ Just Ain't My Day	1968	5.00
❑ 5016	Bring My Baby Home/ Loving You Is Killing Me	1969	5.00
❑ 5061	You're the Reason/Don't Pretend	1970	5.00

CREST

Number	Title (A Side/B Side)	Yr	NM
❑ 1075	You're the Reason/I'm a Fool for Loving You	1961	10.00

MANCO

Number	Title (A Side/B Side)	Yr	NM
❑ 1026	Jealous Heart/I've Lost Everything But the Memories	1962	8.00

MUSICOR

Number	Title (A Side/B Side)	Yr	NM
❑ 1101	A Little Less Heartache/ Within Your Arms	1965	6.00

EDWARDS, DENNIS

45s

INTERNATIONAL SOULVILLE

Number	Title (A Side/B Side)	Yr	NM
❑ 100	Johnny on the Spot/ I Didn't Have To But I Did	196?	1500.

EDWARDS, DEWEY

45s

CAMEO

Number	Title (A Side/B Side)	Yr	NM
❑ 364	Come On Over to My Place/ I Let a Good Thing Go By	1965	20.00

EDWARDS, J.D.

45s

IMPERIAL

Number	Title (A Side/B Side)	Yr	NM
❑ 5245	Crying/Hobo	1953	120.00

EDWARDS, JIMMY

45s

MERCURY

Number	Title (A Side/B Side)	Yr	NM
❑ 71209	Love Bug Crawl/Honey Lovin'	1957	30.00
❑ 71272	My Honey/Golden Ruby Blue	1958	30.00
❑ 71348	Do That Again/Wedding Band	1958	30.00

RCA VICTOR

Number	Title (A Side/B Side)	Yr	NM
❑ 47-7597	A Favor for a Friend/Your Love Is a Good Love	1959	25.00
❑ 47-7717	Rosie Lee/Live and Let Live	1960	20.00
❑ 47-7773	Silver Slippers/What Do You Want from Me	1960	20.00

EDWARDS, JOEY

45s

COLUMBIA

Number	Title (A Side/B Side)	Yr	NM
❑ 4-43620	Trapped/How Big Is Big	1966	12.00
❑ 4-43620 [PS]	Trapped/How Big Is Big	1966	20.00

LILLY

Number	Title (A Side/B Side)	Yr	NM
❑ 501	This Little Girl/Shirley, Shirley	1960	200.00

EDWARDS, JOHNNY, AND THE WHITE CAPS

45s

NORTHLAND

Number	Title (A Side/B Side)	Yr	NM
❑ 90-7002	Rock 'n Roll Saddles/ Why'd You Leave Me?	1957	200.00

EDWARDS, SHIRLEY

45s

SHRINE

Number	Title (A Side/B Side)	Yr	NM
❑ 110	Dream My Heart/It Is Your Love	1966	800.00

EDWARDS, TOM

45s

CORAL

Number	Title (A Side/B Side)	Yr	NM
❑ 61773	What Is a Teen Age Boy/ What Is a Teen Age Girl	1957	12.00
❑ 61826	The Story of Elvis Presley/ What Is Rock 'n' Roll	1957	20.00
❑ 61938	Goodnight Rock 'n' Roll/ The Spirit of Seventeen	1958	10.00

DOT

Number	Title (A Side/B Side)	Yr	NM
❑ 15811	What Is a Boyfriend/All About Girls and Women	1958	10.00

EDWARDS, TYRONE

45s

INVICTUS

Number	Title (A Side/B Side)	Yr	NM
❑ ZS7 1269	Can't Get Enough of You/You Took Me from a World Outside	1974	25.00

EDWARDS, VERN

45s

PROBE

Number	Title (A Side/B Side)	Yr	NM
❑ 100	Cool Baby, Cool/Glenda	1959	200.00

EELY, JACK

Sang lead on THE KINGSMEN's version of "Louie Louie."

45s

BANG

Number	Title (A Side/B Side)	Yr	NM
❑ 520	Louie Louie '66/David's Mood	1966	15.00
❑ 534	Louie Go Home/Ride Ride Baby	1966	15.00

EHRET, BOB

45s

ALADDIN

Number	Title (A Side/B Side)	Yr	NM
❑ 3377	Stop the Clock/So Lonely	1957	150.00

8TH DAY, THE

Probably all the same group.

45s

A&M

Number	Title (A Side/B Side)	Yr	NM
❑ 2539	Call Me Up/I've Got My Heart in the Right Place	1983	4.00
❑ 2595 [DJ]	In the Valley (same on both sides)	1983	4.00

CADET

Number	Title (A Side/B Side)	Yr	NM
❑ 5660	Hear the Grass Grow/ Bring Your Love Back	1969	10.00

CRIB

Number	Title (A Side/B Side)	Yr	NM
❑ 101	Let's Share the Miracle/ It's Christmas Day	19??	4.00

INVICTUS

Number	Title (A Side/B Side)	Yr	NM
❑ 9087	She's Not Just Another Woman/I Can't Fool Myself	1971	5.00
❑ 9098	You've Got to Crawl (Before You Walk)/It's Instrumental to Be Free	1971	5.00
❑ 9107	If I Could See the Light/If I Could See the Light (Part 2)	1971	5.00
❑ 9117	Eeny-Meeny-Miny-Mo (Three's a Crowd)/ Rocks in My Head	1972	5.00
❑ 9124	Good Book/I Gotta Get Home	1972	5.00

KAPP

Number	Title (A Side/B Side)	Yr	NM
❑ 862	Hey Boy (The Girl's in Love with You)/Million Lights	1967	8.00
❑ 862 [PS]	Hey Boy (The Girl's in Love with You)/Million Lights	1967	12.00
❑ 894	Raining Sunshine/That Good Old Fashioned Way	1968	8.00
❑ 916	Glory/Building with a Steeple	1968	8.00

Albums

A&M

Number	Title (A Side/B Side)	Yr	NM
❑ SP-4942	The 8th Day	1983	10.00

INVICTUS

Number	Title (A Side/B Side)	Yr	NM
❑ ST-7306	The 8th Day	1971	12.00
❑ ST-9809	I Gotta Get Home	1973	12.00

KAPP

Number	Title (A Side/B Side)	Yr	NM
❑ KS 3554	On the Eighth Day	1968	15.00

EIRE APPARENT, THE

Produced by JIMI HENDRIX.

45s

BUDDAH

Number	Title (A Side/B Side)	Yr	NM
❑ 67	Yes I Need Someone/ Let Me Stay	1968	15.00

Albums

BUDDAH

Number	Title (A Side/B Side)	Yr	NM
❑ BDS-5031	Sunrise	1969	40.00

EL CAPRIS

45s

ARGYLE

Number	Title (A Side/B Side)	Yr	NM
❑ 1010	Ooh But She Did/(Shimmy, Shimmy) Ko Ko Wop	1961	30.00

BULLSEYE

Number	Title (A Side/B Side)	Yr	NM
❑ 102	Oh But She Did/(Shimmy Shimmy) Ko Ko Wop	1956	150.00
—Note slight difference in A-side title			
❑ 102	Ooh But She Did/(Shimmy Shimmy) Ko Ko Wop	1956	200.00

FEE BEE

Number	Title (A Side/B Side)	Yr	NM
❑ 216	Your Star/To Live Again	1957	40.00

HI-Q

Number	Title (A Side/B Side)	Yr	NM
❑ 5006	Girl of Mine/These Lonely Nights	1958	40.00
—Yellow label			
❑ 5006	Girl of Mine/These Lonely Nights	1958	100.00
—Blue label			

PARIS

Number	Title (A Side/B Side)	Yr	NM
❑ 525	They're Always Laughing at Me/Ivy League Clean	1958	40.00

RING-O

Number	Title (A Side/B Side)	Yr	NM
❑ 308	Safari/Quit Pulling My Woman	1960	30.00

EL CHICANO

45s

GORDO

Number	Title (A Side/B Side)	Yr	NM
❑ 703	Viva Tirado — Part I/ Viva Tirado — Part II	1970	10.00

KAPP

Number	Title (A Side/B Side)	Yr	NM
❑ 2085	Viva Tirado — Part I/ Viva Tirado — Part II	1970	5.00
❑ 2129	Cuban Chant/Viva La Raza	1971	5.00
❑ 2150	Sugar, Sugar/Don't Put Me Down	1971	5.00
❑ 2173	Brown Eyed Girl/Mas Zacate	1972	5.00
❑ 2182	Senor Blues/Satisfy Me Woman	1972	5.00

MCA

Number	Title (A Side/B Side)	Yr	NM
❑ 40021	Last Tango in Paris/ In a Silent Way	1973	5.00
❑ 40104	Tell Her She's Lovely/Chachita	1973	5.00
❑ 40240	El Cayuco/You've Been Wrong So Long	1974	4.00
❑ 40359	Follow the Apollo/You Can Have the Best of Everything	1975	4.00
❑ 40391	Put On a Show/Might As Well	1975	4.00
❑ 40422	Baretta's Theme (Keep Your Eyes on the Sparrow)/ One More Night	1975	4.00
❑ 40457	Michael's Theme/When You Got a Heartache	1975	4.00
❑ 40520	All I Can Remember/Lake Aquabi	1976	4.00

SHADY BROOK

Number	Title (A Side/B Side)	Yr	NM
❑ 45032	Dancin' Mama/Ron Con-Con	1977	6.00
❑ 45039	Little Brother/(B-side unknown)	1977	6.00

Albums

KAPP

Number	Title (A Side/B Side)	Yr	NM
❑ KS-3632	Viva Tirado	1970	12.00
❑ KS-3640	Revolucion	1971	12.00
❑ KS-3663	Celebration	1972	12.00

MCA

Number	Title (A Side/B Side)	Yr	NM
❑ 69	Revolucion	1973	10.00
—Reissue of Kapp 3640			
❑ 312	El Chicano	1973	10.00
❑ 401	Cinco	1974	10.00
❑ 437	The Best of Everything	1975	10.00
❑ 548	Viva Tirado	197?	10.00
—Reissue of Kapp 3632			
❑ 2150	Pyramid of Love	1975	10.00

SHADY BROOK

Number	Title (A Side/B Side)	Yr	NM
❑ SB 33-005	This Is El Chicano	1977	15.00

EL CLOD

45s

CHALLENGE

Number	Title (A Side/B Side)	Yr	NM
❑ 9159	Tijuana Border (Wolverton Mountain)/Pedro's Piano Roll Twist	1962	20.00

MERCURY

Number	Title (A Side/B Side)	Yr	NM
❑ 72082	He's Not a Rebel/ Holiday in Havana	1963	15.00

VEE JAY

Number	Title (A Side/B Side)	Yr	NM
❑ 647	Tijuana Watusi/Gringo	1965	15.00

EL DOMINGOS

45s

CANDLELITE

Number	Title (A Side/B Side)	Yr	NM
❑ 418	Made in Heaven/Lucky Me, I'm in Love	1963	25.00

CHELSEA

Number	Title (A Side/B Side)	Yr	NM
❑ 1009	Made in Heaven/Lucky Me, I'm in Love	1962	200.00

KARMIN

Number	Title (A Side/B Side)	Yr	NM
❑ 1001	Are You Ready to Say "I Do"/ I Want to Know	1964	300.00

EL DORADOS

45s

LOST-NITE

Number	Title (A Side/B Side)	Yr	NM
❑ 263	One More Chance/ Little Miss Love	197?	5.00
—Reissue			
❑ 270	Crazy Little Mama (At My Front Door)/What's Buggin' You Baby	197?	5.00
❑ 278	Now That You've Gone/ Rock 'N' Roll's for Me	197?	5.00
—Reissue			

Except when noted otherwise, VG = 25% of NM, and VG+ = 50% of NM. (Example: VG = $2.00, VG+ = $4.00 and NM = $8.00.)

Number	Title (A Side/B Side)	Yr	NM
❑ 285	I'll Be Forever Lovin' You/ I Began to Realize	197?	5.00
—Reissue			
❑ 293	Bim Bam Boom/ There in the Night	197?	5.00
—Reissue			
❑ 300	Fallen Tear/Chop Ling Soon	197?	5.00
—Reissue			
❑ 308	Tears on My Pillow/ A Rose for My Darling	197?	5.00
—Reissue			

OLDIES 45

Number	Title (A Side/B Side)	Yr	NM
❑ 68	Baby, I Need You/Lovers Never Say Goodbye	1964	8.00
—B-side by the Flamingos			

PAULA

Number	Title (A Side/B Side)	Yr	NM
❑ 347	Looking In from the Outside/ Since You Came Into My Life	1971	10.00
❑ 369	Loose Booty (Part 1)/ Loose Booty (Part 2)	1971	10.00

TORRID

Number	Title (A Side/B Side)	Yr	NM
❑ 100	In Over My Head/You Make My Heart Sing	1970	15.00

VEE JAY

Number	Title (A Side/B Side)	Yr	NM
❑ 115	Baby I Need You/My Loving Baby	1954	80.00
❑ 115	Baby I Need You/My Loving Baby	1954	400.00
—Red vinyl			
❑ 118	Annie's Answer/ Living with Vivian	1954	80.00
❑ 118	Annie's Answer/ Living with Vivian	1954	300.00
—Red vinyl			
❑ 127	One More Chance/ Little Miss Love	1954	200.00
❑ 147	At My Front Door/What's Buggin' You Baby	1955	70.00
❑ 165	I'll Be Forever Lovin' You/ I Began to Realize	1955	60.00
❑ 180	Now That You've Gone/ Rock 'N' Roll's for Me	1956	50.00
❑ 197	Fallen Tear/Chop Ling Soon	1956	50.00
❑ 211	Bim Bam Boom/ There in the Night	1956	80.00
❑ 250	Tears on My Pillow/ A Rose for My Darling	1957	30.00
❑ 263	Three Reasons Why/ Boom Diddle Boom	1958	150.00
❑ 302	Oh What a Girl/The Lights Are Low	1958	150.00

Albums

LOST-NITE

Number	Title (A Side/B Side)	Yr	NM
❑ LLP-20 [10]	The El Dorados	1981	12.00
—Red vinyl			

SOLID SMOKE

Number	Title (A Side/B Side)	Yr	NM
❑ 8025	Low Mileage/High Octane	1984	10.00

VEE JAY

Number	Title (A Side/B Side)	Yr	NM
❑ LP-1001 [M]	Crazy Little Mama	1959	800.00
—Maroon label, thick silver band			
❑ LP-1001 [M]	Crazy Little Mama	1960	400.00
—Maroon label, thin silver band			
❑ LP-1001 [M]	Crazy Little Mama	1962	250.00
—Black label with colorband			
❑ VJLP-1001 [M]	Crazy Little Mama	198?	10.00
—Authorized reissue			

EL RAYS, THE See THE DELLS.

EL VENOS, THE

45s

GROOVE

Number	Title (A Side/B Side)	Yr	NM
❑ 0170	Now We're Together/Geraldine	1956	80.00

RCA VICTOR

Number	Title (A Side/B Side)	Yr	NM
❑ 47-8303	My Heart Beats Faster/ You Won't Be There	1963	25.00

VIK

Number	Title (A Side/B Side)	Yr	NM
❑ 0305	My Heart Beats Faster/ You Must Be True	1957	80.00

ELCHORDS, THE

45s

GOOD

Number	Title (A Side/B Side)	Yr	NM
❑ 544	Peppermint Stick/ Gee, I'm in Love	1958	80.00
—Straight lines on label			
❑ 544	Peppermint Stick/ Gee, I'm in Love	1962	15.00
—No lines on label			
❑ 544	Peppermint Stick/ Gee, I'm in Love	1962	20.00
—Sawtooth lines on label			
❑ 544	Peppermint Stick/ Gee, I'm in Love	1962	60.00
—Red vinyl			

Electric Light Orchestra, "Strange Magic," United Artists XW770, 1976, **$6.**

ELECTRAS, THE John Kerry, senator from Massachusetts and presidential candidate, played bass on this album.

Albums

ELECTRA

Number	Title (A Side/B Side)	Yr	NM
❑ ELT-201	The Electras	1961	450.00

ELECTRIC ELVES, THE Also see RONNIE DIO.

45s

MGM

Number	Title (A Side/B Side)	Yr	NM
❑ K 13839 [DJ]	Hey, Look Me Over/ It Pays to Advertise	1967	50.00
—Stock copy not known to exist; it would probably go for at least twice this amount			

ELECTRIC EXPRESS, THE

45s

AVCO

Number	Title (A Side/B Side)	Yr	NM
❑ 4607	I Can't Believe We Did (The Whole Thing)/Bee Pee	1972	15.00

KEY-VAC

Number	Title (A Side/B Side)	Yr	NM
❑ 2930	Hearsay/(Instrumental)	197?	100.00

LINCO

Number	Title (A Side/B Side)	Yr	NM
❑ 1001	It's the Real Thing - Pt. 1/Pt. 2	1971	10.00
❑ 1002	Where You Coming From - Pt. 1/Pt. 2	1972	20.00
❑ 1003	I Can't Believe We Did (The Whole Thing)/Bee Pee	1972	20.00

ELECTRIC FLAG, THE

45s

ATLANTIC

Number	Title (A Side/B Side)	Yr	NM
❑ 3222	Sweet Soul Music/Every Now and Then	1974	4.00
❑ 3237	Doctor Oh Doctor/The Band Kept Playing	1975	4.00

COLUMBIA

Number	Title (A Side/B Side)	Yr	NM
❑ 44307	Groovin' Is Easy/Over-Lovin' You	1967	8.00
❑ 44307 [PS]	Groovin' Is Easy/Over-Lovin' You	1967	20.00
❑ 44376	Soul Searchin'/Sunny	1967	8.00
❑ 44765	Soul Searchin'/Sunny	1969	6.00

SIDEWALK

Number	Title (A Side/B Side)	Yr	NM
❑ 929	Green and Gold/Peter's Trip	1967	15.00

Albums

ATLANTIC

Number	Title (A Side/B Side)	Yr	NM
❑ SD 18112	The Band Kept Playing	1974	10.00

COLUMBIA

Number	Title (A Side/B Side)	Yr	NM
❑ CS 9597	A Long Time Comin'	1968	15.00
—"360 Sound" label			
❑ CS 9597	A Long Time Comin'	1970	10.00
—Orange label			
❑ PC 9597	A Long Time Comin'	198?	8.00
—Budget-line reissue			
❑ CS 9714	The Electric Flag	1968	15.00
—"360 Sound" label			
❑ CS 9714	The Electric Flag	1970	10.00
—Orange label			
❑ C 30422	The Best of the Electric Flag	1971	10.00

ELECTRIC INDIAN, THE

45s

MARMADUKE

Number	Title (A Side/B Side)	Yr	NM
❑ 4001	Keem-O-Sabe/Broad Street	1969	20.00

UNITED ARTISTS

Number	Title (A Side/B Side)	Yr	NM
❑ 0128	Keem-O-Sabe/Stick Shift	1973	4.00
—"Silver Spotlight Series" reissue; B-side by The Duals			
❑ 50563	Keem-O-Sabe/Broad Street	1969	6.00
❑ 50613	Geronimo/Land of 1,000 Dances	1969	5.00
❑ 50647	Rain Dance/Storm Warning	1970	5.00
❑ 50701	Apotchee/Chicago Hawk	1970	5.00
❑ 50744	Geronimo/My Cherie Amour	1971	5.00

Albums

UNITED ARTISTS

Number	Title (A Side/B Side)	Yr	NM
❑ UAS 6728	Keem-O-Sabe	1969	15.00

ELECTRIC LIGHT ORCHESTRA

Evolved from THE MOVE. Also see JEFF LYNNE; ROY WOOD.

Number	Title (A Side/B Side)	Yr	NM
12-Inch Singles			
CBS ASSOCIATED			
❑ ZAS 2254 [DJ]	Calling America (3:29) (same on both sides)	1986	10.00
45s			
CBS ASSOCIATED			
❑ 05766	Calling America/Caught in a Trap	1986	3.00
❑ 05766 [PS]	Calling America/Caught in a Trap	1986	3.00
❑ 05892	So Serious/Endless Lies	1986	3.00
❑ 05892 [PS]	So Serious/Endless Lies	1986	3.00
JET			
❑ XW 1099	Turn to Stone/Mister Kingdom	1977	4.00
❑ XW 1099 [PS]	Turn to Stone/Mister Kingdom	1977	8.00
❑ XW 1145	Sweet Talkin' Woman/Fire on High	1978	4.00
❑ XW 1145	Sweet Talkin' Woman/Fire on High	1978	5.00
—Purple vinyl			
❑ XW 1145 [PS]	Sweet Talkin' Woman/Fire on High	1978	5.00
❑ 02408	Hold On Tight/When Time Stood Still	1981	4.00
❑ 02559	Twilight/Julie Don't Live Here	1981	4.00
❑ 02693	Rain Is Falling/Another Heart Broke	1982	4.00
❑ 03086	Hold On Tight/Mr. Blue Sky	1982	3.00
—Reissue			
❑ 03964	Rock and Roll Is King/After All	1983	4.00
❑ 04130	Four Little Diamonds/Letter from Spain	1983	4.00
❑ 04208	Stranger/Train of Gold	1983	4.00
❑ 5050	Mr. Blue Sky/One Summer Dream	1978	4.00
❑ 5052	It's Over/The Whale	1978	4.00
❑ 5057	Shine a Little Love/Jungle	1979	4.00
❑ 5057 [PS]	Shine a Little Love/Jungle	1979	8.00
❑ 5060	Don't Bring Me Down/Dreaming of 4000	1979	4.00
❑ 5064	Confusion/Poker	1979	4.00
❑ 5067	Last Train to London/Down Home Town	1979	4.00
MCA			
❑ 41246	I'm Alive/Drum Dreams	1980	4.00
❑ 41246 [PS]	I'm Alive/Drum Dreams	1980	5.00
❑ 41285	Xanadu/Whenever You're Away from Me	1980	4.00
—A-side: Olivia Newton-John/Electric Light Orchestra			
❑ 41289	All Over the World/Drum Dreams	1980	4.00
❑ 41289 [PS]	All Over the World/Drum Dreams	1980	5.00
UNITED ARTISTS			
❑ XW 173	Roll Over Beethoven/Queen of the Hours	1973	6.00
❑ XW 337	Showdown/In Old England Town	1973	6.00
❑ XW 405	Daybreaker/Ma-Ma-Ma-Belle	1974	6.00
❑ XW 513	Roll Over Beethoven/Showdown	1974	4.00
—Reissue			
❑ XW 573	Can't Get It Out of My Head/Illusions in G Major	1974	4.00
❑ XW 573 [PS]	Can't Get It Out of My Head/Illusions in G Major	1974	6.00
❑ XW 634	Boy Blue/Eldorado	1975	5.00
❑ XW 729	Evil Woman/10538 Overture (Live)	1975	4.00
❑ XW 770	Strange Magic/New World Rising	1976	4.00
❑ XW 770 [PS]	Strange Magic/New World Rising	1976	6.00
❑ XW 842	Showdown/Daybreaker (Live)	1976	5.00
❑ XW 888	Livin' Thing/Ma-Ma-Ma-Belle	1976	4.00
❑ XW 939	Do Ya/Nightrider	1977	4.00
❑ XW 1000	Telephone Line/Poorboy (The Greenwood)	1977	4.00
❑ XW 1000	Telephone Line/Poorboy (The Greenwood)	1977	5.00
—Green vinyl			
❑ XW 1000 [PS]	Telephone Line/Poorboy (The Greenwood)	1977	5.00
—Picture sleeves can be found with either green or black vinyl versions, but few black vinyl copies were issued with the picture sleeve			
❑ XW 1176	Can't Get It Out of My Head/Strange Magic	1978	4.00
❑ XW 1177	Evil Woman/Livin' Thing	1978	4.00
❑ XW 1178	Do Ya/Nightrider	1978	4.00
❑ XW 1179	Boy Blue/Telephone Line	1978	4.00
❑ XW 1180	Ma-Ma-Ma-Belle/10538 Overture	1978	4.00
—1176 through 1180 were available for a very short time just before ELO's rights transfered from UA to CBS.			
❑ 50914	10538 Overture/(Battle of) Marston Moor	1972	8.00
Albums			
CBS ASSOCIATED			
❑ FZ 40048	Balance of Power	1986	10.00
JET			
❑ JT-LA823-L2 [(2)]	Out of the Blue	1977	15.00
—Originals include poster and die-cut cardboard "spaceship"			
❑ JT-LA823-L2 [(2)DJ]	Out of the Blue	1977	25.00
—Promo only on blue vinyl			
❑ JZ 35524	No Answer	1978	10.00
❑ PZ 35524	No Answer	1981	8.00
❑ JZ 35525	On the Third Day	1978	10.00
❑ PZ 35525	On the Third Day	1981	8.00
❑ JZ 35526	Eldorado	1978	10.00
❑ PZ 35526	Eldorado	198?	8.00
❑ JZ 35527	Face the Music	1978	10.00
❑ PZ 35527	Face the Music	1981	8.00
❑ JZ 35528	Ole Elo	1978	10.00
❑ PZ 35528	Ole Elo	1981	8.00
❑ JZ 35529	A New World Record	1978	10.00
❑ PZ 35529	A New World Record	1981	8.00
❑ KZ2 35530 [(2)]	Out of the Blue	1978	12.00
❑ JZ 35533	Electric Light Orchestra II	1978	10.00
❑ PZ 35533	Electric Light Orchestra II	1981	8.00
❑ FZ 35769	Discovery	1979	10.00
❑ PZ 35769	Discovery	1987	8.00
❑ FZ 36310	ELO's Greatest Hits	1979	10.00
❑ HZ 36310	ELO's Greatest Hits	1981	40.00
—Half-speed mastered edition			
❑ PZ 36310	ELO's Greatest Hits	1987	8.00
❑ Z4X 36966 [(4)]	A Box of Their Best	1980	25.00
❑ FZ 37371	Time	1981	10.00
❑ PZ 37371	Time	1987	8.00
❑ PZ 38490	Secret Messages	1987	8.00
❑ QZ 38490	Secret Messages	1983	10.00
❑ HZ 45789	Discovery	1980	25.00
—Half-speed mastered edition			
❑ HZ 47371	Time	1982	25.00
—Half-speed mastered edition			
❑ HZ 48490	Secret Messages	1983	30.00
—Half-speed mastered edition			
UNITED ARTISTS			
❑ UA-LA040-F	Electric Light Orchestra II	1973	15.00
—Tan label			
❑ UA-LA040-F	Electric Light Orchestra II	1978	10.00
—Sunrise label			
❑ SP-123 [DJ]	Ole Elo	1976	50.00
—Gold vinyl promo with generic cover			
❑ SP-123 [DJ]	Ole Elo	1976	80.00
—Red, blue or white vinyl promos with generic cover			
❑ SP-123 [DJ]	Ole Elo	1976	100.00
—Gold vinyl, cover similar to the released version except for the single line "Ole Elo" (no "Electric Light Orchestra" underneath) at the top of the front cover			
❑ UA-LA188-F	On the Third Day	1973	15.00
—Tan label			
❑ UA-LA188-F	On the Third Day	1978	10.00
—Sunrise label			
❑ UA-LA318-F	The Night the Light Went On in Long Beach	1974	—
—Canceled			
❑ UA-LA339-G	Eldorado	1974	12.00
—Tan label			
❑ UA-LA339-G	Eldorado	1977	10.00
—Sunrise label			
❑ UA-LA546-DJ [DJ]	Face the Music	1975	25.00
—Promo only, banded for airplay			
❑ UA-LA546-G	Face the Music	1975	12.00
—Tan label			
❑ UA-LA546-G	Face the Music	1978	10.00
—Sunrise label			
❑ UA-LA630-G	Ole Elo	1976	12.00
—Tan label			
❑ UA-LA630-G	Ole Elo	1978	10.00
—Sunrise label			
❑ UA-LA679-G	A New World Record	1976	12.00
—All copies have custom labels			
❑ UAS-5573	No Answer	1972	15.00
—Tan label			
❑ UAS-5573	No Answer	1978	10.00
—Sunrise label			

ELECTRIC PRUNES, THE

Number	Title (A Side/B Side)	Yr	NM
45s			
REPRISE			
❑ PRO 277 [DJ]	Sanctus/Credo	1968	50.00
❑ PRO 305 [DJ]	Help Us (Our Father, Our King)/The Adoration	1968	40.00
❑ 0473	Ain't It Hard/Little Olive	1966	40.00
❑ 0532	I Had Too Much to Dream (Last Night)/Lovin	1966	20.00
❑ 0564	Get Me to the World on Time/Are You Lovin' Me	1967	25.00
❑ 0594	Hideaway/Dr. Do-Good	1967	25.00
❑ 0607	The Great Banana Hoax/Wind-Up Toys	1967	25.00
❑ 0652	You Never Had It So Good/Everybody Knows You're Not in Love	1967	40.00
❑ 0704	I Had Too Much to Dream (Last Night)/Get Me to the World On Time	1968	5.00
—"Back to Back Hits" series — originals have "W7" and "r:" logos			
❑ 0805	Hey, Mr. President/Flowing Smoothly	1969	25.00
❑ 0833	Violent Rose/Sell	1969	40.00
❑ 0858	Love Grows/Finders Keepers, Losers Weepers	1969	25.00
Albums			
REPRISE			
❑ R-6248 [M]	The Electric Prunes	1967	50.00
❑ RS-6248 [S]	The Electric Prunes	1967	40.00
❑ R-6262 [M]	Underground	1967	50.00
❑ RS-6262 [S]	Underground	1967	40.00
❑ R-6275 [M]	Mass in F Minor	1967	40.00
❑ RS-6275 [S]	Mass in F Minor	1967	30.00
❑ RS-6316	Release of an Oath	1968	30.00
❑ RS-6342	Just Good Rock 'n Roll	1969	30.00

ELECTRIC TOILET, THE

Number	Title (A Side/B Side)	Yr	NM
Albums			
NASCO			
❑ 9004	In the Hands of Karma	1968	400.00

ELECTRIC UNDERGROUND, THE

Number	Title (A Side/B Side)	Yr	NM
Albums			
PREMIER			
❑ P-9060 [M]	Guitar Explosion	1967	50.00
❑ PS-9060 [S]	Guitar Explosion	1967	50.00

ELECTRONIC CONCEPT ORCHESTRA

Number	Title (A Side/B Side)	Yr	NM
45s			
LIMELIGHT			
❑ 3090	Aquarius/Grazing in the Grass	1969	6.00
Albums			
LIMELIGHT			
❑ 86070	Moog Groove	1969	10.00
❑ 86072	Electric Love	1969	10.00
MERCURY			
❑ SR-61279	Cinemoog	1970	10.00

ELECTROSONICS, THE

Number	Title (A Side/B Side)	Yr	NM
Albums			
PHILIPS			
❑ PHM 200047 [M]	Electronic Music	1962	70.00
❑ PHS 600047 [S]	Electronic Music	1962	90.00

ELEGANTS, THE

Also see PAT CORDEL.

Number	Title (A Side/B Side)	Yr	NM
45s			
ABC-PARAMOUNT			
❑ 10219	I've Seen Everything/Tiny Cloud	1961	40.00
APT			
❑ 25005	Little Star/Getting Dizzy	1958	40.00
—Black label with rainbow			
❑ 25005	Little Star/Getting Dizzy	1958	50.00
—All-black label			
❑ 25017	Goodnight/Please Believe Me	1958	30.00
❑ 25029	Pay Day/True Love Affair	1959	30.00
BANGAR			
❑ 613	Minor Chaos/Lost Souls	1964	30.00
BIM BAM BOOM			
❑ 121	It's Just a Matter of Time/Lonesome Weekends	1974	4.00
—Black vinyl			
❑ 121	It's Just a Matter of Time/Lonesome Weekends	1974	6.00
—Colored vinyl			
CRYSTAL BALL			
❑ 139	Maybe/Woo Woo Train	197?	5.00
HULL			
❑ 732	Little Boy Blue/Get Well Soon	1960	100.00
LAURIE			
❑ 3283	A Letter from Viet Nam/Barbara Beware	1965	30.00
❑ 3298	Wake Up/Bring Back Wendy	1965	50.00
❑ 3324	Belinda/Lazy Love	1965	25.00
—As "Vito and the Elegants"			
PHOTO			
❑ 2662	Dressin' Up/A Dream Can Come True	1963	50.00
❑ 2662 [PS]	Dressin' Up/A Dream Can Come True	1963	150.00
UNITED ARTISTS			
❑ 230	Speak Low/Let My Prayers Be With You	1960	40.00
❑ 295	Happiness/Spiritual	1961	50.00

Except when noted otherwise, VG = 25% of NM, and VG+ = 50% of NM. (Example: VG = $2.00, VG+ = $4.00 and NM = $8.00.)

Number	Title (A Side/B Side)	Yr	NM

Albums
MURRAY HILL
❑ 210 Little Star 1986 10.00

ELENA
45s
ROULETTE
❑ 4605 Evening Time/Road of Love 1965 15.00

ELEPHANTS MEMORY
45s
APPLE
❑ 1854 Liberation Special/Madness 1972 8.00
❑ 1854 Liberation Special/Power Boogie 1972 400.00
❑ 1854 [PS] Liberation Special/Madness 1972 10.00
ATLANTIC
❑ 3257 Shakedown/Brother Can You Spare Me a Dime 1975 5.00
BUDDAH
❑ 98 Cross Roads of the Stepping Stones/Jungle Gym at the Zoo 1969 8.00
❑ 209 Don't Put Me on Trial No More/Hot Dog 1971 8.00
METROMEDIA
❑ 182 Mongoose/I Couldn't Dream 1970 6.00
❑ 182 [PS] Mongoose/I Couldn't Dream 1970 6.00
❑ 210 Skyscraper Commando/Power 1971 6.00
RCA VICTOR
❑ APBO-0268 Rock and Roll Streaker/Angels Forever 1974 5.00
Albums
APPLE
❑ SMAS-3389 Elephants Memory 1972 25.00
BUDDAH
❑ BDS-5033 Elephants Memory 1969 15.00
❑ BDS-5038 Songs from Midnight Cowboy 1970 15.00
METROMEDIA
❑ MD-1035 Take It to the Streets 1970 20.00
RCA VICTOR
❑ APL1-0569 Angela Forever 1974 15.00

ELEVENTH HOUR, THE
45s
BELL
❑ 45153 Nothin' Comes Easy/Lori 1971 8.00
20TH CENTURY
❑ 2076 So Good/My Bed 1974 6.00
❑ 2114 Far As We Felt Like Goin'/Volcano 1974 8.00
❑ 2215 Hollywood Hot/Hollywood Hotter 1975 6.00
❑ 2278 Get On or Get Off/You'll Never Know Until You Try 1976 8.00
Albums
20TH CENTURY
❑ T-435 Greatest Hits 1974 12.00
❑ T-511 Hollywood Hot 1975 15.00

ELEVENTH HOUSE, THE

ELEVENTH HOUSE, THE (WITH LARRY CORYELL)
45s
ARISTA
❑ 0154 Some Greasy Stuff/(B-side unknown) 1975 4.00
VANGUARD
❑ 35176 The Funky Waltz/Low-Lee-Tah 1974 5.00
Albums
ARISTA
❑ AL 4052 Level One 1975 10.00
❑ AL 4077 Aspects 1976 10.00
VANGUARD
❑ VSQ-40036 [Q] Introducing the Eleventh House with Larry Coryell 1974 25.00
❑ VSD-79342 Introducing the Eleventh House with Larry Coryell 1974 12.00

ELF
Also see RAINBOW; DIO; RONNIE DIO; BLACK SABBATH.
45s
EASTERN ARTISTS
❑ 5015 Sit Down Honey (Everything Will Be Alright)/Gambler, Gambler 1972 50.00
EPIC
❑ 5-10933 Hoochie Koochie Lady/First Avenue 1972 20.00
MGM
❑ M 14752 L.A. 59/(B-side unknown) 1974 15.00
—Stock copy may not exist
Albums
EPIC
❑ KE 31789 Elf 1972 30.00
—Yellow label
❑ KE 31789 Elf 1973 20.00
—Orange label
MGM
❑ M3G 4974 L.A. 59 1974 20.00
❑ M3G 4994 Trying to Burn the Sun 1975 20.00

ELGART, LARRY
12-Inch Singles
RCA
❑ PD-13259 Hooked on Swing (7:07)/Hooked on Astaire (6:37) 1982 10.00
❑ PD-13627 La Cage Aux Folles (5:12)/The Best of Times 1983 10.00
45s
DECCA
❑ 9-29043 More Than You Know/You're Driving Me Crazy (What Did I Do) 1954 12.00
❑ 9-29666 Spanish Lace/What the Thunder Said 1955 10.00
MGM
❑ K12979 Arkansas Holler/This Heart of Mine 1961 8.00
❑ K13012 For the Soul/Green Valley 1961 8.00
❑ K13063 Elgart Twist/Cornelia 1962 8.00
RCA
❑ PB-13219 Hooked on Swing/Hooked on the Big Bands 1982 5.00
❑ PB-13342 Hooked on Astaire/Hooked on the Blues 1982 5.00
❑ PB-13411 Hooked on Dixie/Swingin' the Classics 1982 5.00
❑ PB-13626 La Cage Aux Folles/The Best of Times 1983 5.00
❑ PB-13733 Caravan/The Best of Times 1984 6.00
❑ GB-14071 Hooked on Swing/Caravan 1985 3.00
—"Gold Standard Series" reissue
RCA VICTOR
❑ 47-7461 [M] Nola/Liza 1959 8.00
❑ 47-7575 [M] Honeysuckle Rose/Mountain Greenery 1959 8.00
❑ 47-7651 Have You Heard/Duet from Saratoga-Game of Poker 1959 8.00
❑ 61-7575 [S] Honeysuckle Rose/Mountain Greenery 1959 15.00
—"Living Stereo" on label
Albums
BRUNSWICK
❑ BL 58054 [10] Impressions of Outer Space 1954 60.00
DECCA
❑ DL 5526 [10] The Larry Elgart Band with Strings 1954 100.00
❑ DL 8034 [M] Music for Barefoot Ballerinas 1955 40.00
MGM
❑ E-3891 [M] Sophisticated Sixties 1960 15.00
❑ SE-3891 [S] Sophisticated Sixties 1960 20.00
❑ E-3896 [M] The Shape of Sounds to Come 1961 15.00
❑ SE-3896 [S] The Shape of Sounds to Come 1961 20.00
❑ E-3961 [M] Visions 1961 15.00
❑ SE-3961 [S] Visions 1961 20.00
❑ E-4007 [M] The City 1961 15.00
❑ SE-4007 [S] The City 1961 20.00
❑ E-4028 [M] Music in Motion! 1962 15.00
❑ SE-4028 [S] Music in Motion! 1962 20.00
❑ E-4080 [M] More Music in Motion! 1962 15.00
❑ SE-4080 [S] More Music in Motion! 1962 20.00
PROJECT 3
❑ PR 5102 The Larry Elgart Dance Band 1979 10.00
RCA CAMDEN
❑ CAL-575 [M] Easy Goin' Swing 1960 12.00
❑ CAS-575 [S] Easy Goin' Swing 1960 15.00
❑ CXS-9036 [(2)] That Old Feeling 1972 12.00
RCA VICTOR
❑ LPM-1961 [M] Larry Elgart and His Orchestra 1959 15.00
❑ LSP-1961 [S] Larry Elgart and His Orchestra 1959 20.00
❑ LPM-2045 [M] New Sounds at the Roosevelt 1959 15.00
❑ LSP-2045 [S] New Sounds at the Roosevelt 1959 20.00
❑ LPM-2166 [M] Saratoga 1960 15.00
❑ LSP-2166 [S] Saratoga 1960 20.00
❑ AFL1-4095 Flight of the Condor 1981 10.00
❑ AFL1-4343 Hooked on Swing 1982 10.00
❑ AFL1-4589 Hooked on Swing, Vol. 2 1983 10.00
❑ AFL1-4850 Larry Elgart and His Manhattan Swing Orchestra 1984 10.00
❑ AYL1-5025 Hooked on Swing 1984 8.00
—Budget-line reissue
❑ AYL1-5026 Hooked on Swing, Vol. 2 1984 8.00
—Budget-line reissue
❑ AYL1-7178 (The Theme from) La Cage Aux Folles 1986 8.00

ELGINS, THE (1)
Detroit R&B group.
45s
LUMMTONE
❑ 113 Your Lovely Ways/Finding a Sweetheart 1963 25.00
TAMLA
❑ 54056 Request of a Fool/Your Baby's Back 1962 30.00
—As "The Downbeats"; with "Tamla" in globe at top of label
❑ 54056 Request of a Fool/Your Baby's Back 1962 300.00
—As "The Downbeats"; with "Tamla" circling globe at top of label
V.I.P.
❑ 25029 Darling Baby/Put Yourself in My Place 1965 20.00
❑ 25029 Darling Baby/Put Yourself in My Place 1965 200.00
—First pressings credited "The Downbeats"
❑ 25037 Heaven Must Have Sent You/Stay in My Lonely Arms 1965 20.00
❑ 25043 It's Been a Long, Long Time/I Understand My Man 1966 20.00
❑ 25065 Heaven Must Have Sent You/Stay in My Lonely Arms 1970 10.00
Albums
V.I.P.
❑ 400 [M] Darling Baby 1966 70.00
❑ S-400 [S] Darling Baby 1966 100.00

ELGINS, THE (2)
45s
A.B.S.
❑ 113 Pretending/Lonesome 1961 400.00

ELGINS, THE (3)
45s
CONGRESS
❑ 214 The Times We've Wasted/Ritha Mae 1964 25.00
❑ 225 Here in Your Arms/We're Gonna Have a Good Time 1964 30.00

ELGINS, THE (4)
45s
LUMMTONE
❑ 109 A Winner Never Quits/Johnny I'm Sorry 1962 25.00
❑ 110 You Got Your Magnet on Me Baby/Johnny I'm Sorry 1962 25.00
❑ 112 Finally/I Lost My Love in the Big City 1963 25.00

ELGINS, THE (U)
Some of these may be by group (3) or (4), but not all.
45s
DOT
❑ 16563 Cheryl/Tell Gina 1963 60.00
FLIP
❑ 353 Uncle Sam's Man/Casey Cop 1961 30.00
JOED
❑ 716 Once Upon a Time/The Huddle 1964 700.00
MGM
❑ 12670 A Picture of You/Mademoiselle 1958 60.00
TITAN
❑ 1724 My Illness/Heartache Heartbreak 1962 200.00
❑ 1724 My Illness/Extra, Extra 1962 250.00
VALIANT
❑ 712 Street Scene/You Found Yourself Another Fool 1965 20.00

ELIGIBLES, THE
45s
CAPITOL
❑ 4203 Car Trouble/I Wrote a Song 1959 12.00
❑ 4265 Faker, Faker/24 Hours 1959 12.00
❑ 4304 My First Christmas with You/Little Engine 1959 15.00
❑ 4409 East of West Berlin/Young Is My Lover 1960 12.00
MERCURY
❑ 72000 That Carmen Twist/Come Back, Music 1962 10.00
WARNER BROS.
❑ 5344 Gabie/See What You Can Do For Me 1963 10.00
Albums
CAPITOL
❑ ST 1310 [S] Along the Trail 1960 30.00

Number	Title (A Side/B Side)	Yr	NM
❑ T 1310 [M]	Along the Trail	1960	25.00
❑ ST 1411 [S]	Love Is a Gamble	1960	30.00
❑ T 1411 [M]	Love Is a Gamble	1960	25.00

ELIMINATORS, THE

Number	Title (A Side/B Side)	Yr	NM
Albums			
LIBERTY			
❑ LRP-3365 [M]	Liverpool! Dragsters! Cycles! Surfing!	1964	80.00
❑ LST-7365 [S]	Liverpool! Dragsters! Cycles! Surfing!	1964	100.00

ELIZABETH

Number	Title (A Side/B Side)	Yr	NM
45s			
VANGUARD			
❑ 35070	Mary Anne/The World's For Free	1968	15.00
Albums			
VANGUARD			
❑ VSD-6501	Elizabeth	1968	75.00
—Gold label			

ELLEDGE, JIMMY

Number	Title (A Side/B Side)	Yr	NM
45s			
4 STAR			
❑ 1003	One By One/After You	1975	4.00
❑ 1015	Lady Lover/(B-side unknown)	1976	4.00
HICKORY			
❑ 1313	Follow Every Rainbow/I Just Walked In (Your Heart Last Night)	1965	8.00
❑ 1341	A Good Woman's Love (Not Easy to Find)/World of Lavender Lace	1965	8.00
❑ 1363	A Legend in My Time/Pink Dally Rue	1966	8.00
❑ 1393	Time Is a Thief/I Just Walked In (Your Heart Last Night)	1966	8.00
❑ 1420	Let Me Love You a Little (So I Can Love You a Lot)/She Should Save Some Loving (For a Rainy Day)	1966	8.00
❑ 1452	The Darkest Part of Night (Is Dawn)/She Should Save Some Loving (For a Rainy Day)	1967	8.00
LITTLE DARLIN'			
❑ 0047	Florence Jean/No One Ever Lost More	1968	6.00
RCA VICTOR			
❑ 47-7910	Send Me a Letter/Swanee River Rocket	1961	12.00
❑ 47-7946	Funny How Time Slips Away/Hey Jimmy Joe John Jim Jack	1961	10.00
❑ 47-8012	Can't You See It in My Eyes/What a Laugh	1962	20.00
❑ 47-8042	Bo Diddley/Diamonds	1962	8.00
❑ 47-8081	A Golden Tear/I'll Get By (Don't Worry)	1962	8.00
❑ 47-8136	You Can Have Her/I Miss Her Already	1963	8.00
❑ 47-8191	Please Love Me Forever/A Penny's Worth of Happiness	1963	8.00
❑ 47-8241	I Had to Run Away/There's Nothing There for Me	1963	8.00
❑ 47-8355	Dream of the Year/Gonna Turn My Voodoo On	1964	8.00
❑ 47-8081 [PS]	A Golden Tear/I'll Get By (Don't Worry)	1962	25.00
❑ 47-8191 [PS]	Please Love Me Forever/A Penny's Worth of Happiness	1963	25.00
SIMS			
❑ 204	I Gotta Live Here/Hold My Heart for Awhile	1964	8.00

ELLEN, IVY, & FAMILY

Number	Title (A Side/B Side)	Yr	NM
45s			
FELSTED			
❑ 8609	Go Tell Santa/(Instrumental)	1960	15.00
—B-side by the Reindeers			
❑ 8609 [PS]	Go Tell Santa/(Instrumental)	1960	20.00

ELLEY, MICKEY, AND THE ARISTOCRACY

Number	Title (A Side/B Side)	Yr	NM
45s			
WARNER BROS.			
❑ 7083	Someone Like Me/Yesterday's Rain	1967	50.00

ELLIE POP

Number	Title (A Side/B Side)	Yr	NM
45s			
MAINSTREAM			
❑ 686	Can't Be Love/Seven North Frederick	1968	20.00
Albums			
MAINSTREAM			
❑ S-6115	Ellie Pop	1968	125.00

ELLIMAN, YVONNE

Number	Title (A Side/B Side)	Yr	NM
45s			
DECCA			
❑ 32785	I Don't Know How to Love Him/Overture	1971	5.00
❑ 32870	Everything's Alright/Heaven on Their Minds	1971	5.00
❑ 32949	Can't Find My Way Home/I Would Have Had a Good Time	1972	4.00
❑ 32987	Nothing Rhymed/Speak Your Mind	1972	4.00
❑ 33018	Could We Start Again, Please/Heaven on Their Minds	1972	5.00
—B-side by Ben Vereen			
MCA			
❑ 40121	Hawaii/I Can't Explain	1973	4.00
❑ 40235	Casserole Me Over/Come On Back Where You Belong	1974	4.00
RSO			
❑ 514	Somewhere in the Night/Who's Gonna Save the World	1975	4.00
❑ 517	Walk Right In/Small Town Talk	1975	4.00
❑ 858	Love Me/I Keep Hangin' On (I Don't Know Why)	1976	4.00
❑ 871	Hello Stranger/She'll Be the Home	1977	4.00
❑ 877	I Knew/I Can't Get You Out of My Mind	1977	4.00
❑ 884	If I Can't Have You/Good Sign	1977	4.00
❑ 905	Savannah/Up to the Man in You	1978	4.00
❑ 915	Moment by Moment/Sailing Ships	1978	4.00
❑ 915 [PS]	Moment by Moment/Sailing Ships	1978	4.00
❑ 1007	Love Pains/Rock Me Slowly	1979	4.00
Albums			
DECCA			
❑ DL 75341	Yvonne Elliman	1972	15.00
MCA			
❑ 356	Food of Love	1973	12.00
RSO			
❑ RS-1-3018	Love Me	1977	10.00
❑ RS-1-3031	Night Flight	1978	10.00
❑ RS-1-3038	Yvonne	1979	10.00

ELLINGTON, DUKE

Also see LOUIS ARMSTRONG.

Number	Title (A Side/B Side)	Yr	NM
45s			
BETHLEHEM			
❑ 11007	Indian Summer/The Jeep Is Jumpin'	1958	10.00
❑ 11016	The Blues (Part 1)/The Blues (Part 2)	1959	10.00
❑ 11066	In a Mellow Tone/Jack the Bear	1960	10.00
CAPITOL			
❑ F2458	Satin Doll/Without a Song	1953	12.00
❑ F2503	Ballin' the Blues/Nothin' Nothin' Baby	1953	12.00
❑ F2546	Blue Jean Beguine/Warm Vallen	1953	12.00
❑ F2598	Boo-Dar/Give Me the Right	1953	12.00
❑ F2723	Blue Moon/Ultra Deluxe	1954	12.00
❑ F2817	Isle of Capri/Band Call	1954	12.00
❑ F2875	Bunny Hop Mambo/Is It a Sin	1954	12.00
❑ F2930	Smile/If I Give My Heart to You	1954	12.00
❑ F2980	12th Street Rag Mambo/Chile Bowl	1954	12.00
❑ F3049	Echo Tango/All Day Long	1955	12.00
COLUMBIA			
❑ 31099 [S]	Three J's Blues/Smada	1961	12.00
❑ 31100 [S]	Pie Eye's Blues/Sweet and Pungent	1961	12.00
❑ 31101 [S]	(titles unknown)	1961	12.00
❑ 31102 [S]	(titles unknown)	1961	12.00
❑ 31103 [S]	(titles unknown)	1961	12.00
❑ S7 31433 [S]	I've Just Seen Her/Back to School	1962	12.00
❑ S7 31434 [S]	Which Way?/If I Were You	1962	12.00
❑ S7 31435 [S]	Once Upon a Time/Nightlife	1962	12.00
❑ S7 31436 [S]	(titles unknown)	1962	12.00
❑ S7 31437 [S]	What a Country!/We Speak the Same Language	1962	12.00
—The above five are "Stereo Seven" 33 1/3 rpm jukebox singles from set "JS 7-54" and the album "All American in Jazz"			
❑ S7 31478 [S]	(titles unknown)	1962	12.00
❑ S7 31479 [S]	B D B/Wild Man	1962	12.00
❑ S7 31480 [S]	To You/Jumpin' at the Woodside	1962	12.00
❑ S7 31481 [S]	Take the "A" Train/Until I Met You	1962	12.00
❑ S7 31482 [S]	Segue in C (Part I)/(Part II)	1962	12.00
—The above five are "Stereo Seven" 33 1/3 rpm jukebox singles from set "JS 7-59" and the album "First Time!"			
❑ 39110	Build That Railroad/Love You Madly	1950	15.00
❑ 39496	Monologue/8th Veil	1951	15.00
❑ 39545	Deep Night/Please Be Kind	1951	15.00
❑ 39670	Jam with Sam/V.I.P.'s Boogie	1952	15.00
❑ 39712	Blues at Sundown/Bensonality	1952	15.00
❑ 39942	Rock Skippin' at the Blue Note/The Vulture Song	1953	15.00
❑ 40903	Cop-Out/Rock City Rock	1957	10.00
❑ 41098	My Heart, My Mind, My Everything/Together	1958	10.00
❑ 41180	Duke's Place/Jones	1958	10.00
❑ 41362	Spank No. 1/Spank No. 2	1959	10.00
❑ 41401	Walkin' and Singin' the Blues/Hand Me Down Love	1959	10.00
❑ 41421	Anatomy of a Murder/Flirtbird	1959	10.00
❑ 41689	Blues in Orbit/Villes, Ville Is the Place, Man	1960	10.00
❑ 42144	Asphalt Jungle Theme (Part 1)/Asphalt Jungle Theme (Part 2)	1961	10.00
❑ 42237	Paris Blues (Part 1)/Paris Blues (Part 2)	1962	10.00
❑ 50014	Solitude/Mood Indigo	1954	12.00
—"Hall of Fame Series"			
IMPULSE!			
❑ 210	Limbo Jazz (Part 1)/Limbo Jazz (Part 2)	196?	8.00
RCA VICTOR			
❑ 47-2955	The Sidewalks of New York/Don't Get Around Much Anymore	1949	20.00
❑ 47-3033	Frankie & Johnny/Royal Garden Blues	1949	12.00
❑ 47-3034	Drawing Room Blues/St. Louis Blues	1949	12.00
❑ 47-3035	Beale Street Blues/Pretty Woman	1949	12.00
❑ 47-4281	Jumping Room Only/A Gathering in a Clearing	1951	15.00
❑ 47-4711	Balcony Serenade/Strange Feeling	1952	15.00
❑ 47-4712	Dancers in Love/Coloratura	1952	15.00
REPRISE			
❑ 0545	Satin Doll/Don't Get Around Much Anymore	1967	6.00
7-Inch Extended Plays			
CAPITOL			
❑ EAP 1-477	(contents unknown)	1954	15.00
❑ EAP 1-477 [PS]	The Duke Plays Ellington	1954	15.00
❑ EAP 1-521	Rockin' in Rhythm/Black and Tan Fantasy	1955	15.00
❑ EAP 1-521 [PS]	Ellington '55, Part 1	1955	15.00
❑ EAP 2-521	Stompin' at the Savoy/In the Mood	1955	15.00
❑ EAP 2-521 [PS]	Ellington '55, Part 2	1955	15.00
❑ EAP 3-521	One O'Clock Jump/Honeysuckle Rose	1955	15.00
❑ EAP 3-521 [PS]	Ellington '55, Part 3	1955	15.00
❑ EAP 4-521	Happy Go Lucky Local/Flying Home	1955	15.00
❑ EAP 4-521 [PS]	Ellington '55, Part 4	1955	15.00
❑ EAP 1-679	Harlem Air Shaft/Serious Serenade//Don't Ever Say Goodbye/Big Drag	195?	12.00
❑ EAP 3-679	Blossom/Theme for Trambean//Gonna Tan Your Hide	195?	12.00
❑ EAP 3-679 [PS]	Ellington Showcase, Part 1	195?	12.00
❑ EAP 3-679 [PS]	Ellington Showcase, Part 3	195?	12.00
COLUMBIA			
❑ 5-1405	Skin Deep/The Mooche	195?	15.00
—Alternate numbers are "B 1629-1" and "B 1629-2"			
❑ B-1629 [PS]	Skin Deep/The Mooche	195?	15.00
—Contains record 5-1405			
❑ B-2514	*Solitude/Mood Indigo/Stormy Weather/Sophisticated Lady	195?	12.00
❑ B-2514 [PS]	Duke Ellington and His Orchestra (Hall of Fame Series)	195?	12.00
❑ B-2553	*The Hawk Talks/Monologue/Rock Skippin' at the Blue Note/Jam with Sam	195?	12.00
❑ B-2553 [PS]	Duke Ellington (Hall of Fame Series)	195?	12.00
❑ B-8301	(contents unknown)	1956	12.00
❑ B-8301 [PS]	Hi-Fi Ellington Uptown, Vol. 1	1956	12.00
❑ B-8302	Skin Deep/The Mooche	1956	12.00
❑ B-8302 [PS]	Hi-Fi Ellington Uptown, Vol. 2	1956	12.00
❑ B-8303	(contents unknown)	1956	12.00
❑ B-8303 [PS]	Hi-Fi Ellington Uptown, Vol. 3	1956	12.00
RCA VICTOR			
❑ EPA-5054	Caravan/Sophisticated Lady//Perdido/Mood Indigo	1958	15.00
❑ EPA-5054 [PS]	Caravan (Gold Standard Series)	1958	15.00

Except when noted otherwise, VG = 25% of NM, and VG+ = 50% of NM. (Example: VG = $2.00, VG+ = $4.00 and NM = $8.00.)

Number	Title (A Side/B Side)	Yr	NM
ROYALE			
❑ EP 203	Overture to Jam Session—Part 1/Overture to Jam Session—Part 2//Magenta Haze/Blue Skies	195?	10.00
—Red vinyl			
❑ EP 203 [PS]	Duke Ellington Plays	195?	10.00
Albums			
AAMCO			
❑ ALP-301 [M]	The Royal Concert of Duke Ellington, Vol. 1	196?	30.00
—Reissue of Bethlehem material			
❑ ALP-313 [M]	The Royal Concert of Duke Ellington, Vol. 2	196?	30.00
—Reissue of Bethlehem material			
ABC IMPULSE!			
❑ 9256 [(2)]	Ellingtonia: Reevaluations, The Impulse Years	1973	15.00
❑ 9285 [(2)]	Ellingtonia, Vol. 2	1974	15.00
❑ IA-9350 [(2)]	Great Tenor Encounters	1978	15.00
AIRCHECK			
❑ 4	Duke on the Air	197?	10.00
❑ 29	Duke on the Air, Vol. 2	198?	10.00
ALLEGRO			
❑ 1591 [M]	Duke Ellington and His Orchestra Play	1955	50.00
❑ 3082 [M]	Duke Ellington	1953	50.00
❑ 4014 [10]	Duke Ellington and His Orchestra Play	1954	100.00
❑ 4038 [10]	Duke Ellington and His Orchestra Play	1954	100.00
ATLANTIC			
❑ SD 2-304 [(2)]	The Great Paris Concert	1972	15.00
❑ QD 1580 [Q]	New Orleans Suite	1974	25.00
❑ SD 1580	New Orleans Suite	1971	12.00
❑ SD 1665	Recollections of the Big Band Era	1974	12.00
❑ SD 1688	Jazz Violin Session	1976	12.00
❑ 90043	Recollections of the Big Band Era	1982	10.00
BASF			
❑ 21704	Collages	1973	12.00
BETHLEHEM			
❑ BCP-60 [M]	Historically Speaking, The Duke	1956	60.00
❑ BCP-6005 [M]	Duke Ellington Presents	1956	60.00
❑ 6013	The Bethlehem Years, Vol. 1	197?	10.00
BIOGRAPH			
❑ M-2	Band Shorts (1929-1935)	1978	10.00
BLUE NOTE			
❑ BT-85129	Money Jungle	1986	10.00
—Reissue of United Artists 15017			
BLUEBIRD			
❑ 5659-1-RB [(4)]	Duke Ellington: The Blanton-Webster Band	1986	25.00
❑ 6287-1-RB	And His Mother Called Him Bill	1987	8.00
—Reissue of RCA Victor 3906			
❑ 6641-1-RB [(4)]	Black, Brown and Beige	1988	25.00
❑ 6852-1-RB	Early Ellington	1989	10.00
BOOK-OF-THE-MONTH			
❑ 30-5622 [(3)]	At Fargo, 1940	1978	20.00
BRIGHT ORANGE			
❑ 709	The Stereophonic Sound of Duke Ellington	1973	12.00
BRUNSWICK			
❑ BL 54007 [M]	Early Ellington	1954	50.00
❑ BL 58002 [10]	Ellingtonia, Vol. 1	1950	100.00
❑ BL 58012 [10]	Ellingtonia, Vol. 2	1950	100.00
BULLDOG			
❑ BDL-2021	20 Golden Pieces of Duke Ellington	198?	10.00
CAPITOL			
❑ H 440 [10]	Premiered by Ellington	1953	100.00
❑ H 477 [10]	The Duke Plays Ellington	1954	100.00
❑ T 477 [M]	The Duke Plays Ellington	1954	40.00
—Turquoise label			
❑ T 477 [M]	The Duke Plays Ellington	1958	20.00
—Black label with colorband, logo at left			
❑ T 521 [M]	Ellington '55	1955	40.00
—Turquoise label			
❑ T 521 [M]	Ellington '55	1958	20.00
—Black label with colorband, logo at left			
❑ T 637 [M]	Dance to the Duke	1955	40.00
—Turquoise label			
❑ T 637 [M]	Dance to the Duke	1958	20.00
—Black label with colorband, logo at left			
❑ T 679 [M]	Ellington Showcase	1956	40.00
—Turquoise label			
❑ T 679 [M]	Ellington Showcase	1958	20.00
—Black label with colorband, logo at left			
❑ DT 1602 [R]	The Best of Duke Ellington	1961	12.00
❑ SM-1602	The Best of Duke Ellington	197?	10.00
—Reissue with new prefix			
❑ T 1602 [M]	The Best of Duke Ellington	1961	20.00
❑ M-11058	Piano Reflections	1972	12.00
❑ M-11674	Ellington '55	1977	10.00
❑ N-16172	The Best of Duke Ellington	198?	8.00
—Budget-line reissue			
CIRCLE			
❑ CLP-101	Duke Ellington World Broadcasting Series, Vol. 1	1986	10.00
❑ CLP-102	Duke Ellington World Broadcasting Series, Vol. 2	1986	10.00
❑ CLP-103	Duke Ellington World Broadcasting Series, Vol. 3	1986	10.00
❑ CLP-104	Duke Ellington World Broadcasting Series, Vol. 4	199?	10.00
❑ CLP-105	Duke Ellington World Broadcasting Series, Vol. 5 (1943)	199?	10.00
❑ CLP-106	Duke Ellington World Broadcasting Series, Vol. 6 (1945)	1988	10.00
❑ CLP-108	Duke Ellington World Broadcasting Series, Vol. 8 (1945)	1988	10.00
❑ CLP-109	Duke Ellington World Broadcasting Series, Vol. 9 (1945)	1988	10.00
COLUMBIA			
❑ C3L 27 [(3)M]	The Ellington Era, Vol. 1	1963	40.00
❑ C3L 39 [(3)M]	The Ellington Era, Vol. 2	1964	40.00
❑ CL 558 [M]	The Music of Duke Ellington	1954	50.00
—Maroon label with gold print			
❑ CL 558 [M]	The Music of Duke Ellington	1956	40.00
—Red and black label with six "eye" logos			
❑ CL 558 [M]	The Music of Duke Ellington	1963	15.00
—Red label with "Guaranteed High Fidelity" or "360 Sound Mono"			
❑ CL 663 [M]	Blue Light	1955	40.00
❑ CL 825 [M]	Masterpieces by Ellington	1956	40.00
—Reissue of Columbia Masterworks 4418			
❑ CL 825 [M]	Masterpieces by Ellington	1963	15.00
—Red label with "Guaranteed High Fidelity" or "360 Sound Mono"			
❑ CL 830 [M]	Hi-Fi Ellington Uptown	1956	40.00
❑ CL 830 [M]	Hi-Fi Ellington Uptown	1963	15.00
—Red label with "Guaranteed High Fidelity" or "360 Sound Mono"			
❑ CL 848 [M]	Liberian Suite	1956	40.00
—Reissue of Columbia 6073			
❑ CL 934 [M]	Ellington at Newport '56	1957	40.00
—Red and black label with six "eye" logos			
❑ CL 934 [M]	Ellington at Newport '56	1963	15.00
—Red label with "Guaranteed High Fidelity" or "360 Sound Mono"			
❑ CL 951 [M]	A Drum Is a Woman	1957	40.00
❑ CL 1033 [M]	Such Sweet Thunder	1957	40.00
❑ CL 1085 [M]	Ellington Indigos	1958	25.00
❑ CL 1085 [M]	Ellington Indigos	1963	15.00
—Red label with "Guaranteed High Fidelity" or "360 Sound Mono"			
❑ CL 1162 [M]	Brown, Black and Beige	1958	25.00
❑ CL 1198 [M]	The Cosmic Scene	1959	80.00
❑ CL 1245 [M]	Newport 1958	1959	25.00
❑ CL 1282 [M]	Duke Ellington at the Bal Masque	1959	25.00
❑ CL 1323 [M]	Duke Ellington Jazz Party	1959	25.00
❑ CL 1400 [M]	Festival Session	1960	25.00
❑ CL 1445 [M]	Blues in Orbit	1960	25.00
❑ CL 1541 [M]	The Nutcracker Suite	1960	30.00
❑ CL 1546 [M]	Piano in the Background	1960	30.00
❑ CL 1546 [M]	Piano in the Background	1963	15.00
—Red label with "Guaranteed High Fidelity" or "360 Sound Mono"			
❑ CL 1597 [M]	Peer Gynt Suite/Suite Thursday	1961	25.00
❑ CL 1715 [M]	First Time	1962	25.00
❑ CL 1790 [M]	All American	1962	20.00
❑ CL 1907 [M]	Midnight in Paris	1963	20.00
❑ CL 2522 [10]	Duke's Mixture	1955	80.00
❑ CL 2562 [10]	Here's the Duke	1955	80.00
❑ CL 2593 [10]	Al Hibbler with the Duke	1956	80.00
❑ CL 6024 [10]	Mood Ellington	1949	100.00
❑ CL 6073 [10]	Liberian Suite	1949	100.00
❑ CS 8015 [S]	Brown, Black and Beige	1958	30.00
❑ CS 8053 [S]	Ellington Indigos	1958	30.00
—Red and black label with six "eye" logos			
❑ CS 8053 [S]	Ellington Indigos	1963	15.00
—Red label with "360 Sound Stereo"			
❑ PC 8053	Ellington Indigos	198?	8.00
—Budget-line reissue			
❑ CS 8072 [S]	Newport 1958	1959	30.00
❑ CS 8098 [S]	Duke Ellington at the Bal Masque	1959	30.00
❑ CS 8127 [S]	Duke Ellington Jazz Party	1959	30.00
❑ CS 8241 [S]	Blues in Orbit	1960	30.00
❑ CS 8341 [S]	The Nutcracker Suite	1960	40.00
❑ CS 8346 [S]	Piano in the Background	1960	40.00
❑ CS 8346 [S]	Piano in the Background	1963	15.00
—Red label with "360 Sound Stereo"			
❑ CS 8397 [S]	Peer Gynt Suite/Suite Thursday	1961	30.00
❑ CS 8515 [S]	First Time	1962	30.00
❑ CS 8590 [S]	All American	1962	25.00
❑ CS 8648 [R]	Ellington at Newport	1963	12.00
❑ PC 8648	Ellington at Newport	198?	8.00
—Budget-line reissue			
❑ CS 8829 [S]	Midnight in Paris	1963	25.00
❑ CS 9629	Duke Ellington's Greatest Hits	1969	15.00
❑ KG 32064 [(2)]	Duke Ellington Presents Ivie Anderson	1973	15.00
❑ C 32471	Jazz at the Plaza — Vol. II	1973	12.00
❑ G 32564 [(2)]	The World of Duke Ellington	1974	15.00
❑ KG 33341 [(2)]	The World of Duke Ellington, Vol. 2	1975	15.00
❑ CG 33961 [(2)]	The World of Duke Ellington, Vol. 3	1975	15.00
❑ PC 37340	It Don't Mean a Thing	1981	8.00
—Reissue			
❑ FC 38028	The Girl's Suite & Perfume Suite	1982	10.00
COLUMBIA JAZZ MASTERPIECES			
❑ CJ 40586	First Time	1987	10.00
—Reissue of Columbia 8515			
❑ CJ 40587	Ellington at Newport	1987	10.00
—Reissue of Columbia 934			
❑ CJ 40712	Duke Ellington Jazz Party	1987	10.00
—Reissue of Columbia 8127			
❑ CJ 40836	Uptown	1987	10.00
❑ CJ 44051	Blues in Orbit	1988	10.00
—Reissue of Columbia 8241			
❑ CJ 44444	Ellington Indigos	1989	10.00
—Reissue of Columbia 8053			
COLUMBIA JAZZ ODYSSEY			
❑ PC 36979	The Festival Session	1981	10.00
COLUMBIA MASTERWORKS			
❑ ML 4418 [M]	Masterpieces by Ellington	1951	100.00
❑ ML 4639 [M]	Ellington Uptown	195?	50.00
—Oddly, this exists as a reissue on the red and black "6 eye" label			
❑ ML 4639 [M]	Ellington Uptown	1951	100.00
—Blue or green label, gold print			
COLUMBIA SPECIAL PRODUCTS			
❑ P 13291	Duke Ellington's Greatest Hits (Recorded Live in Concert)	1976	10.00
❑ P 13500	Festival Session	1976	10.00
❑ P 14359	Suite Thursday/Controversial Suite/Harlem Suite	198?	10.00
DAYBREAK			
❑ DR 2017	The Symphonic Ellington	1973	12.00
DECCA			
❑ DL 9224 [M]	Duke Ellington, Vol. 1 — In the Beginning	1958	40.00
—Black label, silver print			
❑ DL 9224 [M]	Duke Ellington, Vol. 1 — In the Beginning	1961	25.00
—Black label with color bars			
❑ DL 9241 [M]	Duke Ellington, Vol. 2 — Hot in Harlem	1959	40.00
—Black label, silver print			
❑ DL 9241 [M]	Duke Ellington, Vol. 2 — Hot in Harlem	1961	25.00
—Black label with color bars			
❑ DL 9247 [M]	Duke Ellington, Vol. 3 — Rockin' in Rhythm	1959	40.00
—Black label, silver print			
❑ DL 9247 [M]	Duke Ellington, Vol. 3 — Rockin' in Rhythm	1961	25.00
—Black label with color bars			
❑ DL 75069	Duke Ellington in Canada	1969	15.00
❑ DL 79224 [R]	Duke Ellington, Vol. 1 — In the Beginning	1958	25.00
—Black label, silver print			
❑ DL 79224 [R]	Duke Ellington, Vol. 1 — In the Beginning	1961	15.00
—Black label with color bars			
❑ DL 79241 [R]	Duke Ellington, Vol. 2 — Hot in Harlem	1959	25.00
—Black label, silver print			
❑ DL 79241 [R]	Duke Ellington, Vol. 2 — Hot in Harlem	1961	15.00
—Black label with color bars			
❑ DL 79247 [R]	Duke Ellington, Vol. 3 — Rockin' in Rhythm	1959	25.00
—Black label, silver print			
❑ DL 79247 [R]	Duke Ellington, Vol. 3 — Rockin' in Rhythm	1961	15.00
—Black label with color bars			
DISCOVERY			
❑ 841	Concert in the Virgin Islands	198?	10.00
—Reissue of Reprise 6185			
❑ 871	Afro Bossa	198?	10.00
—Reissue of Reprise 6069			
DO YOU LIKE JAZZ			
❑ P 13293	Monologue	1973	12.00
DOCTOR JAZZ			
❑ W2X 39137 [(2)]	All-Star Road Band	1984	12.00
❑ W2X 40012 [(2)]	All-Star Road Band, Vol. 2	1985	12.00
❑ FW 40030	Happy Reunion	1985	10.00
❑ FW 40359	New Mood Indigo	1986	10.00
EVEREST ARCHIVE OF FOLK & JAZZ			
❑ 221	Early Duke Ellington	1968	12.00
❑ 249	Early Duke Ellington Vol. 2	1970	12.00
❑ 266	Early Duke Ellington Vol. 3	1972	12.00
❑ 327	Duke Ellington at Carnegie Hall	197?	12.00
FANTASY			
❑ OJC-108	Great Times!	198?	10.00
—Reissue of Riverside 9475			
❑ OJC-446	The Ellington Suites	1990	10.00
—Reissue of Pablo 2310 762			

E

Except when noted otherwise, VG = 25% of NM, and VG+ = 50% of NM. (Example: VG = $2.00, VG+ = $4.00 and NM = $8.00.)

Number	Title (A Side/B Side)	Yr	NM
❑ OJC-469	Latin American Suite	1990	10.00
—Reissue of 8419			
❑ OJC-623	Duke Ellington Featuring Paul Gonsalves	1991	12.00
—Reissue of 9636			
❑ OJC-624	The Intimacy of the Blues	1991	12.00
—Reissue of 9640			
❑ OJC-633	Up in Duke's Workshop	1991	12.00
—Reissue of Pablo 2310 815			
❑ OJC-645	The Afro-Eurasian Eclipse	1991	12.00
—Reissue of 9498			
❑ F-8407/8 [(2)]	Duke Ellington's Second Sacred Concert	1971	15.00
❑ F-8419	Latin American Suite	1971	12.00
❑ F-9433	Yale Concert	1974	12.00
❑ F-9462	The Pianist	1974	12.00
❑ F-9498	Afro-American Eclipse	1976	12.00
❑ F-9636	Duke Ellington Featuring Paul Gonsalves	198?	10.00
❑ F-9640	The Intimacy of the Blues	1986	10.00
FLYING DUTCHMAN			
❑ BXL1-2832	It Don't Mean a Thing	1978	10.00
—Reissue			
❑ 10112	My People	1969	15.00
❑ 10166	It Don't Mean a Thing	1973	12.00
FOLKWAYS			
❑ FJ-2968	First Annual Tour of the Pacific Northwest, Spring, 1952	198?	10.00
GALAXY			
❑ 4807	Duke Ellington and His Famous Orchestra and Soloists	197?	15.00
GNP CRESCENDO			
❑ GNP-9045	The 1953 Pasadena Concert	1986	10.00
❑ GNP-9049	The 1954 Los Angeles Concert	1987	10.00
HALL OF FAME			
❑ 625/6/7 [(3)]	The Immortal Duke Ellington	197?	20.00
HARMONY			
❑ HL 7436 [M]	Fantasies	1967	15.00
❑ HS 11236 [R]	Fantasies	1967	12.00
❑ HS 11323	In My Solitude	1969	12.00
❑ H 30566	Duke Ellington's Greatest Hits Live	1971	12.00
HINDSIGHT			
❑ HSR-125	Duke Ellington 1946	198?	10.00
❑ HSR-126	Duke Ellington 1946, Vol. 2	198?	10.00
❑ HSR-127	Duke Ellington 1946, Vol. 3	198?	10.00
❑ HSR-128	Duke Ellington 1947	198?	10.00
❑ HSR-129	Duke Ellington 1947, Vol. 2	198?	10.00
IAJRC			
❑ LP-45	Fairfield, Connecticut Jazz Fest 1956	198?	8.00
INTERMEDIA			
❑ QS-5002	Sophisticated Duke	198?	10.00
❑ QS-5020	Lullaby of Birdland	198?	10.00
❑ QS-5021	Do Nothin' Till You Hear from Me	198?	10.00
❑ QS-5063	Satin Doll	198?	10.00
JAZZ ODYSSEY			
❑ 32160252	Nutcracker and Peer Gynt Suites	196?	12.00
JAZZ PANORAMA			
❑ 1802 [10]	Duke Ellington — Vol. 1	1951	100.00
❑ 1811 [10]	Duke Ellington — Vol. 2	1951	100.00
❑ 1816 [10]	Duke Ellington — Vol. 3	1951	100.00
JAZZBIRD			
❑ 2009	Meadowbrook to Manhattan	1980	10.00
LONDON			
❑ AL-3551 [10]	The Duke — 1926	195?	100.00
MCA			
❑ 1358	Duke Ellington, Vol. 1 — In the Beginning	198?	8.00
—Reissue of 2075			
❑ 1359	Duke Ellington, Vol. 2 — Hot in Harlem	198?	8.00
—Reissue of 2076			
❑ 1360	Duke Ellington, Vol. 3 — Rockin' in Rhythm	198?	8.00
—Reissue of 2077			
❑ 1374	Brunswick-Vocalion Rarities	198?	10.00
❑ 2075	Duke Ellington, Vol. 1 — In the Beginning	197?	10.00
—Reissue of Decca 79224			
❑ 2076	Duke Ellington, Vol. 2 — Hot in Harlem	197?	10.00
—Reissue of Decca 79241			
❑ 2077	Duke Ellington, Vol. 3 — Rockin' in Rhythm	197?	10.00
—Reissue of Decca 79247			
❑ 4142 [(2)]	Great Tenor Encounters	198?	12.00
—Reissue of Impulse! 9350			
❑ 42325	The Brunswick Era, Vol. 1	1990	12.00
MOBILE FIDELITY			
❑ 1-214	Anatomy of a Murder	1995	40.00
—Audiophile vinyl			
MOSAIC			
❑ MQ8-160 [(8)]	The Complete Capitol Recordings of Duke Ellington	199?	150.00
MUSICRAFT			
❑ 2002	Carnegie Hall Concert	1986	10.00
PABLO			
❑ 2310703	Duke's Big 4	1974	12.00
❑ 2310721	This One's for Blanton	197?	12.00
❑ 2310762	The Ellington Suites	197?	12.00
❑ 2310787	Intimate	197?	12.00
❑ 2310815	Up in Duke's Workshop	1980	10.00
❑ 2405401	The Best of Duke Ellington	198?	10.00
PABLO LIVE			
❑ 2308245	Harlem	198?	10.00
❑ 2308247	In the Uncommon Market	198?	10.00
PAIR			
❑ PDL2-1011 [(2)]	Original Recordings by Duke Ellington	1986	12.00
PICCADILLY			
❑ 3524	Classic Ellington	198?	10.00
PICKWICK			
❑ SPC-3390	We Love You Madly	197?	10.00
PRESTIGE			
❑ 24029 [(2)]	The Golden Duke	1973	15.00
❑ 24045 [(2)]	Duke Ellington's Second Sacred Concert	1974	12.00
—Reissue of Fantasy 8407/8			
❑ 24073 [(2)]	The Carnegie Hall Concerts: December 1944	1977	15.00
❑ 24074 [(2)]	The Carnegie Hall Concerts: January 1946	1977	15.00
❑ 24075 [(2)]	The Carnegie Hall Concerts: December 1947	1977	15.00
❑ 34003 [(3)]	The Carnegie Hall Concerts: January 1943	197?	20.00
RCA CAMDEN			
❑ ACL2-0152 [(2)]	Mood Indigo	1973	15.00
❑ CAL-394 [M]	Duke Ellington at Tanglewood	1958	20.00
❑ CAL-459 [M]	Duke Ellington at the Cotton Club	1959	20.00
❑ ACL-7052	The Duke at Tanglewood	197?	10.00
—Reissue of RCA Red Seal LSC-2857			
RCA VICTOR			
❑ WPT-11 [10]	Duke Ellington	1951	100.00
❑ SP-33-394 [M]	The Duke at Tanglewood	1966	25.00
—"Special Interview Recording for Radio Station Programming"			
❑ LPV-506 [M]	Daybreak Express	1964	20.00
❑ LPV-517 [M]	Jumpin' Punkins	1965	20.00
❑ LPV-541 [M]	Johnny Come Lately	1967	20.00
❑ LPV-553 [M]	Pretty Woman	1968	20.00
❑ LPV-568 [M]	Flaming Youth	1969	20.00
❑ LJM-1002 [M]	Seattle Concert	1954	50.00
❑ LPT-1004 [M]	Ellington's Greatest	1954	40.00
❑ APL1-1023	Eastbourne Performance	1974	12.00
❑ LPM-1092 [M]	Duke and His Men	1955	40.00
❑ LPM-1364 [M]	In a Mellotone	1957	40.00
—Black label, dog at top, "Long Play" at bottom			
❑ LPM-1364 [M]	In a Mellotone	196?	25.00
—Black label, dog at top, "Mono" at bottom			
❑ LPM-1364 [M]	In a Mellotone	1969	20.00
—Orange label			
❑ LPM-1715 [M]	Duke Ellington at His Very Best	1958	40.00
❑ ANL1-2811	Pure Gold	1978	10.00
❑ LPT-3017 [10]	This Is Duke Ellington and His Orchestra	1952	100.00
❑ LPT-3067 [10]	Duke Ellington Plays the Blues	1952	100.00
❑ LPM-3576 [M]	The Popular Duke Ellington	1966	15.00
❑ LSP-3576 [S]	The Popular Duke Ellington	1966	20.00
❑ LPM-3582 [M]	Concert of Sacred Music	1966	15.00
❑ LSP-3582 [S]	Concert of Sacred Music	1966	20.00
❑ LPM-3782 [M]	Far East Suite	1967	25.00
❑ LSP-3782 [S]	Far East Suite	1967	15.00
❑ LPM-3906 [M]	And His Mother Called Him Bill	1968	50.00
❑ LSP-3906 [S]	And His Mother Called Him Bill	1968	15.00
❑ CPL2-4098 [(2)]	Sophisticated Ellington	1983	12.00
❑ LPM-6009 [(2)M]	The Indispensible Duke Ellington	1961	50.00
❑ VPM-6042 [(2)]	This Is Duke Ellington	1972	15.00
RCA VICTOR RED SEAL			
❑ LM-2857 [M]	The Duke at Tanglewood	1966	15.00
❑ LSC-2857 [S]	The Duke at Tanglewood	1966	20.00
REPRISE			
❑ R-6069 [M]	Afro-Bossa	1962	20.00
❑ R9-6069 [S]	Afro-Bossa	1962	20.00
❑ R-6097 [M]	The Symphonic Ellington	1963	20.00
❑ R9-6097 [S]	The Symphonic Ellington	1963	20.00
❑ R-6122 [M]	Ellington '65: Hits of the '60s/This Time by Ellington	1964	20.00
❑ RS-6122 [S]	Ellington '65: Hits of the '60s/This Time by Ellington	1964	20.00
❑ R-6141 [M]	Mary Poppins	1964	20.00
❑ RS-6141 [S]	Mary Poppins	1964	20.00
❑ R-6154 [M]	Ellington '66	1965	20.00
❑ RS-6154 [S]	Ellington '66	1965	15.00
❑ R-6168 [M]	Will Big Bands Ever Come Back?	1965	20.00
❑ RS-6168 [S]	Will Big Bands Ever Come Back?	1965	15.00
❑ R-6185 [M]	Concert in the Virgin Islands	1965	20.00
❑ RS-6185 [S]	Concert in the Virgin Islands	1965	15.00
❑ R-6234 [M]	Duke Ellington's Greatest Hits	1967	20.00
❑ RS-6234 [S]	Duke Ellington's Greatest Hits	1967	15.00
RIVERSIDE			
❑ RLP 12-129 [M]	Birth of Big Band Jazz	195?	30.00
—Blue label with mike logo			
❑ RLP 12-129 [M]	Birth of Big Band Jazz	1956	60.00
—White label, blue print			
❑ RLP-475 [M]	Great Times!	1963	25.00
❑ RS-9475 [S]	Great Times!	1963	25.00
RONDO-LETTE			
❑ A-7 [M]	Duke Ellington and Orchestra	1958	30.00
ROULETTE			
❑ 108 [(2)]	Echoes of an Era	1971	15.00
ROYALE			
❑ 18143 [10]	Duke Ellington and His Orchestra	195?	50.00
❑ 18152 [10]	Duke Ellington Plays Ellington	195?	50.00
SMITHSONIAN COLLECTION			
❑ P6-15079 [(6)]	An Explosion of Genius 1938-1940	1976	50.00
—"Produced in association with Columbia Special Products"			
SOLID STATE			
❑ SM-18022	Money Jungle	1968	15.00
—Reissue of United Artists 15017			
❑ SS-19000 [(2)]	75th Birthday	1970	20.00
STANYAN			
❑ 10105	For Always	197?	12.00
STARDUST			
❑ SD-124 [M]	Duke	196?	12.00
❑ SDS-124 [R]	Duke	196?	12.00
STORYVILLE			
❑ SLP-4003	Duke Ellington and His Orchestra	198?	10.00
SUPER MAJESTIC			
❑ 2000	Duke Ellington	197?	12.00
SUTTON			
❑ SU-276 [M]	Duke Meets Leonard Feather	196?	12.00
TIME-LIFE			
❑ STL-J-02 [(3)]	Giants of Jazz	1978	20.00
❑ STBB-05 [(2)]	Big Bands: Duke Ellington	1983	15.00
❑ STBB-16 [(2)]	Big Bands: Cotton Club Nights	1983	15.00
TREND			
❑ 529	The Symphonic Ellington	1982	20.00
❑ 2004	Carnegie Hall Concert	198?	10.00
UNITED ARTISTS			
❑ UXS-92 [(2)]	Togo Bravo Suite	1972	15.00
❑ UAS-5632	Money Jungle	1972	12.00
—Reissue			
❑ UAJ-14017 [M]	Money Jungle	1962	40.00
❑ UAJS-15017 [S]	Money Jungle	1962	40.00
VEE JAY			
❑ VJS-3061	Love You Madly	198?	10.00
VERVE			
❑ V-8701 [M]	Soul Call	1967	15.00
❑ V6-8701 [S]	Soul Call	1967	12.00
"X"			
❑ LVA-3037 [10]	Duke Ellington Plays	1955	100.00

ELLINGTON, HARVEY

Albums

Number	Title (A Side/B Side)	Yr	NM
STEPHENY			
❑ MF-4010 [M]	I Can't Hide the Blues	1959	80.00

ELLIOT, CASS

Also see THE BIG THREE; THE MAMAS AND THE PAPAS; DAVE MASON; THE MUGWUMPS.

45s

Number	Title (A Side/B Side)	Yr	NM
ABC DUNHILL			
❑ 4145	Dream a Little Dream of Me/Midnight Voyage	1968	8.00
—Label credit: "Featuring Mama Cass with the Mamas and the Papas"			
❑ 4166	California Earthquake/Talkin' to Your Toothbrush	1968	6.00
❑ 4184	Move In a Little Closer, Baby/All for Me	1969	6.00
❑ 4195	It's Getting Better/Who's to Blame	1969	6.00
—The above three as "Mama Cass"			
❑ 4214	Make Your Own Kind of Music/Ladylove	1969	6.00
❑ 4225	New World Coming/Blow Me a Kiss	1970	6.00
❑ 4244	A Song That Never Comes/I Can Dream, Can't I?	1970	6.00
❑ 4253	Good Times Are Coming/Welcome to the World	1970	6.00

Except when noted otherwise, VG = 25% of NM, and VG+ = 50% of NM. (Example: VG = $2.00, VG+ = $4.00 and NM = $8.00.)

Number	Title (A Side/B Side)	Yr	NM
❑ 4264	Don't Let the Good Times Pass You By/A Song That Never Comes	1971	6.00

—The above five as "Mama Cass Elliott"

DUNHILL

Number	Title (A Side/B Side)	Yr	NM
❑ 4145	Dream a Little Dream of Me/Midnight Voyage	1968	25.00

—Label credit: "Featuring Mama Cass with the Mamas and the Papas"; no "ABC" at top of label

RCA VICTOR

Number	Title (A Side/B Side)	Yr	NM
❑ 74-0644	Baby, I'm Yours/Cherries Jubilee	1972	6.00
❑ 74-0693	That Song/When It Doesn't Work Out	1972	6.00
❑ 74-0764	Disney Girls/Break Another Heart	1972	6.00
❑ 74-0830	The Road Is No Place for a Lady/Does Anybody Love You	1972	6.00
❑ 74-0957	I Think a Lot About You/Listen to the World	1973	6.00

7-Inch Extended Plays

ABC DUNHILL

Number	Title (A Side/B Side)	Yr	NM
❑ SP-DS-50040	California Earthquake/Talkin' to Your Toothbrush/Blues for Breakfast//Long Time Loving You/Jane the Insane Dog Lady/Burn Your Hatred	1968	12.00

—As "Mama Cass"; jukebox issue; small hole, plays at 33 1/3 rpm

Number	Title (A Side/B Side)	Yr	NM
❑ SP-DS-50040 [PS]	Dream a Little Dream	1968	12.00

Albums

ABC DUNHILL

Number	Title (A Side/B Side)	Yr	NM
❑ DS-50040	Dream a Little Dream	1968	20.00
❑ DS-50055	Bubble Gum, Lemonade &...Something for Mama	1969	20.00
❑ DS-50071	Make Your Own Kind of Music	1969	15.00

—Reissue of 50055 with new title and one added song

Number	Title (A Side/B Side)	Yr	NM
❑ DS-50093	Mama's Big Ones	1970	15.00

MCA

Number	Title (A Side/B Side)	Yr	NM
❑ 719	Mama's Big Ones	1980	8.00

RCA VICTOR

Number	Title (A Side/B Side)	Yr	NM
❑ APL1-0303	Don't Call Me Mama Anymore	1973	15.00
❑ LSP-4619	Cass Elliot	1971	15.00
❑ LSP-4753	The Road Is No Place for a Lady	1972	15.00

ELLIOTT, BERN, AND THE FENMEN

45s

LONDON

Number	Title (A Side/B Side)	Yr	NM
❑ 9670	New Orleans/Everybody Needs a Little Love	1964	12.00
❑ 9733	Money/Nobody But Me	1965	12.00

ELLIOTT, BILL, AND THE ELASTIC OZ BAND

Also see JOHN LENNON; YOKO ONO.

45s

APPLE

Number	Title (A Side/B Side)	Yr	NM
❑ 1835	God Save Us/Do the Oz	1971	8.00
❑ 1835 [PS]	God Save Us/Do the Oz	1971	10.00
❑ P-1835 [DJ]	God Save Us/Do the Oz	1971	25.00

—Has black star on A-side and unsliced apple on both sides

ELLIOTT, RON

Also see THE BEAU BRUMMELS.

Albums

WARNER BROS.

Number	Title (A Side/B Side)	Yr	NM
❑ WS 1833	Candlestickmaker	1969	15.00

ELLIS, BOBBY

45s

CAMEO

Number	Title (A Side/B Side)	Yr	NM
❑ 354	It's the Talk of the Town/She's Got a Heart of Stone	1965	20.00

CHELTENHAM

Number	Title (A Side/B Side)	Yr	NM
❑ 1007	It's the Talk of the Town/She's Got a Heart of Stone	1965	200.00

ELLIS, JIMMY

Also see ORION.

45s

BOBLO

Number	Title (A Side/B Side)	Yr	NM
❑ 526	Tupelo Woman/The Closer He Gets	1976	4.00
❑ 531	There You Go/Here Comes That Wonderful Feeling	1977	4.00
❑ 532	Movin' On/My Baby's Out of Sight	1977	4.00
❑ 536	I'm Not Trying to Be Like Elvis/Games You've Been Playing	1978	4.00
❑ 536 [PS]	I'm Not Trying to Be Like Elvis/Games You've Been Playing	1978	10.00

DRADCO

Number	Title (A Side/B Side)	Yr	NM
❑ 1892	Don't Count Your Chickens/Love Is But Love	1964	15.00

GOLDBAND

Number	Title (A Side/B Side)	Yr	NM
❑ 1191	Woman in the Picture/What Swinging Doors Did to Me	196?	10.00

KRIS

Number	Title (A Side/B Side)	Yr	NM
❑ 8115	Outskirts of Town (Part 1)/Outskirts of Town (Part 2)	196?	8.00

MCA

Number	Title (A Side/B Side)	Yr	NM
❑ 40060	There Ya Go/Here Comes That Feeling Again	1973	4.00

RIDE

Number	Title (A Side/B Side)	Yr	NM
❑ 146	Baby I Love You/Kiddio	196?	8.00

—As "Jimmie Ellis"; may not be the same performer as the others

SOUTHERN TRACKS

Number	Title (A Side/B Side)	Yr	NM
❑ 1069	I Make the Livin' (You Make the Livin' Worthwhile)/Thank God for America	1986	4.00
❑ 1080	Sunday Fathers/Thank God for America	1987	4.00

SUN

Number	Title (A Side/B Side)	Yr	NM
❑ 1129	That's All Right/Blue Moon of Kentucky	1973	4.00

—Second pressings credit Jimmy Ellis

Number	Title (A Side/B Side)	Yr	NM
❑ 1129	That's All Right/Blue Moon of Kentucky	1973	5.00

—Originals have no artist on label in an attempt to make people believe these were lost Elvis Presley outtakes

Number	Title (A Side/B Side)	Yr	NM
❑ 1131	I Use Her to Remind Me of You/Changing	1974	4.00
❑ 1136	D.O.A./Misty/That's All Right/Blue Moon of Kentucky	1977	4.00

Albums

BOBLO

Number	Title (A Side/B Side)	Yr	NM
❑ 78-829	By Request Jimmy Sings Elvis	1978	100.00

ELLIS, JIMMY (2)

45s

ATLANTIC

Number	Title (A Side/B Side)	Yr	NM
❑ 2572	I Don't Mind/Take the Lord With You	1968	8.00

ELLIS, LARRY

45s

DALE

Number	Title (A Side/B Side)	Yr	NM
❑ 107	Buzz Goes the Bee/Nothing You Can Do	1958	15.00

DART

Number	Title (A Side/B Side)	Yr	NM
❑ 112	I Know the Place/Love That Used to Be	1959	15.00

ROULETTE

Number	Title (A Side/B Side)	Yr	NM
❑ 4195	Hide and Seek/Really and Truly	1959	12.00
❑ 4243	Look, My Love/Nothing You Can Do	1960	12.00

SWAN

Number	Title (A Side/B Side)	Yr	NM
❑ 4007	My Heart Understood/Tennessee	1958	12.00

ELLIS, LLOYD

45s

MERCURY

Number	Title (A Side/B Side)	Yr	NM
❑ 70463X45	Yo-Yo Boogie/Indian Love Call	1954	30.00
❑ 70520X45	Boogie Blues/Blue Champagne	1954	30.00
❑ 70590X45	Cottontail Rag/Sweet and Lovely	1955	30.00

Albums

CARLTON

Number	Title (A Side/B Side)	Yr	NM
❑ LP 12-104 [M]	Fastest Guitar in the World	1958	50.00

FAMOUS DOOR

Number	Title (A Side/B Side)	Yr	NM
❑ HL-100	Las Vegas 3 AM	197?	12.00

TREY

Number	Title (A Side/B Side)	Yr	NM
❑ TLP-902 [M]	So Tall, So Cool, So There!	1960	30.00

ELLIS, LORRAINE

45s

BULLSEYE

Number	Title (A Side/B Side)	Yr	NM
❑ 100	Perfidia/Piano Player Play a Tune	1955	60.00

GEE

Number	Title (A Side/B Side)	Yr	NM
❑ 1	Perfidia/Piano Player Play a Tune	1953	300.00

ELLIS, MATTHEW

Albums

WARNER BROS.

Number	Title (A Side/B Side)	Yr	NM
❑ BS 2610	Matthew Ellis	1972	15.00

ELLIS, RAY

45s

ASCOT

Number	Title (A Side/B Side)	Yr	NM
❑ 2203	A Thousand Clowns/We'll Say Goodbye	1966	8.00

ATCO

Number	Title (A Side/B Side)	Yr	NM
❑ 6389	I'll Never Be Lonely Again/Wait Till We're 65	1965	8.00
❑ 6396	I Got You Babe/King of the Road	1966	8.00

COLUMBIA

Number	Title (A Side/B Side)	Yr	NM
❑ 4-40982	Fascination/Soft Sands	1957	12.00
❑ 4-41094	36-26-36/Come to Me	1958	12.00
❑ 4-41258	Ups 'n' Downs/Milk 'n' Honey	1958	12.00

MGM

Number	Title (A Side/B Side)	Yr	NM
❑ K12770	Sweet Kentucky Belle/Lauralee	1959	10.00
❑ K12797	The Love That Used to Be/I Know the Place	1959	10.00
❑ K12874	Fallout/U.S. Marshal	1960	10.00
❑ K12926	Joey's Theme/Lonely Room	1960	10.00
❑ K12942	Midnight Lace/Theme from "Grand Jury"	1960	10.00

RCA VICTOR

Number	Title (A Side/B Side)	Yr	NM
❑ 37-7888	La Dolce Vita (The Sweet Life)/Parlami Di Me (Speak to Me)	1961	20.00

—"Compact Single 33" (small hole, plays at LP speed)

Number	Title (A Side/B Side)	Yr	NM
❑ 37-7888 [PS]	La Dolce Vita (The Sweet Life)/Parlami Di Me (Speak to Me)	1961	25.00

—Special picture sleeve for "Compact Single 33"

Number	Title (A Side/B Side)	Yr	NM
❑ 47-7888	La Dolce Vita (The Sweet Life)/Parlami Di Me (Speak to Me)	1961	10.00
❑ 47-7888 [PS]	La Dolce Vita (The Sweet Life)/Parlami Di Me (Speak to Me)	1961	12.00
❑ 47-7953	Portofino/Shalom	1961	10.00
❑ 47-8023	The Sheik/Dumpy	1962	10.00
❑ 47-8150	Anything, Anywhere/Rubia	1963	10.00

20TH CENTURY FOX

Number	Title (A Side/B Side)	Yr	NM
❑ 593	Theme from "Von Ryan's Express"/Theme from "Morituri"	1965	8.00

Albums

ATCO

Number	Title (A Side/B Side)	Yr	NM
❑ 33-187 [M]	Big Hits for Swingers	1966	12.00
❑ SD 33-187 [S]	Big Hits for Swingers	1966	15.00

COLUMBIA

Number	Title (A Side/B Side)	Yr	NM
❑ CL 993 [M]	Ellis in Wonderland	1957	15.00
❑ CL 1097 [M]	Let's Get Away from It All	1957	15.00
❑ CL 1122 [M]	Dancing with Gigi	1958	15.00

HARMONY

Number	Title (A Side/B Side)	Yr	NM
❑ HL 7183 [M]	Gigi	1959	12.00
❑ HS 11003 [S]	Gigi	1959	15.00

MGM

Number	Title (A Side/B Side)	Yr	NM
❑ E-3779 [M]	I'm in the Mood for Strings	1959	12.00
❑ SE-3779 [S]	I'm in the Mood for Strings	1959	15.00
❑ E-3813 [M]	The Best of Peter Gunn	1960	12.00
❑ E-3820 [M]	I'm in the Mood to Swing	1960	12.00
❑ SE-3820 [S]	I'm in the Mood to Swing	1960	15.00
❑ E-3842 [M]	The Big Voices, The Big Bands, The Big Songs, The Big Sounds	1960	12.00
❑ SE-3842 [S]	The Big Voices, The Big Bands, The Big Songs, The Big Sounds	1960	15.00
❑ E-3911 [M]	Carnival in Sound	1961	—

—Canceled

Number	Title (A Side/B Side)	Yr	NM
❑ SE-3911 [M]	Carnival in Sound	1961	—

—Canceled

RCA VICTOR

Number	Title (A Side/B Side)	Yr	NM
❑ LPM-2400 [M]	Ray Ellis Plays the Top 20	1961	12.00
❑ LSP-2400 [S]	Ray Ellis Plays the Top 20	1961	15.00
❑ LPM-2410 [M]	La Dolce Vita	1961	12.00
❑ LSP-2410 [S]	La Dolce Vita	1961	15.00
❑ LPM-2493 [M]	How to Succeed in Business Without Really Trying	1961	12.00
❑ LSP-2493 [S]	How to Succeed in Business Without Really Trying	1961	15.00
❑ LPM-2615 [M]	Our Man on Broadway	1963	12.00
❑ LSP-2615 [S]	Our Man on Broadway	1963	15.00

ELLIS, SHIRLEY

45s

COLUMBIA

Number	Title (A Side/B Side)	Yr	NM
❑ 43829	Truly, Truly, Truly/Birds, Bees, Cupids and Bows	1966	8.00
❑ 44021	Soul Time/Waitin'	1967	8.00
❑ 44137	Sugar Let's Shing-a-Ling/How Lonely Is Lonely	1967	8.00

CONGRESS

Number	Title (A Side/B Side)	Yr	NM
❑ 202	The Nitty Gritty/Give Me a List	1963	15.00
❑ 208	(That's) What the Nitty Gritty Is/Get Out	1964	10.00
❑ 210	Shy One/Takin' Care of Business	1964	10.00
❑ 221	Such a Night/Bring It On Home to Me	1964	10.00
❑ 230	The Name Game/Whisper to the Wind	1964	12.00
❑ 230 [PS]	The Name Game/Whisper to the Wind	1964	20.00
❑ 234	The Clapping Song (Clap Pat Clap Slap)/This Is Beautiful	1965	10.00
❑ 234 [PS]	The Clapping Song (Clap Pat Clap Slap)/This Is Beautiful	1965	20.00

Number	Title (A Side/B Side)	Yr	NM
❑ 238	The Puzzle Song (A Puzzle in Song)/I See It, I Like It, I Want It	1965	10.00
❑ 246	I Never Will Forget/I Told You So	1965	10.00
❑ 251	One Sour Note/You Better Be Good, World	1965	10.00
❑ 260	Ever See a Diver Kiss His Wife While the Bubbles Bounce About Above the Water/Stardust	1965	10.00
Albums			
COLUMBIA			
❑ CL 2679 [M]	Sugar, Let's Shing-a-Ling	1967	20.00
❑ CS 9479 [S]	Sugar, Let's Shing-a-Ling	1967	25.00
CONGRESS			
❑ CGL-3002 [M]	Shirley Ellis In Action	1964	25.00
❑ CGS-3002 [S]	Shirley Ellis In Action	1964	30.00
❑ CGL-3003 [M]	The Name Game	1965	25.00
❑ CGS-3003 [S]	The Name Game	1965	30.00

ELLIS, STEVE, AND THE STARFIRES

Number	Title (A Side/B Side)	Yr	NM
Albums			
I.G.L.			
❑ 105	The Steve Ellis Songbook	1967	500.00

ELLISON, LORRAINE

Number	Title (A Side/B Side)	Yr	NM
45s			
LOMA			
❑ 2074	Heart Be Still/Cry Me a River	1967	10.00
❑ 2083	When Love Flies Away/I Want to Be Loved	1967	10.00
❑ 2094	Try (Just a Little Bit Harder)/In My Tomorrow	1968	10.00
MERCURY			
❑ 72472	Don't Let It Go to Your Head/I Dig You Baby	1965	15.00
❑ 72534	Call Me Anytime You Need Some Lovin'/Please Don't Teach Me to Love You	1966	15.00
SHARP			
❑ 635	Open Up Your Heart/This Is the Day	1963	20.00
WARNER BROS.			
❑ GWB 0324	Stay with Me/Heart Be Still	1975	6.00
—"Back to Back Hits" series; "Burbank" palm trees label			
❑ 5850	Stay with Me/I Got My Baby Back	1966	12.00
❑ 5879	Good Love/I'm Over You	1966	12.00
❑ 5895	If I Had a Hammer/Heart and Soul	1967	12.00
❑ 7042	He's My Guy/No Matter How It All Turns Out	1967	10.00
❑ 7302	Only Your Love/What Is a Woman	1969	8.00
❑ 7361	Stay with Me/Try (Just a Little Bit Harder)	1970	8.00
❑ 7394	You've Really Got a Hold on Me/You Don't Know Nothing About Love	1970	8.00
❑ 7700	Many Rivers to Cross/Stormy Weather	1973	8.00
Albums			
WARNER BROS.			
❑ W 1674 [M]	Heart and Soul	1967	40.00
❑ WS 1674 [S]	Heart and Soul	1967	30.00
❑ WS 1821	Stay with Me	1969	40.00
❑ BS 2780 [S]	Lorraine Ellison	1974	15.00

ELMER GANTRY'S VELVET OPERA

Number	Title (A Side/B Side)	Yr	NM
Albums			
EPIC			
❑ BN 26415	Elmer Gantry's Velvet Opera	1968	75.00

ELMO AND ALMO

Number	Title (A Side/B Side)	Yr	NM
45s			
DADDY BEAT			
❑ 2501	When the Good Sun Shines/Part II	1967	8.00

ELVES, THE
Also see RONNIE DIO.

Number	Title (A Side/B Side)	Yr	NM
45s			
DECCA			
❑ 732507	Walking in Different Circles/She's Not the Same	1969	20.00
❑ 732617	Amber Velvet/West Virginia	1970	20.00

EMANONS, THE

Number	Title (A Side/B Side)	Yr	NM
45s			
ABC-PARAMOUNT			
❑ 9913	Dear One/We Teenagers (Know What We Want)	1958	20.00
GEE			
❑ 1005	Change of Time/Hindu Baby	1956	120.00
JOSIE			
❑ 801	Blue Moon/Wish I Had My Baby	1956	100.00
WINLEY			
❑ 226	Dear One/We Teenagers (Know What We Want)	1958	40.00

EMBERS, THE
Several different groups.

Number	Title (A Side/B Side)	Yr	NM
45s			
ATLANTIC			
❑ 2627	Where Did I Go Wrong/You Got What You Want	1969	10.00
BELL			
❑ 664	It Ain't No Big Thing/It Ain't Necessary	1967	20.00
COLUMBIA			
❑ 40287	Sweet Lips/There'll Be No One Else But You	1954	40.00
DOT			
❑ 16101	Wait for Me/Couldn't Wait Any Longer	1960	15.00
❑ 16162	Please Mr. Sun/My Dearest Darling	1960	15.00
EMBER			
❑ 101	Sound of Love/Paradise Hill	1953	800.00
EMPRESS			
❑ 101	Solitaire/I'm Feeling All Right Again	1961	30.00
❑ 104	I Won't Cry Anymore/I Was Too Careful	1961	30.00
❑ 107	Abigail/I Was Too Careful	1962	30.00
❑ 108	What a Surprise/I Was Too Careful	1962	40.00
HERALD			
❑ 410	Sound of Love/Paradise Hill	1953	80.00
—Yellow label			
❑ 410	Sound of Love/Paradise Hill	1953	150.00
—Red vinyl			
❑ 410	Sound of Love/Paradise Hill	1953	200.00
—Black label			
JCP			
❑ 1008	In My Lonely Room/Good Good Lovin'	1964	60.00
LIBERTY			
❑ 55944	Evelyn/And Now I'm Blue	1967	10.00
MGM			
❑ 14167	Watch Out Girl/Far Away Places	1970	30.00
WYNNE			
❑ 101	Peter Gunn Cha Cha/Chinny Chin Cha Cha	1958	15.00
Albums			
EEE			
❑ 1069 [M]	Burn You a New One	1967	200.00
JCP			
❑ 2006 [M]	The Embers Roll Eleven	1965	200.00
❑ 2009 [M]	Just for the Birds	1966	200.00

EMBLEMS, THE
May be two different groups.

Number	Title (A Side/B Side)	Yr	NM
45s			
BAYFRONT			
❑ 107	Would You Still Be Mine/Poor Humpty Dumpty	1962	40.00
—Label has wavy lines or no lines			
❑ 107	Would You Still Be Mine/Poor Humpty Dumpty	1962	100.00
—Label has parallel horizontal lines			
❑ 108	Bang, Bang, Shoot 'Em Daddy/Too Young	1962	100.00
—Black vinyl			
CAMEO			
❑ 293	(It Still Would Be a) Cruel World/Whenever I'm Feelin' Low	1964	15.00

EMBRY, TED

Number	Title (A Side/B Side)	Yr	NM
45s			
ACCENT			
❑ 1057	New Shoes/Teen Age Confession	1958	60.00

EMERALDS, THE
Several different groups.

Number	Title (A Side/B Side)	Yr	NM
45s			
ABC-PARAMOUNT			
❑ 9889	You Belong to My Heart/The One I Adore	1958	25.00
❑ 9948	I'm Dreaming/Confess	1958	25.00
ALLIED			
❑ 10002	Sally Lou/Why Must I Wonder	1958	40.00
BOBBIN			
❑ 107	That's the Way It's Got to Be/Maria's Cha-Cha	1959	50.00
❑ 121	Lover's Cry/Rumblin' Tumblin' Baby	1960	40.00
JUBILEE			
❑ 5474	Dancing Alone/Wanna Make Him Mine	1964	12.00
❑ 5489	Did You Ever Love a Guy/I'm Gonna Ask That Boy to Dance	1964	12.00
KICKS			
❑ 3	Sally Lou/Why Must I Wonder	1954	700.00
KING			
❑ 6078	Baby You've Got Me/Promises	1967	25.00
MOONGLOW			
❑ 230	Ooh Poo Pah Doo/Sally's Snake	1964	30.00
❑ 232	Moonlight Surf/Little D Special	1964	30.00
—Black vinyl			
❑ 232	Moonlight Surf/Little D Special	1964	80.00
—Green vinyl			
REX			
❑ 1004	All the Time/Gotta Be on Time	1959	30.00
❑ 1013	I Kneel at Your Throne/Custer's Last Stand	1960	30.00
TOY			
❑ 7734	Silver/Roadrunner	1961	20.00
VENUS			
❑ 1002	Mademoiselle/The Lover	1959	100.00
❑ 1003	Marsha/You're Driving Me Crazy	1959	150.00
YALE			
❑ 232	The Web/Trapped	1960	20.00

EMERALS, THE

Number	Title (A Side/B Side)	Yr	NM
45s			
TRIPLE X			
❑ 100/101	Please Don't Crush My Dreams/Jukebox Rock	1960	600.00

EMERSON, BILLY

Number	Title (A Side/B Side)	Yr	NM
45s			
CHESS			
❑ 1711	Give Me a Little Love/Woodchuck	1959	20.00
❑ 1728	Holy Mackerel Baby/Believe Me	1959	20.00
❑ 1740	Uh Huh, My Baby/I'll Get to You	1959	20.00
CONSTELLATION			
❑ 148	Aunt Molly (Part 1)/Aunt Molly (Part 2)	1965	15.00
SUN			
❑ 195	No Teasin' Around/If Lovin' Is Believin'	1954	400.00
❑ 203	I'm Not Going Home/The Woodchuck	1954	600.00
❑ 214	Move, Baby, Move/When It Rains, It Pours	1955	50.00
❑ 219	Red Hot/No Greater Love	1955	100.00
❑ 233	Something for Nothing/Little Fine Healthy Thing	1956	50.00
VEE JAY			
❑ 219	Every Woman I Know/Tomorrow Never Comes	1956	30.00
❑ 247	Somebody Show Me/The Pleasure Is All Mine	1957	30.00
❑ 261	You Never Miss the Water/Do Yourself a Favor Billy	1957	30.00

EMERSON, LEE

Number	Title (A Side/B Side)	Yr	NM
45s			
COLUMBIA			
❑ 4-21435	You Call That Waitin'/A Pair of Broken Hearts	1955	20.00
❑ 4-21487	So Little Time/Thank You My Darling	1956	20.00
❑ 4-21525	I'll Know You're Gone/How Long Will It Be	1956	25.00
—With Marty Robbins			
❑ 4-21570	I Thought I Heard You Callin'/My Name/It's So Easy for You to Be Mean	1956	20.00
❑ 4-40868	I Cried Like a Baby/Where D'Ja Go	1957	25.00
—With Marty Robbins			
❑ 4-40985	Start All Over/Do You Think	1957	20.00
❑ 4-41046	What a Night/Catch That Train	1957	25.00

EMERSON, LAKE AND PALMER
Also see GREG LAKE; ASIA.

Number	Title (A Side/B Side)	Yr	NM
45s			
ATLANTIC			
❑ 3398	Fanfare for the Common Man/Brain Salad Surgery	1977	5.00
❑ 3555	All I Want Is You/Tiger in a Spotlight	1979	5.00
❑ 3641	Peter Gunn Theme/Tiger in a Spotlight	1980	5.00
COTILLION			
❑ 44106	Lucky Man/Knife's Edge	1971	6.00

Except when noted otherwise, VG = 25% of NM, and VG+ = 50% of NM. (Example: VG = $2.00, VG+ = $4.00 and NM = $8.00.)

Number	Title (A Side/B Side)	Yr	NM
❑ 44131	A Time and a Place/ Stone of Years	1971	5.00
❑ 44151	Nutrocker/The Great Gates of Kiev	1972	5.00
❑ 44158	From the Beginning/Living Sin	1972	5.00
MANTICORE			
❑ 2003	Still...You Turn Me On/ Brain Salad Surgery	1973	5.00
❑ 2003 [PS]	Still...You Turn Me On/ Brain Salad Surgery	1973	10.00

Albums

Number	Title (A Side/B Side)	Yr	NM
ATLANTIC			
❑ PR 277 [DJ]	Works Vol. 1	1977	15.00
—Promo-only sampler			
❑ PR 281 [DJ]	On Tour with Emerson, Lake and Palmer	1977	40.00
❑ SD 7000 [(2)]	Works Vol. 1	1977	15.00
❑ SD 19120	Emerson, Lake and Palmer	1977	8.00
❑ SD 19121	Tarkus	1977	8.00
❑ SD 19122	Pictures at an Exhibition	1977	8.00
❑ SD 19123	Trilogy	1977	8.00
❑ SD 19124	Brain Salad Surgery	1977	8.00
❑ SD 19147	Works Vol. 2	1977	10.00
❑ SD 19211	Love Beach	1978	10.00
❑ SD 19255	Emerson, Lake and Palmer In Concert	1979	10.00
❑ SD 19283	The Best of Emerson, Lake and Palmer	1980	10.00
COTILLION			
❑ SD 9040	Emerson, Lake and Palmer	1971	12.00
❑ SD 9900	Tarkus	1971	12.00
❑ SD 9903	Trilogy	1972	12.00
❑ ELP 66666	Pictures at an Exhibition	1971	12.00
❑ SMAS-94773	Trilogy	1972	15.00
—Capitol Record Club edition			
MANTICORE			
❑ SD 3-200 [(3)]	Welcome Back, My Friends, to the Show That Never Ends, Ladies and Gentlemen	1974	20.00
❑ ELP 66669	Brain Salad Surgery	1973	12.00
MOBILE FIDELITY			
❑ 1-031	Pictures at an Exhibition	1980	55.00
—Audiophile vinyl			
❑ 1-203	Tarkus	1994	40.00
—Audiophile vinyl			
❑ 1-218	Trilogy	1994	60.00
—Audiophile vinyl			

EMERSON, LAKE AND POWELL That's Cozy Powell of RAINBOW, BLACK SABBATH and MSG fame.

Albums

Number	Title (A Side/B Side)	Yr	NM
POLYDOR			
❑ 829297-1	Emerson, Lake and Powell	1986	10.00

EMERSON'S OLD-TIMEY CUSTARD-SUCKIN' BAND

Albums

Number	Title (A Side/B Side)	Yr	NM
ESP-DISK'			
❑ 2006	Emerson's Old-Timey Custard-Suckin' Band	1970	30.00

EMERY, RALPH

45s

Number	Title (A Side/B Side)	Yr	NM
ABC			
❑ 10920	In the Misty Moonlight/Last Night Morning Sidewalks	1967	10.00
❑ 11001	One More for the Road/ Yodelin' Jim	1967	10.00
ELEKTRA			
❑ 46010	Daddy, Is She Pretty As Mama/ Wrestling Matches	1979	5.00
❑ 46033	Jesus Was a Country Boy/ Kiss and Say Goodbye	1979	5.00
LIBERTY			
❑ 55352	Hello Fool/It's Not a Lot	1961	15.00
❑ 55383	I'll Take Good Care of Your Baby/ Legend of Sleepy Hollow	1961	15.00
❑ 55429	Tough Top Cat/ Two Minutes to Live	1962	15.00
❑ 55524	Christmas Dinner/Christmas Can't Be Far Away	1962	15.00
❑ 55546	Poor Boy/The Touch of the Master's Hand	1963	15.00
MERCURY			
❑ 72295	Sit Down and Write a Letter to Me, Won'tcha Baby/I Cry at Ball Games	1964	12.00
ORLANDO			
❑ 101	Daddy, Is She Pretty As Mama/ Wrestling Matches	1979	10.00

EMOTIONS, THE (1) Female R&B vocal group. Also see EARTH, WIND AND FIRE WITH THE EMOTIONS. These are records by the hit female group. Records on Brainstorm, Calla, Card, Flip, Fury, Kapp, Karate, Laurie 20th Century Fox, and Vardan are not by this Emotions group, thus are outside the scope of this book.

45s

Number	Title (A Side/B Side)	Yr	NM
ARC			
❑ 18-02239	Turn It Out/When You Gonna Wake Up	1981	4.00
❑ 18-02535	Now That I Know/Here You Come Again	1981	4.00
❑ 11134	What's the Name of Your Love?/Layed Back	1979	5.00
❑ 11205	Where Is Your Love?/ Layed Back	1980	5.00
COLUMBIA			
❑ 3-10347	Flowers/I Don't Wanna Lose Your Love	1976	5.00
❑ 3-10544	Best of My Love/A Feeling Is	1977	5.00
❑ 3-10622	Don't Ask My Neighbors/ Love's What's Happenin'	1977	5.00
❑ 3-10791	Smile/Changes	1978	5.00
❑ 3-10828	Whole Lotta Shakin'/ Time Is Passing By	1978	5.00
❑ 3-10874	Walking the Line/Ain't No Doubt About It	1978	5.00
MOTOWN			
❑ 1784	I Can't Wait to Make You Mine/ I'm Gonna Miss Your Love	1985	4.00
❑ 1792	If I Only Knew Then (What I Know Now)/Eternally	1985	4.00
RED LABEL			
❑ 001-1	You're the One/ I Can Do Anything	1984	5.00
❑ 001-2	You're the Best/ (B-side unknown)	1984	5.00
❑ 001-3	Are You Through with My Heart/(B-side unknown)	1984	5.00
STAX			
❑ 1056	What Do The Lonely Do At Christmas?/Santa Claus Wants Some Lovin'	197?	6.00
—B-side by Albert King; reissue			
❑ 3200	Shouting Out Love/ Baby, I'm Through	1977	5.00
❑ 3205	Baby, I'm Through/ Any Way You Look at It	1978	5.00
❑ 3215	What Do the Lonely Do at Christmas/(Instrumental)	1978	5.00
TWIN STACKS			
❑ 126	Somebody New/Brushfire	1968	10.00
❑ 130	I Love You But I'll Leave You/ Brushfire	1968	10.00
VOLT			
❑ 4010	So I Can Love You/ Got to Be the Man	1969	8.00
❑ 4021	The Best Part of a Love Affair/ I Like It	1969	8.00
❑ 4031	Stealing Love/When Tomorrow Comes	1970	8.00
❑ 4045	Heart Association/The Touch of Your Lips	1970	8.00
❑ 4053	Black Christmas/(Instrumental)	1970	10.00
❑ 4054	You Make Me Want to Love You/What You See Is What You Get	1971	7.00
❑ 4062	If You Think It/Love Ain't Easy One-Sided	1971	7.00
❑ 4066	Show Me How/Boss Love Maker	1971	7.00
❑ 4077	My Honey and Me/Blind Alley	1972	7.00
❑ 4083	I Could Never Be Happy/ I've Fallen in Love	1972	7.00
❑ 4088	From Toys to Boys /I Call This Loving You	1972	7.00
❑ 4095	Runnin' Back (And Forth)/ I Wanna Come Back	1973	7.00
❑ 4100	Peace Be Still/Runnin' Back (And Forth)	1973	7.00
❑ 4104	What Do the Lonely Do at Christmas/(Instrumental)	1973	8.00
❑ 4106	Put a Little Love Away/ I Call This Loving You	1974	7.00
❑ 4110	Baby I'm Through/ I Wanna Come Back	1974	7.00
❑ 4113	Any Way You Look At It/There Are More Questions Than Answers	1974	7.00

Albums

Number	Title (A Side/B Side)	Yr	NM
ARC			
❑ JC 36149	Come Into Our World	1979	10.00
❑ FC 37456	New Affair	1981	10.00
COLUMBIA			
❑ PC 34163	Flowers	1976	10.00
—No bar code on cover			
❑ PC 34163	Flowers	198?	8.00
—With bar code on cover			
❑ PC 34762	Rejoice	1977	10.00
—No bar code on cover			
❑ PC 34762	Rejoice	198?	8.00
—With bar code on cover			
❑ JC 35385	Sunbeam	1978	10.00
MOTOWN			
❑ 6136 ML	If I Only Knew	1985	8.00
STAX			
❑ STX-4100	Sunshine	1977	10.00
❑ STX-4110	So I Can Love You	1978	10.00
—Reissue of Volt 6008			
❑ STX-4112	Untouched	1978	10.00
—Reissue of Volt 6015			
❑ STX-4121	Chronicle	1979	10.00
VOLT			
❑ VOS-6008	So I Can Love You	1971	25.00
❑ VOS-6015	Untouched	1972	25.00

E

EMOTIONS, THE (2) Brooklyn-based male vocal group.

45s

Number	Title (A Side/B Side)	Yr	NM
CALLA			
❑ 122	Baby I Need Your Lovin'/ She's My Baby (I Just Can't Let Her Go)	1966	15.00
KAPP			
❑ 490	Echo/Come Dance Baby	1962	25.00
❑ 513	L-O-V-E/A Million Reasons	1963	25.00
20TH FOX			
❑ 430	A Story Untold/One Life. One Love, One You	1963	20.00
❑ 452	Rainbow/Little Miss Blue	1963	20.00
❑ 478	Boomerang/I Love You Madly	1964	20.00
❑ 6623	Heart Strings/Every Time	1966	15.00

EMOTIONS, THE (U) It's unlikely than any of these are group (1). Some of these may be group (2). Others are different.

45s

Number	Title (A Side/B Side)	Yr	NM
BRAINSTORM			
❑ 125	Can't Stand No More Heartaches/You'd Better Get Used to It	1968	8.00
❑ 129	Never Let Me Go/I Can't Control These Emotions	1968	8.00
CARD			
❑ 600	(By the Light of the) Silvery Moon/Do You Love Me	1962	150.00
FLIP			
❑ 356	I Ran to You/Keep Lookin' Your Way	1961	30.00
FURY			
❑ 1010	Candlelight/It's Love	1958	40.00
KARATE			
❑ 506	Hey Baby/I Wonder	1964	20.00
LAURIE			
❑ 3167	Fool's Paradise/Starlit Night	1963	20.00
VARDAN			
❑ 201	Love of a Girl/Do This for Me	1965	20.00

EMPERORS, THE (1) Band from Harrisburg, Pa.

45s

Number	Title (A Side/B Side)	Yr	NM
BRUNSWICK			
❑ 55333	Karate Boogaloo/ Mumble Shing-a-Ling	1967	10.00
MALA			
❑ 543	Karate/I've Got to Have Her	1966	15.00
❑ 554	My Baby Likes to Boogaloo/You Got Me Where You Want Me	1967	12.00
❑ 561	Searchin'/Lookin' for My Baby	1967	12.00

EMPERORS, THE (2) Sometimes called "The Emperors with Rhythm."

45s

Number	Title (A Side/B Side)	Yr	NM
HAVEN			
❑ 511	I May Be Wrong/Come Back, Come Back	1954	4000.
—VG 2000; VG+ 3000			

EMPERORS, THE (3)

45s

Number	Title (A Side/B Side)	Yr	NM
OLIMPIC			
❑ 245	Darlin' in the Moonlight/ Steve Allen	1964	40.00

EMPERORS, THE (4)

45s

Number	Title (A Side/B Side)	Yr	NM
SABRA			
❑ 5555	I Want My Woman/ (B-side unknown)	196?	40.00

EMPIRES, THE (1) LES COOPER was a member of this group.

45s

Number	Title (A Side/B Side)	Yr	NM
AMP 3			
❑ 132	If I'm a Fool/Zippety Zip	1957	100.00
HARLEM			
❑ 2325	Corn Whiskey/My Baby, My Baby	1954	400.00
❑ 2333	Magic Mirror/Make Me or Break Me	1955	400.00
WHIRLIN' DISC			
❑ 104	Linda/Whispering Heart	1957	70.00
WING			
❑ 90023	I Want to Know/Shirley	1955	50.00
❑ 90050	By the Riverside/Tell Me Pretty Baby	1956	40.00
❑ 90080	Don't Touch My Gal/My First Discovery	1956	40.00

EMPIRES, THE (2)

45s

Number	Title (A Side/B Side)	Yr	NM
CALICO			
❑ 121	Definition of Love/Only in My Dreams	1960	20.00
CANDI			
❑ 1026	Love You So Bad/Come Back Girl	1962	25.00
❑ 1033	You're on Top, Girl/Slide On By	1963	40.00
CHAVIS			
❑ 1026	Love You So Bad/Come Back Girl	1962	15.00
COLPIX			
❑ 680	Everyone Knew But Me/Three Little Fishes	1963	20.00
DCP			
❑ 1116	Have Mercy/Love Is Strange	1964	12.00
LAKE			
❑ 711	Over the Summer Vacation/You're So Popular	1961	20.00

EMPIRES, THE (3) Featuring David Blatt, later known as JAY BLACK of JAY AND THE AMERICANS.

45s

Number	Title (A Side/B Side)	Yr	NM
EPIC			
❑ 5-9527	A Time and a Place/Punch Your Nose	1962	40.00

ENALOUISE AND THE HEARTS

45s

Number	Title (A Side/B Side)	Yr	NM
ARGYLE			
❑ 1635	From a Cap and a Gown/A Prisoner to You	1959	50.00

ENCHANTERS, THE (1)

45s

Number	Title (A Side/B Side)	Yr	NM
BALD EAGLE			
❑ 3001	Come On Baby, Let's Do the Stroll/Rock Around	1958	30.00
BAMBOO			
❑ 513	Touch of Love/Cafe Bohemian	1961	25.00
CANDELITE			
❑ 432	Oh Rose Marie/Bewildered	1964	12.00
EP-SOM			
❑ 103	I Need Your Love/Goddess of Love	1962	400.00
J.J. & M.			
❑ 1562	Oh Rose Marie/Bewildered	1962	200.00
MUSITRON			
❑ 1072	I Lied to My Heart/Talk While You Walk	1961	40.00
ORBIT			
❑ 532	Touch of Love/Cafe Bohemian	1959	50.00
SHARP			
❑ 105	We Make Mistakes/The Decision	1960	25.00
STARDUST			
❑ 102	Spellbound by the Moon/Know It All	1956	1500.

ENCHANTERS, THE (2) Also see GARNET MIMMS AND THE ENCHANTERS.

45s

Number	Title (A Side/B Side)	Yr	NM
LOMA			
❑ 2012	I Want to Be Loved/I Paid for the Party	1965	10.00
❑ 2035	You Were Meant to Be My Baby/God Bless the Girl, and Me	1966	10.00
❑ 2054	We Got Love/I've Lost All Communications	1966	10.00
WARNER BROS.			
❑ 5460	I Wanna Thank You/I'm a Good Man	1964	15.00

ENCHANTERS, THE (3)

45s

Number	Title (A Side/B Side)	Yr	NM
CORAL			
❑ 61756	True Love Gone/Wait a Minute Baby	1956	60.00
❑ 61832	There Goes (A Pretty Girl)/Fan Me Baby	1957	25.00
	—Edited version of A-side; matrix number is "102,966"		
❑ 61832	There Goes (A Pretty Girl)/Fan Me Baby	1957	80.00
	—Full-length version of A-side; matrix number is "100,974"		
❑ 61916	Mambo Santa Mambo/Bottle Up and Go	1957	40.00
❑ 62373	True Love Gone/The Day	1963	20.00
❑ 65610	True Love Gone/Today Is Your Birthday	1963	12.00
MERCER			
❑ 992	True Love Gone/Wait a Minute Baby	1956	2000.

ENCHANTERS, THE (4)

45s

Number	Title (A Side/B Side)	Yr	NM
JUBILEE			
❑ 5072	Today Is Your Birthday/How Could You	1952	250.00
❑ 5080	I've Lost/Housewife Blues	1952	200.00

ENCHANTERS, THE (U) May be group (1); may be a fifth different group also.

45s

Number	Title (A Side/B Side)	Yr	NM
TOM TOM			
❑ 301	Surf Blast/Tom Tiki	1963	50.00

ENCHANTMENTS, THE

45s

Number	Title (A Side/B Side)	Yr	NM
FARO			
❑ 620	I'm in Love with Your Daughter/(B-side unknown)	1964	100.00
GONE			
❑ 5130	(I Love You) Sherry/Come On Home	1962	30.00
RITZ			
❑ 17003	I Love You Baby/Pains in My Heart	1963	100.00

ENCHORDS, THE

45s

Number	Title (A Side/B Side)	Yr	NM
LAURIE			
❑ 3089	Zoom Zoom Zoom/I Need You Baby	1961	50.00

ENCORES, THE More than one group.

45s

Number	Title (A Side/B Side)	Yr	NM
BOW			
❑ 302	Barbara/Thank You	1958	100.00
CHECKER			
❑ 760	When I Look at You/Young Girls, Young Girls	1952	4000.
	—VG 2000; VG+ 3000		
HOLLYWOOD			
❑ 1034	Time Is Moving On/Ha-Chi-Bi-Ri-Bi-Ri	1955	80.00
LOOK			
❑ 105	Time Is Moving On/Ha-Chi-Bi-Ri-Bi-Ri	1955	400.00
MGM			
❑ 11947	Chloe/Wa Va Ga Dot	1955	12.00

ENCOUNTERS, THE

45s

Number	Title (A Side/B Side)	Yr	NM
LOST-NITE			
❑ 235	Don't Stop Now/Place in Your Heart	196?	5.00
	—Reissue		
SWAN			
❑ 4206	Don't Stop Now/Place in Your Heart	1964	150.00

END, THE

45s

Number	Title (A Side/B Side)	Yr	NM
LONDON			
❑ 1016	Shades of Orange/Loving, Sacred Loving	1968	20.00
PHILIPS			
❑ 40323	Hey Little Girl/I Can't Get Any Joy	1965	10.00

Albums

Number	Title (A Side/B Side)	Yr	NM
LONDON			
❑ PS 560	Introspection	1969	50.00

ENDEAVORS, THE (1)

45s

Number	Title (A Side/B Side)	Yr	NM
J&S			
❑ 254	Suffering with My Heart/I Got the Feeling	1960	1200.

ENDEAVORS, THE (2) Country group.

45s

Number	Title (A Side/B Side)	Yr	NM
STOP			
❑ 372	Shattered Dreams/I Know You Don't Want Me	1971	10.00

ENDORSERS, THE

45s

Number	Title (A Side/B Side)	Yr	NM
MOON			
❑ 109	Crying/Hold My Hand	1959	2000.

ENEMYS, THE With Cory Wells, later of THREE DOG NIGHT.

45s

Number	Title (A Side/B Side)	Yr	NM
MGM			
❑ 13485	Glitter and Gold/Too Much Monkey Business	1966	15.00
❑ 13525	Hey Joe/My Dues Have Been Paid	1966	15.00
❑ 13573	Mo-Jo Woman/My Dues Have Been Paid	1966	15.00
VALIANT			
❑ 714	Say Goodbye to Donna/Sinner Man	1965	25.00
	—As "Corey Wells and the Enemys"		

ENGEL, SCOTT Also see THE WALKER BROTHERS.

45s

Number	Title (A Side/B Side)	Yr	NM
CHALLENGE			
❑ 9206	Devil Surfer/Your Guess	1963	20.00
LIBERTY			
❑ 55312	Mr. Jones/Anything Will Do	1961	20.00
❑ 55428	Anything Will Do/Forever More	1962	20.00
MARTAY			
❑ 2004	Devil Surfer/Your Guess	1963	40.00
ORBIT			
❑ 506	The Livin' End/Good for Nothin'	1958	20.00
❑ 506 [PS]	The Livin' End/Good for Nothin'	1958	50.00
❑ 511	Charley Bop/All I Do Is Dream	1958	30.00
❑ 511 [PS]	Charley Bop/All I Do Is Dream	1958	60.00
❑ 512	Blue Bell/Paper Doll	1958	20.00
❑ 512 [PS]	Blue Bell/Paper Doll	1958	50.00
❑ 537	The Golden Rule/Sunday	1959	20.00
❑ 537 [PS]	The Golden Rule/Sunday	1959	50.00
❑ 545	Comin' Home/I Don't Wanna Know	1959	20.00
RKO UNIQUE			
❑ 386	Steady As a Rock/When Is a Boy a Man	1957	25.00

ENGEL, SCOTT, AND JOHN STEWART
See THE WALKER BROTHERS.

ENGLAND, BENNY

45s

Number	Title (A Side/B Side)	Yr	NM
SNAP			
❑ 400	Eloping/Some How	1958	300.00

ENGLER, JERRY, AND THE FOUR EKKOS

45s

Number	Title (A Side/B Side)	Yr	NM
BRUNSWICK			
❑ 55037	Sputnik (Satellite Girl)/Unfaithful One	1957	80.00
	—BUDDY HOLLY appears on this record		

ENGLISH, BARBARA Also includes records as "Barbara Jean English." Also see THE FASHIONS (1).

45s

Number	Title (A Side/B Side)	Yr	NM
ALITHIA			
❑ 6040	I'm Living a Lie/All This	1972	6.00
❑ 6041	So Many Ways to Die/(B-side unknown)	1972	6.00
❑ 6042	I'm Sorry/Lil' Baby	1972	6.00
❑ 6046	Baby I'm-a Want You/Don't Make Me Over	1973	6.00
❑ 6053	You're Gonna Need Somebody to Love (While You're Looking for Someone to Love)/All This	1973	6.00
❑ 6059	Comin' or Goin'/Love's Arrangement	1973	6.00
❑ 6064	Breakin' Up a Happy Home/Guess Who	1974	6.00

Except when noted otherwise, VG = 25% of NM, and VG+ = 50% of NM. (Example: VG = $2.00, VG+ = $4.00 and NM = $8.00.)

Number	Title (A Side/B Side)	Yr	NM
AURORA			
❑ 155	Standin' on Tip-Toe/(You Got Me) Sittin' in the Corner	1965	80.00
MALA			
❑ 488	Easy Come, Easy Go/I Don't Deserve a Boy Like You	1964	25.00
REPRISE			
❑ 0290	I've Gotta Date/Shoo Fly	1964	25.00
❑ 0349	Small Town Girl/Tell It Like It Is	1965	25.00
ROULETTE			
❑ 4428	We Need Them/ La-Ta-Tee-Ta-Ta	1962	30.00
❑ 4450	Fever/Bad News	1962	30.00
WARNER BROS.			
❑ 5685	All Because I Love Somebody/ All the Good Times Are Gone	1965	20.00

ENGLISH, SCOTT

Number	Title (A Side/B Side)	Yr	NM
45s			
DOT			
❑ 16099	White Cliffs of Dover/ 4000 Miles Away	1960	30.00
JANUS			
❑ 171	Brandy/Lead Me Back	1971	12.00
—A-side later recorded by Barry Manilow as "Mandy"			
❑ 192	Woman in My Life/ Ballad of the Unloved	1972	5.00
JOKER			
❑ 777	Ugly Pills (You're Takin')/When	1962	50.00
SPOKANE			
❑ 4003	High on a Hill/When	1964	25.00
❑ 4007	Here Comes the Pain/All I Want Is You	1964	40.00
SULTAN			
❑ 1003	High on a Hill/When	1963	50.00

ENGLISH CONGREGATION, THE

Number	Title (A Side/B Side)	Yr	NM
45s			
ATCO			
❑ 6865	Softly Whispering I Love You/ When Susie Takes the Plane	1972	6.00
SIGNPOST			
❑ 70002	Lovers of the World Unite/Love is the Sweetest Thing I Know	1972	6.00
❑ 70004	If I Could Have My Way/Jesahel	1972	6.00
Albums			
SIGNPOST			
❑ SP 7217	Softly Whispering I Love You	1972	12.00
❑ SP 8405	Jesahel	1972	12.00

ENGLISH MUFFINS, THE (1) For the girl group, see THE THREE PENNIES.

ENGLISH MUFFINS, THE (2) Male psychedelic group.

Number	Title (A Side/B Side)	Yr	NM
45s			
GAMA			
❑ 702	Leave or Stay/It's My Pride	1967	40.00

ENJOYABLES, THE

Number	Title (A Side/B Side)	Yr	NM
45s			
CAPITOL			
❑ 5321	Push a Little Harder/We'll Make Our Way	1964	30.00
SHRINE			
❑ 118	Shame/I'll Take You Back	1966	600.00

ENO, BRIAN Also see ROXY MUSIC.

Number	Title (A Side/B Side)	Yr	NM
12-Inch Singles			
OPAL			
❑ 40539	Fractal Zoom (6 versions)/ The Roll, The Choke	1992	8.00
45s			
ISLAND			
❑ 036	The Lion Sleeps Tonight/ I'll Come Running (To Tie Your Shoes)	1975	25.00
❑ 036 [DJ]	The Lion Sleeps Tonight (mono/stereo)	1975	15.00
Albums			
ANTILLES			
❑ AN-7001	No Pussyfooting	1973	15.00
—By Robert Fripp and Eno			
❑ AN-7018	Evening Star	1975	12.00
—By Robert Fripp and Eno			
❑ AN-7030	Discreet Music	1975	12.00
❑ AN-7070	Music for Films	1978	15.00
EDITIONS EG			
❑ ENO-1	Here Come the Warm Jets	1982	10.00
—Reissue			
❑ EGBS-2 [(11)]	Working Backwards: 1983-1973	1984	100.00
—Boxed set of nine albums plus Music For Films II and Rarities 12"			
❑ ENO-2	Taking Tiger Mountain (By Strategy)	1982	10.00
—Reissue			
❑ ENO-3	Another Green World	1982	10.00
—Reissue			
❑ ENO-4	Before and After Science	1982	10.00
—Reissue			
❑ ENO-5	Apollo: Atmospheres and Soundtracks	1983	10.00
❑ EGED-20	Ambient 4 — On Land	1982	10.00
❑ EGED-37	The Pearl	1984	12.00
—By Harold Budd and Brian Eno			
❑ EGS-102	No Pussyfooting	1982	10.00
—By Robert Fripp and Eno; reissue			
❑ EGS-103	Evening Star	1982	10.00
—By Robert Fripp and Eno; reissue			
❑ EGS-105	Music for Films	1982	10.00
—Reissue			
❑ EGS-107	Fourth World Vol. 1: Possible Musics	1980	12.00
—With Jon Hassell			
❑ EGS-201	Ambient #1 — Music for Airports	1982	12.00
—Reissue			
❑ EGS-202	Ambient 2 — The Plateaux of Mirrors	1982	12.00
—By Harold Budd and Brian Eno			
❑ EGS-301	Pavilion of Dreams	1982	12.00
—By Harold Budd and Brian Eno			
❑ EGS-303	Discreet Music	1983	12.00
—Reissue			
ISLAND			
❑ ILPS 9268	Here Come the Warm Jets	1973	18.00
❑ ILPS 9309	Taking Tiger Mountain (By Strategy)	1974	18.00
❑ ILPS 9351	Another Green World	1975	18.00
❑ ILPS 9478	Before and After Science	1977	18.00
—Double the value if four lithographs are included with the package.			
JEM			
❑ ENO DJ [DJ]	Music for Airplay	1981	50.00
—Promo-only 10-track sampler			
OPAL/WARNER BROS.			
❑ 25769	Music for Films, Vol. III	1988	10.00
❑ 26421	Wrong Way Up	1990	10.00
—With John Cale			
PVC			
❑ 7908	Ambient #1 — Music for Airports	1979	12.00

John Entwistle, *John Entwistle's Rigor Mortis Sets In,* Track MCA-321, 1973, **$15.**

ENTWISTLE, JOHN Also see THE WHO.

Number	Title (A Side/B Side)	Yr	NM
45s			
ATCO			
❑ 7337	Too Late the Hero/ Dancin' Master	1981	4.00
❑ 7344	Talk Dirty/Try Me	1982	4.00
DECCA			
❑ 32896	I Believe in Everything/My Size	1971	6.00
❑ 33052	I Wonder/Who Cares	1973	6.00
TRACK			
❑ 40066	Made in Japan/Roller Skate Kate	1973	5.00
Albums			
ATCO			
❑ SD 38-142	Too Late the Hero	1981	10.00
DECCA			
❑ DL 79183	Smash Your Head Against the Wall	1971	25.00
MCA			
❑ 2024	Smash Your Head Against the Wall	1973	12.00
—Reissue of Decca 79183			
TRACK			
❑ MCA-321	Rigor Mortis Sets In	1973	15.00
❑ L33-1926 [DJ]	Who's Ox	1975	50.00
—Promo-only sampler			
❑ MCA-2129	Mad Dog	1975	15.00
❑ DL 79190	Whistle Rymes	1972	25.00

Except when noted otherwise, VG = 25% of NM, and VG+ = 50% of NM. (Example: VG = $2.00, VG+ = $4.00 and NM = $8.00.)

E

Number	Title (A Side/B Side)	Yr	NM

ENYA

12-Inch Singles

GEFFEN

Number	Title (A Side/B Side)	Yr	NM
❑ 21129	Orinoco Flow (Sail Away)/Smaoitim/Out of the Blue	1988	10.00

45s

GEFFEN

Number	Title (A Side/B Side)	Yr	NM
❑ 27633	Orinoco Flow (Sail Away)/Out of the Blue	1988	3.00
❑ 27633 [PS]	Orinoco Flow (Sail Away)/Out of the Blue	1988	3.00

REPRISE

Number	Title (A Side/B Side)	Yr	NM
❑ 7-16719	Only Time/May It Be	2001	3.00
❑ 7-17266	Only If.../Oiche Chiun (Silent Night)	1997	3.00

Albums

GEFFEN

Number	Title (A Side/B Side)	Yr	NM
❑ GHS 24233	Watermark	1988	15.00

EPIC SPLENDOR, THE

45s

HOT BISCUIT

Number	Title (A Side/B Side)	Yr	NM
❑ 1450	A Little Rain Must Fall/Cowboys and Indians	1967	8.00
❑ 1452	It Could Be Wonderful/She's High on Life	1968	8.00
❑ 1452 [PS]	It Could Be Wonderful/She's High on Life	1968	20.00

EPISODE SIX

45s

CHAPTER ONE

Number	Title (A Side/B Side)	Yr	NM
❑ 2902	Lucky Sunday/Mr. Universe	1968	12.00

COMPASS

Number	Title (A Side/B Side)	Yr	NM
❑ 7007	Morning Dew/Sunshine Girl	1967	15.00

ELEKTRA

Number	Title (A Side/B Side)	Yr	NM
❑ 45617	Baby, Baby, Baby/Love-Hate-Revenge	1967	15.00

WARNER BROS.

Number	Title (A Side/B Side)	Yr	NM
❑ 5851	Here, There and Everywhere/Mighty Morris Ten	1966	15.00

EPISODES, THE

45s

FOUR SEASONS

Number	Title (A Side/B Side)	Yr	NM
❑ 1014	The Christmas Tree/Where Is My Love	1965	150.00

EPPS, PRESTON

45s

ADMIRAL

Number	Title (A Side/B Side)	Yr	NM
❑ 901	Bongo Express/Flamenco Bongo	1963	15.00

DONNA

Number	Title (A Side/B Side)	Yr	NM
❑ 1367	Mister Bongo/B'Wana Bongo	1962	15.00

EMBASSY

Number	Title (A Side/B Side)	Yr	NM
❑ 203	Rockin' in the Congo/Sing Donna Go	1961	15.00

JO JO

Number	Title (A Side/B Side)	Yr	NM
❑ 106	Afro Mania/Love Is the Only Good Thing	1969	6.00

MAJESTY

Number	Title (A Side/B Side)	Yr	NM
❑ 1300	Bongo Boogie/Flamenco Bongo	1962	15.00

ORIGINAL SOUND

Number	Title (A Side/B Side)	Yr	NM
❑ 4 [M]	Bongo Rock/Bongo Party	1959	20.00
❑ 4 [S]	Bongo Rock/Bongo Party	1959	50.00
❑ 9	Bongo, Bongo, Bongo/Hully Gully Bongo	1960	20.00
❑ 14	Bongo Shuffle/Bongo in the Congo	1960	15.00
❑ 17	Bongo Rocket/Jungle Drums	1961	15.00

POLO

Number	Title (A Side/B Side)	Yr	NM
❑ 218	Bongo Rock 1965/Bongo Waltz	1965	12.00

TOP RANK

Number	Title (A Side/B Side)	Yr	NM
❑ 2067	Blue Bongo/Bongola	1960	15.00
❑ 2091	Bongo Hop/Caravan	1960	15.00

7-Inch Extended Plays

ORIGINAL SOUND

Number	Title (A Side/B Side)	Yr	NM
❑ EP 1001	Bongo Rock/Doin' the Cha Cha Cha//Bongos in Pastel/Bongo Party	1959	40.00
❑ EP 1001 [PS]	Bongo Rock	1959	40.00

Albums

ORIGINAL SOUND

Number	Title (A Side/B Side)	Yr	NM
❑ LPM-5002 [M]	Bongo, Bongo, Bongo	1960	50.00
❑ LPM-5009 [M]	Surfin' Bongos	1963	40.00
❑ LPS-8851 [S]	Bongo, Bongo, Bongo	1960	80.00
❑ LPS-8872 [S]	Surfin' Bongos	1963	50.00

TOP RANK

Number	Title (A Side/B Side)	Yr	NM
❑ RM-349 [M]	Bongola	1961	40.00
❑ RS-349 [S]	Bongola	1961	50.00

EPSILONS, THE

The Stax record may not be the same group as the others.

45s

HEM

Number	Title (A Side/B Side)	Yr	NM
❑ 1003	Mind in a Bind/It's All Right	196?	150.00

SHRINE

Number	Title (A Side/B Side)	Yr	NM
❑ 106	Mad at the World/I'm So Devoted	1966	250.00

STAX

Number	Title (A Side/B Side)	Yr	NM
❑ 0021	The Echo/Really Rockin'	1969	60.00

EQUADORS, THE

45s

ARGO

Number	Title (A Side/B Side)	Yr	NM
❑ 5353	Say You'll Be Mine/Let Me Sleep, Woman	1959	60.00

MIRACLE

Number	Title (A Side/B Side)	Yr	NM
❑ 7	You're My Desire/Someone to Call My Own	1961	150.00

EQUALLOS, THE

45s

M&M

Number	Title (A Side/B Side)	Yr	NM
❑ 1296	Beneath the Sun/In Between Tears	1962	1500.

EQUALS, THE

45s

BANG

Number	Title (A Side/B Side)	Yr	NM
❑ 582	Ain't Got Nothing to Give You/Black Skin, Blue Eyed Boys	1971	10.00

PRESIDENT

Number	Title (A Side/B Side)	Yr	NM
❑ 103	Fire/I Won't Be There	1967	12.00
❑ 105	My Life Ain't Easy/You Got Too Many Boyfriends	1967	12.00
❑ 108	Giddy Up a Ding-Dong/I Get So Excited	1968	12.00
❑ 109	Lovely Rita/Softly, Softly	1968	12.00
❑ 110	Honey Gun/Michael and the Slipper Tree	1968	12.00
❑ 111	I Can't Let You Go/Viva Bobby Joe	1969	12.00

RCA VICTOR

Number	Title (A Side/B Side)	Yr	NM
❑ 47-9186	Baby Come Back/Hold Me Closer	1967	15.00
❑ 47-9583	Baby Come Back/Hold Me Closer	1968	10.00

SHOUT

Number	Title (A Side/B Side)	Yr	NM
❑ 247	Ain't Got Nothing to Give You/Black Skin, Blue Eyed Boys	1970	12.00

Albums

LAURIE

Number	Title (A Side/B Side)	Yr	NM
❑ LLP-2045 [M]	Unequalled	1967	25.00
❑ SLP-2045 [S]	Unequalled	1967	30.00

PRESIDENT

Number	Title (A Side/B Side)	Yr	NM
❑ PTL-1015	Equal Sensation	1968	25.00
❑ PTL-1020	The Sensational Equals	1968	25.00
❑ PTL-1025	Equals Supreme	1968	25.00
❑ PTL-1030	Strikeback	1969	25.00

RCA VICTOR

Number	Title (A Side/B Side)	Yr	NM
❑ LSP-4078	Baby Come Back	1968	25.00

EQUIPE 84

45s

IMPERIAL

Number	Title (A Side/B Side)	Yr	NM
❑ 66266	The Twenty-Ninth of September/Auschwitz	1967	20.00

ERICA

Albums

ESP-DISK'

Number	Title (A Side/B Side)	Yr	NM
❑ 1099	You Used to Think	1968	200.00

ERLENE AND HER GIRLFRIENDS

45s

OLD TOWN

Number	Title (A Side/B Side)	Yr	NM
❑ 1150	A Guy Is a Guy/My Dada Say	1963	20.00
❑ 1152	Because of You/Casanova	1963	20.00

ERMINES, THE

See CORNEL GUNTER.

ERNIE

See JIM HENSON.

ERNIE AND EDDIE

See EDDIE AND ERNIE.

ERNIE AND THE EMPERORS

45s

REPRISE

Number	Title (A Side/B Side)	Yr	NM
❑ 0414	Got a Lot I Want to Say/Meet Me at the Corner	1965	30.00

ERVIN, SENATOR SAM

45s

COLUMBIA

Number	Title (A Side/B Side)	Yr	NM
❑ 4-45956	Bridge Over Troubled Water/Zeke and the Snake	1973	6.00

Albums

COLUMBIA

Number	Title (A Side/B Side)	Yr	NM
❑ KC 32756	Senator Sam at Home	1973	25.00

ERVIN SISTERS, THE

45s

TRI PHI

Number	Title (A Side/B Side)	Yr	NM
❑ 1014	Changing Baby/Do It Right	1962	60.00
❑ 1022	Every Day's a Holiday/Why I Love Him	1963	80.00

ERWIN, DEE

See BIG DEE IRWIN.

ESCORTS, THE (1)

Group from Rahway State Prison in New Jersey.

45s

ALITHIA

Number	Title (A Side/B Side)	Yr	NM
❑ 6048	All We Need (Is Another Chance) (Short)/All We Need (Is Another Chance) (Long)	1973	6.00
❑ 6052	Look Over Your Shoulder/By the Time I Get to Phoenix	1973	5.00
❑ 6055	I'll Be Sweeter Tomorrow/I'm So Glad I Found You	1973	5.00
❑ 6062	Disrespect Can Wreck/All We Need	1974	5.00
❑ 6066	Let's Make Love (At Home Sometime)/Within Without	1974	5.00

Albums

ALITHIA

Number	Title (A Side/B Side)	Yr	NM
❑ 9104	All We Need Is One More Chance	1973	15.00
❑ 9106	Three Down and Four to Go	1974	15.00

ESCORTS, THE (2)

45s

CORAL

Number	Title (A Side/B Side)	Yr	NM
❑ 62302	Gloria/Seven Wonders of the World	1961	40.00
❑ 62317	As I Love You/Gaudeamus	1962	40.00
❑ 62336	Somewhere/Submarine Race Watching	1962	25.00
❑ 62349	One Hand, One Heart/I Can't Be Free	1963	25.00
❑ 62372	Back Home Again/Something Has Changed Him	1963	25.00
—As "Goldie and the Escorts"			
❑ 62385	Give Me Tomorrow/My Heart Cries for You	1963	25.00

ESCORTS, THE (3)

British group.

45s

FONTANA

Number	Title (A Side/B Side)	Yr	NM
❑ 1512	Come On Home Baby/She Gets No Loving	1965	15.00
❑ 1912	Dizzy Miss Lizzy/All I Want Is You	1964	15.00

ESCORTS, THE (4)

Albums

TEO

Number	Title (A Side/B Side)	Yr	NM
❑ LPM-5000 [M]	The Escorts Bring Down the House	1966	200.00

ESCORTS, THE (U)

None of these are group (1) or (3). Some could be group (2) or (4). More likely, they are more than one other group.

45s

BOOMERANG

Number	Title (A Side/B Side)	Yr	NM
❑ 621	Little Big Horn/Wiped Out	1962	40.00

JUDD

Number	Title (A Side/B Side)	Yr	NM
❑ 1014	My First Year/Clap Happy	1959	15.00

RCA VICTOR

Number	Title (A Side/B Side)	Yr	NM
❑ 47-6834	Bad Boy/Tore Up Over You	1957	15.00
❑ 47-6963	So Hard to Laugh, So Easy to Cry/Lonely Man	1957	15.00
❑ 47-8228	You Can't Even Be My Friend/Itchy Coo	1963	12.00

Except when noted otherwise, VG = 25% of NM, and VG+ = 50% of NM. (Example: VG = $2.00, VG+ = $4.00 and NM = $8.00.)

Number	Title (A Side/B Side)	Yr	NM
❑ 47-8327	The Hurt/No City Folks Allowed	1964	12.00

SCARLET

Number	Title (A Side/B Side)	Yr	NM
❑ 4005	I Will Be Home Again/Leaky Heart and His Red Go-Kart	1960	60.00

SCEPTER

Number	Title (A Side/B Side)	Yr	NM
❑ 1201	Why Why Why/Ugly Duckling	1958	40.00
—With Don Crawford			

SOMA

Number	Title (A Side/B Side)	Yr	NM
❑ 1144	Main Drag/Judy or Jo Ann	1961	25.00

ESQUERITA

45s

CAPITOL

Number	Title (A Side/B Side)	Yr	NM
❑ F4007	Please Come On Home/Oh Baby	1958	30.00
❑ F4058	Rockin' the Joint/Esquerita and the Voola	1958	30.00
❑ F4145	Laid Off/Just Another Lie	1959	30.00

Albums

CAPITOL

Number	Title (A Side/B Side)	Yr	NM
❑ T 1186 [M]	Esquerita	1959	1000.

ESQUIRE BOYS, THE

45s

DOT

Number	Title (A Side/B Side)	Yr	NM
❑ 15380	Guitar Mambo/Dark Eyes	1955	20.00
❑ 15433	Dance with a Rock/ At the Balalaika	1955	20.00

FRANSIL

Number	Title (A Side/B Side)	Yr	NM
❑ 11	Caravan/Pretty Dark Eyes	196?	20.00
❑ 15	Summertime/Sorrento Cha Cha	1961	15.00

GUYDEN

Number	Title (A Side/B Side)	Yr	NM
❑ 601	St. Louis Blues Walk/ Bobbysox Jamboree	195?	25.00
❑ 705	Rock-a-Beatin' Boogie/ St. Louis Blues	1954	25.00

MEDIA

Number	Title (A Side/B Side)	Yr	NM
❑ 1004	Play Me Boogie/Bye Bye Blues	1955	20.00

RAINBOW

Number	Title (A Side/B Side)	Yr	NM
❑ 178	Forgetting You/I Don't Want Everything	1952	20.00
—Black vinyl			
❑ 178	Forgetting You/I Don't Want Everything	1952	30.00
—Red vinyl			
❑ 188	Caravan/We Drifted Apart	1952	20.00
—Black vinyl			
❑ 188	Caravan/We Drifted Apart	1952	30.00
—Red vinyl			
❑ 200	Rock-a-Beatin' Boogie/If It's Love You Want to Borrow	1953	20.00

20TH FOX

Number	Title (A Side/B Side)	Yr	NM
❑ 110	Taboo/Have You Got Good Religion	1958	20.00

ESQUIRES, THE (1)

Milwaukee-based R&B group. Records on Argo, Columbia, Dot, Durco, Epic, Hi-Po and Tower appear to be by other groups with the same name, thus are outside the scope of this book.

45s

BUNKY

Number	Title (A Side/B Side)	Yr	NM
❑ 7750	Get On Up/Listen to Me	1967	10.00
❑ 7752	And Get Away/Everybody's Laughin'	1967	10.00
❑ 7753	You Say/State Fair	1968	10.00
❑ 7755	Why Can't I Stop/The Feeling's Gone	1968	10.00
❑ 7756	How Could It Be/I Know I Can	1968	10.00

CAPITOL

Number	Title (A Side/B Side)	Yr	NM
❑ 2650	Reach Out/Listen to Me	1969	8.00

CIGAR MAN

Number	Title (A Side/B Side)	Yr	NM
❑ 79880	The Show Ain't Over/ What Good Is Music?	1980	6.00

JU-PAR

Number	Title (A Side/B Side)	Yr	NM
❑ 104	Get On Up '76/Feeling's Gone (Also Known As Disco Dancing)	1976	6.00

LAMARR

Number	Title (A Side/B Side)	Yr	NM
❑ 1001	Girls in the City/Ain't Gonna Give It Up	1971	8.00

SCEPTER

Number	Title (A Side/B Side)	Yr	NM
❑ 12232	You've Got the Power/ No Doubt About It	1968	—
—Unreleased? (Possibly reassigned to Wand?)			

WAND

Number	Title (A Side/B Side)	Yr	NM
❑ 1193	You've Got the Power/ No Doubt About It	1968	8.00
❑ 1195	I Don't Know/Part Angel	1969	8.00
❑ 11201	Whip It On Me/It Was Yesterday	1969	8.00

Albums

BUNKY

Number	Title (A Side/B Side)	Yr	NM
❑ 300	Get On Up and Get Away	1968	35.00

ESQUIRES, THE (2)

45s

ARGO

Number	Title (A Side/B Side)	Yr	NM
❑ 5435	Boat of Love/With a Feeling	1963	20.00

ESQUIRES, THE (3)

45s

EPIC

Number	Title (A Side/B Side)	Yr	NM
❑ 5-9024	If You Only Knew What a Three-Cent Stamp Can Do/ Now, Now, Now	1954	1500.
—This does exist on 45			

HI-PO

Number	Title (A Side/B Side)	Yr	NM
❑ 1003	Only the Angels Know/ One Word for This	1955	2000.

ESQUIRES, THE (U)

None of these are groups (1) or (3), but they may not all be the same group, either.

45s

COLUMBIA

Number	Title (A Side/B Side)	Yr	NM
❑ 4-43815	It's a Dirty Shame/Love Hides a Multitude of Sins	1966	20.00

DOT

Number	Title (A Side/B Side)	Yr	NM
❑ 16954	Misfortune/She's My Woman	1966	15.00

DURCO

Number	Title (A Side/B Side)	Yr	NM
❑ 1001	Flashin' Red/What a Burn	1964	40.00

TOWER

Number	Title (A Side/B Side)	Yr	NM
❑ 174	Love's Made a Fool of You/ Summertime	1965	15.00

ESQUIVEL

45s

RCA VICTOR

Number	Title (A Side/B Side)	Yr	NM
❑ 47-5969	Beasme Mucho/Vereda Tropical	1954	20.00
—As "Juan Garcia Esquivel"			
❑ 47-6008	Nocturnal/Amor	1955	20.00
❑ 47-6496	Nightingale/Jungle Drums	1956	15.00
❑ 47-6514	Port Au Prince/To Love Again	1956	15.00
❑ 47-7316	That Old Black Magic/ Cielito Lindo	1958	15.00
❑ 47-7360	It Had to Be You/ Begin the Beguine	1958	15.00
❑ 47-7361	Night and Day/Ballerina	1958	15.00
❑ 47-7462	I Feel Merely Marvelous/ Whatchamacallit	1959	15.00

Albums

BAR NONE

Number	Title (A Side/B Side)	Yr	NM
❑ LP-043	Space Age Bachelor Pad Music	1994	12.00
❑ LP-056	Music for a Sparkling Planet	1995	12.00

RCA VICTOR

Number	Title (A Side/B Side)	Yr	NM
❑ LPM-1345 [M]	To Love Again	1957	50.00
❑ LPM-1749 [M]	Four Corners of the World	1958	25.00
❑ LSP-1749 [S]	Four Corners of the World	1958	50.00
❑ LPM-1753 [M]	Other Worlds, Other Sounds	1959	25.00
❑ LSP-1753 [S]	Other Worlds, Other Sounds	1959	50.00
❑ LPM-1978 [M]	Exploring New Sounds in Hi-Fi	1959	30.00
❑ LSP-1978 [S]	Exploring New Sounds in Hi-Fi	1959	60.00
❑ LPM-1988 [M]	Strings Aflame	1959	25.00
❑ LSP-1988 [S]	Strings Aflame	1959	50.00
❑ LPM-2225 [M]	Infinity in Sound	1960	30.00
❑ LSP-2225 [S]	Infinity in Sound	1960	60.00
❑ LPM-2296 [M]	Infinity in Sound, Vol. 2	1961	30.00
❑ LSP-2296 [S]	Infinity in Sound, Vol. 2	1961	60.00
❑ LPM-2418 [M]	Latin-esque	1962	20.00
❑ LSP-2418 [S]	Latin-esque	1962	40.00
—Standard cover			
❑ LSP-2418 [S]	Latin-esque	1962	60.00
—Die-cut cover that reveals inner sleeve			
❑ LPM-3502 [M]	The Best of Esquivel	1966	20.00
❑ LSP-3502 [S]	The Best of Esquivel	1966	30.00
❑ LPM-3697 [M]	The Genius of Esquivel	1967	20.00
❑ LSP-3697 [S]	The Genius of Esquivel	1967	30.00

REPRISE

Number	Title (A Side/B Side)	Yr	NM
❑ P9-6046 [S]	More of Other World, Other Sounds	1962	30.00
❑ R-6046 [M]	More of Other World, Other Sounds	1962	25.00

ESSEX, DAVID

45s

COLUMBIA

Number	Title (A Side/B Side)	Yr	NM
❑ 10005	America/Dance Little Girl	1974	5.00
❑ 10005 [PS]	America/Dance Little Girl	1974	8.00
❑ 10039	Gonna Make You a Star/Window	1974	5.00
❑ 10183	Rolling Stone/Coconut Ice	1975	5.00
❑ 10183 [PS]	Rolling Stone/Coconut Ice	1975	8.00
❑ 10256	Good Ol' Rock 'N' Roll/ Hold Me Close	1975	5.00
❑ 45940	Rock On/On and On	1973	5.00
❑ 45940 [PS]	Rock On/On and On	1973	10.00
❑ 46041	Lamplight/We're All Insane	1974	5.00
❑ 46041 [PS]	Lamplight/We're All Insane	1974	10.00

RSO

Number	Title (A Side/B Side)	Yr	NM
❑ 1006	Oh What a Circus (From Evita)/ Ships That Pass in the Night	1979	4.00

UNI

Number	Title (A Side/B Side)	Yr	NM
❑ 55020	She's Leaving Home/He's a Better Man Than Me	1967	10.00

Albums

COLUMBIA

Number	Title (A Side/B Side)	Yr	NM
❑ CQ 32560 [Q]	Rock On	1974	30.00
❑ KC 32560	Rock On	1974	20.00
❑ KC 33289	David Essex	1974	15.00
❑ PC 33813	All the Fun of the Fair	1975	15.00

MERCURY

Number	Title (A Side/B Side)	Yr	NM
❑ 812936-1	David Essex	1983	15.00

ESSEX, THE

Also see ANITA HUMES.

45s

BANG

Number	Title (A Side/B Side)	Yr	NM
❑ 537	The Eagle/Moonlight, Music, and You	1966	8.00

ROULETTE

Number	Title (A Side/B Side)	Yr	NM
❑ 4494	Easier Said Than Done/ Are You Going My Way	1963	15.00
❑ 4515	A Walkin' Miracle/What I Don't Know Won't Hurt Me	1963	15.00
❑ 4530	She's Got Everything/Out of Sight, Out of Mind	1964	10.00
❑ 4542	What Did I Do/Curfew Lover	1964	10.00

Albums

ROULETTE

Number	Title (A Side/B Side)	Yr	NM
❑ R-25234 [M]	Easier Said Than Done	1963	40.00
❑ SR-25234 [S]	Easier Said Than Done	1963	50.00
❑ R-25235 [M]	A Walkin' Miracle	1963	40.00
❑ SR-25235 [S]	A Walkin' Miracle	1963	50.00
❑ R-25246 [M]	Young and Lively	1964	40.00
❑ SR-25246 [S]	Young and Lively	1964	50.00

ESTABLISHMENT, THE

45s

KING

Number	Title (A Side/B Side)	Yr	NM
❑ 6320	In My Heart I Am a Free Man/ Stop Fightin' Start Lovin'	1970	6.00
❑ 6349	House of Jack/Why Is She All I See	1971	6.00

Albums

KING

Number	Title (A Side/B Side)	Yr	NM
❑ KS-1123	The Establishment	1971	12.00

ESTELLE

Estelle Bennett, formerly of THE RONETTES.

45s

LAURIE

Number	Title (A Side/B Side)	Yr	NM
❑ 3449	The Year 2000/The Naked Boy	1968	100.00

ESTRADA, ROY, AND THE ROCKETEERS

45s

KING

Number	Title (A Side/B Side)	Yr	NM
❑ 5368	Jungle Dream (Part 1)/ Jungle Dream (Part 2)	1960	50.00

ETERNALS, THE (1)

45s

HOLLYWOOD

Number	Title (A Side/B Side)	Yr	NM
❑ 68	Rockin' in the Jungle/ Rock and Roll Cha Cha	1959	20.00
—Yellow label			
❑ 68	Rockin' in the Jungle/ Rock and Roll Cha Cha	1959	40.00
—Blue label			
❑ 68	Rockin' in the Jungle/ Rock and Roll Cha Cha	1959	60.00
—White label			
❑ 70	Babalu's Wedding Day/My Girl	1959	25.00
—Blue label			
❑ 70	Babalu's Wedding Day/My Girl	1959	50.00
—Red label			

LOST-NITE

Number	Title (A Side/B Side)	Yr	NM
❑ 203	Rockin' in the Jungle/ Rock and Roll Cha Cha	196?	5.00
—Reissue			
❑ 243	Babalu's Wedding Day/My Girl	196?	5.00
—Reissue			

WARWICK

Number	Title (A Side/B Side)	Yr	NM
❑ 611	Blind Date/Today	1961	20.00

ETERNALS, THE (2)

45s

QUALITY

Number	Title (A Side/B Side)	Yr	NM
❑ 1902	Falling Tears/Sticks and Stones	1968	20.00

ETERNITY'S CHILDREN

Number	Title (A Side/B Side)	Yr	NM
45s			
A&M			
❑ 866	Rumors/Wait and See	1967	10.00
LIBERTY			
❑ 56162	Alone Again/From You Unto Us	1970	8.00
TOWER			
❑ 416	Mrs. Bluebird/Little Boy	1968	10.00
❑ 416 [PS]	Mrs. Bluebird/Little Boy	1968	25.00
❑ 439 [PS]	Rupert White/ Sunshine Among Us	1968	10.00
❑ 449	Till I Hear from You/ I Wanna Be with You	1968	10.00
❑ 476	Sidewalks of the Ghetto /Look Away	1969	10.00
❑ 498	Blue Horizon/Lifetime Day	1969	10.00
Albums			
TOWER			
❑ ST-5123 [S]	Eternity's Children	1968	100.00
❑ T-5123 [M]	Eternity's Children	1968	150.00
❑ ST-5144	Timeless	1969	400.00
—Canada only release, but sold into the US.			

ETHERIDGE, MELISSA

Number	Title (A Side/B Side)	Yr	NM
12-Inch Singles			
ISLAND			
❑ PR 2288 [DJ]	Similar Features (Edit) (Album Version)	1988	12.00
❑ PR 2466 [DJ]	Like the Way I Do (Edit) (same on both sides)	1988	15.00
45s			
ISLAND			
❑ 99176	No Souvenirs/(Live Version)	1989	3.00
❑ 99176 [PS]	No Souvenirs/(Live Version)	1989	3.00
❑ 99251	Similar Features/Bring Me Some Water	1989	3.00
❑ 99251 [PS]	Similar Features/Bring Me Some Water	1989	3.00
❑ 99287	Bring Me Some Water/ Occasionally	1988	4.00
❑ 99287 [PS]	Bring Me Some Water/ Occasionally	1988	4.00
❑ 562344-7	Angels Would Fall/Into the Dark	1999	3.00
❑ 854238-7	If I Wanted To/Come to My Window	1995	5.00
❑ 854426-7	Your Little Secret/All American Girl (Live)	1995	4.00
❑ 854580-7	I Want to Come Over/ I'm the Only One	1996	4.00
Albums			
ISLAND			
❑ 90875	Melissa Etheridge	1988	10.00
❑ 91285	Brave and Crazy	1989	12.00
❑ 546591	Breakdown	1999	15.00
—With bonus 7-inch single			

ETHICS, THE (1)
Philadelphia R&B/soul group.

Number	Title (A Side/B Side)	Yr	NM
45s			
GOLDEN FLEECE			
❑ 3252	Good Luck/Who in the World	1974	15.00
VENT			
❑ (no #)	Think About Tomorrow/ Look at Me Now	1968	60.00
—First pressings have no catalog number			
❑ 1001	Think About Tomorrow/ Look at Me Now	1968	20.00
❑ 1004	Sad, Sad Story/Searching	1968	25.00
❑ 1006	Farewell/I Want My Baby Back	1969	30.00
❑ 1007	Tell Me/There'll Still Be a Sweet Tomorrow	1969	30.00
❑ 1008	Standing in the Darkness/ That's the Way Love Goes	1970	50.00

ETHICS, THE (U)
These may or may not be by group (1).

Number	Title (A Side/B Side)	Yr	NM
45s			
DYNAMIC SOUND			
❑ 2001	Confusion/Out of My Mind	1966	40.00
PHALANX			
❑ 1002/3	Hall of Fame/Crazy Horse	196?	40.00

ETRIS, BARRY

Number	Title (A Side/B Side)	Yr	NM
45s			
SIMS			
❑ 141	The Young Ones/ It's Not Too Late	1963	10.00
❑ 141 [PS]	The Young Ones/ It's Not Too Late	1963	15.00

ETTA AND HARVEY
Also see HARVEY; ETTA JAMES.

Number	Title (A Side/B Side)	Yr	NM
45s			
CHESS			
❑ 1760	If I Can't Have You/ My Heart Cries	1960	25.00
❑ 1771	Spoonful/It's a Crying Shame	1960	25.00

ETZEL, ROY

Number	Title (A Side/B Side)	Yr	NM
45s			
HICKORY			
❑ 1197	I Can't Stop Loving You/ I Hate to Love You	1963	8.00
MGM			
❑ 13381	Melancholy/The Silence	1965	8.00
❑ 13801	Mexican Holiday/Vaya Con Dios	1967	8.00
PRESIDENT			
❑ 820	Tell Laura I Love Her/ Reach for the Stars	1961	10.00
TIME			
❑ 1029	Jenny Oh Jenny/Apache Blues	1961	10.00

EUBANKS, JACK

Number	Title (A Side/B Side)	Yr	NM
45s			
MONUMENT			
❑ 434	Chiricahua/What'd I Say	1961	10.00
❑ 451	Searching/Take a Message to Mary	1961	10.00
❑ 462	After the Rain/Since I Met You Baby	1962	10.00
❑ 809	Casino/Te Juana	1963	8.00
❑ 862	Action/Pickin' White Gold	1964	8.00
Albums			
MONUMENT			
❑ LP-8044 [M]	Guitar Sounds of the South	1966	15.00
❑ SLP-18044 [S]	Guitar Sounds of the South	1966	20.00

EUPHONIOUS WAIL

Number	Title (A Side/B Side)	Yr	NM
Albums			
KAPP			
❑ KS-3668	Euphonious Wail	1973	40.00

EUPHORIA (1)

Number	Title (A Side/B Side)	Yr	NM
45s			
BAND BOX			
❑ 393	Somebody Listen/Dedication of Sally and Cher	196?	30.00
MAINSTREAM			
❑ 655	Hungry Women/ No Me Tomorrow	1967	20.00

EUPHORIA (2)

Number	Title (A Side/B Side)	Yr	NM
45s			
HERITAGE			
❑ 831	You Must Forget/ (B-side unknown)	1971	12.00
Albums			
HERITAGE			
❑ HTS 35005	Euphoria	1971	30.00

EUPHORIA (3)

Number	Title (A Side/B Side)	Yr	NM
Albums			
CAPITOL			
❑ SKAO-363	A Gift from Euphoria	1969	200.00

EUPHORIA (4)

Number	Title (A Side/B Side)	Yr	NM
Albums			
RAINBOW			
❑ 1003	Lost in a Trance	1973	300.00

EURYTHMICS

Number	Title (A Side/B Side)	Yr	NM
12-Inch Singles			
ARISTA			
❑ ARDP-3761 [DJ]	17 Again (Peter Rauhofer Mixes) (Vocal 11:52) (Dub 8:10) (Radio)	2000	20.00
❑ ARDP-3766 [DJ]	17 Again (Thunderpuss Mixes) (Vocal 9:37) (Vicious Queen Dub 9:51) (Radio 4:02)	2000	20.00
❑ ARDP-3782 [(2)DJ]	17 Again (Peter Rauhofer Mixes) (Vocal 11:52) (Mixshow 6:16)//(Dub 8:10) (Beats 3:16) (Acappella 3:57)	2000	40.00
—With sticker on cover "Remastered & Repressed for Louder Play"			
RCA			
❑ 5726-1-RDAA [DJ]	When Tomorrow Comes (same on both sides)	1986	15.00
❑ 5771-1-RDAA [DJ]	Thorn in My Side (same on both sides)	1986	10.00
❑ 6808-1-RDAB [DJ]	I Need a Man (LP Version 4:20) (Edited 4:06)	1987	10.00
❑ 6820-1-RD	I Need a Man (Macho Mix 5:56) (Edited 4:06)/(I Love to Listen to) Beethoven (Dance Mix 4:42) (7" Edit 3:46)	1987	8.00
❑ 6986-RDAA [DJ]	You Have Placed a Chill in My Heart (3:52) (same on both sides)	1988	8.00
❑ 7644-1-RD	You Have Placed a Chill in My Heart (Dance Mix 7:52)/Here Comes the Rain Again (Live 7:36)/Wide Eyed Girl (3:31)	1988	10.00
❑ PD-13502	Sweet Dreams (Are Made of This)/I Could Give You (A Mirror)	1983	12.00
❑ JW-13622 [DJ]	Love Is a Stranger (3:43)// Love Is a Stranger (Live 3:44)/The Walk (Live 4:31)	1983	30.00
❑ PW-13629	Love Is a Stranger (Club Mix 3:43)//Let's Just Close Our Eyes (4:13)/Monkey, Monkey (5:20)	1983	12.00
—In generic black cover with a custom sticker			
❑ PW-13629	Love Is a Stranger (Club Mix 3:43)//Let's Just Close Our Eyes (4:13)/Monkey, Monkey (5:20)	1983	40.00
—In picture cover			
❑ PW-13696	Right By Your Side (Extended Mix 12:20) (Special Mix 0:59)/ Plus Something Else (5:35)	1984	8.00
❑ JD-13711 [DJ]	Here Comes the Rain Again (4:54) (same on both sides)	1984	10.00
❑ PW-13726	Here Comes the Rain Again (5:05)//This City Never Sleeps (Live 5:30)/ Paint a Rumour (7:30)	1984	8.00
❑ PW-13801	Who's That Girl? (Remix 6:50)/ /Aqua (4:36)/Jennifer (5:01)	1984	10.00
❑ JD-13803 [DJ]	Who's That Girl? (Long Version 4:46)/(Short Version 3:45)	1984	10.00
❑ JR-13837 [DJ]	Who's That Girl? (Live 5:07) (same on both sides)	1984	12.00
❑ JW-13848 [DJ]	The First Cut (6:34)/Cool Blues (5:58)/Paint a Rumour (7:26)/ Regret (7:34)	1984	10.00
—Remixes from the "Touch Dance" album			
❑ PW-13957	Sexcrime (Nineteen Eighty-Four) (Extended Mix 7:53) (Single Mix 3:59)/I Did It Just the Same (3:26)	1984	10.00
❑ JW-13961 [DJ]	Sexcrime (Nineteen Eighty-Four) (same on both sides)	1984	15.00
❑ PD-14016	Julia (Extended Version 6:37)/ Ministry of Love (Extended Version 3:43)	1985	8.00
❑ PW-14079	Would I Lie to You? (LP Version 4:52) (Extended Remix 4:59)/ Here Comes That Sinking Feeling (5:40)	1985	8.00
❑ JR-14080 [DJ]	Would I Lie to You? (same on both sides)	1985	10.00
❑ JR-14143 [DJ]	I Love You Like a Ball and Chain (same on both sides)	1985	15.00
❑ PD-14161	There Must Be An Angel (Playing with My Heart) (5:22)/Grown Up Girls (4:15)	1985	10.00
❑ PW-14287	It's Alright (Baby's Coming Back)/ /Conditioned Soul/Tout Les Garcons Et Les Filles	1986	10.00
❑ JR-14389 [DJ]	Missionary Man (4:40) (same on both sides)	1986	10.00
❑ JD-14409 [DJ]	Missionary Man (Extended 6:50) (LP Version 4:40)	1986	10.00
❑ PD-14409	Missionary Man (Extended 6:50)/ Take Your Pain Away (4:30)	1986	8.00
45s			
ARISTA			
❑ 2243	Sweet Dreams (Are Made of This) '91/The King and Queen of America	1991	4.00
❑ 9880	Don't Ask Me Why/Rich Girl	1989	3.00
❑ 9880 [PS]	Don't Ask Me Why/Rich Girl	1989	3.00
❑ 9917	Angel/Precious	1989	4.00
❑ 9917 [PS]	Angel/Precious	1989	4.00
❑ 9939	(My, My) Baby's Gonna Cry/ (Acoustic)	1990	6.00
❑ 9939 [PS]	(My, My) Baby's Gonna Cry/ (Acoustic)	1990	6.00
RCA			
❑ 5058-7-R	Thorn in My Side/In This Town	1986	3.00
❑ 5058-7-R [PS]	Thorn in My Side/In This Town	1986	3.00

Except when noted otherwise, VG = 25% of NM, and VG+ = 50% of NM. (Example: VG = $2.00, VG+ = $4.00 and NM = $8.00.)

Number	Title (A Side/B Side)	Yr	NM
❑ 5177-1-RG	Missionary Man/Thorn in My Side	1987	3.00
—Gold Standard Series reissue			
❑ 5361-7-R	I Need a Man/Heaven	1987	3.00
❑ 5361-7-R [PS]	I Need a Man/Heaven	1987	3.00
❑ 7615-7-R	You Have Placed a Chill in My Heart/Wide Eyed Girl	1988	4.00
❑ 7615-7-RAA [DJ]	You Have Placed a Chill in My Heart (same on both sides)	1988	4.00
❑ 7615-7-RX	You Have Placed a Chill in My Heart (Chill Mix)/(3:52)	1988	10.00
❑ 8619-7-RA1 [DJ]	You Have Placed a Chill in My Heart (Chill Mix)/(3:52)	1988	5.00
❑ 8619-7-RA1 [PS]	You Have Placed a Chill in My Heart (Chill Mix)/(3:52)	1988	20.00
❑ PB-13533	Sweet Dreams (Are Made of This)/I Could Give You (A Mirror)	1983	3.00
❑ PB-13533 [PS]	Sweet Dreams (Are Made of This)/I Could Give You (A Mirror)	1983	5.00
❑ PB-13618	Love Is a Stranger/ Monkey, Monkey	1983	3.00
❑ PB-13618 [PS]	Love Is a Stranger/ Monkey, Monkey	1983	15.00
—Sleeve claims the B-side is "I've Got an Angel," though this song was not released as the B-side of the single in the U.S.; this may explain the scarcity of this sleeve			
❑ PB-13695	Right By Your Side/(Party Mix)	1984	3.00
❑ PB-13695 [PS]	Right By Your Side/(Party Mix)	1984	3.00
❑ JB-13725 [DJ]	Here Comes the Rain Again (Long Version 5:05)/ (Short Version 3:50)	1984	6.00
❑ PB-13725	Here Comes the Rain Again/ Paint a Rumour	1984	3.00
—All stock copies have a 5:05 version of A-side			
❑ PB-13725 [PS]	Here Comes the Rain Again/ Paint a Rumour	1984	3.00
❑ GB-13790	Sweet Dreams (Are Made of This)/Love Is a Stranger	1984	3.00
—Gold Standard Series reissue			
❑ PB-13800	Who's That Girl?/Aqua	1984	3.00
❑ PB-13800 [PS]	Who's That Girl?/Aqua	1984	3.00
❑ PB-13956	Sexcrime (Nineteen Eighty-Four)/I Did It Just the Same	1984	3.00
❑ PB-13956 [PS]	Sexcrime (Nineteen Eighty-Four)/I Did It Just the Same	1984	3.00
❑ PB-14015	Julia (Extended)/Theme from 1984 (Sexcrime) (Special Radio Edit)	1985	6.00
❑ PB-14015 [PS]	Julia (Extended)/Theme from 1984 (Sexcrime) (Special Radio Edit)	1985	6.00
❑ GB-14063	Here Comes the Rain Again/ Right By Your Side	1985	3.00
—Gold Standard Series reissue			
❑ PB-14078	Would I Lie to You?/Here Comes That Sinking Feeling	1985	3.00
❑ PB-14078 [PS]	Would I Lie to You?/Here Comes That Sinking Feeling	1985	4.00
❑ PB-14160	There Must Be An Angel (Playing with My Heart)/ Grown Up Girls	1985	3.00
❑ PB-14160 [PS]	There Must Be An Angel (Playing with My Heart)/ Grown Up Girls	1985	3.00
❑ PB-14284	It's Alright (Baby's Coming Back)/Conditioned Soul	1986	3.00
❑ PB-14284 [PS]	It's Alright (Baby's Coming Back)/Conditioned Soul	1986	3.00
❑ GB-14338	Would I Lie to You?/There Must Be An Angel (Playing with My Heart)	1986	3.00
—Gold Standard Series reissue			
❑ PB-14414	Missionary Man/Take Your Pain Away	1986	3.00
❑ PB-14414 [PS]	Missionary Man/Take Your Pain Away	1986	3.00
Albums			
ARISTA			
❑ AL 8606	We Too Are One	1989	12.00
RCA			
❑ 5707-1-RDAA [EP]	Rough and Tough at the Roxy	1986	30.00
—Promo-only 4-song live album			
❑ 6794-1-R	Savage	1987	12.00
RCA VICTOR			
❑ AFL1-4681	Sweet Dreams (Are Made of This)	1983	10.00
❑ AFL1-4917	Touch	1984	12.00
❑ CPL1-5086 [EP]	Touch Dance	1983	12.00
❑ ABL1-5371	1984 (For the Love of Big Brother)	1984	12.00
❑ AJL1-5429	Be Yourself Tonight	1985	12.00
❑ AJL1-5847	Revenge	1986	12.00

EURYTHMICS AND ARETHA FRANKLIN

Number	Title (A Side/B Side)	Yr	NM
12-Inch Singles			
RCA			
❑ JR-14206 [DJ]	Sisters Are Doin' It for Themselves (same on both sides)	1985	10.00
❑ PW-14243	Sisters Are Doin' It for Themselves (5:54) (E.T. Mix 7:56)/I Love You Like a Ball and Chain (4:04)	1985	8.00
—B-side by Eurythmics			
45s			
RCA			
❑ PB-14214	Sisters Are Doin' It for Themselves/I Love You Like a Ball and Chain	1985	3.00
—B-side by Eurythmics			
❑ PB-14214 [PS]	Sisters Are Doin' It for Themselves/I Love You Like a Ball and Chain	1985	3.00

EVANS, BARBARA

Number	Title (A Side/B Side)	Yr	NM
45s			
RCA VICTOR			
❑ 47-7519	Souvenirs/Play for Me, Mother	1959	20.00
❑ 47-7576	Oo La La La La/The Little Girl Cried	1959	20.00
❑ 47-7634	Beatnik Daddy/A Game of Poker	1959	20.00

EVANS, MAUREEN

Number	Title (A Side/B Side)	Yr	NM
45s			
COLUMBIA			
❑ 43189	Get Away/I've Often Wondered	1964	10.00
❑ 43354	Never Let Me Go/Poco Sole	1965	10.00
DOT			
❑ 16678	Time and Time Again/ Tomorrow Is Another Day	1964	10.00
LITTLE DARLIN'			
❑ 0019	Touch My Heart/ (B-side unknown)	1967	10.00
LONDON INT'L.			
❑ 10407	Like I Do/Starlight, Starbright	1963	12.00
❑ 10409	Melancholy Me/Pick the Petals	1963	12.00

EVANS, PAUL

Number	Title (A Side/B Side)	Yr	NM
45s			
ATCO			
❑ 6138	At My Party/Beat Generation	1959	15.00
❑ 6170	Long Gone/Mickey, My Love	1960	15.00
BIG TREE			
❑ 16050	Happy Birthday. America/ You Made Me Over	1975	5.00
CARLTON			
❑ ST 130-4 [S]	Mister Hangman/ British Grenadiers	1961	25.00
—Jukebox issue; small hole, plays at 33 1/3 rpm			
❑ 539	Show Folk/I Love to Make Love to You	1961	15.00
❑ 543	After the Hurricane/Not Me	1961	15.00
❑ 554	Just Because I Love You/ This Pullover	1961	15.00
❑ 558	Over the Mountain, Across the Sea/Sisal Twine	1961	15.00
CINNAMON			
❑ 604	One Night Led to Two/ Hangin' Out and Hangin' In	1980	5.00
COLUMBIA			
❑ 44472	One Red Rose/Bound to Silence	1968	6.00
DECCA			
❑ 30680	I Think About You All the Time/ Oh No	1958	20.00
DOT			
❑ 17463	That's What Loving You Is All About/Do You Remember	1973	5.00
EPIC			
❑ 9726	Bewitched/I Think I'm Gonna Kill Myself	1964	10.00
—By Paul & Mimi Evans			
❑ 9751	Little Miss Tease/ Gina Marina Petunia	1964	10.00
❑ 9842	I Wonder What to Do/Always Thinking of the Roses	1965	10.00
GUARANTEED			
❑ 200	Seven Little Girls Sitting in the Back Seat/Worshipping an Idol	1959	20.00
❑ 205	Midnite Special/Since I Met You Baby	1960	15.00
❑ 208	Happy-Go-Lucky Me/ Fish in the Ocean	1960	15.00
❑ 210	The Brigade of Broken Hearts/ Twins	1960	15.00
❑ 213	Hushabye Little Guitar/Blind Boy	1960	15.00
KAPP			
❑ 473	A Picture of You/Feelin' No Pain	1962	12.00
❑ 486	D-Darling/Gonna Build a Mountain	1962	12.00
❑ 499	The Bell That Couldn't Jingle/ Gilding the Lily	1962	12.00
❑ 520	(Mama and Papa) We've Got Something On You/ What Are the Lips of Janet	1963	12.00
❑ 527	Ten Thousand Years/Evan Tan	1963	12.00
LAURIE			
❑ 3571	Think Summer/For Old Times Sake	1971	6.00
❑ 3581	The Man in a Row Boat/ Here We Go Around Again	1971	6.00
MERCURY			
❑ 73499	But I Was Born in New York City/ Just As Long As You Are There	1974	5.00
❑ 73650	All My Children/Move In with Me	1975	5.00
MUSICOR			
❑ 6305	Roses Are Red Medley/If I Had My Life to Live Over	1977	4.00
RANWOOD			
❑ 928	Try It, You'll Like It/We Liked It	1972	6.00
RCA VICTOR			
❑ 47-6806	What Do You Know/Dorothy	1957	20.00
❑ 47-6924	Looking for a Sweetie/ Any Little Thing	1957	20.00
❑ 47-6992	Caught/Poor Broken Heart	1957	20.00
SPRING			
❑ 183	Hello, This Is Joanie (The Telephone Answering Machine Song)/Lullabye Tissue Paper Company	1978	4.00
❑ 187	Down at the Bluebird/ I'm Givin' Up My Baby	1978	4.00
❑ 193	Disneyland Daddy/Build An Ark	1979	4.00
Albums			
CARLTON			
❑ STLP-129 [S]	Hear Paul Evans in Your Home Tonight	1961	60.00
❑ TLP-129 [M]	Hear Paul Evans in Your Home Tonight	1961	40.00
❑ STLP-130 [S]	Folk Songs of Many Lands	1961	60.00
❑ TLP-130 [M]	Folk Songs of Many Lands	1961	40.00
GUARANTEED			
❑ GUL-1000 [M]	Fabulous Teens	1960	70.00
❑ GUS-1000 [S]	Fabulous Teens	1960	80.00
KAPP			
❑ KL-1346 [M]	21 Years in a Tennessee Jail	1964	25.00
❑ KL-1475 [M]	Another Town, Another Jail	1966	25.00
❑ KS-3346 [S]	21 Years in a Tennessee Jail	1964	40.00
❑ KS-3475 [S]	Another Town, Another Jail	1966	30.00

EVELS, THE

Number	Title (A Side/B Side)	Yr	NM
45s			
TRA-X			
❑ 14	The Magic of Love/ Wonderful Guy	1960	60.00

EVENTUALS, THE

Number	Title (A Side/B Side)	Yr	NM
45s			
OKEH			
❑ 4-7142	Charlie Chan/Just the Things That You Do	1961	15.00
❑ 4-7142 [PS]	Charlie Chan/Just the Things That You Do	1961	30.00

EVER-READY SINGERS, THE

Number	Title (A Side/B Side)	Yr	NM
45s			
CAPITOL			
❑ F2763	I'm a Pilgrim and a Stranger/ One Day While I Was Walking	1954	30.00
❑ F2867	This Heart of Mine/Two Wings	1954	30.00
❑ F2984	I Don't Care What the World May Do/Oh Mary Don't You Weep	1954	40.00

EVERETT, BETTY

Number	Title (A Side/B Side)	Yr	NM
45s			
ABC			
❑ 10829	In Your Arms/Nothing I Wouldn't Do	1966	8.00
❑ 10861	Bye, Bye Baby/Your Love Is Important to Me	1966	8.00
❑ 10919	Love Comes Tumbling Down/ People Around Me	1967	8.00
❑ 10978	I Can't Say/My Baby Loving My Best Friend	1967	8.00

E

Number	Title (A Side/B Side)	Yr	NM
CJ			
❑ 611	Why Did You Have to Go/ Please Come Back	1961	20.00
—As "Bettie Everett & Daylighters"			
❑ 619	Your Lovin' Arms/ Happy I Long to Be	1961	20.00
❑ 674	Days Gone By/Her New Love	1964	15.00
COBRA			
❑ 5019	My Love/My Life Depends on You	1957	30.00
❑ 5024	Ain't Gonna Cry/Killer Diller	1958	25.00
❑ 5031	Weep No More/Tell Me Darling	1959	25.00
FANTASY			
❑ 652	I Got to Tell Somebody/ Why Are You Leaving Me	1970	5.00
❑ 658	Ain't Nothing Gonna Change Me/What Is It?	1971	5.00
❑ 667	I'm a Woman/Prove It	1971	5.00
❑ 687	Black Girl/Innocent Bystanders	1972	5.00
❑ 687	Black Girl/What Is It?	1972	5.00
❑ 696	Danger/Just a Matter of Time Till You're Gone	1973	5.00
❑ 714	Sweet Dan/Who Will Your Next Fool Be	1973	5.00
❑ 725	Try It, You'll Like It/Wondering	1974	5.00
❑ 738	Happy Endings/Keep It Up	1974	5.00
LOST-NITE			
❑ 313	The Shoop Shoop Song (It's In His Kiss)/Hands Off	197?	5.00
—Reissue			
ONE-DERFUL			
❑ 4806	I've Got a Claim on You/ Your Love Is Important to Me	1962	15.00
❑ 4823	I'll Be There/Please Love Me	1964	12.00
UNI			
❑ 55100	Take Me/There'll Come a Time	1968	6.00
❑ 55122	I Can't Say No to You/Better Tomorrow Than Today	1969	6.00
❑ 55141	1900 Yesterday/Maybe	1969	6.00
❑ 55174	Just a Man's Way/ Been a Long Time	1969	6.00
❑ 55189	Sugar/Just Another Winter	1969	6.00
❑ 55219	Unlucky Girl/Better Tomorrow Than Today	1970	6.00
UNITED ARTISTS			
❑ XW1200	True Love (You Took My Heart)/ You Can Do It	1978	4.00
VEE JAY			
❑ 513	By My Side/Prince of Players	1963	15.00
❑ 566	You're No Good/Chained to Your Love	1963	20.00
❑ 585	The Shoop Shoop Song (It's In His Kiss)/Hands Off	1964	20.00
❑ 599	I Can't Hear You/Can I Get to Know You	1964	15.00
❑ 610	It Hurts to Be in Love/ Until You Were Gone	1964	15.00
❑ 628	Getting Mighty Crowded/ Chained to a Memory	1964	15.00
❑ 683	The Real Thing/Gonna Be Ready	1965	15.00
❑ 699	I Don't Hurt Anymore/ Too Hot to Hold	1965	15.00
❑ 716	Trouble Over the Weekend/ My Shoe Won't Fly	1966	15.00
Albums			
FANTASY			
❑ 9447	Love Rhymes	1974	12.00
❑ 9480	Happy Endings	1975	12.00
SUNSET			
❑ SUS-5220	I Need You So	1968	15.00
UNI			
❑ 73048	There'll Come a Time	1969	25.00
VEE JAY			
❑ LP 1077 [M]	It's In His Kiss	1964	30.00
❑ LP 1077 [M]	You're No Good	1964	40.00
❑ SR 1077 [S]	It's In His Kiss	1964	50.00
❑ SR 1077 [S]	You're No Good	1964	70.00
❑ LP 1122 [M]	The Very Best of Betty Everett	1965	40.00
❑ VJLP 1122	The Very Best of Betty Everett	198?	10.00
—Authorized reissue			
❑ VJS 1122 [S]	The Very Best of Betty Everett	1965	50.00

EVERETT, BETTY, AND JERRY BUTLER Also see each artist's individual listings.

Number	Title (A Side/B Side)	Yr	NM
45s			
LOST-NITE			
❑ 299	Let It Be Me/Ain't That Loving You Baby	197?	5.00
—Reissue			
VEE JAY			
❑ 613	Let It Be Me/Ain't That Loving You Baby	1964	12.00
❑ 633	Smile/Love Is Strange	1964	12.00
❑ 676	Since I Don't Have You/ Just Be True	1965	12.00
❑ 691	Fever/The Way You Do the Things You Do	1965	12.00
Albums			
BUDDAH			
❑ BDS-7505	Together	1969	15.00
TRADITION			
❑ 2073	Starring Betty Everett with Jerry Butler	197?	12.00
VEE JAY			
❑ LP 1099 [M]	Delicious Together	1964	20.00
❑ LP-1099 [M]	Delicious Together	1964	20.00
❑ VJLP 1099	Delicious Together	198?	12.00
—Authorized reissue			
❑ VJLP-1099	Delicious Together	198?	10.00
—Reissue of original 1099; has softer vinyl			
❑ VJS 1099 [S]	Delicious Together	1964	25.00
❑ VJS-1099 [S]	Delicious Together	1964	25.00

EVERETT, VINCE

Number	Title (A Side/B Side)	Yr	NM
45s			
ABC-PARAMOUNT			
❑ 10313	Such a Night/Don't Go	1962	60.00
❑ 10360	I Ain't Gonna Be Your Low Down Dog No More/Sugaree	1962	50.00
❑ 10472	Baby, Let's Play House/ Livin' High	1963	80.00
❑ 10538	Sweet Flavors/Box Candy	1964	40.00
❑ 10624	Big Brother/To Have, to Hold and Let Go	1965	40.00
TOWN			
❑ 1964	Buttercup/Land of No Return	1960	40.00

EVERGREEN BLUES, THE

Number	Title (A Side/B Side)	Yr	NM
45s			
ABC			
❑ 11198	Funky Woman/Don't Mess Up My Mind	1969	6.00
❑ 11216	The Moon Is High/Girl I Got Wise	1969	6.00
MERCURY			
❑ 72756	Midnight Confessions/ That's My Baby (Yes)	1967	10.00
❑ 72756 [PS]	Midnight Confessions/ That's My Baby (Yes)	1967	20.00
❑ 72780	Laura (Keep Hangin' On)/ Yesterday's Coming	1968	10.00
❑ 72780 [PS]	Laura (Keep Hangin' On)/ Yesterday's Coming	1968	25.00
❑ 72826	Feelin' Your Love/ Three's a Crowd	1968	10.00
Albums			
ABC			
❑ S-669	Comin' On	1969	15.00
MERCURY			
❑ MG-21157 [M]	7 Do 11	1968	50.00
—Mono is white label promo only			
❑ SR-61157 [S]	7 Do 11	1968	20.00

EVERGREENS, THE

Number	Title (A Side/B Side)	Yr	NM
45s			
CHART			
❑ 605	Very Truly Yours/Guitar Player	1955	150.00

EVERLY, DON Also see THE EVERLY BROTHERS.

Number	Title (A Side/B Side)	Yr	NM
45s			
ABC HICKORY			
❑ 54002	Love at Last Sight/ Oh I'd Like to Go Away	1976	6.00
❑ 54005	Since You Broke My Heart/ Deep Water	1977	6.00
❑ 54012	Brother Juke-Box/ Oh, What a Feeling	1977	6.00
HICKORY/MGM			
❑ 368	Yesterday Just Passed My Way Again/Never Like This	1976	6.00
ODE			
❑ 66009	Only Me/Tumbling Tumbleweeds	1970	8.00
❑ 66046	Warming Up the Band/ Evelyn Swing	1974	8.00
Albums			
ABC HICKORY			
❑ AH-44003	Brother Juke-Box	1977	12.00
ODE			
❑ SP-77005	Don Everly	1970	15.00
❑ SP-77023	Sunset Towers	1974	15.00

EVERLY, PHIL Also see THE EVERLY BROTHERS.

Number	Title (A Side/B Side)	Yr	NM
45s			
CAPITOL			
❑ B-5197	One Way Love/Who's Gonna Keep Me Warm	1983	10.00
CURB			
❑ 02116	Sweet Southern Love/ In Your Eyes	1981	10.00
❑ 5401	Dare to Dream Again/ Lonely Days, Lonely Nights	1980	10.00
ELEKTRA			
❑ 46007	Don't Say You Don't Love Me No More/I Seek the Night	1979	5.00
—A-side: With Sondra Locke; B-side: Sondra Locke solo			
❑ 46519	Living Alone/I Just Don't Feel Like Dancing	1979	5.00
❑ 46556	Buy Me a Beer/You Broke It	1979	5.00
PYE			
❑ 71014	Old Kentucky River/ Summershine	1975	8.00
❑ 71036	New Old Song/Better Than Now	1975	8.00
❑ 71050	You and I Are a Song/ Better Than Now	1975	8.00
❑ 71055	Words in Your Eyes/Back When the Bands Played in Rag Time	1976	8.00
❑ 71056	God Bless Older Ladies/ Sweet Grass Country	1976	6.00
RCA VICTOR			
❑ APBO-0064	God Bless Older Ladies/ Sweet Grass Country	1973	8.00
Albums			
ELEKTRA			
❑ 6E-213	Living Alone	1979	10.00
PYE			
❑ 12104	Phil's Diner	1975	12.00
❑ 12121	Mystic Line	1976	12.00
RCA VICTOR			
❑ APL1-0092	Star Spangled Springer	1973	15.00

EVERLY BROTHERS, THE Also see DON EVERLY; PHIL EVERLY.

Number	Title (A Side/B Side)	Yr	NM
12-Inch Singles			
MERCURY			
❑ PRO 312-1 [DJ]	On the Wings of a Nightingale (same on both sides)	1984	12.00
45s			
BARNABY			
❑ 500	('Til) I Kissed You/ Oh, What a Feeling	197?	5.00
❑ 501	Wake Up Little Susie/ Maybe Tomorrow	197?	5.00
❑ 502	Bye, Bye Love/I Wonder If I Care As Much	197?	5.00
❑ 503	This Little Girl of Mine/ Should We Tell Him?	197?	5.00
❑ 504	Problems/Love of My Life	197?	5.00
❑ 505	Take a Message to Mary/ Poor Jenny	197?	5.00
❑ 506	Let It Be Me/Since You Broke My Heart	197?	5.00
❑ 507	When Will I Be Loved/ Be Bop A-Lula	197?	5.00
❑ 508	Like Strangers/Brand New Heartache	197?	5.00
❑ 509	All I Have to Do Is Dream/ Claudette	197?	5.00
❑ 510	Bird Dog/Devoted to You	197?	5.00
❑ 511	I'm Here to Get My Baby Out of Jail/Lightning Express	197?	5.00
—All Barnaby records are reissues of original Cadence recordings			
CADENCE			
❑ 1315	Bye, Bye Love/I Wonder If I Care As Much	1957	25.00
❑ 1337	Wake Up Little Susie/ Maybe Tomorrow	1957	30.00
❑ 1337 [PS]	Wake Up Little Susie/ Maybe Tomorrow	1957	250.00
❑ 1342	This Little Girl of Mine/ Should We Tell Him?	1958	25.00
❑ 1348	All I Have to Do Is Dream/ Claudette	1958	25.00
❑ 1348	All I Have to Do Is Dream/ Claudette	1961	20.00
—Reissue with red and black label; scarcer than original			
❑ 1350	Bird Dog/Devoted to You	1958	25.00
❑ 1355	Problems/Love of My Life	1958	25.00
❑ 1355 [PS]	Problems/Love of My Life	1958	50.00
❑ 1364	Take a Message to Mary/ Poor Jenny	1959	25.00

Except when noted otherwise, VG = 25% of NM, and VG+ = 50% of NM. (Example: VG = $2.00, VG+ = $4.00 and NM = $8.00.)

Number	Title (A Side/B Side)	Yr	NM
❑ 1369	('Til) I Kissed You/Oh, What a Feeling	1959	25.00
❑ 1369 [PS]	('Til) I Kissed You/Oh, What a Feeling	1959	50.00
❑ 1376	Let It Be Me/Since You Broke My Heart	1959	25.00
❑ 1376 [PS]	Let It Be Me/Since You Broke My Heart	1959	50.00
❑ 1380	When Will I Be Loved/Be Bop A-Lula	1960	25.00
❑ 1388	Like Strangers/Brand New Heartache	1960	25.00
❑ 1429	I'm Here to Get My Baby Out of Jail/Lightning Express	1962	20.00
❑ 1429 [PS]	I'm Here to Get My Baby Out of Jail/Lightning Express	1962	40.00

CAPITOL

Number	Title (A Side/B Side)	Yr	NM
❑ B-44297	Don't Worry Baby/Tequila Dreams	1989	4.00

—A-side with the Beach Boys; B-side by Dave Grusin

Number	Title (A Side/B Side)	Yr	NM
❑ B-44297 [PS]	Don't Worry Baby/Tequila Dreams	1989	10.00

COLUMBIA

Number	Title (A Side/B Side)	Yr	NM
❑ 4-21496	Keep A Lovin' Me/The Sun Keeps Shining	1956	600.00

—Maroon label

Number	Title (A Side/B Side)	Yr	NM
❑ 4-21496 [DJ]	Keep A Lovin' Me/The Sun Keeps Shining	1956	250.00

—White label

MERCURY

Number	Title (A Side/B Side)	Yr	NM
❑ 872098-7	Ride the Wind/Don't Worry Baby	1988	3.00
❑ 872420-7	Ballad of a Teenage Queen/Get Rhythm	1988	3.00

—With Johnny Cash and Roseanne Cash

Number	Title (A Side/B Side)	Yr	NM
❑ 880213-7	On the Wings of a Nightingale/Asleep	1984	5.00

—A-side written and produced by Paul McCartney

Number	Title (A Side/B Side)	Yr	NM
❑ 880423-7	The Story of Me/First in Line	1984	4.00
❑ 884428-7	Don't Say Goodnight/Born Yesterday	1986	4.00
❑ 884694-7	I Know Love/These Shoes	1986	4.00
❑ 884694-7 [PS]	I Know Love/These Shoes	1986	4.00

RCA VICTOR

Number	Title (A Side/B Side)	Yr	NM
❑ 74-0717	Stories We Could Tell/Ridin' High	1972	10.00
❑ 74-0849	Lay It Down/Paradise	1972	10.00
❑ 74-0901	Not Fade Away/Ladies Love Outlaws	1973	10.00
❑ SP-45-409 [DJ]	Pass the Chicken and Listen	1971	30.00

—Promo-only interview record

WARNER BROS.

Number	Title (A Side/B Side)	Yr	NM
❑ GWB 0311	That's Old Fashioned/Bowling Green	197?	4.00

—"Back to Back Hits" series; originals have palm-tree labels

Number	Title (A Side/B Side)	Yr	NM
❑ GWB 0314	Ebony Eyes/Walk Right Back	197?	4.00

—"Back to Back Hits" series; originals have palm-tree labels

Number	Title (A Side/B Side)	Yr	NM
❑ 5151 [DJ]	Cathy's Clown/Always It's You	1960	100.00

—Promo-only gold vinyl pressing

Number	Title (A Side/B Side)	Yr	NM
❑ 5151 [M]	Cathy's Clown/Always It's You	1960	15.00

—Second-pressing stock copies have red labels with arrows

Number	Title (A Side/B Side)	Yr	NM
❑ 5151 [M]	Cathy's Clown/Always It's You	1960	20.00

—Original stock copies have pink labels

Number	Title (A Side/B Side)	Yr	NM
❑ 5151 [PS]	Cathy's Clown/Always It's You	1960	50.00
❑ S-5151 [S]	Cathy's Clown/Always It's You	1960	50.00
❑ 5163	So Sad (To Watch Good Love Go Bad)/Lucille	1960	15.00
❑ 5163 [DJ]	So Sad (To Watch Good Love Go Bad)/Lucille	1960	100.00

—Promo-only gold vinyl pressing

Number	Title (A Side/B Side)	Yr	NM
❑ 5163 [PS]	So Sad (To Watch Good Love Go Bad)/Lucille	1960	50.00
❑ 5199	Ebony Eyes/Walk Right Back	1961	15.00
❑ 5199 [DJ]	Ebony Eyes/Walk Right Back	1961	100.00

—Promo-only gold vinyl pressing

Number	Title (A Side/B Side)	Yr	NM
❑ 5199 [PS]	Ebony Eyes/Walk Right Back	1961	25.00
❑ 5220	Temptation/Stick With Me, Baby	1961	15.00
❑ 5220 [PS]	Temptation/Stick With Me, Baby	1961	30.00
❑ 5250	Crying in the Rain/I'm Not Angry	1961	15.00
❑ 5250 [PS]	Crying in the Rain/I'm Not Angry	1961	20.00
❑ 5273	That's Old Fashioned (That's the Way Love Should Be)/How Can I Meet Her?	1962	15.00
❑ 5273 [PS]	That's Old Fashioned (That's the Way Love Should Be)/How Can I Meet Her?	1962	30.00
❑ 5297	Don't Ask Me to Be Friends/No One Can Make My Sunshine Smile	1962	20.00
❑ 5297 [PS]	Don't Ask Me to Be Friends/No One Can Make My Sunshine Smile	1962	30.00
❑ 5346	(So It Was...So It Is...) So It Always Will Be/Nancy's Minuet	1963	15.00
❑ 5362	I'm Afraid/It's Been Nice	1963	15.00
❑ 5389	Love Her/The Girl Sang the Blues	1963	15.00
❑ 5422	Hello, Amy/Ain't That Loving You, Baby	1964	15.00
❑ 5441	The Ferris Wheel/Don't Forget to Cry	1964	15.00
❑ 5466	You're the One I Love/Ring Around My Rosie	1964	15.00
❑ 5478	Gone, Gone, Gone/Torture	1964	15.00
❑ 5501	Don't Blame Me/Walk Right Back//Muskrat/Lucille	1961	20.00
❑ 5501 [PS]	Don't Blame Me/Walk Right Back//Muskrat/Lucille	1961	40.00

—Part of Warner Bros. "+2" series, with two new songs and excerpts of two prior hits

Number	Title (A Side/B Side)	Yr	NM
❑ 5600	You're My Girl/Don't Let the World Know	1965	12.00
❑ 5611	That'll Be the Day/Give Me a Sweetheart	1965	12.00
❑ 5628	The Price of Love/It Only Costs a Dime	1965	12.00
❑ 5639	I'll Never Get Over You/Follow Me	1965	12.00
❑ 5649	Love Is Strange/A Man with Money	1965	12.00
❑ 5649 [PS]	Love Is Strange/A Man with Money	1965	150.00
❑ 5682	It's All Over/I Used to Love You	1965	12.00
❑ 5698	The Doll House Is Empty/Lovey Kravezit	1966	12.00
❑ 5808	The Power of Love/Leave My Girl Alone	1966	12.00
❑ 5833	Somebody Help Me/Hard, Hard Year	1966	12.00
❑ 5857	Fifi the Flea/Like Every Time Before	1966	20.00

—A-side listed as "Don Everly Brother," B-side as "Phil Everly Brother"

Number	Title (A Side/B Side)	Yr	NM
❑ 5901	She Never Smiles Anymore/Devil Child	1967	12.00
❑ 7020	Bowling Green/I Don't Want to Love You	1967	12.00
❑ 7062	Mary Jane/Talking to the Flowers	1967	12.00
❑ 7088	Love of the Common People/The Voice Within	1967	12.00
❑ 7110	Cathy's Clown/So Sad	1968	8.00

—"Back to Back Hits" series; originals have green "W7" label

Number	Title (A Side/B Side)	Yr	NM
❑ 7111	Crying in the Rain/Lucille	1968	8.00

—"Back to Back Hits" series; originals have green "W7" label

Number	Title (A Side/B Side)	Yr	NM
❑ 7120	Wake Up Little Susie/Bird Dog	1969	8.00

—"Back to Back Hits" series; originals have green "W7" label; re-recordings

Number	Title (A Side/B Side)	Yr	NM
❑ 7121	Bye Bye Love/All I Have to Do Is Dream	1969	8.00

—"Back to Back Hits" series; originals have green "W7" label; re-recordings

Number	Title (A Side/B Side)	Yr	NM
❑ 7192	Empty Boxes/It's My Time	1968	12.00
❑ 7226	Lord of the Manor/Milk Train	1968	12.00
❑ 7262	T for Texas/I Wonder If I Care As Much	1969	12.00
❑ 7290	I'm On My Way Home Again/Cuckoo Bird	1969	12.00
❑ 7326	Carolina on My Mind/My Little Yellow Bird	1969	15.00
❑ 7425	Yves/The Human Race	1970	15.00

7-Inch Extended Plays

CADENCE

Number	Title (A Side/B Side)	Yr	NM
❑ CLLP 33-3	Bye Bye Love/('Til) I Kissed You/Bird Dog//Wake Up Little Susie/When Will I Be Loved/Problems	1961	40.00

—Jukebox issue; small hole, plays at 33 1/3 rpm

Number	Title (A Side/B Side)	Yr	NM
❑ CLLP 33-3 [PS]	Rockin' with the Everly Brothers	1961	60.00

—Cardboard insert in heavy vinyl envelope

Number	Title (A Side/B Side)	Yr	NM
❑ CLLP 33-4	All I Have to Do Is Dream/I Wonder If I Care As Much/Take a Message to Mary//Let It Be Me/Devoted to You/Maybe Tomorrow	1961	40.00

—Jukebox issue; small hole, plays at 33 1/3 rpm

Number	Title (A Side/B Side)	Yr	NM
❑ CLLP 33-4 [PS]	Dream with the Everly Brothers	1961	60.00

—Cardboard insert in heavy vinyl envelope

Number	Title (A Side/B Side)	Yr	NM
❑ CEP-104	Wake Up Little Susie/Maybe Tomorrow//Bye Bye Love/I Wonder If I Care As Much	1957	50.00
❑ CEP-104 [PS]	The Everly Brothers	1957	50.00
❑ CEP-105	This Little Girl of Mine/Leave My Woman Alone//Should We Tell Him/Be-Bop-a-Lula	1957	50.00
❑ CEP-105 [PS]	The Everly Brothers	1957	50.00
❑ CEP-107	Brand New Heartache/Keep a Knockin'//Rip It Up/Hey Doll Baby	1957	50.00
❑ CEP-107 [PS]	The Everly Brothers	1957	50.00
❑ CEP-108	Roving Gambler/Oh So Many Years//Put My Little Shoes Away/That Silver Haired Daddy Of Mine	1958	50.00
❑ CEP-108 [PS]	Songs Our Daddy Taught Us, Vol. 1	1958	50.00
❑ CEP-109	Barbara Allen/Long Time Gone//Lightning Express/Who's Gonna Shoe Your Pretty Little Feet	1958	50.00
❑ CEP-109 [PS]	Songs Our Daddy Taught Us, Vol. 2	1958	50.00
❑ CEP-110	*Down in the Willow Garden/Kentucky/I'm Here to Get My Baby Out of Jail/Rockin' Alone in My Old Rockin' Chair	1958	50.00
❑ CEP-110 [PS]	Songs Our Daddy Taught Us, Vol. 3	1958	50.00
❑ CEP-111	Bird Dog/Devoted to You//All I Have to Do Is Dream/Claudette	1959	50.00
❑ CEP-111 [PS]	The Everly Brothers	1959	50.00
❑ CEP-118	(contents unknown)	1959	50.00
❑ CEP-118 [PS]	The Everly Brothers	1959	50.00
❑ CEP-121	Let It Be Me/Since You Broke My Heart//'Til I Kissed You/Oh, What a Feeling	1960	25.00
❑ CEP-121 [PS]	The Very Best of the Everly Brothers	1960	25.00

WARNER BROS.

Number	Title (A Side/B Side)	Yr	NM
❑ PRO 135 [DJ]	My Gal Sal/Grandfather's Clock/Bully of the Town/The Wayward Wind/Chlo-E//Hi-Lili, Hi-Lo/Don't Blame Me/Now Is the Hour/When I Grow Too Old to Dream/Love Is Where You Find It	1961	60.00

—7-inch record, large hole, with excerpts from each of the above songs

Number	Title (A Side/B Side)	Yr	NM
❑ PRO 135 [PS]	Souvenir Sampler	1961	100.00

—Back cover of sleeve has a coupon for LP W/WS 1418

Number	Title (A Side/B Side)	Yr	NM
❑ EA 1381	So Sad (To Watch Good Love Go Bad)/You Thrill Me (Through and Through)//Memories Are Made of This/Oh, True Love	1960	40.00
❑ EA 1381 [PS]	Foreverly Yours	1960	40.00
❑ EB 1381	Sleepless Nights/Carol Jane//Nashville Blues/That's What You Do to Me	1960	40.00
❑ EB 1381 [PS]	Especially for You	1960	40.00
❑ S 1471	That's Old Fashioned (That's the Way Love Should Be)/Crying in the Rain/Lucille//Cathy's Clown/Walk Right Back/So Sad (To Watch Good Love Go Bad)	1963	25.00

—Stereo jukebox issue; small hole, plays at 33 1/3 rpm

Number	Title (A Side/B Side)	Yr	NM
❑ S 1471 [PS]	The Golden Hits of the Everly Brothers	1963	25.00
❑ 2S 1858	('Til) I Kissed You/Wake Up Little Susie/Cathy's Clown//Mama Tried/Bowling Green/Walk Right Back	1970	15.00

—Stereo jukebox issue; small hole, plays at 33 1/3 rpm

Number	Title (A Side/B Side)	Yr	NM
❑ 2S 1858 [PS]	The Everly Brothers Show	1970	15.00

—Part of "Little LP" series (#120)

Albums

ARISTA

Number	Title (A Side/B Side)	Yr	NM
❑ AL9-8207 [(2)]	24 Original Classics	1985	15.00

BARNABY

Number	Title (A Side/B Side)	Yr	NM
❑ BGP-350 [(2)]	The Everly Brothers' Original Golden Hits	1970	20.00
❑ 4004	Greatest Hits, Vol. 1	1977	10.00
❑ 4005	Greatest Hits, Vol. 2	1977	10.00
❑ 4006	Greatest Hits, Vol. 3	1977	10.00
❑ BR-6006 [(2)]	The Everly Brothers' Greatest Hits	1974	15.00
❑ BR-15008 [(2)]	History of the Everly Brothers	1973	15.00
❑ ZG 30260 [(2)]	End of an Era	1971	15.00

CADENCE

Number	Title (A Side/B Side)	Yr	NM
❑ CLP-3003 [M]	The Everly Brothers	1958	100.00

—Maroon label with metronome logo

Number	Title (A Side/B Side)	Yr	NM
❑ CLP-3003 [M]	The Everly Brothers	1962	60.00

—Red label with black border

Number	Title (A Side/B Side)	Yr	NM
❑ CLP-3016 [M]	Songs Our Daddy Taught Us	1958	100.00

—Maroon label with metronome logo

Number	Title (A Side/B Side)	Yr	NM
❑ CLP-3016 [M]	Songs Our Daddy Taught Us	1962	60.00

—Red label with black border

Number	Title (A Side/B Side)	Yr	NM
❑ CLP-3025 [M]	The Everly Brothers' Best	1959	90.00

—Maroon label with metronome logo

Number	Title (A Side/B Side)	Yr	NM
❑ CLP-3025 [M]	The Everly Brothers' Best	1962	60.00

—Red label with black border

Number	Title (A Side/B Side)	Yr	NM
❑ CLP-3040 [M]	The Fabulous Style of the Everly Brothers	1960	80.00

—Maroon label with metronome logo

Number	Title (A Side/B Side)	Yr	NM
❑ CLP-3040 [M]	The Fabulous Style of the Everly Brothers	1962	50.00

—Red label with black border

Number	Title (A Side/B Side)	Yr	NM
❑ CLP-3059 [M]	Folk Songs of the Everly Brothers	1963	50.00

—Reissue of 3016

Number	Title (A Side/B Side)	Yr	NM
❑ CLP-3062 [M]	15 Everly Hits 15	1963	40.00
❑ CLP-25040 [P]	The Fabulous Style of the Everly Brothers	1960	120.00

—Maroon label with metronome logo

Number	Title (A Side/B Side)	Yr	NM
❑ CLP-25040 [P]	The Fabulous Style of the Everly Brothers	1962	60.00

—Red label with black border

Number	Title (A Side/B Side)	Yr	NM
❑ CLP-25059 [R]	Folk Songs of the Everly Brothers	1963	40.00
❑ CLP-25062 [P]	15 Everly Hits 15	1963	50.00

Number	Title (A Side/B Side)	Yr	NM
HARMONY			
❑ HS 11304	Wake Up Little Susie	1969	12.00
❑ HS 11350	Christmas with the Everly Brothers and the Boys Town Choir	1969	20.00
❑ KH 11388	Chained to a Memory	1970	12.00
MERCURY			
❑ 822431-1	EB 84	1984	10.00
❑ 826142-1	Born Yesterday	1986	10.00
❑ 832520-1	Some Hearts	1989	12.00
PAIR			
❑ PDL1-1063 [(2)]	Living Legends	1986	12.00
PASSPORT			
❑ 11001 [(2)]	The Everly Brothers Reunion Concert	1984	15.00
RCA VICTOR			
❑ LSP-4620	Stories We Could Tell	1972	15.00
❑ LSP-4781	Pass the Chicken and Listen	1972	15.00
❑ AFL1-5401	Home Again	1985	10.00
RHINO			
❑ RNLP-211	The Everly Brothers	1985	10.00
❑ RNLP-212	Songs Our Daddy Taught Us	1985	10.00
❑ RNLP-213	The Fabulous Style of the Everly Brothers	1985	10.00
❑ RNLP-214	All They Had to Do Was Dream	1985	10.00
❑ RNDF-258 [PD]	Heartaches and Harmonies	1985	20.00
❑ RNLP-70173	The Best of the Everly Brothers (Golden Archive Series)	1987	10.00
TIME-LIFE			
❑ SRNR-09 [(2)]	The Everly Brothers: 1957-1962	1986	20.00
—Part of "The Rock 'n' Roll Era" series; box set with insert			
WARNER BROS.			
❑ PRO 134 [10]	It's Everly Time!	1960	600.00
—Promo "souvenir sampler" from their debut on WB			
❑ W 1381 [M]	It's Everly Time!	1960	30.00
❑ WS 1381 [S]	It's Everly Time!	1960	40.00
❑ W 1395 [M]	A Date with the Everly Brothers	1960	40.00
—Gatefold edition without poster or photos			
❑ W 1395 [M]	A Date with the Everly Brothers	1960	50.00
—Gatefold edition with poster and wallet-size photos			
❑ W 1395 [M]	A Date with the Everly Brothers	1961	30.00
—Regular edition			
❑ WS 1395 [S]	A Date with the Everly Brothers	1960	50.00
—Gatefold edition without poster or photos			
❑ WS 1395 [S]	A Date with the Everly Brothers	1960	75.00
—Gatefold edition with poster and wallet-size photos			
❑ WS 1395 [S]	A Date with the Everly Brothers	1961	40.00
—Regular edition			
❑ W 1418 [M]	Both Sides of an Evening	1961	30.00
❑ WS 1418 [S]	Both Sides of an Evening	1961	40.00
❑ W 1430 [M]	Instant Party!	1962	30.00
❑ WS 1430 [S]	Instant Party!	1962	40.00
❑ W 1471 [M]	The Golden Hits of the Everly Brothers	1962	30.00
❑ WS 1471	The Golden Hits of the Everly Brothers	1967	20.00
—Green "W7" label			
❑ WS 1471	The Golden Hits of the Everly Brothers	1970	15.00
—Green "WB" label			
❑ WS 1471	The Golden Hits of the Everly Brothers	1973	12.00
—"Burbank" palm-tree label			
❑ WS 1471	The Golden Hits of the Everly Brothers	1979	10.00
—White or tan label			
❑ WS 1471 [S]	The Golden Hits of the Everly Brothers	1962	40.00
—Gold label			
❑ W 1483 [M]	Christmas with the Everly Brothers and the Boys Town Choir	1962	40.00
❑ WS 1483 [S]	Christmas with the Everly Brothers and the Boys Town Choir	1962	50.00
❑ W 1513 [M]	Great Country Hits	1963	40.00
❑ WS 1513 [S]	Great Country Hits	1963	50.00
❑ W 1554 [M]	The Very Best of the Everly Brothers	1964	30.00
—Originals have yellow covers			
❑ W 1554 [M]	The Very Best of the Everly Brothers	1965	20.00
—Later pressings have white covers			
❑ WS 1554	The Very Best of the Everly Brothers	1967	20.00
—Green "W7" label			
❑ WS 1554	The Very Best of the Everly Brothers	1970	15.00
—Green "WB" label			
❑ WS 1554	The Very Best of the Everly Brothers	1973	12.00
—"Burbank" palm-tree label			
❑ WS 1554	The Very Best of the Everly Brothers	1979	10.00
—White or tan label			
❑ WS 1554 [S]	The Very Best of the Everly Brothers	1964	40.00
—Originals have yellow covers			
❑ WS 1554 [S]	The Very Best of the Everly Brothers	1965	25.00
—White cover; gold label			
❑ W 1578 [M]	Rock & Soul	1964	40.00
❑ WS 1578 [S]	Rock & Soul	1964	50.00
❑ W 1585 [M]	Gone, Gone, Gone	1965	40.00
❑ WS 1585 [S]	Gone, Gone, Gone	1965	50.00
❑ W 1605 [M]	Beat & Soul	1965	40.00
❑ WS 1605 [S]	Beat & Soul	1965	50.00
❑ W 1620 [M]	In Our Image	1966	40.00
❑ WS 1620 [S]	In Our Image	1966	50.00
❑ W 1646 [M]	Two Yanks in England	1966	40.00
❑ WS 1646 [S]	Two Yanks in England	1966	50.00
❑ W 1676 [M]	The Hit Sound of the Everly Brothers	1967	50.00
❑ WS 1676 [S]	The Hit Sound of the Everly Brothers	1967	40.00
❑ W 1708 [M]	The Everly Brothers Sing	1967	50.00
❑ WS 1708 [S]	The Everly Brothers Sing	1967	40.00
❑ WS 1752	Roots	1968	40.00
❑ WS 1858	The Everly Brothers Show	1970	30.00
❑ ST-91343 [S]	The Very Best of the Everly Brothers	1967	40.00
—Capitol Record Club edition			
❑ ST-91601	Roots	1968	50.00
—Capitol Record Club edition			
❑ STAO-93286	The Everly Brothers Show	1970	40.00
—Capitol Record Club edition			

EVERPRESENT FULLNESS, THE

Number	Title (A Side/B Side)	Yr	NM
45s			
WHITE WHALE			
❑ 233	Wild About My Lovin'/Doin' a Number	1966	15.00
❑ 233	Wild About My Lovin'/Fine and Dandy	1966	15.00
❑ 248	Darlin' You Can Count On Me/Yeah	1967	15.00
Albums			
WHITE WHALE			
❑ 7132	The Everpresent Fullness	1970	75.00

EVERY FATHER'S TEENAGE SON

Number	Title (A Side/B Side)	Yr	NM
45s			
BUDDAH			
❑ 25	A Letter to Dad/Josephine's Song	1968	8.00

EVERY MOTHERS' SON

Number	Title (A Side/B Side)	Yr	NM
45s			
MGM			
❑ 13733	Come On Down to My Boat/I Believe in You	1967	10.00
❑ 13788	Put Your Mind at Ease/Proper Four Leaf Clover	1967	8.00
❑ 13788 [PS]	Put Your Mind at Ease/Proper Four Leaf Clover	1967	12.00
❑ 13844	Pony with the Golden Mane/Dolls in the Clock	1967	8.00
❑ 13887	No One Knows/What Became of Mary	1968	8.00
❑ 13987	Rainflowers/For Brandy	1968	8.00
Albums			
MGM			
❑ E-4471 [M]	Every Mothers' Son	1967	20.00
❑ SE-4471 [S]	Every Mothers' Son	1967	20.00
❑ E-4504 [M]	Every Mothers' Son's Back	1967	20.00
❑ SE-4504 [S]	Every Mothers' Son's Back	1967	20.00

EVERYTHING IS EVERYTHING

Number	Title (A Side/B Side)	Yr	NM
45s			
VANGUARD APOSTOLIC			
❑ 35082	Witchi Tai To/Ooh Baby	1969	8.00
❑ 35097	Ya Hay Ho/You Don't Need No Music	1969	8.00
Albums			
VANGUARD			
❑ VSD-6512	Everything Is Everything	1969	25.00

EVIL, THE

Number	Title (A Side/B Side)	Yr	NM
45s			
CAPITOL			
❑ 2038	Whatcha Gonna Do About It/Always Runnin' Around	1967	20.00
LIVING LEGEND			
❑ 108	Whatcha Gonna Do About It/Always Runnin' Around	1967	40.00

EVIL ENCORPORATED

Number	Title (A Side/B Side)	Yr	NM
45s			
SCENE			
❑ 101	Hey You/The Thing Is...	1967	30.00
❑ 102	Baby It's You/All I Really Want to Do	1967	30.00

EXCALIBURS, THE

Number	Title (A Side/B Side)	Yr	NM
45s			
TRENT TOWN			
❑ 1017	Christmas Dreaming/Peace On Earth	19??	100.00

EXCELLENTS, THE

Number	Title (A Side/B Side)	Yr	NM
45s			
BLAST			
❑ 205	Coney Island Baby/You Baby You	1962	20.00
—Red and white label			
❑ 205	Coney Island Baby/You Baby You	1962	30.00
—All-red label			
❑ 205	Coney Island Baby/You Baby You	1965	25.00
—Purple label			
❑ 207	I Hear a Rhapsody/Why Did You Laugh	1963	60.00
MERMAID			
❑ 106	Love No One But You/Red Red Robin	1961	50.00
—No mermaid on label			
❑ 106	Love No One But You/Red Red Robin	1961	200.00
—With mermaid on label			

EXCELS, THE (1)

Number	Title (A Side/B Side)	Yr	NM
45s			
GONE			
❑ 5094	My Foolish Heart/Just You and I Together	1960	25.00
RSVP			
❑ 111	Can't Help Lovin' That Girl of Mine/Till You	1961	50.00

EXCELS, THE (2)

Number	Title (A Side/B Side)	Yr	NM
45s			
CARLA			
❑ 1901	Little Innocent Girl/Some Kind of Fun	1968	20.00
❑ 2529	Gonna Make You Mine Girl/Goodbye Poor Boy	1966	20.00
❑ 2534	I Wanna Be Free/Too Much Too Soon	1967	20.00
❑ 2536	California on My Mind/Arrival of Mary	1967	20.00

EXCELS, THE (3)

Number	Title (A Side/B Side)	Yr	NM
45s			
CENTRAL			
❑ 2601	You're Mine Forever/Baby Doll	1957	50.00
RELIC			
❑ 1007	You're Mine Forever/Baby Doll	1965	10.00

EXCEPTION, THE

Peter Cetera (later of CHICAGO) was a member of this group. See THE EXCEPTIONS (1).

Number	Title (A Side/B Side)	Yr	NM
45s			
❑			—

EXCEPTIONS, THE (1)

Members of this group would later appear in THE BUCKINGHAMS; CHICAGO; THE ILLINOIS SPEED PRESS and NEW COLONY SIX.

Number	Title (A Side/B Side)	Yr	NM
45s			
CAPITOL			
❑ 2046	Business As Usual/My Mind Goes Traveling	1967	12.00
—As "The Exception"			
❑ 2120	You Always Hurt Me/You Don't Know Like I Know	1968	12.00
—As "The Exception"			
❑ 5982	The Girl from New York City/As Far As I Can See	1967	12.00
—As "The Exception"			
MERCURY			
❑ 72562	Ask Me If I Care/Do-Do-Do Bah	1966	40.00
QUILL			
❑ 114	As Far As I Can See/Girl from New York	1966	30.00
TOLLIE			
❑ 9007	Searchin'/Daydreaming of You	1964	20.00
—As "Kal David and the Exceptions"			
❑ 9043	Come On Home/Dancing Danny	1965	20.00
—As "Kal David and the Exceptions"			

Except when noted otherwise, VG = 25% of NM, and VG+ = 50% of NM. (Example: VG = $2.00, VG+ = $4.00 and NM = $8.00.)

Number	Title (A Side/B Side)	Yr	NM
7-Inch Extended Plays			
FLAIR			
❑ 6444	Lord Have Mercy/Glory to God/ /Holy, Holy, Holy/Our Father/ Lamb of God	1966	50.00
—7-inch 33 1/3 rpm single with small hole			
❑ 6444 [PS]	Rock 'n' Roll Mass	1966	50.00

EXCEPTIONS, THE (2) Different group from (1).

Number	Title (A Side/B Side)	Yr	NM
45s			
CAMEO			
❑ 378	Down by the Ocean/ Pancho's Villa	1965	20.00

EXCITERS, THE

Number	Title (A Side/B Side)	Yr	NM
45s			
BANG			
❑ 515	A Little Bit of Soap/I'm Gonna Get Him Someday	1966	12.00
❑ 518	You Better Come Home/ Weddings Make Me Cry	1966	30.00
FARGO			
❑ 1400	Alone Again, Naturally/ (B-side unknown)	1972	8.00
RCA VICTOR			
❑ 47-9633	Take One Step (I'll Take Two)/ If You Want My Love	1968	30.00
❑ 47-9723	You Don't Know What You're Missing ('Til It's Gone!)/ Blowing Up My Mind	1969	30.00
❑ 48-1035	You Don't Know What You're Missing ('Til It's Gone!)/ Blowing Up My Mind	1972	15.00
ROULETTE			
❑ 4591	I Want You to Be My Boy/ Tonight, Tonight	1965	12.00
❑ 4591 [PS]	I Want You to Be My Boy/ Tonight, Tonight	1965	50.00
❑ 4594	Are You Satisfied/Just Not Ready	1965	12.00
❑ 4614	My Father/Run Mascara	1965	12.00
❑ 4632	I Knew You Would/ There They Go	1965	12.00
SHOUT			
❑ 205	Number One/You Got Love	1966	10.00
❑ 214	Soulmotion/You Know It Ain't Right	1967	10.00
TODAY			
❑ 1002	Learning How to Fly/Life, Love and Peace	1970	8.00
UNITED ARTISTS			
❑ 0029	Tell Him/Do Wah Diddy	1973	4.00
—"Silver Spotlight Series" reissue			
❑ 544	Tell Him/Hard Way to Go	1963	15.00
❑ 572	Drama of Love/He's Got the Power	1963	12.00
❑ 604	Get Him/It's So Exciting	1963	12.00
❑ 662	Do-Wah-Diddy/If Love Came Your Way	1963	12.00
❑ 721	Having My Fun/We Were Lovers (When the Party Began)	1964	12.00
❑ 830	Having My Fun/We Were Lovers (When the Party Began)	1965	10.00
Albums			
ROULETTE			
❑ R 25326 [M]	The Exciters	1966	30.00
❑ SR 25326 [S]	The Exciters	1966	40.00
TODAY			
❑ 1001	Black Beauty	1971	20.00
UNITED ARTISTS			
❑ UAL-3264 [M]	Tell Him	1963	70.00
❑ UAS-6264 [S]	Tell Him	1963	150.00

EXILE

Number	Title (A Side/B Side)	Yr	NM
45s			
ARISTA			
❑ 2009	Nobody's Talking/Don't Hang Up (Girl)	1990	3.00
❑ 2075	Yet/Show Me	1990	3.00
❑ 2139	There You Go/I'm Still Standing	1990	3.00
❑ 2228	Even Now/One Too Many Times	1991	3.00
❑ 9911	Keep It in the Middle of the Road/ Yet	1989	3.00
❑ 12351	Nothing at All/What You See	1991	3.00
ATCO			
❑ 7072	Try It On/Show Me What You Got	1977	5.00
COLUMBIA			
❑ 4-44972	Church Street Soul Revival/ Your Day Is Comin'	1969	8.00
—As "The Exiles"			
❑ 4-45210	Put Your Hands Together/ Your Day Is Comin'	1970	8.00
—As "The Exiles"			
EPIC			
❑ 34-04041	High Cost of Leaving/Like a Fool's Supposed to Do	1983	3.00
❑ 34-04247	Woke Up in Love/ First Things First	1983	4.00
❑ 34-04421	I Don't Want to Be a Memory/ After All These Years (I'm Still Chasing You)	1984	3.00
❑ 34-04567	Give Me One More Chance/ Ain't That a Pity	1984	3.00
❑ 34-04567 [PS]	Give Me One More Chance/ Ain't That a Pity	1984	4.00
❑ 34-04722	Crazy for Your Love/ Just in Case	1984	3.00
❑ 34-04864	She's a Miracle/I've Never Seen Anything	1985	3.00
❑ 34-05580	Hang On to Your Heart/ She Loves Her Lovin'	1985	3.00
❑ 34-05723	I Could Get Used to You/ Practice Makes Perfect	1985	3.00
❑ 34-05860	Super Love/Proud to Be Your Man	1986	3.00
❑ 34-06229	It'll Be Me/Music	1986	3.00
❑ 34-07135	She's Too Good to Be True/ Promises, Promises	1987	3.00
❑ 34-07597	I Can't Get Close Enough/As Long As I Have Your Memory	1987	3.00
❑ 34-07710	Feel Like Foolin' Around/ Showdown	1988	3.00
❑ 34-0 7775	Just One Kiss/As Long As I Have Your Memory	1988	3.00
❑ 34-08020	It's You Again/The Girl Can't Help It	1988	3.00
MCA CURB			
❑ 52551	Stay with Me/Kiss You All Over	1985	3.00
❑ 52596	Dixie Girl/Someone Like You	1985	3.00
SSS INTERNATIONAL			
❑ 848	Got to Be All Right/Second Hand Lady	197?	8.00
—As "Exiles"			
WARNER BROS.			
❑ 8589	Kiss You All Over/Don't Do It	1978	4.00
❑ 8711	You Thrill Me/One Step at a Time	1978	4.00
❑ 8796	How Could This Go Wrong/Being in Love with You Is Easy	1979	4.00
❑ 8848	Part of Me That Needs You Most/ Let's Do It All Over Again	1979	4.00
❑ 49048	Too Proud to Cry/Destiny	1979	4.00
❑ 49245	You're Gone for Me/Let's Do It All Over Again	1980	4.00
❑ 49548	Take Me Down/It Takes Love to Make Love	1980	6.00
—A-side was later a hit for Alabama			
❑ 49794	Heart and Soul/Your Love Is Everything	1981	4.00
❑ 49863	Till the Very End/What Kind of Love Is This	1981	4.00
WOODEN NICKEL			
❑ BWBO-0006	Do What You Think You Should/ Hold Tight Sweet Woman	1973	7.00
❑ 65-0115	Devil's Rite/Mabel	1973	7.00
Albums			
ARISTA			
❑ AL-9624	Still Standing	1990	15.00
EPIC			
❑ B6E 39154	Exile	1983	8.00
❑ FE 39424	Kentucky Hearts	1984	8.00
❑ BFE 40000	Hang On to Your Heart	1985	8.00
❑ FE 40401	Greatest Hits	1986	8.00
❑ FE 40901	Shelter from the Night	1987	8.00
MCA CURB			
❑ 946	All There Is	1986	8.00
❑ 947	Heart and Soul	1986	8.00
❑ 963	Mixed Emotions	1986	8.00
❑ 964	Don't Leave Me This Way	1986	8.00
❑ 1456	More of the Best of Exile	1986	8.00
❑ 5581	Best of Exile	1985	8.00
RCA VICTOR			
❑ AFL1-3086	Exile	1978	12.00
❑ AFL1-3087	Stage Pass	1978	12.00
WARNER BROS.			
❑ BSK 3205	Mixed Emotions	1978	10.00
❑ BSK 3323	All There Is	1979	10.00
❑ BSK 3437	Don't Leave Me This Way	1980	10.00
❑ BSK 3588	Heart and Soul	1981	10.00
WOODEN NICKEL			
❑ BWL1-0120	Exile	1973	15.00

EXITS, THE

Number	Title (A Side/B Side)	Yr	NM
45s			
GEMINI			
❑ 1004	Under the Street Lamp/ You Got to Have Money	1967	80.00
❑ 1006	I Don't Want to Hear It/ (Instrumental)	1967	50.00
KAPP			
❑ 2028	Another Sundown in Watts/I'm So Bad	1969	500.00

EXODUS

Number	Title (A Side/B Side)	Yr	NM
45s			
JAMIE			
❑ 1442	Four Seasons Medley (mono/stereo)	1981	5.00
—As "Exodus II"			
WAND			
❑ 11248	M&M/Silhouettes-You Cheated	1972	30.00
—Multi-colored label			
❑ 11248	M&M/Silhouettes-You Cheated	1972	100.00
—Black and white label			

EXOTIC GUITARS AL CASEY was guitarist for this studio group.

Number	Title (A Side/B Side)	Yr	NM
45s			
RANWOOD			
❑ 804	Spanish Eyes/C'est Si Bon	1968	5.00
❑ 811	I Will Wait for You/Blueberry Hill	1968	5.00
❑ 830	I Walk Alone/Twilight Time	1969	5.00
❑ 843	Indian Love Call/Trying	1969	5.00
❑ 856	To Rome with Love/ Peg o' My Heart	1969	5.00
❑ 863	I Was Kaiser Bill's Batman/ Now Is the Hour	1970	5.00
❑ 871	Holly Holy/High Noon	1970	5.00
❑ 882	Orange Blossom Special/ San Antonio Rose	1970	5.00
❑ 898	Till Love Touches Your Life/I Can't Stop Loving You	1971	4.00
❑ 914	Memphis/Maria Elena	1971	4.00
❑ 936	Crusing Down the River/ You Can't Be True Dear	1971	4.00
Albums			
RANWOOD			
❑ 8002	The Exotic Guitars	1968	12.00
❑ 8040	Those Were the Days	1968	12.00
❑ 8051	Indian Love Call	1969	12.00
❑ 8061	Everybody's Talkin'	1970	10.00
❑ 8073	Holly Holy	1970	10.00
❑ 8080	Country Music	1970	10.00
❑ 8085	I Can't Stop Loving You	1971	10.00
❑ 8090	All the Guitar Hits	1971	10.00
❑ 8171	300 Watt Music Box	1975	10.00

EXOTICS, THE More than one group.

Number	Title (A Side/B Side)	Yr	NM
45s			
BOLO			
❑ 722	Oasis/Chattanooga Choo Choo	1962	12.00
CORAL			
❑ 62268	That's My Desire/Darking, I Want to Get Married	1961	20.00
❑ 62289	The Gang That Sang (Heart of My Heart)/Hotcha Mighty Knows	1961	20.00
❑ 62310	Fortune Hunter/Manpower	1962	20.00
❑ 62343	My Life's Desire (Part 1)/ My Life's Desire (Part 2)	1963	15.00
❑ 62399	Let's Get Together/ Sad, Sad Song	1964	15.00
❑ 62439	Like You Hurt Me/ Big Time Charlie	1964	20.00
EXCELLO			
❑ 2284	Boogaloo Investigator/I Won't Ever Stop Loving You	1967	8.00
❑ 2292	Let Me Be a Part of You/Let's Try to Build a Love Affair	1968	8.00
JERDEN			
❑ 106	Four Banger/Cat Hairs	1960	15.00
MONUMENT			
❑ 984	Fire Engine Red/Morning Sun	1966	12.00
SEAFAIR			
❑ 108	Ginger Snap/(B-side unknown)	1962	10.00
❑ 113	Jerk Time/For the Winds	1965	10.00
SPRINGBOARD			
❑ 101	Gee/Lorraine	1963	20.00
❑ 101 [PS]	Gee/Lorraine	1963	40.00

EXPLORERS, THE

Number	Title (A Side/B Side)	Yr	NM
45s			
CORAL			
❑ 62147	Vision of Love/On a Clear Night	1959	60.00

Number	Title (A Side/B Side)	Yr	NM
❑ 62175	Don't Be a Fool/In the Wee Small Hours of the Morning	1960	100.00
❑ 62295	Remember/Every Road (I Walk Along)	1961	60.00

—As "Dennis and the Explorers"

Number	Title (A Side/B Side)	Yr	NM
❑ 65575	Don't Be a Fool/Vision of Love	196?	30.00

—Was listed in the last edition under "The Visions"

EXPORTS, THE

45s

KING

Number	Title (A Side/B Side)	Yr	NM
❑ 5917	Car Hop/Seat Belts Please	1964	25.00
❑ 5985	Mustang '65/Always It's You	1965	25.00

EXPRESSIONS, THE

45s

ARLISS

Number	Title (A Side/B Side)	Yr	NM
❑ 1012	My Love, My Love/The Sign of Happiness	1962	50.00

FEDERAL

Number	Title (A Side/B Side)	Yr	NM
❑ 12533	You Better Know It/Out of My Life	1964	10.00

GUYDEN

Number	Title (A Side/B Side)	Yr	NM
❑ 2122	Be-Bop-a-Lula/Skinnie Minnie	1965	15.00

—As "J-D and the Expressions"

PARKWAY

Number	Title (A Side/B Side)	Yr	NM
❑ 892	On the Corner/To Cry	1963	15.00

REPRISE

Number	Title (A Side/B Side)	Yr	NM
❑ 0360	Playboy/One Plus One	1965	20.00

SMASH

Number	Title (A Side/B Side)	Yr	NM
❑ 1848	Karen/Thrill	1963	15.00

TEEN

Number	Title (A Side/B Side)	Yr	NM
❑ 101	Now That You've Gone/Crazy	1957	200.00

EXTERMINATORS, THE

45s

CHANCELLOR

Number	Title (A Side/B Side)	Yr	NM
❑ 1143	The Beetle Bomb/Stomp 'Em Out	1963	25.00
❑ 1148	Beatle Stomp/Stomp 'Em Out	1964	15.00

—A-sides are the same song with different titles

GOLDEN WEST

Number	Title (A Side/B Side)	Yr	NM
❑ 1002	Beatle Stomp/Stomp 'Em Out	1964	20.00

EXTREMES, THE

45s

EVERLAST

Number	Title (A Side/B Side)	Yr	NM
❑ 5013	Come Next Spring/Let's Elope	1958	150.00

PARO

Number	Title (A Side/B Side)	Yr	NM
❑ 733	The Bells/That's All I Want	1962	300.00

EYES OF BLUE

45s

DERAM

Number	Title (A Side/B Side)	Yr	NM
❑ 85001	Heart Trouble/Up and Down	1967	8.00
❑ 85003	Don't Ask Me to Mend Your Broken Heart/Supermarket Full of Cans	1967	8.00

MERCURY

Number	Title (A Side/B Side)	Yr	NM
❑ 72911	Apache '69/QIII	1969	8.00

Albums

MERCURY

Number	Title (A Side/B Side)	Yr	NM
❑ SR-61184	Crossroads of Time	1968	30.00
❑ SR-61220	In Fields of Ardath	1969	30.00

F

FABARES, SHELLEY

45s

COLPIX

Number	Title (A Side/B Side)	Yr	NM
❑ 621	Johnny Angel/Where's It Gonna Get Me	1962	20.00
❑ 621 [PS]	Johnny Angel/Where's It Gonna Get Me	1962	500.00
❑ 631	What Did They Do Before Rock and Roll/Very Unlikely	1962	20.00

—With Paul Petersen

Number	Title (A Side/B Side)	Yr	NM
❑ 631 [PS]	What Did They Do Before Rock and Roll/Very Unlikely	1962	400.00
❑ 636	Johnny Loves Me/I'm Growing Up	1962	20.00
❑ 636 [PS]	Johnny Loves Me/I'm Growing Up	1962	120.00
❑ 654	The Things We Did Last Summer/Breaking Up Is Hard to Do	1962	20.00
❑ 667	Big Star/Telephone (Don't You Ring)	1962	20.00
❑ 682	Ronnie, Call Me When You Get a Chance/I Left a Note to Say Goodbye	1963	20.00
❑ 705	Welcome Home/Billy Boy	1963	20.00
❑ 721	Football Season's Over/He Don't Love Me	1963	100.00

—Produced by Jan Berry of Jan and Dean

DUNHILL

Number	Title (A Side/B Side)	Yr	NM
❑ 4001	My Prayer/Pretty Please	1965	30.00
❑ 4041	See Ya 'Round on the Rebound/Pretty Please	1966	30.00

VEE JAY

Number	Title (A Side/B Side)	Yr	NM
❑ 632	I Know You'll Be There/Lost Summer Love	1964	40.00

Albums

COLPIX

Number	Title (A Side/B Side)	Yr	NM
❑ CP-426 [M]	Shelley!	1962	150.00
❑ SCP-426 [S]	Shelley!	1962	600.00
❑ CP-431 [M]	The Things We Did Last Summer	1962	100.00
❑ SCP-431 [S]	The Things We Did Last Summer	1962	400.00

FABIAN

45s

CHANCELLOR

Number	Title (A Side/B Side)	Yr	NM
❑ 1020	I'm in Love/Shivers	1958	25.00
❑ 1024	Be My Steady Date/Lilly Lou	1958	25.00
❑ 1029 [M]	I'm a Man/Hypnotized	1959	20.00
❑ 1029 [PS]	I'm a Man/Hypnotized	1959	40.00
❑ 1029 [PS]	I Am a Man/Hypnotized	1959	50.00

—Incorrect title on A-side of sleeve

Number	Title (A Side/B Side)	Yr	NM
❑ S-1029 [S]	I'm a Man/Hypnotized	1959	50.00
❑ 1033 [M]	Turn Me Loose/Stop Thief!	1959	20.00
❑ 1033 [PS]	Turn Me Loose/Stop Thief!	1959	40.00
❑ S-1033 [S]	Turn Me Loose/Stop Thief!	1959	50.00
❑ 1037 [M]	Tiger/Mighty Cold (To a Warm, Warm Heart)	1959	20.00
❑ 1037 [PS]	Tiger/Mighty Cold (To a Warm, Warm Heart)	1959	40.00
❑ S-1037 [S]	Tiger/Mighty Cold (To a Warm, Warm Heart)	1959	50.00
❑ 1041 [M]	Come On and Get Me/Got the Feeling	1959	20.00
❑ 1041 [PS]	Come On and Get Me/Got the Feeling	1959	40.00
❑ S-1041 [S]	Come On and Get Me/Got the Feeling	1959	50.00
❑ 1044	Hound Dog Man/Friendly World	1959	25.00
❑ 1044 [M]	Hound Dog Man/This Friendly World	1959	20.00

—Note difference in B-side title

Number	Title (A Side/B Side)	Yr	NM
❑ 1044 [PS]	Hound Dog Man/This Friendly World	1959	40.00
❑ S-1044 [S]	Hound Dog Man/This Friendly World	1959	50.00
❑ 1047 [M]	About This Thing Called Love/String Along	1960	12.00
❑ 1047 [PS]	About This Thing Called Love/String Along	1960	30.00
❑ S-1047 [S]	About This Thing Called Love/String Along	1960	50.00
❑ 1051	I'm Gonna Sit Right Down and Write Myself a Letter/Strollin' in the Springtime	1960	12.00
❑ 1051 [PS]	I'm Gonna Sit Right Down and Write Myself a Letter/Strollin' in the Springtime	1960	30.00
❑ 1055	Tomorrow/King of Love	1960	12.00
❑ 1055 [PS]	Tomorrow/King of Love	1960	30.00
❑ 1061	Kissin' and Twistin'/Long Before	1960	12.00
❑ 1061 [PS]	Kissin' and Twistin'/Long Before	1960	30.00
❑ 1067	You Know You Belong to Someone Else/Hold On	1961	12.00
❑ 1067 [PS]	You Know You Belong to Someone Else/Hold On	1961	30.00
❑ 1072	Grapevine/David and Goliath	1961	12.00
❑ 1079	The Love That I'm Giving to You/You're Only Young Once	1961	15.00
❑ 1079 [PS]	The Love That I'm Giving to You/You're Only Young Once	1961	40.00
❑ 1084	A Girl Like You/Dream Factory	1961	12.00
❑ 1084 [PS]	A Girl Like You/Dream Factory	1961	30.00
❑ 1086	Tongue-Tied/Kansas City	1961	20.00
❑ 1092	Wild Party/Made You	1961	20.00
❑ 1092	Wild Party/The Gospel Truth	1961	25.00
❑ 1092 [PS]	Wild Party/Made You	1961	40.00

CREAM

Number	Title (A Side/B Side)	Yr	NM
❑ 7717	Ease On (Into My Life)/The American East	1977	5.00
❑ 7717 [PS]	Ease On (Into My Life)/The American East	1977	5.00

DOT

Number	Title (A Side/B Side)	Yr	NM
❑ 16413	Break Down and Cry/She's Staying Inside with Me	1963	10.00

7-Inch Extended Plays

CHANCELLOR

Number	Title (A Side/B Side)	Yr	NM
❑ A-301	*Hound Dog Man/This Friendly World/Pretty Little Girl/I'm Growin' Up/Single	1960	50.00
❑ A-301 [PS]	5 Songs from Hound Dog Man	1960	50.00
❑ A-5003	*Hold Me (In Your Arms)/Just One More Time/Please Don't Stop/Ooh, What You Do!	1959	60.00
❑ A-5003 [PS]	Hold That Tiger! Vol. 1	1959	60.00
❑ B-5003	(contents unknown)	1959	60.00
❑ B-5003 [PS]	Hold That Tiger! Vol. 2	1959	60.00
❑ C-5003	Turn Me Loose/Steady Date//Don't You Think It's Time?/Cuddle Up a Little Closer	1959	60.00
❑ C-5003 [PS]	Hold That Tiger! Vol. 3	1959	60.00
❑ A-5005	Remember Me/I'm Sincere//Everything Is Just Right/You'll Never Tame Me	1959	60.00
❑ A-5005 [PS]	The Fabulous Fabian, Vol. 1	1959	60.00
❑ B-5005	(contents unknown)	1959	60.00
❑ B-5005 [PS]	The Fabulous Fabian, Vol. 2	1959	60.00
❑ C-5005	(contents unknown)	1959	60.00
❑ C-5005 [PS]	The Fabulous Fabian, Vol. 3	1959	60.00
❑ A-9802	Young and Wonderful/Think of Me//Take Me/Exactly Like You	1960	50.00
❑ A-9802 [PS]	Young and Wonderful	1960	50.00

Albums

ABC

Number	Title (A Side/B Side)	Yr	NM
❑ X-806	16 Greatest Hits	1973	12.00

CHANCELLOR

Number	Title (A Side/B Side)	Yr	NM
❑ CHL-5003 [M]	Hold That Tiger!	1959	50.00

—Black label

Number	Title (A Side/B Side)	Yr	NM
❑ CHL-5003 [M]	Hold That Tiger!	1959	100.00

—Pink label

Number	Title (A Side/B Side)	Yr	NM
❑ CHLS-5003 [S]	Hold That Tiger!	1959	75.00

—Black label

Number	Title (A Side/B Side)	Yr	NM
❑ CHLS-5003 [S]	Hold That Tiger!	1959	150.00

—Pink label

Number	Title (A Side/B Side)	Yr	NM
❑ CHL-5005 [M]	Fabulous Fabian	1959	50.00
❑ CHLS-5005 [S]	Fabulous Fabian	1959	75.00
❑ CHL-5012 [M]	The Good Old Summertime	1960	50.00
❑ CHLS-5012 [S]	The Good Old Summertime	1960	75.00
❑ CHL-5019 [M]	Rockin' Hot	1961	75.00
❑ CHL-5024 [M]	Fabian's 16 Fabulous Hits	1962	75.00
❑ CHL-69802 [M]	The Fabian Facade: Young and Wonderful	1960	80.00

—Felt gatefold cover with die-cut window

MCA

Number	Title (A Side/B Side)	Yr	NM
❑ 27095	The Best of Fabian	1985	8.00

UNITED ARTISTS

Number	Title (A Side/B Side)	Yr	NM
❑ UA-LA449-E	The Very Best of Fabian	1975	12.00

FABIAN / FRANKIE AVALON

Albums

CHANCELLOR

Number	Title (A Side/B Side)	Yr	NM
❑ CHL-5009 [M]	The Hit Makers	1960	100.00

FABRIC, BENT

Also see ACKER BILK.

45s

ATCO

Number	Title (A Side/B Side)	Yr	NM
❑ 6226	Alley Cat/Marking Time	1962	8.00
❑ 6245	Chicken Feed/That Certain Party	1962	8.00
❑ 6271	The Happy Puppy/Sermonette	1963	8.00
❑ 6304	The Organ Grinder's Swing/Goofus	1964	8.00
❑ 6333	The Old Piano Roll Blues/Titena	1964	8.00
❑ 6363	The Drunken Penguin/Alley Cat	1965	8.00
❑ 6401	Sweet Charity Theme/Can't You See	1966	8.00

Albums

ATCO

Number	Title (A Side/B Side)	Yr	NM
❑ 33-148 [M]	Alley Cat	1962	15.00
❑ SD 33-148 [S]	Alley Cat	1962	20.00
❑ 33-155 [M]	The Happy Puppy	1963	12.00
❑ SD 33-155 [S]	The Happy Puppy	1963	15.00
❑ 33-164 [M]	Organ Grinder's Swing	1964	12.00
❑ SD 33-164 [S]	Organ Grinder's Swing	1964	15.00
❑ 33-173 [M]	The Drunken Penguin	1965	12.00
❑ SD 33-173 [S]	The Drunken Penguin	1965	15.00
❑ 33-185 [M]	Never Tease Tigers	1966	12.00
❑ SD 33-185 [S]	Never Tease Tigers	1966	15.00
❑ 33-202 [M]	Operation Lovebirds	1967	12.00
❑ SD 33-202 [S]	Operation Lovebirds	1967	15.00
❑ 33-221 [M]	Relax	1967	15.00
❑ SD 33-221 [S]	Relax	1967	12.00

FABS, THE

45s

COTTON BALL

Number	Title (A Side/B Side)	Yr	NM
❑ 1005	That's the Bag I'm In/Dinah Wants Religion	1966	150.00

Except when noted otherwise, VG = 25% of NM, and VG+ = 50% of NM. (Example: VG = $2.00, VG+ = $4.00 and NM = $8.00.)

FABULAIRES, THE

45s

EASTWEST

Number	Title (A Side/B Side)	Yr	NM
❑ 103	While Walking/No No	1957	300.00

LOST-NITE

Number	Title (A Side/B Side)	Yr	NM
❑ 184	While Walking/No No	196?	6.00

—Reissue

MAIN LINE

Number	Title (A Side/B Side)	Yr	NM
❑ 103	While Walking/No No	1958	200.00

FABULONS, THE (1)

45s

EMBER

Number	Title (A Side/B Side)	Yr	NM
❑ 1069	Smoke From Your Cigarette/ Give Me Back My Ring	1960	25.00

—Black label

Number	Title (A Side/B Side)	Yr	NM
❑ 1069	Smoke From Your Cigarette/ Give Me Back My Ring	1960	50.00

—White label

FABULONS, THE (2) Also see THE TIKIS AND THE FABULONS.

45s

TOWER

Number	Title (A Side/B Side)	Yr	NM
❑ 259	Since You've Been Gone/Don't Ask Me	1966	15.00

FABULOUS CONTINENTALS

45s

CB

Number	Title (A Side/B Side)	Yr	NM
❑ 5003	Undertow/Return to Me	1963	20.00
❑ 5007	Let's Get Goin'/New York Walk	1964	15.00

RORI

Number	Title (A Side/B Side)	Yr	NM
❑ 709	Venus/Breakin' Up	1962	15.00

FABULOUS COUNTS, THE

45s

MOIRA

Number	Title (A Side/B Side)	Yr	NM
❑ 103	Jan Jan/Girl from Kenya	1969	10.00
❑ 105	Dirty Red/Scrambled Eggs	1970	15.00
❑ 108	Get Down People/Lunar Funk	1970	10.00

Albums

COTILLION

Number	Title (A Side/B Side)	Yr	NM
❑ SD 9011	Jan Jan	1969	100.00
❑ SD 9011	Jan Jan	199?	12.00

—Reissue; superficially almost identical to original

FABULOUS FARQUAHR See FARQUAHR.

FABULOUS FIVE, THE

45s

KING

Number	Title (A Side/B Side)	Yr	NM
❑ 5220	Janie Made a Monster/Gettin' Old	1959	15.00

FABULOUS FLAMES, THE (1)

45s

BAY-TONE

Number	Title (A Side/B Side)	Yr	NM
❑ 102	Do You Remember/ Get to Stepping	1961	40.00
❑ 105	Lover/I'm So All Alone	1961	50.00

REX

Number	Title (A Side/B Side)	Yr	NM
❑ 3000	Josephine/My Joan	1958	120.00

FABULOUS FLAMES, THE (2) For records on Harlem, see THE FLAMES.

FABULOUS FLIPPERS, THE

45s

CAMEO

Number	Title (A Side/B Side)	Yr	NM
❑ 439	Harlem Shuffle/I Don't Want to Cry	1966	30.00
❑ 454	Shout/Turn On Your Love Light	1967	20.00

FONA

Number	Title (A Side/B Side)	Yr	NM
❑ 307	Don't Fight It/(B-side unknown)	196?	30.00
❑ 312	West Side Story/Women Ain't Good for Me	196?	30.00

QUILL

Number	Title (A Side/B Side)	Yr	NM
❑ 110	Dry My Eyes/Women Ain't Good for Me	1966	40.00
❑ 111	Harlem Shuffle/I Don't Want to Cry	1966	40.00

Albums

VERITAS

Number	Title (A Side/B Side)	Yr	NM
❑ VS-2570	Something Tangible	1970	25.00

FABULOUS FOUR, THE

45s

BRASS

Number	Title (A Side/B Side)	Yr	NM
❑ 311	Now You Cry/Got to Get Her Back	1964	20.00
❑ 314	Who Could It Be/Happy	1964	20.00
❑ 316	I'm Always Doing Something Wrong/Young Blood	1964	20.00

CHANCELLOR

Number	Title (A Side/B Side)	Yr	NM
❑ 1062	In the Chapel in the Moonlight/ Mr. Twist	1960	25.00
❑ 1068	Let's Try Again/ Precious Moments	1961	25.00
❑ 1078	Why Do Fools Fall in Love/ Sounds of Summer	1961	40.00
❑ 1085	Prisoner of Love/Betty Ann	1961	80.00
❑ 1090	Everybody Knows/ I'm Coming Home	1961	20.00
❑ 1098	Mr. Twist/Everybody Knows	1961	20.00
❑ 1102	Forever/(It's No) Sin	1962	25.00

CORAL

Number	Title (A Side/B Side)	Yr	NM
❑ 62479	Now You Cry/Got to Get Her Back	1966	15.00

MELIC

Number	Title (A Side/B Side)	Yr	NM
❑ 4114	Welcome Me Home/ Oop Shoobee Doop	1962	50.00

FABULOUS JOKERS, THE

Albums

MONUMENT

Number	Title (A Side/B Side)	Yr	NM
❑ MLP-8059 [M]	Guitars Extraordinaire	1966	100.00
❑ SLP-18059 [S]	Guitars Extraordinaire	1966	150.00

FABULOUS PACK, THE See TERRY KNIGHT AND THE PACK.

FABULOUS PEARL DEVINES, THE

45s

ALCO

Number	Title (A Side/B Side)	Yr	NM
❑ 101	You've Been Gone/So Lonely	1963	400.00

FABULOUS PEPS, THE

45s

D-TOWN

Number	Title (A Side/B Side)	Yr	NM
❑ 1049	You Never Had It So Good/ Detroit, Michigan	1965	40.00

—As "The Peps"

Number	Title (A Side/B Side)	Yr	NM
❑ 1060	Thinking About You/This I Pray	1965	40.00

—As "The Peps"

Number	Title (A Side/B Side)	Yr	NM
❑ 1065	My Love Looks Good on You/ Speak Your Peace	1966	50.00

GE GE

Number	Title (A Side/B Side)	Yr	NM
❑ 503	This Love I Have for You/ She's Going to Leave You	1965	40.00

PREMIUM STUFF

Number	Title (A Side/B Side)	Yr	NM
❑ 1	Why Are You Blowing My Mind/ I Can't Get Right	1967	40.00
❑ 3	So Fine/I'll Never Be the Same Again	1967	40.00
❑ 7	Gypsy Woman/Why Are You Blowing My Mind	1967	40.00

WEE-3

Number	Title (A Side/B Side)	Yr	NM
❑ 233	With These Eyes/ I've Been Trying	1967	30.00

WHEELSVILLE

Number	Title (A Side/B Side)	Yr	NM
❑ 109	With These Eyes/Light of My Life	1968	12.00

FABULOUS POODLES

12-Inch Singles

EPIC

Number	Title (A Side/B Side)	Yr	NM
❑ AS 718 [DJ]	Pink City Twist/Bionic Man	1979	10.00

45s

EPIC

Number	Title (A Side/B Side)	Yr	NM
❑ 8-50666	Mirror Star/Tit Photographer Blues	1979	5.00
❑ 8-50720	Work Shy/Toytown People	1979	5.00
❑ 9-50823	Man with Money/B Movies	1980	5.00
❑ 9-50835	Bionic Man/Suicide Bridge	1980	5.00

Albums

EPIC

Number	Title (A Side/B Side)	Yr	NM
❑ JE 35666	Mirror Stars	1978	10.00
❑ JE 35666 [DJ]	Mirror Stars	1978	16.00

—White label promo on pink vinyl

Number	Title (A Side/B Side)	Yr	NM
❑ JE 36256	Think Pink	1979	10.00

FABULOUS RHINESTONES, THE

45s

JUST SUNSHINE

Number	Title (A Side/B Side)	Yr	NM
❑ 500	What a Wonderful Thing We Have/Nothing New	1972	5.00
❑ 500 [PS]	What a Wonderful Thing We Have/Nothing New	1972	6.00
❑ 501	Free/Live It Out to the End	1972	5.00
❑ 509	Freewheelin'/Whitecaps	1973	5.00

Albums

JUST SUNSHINE

Number	Title (A Side/B Side)	Yr	NM
❑ 1	The Fabulous Rhinestones	1972	12.00
❑ 9	Freewheelin'	1973	12.00

FABULOUS THUNDERBIRDS, THE

12-Inch Singles

CBS ASSOCIATED

Number	Title (A Side/B Side)	Yr	NM
❑ ZAS 1537 [DJ]	Rock This Place (same on both sides)	1989	6.00
❑ ZAS 2276 [DJ]	Tuff Enuff (same on both sides)	1986	8.00
❑ ZAS 2313 [DJ]	Wrap It Up/Why Get Up?	1986	8.00
❑ ZAS 2451 [DJ]	Look at That, Look at That (same on both sides)	1987	10.00
❑ ZAS 2735 [DJ]	Stand Back (same on both sides)	1987	6.00

CHRYSALIS

Number	Title (A Side/B Side)	Yr	NM
❑ CHS-26 [DJ]	Ones Too Many (same on both sides)	1981	8.00

ELEKTRA

Number	Title (A Side/B Side)	Yr	NM
❑ ED 5316 [DJ]	Powerful Stuff (LP Version) (Edit)	1988	6.00

45s

CBS ASSOCIATED

Number	Title (A Side/B Side)	Yr	NM
❑ ZS4 05838	Tuff Enuff/Look at That, Look at That	1986	3.00
❑ ZS4 05838 [PS]	Tuff Enuff/Look at That, Look at That	1986	3.00
❑ ZS4 06270	Wrap It Up/True Love	1986	3.00
❑ ZS4 06270 [PS]	Wrap It Up/True Love	1986	3.00
❑ ZS4 06396	Why Get Up/I Don't Care	1986	3.00
❑ ZS4 07230	Stand Back/It Takes a Big Man to Cry	1987	3.00
❑ ZS4 07230 [PS]	Stand Back/It Takes a Big Man to Cry	1987	3.00
❑ ZS4 07602	How Do You Spell Love/ Love in Common	1987	3.00
❑ ZS4 07649	Wasted Tears/It Comes to Me Naturally	1987	3.00
❑ ZS4 68880	Knock Yourself Out/Emergency	1989	3.00

ELEKTRA

Number	Title (A Side/B Side)	Yr	NM
❑ 69384	Powerful Stuff/Tutti Frutti	1988	3.00

—B-side by Little Richard

EPIC

Number	Title (A Side/B Side)	Yr	NM
❑ ES7 2594 [DJ]	Merry Christmas Darling/ (Rockin') Winter Wonderland	1983	5.00

Albums

CBS ASSOCIATED

Number	Title (A Side/B Side)	Yr	NM
❑ BFZ 40304	Tuff Enuff	1986	10.00
❑ FZ 40304	Tuff Enuff	1986	8.00

—Reissue with new prefix

Number	Title (A Side/B Side)	Yr	NM
❑ FZ 40818	Hot Number	1987	8.00
❑ OZ 45094	Powerful Stuff	1989	10.00

CHRYSALIS

Number	Title (A Side/B Side)	Yr	NM
❑ CHR 1287	What's the Word	1980	12.00
❑ CHR 1319	Butt Rockin'	1981	12.00
❑ CHR 1395	T-Bird Rhythm	1982	12.00
❑ PV 41250	The Fabulous Thunderbirds	198?	8.00

—Reissue of Takoma 7068

Number	Title (A Side/B Side)	Yr	NM
❑ PV 41287	What's the Word	198?	8.00

—Reissue of 1287

Number	Title (A Side/B Side)	Yr	NM
❑ PV 41319	Butt Rockin'	198?	8.00

—Reissue of 1319

Number	Title (A Side/B Side)	Yr	NM
❑ FV 41395	T-Bird Rhythm	1983	10.00

—Reissue of 1395

Number	Title (A Side/B Side)	Yr	NM
❑ PV 41395	T-Bird Rhythm	198?	8.00

—Reissue with new prefix

TAKOMA

Number	Title (A Side/B Side)	Yr	NM
❑ TAK 7068	The Fabulous Thunderbirds	1979	12.00

FABULOUS UPTONES, THE

45s

TULIP

Number	Title (A Side/B Side)	Yr	NM
❑ 100	New Love I've Found/Turtle	1962	300.00

FABULOUS VALIENTS, THE

45s

HOLIDAY

Number	Title (A Side/B Side)	Yr	NM
❑ 61005	Your Golden Teardrops/ Carmelita	1962	250.00

FACENDA, JOHN (NARRATOR)

Albums

MANUSCRIPT

Number	Title (A Side/B Side)	Yr	NM
❑ MLP-571 [M]	The Nativity	1957	40.00

—Original Philadelphia-area issue; gatefold with 12-page booklet

RCA VICTOR

Number	Title (A Side/B Side)	Yr	NM
❑ LOP-1504 [M]	The Nativity	1958	30.00

—National reissue of Manuscript LP; very similar to original issue

FACENDA, TOMMY

45s

ATLANTIC

Number	Title (A Side/B Side)	Yr	NM
❑ 45-51	High School U.S.A.-Virginia/ Plea of Love	1959	40.00
❑ 45-52	High School U.S.A.-New York City/Plea of Love	1959	40.00

Number	Title (A Side/B Side)	Yr	NM
❑ 45-53	High School U.S.A.-North & South Carolina/Plea of Love	1959	40.00
❑ 45-54	High School U.S.A.-Washington, D.C./Plea of Love	1959	40.00
❑ 45-55	High School U.S.A.-Philadelphia/Plea of Love	1959	40.00
❑ 45-56	High School U.S.A.-Detroit/Plea of Love	1959	40.00
❑ 45-57	High School U.S.A.-Pittsburgh/Plea of Love	1959	40.00
❑ 45-58	High School U.S.A.-Minneapolis-St. Paul/Plea of Love	1959	40.00
❑ 45-59	High School U.S.A.-Florida/Plea of Love	1959	40.00
❑ 45-60	High School U.S.A.-Newark, N.J./Plea of Love	1959	40.00
❑ 45-61	High School U.S.A.-Boston/Plea of Love	1959	40.00
❑ 45-62	High School U.S.A.-Cleveland/Plea of Love	1959	40.00
❑ 45-63	High School U.S.A.-Buffalo/Plea of Love	1959	40.00
❑ 45-64	High School U.S.A.-Hartford, Conn./Plea of Love	1959	40.00
❑ 45-65	High School U.S.A.-Nashville/Plea of Love	1959	40.00
❑ 45-66	High School U.S.A.-Indianapolis/Plea of Love	1959	40.00
❑ 45-67	High School U.S.A.-Chicago/Plea of Love	1959	40.00
❑ 45-68	High School U.S.A.-New Orleans/Plea of Love	1959	40.00
❑ 45-69	High School U.S.A.-St. Louis & Kansas City/Plea of Love	1959	40.00
❑ 45-70	High School U.S.A.-Georgia, Alabama/Plea of Love	1959	40.00
❑ 45-71	High School U.S.A.-Cincinnati/Plea of Love	1959	40.00
❑ 45-72	High School U.S.A.-Memphis/Plea of Love	1959	40.00
❑ 45-73	High School U.S.A.-Los Angeles/Plea of Love	1959	40.00
❑ 45-74	High School U.S.A.-San Francisco/Plea of Love	1959	40.00
❑ 45-75	High School U.S.A.-Texas/Plea of Love	1959	40.00
❑ 45-76	High School U.S.A.-Seattle, Portland/Plea of Love	1959	40.00
❑ 45-77	High School U.S.A.-Denver/Plea of Love	1959	40.00
❑ 45-78	High School U.S.A.-Oklahoma/Plea of Love	1959	40.00
❑ 2057	Bubba Ditty/I Don't Know	1960	20.00

LEGRAND

Number	Title (A Side/B Side)	Yr	NM
❑ 1001	High School U.S.A./Give Me Another Chance	1959	25.00
—Original pressings have purple labels			
❑ 1001	High School U.S.A./Give Me Another Chance	196?	15.00
—Later pressings have red and gold labels			

NASCO

Number	Title (A Side/B Side)	Yr	NM
❑ 6018	Little Baby/You Are My Everything	1958	25.00

FACES
Also see SMALL FACES; ROD STEWART; RONNIE WOOD.

45s

WARNER BROS.

Number	Title (A Side/B Side)	Yr	NM
❑ 7393	Around the Phynth/Wicked Messenger	1970	10.00
—As "Small Faces"			
❑ 7442	Real Good Time/Real Wheel Skid	1970	10.00
❑ 7483	Maybe I'm Amazed/Oh Lord I'm Browned Off	1971	8.00
❑ 7545	Stay with Me/You're So Rude	1971	6.00
❑ 7681	Cindy Incidentally/Skewiff (Mend the Fuse)	1973	5.00
❑ 7681 [PS]	Cindy Incidentally/Skewiff (Mend the Fuse)	1973	6.00
❑ 7711	Ooh-La-La/Borstal Boys	1973	5.00

Albums

WARNER BROS.

Number	Title (A Side/B Side)	Yr	NM
❑ WS 1851	First Step	197?	12.00
—Later pressings have "faces." on front cover			
❑ WS 1851	First Step	1970	20.00
—First pressings have "small faces." on front cover			
❑ WS 1892	Long Player	1971	15.00
❑ BS 2574	A Nod Is As Good As a Wink...To a Blind Horse	1971	15.00
—Green label			
❑ BS 2574	A Nod Is As Good As a Wink...To a Blind Horse	1973	12.00
—"Burbank" palm trees label			
❑ BS 2665	Ooh La La	1973	12.00
—"Burbank" palm trees label			
❑ BS 2665	Ooh La La	1973	15.00
—Green label			
❑ BS 2897	Snakes and Ladders: The Best of Faces	1976	12.00
❑ ST-93718	Long Player	1971	20.00
—Capitol Record Club edition			

FACES, THE

45s

IGUANA

Number	Title (A Side/B Side)	Yr	NM
❑ 601	Christmas/New Year's Resolution	1965	100.00

REGINA

Number	Title (A Side/B Side)	Yr	NM
❑ 326	Skier Jones/What Is This Dream (I Have)	1965	25.00
❑ 328	I'll Walk Alone/I Didn't Want Her	1965	25.00

FACTORY, THE
Lowell George was in this group before LITTLE FEAT.

45s

UNI

Number	Title (A Side/B Side)	Yr	NM
❑ 55005	Smile, Let Your Life Begin/When I Was An Apple	1967	12.00

FAGAN, SCOTT

45s

BANG

Number	Title (A Side/B Side)	Yr	NM
❑ 530	Give Love a Chance/Tutsie	1966	12.00

BOURNEFIELD

Number	Title (A Side/B Side)	Yr	NM
❑ 800	Sandy the Blue-Nosed Reindeer/The Story of Sandy the Blue-Nosed Reindeer	1979	6.00

EPIC

Number	Title (A Side/B Side)	Yr	NM
❑ 5-10570	Kings and Pawns/Ashes	1970	10.00
❑ 5-10619	I Am/Where My Lover Has Gone	1970	10.00

RCA VICTOR

Number	Title (A Side/B Side)	Yr	NM
❑ PB-10678	Surrender to the Sun/Many Sunny Places	1976	6.00

Albums

ATCO

Number	Title (A Side/B Side)	Yr	NM
❑ SD 33-267	South Atlantic Blues	1968	20.00

RCA VICTOR

Number	Title (A Side/B Side)	Yr	NM
❑ APL1-1185	Many Sunny Places	1976	15.00

FAGEN, DONALD

12-Inch Singles

WARNER BROS.

Number	Title (A Side/B Side)	Yr	NM
❑ PRO-A-1092 [DJ]	New Frontier/The Goodbye Look	1983	20.00

45s

FULL MOON/ASYLUM

Number	Title (A Side/B Side)	Yr	NM
❑ 47244	True Companion/All of You	1981	5.00
—B-side by Don Felder			

REPRISE

Number	Title (A Side/B Side)	Yr	NM
❑ 18502	Tomorrow's Girls/Confide in Me	1993	3.00

WARNER BROS.

Number	Title (A Side/B Side)	Yr	NM
❑ 27972	Century's End/Shanghai Confidential	1988	5.00
❑ 27972 [PS]	Century's End/Shanghai Confidential	1988	5.00
❑ 29792	New Frontier/Maxine	1983	4.00
❑ 29900	I.G.Y. (What a Beautiful World)/Walk Between Raindrops	1982	4.00
❑ 29900 [PS]	I.G.Y. (What a Beautiful World)/Walk Between Raindrops	1982	5.00

Albums

MOBILE FIDELITY

Number	Title (A Side/B Side)	Yr	NM
❑ 1-120	The Nightfly	1982	40.00
—Audiophile vinyl			

WARNER BROS.

Number	Title (A Side/B Side)	Yr	NM
❑ 23696	The Nightfly	1982	8.00

FAHEY, JOHN

45s

VANGUARD

Number	Title (A Side/B Side)	Yr	NM
❑ 35076	A March for Martin Luther King/Singing Bridge	1968	12.00

Albums

REPRISE

Number	Title (A Side/B Side)	Yr	NM
❑ MS 2089	Of Rivers and Religions	1972	20.00
❑ MS 2145	After the Ball	1973	20.00

RIVERBOAT

Number	Title (A Side/B Side)	Yr	NM
❑ RB-1 [M]	The Transfiguration of Blind Joe Death	1965	200.00
—Original issue of 50 copies with booklet, hand-written labels and no "Vol. 5" anywhere on the cover			
❑ RB-1 [M]	The Transfiguration of Blind Joe Death	1967	60.00
—Green cover with booklet; "Vol. 5" added to back cover			

SHANACHIE

Number	Title (A Side/B Side)	Yr	NM
❑ 97006	God, Time and Causality	1990	15.00

TABLE OF THE ELEMENTS

Number	Title (A Side/B Side)	Yr	NM
❑ 38 [(2)]	Georgia Stomps, Atlanta Struts, and Other Contemporary Dance Favorites	1999	20.00

TAKOMA

Number	Title (A Side/B Side)	Yr	NM
❑ (# unknown)	Blind Joe Death	1959	200.00
—Original edition of 1,000 has a white cover with "Blind Joe Death" on one side and "John Fahey" on the other; possibly pressed by RCA Victor Custom Division; no Berkeley, California address on cover			
❑ C-1002	Blind Joe Death	1964	50.00
—White cover, similar to first edition, except it has a Berkeley, California address on cover; six tracks were re-recorded for this edition			
❑ C-1002	Vol. 1: Blind Joe Death	1967	40.00
—Psychedelic gold and blue cover; the entire album was re-recorded for this edition, including the six songs re-recorded for the first Berkeley edition and one song not on the white-cover editions, "I'm Gonna Do All I Can For My Lord"			
❑ C-1002	Vol. 1: Blind Joe Death	1968	15.00
—Blue and white cover with "Stereo" added to upper left			
❑ C-1003	Death Chants, Break Downs & Military Waltzes	1964	60.00
—First cover is white with block print with title on cover as above			
❑ C-1003	Death Chants, Breakdowns and Military Waltzes Vol. II	1965	50.00
—Second cover is white with what looks like handwritten print; title is as listed above and "Vol. II" is added to the lower left corner			
❑ C-1003	Vol. 2: Death Chants, Breakdowns & Military Waltzes	1967	40.00
—Psychedelic gold and orange cover; most of the album was re-recorded for this edition			
❑ C-1003	Vol. 2: Death Chants, Breakdowns & Military Waltzes	1968	15.00
—Orange and white cover with orange lettering			
❑ C-1004	Dance of Death & Other Plantation Favorites/John Fahey Vol. 3	1964	60.00
—White cover with block lettering			
❑ C-1004	Vol. 3: The Dance of Death & Other Plantation Favorites	1967	40.00
—Psychedelic gold and brown cover			
❑ C-1004	Vol. 3: The Dance of Death & Other Plantation Favorites	1968	15.00
—Brown and white cover			
❑ C-1008	Vol. 4: The Great San Bernardino Birthday Party	1966	30.00
—First pressings have a discography on the back cover			
❑ C-1008	Vol. 4: The Great San Bernardino Birthday Party	1968	12.00
—Without discography on back cover			
❑ C-1014	Days Have Gone By Vol. 6	1967	30.00
—With booklet			
❑ C-1014	Days Have Gone By Vol. 6	1968	12.00
—Without booklet			
❑ C-1019	The Voice of the Turtle	197?	15.00
—Later pressings with no gatefold			
❑ C-1019	The Voice of the Turtle	1971	30.00
—With gatefold jacket and booklet			
❑ C-1020	The New Possibility: John Fahey's Guitar Soli Christmas Album	1968	25.00
—Originals with back cover liner notes			
❑ C-1020	The New Possibility: John Fahey's Guitar Soli Christmas Album	197?	15.00
—Later pressings with no liner notes			
❑ C-1030	America	197?	15.00
—Later pressings with no gatefold			
❑ C-1030	America	1972	25.00
—With gatefold jacket and booklet			
❑ C-1035	Fare Forward Voyagers	1973	20.00
❑ C-1043	Old Fashioned Love	1975	15.00
❑ C-1045	Christmas with John Fahey, Vol. 2	1975	15.00
❑ C-1058	The Best of John Fahey 1959-1977	1977	15.00
❑ TAK-7002	Blind Joe Death	1979	12.00
—Reissue of 1002			
❑ TAK-7003	Death Chants, Breakdowns and Military Waltzes	198?	12.00
—Reissue of 1003			
❑ TAK-7004	Dance of Death and Other Plantation Favorites	198?	12.00
—Reissue of 1004			
❑ TAK-7015	The Transfiguration of Blind Joe Death	198?	12.00
—Reissue of 9015			
❑ TAK-7020	The New Possibility: John Fahey's Guitar Soli Christmas Album	198?	12.00
—Reissue of 1020			
❑ TAK-7035	Fare Forward Voyagers	198?	12.00
—Reissue of 1035			
❑ TAK-7043	Old Fashioned Love	198?	12.00
—Reissue of 1043			

Except when noted otherwise, VG = 25% of NM, and VG+ = 50% of NM. (Example: VG = $2.00, VG+ = $4.00 and NM = $8.00.)

Number	Title (A Side/B Side)	Yr	NM
❑ TAK-7045	Christmas with John Fahey, Vol. 2	198?	12.00
—Reissue of 1045			
❑ TAK-7058	The Best of John Fahey 1959-1977	198?	12.00
—Reissue of 1058			
❑ TAK-7069	John Fahey Visits Washington, D.C.	1979	12.00
❑ TAK-7085	Yes! Jesus Loves Me	1980	12.00
❑ TAK-7089	Live in Tasmania	198?	12.00
❑ TAK-7102	Railroads I	1981	12.00
❑ R-9015	The Transfiguration of Blind Joe Death	1969	20.00
—Reissue of Riverboat RB-1; logo added to lower right front cover, and the drawing in the center is much more green than on 1967 Riverboat covers			
TERRA			
❑ T-2	Requia	1985	10.00
—Reissue of Vanguard 79259			
VANGUARD			
❑ VSD 55/56 [(2)]	Essential John Fahey	1974	20.00
❑ VRS-9259 [M]	Requia	1968	25.00
❑ VSD-79259 [S]	Requia	1968	20.00
❑ VSD-79293	The Yellow Princess	1969	20.00
VARRICK			
❑ VR-002	John Fahey Christmas Guitar, Vol. 1	1982	15.00
❑ VR-008	Let Go	1983	15.00
❑ VR-012	Popular Songs of Christmas and New Year's	1983	15.00
❑ VR-019	Rain Forests, Oceans & Other Themes	1985	12.00
❑ VR-028	I Remember Blind Joe Death	1987	12.00

FAIR, YVONNE

Number	Title (A Side/B Side)	Yr	NM
45s			
DADE			
❑ 1851	Straighten Up/Say Yeah Yeah	1963	12.00
❑ 5006	Straighten Up/Say Yeah Yeah	1963	20.00
KING			
❑ 5594	I Found You/If I Knew	1962	15.00
—With the James Brown Band			
❑ 5654	Tell Me Why/Say So Long	1962	15.00
—With James Brown			
❑ 5687	It Hurts to Be in Love/You Can Make It If You Try	1962	15.00
—With James Brown			
❑ 6017	Tell Me Why/You Can Make It If You Try	1966	8.00
MOTOWN			
❑ 1306	Funky Music Sho Nuff Turns Me On/Let Your Hair Down	1974	7.00
❑ 1323	Walk Out the Door If You Wanna/It Should Have Been Me	1974	7.00
❑ 1323 [PS]	Walk Out the Door If You Wanna/It Should Have Been Me	1974	10.00
❑ 1344	It's Bad for Me to See You/You Can't Judge a Book By Its Cover	1975	7.00
❑ 1354 [PS]	Love Ain't No Toy/It's Bad for Me to See You	1975	7.00
❑ 1384	It Should Have Been Me/Tell Me Something Good	1976	6.00
SMASH			
❑ 2030	Just As Sure (As You Play, You Must Pay)/Baby, Baby, Baby	1966	10.00
SOUL			
❑ 35075	Stay a Little Longer/We Should Never Be Lonely My Love	1970	8.00
Albums			
MOTOWN			
❑ M6-832S1	The Bitch Is Black	1975	30.00

FAIRLANES, THE

Number	Title (A Side/B Side)	Yr	NM
45s			
ARGO			
❑ 5357	Little Girl, Little Girl/Comin' After You	1960	30.00
CONTINENTAL			
❑ 1001	Writing This Letter/Playboy	1961	300.00
DART			
❑ 109	Just for Me/Bullseye	1959	80.00
LUCKY SEVEN			
❑ 102	Seventeen Steps/Johnny Rhythm	1959	60.00
MINARET			
❑ 103	The Dagwood/I'm Not the Kind of Guy	1962	20.00
RADIANT			
❑ 101	Baby Baby/Tell Me	1964	250.00
REPRISE			
❑ 20213	Surf Train/Lonely Weekends	1963	30.00

FAIRPORT CONVENTION

Also see SANDY DENNY; RICHARD THOMPSON.

Number	Title (A Side/B Side)	Yr	NM
45s			
A&M			
❑ 1108	Fotheringay/I'll Keep It with Mine	1969	12.00
❑ 1155	Genesis Hall/Si Tu Dois Partie	1969	12.00
❑ 1333	Journeyman's Grace/The World Has Surely Lost Its Head	1972	8.00
❑ 1348	John Lee/The Time Is Near	1972	8.00
Albums			
A&M			
❑ SP-3530 [(2)]	The Fairport Chronicles	1976	15.00
❑ SP-3603	Fairport Nine	1974	12.00
—Early reissue of 4407			
❑ SP-4185	Fairport Convention	1969	15.00
—Not a reissue of Cotillion LP, but the US issue of the second UK LP "What We Did On Our Holidays"			
❑ SP-4206	Unhalfbricking	1969	15.00
❑ SP-4257	Liege and Lief	1970	15.00
❑ SP-4265	Full House	1970	15.00
❑ SP-4316	Angel Delight	1971	15.00
❑ SP-4333	"Babbacombe" Lee	1972	15.00
❑ SP-4383	Rosie	1973	15.00
❑ SP-4407	Fairport Nine	1973	15.00
❑ SP-6016 [(2)]	The Fairport Chronicles	198?	12.00
—Reissue of 3530			
ANTILLES			
❑ 7054	Gottle O' Geer	1976	12.00
CARTHAGE			
❑ CGLP-4417	Full House	198?	10.00
—Reissue of A&M 4265			
❑ CGLP-4418	Unhalfbricking	198?	10.00
—Reissue of A&M 4206			
❑ CGLP-4430	What We Did on Our Holidays	198?	10.00
—Reissue of A&M 4185 with UK title restored			
COTILLION			
❑ 9024 [M]	Fairport Convention	1968	80.00
—Mono is white label promo only; "DJ Copy Monaural" sticker on front cover			
❑ SD 9024 [S]	Fairport Convention	1968	30.00
HANNIBAL			
❑ HNBL-1319	House Full	1986	10.00
❑ HNBL-1329	Heyday	1987	10.00
ISLAND			
❑ ILPS-9285	Fairport Live/A Movable Feast	1974	12.00
❑ ILPS-9313	Rising for the Moon	1975	12.00
❑ 90678	In Real Time — Live '87	1987	10.00
VARRICK			
❑ VR-023	Gladys' Leap	1986	10.00
❑ VR-029	Expletive Delighted!	1987	10.00

FAITH, ADAM

Number	Title (A Side/B Side)	Yr	NM
45s			
AMY			
❑ 895	The First Time/So Long Baby	1964	15.00
❑ 899	We Are in Love/What Now	1964	15.00
❑ 913	It's Alright/I Just Don't Know	1964	15.00
❑ 922	Talk About Love/Stop Feeling Sorry for Yourself	1965	15.00
❑ 936	Don't You Know/Someone's Taken Marie Away	1965	15.00
CAPITOL			
❑ 5543	I'm Used to Losing You/I Don't Need That Kind of Lovin'	1965	10.00
❑ 5699	To Make a Big Man Cry/Here's Another Day	1966	10.00
CUB			
❑ 9061	What Do You Want/From Now Until September	1960	20.00
❑ 9068	Poor Me/The Reason	1960	20.00
❑ 9074	I Did What You Told Me/When Johnny Comes Marching Home	1960	20.00
DOT			
❑ 16405	Don't That Beat All/Mix Me a Person	1962	15.00
LAURIE			
❑ 3455	Daddy, What'll Happen to Me/Cowman, Milk Your Cow	1968	8.00
Albums			
AMY			
❑ 8005 [M]	Adam Faith	1965	25.00
❑ S-8005 [S]	Adam Faith	1965	30.00
MGM			
❑ E-3951 [M]	England's Top Singer	1961	40.00
❑ SE-3951 [S]	England's Top Singer	1961	50.00

FAITH, PERCY

Number	Title (A Side/B Side)	Yr	NM
45s			
COLUMBIA			
❑ 1-607	I Cross My Fingers/Valencia	1950	20.00
—Microgroove 33 1/3 rpm 7-inch single			
❑ 1-619 (?)	Violins from Nowhere/Tzin-Tzun-Tzan	1950	20.00
—Microgroove 33 1/3 rpm 7-inch single			
❑ 1-681 (?)	They Can't Take That Away from Me/If I Had a Magic Carpet	1950	20.00
—Microgroove 33 1/3 rpm 7-inch single			
❑ 1-699 (?)	I Was Dancing with Someone/Friendly Star	1950	20.00
—Microgroove 33 1/3 rpm 7-inch single			
❑ 1-752	All My Love/This Is the Time	1950	18.00
—Microgroove 33 1/3 rpm 7-inch single			
❑ 6-752	All My Love/This Is the Time	1950	15.00
❑ 1-812 (?)	Brazilian Sleighride/What Is This Thing Called Love	1950	20.00
—Microgroove 33 1/3 rpm 7-inch single			
❑ 6-812 (?)	Brazilian Sleighride/What Is This Thing Called Love	1950	15.00
❑ 1-835	Green Grass/I'm in the Middle of a Riddle	1950	18.00
—Microgroove 33 1/3 rpm 7-inch single			
❑ 6-835	Green Grass/I'm in the Middle of a Riddle	1950	15.00
❑ 1-841 (?)	Christmas in My Heart/Sleigh Ride	1950	20.00
—Microgroove 33 1/3 rpm 7-inch single			
❑ 6-841 (?)	Christmas in My Heart/Sleigh Ride	1950	15.00
❑ 1-899	Christmas In Killarney/Norah	1950	20.00
—Microgroove 33 1/3 rpm 7-inch single			
❑ 6-899	Christmas In Killarney/Norah	1950	15.00
❑ 10010	Theme from "Chinatown"/Tubular Bells	1974	4.00
❑ 10098	Orange Blossom Special/1,2,3,4	1975	4.00
❑ 10165	El Bimbo/Cherry Cherry	1975	4.00
❑ 10233	Summer Place '76/Chompin'	1975	4.00
❑ 10301	Emmanuelle-The Joys of a Woman/Ding Dong	1976	4.00
❑ 31500 [S]	Non Dimenticar/Tropical Merengue	1962	8.00
❑ 31501 [S]	The Syncopated Clock/Delicado	1962	8.00
❑ 31502 [S]	The Rain in Spain/Till	1962	8.00
❑ 31503 [S]	Jamaican Rhumba/They Can't Take That Away from Me	1962	8.00
❑ 31504 [S]	Swedish Rhapsody/All My Love	1962	8.00
❑ 31536 [S]	(contents unknown)	1962	8.00
❑ 31537 [S]	(contents unknown)	1962	8.00
❑ 31538 [S]	(contents unknown)	1962	8.00
❑ 31539 [S]	Maxine/The Minute Samba	1962	8.00
❑ 31540 [S]	(contents unknown)	1962	8.00
—The above 10 are Columbia "Stereo 7" singles			
❑ 39155	Zing Zing/Kiss and Promise	1951	15.00
❑ 39192	The Loveliest Night of the Year/You Are the One	1951	15.00
❑ 39257	No One But You/Goodbye John	1951	15.00
❑ 39329	Nervous Gavotte/Hot Canary	1951	15.00
❑ 39356	Carousel Waltz/When I'm Not Near the Girl I Love	1951	12.00
❑ 39357	While We're Young/The Girl That I Marry	1951	12.00
❑ 39358	A Kiss in the Dark/Valse Huguette	1951	12.00
❑ 39359	Waltz in Swingtown/I'll Take Romance	1951	12.00
—The above four comprise a box set			
❑ 39426	Black Ball Perry Line/Wondrous Word	1951	15.00
❑ 39491	Fiddle Derby/March of the Siamese Children	1951	15.00
❑ 39528	When the Saints Go Marching In/I Want to Be Near You	1951	15.00
❑ 39559	Sleigh Ride/Christmas in Killarney	1951	15.00
❑ 39613	If I Loved You/Dizzy Fingers	1951	15.00
❑ 39638	Would You/I Talk to the Trees	1952	12.00
❑ 39640	Flight 33 1/3/Ba-Tu-Ca-Da	1952	10.00
❑ 39641	One Night of Love/My Shawl	1952	10.00
❑ 39642	Brazilian Sleighride/What Is This Thing Called Love	1952	10.00
❑ 39643	Beautiful Love/Nightingale	1952	10.00
—The above four comprise a box set			
❑ 39664	Carefree/Invitation	1952	12.00
❑ 39708	Delicado/Festival	1952	12.00
❑ 39732	Delicado/The Gandy Dancers' Ball	1952	10.00
—B-side by Frankie Laine; this is part of a various-artists box set			
❑ 39781	Enlloro/Jungle Fantasy	1952	10.00
❑ 39782	Caribbean Night/Cu-Tu-Gu-Ru	1952	10.00
❑ 39783	Minute Samba/The Girl with the Spanish Drawl	1952	10.00
❑ 39784	Oye Negra/Jamaican Rhumba	1952	10.00
—The above four comprise a box set			

Number	Title (A Side/B Side)	Yr	NM
39790	Jamaican Rhumba/Dadu	1952	12.00
39874	Amorada/Funny Fellow	1952	12.00
39907	Over the Mountain/Caress	1952	12.00
39944	The Song from Moulin Rouge (Where Is Your Heart)/Swedish Rhapsody	1953	10.00
—Vocal on A-side by Felicia Sanders			
39998	Return to Paradise (Part 1)/Return to Paradise (Part 2)	1953	10.00
40029	Tropic Holiday/Gaviotta	1953	10.00
40076	Many Times/In Love	1953	10.00
40115	Ev'rybody Loves Saturday Night/True or False	1953	10.00
40124	Genevieve/Suddenly	1953	10.00
40155	Non Dimenticar (Don't Forget)/They Can't Take That Away from Me	1954	10.00
40174	Baubles, Bangles and Beads/And This Is My Beloved	1954	10.00
40185	Eleanora/Dream, Dream, Dream	1954	10.00
4-40277	Song for Sweethearts/Bubbling Over	1954	10.00
40323	Rainfall/The Bandit	1954	10.00
40390	Ching-Ching-a-Ling/Petite	1954	10.00
40428	If Hearts Could Talk/Blue Mirage	1955	10.00
40482	Land of the Pharaohs/The World Is Mine	1955	10.00
40512	The Fiddling Bullfighter/Not As a Stranger	1955	10.00
40543	Tropical Merengue/We Won't Say Goodbye	1955	10.00
40588	The Rose Tattoo/Tambora	1955	10.00
40633	Valley Valparaiso/Bluebell	1956	10.00
40644	We All Need Love/Carmelita	1956	10.00
40696	With a Little Bit of Luck/The Rain in Spain	1956	10.00
40719	Wouldn't It Be Loverly/Sierra Madre	1956	10.00
40764	Baby Doll/Vagabond Waltz King	1956	10.00
40826	Till/The Last Dance	1957	10.00
40900	Italiano!/Bahama Lullaby	1957	10.00
40949	Hey Jose/What's It Like in Paree?	1957	10.00
41024	Never Till Now/Katsumi Love Theme	1957	10.00
41095	Maria/The Stars	1958	8.00
41126	The Impala Theme/Pizzicato Polka	1958	8.00
41181	Same Old Moon/Indiscreet	1958	8.00
41271	The Pyramid Dance/Quia Quia	1958	8.00
41328	Goin' Home Train/Isle of Paradise	1959	8.00
41490	Theme from "A Summer Place"/Go-Go-Po-Go	1959	8.00
41490 [PS]	Theme from "A Summer Place"/Go-Go-Po-Go	1959	15.00
41655	Theme for Young Lovers/Bimini Goombay	1960	8.00
41731	Sons and Lovers/Hawaiian Lullaby	1960	8.00
41796	Theme from "The Dark at the Top of the Stairs"/Our Language of Love	1960	8.00
41978	The Bilbao Song/Lover's Prelude	1961	8.00
42011	At Last-Angel Face/Tammy Tell Me True	1961	8.00
3-42239	The Brass Ring/I Just Can't Wait	1961	12.00
—"Columbia Single 33" with small hole; orange label			
4-42239	The Brass Ring/I Just Can't Wait	1961	8.00
42333	Love Theme from "The Four Horsemen of the Apocalypse"/Theme from "Light in the Piazza"	1962	6.00
42423	Advise and Consent/Jacqueline's Journey	1962	6.00
42844	The Sound of Surf/Our Love	1963	6.00
42979	The Virginian/Melody from "Mahogany"	1964	6.00
42991	Sloop John B/This Train	1964	6.00
43116	Judy/Love Goddess	1964	6.00
43208	Kahlua/Insensatez	1965	6.00
43326	Love Me/We're Gonna Be Alright	1965	6.00
43555	Song from "The Oscar"/Glass Mountain	1966	6.00
43642	Cheryl/Swingin' Village	1966	6.00
43746	Tropic Holiday/Reza	1966	6.00
43846	Christmas Is.../Silver Bells	1966	6.00
44086	A Man and a Woman/This Hotel	1967	5.00
44166	Kahlua/Yellow Days	1967	5.00
44319	Can't Take My Eyes Off You/Windy	1967	5.00

Number	Title (A Side/B Side)	Yr	NM
44412	Theme from "The Dark at the Top of the Stairs"/Tara's Theme (From "Gone with the Wind")	1967	5.00
44446	For Those in Love/There Was a Time	1968	5.00
44585	MacArthur Park/Elvira Madigan Theme	1968	5.00
44734	Zorba/A Quiet Day	1969	5.00
44876	The Windmills of Your Mind/Theme from "The Fox"	1969	4.00
44932	Theme from "A Summer Place"/Hello Tomorrow	1969	5.00
44987	Spinning Wheel/April Fools	1969	4.00
45051	Peppermint Hill and Strawberry Lane/The Time for Love Is Anytime	1969	4.00
45114	Airport Love Theme/Theme for Young Lovers	1970	4.00
45297	I Don't Know How to Love Him/Everything's Alright	1971	4.00
45374	Anytime of the Year/I Can Hear the Music	1971	4.00
45401	Theme from "Summer of '42"/Tres	1971	4.00
45525	Diamonds Are Forever/Love Theme from "Mary Queen of Scots"	1972	4.00
45563	Love Theme from "The Godfather"/Godfather Waltz	1972	5.00
45619	Theme from "Kotch"/Back's Lunch	1972	4.00
45868	Viva Vivaldi/We Were Having Some Fun at the Conservatory, When ...	1973	4.00
45945	Corazon/Crunchy Granola Suite	1973	4.00
46013	Euterpe/Hill Where the Lord Hides	1974	4.00
JZSP 75661/2 [DJ]	I Will Follow You/Theme for Young Lovers	1963	12.00
—Promo-only "Special Album Excerpt"			
JZSP 111903/4 [DJ]	Away In A Manger/We Three Kings Of Orient Are	1965	12.00
—Promo only on green vinyl			
JZSP 119961/2 [DJ]	Christmas Is . . ./Happy Holiday	1966	10.00
—Yellow label			
JZSP 119961/2 [DJ]	Christmas Is . . ./Happy Holiday	1967	10.00
—White label			
JZSP 119961/2 [PS]	Christmas Is . . ./Happy Holiday	1967	15.00
—Sleeve announces this as the 1967 Christmas Seals Record			
DECCA			
27542	I Love You/Long Ago (and Far Away)	1951	12.00
27543	I'll Close My Eyes/There's No Holding Me	1951	12.00
—With Hildegarde			
27544	Amor/Spring Will Be a Little Late This Year	1951	12.00
RCA VICTOR			
47-3004	Deep Purple/Oodles of Noodles	1949	15.00
47-3063	Whirlwind/My Dream Concerto	1949	15.00
47-4001	Perpetual Motion/Solitude	1950	15.00
47-4002	Body and Soul/Cumana	1950	15.00
47-4003	Beyond the Sea/El Cumbanchero	1950	15.00

7-Inch Extended Plays

Number	Title (A Side/B Side)	Yr	NM
COLUMBIA			
B-1610	Would You/I Talk to the Trees//If I Loved You/Easy to Love	195?	10.00
B-1610 [PS]	Percy Faith's Magic Voices	195?	10.00
B-1805	La Ronde (Love Makes the World Go Round)/Many Times//If You Said Goodbye/April in Portugal	195?	10.00
B-1805 [PS]	Percy Faith Plays Continental Music Vol. II	195?	10.00
B-2529	*The Song from Moulin Rouge/Swedish Rhapsody/Delicado/Invitation	1958	10.00
B-2529 [PS]	Percy Faith (Hall of Fame Series)	1958	10.00
B-2623	Mademoiselle De Paree/Under the Bridges of Paris//Non Dimenticar/April in Portugal	195?	10.00
B-2623 [PS]	(title unknown)	195?	10.00
B-9553	If I Had My Druthers/Oh Happy Day//Matrimonial Stomp/Namely You	195?	10.00
B-9553 [PS]	Li'l Abner, Vol. 3	195?	10.00
B-11871	Hallelujah Chorus/Carol of the Bells//I Wonder As I Wander/What Child Is This (Greensleeves)	195?	10.00
B-11871 [PS]	Hallelujah!	195?	10.00

Albums

Number	Title (A Side/B Side)	Yr	NM
COLUMBIA			
GP 1 [(2)]	Forever Young	1968	15.00
C2L 15 [(2)M]	The Columbia Album of Christmas Music	1958	30.00
—Combines CL 588 and CL 1187 into one gatefold package			
CL 525 [M]	Continental Music	1955	20.00
CL 550 [M]	Kismet	1955	20.00
CL 577 [M]	Music from Hollywood	1955	20.00
CL 588 [M]	Music of Christmas	1955	25.00
CL 640 [M]	House of Flowers	1956	20.00
CL 681 [M]	Delicado	1956	20.00
CL 705 [M]	Music for Her	1956	20.00
CL 880 [M]	Passport to Romance	1956	20.00
CL 895 [M]	My Fair Lady	1957	20.00
CL 955 [M]	L'il Abner	1957	20.00
CL 1010 [M]	Adventure in the Sun	1957	20.00
CS 1019	Held Over! Today's Great Movie Themes	1970	12.00
CL 1075 [M]	Viva!	1957	20.00
CL 1105 [M]	South Pacific	1957	15.00
CL 1182 [M]	Touchdown!	1957	20.00
CL 1187 [M]	Hallelujah!	1957	20.00
CL 1188 [M]	Jubliation!	1957	20.00
CL 1267 [M]	Malaguena	1958	20.00
CL 1298 [M]	Porgy and Bess	1958	15.00
CL 1302 [M]	A Night with Sigmund Romberg	1959	15.00
CL 1322 [M]	Bouquet	1959	15.00
CL 1381 [M]	Music of Christmas	1959	20.00
—Re-recorded version of CL 588 with same track order			
CL 1386 [M]	A Night with Jerome Kern	1959	15.00
CL 1417 [M]	Bon Voyage!	1960	15.00
CL 1418 [M]	The Sound of Music	1960	15.00
CL 1493 [M]	Percy Faith's Greatest Hits	1960	15.00
CL 1501 [M]	Jealousy	1960	12.00
CL 1570 [M]	Camelot	1960	12.00
CL 1627 [M]	Tara's Theme from "Gone with the Wind" and Other Themes	1961	12.00
CL 1639 [M]	Mucho Gusto! More Music of Brazil	1961	12.00
CL 1681 [M]	Bouquet of Love	1962	12.00
CL 1783 [M]	Hollywood's Great Themes	1962	12.00
CL 1822 [M]	The Music of Brazil!	1962	12.00
CL 1902 [M]	Exotic Strings	1963	12.00
CL 1957 [M]	American Serenade	1963	12.00
CL 2023 [M]	Themes for Young Lovers	1963	12.00
CL 2024 [M]	Shangri-La!	1963	12.00
CL 2108 [M]	Great Folk Themes	1964	12.00
CL 2167 [M]	More Themes for Young Lovers	1964	12.00
CL 2209 [M]	Love Goddess	1966	12.00
CL 2279 [M]	Latin Themes for Young Lovers	1966	12.00
CL 2317 [M]	Do I Hear a Waltz	1965	12.00
CL 2356 [M]	Broadway Bouquet	1965	12.00
CL 2405 [M]	Music of Christmas, Vol. 2	1965	12.00
CL 2441 [M]	Themes for the "In" Crowd	1966	12.00
CL 2529 [M]	Bim Bam Boom	1966	12.00
CL 2577 [M]	Christmas Is...	1966	12.00
CL 2650 [M]	The Academy Award Winner and Other Great Movie Themes	1967	15.00
CL 2704 [M]	Today's Themes for Young Lovers	1967	15.00
CL 2810 [M]	For Those in Love	1968	20.00
CL 2906 [M]	Angel of the Morning (Hit Themes for Young Lovers)	1968	20.00
CL 6148 [10]	Football Songs	1950	40.00
CS 8005 [S]	South Pacific	1958	25.00
CS 8033 [S]	Hallelujah!	1958	25.00
CS 8038 [S]	Viva!	1958	25.00
CS 8081 [S]	Malaguena	1958	25.00
CS 8105 [S]	Porgy and Bess	1959	20.00
CS 8108 [S]	A Night with Sigmund Romberg	1959	20.00
CS 8124 [S]	Bouquet	1959	15.00
CS 8176 [S]	Music of Christmas	1959	15.00
CS 8181 [S]	A Night with Jerome Kern	1959	20.00
CS 8214 [S]	Bon Voyage!	1960	15.00
CS 8215 [S]	The Sound of Music	1960	15.00
CS 8292 [S]	Jealousy	1960	15.00
CS 8370 [S]	Camelot	1960	15.00
CS 8427 [S]	Tara's Theme from "Gone with the Wind" and Other Themes	1961	15.00
CS 8439 [S]	Mucho Gusto! More Music of Brazil	1961	15.00
CS 8481 [S]	Bouquet of Love	1962	15.00
CS 8583 [S]	Hollywood's Great Themes	1962	15.00
CS 8622 [S]	The Music of Brazil!	1962	15.00
CS 8637 [R]	Percy Faith's Greatest Hits	1963	10.00
PC 8637 [R]	Percy Faith's Greatest Hits	198?	8.00
—Budget-line reissue			
CS 8642 [R]	Kismet	1963	10.00
CS 8702 [S]	Exotic Strings	1963	12.00
CS 8757 [S]	American Serenade	1963	12.00
CS 8823 [S]	Themes for Young Lovers	1963	12.00
CS 8824 [S]	Shangri-La!	1963	12.00
CS 8908 [S]	Great Folk Themes	1964	12.00
CS 8967 [S]	More Themes for Young Lovers	1964	12.00
CS 9004 [R]	My Fair Lady	1964	12.00
CS 9009 [S]	Love Goddess	1964	12.00
CS 9079 [S]	Latin Themes for Young Lovers	1965	12.00
CS 9117 [S]	Do I Hear a Waltz	1965	12.00

Number	Title (A Side/B Side)	Yr	NM
❑ CS 9156 [S]	Broadway Bouquet	1965	12.00
❑ CS 9205 [S]	Music of Christmas, Vol. 2	1965	12.00
❑ CS 9241 [S]	Themes for the "In" Crowd	1966	12.00
❑ CS 9329 [S]	Bim Bam Boom	1966	12.00
❑ 3C 9377	Christmas Is...	198?	8.00
—Budget-line reissue			
❑ CS 9377 [S]	Christmas Is...	1966	12.00
❑ CS 9450 [S]	The Academy Award Winner and Other Great Movie Themes	1967	12.00
❑ CS 9504 [S]	Today's Themes for Young Lovers	1967	12.00
❑ CS 9610 [S]	For Those in Love	1968	12.00
❑ CS 9706 [S]	Angel of the Morning (Hit Themes for Young Lovers)	1968	12.00
❑ CS 9762	Those Were the Days	1969	12.00
❑ CS 9835	Windmills of Your Mind	1969	12.00
❑ CS 9906	Love Theme from "Romeo & Juliet"	1969	12.00
❑ CS 9983	Leaving on a Jet Plane	1970	12.00
❑ C 30097	The Beatles Album	1970	12.00
❑ G 30330 [(2)]	A Time for Love	1971	15.00
❑ C 30502	I Think I Love You	1971	10.00
❑ CQ 30502 [Q]	I Think I Love You	1971	15.00
❑ C 30800	Black Magic Woman	1971	10.00
❑ CQ 31004 [Q]	Love Theme from "Romeo & Juliet"	1971	15.00
❑ C 31042	Jesus Christ Superstar	1971	10.00
❑ C 31301	Joy	1972	10.00
❑ CQ 31301 [Q]	Joy	1972	15.00
❑ KG 31588 [(2)]	All-Time Greatest Hits	1972	12.00
❑ PG 31588 [(2)]	All-Time Greatest Hits	198?	10.00
—Budget-line reissue			
❑ CQ 31627 [Q]	Day By Day	1972	15.00
❑ KC 31627	Day By Day	1972	10.00
❑ CQ 32164 [Q]	Clair	1973	15.00
❑ KC 32164	Clair	1973	10.00
❑ KC 32380	My Love	1973	10.00
❑ C 32585	Remembering the Hits of the 60's	1973	10.00
❑ KC 32714	Corazon	1974	10.00
❑ CQ 32803 [Q]	A New Thing	1974	15.00
❑ KC 32803	A New Thing	1974	10.00
❑ PCQ 33006 [Q]	The Entertainer	1974	15.00
❑ KC 33142	Country Bouquet	1975	10.00
❑ CQ 33244 [Q]	Chinatown (Featuring "The Entertainer")	1974	15.00
❑ KC 33244	Chinatown (Featuring "The Entertainer")	1974	10.00
❑ KC 33549	Disco Party	1975	10.00
❑ CG 33606 [(2)]	Viva!/Mucho Gusto!	1975	12.00
❑ CG 33895 [(2)]	Great Moments of Percy Faith	1976	12.00
❑ KC 33915	Summer of '76	1976	10.00
❑ PC 38302	Music of Christmas	1983	8.00
❑ PC 39471	Christmas Melodies	1984	8.00
—Repackage of previously released material			

COLUMBIA LIMITED EDITION

Number	Title (A Side/B Side)	Yr	NM
❑ LE 10004	Tara's Theme from "Gone with the Wind" and Other Themes	197?	10.00
❑ LE 10015	Windmills of Your Mind	197?	10.00
❑ LE 10041	Themes for the "In" Crowd	197?	10.00
❑ LE 10042	Bouquet	197?	10.00
❑ LE 10082	Music of Christmas	197?	10.00
—Brown label "Limited Edition" series; same contents as CS 8176			
❑ LE 10088	Music of Christmas, Vol. 2	197?	10.00
❑ LE 10095	Great Folk Themes	197?	10.00
❑ LE 10131	Jealousy	197?	10.00
❑ LE 10185	Those Were the Days	197?	10.00
❑ LE 10350	Hallelujah!	197?	10.00

COLUMBIA SPECIAL PRODUCTS

Number	Title (A Side/B Side)	Yr	NM
❑ P 13091	Broadway Bouquet	197?	8.00
❑ P 13277	Leaving on a Jet Plane	197?	8.00
❑ P2 13719 [(2)]	The Columbia Album of George Gershwin	197?	12.00
❑ P 13827	American Serenade	197?	8.00

HARMONY

Number	Title (A Side/B Side)	Yr	NM
❑ HS 11348	Sounds of Music	1969	10.00
❑ H 30020	Younger Than Springtime	1970	10.00
❑ KH 30607	A Summer Place	1971	10.00
❑ KH 30977	Raindrops Keep Fallin'	1971	10.00
❑ KH 31777	Every Night at the Movies	1972	10.00

VOCALION

Number	Title (A Side/B Side)	Yr	NM
❑ VL 3600 [M]	North and South of the Border	1958	15.00

FAITH BAND

45s

MERCURY

Number	Title (A Side/B Side)	Yr	NM
❑ 74037	Dancin' Shoes/Desire	1978	5.00
❑ 74068	You're My Weakness/Forever	1979	5.00
❑ 74090	Big City Lights/Touchy Situation	1979	5.00
❑ 76024	Paradise/Is It for Real	1979	5.00

VILLAGE

Number	Title (A Side/B Side)	Yr	NM
❑ 202	Dancin' Shoes/Desire	1978	10.00

Albums

MERCURY

Number	Title (A Side/B Side)	Yr	NM
❑ SRM-1-3759	Rock'n Romance	1978	12.00
❑ SRM-1-3770	Face to Face	1979	12.00
❑ SRM-1-3807	Vital Signs	1979	10.00

VILLAGE

Number	Title (A Side/B Side)	Yr	NM
❑ VR 7703	Excuse Me... I Just Cut an Album	1977	20.00
❑ VR 7805	Rock'n Romance	1978	20.00

FAITH HOPE & CHARITY

45s

MAXWELL

Number	Title (A Side/B Side)	Yr	NM
❑ 805	So Much Love/Let's Try It Over	1970	6.00
❑ 808	Baby Don't Take Your Love/Make Love to Me	1970	6.00

RCA

Number	Title (A Side/B Side)	Yr	NM
❑ PB-10749	You're My Peace of Mind/Rescue Me	1976	5.00
❑ PB-10865	Life Goes On/You've Gotta Tell Her	1976	5.00

RCA VICTOR

Number	Title (A Side/B Side)	Yr	NM
❑ PB-10343	To Each His Own/Find a Way	1975	5.00
❑ PB-10542	Don't Go Looking for Love/Disco Dan	1976	5.00

SUSSEX

Number	Title (A Side/B Side)	Yr	NM
❑ 216	Come Back and Finish What You Started/I Worship the Very Ground You Walk On	1971	5.00
❑ 224	No Trespassing/Ghosts Keep Haunting Me	1971	5.00
❑ 231	We Can Change the World/God Bless the World	1972	5.00
❑ 243	I Was There/Who Could Love You More Than I	1972	5.00
❑ 252	Who Made You Go/Heavy Love	1973	5.00

20TH CENTURY

Number	Title (A Side/B Side)	Yr	NM
❑ 2370	Don't Pity Me/Find What You Need	1978	4.00
❑ 2391	How Can I Help But Love You/Keep Me Baby	1978	4.00

Albums

RCA VICTOR

Number	Title (A Side/B Side)	Yr	NM
❑ APL1-1100	Faith, Hope & Charity	1975	12.00
❑ APL1-1827	Life Goes	1976	12.00

SUSSEX

Number	Title (A Side/B Side)	Yr	NM
❑ SXSB-7019	Heavy Love	1972	15.00

FAITH NO MORE MR. BUNGLE and FANTOMAS related.

12-Inch Singles

SLASH

Number	Title (A Side/B Side)	Yr	NM
❑ PRO-A-2702 [DJ]	We Care a Lot (Make Love Not War Mix) (LP Mix)/Anne's Song	1987	12.00
❑ PRO-A-2823 [DJ]	Chinese Arithmetic (Radio Mix) (Kick and Scream Mix)	1987	10.00
❑ PRO-A-3559 [DJ]	From Out of Nowhere (same on both sides)	1989	8.00
❑ PRO-A-5757 [DJ]	A Small Victory (Sundown Mix) (Sundown Instrumental) (R-Evolution 23 Full Moon Mix)/Malpractice (LP Version)	1992	12.00

45s

REPRISE

Number	Title (A Side/B Side)	Yr	NM
❑ 18569	Easy/Das Schutzenfest	1993	4.00

SLASH

Number	Title (A Side/B Side)	Yr	NM
❑ 17868	Evidence/Get Out	1995	4.00
❑ 18891	Epic/Falling to Pieces	1993	5.00
—Reissue; first appearance of B-side on U.S. 45			
❑ 19813	Epic/Edge of the World	1990	4.00
❑ 28287	We Care a Lot/Spirit	1987	6.00

WARNER BROS.

Number	Title (A Side/B Side)	Yr	NM
❑ PRO-S-5847 [DJ]	Easy/Slide (Live)	1992	10.00
—"Soil X Samples" 8; green vinyl; B-side by L7			
❑ PRO-S-5847 [PS]	Easy/Slide (Live)	1992	10.00
—"Season's Greetings from..." sleeve with photos of both Faith No More and L7			

Albums

MORDAM

Number	Title (A Side/B Side)	Yr	NM
❑ FNM 1	We Care a Lot	1985	25.00

SLASH

Number	Title (A Side/B Side)	Yr	NM
❑ 25559	Introduce Yourself	1987	15.00
❑ 25878	The Real Thing	1989	20.00
❑ 45723 [(2)]	King for a Day/Fool for a Lifetime	1995	25.00

TPM/RHINO EXCLUSIVE

Number	Title (A Side/B Side)	Yr	NM
❑ 2310	Angel Dust	2008	40.00

FAITHFULL, MARIANNE

12-Inch Singles

ANTILLES

Number	Title (A Side/B Side)	Yr	NM
❑ AN 801	Broken English (5:59)/Why D'Ya Do It	1979	10.00

ISLAND

Number	Title (A Side/B Side)	Yr	NM
❑ DMD 627 [DJ]	Blue Millionaire (Long)/Blue Millionaire (Short)	1983	8.00

45s

COLLECTABLES

Number	Title (A Side/B Side)	Yr	NM
❑ 2605	Broken English/Why D'Ya Do It	199?	3.00
—Reissue			
❑ 4238	As Tears Go By/Gloria	199?	3.00
—Reissue; B-side by Them			

ISLAND

Number	Title (A Side/B Side)	Yr	NM
❑ 49121	Broken English/Brain Drain	1979	5.00
❑ 49873	Sweetheart/For Beauty's Sake	1981	4.00
❑ 94997	Broken English/Why D'Ya Do It?	198?	10.00
—Gold label "Revival of the Fittest" series			
❑ 99888 [DJ]	Running for Our Lives/Running for Our Lives	1983	6.00

LONDON

Number	Title (A Side/B Side)	Yr	NM
❑ 1022	Sister Morphine/Something Better	1969	100.00
—Promo worth about 50% of these values.			
❑ 9697	As Tears Go By/Greensleeves	1964	12.00
❑ 9731	Come and Stay with Me/What Have I Done Wrong	1965	10.00
❑ 9759	This Little Bird/Morning Sun	1965	10.00
❑ 9780	Summer Nights/The Sha-La-La Song	1965	10.00
❑ 9802	Go Away from My World/Oh Look Around You	1965	10.00
❑ 9802 [PS]	Go Away from My World/Oh Look Around You	1965	20.00
❑ 20012	Counting/Tomorrow's Calling	1966	10.00
❑ 20012 [PS]	Counting/Tomorrow's Calling	1966	20.00
❑ 20020	Is This What I Get for Loving You/Tomorrow's Calling	1966	10.00

Albums

ABKCO

Number	Title (A Side/B Side)	Yr	NM
❑ 75471	Greatest Hits	1988	10.00
—Reissue of London PS 547			

ISLAND

Number	Title (A Side/B Side)	Yr	NM
❑ PRO 794 [EP]	Blazing Away Sampler	1990	20.00
—Promo-only sampler for radio			
❑ ILPS 9570	Broken English	1979	10.00
❑ ILPS 9648	Dangerous Acquaintances	1981	10.00
❑ 90039	Broken English	1983	8.00
—Reissue			
❑ 90066	A Child's Adventure	1983	10.00
❑ 90066 [DJ]	A Child's Adventure	1983	15.00
—Promo-only Quiex II audiophile pressing			
❑ 90613	Strange Weather	1987	10.00

LONDON

Number	Title (A Side/B Side)	Yr	NM
❑ PS 423 [R]	Marianne Faithfull	1965	15.00
❑ PS 452 [S]	Go Away from My World	1965	20.00
❑ PS 482 [S]	Faithfull Forever	1966	20.00
❑ PS 547	Greatest Hits	1969	15.00
❑ LL 3423 [M]	Marianne Faithfull	1965	20.00
❑ LL 3452 [M]	Go Away from My World	1965	20.00
—With Oldham credit.			
❑ LL 3452 [M]	Go Away from My World	1965	30.00
—No Oldham credit.			
❑ LL 3482 [M]	Faithfull Forever	1966	15.00

MOBILE FIDELITY

Number	Title (A Side/B Side)	Yr	NM
❑ 1-235	Broken English	1995	45.00
—Audiophile vinyl			

FALCONS, THE (1) Detroit R&B group. Also see EDDIE FLOYD; WILSON PICKETT.

45s

ANNA

Number	Title (A Side/B Side)	Yr	NM
❑ 1110	Just for Your Love/This Heart of Mine	1959	100.00

ATLANTIC

Number	Title (A Side/B Side)	Yr	NM
❑ 2153	Darling/Lah-Tee-Lah-Tah	1962	20.00
❑ 2179	Let's Kiss and Make Up/Take This Love I've Got	1963	20.00
❑ 2207	Oh Baby/Fine, Fine, Fine	1963	20.00

BIG WHEEL

Number	Title (A Side/B Side)	Yr	NM
❑ 321	I Must Love You/Love, Love, Love	1966	20.00
❑ 323/4	I Can't Help It/Standing on Guard	1966	20.00
❑ 1967	Standing On Guard/I Can't Help It	1966	20.00
❑ 1972	Good Good Feeling/You Like You Never Been Loved	1966	20.00

CHESS

Number	Title (A Side/B Side)	Yr	NM
❑ 1743	Just for Your Love/This Heart of Mine	1959	25.00

FALCON

Number	Title (A Side/B Side)	Yr	NM
❑ 1006	Now That It's Over/My Only Love	1957	200.00

FLICK

Number	Title (A Side/B Side)	Yr	NM
❑ 001	You're So Fine/Goddess of Angels	1959	400.00
❑ 008	You Must Know I Love You/That's What I Aim to Do	1960	120.00

KUDO

Number	Title (A Side/B Side)	Yr	NM
❑ 661	This Heart of Mine/Romanita	1958	400.00

Number	Title (A Side/B Side)	Yr	NM
LUPINE			
❑ 103	I Found a Love/Swim	1962	50.00
❑ 124	Lonely Nights/Has It Happened to You	1962	100.00
❑ 1003	I Found a Love/Swim	1962	50.00
❑ 1024	Lonely Nights/Has It Happened to You	1962	40.00
UNART			
❑ 2013 [M]	You're So Fine/Goddess of Angels	1959	30.00
❑ 2013-S [S]	You're So Fine/Goddess of Angels	1959	100.00
—Though labeled as stereo, this seems to be rechanneled			
❑ 2022	You're Mine/Country Shack	1959	25.00
UNITED ARTISTS			
❑ 0108	You're So Fine/Showtime	1973	4.00
—"Silver Spotlight Series" reissue			
❑ 229	The Teacher/Waiting for You	1960	20.00
❑ 255	I Plus Love Plus You/Wonderful Love	1960	20.00
❑ 289	Pow! You're in Love/Workin' Man's Song	1961	20.00
❑ 420	You're So Fine/Goddess of Angels	1962	20.00
❑ 1624	You're So Fine/Goddess of Angels	196?	8.00
—"Silver Spotlight Series" issue			
7-Inch Extended Plays			
UNITED ARTISTS			
❑ UAE 10010	*The Teacher/Waiting for You/You're So Fine/Goddess of Angels	1960	300.00
❑ UAE 10010 [PS]	The Falcons	1960	300.00
Albums			
RELIC			
❑ 8005	You're So Fine (The Falcons' Story Part One: 1956-1959)	1987	12.00
❑ 8006	I Found a Love (The Falcons' Story Part Two: 1960-1964)	1987	12.00

FALCONS, THE (2)

Number	Title (A Side/B Side)	Yr	NM
45s			
CASH			
❑ 1002	Tell Me Why/I Miss You Darling	1955	500.00
FLIP			
❑ 301	Stay Mine/Du-Bi-A-Do	1954	200.00
❑ 302	You Are the Only One/Mambo Baby Tonight	1954	200.00

FALCONS, THE (U)
These may be by group (1) or by group (2) or by neither.

Number	Title (A Side/B Side)	Yr	NM
45s			
MERCURY			
❑ 70940	Baby That's It/This Day	1956	60.00
SILHOUETTE			
❑ 522	Can This Be Christmas/Sent Up	1957	300.00

FALL, THE
Featuring Mark E. Smith.

Number	Title (A Side/B Side)	Yr	NM
12-Inch Singles			
PVC			
❑ 5909	Rollin' Danny/Couldn't Get Ahead/Vixen/Barmy	1986	8.00
RCA			
❑ 7617-1 [DJ]	Victoria (same on both sides)	1988	6.00
❑ 8826-1-HDAA [DJ]	New Big Prinz (same on both sides)	1988	6.00
Albums			
BEGGARS BANQUET			
❑ 2430-1-H	458489	1990	10.00
❑ 6897-1-H	The Frenz Experiment	1988	10.00
❑ 9582-1-H	I Am Kurious Oranj	1988	10.00
❑ 9807-1-H	Seminal Live	1989	10.00
I.R.S.			
❑ SP-003	Live at the Witch Trials	1979	20.00
I.R.S./FAULTY			
❑ COPE-2	Early Years 77-79	1981	15.00
MATADOR			
❑ OLE 55-1	The Infotainment Scan	1993	10.00
❑ OLE 95-1	Middle Class Revolt	1994	10.00
PVC			
❑ 8932	The Wonderful and Frightening World of The Fall	1984	16.00
❑ 8940	This Nation's Saving Grace	1985	15.00
ROUGH TRADE			
❑ TRADE 3/10 [10]	Slates	1981	12.00
—10-inch EP			
❑ ROUGH US-8	Grotesque (After the Gramme)	1981	15.00

FALL OUT BOY

Number	Title (A Side/B Side)	Yr	NM
Albums			
ISLAND			
❑ 1219601	Folie a Deux	2008	30.00

FALLEN ANGELS, THE

Number	Title (A Side/B Side)	Yr	NM
45s			
LAURIE			
❑ 3343	Eveytime I Fall in Love/I Have Found	1966	25.00
❑ 3369	Have You Ever Lost a Love/A Little Love from You Will Do	1966	25.00
PHILCO-FORD			
❑ HP-23	Room at the Top/Most Children Do	1968	20.00
—4-inch plastic "Hip Pocket Record" with color sleeve			
ROULETTE			
❑ 4770	Room at the Top/Your Friends Here in Dunderville	1967	20.00
❑ 4785	Most Children Do/Hello Girl	1967	20.00
TOLLIE			
❑ 9049	Up on the Mountain/So Young, So Fine	1965	25.00
Albums			
ROULETTE			
❑ R 25358 [M]	The Fallen Angels	1967	30.00
❑ SR 25358 [S]	The Fallen Angels	1967	40.00
❑ SR 42011	It's a Long Way Down	1968	400.00

FALLENROCK

Number	Title (A Side/B Side)	Yr	NM
45s			
CAPRICORN			
❑ 0211	Sayin' It's So Don't Make It So/She's a Mystery	1974	5.00
❑ 0227	Mary Anne/My World Begins and Ends with You	1975	5.00
Albums			
CAPRICORN			
❑ CP 0143	Watch for Fallenrock	1974	10.00

FALLING PEBBLES, THE
Early version of THE BUCKINGHAMS.

Number	Title (A Side/B Side)	Yr	NM
45s			
ALLEY CAT			
❑ 201	Lawdy Miss Clawdy/Virginia Wolf	1964	25.00

FALLOWS, SCOTT, AND THE EBBTONES

Number	Title (A Side/B Side)	Yr	NM
45s			
DOT			
❑ 16577	Surfing Boop-Boop-A-Do/King of Lovers	1964	20.00

FAME, GEORGIE

Number	Title (A Side/B Side)	Yr	NM
45s			
EPIC			
❑ 10166	Because I Love You/Bidin' My Time ('Cos I Love You)	1967	8.00
❑ 10283	The Ballad of Bonnie and Clyde/Beware of the Dog	1968	10.00
❑ 10347	Hideaway/Runaway Child	1968	6.00
❑ 10402	Someone to Watch Over Me/For Your Pleasure	1968	6.00
❑ 10477	I'll Be Your Baby Tonight/Down Along the Cove	1969	6.00
❑ 10546	Peaceful/Hideaway	1969	6.00
❑ 10640	Fire and Rain/The Movie Star Song	1970	6.00
IMPERIAL			
❑ 66086	Yeh, Yeh/Preach and Teach	1965	12.00
❑ 66104	Let the Sunshine In/In the Meantime	1965	10.00
❑ 66125	Blue Monday/Like We Used to Be	1965	10.00
❑ 66189	El Bandido/Get Away	1966	10.00
❑ 66220	Last Night/Sitting in the Park	1966	10.00
❑ 66299	Funny How Time Slips Away/Last Night	1968	8.00
ISLAND			
❑ 035	Everlovin' Woman/Ozone	1975	5.00
7-Inch Extended Plays			
EPIC			
❑ 5-26368	The Ballad of Bonnie & Clyde/Ask Me Nice/Exactly Like You//Someone to Watch Over Me/Blue Prelude/Side by Side	1968	20.00
—Jukebox issue; small hole, plays at 33 1/3 rpm			
❑ 5-26368 [PS]	The Ballad of Bonnie & Clyde	1968	20.00
Albums			
EPIC			
❑ BN 26368	The Ballad of Bonnie and Clyde	1968	25.00
❑ BN 26563	Shorty Featuring Georgie Fame	1968	25.00
IMPERIAL			
❑ LP-9282 [M]	Yeh, Yeh	1965	25.00
❑ LP-9331 [M]	Get Away	1966	25.00
❑ LP-12282 [P]	Yeh, Yeh	1965	30.00
—Entire album is stereo except "Yeh, Yeh" (rechanneled)			
❑ LP-12331 [R]	Get Away	1966	20.00
ISLAND			
❑ ILPS 9293	Georgie Fame	1975	10.00

FAME, GEORGIE, AND ANNIE ROSS

Number	Title (A Side/B Side)	Yr	NM
Albums			
DRG			
❑ 5197	Georgie Fame and Annie Ross in Hoagland	198?	12.00

FAME & PRICE — PRICE & FAME TOGETHER
GEORGIE FAME and ALAN PRICE.

Number	Title (A Side/B Side)	Yr	NM
45s			
REPRISE			
❑ 1014	John and Mary/Rosetta	1971	5.00

FAMILY

Number	Title (A Side/B Side)	Yr	NM
45s			
REPRISE			
❑ 0786	Hey Mr. Policeman/Old Songs, New Songs	1968	8.00
❑ 0809	Second Generation Woman/Hometown	1969	8.00
❑ 0881	Good Friend of Mine/No Mule Fool	1969	8.00
UNITED ARTISTS			
❑ XW171	My Friend the Sun/Glove	1973	5.00
❑ XW416	Suspicion/It's Only a Movie	1974	5.00
❑ 50832	Seasons/In My Own Time	1971	6.00
❑ 50882	Between Blue and Me/Laff and Sing	1972	5.00
Albums			
REPRISE			
❑ RS-6313	Music in a Doll's House	1968	20.00
❑ RS-6340	Family Entertainment	1969	15.00
❑ RS-6384	A Song for Me	1970	15.00
UNITED ARTISTS			
❑ UA-LA181-F	It's Only a Movie	1974	12.00
❑ UAS-5527	Anyway	1971	15.00
❑ UAS-5562	Fearless	1972	15.00
❑ UAS-5644	Bandstand	1972	15.00

FAMILY DOGG

Number	Title (A Side/B Side)	Yr	NM
45s			
BELL			
❑ 848	Arizona/The House and the Heather	1969	6.00
❑ 863	Moonshine Mary/Sympathy	1970	6.00
❑ 885	This Unhappy Heart of Mine/When Tomorrow Becomes Tomorrow	1970	6.00
❑ 939	This Unhappy Heart of Mine/(B-side unknown)	1970	5.00
Albums			
BUDDAH			
❑ BDS-5100	The View from Rowland's Head	1972	25.00

FAMILY TREE, THE

Number	Title (A Side/B Side)	Yr	NM
45s			
MIRA			
❑ 228	Prince of Dreams/Live Your Own Life	1966	10.00
PAULA			
❑ 329	Electric Kangaroo/Terry Tommy	1970	6.00
RCA VICTOR			
❑ 47-9184	Do You Have the Time/Keepin' a Secret	1967	8.00
Albums			
RCA VICTOR			
❑ LSP-3955	Miss Butters	1968	15.00

FAMOUS FLAMES, THE
Backing group for JAMES BROWN.

Number	Title (A Side/B Side)	Yr	NM
45s			
KING			
❑ 6341	Nobody Knows But My Baby and Me/Who Am I	1970	8.00

FANADOS, THE

Number	Title (A Side/B Side)	Yr	NM
45s			
CARTER			
❑ 2050	The One I Love/She Must Be from a Different Planet	195?	800.00

Except when noted otherwise, VG = 25% of NM, and VG+ = 50% of NM. (Example: VG = $2.00, VG+ = $4.00 and NM = $8.00.)

FANCY (1) British pop group.

Number	Title (A Side/B Side)	Yr	NM
45s			
BIG TREE			
❑ 15004	Wild Thing/Fancy	1974	5.00
❑ 16026	Touch Me/I Don't Need Your Love	1974	5.00
Albums			
BIG TREE			
❑ BT 89502	Wild Thing	1974	12.00
RCA VICTOR			
❑ APL1-1482	Fancy Turns You On	1976	12.00

FANCY (2) Rock band from Connecticut.

Number	Title (A Side/B Side)	Yr	NM
45s			
POISON RING			
❑ PR-716	All My Best (Sweet Mary)/Goin' Down to the Sea	1971	20.00
Albums			
POISON RING			
❑ PRR-2238	Meeting You Here	1971	80.00

FANCY (3)

Number	Title (A Side/B Side)	Yr	NM
12-Inch Singles			
PERSONAL			
❑ P 49812	Come Inside (Long Version 9:00) (Short Version 4:10)/Chinese Eyes (5:58)	1985	8.00
❑ P 49818	Check It Out (6:00)//Get Lost Tonight (5:38)/Burnin' Out the Light (5:08)	1985	8.00

FANNY

Number	Title (A Side/B Side)	Yr	NM
45s			
CASABLANCA			
❑ 0009	I've Had It/First Time	1974	5.00
❑ 814	Butter Boy/Beggar Man	1974	5.00
REPRISE			
❑ 0901	Ladies' Choice/New Day	1970	6.00
❑ 0938	One Step at a Time/Nowhere to Run	1970	6.00
❑ 0963	Changing Horses/Conversation with a Copy	1970	6.00
❑ 1033	Charity Ball/Place in the Country	1971	6.00
❑ 1080	Ain't That Peculiar/Think About the Children	1972	6.00
❑ 1097	Rock Bottom Blues/Wonderful Feeling	1972	6.00
❑ 1119	Knock on My Door/Young and Dumb	1972	6.00
❑ 1148	All Mine/I Need You Need Me	1972	6.00
❑ 1162	Last Night I Had a Dream/Beside Myself	1973	6.00
Albums			
CASABLANCA			
❑ NBLP 7007	Rock & Roll Survivors	1974	12.00
REPRISE			
❑ MS-2058	Fanny Hill	1972	15.00
❑ MS-2137	Mother's Pride	1973	15.00
❑ RS-6416	Fanny	1970	15.00
❑ RS-6456	Charity Ball	1971	15.00

FANS, THE

Number	Title (A Side/B Side)	Yr	NM
45s			
DOT			
❑ 16688	I Want a Beatle for Christmas/How Far Should I Let My Heart Go Tonight	1964	15.00

FANTASIES, THE

Number	Title (A Side/B Side)	Yr	NM
45s			
HIT			
❑ 84	Mickey's Monkey/Cry Baby	1963	8.00

FANTASTIC BAGGYS, THE Also see STEVE BARRI; P.F. SLOAN.

Number	Title (A Side/B Side)	Yr	NM
45s			
IMPERIAL			
❑ 66047	Tell 'Em I'm Surfin'/Surfer Boy's Dream	1964	70.00
❑ 66072	Anywhere the Girls Are/Debbie Be True	1964	50.00
❑ 66092	Alone on the Beach/It Was I	1965	50.00
Albums			
IMPERIAL			
❑ LP-9270 [M]	Tell 'Em I'm Surfin'	1964	150.00
❑ LP-12270 [S]	Tell 'Em I'm Surfin'	1964	300.00
LIBERTY			
❑ LN-10192	Tell 'Em I'm Surfin'	1982	10.00

FANTASTIC DEE JAYS, THE

Number	Title (A Side/B Side)	Yr	NM
Albums			
STONE			
❑ SLP-4003	The Fantastic Dee Jays	1966	1000.

FANTASTIC FOUR, THE

Number	Title (A Side/B Side)	Yr	NM
12-Inch Singles			
WESTBOUND			
❑ DSKO 136	Sexy Lady (Vocal 7:04) (same on both sides)	1978	20.00
❑ DSKO 152	BYOF (Bring Your Own Funk) (6:06) (same on both sides)	1978	15.00
45s			
EASTBOUND			
❑ 609	I Had the Whole World to Choose From/If You Need Me	1973	8.00
❑ 620	I'm Falling in Love (I Feel Good All Over)/I Believe in Miracles	1974	10.00
RIC-TIC			
❑ 113	Can't Stop Looking for My Baby/Can't Stop Looking for My Baby (Part 2)	1966	200.00
❑ 119	Girl Have Pity/Live Up to What She Thinks	1967	20.00
❑ 121	Can't Stop Looking for My Baby/Just the Lonely	1967	100.00
❑ 122	The Whole World Is a Stage/Ain't Love Wonderful	1967	15.00
❑ 128	You Gave Me Something (And Everything's Alright)/I Don't Wanna Live Without You	1967	15.00
❑ 130	To Share Your Love/As Long As I Live (I Live for You)	1967	15.00
❑ 134	Goddess of Love/As Long As the Feeling Is There	1968	15.00
❑ 136	Love Is a Many-Splendored Thing/Goddess of Love	1968	15.00
❑ 137	No Love Like Your Love/A Man in Love	1968	15.00
❑ 139	I've Got to Have You/Win or Lose	1968	15.00
❑ 144	I Love You Madly/(Instrumental)	1968	20.00
SOUL			
❑ 35052	I Love You Madly/(Instrumental)	1968	12.00
❑ 35058	I Feel Like I'm Falling in Love/Pin Point It Out	1969	15.00
❑ 35065	Just Another Lonely Night/I Don't Care Why You Want Me	1969	15.00
❑ 35072	On the Brighter Side of a Blue World/I'm Gonna Hurry On	1970	12.00
WESTBOUND			
❑ 5009	Alvin Stone (The Birth & Death of a Gangster)/I Believe in Miracles, I Believe in You	1975	7.00
❑ 5017	Have a Little Mercy/County Line	1975	5.00
❑ 5030	Don't Risk Your Happiness On Foolish Things/They Took the Show on the Road	1976	5.00
❑ 5032	Hideaway/They Took the Show on the Road	1976	5.00
❑ 55403	I Got to Have Your Love/Ain't I Been Good to You	1977	5.00
❑ 55408	Mixed Up Moods and Attitudes/Disco Fool Blues	1978	5.00
❑ 55417	Sexy Lady/If This Is Love	1979	5.00
❑ 55419	BYOF (Bring Your Own Funk)/If This Is Love	1979	5.00
Albums			
SOUL			
❑ SS-717	The Best of the Fantastic Four	1969	40.00
❑ SS-722	How Sweet He Is	1970	—
—Canceled			
WESTBOUND			
❑ W 201	Alvin Stone (The Birth and Death of a Gangster)	1975	15.00
❑ W 226	Night People	1976	15.00
❑ WT 306	Got to Have Your Love	1977	15.00
❑ WT 6108	BYOF (Bring Your Own Funk)	1978	15.00

FANTASTIC JOHNNY C, THE

Number	Title (A Side/B Side)	Yr	NM
45s			
KAMA SUTRA			
❑ 511	Let's Do It Together/Peace Treaty	1970	5.00
❑ 515	Good Love/You Got Your Hooks in Me	1970	5.00
PHIL.-LA OF SOUL			
❑ 305	Boogaloo Down Broadway/Look What Love Can Make You Do	1967	8.00
❑ 309	Got What You Need/New Love	1968	6.00
❑ 315	Hitch It to the Horse/Cool Broadway	1968	6.00
❑ 320	Baby I Need You/Some Kind of Wonderful	1968	6.00
❑ 327	Is There Anything Better Than Making Love/New Love	1969	6.00
❑ 361	Don't Depend on Me/Waitin' for the Rain	1973	4.00
❑ 363	Just Say the Word/I'm a Man	1973	4.00
PHILCO-FORD			
❑ HP-39	Boogaloo Down Broadway/Got What You Need	1969	20.00
—4-inch plastic "Hip Pocket Record" with color sleeve			
Albums			
PHIL-LA OF SOUL			
❑ 4000	Boogaloo Down Broadway	1968	80.00

FANTASTICS, THE (1) Male R&B group.

Number	Title (A Side/B Side)	Yr	NM
45s			
BELL			
❑ 977	Something Old, Something New/High and Dry	1971	20.00
❑ 45157	(Love Me) Love the Life I Lead/Old Rags and Tatters	1971	15.00
DERAM			
❑ 7528	Face to Face with Heartache/This Must Be My Rainy Day	1970	15.00

FANTASTICS, THE (2)

Number	Title (A Side/B Side)	Yr	NM
45s			
RCA VICTOR			
❑ 47-7572	There Goes My Love/Millionaire Hobo	1959	40.00
—Black label, dog on top			
❑ 47-7572	There Goes My Love/I Wanna Be a Millionaire Hobo	1965	15.00
—Evidenly, a reissue with the same number, but the dog on side of label rather than on top, exists			
❑ 47-7664	This Is My Wedding Day/I Got a Zero	1960	40.00
UNITED ARTISTS			
❑ 309	Dancing Doll/I Told You Once	1961	50.00

FANTASTICS, THE (3) Nashville studio group.

Number	Title (A Side/B Side)	Yr	NM
45s			
HIT			
❑ 289	Bernadette/I Never Loved a Man the Way I Love You	1967	8.00
—B-side by Odessa Crawford			
❑ 293	Here Comes My Baby/I Got Rhythm	1967	8.00
—B-side by the Jalopy Five			
❑ 297	A Whiter Shade of Pale/San Francisco (Be Sure to Wear Flowers in Your Hair)	1967	8.00
—B-side by Bobby Sims			
❑ 302	Light My Fire./Mercy, Mercy, Mercy	1967	8.00
—B-side by the Chords (2)			
❑ 309	People Are Strange/Please Love Me Forever	1967	8.00
—B-side by Bobby Sims			
❑ 314	Pata Pata/Massachusetts	1967	8.00
—B-side by the Chords (2)			
❑ 324	Cowboys to Girls/Tighten Up	1968	8.00
—B-side by the Classmates			
❑ 329	Mony Mony/I Wanna Live	1968	8.00
—B-side by Ed Hardin			
❑ 336	Stoned Soul Picnic/Hurdy Gurdy Man	1968	8.00
—B-side by the Jalopy Five			
❑ 340	1-2-3, Red Light/The House That Jack Built	1968	8.00
—B-side by Kathy Shannon			
❑ 344	Over You/My Special Angel	1968	8.00
—B-side by the Chords (2)			
❑ 348	White Room/Who's Making Love	1968	8.00
—B-side by Bobby Sims			
❑ 352	Touch Me/Everyday People	1969	8.00
—B-side by the Jalopy Five			
❑ 355	You Showed Me/Soulful Strut	1969	8.00
—B-side by the New Society Group			

FANTASTICS, THE (U) Neither group (1) nor group (2), but are they both the same?

Number	Title (A Side/B Side)	Yr	NM
45s			
SCORPIO			
❑ 407	Malaguena/Dance for an Unnamed Gypsy Queen	1966	25.00
SOUND STAGE 7			
❑ 2565	Have a Little You/Me and You	1966	12.00

FANTASY

Number	Title (A Side/B Side)	Yr	NM
45s			
IMPERIAL			
❑ 66394	Painted Horse/I Got the Fever	1969	10.00
LIBERTY			
❑ 56190	Stoned Cowboy/Understand	1970	8.00

Number	Title (A Side/B Side)	Yr	NM
Albums			
LIBERTY			
❑ LSP-7643	Fantasy	1970	20.00

FAPARDOKLY

Number	Title (A Side/B Side)	Yr	NM
Albums			
U.I.P.			
❑ 2250	Fapardokly	1967	500.00

FAR CRY

Number	Title (A Side/B Side)	Yr	NM
45s			
VANGUARD			
❑ 35085	Shapes/Hellhound	1969	10.00
Albums			
VANGUARD APOSTOLIC			
❑ VSD-6510	Far Cry	1968	75.00

FARBER, BURT

Number	Title (A Side/B Side)	Yr	NM
45s			
FRATERNITY			
❑ F-796	Never a Day Goes By/Mon Reve	1958	20.00

FARDON, DON

Number	Title (A Side/B Side)	Yr	NM
45s			
CAPITOL			
❑ 3929	St. Matthew, St. Mark, St. Luke and St. John/Lola	1974	5.00
CHELSEA			
❑ 78-0115	Delta Queen/Home Town Baby	1973	6.00
DECCA			
❑ 32696	Belfast Boy/Echoes of the Cheers	1970	6.00
GNP CRESCENDO			
❑ 405	(The Lament of the Cherokee) Indian Reservation/ Dreaming Room	1968	8.00
❑ 418	Take a Heart/How Do You Break a Broken Heart	1968	6.00
❑ 421	Sally Goes 'Round the Moon/ How Do You Break a Broken Heart	1969	6.00
❑ 424	Running Bear/Ruby's Picture	1969	6.00
ROXBURY			
❑ BRBO-0159	Louisiana/Lady Zelda	1973	5.00
Albums			
DECCA			
❑ DL 75225	I've Paid My Dues	1970	15.00
GNP CRESCENDO			
❑ GNPS-2044	Indian Reservation	1968	20.00

FARGO, DONNA

Number	Title (A Side/B Side)	Yr	NM
45s			
ABC/DOT			
❑ 17523	U.S. of A./A Woman's Prayer	1974	5.00
❑ 17541	If Do Feel Good/Only the Strong	1974	5.00
❑ 17557	Hello Little Bluebird/2 Sweet 2 Be 4 Gotten	1975	5.00
❑ 17579	Whatever I Say/Rain Song	1975	5.00
❑ 17586	What Will the New Year Bring/ A Woman's Prayer	1975	5.00
❑ 17609	You're Not Charlie Brown (And I'm Not Raggedy Ann)/ Sing, Sing, Sing	1976	4.00
❑ 17660	Don't Be Angry/You Don't Mess Around with Jim	1976	4.00
❑ 17692	I'd Love You to Want Me/ How Close You Came (To Being Gone)	1977	4.00
CHALLENGE			
❑ 59387	Daddy/Sticks and Stones	1968	10.00
❑ 59391	Wishful Thinking/All That's Keeping Me Alive	1968	10.00
CLEVELAND INTERNATIONAL			
❑ 1	My Heart Will Always Belong to You/Reasons to Be	1984	4.00
❑ 10	Soldier Boy/Stand Tall	1991	5.00
COLUMBIA			
❑ 04097	The Sign of the Times/ Reasons to Be	1983	4.00
COUNTRY HEARTS			
❑ CH-001 [DJ]	My Side of the Bed/ Country Singer's Wife	1970	30.00
—Promo-only release			
DECCA			
❑ 33001	Daddy/Sticks and Stones	1972	8.00
DOT			
❑ 17409	The Happiest Girl in the Whole U.S.A./The Awareness of Nothing	1972	6.00
❑ 17409 [PS]	The Happiest Girl in the Whole U.S.A./The Awareness of Nothing	1972	8.00
❑ 17429	Funny Face/How Close You Came (To Being Gone)	1972	6.00
❑ 17444	Superman/Forever Is As Far As I Could Go	1973	5.00
❑ 17460	You Were Always There/ He Can Have All He Wants	1973	5.00
❑ 17476	Little Girl Gone/Just Call Me	1973	5.00
❑ 17476 [PS]	Little Girl Gone/Just Call Me	1973	8.00
❑ 17491	I'll Try a Little Bit Harder/ All About a Feeling	1973	5.00
❑ 17506	You Can't Be a Beacon (If Your Light Don't Shine)/ Just a Friend of Mine	1974	5.00
MCA			
❑ 51209	Say "I Do"/All About a Feeling	1981	4.00
MERCURY			
❑ 884712-7	Woman of the 80's/You Were Always There	1986	3.00
❑ 888043-7	Winners/I've Laid Too Many Eggs	1986	3.00
❑ 888093-7	Me and You/I've Laid Too Many Eggs	1986	3.00
❑ 888680-7	Members Only/Funny Face	1987	3.00
—A-side: With Billy Joe Royal			
RAMCO			
❑ 1982	You Make Me Feel Like a Woman/Would You Believe a Lifetime	1967	15.00
❑ 1988	Who's Been Playin' House/ You Reach for the Bottle	1967	15.00
❑ 1991	Kind of Glad I'm Me/Then You Haven't Lied	1967	15.00
RCA			
❑ PB-13264	It's Hard to Be the Dreamer/I Just Saw My Reflection in You	1982	4.00
❑ PB-13329	Did We Have to Go This Far (To Say Goodbye)/All I Need to Know	1982	4.00
WARNER BROS.			
❑ 8186	Mr. Doodles/If You Can't Love All of Me	1976	5.00
❑ 8227	I've Loved You All the Way/ One of God's Children	1976	5.00
❑ 8305	Mockingbird Hill/Second Chance	1976	5.00
❑ 8375	That Was Yesterday/ Cricket Song	1977	5.00
❑ 8431	Shame on Me/Hey, Mister Music Man	1977	5.00
❑ 8509	Do I Love You (Yes in Every Way)/Dee Dee	1977	5.00
❑ 8578	Ragamuffin Girl/ Everybody's Girl	1978	4.00
❑ 8643	Another Goodbye/ Changes in My Life	1978	4.00
❑ 8722	Somebody Special/ Changes in My Life	1978	4.00
❑ 8867	Daddy/For the Rest of My Life	1979	4.00
❑ 49093	Preacher Berry/I Don't Know What to Do	1979	4.00
❑ 49183	Walk On By/I Wrote This Song Just for You	1980	4.00
❑ 49514	Land of Cotton/I Still Believe in You	1980	4.00
❑ 49575	Seeing Is Believing/Look What You've Done	1980	4.00
❑ 49757	Lonestar Cowboy/Utah Song	1981	4.00
❑ 49757 [PS]	Lonestar Cowboy/Utah Song	1981	6.00
❑ 49852	Jacamo/Song to Celebrate Life	1981	4.00
7-Inch Extended Plays			
DOT			
❑ JBA 26000	Would Have Been Just Perfect/ Daddy Dumplin'/Manhattan, Kansas//Johnny B. Goode/A Little Somethin' (To Hang On To)/Society's Got Us	1972	10.00
—Jukebox issue; small hole, plays at 33 1/3 rpm			
❑ JBA 26000 [PS]	The Happiest Girl in the Whole U.S.A	1972	10.00
Albums			
ABC/DOT			
❑ DOSD-2002	Miss Donna Fargo	1974	12.00
❑ DOSD-2029	Whatever I Say Means I Love You	1975	12.00
❑ DO-2075	The Best of Donna Fargo	1977	12.00
DOT			
❑ DOS-26000	The Happiest Girl in the Whole U.S.A.	1972	12.00
❑ DOS-26006	My Second Album	1973	12.00
❑ DOS-26019	All About a Feeling	1973	12.00
MCA			
❑ 667	The Happiest Girl in the Whole U.S.A.	198?	8.00
—Budget-line reissue			
❑ 37108	The Best of Donna Fargo	198?	8.00
—Budget-line reissue			
MERCURY			
❑ 830236-1	Winners	1986	12.00
❑ 832507-1	Winners	1987	8.00
—Reissue with two songs deleted and one added from above			
PICKWICK			
❑ SPC-6187	Superman	197?	8.00
SONGBIRD			
❑ 5203	Brotherly Love	1982	10.00
WARNER BROS.			
❑ BS 2926	On the Move	1976	10.00
❑ BS 2996	Donna Fargo Country	1977	10.00
❑ BS 3099	Shame on Me	1977	10.00
❑ BSK 3191	Dark Eyed Lady	1978	10.00
❑ BSK 3377	Just for You	1979	10.00
❑ BSK 3470	Fargo	1980	10.00

FARLOWE, CHRIS

Number	Title (A Side/B Side)	Yr	NM
45s			
GENERAL AMERICAN			
❑ 718	What You Gonna Do/ Just a Dream	1964	15.00
IMMEDIATE			
❑ 5002	Paint It Black/ You're So Good to Me	1967	10.00
❑ 5005	Handbags and Gladrags/ Everyone Makes a Mistake	1968	10.00
❑ 5011	What Have I Been Doing/ Paint It Black	1968	10.00
MGM			
❑ 13567	Out of Time/ Baby Make It Soon	1966	20.00
—A-side is a Mick Jagger-Keith Richards composition only later recorded by the Rolling Stones.			
POLYDOR			
❑ 14008	Circles 'Round the Sun/Save Your Tears	1969	8.00
❑ 14013	Medicated Goo/Betty Lou	1970	8.00
Albums			
COLUMBIA			
❑ CL 2593 [M]	The Fabulous Chris Farlowe	1966	40.00
❑ CS 9393 [R]	The Fabulous Chris Farlowe	1966	25.00
IMMEDIATE			
❑ Z12 52010	Paint It Farlowe	1968	20.00
POLYDOR			
❑ 24-4041	From Here to Mama Rosa with the Hill	1970	12.00

FARM BAND, THE

Number	Title (A Side/B Side)	Yr	NM
Albums			
MANTRA			
❑ 777 [(2)]	The Farm Band	1972	75.00
—With poster			

FARMER BOYS, THE

Number	Title (A Side/B Side)	Yr	NM
45s			
CAPITOL			
❑ F3077	You're a Humdinger/ I'm Just Too Lazy	1955	20.00
❑ F3162	Lend a Helping Hand/ Onions, Onions	1955	20.00
❑ F3246	You Lied/It Pays to Advertise	1955	20.00
❑ F3322	Flip Flop/Charming Betsy	1956	20.00
❑ F3476	My Baby Done Left Me/ Somehow, Someway, Someday	1956	20.00
❑ F3569	Cool Down Mame/ Oh How It Hurts	1956	20.00
❑ F3732	Flash, Crash and Thunder/ Someone to Love	1957	20.00
❑ F3827	Yearning, Burning Heart/ No One	1957	20.00

FARNER, MARK Of GRAND FUNK RAILROAD.

Number	Title (A Side/B Side)	Yr	NM
45s			
ATLANTIC			
❑ 3448	You and Me Baby/Second Chance to Dance	1977	4.00
❑ 3510	When a Man Loves a Woman/ If It Took All Day	1978	4.00
❑ 3529	Just One Look/Crystal Eyes	1978	4.00
LUCKY ELEVEN			
❑ 352	Down in the Valley/I Got News for You	1968	10.00

Except when noted otherwise, VG = 25% of NM, and VG+ = 50% of NM. (Example: VG = $2.00, VG+ = $4.00 and NM = $8.00.)

Number	Title (A Side/B Side)	Yr	NM
Albums			
ATLANTIC			
❑ SD 18232	Mark Farner	1977	10.00
❑ SD 19196	No Frills	1978	10.00

FARNER, MARK, AND DON BREWER
Both later of GRAND FUNK RAILROAD.

Number	Title (A Side/B Side)	Yr	NM
45s			
LUCKY ELEVEN			
❑ 366	Does It Matter to You Girl/We Gotta Have Love	1968	12.00
❑ 366 [PS]	Does It Matter to You Girl/We Gotta Have Love	1968	40.00
Albums			
QUADICO			
❑ 7401	Monumental Funk	1977	10.00
❑ 7401 [PD]	Monumental Funk	1977	20.00
—Picture disc			

FARNHAM, JOHN

Number	Title (A Side/B Side)	Yr	NM
12-Inch Singles			
MCA CURB			
❑ L33-1206 [DJ]	Justice for One/Innocent Hearts	1984	12.00
45s			
CAPITOL			
❑ 2128	Sadie the Cleaning Lady/ In My Room	1968	10.00
—As "Johnny Farnham"			
❑ 3522	Don't You Know It's Magic/ Sweet Cherry Wine	1973	10.00
—As "Johnny Farnham"			
MCA			
❑ 52798	Break the Ice/Thunder in Your Heart	1986	4.00
MCA CURB			
❑ 52580	Love (It's Just the Way It Goes)/ Ragtop Day	1984	5.00
—A-side with Sarah M. Taylor			
RCA			
❑ 5146-7-R	You're the Voice/ Going, Going, Gone	1986	4.00
❑ 5264-7-R	Pressure Down/Trouble	1986	4.00
❑ 8915-7-R	Two Strong Hearts/ Some Do, Some Don't	1988	4.00
Albums			
RCA			
❑ 6300-1-R	Whispering Jack	1986	10.00

FARON'S FLAMINGOS

Number	Title (A Side/B Side)	Yr	NM
45s			
COLUMBIA			
❑ 43018	Let's Stomp/I Can Tell	1964	25.00
—B-side by Rory Storm and the Hurricanes			

FARQUAHR

Number	Title (A Side/B Side)	Yr	NM
45s			
ELEKTRA			
❑ 45735	Holy Moses/My Island	1971	6.00
VERVE FORECAST			
❑ 5077	My Eggs Don't Taste the Same Without You/Sister Theresa's East River Orphanage	1968	8.00
❑ 5085	Teddy Bear Days/My Island	1968	8.00
WARNER BROS.			
❑ 7354	Kiss the Wind Goodbye/ Neither Here Nor There	1969	6.00
Albums			
ELEKTRA			
❑ EKS-74083	Farquahr	1970	12.00
VERVE FORECAST			
❑ FTS-3053	Fabulous Farquahr	1969	12.00

FARR, GARY, AND THE T-BONES

Number	Title (A Side/B Side)	Yr	NM
45s			
EPIC			
❑ 9832	Don't Stop and Stare/ Give All She's Got	1965	12.00

FARR, LITTLE JOEY

Number	Title (A Side/B Side)	Yr	NM
45s			
BAND BOX			
❑ 286	Rock & Roll Santa/ Big White Cadillac	196?	50.00

FARRELL AND THE FLAMES

Number	Title (A Side/B Side)	Yr	NM
45s			
FRANSIL			
❑ 14	Dreams and Memories/ You'll Be Sorry	1961	400.00

FASCINATIONS, THE (1) Female vocal group.

Number	Title (A Side/B Side)	Yr	NM
45s			
ABC-PARAMOUNT			
❑ 10387	Mama Didn't Lie/ Someone Like You	1962	20.00
—Some of the ABC-Paramount pressings are misspelled "Fasinations"			
❑ 10443	Tears In My Eyes/ You're Gonna Be Sorry	1963	25.00
MAYFIELD			
❑ 7711	(Say It Isn't So) Say You'd Never Go/I'm So Lucky	1966	10.00
❑ 7714	Girls Are Out to Get You/You'll Be Sorry	1966	10.00
❑ 7716	I Can't Stay Away from You/ (B-side unknown)	1967	10.00

FASCINATIONS, THE (2)

Number	Title (A Side/B Side)	Yr	NM
45s			
DORE			
❑ 593	If I Had Your Love/Why	1961	50.00
PAXLEY			
❑ 750	If I Had Your Love/Why	1960	150.00

FASCINATIONS, THE (U) It's doubtful that any of these are group (1), but they could be group (2).

Number	Title (A Side/B Side)	Yr	NM
45s			
A&G			
❑ 101	I'm Gonna Cry/Since You Went Away	1972	20.00
SURE			
❑ 106	It's Midnight/Boom Bada Boom	1960	80.00
❑ 106	Midnight/Boom Bada Boom	1960	120.00

FASCINATORS, THE (1)

Number	Title (A Side/B Side)	Yr	NM
45s			
BIM BAM BOOM			
❑ 110	Oh, Rose Marie/Forgive Me, My Darling	1974	10.00
CAPITOL			
❑ F-4053	Chapel Bells/I Wonder Who	1958	150.00
❑ F-4137	Come to Paradise/Who Do You Think You Are	1959	200.00
❑ F-4247	Oh Rose Marie/Fried Chicken and Macaroni	1959	200.00
❑ 4544	Chapel Bells/I Wonder Who	1961	80.00

FASCINATORS, THE (2)

Number	Title (A Side/B Side)	Yr	NM
45s			
BLUE LAKE			
❑ 112	Can't Stop/Don't Give My Love Away	1953	2000.

FASCINATORS, THE (3)

Number	Title (A Side/B Side)	Yr	NM
45s			
BURN			
❑ 845	I'll Be Gone/Can't You See I'm Lonely	1965	20.00

FASCINATORS, THE (4)

Number	Title (A Side/B Side)	Yr	NM
45s			
DOOTO			
❑ 441	Teardrop Eyes/ Shivers and Shakes	1958	60.00

FASCINATORS, THE (5)

Number	Title (A Side/B Side)	Yr	NM
45s			
YOUR COPY			
❑ 1135	The Bells of My Heart/ Sweet Baby	1954	1000.
—Black vinyl			
❑ 1135	The Bells of My Heart/ Sweet Baby	1954	2000.
—Red vinyl			
❑ 1136	My Beauty, My Own/ Don't Give It Away	1954	1000.

FASCINATORS, THE (U) If these are not completely different groups, these are most likely by group (3) or (4).

Number	Title (A Side/B Side)	Yr	NM
45s			
KING			
❑ 5119	Cuddle Up with Carolyn/Tee Hee	1958	50.00
TRANS ATLAS			
❑ 688	You're to Blame/Revived	196?	30.00

FASHIONS, THE (1) BARBARA ENGLISH was a member of this group.

Number	Title (A Side/B Side)	Yr	NM
45s			
CAMEO			
❑ 331	Baby That's Me/ Nick and Joe Callin'	1964	10.00
ELMOR			
❑ 301	Please Let It Be Me/Fairy Tales	1961	25.00
EMBER			
❑ 1084	I Just Got a Letter/Try My Love	1962	12.00
V-TONE			
❑ 202	I'm Dreaming of You/ I Love You So	1959	20.00
—Blue label			
❑ 202	I'm Dreaming of You/ I Love You So	1959	30.00
—Orange label			
❑ 202	I'm Dreaming of You/ Lonesome Road	1959	50.00
WARWICK			
❑ 646	All I Want/Dearest One	1961	20.00

FASHIONS, THE (2)

Number	Title (A Side/B Side)	Yr	NM
45s			
FELSTED			
❑ 8689	Surfer's Memories/Surfin' Back to School	1964	30.00

FASHIONS, THE (3)

Number	Title (A Side/B Side)	Yr	NM
45s			
PHIL-L.A. OF SOUL			
❑ 354	I Don't Mind Doin' It/What Goes Up (Must Come Down)	1972	6.00

FASHIONS, THE (4)

Number	Title (A Side/B Side)	Yr	NM
45s			
20TH CENTURY FOX			
❑ 6710	Lover's Stand/ Only Those in Love	1968	8.00

FASTBACKS, THE

Number	Title (A Side/B Side)	Yr	NM
45s			
NO THREES			
❑ 005	It's Your Birthday/ You Can't Be Happy	1981	30.00
—With drummer Duff McKagan, pre-Guns N' Roses			
❑ 005 [PS]	It's Your Birthday/ You Can't Be Happy	1981	30.00
SUB POP			
❑ 104 [(2)]	Impatience/Whatever Happened To/Above the Sunrise/ My Letters	1991	7.50
—Two black vinyl records			
❑ 104 [(2)]	Impatience/Whatever Happened To/Above the Sunrise/ My Letters	1991	22.50
—One red, one green vinyl record			
❑ 104 [PS]	Impatience/Whatever Happened To/Above the Sunrise/ My Letters	1991	7.50
—Fold-out poster sleeve			
7-Inch Extended Plays			
NO THREES			
❑ 009	In the Summer/You Can't Be Happy/Everything That I Don't Need/Queen of Eyes	1989	7.50
❑ 009 [PS]	In the Summer/You Can't Be Happy/Everything That I Don't Need/Queen of Eyes	1989	7.50
SMILIN' EARS			
❑ 009 [(2)]	Live in America	199?	7.50
❑ 009 [PS]	Live in America	199?	7.50

FASTER PUSSYCAT

Number	Title (A Side/B Side)	Yr	NM
12-Inch Singles			
ELEKTRA			
❑ ED 5240 [DJ]	Don't Change That Song (same on both sides)	1987	7.00
❑ ED 5261 [DJ]	Bathroom Wall (Remix) (Remix with Pussycat Intro)	1987	8.00
❑ ED 5284 [DJ]	Babylon (same on both sides)	1988	7.00
❑ ED 5402 [DJ]	Poison Ivy (Edit) (LP Version)	1989	7.00
❑ ED 5430 [DJ]	House of Pain (LP Version) (Edit)	1989	10.00
45s			
ELEKTRA			
❑ 64995	House of Pain/Slip of the Tongue	1990	5.00
❑ 69274	Poison Ivy/Tattoo	1989	4.00
❑ 69413	Babylon/Smash House	1988	4.00
❑ 69413 [PS]	Babylon/Smash House	1988	4.00
❑ 69437	Bathroom Wall/Cathouse	1987	6.00
Albums			
ELEKTRA			
❑ 60730	Faster Pussycat	1987	8.00
❑ 60883	Wake Me When It's Over	1989	10.00

FASTEST GROUP ALIVE, THE

45s

Number	Title (A Side/B Side)	Yr	NM
TEEN			
❑ 100	The Bears/Beside	1966	30.00
VALIANT			
❑ 754	The Bears/Beside	1966	20.00
❑ 759	Lullabye/5:15 Sports	1967	20.00

FAT CITY
Also see JOHN DENVER.

45s

Number	Title (A Side/B Side)	Yr	NM
ABC PROBE			
❑ 469	Wall Street/City Cat	1969	6.00
PARAMOUNT			
❑ 0162	I Guess He'd Rather Be in Colorado/Morning Go Away	1972	6.00
❑ 0176	Workingman's Day/Hey, Loretta	1972	5.00

Albums

Number	Title (A Side/B Side)	Yr	NM
ABC PROBE			
❑ 4508	Reincarnation	1969	20.00
PARAMOUNT			
❑ PAS-6028	Welcome to Fat City	1972	15.00

FAT MATTRESS

Albums

Number	Title (A Side/B Side)	Yr	NM
ATCO			
❑ 33-309 [M]	Fat Mattress	1969	40.00
—White label promo only; "DJ Copy Monaural" sticker on cover			
❑ SD 33-309 [S]	Fat Mattress	1969	20.00
❑ 33-347 [M]	Fat Mattress II	1970	40.00
—White label promo only; "DJ Copy Monaural" sticker on cover			
❑ SD 33-347 [S]	Fat Mattress II	1970	15.00

FATBACK
Includes records as "Fatback Band."

12-Inch Singles

Number	Title (A Side/B Side)	Yr	NM
COTILLION			
❑ PR 763 [DJ]	You've Got That Magic (6:43)/You've Got That Magic (3:55)	1984	8.00
SPRING			
❑ PRO 184 [DJ]	On the Floor (same on both sides)	1982	8.00
❑ 402	King Tim III (Personalty Jock)/You're My Candy Sweet	1979	10.00
❑ 409	The Girl Is Fine (So Fine)/(B-side unknown)	1983	8.00
❑ 414	Spread Love/(B-side unknown)	1984	6.00

45s

Number	Title (A Side/B Side)	Yr	NM
COTILLION			
❑ 99642	Lover Undercover/(B-side unknown)	1985	3.00
❑ 99665	Girls on My Mind/Osiris (There's a Party Goin' On)	1985	3.00
❑ 99730	You've Got That Magic/(B-side unknown)	1984	3.00
❑ 99749	Call Out My Name/I Love You So	1984	3.00
EVENT			
❑ 217	Keep On Steppin'/Breakin' Up Is Hard to Do	1974	5.00
❑ 219	Wicki-Wacky/Can't Fight the Flame	1974	5.00
❑ 224	(Hey I) Feel Real Good (Part 1)/(Hey I) Feel Real Good (Part 2)	1975	5.00
❑ 226	Yum Yum (Gimme Some)/Let the Drums Speak	1975	5.00
❑ 227	(Are You Ready) Do the Bus Stop/Gotta Learn to Dance	1975	5.00
❑ 229	Spanish Hustle/Put Your Love (In My Tender Care)	1976	5.00
PERCEPTION			
❑ 520	Soul March/To Be with You	1973	5.00
❑ 526	Street Dance/Goin' to See My Baby	1973	5.00
❑ 540	Nija (Nija) Walk (Street Walk)/Soul Man	1973	5.00
SPRING			
❑ 165	Party Time/Groovy Kind of Day	1976	5.00
❑ 168	The Booty/If That's the Way You Want It	1976	5.00
❑ 171	Double Dutch/Spank the Baby	1977	5.00
❑ 174	NYCNY USA (Nik-Ne-Yoo-Sa)/Soulfinger	1977	5.00
❑ 177	Master Booty/Zodiac Man	1977	5.00
❑ 180	Mile High/Midnight Freak	1978	5.00
❑ 181	I Like Girls/Get Out on the Dance Floor	1978	5.00
❑ 188	Boogie Freak/I'm Fired Up	1978	5.00
❑ 191	Freak the Freak the Funk (Rock)/Wild Dreams	1979	5.00
❑ 195	(Do the) Boogie Woogie/Hesitation	1979	5.00
❑ 199	King Tim III (Personality Jock)/You're My Candy Sweet	1979	6.00
❑ 3005	Love in Perfect Harmony/Disco Bass	1979	4.00
❑ 3008	Gotta Get My Hands on Some (Money)/Street Band	1980	4.00
❑ 3012	Backstrokin'/Love Spell	1980	4.00
❑ 3015	Let's Do It Again/Come and Get the Love	1980	4.00
❑ 3016	Angel/Concrete Jungle	1981	4.00
❑ 3018	Take It Any Way You Want It/Lady Groove	1981	4.00
❑ 3020	Kool Whip/Keep Your Fingers Out of the Jam	1981	4.00
❑ 3022	Rockin' to the Beat/Wanna Dance	1981	4.00
❑ 3023	Na Na Hey Hey Kiss Her Goodbye/I'm So in Love	1982	4.00
❑ 3025	On the Floor/Chillin' Out	1982	4.00
❑ 3026	She's My Shining Star/UFO (Unidentified Funk Object)	1982	4.00
❑ 3030	The Girl Is Fine (So Fine)/(B-side unknown)	1983	4.00
❑ 3032	Is This the Future/Double Love Affair	1983	4.00
❑ 3033	Up Against the Wall/With Love	1983	4.00
❑ 3037	I Wanna Be Your Lover/(B-side unknown)	1984	4.00

Albums

Number	Title (A Side/B Side)	Yr	NM
COTILLION			
❑ 90168	Phoenix	1984	8.00
❑ 90253	So Delicious	1985	8.00
EVENT			
❑ 6902	Keep On Steppin'	1974	15.00
—As "The Fatback Band"			
❑ 6904	Yum Yum	1975	15.00
—As "The Fatback Band"			
❑ 6905	Raising Hell	1976	15.00
—As "The Fatback Band"			
SPRING			
❑ 6711	Night Fever	1976	12.00
—As "The Fatback Band"			
❑ 6714	NYCNYUSA	1977	12.00
—As "The Fatback Band"			
❑ 6717	Man with a Plan	1978	12.00
—As "The Fatback Band"			
❑ 6718	Fired Up 'N' Kickin'	1978	10.00
❑ 6721	Bright Lites, Big City	1979	10.00
❑ 6723	Fatback XII	1979	10.00
❑ 6726	Hot Box	1980	10.00
❑ 6729	14 Karat	1980	10.00
❑ 6731	Tasty Jam	1981	10.00
❑ 6734	Gigolo	1981	10.00
❑ 6736	On the Floor	1982	10.00

FATBACK BAND, THE
See FATBACK.

FATHER YOD AND THE SPIRIT OF '76
See YA HO WA 13.

FAUN

45s

Number	Title (A Side/B Side)	Yr	NM
GREGAR			
❑ 7000	Better Dig What You Find/I Asked My Mother	1969	20.00
❑ 7001	Son of a Literate Man/Yes I'm Really Lonely	1969	20.00

Albums

Number	Title (A Side/B Side)	Yr	NM
GREGAR			
❑ 7000	Faun	1969	100.00

FAWNS, THE

45s

Number	Title (A Side/B Side)	Yr	NM
APT			
❑ 25015	Come On/Until I Die	1958	25.00

FEAR

45s

Number	Title (A Side/B Side)	Yr	NM
CRIMINAL RECORDS			
❑ (no #)	I Love Livin' in the City/Now Your Dead	1978	250.00
❑ (no #) [PS]	I Love Livin' in the City/Now Your Dead	1978	250.00
SLASH			
❑ 900	Fuck Christmas/*Uck Christmas	1979	40.00
—Not issued with picture sleeve; add 20% for plain white sleeve rubber-stamped with Christmas tree			

Albums

Number	Title (A Side/B Side)	Yr	NM
RESTLESS			
❑ 72039	More Beer	1985	15.00
SLASH			
❑ SR 111	The Record	1982	20.00
❑ 23933	The Record	1982	15.00

FEAR ITSELF

45s

Number	Title (A Side/B Side)	Yr	NM
DOT			
❑ 17278	The Letter/Born Under a Bad Sign	1969	8.00

Albums

Number	Title (A Side/B Side)	Yr	NM
DOT			
❑ DLP-25942	Fear Itself	1969	30.00

FEATHER

45s

Number	Title (A Side/B Side)	Yr	NM
COLUMBIA			
❑ 4-45231	The Fifth Stone/No Time for Sorrow	1970	8.00
❑ 4-45405	Choo Choo Nairobi/Down to the Wire	1971	8.00
VIVA			
❑ 635	Kiss of Fire/Moccasin	1969	10.00
WHITE WHALE			
❑ 353	Friends/Salli	1970	6.00

Albums

Number	Title (A Side/B Side)	Yr	NM
COLUMBIA			
❑ C 30137	Friends by Feather	1970	15.00

FEATHERBED
Early BARRY MANILOW.

45s

Number	Title (A Side/B Side)	Yr	NM
BELL			
❑ 971	Amy/Morning	1971	60.00
—Stock copies are much scarcer than promo copies			
❑ 45133 [DJ]	Could It Be Magic (mono/stereo)	1971	100.00
—Stock copy may not exist			

FEATHERS, CHARLIE

45s

Number	Title (A Side/B Side)	Yr	NM
FLIP			
❑ 503	I've Been Deceived/Peeping Eyes	1955	500.00
HOLIDAY INN			
❑ 114	Deep Elm Blues/Nobody's Darling	1962	200.00
KAY			
❑ 1001	Jungle Fever/Why Don't You	1960	200.00
KING			
❑ 4971	Can't Hardly Stand It/Everybody's Lovin' My Baby	1956	600.00
❑ 4997	One Hand Loose/Bottle to the Baby	1956	500.00
❑ 5022	Nobody's Woman/When You Decide	1957	400.00
❑ 5043	When You Come Around/Too Much Alike	1957	400.00
MEMPHIS			
❑ 103	Wild, Wild Party/Today and Tomorrow	1961	100.00
METEOR			
❑ 5032	Tongue-Tied Jill/Get With It	1956	400.00
—Blue label			
❑ 5032	Tongue-Tied Jill/Get With It	1956	1500.
—Maroon label			
PHILWOOD			
❑ 223	Tear It Up/Stutterin' Cindy	197?	8.00
POMPADOUR			
❑ 231	Uh-Huh Honey/A Wedding Gown of White	1974	8.00
ROLLIN' ROCK			
❑ 45-025	That Certain Female/She Set Me Free	1978	8.00
SUN			
❑ 231	Defrost Your Heart/Wedding Gown of White	1956	600.00
❑ 503	I've Been Deceived/Peeping Eyes	1956	600.00
WAL-MAY			
❑ 101	Dinky John/South of Chicago	1960	200.00

FEATHERS, THE (1)

45s

Number	Title (A Side/B Side)	Yr	NM
ALADDIN			
❑ 3267	Johnny Darling/Shake 'Em Up	1954	200.00
❑ 3277	I Need a Girl/Standing Right There	1955	200.00
HOLLYWOOD			
❑ 1051	Dear One/Lonesome Tonight	1956	3000.
—VG 1000; VG+ 2000			
SHOW TIME			
❑ 1104	Nona/Johnny Darling	1954	300.00
❑ 1105	Why Don't You Write Me/Where Did Caledonia Go	1954	150.00

Except when noted otherwise, VG = 25% of NM, and VG+ = 50% of NM. (Example: VG = $2.00, VG+ = $4.00 and NM = $8.00.)

Number	Title (A Side/B Side)	Yr	NM
❑ 1105	Why Don't You Write Me/Busy as a Bee	1954	200.00
❑ 1106	Love Only You/ Crashing the Party	1955	200.00

FEATHERS, THE (2)

45s

KAPP

Number	Title (A Side/B Side)	Yr	NM
❑ 887	Give Him Love/To Be Loved by You	1968	150.00

FEATHERS, THE (U) May or may not be by group (2).

45s

VEEP

Number	Title (A Side/B Side)	Yr	NM
❑ 1200	The Dummy/Them Onions	1964	8.00

FEDERALS, THE (1) British group.

45s

CAPITOL

Number	Title (A Side/B Side)	Yr	NM
❑ 5526	Bucketful of Love/Leah	1965	10.00

FEDERALS, THE (2)

45s

DELUXE

Number	Title (A Side/B Side)	Yr	NM
❑ 6112	Come Go with Me/Cold Cash	1957	80.00

FURY

Number	Title (A Side/B Side)	Yr	NM
❑ 1005	While Our Hearts Are Young/ You're the One I Love	1957	100.00
❑ 1009	Dear Lorraine/She's My Girl	1958	100.00

FEELIES, THE

12-Inch Singles

A&M

Number	Title (A Side/B Side)	Yr	NM
❑ SP-17627 [DJ]	Away (Edit)/Dancing Barefoot	1988	8.00

Albums

A&M

Number	Title (A Side/B Side)	Yr	NM
❑ SP-5214	Only Life	1988	15.00
❑ 75021 5344-1	Time for a Witness	1991	15.00
❑ 75021 7403-1 [DJ]	Paint It Black + 5	1990	18.00

—Promo-only 6-song sampler

COYOTE/TWINTONE

Number	Title (A Side/B Side)	Yr	NM
❑ TTC 8673	The Good Earth	1986	15.00

STIFF

Number	Title (A Side/B Side)	Yr	NM
❑ USE-4	Crazy Rhythms	1980	40.00

—Price is for an actual U.S. pressing. Most copies sold in U.S. were U.K. copies with stickers.

FELDER, DON Also see EAGLES.

45s

ASYLUM

Number	Title (A Side/B Side)	Yr	NM
❑ 69673	Winters/(B-side unknown)	1984	3.00
❑ 69743	Who Tonight/Winners	1984	3.00
❑ 69784	Bad Girls/Night Owl	1983	4.00
❑ 69976	Never Surrender/ Raised on the Radio	1982	4.00

—B-side by Ravyns

Number	Title (A Side/B Side)	Yr	NM
❑ 69976 [PS]	Never Surrender/ Raised on the Radio	1982	4.00

FULL MOON/ASYLUM

Number	Title (A Side/B Side)	Yr	NM
❑ 47175	Heavy Metal (Takin' a Ride)/ All of You	1981	4.00
❑ 47175 [PS]	Heavy Metal (Takin' a Ride)/ All of You	1981	4.00
❑ 47244	All of You/True Companion	1981	4.00

—B-side by Donald Fagen

Albums

ASYLUM

Number	Title (A Side/B Side)	Yr	NM
❑ 60295	Airborne	1983	10.00

FELDERS ORIOLES

45s

MERCURY

Number	Title (A Side/B Side)	Yr	NM
❑ 72480	Down Home Girl/Misty	1965	10.00

FELDMAN, VICTOR

45s

AVA

Number	Title (A Side/B Side)	Yr	NM
❑ 123	Theme from "Lawrence of Arabia"/Theme from "David & Lisa"	1963	10.00

INFINITY

Number	Title (A Side/B Side)	Yr	NM
❑ 020	A Taste of Honey/Valerie	1962	10.00
❑ 025	New Dell High/John Brown's Battle Hymn	1962	10.00
❑ 030	Moon River/Theme from 9073	1963	10.00

PACIFIC JAZZ

Number	Title (A Side/B Side)	Yr	NM
❑ 88127	Do the Jake/Have a Heart	1966	8.00

VEE JAY

Number	Title (A Side/B Side)	Yr	NM
❑ 630	Hard to Find/Make Me a Present of You	1964	10.00
❑ 662	Green Dolphin Street/Overfat Cat	1965	10.00

Albums

AVA

Number	Title (A Side/B Side)	Yr	NM
❑ A-19 [M]	Soviet Jazz Themes	1963	25.00
❑ AS-19 [S]	Soviet Jazz Themes	1963	25.00

CHOICE

Number	Title (A Side/B Side)	Yr	NM
❑ CRS 1005 [M]	Your Smile	1974	15.00

COHEARANT

Number	Title (A Side/B Side)	Yr	NM
❑ CSR 1001	In My Pocket	1977	40.00

CONCORD JAZZ

Number	Title (A Side/B Side)	Yr	NM
❑ CJ-38	The Artful Dodger	1977	12.00

CONTEMPORARY

Number	Title (A Side/B Side)	Yr	NM
❑ C-3541 [M]	Suite Sixteen	1957	40.00
❑ C-3549 [M]	The Arrival of Victor Feldman	1958	40.00
❑ M-5005 [M]	Latinsville	1960	150.00
❑ S-7541 [S]	Suite Sixteen	1959	30.00
❑ S-7549 [S]	The Arrival of Victor Feldman	1959	30.00
❑ S-9005 [S]	Latinsville	1960	100.00

FANTASY

Number	Title (A Side/B Side)	Yr	NM
❑ OJC-268	The Arrival of Victor Feldman	1987	10.00
❑ OJC-402	Merry Olde Soul	1989	12.00

INFINITY

Number	Title (A Side/B Side)	Yr	NM
❑ 5000 [M]	A Taste of Honey and a Taste of Bossa Nova	1962	25.00

INTERLUDE

Number	Title (A Side/B Side)	Yr	NM
❑ MO-510 [M]	With Mallets Aforethought	1959	40.00

—Reissue of Mode LP

MODE

Number	Title (A Side/B Side)	Yr	NM
❑ LP-120 [M]	Victor Feldman on Vibes	1957	60.00

NAUTILUS

Number	Title (A Side/B Side)	Yr	NM
❑ NR-50	The Secret of the Andes	1982	20.00

—Audiophile vinyl

PACIFIC JAZZ

Number	Title (A Side/B Side)	Yr	NM
❑ PJ-10121 [M]	Victor Feldman Plays Everything in Sight	196?	20.00
❑ ST-20121 [S]	Victor Feldman Plays Everything in Sight	196?	25.00
❑ PJ-20128 [M]	Venezuela Joropo	196?	25.00
❑ ST-20128 [S]	Venezuela Joropo	196?	25.00

PALO ALTO

Number	Title (A Side/B Side)	Yr	NM
❑ PA-8053	The Secret of the Andes	1982	10.00
❑ PA-8056	To Chopin with Love	1983	10.00
❑ PA-8066	Fiesta	1984	10.00

RIVERSIDE

Number	Title (A Side/B Side)	Yr	NM
❑ RLP-366 [M]	Merry Ole Soul	1961	25.00
❑ RS-9366 [S]	Merry Ole Soul	1961	25.00

VEE JAY

Number	Title (A Side/B Side)	Yr	NM
❑ LP-1096 [M]	Love Me with All Your Heart	1964	30.00
❑ LP-2507 [M]	It's a Wonderful World	1965	20.00

WORLD PACIFIC

Number	Title (A Side/B Side)	Yr	NM
❑ ST-1807 [S]	Stop the World, I Want to Get Off	1962	20.00

—Black vinyl

Number	Title (A Side/B Side)	Yr	NM
❑ ST-1807 [S]	Stop the World, I Want to Get Off	1962	50.00

—Yellow vinyl

FELICITY Either Don Henley or Glenn Frey was a member of this group (sources conflict).

45s

WILSON

Number	Title (A Side/B Side)	Yr	NM
❑ 101	Hurtin'/I'll Try It	1965	30.00

FELIX AND THE ESCORTS An early version of THE (YOUNG) RASCALS. "Felix" is FELIX CAVALIERE.

45s

JAG

Number	Title (A Side/B Side)	Yr	NM
❑ 685	The Syracuse/Save	1964	150.00

FELT

Albums

NASCO

Number	Title (A Side/B Side)	Yr	NM
❑ 9006	Felt	1971	500.00

FEMALE BEATLES, THE

45s

20TH FOX

Number	Title (A Side/B Side)	Yr	NM
❑ 531	I Don't Want to Cry/I Want You	1964	20.00

FEMININE COMPLEX, THE

45s

ATHENA

Number	Title (A Side/B Side)	Yr	NM
❑ 5003	Six O'Clock in the Morning/I've Been Workin' on You	1969	12.00
❑ 5006	I Won't Run/Forgetting	1969	12.00
❑ 5008	Are You Lonesome Like Me/ Run That Through Your Mind	1969	12.00

Albums

ATHENA

Number	Title (A Side/B Side)	Yr	NM
❑ 6001	Livin' Love	1969	75.00

FENDER IV

45s

IMPERIAL

Number	Title (A Side/B Side)	Yr	NM
❑ 66061	Mar-Gaya/You Better Tell Me Now	1964	50.00
❑ 66098	Malibu Run/Everybody Up	1965	50.00

FENDERMEN, THE

45s

CUCA

Number	Title (A Side/B Side)	Yr	NM
❑ 1003	Mule Skinner Blues/Torture	1960	200.00

SOMA

Number	Title (A Side/B Side)	Yr	NM
❑ 1137	Mule Skinner Blues/Torture	1960	25.00
❑ 1142	Don't You Just Know It/ Beach Party	1960	20.00
❑ 1155	Heartbreakin' Special/ Can't You Wait	1960	20.00

Albums

BEAT ROCKET

Number	Title (A Side/B Side)	Yr	NM
❑ BR 116	Mule Skinner Blues	2000	15.00

KOALA

Number	Title (A Side/B Side)	Yr	NM
❑ 14565	Poison Ivy	1980	50.00

SOMA

Number	Title (A Side/B Side)	Yr	NM
❑ MG-1240 [M]	Mule Skinner Blues	1960	1200.

—Black vinyl

Number	Title (A Side/B Side)	Yr	NM
❑ MG-1240 [M]	Mule Skinner Blues	1960	4000.

—Blue vinyl; VG value 2000; VG+ value 3000

FENTON, SHANE, AND THE FENTONES

45s

LAURIE

Number	Title (A Side/B Side)	Yr	NM
❑ 3287	Don't Do That/I'll Know	1965	10.00

20TH FOX

Number	Title (A Side/B Side)	Yr	NM
❑ 439	Don't Do That/I'll Know	1963	15.00

FENWAYS, THE

45s

BEVMAR

Number	Title (A Side/B Side)	Yr	NM
❑ 401	Humpty Dumpty/Nothing to Offer You	1964	25.00
❑ 402	Be Careful Little Girl/ (Instrumental)	1964	40.00

BLUE CAT

Number	Title (A Side/B Side)	Yr	NM
❑ 116	The Fight/Hard Road Ahead	1965	80.00

CHESS

Number	Title (A Side/B Side)	Yr	NM
❑ 1901	Humpty Dumpty/Nothing to Offer You	1964	20.00

CO & CE

Number	Title (A Side/B Side)	Yr	NM
❑ 233	Satisfied/I'm a Mover	1966	25.00
❑ 237	Love Me for Myself/Satisfied	1966	25.00
❑ 243	I'm Your Toy/Theme for Pammy	1967	15.00

IMPERIAL

Number	Title (A Side/B Side)	Yr	NM
❑ 66082	The Walk/Whip and Jerk	1964	20.00

ROULETTE

Number	Title (A Side/B Side)	Yr	NM
❑ 4573	Be Careful Little Girl/ (Instrumental)	1964	30.00

FERG, JOHNNY May be the same person as JOHNNY FERGUSON.

45s

DECCA

Number	Title (A Side/B Side)	Yr	NM
❑ 30572	Candy Love/Sad, Sad Day	1958	30.00

FERGUSON, HELEN

45s

20TH CENTURY-FOX

Number	Title (A Side/B Side)	Yr	NM
❑ 485	One Last Chance/ Forgetfulness	1964	8.00

FERGUSON, HELENA

45s

COMPASS

Number	Title (A Side/B Side)	Yr	NM
❑ 7009	Where Is the Party/My Terms	1967	20.00
❑ 7017	Don't Spoil Our Good Thing/ The Loneliness	1968	20.00

CONGRESS

Number	Title (A Side/B Side)	Yr	NM
❑ 6009	I'm So Glad/I'd Rather Go Blind	1970	60.00

FERGUSON, JAY

12-Inch Singles

CAPITOL

Number	Title (A Side/B Side)	Yr	NM
❑ SPRO-9745 [DJ]	White Noise (same on both sides)	1982	12.00

45s

ASYLUM

Number	Title (A Side/B Side)	Yr	NM
❑ 45444	Thunder Island/Magic Moment	1977	4.00
❑ 45480	Losing Control/ Happy Birthday Baby	1978	4.00

Number	Title (A Side/B Side)	Yr	NM
❑ 46041	Shakedown Cruise/City of Angels	1979	4.00
❑ 46508	Paying Time/Too Late to Save Your Heart	1979	4.00

CAPITOL

Number	Title (A Side/B Side)	Yr	NM
❑ 4923	Modern Girl/My Baby's Eyes	1980	4.00
❑ B-5111	Empty Sky/Tonite	1982	4.00
❑ B-5130	I Come Alive/Inside Out	1982	4.00

Albums

ASYLUM

Number	Title (A Side/B Side)	Yr	NM
❑ 6E-158	Real Life Ain't This Way	1979	10.00
❑ 7E-1063	All Alone in the End Zone	1976	10.00
❑ 7E-1115	Thunder Island	1978	10.00

CAPITOL

Number	Title (A Side/B Side)	Yr	NM
❑ ST-12083	Terms and Conditions	1980	10.00
❑ ST-12196	White Noise	1982	10.00

FERGUSON, JOHNNY
Also see JOHNNY FERG.

45s

DECCA

Number	Title (A Side/B Side)	Yr	NM
❑ 30731	Last Date/Til School Starts Again	1959	20.00

MGM

Number	Title (A Side/B Side)	Yr	NM
❑ 12789	Afterglow/Waitin' for the Sandman	1959	30.00
❑ 12855	Angela Jones/Blue Serge and White Lace	1959	20.00
❑ 12905	I Understand Just How You Feel/Flutter Flutter	1960	30.00
❑ 12960	No One Can Love You (Like I Do)/Valley of Love	1960	15.00

FERGUSON, MAYNARD

12-Inch Singles

COLUMBIA

Number	Title (A Side/B Side)	Yr	NM
❑ 10546	Gonna Fly Now (Theme from "Rocky")/The Fly	1977	10.00
❑ 43-11039	Rocky II Disco/Gabriel	1979	10.00

45s

CAMEO

Number	Title (A Side/B Side)	Yr	NM
❑ 261	Antony & Cleopatr/Theme from Naked City	1963	8.00
❑ 275	Blues for a Four-String Guitar/Groove	1963	8.00

CAPITOL

Number	Title (A Side/B Side)	Yr	NM
❑ F1269	Love Locked Out/Band Ain't Draggin'	1950	15.00
❑ F1713	Hot Canary/What's New	1951	15.00

COLUMBIA

Number	Title (A Side/B Side)	Yr	NM
❑ 10468	Gonna Fly Now (Theme from "Rocky")/The Fly	1977	4.00
❑ 10595	Main Title (From the 20th Century Fox Film Star Wars)/Oasis	1977	4.00
❑ 10678	Maria/Oasis	1978	4.00
❑ 10823	Theme from "Battlestar Galactica"/M.F. Carnival	1978	4.00
❑ 11037	Rocky II Disco/Gabriel	1979	4.00
❑ 11151	Theme from Star Trek/Topa-Topa Woman	1979	4.00
❑ 11183	Main Theme from Star Trek The Motion Picture/Naima	1980	4.00
❑ 11411	An Offering of Love Pt. 1/Dance to Your Heart	1980	4.00
❑ 45352	Eli's Coming/MacArthur Park	1971	5.00

MAINSTREAM

Number	Title (A Side/B Side)	Yr	NM
❑ 603	People/Marcarena	1965	8.00
❑ 604	Marcarena (Part 1)/Marcarena (Part 2)	1965	8.00

MERCURY

Number	Title (A Side/B Side)	Yr	NM
❑ 70355	The Way You Look Tonight/Lonely Town	1954	12.00
❑ 70686	Autumn Leaves/Finger-Snappin'	1955	12.00

ROULETTE

Number	Title (A Side/B Side)	Yr	NM
❑ 4207	Hey There/Let's Fall in Love	1959	10.00
❑ 4250	Doin' the Madison (Part 1)/Doin' the Madison (Part 2)	1960	10.00
❑ 4317	Christmas for Moderns (Part 1)/Christmas for Moderns (Part 2)	1960	12.00
❑ 4421	Hip Twist/Maria	1962	10.00

7-Inch Extended Plays

ROULETTE

Number	Title (A Side/B Side)	Yr	NM
❑ SEPR-1-333	Send for Me/When the Sun Comes Out/Can't Get Out of This Mood//(B-side unknown)	196?	20.00
❑ SEPR-1-333 [PS]	(title unknown)	196?	20.00

—With Chris Connor

Albums

BASF

Number	Title (A Side/B Side)	Yr	NM
❑ 20662	Trumpet Rhapsody	1973	12.00

BLACK HAWK

Number	Title (A Side/B Side)	Yr	NM
❑ BKH-50101	Body and Soul	1986	10.00

BLUEBIRD

Number	Title (A Side/B Side)	Yr	NM
❑ 6455-1-RB	The Bluebird Dreamband	1987	10.00

CAMEO

Number	Title (A Side/B Side)	Yr	NM
❑ C-1046 [M]	The New Sounds of Maynard Ferguson	1963	20.00
❑ SC-1046 [S]	The New Sounds of Maynard Ferguson	1963	25.00
❑ C-1066 [M]	Come Blow Your Horn	1964	20.00
❑ SC-1066 [S]	Come Blow Your Horn	1964	25.00

COLUMBIA

Number	Title (A Side/B Side)	Yr	NM
❑ C 30466	M.F. Horn	1971	12.00
❑ PC 30466	M.F. Horn	198?	8.00
—Budget-line reissue			
❑ C 31117	Alive and Well in London	1972	12.00
❑ PC 31117	Alive and Well in London	198?	8.00
—Budget-line reissue			
❑ KC 31709	M.F. Horn Two	1972	12.00
❑ PC 31709	M.F. Horn Two	198?	8.00
—Budget-line reissue			
❑ KC 32403	M.F. Horn/3	1973	12.00
❑ PC 32403	M.F. Horn/3	198?	8.00
—Budget-line reissue			
❑ KG 32732 [(2)]	M.F. Horn 4 & 5/Live at Jimmy's	1973	15.00
❑ PG 32732 [(2)]	M.F. Horn 4 & 5/Live at Jimmy's	198?	10.00
—Budget-line reissue			
❑ KC 33007	Chameleon	1974	12.00
❑ PC 33007	Chameleon	1975	10.00
—Early reissue of KC 33007; no bar code			
❑ PC 33007	Chameleon	1980	8.00
—Budget-line reissue with bar code			
❑ CG 33660 [(2)]	M.F. Horn/M.F. Horn Two	1975	15.00
❑ PC 33953	Primal Scream	1976	10.00
—No bar code			
❑ PC 34457	Conquistador	1977	10.00
—No bar code			
❑ PC 34457	Conquistador	1980	8.00
—Budget-line reissue with bar code			
❑ PCQ 34457 [Q]	Conquistador	1977	20.00
❑ JC 34971	New Vintage	1977	10.00
❑ JC 35480	Carnival	1978	10.00
❑ PC 35480	Carnival	1980	8.00
—Budget-line reissue			
❑ JC 36124	Hot	1979	10.00
❑ JC 36361	The Best of Maynard Ferguson	1980	10.00
❑ PC 36361	The Best of Maynard Ferguson	1986	8.00
—Budget-line reissue			
❑ JC 36766	It's My Time	1980	10.00
❑ PC 36978	Maynard Ferguson	1981	10.00
❑ FC 37713	Hollywood	1982	10.00
❑ HC 44457	Conquistador	1982	50.00
—Half-speed mastered edition			

EMARCY

Number	Title (A Side/B Side)	Yr	NM
❑ EMS-2-406 [(2)]	Stratospheric	1976	12.00
❑ MG-26017 [10]	Maynard Ferguson's Hollywood Party	1954	100.00
❑ MG-26024 [10]	Dimensions	1954	100.00
❑ MG-36009 [M]	Jam Session Featuring Maynard Ferguson	1955	50.00
❑ MG-36021 [M]	Maynard Ferguson Octet	1955	60.00
❑ MG-36044 [M]	Dimensions	1956	50.00
❑ MG-36046 [M]	Maynard Ferguson's Hollywood Party	1956	50.00
❑ MG-36076 [M]	Around the Horn with Maynard Ferguson	1956	50.00
❑ MG-36114 [M]	Boy with Lots of Brass	1957	50.00

EMUS

Number	Title (A Side/B Side)	Yr	NM
❑ ES-12024 [S]	Maynard	197?	10.00
—Reissue of Roulette material			

ENTERPRISE

Number	Title (A Side/B Side)	Yr	NM
❑ S-13-101	Ridin' High	1968	15.00

FORUM

Number	Title (A Side/B Side)	Yr	NM
❑ F-9035 [M]	Jazz for Dancing	196?	12.00
❑ SF-9035 [S]	Jazz for Dancing	196?	15.00

INTIMA

Number	Title (A Side/B Side)	Yr	NM
❑ SJ-73279	High Voltage	1987	12.00
❑ D1-73390	Big Bop Nouveau	1990	12.00

MAINSTREAM

Number	Title (A Side/B Side)	Yr	NM
❑ MRL-316	Screamin' Blue	1971	12.00
❑ MRL-359	Dues	1972	12.00
❑ MRL-372	6 By 6	1973	12.00
❑ 805 [(2)]	Big "F"	1974	15.00
❑ S-6031 [S]	Color Him Wild	1965	20.00
❑ S-6045 [S]	The Blues Roar	1965	20.00
❑ S-6060 [S]	Maynard Ferguson Sextet	1966	20.00
❑ 56031 [M]	Color Him Wild	1965	15.00
❑ 56045 [M]	The Blues Roar	1965	15.00
❑ 56060 [M]	Maynard Ferguson Sextet	1966	15.00

MERCURY

Number	Title (A Side/B Side)	Yr	NM
❑ MG-20556 [M]	Boy with Lots of Brass	1960	30.00
❑ SR-60124 [S]	Boy with Lots of Brass	1960	30.00

MOSAIC

Number	Title (A Side/B Side)	Yr	NM
❑ MQ14-156 [(14)]	The Complete Roulette Recordings of the Maynard Ferguson Orchestra	1994	250.00

NAUTILUS

Number	Title (A Side/B Side)	Yr	NM
❑ NR-57	Storm	1983	40.00
—Audiophile vinyl			

PALO ALTO

Number	Title (A Side/B Side)	Yr	NM
❑ PA-8052	Storm	1983	10.00
❑ PA-8077	Live from San Francisco	1985	10.00

PAUSA

Number	Title (A Side/B Side)	Yr	NM
❑ 7037	Trumpet Rhapsody	1980	10.00
—Reissue of BASF LP			

PRESTIGE

Number	Title (A Side/B Side)	Yr	NM
❑ PRLP-7636	Maynard Ferguson 1969	1969	15.00

ROULETTE

Number	Title (A Side/B Side)	Yr	NM
❑ SK-101 [(2)]	The Ferguson Years	197?	15.00
❑ RE-116 [(2)]	A Message from Newport/Newport Suite	1972	15.00
—Reissue of 52012 and 52047 in one package			
❑ RE-122 [(2)]	Maynard '61/Si! Si! M.F.	1973	15.00
—Reissue of 52064 and 52084 in one package			
❑ R 52012 [M]	A Message from Newport	1958	25.00
❑ SR 52012 [S]	A Message from Newport	1958	25.00
❑ R 52027 [M]	A Message from Birdland	1959	25.00
❑ SR 52027 [S]	A Message from Birdland	1959	25.00
❑ R 52038 [M]	Maynard Ferguson Plays Jazz for Dancing	1959	25.00
❑ SR 52038 [S]	Maynard Ferguson Plays Jazz for Dancing	1959	25.00
❑ R 52047 [M]	Newport Suite	1960	25.00
❑ SR 52047 [S]	Newport Suite	1960	25.00
❑ R 52055 [M]	Let's Face the Music and Dance	1960	25.00
❑ SR 52055 [S]	Let's Face the Music and Dance	1960	25.00
❑ R 52058 [M]	Swingin' My Way Through College	1960	25.00
❑ SR 52058 [S]	Swingin' My Way Through College	1960	25.00
❑ R 52064 [M]	Maynard '61	1961	25.00
❑ SR 52064 [S]	Maynard '61	1961	25.00
❑ R 52083 [M]	Maynard '62	1962	15.00
❑ SR 52083 [S]	Maynard '62	1962	20.00
❑ R 52084 [M]	Si! Si! M.F.	1962	15.00
❑ SR 52084 [S]	Si! Si! M.F.	1962	20.00
❑ R 52097 [M]	Maynard '63	1963	15.00
❑ SR 52097 [S]	Maynard '63	1963	20.00
❑ R 52107 [M]	Maynard '64	1964	15.00
❑ SR 52107 [S]	Maynard '64	1964	20.00
❑ R 52110 [M]	The World of Maynard Ferguson	1964	15.00
❑ SR 52110 [S]	The World of Maynard Ferguson	1964	20.00

TRIP

Number	Title (A Side/B Side)	Yr	NM
❑ 5507	Dimensions	197?	8.00
❑ 5525	Jam Session Featuring Maynard Ferguson	197?	8.00
❑ 5558	Around the Horn with Maynard Ferguson	197?	8.00

VIK

Number	Title (A Side/B Side)	Yr	NM
❑ LX-1070 [M]	Birdland Dream Band, Vol. 1	1957	40.00
❑ LX-1077 [M]	Birdland Dream Band, Vol. 2	1957	40.00

FERGUSON, SHEILA

45s

LANDA

Number	Title (A Side/B Side)	Yr	NM
❑ 706	How Did That Happen/Little Red Riding Hood	1965	30.00

SWAN

Number	Title (A Side/B Side)	Yr	NM
❑ 4217	I Weep for You/Don't (Leave Me Lover)	1965	40.00
❑ 4225	And In Return/Are You Satisfied	1965	30.00
❑ 4234	Signs of Love/Heartbroken Memories	1965	40.00

FERGUSON, DAVIS AND JONES

45s

EPIC

Number	Title (A Side/B Side)	Yr	NM
❑ 5-10592	I Think I'm Gonna Cry/Up Grade	1970	30.00
❑ 5-10661	Canterbury Road/Happy and Free (Out in the Country)	1970	30.00

FERGUSON, DAVIS AND LEE

45s

CHESS

Number	Title (A Side/B Side)	Yr	NM
❑ 2138	She's Gone/She's Not an Ordinary Girl	1973	25.00

GRT

Number	Title (A Side/B Side)	Yr	NM
❑ 51	Must Be Going Out of My Head/Please Don'tcha Mention	1974	25.00

FERLINGHETTI, LAWRENCE

Albums

FANTASY

Number	Title (A Side/B Side)	Yr	NM
❑ 7004 [M]	The Impeachment of Eisenhower	1958	100.00
—Black vinyl			
❑ 7004 [M]	The Impeachment of Eisenhower	1958	200.00
—Red vinyl			

Except when noted otherwise, VG = 25% of NM, and VG+ = 50% of NM. (Example: VG = $2.00, VG+ = $4.00 and NM = $8.00.)

F

FERRE, CLIFF

45s

KEM

Number	Title (A Side/B Side)	Yr	NM
❑ 127	Hawaiian Tale/Joe's Joint	195?	12.00
❑ 128	Ain't It a Beauty/The Greatest Broad-Jumper	195?	12.00
❑ 129	Cocky Cowboy/House with the Little Red Light	195?	12.00
❑ 130	Rosie Don't Bang on the Piano/Favorite Indoor Sport	195?	20.00
❑ 132	That No Good!/Pirate's Poop	195?	12.00

Albums

KEM

Number	Title (A Side/B Side)	Yr	NM
❑ LP-100 [M]	Looks Like Fun	195?	25.00

FERRIER, GARRY

45s

ACADEMY

Number	Title (A Side/B Side)	Yr	NM
❑ 112	Ringo-Deer/Just My Luck	1964	20.00

FERRIS AND THE WHEELS

45s

BAMBI

Number	Title (A Side/B Side)	Yr	NM
❑ 801	I Want to Dance (Every Night)/Chop Chop	1961	25.00

UNITED ARTISTS

Number	Title (A Side/B Side)	Yr	NM
❑ 458	Moments Like This/He Was a Fortune Teller	1962	100.00

FERRY, BRYAN

Also see ROXY MUSIC.

12-Inch Singles

MCA

Number	Title (A Side/B Side)	Yr	NM
❑ 23620	Is Your Love Strong Enough (2 versions)/Windswept	1986	8.00

REPRISE

Number	Title (A Side/B Side)	Yr	NM
❑ PRO-A-2852 [DJ]	The Right Stuff (same on both sides)	1987	6.00
❑ 20799	The Right Stuff (3 mixes)	1987	6.00
❑ 20841	Kiss and Tell (3 versions)/Zamba	1988	10.00

—With picture cover; deduct 40% if cover is missing

Number	Title (A Side/B Side)	Yr	NM
❑ 20846	Limbo (2 versions)/Bete Noire	1989	10.00

WARNER BROS.

Number	Title (A Side/B Side)	Yr	NM
❑ PRO-A-2304 [DJ]	Slave to Love (Long)/Slave to Love (Short)	1985	8.00
❑ PRO-A-2352 [DJ]	Don't Stop the Dance/Don't Stop the Dance (Edit)	1985	8.00
❑ PRO-A-2577 [DJ]	Help Me (same on both sides)	1986	12.00
❑ 20385	Don't Stop the Dance/Slave to Love	1985	6.00

45s

ATLANTIC

Number	Title (A Side/B Side)	Yr	NM
❑ 3017	A Hard Rain's Gonna Fall/2 HB	1974	5.00
❑ 3351	Let's Stick Together (Let's Work Together)/Sea Breezes	1976	4.00
❑ 3364	Heart on My Sleeve/Re-Make, Re-Model	1976	4.00
❑ 3399	Tokyo Joe/As the World Turns	1977	4.00
❑ 3539	Sign of the Times/Can't Let Go	1978	4.00

MCA

Number	Title (A Side/B Side)	Yr	NM
❑ 52788	Is Your Love Strong Enough/Windswept	1986	3.00
❑ 52788 [PS]	Is Your Love Strong Enough/Windswept	1986	3.00

REPRISE

Number	Title (A Side/B Side)	Yr	NM
❑ 28116	Limbo (Brooklyn Version)/Limbo (Latin Version)	1988	3.00
❑ 28116 [PS]	Limbo (Brooklyn Version)/Limbo (Latin Version)	1988	3.00
❑ 28117	Kiss and Tell/Zamba	1988	3.00
❑ 28117 [PS]	Kiss and Tell/Zamba	1988	3.00
❑ 28172	The Right Stuff/The Right Stuff (Brooklyn Mix)	1987	3.00

VIRGIN

Number	Title (A Side/B Side)	Yr	NM
❑ S7-18133	Mamouna/Don't Stop the Dance (Live)	1994	4.00
❑ 38684	As Time Goes By/Falling in Love Again	1999	3.00

WARNER BROS.

Number	Title (A Side/B Side)	Yr	NM
❑ 28582	Help Me/Broken Wings	1986	3.00
❑ 28582 [PS]	Help Me/Broken Wings	1986	3.00
❑ 28887	Don't Stop the Dance/Nocturne	1985	3.00
❑ 28887 [PS]	Don't Stop the Dance/Nocturne	1985	3.00
❑ 28990	Slave to Love/Valentine	1985	3.00
❑ 28990 [PS]	Slave to Love/Valentine	1985	3.00

Albums

ATLANTIC

Number	Title (A Side/B Side)	Yr	NM
❑ SD 7304	These Foolish Things	1973	15.00
❑ SD 18113	Another Time, Another Place	1974	15.00
❑ SD 18187	Let's Stick Together	1976	12.00
❑ SD 18216	In Your Mind	1977	12.00
❑ SD 19205	The Bride Stripped Bare	1978	12.00

REPRISE

Number	Title (A Side/B Side)	Yr	NM
❑ 25598	Bete Noire	1988	12.00

WARNER BROS.

Number	Title (A Side/B Side)	Yr	NM
❑ 25082	Boys and Girls	1985	12.00

FESTIVALS, THE

45s

BLUE ROCK

Number	Title (A Side/B Side)	Yr	NM
❑ 4076	Hey Girl/Checkin' Out	1969	8.00

COLOSSUS

Number	Title (A Side/B Side)	Yr	NM
❑ 122	You're Gonna Make It/So in Love	1970	7.00
❑ 136	Baby Show It/Take Your Time	1971	7.00
❑ 146	Gee Baby/Give Her Up	1971	7.00

GORDY

Number	Title (A Side/B Side)	Yr	NM
❑ 7120	Green Grows the Lilacs/So in Love	1972	6.00

SMASH

Number	Title (A Side/B Side)	Yr	NM
❑ 2056	I'll Always Love You/Music	1966	8.00
❑ 2196	Hey GIrl/Not Gonna Let Her	1968	8.00

FEVER TREE

45s

AMPEX

Number	Title (A Side/B Side)	Yr	NM
❑ 11013	She Comes in Colors/You're Not the Same Baby	1970	15.00
❑ 11028	I Put a Spell on You/Hey Joe, Where You Gonna Go	1970	15.00

MAINSTREAM

Number	Title (A Side/B Side)	Yr	NM
❑ 661	Hey Mister/I Can Beat Your Drum	1967	12.00
❑ 665	Girl, Oh Girl (Don't Push Me)/Steve Lenore	1967	12.00

UNI

Number	Title (A Side/B Side)	Yr	NM
❑ 55060	San Fransisco Girls (Return of the Native)/Come with Me	1968	12.00
❑ 55060 [DJ]	San Fransisco Girls (Return of the Native) (same on both sides)	1968	40.00

—Promo only on blue vinyl

Number	Title (A Side/B Side)	Yr	NM
❑ 55095	What Time Did You Say It Is in Salt Lake City/Where Do You Go	1968	15.00
❑ 55146	Love Makes the Sun Rise/Filigree and Shadow	1969	15.00
❑ 55172	The Sun Also Rises/Clancey	1969	15.00
❑ 55202	Catcher in the Rye/What Time Did You Say It Is in Salt Lake City?	1970	20.00
❑ 55228	I Am/Grand Candy Young Sweet	1970	20.00

Albums

AMPEX

Number	Title (A Side/B Side)	Yr	NM
❑ A-10113	For Sale	1970	25.00

MCA

Number	Title (A Side/B Side)	Yr	NM
❑ 551	Fever Tree	197?	10.00

UNI

Number	Title (A Side/B Side)	Yr	NM
❑ 73024	Fever Tree	1968	25.00
❑ 73040	Another Time, Another Place	1968	25.00
❑ 73067	Creation	1970	25.00

FI-TONES, THE

45s

ANGLE TONE

Number	Title (A Side/B Side)	Yr	NM
❑ 525	You'll Be the Last/Wake Up	1958	100.00
❑ 530	It Wasn't a Lie/What Am I Goin' to Do	1958	80.00
❑ 536	Deep In My Heart/Minnie	1959	60.00

ATLAS

Number	Title (A Side/B Side)	Yr	NM
❑ 1050	Foolish Dreams/Let's Fall in Love	1955	100.00

—Second pressings identify label as "Atlas Records" and have Atlas logo at left side

Number	Title (A Side/B Side)	Yr	NM
❑ 1050	Foolish Dreams/Let's Fall in Love	1955	400.00

—Originals identify label as "Atlas Record Company" and have Atlas logo at far upper left

Number	Title (A Side/B Side)	Yr	NM
❑ 1051	It Wasn't a Lie/Lots and Lots of Love	1955	100.00
❑ 1052	I Call to You/Love You Baby	1955	100.00
❑ 1055	I Belong to You/Silly and Happy	1956	100.00
❑ 1056	Waiting for Your Call/My Tired Feet	1956	100.00

OLD TOWN

Number	Title (A Side/B Side)	Yr	NM
❑ 1042	My Faith/My Heart	1957	400.00

FIDELITY'S, THE

BUDDY MILES was in this group.

45s

BATON

Number	Title (A Side/B Side)	Yr	NM
❑ 252	The Things I Love/Hold On to Whatcha Got	1958	25.00
❑ 256	Memories of You/Can't You Come Out	1958	25.00
❑ 261	Captain of My Ship/My Greatest Thrill	1958	25.00

SIR

Number	Title (A Side/B Side)	Yr	NM
❑ 271	Marie/The Invitation	1959	20.00
❑ 274	Walk with the Wind/Only to You	1959	20.00
❑ 276	Where in the World/This Girl of Mine	1960	20.00
❑ 277	Wishing Star/Broken Love	1960	30.00

FIELD, JERRY, AND THE LAWYERS

45s

PARKWAY

Number	Title (A Side/B Side)	Yr	NM
❑ 801	The Trial/Easy Steppin'	1958	20.00

—White label. This is actually a cover of a break-in record (for the original, see HERB B. LOU AND THE LEGAL EAGLES).

Number	Title (A Side/B Side)	Yr	NM
❑ 801	The Trial/Easy Steppin'	1958	30.00

—Blue label

FIELD, SALLY

45s

COLGEMS

Number	Title (A Side/B Side)	Yr	NM
❑ 66-1008	Felicidad/Find Yourself a Rainbow	1967	10.00
❑ 66-1008 [PS]	Felicidad/Find Yourself a Rainbow	1967	15.00
❑ 66-1014	Golden Days/You're a Grand Old Flag	1967	8.00

Albums

COLGEMS

Number	Title (A Side/B Side)	Yr	NM
❑ COM-106 [M]	The Flying Nun	1967	30.00
❑ COS-106 [S]	The Flying Nun	1967	25.00

FIELDS, BOBBY

45s

ACE

Number	Title (A Side/B Side)	Yr	NM
❑ 504	Pity Poor Me/Give Me a Helping Hand	1955	60.00

FIELDS, ERNIE

45s

CAPITOL

Number	Title (A Side/B Side)	Yr	NM
❑ 5161	St. Louis Blues/Lilies of the Field	1964	8.00
❑ 5326	Swanne River/Chloe	1964	8.00

RENDEZVOUS

Number	Title (A Side/B Side)	Yr	NM
❑ 110	In the Mood/Christopher Columbus	1959	12.00
❑ 117	Chattanooga Choo Choo/Workin' Out	1960	10.00
❑ 122	Begin the Beguine/Things Ain't What They Used to Be	1960	10.00
❑ 129	Teen Flip/Sweet Slumber	1960	10.00
❑ 138	The Honeydripper/Monkey	1960	10.00
❑ 142	The Happy Whistler/Honky Tonk	1961	10.00
❑ 148	Be Anything (But Be Mine)/Fallin'	1961	10.00
❑ 150	The Charleston/12th Street Rag	1961	10.00
❑ 161	A String of Pearls/Castle Rock	1961	10.00
❑ 170	Hucklebuck (Twist)/Ernie's Tune	1962	8.00
❑ 181	Theme from Perry Mason/Me and My Shadow	1962	10.00

Albums

RENDEZVOUS

Number	Title (A Side/B Side)	Yr	NM
❑ 1309 [M]	In the Mood	1960	60.00

FIELDS, GRACIE

Albums

LIBERTY

Number	Title (A Side/B Side)	Yr	NM
❑ LRP-3059 [M]	Our Gracie	1957	40.00

FIELDS, THE

45s

UNI

Number	Title (A Side/B Side)	Yr	NM
❑ 55106	Bide My Time/Take You Home	1969	10.00

Albums

UNI

Number	Title (A Side/B Side)	Yr	NM
❑ 73050	Fields	1969	50.00

FIESTAS, THE

45s

CHIMNEYVILLE

Number	Title (A Side/B Side)	Yr	NM
❑ 10216	Tina, the Disco Queen/I'm No Better Than You	1977	12.00
❑ 10221	Is That Long Enough for You/I'm Gonna Make Myself	1977	12.00

The Fifth Dimension, "Go Where You Wanna Go," Soul City 753, 1967, **$20.**

Number	Title (A Side/B Side)	Yr	NM
COTILLION			
❑ 44117	So Fine/Broken Heart	1971	25.00
OLD TOWN			
❑ 1062	So Fine/Last Night I Dreamed	1958	30.00
—Standard version; no "ZTSP" on label			
❑ 1062	So Fine/Last Night I Dreamed	1958	50.00
—Versions pressed by Columbia have a piano intro not available elsewhere. Look for "ZTSP" on label			
❑ 1067	Grandma Gave a Party/ I'm Your Slave	1959	25.00
❑ 1069	Our Anniversary/I'm Your Slave	1959	25.00
❑ 1074	Good News/That Was Me	1959	25.00
❑ 1080	Dollar Bill/It Don't Make Sense	1960	25.00
❑ 1090	So Nice/You Could Be My Girlfriend	1960	25.00
❑ 1104	Look at That Girl/ Mr. Dillon, Mr. Dillon	1961	25.00
❑ 1111	Hobo's Prayer/She's Mine	1961	40.00
❑ 1122	Broken Heart/Railroad Song	1962	20.00
❑ 1127	I Feel Good All Over/ Look at That Girl	1962	20.00
❑ 1134	The Gypsy Said/Mama Put the Law Down	1963	20.00
❑ 1140	The Party's Over/Try It One More Time	1963	20.00
❑ 1148	Foolish Dreamer/ Rock-a-By Baby	1963	20.00
❑ 1166	All That's Good/ Rock-a-By Baby	1964	20.00
❑ 1178	Think Smart/Anna	1965	80.00
❑ 1187	Love Is Strange/Love Is Good to Me	1965	15.00
❑ 1189	Ain't She Sweet/I Gotta Have Your Lovin'	1965	15.00
RESPECT			
❑ 2509	I Can't Shake Your Love (Can't Shake You Loose)/ A Sometimes Storm	1972	8.00
STRAND			
❑ 25046	Come On Everybody/Julia	1961	40.00

Number	Title (A Side/B Side)	Yr	NM
VIGOR			
❑ 712	So Fine/Darling You've Changed	1974	8.00

FIFTH DIMENSION, THE Also see BILLY DAVIS.

45s

Number	Title (A Side/B Side)	Yr	NM
ABC			
❑ 12136	Magic in My Life/Lean On Me Always	1975	4.00
❑ 12168	Walk Your Feet in the Sunshine/ Speaking with My Heart	1976	4.00
❑ 12181	Love Hangover/Will You Be There	1976	4.00
ARISTA			
❑ 0101	No Love in the Room/I Don't Know How to Look for Love	1975	4.00
BELL			
❑ 860	Medley: A Change Is Gonna Come & People Gotta Be Free/The Declaration	1970	5.00
❑ 880	Puppet Man/A Love Like Ours	1970	5.00
❑ 895	Save the Country/Dimension 5	1970	5.00
❑ 913	On the Beach (In the Summertime)/This Is Your Life	1970	5.00
❑ 940	One Less Bell to Answer/ Feelin' Alright?	1970	5.00
❑ 965	Love's Lines, Angles and Rhymes/The Singer	1971	5.00
❑ 999	Light Sings/Viva Tirado	1971	5.00
❑ 45134	Never My Love/A Love Like Ours	1971	5.00
❑ 45170	Together Let's Find Love/I Just Wanta Be Your Friend	1972	5.00
❑ 45195	(Last Night) I Didn't Get to Sleep at All/The River Witch	1972	5.00
❑ 45261	If I Could Reach You/Tomorrow Belongs to the Children	1972	5.00
❑ 45310	Living Together, Growing Together/What Do I Need to Be Me	1973	4.00
❑ 45338	Everything's Been Changed/ There Never Was a Day	1973	4.00
❑ 45380	Ashes to Ashes/The Singer	1973	4.00
❑ 45425	Flashback/Diggin' for a Livin'	1973	4.00
❑ 45612	Harlem/My Song	1974	4.00
MOTOWN			
❑ 1437	You Are the Reason (I Feel Like Dancing)/Slipping Into Something New	1978	4.00
❑ 1453	Everybody's Got to Give It Up/ You're My Star	1978	4.00
SOUL CITY			
❑ 752	I'll Be Loving You Forever/ Train, Keep On Moving	1966	60.00
❑ 753	Go Where You Wanna Go/ Too Poor to Die	1967	8.00
❑ 753 [PS]	Go Where You Wanna Go/ Too Poor to Die	1967	20.00
❑ 755	Another Day, Another Heartache/Rosecrans Blvd.	1967	10.00
❑ 755 [PS]	Another Day, Another Heartache/Rosecrans Blvd.	1967	20.00
❑ 756	Up-Up and Away/Which Way to Nowhere	1967	8.00
❑ 760	Paper Cup/Poor Side of Town	1967	8.00
❑ 762	Carpet Man/Magic Garden	1968	8.00
❑ 766	Stoned Soul Picnic/ The Saliboat Song	1968	8.00
❑ 766 [PS]	Stoned Soul Picnic/ The Saliboat Song	1968	15.00
❑ 768	Sweet Blindness/Bobby's Blues	1968	8.00
❑ 768 [PS]	Sweet Blindness/Bobby's Blues	1968	15.00
❑ 770	California Soul/It'll Never Be the Same	1968	8.00
❑ 772	Aquarius/Let the Sunshine In (The Flesh Failures)//Don'tcha Hear Me Callin' To Ya	1969	8.00
❑ 772 [DJ]	Aquarius/Let the Sunshine In (The Flesh Failures) (same on both sides?)	1969	15.00
—Promo only on yellow vinyl			
❑ 772 [PS]	Aquarius/Let the Sunshine In (The Flesh Failures)//Don'tcha Hear Me Callin' To Ya	1969	15.00
❑ 776	Workin' on a Groovy Thing/ Broken Wing Bird	1969	8.00
❑ 779	Wedding Bell Blues/Lovin' Stew	1969	8.00
❑ 780	Blowing Away/Skinny Man	1970	6.00
❑ 781	The Girls' Song/It'll Never Be the Same Again	1970	6.00
SUTRA			
❑ 122	Surrender/Fantasy	1983	4.00
Albums			
ABC			
❑ D-897	Earthbound	1975	10.00
ARISTA			
❑ ABM-1106	Greatest Hits on Earth	1975	8.00
—Reissue of Bell 1106			
❑ AL 8335	Greatest Hits on Earth	198?	8.00
—Reissue of Arista 1106			
BELL			
❑ 1106	Greatest Hits on Earth	1972	10.00
❑ 1116	Living Together, Growing Together	1973	10.00
❑ 1315	Soul and Inspiration	1974	10.00
❑ 6045	Portrait	1970	12.00
❑ 6060	Love's Lines, Angles and Rhymes	1971	12.00
❑ 6065	Reflections	1971	10.00
❑ 6073	Individually & Collectively	1972	10.00
❑ 9000 [(2)]	The 5th Dimension/Live!!	1971	12.00
MOTOWN			
❑ M7-896	Star	1978	10.00
PAIR			
❑ PDL2-1108 [(2)]	The Glory Days	1986	12.00
RHINO			
❑ RNDA-71104 [(2)]	The 5th Dimension Anthology	1986	12.00
SOUL CITY			
❑ SCS-33900	The 5th Dimension/Greatest Hits	1970	12.00
❑ SCS-33901	The July 5th Album	1970	12.00
❑ SCM-91000 [M]	Up, Up and Away	1967	20.00
❑ SCM-91001 [M]	The Magic Garden	1967	20.00
❑ SCS-92000 [S]	Up, Up and Away	1967	15.00
❑ SCS-92001 [S]	The Magic Garden	1967	15.00
❑ SCS-92002	Stoned Soul Picnic	1968	15.00
❑ SCS-92005	The Age of Aquarius	1969	15.00

FIFTH ESTATE, THE Also see THE D-MEN.

45s

Number	Title (A Side/B Side)	Yr	NM
JUBILEE			
❑ 5573	Ding! Dong! The Witch Is Dead/ The Rub-a-Dub	1967	12.00
❑ 5588	Lost Generation/ The Goofin' Song	1967	8.00
❑ 5595	Heigh-Ho/It's Waiting There for You	1967	8.00

Except when noted otherwise, VG = 25% of NM, and VG+ = 50% of NM. (Example: VG = $2.00, VG+ = $4.00 and NM = $8.00.)

Number	Title (A Side/B Side)	Yr	NM
❑ 5607	Morning, Morning/Tomorrow Is My Turn	1967	8.00
❑ 5617	Do Drop Inn/That's Love	1968	8.00
❑ 5627	Coney Island Sally/Tomorrow Is My Turn	1968	8.00
❑ 5655	Mickey Mouse Club March/I Knew You Before I Met You	1969	8.00
❑ 5683	Parade of the Wooden Soldiers/I Knew You Before I Met You	1969	25.00
❑ 5683 [DJ]	Parade of the Wooden Soldiers (mono/stereo)	1969	10.00
RED BIRD			
❑ 10-064	Love Is All a Game/Like I Love You	1966	15.00
Albums			
JUBILEE			
❑ JGM-8005 [M]	Ding Dong! The Witch Is Dead	1967	25.00
❑ JGS-8005 [S]	Ding Dong! The Witch Is Dead	1967	50.00

FIFTY FOOT HOSE

Number	Title (A Side/B Side)	Yr	NM
Albums			
LIMELIGHT			
❑ 86062	Cauldron	1968	200.00

FILETS OF SOUL

Number	Title (A Side/B Side)	Yr	NM
45s			
SAVOY			
❑ 1630	Since I Fell for You/C'mon Let's Dance	1968	25.00
Albums			
SQUID			
❑ 4857	Freedom	1968	200.00

FINCHLEY BOYS, THE

Number	Title (A Side/B Side)	Yr	NM
Albums			
GOLDEN THROAT			
❑ 200-19	Everlasting Tribute	1972	100.00

FINDERS KEEPERS

Number	Title (A Side/B Side)	Yr	NM
45s			
CHALLENGE			
❑ 59338	Lavender Blue/Raggedy Ann	1966	15.00
❑ 59364	Don't Give In to Him/I've Done All I Can	1967	15.00
FONTANA			
❑ 1609	Friday Kind of Monday/On the Beach	1968	12.00

FINN, MICKY

Number	Title (A Side/B Side)	Yr	NM
45s			
CHATTAHOOCHIE			
❑ 663	I Still Want You/Reelin' and Rockin'	1965	12.00
WORLD ARTISTS			
❑ 1048	Night Comes Down/This Sporting Life	1965	12.00

FINNEGAN, LARRY

Number	Title (A Side/B Side)	Yr	NM
45s			
CORAL			
❑ 62313	I'll Be Back, Jack/There Ain't Nothin' in This World	1962	10.00
OLD TOWN			
❑ 1113	Dear One/Candy Lips	1961	12.00
❑ 1120	Pretty Susie Sunshine/It's Walkin' Talkin' Time	1962	10.00
❑ 1136	A Kiss and a Dozen Roses/Pick Up the Pieces	1963	10.00
RIC			
❑ 146	The Other Ringo (A Tribute to Ringo Starr)/When My Love Passes By	1964	15.00

FINNEGAN, MIKE, AND THE SERFS

Number	Title (A Side/B Side)	Yr	NM
45s			
PARKWAY			
❑ 113	Help Me Somebody/Bread and Water	1966	20.00

FINSTER, WERBLEY

See JOSE FELICIANO.

FIRE

Number	Title (A Side/B Side)	Yr	NM
Albums			
ABC			
❑ ABCS-661	Fire	1969	20.00

FIRE & ICE LTD.

Number	Title (A Side/B Side)	Yr	NM
45s			
CAPITOL			
❑ 2587	Music Man/For the Money	1969	8.00
—As "Fire & Ice"			

Number	Title (A Side/B Side)	Yr	NM
Albums			
CAPITOL			
❑ ST 2577 [S]	The Happening	1966	40.00
❑ T 2577 [M]	The Happening	1966	30.00

FIRE AND RAIN

Number	Title (A Side/B Side)	Yr	NM
45s			
MERCURY			
❑ 73358	Alright Tonight/Home to You	1973	10.00
❑ 73373	Hello Stranger/Somebody to Love	1973	40.00
❑ 73420	Take Me for a Little While/Touch Me	1973	10.00
20TH CENTURY			
❑ 2240	Don't Throw It All Away/Layin' in Your Arms (Before Daybreak)	1975	6.00
❑ 2280	Dance for Me/Make Love to Me	1976	6.00
Albums			
MERCURY			
❑ SRM-1-654	Fire and Rain	1973	15.00

FIRE ESCAPE, THE

Number	Title (A Side/B Side)	Yr	NM
45s			
GNP CRESCENDO			
❑ 384	Blood Beat/Love Special Delivery	1967	12.00
Albums			
GNP CRESCENDO			
❑ GNP-2034 [M]	Psychotic Reaction	1967	40.00
—Mono pressings are all original first pressings.			
❑ GNPS-2034 [S]	Psychotic Reaction	1967	30.00
—Stereo pressings in circulation are various re-pressings.			

FIREBALLET

Number	Title (A Side/B Side)	Yr	NM
45s			
PASSPORT			
❑ 7908	Desiree/Carrollon	1975	5.00
Albums			
PASSPORT			
❑ 98010	Night on Bald Mountain	1975	12.00
❑ 98016	Two, Too…	1976	12.00

FIREBALLS, THE

Includes records credited to "Jimmy Gilmer and the Fireballs." Also see JIMMY GILMER.

Number	Title (A Side/B Side)	Yr	NM
45s			
ASTRA			
❑ 1021	Torquay/Sweet Walk	1966	10.00
ATCO			
❑ 6491	Bottle of Wine/Can't You See I'm Tryin'	1967	10.00
❑ 6569	Goin' Away/Groovy Motions	1968	8.00
❑ 6595	Chicken Little/Three Minutes' Time	1968	8.00
❑ 6614	Come On, React!/Woman Help Me	1968	8.00
❑ 6651	Long Green/Light in the Window	1969	8.00
❑ 6678	Watch Her Walk/Good Morning Shame	1969	8.00
DOT			
❑ 16487	Sugar Shack/My Heart Is Free	1963	15.00
—Jimmy Gilmer and the Fireballs			
❑ 16493	Torquay Two/Peg Leg	1963	15.00
❑ 16539	Daisy Petal Pickin'/When My Tears Have Dried	1963	12.00
—Jimmy Gilmer and the Fireballs			
❑ 16583	Ain't Gonna Tell Anybody/Young Am I	1964	12.00
—Jimmy Gilmer and the Fireballs			
❑ 16591	Daytona Drag/Gently, Gently	1964	15.00
❑ 16609	I'll Send for You/Look at Me	1964	10.00
—Jimmy Gilmer and the Fireballs			
❑ 16642	Wishing/What Kinda Love	1964	10.00
—Jimmy Gilmer and the Fireballs			
❑ 16661	Dumbo/Mr. Reed	1964	15.00
❑ 16666	Cry Baby/Thunder 'N' Lightnin'	1964	10.00
—Jimmy Gilmer and the Fireballs			
❑ 16687	Break His Heart for Me/Cinnamon Cindy	1965	10.00
—Jimmy Gilmer and the Fireballs			
❑ 16692	Yummie Yama Papa/Baby, What's Wrong	1965	15.00
❑ 16714	Born to Be with You/Lonesome Tears	1965	10.00
—Jimmy Gilmer and the Fireballs			
❑ 16715	More Than I Can Say/Beating of My Heart	1965	15.00
❑ 16743	The Fool/Somebody Stole My Watermelon	1965	10.00
—Jimmy Gilmer and the Fireballs			
❑ 16745	Ahhh, Soul/Campusology	1965	15.00
❑ 16768	Codine/Come to Me	1965	10.00
—Jimmy Gilmer and the Fireballs			
❑ 16786	She Belongs to Me/Rambler's Blues	1965	10.00
—Jimmy Gilmer and the Fireballs			
❑ 16833	Hungry, Hungry, Hungry/Wild Roses	1966	10.00
—Jimmy Gilmer and the Fireballs			
❑ 16834	Jada/What I Am	1966	15.00
❑ 16881	All I Do Is Dream of You/Ain't That Rain	1966	10.00
—Jimmy Gilmer and the Fireballs			
❑ 16918	Torquay Two/Say I Am	1966	15.00
❑ 16979	Sugar Shack/Daisy Petal Pickin'	1966	10.00
—Jimmy Gilmer and the Fireballs			
❑ 16992	Shy Girl/I Think I'll Catch a Bus	1967	10.00
—Jimmy Gilmer and the Fireballs			
HAMILTON			
❑ 50036	Blacksmith Blues/Tuff-a-Nuff	1960	20.00
JARO			
❑ 77029	Long, Long Ponytail/Let There Be Love	1960	80.00
—Chuck Tharp and the Fireballs			
KAPP			
❑ 248	Fireball/I Don't Know	1958	100.00
—Chuck Tharp and the Fireballs			
7 ARTS			
❑ 714	Callin' the Sheriff/Don't Stop	1961	—
—Evidently, record was never released, though its picture sleeve exists			
❑ 714 [PS]	Callin' the Sheriff/Don't Stop	1961	50.00
TOP RANK			
❑ 2008	Torquay/Cry Baby	1959	20.00
❑ 2026 [M]	Bulldog/Nearly Sunrise	1959	20.00
❑ 2026ST [S]	Bulldog/Nearly Sunrise	1959	50.00
❑ 2038 [M]	Foot Patter/Kissin'	1959	20.00
❑ 2038ST [S]	Foot Patter/Kissin'	1959	50.00
❑ 2054	Vaquero/Chief Whoopin'-Koff	1960	20.00
❑ 2081	Almost Paradise/Sweet Talk	1960	20.00
❑ 3003	Rick-a-Tic/Tacky Doo	1961	20.00
WARWICK			
❑ 630	Rik-A-Tik/Yackey-Doo	1961	16.00
❑ 644	Quite a Party/Gunshot	1961	16.00
7-Inch Extended Plays			
TOP RANK			
❑ REX 1000	Bulldog/Torquay//Kissin'/Foot Patter	196?	150.00
❑ REX 1000 [PS]	The Fireballs	196?	150.00
Albums			
ATCO			
❑ 33-239 [M]	Bottle of Wine	1968	40.00
❑ SD 33-239 [S]	Bottle of Wine	1968	25.00
❑ SD 33-275	Come On, React!	1969	25.00
CROWN			
❑ CST-376 [R]	Jimmy Gilmer and the Fireballs & The Sugar Shackers	1963	25.00
❑ CST-387 [R]	The Sensational Jimmy Gilmer & The Fireballs	1964	25.00
❑ CLP-5376 [M]	Jimmy Gilmer and the Fireballs & The Sugar Shackers	1963	25.00
❑ CLP-5387 [M]	The Sensational Jimmy Gilmer & The Fireballs	1964	25.00
DOT			
❑ DLP-3512 [M]	Torquay	1963	50.00
❑ DLP-3545 [M]	Sugar Shack	1963	40.00
—Jimmy Gilmer and the Fireballs			
❑ DLP-3577 [M]	Buddy's Buddy	1964	50.00
—Jimmy Gilmer and the Fireballs			
❑ DLP-3643 [M]	Lucky 'Leven	1965	30.00
❑ DLP-3668 [M]	Folkbeat	1965	30.00
❑ DLP-3709 [M]	Campusology	1966	30.00
❑ DLP-3856 [M]	Firewater	1968	50.00
—Stereo cover with "Monaural" and "Promotional Copy Not for Sale" stickers, but the record is stock mono			
❑ DLP-25512 [S]	Torquay	1963	80.00
❑ DLP-25545 [S]	Sugar Shack	1963	60.00
—Jimmy Gilmer and the Fireballs			
❑ DLP-25577 [S]	Buddy's Buddy	1964	80.00
—Jimmy Gilmer and the Fireballs			
❑ DLP-25643 [S]	Lucky 'Leven	1965	40.00
❑ DLP-25668 [S]	Folkbeat	1965	40.00
❑ DLP-25709 [S]	Campusology	1966	40.00
❑ DLP-25856 [S]	Firewater	1968	25.00
SUNDAZED			
❑ LP-5016	The Fireballs	1995	10.00
❑ LP-5017	Torquay	1995	10.00
❑ LP-5018	Gunshot!	1995	10.00
TOP RANK			
❑ RM-324 [M]	The Fireballs	1960	150.00
❑ RM-343 [M]	Vaquero	1960	150.00
❑ RS-643 [S]	Vaquero	1960	200.00
WARWICK			
❑ W-2042 [M]	Here Are the Fireballs	1961	150.00
❑ WST-2042 [S]	Here Are the Fireballs	1961	250.00

FIREBIRDS, THE

Albums

CROWN

Number	Title (A Side/B Side)	Yr	NM
❑ CST-589	Light My Fire	1968	70.00

FIREFLIES, THE

45s

CANADIAN AMERICAN

Number	Title (A Side/B Side)	Yr	NM
❑ 117	Marianne/Give All Your Love to Me	1960	20.00

RIBBON

Number	Title (A Side/B Side)	Yr	NM
❑ 6901	You Were Mine/Stella Got a Fella	1959	25.00
—With "Ribbon" encased in a ribbon on label			
❑ 6901	You Were Mine/Stella Got a Fella	1959	30.00
—With "Ribbon" standing alone on label			
❑ 6904	I Can't Say Goodbye/ What Did I Do Wrong	1959	20.00
❑ 6906	My Girl/Because of My Pride	1960	20.00

TAURUS

Number	Title (A Side/B Side)	Yr	NM
❑ 355	One O'Clock Twist/ You Were Mine for Awhile	1962	20.00
❑ 366	Good Friends/My Prayer for You	1964	20.00
❑ 376	Runaround/Could You Mean More	1965	20.00
❑ 380	Tonight/A Time for Us	1965	20.00

Albums

TAURUS

Number	Title (A Side/B Side)	Yr	NM
❑ 1002 [M]	You Were Mine	196?	100.00
❑ S-1002 [S]	You Were Mine	196?	300.00

FIREFLY (1)

45s

A&M

Number	Title (A Side/B Side)	Yr	NM
❑ 1736	Hey There Little Firefly Part I/ Part II	1975	5.00
❑ 1798	If You Ever Stopped Callin' Me Baby Part I/Part II	1976	6.00

POLYDOR

Number	Title (A Side/B Side)	Yr	NM
❑ 14496	My Jole Part I/Part II	1978	10.00

FIREHOSE Also see MINUTEMEN.

12-Inch Singles

SST

Number	Title (A Side/B Side)	Yr	NM
❑ PRO 235 [DJ]	Time with You (same on both sides)	1989	10.00

45s

CO & CE

Number	Title (A Side/B Side)	Yr	NM
❑ 241	A-Go-Go/I Move Around	1966	25.00

SST

Number	Title (A Side/B Side)	Yr	NM
❑ PSST-079 [DJ]	Brave Captain/Perfect Pairs	1986	10.00
—Not issued with picture sleeve			

7-Inch Extended Plays

(NO LABEL)

Number	Title (A Side/B Side)	Yr	NM
❑ fHYPE-1 [DJ]	Flyin' the Flannel/Epoxy, For Example/O'er the Town of Pedro/Too Long	1991	8.00
—Not issued with picture sleeve			

Albums

COLUMBIA

Number	Title (A Side/B Side)	Yr	NM
❑ C 47839	Flyin' the Flannel	1991	12.00

SST

Number	Title (A Side/B Side)	Yr	NM
❑ 079	Ragin' Full-On	1986	12.00
❑ 115	If'n	1987	12.00
❑ 131 [EP]	Sometimes	1988	6.00
❑ 235	fROMOHIO	1989	12.00

FIREHOUSE

45s

EPIC

Number	Title (A Side/B Side)	Yr	NM
❑ 34-73676	Don't Treat Me Bad/ Overnight Sensation	1991	3.00
❑ 34-73771	Love of a Lifetime/ Don't Treat Me Bad	1991	4.00
❑ 34-73984	All She Wrote/Love of a Lifetime (Extremely Acoustic Version)	1991	3.00
❑ 34-74323	Sleeping with You/ (Acoustic Version)	1992	3.00
❑ 34-74335	Reach for the Sky/ Shake and Tumble (Live)	1992	3.00
❑ 34-74440	When I Look Into Your Eyes/ Life in the Real World	1992	3.00
❑ 34-77812	I Live My Life for You/ Love of a Lifetime (Acoustic)	1995	3.00

FIRESIDERS, THE

45s

SWAN

Number	Title (A Side/B Side)	Yr	NM
❑ 4074	(I'll Remember) One and All/ No One Cares for Me	1961	20.00

FIRESIGN THEATRE, THE

45s

COLUMBIA

Number	Title (A Side/B Side)	Yr	NM
❑ 45052	Forward Into the Past/ Station Break	1969	10.00
❑ 45052 [PS]	Forward Into the Past/ Station Break	1969	40.00

Albums

BUTTERFLY

Number	Title (A Side/B Side)	Yr	NM
❑ 001	Jost Folks...A Firesign Chat	1977	10.00

COLUMBIA

Number	Title (A Side/B Side)	Yr	NM
❑ CL 2718 [M]	Waiting for the Electrician or Someone Like Him	1968	25.00
❑ CS 9518 [S]	Waiting for the Electrician or Someone Like Him	1968	15.00
—"360 Sound" label			
❑ CS 9884	How Can You Be in Two Places at Once When You're Not Anywhere at All	1969	15.00
—"360 Sound" label			
❑ C 30102	Don't Crush That Dwarf, Hand Me the Pliers	1970	15.00
❑ C 30737	I Think We're All Bozos on This Bus	1971	15.00
❑ CQ 30737 [Q]	I Think We're All Bozos on This Bus	1972	20.00
❑ KG 31099 [(2)]	Dear Friends	1972	20.00
❑ KC 31585	Not Insane or Anything You Want To	1972	15.00
❑ KC 32411	David Ossman's How Time Flys	1973	12.00
❑ KC 32730	The Tale of the Giant Rat of Sumatra	1974	12.00
❑ CQ 33141 [Q]	Everything You Know Is Wrong	1974	20.00
❑ KC 33141	Everything You Know Is Wrong	1974	12.00
❑ PC 33475	In the Next World You're On Your Own	1975	12.00
❑ PG 34391 [(2)]	Forward Into the Past (An Anthology)	1977	15.00

MERCURY

Number	Title (A Side/B Side)	Yr	NM
❑ 826452-1	Eat or Be Eaten	1985	10.00

RHINO

Number	Title (A Side/B Side)	Yr	NM
❑ RNLP-018	Fighting Clowns	1979	12.00
❑ RNEP-506 [EP]	Nick Danger, Third Eye	1983	10.00
❑ RNLP-806	Lawyer's Hospital	1981	12.00
❑ RNLP-807	Shakespeare's Lost Comedie	1982	12.00
❑ RNLP-812	Nick Danger In: The Three Faces of Al	1984	12.00
❑ RNLP-904	Reagan/Carter	1980	12.00

FIRM, THE Supergroup featuring Jimmy Page of LED ZEPPELIN and Paul Rodgers of BAD COMPANY.

12-Inch Singles

ATLANTIC

Number	Title (A Side/B Side)	Yr	NM
❑ PR 698 [DJ]	Radioactive (LP Version 2:49) (same on both sides)	1985	10.00
❑ PR 714 [DJ]	Radioactive (LP Version 2:49) (Special Extended Remix 5:52)	1985	12.00
❑ PR 721 [DJ]	Satisfaction Guaranteed (same on both sides)	1985	12.00
❑ PR 735 [DJ]	Someone to Love (same on both sides)	1985	10.00
❑ PR 834 [DJ]	All the King's Horses (3:15) (same on both sides)	1986	12.00
❑ PR 878 [DJ]	Live in Peace (5:05) (same on both sides)	1986	12.00
❑ 86896	Radioactive (Special Extended Remix 5:52)//City Sirens (Live)/Live in Peace (Live)	1985	10.00

45s

ATLANTIC

Number	Title (A Side/B Side)	Yr	NM
❑ 89421	Live in Peace/Free to Live	1986	3.00
❑ 89458	All the King's Horses/ Fortune Hunter	1986	3.00
❑ 89458 [PS]	All the King's Horses/ Fortune Hunter	1986	4.00
❑ 89561	Satisfaction Guaranteed/Closer	1985	3.00
❑ 89561 [PS]	Satisfaction Guaranteed/Closer	1985	4.00
❑ 89586	Radioactive/Together	1985	3.00
❑ 89586 [PS]	Radioactive/Together	1985	4.00

Albums

ATLANTIC

Number	Title (A Side/B Side)	Yr	NM
❑ PR 883 [DJ]	Talks Business	1985	20.00
—Promo-only music and interview album			
❑ 81239	The Firm	1985	8.00
❑ 81628	Mean Business	1986	8.00

FIRST CHOICE

12-Inch Singles

GOLD MIND

Number	Title (A Side/B Side)	Yr	NM
❑ GG-401	Hold Your Horses (5:50) (2:44)	1978	20.00
❑ GG-405	Double Cross (6:59) (B-side unknown)	1979	20.00
❑ GG-502	Love Thang (8:04)/ Great Expectations	1980	20.00
❑ GG-504	Breakaway (6:56) (Instrumental 6:56)	1980	20.00
❑ 12G-4004	Doctor Love (7:35) (2:38)	1977	25.00

SALSOUL

Number	Title (A Side/B Side)	Yr	NM
❑ SG 397	Let No Man Put Asunder (Vocal 7:25) (Instrumental) (Vocal 7:00)	1982	50.00
—A-side remixed by Shep Pettibone; B-side remixed by Frankie Knuckles			
❑ SG 404	Double Cross (unknown versions)	1983	50.00
❑ SG 419	Doctor Love (7:47) (Mega Dub Remix 8:15)	1983	40.00
—Remixed by Shep Pettibone			
❑ 2571-1	Let No Man Put Asunder (Vocal Dub 6:57) (90's Dub 6:59) (Masters at Work Remix 5:54) (90's Mix 6:56) (Vocal 6:59)	1993	15.00
❑ 2573-1	Doctor Love (Love Mix 12:14) (Radio Edit 3:38) (David's Jam 11:55) (David's Theme 4:38)	1993	15.00
❑ 2574-1 [(2)]	Doctor Love (Love Mix 12:14) (Robapella Mix 5:52) (David's Jam 11:55) (C & C Theme 6:40) (Dr. Dub 8:37) (Acapella Mix 5:54) (LP Version 7:25) (Radio Version 3:38) (David's Theme 4:38)	1993	25.00
❑ 5599-1	Double Cross (Club Mix 6:06) (Swing Mix 8:27) (Techno Mix 5:55) (Flute Dub 6:04) (Percapella Mix 5:59) (Traxx Mix 5:50)	1993	15.00
—Remixes of the original version			

45s

GOLD MIND

Number	Title (A Side/B Side)	Yr	NM
❑ 4004	Doctor Love/I Love You More Than Before	1977	5.00
❑ 4009	Love Having You Around/ Indian Giver	1977	5.00
❑ 4017	Hold Your Horses/Now I've Thrown It All Away	1978	5.00
❑ 4019	Double Cross/Game of Love	1979	5.00
❑ 4022	Love Thang/Great Expectations	1980	5.00
❑ 4023	Breakaway/House for Sale	1980	5.00

PHILLY GROOVE

Number	Title (A Side/B Side)	Yr	NM
❑ 175	Armed and Extremely Dangerous/Gonna Keep On Lovin' Him	1973	5.00
❑ 179	Smarty Pants/One Step Away	1973	6.00
❑ 183	Newsy Neighbors/This Little Woman	1974	6.00
❑ 200	The Player — Part 1/ The Player — Part 2	1974	6.00
❑ 202	Guilty/Wake Up to Me	1974	6.00
❑ 204	Love Freeze/A Boy Named Junior	1975	10.00

SCEPTER

Number	Title (A Side/B Side)	Yr	NM
❑ 12347	This Is the House (Where Love Died)/One Step Away	1972	50.00

WARNER BROS.

Number	Title (A Side/B Side)	Yr	NM
❑ 8214	Gotta Get Away (From You Baby)/Yes, Maybe Not	1976	8.00
❑ 8251	First Choice Theme/Let Him Go	1976	8.00

Albums

GOLD MIND

Number	Title (A Side/B Side)	Yr	NM
❑ 7501	Delusions	1977	15.00
❑ GA 9502	Hold Your Horses	1979	20.00
❑ GA 9505	Breakaway	1980	30.00

PHILLY GROOVE

Number	Title (A Side/B Side)	Yr	NM
❑ 1400	Armed and Extremely Dangerous	1973	15.00
❑ 1502	The Player	1974	20.00

WARNER BROS.

Number	Title (A Side/B Side)	Yr	NM
❑ BS 2934	So Let Us Entertain You	1976	15.00

FIRST CLASS (1) British studio group featuring Tony Burrows on vocals.

45s

UK

Number	Title (A Side/B Side)	Yr	NM
❑ 49022	Beach Baby/Both Sides of the Story	1974	5.00
—Most stock copies have the full-length (4:59) version of the A-side			
❑ 49022	Beach Baby/Both Sides of the Story	1974	6.00
—Some stock copies have a short version of the A-side			
❑ 49028	Dreams Are Ten a Penny/ Lavender Man	1974	4.00
❑ 49033	Funny How Love Can Be/ Surfer Queen	1975	4.00

Except when noted otherwise, VG = 25% of NM, and VG+ = 50% of NM. (Example: VG = $2.00, VG+ = $4.00 and NM = $8.00.)

Number	Title (A Side/B Side)	Yr	NM
Albums			
UK			
❑ 53108	The First Class	1974	15.00

FIRST CLASS (2)
U.S. R&B group.

Number	Title (A Side/B Side)	Yr	NM
45s			
ALL PLATINUM			
❑ 2365	Me and My Gemini/Me and My Gemini (Part 2)	1976	5.00
❑ 2368	This Is It/Filled with Desire	1977	5.00
❑ 2372	Coming Back to You/This Is It	1977	5.00
EBONY SOUNDS			
❑ 187	The Beginning of My End/(B-side unknown)	1975	5.00
TODAY			
❑ 1528	What About Me/Outside Your World	1974	5.00

FIRST CLASS (U)
This is either group (1) or group (2).

Number	Title (A Side/B Side)	Yr	NM
45s			
PRIVATE STOCK			
❑ 45,093	Ain't No Love/Long Time Gone	1976	4.00

FIRST EDITION, THE
Includes "Kenny Rogers and the First Edition." Also see KENNY ROGERS.

Number	Title (A Side/B Side)	Yr	NM
45s			
JOLLY ROGERS			
❑ 1001	Lady, Play Your Symphony/There's An Old Man in Our Town	1973	5.00
❑ 1003	(Do You Remember) The First Time/Indian Joe	1973	5.00
❑ 1004	Today I Started Loving You Again/She Thinks I Still Care	1973	5.00
❑ 1006	Whatcha Gonna Do/Something About Your Song	1973	5.00
❑ 1007	A Stranger in My Place/Makin' Music for Money	1974	5.00
—All of the above as "Kenny Rogers and the First Edition"			
REPRISE			
❑ 0628	Ticket to Nowhere/I Found a Reason	1967	8.00
❑ 0655	Just Dropped In (To See What Condition My Condition Was In)/Shadow in the Corner of Your Mind	1967	10.00
—Second pressing has lighter orange "steamboat" Reprise/W7 label			
❑ 0655	Just Dropped In (To See What Condition My Condition Was In)/Shadow in the Corner of Your Mind	1967	12.00
—Original pressing has orange and brown label			
❑ 0683	Dream On/Only Me	1968	6.00
❑ 0693	Look Around, I'll Be There/Charlie the Fer-De-Lance	1968	6.00
❑ 0737	Just Dropped In (To See What Condition My Condition Was In)/But You Know I Love You	1971	4.00
—As "Kenny Rogers and the First Edition"; "Back to Back Hits" series			
❑ 0738	Ruby, Don't Take Your Love to Town/Reuben James	1971	4.00
—As "Kenny Rogers and the First Edition"; "Back to Back Hits" series			
❑ 0747	Something's Burning/Someone Who Cares	1972	4.00
—As "Kenny Rogers and the First Edition"; "Back to Back Hits" series			
❑ 0748	Tell It All Brother/Heed the Call	1972	4.00
—As "Kenny Rogers and the First Edition"; "Back to Back Hits" series			
❑ 0773	If I Could Only Change Your Mind/Are My Thoughts With You	1968	6.00
❑ 0799	But You Know I Love You/Homemade Lies	1968	6.00
❑ 0822	Good Time Liberator/Once Again She's All Alone	1969	5.00
—Starting above, by "Kenny Rogers and the First Edition"			
❑ 0829	Ruby, Don't Take Your Love to Town/Girl Get a Hold of Yourself	1969	5.00
❑ 0854	Reuben James/Sunshine	1969	5.00
❑ 0854	Ruben James/Sunshine	1969	5.00
❑ 0888	Something's Burning/Mama's Waiting	1970	5.00
❑ 0923	Tell It All Brother/Just Remember You're My Sunshine	1970	5.00
❑ 0953	Heed the Call/A Stranger in My Place	1970	5.00
❑ 0999	Someone Who Cares/Mission of San Mohera	1971	5.00
❑ 1018	Take My Hand/All God's Lonely Children	1971	5.00
❑ 1053	Where Does Rosie Go/What Am I Gonna Do	1971	5.00
❑ 1069	School Teacher/Trigger Happy Kid	1972	5.00
7-Inch Extended Plays			
REPRISE			
❑ PRO 399 [DJ]	Radio Spot for: Something's Burning	1970	15.00
—White label; each side has two 60-second radio ads; not issued with cover			
Albums			
JOLLY ROGERS			
❑ 5001	Backroads	1973	15.00
❑ 5003	Rollin'	1974	15.00
❑ 5004	Monumental	1974	15.00
—All the above as "Kenny Rogers and the First Edition"			
MCA			
❑ 912	Love Songs	1984	8.00
❑ 913	Country Songs	1984	8.00
❑ 942	Hits and Pieces	1985	8.00
❑ 943	The 60's Revisited	1985	8.00
❑ 944	Pieces of Calico Silver	1985	8.00
❑ 1460	Greatest Hits	1985	8.00
—Reissue of Reprise 6437			
REPRISE			
❑ MS 2039	Transition	1971	20.00
—As "Kenny Rogers and the First Edition"			
❑ R-6276 [M]	The First Edition	1967	30.00
❑ RS-6276 [S]	The First Edition	1967	25.00
❑ RS-6302	The First Edition's Second	1968	25.00
❑ RS-6328	The First Edition '69	1969	25.00
❑ RS-6352	Ruby, Don't Take Your Love to Town	1969	20.00
—Starting above, as "Kenny Rogers and the First Edition"			
❑ RS-6385	Something's Burning	1970	20.00
❑ RS-6412	Tell It All Brother	1970	20.00
❑ RS-6437	Greatest Hits	1971	20.00
❑ 2XS 6476 [(2)]	The Ballad of Calico	1972	25.00
❑ ST-92060	Ruby, Don't Take Your Love to Town	1969	25.00
—Capitol Record Club edition			
WARNER SPECIAL PRODUCTS			
❑ OP-2514 [(2)]	Kenny Rogers and the First Edition	1979	15.00
—Manufactured for Lakeshore Music			

FISCHER, WILD MAN

Number	Title (A Side/B Side)	Yr	NM
45s			
REPRISE			
❑ 0781	Merry-Go-Round/The Circle	1968	20.00
Albums			
REPRISE			
❑ 2XS 6332 [(2)]	An Evening with Wild Man Fischer	1969	50.00
RHINO			
❑ RNLP-001	Wildmania	1978	15.00
❑ RNLP-021	Pronounced Normal	1981	10.00
❑ RNLP-022	Nothing Scary	1981	12.00

FISCHER, WILLIAM S.

Number	Title (A Side/B Side)	Yr	NM
Albums			
EMBRYO			
❑ 529	Circles	1970	12.00

FISCHOFF, GEORGE

Number	Title (A Side/B Side)	Yr	NM
12-Inch Singles			
COLUMBIA			
❑ AS 339 [DJ]	Piano Dancing (stereo/mono)	1977	25.00
45s			
AVALANCHE			
❑ XW231	That Summer Night/For Gladys	1973	6.00
DRIVE			
❑ 6273	The Piano Picker/Love Dust	1979	5.00
GNP CRESCENDO			
❑ 491	That Great Old Song/Blue Night	1975	5.00
HERITAGE			
❑ 300	Little Ballerina Blue/Foxy	197?	6.00
LISA			
❑ 1	That Great Old Song/Blue Night	1975	7.00
❑ 17315	Starry Night/(B-side unknown)	198?	5.00
MMG			
❑ 006	Carnival Island/(B-side unknown)	198?	5.00
❑ 13365	Summer Love/(B-side unknown)	198?	5.00
P.I.P.			
❑ 6503	New Kingston/Waterflower	1975	6.00
RANWOOD			
❑ 1053	Funky Doodle/Quiet Time	1976	5.00
REWARD			
❑ WS4-04354	Boogie Piano Man/Blues for the Boogie Man	1984	4.00
Albums			
MMG			
❑ 1140	Pretty Kitty: The Piano Magic of George Fischoff	1982	20.00

FISHBONE

Number	Title (A Side/B Side)	Yr	NM
12-Inch Singles			
COLUMBIA			
❑ AS 2076 [DJ]	? (Modern Industry) (Dance Mix) (Original Version)	1985	8.00
❑ CAS 3082 [DJ]	Sunless Saturday/Fishy Swa Ska/Understand Me	1991	8.00
❑ 44-05223	? (Modern Industry) (3 versions)	1984	8.00
❑ CAS 5252 [DJ]	Swim (3 versions)	1993	12.00
❑ 44-05326	Party at Ground Zero (Vapor Mix 7:02) (Visual Mix 4:50)/Skankin' to the Beat	1985	10.00
❑ 44-05984	When Problems Arise (The Mix Is Risen) (Album Mix) (Problematic Mix)	1986	10.00
❑ 44-08172	Freddie's Dead (12" Mix) (Urban Mix) (Single Mix) (Zeoniquz Mix) (Zeoniquz Mix Instrumental)	1988	8.00
45s			
COLUMBIA			
❑ 38-04922	? (Modern Industry)/V.T.T.L.O.T.S.D.G.F.	1985	4.00
❑ 38-08500	Freddie's Dead/Question of Life	1988	4.00
WTG			
❑ 31-68936	Skankin' to the Beat/In Your Eyes	1989	4.00
—B-side by Peter Gabriel			
Albums			
COLUMBIA			
❑ CAS 1416 [DJ]	Interchords	198?	25.00
—Promo-only music and interviews			
❑ CAS 2235 [EP]	New and Improved Bonin'	1990	12.00
—Promo-only five-song sampler			
❑ B6C 40032 [EP]	Fishbone	1985	12.00
❑ BFC 40333	In Your Face	1986	12.00
❑ FC 40891	Truth and Soul	1988	12.00
❑ 4C 44097 [EP]	It's a Wonderful Life (Gonna Have a Good Time)	1987	10.00
❑ C 46142 [(2)]	The Reality of My Surroundings	1991	15.00

FISHBONE AND CURTIS MAYFIELD

Number	Title (A Side/B Side)	Yr	NM
12-Inch Singles			
ARISTA			
❑ 9812	He's a Flyguy (3 versions)	1988	6.00
45s			
ARISTA			
❑ 9806	He's a Flyguy/(Instrumental)	1989	2.00
❑ 9806 [PS]	He's a Flyguy/(Instrumental)	1989	3.00

FISHER, JERRY

Number	Title (A Side/B Side)	Yr	NM
45s			
NEW DESIGN			
❑ ZS7 1003	A New Day's Comin'/Do It If You Want To	1971	8.00
❑ ZS7 1007	I Never Had It So Good/Yonder Stands Little Maggie	1972	8.00

FISHER, MARY ANN

Number	Title (A Side/B Side)	Yr	NM
45s			
FIRE			
❑ 1002	Put On My Shoes/Wild As You Can Be	1959	25.00
❑ 1010	Only Yesterday/Wild As You Can Be	1960	25.00
IMPERIAL			
❑ 5853	I Keep Comin' Back for More/It's a Man's World	1962	20.00
SEG-WAY			
❑ 1001	I Can't Take It/Forever More	1961	20.00
❑ 1007	Can't Take the Heartbreak/Give	1961	20.00

FISHER, TONI

Number	Title (A Side/B Side)	Yr	NM
45s			
BIG TOP			
❑ 3097	West of the Wall/What Did I Do	1962	12.00
❑ 3124	The Music from the House Next Door/Quickly My Love	1962	12.00
CAPITOL			
❑ 5901	Train of Love/A Million Heartbeats from Now	1967	8.00
COLUMBIA			
❑ 42066	If I Loved You/Love Big	1961	12.00
SIGNET			
❑ 275	The Big Hurt/Memphis Belle	1959	15.00
❑ 276	How Deep Is the Ocean/Blue, Blue, Blue	1960	12.00

Number	Title (A Side/B Side)	Yr	NM
❑ 279	Everlasting Love/The Red Sea of Mars	1960	12.00
❑ 364	You Never Told Me/ Toot Toot Amore	1964	8.00
❑ 400	A Man That's Steady/ You Never Told Me	196?	8.00
❑ 664	Springtime of Love/Train of Love	1964	8.00
SMASH			
❑ 1797	Hold Me/Laugh or Cry	1963	10.00
❑ 1820	Cry a Little for Me/365 Disappointments	1963	10.00
❑ 1832	Lovers, Dreamers, Fools/ You Won't Forget Me	1963	10.00
❑ 1847	Your Royal Majesty/ Billy, Marry Me	1963	10.00

Albums

Number	Title (A Side/B Side)	Yr	NM
SIGNET			
❑ WP-509 [S]	The Big Hurt	1960	50.00
—Issued in "Stereomonic"			

FITZGERALD, ELLA

45s

Number	Title (A Side/B Side)	Yr	NM
CAPITOL			
❑ 2099	Born to Lose/I Taught Him Everything He Knows	1968	8.00
❑ 2212	Brighten the Corner/ It's Up to Me and You	1968	8.00
❑ 2267	Hawaiian War Chant/ It's Only Love	1968	8.00
❑ 5946	Just a Closer Walk with Thee/I Shall Not Be Moved	1967	8.00
DECCA			
❑ 27061	Mississippi/I Don't Want the World (With a Fence Around It)	1950	20.00
❑ 27120	I've Got the World on a String/ Peas and Rice	1950	20.00
❑ 27200	Ain't Nobody's Business If I Do/ I'll Never Be Free	1950	20.00
—With Louis Jordan			
❑ 27255	Santa Claus Got Stuck (In My Chimney)/Molasses, Molasses (It's Icky Sticky Goo)	1950	20.00
❑ 27368	My One and Only/Someone to Watch Over Me	1951	15.00
❑ 27369	But Not for Me/Looking for a Boy	1951	15.00
❑ 27370	I've Got a Crush on You/How Long Has This Been Going On	1951	15.00
❑ 27371	Soon/Maybe	1951	15.00
—The above four comprise a box set			
❑ 27419	Little Small Town/I Still Feel the Same About You	1951	20.00
—With the Ink Spots			
❑ 27453	The Beanbag Song/ Lonesome Gal	1951	20.00
❑ 27578	The Hot Canary/Two Little Men	1951	20.00
❑ 27602	The Chesapeake and Ohio/ Because of Rain	1951	20.00
❑ 27634	Do You Really Love Me/ Even As You and I	1951	20.00
❑ 27680	Come On-a My House/ Mixed Emotions	1951	20.00
❑ 27693	Smooth Sailing/Love You Madly	1951	20.00
❑ 27724	Give a Little — Get a Little/ There Never Was a Baby (Like My Baby)	1951	20.00
❑ 27900	Baby Doll/Lady Bug	1951	20.00
❑ 27901	Oops!/Necessary Evil	1951	20.00
❑ 27948	I Don't Want to Take a Chance/ Rough Ridin'	1952	15.00
❑ 28034	Lazy Day/What Does It Take	1952	15.00
❑ 28049	A Guy Is a Guy/That Old Feeling	1952	15.00
❑ 28126	Goody Goody/Air Mail Special	1952	15.00
❑ 28181	I Hadn't Anyone Till You/Gee, But I'm Glad to Know You Love Me	1952	15.00
❑ 28321	Ding-Dong Boogie/Preview	1952	15.00
❑ 28375	Trying/My Bonnie Lies Over the Ocean	1952	15.00
❑ 28433	My Favorite Song/Walkin' by the River	1952	15.00
❑ 28589	I Can't Lie to Myself/Don't Wake Me Up	1953	15.00
❑ 28671	Careless/Blue Lou	1953	15.00
❑ 28707	Angel Eyes/Nowhere Guy	1953	15.00
❑ 28762	Crying in the Chapel/When the Hands of the Clock Pray at Midnite	1953	15.00
❑ 28774	You'll Have to Swing It (Part 1)/ You'll Have to Swing It (Part 2)	1953	15.00
❑ 28930	The Greatest There Is/I Wonder What Kind of Guy You'd Be	1953	15.00
❑ 28993	A Sunday Kind of Love/ That's My Desire	1954	15.00
❑ 29008	Somebody Bad Stole De Wedding Bell/Melancholy Me	1954	15.00
❑ 29108	Baby/I Need	1954	15.00
❑ 29136	(I Love You) For Sentimental Reasons/It's Only a Paper Moon	1954	15.00
—With the Delta Rhythm Boys			
❑ 29137	Who's Afraid/I Wished on the Moon	1954	15.00
❑ 29198	Lullaby of Birdland/Later	1954	15.00
❑ 29259	Empty Ballroom/If You Don't, I Know Who Will	1954	15.00
❑ 29475	Moanin' Low/Take a Chance on Love	1955	12.00
❑ 29580	Old Devil Moon/ Lover, Come Back to Me	1955	12.00
❑ 29609	Pete Kelly's Blues/ Hard Hearted Hannah	1955	12.00
❑ 29648	Soldier Boy/A Satisfied Mind	1955	12.00
❑ 29665	The Impatient Years/ But Not Like Mine	1955	12.00
❑ 29746	(Love Is) The Tender Trap/ My One and Only Love	1955	12.00
❑ 29810	Early Autumn/Ella's Contribution to the Blues	1956	12.00
❑ 30222	Stone Cold Dead in the Market/ Peas and Rice	1957	12.00
❑ 30405	Goody Goody/It's Too Soon to Know	1957	25.00
—Reissued to compete with Frankie Lymon's remake, this is scarcer than the original on 28126			
❑ 31142	How High the Moon/ Smooth Sailing	1960	10.00
PRESTIGE			
❑ 715	Hey Jude/Sunshine of Your Love	1969	8.00
REPRISE			
❑ 0850	Get Ready/Open Your Window	1969	6.00
❑ 0875	I'll Never Fall in Love Again/ Savoy Truffle	1969	6.00
❑ 0922	Yellow Man/Try a Little Bit	1970	6.00
❑ 0995	I Wonder Why/Ooo Baby Baby	1971	6.00
VERVE			
❑ 2002	It's Only a Man/Too Young for the Blues	1956	12.00
❑ 2012	A Beautiful Friendship/Stay There	1956	12.00
❑ 2021	The Silent Treatment/The Sun Forgot to Shine This Morning	1956	12.00
❑ 10031	Hotta Chocolatta/Hear My Heart	1957	12.00
❑ 10050	Let's Do It (Let's Fall in Love)/ Manhattan	1957	12.00
❑ 10077	All of Me/It's All Right with Me	1957	12.00
❑ 10111	What Will I Tell My Heart/ Midnight Sun	1958	10.00
❑ 10130	Beale Street Blues/St. Louis Blues	1958	10.00
❑ 10132	Swingin' Shepherd Blues/ Teach Me How to Cry	1958	10.00
❑ 10143	Trav'lin' Light/Your Red Wagon	1958	10.00
❑ 10158	Oh What a Night for Love/ Dreams Are Made for Children	1959	10.00
❑ 10166	Teardrops from My Eyes/A Little Jazz	1959	10.00
❑ 10171	Stairway to the Stars/I'm Through with Love	1959	10.00
❑ 10180	But Not for Me/You Make Me Feel So Young	1959	10.00
❑ 10186	The Christmas Song/The Secret of Christmas	1959	15.00
❑ 10189	Like Young/Beat Me Daddy, Eight to the Bar	1959	10.00
❑ 10209	Mack the Knife/Lorelei	1960	10.00
❑ 10220	How High the Moon (Part 1)/ How High the Moon (Part 2)	1960	10.00
❑ 10222	I Can't Give You Anything But Love/Reach for Tomorrow	1960	10.00
❑ 10224	Jingle Bells/Good Morning Blues	1960	15.00
❑ 10237	(You'll Have to Swing It) Mr. Paganini/You're Driving Me Crazy	1961	10.00
❑ 10237 [DJ]	(You'll Have to Swing It) Mr. Paganini/You're Driving Me Crazy	1961	25.00
—Promo copy on gold vinyl			
❑ 10237 [PS]	(You'll Have to Swing It) Mr. Paganini/You're Driving Me Crazy	1961	30.00
—Sleeve may be promo only			
❑ 10241	Clap Hands (Here Come Charlie!)/Cry Me a River	1961	10.00
❑ 10241 [PS]	Clap Hands (Here Come Charlie!)/Cry Me a River	1961	20.00
❑ 10248	What Is This Thing Called Love/ Call Me Darling	1962	8.00
❑ 10274	Desafinado (Slightly Out of Tune)/Stardust Bossa Nova	1962	8.00
❑ 10288	Bill Bailey, Won't You Please Come Home/Ol' Man Mose	1963	8.00
❑ 10305	Shiny Stockings/Into Each Love Some Rain Must Fall	1963	8.00
❑ 10319	See See Rider/Trouble in Mind	1964	8.00
❑ 10324	Can't Buy Me Love/Hello, Dolly!	1964	10.00
❑ 10337	I've Grown Accustomed to Your Face/I Could Have Danced All Night	1964	8.00
❑ 10340	Ringo Beat/I'm Falling in Love	1964	15.00
❑ 10341	All the Livelong Day/ (B-side unknown)	1965	8.00
❑ 10359	Mae (She's Just a Quiet Girl)/ We Three	1965	8.00
❑ 10368	A Hard Day's Night/ And the Angels Sing	1965	10.00
❑ 10379	Imagine My Frustration (Part 1)/ Imagine My Frustration (Part 2)	1966	8.00
❑ 10408	Love Theme from "Thez Sandpiper"/Duke's Place	1966	8.00

7-Inch Extended Plays

Number	Title (A Side/B Side)	Yr	NM
DECCA			
❑ ED 2014	It's Only a Paper Moon/ (I Love You) For Sentimental Reasons//Guilty/Stairway to the Stars	195?	20.00
❑ ED 2014 [PS]	Ella Fitzgerald Sings — Vol. 1	195?	20.00
❑ ED 2028	Smooth Sailing/Flying Home// Oh, Lady Be Good/How High the Moon	195?	20.00
❑ ED 2028 [PS]	Smooth Sailing	195?	20.00
❑ ED 2049	(contents unknown)	195?	20.00
❑ ED 2049 [PS]	Ella Fitzgerald Sings — Vol. 2	195?	20.00
❑ ED 2253	Moanin' Low/Taking a Chance on Love//(If You Can't Sing It) You'll Have to Swing It (Part 1) (Part 2)	195?	20.00
❑ ED 2253 [PS]	Sweet and Hot, Part 3	195?	20.00
❑ ED 2269	(contents unknown)	1955	20.00
❑ ED 2269 [PS]	Pete Kelly's Blues	1955	20.00
❑ 34244 [PS]	Early Ella	196?	12.00
❑ 34244 [S]	Mixed Emotions/It's Too Soon to Know/Walkin' by the River// Baby Doll/I Hadn't Anyone Till You/So Long	196?	12.00
—33 1/3 rpm, small hole			
VERVE			
❑ SLV 4055	Sweet and Slow/Street of Dreams/The Very Thought of You//It's a Blue World/ I Wished on the Moon/ Body and Soul	196?	20.00
—Jukebox issue; small hole, plays at 33 1/3 rpm			
❑ SLV 4055 [PS]	Ella Fitzgerald Swings Gently with Nelson Riddle	196?	20.00

Albums

Number	Title (A Side/B Side)	Yr	NM
AMERICAN RECORDING SOCIETY			
❑ G-433 [M]	Ella Fitzgerald At Newport	195?	40.00
ATLANTIC			
❑ SD 1631	Ella Loves Cole	1972	12.00
BAINBRIDGE			
❑ 6223	Things Ain't What They Used to Be	1982	10.00
—Reissue of Reprise 6432			
BASF			
❑ 20712	Watch What Happens	1972	12.00
CAPITOL			
❑ ST 2685 [S]	Brighten the Corner	1967	15.00
❑ T 2685 [M]	Brighten the Corner	1967	20.00
❑ ST 2805 [S]	Ella Fitzgerald's Christmas	1967	12.00
—Same as above, but in stereo			
❑ T 2805 [M]	Ella Fitzgerald's Christmas	1967	20.00
❑ ST 2888	Misty Blue	1968	15.00
❑ ST 2960	Thirty by Ella	1968	15.00
❑ SM-11793	Brighten the Corner	1978	10.00
❑ SN-16276	Thirty by Ella	1983	10.00
—Budget-line reissue			
CLASSICS RECORD LIBRARY/VERVE			
❑ 80-55713 [(4)]	Ella Fitzgerald Sings the George and Ira Gershwin Songbook	1978	40.00
—Reissue of the entire set for Book-of-the-Month Club			
COLUMBIA			
❑ KG 32557 [(2)]	Carnegie Hall & Newport Jazz Festival 1973	1973	15.00
DECCA			
❑ DXB 156 [(2)M]	The Best of Ella	1959	40.00
—Black labels, silver print			
❑ DXB 156 [(2)M]	The Best of Ella	1961	25.00
—Black labels with color bars			
❑ DL 4129 [M]	Golden Favorites	1961	20.00
❑ DL 4446 [M]	Stairway to the Stars	1964	15.00
❑ DL 4447 [M]	Early Ella	1964	15.00
❑ DL 4451 [M]	Ella Sings Gershwin	1964	15.00
❑ DL 4887 [M]	Smooth Sailing	1967	15.00
❑ DL 5084 [10]	Souvenir Album	1950	120.00

Except when noted otherwise, VG = 25% of NM, and VG+ = 50% of NM. (Example: VG = $2.00, VG+ = $4.00 and NM = $8.00.)

Number	Title (A Side/B Side)	Yr	NM
❑ DL 5300 [10]	Ella Fitzgerald Sings Gershwin Songs	1951	120.00
❑ DXSB 7156 [(2)R]	The Best of Ella	196?	20.00
❑ DL 8068 [M]	Songs in a Mellow Mood	1954	50.00
❑ DL 8149 [M]	Lullabies of Birdland	1955	50.00
❑ DL 8155 [M]	Sweet and Hot	1955	50.00
❑ DL 8378 [M]	Ella Sings Gershwin	1957	40.00
❑ DL 8477 [M]	Ella and Her Fellas	1957	40.00
❑ DL 8695 [M]	The First Lady of Song	1958	40.00
❑ DL 8696 [M]	Miss Ella Fitzgerald and Mr. Nelson Riddle Invite You to Listen and Relax	1958	40.00
❑ DL 8832 [M]	For Sentimental Reasons	1958	40.00
❑ DL 74129 [R]	Golden Favorites	1961	12.00
❑ DL 74446 [R]	Stairway to the Stars	1964	12.00
❑ DL 74447 [R]	Early Ella	1964	12.00
❑ DL 74451 [R]	Ella Sings Gershwin	1964	12.00
❑ DL 74887 [R]	Smooth Sailing	1967	12.00

EVEREST ARCHIVE OF FOLK & JAZZ

Number	Title (A Side/B Side)	Yr	NM
❑ 276	Ella Fitzgerald	1973	12.00

FANTASY

Number	Title (A Side/B Side)	Yr	NM
❑ OJC-376	Montreux '77	1989	12.00
—Reissue of Pablo Live 2308 206			
❑ OJC-442	Ella & Nice	1990	12.00
—Reissue of Pablo Live 2308 234			

INTERMEDIA

Number	Title (A Side/B Side)	Yr	NM
❑ QS-5049	Ella by Starlight	198?	10.00

MCA

Number	Title (A Side/B Side)	Yr	NM
❑ 215	Ella Sings Gershwin	1973	10.00
❑ 734	Memories	198?	10.00
❑ 4016 [(2)]	The Best of Ella Fitzgerald, Vol. II	1973	15.00
❑ 4047 [(2)]	The Best of Ella	197?	15.00

METRO

Number	Title (A Side/B Side)	Yr	NM
❑ M-500 [M]	Ella Fitzgerald	1965	12.00
❑ MS-500 [S]	Ella Fitzgerald	1965	12.00
❑ M-567 [M]	The World of Ella Fitzgerald	1966	12.00
❑ MS-567 [S]	The World of Ella Fitzgerald	1966	12.00

MGM

Number	Title (A Side/B Side)	Yr	NM
❑ GAS-130	Ella Fitzgerald (Golden Archive Series)	1970	15.00

PABLO

Number	Title (A Side/B Side)	Yr	NM
❑ 2310702	Take Love Easy	1974	12.00
❑ 2310711	Ella in London	1974	12.00
❑ 2310751	Montreux '75	1976	12.00
❑ 2310759	Ella and Oscar	1976	12.00
❑ 2310772	Again	1977	12.00
❑ 2310814	Dream Dancing	1978	12.00
❑ 2310825	Lady Time	1978	12.00
❑ 2310829	Fine and Mellow	1979	12.00
❑ 2310888	Speak Love	1983	10.00
❑ 2310921	Easy Living	1987	10.00
❑ 2310938	All That Jazz	1990	12.00
❑ 2405421	The Best of Ella Fitzgerald	198?	10.00

PABLO LIVE

Number	Title (A Side/B Side)	Yr	NM
❑ 2308206	Montreux '77	1978	12.00
❑ 2308234	Ella & Nice	197?	15.00

PABLO TODAY

Number	Title (A Side/B Side)	Yr	NM
❑ 2312132	A Classy Pair	1983	10.00
❑ 2312138	The Best Is Yet to Come	1982	10.00
❑ 2312140	Nice Work If You Can Get It	198?	10.00
❑ 2630201 [(2)]	Ella Abraca Jobim: Ella Fitzgerald Sings the Antonio Carlos Jobim Song Book	1981	15.00

PAUSA

Number	Title (A Side/B Side)	Yr	NM
❑ 7130	Love You Madly	198?	10.00

PICKWICK

Number	Title (A Side/B Side)	Yr	NM
❑ SPC-3259	Misty Blues	1974	10.00

PRESTIGE

Number	Title (A Side/B Side)	Yr	NM
❑ PRLP-7685	Sunshine of Your Love	1970	15.00

REPRISE

Number	Title (A Side/B Side)	Yr	NM
❑ RS-6354	Ella	1969	15.00
❑ RS-6432	Things Ain't What They Used to Be	1971	12.00

SUNBEAM

Number	Title (A Side/B Side)	Yr	NM
❑ 205	Ella Fitzgerald and Her Orchestra, 1940	197?	10.00

TIME-LIFE

Number	Title (A Side/B Side)	Yr	NM
❑ SLGD-03 [(2)]	Legendary Singers: Ella Fitzgerald	1985	15.00

VERVE

Number	Title (A Side/B Side)	Yr	NM
❑ V-10-4 [(4)M]	Ella Fitzgerald Sings the Duke Ellington Song Book	196?	50.00
❑ V-29-5 [(5)M]	Ella Fitzgerald Sings the George and Ira Gershwin Song Book	196?	100.00
—Reissue of MGV-4029			
❑ V6-29-5 [(5)S]	Ella Fitzgerald Sings the George and Ira Gershwin Song Book	196?	100.00
—Reissue of MGVS-6082			
❑ VE-2-2511 [(2)]	The Cole Porter Song Book	197?	15.00
❑ VE-2-2519 [(2)]	The Rodgers and Hart Song Book	197?	15.00
❑ VE-2-2525 [(2)]	The George Gershwin Song Book	1978	15.00
❑ VE-2-2535 [(2)]	The Duke Ellington Song Book	1979	15.00
❑ VE-1-2539	Ella Wishes You a Swinging Christmas	198?	12.00
—Reissue			
❑ VE-2-2540 [(2)]	The Duke Ellington Song Book, Vol. 2	1982	15.00
❑ MGV-4001-2 [(2)M]	Ella Fitzgerald Sings the Cole Porter Song Book	1956	80.00
❑ V-4001-2 [(2)M]	Ella Fitzgerald Sings the Cole Porter Song Book	1961	25.00
❑ MGV-4002-2 [(2)M]	Ella Fitzgerald Sings the Rodgers & Hart Song Book	1956	80.00
❑ V-4002-2 [(2)M]	Ella Fitzgerald Sings the Rodgers and Hart Song Book	1961	25.00
❑ MGV-4004 [M]	Like Someone in Love	1957	50.00
❑ V-4004 [M]	Like Someone in Love	1961	20.00
❑ V6-4004 [S]	Like Someone in Love	1961	20.00
❑ MGV-4008-2 [(2)M]	Ella Fitzgerald Sings the Duke Ellington Song Book, Vol. 1	1957	80.00
❑ V-4008-2 [(2)M]	Ella Fitzgerald Sings the Duke Ellington Song Book, Vol. 1	1961	25.00
❑ MGV-4009-2 [(2)M]	Ella Fitzgerald Sings the Duke Ellington Song Book, Vol. 2	1957	80.00
❑ V-4009-2 [(2)M]	Ella Fitzgerald Sings the Duke Ellington Song Book, Vol. 2	1961	25.00
❑ MGV-4010-4 [(4)M]	Ella Fitzgerald Sings the Duke Ellington Song Book	1957	150.00
—Combines 4008 and 4009 into one package			
❑ MGV-4013 [M]	Ella Fitzgerald Sings the Gershwin Song Book	1957	50.00
❑ MGV-4019-2 [(2)M]	Ella Fitzgerald Sings the Irving Berlin Song Book	1958	80.00
❑ V-4019-2 [(2)M]	Ella Fitzgerald Sings the Irving Berlin Song Book	1961	25.00
❑ V6-4019-2 [(2)S]	Ella Fitzgerald Sings the Irving Berlin Song Book	1961	25.00
❑ MGV-4021 [M]	Ella Swings Lightly	1958	50.00
❑ V-4021 [M]	Ella Swings Lightly	1961	20.00
❑ V6-4021 [S]	Ella Swings Lightly	1961	20.00
❑ MGV-4022 [M]	Ella Fitzgerald Sings the Rodgers & Hart Song Book, Vol. 1	1959	50.00
❑ V-4022 [M]	Ella Fitzgerald Sings the Rodgers & Hart Song Book, Vol. 1	1961	20.00
❑ V6-4022 [S]	Ella Fitzgerald Sings the Rodgers & Hart Song Book, Vol. 1	1961	20.00
❑ MGV-4023 [M]	Ella Fitzgerald Sings the Rodgers & Hart Song Book, Vol. 2	1959	50.00
❑ V-4023 [M]	Ella Fitzgerald Sings the Rodgers & Hart Song Book, Vol. 2	1961	20.00
❑ V6-4023 [S]	Ella Fitzgerald Sings the Rodgers & Hart Song Book, Vol. 2	1961	20.00
❑ MGV-4024 [M]	Ella Fitzgerald Sings the George and Ira Gershwin Song Book, Vol. 1	1959	50.00
❑ V-4024 [M]	Ella Fitzgerald Sings the George and Ira Gershwin Song Book, Vol. 1	1961	20.00
❑ V6-4024 [S]	Ella Fitzgerald Sings the George and Ira Gershwin Song Book, Vol. 1	1961	20.00
❑ MGV-4025 [M]	Ella Fitzgerald Sings the George and Ira Gershwin Song Book, Vol. 2	1959	50.00
❑ V-4025 [M]	Ella Fitzgerald Sings the George and Ira Gershwin Song Book, Vol. 2	1961	20.00
❑ V6-4025 [S]	Ella Fitzgerald Sings the George and Ira Gershwin Song Book, Vol. 2	1961	20.00
❑ MGV-4026 [M]	Ella Fitzgerald Sings the George and Ira Gershwin Song Book, Vol. 3	1959	50.00
❑ V-4026 [M]	Ella Fitzgerald Sings the George and Ira Gershwin Song Book, Vol. 3	1961	20.00
❑ V6-4026 [S]	Ella Fitzgerald Sings the George and Ira Gershwin Song Book, Vol. 3	1961	20.00
❑ MGV-4027 [M]	Ella Fitzgerald Sings the George and Ira Gershwin Song Book, Vol. 4	1959	50.00
❑ V-4027 [M]	Ella Fitzgerald Sings the George and Ira Gershwin Song Book, Vol. 4	1961	20.00
❑ V6-4027 [S]	Ella Fitzgerald Sings the George and Ira Gershwin Song Book, Vol. 4	1961	20.00
❑ MGV-4028 [M]	Ella Fitzgerald Sings the George and Ira Gershwin Song Book, Vol. 5	1959	50.00
❑ V-4028 [M]	Ella Fitzgerald Sings the George and Ira Gershwin Song Book, Vol. 5	1961	20.00
❑ V6-4028 [S]	Ella Fitzgerald Sings the George and Ira Gershwin Song Book, Vol. 5	1961	20.00
❑ MGV-4029-5 [(5)M]	Ella Fitzgerald Sings the George and Ira Gershwin Song Book	1959	250.00
—Box set with 4024 through 4028 plus bonus 10-inch LP			
❑ MGV-4029-5 [(5)M]	Ella Fitzgerald Sings the George and Ira Gershwin Song Book	1959	500.00
—Box set with 4024 through 4028 plus bonus 10-inch LP, all in walnut box with leather pockets			
❑ MGV-4030 [M]	Ella Fitzgerald Sings the Irving Berlin Song Book, Vol. 1	1959	50.00
❑ V-4030 [M]	Ella Fitzgerald Sings the Irving Berlin Song Book, Vol. 1	1961	20.00
❑ V6-4030 [S]	Ella Fitzgerald Sings the Irving Berlin Song Book, Vol. 1	1961	20.00
❑ MGV-4031 [M]	Ella Fitzgerald Sings the Irving Berlin Song Book, Vol. 2	1959	50.00
❑ V-4031 [M]	Ella Fitzgerald Sings the Irving Berlin Song Book, Vol. 2	1961	20.00
❑ V6-4031 [S]	Ella Fitzgerald Sings the Irving Berlin Song Book, Vol. 2	1961	20.00
❑ MGV-4032 [M]	Sweet Songs for Swingers	1959	50.00
❑ V-4032 [M]	Sweet Songs for Swingers	1961	20.00
❑ V6-4032 [S]	Sweet Songs for Swingers	1961	20.00
❑ MGV-4034 [M]	Hello, Love	1959	50.00
❑ V-4034 [M]	Hello, Love	1961	20.00
❑ V6-4034 [S]	Hello, Love	1961	20.00
❑ MGV-4036 [M]	Get Happy!	1960	40.00
❑ V-4036 [M]	Get Happy!	1961	20.00
❑ V6-4036 [S]	Get Happy!	1961	20.00
❑ MGV-4041 [M]	Mack the Knife — Ella in Berlin	1960	40.00
❑ V-4041 [M]	Mack the Knife — Ella in Berlin	1961	20.00
❑ V6-4041 [S]	Mack the Knife — Ella in Berlin	1961	20.00
❑ MGV-4042 [M]	Ella Wishes You a Swinging Christmas	1960	50.00
❑ V-4042 [M]	Ella Wishes You a Swinging Christmas	1961	40.00
❑ V6-4042 [S]	Ella Wishes You a Swinging Christmas	1961	50.00
❑ MGV-4043 [M]	Let No Man Write My Epitaph	1961	40.00
❑ V-4043 [M]	Let No Man Write My Epitaph	1961	20.00
❑ V6-4043 [S]	Let No Man Write My Epitaph	1961	20.00
❑ MGV-4046-2 [(2)M]	Ella Fitzgerald Sings the Harold Arlen Song Book	1961	60.00
❑ MGV-4049 [M]	Ella Fitzgerald Sings Cole Porter	1961	40.00
❑ V-4049 [M]	Ella Fitzgerald Sings Cole Porter	1961	20.00
❑ MGV-4050 [M]	Ella Fitzgerald Sings More Cole Porter	1961	40.00
❑ V-4050 [M]	Ella Fitzgerald Sings More Cole Porter	1961	20.00
❑ MGV-4052 [M]	Ella in Hollywood	1961	40.00
❑ V-4052 [M]	Ella in Hollywood	1961	20.00
❑ V-4053 [M]	Clap Hands, Here Comes Charley	1962	40.00
❑ V6-4053 [S]	Clap Hands, Here Comes Charley	1962	150.00
❑ V-4054 [M]	Ella Swings Brightly with Nelson	1962	30.00
❑ V6-4054 [S]	Ella Swings Brightly with Nelson	1962	30.00
❑ V-4055 [M]	Ella Swings Gently with Nelson	1962	30.00
❑ V6-4055 [S]	Ella Swings Gently with Nelson	1962	30.00
❑ V-4056 [M]	Rhythm Is My Business	1962	30.00
❑ V6-4056 [S]	Rhythm Is My Business	1962	30.00
❑ V-4057 [M]	Ella Fitzgerald Sings the Harold Arlen Song Book, Vol. 1	1962	30.00
❑ V6-4057 [S]	Ella Fitzgerald Sings the Harold Arlen Song Book, Vol. 1	1962	30.00
❑ V-4058 [M]	Ella Fitzgerald Sings the Harold Arlen Song Book, Vol. 2	1962	30.00
❑ V6-4058 [S]	Ella Fitzgerald Sings the Harold Arlen Song Book, Vol. 2	1962	30.00
❑ V-4059 [M]	Ella Sings Broadway	1963	25.00
❑ V6-4059 [S]	Ella Sings Broadway	1963	25.00
❑ V-4060 [M]	Ella Fitzgerald Sings the Jerome Kern Song Book	1963	25.00
❑ V6-4060 [S]	Ella Fitzgerald Sings the Jerome Kern Song Book	1963	25.00
❑ V-4062 [M]	These Are the Blues	1963	25.00
❑ V6-4062 [S]	These Are the Blues	1963	25.00
❑ V-4063 [M]	The Best of Ella Fitzgerald	1964	15.00
❑ V6-4063 [S]	The Best of Ella Fitzgerald	1964	15.00
❑ V-4064 [M]	Hello, Dolly!	1964	25.00
❑ V6-4064 [S]	Hello, Dolly!	1964	25.00
❑ V-4065 [M]	Ella at Juan Les Pins	1964	25.00
❑ V6-4065 [S]	Ella at Juan Les Pins	1964	25.00
❑ V-4066 [M]	A Tribute to Cole Porter	1964	25.00
❑ V6-4066 [S]	A Tribute to Cole Porter	1964	25.00
❑ V-4067 [M]	Ella Fitzgerald Sings the Johnny Mercer Song Book	1965	20.00
❑ V6-4067 [S]	Ella Fitzgerald Sings the Johnny Mercer Song Book	1965	20.00
❑ V-4068 [M]	Porgy & Bess	1965	20.00
❑ V6-4068 [S]	Porgy & Bess	1965	20.00
❑ V-4069 [M]	Ella in Hamburg	1966	20.00

F

Number	Title (A Side/B Side)	Yr	NM
❑ V6-4069 [S]	Ella in Hamburg	1966	20.00
❑ V-4070 [M]	Ella at Duke's Place	1966	20.00
❑ V6-4070 [S]	Ella at Duke's Place	1966	20.00
❑ V-4071 [M]	Whisper Not	1966	20.00
❑ V6-4071 [S]	Whisper Not	1966	20.00
❑ V-4072 [(2)M]	Ella & Duke at Cote d'Azur	1967	40.00
❑ V6-4072 [(2)S]	Ella & Duke at Cote d'Azur	1967	25.00
❑ MGVS-6000 [S]	Like Someone in Love	1960	40.00
❑ MGVS-6005-2 [(2)S]	Ella Fitzgerald Sings the Irving Berlin Song Book	1960	60.00
❑ MGVS-6009 [S]	Ella Fitzgerald Sings the Rodgers & Hart Song Book, Vol. 1	1960	40.00
❑ MGVS-6010 [S]	Ella Fitzgerald Sings the Rodgers & Hart Song Book, Vol. 2	1960	40.00
❑ MGVS-6019 [S]	Ella Swings Lightly	1960	40.00
❑ MGVS-6026 [S]	Ella Fitzgerald at the Opera House	1960	40.00
❑ MGVS-6052 [S]	Ella Fitzgerald Sings the Irving Berlin Song Book, Vol. 1	1960	40.00
❑ MGVS-6053 [S]	Ella Fitzgerald Sings the Irving Berlin Song Book, Vol. 2	1960	40.00
❑ MGVS-6072 [S]	Sweet Songs for Swingers	1960	40.00
❑ MGVS-6077 [S]	Ella Fitzgerald Sings the George and Ira Gershwin Song Book, Vol. 1	1960	40.00
❑ MGVS-6078 [S]	Ella Fitzgerald Sings the George and Ira Gershwin Song Book, Vol. 2	1960	40.00
❑ MGVS-6079 [S]	Ella Fitzgerald Sings the George and Ira Gershwin Song Book, Vol. 3	1960	40.00
❑ MGVS-6080 [S]	Ella Fitzgerald Sings the George and Ira Gershwin Song Book, Vol. 4	1960	40.00
❑ MGVS-6081 [S]	Ella Fitzgerald Sings the George and Ira Gershwin Song Book, Vol. 5	1960	40.00
❑ MGVS-6082-5 [(5)S]	Ella Fitzgerald Sings the George and Ira Gershwin Song Book	1960	200.00
—Box set with 6077 through 6081 plus bonus 10-inch LP			
❑ MGVS-6100 [S]	Hello, Love	1960	40.00
❑ MGVS-6102 [S]	Get Happy!	1960	40.00
❑ MGVS-6163 [S]	Mack the Knife — Ella in Berlin	1960	40.00
❑ MGVS-7000 [S]	Ella Fitzgerald Sings the Gershwin Song Book	1959	50.00
❑ MGV-8264 [M]	Ella Fitzgerald at the Opera House	1958	50.00
❑ V-8264 [M]	Ella Fitzgerald at the Opera House	1961	20.00
❑ V6-8264 [S]	Ella Fitzgerald at the Opera House	1961	20.00
❑ MGV-8288 [M]	One O'Clock Jump	1958	50.00
❑ V-8288 [M]	One O'Clock Jump	1961	20.00
❑ V-8670 [M]	Ella Fitzgerald Sings the Jerome Kern Song Book	1967	—
—Canceled reissue			
❑ V-8720 [M]	The Best of Ella Fitzgerald	1967	15.00
❑ V6-8720 [S]	The Best of Ella Fitzgerald	1967	12.00
❑ V-8745 [M]	Ella "Live"	1968	30.00
❑ V6-8745 [S]	Ella "Live"	1968	15.00
❑ V6-8795	The Best of Ella Fitzgerald, Vol. 2	1969	12.00
❑ V6-8817 [(2)]	History	1973	15.00
❑ MGVS-64041 [S]	Mack the Knife — Ella in Berlin	1960	50.00
❑ MGVS-64042 [S]	Ella Wishes You a Swinging Christmas	1960	60.00
❑ SMAS-90644 [S]	Ella at Duke's Place	1966	25.00
—Capitol Record Club edition			
❑ 817526-1 [(2)]	The Harold Arlen Song Book	1984	15.00
❑ 821693-1 [(2)]	The Rodgers and Hart Song Book	198?	12.00
❑ 823247-1	The Johnny Mercer Song Book	1985	10.00
❑ 823278-1 [(2)]	The Cole Porter Song Book	198?	12.00
❑ 823279-1 [(2)]	The George and Ira Gershwin Songbook (Highlights)	198?	12.00
❑ 825024-1 [(5)]	The George and Ira Gershwin Songbook (Complete)	198?	25.00
❑ 825098-1	Lady Be Good	1985	10.00
❑ 825669-1	The Jerome Kern Song Book	1985	10.00
❑ 825670-1	Mack the Knife — Ella in Berlin	1985	10.00
❑ 827150-1	Ella Wishes You a Swinging Christmas	198?	10.00
❑ 827163-1 [(2)]	The Duke Ellington Song Book, Vol. 1	198?	12.00
❑ 827169-1 [(2)]	The Duke Ellington Song Book, Vol. 2	198?	12.00
❑ 829533-1 [(2)]	The Irving Berlin Song Book	1988	12.00
❑ 835454-1	Ella in Rome: The Birthday Concert	1988	10.00
VOCALION			
❑ VL 3797 [M]	Ella Fitzgerald	1967	12.00
❑ VL 73797 [R]	Ella Fitzgerald	1967	12.00

FITZGERALD, ELLA, AND LOUIS ARMSTRONG

Also see each artist's individual listings.

45s

Number	Title (A Side/B Side)	Yr	NM
DECCA			
❑ 27209	Can Anyone Explain? (No, No, No)/Dream a Little Dream of Me	1950	20.00
❑ 28552	Who Walks In When I Walk Out/Would You Like to Take a Walk	1953	15.00
VERVE			
❑ 2023	Stars Fell on Alabama/Can't We Be Friends	1956	12.00
❑ 10079	Goody Goody/A-Tisket, A-Tasket	1957	20.00

7-Inch Extended Plays

Number	Title (A Side/B Side)	Yr	NM
DECCA			
❑ ED 2027	You Won't Be Satisfied/Dream a Little Dream of Me//Would You Like to Take a Walk/The Frim-Fram Sauce	195?	15.00
❑ ED 2027 [PS]	Ella Fitzgerald and Louis Armstrong, Vol. 1	195?	15.00

Albums

Number	Title (A Side/B Side)	Yr	NM
METRO			
❑ M-601 [M]	Louis and Ella	1967	12.00
❑ MS-601 [S]	Louis and Ella	1967	12.00
MOBILE FIDELITY			
❑ 2-248 [(2)]	Ella and Louis Again	1996	150.00
—Audiophile vinyl			
VERVE			
❑ VE-1-2507	Porgy and Bess	197?	10.00
❑ MGV-4003 [M]	Ella and Louis	1956	50.00
❑ V-4003 [M]	Ella and Louis	1961	20.00
❑ MGV-4006-2 [(2)M]	Ella and Louis Again	1956	80.00
❑ V-4006-2 [(2)M]	Ella and Louis Again	1961	25.00
❑ MGV-4011-2 [(2)M]	Porgy and Bess	1957	80.00
❑ V-4011-2 [(2)M]	Porgy and Bess	1961	25.00
❑ V6-4011-2 [(2)S]	Porgy and Bess	1961	25.00
❑ MGV-4017 [M]	Ella and Louis Again, Vol. 1	1958	50.00
❑ V-4017 [M]	Ella and Louis Again, Vol. 1	1961	20.00
❑ MGV-4018 [M]	Ella and Louis Again, Vol. 2	1958	50.00
❑ V-4018 [M]	Ella and Louis Again, Vol. 2	1961	20.00
❑ MGVS-6040-2 [(2)S]	Porgy and Bess	1960	60.00
❑ V6-8811 [(2)]	Ella and Louis	1972	15.00
❑ 827475-1 [(2)]	Porgy and Bess	198?	12.00

FITZGERALD, ELLA, AND COUNT BASIE

Albums

Number	Title (A Side/B Side)	Yr	NM
PABLO TODAY			
❑ 2312110	A Perfect Match	1980	12.00
—Red vinyl			
VERVE			
❑ V-4061 [M]	Ella and Basie!	1963	25.00
❑ V6-4061 [S]	Ella and Basie!	1963	25.00
❑ ST-90028 [S]	Ella and Basie!	1964	30.00
—Capitol Record Club edition			
❑ T-90028 [M]	Ella and Basie!	1964	30.00
—Capitol Record Club edition			

FITZGERALD, ELLA, AND DUKE ELLINGTON

Albums

Number	Title (A Side/B Side)	Yr	NM
PABLO LIVE			
❑ 2308242	The Stockholm Concert 1966	1984	10.00

FITZGERALD, ELLA, AND BILLIE HOLIDAY

Also see each artist's individual listings.

Albums

Number	Title (A Side/B Side)	Yr	NM
AMERICAN RECORDING SOCIETY			
❑ G-433 [M]	Ella Fitzgerald and Billie Holiday at Newport	1957	40.00
VERVE			
❑ MGVS-6022 [S]	Ella Fitzgerald and Billie Holiday at Newport	1960	40.00
❑ MGV-8234 [M]	Ella Fitzgerald and Billie Holiday at Newport	1958	50.00
❑ V-8234 [M]	Ella Fitzgerald and Billie Holiday at Newport	1961	20.00
❑ V6-8234 [S]	Ella Fitzgerald and Billie Holiday at Newport	1961	20.00
❑ V-8826	Newport Years	1973	12.00

FI-DELLS, THE

45s

Number	Title (A Side/B Side)	Yr	NM
IMPERIAL			
❑ 5780	What Is Love/Don't Let Me Love You	1961	25.00
WARNER			
❑ 1014	No Other Love/Come Back to Me	1957	20.00

FIVE AMERICANS, THE

45s

Number	Title (A Side/B Side)	Yr	NM
ABC-PARAMOUNT			
❑ 10686	Show Me/Love, Love, Love	1965	15.00
ABNAK			
❑ 106	Say That You Love Me/Without You	1965	10.00
❑ 106 [DJ]	Say That You Love Me/Without You	1965	25.00
—Promo only on yellow vinyl			
❑ 109	I See the Light/The Outcast	1965	20.00
❑ 109 [DJ]	I See the Light/The Outcast	1965	25.00
—Promo only on yellow vinyl			
❑ 114	Reality/Sympathy	1966	10.00
❑ 114 [DJ]	Reality/Sympathy	1966	25.00
—Promo only on yellow vinyl			
❑ 116	If I Could/Now That It's Over	1966	10.00
❑ 116 [DJ]	If I Could/Now That It's Over	1966	25.00
—Promo only on yellow vinyl			
❑ 118	Western Union/Now That It's Over	1967	12.00
❑ 118 [DJ]	Western Union/Now That It's Over	1967	25.00
—Promo only on yellow vinyl			
❑ 120	Sound of Love/Sympathy	1967	8.00
❑ 120 [DJ]	Sound of Love/Sympathy	1967	25.00
—Promo only on yellow vinyl			
❑ 123	Zip Code/Sweet Bird of Youth	1967	8.00
❑ 123 [DJ]	Zip Code/Sweet Bird of Youth	1967	25.00
—Promo only on yellow vinyl			
❑ 125	Stop Light/Tell Ann I Love Her	1967	8.00
❑ 125 [DJ]	Stop Light/Tell Ann I Love Her	1967	25.00
—Promo only on yellow vinyl			
❑ 125 [PS]	Stop Light/Tell Ann I Love Her	1967	15.00
❑ 126	7:30 Guided Tour/See Saw Baby	1967	8.00
❑ 126 [DJ]	7:30 Guided Tour/See Saw Baby	1967	25.00
—Promo only on yellow vinyl			
❑ 126 [PS]	7:30 Guided Tour/See Saw Baby	1967	15.00
❑ 128	The Rain Maker/No Communication	1968	8.00
❑ 128 [DJ]	The Rain Maker/No Communication	1968	25.00
—Promo only on yellow vinyl			
❑ 131	Con Man/Lovin' Is Lovin'	1968	8.00
❑ 131 [DJ]	Con Man/Lovin' Is Lovin'	1968	25.00
—Promo only on yellow vinyl			
❑ 132	Generation Gap/The Source	1968	8.00
❑ 132 [DJ]	Generation Gap/The Source	1968	25.00
—Promo only on yellow vinyl			
❑ 134	Virginia Girl/Call on Me	1969	8.00
❑ 134 [DJ]	Virginia Girl/Call on Me	1969	25.00
—Promo only on yellow vinyl			
❑ 137	Scrooge/Ignert Woman	1969	8.00
❑ 137 [DJ]	Scrooge/Ignert Woman	1969	25.00
—Promo only on yellow vinyl			
❑ 139	I See the Light '69/Red Cape	1969	8.00
—As "Michael Rabon and the Five Americans"			
❑ 139 [DJ]	I See the Light '69/Red Cape	1969	25.00
—As "Michael Rabon and the Five Americans"; promo only on yellow vinyl			
❑ 142	She's Too Good to Me/Molly Black	1969	8.00
❑ 142 [DJ]	She's Too Good to Me/Molly Black	1969	25.00
—Promo only on yellow vinyl			
HANNA-BARBERA			
❑ 454	I See the Light/The Outcast	1965	12.00
❑ 468	Evol-Not Love/Don't Blame Me	1966	12.00
❑ 468 [PS]	Evol-Not Love/Don't Blame Me	1966	15.00
❑ 483	Good Times/The Losing Game	1966	12.00
JETSTAR			
❑ 104	It's You Girl/I'm Gonna Leave You	1966	25.00
❑ 105	I'm Feeling OK/Slippin' and Slidin'	1966	30.00
PHILCO-FORD			
❑ HP-10	Western Union/Sounds of Love	1968	20.00
—4-inch plastic "Hip Pocket Record" with color sleeve			

Albums

Number	Title (A Side/B Side)	Yr	NM
ABNAK			
❑ AB-1967 [M]	Western Union/Sound of Love	1967	20.00
❑ AB-1969 [M]	Progressions	1967	40.00
❑ ABST-2067 [S]	Western Union/Sound of Love	1967	30.00
❑ ABST-2069 [S]	Progressions	1967	60.00
❑ ABST-2071 [(2)]	Now and Then	1968	25.00
HANNA-BARBERA			
❑ HLP-8503 [M]	I See the Light	1966	40.00
❑ HST-9503 [S]	I See the Light	1966	75.00

FIVE BARS, THE

45s

Number	Title (A Side/B Side)	Yr	NM
MONEY			
❑ 224	Stormy Weather/Somebody Else's Fool	1957	60.00

Except when noted otherwise, VG = 25% of NM, and VG+ = 50% of NM. (Example: VG = $2.00, VG+ = $4.00 and NM = $8.00.)

FIVE BELLS, THE

45s

Number	Title (A Side/B Side)	Yr	NM
BRUNSWICK			
❑ 84002	Till I Waltz Again with You/Can't Wait for Tomorrow	1952	500.00
❑ 84004	Till Dawn and Tomorrow/Waiting, Waiting	1952	500.00

FIVE BLOBS, THE

45s

Number	Title (A Side/B Side)	Yr	NM
COLUMBIA			
❑ 4-41250	The Blob/Saturday Night in Tiajuana	1958	25.00
JOY			
❑ 226	Rockin' Pow Wow/From the Top of Your Guggle	1959	20.00
❑ 230	Juliet/Young and Wild	1959	20.00

FIVE BLUE FLAMES, THE

See CHRIS POWELL AND THE FIVE BLUE FLAMES.

FIVE BLUE NOTES, THE

45s

Number	Title (A Side/B Side)	Yr	NM
SABRE			
❑ 103	My Gal Is Gone/Ooh Baby	1953	1000.
❑ 108	The Beat of Our Hearts/You Gotta Go Baby	1954	2500.

FIVE BUDDS, THE

45s

Number	Title (A Side/B Side)	Yr	NM
RAMA			
❑ 1	I Was Such a Fool (To Fall in Love with You)/Midnight	1953	500.00
❑ 2	I Guess It's All Over Now/I Want Her Back	1953	500.00

FIVE BY FIVE

45s

Number	Title (A Side/B Side)	Yr	NM
PAULA			
❑ 261	Shake a Tail Feather/Tell Me What to Do	1967	12.00
❑ 283	Harlem Shuffle/You Really Got a Hold on Me	1967	12.00
❑ 302	Fire/Hang Up	1968	15.00
❑ 311	Ain't Gonna Be Your Fool No More/She Digs My Love	1968	12.00
❑ 319	Apple Cider/Fruitstand Man	1970	10.00
❑ 322	Too Much Tomorrow/Ain't Gonna Be Your Fool No More	1970	10.00
❑ 326	15 Going on 20/Penthouse Pauper	1970	10.00
❑ 328	Never/Good Connection	1970	10.00

FIVE CAMPBELLS, THE

45s

Number	Title (A Side/B Side)	Yr	NM
MUSIC CITY			
❑ 794	Hey Baby/Morrine	1956	500.00

FIVE CARD STUD

45s

Number	Title (A Side/B Side)	Yr	NM
RED BIRD			
❑ 10-082	Be-Bop-A-Lula/Everybody Needs Somebody	1967	15.00
SMASH			
❑ 2080	Bag Me/Once	1967	15.00

FIVE CATS, THE

45s

Number	Title (A Side/B Side)	Yr	NM
RCA VICTOR			
❑ 47-5885	He Follows She/Santa Lucia	1954	25.00
❑ 47-6012	Rockin' Chair/Mine, Mine, Mine	1955	30.00
❑ 47-6181	I Was So Wrong/Someone's Gonna Cry	1955	40.00

FIVE CHANCES, THE

45s

Number	Title (A Side/B Side)	Yr	NM
ATOMIC			
❑ 2494	Make Love to Me/California	1977	12.00
BLUE LAKE			
❑ 115	All I Want/Shake-a-Link	1955	800.00
CHANCE			
❑ 1157	I May Be Small/Nagasaki	1954	1000.
FEDERAL			
❑ 12303	My Days Are Blue/Tell Me Why	1957	500.00
P.S.			
❑ 1510	Is This Love/Need Your Love	1960	300.00
STATES			
❑ 156 *—Black vinyl*	Gloria/Sugar Lips	1956	800.00
❑ 156 *—Red vinyl*	Gloria/Sugar Lips	1956	1200.

FIVE CHANELS, THE

45s

Number	Title (A Side/B Side)	Yr	NM
DEB			
❑ 500 *—As "The Five Chanels"*	The Reason/Skiddily Doo	1958	40.00
❑ 500 *—As "The Chanels"*	The Reason/Skiddily Doo	1958	80.00

FIVE DEBONAIRES, THE

See THE DEBONAIRES.

FIVE DELIGHTS, THE

45s

Number	Title (A Side/B Side)	Yr	NM
ABEL			
❑ 228	The Thought of Losing You/That Love Affair	1959	300.00
NEWPORT			
❑ 7002	There'll Be No Goodbye/Okey Dokey Mama	1958	150.00
UNART			
❑ 2003	There'll Be No Goodbye/Okey Dokey Mama	1958	30.00

FIVE DEMARCO SISTERS, THE

45s

Number	Title (A Side/B Side)	Yr	NM
DECCA			
❑ 9-29299	Love Me/Just a Girl That Men Forget	1954	12.00
❑ 9-29388	Mumbo Is the Word/This Love of Mine	1954	12.00
❑ 9-29470	Dreamboat/Two Hearts, Two Kisses	1955	12.00
❑ 9-29470	Sailor Boys Have to Talk to Me in English/The Hot Barcarolle	1955	12.00
❑ 9-29758	Romance Me/Say You Care	1955	12.00
❑ 9-30181	Five Little Misses/I'm Through with Love	1957	10.00

FIVE DISCS, THE

Evidently these are all the same group or closely related. Also see DAWN (3).

45s

Number	Title (A Side/B Side)	Yr	NM
CALO			
❑ 202 *—Green label*	Adios/My Baby Loves Me	1961	150.00
❑ 202 *—White label*	Adios/My Baby Loves Me	1962	100.00
CHEER			
❑ 1000 *—Red label*	Never Let You Go/That Was the Time	1962	50.00
❑ 1000 *—Black label*	Never Let You Go/That Was the Time	1962	100.00
❑ 1000 [DJ] *—White label, promo only*	Never Let You Go/That Was the Time	1962	300.00
CRYSTAL BALL			
❑ 114	Mirror Mirror/Most of All I Wonder Why	1978	10.00
❑ 120	Unchained Melody/The Shrine of St. Cecelia	1978	10.00
❑ 136	Playing a Game of Love/Bells	1979	8.00
❑ 141	This Love of Ours/To the Fair	1979	8.00
DWAIN			
❑ 803	My Chinese Girl/Roses	1959	150.00
❑ 803 *—As "Mario and the Five Discs"*	My Chinese Girl/Roses	1959	200.00
❑ 6072	My Chinese Girl/Roses	1959	2000.
EMGE			
❑ 1004	I Remember/The World Is a Beautiful Place	1958	400.00
LAURIE			
❑ 3601	Rock and Roll Revival/Gypsy Women	1973	15.00
MELLO MOOD			
❑ 1002	My Chinese Girl/Roses	1964	15.00
PYRAMID			
❑ 166	Let's Fall in Love/That Was the Time	197?	6.00
RUST			
❑ 5027	I Remember/The World Is a Beautiful Place	1961	25.00
VIK			
❑ 0327	I Remember/The World Is a Beautiful Place	1958	80.00
YALE			
❑ 240	When Love Comes Knocking/Go-Go	1961	400.00
❑ 243/4	Come On Baby/I Don't Know What to Do	1961	400.00

Albums

Number	Title (A Side/B Side)	Yr	NM
CRYSTAL BALL			
❑ 119	Unchained	1978	15.00
MAGIC CARPET			
❑ 1002 *—Dark blue cover*	The Five Discs Sing Again	1991	20.00

FIVE DOLLARS, THE

45s

Number	Title (A Side/B Side)	Yr	NM
FORTUNE			
❑ 821	Harmony of Love/Doctor Baby	1955	100.00
❑ 826	So Strange/You Know I Can't Refuse	1956	100.00
❑ 830	I Will Wait/Hard Working Mama	1956	100.00
❑ 833	You Fool/How Do You Do the Bacon Fat	1957	80.00
❑ 854	That's the Way It Goes/My Baby-O	1960	50.00
FRATERNITY			
❑ 821	Harmony of Love/Doctor Baby	1958	40.00

FIVE DU-TONES, THE

45s

Number	Title (A Side/B Side)	Yr	NM
LOST-NITE			
❑ 196 *—Reissue of One-derful 4815*	Shake a Tail Feather/Divorce Court	196?	6.00
ONE-DERFUL			
❑ 4811	The Flea/Please Change Your Mind	1963	15.00
❑ 4814	Dry Your Eyes/Come Back Baby	1963	15.00
❑ 4815	Shake a Tail Feather/Divorce Court	1963	15.00
❑ 4818	The Gouster/Monkey See-Monkey Do	1963	15.00
❑ 4821	Nobody But (My Baby)/That's How I Love You	1964	15.00
❑ 4824	The Cool Bird/The Chicken Astronaut	1964	15.00
❑ 4828	Sweet Lips/Let Me Love You	1964	30.00
❑ 4831	We Want More/The Woodbine Twine	1965	15.00
❑ 4836	Mountain of Love/Outside the Record Hop	1965	15.00

FIVE ECHOES, THE

45s

Number	Title (A Side/B Side)	Yr	NM
SABRE			
❑ 102 *—Black vinyl*	Baby Come Back to Me/Lonely Mood	1953	600.00
❑ 102 *—Red vinyl*	Baby Come Back to Me/Lonely Mood	1953	1500.
❑ 105 *—Black vinyl*	So Lonesome/Broke	1954	600.00
❑ 105 *—Red vinyl*	So Lonesome/Broke	1954	1500.
VEE JAY			
❑ 129	I Really Do/Tell Me Baby	1954	300.00
❑ 156	Fool's Prayer/Tastee Freeze	1955	1000.
❑ 190	Soldier Boy/Pledging to You	1956	200.00

FIVE EMBERS, THE

45s

Number	Title (A Side/B Side)	Yr	NM
GEM			
❑ 224	Please Come Home/(B-side unknown)	1954	800.00

FIVE EMERALDS, THE

45s

Number	Title (A Side/B Side)	Yr	NM
S.R.C.			
❑ 106 *—Label spells out "Five" in group name, and "S-R-C" has hyphens in it*	I'll Beg/Let Me Take You Out Tonight	1953	1000.
❑ 106 *—Label uses numeral "5" in group name, and "S.R.C." has periods in it*	I'll Beg/Let Me Take You Out Tonight	1953	1000.
❑ 107	Darling/Pleasure Me	1954	1200.

FIVE EMPREES, THE

45s

Number	Title (A Side/B Side)	Yr	NM
FREEPORT			
❑ 1001	Little Miss Sad/Hey Lover	1965	12.00
❑ 1001 *—Originally released as "The Five Empressions"*	Little Miss Sad/Hey Lover	1965	25.00
❑ 1002	Hey Baby/Why	1965	12.00
❑ 1007	Little Miss Happiness/Over the Mountain	1966	12.00
❑ 1009	Pretty Face (Part 1)/Pretty Face (Part 2)	1966	12.00
❑ 1010	Johnny B. Goode/Hey Lover	1966	12.00

Number	Title (A Side/B Side)	Yr	NM
SMASH			
❑ 2065	Gone from My Mind/ Hey Diddle Diddle	1966	10.00
Albums			
FREEPORT			
❑ 3001 [M]	The Five Emprees	1965	150.00
❑ 3001 [M]	Little Miss Sad	1966	150.00
—Same LP, new title			
❑ 3001 [S]	The Five Emprees	1965	100.00
❑ 4001 [S]	Little Miss Sad	1966	100.00
—Same LP, new title			

FIVE EMPRESSIONS, THE
See THE FIVE EMPREES.

FIVE FLIGHTS UP

Number	Title (A Side/B Side)	Yr	NM
45s			
T-A			
❑ 202	Do What You Wanna Do/ Black Cat	1970	8.00
❑ 207	After the Feeling Is Gone/ Where Are You Going, Girl?	1970	8.00
❑ 212	Like Monday Follows Sunday/ California Girl	1971	8.00

FIVE FORTUNES, THE

Number	Title (A Side/B Side)	Yr	NM
45s			
RANSOM			
❑ 103	You Are My Only Love/ Time Out for Love	1958	1000.

FIVE JETS, THE

Number	Title (A Side/B Side)	Yr	NM
45s			
DELUXE			
❑ 6018	I Am in Love/Not a Hand to Shake	1953	150.00
❑ 6053	I'm Stuck/I Want a Woman	1954	150.00
❑ 6058	Tell Me You're Mine/Give In	1954	200.00
❑ 6064	Crazy Chicken/Everybody Do the Chicken	1954	60.00
❑ 6071	Down Slow/Please Love Me Baby	1955	120.00
KING			
❑ 6058	Tell Me You're Mine/Give In	1966	20.00

FIVE KEYS, THE

Number	Title (A Side/B Side)	Yr	NM
45s			
ALADDIN			
❑ 3085	With a Broken Heart/Too Late	1951	—
—Unconfirmed on 45 rpm			
❑ 3099	The Glory of Love/ Hucklebuck with Jimmy	1951	1000.
❑ 3113	It's Christmas Time/ Old Mac Donald	1951	1000.
❑ 3118	Yes Sir That's My Baby/Old Mac Donald	1952	1000.
❑ 3119	Darling/Goin' Downtown	1952	1000.
❑ 3127	Red Sails in the Sunset/ Be Anything, But Be Mine	1952	6000.
—VG 3000; VG+ 4500			
❑ 3131	How Long/Mistakes	1952	1200.
❑ 3136	Hold Me/I Hadn't Anyone Till You	1952	800.00
❑ 3158	I Cried for You/Serve Another Round	1953	900.00
❑ 3167	Can't Keep From Crying/ Come Go My Bail, Louise	1953	800.00
❑ 3175	There Ought to Be a Law/ Mama (Your Daughter Told a Lie on Me)	1953	800.00
❑ 3182	I'll Always Be in Love with You/ Rocking and Crying Blues	1953	800.00
❑ 3190	These Foolish Things/ Lonesome Old Story	1953	4000.
❑ 3204	Teardrops in Your Eyes/ I'm So High	1953	800.00
❑ 3214	My Saddest Hour/Oh! Babe!	1953	800.00
❑ 3228	Someday Sweetheart/ Love My Loving	1954	800.00
❑ 3245	Deep in My Heart/How Do You Expect Me to Get It	1954	800.00
❑ 3263	My Love/Why, Oh Why	1954	300.00
❑ 3312	Story of Love/ Serve Another Round	1956	300.00
❑ S7-19768	Every Heart Is Home at Christmas/Frosty the Snowman	1997	5.00
—B-side by Fats Domino on The Right Stuff			
BANGAR			
❑ 661	Run-Around/I Tell My Heart	1965	15.00
CAPITOL			
❑ F-2945	Ling, Ting, Tong/I'm Alone	1954	40.00
❑ F-3032	Close Your Eyes/Doggone It, You Did It	1955	40.00
❑ F-3127	The Verdict/Me Make Um Pow Wow	1955	40.00
❑ F-3185	Don't You Know I Love You/ I Wish I'd Never Learned to Read	1955	40.00
❑ F-3267	'Cause You're My Lover/ Gee Whittakers	1955	40.00
❑ F-3318	You Broke the Rules of Love/ What Goes On	1956	40.00
❑ F-3392	She's the Most/I Dreamt I Dwelt in Heaven	1956	40.00
—Regular large hole			
❑ F-3392	She's the Most/I Dreamt I Dwelt in Heaven	1956	70.00
—Small hole			
❑ F-3455	My Pigeon's Gone/ Peace and Love	1956	40.00
❑ F-3502	Out of Sight, Out of Mind/ That's Right	1956	30.00
❑ F-3597	Wisdom of a Fool/Now Don't That Prove I Love You	1956	30.00
❑ F-3660	Tiger Lily/Let There Be You	1957	25.00
❑ F-3710	Four Walls/It's a Groove	1957	25.00
❑ F-3738	This I Promise You/The Blues Don't Care	1957	25.00
❑ F-3786	Boom Boom/Face of An Angel	1957	25.00
❑ F-3830	Do Anything/It's a Cryin' Shame	1957	25.00
❑ F-3861	From Me to You/Whippety Whirl	1957	25.00
❑ F-3948	You're for Me/With All My Love	1958	25.00
❑ F-4009	Emily Please/Handy Andy	1958	25.00
❑ F-4092	One Great Love/ Really-O, Truly-O	1958	25.00
❑ 4828	Out of Sight, Out of Mind/ From the Bottom of My Heart	1962	20.00
CLASSIC ARTISTS			
❑ 115	I Want You For Christmas/ Express Yourself Back Home	1989	5.00
—As "Rudy West and the Five Keys"			
GROOVE			
❑ 0031	I'll Follow You/Lawdy Miss Mary	1954	4000.
—There is some debate about whether this record actually exists on 45.. VG 2000; VG+ 3000			
INFERNO			
❑ 4500	Hey Girl/No Matter	1967	20.00
KING			
❑ 5251	I Took Your Love for a Toy/Ziggus	1959	30.00
❑ 5273	Dancing Senorita/Dream On	1959	20.00
❑ 5302	How Can I Forget You/ I Burned Your Letter	1960	20.00
❑ 5330	Gonna Be Too Late/Rosetta	1960	20.00
❑ 5358	I Didn't Know/No, Says My Heart	1960	20.00
❑ 5398	Bimbo/Valley of Love	1960	20.00
❑ 5446	You Broke the Only Heart/That's What You're Doing to Me	1961	20.00
❑ 5496	Do Something for Me/ Stop Your Crying	1961	20.00
❑ 5877	I'll Never Stop Loving You/ I Can't Escape from You	1964	12.00
LIBERTY			
❑ 1394	It's Christmas Time/It's Christmas	1980	8.00
—B-side by Marvin and Johnny			
OWL			
❑ 321	A Dreamer/Your Teeth and Your Tongue	1973	8.00
SEG-WAY			
❑ 1008	Out of Sight, Out of Mind /You're the One	1962	15.00
UNITED ARTISTS			
❑ 0150	The Glory of Love/My Saddest Hour	1973	4.00
—"Silver Spotlight Series" reissue			
7-Inch Extended Plays			
CAPITOL			
❑ EAP 1-572	Ling Ting Tong/I'm Alone// Close Your Eyes/Doggone It, You Did It	1955	100.00
❑ EAP 1-572 [PS]	The Five Keys	1955	100.00
❑ EAP 1-828	(contents unknown)	1957	100.00
❑ EAP 1-828 [PS]	The Five Keys On Stage! Vol. 1	1957	100.00
—On cover, the far left singer's "offending" thumb is airbrushed out			
❑ EAP 1-828 [PS]	The Five Keys On Stage! Vol. 1	1957	150.00
—On cover, the far left singer has his thumb sticking out (inadvertently?) in a phallic way			
❑ EAP 2-828	(contents unknown)	1957	100.00
❑ EAP 2-828 [PS]	The Five Keys On Stage! Vol. 2	1957	100.00
—On cover, the far left singer's "offending" thumb is airbrushed out			
❑ EAP 2-828 [PS]	The Five Keys On Stage! Vol. 2	1957	150.00
—On cover, the far left singer has his thumb sticking out (inadvertently?) in a phallic way			
❑ EAP 3-828	C'est La Vie/Dream//Let There Be You/All I Need Is You	1957	100.00
❑ EAP 3-828 [PS]	The Five Keys On Stage! Vol. 3	1957	100.00
—On cover, the far left singer's "offending" thumb is airbrushed out			
❑ EAP 3-828 [PS]	The Five Keys On Stage! Vol. 3	1957	150.00
—On cover, the far left singer has his thumb sticking out (inadvertently?) in a phallic way			
Albums			
ALADDIN			
❑ LP-806 [M]	The Best of the Five Keys	1956	2000.
—Copies of Aladdin 806 entitled "On the Town" are bootlegs made in the 1970s; VG value 1000; VG+ value 1500			
CAPITOL			
❑ T 828 [M]	The Five Keys On Stage!	1957	300.00
—On cover, the far left singer has his thumb sticking out (inadvertently?) in a phallic way			
❑ T 828 [M]	The Five Keys On Stage!	1957	500.00
—On cover, the far left singer's "offending" thumb is airbrushed out			
❑ M-1769	The Fantastic Five Keys	1977	20.00
—Reissue with new prefix			
❑ T 1769 [M]	The Fantastic Five Keys	1962	300.00
HARLEM HIT PARADE			
❑ 5004	The Five Keys	1972	15.00
KING			
❑ 688 [M]	The Five Keys	1960	800.00
❑ 692 [M]	Rhythm and Blues Hits, Past and Present	1960	600.00
❑ 5013	14 Hits	1978	12.00
SCORE			
❑ LP-4003 [M]	The Five Keys On the Town	1957	800.00
—Reissue of Aladdin 806.			

FIVE KIDS, THE

Number	Title (A Side/B Side)	Yr	NM
45s			
MAXWELL			
❑ 101	Carolyn/Oh Baby	1955	3000.
—VG 1000; VG+ 2000			

FIVE LYRICS, THE

Number	Title (A Side/B Side)	Yr	NM
45s			
MUSIC CITY			
❑ 799	I'm Traveling Light/ My Honeysweet Pea	1956	1500.

FIVE MAN ELECTRICAL BAND

Number	Title (A Side/B Side)	Yr	NM
45s			
CAPITOL			
❑ 2368	It Never Rains on Maple Lane/ Private Train	1968	6.00
❑ 2517	Baby/Lovin' Look	1969	6.00
❑ 2562	Sunrise to Sunset/ Little Bit of Love	1969	6.00
❑ 2628	Riverboat/Good	1969	6.00
LION			
❑ 112	Coming of Age/The Devil and Miss Lucy	1972	5.00
❑ 127	Money Back Guarantee/ Find the One	1972	5.00
❑ 149	I'm a Stranger Here/Doin' The Best We Can Rag	1973	5.00
❑ 160	Sweet Paradise/Baby Wanna Boogie	1973	5.00
LIONEL			
❑ 3213	Signs/Hello Melinda Goodbye	1971	6.00
—Lists no A and B sides and contains an edited version (3:20) of "Signs"			
❑ 3213	Signs/Hello Melinda Goodbye	1971	8.00
—Lists "Hello Melinda Goodbye" as the A-side and contains the full-length version of "Signs"			
❑ 3220	Absolutely Right/Butterfly	1971	5.00
❑ 3224	Friends and Family/Julianna	1971	5.00
MGM			
❑ 14149	Moonshine/Forever Together	1970	6.00
❑ 14182 [DJ]	Hello Melinda Goodbye/Signs	1970	10.00
—Evidently only exists as a promo			
POLYDOR			
❑ 14221	Werewolf/Country Angel	1974	4.00
❑ 14263	Johnnie Get a Gun/And the World Goes Round	1974	6.00
Albums			
CAPITOL			
❑ ST-165	Five Man Electrical Band	1969	20.00
LION			
❑ LN-1009	Sweet Paradise	1973	20.00
LIONEL			
❑ LRS-1100	Good-Byes & Butterflies	1970	30.00
❑ LRS-1101	Coming of Age	1971	20.00
MGM			
❑ SE-4725	Good-Byes & Butterflies	1970	50.00
PICKWICK			
❑ SPC-3289	Five Man Electrical Band	1973	10.00
—Reissue of Capitol material			

FIVE NOTES, THE

Number	Title (A Side/B Side)	Yr	NM
45s			
CHESS			
❑ 1614	Show Me the Way/ Park Your Lover	1955	150.00

Except when noted otherwise, VG = 25% of NM, and VG+ = 50% of NM. (Example: VG = $2.00, VG+ = $4.00 and NM = $8.00.)

Number	Title (A Side/B Side)	Yr	NM
JEN D			
❑ 4185	You Are So Beautiful/ Broken Hearted Baby	1955	500.00
JOSIE			
❑ 784	You Are So Beautiful/ Broken Hearted Baby	1955	80.00

FIVE PLAYBOYS, THE

Number	Title (A Side/B Side)	Yr	NM
45s			
DOT			
❑ 15605	When We Were Young/ Pages of My Scrapbook	1957	25.00
FEE BEE			
❑ 213	When We Were Young/ Pages of My Scrapbook	1958	50.00
❑ 232	Angel Mine/She's My Baby	1959	100.00
MERCURY			
❑ 71269	Time Will Allow/Why Be a Fool	1958	25.00
PETITE			
❑ 504	She's My Baby/Mr. Echo	1959	40.00

FIVE ROVERS, THE

Number	Title (A Side/B Side)	Yr	NM
45s			
MUSIC CITY			
❑ 798	Down to the Sea/Change Your Mind	1956	120.00

FIVE ROYALES, THE

Also includes "The Five Royals" and "The '5' Royales."

Number	Title (A Side/B Side)	Yr	NM
45s			
ABC-PARAMOUNT			
❑ 10348	Catch That Teardrop/Goof Ball	1962	10.00
❑ 10368	What's In Your Heart/I Want It Like That	1962	10.00
APOLLO			
❑ 441	Courage to Love/You Know I Know	1952	100.00
—Black vinyl			
❑ 441	Courage to Love/You Know I Know	1952	400.00
—Red vinyl			
❑ 443	Baby Don't Do It/Take All of Me	1952	100.00
—Black vinyl			
❑ 443	Baby Don't Do It/Take All of Me	1952	400.00
—Red vinyl			
❑ 446	Help Me, Somebody/ Crazy, Crazy, Crazy	1953	100.00
❑ 448	Too Much Lovin' (Much Too Much)/Laundromat Blues	1953	120.00
❑ 449	I Want to Thank You/All Righty	1953	80.00
❑ 452	I Do/Good Things	1954	80.00
❑ 454	Cry Some More/I Like It Like That	1954	80.00
❑ 458	What's That/Let Me Come Back Home	1954	70.00
❑ 467	With All Your Heart/6 O'Clock in the Morning	1955	70.00
HOME OF THE BLUES			
❑ 112	Please, Please, Please/ I Got to Know	1960	15.00
❑ 218	If You Don't Need Me/ I'm Gonna Tell Them	1961	15.00
❑ 232	Take Me With You Baby/ Not Going to Cry	1961	15.00
❑ 234	Nuch in Need/They Don't Know	1962	15.00
❑ 243	Catch That Teardrop/Goof Ball	1962	700.00
KING			
❑ 4740	I'm Gonna Run It Down/ Behave Yourself	1954	80.00
❑ 4744	Monkey Hips and Rice/ Devil with the Rest	1954	80.00
❑ 4762	School Girl/One Mistake	1955	80.00
❑ 4770	Every Dog Has His Day/You Didn't Learn It at Home	1955	80.00
❑ 4785	How I Wonder/Mohawk Squaw	1955	80.00
❑ 4806	I Need Your Lovin'/ When I Get Like This	1955	50.00
❑ 4819	Women About to Make Me Go Crazy/Do Unto You	1955	50.00
❑ 4830	I Ain't Gettin' Caught/Someone Made You for Me	1955	50.00
❑ 4869	When You Walked Through the Door/Right Around the Corner	1956	50.00
❑ 4901	I Could Love You/ My Wants for Love	1956	50.00
❑ 4952	Get Something Out of It/ Come On and Save Me	1956	50.00
❑ 4973	Just As I Am/Mine Forevermore	1956	50.00
❑ 5032	Tears of Joy/Thirty Second Lover	1957	40.00
❑ 5053	Think/I'd Better Make a Move	1957	40.00
❑ 5082	Messin' Up/Say It	1957	40.00
❑ 5098	Dedicated to the One I Love/ Don't Be Ashamed	1958	40.00
❑ 5131	Do the Cha Cha Cherry/ The Feeling Is Real	1958	25.00
❑ 5141	Tell the Truth/Double or Nothing	1958	25.00
❑ 5153	The Slummer the Slum/ Don't Let It Be in Vain	1958	25.00
❑ 5162	Your Only Love/The Real Thing	1958	25.00
❑ 5191	Miracle of Love/I Know It's Hard, But It's Fair	1959	25.00
❑ 5237	Tell Me You Care/Wonder Where Your Love Has Gone	1959	25.00
❑ 5266	My Sugar Sugar/It Hurts Inside	1959	25.00
❑ 5329	Don't Give No More Than You Can Take/I'm with You	1960	25.00
❑ 5357	Why/Within My Heart	1960	25.00
❑ 5453	Dedicated to the One I Love/ Miracle of Love	1961	15.00
❑ 5756	Dedicated to the One I Love/ Tears of Joy	1963	15.00
❑ 5892	I Wonder Where Your Love Has Gone/I Need Your Lovin' Baby	1964	15.00
—The Five Royals			
SMASH			
❑ 1936	Baby Don't Do It/I Like It Like That	1964	10.00
❑ 1963	Never Turn Your Back/Faith	1965	10.00
TODD			
❑ 1086	I'm Standing in the Shadows/ Doin' Everything	1963	10.00
❑ 1088	Baby Don't Do It/There's Somebody Over There	1963	10.00
VEE JAY			
❑ 412	Much in Need/They Don't Know	1961	15.00
❑ 431	Help Me Somebody/Talk About My Woman	1962	15.00
Albums			
APOLLO			
❑ LP-488 [M]	The Rockin' 5 Royales	1956	1000.
—Yellow label			
❑ LP-488 [M]	The Rockin' 5 Royales	1956	2000.
—Green label; VG value 1000; VG+ value 1500			
❑ LP-488 [M]	The Rockin' 5 Royales	1956	4000.
—Purple label; VG value 2000; VG+ value 3000			
KING			
❑ 580 [M]	Dedicated to You	1957	500.00
❑ 616 [M]	The 5 Royales Sing for You	1959	400.00
❑ 678 [M]	The Five Royales	1960	250.00
❑ 955 [M]	24 All Time Hits	1966	100.00
❑ 5014	17 Hits	197?	12.00

FIVE SATINS, THE

Also see FRED PARRIS; THE WILDWOODS.

Number	Title (A Side/B Side)	Yr	NM
45s			
BUDDAH			
❑ 477	Everybody Stand and Clap Your Hands/Hey There Pretty Lady	1975	5.00
—As "Black Satin"			
CANDELITE			
❑ 411	She's Gone (With the Wind)/ Somewhere a Voice Is Calling	1974	6.00
CHANCELLOR			
❑ 1110	The Masquerade Is Over/ Raining in My Heart	1962	20.00
❑ 1121	Do You Remember/Downtown	1962	20.00
CUB			
❑ 9071	Your Memory/I Didn't Know	1960	25.00
❑ 9077	These Foolish Things/ A Beggar with a Dream	1960	25.00
❑ 9090	Golden Earrings/Can I Come Over Tonight	1961	25.00
ELEKTRA			
❑ 47411	Memories of Days Gone By Medley/Loving You (Would Be the Sweetest Thing)	1982	20.00
—As "Fred Parris and the Five Satins"			
❑ 69888	Didn't I (Blow Your Mind)/ Loving You (Would Be the Sweetest Thing)	1982	5.00
❑ 69938	Breaking Up/Loving You (Would Be the Sweetest Thing)	1982	5.00
❑ 69984	I'll Be Seeing You/Loving You (Would Be the Sweetest Thing)	1982	5.00
EMBER			
❑ 1005	I'll Remember (In the Still of the Nite)/The Jones Girl	1956	30.00
—Red label			
❑ 1005	In the Still of the Nite/ The Jones Girl	1956	30.00
—Red label; has "E-1005" in the trail-off vinyl			
❑ 1005	In the Still of the Nite/ The Jones Girl	1956	50.00
—Red label; has "E-2105-45" in the trail-off vinyl			
❑ 1005	In the Still of the Nite/ The Jones Girl	1956	200.00
—Red label; has "6106A" in the trail-off vinyl			
❑ 1005	I'll Remember (In the Still of the Nite)/The Jones Girl	1959	30.00
—Multi-color "logs" label; no "Special Demand Release"			
❑ 1005	In the Still of the Nite/ The Jones Girl	1959	40.00
—Multi-color "logs" label with original A-side title			
❑ 1005	I'll Remember (In the Still of the Nite)/The Jones Girl	1959	50.00
—Multi-color "logs" label; reads "Special Demand Release"			
❑ 1005	In the Still of the Night "I'll Remember"/The Jones Girl	1961	30.00
—Black label, white logo and red flames at left; A-side title revised yet again			
❑ 1008	Weeping Willow/Wonderful Girl	1956	40.00
❑ 1014	Our Love Is Forever/ Oh Happy Day	1957	40.00
❑ 1019	To the Aisle/Wish I Had My Baby	1957	40.00
—Red label			
❑ 1019	To the Aisle/Wish I Had My Baby	1960	30.00
—Multi-color "logs" label			
❑ 1019	To the Aisle/Wish I Had My Baby	1961	20.00
—Black label			
❑ 1025	Our Anniversary/Pretty Baby	1957	20.00
—Black label			
❑ 1025	Our Anniversary/Pretty Baby	1957	40.00
—Red label			
❑ 1028	A Million to One/Love with No Love in Return	1957	40.00
❑ 1038	A Night to Remember/ Senorita Lolita	1958	30.00
—As "Fred Parris and the Satins"			
❑ 1056	Shadows/Toni My Love	1959	30.00
❑ 1061	I'll Be Seeing You/ A Night Like This	1960	30.00
❑ 1066	Candlelight/The Time	1960	25.00
❑ 1070	Wishing Ring/Tell Me Dear	1961	25.00
FIRST			
❑ 104	When Your Love Comes Along/ Skippity Doo	1959	25.00
—Green label			
❑ 104	When Your Love Comes Along/ Skippity Doo	1959	40.00
—Orange label			
GLENVILLE MUSIC			
❑ 106	(I'll Remember) In the Still of the Night/The Jones Girl	196?	8.00
—Reissue			
KIRSHNER			
❑ 4251	Very Precious Oldies/ You Are Love	1974	10.00
❑ 4252	Two Different Worlds/Love Is Such a Beautiful Thing	1974	10.00
KLIK			
❑ 1020	I Love You So/Story to You	1973	10.00
LANA			
❑ 106	In the Still of the Nite/ The Jones Girl	196?	8.00
—Oldies reissue			
LOST-NITE			
❑ 151	All Mine/Rose Mary	196?	6.00
—Reissue			
❑ 202	To the Aisle/Just to Be Near You	196?	5.00
—Reissue			
❑ 411	In the Still of the Nite/ The Jones Girl	197?	5.00
—Reissue			
❑ 423	Our Love Is Forever/ Oh Happy Day	197?	5.00
—Reissue			
❑ 426	To the Aisle/Wish I Had My Baby	197?	5.00
—Reissue			
❑ 428	Our Anniversary/Pretty Baby	197?	5.00
—Reissue			
❑ 431	Weeping Willow/Wonderful Girl	197?	5.00
—Reissue			
❑ 434	Shadows/Toni My Love	197?	5.00
—Reissue			
MAMA SADIE			
❑ 1001	In the Still of the Night "67"/Heck No (Instrumental)	1967	12.00
MUSICTONE			
❑ 1108	To the Aisle/Just to Be Near You	1961	25.00
NIGHTRAIN			
❑ 901	All Mine/The Voice	1970	10.00
RCA			
❑ 6989-7-R	In the Still of the Night/Yes	1988	3.00
—B-side by Merry Clayton			
RCA VICTOR			
❑ 74-0478	Summer in New York/Dark at the Top of My Heart	1971	10.00
ROULETTE			
❑ 4563	Ain't Gonna Cry/You Can Count on Me	1964	10.00

Number	Title (A Side/B Side)	Yr	NM
SAMMY			
❑ 103	No One Knows/Musical Chairs	196?	30.00
SIGNATURE			
❑ 001	Everybody's Got a Home But Me/Heartache	1990	5.00
STANDORD			
❑ 100	All Mine/Rose Mary	1956	700.00
—Red label			
❑ 100	All Mine/Rose Mary	1962	200.00
—Maroon label			
❑ 200	In the Still of the Nite/ The Jones Girl	1956	900.00
❑ 200	In the Still of the Nite/ The Jones Girl	1956	2000.
—With "Produced by Martin Kuegell" credit. VG 1000; VG+ 1500			
TIME MACHINE			
❑ 570	Wonder Why/No One Knows	1962	8.00
❑ 571	The Masquerade Is Over/ Lonely Hearts	1962	8.00
TIMES SQUARE			
❑ 4	All Mine/Rose Mary	1962	20.00
—Blue vinyl			
❑ 21	Paradise on Earth/ Monkey Business	1963	20.00
❑ 94	Paradise on Earth/ Monkey Business	1964	15.00
UNITED ARTISTS			
❑ 368	On a Lover's Island/Till the End	1961	25.00
WARNER BROS.			
❑ 5367	Remember Me/Kangaroo	1963	12.00
X-BAT			
❑ 1000	When the Swallows Come Back to Capistrano/ Dance Girl Dance	1995	5.00
—Red vinyl			
❑ 1000 [PS]	When the Swallows Come Back to Capistrano/ Dance Girl Dance	1995	5.00

7-Inch Extended Plays

Number	Title (A Side/B Side)	Yr	NM
EMBER			
❑ EEP-100	I'll Remember/The Jones Girl// Wonderful Girl/Pretty Baby	1957	200.00
❑ EEP-100 [PS]	The Five Satins Sing (Vol. 1)	1957	200.00
❑ EEP-101	To the Aisle/Sugar//Our Love Is Forever/Weeping Willow	1957	200.00
❑ EEP-101 [PS]	The Five Satins Sing (Vol. 2)	1957	200.00
❑ EEP-102	Our Anniversary/I'll Get Along/ /Wish I Had My Baby/ Moonlight and I	1957	200.00
❑ EEP-102 [PS]	The Five Satins Sing (Vol. 3)	1957	200.00

Albums

Number	Title (A Side/B Side)	Yr	NM
BUDDAH			
❑ BDS-5654	Black Satin	1976	15.00
—As "Black Satin"			
CELEBRITY SHOWCASE			
❑ JB-7671	The Best of the Five Satins	1970	20.00
COLLECTABLES			
❑ COL-5017	The Five Satins Sing Their Greatest Hits	198?	10.00
ELEKTRA			
❑ 60152	Fred Parris and the Satins	1982	20.00
EMBER			
❑ ELP-100 [M]	The Five Satins Sing	1957	600.00
—Red label; group pictured on front cover; black vinyl			
❑ ELP-100 [M]	The Five Satins Sing	1957	2000.
—Red label; group pictured on front cover; blue vinyl; VG value 1000; VG+ value 1500			
❑ ELP-100 [M]	The Five Satins Sing	1959	200.00
—Mostly white "logs" label; no picture on cover			
❑ ELP-100 [M]	The Five Satins Sing	1959	300.00
—Mostly white "logs" label; group pictured on front cover			
❑ ELP-100 [M]	The Five Satins Sing	1961	100.00
—Black label; no picture on cover			
❑ ELP-401 [M]	The Five Satins Encore	1960	200.00
—Mostly white "logs" label			
❑ ELP-401 [M]	The Five Satins Encore	1961	100.00
—Black label			
LOST-NITE			
❑ LLP-8 [10]	The Five Satins	1981	10.00
—Red vinyl			
❑ LLP-9 [10]	The Five Satins	1981	10.00
—Red vinyl			
MOUNT VERNON			
❑ 108	The Five Satins Sing	196?	30.00
RELIC			
❑ 5008	The Five Satins' Greatest Hits (1956-1959), Vol. 1	198?	10.00
❑ 5013	The Five Satins' Greatest Hits (1956-1959), Vol. 2	198?	10.00
❑ 5024	The Five Satins' Greatest Hits (1956-1959), Vol. 3	198?	10.00

FIVE SCALDERS, THE

45s

Number	Title (A Side/B Side)	Yr	NM
DRUMMOND			
❑ 3000	If Only You Were Mine/ There Will Come a Time	1956	1000.
❑ 3001	Girl Friend/Willow Blues	1956	1000.
—Maroon label			
❑ 3001	Girl Friend/Willow Blues	1956	1500.
—Blue label			
SUGAR HILL			
❑ 3000	If Only You Were Mine/ There Will Come a Time	1956	2000.

FIVE SECRETS, THE

45s

Number	Title (A Side/B Side)	Yr	NM
DECCA			
❑ 30350	See You Next Year/Queen Bee	1957	40.00
—As "The Secrets"			
❑ 30350	See You Next Year/Queen Bee	1957	80.00

FIVE SHARKS, THE

45s

Number	Title (A Side/B Side)	Yr	NM
AMBER			
❑ 852	The Lion Sleeps Tonight/ Land of 1000 Dances	1966	10.00
LOST-NITE			
❑ 404	Stormy Weather/If You Love Me	197?	6.00
—Reissue			
OLD TIMER			
❑ 604	Gloria/Flames	1964	20.00
❑ 605	Stand By Me/I'll Never Let You Go	1964	16.00
—Blue vinyl			
❑ 605	Stand By Me/I'll Never Let You Go	1964	20.00
—Gold vinyl			
❑ 611	Gloria/Flames	1965	15.00
—Black vinyl			
❑ 611	Gloria/Flames	1965	20.00
—Red vinyl			
RELIC			
❑ 525	Stormy Weather (2:45)/ If You Love Me	1965	10.00
SIAMESE			
❑ 404	Gloria/Flames	1965	12.00
TIMES SQUARE			
❑ 35	Stormy Weather (2:45)/ If You Love Me	1964	30.00
❑ 35	Stormy Weather (3:45)/ If You Love Me	1964	40.00
—Black vinyl			
❑ 35	Stormy Weather (3:45)/ If You Love Me	1964	60.00
—Blue vinyl			

FIVE SHARPS, THE (1)

45s

Number	Title (A Side/B Side)	Yr	NM
BIM BAM BOOM			
❑ 103	Stormy Weather/Sleepy Cowboy	1972	8.00
—Reissue mastered off the cracked Jubilee 78 (see below); the original master has long since disappeared			
JUBILEE			
❑ 5104	Stormy Weather/Sleepy Cowboy	1952	—
—Unknown on 45 RPM (3 known copies, one of which is cracked, exist on 78); all known 45s are counterfeits. Known counterfeits do not match the proper typeface of the era for the label, and the blue labels are too bright compared to authentic Jubilee 45s of the early 1950s. If a legitimate 45 would be confirmed, it could sell for more than any record ever made!			

FIVE SHARPS, THE (2)

A completely different group than (1), they were assembled by Jubilee to record a new version of "Stormy Weather" in the midst of the hubbub about the first Five Sharps version. (For the full story, see The Complete Book of Doo-Wop by Gribin and Schiff, Krause Publications, 2000.)

45s

Number	Title (A Side/B Side)	Yr	NM
JUBILEE			
❑ 5478	Stormy Weather/ Mammy Jammy	1964	12.00

FIVE SHITS

45s

Number	Title (A Side/B Side)	Yr	NM
CHANCE			
❑ 1163	My Pretty Little Girl/ Stormy Weather	1974	20.00
—This was not released in the 1950s; this used the classic 1950s label, either as a lark or an attempt to fool gullible collectors. (Come on; would a group called the Five Shits ever made it onto record in the 1950s?)			
LOST-CAUSE			
❑ 100	Dreaming of You/Let Me Tell You	1974	20.00
—Blue vinyl			

FIVE STAIRSTEPS, THE

Includes records by "Five Stairsteps and Cubie" and "Stairsteps."

45s

Number	Title (A Side/B Side)	Yr	NM
BUDDAH			
❑ 20	Something's Missing/ Tell Me Who	1967	8.00
—As "Five Stairsteps and Cubie"			
❑ 20 [PS]	Something's Missing/ Tell Me Who	1967	15.00
❑ 26	A Million to One/You Make Me So Mad	1968	8.00
—As "Five Stairsteps and Cubie"			
❑ 26 [PS]	A Million to One/You Make Me So Mad	1968	15.00
❑ 35	The Shadow of Your Love/ Bad News	1968	8.00
❑ 165	O-o-h Child/Who Do You Belong To	1970	6.00
❑ 165	Dear Prudence/O-o-h Child	1970	8.00
❑ 188	Because I Love You/ America Standing	1970	5.00
❑ 213	Didn't It Look So Easy/ Peace Is Gonna Come	1971	5.00
—Starting with the above, as "Stairsteps"			
❑ 222	Snow/Look Out	1971	5.00
❑ 277	I Love You-Stop/I Feel a Song (In My Heart Again)	1972	5.00
❑ 291	Hush Child/The Easy Way	1972	5.00
❑ 320	Every Single Way/ Two Weeks' Notice	1972	5.00
CURTOM			
❑ 1931	Don't Change Your Love/ New Dance Craze	1968	6.00
—Curtom releases as "Five Stairsteps and Cubie"			
❑ 1933	I Made a Mistake/ Stay Close to Me	1968	6.00
❑ 1936	Baby Make Me Feel So Good/ Little Young Lover	1969	6.00
❑ 1944	Madame Mary/Little Boy Blue	1969	6.00
❑ 1945	We Must Be in Love/ Little Young Lover	1969	6.00
DARK HORSE			
❑ 10005	From Us to You/Time	1975	5.00
❑ 10005 [PS]	From Us to You/Time	1975	6.00
❑ 10009	Tell Me Why/Salaam	1976	5.00
WINDY "C"			
❑ 601	You Waited Too Long/ Don't Waste Your Time	1966	10.00
❑ 602	World of Fantasy/Playgirl's Love	1966	10.00
❑ 603	Come Back/You Don't Love Me	1966	10.00
❑ 604	Danger, She's a Stranger/ Behind Curtains	1967	10.00
❑ 605	Ain't Gonna Rest (Till I Get You)/You Can't See	1967	10.00
❑ 607	Oooh, Baby Baby/The Girl I Love	1967	10.00
❑ 608	The Touch of You/ Change of Face	1967	10.00

Albums

Number	Title (A Side/B Side)	Yr	NM
BUDDAH			
❑ BDS-5008	Our Family Portrait	1967	20.00
❑ BDS-5061	Stairsteps	1970	15.00
—As "Stairsteps"			
❑ BDS-5068	Step by Step by Step	1970	15.00
—As "Stairsteps"			
COLLECTABLES			
❑ COL-5023	Greatest Hits	1985	10.00
CURTOM			
❑ 8002	Love's Happening	1969	20.00
WINDY C			
❑ 6000 [M]	The Five Stairsteps	1967	25.00
❑ S-6000 [S]	The Five Stairsteps	1967	25.00

FIVE STARS, THE (1)

45s

Number	Title (A Side/B Side)	Yr	NM
ABC-PARAMOUNT			
❑ 9911	Pickin' on the Wrong Chicken/ Dreaming	1958	25.00
HUNT			
❑ 318	Pickin' on the Wrong Chicken/ Dreaming	1959	20.00
NOTE			
❑ 10011	Pickin' on the Wrong Chicken/ Dreaming	1958	30.00
❑ 10016	My Paradise/Friction	1958	40.00
❑ 10031	Am I Wasting My Time/ Gamblin' Man	1959	30.00

FIVE STARS, THE (2)

45s

Number	Title (A Side/B Side)	Yr	NM
SHOW TIME			
❑ 1102	Where Did Caledonia Go?/ Walkin' An' Talkin'	1954	250.00

Except when noted otherwise, VG = 25% of NM, and VG+ = 50% of NM. (Example: VG = $2.00, VG+ = $4.00 and NM = $8.00.)

FIVE STARS, THE (U)
Many of these are probably group (1); the Treat release may be group (2).

Number	Title (A Side/B Side)	Yr	NM
45s			
ATCO			
❑ 6065	Take Five/Humpty Dump	1956	30.00
BLUES BOYS KINGDOM			
❑ 106	So Lonely, Baby/Hey Juanita	1957	200.00
COLUMBIA			
❑ 4-42056	Baby Baby/Blabber Mouth	1961	60.00
END			
❑ 1028	Baby Baby/Blabber Mouth	1958	80.00
KERNEL			
❑ 3195	Atom Bomb Baby/You Sweet Little Thing	1957	100.00
MARK-X			
❑ 7006	Dead Wrong/Ooh Shucks	1957	100.00
TREAT			
❑ 505	Let's Fall in Love/We Danced in the Moonlight	1955	2000.

FIVE SUPERIORS, THE

Number	Title (A Side/B Side)	Yr	NM
45s			
GARPAX			
❑ 44170	There's a Fool Born Every Day/Big Shot	1962	150.00

FIVE SWANS, THE

Number	Title (A Side/B Side)	Yr	NM
45s			
MUSIC CITY			
❑ 795	Little Girl of My Dreams/Little Tipa Tins	1956	300.00

5000 VOLTS

Number	Title (A Side/B Side)	Yr	NM
45s			
PHILIPS			
❑ 40801	I'm on Fire/Still on Fire	1975	6.00
❑ 40804	Bye Love/Look Out I'm Coming	1976	6.00
PRIVATE STOCK			
❑ 45,114	Doctor Kiss-Kiss/Thunderfire	1976	8.00

FIVE THRILLS, THE

Number	Title (A Side/B Side)	Yr	NM
45s			
LOST-NITE			
❑ 152	My Baby's Gone/Feel So Good	196?	6.00
—Reissue			
❑ 157	Gloria/Wee Wee Baby	196?	6.00
—Reissue			
PARROT			
❑ 796	My Baby's Gone/Feel So Good	1954	800.00
❑ 800	Gloria/Wee Wee Baby	1954	4000.
—Red vinyl			
❑ 800	Gloria/Wee Wee Baby	1954	2000.
—Black vinyl. VG 1000; VG+ 1500			

FIVE TINOS, THE

Number	Title (A Side/B Side)	Yr	NM
45s			
SUN			
❑ 222	Sitting By My Window/Don't Do That	1955	1200.

FIVE TRUMPETS, THE

Number	Title (A Side/B Side)	Yr	NM
45s			
GOTHAM			
❑ 681	Stand By Me/Jesus Is Here Today	1951	60.00
❑ 693	My Chains Fell Off/The Lord Knows What I Need	1952	60.00
❑ 696	No Not One/A Hand I Can See	1952	60.00
RCA VICTOR			
❑ 50-0014	Oh Lord/Don't Let Nobody Turn You Around	1949	70.00
—Orange vinyl			
❑ 50-0034	Swing Low Sweet Chariot/Sign of the Judgment	1949	70.00
—Orange vinyl			
❑ 50-0080	When the Saints Go Marching In/Preach My Word	1950	70.00
—Orange vinyl			
SAVOY			
❑ 4060	Amazing Grace/Lord I Want to Be a Christian	1955	25.00
❑ 4072	I've Got Jesus/I Shall Not Be Moved	1956	25.00

FIVE WHISPERS, THE

Number	Title (A Side/B Side)	Yr	NM
45s			
DOLTON			
❑ 61	Midnight Sun/Moon in the Afternoon	1962	15.00
❑ 69	Awake of Asleep/Especially for You	1963	15.00
❑ 90	Can't Face the Crowd/Sleep Walker	1964	15.00

FIVE WILLOWS, THE

Number	Title (A Side/B Side)	Yr	NM
45s			
ALLEN			
❑ 1000	My Dear, Dearest Darling/Rock, Little Francis	1953	300.00
❑ 1002	Delores/All Night Long	1953	600.00
❑ 1003	The White Cliffs of Dover/With These Hands	1953	700.00
HERALD			
❑ 433	Baby Come a Little Closer/Lay Your Head on My Shoulder	1954	300.00
❑ 442	Look Me in the Eyes/So Help Me	1954	400.00
LOST-NITE			
❑ 174	My Dear, Dearest Darling/Rock, Little Francis	196?	6.00
❑ 183	Delores/All Night Long	196?	6.00
❑ 187	The White Cliffs of Dover/With These Hands	196?	6.00
—Lost-Nite records are reissues			
❑ 192	Love Bells/Please Baby	196?	6.00
PEE DEE			
❑ 290	Love Bells/Please, Baby	1953	1500.

FIVE WINGS, THE

Number	Title (A Side/B Side)	Yr	NM
45s			
KING			
❑ 4778	Johnny Has Gone/Johnny's Still Singing	1955	200.00
❑ 4781	Teardrops Are Falling/Rock-A-Locka	1955	400.00
—Later released on King 5199 as The Checkers.			

FIXX, THE

Number	Title (A Side/B Side)	Yr	NM
12-Inch Singles			
IMPACT			
❑ L33-1429 [DJ]	How Much Is Enough (12-Inch Lorber Dance Mix 6:24) (Percussapella 4:18) (Instrumental) (7-Inch Edit 3:58)	1991	12.00
MCA			
❑ L33-1102 [DJ]	Red Skies (LP Version) (Live Version)	1983	15.00
—Red vinyl			
❑ L33-1109 [DJ]	Saved by Zero (Extended Remix 4:24)/Outside	1983	15.00
❑ L33-1128 [DJ]	One Thing Leads to Another (8:00) (3:23)/The Sign of Fire	1983	15.00
—Black vinyl			
❑ L33-1128 [DJ]	One Thing Leads to Another (8:00) (3:23)/The Sign of Fire	1983	30.00
—Blue vinyl			
❑ L33-1146 [DJ]	The Sign of Fire/One Thing Leads to Another (Live)/Saved by Zero (Live)	1983	12.00
❑ L33-1184 [DJ]	Deeper and Deeper (6:30) (3:45)//Sorcerer/Tonight I Know What It Means to Be Young	1984	8.00
—B-side tracks by Marilyn Martin and Fire Inc., respectively			
❑ L33-1186 [DJ]	Deeper and Deeper (same on both sides)	1984	6.00
❑ L33-1230 [DJ]	Less Cities, More Moving People (7:09) (same on both sides)	1984	10.00
❑ L33-1252 [DJ]	Sunshine in the Shade (Live) (same on both sides)	1984	8.00
❑ 13979	One Thing Leads to Another (12" Extended Mix 8:00)/The Sign of Fire	1983	15.00
❑ L33-17027 [DJ]	A Letter to Both Sides (same on both sides)	1985	8.00
❑ L33-17175 [DJ]	Built for the Future (same on both sides)	1986	7.00
❑ L33-17181 [DJ]	Bulit for the Future (Rock Version) (Album Version) (No Familiarity Son Version)	1986	8.00
❑ L33-17304 [DJ]	Red Skies (Long Version) (Short Version)	1987	8.00
❑ L33-17328 [DJ]	Don't Be Scared (3:51) (5:00)	1987	6.00
45s			
AMERICAN PIE			
❑ 9116	One Thing Leads to Another/Saved by Zero	199?	3.00
—Reissue			
MCA			
❑ 52106	Stand or Fall/Sinking Island	1982	4.00
❑ 52167	Red Skies/Is It By Instinct	1982	5.00
❑ 52213	Saved by Zero/Going Overboard	1983	4.00
❑ 52213 [PS]	Saved by Zero/Going Overboard	1983	4.00
❑ 52264	One Thing Leads to Another/Opinions	1983	4.00
❑ 52264 [PS]	One Thing Leads to Another/Opinions	1983	4.00
❑ 52316	The Sign of Fire/Saved by Zero (Live)	1983	4.00
❑ 52316	The Sign of Fire/One Thing Leads to Another (Live)	1983	5.00
❑ 52316 [PS]	The Sign of Fire	1983	4.00
—Most copies of this sleeve had a "Sealed for Your Protection" sticker that kept the record from being removed; the same sleeve was used for both variations of the record			
❑ 52444	Are We Ourselves?/Deeper and Deeper	1984	3.00
❑ 52444 [PS]	Are We Ourselves?/Deeper and Deeper	1984	3.00
❑ 52498	Sunshine in the Shade/Question	1984	4.00
❑ 52498 [DJ]	Sunshine in the Shade (same on both sides)	1984	10.00
—Promo only on yellow vinyl (black vinyl promos are about the same as a stock copy in value)			
❑ 52498 [PS]	Sunshine in the Shade/Question	1984	4.00
❑ 52529	Less Cities, More Moving People/Woman on a Train	1984	4.00
❑ 52529 [PS]	Less Cities, More Moving People/Woman on a Train	1984	4.00
❑ 52832	Secret Separation/Sense of Adventure	1986	4.00
❑ 52902	Built for the Future/Camphor	1986	4.00
❑ 52902 [PS]	Built for the Future/Camphor	1986	8.00
❑ 53066	Red Skies/Built for the Future (Live)	1987	4.00
❑ 53066 [PS]	Red Skies/Built for the Future (Live)	1987	4.00
RCA			
❑ 8837-7-R	Driven Out/Shred of Evidence	1988	3.00
❑ 8837-7-R [PS]	Driven Out/Shred of Evidence	1988	3.00
Albums			
IMPACT			
❑ 10205	Ink	1991	12.00
MCA			
❑ L33-1212 [DJ]	Phantoms	1984	15.00
—Promo sampler; contains three complete songs, "Are We Ourselves?", "Sunshine in the Shade" and "Less Cities, More Morving People," plus spoken introductions for all the songs on the album			
❑ L33-1213 [DJ]	Phantoms	1984	12.00
—Advance version; no interviews			
❑ 5345	Shuttered Room	1982	10.00
❑ 5417	Reach the Beach	1983	8.00
—Reissue			
❑ 5507	Phantoms	1984	8.00
❑ 5705	Walkabout	1986	8.00
❑ 39001	Reach the Beach	1983	12.00
—Original issue			
❑ 42008	React	1987	10.00
❑ 42316	Greatest Hits	1989	15.00
❑ R 153353	Phantoms	1984	10.00
—RCA Music Service edition			
❑ R 164166	React	1987	10.00
—BMG Direct Marketing edition			
❑ R 164380	Walkabout	1986	10.00
—RCA Music Service edition			
RCA			
❑ 8566-1-R	Calm Animals	1989	10.00

FLACK, ROBERTA

Number	Title (A Side/B Side)	Yr	NM
12-Inch Singles			
ATLANTIC			
❑ 85501	Killing Me Softly with His Song (unknown versions)	1996	15.00
❑ 86414	Shock to My System (Extended) (Dub)	1989	8.00
❑ 86453	Uh-Uh Ooh-Ooh Look Out (Here It Comes) (Arthur Baker's Dance Mix) (Arthur Baker's Dub) (Steve Hurley's House Mix)	1989	8.00
❑ 86502	Oasis (LP Version) (Radio Version)/You Know What It's Like (LP Version)	1988	8.00
45s			
ANGEL			
❑ S7-19773	The Christmas Song (Chestnuts Roasting on an Open Fire)/25th of Last December	1997	4.00
ATLANTIC			
❑ 2665	Compared to What/That's No Way to Say Goodbye	1969	8.00
❑ 2730	How Many Broken Wings/Baby Baby	1970	6.00
—With Les McCann			
❑ 2758	Reverend Lee/Business Goes On As Usual	1970	6.00
❑ 2785	Let It Be Me/Do What Cha Gotta Do	1971	6.00

Number	Title (A Side/B Side)	Yr	NM
❑ 2851	Will You Still Love Me Tomorrow/Go Up Moses	1972	5.00
❑ 2864	The First Time Ever I Saw Your Face/Trade Winds	1972	5.00
❑ 2940	Killing Me Softly with His Song/Just Like a Woman	1973	5.00
❑ 2982	Jesse/No Tears	1973	5.00
❑ 3025	Feel Like Makin' Love/When You Smile	1974	5.00
❑ 3203	Feel Like Makin' Love/When You Smile	1974	4.00
❑ 3271	Feelin' That Glow/Some Gospel According to Matthew	1975	4.00
❑ 3441	The 25th of Last December/Move In with Me	1977	4.00
❑ 3483	If Ever I See You Again/I'd Like to Be a Baby to You	1978	4.00
❑ 3521	When It's Over/Come Share My Love	1978	4.00
❑ 3560	You Are Everything/Knowing That We're Made for Each Other	1979	4.00
❑ 3627	You Are My Heaven/I'll Love You Forever and Ever	1979	4.00
❑ 3753	Don't Make Me Wait Too Long/Only Heaven Can Wait (For Love)	1980	4.00
❑ 4005	Making Love/Jesse	1982	4.00
❑ 4005 [PS]	Making Love/Jesse	1982	6.00
❑ 4068	I'm the One/'Til the Morning Comes	1982	4.00
❑ 87607	Set the Night to Music/Natural Thing	1991	4.00
—A-side: With Maxi Priest			
❑ 88898	Shock to My System/You Know What It's Like	1989	3.00
❑ 88941	Uh-Uh Ooh-Ooh Look Out (Here It Comes)/You Know What It's Like	1989	3.00
❑ 88941 [PS]	Uh-Uh Ooh-Ooh Look Out (Here It Comes)/You Know What It's Like	1989	3.00
❑ 88996	Oasis/You Know What It's Like	1988	3.00
❑ 88996 [PS]	Oasis/You Know What It's Like	1988	3.00
❑ 89295	We Shall Overcome/We Shall Overcome	1987	3.00
❑ 89440	Let Me Be a Light to Shine/We Shall Overcome	1986	3.00
—With Howard Hewett			
❑ 89931	Our Love Will Stop the World/Only Heaven Can Wait (For Love)	1982	4.00
—A-side: With Eric Mercury			
❑ 89932	In the Name of Love/Happiness	1982	4.00

COLUMBIA

Number	Title (A Side/B Side)	Yr	NM
❑ 44050	Si, Si, Senor/This Year	1967	10.00
❑ 44448	Cold, Cold Winter/If You Ever Leave Me Now	1968	10.00

MCA

Number	Title (A Side/B Side)	Yr	NM
❑ 51126	You Stopped Loving Me/Qual E Maundrinio	1981	4.00
❑ 51173	Lovin' You/Hittin' Me Where It Hurts	1981	4.00

VIVA

Number	Title (A Side/B Side)	Yr	NM
❑ 29401	This Side of Forever/Robbery Suspects	1983	4.00

—B-side by The Enforcers

7-Inch Extended Plays

ATLANTIC

Number	Title (A Side/B Side)	Yr	NM
❑ SD 7-7271	I'm the Girl/Conversation Love//River/When You Smile	1973	8.00
—Jukebox issue; small hole, plays at 33 1/3 rpm			
❑ SD 7-7271 [PS]	Killing Me Softly	1973	8.00

Albums

ATLANTIC

Number	Title (A Side/B Side)	Yr	NM
❑ SD 1569	Chapter Two	1970	10.00
❑ SD 1594	Quiet Fire	1971	10.00
❑ QD 7271 [Q]	Killing Me Softly	1973	15.00
❑ SD 7271	Killing Me Softly	1973	10.00
❑ SD 8230	First Take	1969	10.00
—Red and green label (second edition)			
❑ SD 8230	First Take	1969	20.00
—Brown and purple label (first edition)			
❑ SD 16013	Roberta Flack Featuring Donny Hathaway	1980	10.00
—Only two tracks feature Mr. Hathaway			
❑ SD 18131	Feel Like Makin' Love	1974	10.00
❑ SD 19149	Blue Lights in the Basement	1977	10.00
❑ SD 19154	Killing Me Softly	1978	8.00
—Reissue of 7271			
❑ SD 19186	Roberta Flack	1978	10.00
❑ SD 19317	The Best of Roberta Flack	1981	10.00
❑ SD 19354	I'm the One	1982	10.00
❑ 81916	Oasis	1988	10.00
❑ SW-94346	First Take	1972	15.00
—Capitol Record Club edition			

MCA

Number	Title (A Side/B Side)	Yr	NM
❑ 5141	Bustin' Loose	1981	10.00

FLACK, ROBERTA, AND DONNY HATHAWAY

Also see each artist's individual listings.

45s

ATLANTIC

Number	Title (A Side/B Side)	Yr	NM
❑ 2808	You've Got a Friend/Gone Away	1971	5.00
❑ 2837	You've Lost That Lovin' Feeling/Be Real Black for Me	1971	5.00
❑ 2879	Where Is the Love/Mood	1972	5.00
❑ 3463	The Closer I Get to You/Love Is the Healing	1978	4.00
—B-side by Flack alone			
❑ 3661	Back Together Again/God Don't Like Ugly	1980	4.00

Albums

ATLANTIC

Number	Title (A Side/B Side)	Yr	NM
❑ SD 7216	Roberta Flack and Donny Hathaway	1972	10.00

FLAGG, BILL

45s

MGM

Number	Title (A Side/B Side)	Yr	NM
❑ 12637	Doin' My Time/I Will Always Love You	1958	100.00

TETRA

Number	Title (A Side/B Side)	Yr	NM
❑ 4445	Go Cat, Go/A Good Woman's Leaving	1956	150.00
❑ 4448	Guitar Rock/I'm So Lonely	1957	150.00

FLAGG, FANNIE

Albums

RCA VICTOR

Number	Title (A Side/B Side)	Yr	NM
❑ LPM-3856 [M]	Rally 'Round the Flagg	1967	20.00
❑ LSP-3856 [S]	Rally 'Round the Flagg	1967	15.00

FLAIRS, THE (1)

Also see CORNEL GUNTER; SHIRLEY GUNTER.

45s

ABC-PARAMOUNT

Number	Title (A Side/B Side)	Yr	NM
❑ 9740	Aladdin's Lamp/Steppin' Out	1956	40.00

FLAIR

Number	Title (A Side/B Side)	Yr	NM
❑ 1012	I Had a Love/She Wants to Rock	1953	400.00
❑ 1019	Tell Me You Love Me/You Should Care for Me	1953	400.00
❑ 1028	Love Me Girl/Gettin' High	1954	400.00
❑ 1041	Baby Wants/You Were Untrue	1954	400.00
❑ 1044	This Is the Night for Love/Let's Make with Some Love	1954	400.00
❑ 1051	Love Me, Love Me, Love Me/My Heart's Crying for You	1954	400.00
—As "The Chimes"			
❑ 1056	I'll Never Let You Go/Hold Me, Thrill Me, Chill Me	1955	400.00
❑ 1067	She Loves to Dance/My Darling, My Sweet	1955	400.00

Albums

CROWN

Number	Title (A Side/B Side)	Yr	NM
❑ CLP-5356 [M]	The Flairs	1963	80.00

FLAIRS, THE (2)

For records on Epic, see THE REDWOODS.

FLAIRS, THE (3)

For records on Jamie and Palms, see THE VELAIRES.

FLAME, THE

With Rikki Fataar and Blondie Chaplin, who later spent time in THE BEACH BOYS. (Fataar also was with The Rutles in the studio.)

45s

BROTHER

Number	Title (A Side/B Side)	Yr	NM
❑ 3501	See the Light/Got Your Mind Made Up	1970	15.00
❑ 3502	Another Day Like Heaven/I'm So Happy	1970	15.00

Albums

BROTHER

Number	Title (A Side/B Side)	Yr	NM
❑ BR-2500	The Flame	1970	30.00

—Deduct 1/3 if poster is missing

FLAMES, THE

More than one group. Also see THE HOLLYWOOD FLAMES.

45s

HARLEM

Number	Title (A Side/B Side)	Yr	NM
❑ 114	So Long My Darling/I'm Going to Try to Live My Life All Over	1960	800.00
—As "The Flames"			
❑ 114	So Long My Darling/I'm Going to Try to Live My Life All Over	1960	3000.
—As "The Fabulous Flames." VG 1500; VG+ 2250			

FLAMIN' GROOVIES, THE

45s

BOMP!

Number	Title (A Side/B Side)	Yr	NM
❑ 101	You Tore Me Down/Him or Me (What's It Gonna Be?)	1975	8.00

EPIC

Number	Title (A Side/B Side)	Yr	NM
❑ 10507	Rockin' Pneumonia & The Boogie Woogie Flu/The First One's Free	1969	10.00
❑ 10564	Somethin' Else/Laurie Did It	1969	10.00

KAMA SUTRA

Number	Title (A Side/B Side)	Yr	NM
❑ 527	Have You Seen My Baby/Yesterday's Numbers	1971	10.00

RCA

Number	Title (A Side/B Side)	Yr	NM
❑ PB-11266	Too Many Cooks/Watch Me Run	1978	6.00

SIRE

Number	Title (A Side/B Side)	Yr	NM
❑ 731	I Can't Hide/Teenage Confidential	1976	6.00

Albums

BUDDAH

Number	Title (A Side/B Side)	Yr	NM
❑ BDS-5683	Shill Shakin'	1977	15.00

EPIC

Number	Title (A Side/B Side)	Yr	NM
❑ BN 26487	Supersnazz	1969	50.00

KAMA SUTRA

Number	Title (A Side/B Side)	Yr	NM
❑ KSBS-2021	Flamingo	1970	30.00
—Pink label			
❑ KSBS-2021	Flamingo	1972	15.00
—Blue label			
❑ KSBS-2031	Teenage Head	1971	30.00
—Pink label			
❑ KSBS-2031	Teenage Head	1972	15.00
—Blue label			

SIRE

Number	Title (A Side/B Side)	Yr	NM
❑ SRK 6059	The Flamin' Groovies Now	1978	12.00
—Reissues have 14 tracks			
❑ SRK 6059	The Flamin' Groovies Now	1978	15.00
—Originals have 12 tracks			
❑ SRK 6067	Jumpin' in the Night	1979	12.00
❑ SASD-7521	Shake Some Action	1976	15.00

SNAZZ

Number	Title (A Side/B Side)	Yr	NM
❑ R-2371 [10]	Sneekers	1969	200.00

—Beware - this album has been counterfeited.

FLAMING EMBER, THE

45s

FORTUNE

Number	Title (A Side/B Side)	Yr	NM
❑ 869	Gone, Gone, Gone/You Can Count on Me	1965	60.00

HOT WAX

Number	Title (A Side/B Side)	Yr	NM
❑ 6902	Mind, Body and Soul/Filet de Soul	1969	6.00
❑ 6907	Shades of Green/Don't You Wanna Wanna	1969	6.00
❑ 7003	Westbound #9/Why Don't You Stay	1970	6.00
❑ 7006	I'm Not My Brothers Keeper/Deserted Village	1970	6.00
❑ 7010	Stop the World and Let Me Off/Robot in a Robot's World	1970	6.00
❑ 7103	Sunshine/1200 Miles	1971	6.00
❑ 7109	If It's Good to You (Part 1)/If It's Good to You (Part 2)	1971	6.00

RIC-TIC

Number	Title (A Side/B Side)	Yr	NM
❑ 129	Let's Have a Love-In (Vocal)/Let's Have a Love-In (Instrumental)	1967	20.00
—B-side credited to Wingate's Love-In Strings			
❑ 131	She's a Real Live Wire/Let's Have a Love-In (Instrumental)	1967	20.00
—B-side credited to Wingate's Love-In Strings			
❑ 132	Hey Mama/Let's Have a Love-In	1967	20.00
❑ 140	Bless You (My Love) (Instrumental)/Bless You (My Love) (Vocal)	1968	15.00
—B-side by Al Kent			
❑ 143	Children (Vocal)/Children (Instrumental)	1968	15.00
❑ 145	Tell It Like It Is/Just Like Children	1968	15.00

Albums

HOT WAX

Number	Title (A Side/B Side)	Yr	NM
❑ HA-702	Westbound #9	1970	15.00
❑ HA-705	Sunshine	1971	15.00

FLAMING LIPS, THE

45s

SUB POP

Number	Title (A Side/B Side)	Yr	NM
❑ SP 28	Drug Machine//Strychnine/What's So Funny 'Bout Peace, Love and Understanding	1989	25.00

—1500 copies, all on black vinyl

Number	Title (A Side/B Side)	Yr	NM
❑ SP 28 [PS]	Drug Machine//Strychnine/What's So Funny 'Bout Peace, Love and Understanding	1989	25.00
—Sub Pop Singles Club release for January 1989 (#3)			
WARNER BROS.			
❑ PRO-S-5452 [DJ]	Ballrooms of Mars/Sudden Death	1991	25.00
—"Soil Samples #6" on gray vinyl; B-side by Mr. Bungle			
❑ PRO-S-7918 [DJ]	What's the New Mary Jane?/Under Pressure	1995	25.00
❑ 16659	Fight Test/Thank You Jack White (For the Fiber Optic Jesus)	2003	10.00
—Picture disc in plastic sleeve			
❑ 16682	Yoshimi Battles the Pink Robots Part 1 (Album Version)/(AOL Sessions Version)	2003	10.00
—Picture disc in plastic sleeve			
❑ 16691	Do You Realize?/Up Above the Daily Hum	2002	10.00
—Picture disc in plastic sleeve			
❑ 17897	Turn It On/Moth in the Incubator	1995	6.00
❑ 18131	She Don't Use Jelly/Turn It On	1994	4.00
❑ PRO-S-100498 [DJ]	White Christmas (Demo for Tom Waits)/(Moogy Moogy Mallow Mix with Synthesizer No. 13)	2000	15.00
—Green vinyl			
❑ PRO-S-100498 [PS]	White Christmas (Demo for Tom Waits)/(Moogy Moogy Mallow Mix with Synthesizer No. 13)	2000	15.00
Albums			
ATAVISTIC			
❑ ALP-04 [EP]	Unconsciously Screamin'	1991	25.00
LOVELY SORTS OF DEATH			
❑ (# unknown) [EP]	The Flaming Lips (Bag Full of Thoughts)	1984	80.00
—Red vinyl; black background on jacket			
❑ (# unknown) [EP]	The Flaming Lips (Bag Full of Thoughts)	1984	120.00
—Green vinyl; dark brown background on jacket			
PINK DUST			
❑ 72173	Hear It Is	1986	40.00
—Originals on white vinyl			
❑ 72188 [EP]	The Flaming Lips	1985	40.00
—Originals on lavender vinyl; reissue of Lovely Sorts of Death EP			
PLAIN			
❑ 111	Hear It Is	2006	15.00
—Reissue on white vinyl			
❑ 112	Oh My Gawd!!!... The Flaming Lips	2006	15.00
—Reissue on clear vinyl			
❑ 113 [(2)]	Telepathic Surgery	2006	15.00
—Reissue on blue vinyl			
❑ 114 [(2)]	In a Priest Driven Ambulance	2006	15.00
—Reissue on pink vinyl			
RESTLESS			
❑ 72207	Oh My Gawd, The Flaming Lips	1987	40.00
—Clear vinyl			
❑ 72350	Telepathic Surgery	1989	25.00
❑ 72359	In a Priest Driven Ambulance	1990	25.00
—Pink vinyl			
WARNER BROS.			
❑ 1-44250 [(2)]	At War with the Mystics	2006	30.00
—180-gram edition on black vinyl			
❑ 45334	Transmissions from the Satellite Heart	1993	20.00
❑ 45911	Clouds Taste Metallic	1995	15.00
❑ 48141	Yoshimi Battles the Pink Robots	2002	20.00
❑ 1-49966 [(2)]	At War with the Mystics	2006	25.00
—150-gram edition; one record is on orange vinyl, the other is on turquoise vinyl			

FLAMING YOUTH

Phil Collins was in this group.

Number	Title (A Side/B Side)	Yr	NM
Albums			
UNI			
❑ 73075	Ark 2	1969	40.00

FLAMINGOS, THE

Number	Title (A Side/B Side)	Yr	NM
45s			
CHANCE			
❑ 1133	If I Can't Have You/Someday, Somehow	1953	800.00
—Black vinyl			
❑ 1133	If I Can't Have You/Someday, Somehow	1953	2000.
—Red vinyl. VG 1000; VG+ 1500			
❑ 1140	That's My Desire/Hurry Home Baby	1953	600.00
—Black vinyl			
❑ 1140	That's My Desire/Hurry Home Baby	1953	1500.
—Red vinyl			
❑ 1145	Golden Teardrops/Carried Away	1953	1000.
—Black vinyl			
❑ 1145	Golden Teardrops/Carried Away	1953	3000.
—Red vinyl			
❑ 1149	Plan for Love/You Ain't Ready	1953	800.00
—Blue and silver label			
❑ 1149	Plan for Love/You Ain't Ready	1953	2000.
—Yellow and black label			
❑ 1154	Cross Over the Bridge/Listen to My Plea	1954	1000.
❑ 1162	Jump Children/Blues in the Letter	1954	600.00
CHECKER			
❑ 815	That's My Baby (Chick-a-Boom)/When	1955	80.00
❑ 821	I Want to Love You/Please Come Back Home	1955	80.00
❑ 830	I'll Be Home/Need Your Love	1956	80.00
❑ 837	A Kiss from Your Lips/Get With It	1956	80.00
❑ 846	The Vow/Shilly Dilly	1956	80.00
❑ 853	Just for a Kick/Would I Be Crying	1957	80.00
—Originals of above Checker singles are maroon with a checkerboard at top of label			
❑ 915	Whispering Stars/Dream of a Lifetime	1959	50.00
❑ 1084	Lover Come Back to Me/Your Little Guy	1964	15.00
❑ 1091	Goodnight Sweetheart/Does It Really Matter	1964	15.00
DECCA			
❑ 30335	The Ladder of Love/Let's Make Up	1957	30.00
❑ 30454	Helpless/My Faith in You	1957	30.00
❑ 30687	Rock and Roll March/Where Mary Go	1958	30.00
❑ 30880	Kiss-A Me/Ever Since I Met Lucy	1959	30.00
❑ 30948	Jerri-Lee/Hey Now	1959	30.00
END			
❑ 1035	Lovers Never Say Goodbye/That Love Is You	1958	40.00
—A-sides of End 1035 are the same song, the titles were changed			
❑ 1035	Please Wait for Me/That Love Is You	1958	60.00
❑ 1040	I Shed a Tear at Your Wedding/But Not for Me	1959	30.00
❑ 1044	At the Prom/Love Walked In	1959	40.00
❑ 1046 [M]	I Only Have Eyes for You/At the Prom	1959	25.00
❑ 1046 [M]	I Only Have Eyes for You/Love Walked In	1959	25.00
❑ 1046 [M]	I Only Have Eyes for You/Goodnight Sweetheart	1959	30.00
❑ 1046 [S]	I Only Have Eyes for You/At the Prom	1959	50.00
—This B-side has been confirmed for the stereo version; others are not yet known			
❑ 1055 [M]	Yours/Love Walked In	1959	25.00
❑ 1055 [S]	Yours/Love Walked In	1959	50.00
❑ 1062	I Was Such a Fool/Heavenly Angel	1959	25.00
❑ 1065	Mio Amore/You, Me and the Sea	1960	25.00
❑ 1068	Nobody Loves Me Like You/You, Me and the Sea	1960	25.00
❑ 1068	Nobody Loves Me Like You/Besame Mucho	1960	30.00
❑ 1070	Besame Mucho/You, Me and the Sea	1960	25.00
❑ 1073	Mio Amore/At Night	1960	20.00
❑ 1079	Beside You/When I Fall in Love	1960	20.00
❑ 1081	Your Other Love/Lovers Gotta Cry	1960	20.00
❑ 1085	Thatr's Why I Love You/Ko Ko Mo	1961	20.00
❑ 1092	Time Was/Dream Girl	1961	20.00
❑ 1099	My Memories of You/I Want to Love You	1961	20.00
❑ 1111	It Must Be Love/I'm No Fool Anymore	1962	20.00
❑ 1116	For All We Know/Near You	1962	20.00
❑ 1121	I Know Better/Flame of Love	1963	20.00
❑ 1124	(Talk About) True Love/Come to My Party	1963	20.00
JULMAR			
❑ 506	Dealin' All the Way/Dealin' (Groovin' with Feelin')	1969	10.00
LOST-NITE			
❑ 149	Dream of a Lifetime/On My Merry Way	196?	6.00
—Reissue			
❑ 154	I'm Yours/Ko Ko Mo	196?	6.00
—Reissue			
❑ 161	I Really Don't Want to Know/Get With It	196?	6.00
—Reissue			
❑ 269	If I Can't Have You/Plan for Love	197?	5.00
❑ 287	That's My Desire/Cross Over the Bridge	197?	5.00
❑ 294	Golden Teardrops/Secret Love	197?	5.00
—B-side by the Moonglows; reissue			
❑ 316	September Song/Vooit Vooit	197?	5.00
MERCURY			
❑ 72455	Temptation/Call Her on the Phone	1965	—
—Cancelled			
OLDIES 45			
❑ 35	Golden Teardrops/Carried Away	1963	8.00
❑ 43	I Only Have Eyes for You/At the Prom	1963	8.00
❑ 68	Lovers Never Say Goodbye/Baby, I Need You	1964	8.00
—B-side by the El Dorados			
PARROT			
❑ 808	Dream of a Lifetime/On My Merry Way	1954	800.00
—Black vinyl			
❑ 808	Dream of a Lifetime/On My Merry Way	1954	1600.
—Red vinyl			
❑ 811	I Really Don't Want to Know/Get With It	1955	5000.
—Black vinyl. VG 2500; VG+ 2750			
❑ 811	I Really Don't Want to Know/Get With It	1955	8000.
—Red vinyl. VG 4000; VG+ 6000			
❑ 812	I'm Yours/Ko Ko Mo	1955	800.00
—Black vinyl			
❑ 812	I'm Yours/Ko Ko Mo	1955	1600.
—Red vinyl			
PHILIPS			
❑ 40308	Temptation/Call Her on the Phone	1965	15.00
❑ 40347	The Boogaloo Party/The Nearness of You	1965	15.00
❑ 40378	Brooklyn Boogaloo/Since My Baby Put Me Down	1966	15.00
❑ 40413	Itty Bitty Baby/She Shook My World	1966	15.00
❑ 40452	Koo Koo/It Keeps the Doctor Away	1967	15.00
❑ 40496	Oh Mary Don't You Worry/Do It, Do It	1967	15.00
POLYDOR			
❑ 14019	Buffalo Soldier (Long)/Buffalo Soldier (Short)	1970	10.00
❑ 14044	Straighten It Up (Get It Together)/Lover Come Back to Me	1970	10.00
RONZE			
❑ 111	Welcome Home/Gotta Have All Your Lovin'	1971	5.00
❑ 115	Someone to Watch Over Me/Heavy Hips	1972	5.00
❑ 116	Love Keeps the Doctor Away (Long)/Love Keeps the Doctor Away (Short)	1972	5.00
ROULETTE			
❑ 4524	Ol' Man River (Part 1)/Ol' Man River (Part 2)	1963	20.00
SKYLARK			
❑ 541	If I Could Love You/I Found a New Baby	197?	5.00
TIMES SQUARE			
❑ 102	A Lovely Way to Spend an Evening/Walking My Baby Back Home	1964	15.00
VEE JAY			
❑ 384	Golden Teardrops/Carried Away	1961	25.00
WORLDS			
❑ 103	Think About Me/(Instrumental)	1974	5.00
7-Inch Extended Plays			
END			
❑ 205	Goodnight Sweetheart/Music Maestro Please//I Only Have Eyes for You/I'm in the Mood for Love	1959	200.00
❑ 205 [PS]	The Flamingos	1959	200.00
Albums			
CHECKER			
❑ LP-1433 [M]	The Flamingos	1959	400.00
—Black label			
❑ LP-1433 [M]	The Flamingos	196?	150.00
—Blue label			
❑ LPS-3005 [R]	The Flamingos	1966	25.00
—Rechanneled reissue of 1433			
CONSTELLATION			
❑ CS-3 [M]	Collectors Showcase: The Flamingos	1964	50.00
—With more restrained pink lettering on cover			
❑ CS-3 [M]	Collectors Showcase: The Flamingos	1964	100.00
—With hot pink lettering on cover			

F

Number	Title (A Side/B Side)	Yr	NM
END			
❑ LP-304 [M]	Flamingo Serenade	1959	200.00
—Gray label with dog			
❑ LP-304 [M]	Flamingo Serenade	1959	400.00
—Black label with shadow print logo			
❑ LPS-304 [S]	Flamingo Serenade	1959	500.00
—Cover says "Stereo"			
❑ LPS-304 [S]	Flamingo Serenade	196?	200.00
—Cover says "Rechanneled Stereo" (only one track is)			
❑ LP-307 [M]	Flamingo Favorites	1960	100.00
❑ LPS-307 [R]	Flamingo Favorites	1960	70.00
❑ LP-308 [M]	Requestfully Yours	1960	100.00
❑ LPS-308 [R]	Requestfully Yours	1960	70.00
❑ LP-316 [M]	The Sound of the Flamingos	1962	100.00
❑ LPS-316 [R]	The Sound of the Flamingos	1962	70.00
❑ LPS-316 [S]	The Sound of the Flamingos	1962	200.00
—"Stereo" at upper right corner of front cover			
LOST-NITE			
❑ LLP-7 [10]	The Flamingos	1981	10.00
—Red vinyl			
PHILIPS			
❑ PHM 200206 [M]	Their Hits — Then and Now	1966	25.00
❑ PHS 600206 [S]	Their Hits — Then and Now	1966	30.00
RONZE			
❑ RLP-1001	The Flamingos Today	1972	15.00
SOLID SMOKE			
❑ 8018	Golden Teardrops	198?	10.00

FLAMINGOS, THE, AND THE MOONGLOWS

Number	Title (A Side/B Side)	Yr	NM
Albums			
VEE JAY			
❑ LP-1052 [M]	The Flamingos Meet the Moonglows on the Dusty Road of Hits	1962	150.00
❑ VJLP-1052 [M]	The Flamingos Meet the Moonglows on the Dusty Road of Hits	198?	12.00
—Authorized reissue			

FLARES, THE

Number	Title (A Side/B Side)	Yr	NM
45s			
FELSTED			
❑ 8604	Loving You/Hotcha Cha-Cha Brown	1960	20.00
❑ 8607	What Do You Want If You Don't Want Love/Jump and Hump	1960	20.00
❑ 8624	Foot Stomping — Part 1/Foot Stomping — Part 2	1961	20.00
PRESS			
❑ 2800	Rock and Roll Heaven — Part 1/Rock and Roll Heaven — Part 2	1962	15.00
❑ 2802	Doing the Hully Gully/Truck and Trailer	1962	15.00
❑ 2803	Madhouse/Make It Be Me	1962	15.00
❑ 2807	Do It with Me/Yon He Go	1963	15.00
❑ 2808	Hand Clappin'/Shimmy and Stomp	1963	15.00
❑ 2810	Monkey Walk/Do It If You Wanna	1963	15.00
❑ 2814	I Didn't Lose a Doggone Thing/Write a Song About Me	1964	15.00
Albums			
PRESS			
❑ PR 73001 [M]	Encore of Foot Stompin' Hits	196?	80.00
❑ PRS 83001 [S]	Encore of Foot Stompin' Hits	196?	120.00

FLASH Also see YES.

Number	Title (A Side/B Side)	Yr	NM
45s			
CAPITOL			
❑ 3345	Small Beginnings/Morning Haze	1972	5.00
Albums			
SOVEREIGN/CAPITOL			
❑ SMAS-11040	Flash	1972	12.00
❑ SMAS-11115	Flash in the Can	1972	12.00
❑ SMAS-11218	Out of Our Hands	1973	12.00

FLASH CADILLAC AND THE CONTINENTAL KIDS

Number	Title (A Side/B Side)	Yr	NM
45s			
EPIC			
❑ 10930	Muleskinner Blues/Teenage Eyes	1972	5.00
❑ 11043	At the Hop/She's So Fine	1973	5.00
❑ 11102	The Way I Feel Tonight/Dancin'	1974	5.00
PRIVATE STOCK			
❑ 45,006	Good Times, Rock and Roll/It's Hard	1974	4.00
❑ 45,026	Hot Summer Girls/Time Will Tell	1975	4.00
❑ 45,079	Did You Boogie (With Your Baby)/Maybe It's All in My Mind	1976	4.00
❑ 45,134	See My Baby Jive/Brown Water	1977	4.00
Albums			
EPIC			
❑ KE 31787	Flash Cadillac and the Continental Kids	1972	15.00
—Yellow label			
❑ KE 31787	Flash Cadillac and the Continental Kids	1973	12.00
—Orange label			
❑ KE 32488	There's No Face Like Chrome	1974	12.00
PRIVATE STOCK			
❑ PS 2003	Sons of Beaches	1975	12.00

FLAT EARTH SOCIETY, THE

Number	Title (A Side/B Side)	Yr	NM
Albums			
FLEETWOOD			
❑ 3027	Waleeco	1968	400.00

FLATT AND SCRUGGS Also includes records credited to "Lester Flatt and Earl Scruggs."

Number	Title (A Side/B Side)	Yr	NM
45s			
COLUMBIA			
❑ 20777	Come Back Darling/I'm Waiting to Hear You Call Me Darling	1951	20.00
❑ 20805	We Can't Be Darlings/I'm Head Over Heels in Love	1951	20.00
❑ 20830	Jimmy Brown the Newsboy/Somehow Tonight	1951	20.00
❑ 20854	Don't Get Above Your Raisin'/I've Lost You	1951	20.00
❑ 20886	'Tis Sweet to Be Remembered/Earl's Breakdown	1952	20.00
❑ 20915	Brother I'm Getting Ready to Go/Get in Line Brother	1952	20.00
❑ 20957	I'll Stay Around/Old Home Town	1952	20.00
❑ 21002	Over the Hills to the Poorhouse/My Darling's Last Goodbye	1952	20.00
❑ 21043	I'm Gonna Settle Down/I'm Lonesome and Blue	1952	20.00
❑ 21054	Dim Lights Thick Smoke/Flint Hill Special	1952	20.00
❑ 21091	Why Did You Wander/Thinking About You	1953	20.00
❑ 21125	Dear Old Dixie/If I Should Wander Back	1953	20.00
❑ 21147	I'm Workin' on a Road/He Took Your Place	1953	20.00
❑ 21179	Foggy Mountain Chimes/I'll Go Steppin' Too	1953	20.00
❑ 21209	Be Ready/Mother Prays Loud	1954	20.00
❑ 21248	Somebody Took My Place with You/I'd Rather Be Alone	1954	20.00
❑ 21295	Foggy Mountain Breakdown/You're Not a Drop in the Bucket	1954	20.00
❑ 21334	Till the End of the World Rolls Around/Don't This Road Look Rough	1954	20.00
❑ 21370	You Can Feel It in Your Soul/Old Fashioned Preacher	1955	15.00
❑ 21412	I'm Gonna Sleep with One Eye Open/Before I Met You	1955	15.00
❑ 21460	Gone Home/Bubbling in My Soul	1955	15.00
❑ 21501	Randy Lynn Rag/On My Mind	1956	15.00
❑ 21536	Joy Bells/Give Mother My Crown	1956	15.00
❑ 21561	No Doubt About It/What's Good for You	1956	15.00
❑ S7 30904 [S]	Ground Speed/Home Sweet Home	1960	15.00
❑ S7 30905 [S]	Sally Ann/Reuben	1960	15.00
❑ S7 30906 [S]	Cripple Creek/Lonesome Road Blues	1960	15.00
❑ S7 30907 [S]	John Henry/Fire Ball Mail	1960	15.00
❑ S7 30908 [S]	Bugle Call Rag/Cumberland Gap	1960	15.00
—The above five are "Stereo Seven" 33 1/3 rpm jukebox singles from "JS7-19"			
❑ 40853	Shuckin' the Corn/Six White Horses	1957	15.00
❑ 40928	Give Me Flowers While I'm Living/Is There Room for Me?	1957	15.00
❑ 40990	Don't Let Your Deal Go Down/Let Those Brown Eyes Smile at Me	1957	15.00
❑ 41064	A Hundred Years from Now/I Won't Be Hanging Around	1957	15.00
❑ 41125	Big Black Train/Crying Alone	1958	15.00
❑ 41184	Building on Sand/Heaven	1958	15.00
❑ 41244	Mama's and Daddy's Little Girl/I Don't Care Anymore	1958	15.00
❑ 41336	A Million Years in Glory/Jesus Savior, Pilot Me	1959	15.00
❑ 41389	Cabin in the Hills/Someone You Have Forgotten	1959	15.00
❑ 41518	Crying My Heart Out Over You/Foggy Mountain Rock	1959	15.00
❑ 41708	The Great Historical Bum/All I Want Is You	1960	15.00
❑ 41786	Polka on a Banjo/Shuckin' the Corn	1960	15.00
❑ 41983	I Ain't Going to Work Tomorrow/I Should Wander Back Tonight	1961	15.00
❑ 42141	Go Home/Where Will I Shelter My Sheep	1961	12.00
❑ 42280	Just Ain't/Cold, Cold Loving	1962	12.00
❑ 42413	The Legend of the Johnson Boys/Hear the Whistle Blow a Hundred Miles	1962	12.00
❑ 42606	The Ballad of Jed Clampett/Coal Loadin' Johnny	1962	15.00
❑ 42606 [PS]	The Ballad of Jed Clampett/Coal Loadin' Johnny	1962	20.00
❑ 4-42606 [DJ]	The Ballad of Jed Clampett (same on both sides)	1962	30.00
—Promo only on red vinyl			
❑ 42755	Pearl Pearl Pearl/Hard Travelin'	1963	12.00
❑ 42755 [PS]	Pearl Pearl Pearl/Hard Travelin'	1963	15.00
❑ 42840	New York Town/Mama Don't Allow It	1963	12.00
❑ 42954	You Are My Flower/My Saro Jane	1964	10.00
❑ 42982	Petticoat Junction/Have You Seen My Dear Companion	1964	15.00
❑ 43080	Workin' It Out/Fireball	1964	10.00
❑ 43135	Sally Don't You Grieve/Little Birdie	1964	10.00
❑ 43204	I Still Miss Someone/Father's Table Grace	1964	10.00
❑ 43259	Rock Salt and Nails/Gonna Have Myself a Ball	1965	10.00
❑ 43412	Memphis/Foggy Mountain Breakdown	1965	10.00
❑ 43497	Green Acres/I Had a Dream	1965	15.00
—With June Carter			
❑ 43627	For Lovin' Me/Colours	1966	10.00
❑ 43803	The Last Thing on My Mind/Mama You Been on My Mind	1966	10.00
❑ 43973	It Was Only the Wind/Why Can't I Find Myself with You	1967	10.00
❑ 44040	Nashville Cats/Roust-A-Bout	1967	10.00
❑ 44194	California Up Tight Band/Last Train to Clarksville	1967	10.00
❑ 44194 [PS]	California Up Tight Band/Last Train to Clarksville	1967	15.00
❑ 44380	Foggy Mountain Breakdown/Down in the Flood	1967	12.00
❑ 44380 [PS]	Foggy Mountain Breakdown/Down in the Flood	1967	12.00
❑ 44623	Like a Rolling Stone/I'd Like to Say a Word About Texas	1968	10.00
❑ 44731	I'll Be Your Baby Tonight/Universal Soldier	1969	10.00
❑ 45030	Maggie's Farm/Tonight We'll Be Fine	1969	10.00
MERCURY			
❑ 6161	God Loves His Children/I'm Going to Make Heaven My Home	1950	30.00
—Note: Earlier Mercury 45s by Flatt and Scruggs may exist			
❑ 6211	Down the Road/Why Don't You Tell Me So	1950	30.00
❑ 6268	Is It Too Late Now/So Happy I'll Be	1950	30.00
❑ 6287	I'll Never Love Another/My Little Girl in Tennessee	1950	30.00
❑ 6302	That Little Old Country Church House/Cora Is Gone	1951	25.00
❑ 6317	Pain in My Heart/Take Me in a Lifeboat	1951	25.00
❑ 6333	Doin' My Time/Farewell Blues	1951	25.00
❑ 6372	Roll in My Sweet Baby's Arms/I'll Just Pretend	1952	25.00
❑ 6396	Pike County Breakdown/Old Salty Dog Blues	1952	25.00
❑ 70016	Preachin', Prayin', Singin'/Will Roses Bloom	1952	20.00
❑ 70064	God Loves His Children/Back to the Cross	1953	20.00
❑ 72739	Theme from Bonnie & Clyde (Foggy Mountain Breakdown)/My Cabin in Caroline	1967	10.00
❑ 72739 [PS]	Theme from Bonnie & Clyde (Foggy Mountain Breakdown)/My Cabin in Caroline	1967	15.00
7-Inch Extended Plays			
COLUMBIA			
❑ B-2823	Jimmy Brown, The Newsboy/Mother Prays Loud in Her Sleep//I'll Go Stepping Too/Randy Lynn Rag	195?	25.00
❑ B-2823 [PS]	(title unknown)	195?	25.00
Albums			
COLUMBIA			
❑ GP 30 [(2)]	20 All-Time Great Recordings	1970	20.00
❑ CL 1019 [M]	Foggy Mountain Jamboree	1957	50.00
❑ CL 1424 [M]	Songs of Glory	1960	20.00
❑ CL 1564 [M]	Foggy Mountain Banjo	1961	20.00

Except when noted otherwise, VG = 25% of NM, and VG+ = 50% of NM. (Example: VG = $2.00, VG+ = $4.00 and NM = $8.00.)

Number	Title (A Side/B Side)	Yr	NM
❑ CL 1664 [M]	Songs of the Famous Carter Family	1961	20.00
❑ CL 1830 [M]	Folk Songs of Our Land	1962	20.00
❑ CL 1951 [M]	Hard Travelin' Featuring The Ballad of Jed Clampett	1963	20.00
❑ CL 2045 [M]	Flatt and Scruggs at Carnegie Hall	1963	20.00
❑ CL 2134 [M]	Recorded Live at Vanderbilt University	1964	20.00
❑ CL 2255 [M]	The Fabulous Sound of Flatt & Scruggs	1964	20.00
❑ CL 2354 [M]	Pickin' Strummin' and Singin'	1965	15.00
❑ CL 2443 [M]	Town and Country	1966	15.00
❑ CL 2513 [M]	When the Saints Go Marching In	1966	15.00
❑ CL 2570 [M]	Flatt and Scruggs' Greatest Hits	1966	15.00
❑ CL 2643 [M]	Strictly Instrumental	1967	20.00
❑ CL 2686 [M]	Hear the Whistle Blow	1967	20.00
❑ CL 2796 [M]	Changin' Times Featuring Foggy Mountain Breakdown	1968	40.00
❑ CS 8221 [S]	Songs of Glory	1960	25.00
❑ CS 8364 [S]	Foggy Mountain Banjo	1961	25.00
❑ CS 8464 [S]	Songs of the Famous Carter Family	1961	25.00
❑ CS 8630 [S]	Folk Songs of Our Land	1962	25.00
❑ CS 8751 [S]	Hard Travelin' Featuring The Ballad of Jed Clampett	1963	25.00
❑ CS 8845 [S]	Flatt and Scruggs at Carnegie Hall	1963	25.00
❑ PC 8845	Flatt and Scruggs at Carnegie Hall	198?	8.00
—Budget-line reissue			
❑ CS 8934 [S]	Recorded Live at Vanderbilt University	1964	25.00
❑ CS 9055 [S]	The Fabulous Sound of Flatt & Scruggs	1964	25.00
❑ CS 9154 [S]	Pickin' Strummin' and Singin'	1965	20.00
❑ CS 9243 [S]	Town and Country	1966	20.00
❑ CS 9313 [S]	When the Saints Go Marching In	1966	20.00
❑ CS 9370 [S]	Flatt and Scruggs' Greatest Hits	1966	20.00
❑ PC 9370	Flatt and Scruggs' Greatest Hits	198?	8.00
—Budget-line reissue			
❑ CS 9443 [S]	Strictly Instrumental	1967	20.00
❑ CS 9486 [S]	Hear the Whistle Blow	1967	20.00
❑ CS 9596	Changin' Times Featuring Foggy Mountain Breakdown	1970	12.00
—Orange label with six "Columbia"s along edge			
❑ CS 9596 [S]	Changin' Times Featuring Foggy Mountain Breakdown	1968	20.00
—Red "360 Sound" label			
❑ CS 9649 [M]	The Story of Bonnie & Clyde	1968	40.00
—White label promo with "Special Mono Radio Station Copy" sticker and timing strip on front cover			
❑ CS 9649 [S]	The Story of Bonnie & Clyde	1968	20.00
❑ CS 9741	Nashville Airplane	1969	20.00
❑ CS 9945	Final Fling	1970	15.00
❑ C 30347	Breaking Out	1971	12.00
❑ CG 31964 [(2)]	The World of Flatt and Scruggs	1972	15.00
❑ C 32244	A Boy Named Sue	1973	12.00
❑ FC 37469	Lester Flatt & Earl Scruggs	1981	10.00
COLUMBIA LIMITED EDITION			
❑ LE 10149	Breaking Out	197?	10.00
COLUMBIA MUSICAL TREASURY			
❑ DS 493	Detroit City	1969	15.00
COUNTY			
❑ CCS-111	You Can Feel It in Your Soul	1988	10.00
EVEREST ARCHIVE OF FOLK & JAZZ			
❑ 259	Lester Flatt & Earl Scruggs	197?	10.00
HARMONY			
❑ HL 7250 [M]	Lester Flatt & Earl Scruggs	1960	15.00
❑ HL 7340 [M]	Great Original Recordings	1965	15.00
❑ HL 7402 [M]	Sacred Songs	1967	15.00
❑ HL 7465 [M]	Songs to Cherish	1968	15.00
❑ HS 11202 [S]	Sacred Songs	1967	12.00
❑ HS 11265 [S]	Songs to Cherish	1968	12.00
❑ HS 11401	Foggy Mountain Chimes	1970	12.00
❑ H 30932	Wabash Cannonball	197?	10.00
MERCURY			
❑ MG-20358 [M]	Country Music	1958	40.00
❑ MG-20542 [M]	Lester Flatt & Earl Scruggs	1959	40.00
❑ MG-20773 [M]	The Original Sound of Flatt & Scruggs	1963	25.00
❑ SR-60773 [R]	The Original Sound of Flatt & Scruggs	1963	15.00
❑ SR-61162	Original Theme from Bonnie & Clyde	1968	20.00
NASHVILLE			
❑ 2087	The Best of Flatt and Scruggs	1970	12.00
PICKWICK			
❑ 6093	Foggy Mountain Breakdown	197?	12.00
❑ 6140	Blue Grass Banjos	197?	10.00
POWER PAK			
❑ 297	Golden Hits	197?	10.00
ROUNDER			
❑ SS-05	The Golden Era	198?	10.00
❑ SS-08	Don't Get Above Your Raisin'	198?	10.00
❑ SS-18	The Mercury Sessions, Vol. 1	1985	10.00
❑ SS-19	The Mercury Sessions, Vol. 2	1985	10.00
STARDAY			
❑ SLP-365 [M]	Stars of the Grand Ol' Opry	1966	25.00
—With Jim and Jesse			
WING			
❑ SRW-16376	The Original Foggy Mountain Breakdown	1968	12.00

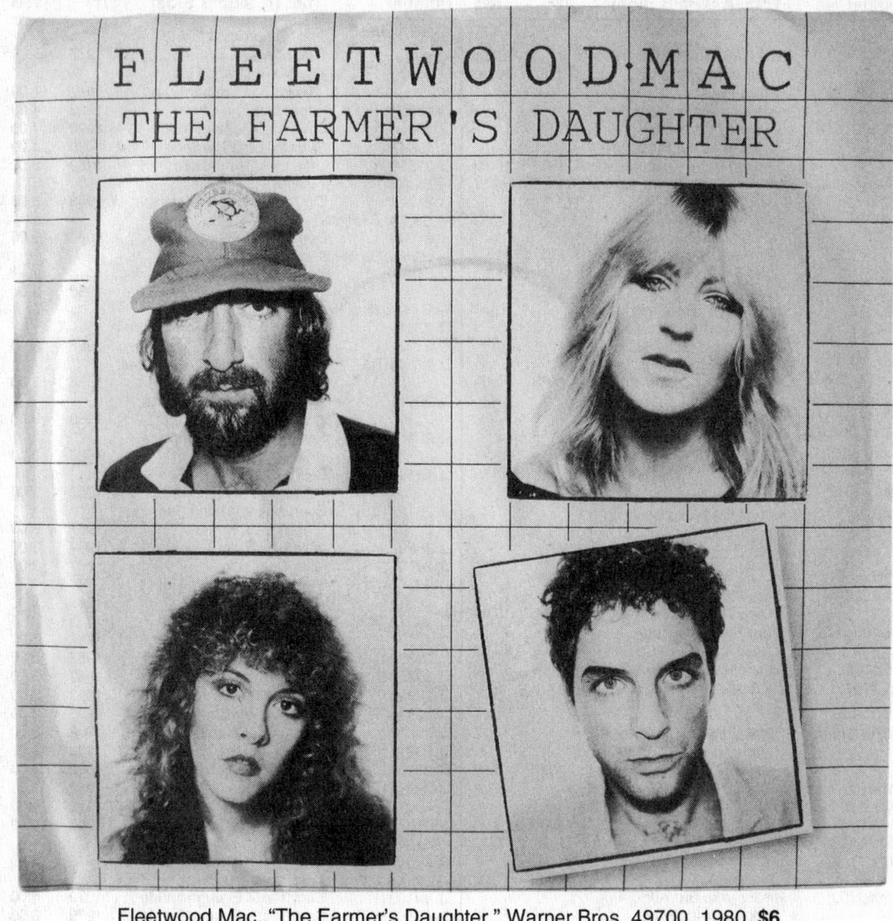

Fleetwood Mac, "The Farmer's Daughter," Warner Bros. 49700, 1980, **$6.**

FLAVOR May be two different groups.

Number	Title (A Side/B Side)	Yr	NM
45s			
BUNKY			
❑ 711	Don't Freeze Up/(Instrumental)	1976	10.00
COLUMBIA			
❑ 4-44521	Sally Had a Party/Shop Around	1968	8.00
❑ 4-44673	Heart Teaser/Yeah, I'm Hip	1968	8.00
❑ 4-44881	Comin' On Home/Dancing in the Streets	1969	12.00
JU-PAR			
❑ 8001	Don't Freeze Up/(Instrumental)	1976	8.00
Albums			
JU-PAR			
❑ JP6-1002S1	In Good Taste	1976	20.00

FLEAS, THE All-star studio group supposedly with DAVE BURGESS, GLEN CAMPBELL, JERRY FULLER and RICK NELSON!

Number	Title (A Side/B Side)	Yr	NM
45s			
CHALLENGE			
❑ 9115	Scratchin'/Tears	1961	40.00

FLEETWOOD, MICK

Number	Title (A Side/B Side)	Yr	NM
12-Inch Singles			
RCA			
❑ JR-13616 [DJ]	I Want You Back (same on both sides)	1983	6.00
❑ JR-13744 [DJ]	Angel Come Home (same on both sides)	1984	6.00
45s			
RCA			
❑ PB-12308	You Weren't in Love/O'Niamali	1981	4.00
❑ PB-13621	I Want You Back/Put Me Right	1983	4.00
❑ PB-13621 [PS]	I Want You Back/Put Me Right	1983	4.00
❑ PB-13739	Angel Come Home/I Give	1984	4.00
Albums			
RCA VICTOR			
❑ AFL1-4080	The Visitor	1981	8.00
❑ DJL1-4106 [EP]	The Visitor	1981	8.00
—Four-song promo sampler from LP			
❑ AFL1-4652	I'm Not Me	1983	8.00

FLEETWOOD MAC Also see LINDSEY BUCKINGHAM; BUCKINGHAM NICKS; BILLY BURNETTE; MICK FLEETWOOD; DANNY KIRWAN; DAVE MASON; CHRISTINE McVIE; STEVIE NICKS; JEREMY SPENCER; BOB WELCH.

Number	Title (A Side/B Side)	Yr	NM
12-Inch Singles			
REPRISE			
❑ 44540	Landslide (Remix) (String Mix) (Analog Mix) (Live LP Version)	1998	10.00
WARNER BROS.			
❑ PRO-A-652 [DJ]	Go Your Own Way/Silver Springs	1977	15.00
❑ PRO-A-831 [DJ]	Tusk/Never Make Me Cry	1979	12.00
❑ PRO-A-845 [DJ]	Sara (Edit) (same on both sides)	1979	10.00
❑ PRO-A-853 [DJ]	Think About Me (Remix)/ Save Me a Place	1980	20.00
❑ PRO-A-932 [DJ]	Fireflies (Remix Long Version 4:05)(Remix Edit 3:22)	1981	15.00
❑ PRO-A-1040 [DJ]	Hold Me (same on both sides)	1982	10.00
❑ PRO-A-2688 [DJ]	Big Love (same on both sides)	1987	8.00
❑ PRO-A-2723 [DJ]	Big Love (Extended Remix)/ (Remix Edit)	1987	10.00
❑ PRO-A-2728 [DJ]	Tango in the Night (same on both sides)	1987	10.00

Number	Title (A Side/B Side)	Yr	NM
❑ PRO-A-2773 [DJ]	Isn't It Midnight (same on both sides)	1987	10.00
❑ PRO-A-2884 [DJ]	Everywhere (same on both sides)	1987	8.00
❑ 20683	Big Love (Extended Remix)/(House on the Hill Dub)//(Piano Dub)/You and I, Part I	1987	10.00
—Record is labeled "You and I, Part I" but actually plays the LP version of "You and I, Part II"			
❑ 20746	Seven Wonders (Extended Version)//(Dub)/Book of Miracles	1987	10.00
❑ 20761	Little Lies (Extended Version)//(Dub)/Ricky	1987	10.00
❑ 20842	Family Man (Extended Vocal Remix)/(I'm a Jazz Man Dub)//(Extended Guitar Remix)/Family Party (Bonus Beats)/Down Endless Street	1988	10.00

45s

BLUE HORIZON

Number	Title (A Side/B Side)	Yr	NM
❑ 304	Hungry Country Woman/Walkin'	1970	12.00
—A-side by Otis Spann with Fleetwood Mac; B-side by Otis Spann			

DJM

Number	Title (A Side/B Side)	Yr	NM
❑ 1007	Man of the World/Best Girl in the World	1976	10.00
—B-side by Danny Kirwan			

EPIC

Number	Title (A Side/B Side)	Yr	NM
❑ 5-10351	Black Magic Woman/Long Grey Mare	1968	15.00
❑ 5-10368	Stop Messin' Around/Need Your Love So Bad	1968	12.00
❑ 5-10436	Albatross/Jigsaw Puzzle Blues	1969	12.00
❑ 5-11029	Albatross/Black Magic Woman	1973	8.00

REPRISE

Number	Title (A Side/B Side)	Yr	NM
❑ GRE 0108	Oh Well, Part 1/The Green Manalishi (With the Two-Prong Crown)	1972	5.00
—"Back to Back Hits" reissue			
❑ GRE 0119	Rhiannon (Will You Ever Win)/Over My Head	1978	3.00
—"Back to Back Hits" series			
❑ 0860	Rattlesnake Shake/Coming Your Way	1969	25.00
❑ 0860 [DJ]	Rattlesnake Shake/Coming Your Way	1969	10.00
❑ 0883	Oh Well, Part 1/Part 2	1970	20.00
❑ 0883 [DJ]	Oh Well, Part 1/Part 2	1970	10.00
❑ 0925	The Green Manalishi (With the Two-Prong Crown)/World In Harmony	1970	20.00
❑ 0925 [DJ]	The Green Manalishi (With the Two-Prong Crown)/World In Harmony	1970	10.00
❑ 0984	Jewel-Eyed Judy/Station Man	1971	15.00
❑ 0984 [DJ]	Jewel-Eyed Judy/Station Man	1971	10.00
❑ 1057	Sands of Time/Lay It All Down	1971	10.00
❑ 1077	Oh Well, Part 1/The Green Manalishi (With the Two-Prong Crown)	1971	8.00
—"Back to Back Hits" reissue			
❑ 1093	Sentimental Lady/Sunny Side of Heaven	1972	20.00
❑ 1093 [DJ]	Sentimental Lady/Sunny Side of Heaven	1972	12.00
❑ 1159	Remember Me/Dissatisfied	1973	10.00
❑ 1172	Did You Ever Love Me/Revelation	1973	12.00
❑ 1172 [DJ]	Did You Ever Love Me (stereo/mono)	1973	8.00
❑ 1188	For Your Love/Hypnotized	1973	15.00
❑ 1188 [DJ]	For Your Love (stereo/mono)	1973	10.00
❑ 1317	Heroes Are Hard to Find/Born Enchanter	1974	8.00
❑ 1339	Over My Head/I'm So Afraid	1975	5.00
❑ 1345	Rhiannon (Will You Ever Win)/Sugar Daddy	1976	5.00
❑ 1356	Say You Love Me (Edited)/Monday Morning	1976	5.00
—The A-sides of Reprise 1339, 1345 and 1356 feature significantly different mixes than those on their parent album, "Fleetwood Mac."			
❑ 17300	Silver Springs/Go Your Own Way	1997	4.00
❑ 17300 [PS]	Silver Springs/Go Your Own Way	1997	4.00

WARNER BROS.

Number	Title (A Side/B Side)	Yr	NM
❑ GWB 0348	Go Your Own Way/Dreams	1979	3.00
—"Back to Back Hits" series			
❑ GWB 0388	Tusk/Sara	1981	3.00
—"Back to Back Hits" series			
❑ GWB 0439	Hold Me/Gypsy	1984	3.00
—"Back to Back Hits" series			
❑ 8304	Go Your Own Way/Silver Springs	1976	8.00
—Sought-after because of its non-LP B-side			
❑ 8371	Dreams/Songbird	1977	4.00
❑ 8413	Don't Stop/Never Going Back Again	1977	4.00
❑ 8413 [PS]	Don't Stop/Never Going Back Again	1977	5.00
❑ 8483	You Make Loving Fun/Gold Dust Woman	1977	4.00
❑ 18661	Paper Doll/The Chain	1993	4.00
❑ 19866	Save Me/Another Woman	1990	4.00
❑ 19867	Skies the Limit/The Second Time	1990	4.00
❑ 21888	Little Lies/Everywhere	1989	3.00
—"Back to Back Hits" series			
❑ 21943	Big Love/Seven Wonders	1988	3.00
—"Back to Back Hits" series			
❑ 21990	Don't Stop/Silver Springs	1988	3.00
—"Back to Back Hits" series			
❑ 21991	You Make Loving Fun/Say You Love Me	1988	3.00
—"Back to Back Hits" series			
❑ 27644	As Long As You Follow/Oh Well (Live)	1988	3.00
❑ 27644 [PS]	As Long As You Follow/Oh Well (Live)	1988	3.00
❑ 28114	Family Man/Down Endless Street	1988	3.00
❑ 28114 [PS]	Family Man/Down Endless Street	1988	3.00
❑ 28143	Everywhere/When I See You Again	1987	3.00
❑ 28143 [PS]	Everywhere/When I See You Again	1987	3.00
❑ 28291	Little Lies/Ricky	1987	3.00
❑ 28291 [PS]	Little Lies/Ricky	1987	3.00
❑ 28317	Seven Wonders/Book of Miracles	1987	3.00
❑ 28317 [PS]	Seven Wonders/Book of Miracles	1987	3.00
❑ 28398	Big Love/You and I, Part 1	1987	3.00
❑ 28398 [PS]	Big Love/You and I, Part 1	1987	3.00
❑ 29698	Oh Diane/That's Alright	1983	3.00
❑ 29848	Love in Store/Can't Go Back	1983	3.00
❑ 29918	Gypsy/Cool Water	1982	3.00
❑ 29918 [PS]	Gypsy/Cool Water	1982	3.00
❑ 29966	Hold Me/Eyes of the World	1982	3.00
❑ 29966 [PS]	Hold Me/Eyes of the World	1982	3.00
❑ 49077	Tusk/Never Make Me Cry	1979	4.00
❑ 49077 [PS]	Tusk/Never Make Me Cry	1979	4.00
—Version 2: Black print, large dog photo			
❑ 49077 [PS]	Tusk/Never Make Me Cry	1979	5.00
—Version 1: Brown print, small dog photo			
❑ 49150	Sara/That's Enough for Me	1979	4.00
❑ 49150 [PS]	Sara/That's Enough for Me	1979	6.00
❑ 49196	Think About Me/Save Me a Place	1980	4.00
❑ 49196 [PS]	Think About Me/Save Me a Place	1980	6.00
❑ 49500	Sisters of the Moon/Walk a Thin Line	1980	10.00
—Scarce on stock copy; A-side is a different mix than the LP version			
❑ 49660	Fireflies/Over My Head (Live)	1981	4.00
❑ 49660 [PS]	Fireflies/Over My Head (Live)	1981	4.00
❑ 49700	The Farmer's Daughter/Monday Morning (Live)	1982	6.00
❑ 49700 [PS]	The Farmer's Daughter/Monday Morning (Live)	1982	6.00

Albums

BLUE HORIZON

Number	Title	Yr	NM
❑ BH-3801 [(2)]	Fleetwood Mac in Chicago	1970	30.00
❑ BH-4802	Blues Jam in Chicago, Vol. 1	1970	15.00
❑ BH-4803	Blues Jam in Chicago, Vol. 2	1970	15.00

EPIC

Number	Title	Yr	NM
❑ LN 24402 [M]	Fleetwood Mac	1968	100.00
—White label promo only			
❑ LN 24446 [M]	English Rose	1969	100.00
—White label promo only			
❑ BN 26402 [S]	Fleetwood Mac	1968	30.00
❑ BN 26446 [S]	English Rose	1969	30.00
❑ KE 30632 [(2)]	Black Magic Woman	1971	20.00
❑ KE 33740 [(2)]	Fleetwood Mac/English Rose	1974	15.00

MOBILE FIDELITY

Number	Title	Yr	NM
❑ 1-012	Fleetwood Mac	1980	55.00
—Audiophile vinyl			
❑ 1-119	Mirage	1984	45.00
—Audiophile vinyl			

NAUTILUS

Number	Title	Yr	NM
❑ NR-8	Rumours	1980	40.00
—Audiophile vinyl			

REPRISE

Number	Title	Yr	NM
❑ MS 2080	Bare Trees	197?	15.00
—Without brown line on front cover; uncommon with the MS 2080 number			
❑ MS 2080	Bare Trees	1972	12.00
—With brown line near all four edges of the front cover			
❑ MS 2138	Penguin	1973	15.00
❑ MS 2158	Mystery to Me	1973	12.00
—With "For Your Love" listed correctly on the back cover			
❑ MS 2158	Mystery to Me	1973	20.00
—With "Good Things (Come to Those Who Wait)" listed on the album cover; it was replaced at the last minute by "For Your Love"			
❑ MS 2196	Heroes Are Hard to Find	1974	12.00
❑ MS 2225	Fleetwood Mac	1975	10.00
❑ MSK 2278	Bare Trees	1977	8.00
—Reissue; no brown line on the front cover			
❑ MSK 2279	Mystery to Me	1977	8.00
❑ MSK 2281	Fleetwood Mac	1977	8.00
❑ RS 6368	Then Play On	1969	25.00
—First pressings include "When You Say" and "My Dream"			
❑ RS 6368	Then Play On	1970	15.00
—Later pressings replace above two tracks with "Oh Well (Parts 1 and 2)."			
❑ RS 6408	Kiln House	1970	15.00
❑ RS 6465	Future Games	1971	25.00
—Originals have a pale yellow cover			
❑ RS 6465	Future Games	1972	15.00
—Later pressings have a pale green cover			

SIRE

Number	Title	Yr	NM
❑ SASH-3706 [(2)]	Vintage Years	1975	15.00
❑ SASH-3715 [(2)]	Fleetwood Mac in Chicago	1975	15.00
—Reissue of Blue Horizon 3801			
❑ 2XS-6006 [(2)]	Vintage Years	1977	12.00
❑ 2XS-6009 [(2)]	Fleetwood Mac in Chicago	1977	12.00
❑ 2XS-6045 [(2)]	The Original Fleetwood Mac	1977	12.00

VARRICK

Number	Title	Yr	NM
❑ VR-020	Jumping at Shadows	1985	12.00

WARNER BROS.

Number	Title	Yr	NM
❑ PRO-A-866 [DJ]	Tusk Remix	1979	20.00
—Promo-only EP			
❑ BSK 3010	Rumours	1977	8.00
—With long version (2:16) of "Never Going Back Again"; we do not yet know how to identify these without playing them			
❑ BSK 3010	Rumours	1977	10.00
—With short version (2:02) of "Never Going Back Again"; we do not yet know how to identify these without playing them			
❑ BSK3010	Rumours	1979	6.00
—White label reissue			
❑ 2HS 3350 [(2)]	Tusk	1979	15.00
❑ 2WB 3500 [(2)]	Fleetwood Mac Live	1980	12.00
❑ 23607	Mirage	1982	10.00
❑ 23607 [DJ]	Mirage	1982	20.00
—Promo on Quiex II vinyl			
❑ 25471	Tango in the Night	1987	10.00
❑ 25801	Greatest Hits	1989	10.00
❑ 26111	Behind the Mask	1990	15.00

FLEETWOODS, THE

45s

DOLPHIN

Number	Title (A Side/B Side)	Yr	NM
❑ 1	Come Softly to Me/I Care So Much	1959	25.00

DOLTON

Number	Title (A Side/B Side)	Yr	NM
❑ 3	Graduation's Here/Oh Lord, Let It Be	1959	20.00
❑ S-3 [S]	Graduation's Here/Oh Lord, Let It Be	1959	50.00
❑ 5	Mr. Blue/You Mean Everything to Me	1959	20.00
❑ 15	Outside My Window/Magic Star	1960	20.00
❑ 22	Runaround/Truly Do	1960	20.00
❑ 22 [PS]	Runaround/Truly Do	1960	50.00
❑ 27	The Last One to Know/Dormilona	1960	15.00
❑ 30	Confidential/I Love You So	1960	15.00
❑ 40	Tragedy/Little Miss Sad One	1961	15.00
❑ 45	(He's) The Great Impostor/Poor Little Girl	1961	15.00
❑ 49	Billy Old Buddy/Trouble	1962	15.00
❑ 62	They Tell Me It's Summer/Lovers by Night, Strangers by Day	1962	15.00
❑ 74	You Should Have Been There/Sure Is Lonesome Downtown	1963	15.00
❑ 75	Goodnight My Love/Jimmy Beware	1963	15.00
❑ 86	Baby Bye-O/What'll I Do	1963	10.00
❑ 93	Lonesome Town/Ruby Red Baby Blue	1964	10.00
❑ 97	Ten Times Blue/Ska Light Ska Bright	1964	10.00
❑ 98	Mr. Sandman/This Is My Prayer	1964	10.00
❑ 302	Before and After (Losing You)/Lonely Is As Lonely Does	1964	10.00
❑ 307	Come Softly to Me/I'm Not Jimmy	1965	10.00
❑ 310	Rainbow/Just As I Need You	1965	10.00
❑ 315	For Lovin' Me/This Is Where I See Her	1965	10.00

LIBERTY

Number	Title (A Side/B Side)	Yr	NM
❑ 62	They Tell Me It's Summer/Lovers by Night, Strangers by Day	1970	15.00
—Odd reissue keeping the Dolton number			
❑ 55188 [M]	Come Softly to Me/I Care So Much	1959	25.00
❑ 77188 [S]	Come Softly to Me/I Care So Much	1959	50.00

UNITED ARTISTS

Number	Title (A Side/B Side)	Yr	NM
❑ 0038	Come Softly to Me/Runaround	1973	4.00
❑ 0039	Mr. Blue/Tragedy	1973	4.00
❑ 0040	He's the Great Impostor/Goodnight My Love	1973	4.00
—0038, 0039 and 0040 are "Silver Spotlight Series" reissues			

Number	Title (A Side/B Side)	Yr	NM
❑ XW515	(He's) The Great Impostor/Goodnight My Love	1974	4.00
—Reissue			
7-Inch Extended Plays			
DOLTON			
❑ BEP-502	Runaround/Mr. Blue//Outside My Window/Come Softly to Me	1960	60.00
❑ BEP-502 [PS]	The Fleetwoods	1960	90.00
Albums			
DOLTON			
❑ BLP-2001 [M]	Mr. Blue	1959	80.00
—Pale blue label with dolphins on top			
❑ BLP-2001 [M]	Mr. Blue	1963	20.00
—Dark label, logo on left			
❑ BLP-2002 [M]	The Fleetwoods	1960	50.00
—Pale blue label with dolphins on top			
❑ BLP-2002 [M]	The Fleetwoods	1963	20.00
—Dark label, logo on left			
❑ BLP-2005 [M]	Softly	1961	50.00
—Pale blue label with dolphins on top			
❑ BLP-2005 [M]	Softly	1963	20.00
—Dark label, logo on left			
❑ BLP-2007 [M]	Deep in a Dream	1961	40.00
—Pale blue label with dolphins on top			
❑ BLP-2007 [M]	Deep in a Dream	1963	20.00
—Dark label, logo on left			
❑ BLP-2011 [M]	The Best of the Oldies	1962	40.00
—Pale blue label with dolphins on top			
❑ BLP-2011 [M]	The Best of the Oldies	1963	20.00
—Dark label, logo on left			
❑ BLP-2018 [M]	The Fleetwoods' Greatest Hits	1962	25.00
❑ BLP-2020 [M]	The Fleetwoods Sings for Lovers by Night	1963	30.00
❑ BLP-2025 [M]	Goodnight My Love	1963	30.00
❑ BLP-2030 [M]	Before and After	1965	30.00
❑ BLP-2039 [M]	Folk Rock	1965	30.00
❑ BST-8001 [S]	Mr. Blue	1959	100.00
—Pale blue label with dolphins on top			
❑ BST-8001 [S]	Mr. Blue	1963	25.00
—Dark label, logo on left			
❑ BST-8002 [S]	The Fleetwoods	1960	70.00
—Pale blue label with dolphins on top			
❑ BST-8002 [S]	The Fleetwoods	1963	25.00
—Dark label, logo on left			
❑ BST-8005 [S]	Softly	1961	70.00
—Pale blue label with dolphins on top			
❑ BST-8005 [S]	Softly	1963	25.00
—Dark label, logo on left			
❑ BST-8007 [S]	Deep in a Dream	1961	50.00
—Pale blue label with dolphins on top			
❑ BST-8007 [S]	Deep in a Dream	1963	25.00
—Dark label, logo on left			
❑ BST-8011 [S]	The Best of the Oldies	1962	50.00
—Pale blue label with dolphins on top			
❑ BST-8011 [S]	The Best of the Oldies	1963	25.00
—Dark label, logo on left			
❑ BST-8018 [S]	The Fleetwoods' Greatest Hits	1962	30.00
❑ BST-8020 [S]	The Fleetwoods Sings for Lovers by Night	1963	40.00
❑ BST-8025 [S]	Goodnight My Love	1963	40.00
❑ BST-8030 [S]	Before and After	1965	40.00
❑ BST-8039 [S]	Folk Rock	1965	40.00
LIBERTY			
❑ LN-10159	The Fleetwoods' Greatest Hits	1982	8.00
❑ LN-10160	The Best Goodies of the Oldies	1982	8.00
❑ LN-10199	Buried Treasure	1983	8.00
SUNSET			
❑ SUM-1131 [M]	In a Mellow Mood	1966	12.00
❑ SUS-5131 [S]	In a Mellow Mood	1966	15.00
UNITED ARTISTS			
❑ UA-LA334-E	The Very Best of the Fleetwoods	1975	12.00

FLEMONS, WADE

Also see EARTH, WIND AND FIRE.

Number	Title (A Side/B Side)	Yr	NM
45s			
RAMSEL			
❑ 1001	Jeanette/What a Price to Pay	196?	500.00
❑ 1002	Two of a Kind/I Knew You'd Be Mine	196?	600.00
VEE JAY			
❑ 295	Here I Stand/My Baby Likes to Rock	1958	30.00
❑ 309	Hold Me Close/You'll Remain Forever	1959	30.00
❑ 321	Slow Motion/Wailing by the River	1959	30.00
❑ 335	Goodnite, It's Time To Go/What's Happening	1959	30.00
❑ 344	Easy Lovin'/Woops Now	1960	30.00
❑ 368	Ain't That Lovin' You Baby/I'll Come Runnin'	1960	30.00
❑ 377	At the Party/Devil in Your Soul	1961	30.00
❑ 389	Please Send Me Someone to Love/Keep On Loving Me	1961	30.00
❑ 427	Half a Love/Welcome Stranger	1962	20.00
❑ 471	Ain't These Tears/I Hope, I Think, I Wish	1962	20.00
❑ 533	That Time of the Year/I Came Running	1963	50.00
❑ 578	When It Rains, It Pours/Watch Over Her	1964	40.00
—The Four Seasons sing backup on this record			
❑ 614	I Knew You When/That Other Place	1964	300.00
❑ 668	Where Did You Go Last Night/Empty Balcony	1965	20.00
Albums			
VEE JAY			
❑ LP-1011 [M]	Wade Flemons	1959	150.00
—Maroon label			
❑ LP-1011 [M]	Wade Flemons	196?	80.00
—Black label			

FLESH GORDON AND THE NUDE HOLLYWOOD ARGYLES

Also see THE HOLLYWOOD ARGYLES.

Number	Title (A Side/B Side)	Yr	NM
45s			
PARAMOUNT			
❑ 0289	Superstreaker/Naked	1974	12.00

FLESHEATERS

Number	Title (A Side/B Side)	Yr	NM
7-Inch Extended Plays			
UPSETTER			
❑ (no #)	Flesheaters	1978	30.00
Albums			
HOMESTEAD			
❑ (# unknown)	Prehistoric Hits Vol. 1	198?	12.00
❑ 124-1	Live	1988	10.00
RUBY			
❑ JRR-101	A Minute to Pray, a Second to Die	1981	20.00
❑ JRR 805	Forever Came Today	1982	20.00
SST			
❑ 094	Greatest Hits	1986	12.00
❑ 094	Destroyed by Fire/Greatest Hits	1991	10.00
—Reissue with new name			
❑ 264	Prehistoric Fits	1990	12.00
❑ 273 [(2)]	Dragstrip Riot	1991	12.00

FLETCHER, DARROW

Number	Title (A Side/B Side)	Yr	NM
45s			
ATCO			
❑ 7083	Improve/Let's Get Together	1977	20.00
ATLANTIC			
❑ 3600	The Rising Cost of Love/Honey Can I	1979	10.00
CONGRESS			
❑ 6011	I Think I'm Gonna Write a Song/Sitting There That Night	1970	15.00
CROSSOVER			
❑ 980	It's No Mistake/Try Something New	1975	40.00
❑ 983	We've Got to Get an Understanding/This Time (I'll Be the Fool)	1976	10.00
GROOVY			
❑ 3001	The Pain Gets a Little Deeper/My Judgement Day	1965	25.00
❑ 3004	My Young Misery/I've Gotta Know Why	1966	20.00
❑ 3007	Gotta Draw the Line/I've Gotta Know Why	1966	20.00
❑ 3009	That Certain Little Something/My Judgement Day	1966	20.00
JACKLYN			
❑ 1002	What Have I Got Now/Sitting There That Night	1966	50.00
❑ 1003	Infatuation/Little Girl	1966	20.00
❑ 1006	What Good Am I Without You/Little Girl	1967	20.00
REVUE			
❑ 11008	I Like the Way I Feel/The Way of a Man	1967	15.00
❑ 11023	Gonna Keep Loving You/We Can't Go On This Way	1967	15.00
❑ 11035	Those Hanging Heartaches/Sitting There That Night	1968	20.00
UNI			
❑ 55244	Changing by the Minute/When Love Calls	1970	12.00
❑ 55270	Dolly Baby/What Is This	1971	12.00

FLETCHER, LOIS

Number	Title (A Side/B Side)	Yr	NM
45s			
COLUMBIA			
❑ 4-43633	Winken, Blinken and Nod/Until I Get Over You	1966	10.00
PLAYBOY			
❑ 6003	Ever Lovin' Sunshine/Man Smart, Woman Smarter	1974	6.00
❑ 50049	I Am What I Am/One More Time	1974	6.00

FLETCHER, SAM

Number	Title (A Side/B Side)	Yr	NM
45s			
CUB			
❑ 9032	No Such Luck/Time Has a Way	1959	30.00
❑ 9048	Only Heaven Knows/Beyond My Wildest Dreams	1959	30.00
METRO			
❑ 20013	Before/Torn Between Two Loves	1959	25.00
❑ 20022	Out in the Cold Again/If You Love Me	1959	25.00
RCA VICTOR			
❑ 47-7676	Take Me in Your Arms/I Just Had to Tell Someone	1960	25.00
❑ 47-7817	Tall Hope/Far Away from Home	1960	20.00
❑ 47-7872	Hold Me/You Did It	1961	15.00
❑ 47-7972	I Believe in You/Sweet Slumber	1961	15.00
❑ 47-8027	My Girl/This One Night	1962	20.00
❑ 47-8076	The Answer to Everything/Me and the One I Love	1962	20.00
TOLLIE			
❑ 9012	I'd Think It Over/Friday Night	1964	200.00
VAULT			
❑ 502	More Today Than Yesterday/What'll I Do	197?	25.00
❑ 934	The Look of Love/You Better Come Home	1967	15.00
VEE JAY			
❑ 623	Guess Who/The Sinner	1964	12.00
WARNER BROS.			
❑ 5384	As Time Goes By/My Wish	1963	15.00

FLINT, SHELBY

Number	Title (A Side/B Side)	Yr	NM
45s			
CADENCE			
❑ 1352	Oh, I Miss Him So/I Will Love You	1958	15.00
VALIANT			
❑ 701	Angel on My Shoulder/I Will Love You	1965	8.00
❑ 716	Joy in the Morning/Lonely Cinderella	1965	8.00
❑ 743	Cast Your Fate to the Wind/The Lily	1966	8.00
❑ 6001	Angel on My Shoulder/Someday	1960	12.00
❑ 6010	I Will Love You/Every Night	1961	10.00
❑ 6014	A Broken Vow/Magic Wand	1961	10.00
❑ 6017	The Riddle Song/I Love a Wanderer	1962	10.00
❑ 6022	The Boy I Love/Ugly Duckling	1962	10.00
❑ 6031	Little Dancing Doll/It Really Wouldn't Matter	1963	10.00
❑ 6052	Wonderland/Pipes of Keith	1964	10.00
❑ 6060	I've Grown Accustomed to Her (Your) Face/Our Town	1964	10.00
Albums			
MAD SATYR			
❑ MSR-101	You've Been On My Mind	1982	25.00
VALIANT			
❑ LP-401 [M]	Shelby Flint — The Quiet Girl	1961	40.00
❑ LP-403 [M]	Shelby Flint Sings Folk	1962	40.00
❑ LPS-403 [S]	Shelby Flint Sings Folk	1962	50.00
❑ VL-5003 [M]	Cast Your Fate to the Wind	1966	25.00
❑ VLS-25003 [S]	Cast Your Fate to the Wind	1966	30.00

FLINTSTONE, FRED

Number	Title (A Side/B Side)	Yr	NM
45s			
EPIC			
❑ 9475	Bedrock Beat/Stone Age Roll	1961	20.00

FLIPPER

Number	Title (A Side/B Side)	Yr	NM
45s			
SUBTERRANEAN			
❑ SUB 23	Sexbomb/Brainwash	1981	6.00
❑ SUB 23 [PS]	Sexbomb/Brainwash	1981	6.00
❑ SUB 35	Get Away/The Old Lady That Swallowed the Fly	1982	6.00
❑ SUB 35 [PS]	Get Away/The Old Lady That Swallowed the Fly	1982	6.00
THERMIDOR/SUBTERRANEAN			
❑ T 1/SUB 7	Love Canal/Ha Ha Ha	1980	6.00
❑ T 1/SUB 7 [PS]	Love Canal/Ha Ha Ha	1980	6.00
Albums			
SUBTERRANEAN			
❑ SUB 25	Generic Flipper	1981	12.00
❑ SUB 42	Gone Fishin'	1982	12.00
❑ SUB 53	Public Flipper Ltd.	1985	12.00

Number	Title (A Side/B Side)	Yr	NM
FLIRTATIONS, THE (1) Female vocal group.			
45s			
DERAM			
❑ 7531	Give Me Love, Love, Love/This Must Be the End	1970	8.00
❑ 85036	Christmas Time Is Here Again/Nothing But a Heartache	1968	8.00
❑ 85038	Nothing But a Heartache/How Can You Tell Me	1969	6.00
❑ 85048	Need Your Loving/South Caroline	1969	6.00
❑ 85057	I Wanna Be There/Keep On Searching	1970	6.00
❑ 85062	Can't Stop Lovin' You/Everybody Needs Somebody	1970	6.00
PARROT			
❑ 40028	Somewhere Out There/How Can You Tell Me	1968	12.00
Albums			
DERAM			
❑ DES-18028	Nothing But a Heartache	1969	20.00
FLIRTATIONS, THE (2) Male vocal group.			
45s			
FESTIVAL			
❑ 705	Stronger Than Her Love/Settle Down	1967	60.00
FLIRTATIONS, THE (U) May be group (2), or perhaps a completely different group.			
45s			
JOSIE			
❑ 956	Natural Born Lover/Change My Darkness Into Light	1965	15.00
FLO AND EDDIE Also see THE TURTLES.			
45s			
COLUMBIA			
❑ 10028	Come to My Rescue, Webelos/Let Me Make Love to You	1974	6.00
❑ 10204	Come to My Rescue, Webelos/Let Me Make Love to You	1975	5.00
❑ 10264	Illegal, Immoral and Fattening/Rebecca	1975	5.00
❑ 10425	Elenore/The Love You Gave Away	1976	5.00
❑ 10458	Keep It Warm/Hot	1976	5.00
REPRISE			
❑ 1113	Nikki Hoi/Godbye Surprise	1972	5.00
❑ 1142	Afterglow/Original Soundtract from "Carlos & De Bull"	1972	5.00
❑ 1160	If We Only Had the Time/You're a Lady	1973	5.00
Albums			
COLUMBIA			
❑ PC 33554	Illegal, Immoral and Fattening	1975	12.00
❑ PC 34262	Moving Targets	1976	12.00
EPIPHANY			
❑ ELP-4010	Rock Steady with Flo & Eddie	1981	10.00
REPRISE			
❑ MS 2099	The Phlorescent Leech and Eddie	1972	20.00
❑ MS 2141	Flo and Eddie	1973	20.00
RHINO			
❑ RNTA-1999 [(3)]	History of Flo & Eddie	198?	20.00
FLOATERS, THE			
12-Inch Singles			
ABC			
❑ DM-13 [DJ]	Magic (We Thank You) (11:33)/I Just Want to Be with You (5:23)	1978	15.00
MCA			
❑ L33-1834 [DJ]	Levitation (2 versions)	1979	12.00
45s			
ABC			
❑ 12237	I Am So Glad I Took My Time/Take One Step at a Time	1976	4.00
❑ 12284	Float On/Everything Happens for a Reason	1977	4.00
❑ 12284 [PS]	Float On/Everything Happens for a Reason	1977	6.00
❑ 12314	You Don't Have to Say You Love Me/Take One Step at a Time	1977	4.00
❑ 12364	I Just Want to Be with You/Whatever Your Sign	1978	4.00
❑ 12399	Let's Try Love/The Time Is Now	1978	4.00
FEE			
❑ 311	I Am So Glad I Took My Time/Take One Step at a Time	1976	8.00
❑ 2080	For Your Love/Glass House	1980	10.00
❑ 2661	Get Ready/For Your Love	1981	10.00
MCA			
❑ 41063	Levitation/Best of Our Love	1979	4.00
❑ 41063 [PS]	Levitation/Best of Our Love	1979	8.00
Albums			
ABC			
❑ AB-1030	Floaters	1977	10.00
❑ AA-1047	Magic	1978	10.00
FEE			
❑ WW-711	Get Ready for the Floaters and Shu-Ga	1981	30.00
MCA			
❑ 3093	Into the Future	1979	10.00
FLOATING BRIDGE, THE			
45s			
VAULT			
❑ 947	Watch Your Step/Brought Up Wrong	1969	10.00
❑ 953	Don't Mean a Thing/Mr. Jaybird	1969	10.00
Albums			
VAULT			
❑ VS-124	The Floating Bridge	1969	100.00
FLOCK, THE			
45s			
COLUMBIA			
❑ 45021	Tired of Waiting/Store Bought Store Thought	1969	8.00
❑ 45295	Mermaid/Crabfoot	1971	8.00
DESTINATION			
❑ 628	Can't You See/Hold On to My Mind	1966	10.00
❑ 631	Are You the Kind/I Like You	1966	10.00
❑ 635	Take Me Back/Each Day Is a Lonely Night	1967	10.00
U.S.A.			
❑ 910	Magical Winds/What Would You Do If the Sun Died?	1968	8.00
Albums			
COLUMBIA			
❑ CS 9911	The Flock	1969	20.00
—"360 Sound" label			
❑ CS 9911	The Flock	1970	15.00
—Orange label			
❑ C 30007	Dinosaur Swamps	1970	15.00
—Orange label			
❑ C 30007	Dinosaur Swamps	1970	20.00
—"360 Sound" label			
MERCURY			
❑ SRM-1-1035	Inside Out	1975	15.00
FLOOD, DICK			
45s			
EPIC			
❑ 5-9479	Hellbound Train/Judy Lynn	1961	12.00
❑ 5-9500	King or Clown/Never Has So Much Been Lost	1962	12.00
❑ 5-9556	Another Stretch of Track/Outside Your Door (Someone Was Standing)	1962	12.00
KAPP			
❑ 640	These Things Make a Heartache/I Need All the Friends	1965	10.00
❑ 681	Between Two Worlds/From Warm to Cool to Cold	1965	10.00
❑ 754	Don't Sweetheart Me/Trouble's Back in Town	1966	10.00
MONUMENT			
❑ 45-408	The Three Bells (The Jimmy Brown Story)/Far Away	1959	15.00
❑ 45-414	It's My Way/It Only Costs a Dime	1960	15.00
❑ 45-427	Carita/Cowpoke	1960	15.00
NASCO			
❑ 025	Slow It Down/Speak My Name	1971	8.00
NUGGET			
❑ 1026	Home Was Never Like This/Woman Leave Me Alone	1968	8.00
TOTEM			
❑ 7	Sure Gets Dark/(B-side unknown)	1967	8.00
FLORIDIANS, THE			
45s			
ABC-PARAMOUNT			
❑ 10185	That Lucky Old Sun/I Love Marie	1961	50.00
FLOW			
45s			
CTI			
❑ 503	Mr. Invisible/Daddy	1970	6.00
Albums			
CTI			
❑ 1003	Flow	1970	20.00
FLOWER SISTERS, THE			
45s			
HIT			
❑ 120	Chapel of Love/A World Without Love	1964	8.00
—B-side by Bobby Brooks			
❑ 136	People Say/C'Mon and Swim	1964	8.00
—B-side by Leroy Jones			
FLOWERPOT MEN, THE			
45s			
DERAM			
❑ 7513	Let's Go to San Francisco/Let's Go to San Francisco, Part 2	1967	15.00
—As "The Flower Pots"			
❑ 7516	Am I Losing You/A Walk in the Sky	1968	15.00
❑ 85051	A Moment of Madness/Young Birds Fly	1969	12.00
FLOWERS, THE			
45s			
HIT			
❑ 310	The Rain, the Park, and Other Things/It Must Be Him	1967	8.00
—B-side by Kathy Shannon			
FLOYD, EDDIE Also see THE FALCONS.			
45s			
ATLANTIC			
❑ 2275	Hush Hush/Drive On	1965	12.00
LUPINE			
❑ 115	Set My Soul on Fire/Will I Be the One	1963	15.00
MALACO			
❑ 1032	Somebody Touch Me/Never Too Old	1976	5.00
❑ 1035	Chi-Town Hustler/In Paradise	1976	5.00
❑ 1039	Special Christmas Day/Mother, My Dear Mother	1976	5.00
❑ 1040	We Should Really Be in Love/I'll Never Be Loved	1977	5.00
—With Dorothy Moore			
❑ 1043	You're Gonna Walk Out on Me/Prove It to Me	1977	5.00
MERCURY			
❑ 73964	If You Really Love Me/It's Me	1977	4.00
❑ 74003	Disco Summer/Do It in the Water	1978	4.00
SAFICE			
❑ 336	Can This Be Christmas/I'll Be Home For Christmas	1964	12.00
STAX			
❑ 0002	I've Never Found a Girl (To Love Me Like You Do)/I'm Just the Kind of Fool	1968	6.00
❑ 0012	Bring It On Home to Me/The Sweet Things You Do	1968	6.00
❑ 0025	I've Got to Have Your Love/Girl I Love You	1969	6.00
❑ 0036	Don't Tell Your Mama (Where You've Been)/Consider Me	1969	6.00
❑ 0041	Never Never Let You Go/Ain't That Good	1969	6.00
—With Mavis Staples			
❑ 0051	Why Is the Wine Sweeter (On the Other Side)/People Get It Together	1969	6.00
❑ 0060	California Girl/The Woodman	1970	6.00
❑ 0072	My Girl/Laurie	1970	6.00
❑ 0077	The Best Years of My Life/My Little Girl	1970	6.00
❑ 0087	Oh How It Rained/When My Baby Said Goodbye	1971	6.00
❑ 0095	Blood Is Thicker Than Water/Have You Heard the Word	1971	6.00
❑ 0109	Yum Yum Yum (I Want Some)/Tears of Joy	1971	6.00
❑ 0134	You're Good Enough (To Be My Baby)/Spend All You Have on Love	1972	6.00
❑ 0158	Knock on Wood/Lay Your Loving on Me	1973	6.00
❑ 0171	Baby Lay Your Head Down (Gently on My Bed)/Check Me Out	1973	6.00

Number	Title (A Side/B Side)	Yr	NM
❑ 187	Things Get Better/Good Love, Bad Love	1966	12.00
❑ 0188	I Wanna Do Things for You/ We've Been Through Too Much Together	1973	6.00
❑ 194	Knock on Wood/Got to Make a Comeback	1966	15.00
❑ 208	Raise Your Hand/I've Just Been Feeling Bad	1967	10.00
❑ 0209	Guess Who/Something to Write Home About	1974	6.00
❑ 0216	Soul Street/Highway Man	1974	6.00
❑ 219	Don't Rock the Boat/This House	1967	10.00
❑ 223	Love Is a Doggone Good Thing/ Hey Now	1967	10.00
❑ 0232	Stealing Love/I Got a Reason to Smile	1974	6.00
❑ 233	On a Saturday Night/ Under My Nose	1967	10.00
❑ 0239	Talk to the Man/I Got a Reason to Smile	1975	6.00
❑ 246	Holding On with Both Hands/ Big Bird	1968	10.00
❑ 0251	I'm So Glad I Met You/ I'm So Grateful	1975	6.00

Albums

MALACO

Number	Title	Yr	NM
❑ 6352	Experience	1977	12.00

STAX

Number	Title	Yr	NM
❑ 714 [M]	Knock on Wood	1967	70.00
❑ ST 714 [S]	Knock on Wood	1967	70.00
❑ STS-2002	I've Never Found a Girl	1968	30.00
❑ STS-2011	Rare Stamps	1969	25.00
❑ STS-2017	You've Got to Have Eddie	1969	25.00
❑ STS-2029	California Girl	1970	25.00
❑ STS-2041	Down to Earth	1971	25.00
❑ STS-3016	Baby Lay Your Head Down	1973	25.00
❑ STX-4122	Chronicle	1979	12.00
❑ STS-5512	Soul Street	1974	25.00
❑ MPS-8527	Soul Street	198?	10.00

FLOYD, KING

45s

CHIMNEYVILLE

Number	Title (A Side/B Side)	Yr	NM
❑ 435	Groove Me/What Our Love Needs	1970	6.00
❑ 437	Baby Let Me Kiss You/Please Don't Leave Me Lonely	1971	5.00
❑ 437 [PS]	Baby Let Me Kiss You/Please Don't Leave Me Lonely	1971	8.00
❑ 439	Got to Have Your Lovin'/ Let Us Be	1971	5.00
❑ 442	It's Wonderful/Let Me See You Do That Thing	1971	5.00
❑ 443	Woman Don't Go Astray/ Everybody Needs Somebody	1972	5.00
❑ 446	Think About It/Here It Is	1973	5.00
❑ 1779	So Much Confusion/So Much Confusion (Part 2)	1973	5.00
❑ 10202	I Feel Like Dynamite/ Handle with Care	1974	5.00
❑ 10205	Don't Cry No More/ I'm Missing You	1974	5.00
❑ 10206	Can't Give It Up/I'm Gonna Fall in Love with You	1975	5.00
❑ 10207	We Can Love/Making Love	1975	6.00
—With Dorothy Moore			
❑ 10209	Hey Baby/I Really Love You	1976	5.00
❑ 10212	Body English/I Really Love You	1976	5.00
❑ 10218	Stop, Look and Listen/Trouble	1977	5.00
❑ 10222	So True/Doing That No More	197?	5.00
❑ 10224	I Wanna Slow Dance Wit 'Cha/ Stop, Look and Listen	197?	5.00

DIAL

Number	Title	Yr	NM
❑ 1027	Can You Dig It/Learning to Forget You	1974	6.00

ORIGINAL SOUND

Number	Title	Yr	NM
❑ 52	Why Did She Leave Me/ Walkin' and Thinkin'	1964	15.00

PULSAR

Number	Title	Yr	NM
❑ 2401	Times Have Changed/ Groov-a-Ling	1969	10.00
—With the Three Queens			
❑ 2406	Together We Can Do It/ You Got the Love I Need	1969	10.00

UPTOWN

Number	Title	Yr	NM
❑ 719	Love Makes the World Go Round/Walkin' and Thinkin'	1965	12.00
❑ 733	Come On Home (Where You Belong)/I Don't Care (No More)	1966	12.00

V.I.P.

Number	Title	Yr	NM
❑ 25061	Heartaches/Together We Can Do Anything	1970	20.00

Albums

CHIMNEYVILLE

Number	Title	Yr	NM
❑ SD 9047	King Floyd	1971	15.00

PULSAR

Number	Title	Yr	NM
❑ 10602	A Man in Love	1969	20.00

V.I.P.

Number	Title	Yr	NM
❑ 407	The Heart of the Matter	1970	40.00

FLYERS, THE

45s

ATCO

Number	Title	Yr	NM
❑ 6088	On Bended Knee/ My Only Desire	1957	40.00

FLYING BURRITO BROTHERS, THE

Also includes records as "Burrito Brothers." Also see GRAM PARSONS; EARL SCRUGGS.

45s

A&M

Number	Title	Yr	NM
❑ 1067	Train Song/Hot Burrito #1	1969	8.00
❑ 1166	If You Gotta Go, Go Now/ Cody, Cody	1970	8.00
❑ 1189	Down in the Churchyard/ Older Guys	1970	8.00
❑ 1277	White Line Fever/Colorado	1971	8.00
❑ 1277 [PS]	White Line Fever/Colorado	1971	15.00

COLUMBIA

Number	Title	Yr	NM
❑ 10229	Building Fires/Hot Burrito No. 3	1975	5.00
❑ 10287	Bon Soir Blues/Hot Burrito No. 3	1976	5.00
❑ 10389	Big Bayou/Waiting for Love t o Begin	1976	5.00

CURB

Number	Title	Yr	NM
❑ 01011	Does She Wish She Was Single Again/Oh Lonesome Me	1981	4.00
—As "Burrito Brothers"			
❑ 02243	She Belongs to Everyone But Me/ Why Must the Ending Always Be So Sad	1981	4.00
—As "Burrito Brothers"			
❑ 02641	If Something Should Come Between Us/Damned If I'll Be Lonely Tonight	1981	4.00
—As "Burrito Brothers"			
❑ 02667	If Something Should Come Between Us	1982	4.00
—As "Burrito Brothers"			
❑ 02835	Closer to You/Coast to Coast	1982	4.00
—As "Burrito Brothers"			
❑ 03023	I'm Drinkin' Canada Dry/ How'd We Ever Get This Way	1982	4.00
—As "Burrito Brothers"			
❑ 03314	Blue and Broken Hearted Me/ Our Roots Are Country Music	1982	4.00
—As "Burrito Brothers"			
❑ 5402	She's a Friend of a Friend/ (B-side unknown)	1981	4.00
—As "Burrito Brothers"			

MCA CURB

Number	Title	Yr	NM
❑ 52329	Almost Saturday Night/ Juke Box Kind of Night	1983	3.00
—As "Burrito Brothers"			
❑ 52379	My Kind of Lady/Dream Chaser	1984	3.00
—As "Burrito Brothers"			

REGENCY

Number	Title	Yr	NM
❑ 45001	White Line Fever/ (B-side unknown)	1980	6.00

Albums

A&M

Number	Title	Yr	NM
❑ SP-3122	The Gilded Palace of Sin	198?	8.00
—Budget-line reissue			
❑ SP-3631 [(2)]	Close Up the Honky-Tonks	1974	15.00
❑ SP-4175	The Gilded Palace of Sin	1969	20.00
—Brown label			
❑ SP-4175	The Gilded Palace of Sin	1974	12.00
—Silvery label			
❑ SP-4258	Burrito Deluxe	1970	15.00
—Brown label			
❑ SP-4258	Burrito Deluxe	1974	12.00
—Silvery label			
❑ SP-4295	The Flying Burrito Bros.	1971	15.00
—Brown label			
❑ SP-4295	The Flying Burrito Bros.	1974	12.00
—Silvery label			
❑ SP-4343	Last of the Red Hot Burritos	1972	15.00
—Brown label			
❑ SP-4343	Last of the Red Hot Burritos	1974	12.00
—Silvery label			
❑ SP-4578	Sleepless Nights	1976	12.00
—As "Gram Parsons/The Flying Burrito Bros."			
❑ SP-6510 [(2)]	Close Up the Honky-Tonks	198?	12.00
—Reissue of 3631			
❑ SP-8070 [DJ]	Hot Burrito	1975	40.00
—Promo-only issue with poster			

COLUMBIA

Number	Title	Yr	NM
❑ PC 33817	Flying Again	1975	12.00
❑ PC 34222	Airborne	1976	12.00

CURB

Number	Title	Yr	NM
❑ JZ 37004	Hearts on the Line	1981	10.00
—As "Burrito Brothers"			
❑ FZ 37705	Sunset Sundown	1982	10.00
—As "Burrito Brothers"			

REGENCY

Number	Title	Yr	NM
❑ REG-79001	Live from Tokyo	1980	10.00

FLYING MACHINE, THE

This is a British group, no relation to the American group that featured JAMES TAYLOR.

45s

CONGRESS

Number	Title	Yr	NM
❑ 6000	Smile a Little Smile for Me/ Maybe We've Been Loving Too Long	1969	8.00
❑ 6012	There She Goes/Baby Make It Soon	1970	6.00

JANUS

Number	Title	Yr	NM
❑ 121	Hanging on the Edge of Sadness/ My Baby's Coming Home	1970	6.00
❑ 137	Hey Little Girl/The Devil Has Possession of My Mind	1971	6.00

Albums

JANUS

Number	Title	Yr	NM
❑ JLS-3007	The Flying Machine	1969	20.00

FOCUS

Also see JAN AKKERMAN. The "Focus" that appeared on EMI America in the mid-1980s was an R&B group from the United States and not this group.

45s

ATCO

Number	Title	Yr	NM
❑ 7002	Harem Scarem/Birth	1974	6.00

SIRE

Number	Title	Yr	NM
❑ 352	House of the King/Black Beauty	1971	8.00
❑ 704	Hocus Pocus/Hocus Pocus II	1973	6.00
❑ 708	Sylvia/Love Remembered	1973	5.00

Albums

ATCO

Number	Title	Yr	NM
❑ SD 36-100	Hamburger Concerto	1974	12.00
❑ SD 36-117	Mother Focus	1975	12.00

HARVEST

Number	Title	Yr	NM
❑ ST-11721	Focus Con Proby	1978	12.00
—With P.J. Proby			

MERCURY

Number	Title	Yr	NM
❑ 824524-1	Focus: Jan Akkerman and Thijs Van Leer	1986	12.00

SIRE

Number	Title	Yr	NM
❑ SAS-3901 [(2)]	Focus 3	1973	15.00
❑ SAS-7401	Moving Waves	1972	12.00
❑ SAS-7404	In and Out of Focus	1973	12.00
—Reissue of 97027			
❑ SAS-7408	Live at the Rainbow	1973	12.00
❑ SASD-7505	Dutch Masters — A Selection of Their Finest Recordings 1969-1973	1975	12.00
❑ SASD-7531	Ship of Memories	1977	12.00
❑ SES-97027	In and Out of Focus	1970	20.00
—Original issue			

FOGELBERG, DAN

12-Inch Singles

FULL MOON/EPIC

Number	Title	Yr	NM
❑ AS 392 [DJ]	Nether Lands (Stereo) (Mono)	1977	30.00
❑ AS 703 [DJ]	Longer//Face the Fire/Phoenix	1979	25.00
❑ AS 1812 [DJ]	The Language of Love (same on both sides)	1984	7.00
❑ EAS 2039 [DJ]	Go Down Easy (same on both sides)	1985	6.00

45s

COLUMBIA

Number	Title	Yr	NM
❑ 4-45764	Anyway I Love You/ Looking for a Lady	1973	8.00

FULL MOON/EPIC

Number	Title	Yr	NM
❑ ES7 2142 [DJ]	High Country Snows (same on both sides)	1985	5.00
❑ 15-02155	Longer/Heart Hotels	1981	4.00
—Reissue			
❑ 14-02488	Hard to Say/The Innocent Age	1981	4.00
❑ 14-02647	Leader of the Band/ Times Like These	1981	4.00
❑ 14-02821	Run for the Roses/ The Sand and the Foam	1982	4.00
❑ 15-03087	Same Old Lang Syne/ Hard to Say	1982	3.00
—Reissue			
❑ 34-03289	Missing You/Hearts and Crafts	1982	4.00
❑ ENR-03323	Missing You/(B-side blank)	1982	8.00
—One-sided budget release			
❑ 34-03525	Make Love Stay/ Hearts and Crafts	1983	4.00

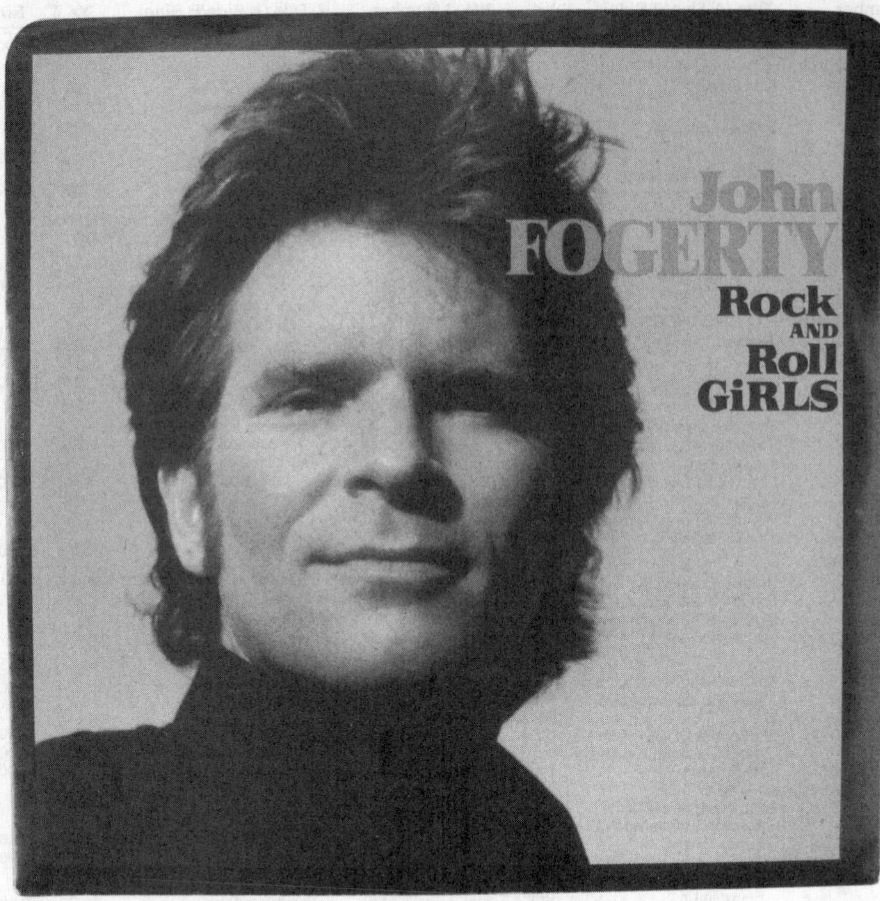

John Fogerty, "Rock and Roll Girls," Warner Bros. 29053, 1985, **$4.**

Number	Title (A Side/B Side)	Yr	NM
❑ ENR-03570	Make Love Stay/(B-side blank)	1983	6.00
—One-sided budget release			
❑ 15-03843	Leader of the Band/Run for the Roses	1983	3.00
—Reissue			
❑ 34-04314	The Language of Love/Windows and Walls	1984	3.00
❑ 34-04314 [PS]	The Language of Love/Windows and Walls	1984	3.00
❑ 34-04447	Believe in Me/Windows and Walls	1984	4.00
❑ 34-04660	Sweet Magnolia and the Traveling Salesman/The Loving Cup	1984	4.00
❑ 34-04835	Go Down Easy/High Country Snows	1985	4.00
❑ 34-05446	Down the Road-Mountain Pass/High Country Snows	1985	4.00
❑ 15-05498	Missing You/Make Love Stay	1985	3.00
—Reissue			
❑ 34-07044	She Don't Look Back/It Doesn't Matter	1987	3.00
❑ 34-07044 [PS]	She Don't Look Back/It Doesn't Matter	1987	3.00
❑ 34-07275	Lonely in Love/Beyond the Edge	1987	4.00
❑ 34-07275 [PS]	Lonely in Love/Beyond the Edge	1987	4.00
❑ 34-07640	Seeing You Again/Hearts in Decline	1987	4.00
❑ 34-07756	The Way It Must Be/What You're Doing	1988	4.00
❑ 8-50055	Part of the Plan/Song from Half Mountain	1974	5.00
❑ 8-50108	Changing Horses/Morning Sky	1975	6.00
❑ 8-50165	Captured Angel/Next Time	1975	6.00
❑ 8-50189	Below the Surface/Comes and Goes	1976	6.00
❑ 8-50234	Old Tennessee/The Crow	1976	6.00
❑ 8-50412	Love Gone By/Scarecrow's Dream	1977	6.00
❑ 8-50462	Nether Lands/False Faces	1977	5.00
❑ 8-50462 [PS]	Nether Lands/False Faces	1977	8.00
❑ 8-50536	Sketches/Promises Made	1978	6.00
❑ 8-50577	There's a Place in the World for a Gambler/Souvenirs	1978	6.00
❑ 9-50824	Longer/Along the Road	1980	4.00
❑ 9-50862	Heart Hotels/Beggar's Game	1980	5.00
❑ 19-50961	Same Old Lang Syne/Hearts and Crafts	1980	4.00
❑ 19-50961 [PS]	Same Old Lang Syne/Hearts and Crafts	1980	6.00
❑ 34-73513	Rhythm of the Rain-Rain/Ever On	1990	5.00

Albums

COLUMBIA

Number	Title	Yr	NM
❑ KC 31751	Home Free	1972	12.00
❑ PC 31751	Home Free	197?	8.00
—Reissue with new prefix			

FULL MOON/EPIC

Number	Title	Yr	NM
❑ AS 1284 [DJ]	The Innocent Age Sampler	1982	12.00
—Promo only; 6 songs			
❑ A2S 1335 [(2)DJ]	Interchords	1982	25.00
—Promo-only release			
❑ KE 33137	Souvenirs	1974	12.00
—First pressings have orange Epic label with small Full Moon logo			
❑ KE 33137	Souvenirs	1975	10.00
—Second pressings have dark blue/black Full Moon label			
❑ PE 33137	Souvenirs	197?	8.00
—Reissue with new prefix			
❑ PE 33499	Captured Angel	1975	10.00
—No bar code on cover			
❑ PE 33499	Captured Angel	198?	8.00
—With bar code on cover			
❑ PEQ 33499 [Q]	Captured Angel	1975	20.00
❑ PE 34185	Nether Lands	1977	10.00
—No bar code on cover			
❑ PE 34185	Nether Lands	198?	8.00
—With bar code on cover			
❑ PE 35364	Phoenix	198?	8.00
—Budget-line reissue			
❑ FE 35634	Phoenix	1979	10.00
❑ KE2 37393 [(2)]	The Innocent Age	1981	12.00
❑ QE 38308	Dan Fogelberg/Greatest Hits	1982	10.00
❑ QE 39004	Windows and Walls	1984	10.00
❑ FE 39616	High Country Snows	1985	10.00
❑ OE 40271	Exiles	1987	10.00
❑ HE 45634	Phoenix	1981	30.00
—Half-speed mastered edition			
❑ HE 48308	Dan Fogelberg/Greatest Hits	1983	30.00
—Half-speed mastered edition			

FOGELBERG, DAN, AND TIM WEISBERG

12-Inch Singles

FULL MOON/EPIC

Number	Title (A Side/B Side)	Yr	NM
❑ AS 550 [DJ]	Tell Me to My Face (7:15) (4:09)	1978	25.00

45s

FULL MOON/EPIC

Number	Title (A Side/B Side)	Yr	NM
❑ 8-50605	Tell Me to My Face/Hurtwood Alley	1978	6.00
❑ 8-50606	The Power of Gold/Lahaina Luna	1978	4.00

Albums

FULL MOON/EPIC

Number	Title	Yr	NM
❑ JE 35339	Twin Sons of Different Mothers	1978	10.00
❑ PE 35339	Twin Sons of Different Mothers	198?	8.00
—Budget-line reissue			
❑ HE 45339	Twin Sons of Different Mothers	198?	30.00
—Half-speed mastered edition			

FOGERTY, JOHN

Includes records as "The Blue Ridge Rangers." Also see CREEDENCE CLEARWATER REVIVAL; TOMMY FOGERTY AND THE BLUE VELVETS; THE GOLLIWOGS.

12-Inch Singles

WARNER BROS.

Number	Title (A Side/B Side)	Yr	NM
❑ PRO-A-2234 [DJ]	The Old Man Down the Road (same on both sides)	1984	8.00
❑ PRO-A-2267 [DJ]	Rock and Roll Girls/Centerfield	1985	8.00
❑ PRO-A-2337 [DJ]	I Can't Help Myself (same on both sides)	1985	8.00
❑ PRO-A-2362 [DJ]	Vanz Kant Danz (edit)/(LP)	1985	8.00
❑ PRO-A-2514 [DJ]	Eye of the Zombie (same on both sides)	1986	8.00
❑ PRO-A-2595 [DJ]	Change in the Weather (edit)/(LP)	1986	8.00
❑ PRO-A-2637 [DJ]	Knockin' on Your Door (same on both sides)	1986	8.00

45s

ASYLUM

Number	Title (A Side/B Side)	Yr	NM
❑ 45274	Rockin' All Over the World/The Wall	1975	6.00
❑ 45293	Almost Saturday Night/Sea Cruise	1975	6.00
❑ 45309	You Got the Magic/Evil Thing	1976	15.00
❑ 45309 [DJ]	You Got the Magic (stereo/mono)	1976	10.00

ELEKTRA

Number	Title (A Side/B Side)	Yr	NM
❑ 45309 [DJ]	You Got the Magic (stereo/mono)	1976	20.00
—Promo-only version with wrong label (promos also exist on Asylum)			

FANTASY

Number	Title (A Side/B Side)	Yr	NM
❑ 683	Blue Ridge Mountain Blues/Have Thine Own Way, Lord	1972	5.00
—As "The Blue Ridge Rangers"			
❑ 683 [PS]	Blue Ridge Mountain Blues/Have Thine Own Way, Lord	1972	15.00
—As "The Blue Ridge Rangers"			
❑ 689	Jambalaya (On the Bayou)/Workin' on a Building	1972	6.00
—As "The Blue Ridge Rangers"; green, red and orange label			
❑ 689	Jambalaya (On the Bayou)/Workin' on a Building	1973	5.00
—As "The Blue Ridge Rangers"; brown label			
❑ 700	Hearts of Stone/Somewhere Listening	1973	5.00
—As "The Blue Ridge Rangers"			
❑ 710	Back in the Hills/You Don't Own Me	1973	5.00
—As "The Blue Ridge Rangers"			
❑ 717	Coming Down the Road/Ricochet	1973	5.00

REPRISE

Number	Title (A Side/B Side)	Yr	NM
❑ 17191	Premonition/Born on the Bayou	1998	3.00
❑ 17192	Almost Saturday Night/Who'll Stop the Rain	1998	3.00

WARNER BROS.

Number	Title (A Side/B Side)	Yr	NM
❑ PRO-S-2363 [DJ]	Vanz Kant Danz (edit)/(LP)	1985	10.00
❑ 17283	Blueboy/Bad Bad Boy	1997	3.00
❑ 28535	Change in the Weather/My Toot Toot	1986	4.00
❑ 28535 [PS]	Change in the Weather/My Toot Toot	1986	5.00
❑ 28657	Eye of the Zombie/I Confess	1986	4.00
❑ 28657 [PS]	Eye of the Zombie/I Confess	1986	5.00
❑ 29053	Rock and Roll Girls/Centerfield	1985	4.00
❑ 29053 [PS]	Rock and Roll Girls/Centerfield	1985	5.00
❑ 29100	The Old Man Down the Road/Big Train (From Memphis)	1985	4.00

Number	Title (A Side/B Side)	Yr	NM
❑ 29100 [PS]	The Old Man Down the Road/ Big Train (From Memphis)	1985	5.00

Albums

ASYLUM

Number	Title (A Side/B Side)	Yr	NM
❑ 7E-1046	John Fogerty	1975	12.00
❑ 7E-1081	Hoodoo	1976	—

—Canceled; poor quality bootleg cassettes exist

FANTASY

Number	Title (A Side/B Side)	Yr	NM
❑ MPF-4502	John Fogerty: The Blue Ridge Rangers	1981	10.00
—Reissues prominently place John Fogerty's name on the cover			
❑ F-9415	The Blue Ridge Rangers	1973	15.00
—As "The Blue Ridge Rangers"			
❑ FLP-30523	Revival	2007	15.00

WARNER BROS.

Number	Title (A Side/B Side)	Yr	NM
❑ 25203	Centerfield	1985	15.00
—Originals have the last song on side 2 as "Zanz Kant Danz"			
❑ 25203	Centerfield	1986	10.00
—Later editions have the last song on side 2 re-recorded and listed as "Vanz Kant Danz"			
❑ 25203 [DJ]	Centerfield	1985	30.00
—Promo versions on Quiex II audiophile vinyl			
❑ 25449	Eye of the Zombie	1986	10.00

FOGERTY, TOM

Also see CREEDENCE CLEARWATER REVIVAL; TOMMY FOGERTY AND THE BLUE VELVETS; THE GOLLIWOGS.

45s

FANTASY

Number	Title (A Side/B Side)	Yr	NM
❑ 661	Goodbye, Media Man/ Goodbye, Media Man (Part 2)	1971	5.00
❑ 661 [PS]	Goodbye, Media Man/ Goodbye, Media Man (Part 2)	1971	10.00
❑ 680	Cast the First Stone/ Lady of Fatima	1972	5.00
❑ 691	Forty Years/Faces, Places, People	1972	5.00
❑ 702	Heartbeat/Joyful Resurrection	1973	5.00
❑ 715	Mystic Island Avalon/Reggie	1973	5.00
❑ 726	It's Been a Good Day/Money	1974	5.00
❑ 737	Sweet Things to Come/ There Was a Time	1974	5.00

Albums

FANTASY

Number	Title (A Side/B Side)	Yr	NM
❑ 9407	Tom Fogerty	1972	15.00
❑ 9413	Excalibur	1972	15.00
❑ 9448	Zephyr National	1974	12.00
❑ 9469	Myopia	1974	12.00
❑ 9611	Deal It Out	1981	10.00

FOGERTY, TOMMY, AND THE BLUE VELVETS

Early version of THE GOLLIWOGS, which was an early version of CREEDENCE CLEARWATER REVIVAL.

45s

ORCHESTRA

Number	Title (A Side/B Side)	Yr	NM
❑ (# unknown)	Yes, You Did/Now You're Not Mine	1962	—
—This record may not exist; when the "complete" Creedence Clearwater Revival box set was compiled in 2001, no copy could be found			
❑ 1010	Have You Ever Been Lonely/ Bonita	1961	80.00
❑ 6177	Come On Baby/Oh! My Love	1961	80.00

FOGHAT

Also see SAVOY BROWN.

12-Inch Singles

BEARSVILLE

Number	Title (A Side/B Side)	Yr	NM
❑ PRO-A-725 [DJ]	Stone Blue (Edit) (LP Version)	1978	15.00

—Blue vinyl

45s

BEARSVILLE

Number	Title (A Side/B Side)	Yr	NM
❑ 0008	I Just Want to Make Love to You/Hole to Hide In	1973	5.00
❑ 0014	What a Shame/Helping Hand	1973	5.00
❑ 0019	That'll Be the Day/Wild Cherry	1974	5.00
❑ 0021	Maybelline/Step Outside	1974	5.00
❑ 0306	Slow Ride/Save Your Loving	1975	5.00
❑ 0307	Fool for the City/Take It or Leave It	1976	5.00
❑ 0313	Drivin' Wheel/Night Shift	1976	4.00
❑ 0315	I'll Be Standing By/Take Me to the River	1977	4.00
❑ 0319	I Just Want to Make Love to You (Live)/Fool for the City (Live)	1977	4.00
❑ 0325	Stone Blue/Chevrolet	1978	4.00
❑ 0329	High on Love/Sweet Home Chicago	1978	4.00
❑ PRO-S-780 [DJ]	Run, Run, Rudolph (same on both sides)	1978	10.00
❑ PRO-S-1002 [DJ]	All I Want for Christmas Is You (same on both sides)	1981	10.00
❑ 29612	Seven Day Weekend/ That's What Love Can Do	1983	4.00
❑ 29860	Slipped, Tripped, Fell in Love/ And I Do Just What I Want	1982	4.00
❑ 49125	Third Time Lucky (First Time I Was a Fool)/Love in Motion	1979	4.00
❑ 49125 [PS]	Third Time Lucky (First Time I Was a Fool)/Love in Motion	1979	5.00
❑ 49510	Stranger in My Home Town/ Be My Woman	1980	4.00
❑ 49779	Wide Boy/Love Zone	1981	4.00
❑ 49779 [PS]	Wide Boy/Love Zone	1981	7.00

FOGHAT

Number	Title (A Side/B Side)	Yr	NM
❑ 1069	Goin' Home For Christmas/ Santa Claus Is Back In Town	1986	6.00
❑ 1069 [PS]	Goin' Home For Christmas/ Santa Claus Is Back In Town	1986	7.00

Albums

BEARSVILLE

Number	Title (A Side/B Side)	Yr	NM
❑ BR 2077	Foghat	1972	12.00
❑ BR 2136	Foghat	1973	12.00
❑ BRK 3578	Girls to Chat & Boys to Bounce	1981	10.00
❑ BR 6950	Energized	1974	10.00
❑ BR 6956	Rock and Roll Outlaws	1974	10.00
❑ BR 6959	Fool for the City	1975	10.00
❑ BR 6962	Night Shift	1976	10.00
❑ BRK 6971	Foghat Live	1977	10.00
❑ BRK 6977	Stone Blue	1978	10.00
❑ BRK 6980	Fool for the City	1978	8.00
—Reissue of 6959			
❑ BHS 6990	Boogie Motel	1979	10.00
❑ BHS 6999	Tight Shoes	1980	10.00
❑ 23747	In the Mood for Something Rude	1982	10.00
❑ 23888	Zig-Zag Walk	1983	10.00

RHINO

Number	Title (A Side/B Side)	Yr	NM
❑ R1-70088	The Best of Foghat	1989	10.00
❑ RNLP-70881	Stone Blue	1987	8.00
—Reissue of Bearsville 6977			
❑ RNLP-70882	Fool for the City	1987	8.00
—Reissue of Bearsville 6980			
❑ RNLP-70883	Energized	1988	8.00
—Reissue of Bearsville 6950			
❑ RNLP-70884	Foghat Live	1988	8.00
—Reissue of Bearsville 6971			
❑ RNLP-70887	Foghat	1988	8.00
—Reissue of Bearsville 2077			
❑ RNLP-70888	Night Shift	1988	8.00
—Reissue of Bearsville 6962			
❑ R1-70889	Rock and Roll Outlaws	1988	8.00
—Reissue of Bearsville 6956			
❑ R1-70890	Foghat	1988	8.00
—Reissue of Bearsville 2136			

TPM/RHINO EXCLUSIVE

Number	Title (A Side/B Side)	Yr	NM
❑ 295	Fool for the City	2008	20.00

FOLEY, BRIAN

45s

DOT

Number	Title (A Side/B Side)	Yr	NM
❑ 16889	Where Are We Going in Such a Hurry/Time and Tide	1966	10.00

KAPP

Number	Title (A Side/B Side)	Yr	NM
❑ 861	Love Was Here Before the Stars/ Love Me, Please Love Me	1967	8.00
❑ 861 [PS]	Love Was Here Before the Stars/ Love Me, Please Love Me	1967	12.00
❑ 885	Love Never Changes/Once There Was a Time	1968	8.00
❑ 924	Elvira Madigan Theme/Let's Go	1968	8.00

FOLEY, WEBB

45s

EMERALD

Number	Title (A Side/B Side)	Yr	NM
❑ 2011	Little Town/It Wasn't Faith	1956	400.00
❑ 2013	Bee Bop Baby/You Oughta Make Records	1956	600.00

FOX

Number	Title (A Side/B Side)	Yr	NM
❑ 100	The Look/Strange Little Girl	198?	5.00
❑ 101	George Jones, Jack Daniels, and Me/Vacation Time	198?	5.00
❑ 102	Ma Bell/The Orange and the Green	198?	4.00
❑ 103	The Last Thing on My Mind/ Beer and Popcorn	198?	4.00
❑ 106	Red Ridin' Hood/Time to Do	198?	4.00

M

Number	Title (A Side/B Side)	Yr	NM
❑ 550	You'll Come Back/Adios You All	197?	10.00
❑ 552	Strange Little Girl/One by One	197?	10.00
❑ 553	I Wish It Was Only a Dream/ Time to Do	197?	10.00
❑ 602	Out of My Mind/You and Me	197?	8.00
—With Dixie Lee			
❑ 660	Think About Livin'/Mr. Bottle, Mr. Glass	197?	6.00
❑ 666	Littletown Christmas/ Extra Christmas	197?	5.00
❑ 668	Marlene/Always a Few Things	197?	10.00
❑ 670	Back to Back/Marlene	197?	10.00
❑ 770	Footprints in the Snow/ Vacation Time	197?	10.00
❑ 800	Another Day, Another Heartache/Thirty More Steps	197?	10.00
❑ 1000	The Look/Let George Do It	197?	10.00
❑ 1006	I Love Them, Everyone/ I'm an American	197?	10.00
❑ 1012	Everybody Wants to Get to Heaven/Snodgrass & Me	197?	10.00
❑ 1015	Just Talkin' Baseball/Darling	197?	10.00
❑ 1021	Willie Nelson/Vacation Time	197?	10.00

7-Inch Extended Plays

EMERALD

Number	Title (A Side/B Side)	Yr	NM
❑ 750	Makin' a Plan/Pinkey// They Never Should'a Done It/ Little Bitty Mama	1957	300.00
❑ 750 [PS]	Webb Foley Sings	1957	300.00

FOLKSWINGERS, THE

45s

WORLD PACIFIC

Number	Title (A Side/B Side)	Yr	NM
❑ 391	This Train/Black Mountain Rag	1963	10.00
❑ 396	12 String Special/Amor A Todos	1963	10.00
❑ 77831	Norwegian Wood/Raga Rock	1966	8.00

Albums

WORLD PACIFIC

Number	Title (A Side/B Side)	Yr	NM
❑ ST-1812 [S]	12 String Guitar!	1963	30.00
—Black vinyl			
❑ ST-1812 [S]	12 String Guitar!	1963	60.00
—Red vinyl			
❑ WP-1812 [M]	12 String Guitar!	1963	25.00
❑ ST-1814 [S]	12 String Guitar, Vol. 2	1963	30.00
❑ WP-1814 [M]	12 String Guitar, Vol. 2	1963	25.00
❑ ST-1846 [S]	Raga Rock	1966	75.00
❑ WP-1846 [M]	Raga Rock	1966	75.00

FONTAINE, EDDIE

45s

ARGO

Number	Title (A Side/B Side)	Yr	NM
❑ 5309	Nothin' Shakin'/Don't Ya Know	1958	25.00

CHANCELLOR

Number	Title (A Side/B Side)	Yr	NM
❑ 1018	Goodness, It's Gladys/ Middle of the Road	1958	20.00

DECCA

Number	Title (A Side/B Side)	Yr	NM
❑ 30042	Cool It Baby/Into Each Life Some Rain Must Fall	1956	25.00
❑ 30108	A Rose and a Baby Ruth/ The Years Before	1956	25.00
❑ 30121	As Far As I'm Concerned/ 'Til Tonight	1956	25.00
—With Karen Chandler			
❑ 30202	I'll Be There/East of Mississippi	1957	25.00
❑ 30256	Money/Homesick Blues	1957	25.00
❑ 30338	Hey Marie, Rock with Me/ The One and Only	1957	25.00
❑ 30446	Fun Lovin'/Honky Tonk Man	1957	25.00

JALO

Number	Title (A Side/B Side)	Yr	NM
❑ 102	Where Is Da Woman/It Ain't Gonna Happen No More	1956	80.00

LIBERTY

Number	Title (A Side/B Side)	Yr	NM
❑ 55776	Blue Roses/Way Down Home	1965	10.00
❑ 55823	I Need You/It Can Happen to You	1965	10.00

SUNBEAM

Number	Title (A Side/B Side)	Yr	NM
❑ 105	Nothin' Shakin'/ Oh, Wonderful Night	1958	40.00
❑ 112	Nobody Can Handle This Job/ I'm Ready As I'll Ever Be	1958	25.00
—B-side by Gerry Granahan			
❑ 118	Love Eyes/Something Cha Cha	1958	25.00

VIK

Number	Title (A Side/B Side)	Yr	NM
❑ 0184	Turn the Light On/ Boom-De-De-Boom	1955	25.00
❑ 0193	Here 'Tis/I Look at You	1956	25.00
❑ 0203	Stand On That Rock/ Baby You Did This to Me	1956	25.00

WARNER BROS.

Number	Title (A Side/B Side)	Yr	NM
❑ 5313	My Heart Belongs to You/ I'm Gonna Settle Down	1962	15.00
❑ 5345	(It's No) Sin/All I Want Is You	1963	15.00

"X"

Number	Title (A Side/B Side)	Yr	NM
❑ 0096	Rock Love/All My Love Belongs to You	1955	30.00
❑ 0108	On Bended Knees/ I Miss You So	1955	30.00
❑ 0128	Rollin' Stone/I'm Through Chasin' After You	1955	30.00
❑ 0151	Poor Little Monday/ The Rain Song	1955	30.00
❑ 0184	Turn the Light On/ Boom-De-De-Boom	1955	30.00
❑ 0193	Here 'Tis/I Look at You	1956	30.00
❑ 0203	Stand On That Rock/ Baby You Did This to Me	1956	30.00

Number | Title (A Side/B Side) | Yr | NM

FONTANA, WAYNE Also see WAYNE FONTANA AND THE MINDBENDERS.

45s

BRUT
❑ 812 Sweet America/Interested 1973 5.00

METROMEDIA
❑ 133 Say Goodbye to Yesterday/Dayton, Ohio 1969 6.00

MGM
❑ 13456 It Was Easier to Hurt Her/You Made Me What I Am Today 1966 8.00
❑ 13516 Come On Home/My Eyes 1966 8.00
❑ 13661 Pamela, Pamela/Something Keeps Calling Me Back 1967 6.00
❑ 13762 From a Boy to a Girl/24 Sycamore 1967 6.00

Albums

MGM
❑ E-4459 [M] Wayne Fontana 1967 20.00
❑ SE-4459 [S] Wayne Fontana 1967 25.00

FONTANA, WAYNE, AND THE MINDBENDERS Also see WAYNE FONTANA; THE MINDBENDERS.

45s

A&M
❑ 3010 Game of Love/What a Wonderful World 1988 4.00
—B-side by Louis Armstrong
❑ 3010 [PS] Game of Love/What a Wonderful World 1988 4.00
—"Good Morning Vietnam" sleeve

FONTANA
❑ 1503 Game of Love/Since You've Been Gone 1965 15.00
❑ 1509 Game of Love/One More Time 1965 12.00
❑ 1514 It's Just a Little Bit Too Late/Long Time Comin' 1965 10.00
❑ 1524 She Needs Love/Like I Do 1965 10.00
❑ 1917 Stop, Look, Listen/Road Runner 1964 12.00
❑ 1945 Um, Um, Um, Um, Um, Um/First Taste of Love 1964 12.00

Albums

FONTANA
❑ MGF-27542 [M] The Game of Love 1965 30.00
❑ SRF-67542 [R] The Game of Love 1965 25.00

FOOD

Albums

CAPITOL
❑ ST-304 Forever Is a Dream 1969 140.00

FOOL, THE

45s

MERCURY
❑ 72896 Lay It Down/Rainbow Man 1969 8.00
❑ 72918 We Are One/Shining Light 1969 8.00

Albums

MERCURY
❑ SR-61178 The Fool 1968 30.00

FOOLS, THE

12-Inch Singles

PVC
❑ 3902 Life Sucks, Then You Die (LP Version) (Bleeped Version) 1984 12.00
❑ 4908 World Dance Party//Do Wah Diddy/Psycho Chicken 1985 12.00
—Also known as 'The 12" Fools'

45s

EMI AMERICA
❑ 8036 It's a Night for Beautiful Girls/Sold Out 1980 5.00
❑ 8046 Easy for You/I Won't Grow Up 1980 6.00
❑ 8072 Running Scared/Alibi 1981 5.00
❑ 8081 Lost Number/Local Talent 1981 6.00
❑ SPRO-9324 [DJ] It's a Night for Beautiful Girls/Sold Out 1980 8.00
—Promo-only picture disc in plastic sleeve
❑ SPRO-9330/1 [DJ] Psycho Chicken (Beeped)/(Clucked) 1980 10.00
—Promo only on yellow vinyl

Albums

EMI AMERICA
❑ SPRO-9393/4 [DJ] The First Annual Official Unofficial April Fools Day Live Bootleg... 1980 20.00
❑ SW-17024 Sold Out 1980 12.00
❑ SW-17046 Heavy Mental 1981 12.00

Number | Title (A Side/B Side) | Yr | NM

PVC
❑ 8930 World Dance Party 1985 15.00
❑ 8962 Wake Up ... It's Alive!!! 1987 15.00
❑ 8962 Wake Up... It's Alive 1987 15.00

FOOTPRINTS

45s

CAPITOL
❑ 2052 Never Say Die/Mama Rand's 1967 15.00

FORBES, GRAHAM

Albums

PHILLIPS INTERNATIONAL
❑ PLP-1955 [M] The Martini Set 1959 800.00

FORCE FIVE, THE

45s

ASCOT
❑ 2206 Gee Too Tiger/I Want You Babe 1966 50.00

FORD, BILLY Of BILLY AND LILLIE.

45s

JOSIE
❑ 775 String of Pearls/Stop Lyin' on Me 1955 40.00

REPRISE
❑ 0265 This Is Worth Fighting For/My Girl 1964 12.00

UNITED
❑ 142 Smooth Rocking/You Foxie Thing 1954 30.00
❑ 167 Confessing/Old Age 1955 30.00

VIK
❑ 0263 How Can I Be Sure/Billy Boy Blow 1957 25.00

FORD, DEE DEE Also see DON GARDNER AND DEE DEE FORD.

45s

ABC-PARAMOUNT
❑ 10503 Just Like a Fool (I Keep Hopin')/Shoo-Fly Pie 1963 12.00

BRIAR
❑ 142 Good Morning Blues/I Just Can't Believe 1962 12.00

TODD
❑ 1049 Good Morning Blues/I Just Can't Believe 1959 15.00

FORD, EMILE, AND THE CHECKMATES

45s

ANDIE
❑ 5018 Don't Tell Me Your Troubles/What Do You Want to Make Those Eyes at Me For 1960 15.00

FORD, FRANKIE

45s

ABC
❑ 11431 All Alone Am I/Blue Monday 1974 5.00

ACE
❑ 549 The Last One to Cry/Cheatin' Woman 1958 25.00
❑ 554 Sea Cruise/Roberta 1959 30.00
❑ 566 Alimony/Can't Tell My Heart (What to Do) 1959 25.00
❑ 580 Time After Time/Want to Be Your Man 1960 25.00
❑ 592 Chinatown/What's Goin' On 1960 25.00
❑ 592 [PS] Chinatown/What's Goin' On 1960 50.00
❑ 8009 Ocean Full of Tears/Hour of Need 1963 15.00

BRIARMEADE
❑ 7600 I've Found Someone of My Own/Battle Hymn of the Republic 1976 5.00
❑ 7701 Desperado/Mardi Gras in New Orleans 1977 5.00
❑ 7901 Halfway to Paradise/I'm Proud of What I Am 1979 5.00

CINNAMON
❑ 752 When I Stop Dreamin'/I'm Proud of What I Am 1972 5.00
❑ 767 Talk to a Carpenter/When I Stop Dreamin' 1973 5.00

CONSTELLATION
❑ 101 Chinatown/Ocean Full of Tears 1963 15.00

DOUBLOON
❑ 101 Half a Crown/I Can't Face Tomorrow 1967 10.00

IMPERIAL
❑ 5686 You Talk Too Much/If You've Got Troubles 1960 15.00
❑ 5706 My Southern Belle/The Groom 1960 15.00
❑ 5735 Seventenn/Doghouse 1961 15.00

Number | Title (A Side/B Side) | Yr | NM

❑ 5749 Saturday Night Fish Fry/Love Don't Love Nobody 1961 15.00
❑ 5776 Let 'Em Talk/What Happened to You 1961 15.00
❑ 5819 They Said It Couldn't Be Done/A Man Only Does 1962 15.00

PAULA
❑ 351 Peace of Mind/I'm Proud of What I Am 1971 8.00

STARFIRE
❑ 119 Time After Time/Cheatin' Woman 1979 5.00

SYC
❑ 1227 Growing Pains/Ups and Downs 1982 4.00
❑ 1228 My Prayer/Gospel Ship 1983 4.00

7-Inch Extended Plays

ACE
❑ 105 [PS] The Best of Frankie Ford 1959 150.00
❑ 105 Chinatown My Chinatown/Time After Time//Sea Cruise/Roberta 1959 150.00

Albums

ACE
❑ LP 1005 [M] Let's Take a Sea Cruise 1959 300.00

BRIARMEADE
❑ BR-5002 Frankie Ford 1976 12.00

FORD, LITA

12-Inch Singles

RCA
❑ 8641-1-RDA [DJ] Back to the Cave (same on both sides) 1988 20.00

45s

RCA
❑ 6866-7-R Kiss Me Deadly/Broken Dreams 1988 3.00
❑ 6866-7-R [PS] Kiss Me Deadly/Broken Dreams 1988 3.00
❑ 8640-7-R Back to the Cave/Under the Gun 1988 3.00
❑ 8640-7-R [PS] Back to the Cave/Under the Gun 1988 4.00
❑ 8899-7-R Close My Eyes Forever/Under the Gun 1989 3.00
—A-side with Ozzy Osbourne
❑ 8899-7-R [PS] Close My Eyes Forever/Under the Gun 1989 3.00
❑ 9008-7-R Falling In and Out of Love/Fatal Passion 1989 3.00
❑ 9008-7-R [PS] Falling In and Out of Love/Fatal Passion 1989 3.00

Albums

MERCURY
❑ 810331-1 Out for Blood 1984 8.00
—Reissue cover has a different photo of Lita holding a non-bloody guitar
❑ 810331-1 Out for Blood 1984 25.00
—Original cover has Lita holding a bloody, gored guitar
❑ 818864-1 Dancin' on the Edge 1984 10.00

RCA
❑ 2090-1-R Stiletto 1990 10.00
❑ 6397-1-R Lita 1988 8.00

FORD, NEAL, AND THE FANATICS

45s

ABC
❑ 11184 You Made Me a Man/I've Got to Find Me a Woman 1969 30.00
—As "The Neal Ford Factory"

HICKORY
❑ 1433 Gonna Be My Girl/Shame on You 1967 20.00
❑ 1468 Get Together with Me/Pain 1967 20.00
❑ 1490 I Have Thoughts of You/That Girl of Mine 1967 20.00
❑ 1500 Movin' Along/Little World Girl 1968 20.00
❑ 1506 The Jones/Mary Wanna Marry Me 1968 20.00
❑ 1516 I'll Put My Boots On Backwards/Buttercup 1968 20.00

TANTARA
❑ 1101 Don't Tie Me Down/Bitter Bells 1966 30.00
❑ 1104 Searchin'/All I Have to Do Is Dream 1966 30.00
❑ 1107 I Will If You Want/(B-side unknown) 1966 30.00

Albums

HICKORY
❑ LPS-141 Neal Ford and the Fanatics 1968 35.00

FORD, ROCKY BILLY

Albums

AUDIO LAB
❑ AL-1561 [M] A New Singing Star 1960 150.00

Except when noted otherwise, VG = 25% of NM, and VG+ = 50% of NM. (Example: VG = $2.00, VG+ = $4.00 and NM = $8.00.)

F

FORD THEATRE, THE

45s

ABC

Number	Title (A Side/B Side)	Yr	NM
❑ 11118	Theme for the Masses/ I Can't Help It Baby	1968	10.00
❑ 11227	I've Got the Fever/ Jefferson Airplane	1969	10.00

Albums

ABC

Number	Title (A Side/B Side)	Yr	NM
❑ S-658	Trilogy	1968	75.00
❑ S-681	Time Changes	1969	20.00

FOREHAND, EDDIE "BUSTER"

45s

JOSIE

Number	Title (A Side/B Side)	Yr	NM
❑ 981	I'm So Lonely/But I Do	1967	30.00
❑ 993	You Were Meant for Me/ Young Boy Blues	1968	30.00

MINIT

Number	Title (A Side/B Side)	Yr	NM
❑ 32076	City of Blues/Cry Me a River	1969	25.00

FOREIGNER

Also see BLACK SHEEP; SPOOKY TOOTH; MICK JONES; LOU GRAMM.

12-Inch Singles

ATLANTIC

Number	Title (A Side/B Side)	Yr	NM
❑ PR 393 [DJ]	Urgent (same on both sides)	1981	10.00
❑ PR 440 [DJ]	Break It Up/Head Games (Live)	1982	15.00
❑ PR 475 [DJ]	Hot Blooded (Live) (same on both sides)	1982	15.00
❑ PR 708 [DJ]	That Was Yesterday (same on both sides)	1985	8.00
❑ PR 770 [DJ]	Down on Love (same on both sides)	1985	8.00
❑ DMD 827 [DJ]	That Was Yesterday (Vocal/Extended Version) (Instrumental Version) (Orchestral Version)	1985	8.00
❑ DMD 853 [DJ]	Reaction to Action (Vocal Long Version 7:17) (Instrumental 5:48) (Vocal Edit 4:53)	1985	8.00
❑ PR 2259 [DJ]	I Don't Want to Live Without You (same on both sides)	1988	8.00

45s

ATLANTIC

Number	Title (A Side/B Side)	Yr	NM
❑ 3394	Feels Like the First Time/ Woman, Oh Woman	1977	4.00
❑ 3410	Cold As Ice/I Need You	1977	4.00
—Has a different mix (with strings) than the LP version			
❑ 3439	Long, Long Way from Home/ The Damage Is Done	1977	4.00
—Has a different vocal with slightly altered lyrics from the LP version			
❑ 3488	Hot Blooded/Tramontaine	1978	4.00
❑ 3514	Double Vision/Lonely Children	1978	4.00
❑ 3514 [PS]	Double Vision/Lonely Children	1978	5.00
❑ 3543	Blue Morning, Blue Day/ I Have Waited So Long	1978	4.00
❑ 3543 [DJ]	Blue Morning, Blue Day (same on both sides)	1978	10.00
—Promo only on blue vinyl			
❑ 3618	Dirty White Boy/Rev on the Red Line	1979	4.00
❑ 3618 [PS]	Dirty White Boy/Rev on the Red Line	1979	5.00
❑ 3633	Head Games/Do What You Like	1979	4.00
❑ 3633 [PS]	Head Games/Do What You Like	1979	5.00
❑ 3651	Women/The Modern Day	1980	4.00
❑ 3831 [PS]	Urgent/Girl on the Moon	1981	4.00
❑ 3831	Urgent/Girl on the Moon	1981	3.00
❑ 3868 [PS]	Waiting for a Girl Like You/ I'm Gonna Win	1981	5.00
❑ 3868	Waiting for a Girl Like You/ I'm Gonna Win	1981	3.00
❑ 4017 [PS]	Juke Box Hero/Night Life	1982	4.00
❑ 4017	Juke Box Hero/Night Life	1982	3.00
❑ 4044	Break It Up/Head Games (Live)	1982	4.00
❑ 4044 [PS]	Break It Up/Head Games (Live)	1982	4.00
❑ 4044 [DJ]	Break It Up (Edit)/(LP Version)	1982	6.00
❑ 4072	Luanne/Fool For You Anyway	1982	4.00
❑ 89046	Heart Turns to Stone/ Counting Every Minute	1988	3.00
❑ 89046 [PS]	Heart Turns to Stone/ Counting Every Minute	1988	3.00
❑ 89101	I Don't Want to Live Without You/Face to Face	1988	3.00
❑ 89101 [PS]	I Don't Want to Live Without You/Face to Face	1988	3.00
❑ 89169	Say You Will/A Night to Remember	1987	3.00
❑ 89169 [PS]	Say You Will/A Night to Remember	1987	3.00
❑ 89493	Down on Love/Growing Up the Hard Way	1985	3.00
❑ 89542	Reaction to Action/ She's Too Tough	1985	3.00
❑ 89542 [PS]	Reaction to Action/ She's Too Tough	1985	3.00
❑ 89571	That Was Yesterday/ Two Different Worlds	1985	3.00
❑ 89571 [PS]	That Was Yesterday/ Two Different Worlds	1985	3.00
❑ 89596	I Want to Know What Love Is/ Street Thunder	1984	3.00
—Custon black and colorblocked label			
❑ 89596	I Want to Know What Love Is/ Street Thunder	1984	4.00
—Generic red and black Atlantic label			
❑ 89596 [PS]	I Want to Know What Love Is/ Street Thunder	1984	4.00

ATLANTIC OLDIES SERIES

Number	Title (A Side/B Side)	Yr	NM
❑ OS 13208	Feels Like the First Time/ Cold As Ice	1980	3.00
—Reissue			
❑ OS 13209	Hot Blooded/Double Vision	1980	3.00
—Reissue			
❑ OS 13218	Dirty White Boy/Head Games	1981	3.00
—Reissue			
❑ OS 13232	Urgent/Waiting for a Girl Like You	1982	3.00
—Reissue			
❑ OS 13267	Juke Box Hero/Women	1983	3.00
—Reissue			
❑ 84924	Say You Will/I Don't Want to Live Without You	1989	3.00
—Reissue			
❑ 84973	I Want to Know What Love Is/ That Was Yesterday	1987	3.00
—Reissue			

Albums

ATLANTIC

Number	Title (A Side/B Side)	Yr	NM
❑ SD 16999	4	1981	10.00
—First pressings have a hologram sticker on the upper back cover			
❑ SD 16999	4	1982	8.00
—No hologram sticker on back cover			
❑ SD 18215	Foreigner	1977	10.00
❑ SD 19109	Foreigner	1977	8.00
—Reissue of 18215			
❑ SD 19999	Double Vision	1978	10.00
—Second cover has a blue tint with the words "Double Vision" right under the band name			
❑ SD 19999	Double Vision	1978	12.00
—Original cover is mostly brown with the words "Double Vision" barely visible along the bottom edge of front cover			
❑ SD 19999	Double Vision	1979	8.00
—Third cover is the same as the second cover, but has a red tint			
❑ SD 29999	Head Games	1979	10.00
❑ 80999	Records	1982	10.00
❑ 81808	Inside Information	1988	8.00
❑ 81999	Agent Provocateur	1984	8.00
❑ A1-82299	Unusual Heat	1990	25.00
—U.S. vinyl available only through Columbia House			

MOBILE FIDELITY

Number	Title (A Side/B Side)	Yr	NM
❑ 1-052	Double Vision	1981	50.00
—Audiophile vinyl			

Foreigner, "Urgent," Atlantic 3831, 1981, $4.

FOREST

Albums

HARVEST

Number	Title (A Side/B Side)	Yr	NM
❑ SKAO-419	Forest	1970	50.00

FOREVER MORE

45s

RCA VICTOR

Number	Title (A Side/B Side)	Yr	NM
❑ 74-0277	Home Country Blues/ Back in the States Again	1969	8.00
❑ 74-0335	Beautiful Afternoon/ One O'Clock and All's Well	1970	8.00

Albums

RCA VICTOR

Number	Title (A Side/B Side)	Yr	NM
❑ LSP-4272	Yours Forever More	1970	15.00
❑ LSP-4425	Words on Black Plastic	1971	15.00

FORGOTTEN CHILD

Albums

BLUE LAMPION

Number	Title (A Side/B Side)	Yr	NM
❑ BLM 10001	Forgotten Child	1986	60.00

Number	Title (A Side/B Side)	Yr	NM
FORMATIONS, THE			
45s			
BANK			
❑ 1007	At the Top of the Stairs/ Magic Melody	1968	30.00
MGM			
❑ 13899	At the Top of the Stairs/ Magic Melody	1968	10.00
❑ 13963	Love's Not Only for the Heart/ Lonely Voice of Love	1968	20.00
❑ 14009	Don't Get Close/ There's No Room	1968	12.00
FORREST, SONNY			
45s			
ATCO			
❑ 6157	Diddy Bop/Knockdown	1960	40.00
RED TOP			
❑ 128	Mama, Keep My Wife at Home/ Madame Bootie Green	1960	40.00
VERVE			
❑ 10306	Travelin'/Now That I'm Lonely	1963	30.00
—As "Sonny Forest"			

FORTUNE Group of studio musicians who appear to have specialized in recording "song poems," lyrics sent in by unwitting members of the public in reply to ads in the backs of magazines.

Number	Title (A Side/B Side)	Yr	NM
45s			
SONGUILD			
❑ 926	Christmas Without You/ For One Moment in Time You Were Mine	197?	5.00
❑ 931	Astrologer/A Poet	197?	5.00
—B-side by Dick Charles			
❑ 932	Ho Chi Minh Trail/ You're Coming Back to Me	197?	5.00
❑ 935	Be Good to Your Baby/ To My Beloved Myrtle	197?	5.00
❑ 936	Traffic Lights/Spring	197?	5.00
❑ 937	Your Song/Race Horses Have Funny Names	197?	5.00
❑ 938	A Little Bit North and Way Out West/Mary Jane	197?	5.00
❑ 942	Blue Bird Blues/Jakey Stuff	197?	5.00
❑ 945	Red Headed Baby Doll/ That Gray Haired Sweetheart of Mine	197?	5.00
❑ 946	One and Only/ Them Wailin' Blues	197?	5.00
❑ 947	I Saw The Light/ Grapes Born of Vine	197?	5.00
❑ 956	Last Bus To Memphis/ A Place in Your Memory	197?	5.00
❑ 957	Walk a Tight Rope/ Luxury of Lies	197?	5.00
❑ 969	Something of Value/ The Key Is Still There	197?	5.00
—B-side by Bobbi Blake			
FORTUNE, JOHNNY			
45s			
ARENA			
❑ 102	I'm a Fool for You/ Gee But I Miss You	1963	20.00
ARHAVEN			
❑ 1001	I'm a Fool for You/ Gee But I Miss You	1962	25.00
BEAVER			
❑ 111	I'm Requesting a Love Song/ Stay Just One More Day	1966	15.00
CRUSADER			
❑ 104	If You Love Me/Gee But I Miss You	1964	15.00
CURRENT			
❑ 101	Say You Will/Come On and Love Me	1965	15.00
❑ 104	Dan Stole My Girl/You Want Me to Be Your Baby	1965	15.00
❑ 105	I Am Lonely for You/I'll Never Let You Go	1965	15.00
EMMY			
❑ 1001	If You Love Me/Alone and Crying	1960	30.00
❑ 1002	I'm in Heaven (When You Kiss Me)/Gee But I Miss You	1960	30.00
PARK AVENUE			
❑ 104	Need You/One Less Angel	1963	15.00
❑ 110	Midnight Surf/Soul Surfer	1963	15.00
❑ 126	Surfer's Trip/Soul Traveler	1963	15.00
❑ 130	Dragster/Siboney	1963	15.00
❑ 4905	I'm Talkin' About You/ My Wandering Love	1963	15.00
UNITED ARTISTS			
❑ 720	Juarez/It Ain't Necessarily So	1964	15.00
❑ 780	Don't You Lie to Me/Don't Stay Out After Midnight	1964	15.00
VAULT			
❑ 954	Your True Love/Tell me You Love Me	1969	10.00

FORTUNES, THE (1) British band. Records on Argo, Checker, Cub, Decca, DRA, Lake, Queen, Top Rank and Yucca are by at least one different group with the same name; they are outside the scope of this book.

Number	Title (A Side/B Side)	Yr	NM
45s			
CAPITOL			
❑ 3086	Here Comes That Rainy Day Feeling Again/I Gotta Dream	1971	6.00
❑ 3086	Here Comes That Rainy Day Feeling Again/Bad Side of Town	1971	10.00
❑ 3179	Freedom Comes, Freedom Goes/There's a Man	1971	5.00
❑ 3248	Storm in a Teacup/ I'm Not Following You	1971	5.00
❑ 3445	Wait Until September/ Don't Sing to Me	1972	5.00
❑ 3514	I Can't Remember When the Sun Went In/Secret Love	1973	5.00
❑ 3626	Give Me Some Room/ Whenever It's a Sunday	1973	5.00
PRESS			
❑ 9773	You've Got Your Troubles/ I've Gotta Go	1965	12.00
—Purple label			
❑ 9773	You've Got Your Troubles/ I've Gotta Go	1965	16.00
—White label stock copy			
❑ 9798	Here It Comes Again/Things I Should Have Known	1965	10.00
—Purple label			
❑ 9798	Here It Comes Again/Things I Should Have Known	1965	15.00
—White label stock copy			
❑ 9811	This Golden Ring/ Someone to Care	1966	10.00
❑ 60001	Gone from My Mind/Silent Street	1966	10.00
UNITED ARTISTS			
❑ 50211	The Idol/His Smile Was a Lie	1967	10.00
❑ 50280	Painting a Shadow/Fire Brigade	1968	10.00
WORLD PACIFIC			
❑ 77937	That Same Old Feeling/ Lifetime of Love	1970	8.00
Albums			
CAPITOL			
❑ ST-647	Freedom	1971	—
—Canceled			
❑ ST-809	Here Comes That Rainy Day Feeling Again	1971	20.00
❑ ST-11041	Storm in a Teacup	1972	15.00
—Contains the canceled "Freedom" LP with one track deleted, plus the title song added			
COCA-COLA			
❑ (no #) [DJ]	It's the Real Thing	1969	60.00
PRESS			
❑ PR 73002 [M]	The Fortunes	1965	35.00
❑ PRS 83002 [S]	The Fortunes	1965	50.00
WORLD PACIFIC			
❑ WPS-21904	That Same Old Feeling	1970	15.00

FORTUNES, THE (U) None of these are by group (1), but exactly which ones are by the same group as others, we have not yet determined.

Number	Title (A Side/B Side)	Yr	NM
45s			
ARGO			
❑ 5364	Congratulations/Look at Me, Look at You	1960	60.00
CHECKER			
❑ 818	Believe in Me/My Baby Is Fine	1955	60.00
CUB			
❑ 9123	The Ghoul in School/ You Don't Know (What I've Been Through)	1963	15.00
DECCA			
❑ 30541	Tarnished Angel/Who Cares?	1958	60.00
❑ 30688	How Clever of You/Trees	1958	50.00
DRA			
❑ 320	Tell Me/Running Away from Love	1962	300.00
LAKE			
❑ 704	St. John's Cha Cha/Runnin'	196?	15.00
QUEEN			
❑ 24010	Nothing Matters Anymore/ Ugly Duckling	1962	25.00
TOP RANK			
❑ 2019	Steady Vows/In the Night	1959	40.00
YUCCA			
❑ 168	Laugh of the Train/Chi Wawa	1964	30.00
❑ 170	Lonely Teardrops/This Is Love	1964	40.00
49TH PARALLEL, THE			
45s			
MAVERICK			
❑ 1004	Close the Barn Door/ Twilight Woman	1968	20.00
❑ 1011	(Come On Little Child and) Talk to Me/Now That I'm a Man	1968	20.00
Albums			
MAVERICK			
❑ MAS-7001	The 49th Parallel	1969	250.00
FORUM, THE			
45s			
MIRA			
❑ 232	The River Is Wide/I Fall in Love	1967	12.00
❑ 243	Trip on Me/It's Sunday	1967	12.00
❑ 248	A Girl Without a Boy/Go Try to Put Out the Sun	1968	12.00
PENTHOUSE			
❑ 504	The River Is Wide/ (B-side unknown)	1966	20.00
Albums			
MIRA			
❑ MLP-301 [M]	The River Is Wide	1967	15.00
❑ MLPS-301 [S]	The River Is Wide	1967	20.00
FOSTER, CELL, AND THE AUDIOS			
45s			
ULTRA			
❑ 105	Honest I Do/I Prayed for You	1956	250.00
—Maroon label			
❑ 105	Honest I Do/I Prayed for You	1956	400.00
—Yellow label			
FOSTER, DAVID			
12-Inch Singles			
ATLANTIC			
❑ DMD 914 [DJ]	Tap Dance (Instrumental Extended Version 6:40) (Instrumental Version 4:40)	1985	15.00
45s			
ATLANTIC			
❑ 87788	Grown-Up Christmas List/ Freedom	1990	5.00
—A-side with Natalie Cole			
❑ 89140	Winter Games/Piano Concerto in G	1988	3.00
❑ 89140 [PS]	Winter Games/Piano Concerto in G	1988	3.00
❑ 89323	Rendez-Vous/Flight of the Snowbirds	1986	4.00
❑ 89376	Who's Gonna Love You Tonight/Playing with Fire	1986	3.00
❑ 89420	The Best of Me/Saje	1986	3.00
—A-side with Olivia Newton-John			
❑ 89420 [PS]	The Best of Me/Saje	1986	3.00
❑ 89528	Love Theme from St. Elmo's Fire/Georgetown	1985	3.00
❑ 89528 [PS]	Love Theme from St. Elmo's Fire/Georgetown	1985	3.00
—With David Foster's name on front of sleeve in place of "Georgetown"			
❑ 89528 [PS]	Love Theme from St. Elmo's Fire/Georgetown	1985	5.00
—With "Georgetown" listed on front of sleeve			
Albums			
ATLANTIC			
❑ 81642	David Foster	1986	8.00
❑ 81799	The Symphony Sessions	1988	8.00
MOBILE FIDELITY			
❑ 1-123	The Best of Me	1982	30.00
—Audiophile vinyl			
FOSTER, JOHN, AND SONS BLACK DYKE MILLS BAND			
45s			
APPLE			
❑ 1800	Thingumybob/Yellow Submarine	1968	100.00
—With "Thingumybob" on uncut apple side			
❑ 1800	Thingumybob/Yellow Submarine	1968	100.00
—With "Yellow Submarine" on uncut apple side			

Except when noted otherwise, VG = 25% of NM, and VG+ = 50% of NM. (Example: VG = $2.00, VG+ = $4.00 and NM = $8.00.)

Number	Title (A Side/B Side)	Yr	NM
❑ 1800	Thingumybob/Yellow Submarine	1968	120.00

—With black star on uncut apple side

FOTHERINGAY Also see SANDY DENNY.

Albums

A&M

Number	Title	Yr	NM
❑ SP-4289	Fotheringay	1970	15.00

FOTO-FI FOUR, THE Some sources say Harry NILSSON is on this recording.

45s

FOTO-FI

Number	Title (A Side/B Side)	Yr	NM
❑ 107	Stand Up and Holler!/Ismael	1964	25.00
❑ 107 [PS]	Stand Up and Holler!/Ismael	1964	50.00

—Sleeve states: "The Beatles arrive in America! Have fun running the film with this specially scored recording." Price does not include film.

FOUL DOGS, THE

Albums

RHYTHM SOUND

Number	Title	Yr	NM
❑ GA-481	No. 1	1966	400.00

FOUNDATIONS, THE

45s

UNI

Number	Title (A Side/B Side)	Yr	NM
❑ 55038	Baby, Now That I've Found You/Come On Back to Me	1967	8.00
❑ 55058	Back on My Feet Again/I Can Take or Leave Your Loving	1968	6.00
❑ 55073	We Are Happy People/Any Old Time	1968	6.00
❑ 55101	Build Me Up Buttercup/New Direction	1968	8.00
❑ 55117	In the Bad, Bad Old Days (Before You Loved Me)/Give Me Love	1969	6.00
❑ 55137	My Little Chickadee/Solomon Grundy	1969	6.00
❑ 55162	Why Did You Cry/Born to Live, Born to Die	1969	6.00
❑ 55210	Take a Girl Like You/I'm Gonna Be a Rich Man	1970	6.00
❑ 55315	I'll Give You Love/Stoney Ground	1972	6.00

Albums

UNI

Number	Title	Yr	NM
❑ 73016	Baby Now That I've Found You	1968	30.00
❑ 73043	Build Me Up Buttercup	1969	30.00
❑ 73058	Digging the Foundations	1969	30.00

FOUNTAIN, CAPT. JESSE

45s

CAMEO

Number	Title (A Side/B Side)	Yr	NM
❑ 457	When It Rains Love (It Pours)/I'm Marchin'	1967	20.00

NEW ART

Number	Title (A Side/B Side)	Yr	NM
❑ 1002	This Love of Mine/If I Had the Power	196?	10.00

—As "Jessie Fountain"

FOUNTAIN, PETE

45s

CORAL

Number	Title (A Side/B Side)	Yr	NM
❑ 7-38090 [S]	While We Danced at the Mardi Gras/A Closer Walk	196?	10.00
—Small hole, plays at 33 1/3 rpm			
❑ 7-38091 [S]	When the Saints Go Marching In/When It's Sleepy Time Down South	196?	10.00
—Small hole, plays at 33 1/3 rpm			
❑ 7-38092 [S]	Ol' Man River/Do You Know What It Means to Miss New Orleans	196?	10.00
—Small hole, plays at 33 1/3 rpm			
❑ 7-38093 [S]	Lazy River/Basin Street Blues	196?	10.00
—Small hole, plays at 33 1/3 rpm			
❑ 7-38094 [S]	Tin Roof Blues/Way Down Yonder in New Orleans	196?	10.00
—Small hole, plays at 33 1/3 rpm			
❑ 62107	My Inspiration/Japansy	1959	8.00
❑ 62154	A Closer Walk/Do You Know What It Means to Miss New Orleans	1959	8.00
❑ 62211	Sentimental Journey/Columbus Stockade Blues	1960	8.00
❑ 62243	Alone Together/Forbidden Love	1961	8.00
❑ 62266	Oh, Didn't He Ramble/Allison's Theme from Parrish	1962	8.00
❑ 62350	The Grasshopper/Lonely Little Tune	1963	6.00
❑ 62365	Casablanca/Lost Love	1963	6.00
❑ 62376	China Nights/Theme from "Women of the World"	1963	6.00
❑ 62413	Licorice Stick/Estrellita	1964	6.00
❑ 62427	The Horny Wind Blows/Humbug	1964	6.00
❑ 62441	Mr. Stick Man/Amazon	1965	6.00
❑ 62446	Whipped Cream/Midnight Pete	1965	6.00
❑ 62454	Mae/Gotta Travel On	1965	6.00
❑ 62460	Rave On/The Whippenpoof Song	1965	6.00
❑ 62474	Juliet's Theme/Walking the Floor Over You	1965	6.00
❑ 62496	Mood Indigo/Sleepy Serenade	1966	5.00
❑ 62516	Thoroughly Modern Millie/Jimmy	1967	5.00
❑ 62527	Music to Turn You On/(Carol's Theme) The Eyes of Love	1967	5.00
❑ 62545	For Pete's Sake/Danke Schoen	1967	5.00
❑ 62557	Les Bicyclettes De Belsize/Puddin	1969	5.00
❑ 62561	Aquarius/The Flesh Failures	1969	5.00
❑ 62564	Sunday in the Country/Applause	1970	4.00
❑ 62565	Night Train to Memphis/San Antonio Rose	1970	4.00
❑ 65545	San Antonio Rose/Dixie	1961	8.00
❑ 65549	Yes Indeed/While We Danced at the Mardi Gras	1962	8.00
❑ 65563	Corrine, Corrina/Talkin' 'Bout You	196?	6.00
❑ 65566	Shine/Mighty Like the Blues	196?	6.00
❑ 65577	Sugar Bowl Parade/Marching 'Round the Mountain	196?	6.00
❑ 65579	Birth of the Blues/Begin the Beguine	196?	6.00
❑ 65586	Hello, Dolly!/Tippin' In	1964	6.00
❑ 65601	Born to Lose/I Love You So Much It Hurts	196?	5.00
❑ 65602	Tiger Rag/I Love You So Much It Hurts	196?	5.00
❑ 65605	The Christmas Song (Merry Christmas To You)/Santa Claus Medley	1966	8.00
❑ 65606	Fountain in the Rain/Over the Waves	196?	5.00
❑ 65612	My Blue Heaven/Tiger Rag	196?	5.00
❑ 65614	Swing Low, Sweet Chariot/Walking Through New Orleans	196?	5.00
❑ 65616	Maria Elena/Put On Your Old Grey Bonnet	196?	5.00
❑ 65617	When the Saints Go Marching In March/Mardi Gras Walking Club	196?	5.00
❑ 65619	Make Your Own Kind of Music/Early in the Morning	1970	4.00

7-Inch Extended Plays

CORAL

Number	Title	Yr	NM
❑ EC 81177	*La Vie En Rose/If I Had You/That Old Feeling/Tiger Rag	195?	10.00
❑ EC 81177 [PS]	Lawrence Welk Presents Pete Fountain	195?	10.00
❑ EC 81190	Yes Indeed/Dis Ol' Train//Nobody Knows the Trouble I've Seen/Sing You Sinners	195?	10.00
❑ EC 81190 [PS]	Yes Indeed	195?	10.00
❑ 7-98109	Bye Bye Bill Bailey/I Wish I Could Shimmy Like My Sister Kate/Song of the Wanderer (Where Shall I Go?)//Struttin' with Some Barbeque/When You're Smiling (The Whole World Smiles With You)/Hallelujah	196?	10.00
—Stereo jukebox issue; small hole, plays at 33 1/3 rpm			
❑ 7-98109 [PS]	Pete Fountain's Music from Dixie	196?	10.00
❑ 7-98118	Medley: Stardust-Is It True What They Say About Dixie?-When the Saints Go Marching In-Dixie//Jazz Me Blues/Blue Skies	196?	10.00
—Stereo jukebox issue; small hole, plays at 33 1/3 rpm			
❑ 7-98118 [PS]	Plenty of Pete	196?	10.00

Albums

CAPITOL

Number	Title	Yr	NM
❑ SN-16224	Pete Fountain and Friends	1982	8.00
❑ SN-16225	Way Down Yonder in New Orleans	1982	8.00

CORAL

Number	Title	Yr	NM
❑ CXS-710 [(2)]	The Best of Pete Fountain	1969	15.00
❑ CRL 57200 [M]	Lawrence Welk Presents Pete Fountain	1958	20.00
❑ CRL 57282 [M]	Pete Fountain's New Orleans	1959	15.00
❑ CRL 57284 [M]	The Blues	1959	15.00
❑ CRL 57313 [M]	Pete Fountain Day	1960	15.00
❑ CRL 57314 [M]	Pete Fountain at the Bateau Lounge	1960	15.00
❑ CRL 57333 [M]	Pete Fountain Salutes the Great Clarinetists	1960	15.00
❑ CRL 57357 [M]	Pete Fountain On Tour	1961	15.00
❑ CRL 57359 [M]	Pete Fountain's French Quarter	1961	15.00
❑ CRL 57378 [M]	I Love Paris	1961	15.00
❑ CRL 57394 [M]	Swing Low Sweet Chariot	1962	15.00
❑ CRL 57401 [M]	Pete Fountain's Music from Dixie	1962	15.00
❑ CRL 57419 [M]	New Orleans Scene	1963	15.00
❑ CRL 57424 [M]	Plenty of Pete	1963	12.00
❑ CRL 57429 [M]	New Orleans at Midnight	1964	12.00
❑ CRL 57440 [M]	South Rampart Street Parade	1963	12.00
❑ CRL 57453 [M]	Pete's Place	1964	12.00
❑ CRL 57460 [M]	Licorice Stick	1964	12.00
❑ CRL 57473 [M]	Mr. Stick Man	1965	12.00
❑ CRL 57474 [M]	Standing Room Only	1965	12.00
❑ CRL 57484 [M]	Mood Indigo	1966	12.00
❑ CRL 57486 [M]	A Taste of Honey	1966	12.00
❑ CRL 57487 [M]	Candy Clarinet — Merry Christmas from Pete Fountain	1966	12.00
❑ CRL 57488 [M]	I've Got You Under My Skin	1967	12.00
❑ CRL 57496 [M]	Music to Turn You On	1967	15.00
❑ CRL 57499 [M]	Pete Fountain Plays Bert Kaempfert	1968	15.00
❑ CRL 757282 [S]	Pete Fountain's New Orleans	1959	20.00
❑ CRL 757284 [S]	The Blues	1959	20.00
❑ CRL 757313 [S]	Pete Fountain Day	1960	20.00
❑ CRL 757314 [S]	Pete Fountain at the Bateau Lounge	1960	20.00
❑ CRL 757333 [S]	Pete Fountain Salutes the Great Clarinetists	1960	20.00
❑ CRL 757357 [S]	Pete Fountain On Tour	1961	20.00
❑ CRL 757359 [S]	Pete Fountain's French Quarter	1961	20.00
❑ CRL 757378 [S]	I Love Paris	1961	20.00
❑ CRL 757394 [S]	Swing Low Sweet Chariot	1962	20.00
❑ CRL 757401 [S]	Pete Fountain's Music from Dixie	1962	20.00
❑ CRL 757419 [S]	New Orleans Scene	1963	20.00
❑ CRL 757424 [S]	Plenty of Pete	1963	15.00
❑ CRL 757429 [S]	New Orleans at Midnight	1964	15.00
❑ CRL 757440 [S]	South Rampart Street Parade	1963	15.00
❑ CRL 757453 [S]	Pete's Place	1964	15.00
❑ CRL 757460 [S]	Licorice Stick	1964	15.00
❑ CRL 757473 [S]	Mr. Stick Man	1965	15.00
❑ CRL 757474 [S]	Standing Room Only	1965	15.00
❑ CRL 757484 [S]	Mood Indigo	1966	15.00
❑ CRL 757486 [S]	A Taste of Honey	1966	15.00
❑ CRL 757487 [S]	Candy Clarinet — Merry Christmas from Pete Fountain	1966	15.00
❑ CRL 757488 [S]	I've Got You Under My Skin	1967	15.00
❑ CRL 757496 [S]	Music to Turn You On	1967	12.00
❑ CRL 757499 [S]	Pete Fountain Plays Bert Kaempfert	1968	12.00
❑ CRL 757503	Walking Through New Orleans	1968	12.00
❑ CRL 757505	Those Were the Days	1969	12.00
❑ CRL 757507	Both Sides Now	1969	12.00
❑ CRL 757510	Make Your Own Kind of Music	1970	12.00
❑ CRL 757511	Golden Favorites	1970	12.00
❑ CRL 757513	Dr. Fountain's Magical Licorice Stick	1971	12.00
❑ CRL 757516	Something/Misty	1971	12.00
❑ CRL 757517	New Orleans Tennessee	1971	12.00

DECCA

Number	Title	Yr	NM
❑ DL 75374	Pete Fountain's New Orleans	1972	12.00
—Reissue of Coral 757282			
❑ DL 75375	The Blues	1972	12.00
—Reissue of Coral 757284			
❑ DL 75377	Mr. New Orleans	1972	12.00
❑ DL 75378	Dr. Fountain's Magical Licorice Stick	1972	10.00
—Reissue of Coral 757513			
❑ DL 75379	Something/Misty	1972	10.00
—Reissue of Coral 757516			
❑ DL 75380	New Orleans Tennessee	1972	12.00
—Reissue of Coral 757517			

EVEREST ARCHIVE OF FOLK & JAZZ

Number	Title	Yr	NM
❑ 257	New Orleans All-Stars	197?	10.00

FIRST AMERICAN

Number	Title	Yr	NM
❑ 7706	New Orleans Jazz	1978	10.00

INTERMEDIA

Number	Title	Yr	NM
❑ QS-5038	Down on Rampart Street	198?	8.00

JUCU

Number	Title	Yr	NM
❑ JMK-12S	Pete Fountain's Jazz Reunion	1976	12.00

MCA

Number	Title	Yr	NM
❑ 165	Mr. New Orleans	1973	10.00
—Reissue of Decca 75377			
❑ 176	Something/Misty	1973	10.00
—Reissue of Decca 75379			
❑ 336	Crescent City	1974	10.00
❑ 505	Pete Fountain's New Orleans	1974	10.00
—Reissue of Decca 75374			
❑ 506	The Blues	1974	10.00
—Reissue of Decca 75375			
❑ 507	Dr. Fountain's Magical Licorice Stick	1974	10.00
—Reissue of Decca 75378			
❑ 508	New Orleans Tennessee	1974	10.00
—Reissue of Decca 75380			
❑ 2-4032 [(2)]	The Best of Pete Fountain	1974	12.00
—Reissue of Coral 710			
❑ 2-4095 [(2)]	The Best of Pete Fountain, Vol. 2	1976	12.00
—Black labels with rainbow			
❑ 2-4095 [(2)]	The Best of Pete Fountain, Vol. 2	1977	10.00
—Tan labels			

PICKWICK

Number	Title	Yr	NM
❑ SPC-3024	Pete Fountain	196?	12.00
❑ SPC-3201	High Society	1971	10.00

RCA CAMDEN

Number	Title	Yr	NM
❑ CAL-727 [M]	Dixieland	1962	12.00

Number	Title (A Side/B Side)	Yr	NM
❑ CAS-727 [R]	Dixieland	1962	10.00

RCA VICTOR

Number	Title (A Side/B Side)	Yr	NM
❑ LPM-2097 [M]	Pete Fountain at the Jazz Band Ball	1960	15.00
❑ LSP-2097 [S]	Pete Fountain at the Jazz Band Ball	1960	20.00

VOCALION

Number	Title (A Side/B Side)	Yr	NM
❑ VL 3803 [M]	And the Angels Sing	1967	12.00
❑ VL 73803 [S]	And the Angels Sing	1967	12.00

FOUNTAIN, PETE, AND AL HIRT

Also see each artist's individual listings.

45s

CORAL

Number	Title (A Side/B Side)	Yr	NM
❑ 65544	March of the Bob Cats/ Farewell Blues	1962	8.00

Albums

CORAL

Number	Title (A Side/B Side)	Yr	NM
❑ CRL 57389 [M]	Bourbon Street	1962	15.00
❑ CRL 757389 [S]	Bourbon Street	1962	20.00

MGM

Number	Title (A Side/B Side)	Yr	NM
❑ E-4216 [M]	The Very Best of Al Hirt and Pete Fountain	1964	12.00
❑ SE-4216 [S]	The Very Best of Al Hirt and Pete Fountain	1964	15.00

MONUMENT

Number	Title (A Side/B Side)	Yr	NM
❑ 8602 [(2)]	Super I	1975	10.00

FOUNTAIN, PETE, AND "BIG" TINY LITTLE

45s

CORAL

Number	Title (A Side/B Side)	Yr	NM
❑ 65557	Ain't Misbehavin'/ American Patrol	196?	6.00
❑ 65598	Honeysuckle Rose/ Darktown Strutters' Ball	196?	5.00

Albums

CORAL

Number	Title (A Side/B Side)	Yr	NM
❑ CRL 57334 [M]	Mr. New Orleans Meets Mr. Honky Tonk	1961	15.00
❑ CRL 757334 [S]	Mr. New Orleans Meets Mr. Honky Tonk	1961	20.00

FOUNTAIN, ROOSVELT, AND PENS OF RHYTHM

45s

M&M

Number	Title (A Side/B Side)	Yr	NM
❑ 331	I'm Gonna Be with You/ One Night	196?	100.00

PRINCE-ADAMS

Number	Title (A Side/B Side)	Yr	NM
❑ 45-447	Red Pepper I/Red Pepper II	1962	20.00

FOUNTAIN OF YOUTH

45s

COLGEMS

Number	Title (A Side/B Side)	Yr	NM
❑ 66-1020	Livin' Too Fast/(Angie, Love Me) Make the Hurt Go Away	1968	20.00
❑ 66-1024	Take a Giant Step/Don't Blame Me (For Trying)	1968	20.00
❑ 66-1032	The Day Don't Come/Sunshine on a Cold Morning	1969	15.00
❑ 66-5003	Liza Jane/Mistress People	1969	15.00

FOUR ACES

Also see AL ALBERTS.

45s

ABC-PARAMOUNT

Number	Title (A Side/B Side)	Yr	NM
❑ 10166	Searching/Dolce Par Niente	1960	10.00
❑ 10183	Me Without You/The Ballad of Patrick Henry	1961	10.00

DECCA

Number	Title (A Side/B Side)	Yr	NM
❑ 27860	Tell Me Why/A Garden in the Rain	1951	20.00
❑ 27937	Perfidia/You Brought Me Love	1952	20.00
❑ 28073	My Hero/Spring Is a Wonderful Thing	1952	20.00
❑ 28162	I'm Yours/I Understand	1952	20.00
❑ 28323	Should I/There's Only Tonight	1952	20.00
❑ 28390	Heart and Soul/Just Squeeze Me	1952	20.00
❑ 28391	I'll Never Smile Again/My Devotion	1952	20.00
❑ 28392	Tip-Pi-Tin/Heaven Can Wait	1952	20.00
❑ 28393	La Rosita/Take Me in Your Arms	1952	20.00
❑ 28560	You Fooled Me/If You Take My Heart Away	1953	15.00
❑ 28691	Organ Grinder's Swing/Honey in the Horn	1953	15.00
❑ 28744	Don't Forget Me/False Love	1953	15.00
❑ 28843	Laughing on the Outisde (Crying on the Inside)/I've Been Waiting a Lifetime	1953	15.00
❑ 28927	The Gang That Sang "Heart of My Heart"/Stranger in Paradise	1953	15.00
❑ 28979	Bandera (Texas Polka)/What More Is There	1954	15.00
❑ 29036	Amor/So Long	1954	15.00
❑ 29123	Three Coins in the Fountain/ Wedding Bells (Are Breaking Up That Old Gang of Mine)	1954	15.00
❑ 29217	Dream/It Shall Come to Pass	1954	15.00
❑ 29269	It's a Woman's World/The Cuckoo Bird in the Pickle Tree	1954	15.00
❑ 29344	Mister Sandman/(I'll Be With You) In Apple Blossom Time	1954	15.00
❑ 29395	Melody of Love/There Is a Tavern in the Town	1954	15.00
❑ 29435	There Goes My Heart/ You'll Always Be the One	1955	12.00
❑ 29476	Heart/Sluefoot	1955	12.00
❑ 29625	Love is a Many-Splendored Thing/Shine On Harvest Moon	1955	12.00
❑ 29702	The Christmas Song (Merry Christmas to You)/Jingle Bells	1955	12.00
❑ 29712	O Holy Night/Silent Night	1955	12.00
❑ 29725	A Woman in Love/ Of This I'm Sure	1955	12.00
❑ 29809	If You Can Dream/The Gal with the Yaller Shoes	1956	12.00
❑ 29889	To Love Again/Charlie Was a Boxer	1956	12.00
❑ 29989	I Only Know I Love You/Dreamer	1956	12.00
❑ 30041	Friendly Persuasion (Thee I Love)/You Can't Run Away from It	1956	12.00
❑ 30123	Someone to Love/ Written on the Wind	1956	12.00
❑ 30242	Bahama Mama/You're Mine	1957	12.00
❑ 30348	Three Sheets to the Wind/ Yes Sir, That's My Baby	1957	12.00
❑ 30384	Half of My Heart/When My Sugar Walks Down the Street	1957	12.00
❑ 30466	How Do You Say Goodbye?/ I Would Love You Still	1957	12.00
❑ 30575	Rock and Roll Rhapsody/ I Wish I May, I Wish I Might	1958	12.00
❑ 30649	Saturday Swing-Out/ Take My Heart	1958	12.00
❑ 30695	Two Arms, Two Lips, One Heart/Heartache in Costume	1958	12.00
❑ 30721	Roses of Rio/Hangin' Up a Horseshoe	1958	12.00
❑ 30764	The World Outside/How Can You Forget	1958	12.00
❑ 30775	Ol' Fatso/Christmas Tree	1958	12.00
❑ 30822	No Other Arms, No Other Lips/ The Inn of the Sixth Happiness	1959	10.00
❑ 30874	Ciao, Ciao Bambino/ Paradise Island	1959	10.00
❑ 30897	The Five Pennies/ Anyone Would Love You	1959	10.00
❑ 30989	Waltzing Matilda/The Wonder of It All	1959	10.00
❑ 31027	I Love Paris/Till Tomorrow	1959	10.00
❑ 31081	Poor Butterfly/You Are Music	1960	10.00

FLASH

Number	Title (A Side/B Side)	Yr	NM
❑ 103	Who's to Blame/Two Little Kisses	1950	30.00

JUBILEE

Number	Title (A Side/B Side)	Yr	NM
❑ 5416	It's All Over But the Crying/ Lonely Hill	1962	8.00

RADNOR

Number	Title (A Side/B Side)	Yr	NM
❑ 301	Always Keep Me in Your Heart/ Didn't We	1968	5.00
❑ 302	I Started a Joke/Summer Won't Be Summer	1969	5.00

VICTORIA

Number	Title (A Side/B Side)	Yr	NM
❑ 101	Sin/Arizona Moon	1951	25.00
—Black vinyl			
❑ 101	Sin/Arizona Moon	1951	60.00
—Red vinyl			
❑ 102	There's a Christmas Tree in Heaven/There's a Small Hotel	1951	30.00

7-Inch Extended Plays

DECCA

Number	Title (A Side/B Side)	Yr	NM
❑ ED 2004	Tell Me Why/Perfidia// I Understand/My Hero	195?	15.00
❑ ED 2004 [PS]	The Four Aces, Vol. 1	195?	15.00
❑ ED 2170	*I Don't Know Why/(I'll Be With You) In Apple Blossom Time/ Dream/Among My Souvenirs	195?	15.00
❑ ED 2170 [PS]	Dream	195?	15.00
❑ ED 2211	I'm in the Mood for Love/What a Difference a Day Makes//Stars Fell on Alabama/Pennies from Heaven	195?	12.00
❑ ED 2211 [PS]	Mood for Love, Vol. 1	195?	12.00
❑ ED 2212	Let's Fall in Love/Don't Take Your Love from Me//It's the Talk of the Town/I'm Sitting on Top of the World	195?	12.00
❑ ED 2212 [PS]	Mood for Love, Vol. 2	195?	12.00
❑ ED 2213	There Goes My Heart/Melody of Love//Three Coins in the Fountain/Stranger in Paradise	195?	12.00
❑ ED 2213 [PS]	Mood for Love, Vol. 3	195?	12.00
❑ ED 2309	White Christmas/The Christmas Song//Silent Night/O Little Town of Bethlehem/Joy to the World	1956	12.00
❑ ED 2309 [PS]	A Merry Christmas with the Four Aces, Part 1	1956	12.00
❑ ED 2310	Silver Bells/Jingle Bells//O Come All Ye Faithful/Hark! The Herald Angels Sing/We Three Kings of Orient Are	1956	12.00
❑ ED 2310 [PS]	A Merry Christmas with the Four Aces, Part 2	1956	12.00
❑ ED 2311	Santa Claus Is Comin' to Town/ Rudolph the Red-Nosed Reindeer//O Holy Night (Cantique de Noel)/The First Nowell/Deck the Hall	1956	12.00
❑ ED 2311 [PS]	A Merry Christmas with the Four Aces, Part 3	1956	12.00
❑ ED 2323	The Gang That Sang "Heart of My Heart"/Wedding Bells (Are Breaking Up That Old Gang of Mine)//Mister Sandman/There Is a Tavern in the Town	195?	12.00
❑ ED 2323 [PS]	Heart of My Heart	195?	12.00
❑ ED 2324	Amor/I'm Yours//Organ Grinder's Swing/So Long	195?	12.00
❑ ED 2324 [PS]	Amor	195?	12.00
❑ ED 2529	(It's No) Sin/Somebody Else Is Taking My Place//Have You Ever Been Lonely (Have You Ever Been Blue)/There I've Said It Again	195?	12.00
❑ ED 2529 [PS]	Shufflin' Along, Vol. 1	195?	12.00
❑ ED 2565	(contents unknown)	195?	12.00
❑ ED 2565 [PS]	Hits from Hollywood	195?	12.00
❑ ED 2675	(contents unknown)	1959	12.00
❑ ED 2675 [PS]	Beyond the Blue Horizon	1959	12.00

Albums

DECCA

Number	Title (A Side/B Side)	Yr	NM
❑ DL 4013 [M]	The Golden Hits of the Four Aces	1960	20.00
❑ DL 5429 [10]	The Four Aces	1952	80.00
❑ DL 8122 [M]	The Mood for Love	1955	50.00
—All-black label, silver print			
❑ DL 8122 [M]	The Mood for Love	196?	20.00
—Black label with color bars			
❑ DL 8191 [M]	Merry Christmas	1956	50.00
❑ DL 8227 [M]	Sentimental Souvenirs	1956	50.00
—All-black label, silver print			
❑ DL 8227 [M]	Sentimental Souvenirs	196?	20.00
—Black label with color bars			
❑ DL 8228 [M]	Heart and Soul	1956	50.00
—All-black label, silver print			
❑ DL 8228 [M]	Heart and Soul	196?	20.00
—Black label with color bars			
❑ DL 8312 [M]	She Sees All the Hollywood Hits	1957	50.00
❑ DL 8567 [M]	Shuffling Along	1957	50.00
—All-black label, silver print			
❑ DL 8567 [M]	Shuffling Along	196?	20.00
—Black label with color bars			
❑ DL 8693 [M]	Hits from Hollywood	1958	50.00
—All-black label, silver print			
❑ DL 8693 [M]	Hits from Hollywood	196?	20.00
—Black label with color bars			
❑ DL 8766 [M]	The Swingin' Aces	1958	40.00
—All-black label, silver print			
❑ DL 8766 [M]	The Swingin' Aces	196?	20.00
—Black label with color bars			
❑ DL 8855 [M]	Hits from Broadway	1959	40.00
—All-black label, silver print			
❑ DL 8855 [M]	Hits from Broadway	196?	20.00
—Black label with color bars			
❑ DL 8944 [M]	Beyond the Blue Horizon	1959	40.00
—All-black label, silver print			
❑ DL 8944 [M]	Beyond the Blue Horizon	196?	20.00
—Black label with color bars			
❑ DL 74013 [S]	The Golden Hits of the Four Aces	1960	25.00
❑ DL 78766 [S]	The Swingin' Aces	1958	50.00
—All-black label, silver print			
❑ DL 78766 [S]	The Swingin' Aces	196?	25.00
—Black label with color bars			
❑ DL 78855 [S]	Hits from Broadway	1959	50.00
—All-black label, silver print			
❑ DL 78855 [S]	Hits from Broadway	196?	25.00
—Black label with color bars			
❑ DL 78944 [S]	Beyond the Blue Horizon	1959	50.00
—All-black label, silver print			
❑ DL 78944 [S]	Beyond the Blue Horizon	196?	25.00
—Black label with color bars			

MCA

Number	Title (A Side/B Side)	Yr	NM
❑ 4033 [(2)]	The Best of the Four Aces	197?	15.00

PICKWICK

Number	Title (A Side/B Side)	Yr	NM
❑ SPC-3527	Love Is a Many-Splendored Thing	197?	10.00

UNITED ARTISTS

Number	Title (A Side/B Side)	Yr	NM
❑ UAL-3337 [M]	Record Oldies	1963	20.00
❑ UAS-6337 [S]	Record Oldies	1963	25.00

VOCALION

Number	Title (A Side/B Side)	Yr	NM
❑ VL 3604 [M]	The Four Aces Sing	196?	15.00
❑ VL 73881	There Goes My Heart	1969	12.00
❑ VL 73902	Written on the Wind	1970	12.00

FOUR AIMS, THE
See FOUR TOPS.

FOUR BARS, THE

45s

JOSIE

Number	Title (A Side/B Side)	Yr	NM
❑ 762	Grief by Day, Grief by Night/Hey Baby	1954	300.00
❑ 768	If I Give My Heart to You/Stop It! Quit It!	1954	300.00
❑ 783	Let Me Live/Why Do You Treat Me This Way	1955	600.00

REPUBLIC

Number	Title (A Side/B Side)	Yr	NM
❑ 7101	Memories of You/When Did You Leave Heaven	1954	600.00

FOUR BELLS, THE

45s

GEM

Number	Title (A Side/B Side)	Yr	NM
❑ 207	Please Tell It to Me/Long Way to Go	1953	800.00
❑ 220	Only a Miracle/My Tree	1954	800.00

FOUR BROTHERS AND A COUSIN

45s

JAGUAR

Number	Title (A Side/B Side)	Yr	NM
❑ 3003	Trust in Me/Whistle Stop Blues	1954	400.00
❑ 3005	Whispeing Wind/Can It Be	1954	500.00

FOUR BUDDIES, THE (1)
Vocal group from Baltimore.

45s

SAVOY

Number	Title (A Side/B Side)	Yr	NM
❑ 769	I Will Wait/Just to See You Smile Again	1951	400.00
❑ 769	I Will Wait/Just to See You Smile Again	1951	500.00
—As "The Four Buds"			
❑ 779	Don't Leave Me Now/Sweet Slumber	1951	400.00
❑ 789	My Summer's Gone/Why at a Time Like This	1951	300.00
❑ 817	Heart and Soul/Sin	1951	300.00
❑ 823	Window Eyes/Simply Say Goodbye	1951	300.00
❑ 845	You're Part of Me/Story Blues	1952	300.00
❑ 866	What's the Matter with Me/Sweet Tooth for My Baby	1952	300.00
❑ 888	My Mother's Eyes/Ooh Ow	1953	300.00
❑ 891	I'd Climb the Highest Mountain/I Wanna Know	1953	300.00
—B-side by Dolly Cooper			

FOUR BUDDIES, THE (2)
Vocal group from Chicago.

45s

CLUB 51

Number	Title (A Side/B Side)	Yr	NM
❑ 105	Delores/Look Out	1956	200.00
—Black vinyl			
❑ 105	Delores/Look Out	1956	4000.
—Red vinyl			

FOUR BUDDIES, THE (3)

45s

CORAL

Number	Title (A Side/B Side)	Yr	NM
❑ 62217	Hurt/Moonglow & Theme from Picnic	1960	20.00
❑ 62325	The Light/Cin Cin (Che Bell)	1962	20.00

IMPERIAL

Number	Title (A Side/B Side)	Yr	NM
❑ 66018	I Want to Be the Boy You Love/Just Enough of Your Love	1964	60.00

PHILIPS

Number	Title (A Side/B Side)	Yr	NM
❑ 40122	Lonely Summer/Slow Locomotion	1963	20.00

FOUR CAL-QUETTES, THE

45s

CAPITOL

Number	Title (A Side/B Side)	Yr	NM
❑ 4534	Sparkle and Shine/In This World	1961	30.00
—As "The Four Coquettes"			
❑ 4574	Billy, My Billy/Star Bright	1961	30.00
❑ 4657	Most of All/I'm Gonna Love Him Anyway	1961	30.00
❑ 4725	I'll Never Come Back (Silly Boy)/Again	1962	30.00

LIBERTY

Number	Title (A Side/B Side)	Yr	NM
❑ 55549	I Cried/Movie Magazines	1963	15.00

FOUR CASTS, THE

45s

ATLANTIC

Number	Title (A Side/B Side)	Yr	NM
❑ 2228	Stormy Weather/Workin' at the Factory	1964	12.00

FOUR CHEERS, THE

45s

END

Number	Title (A Side/B Side)	Yr	NM
❑ 1034	Fatal Charms of Love/Periwinkle Blue	1958	200.00

FOUR CHELLOWS, THE
See THE CHELLOWS.

FOUR CHEVELLES, THE

45s

BAND BOX

Number	Title (A Side/B Side)	Yr	NM
❑ 357	This Is Our Wedding Day/Darling Forever	1957	20.00
❑ 358	I Can't Believe/I Know	1957	20.00

DELFT

Number	Title (A Side/B Side)	Yr	NM
❑ 357	This Is Our Wedding Day/Darling Forever	1957	600.00

FOUR CHICADEES, THE

45s

CHECKER

Number	Title (A Side/B Side)	Yr	NM
❑ 849	Ding Dong/Teenage Blues	1956	60.00

FOUR COINS, THE

45s

COLUMBIA

Number	Title (A Side/B Side)	Yr	NM
❑ 44006	If You Love Me (Really Love Me)/Learning to Live Without Your Love	1967	6.00

EPIC

Number	Title (A Side/B Side)	Yr	NM
❑ 9074	Once More/We'll Be Married...	1954	15.00
❑ 9082	I Love You Madly/Maybe	1954	15.00
❑ 9091	My Anxious Heart/Oh Mother Dear	1955	15.00
❑ 9104	Promises, Promises/That's the Way	1955	15.00
❑ 9107	A Story Untold/Magnolia	1955	15.00
❑ 9116	The Song That Brought Us Together/Need You	1955	15.00
❑ 9129	Memories of You/Tear Down the Fence	1955	15.00
❑ 9148	The Song That God Sings/The Old Professor	1956	12.00
❑ 9164	Cherry Lips/All My Tomorrows	1956	12.00
❑ 9171	This I Offer You/One Kiss (Is Worth a Thousand Words)	1956	12.00
❑ 9183	Manhattan Serenade/Too Late	1956	12.00
❑ 9192	Destination Love/The Time of the Year	1956	12.00
❑ 9200	Falling Star/My Love Is a Little Kitten	1957	12.00
❑ 9213	Shangri-La/First in Line	1957	12.00
❑ 9229	My One Sin/This Life	1957	12.00
❑ 9253	Follow Your Heart/A Broken Promise	1957	12.00
❑ 9258	My Love Loves Me/New World	1957	12.00
❑ 9276	Dream World/One Life, One Love	1958	10.00
❑ 9286	Wendy, Wendy/Be Still My Heart	1958	10.00
❑ 9295	The World Outside/Roselle	1958	10.00
❑ 9306	Angel of Love/Who Are You	1959	10.00
❑ 9314	My First Love/One Love, One Heart	1959	10.00
❑ 9337	Angel in the Rain/First Signs of Love	1959	10.00
❑ 9348	Buon Natale/Serenade of the Bells	1959	10.00
❑ 9383	My Only Love/You're Breaking My Heart	1960	10.00

JOY

Number	Title (A Side/B Side)	Yr	NM
❑ 284	Love Me with All Your Heart (Cuando Calienta El Sol)/Boys Cry	1964	8.00
❑ 287	Answer Me, My Love/Joanna	1964	8.00

JUBILEE

Number	Title (A Side/B Side)	Yr	NM
❑ 5411	Gee, Officer Krupki/The Miracle of St. Marie	1961	8.00
❑ 5419	Come a Little Closer/Windows of Heaven	1962	8.00
❑ 5429	One Red Rose/I Wish You Were Here	1962	8.00

LAURIE

Number	Title (A Side/B Side)	Yr	NM
❑ 3331	I'll Never Love Again/Try Your Luck	1966	6.00
❑ 3360	Shout Shout (Knock Yourself Out)/People Get Jealous	1966	6.00

MGM

Number	Title (A Side/B Side)	Yr	NM
❑ 12951	Pledging My Love/I Want a Little Girl	1960	8.00
❑ 12977	Love Is Where You Find It/Beat on Your Drum Little Susan	1961	8.00
❑ 13003	To Love/From Your Very Own Lips	1961	8.00
❑ 13031	Pretty Nina/Moon of Manakoora	1961	8.00

VEE JAY

Number	Title (A Side/B Side)	Yr	NM
❑ 474	They Say/Jimmy San	1962	8.00
❑ 551	Take a Bow (Little Darlin')/Nina	1963	8.00

7-Inch Extended Plays

EPIC

Number	Title (A Side/B Side)	Yr	NM
❑ EG-7121	(contents unknown)	195?	12.00
❑ EG-7121 [PS]	The Four Coins	195?	12.00
❑ EG-7186	(contents unknown)	195?	12.00
❑ EG-7186 [PS]	The Four Coins in Shangri-La	195?	12.00
❑ EG-7196	(contents unknown)	195?	10.00
❑ EG-7196 [PS]	The Four Coins Sing	195?	10.00
❑ EG-7197	(contents unknown)	195?	10.00
❑ EG-7197 [PS]	The Four Coins Sing	195?	10.00

Albums

EPIC

Number	Title (A Side/B Side)	Yr	NM
❑ LN 1104 [M]	The Four Coins	1955	50.00
❑ LN 3445 [M]	The Four Coins in Shangri-La	1958	30.00

MGM

Number	Title (A Side/B Side)	Yr	NM
❑ E-3944 [M]	Greek Songs	1961	15.00
❑ SE-3944 [S]	Greek Songs	1961	20.00

ROULETTE

Number	Title (A Side/B Side)	Yr	NM
❑ R-25288 [M]	Greek Songs Mama Never Taught Me	1965	15.00
❑ SR-25288 [S]	Greek Songs Mama Never Taught Me	1965	20.00

FOUR COQUETTES, THE
See THE FOUR CAL-QUETTES.

FOUR DATES, THE

45s

CHANCELLOR

Number	Title (A Side/B Side)	Yr	NM
❑ 1014	I'm Happy/Eloise	1958	20.00
❑ 1019	I say babe/Hey Roly Poly	1958	20.00
❑ 1027	Feel Good/Teenage Neighbor	1958	25.00

FOUR DEALS, THE

45s

CAPITOL

Number	Title (A Side/B Side)	Yr	NM
❑ F1313	It's Too Late Now/There Ain't No Bears	1950	100.00

FOUR DEEP TONES, THE

45s

CORAL

Number	Title (A Side/B Side)	Yr	NM
❑ 65061	Just in Case You Change Your Mind/Castle Rock	1951	200.00
❑ 65062	The Night You Said Goodbye/When the Saints Go Marching In	1951	200.00

FOUR DEUCES, THE

45s

EVEREST

Number	Title (A Side/B Side)	Yr	NM
❑ 19311	Polly/Yella Shoes	1959	30.00

MUSIC CITY

Number	Title (A Side/B Side)	Yr	NM
❑ 790	W-P-L-J/Here Lies My Love	1955	40.00
—Black label			
❑ 790	W-P-L-J/Here Lies My Love	1955	150.00
—Maroon label			
❑ 796	Down It Went/Goose Is Gone	1955	60.00

FOUR DIRECTIONS, THE

45s

CORAL

Number	Title (A Side/B Side)	Yr	NM
❑ 62456	(Doin' the) Arthur/Tonight We Love	1965	30.00

FOUR DUKES, THE (1)

45s

DUKE

Number	Title (A Side/B Side)	Yr	NM
❑ 116	Crying in the Chapel/I Done Done It	1953	800.00

FOUR DUKES, THE (2)

45s

IMPERIAL

Number	Title (A Side/B Side)	Yr	NM
❑ 5653	Baby Won't You Please Come Home/John Henry	1960	30.00

FOUR EPICS, THE

45s

HERITAGE

Number	Title (A Side/B Side)	Yr	NM
❑ 109	I'm On My Way to Love/When the Music Ends	1962	100.00

Number	Title (A Side/B Side)	Yr	NM
LAURIE			
❑ 3155	Again/I Love You Diane	1963	25.00
❑ 3183	How I Wish I Was Single Again/Dance Joanne	1963	25.00
FOUR ESQUIRES, THE			
45s			
CADENCE			
❑ 1260	Three Things/The Sphinx Won't Tell	1955	20.00
❑ 1277	Adorable/Thunderbolt	1955	20.00
LONDON			
❑ 1652	Look Homeward Angel/Santo Domingo	1956	25.00
PARIS			
❑ 501	Song of April/Everyone's Sweet on My Sugar	1957	20.00
❑ 505	The Chopstick Rock/Never Look for Love	1957	20.00
❑ 509	Love Me Forever/I Ain't Been Right Since You Left	1957	20.00
❑ 512	Always and Forever/I Walk Down the Street	1958	20.00
❑ 515	All Around the Clock/The Big Dance	1958	20.00
❑ 520	Hideaway/Repeat After Me	1958	20.00
—With Rosemary June			
❑ 526	Follow Me/The Land of You and Me	1958	20.00
❑ 531	Lucky Old Sun/Non E Cosi	1959	20.00
❑ 535	Act Your Age/So Ends the Night	1959	20.00
❑ 539	Wonderful One/Wouldn't It Be Wonderful	1959	20.00
❑ 544	Make Them Mine/Peg O' My Heart	1960	20.00
❑ 549	Sweet Sixteen She'll Never Be/The Chopstick Rock	1960	20.00
PILGRIM			
❑ 717	Follow Me/Summer Vacation	1956	25.00
TERRACE			
❑ 7502	Can't Help Falling in Love/Merry-Go-Round of Love	1961	15.00
❑ 7516	The James Bond Theme (Double-O-Seven)/Summer Vacation	1963	25.00
—Betcha didn't know this had lyrics...			
FOUR-EVERS, THE			
45s			
CHATTAHOOCHIE			
❑ 630	Colors/Come Up in the World	1963	15.00
COLUMBIA			
❑ 42303	You Belong to Me/Such a Good Night for Dreaming	1962	60.00
❑ 43886	A Lovely Way to Say Goodnight/The Girl I Wanna Bring Home	1966	20.00
CONSTELLATION			
❑ 151	Stormy/Out of the Crowd	1965	30.00
JAMIE			
❑ 1247	Everybody South Street/One More Time	1963	15.00
RED BIRD			
❑ 10-078	You Never Had It So Good/What a Scene	1966	25.00
SMASH			
❑ 1853	Lover Come Back to Me/It's Love	1963	15.00
❑ 1887	Be My Girl/If I Were a Magician	1964	15.00
—Same A-side, different title			
❑ 1887	Please Be Mine/If I Were a Magician	1964	30.00
❑ 1921	(Say I Love You) Doo Bee Dum/Everlasting	1964	15.00
FOUR EXCEPTIONS, THE			
45s			
PARKWAY			
❑ 986	You Got the Power/A Sad Goodbye	1966	50.00
FOUR FELLOWS, THE			
45s			
DERBY			
❑ 862	I Tried/Bend of the River	1954	400.00
GLORY			
❑ 231	I Wish I Didn't Know You/I Know Love	1955	80.00
❑ 234	Soldier Boy/Take Me Back Baby	1955	60.00
❑ 236	Angels Say/In the Rain	1955	60.00
❑ 238	Fallen Angel/Hold 'Em Joe	1956	60.00
❑ 242	Darling You/Please Don't Deprive Me of My Love	1956	80.00
❑ 244	I Sit in My Window/Please Play My Song	1956	60.00
❑ 248	You Don't Know Me/Sweet Girl	1956	60.00
❑ 250	Loving You, Darling/Give Me Back My Broken Heart	1957	60.00
NESTOR			
❑ 27	Remember/That Kiss You Gave Me	1958	300.00
FOUR FIFTHS, THE			
45s			
COLUMBIA			
❑ 43913	If You Still Want Me/Have You Ever Loved a Girl	1966	12.00
HUDSON			
❑ 8101	After Graduation/Come On Girl	1963	150.00
—Black vinyl			
❑ 8101	After Graduation/Come On Girl	1963	400.00
—Blue vinyl			
FOUR FRESHMEN, THE			
45s			
CAPITOL			
❑ F1293	Mr. B's Blues/Then I'll Be Happy	1950	15.00
❑ F1377	Now You Know/Pick Up Tears	1951	15.00
❑ F2152	It's a Blue World/Tuxedo Junction	1952	12.00
❑ F2286	Stormy Weather/The Day Isn't Long Enough	1952	12.00
❑ F2398	Baltimore Oriole/Poinciana	1953	12.00
❑ F2564	Holiday/It Happened Once Before	1953	12.00
❑ F2745	Seems Like Old Times/Crazy Bones	1954	12.00
❑ F2832	I'll Be Seeing You/Please Remember	1954	12.00
❑ F2898	We'll Be Together Again/My Heart Stood Still	1954	12.00
❑ F2961	Mood Indigo/Love Turns Winter to Spring	1954	12.00
❑ F3070	It Never Occurred to Me/Malaya	1955	10.00
❑ F3154	Day by Day/How Can I Tell Her	1955	10.00
❑ F3292	Charmaine/In This Whole Wide World	1955	10.00
❑ F3359	Angel Eyes/Love Is Just Around the Corner	1956	10.00
❑ F3410	Graduation Day/Lonely Night in Paris	1956	15.00
❑ F3532	You're So Far Above Me/He Who Loves and Runs Away	1956	10.00
❑ F3652	That's the Way I Feel/What's It Gonna Be	1957	10.00
❑ F3779	Julie Is Her Name/Sometimes I'm Happy	1957	10.00
❑ F3832	Grenada/How Can I Begin to Tell	1957	10.00
❑ F3930	Whistle Me Some Blues/Nights Are Longer	1958	10.00
❑ 4341	Candy/Route 66	1960	8.00
❑ 4749	Shangri-La/Teach Me Tonight	1962	8.00
❑ 4824	I'm Gonna Go Fishin'/Taps Miller	1962	8.00
❑ 5007	Summertime/Baby Won't You Please Come Home	1963	8.00
❑ 5007 [PS]	Summertime/Baby Won't You Please Come Home	1963	15.00
❑ 5083	Charade/Funny How Time Slips Away	1963	8.00
❑ 5151	Don't Make Me Sorry/My Baby's Gone	1964	8.00
❑ 5401	When I Stop Lovin' You/Nights Are Long	1965	8.00
❑ 5471	Those Magnificent Men in Their Flying Machines/Old Cape Cod	1965	10.00
DECCA			
❑ 32070	Cry/Nowhere to Go	1966	6.00
LIBERTY			
❑ 56047	Cherish-Windy/Come Fly with Me-Up Up and Away	1968	6.00
❑ 56099	By the Time I Get to Phoenix-My Special Angel/It's a Blue World	1969	6.00
7-Inch Extended Plays			
CAPITOL			
❑ EAP 1-433	It's a Blue World/Stormy Weather//Tuxedo Junction/Mr. B's Blues	195?	15.00
❑ EAP 1-433 [PS]	The Four Freshmen	195?	15.00
❑ EAP 1-522	After You/Over the Rainbow//My Heart Stood Still/The Nearness of You	195?	15.00
❑ EAP 1-522 [PS]	Voices in Modern, Part 1	195?	15.00
❑ EAP 2-522	Street of Dreams/We'll Be Together Again//Circus/Mood Indigo	195?	15.00
❑ EAP 2-522 [PS]	Voices in Modern, Part 2	195?	15.00
❑ EAP 1-683	(contents unknown)	1956	12.00
❑ EAP 1-683 [PS]	Four Freshmen and Five Trombones, Part 1	1956	12.00
❑ EAP 2-683	Mam'selle/Speak Low//Love/Love Is Here to Stay	1956	12.00
❑ EAP 2-683 [PS]	Four Freshmen and Five Trombones, Part 2	1956	12.00
❑ EAP 3-683	(contents unknown)	1956	12.00
❑ EAP 3-683 [PS]	Four Freshmen and Five Trombones, Part 3	1956	12.00
❑ EAP 1-743	(contents unknown)	1957	10.00
❑ EAP 1-743 [PS]	Freshmen Favorites, Part 1	1957	10.00
❑ EAP 2-743	Graduation Day/Poinciana//Lonely Night in Paris/Seems Like Old Times	1957	10.00
❑ EAP 2-743 [PS]	Freshmen Favorites, Part 2	1957	10.00
❑ EAP 3-743	(contents unknown)	1957	10.00
❑ EAP 3-743 [PS]	Freshmen Favorites, Part 3	1957	10.00
❑ EAP 1-763	After You've Gone/Ev'ry Time We Say Goodbye//Easy Street/Good Night Sweetheart	1957	10.00
❑ EAP 1-763 [PS]	4 Freshmen and 5 Trumpets, Part 1	1957	10.00
❑ EAP 2-763	(contents unknown)	1957	10.00
❑ EAP 2-763 [PS]	4 Freshmen and 5 Trumpets, Part 2	1957	10.00
❑ EAP 3-763	(contents unknown)	1957	10.00
❑ EAP 3-763 [PS]	4 Freshmen and 5 Trumpets, Part 3	1957	10.00
❑ EAP 1-844	'Liza/You've Got Me Cryin' Again/This Love of Mine/I Get Along Without You Very Well	1957	10.00
❑ EAP 1-844 [PS]	Four Freshmen and Five Saxes, Part 1	1957	10.00
❑ EAP 2-844	(contents unknown)	1957	10.00
❑ EAP 2-844 [PS]	Four Freshmen and Five Saxes, Part 2	1957	10.00
❑ EAP 3-844	(contents unknown)	1957	10.00
❑ EAP 3-844 [PS]	Four Freshmen and Five Saxes, Part 3	1957	10.00
❑ EAP 1-922	(contents unknown)	1958	10.00
❑ EAP 1-922 [PS]	Voices in Latin, Part 1	1958	10.00
❑ EAP 2-922	(contents unknown)	1958	10.00
❑ EAP 2-922 [PS]	Voices in Latin, Part 2	1958	10.00
❑ EAP 3-922	What's New/Chelsea Bridge//Tangerine/Brazil	1958	10.00
❑ EAP 3-922 [PS]	Voices in Latin, Part 3	1958	10.00
❑ EAP 1-1255	(contents unknown)	1959	10.00
❑ EAP 1-1255 [PS]	The Four Freshmen and Five Guitars, Part 1	1959	10.00
❑ EAP 2-1255	(contents unknown)	1959	10.00
❑ EAP 2-1255 [PS]	The Four Freshmen and Five Guitars, Part 2	1959	10.00
❑ EAP 3-1255	(contents unknown)	1959	10.00
❑ EAP 3-1255 [PS]	The Four Freshmen and Five Guitars, Part 3	1959	10.00
Albums			
CAPITOL			
❑ H 522 [10]	Voices in Modern	1955	50.00
❑ T 522 [M]	Voices in Modern	1955	40.00
❑ T 683 [M]	Four Freshmen and Five Trombones	1956	40.00
❑ DT 743 [R]	Freshmen Favorites	196?	12.00
❑ SM-743	Freshmen Favorites	197?	10.00
❑ T 743 [M]	Freshmen Favorites	1956	40.00
❑ T 763 [M]	4 Freshmen and 5 Trumpets	1957	40.00
❑ T 844 [M]	Four Freshmen and Five Saxes	1957	40.00
❑ T 992 [M]	Voices in Latin	1958	30.00
❑ ST 1008 [S]	The Four Freshmen In Person	1958	40.00
❑ T 1008 [M]	The Four Freshmen In Person	1958	30.00
❑ ST 1074 [S]	Voices in Love	1958	30.00
❑ T 1074 [M]	Voices in Love	1958	20.00
❑ ST 1103 [S]	Freshmen Favorites, Vol. 2	1959	30.00
❑ T 1103 [M]	Freshmen Favorites, Vol. 2	1959	20.00
❑ ST 1189 [S]	Love Lost	1959	30.00
❑ T 1189 [M]	Love Lost	1959	20.00
❑ ST 1255 [S]	The Four Freshmen and Five Guitars	1959	30.00
❑ T 1255 [M]	The Four Freshmen and Five Guitars	1959	20.00
❑ ST 1295 [S]	Voices and Brass	1960	30.00
❑ T 1295 [M]	Voices and Brass	1960	20.00
❑ ST 1378 [S]	First Affair	1960	30.00
❑ T 1378 [M]	First Affair	1960	20.00
❑ ST 1485 [S]	Freshmen Year	1961	25.00
❑ T 1485 [M]	Freshmen Year	1961	20.00
❑ ST 1543 [S]	Voices in Fun	1961	25.00
❑ T 1543 [M]	Voices in Fun	1961	20.00
❑ ST 1640 [S]	The Best of the Four Freshmen	1962	25.00
❑ T 1640 [M]	The Best of the Four Freshmen	1962	20.00
❑ ST 1682 [S]	Stars in Our Eyes	1962	25.00
❑ T 1682 [M]	Stars in Our Eyes	1962	20.00
❑ ST 1753 [S]	Swingers	1963	20.00
❑ T 1753 [M]	Swingers	1963	15.00
❑ ST 1860 [S]	The Four Freshmen In Person, Vol. 2	1963	20.00
❑ T 1860 [M]	The Four Freshmen In Person, Vol. 2	1963	15.00

Number	Title (A Side/B Side)	Yr	NM
❑ ST 1950 [S]	Got That Feelin'	1963	20.00
❑ T 1950 [M]	Got That Feelin'	1963	15.00
❑ ST 2067 [S]	Funny How Time Slips Away	1964	20.00
❑ T 2067 [M]	Funny How Time Slips Away	1964	15.00
❑ ST 2168 [S]	More Four Freshmen and Five Trombones	1964	20.00
❑ T 2168 [M]	More Four Freshmen and Five Trombones	1964	15.00
❑ SM-11639	Four Freshmen and Five Trombones	1977	10.00
❑ SM-11965	Best of the Four Freshmen	1978	10.00

CREATIVE WORLD

Number	Title (A Side/B Side)	Yr	NM
❑ ST-1059 [(2)]	Stan Kenton and the Four Freshmen at Butler University	1972	20.00

LIBERTY

Number	Title (A Side/B Side)	Yr	NM
❑ LST-7563	Today Is Tomorrow	1968	15.00
❑ LST-7590	In a Class By Themselves	1969	15.00
❑ LST-7630	Different Strokes	1969	15.00
❑ LN-10181	In a Class By Themselves	198?	8.00

PAUSA

Number	Title (A Side/B Side)	Yr	NM
❑ PR-7193	Fresh!	1986	10.00
❑ PR-9029	The Four Freshmen and Five Guitars	198?	10.00
❑ PR-9040	4 Freshmen and 5 Trumpets	1985	10.00

PICKWICK

Number	Title (A Side/B Side)	Yr	NM
❑ SPC-3080	The Fabulous Four Freshmen	196?	12.00
❑ SPC-3563	A Taste of Honey	1977	10.00

SUNSET

Number	Title (A Side/B Side)	Yr	NM
❑ SUS-5289	My Special Angel	1970	12.00

FOUR GRADUATES, THE

45s

CRYSTAL BALL

Number	Title (A Side/B Side)	Yr	NM
❑ 116	May I Have This Dance/ Caught in a Lie	1978	4.00
❑ 119	Your Initials/Every Year About This Time	1978	4.00

RUST

Number	Title (A Side/B Side)	Yr	NM
❑ 5062	Picture of An Angel/A Lovely Way to Spend An Evening	1963	100.00
❑ 5084	Candy Queen/A Girl in Love	1964	180.00

FOUR HAVEN KNIGHTS, THE

45s

ANGLETONE

Number	Title (A Side/B Side)	Yr	NM
❑ 1066	In My Lonely Room/ I'm Just a Dreamer	1958	50.00
❑ 1092	Just to Be in Love/ Why Go On Pretending	1958	50.00

ATLAS

Number	Title (A Side/B Side)	Yr	NM
❑ 1066	In My Lonely Room/ I'm Just a Dreamer	1957	150.00
❑ 1092	Just to Be in Love/ Why Go On Pretending	1957	150.00

JOSIE

Number	Title (A Side/B Side)	Yr	NM
❑ 824	In My Lonely Room/ I'm Just a Dreamer	1957	30.00

FOUR HOLIDAYS, THE

45s

UNITED ARTISTS

Number	Title (A Side/B Side)	Yr	NM
❑ 163	Who Can Say/Nobody Loves You Like-a Me	1959	30.00

VERVE

Number	Title (A Side/B Side)	Yr	NM
❑ 10204	I Don't Wanna Go to School/ Love Ya' Baby	1960	15.00

FOUR HUES, THE

45s

CORAL

Number	Title (A Side/B Side)	Yr	NM
❑ 61617	Ivory Tower/Sister Jenny	1956	30.00

CROWN

Number	Title (A Side/B Side)	Yr	NM
❑ 159	Rock-a-Bye/Take Me Out of Your Heart	1955	40.00

FOUR IMPERIALS, THE

45s

CHANT

Number	Title (A Side/B Side)	Yr	NM
❑ 10067	My Girl/Teen Age Fool	1958	50.00

DIAL

Number	Title (A Side/B Side)	Yr	NM
❑ 101	Valley of Tears/Time Out	1959	150.00

DOT

Number	Title (A Side/B Side)	Yr	NM
❑ 15737	Lazy Bonnie/Let's Make a Scene	1958	25.00

FOX

Number	Title (A Side/B Side)	Yr	NM
❑ 102	Give Me One More Chance/ Look Up and Live	1958	80.00

LORELEI

Number	Title (A Side/B Side)	Yr	NM
❑ 4444	Lazy Bonnie/Let's Make a Scene	1958	100.00

TWIRL

Number	Title (A Side/B Side)	Yr	NM
❑ 2005	Santa's Got a Coupe de Ville/ Seven Lonely Days	1960	25.00

FOUR J'S, THE

45s

CONGRESS

Number	Title (A Side/B Side)	Yr	NM
❑ 6003	Dreamin'/Love My Life	1969	10.00

4-J

Number	Title (A Side/B Side)	Yr	NM
❑ 506	Will You Be My Love/Nursery	1963	15.00

HERALD

Number	Title (A Side/B Side)	Yr	NM
❑ 528	Kissin' at the Drive-In/ Dreams Are a Dime a Dozen	1958	30.00

JAMIE

Number	Title (A Side/B Side)	Yr	NM
❑ 1267	Here I Am Broken-Hearted/ She Said That She Loved Me	1964	25.00
❑ 1274	By Love Possessed/ My Love, My Love	1964	25.00

UNITED ARTISTS

Number	Title (A Side/B Side)	Yr	NM
❑ 125	Rock and Roll Age/ Be Nice, Don't Fight	1958	40.00

FOUR J'S, THE, AND THE FABULOUS IMPERIALS

45s

MGM

Number	Title (A Side/B Side)	Yr	NM
❑ 12687	Class Ring/Weird	1958	80.00

FOUR JACKS, THE

45s

FEDERAL

Number	Title (A Side/B Side)	Yr	NM
❑ 12075	You Met a Fool/Goodbye Baby	1952	800.00
❑ 12087	The Last of the Good Rockin' Men/I'll Be Home Again	1952	500.00

MGM

Number	Title (A Side/B Side)	Yr	NM
❑ 11179	You're in Love with Someone Else/Darling, Lonesome for You	1952	20.00

FOUR JACKS AND A JILL (1)

45s

RCA VICTOR

Number	Title (A Side/B Side)	Yr	NM
❑ 47-9473	Master Jack/I Looked Back	1968	8.00
❑ 47-9572	Mister Nico/Hamba Liliwam	1968	6.00
❑ 47-9655	Hey Mister/Sad Little Pigeon	1968	6.00
❑ 47-9728	Stone in My Shoe/ Grandfather Dugan	1969	6.00

Albums

RCA VICTOR

Number	Title (A Side/B Side)	Yr	NM
❑ LPM-4019 [M]	Master Jack	1968	30.00
❑ LSP-4019 [S]	Master Jack	1968	15.00
❑ LSP-4103	Fables	1968	15.00

FOUR JACKS AND A JILL (2)

45s

FORTUNE

Number	Title (A Side/B Side)	Yr	NM
❑ 507	Love's Not Love Without You/ I'm in Love with Someone	1955	30.00

FOUR JACKS AND A JILL (U)

45s

HEART SONG

Number	Title (A Side/B Side)	Yr	NM
❑ 103	It's Christmas Time Again/ (B-side unknown)	19??	10.00

FOUR JETS, THE

See THE SHADOWS.

FOUR JEWELS, THE

45s

CHECKER

Number	Title (A Side/B Side)	Yr	NM
❑ 1039	Dapper Dan/Loaded with Goodies	1963	20.00
❑ 1069	Time for Love/That's What They Put Erasers on Pencils For	1964	20.00

START

Number	Title (A Side/B Side)	Yr	NM
❑ 638	Johnny Jealousy/ Someone Special	1963	30.00
❑ 638	Loaded with Goodies/Fire	1963	40.00
❑ 641	All That's Good/I Love Me Some You	1963	30.00

TEC

Number	Title (A Side/B Side)	Yr	NM
❑ 3007	Baby It's You/She's Wrong for You Baby	1964	25.00

FOUR JOKERS, THE (1)

45s

AMY

Number	Title (A Side/B Side)	Yr	NM
❑ 832	She's a Flirt/Uggaboo	1961	20.00

FOUR JOKERS, THE (2)

45s

CRYSTALLETTE

Number	Title (A Side/B Side)	Yr	NM
❑ 730	Your Decision/We Met in Catalina	1959	15.00
❑ 733	Beyond the Reef/That's the Way	1959	15.00

FOUR JOKERS, THE (3)

Jimmy Drake, a.k.a. NERVOUS NORVUS, was in this group.

45s

DIAMOND

Number	Title (A Side/B Side)	Yr	NM
❑ 3004	Transfusion/You Dig	1956	30.00

FOUR JOKERS, THE (4)

45s

MGM

Number	Title (A Side/B Side)	Yr	NM
❑ 11815	Tell Me Now/Caring	1954	30.00

FOUR JOKERS, THE (5)

45s

SUE

Number	Title (A Side/B Side)	Yr	NM
❑ 703	Written in the Stars/ The Run-Around	1958	60.00

FOUR JUST MEN

Also see FREDDIE AND THE DREAMERS.

45s

TOWER

Number	Title (A Side/B Side)	Yr	NM
❑ 118	That's My Baby/Things Will Never Be the Same	1965	12.00

FOUR KNIGHTS, THE

45s

CAPITOL

Number	Title (A Side/B Side)	Yr	NM
❑ F1587	I Love the Sunshine of Your Smile/Sentimental Fool	1951	50.00
❑ F1707	Walkin' and Whistlin' Blues/ Who Am I	1951	40.00
❑ F1787	I Go Crazy/Get Her Off My Hands	1951	40.00
❑ F1806	It's No Sin/The Glory of Love	1951	40.00
❑ F1875	Cry/Charmaine	1951	40.00
❑ F1914	Marshmallow Moon/Five Foot Two, Eyes of Blue	1951	30.00
❑ F1930	The Way I Feel/I Wish I Had a Girl	1952	30.00
❑ F1971	There Are Two Sides to Every Heartache/Walkin' in Sunshine	1952	30.00
❑ F1998	The More I Go Out with Somebody Else/The Doll with the Sawdust Heart	1952	30.00
❑ F2087	I'm the World's Biggest Fool/ It's a Sin to Tell a Lie	1952	30.00
❑ F2127	Win or Lose/Do-Wacka-Do	1952	30.00
❑ F2195	Say No More/That's the Way It's Gonna Be	1952	30.00
❑ F2234	Lies/One Way Kisses	1952	30.00
❑ F2315	Oh Happy Day/A Million Tears	1953	25.00
❑ F2403	Anniversary Song/ A Few Kind Words	1953	25.00
❑ F2517	Baby Doll/Tennessee Train	1953	25.00
❑ F2654	I Get So Lonely (When I Dream About You)/I Couldn't Stay Away from You	1953	20.00
❑ F2654	Oh Baby Mine/I Couldn't Stay Away from You	1953	40.00
❑ F2782	I Was Meant for You/They Tell Me	1954	20.00
❑ F2847	How Wrong Can You Be/Period	1954	20.00
❑ F2894	In the Chapel in the Moonlight/ Easy Street	1954	20.00
❑ F2938	I Don't Wanna See You Cryin'/ Saw Your Eyes	1954	20.00
❑ F3024	Write Me Baby/Honey Bunch	1955	20.00
❑ F3093	Foolishly Yours/Inside You	1955	20.00
❑ F3155	Gratefully Yours/Me	1955	20.00
❑ F3192	Don't Sit Under the Apple Tree/ Believing You	1955	20.00
❑ F3250	Perdido/After	1955	20.00
❑ F3279	Guilty/You	1955	20.00
❑ F3339	I Love You Still/Happy Birthday Baby	1956	15.00
❑ F3386	Bottle Up the Moonlight/Mistaken	1956	15.00
❑ F3494	Don't Depend on Me/ You're a Honey	1956	15.00
❑ F3689	It Doesn't Cost Money/ How Can You Not Believe	1957	15.00
❑ F3730	Walkin' and Whistlin' Blues/I Love That Song	1957	15.00
❑ F15895	I Ain't Got Nobody/When My Baby Smiles at Me	1952	30.00
❑ F15896	Easy Street/Ida, Sweet As Apple Cider	1952	30.00
❑ F15897	Georgia on My Mind/ Sentimental Journey	1952	30.00

CORAL

Number	Title (A Side/B Side)	Yr	NM
❑ 61936	The Four Minute Mile/ When Your Lover Has Gone	1958	12.00

Number	Title (A Side/B Side)	Yr	NM
❑ 61981	Yes I Do/If You Ever Change Your Mind	1958	12.00
❑ 62045	O Falling Star/Foolish Tears	1959	12.00
❑ 62110	Where Is the Love/ Things to Do Today	1959	12.00

DECCA

Number	Title (A Side/B Side)	Yr	NM
❑ 9-48018	He'll Understand and Say Well Done/Lead Me to That Rock	1952	100.00

—Reissue of original 78 from 1947 (Decca 48014 and 48026 are known to exist only on 78s)

DECCA FAITH SERIES

Number	Title (A Side/B Side)	Yr	NM
❑ 9-14524	He'll Understand and Say Well Done/Lead Me to That Rock	195?	50.00

—Later pressing; black Decca label with the words "Faith Series" where the star would normally be on the label

Number	Title (A Side/B Side)	Yr	NM
❑ 9-14524	He'll Understand and Say Well Done/Lead Me to That Rock	1950	120.00

—Purple label

7-Inch Extended Plays

CAPITOL

Number	Title (A Side/B Side)	Yr	NM
❑ EAP 1-414	*(It's No) Sin/The Glory of Love/ Cry/Charmaine	1953	40.00
❑ EAP 1-414 [PS]	The Four Knights Sing	1953	40.00
❑ EAP 1-506	I Get So Lonely/Tennessee Train//Till Then/Anniversary Song	1954	40.00
❑ EAP 1-506 [PS]	I Get So Lonely	1954	40.00

MONOGRAM

Number	Title (A Side/B Side)	Yr	NM
❑ 2	Speaking of Angels/What Are You Doing New Year's Eve// + 2	19??	10.00

Albums

CAPITOL

Number	Title (A Side/B Side)	Yr	NM
❑ H 346 [10]	Spotlight Songs	1953	200.00
❑ T 346 [M]	Spotlight Songs	1956	150.00

CORAL

Number	Title (A Side/B Side)	Yr	NM
❑ CRL 57221 [M]	The Four Knights	1959	100.00
❑ CRL 57309 [M]	Million Dollar Baby	1960	60.00
❑ CRL 757309 [S]	Million Dollar Baby	1960	80.00

FOUR LADS, THE

45s

COLUMBIA

Number	Title (A Side/B Side)	Yr	NM
❑ 39865	Somebody Loves Me/ Thanks to You	1952	15.00
❑ 39902	Blackberry Boogie/ Girl on the Shore	1952	15.00
❑ 39958	He Who Has Love/I Wonder, I Wonder, I Wonder	1953	15.00
❑ 40005	Down By the Riverside/ Take Me Back	1953	15.00
❑ 40082	Istanbul (Not Constantinople)/ I Should Have Told You Long Ago	1953	15.00
❑ 40140	Harmony Brown/Gotta Go to the Fais Do Do	1953	15.00
❑ 40204	Long John/The Place Where I Worship	1954	15.00
❑ 40220	What Can I Lose by Letting You Know/Oh That'll Be Joyful	1954	15.00
❑ 40236	Gilly Gilly Ossenfeffer Katzenelle Bogen by the Sea/ I Hear It Everywhere	1954	15.00
❑ 40306	Skokiaan (South African Song)/ Why Should I Love You So	1954	15.00
❑ 40402	Two Ladies in De Shade of De Banana Tree/Dance Calinda	1954	15.00
❑ 40436	Pledging My Love/I've Been Thinking	1955	12.00
❑ 40490	Too Much! Baby, Baby/ The Average Giraffe	1955	12.00
❑ 40539	Moments to Remember/Dream On, My Love, Dream On	1955	12.00
❑ 40629	No, Not Much!/I'll Never Know	1955	12.00
❑ 40674	Standing on the Corner/ My Little Angel	1956	12.00
❑ 40736	The Bus Stop Song (A Paper of Pins)/A House with Love In It	1956	12.00
❑ 40788	Mary's Little Boy Child/ The Stingiest Man in Town	1956	12.00
❑ 40811	Who Needs You/It's So Easy to Forget	1956	12.00
❑ 40811 [PS]	Who Needs You/It's So Easy to Forget	1956	20.00
❑ 40914	I Just Don't Know/Golly	1957	12.00
❑ 40974	The Eyes of God/ His Invisible Hand	1957	12.00
❑ 41058	Put a Light in the Window/The Things We Did Last Summer	1957	10.00
❑ 41136	There's Only One of You/ Blue Tattoo	1958	10.00
❑ 41194	Enchanted Island/Guess What the Neighbors'll Say	1958	10.00
❑ 41194 [PS]	Enchanted Island/Guess What the Neighbors'll Say	1958	15.00
❑ 41266	The Mocking Bird/I May Hate Myself in the Morning	1958	10.00
❑ 41310	The Girl on Page 44/Sunday	1958	10.00
❑ 41365	The Fountain of Youth/Meet Me Tonight in Dreamland	1959	10.00
❑ 41409	The Chosen Few/Together Wherever We Go	1959	10.00
❑ 41443	Got a Locket in My Pocket/ Real Thing	1959	10.00
❑ 41497	Happy Anniversary/Who Do You Think You Are	1959	10.00
❑ 41497 [PS]	Happy Anniversary/Who Do You Think You Are	1959	15.00
❑ 41629	You're Nobody 'Til Somebody Loves You/Goona Goona	1960	10.00
❑ 41682	Our Lady of Fatima (Vocal)/Our Lady of Fatima (Recitation)	1960	10.00
❑ 41733	Two Other People/The Sheik of Chicago (Mustafa)	1960	10.00

DOT

Number	Title (A Side/B Side)	Yr	NM
❑ 16328	Don't Fly Away, Flamingo/ Winter Snow	1962	8.00
❑ 16373	The Exodus Song/Never on Sunday	1962	8.00
❑ 16390	That's What I Like/Sweet Mama Tree-Top Tall	1962	8.00
❑ 16412	Beyond My Heart/Not That I Care	1962	8.00

EPIC

Number	Title (A Side/B Side)	Yr	NM
❑ 9150	The Mocking Bird/I May Hate Myself in the Morning	1956	12.00

FONA

Number	Title (A Side/B Side)	Yr	NM
❑ 1000	You'll Never Know/ (B-side unknown)	1977	4.00
❑ 1001	Moments to Remember/ Skokiaan	1977	4.00

KAPP

Number	Title (A Side/B Side)	Yr	NM
❑ 359	Just Young/Goodbye Mr. Love	1960	8.00
❑ 359 [PS]	Just Young/Goodbye Mr. Love	1960	10.00
❑ 404	555 Times/I Should Know Better	1961	8.00
❑ 412	Giuggigla/Oceans of Love	1961	8.00

OKEH

Number	Title (A Side/B Side)	Yr	NM
❑ 6885	The Mocking Bird/I May Hate Myself in the Morning	1952	20.00

REPRISE

Number	Title (A Side/B Side)	Yr	NM
❑ 20163	My Home Town/Cornflower Blue	1963	8.00

UNITED ARTISTS

Number	Title (A Side/B Side)	Yr	NM
❑ 653	It's a Mad, Mad, Mad, Mad World/Stolen Hours	1963	6.00
❑ 702	Love Theme from "Tom Jones"/ Theme from "Lilies of the Field"	1964	6.00
❑ 760	Memories of You/Always Thinking of the Roses	1964	6.00
❑ 852	Thanks, Mr. Florist/Barabanchik	1965	6.00
❑ 893	With My Eyes Wide Open/I'm Not a Run-Around	1965	6.00
❑ 962	Give Her My Love/All the Winds	1965	6.00
❑ 50006	No, Not Much/Standing on the Corner	1966	5.00
❑ 50339	Where Do I Go/A Woman	1968	5.00
❑ 50517	My Heart's Symphony/ Pardon Me Kiss	1969	5.00
❑ 50585	Moments to Remember/ Free Again	1969	5.00

7-Inch Extended Plays

COLUMBIA

Number	Title (A Side/B Side)	Yr	NM
❑ B-2538	*Moments to Remember/ No, Not Much!/Istanbul (Not Constantinople)/ Down by the River Side	195?	15.00
❑ B-2538 [PS]	The Four Lads (Hall of Fame Series)	195?	15.00
❑ B-2557	*Standing on the Corner/Take Me Back/Skokiaan/ Who Needs You	1958	15.00
❑ B-2557 [PS]	The Four Lads (Hall of Fame Series)	1958	15.00
❑ B-9121	On the Sunny Side of the Street/ The Things We Did Last Summer//Taking a Chance on Love/Bidin' My Time	1956	12.00
❑ B-9121 [PS]	On the Sunny Side, Vol. 1	1956	12.00
❑ B-9122	(contents unknown)	1956	12.00
❑ B-9122 [PS]	On the Sunny Side, Vol. 2	1956	12.00
❑ B-9123	(contents unknown)	1956	12.00
❑ B-9123 [PS]	On the Sunny Side, Vol. 3	1956	12.00

Albums

COLUMBIA

Number	Title (A Side/B Side)	Yr	NM
❑ CL 861 [M]	The Four Lads with Frankie Laine	1956	40.00
❑ CL 912 [M]	On the Sunny Side	1956	40.00
❑ CL 1045 [M]	The Four Lads Sing Frank Loesser	1957	40.00
❑ CL 1111 [M]	Four on the Aisle	1958	25.00
❑ CL 1223 [M]	Breezin' Along	1958	25.00
❑ CL 1235 [M]	The Four Lads' Greatest Hits	1958	25.00
❑ CL 1299 [M]	The Four Lads Swing Along	1959	25.00
❑ CL 1407 [M]	High Spirits!	1959	25.00
❑ CL 1502 [M]	Love Affair	1960	15.00
❑ CL 1550 [M]	Everything Goes	1960	15.00
❑ CL 2545 [10]	The Four Lads Sing Frank Loesser	1956	50.00
❑ CL 2577 [10]	Stage Show	1956	50.00
❑ CL 6329 [10]	Stage Show	1954	50.00
❑ CS 8035 [S]	Breezin' Along	1958	30.00
❑ CS 8047 [S]	Four on the Aisle	1958	30.00
❑ CS 8106 [S]	The Four Lads Swing Along	1959	30.00
❑ CS 8203 [S]	High Spirits!	1959	30.00
❑ CS 8293 [S]	Love Affair	1960	20.00
❑ CS 8350 [S]	Everything Goes	1960	20.00

DOT

Number	Title (A Side/B Side)	Yr	NM
❑ DLP-3438 [M]	Hits of the 60's	1962	15.00
❑ DLP-3533 [M]	Oh Happy Day	1963	15.00
❑ DLP-25438 [S]	Hits of the 60's	1962	20.00
❑ DLP-25533 [S]	Oh Happy Day	1963	20.00

HARMONY

Number	Title (A Side/B Side)	Yr	NM
❑ HS 11369	Moments to Remember	1970	12.00

KAPP

Number	Title (A Side/B Side)	Yr	NM
❑ KL-1224 [M]	Twelve Hits	1961	15.00
❑ KL-1254 [M]	Dixieland Doin's	1961	15.00
❑ KS-3224 [S]	Twelve Hits	1961	20.00
❑ KS-3254 [S]	Dixieland Doin's	1961	20.00

UNITED ARTISTS

Number	Title (A Side/B Side)	Yr	NM
❑ UAL-3356 [M]	This Year's Top Movie Hits	1964	15.00
❑ UAL-3399 [M]	Songs of World War I	1964	15.00
❑ UAS-6356 [S]	This Year's Top Movie Hits	1964	20.00
❑ UAS-6399 [S]	Songs of World War I	1964	20.00

FOUR LARKS, THE

45s

TOWER

Number	Title (A Side/B Side)	Yr	NM
❑ 364	Rain/Another Chance	1967	30.00
❑ 402	I Still Love You (From the Bottom of My Heart)/ Groovin' at the Go-Go	1968	40.00
❑ 450	Can I Have Another Helping, Please/I've Got Plenty	1968	10.00

UPTOWN

Number	Title (A Side/B Side)	Yr	NM
❑ 748	You and Me/That's All That Counts	1967	40.00

FOUR LOVERS, THE

Also see THE FOUR SEASONS; FRANKIE VALLI.

45s

EPIC

Number	Title (A Side/B Side)	Yr	NM
❑ 9255	My Life for Your Love/Pucker Up	1957	2000.

RCA VICTOR

Number	Title (A Side/B Side)	Yr	NM
❑ 47-6518	You're the Apple of My Eye/ The Girl of My Dreams	1956	40.00
❑ 47-6519	Honey Love/Please Don't Leave Me	1956	40.00
❑ 47-6646	Be Lovey Dovey/Jambalaya	1956	30.00
❑ 47-6768	Happy Am I/Never Never	1956	30.00
❑ 47-6812	Shake a Hand/The Stranger	1957	40.00
❑ 47-6819	Night Train/The Stranger	1957	40.00

7-Inch Extended Plays

RCA VICTOR

Number	Title (A Side/B Side)	Yr	NM
❑ EPA-869	Diddley Diddley Babe/Shake a Hand//The Stranger/ Night Train	1956	150.00
❑ EPA-869 [PS]	The Four Lovers	1956	150.00
❑ EPA-871	I Want a Girl Just Like the Girl That Married Dear Old Dad/ (I Love You) For Sentimental Reasons//This Is My Story/ Memories of You	1956	150.00
❑ EPA-871 [PS]	Joyride	1956	150.00

Albums

RCA VICTOR

Number	Title (A Side/B Side)	Yr	NM
❑ LPM-1317 [M]	Joyride	1956	700.00

FOUR NATURALS, THE

45s

RED TOP

Number	Title (A Side/B Side)	Yr	NM
❑ 113	How Strange/Blue Moon	1958	50.00

—As "The Naturals"

Number	Title (A Side/B Side)	Yr	NM
❑ 119	I Hear a Rhapsody/When I'm In Your Arms	1959	50.00
❑ 125	The Thought of You Darling/ Long Long Ago	1959	80.00

FOUR OF A KIND

More than one group.

45s

BOMARC

Number	Title (A Side/B Side)	Yr	NM
❑ 302	It's Better That Way/ I Care for You	1959	20.00

CAMEO

Number	Title (A Side/B Side)	Yr	NM
❑ 154	You Were Made T'Love/Love Every Moment You Love	1958	20.00

Except when noted otherwise, VG = 25% of NM, and VG+ = 50% of NM. (Example: VG = $2.00, VG+ = $4.00 and NM = $8.00.)

Number	Title (A Side/B Side)	Yr	NM
LAURIE			
❑ 3309	Chippies' Playground/ Prance Around	1965	10.00
MELBA			
❑ 110	I'm Gonna Rock My Heart/ Our Song Dedicated to You	1957	25.00
❑ 117	Dreamy Eyes/Fools Fall in Love	1957	25.00

FOUR PEARLS, THE

45s

Number	Title (A Side/B Side)	Yr	NM
DOLTON			
❑ 26	Look at Me/It's Almost Tomorrow	1960	200.00

FOUR PENNIES, THE (1) See THE CHIFFONS.

FOUR PENNIES, THE (2) British group.

45s

Number	Title (A Side/B Side)	Yr	NM
PHILIPS			
❑ 40202	Juliet/Tell Me Girl. What Are You Gonna Do	1964	15.00
❑ 40333	Until It's Time for You to Go/ Till Another Day	1965	15.00

FOUR PENNIES, THE (U) May also be by group (2), but we're not sure.

45s

Number	Title (A Side/B Side)	Yr	NM
BRUNSWICK			
❑ 55304	You Have No Time to Lose/ You're a Gas with Your Trash	1966	10.00
❑ 55324	Shake a Hand/'Tis the Season	1967	20.00

FOUR REPUTATIONS, THE

45s

Number	Title (A Side/B Side)	Yr	NM
MILLAGE			
❑ 105	Call on Me/(B-side unknown)	196?	800.00

FOUR SEASONS, THE Also see THE FOUR LOVERS; FRANKIE VALLI.

45s

Number	Title (A Side/B Side)	Yr	NM
COLUMBIA			
❑ (# unknown)	Big Man's World	1964	30.00
—One-sided cardboard soundsheet, a promo for the Columbia Record Club. Number has been reported as both 6675 and 6724.			
CREWE			
❑ 333	And That Reminds Me (My Heart Reminds Me)/ The Singles Game	1969	8.00
❑ 333 [PS]	And That Reminds Me (My Heart Reminds Me)/ The Singles Game	1969	10.00
—No shadow behind Frankie Valli's and Joe Long's heads			
❑ 333 [PS]	And That Reminds Me (My Heart Reminds Me)/ The Singles Game	1969	12.00
—With shadow behind Frankie Valli's and Joe Long's heads			
FBI			
❑ 7701	East Meets West/Rhapsody	1986	20.00
—With the Beach Boys			
FOUR SEASONS			
❑ 0019	I Saw Mommy Kissing Santa Claus/Santa Claus Is Coming to Town	198?	4.00
GONE			
❑ 5122	Bermuda/Spanish Lace	1961	80.00
❑ 5122 [DJ]	Bermuda/Spanish Lace	1961	60.00
MCA/CURB			
❑ 52618	Streetfighter/Deep Inside Your Love	1985	4.00
❑ 52724	Moonlight Memories/What About Tomorrow	1985	4.00
❑ 52871	Book of Love/What About Tomorrow	1986	4.00
❑ 53440	Big Girls Don't Cry (Enhanced Original Mix)/Big Girls Don't Cry (Dirty Dancing Rap)	1988	4.00
MOTOWN			
❑ 1255	How Come/Life and Breath	1973	10.00
❑ 1288	Hickory/Charisma	1973	10.00
MOWEST			
❑ 5026	Walk On, Don't Look Back/ Sun Country	1972	10.00
OLDIES 45			
❑ 18	Sherry/I've Cried Before	1964	8.00
❑ 47	Big Girls Don't Cry/Connie-O	1964	8.00
❑ 60	Walk Like a Man/Lucky Ladybug	1964	8.00
❑ 116	Candy Girl/Marlena	1964	8.00
❑ 319	Stay/Goodnight My Love	1965	8.00
PHILIPS			
❑ 40166	Dawn (Go Away)/ No Surfin' Today	1964	15.00
—Black label			

The Four Seasons, "Something's On Her Mind," Philips 40597, 1969, **$10.**

Number	Title (A Side/B Side)	Yr	NM
❑ 40166	Dawn (Go Away)/ No Surfin' Today	1967	8.00
—Light blue label with "S" stamp			
❑ 40185	Ronnie/Born to Wander	1964	12.00
❑ 40185 [PS]	Ronnie/Born to Wander	1964	30.00
❑ 40211	Rag Doll/Silence Is Golden	1964	15.00
—Black label			
❑ 40211	Rag Doll/Silence Is Golden	1967	8.00
—Light blue label with "S" stamp			
❑ 40211 [PS]	Rag Doll/Silence Is Golden	1964	30.00
—Green sleeve			
❑ 40211 [PS]	Rag Doll/Silence Is Golden	1964	30.00
—Yellow sleeve			
❑ 40225	Save It for Me/Funny Face	1964	10.00
❑ 40238	Big Man in Town/Little Angel	1964	10.00
❑ 40238 [PS]	Big Man in Town/Little Angel	1964	25.00
❑ 40260	Bye, Bye Baby (Baby Goodbye)/ Searching Wind	1965	10.00
❑ 40260 [PS]	Bye, Bye Baby (Baby Goodbye)/ Searching Wind	1965	25.00
❑ 40278	Toy Soldier/Betrayed	1965	10.00
❑ 40278 [PS]	Toy Soldier/Betrayed	1965	25.00
❑ 40305	Girl Come Running/ Cry Myself to Sleep	1965	10.00
❑ 40305 [PS]	Girl Come Running/ Cry Myself to Sleep	1965	25.00
❑ 40317	Let's Hang On!/On Broadway Tonight	1965	10.00
—Black label			
❑ 40317	Let's Hang On!/On Broadway Tonight	1967	8.00
—Light blue label with "S" stamp			
❑ 40324	Don't Think Twice/Sassy	1965	10.00
❑ 40324 [PS]	Don't Think Twice/Sassy	1965	25.00
—Philips 40324 by "The Wonder Who?"			
❑ 40350	Working My Way Back to You/ Too Many Memories	1966	10.00
❑ 40370	Opus 17 (Don't You Worry 'Bout Me)/Beggar's Paradise	1966	10.00
❑ 40370 [PS]	Opus 17 (Don't You Worry 'Bout Me)/Beggar's Paradise	1966	25.00
❑ 40380	On the Good Ship Lollipop/ You're Nobody Until Somebody Loves You	1966	10.00
❑ 40380 [PS]	On the Good Ship Lollipop/ You're Nobody Until Somebody Loves You	1966	25.00
—Philips 40380 by "The Wonder Who?"			
❑ 40393	I've Got You Under My Skin/ Huggin' My Pillow	1966	10.00
❑ 40393 [PS]	I've Got You Under My Skin/ Huggin' My Pillow	1966	25.00
❑ 40412	Tell It to the Rain/Show Girl	1966	10.00
❑ 40412 [PS]	Tell It to the Rain/Show Girl	1966	25.00
❑ 40433	Beggin'/Dody	1967	8.00
—Light blue label			
❑ 40433	Beggin'/Dody	1967	10.00
—Black label			
❑ 40433 [PS]	Beggin'/Dody	1967	25.00
❑ 40460	C'mon Marianne/ Let's Ride Again	1967	10.00
—Black label			
❑ 40460	C'mon Marianne/ Let's Ride Again	1967	12.00
—Blue label; contains a noticeably different, slowed-down mix of A-side			
❑ 40460 [PS]	C'mon Marianne/ Let's Ride Again	1967	25.00
❑ 40471	Lonesome Road/ Around and Around	1967	10.00
❑ 40471 [PS]	Lonesome Road/ Around and Around	1967	25.00
—Philips 40471 by "The Wonder Who?"; B-side listed as The Four Seasons			
❑ 40490	Watch the Flowers Grow/Raven	1967	10.00
❑ 40490 [PS]	Watch the Flowers Grow/Raven	1967	25.00
❑ 40500	Donneybrook/Around and Around	1968	20.00
—Only released in Canada			
❑ 40523	Will You Love Me Tomorrow/ Around and Around	1968	10.00
—Blue label			
❑ 40523	Will You Love Me Tomorrow/ Around and Around	1968	12.00
—Black label			
❑ 40542	Saturday's Father/Good-Bye Girl	1968	6.00
❑ 40542 [PS]	Saturday's Father/Good-Bye Girl	1968	10.00
—Standard sleeve			

Number	Title (A Side/B Side)	Yr	NM
❑ 40542 [PS]	Saturday's Father/Good-Bye Girl	1968	15.00
—Fold-open sleeve			
❑ 40577	Electric Stories/Pity	1968	6.00
❑ 40597	Something's On Her Mind/Idaho	1969	6.00
❑ 40597 [PS]	Something's On Her Mind/Idaho	1969	10.00
❑ 40662	Patch of Blue/She Gives Me Light	1970	8.00
—As "Frankie Valli & THE 4 SEASONS"			
❑ 40662 [PS]	Patch of Blue/She Gives Me Light	1970	10.00
❑ 40688	Lay Me Down (Wake Me Up)/ Heartaches and Rainbows	1970	25.00
❑ 40688 [DJ]	Lay Me Down (Wake Me Up) (mono/stereo)	1970	15.00
❑ 40694	Where Are My Dreams?/Any Day Now-Oh Happy Day	1971	25.00
❑ 40694 [DJ]	Where Are My Dreams? (mono/stereo)	1971	15.00

F

SEASONS 4-EVER

Number	Title (A Side/B Side)	Yr	NM
❑ 777	Trance/I Am All Alone	1971	8.00
—As "Billy Dixon and the Topics"; green vinyl			
❑ 777	Trance/I Am All Alone	1971	15.00
—As "Billy Dixon and the Topics"; blue vinyl			

TOPIX

Number	Title (A Side/B Side)	Yr	NM
❑ 6000	Too Young to Start/Red Lips	1960	100.00
—As "The Village Voices"; yellow, black and white label			
❑ 6000	Too Young to Start/Red Lips	1960	150.00
—As "The Village Voices"; yellow and black label			
❑ 6002	I Am All Alone/Trance	1961	150.00
—As "Billy Dixon and the Topics"			
❑ 6008	Lost Lullaby/Trance	1961	200.00
—As "Billy Dixon and the Topics"			

VEE JAY

Number	Title (A Side/B Side)	Yr	NM
❑ 456	Sherry/I've Cried Before	1962	25.00
—A later pressing has an all-black label			
❑ 456	Sherry/I've Cried Before	1962	25.00
—First pressings have black rainbow labels with oval logo			
❑ 465	Big Girls Don't Cry/Connie-O	1962	20.00
—First pressings have black rainbow labels with oval logo			
❑ 465	Big Girls Don't Cry/Connie-O	1962	25.00
—A later pressing has an all-black label			
❑ 478	Santa Claus Is Coming to Town/Christmas Tears	1962	25.00
❑ 485	Walk Like a Man/Lucky Ladybug	1963	15.00
❑ 512	Ain't That a Shame!/Soon (I'll Be Home Again)	1963	20.00
❑ 539	Candy Girl/Marlena	1963	15.00
❑ 539 [PS]	Candy Girl/Marlena	1963	—
—Rumored to exist, but without conclusive evidence, we will delete this from future editions			
❑ 562	New Mexican Rose/ That's the Only Way	1963	15.00
❑ 562	New Mexican Rose/ That's the Way It Goes	1963	60.00
—Wrong title on B-side; stock copy			
❑ 562 [DJ]	New Mexican Rose/ That's the Way It Goes	1963	30.00
—Wrong title on B-side; white label promo			
❑ 576	Peanuts/Stay	1963	100.00
❑ 576 [DJ]	Peanuts/Stay	1963	60.00
❑ 582	Stay/Goodnight My Love	1964	15.00
❑ 597	Alone/Long, Lonely Nights	1964	15.00
—Black rainbow label			
❑ 597	Alone/Long, Lonely Nights	1964	25.00
—Plain black label			
❑ 597	Alone/Long, Lonely Nights	1964	30.00
—Yellow label			
❑ 597 [PS]	Alone/Long, Lonely Nights	1964	50.00
❑ 608	Sincerely/One Song	1964	20.00
❑ 618	Happy, Happy Birthday Baby/ You're the Apple of My Eye	1964	20.00
❑ 626	I Saw Mommy Kissing Santa Claus/Christmas Tears	1964	20.00
❑ 626 [PS]	I Saw Mommy Kissing Santa Claus/Christmas Tears	1964	50.00
❑ 639	Never on Sunday/Connie-O	1965	20.00
❑ 664	Since I Don't Have You/ Tonite, Tonite	1965	30.00
❑ 713	Little Boy (In Grown Up Clothes)/ Silver Wings	1965	20.00
—Maroon label			
❑ 713	Little Boy (In Grown Up Clothes)/ Silver Wings	1965	30.00
—Black label			
❑ 717	Peanuts/My Sugar	1966	30.00
—As "The Wonder Who"			
❑ 719	My Mother's Eyes/Stay	1966	15.00
❑ 901 [DJ]	Peanuts	1963	100.00
—One-sided promo from EP 901			

WABC RADIO

Number	Title (A Side/B Side)	Yr	NM
❑ 77	Cousin Brucie Go Go	1964	150.00
—One-sided yellow vinyl; theme song for Cousin Brucie's radio show			

WARNER BROS.

Number	Title (A Side/B Side)	Yr	NM
❑ 8122	Who Loves You/Who Loves You (Disco Version)	1975	5.00
❑ 8168	December, 1963 (Oh, What a Night)/Slip Away	1975	5.00
❑ 8203	Silver Star/Mystic Mr. Sam	1976	5.00
❑ 8407	Down the Hall/I Believe in You	1977	8.00
❑ 49585	Heaven Must Have Sent You (Here in the Night)/Silver Star	1981	8.00
❑ 49597	Spend the Night in Love/ Slip Away	1980	8.00

WIBBAGE

Number	Title (A Side/B Side)	Yr	NM
❑ WIBG-	Joey Reynolds Theme/ Rats in My Room	1965	100.00
—Custom pressing for Philadelphia radio station; B-side by Joey and Danny			

WXYZ DETROIT

Number	Title (A Side/B Side)	Yr	NM
❑ 121003	Joey Reynolds Theme (same on both sides)	1965	100.00
—Custom pressing for Detroit radio station			

7-Inch Extended Plays

PHILIPS

Number	Title (A Side/B Side)	Yr	NM
❑ PHS 810-C	Dawn/Rag Doll/Bye Bye Baby// Let's Hang On!/Big Man in Town/Save It for Me	1966	15.00
—Jukebox issue; small hole, plays at 33 1/3 rpm			
❑ PHS 810-C [PS]	The 4 Seasons' Gold Vault of Hits	1966	15.00
❑ PL-2704	Wall Street Village Day/Mrs. Stately's Garden//Idaho/ Something's On Her Mind/ Wonder What You'll Be	1968	15.00
—Stereo jukebox issue; small hole, plays at 33 1/3 rpm			
❑ PL-2704 [PS]	Genuine Imitation Life Gazette	1968	15.00
❑ PL-2705	Sherry/Big Girls Don't Cry/Will You Still Love Me Tomorrow// I've Got You Under My Skin/ Silence Is Golden/Walk Like a Man	1968	15.00
—Stereo jukebox issue; small hole, plays at 33 1/3 rpm			
❑ PL-2705 [PS]	Edizione D'Oro	1968	15.00

VEE JAY

Number	Title (A Side/B Side)	Yr	NM
❑ EP 1-901	Never on Sunday/Peanuts// I Can't Give You Anything But Love/La Dee Dah	1962	25.00
❑ EP 1-901 [PS]	The Four Seasons Sing	1962	25.00
❑ EP 1-902	Why Do Fools Fall in Love/ Silhouettes//Since I Don't Have You/Alone	1963	25.00
❑ EP 1-902 [PS]	The Four Seasons Sing	1963	25.00

Albums

MCA/CURB

Number	Title (A Side/B Side)	Yr	NM
❑ 5632	Starfighter	1985	10.00

MOTOWN

Number	Title (A Side/B Side)	Yr	NM
❑ 788	Inside Out	1973	—
—Canceled			

MOWEST

Number	Title (A Side/B Side)	Yr	NM
❑ MW 108L	Chameleon	1972	12.00

PHILIPS

Number	Title (A Side/B Side)	Yr	NM
❑ PHS-2-6501 [(2)]	Edizione d'Oro	1968	25.00
—Number "4" on cover is red on gold foil			
❑ PHS-2-6501 [(2)]	Edizione d'Oro	1968	30.00
—Number "4" on cover is white on gold foil			
❑ PHS-2-6501 [(2)]	Edizione d'Oro	1969	25.00
—Number "4" on cover is white on gold board			
❑ PHM 200124 [M]	Dawn (Go Away) and 11 Other Great Songs	1964	20.00
❑ PHM 200129 [M]	Born to Wander	1964	20.00
❑ PHM 200146 [M]	Rag Doll	1964	20.00
—With yellow seal noting presence of "Save It For Me"			
❑ PHM 200146 [M]	Rag Doll	1964	20.00
—Without yellow seal noting presence of "Save It For Me"			
❑ PHM 200150 [M]	All the Song Hits of the Four Seasons	1964	20.00
❑ PHM 200164 [M]	The 4 Seasons Entertain You	1965	15.00
—With blue seal noting presence of "Bye Bye Baby" and "Toy Soldier"			
❑ PHM 200164 [M]	The 4 Seasons Entertain You	1965	20.00
—With orange seal noting presence of "Bye Bye Baby" and "Toy Soldier"			
❑ PHM 200164 [M]	The 4 Seasons Entertain You	1965	20.00
—With orange seal noting presence of "Bye Bye Baby"			
❑ PHM 200193 [M]	Big Hits by Burt Bacharach...Hal David...Bob Dylan	1965	20.00
—"Open book" cover			
❑ PHM 200193 [M]	Big Hits by Burt Bacharach... Hal David...Bob Dylan	1966	30.00
—Group photos on cover			
❑ PHM 200196 [M]	The 4 Seasons' Gold Vault of Hits	196?	12.00
—Title in all-black print			
❑ PHM 200196 [M]	The 4 Seasons' Gold Vault of Hits	1965	15.00
—Title in red print with black border			
❑ PHM 200196 [M]	The 4 Seasons' Gold Vault of Hits	1965	20.00
—Title in red print with no border			
❑ PHM 200201 [M]	Working My Way Back to You	1966	20.00
❑ PHM 200221 [M]	2nd Vault of Golden Hits	1966	15.00
❑ PHM 200222 [M]	Lookin' Back	1966	20.00
❑ PHM 200223 [M]	The Four Seasons' Christmas Album	1966	25.00
—Reissue of Vee Jay album (same contents and order) with new cover			
❑ PHM 200243 [M]	New Gold Hits	1967	20.00
❑ PHS 600124 [S]	Dawn (Go Away) and 11 Other Great Songs	1964	25.00
❑ PHS 600129 [S]	Born to Wander	1964	25.00
❑ PHS 600146 [S]	Rag Doll	1964	25.00
—With yellow seal noting presence of "Save It For Me"			
❑ PHS 600146 [S]	Rag Doll	1964	25.00
—Without yellow seal noting presence of "Save It For Me"			
❑ PHS 600150 [S]	All the Song Hits of the Four Seasons	1964	25.00
❑ PHS 600164 [S]	The 4 Seasons Entertain You	1965	20.00
—With blue seal noting presence of "Bye Bye Baby" and "Toy Soldier"			
❑ PHS 600164 [S]	The 4 Seasons Entertain You	1965	25.00
—With orange seal noting presence of "Bye Bye Baby" and "Toy Soldier"			
❑ PHS 600164 [S]	The 4 Seasons Entertain You	1965	25.00
—With orange seal noting presence of "Bye Bye Baby"			
❑ PHS 600193 [S]	Big Hits by Burt Bacharach... Hal David...Bob Dylan	1965	25.00
—"Open book" cover			
❑ PHS 600193 [S]	Big Hits by Burt Bacharach... Hal David...Bob Dylan	1966	40.00
—Group photos on cover			
❑ PHS 600196 [S]	The 4 Seasons' Gold Vault of Hits	196?	15.00
—Title in all-black print			
❑ PHS 600196 [S]	The 4 Seasons' Gold Vault of Hits	1965	20.00
—Title in red print with black border			
❑ PHS 600196 [S]	The 4 Seasons' Gold Vault of Hits	1965	25.00
—Title in red print with no border			
❑ PHS 600201 [S]	Working My Way Back to You	1966	25.00
❑ PHS 600221 [S]	2nd Vault of Golden Hits	1966	20.00
❑ PHS 600222 [S]	Lookin' Back	1966	25.00
❑ PHS 600223 [S]	The Four Seasons' Christmas Album	1966	30.00
❑ PHS 600243 [S]	New Gold Hits	1967	25.00
❑ PHS 600290	The Genuine Imitation Life Gazette	1969	15.00
—White newspaper			
❑ PHS 600290	The Genuine Imitation Life Gazette	1969	25.00
—Yellow newspaper			
❑ PHS 600341	Half & Half	1970	20.00

PICKWICK

Number	Title (A Side/B Side)	Yr	NM
❑ SPC-3223	Brotherhood of Man	1970	12.00
—Mass-market version of Sears 609			

PRIVATE STOCK

Number	Title (A Side/B Side)	Yr	NM
❑ PS-7000 [(2)]	The Four Seasons Story	1975	15.00

RHINO

Number	Title (A Side/B Side)	Yr	NM
❑ RNLP 70234	The Four Seasons' Christmas Album	1987	12.00
—Reissue of Philips album (same contents and order)			
❑ R1-70247	Working My Way Back to You	1988	10.00
—Reissue of Philips 600-201			
❑ R1-70249	The Genuine Imitation Life Gazette	1988	10.00
—Reissue of Philips 600-290			
❑ R1-71248	Big Hits by Burt Bacharach... Hal David...Bob Dylan	1988	10.00
—Reissue of Philips 600-193			
❑ R1-71490 [(2)]	Anthology	1988	12.00
❑ RNRP-72998 [(4)]	25th Anniversary Collection	1987	25.00

SEARS

Number	Title (A Side/B Side)	Yr	NM
❑ SPS-609	Brotherhood of Man	1970	25.00

VEE JAY

Number	Title (A Side/B Side)	Yr	NM
❑ LP-1053 [M]	Sherry & 11 Others	1962	40.00
❑ SR-1053 [S]	Sherry & 11 Others	1962	60.00
❑ LP 1055 [M]	The Four Seasons Greetings	1962	30.00
❑ SR 1055 [S]	The Four Seasons Greetings	1962	40.00
❑ LP-1056 [M]	Big Girls Don't Cry and Twelve Others	1963	30.00
❑ SR-1056 [S]	Big Girlzs Don't Cry and Twelve Others	1963	40.00
❑ LP-1059 [M]	Ain't That a Shame and 11 Others	1963	30.00
❑ SR-1059 [S]	Ain't That a Shame and 11 Others	1963	40.00
❑ LP-1065 [M]	Golden Hits of the Four Seasons	1963	30.00
❑ SR-1065 [S]	Golden Hits of the Four Seasons	1963	40.00
❑ LP-1082 [M]	Stay & Other Great Hits	1964	25.00
—Retitled version of Folk-Nanny			
❑ LP-1082 [M]	Folk-Nanny	1964	30.00
❑ SR-1082 [S]	Stay & Other Great Hits	1964	30.00
—Retitled version of Folk-Nanny			
❑ SR-1082 [S]	Folk-Nanny	1964	40.00
❑ LP-1088 [M]	More Golden Hits by the Four Seasons	1964	20.00
—With "Apple of My Eye" on record			
❑ LP-1088 [M]	More Golden Hits by the Four Seasons	1964	30.00
—With "Long Lonely Nights" on record			
❑ SR-1088 [S]	More Golden Hits by the Four Seasons	1964	25.00
—With "Apple of My Eye" on record			
❑ SR-1088 [S]	More Golden Hits by the Four Seasons	1964	40.00
—With "Long Lonely Nights" on record			
❑ LP-1121 [M]	We Love Girls	1965	30.00
❑ LPS-1121 [S]	We Love Girls	1965	40.00
❑ LP-1154 [M]	Recorded Live on Stage	1965	30.00
❑ LPS-1154 [S]	Recorded Live on Stage	1965	40.00

Except when noted otherwise, VG = 25% of NM, and VG+ = 50% of NM. (Example: VG = $2.00, VG+ = $4.00 and NM = $8.00.)

WARNER BROS.

Number	Title (A Side/B Side)	Yr	NM
❑ BS 2900	Who Loves You	1975	12.00
❑ BS 3016	Helicon	1977	12.00
❑ 2WB 3497 [(2)]	Reunited Live	1980	15.00

FOUR SEASONS, THE (2)
Not the same as the better-known group.

45s

ALANNA

Number	Title (A Side/B Side)	Yr	NM
❑ 555	Don't Sweat It Baby/That's the Way the Ball Bounces	1959	40.00
❑ 555	I'm Still in Love with You, Baby/That's the Way the Ball Bounces	1959	60.00
❑ 558	Love Knows No Season/Hot Water Bottle	1959	30.00

ROBBEE

Number	Title (A Side/B Side)	Yr	NM
❑ 106	Mirage/Nancy's Trampoline	1960	150.00

FOUR SONICS, THE

45s

JMC

Number	Title (A Side/B Side)	Yr	NM
❑ 141	If It Wasn't for My Baby/There's No Love	197?	15.00

SEPIA

Number	Title (A Side/B Side)	Yr	NM
❑ 1	Tell Me You're Mine/Lost Without You	196?	40.00

—As "The Four Sonics Plus One"

SPORT

Number	Title (A Side/B Side)	Yr	NM
❑ 110	You Don't Have to Say You Love Me/It Takes Two	1968	15.00
❑ 111	Easier Said Than Done/The Greatest Love	1968	20.00

TRIPLE B

Number	Title (A Side/B Side)	Yr	NM
❑ 0002	Where Are You/Blue Velvet	196?	60.00

FOUR SPARKS, THE

45s

ABC-PARAMOUNT

Number	Title (A Side/B Side)	Yr	NM
❑ 9906	My Sweet Juanita/Out of This World	1958	20.00

FOUR SPEEDS, THE

45s

CHALLENGE

Number	Title (A Side/B Side)	Yr	NM
❑ 9187	R.P.M./My Sting Ray	1963	40.00
❑ 9202	Four on the Floor/Cheater Slicks	1963	40.00

FEDERAL

Number	Title (A Side/B Side)	Yr	NM
❑ 6070	I Need You Baby/The Girls Back Home	1954	80.00

FOUR SPORTSMEN, THE

45s

SUNNYBROOK

Number	Title (A Side/B Side)	Yr	NM
❑ 1	Surrender/Franklin Delano Brown	1960	60.00
❑ 2	Lucille/Mother-in-Law	1961	30.00
❑ 4	Pitter-Patter/Git Up Paint	1961	30.00
❑ 5	Sixty Minute Man/Jellyroll Brown	1961	30.00
❑ 6	If Your Heart Can Take It/Records, Records, Records	1961	40.00

FOUR STUDENTS, THE

45s

GROOVE

Number	Title (A Side/B Side)	Yr	NM
❑ 0110	So Near and Yet So Far/Hot Rotten Soda Pop	1955	50.00

FOUR TEENS, THE

45s

CHALLENGE

Number	Title (A Side/B Side)	Yr	NM
❑ 59021	Go Little Go Cat/Spark Plug	1958	60.00

FOUR TEMPTATIONS, THE

45s

ABC-PARAMOUNT

Number	Title (A Side/B Side)	Yr	NM
❑ 9920	Cathy/Rock and Roll Baby	1958	30.00

FOUR TOPS, THE
Also see DELORES CARROLL AND THE FOUR TOPS.

12-Inch Singles

ABC

Number	Title (A Side/B Side)	Yr	NM
❑ DM-21 [DJ]	H.E.L.P. (stereo/mono)	1978	10.00

ARISTA

Number	Title (A Side/B Side)	Yr	NM
❑ AD1-9705	Indestructible (4 versions)/Are You With Me	1988	8.00

CASABLANCA

Number	Title (A Side/B Side)	Yr	NM
❑ NBD 20239	Let Me Set You Free (4:24) (same on both sides)	1981	10.00

RELIANT

Number	Title (A Side/B Side)	Yr	NM
❑ REG 3691	I'm Here Again (2 versions)	1983	8.00

45s

ABC

Number	Title (A Side/B Side)	Yr	NM
❑ 12096	Seven Lonely Nights/I Can't Hold Out Much Longer	1975	4.00
❑ 12123	We All Gotta Stick Together/(It Would Almost) Drive Me Out of My Mind	1975	4.00
❑ 12155	I'm Glad You Walked Into My Life/Mama, You're All Right with Me	1975	4.00
❑ 12214	Catfish/Look at My Baby	1976	4.00
❑ 12223	Look at My Baby/Catfish	1976	4.00
❑ 12236	Feel Free/I Know You Like It	1976	4.00
❑ 12267	Strung Out for Your Love/You Can't Hold Back on Love	1977	4.00
❑ 12315	Runnin' From Your Love/The Show Must Go On	1977	4.00
❑ 12427	Inside a Brokenhearted Man/H.E.L.P.	1978	4.00
❑ 12457	Just in Time/This House	1978	4.00

ABC DUNHILL

Number	Title (A Side/B Side)	Yr	NM
❑ 4330	Keeper of the Castle/Jubilee with Soul	1972	5.00
❑ 4334	Guardian De Tu Castle/Jubilee with Soul	1972	5.00
❑ 4339	Ain't No Woman (Like the One I've Got)/The Good Lord Knows	1973	5.00
❑ 4354	Are You Man Enough/Peace of Mind	1973	5.00
❑ 4366	Sweet Understanding Love/Main Street People	1973	5.00
❑ 4377	I Just Can't Get You Out of My Mind/Am I My Brother's Keeper?	1973	5.00
❑ 4386	One Chain Don't Make No Prison/Light of Your Love	1974	5.00
❑ 15005	Midnight Flower/All My Love	1974	5.00

ARISTA

Number	Title (A Side/B Side)	Yr	NM
❑ 9706	Indestructible/Are You With Me	1988	3.00
❑ 9706 [PS]	Indestructible/Are You With Me	1988	3.00
❑ 9766	If Ever a Love There Was/Indestructible	1988	3.00

—A-side with Aretha Franklin

Number	Title (A Side/B Side)	Yr	NM
❑ 9766 [PS]	If Ever a Love There Was/Indestructible	1988	3.00
❑ 9801	Change of Heart/Loco in Acapulco	1989	3.00

CASABLANCA

Number	Title (A Side/B Side)	Yr	NM
❑ 2338	When She Was My Girl/Something to Remember	1981	4.00
❑ 2344	Let Me Set You Free/From a Distance	1981	4.00
❑ 2345	Tonight I'm Gonna Love You All Over/I'll Never Leave Again	1981	4.00
❑ 2353	Sad Hearts/I Believe in You and Me	1982	4.00

CHESS

Number	Title (A Side/B Side)	Yr	NM
❑ 1623	Could It Be You?/Kiss Me, Baby	1956	200.00

COLUMBIA

Number	Title (A Side/B Side)	Yr	NM
❑ 41755	Ain't That Love/Lonely Summer	1960	60.00
❑ 43356	Ain't That Love/Lonely Summer	1965	25.00

GRADY

Number	Title (A Side/B Side)	Yr	NM
❑ 012	If Only I Had Known/(B-side unknown)	1956	600.00

—As "The Four Aims"

MOTOWN

Number	Title (A Side/B Side)	Yr	NM
❑ 1062	Baby I Need Your Loving/Call On Me	1964	15.00
❑ 1069	Without the One You Love (Life's Not Worth While)/Love Has Gone	1964	12.00
❑ 1073	Ask the Lonely/Where Did You Go	1965	15.00
❑ 1073 [PS]	Ask the Lonely/Where Did You Go	1965	80.00
❑ 1076	I Can't Help Myself/Sad Souvenirs	1965	15.00
❑ 1081	It's the Same Old Song/Your Love Is Amazing	1965	15.00
❑ 1084	Something About You/Darling, I Hum Our Song	1965	15.00
❑ 1090	Shake Me, Wake Me (When It's Over)/Just As Long As You Need Me	1966	15.00
❑ 1096	Loving You Is Sweeter Than Ever/I Like Everything About You	1966	15.00
❑ 1098	Reach Out I'll Be There/Until You Love Someone	1966	15.00
❑ 1098 [PS]	Reach Out I'll Be There/Until You Love Someone	1966	80.00
❑ 1102	Standing in the Shadows of Love/Since You've Been Gone	1966	15.00
❑ 1104	Bernadette/I Got a Feeling	1967	12.00
❑ 1110	7-Rooms of Gloom/I'll Turn to Stone	1967	12.00
❑ 1113	You Keep Running Away/If You Don't Want My Love	1967	12.00
❑ 1119	Walk Away Renee/Your Love Is Wonderful	1968	12.00
❑ 1124	If I Were a Carpenter/Wonderful Baby	1968	12.00
❑ 1127	Yesterday's Dreams/For Once in My Life	1968	8.00
❑ 1132	I'm in a Different World/Remember When	1968	8.00
❑ 1147	What Is a Man/Don't Bring Back Memories	1969	8.00
❑ 1159	Don't Let Him Take Your Love from Me/The Key	1969	8.00
❑ 1164	It's All in the Game/Love (Is the Answer)	1970	8.00
❑ 1164 [PS]	It's All in the Game/Love (Is the Answer)	1970	20.00
❑ 1170	Still Water (Love)/Still Water (Peace)	1970	6.00
❑ 1175	Just Seven Numbers (Can Straighten Out My Life)/I Wish I Were Your Mirror	1971	6.00
❑ 1175 [PS]	Just Seven Numbers (Can Straighten Out My Life)/I Wish I Were Your Mirror	1971	20.00
❑ 1185	In These Changing Times/Right Before My Eyes	1971	6.00
❑ 1189	MacArthur Park (Part 2)/MacArthur Park (Part 1)	1971	6.00
❑ 1196	A Simple Game/L.A. My Town	1972	6.00
❑ 1198	I Can't Quit Your Love/Happy (Is a Bumpy Road)	1972	6.00
❑ 1210	(It's the Way) Nature Planned It/I'll Never Change	1972	6.00
❑ 1254	Hey Man-We Gotta Get You a Woman/How Can I Forget You	1973	—

—Unreleased

Number	Title (A Side/B Side)	Yr	NM
❑ 1706	I Just Can't Walk Away/Hang	1983	3.00
❑ 1718	Make Yourself Right at Home/Sing a Song of Yesterday	1984	3.00
❑ 1790	Sexy Ways/Body and Soul	1985	3.00
❑ 1811	Don't Tell Me That It's Over/I'm Ready for Love	1985	3.00
❑ 1854	Hot Nights/Again	1986	3.00

RELIANT

Number	Title (A Side/B Side)	Yr	NM
❑ 1691	I'm Here Again/(Instrumental)	1983	4.00

RIVERSIDE

Number	Title (A Side/B Side)	Yr	NM
❑ 4534	Pennies from Heaven/Where Are You?	1962	75.00

RSO

Number	Title (A Side/B Side)	Yr	NM
❑ 1069	Back to School Again/Rock-a-Hula Luau	1982	3.00
❑ 1069 [PS]	Back to School Again/Rock-a-Hula Luau	1982	3.00

—B-side: by The Cast (from the movie Grease 2)

TOPPS/MOTOWN

Number	Title (A Side/B Side)	Yr	NM
❑ 5	I Can't Help Myself	1967	75.00
❑ 9	Baby I Need Your Loving	1967	75.00

—These are cardboard discs

Albums

ABC

Number	Title (A Side/B Side)	Yr	NM
❑ D-862	Night Lights Harmony	1975	12.00
❑ D-968	Catfish	1976	12.00
❑ D-1014	The Show Must Go On	1977	12.00
❑ AA-1092	At the Top	1978	12.00

ABC DUNHILL

Number	Title (A Side/B Side)	Yr	NM
❑ DSX-50129	Keeper of the Castle	1972	12.00
❑ DSX-50144	Main Street People	1973	12.00
❑ DSX-50166	Meeting of the Minds	1974	12.00
❑ DSX-50188	Live & In Concert	1974	12.00

ARISTA

Number	Title (A Side/B Side)	Yr	NM
❑ AL-8492	Indestructible	1988	8.00

CASABLANCA

Number	Title (A Side/B Side)	Yr	NM
❑ NBLP 7258	Tonight!	1981	10.00
❑ NBLP 7266	One More Mountain	1982	10.00

COMMAND

Number	Title (A Side/B Side)	Yr	NM
❑ CQD-40011 [Q]	Keeper of the Castle	1974	20.00
❑ CQD-40012 [Q]	Main Street People	1974	20.00

MCA

Number	Title (A Side/B Side)	Yr	NM
❑ 27019	Greatest Hits	198?	10.00

MOTOWN

Number	Title (A Side/B Side)	Yr	NM
❑ M5-114V1	Superstar Series, Vol. 14	1981	10.00
❑ M5-122V1	Four Tops	1981	8.00

—Reissue of 622

Number	Title (A Side/B Side)	Yr	NM
❑ M5-149V1	Four Tops Reach Out	1981	8.00

—Reissue of 660

Number	Title (A Side/B Side)	Yr	NM
❑ M5-209V1	The Four Tops' Greatest Hits	1981	8.00

—Reissue of 662

Number	Title (A Side/B Side)	Yr	NM
❑ 622 [M]	Four Tops	1964	30.00
❑ MS-622 [S]	Four Tops	1964	40.00
❑ 634 [M]	Four Tops Second Album	1965	25.00

Number	Title (A Side/B Side)	Yr	NM
❑ MS-634 [S]	Four Tops Second Album	1965	30.00
❑ 647 [M]	4 Tops On Top	1966	25.00
❑ MS-647 [S]	4 Tops On Top	1966	30.00
❑ 654 [M]	Four Tops Live!	1966	25.00
❑ MS-654 [S]	Four Tops Live!	1966	30.00
❑ 657 [M]	4 Tops on Broadway	1967	25.00
❑ MS-657 [S]	4 Tops on Broadway	1967	30.00
❑ 660 [M]	Four Tops Reach Out	1967	30.00
❑ MS-660 [S]	Four Tops Reach Out	1967	25.00
❑ 662 [M]	The Four Tops Greatest Hits	1967	30.00
❑ MS-662 [S]	The Four Tops Greatest Hits	1967	20.00
❑ 669 [M]	Yesterday's Dreams	1968	30.00
❑ MS-669 [S]	Yesterday's Dreams	1968	20.00
❑ MS-675	Four Tops Now!	1969	20.00
❑ MS-695	Soul Spin	1969	20.00
❑ MS-704	Still Waters Run Deep	1970	20.00
❑ MS-721	Changing Times	1970	20.00
❑ M-740L	Four Tops Greatest Hits, Vol. 2	1971	20.00
❑ M-748L	Nature Planned It	1972	20.00
❑ M-764D [(2)]	The Best of the 4 Tops	1973	15.00
❑ M9-809A3 [(3)]	Anthology	1974	20.00
❑ 5224 ML	Still Waters Run Deep	1982	8.00
—Reissue of 704			
❑ 5258 ML	Four Tops Live!	1983	8.00
—Reissue of 654			
❑ 5314 ML	Great Songs	1983	10.00
❑ 6066 ML	Back Where I Belong	1983	10.00
❑ 6130 ML	Magic	1985	10.00
UNIVERSAL MOTOWN			
❑ 5315998 [S]	Four Tops Reach Out	2009	20.00
WORKSHOP JAZZ			
❑ 217 [M]	Breakin' Through	1962	—

—This album is pictured on some early Motown inner sleeves, but is not known to exist

FOUR TUNES, THE

45s

Number	Title (A Side/B Side)	Yr	NM
JUBILEE			
❑ 5128	Marie/I Gambled with Love	1953	40.00
❑ 5132	I Understand Just How You Feel/Sugar Lump	1953	30.00
❑ 5135	My Wild Irish Rose/ Do-Do-Do It Again	1954	30.00
❑ 5152	Lonesome/The Greatest Feeling in the World	1954	30.00
❑ 5165	Don't Cry Darling/L'Amour Toujours, L'Amour	1954	30.00
❑ 5174	I Sold My Heart to the Junkman/ Good News	1954	30.00
❑ 5174	I Sold My Heart to the Junkman/ Let Me Go Lover	1954	30.00
❑ 5183	I Hope/I Close My Eyes	1955	25.00
❑ 5200	Tired of Waitin'/ Time Out for Texas	1955	25.00
❑ 5212	Brooklyn Bridge/ Three Little Chickens	1955	25.00
❑ 5218	You Are My Love/At the Steamboat River Ball	1955	25.00
❑ 5232	Rock and Roll Call/Our Love	1956	20.00
❑ 5239	I Gotta Go/Hold Me Closer	1956	20.00
❑ 5245	Far Away Places/Dancing with Tears in My Eyes	1956	20.00
❑ 5255	The Ballad of James Dean/ Japanses Farewell	1956	20.00
❑ 5276	Cool Water/A Little on the Lonely Side	1957	20.00
❑ 6000	I Understand/Marie	196?	10.00
KAY-RON			
❑ 1000	I Want to Be Loved/ Savannah Sings the Blues	1953	40.00
❑ 1005	I Understand/Just in Case You Change Your Mind	1953	40.00
RCA VICTOR			
❑ 47-3881	Say When/Do I Worry?	1950	50.00
❑ 47-3967	How Can You Say That I Don't Care/Cool Water	1950	40.00
❑ 47-4102	Wishing You Were Here Tonight/The Last Roundup	1951	40.00
❑ 47-4198	Cool Water/Carry Me Back to the Lone Prairie	1951	40.00
❑ 47-4241	The Prisoner's Song/ I Married An Angel	1951	30.00
❑ 47-4305	My Buddy/Early in the Morning	1951	30.00
❑ 47-4427	Tell Me Why/I'll See You in My Dreams	1951	40.00
❑ 47-4489	Greatest Song I Ever Heard/ Come What May	1952	25.00
❑ 47-4663	I Wonder/Can I Say Any More?	1952	25.00
❑ 47-4828	They Don't Understand/Why Did You Do This	1952	25.00
❑ 47-4968	I Don't Want to Set the World On Fire/Let's Give Love Another Chance	1952	40.00
❑ 47-5532	Don't Get Around Much Anymore/Water Boy	1953	30.00
❑ 50-0008	You're Heartless/Careless Love	1949	200.00
—Gray label, orange vinyl			
❑ 50-0016	My Last Affair/I'm the Guy	1949	200.00
—Gray label, orange vinyl			
❑ 50-0042	I'm Just a Fool in Love/ The Lonesome Road	1949	200.00
—Gray label, orange vinyl			
❑ 50-0072	There Goes My Heart/Am I Blue	1950	150.00
—Gray label, orange vinyl			
❑ 50-0085	Old Fashioned Love/ Kentucky Babe	1950	150.00
—Gray label, orange vinyl			
❑ 50-0131	May That Day Never Come/Carry Me Back to the Lone Prairie	1951	150.00
—Gray label, orange vinyl			

7-Inch Extended Plays

Number	Title (A Side/B Side)	Yr	NM
RCA VICTOR			
❑ EPA-586	(contents unknown)	1954	40.00
❑ EPA-586 [PS]	The Four Tunes	1954	40.00

FOUR UPSETTERS, THE

45s

Number	Title (A Side/B Side)	Yr	NM
SUN			
❑ 381	Crazy Arms/Midnight Soiree	1962	20.00
❑ 386	Surfin' Calliope/Wabash Cannonball	1963	30.00

FOUR WINDS, THE (1)

Also see THE TOKENS, to which they are related.

45s

Number	Title (A Side/B Side)	Yr	NM
B.T. PUPPY			
❑ 555	Let It Ride/One Face in the Crowd	1970	10.00
CRYSTAL BALL			
❑ 102	Come Softly to Me/Judy	1978	5.00
❑ 105	Arlene/Goodbye, Maureen	1978	5.00
—Black vinyl			
❑ 105	Arlene/Goodbye, Maureen	1978	10.00
—Red vinyl			
SWING			
❑ 100	Remember Last Summer/ Strange, Strange Feeling	1964	20.00

FOUR WINDS, THE (U)

None of these are group (1), but they aren't all the same group, either.

45s

Number	Title (A Side/B Side)	Yr	NM
CHATTAHOOCHIE			
❑ 655	Down and Out/To Love or Not to Love	1964	15.00
DECOR			
❑ 175	Short Shorts/Five Minutes More	1961	20.00
DERBY			
❑ 10022	Playgirl/Jennifer	1964	30.00
DIAL			
❑ 3006	Woe Is Me/Promised Land	1962	15.00
FELSTED			
❑ 8703	Playgirl/Jennifer	1964	20.00
HIDE-A-WAY			
❑ 101	Mission by the Sea/These Hearts Were Mine	1958	20.00
VIK			
❑ 0221	Colorado Moon/ Find Someone New	1956	20.00
WARWICK			
❑ 633	Daddy's Home/ Bull-Moose Stomp	1961	40.00

FOURMOST, THE

45s

Number	Title (A Side/B Side)	Yr	NM
ATCO			
❑ 6280	Hello Little Girl/Just in Case	1963	20.00
❑ 6285	I'm in Love/Respectable	1964	15.00
❑ 6307	If You Cry/Little Bit of Loving	1964	15.00
❑ 6317	How Can I Tell Her/ You Got That Way	1964	15.00
CAPITOL			
❑ 5591	Girls, Girls, Girls/Why Do Fools Fall in Love	1966	12.00
❑ 5738	Here, There and Everywhere/ You've Changed	1966	20.00

FOURTH CEKCION, THE

Albums

Number	Title (A Side/B Side)	Yr	NM
SOLAR			
❑ 110	The Fourth Cekcion	1970	60.00

FOURTH WAY, THE

45s

Number	Title (A Side/B Side)	Yr	NM
CAPITOL			
❑ 2619	Buckleheggin'/Clouds	1969	8.00
SOUL CITY			
❑ 765	Far Side of Your Moon/ Pink Cloud	1968	8.00

Albums

Number	Title (A Side/B Side)	Yr	NM
CAPITOL			
❑ ST-317	The Fourth Way	1969	25.00
HARVEST			
❑ SKAO-423	The Sun and Moon Have Come Together	1970	20.00
❑ ST-666	Werewolf	1971	20.00

FOWLER, RAY

45s

Number	Title (A Side/B Side)	Yr	NM
HIT			
❑ 09	What'd I Say/Soul Twist	1962	8.00
—B-side by the Hit Combo			

FOWLEY, KIM

Instrumental in the career of THE RUNAWAYS.

45s

Number	Title (A Side/B Side)	Yr	NM
CAPITOL			
❑ 3403	Forbidden Love/I'm Bad	1972	6.00
❑ 3534	International Heroes/ E.S.P. Reader	1973	6.00
❑ 3662	A Born Dancer/Something New	1973	6.00
IMPERIAL			
❑ 66326	Born to Be Wild/Space Odyssey	1968	10.00
❑ 66349	Bubble Gum/Wildfire	1969	10.00
LIVING LEGEND			
❑ 721	Mr. Responsibility/ My Foolish Heart	1965	15.00
❑ 725	Underground Lady/Pop Art '66	1966	15.00
LOMA			
❑ 2064	Lights/Something New and Different	1966	10.00
MIRA			
❑ 209	American Dream/The Statue	1965	10.00
ORIGINAL SOUND			
❑ 98	Thunder Road/Born to Make You Cry	1970	10.00
RCA VICTOR			
❑ 74-0511	Citizen Kane/The Sky Is On Fire	1971	—
—Canceled			
REPRISE			
❑ 0569	Don't Be Cruel/Strangers from the Sky	1967	10.00
TOWER			
❑ 342	Love Is Alive and Well/ Reincarnation	1967	10.00

Albums

Number	Title (A Side/B Side)	Yr	NM
ANTILLES			
❑ AN-7075	Snake Document Masquerade	1979	12.00
CAPITOL			
❑ ST-11075	I'm Bad	1972	20.00
❑ ST-11159	International Heroes	1973	20.00
❑ ST-11248	Automatic	1974	20.00
GNP CRESCENDO			
❑ GNPS-2132	Hollywood Confidential	197?	12.00
IMPERIAL			
❑ LP-12413	Born to Be Wild	1968	40.00
❑ LP-12423	Outrageous	1969	40.00
❑ LP-12443	Good Clean Fun	1969	40.00
PVC			
❑ 7906	Sunset Boulevard	1978	12.00
TOWER			
❑ ST 5080 [S]	Love Is Alive and Well	1967	40.00
❑ T 5080 [M]	Love Is Alive and Well	1967	30.00

FOX

45s

Number	Title (A Side/B Side)	Yr	NM
ARIOLA AMERICA			
❑ 7601	Only You Can/Out of My Body	1975	6.00
❑ 7608	Imagine Me Imagine You/If I Point at the Moon	1975	6.00
GTO			
❑ 1003	Only You Can/Out of My Body	1975	10.00
—Original issue			

Albums

Number	Title (A Side/B Side)	Yr	NM
ARIOLA AMERICA			
❑ ST-50001	Fox	1975	12.00

FOX, BARNEY

45s

Number	Title (A Side/B Side)	Yr	NM
HIT			
❑ 30	Teenage Idol/Sherry	1962	8.00
—B-side by the Four Chellows			

FOX, NORMAN, AND THE ROB ROYS

45s

Number	Title (A Side/B Side)	Yr	NM
BACK BEAT			
❑ 499	Lover Doll/Little Star	197?	4.00
—Bootleg			

Except when noted otherwise, VG = 25% of NM, and VG+ = 50% of NM. (Example: VG = $2.00, VG+ = $4.00 and NM = $8.00.)

Number	Title (A Side/B Side)	Yr	NM
❑ 501	Tell Me Why/Audry	1957	40.00
—Red label			
❑ 501	Tell Me Why/Audry	1957	80.00
—White label			
❑ 508	Dance Girl Dance/ My Dearest One	1958	80.00
CAPITOL			
❑ F4128	Dream Girl/Pizza Pie	1959	700.00
HAMMER			
❑ 544	Dream Girl/Pizza Pie	1958	30.00

FOX, SAMMY

Number	Title (A Side/B Side)	Yr	NM
45s			
HIT			
❑ 80	The Monkey Time/ My Boyfriend's Back	1963	8.00
—B-side by Dot Hester			

FOXX, INEZ (AND CHARLIE)

Number	Title (A Side/B Side)	Yr	NM
45s			
DYNAMO			
❑ 102	Baby Take It All/Tightrope	1967	8.00
❑ 104	I Stand Accused/Guilty	1967	8.00
❑ 109	You Are the Man/Hard to Get	1967	8.00
❑ 112	(1-2-3-4-5-6-7) Count the Days/A Stranger I Don't Know	1967	8.00
❑ 117	Undecided/I Ain't Goin' for That	1968	8.00
❑ 119	Vaya Con Dios/ Fellows in Vietnam	1968	8.00
❑ 126	Come On In/Baby Drop a Dime	1968	8.00
❑ 127	Baby Give It to Me/You Fixed My Heartache	1968	8.00
❑ 134	We Got a Chance to Be Free/ Speed Ticket	1969	8.00
❑ 138	North Carolina (South Carolina)/I Got It	1970	8.00
❑ 144	You Shouldn't Have Set My Soul on Fire/Live for Today	1970	8.00
LANA			
❑ 148	Mockingbird/Jaybirds	196?	8.00
—Oldies reissue			
MUSICOR			
❑ 1201	No Stranger to Love/ Come By Here	1966	10.00
SYMBOL			
❑ 20-001	Hurt by Love/Confusion	1964	12.00
❑ 201	La De Da, I Love You/ Yankee Doodle Dandy	1964	12.00
❑ 204	Don't Do It No More/I Fancy You	1964	12.00
❑ 206	I Feel Alright/My Mama Told Me	1965	12.00
❑ 208	I've Come to One Conclusion/ Down by the Seashore	1965	12.00
❑ 213	Hummingbird/If I Need Anyone	1966	12.00
❑ 919	Mockingbird/Jaybirds	1963	25.00
❑ 922	Broken Hearted Fool/ He's the One You Love	1963	15.00
❑ 924	Hi Diddle Diddle/Talk with Me	1963	15.00
❑ 926	Ask Me/I See You My Love	1963	15.00
UNITED ARTISTS			
❑ XW516	Mockingbird/I Know (You Don't Love Me No More)	1974	4.00
—Reissue; B-side by Barbara George			
VOLT			
❑ 4087	Watch the Dog/You Hurt Me for the Last Time	1972	6.00
❑ 4093	One Woman's Man/The Time	1973	6.00
❑ 4096	Crossing Over That Bridge/ You're Saving Me for a Rainy Day	1973	6.00
❑ 4101	I Had a Talk with My Man/ The Lady, The Doctor and the Prescription	1973	6.00
❑ 4107	Circuit's Overloaded/There's a Hand That's Reading Out	1974	6.00
Albums			
DYNAMO			
❑ DM-7000 [M]	Come By Here	1967	30.00
❑ DM-7002 [M]	Inez and Charlie Foxx's Greatest Hits	1967	30.00
❑ DS-8000 [S]	Come By Here	1967	40.00
❑ DS-8002 [S]	Inez and Charlie Foxx's Greatest Hits	1967	40.00
❑ DS-8003	Swingin' Mockin' Band	1968	30.00
SUE			
❑ LP-1027 [M]	Mockingbird	1966	100.00
SYMBOL			
❑ SYM-4400 [M]	Mockingbird	1963	150.00
VOLT			
❑ VOS-6022	Inez Foxx at Memphis	1973	15.00

Peter Frampton
"SHOW ME THE WAY"

Produced by Peter Frampton

AM-1795

From the A&M album "Frampton Comes Alive!"
(SP-3703)

Peter Frampton, "Show Me the Way," A&M 1795, 1976, **$6.**

FRACTION

Number	Title (A Side/B Side)	Yr	NM
45s			
ANGELUS			
❑ 5005	Sanc Divided/(B-side unknown)	1971	100.00
Albums			
ANGELUS			
❑ 571	Moon Blood	1971	2000.
—VG value 1000; VG+ value 1500			

FRAGGIES, THE

Number	Title (A Side/B Side)	Yr	NM
45s			
CAMEO			
❑ 410	Stick with You/I Wanna Love You	1966	15.00

FRAMPTON, PETER Also see THE HERD; HUMBLE PIE.

Number	Title (A Side/B Side)	Yr	NM
12-Inch Singles			
ATLANTIC			
❑ PR 826 [DJ]	Lying (Edit 4:11) (LP Version 5:40)	1985	10.00
45s			
A&M			
❑ 1379	Jumping Jack Flash/ Oh for Another Day	1972	10.00
❑ 1456	All Night Long/Don't Fade Away	1973	6.00
—As "Frampton's Camel"			
❑ 1470	I Believe (When I Fall in Love It Will Be Forever)/Which Way the Wind Blows	1973	8.00
—As "Frampton's Camel"			
❑ 1506	Somethin's Happening/ I Wanna Go to the Sun	1974	6.00
❑ 1693	Show Me the Way/Crying Clown	1975	8.00
❑ 1738	Baby I Love Your Way/ (I'll Give You) Money	1975	8.00
❑ 1763	(I'll Give You) Money/ Nowhere's Too Far (For My Baby)	1975	6.00
❑ 1795	Show Me the Way/Shine On	1976	4.00
❑ 1795 [PS]	Show Me the Way/Shine On	1976	6.00
❑ 1832	Baby, I Love Your Way/ It's a Plain Shame	1976	4.00
❑ 1832 [PS]	Baby, I Love Your Way/ It's a Plain Shame	1976	6.00
❑ 1867	Do You Feel Like We Do/ Penny for Your Thoughts	1976	4.00
❑ 1941	I'm in You/St. Thomas (Don't You Know How I Feel)	1977	4.00
❑ 1941	I'm in You/St. Thomas (Know How I Feel)	1977	5.00
❑ 1941 [PS]	I'm in You/St. Thomas (Don't You Know How I Feel)	1977	6.00
❑ 1941 [PS]	I'm in You/St. Thomas (Know How I Feel)	1977	7.00
❑ 1972	Signed, Sealed, Delivered (I'm Yours)/Rocky's Hot Club	1977	4.00
❑ 1972 [PS]	Signed, Sealed, Delivered (I'm Yours)/Rocky's Hot Club	1977	6.00
❑ 1988	Tried to Love/You Don't Have to Worry	1977	4.00
❑ 1988 [PS]	Tried to Love/You Don't Have to Worry	1977	6.00
❑ 2070	The Long and Winding Road/ Tried to Love	1978	6.00
❑ 2148	I Can't Stand It No More/ Where Should I Be	1979	4.00
❑ 2148 [PS]	I Can't Stand It No More/ Where Should I Be	1979	5.00
❑ 2174	She Don't Reply/St. Thomas (Don't You Know How I Feel)	1979	4.00
❑ 2350	Breaking All the Rules/ Night Town	1981	4.00
❑ 2350 [PS]	Breaking All the Rules/ Night Town	1981	6.00
❑ 2362	You Kill Me/Wasting the Night Away	1981	6.00
❑ 2442	Sleepwalk/Theme from Nivram	1982	8.00
❑ 8595	Show Me the Way/Baby, I Love Your Way	1977	4.00
—"Forget Me Nots" reissue; green and gold label			
❑ 8595 [PS]	Show Me the Way/Baby, I Love Your Way	1977	10.00

Number	Title (A Side/B Side)	Yr	NM
❑ 8604	I'm in You/Do You Feel Like We Do	1978	4.00
—"Forget Me Nots" reissue; green and gold label			

ATLANTIC

Number	Title (A Side/B Side)	Yr	NM
❑ 88820	Holding On to You/Give Me a Love That's Real	1990	3.00
❑ 89395	Hiding from a Heartache/Into View	1986	3.00
❑ 89426	All Eyes on You/So Far Away	1986	3.00
❑ 89426 [PS]	All Eyes on You/So Far Away	1986	3.00
❑ 89463	Lying/Into View	1985	3.00
❑ 89463 [PS]	Lying/Into View	1985	3.00

Albums

A&M

Number	Title (A Side/B Side)	Yr	NM
❑ SP-3133	Wind of Change	198?	8.00
—Budget-line reissue			
❑ SP-3619	Somethin's Happening	1974	12.00
❑ PR-3703	Frampton Comes Alive!	1976	20.00
—Single-record picture disc of highlights			
❑ SP-3703 [(2)]	Frampton Comes Alive!	1976	12.00
❑ SP-3710	Where I Should Be	1979	10.00
❑ SP-3722	Breaking All the Rules	1981	10.00
❑ SP-4348	Wind of Change	1972	12.00
—Brown label			
❑ SP-4348	Wind of Change	1974	10.00
—Silvery label			
❑ SP-4389	Frampton's Camel	1973	12.00
—Brown label			
❑ SP-4389	Frampton's Camel	1974	10.00
—Silvery label			
❑ SP-4512	Frampton	1975	10.00
❑ SP-4704	I'm In You	1977	10.00
❑ SP-4704 [DJ]	I'm In You	1977	40.00
—Promo-only picture disc			
❑ SP-4905	The Art of Control	1982	10.00
❑ SP-6505 [(2)]	Frampton Comes Alive!	198?	10.00
—Budget-line reissue			
❑ SP-17100 [DJ]	Peter Frampton Radio Special	1979	20.00
—Promo-only interview record			

ATLANTIC

Number	Title (A Side/B Side)	Yr	NM
❑ PR 848 [DJ]	Frampton Is Alive!	1986	20.00
—Promo-only interview record			
❑ PR 3093 [DJ]	Perfect Fit: A Candid Interview	1989	20.00
—Promo-only album			
❑ 81290	Premonition	1986	8.00
❑ 82030	Where All the Pieces Fit	1989	8.00

MOBILE FIDELITY

Number	Title (A Side/B Side)	Yr	NM
❑ 2-262 [(2)]	Frampton Comes Alive!	1996	40.00
—Audiophile vinyl			

SWEET THUNDER

Number	Title (A Side/B Side)	Yr	NM
❑ 6 [(2)]	Frampton Comes Alive!	198?	100.00
—Audiophile edition			

FRANCESCO

45s

DATE

Number	Title (A Side/B Side)	Yr	NM
❑ 2-1625	You Want to Be Americano (Tu Vuo' Da L'Americano)/Taxi, Taxi Italiano	1968	8.00

FRANCHI, SERGIO

12-Inch Singles

LAX

Number	Title (A Side/B Side)	Yr	NM
❑ L33-1836 [DJ]	Laugh You Silly Clown/More (Theme from Mondo Cane)	1979	10.00

45s

LAX

Number	Title (A Side/B Side)	Yr	NM
❑ 41164	Laugh You Silly Clown/(B-side unknown)	1979	4.00

METROMEDIA

Number	Title (A Side/B Side)	Yr	NM
❑ 238	If/Somehow	1971	4.00

RCA VICTOR

Number	Title (A Side/B Side)	Yr	NM
❑ 47-8103	I Mustn't Say I Love You/Once	1962	8.00
❑ 47-8103	I Mustn't Say I Love Her/Once	1962	10.00
—Some copies of the record have this incorrect title			
❑ 47-8103 [PS]	I Mustn't Say I Love You/Once	1962	15.00
❑ 47-8149	The Good Life/Bella Nina	1963	8.00
❑ 47-8315	Cuando Caliente El Sol/Chicago	1964	6.00
❑ 47-8409	No Arms Can Ever Hold You/Seventh Dawn	1964	6.00
❑ 47-8552	Someone Like You/Take the Moment	1965	6.00
❑ 47-8686	Ciao, Ciao (So Long for Now)/Moon Over Naples	1965	6.00
❑ 47-9124	What Will Tomorrow Bring/Maybe It's Time for Me	1967	6.00
❑ 47-9277	I Should Care/No One Else	1967	6.00
❑ 47-9471	Time Alone Will Tell/I'm a Fool to Want You	1968	6.00

UNITED ARTISTS

Number	Title (A Side/B Side)	Yr	NM
❑ 50612	Hold Me/Song of Santa Vittoria	1969	5.00
❑ 50630	Granada/Within Me	1970	5.00
❑ 50664	More Than Strangers/Buona Fortuna, Addio Bambino	1970	5.00
❑ 50681	Here We Go Again/Love Is All	1970	5.00

Albums

4 CORNERS OF THE WORLD

Number	Title (A Side/B Side)	Yr	NM
❑ FCL-4221 [M]	La Bella Italia	196?	12.00
❑ FCS-4221 [S]	La Bella Italia	196?	15.00
❑ FCL 4223 [M]	Buon Natale	196?	12.00
❑ FCS 4223 [S]	Buon Natale	196?	15.00
❑ FCL-4228 [M]	Il Fantastico	196?	12.00
❑ FCS-4228 [S]	Il Fantastico	196?	15.00

METROMEDIA

Number	Title (A Side/B Side)	Yr	NM
❑ MD 1047	Sergio Franchi	1971	10.00

RCA VICTOR

Number	Title (A Side/B Side)	Yr	NM
❑ ANL1-1070	The Best of Sergio Franchi	1975	10.00
❑ APL1-2132	Volare	1976	10.00
❑ ANL1-2643	Songs of Richard Rodgers	1977	8.00
—Reissue of LSP-3365			
❑ LPM-2943 [M]	The Exciting Voice of Sergio Franchi	1964	12.00
❑ LSP-2943 [S]	The Exciting Voice of Sergio Franchi	1964	15.00
❑ LPM-3310 [M]	Live at the Cocoanut Grove	1965	10.00
❑ LSP-3310 [S]	Live at the Cocoanut Grove	1965	12.00
❑ LPM-3365 [M]	Songs of Richard Rodgers	1965	10.00
❑ LSP-3365 [S]	Songs of Richard Rodgers	1965	12.00
❑ LPM-3437 [M]	The Heart of Christmas (Cuor' di Natale)	1965	12.00
❑ LSP-3437 [S]	The Heart of Christmas (Cuor' di Natale)	1965	15.00
❑ LPM-3500 [M]	La Dolce Italy	1966	10.00
❑ LSP-3500 [S]	La Dolce Italy	1966	12.00
❑ LPM-3654 [M]	From Sergio — With Love	1966	10.00
❑ LSP-3654 [S]	From Sergio — With Love	1966	12.00
❑ LPM-3810 [M]	There Goes My Heart	1967	10.00
❑ LSP-3810 [S]	There Goes My Heart	1967	12.00
❑ LPM-3933 [M]	I'm a Fool to Want You	1968	15.00
❑ LSP-3933 [S]	I'm a Fool to Want You	1968	12.00
❑ AFL1-4018	Wine and Song	1977	8.00
—Reissue of LSP-4018			
❑ LPM-4018 [M]	Wine and Song	1968	20.00
❑ LSP-4018 [S]	Wine and Song	1968	12.00
❑ VPS-6082 [(2)]	This Is Sergio Franchi	1972	12.00

RCA VICTOR RED SEAL

Number	Title (A Side/B Side)	Yr	NM
❑ LM-2640 [M]	Romantic Italian Songs	1962	12.00
❑ LSC-2640 [S]	Romantic Italian Songs	1962	15.00
❑ LM-2657 [M]	Our Man from Italy	1963	12.00
❑ LSC-2657 [S]	Our Man from Italy	1963	15.00
❑ LM-2674 [M]	Broadway...I Love You	1963	12.00
❑ LSC-2674 [S]	Broadway...I Love You	1963	15.00
❑ LM-2675 [M]	The Dream Duet	1963	12.00
—With Anna Moffo			
❑ LSC-2675 [S]	The Dream Duet	1963	15.00
—With Anna Moffo			
❑ LM-2696 [M]	The Women in My Life	1964	12.00
❑ LSC-2696 [S]	The Women in My Life	1964	15.00

UNITED ARTISTS

Number	Title (A Side/B Side)	Yr	NM
❑ UAS-6727	Within Me	1970	10.00

FRANCIS, CONNIE

45s

GSF

Number	Title (A Side/B Side)	Yr	NM
❑ 6901	The Answer (Should I Tie a Yellow Ribbon Round the Ole Oak Tree?)/Paint the Rain	1973	5.00

IVANHOE

Number	Title (A Side/B Side)	Yr	NM
❑ 508	I Don't Wanna Walk Without You/Don't Turn Around	197?	5.00

MGM

Number	Title (A Side/B Side)	Yr	NM
❑ CS6-5	Celebrity Scene: Connie Francis	1967	60.00
—Box set of five singles (13708-13712). Price includes box, all 5 singles, jukebox title strips, bio. Records are sometimes found by themselves, so they are also listed separately.			
❑ SB-9 [S]	Rock-A-Bye Your Baby with a Dixie Melody/Ciao Ciao Bambino	1960	50.00
❑ SB-10 [S]	I Almost Lost My Mind/Come Back to Sorrento	1960	50.00
❑ 126	Stupid Cupid/I'm Sorry I Made You Cry	196?	8.00
—Reissue			
❑ 129	Who's Sorry Now/You Were Only Fooling	196?	8.00
—Reissue			
❑ 135	Mama/You're Gonna Miss Me	196?	8.00
—Reissue			
❑ 136	Among My Souvenirs/God Bless America	196?	8.00
—Reissue			
❑ 139	Lipstick on Your Collar/Frankie	196?	8.00
—Reissue			
❑ 141	My Happiness/If I Didn't Care	196?	8.00
—Reissue			
❑ 148	My Heart Has a Mind of Its Own/Malaguena	196?	8.00
—Reissue			
❑ 150	Where the Boys Are/No One	196?	8.00
—Reissue			
❑ 153	Breakin' In a Brand New Broken Heart/Somebody Else's Boy	196?	8.00
—Reissue			
❑ 155	Together/Too Many Rules	196?	8.00
—Reissue			
❑ 156	Many Tears Ago/Senza Mama E Numerata	196?	8.00
—Reissue			
❑ 157	Don't Break the Heart That Loves You/Second Hand Love	196?	8.00
—Reissue			
❑ 165	Everybody's Somebody's Fool/Al Di La	196?	8.00
—Reissue			
❑ 169	Jealous Heart/Forget Domani	196?	8.00
—Reissue			
❑ 511	Who's Sorry Now/Stupid Cupid	197?	5.00
—Reissue			
❑ 512	Lipstick on Your Collar/Mama	197?	5.00
—Reissue			
❑ 513	Everybody's Somebody's Fool/Al Di La	197?	5.00
—Reissue			
❑ 524	My Happiness/If I Didn't Care	197?	5.00
—Reissue			
❑ 12015	Freddy/Didn't I Love You Enough	1955	50.00
❑ 12056	Oh Please Make Him Jealous/Goody Goodbye	1955	50.00
❑ 12122	Are You Satisfied/My Treasure	1956	25.00
❑ 12191	My First Real Love/Believe in Me	1956	60.00
❑ 12251	Send for My Baby/Forgetting	1956	25.00
❑ 12335	My Sailor Boy/Everyone Needs Someone	1956	25.00
❑ 12375	I Never Had a Sweetheart/Little Blue Wren	1957	25.00
❑ 12440	No Other One/I Leaned on a Man	1957	25.00
❑ 12490	Eighteen/Faded Orchid	1957	25.00
❑ 12588	Who's Sorry Now?/You Were Only Fooling	1958	20.00
❑ 12647	I'm Sorry I Made You Cry/Lock Up Your Heart	1958	20.00
❑ 12669	Heartaches/I Miss You So	1958	50.00
❑ 12683	Stupid Cupid/Carolina Moon	1958	20.00
❑ 12713	Fallin'/Happy Days and Lonely Nights	1958	20.00
❑ 12738 [M]	My Happiness/Never Before	1958	20.00
❑ 12738 [PS]	My Happiness/Never Before	1958	30.00
—Pink sleeve			
❑ 12738 [PS]	My Happiness/Never Before	1958	40.00
—White sleeve			
❑ 12769	If I Didn't Care/Toward the End of the Day	1959	20.00
❑ 12769 [PS]	If I Didn't Care/Toward the End of the Day	1959	30.00
❑ 12793 [M]	Lipstick on Your Collar/Frankie	1959	20.00
❑ 12824 [M]	You're Gonna Miss Me/Plenty Good Lovin'	1959	20.00
❑ 12841 [M]	Among My Souvenirs/God Bless America	1959	20.00
—Second pressing has a black label			
❑ 12841 [M]	Among My Souvenirs/God Bless America	1959	30.00
—First pressing has a yellow label			
❑ 12878	Mama/Teddy	1960	15.00
❑ 12899	Everybody's Somebody's Fool/Jealous of You	1960	15.00
❑ 12899 [PS]	Everybody's Somebody's Fool/Jealous of You	1960	20.00
❑ 12923	My Heart Has a Mind of Its Own/Malaguena	1960	15.00
❑ 12923 [PS]	My Heart Has a Mind of Its Own/Malaguena	1960	20.00
❑ 12964	Many Tears Ago/Senza Mama (With No One)	1960	15.00
❑ 12964 [PS]	Many Tears Ago/Senza Mama (With No One)	1960	20.00
❑ 12971	Where the Boys Are/No One	1961	15.00
❑ 12971 [PS]	Where the Boys Are/No One	1961	20.00
❑ 12995	Breakin' In a Brand New Broken Heart/Someone Else's Boy	1961	15.00
❑ 12995 [PS]	Breakin' In a Brand New Broken Heart/Someone Else's Boy	1961	20.00
❑ 13005	Atashi-No/Swanee	1961	30.00
❑ 13019	Together/Too Many Rules	1961	15.00
❑ 13019 [PS]	Together/Too Many Rules	1961	20.00
❑ 13039	(He's My) Dreamboat/Hollywood	1961	15.00
❑ 13039 [PS]	(He's My) Dreamboat/Hollywood	1961	20.00
❑ 13051	When the Boy in Your Arms (Is the Boy in Your Heart)/Baby's First Christmas	1961	15.00
❑ 13051 [PS]	When the Boy in Your Arms (Is the Boy in Your Heart)/Baby's First Christmas	1961	20.00
❑ 13059	Don't Break the Heart That Loves You/Drop It, Joe	1962	15.00

Number	Title (A Side/B Side)	Yr	NM
13059 [PS]	Don't Break the Heart That Loves You/Drop It, Joe	1962	20.00
13074	Second Hand Love/Gonna Git That Man	1962	20.00
—A-side is said to have been produced by Phil Spector, though Connie Francis disputes this; regardless, Spector did co-write the song			
13074 [PS]	Second Hand Love/Gonna Git That Man	1962	25.00
13087	Vacation/The Biggest Sin of All	1962	15.00
13087 [PS]	Vacation/The Biggest Sin of All	1962	20.00
13096	I Was Such a Fool (To Fall in Love with You)/He Thinks I Still Care	1962	12.00
13096 [PS]	I Was Such a Fool (To Fall in Love with You)/He Thinks I Still Care	1962	16.00
13116	I'm Gonna' Be Warm This Winter/Al Di La	1962	12.00
13116 [PS]	I'm Gonna' Be Warm This Winter/Al Di La	1962	16.00
13127	Follow the Boys/Waiting for Billy	1962	12.00
13127 [PS]	Follow the Boys/Waiting for Billy	1962	16.00
13143	If My Pillow Could Talk/You're the Only One Can Hurt Me	1963	12.00
13143 [PS]	If My Pillow Could Talk/You're the Only One Can Hurt Me	1963	16.00
13160	Drownin' My Sorrows/Mala Femmena	1963	12.00
13160 [PS]	Drownin' My Sorrows/Mala Femmena	1963	16.00
13176	Your Other Love/Whatever Happened to Rosemarie?	1963	12.00
13176 [PS]	Your Other Love/Whatever Happened to Rosemarie?	1963	16.00
13203	In the Summer of His Years/My Buddy	1963	12.00
13203 [PS]	In the Summer of His Years/My Buddy	1963	40.00
13214	Blue Winter/You Know You Don't Want Me (So Why Don't You Leave Me Alone)	1964	12.00
13214 [PS]	Blue Winter/You Know You Don't Want Me (So Why Don't You Leave Me Alone)	1964	16.00
13237	Be Anything (But Be Mine)/Tommy	1964	12.00
13237 [PS]	Be Anything (But Be Mine)/Tommy	1964	16.00
13256	Looking for Love/This Is My Happiest Moment	1964	12.00
13256 [PS]	Looking for Love/This Is My Happiest Moment	1964	16.00
13287	Don't Ever Leave Me/We Have Something More (Than a Summer Love)	1964	12.00
13287 [PS]	Don't Ever Leave Me/We Have Something More (Than a Summer Love)	1964	16.00
13303	Whose Heart Are You Breaking Tonight/Come On Jerry	1965	10.00
13303 [PS]	Whose Heart Are You Breaking Tonight/Come On Jerry	1965	12.00
13325	For Mama (La Mamma)/She'll Be Coming 'Round the Mountain	1965	12.00
13331	Wishing It Was You/You're Mine (Just When You're Lonely)	1965	10.00
13331 [PS]	Wishing It Was You/You're Mine (Just When You're Lonely)	1965	12.00
13363	Forget Domani/No One Sends Me Roses	1965	10.00
13389	Roundabout/Bossa Nova Hand Dance	1965	10.00
13420	Jealous Heart/Can I Rely on You	1965	10.00
13470	Love Is Me, Love Is You/I'd Let You Break My Heart All Over Again	1966	10.00
13470 [PS]	Love Is Me, Love Is You/I'd Let You Break My Heart All Over Again	1966	12.00
13505	It's a Different World/Empty Chapel	1966	10.00
13505 [PS]	It's a Different World/Empty Chapel	1966	20.00
13545	A Letter from a Soldier (Dear Mama)/Somewhere, My Love	1966	10.00
13550 [DJ]	A Nurse in the U.S. Army (same on both sides)	1966	30.00
—Promotional item for the U.S. Army			
13578	All the Love in the World/So Nice	1966	10.00
13610	Spanish Nights and You/Games That Lovers Play	1966	10.00
13610 [PS]	Spanish Nights and You/Games That Lovers Play	1966	20.00
13665	Another Page/Souvenir d'Italie	1967	10.00
13708	Mama/Never on Sunday	1967	10.00
—Part of Celebrity Series CS-5			
13709	My Happiness/Al Di La	1967	10.00
—Part of Celebrity Series CS-5			
13710	Malaguena/I Love You Much Too Much	1967	10.00
—Part of Celebrity Series CS-5			
13711	Once in a Lifetime/Oh Lonesome Me	1967	10.00
—Part of Celebrity Series CS-5			
13712	Jealous Heart/Will You Still Be Mine	1967	10.00
—Part of Celebrity Series CS-5			
13718	Time Alone Will Tell/Born Free	1967	10.00
13773	My Heart Cries for You/Someone Took the Sweetness Out of Sweetheart	1967	10.00
13773 [PS]	My Heart Cries for You/Someone Took the Sweetness Out of Sweetheart	1967	20.00
13814	Lonely Again/When You Care a Lot for Someone	1967	10.00
13876	My World Is Slipping Away/Till We're Together	1967	10.00
13923	Why Say Goodbye/Adios, Me Amore	1968	8.00
13948	Somebody Else Is Taking My Place/Brother, Can You Spare a Dime?	1968	8.00
14004	I Don't Wanna Play House/The Welfare Check	1968	8.00
14034	The Wedding Cake/Over Hill, Under Ground	1969	8.00
14058	Gone Like the Wind/Am I Blue?	1969	8.00
14058 [PS]	Gone Like the Wind/Am I Blue?	1969	20.00
14089	Invierno Trieste/Noches Espanolas Y Tu	1969	—
—Not known to exist			
14091	Mr. Love/Zingara	1969	8.00
14091 [PS]	Mr. Love/Zingara	1969	20.00
14853	I'm Me Again/Comme Si, Comme Sa	1976	6.00
SK-50117 [S]	My Happiness/Never Before	1958	50.00
SK-50121 [S]	Lipstick on Your Collar/Frankie	1959	60.00
SK-50129 [S]	You're Gonna Miss Me/Plenty Good Lovin'	1959	50.00
SK-50133 [S]	Among My Souvenirs/God Bless America	1959	50.00

POLYDOR

Number	Title (A Side/B Side)	Yr	NM
2143	I'm Me Again/Comme Si, Comme Sa	1981	5.00
810087-7	There's Still a Few Good Love Songs Left in Me/Let's Make It Love Tonight	1983	5.00

7-Inch Extended Plays

MGM

Number	Title (A Side/B Side)	Yr	NM
HC5-6 [DJ]	Heart Circuit Interview	1959	100.00
X-1599	Who's Sorry Now/You Were Only Fooling (While I Was Falling in Love)//Eighteen/Faded Orchid	1958	40.00
X-1599 [PS]	Connie Francis	1958	40.00
X-1603	(contents unknown)	1958	40.00
X-1603 [PS]	Who's Sorry Now Vol. I	1958	40.00
X-1604	(contents unknown)	1958	40.00
X-1604 [PS]	Who's Sorry Now Vol. II	1958	40.00
X-1605	*You Always Hurt the One You Love/If I Had You/How Deep Is the Ocean?/I'll Get By	1958	40.00
X-1605 [PS]	Who's Sorry Now Vol. III	1958	40.00
X-1655	My Happiness/No Other One//You're My Everything/Never Before	1958	40.00
X-1655 [PS]	My Happiness	1958	40.00
X-1662	If I Didn't Care/Toward the End of the Day//Don't Speak of Love/If You Loved Me Tonight	1959	40.00
X-1662 [PS]	If I Didn't Care	1959	40.00
SX-1663 [PS]	The Exciting Connie Francis Vol. 1	1959	80.00
—A stereo copy of the above has recently emerged. We presume that Vol. 2 and Vol. 3 of the same title also were made in stereo, but we don't have concrete proof, so we don't list them yet.			
SX-1663 [S]	*Come Rain or Come Shine/Time After Time/Hallelujah, I Love Him So/How Did He Look	1959	80.00
X-1663	*Come Rain or Come Shine/Time After Time/Hallelujah, I Love Him So/How Did He Look	1959	40.00
X-1663 [PS]	The Exciting Connie Francis Vol. 1	1959	40.00
X-1664	(contents unknown)	1959	40.00
X-1664 [PS]	The Exciting Connie Francis Vol. 2	1959	40.00
X-1665	(contents unknown)	1959	40.00
X-1665 [PS]	The Exciting Connie Francis Vol. 3	1959	40.00
X-1687	You're Gonna Miss Me/Plenty Good Lovin'//Frankie/Lipstick on Your Collar	1959	30.00
X-1687 [PS]	Connie Francis	1959	30.00
X-1688	Who's Sorry Now/Fallin'//Happy Days and Lonely Nights/Stupid Cupid	1960	30.00
X-1688 [PS]	Connie's Greatest Hits (Part 1)	1960	30.00
X-1689	(contents unknown)	1960	30.00
X-1689 [PS]	Connie's Greatest Hits (Part 2)	1960	30.00
X-1690	(contents unknown)	1960	30.00
X-1690 [PS]	Connie's Greatest Hits (Part 3)	1960	30.00
X-1691	(contents unknown)	1960	30.00
X-1691 [PS]	Rock 'N Roll Million Sellers (Part 1)	1960	30.00
X-1692	(contents unknown)	1960	30.00
X-1692 [PS]	Rock 'N Roll Million Sellers (Part 2)	1960	30.00
X-1693	(contents unknown)	1960	30.00
X-1693 [PS]	Rock 'N Roll Million Sellers (Part 3)	1960	30.00
X-1694	(contents unknown)	1960	30.00
X-1694 [PS]	Country & Western Golden Hits (Part 1)	1960	30.00
X-1695	(contents unknown)	1960	30.00
X-1695 [PS]	Country & Western Golden Hits (Part 2)	1960	30.00
X-1696	(contents unknown)	1960	30.00
X-1696 [PS]	Country & Western Golden Hits (Part 3)	1960	30.00
X-1703	Valentino/You Made Me Love You//Because of You/Young at Heart	1961	30.00
X-1703 [PS]	Connie Francis	1961	30.00
—Has paper sleeve rather than a cardboard sleeve			
X-1706	Don't Break the Heart That Loves You/It Happened Last Night//Too Many Rules/Kiss 'N' Twist	1962	40.00
X-1706 [PS]	Connie Francis	1962	40.00
—Paper sleeve rather than the typical cardboard EP sleeve			
SLM-4079	I'm Movin' On/She'll Have to Go/I'm a Fool to Care/I Really Don't Want to Know/Someday (You'll Want Me to Want You)/He Thinks I Still Care	196?	25.00
—Jukebox issue; small hole, plays at 33 1/3 rpm			
SLM-4079 [PS]	Country Music Connie Style	196?	25.00

Albums

LEO

Number	Title	Yr	NM
LE-903 [M]	Connie Francis and the Kids Next Door	1967	50.00
LES-903 [S]	Connie Francis and the Kids Next Door	1967	60.00

MATI-MOR

Number	Title	Yr	NM
8002 [M]	Sing Along wth Connie Francis	1961	40.00
—Made for Brylcreem			

METRO

Number	Title	Yr	NM
M-519 [M]	Connie Francis	1964	20.00
MS-519 [S]	Connie Francis	1964	25.00
M-538 [M]	Folk Favorites	1965	20.00
MS-538 [S]	Folk Favorites	1965	25.00
M-571 [M]	Songs of Love	1966	20.00
MS-571 [S]	Songs of Love	1966	25.00
M-603 [M]	The Incomparable Connie Francis	1967	20.00
MS-603 [S]	The Incomparable Connie Francis	1967	25.00

MGM

Number	Title	Yr	NM
GAS-109	Greatest Golden Groovie Goodies (Golden Archive Series)	1970	25.00
E-3686 [M]	Who's Sorry Now?	1958	100.00
—Yellow label			
E-3686 [M]	Who's Sorry Now?	1960	40.00
—Black label			
E-3761 [M]	The Exciting Connie Francis	1959	30.00
—Black label			
E-3761 [M]	The Exciting Connie Francis	1959	80.00
—Yellow label			
SE-3761 [S]	The Exciting Connie Francis	1959	40.00
—Black label			
SE-3761 [S]	The Exciting Connie Francis	1959	100.00
—Yellow label			
E-3776 [M]	My Thanks to You	1959	30.00
SE-3776 [S]	My Thanks to You	1959	40.00
E-3791 [M]	Italian Favorites	1959	30.00
SE-3791 [S]	Italian Favorites	1959	40.00
E-3792 [M]	Christmas in My Heart	1959	30.00
SE-3792 [S]	Christmas in My Heart	1959	40.00
—Same as above, but in stereo			
E-3793 [M]	Connie's Greatest Hits	1960	30.00
E-3794 [M]	Rock 'N' Roll Million Sellers	1960	30.00
SE-3794 [S]	Rock 'N' Roll Million Sellers	1960	40.00
E-3795 [M]	Country and Western Golden Hits	1960	30.00
SE-3795 [S]	Country and Western Golden Hits	1960	40.00
E-3853 [M]	Spanish and Latin American Favorites	1960	30.00
SE-3853 [S]	Spanish and Latin American Favorites	1960	40.00

Number	Title (A Side/B Side)	Yr	NM
❑ E-3869 [M]	Jewish Favorites	1961	30.00
❑ SE-3869 [S]	Jewish Favorites	1961	40.00
❑ E-3871 [M]	More Italian Favorites	1960	30.00
❑ SE-3871 [S]	More Italian Favorites	1960	40.00
❑ E-3893 [M]	Songs to a Swinging Band	1961	30.00
❑ SE-3893 [S]	Songs to a Swinging Band	1961	40.00
❑ E-3913 [M]	Connie Francis at the Copa	1961	30.00
❑ SE-3913 [S]	Connie Francis at the Copa	1961	40.00
❑ E-3942 [M]	More Greatest Hits	1961	30.00
❑ SE-3942 [S]	More Greatest Hits	1961	40.00
❑ E-3965 [M]	Never on Sunday and Other Title Songs from Motion Pictures	1961	30.00
❑ SE-3965 [S]	Never on Sunday and Other Title Songs from Motion Pictures	1961	40.00
❑ E-3969 [M]	Folk Song Favorites	1961	30.00
❑ SE-3969 [S]	Folk Song Favorites	1961	40.00
❑ E-4013 [M]	Irish Favorites	1962	30.00
❑ SE-4013 [S]	Irish Favorites	1962	40.00
❑ E-4022 [M]	Dance Party	196?	25.00
—Retitled version of "Do the Twist"			
❑ E-4022 [M]	Do the Twist	1962	30.00
❑ SE-4022 [S]	Dance Party	196?	30.00
—Retitled version of "Do the Twist"			
❑ SE-4022 [S]	Do the Twist	1962	40.00
❑ E-4023 [M]	Fun Songs for Children	1962	50.00
❑ E-4048 [M]	Award Winning Motion Picture Hits	1963	25.00
❑ SE-4048 [S]	Award Winning Motion Picture Hits	1963	30.00
❑ E-4049 [M]	Connie Francis Sings Second Hand Love and Other Hits	1962	25.00
❑ SE-4049 [S]	Connie Francis Sings Second Hand Love and Other Hits	1962	30.00
❑ E-4079 [M]	Country Music Connie Style	1962	25.00
❑ SE-4079 [S]	Country Music Connie Style	1962	30.00
❑ E-4102 [M]	Modern Italian Hits	1963	25.00
❑ SE-4102 [S]	Modern Italian Hits	1963	30.00
❑ E-4123 [M]	Follow the Boys	1963	25.00
❑ SE-4123 [S]	Follow the Boys	1963	30.00
❑ E-4124 [M]	German Favorites	1963	25.00
❑ SE-4124 [S]	German Favorites	1963	30.00
❑ E-4145 [M]	Greatest American Waltzes	1963	25.00
❑ SE-4145 [S]	Greatest American Waltzes	1963	30.00
❑ E-4161 [M]	Mala Femmena & Connie's Big Hits from Italy	1963	25.00
❑ SE-4161 [S]	Mala Femmena & Connie's Big Hits from Italy	1963	30.00
❑ E-4167 [M]	The Very Best of Connie Francis	1963	25.00
❑ SE-4167 [S]	The Very Best of Connie Francis	1963	30.00
❑ E-4210 [M]	In the Summer of His Years	1964	25.00
❑ SE-4210 [S]	In the Summer of His Years	1964	30.00
❑ E-4229 [M]	Looking for Love	1964	25.00
❑ SE-4229 [S]	Looking for Love	1964	30.00
❑ E-4253 [M]	A New Kind of Connie	1964	25.00
❑ SE-4253 [S]	A New Kind of Connie	1964	30.00
❑ E-4294 [M]	Connie Francis Sings For Mama	1965	25.00
❑ SE-4294 [S]	Connie Francis Sings For Mama	1965	30.00
❑ E-4298 [M]	All Time International Hits	1965	25.00
❑ SE-4298 [S]	All Time International Hits	1965	30.00
❑ E-4355 [M]	Jealous Heart	1966	25.00
❑ SE-4355 [S]	Jealous Heart	1966	30.00
❑ E-4382 [M]	Movie Greats of the 60's	1966	25.00
❑ SE-4382 [S]	Movie Greats of the 60's	1966	30.00
❑ E-4399 [M]	Connie's Christmas	1966	25.00
❑ SE-4399 [S]	Connie's Christmas	1966	30.00
❑ E-4411 [M]	Live at the Sahara in Las Vegas	1967	25.00
❑ SE-4411 [S]	Live at the Sahara in Las Vegas	1967	30.00
❑ E-4448 [M]	Love, Italian Style	1967	25.00
❑ SE-4448 [S]	Love, Italian Style	1967	30.00
❑ E-4472 [M]	Connie Francis On Broadway Today	1967	25.00
❑ SE-4472 [S]	Connie Francis On Broadway Today	1967	30.00
❑ E-4474 [M]	Grandes Exitos del Cine de los Anos 60	1967	25.00
❑ SE-4474 [S]	Grandes Exitos del Cine de los Anos 60	1967	30.00
❑ E-4487 [M]	My Heart Cries for You	1967	30.00
❑ SE-4487 [S]	My Heart Cries for You	1967	25.00
❑ E-4522 [M]	Hawaii: Connie	1968	100.00
❑ SE-4522 [S]	Hawaii: Connie	1968	25.00
❑ E-4573 [M]	Connie & Clyde	1968	150.00
—Yellow label "Special Disc Jockey Record" in stereo cover with "Mono" sticker			
❑ SE-4573 [S]	Connie & Clyde	1968	25.00
❑ SE-4585	Connie Francis Sings Bacharach & David	1968	25.00
❑ SE-4637	The Wedding Cake	1969	25.00
❑ SE-4655	The Songs of Les Reed	1969	25.00
❑ MG-1-5406	I'm Me Again	198?	12.00
❑ MG-1-5410	Greatest Hits	198?	12.00
❑ MG-1-5411	Greatest Jewish Hits	198?	12.00
❑ ST-90027 [S]	Award Winning Motion Picture Hits	196?	30.00
—Capitol Record Club edition			
❑ T-90027 [M]	Award Winning Motion Picture Hits	196?	30.00
—Capitol Record Club edition			
❑ ST-90068 [S]	A New Kind of Connie	1964	35.00
—Capitol Record Club issue			
❑ T-90068 [M]	A New Kind of Connie	1964	30.00
—Capitol Record Club issue			
❑ ST 90510 [S]	The Very Best of Connie Francis	1965	40.00
—Capitol Record Club edition			
❑ T 90510 [M]	The Very Best of Connie Francis	1965	40.00
—Capitol Record Club edition			
❑ ST-90592 [S]	Never on Sunday and Other Title Songs from Motion Pictures	1965	25.00
—Capitol Record Club edition			
❑ ST-91145	My Best to You	1968	30.00
—Capitol Record Club			
POLYDOR			
❑ 827569-1	The Very Best of Connie Francis	1985	10.00
❑ 827582-1	Greatest Hits	1985	10.00
❑ 827584-1	Greatest Jewish Hits	1985	10.00
❑ 839922-1	Lo Mejor De Su Repertorio	198?	10.00
❑ 839923-1	12 Exitos De Connie Francis	198?	10.00

FRANCIS, CONNIE, AND MARVIN RAINWATER

Also see each artist's individual listings.

45s

Number	Title (A Side/B Side)	Yr	NM
MGM			
❑ 12555	You, My Darlin', You/ The Majesty of Love	1957	25.00

FRANCIS, CONNIE, AND HANK WILLIAMS, JR.

Also see each artist's individual listings.

Albums

Number	Title (A Side/B Side)	Yr	NM
MGM			
❑ E-4251 [M]	Connie Francis & Hank Williams, Jr. Sing Great Country Favorites	1964	30.00
❑ SE-4251 [S]	Connie Francis & Hank Williams, Jr. Sing Great Country Favorites	1964	40.00

FRANCISCUS, JAMES

45s

Number	Title (A Side/B Side)	Yr	NM
MGM			
❑ K 13319	Droppity Dropouts/ On Friday Day	1965	10.00
—B-side by Vince Howard			
❑ K 13319 [PS]	Droppity Dropouts/ On Friday Day	1965	25.00

FRANK, JOE, AND THE KNIGHTS

45s

Number	Title (A Side/B Side)	Yr	NM
ABC-PARAMOUNT			
❑ 10782	Can't Find a Way/ Won't You Come Home	1966	20.00

FRANK AND JACK

45s

Number	Title (A Side/B Side)	Yr	NM
BERGEN			
❑ 100	'Twas The Night Before Christmas/Jingle Bells	1957	20.00
JOSIE			
❑ 827	Twas the Night Before Christmas (Breaking Thru the Sound Barrier)/Jingle Bells (From the Sound Track)	1957	15.00

FRANKIE AND JOHNNY

Probably more than one group.

45s

Number	Title (A Side/B Side)	Yr	NM
EPIC			
❑ 5-10010	Over the Rainbow/ Two's Company	1966	12.00
HICKORY			
❑ 1391	I'll Hold You/(I'm) Never Gonna Leave You	1966	120.00
INTERNATIONAL ARTISTS			
❑ 112	Sweet Thang/Times Gone By	1968	40.00
❑ 117	A Present of the Past/ Right String Baby	1968	20.00
LIBERTY			
❑ 55271	Do You Love Me/My First Love	1960	15.00
LIDO			
❑ 604	Big Clem/Together Tonight	1959	40.00
MERCURY			
❑ 72955	Hometown, U.S.A./ Lucille-Slippin' and Slidin'	1969	12.00
SABRINA			
❑ 331	Do You Love Me/My First Love	1959	20.00
WARNER BROS.			
❑ 7684	Life Line/Mr. R.M.	1973	8.00

Albums

Number	Title (A Side/B Side)	Yr	NM
WARNER BROS.			
❑ BS 2675	The Sweetheart Sampler	1973	20.00

FRANKIE AND THE C-NOTES

45s

Number	Title (A Side/B Side)	Yr	NM
RICHIE			
❑ 2	Forever and Ever/Fade Out	1959	400.00

FRANKLIN, ALAN, EXPLOSION

Albums

Number	Title (A Side/B Side)	Yr	NM
ALADDIN			
❑ 104049	Come Home Baby	1969	80.00
HORNE			
❑	Climax	1970	250.00
—Pre-release or demo versions of tracks from The Blues Climax.			
❑ JC-888	The Blues Climax	1970	100.00

FRANKLIN, ARETHA

12-Inch Singles

Number	Title (A Side/B Side)	Yr	NM
ARISTA			
❑ SP-103 [DJ]	What a Fool Believes (Long Version) (Short Version)	1980	12.00
❑ SP-138 [DJ]	Jump To It (6:40) (3:58)/ Just My Daydream	1982	10.00
❑ SP-147 [DJ]	Love Me Right (Dance Version) (Short Version)	1982	15.00
❑ CP 718	Jump to It (Extended Version 6:40) (Single Version 3:58)/ Just My Daydream	1982	20.00
❑ 2240	Everyday People (People Remix) (Bonus Beats)/ (Everyday Remix) (People Dub)	1991	10.00
❑ ADP 2651 [(3)DJ]	A Deeper Love (9 versions)	1994	20.00
❑ ADP 2703 [DJ]	Jump To It (CJ's Masta Mix) (Gorda Dub) (Original Extended Version)	1994	15.00
❑ ADP 3455 [DJ]	A Rose Is Still a Rose (Without Intro) (With Intro)	1998	10.00
❑ ADP 3484 [(2)DJ]	A Rose Is Still a Rose (Hex Hector Club Mix 8:55) (Album Version 4:29)/(Johnny Vicious Dub 9:28) (Love to Infinity Kick Mix 7:11)//(Johnny Vicious Club Mix 10:44) (HEx Hector Drums 3:50)/(Love to Infinity Club Mix) (Love to Infinity Rhythm Radio Mix) (Album Version Instrumental)	1998	15.00
—Promo version of 13484			
❑ ADP 3486 [DJ]	A Rose Is Still a Rose (Yogi's Bystorm Remix) (Yogi's Bystorm Remix Instrumental) (Yogi's Bystorm Remix Acappella) (Desert Eagle Remix) (Desert Eagle Remix Instrumental) (Original Radio Edit)	1998	20.00
❑ ADP 3493 [DJ]	Here We Go Again (LP Version) (Instrumental) (Acappella)	1998	10.00
❑ ADP 3513 [(2)DJ]	Here We Go Again (Morales Classic Mix) (Razor-N-Guido Mix) (Morales Rascal Dub) (Razor-N-Guido Key Line) (Morales Def Zone Dub) (Mixologist Bass Mix) (Morales Bass Dub) (Album Version)	1998	25.00
❑ ADP 3514 [DJ]	Here We Go Again (Bump Mix) (Mixologist Bass Rap) (Acappella) (Bass Mix) (Instrumental)	1998	15.00
❑ AD1-9043	Get It Right (Long Version 6:22)/(Instrumental 6:31)	1983	10.00
❑ AD1-9355	Freeway of Love (Rock Mix)/ (Radio Mix) (Extended Remix)	1985	8.00
❑ AD1-9411	Who's Zoomin' Who (Dance Mix) (Dub Mix)/(Radio Mix) (Acappella Mix)	1985	8.00
❑ AD1-9454	Another Night (Dance Mix 6:40) (Dub 6:57)/(Radio Mix 5:02) (7" Edit 4:03)	1985	8.00
❑ AD1-9473	Ain't Nobody Ever Loved You (Remix 6:22) (Dub 6:59) (Single Edit 4:16) (Percapella)	1986	8.00
❑ AD1-9529	Jumpin' Jack Flash (LP Mix) (Street Mix)/(Street Mix Radio Edit) (Master Dub Mix) (Beat Dub)	1986	10.00
❑ AD1-9547	Jimmy Lee (Extended Remix 7:16) (Single Version 5:47) (Dub Mix 6:14)/Aretha Megamix	1986	8.00

Except when noted otherwise, VG = 25% of NM, and VG+ = 50% of NM. (Example: VG = $2.00, VG+ = $4.00 and NM = $8.00.)

Number	Title (A Side/B Side)	Yr	NM
❑ AD1-9560	I Knew You Were Waiting (For Me) (Edited Remix) (Percapella)/(LP Version) (Extended Remix)	1987	8.00
—With George Michael			
❑ AD1-9575	Rock-a-Lott (Street Mix) (Single Version) (Street Mix Radio Edit) (Dub Mix) (Acappella)	1987	8.00
❑ ADP 9682 [DJ]	Oh Happy Day/The Lord's Prayer//I've Been in the Storm Too Long/Packing Up, Getting Ready to Go	1988	15.00
❑ AD1-9851	It Isn't, It Wasn't, It Ain't Never Gonna Be (Extended Radio) (House Radio Mix)/(Hip Hop Radio) (New Jack Swing Dub)/Think '89	1989	8.00
—With Whitney Houston			
❑ ADP 9877 [DJ]	It Isn't, It Wasn't, It Ain't Never Gonna Be (Extended Radio Mix 6:12) (Dub Mix 6:20)//(After Hours Club Mix 7:35) (1989 Vogue Dub Mix 5:36)	1989	15.00
—With Whitney Houston			
❑ AD1-9885	Gimme Your Love (Single Edit) (Extended Remix)/Think '89	1989	8.00
—With James Brown			
❑ ADP 9906 [DJ]	Gimme Your Love (Single Edit) (Extended Remix)/Interview	1989	15.00
—With James Brown			
❑ 12702	Willing to Forgive/Jump to It (2 versions)	1994	10.00
❑ 13484 [(2)]	A Rose Is Still a Rose (Hex Hector Club Mix 8:55) (Album Version 4:29)/(Johnny Vicious Dub 9:28) (Love to Infinity Kick Mix 7:11)//(Johnny Vicious Club Mix 10:44) (HEx Hector Drums 3:50)/(Love to Infinity Club Mix) (Love to Infinity Rhythm Radio Mix) (Album Version Instrumental)	1998	12.00
❑ 13503	Here We Go Again (Morales Classic Mix 9:25) (Album Version 3:30) (Razor-N-Guide KeyLine 1:31) (Razor-N-Guido Mix 9:41) (Mixologist Bass Mix 3:26)	1999	10.00

45s

ARISTA

Number	Title (A Side/B Side)	Yr	NM
❑ 0569	United Together/Take Me With You	1980	4.00
❑ 0591	What a Fool Believes/Love Me Forever	1980	4.00
❑ 0600	Come to Me/School Days	1981	4.00
❑ 0624	Love All the Hurt Away/Whole Lotta Me	1981	4.00
—Aretha Franklin and George Benson			
❑ 0646	It's My Turn/Kind of Man	1981	4.00
❑ 0665	Livin' in the Streets/There's a Star for Everyone	1982	4.00
❑ 0699	Jump To It/Just My Daydream	1982	4.00
❑ 1023	Love Me Right/(It's Just) Your Love	1982	4.00
❑ 1043	This Is for Real/I Just Want to Make It Up to You	1983	4.00
❑ 2239	Everyday People/You Can't Take Me for Granted	1991	5.00
❑ 9034	Get It Right/Giving In	1983	4.00
❑ 9095	Every Girl (Wants My Guy)/I Got Your Love	1983	4.00
❑ 9354	Freeway of Love/Until You Say You Love Me	1985	3.00
❑ 9354 [DJ]	Freeway of Love (Short) (Long)	1985	20.00
—Promo only on pink vinyl			
❑ 9354 [PS]	Freeway of Love/Until You Say You Love Me	1985	3.00
❑ 9410	Who's Zoomin' Who/Sweet Bitter Love	1985	3.00
❑ 9410 [PS]	Who's Zoomin' Who/Sweet Bitter Love	1985	3.00
❑ 9453	Another Night/Kind of Man	1986	3.00
❑ 9474	Ain't Nobody Ever Loved You/Push	1986	3.00
—B-side with Peter Wolf			
❑ 9528	Jumpin' Jack Flash/Integrity	1986	3.00
—Second pressing on black vinyl			
❑ 9528	Jumpin' Jack Flash/Integrity	1986	5.00
—Original stock pressings on clear vinyl			
❑ 9528 [DJ]	Jumpin' Jack Flash (Long Version) (Short Version)	1986	10.00
—Promo on clear vinyl			
❑ 9528 [PS]	Jumpin' Jack Flash/Integrity	1986	3.00
—Picture sleeve with black vinyl pressing lists catalog number as AL-9528			
❑ 9528 [PS]	Jumpin' Jack Flash/Integrity	1986	5.00
—Picture sleeve with clear vinyl pressing lists catalog number as ALC-9528			
❑ 9541	Jumpin' Jack Flash/(Street Mix Radio Edit)	1986	4.00
❑ 9541 [PS]	Jumpin' Jack Flash/(Street Mix Radio Edit)	1986	5.00
❑ 9546	Jimmy Lee/If You Need My Love Tonight	1986	4.00
❑ 9546 [DJ]	Jimmy Lee (Short Version 4:10)/(Long Version 5:47)	1986	4.00
❑ 9546 [PS]	Jimmy Lee/If You Need My Love Tonight	1986	4.00
—B-side by Larry Graham			
❑ 9557	Jimmy Lee/An Angel Cries	1986	3.00
❑ 9557 [PS]	Jimmy Lee/An Angel Cries	1986	3.00
❑ 9559	I Knew You Were Waiting (For Me)/(Instrumental)	1987	3.00
—With George Michael			
❑ 9559 [PS]	I Knew You Were Waiting (For Me)/(Instrumental)	1987	3.00
—With George Michael			
❑ 9574	Rock-A-Lott/Look to the Rainbow	1987	3.00
❑ 9574 [PS]	Rock-A-Lott/Look to the Rainbow	1987	3.00
❑ 9623	If You Need My Love Tonight/He'll Come Along	1987	3.00
—A-side with Larry Graham			
❑ 9672	Oh Happy Day/The Lord's Prayer	1988	5.00
❑ 9672 [PS]	Oh Happy Day/The Lord's Prayer	1988	5.00
❑ 9809	Through the Storm/Come to Me	1989	3.00
—A-side with Elton John			
❑ 9809 [PS]	Through the Storm/Come to Me	1989	3.00
❑ 9850	It Isn't, It Wasn't, It Ain't Never Gonna Be/If Ever a Love There Was	1989	3.00
—A-side with Whitney Houston; B-side with the Four Tops			
❑ 9850 [PS]	It Isn't, It Wasn't, It Ain't Never Gonna Be/If Ever a Love There Was	1989	3.00
—A-side with Whitney Houston; B-side with the Four Tops			
❑ 9884	Gimme Your Love/Think	1989	3.00
—With James Brown			
❑ 9884 [PS]	Gimme Your Love/Think	1989	3.00
—With James Brown			
❑ 55977	The Only Thing Missin'/Wonderful	2003	3.00

ATLANTIC

Number	Title (A Side/B Side)	Yr	NM
❑ 2386	I Never Loved a Man (The Way I Love You)/Do Right Woman, Do Right Man	1967	12.00
❑ 2403	Respect/Dr. Feelgood	1967	12.00
❑ 2427	Baby I Love You/Going Down Now	1967	12.00
❑ 2441	(You Make Me Feel Like) A Natural Woman/Baby, Baby, Baby	1967	12.00
❑ 2464	Chain of Fools/Prove It	1967	12.00
❑ 2486	(Sweet Sweet Baby) Since You've Been Gone/Ain't No Way	1968	12.00
❑ 2518	Think/You Send Me	1968	12.00
❑ 2546	I Say a Little Prayer/The House That Jack Built	1968	12.00
❑ 2574	See Saw/My Song	1968	10.00
❑ 2603	The Weight/Tracks of My Tears	1969	10.00
❑ 2619	I Can't See Myself Leaving You/Gentle On My Mind	1969	10.00
❑ 2650	Share Your Love with Me/Pledging My Love-The Clock	1969	10.00
❑ 2683	Eleanor Rigby/It Ain't Fair	1969	10.00
❑ 2706	Call Me/Son of a Preacher Man	1970	10.00
❑ 2731	Spirit in the Dark/The Thrill Is Gone	1970	10.00
❑ 2751	Don't Play That Song/Let It Be	1970	10.00
❑ 2772	Border Song (Holy Moses)/You and Me	1970	10.00
❑ 2787	You're All I Need to Get By/Pullin'	1971	8.00
❑ 2796	Bridge Over Troubled Water/Brand New Me	1971	8.00
❑ 2817	Spanish Harlem/Lean On Me	1971	8.00
❑ 2838	Rock Steady/Oh Me Oh My (I'm a Fool for You Baby)	1971	8.00
❑ 2866	Day Dreaming/I've Been Loving You Too Long	1972	8.00
❑ 2883	All the King's Horses/April Fools	1972	8.00
❑ 2901	Wholy Holy/Give Yourself to Jesus	1972	8.00
❑ 2941	Master of Eyes (The Deepness of Your Eyes)/Moody's Mood for You	1973	8.00
❑ 2969	Angel/Hey Hey Now (Sister from Texas)	1973	8.00
❑ 2995	Until You Come Back to Me (That's What I'm Gonna Do)/If You Don't Think	1973	8.00
❑ 2999	I'm in Love/Oh Baby	1974	8.00
❑ 3200	Ain't Nothing Like the Real Thing/Eight Days on the Road	1974	8.00
❑ 3224	Without Love/Don't Go Breaking My Heart	1974	8.00
❑ 3249	With Everything I Feel in Me/Sing It Again, Say It Again	1975	8.00
❑ 3289	Mr. D.J. (5 for the D.J.)/As Long As You Are There	1975	8.00
❑ 3311	You/Without You	1975	8.00
❑ 3326	Something He Can Feel/Loving You, Baby	1976	8.00
❑ 3358	Jump/Hooked on Your Love	1976	8.00
❑ 3373	Look Into Your Heart/Rock with Me	1977	8.00
❑ 3393	Break It To Me Gently/Meadows of Springtime	1977	8.00
❑ 3418	When I Think About You/Touch Me Up	1978	8.00
❑ 3468	Almighty Fire (Woman of the Future)/I'm Your Speed	1978	8.00
❑ 3495	More Than Just a Joy/This You Can Believe	1979	8.00
❑ 3605	Ladies Only/What If I Should Ever Need You	1979	6.00
❑ 3632	Half a Love/Only Star	1979	6.00

CHECKER

Number	Title (A Side/B Side)	Yr	NM
❑ 861	Never Grow Old/You Grow Closer	1957	20.00
❑ 941	Precious Lord, Part 1/Precious Lord, Part 2	1960	15.00

COLUMBIA

Number	Title (A Side/B Side)	Yr	NM
❑ S7 31202 [S]	Won't Be Long/Love Is the Only Thing	1961	12.00
❑ S7 31203 [S]	Sweet Lover/All Night Long	1961	12.00
❑ S7 31204 [S]	Who Needs You?/Right Now	1961	12.00
❑ S7 31205 [S]	Maybe I'm a Fool/It Ain't Necessarily So	1961	12.00
❑ S7 31206 [S]	(Blue) By Myself/Today I Sing the Blues	1961	12.00
—The above five are "Stereo Seven" 33 1/3 rpm jukebox singles from set "JS 7-38" entitled "Aretha (with the Ray Bryant Combo)"			
❑ 41793	Today I Sing the Blues/Love Is the Only Thing	1960	12.00
❑ 41923	Won't Be Long/Right Now	1961	12.00
❑ 41965	Are You Sure/Maybe I'm a Fool	1961	12.00
❑ 42157	Rock-A-Bye Your Baby with a Dixie Melody/Operation Heartbreak	1961	12.00
❑ 42266	I Surrender, Dear/Rough Lover	1962	10.00
❑ 42266 [PS]	I Surrender, Dear/Rough Lover	1962	30.00
❑ 42456	Don't Cry, Baby/Without the One You Love	1962	10.00
❑ 42456 [PS]	Don't Cry, Baby/Without the One You Love	1962	30.00
❑ 42520	Try a Little Tenderness/Just for a Thrill	1962	10.00
❑ 42520 [PS]	Try a Little Tenderness/Just for a Thrill	1962	25.00
❑ 42625	Trouble in Mind/God Bless the Child	1962	10.00
❑ 42796	Here's Where I Came In/Say It Isn't So	1963	10.00
❑ 42796 [PS]	Here's Where I Came In/Say It Isn't So	1963	30.00
❑ 42874	Skylark/You've Got Her	1963	10.00
❑ 42933	Johnny/Kissin' by the Mistletoe	1963	10.00
❑ 43009	Soulville/Evil Gal Blues	1964	10.00
❑ 43113	Runnin' Out of Fools/It's Just a Matter of Time	1964	10.00
❑ 43177	Winter Wonderland/The Christmas Song (Chestnuts Roasting on an Open Fire)	1964	10.00
❑ 43203	Can't You Just See Me/Little Miss Raggedy Ann	1965	10.00
❑ 43241	One Step Ahead/I Can't Wait Until I See My Baby's Face	1965	10.00
❑ 43333	(No, No) I'm Losing You/Sweet Bitter Love	1965	10.00
❑ 43442	You Made Me Love You/There Is No Greater Love	1966	10.00
❑ 43515	Hands Off/Tighten Up Your Tie, Button Up Your Jacket	1966	10.00
❑ 43637	Until You Were Gone/Swanee	1966	10.00
❑ 43827	Cry Like a Baby/Swanee	1966	10.00
❑ 44181	Until You Were Gone/Lee Cross	1967	10.00
❑ 44270	Take a Look/Follow Your Heart	1967	10.00
❑ 44381	Mockingbird/A Mother's Love	1967	8.00
❑ 44441	Soulville/If Ever I Would Leave You	1968	8.00
❑ 44851	Friendly Persuasion/Jim	1969	8.00
❑ 44951	Today I Sing the Blues/People	1969	8.00

JVB

Number	Title (A Side/B Side)	Yr	NM
❑ 47	Never Grow Old/You Grow Closer	1957	30.00
❑ 75	Precious Lord, Part 1/Precious Lord, Part 2	1959	30.00

PHILCO-FORD

Number	Title (A Side/B Side)	Yr	NM
❑ HP-24	Respect/Soul Serenade	1968	25.00
—4-inch plastic "Hip Pocket Record" with color sleeve			

Number	Title (A Side/B Side)	Yr	NM
7-Inch Extended Plays			
ATLANTIC			
❑ A 1025 [DJ]	Precious Lord, Take My Hand/ You've Got a Friend/Precious Memories//Wholy❑ Holy/ Mary, Don't You Weep	1972	15.00
—Mono; white label promo sampler			
❑ A 1025 [PS]	Amazing Grace	1972	20.00
❑ SD 7-7265	Somewhere/Moody's Mood// Hey Now Hey/So Swell When You're Well	1973	10.00
—Jukebox issue; small hole, plays at 33 1/3 rpm			
❑ SD 7-7265 [PS]	Hey Now Hey	1973	10.00
❑ SD 7-8207	Satisfaction/Baby, I Love You/ Groovin'//Soul Serenade/Dr. Feelgood	196?	15.00
—Jukebox issue; small hole, plays at 33 1/3 rpm			
❑ SD 7-8207 [PS]	Aretha in Paris	196?	15.00
❑ SD 7-8248	Let It Be/The Weight/Eleanor Rigby//This Girl's in Love with You/Share Your Love with Me	1970	12.00
—Jukebox issue; small hole, plays at 33 1/3 rpm			
❑ SD 7-8248 [PS]	This Girl's in Love with You	1970	12.00
❑ SD 77205	Spirit in the Dark (with Ray Charles)//Respect/Love the One You're With	1971	12.00
—Stereo jukebox issue; small hole, plays at 33 1/3 rpm			
❑ SD 77205 [PS]	Aretha Live at Fillmore West	1971	12.00
Albums			
ARISTA			
❑ AL8-8019	Get It Right	1983	10.00
❑ AL8-8286	Who's Zoomin' Who	1985	10.00
❑ AL-8344	Jump To It	1985	8.00
—Budget-line reissue			
❑ AL-8368	Love All the Hurt Away	1985	8.00
—Budget-line reissue			
❑ AL-8442	Aretha	1986	10.00
—Different album than 9538			
❑ A2L-8497 [(2)]	One Lord, One Faith, One Baptism	1987	20.00
❑ AL-8572	Through the Storm	1989	10.00
❑ AL-9538	Aretha	1980	10.00
❑ AL-9552	Love All the Hurt Away	1981	10.00
❑ AL-9602	Jump To It	1982	10.00
ATLANTIC			
❑ SD 2-906 [(2)]	Amazing Grace	1972	20.00
❑ 7205 [M]	Aretha Live at Fillmore West	1971	40.00
—Mono is white label promo only with "d/j copy monaural" sticker on front cover			
❑ QD 7205 [Q]	Aretha Live at Fillmore West	1973	25.00
❑ SD 7205 [S]	Aretha Live at Fillmore West	1971	15.00
❑ 7213 [M]	Young, Gifted & Black	1972	40.00
—Mono is promo only; "d/j copy monaural" sticker on front cover			
❑ SD 7213 [S]	Young, Gifted & Black	1972	15.00
❑ SD 7265	Hey Now Hey (The Other Side of the Sky)	1973	12.00
❑ SD 7292	Let Me in Your Life	1974	12.00
❑ 8139 [M]	I Never Loved a Man the Way I Love You	1967	25.00
❑ SD 8139	I Never Loved a Man the Way I Love You	1969	12.00
—Green and red label			
❑ SD 8139 [S]	I Never Loved a Man the Way I Love You	1967	20.00
—Green and blue label			
❑ 8150 [M]	Aretha Arrives	1967	25.00
❑ SD 8150	Aretha Arrives	1969	12.00
—Green and red label			
❑ SD 8150 [S]	Aretha Arrives	1967	20.00
—Green and blue label			
❑ 8176 [M]	Aretha: Lady Soul	1968	30.00
❑ SD 8176	Aretha: Lady Soul	1969	12.00
—Green and red label			
❑ SD 8176 [S]	Aretha: Lady Soul	1968	20.00
—Green and blue label			
❑ SD 8186	Aretha Now	1968	20.00
—Green and blue label			
❑ SD 8186	Aretha Now	1969	12.00
—Green and red label			
❑ SD 8207	Aretha in Paris	1968	15.00
❑ 8212 [M]	Aretha Franklin: Soul '69	1969	50.00
—White label promo; no stock copies in mono			
❑ SD 8212 [S]	Aretha Franklin: Soul '69	1969	15.00
❑ SD 8227	Aretha's Gold	1969	15.00
❑ 8248 [M]	This Girl's in Love with You	1970	40.00
—Mono is white label promo only; cover has "d/j copy monaural" sticker on front			
❑ SD 8248 [S]	This Girl's in Love with You	1970	15.00
❑ 8265 [M]	Spirit in the Dark	1970	40.00
—Mono is white label promo only in stereo cover with "d/j monaural" sticker			
❑ SD 8265 [S]	Spirit in the Dark	1970	15.00
❑ 8295 [M]	Aretha's Greatest Hits	1971	40.00
—Mono is white label promo only in stereo cover with "d/j monaural" sticker			
❑ SD 8295 [S]	Aretha's Greatest Hits	1971	15.00
❑ QD 8305 [Q]	The Best of Aretha Franklin	1974	20.00
❑ SD 18116	With Everything I Feel in Me	1974	12.00
❑ SD 18151	You	1975	12.00
❑ SD 18176	Sparkle	1976	12.00
❑ SD 18204	Ten Years of Gold	1976	12.00
❑ SD 19102	Sweet Passion	1977	12.00
❑ SD 19161	Almighty Fire	1978	12.00
❑ SD 19248	La Diva	1979	12.00
❑ 81230	Aretha's Jazz	1984	10.00
❑ 81280	The Best of Aretha Franklin	1985	10.00
❑ 81668 [(2)]	30 Greatest Hits	1986	15.00
❑ STAO-95151	Hey Now Hey (The Other Side of the Sky)	1973	15.00
—Capitol Record Club edition			
CHECKER			
❑ 10009 [M]	Songs of Faith	1965	500.00
—Original issue of this album; cover has Aretha sitting at a piano			
❑ 10009 [M]	Gospel Soul	1967	20.00
—Reissue with new title and cover			
COLUMBIA			
❑ GP 4 [(2)]	Two All-Time Great Albums in One Great Package	196?	25.00
—Contains CS 9081 and CS 9429			
❑ CL 1612 [M]	Aretha	1961	50.00
—Red and black label with six "eye" logos			
❑ CL 1612 [M]	Aretha	1963	20.00
—"Guaranteed High Fidelity" on label			
❑ CL 1612 [M]	Aretha	1965	15.00
—"360 Sound Mono" on label			
❑ CL 1761 [M]	The Electrifying Aretha Franklin	1962	40.00
—Red and black label with six "eye" logos			
❑ CL 1761 [M]	The Electrifying Aretha Franklin	1963	20.00
—"Guaranteed High Fidelity" on label			
❑ CL 1761 [M]	The Electrifying Aretha Franklin	1965	15.00
—"360 Sound Mono" on label			
❑ CL 1876 [M]	The Tender, The Moving, The Swinging Aretha Franklin	1962	40.00
—Red and black label with six "eye" logos			
❑ CL 1876 [M]	The Tender, The Moving, The Swinging Aretha Franklin	1963	20.00
—"Guaranteed High Fidelity" on label			
❑ CL 1876 [M]	The Tender, The Moving, The Swinging Aretha Franklin	1965	15.00
—"360 Sound Mono' on label			
❑ CL 2079 [M]	Laughing on the Outside	1963	20.00
—"Guaranteed High Fidelity" on label			
❑ CL 2079 [M]	Laughing on the Outside	1965	15.00
—"360 Sound Mono" on label			
❑ CL 2163 [M]	Unforgettable	1964	20.00
—"Guaranteed High Fidelity" on label			
❑ CL 2163 [M]	Unforgettable	1965	15.00
—"360 Sound Mono" on label			
❑ CL 2281 [M]	Runnin' Out of Fools	1964	20.00
—"Guaranteed High Fidelity" on label			
❑ CL 2281 [M]	Runnin' Out of Fools	1965	15.00
—"360 Sound Mono" on label			
❑ CL 2351 [M]	Yeah!!!	1965	20.00
—"Guaranteed High Fidelity" on label			
❑ CL 2351 [M]	Yeah!!!	1966	15.00
—"360 Sound Mono" on label			
❑ CL 2521 [M]	Soul Sister	1966	20.00
❑ CL 2629 [M]	Take It Like You Give It	1967	25.00
❑ CL 2673 [M]	Aretha Franklin's Greatest Hits	1967	25.00
❑ CL 2754 [M]	Take a Look	1967	30.00
❑ CS 8412 [S]	Aretha	1961	80.00
—Red and black label with six "eye" logos			
❑ CS 8412 [S]	Aretha	1963	25.00
—"360 Sound Stereo" on label			
❑ CS 8561 [S]	The Electrifying Aretha Franklin	1962	50.00
—Red and black label with six "eye" logos			
❑ CS 8561 [S]	The Electrifying Aretha Franklin	1963	25.00
—"360 Sound Stereo" on label			
❑ CS 8676 [S]	The Tender, The Moving, The Swinging Aretha Franklin	1962	50.00
—Red and black label with six "eye" logos			
❑ CS 8676 [S]	The Tender, The Moving, The Swinging Aretha Franklin	1963	25.00
—"360 Sound Stereo" on label			
❑ CS 8879 [S]	Laughing on the Outside	1963	25.00
—"360 Sound Stereo" on label			
❑ CS 8963 [S]	Unforgettable	1964	25.00
—"360 Sound Stereo" on label			
❑ CS 9081 [S]	Runnin' Out of Fools	1964	25.00
—"360 Sound Stereo" on label			
❑ CS 9151 [S]	Yeah!!!	1965	25.00
—"360 Sound Stereo" on label			
❑ CS 9321 [S]	Soul Sister	1966	25.00
—"360 Sound Stereo" on label			
❑ CS 9429 [S]	Take It Like You Give It	1967	20.00
—"360 Sound Stereo" on label			
❑ CS 9473 [S]	Aretha Franklin's Greatest Hits	1967	20.00
—"360 Sound Stereo" on label			
❑ CS 9554 [S]	Take a Look	1967	20.00
—"360 Sound Stereo" on label			
❑ CS 9601	Aretha Franklin's Greatest Hits, Vol. 2	1968	20.00
—"360 Sound Stereo" on label			
❑ CS 9776	Soft and Beautiful	1969	20.00
—"360 Sound Stereo" on label			
❑ CS 9956	Today I Sing the Blues	1970	15.00
—"360 Sound Stereo" on label			
❑ KG 31355 [(2)]	In the Beginning/The World of Aretha Franklin 1960-1967	1972	20.00
❑ KC 31953	The First 12 Sides	1973	12.00
❑ C2 37377 [(2)]	The Legendary Queen of Soul	1981	12.00
❑ PC 38042	Sweet Bitter Love	1982	10.00
❑ FC 40105	Aretha Franklin Sings the Blues	1985	10.00
❑ FC 40708	Aretha After Hours	1987	10.00
COLUMBIA SPECIAL PRODUCTS			
❑ C 10589	Take a Look	1971	12.00
❑ C 11282	Runnin' Out of Fools	1972	12.00
4 MEN WITH BEARDS			
❑ 4M 101	I Never Loved a Man the Way I Love You	2001	15.00
—Reissue on 180-gram vinyl			
❑ 4M 111	Soul '69	2002	15.00
—Reissue on 180-gram vinyl			
❑ 4M 114	Spirit in the Dark	2003	15.00
—Reissue on 180-gram vinyl			
❑ 4M 115	Aretha Live at Fillmore West	2003	15.00
—Reissue on 180-gram vinyl			
❑ 4M 130	Lady Soul	2006	15.00
—Reissue on 180-gram vinyl			
❑ 4M 131	Aretha Now	2006	15.00
—Reissue on 180-gram vinyl			
HARMONY			
❑ HS 11349	Once in a Lifetime	1969	12.00
❑ HS 11418	Two Sides of Love	1970	12.00
❑ KH 30606	Greatest Hits 1960-1965	1971	12.00
❑ KH 30606	Greatest Hits 1960-1966	1972	12.00

FRANKLIN, CAROLYN

Number	Title (A Side/B Side)	Yr	NM
45s			
RCA VICTOR			
❑ 47-9734	The Boxer/I Don't Want to Lose You	1969	6.00
❑ 74-0188	Reality/It's True I'm Gonna Miss You	1969	6.00
❑ 74-0289	Ain't That Groovy/All I Want Is to Be Your Woman	1969	6.00
❑ 74-0314	Everybody's Talkin'/ Chain Reaction	1970	5.00
❑ 74-0373	You Really Didn't Mean It/All I Want Is to Be Your Woman	1970	5.00
❑ 74-0783	As Long As You're There/ I Want to Be With You	1972	5.00
❑ APBO-0022	You Are Everything/ If You Want Me	1973	5.00
❑ PB-10688	I Can't Help My Feeling So Blue/If You Want Me	1976	4.00
Albums			
RCA VICTOR			
❑ LSP-4160	Baby Dynamite	1969	20.00
❑ LSP-4317	Chain Reaction	1970	20.00
❑ LSP-4411	I'd Rather Be Lonely	1973	20.00

FRANKLIN, DOUG, AND THE BLUENOTES

Number	Title (A Side/B Side)	Yr	NM
45s			
COLONIAL			
❑ 7777	My Lucky Love/Drizzlin' Rain	1958	20.00
❑ 7779	Christmas Chimes/Let Her Know	1958	25.00
❑ 8888	I Used to Wonder/I Wonder Who's Kissing Her Now	1959	20.00
❑ 9999	Darling of Mine/ Never Never Land	1959	20.00

FRANKLIN, ERMA

Number	Title (A Side/B Side)	Yr	NM
45s			
BRUNSWICK			
❑ 55403	Change My Thoughts from You/Gotta Find Me a Lover	1969	8.00
❑ 55415	Saving My Love/You've Been Cancelled	1969	8.00
❑ 55424	I Just Don't Need You (At All)/ It Could've Been Me	1969	8.00
❑ 55430	Whispers (Gettin' Louder)/ (I Get the) Swetest Feeling	1970	8.00
EPIC			
❑ 5-9468	Don't Blame Me/What Kind of Girl (Do You Think I Am)	1961	20.00
❑ 5-9488	Hello Again/It's Over	1962	20.00
❑ 5-9511	Each Night I Cry/Time After Time	1962	20.00
❑ 5-9516	Dear Mama/Never Again	1962	20.00
❑ 5-9559	Don't Wait Too Long/ Time After Time	1962	20.00
❑ 5-9594	Have You Ever Had the Blues/ I Don't Want No Mama's Boy	1963	15.00
❑ 5-9610	Abracadabra/Love Is Blind	1963	15.00
SHOUT			
❑ 218	Big Boss Man/Didn't Catch the Dog's Bone	1967	10.00
❑ 221	Piece of My Heart/Baby What You Want Me to Do	1967	12.00
❑ 230	Open Up Your Soul/I'm Just Not Ready for Love	1967	10.00
❑ 234	Right to Cry/I'm Just Not Ready for Love	1968	10.00

Except when noted otherwise, VG = 25% of NM, and VG+ = 50% of NM. (Example: VG = $2.00, VG+ = $4.00 and NM = $8.00.)

Number	Title (A Side/B Side)	Yr	NM
Albums			
BRUNSWICK			
❑ BL 754147	Soul Sister	1969	20.00
EPIC			
❑ BN 619 [S]	Her Name Is Erma	1962	40.00
❑ LN 3824 [M]	Her Name Is Erma	1962	30.00

FRANKS, MICHAEL

Number	Title (A Side/B Side)	Yr	NM
12-Inch Singles			
REPRISE			
❑ PRO-A-4084 [DJ]	The Art of Love (same on both sides)	1990	8.00
❑ PRO-A-4564 [DJ]	Speak to Me (4 versions)	1990	15.00
❑ PRO-A-6175 [DJ]	Practice Makes Perfect (4 versions)	1993	7.00
WARNER BROS.			
❑ PRO-A-2834 [DJ]	Doctor Sax/Face to Face	1987	6.00
45s			
BRUT			
❑ 809	Can't Seem to Shake This Rock 'n' Roll/King of Oklahoma	1973	15.00
JOHN HAMMOND			
❑ WS4 03794	Can't Seem to Shake This Rock 'n' Roll/Just Like Key Largo	1983	5.00
❑ WS4 03794 [PS]	Can't Seem to Shake This Rock 'n' Roll/Just Like Key Largo	1983	5.00
REPRISE			
❑ 1360	Popsicle Toes/I Don't Know Why I'm So Happy I'm Sad	1976	5.00
WARNER BROS.			
❑ 8583	When the Cookie Jar Is Empty/Burchfield Nines	1978	5.00
❑ 8811	When It's Over/(B-side unknown)	1979	5.00
❑ 27997	The Camera Never Lies/Innuendo	1988	5.00
❑ 28184	Face to Face/Innuendo	1987	5.00
❑ 28285	Island Life/Innuendo	1987	5.00
❑ 28819	When I Give My Love to You/When She Is Mine	1986	4.00
—With Brenda Russell			
❑ 28819 [PS]	When I Give My Love to You/When She Is Mine	1986	4.00
❑ 28928	Your Secret's Safe with Me/Please Don't Say Goodnight	1985	4.00
❑ 29004	Queen of the Underground/Now I Know Why	1985	5.00
❑ 29400	When Sly Calls/Never Satisfied	1983	8.00
❑ 29989	Jealousy/Wonderland	1982	5.00
❑ 49271	One Bad Habit/Still Lifes	1980	5.00
❑ 49556	Baseball/Loving You More and More	1980	4.00
❑ 50025	Love Duet/No One But You	1982	5.00
—With S. Renee Diggs			
Albums			
BRUT			
❑ 6005	Michael Franks	1973	20.00
DIRECT DISK			
❑ SD-16611	Tiger in the Rain	1980	30.00
—Audiophile vinyl			
DRG			
❑ SL-5210	Previously Unavailable	1989	12.00
—Reissue of John Hammond LP			
JOHN HAMMOND			
❑ BFW 38664	Previously Unavailable	1983	15.00
REPRISE			
❑ MS 2230	The Art of Tea	1975	10.00
WARNER BROS.			
❑ BS 3004	Sleeping Gypsy	1977	10.00
❑ BSK 3167	Burchfield Nines	1978	10.00
❑ BSK 3294	Tiger in the Rain	1979	10.00
❑ BSK 3427	One Bad Habit	1980	10.00
❑ BSK 3648	Objects of Desire	1981	10.00
❑ 23962	Passion Fruit	1983	8.00
❑ 25275	Skin Dive	1985	8.00
❑ 25570	The Camera Never Lies	1987	8.00

FRANLKIN, DOUG, WITH THE BLUENOTES

Number	Title (A Side/B Side)	Yr	NM
45s			
COLONIAL			
❑ 7777	My Lucky Love/Drizzin' Rain	1958	20.00

FRANTIC

Number	Title (A Side/B Side)	Yr	NM
45s			
LIZARD			
❑ 21002	Midnight to Six Man/Shady Sam	1970	15.00
Albums			
LIZARD			
❑ 20103	Conception	1971	25.00

FRANTICS, THE

Number	Title (A Side/B Side)	Yr	NM
45s			
BOLO			
❑ 728	Pony Moronie/Meet Me in Seattle Twist	1962	10.00
❑ 736	Oh Yeah/Let Our Love Roll On	1962	10.00
DOLTON			
❑ 2	Straight Flush/Young Blues	1959	20.00
❑ 6	Fog Cutter/Black Sapphire	1959	20.00
❑ 13	Checkerboard/Werewolf	1959	20.00
❑ 16	Werewolf/No Werewolf	1960	15.00
❑ 24	The Whip/Delilah	1960	15.00
❑ 31	Yankee Doodlin'/One Minute of Flamenco	1961	15.00
❑ 33	San Antonio Rose/Trees	1961	15.00
SEAFAIR			
❑ 111	San Francisco Swim/Blue Day	1964	10.00

FRATERNITY OF MAN, THE

Number	Title (A Side/B Side)	Yr	NM
45s			
ABC			
❑ 11106	Don't Bogart Me/Wispy Paisley Skies	1968	8.00
Albums			
ABC			
❑ S-647	The Fraternity of Man	1968	30.00
DOT			
❑ DLP-25955	Get It On	1969	25.00

FRAWLEY, WILLIAM

Number	Title (A Side/B Side)	Yr	NM
Albums			
DOT			
❑ DLP-3061 [M]	William Frawley Sings the Old Ones	1958	40.00

FRAZIER, DALLAS

Number	Title (A Side/B Side)	Yr	NM
45s			
CAPITOL			
❑ 2011	Everybody Oughta Sing a Song/Only a Fool	1967	10.00
❑ 2133	The Sunshine of My World/Lonelier and More in Love	1968	10.00
❑ 2257	I Hope I Like Mexico Blues/I Just Thought That I Love Her ('Till I Lost You)	1968	10.00
❑ 2402	The Conspiracy of Homer Jones/Sundown of My Mind	1969	10.00
❑ F2813	Space Command/Ain't You Had No Bringin' Up at All	1954	20.00
❑ F2895	Love Life at 14/I'm Gonna Move Over Yonder	1954	20.00
❑ F2956	My Birthday Comes on Christmas/Jingle o' the Brownie	1954	20.00
—With Joe "Fingers" Carr			
❑ 5444	King of the Jungle/Make Believe You're Here with Me	1965	12.00
❑ 5560	Elvira/That Ain't No Stuff	1966	15.00
❑ 5670	Walkin' Wonder/Just a Little Bit of You	1966	12.00
❑ 5728	Tennessee Sue/Especially for You	1966	12.00
❑ 5862	My Woman Up't and Gone/Clawhammer Clyde	1967	12.00
JAMIE			
❑ 1135	Can't Go On/Without Your Love	1959	20.00
MERCURY			
❑ 72279	My Little Swing Broke Down/Money Greases the Wheels	1964	12.00
RCA VICTOR			
❑ 47-9881	The Birthmark Henry Thompson Talks About/If My Heart Had Windows	1970	8.00
❑ 47-9950	Big Mable Murphy/White Fences and Evergreen Trees	1971	8.00
❑ 47-9991	My Baby Packed Up My Mind and Left Me/I'm Finally Over You	1971	8.00
❑ 74-0259	California Cotton Fields/Sweetheart Don't Throw Yourself Away	1969	8.00
❑ 74-0569	Common, Broke Elastic, Rotten Cotton, Hound Dog Snoopin', Ankle Droopin', Funky Fuzzy, White Sock Blues No. 2/High Steppin' Mama	1971	8.00
❑ 74-0748	North Carolina/The Last Time I Called Somebody Darlin'	1972	8.00
❑ 74-0903	This Time the Hurtin's on Me/Lonesome Fiddle Man	1973	8.00
20TH CENTURY			
❑ 2171	Cash on Delivery/Watching My World Walk Away	1975	6.00
❑ 2199	Liberal Acres/Heaven Hangin' Over My Head	1975	6.00
Albums			
CAPITOL			
❑ ST 2552 [S]	Elvira	1966	25.00
❑ T 2552 [M]	Elvira	1966	20.00
❑ ST 2764 [S]	Tell It Like It Is	1967	20.00
❑ T 2764 [M]	Tell It Like It Is	1967	25.00

FREAK SCENE, THE

Number	Title (A Side/B Side)	Yr	NM
45s			
COLUMBIA			
❑ 4-44056	A Million Grains of Sand/Behind the Mind	1967	25.00
Albums			
COLUMBIA			
❑ CL 2656 [M]	Psychedelic Psoul	1967	70.00
❑ CS 9456 [S]	Psychedelic Psoul	1967	100.00

FRED, JOHN, AND HIS PLAYBOY BAND

Number	Title (A Side/B Side)	Yr	NM
45s			
BELL			
❑ 45382	I'm in Love Again/In the Mood	1973	5.00
—As "John Fred and the Creepers"			
JEWEL			
❑ 730	The Fool/There'll Be No Teardrops Tonight	1964	10.00
❑ 736	Lenne/You're Mad at Me	1964	10.00
❑ 737	Boogie Children/My First Love	1964	10.00
—As "The Playboys"			
❑ 743	Wrong to Me/How Can I Prove	1965	10.00
MONTEL			
❑ 904	Down in New Orleans/I Love You	1959	15.00
❑ 1002	Shirley/My Love for You	1959	15.00
❑ 1007	Good Lovin'/You Know You Made Me Cry	1961	10.00
❑ 2001	Mirror Mirror (On the Wall)/To Have and to Hold	1962	10.00
N-JOY			
❑ 1005	Boogie Children/My First Love	1965	10.00
PAULA			
❑ 225	Fortune Teller/Making Love to You	1965	8.00
❑ 234	Can't I Get a Word In/Sun City	1966	8.00
❑ 244	Doin' the Best I Can/Leave Her Never	1966	8.00
❑ 247	Outta My Head/Love Comes in Time	1966	8.00
❑ 259	Up and Down/Wind-Up Doll	1967	8.00
❑ 273	Agnes English/Sad Story	1967	8.00
❑ 282	Judy in Disguise (With Glasses)/When the Lights Go Out	1967	8.00
—Pink label			
❑ 282	Judy in Disguise (With Glasses)/When the Lights Go Out	1967	10.00
—Yellow label			
❑ 282	Judy in Disguise (With Glasses)/When the Lights Go Out	1967	12.00
—White label			
❑ 294	Hey Hey Bunny/No Letter Today	1968	8.00
❑ 303	Lonely Are the Lonely/We Played Games	1968	8.00
❑ 310	Tissue Paper/Little Dum Dum	1968	8.00
❑ 315	What Is Happiness/Sometimes You Just Can't Win	1968	8.00
PHILCO-FORD			
❑ HP-25	Judy in Disguise/No Letter Today	1968	20.00
—4-inch plastic "Hip Pocket Record" with color sleeve			
SUGARCANE			
❑ 1001	Keep It Hid/You Had to Be a Woman	1975	4.00
❑ 1002	Jukebox Shirley/Hey, Good Lookin'	1975	4.00
UNI			
❑ 55135	Back in the U.S.S.R./Silly Sarah Carter	1969	6.00
❑ 55160	Open Doors/Three Deep Is a Feeling	1969	6.00
❑ 55187	Love My Soul/Julia Julia	1969	6.00
❑ 55220	Come with Me/Where's Everybody Going	1970	6.00
Albums			
GUINNESS			
❑ GNS 36022	Juke Box	1977	40.00
JIN			
❑ 9027	The Best of John Fred and His Playboys	198?	10.00
PAULA			
❑ LP-2191 [M]	John Fred and His Playboys	1966	20.00
❑ LPS-2191 [S]	John Fred and His Playboys	1966	35.00

Number	Title (A Side/B Side)	Yr	NM
❑ LP-2193 [M]	34:40 of John Fred and His Playboys	1967	20.00
❑ LPS-2193 [S]	34:40 of John Fred and His Playboys	1967	35.00
❑ LP-2197 [M]	Agnes English	1967	25.00
❑ LPS-2197 [S]	Agnes English	1967	35.00
❑ LPS-2197 [S]	Judy in Disguise with Glasses	1968	20.00

—Retitled version of "Agnes English"

Number	Title (A Side/B Side)	Yr	NM
❑ LPS-2201	Permanently Stated	1969	35.00

UNI

Number	Title (A Side/B Side)	Yr	NM
❑ 73077	Love in My Soul	1970	30.00

FREDDIE AND THE DREAMERS

45s

CAPITOL

Number	Title (A Side/B Side)	Yr	NM
❑ 5053	I'm Telling You Now/What Have I Done to You	1963	20.00
❑ 5137	You Were Made for Me/Send a Letter to Me	1964	20.00

MERCURY

Number	Title (A Side/B Side)	Yr	NM
❑ 72285	I Love You Baby/Don't Make Me Cry	1965	10.00
❑ 72285 [PS]	I Love You Baby/Don't Make Me Cry	1965	20.00
❑ 72327	Don't Do That to Me/Just for You	1965	10.00
❑ 72377	I Understand (Just How You Feel)/I Will	1965	10.00
❑ 72428	Do the Freddie/Tell Me When	1965	10.00
❑ 72428	Do the Freddie/A Love Like You	1965	12.00
❑ 72462	A Little You/Things I'd Like to Say	1965	10.00
❑ 72487	I Don't Know/Windmill in Old Amsterdam	1965	10.00
❑ 72487 [PS]	I Don't Know/Windmill in Old Amsterdam	1965	20.00
❑ 72548	When I'm Home with You/If You Got a Minute Baby	1966	10.00
❑ 72604	Some Day/Short Shorts	1966	10.00

SUPER K

Number	Title (A Side/B Side)	Yr	NM
❑ 146	She Needs Me/Susan's Tuba	1970	8.00

TOWER

Number	Title (A Side/B Side)	Yr	NM
❑ 125	I'm Telling You Now/What Have I Done to You	1964	15.00
❑ 127	You Were Made for Me/So Fine	1965	15.00

—B-side: "Introducing the Beat Merchants"

Number	Title (A Side/B Side)	Yr	NM
❑ 127	You Were Made for Me/Send a Letter to Me	1965	20.00
❑ 163	Send a Letter to Me/There's Not One Thing	1965	15.00

—B-side by 4 Just Men

UNITED ARTISTS

Number	Title (A Side/B Side)	Yr	NM
❑ 50239	Come Back When You Grow Up/Oh What a Lovely Day	1967	—

—Unreleased

7-Inch Extended Plays

MERCURY

Number	Title (A Side/B Side)	Yr	NM
❑ SRC 661-C	Thou Shalt Not Steal/Funny Over You/He Got What He Wanted//I Fell in Love with Your Picture/I Think of You/Some Other Guy	1965	20.00

—Jukebox mini-LP

Number	Title (A Side/B Side)	Yr	NM
❑ SRC 661-C [PS]	Fun Lovin' Freddie	1965	20.00

Albums

CAPITOL

Number	Title (A Side/B Side)	Yr	NM
❑ SM-11896 [B]	The Best of Freddie and the Dreamers	1976	10.00

—"I'm Telling You Now," "You Were Made for Me," "I Just Don't Understand," "A Little You" and "Over You" are in stereo, the rest are mono.

MERCURY

Number	Title (A Side/B Side)	Yr	NM
❑ MG-21017 [M]	Freddie and the Dreamers	1965	25.00
❑ MG-21026 [M]	Do the Freddie	1965	20.00
❑ MG-21031 [M]	Seaside Swingers	1965	20.00
❑ MG-21053 [M]	Frantic Freddie	1965	15.00
❑ MG-21061 [M]	Fun Lovin' Freddie	1966	15.00
❑ SR-61017 [R]	Freddie and the Dreamers	1965	20.00
❑ SR-61026 [S]	Do the Freddie	1965	25.00
❑ SR-61031 [S]	Seaside Swingers	1965	25.00
❑ SR-61053 [S]	Frantic Freddie	1965	20.00
❑ SR-61061 [S]	Fun Lovin' Freddie	1966	20.00

TOWER

Number	Title (A Side/B Side)	Yr	NM
❑ DT 5003 [R]	I'm Telling You Now	1965	20.00

—Contains only two Freddie and the Dreamers songs, but the group's picture is on the cover. Also includes Four Just Men (2), Heinz (2), Linda Laine and the Sinners (2), Mike Rabin and the Demons (2) and The Toggery Five (2)

Number	Title (A Side/B Side)	Yr	NM
❑ T 5003 [M]	I'm Telling You Now	1965	25.00

—Contains only two Freddie and the Dreamers songs, but the group's picture is on the cover. Also includes Four Just Men (2), Heinz (2), Linda Laine and the Sinners (2), Mike Rabin and the Demons (2) and The Toggery Five (2)

FREDDIE AND THE PARLIAMENTS

45s

TWIRL

Number	Title (A Side/B Side)	Yr	NM
❑ 1003	Darlene/That Girl	1959	100.00

FREDRIC

45s

EVOLUTION

Number	Title (A Side/B Side)	Yr	NM
❑ 1001	Five O'Clock Traffic/Red Pier	1968	25.00

FORTE

Number	Title (A Side/B Side)	Yr	NM
❑ 3001	Five O'Clock Traffic/Red Pier	1968	40.00

Albums

FORTE

Number	Title (A Side/B Side)	Yr	NM
❑ 80461	Phases and Faces	1968	800.00

FREE Also see PAUL KOSSOFF; BAD COMPANY; THE FIRM.

45s

A&M

Number	Title (A Side/B Side)	Yr	NM
❑ 1099	I'm a Mover/Worry	1969	4.00
❑ 1172	I'll Be Creepin'/Mouthful of Grass	1970	4.00
❑ 1206	All Right Now/Mouthful of Grass	1970	5.00
❑ 1230	Stealer/Broad Daylight	1970	4.00
❑ 1230 [PS]	Stealer/Lying in the Sunshine	1970	10.00

—Picture sleeve lists a different B-side than is on the record

Number	Title (A Side/B Side)	Yr	NM
❑ 1248	Highway Song/Love You So	1971	4.00
❑ 1266	Mr. Big/I'll Be Creepin'	1971	4.00
❑ 1276	My Brother Jake/Only My Soul	1971	4.00
❑ 1352	Little Bit of Love/Sail On	1972	4.00
❑ 1720	All Right Now/Stealer	1975	4.00

ISLAND

Number	Title (A Side/B Side)	Yr	NM
❑ 1212	Wishing Well/Let Me Show You	1972	4.00

Albums

A&M

Number	Title (A Side/B Side)	Yr	NM
❑ SP-3126	Fire and Water	198?	8.00

—Budget-line reissue

Number	Title (A Side/B Side)	Yr	NM
❑ SP-3663	Best of Free	1975	12.00
❑ SP-4198	Tons of Sobs	1969	15.00
❑ SP-4204	Free	1969	15.00
❑ SP-4268	Fire and Water	1970	15.00
❑ SP-4287	Highway	1971	15.00
❑ SP-4306	Free Live!	1971	15.00
❑ SP-4349	Free at Last	1972	15.00
❑ 5318185	Fire and Water	2009	20.00

ISLAND

Number	Title (A Side/B Side)	Yr	NM
❑ ILSD 4 [(2)]	The Free Story	1975	15.00
❑ ILPS 9217	Heartbreaker	1975	10.00

—U.S. reissue with same number as original U.K. issue

Number	Title (A Side/B Side)	Yr	NM
❑ SW-9324	Heartbreaker	1973	12.00

—Original U.S. number, distributed by Capitol

PICKWICK

Number	Title (A Side/B Side)	Yr	NM
❑ SPC-3706	Free at Last	197?	10.00

FREE BAND, THE

Albums

VANGUARD

Number	Title (A Side/B Side)	Yr	NM
❑ VSD-6507	The Free Band	1969	20.00

FREE DESIGN, THE

45s

PROJECT 3

Number	Title (A Side/B Side)	Yr	NM
❑ 1324	Kites Are Fun/Proper Ornaments	1967	8.00
❑ 1331	You Be You and I'll Be Me/Never Tell the World	1967	8.00
❑ 1336	I Found Love/Umbrellas	1968	8.00
❑ 1345	Eleanor Rigby/Make the Madness Stop	1968	8.00
❑ 1347 [DJ]	Close Your Mouth (It's Christmas)/Christmas Is The Day	1968	10.00

—Stock copy may not exist

Number	Title (A Side/B Side)	Yr	NM
❑ 1350	You Could Be Born Again/A Leaf Has Veins	1968	8.00
❑ 1356	Where Do I Go/Girls Alone	1969	8.00
❑ 1358	Summertime/Dorian Benediction	1969	8.00
❑ 1360	If I Were a Carpenter/Now Is the Time	1969	8.00
❑ 1366	2002: A Hit Song/Hurry Sundown	1969	8.00
❑ 1370	Butterflies Are Free/(B-side unknown)	1970	8.00
❑ 1375	I'm a Yogi/Bubbles	1970	8.00
❑ 1383	Tomorrow Is the First Day of the Rest of My Life/Kije's Ouija	1970	8.00
❑ 1393	Felt So Good/You Are My Sunshine	1971	8.00
❑ 1404	Stay Off of Your Frown/Friendly Man	1971	8.00

Albums

AMBROTYPE

Number	Title (A Side/B Side)	Yr	NM
❑ 1016	There Is a Song	1972	150.00

PROJECT 3

Number	Title (A Side/B Side)	Yr	NM
❑ PR 4006 SD	The Free Design Sing for Very Important People	1970	25.00
❑ PR-5019 QD [Q]	Kites Are Fun	197?	40.00
❑ PR-5019 SD	Kites Are Fun	1967	25.00
❑ PR-5031 SD	You Could Be Born Again	1968	25.00
❑ PR-5037 SD	Heaven/Earth	1969	25.00
❑ PR-5045 SD	Stars/Times/Bubbles/Love	1971	25.00
❑ PR-5061 SD	One By One	1971	25.00

FREE MOVEMENT, THE

45s

COLUMBIA

Number	Title (A Side/B Side)	Yr	NM
❑ 45512	The Harder I Try (The Bluer I Get)/Comin' Home	1972	5.00
❑ 45567	Could You Believe in a Dream/Love the One You're With	1972	5.00
❑ 45778	Every Step of the Way/I Can't Move No Mountains	1973	5.00

DECCA

Number	Title (A Side/B Side)	Yr	NM
❑ 32818	I've Found Someone of My Own/I Can't Convince My Heart	1971	6.00

Albums

COLUMBIA

Number	Title (A Side/B Side)	Yr	NM
❑ KC 31136	I've Found Someone of My Own	1972	15.00

FREEBORNE

Albums

MONITOR

Number	Title (A Side/B Side)	Yr	NM
❑ MPS-607	Peak Impressions	1967	150.00

FREED, ALAN Also see VARIOUS ARTISTS COLLECTIONS.

45s

CORAL

Number	Title (A Side/B Side)	Yr	NM
❑ 61626	Right Now, Right Now/Tina's Cantine	1956	30.00
❑ 61660	THe Camel Rock/I Don't Need Lotsa Money	1956	30.00
❑ 61693	The Space Man/Jazzbo's Theory	1956	30.00

—With Al "Jazzbo" Collins and the Modernaires

Number	Title (A Side/B Side)	Yr	NM
❑ 61749	Rock 'N' Roll Boogie/The Grey Bear	1956	40.00
❑ 61818	Sentimental Journey/Stop! Look! and Run!	1957	40.00

Albums

BRUNSWICK

Number	Title (A Side/B Side)	Yr	NM
❑ BL 54043 [M]	The Alan Freed Rock 'n' Roll Show	1959	150.00

CORAL

Number	Title (A Side/B Side)	Yr	NM
❑ CRL 57063 [M]	Alan Freed's Rock 'n' Roll Dance Party, Vol. 1	1956	150.00
❑ CRL 57115 [M]	Alan Freed's Rock 'n' Roll Dance Party, Vol. 2	1957	150.00
❑ CRL 57177 [M]	Go Go Go — Alan Freed's TV Record Hop	1957	150.00
❑ CRL 57213 [M]	Rock Around the Block	1958	150.00
❑ CRL 57216 [M]	Alan Freed Presents the King's Henchmen	1958	150.00

MGM

Number	Title (A Side/B Side)	Yr	NM
❑ E-293 [10]	The Big Beat	195?	200.00

FREEMAN, ART

45s

FAME

Number	Title (A Side/B Side)	Yr	NM
❑ 1008	I Can't Get You Out of My Mind/Slippin' Around with You	1966	50.00
❑ 1012	A Piece of My Heart/Everybody's Got to Cry Sometime	1966	30.00

FREEMAN, ARTHUR

45s

EXCELLO

Number	Title (A Side/B Side)	Yr	NM
❑ 2322	Here I Am/Played Out Play Girl	1971	20.00

FREEMAN, BOBBY

45s

AUTUMN

Number	Title (A Side/B Side)	Yr	NM
❑ 1	Come to Me/Let's Surf Again	1964	20.00
❑ 2	C'mon and Swim/C'mon and Swim — Part 2	1964	10.00

—Tan label

Number	Title (A Side/B Side)	Yr	NM
❑ 2	C'mon and Swim/C'mon and Swim — Part 2	1964	12.00

—White label, red print

Number	Title (A Side/B Side)	Yr	NM
❑ 5	S-W-I-M/That Little Old Heartbreaker	1964	10.00
❑ 9	I'll Never Fall in Love Again/Friends	1965	10.00
❑ 25	Cross My Heart/The Duck	1965	10.00

DOUBLE SHOT

Number	Title (A Side/B Side)	Yr	NM
❑ 139	There Oughta Be a Law/Everybody's Got a Hang-Up	1969	6.00
❑ 144	Susie Sunshine/Four Piece Funky Nitty Gritty Junky Band	1969	6.00

Except when noted otherwise, VG = 25% of NM, and VG+ = 50% of NM. (Example: VG = $2.00, VG+ = $4.00 and NM = $8.00.)

Number	Title (A Side/B Side)	Yr	NM
❑ 148	Can You Stand the Pressure/ Put Another Dime in the Parking Meter	1970	6.00
❑ 152	Do You Wanna Dance 1970/ Society for the Prevention of Cruelty to People	1970	6.00

JOSIE

Number	Title (A Side/B Side)	Yr	NM
❑ 835	Do You Want to Dance/ Big Fat Woman	1958	20.00
❑ 841	Betty Lou Got a New Pair of Shoes/Starlight	1958	20.00
❑ 844	Need Your Love/Shame On You, Miss Johnson	1958	15.00
❑ 855	A Love to Last a Lifetime/ When You're Smiling	1959	15.00
❑ 863	Love Me/Mary Ann Thomas	1959	15.00
❑ 867	My Guardian Angel/ Where Did My Baby Go	1959	15.00
❑ 872	Ebb Tide/Sinbad	1959	15.00
❑ 879	I Need Someone/ First Day of Spring	1960	12.00
❑ 886	Miss You So/Baby What Would You Do	1961	12.00
❑ 887	The Mess Around/So Much to Do	1961	12.00
❑ 889	Put You Down/She Said She Wants to Dance	1961	12.00
❑ 896	Love Me/Little Girl Don't You Understand	1962	12.00
❑ 928	The Mess Around/Little Girl Don't You Understand	1965	10.00

KING

Number	Title (A Side/B Side)	Yr	NM
❑ 5373	(I Do the) Shimmy Shimmy/ You Don't Understand Me	1960	12.00
❑ 5953	Fever/What Can I Do	1964	10.00
❑ 5962	Somebody, Somewhere/ Be My Little Chick-A-Dee	1964	10.00
❑ 5975	Come to Me/There's Gonna Be a Change	1965	10.00

LOMA

Number	Title (A Side/B Side)	Yr	NM
❑ 2056	Shadow of Your Love/ Soulful Sound of Music	1966	8.00
❑ 2080	I Got a Good Thing/Lies	1967	8.00

PARKWAY

Number	Title (A Side/B Side)	Yr	NM
❑ 875	She's a Hippy/Whip It Up Baby	1963	12.00

RHINO

Number	Title (A Side/B Side)	Yr	NM
❑ 4508	S-W-I-M/C'mon and Swim	198?	4.00
❑ 4508 [PS]	S-W-I-M/C'mon and Swim	198?	4.00

Albums

AUTUMN

Number	Title (A Side/B Side)	Yr	NM
❑ LP 102 [M]	C'mon and S-W-I-M	1964	50.00

JOSIE

Number	Title (A Side/B Side)	Yr	NM
❑ JM-4007 [M]	Get In the Swim with Bobby Freeman	1965	30.00
❑ JS-4007 [R]	Get In the Swim with Bobby Freeman	1965	25.00

JUBILEE

Number	Title (A Side/B Side)	Yr	NM
❑ JLP-1086 [M]	Do You Wanna Dance?	1959	140.00
❑ JLPS-1086 [S]	Do You Wanna Dance?	1959	200.00
❑ JGM-5010 [M]	Twist with Bobby Freeman	1962	100.00

KING

Number	Title (A Side/B Side)	Yr	NM
❑ 930 [M]	The Lovable Style of Bobby Freeman	1965	250.00

FREEMAN, GEORGE

45s

EPIC

Number	Title (A Side/B Side)	Yr	NM
❑ 5-10668	I'll Be Long Gone (Make My Life Shine)/Stop Now (There's Still Time)	1971	12.00

GARDENA

Number	Title (A Side/B Side)	Yr	NM
❑ 129	Sugar Lips/If I Told You	1962	20.00

GROOVE MERCHANT

Number	Title (A Side/B Side)	Yr	NM
❑ 1016	Guitar Lover Man/ (B-side unknown)	197?	12.00

OKEH

Number	Title (A Side/B Side)	Yr	NM
❑ 4-7333	All Right Now/You Lied, I Cried, Love Died	1969	25.00

SHOUT

Number	Title (A Side/B Side)	Yr	NM
❑ 201	Why Are You Doing This to Me/ I'm Like a Fish	1966	25.00

VALIANT

Number	Title (A Side/B Side)	Yr	NM
❑ 6035	Come to Me/You Guessed It	1963	20.00
❑ 6039	Down and Out/The Quiver	1963	250.00
❑ 6057	One Last Dance/You're Guilty	1964	25.00

FREEMAN BROTHERS, THE

45s

MALA

Number	Title (A Side/B Side)	Yr	NM
❑ 553	I'm Counting on You/ Everyday It's You	1966	25.00

SOUL

Number	Title (A Side/B Side)	Yr	NM
❑ 35011	My Baby/Beautiful Brown Eyes	1965	40.00

FREEPORT

45s

MAINSTREAM

Number	Title (A Side/B Side)	Yr	NM
❑ 730	I Need Your Lovin'/ (B-side unknown)	1970	10.00
❑ 732	Now That She's Gone/ Misunderstood	1970	10.00

Albums

MAINSTREAM

Number	Title (A Side/B Side)	Yr	NM
❑ S-6130	Freeport	1970	50.00

FREEWHEELERS, THE

45s

EPIC

Number	Title (A Side/B Side)	Yr	NM
❑ 9664	Walk, Walk/The Best of It	1964	20.00
❑ 9700	San Francisco Bay Blues/Susu	1964	20.00
❑ 9725	Beach Boy/Annie	1964	15.00

FREHLEY, ACE

45s

ATLANTIC

Number	Title (A Side/B Side)	Yr	NM
❑ 89072	Insane/The Acorn Is Spinning	1988	3.00
—As "Frehley's Comet"			
❑ 89072 [PS]	Insane/The Acorn Is Spinning	1988	4.00
—As "Frehley's Comet"			
❑ 89255 [PS]	Into the Night/Fractured Too	1987	4.00

CASABLANCA

Number	Title (A Side/B Side)	Yr	NM
❑ 941	New York Groove/Snowblind	1978	6.00
—"Casablanca Record and FilmWorks" label			
❑ 941	New York Groove/Snowblind	1978	12.00
—Tan label with camel			

Albums

CASABLANCA

Number	Title (A Side/B Side)	Yr	NM
❑ NBLP-7121	Ace Frehley	1978	18.00
❑ NBPIX-7121 [PD]	Ace Frehley	1978	50.00

MEGAFORCE/ATLANTIC

Number	Title (A Side/B Side)	Yr	NM
❑ 81749	Frehley's Comet	1987	8.00
❑ 81826	Live + 1	1988	8.00
❑ 81862	Second Sighting	1988	8.00
❑ 82042	Trouble Walkin'	1989	14.00

FRENCH, DON

45s

LANCER

Number	Title (A Side/B Side)	Yr	NM
❑ 104	Lonely Saturday Night/ Goldilocks	1959	25.00
❑ 105	Little Blonde Girl/I Look Into My Heart	1959	30.00

FRENCH, LISA

45s

HIT

Number	Title (A Side/B Side)	Yr	NM
❑ 181	The Name Game/You Don't Want My Love	1965	8.00
—B-side by Leroy Jones			
❑ 200	You Can't Trust a Friend/Send Me the Pillow You Dream On	1965	8.00
—B-side by Marty Wood			

FREY, GLENN

12-Inch Singles

MCA

Number	Title (A Side/B Side)	Yr	NM
❑ L33-1256 [DJ]	The Heat Is On (3:45) (same on both sides)	1984	8.00
❑ L33-17035 [DJ]	You Belong to the City (Long Version 5:51) (Short Version 4:22)	1985	7.00
❑ L33-17583 [DJ]	True Love (same on both sides)	1988	6.00
❑ 23540	The Heat Is On ((Extended 6:04) (Dub Version 2:39) (Dance Version 5:40)	1984	8.00

45s

ASYLUM

Number	Title (A Side/B Side)	Yr	NM
❑ 47466	I Found Somebody/ She Can't Let Go	1982	4.00
❑ 47466 [PS]	I Found Somebody/ She Can't Let Go	1982	5.00
❑ 69857	All Those Lies/That Girl	1982	4.00
❑ 69974	The One You Love/All Those Lies	1982	4.00

MCA

Number	Title (A Side/B Side)	Yr	NM
❑ 52413	Sexy Girl/Better in the U.S.A.	1984	3.00
❑ 52413 [PS]	Sexy Girl/Better in the U.S.A.	1984	3.00
❑ 52461	The Allnighter/Smuggler's Blues	1984	3.00
❑ 52461 [PS]	The Allnighter/Smuggler's Blues	1984	3.00
❑ 52512	The Heat Is On/Shoot Out	1984	3.00
❑ 52512 [PS]	The Heat Is On/Shoot Out	1984	3.00
—B-side by Harold Faltermeyer			
❑ 52546	Smuggler's Blues/New Love	1985	3.00
❑ 52546 [PS]	Smuggler's Blues/New Love	1985	3.00
❑ 52651	You Belong to the City/ Smuggler's Blues	1985	3.00
❑ 52651 [PS]	You Belong to the City/ Smuggler's Blues	1985	3.00
❑ 52651 [DJ]	You Belong to the City (Long Version)/(Short Version)	1985	5.00
❑ 53363	True Love/Working Man	1988	3.00
❑ 53363 [PS]	True Love/Working Man	1988	3.00
❑ 53452	Soul Searchin'/It's Cold in Here	1988	3.00
❑ 53497	Livin' Right/Soul Searchin'	1989	3.00
❑ 53684	Two Hearts/Some Kind of Blue	1989	3.00
❑ 54461	River of Dreams/He Took Advantage (Blues for Ronald Reagan)	1992	3.00

Albums

ASYLUM

Number	Title (A Side/B Side)	Yr	NM
❑ E1-60129	No Fun Aloud	1982	10.00

MCA

Number	Title (A Side/B Side)	Yr	NM
❑ 5501	The Allnighter	1984	10.00
❑ 6239	Soul Searchin'	1988	10.00

FRIAR TUCK

Curt Boetcher was in the group.

45s

BANSHEE

Number	Title (A Side/B Side)	Yr	NM
❑ 100	The Return of Robin Hood/ (B-side unknown)	196?	15.00

MERCURY

Number	Title (A Side/B Side)	Yr	NM
❑ 72684	Alley-Oop/Sweet Pea	1967	10.00

Albums

MERCURY

Number	Title (A Side/B Side)	Yr	NM
❑ MG-21111 [M]	Friar Tuck and His Psychedelic Guitar	1967	40.00
❑ SR-61111 [S]	Friar Tuck and His Psychedelic Guitar	1967	50.00

FRIEDMAN, KINKY

45s

ABC

Number	Title (A Side/B Side)	Yr	NM
❑ 12073	Lover Please/Autograph	1975	6.00
❑ 12107	Wild Man from Borneo/ Popeye the Sailor Man	1975	6.00

EPIC

Number	Title (A Side/B Side)	Yr	NM
❑ 50299	Catfish/Dear Abby	1976	5.00

SUNRISE

Number	Title (A Side/B Side)	Yr	NM
❑ 41932	Twirl/Hello, Good Mornin'	1983	6.00
—B-side with Ronee Blakely			

VANGUARD

Number	Title (A Side/B Side)	Yr	NM
❑ 35173	Sold American/ Western Union Wire	1973	8.00

Albums

ABC

Number	Title (A Side/B Side)	Yr	NM
❑ X-829	Kinky Friedman	1974	10.00

EPIC

Number	Title (A Side/B Side)	Yr	NM
❑ PE 34304	Lasso from El Paso	1976	10.00

VANGUARD

Number	Title (A Side/B Side)	Yr	NM
❑ VSD-79333	Sold American	1973	12.00

FRIEND AND LOVER

45s

ABC

Number	Title (A Side/B Side)	Yr	NM
❑ 10910	Town Called Love/If Tomorrow	1967	12.00

CADET CONCEPT

Number	Title (A Side/B Side)	Yr	NM
❑ 7019	Hard Lovin'/Colorado Exile	1970	6.00
❑ 7019 [PS]	Hard Lovin'/Colorado Exile	1970	15.00

VERVE FORECAST

Number	Title (A Side/B Side)	Yr	NM
❑ 5069	Reach Out of the Darkness/ Time on Your Side (You're Only 15 Years Old)	1967	10.00
❑ 5091	If Love Is In Your Heart/Zig Zag	1968	8.00
❑ 5100	I Want to Be Free/Circus	1968	8.00
❑ 5106	Ode to a Dandelion/A Wise Man Changes His Mind	1969	6.00

Albums

VERVE FORECAST

Number	Title (A Side/B Side)	Yr	NM
❑ FTS-3055	Reach Out of the Darkness	1968	20.00

FRIENDLY TORPEDOES, THE

45s

ORIGINAL SOUND

Number	Title (A Side/B Side)	Yr	NM
❑ 95	Nothing's Too Good for My Car/ So Long Ago	1970	25.00

FRIENDS, THE

45s

MGM

Number	Title (A Side/B Side)	Yr	NM
❑ 14646	Gonna Have a Good Time/ Would You Laugh	1973	6.00
❑ 14646 [PS]	Gonna Have a Good Time/ Would You Laugh	1973	12.00

F

Except when noted otherwise, VG = 25% of NM, and VG+ = 50% of NM. (Example: VG = $2.00, VG+ = $4.00 and NM = $8.00.)

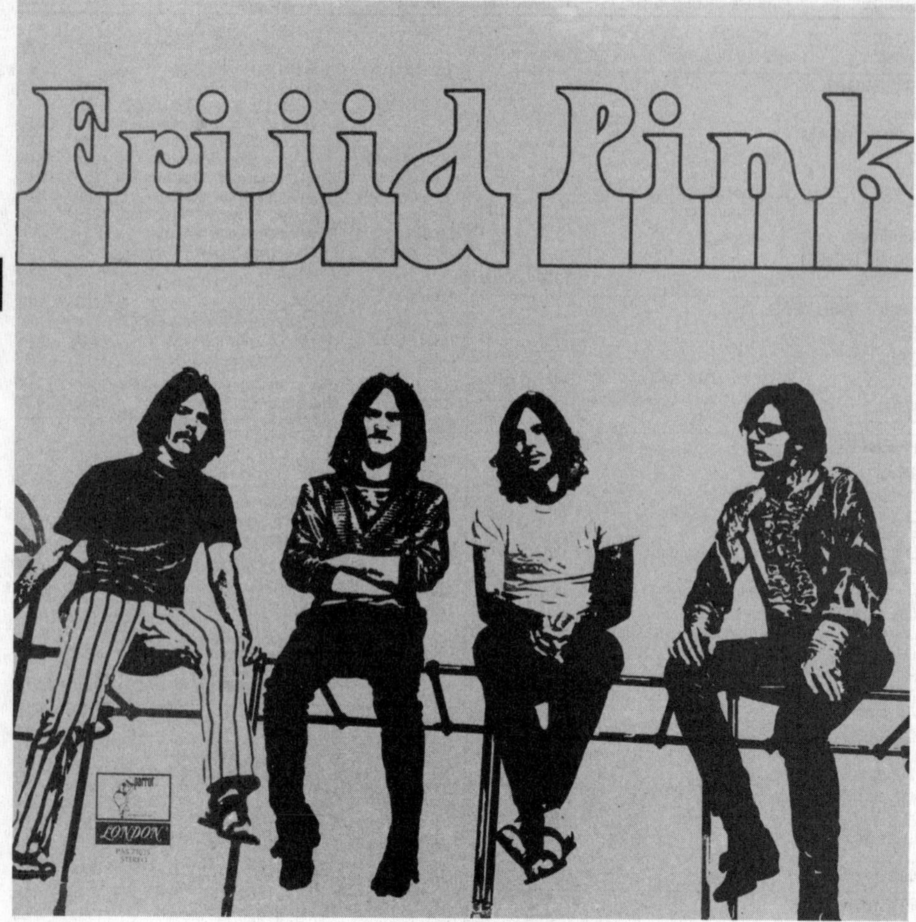

Frijid Pink, *Frijid Pink,* Parrot PAS 71033, 1970, **$25.**

Number	Title (A Side/B Side)	Yr	NM
Albums			
MGM			
❑ SE-4901	The Friends	1973	12.00
FRIENDS OF DISTINCTION, THE			
45s			
RCA VICTOR			
❑ 74-0107	Grazing in the Grass/ I Really Hope You Do	1969	6.00
❑ 74-0204	Going in Circles/Let Yourself Go	1969	6.00
❑ 74-0319	Love Or Let Me Be Lonely/ This Generation	1970	6.00
❑ 74-0385	Time Waits for No One/ Mother Nature	1970	5.00
❑ 74-0416	Check It Out/I Need You	1971	5.00
❑ 74-0516	It Don't Matter to Me/Down I Go	1971	5.00
❑ 74-0562	Let Me Be/Long Time Comin' My Way	1971	5.00
❑ 74-0679	Love Is the Way of Life/ Jenny Wants to Know	1972	5.00
❑ 74-0787	Now Is the Time/Thumb Tripping	1972	5.00
❑ 74-0888	Ain't No Woman (Like the One I've Got)/Easy Evil	1973	5.00
❑ 74-0956	Check It Out/Love Can Make It Easier	1973	5.00
❑ PB-10197	Honey Baby Theme Part 1/ Honey Baby Theme Part 2	1975	4.00
❑ PB-10220	Love Shack Part 1/Love Shack Part 2	1975	4.00
Albums			
RCA VICTOR			
❑ APD1-0276 [Q]	Greatest Hits	1973	20.00
❑ LSP-4149	Grazin'	1969	15.00
❑ LSP-4212	Highly Distinct	1969	15.00
❑ LSP-4313	Real Friends	1970	15.00
❑ LSP-4408	Whatever	1970	15.00
❑ LSP-4492	Friends & People	1971	15.00
❑ LSP-4819	Greatest Hits	1972	12.00
❑ LSP-4829	Love Can Make It Easier	1973	12.00

Number	Title (A Side/B Side)	Yr	NM
FRIJID PINK			
45s			
LION			
❑ 115	Earth Omen/Lazy Day	1972	8.00
❑ 136	Go Now/Lazy Day	1972	8.00
❑ 158	Big Betty/Shady Lady	1973	6.00
PARROT			
❑ 334	Tell Me Why/Cryin' Shame	1969	6.00
❑ 340	God Gave Me You/Drivin' Blues	1970	6.00
❑ 341	House of the Rising Sun/ Drivin' Blues	1970	8.00
❑ 349	Sing a Song for Freedom/ End of the Line	1970	6.00
❑ 352	Heartbreak Hotel/Bye Bye Blues	1970	6.00
❑ 355	Music for the People/Sloony	1971	6.00
❑ 358	We're Gonna Be There/ Shorty Kline	1971	6.00
❑ 360	Lost Son/I Love Her	1971	6.00
Albums			
FANTASY			
❑ 9464	All Pink Inside	1974	15.00
LION			
❑ LN-1004	Earth Omen	1972	20.00
PARROT			
❑ PAS 71033	Frijid Pink	1970	25.00
❑ PAS 71041	Defrosted	1970	25.00
FROGGIE BEAVER			
Albums			
FROGGIE BEAVER			
❑ 7301	From the Pond	1973	50.00
FROGMEN, THE			
45s			
ASTRA			
❑ 1009	Underwater/The Mad Rush	196?	50.00
❑ 1010	Beware Below/Tioga	196?	50.00
—The above two are East Coast reissues			

Number	Title (A Side/B Side)	Yr	NM
CANDIX			
❑ 314	Underwater/The Mad Rush	1961	25.00
❑ 326	Beware Below/Tioga	1961	25.00
SCOTT			
❑ 101	Seahorse Flats/Tioga	1961	50.00
❑ 102	Underwater/Beware Below	1961	50.00
TEE JAY			
❑ 131	Sea Haunt/Diamond Back	1964	80.00
—Blue vinyl			
FROLIC, HARVEY			
45s			
HIT			
❑ 23	Things/Heart in Hand	1962	8.00
—B-side by Connie Landers			
❑ 74	Ring of Fire/On Top of Spaghetti	1963	8.00
❑ 91	The Matador/Maria Elena	1963	8.00
—B-side by the Music City Five			
❑ 105	Talking About My Baby/ You Don't Know Me	1964	8.00
—B-side by Bill Austin			
❑ 131	Dang Me/The Girl from Ipanema	1964	8.00
—B-side by Betty Coleson			
❑ 148	Chug-a-Lug/Lonesome Fool	1964	8.00
—B-side by Joanne Kay			
❑ 181	Midnight Special/Sha La La	1965	12.00
—B-side by the Spartas			
FROLIC, ROGER			
45s			
HIT			
❑ 267	My Uncle Used to Love Me But She Died/Almost Persuaded	1966	8.00
—B-side by Leroy Jones			
FROLK HAVEN			
Albums			
LRS			
❑ RT-6023	At the Apex of High	1972	180.00
FRONT PAGE NEWS			
45s			
DIAL			
❑ 4052	Thoughts/You Better Behave	1967	25.00
FROST, FRANK			
45s			
JEWEL			
❑ 765	My Back Scratcher/ Harp and Soul	1966	15.00
❑ 771	Things You Do/Harpin' On It	1966	15.00
❑ 778	Pocketful of Money/Ride with Your Daddy Tonight	1967	20.00
PHILLIPS INTERNATIONAL			
❑ 3578	Jelly Roll King/Crawlback	1962	20.00
Albums			
EARWIG			
❑ 4901	Rockin' the Juke Joint Down	1986	10.00
❑ 4914	Midnight Prowler	1990	10.00
JEWEL			
❑ LPS-5013	Frank Frost	1973	15.00
PHILLIPS INTERNATIONAL			
❑ PLP-1975 [M]	Hey Boss Man!	1962	3000.
—VG value 1500; VG+ value 2250			
FROST, MAX, AND THE TROOPERS			
45s			
SIDEWALK			
❑ 938	There Is a Party Going On/ Stomper's Ride	1968	15.00
TOWER			
❑ 419	Shape of Things to Come/ Free Lovin'	1968	15.00
❑ 419 [PS]	Shape of Things to Come/ Free Lovin'	1968	50.00
—Promo-only sleeve with message to DJs on back			
❑ 452	52%/Max Frost Theme	1968	15.00
❑ 452 [PS]	52%/Max Frost Theme	1968	20.00
❑ 478	Paxton Quigley's Had the Course/Sittin' in Circles	1969	15.00
❑ 478 [PS]	Paxton Quigley's Had the Course/Sittin' in Circles	1969	20.00
Albums			
TOWER			
❑ ST-5147	Shape of Things to Come	1968	50.00
FROST, THE Featuring Dick Wagner.			
45s			
DATE			
❑ 1577	Bad Girl/Rainy Day	1967	12.00
—As "Dick Wagner and the Frosts"			

Except when noted otherwise, VG = 25% of NM, and VG+ = 50% of NM. (Example: VG = $2.00, VG+ = $4.00 and NM = $8.00.)

Number	Title (A Side/B Side)	Yr	NM
❑ 1596	Little Girl/Sunshine	1968	12.00
—As "Dick Wagner and the Frosts"			
VANGUARD			
❑ 35099	Linda/Sweet Lady Love	1969	8.00
❑ 35111	Rock and Roll Music/ Donny's Blues	1969	8.00
❑ 35115	A Long Way from Home/ Black As Night	1970	8.00
Albums			
VANGUARD			
❑ VSD-6520	Frost Music	1969	20.00
❑ VSD-6541	Rock and Roll Music	1969	20.00
❑ VSD-6556	Through the Eyes of Love	1970	20.00
❑ VSD-79392	Early Frost	1978	15.00

FROST, THOMAS AND RICHARD

Number	Title (A Side/B Side)	Yr	NM
45s			
IMPERIAL			
❑ 66405	She's Got Love/The Word Is Love	1969	8.00
❑ 66426	With Me My Love/Gotta Find a New Place to Stay	1969	10.00
❑ 66451	Hello Stranger/Fairy Tale Affair	1970	10.00
UNI			
❑ 55320	Got to Find the Light/ St. Petersburg	1972	10.00
❑ 55320	Mona Lisas and Mad Hatters/ Kentucky Moon	1972	10.00
Albums			
UNI			
❑ 73124	Thomas and Richard Frost	1972	15.00

FRUMIOUS BANDERSNATCH

Number	Title (A Side/B Side)	Yr	NM
7-Inch Extended Plays			
MUGGLES GRAMOPHONE WORKS			
❑ (no #)	Hearts to Cry/Misty Cloudy// Cheshire	1967	250.00
—Legitimate copies show purple vinyl when held to a light; all others are counterfeits			
❑ (no #) [PS]	Frumious Bandersnatch	1967	250.00

FRUMMOX

Number	Title (A Side/B Side)	Yr	NM
45s			
PROBE			
❑ 470	Mary Martin/There You Go	1970	8.00
Albums			
PROBE			
❑ 4511	From Here to There	1970	15.00

FRUT

Number	Title (A Side/B Side)	Yr	NM
45s			
WESTBOUND			
❑ 189	Prison of Love/Send Me Down	1972	10.00
Albums			
TRASH			
❑ (# unknown)	Keep On Truckin'	1971	80.00
—Originals on yellow vinyl			
WESTBOUND			
❑ WB-2005	Keep On Truckin'	1971	30.00
—Reissue of Trash LP			
❑ WB-2008	Spoiled Rotten	1972	30.00

FRYE, DAVID

Number	Title (A Side/B Side)	Yr	NM
45s			
BUDDAH			
❑ 378 [DJ]	Nixon Meets the Godfather (mono/stereo)	1973	10.00
—Promo only?			
ELEKTRA			
❑ 45722	My Way/Farm Report	1971	10.00
Albums			
BUDDAH			
❑ 1600	Richard Nixon: A Fantasy	1973	12.00
❑ BDS-5097	Richard Nixon: Superstar	1971	12.00
ELEKTRA			
❑ EKS-74085	Radio Free Nixon	1971	12.00
❑ EKS-75006	I Am the President	1969	12.00
FRYE			
❑ DFP-80	The Great Debate	1980	15.00

FUGAZI

Number	Title (A Side/B Side)	Yr	NM
45s			
DISCHORD			
❑ 43 [PS]	Joe #1/Break In/Song #1	1990	2.00
❑ 43	Joe #1/Break In/Song #1	1990	5.00
SUB POP			
❑ 52	Joe #1/Break In/Song #1	1989	25.00
—Black vinyl pressing of 800			
❑ 52	Joe #1/Break In/Song #1	1989	65.00
—Green vinyl pressing of 1,200			
❑ 52 [PS]	Joe #1/Break In/Song #1	1989	25.00
—#14 in Sub Pop Singles Club series			
Albums			
DISCHORD			
❑ 30 [EP]	Fugazi	1988	10.00
❑ 35 [EP]	Margin Walker	1989	10.00
❑ 44	Repeater	1990	12.00
❑ 60	Steady Diet of Nothing	1991	12.00
❑ 70	In On the Kill Taker	1993	12.00
❑ 90-V	Red Medicine	1995	12.00

FUGS, THE

Number	Title (A Side/B Side)	Yr	NM
45s			
ESP-DISK'			
❑ 4507	Frenzy/I Want to Know	1966	15.00
Albums			
BROADSIDE			
❑ 304 [M]	The Village Fugs Sing Ballads of Contemporary Protest, Point of View, and General Dissatisfaction	1965	400.00
—Without insert			
❑ 304 [M]	The Village Fugs Sing Ballads of Contemporary Protest, Point of View, and General Dissatisfaction	1965	500.00
—With insert			
ESP-DISK			
❑ 1018 [M]	The Fugs First Album	1966	40.00
—"Reissue of Broadside 304" on cover			
❑ 1018 [M]	The Fugs First Album	1966	150.00
—Turquoise and black cover, different from all other versions			
❑ 1018 [M]	The Fugs First Album	1967	30.00
—No reference to reissue on cover			
❑ 1028 [S]	The Fugs	1966	30.00
—Black and white cover, back cover photos aligned			
❑ 1028 [S]	The Fugs	1966	50.00
—Black and white cover, back cover photos staggered			
❑ 1028 [S]	The Fugs	1966	80.00
—Psychedelic color shield on cover			
❑ 1038 [S]	Virgin Fugs	1967	30.00
—"For Adult Minds" printed on cover			
❑ 1038 [S]	Virgin Fugs	1967	50.00
—"For Adult Minds" stamped on cover			
❑ 1038 [S]	Virgin Fugs	1967	50.00
—"For Adult Minds" sticker, no inserts			
❑ 1038 [S]	Virgin Fugs	1967	100.00
—"For Adult Minds" sticker on cover; with poster, book and stickers			
❑ 2018	Fugs 4, Rounders Score	196?	80.00
PVC			
❑ 8914	Proto Punk: The Fugs Greatest Hits, Vol. 1	1982	15.00
REPRISE			
❑ R-6280 [M]	Tenderness Junction	1968	40.00
❑ RS-6280 [S]	Tenderness Junction	1968	30.00
❑ RS-6305	It Crawled Into My Hand, Honest	1968	25.00
❑ RS-6359	Belle of Avenue A	1969	25.00
❑ RS-6396	Golden Fifth	1970	25.00

FULL MOON

Number	Title (A Side/B Side)	Yr	NM
45s			
DOUGLAS			
❑ ZS7 6506	To Know/(B-side unknown)	1972	8.00
Albums			
DOUGLAS			
❑ KZ 31904	Full Moon	1972	15.00

FULLER, BOBBY, FOUR

Number	Title (A Side/B Side)	Yr	NM
45s			
CAPITOL			
❑ 3038	The Only God I Know/ A Name Like Watermelon	1971	20.00
DONNA			
❑ 1403	Those Memories of You/ Our Favorite Martian	1965	200.00
—As "Bobby Fuller and the Fantastics"			
EASTWOOD			
❑ 345	Not Fade Away/ Nervous Breakdown	1962	100.00
EXETER			
❑ 122	King of the Beach/ Wine, Wine, Wine	1964	200.00
❑ 124	I Fought the Law/She's My Girl	1964	350.00
❑ 126	Fool of Love/Shakedown	1964	120.00
LIBERTY			
❑ 55812	Let Her Dance/Another Sad and Lonely Night	1965	30.00
LOST-NITE			
❑ 257	I Fought the Law/Little Annie Lou	196?	5.00
—Reissue			
MUSTANG			
❑ 3004	She's My Girl/Take My Hand	1965	25.00
❑ 3006	Let Her Dance/Another Sad and Lonely Night	1965	15.00
❑ 3011	Never to Be Forgotten/ You Kissed Me	1965	25.00
❑ 3012	Let Her Dance/Another Sad and Lonely Night	1965	15.00
❑ 3014	I Fought the Law/Little Annie Lou	1966	15.00
❑ 3016	Love's Made a Fool of You/ Don't Ever Let Me Know	1966	15.00
❑ 3018	Magic Touch/My True Love	1966	12.00
TODD			
❑ 1090	Saturday Night/The Stinger	1963	100.00
YUCCA			
❑ 140	You're in Love/Guess We'll Fall in Love	1961	40.00
—Fast version			
❑ 140	You're in Love/Guess We'll Fall in Love	1961	80.00
—Slow version			
❑ 144	My Heart Jumped/ Gently My Love	1961	80.00
Albums			
MUSTANG			
❑ M-900 [M]	KRLA King of the Wheels	1965	150.00
❑ MS-900 [S]	KRLA King of the Wheels	1965	200.00
❑ M-901 [M]	I Fought the Law	1966	80.00
❑ MS-901 [S]	I Fought the Law	1966	150.00
RHINO			
❑ RNLP-057	The Bobby Fuller Tapes, Vol. 1	1983	10.00
❑ RNDF-201	The Best of the Bobby Fuller Four	1981	12.00
❑ RNLP 70174	The Best of the Bobby Fuller Four (Golden Archive Series)	1987	10.00
VOXX			
❑ VXS 200028	The Bobby Fuller Tapes, Vol. 2	1984	10.00

FULLER, JERRY

Also see THE FLEAS; THE FULLER BROTHERS.

Number	Title (A Side/B Side)	Yr	NM
45s			
ABC			
❑ 12436	Salt on the Wound/No Time	1978	4.00
BELL			
❑ 45233	Rhyme/Thumb Tripping	1972	5.00
❑ 45295	Bookends/(B-side unknown)	1972	5.00
❑ 45349	Lazy Susan/How Do We Stand	1973	5.00
❑ 45433	Arianne/(B-side unknown)	1974	5.00
CHALLENGE			
❑ 9114	Guilty of Loving You/ First Love Never Dies	1961	20.00
❑ 9128	The Place Where I Cry/ Poor Little Heart	1961	20.00
❑ 9132	Wake Up Sleeping Beauty/ Trust Me	1962	20.00
❑ 9148	Too Many People/ Willingly, I'll Let You Go	1962	20.00
❑ 9161	Why Do They Say Goodbye/ Let Me Be with You	1962	20.00
❑ 9184	Give My Love to Christy/ Dear Teresa	1963	20.00
❑ 59052	Betty My Angel/Memories of You	1959	30.00
❑ 59057	Tennessee Waltz/Charlene	1959	20.00
❑ 59068	Two Loves Have I/I Dreamed About My Lover	1960	20.00
❑ 59074	Above and Beyond/One Heart	1960	20.00
—With Diane Maxwell			
❑ 59085	Gone for the Summer/ Anna from Louisiana	1960	20.00
❑ 59104	Shy Away/Heavenly	1961	20.00
❑ 59217	I Only Came to Dance with You/ Young Land	1963	20.00
❑ 59235	Footprints in the Snow/ Hollywood Star	1964	15.00
❑ 59252	Don't Let Go/Roses Love Sunshine	1964	15.00
❑ 59269	The Killer/Mi Amora Mi Vidor	1965	15.00
❑ 59279	I Get Carried Away/Am I That Easy to Forget	1965	30.00
❑ 59307	Don't Look at Me Like That/ What Happened to the Music	1965	15.00
❑ 59315	Man in Black/Master Plan	1965	15.00
❑ 59329	Double Life/Turn to Me	1966	25.00
COLUMBIA			
❑ 4-45131	Could It Be/I Know We Can Make It	1970	8.00
❑ 4-45209	Go/If I Had a Mind To	1970	8.00
LIN			
❑ 5011	Blue Memories/I Found a New Love	1958	30.00
❑ 5012	Do You Love Me/Teenage Love	1958	30.00
❑ 5015	A Certain Smile/ Angel from Above	1958	30.00
❑ 5016	The Door Is Open/ Through Eternity	1958	30.00
❑ 5019	Lipstick and Rouge/Mother Goose at the Bandstand	1959	30.00

Number	Title (A Side/B Side)	Yr	NM
MCA			
❑ 41022	Lines/Over You	1979	4.00
❑ 41114	Don't Do Anything/Don't Tell Me	1979	4.00
Albums			
LIN			
❑ 100 [M]	Teenage Love	1960	250.00
MCA			
❑ 3170	My Turn Now	1979	12.00

FULLER, JOHNNY

Number	Title (A Side/B Side)	Yr	NM
45s			
ALADDIN			
❑ 3278	Johnny Ace's Last Letter/ Fools Paradise	1955	80.00
❑ 3286	Cruel, Cruel World/ My Heart Beats for You	1955	60.00
ART TONE			
❑ 828	No More/The Power	1962	20.00
CHECKER			
❑ 899	You Got Me Whistling/ All Night Long	1958	25.00
FLAIR			
❑ 1054	Buddy/Hard Times	1955	150.00
HOLLYWOOD			
❑ 1043	Train Train Blues/ Bad Luck Overtook Me	1955	80.00
❑ 1057	Mean Old World/How Long	1956	80.00
❑ 1063	Comin' Round the Corner/ Roughest Place in Town	1956	80.00
❑ 1077	My Mama Told Me/Too Late to Change My Mind	1956	80.00
❑ 1084	Sunny Road/I Can't Succeed	1957	80.00
IMPERIAL			
❑ 5580	Heavenly Love/Whispering Wind	1959	20.00
❑ 5697	Miss You/Stop, Look and Listen	1960	20.00
IRMA			
❑ 106	Weeping and Mourning/ Strange Land	1958	80.00
❑ 110	First Stage of the Blues/ No More, No More	1958	80.00
❑ 112	You Got Me Whistling/ All Night Long	1958	60.00
MONEY			
❑ 206	I Walk All Night/ These Young Girls	1955	60.00
SPECIALTY			
❑ 655	Haunted House/ The Mighty Hand	1959	20.00
❑ 671	Swingin' at the Creek/Many Rivers, Mighty Seas	1959	20.00

FULLER BROTHERS, THE Also see JERRY FULLER.

Number	Title (A Side/B Side)	Yr	NM
45s			
CHALLENGE			
❑ 9119	Moon River/Framed, Convicted and Condemned	1961	20.00
❑ 9145	Ballad of the Midnight Special/ The Gallows Tree	1962	20.00

FULSON, LOWELL Also recorded as "Lowell Folsom" and "Lowell Fulsom," both included below.

Number	Title (A Side/B Side)	Yr	NM
45s			
ALADDIN			
❑ 3088	Double Trouble/ Good Woman Blues	1951	150.00
❑ 3104	Night and Day/ Stormin' and Rainin'	1951	100.00
—Black vinyl			
❑ 3104	Night and Day/ Stormin' and Rainin'	1951	1000.
—Green vinyl			
❑ 3217	Don't Leave Me Baby/ Check with the Boys	1954	80.00
❑ 3233	Blues Never Fail/ You've Gotta Reap	1954	80.00
CASH			
❑ 1051	Love Society Blues/ Blue Shadows	1957	40.00
CHECKER			
❑ 804	Reconsider Baby/I Believe I'll Give It Up	1954	40.00
❑ 812	Loving You (Is All I Crave)/ Check Yourself	1955	40.00
❑ 820	Lonely Hours/Do Me Right	1955	30.00
❑ 829	Trouble, Trouble/I Still Love You Baby	1955	30.00
❑ 841	It's Your Fault, Baby/Tollin' Bells	1956	30.00
❑ 854	Blues Rhumba/Please Don't Go	1957	25.00
❑ 865	Don't Drive Me, Baby/ You're Gonna Miss Me	1957	25.00
❑ 882	I Want to Make Love to You/ Rock This Morning	1958	25.00
❑ 937	It Took a Long Time/That's Alright	1960	20.00
❑ 952	Comin' Home/Have You Changed Your Mind	1960	20.00
❑ 959	I'm Glad You Reconsidered/ Blue Shadows	1960	20.00
❑ 972	I Want to Know (Part 1)/ I Want to Know (Part 2)	1961	15.00
❑ 992	So Many Tears/Hung Down Head	1961	15.00
❑ 1027	Shed No Tears/Can She	1962	15.00
❑ 1046	Trouble with the Blues/ Love Grows Cold	1963	15.00
GRANITE			
❑ 533	Do You Love Me/A Step at a Time	1975	5.00
❑ 538	The Old Blues Singer/ Monday Morning Blues	1976	5.00
HOLLYWOOD			
❑ 567-242	The Original Lonesome Christmas Part 1/ The Original Lonesome Christmas Part 2	196?	10.00
❑ 1022	The Original Lonesome Christmas Part 1/ The Original Lonesome Christmas Part 2	1955	20.00
❑ 1029	Everyday I Have the Blues/ Guitar Shuffle	1955	50.00
❑ 1103	Everyday I Have the Blues/ Guitar Shuffle	1962	15.00
JEWEL			
❑ 801	Letter Home/Lady in the Rain	1969	8.00
❑ 802	Why Don't We Do It in the Road/ Too Soon	1969	10.00
❑ 805	How Do You Want Your Man/ Sleeper	1969	8.00
❑ 808	Don't Leave Me/Thug	1970	8.00
❑ 811	Do You Feel It/Don't Destroy Me	1970	8.00
❑ 813	Lonesome Christmas (Part 1)/ Lonesome Christmas (Part 2)	1970	6.00
❑ 818	My Baby/Bluesway	1971	6.00
❑ 820	Teach Me/Man of Motion	1971	6.00
❑ 827	Change of Heart/Every Second a Fool Is Born	1972	6.00
❑ 832	Look at You Baby/Fed Up	1972	6.00
KENT			
❑ 395	Every Time It Rains/ Just One More Time	1964	12.00
❑ 395	Every Time It Rains/ My Heart Belongs to You	1964	12.00
❑ 401	Key to My Heart/ Too Many Drivers	1964	12.00
❑ 410	Strange Feeling/ What's Gonna Be	1965	12.00
❑ 422	No More (Part 1)/No More (Part 2)	1965	12.00
❑ 431	Black Nights/Little Angel	1965	10.00
❑ 440	Sittin' Here Thinkin'/ Shattered Dreams	1966	10.00
❑ 443	Blues Around Midnight/ Talkin' Woman	1966	10.00
❑ 448	Change Your Ways/ My Aching Back	1966	10.00
❑ 452	The Trouble I'm In/ Ask at Any Door in Town	1966	10.00
❑ 456	Tramp/Pico	1966	10.00
❑ 463	Make a Little Love/I'm Sinking	1967	10.00
❑ 463 [PS]	Make a Little Love/I'm Sinking	1967	20.00
❑ 466	Everyday I Have the Blues/ No Hard Feelings	1967	10.00
❑ 471	I Cried/The Thing	1967	10.00
❑ 474	I'm a Drifter/Hobo Meetin'	1967	10.00
❑ 477	I Wanna Spend Christmas with You Part 1/I Wanna Spend Christmas with You Part 2	1967	12.00
❑ 479	Tomorrow/Push Me	1968	10.00
❑ 486	The Letter/Let's Go Get Stoned	1968	10.00
❑ 489	Blues Pain/Mellow Together	1968	10.00
❑ 497	Sweetest Thing/What the Heck	1968	10.00
❑ 505	Lovin' Touch/Price for Love	1969	10.00
❑ 4535	Let's Go Get Stoned/ Funky Broadway	1970	8.00
MOVIN'			
❑ 128	Stop and Think/Baby	1964	12.00
PARROT			
❑ 787	I've Been Mistreated/ Juke Box Shuffle	1953	100.00
—Black vinyl			
❑ 787	I've Been Mistreated/ Juke Box Shuffle	1953	200.00
—Red vinyl			
SWING TIME			
❑ 242	Lonesome Christmas (Part 1)/ Lonesome Christmas (Part 2)	1951	60.00
—78 released in 1950; 45 released in 1951			
❑ 243	I'm a Night Owl (Part 1)/ I'm a Night Owl (Part 2)	1951	100.00
❑ 272	Why Can't You Cry for Me/ Blues with a Feeling	1951	150.00
—This has been confirmed to exist on 45			
❑ 289	Let's Live Right/Best Wishes	1952	50.00
❑ 290	Three O'Clock in the Morning Blues/I'm Wild About You Baby	1952	—
—Unreleased on 45 rpm?			
❑ 295	Guitar Shuffle/Mean Old Lonesome Song	1952	50.00
❑ 308	Black Widow Spider/Midnight Showers of Rain	1953	50.00
❑ 315	Raggedy Daddy Blues/Goodbye	1953	50.00
❑ 320	Ride Until the Sun Goes Down/ Good Party Shuffle	1953	50.00
❑ 325	Upstairs/Let Me Ride Your Automobile	1953	50.00
❑ 330	The Blues Come Rollin' In/ I Love My Baby	1954	50.00
❑ 335	Cash Box Boogie/ My Daily Prayer	1954	50.00
❑ 338	I've Been Mistreated/ Juke Box Shuffle	1954	50.00
Albums			
ARHOOLIE			
❑ R-2003	Early Recordings	1962	30.00
BIG TOWN			
❑ 1008	Lovemaker	1978	12.00
CHESS			
❑ 408	Hung Down Head	197?	15.00
GRANITE			
❑ 1006	Ol' Blues Singer	1976	15.00
JEWEL			
❑ LPS-5003	In a Heavy Bag	1970	15.00
❑ LPS-5009	I've Got the Blues	1973	15.00
KENT			
❑ KST-516 [S]	Lowell Fulsom	1965	40.00
❑ KST-520 [S]	Tramp	1967	40.00
❑ KST-531	Lowell Fulsom Now	1969	30.00
❑ KLP-5016 [M]	Lowell Fulsom	1965	30.00
❑ KLP-5020 [M]	Tramp	1967	30.00
ROUNDER			
❑ 2088	It's a Good Day	198?	12.00

FUN AND GAMES

Number	Title (A Side/B Side)	Yr	NM
45s			
UNI			
❑ 55086	Elephant Candy/The Way She Smiles	1968	12.00
❑ 55098	The Grooviest Girl in the World/ It Must Have Been the Wind	1968	12.00
❑ 55128	Gotta Say Goodbye/We	1969	12.00
Albums			
UNI			
❑ 73042	Elephant Candy	1968	25.00

FUN SONS, THE

Number	Title (A Side/B Side)	Yr	NM
45s			
CAMEO			
❑ 478	Hang Ten/Don't Hold It Against Me	1967	25.00

FUNK INC.

Number	Title (A Side/B Side)	Yr	NM
45s			
PRESTIGE			
❑ 752	Whipper (Part 1)/Whipper (Part 2)	1972	6.00
❑ 754	The Thrill Is Gone/Bowlegs	1973	6.00
❑ 759	Dirty Red (Part 1)/Dirty Red (Part 2)	197?	6.00
❑ 762	Goodbye, So Long/Just Don't Mean a Thing	197?	6.00
Albums			
PRESTIGE			
❑ 10031	Funk Inc.	1971	15.00
❑ 10043	Chicken Lickin'	1972	15.00
❑ 10059	Hangin' Out	1973	15.00
❑ 10071	Superfunk	1973	15.00
❑ 10087	Priced to Sell	1974	15.00

FUNKADELIC Also see GEORGE CLINTON; FUNKADELIC (2); PARLIAMENT; THE PARLIAMENTS.

Number	Title (A Side/B Side)	Yr	NM
12-Inch Singles			
MCA			
❑ L33-17955 [DJ]	By Way of the Drum (Extended Version 9:15) (Acappella 5:50) (Radio Edit 6:00) (Basstrumental 6:10) (Dub 6:55) (Drum Beats 3:59)	1989	10.00
❑ 23953	By Way of the Drum (Extended Version) (Dub) (Basstrumental)	1989	8.00

Except when noted otherwise, VG = 25% of NM, and VG+ = 50% of NM. (Example: VG = $2.00, VG+ = $4.00 and NM = $8.00.)

Number	Title (A Side/B Side)	Yr	NM
WARNER BROS.			
❑ PRO-A- 766 [DJ]	One Nation Under a Groove (11:26) (Instrumental 5:26)	1978	150.00
❑ PRO-A-829 [DJ]	(Not Just) Knee Deep (unknown versions)	1979	100.00
❑ WBSD 8803	One Nation Under a Groove (Part 1) (Part 2)	1979	25.00
45s			
MCA			
❑ 53654	By Way of the Drum/ (Instrumental)	1989	3.00
WARNER BROS.			
❑ 8618	One Nation Under a Groove (Part 1)/One Nation Under a Groove (Part 2)	1978	5.00
❑ 8618 [PS]	One Nation Under a Groove (Part 1)/One Nation Under a Groove (Part 2)	1978	5.00
❑ 8735	Cholly (Funk Getting Ready to Roll)/Into You	1979	5.00
❑ 49040	(Not Just) Knee Deep — Part 1/ (Not Just) Knee Deep — Part 2	1979	5.00
❑ 49117	Uncle Jam (Part 1)/Uncle Jam (Part 2)	1979	5.00
❑ 49667	The Electric Spanking of War Babies/The Electric Spanking of War Babies (Part 2)	1981	4.00
❑ 49667 [PS]	The Electric Spanking of War Babies/The Electric Spanking of War Babies (Part 2)	1981	5.00
❑ 49807	Shockwaves/Bullino's Bounce	1981	4.00
WESTBOUND			
❑ 148	Music for My Mother/ (Instrumental)	1969	10.00
❑ 150	I'll Bet You/Open Your Eyes	1969	10.00
❑ 158	I Got a Thing, You Got a Thing, Everybody's Got a Thing/ Fish, Chips and Sweat	1970	10.00
❑ 167	I Wanna Know If It's Good to You?/I Wanna Know If It's Good to You? (Part 2)	1970	10.00
❑ 175	You and Your Folks, Me and My Folks/Funky Dollar Bill	1971	10.00
❑ 185	Can You Get to That/ Back in Our Minds	1971	10.00
❑ 197	I Miss My Baby/Baby I Owe You Something Good	1972	10.00
—As "U.S. Music with Funkadelic"			
❑ 198	Hit It and Quit It/ A Whole Lot of B.S.	1972	10.00
❑ 205	A Joyful Process/Loose Booty	1972	10.00
❑ 218	Cosmic Slop/If You Don't Like the Effects, Don't Produce the Cause	1973	10.00
❑ 224	Standing on the Verge of Getting It On/Jimmy's Got a Little Bit of Bitch in Him	1974	10.00
❑ 5000	Red Hot Momma/Vital Juices	1975	8.00
❑ 5014	Better by the Pound/ Stuffs and Things	1975	8.00
❑ 5026	Let's Take It to the Stage/ Bilogical Speculation	1976	8.00
❑ 5029	Undisco Kidd/How Do Yeau View You	1976	8.00
Albums			
SCARFACE/PRIORITY			
❑ 53872	One Nation Under a Groove	1993	15.00
—Limited-edition reissue of Warner Bros. 3209			
❑ 53873	Hardcore Jollies	1993	15.00
—Limited-edition reissue of Warner Bros. 2973			
❑ 53874	The Electric Spanking of War Babies	1993	15.00
—Limited-edition reissue of Warner Bros. 3482			
❑ 53875	Uncle Jam Wants You	1993	15.00
—Limited-edition reissue of Warner Bros. 3371			
WARNER BROS.			
❑ BS 2973	Hardcore Jollies	1976	25.00
❑ BS 3209	One Nation Under a Groove	1978	25.00
—Includes bonus 7-inch single with small hole (deduct 20% if missing)			
❑ BSK 3371	Uncle Jam Wants You	1979	25.00
❑ BSK 3482	The Electric Spanking of War Babies	1981	25.00
WESTBOUND			
❑ 208	Standing on the Verge of Getting It On	1975	25.00
—Reissue of Westbound 1001			
❑ 215	Let's Take It to the Stage	1975	50.00
❑ 215	Let's Take It to the Stage	1992	15.00
—Reissue with bar code			
❑ 216	Funkadelic	1975	30.00
—Reissue of Westbound 2000			
❑ 217	Free Your Mind...And Your Ass Will Follow	1975	25.00
—Reissue of Westbound 2001			
❑ 218	Maggot Brain	1975	25.00
—Reissue of Westbound 2007			
❑ 221 [(2)]	America Eats Its Young	1976	25.00
—Reissue of Westbound 2020			
❑ 223	Cosmic Slop	1976	25.00
—Reissue of Westbound 2022			
❑ 227	Tales of Kidd Funkadelic	1976	50.00
❑ 227	Tales of Kidd Funkadelic	1992	15.00
—Reissue with bar code			
❑ 303	Best of the Early Years	197?	40.00
❑ 1001	Standing on the Verge of Getting It On	1974	50.00
❑ 1001	Standing on the Verge of Getting It On	1991	15.00
—Reissue with bar code			
❑ 1004	Funkadelic's Greatest Hits	1975	50.00
❑ 2000	Funkadelic	1970	50.00
❑ 2000	Funkadelic	1990	15.00
—Reissue with bar code			
❑ 2001	Free Your Mind...And Your Ass Will Follow	1970	50.00
❑ 2001	Free Your Mind...And Your Ass Will Follow	1990	15.00
—Reissue with bar code			
❑ 2007	Maggot Brain	1971	50.00
❑ 2007	Maggot Brain	1990	15.00
—Reissue with bar code			
❑ 2020 [(2)]	America Eats Its Young	1972	60.00
❑ 2020 [(2)]	America Eats Its Young	1991	20.00
—Reissue with bar code			
❑ 2022	Cosmic Slop	1973	50.00
❑ 2022	Cosmic Slop	1991	15.00
—Reissue with bar code			

FUNKADELIC (2) Splinter group from the original band, listed separately because GEORGE CLINTON is not involved.

Number	Title (A Side/B Side)	Yr	NM
45s			
LAX			
❑ 70055	Connections and Disconnections/The Witch	1981	4.00
Albums			
LAX			
❑ FW 37087	Connections and Disconnections	1981	10.00

FURAY, RICHIE

Number	Title (A Side/B Side)	Yr	NM
45s			
ASYLUM			
❑ 45351	Still Rolling Stones/Starlight	1976	6.00
❑ 45487	This Magic Moment/ Bittersweet Love	1978	5.00
❑ 45520	Dance a Little Light/Ooh Dreamer	1978	5.00
❑ 46534	I Still Have Dreams/ Headin' South	1979	5.00
❑ 46534 [DJ]	Lonely Too Long (stereo/mono)	1979	8.00
—Promo only; appears to have been the originally planned first single from the "I Still Have Dreams" LP but was changed in favor of the title song			
❑ 46599	Oooh Child/Come On	1980	5.00
Albums			
ASYLUM			
❑ 6E-115	Dance a Little Light	1978	10.00
❑ 6E-231	I Still Have Dreams	1979	10.00
❑ 7E-1067	I've Got a Reason	1976	15.00
MYRRH			
❑ MSB-6672	I've Got a Reason	1981	20.00
—Christian-market reissue of Asylum 7E-1067			
❑ MSB-6695	Seasons of Change	1982	10.00

FURY, BILLY

Number	Title (A Side/B Side)	Yr	NM
45s			
LONDON			
❑ 1857	Maybe Tomorrow/ Gonna Type a Letter	1959	20.00
❑ 1925	Colette/Baby How I Cried	1960	20.00
❑ 1991	Halfway to Paradise/ Cross My Heart	1961	20.00
❑ 2004	Stick Around/Coming Up in the World	1961	20.00
❑ 9515	I'll Never Find Another You/ Don't Jump	1962	15.00
❑ 9548	Once Upon a Dream/ Running Around	1962	15.00
❑ 9594	Because of Love/Like I've Never Loved Before	1963	15.00
❑ 9615	Don't Walk Away/When Will I Say I Love You	1963	15.00
❑ 9662	Hippy Hippy Shake/ Glad All Over	1964	15.00
❑ 9675	I Will/What Am I Living For	1964	15.00
❑ 9740	I'm Lost Without You/ Go Ahead and Ask Her	1965	15.00
MALA			
❑ 569	Loving You/I'll Go Along With It	1967	10.00
❑ 583	Suzanne in the Mirror/ It Just Don't Matter Now	1968	10.00
❑ 595	Beyond the Shadow of a Doubt/ Baby Do You Love Me	1968	10.00
❑ 12018	Silly Boy Blue/One Minute Woman	1968	10.00
PARROT			
❑ 9692	Baby What You Want Me to Do/ It's Only Make Believe	1964	15.00
UNITED ARTISTS			
❑ 968	In Thoughts of You/ Away from You	1966	12.00
❑ 50061	She's So Far Out She's In/ Give Me Your Word	1966	12.00

FURYS, THE (1) Doo-wop/R&B group. These were the only Furys to have a chart hit.

Number	Title (A Side/B Side)	Yr	NM
45s			
EDSEL			
❑ 786	So Tough/I've Got a Pain in My Head (Over You)	1961	60.00
LIBERTY			
❑ 55692	Baby You Can Bet Your Boots/ The Man Who Has Everything	1964	50.00
❑ 55719	If I Didn't Have a Dime/Dream	1964	50.00
MACK IV			
❑ 112	Zing! Went the Strings of My Heart/Never More	1962	30.00
❑ 114	If There's a Next Time/ Another Fella	1963	30.00
❑ 115	I Really Feel So Good/Always	1963	40.00
❑ 118	What Is Soul/I Lost My Baby	1963	40.00
WORLD PACIFIC			
❑ 386	Cat 'n Mouse/Anything for You	1964	30.00

FURYS, THE (2) Rock band, probably from Wisconsin.

Number	Title (A Side/B Side)	Yr	NM
45s			
CUCA			
❑ 1010	This Way Out/St. Louis Blues	1960	30.00
❑ 1097	Run to Him/Jenny	1962	25.00

FURYS, THE (3) Band probably from the Boston, Massachusetts area.

Number	Title (A Side/B Side)	Yr	NM
45s			
FLEETWOOD			
❑ 4569	I Walk Away/Gone in the Night	1966	30.00
LAURIE			
❑ 3382	I Walk Away/Gone in the Night	1967	12.00

FURYS, THE (4) Pacific Northwest band from Springfield, Oregon.

Number	Title (A Side/B Side)	Yr	NM
45s			
LAVENDER			
❑ 1806	Parchman Farm/Beachin'	1962	20.00
❑ 1926	Merryman/Sand Flea	1963	20.00

FURYS, THE (5) Band from Rochester, Minnesota.

Number	Title (A Side/B Side)	Yr	NM
45s			
STUDIO CITY			
❑ 1026	Baby What's Wrong/ Little Queenie	1965	30.00

FURYS, THE (U)

Number	Title (A Side/B Side)	Yr	NM
45s			
AURA			
❑ 395	Cover Girl/Where My Money Goes	196?	50.00
DIAMOND			
❑ 242	That's All Right You're in Love/ You're My Little Baby	1968	12.00

FUSE Early version of CHEAP TRICK. Early version of Cheap Trick.

Number	Title (A Side/B Side)	Yr	NM
45s			
EPIC			
❑ 10514	Cruisin' for Burgers/Hound Dog	1969	25.00
Albums			
EPIC			
❑ BN 26502	Fuse	1970	80.00

FUT, THE Maurice Gibb was in this group, whose single often was bootlegged as a "lost" Beatles track. It has no Beatles involvement whatsoever.

Number	Title (A Side/B Side)	Yr	NM
45s			
BEACON			
❑ 160	Have You Heard the Word/ Futting	1970	10.00
FUT			
❑ 160	Have You Heard the Word/ Futting	1976	5.00

FUTURE, FREDDY

Number	Title (A Side/B Side)	Yr	NM
45s			
PARKWAY			
❑ 832	Don't Forget Me/Like Soiree	1961	12.00

Peter Gabriel, "Sledgehammer," Geffen 7-28718, 1986, **$3.**

Number	Title (A Side/B Side)	Yr	NM
FUTURE, THE			
45s			
UNI			
❑ 55082	The Shape of Things to Come/ 52%	1968	8.00
Albums			
SHAMLEY			
❑ 703	Down the Country Road	1969	20.00
FUTURES, THE			
12-Inch Singles			
PHILADELPHIA INT'L.			
❑ 3665	Party Time Man (6:05)/You Got It (The Love That I Need) (5:38)	1978	100.00
45s			
AMJO			
❑ 3033	Breaking Up/Our Thing	1971	30.00
AVALANCHE			
❑ 36000	Breaking Up/Our Thing	1971	25.00
BUDDAH			
❑ 404	(That's) The Way of a Woman in Love/(B-side unknown)	1974	100.00
❑ 417	No One Could Compare/You Better Be Certain	1974	40.00
❑ 462	Castles/(I Feel the) Ice Breaking	1975	15.00
GAMBLE			
❑ ZS7 2502	Love Is Here/Stay with Me	1972	20.00
PHILADELPHIA INT'L.			
❑ 3119	Silhouettes/We're Gonna Make It Somehow	1980	20.00
❑ ZS8 3661	Party Time Man/You Got It (The Love That I Need)	1978	60.00
❑ ZS8 3674	Ain't No Time Fa Nothin'/ Someone Special (You're the One)	1979	40.00
❑ 3747	In Answer to Your Question/ Let's Dance Together	1980	50.00

Number	Title (A Side/B Side)	Yr	NM
Albums			
BUDDAH			
❑ BDS-5630	Castles in the Sky	1975	100.00
PHILADELPHIA INT'L.			
❑ JZ 35458	Past, Present and the Futures	1979	50.00
❑ JZ 36414	Greetings of Peace	1980	60.00
FUZZ, THE			
45s			
CALLA			
❑ 174	I Love You for All Seasons/I Love You for All Seasons (Part 2)	1970	6.00
❑ 177	Like an Open Door/Leave It All Behind Me	1971	6.00
❑ 179	I'm So Glad/All About Love	1971	6.00
❑ 183	Mr. Heartache and Miss Tears/ Do Just What You Can	1971	6.00
Albums			
CALLA			
❑ SD 2001	The Fuzz	1971	15.00

G

Number	Title (A Side/B Side)	Yr	NM
G-CLEFS, THE			
45s			
LOMA			
❑ 2034	Party '66/Little Lonely Boy	1966	10.00
❑ 2048	I Can't Stand It/Whirlwind	1966	10.00
PARIS			
❑ 502	Symbol of Love/Love Her in the Mornin'	1957	30.00
❑ 506	Zing Zang Zoo/Is This the Way	1957	25.00
PILGRIM			
❑ 715 —*Red label*	Ka-Ding-Dong/Darla My Darlin'	1956	20.00
❑ 715 —*Purple label*	Ka-Ding-Dong/Darla My Darlin'	1956	30.00
❑ 720	'Cause You're Mine/Please Write While I'm Away	1956	30.00
REGINA			
❑ 1314	To the Winner Goes the Prize/ I Believe in All I Feel	1964	30.00
❑ 1319	Angel Listen to Me/ Nobody But Betty	1964	20.00
TERRACE			
❑ 7500	I Understand (Just How You Feel)/Little Girl I Love You	1961	20.00
❑ 7503	Girl Has to Know/Lad (There Never Was a Dog Like You)	1962	20.00
❑ 7507	Make Up Your Mind/ They'll Call Me Away	1962	20.00
❑ 7510	A Lover's Prayer/ Sitting in the Moonlight	1962	25.00
❑ 7514	All My Trials/Big Train	1963	25.00
VEEP			
❑ 1218	I Have/On the Other Side of Town	1965	15.00
❑ 1226	This Time/On the Other Side of Town	1965	15.00
G.T.O.'S, THE (1) Also see JOEY AND THE CONTINENTALS.			
45s			
CLARIDGE			
❑ 312	She Rides with Me/Rudy Vahoo	1966	20.00
—*Reissue of Claridge 304 by "Joey and the Continentals"*			
PARKWAY			
❑ 108	Girl from New York City/ Missing Out on the Fun	1966	15.00
G.T.O.'S, THE (2) Short for "Girls Together Outrageously."			
Albums			
REPRISE			
❑ RS 6390 —*Without booklet*	Permanent Damage	1970	50.00
❑ RS 6390 —*With booklet*	Permanent Damage	1970	70.00
STRAIGHT			
❑ STS-1059 —*Without booklet*	Permanent Damage	1969	80.00
❑ STS-1059 —*With booklet*	Permanent Damage	1969	100.00
GABRIEL, PETER Also see GENESIS.			
12-Inch Singles			
ATLANTIC			
❑ PR 310 [DJ]	Do It Yourself (D.I.Y.) (same on both sides)	1978	25.00
❑ PR 609 [DJ]	Walk Through the Fire (Remix) (same on both sides)	1984	12.00
GEFFEN			
❑ PRO-A-1062 [DJ]	Shock the Monkey/I Have the Touch/Kiss of Life	1982	10.00
❑ PRO-A-2044 [DJ]	I Go Swimming (Live)/No Self Control (Live)/D.I.Y. (Live)/ I Don't Remember (Live)	1984	12.00
❑ PRO-A-2462 [DJ]	Sledgehammer (Edit) (LP Version)	1986	12.00
❑ PRO-A-2527 [DJ]	Red Rain (same on both sides)	1986	12.00
❑ PRO-A-2529 [DJ]	That Voice Again (same on both sides)	1986	12.00
❑ PRO-A-2558 [DJ]	In Your Eyes (2 versions)/Biko	1986	10.00
❑ PRO-A-2625 [DJ]	Big Time (same on both sides)	1986	10.00
❑ PRO-A-2689 [DJ]	Don't Give Up (Edit) (LP Version)	1986	10.00
❑ PRO-A-4488 [DJ]	Steam (4 versions)	1992	15.00
❑ 20456	Sledgehammer (2 remixes)/ Don't Break this Rhythm/ I Have the Touch (Remix)	1986	10.00
❑ 20535	In Your Eyes (2 versions)/Biko	1986	8.00
❑ 20600	Big Time (Dance Mix)/In Your Eyes (Special Mix)/ We Do What We're Told	1986	8.00
❑ 20749	Red Rain/Ga Ga/ Walk Through the Fire	1987	8.00
❑ 20804	Biko (Video Mix)/Biko (Edit)/ No More Apartheid	1987	12.00
❑ 29863	Shock the Monkey (Long) (Short)	1982	12.00
MERCURY			
❑ MK 157 [DJ]	I Don't Remember/ And Through the Wire	1980	30.00

Except when noted otherwise, VG = 25% of NM, and VG+ = 50% of NM. (Example: VG = $2.00, VG+ = $4.00 and NM = $8.00.)

45s

ATCO

Number	Title (A Side/B Side)	Yr	NM
❑ 7079	Solsbury Hill/Moribund the Burgermeister	1977	10.00

ATLANTIC

Number	Title (A Side/B Side)	Yr	NM
❑ 3479	D.I.Y. (Do It Yourself)/Mother of Violence	1978	10.00
❑ 7-89668	Walk Through the Fire/Making a Big Mistake	1984	4.00
❑ 7-89668 [PS]	Walk Through the Fire/Making a Big Mistake	1984	4.00

GEFFEN

Number	Title (A Side/B Side)	Yr	NM
❑ GGEF 0481	Shock the Monkey/Solsbury Hill (Live)	198?	3.00
—Reissue			
❑ PRO-S-2602 [DJ]	In Your Eyes (LP Version) (same on both sides)	1986	10.00
❑ 19136	Digging in the Dirt/Quiet Steam	1992	4.00
❑ 19145	Steam/Games Without Frontiers (DB Mix)	1992	4.00
❑ 28247	Red Rain/I Go Swimming	1987	3.00
❑ 28247 [PS]	Red Rain/I Go Swimming	1987	3.00
❑ 28463	Don't Give Up/Curtains	1987	3.00
—A-side: Peter Gabriel/Kate Bush			
❑ 28463 [PS]	Don't Give Up/Curtains	1987	3.00
❑ 28503	Big Time/We Do What We're Told (milgram's 37)	1986	3.00
❑ 28503 [PS]	Big Time/We Do What We're Told (milgram's 37)	1986	3.00
❑ 28622	In Your Eyes/In Your Eyes (Special Mix)	1986	3.00
❑ 28622 [PS]	In Your Eyes/In Your Eyes (Special Mix)	1986	3.00
❑ 28718	Sledgehammer/Don't Break This Rhythm	1986	3.00
❑ 28718 [PS]	Sledgehammer/Don't Break This Rhythm	1986	3.00
❑ 29542	Solsbury Hill (Live)/I Go Swimming	1983	5.00
❑ 29883	Shock the Monkey/Soft Dog	1982	5.00

MERCURY

Number	Title (A Side/B Side)	Yr	NM
❑ 76063	Games Without Frontiers/Lead a Normal Life	1980	4.00
❑ 76063 [PS]	Games Without Frontiers/Lead a Normal Life	1980	12.00
❑ 76086	I Don't Remember/Shosholoza	1980	15.00
❑ 76086 [DJ]	I Don't Remember (same on both sides)	1980	8.00
—Promos are much more common than stock copies			

WTG

Number	Title (A Side/B Side)	Yr	NM
❑ 68936	In Your Eyes/Skankin' to the Beat	1989	4.00
—B-side by Fishbone			
❑ 68977	In Your Eyes/In Your Eyes (Live Version)	1989	3.00

Albums

ATCO

Number	Title (A Side/B Side)	Yr	NM
❑ SD 36-147	Peter Gabriel	1977	15.00
—(The "Solsbury Hill" album) — Original pressing has yellow labels			
❑ SD 36-147	Peter Gabriel	1980	10.00
—(The "Solsbury Hill" album) — Other than yellow labels			

ATLANTIC

Number	Title (A Side/B Side)	Yr	NM
❑ SD-19181	Peter Gabriel	1978	15.00
—(The "D.I.Y." album)			

DIRECT DISK

Number	Title (A Side/B Side)	Yr	NM
❑ SD-16615	Peter Gabriel	1980	80.00
—The "Solsbury Hill" album; contains a long version of "Slowburn" not available elsewhere			

GEFFEN

Number	Title (A Side/B Side)	Yr	NM
❑ GHS 2011	Peter Gabriel (Security)	1982	10.00
❑ GHS 2011 [DJ]	Peter Gabriel (Security)	1982	15.00
—Promo-only Quiex II audiophile pressing			
❑ GHSP 2035	Peter Gabriel	1983	10.00
—Reissue of Mercury album			
❑ 2GHS 4012 [(2)]	Plays Live	1983	15.00
❑ GHS 24070	Birdy (Soundtrack)	1985	10.00
❑ GHS 24088	So	1986	10.00
❑ GHS 24206	Passion: Music for "The Last Temptation of Christ"	1989	15.00
❑ R 114764	So	1986	12.00
—BMG Direct Marketing edition			
❑ R 153801	Peter Gabriel (Security)	1982	12.00
—RCA Music Service edition			
❑ R 243372 [(2)]	Plays Live	1983	18.00
—RCA Music Service edition			

MERCURY

Number	Title (A Side/B Side)	Yr	NM
❑ SRM-1-3848	Peter Gabriel	1980	12.00
—(The "Games Without Frontiers" album)			

REAL WORLD

Number	Title (A Side/B Side)	Yr	NM
❑ PGDLP-1	Peter Gabriel	2002	25.00
—(The "Solsbury Hill" album) — Classic Records audiophile issue			
❑ PGDLP-2	Peter Gabriel	2002	25.00
—(The "D.I.Y." album) — Classic Records audiophile issue			
❑ PGDLP-3	Peter Gabriel	2003	25.00
—(The "Games Without Frontiers" album) — Classic Records audiophile issue			
❑ PGDLP-4	Peter Gabriel (Security)	2003	25.00
—Classic Records audiophile edition			
❑ PGDLP 5 [(2)]	Plays Live	2004	40.00
—Classic Records audiophile issue			
❑ PGDLP-6	Birdy (Soundtrack)	2004	25.00
—Classic Records reissue on 200-gram vinyl			
❑ PGDLP-7	So	2003	25.00
—Classic Records audiophile edition			
❑ PGDLP-8	Passion: Music for "The Last Temptation of Christ"	2004	30.00
—Classic Records reissue on 200-gram vinyl			
❑ PGDLP-9 [(2)]	Us	2004	40.00
—Classic Records edition on 200-gram vinyl			
❑ PGDLP 11 [(2)]	Up	2002	40.00
—Classic Records audiophile issue; includes bonus 45 in picture sleeve			

GABRIEL AND THE ANGELS

45s

AMY

Number	Title (A Side/B Side)	Yr	NM
❑ 802	Chumba/Hey	1960	20.00
❑ 823	Zing Went the Strings of My Heart/The Rooster	1961	40.00

APRIL

Number	Title (A Side/B Side)	Yr	NM
❑ 1102	Chumba/Hey	1960	50.00

NORMAN

Number	Title (A Side/B Side)	Yr	NM
❑ 506	I'm Gabriel/Ginza	1961	15.00
❑ 510	Gabriel, Blow Your Horn (Part 1)/Gabriel, Blow Your Horn (Part 2)	1961	15.00
❑ 514	Miss You So/See See Rider	1962	15.00
—As "Gabriel and His Trumpet"			

SWAN

Number	Title (A Side/B Side)	Yr	NM
❑ 4118	That's Life (That's Tough)/Don't Wanna Twist No More	1962	12.00
❑ 4118	That's Life/Don't Wanna Twist No More	1962	15.00
—No subtitle on A-side			
❑ 4133	The Peanut Butter Song/All Work and No Play	1963	12.00

GABRIEL BONDAGE

Albums

DHARMA

Number	Title (A Side/B Side)	Yr	NM
❑ D-804	Angel Dust	1975	50.00
❑ D-808	Another Trip to Earth	1977	20.00
—Exists on white, red, or blue vinyl; each of similar value			

GADABOUTS, THE

45s

JARO

Number	Title (A Side/B Side)	Yr	NM
❑ 77022	Caress Me/Deep Are the Roots of a Happy Home	1960	15.00

MERCURY

Number	Title (A Side/B Side)	Yr	NM
❑ 70495	By the Waters of the Minnetonka/Giuseppe Mandolino	1954	25.00
❑ 70581	Go Boom Boom/Oochi Pachi	1955	25.00
❑ 70823	Busy Body Rock/All My Love Belongs to You	1956	25.00
❑ 70898	Stranded in the Jungle/Blues Train	1956	25.00
❑ 70978	Too Much Monkey Business/To Be with You	1956	25.00

WING

Number	Title (A Side/B Side)	Yr	NM
❑ 90008	Two Things I Love/Glass Heart	1955	25.00
❑ 90043	Teenage Rock/If You Only Had a Heart	1955	25.00
❑ 90062	Busy Body Rock/All My Love Belongs to You	1956	20.00

GADDY, BOB

45s

DOT

Number	Title (A Side/B Side)	Yr	NM
❑ 1185	Honey Stealin' Blues/Hold That Train, Conductor	1954	100.00
—As "Doctor Gaddy and His Orchestra"			

HARLEM

Number	Title (A Side/B Side)	Yr	NM
❑ 2330	The Blues Has Walked in My Room/Slow Down Baby	1954	150.00

JAX

Number	Title (A Side/B Side)	Yr	NM
❑ 308	No Help Wanted/Little Girls Boogie	1952	300.00

OLD TOWN

Number	Title (A Side/B Side)	Yr	NM
❑ 1031	I Love My Baby/Operator	1956	25.00
❑ 1039	Paper Lady/Out of My Name	1957	25.00
❑ 1050	Woe, Woe Is Me/Rip and Run	1958	25.00
❑ 1057	You Are the One/Take My Advice	1958	25.00
❑ 1064	What Would I Do/Paper Lady	1959	20.00
❑ 1070	Till the Day I Die/I'll Go My Way	1959	20.00
❑ 1077	Early One Morning/What Wrong Did I Do	1960	20.00
❑ 1085	Don't Tell Her/Could I	1960	20.00
❑ 1162	I Love My Baby/Operator	1964	12.00

GADDY, DOCTOR

See BOB GADDY.

GAILTONES, THE

45s

DECCA

Number	Title (A Side/B Side)	Yr	NM
❑ 30726	Lover Boy/Please Don't Go	1958	40.00

GAINES, PEGGY

45s

HIT

Number	Title (A Side/B Side)	Yr	NM
❑ 17	Playboy/A Steel Guitar and a Glass of Wine	1962	8.00
—B-side by Joe Cash			
❑ 19	Gravy (For My Mashed Potatoes)/Roses Are Red (My Love)	1962	8.00
—B-side by Jimmy Lucas			
❑ 24	The Loco-Motion/Bring It On Home to Me	1962	8.00
—B-side by Herbert Hunter			
❑ 40	Ride!/Bobby's Girl	1962	8.00
—B-side by Connie Landers			
❑ 45	Tell Him/It's Up to You	1962	8.00
—B-side by Bill Carmichael			
❑ 124	Every Little Bit Hurts/What'd I Say	1964	8.00
—B-side by Jerry Poncher			

GAINES, ROY

45s

CHART

Number	Title (A Side/B Side)	Yr	NM
❑ 606	Loud Mouth Lucy/I'm Setting You Free	1955	60.00

DEL-FI

Number	Title (A Side/B Side)	Yr	NM
❑ 4169	What Is This Thing Called Love/Lizzie	1961	15.00

DELUXE

Number	Title (A Side/B Side)	Yr	NM
❑ 6119	Isabella/Gainesville	1957	25.00
❑ 6132	You're Right, I'm Left/Stolen Moments	1957	25.00
❑ 6147	Annabelle/Night Beat	1957	25.00

GROOVE

Number	Title (A Side/B Side)	Yr	NM
❑ 0146	Right Now Baby/De Dat De Dum Dum	1956	30.00
❑ 0161	Worried 'Bout You Baby/All My Life	1956	30.00

RCA VICTOR

Number	Title (A Side/B Side)	Yr	NM
❑ 47-7243	Skippy Is a Sissy/Weeping Willow	1958	60.00

GALAHADS, THE

Albums

LIBERTY

Number	Title (A Side/B Side)	Yr	NM
❑ LRP-3371 [M]	Hello, Galahads	1964	20.00
❑ LST-7371 [S]	Hello, Galahads	1964	25.00

GALAXYS, THE

45s

CARTHAY

Number	Title (A Side/B Side)	Yr	NM
❑ 103	A Lover's Prayer/Jelly Bean	1959	1500.

GALBRAITH, ROB

45s

COLUMBIA

Number	Title (A Side/B Side)	Yr	NM
❑ 4-44997	Willie Was a Honkie/Maggie McGhee, the Preacher's Daughter	1969	8.00
❑ 4-45156	Jezebel of the Morning/Mudflap Cadillac	1970	8.00

RCA

Number	Title (A Side/B Side)	Yr	NM
❑ PB-11051	No Pride/One on One with You	1977	5.00

Albums

COLUMBIA

Number	Title (A Side/B Side)	Yr	NM
❑ CS 1057	Nashville Dirt	1970	20.00

GALE, BARBARA

45s

LLOYDS

Number	Title (A Side/B Side)	Yr	NM
❑ 107	Lonely Weather/So Long, Good-Bye Joe	1953	120.00
❑ 109	Once Again/Fool Fool Me	1953	120.00
❑ 111	When You're Near/Who Walks In	1954	300.00
—With the Larks			
❑ 115	Johnny Darlin'/You're Gonna Lose That Gal	1954	300.00
—With the Larks			

GALE, SUNNY

45s

BLAINE

Number	Title (A Side/B Side)	Yr	NM
❑ 4002	Stay/Once in Every Lifetime	1965	6.00

Number	Title (A Side/B Side)	Yr	NM
❑ 4003	March of the Angels/Let the Rest of the World Go By	1965	6.00
CANADIAN AMERICAN			
❑ 163	Too Bad for You/I'm Telling My Heart	1963	8.00
❑ 171	I Wish I Didn't Love You So/ I'm Not Sorry	1964	8.00
❑ 176	I Really Loved Him So/ I'm Telling My Heart	1964	8.00
DECCA			
❑ 9-30063	One Kiss Led to Another/ Two Hearts	1956	10.00
❑ 9-30125	Hot Dog! That Made Him Mad/ Welcome to My Heart	1956	10.00
❑ 9-30157	I Have You/Maybe You'll Be There	1956	10.00
❑ 9-30231	Come Go with Me/Please Go	1957	10.00
❑ 9-30319	Let's Be Friendly/Mirror	1957	10.00
❑ 9-30391	My Arms Are a House/ Don't Worry 'Bout Me	1957	10.00
❑ 9-30518	A Meeting of the Eyes/ Who Are We to Say?	1957	10.00
❑ 9-30597	For Crying Out Loud/I Don't Want Your Greenback Dollars	1958	10.00
❑ 9-30670	A Certain Smile/Just Friends	1958	10.00
❑ 9-30791	Wheel of Fortune/Three O'Clock	1958	10.00
❑ 9-30837	The Gypsy Told Me So/ Oh What It Seemed to Be	1959	10.00
RCA VICTOR			
❑ 47-4789	I Laughed at Love/Father Time	1952	12.00
❑ 47-4901	Tossin' and Turnin'/You Could Make Me Smile Again	1952	12.00
❑ 47-5103	Teardrops on My Pillow/ A Stolen Waltz	1952	12.00
❑ 47-5216	How Could You/I Feel Like I'm Gonna Live Forever	1953	12.00
❑ 47-5306	Send My Baby Back to Me/ Meanwhile	1953	12.00
❑ 47-5424	Love Me Again/ Before It's Too Late	1953	12.00
❑ 47-5543	The Note in the Bottle/ Mama's Gone Goodbye	1953	40.00
—With the Du Droppers			
❑ 47-5609	Close to Me/Just in Case You Change Your Mind	1954	12.00
❑ 47-5677	Dream, Dream, Dream/ Don't Cry Mama	1954	12.00
❑ 47-5746	Goodnight, Sweetheart, Goodnight/Call Off the Wedding	1954	12.00
❑ 47-5836	Smile/An Old Familiar Love Song	1954	12.00
❑ 47-5952	Let Me Go, Lover!/ Unsuspecting Heart	1954	12.00
❑ 47-6160	Constantly/A Little You	1955	10.00
❑ 47-6227	Soldier Boy/Certainly Baby	1955	10.00
❑ 47-6286	C'est La Vie/Looking Glass	1955	10.00
❑ 47-6398	On the Way to Your Heart/ Devotion	1956	10.00
❑ 47-6479	Rock and Roll Wedding/ Winner Take All	1956	10.00
❑ 47-6588	If You Really Want to Know/Try a Little Prayer	1956	10.00
❑ 47-9580	Our Love Is a Sad Song/ Georgie Porgie	1968	7.00
TERRACE			
❑ 7505	Crying in the Chapel/ Love Me Again	1962	8.00
THIMBLE			
❑ THS 009	Birningham Rag/Sunshine State	1974	6.00
WARWICK			
❑ 526	Falling Star/What Do You Want to Make Those Eyes at Me For	1960	8.00
❑ 540	Church Bells May Ring/ My Foolish Heart	1960	8.00
❑ 578	It's Your Turn/Where Have You Been All My Life	1960	8.00
❑ 626	Please Love Me Forever/Sunny	1961	10.00
❑ 648	Near You/Please Don't Tell Him I Love Him	1961	8.00
Albums			
ROYALE			
❑ 18123 [10]	Sunny Gale and Jazz Orchestra	1954	50.00
THIMBLE			
❑ TLP-10	Sunny Sings Dixieland and Blues	1974	20.00

GALENS, THE

Number	Title (A Side/B Side)	Yr	NM
45s			
CHALLENGE			
❑ 59212	Baby I Do Love You/Love Bells	1963	15.00
❑ 59253	Stranger in Paradise/ Chinese Lanterns	1964	15.00
❑ 59302	Young Dreams/I Love You More Than You Know	1965	15.00

GALES, THE

Number	Title (A Side/B Side)	Yr	NM
45s			
DEBRA			
❑ 1002	Tommy/Around the Clock with You	1963	40.00
J.O.B.			
❑ 3001	Darling Patricia/All Is Well, All Is Well	1956	200.00
JVB			
❑ 34	His Eyes Keep Me in Trouble/ Don't Let the Sun Catch You Cryin'	1955	3000.
—VG 1000; VG+ 2000			
❑ 35	Darling Patricia/All Is Well, All Is Well	1955	500.00
MEL-O			
❑ 111	Guiding Angel/Boy Come Home	1958	250.00
❑ 113	Josephine/If I Could Forget	1958	250.00
WINN			
❑ 916	I Love You/Squeeze Me	1960	500.00

GALLAGHER, BRIAN

Number	Title (A Side/B Side)	Yr	NM
Albums			
CYPRESS			
❑ 0126	Coming Home	1989	12.00

GALLAGHER, JAMES

Number	Title (A Side/B Side)	Yr	NM
45s			
DECCA			
❑ 29984	Crazy Chicken/Just for You	1956	120.00

GALLAGHER, RORY

Also see TASTE.

Number	Title (A Side/B Side)	Yr	NM
Albums			
ATCO			
❑ SD 33-368	Rory Gallagher	1971	15.00
❑ SD 7004	Deuce	1971	15.00
CHRYSALIS			
❑ CHR 1098	Against the Grain	1975	10.00
❑ CHR 1124	Calling Card	1976	10.00
❑ CHR 1170	Photo-Finish	1978	10.00
❑ CHR 1235	Top Priority	1979	10.00
❑ CHR 1280	Stage Struck	1980	10.00
MERCURY			
❑ SRM-1-4051	Jinx	1982	10.00
POLYDOR			
❑ PD-5513	Rory Gallagher/Live!	1972	12.00
❑ PD-5522	Blueprint	1973	12.00
❑ PD-5539	Tattoo	1973	12.00
❑ PD-1-6510	Sinner...And Saint	1975	12.00
❑ PD-1-6519	The Story So Far	1975	12.00
❑ PD-9501 [(2)]	Irish Tour '74	1974	12.00
SPRINGBOARD			
❑ SPB-4056	Take It Easy Baby	1976	10.00

GALLAHADS, THE (1)

Number	Title (A Side/B Side)	Yr	NM
45s			
CAPITOL			
❑ F-3060	Ooh Ah/Careless	1955	25.00
❑ F-3175	Do You Believe Me/ If It Wasn't for You	1955	25.00
JUBILEE			
❑ 5252	The Fool/The Morning Mail	1956	30.00
❑ 5259	Take My Love/I Give You My Word	1956	25.00

GALLAHADS, THE (2)

Number	Title (A Side/B Side)	Yr	NM
45s			
DEL-FI			
❑ 4137	Lonely Guy/Jo Jo the Big Wheel	1960	20.00
—Black label			
❑ 4137	Lonely Guy/Jo Jo the Big Wheel	1960	40.00
—Green label			
❑ 4148	Be Fair/I'm Without a Girl Friend	1960	20.00
—Black label			
❑ 4148	Be Fair/I'm Without a Girl Friend	1960	40.00
—Green label			
DONNA			
❑ 1322	Lonely Guy/Jo Jo the Big Wheel	1960	40.00
❑ 1361	This Letter to You/The Answer to Love	1962	50.00
LOST-NITE			
❑ 205	Be Fair/I'm Without a Girl Friend	196?	5.00
—Reissue			

GALLAHADS, THE (U)

It's unlikely any of these are group (1). Some of these are probably group (2). Others could be by different groups.

Number	Title (A Side/B Side)	Yr	NM
45s			
BEECHWOOD			
❑ 3001	Keeper of Dreams/Sad Girl	1960	120.00
—More than one group.			
NITE OWL			
❑ 20	Gone/So Long	1961	60.00
RENDEZVOUS			
❑ 153	Gone/Why Do Fools Fall in Love	1961	40.00
SEA CREST			
❑ 6005	Have Love, Will Travel/ My Offering	1964	40.00
STARLA			
❑ 15	Keeper of Dreams/Sad Girl	1960	20.00

GALLANT, RONNIE

Number	Title (A Side/B Side)	Yr	NM
45s			
ATLANTIC			
❑ 2169	Shake Shake Baby/Shadows	1962	12.00
WARNER BROS.			
❑ 5251	Hole in the Wall/In the Night	1962	12.00

GALLERY

Number	Title (A Side/B Side)	Yr	NM
45s			
SUSSEX			
❑ 232	Nice to Be with You/Ginger Haired Man	1972	5.00
❑ 239	I Believe in Music/Someone	1972	5.00
❑ 239 [PS]	I Believe in Music/Someone	1972	8.00
❑ 248	Big City Miss Ruth Ann/ Lover's Hideaway	1972	5.00
❑ 255	Rest in Peace/Riverboat Captain	1973	5.00
❑ 259	Maybe Baby/Lady Luck	1973	5.00
❑ 512	Friends/I Love Every Little Thing About You	1974	4.00
❑ 630	Living Next Door to Alice/ Captain Sam	1975	4.00
❑ 639	Power to All Our Friends/ (B-side unknown)	1975	4.00
Albums			
SUSSEX			
❑ SUX-7017	Nice to Be with You	1972	12.00
❑ SUX-7026	Jim Gold and Gallery	1973	12.00

GALLERY (2)

Number	Title (A Side/B Side)	Yr	NM
Albums			
ECM			
❑ 1206	Gallery	1982	12.00

GALLICOS, THE

Number	Title (A Side/B Side)	Yr	NM
45s			
HIT			
❑ 260	Hungry/Hanky Panky	1966	10.00
—B-side by the McCalls			

GALLOP, FRANK

Number	Title (A Side/B Side)	Yr	NM
45s			
ABC-PARAMOUNT			
❑ 9931	Got a Match?/I Beg Your Pardon	1958	12.00
KAPP			
❑ 745	The Ballad of Irving/Would You Believe It	1966	10.00
—B-side by Phil Leeds			
MUSICOR			
❑ 1191	Son of Irving/One Love I'll Never Forget	1966	8.00
❑ 1191 [PS]	Son of Irving/One Love I'll Never Forget	1966	12.00
Albums			
MUSICOR			
❑ MM-2110 [M]	Frank Gallop Sings	1966	15.00
❑ MS-3110 [S]	Frank Gallop Sings	1966	20.00

GAMBLE, DEE DEE SHARP

See DEE DEE SHARP.

GAMBLE, KENNY

Number	Title (A Side/B Side)	Yr	NM
45s			
ARCTIC			
❑ 107	Down by the Seashore (Part 1)/ Down by the Seashore (Part 2)	1965	50.00
❑ 114	Ain't It Baby (Part 1)/ Ain't It Baby (Part 2)	1965	150.00
❑ 123	The Joke's on You/ Don't Stop Loving Me	1966	40.00
—Styrene			
❑ 123	The Joke's on You/ Don't Stop Loving Me	1966	1500.
—Vinyl			

Except when noted otherwise, VG = 25% of NM, and VG+ = 50% of NM. (Example: VG = $2.00, VG+ = $4.00 and NM = $8.00.)

Number	Title (A Side/B Side)	Yr	NM
COLUMBIA			
❑ 43132	Our Love/You Don't Know What You Got Until You Lose It	1964	75.00
EPIC			
❑ 9636	Standing in the Shadows/ No Mail on Monday	1963	300.00

GAMBLERS, THE (1)
BRUCE JOHNSTON and SANDY NELSON were in this group.

45s

Number	Title (A Side/B Side)	Yr	NM
LAST CHANCE			
❑ 2	Teen Machine/Tonky	1961	40.00
❑ 108	Teen Machine/Tonky	1962	25.00
WORLD PACIFIC			
❑ 815	Moon Dawg/LSD-25	1960	60.00

GAMBLERS, THE (2)
British group.

45s

Number	Title (A Side/B Side)	Yr	NM
CORAL			
❑ 62525	Cry Me a River/Who Will Buy	1967	8.00
PRESS			
❑ 9739	Now I'm All Alone/Find Out What's Happening	1965	12.00

GAME

45s

Number	Title (A Side/B Side)	Yr	NM
EVOLUTION			
❑ 1042	Fat Mama/The Girl Next Door	1970	6.00
❑ 1053	Two Songs for the Senorita/ (B-side unknown)	1971	6.00

Albums

Number	Title (A Side/B Side)	Yr	NM
EVOLUTION			
❑ 2021	Game	1970	12.00
❑ 3008	Long Hot Summer	1971	12.00
FAITHFUL VIRTUE			
❑ 2003	Game	1969	20.00

GAMMA
Also see MONTROSE; ROBIN TROWER.

Albums

Number	Title (A Side/B Side)	Yr	NM
ELEKTRA			
❑ E 219	1	1979	14.00
❑ E 288	2	1980	14.00
❑ E 160034	3	1982	10.00

GAMMA GOOCHEE

45s

Number	Title (A Side/B Side)	Yr	NM
COLPIX			
❑ 786	I'm Gonna Buy Me a Dog/(You Got the) Gamma Goochee	1965	40.00
❑ 804	I'm So Glad/Sweet Violets	1966	40.00
MGM			
❑ 13874	Booga-Loo/Everybody's Somebody's Fool	1967	30.00

GANDALF

45s

Number	Title (A Side/B Side)	Yr	NM
CAPITOL			
❑ 2400	Golden Earrings/Never Too Far	1969	25.00

Albums

Number	Title (A Side/B Side)	Yr	NM
CAPITOL			
❑ ST-121	Gandalf	1969	240.00

GANDALF THE GREY

Albums

Number	Title (A Side/B Side)	Yr	NM
G.W.R.			
❑ 7	The Grey Wizard Am I	1972	675.00

GANEY, JERRY

45s

Number	Title (A Side/B Side)	Yr	NM
MGM			
❑ 13697	Hi-Heel Sneakers/ You Don't Love Me	1967	200.00
VERVE			
❑ 10454	Who Am I/Just a Fool	1966	200.00

GANG OF FOUR

12-Inch Singles

Number	Title (A Side/B Side)	Yr	NM
POLYDOR			
❑ 922 [DJ]	Cadillac (2 versions)/Favourites	1991	8.00
❑ 925 [DJ]	Don't Fix What Ain't Broke (same on both sides)	1991	8.00
WARNER BROS.			
❑ PRO-A-1050 [DJ]	I Love a Man in a Uniform (2 versions)/Call Me Up	1982	7.00
❑ PRO-A-2081 [DJ]	Is It Love (Long Mix)/Is It Love (Short)/Man with a Good Car	1983	7.00
❑ 20174	Is It Love (Remix)/(Instrumental)	1983	6.00
❑ 29907	I Love a Man in a Uniform (Remix)/I Love a Man in a Uniform (Dub)	1982	8.00

45s

Number	Title (A Side/B Side)	Yr	NM
WARNER BROS.			
❑ 29449	Is It Love/Arabic	1983	4.00
❑ 29921	I Love a Man in a Uniform/ I Will Be a Good Boy	1982	4.00

Albums

Number	Title (A Side/B Side)	Yr	NM
WARNER BROS.			
❑ BSK 3446	Entertainment!	1980	14.00
❑ BSK 3494	Gang of Four	1980	10.00
❑ BSK 3565	Solid Gold	1981	10.00
❑ MINI 3646 [EP]	Another Day, Another Dollar	1982	8.00
❑ 23683	Songs of the Free	1982	10.00
❑ 23936	Hard	1983	10.00

GANT, CECIL

45s

Number	Title (A Side/B Side)	Yr	NM
DECCA			
❑ 9-30320	I Wonder/Cecil's Boogie	1957	30.00
❑ 9-48167	Goodnight Irene/My House Fell Down	1950	50.00
—As "Gunter Lee Carr"			
❑ 9-48170	We're Gonna Rock/Yesterday	1950	50.00
—As "Gunter Lee Carr"			
❑ 9-48171	Someday You'll Be Sorry (Part 1)/ Someday You'll Be Sorry (Part 2)	1950	40.00
❑ 9-48185	It's Christmas Time Again/ Hello Santa Claus	1950	40.00
❑ 9-48191	Train Time Blues No. 2/ It Ain't Gonna Be Like That	1951	40.00
❑ 9-48200	Shot Gun Boogie/ Rock Little Baby	1951	50.00
❑ 9-48212	Don't You Worry/My Little Baby	1951	40.00
❑ 9-48231	Owl Stew/Playin' Myself the Blues	1951	40.00
❑ 9-48249	God Bless My Daddy/The Grass Is Gettin' Greener	1951	40.00
DOT			
❑ 1112	All By Myself/It Hurts Me Too	1952	40.00
—Earlier singles on Dot may not exist on 45s			
❑ 1121	Sloppy Joes/Train Time Blues	1952	40.00
GILT EDGE			
❑ 5090	I Wonder/Cecil's Boogie	1955	40.00
—Reissue of 78 first released in 1944			

Albums

Number	Title (A Side/B Side)	Yr	NM
KING			
❑ 671 [M]	Cecil Gant	1960	80.00
RED MILL			
❑ (no #) [M]	Cecil Gant	1956	500.00
—Red vinyl			
SOUND			
❑ 601 [M]	The Incomparable Cecil Gant	1958	100.00

GANTS, THE

45s

Number	Title (A Side/B Side)	Yr	NM
ALADDIN			
❑ 3387	My Unfaithful Love/ Happening After School	1957	60.00
LIBERTY			
❑ 55829	Road Runner/ My Baby Don't Care	1965	15.00
❑ 55853	Smoke Rings/Little Boy Sad	1966	10.00
❑ 55884	Dr. Feelgood/Crackin' Up	1966	10.00
❑ 55903	I Want Your Lovin'/ A Spoonful of Sugar	1966	10.00
❑ 55940	Greener Days/I Wonder	1967	10.00
❑ 55965	Drifter's Sunrise/ Just a Good Show	1967	10.00
STATUE			
❑ 605	Road Runner/ My Baby Don't Care	1965	50.00
❑ 608	What's Happening/ Careless Hands	1965	25.00
—B-side by the Niteliters			

Albums

Number	Title (A Side/B Side)	Yr	NM
LIBERTY			
❑ LRP-3432 [M]	Road Runner	1965	30.00
❑ LRP-3455 [M]	The Gants Galore	1966	30.00
❑ LRP-3473 [M]	The Gants Again	1966	30.00
❑ LST-7432 [S]	Road Runner	1965	40.00
❑ LST-7455 [S]	The Gants Galore	1966	40.00
❑ LST-7473 [S]	The Gants Again	1966	40.00

GAP BAND, THE

12-Inch Singles

Number	Title (A Side/B Side)	Yr	NM
ARISTA			
❑ AD1-9777	I'm Gonna Git Ya Sucka (Extended Version 6:13) (Sugar Shack Version 6:00)/ (Single Version 3:34) (Extended Edit 3:58) (Tripped Out Dub Version 6:00)	1988	7.00
CAPITOL			
❑ V-15493	All of My Love (Extended Mix) (Instrumental) (Just Coolin' Mix) (Radio Mix) (Percussapella) (Bonus Beats)	1989	7.00
❑ V-15534	Addicted to Your Love (Extended Mix) (Instrumental) (Silly Stoopid Crazy Over You Mix)/ (I'll Groove 4 U Remix) (I'll Groove 4 U Rap) (I'll Groove 4 U Instrumental)	1990	8.00
MERCURY			
❑ MK 86 [DJ]	Baby Baba Boogie (7:32)/Shake	1979	12.00
❑ MK 124 [DJ]	Steppin' (Out) (same on both sides)	1979	8.00
❑ MK 138 [DJ]	Party Lights (2 versions)	1980	12.00
❑ MK 175 [DJ]	Yearning for Your Love/Humpin'	1980	8.00
❑ MDS 4006	Shake/Baby Baba Boogie	1979	10.00
❑ 884662-1	You Dropped a Bomb on Me/ Party Train	1986	12.00
—Reissue in conjunction with 'The 12" Collection' LP			
PASSPORT			
❑ PB-4005	Not Guilty/Knucklehead Funkin'/ Listen to the Music	1983	8.00
RAGING BULL			
❑ RB 5023	Got It Goin' On (Extended BATT Edit) (Radio Edit)	1995	8.00
❑ RB 8013	First Lover (4 versions)	1995	8.00
TOTAL EXPERIENCE			
❑ TK 214 [DJ]	You Dropped a Bomb on Me (Long Version 13:05) (LP Version 5:12)	1982	12.00
❑ TED-701	Early in the Morning (Short Version 6:30) (Long Version 7:33)	1982	8.00
❑ TED-702	You Dropped a Bomb on Me (13:05)/Humpin' (5:06)	1982	15.00
❑ TED-704	Outstanding (unknown versions)	1982	8.00
❑ TED-706	Party Train (5:55) (6:10)	1983	10.00
❑ TED-707	I'm Ready (If You're Ready) (5:51)/Shake a Leg	1983	7.00
❑ TED 1003	Straight from the Heart (Cardiac Mix) (Radio Mix) (Pump the Heart Dub Mix) (Thump Thump Instrumental)	1988	6.00
❑ TED 1005	All the Way Yours (unknown versions)	1988	6.00
❑ TED1-2606	Beep a Freak (Short Version, To Be LP Mix 5:10) (Dance Mix 7:47) (Instrumental)	1984	8.00
❑ TED1-2615	Disrespect (Extended LP Version with Breakdown) (LP Version) (Club Mix)	1985	8.00
❑ TED1-2624	Desire (Special Remix) (LP Version) (Dub Version)	1985	8.00
❑ TED1-2632	Going in Circles (4:31)/ I Believe (4:28)	1985	7.00
❑ TED1-2636	Automatic Brain (Main Radio and Club Mix Vocal 7:40) (Acapella 5:10) (Dub Version 5:55) (Rap Version)	1986	8.00
❑ 2701-1-TD	Big Fun (Radio Mix) (Serious Dub Mix) (Acapella Mix) (Mega Mix) (Bandolero Mix)	1986	7.00
❑ 2705-1-TD	Zibble, Zibble (Get the Money) (aka: Get Loose Get Funky) (Album Mix 5:27) (Radio Short Mix 4:04) (Dub-Zibble Money Mix 5:37)	1986	8.00

45s

Number	Title (A Side/B Side)	Yr	NM
A&M			
❑ 1788	Hard Time Charlie/This Place Called Heaven	1976	5.00
ARISTA			
❑ 9788	I'm Gonna Git Ya Sucka/ Clean Up Your Act	1988	3.00
—B-side by Jermaine Jackson			
❑ 9788 [PS]	I'm Gonna Git Ya Sucka/ Clean Up Your Act	1988	3.00
CAPITOL			
❑ B-44418	All of My Love (7" Version)/ (Radio Mix)	1989	4.00
❑ 7PRO-79045 [DJ]	We Can Make It Alright (same on both sides)	1990	6.00
—Vinyl is promo only			
COLLECTABLES			
❑ 4391	Early in the Morning/ Open Your Mind (Wide)	199?	3.00
❑ 4478	Steppin' (Out)/Shake	199?	3.00
MEGA			
❑ 4005	Not Guilty/(B-side unknown)	1984	5.00
MERCURY			
❑ DJ-568 [DJ]	The Boys Are Back in Town (stereo/mono?)	1980	8.00

Number	Title (A Side/B Side)	Yr	NM
❑ 74053	Shake/Got to Get Away	1979	4.00
❑ 74080	Open Up Your Mind (Wide)/ I Can Sing	1979	4.00
❑ 76021	Steppin' (Out)/You Are My High	1979	4.00
❑ 76037	I Don't Believe You Want to Get Up and Dance (Oops, Up Side Your Head)/Who Do You Call	1980	4.00
❑ 76062	Party Lights/The Boys Are Back in Town	1980	4.00
❑ 76091	Burn Rubber (Why You Wanna Hurt Me)/Nothin' Comes to a Sleeper	1980	4.00
❑ 76101	Yearning for Your Love/ When I Look in Your Eyes	1981	4.00
❑ 76114	Humpin'/No Hiding Place	1981	4.00
❑ 811357-7	Burn Rubber/Yearning for Your Love	1983	3.00
—Reissue			
❑ 884662-7	You Dropped a Bomb on Me/ Party Train	1986	5.00
—Reissue in conjunction with 'The 12" Collection' LP			

RCA

Number	Title (A Side/B Side)	Yr	NM
❑ 5035-7-R	Sweeter Than Candy (Penitentiary III)/(Instrumental)	1986	4.00

SHELTER

Number	Title (A Side/B Side)	Yr	NM
❑ 40228	Backbone/Loving You Is Everything	1974	6.00
❑ 40295	I-Yike-It/Tommy's Groove	1974	6.00

TATTOO

Number	Title (A Side/B Side)	Yr	NM
❑ TB-10884	Out of the Blue (Can You Feel It)/Silly Grin	1977	5.00
❑ TB-10990	Little Bit of Love/ Knucklehead Sunckin'	1977	5.00

TOTAL EXPERIENCE

Number	Title (A Side/B Side)	Yr	NM
❑ 101	Straight from the Heart/(Dub Mix)	1988	3.00
❑ 101 [PS]	Straight from the Heart/(Dub Mix)	1988	4.00
❑ 2405	Beep a Freak/(Dub Version)	1984	3.00
❑ 2405 [PS]	Beep a Freak/(Dub Version)	1984	4.00
❑ 2412	I Found My Baby/(Instrumental)	1985	3.00
❑ 2418	Disrespect/(Instrumental)	1985	3.00
❑ 2427	Desire/(Album Version)	1985	3.00
❑ 2428	Automatic Brain/(Instrumental)	1986	4.00
❑ 2435	The Christmas Song (Chestnuts Roasting on an Open Fire)/ Joy to the World	1985	5.00
—B-side by Oliver Scott			
❑ 2436	Going in Circles/I Believe	1986	3.00
❑ 2436 [DJ]	Going in Circles (Remix 3:59)/ (Remix Instrumental with Harmonica 5:15)	1986	6.00
❑ 2440	Automatic Brain/(With Rap)	1986	3.00
❑ 2700	Big Fun/(Ooh Ah Dub)	1986	3.00
❑ 2703	Zibble, Zibble (Get the Money) (aka: Get Loose, Get Funky)/ (Instrumental)	1987	3.00
❑ 8201	Early in the Morning/I'm in Love	1982	4.00
❑ 8201 [PS]	Early in the Morning/I'm in Love	1982	5.00
❑ 8203	You Dropped a Bomb on Me/ Lonely Like Me	1982	4.00
❑ 8205	Outstanding/The Blues Are Back in Town	1982	4.00
❑ 8209	Party Train/The Special Party Train Dance Mix	1983	4.00
❑ 8210	Jam the Motha' (Party Mix)/ (Munchkin People)	1983	4.00
❑ 8211	I'm Ready (If You're Ready)/ Shake a Leg	1984	4.00

Albums

CAPITOL

Number	Title	Yr	NM
❑ C1-90799	Round Trip	1989	10.00

MERCURY

Number	Title	Yr	NM
❑ SRM-1-3758	The Gap Band	1979	10.00
❑ SRM-1-3804	The Gap Band II	1979	10.00
❑ SRM-1-4003	The Gap Band III	1980	10.00
❑ 822788-1	The Gap Band III	198?	8.00
—Reissue			
❑ 826808-1	The 12" Collection	1986	8.00

PASSPORT

Number	Title	Yr	NM
❑ PB-6026	Strike a Groove	1983	10.00

SHELTER

Number	Title	Yr	NM
❑ 2111	Magicians' Holiday	1974	15.00

TATTOO

Number	Title	Yr	NM
❑ BJL1-2168	The Gap Band	1977	15.00

TOTAL EXPERIENCE

Number	Title	Yr	NM
❑ 2700-1-T	Gap Band 8	1986	8.00
❑ 2710-1-T	Straight from the Heart	1987	8.00
❑ TE-1-3001	Gap Band IV	1982	8.00
❑ TE-1-3004	Gap Band V — Jammin'	1983	8.00
❑ TEL8-5705	Gap Band VI	1984	8.00
❑ TEL8-5714	Gap Band VII	1986	8.00
❑ 812186-1	Gap Band V — Jammin'	198?	6.00
—Reissue			
❑ 822794-1	Gap Band IV	198?	6.00
—Reissue			

Number	Title (A Side/B Side)	Yr	NM
❑ 824343-1	Gap Gold/Best of the Gap Band	1985	8.00

GARAGIOLA, JOE

Albums

UNITED ARTISTS

Number	Title	Yr	NM
❑ UAL-3032 [M]	That Holler Guy!	1959	40.00
❑ UAS-6032 [S]	That Holler Guy!	1959	50.00

GARCIA, JERRY

Also see THE GRATEFUL DEAD; NEW RIDERS OF THE PURPLE SAGE; OLD & IN THE WAY.

45s

ROUND

Number	Title (A Side/B Side)	Yr	NM
❑ 4504	Let It Rock/Midnight Town	1974	9.00

WARNER BROS.

Number	Title (A Side/B Side)	Yr	NM
❑ PRO 514 [DJ]	Deal/The Wheel	1972	15.00
—White label, small hole, plays at 33 1/3 rpm			
❑ PRO 514 [PS]	Deal/The Wheel	1972	30.00
—Title sleeve with the above promo			
❑ 7551	Deal/The Wheel	1972	9.00
❑ 7569	Deep Hour/Sugaree	1972	9.00

Albums

ARISTA

Number	Title	Yr	NM
❑ AB 4160	Cats Under the Stars	1978	16.00
❑ AL 8364	Run for the Roses	198?	8.00
—Reissue of 9603			
❑ AL 9603	Run for the Roses	1982	12.00

ROUND

Number	Title	Yr	NM
❑ RX-102	Garcia	1974	25.00
❑ RX-107	Reflections	1975	30.00
❑ RN-LA565-G	Reflections	1976	20.00
—Reissue of Round 107 with United Artists distribution			

WARNER BROS.

Number	Title	Yr	NM
❑ BS 2582	Garcia	1972	40.00
—Green label with "WB" logo			

GARDENIAS, THE (1)

45s

FEDERAL

Number	Title (A Side/B Side)	Yr	NM
❑ 12284	Flaming Love/My Baby's Tops	1956	120.00

GARDENIAS, THE (2)

45s

FAIRLANE

Number	Title (A Side/B Side)	Yr	NM
❑ 21019	Darling It's You, You, You/ What's the Matter with Me	1962	25.00

GARDNER, BROTHER DAVE

Includes records as "Dave Gardner."

45s

DECCA

Number	Title (A Side/B Side)	Yr	NM
❑ 30548	Hop Along Rock/All By Myself	1958	20.00
❑ 30627	Slick Slacks/Wild Streak	1958	40.00

OJ

Number	Title (A Side/B Side)	Yr	NM
❑ 1002	White Silver Sands/Fat Charlie	1957	15.00
❑ 1006	Love Is My Business/Mad Witch	1958	15.00

RCA VICTOR

Number	Title (A Side/B Side)	Yr	NM
❑ 47-7876	Coward at the Alamo/ You Are My Love	1961	10.00

Albums

CAPITOL

Number	Title	Yr	NM
❑ ST 1867 [S]	It Don't Make No Difference	1963	25.00
❑ T 1867 [M]	It Don't Make No Difference	1963	20.00
❑ ST 2055 [S]	It's All in How You Look at It	1964	25.00
❑ T 2055 [M]	It's All in How You Look at It	1964	20.00

4 STAR

Number	Title	Yr	NM
❑ 4S 75003	Brother Dave Gardner's New Comedy Album	1976	20.00

RCA VICTOR

Number	Title	Yr	NM
❑ LPM-2083 [M]	Rejoice, Dear Hearts!	1960	20.00
❑ LSP-2083(e) [S]	Rejoice, Dear Hearts!	196?	25.00
❑ LPM-2239 [M]	Kick Thy Own Self	1960	20.00
❑ LSP-2239(e) [S]	Kick Thy Own Self	196?	25.00
❑ LPM-2335 [M]	Ain't That Weird?	1961	20.00
❑ LSP-2335 [S]	Ain't That Weird?	1961	25.00
❑ LPM-2498 [M]	Did You Ever?	1962	20.00
❑ LSP-2498 [S]	Did You Ever?	1962	25.00
❑ LPM-2628 [M]	All Seriousness Aside	1963	20.00
❑ LSP-2628 [S]	All Seriousness Aside	1963	25.00
❑ LPM-2761 [M]	It's Bigger Than Both of Us	1963	20.00
❑ LSP-2761 [S]	It's Bigger Than Both of Us	1963	25.00
❑ LPM-2852 [M]	Best of Dave Gardner	1964	20.00
❑ LSP-2852 [S]	Best of Dave Gardner	1964	25.00

TONKA

Number	Title	Yr	NM
❑ TLP 713	Out Front	1969	20.00

TOWER

Number	Title	Yr	NM
❑ ST 5050 [S]	Hip-ocracy	1966	20.00
❑ T 5050 [M]	Hip-ocracy	1966	15.00
❑ ST 5075 [S]	It Don't Make No Difference	1967	20.00
❑ T 5075 [M]	It Don't Make No Difference	1967	15.00

GARDNER, DON

Also see DON GARDNER AND DEE DEE FORD.

45s

BRUCE

Number	Title (A Side/B Side)	Yr	NM
❑ 105	How Do You Speak to an Angel/ Sonotone Bounce	1954	60.00
❑ 108	I'll Walk Alone/Going Down Mary	1954	50.00
❑ 127	It's a Sin to Tell a Lie/ I Hear a Rhapsody	1955	50.00

CAMEO

Number	Title (A Side/B Side)	Yr	NM
❑ 102	Love Only Brings Happiness/ Sneakin' In	1957	40.00

DELUXE

Number	Title (A Side/B Side)	Yr	NM
❑ 6133	This Nearly Was Mine/ A Dagger in My Chest	1957	25.00
❑ 6155	There! I've Said It Again/ I Don't Want to Go Home	1958	25.00

JUBILEE

Number	Title (A Side/B Side)	Yr	NM
❑ 5482	I Really Love You Baby/ Talking About You	1964	20.00
❑ 5484	The Bitter with the Sweet/I Don't Know What I'm Gonna Do	1964	25.00
❑ 5493	Little Girl Blue/I'm In Such Misery	1964	20.00

JUNIOR

Number	Title (A Side/B Side)	Yr	NM
❑ 393	High School Baby/ Crying All Alone	1957	40.00
❑ 394	Dark Alley/Up the Street	1957	30.00

KAISER

Number	Title (A Side/B Side)	Yr	NM
❑ 399	Ask Anything/Humility	1958	25.00
❑ 402	At Last/The Hump	1959	25.00

MR. G

Number	Title (A Side/B Side)	Yr	NM
❑ 824	Your Love Is Driving Me Crazy/ There Ain't Gonna Be No Loving	1969	75.00

SEDGRICK

Number	Title (A Side/B Side)	Yr	NM
❑ 3001	Cheatin' Kind/(B-side unknown)	196?	10000.
—VG 2000; VG+ 3000			

VERVE

Number	Title (A Side/B Side)	Yr	NM
❑ 10582	You Babe/I'm a Practical Guy	1967	15.00

GARDNER, DON, AND DEE DEE FORD

Also see each artist's individual listings.

45s

FIRE

Number	Title (A Side/B Side)	Yr	NM
❑ 508	I Need Your Loving/Tell Me	1962	15.00
—Multicolor label			
❑ 508	I Need Your Loving/Tell Me	1962	20.00
—Red label			
❑ 513	Don't You Worry/I'm Coming Home to Stay	1962	15.00
❑ 517	Lead Me On/TCB (Taking Care of Business)	1962	15.00

KC

Number	Title (A Side/B Side)	Yr	NM
❑ 196	Glory of Love/'Deed I Do	1963	12.00

LOST-NITE

Number	Title (A Side/B Side)	Yr	NM
❑ 384	I Need Your Loving/Tell Me	197?	5.00
—Reissue			

LUDIX

Number	Title (A Side/B Side)	Yr	NM
❑ 104	You Upset My Soul/Son My Son	1963	12.00

Albums

COLLECTABLES

Number	Title	Yr	NM
❑ COL-5155	Golden Classics: Need Your Lovin'	198?	12.00

FIRE

Number	Title	Yr	NM
❑ LP-105 [M]	Need Your Lovin'	1962	400.00

SUE

Number	Title	Yr	NM
❑ LP-1044 [M]	Don Gardner and Dee Dee Ford In Sweden	1965	120.00

GARDNERS, THE

Albums

PRESTIGE INT'L.

Number	Title	Yr	NM
❑ PRLP-13062 [M]	Folk Songs Far and Near	1962	30.00

GARFUNKEL, ART

Also see SIMON AND GARFUNKEL.

45s

COLUMBIA

Number	Title (A Side/B Side)	Yr	NM
❑ 02307	A Heart in New York/Is This Love	1981	4.00
❑ 02307 [PS]	A Heart in New York/Is This Love	1981	4.00
❑ 02627	Bright Eyes/The Romance	1981	4.00
❑ 06590	Carol of the Birds/The Decree	1986	3.00
—With Amy Grant			
❑ 06590 [PS]	Carol of the Birds/The Decree	1986	3.00
❑ 07711	So Much in Love/King of Tonga	1988	3.00
❑ 07949	This Is the Moment/ Slow Breakup	1988	3.00
❑ 08511	When a Man Loves a Woman/ I Have a Love	1988	3.00
❑ 10020	Second Avenue/Woyaya	1974	5.00
—As "Garfunkel"			

Except when noted otherwise, VG = 25% of NM, and VG+ = 50% of NM. (Example: VG = \$2.00, VG+ = \$4.00 and NM = \$8.00.)

Number	Title (A Side/B Side)	Yr	NM
❑ 10190	I Only Have Eyes for You/ Looking for the Right One	1975	5.00
❑ 10274	Breakaway/Disney Girls	1975	5.00
❑ 10608	Crying in My Sleep/ Mr. Shuck 'N' Jive	1977	5.00
❑ 10676	(What a) Wonderful World/ Wooden Planes	1978	6.00

—A-side: Art Garfunkel with Paul Simon and James Taylor

Number	Title (A Side/B Side)	Yr	NM
❑ 10933	In a Little While (I'll Be On My Way)/And I Know	1979	4.00
❑ 10999	Since I Don't Have You/When Someone Doesn't Want You	1979	4.00
❑ 11050	Bright Eyes/Sail on a Rainbow	1979	4.00
❑ 45926	All I Know/Mary Was An Only Child	1973	5.00

—As "Art Garfunkel"

Number	Title (A Side/B Side)	Yr	NM
❑ 45926	All I Know/Mary Was An Only Child	1973	5.00

—As "Garfunkel"

Number	Title (A Side/B Side)	Yr	NM
❑ 45926 [DJ]	All I Know (mono/stereo)	1973	8.00

—As "Garfunkel"; mono version is about 10 seconds longer than any other version of this song (longer piano fade at the end)

Number	Title (A Side/B Side)	Yr	NM
❑ 45926 [Q]	All I Know/Mary Was An Only Child	1973	10.00

—As "Garfunkel"; promo-only quadraphonic pressing

Number	Title (A Side/B Side)	Yr	NM
❑ 45983	I Shall Sing/Feuilles-Oh: Do Space Men Pass Dead Souls on Their Way to the Moon	1973	5.00

—As "Garfunkel"

Number	Title (A Side/B Side)	Yr	NM
❑ 46030	Traveling Boy/Old Men	1974	5.00

—As "Garfunkel"

OCTAVIA

Number	Title (A Side/B Side)	Yr	NM
❑ 8002	Forgive Me/Private World	1960	40.00

—As "Artie Garr"

WARWICK

Number	Title (A Side/B Side)	Yr	NM
❑ 515	Beat Love/Dream Alone	1959	40.00

—As "Artie Garr"

Albums

COLUMBIA

Number	Title (A Side/B Side)	Yr	NM
❑ CQ 31474 [Q]	Angel Clare	1973	20.00
❑ KC 31474	Angel Clare	1973	12.00
❑ PC 31474	Angel Clare	197?	8.00

—Reissue

Number	Title (A Side/B Side)	Yr	NM
❑ PC 33700	Breakaway	197?	8.00

—With bar code on cover

Number	Title (A Side/B Side)	Yr	NM
❑ PC 33700	Breakaway	1975	12.00

—Originals have no bar code

Number	Title (A Side/B Side)	Yr	NM
❑ PCQ 33700 [Q]	Breakaway	1975	20.00
❑ JC 34975	Watermark	1978	12.00

—Stock copy with "(What a) Wonderful World" on side 2

Number	Title (A Side/B Side)	Yr	NM
❑ JC 34975	Watermark	1978	100.00

—Stock copy with "Fingerpaint" on side 2

Number	Title (A Side/B Side)	Yr	NM
❑ JC 34975 [DJ]	Watermark	1978	60.00

—Test pressing or white label promo with "Fingerpaint" on side 2

Number	Title (A Side/B Side)	Yr	NM
❑ PC 34975	Watermark	198?	8.00

—Reissue

Number	Title (A Side/B Side)	Yr	NM
❑ JC 35780	Fate for Breakfast	1979	12.00

—With six different covers, each illustrating Art Garfunkel at a different stage of eating breakfast. No difference in value.

Number	Title (A Side/B Side)	Yr	NM
❑ FC 37392	Scissors Cut	1981	10.00
❑ FC 40212	The Animals' Christmas By Jimmy Webb	1986	10.00

—With Amy Grant

Number	Title (A Side/B Side)	Yr	NM
❑ FC 40942	Lefty	1988	8.00
❑ OC 45008	Garfunkel	1989	10.00

GARI, FRANK

45s

ATLANTIC

Number	Title (A Side/B Side)	Yr	NM
❑ 2171	Ain't That Fun/You Make Me Wanna Dance	1962	12.00

CAPITOL

Number	Title (A Side/B Side)	Yr	NM
❑ 2101	April/Love That's Where It's At	1968	8.00

CRUSADE

Number	Title (A Side/B Side)	Yr	NM
❑ 1020	Utopia/I Ain't Got a Girl	1960	15.00
❑ 1021	Lullaby of Love/Tonight Is Our Last Night	1961	15.00
❑ 1021 [PS]	Lullaby of Love/Tonight Is Our Last Night	1961	25.00
❑ 1022	Princess/The Last Bus Left at Midnight	1961	15.00
❑ 1022 [PS]	Princess/The Last Bus Left at Midnight	1961	25.00
❑ 1024	You Better Keep Runnin'/ There's Lots More Where This Came From	1962	15.00
❑ 1024 [PS]	You Better Keep Runnin'/ There's Lots More Where This Came From	1962	30.00

RIBBON

Number	Title (A Side/B Side)	Yr	NM
❑ 6903	Lil' Girl/Your Only Love	1958	15.00

GARI AND THE PRISTINES

45s

CAMEO

Number	Title (A Side/B Side)	Yr	NM
❑ 408	Losers Club/Let Me Go Lover	1966	40.00

Art Garfunkel, "A Heart in New York," Columbia 02307, 1981, $4.

GARLAND, JUDY

45s

ABC

Number	Title (A Side/B Side)	Yr	NM
❑ 10973	I Feel a Song Coming On/ What Now My Love	1967	8.00

CAPITOL

Number	Title (A Side/B Side)	Yr	NM
❑ X3-1569 [S]	After You've Gone/Chicago	196?	20.00

—Small hole, plays at 33 1/3 rpm

Number	Title (A Side/B Side)	Yr	NM
❑ 4624	Rock-a-Bye Your Baby with a Dixie Melody/Zing Went the Strings of My Heart	1961	10.00
❑ 4656	Sweet Danger/Comes Once in a Lifetime	1961	10.00
❑ 4938	Hello Bluebird/I Could Go On Singing	1963	10.00

CAPITOL STARLINE

Number	Title (A Side/B Side)	Yr	NM
❑ 6125	San Francisco/Chicago	1968	8.00

—Originals have red and white "target" labels

Number	Title (A Side/B Side)	Yr	NM
❑ 6126	The Man That Got Away/ April Showers	1968	8.00

—Originals have red and white "target" labels

Number	Title (A Side/B Side)	Yr	NM
❑ 6127	Rock-a-Bye Your Baby with a Dixie Melody/Come Rain or Come Shine	1968	8.00

—Originals have red and white "target" labels

Number	Title (A Side/B Side)	Yr	NM
❑ 6128	Over the Rainbow/ Maybe I'll Come Back	1968	8.00

—Originals have red and white "target" labels

Number	Title (A Side/B Side)	Yr	NM
❑ 6129	That's Entertainment/Swanee	1968	8.00

—Originals have red and white "target" labels

COLUMBIA

Number	Title (A Side/B Side)	Yr	NM
❑ 40010	Send My Baby Back to Me/ Without a Memory	1953	15.00
❑ 40023	Go Home Joe/Heartbroken	1953	15.00
❑ 40270	The Man That Got Away/ Here's What I'm Here For	1954	15.00

DECCA

Number	Title (A Side/B Side)	Yr	NM
❑ 23658	The Birthday of a King/ The Star of the East	195?	15.00
❑ 29295	Have Yourself a Merry Little Christmas/You'll Never Walk Alone	1954	15.00

MGM

Number	Title (A Side/B Side)	Yr	NM
❑ 166	Over the Rainbow/You Made Me Love You	196?	8.00
❑ 505	Over the Rainbow/You Made Me Love You	1969	8.00

WARNER BROS.

Number	Title (A Side/B Side)	Yr	NM
❑ 5310	Little Drops of Rain/ Paris Is a Lonely Town	1962	10.00

7-Inch Extended Plays

CAPITOL

Number	Title (A Side/B Side)	Yr	NM
❑ EAP 1-676	This Is the Time of the Evening/ While We're Young// Over the Rainbow	195?	12.00
❑ EAP 1-676 [PS]	Miss Show Business, Part 1	195?	12.00
❑ EAP 2-676	Medley: You Made Me Love You/ For Me and My Gal/The Boy Next Door/The Trolley Song// Danny Boy/After You've Gone	195?	12.00
❑ EAP 2-676 [PS]	Miss Show Business, Part 2	195?	12.00
❑ EAP 3-676	A Pretty Girl Milking Her Cow/ Rock-a-Bye Your Baby with a Dixie Melody//Carolina in the Morning	195?	12.00
❑ EAP 3-676 [PS]	Miss Show Business, Part 3	195?	12.00
❑ EAP 4-676	Happiness Is a Thing Called Joe/ /Judy at the Palace—Shine On Harvest Moon/Some of These Days/My Man/I Don't Care	195?	12.00
❑ EAP 4-676 [PS]	Miss Show Business, Part 4	195?	12.00
❑ EDM-676 [PS]	Miss Show Business	195?	15.00

—Box only; used for some editions of all four 676 records

DECCA

Number	Title (A Side/B Side)	Yr	NM
❑ ED 2022	Embraceable You/Bidin' My Time//But Not for Me/ I Got Rhythm	195?	15.00
❑ ED 2022 [PS]	Judy Garland	195?	15.00

Number	Title (A Side/B Side)	Yr	NM
❑ ED 2050	Smilin' Through/You'll Never Walk Alone//The Boy Next Door/I'm Always Chasing Rainbows	195?	15.00
❑ ED 2050 [PS]	Judy Garland Vol. 2	195?	15.00
MGM			
❑ X1038	Get Happy/Love of My Life//Johnny One Note/Who?	1953	25.00
❑ X1038 [PS]	Get Happy	1953	25.00
Albums			
A.E.I.			
❑ 2108	Judy Garland Vol. 1: Born in a Trunk	198?	10.00
❑ 2109 [M]	Judy Garland Vol. 2: Stardom 1940-45	1980	10.00
❑ 2110	Judy Garland Vol. 3: Superstar 1945-50	198?	10.00
ABC			
❑ 620 [M]	Judy Garland At Home at the Palace — Opening Night	1967	20.00
❑ S-620 [S]	Judy Garland At Home at the Palace — Opening Night	1967	25.00
❑ AC-30007	The ABC Collection	1976	15.00
CAPITOL			
❑ DW 676 [R]	Miss Show Business	1963	12.00
❑ W 676 [M]	Miss Show Business	1955	40.00
❑ DT 734 [R]	Judy	1963	15.00
❑ T 734 [M]	Judy	1956	40.00
❑ DT 835 [R]	Alone	1963	15.00
❑ T 835 [M]	Alone	1957	40.00
❑ ST 1036 [S]	Judy in Love	1959	40.00
❑ T 1036 [M]	Judy in Love	1958	25.00
❑ ST 1118 [S]	Garland at the Grove	1959	40.00
❑ T 1118 [M]	Garland at the Grove	1959	25.00
❑ ST 1188 [S]	The Letter	1959	40.00
—Add 80% if letter is on cover			
❑ T 1188 [M]	The Letter	1959	25.00
—Add 80% if letter is on cover			
❑ ST 1467 [S]	Judy — That's Entertainment	196?	20.00
—Black rainbow label, Capitol logo at top			
❑ ST 1467 [S]	Judy — That's Entertainment	1960	40.00
—Black rainbow label, Capitol logo at left			
❑ T 1467 [M]	Judy — That's Entertainment	196?	15.00
—Black rainbow label, Capitol logo at top			
❑ T 1467 [M]	Judy — That's Entertainment	1960	25.00
—Black rainbow label, Capitol logo at left			
❑ SWBO 1569 [(2)S]	Judy at Carnegie Hall	1961	50.00
❑ WBO 1569 [(2)M]	Judy at Carnegie Hall	1961	40.00
❑ SW 1710 [S]	The Garland Touch	1962	30.00
❑ W 1710 [M]	The Garland Touch	1962	20.00
❑ SW 1861 [P]	I Could Go On Singing	1963	60.00
—"I Am the Monarch of the Sea" and "It Never Was You" are rechanneled			
❑ W 1861 [M]	I Could Go On Singing	1963	40.00
❑ ST 1941 [S]	Our Love Letter	1963	30.00
—Reissue of ST 1188			
❑ T 1941 [M]	Our Love Letter	1963	20.00
—Reissue of T 1188			
❑ SM-1999	The Hits of Judy Garland	197?	10.00
—Reissue			
❑ ST 1999 [P]	The Hits of Judy Garland	1964	30.00
—"Over the Rainbow," "Come Rain or Come Shine" and "April Showers" are rechanneled			
❑ T 1999 [M]	The Hits of Judy Garland	1964	20.00
❑ DW 2062 [R]	Just for Openers	1964	15.00
❑ W 2062 [M]	Just for Openers	1964	20.00
❑ STCL 2988 [(3)]	The Judy Garland Deluxe Set	1968	40.00
❑ DNFR-7632 [(6)]	The Magic of Judy Garland	196?	40.00
—Box set with 4-page insert; 20 of the 60 tracks are rechanneled			
❑ SM-11763	Alone	1978	10.00
—Edited reissue of 835			
❑ SM-11876	Judy — That's Entertainment	1978	10.00
—Edited reissue			
❑ M-12034	Just for Openers	1979	10.00
—Edited reissue			
❑ SN-16175	The Hits of Judy Garland	198?	8.00
—Budget-line reissue			
DECCA			
❑ DXB 172 [(2)M]	The Best of Judy Garland	1963	20.00
❑ DL 4199 [M]	The Magic of Judy Garland	1961	30.00
❑ DL 6020 [10]	Judy at the Palace	1952	100.00
❑ DXSB 7172 [(2)R]	The Best of Judy Garland	1963	20.00
❑ DL 8190 [M]	Judy Garland's Greatest Performances	1955	40.00
—Black label, silver print			
❑ DL 8190 [M]	Judy Garland's Greatest Performances	196?	25.00
—Black label with color bars			
❑ DL 75150 [R]	Judy Garland's Greatest Hits	1969	12.00
DRG			
❑ SL 5179	The Wit and the Wonder of Judy Garland	1977	15.00
❑ SL-5187	The Beginning	1979	15.00

Number	Title (A Side/B Side)	Yr	NM
LONGINES SYMPHONETTE			
❑ SY 5217 [(5)]	The Magic of Judy Garland	197?	30.00
MARK 56			
❑ 632 [PD]	In Concert: San Francisco	1978	60.00
MCA			
❑ 907	From the Decca Vaults	1984	10.00
❑ 4003 [(2)]	The Best of Judy Garland	1973	15.00
—Black label with rainbow			
❑ 4003 [(2)]	The Best of Judy Garland	1980	10.00
—Blue label with rainbow			
❑ 4046 [(2)]	Collector's Items (1936-45)	197?	12.00
❑ 25165	The Best of Judy Garland from MGM Classic Films	1988	12.00
METRO			
❑ M-505 [M]	Judy Garland	1965	15.00
❑ MS-505 [S]	Judy Garland	1965	20.00
❑ M-581 [M]	Judy Garland in Song	1966	15.00
❑ MS-581 [S]	Judy Garland in Song	1966	20.00
MGM			
❑ SDP-1 [(2)]	Golden Years at MGM	1969	30.00
❑ E-82 [10]	Judy Garland Sings	1951	100.00
❑ PX 102	Forever Judy	1969	25.00
—White label "Limited Edition" with poster			
❑ E-3149 [M]	If You Feel Like Singing, Sing	1955	60.00
❑ E-3989 [M]	The Judy Garland Story Vol. 1: The Star Years	1961	30.00
❑ E-4005 [M]	The Judy Garland Story Vol. 2: The Hollywood Years	1962	30.00
❑ E-4204 [M]	The Very Best of Judy Garland	1964	30.00
❑ SE-4204 [R]	The Very Best of Judy Garland	1964	10.00
—Blue and gold label			
❑ SE-4204 [R]	The Very Best of Judy Garland	1964	15.00
—Black label			
MINERVA			
❑ LP-6JG-FNJ	Judy Garland and Friends	1982	10.00
❑ LP-6JG-FST	The Judy Garland Show: Mutual Admiration Society	1982	10.00
PAIR			
❑ PDL2-1030 [(2)]	Golden Memories	1986	12.00
❑ PDL2-1127 [(2)]	The Legendary Judy Garland	1986	12.00
PICKWICK			
❑ PTP-2010 [(2)]	Her Greatest Hits	197?	12.00
❑ SPC-3053	I Feel a Song Coming On	197?	12.00
SPRINGBOARD			
❑ SPB-4054	Over the Rainbow	197?	8.00
STANYAN			
❑ POW-3001	More Than a Memory	198?	10.00
—Reissue of 10095			
❑ 10095	More Than a Memory	1974	10.00
TIME-LIFE			
❑ SLGD-12 [(2)]	Legendary Singers: Judy Garland	1986	20.00
TROPHY			
❑ TR-7-2145 [(2)]	Judy Garland Concert	1974	15.00

GARLAND, JUDY, AND LIZA MINNELLI Also see each artist's individual listings.

Number	Title (A Side/B Side)	Yr	NM
45s			
CAPITOL			
❑ 5497	Hello Dolly/He's Got the Whole World In His Hands	1965	8.00
Albums			
CAPITOL			
❑ SWBO 2295 [(2)S]	"Live" at the London Palladium	1965	30.00
❑ WBO 2295 [(2)M]	"Live" at the London Palladium	1965	25.00
❑ ST-11191	"Live" at the London Palladium	1973	12.00
—Condensation of above 2-record set			
MOBILE FIDELITY			
❑ 1-048	"Live" at the London Palladium	1981	25.00
—Audiophile vinyl			

GARNER, ERROLL

Number	Title (A Side/B Side)	Yr	NM
45s			
ABC-PARAMOUNT			
❑ 10260	Dreamstreet/When You're Smiling	1961	8.00
❑ 10301	You Do Something to Me/Some of These Days	1962	8.00
COLUMBIA			
❑ 1-869	When Johnny Comes Marching Home/I Don't Know Why	1950	20.00
—Microgroove 33 1/3 rpm 7-inch single			
❑ 6-869	When Johnny Comes Marching Home/I Don't Know Why	1950	15.00
❑ 1-874	Petite Waltz Bounce/Petite Waltz	1950	20.00
—Microgroove 33 1/3 rpm 7-inch single			
❑ 6-874	Petite Waltz Bounce/Petite Waltz	1950	15.00
❑ 39100	People Will Say We're in Love/Lover	1950	15.00
❑ 39145	How High the Moon/Poor Butterfly	1951	15.00
❑ 39165	When Johnny Comes Marching Home/My Heart Stood Still	1951	12.00
❑ 39166	Poor Butterfly/Long Ago and Far Away	1951	12.00
❑ 39167	When You're Smiling/Spring Is Here	1951	12.00
❑ 39168	It Could Happen to You/I Don't Know Why	1951	12.00
—The above four comprise a box set			
❑ 39249	Honeysuckle Rose/My Heart Stood Still	1951	15.00
❑ 39273	I Cover the Waterfront/Laura	1951	12.00
❑ 39274	I'm in the Mood for Love/Body and Soul	1951	12.00
❑ 39275	The Way You Look Tonight/Indiana	1951	12.00
❑ 39276	Penthouse Serenade/Play, Piano, Play	1951	12.00
—The above four comprise a box set			
❑ 39580	It's the Talk of the Town/Robbins' Nest	1951	15.00
❑ 39615	Sophisticated Lady/Fine and Dandy	1951	15.00
❑ 39681	Ain't She Sweet/Please Don't Talk About Me When I'm Gone	1952	12.00
❑ 39713	Ja Da/Oh Lady Be Good	1952	12.00
❑ 39734	Out of Nowhere/Music, Maestro, Please	1952	12.00
❑ 39746	Cocktails for Two/Dancing in the Dark	1952	10.00
❑ 39747	Willow Weep for Me/I Don't Hear a Thing	1952	10.00
❑ 39748	Chopin Impressions/How Come You Do	1952	10.00
❑ 39749	With Every Breath I Take/Love Me or Leave Me	1952	10.00
—The above four comprise a box set			
❑ 39888	Summertime/What's New	1952	12.00
❑ 39918	Am I Blue/I Never Knew	1953	12.00
❑ 39996	Lullaby of Birdland/Easy to Love	1953	12.00
❑ 40043	St. Louis Blues/My Ideal	1953	12.00
❑ 40074	Frenesi/Mean to Me	1953	12.00
❑ 40172	You're Driving Me Crazy/Oh, What a Beautiful Morning	1954	12.00
❑ 40766	On the Street Where You Live/Dreamy	1956	10.00
❑ 40899	Way Back Blues (Part 1)/Way Back Blues (Part 2)	1957	10.00
❑ 41067	Misty/Moment's Delight	1957	12.00
❑ 41231	I Can't Get Started/Just Blues	1958	10.00
❑ 41482	Misty/Solitude	1959	10.00
MERCURY			
❑ 1001	Embraceable You/Lover Come Back to Me	195?	15.00
❑ 70442	Misty/Exactly Like You	1954	15.00
❑ 70487	Rosalie/There's a Small Hotel	1954	12.00
❑ 70649	That Old Black Magic/Night and Day	1955	12.00
❑ 72192	Mimi/Theme from "A New Kind of Love"	1963	8.00
❑ 73177	For Once in My Life/Mood Island	1971	4.00
MGM			
❑ 13471	As Time Goes By/You Made Me Love You	1966	6.00
❑ 13547	Affinidad/That's My Kick	1966	6.00
❑ 13677	More/It Ain't Necessarily So	1967	6.00
❑ 13677 [PS]	More/It Ain't Necessarily So	1967	15.00
❑ 13834	Nervous Waltz/As Time Goes By	1967	6.00
❑ 13870	Blue Moon/Like It Is	1967	6.00
❑ 13916	Watermelon Man/Gaslight	1968	5.00
❑ 13988	Coffee Song/Up in Erroll's Room	1968	5.00
❑ 14043	Cheek to Cheek/It's the Talk of the Town	1969	5.00
OKEH			
❑ 6898	Laura/Penthouse Serenade	1952	20.00
RCA VICTOR			
❑ 47-4723	Stariway to the Stars/I Can't Escape from You	1952	15.00
REPRISE			
❑ 20179	Moritat/Sweet and Lovely	1963	8.00
7-Inch Extended Plays			
COLUMBIA			
❑ 5-1497	Caravan/(There Is) No Greater Love	195?	15.00
—Alternate numbers are "B-1656-1" and "B-1656-2"			
❑ B-1656 [PS]	Erroll Garner	195?	15.00
—Contains record 5-1497			
❑ B-1678	Lullaby of Birdland/Memories of You	195?	15.00
❑ B-1678 [PS]	Lullaby of Birdland/Memories of You	195?	15.00
❑ B-1700	I've Got My Love to Keep Me Warm/Stompin' at the Savoy//Cheek to Cheek	195?	15.00

Number	Title (A Side/B Side)	Yr	NM
❑ B-1700 [PS]	Erroll Garner Plays for Dancing	195?	15.00
❑ B-1971	*Lullaby in Rhythm/Bewitched/ Once in a While	195?	15.00
❑ B-1971 [PS]	Gone — Garner — Gonest	195?	15.00
❑ B-2549	*Laura/Body and Soul/Fine and Dandy/Oh, Lady Be Good!	195?	12.00
❑ B-2549 [PS]	Erroll Garner (Hall of Fame Series)	195?	12.00
❑ B-2586	*Penthouse Serenade/The Way You Look Tonight/I'm in the Mood for Love/Indiana	1959	12.00
❑ B-2586 [PS]	Erroll Garner (Hall of Fame Series)	1959	12.00

Albums

ABC-PARAMOUNT

Number	Title (A Side/B Side)	Yr	NM
❑ 365 [M]	Dreamstreet	1961	20.00
❑ S-365 [S]	Dreamstreet	1961	25.00
❑ 395 [M]	Closeup in Swing	1961	20.00
❑ S-395 [S]	Closeup in Swing	1961	25.00

ATLANTIC

Number	Title (A Side/B Side)	Yr	NM
❑ ALR-109 [10]	Rhapsody	1950	200.00
❑ ALR-112 [10]	Erroll Garner at the Piano	1951	200.00
❑ ALR-128 [10]	Passport to Fame	1952	200.00
❑ ALR-135 [10]	Piano Solos, Vol. 2	1952	200.00
❑ 1227 [M]	The Greatest Garner	1956	40.00
—Black label			
❑ 1227 [M]	The Greatest Garner	196?	12.00
—Multi-color label with black "fan" logo			
❑ 1227 [M]	The Greatest Garner	1961	15.00
—Multi-color label with white "fan" logo			
❑ 1315 [M]	Perpetual Motion	1959	40.00
—Black label			

BARONET

Number	Title (A Side/B Side)	Yr	NM
❑ B-109 [M]	Informal Piano Improvisations	1962	12.00
❑ BS-109 [R]	Informal Piano Improvisations	1962	10.00

BLUE NOTE

Number	Title (A Side/B Side)	Yr	NM
❑ BLP-5007 [10]	Overture to Dawn, Vol. 1	1952	500.00
❑ BLP-5008 [10]	Overture to Dawn, Vol. 2	1952	500.00
❑ BLP-5014 [10]	Overture to Dawn, Vol. 3	1953	500.00
❑ BLP-5015 [10]	Overture to Dawn, Vol. 4	1953	500.00
❑ BLP-5016 [10]	Overture to Dawn, Vol. 5	1953	500.00

CLARION

Number	Title (A Side/B Side)	Yr	NM
❑ 610 [M]	Serenade in Blue	1966	12.00
❑ SD 610 [S]	Serenade in Blue	1966	12.00

COLUMBIA

Number	Title (A Side/B Side)	Yr	NM
❑ C2L 9 [(2)M]	Paris Impressions	1958	40.00
❑ CL 535 [M]	Erroll Garner	1953	60.00
—Red label with gold print			
❑ CL 535 [M]	Erroll Garner	1956	30.00
—Red and black label with six "eye" logos			
❑ CL 583 [M]	Gems	1954	60.00
—Red label with gold print			
❑ CL 583 [M]	Gems	1956	30.00
—Red and black label with six "eye" logos			
❑ CL 617 [M]	Gone Garner Gonest	1955	60.00
—Red label with gold print			
❑ CL 617 [M]	Gone Garner Gonest	1956	30.00
—Red and black label with six "eye" logos			
❑ CL 667 [M]	Erroll Garner Plays for Dancing	1956	30.00
❑ CL 883 [M]	Concert by the Sea	1956	30.00
❑ CL 939 [M]	The Most Happy Piano	1957	30.00
❑ CL 1014 [M]	Other Voices	1957	30.00
—Red and black label wirh six "eye" logos			
❑ CL 1060 [M]	Soliloquy	1957	30.00
❑ CL 1141 [M]	Encores in Hi-Fi	1958	30.00
❑ CL 1216 [M]	Paris Impressions, Vol. 1	1958	20.00
❑ CL 1217 [M]	Paris Impressions, Vol. 2	1958	20.00
❑ CL 1452 [M]	The One and Only Erroll Garner	1960	20.00
❑ CL 1512 [M]	Swinging Solos	1960	20.00
❑ CL 1587 [M]	The Provocative Erroll Garner	1961	20.00
❑ CL 2540 [10]	Garnerland	1955	60.00
❑ CL 2606 [10]	He's Here! He's Gone! He's Garner!	1956	60.00
❑ CL 6139 [10]	Piano Moods	1950	80.00
❑ CL 6173 [10]	Gems	1951	80.00
❑ CL 6209 [10]	Solo Flight	1952	80.00
❑ CL 6259 [10]	Erroll Garner Plays for Dancing	1953	80.00
❑ CS 8131 [S]	Paris Impressions, Vol. 1	1958	30.00
❑ CS 8252 [S]	The One and Only Erroll Garner	1960	25.00
❑ CS 8312 [S]	Swinging Solos	1960	25.00
❑ CS 8387 [S]	The Provocative Erroll Garner	1961	25.00
❑ CS 9820 [R]	Other Voices	1970	12.00
❑ CS 9821 [R]	Concert by the Sea	1970	12.00
❑ PG 33424 [(2)]	Play It Again, Erroll!	1975	12.00

COLUMBIA JAZZ MASTERPIECES

Number	Title (A Side/B Side)	Yr	NM
❑ CJ 40863	Long Ago and Far Away	1987	12.00

COLUMBIA SPECIAL PRODUCTS

Number	Title (A Side/B Side)	Yr	NM
❑ P 14386	Dreamy	1978	10.00

DIAL

Number	Title (A Side/B Side)	Yr	NM
❑ LP-205 [10]	Erroll Garner, Vol. 1	1950	200.00
❑ LP-902 [M]	Free Piano Improvisations Recorded by Baron Timme Rosenkranz at One of His Famous Gaslight Jazz Sessions	1949	300.00

EMARCY

Number	Title (A Side/B Side)	Yr	NM
❑ MG-26016 [10]	Garnering	1954	80.00
❑ MG-26042 [10]	Gone with Garner	1954	80.00
❑ MG-36001 [M]	Contrasts	1955	30.00
❑ MG-36026 [M]	Garnering	1955	30.00
❑ MG-36069 [M]	Erroll!	1956	30.00
❑ 826224-1	Erroll Garner Plays Gershwin and Kern	1986	10.00
❑ 832994-1	The Erroll Garner Collection Vol. 1: Easy to Love	1988	10.00
❑ 834935-1	The Erroll Garner Collection Vol. 2: Dancing on the Ceiling	1989	10.00

EVEREST ARCHIVE OF FOLK & JAZZ

Number	Title (A Side/B Side)	Yr	NM
❑ 245	Erroll Garner	1970	10.00

GUEST STAR

Number	Title (A Side/B Side)	Yr	NM
❑ G 1403 [M]	Piano Greats	196?	12.00
—With tracks by Art Tatum and Mike Di Napoli			
❑ GS 1403 [S]	Piano Greats	196?	10.00
—With tracks by Art Tatum and Mike Di Napoli			

HALL OF FAME

Number	Title (A Side/B Side)	Yr	NM
❑ 610	Early Erroll	198?	10.00

HARMONY

Number	Title (A Side/B Side)	Yr	NM
❑ HS 11268	One More Time	1968	12.00

JAZZTONE

Number	Title (A Side/B Side)	Yr	NM
❑ J-1269 [M]	Early Erroll	1957	40.00

KING

Number	Title (A Side/B Side)	Yr	NM
❑ 295-17 [10]	Piano Stylist	1952	80.00
❑ 395-540 [M]	Piano Variations	1958	150.00

LONDON

Number	Title (A Side/B Side)	Yr	NM
❑ XPS 617	Gemini	1972	12.00
❑ APS 640	Magician	1973	12.00

MERCURY

Number	Title (A Side/B Side)	Yr	NM
❑ MG-20009 [M]	Erroll Garner at the Piano	1953	50.00
❑ MG-20055 [M]	Mambo Moves Garner	1954	50.00
❑ MG-20063 [M]	Solitaire	1954	50.00
❑ MG-20090 [M]	Afternoon of an Elf	1955	50.00
❑ MG-20662 [M]	Erroll Garner Plays Misty	1962	15.00
❑ MG-20803 [M]	The Best of Erroll Garner	1963	15.00
❑ MG-20859 [M]	New Kind of Love	1963	15.00
❑ MG-21308 [M]	Feeling Is Believing	1964	15.00
❑ MG-25117 [10]	Erroll Garner at the Piano	1951	80.00
❑ MG-25157 [10]	Gone with Garner	1951	80.00
❑ SR-60662	Erroll Garner Plays Misty	1975	10.00
—Chicago skyline label			
❑ SR-60662	Erroll Garner Plays Misty	1983	8.00
—Black label, neon-style "mercury" logo			
❑ SR-60662 [S]	Erroll Garner Plays Misty	1962	20.00
—Black label, all-silver print			
❑ SR-60662 [S]	Erroll Garner Plays Misty	1965	12.00
—Red label, "MERCURY" in all caps at top			
❑ SR-60803 [S]	The Best of Erroll Garner	1963	20.00
❑ SR-60859 [S]	New Kind of Love	1963	20.00
❑ SR-61308 [S]	Feeling Is Believing	1964	20.00
❑ SR-61308 [S]	Feeling Is Believing	1970	12.00
—Newer Mercury logo on cover			
❑ 826457-1	Afternoon of an Elf	1986	10.00
—Reissue			

MGM

Number	Title (A Side/B Side)	Yr	NM
❑ E-4335 [M]	Now Playing: Erroll Garner	1966	12.00
❑ SE-4335 [S]	Now Playing: Erroll Garner	1966	15.00
❑ E-4361 [M]	Campus Concert	1966	12.00
❑ SE-4361 [S]	Campus Concert	1966	15.00
❑ E-4463 [M]	That's My Kick	1967	15.00
❑ SE-4463 [S]	That's My Kick	1967	12.00
❑ E-4520 [M]	Up in Erroll's Room	1967	15.00
❑ SE-4520 [S]	Up in Erroll's Room	1967	12.00

PICKWICK

Number	Title (A Side/B Side)	Yr	NM
❑ SPC-3254	Deep Purple	197?	10.00

REPRISE

Number	Title (A Side/B Side)	Yr	NM
❑ R 6080 [DJ]	One World Concert	1963	40.00
—Six-song sampler — three on each side — on a 12-inch record that plays at 45 rpm. This comes in a different cover than the stock copy; this is clearly marked "Special 45 RPM Preview Record" on the top front.			
❑ R 6080 [M]	One World Concert	1963	20.00
❑ RS 6080 [S]	One World Concert	1963	25.00

RONDO-LETTE

Number	Title (A Side/B Side)	Yr	NM
❑ A-15 [M]	Erroll Garner	1958	25.00

SAVOY

Number	Title (A Side/B Side)	Yr	NM
❑ SJC-411	Penthouse Serenade	1985	10.00
❑ SJL-1118	Yesterdays	198?	10.00
❑ SJL-2207 [(2)]	Elf	198?	12.00
❑ MG-12002 [M]	Penthouse Serenade	1955	30.00
❑ MG-12003 [M]	Serenade to "Laura"	1955	30.00
❑ MG-15000 [10]	Erroll Garner Plays Piano Solos	1950	80.00
❑ MG-15001 [10]	Erroll Garner Plays Piano Solos, Vol. 2	1950	80.00
❑ MG-15002 [10]	Erroll Garner Plays Piano Solos, Vol. 3	1950	80.00
❑ MG-15003 [10]	Erroll Garner Plays Piano Solos, Vol. 4	1950	80.00
❑ MG-15026 [10]	Erroll Garner at the Piano	1953	80.00

TRIP

Number	Title (A Side/B Side)	Yr	NM
❑ 5519	Garnering	197?	10.00

WING

Number	Title (A Side/B Side)	Yr	NM
❑ MGW 12134	Erroll Garner Moods	196?	12.00

GARNER, ERROLL/PETE JOHNSON

Albums

GRAND AWARD

Number	Title (A Side/B Side)	Yr	NM
❑ GA 33-321 [M]	Jazz Piano	1956	25.00
—Without removable cover			
❑ GA 33-321 [M]	Jazz Piano	1956	80.00
—With removable David Stone Martin cover still attached			

GARNER, ERROLL/OSCAR PETERSON/ART TATUM

Albums

RCA CAMDEN

Number	Title (A Side/B Side)	Yr	NM
❑ CAL-882 [M]	Great Jazz Pianists of Our Time	196?	15.00
❑ CAS-882 [R]	Great Jazz Pianists of Our Time	196?	12.00

GARNER, ERROLL/BILLY TAYLOR

Albums

SAVOY

Number	Title (A Side/B Side)	Yr	NM
❑ MG-12008 [M]	Erroll Garner/Billy Taylor	1955	50.00

GARNER, JOHNNY

45s

IMPERIAL

Number	Title (A Side/B Side)	Yr	NM
❑ 5536	Kiss Me Sweet/Little Starry Eyes	1958	25.00
❑ 5548	Didi Didi/The Fool	1958	50.00

GARR, ARTIE See ART GARFUNKEL.

GARRETT, SCOTT

45s

LAURIE

Number	Title (A Side/B Side)	Yr	NM
❑ 3023	House of Love/So Far So Good	1959	20.00
❑ 3029	Love Story/Graduation Souvenir	1959	50.00
—With vocal backing by the Mystics			
❑ 3034	Where Are You/ Jumpin' Blue Blazes	1959	20.00

OKEH

Number	Title (A Side/B Side)	Yr	NM
❑ 7104	In My Heart/The Day I Died	1960	20.00

GARRETT, TOMMY, 50 GUITARS OF

Better known as "Snuff" Garrett, longtime producer.

45s

LIBERTY

Number	Title (A Side/B Side)	Yr	NM
❑ 55731	Stranger from Durango/Juarez	1964	6.00
❑ 55797	Corcovado/La Violettra	1965	6.00
❑ 55868	Our Man Flint/Tender Moments	1966	6.00
❑ 55888	La Cucaracha/Spanish Lights	1966	6.00
❑ 55969	Theme for Someone in Love/ Courtin'	1967	6.00
❑ 56046	Hang 'Em High/Spanish Pearls	1968	5.00
❑ 56129	Flamenco Funk/ Mexican Standoff	1969	5.00

Albums

LIBERTY

Number	Title (A Side/B Side)	Yr	NM
❑ L-5507 [M]	Limited Edition	196?	12.00
❑ S-6607 [S]	Limited Edition	196?	15.00
❑ LMM-13005 [M]	50 Guitars Go South of the Border	1961	12.00
❑ LMM-13016 [M]	50 Guitars Go South of the Border, Vol. 2	1962	12.00
❑ LMM-13022 [M]	50 Guitars Visit Hawaii	1962	12.00
❑ LMM-13025 [M]	50 Guitars Go Country	1963	12.00
❑ LMM-13028 [M]	50 Guitars Go Italiano	1964	12.00
❑ LMM-13030 [M]	Maria Elena	1963	12.00
❑ LMM-13031 [M]	Bordertown Bandito	1964	12.00
❑ LMM-13032 [M]	Espana	1964	12.00
❑ LMM-13033 [M]	Return to Paradise	1965	12.00
❑ LMM-13035 [M]	Love Songs from South of the Border	1965	12.00
❑ LMM-13036 [M]	Viva Mexico	1966	12.00
❑ LMM-13037 [M]	50 Guitars in Love	1966	12.00
❑ LMM-13039 [M]	More 50 Guitars in Love	1967	12.00
❑ LSS-14005 [S]	50 Guitars Go South of the Border	1961	15.00
❑ LSS-14016 [S]	50 Guitars Go South of the Border, Vol. 2	1962	15.00
❑ LSS-14022 [S]	50 Guitars Visit Hawaii	1962	15.00
❑ LSS-14025 [S]	50 Guitars Go Country	1963	15.00
❑ LSS-14028 [S]	50 Guitars Go Italiano	1964	15.00
❑ LSS-14030 [S]	Maria Elena	1963	15.00
❑ LSS-14031 [S]	Bordertown Bandito	1964	15.00
❑ LSS-14032 [S]	Espana	1964	15.00
❑ LSS-14033 [S]	Return to Paradise	1965	15.00
❑ LSS-14035 [S]	Love Songs from South of the Border	1965	15.00
❑ LSS-14036 [S]	Viva Mexico	1966	15.00
❑ LSS-14037 [S]	50 Guitars in Love	1966	15.00
❑ LSS-14039 [S]	More 50 Guitars in Love	1967	12.00
❑ LSS-14045	The Best of the 50 Guitars of Tommy Garrett	1969	12.00
❑ LSS-14046	Mexican Leather	1969	12.00
❑ LSS-14047	For Midnight Lovers	1970	12.00

Number	Title (A Side/B Side)	Yr	NM
❑ LSS-35001 [(2)]	The Best of the 50 Guitars of Tommy Garrett, Vol.s 2 & 3	1970	15.00
MUSICOR			
❑ 4606 [(2)]	The Best of the 50 Guitars of Tommy Garrett	1976	12.00
PICKWICK			
❑ SPC-3585	In Love	197?	8.00
❑ SPC-3615	Brazilian Mood	197?	8.00
SUNSET			
❑ SUS-5282	The Fabulous 50 Guitars of Tommy Garrett	197?	10.00
UNITED ARTISTS			
❑ UA-LA039-F	You're a Lady	1973	10.00
❑ UXS-79 [(2)]	Tommy Garrett Superpak	1972	12.00
❑ UAS-5528	50 Guitars Go South of the Border, Vol. 3	1971	10.00
❑ UAS-5569	The Way of Love	1972	10.00

GARRIGAN, EDDIE

45s

Number	Title (A Side/B Side)	Yr	NM
FONTANA			
❑ 1575	I Wish I Was/Mail Call	1966	100.00

GARRISON, GLEN

45s

Number	Title (A Side/B Side)	Yr	NM
CREST			
❑ 1047	Lovin' Lorene/You're My Darling	1958	60.00
IMPERIAL			
❑ 66191	Green to Blue/You Can't Win 'Em All	1966	10.00
❑ 66215	Where Do I Go from Here/Strong and Handsome, Sweet and Simple Side	1966	10.00
❑ 66230	Listen, They're Playing My Song/My New Creation	1967	10.00
❑ 66257	Goodbye Swingers/Hello Mama	1967	10.00
❑ 66279	Your Side of Me/If I Lived Here (I'd Be Home Now)	1968	8.00
❑ 66300	I'll Be Your Baby Tonight/You Know I Love You	1968	8.00
❑ 66333	That Lucky Old Sun/She Thinks I Still Care	1968	8.00
❑ 66401	Goodnight Irene/Change Me	1969	8.00
LODE			
❑ 106	Pony Tail Girl/Ballad of Hank Gordon	1959	60.00

GARROWAY, DAVE

Albums

Number	Title (A Side/B Side)	Yr	NM
CAMEO			
❑ C-1001 [M]	An Adventure in Hi-Fi Music	1958	40.00
—Black label, brown print, cameo figure at top			

GARSON, MIKE

Albums

Number	Title (A Side/B Side)	Yr	NM
CONTEMPORARY			
❑ C-14003	Avant Garson	1979	12.00
JAZZ HOUNDS			
❑ 0005	Jazzical	1982	12.00
REFERENCE RECORDINGS			
❑ RR-20	Serendipity	1987	15.00
❑ RR-37	The Oxnard Sessions	1991	20.00
❑ RR-53 [(2)]	The Oxnard Sessions, Vol. Two	1993	25.00

GARSON, MIKE, AND JIM WALKER

Albums

Number	Title (A Side/B Side)	Yr	NM
REFERENCE RECORDINGS			
❑ RR-18	Reflections	1987	15.00

GARY, JOHN

45s

Number	Title (A Side/B Side)	Yr	NM
ACE			
❑ 861	First Lady Waltz/A River of Silver	1962	12.00
FRATERNITY			
❑ 799	How Many Tear Drops/Little People	1958	15.00
❑ 844	Let Them Talk/Tell My Love	1959	15.00
❑ 858	Little Things Mean a Lot/Ever Since I Met Lucy	1959	15.00
❑ 860	Thank the Lord (For This Thanksgiving Day)/The Rest of My Days	1959	15.00
❑ 864	The Shrine of St. Cecelia/When I'm Alone	1960	12.00
❑ 870	The Bell Rings/Forget It	1960	12.00
❑ 958	Let Them Talk/Tell My Love	1966	6.00
RCA VICTOR			
❑ 47-8292	That's Life/Ciumanchella	1963	8.00
❑ 47-8386	Warm and Willing/Friend and Lover	1964	8.00
❑ 47-8413	Soon I'll Wed My Love/The Young Lovers	1964	8.00
❑ 47-8475	Do You Hear What I Hear/Little Snow Girl	1964	12.00
❑ 47-8479	Sunrise, Sunset/The Bell Rings	1964	8.00
❑ 47-8526	Color of Love/My First Love Song	1965	6.00
❑ 47-8617	Joy in the Morning/Linger Awhile	1965	6.00
❑ 47-8677	Don't Throw Those Roses Away/Give Me This Moment	1965	6.00
❑ 47-8731	Ashamed/She Wasn't You	1965	6.00
❑ 47-8806	You Don't Know Me/Don't Let the Music Play	1966	6.00
❑ 47-8890	Sunrise, Sunset/The Bell Rings	1966	6.00
❑ 47-8993	Mine/You've Never Kissed Her	1966	6.00
❑ 47-9119	Hang On to Me/Sleeping Beauty	1967	6.00
❑ 47-9213	Everybody Say Peace/Spanish Moonlight	1967	6.00
❑ 47-9361	Cold/Imagine	1967	6.00
❑ 47-9456	A Certain Girl/The End of Time	1968	5.00
❑ 47-9540	Let There Be Peace on Earth/Give Some Time to Be Happy	1968	5.00
❑ 47-9868	In the Morning/In the Wind	1970	5.00
❑ 74-0149	The Windmills of Your Mind/Then She's a Lover	1969	5.00
❑ 74-0218	Natalie/Summer Me, Winter Me	1969	5.00
TAP			
❑ 7033	I Thought I Had You/The Bell Rings	197?	5.00
❑ 7033 [PS]	I Thought I Had You/The Bell Rings	197?	5.00

Albums

Number	Title (A Side/B Side)	Yr	NM
CHURCHILL			
❑ 67236	In a Class By Himself	1977	10.00
LA BREA			
❑ 8010 [M]	John Gary	1961	25.00
❑ S-8010 [S]	John Gary	1961	30.00
METRO			
❑ M-522 [M]	John Gary	1966	10.00
❑ MS-522 [S]	John Gary	1966	12.00
PICKWICK			
❑ SPC-3025	John Gary	197?	10.00
RCA CAMDEN			
❑ CAL-983 [M]	The One and Only John Gary	1966	10.00
❑ CAS-983 [S]	The One and Only John Gary	1966	12.00
RCA VICTOR			
❑ LOC-1139 [M]	The John Gary Carnegie Hall Concert	1967	20.00
❑ LSO-1139 [S]	The John Gary Carnegie Hall Concert	1967	12.00
❑ ANL1-2342	Pure Gold	1977	10.00
❑ ANL1-2672	A Little Bit of Heaven	1978	10.00
—Reissue of LSP-2994			
❑ LPM-2745 [M]	Catch a Rising Star	1963	15.00
❑ LSP-2745 [S]	Catch a Rising Star	1963	20.00
❑ LPM-2804 [M]	Encore	1964	15.00
❑ LSP-2804 [S]	Encore	1964	20.00
❑ LPM-2922 [M]	So Tenderly	1964	15.00
❑ LSP-2922 [S]	So Tenderly	1964	20.00
❑ LPM-2940 [M]	The John Gary Christmas Album	1964	15.00
❑ LSP-2940 [S]	The John Gary Christmas Album	1964	20.00
❑ LPM-2994 [M]	A Little Bit of Heaven	1965	12.00
❑ LSP-2994 [S]	A Little Bit of Heaven	1965	15.00
❑ LPM-3349 [M]	The Nearness of You	1965	12.00
❑ LSP-3349 [S]	The Nearness of You	1965	15.00
❑ LPM-3411 [M]	Your All-Time Favorite Songs	1965	12.00
❑ LSP-3411 [S]	Your All-Time Favorite Songs	1965	15.00
❑ LPM-3501 [M]	Choice	1966	12.00
❑ LSP-3501 [S]	Choice	1966	15.00
❑ LPM-3570 [M]	Your All-Time Country Favorites	1966	12.00
❑ LSP-3570 [S]	Your All-Time Country Favorites	1966	15.00
❑ LPM-3666 [M]	A Heart Filled with Song	1966	12.00
❑ LSP-3666 [S]	A Heart Filled with Song	1966	15.00
❑ LPM-3695 [M]	Especially for You	1967	15.00
❑ LSP-3695 [S]	Especially for You	1967	12.00
❑ LPM-3730 [M]	The Best of John Gary	1967	15.00
❑ LSP-3730 [S]	The Best of John Gary	1967	12.00
❑ LPM-3785 [M]	Spanish Moonlight	1967	15.00
❑ LSP-3785 [S]	Spanish Moonlight	1967	12.00
❑ LPM-3928 [M]	John Gary On Broadway	1968	20.00
❑ LSP-3928 [S]	John Gary On Broadway	1968	12.00
❑ LPM-3992 [M]	John Gary Sings/John Gary Swings	1968	20.00
❑ LSP-3992 [S]	John Gary Sings/John Gary Swings	1968	12.00
❑ LSP-4075	Holding Your Mind	1969	12.00
❑ LSP-4134	Love of a Gentle Woman	1970	12.00
❑ LSP-4233	That's the Way It Was	1971	12.00
❑ VPS-6041 [(2)]	This Is John Gary	1971	15.00

GARY AND CLYDE

See SKIP AND FLIP.

GARY AND DAVE

45s

Number	Title (A Side/B Side)	Yr	NM
LONDON			
❑ 200	Could You Ever Love Me Again/Where Do We Go from Here	1973	6.00
❑ 204	I Fell in Love with You Sometime/For You	1974	6.00
❑ 207	It Might As Well Rain Until September/(B-side unknown)	1974	20.00

GARY AND THE CASUALS

45s

Number	Title (A Side/B Side)	Yr	NM
VANDAN			
❑ 609	My Own Desire/Someone Like You	1959	60.00

GARY AND THE HORNETS

45s

Number	Title (A Side/B Side)	Yr	NM
SMASH			
❑ 2061	Hi, Hi, Hazel/Patty Girl	1966	15.00
❑ 2061 [PS]	Hi, Hi, Hazel/Patty Girl	1966	25.00
❑ 2078	A Kind of Hush/That's All for Now Sugar Baby	1967	12.00
❑ 2078 [PS]	A Kind of Hush/That's All for Now Sugar Baby	1967	15.00
❑ 2090	Baby It's You/Tell Tale	1967	12.00
❑ 2145	Turn the World On/Holdin' Back	1968	12.00

GARY AND THE KNIGHT-LITES

Evolved into THE AMERICAN BREED.

45s

Number	Title (A Side/B Side)	Yr	NM
BELL			
❑ 643	Lonely Soldier's Pledge/So Far Away from Home	1966	15.00
NIKE			
❑ 1020	I'm Glad She's Mine/How Can I Forget Her	1963	40.00
PRIMA			
❑ 1016	I Can't Love You Anymore/Will You Go Steady	1963	100.00
SEEBURG			
❑ 3016	Sweet Little Sixteen/Take Me Back	1965	25.00
❑ 3017	Bony Moronie/Glad You're Mine	1965	25.00
U.S.A.			
❑ 833	Bid Bad Wolf/I Don't Need Your Help	1966	40.00

GAS AND FUNK FACTORY, THE

45s

Number	Title (A Side/B Side)	Yr	NM
BRUNSWICK			
❑ 55434	Goodnight Song/Everybody Get Some Love	1970	30.00

GAS MASK

Albums

Number	Title (A Side/B Side)	Yr	NM
TONSIL			
❑ 4001	Gas Mask	1970	20.00

GASCA, LUIS

Albums

Number	Title (A Side/B Side)	Yr	NM
ATLANTIC			
❑ SD 1527	Little Giants	1970	25.00
BLUE THUMB			
❑ BTS-37	Luis Gasca	1972	25.00
FANTASY			
❑ F-9461	Born to Love You	1974	30.00
❑ F-9504	Collage	1976	30.00
—Brown label (original)			

GASSAWAY, SENATOR BOLLIVAR E.

45s

Number	Title (A Side/B Side)	Yr	NM
RCA VICTOR			
❑ 47-7743	Senator Bollivar E. Gassaway for President/Senator Bolivar E. Gassaway Visits Russia	1960	12.00
❑ 47-7743 [PS]	Senator Bollivar E. Gassaway for President/Senator Bolivar E. Gassaway Visits Russia	1960	20.00

GATEMEN, THE

45s

Number	Title (A Side/B Side)	Yr	NM
COLPIX			
❑ 671	Silent Night/White Christmas	1962	20.00
MAY			
❑ 141	Goodnight Irene/The Klan	1963	20.00

GATES, HEN

Albums

Number	Title (A Side/B Side)	Yr	NM
MASTERSEAL			
❑ MLP-700 [M]	Let's All Dance to Rock and Roll	1956	100.00
PALACE			
❑ P-700 [M]	Let's All Dance to Rock and Roll	1958	60.00
—Reissue of Masterseal 700			
❑ PST-700 [S]	Let's All Dance to Rock and Roll	1958	80.00
—Labeled stereo, but plays in mono			

Number	Title (A Side/B Side)	Yr	NM
PARIS			
❑ 101 [M]	Rock and Roll Festival	1957	60.00
PLYMOUTH			
❑ R12-144 [M]	Rock and Roll	1956	60.00
❑ R12-149 [M]	Rock and Roll, No. 2	1957	60.00
GATES, WALTER			
45s			
SWAN			
❑ 4160	I Remember Papa/ That's My Boy	1963	8.00
❑ 4180	My Man/Rose of Washington Square	1964	8.00
❑ 4190	Ace in the Hole/Never Before	1964	8.00
GATEWAY SINGERS, THE			
45s			
DECCA			
❑ 29972	The Midnight Special/ Puttin' On the Style	1956	12.00
❑ 30088	Bury Me in My Overalls/Monaco	1956	12.00
❑ 30630	Hey Li Lee/Come to the Dance	1958	10.00
MGM			
❑ 12927	Billy Boy/Goin' Down the Road	1960	8.00
❑ 12939	Wait for the Wagon/ Kingston Market	1960	8.00
WARNER BROS.			
❑ 5073	The M.T.A./Keep a-Movin'	1959	10.00
Albums			
DECCA			
❑ DL 8413 [M]	Puttin' On the Style	1956	40.00
❑ DL 8671 [M]	The Gateway Singers at the Hungry I	1958	30.00
❑ DL 8742 [M]	The Gateway Singers in Hi-Fi	1958	30.00
MGM			
❑ E-3905 [M]	Down in the Valley	1961	20.00
❑ SE-3905 [S]	Down in the Valley	1961	25.00
❑ E-4154 [M]	Hootenanny	1963	20.00
❑ SE-4154 [S]	Hootenanny	1963	25.00
WARNER BROS.			
❑ W 1295 [M]	The Gateway Singers on the Lot	1959	25.00
❑ WS 1295 [S]	The Gateway Singers on the Lot	1959	30.00
❑ W 1334 [M]	Wagons West	1960	25.00
❑ WS 1334 [S]	Wagons West	1960	30.00
GATEWAY TRIO, THE			
45s			
CAPITOL			
❑ 5045	Soldiers Who Want to Be Heroes/ Poor Man's Travellin' Blues	1963	15.00
❑ 5286	Coney Island/All the Good Times	1964	15.00
Albums			
CAPITOL			
❑ ST 1868 [S]	The Mad, Mad, Mad Gateway Trio	1963	20.00
❑ T 1868 [M]	The Mad, Mad, Mad Gateway Trio	1963	15.00
❑ ST 2184 [S]	The Gateway Trio	1964	20.00
❑ T 2184 [M]	The Gateway Trio	1964	15.00
GATOR CREEK			
Albums			
MERCURY			
❑ SR-61311	Gator Creek	1970	12.00
GAUCHOS, THE See JIM DOVAL AND THE GAUCHOS.			
GAUDET, JOHN, AND THE LAURELS			
45s			
MARY GLEN			
❑ 1001/2	Christmas Will Soon Be Here/ Your Name Shall Be Remembered	1961	50.00
GAULT, JONNA, AND HER SYMPHONOPOP SCENE			
45s			
RCA VICTOR			
❑ 47-9440	Wonder Why, I Guess/ What If They Gave a War and No One Came?	1968	12.00
❑ 47-9704	Watch Me/The Answer Has to Come from Within	1968	8.00
Albums			
RCA VICTOR			
❑ LSP-4081	Watch Me	1968	25.00
GAVIN, TONY			
45s			
20TH FOX			
❑ 228	Ever Lovin' Baby/ I Just Don't Know	1960	40.00

Number	Title (A Side/B Side)	Yr	NM
GAY KNIGHTS, THE			
45s			
PET			
❑ 801	The Loudness of My Heart/ Angel	1958	40.00
GAY NOTES, THE			
45s			
DREXEL			
❑ 905	For Only a Moment/ Pu-Pu-Pa-Doo	1955	600.00
POST			
❑ 2006	Crossroads/Hear My Plea	1955	60.00
VIM			
❑ 501	Something Special/Cherie	1959	60.00
GAYE, MARVIN Also see THE MARQUEES (5); DIANA ROSS AND MARVIN GAYE.			
12-Inch Singles			
COLUMBIA			
❑ AS 1566 [DJ]	Sexual Healing (Long Version 5:10) (Short Version 3:52)	1982	60.00
❑ CAS 2124 [DJ]	Masochistic Beauty (Vocal 4:39) (Instrumental 4:39)	1985	8.00
❑ 44-03934	Joy (2 versions?)	1983	8.00
❑ 44-05188	Sanctified Lady/(Instrumental)	1985	8.00
❑ 44H-69170	Sexual Healing/The Groove	1989	8.00
—"Mixed Masters" reissue; B-side by Rodney Franklin			
MOTOWN			
❑ M 00014D1	A Funky Space Reincarnation (8:15) (Instrumental 8:19)	1978	20.00
❑ PR-129 [DJ]	I Heard It Through the Grapevine (5:03)//The Tracks of My Tears/ I Second That Emotion	1983	10.00
—B-side by Smokey Robinson and the Miracles; promo-only item issued in conjunction with the movie "The Big Chill"			
REPRISE			
❑ PRO-A-8343 [DJ]	Piece of Clay (Edit) (LP Version)	1996	10.00
TAMLA			
❑ PR-16 [DJ]	I Want You (Vocal 4:33) (Instrumental 4:36)/ Love Hangover (7:49)	1976	200.00
—B-side by Diana Ross on Motown label			
❑ PR-46 [DJ]	A Funky Space Reincarnation (8:15) (same on both sides)	1979	30.00
❑ PR-178 [DJ]	The World Is Rated X (12-Inch Version 6:28)/(Single Version 3:58)/Dark Side of the World/ Lonely Lover/I'm Going Home	1986	15.00
45s			
COLUMBIA			
❑ 38-03302	Sexual Healing/(Instrumental)	1982	4.00
❑ CNR-03344	Sexual Healing/(B-side blank)	1982	6.00
—One-sided budget release			
❑ 13-03585	Sexual Healing/(Instrumental)	1983	3.00
—Reissue			
❑ 38-03589	'Til Tomorrow/ Rockin' After Midnight	1983	4.00
❑ 38-03860	Joy/(Instrumental)	1983	—
—Canceled? (Replaced by 38-03935?)			
❑ 38-03870	Star Spangled Banner/ Turn On Some Music	1983	—
—Canceled?			
❑ 38-03935	Joy/Turn On Some Music	1983	4.00
❑ 38-04861	Sanctified Lady/(Instrumental)	1985	4.00
❑ 38-05442	It's Madness/Ain't It Funny (How Things Turn Around)	1985	4.00
❑ 38-05791	Just Like/More	1986	4.00
DETROIT FREE PRESS			
❑ (no #) [DJ]	The Teen Beat Song/Loraine Alterman Interviews Marvin Gaye	1966	200.00
TAMLA			
❑ (no #) [DJ]	Masquerade (Is Over)/Witchcraft	1962	600.00
—As "Marvin Gay"; label states "Single Not Available extracted from Album (TM-221)"			
❑ S4KM 0741/2 [DJ]	This Is the Life/My Way	1965	50.00
❑ 1836	The World Is Rated X/ No Greater Love	1986	5.00
❑ 1836 [PS]	The World Is Rated X/ No Greater Love	1986	5.00
❑ 54041	Let Your Conscience Be Your Guide/Never Let You Go	1961	200.00
❑ 54055	Sandman/I'm Yours, You're Mine	1962	60.00
❑ 54062	Masquerade (Is Over)/Witchcraft	1962	—
—Unreleased			
❑ 54063	Soldier's Plea/Taking My Time	1962	40.00
—With label credit "Marvin Gaye Love Tones"			
❑ 54063	Soldier's Plea/Taking My Time	1962	50.00
—With label credit "Marvin Gaye"			
❑ 54068	Stubborn Kind of Fellow/ It Hurts Me Too	1962	30.00
❑ 54075	Hitch Hike/Hello There Angel	1963	20.00

Number	Title (A Side/B Side)	Yr	NM
❑ 54079	Pride and Joy/One of These Days	1963	20.00
❑ 54087	Can I Get a Witness/ I'm Crazy 'Bout My Baby	1963	20.00
❑ 54093	You're a Wonderful One/ When I'm Alone I Cry	1964	15.00
❑ 54095	Try It Baby/If My Heart Could Sing	1964	15.00
❑ 54095 [PS]	Try It Baby/If My Heart Could Sing	1964	60.00
❑ 54101	Baby Don't You Do It/ Walk on the Wild Side	1964	15.00
❑ 54101 [PS]	Baby Don't You Do It/ Walk on the Wild Side	1964	60.00
❑ 54107	How Sweet It Is To Be Loved By You/Forever	1964	15.00
❑ 54112	I'll Be Doggone/You've Been a Long Time Coming	1965	15.00
❑ 54117	Pretty Little Baby/Now That You've Won Me	1965	15.00
❑ 54122	Ain't That Peculiar/ She's Got to Be Real	1965	15.00
❑ 54129	One More Heartache/ When I Had Your Love	1966	12.00
❑ 54132	Take This Heart of Mine/Need Your Lovin' (Want You Back)	1966	12.00
❑ 54138	Little Darling, I Need You/ Hey Diddle Diddle	1966	12.00
❑ 54153	Your Unchanging Love/ I'll Take Care of You	1967	10.00
❑ 54160	You/Change What You Can	1967	10.00
❑ 54170	Chained/At Last I Found a Love	1968	10.00
❑ 54176	I Heard It Through the Grapevine/ You're What's Happening (In the World Today)	1968	10.00
❑ 54181	Too Busy Thinking About My Baby/Wherever I Lay My Hat (That's My Home)	1969	8.00
❑ 54185	That's the Way Love Is/ Gonna Keep On Tryin' Till I Win Your Love	1969	8.00
❑ 54190	Gonna Give Her All the Love I've Got/How Can I Forget You	1970	8.00
❑ 54195	The End of Our Road/ Me and My Lonely Room	1970	8.00
❑ 54201	What's Going On/God Is Love	1971	6.00
❑ 54207	Mercy Mercy Me (The Ecology)/ Sad Tomorrows	1971	6.00
❑ 54209	Inner City Blues (Make Me Wanna Holler)/Wholly Holy	1971	6.00
❑ 54221	You're the Man (Part 1)/ You're the Man (Part 2)	1972	6.00
❑ 54228	Trouble Man/Don't Mess With Mister "T"	1972	6.00
❑ 54229	Christmas in the City/I Want to Come Home for Christmas	1972	—
—Canceled			
❑ 54234	Let's Get It On/I Wish It Would Rain	1973	4.00
❑ 54241	Come Get to This/Distant Lover	1973	4.00
❑ 54244	You Sure Love to Ball/ Just to Keep You Satisfied	1974	4.00
❑ 54253	Distant Lover/Trouble Man	1974	4.00
❑ 54264	I Want You/I Want You (Instrumental)	1975	4.00
❑ 54273	After the Dance/ Feel All My Love Inside	1976	4.00
❑ 54280	Got to Give It Up — Pt. 1/ Got to Give It Up — Pt. 2	1977	4.00
❑ 54280 [PS]	Got to Give It Up — Pt. 1/ Got to Give It Up — Pt. 2	1977	10.00
❑ 54298	Funky Space Reincarnation — Pt. 1/Funky Space Reincarnation — Pt. 2	1979	4.00
❑ 54300	Time to Get It Together/Anger	1979	10.00
—Only released in Canada			
❑ 54305	Ego Tripping Out/ (Instrumental)	1979	4.00
❑ 54322	Funk Me/Praise	1981	4.00
❑ 54326	Heavy Love Affair/Far Cry	1981	4.00
TOPPS/MOTOWN			
❑ 6	How Sweet It Is	1967	75.00
—Cardboard record			
Albums			
COLUMBIA			
❑ FC 38197	Midnight Love	1982	10.00
❑ PC 38197	Midnight Love	1986	8.00
—Budget-line reissue			
❑ FC 39916	Dream of a Lifetime	1985	10.00
❑ 9C9 40133 [PD]	Dream of a Lifetime	1985	20.00
❑ FC 40208	Romantically Yours	1986	10.00
❑ HC 48197	Midnight Love	1984	40.00
—Half-speed mastered edition			
MOTOWN			
❑ M5-115V1	Motown Superstar Series, Vol. 15	1981	10.00
❑ M5-125V1	M.P.G.	1981	10.00
—Reissue of Tamla 292			
❑ M5-181V1	Marvin Gaye Live!	1981	10.00
—Reissue of Tamla 333			
❑ M5-191V1	Marvin Gaye's Greatest Hits	1981	10.00
—Reissue of Tamla 348			

G

G

Number	Title (A Side/B Side)	Yr	NM
❑ M5-192V1	Let's Get It On	1981	10.00
—Reissue of Tamla 329			
❑ M5-216V1	A Tribute to the Great Nat King Cole	1981	10.00
—Reissue of Tamla 261			
❑ M5-218V1	That Stubborn Kinda' Fellow	1981	10.00
—Reissue of Tamla 239			
❑ M9-791A3 [(3)]	Anthology	1974	20.00
❑ 37463 1296-1 [DJ]	The Master 1961-1984	1995	20.00
—Vinyl is promo only; 8-song sampler from box set			
❑ 5259 ML [(2)]	Marvin Gaye Live at the London Palladium	1983	12.00
—Reissue of Tamla 352			
❑ 5306 ML	Super Hits	198?	10.00
❑ 5339 ML	What's Going On	198?	10.00
—Reissue of Tamla 322			
❑ 6058 ML	Every Great Motown Hit of Marvin Gaye	1983	10.00
❑ 6255 ML [(2)]	A Musical Testament 1964-1984	1988	12.00
❑ 952921	I Want You	2008	20.00

NATURAL RESOURCES

Number	Title (A Side/B Side)	Yr	NM
❑ NR 4007T1	The Soulful Moods of Marvin Gaye	1978	12.00
—Reissue of Tamla 221			

TAMLA

Number	Title (A Side/B Side)	Yr	NM
❑ TM 221 [M]	The Soulful Moods of Marvin Gaye	1961	1000.
❑ T 239 [M]	That Stubborn Kinda' Fella	1963	600.00
❑ T 242 [M]	Recorded Live — Marvin Gaye on Stage	1963	300.00
❑ T 251 [M]	When I'm Alone I Cry	1964	250.00
❑ T 252 [M]	Marvin Gaye/Greatest Hits	1964	30.00
❑ TS 252 [S]	Marvin Gaye/Greatest Hits	1964	40.00
❑ T 258 [M]	How Sweet It Is to Be Loved by You	1965	40.00
❑ TS 258 [S]	How Sweet It Is to Be Loved by You	1965	50.00
❑ T 259 [M]	Hello Broadway, This Is Marvin	1965	40.00
❑ TS 259 [S]	Hello Broadway, This Is Marvin	1965	50.00
❑ T 261 [M]	A Tribute to the Great Nat King Cole	1965	40.00
❑ TS 261 [S]	A Tribute to the Great Nat King Cole	1965	50.00
❑ T 266 [M]	Moods of Marvin Gaye	1966	40.00
❑ TS 266 [S]	Moods of Marvin Gaye	1966	50.00
❑ T 278 [M]	Marvin Gaye/Greatest Hits, Vol. 2	1967	25.00
❑ TS 278 [S]	Marvin Gaye/Greatest Hits, Vol. 2	1967	20.00
❑ T 285 [M]	In the Groove	1968	50.00
❑ TS 285 [S]	In the Groove	1968	25.00
❑ TS 285 [S]	I Heard It Through the Grapevine	1969	20.00
—Retitled version of "In the Groove"			
❑ TS 292	M.P.G.	1969	20.00
❑ TS 293	Marvin Gaye and His Girls	1969	20.00
—Includes duets with Tammi Terrell, Mary Wells, Kim Weston			
❑ TS 299	That's the Way Love Is	1969	20.00
❑ TS 300	Marvin Gaye Super Hits	1970	20.00
❑ T5-310	What's Going On	1971	15.00
❑ T5-322	Trouble Man	1972	15.00
❑ T6-329	Let's Get It On	1973	15.00
❑ T6-333	Marvin Gaye Live!	1974	15.00
❑ T6-342	I Want You	1976	15.00
❑ T6-348	Marvin Gaye's Greatest Hits	1976	15.00
❑ T7-352 [(2)]	Marvin Gaye Live at the London Palladium	1977	15.00
❑ T13-364 [(2)]	Here, My Dear	1978	15.00
❑ T8-374	In Our Lifetime	1981	10.00
❑ 6172 TL	Motown Remembers Marvin Gaye	1986	10.00

UNIVERSAL MOTOWN

Number	Title (A Side/B Side)	Yr	NM
❑ 5300221	What's Going On	2008	20.00

GAYE, MARVIN, AND TAMMI TERRELL

Also see each artist's individual listings.

45s

TAMLA

Number	Title (A Side/B Side)	Yr	NM
❑ 54149	Ain't No Mountain High Enough/Give a Little Love	1967	8.00
❑ 54156	Your Precious Love/Hold Me Oh My Darling	1967	8.00
❑ 54161	If I Could Build My Whole World Around You/If This World Were Mine	1967	8.00
❑ 54163	Ain't Nothing Like the Real Thing/Little Ole Boy, Little Ole Girl	1968	8.00
❑ 54169	You're All I Need to Get By/Two Can Have a Party	1968	8.00
❑ 54173	You Ain't Livin' Till You're Lovin'/Keep On Lovin' Me Honey	1968	6.00
❑ 54179	Good Lovin' Ain't Easy to Come By/Satisfied Feelin'	1969	6.00
❑ 54179 [PS]	Good Lovin' Ain't Easy to Come By/Satisfied Feelin'	1969	20.00
❑ 54187	What You Gave Me/How You Gonna Keep It	1969	6.00
❑ 54192	The Onion Song/California Soul	1970	6.00

Albums

MOTOWN

Number	Title (A Side/B Side)	Yr	NM
❑ M5-102V1	Motown Superstar Series, Vol. 2	1981	10.00
❑ M5-142V1	You're All I Need	1981	10.00
—Reissue of Tamla 284			
❑ M5-200V1	United	1981	10.00
—Reissue of Tamla 277			

TAMLA

Number	Title (A Side/B Side)	Yr	NM
❑ T 277 [M]	United	1967	30.00
❑ TS 277 [S]	United	1967	25.00
❑ T 284 [M]	You're All I Need	1968	50.00
❑ TS 284 [S]	You're All I Need	1968	20.00
❑ TS 294	Easy	1969	20.00
❑ TS 302	Marvin Gaye & Tammi Terrell/Greatest Hits	1970	20.00

GAYE, MARVIN, AND MARY WELLS

Also see each artist's individual listings.

45s

MOTOWN

Number	Title (A Side/B Side)	Yr	NM
❑ 1057	Once Upon a Time/What's the Matter with You Baby	1964	15.00
❑ 1057 [PS]	Once Upon a Time/What's the Matter with You Baby	1964	60.00

Albums

MOTOWN

Number	Title (A Side/B Side)	Yr	NM
❑ M 613 [M]	Together	1964	50.00
❑ 5260 ML	Together	1982	10.00

GAYE, MARVIN, AND KIM WESTON

Also see each artist's individual listings.

45s

TAMLA

Number	Title (A Side/B Side)	Yr	NM
❑ 54104	What Good Am I Without You/I Want You 'Round	1964	15.00
❑ 54141	It Takes Two/It's Got to Be a Miracle	1966	12.00

Albums

TAMLA

Number	Title (A Side/B Side)	Yr	NM
❑ T/TS 260	Side by Side	1965	—
—Canceled			
❑ T 270 [M]	Take Two	1966	30.00
❑ TS 270 [S]	Take Two	1966	40.00

GAYLARKS, THE

45s

MUSIC CITY

Number	Title (A Side/B Side)	Yr	NM
❑ 792	Tell Me Darling/Whole Lot of Love	1956	120.00
—B-side by the Rovers			
❑ 793	Romantic Memories/Li'l Dream Girl	1956	120.00
❑ 805	My Greatest Sin/Teenage Mambo	1957	100.00
❑ 809	Church on the Hill/Mr. Rock-n-Roll	1957	120.00
❑ 812	Just One More Chance/Somewhere in This World	1957	60.00
❑ 819	Ivy League Clothes/Rockin' Satellite	1958	50.00

GAYLES, BILLY, WITH IKE TURNER'S RHYTHM ROCKERS

45s

FEDERAL

Number	Title (A Side/B Side)	Yr	NM
❑ 12265	I'm Tore Up/If I Had Never Known You	1956	40.00
❑ 12272	Let's Call It a Day/Take Your Fine Frame Home	1956	40.00
❑ 12282	No Coming Back/Do Right Baby	1956	40.00
❑ 12287	Just One More Time/Sad as a Man Can Be	1957	40.00

GAYLES, THE

45s

ABC-PARAMOUNT

Number	Title (A Side/B Side)	Yr	NM
❑ 9707	Shortnin' Bread Rock/You Fool	1956	25.00

KING

Number	Title (A Side/B Side)	Yr	NM
❑ 4846	My Boy, Flat Top/I Get So Happy	1955	20.00
❑ 4860	I Had to Love You/Too Late I Learned	1955	20.00

GAYLORDS, THE

45s

MERCURY

Number	Title (A Side/B Side)	Yr	NM
❑ 70030	Tell Me You're Mine/Cuban Love Song	1952	15.00
❑ 70067	Tell Me You're Mine/Aye Aye Aye	1952	12.00
❑ 70112	Ramona/Spinning a Web	1953	12.00
❑ 70170	Tell Me That You Love Me/Coquette	1953	12.00
❑ 70235	Wonderin'/Sweet Sue	1953	12.00
❑ 70258	The Strings of My Heart/Mama Papa Polka	1953	12.00
❑ 70286	Stolen Moments/Patzo for Pizza	1954	12.00
❑ 70296	From the Vine Came the Grape/Stolen Moments	1954	12.00
❑ 70308	From the Vine Came the Grape/Patzo for Pizza	1954	10.00
❑ 70350	Isle of Capri/Love I You	1954	12.00
❑ 70403	The Little Shoemaker/Masque, Masque	1954	12.00
❑ 70427	Veni, Vida, Vida/A Kiss to Call My Own	1954	12.00
❑ 70479	Wonderful Lips/Pupalina	1954	12.00
❑ 70543	Chow Mein/Poppa Poppadopolis	1955	10.00
❑ 70586	The Woodpecker Song/My Babe	1955	10.00
❑ 70589	Mambo Rock/Plantation Boogie	1955	10.00
❑ 70630	Chee Chee O-Chee/Who's Got the Pain	1955	10.00
❑ 70660	Happy Time Medley (1. Minnie the Mermaid; 2. The Man Who Broke the Bank at Monte Carlo; 3. Goodbye My Coney Island Baby; 4. If You Knew Susie)/Madalaina	1955	10.00
❑ 70706	No Arms Can Ever Hold You/Bring Me a Bluebird	1955	10.00
❑ 70778	Molly-O/Vino Vino	1956	10.00
❑ 70834	Bella Bambinella/Who's Gonna Take You to the Prom	1956	10.00
❑ 70891	First Row Balcony/One Night Only	1956	10.00
❑ 70979	A Little Love, A Little Kiss/The Mountain Climber	1956	10.00
❑ 71051	The Dum-De-Dum Song/Open the Letter	1957	10.00
❑ 71186	Satin Doll/Wandering Heart	1957	10.00
❑ 71236	O Mari/Magic Song	1957	10.00
❑ 71265	Love/Each Time I Love You More	1958	8.00
❑ 71337	Ma Ma Ma Marie/Buona Sera	1958	8.00
❑ 71369	Flamingo L'Amore/I'm Longing for Love	1958	8.00
❑ 71399	Again/How About Me	1959	8.00
❑ 71450	Sweeter Than You/Homin' Pigeon	1959	8.00
❑ 71503	Jesse James/The Shovel	1959	8.00
❑ 71569	She's Gone/Please Consider	1960	8.00
❑ 71601	Love Me Now and Forever/Whip of the Wind	1960	8.00
❑ 71625	Sensation/Carina	1960	8.00
❑ 71762	Daisy, You're Driving Me Crazy/Born to Be Loved	1961	8.00
❑ 71832	Oh Lonesome Me/Yakety Yak	1961	8.00
❑ 71902	It Hurts Me More (The Second Time Around)/American 100%	1961	8.00
❑ 71970	How About Me/Two-Ton Tessie	1962	8.00

7-Inch Extended Plays

MERCURY

Number	Title (A Side/B Side)	Yr	NM
❑ EP-1-3210	Wonderin'/Coquette//Cuban Love Song/The Strings of My Heart	195?	20.00
❑ EP-1-3210 [PS]	(title unknown)	195?	20.00
❑ EP-1-3263	A Kiss to Call My Own/It//Serenade in the Night/Frivolette	195?	20.00
❑ EP-1-3263 [PS]	(title unknown)	195?	20.00
❑ EP-1-3288	Pupalina/Wonderful Lips//The Little Shoemaker/Mecque, Mecque	195?	20.00
❑ EP-1-3288 [PS]	(title unknown)	195?	20.00

Albums

MERCURY

Number	Title (A Side/B Side)	Yr	NM
❑ MG-20186 [M]	Italia	1957	30.00
❑ MG-20213 [M]	Collection of Golden Hits	1957	30.00
❑ MG-20356 [M]	Let's Have a Pizza Party	1958	20.00
❑ MG-20430 [M]	That's Amore	1959	20.00
❑ MG-20620 [M]	American Hits in Italian	1961	20.00
❑ MG-20695 [M]	The Gaylords at the Shamrock	1962	20.00
❑ MG-20742 [M]	Party Style	1963	20.00
❑ MG-25198 [10]	By Request	1955	50.00
❑ SR-60075 [S]	Let's Have a Pizza Party	1959	30.00
❑ SR-60102 [S]	That's Amore	1959	30.00
❑ SR-60620 [S]	American Hits in Italian	1961	30.00
❑ SR-60695 [S]	The Gaylords at the Shamrock	1962	25.00
❑ SR-60742 [S]	Party Style	1963	25.00

TIME

Number	Title (A Side/B Side)	Yr	NM
❑ S-2109 [S]	Live at Lake Tahoe	196?	20.00
❑ S-2127 [S]	Bella Italia	196?	20.00
❑ 52109 [M]	Live at Lake Tahoe	196?	15.00
❑ 52127 [M]	Bella Italia	196?	15.00

WING

Number	Title (A Side/B Side)	Yr	NM
❑ MGW-12139 [M]	Italiano Favorites	196?	12.00
❑ MGW-12278 [M]	Let's Have a Pizza Party	196?	12.00
❑ SRW-16139 [S]	Italiano Favorites	196?	12.00
❑ SRW-16278 [S]	Let's Have a Pizza Party	196?	12.00

Except when noted otherwise, VG = 25% of NM, and VG+ = 50% of NM. (Example: VG = $2.00, VG+ = $4.00 and NM = $8.00.)

Number	Title (A Side/B Side)	Yr	NM
GAYTEN, PAUL Also see THE TUNE WEAVERS.			
45s			
ANNA			
❑ 1106	The Hunch/Hot Cross Buns	1959	20.00
❑ 1112	Beatnick Beat/Scratch Back	1960	20.00
ARGO			
❑ 5257	The Music Goes Round and Round/Be My Baby	1956	25.00
❑ 5263	Driving Home Part 1/ Driving Home Part 2	1957	25.00
❑ 5267	Old Buttermilk Sky/The Sweeper	1957	25.00
❑ 5277	Nervous Boogie/Flatfoot Sam	1957	25.00
—B-side by Oscar Wiles			
❑ 5300	Windy/Tickle Toe	1958	25.00
CHECKER			
❑ 801	I'm Tired/Get It	1954	25.00
❑ 836	You Better Believe It/ Mother Roux	1956	25.00
OKEH			
❑ 6847	Lonesome for My Baby/ All Alone and Lovely	1952	30.00
❑ 6870	Give Me Liberty or Give Me Death/Happy Days	1952	30.00
❑ 6908	True (You Don't Love Me)/ They All Ask for You	1952	30.00
❑ 6934	Yes You Do, Yes You Do/ Don't Worry Me	1953	30.00
❑ 6972	Time Is a-Passin'/Ain't Nothin' Happenin'	1953	30.00
❑ 6982	Cow Cow Blues/Ooh-Boo	1953	30.00
❑ 7003	Hurry Home/Sugar Baby	1953	30.00
❑ 7019	Mule Face/It's Over	1954	30.00
❑ 7068	True (You Don't Love Me)/ Cow Cow Blues	1956	25.00
GAYTUNES, THE			
45s			
JOYCE			
❑ 101	I Love You/You Left Me	1957	200.00
❑ 106	Pen Pal/Plea in the Moonlight	199?	8.00
—Black vinyl			
❑ 106	Pen Pal/Plea in the Moonlight	199?	10.00
—Red vinyl			
LOST-NITE			
❑ 244	I Love You/You Left Me	196?	5.00
—Reissue			
GAZELLES, THE			
45s			
GOTHAM			
❑ 315	Honest/Pretty Baby, Baby	1956	300.00
GEARS, THE			
45s			
FOUR SPEED			
❑ (# unknown)	Let's Go to the Beach/Hard Rock/Don't Be Afraid to Pogo	1979	100.00
❑ (# unknown) [PS]	Let's Go to the Beach/Hard Rock/Don't Be Afraid to Pogo	1979	100.00
Albums			
PLAYGEMS			
❑ GS 6471	Rockin' at Ground Zero	1980	30.00
GEDDES, DAVID			
45s			
ATCO			
❑ 7028	Run Joey Run/Honey Don't Blow It	1975	—
—Canceled?			
BIG TREE			
❑ 16044	Run Joey Run/Honey Don't Blow It	1975	4.00
❑ 16052	The Last Game of the Season (A Blind Man in the Bleachers)/Wake Up Girl	1975	4.00
❑ 16059	Stephanie/Changing Colours	1976	4.00
❑ 16067	Trouble/Wait for Me	1976	4.00
H&L			
❑ 4684	Rocky's Girl/Changing Colours	1977	4.00
ZODIAC			
❑ 1019	Rocky's Girl/Changing Colours	1977	4.00
Albums			
BIG TREE			
❑ BT 89511	Run Joey Run	1975	12.00

The J. Geils Band, "One Last Kiss," EMI America 8007, 1978, **$6.**

Number	Title (A Side/B Side)	Yr	NM
GEE, ELLIE See ELLIE GREENWICH.			
GEE, JOEY			
45s			
ABC-PARAMOUNT			
❑ 10781	Don't Blow Your Cool/ It's More Than I Deserve	1966	400.00
SARA			
❑ 6599	She's Mean/You Know Till the End of Time	1965	20.00
GEE CEES, THE Also see THE KELLY FOUR.			
45s			
CREST			
❑ 1088	Buzz Saw/Annie Had a Party	1961	40.00
—Glen Campbell is on A-side; Eddie Cochran is on B-side			
❑ 1088	Buzz Saw Twist/ Annie Had a Party	1962	30.00
GEILS, J., BAND Featuring Peter Wolf.			
45s			
ATLANTIC			
❑ 2784	First I Look at the Purse/ Homework	1971	8.00
❑ 2802	Cruisin' for a Love/Wait	1971	6.00
❑ 2843	Dead Presidents/I Don't Need You No More	1971	6.00
❑ 2844	Looking for a Love/What's Your Whammer Jammer	1971	6.00
❑ 2929	Hard Drivin' Man/ Whammer Jammer	1972	6.00
❑ 2953	Give It To Me/Hold Your Loving	1973	5.00
❑ 2974	Make Up Your Mind/ Southside Shuffle	1973	5.00
❑ 2974 [PS]	Make Up Your Mind/ Southside Shuffle	1973	10.00
❑ 3007	Did You No Wrong/That's Why I'm Thinking of You	1974	5.00
❑ 3214	Must of Got Lost/Funky Judge	1974	5.00
❑ 3251	Givin' It All Up/Gettin' Out	1975	5.00
❑ 3301	Think It Over/Love-Itis	1975	5.00
❑ 3320	Where Did Our Love Go/ What's Your Hurry	1976	5.00
❑ 3350	(Ain't Nothing But a) House Party/Give It To Me	1976	5.00
❑ 3378	Peanut Buuter/Magic's Mood	1976	5.00
❑ 3411	You're the Only One/Wreckage	1977	5.00
—As "Geils"			
❑ 3438	Monkey Island (Part 1)/Surrender	1977	5.00
—As "Geils"			
❑ 3454	I Do/Trying to Live My Life Without You	1978	5.00
—As "Geils"			
❑ 3454 [PS]	I Do/Trying to Live My Life Without You	1978	8.00
—As "Geils"			
EMI AMERICA			
❑ 8007	One Last Kiss/Revenge	1978	4.00
❑ 8007 [PS]	One Last Kiss/Revenge	1978	6.00
❑ 8012	Take It Back/I Can't Believe You	1979	4.00
❑ 8016	Wild Man/Just Can't Stop Me	1979	4.00
❑ 8016 [PS]	Wild Man/Just Can't Stop Me	1979	10.00
❑ 8032	Come Back/Takin' You Down	1980	4.00
❑ 8032 [DJ]	Come Back (Long)/ Come Back (Edit)	1980	5.00
❑ 8039	Love Stinks/Till the Walls Come Tumblin' Down	1980	4.00
❑ 8039 [PS]	Love Stinks/Till the Walls Come Tumblin' Down	1980	5.00
❑ 8047	Just Can't Wait/No Anchovies, Please	1980	4.00
❑ 8100	Angel in Blue/Rage in the Cage	1982	3.00
❑ 8100 [PS]	Angel in Blue/Rage in the Cage	1982	4.00
❑ 8102	Centerfold/Rage in the Cage	1981	3.00
—Custom pink label			
❑ 8102	Centerfold/Rage in the Cage	1981	5.00
—Regular gray EMI America label			
❑ 8102 [PS]	Centerfold/Rage in the Cage	1981	10.00
❑ 8108	Freeze-Frame/Flamethrower	1982	3.00
❑ 8108 [PS]	Freeze-Frame/Flamethrower	1982	6.00
❑ 8148	I Do/Sanctuary	1982	3.00
❑ 8148 [PS]	I Do/Sanctuary	1982	4.00
❑ 8156	Land of 1000 Dances/ Jus' Can't Stop Me	1983	3.00

Number	Title (A Side/B Side)	Yr	NM
❑ 8242	Concealed Weapons/Tell 'Em Jonsey	1984	3.00
❑ 8242 [PS]	Concealed Weapons/Tell 'Em Jonsey	1984	4.00
❑ 8260	Eenie Meenie Miney Mo/I Will Carry You Home	1985	3.00
PRIVATE I			
❑ 05462	Fright Night/Boppin' Tonight	1985	3.00
—B-side by The Fabulous Fontaines			
❑ 05462 [PS]	Fright Night/Boppin' Tonight	1985	4.00
SILVER SPOTLIGHT SERIES			
❑ X-7106	Centerfold/I Do (Live Version)	1983	5.00
—Unusual reissue			
7-Inch Extended Plays			
ATLANTIC			
❑ SD 7-7260	House Party/Give It to Me//Start All Over Again/Make Up Your Mind	1973	15.00
—Jukebox issue; small hole, plays at 33 1/3 rpm			
❑ SD 7-7260 [PS]	Bloodshot	1973	15.00
—Part of "Little LP" series (LLP #219)			
Albums			
ATLANTIC			
❑ SD 2-507 [(2)]	Live — Blow Your Face Out	1976	15.00
❑ SD 7241	"Live" — Full House	1972	12.00
❑ QD 7260 [Q]	Bloodshot	1973	20.00
❑ SD 7260	Bloodshot	1973	12.00
—Black vinyl			
❑ SD 7260	Bloodshot	1973	20.00
—Red vinyl			
❑ QD 7286 [Q]	Ladies Invited	1973	—
—Not released			
❑ SD 7286	Ladies Invited	1973	12.00
❑ 8275 [M]	The J. Geils Band	1970	40.00
—Mono is white label promo only; stereo cover with "dj copy monaural" sticker			
❑ SD 8275 [S]	The J. Geils Band	1970	15.00
❑ 8297 [M]	The Morning After	1971	40.00
—Mono version is white label promo only with "d/j copy monaural" stucker on front cover			
❑ SD 8297 [S]	The Morning After	1971	12.00
❑ QD 18107 [Q]	Nightmares and Other Tales from the Vinyl Jungle	1974	20.00
❑ SD 18107	Nightmares and Other Tales from the Vinyl Jungle	1974	12.00
❑ SD 18147	Hotline	1975	12.00
❑ SD 19103	Monkey Island	1977	12.00
—As "Geils"			
❑ SD 19234	Best of the J. Geils Band	1979	10.00
❑ SD 19284	Best of the J. Geils Band — 2	1980	10.00
EMI AMERICA			
❑ SN-16316	Sanctuary	1985	8.00
—Reissue			
❑ SN-16373	Showtime!	1986	8.00
—Reissue			
❑ SN-16374	Freeze-Frame	1986	8.00
—Reissue			
❑ SN-16375	Love Stinks	1986	8.00
—Reissue			
❑ SO-17006	Sanctuary	1978	10.00
❑ SOO-17016	Love Stinks	1980	10.00
❑ SOO-17062	Freeze-Frame	1981	10.00
❑ SO-17087	Showtime!	1982	10.00
❑ SJ-17137	You're Gettin' Even While I'm Gettin' Odd	1984	8.00
❑ ST-17174	Flashback — The Best of the J. Geils Band	1985	8.00
NAUTILUS			
❑ NR-25	Love Stinks	1982	20.00
—Audiophile vinyl			

GEMS, THE (1)

Number	Title (A Side/B Side)	Yr	NM
45s			
CHESS			
❑ 1863	One More Year/Let Your Hair Down	1963	12.00
❑ 1875	If It's the Last Thing I Do/A Girl's Impression	1963	12.00
❑ 1882	A Love of Mine/That's Why They Put Erasers On	1964	40.00
❑ 1908	I Can't Help Myself/Can't You Take a Hint	1964	40.00
❑ 1917	Love For Christmas/All Of It	1964	15.00
❑ 1930	He Makes Me Feel So Good/Happy New Love	1965	40.00
❑ 2104	Girls Can Do It/Ain't That Loving You	1971	20.00

GEMS, THE (2)

Number	Title (A Side/B Side)	Yr	NM
45s			
DREXEL			
❑ 901	Deed I Do/Talk About the Weather	1954	400.00
—Black vinyl			
❑ 901	Deed I Do/Talk About the Weather	1954	2500.
—Red vinyl			
❑ 903	I Thought You'd Care/Kitty from New York City	1954	300.00
—Black vinyl			
❑ 903	I Thought You'd Care/Kitty from New York City	1954	600.00
—Red vinyl			
❑ 904	You're Tired of Love/Ol' Man River	1954	300.00
—Black vinyl			
❑ 904	You're Tired of Love/Ol' Man River	1954	600.00
—Red vinyl			
❑ 909	One Woman Man/The Darkest Night	1955	400.00
❑ 915	Till the Day I Die/Monkey Face Baby	1956	400.00

GEMS, THE (U) These probably are neither group (1) nor (2).

Number	Title (A Side/B Side)	Yr	NM
45s			
MERCURY			
❑ 71819	Crazy Chicken/Hippy Dippy	1961	10.00
PAT			
❑ 101	There's No One Like My Love/School Rock	1961	30.00
RECORTE			
❑ 407	Waiting/Please Change Your Mind	1959	50.00
RIVERSIDE			
❑ 4590	I'll Be There/I Miss Him	1967	30.00
WIN			
❑ 701	Nursery Rhymes/The Night Is Over	1958	300.00

GENE AND DEBBE Also see GENE THOMAS.

Number	Title (A Side/B Side)	Yr	NM
45s			
HICKORY			
❑ 1643	Lovin' Season/Then You Can Tell Me Goodbye	1972	7.00
SAN			
❑ 1519	Go with Me/The Torch I Carry	1967	20.00
TRX			
❑ 5002	Go with Me/The Torch I Carry	1967	8.00
❑ 5006	Playboy/I'll Come Running	1967	10.00
❑ 5010	Lovin' Season/Love Will Give Us Wings	1968	8.00
❑ 5014	Rings of Gold/Make a Noise Like Love	1968	8.00
❑ 5017	Memories Are Made of This/The Sun Won't Shine Again	1969	8.00
❑ 5021	I'm Only Human/Loan Some	1969	8.00
Albums			
TRX			
❑ 1001	Here and Now	1968	25.00

GENE AND EUNICE

Number	Title (A Side/B Side)	Yr	NM
45s			
ALADDIN			
❑ 3276	Ko Ko Mo (I Need You So)/You and Me	1954	25.00
❑ 3282	This Is My Story/Move It Over Baby	1954	25.00
❑ 3292	Flim Flam/Can We Forget It	1954	25.00
❑ 3305	I Gotta Go Home/Have You Changed Your Mind	1954	25.00
❑ 3315	Hootchy Kootchy/I'll Never Believe in You	1955	20.00
❑ 3321	Let's Get Together/I'm So in Love with You	1955	20.00
❑ 3351	Bom Bom Lulu/Hi Diddle Diddle	1956	20.00
❑ 3374	The Vow/Strange World	1957	20.00
❑ 3376	Doodle Doodle Doo/Don't Treat Me This Way	1957	20.00
❑ 3414	I Mean Love/The Angels Gave You to Me	1958	20.00
CASE			
❑ 1001	Poco-Loco/Go-On Kokomo	1959	30.00
❑ 1002	Ah! Ah!/You Think I'm Not Thinking	1959	30.00
❑ 1005	Without Love/(B-side unknown)	1959	25.00
❑ 1007	Sugar Babe/Let's Play the Game	1960	25.00
COMBO			
❑ 64	Ko Ko Mo (I Need You So)/You and Me	1954	30.00
LILLY			
❑ 512	Everlovin' Baby/Got a Right to Know	1962	15.00
UNITED ARTISTS			
❑ 0151	Ko Ko Mo (I Love You So)/This Is My Story	1973	4.00
—"Silver Spotlight Series" reissue			

GENE AND TOMMY Real names: TERRY CASHMAN; TOMMY WEST.

Number	Title (A Side/B Side)	Yr	NM
45s			
ABC			
❑ 10981	Richard and Me/Can't Get to Stopping	1967	8.00

GENE LOVES JEZEBEL

Number	Title (A Side/B Side)	Yr	NM
12-Inch Singles			
GEFFEN			
❑ PRO2800 [DJ]	Suspicion (same on both sides)	1987	10.00
❑ PRO2998 [DJ]	Twenty Killer Hurts (3 versions)	1987	8.00
❑ PRO-A-2800 [DJ]	Suspicion (same on both sides)	1987	10.00
❑ PRO-A-2998 [DJ]	Twenty Killer Hurts (Killer 12") (Killer Dub) (Killer Instrumental)	1987	10.00
❑ 4157 [DJ]	Tangled Up in You (2 mixes)/Jealous (2 mixes)	1990	10.00
❑ PRO-A-4157 [DJ]	Tangled Up in You (2 versions)/Jealous (2 versions)	1990	10.00
❑ 20519	Heartache (LP Version) (Extended Version)/Before Doubt/Deli Babies	1986	8.00
❑ 20568	Desire (Come and Get It) (Dance Mix)/Sapphire Scavenger/New Horizons/Message	1986	8.00
❑ 20744	The Motion of Love (LP Version) (Jezebel Mix)/Vagabond (A New Adventure)/Bugg's Bruises	1987	8.00
❑ 20929	Suspcion (Jezebel Mix) (LP Version)/Twenty Killer Hurts (Killer 12")	1987	8.00
45s			
GEFFEN			
❑ 28104	Suspicion/Drowning Crazy	1988	4.00
❑ 28104 [PS]	Suspicion/Drowning Crazy	1988	4.00
❑ 28183	The Motion of Love/Bugg's Bruises	1987	4.00
❑ 28183 [PS]	The Motion of Love/Bugg's Bruises	1987	4.00
Albums			
GEFFEN			
❑ 141 [DJ]	Discover Interview	1986	25.00
❑ 4192 [EP]	Remix Sampler	1990	20.00
—Promo-only collection			
❑ GHS 24118	Discover	1986	10.00
❑ GHS 24165	Promise	1988	10.00
—First American issue of 1983 U.K. debut			
❑ GHS 24171	The House of Dolls	1988	10.00
❑ GHS 24260	Kiss of Life	1990	12.00
RELATIVITY			
❑ EMC 8036	Immigrant	1985	12.00
❑ EMC 8075 [EP]	Desire	1985	8.00
WARNER BROS.			
❑ WBMS-141 [DJ]	Discover Interview	1986	20.00
—Part of "The Warner Bros. Music Show" series; in die-cut cover			

GENERATION X Also see BILLY IDOL.

Number	Title (A Side/B Side)	Yr	NM
Albums			
CHRYSALIS			
❑ CHR 1169	Generation X	1978	25.00
❑ CHR 1193	Valley of the Dolls	1979	30.00
❑ CHR 1327	Kiss Me Deadly	1981	25.00
❑ PV 41169	Generation X	1984	15.00
—Reissue			
❑ PV 41193	Valley of the Dolls	1984	20.00
—Reissue			
❑ PV 41327	Kiss Me Deadly	1985	15.00
—Reissue			

GENESIS Also see PHIL COLLINS; PETER GABRIEL; STEVE HACKETT; MIKE RUTHERFORD; PETER BANKS. Records on Buddah, Mercury, Ripchord and Scepter are all by different groups, thus outside the scope of this book. Also see PHIL COLLINS; PETER GABRIEL.

Number	Title (A Side/B Side)	Yr	NM
12-Inch Singles			
ATLANTIC			
❑ PR 311 [DJ]	Go West Young Man (Deep in the Motherlode) (same on both sides)	1978	25.00
❑ PR 369 [DJ]	Turn It On Again (Studio Version 3:27) (Live Version 4:47)	1980	20.00
❑ PR 404 [DJ]	No Reply at All (4:37) (4:00)	1981	12.00
❑ PR 416 [DJ]	Abacab (same on both sides)	1981	12.00
❑ PR 425 [DJ]	Man on the Corner (same on both sides)	1981	12.00
❑ PR 442 [DJ]	Paperlate (same on both sides)	1982	10.00
❑ PR 535 [DJ]	Mama (same on both sides)	1983	10.00

Except when noted otherwise, VG = 25% of NM, and VG+ = 50% of NM. (Example: VG = $2.00, VG+ = $4.00 and NM = $8.00.)

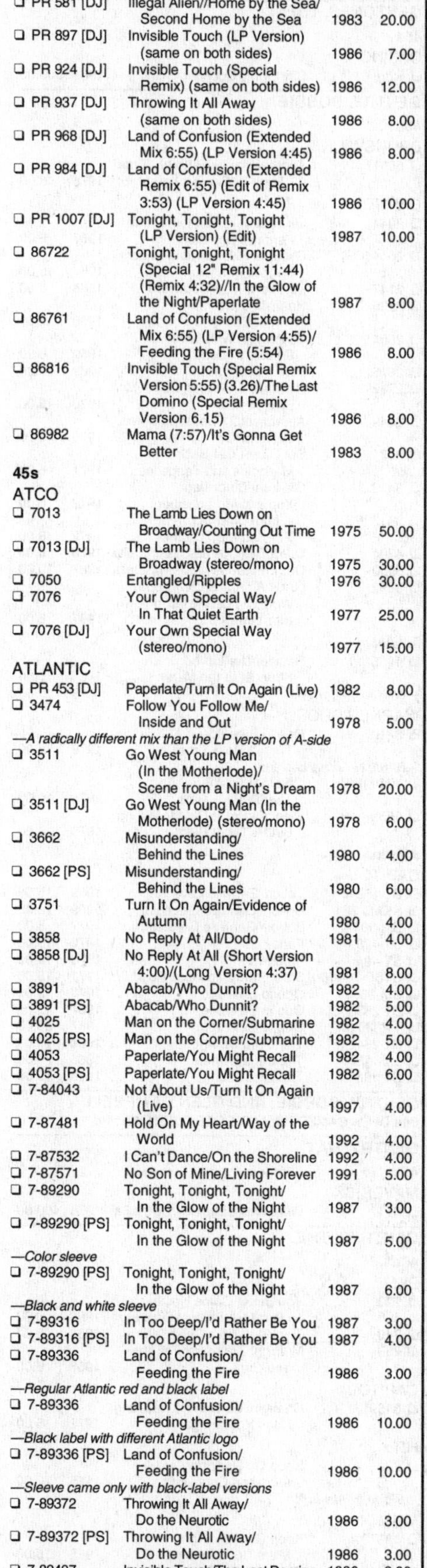

Number	Title (A Side/B Side)	Yr	NM
❑ PR 581 [DJ]	Illegal Alien//Home by the Sea/ Second Home by the Sea	1983	20.00
❑ PR 897 [DJ]	Invisible Touch (LP Version) (same on both sides)	1986	7.00
❑ PR 924 [DJ]	Invisible Touch (Special Remix) (same on both sides)	1986	12.00
❑ PR 937 [DJ]	Throwing It All Away (same on both sides)	1986	8.00
❑ PR 968 [DJ]	Land of Confusion (Extended Mix 6:55) (LP Version 4:45)	1986	8.00
❑ PR 984 [DJ]	Land of Confusion (Extended Remix 6:55) (Edit of Remix 3:53) (LP Version 4:45)	1986	10.00
❑ PR 1007 [DJ]	Tonight, Tonight, Tonight (LP Version) (Edit)	1987	10.00
❑ 86722	Tonight, Tonight, Tonight (Special 12" Remix 11:44) (Remix 4:32)//In the Glow of the Night/Paperlate	1987	8.00
❑ 86761	Land of Confusion (Extended Mix 6:55) (LP Version 4:55)/ Feeding the Fire (5:54)	1986	8.00
❑ 86816	Invisible Touch (Special Remix Version 5:55) (3.26)/The Last Domino (Special Remix Version 6.15)	1986	8.00
❑ 86982	Mama (7:57)/It's Gonna Get Better	1983	8.00
45s			
ATCO			
❑ 7013	The Lamb Lies Down on Broadway/Counting Out Time	1975	50.00
❑ 7013 [DJ]	The Lamb Lies Down on Broadway (stereo/mono)	1975	30.00
❑ 7050	Entangled/Ripples	1976	30.00
❑ 7076	Your Own Special Way/ In That Quiet Earth	1977	25.00
❑ 7076 [DJ]	Your Own Special Way (stereo/mono)	1977	15.00
ATLANTIC			
❑ PR 453 [DJ]	Paperlate/Turn It On Again (Live)	1982	8.00
❑ 3474	Follow You Follow Me/ Inside and Out	1978	5.00
—A radically different mix than the LP version of A-side			
❑ 3511	Go West Young Man (In the Motherlode)/ Scene from a Night's Dream	1978	20.00
❑ 3511 [DJ]	Go West Young Man (In the Motherlode) (stereo/mono)	1978	6.00
❑ 3662	Misunderstanding/ Behind the Lines	1980	4.00
❑ 3662 [PS]	Misunderstanding/ Behind the Lines	1980	6.00
❑ 3751	Turn It On Again/Evidence of Autumn	1980	4.00
❑ 3858	No Reply At All/Dodo	1981	4.00
❑ 3858 [DJ]	No Reply At All (Short Version 4:00)/(Long Version 4:37)	1981	8.00
❑ 3891	Abacab/Who Dunnit?	1982	4.00
❑ 3891 [PS]	Abacab/Who Dunnit?	1982	5.00
❑ 4025	Man on the Corner/Submarine	1982	4.00
❑ 4025 [PS]	Man on the Corner/Submarine	1982	5.00
❑ 4053	Paperlate/You Might Recall	1982	4.00
❑ 4053 [PS]	Paperlate/You Might Recall	1982	6.00
❑ 7-84043	Not About Us/Turn It On Again (Live)	1997	4.00
❑ 7-87481	Hold On My Heart/Way of the World	1992	4.00
❑ 7-87532	I Can't Dance/On the Shoreline	1992	4.00
❑ 7-87571	No Son of Mine/Living Forever	1991	5.00
❑ 7-89290	Tonight, Tonight, Tonight/ In the Glow of the Night	1987	3.00
❑ 7-89290 [PS]	Tonight, Tonight, Tonight/ In the Glow of the Night	1987	5.00
—Color sleeve			
❑ 7-89290 [PS]	Tonight, Tonight, Tonight/ In the Glow of the Night	1987	6.00
—Black and white sleeve			
❑ 7-89316	In Too Deep/I'd Rather Be You	1987	3.00
❑ 7-89316 [PS]	In Too Deep/I'd Rather Be You	1987	4.00
❑ 7-89336	Land of Confusion/ Feeding the Fire	1986	3.00
—Regular Atlantic red and black label			
❑ 7-89336	Land of Confusion/ Feeding the Fire	1986	10.00
—Black label with different Atlantic logo			
❑ 7-89336 [PS]	Land of Confusion/ Feeding the Fire	1986	10.00
—Sleeve came only with black-label versions			
❑ 7-89372	Throwing It All Away/ Do the Neurotic	1986	3.00
❑ 7-89372 [PS]	Throwing It All Away/ Do the Neurotic	1986	3.00
❑ 7-89407	Invisible Touch/The Last Domino	1986	3.00
❑ 7-89407 [PS]	Invisible Touch/The Last Domino	1986	3.00
❑ 7-89656	Taking It All Too Hard/ Silver Rainbow	1984	3.00

Genesis, "Tonight, Tonight, Tonight," Atlantic 7-89290, 1987, black and white sleeve, **$6.**

Number	Title (A Side/B Side)	Yr	NM
❑ 7-89656 [PS]	Taking It All Too Hard/ Silver Rainbow	1984	6.00
❑ 7-89698	Illegal Alien/Turn It On Again (Live in Philadelphia)	1984	4.00
❑ 7-89698 [DJ]	Illegal Alien (Edit)/(LP Version)	1984	6.00
❑ 7-89698 [PS]	Illegal Alien/Turn It On Again (Live in Philadelphia)	1984	4.00
❑ 7-89724	That's All/Second Home by the Sea	1983	3.00
—With custom labels			
❑ 7-89724 [PS]	That's All/Second Home by the Sea	1983	4.00
—Brown title sleeve with center cut-out			
❑ 7-89724 [PS]	That's All/Second Home by the Sea	1983	5.00
—Brown title sleeve with no center cut-out			
❑ 7-89770	Mama/It's Gonna Get Better	1983	3.00
❑ 7-89770 [PS]	Mama/It's Gonna Get Better	1983	4.00
ATLANTIC OLDIES SERIES			
❑ OS 13239	I Know What I Like (In Your Wardrobe)/The Lamb Lies Down on Broadway	1984	10.00
—Reissue			
❑ OS 13251	Your Own Special Way/ Go West Young Man (In the Motherlode)	1984	7.00
—Reissue; black and gold label			
❑ OS 13252	Misunderstanding/ Turn It On Again	1984	5.00
—Reissue; black and gold label			
❑ OS 13253	No Reply at All/Abacab	1984	5.00
—Reissue; black and gold label			
❑ OS 13254	Paperlate/Man on the Corner	1984	5.00
—Reissue; black and gold label			
❑ 7-84956	In Too Deep/Mama	1987	3.00
—Reissue			
❑ 7-84957	Follow You Follow Me /Illegal Alien	1987	3.00
—Reissue			
❑ 7-84958	Land of Confusion/ Tonight, Tonight, Tonight	1987	3.00
—Reissue			

Number	Title (A Side/B Side)	Yr	NM
❑ 7-84959	Invisible Touch/ Throwing It All Away	1987	3.00
—Reissue			
❑ 7-84996	That's All/Taking It All Too Hard	1987	3.00
—Reissue			
CHARISMA			
❑ 103	Watcher of the Skies/ Willow Farm	1973	80.00
❑ 26002	I Know What I Like (In Your Wardrobe)/ Twilight Ale House	1973	50.00
❑ 26002 [DJ]	I Know What I Like (In Your Wardrobe) (stereo/mono)	1973	30.00
PARROT			
❑ 3018	Silent Sun/That's Me	1968	400.00
—Stock copy with black label and green and yellow bird			
❑ 3018 [DJ]	Silent Sun/That's Me	1968	100.00
—Promotional copy; orangeish label with black bird			
Albums			
ABC			
❑ ABCX-816	Trespass	1971	15.00
—Reissue of Impulse album; black label			
❑ ABCX-816	Trespass	1974	12.00
—Reissue; concentric yellow/orange/purple "target" label			
ABC IMPULSE!			
❑ ASD-9205	Trespass	1971	30.00
ATCO			
❑ SD 38-100	Wind & Wuthering	1978	10.00
—Reissue of SD 36-144			
❑ SD 38-101	A Trick of the Tail	1978	10.00
—Reissue of SD 36-129			
❑ SD 36-129	A Trick of the Tail	1976	12.00
❑ SD 36-144	Wind & Wuthering	1977	12.00
❑ SD 2-401 [(2)]	The Lamb Lies Down on Broadway	1974	15.00
—Originals have yellow labels (other labels worth less)			
ATLANTIC			
❑ PR 965 [DJ]	Tonight, Tonight, Tonight — Exclusive Candid Interview	1986	30.00
—Promo-only music and interviews; came with cover letter and cue sheet (deduct 1/3 if missing)			

Number	Title (A Side/B Side)	Yr	NM
❑ SD 2-2000 [(2)]	Three Sides Live	1982	12.00
❑ SD 2-9002 [(2)]	Seconds Out	1977	12.00
❑ SD 16014	Duke	1980	10.00
❑ SD 19173	...And Then There Were Three	1978	10.00
❑ SD 19277	Selling England by the Pound	1981	8.00
—Reissue of Charisma LP of same name			
❑ SD 19313	Abacab	1981	10.00
—Released with four different covers, lettered "A" through "D" on the upper part of the spine; no difference in value			
❑ 80030	Nursery Cryme	1982	8.00
—Reissue of Charisma LP of same name			
❑ 80116	Genesis	1983	8.00
❑ 81641	Invisible Touch	1986	8.00
❑ 81848	Foxtrot	1988	10.00
—Reissue of Charisma LP of the same name			
❑ 81855	Genesis Live	1988	10.00
—Reissue of Charisma LP of the same name			

BUDDAH

Number	Title (A Side/B Side)	Yr	NM
❑ BDS-5659 [(2)]	The Best ... Genesis	1976	20.00
—Reissue of "Nursery Cryme" and "Foxtrot" in one set			

CHARISMA

Number	Title (A Side/B Side)	Yr	NM
❑ CAS-1052	Nursery Cryme	1971	15.00
❑ CAS-1052	Nursery Cryme	2000	25.00
—Classic Records reissue on 180-gram vinyl			
❑ CAS-1058	Foxtrot	1972	15.00
❑ CAS-1058	Foxtrot	2001	25.00
—Classic Records reissue on 180-gram vinyl			
❑ CAS-1666	Genesis Live	1974	15.00
❑ CAS-1666	Genesis Live	2001	25.00
—Classic Records reissue on 180-gram vinyl			
❑ CA2-2701 [(2)]	Nursery Cryme/Foxtrot	1976	15.00
—Repackage of the individual albums of these names			
❑ FC-6060	Selling England by the Pound	1973	15.00
❑ FC-6060	Selling England by the Pound	2001	25.00
—Classic Records reissue on 180-gram vinyl			

LONDON

Number	Title (A Side/B Side)	Yr	NM
❑ PS 643	From Genesis to Revelation	1974	25.00
—First US release of debut album			
❑ LC-50006	In the Beginning	1977	12.00
❑ 820322-1	In the Beginning	198?	10.00
—Reissue of London 50006			

MCA

Number	Title (A Side/B Side)	Yr	NM
❑ ABCX-816	Trespass	1979	10.00
—Reissue of ABC ABCX-816			
❑ 37151	Trespass	198?	8.00
—Reissue of MCA 816			

MOBILE FIDELITY

Number	Title (A Side/B Side)	Yr	NM
❑ 1-062	A Trick of the Tail	1981	50.00
—Audiophile vinyl			

GENESIS (2)

45s

BUDDAH

Number	Title (A Side/B Side)	Yr	NM
❑ 132	Journey to the Moon (Part 1)/ Journey to the Moon (Part 2)	1969	15.00

GENESIS (3)

45s

MERCURY

Number	Title (A Side/B Side)	Yr	NM
❑ 72806	Angeline/Suzanne	1968	12.00
❑ 72869	Gloomy Sunday/ What's It All About	1968	10.00

Albums

MERCURY

Number	Title (A Side/B Side)	Yr	NM
❑ SR 61175	In the Beginning	1968	100.00
—First pressing is textured cover, red label.			
❑ SR 61175	In the Beginning	197?	18.00
—Second pressing is non-textured cover, skyline label.			

GENESIS (4)

45s

RIPCHORD

Number	Title (A Side/B Side)	Yr	NM
❑ 004	Window of Sand/ Would You Like To	1967	25.00

GENESIS (5)

45s

SCEPTER

Number	Title (A Side/B Side)	Yr	NM
❑ 12341	Second Coming/Double Bubble	1972	5.00

GENIES, THE (1)

45s

HOLLYWOOD

Number	Title (A Side/B Side)	Yr	NM
❑ 69	No More Knockin'/ On the Edge of Town	1959	20.00

SHAD

Number	Title (A Side/B Side)	Yr	NM
❑ 5002	Who's That Knocking/ The First Time	1959	15.00
—Blue label			
❑ 5002	Who's That Knocking/ The First Time	1959	25.00
—Pink label			

WARWICK

Number	Title (A Side/B Side)	Yr	NM
❑ 573	Crazy Love/There Goes That Rain	1960	15.00
❑ 607	Just Like the Bluebird/ Twistin' Pneumonia	1960	15.00
❑ 643	Little Young Girl/Crazy Feeling	1961	15.00

GENIES, THE (2)

45s

RONN

Number	Title (A Side/B Side)	Yr	NM
❑ 50	Anybody Here Know How to Pray/Take Me There	1971	6.00
❑ 56	No News Is Good News/ Sunday Morning People	1971	6.00
❑ 68	Know Whatr to Do When You Get It/Prove It	197?	6.00

GENTEELS, THE

45s

CAPITOL

Number	Title (A Side/B Side)	Yr	NM
❑ 4798	Take It Off/Hitchhiker	1962	25.00

STAG

Number	Title (A Side/B Side)	Yr	NM
❑ 2930/1	Take It Off/Hitch Hiker	1962	50.00
❑ 4949/50	The Force of Gravity/ Springboard	1962	50.00

GENTLE GIANT

45s

CAPITOL

Number	Title (A Side/B Side)	Yr	NM
❑ 4484	Cogs in Cogs/I'm Turning Around	1977	5.00
❑ 4652	Spooky Boogie/Words from the Wise	1978	5.00

Albums

CAPITOL

Number	Title (A Side/B Side)	Yr	NM
❑ ST-11337	The Power and the Glory	1974	10.00
❑ ST-11428	Free Hand	1975	10.00
❑ ST-11532	Interview	1976	10.00
❑ SKBB-11592 [(2)]	The Official "Live" Gentle Giant — Playing the Fool	1977	12.00
❑ ST-11696	The Missing Piece	1977	10.00
❑ SW-11813	Giant for a Day	1978	10.00
❑ SN-16044	The Power and the Glory	1980	8.00
—Budget-line reissue			
❑ SN-16045	Giant for a Day	1980	8.00
—Budget-line reissue			
❑ SN-16046	The Missing Piece	1980	8.00
—Budget-line reissue			
❑ SN-16047	Interview	1980	8.00
—Budget-line reissue			
❑ SN-16048	Free Hand	1980	8.00
—Budget-line reissue			

COLUMBIA

Number	Title (A Side/B Side)	Yr	NM
❑ KC 31649	Three Friends	1972	12.00
❑ PC 31649	Three Friends	197?	8.00
—Reissue			
❑ KC 32022	Octopus	1973	12.00
❑ PC 32022	Octopus	197?	8.00
—Reissue			
❑ JC 36341	Civilian	1980	10.00

VERTIGO

Number	Title (A Side/B Side)	Yr	NM
❑ VE-1005	Acquiring the Taste	1971	15.00

GENTLE SOUL, THE

45s

COLUMBIA

Number	Title (A Side/B Side)	Yr	NM
❑ 4-43952	Tell Me Love/You Move Me	1966	20.00
❑ 4-43952 [PS]	Tell Me Love/You Move Me	1966	40.00
❑ 4-44152	Song for Three/ Our National Anthem	1967	20.00

EPIC

Number	Title (A Side/B Side)	Yr	NM
❑ 5-10448	Reelin'/2:30 Train	1969	20.00

Albums

EPIC

Number	Title (A Side/B Side)	Yr	NM
❑ BN 26374	The Gentle Soul	1969	200.00
—Reproductions exist			

GENTLEMEN, THE

45s

APOLLO

Number	Title (A Side/B Side)	Yr	NM
❑ 464	Something to Remember Me By/ Tired of You	1954	200.00
❑ 470	Don't Leave Me Baby/ Baby Don't Go	1955	100.00

CAMEO

Number	Title (A Side/B Side)	Yr	NM
❑ 419	Come On (If You Can)/Only Me	1966	20.00

GENTLEMEN FOUR, THE

45s

WAND

Number	Title (A Side/B Side)	Yr	NM
❑ 1184	It Won't Hurt Baby/You Can't Keep a Good Man Down	1968	600.00

GENTONES, THE

45s

CASINO

Number	Title (A Side/B Side)	Yr	NM
❑ 52261	City Lights/Counting Stars	1961	500.00

GENTRY, BOBBIE

45s

BRUNSWICK

Number	Title (A Side/B Side)	Yr	NM
❑ 55517	Another Place — Another Time/ I Think I'll Cry Out Loud	1975	6.00

CAPITOL

Number	Title (A Side/B Side)	Yr	NM
❑ 2044	Okolona River Bottom Band/ Penduli Pendulum	1967	8.00
❑ 2044 [PS]	Okolona River Bottom Band/ Penduli Pendulum	1967	15.00
❑ 2147	Louisiana Man/Courtyard	1968	8.00
❑ 2295	Hushabye Mountain/ Sweet Peony	1968	8.00
❑ 2501	Touch 'Em With Love/ Casket Vignette	1969	6.00
❑ 2675	Fancy/Courtyard	1969	6.00
❑ 2788	He Made a Woman Out of Me/ Billy the Kid	1970	6.00
❑ 2849	Apartment 21/Seasons Come, Seasons Go	1970	6.00
❑ 3071	But I Can't Get Back/ Marigolds and Tangerines	1971	6.00
❑ 3413	Girl from Cincinnati/ You and Me Together	1972	6.00
❑ 3413 [PS]	Girl from Cincinnati/ You and Me Together	1972	8.00
❑ 4294	Ode to Billie Joe/Mississippi Delta	1976	5.00
❑ 5950	Ode to Billie Joe/Mississippi Delta	1967	10.00
❑ 5992	I Saw An Angel Die/Poppa, Won'tcha Let Me Go to Town with You	1967	8.00

TITAN

Number	Title (A Side/B Side)	Yr	NM
❑ 1736	Requiem for Love/ Stranger in the Mirror	1963	15.00
—With Jody Reynolds			

WARNER BROS.

Number	Title (A Side/B Side)	Yr	NM
❑ 8210	Ode to Billie Joe/ There'll Be a Time	1976	5.00
—B-side by Michel Legrand			
❑ 8210 [PS]	Ode to Billie Joe/ There'll Be a Time	1976	10.00
❑ 8532	Steal Away/He Did Me Wrong But He Did It Right	1978	4.00

Albums

CAPITOL

Number	Title (A Side/B Side)	Yr	NM
❑ ST-155	Touch 'Em with Love	1969	15.00
❑ SKAO-381	Bobbie Gentry's Greatest!	1969	15.00
❑ SM-381	Bobbie Gentry's Greatest!	197?	8.00
❑ ST-428	Fancy	1970	15.00
❑ ST-494	Patchwork	1970	15.00
❑ STBB-704 [(2)]	Sittin' Pretty/Tobacco Road	1971	15.00
❑ SM-2830	Ode to Billie Joe	197?	8.00
❑ ST 2830 [S]	Ode to Billie Joe	1967	15.00
❑ T 2830 [M]	Ode to Billie Joe	1967	20.00
❑ ST 2842 [S]	The Delta Sweete	1968	15.00
❑ T 2842 [M]	The Delta Sweete	1968	25.00
❑ ST 2964	The Local Gentry	1968	15.00

GENTRY, BOBBIE, AND GLEN CAMPBELL

See GLEN CAMPBELL AND BOBBIE GENTRY.

GENTRY, RAY

45s

MAVERICK

Number	Title (A Side/B Side)	Yr	NM
❑ 614	Willie Was a Bad Boy/Do the Fly	1958	400.00

GENTRYS, THE

45s

BELL

Number	Title (A Side/B Side)	Yr	NM
❑ 720	You Better Come Home/ I Can't Go Back to Denver	1968	6.00
❑ 740	Thinking Like a Child/Silky	1968	6.00
❑ 753	Midnight Train/You Tell Me You Care	1968	6.00

CAPITOL

Number	Title (A Side/B Side)	Yr	NM
❑ 3459	Changin'/Let Me Put This Ring Upon Your Finger	1972	5.00

HIT

Number	Title (A Side/B Side)	Yr	NM
❑ 229	Keep On Dancing/ A Lover's Concerto	1965	20.00
—B-side by Alpha Zoe			

MGM

Number	Title (A Side/B Side)	Yr	NM
❑ 13379	Keep On Dancing/ Make Up Your Mind	1965	15.00
❑ 13432	Spread It On Thick/ Brown Paper Sack	1965	12.00
❑ 13432 [PS]	Spread It On Thick/ Brown Paper Sack	1965	16.00

Except when noted otherwise, VG = 25% of NM, and VG+ = 50% of NM. (Example: VG = $2.00, VG+ = $4.00 and NM = $8.00.)

Number	Title (A Side/B Side)	Yr	NM
❑ 13495	Everyday I Have to Cry/ Don't Let It Be (This Time)	1966	12.00
❑ 13561	There Are Two Sides to Every Story/Woman of the World	1966	12.00
❑ 13690	There's a Love/You Make Me Feel So Good	1967	25.00
❑ 13749	I Can See/90 Pound Weakling	1967	10.00

STAX

Number	Title (A Side/B Side)	Yr	NM
❑ 0223	All Hung Up on You/ Little Gold Band	1974	4.00
❑ 0242	High Flyer/Little Gold Band	1975	4.00

SUN

Number	Title (A Side/B Side)	Yr	NM
❑ 1108	I Need Love/Why Should I Cry	1969	5.00
❑ 1114	Cinnamon Girl/I Just Got the News	1970	5.00
❑ 1114 [DJ]	Cinnamon Girl/I Just Got the News	1970	10.00
—Promo only on blue vinyl			
❑ 1118	I Hate to See You Go/ He'll Never Love Me	1970	5.00
❑ 1120	Friends/Goddess of Love	1970	30.00
❑ 1122	Wild World/Sunshine	1971	5.00
❑ 1126	God Save Our Country/ Love You All My Life	1971	5.00

YOUNGSTOWN

Number	Title (A Side/B Side)	Yr	NM
❑ 600	Sometimes/Little Drops of Water	1965	25.00
❑ 601	Keep On Dancing/ Make Up Your Mind	1965	30.00

Albums

MGM

Number	Title (A Side/B Side)	Yr	NM
❑ GAS-127	The Gentrys (Golden Archive Series)	1970	20.00
❑ E-4336 [M]	Keep On Dancing	1965	25.00
❑ SE-4336 [P]	Keep On Dancing	1965	30.00
❑ E-4346 [M]	Gentry Time	1966	20.00
❑ SE-4346 [S]	Gentry Time	1966	25.00

SUN

Number	Title (A Side/B Side)	Yr	NM
❑ LP-117	The Gentrys	1970	30.00

GEORDIE
Includes Brian Johnson, later of AC/DC.

45s

MGM

Number	Title (A Side/B Side)	Yr	NM
❑ 14539	Ain't It Just Like a Woman/ All Because of You	1973	6.00

Albums

MGM

Number	Title (A Side/B Side)	Yr	NM
❑ SE-4903	Hope You Like It	1973	30.00

GEORGE, LLOYD

45s

IMPERIAL

Number	Title (A Side/B Side)	Yr	NM
❑ 5837	Twistville/Young Date	1962	15.00
❑ 5896	Come On Train/Frog Hunt	1962	15.00

GEORGE, LOWELL
Also see LITTLE FEAT.

45s

WARNER BROS.

Number	Title (A Side/B Side)	Yr	NM
❑ 8847	What Do You Want the Girl to Do/A Million Things	1979	5.00

Albums

WARNER BROS.

Number	Title (A Side/B Side)	Yr	NM
❑ 3194	Thanks I'll Eat it Here	1979	15.00

GEORGE AND EARL

45s

MERCURY

Number	Title (A Side/B Side)	Yr	NM
❑ 70605	Got Anything Good/Can I?	1955	25.00
❑ 70632	Goin' Steady with the Blues/ Sweet Little Miss Blue Eyes	1955	25.00
❑ 70683	Heartaches/Don't, Don't, Don't	1955	25.00
❑ 70773	Cry, Baby, Cry/Take a Look at My Darlin'	1956	25.00
❑ 70852	Done Gone/Better Stop, Look and Listen	1956	60.00
❑ 70935	Eleven Roses/Remember and Regret	1956	25.00

GEORGE AND GREER

45s

GOLDWAX

Number	Title (A Side/B Side)	Yr	NM
❑ 313	You Don't Know It, But You Had Me/Good Times	1966	30.00
—Reissue as "George Jackson and Dan Greer"			
❑ 313	You Don't Know It, But You Had Me/Good Times	1966	75.00

GEORGE AND LOUIS

45s

SUN

Number	Title (A Side/B Side)	Yr	NM
❑ 301	The Return of Jerry Lee/The Return of Jerry Lee, Part 2	1958	25.00
❑ 301	The Return of Jerry Lee/ Lewis Boogie	1958	30.00
—B-side by Jerry Lee Lewis			

GEORGETTES, THE
See GERRY AND THE GEORGETTES.

GEORGIA SATELLITES, THE

12-Inch Singles

ELEKTRA

Number	Title (A Side/B Side)	Yr	NM
❑ ED 5181 [DJ]	Keep Your Hands to Yourself (same on both sides)	1986	10.00
❑ ED 5197 [DJ]	Battleship Chains (same on both sides)	1987	6.00
❑ ED 5231 [DJ]	Myth of Love (LP Version 4:11) (Live 4:33)	1987	12.00
❑ ED 5310 [DJ]	Open All Night (same on both sides)	1988	8.00
❑ ED 5326 [DJ]	Don't Pass Me By (same on both sides)	1988	8.00
❑ ED 5334 [DJ]	Hippy Hippy Shake (same on both sides)	1988	12.00
❑ ED 5350 [DJ]	Sheila (Remix) (LP Version)	1988	8.00
❑ ED 5408 [DJ]	Another Chance (Edit 3:58) (same on both sides)	1989	8.00
❑ ED 5426 [DJ]	All Over But the Cryin' (same on both sides)	1989	8.00
❑ ED 5449 [DJ]	Shake That Thing (same on both sides)	1989	8.00

45s

ELEKTRA

Number	Title (A Side/B Side)	Yr	NM
❑ 7-69267	Another Chance/Saddle Up	1989	3.00
❑ 7-69328	Sheila/Hippy Hippy Shake	1988	3.00
❑ 7-69328 [PS]	Sheila/Hippy Hippy Shake	1988	3.00
❑ 7-69366	Hippy Hippy Shake/ Hand to Mouth	1988	3.00
❑ 7-69393	Open All Night/Dunk 'N' Dine	1988	3.00
❑ 7-69393 [PS]	Open All Night/Dunk 'N' Dine	1988	3.00
❑ 7-69497	Battleship Chains/Golden Light	1987	3.00
❑ 7-69497 [PS]	Battleship Chains/Golden Light	1987	3.00
❑ 7-69502	Keep Your Hands to Yourself/ Can't Stand the Pain	1986	3.00
❑ 7-69502 [PS]	Keep Your Hands to Yourself/ Can't Stand the Pain	1986	3.00

ELEKTRA SPUN GOLD

Number	Title (A Side/B Side)	Yr	NM
❑ 7-65971	Keep Your Hands to Yourself/ Battleship Chains	199?	3.00
—Reissue			

Albums

ELEKTRA

Number	Title (A Side/B Side)	Yr	NM
❑ 60496	Georgia Satellites	1986	10.00
❑ 60793	Open All Night	1988	10.00
❑ 60887	In the Land of Salvation and Sin	1989	12.00

GERARD, DANYEL

45s

COLUMBIA

Number	Title (A Side/B Side)	Yr	NM
❑ 4-45468	Butterfly/One White Rose	1971	8.00

MGM VERVE

Number	Title (A Side/B Side)	Yr	NM
❑ 10670	Butterfly/Let's Love	1972	6.00
❑ 10670 [PS]	Butterfly/Let's Love	1972	10.00
❑ 10685	Elie Lama Sabacthani/The Gun	1972	6.00

Albums

MGM VERVE

Number	Title (A Side/B Side)	Yr	NM
❑ MV 5081	Danyel Gerard	1972	12.00

GERMS, THE

45s

ILOKI

Number	Title (A Side/B Side)	Yr	NM
❑ ILSO 101	Forming/Sexboy	1990	7.50
—1,000 copies, all on clear vinyl			
❑ ILSO 101 [PS]	Forming/Sexboy	1990	7.50

SLASH

Number	Title (A Side/B Side)	Yr	NM
❑ 101	Lexicon Devil/Circle One/No God	1978	20.00
❑ 101 [PS]	Lexicon Devil/Circle One/No God	1978	20.00

WHAT

Number	Title (A Side/B Side)	Yr	NM
❑ 01	Forming/Sex Boy	1977	20.00
❑ 01 [PS]	Forming/Sex Boy	1977	20.00
—With lyric insert			

Albums

MOHAWK

Number	Title (A Side/B Side)	Yr	NM
❑ SCALP-001	Recorded Live at the Whiskey, June, 1977	1981	20.00
—Second edition: Un-numbered edition, with sticker			
❑ SCALP-001	Recorded Live at the Whiskey, June, 1977	1981	50.00
—First edition: Numbered edition, with sticker			

RHINO

Number	Title (A Side/B Side)	Yr	NM
❑ R1-78602	(GI)	2005	15.00
—Reissue on 180-gram vinyl			

SLASH

Number	Title (A Side/B Side)	Yr	NM
❑ SR-103	(GI)	1981	15.00
❑ SREP 108	What We Do Is Secret	1981	15.00
❑ 23932	(GI)	1983	12.00
—Reissue			

GERMZ, THE

45s

VERTIGO

Number	Title (A Side/B Side)	Yr	NM
❑ 8001	Boy-Girl Love/No Easy Way Down	1967	15.00

GERONIMO BLACK
Also see FRANK ZAPPA, as this band included members of the Mothers of Invention.

45s

UNI

Number	Title (A Side/B Side)	Yr	NM
❑ 55339	Let Us Live/'59 Chevy	1972	10.00

Albums

UNI

Number	Title (A Side/B Side)	Yr	NM
❑ 73132	Geronimo Black	1972	25.00

GERRY AND THE GEORGETTES

45s

HIT

Number	Title (A Side/B Side)	Yr	NM
❑ 83	Be My Baby/Sally Go 'Round the Roses	1963	8.00
—As "The Georgettes"; B-side by the Belles			
❑ 97	Quicksand/Loddy Lo	1963	8.00
—B-side by Leroy Jones			

GERRY AND THE PACEMAKERS

45s

LAURIE

Number	Title (A Side/B Side)	Yr	NM
❑ 3162	How Do You Do It/ Away From You	1963	20.00
❑ 3196	I Like It/It Happened to Me	1963	20.00
❑ 3218	You'll Never Walk Alone/ It's All Right	1964	20.00
❑ 3233	I'm the One/How Do You Do It	1964	15.00
❑ 3233	I'm the One/It's All Right	1964	15.00
❑ 3233	I'm the One/You've Got What I Like	1964	20.00
❑ 3251	Don't Let the Sun Catch You Crying/Away from You	1964	15.00
❑ 3261	How Do You Do It/ You'll Never Walk Alone	1964	12.00
❑ 3271	I Like It/Jambalaya	1964	12.00
❑ 3279	I'll Be There/You, You, You	1964	12.00
❑ 3284	Ferry Across the Mersey/Pretend	1965	12.00
❑ 3293	It's Gonna Be Alright/ Skinny Minnie	1965	10.00
❑ 3302	You'll Never Walk Alone/ Away from You	1965	10.00
❑ 3313	Give All Your Love to Me/ You're the Reason	1965	10.00
❑ 3323	Dreams/Walk Hand in Hand	1965	10.00
❑ 3337	La La La/Without You	1966	10.00
❑ 3354	Girl on a Swing/The Way You Look Tonight	1966	10.00
❑ 3370	The Big Bright Green Pleasure Machine/Looking for My Life	1966	12.00

Albums

CAPITOL

Number	Title (A Side/B Side)	Yr	NM
❑ SM-11898 [B]	The Best of Gerry and the Pacemakers	1979	8.00
—All stereo except "I Like It," "Away from You" and "I'm the One," which are mono.			

LAURIE

Number	Title (A Side/B Side)	Yr	NM
❑ LLP-2024 [M]	Don't Let the Sun Catch You Crying	1964	30.00
❑ SLP-2024 [R]	Don't Let the Sun Catch You Crying	1964	25.00
❑ LLP-2027 [M]	Gerry and the Pacemakers' Second Album	1964	30.00
❑ SLP-2027 [R]	Gerry and the Pacemakers' Second Album	1964	25.00
❑ LLP-2030 [M]	I'll Be There	1964	30.00
❑ SLP-2030 [R]	I'll Be There	1964	25.00
❑ LLP-2031 [M]	Greatest Hits	1965	25.00
❑ SLP-2031 [R]	Greatest Hits	1965	15.00
❑ LLP-2037 [M]	Girl on a Swing	1966	25.00
❑ SLP-2037 [S]	Girl on a Swing	1966	20.00
❑ DT 90384 [R]	Greatest Hits	1965	25.00
—Capitol Record Club edition			
❑ T 90384 [M]	Greatest Hits	1965	25.00
—Capitol Record Club edition			
❑ DT 90555 [R]	Don't Let the Sun Catch You Crying	1964	30.00
—Capitol Record Club edition			
❑ T 90555 [M]	Don't Let the Sun Catch You Crying	1964	40.00
—Capitol Record Club edition			

UNITED ARTISTS

Number	Title (A Side/B Side)	Yr	NM
❑ UAL 3387 [M]	Ferry Cross the Mersey	1965	25.00
—Also contains incidental music by George Martin			
❑ UAS 6387 [S]	Ferry Cross the Mersey	1965	40.00
❑ ST 90812 [S]	Ferry Cross the Mersey	1965	50.00
—Capitol Record Club edition			

Number	Title (A Side/B Side)	Yr	NM
❑ T 90812 [M]	Ferry Cross the Mersey	1965	40.00
—Capitol Record Club edition			
GESTURES, THE			
45s			
SOMA			
❑ 1417	Run, Run, Run/It Seems to Me	1964	15.00
❑ 1426	Don't Mess Around/Candlelight	1965	25.00
GETZ, STAN			
45s			
CLEF			
❑ 89090	Rustie Hop/Cool Mix	1954	15.00
❑ 89193	Nature Boy/'Round Midnight	195?	15.00
COLUMBIA			
❑ 10132	La Fiesta/(B-side unknown)	1975	5.00
DAWN			
❑ 204	Pennies from Heaven/ It's the Talk of the Town	1954	15.00
MERCURY			
❑ 89042	'Tis Autumn/Lover Come Back to Me	1953	15.00
❑ 89059	Erudition/Have You Met Miss Jones	1953	15.00
MGM			
❑ 13430	Once Upon a Time/ Taste of Living	1965	6.00
❑ 13430 [PS]	Once Upon a Time/ Taste of Living	1965	15.00
PRESTIGE			
❑ 240	My Old Flame/The Lady in Red	1962	10.00
—Reissue of 712			
❑ 708	I've Got You Under My Skin/ There's a Small Hotel	195?	15.00
❑ 710	Long Island Sound/Mar-Cia	195?	15.00
❑ 712	My Old Flame/The Lady in Red	195?	15.00
❑ 724	Wrap Your Troubles in Dreams/ Battle of Saxes	195?	15.00
❑ 729	Too Marvelous for Words/ Michelle	195?	15.00
—B-side by Terry Gibbs			
❑ 740	What's New/Indian Summer	195?	15.00
❑ 800	T & S/Terry's Tune	195?	12.00
❑ 802	Four and One More/ Five Brothers	195?	12.00
❑ 811	Speedway/Crazy Chords	195?	12.00
❑ 818	Battleground/Preservation	195?	12.00
❑ 867	Into It/You Stepped Out of a Dream	195?	12.00
VERVE			
❑ 10251	I Remember When/ I'm Late-I'm Late	1962	8.00
❑ 10279	Balanco No Samba/ Mahna de Carnaval	1963	8.00
❑ 10291	O Morro/Sambalero	1963	8.00
❑ 10321	Reflections/Blowin' in the Wind	1964	10.00
❑ 10557	Midnight Samba/Once	1967	6.00
❑ 10571	My Own True Love/ A Tribute to Stan	1967	6.00
❑ 10676	Communication '72/Back to Bach	1972	5.00
7-Inch Extended Plays			
CLEF			
❑ EP-149	Stars Fell on Alabama/The Way You Look Tonight//'Tis Autumn/Lover Come Back to Me	195?	20.00
❑ EP-149 [PS]	(title unknown)	195?	20.00
PRESTIGE			
❑ PREP-1310	Indian Summer/Crazy Chords// Long Island Sound/Mar-Cie	195?	20.00
❑ PREP-1310 [PS]	Stan Getz Quartet, Vol. 1	195?	20.00
SAVOY			
❑ XP-8021	Stan Gets Along/Opus de Bop// Stan's Mood/Don't Worry About Me	195?	20.00
❑ XP-8021 [PS]	New Trends of Jazz, Vol. 2	195?	20.00
Albums			
A&M			
❑ SP-5297	Apasionado	1990	15.00
AMERICAN RECORDING SOCIETY			
❑ G-407 [M]	Cool Jazz of Stan Getz	1956	40.00
❑ G-428 [M]	Intimate Portrait	1957	40.00
❑ G-443 [M]	Stan Getz '57	1957	40.00
BLACKHAWK			
❑ BKH-51101	Voyage	1986	10.00
BLUE RIBBON			
❑ BR-8012 [M]	Rhythms	1961	20.00
❑ BS-8012 [R]	Rhythms	1961	10.00
CLEF			
❑ MGC-137 [10]	Stan Getz Plays	1953	200.00
❑ MGC-143 [10]	The Artistry of Stan Getz	1953	200.00

Number	Title (A Side/B Side)	Yr	NM
COLUMBIA			
❑ PC 32706	Captain Marvel	1974	15.00
❑ PC 33703	Best of Two Worlds	1975	15.00
❑ JC 34873	The Peacocks	1977	12.00
❑ JC 35992	Children of the World	1979	12.00
❑ JC 36403	The Best of Stan Getz	1980	12.00
❑ FC 38272	The Master	1983	10.00
❑ CJ 44047	The Lyrical Stan Getz	1988	12.00
CONCORD JAZZ			
❑ CJ-158	The Dolphin	198?	12.00
❑ CJ-188	Pure Getz	1983	12.00
CROWN			
❑ CLP-5002 [M]	Groovin' High	1957	40.00
—Reissue of Modern 1202			
❑ CLP-5284 [M]	Groovin' High	196?	20.00
—Reissue of 5002			
DALE			
❑ 21 [10]	In Retrospect	1951	300.00
EMARCY			
❑ 838771-1	Billy Highstreet Samba	1990	12.00
FANTASY			
❑ OJC-121	Stan Getz Quartets	198?	10.00
—Reissue of Prestige 7002			
HALL OF FAME			
❑ 606	Stan Getz and His Tenor Sax	197?	12.00
INNER CITY			
❑ 1040 [(2)]	Gold	1977	12.00
INTERMEDIA			
❑ QS-5057	Stella by Starlight	198?	10.00
JAZZ MAN			
❑ 5014	Forrest Eyes	1982	12.00
JAZZTONE			
❑ J-1230 [M]	Stan Getz	1956	40.00
❑ J-1240 [M]	Stan Getz '57	1957	40.00
METRO			
❑ M-501 [M]	The Melodic Stan Getz	1965	12.00
❑ MS-501 [S]	The Melodic Stan Getz	1965	15.00
METRONOME			
❑ BLP-6 [M]	The Sound	1956	50.00
MGM			
❑ SE-4696	Marrakesh Express	1970	15.00
MODERN			
❑ MLP-1202 [M]	Groovin' High	1956	150.00
MOSAIC			
❑ MR4-131 [(4)]	The Complete Recordings of the Stan Getz Quintet with Jimmy Raney	199?	60.00
NEW JAZZ			
❑ NJLP-8214 [M]	Long Island Sound	1959	60.00
—Reissue of Prestige 7002; purple label			
❑ NJLP-8214 [M]	Long Island Sound	1965	25.00
—Blue label with trident logo on right			
NORGRAN			
❑ MGN-1000 [M]	Interpretations by the Stan Getz Quintet	1954	120.00
❑ MGN-1008 [M]	Interpretations by the Stan Getz Quintet #2	1954	120.00
❑ MGN-1029 [M]	Interpretations by the Stan Getz Quintet #3	1955	150.00
❑ MGN-1032 [M]	West Coast Jazz	1955	150.00
❑ MGN-1042 [M]	Stan Getz Plays	1955	100.00
—Reissue of Clef 137 and 143 on one 12-inch LP			
❑ MGN-1087 [M]	Stan Getz '56	1956	100.00
❑ MGN-1088 [M]	More West Coast Jazz with Stan Getz	1956	100.00
❑ MGN-2000-2 [(2)M]	Stan Getz at the Shrine	1955	200.00
—Boxed set with booklet			
PICKWICK			
❑ SPC-3031	Stan Getz In Concert	197?	10.00
PRESTIGE			
❑ PRLP-102 [10]	Stan Getz and the Tenor Sax Stars	1951	200.00
❑ PRLP-104 [10]	Stan Getz, Vol. 2	1951	200.00
❑ PRLP-108 [10]	Stan Getz-Lee Konitz	1951	200.00
❑ PRLP-7002 [M]	Stan Getz Quartets	1955	100.00
❑ PRLP-7255 [M]	Early Stan	1963	40.00
❑ PRST-7255 [R]	Early Stan	1963	20.00
❑ PRLP-7256 [M]	Stan Getz' Greatest Hits	1963	40.00
❑ PRST-7256 [R]	Stan Getz' Greatest Hits	1963	20.00
❑ PRLP-7337 [M]	Stan Getz' Greatest Hits	1967	25.00
—Reissue of PRLP 7256			
❑ PRST-7337 [R]	Stan Getz' Greatest Hits	1967	15.00
—Reissue of PRST 7256			
❑ PRLP-7434 [M]	Getz Plays Jazz Classics	1967	25.00
—Reissue of PRLP 7255			
❑ PRST-7434 [R]	Getz Plays Jazz Classics	1967	15.00
—Reissue of PRST 7255			
❑ PRLP-7516 [M]	Preservation	1967	25.00
❑ PRST-7516 [R]	Preservation	1967	15.00

Number	Title (A Side/B Side)	Yr	NM
❑ 24019 [(2)]	Stan Getz	197?	15.00
❑ 24088 [(2)]	Early Getz	197?	12.00
ROOST			
❑ RK-103 [(2)M]	The Stan Getz Years	1964	40.00
❑ SRK-103 [(2)R]	The Stan Getz Years	1964	25.00
❑ R-402 [10]	Stan Getz	1950	200.00
❑ R-404 [10]	Stan Getz and the Swedish All Stars	1951	200.00
❑ R-407 [10]	Jazz at Storyville	1952	150.00
❑ R-411 [10]	Jazz at Storyville, Vol. 2	1952	150.00
❑ R-417 [10]	Chamber Music	1953	150.00
❑ R-420 [10]	Jazz at Storyville, Vol. 3	1954	150.00
❑ R-423 [10]	Split Kick	1954	150.00
❑ LP-2207 [M]	The Sounds of Stan Getz	1956	80.00
—Reissue of R-402			
❑ LP-2209 [M]	Storyville	1956	80.00
—Reissue of R-407 and half of R-411			
❑ LP-2225 [M]	Storyville, Vol. 2	1957	80.00
—Reissue of R-423 and the other half of R-411			
❑ LP-2249 [M]	The Greatest of Stan Getz	1963	30.00
❑ SLP-2249 [R]	The Greatest of Stan Getz	1963	15.00
❑ LP-2251 [M]	Moonlight in Vermont	1963	30.00
❑ SLP-2251 [R]	Moonlight in Vermont	1963	15.00
❑ LP-2255 [M]	Modern World	1963	30.00
❑ SLP-2255 [R]	Modern World	1963	15.00
❑ LP-2258 [M]	Getz Age	1963	30.00
❑ SLP-2258 [R]	Getz Age	1963	15.00
ROULETTE			
❑ RE-119 [(2)]	The Best of Stan Getz	1972	15.00
❑ RE-123 [(2)]	Stan Getz/Sonny Stitt	1973	15.00
SAVOY			
❑ SJL-1105	Opus de Bop	1977	12.00
❑ MG-9004 [10]	New Sounds in Modern Music	1951	300.00
STEEPLECHASE			
❑ SCS-1073/4 [(2)]	Live at Montmartre	1986	12.00
VERVE			
❑ VSP-2 [M]	Eloquence	1966	15.00
❑ VSPS-2 [R]	Eloquence	1966	10.00
❑ VSP-22 [M]	Another Time, Another Place	1966	15.00
❑ VSPS-22 [R]	Another Time, Another Place	1966	10.00
❑ VSP-31 [M]	Stan Getz Plays Blues	1966	15.00
❑ VSPS-31 [R]	Stan Getz Plays Blues	1966	10.00
❑ V6S-200 [S]	An Introduction to the World of Stan Getz	1964	20.00
—Sampler of material from five LPs plus one single-only track			
❑ VS-200 [M]	An Introduction to the World of Stan Getz	1964	15.00
❑ UMV-2071	Focus	198?	10.00
—Reissue			
❑ UMV-2075	Getz Au Go Go	198?	10.00
—Reissue			
❑ UMV-2100	Jazz Samba Encore	198?	10.00
—Reissue			
❑ VE-2-2510 [(2)]	The Corea/Evans Sessions	1976	15.00
❑ VR-1-2528	Focus	1977	10.00
—Reissue of 8412			
❑ UMV-2614	Stan Getz in Stockholm	198?	10.00
—Reissue			
❑ MGVS-6160 [S]	Cool Velvet — Stan Getz and Strings	1960	—
—Unreleased			
❑ MGV-8028 [M]	West Coast Jazz	1957	50.00
—Reissue of Norgran 1032			
❑ V-8028 [M]	West Coast Jazz	1961	20.00
—Reissue of MGV-8028			
❑ V6-8028 [R]	West Coast Jazz	196?	12.00
❑ MGV-8029 [M]	Stan Getz '57	1957	50.00
—Reissue of Norgran 1087 with revised title			
❑ V-8029 [M]	Stan Getz '57	1961	20.00
—Reissue of MGV-8029			
❑ MGV-8122 [M]	Interpretations by the Stan Getz Quintet #3	1957	50.00
—Reissue of Norgran 1029			
❑ V-8122 [M]	Interpretations by the Stan Getz Quintet #3	1961	20.00
—Reissue of MGV-8122			
❑ MGV-8133 [M]	Stan Getz Plays	1957	50.00
—Reissue of Norgran 1042			
❑ V-8133 [M]	Stan Getz Plays	1961	20.00
—Reissue of MGV-8133			
❑ V6-8133 [R]	Stan Getz Plays	196?	12.00
❑ MGV-8177 [M]	More West Coast Jazz with Stan Getz	1957	50.00
—Reissue of Norgran 1088			
❑ V-8177 [M]	More West Coast Jazz with Stan Getz	1961	20.00
—Reissue of MGV-8177			
❑ V6-8177 [R]	More West Coast Jazz with Stan Getz	196?	12.00
❑ MGV-8188-2 [M]	Stan Getz at the Shrine	1957	100.00
—Reissue of Norgran 2000-2			
❑ V-8188-2 [(2)M]	Stan Getz at the Shrine	1961	25.00
—Reissue of MGV-8188-2			
❑ V6-8188-2 [(2)R]	Stan Getz at the Shrine	196?	15.00
❑ MGV-8200 [M]	Stan Getz and the Cool Sounds	1957	50.00
—Reissue of American Recording Society 407 with new name			
❑ V-8200 [M]	Stan Getz and the Cool Sounds	1961	20.00
—Reissue of MGV-8200			

Except when noted otherwise, VG = 25% of NM, and VG+ = 50% of NM. (Example: VG = $2.00, VG+ = $4.00 and NM = $8.00.)

Number	Title (A Side/B Side)	Yr	NM
❑ V6-8200 [R]	Stan Getz and the Cool Sounds	196?	12.00
❑ MGV-8213 [M]	Stan Getz in Stockholm	1958	50.00
—Reissue of American Recording Society 428 with new name			
❑ V-8213 [M]	Stan Getz in Stockholm	1961	20.00
—Reissue of MGV-8213			
❑ V6-8213 [R]	Stan Getz in Stockholm	196?	12.00
❑ MGV-8263 [M]	Stan Meets Chet	1958	60.00
—With Chet Baker			
❑ V-8263 [M]	Stan Meets Chet	1961	20.00
—Reissue of MGV-8263			
❑ V6-8263 [R]	Stan Meets Chet	196?	12.00
❑ MGV-8294 [M]	The Steamer	1959	50.00
❑ V-8294 [M]	The Steamer	1961	20.00
—Reissue of MGV-8294			
❑ V6-8294 [R]	The Steamer	196?	12.00
❑ MGV-8296 [M]	Award Winner	1959	50.00
❑ V-8296 [M]	Award Winner	1961	20.00
—Reissue of MGV-8296			
❑ V6-8296 [R]	Award Winner	196?	12.00
❑ MGV-8321 [M]	The Soft Swing	1959	50.00
❑ V-8321 [M]	The Soft Swing	1961	20.00
—Reissue of MGV-8321			
❑ V6-8321 [R]	The Soft Swing	196?	12.00
❑ MGV-8331 [M]	Imported from Europe	1959	50.00
❑ V-8331 [M]	Imported from Europe	1961	20.00
—Reissue of MGV-8331			
❑ V6-8331 [R]	Imported from Europe	196?	12.00
❑ MGV-8356 [M]	Stan Getz Quintet	1960	—
—Unreleased			
❑ MGV-8379 [M]	Cool Velvet — Stan Getz and Strings	1960	50.00
❑ V-8379 [M]	Cool Velvet — Stan Getz and Strings	1961	20.00
—Reissue of MGV-8379			
❑ V6-8379 [S]	Cool Velvet — Stan Getz and Strings	1961	20.00
❑ MGV-8393-2 [(2)M]	Stan Getz At Large	1960	60.00
❑ V-8393-2 [(2)M]	Stan Getz At Large	1961	25.00
—Reissue of MGV-8393-2			
❑ V6-8393-2 [(2)R]	Stan Getz At Large	1961	15.00
❑ MGV-8401 [M]	Stan Getz At Large, Vol. 1	1960	—
—Unreleased			
❑ MGV-8402 [M]	Stan Getz At Large, Vol. 2	1960	—
—Unreleased			
❑ V-8412 [M]	Focus	1961	25.00
❑ V6-8412 [S]	Focus	1961	20.00
❑ V-8494 [M]	Big Band Bossa Nova	1962	20.00
❑ V6-8494 [S]	Big Band Bossa Nova	1962	25.00
❑ V-8523 [M]	Jazz Samba Encore!	1963	20.00
—With Luiz Bonfa			
❑ V6-8523 [S]	Jazz Samba Encore!	1963	25.00
—With Luiz Bonfa			
❑ V-8554 [M]	Reflections	1964	15.00
❑ V6-8554 [S]	Reflections	1964	20.00
❑ V-8600 [M]	Getz Au Go Go	1964	15.00
❑ V6-8600 [S]	Getz Au Go Go	1964	20.00
❑ V-8693 [M]	Sweet Rain	1967	25.00
❑ V6-8693 [S]	Sweet Rain	1967	15.00
❑ V-8707 [M]	Voices	1967	25.00
❑ V6-8707 [S]	Voices	1967	15.00
❑ V-8719 [M]	The Best of Stan Getz	1967	25.00
❑ V6-8719 [S]	The Best of Stan Getz	1967	15.00
❑ V-8752 [M]	What the World Needs Now — Stan Getz Plays Bacharach and David	1968	30.00
❑ V6-8752 [S]	What the World Needs Now — Stan Getz Plays Bacharach and David	1968	15.00
❑ V6-8780	Didn't We	1969	15.00
❑ V6-8802-2 [(2)]	Dynasty	1971	20.00
❑ V6-8807	Communications '72	1972	15.00
❑ V6-8815-2 [(2)]	History of Stan Getz	1973	15.00
❑ V3HB-8844 [(2)]	Return Engagement	1974	15.00
❑ MGVS-68379 [S]	Cool Velvet — Stan Getz and Strings	1960	50.00
❑ 815239-1	Stan the Man	1983	10.00
❑ 821725-1	Getz Au Go Go	198?	10.00
—Reissue			
❑ 823242-1 [(2)]	The Corea/Evans Sessions	198?	12.00
—Reissue			
❑ 823611-1 [(5)]	The Girl from Ipamena: The Bossa Nova Years	1984	50.00
❑ 823613-1	Jazz Samba Encore	198?	10.00
—Reissue			

GETZ, STAN, AND LAURINDO ALMEIDA

45s

VERVE

Number	Title (A Side/B Side)	Yr	NM
❑ 10468	Winter Moon/Menina Moca	1966	6.00

Albums

VERVE

Number	Title (A Side/B Side)	Yr	NM
❑ V-8665 [M]	Stan Getz with Guest Artist Laurindo Almeida	1965	15.00
❑ V6-8665 [S]	Stan Getz with Guest Artist Laurindo Almeida	1965	20.00

GETZ, STAN, AND CHET BAKER

Albums

STORYVILLE

Number	Title (A Side/B Side)	Yr	NM
❑ 4090	Line for Lyons	1984	10.00

GETZ, STAN, AND BOB BROOKMEYER

Albums

VERVE

Number	Title (A Side/B Side)	Yr	NM
❑ V-8418 [M]	Stan Getz and Bob Brookmeyer (Recorded Fall 1961)	1961	20.00
❑ V6-8418 [S]	Stan Getz and Bob Brookmeyer (Recorded Fall 1961)	1961	20.00

GETZ, STAN, AND CHARLIE BYRD

45s

VERVE

Number	Title (A Side/B Side)	Yr	NM
❑ 10260	Desafinado/Theme from Dr. Kildare	1962	8.00

7-Inch Extended Plays

VERVE

Number	Title (A Side/B Side)	Yr	NM
❑ SLV 8432	Desafinado/O Pato//Samba Dees Days/Samba Triste	196?	12.00
—Jukebox issue; small hole, plays at 33 1/3 rpm			
❑ SLV 8432 [PS]	Jazz Samba	196?	12.00

Albums

DCC COMPACT CLASSICS

Number	Title (A Side/B Side)	Yr	NM
❑ LPZ-2011	Jazz Samba	1995	25.00
—Audiophile vinyl			

VERVE

Number	Title (A Side/B Side)	Yr	NM
❑ UMJ-3158	Jazz Samba	198?	10.00
❑ V-8432 [M]	Jazz Samba	1962	20.00
❑ V6-8432 [S]	Jazz Samba	1962	25.00
—With "MGM Records" on label print			
❑ V6-8432 [S]	Jazz Samba	1976	12.00
—"Manufactured and Marketed by Polydor Incorporated" on label			
❑ 810061-1	Jazz Samba	198?	10.00
—Reissue			

GETZ, STAN, AND ALBERT DAILEY

Albums

ELEKTRA/MUSICIAN

Number	Title (A Side/B Side)	Yr	NM
❑ 60370	Poetry	1985	10.00

GETZ, STAN, AND BILL EVANS

Albums

VERVE

Number	Title (A Side/B Side)	Yr	NM
❑ V3G-8833	Previously Unreleased Recordings	1974	12.00

GETZ, STAN, AND JOAO GILBERTO

45s

VERVE

Number	Title (A Side/B Side)	Yr	NM
❑ 10322	The Girl from Ipanema/Corcovado	1964	10.00
❑ 10323	The Girl from Ipanema/Blowin' in the Wind	1964	8.00
❑ 10336	Only Trust Your Heart/Telephone Song	1964	8.00

Albums

MOBILE FIDELITY

Number	Title (A Side/B Side)	Yr	NM
❑ 1-208	Getz/Gilberto	1994	50.00
—Audiophile vinyl			

VERVE

Number	Title (A Side/B Side)	Yr	NM
❑ UMV-2099	Getz/Gilberto	198?	10.00
—Reissue			
❑ V-8545 [M]	Getz/Gilberto	1964	15.00
❑ V6-8545 [S]	Getz/Gilberto	1964	20.00
❑ V-8623 [M]	Getz/Gilberto #2	1965	15.00
❑ V6-8623 [S]	Getz/Gilberto #2	1965	20.00
❑ 810048-1	Getz/Gilberto	198?	10.00
—Reissue			

GETZ, STAN; DIZZY GILLESPIE; SONNY STITT

Albums

VERVE

Number	Title (A Side/B Side)	Yr	NM
❑ MGV-8198 [M]	For Musicians Only	1958	80.00
❑ V-8198 [M]	For Musicians Only	1961	25.00

GETZ, STAN, AND WARDELL GRAY

Albums

DAWN

Number	Title (A Side/B Side)	Yr	NM
❑ DLP-1126 [M]	Tenors Anyone?	1958	120.00

SEECO

Number	Title (A Side/B Side)	Yr	NM
❑ SLP-7 [10]	Highlights in Modern Jazz	1954	200.00

GETZ, STAN, AND J.J. JOHNSON

Albums

VERVE

Number	Title (A Side/B Side)	Yr	NM
❑ MGVS-6027 [S]	Stan Getz and J.J. Johnson at the Opera House	1960	40.00
❑ MGV-8265 [M]	Stan Getz and J.J. Johnson at the Opera House	1958	50.00
❑ V-8265 [M]	Stan Getz and J.J. Johnson at the Opera House	1961	20.00
❑ V6-8265 [S]	Stan Getz and J.J. Johnson at the Opera House	1961	15.00
❑ MGV-8405 [M]	Stan Getz and J.J. Johnson	1961	—
—Unreleased			
❑ V-8490 [M]	Stan Getz and J.J. Johnson at the Opera House	1962	15.00
❑ V6-8490 [S]	Stan Getz and J.J. Johnson at the Opera House	1962	15.00

GETZ, STAN, AND GERRY MULLIGAN

Albums

MAINSTREAM

Number	Title (A Side/B Side)	Yr	NM
❑ MRL 364	Yesterday	1972	15.00

GETZ, STAN, AND OSCAR PETERSON

Albums

VERVE

Number	Title (A Side/B Side)	Yr	NM
❑ UMV-2665	Stan Getz and the Oscar Peterson Trio	198?	10.00
—Reissue			
❑ MGV-8251 [M]	Stan Getz and the Oscar Peterson Trio	1958	50.00
❑ V-8251 [M]	Stan Getz and the Oscar Peterson Trio	1961	20.00
—Reissue of MGV-8251			
❑ V6-8251 [R]	Stan Getz and the Oscar Peterson Trio	196?	12.00
❑ MGV-8348 [M]	Stan Getz with Gerry Mulligan and the Oscar Peterson Trio	1959	50.00
❑ V-8348 [M]	Stan Getz with Gerry Mulligan and the Oscar Peterson Trio	1961	20.00
—Reissue of MGV-8348			
❑ V6-8348 [R]	Stan Getz with Gerry Mulligan and the Oscar Peterson Trio	1961	12.00

GETZ, STAN, AND HORACE SILVER

Albums

BARONET

Number	Title (A Side/B Side)	Yr	NM
❑ B-102 [M]	A Pair of Kings	1962	15.00
❑ BS-102 [R]	A Pair of Kings	196?	10.00

GETZ, STAN, AND ZOOT SIMS

Albums

FANTASY

Number	Title (A Side/B Side)	Yr	NM
❑ OJC-008	The Brothers	1982	12.00

PRESTIGE

Number	Title (A Side/B Side)	Yr	NM
❑ PRLP-7022 [M]	The Brothers	1956	400.00
—Yellow label with W. 50th St. address			
❑ PRLP-7252 [M]	The Brothers	1963	100.00
—Yellow label with Bergenfield, N.J. address			

GHOULS, THE

Albums

CAPITOL

Number	Title (A Side/B Side)	Yr	NM
❑ ST 2215 [S]	Dracula's Deuce	1965	150.00
❑ T 2215 [M]	Dracula's Deuce	1965	120.00

GIANT CRAB, THE

45s

UNI

Number	Title (A Side/B Side)	Yr	NM
❑ 55094	Hi Ho Silver Lining/Hot Line Conversation	1968	8.00
❑ 55103	Believe It or Not/The Color Purple	1968	8.00
❑ 55134	Cool It/Intensify My Soul	1969	8.00
❑ 55155	ESP/Hot Line Conversation	1969	8.00

Albums

UNI

Number	Title (A Side/B Side)	Yr	NM
❑ 73037	A Giant Crab Comes Forth	1968	25.00
❑ 73057	Cool It, Helios	1969	25.00

GIBB, BARRY

Also see BEE GEES; BARBRA STREISAND.

45s

ATCO

Number	Title (A Side/B Side)	Yr	NM
❑ 6786	One Bad Thing/The Day Your Eyes Met Mine	1970	—
—May not exist as a US pressing			

MCA

Number	Title (A Side/B Side)	Yr	NM
❑ 52443	Shine Shine/She Says	1984	3.00
❑ 52443 [PS]	Shine Shine/She Says	1984	3.00
❑ 52501	Fine Line/Stay Alone	1984	3.00
❑ 52501 [PS]	Fine Line/Stay Alone	1984	4.00

GIBB, MAURICE

Also see BEE GEES; THE FUT.

45s

ATCO

Number	Title (A Side/B Side)	Yr	NM
❑ 6757	Railroad/I've Come Back	1970	30.00
—Possibly only issued in Canada			

G

GIBB, ROBIN Also see BEE GEES.

Number	Title (A Side/B Side)	Yr	NM
12-Inch Singles			
MIRAGE			
❑ DMD 740 [DJ]	Boys Do Fall in Love (Long Version 5:20) (Short Version 3:50)	1984	20.00
❑ DMD 775 [DJ]	Secret Agent/Robot	1984	10.00
45s			
ATCO			
❑ 6698	Saved by the Bell/Mother and Jack	1969	10.00
❑ 6727	One Million Years/Weekend	1969	12.00
❑ 6737	August October/Give Me a Smile	1970	12.00
EMI AMERICA			
❑ B-8291	Like a Fool/Possession	1985	3.00
❑ B-8291 [PS]	Like a Fool/Possession	1985	4.00
❑ B-8304	Toys/Do You Love Her	1986	3.00
❑ B-8304 [PS]	Toys/Do You Love Her	1986	4.00
MIRAGE			
❑ 99688 [DJ]	In Your Diary (same on both sides)	1984	8.00
—Stock copy unknown			
❑ 99712	Secret Agent/Robot	1984	3.00
❑ 99743	Boys Do Fall in Love/Diamonds	1984	3.00
❑ 99743 [PS]	Boys Do Fall in Love/Diamonds	1984	3.00
POLYDOR			
❑ 810895-7	Juliet/Hearts on Fire	1983	3.00
❑ 810895-7 [PS]	Juliet/Hearts on Fire	1983	4.00
RSO			
❑ 907	Oh Darling/She's Leaving Home	1978	4.00
—B-side by The Bee Gees			
❑ 1047	Help Me!/(Instrumental)	1980	4.00
—With Marcy Levy			
❑ 1047 [PS]	Help Me!/(Instrumental)	1980	4.00
SESAME STREET			
❑ 99070	Sesame Street Fever/Trash	1978	5.00
❑ 99070 [PS]	Sesame Street Fever/Trash	1978	6.00
Albums			
ATCO			
❑ SD 33-323	Robin's Reign	1969	40.00
MIRAGE			
❑ 90170	Secret Agent	1984	8.00
POLYDOR			
❑ 810896-1	How Old Are You?	1983	10.00

GIBSON, ALTHEA

Number	Title (A Side/B Side)	Yr	NM
45s			
DOT			
❑ 15758	Around the World/So Much to Live For	1958	15.00
Albums			
DOT			
❑ DLP-3105 [M]	Althea Gibson Sings	1959	40.00
❑ DLP-25105 [S]	Althea Gibson Sings	1959	50.00

GIBSON, BOBBY, AND THE VOYAGERS

Number	Title (A Side/B Side)	Yr	NM
45s			
GIBSON			
❑ 6003	B-52/Samoa	1959	50.00

GIBSON, DAVE

Number	Title (A Side/B Side)	Yr	NM
45s			
HIT			
❑ 50	I Saw Linda Yesterday/Hey Paula	1963	8.00
—B-side by Bob and Bobbie			

GIBSON, GINNY

Number	Title (A Side/B Side)	Yr	NM
45s			
ABC-PARAMOUNT			
❑ 9739	Miracle of Love/Two Innocent Hearts	1956	15.00
❑ 9786	I Pledge Allegiance to Your Heart/Pair of Fools	1957	15.00
❑ 9872	Homing Pigeon/September Till June	1957	15.00
DAVIS			
❑ 442	Mommy's Little Angel/Wanting You	1955	15.00
DERBY			
❑ 810	Mommy's Little Angel/Wanting You	195?	20.00
KAMA			
❑ 500	You Pass This Way (Only Once)/Bluesville	1962	10.00
MGM			
❑ K10661	Where in the World/You're Finding Out How Much I Love You	1950	25.00
❑ K11383	You Blew Me a Kiss/Too Far Between Kisses	1952	20.00
❑ K11435	Condemned Without a Trial/Kiss	1953	20.00
❑ K11499	Lonely Lover/Unless You're Really Mine	1953	20.00
❑ K11571	Dansero/No More Tears	1953	20.00
❑ K11672	Baton Rouge/Don't Stop Kissing Me Goodnight	1954	20.00
❑ K11736	Aye, Aye, Aye, Aye/Serenade to Spring	1954	20.00
❑ K11814	There's a Small Hotel/The Song That Broke My Heart	1954	20.00
❑ K11913	Like M-A-D/Once There Was a Little Girl	1955	20.00
❑ K11961	Whatever Lola Wants/If Anything Should Happen to You	1955	20.00
❑ K12019	Am I Asking Too Much/Chihuahua Choo-Choo	1955	20.00
❑ K12113	Ooh (How I Love Ya)/If You Want to Make Me Happy	1955	20.00

GIBSON, JILL For a very brief time in late 1966, she was a member of THE MAMAS AND THE PAPAS.

Number	Title (A Side/B Side)	Yr	NM
45s			
IMPERIAL			
❑ 66068	It's as Easy as 1,2,3/Jilly's Flip Side	1964	60.00
—Produced by Jan Berry			

GIBSON, JOHNNY

Number	Title (A Side/B Side)	Yr	NM
45s			
BIG TOP			
❑ 3088	Midnight/Chuck-a-Luck	1961	20.00
❑ 3118	After Midnight/Walking On Down	1962	20.00
❑ 3149	Summer Holiday/Ooh Poo Pa Doo	1963	20.00
LAURIE			
❑ 3256	Beachcomber/Swanky	1964	25.00
—As "The Johnny Gibson Trio"			
TWIRL			
❑ 2012	Beachcomber/Swanky	1964	40.00
—As "The Johnny Gibson Trio"			

GIBSON, STEVE, AND THE RED CAPS

Number	Title (A Side/B Side)	Yr	NM
45s			
ABC-PARAMOUNT			
❑ 9702	Love Me Tenderly/Rock and Roll Stomp	1956	20.00
❑ 9750	Write to Me/Cuacho Serenade	1956	20.00
❑ 9796	You've Got Me Dizzy/You May Not Love Me	1957	20.00
❑ 9856	Silhouettes/Flamingo	1957	20.00
❑ 10105	I Went to Your Wedding/Together	1960	15.00
BAND BOX			
❑ 325	No More/Peppermint Baby	1962	12.00
HUNT			
❑ 326	Bless You/Cheryl Lee	1959	15.00
❑ 330	Where Are You/San Antonio Rose	1959	15.00
JAY DEE			
❑ 796	It Hurts Me But I Like It/Ouch!	1954	40.00
MERCURY			
❑ 5380	I'll Never Love Anyone Else/(B-side unknown)	1950	150.00
❑ 8146	Blueberry Hill/I Love You	1951	80.00
—78 released in 1949			
❑ 70389	Wedding Bells (Are Breaking Up That Old Gang of Mine)/Second Hand Romance	1954	50.00
RCA VICTOR			
❑ 47-3986	The Thing/Am I To Blame?	1950	60.00
❑ 47-4076	Did Ya Eat Yet, Joe/$3.98	1951	50.00
❑ 47-4294	Shame/Boogie Woogie on Saturday Night	1951	50.00
❑ 47-4670	Two Little Kisses/I May Hate Myself in the Morning	1952	40.00
❑ 47-4835	I Went to Your Wedding/Wait	1952	40.00
❑ 47-5013	Why Don't You Love Me/Truthfully	1952	40.00
❑ 47-5130	Big Game Hunter/Do I, Do I, Do I	1953	40.00
❑ 47-6096	Nuff of That Stuff/Feelin' Kinda Happy	1955	20.00
—B-side by Damita Jo			
❑ 47-6345	How I Cry/Bobbin'	1955	20.00
❑ 50-0127	I'm to Blame/Sidewalk Shuffle	1951	60.00
❑ 50-0138	Would I Mind/When You Come Back to Me	1951	60.00
7-Inch Extended Plays			
MERCURY			
❑ EP1-3215	(contents unknown)	1952	200.00
❑ EP1-3215 [PS]	Blueberry Hill	1952	200.00
Albums			
MERCURY			
❑ MG-25115 [10]	You're Driving Me Crazy (Harmony Time)	1952	400.00
❑ MG-25116 [10]	Blueberry Hill (Singing & Swinging)	1952	400.00

GIGOLOS, THE

Number	Title (A Side/B Side)	Yr	NM
45s			
BROADWAY			
❑ 1000	Movin' Out/Black and Blue	1961	30.00
CHESS			
❑ 1715	Luna Rock/La Companola	1959	30.00
DAYNITE			
❑ 1	Swingin' Saints/Night Crawlers	1960	50.00
ENTERPRISE			
❑ 5000	Don't You Just Know It/Movin' Out	1965	15.00

GILBERTO, ASTRUD

Number	Title (A Side/B Side)	Yr	NM
45s			
PERCEPTION			
❑ 524	Make Love to Me/General Da Banda	1973	5.00
VERVE			
❑ CS?-5	Celebrity Scene: Astrud Gilberto	1967	50.00
—Box set of five singles (10531-10535). Price includes box, all 5 singles, jukebox title strips, bio. Records are sometimes found by themselves, so they are also listed separately.			
❑ 10339	Who Can I Turn To/Funny World	1965	8.00
❑ 10347	Day by Day/Ecco Homo	1965	8.00
❑ 10358	The Shadow of Your Smile/O Gauso	1965	8.00
❑ 10414	Don't Go Breaking My Heart/Wish Me a Rainbow	1966	6.00
❑ 10457	Who Needs Forever/Main Theme "The Deadly Affair"	1966	6.00
❑ 10480	A Certain Smile/A Certain Sadness	1967	6.00
—With Walter Wanderley			
❑ 10531 [DJ]	Once Upon a Summertime/Once I Loved	1967	8.00
❑ 10532 [DJ]	Aruanda/Dindi	1967	8.00
❑ 10533 [DJ]	Manha De Carnival/Berimbau	1967	8.00
❑ 10534 [DJ]	Look to the Rainbow/Lugar Bonita	1967	8.00
❑ 10535 [DJ]	So Nice/Wish Me a Rainbow	1967	8.00
❑ 10548	Stay/I Had the Craziest Dream	1967	6.00
❑ 10554	A Banda/You Didn't Have to Be So Nice	1967	6.00
❑ 10580	Come Softly to Me-Hushabye/Lilies by Monet	1968	6.00
❑ 10638	I Haven't Got Anything Better to Do/The Sea Is My Soul	1969	5.00
❑ 10643	Love Theme from "Romeo and Juliet"/The Thought of Loving You	1969	5.00
❑ 10651	Holiday/Let's Have the Morning After	1970	5.00
Albums			
CTI			
❑ CTS-6008	Astrud Gilberto with Stanley Turrentine	1970	12.00
ELEKTRA/MUSICIAN			
❑ 60760	Live in Montreux	1988	10.00
PERCEPTION			
❑ 29	Now	1973	10.00
VERVE			
❑ V-8608 [M]	The Astrud Gilberto Album	1965	12.00
❑ V6-8608 [S]	The Astrud Gilberto Album	1965	15.00
❑ V-8629 [M]	The Shadow of Your Smile	1965	12.00
❑ V6-8629 [S]	The Shadow of Your Smile	1965	15.00
❑ V-8643 [M]	Look to the Rainbow	1966	12.00
❑ V6-8643 [S]	Look to the Rainbow	1966	15.00
❑ V-8673 [M]	A Certain Smile, A Certain Sadness	1966	12.00
❑ V6-8673 [S]	A Certain Smile, A Certain Sadness	1966	15.00
❑ V-8708 [M]	Beach Samba	1967	12.00
❑ V6-8708 [S]	Beach Samba	1967	15.00
❑ V6-8754	Windy	1968	12.00
❑ V6-8776	I Haven't Got Anything Better to Do	1969	12.00
❑ V6-8793	September 17, 1969	1969	12.00
❑ SW-90649 [S]	The Shadow of Your Smile	1965	20.00
—Capitol Record Club edition			
❑ 821566-1	Look to the Rainbow	1986	10.00
—Reissue of V6-8643			

Except when noted otherwise, VG = 25% of NM, and VG+ = 50% of NM. (Example: VG = $2.00, VG+ = $4.00 and NM = $8.00.)

GILES, GILES & FRIPP Also see KING CRIMSON.

Albums

DERAM

Number	Title (A Side/B Side)	Yr	NM
❑ DES 18019	The Cheerful Insanity of Giles, Giles & Fripp	1968	75.00

GILLAN Also see BLACK SABBATH; DEEP PURPLE; IAN GILLAN BAND.

Albums

VIRGIN

Number	Title (A Side/B Side)	Yr	NM
❑ 2196	Future Shock	1981	12.00
❑ 13146	Glory Road	1980	12.00

GILLAN BAND, IAN Also see BLACK SABBATH, DEEP PURPLE, GILLAN.

Albums

ISLAND

Number	Title (A Side/B Side)	Yr	NM
❑ ILPS 9500	Clear Air Turbulence	1977	14.00
❑ ILPS 9511	Scarabus	1978	15.00

—Different cover from UK issue

OYSTER

Number	Title (A Side/B Side)	Yr	NM
❑ OY 11602	Child In Time	1976	14.00

GILLAN, IAN, & ROGER GLOVER Also see DEEP PURPLE.

Albums

VIRGIN

Number	Title (A Side/B Side)	Yr	NM
❑ 90953	Accidentally on Purpose	1988	12.00

GILLESPIE, DANA

45s

JERDEN

Number	Title (A Side/B Side)	Yr	NM
❑ 764	Donna Donna/It's No Use Saying If	1965	12.00

Albums

LONDON

Number	Title (A Side/B Side)	Yr	NM
❑ PS 540	Foolish Seasons	1968	40.00

GILLESPIE, DARLENE

45s

CORAL

Number	Title (A Side/B Side)	Yr	NM
❑ 62178	I Loved, I Laughed, I Cried/Ring the Bell, Beat the Drum	1960	15.00

DISNEYLAND

Number	Title (A Side/B Side)	Yr	NM
❑ F-050	Sittin' in the Balcony/Too Much	1957	30.00
❑ F-051	Butterfly/Seven Days	1957	30.00
❑ F-052	I've Never Been in Love/Rock-a-Billy	1957	30.00
❑ F-060	Together Time/Now to Sleep	1957	25.00

—A-side with Jimmie Dodd

Number	Title (A Side/B Side)	Yr	NM
❑ F-061	Break of Day/Perri	1957	25.00

—With Jimmie Dodd

Albums

DISNEYLAND

Number	Title (A Side/B Side)	Yr	NM
❑ WDL-1010 [M]	Top Tunes of the '50's—Darlene Gillespie Sings TV Favorites	1959	40.00

—Reissue of 3010

Number	Title (A Side/B Side)	Yr	NM
❑ DQ-1228 [M]	Sleeping Beauty	1962	20.00

—Cover is black and white; later pressings, which go for less, are shaded blue on the back

Number	Title (A Side/B Side)	Yr	NM
❑ WDL-3010 [M]	Darlene of the Teens	1957	80.00
❑ WDL-3010 [M]	Top Tunes of the '50's—Darlene Gillespie Sings TV Favorites	1958	50.00

—Reissue with new title and cover

MICKEY MOUSE CLUB

Number	Title (A Side/B Side)	Yr	NM
❑ MM-32 [M]	Sleeping Beauty	1959	40.00

GILLESPIE, DIZZY

Albums

PHILIPS

Number	Title (A Side/B Side)	Yr	NM
❑ PHM 200138 [M]	The Cool World	1964	50.00
❑ PHS 600138 [S]	The Cool World	1964	80.00

GILMER, JIMMY Also see THE FIREBALLS.

45s

ATCO

Number	Title (A Side/B Side)	Yr	NM
❑ 6583	Three Squares (And a Place to Lay Your Head)/Baby	1968	8.00
❑ 6716	Sugar in the Woods/Model Child	1969	8.00

DECCA

Number	Title (A Side/B Side)	Yr	NM
❑ 30942	Look Alive/Because I Need You	1959	25.00

HAMILTON

Number	Title (A Side/B Side)	Yr	NM
❑ 50037	Won't Be Long/I'm Gonna Go Walkin'	1960	15.00

WARWICK

Number	Title (A Side/B Side)	Yr	NM
❑ 592	Good Good Lovin'/Do You Think	1960	20.00

GILMER, JIMMY, AND THE FIREBALLS
See THE FIREBALLS.

GILMORE, JIMMIE DALE

45s

HIGHTONE

Number	Title (A Side/B Side)	Yr	NM
❑ 504	White Freight Liner Blues/Trying to Get to You	1988	5.00
❑ 510	Honky Tonk Song/(B-side unknown)	1989	5.00

Albums

HIGHTONE

Number	Title (A Side/B Side)	Yr	NM
❑ HT-8011	Fair and Square	1988	10.00
❑ HT-8018	Jimmie Dale Gilmore	1989	10.00

GILREATH, JAMES

45s

JOY

Number	Title (A Side/B Side)	Yr	NM
❑ 274	Little Band of Gold/I'll Walk with You	1963	12.00
❑ 278	Lollipops, Lace and Lipstick/Mean Ole River	1963	15.00
❑ 286	Blue Is My Color/Keep Her Out of Sight	1964	10.00

GILSON, PATTI

45s

GOLDEN WORLD

Number	Title (A Side/B Side)	Yr	NM
❑ 6	Don't You Tell a Lie/Pulling Petals from a Daisy	1964	300.00

GILSTRAP, JIM

45s

BELL

Number	Title (A Side/B Side)	Yr	NM
❑ 45435	Airport/(B-side unknown)	1974	5.00
❑ 45474	When You Come Back Down/(B-side unknown)	1974	5.00

ROXBURY

Number	Title (A Side/B Side)	Yr	NM
❑ 2006	Swing Your Daddy/Swing Your Daddy (Part 2)	1975	4.00
❑ 2013	House of Strangers/Take Your Daddy for a Ride	1975	4.00
❑ 2016	I'm on Fire/I'm on Fire (Part 2)	1975	4.00
❑ 2026	Move Me/Move Me (Part 2)	1976	4.00
❑ 2029	Love Talk/Love Talk (Part 2)	1976	4.00
❑ 2032	Hello It's Me/Never Stop Your Loving Me	1976	4.00

Albums

ROXBURY

Number	Title (A Side/B Side)	Yr	NM
❑ 102	Swing Your Daddy	1975	10.00
❑ 105	Love Talk	1976	10.00

GIN BLOSSOMS

45s

A&M

Number	Title (A Side/B Side)	Yr	NM
❑ 31458 0418 7	Found Out About You/Hey Jealousy	1993	5.00
❑ 31458 0862 7	Allison Road/Until I Fall Away	1994	3.00
❑ 31458 1380 7	Follow You Down/Til I Hear It from You	1996	3.00
❑ 31458 1672 7	As Long As It Matters/Allison Road (Live)	1996	3.00
❑ 74021 8735 7	Hey Jealousy/Found Out About You	1996	3.00

—Oldies reissue

Albums

A&M

Number	Title (A Side/B Side)	Yr	NM
❑ 75021 5369 1 [EP]	Up and Crumbling	1991	15.00

SAN JACINTO

Number	Title (A Side/B Side)	Yr	NM
❑ DRAM 019	Dusted	1989	20.00

—With picture insert and biographical material

GINGER Also see GINGER AND THE SNAPS; THE HONEYS.

45s

TITAN

Number	Title (A Side/B Side)	Yr	NM
❑ 1717	Dry Tears/Spare Time	1961	100.00

GINGER AND THE CHIFFONS

45s

GROOVE

Number	Title (A Side/B Side)	Yr	NM
❑ 58-0003	She/Where Were You Last Night	1963	30.00

GINGER AND THE SNAPS Also see GINGER.

45s

MGM

Number	Title (A Side/B Side)	Yr	NM
❑ 13413	Growing Up Is Hard to Do/Seven Days in September	1965	150.00

TORE

Number	Title (A Side/B Side)	Yr	NM
❑ 1008	Love Me the Way That I Love You/Truly	1961	75.00

GINGER-SNAPS, THE

45s

DUNHILL

Number	Title (A Side/B Side)	Yr	NM
❑ 4003	The Sh-Down-Down Song/I've Got Faith in Him	1965	20.00

GINGOLEERS, THE

45s

BRUNSWICK

Number	Title (A Side/B Side)	Yr	NM
❑ 55108	Jingle Bell Rock/Christmas Morn	1958	15.00

GINNY AND THE GALLIONS

45s

DOWNEY

Number	Title (A Side/B Side)	Yr	NM
❑ 110	Hava Nagila/Hava Nagila Part 2	1963	12.00
❑ 112	Wheel of Fortune/Hava Nagila	1963	12.00

Albums

DOWNEY

Number	Title (A Side/B Side)	Yr	NM
❑ D-1003 [M]	Two Sides of Ginny and the Gallions	1964	30.00
❑ DS-1003 [S]	Two Sides of Ginny and the Gallions	1964	40.00

GINO AND GINA

45s

BRUNSWICK

Number	Title (A Side/B Side)	Yr	NM
❑ 55215	I Hope You're Satisfied/Why Do You Make Believe	1961	20.00

MERCURY

Number	Title (A Side/B Side)	Yr	NM
❑ 71283X45	Pretty Baby/Love's a Carousel	1958	15.00
❑ 71283X45	(It's Been a Long Time) Pretty Baby/Love's a Carousel	1958	20.00
❑ 71346X45	She Belongs to Me/Rainin' and Rainin'	1958	20.00
❑ 71370X45	Brand New Penny/I Don't Love You	1958	20.00
❑ 71398X45	Kooka Dong/You're Mine Alone	1959	25.00
❑ 71483X45	I Don't Need a Ring Around Your Finger/Charlie	1959	25.00

WARWICK

Number	Title (A Side/B Side)	Yr	NM
❑ 554	I'm Bugged Over You/Come On Legs	1960	20.00

GINO AND THE DELLS

45s

GOLDEN CREST

Number	Title (A Side/B Side)	Yr	NM
❑ 567	Altar of Dreams/Baby Don't Go Now	1962	40.00
❑ 576	We'll Make It Someday/I'm a Boy in Love	1963	40.00
❑ 581	It's Only a Paper Moon/Home Sweet Home	1963	150.00

GINSBERG, ALLEN

Albums

ATLANTIC

Number	Title (A Side/B Side)	Yr	NM
❑ 4001 [M]	Allen Ginsburg Reads Kaddish	1966	30.00

FANTASY

Number	Title (A Side/B Side)	Yr	NM
❑ F-7006 [M]	Howl and Other Poems	1959	200.00

—Black non-flexible vinyl

Number	Title (A Side/B Side)	Yr	NM
❑ F-7006 [M]	Howl and Other Poems	1959	400.00

—Red vinyl

GIORDANO, LOU

45s

BRUNSWICK

Number	Title (A Side/B Side)	Yr	NM
❑ 55115	Stay Close to Me/Don'Cha Know	1959	1200.

—With Buddy Holly on guitar

GIOVANNI, NIKKI

Albums

NIKTOM

Number	Title (A Side/B Side)	Yr	NM
❑ NK 4200	Like a Ripple on a Pond	1973	10.00
❑ NK 4201	The Way I Feel	1975	10.00

RIGHT-ON

Number	Title (A Side/B Side)	Yr	NM
❑ 5001	Truth Is On Its Way	1971	10.00

GIRLFRIENDS, THE

45s

COLPIX

Number	Title (A Side/B Side)	Yr	NM
❑ 712	My One and Only Jimmy Boy/For My Sake	1963	20.00
❑ 744	Baby Don't Cry/I Don't Believe in You	1964	20.00

MELIC

Number	Title (A Side/B Side)	Yr	NM
❑ 4125	No More Tears/I Want to Be Happy	1963	15.00

PIONEER

Number	Title (A Side/B Side)	Yr	NM
❑ 71833	Four Shy Girls (In Their Itsy Bitsy Teeny Weeny Yellow Polka Dot Bikinis)/Jackie	1961	20.00

Number	Title (A Side/B Side)	Yr	NM

GIRLS, THE

45s

CAPITOL

❑ 5528 My Baby/My Love 1965 30.00
❑ 5675 Chico's Girl/The Dumb Song 1966 20.00

SCEPTER

❑ 12242 Perfect Love/Mr. Poster 1969 8.00

20TH CENTURY FOX

❑ 6651 Way, Way Out/Modesty Blaise 1966 20.00

GITS, THE

45s

BIG FLAMING EGO

❑ 06 Precious Blood/Seaweed/Kings and Queens 1990 10.00
❑ 06 [PS] Precious Blood/Seaweed/Kings and Queens 1990 10.00

BROKEN REKIDS

❑ SKIP 4 Second Skin/Social Love 1991 8.00
—Purple vinyl
❑ SKIP 4 [PS] Second Skin/Social Love 1991 8.00

Albums

BROKEN REKIDS

❑ SKIP 44 Kings & Queens 1995 15.00
❑ SKIP 87 Seafish Louisville 2000 15.00

C/Z

❑ 051 Frenching the Bully 1992 25.00
—Originals on red vinyl

GLACIERS, THE

Albums

MERCURY

❑ MG-20895 [M] From Sea to Ski 1964 50.00
❑ SR-60895 [S] From Sea to Ski 1964 60.00

GLAD, THE Timothy Schmit, later of POCO and EAGLES, was in this group.

45s

ABC

❑ 11163 Johnny Silver's Ride/Love Needs the World 1969 12.00

EQUINOX

❑ 70004 See What You Mean/Bedtime Story 1968 20.00
❑ 70006 A New Tomorrow/Pickin' Up the Pieces 1968 20.00

Albums

ABC

❑ S-655 Feelin' Glad 1969 25.00

GLADIATORS, THE

45s

DIG

❑ 135 Girl of My Heart/My Baby Doll 1957 300.00

GLADIOLAS, THE Evolved into MAURICE WILLIAMS AND THE ZODIACS.

45s

EXCELLO

❑ 2101 Little Darlin'/Sweetheart, Please Don't Go 1957 75.00
❑ 2110 Run, Run, Little Joe/Comin' Home to You 1957 50.00
❑ 2120 Hey Little Girl/I Wanta Know 1957 50.00
❑ 2136 Shoop Shoop/Say You'll Be Mine 1958 50.00

GLADSTONE

45s

ABC

❑ 11327 A Piece of Paper/Livin' in the Country 1972 6.00
❑ 11340 Marietta Station/Lady Eyes 1972 6.00
❑ 11361 Natural Inclination/Here Comes That Feeling 1973 6.00

Albums

ABC

❑ ABCX-751 From Down Home in Tyler, Texas, U.S.A. 1972 12.00
❑ ABCX-778 Lookin' for a Smile 1973 12.00

GLAHE, WILL

45s

LONDON

❑ 1523 Came the Morning/Rose of the Wildwood 1954 10.00
❑ 1673 The March Hare/The Peanut Polka 1956 10.00
❑ 1693 Beer Barrel Polka/Hearts and Heartaches 1957 10.00
❑ 1755 Liechtensteiner Polka/Schweizer Kanton Polka 1957 10.00
❑ 1788 Sweet Elizabeth/Tavern in the Town 1958 10.00
❑ 1818 Duschka/The Pretzel Waltz 1958 10.00
❑ 1859 In Einen Weindorf/The 30th of May 1959 10.00
❑ 1900 Flower on Your Hat/Swedish Punch 196? 8.00
❑ 1915 Ei, Ei, Wat Hat Du Da/In Pfaffenhofen 196? 8.00
❑ 10037 I Want to Marry a Cowboy/America 196? 12.00

LONDON INT'L.

❑ 10023 Just Because/Seven Roses 196? 10.00
❑ 10029 I'd Rather Buy Myself a Tyrolean Hat/(Instrumental) 196? 10.00

Albums

LONDON

❑ PS 146 [S] Christmas Greetings from Germany 195? 20.00
❑ PS 150 [S] Old Heidelberg 196? 15.00
❑ LB 311 [10] Beer Garden Rhythms 195? 25.00
❑ PS 344 [S] Big Polka Band Hits 196? 15.00
❑ PS 397 [S] Happy Days Are Here Again 196? 15.00
❑ LL 1710 [M] Beer Garden Music 195? 20.00
❑ LL 3021 [M] Beer Garden Musik 195? 15.00
❑ LL 3046 [M] The Polka King 195? 15.00
❑ LL 3099 [M] Old Heidelberg 196? 15.00
❑ LL 3344 [M] Big Polka Band Hits 196? 12.00
❑ LL 3397 [M] Happy Days Are Here Again 196? 15.00
❑ TW 91223 [M] Christmas Greetings from Germany 195? 15.00
❑ TW 91225 [M] Cafe International 195? 15.00
❑ TW 91227 [M] Old Heidelberg 196? 12.00
❑ SW 99009 [S] German Sing-a-Long 195? 15.00
❑ SW 99227 [S] Old Heidelberg 196? 12.00
❑ SW 99419 [S] More German Sing-a-Long 196? 12.00

LONDON PHASE 4

❑ SP-44069 New Beer Barrel Polka 196? 15.00
❑ SP-44122 Strictly Oompah 1969 15.00
❑ SP-44145 Oktoberfest! 1970 15.00
❑ SP-44224 The Polka King, Vol. 1 197? 15.00
❑ SP-44226 The Polka King, Vol. 2 197? 15.00
❑ SP-44257 Bavarian Merry-Go-Round 1976 15.00

RICHMOND

❑ B 20016 [M] Polka Hits 196? 12.00

GLASS BOTTLE, THE

45s

AVCO

❑ 4584 The Girl Who Loved Me When/Because She's Mine Again 1971 6.00
❑ 4592 Don't It Make You Feel So Good/(B-side unknown) 1972 5.00
❑ 4597 Pretty Thing/(B-side unknown) 1972 5.00
—Both of the above credit lead singer Gary Criss

AVCO EMBASSY

❑ 4575 I Ain't Got Time Anymore/The First Time 1971 6.00

Albums

AVCO

❑ 33012 The Glass Bottle 1971 15.00

GLASS HARP Christian rock pioneer Phil Keaggy was in this group.

45s

DECCA

❑ 32830 Children's Fantasy/Village Queen 1971 10.00
❑ 32915 The Answer/Just Always 1972 10.00
❑ 32995 La De Da/(B-side unknown) 1972 10.00

Albums

DECCA

❑ DL 75261 Glass Harp 1971 25.00
❑ DL 75306 Synergy 1971 25.00
❑ DL 75358 It Makes Me Glad 1972 25.00

MCA

❑ 293 Glass Harp 1974 10.00
—Reissue of Decca 75261

GLASS HOUSE, THE

45s

INVICTUS

❑ 9071 Crumbs Off the Table/Bad Bill of Goods 1969 6.00
❑ 9076 I Can't Be You (You Can't Be Me)/He's In My Life 1970 6.00
❑ 9082 Stealing Moments From Another Woman's Life/If It Ain't Love, It Don't Matter 1970 6.00
❑ 9090 Touch Me Jesus/If It Ain't Love, It Don't Matter 1971 6.00
❑ 9097 Look What We've Done to Love/Heaven's There to Guide Us 1971 6.00
❑ 9111 Let It Flow/Playing Games 1972 6.00
❑ 9129 Thanks I Needed That/I Don't See Me in Your Eyes Anymore 1972 6.00

Albums

INVICTUS

❑ ST-7305 Inside the Glass House 1971 12.00
❑ ST-9810 Thanks I Needed That 1972 12.00

GLASS PRISM, THE

45s

RCA VICTOR

❑ 74-0205 The Raven/El Dorado 1969 6.00

Albums

RCA VICTOR

❑ LSP-4201 Poe Through the Glass Prism 1969 15.00
❑ LSP-4270 On Joy and Sorrow 1970 15.00

GLEAMS, THE

45s

HIT

❑ 36 He's a Rebel/Next Door to an Angel 1962 10.00
—B-side by Ward Oliver

J-V

❑ 101 Bad Boy/Give Me a Chance 1961 300.00

GLEEMS, THE

45s

PARKWAY

❑ 893 Sandra Baby/You Are the One 1964 20.00

GLENCOVES, THE

45s

SELECT

❑ 724 Hootenanny/It's Sister Ginny's Turn to Throw the Bomb 1963 10.00
❑ 726 Don't Knock/Ginny's Come Home 1963 10.00
❑ 727 Devil's Waitin'/Better Think Twice 1963 10.00
❑ 729 Keep Away from My Gal/Keep On Truckin' Mama 1964 12.00

GLENN, GLEN

45s

DORE

❑ 523 Goofin' Around/Susie Green from Abilene 1959 15.00

ERA

❑ 1061 Everybody's Movin'/I'm Glad My Baby's Gone 1957 60.00
❑ 1074 One Cup of Coffee/Laurie Ann 1958 50.00

GLENN, LLOYD

45s

ALADDIN

❑ 3268 Nite Flite/Still Waters 1954 25.00
❑ 3288 Footloose/Glen's Glide 1955 25.00
❑ 3307 Sunrise/Tiddly Winks 1955 25.00
❑ 3327 Southbound Special/Blue Ivories 1956 20.00
❑ 3346 After Hours (Part 1)/After Hours (Part 2) 1956 20.00
❑ 3353 Chica-Boo/Old Time Shuffle 1957 20.00
❑ 3378 The Vamp/Ballroom Shuffle 1957 20.00
❑ 3400 Hyde Park/Love for Sale 1957 20.00
❑ 3407 Cute-Tee/Black Fantasy 1958 20.00
❑ 3446 Petite Fleur/Honky Tonk Train 1959 15.00
❑ 3459 Long Gone (Part 1)/Long Gone (Part 2) 1959 15.00

HOLLYWOOD

❑ 1021 Merry Christmas Baby/Sleigh Ride 1954 20.00
—B-side by Charles Brown; red label
❑ 1021 Merry Christmas Baby/Sleigh Ride 196? 8.00
—B-side by Charles Brown; color label
❑ 1021 Merry Christmas Baby/Sleigh Ride 197? 5.00
—B-side by Charles Brown; black label
❑ 1028 Chica-Boo/Old Time Shuffle 1954 25.00
❑ 1033 Sleigh Ride/China Doll 1954 25.00

IMPERIAL

❑ 5839 Twistville/Young Date 1962 12.00

SWING TIME

❑ 254 Chica-Boo/Jungle Town Jubilee 1951 30.00
❑ 271 Sleigh Ride/Savage Boy 1951 30.00
❑ 277 Day Break Stomp/Jungle Twilight 1952 30.00
❑ 278 Cute-Tee/Rhumba 1952 30.00
❑ 292 After Hours/Yancey Special 1952 30.00
❑ 293 Honky Tonk Train/Pine Top Boogie Woogie 1952 30.00
❑ 296 Angora/Cuba Doll 1952 30.00

Except when noted otherwise, VG = 25% of NM, and VG+ = 50% of NM. (Example: VG = $2.00, VG+ = $4.00 and NM = $8.00.)

Number | Title (A Side/B Side) | Yr | NM

❑ 311 Boogie Woogie on St. Louis Blues/Ugh 1953 30.00
❑ 324 Night Time/It Moves Me 1953 30.00
❑ 336 Not the Girl for Me/Black Fantasy 1954 30.00

Albums

ALADDIN
❑ LP-808 [M] Chica-Boo 1956 1000.
—Black vinyl
❑ LP-808 [M] Chica-Boo 1956 2000.
—Red vinyl; VG value 1000; VG+ value 1500

BLACK & BLUE
❑ 33077 Old Time Shuffle 1977 12.00

IMPERIAL
❑ LP-9174 [M] Chica-Boo 1962 150.00
❑ LP-9175 [M] After Hours 1962 150.00
❑ LP-12174 [S] Chica-Boo 1962 200.00
❑ LP-12175 [S] After Hours 1962 200.00

SCORE
❑ SLP-4006 [M] Lloyd Glenn 1957 1000.
❑ SLP-4020 [M] After Hours 1958 1000.

SWING TIME
❑ 1901 [10] Lloyd Glenn Presents All Time Favorites 1954 3000.
—VG value 1500; VG+ value 2250

GLITTER, GARY

45s

ARISTA
❑ 0173 I Love You Love Me Love/Hands Up! It's a Stick-Up 1976 5.00

BELL
❑ 45237 Rock and Roll, Part 2/Rock and Roll, Part 1 1972 6.00
❑ 45276 I Didn't Know I Loved You (Till I Saw You Rock and Roll)/Shakey Sue 1972 5.00
❑ 45326 Do You Wanna Touch Me (Oh Yeah)/I Would If I Could But I Can't 1973 5.00
❑ 45345 Baby Please Don't Go/I.O.U. 1973 5.00
❑ 45375 Come On, Come In/Happy Birthday 1973 5.00
❑ 45398 (I'm the) Leader of the Gang (I Am)/(B-side unknown) 1973 5.00
❑ 45438 I Love You Love Me Love/(B-side unknown) 1974 5.00

DECCA
❑ 32714 Goodbye Seattle/Wait for Me 1970 15.00
—As "Paul Raven"

TOMMY BOY
❑ 639 Rock 'N' Roll Part 2...The Hey Song (same on both sides) 1995 3.00
—Original recording with overdubbed crowd sounds

Albums

BELL
❑ 1108 Glitter 1972 15.00
❑ 6082 Gary Glitter 1973 15.00

EPIC
❑ PE 39299 The Leader 1984 15.00

EPIC/NU-DISK
❑ 3E 36848 [10] Glitter & Gold 1981 12.00

GLITTERHOUSE

45s

DYNOVOICE
❑ 925 I Lost Me a Friend/Tinkerbell's Mind 1968 10.00
❑ 927 Barbarella/Love Drags Me Down 1968 12.00

Albums

DYNOVOICE
❑ 31905 Color Bland 1968 20.00

GLOBETROTTERS, THE

45s

BUDDAH
❑ 309 Don't Rock the Boat/Hatfield Small 1972 10.00

KIRSHNER
❑ 63-5006 Cheer Me Up/Gravy 1970 12.00
❑ 63-5006 [PS] Cheer Me Up/Gravy 1970 15.00
❑ 63-5008 Rainy Day Bells/Meadowlark 1970 15.00
❑ 63-5012 Duke of Earl/Everybody's Got Hot Pants 1971 12.00
❑ 63-5016 Everybody Needs Love/ESP 1971 12.00

Albums

KIRSHNER
❑ KES-108 The Globetrotters 1970 20.00

GLORIES, THE

45s

DATE
❑ 1553 I Stand Accused (Of Loving You)/Wish They Could Write a Song 1967 10.00
❑ 1571 Give Me My Freedom/Security 1967 25.00
❑ 1579 Sing Me a Love Song/Ooh, That's Love, Baby 1967 25.00
❑ 1593 Stand By (I'm Coming Home)/My Sweet, Sweet Baby 1968 25.00
❑ 1593 [PS] Stand By (I'm Coming Home)/My Sweet, Sweet Baby 1968 50.00
❑ 1615 I Worship You Baby/Don't Dial My Number 1968 150.00
❑ 1622 No News/Oh Baby That's Love 1968 25.00
❑ 1636 Try a Little Tenderness/There He Is 1969 25.00
❑ 1647 Don't Make the Good Girls Go Bad/The Dark End of the Street 1969 20.00

GLORY (1)

45s

AVALANCHE
❑ XW-289 Find Out Lover/Mrs. Walter 1973 6.00

Albums

AVALANCHE
❑ AV-LA148-F Glory 1973 15.00

GLORY (2)

Albums

TEXAS REVOLUTION
❑ CFS-2531 A Meat Music Sampler 1969 100.00

GLORYTONES, THE

45s

EPIC
❑ 9243 You Only Came Back to Hurt Me/Was That the Right Thing to Do 1957 40.00

GLOWTONES, THE

45s

ATLANTIC
❑ 1156 The Girl I Love/Ping Pong 1957 —
—Only known on 78 rpm; 45 rpm release was on EastWest 101

EASTWEST
❑ 101 The Girl I Love/Ping Pong 1957 30.00

GO-GO'S, THE

No relation to the 1980s girl group.

45s

RCA VICTOR
❑ 47-8370 Lonely Girl/Chicken of the Sea 1964 15.00
❑ 47-8435 The Wild One/Saturday's Hero 1964 30.00

Albums

RCA VICTOR
❑ LPM-2930 [M] Swim with the Go-Go's 1964 25.00
❑ LSP-2930 [S] Swim with the Go-Go's 1964 30.00

GODCHAUX, KEITH AND DONNA

See KEITH AND DONNA.

GODDARD, GEOFF

45s

LAWN
❑ 235 Walk With My Angel/Sky Men 1964 12.00

GODFREY, RAY

45s

ABC
❑ 10999 I Can't Go On Living Like This/Right Straight in the Eye 1967 10.00

COLUMBIA
❑ 4-43398 Old Love/There's Always Room (For One More Fool Like Me) 1965 10.00
❑ 4-43618 I Can Live It Down/Keep Your Chin Up, Soldier 1966 10.00
❑ 4-43618 [PS] I Can Live It Down/Keep Your Chin Up, Soldier 1966 12.00
❑ 4-43785 Winner Take All/Please Don't Mention My Name 1966 10.00
❑ 4-44071 Three Little Words from You/The Difference in Me 1967 10.00

J&J
❑ 001 The Picture/The Overall Song 1960 40.00

PEACH
❑ 757 Let's Move to the City/Wait, Weep and Wonder 1961 20.00

SAVOY
❑ 3021 The Picture/The Overall Song 1960 25.00

SIMS
❑ 130 Better Times a-Comin'/Ten Silver Dollars 1962 20.00

SPRING
❑ 104 I Gotta Get Away/Sherry Washington 1970 8.00
❑ 135 Candy Clown/I Want to Be Your Only Love 1973 6.00

GODSPELL

45s

BELL
❑ 45147 By My Side/Crucifixion, Resurrection 1971 5.00
❑ 45210 Day By Day/Bless the Lord 1972 4.00
❑ 45240 We Beseech Thee/On the Willows 1972 5.00
❑ 45275 By My Side/(B-side unknown) 1972 5.00
❑ 45351 Beautiful City/Bless the Lord 1973 5.00

GODZ, THE

No relation to the late-1970s punk/metal band of the same name.

45s

ESP-DISK'
❑ 4503 Lay in the Sun/I Want a Word with You 1966 10.00

Albums

ESP-DISK'
❑ 1037 [M] Contact High with the Godz 1967 60.00
❑ S-1037 [S] Contact High with the Godz 1967 50.00
❑ 1047 Godz 2 1968 50.00
❑ 1077 Third Testament 1969 50.00
❑ 2017 Godzundheit 1970 50.00

GOGGLES, THE

45s

AUDIO FIDELITY
❑ 168 Don't Say You Don't Remember/We All Live on a Rainbow 1971 5.00

Albums

AUDIO FIDELITY
❑ AFSD-6244 The Goggles 1971 15.00

GOINS, HERBIE, AND THE NIGHT-RIDERS

45s

CAPITOL
❑ 5978 Coming Home to You/The Incredible Miss Brown 1967 40.00

GOLD, ANDREW

Also see BRYNDLE.

45s

ASYLUM
❑ 45286 That's Why I Love You/A Note from You 1975 4.00
❑ 45339 Stay/Firefly 1976 4.00
❑ 45378 Angel Woman/Do Wah Diddy 1976 4.00
❑ 45384 Lonely Boy/Must Be Crazy 1977 4.00
❑ 45384 [PS] Lonely Boy/Must Be Crazy 1977 5.00
❑ 45417 One of Them Is Me/Passing Thing 1977 4.00
❑ 45439 Go Back Home Again/Firefly 1977 4.00
❑ 45456 Thank You for Being a Friend/Still You Linger On 1978 4.00
❑ 45489 Never Let Her Slip Away/Genevieve 1978 4.00
❑ 45489 [PS] Never Let Her Slip Away/Genevieve 1978 5.00
❑ 45521 Looking for My Love/How Can This Be Love 1978 4.00
❑ 45522 I'm On My Way/Always for You 1978 4.00
❑ 46626 Kiss This One Goodbye/Make Up Your Mind 1980 4.00

Albums

ASYLUM
❑ 6E-116 All This and Heaven Too 1978 10.00
❑ 6E-264 Whirlwind 1979 10.00
❑ 7E-1047 Andrew Gold 1975 10.00
❑ 7E-1086 What's Wrong with This Picture? 1977 10.00

GOLD, MARTY

45s

KAPP
❑ 244 Hey! Paesano Cha Cha Cha/I'm Not Afraid Anymore 1958 10.00

RCA VICTOR
❑ 47-7696 Lissabon/Music of Home 1960 8.00
❑ 47-7722 Lonely Guitar/Home from the Hill 1960 8.00
❑ 47-7822 The Breeze and I/Cry Like the Wind 1960 8.00
❑ 47-7856 Carnival in Rome/My Romance 1961 8.00

Albums

KAPP
❑ KL-1125 [M] By the Waters of the Minnetonka 1959 15.00

Number	Title (A Side/B Side)	Yr	NM
PICKWICK			
❑ ACL-9003	Songs from "How the Grinch Stole Christmas" and Other Children's Christmas Songs	197?	8.00
RCA VICTOR			
❑ LPM-2290 [M]	It's Magic	1961	12.00
❑ LSP-2290 [S]	It's Magic	1961	15.00
❑ LSP-2381 [S]	Stereo Action Goes Hollywood	1962	12.00
❑ LPM-2620 [M]	Soundpower!	1963	12.00
❑ LSP-2620 [S]	Soundpower!	1963	15.00
❑ LSP-3599 [S]	Soundaroundus	1966	12.00
VIK			
❑ LX-1069 [M]	Organized for Hi-Fi	1957	15.00

GOLD, SANDY

45s

Number	Title (A Side/B Side)	Yr	NM
HIT			
❑ 27	Sheila/She's Not You	1962	8.00
—B-side by George Killebrew			

GOLD BUGS, THE

45s

Number	Title (A Side/B Side)	Yr	NM
CORAL			
❑ 62453	Stop That Wedding/It's So Nice	1965	40.00

GOLDBERG, BARRY
Also see GOLDBERG-MILLER BLUES BAND.

45s

Number	Title (A Side/B Side)	Yr	NM
ATCO			
❑ 6946	(I've Got to Use My) Imagination/Dusty Country	1973	10.00
—A-side co-produced by Bob Dylan			
BUDDAH			
❑ 59	Sittin' in Circles/Hole in My Pocket	1968	10.00
❑ 103	Jimi the Fox/On the Road Again	1969	10.00
EPIC			
❑ 10007	Blowing My Mind/Think	1966	15.00
❑ 10033	Ginger Man/Whole Lotta Shakin' Goin' On	1966	15.00

Albums

Number	Title (A Side/B Side)	Yr	NM
ATCO			
❑ SD 7040	Barry Goldberg	1974	12.00
BUDDAH			
❑ BDM-1012 [M]	The Barry Goldberg Reunion	1968	50.00
—White-label promo in stereo cover with "mono" sticker			
❑ BDS-5012 [S]	The Barry Goldberg Reunion	1968	25.00
❑ BDS-5029	Two Jews Blues	1969	25.00
❑ BDS-5051	Street Man	1970	15.00
❑ BDS-5081	Blast from My Past	1974	15.00
EPIC			
❑ LN 24199 [M]	Blowing My Mind	1966	30.00
❑ BN 26199 [S]	Blowing My Mind	1966	40.00
RECORD MAN			
❑ CR 5015	Barry Goldberg and Friends	1972	15.00

GOLDBERG-MILLER BLUES BAND
Also see BARRY GOLDBERG; STEVE MILLER.

45s

Number	Title (A Side/B Side)	Yr	NM
EPIC			
❑ 9865	More Soul Than Soulful/Mother Song	1965	15.00
❑ 9865 [DJ]	More Soul Than Soulful/Mother Song	1965	25.00
—Promo only on blue vinyl			
❑ 9865 [PS]	More Soul Than Soulful/Mother Song	1965	50.00
—Promo only			

GOLDDIGGERS, THE
DEAN MARTIN's girl group from his TV show.

45s

Number	Title (A Side/B Side)	Yr	NM
METROMEDIA			
❑ 141	I Wanna Be Loved/It's Fun to Be Young	1969	5.00
❑ 156	We Need A Little Christmas/I Just Want You For Christmas	1969	6.00
RCA VICTOR			
❑ 74-0670	A-Flat Cricket and B-Flat Frog/Nobody Else But You	1972	5.00

Albums

Number	Title (A Side/B Side)	Yr	NM
METROMEDIA			
❑ MD 1009	The Golddiggers	1969	12.00
❑ MD 1012	We Need a Little Christmas	1969	15.00
RCA VICTOR			
❑ LSP-4643	The Golddiggers Today!	1972	12.00

GOLDEBRIARS, THE
Curt Boetcher was a member of this group.

45s

Number	Title (A Side/B Side)	Yr	NM
EPIC			
❑ 9673	Pretty Girls and Rolling Stones/Shenandoah	1964	12.00
❑ 9719	The Castle in the Corner/I've Got to Love Somebody	1964	12.00
❑ 9806	Don't Want Your Love/Give Me Lovin'	1965	12.00

Albums

Number	Title (A Side/B Side)	Yr	NM
EPIC			
❑ LN 24087 [M]	The Goldebriars	1964	15.00
❑ LN 24114 [M]	Straight Ahead	1964	15.00
❑ BN 26087 [S]	The Goldebriars	1964	20.00
❑ BN 26114 [S]	Straight Ahead	1964	20.00

GOLDEN DAWN

Albums

Number	Title (A Side/B Side)	Yr	NM
INTERNATIONAL ARTISTS			
❑ 4	Power Plant	1968	300.00
❑ 4	Power Plant	1979	15.00
—Reissue with "Masterfonics" in trail-off wax			

GOLDEN EARRING

45s

Number	Title (A Side/B Side)	Yr	NM
ATLANTIC			
❑ 2710	Eight Miles High/One Huge Road	1970	6.00
DWARF			
❑ 2001	Back Home/As Long As the Wind Blows	1969	10.00
❑ 2001 [PS]	Back Home/As Long As the Wind Blows	1969	20.00
MCA			
❑ 40513	Babylon/Sleep Walkin'	1976	4.00
❑ 40802	Radar Love (Live)/Radar Love (Studio)	1977	4.00
POLYDOR			
❑ 2004	Weekend Love/Tiger Bay	1979	4.00
❑ 14001	It's Alright, But I Admit It Could Be Better/Song of a Devil's Servant	1969	10.00
❑ 14581	Weekend Love/Tiger Bay	1979	—
—Unreleased			
TRACK			
❑ 40202	Radar Love/Just Like Vince Taylor	1974	6.00
❑ 40309	Candy's Going Bad/She Flies on Strange Wings	1974	5.00
❑ 40369	Ce Soir/Lucky Numbers	1975	5.00
❑ 40412	The Switch/Lonesome D.J.	1975	5.00
21 RECORDS			
❑ 103	Twilight Zone/King Dark	1982	4.00
❑ 108	The Devil Made Me Do It/Chargin' Batteries	1983	4.00
❑ 112	When the Lady Smiles/Orwell's Ear	1984	3.00
❑ 112 [PS]	When the Lady Smiles/Orwell's Ear	1984	5.00
❑ 113	Fist in Glove/One Night Moonlight	1984	3.00
❑ 99515	Love in Motion/Why Do I	1986	3.00
❑ 99533	Quiet Eyes/Love in Motion	1986	3.00
❑ 99533 [PS]	Quiet Eyes/Love in Motion	1986	4.00
❑ 881415-7	Something Heavy Going Down/Enough Is Enough	1984	3.00

Albums

Number	Title (A Side/B Side)	Yr	NM
ATLANTIC			
❑ SD 8244	Eight Miles High	1970	35.00
CAPITOL			
❑ ST-164	Miracle Mirror	1969	50.00
❑ ST 2823 [S]	Winter Harvest	1967	150.00
❑ T 2823 [M]	Winter Harvest	1967	175.00
❑ ST-11315	The Golden Earring	1974	12.00
DWARF			
❑ 2000	Golden Earring	1971	35.00
MCA			
❑ 703	Grab It For a Second	198?	8.00
—Reissue of 3057			
❑ 827	Switch	198?	8.00
—Reissue of 2139			
❑ 2139	Switch	197?	10.00
—Reissue of Track 2139			
❑ 2183	To the Hilt	1976	12.00
❑ 2254	Mad Love	1977	12.00
❑ 2352	Moontan	1978	10.00
—Reissue of Track 396			
❑ 3057	Grab It For a Second	1978	12.00
❑ 6004 [(2)]	Golden Earring Live!	198?	10.00
—Reissue of 8009			
❑ 8009 [(2)]	Golden Earring Live!	1977	15.00
❑ 37172	Moontan	198?	8.00
—Reissue of 2352			
POLYDOR			
❑ PD-1-6223	No Promises...No Debts	1979	12.00
❑ PD-1-6303	Long Blond Animal	1980	12.00
TRACK			
❑ 396	Moontan	1974	15.00
—Reissue cover with close-up of earring in ear			
❑ 396	Moontan	1974	25.00
—Original cover with nude dancer			
❑ 2139	Switch	1975	15.00
21 RECORDS			
❑ T1-1-9004	Cut	1982	10.00
❑ T1-1-9008	N.E.W.S.	1984	10.00
❑ 90514	The Hole	1986	10.00
❑ 817585-1	Cut	1985	8.00
—Reissue			
❑ 823717-1	Something Heavy Going Down—Live from the Twilight Zone	1984	10.00

GOLDEN NUGGETS, THE

45s

Number	Title (A Side/B Side)	Yr	NM
FUTURA			
❑ 1691	I Was a Fool/Teenage Josephine	1959	600.00
HAWK			
❑ 107/8	Surf Everybody/Everybody Bird	1963	40.00

GOLDENROD

Albums

Number	Title (A Side/B Side)	Yr	NM
CHARTMAKER			
❑ CSG-1101	Goldenrod	1968	400.00

GOLDENRODS, THE

45s

Number	Title (A Side/B Side)	Yr	NM
VEE JAY			
❑ 307	Wish I Was Back in School/Color Cartoons	1959	250.00

GOLDIE, DAN

45s

Number	Title (A Side/B Side)	Yr	NM
TEARDROP			
❑ 3070	Take Our Last Walk Tonight/Walking the Streets	1966	25.00
—The Sir Douglas Quintet is the backing band			

GOLDTONES, THE
Two different groups?

45s

Number	Title (A Side/B Side)	Yr	NM
A&R			
❑ 714	Strike/Gutterball	1963	30.00
❑ 714 [PS]	Strike/Gutterball	1963	50.00

Albums

Number	Title (A Side/B Side)	Yr	NM
LABREA			
❑ L-8011 [M]	The Goldtones	1961	40.00
❑ LS-8011 [S]	The Goldtones	1961	50.00

GOLLIWOGS, THE
Early CREEDENCE CLEARWATER REVIVAL. Also see TOMMY FOGERTY AND THE BLUE VELVETS.

45s

Number	Title (A Side/B Side)	Yr	NM
FANTASY			
❑ 590	Don't Tell Me No Lies/Little Girl, Does Your Mama Know	1964	60.00
❑ 597	Where You Been/You Came Walking	1965	60.00
❑ 599	You Got Nothin' on Me/You Can't Be True	1965	50.00
SCORPIO			
❑ 404	Brown Eyed Girl/You Better Be Careful	1967	50.00
❑ 405	Fragile Child/Fight Fire	1967	50.00
❑ 408	Walking on the Water/You Better Get It Before It Gets You	1967	50.00
❑ 412 [DJ]	Porterville/Call It Pretending	1968	60.00
—Only promos credit the Golliwogs; all known stock copies credit Creedence Clearwater Revival.			

Albums

Number	Title (A Side/B Side)	Yr	NM
FANTASY			
❑ F-9474	Pre-Creedence	1975	30.00
—Reissue of Fantasy and Scorpio sides			

GONE ALL STARS

45s

Number	Title (A Side/B Side)	Yr	NM
GONE			
❑ 5016	7-11/Down Yonder Rock	1957	25.00

GONKS, THE

45s

Number	Title (A Side/B Side)	Yr	NM
LONDON			
❑ 9696	The Gonk Song/Take Care	1964	12.00

Number	Title (A Side/B Side)	Yr	NM

GONN

45s

EMIR

Number	Title (A Side/B Side)	Yr	NM
❑ SS-9217-01	Blackout of Gretley/ Pain in My Heart	1966	800.00

EMIR/MCCM

Number	Title (A Side/B Side)	Yr	NM
❑ 88-9217	Blackout of Gretley/ Pain in My Heart	1988	5.00
—Black vinyl			
❑ 88-9217	Blackout of Gretley/ Pain in My Heart	1988	15.00
—Red vinyl			
❑ 88-9217 [PS]	Blackout of Gretley/ Pain in My Heart	1988	10.00

MERRY JAINE

Number	Title (A Side/B Side)	Yr	NM
❑ IT-2316	Come with Me (To the Stars)/ You're Looking Fine	1967	100.00

GONZALES, FRANK

45s

F-G

Number	Title (A Side/B Side)	Yr	NM
❑ 1001	Sweet Surfing Little Girl/ Let's Make Up	1961	250.00

GONZALES, NITOY

Albums

CAPITOL

Number	Title (A Side/B Side)	Yr	NM
❑ ST 10305 [S]	Christmas in the Philippines	196?	15.00
❑ T 10305 [M]	Christmas in the Philippines	196?	12.00

GOO GOO DOLLS

45s

WARNER BROS.

Number	Title (A Side/B Side)	Yr	NM
❑ 16663	Sympathy/Think About Me	2003	3.00
❑ 16705	Here Is Gone/Big Machine	2002	3.00
❑ 16946	Black Balloon/Slide (Live)	1999	3.00
❑ 18512	We Are the Normal/Another Second Time Around	1993	3.00

Albums

ENIGMA

Number	Title (A Side/B Side)	Yr	NM
❑ 7 73406-1	JED	1989	20.00

MERCENARY

Number	Title (A Side/B Side)	Yr	NM
❑ MER-2102	Goo Goo Dolls	1987	75.00

GOOBERS, THE

45s

SURF

Number	Title (A Side/B Side)	Yr	NM
❑ 1001	Hawaiian Holiday/Buyer Beware	1963	50.00

GOOD, TOMMY

45s

GORDY

Number	Title (A Side/B Side)	Yr	NM
❑ 7034	Baby I Miss You/Leaving Here	1964	100.00

GOOD AND PLENTY

45s

SENATE

Number	Title (A Side/B Side)	Yr	NM
❑ 2105	Living in a World of Make Believe/I Played My Part Well	1967	10.00
❑ 2106	Sunny and Me/Children Dreamin'	1967	10.00

Albums

SENATE

Number	Title (A Side/B Side)	Yr	NM
❑ LP-21001 [M]	The World of Good and Plenty	1967	30.00
❑ LPS-21001 [S]	The World of Good and Plenty	1967	30.00

GOOD GUYS, THE

45s

GNP CRESCENDO

Number	Title (A Side/B Side)	Yr	NM
❑ 326	Asphalt Wipe Out/Scratch	1964	20.00

Albums

GNP CRESCENDO

Number	Title (A Side/B Side)	Yr	NM
❑ GNP-2001 [M]	Sidewalk Surfing	1964	30.00
❑ GNPS-2001 [S]	Sidewalk Surfing	1964	40.00

UNITED ARTISTS

Number	Title (A Side/B Side)	Yr	NM
❑ UAL-3370 [M]	The Good Guys Sing	1964	15.00
❑ UAS-6370 [S]	The Good Guys Sing	1964	20.00

GOOD RATS, THE

45s

KAPP

Number	Title (A Side/B Side)	Yr	NM
❑ 946	The Hobo/Truth Is Gone	1968	12.00

PASSPORT

Number	Title (A Side/B Side)	Yr	NM
❑ 7912	Just Found a Lady/Coo Coo Coo Blues	1978	5.00

Albums

KAPP

Number	Title (A Side/B Side)	Yr	NM
❑ KS-3580	The Good Rats	1969	40.00

PASSPORT

Number	Title (A Side/B Side)	Yr	NM
❑ SP-20 [DJ]	Rats the Way You Like It (Live)	1978	45.00
❑ PB-9825	From Rats to Riches	1978	12.00
❑ PB-9830	Birth Comes to Us All	1978	12.00

RAT CITY

Number	Title (A Side/B Side)	Yr	NM
❑ 998 [(2)]	Live at Last	1979	15.00
❑ RCR-8001	Rat City in Blue	1975	20.00
❑ RCR-8002	Tasty	1978	12.00
❑ RCR-8003	Great American Music	1981	12.00

RAT CITY/GEMM

Number	Title (A Side/B Side)	Yr	NM
❑ RCR-8004	Rat City in Blue	1976	20.00
—Reissue with extra track			

WARNER BROS.

Number	Title (A Side/B Side)	Yr	NM
❑ BS 2813	Tasty	1974	30.00

GOOD ROCKIN' SAM

45s

EXCELLO

Number	Title (A Side/B Side)	Yr	NM
❑ 2059	Baby I'm Fool Proof/ Thing-a-Ma-Jig	1955	50.00

GOOD TIMES, THE

45s

KAMA SUTRA

Number	Title (A Side/B Side)	Yr	NM
❑ 215	That's When Your Heartaches Begin/Good Life	1966	8.00
❑ 247	You Got the Fever/Mr. & Mrs. Arthur Thompson Request (Your Presence at the Marriage of Their Daughter Lorna Beth)	1968	8.00

Albums

KAMA SUTRA

Number	Title (A Side/B Side)	Yr	NM
❑ KLP-8052 [M]	The Good Times	1966	15.00
❑ KSLP-8052 [S]	The Good Times	1966	20.00

GOODEES, THE

45s

HIP

Number	Title (A Side/B Side)	Yr	NM
❑ 109	For a Little While/ Would You, Could You	1968	8.00
❑ 8005	Condition Red/Didn't Know Love Was So Good	1968	10.00
❑ 8010	Jilted/Love Is Here	1969	8.00
❑ 8016	He's a Rebel/Goodies	1969	8.00

Albums

HIP

Number	Title (A Side/B Side)	Yr	NM
❑ HIS-7002	Candy Coated Goodees	1969	30.00

GOODIES, THE

45s

20TH CENTURY

Number	Title (A Side/B Side)	Yr	NM
❑ 2189	The Funky Gibbon/ The Inbetweenies	1975	7.00

GOODMAN, DICKIE

Also see BUCHANAN AND GOODMAN; JOHN AND ERNEST; SPENCER AND SPENCER.

45s

ASI

Number	Title (A Side/B Side)	Yr	NM
❑ 1013	Rocky and the Angel/Pug Rock	1977	6.00
—As "Dickie G. and the Don'ts"			

AUDIO SPECTRUM

Number	Title (A Side/B Side)	Yr	NM
❑ 75	Presidential Interview (Flying Saucer '64)/Paul Revere	1964	40.00

CASH

Number	Title (A Side/B Side)	Yr	NM
❑ 451	Mr. Jaws/Irv's Theme	1975	5.00
❑ 451	Mr. Jaws/Irv's Theme	1975	50.00
—Clear purple vinyl, possibly an "after-hours" edition; at least two, and probably more, exist			

COTIQUE

Number	Title (A Side/B Side)	Yr	NM
❑ 158	On Campus/Mombo Suzie	1969	6.00
—B-side by Johnny Colo			
❑ 173	Luna Trip/My Victrola	1969	6.00
—B-side by Joey Pastrana			

DAVY JONES

Number	Title (A Side/B Side)	Yr	NM
❑ 663	White House Happening/ President Johnson	1967	25.00
❑ 663 [PS]	White House Happening/ President Johnson	1967	40.00

DIAMOND

Number	Title (A Side/B Side)	Yr	NM
❑ 119	Ben Crazy/Flip Side	1962	15.00

EXTRAN

Number	Title (A Side/B Side)	Yr	NM
❑ 601	Hey, E.T./Get a Job	1982	5.00

GOODNAME

Number	Title (A Side/B Side)	Yr	NM
❑ 7100	Safe Sex Report/Safety First	1987	15.00
—His last record			

HOT LINE

Number	Title (A Side/B Side)	Yr	NM
❑ 1017	Energy Crisis '79/Pain	1979	6.00
—Common version has a light green label and "Hot Line" as two words			
❑ 1017	Energy Crisis '79/Pain	1979	8.00
—Less common version has a reddish label and the label as "Hotline" (one word)			

J.M.D.

Number	Title (A Side/B Side)	Yr	NM
❑ 001	Ben Crazy/Flip Side	1962	25.00

JANUS

Number	Title (A Side/B Side)	Yr	NM
❑ 271	Star Warts/The Boys Tune	1977	5.00

M.D.

Number	Title (A Side/B Side)	Yr	NM
❑ 101	Schmonanza/Backwards Theme	1961	20.00

MARK-X

Number	Title (A Side/B Side)	Yr	NM
❑ 8009	The Touchables/Martian Melody	1961	20.00
—Black label			
❑ 8009	The Touchables/Martian Melody	1961	30.00
—Yellow label			
❑ 8010	The Touchables in Brooklyn/ Mystery	1961	20.00

MONTAGE

Number	Title (A Side/B Side)	Yr	NM
❑ 1220	Hey, E.T./The Ride of Paul Revere	1982	15.00
❑ 1220 [DJ]	Hey, E.T. (same on both sides)	1982	5.00

ORON

Number	Title (A Side/B Side)	Yr	NM
❑ 101	Washington Uptight/The Cat	1967	25.00
—As "The Pennsylvania Players"			

PRELUDE

Number	Title (A Side/B Side)	Yr	NM
❑ 8018	Election '80 (same on both sides)	1980	5.00

RAINY WEDNESDAY

Number	Title (A Side/B Side)	Yr	NM
❑ 202	Watergrate/Friends	1973	20.00
❑ 204	Purple People Eater/ Ruthie's Theme	1973	6.00
❑ 205	The Constitution/The End	1973	6.00
❑ 206	Energy Crisis '74/The Mistake	1974	6.00
❑ 206	Energy Crisis '74/ Ruthie's Theme	1974	8.00
❑ 207	Mr. President/Popularity	1974	6.00
❑ 208	Gerry Ford, A Special Report/ Robert	1974	6.00
❑ 209	Inflation in the Nation/ Jon and Jed's Theme	1975	6.00

RAMGO

Number	Title (A Side/B Side)	Yr	NM
❑ 501	Speaking of Ecology/ Dayton's Theme	1970	25.00

RED BIRD

Number	Title (A Side/B Side)	Yr	NM
❑ 10-058	Batman & His Grandmother/ Suspense	1966	20.00

RHINO

Number	Title (A Side/B Side)	Yr	NM
❑ 019	Radio Russia/Washington Inside Out	1984	4.00

RORI

Number	Title (A Side/B Side)	Yr	NM
❑ 601	Horror Movies/Whoa, Mule	1961	25.00
❑ 602	The Berlin Top Ten/Little Tiger	1961	25.00
❑ 701	Santa and the Touchables/ North Pole Rock	1961	25.00

SCEPTER

Number	Title (A Side/B Side)	Yr	NM
❑ 12339	Speaking of Ecology/ Dayton's Theme	1971	12.00

SHARK

Number	Title (A Side/B Side)	Yr	NM
❑ 1001	Mrs. Jaws/(B-side unknown)	1979	20.00
❑ 1002	Super Superman/ Chomp Chomp	1979	15.00

SHELL

Number	Title (A Side/B Side)	Yr	NM
❑ 711	Election '84/Herb's Theme	1984	4.00

SHOCK

Number	Title (A Side/B Side)	Yr	NM
❑ 6	Kong/Ed's Tune	1977	5.00

20TH FOX

Number	Title (A Side/B Side)	Yr	NM
❑ 443	Senate Hearing/Lock-Up	1963	15.00

TWIRL

Number	Title (A Side/B Side)	Yr	NM
❑ 2015	James Bomb/Seventh Theme	1966	15.00

WACKO

Number	Title (A Side/B Side)	Yr	NM
❑ 1001	Mr. President/Dancin' U.S.A.	1981	5.00
❑ 1002	Super-Duper Man/Robert's Tune	1981	5.00
❑ 1381	America '81 (two different versions)	1981	8.00

Z-100

Number	Title (A Side/B Side)	Yr	NM
❑ 100 [DJ]	Attack of the Z Monster/Mystery	1984	10.00
—Promo item for New York radio station			

Albums

CASH

Number	Title (A Side/B Side)	Yr	NM
❑ CR 6000	Mr. Jaws and Other Fables	1975	25.00

COMET

Number	Title (A Side/B Side)	Yr	NM
❑ 69	My Son, the Joke	1963	40.00

IX CHAINS

Number	Title (A Side/B Side)	Yr	NM
❑ NCS 9000	The Original Flying Saucers	1973	40.00

RHINO

Number	Title (A Side/B Side)	Yr	NM
❑ RNLP-811	Dickie Goodman's Greatest Hits	1983	15.00

RORI

Number	Title (A Side/B Side)	Yr	NM
❑ 3301	The Many Heads of Dickie Goodman	1962	80.00

GOODMAN, JERRY, AND JAN HAMMER

Number	Title (A Side/B Side)	Yr	NM
Albums			
NEMPEROR			
❑ SD 430	Like Children	1975	10.00

GOODMAN, SHIRLEY Of SHIRLEY AND LEE; also of SHIRLEY (AND COMPANY).

Number	Title (A Side/B Side)	Yr	NM
45s			
IMPERIAL			
❑ 5944	When a Boy Meets a Girl/ Don't Marry Too Soon	1963	12.00

GOODMAN, STEVE

Number	Title (A Side/B Side)	Yr	NM
45s			
ASYLUM			
❑ 45284	Jessie's Jig (Rob's Romp, Beth's Bounce)/It's a Sin to Tell a Lie	1975	6.00
❑ 45331	Between the Lines/ Can't Go Back	1976	6.00
❑ 45481	Video Tape/My Old Man	1978	6.00
❑ 46012	Men Who Love Women Who Love Men/The One That Got Away	1979	6.00
❑ 46522	Men Who Love Women Who Love Men/The One That Got Away	1979	5.00
❑ 47107	Bobby Don't Stop/Trust Me	1981	5.00
BUDDAH			
❑ 270	City of New Orleans/ (B-side unknown)	1971	12.00
❑ 326	Election Year Rag/Someone Else's Troubles	1972	10.00
❑ 348	The Dutchman/Song for David	1973	10.00
RED PAJAMA			
❑ 1001	A Dying Cub Fan's Last Request/ Take Me Out to the Ball Game	1981	15.00
WGN			
❑ 784	Go Cubs Go (WGN Radio Cubs Theme) (same on both sides)	1984	12.00
Albums			
ASYLUM			
❑ 6E-174	High and Outside	1979	12.00
❑ 6E-297	Hot Spot	1980	12.00
❑ 7E-1037	Jessie's Jig & Other Favorites	1975	12.00
❑ 7E-1061	Words We Can Dance To	1976	12.00
❑ 7E-1118	Say It in Private	1977	12.00
BUDDAH			
❑ BDS 5096	Steve Goodman	1971	15.00
❑ BDS 5121	Somebody Else's Troubles	1972	15.00
❑ BDS 5665 [(2)]	The Essential Steve Goodman	1976	15.00
RED PAJAMAS			
❑ RPJ-001	Artistic Hair	1982	12.00
❑ RPJ-002	Affordable Art	1983	12.00
❑ RPJ-003	Santa Ana Winds	1984	12.00
❑ RPJ-005	Unfinished Business	1985	12.00
❑ RPJ-006	Best of the Asylum Years, Vol. 1	198?	12.00
❑ RPJ-007	Best of the Asylum Years, Vol. 2	198?	12.00

GOODMAN, STEVE, AND PHOEBE SNOW Also see each artist's individual listings.

Number	Title (A Side/B Side)	Yr	NM
45s			
ASYLUM			
❑ 47069	Sometimes Love Forgets/Can't Find My Heart	1980	5.00

GOODTIMERS, THE See DON COVAY.

GOODWIN, DON

Number	Title (A Side/B Side)	Yr	NM
45s			
SILVER BLUE			
❑ 806	This Is Your Song/Help It Along	1973	7.00
❑ 808	Time to Cry/Good Good Lovin'	1974	7.00
❑ 821	Diana/I'll Never Be Away from You	1974	7.00
❑ 822	Baby, Baby Do It/ (B-side unknown)	1974	8.00

GOODWIN, RON

Number	Title (A Side/B Side)	Yr	NM
45s			
CAPITOL			
❑ F3708	The Headless Horseman/ When I Fall in Love	1957	10.00
❑ F3748	Swinging Sweethearts/ I'll Find You	1957	10.00
❑ F3834	Lingering Lovers/Swedish Polka	1957	10.00
❑ F3927	Red Cloak/Laughing Sailor	1958	10.00
❑ F4139	Wagon Train/Latin Lovers	1959	10.00
❑ F4201	The Venus Waltz/Martians on Parade	1959	10.00
KING			
❑ 45-5509	Romanoff and Juliet/El Morocco Tea Rooms	1961	12.00
Albums			
CAPITOL			
❑ T 10078 [M]	It Can't Be Wrong	1957	20.00
❑ T 10177 [M]	Swinging Sweethearts	1958	20.00
❑ ST 10188 [S]	Music in Orbit	1958	40.00
❑ T 10188 [M]	Music in Orbit	1958	30.00
❑ ST 10251 [S]	Music for an Arabian Night	1959	30.00
❑ T 10251 [M]	Music for an Arabian Night	1959	25.00
❑ SP-10560	Jet Flight to Beirut	196?	20.00
❑ ST-11012	Ron Goodwin Plays Someone Named Burt Bacharach	1972	10.00

GOONS, THE

Number	Title (A Side/B Side)	Yr	NM
45s			
LONDON			
❑ 1684	I'm Walking Backwards for Christmas/Bluebottle Blues	1956	25.00

GOOSE CREEK SYMPHONY

Number	Title (A Side/B Side)	Yr	NM
45s			
CAPITOL			
❑ 2729	Big Time Saturday Nite/ Beautiful Bertha	1970	6.00
❑ 2853	Charlie's Tune/No News Is Good News	1970	6.00
❑ 3246	(Oh Lord Won't You Buy Me a) Mercedes Benz/Rich on Love	1971	5.00
❑ 3371	Guitars Pickin', Fiddles Playin'/ Broken Creek Goose Down	1972	5.00
COLUMBIA			
❑ 10062	Hot Dog Daddy/Plans of the Lord	1974	5.00
Albums			
CAPITOL			
❑ SM-444	Goose Creek Symphony	197?	10.00
—Reissue			
❑ ST-444	Goose Creek Symphony	1970	15.00
❑ ST-690	Welcome to Goose Creek	1971	15.00
❑ ST-11044	Words of Earnest	1972	15.00
COLUMBIA			
❑ KC 32918	Do Your Thing But Don't Touch Mine	1974	12.00

GORDIAN KNOT, THE JIM WEATHERLY was in this group.

Number	Title (A Side/B Side)	Yr	NM
45s			
VERVE			
❑ 10595	Year of the Sun/If Only I Could Cry	1968	10.00
❑ 10612	Broken Down Old Merry-Go-Round/We Must Be Doin' Something Right	1968	10.00
Albums			
VERVE			
❑ V-5062 [M]	Tones	1968	30.00
—White label promo only (no stock copies were issued in mono)			
❑ V6-5062 [S]	Tones	1968	15.00

GORDON, BARRY

Number	Title (A Side/B Side)	Yr	NM
45s			
ABC			
❑ 11113	The Girl I Left Behind/ A House Built on Sand	1968	8.00
ABC DUNHILL			
❑ 4126	Days of Pearly Spencer/ Ramshackle Guy	1968	8.00
❑ 4141	The Girl I Left Behind/A House Built on Sand	1968	8.00
❑ 4188	You Can't Love a Child Like a Woman/Take Off the Veil	1969	7.00
CADENCE			
❑ 1431	You Can't Lie to a Liar/ You Can't See the Trees	1962	10.00
DUNHILL			
❑ 4110	Angelica/Take Off the Veil	1967	8.00
❑ 4126	Days of Pearly Spencer/ Ramshackle Guy	1968	15.00
—No "ABC" logo next to "Dunhill" at top of label			
ERA			
❑ 1084	Katy/They	1958	12.00
❑ 1092	Bluebird Song/Rabbit Habit	1959	12.00
MERCURY			
❑ 71878	Sad Little Girl/She's Got Soul	1961	12.00
MGM			
❑ K12166	Rock Around Mother Goose/ Seven	1956	20.00
❑ K12222	I Can't Whistle/ The Milkman's Polka	1956	20.00
❑ K12276	How Do We Look to the Monkeys/Ten Years to Go	1956	20.00
❑ K12373	Rock Little Chillun/That Pretty Little Girl Next Door	1956	20.00
❑ K12468	The Thief/Yes, We Have No Bananas	1957	15.00
UNITED ARTISTS			
❑ 730	Go Back Little Tear/Susan	1964	10.00
❑ 795	True Love Can Never Die/ The Two of Them	1964	10.00
❑ 876	Sealed with a Kiss/ Talk, Talk, Talk	1965	10.00
❑ 950	Let Me Try/The World Is Mine	1965	10.00
❑ 50019	Yes Sir, That's My Baby/ True Love Can Never Die	1966	10.00
Albums			
CAPITOL			
❑ ST-805	Pieces of Time	1971	12.00
UNITED ARTISTS			
❑ UAL 3491 [M]	Yes Sir, That's My Baby	1966	15.00
❑ UAS 6491 [S]	Yes Sir, That's My Baby	1966	20.00

GORDON, DEXTER

Number	Title (A Side/B Side)	Yr	NM
Albums			
COLUMBIA			
❑ JC 36853	Gotham City	2000	12.00
—180-gram reissue			

GORDON, JUSTIN

Number	Title (A Side/B Side)	Yr	NM
Albums			
DOT			
❑ DLP-3214 [M]	Justin Gordon Swings	1959	40.00

GORDON, MIKE, AND THE AGATES

Number	Title (A Side/B Side)	Yr	NM
45s			
DORE			
❑ 681	Rumble at Newport Beach/ Last Call for Dinner	1963	30.00
❑ 780	Curfew on the Strip/Last Call for Dinner	1966	15.00

GORDON, MIKE, AND THE EL TEMPOS

Number	Title (A Side/B Side)	Yr	NM
45s			
CAT			
❑ 101	Why Don't You Do Right/ You Got to Give	1954	50.00

GORDON, ROBERT

Number	Title (A Side/B Side)	Yr	NM
45s			
PRIVATE STOCK			
❑ 45,156	Red Hot/Sweet Surrender	1977	6.00
❑ 45,191	Sea Cruise/If This Is Wrong	1978	6.00
—With Link Wray			
❑ 45,203	Fire/If This Is Wrong	1979	6.00
❑ 45,203 [PS]	Fire/If This Is Wrong	1979	12.00
RCA			
❑ JH-11452 [DJ]	Blue Christmas (mono/stereo)	1978	6.00
❑ PB-11452	Blue Christmas/Fire	1978	5.00
—With Link Wray			
❑ PB-11471	It's Only Make Believe/ Rock Billy Boogie	1979	5.00
❑ PB-11608	Walk On By/Black Slacks	1979	5.00
❑ PB-11919	Born to Lose/Need You	1980	5.00
❑ PB-12239	Someday, Someway/ Drivin' Wheel	1981	5.00
❑ PB-13399	Something's Gonna Happen/ Flying Saucers Rock and Roll	1982	5.00
Albums			
PRIVATE STOCK			
❑ PS-2030	Robert Gordon with Link Wray	1977	16.00
—Formerly with Tuff Darts			
❑ PS-7008	Fresh Fish Special	1978	16.00
RCA VICTOR			
❑ DJL1-3411 [DJ]	Essential Robert Gordon	1979	30.00
—Promo-only live album with tracks from Tuff Darts			
❑ AFL1-3294	Rock Billy Boogie	1979	12.00
❑ AFL1-3294	Rock Billy Boogie	1979	20.00
—Original pressing on white vinyl			
❑ AFL1-3296	Robert Gordon with Link Wray	1979	12.00
—Reissue			
❑ AFL1-3299	Fresh Fish Special	1979	12.00
—Reissue			
❑ DJL1-3411 [DJ]	Essential Robert Gordon	1979	30.00
—Promo-only live album with tracks from Tuff Darts			
❑ AFL1-3523	Bad Boy	1980	12.00
❑ AFL1-3773	Are You Gonna Be the One	1981	12.00
❑ AFL1-4380	Too Fast to Live, Too Young to Die	1982	12.00

GORDON, ROSCOE

Number	Title (A Side/B Side)	Yr	NM
45s			
ABC-PARAMOUNT			
❑ 10351	A Girl to Love/As You Walk Away	1962	75.00
❑ 10407	A Little Bit of Magic/ I Want Revenge	1963	40.00

Number	Title (A Side/B Side)	Yr	NM
❑ 10501	I Don't Stand a Chance/ That's What You Did	1963	40.00

—As "Barbara & Roscoe Gordon"

CALLA

Number	Title (A Side/B Side)	Yr	NM
❑ 145	Just a Little Bit/I Really Love You	1968	30.00

CHESS

Number	Title (A Side/B Side)	Yr	NM
❑ 1487	Booted/I Love You Till the Day I Die	1951	1500.

DUKE

Number	Title (A Side/B Side)	Yr	NM
❑ 101	Tell Daddy/Hey Fat Girl	1952	100.00
❑ 106	T-Model Boogie/ New Orleans Woman	1953	50.00
❑ 109	Too Many Women/ Wise to You, Baby	1953	50.00
❑ 114	Ain't No Use/Roscoe's Mambo	1953	50.00
❑ 129	Three Can't Love/ You Figure It Out	1954	50.00
❑ 165	Keep On Doggin'/Bad Dream	1957	30.00
❑ 173	I've Loved and Lost/ Tummer Tee	1957	30.00
❑ 320	Dilly Bop/You'll Never Know	1960	15.00

FLIP

Number	Title (A Side/B Side)	Yr	NM
❑ 227	Weeping Blues/Just Love Me, Baby	1956	300.00
❑ 237	The Chicken (Dance with You)/ Love for You Baby	1956	50.00

OLD TOWN

Number	Title (A Side/B Side)	Yr	NM
❑ 1167	Gotta Keep Rollin'/ Just a Little at a Time	1964	20.00
❑ 1175	It Ain't Right/Could This Be Love	1965	10.00

—As "Roscoe and Barbara"

RPM

Number	Title (A Side/B Side)	Yr	NM
❑ 324	Saddled the Cow/ Ouch, Pretty Baby	1951	400.00
❑ 336	Dime a Dozen/A New Remedy for Love	1951	250.00
❑ 344	Booted/Cold, Cold Winter	1952	200.00
❑ 350	No More Doggin'/Maria	1952	200.00
❑ 358	New Orleans Woman/I Remember Your Kisses	1952	100.00
❑ 365	What You Got on Your Mind/ Two Kinds of Women	1952	100.00
❑ 369	Trying/Dream Baby	1952	60.00
❑ 373	Lucille/Blues for My Baby	1953	60.00
❑ 379	I'm in Love/Just In from Texas	1953	60.00
❑ 384	We're All Loaded/Tomorrow May Be Too Late	1953	60.00

SUN

Number	Title (A Side/B Side)	Yr	NM
❑ 227	Weeping Blues/Just Love Me, Baby	1956	500.00
❑ 237	The Chicken (Dance with You)/ Love for You Baby	1956	200.00
❑ 257	Shoobie Oobie/Cheese and Crackers	1956	50.00
❑ 305	Sally Jo/Torro	1958	25.00

VEE JAY

Number	Title (A Side/B Side)	Yr	NM
❑ 316	A Fool in Love/No More Doggin'	1959	15.00
❑ 332	Just a Little Bit/Goin' Home	1959	15.00
❑ 348	Surely I Love You/ What You Do to Me	1960	15.00
❑ 385	What I Wouldn't Do/Let 'Em Try	1961	12.00

GORDON 'N ROGERS' INTER-URBAN ELECTRIC A&E PIT CREW & RHYTHM BAND

Albums

CAPITOL

Number	Title (A Side/B Side)	Yr	NM
❑ STAO-276	Bug In!	1969	20.00

GORE, LESLEY

45s

A&M

Number	Title (A Side/B Side)	Yr	NM
❑ 1710	Give It to Me, Sweet Thing/ Immortality	1975	5.00
❑ 1710 [PS]	Give It to Me, Sweet Thing/ Immortality	1975	6.00
❑ 1830	Sometimes/Give It To Me, Sweet Thing	1976	5.00

CREWE

Number	Title (A Side/B Side)	Yr	NM
❑ 338	Why Doesn't Love Make Me Happy/Tomorrow's Children	1970	10.00
❑ 344	When Yesterday Was Tomorrow/Why Me, Why You	1970	10.00
❑ 601	Back Together/Quiet Love	1971	10.00

MANHATTAN

Number	Title (A Side/B Side)	Yr	NM
❑ 50039	Since I Don't Have You-It's Only Make Believe/ Our Love Was Meant to Be	1986	8.00

—With Lou Christie

MERCURY

Number	Title (A Side/B Side)	Yr	NM
❑ 72119	It's My Party/Danny	1963	15.00
❑ 72119 [PS]	It's My Party/Danny	1963	30.00
❑ 72143	Judy's Turn to Cry/ Just Let Me Cry	1963	15.00
❑ 72143 [PS]	Judy's Turn to Cry/ Just Let Me Cry	1963	25.00
❑ 72180	She's a Fool/The Old Crowd	1963	15.00
❑ 72180 [PS]	She's a Fool/The Old Crowd	1963	25.00
❑ 72206	You Don't Own Me/ Run, Bobby, Run	1963	15.00
❑ 72206 [PS]	You Don't Own Me/ Run, Bobby, Run	1963	40.00

—With insert (deduct 25% if missing)

Number	Title (A Side/B Side)	Yr	NM
❑ 72245	Je Ne Sais Plus/Je N'ose Pas	1964	20.00
❑ 72259	That's the Way Boys Are/That's the Way the Ball Bounces	1964	10.00
❑ 72259 [PS]	That's the Way Boys Are/That's the Way the Ball Bounces	1964	20.00
❑ 72270	I Don't Wanna Be a Loser/ It's Gotta Be You	1964	10.00
❑ 72270 [PS]	I Don't Wanna Be a Loser/ It's Gotta Be You	1964	20.00
❑ 72309	Maybe I Know/Wonder Boy	1964	10.00
❑ 72309 [PS]	Maybe I Know/Wonder Boy	1964	20.00
❑ 72352	Hey Now/Sometimes I Wish I Were a Boy	1964	10.00
❑ 72352 [PS]	Hey Now/Sometimes I Wish I Were a Boy	1964	20.00
❑ 72372	Look of Love/Little Girl Gone Home	1964	10.00
❑ 72372 [PS]	Look of Love/Little Girl Gone Home	1964	20.00
❑ 72412	All of My Life/I Cannot Hope for Anything	1965	10.00
❑ 72412 [PS]	All of My Life/I Cannot Hope for Anything	1965	20.00
❑ 72433	Sunshine, Lollipops and Rainbows/You've Come Back	1965	10.00
❑ 72433 [PS]	Sunshine, Lollipops and Rainbows/You've Come Back	1965	20.00
❑ 72475	My Town, My Guy and Me/ Girl in Love	1965	10.00
❑ 72475 [PS]	My Town, My Guy and Me/ Girl in Love	1965	20.00
❑ 72513	I Won't Love You Anymore (Sorry)/No Matter What You Do	1966	10.00
❑ 72513 [PS]	I Won't Love You Anymore (Sorry)/No Matter What You Do	1966	20.00
❑ 72530	We Know We're in Love/ That's What We'll Do	1966	10.00
❑ 72553	Young Love/I Just Don't Know If I Can	1966	10.00
❑ 72580	Off and Running/I Don't Care	1966	10.00
❑ 72611	Maybe Now/Treat Me Like a Lady	1966	10.00
❑ 72649	California Nights/I'm Goin' Out	1967	10.00
❑ 72649 [PS]	California Nights/I'm Goin' Out	1967	—

—Rumored to exist, but without conclusive evidence, we will delete this from future editions

Number	Title (A Side/B Side)	Yr	NM
❑ 72683	Summer and Sandy/ I'm Fallin' Down	1967	10.00
❑ 72683 [PS]	Summer and Sandy/ I'm Fallin' Down	1967	20.00
❑ 72726	Brink of Disaster/On a Day Like This	1967	10.00
❑ 72759	It's a Happening/Magic Colors	1967	10.00
❑ 72787	Small Talk/Say What You See	1968	12.00
❑ 72819	He Gives Me Love (La, La, La)/ Brand New Me	1968	12.00
❑ 72842	Where Can I Go/I Can't Make It Without You	1968	12.00
❑ 72867	Look the Other Way/ I'll Be Standing By	1968	12.00
❑ 72892	Take Good Care (Of My Heart)/ I Can't Make It Without You	1969	12.00
❑ 72892	Take Good Care (Of My Heart)/ You Sent Me Silver Bells	1969	12.00
❑ 72931	Summer Symphony/ 98.6-Lazy Day	1969	15.00
❑ 72969	Wedding Bell Blues/One by One	1969	15.00

MOWEST

Number	Title (A Side/B Side)	Yr	NM
❑ 5029	The Road I Walk/She Said That	1972	10.00
❑ 5042	Give It to Me, Sweet Thing/ Don't Want to Be One	1973	—

—Unreleased

PHILCO-FORD

Number	Title (A Side/B Side)	Yr	NM
❑ HP-21	You Don't Own Me/That's the Way Boys Are	1968	15.00

—4-inch plastic "Hip Pocket Record" with color sleeve

Albums

A&M

Number	Title (A Side/B Side)	Yr	NM
❑ SP-4564	Love Me by Name	1975	15.00

MERCURY

Number	Title (A Side/B Side)	Yr	NM
❑ ML-8016	I'll Cry If I Want To	1980	10.00

—Reissue of 60805

Number	Title (A Side/B Side)	Yr	NM
❑ MG 20805 [M]	I'll Cry If I Want To	1963	30.00

—With no blurb for "It's My Party"

Number	Title (A Side/B Side)	Yr	NM
❑ MG 20805 [M]	I'll Cry If I Want To	1964	20.00

—With blurb for "It's My Party"

Number	Title (A Side/B Side)	Yr	NM
❑ MG 20849 [M]	Lesley Gore Sings of Mixed-Up Hearts	1963	30.00
❑ MG 20901 [M]	Boys, Boys, Boys	1964	30.00
❑ MG 20943 [M]	Girl Talk	1964	30.00
❑ MG 21024 [M]	The Golden Hits of Lesley Gore	1965	30.00
❑ MG 21042 [M]	My Town, My Guy & Me	1965	30.00
❑ MG 21066 [M]	All About Love	1966	30.00
❑ MG 21120 [M]	California Nights	1967	30.00
❑ SR 60805 [S]	I'll Cry If I Want To	1963	40.00

—With no blurb for "It's My Party"

Number	Title (A Side/B Side)	Yr	NM
❑ SR 60805 [S]	I'll Cry If I Want To	1964	30.00

—With blurb for "It's My Party"

Number	Title (A Side/B Side)	Yr	NM
❑ SR 60849 [S]	Lesley Gore Sings of Mixed-Up Hearts	1963	40.00
❑ SR 60901 [S]	Boys, Boys, Boys	1964	40.00
❑ SR 60943 [S]	Girl Talk	1964	40.00
❑ SR 61024 [S]	The Golden Hits of Lesley Gore	196?	15.00

—Reissues have 10 tracks

Number	Title (A Side/B Side)	Yr	NM
❑ SR 61024 [S]	The Golden Hits of Lesley Gore	1965	40.00

—Originals have 12 tracks

Number	Title (A Side/B Side)	Yr	NM
❑ SR 61042 [S]	My Town, My Guy & Me	1965	40.00
❑ SR 61066 [S]	All About Love	1966	40.00

—Stereo version has a different cover and liner notes than the mono version

Number	Title (A Side/B Side)	Yr	NM
❑ SR 61120 [S]	California Nights	1967	40.00
❑ SR 61185	Golden Hits Vol. 2	1968	40.00
❑ 810370-1	The Golden Hits of Lesley Gore	1983	10.00

—Reissue of 61024

MOWEST

Number	Title (A Side/B Side)	Yr	NM
❑ MW 117L	Someplace Else Now	1972	15.00

RHINO

Number	Title (A Side/B Side)	Yr	NM
❑ RNFP-71496 [(2)]	The Lesley Gore Anthology (1963-1968)	1986	15.00

WING

Number	Title (A Side/B Side)	Yr	NM
❑ PRW-2-119 [(2)]	The Sound of Young Love	1969	20.00
❑ SRW-16350	Girl Talk	1968	15.00
❑ SRW-16382	Love, Love, Love	1968	15.00

GORMAN, FREDDIE

45s

MIRACLE

Number	Title (A Side/B Side)	Yr	NM
❑ 11	The Day Will Come/Just for You	1962	100.00

RIC-TIC

Number	Title (A Side/B Side)	Yr	NM
❑ 101	In a Bad Way/There Can Be Too Much	1964	30.00
❑ 102	Take Me Back/Can't Get It Out of My Mind	1965	50.00

GOSPEL STARS, THE

45s

TAMLA

Number	Title (A Side/B Side)	Yr	NM
❑ 54037	He Lifted Me/Behold the Saints of God	1961	60.00

—Globe logo

Number	Title (A Side/B Side)	Yr	NM
❑ 54037	He Lifted Me/Behold the Saints of God	1961	150.00

—Horizontal lines logo

Albums

TAMLA

Number	Title (A Side/B Side)	Yr	NM
❑ TM-222 [M]	The Great Gospel Stars	1961	3000.

—VG value 1000; VG+ value 2000

GOTHAM CITY CRIME FIGHTERS, THE

45s

BATWING

Number	Title (A Side/B Side)	Yr	NM
❑ 1001	Who Stole the Batmobile/ That's Life	1966	30.00

GOULDMAN, GRAHAM

Also see THE MOCKINGBIRDS; 10CC.

45s

A&M

Number	Title (A Side/B Side)	Yr	NM
❑ 2251	Away from It All/Bionic Boar	1980	4.00

RCA VICTOR

Number	Title (A Side/B Side)	Yr	NM
❑ 47-9453	Impossible Years/No Milk Today	1968	12.00
❑ 47-9584	For Your Love/Pamela, Pamela	1968	12.00

Albums

RCA VICTOR

Number	Title (A Side/B Side)	Yr	NM
❑ LPM-3954 [M]	The Graham Gouldman Thing	1968	50.00
❑ LSP-3954 [S]	The Graham Gouldman Thing	1968	50.00

GOWENS, SAMMY

45s

UNITED ARTISTS

Number	Title (A Side/B Side)	Yr	NM
❑ 114	Kissin' at the Drive-In/ Rockin' By Myself	1958	100.00

GRACIE, CHARLIE

45s

CADILLAC

Number	Title (A Side/B Side)	Yr	NM
❑ 141	Boogie Boogie Blues/I'm Gonna Sit Right Down and Write Myself a Letter	1953	150.00
❑ 144	Rockin' and Rollin'/ (B-side unknown)	1954	150.00

Except when noted otherwise, VG = 25% of NM, and VG+ = 50% of NM. (Example: VG = $2.00, VG+ = $4.00 and NM = $8.00.)

Number	Title (A Side/B Side)	Yr	NM
CAMEO			
❑ 105	Butterfly/Ninety-Nine Ways	1957	25.00
❑ 107	Fabulous/Just Lookin'	1957	20.00
❑ 111	I Love You So Much It Hurts/ Wandering Eyes	1957	20.00
❑ 118	Cool Baby/You've Got a Heart Like a Rock	1957	20.00
❑ 127	Crazy Girl/Dressin' Up	1958	20.00
❑ 141	Love Bird/Trying	1958	20.00
CORAL			
❑ 62073	Hurry Up Buttercup/Doodlebug	1959	15.00
❑ 62115	Angel of Love/I'm a Fool, That's Why	1959	15.00
❑ 62141	Oh-Well-a/Because I Love You So	1959	15.00
DIAMOND			
❑ 178	He'll Never Love You Like I Do/ Keep My Love Next to Your Heart	1965	100.00
FELSTED			
❑ 8629	W-Wow/Makin' Whoopee	1961	15.00
PRESIDENT			
❑ 825	Pretty Baby/Night and Day U.S.A.	1962	15.00
❑ 828	Count to Three/Just Like Us	1963	15.00
ROULETTE			
❑ 4255	I Look for You/The Race	1960	15.00
❑ 4312	Sorry for You/Scenery	1960	15.00
20TH CENTURY			
❑ 5033	Head Home, Honey/My Baby Loves Me	1955	50.00
❑ 5035	Honey Honey/Wildwood Boogie	1955	60.00

GRACIOUS PAUL DAVIS was in this group.

Number	Title (A Side/B Side)	Yr	NM
Albums			
CAPITOL			
❑ ST-602	Gracious	1970	40.00

GRADS, THE

Number	Title (A Side/B Side)	Yr	NM
45s			
A&M			
❑ 797	Everything in the Garden/ Stage Door	1966	10.00
MERCURY			
❑ 72346	Cool One/Wild One	1964	20.00
MGM			
❑ 13216	Their Hearts Were Full of Spring/ It Happened Once Before	1964	10.00
VALIANT			
❑ 6023	Once Again/White Steeple	1962	15.00

GRADUATES, THE (1)

Number	Title (A Side/B Side)	Yr	NM
45s			
CORSICAN			
❑ 0058	What Good Is Graduation/Lonely	1959	40.00
LAWN			
❑ 208	Ballad of a Girl and Boy/ Goodbye My Love	1963	20.00
SHAN-TODD			
❑ 0055	Ballad of a Girl and Boy/Care	1959	30.00

GRADUATES, THE (2)

Number	Title (A Side/B Side)	Yr	NM
45s			
GNP CRESCENDO			
❑ 404	(The Shape of) Things to Come/Listen to the Music	1968	10.00

GRADUATES, THE (U) Definitely not group (1); might not be group (2), either.

Number	Title (A Side/B Side)	Yr	NM
45s			
RISING SONS			
❑ 712	If Ever I Get Out of This Mess I'm In/Seventh Generation Breakthrough	1968	40.00

GRADY, DON

Number	Title (A Side/B Side)	Yr	NM
45s			
CANTERBURY			
❑ 501	The Children of St. Monica/ A Good Man to Have Around the House	1967	12.00
❑ 501 [PS]	The Children of St. Monica/ A Good Man to Have Around the House	1967	15.00
❑ 507	Impressions with Syvonne/ Leaving It Up to You	1967	12.00
CAPITOL			
❑ 5181	I Think You're Through/ A Broken Heart Knows Better	1964	12.00
❑ 5362	It's Better This Way/One Good Turn Deserves Another	1965	12.00
CHALLENGE			
❑ 59328	Don't Let It Happen/Out	1966	12.00
ELEKTRA			
❑ 45846 —*As "Don Agrati"*	One Man Woman/Story	1973	6.00
❑ 45860 —*As "Don Agrati"*	Bloodstream/Two-Bit Afternoon	1973	6.00
ORANGE EMPIRE			
❑ 91647	Summertime Game/Little People	1965	20.00
Albums			
ELEKTRA			
❑ EKS-75057 —*As "Don Agrati"*	Homegrown	1973	15.00

GRAFFITI

Number	Title (A Side/B Side)	Yr	NM
45s			
ABC			
❑ 11123	He's Got the Knack/Love In Spite	1968	30.00
Albums			
ABC			
❑ S-663	Graffiti	1968	60.00

GRAHAM, DAVY

Number	Title (A Side/B Side)	Yr	NM
Albums			
LONDON			
❑ PS 552	Large As Life and Twice As Natural	1968	25.00

GRAHAM, ED

Number	Title (A Side/B Side)	Yr	NM
Albums			
M&K REALTIME			
❑ 106	Hot Stix	1980	40.00

—Direct-to-disc recording; plays at 45 rpm

GRAHAM, JIMMY

Number	Title (A Side/B Side)	Yr	NM
45s			
REVUE			
❑ 11044	Soul Walk In/Soul Walk	1969	30.00
❑ 11065	Love Can't Be Modernized/ We Shall Overcome	1970	40.00

GRAHAM, LARRY Also see GRAHAM CENTRAL STATION; SLY AND THE FAMILY STONE.

Number	Title (A Side/B Side)	Yr	NM
12-Inch Singles			
WARNER BROS.			
❑ PRO-A-1027 [DJ]	Don't Stop When You're Hot (edit)/(LP version)	1982	8.00
❑ PRO-A-1046 [DJ]	Sooner or Later/(Instrumental)	1982	8.00
❑ PRO-A-2065 [DJ]	I'm Sick and Tired (same on both sides)	1983	8.00
45s			
WARNER BROS.			
❑ 29003	What We All Need Is More Love/Tearing Out My Heart	1985	3.00
❑ 29529	I'm Sick and Tired/I'd Rather Be Loving You	1983	4.00
❑ 29620	I Never Forgot Your Eyes/ Movin' Inside Your Love	1983	4.00
❑ 29884	Let Me Come Into Your Life/ What You Are Inside	1982	4.00
❑ 29956	Sooner or Later/I Feel Good	1982	4.00
❑ 29956 [PS]	Sooner or Later/I Feel Good	1982	5.00
❑ 49221	One in a Million You/ The Entertainer	1980	4.00
❑ 49221 [PS]	One in a Million You/ The Entertainer	1980	5.00
❑ 49581	When We Get Married/Tonight	1980	4.00
❑ 49744	Just Be My Lady/Feels Like Love	1981	4.00
❑ 49833	Guess Who/Sweetheart	1981	4.00
❑ 50068	Don't Stop When You're Hot/ I Love Loving You	1982	4.00
❑ 50068 [PS]	Don't Stop When You're Hot/ I Love Loving You	1982	5.00
Albums			
WARNER BROS.			
❑ BSK 3447	One in a Million You	1980	8.00
❑ BSK 3554	Just Be My Lady	1981	8.00
❑ BSK 3668	Sooner or Later	1982	8.00
❑ 23878	Victory	1983	8.00
❑ 25307	Fired Up	1985	8.00

GRAHAM, LOU

Number	Title (A Side/B Side)	Yr	NM
45s			
CLYMAX			
❑ 318	Wee Willie Brown/ You Were Mean Baby	1957	300.00
CORAL			
❑ 61931	Wee Willie Brown/ You Were Mean Baby	1958	100.00

GRAHAM CENTRAL STATION Also see LARRY GRAHAM.

Number	Title (A Side/B Side)	Yr	NM
12-Inch Singles			
WARNER BROS.			
❑ PRO-A-639 [DJ]	Entrow (2 versions)	1976	15.00
❑ PRO-A-673 [DJ]	Now Do U Wanta Dance (same on both sides)	1977	15.00
45s			
WARNER BROS.			
❑ 7782	Can You Handle It/Ghetto	1974	5.00
❑ 8025	Release Yourself/ 'Tis Your Kind of Music	1974	5.00
❑ 8061	Feel the Need/We Be's Gettin' Down	1974	5.00
❑ 8105	Your Love/I Believe in You	1975	4.00
❑ 8148	It's Alright/Luckiest People	1975	4.00
❑ 8175	The Jam/The Jam (Disco Version)	1975	4.00
❑ 8205	Love/Why	1976	4.00
❑ 8235	Entrow—Part 1/Entrow—Part 2	1976	4.00
❑ 8288	Do Yah/I Got a Reason	1976	4.00
❑ 8378	Now Do-U-Wanta Dance/ (B-side unknown)	1977	4.00
❑ 8417	Stomped Beat-Up and Whooped/Ole Smokey	1977	4.00
❑ 8464	Crazy Chicken/Saving My Love for You	1977	4.00
❑ 8602	My Radio Sure Sounds Good to Me/Turn It Out	1978	4.00
❑ 8665	Is It Love?/Are You Happy?	1978	4.00
❑ 8816	(You're a) Foxy Lady/Tonight	1979	4.00
❑ 49011	Star Walk/Boogie Baby	1979	4.00
❑ 49067	Sneaky Freak/Boogie Baby	1979	4.00
Albums			
WARNER BROS.			
❑ BS 2763	Graham Central Station	1974	10.00
❑ BS4 2763 [Q]	Graham Central Station	1974	15.00
❑ BS 2814	Release Yourself	1974	10.00
❑ BS 2876	Ain't No 'Bout-a-Doubt It	1975	10.00
❑ BS4 2876 [Q]	Ain't No 'Bout-a-Doubt It	1975	15.00
❑ BS 2937	Mirror	1976	10.00
❑ BS 3041	Now Do U Wanta Dance	1977	10.00
❑ BSK 3175 —*As "Larry Graham and Graham Central Station"*	My Radio Sure Sounds Good to Me	1978	10.00
❑ BSK 3322 —*As "Larry Graham and Graham Central Station"*	Star Walk	1979	10.00

GRAMM, LOU

Number	Title (A Side/B Side)	Yr	NM
45s			
ATLANTIC			
❑ 88781	Just Between You and Me/ Tin Soldier	1989	4.00
❑ 89236	Lost in the Shadows (The Lost Boys)/Power Play	1987	3.00
❑ 89236 [PS]	Lost in the Shadows (The Lost Boys)/Power Play	1987	3.00
❑ 89269	Ready Or Not/Lover Come Back	1987	3.00
❑ 89269 [PS]	Ready Or Not/Lover Come Back	1987	3.00
❑ 89304	Midnight Blue/Chains of Love	1987	3.00
❑ 89304 [PS]	Midnight Blue/Chains of Love	1987	3.00

GRANAHAN, GERRY Also see JERRY GRANT.

Number	Title (A Side/B Side)	Yr	NM
45s			
ATCO			
❑ 6122	Sweet Affection/Confess It to Your Heart	1958	30.00
CANADIAN AMERICAN			
❑ 116	When Irish Eyes Are Smiling/ In My Heart	1960	20.00
❑ 119	You'll Never Walk Alone/ Where's the Girl	1960	20.00
❑ 121	Short Skirts/I'm Afraid You'll Never Know	1960	20.00
CAPRICE			
❑ 106	Unchained Melody/Dancing Man	1961	20.00
❑ 108	Too Big for Her Bikini/ Dance, Girl, Dance	1961	100.00

—With backing by the Belmonts or the Five Satins (sources disagree)

Number	Title (A Side/B Side)	Yr	NM
GONE			
❑ 5065	Let the Rumors Fly/ Put Me Anywhere	1959	20.00
❑ 5081	It Hurts/Look for Me	1959	20.00
❑ 5081 [PS]	It Hurts/Look for Me	1959	60.00
MARK			
❑ 121	Love's Young Dream/Oh Well- A Watch-A Gonna Do	1957	35.00

Except when noted otherwise, VG = 25% of NM, and VG+ = 50% of NM. (Example: VG = $2.00, VG+ = $4.00 and NM = $8.00.)

Number	Title (A Side/B Side)	Yr	NM
SUNBEAM			
❑ 102	No Chemise, Please/ Girl of My Dreams	1958	30.00
❑ 108	Baby Wait/Completely	1958	25.00
❑ 112	I'm Ready As I'll Ever Be/ Nobody Can Handle This Job	1958	25.00
—B-side by Eddie Fontaine			
❑ 122	King Size/I'm Afraid You'll Never Know	1958	25.00
❑ 127	A Ring, a Bracelet, a Heart/ You're Adorable	1959	25.00
20TH CENTURY FOX			
❑ 425	Hang Up the Phone/ Too Weak to Win	1963	15.00
❑ 541	Racing Fever: Title/Racing Fever: Mainstream	1964	15.00
—B-side by Arnold Goland and His Orchestra			
VEEP			
❑ 1205	All the Live-Long Day/Sophia	1965	12.00

GRANATA, ROCCO

45s

Number	Title (A Side/B Side)	Yr	NM
EPIC			
❑ 5-9401	E Primavera/Oh Oh Rose	1960	10.00
LAURIE			
❑ 3041	Marina/Manuela	1959	12.00
❑ 3041 [PS]	Marina/Manuela	1959	15.00
—All black and white sleeve			
❑ 3041 [PS]	Marina/Manuela	1959	20.00
—Pink title strip on otherwise black and white sleeve			
❑ 3048	Lo Bella/Torna A Sorriento	1960	12.00

GRAND CANYON

45s

Number	Title (A Side/B Side)	Yr	NM
BANG			
❑ 713	Evil Boll-Weevil/Got to Find My Way Back	1974	8.00

GRAND FUNK RAILROAD

Includes records as "Grand Funk." Also see MARK FARNER; MARK FARNER AND DON BREWER; TERRY KNIGHT AND THE PACK.

45s

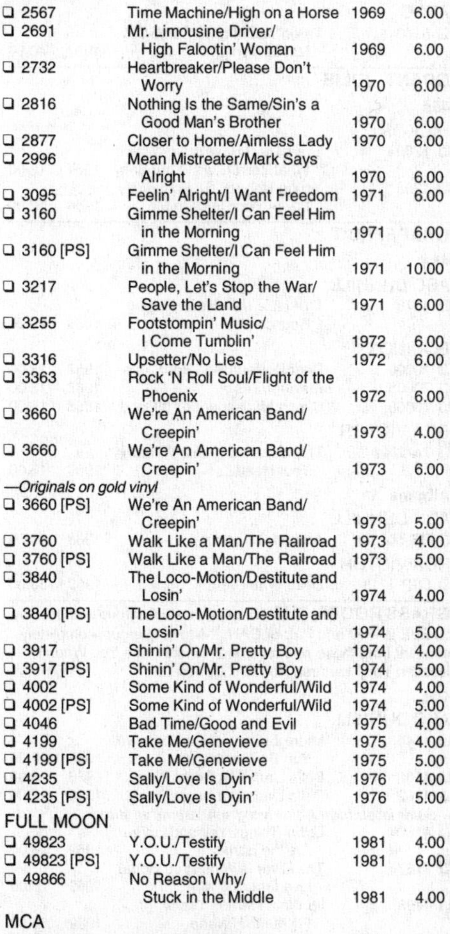

Number	Title (A Side/B Side)	Yr	NM
CAPITOL			
❑ 2567	Time Machine/High on a Horse	1969	6.00
❑ 2691	Mr. Limousine Driver/ High Falootin' Woman	1969	6.00
❑ 2732	Heartbreaker/Please Don't Worry	1970	6.00
❑ 2816	Nothing Is the Same/Sin's a Good Man's Brother	1970	6.00
❑ 2877	Closer to Home/Aimless Lady	1970	6.00
❑ 2996	Mean Mistreater/Mark Says Alright	1970	6.00
❑ 3095	Feelin' Alright/I Want Freedom	1971	6.00
❑ 3160	Gimme Shelter/I Can Feel Him in the Morning	1971	6.00
❑ 3160 [PS]	Gimme Shelter/I Can Feel Him in the Morning	1971	10.00
❑ 3217	People, Let's Stop the War/ Save the Land	1971	6.00
❑ 3255	Footstompin' Music/ I Come Tumblin'	1972	6.00
❑ 3316	Upsetter/No Lies	1972	6.00
❑ 3363	Rock 'N Roll Soul/Flight of the Phoenix	1972	6.00
❑ 3660	We're An American Band/ Creepin'	1973	4.00
❑ 3660	We're An American Band/ Creepin'	1973	6.00
—Originals on gold vinyl			
❑ 3660 [PS]	We're An American Band/ Creepin'	1973	5.00
❑ 3760	Walk Like a Man/The Railroad	1973	4.00
❑ 3760 [PS]	Walk Like a Man/The Railroad	1973	5.00
❑ 3840	The Loco-Motion/Destitute and Losin'	1974	4.00
❑ 3840 [PS]	The Loco-Motion/Destitute and Losin'	1974	5.00
❑ 3917	Shinin' On/Mr. Pretty Boy	1974	4.00
❑ 3917 [PS]	Shinin' On/Mr. Pretty Boy	1974	5.00
❑ 4002	Some Kind of Wonderful/Wild	1974	4.00
❑ 4002 [PS]	Some Kind of Wonderful/Wild	1974	5.00
❑ 4046	Bad Time/Good and Evil	1975	4.00
❑ 4199	Take Me/Genevieve	1975	4.00
❑ 4199 [PS]	Take Me/Genevieve	1975	5.00
❑ 4235	Sally/Love Is Dyin'	1976	4.00
❑ 4235 [PS]	Sally/Love Is Dyin'	1976	5.00
FULL MOON			
❑ 49823	Y.O.U./Testify	1981	4.00
❑ 49823 [PS]	Y.O.U./Testify	1981	6.00
❑ 49866	No Reason Why/ Stuck in the Middle	1981	4.00
MCA			
❑ 40590	Can You Do It/1976	1976	5.00
❑ 40590 [PS]	Can You Do It/1976	1976	6.00
❑ 40641	Out to Get You/Just Couldn't Wait	1976	5.00
—The MCA sides were produced by Frank Zappa			

Grand Funk, "Walk Like a Man," Capitol 3760, 1973, **$5.**

Albums

Number	Title (A Side/B Side)	Yr	NM
CAPITOL			
❑ ST-307	On Time	1969	15.00
❑ SKAO-406	Grand Funk	1970	15.00
❑ SKAO-471	Closer to Home	1970	15.00
❑ SWBB-633 [(2)]	Live Album	1970	15.00
—Includes poster			
❑ SW-764	Survival	1971	12.00
—Red "target" label; add $5 if individual photos of the band members are included			
❑ SW-764	Survival	1971	15.00
—Lime-green label; add $5 if individual photos of the band members are included			
❑ SW-764	Survival	1973	10.00
—Orange label, "Capitol" at bottom			
❑ SW-853	E Pluribus Funk	1971	50.00
—Round cover designed like a coin; price reflects rarity in NM condition			
❑ SABB-11042 [(2)]	Mark, Don and Mel 1969-71	1972	15.00
❑ SMAS-11099	Phoenix	1972	12.00
❑ SMAS-11207	We're An American Band	1973	10.00
—Black vinyl			
❑ SMAS-11207	We're An American Band	1973	20.00
—Gold vinyl without sheet of four stickers			
❑ SMAS-11207	We're An American Band	1973	30.00
—Gold vinyl with sheet of four stickers			
❑ SWAE-11278	Shinin' On	1974	8.00
—With 3-D glasses missing and no poster			
❑ SWAE-11278	Shinin' On	1974	30.00
—With 3-D glasses attached to cover and with 3-D poster			
❑ SO-11356	All the Girls in the World Beware!!!	1974	15.00
—With poster (deduct 33% if missing)			
❑ SABB-11445	Caught in the Act	1975	10.00
❑ ST-11482	Born to Die	1976	10.00
❑ ST-11579	Grand Funk Hits	1976	10.00
❑ SN-16138	Grand Funk Hits	1981	8.00
❑ SN-16176	Closer to Home	1981	8.00
❑ SN-16177	Grand Funk	1981	8.00
❑ SN-16178	On Time	1981	8.00
❑ 21692	We're An American Band	1999	25.00
—Limited-edition reissue on 180-gram gold vinyl with original 1973 packaging			
FULL MOON			
❑ HS 3625	Grand Funk Lives	1981	10.00
❑ 23750	What's Funk	1983	10.00
MCA			
❑ 2216	Good Singin' Good Playin'	1976	12.00
—Produced by Frank Zappa			

GRANDMA'S ROCKERS

Albums

Number	Title (A Side/B Side)	Yr	NM
FREDLO			
❑ 6727	Homemade Apple Pie	1967	1500.
—VG value 500; VG+ value 1000			

GRANDMASTER FLASH

12-Inch Singles

Number	Title (A Side/B Side)	Yr	NM
ELEKTRA			
❑ ED 5024 [DJ]	Sign of the Times (6:05) (Instrumental 5:59) (Edit of LP Version)/Larry's Dance Theme	1985	15.00
❑ ED 5052 [DJ]	Girls Love the Way He Spins (unknown versions)	1985	10.00
❑ ED 5079 [DJ]	Alternate Groove (LP Version 5:20) (Vocal Edit 3:56) (Instrumental 5:27)	1985	20.00
❑ ED 5134 [DJ]	Style (Peter Gunn Theme) (Extended Remixed Version) (Edit of LP Version) (Instrumental Version)	1986	15.00
❑ ED 5154 [DJ]	Behind Closed Doors (Extended Remix Version 5:28) (LP Version 3:38)	1986	15.00
❑ ED 5205 [DJ]	U Know What Time It Is (2 versions)	1987	12.00
❑ ED 5233 [DJ]	All Wrapped Up (Vocal Extended Mix) (Instrumental)/ Kid Named Flash	1987	15.00
❑ ED 5279 [DJ]	Gold (6 versions)	1988	20.00
❑ ED 5301 [DJ]	Fly Girl (6 versions)	1988	12.00

Number	Title (A Side/B Side)	Yr	NM
❑ ED 5319 [DJ]	Magic Carpet Ride (Chep-O-Matic Mix) (LP Version) (Instrumental)	1988	12.00
❑ 66749	Magic Carpet Ride (unknown versions)/On the Strength	1988	12.00
❑ 66777	Gold (Extended Version) (Acapella Dub Version) (Edit of LP Version) (Acapella Version) (Instrumental)	1988	15.00
❑ 66801	All Wrapped Up (Extended 5:08) (Instrumental)/Kid Named Flash	1987	20.00
❑ 66825	U Know What Time It Is (Extended Scratch Mix) (Instrumental)/Bus Dis (Woo)	1987	8.00
❑ 66842	Behind Closed Doors (Extended Remix Version 5:28) (LP Version 3:38)/Lies	1986	15.00
❑ 66857	Style (Peter Gunn Theme) (Extended Remixed Version) (Edit of LP Version) (Instrumental Version)	1986	10.00
❑ 66908	Girls Love the Way He Spins/Larry's Dance Theme (2 versions)	1985	15.00
❑ 66922	Sign of the Times (Vocal) (Instrumental)	1985	12.00

ENJOY

Number	Title (A Side/B Side)	Yr	NM
❑ 6001	Superappin' (12:03)/Superappin' Theme (12:01)	1979	300.00

SUGAR HILL

Number	Title (A Side/B Side)	Yr	NM
❑ SH 457	New York, New York (Vocal) (Instrumental)	1983	12.00
❑ SH 465	White Lines (Don't Don't Do It) (4 versions)	1983	20.00
—As "Grandmaster and Melle Mel"			
❑ SH 549	Freedom (Vocal 8:13) (Instrumental 8:13)	1980	20.00
—A wide range of prices has been noted on this record			
❑ SH 555	The Birthday Party (2 versions)	1981	15.00
❑ SH 557	The Adventures of Grandmaster Flash on the Wheels of Steel/The Party Mix	1981	40.00
❑ SH 558	Showdown (Vocal 5:52) (Instrumental 5:52)	1981	40.00
—As "The Furious Five Meets the Sugarhill Gang"			
❑ SH 569	It's Nasty (Genius of Love) (7:49) (8:15)	1982	15.00
❑ SH 574	Flash to the Beat (Part 1 and 2)	1982	20.00
❑ SH 584	The Message (Vocal 7:11) (Instrumental)	1982	15.00
❑ SH 590	Scorpio (unknown versions)	1982	20.00
❑ SH 32504	Freedom/New York, New York	1985	12.00
—"Old Gold" reissue			
❑ 32505	The Message/The Birthday Party	1985	12.00
—"Old Gold" reissue			
❑ 32508	White Lines (Don't Don't Do It)/Scorpio	1985	10.00
—"Old Gold" reissue			

45s

ELEKTRA

Number	Title (A Side/B Side)	Yr	NM
❑ 69380	Magic Carpet Ride/On the Strength	1988	6.00
❑ 69400	Fly Girl/Gold In Effect	1988	6.00
❑ 69416	Gold/Back in the Old Days of Hip-Hop	1988	5.00
❑ 69459	All Wrapped Up/Kid Named Flash	1987	3.00
❑ 69490	U Know What Time It Is/Bus Dis (Woo)	1987	6.00
❑ 69530	Behind Closed Doors/Lies	1986	5.00
❑ 69552	Style (Peter Gunn Theme)/(Instrumental)	1986	6.00
❑ 69617	Alternate Groove/Who's That Lady?	1985	5.00
❑ 69643	Girls Love the Way He Spins/Larry's Dance Theme	1985	6.00
❑ 69677	Sign of the Times/Larry's Dance Theme	1984	6.00

SUGAR HILL

Number	Title (A Side/B Side)	Yr	NM
❑ 756	Freedom/(Instrumental)	1980	15.00
❑ 759	The Birthday Party/(Instrumental)	1981	15.00
❑ 775	It's Nasty (Genius of Love)/(Instrumental)	1982	15.00

Albums

ELEKTRA

Number	Title (A Side/B Side)	Yr	NM
❑ 60389	They Said It Couldn't Be Done	1985	12.00
❑ 60723	Ba-Dop-Boom-Bang	1987	10.00
❑ 60769	On the Strength	1988	12.00

SUGAR HILL

Number	Title (A Side/B Side)	Yr	NM
❑ SH 268	The Message	1982	20.00
—Note: This album has been reissued to look like the original			
❑ SH 9121	Greatest Messages	1984	20.00

GRANT, CARY

45s

COLUMBIA

Number	Title (A Side/B Side)	Yr	NM
❑ 4-44377	Christmas Lullaby/Here's to You	1967	30.00

GRANT, ESTHER

45s

WILSTONE

Number	Title (A Side/B Side)	Yr	NM
❑ 001	Let's Make the Most Out of Love/Take Me Now or Leave Me Be	196?	5000.

GRANT, GEORGE, AND THE CASTELLES

See THE CASTELLES.

GRANT, GOGI

45s

ERA

Number	Title (A Side/B Side)	Yr	NM
❑ 1003	Suddenly There's a Valley/Love Is	1955	15.00
❑ 1008	Who Are We/We Believe in Love	1955	15.00
❑ 1013	The Wayward Wind/No More Than Forever	1956	16.00
❑ 1019	You're in Love/When the Tide Is High	1956	15.00
❑ 1053	The Golden Ladder/All of Me	1957	12.00
❑ 1062	I Gave You My Heart/I Don't Want to Walk Without You	1957	12.00
❑ 3046	The Wayward Wind/The Tide Is High	1961	8.00
❑ 3205	The Wayward Wind/Suddenly There's a Valley	1969	5.00

LIBERTY

Number	Title (A Side/B Side)	Yr	NM
❑ 55214	If and When/I'll Never Smile Again	1959	10.00
❑ 55229	Goin' Home/All God's Children Got Shoes	1959	10.00
❑ 55252	I Never Meant to Fall in Love/Stay Here with Me	1960	10.00
❑ 55286	Two Lovers by the Sea/In a Sentimental Mood	1960	10.00
❑ 55316	That One Kiss/Adrift on a Star	1961	10.00

MONUMENT

Number	Title (A Side/B Side)	Yr	NM
❑ 986	Don't Touch Me/Pathfinder	1966	6.00
❑ 1005	The Sea/How Much Will I Love You	1967	6.00

PETE

Number	Title (A Side/B Side)	Yr	NM
❑ 701	Down Here on the Ground/The Magic of People	1968	5.00
❑ 708	Buy Me Penny Candy/Paradise	1968	5.00
❑ 717	Yesterday, When I Was Young/(B-side unknown)	1969	5.00
❑ 718	On the Mountain/Faure	1969	5.00

RCA VICTOR

Number	Title (A Side/B Side)	Yr	NM
❑ 47-4994	Forget Me Not/Where There's Smoke, There's Fire	1952	20.00
❑ 47-5053	Mommy's Little Angel/My Tormented Heart	1952	20.00
—B-side by the Three Suns			
❑ 47-5436	Everyone Knows I Love You/Ricochet	1953	20.00
❑ 47-5512	Secret Love/Ricochet	1953	20.00
❑ 47-6996	That's the Life for Me/It's a Wonderful Thing to Be Loved	1957	10.00
❑ 47-7082	Johnny's Dream/What a Beautiful Combination	1957	10.00
❑ 47-7146	Chinese Nightingale/Bonjour Tristesse	1958	10.00
❑ 47-7215	My Secret Prayer/How Do We Know We're in Love	1958	10.00
❑ 47-7294	Strange Are the Ways of Love/Marjolaino	1958	10.00
❑ 47-7438	Two Dreams/(Kiss Me) Honey Honey (Kiss Me)	1959	10.00
❑ 47-7492	The Ride Back from Boot Hill/A Restless Pair	1959	10.00

20TH FOX

Number	Title (A Side/B Side)	Yr	NM
❑ 284	Johnny, I Hardly Knew Ye/The Second Time Around	1961	10.00
❑ 297	Magic Music/Tender Is the Night	1962	10.00
❑ 403	Magic Music/Tender Is the Night	1963	8.00

Albums

ERA

Number	Title (A Side/B Side)	Yr	NM
❑ EL-106 [M]	The Wayward Wind	196?	25.00
❑ 20001 [M]	Suddenly There's Gogi Grant	1956	60.00
—Black vinyl			
❑ 20001 [M]	Suddenly There's Gogi Grant	1956	100.00
—Red vinyl			

LIBERTY

Number	Title (A Side/B Side)	Yr	NM
❑ LRP-3144 [M]	If You Want to Get to Heaven, Shout	1960	30.00
❑ LST-7144 [S]	If You Want to Get to Heaven, Shout	1960	40.00

PETE

Number	Title (A Side/B Side)	Yr	NM
❑ S-1101	Gogi Grant	1968	15.00
❑ S-1111	The Way a Woman Feels	1970	15.00

RCA VICTOR

Number	Title (A Side/B Side)	Yr	NM
❑ LOC-1030 [M]	The Helen Morgan Story	1957	60.00
❑ LPM-1717 [M]	Welcome to My Heart	1958	40.00
❑ LPM-1940 [M]	Torch Time	1959	30.00
❑ LSP-1940 [S]	Torch Time	1959	40.00
❑ LPM-2000 [M]	Granted... It's Gogi	1960	30.00
❑ LSP-2000 [S]	Granted... It's Gogi	1960	40.00

GRANT, JANIE

45s

CAPRICE

Number	Title (A Side/B Side)	Yr	NM
❑ 104	Triangle/She's Going Steady with You	1961	15.00
❑ 109	Romeo/Roller Coaster	1961	15.00
❑ 111	I Wonder Who's Kissing You Now/Unhappy	1961	15.00
❑ 113	Oh Johnny/Oh My Love	1962	15.00
❑ 115	That Greasy Kid Stuff/Trying to Forget You	1962	15.00
❑ 119	Peggy Got Engaged/Two Is Company and Three's a Crowd	1962	15.00

PARKWAY

Number	Title (A Side/B Side)	Yr	NM
❑ 982	My Heart, Your Heart/And That Reminds Me of You	1966	200.00

UNITED ARTISTS

Number	Title (A Side/B Side)	Yr	NM
❑ 616	Tell Me Mama/Whose Heart Are You Breaking Now	1963	12.00
❑ 649	That Kind of Boy/Priceless Persuasion	1963	12.00
❑ 731	Ribbons and Roses/Too Young for Me	1964	12.00
❑ 775	After Last Night/All I Did Was Fall in Love	1964	12.00
❑ 843	I Shouldn't Care (If You're Using Me)/There Ain't No Party Tonight	1965	12.00

GRANT, JERRY

Probably the artist who later recorded as GERRY GRANAHAN.

45s

ATCO

Number	Title (A Side/B Side)	Yr	NM
❑ 6100	Talkin' About Love/Some Day, Maybe Tonight	1957	40.00

GRANT, JULIE

45s

HICKORY

Number	Title (A Side/B Side)	Yr	NM
❑ 1260	Every Day I Have to Cry/Watch What You Do with Your Baby	1964	12.00
❑ 1288	You're Nobody 'Til Somebody Loves You/Come to Me	1964	12.00

GRAPEFRUIT

45s

ABC DUNHILL

Number	Title (A Side/B Side)	Yr	NM
❑ 4178	This Little Man/Round Going Round	1968	10.00

EQUINOX

Number	Title (A Side/B Side)	Yr	NM
❑ 70000	Dear Delilah/Dead Boot	1967	15.00
❑ 70005	Elevator/Yes	1968	15.00
❑ 70008	C'mon Marianne/Ain't It Good	1968	15.00

RCA VICTOR

Number	Title (A Side/B Side)	Yr	NM
❑ 74-0241	Thunder and Lightning/Blues in Your Head	1969	15.00

Albums

ABC DUNHILL

Number	Title (A Side/B Side)	Yr	NM
❑ DS-50050	Around Grapefruit	1968	40.00

RCA VICTOR

Number	Title (A Side/B Side)	Yr	NM
❑ LSP-4215	Deep Water	1969	30.00

GRASS ROOTS, THE

Originally a studio group produced by STEVE BARRI and P.F. SLOAN; the touring group, completely different from those who recorded "Where Were You When I Needed You," featured Rob Grill on vocals.

45s

ABC DUNHILL

Number	Title (A Side/B Side)	Yr	NM
❑ 4144	Midnight Confessions/Who Will You Be Tomorrow	1968	8.00
❑ 4162	Bella Linda/Hot Bright Blues	1968	8.00
❑ 4162	Della Linda/Hot Bright Blues	1968	12.00
—Some labels have A-side typographical error as shown			
❑ 4180	Lovin' Things/You and Love Are the Same	1969	8.00
❑ 4187	The River Is Wide/(You Gotta) Live for Love	1969	8.00
❑ 4198	I'd Wait a Million Years/Fly Me to Havana	1969	6.00
❑ 4217	Heaven Knows/Don't Remind Me	1969	6.00

Except when noted otherwise, VG = 25% of NM, and VG+ = 50% of NM. (Example: VG = $2.00, VG+ = $4.00 and NM = $8.00.)

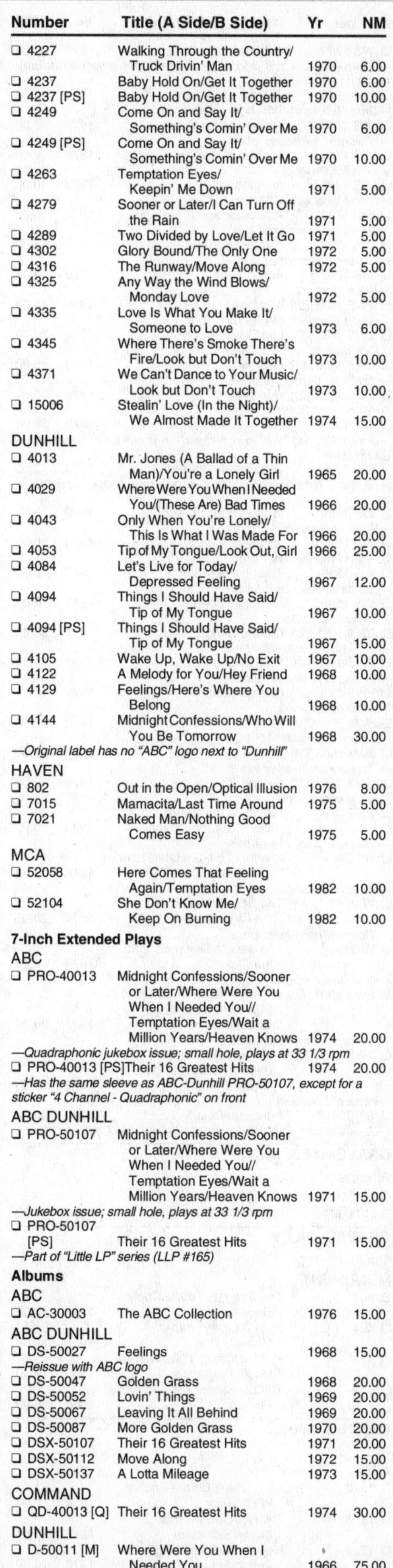

Number	Title (A Side/B Side)	Yr	NM
❑ 4227	Walking Through the Country/ Truck Drivin' Man	1970	6.00
❑ 4237	Baby Hold On/Get It Together	1970	6.00
❑ 4237 [PS]	Baby Hold On/Get It Together	1970	10.00
❑ 4249	Come On and Say It/ Something's Comin' Over Me	1970	6.00
❑ 4249 [PS]	Come On and Say It/ Something's Comin' Over Me	1970	10.00
❑ 4263	Temptation Eyes/ Keepin' Me Down	1971	5.00
❑ 4279	Sooner or Later/I Can Turn Off the Rain	1971	5.00
❑ 4289	Two Divided by Love/Let It Go	1971	5.00
❑ 4302	Glory Bound/The Only One	1972	5.00
❑ 4316	The Runway/Move Along	1972	5.00
❑ 4325	Any Way the Wind Blows/ Monday Love	1972	5.00
❑ 4335	Love Is What You Make It/ Someone to Love	1973	6.00
❑ 4345	Where There's Smoke There's Fire/Look but Don't Touch	1973	10.00
❑ 4371	We Can't Dance to Your Music/ Look but Don't Touch	1973	10.00
❑ 15006	Stealin' Love (In the Night)/ We Almost Made It Together	1974	15.00
DUNHILL			
❑ 4013	Mr. Jones (A Ballad of a Thin Man)/You're a Lonely Girl	1965	20.00
❑ 4029	Where Were You When I Needed You/(These Are) Bad Times	1966	20.00
❑ 4043	Only When You're Lonely/ This Is What I Was Made For	1966	20.00
❑ 4053	Tip of My Tongue/Look Out, Girl	1966	25.00
❑ 4084	Let's Live for Today/ Depressed Feeling	1967	12.00
❑ 4094	Things I Should Have Said/ Tip of My Tongue	1967	10.00
❑ 4094 [PS]	Things I Should Have Said/ Tip of My Tongue	1967	15.00
❑ 4105	Wake Up, Wake Up/No Exit	1967	10.00
❑ 4122	A Melody for You/Hey Friend	1968	10.00
❑ 4129	Feelings/Here's Where You Belong	1968	10.00
❑ 4144	Midnight Confessions/Who Will You Be Tomorrow	1968	30.00
—Original label has no "ABC" logo next to "Dunhill"			
HAVEN			
❑ 802	Out in the Open/Optical Illusion	1976	8.00
❑ 7015	Mamacita/Last Time Around	1975	5.00
❑ 7021	Naked Man/Nothing Good Comes Easy	1975	5.00
MCA			
❑ 52058	Here Comes That Feeling Again/Temptation Eyes	1982	10.00
❑ 52104	She Don't Know Me/ Keep On Burning	1982	10.00
7-Inch Extended Plays			
ABC			
❑ PRO-40013	Midnight Confessions/Sooner or Later/Where Were You When I Needed You// Temptation Eyes/Wait a Million Years/Heaven Knows	1974	20.00
—Quadraphonic jukebox issue; small hole, plays at 33 1/3 rpm			
❑ PRO-40013 [PS]	Their 16 Greatest Hits	1974	20.00
—Has the same sleeve as ABC-Dunhill PRO-50107, except for a sticker "4 Channel - Quadraphonic" on front			
ABC DUNHILL			
❑ PRO-50107	Midnight Confessions/Sooner or Later/Where Were You When I Needed You// Temptation Eyes/Wait a Million Years/Heaven Knows	1971	15.00
—Jukebox issue; small hole, plays at 33 1/3 rpm			
❑ PRO-50107 [PS]	Their 16 Greatest Hits	1971	15.00
—Part of "Little LP" series (LLP #165)			
Albums			
ABC			
❑ AC-30003	The ABC Collection	1976	15.00
ABC DUNHILL			
❑ DS-50027	Feelings	1968	15.00
—Reissue with ABC logo			
❑ DS-50047	Golden Grass	1968	20.00
❑ DS-50052	Lovin' Things	1969	20.00
❑ DS-50067	Leaving It All Behind	1969	20.00
❑ DS-50087	More Golden Grass	1970	20.00
❑ DSX-50107	Their 16 Greatest Hits	1971	20.00
❑ DSX-50112	Move Along	1972	15.00
❑ DSX-50137	A Lotta Mileage	1973	15.00
COMMAND			
❑ QD-40013 [Q]	Their 16 Greatest Hits	1974	30.00
DUNHILL			
❑ D-50011 [M]	Where Were You When I Needed You	1966	75.00

The Grass Roots, Golden Grass, ABC-Dunhill DS-50047, 1968, **$20.**

Number	Title (A Side/B Side)	Yr	NM
❑ DS-50011 [S]	Where Were You When I Needed You	1966	100.00
❑ D-50020 [M]	Let's Live for Today	1967	25.00
❑ DS-50020 [S]	Let's Live for Today	1967	30.00
❑ D-50027 [M]	Feelings	1968	30.00
❑ DS-50027 [S]	Feelings	1968	20.00
HAVEN			
❑ ST-9204	The Grass Roots	1975	15.00
MCA			
❑ 5331	Powers of the Night	1982	12.00
❑ 37154	Their 16 Greatest Hits	198?	8.00
—Budget-line reissue of ABC Dunhill 50107			

GRATEFUL DEAD, THE Also see JERRY GARCIA; MICKEY HART; KEITH AND DONNA; BOB WEIR.

Number	Title (A Side/B Side)	Yr	NM
12-Inch Singles			
ARISTA			
❑ ADP 9757 [DJ]	Throwing Stones (Ashes Ashes) (LP version)/(Edit Remix)	1987	12.00
45s			
ARISTA			
❑ 0276	Dancin' in the Streets/ Terrapin Station	1977	6.00
❑ 0291	Passenger/Terrapin Station	1977	6.00
❑ 0383	Good Lovin'/Stagger Lee	1978	6.00
❑ 0383 [PS]	Good Lovin'/Stagger Lee	1978	600.00
❑ 0410	France/Shakedown Street	1979	6.00
❑ 0519	Alabama Getaway/Far from Me	1980	5.00
❑ 0519 [PS]	Alabama Getaway/Far from Me	1980	8.00
❑ 0546	Don't Ease Me In/Far from Me	1980	5.00
❑ 9606	Touch of Grey/My Brother Esau	1987	3.00
—Black vinyl (not issued with picture sleeve)			
❑ 9606	Touch of Grey/My Brother Esau	1987	5.00
—Grey vinyl			
❑ 9606 [PS]	Touch of Grey/My Brother Esau	1987	7.00
—Fold-open poster sleeve (add $2 for sticker attached to original shrink wrap)			
❑ 9643	Throwing Stones (Ashes Ashes) Edit/Throwing Stones (Ashes Ashes) LP Version	1987	3.00
❑ 9643 [PS]	Throwing Stones (Ashes Ashes) Edit/Throwing Stones (Ashes Ashes) LP Version	1987	7.00
❑ 9899	Foolish Heart/We Can Run	1989	4.00
❑ 9899 [PS]	Foolish Heart/We Can Run	1989	4.00
GRATEFUL DEAD			
❑ 01	Here Comes Sunshine/Let Me Sing Your Blues Away	1973	12.00
❑ 02	Eyes of the World/Weather Report (Part 1)	1974	12.00
❑ 03	U.S. Blues/Loose Lucy	1974	10.00
❑ 03 [PS]	U.S. Blues/Loose Lucy	1974	25.00
❑ XW-718	The Music Never Stopped/ Help on the Way	1975	15.00
❑ XW-762	Franklin's Tower/ Help on the Way	1976	25.00
SCORPIO			
❑ 201	Stealin'/Don't Ease Me In	1966	1000.
WARNER BROS.			
❑ 7016	The Golden Road (To Unlimited Devotion)/Cream Puff War	1967	25.00
❑ 7186	Dark Star/Born Cross-Eyed	1968	25.00
❑ 7186 [PS]	Dark Star/Born Cross-Eyed	1968	500.00
❑ 7324	Dupree's Diamond Blues/ Cosmic Charlie	1969	25.00
❑ 7410	Uncle John's Band/ New Speedway Boogie	1970	15.00
—A picture sleeve for this is rumored to exist			
❑ 7464	Truckin'/Ripple	1971	15.00
❑ 7627	Johnny B. Goode/So Fine	1972	20.00
—B-side by Elvin Bishop Group			
❑ 7653	Truckin'/Johnny B. Goode	1973	8.00
—"Back to Back Hits" series			
❑ 7667	Sugar Magnolia/Mr. Charlie	1972	15.00
7-Inch Extended Plays			
WARNER BROS.			
❑ S 1893	Sugar Magnolia/Operator/ Till the Morning Comes// Truckin'/Friend of the Devil	1973	20.00
—Jukebox issue, small hole, plays at 33 1/3 rpm			

Grateful Dead, *American Beauty*, Warner Bros. WS 1893, 1971, green label, **$25.**

Number	Title (A Side/B Side)	Yr	NM
❑ S 1893 [PS]	American Beauty	1973	30.00
—Part of Little LP series (LLP #226)			

Albums

ARISTA

Number	Title (A Side/B Side)	Yr	NM
❑ SP-35 [DJ]	Grateful Dead Sampler	1978	30.00
❑ AB 4198	Shakedown Street	1978	12.00
❑ AL 7001	Terrapin Station	1977	15.00
❑ AL 7001 [DJ]	Terrapin Station	1977	50.00
—Radio station promos are banded for airplay			
❑ AL 8112 [(2)]	Dead Set	198?	18.00
—Budget-line reissue of 8606			
❑ AL 8321	Shakedown Street	198?	10.00
—Budget-line reissue of 4198			
❑ AL 8329	Terrapin Station	198?	10.00
—Budget-line reissue of 7001			
❑ AL 8332	Go to Heaven	198?	10.00
—Budget-line reissue of 9508			
❑ AL 8452	In the Dark	1987	15.00
❑ AL 8575	Built to Last	1989	15.00
❑ A2L 8604 [(2)]	Reckoning	1981	15.00
❑ A2L 8606 [(2)]	Dead Set	1981	15.00
❑ AL3 8634 [(3)]	Without a Net	1990	25.00
❑ AL 9508	Go to Heaven	1980	12.00

DIRECT DISK

Number	Title (A Side/B Side)	Yr	NM
❑ SD-16619	Terrapin Station	1980	100.00
—Audiophile vinyl			

GRATEFUL DEAD

Number	Title (A Side/B Side)	Yr	NM
❑ GD-01	Wake of the Flood	1973	20.00
—With no contributing artists on back cover			
❑ GD-01	Wake of the Flood	1975	15.00
—With contributing artists on back cover and United Artists distribution			
❑ GD-01 [DJ]	Wake of the Flood	1973	400.00
—Green vinyl meant for fan-club members; ironically, most copies were damaged in a flood before distribution			
❑ GD-102	Grateful Dead from the Mars Hotel	1974	20.00
—Without United Artists distribution			
❑ GD-102	Grateful Dead from the Mars Hotel	1975	15.00
—With United Artists distribution and "Grateful Dead" label			
❑ GD-LA494-G	Blues for Allah	1975	20.00
❑ GD-LA620-J2 [(2)]	Steal Your Face	1976	25.00

MOBILE FIDELITY

Number	Title (A Side/B Side)	Yr	NM
❑ 1-014	American Beauty	1980	80.00
—Audiophile vinyl			
❑ 1-172	Grateful Dead from the Mars Hotel	1984	75.00
—Audiophile vinyl			

PAIR

Number	Title (A Side/B Side)	Yr	NM
❑ PDL2-1053 [(2)]	For the Faithful...	1986	12.00

RHINO

Number	Title (A Side/B Side)	Yr	NM
❑ R1-74395 [(2)]	Live/Dead	2003	30.00
—Reissue on 180-gram vinyl			
❑ R1-74396	Workingman's Dead	2003	20.00
—Reissue on 180-gram vinyl			
❑ R1-74397	American Beauty	2003	20.00
—Reissue on 180-gram vinyl			

SUNFLOWER

Number	Title (A Side/B Side)	Yr	NM
❑ SUN-5001	Vintage Dead	1970	40.00
—Album has been counterfeited, but bogus covers are 1/4" shorter than normal LP cover			
❑ SNF-5004	Historic Dead	1971	40.00

UNITED ARTISTS

Number	Title (A Side/B Side)	Yr	NM
❑ GD-102	Grateful Dead from the Mars Hotel	1978	15.00
—With United Artists "sunrise" label			

WARNER BROS.

Number	Title (A Side/B Side)	Yr	NM
❑ W 1689 [M]	The Grateful Dead	1967	200.00
❑ WS 1689 [S]	The Grateful Dead	1967	80.00
—Gold label			
❑ WS 1689 [S]	The Grateful Dead	1968	25.00
—Green label with "W7" logo			
❑ WS 1689 [S]	The Grateful Dead	1970	15.00
—Green label with "WB" logo			
❑ WS 1689 [S]	The Grateful Dead	1973	12.00
—"Burbank" palm-trees label			
❑ WS 1689 [S]	The Grateful Dead	1979	8.00
—White or tan label			
❑ WS 1749	Anthem of the Sun	1968	30.00
—Green label with "W7" logo			
❑ WS 1749	Anthem of the Sun	197?	50.00
—Green label with "WB" logo, white background on cover with radically remixed version of LP			
❑ WS 1749	Anthem of the Sun	1970	15.00
—Green label with "WB" logo, purple cover			
❑ WS 1749	Anthem of the Sun	1973	12.00
—"Burbank" palm-trees label			
❑ WS 1749	Anthem of the Sun	1979	8.00
—White or tan label			
❑ WS 1790	Aoxomoxoa	1969	30.00
—Green label with "W7" logo			
❑ WS 1790	Aoxomoxoa	1970	15.00
—Green label with "WB" logo			
❑ WS 1790	Aoxomoxoa	1973	12.00
—"Burbank" palm-trees label			
❑ WS 1790	Aoxomoxoa	1979	8.00
—White or tan label			
❑ 2WS 1830 [(2)]	Live/Dead	1969	40.00
—Green labels with "W7" logo			
❑ 2WS 1830 [(2)]	Live/Dead	1970	20.00
—Green labels with "WB" logo			
❑ 2WS 1830 [(2)]	Live/Dead	1973	15.00
—"Burbank" palm-trees labels			
❑ 2WS 1830 [(2)]	Live/Dead	1979	10.00
—White or tan labels			
❑ WS 1869	Workingman's Dead	1970	25.00
—Green label with "WB" logo; textured cover with back cover slick upside down			
❑ WS 1869	Workingman's Dead	1973	12.00
—"Burbank" palm-trees label; standard cover with back cover right side up			
❑ WS 1869	Workingman's Dead	1979	8.00
—White or tan label			
❑ WS 1893	American Beauty	1970	25.00
—Green label with "WB" logo			
❑ WS 1893	American Beauty	1973	12.00
—"Burbank" palm-trees label			
❑ WS 1893	American Beauty	1979	8.00
—White or tan label			
❑ 2WS 1935 [(2)]	Grateful Dead	1971	30.00
—Green labels with "WB" logo			
❑ 2WS 1935 [(2)]	Grateful Dead	1973	15.00
—"Burbank" palm-trees labels			
❑ 2WS 1935 [(2)]	Grateful Dead	1979	10.00
—White or tan labels			
❑ 3WX 2668 [(3)]	Europe '72	1972	40.00
—Green labels with "WB" logo			
❑ 3WX 2668 [(3)]	Europe '72	1973	20.00
—"Burbank" palm-trees labels			
❑ 3WX 2668 [(3)]	Europe '72	1979	12.00
—White or tan labels			
❑ BS 2721	History of the Grateful Dead, Vol. 1 (Bear's Choice)	1973	20.00
—"Burbank" palm-trees labels			
❑ BS 2721	History of the Grateful Dead, Vol. 1 (Bear's Choice)	1978	8.00
—White or tan labels			
❑ W 2764	The Best of/Skeletons from the Closet	1974	20.00
—"Burbank" palm-trees labels			
❑ W 2764	The Best of/Skeletons from the Closet	1979	8.00
—White or tan labels			
❑ 2WS 3091 [(2)]	What a Long Strange Trip It's Been: The Best of the Grateful Dead	1977	20.00
—"Burbank" palm-trees labels			
❑ 2WS 3091 [(2)]	What a Long Strange Trip It's Been: The Best of the Grateful Dead	1979	10.00
—White or tan labels			
❑ ST-93416	American Beauty	1970	50.00
—Capitol Record Club edition; green label with "W7" logo			

GRAVENITES, NICK

Albums

COLUMBIA

Number	Title (A Side/B Side)	Yr	NM
❑ CS 9899	My Labors	1969	15.00

GRAVES, BILLY

45s

MONUMENT

Number	Title (A Side/B Side)	Yr	NM
❑ 401	The Shag (Is Totally Cool)/ Uncertain	1958	20.00
❑ 404	Long Journey Home/ Midnight Bus	1959	15.00
❑ 418	Right or Wrong (I'll Be With You)/ Mount Fujiyama	1960	12.00
❑ 992	The Lonesome Ape/I've Got a Feeling	1966	8.00

GRAVES, CARL

45s

A&M

Number	Title (A Side/B Side)	Yr	NM
❑ 1620	Baby, Hang Up the Phone/ Walk Softly	1974	10.00
❑ 1673	The Next Best Thing/ Brown Skin Love	1975	10.00
❑ 1716	Hey Radio/Something's Telling Me	1975	10.00

Except when noted otherwise, VG = 25% of NM, and VG+ = 50% of NM. (Example: VG = $2.00, VG+ = $4.00 and NM = $8.00.)

Number	Title (A Side/B Side)	Yr	NM
❑ 1757	Heart Be Still/Breaking Up Is Hard to Do	1975	10.00
❑ 1799	My Whole World Ended (The Moment You Left Me)/ Baby Don't Knock	1976	10.00
ARIOLA AMERICA			
❑ 7660	Sad Girl/Walk in Love	1977	10.00

GRAVES, JOE

45s

Number	Title (A Side/B Side)	Yr	NM
PARKWAY			
❑ 103	Debbie/A Boy and a Girl Fall in Love	1966	50.00
❑ 964	See Saw/Beautiful Girl	1965	30.00

GRAVITY ADJUSTERS EXPANSION BAND

Albums

Number	Title (A Side/B Side)	Yr	NM
NOCTURNE			
❑ NRS-302	One	1973	300.00

GRAY, BARRY, AND THE SPACEMAKERS

45s

Number	Title (A Side/B Side)	Yr	NM
ABC-PARAMOUNT			
❑ 10424	Fireball/XL 5	1963	12.00

GRAY, BILLY

45s

Number	Title (A Side/B Side)	Yr	NM
DECCA			
❑ 29489	Okie Blondie/I've Had At My Heart	1955	30.00
❑ 29678	Harbor of Love/Girls, Girls, Girls	1955	30.00
❑ 29800	Tennessee Toddy/It Could Have Been Me	1956	40.00
LIBERTY			
❑ 55599	I'll Never Live Long Enough/I Left My Heart in San Francisco	1963	12.00
❑ 55712	Last Call for Alcohol/ Late Last Night	1964	10.00

GRAY, CLAUDE

45s

Number	Title (A Side/B Side)	Yr	NM
COLUMBIA			
❑ 4-43150	Too Many Rivers/House of Tears	1964	10.00
❑ 4-43294	Thank You Neighbor/ Kinderhook Bill	1965	10.00
❑ 4-43443	For Losing You/ Thank You for the Ride	1965	10.00
❑ 4-43614	Mean Old Woman/ Then Cry You Away	1966	10.00
COUNTRY INT'L.			
❑ 158	Every Night Sensation/ (B-side unknown)	1980	6.00
❑ 164	Pride Goes Before a Fall/ Every Night Sensation	1980	6.00
❑ 169	He's Just an Illusion/ Every Night Sensation	1981	6.00
❑ 208	Sweet Caroline/Half a Mind	1986	6.00
D			
❑ 1059	Letter Overdue/I'm Not Supposed	1959	25.00
❑ 1093	Best Part of Me/Loneliness	1959	25.00
❑ 1118	Family Bible/Crying in the Night	1960	25.00
❑ 1144	My Party's Over/Leave Alone	1960	20.00
❑ 1154	When the Light Shines in the Valley/Homecoming in Heaven	1960	20.00
DECCA			
❑ 32039	I Never Had the One I Wanted/ Effects Your Leaving Had on Me	1966	8.00
❑ 32122	Because of Him/If I Ever Need a Lady (I'll Call You)	1967	7.00
❑ 32180	How Fast Them Trucks Can Go/Next Time You See Me	1967	7.00
❑ 32266	Easy Way Out/Your Devil Memory	1968	6.00
❑ 32312	Night Life/Just Between Us Tears	1968	6.00
❑ 32393	The Love of a Woman/ The Kind You Find Tonight Forget Tomorrow	1968	6.00
❑ 32456	Don't Give Me a Chance/ Once in Every Lifetime	1969	6.00
❑ 32566	Take Off Time/Sherry Ann	1969	6.00
❑ 32648	The Cleanest Man in Cincinnati/Crazy Arms	1970	6.00
❑ 32697	Everything Will Be Alright/ Apartment No. 9	1970	6.00
❑ 32786	Angel/Save My Mind	1971	6.00
❑ 32852	Baton Rouge/Your Devil Memory	1971	6.00
GRANNY WHITE			
❑ 10001	Rockin' My Memories (To Sleep)/But That's All Right	1976	7.00
❑ 10002	We Fell in Love That Way/ That's My Baby	1976	7.00
❑ 10003	It'll Do/Vin Rose	1977	7.00

Grateful Dead, "Good Lovin'," Arista 0383, 1978, **$6.**

Number	Title (A Side/B Side)	Yr	NM
❑ 10005	Slow Dancing/Late Cup of Coffee	1977	7.00
❑ 10006	If I Ever Need a Lady/The Bar	1978	7.00
❑ 10007	I Never Had the One I Wanted/ Late Cup of Coffee	1978	7.00
❑ 10009	Let's Go All the Way/We Climbed a Mountain Last Night	1982	7.00
—With Norma Jean			
❑ 10010	So Sad (To Watch Good Love Go Bad)/Who Sent My Ex to Texas	1982	7.00
❑ 10011	Old Flames Can't Hold a Candle to You/How Fast Them Trucks Can Go	198?	7.00
LITTLE DARLIN'			
❑ 7924	It Ain't the Wakin' Up/The Effects Your Leaving Had on Me	1979	7.00
MERCURY			
❑ 71732	I'll Just Have a Cup of Coffee (Then I'll Go)/I Just Want to Be Alone	1960	12.00
❑ 71826	My Ears Should Burn (When Fools Are Talked About)/ Crying in the Night	1961	12.00
❑ 71898	Let's End It Before It Begins/ Talk to Me Old Lonesome Heart	1961	12.00
❑ 71936	You Take the Table (I'll Take the Chairs)/Stone Heart	1962	12.00
❑ 72001	Daddy Stopped In/Three Times	1962	12.00
❑ 72063	Knock Again, True Love/ Call of the Wild	1962	12.00
❑ 72088	First Love Never Dies/ Heartbreak Eve	1963	12.00
❑ 72156	Go Home Cheater/ I'm Gonna Lie Again	1963	12.00
❑ 72236	Eight Years (And Two Children Later)/Lonesome	1964	12.00
MILLION			
❑ 3	Straight Down to Heaven/ Jeannie	1972	8.00
❑ 18	What Every Woman Wants to Hear/There's You	1972	8.00
❑ 31	Woman Ease My Mind/ Don't Fight the Feeling	1972	8.00
❑ 36	Loving You Is a Habit I Can't Break/We Could	1973	8.00

Albums

Number	Title (A Side/B Side)	Yr	NM
DECCA			
❑ DL 4882 [M]	Claude Gray Sings	1967	25.00
❑ DL 74882 [S]	Claude Gray Sings	1967	20.00
❑ DL 74963	The Easy Way of Claude Gray	1968	20.00
HILLTOP			
❑ JM-6051 [M]	Treasure of Love	1967	15.00
❑ JS-6051 [S]	Treasure of Love	1967	12.00
MERCURY			
❑ MG-20658 [M]	Songs of Broken Love Affairs	1962	20.00
❑ MG-20718 [M]	Country Goes to Town	1962	20.00
❑ SR-60658 [S]	Songs of Broken Love Affairs	1962	25.00
❑ SR-60718 [S]	Country Goes to Town	1962	25.00

GRAY, DOBIE

12-Inch Singles

Number	Title (A Side/B Side)	Yr	NM
INFINITY			
❑ INF-16001	You Can Do It/Thank You for Tonight	1979	12.00

45s

Number	Title (A Side/B Side)	Yr	NM
ANTHEM			
❑ 200	Guess Who?/Bits and Pieces	1972	5.00
ARISTA			
❑ 1047	One Can Fake It/ (B-side unknown)	1983	4.00
CAPITOL			
❑ 2241	We the People/ Funny and Groovy	1968	10.00
❑ B-5562	Gonna Be a Long Night/ That's One to Grown On	1986	3.00
❑ B-5596	The Dark Side of Life/A Night in the Life of a Country Boy	1986	3.00
❑ B-5647	From Where I Stand/ So Far So Good	1986	3.00

Except when noted otherwise, VG = 25% of NM, and VG+ = 50% of NM. (Example: VG = $2.00, VG+ = $4.00 and NM = $8.00.)

Number	Title (A Side/B Side)	Yr	NM
❑ 5853	River Deep, Mountain High/Tennessee Waltz	1967	15.00
❑ B-44087	Take It Real Easy/You Must Have Been Reading My Heart	1987	3.00
❑ B-44126	Love Letters/Steady As She Goes	1988	3.00
CAPRICORN			
❑ 0249	If Love Must Go/Lover's Sweat	1975	4.00
❑ 0259	Find 'Em, Fool 'Em and Forget 'Em/Mellow Man	1976	4.00
❑ 0267	Let Go/Mellow Man	1976	4.00
CHARGER			
❑ 105	The "In" Crowd/Be a Man	1964	15.00
❑ 107	See You at the "Go-Go"/Walk with Love	1965	10.00
❑ 109	In Hollywood/Mr. Engineer	1965	10.00
❑ 113	Monkey Jerk/My Baby	1965	10.00
❑ 115	No Room to Cry/Out on the Floor	1966	10.00
CORDAK			
❑ 1602	Look at Me/Walkin' and Whistlin'	1962	20.00
DECCA			
❑ 33057	Drift Away/City Stars	1973	5.00
INFINITY			
❑ 50003	You Can Do It/Sharing the Night Together	1978	4.00
❑ 50010	Who's Lovin' You/Thank You for Tonight	1979	4.00
❑ 50020	Spending Time, Making Love, and Going Crazy/Let This Man Take Hold of Your Life	1979	4.00
❑ 50043	The In Crowd/Let This Man Take Hold of Your Life	1979	4.00
LANA			
❑ 138	The "In" Crowd/Be a Man	196?	6.00
—Oldies reissue			
MCA			
❑ 40100	Loving Arms/Now That I'm Without You	1973	4.00
❑ 40153	Good Old Song/Reachin' for the Feelin'	1973	4.00
❑ 40188	Rose/Lovin' the Easy Way	1974	4.00
❑ 40201	There's a Honky Tonk Angel (Who'll Take Me Back In)/Lovin' the Easy Way	1974	4.00
❑ 40268	Watch Out for Lucy/Turning On You	1974	4.00
❑ 40315	The Music's Real/Roll On Sweet Mississippi	1974	4.00
ROBOX			
❑ RRS-117	Decorate the Night (same on both sides)	1979	5.00
WHITE WHALE			
❑ 300	Rose Garden/Where's the Girl Gone	1969	10.00
❑ 330	What a Way to Go/Do You Really Have a Heart	1969	500.00
❑ 342	Honey, You Can't Take It Back	1970	150.00
Albums			
CAPITOL			
❑ ST-12489	From Where I Stand	1986	10.00
CAPRICORN			
❑ CP 0163	New Ray of Sunshine	1976	10.00
CHARGER			
❑ CHR-M-2002 [M]	Dobie Gray Sings for "In" Crowders That Go "Go Go"	1965	40.00
❑ CHR-S-2002 [S]	Dobie Gray Sings for "In" Crowders That Go "Go Go"	1965	120.00
DECCA			
❑ DL 75397	Drift Away	1973	12.00
INFINITY			
❑ INF-9001	Midnight Diamond	1979	10.00
MCA			
❑ 371	Loving Arms	1973	10.00
❑ 449	Hey Dixie	1974	10.00
❑ 515	Drift Away	1974	10.00
—Reissue of Decca 75397			
ROBOX			
❑ RBX 8102	Welcome Home	1981	10.00
STRIPE			
❑ LPM 2001 [M]	Look — Dobie Gray	1963	100.00

GRAY, DOLORES

Number	Title (A Side/B Side)	Yr	NM
45s			
CAPITOL			
❑ F3774	I'm Innocent/My Mama Likes You	1957	10.00
DECCA			
❑ 9-27832	Shrimp Boats/More, More, More	1951	15.00
❑ 9-27942	I Got a Feelin' You're Foolin'/Did Anybody Call	1952	12.00
❑ 9-28032	Beware/Frankie	1952	12.00
❑ 9-28051	To Be Loved by You/If Someone Had Told Me	1952	12.00
❑ 9-28218	Dancing on the Grapes/A Diamond Mine in Madagascar	1952	12.00
❑ 9-28469	Two Other People/I Don't Care	1952	12.00
❑ 9-28582	Kaw-Liga/My Heart Is a Kingdom	1953	12.00
❑ 9-28676	Big Mamou/Say You're Mine Again	1953	12.00
❑ 9-28755	Call of the Far-Away Hills/Darling, the Moon Is So Bright	1953	12.00
❑ 9-28783	L-O-V-E/That's Love I Guess	1953	15.00
❑ 9-28968	Face to Face/Poppa Piccolino	1954	12.00
❑ 9-29031	Sweet Cheat/Flowers for the Lady	1954	12.00
❑ 9-29064	Happy Habit/Hang Up	1954	12.00
❑ 9-29109	In Paris and In Love/Lost in Loneliness	1954	12.00
❑ 9-29205	Too Bad/One	1954	12.00
❑ 9-29353	Without Love/The Finger of Suspicion Points at You	1954	12.00
❑ 9-29380	Heat Wave/After You Get What You Want	1954	12.00
❑ 9-29430	Rock Love/It May Sound Silly	1955	10.00
Albums			
CAPITOL			
❑ T 897 [M]	Warm Brandy	1957	30.00

GRAY, GENE, AND THE STINGRAYS

Number	Title (A Side/B Side)	Yr	NM
45s			
DOT			
❑ 16478	Surf Bunny/Surfer's Mood	1963	20.00
LINDA			
❑ 110	Surf Bunny/Surfer's Mood	1963	40.00

GRAY, GLEN

Number	Title (A Side/B Side)	Yr	NM
45s			
CAPITOL			
❑ SXE-1739 [S]	Blowin' Up a Storm/Farewell Blues	196?	10.00
—Small hole, plays at 33 1/3 rpm			
7-Inch Extended Plays			
CAPITOL			
❑ EAP 1-747	No Name Jive//Black Jazz/Smoke Rings	1956	10.00
—Sides 1 and 8 of "Album 747"			
❑ EAP 1-747 [PS]	Casa Loma in Hi-Fi! Part 1	1956	10.00
❑ EAP 2-747	Memories of You/White Jazz//Dance of the Lame Duck/For You	1956	10.00
—Sides 2 and 7 of "Album 747"			
❑ EAP 2-747 [PS]	Casa Loma in Hi-Fi! Part 2	1956	10.00
❑ EAP 3-747	(contents unknown)	1956	10.00
—Sides 3 and 6 of "Album 747"			
❑ EAP 3-747 [PS]	Casa Loma in Hi-Fi! Part 3	1956	10.00
❑ EAP 4-747	Sunrise Serenade/Maniac's Ball//Casa Loma Stomp/Just an Old Manuscript	1956	10.00
—Sides 4 and 5 of "Album 747"			
❑ EAP 4-747 [PS]	Casa Loma in Hi-Fi! Part 4	1956	10.00
❑ EAP 1-856	Drifting Apart/The World Is Waiting for the Sunrise//Out of Space/Under a Blanket of Blue	195?	10.00
❑ EAP 1-856 [PS]	Casa Loma Caravan, Part 1	195?	10.00
❑ EAP 2-856	(contents unknown)	195?	10.00
❑ EAP 2-856 [PS]	Casa Loma Caravan, Part 2	195?	10.00
❑ EAP 3-856	(contents unknown)	195?	10.00
❑ EAP 3-856 [PS]	Casa Loma Caravan, Part 3	195?	10.00
❑ EAP 1-1022	(contents unknown)	195?	10.00
❑ EAP 1-1022 [PS]	Sounds of the Great Bands, Part 1	195?	10.00
❑ EAP 2-1022	One O'Clock Jump/Contrasts//Boogie Woogie on St. Louis Blues/String of Pearls	195?	10.00
❑ EAP 2-1022 [PS]	Sounds of the Great Bands, Part 2	195?	10.00
DECCA			
❑ 7-34556	Smoke Rings/Casa Loma Stomp/It's the Talk of the Town//No Name Jive (Part 1 & 2)	1968	10.00
—Jukebox issue; small hole, plays at 33 1/3 rpm			
❑ 7-34556 [PS]	Glen Gray and the Original Casa Loma Orchestra's Greatest Hits	1968	10.00
Albums			
CAPITOL			
❑ W 747 [M]	Casa Loma in Hi-Fi!	1956	25.00
❑ T 856 [M]	Casa Loma Caravan	1957	20.00
—Turquoise label			
❑ SM-1022	Sounds of the Great Bands!	197?	10.00
—Reissue			
❑ SW 1022 [S]	Sounds of the Great Bands!	1959	15.00
❑ W 1022 [M]	Sounds of the Great Bands!	1959	12.00
❑ SM-1067	Sounds of the Great Bands Vol. 2	197?	10.00
—Reissue			
❑ ST 1067 [S]	Sounds of the Great Bands Vol. 2	1959	15.00
❑ T 1067 [M]	Sounds of the Great Bands Vol. 2	1959	12.00
❑ ST 1234 [S]	Solo Spotlight	1960	15.00
❑ T 1234 [M]	Solo Spotlight	1960	12.00
❑ ST 1289 [S]	Swingin' Decade	1960	15.00
❑ T 1289 [M]	Swingin' Decade	1960	12.00
❑ ST 1400 [S]	Swingin' Southern Style	1961	15.00
❑ T 1400 [M]	Swingin' Southern Style	1961	12.00
❑ ST 1506 [S]	Please Mr. Gray...More Sounds of the Great Bands	1961	15.00
❑ T 1506 [M]	Please Mr. Gray...More Sounds of the Great Bands	1961	12.00
❑ DT 1588 [R]	Sounds of the Great Casa Loma Band	1961	12.00
❑ SM-1588	Sounds of the Great Casa Loma Band	197?	10.00
—Reissue			
❑ T 1588 [M]	Sounds of the Great Casa Loma Band	1961	15.00
❑ ST 1615 [S]	Shall We Swing?	1961	15.00
❑ T 1615 [M]	Shall We Swing?	1961	12.00
❑ ST 1739 [S]	Sounds of the Great Bands Vol. 5: They All Swung the Blues	1962	15.00
❑ T 1739 [M]	Sounds of the Great Bands Vol. 5: They All Swung the Blues	1962	12.00
❑ SM-1812	Themes of the Great Bands	197?	10.00
—Reissue			
❑ ST 1812 [S]	Themes of the Great Bands	1963	15.00
❑ T 1812 [M]	Themes of the Great Bands	1963	12.00
❑ ST 1938 [S]	Sounds of the Great Bands Vol. 7: Today's Best	1963	12.00
❑ T 1938 [M]	Sounds of the Great Bands Vol. 7: Today's Best	1963	10.00
❑ ST 2014 [S]	Sounds of the Great Bands Vol. 8: More of Today's Best	1964	12.00
❑ T 2014 [M]	Sounds of the Great Bands Vol. 8: More of Today's Best	1964	10.00
❑ ST 2131 [S]	Sounds of the Great Bands in Latin	1964	12.00
❑ T 2131 [M]	Sounds of the Great Bands in Latin	1964	10.00
CIRCLE			
❑ 16	Glen Gray and the Casa Loma Orchestra	198?	10.00
CORAL			
❑ CRL 56006 [10]	Hoagy Carmichael Songs	1950	50.00
❑ CRL 56009 [10]	Glen Gray Souvenirs	1950	50.00
CREATIVE WORLD			
❑ ST-1055	Shall We Swing?	197?	10.00
DECCA			
❑ DL 5089 [10]	Musical Smoke Rings	1950	50.00
❑ DL 5397 [10]	No-Name Jive	1953	50.00
❑ DL 8570 [M]	Smoke Rings	1957	20.00
❑ DL 75016 [R]	Greatest Hits	1968	12.00
HARMONY			
❑ HL 7045 [M]	The Great Recordings of Glen Gray	1957	20.00
HINDSIGHT			
❑ HSR-104	Glen Gray and the Casa Loma Orchestra, 1939-1940	198?	10.00
❑ HSR-120	Glen Gray and the Casa Loma Orchestra, 1943-1946	198?	10.00
INSIGHT			
❑ 214	Glen Gray and the Casa Loma Orchestra, 1939-1946	198?	10.00
MCA			
❑ 122	Greatest Hits	1973	10.00
—Reissue of Decca 75016			
❑ 4076 [(2)]	The Best of Glen Gray	197?	12.00
❑ 20199	Smoke Rings	198?	8.00

GRAY, MAUREEN

Number	Title (A Side/B Side)	Yr	NM
45s			
CHANCELLOR			
❑ 1082	Crazy Over You/Today's the Day	1961	25.00
❑ 1091	Come On and Dance/I Don't Want to Cry	1961	25.00
❑ 1100	I'm So Young/There's a Boy	1962	25.00
LANDA			
❑ 689	Dancin' the Strand/Oh My	1962	15.00
❑ 692	People Are Talking/Oh My	1962	15.00
MERCURY			
❑ 72131	Story of My Love/Summertime Is Near	1963	12.00
❑ 72227	I'm a Happy Girl (Tra La La)/Goodbye Baby	1964	12.00

GRAY, RUDY See RUDY GRAYZELL.

GRAYZELL, RUDY

45s

ABBOTT

Number	Title (A Side/B Side)	Yr	NM
❑ 147	Bonita Chiquita/I'm Gone Again	1953	80.00
❑ 157	Ocean Paradise/It Ain't My Baby	1954	80.00

CAPITOL

Number	Title (A Side/B Side)	Yr	NM
❑ F2946	Hearts Made of Stone/ There's Gonna Be a Ball	1954	40.00
❑ F3044	You Better Believe It/Ca-Razy	1955	40.00
❑ F3149	Please Big Mama/My Heart Is Willing	1955	40.00

—Capitol titles as "Rudy Gray"

MERCURY

Number	Title (A Side/B Side)	Yr	NM
❑ 71138	Let's Get Wild/I Love You So	1957	80.00

STARDAY

Number	Title (A Side/B Side)	Yr	NM
❑ 229	The Moon Is Up/Day by Day	1956	80.00
❑ 241	Duck Dail/You're Gone	1956	80.00
❑ 270	You Hurt Me So/Jig-Ga-Lee-Ga	1956	80.00
❑ 321	Let's Get Wild/I Love You So	1957	100.00

SUN

Number	Title (A Side/B Side)	Yr	NM
❑ 290	Judy/I Think of You	1958	50.00

GREAN, CHARLES RANDOLPH

45s

RANWOOD

Number	Title (A Side/B Side)	Yr	NM
❑ 840	Quentin's Theme/#1 at the Blue Whale	1969	7.00
❑ 858	Josette's Music Box/ Back at the Blue Whale	1969	5.00
❑ 864	Peter and the Wolf/Georgy	1970	5.00
❑ 872	Marcus Welby, M.D. Theme/ Come Touch the Sun	1970	6.00
❑ 880	The Odd Couple/Theme from "Borsalino"	1970	6.00
❑ 891	Bullfrog/Singalong Junk	1970	5.00
❑ 901	Any Time of the Year/ Although You Make Me Cry	1971	5.00
❑ 907	Johnny, Harvey, Charlie, Herbie, Etc. (Part 1 & 2)	1971	5.00
❑ 918	Concerto for Knives, Forks, Spoons and Soup Ladle/ Gymnopedie	1971	5.00
❑ 938	Theme from Star Trek/ Rayo de Sol	1972	5.00
❑ 952	The Old Piano Roll Blues/ Rag-a-Muffin	1972	5.00
❑ 973	Karamoja Krackerjack/ Two Men of Karamoja	1973	5.00
❑ 1010	Very, Very Blue Danube/Now	1974	4.00
❑ 1044	Star Trek/Love Theme from "Hustle"	1975	4.00
❑ 1064	The $128,000 Question/ Sentimentale	1976	4.00
❑ 1088	The Masterpiece/Solitary Joe	197?	4.00

Albums

HARMONY

Number	Title (A Side/B Side)	Yr	NM
❑ KH 31389	Vol. 2	1972	10.00

RANWOOD

Number	Title (A Side/B Side)	Yr	NM
❑ 8055	Quentin's Theme	1969	12.00
❑ 8075	The Charles Randolph Grean Sounde	1970	12.00
❑ 8105	Masterpiece	1972	12.00

GREASE BAND

45s

SHELTER

Number	Title (A Side/B Side)	Yr	NM
❑ 7304	Let It Be Gone/Laughed at the Judge	1971	6.00
❑ 7310	All I Wanna Do/Jesse James	1971	6.00

Albums

SHELTER

Number	Title (A Side/B Side)	Yr	NM
❑ SW-8904	Grease Band	1971	12.00

GREAT JAZZ TRIO, THE

Albums

EAST WIND

Number	Title (A Side/B Side)	Yr	NM
❑ 10005	Direct from L.A.	1978	25.00

—Direct-to-disc recording

INNER CITY

Number	Title (A Side/B Side)	Yr	NM
❑ IC-6003	Love for Sale	1976	12.00
❑ IC-6013	The Great Jazz Trio at the Village Vanguard	1977	12.00
❑ IC-6023	Kindness, Joy, Love and Happiness	1978	12.00
❑ IC-6030	Milestones	1979	12.00

GREAT LOVE TRIP, THE

45s

UNI

Number	Title (A Side/B Side)	Yr	NM
❑ 55163	Why Can't We Be/Noah	1969	10.00

GREAT SCOTTS, THE

45s

EPIC

Number	Title (A Side/B Side)	Yr	NM
❑ 9805	Don't Want Your Love/ Give Me Lovin'	1965	20.00
❑ 9866	That's My Girl (Rotten to the Core)/Lost in Conversation	1965	40.00

TRIUMPH

Number	Title (A Side/B Side)	Yr	NM
❑ 66	Ball and Chain/Run, Run for Your Life	1966	30.00
❑ 67	Light Hurts My Eyes/You Know What You Can Do	1966	30.00

GREAT SOCIETY, THE Also see GRACE SLICK.

45s

COLUMBIA

Number	Title (A Side/B Side)	Yr	NM
❑ 44583	Sally Go 'Round the Roses/ Didn't Think So	1968	20.00

NORTH BEACH

Number	Title (A Side/B Side)	Yr	NM
❑ 1001	Someone to Love/Free Advice	1966	250.00

—As "The Great!! Society!!"

Albums

COLUMBIA

Number	Title (A Side/B Side)	Yr	NM
❑ CS 9627 [M]	Conspicuous Only In Its Absence	1968	50.00

—White label promo only; "Special Mono Radio Station Copy" sticker on front; same number as stereo version

Number	Title (A Side/B Side)	Yr	NM
❑ CS 9627 [S]	Conspicuous Only In Its Absence	1968	25.00

—Red label, "360 Sound Stereo"

Number	Title (A Side/B Side)	Yr	NM
❑ CS 9702	How It Was	1968	25.00

—Red label, "360 Sound Stereo"

Number	Title (A Side/B Side)	Yr	NM
❑ G 30459 [(2)]	The Great Society Collectors Item	1971	15.00

HARMONY

Number	Title (A Side/B Side)	Yr	NM
❑ KH 30391	Somebody to Love	1970	12.00

GREAT SPECKLED BIRD

45s

AMPEX

Number	Title (A Side/B Side)	Yr	NM
❑ 11003	We Sail/Disappearing Woman	1970	8.00
❑ 11006	Trucker's Café/Smiling Wine	1970	8.00

Albums

AMPEX

Number	Title (A Side/B Side)	Yr	NM
❑ A-10103	Great Speckled Bird	1970	20.00

GREATS, THE

45s

EBB

Number	Title (A Side/B Side)	Yr	NM
❑ 145	Marching Elvis/Fiddler's Rock	1958	50.00

GRECH, RICH

Albums

RSO

Number	Title (A Side/B Side)	Yr	NM
❑ SO 876	The Last Five Years	1973	12.00

—Compiles his work with such groups as Family, Traffic, Blind Faith, Ginger Baker's Air Force and KGB

GRECO, BUDDY

45s

CORAL

Number	Title (A Side/B Side)	Yr	NM
❑ 9-60573	I Ran All the Way Home/ The Glory of Love	1951	15.00
❑ 9-60623	Take Me Back/'Til the Stars Fall	1952	12.00
❑ 9-60672	It's a Sin to Tell a Lie/ Never Leave Your Sugar	1952	12.00
❑ 9-60904	I'll Always Love You Some/ And So Goodbye	1953	12.00
❑ 9-60979	You're Driving Me Crazy (What Did I Do)/I Predict	1953	12.00
❑ 9-61038	Don't Say Goodbye/ How Do You Think I Feel	1953	12.00
❑ 9-61128	Up the Chimney in Smoke/ The Sheik of Araby	1954	12.00
❑ 9-61190	What Word Is Sweeter Than Sweetheart/Lulu's Back in Town	1954	12.00
❑ 9-61236	If I Give My Heart to You/ Cold Glass of Water	1954	12.00
❑ 9-61265	Paris Loves Lovers/ Ain't No In-Between	1954	12.00
❑ 9-61409	Tonight/Truly	1955	10.00
❑ 9-61483	Why Don't You Write Me/ Pennies from Heaven	1955	12.00

EPIC

Number	Title (A Side/B Side)	Yr	NM
❑ 5-9377	The Lady Is a Tramp/ The More I See You	1960	8.00
❑ 5-9378	Like Young/Something's Gotta Give	1960	8.00
❑ 5-9379	Cheek to Cheek/How About You	1960	8.00
❑ 5-9380	(I Don't Care) Only Love Me/Misty	1960	8.00
❑ 5-9381	Just in Time/I Laughed at Love	1960	8.00

—The above five presumably are stereo jukebox singles from the album "My Buddy"

Number	Title (A Side/B Side)	Yr	NM
❑ 5-9387	The Lady Is a Tramp/Like Young	1960	8.00
❑ 5-9387 [PS]	The Lady Is a Tramp/Like Young	1960	10.00
❑ 5-9404	Oooh Look-a-There, Ain't She Pretty/This Could Be the Start of Something	1960	8.00
❑ 5-9404 [PS]	Oooh Look-a-There, Ain't She Pretty/This Could Be the Start of Something	1960	10.00
❑ 5-9408	(titles unknown)	1960	8.00
❑ 5-9409	(titles unknown)	1960	8.00
❑ 5-9410	(titles unknown)	1960	8.00
❑ 5-9411	(titles unknown)	1960	8.00
❑ 5-9412	(titles unknown)	1960	8.00

—The above five presumably are stereo jukebox singles from the album "Songs for Swinging Losers"

Number	Title (A Side/B Side)	Yr	NM
❑ 5-9439	I Could Write a Book/ They Took John Away	1961	8.00
❑ 5-9451	Around the World/Hey There	1961	8.00
❑ 5-9455	(titles unknown)	1961	8.00
❑ 5-9456	(titles unknown)	1961	8.00
❑ 5-9457	(titles unknown)	1961	8.00
❑ 5-9458	(titles unknown)	1961	8.00
❑ 5-9459	(titles unknown)	1961	8.00

—The above five presumably are stereo jukebox singles from the album "I Like It Swinging"

Number	Title (A Side/B Side)	Yr	NM
❑ 5-9472	Roses of Picardy/Hallelujah! I Love Her So	1961	8.00
❑ 5-9499	Let Me Love You/ Twistin' to the Blues	1962	8.00
❑ 5-9499 [PS]	Let Me Love You/ Twistin' to the Blues	1962	10.00
❑ 5-9536	Mr. Lonely/Sentimental Fool	1962	8.00

—A-side has the same backing track as Bobby Vinton's 1964 hit version of the song

Number	Title (A Side/B Side)	Yr	NM
❑ 5-9563	Stranger/Just Walk Away	1962	8.00
❑ 5-9563 [PS]	Stranger/Just Walk Away	1962	10.00
❑ 5-9588	Make Up Your Mind/ What Now My Love	1963	8.00
❑ 5-9588 [PS]	Make Up Your Mind/ What Now My Love	1963	10.00
❑ 5-9627	The Magic of a Girl/ Miss Kiss and Run	1963	8.00
❑ 5-9657	Ciumachella (Tender Flower)/ I'll Be a Fool	1964	8.00
❑ 5-9666	More/It Had Better Be Tonight	1964	8.00
❑ 5-9713	It's Such a Happy Day/ Zip-a-Dee Do-Dah	1964	8.00
❑ 5-9750	I Can't Help It (If I'm Still in Love with You)/Jambalaya	1965	8.00
❑ 5-9786	The Most Beautiful Girl in the World/You Win Again	1965	8.00
❑ 5-9817	I Can't Begin to Tell You/When the Subject Was Roses	1965	8.00
❑ 5-9834	The Best Is Yet to Come/Time's a-Wastin' While You're Gone	1965	8.00
❑ 5-9864	That Darn Cat/I'm Gonna Laugh You Out of My Life	1965	8.00
❑ 5-9864 [PS]	That Darn Cat/I'm Gonna Laugh You Out of My Life	1965	10.00

HERALD

Number	Title (A Side/B Side)	Yr	NM
❑ 545	Ooh Baby/Ask Her	1959	12.00

KAPP

Number	Title (A Side/B Side)	Yr	NM
❑ 155	In Time to Come/Love Don't Be a Stranger	1956	10.00
❑ 165	Holiday Romance/You're the Love of My Love	1956	10.00
❑ 170	Wow/Pink Flamingo and Dancing Crane	1957	10.00
❑ 183	Game of Love/With All My Heart	1957	10.00
❑ 192	You Are Mine/Leona	1957	10.00

MGM

Number	Title (A Side/B Side)	Yr	NM
❑ 14235	How Can I Live Without Your Love/Mountain Girl	1971	5.00
❑ 14269	Days of Icy Fingers/ You Can Close Your Eyes	1971	5.00
❑ 14325	Keep the Customer Satisfied/ Your Love's Return	1972	5.00

REPRISE

Number	Title (A Side/B Side)	Yr	NM
❑ 0474	Keep the Lovin' Feelin'/You Don't Have to Say You Love Me	1966	7.00
❑ 0495	Put Yourself in My Place/Be Anything (But Be Mine)	1966	7.00
❑ 0515	Walking on New Grass/ What Am I	1966	7.00
❑ 0551	Dani/Where's the Girl	1967	6.00
❑ 0562	There She Goes/Your Name	1967	6.00
❑ 0584	Love's Gonna Live Here Again/ Bonita	1967	6.00
❑ 0605	I Will Wait for You/ She's a Cariocia	1967	6.00
❑ 0638	Good Times/Is All That Bright and Beautiful	1967	6.00
❑ 0657	Girl Talk/This Is Your Life	1968	6.00

SCEPTER

Number	Title (A Side/B Side)	Yr	NM
❑ 12260	From Atlanta to Goodbye/ Love Is a Hurtin' Thing	1969	6.00
❑ 12270	Distant Carolina/Double Life	1970	6.00

Number	Title (A Side/B Side)	Yr	NM
❑ 12278	Let It Be/Walking Backwards Down the Road	1970	6.00
❑ 12287	My God and I/Walking Backwards Down the Road	1970	6.00

Albums

APPLAUSE

Number	Title (A Side/B Side)	Yr	NM
❑ APLP-1004	Hot Nights	1982	10.00

BAINBRIDGE

Number	Title (A Side/B Side)	Yr	NM
❑ 8004 [(2)]	Greatest Hits	198?	15.00

EPIC

Number	Title (A Side/B Side)	Yr	NM
❑ BN 557 [S]	My Buddy	1960	15.00
❑ BN 585 [S]	Songs for Swinging Losers	1960	15.00
❑ BN 593 [S]	Buddy's Back in Town	1961	15.00
❑ BN 602 [S]	I Like It Swinging	1961	15.00
❑ BN 615 [S]	Let's Love	1961	15.00
❑ LN 3660 [M]	My Buddy	1960	12.00
❑ LN 3746 [M]	Songs for Swinging Losers	1960	12.00
❑ LN 3771 [M]	Buddy's Back in Town	1961	12.00
❑ LN 3793 [M]	I Like It Swinging	1961	12.00
❑ LN 3820 [M]	Let's Love	1961	12.00
❑ LN 24010 [M]	Buddy and Soul	1962	12.00
❑ LN 24032 [M]	Soft and Gentle	1962	12.00
❑ LN 24043 [M]	Buddy Greco's Greatest Hits	1963	12.00
❑ LN 24057 [M]	Buddy Greco Sings for Intimate Moments	1963	12.00
❑ LN 24088 [M]	My Last Night in Rome	1964	12.00
❑ LN 24116 [M]	On Stage	1964	12.00
❑ LN 24130 [M]	Modern Sounds of Hank Williams	1965	12.00
❑ LN 24181 [M]	From the Wrists Down	1965	12.00
❑ BN 26010 [S]	Buddy and Soul	1962	15.00
❑ BN 26032 [S]	Soft and Gentle	1962	15.00
❑ BN 26043 [S]	Buddy Greco's Greatest Hits	1963	15.00
❑ BN 26057 [S]	Buddy Greco Sings for Intimate Moments	1963	15.00
❑ BN 26088 [S]	My Last Night in Rome	1964	15.00
❑ BN 26116 [S]	On Stage	1964	15.00
❑ BN 26130 [S]	Modern Sounds of Hank Williams	1965	15.00
❑ BN 26181 [S]	From the Wrists Down	1965	15.00

HARMONY

Number	Title (A Side/B Side)	Yr	NM
❑ HL 7448 [M]	You're Something Else	196?	10.00
❑ HS 11248 [S]	You're Something Else	196?	12.00

KAPP

Number	Title (A Side/B Side)	Yr	NM
❑ KL-1033 [M]	Broadway Melodies	1956	20.00
❑ KL-1107 [M]	Buddy	1958	20.00
❑ KL-1231 [M]	The Best of Buddy Greco	1961	15.00

PROJECT 3

Number	Title (A Side/B Side)	Yr	NM
❑ PR 5105	For Once in My Life: In Concert	1980	10.00

REPRISE

Number	Title (A Side/B Side)	Yr	NM
❑ R-6220 [M]	Big Band and Ballads	1966	12.00
❑ RS-6220 [S]	Big Band and Ballads	1966	15.00
❑ R-6230 [M]	Buddy's in a Brand New Bag	1966	12.00
❑ RS-6230 [S]	Buddy's in a Brand New Bag	1966	15.00
❑ R-6256 [M]	Away We Go!	1967	15.00
❑ RS-6256 [S]	Away We Go!	1967	12.00

SCEPTER

Number	Title (A Side/B Side)	Yr	NM
❑ SPS-579	Let the Sunshine In	1969	12.00

SUTTON

Number	Title (A Side/B Side)	Yr	NM
❑ SSU 282 [M]	All Time Favorites Featuring Buddy Greco	196?	10.00

VOCALION

Number	Title (A Side/B Side)	Yr	NM
❑ VL 3706 [M]	Here's Buddy Greco	1964	12.00
❑ VL 73706 [R]	Here's Buddy Greco	1964	10.00

GRECO, JOHNNY

45s

PAGEANT

Number	Title (A Side/B Side)	Yr	NM
❑ 602	Rocket Ride/(B-side unknown)	1963	150.00

GREEN

45s

ATCO

Number	Title (A Side/B Side)	Yr	NM
❑ 6833	Big Dipper/All My Bells	1971	5.00

Albums

ATCO

Number	Title (A Side/B Side)	Yr	NM
❑ SD 33-282	Green	1969	15.00
❑ SD 33-366	To Help Somebody	1971	12.00

GREEN, AL

12-Inch Singles

A&M

Number	Title (A Side/B Side)	Yr	NM
❑ 12311	As Long As We're Together (4 versions)	1989	6.00
❑ 12323	The Message Is Love (6 versions)	1989	6.00

HI

Number	Title (A Side/B Side)	Yr	NM
❑ 78510	I Feel Good (7:30)/I Feel Good (3:17)	1978	15.00

45s

A&M

Number	Title (A Side/B Side)	Yr	NM
❑ 1427	As Long As We're Together/Blessed	1989	3.00
❑ 2786	Going Away/Building Up	1985	4.00
❑ 2807	True Love/He Is the Light	1986	4.00
❑ 2919	Everything's Gonna Be Alright/So Real to Me	1987	3.00
❑ 2952	You Know and I Know/True Love	1987	3.00
❑ 2962	Soul Survivor/Jesus Will Fix It	1987	3.00

BELL

Number	Title (A Side/B Side)	Yr	NM
❑ 45258	Guilty/Let Me Help You	1972	20.00
❑ 45305	Hot Wire/Don't Leave Me	1973	20.00

CAPITOL

Number	Title (A Side/B Side)	Yr	NM
❑ S7-18869	Tired of Being Alone/Walk On By	1995	3.00

—B-side by Isaac Hayes

HI

Number	Title (A Side/B Side)	Yr	NM
❑ 2159	I Want to Hold Your Hand/What Am I Gonna Do with Myself	1969	8.00
❑ 2164	One Woman/Tomorrow's Dream	1969	8.00
❑ 2172	You Say It/Gotta Find a New World	1969	30.00
❑ 2177	Right Now, Right Now/All Because I'm a Foolish One	1970	6.00
❑ 2182	I Can't Get Next to You/Ride Sally Ride	1970	6.00
❑ 2188	Driving Wheel/True Love	1971	6.00
❑ 2194	Tired of Being Alone/Get Back Baby	1971	5.00
❑ 2202	Let's Stay Together/Tomorrow's Dream	1971	5.00
❑ 2211	Look What You Done for Me/La La for You	1972	5.00
❑ 2216	I'm Still in Love with You/Old Time Lovin'	1972	5.00
❑ 2227	You Ought to Be with Me/What Is This Feeling	1972	5.00
❑ 2235	Call Me (Come Back Home)/What a Wonderful Thing Love Is	1973	5.00
❑ 2247	Here I Am (Come and Take Me)/I'm Glad You're Mine	1973	5.00
❑ 2257	Livin' for You/It Ain't No Fun to Me	1973	5.00
❑ 2262	Let's Get Married/So Good to Be Here	1974	5.00
❑ 2274	Sha-La-La (Make Me Happy)/School Days	1974	5.00
❑ 2282	L-O-V-E (Love)/I Wish You Were Here	1975	5.00
❑ 2288	Oh Me, Oh My (Dreams in My Arms)/Strong As Death (Sweet As Love)	1975	5.00
❑ 2300	Full of Fire/Could I Be the One	1975	5.00
❑ 2306	Let It Shine/There's No Way	1976	5.00
❑ 2319	Keep Me Cryin'/There Is Love	1976	5.00
❑ 2322	I Tried to Tell Myself/Something	1977	10.00
❑ 2324	Love and Happiness/Glory Glory	1977	5.00
❑ 77505	Belle/Chariots of Fire	1977	4.00
❑ 77505 [PS]	Belle/Chariots of Fire	1977	6.00
❑ 77680	White Christmas/Winter Wonderland	2001	5.00

—Clear vinyl

Number	Title (A Side/B Side)	Yr	NM
❑ 78511	I Feel Good/Feels Like Summer	1978	4.00
❑ 78522	Wait Here/To Sir with Love	1978	4.00
❑ 78522 [PS]	Wait Here/To Sir with Love	1978	6.00

HOT LINE JOURNAL

Number	Title (A Side/B Side)	Yr	NM
❑ 15000	Back Up Train/Don't Leave Me	1967	30.00
❑ 15001	Don't Hurt Me No More/Get Yourself Together	1967	20.00
❑ 15002	I'll Be Good to You/Lover's Hideaway	1967	20.00

THE RIGHT STUFF

Number	Title (A Side/B Side)	Yr	NM
❑ S7-17524	Let's Stay Together/I'm Still in Love with You	1993	3.00
❑ S7-18217	I'll Be Home for Christmas/It Feels Like Christmas	1994	5.00

7-Inch Extended Plays

HI

Number	Title (A Side/B Side)	Yr	NM
❑ SBG 81	How Can You Mend a Broken Heart/So You're Leaving//I've Never Found a Girl/What Is This Feeling/It Ain't No Fun to Me	1972	10.00

—Jukebox issue; small hole, plays at 33 1/3 rpm

Number	Title (A Side/B Side)	Yr	NM
❑ SBG 81 [PS]	Let's Stay Together	1972	10.00
❑ SBG 87	Funny How Time Slips Away/Love Is Like the Morning Sun//Have You Been Making Out O.K./Stand Up	1973	10.00

—Jukebox issue; small hole, plays at 33 1/3 rpm

Number	Title (A Side/B Side)	Yr	NM
❑ SBG 87 [PS]	Call Me	1973	10.00

Albums

A&M

Number	Title (A Side/B Side)	Yr	NM
❑ SP-5150	Soul Survivor	1987	10.00
❑ SP-5228	I Get Joy	1989	10.00

BELL

Number	Title (A Side/B Side)	Yr	NM
❑ 6076	Al Green	1972	20.00

—Reissue of Hot Line LP

BLUE NOTE

Number	Title (A Side/B Side)	Yr	NM
❑ BTE 74584	Everything's OK	2005	15.00
❑ 93556 [(2)]	I Can't Stop	2003	15.00

DCC COMPACT CLASSICS

Number	Title (A Side/B Side)	Yr	NM
❑ LPZ-2058	Greatest Hits	1998	30.00

—Audiophile vinyl

HI

Number	Title (A Side/B Side)	Yr	NM
❑ 6004	The Belle Album	1977	12.00
❑ 6009	Truth 'N' Time	1978	12.00
❑ 8000	Tired of Being Alone	1977	12.00
❑ 8001	Al Green Gets Next to You	1977	12.00
❑ 8007	Let's Stay Together	1977	12.00
❑ SHL-32055	Green Is Blues	1969	15.00
❑ SHL-32062	Al Green Gets Next to You	1971	15.00
❑ SHL-32070	Let's Stay Together	1972	15.00
❑ SHL-32074	I'm Still in Love with You	1972	15.00
❑ SHL-32077	Call Me	1973	15.00
❑ SHL-32082	Livin' for You	1973	15.00
❑ SHL-32087	Al Green Explores Your Mind	1974	15.00
❑ SHL-32089	Al Green/Greatest Hits	1975	15.00
❑ SHL-32092	Al Green Is Love	1975	15.00
❑ SHL-32097	Full of Fire	1976	15.00
❑ SHL-32103	Have a Good Time	1976	15.00
❑ SHL-32105	Al Green's Greatest Hits, Vol. II	1977	15.00

HOT LINE

Number	Title (A Side/B Side)	Yr	NM
❑ 1500 [M]	Back Up Train	1967	50.00

—As "Al Greene"

Number	Title (A Side/B Side)	Yr	NM
❑ S-1500 [S]	Back Up Train	1967	80.00

—As "Al Greene"

KORY

Number	Title (A Side/B Side)	Yr	NM
❑ 1005	Al Green	1977	10.00

—Reissue of Bell LP

MCA

Number	Title (A Side/B Side)	Yr	NM
❑ 42308	Love Ritual	1988	10.00

MOTOWN

Number	Title (A Side/B Side)	Yr	NM
❑ 5283 ML	Al Green/Greatest Hits	198?	10.00

—Reissue of Hi 32089

Number	Title (A Side/B Side)	Yr	NM
❑ 5284 ML	I'm Still in Love with You	198?	10.00

—Reissue of Hi 32074

Number	Title (A Side/B Side)	Yr	NM
❑ 5290 ML	Let's Stay Together	198?	10.00

—Reissue of Hi 32070

Number	Title (A Side/B Side)	Yr	NM
❑ 5291 ML	Al Green's Greatest Hits, Vol. II	198?	10.00

—Reissue of Hi 32105

Number	Title (A Side/B Side)	Yr	NM
❑ 5317 ML	Truth N' Time	198?	10.00

MYRRH

Number	Title (A Side/B Side)	Yr	NM
❑ MSB-6661	The Lord Will Make a Way	1980	10.00
❑ MSB-6671	Higher Plane	1981	10.00
❑ MSB-6702	Precious Lord	1981	10.00
❑ MSB-6747	I'll Rise Again	1982	10.00
❑ MSB-6774	Al Green and the Full Gospel Tabernacle Choir	1984	10.00
❑ WR-8113	The Lord Will Make a Way	1985	8.00

—Reissue with new number and A&M logo

Number	Title (A Side/B Side)	Yr	NM
❑ WR-8114	Higher Plane	1985	8.00

—Reissue with new number and A&M logo

Number	Title (A Side/B Side)	Yr	NM
❑ WR-8115	Precious Lord	1985	8.00

—Reissue with new number and A&M logo

Number	Title (A Side/B Side)	Yr	NM
❑ WR-8116	I'll Rise Again	1985	8.00

—Reissue with new number and A&M logo

Number	Title (A Side/B Side)	Yr	NM
❑ WR-8117	White Christmas	1985	10.00

—Reissue with new number and A&M logo

Number	Title (A Side/B Side)	Yr	NM
❑ WR-8118	Trust in God	1985	8.00

—Reissue with new number and A&M logo

Number	Title (A Side/B Side)	Yr	NM
❑ WR-8209	Al Green and the Full Gospel Tabernacle Choir	1986	8.00

—Reissue with new number and A&M logo

Number	Title (A Side/B Side)	Yr	NM
❑ 7-01-678006-6	White Christmas	1984	12.00
❑ 7-01-678306-?	Trust in God	1984	10.00

THE RIGHT STUFF

Number	Title (A Side/B Side)	Yr	NM
❑ T1-27121	Let's Stay Together	1995	15.00

—Green vinyl reissue

Number	Title (A Side/B Side)	Yr	NM
❑ T1-27627	I'm Still in Love with You	1995	15.00

—Green vinyl reissue

WORD

Number	Title (A Side/B Side)	Yr	NM
❑ E 77000	One in a Million	1991	12.00

GREEN, BARBARA

See BARBARA GREENE.

GREEN, BERNIE

Albums

RCA VICTOR

Number	Title (A Side/B Side)	Yr	NM
❑ LPM-1929 [M]	Musically Mad	1959	60.00
❑ LSP-1929 [S]	Musically Mad	1959	100.00
❑ LSA-2376 [S]	Futura	1961	50.00

SAN FRANCISCO

Number	Title (A Side/B Side)	Yr	NM
❑ M-33015 [M]	Bernie Green Plays More Than You Can Stand in Hi-Fi	1957	50.00

GREEN, FRED

45s

BOBBIN

Number	Title (A Side/B Side)	Yr	NM
❑ 111	Wham Slam Baby/It's Funny	1959	100.00
❑ 123	Don't Make a Fool Out of Me/If You Ever Try to Leave Me	1960	100.00

Except when noted otherwise, VG = 25% of NM, and VG+ = 50% of NM. (Example: VG = $2.00, VG+ = $4.00 and NM = $8.00.)

G

GREEN, FRED, AND THE MELLARDS

45s

Number	Title (A Side/B Side)	Yr	NM
BALLAD			
❑ 1012	My Sweetheart/You Can't Keep Love in a Broken Heart	1955	300.00
❑ 1016	Love Me Crazy/That's Life	1955	200.00

GREEN, GARLAND

45s

Number	Title (A Side/B Side)	Yr	NM
CASINO			
❑ 056	I.O.U./It's a Backdoor World	1976	5.00
COTILLION			
❑ 44098	Plain and Simple Girl/Hey Cloud	1971	6.00
OCEAN-FRONT			
❑ 2000	Tryin' to Hold On/(B-side unknown)	1983	4.00
RCA			
❑ PB-10889	Don't Let Love Walk Out on Us/Ask Me for What You Want	1977	6.00
❑ PB-11023	Shake Your Shaker/Lovin' You Baby	1977	5.00
❑ PB-11126	Let's Celebrate/Let Me Be Your Pacifier	1977	5.00
REVUE			
❑ 11001	Girl I Love You/It Rained Forty Days and Nights	1967	80.00
❑ 11020	Mr. Misery/You Played on a Prayer	196?	12.00
❑ 11030	Love Now, Pay Later/Ain't That Good Enough	196?	80.00
SPRING			
❑ 142	He Didn't Know (He Kept On Talkin')/Please Come Home	1973	5.00
❑ 146	Sweet Loving Woman/Sending My Best Friend	1974	5.00
❑ 151	Let the Good Times Roll/You and I Go Good Together	1974	5.00
❑ 158	Bumpin' and Stompin'/Nothing Can Take You from Me	1975	5.00
❑ 160	Just Loving You/Nothing Can Take You from Me	1975	5.00
UNI			
❑ 55143	Jealous Kind of Fella/I Can't Believe You Quit Me	1969	8.00
❑ 55188	Don't Think That I Am a Violent Guy/All She Said (Was Goodbye to Me)	1969	8.00
❑ 55213	Angel Baby/You Played On a Player	1970	8.00

Albums

Number	Title (A Side/B Side)	Yr	NM
RCA VICTOR			
❑ APL1-2351	Love Is What We Came Here For	1977	12.00
UNI			
❑ 73073	Jealous Kind of Fellow	1969	20.00

GREEN, GRANT

45s

Number	Title (A Side/B Side)	Yr	NM
BLUE NOTE			
❑ 1960	Ain't It Funky Now (Part 1)/Ain't It Funky Now (Part 2)	1970	5.00
❑ 1965	Sookie, Sookie/Time to Remember	1971	5.00
❑ 1969	Does Anybody Really Know What Time It Is?/Never Can Say Goodbye	1971	5.00
❑ 1972	The Battle (Part 1)/The Battle (Part 2)	1972	5.00
❑ 1983	Afro Party/Father's Lament	1972	5.00
VERVE			
❑ 10361	Cantaloupe Woman/Daddy Grapes	1965	8.00

Albums

Number	Title (A Side/B Side)	Yr	NM
BLUE NOTE			
❑ BN-LA037-G2 [(2)]	Live at the Lighthouse	1973	50.00
❑ LT-990	Solid	1980	40.00
❑ LT-1032	Nigeria	1980	50.00
❑ BLP-4064 [M]	Grant's First Stand	1961	200.00
—With W. 63rd St. address on label			
❑ BLP-4064 [M]	Grant's First Stand	1963	50.00
—With New York, USA address on label			
❑ BLP-4071 [M]	Green Street	1961	200.00
—With W. 63rd St. address on label			
❑ BLP-4071 [M]	Green Street	1963	60.00
—With New York, USA address on label			
❑ BLP-4086 [M]	Grant Stand	1962	200.00
—With W. 63rd St. address on label			
❑ BLP-4086 [M]	Grant Stand	1963	100.00
—With New York, USA address on label			
❑ BLP-4099 [M]	Sunday Mornin'	1962	200.00
—With W. 63rd St. address on label			
❑ BLP-4099 [M]	Sunday Mornin'	1963	150.00
—With New York, USA address on label			
❑ BLP-4111 [M]	The Latin Bit	1962	100.00
—With "New York, USA" on label			
❑ BLP-4132 [M]	Feelin' the Spirit	1963	40.00
❑ BLP-4139 [M]	Am I Blue	1963	100.00
—With "New York, USA" on label			
❑ BLP-4154 [M]	Idle Moments	1964	40.00
❑ BLP-4183 [M]	Talkin' About!	1964	40.00
❑ BLP-4202 [M]	I Want to Hold Your Hand	1964	40.00
❑ BLP-4253 [M]	Street of Dreams	1967	100.00
—"A Division of Liberty Records" on label			
❑ BLP-84064 [S]	Grant's First Stand	1961	150.00
—With W. 63rd St. addresss on label			
❑ BLP-84064 [S]	Grant's First Stand	1963	80.00
—With New York, USA address on label			
❑ BLP-84064 [S]	Grant's First Stand	1968	25.00
—With "A Division of Liberty Records" on label			
❑ BLP-84071 [S]	Green Street	1961	150.00
—With W. 63rd St. address on label			
❑ BLP-84071 [S]	Green Street	1963	60.00
—With New York, USA address on label			
❑ BLP-84071 [S]	Green Street	1968	25.00
—With "A Division of Liberty Records" on label			
❑ BLP-84086 [S]	Grant Stand	1962	150.00
—With W. 63rd St. address on label			
❑ BLP-84086 [S]	Grant Stand	1963	100.00
—With New York, USA address on label			
❑ BLP-84086 [S]	Grant Stand	1968	30.00
—With "A Division of Liberty Records" on label			
❑ BLP-84086 [S]	Grant Stand	197?	20.00
—Dark blue label with white stylized "b" at upper right			
❑ BLP-84099 [S]	Sunday Mornin'	1962	150.00
—With W. 63rd St. address on label			
❑ BLP-84099 [S]	Sunday Mornin'	1963	120.00
—With New York, USA address on label			
❑ BLP-84099 [S]	Sunday Mornin'	1968	20.00
—With "A Division of Liberty Records" on label			
❑ BLP-84111 [S]	The Latin Bit	1962	100.00
—With New York, USA address on label; reproductions exist			
❑ BLP-84111 [S]	The Latin Bit	1968	25.00
—With "A Division of Liberty Records" on label			
❑ BLP-84132 [S]	Feelin' the Spirit	1963	100.00
—With New York, USA address on label			
❑ BLP-84132 [S]	Feelin' the Spirit	1968	25.00
—With "A Division of Liberty Records" on label			
❑ BLP-84139 [S]	Am I Blue	1963	100.00
—With New York, USA address on label			
❑ BLP-84139 [S]	Am I Blue	1968	25.00
—With "A Division of Liberty Records" on label			
❑ BLP-84154 [S]	Idle Moments	1964	100.00
—With New York, USA address on label			
❑ BLP-84154 [S]	Idle Moments	1968	25.00
—With "A Division of Liberty Records" on label			
❑ BLP-84183 [S]	Talkin' About!	1964	100.00
—With New York, USA address on label			
❑ BLP-84183 [S]	Talkin' About!	1968	25.00
—With "A Division of Liberty Records" on label			
❑ BLP-84202 [S]	I Want to Hold Your Hand	1964	100.00
—With New York, USA address on label			
❑ BLP-84202 [S]	I Want to Hold Your Hand	1968	25.00
—With "A Division of Liberty Records" on label			
❑ BLP-84253 [S]	Street of Dreams	1967	80.00
—"A Division of Liberty Records" on label			
❑ BLP-84310	Goin' West	1969	100.00
—"A Division of Liberty Records" on label			
❑ BLP-84327	Carryin' On	1969	100.00
—"A Division of Liberty Records" on label			
❑ BLP-84342	Green Is Beautiful	1970	60.00
—"A Division of Liberty Records" on label			
❑ BLP-84360	Alive!	1970	60.00
—We're not sure what the original label is; it could be the blue and white label with "A Division of Liberty Records," the mostly black label with "Liberty/UA," or the blue and white label with "A Division of United Artists Records"			
❑ BLP-84360	Alive!	1973	25.00
—Dark blue label with black stylized "b" at upper right			
❑ BLP-84373	Visions	1971	80.00
❑ BLP-84413	Shades of Green	1972	80.00
—"A Division of United Artists Records" on blue and white label			
❑ BLP-84415	The Final Comedown	1972	80.00
—"A Division of United Artists Records" on blue and white label			
❑ BLP-84432	Born to Be Blue	1985	50.00
COBBLESTONE			
❑ CST-9002	Iron City	1972	100.00
—Reproductions exist			
DELMARK			
❑ DL-404 [M]	All the Gin Is Gone	1966	25.00
❑ DS-404 [S]	All the Gin Is Gone	1966	25.00
❑ DL-427 [M]	Black Forrest	1966	25.00
❑ DS-427 [S]	Black Forrest	1966	25.00
KUDU			
❑ KU-29	The Main Attraction	1976	25.00
MOSAIC			
❑ MR5-133 [(5)]	The Complete Blue Note Recordings of Grant Green with Sonny Clark	199?	300.00
MUSE			
❑ MR-5014	Green Blues	1973	25.00
❑ MR-5120	Iron City	197?	25.00
VERSATILE			
❑ MSG-6002	Easy	1978	20.00
VERVE			
❑ V-8627 [M]	His Majesty, King Funk	1965	100.00
❑ V6-8627 [S]	His Majesty, King Funk	1965	120.00

GREEN, JANICE (THE "OH JULIE" GIRL)

45s

Number	Title (A Side/B Side)	Yr	NM
NASCO			
❑ 6013	With All My Heart/Jackie	1958	20.00

GREEN, KEITH

45s

Number	Title (A Side/B Side)	Yr	NM
DECCA			
❑ 31799	A Go-Go Letter/The Way I Used to Be	1965	20.00
❑ 31859	Girl Don't Tell Me/How to Be Your Guy	1965	25.00
❑ 31973	Home Town Girls/Hear What's Happening, Baby	1966	20.00
ERA			
❑ 108	Sgt. Pepper's Epitaph/Country Store	1970	10.00
❑ 3210	Fantastic/L.A. City Smog Blues	1969	10.00

Albums

Number	Title (A Side/B Side)	Yr	NM
PRETTY GOOD			
❑ PGR-1	So You Wanna Go Back to Egypt	1980	12.00
SPARROW			
❑ SPR-1015	For Him Who Has Ears to Hear	1977	12.00
❑ SPR-1024	No Compromise	1978	12.00
❑ SP-9901	For Him Who Has Ears to Hear	198?	8.00
—Reissue of 1015			
❑ SP-9904	No Compromise	198?	8.00
—Reissue of 1024			
❑ SP-9927	The Collection	198?	10.00

GREEN, LIL

45s

Number	Title (A Side/B Side)	Yr	NM
ATLANTIC			
❑ 951	Every Time/I've Got That Feeling	1952	100.00

GREEN, LLOYD

45s

Number	Title (A Side/B Side)	Yr	NM
MONUMENT			
❑ 8648	I Can Help/Theme from A Summer Place	1975	5.00
—With Charlie McCoy			

GREEN, PETER

Also see FLEETWOOD MAC.

45s

Number	Title (A Side/B Side)	Yr	NM
SAIL			
❑ 116	In the Skies/(B-side unknown)	1979	10.00

Albums

Number	Title (A Side/B Side)	Yr	NM
REPRISE			
❑ RS 6436	The End of the Game	1970	20.00
SAIL			
❑ 0110	In the Skies	1979	10.00
❑ 0112	Little Dreamer	1980	10.00

GREEN, RUDY

See RUDY GREENE.

GREEN, VERNON, AND THE MEDALLIONS

See THE MEDALLIONS.

GREEN BULLFROG

Albums

Number	Title (A Side/B Side)	Yr	NM
DECCA			
❑ DL 75269	Green Bullfrog	1971	25.00

GREEN DAY

10-Inch Singles

Number	Title (A Side/B Side)	Yr	NM
REPRISE			
❑ 41656	Longview/Going to Pasalaqua (Live)//F.O.D. (Live)/Christy Road (Live)	1994	10.00
—Green vinyl 10-inch single in clear plastic sleeve with sticker			

45s

Number	Title (A Side/B Side)	Yr	NM
ADELINE			
❑ AR 014	Warning//Scumbag/Outsider	2001	5.00
—Small hole, yellow vinyl			
❑ AR 014 [PS]	Warning//Scumbag/Outsider	2001	5.00
—Sleeve also includes an insert			
❑ AR 019	Waiting/Maria	2001	5.00
—Large hole, pink marbled vinyl			
❑ AR 019 [PS]	Waiting/Maria	2001	5.00
—Sleeve includes lyric insert and record company fold-open flyer			
REPRISE			
❑ 16819	Minority/Jackass	2000	6.00
❑ 17941	When I Come Around/Basket Case	1995	6.00

Number	Title (A Side/B Side)	Yr	NM
7-Inch Extended Plays			
ADELINE			
❑ AR 013	Minority (Radio Version)/ Brat (Live)//Jackass/86 (Live)	2000	5.00
—Small hole, black vinyl			
❑ AR 013	Minority (Radio Version)/ Brat (Live)//Jackass/86 (Live)	2000	6.00
—Small hole, green vinyl			
❑ AR 013	Minority (Radio Version)/ Brat (Live)//Jackass/86 (Live)	2000	10.00
—Small hole, red vinyl			
❑ AR 013 [PS]	Minority	2000	6.00
LOOKOUT!			
❑ 17 [PS]	1,000 Hours	1989	3.00
❑ 17	1,000 Hours/Dry Ice//Only of You/The One I Want	1989	7.00
❑ 35	Paper Lanterns/Why Do You Want Him?//409 In Your Coffeemaker/Knowledge	1990	20.00
—First pressing of 1,000 on blue vinyl			
❑ 35	Paper Lanterns/Why Do You Want Him?//409 In Your Coffeemaker/Knowledge	1990	5.00
❑ 35 [PS]	Slappy	1990	7.00
Albums			
ADELINE			
❑ 012-1	Warning:	2000	18.00
❑ AR033-1 [(2)]	American Idiot	2006	30.00
LOOKOUT!			
❑ 22	39/Smooth	1990	16.00
❑ 46	Kerplunk	1992	20.00
REPRISE			
❑ 45529 [DJ]	Dookie	1994	35.00
—Promo version on clear green vinyl in plain white cover			
❑ 45529	Dookie	1994	20.00
—Original stock issue on black vinyl			
❑ 45529	Dookie	1995	20.00
—Reissue on pink vinyl			
❑ 45529 [DJ]	Dookie	1994	30.00
—Promo version on milky pale-green vinyl			
❑ 46046	Insomniac	1995	22.00

GREEN RIVER
Members of this band later joined MOTHER LOVE BONE, MUDHONEY and PEARL JAM.

Number	Title (A Side/B Side)	Yr	NM
45s			
TASQUE FORCE			
❑ ICP 01	Together We'll Never/ Ain't Nothing to Do	1984	130.00
—500 pressed on green vinyl; no picture sleeve			
Albums			
HOMESTEAD			
❑ 031	Come On Down	1985	16.00
—Originals do not have a UPC code (deduct 25% if UPC is there)			
SUB POP			
❑ 11 [EP]	Dry as a Bone	1987	35.00
—Later copies have pink inserts			
❑ 11 [EP]	Dry as a Bone	1987	50.00
—First 2,000 copies have yellow inserts			
❑ 15 [EP]	Rehab Doll	1988	25.00
❑ 15 [EP]	Rehab Doll	1988	35.00
—First 1,000 copies on green vinyl			

GREEN SLIME, THE

Number	Title (A Side/B Side)	Yr	NM
45s			
MGM			
❑ K14052	The Green Slime/Far Beyond the Stars	1969	10.00
❑ K14052 [PS]	The Green Slime/Far Beyond the Stars	1969	50.00

GREENBAUM, NORMAN
Also see DR. WEST'S MEDICINE SHOW AND JUG BAND.

Number	Title (A Side/B Side)	Yr	NM
45s			
GREGAR			
❑ 71-0107	Nancy Whiskey/Twentieth Century Fox	1969	10.00
REPRISE			
❑ 0739	Spirit in the Sky/Canned Ham	1971	4.00
—"Back to Back Hits" series			
❑ 0752	Children of Paradise/ School for Sweet Talk	1968	10.00
❑ 0818	Marcy/Children of Paradise	1969	10.00
❑ 0846	Jubilee/Skyline	1969	10.00
❑ 0885	Spirit in the Sky/Milk Cow	1969	8.00
❑ 0919	Canned Ham/Junior Cadillac	1970	6.00
❑ 0956	Rhode Island Red/I.J. Foxx	1970	6.00
❑ 0956 [PS]	Rhode Island Red/I.J. Foxx	1970	30.00
❑ 1008	California Earthquake/ Rhode Island Red	1971	6.00
❑ 1134	Dairy Queen/Petaluma	1972	6.00
Albums			
REPRISE			
❑ MS 2048	Petaluma	1972	25.00
❑ RS 6365	Spirit in the Sky	1969	15.00
❑ RS 6422	Back Home Again	1970	15.00

GREENBEATS, THE

Number	Title (A Side/B Side)	Yr	NM
45s			
JERDEN			
❑ 757	You Must Be the One/ If This World Were Mine	1965	12.00
❑ 763	So Sad/I'm on Fire	1965	12.00
PARKWAY			
❑ 939	You Must Be the One/ If This World Were Mine	1965	15.00

GREENBERG, STEVE

Number	Title (A Side/B Side)	Yr	NM
45s			
TRIP			
❑ 3000	Big Bruce/Run to You	1969	10.00

GREENE, BARBARA

Number	Title (A Side/B Side)	Yr	NM
45s			
ATCO			
❑ 6250	Long Tall Sally/Slippin' and Slidin'	1963	30.00
RENEE			
❑ 5001	Young Boy/I Should Have Treated You Right	1968	20.00
❑ 5004	A Lover's Plea/Our Love Is No Secret Now	1968	50.00
VIVID			
❑ 105	Young Boy/I Should Have Treated You Right	1968	25.00
—As "Barbara Green"			

GREENE, JACK

Number	Title (A Side/B Side)	Yr	NM
45s			
DECCA			
❑ 31768	Don't You Ever Get Tired/ The Hurt's On Me	1965	10.00
❑ 31856	Ever Since My Baby Went Away/ Room for One More Heartache	1965	8.00
❑ 32023	There Goes My Everything/ The Hardest Easy Thing	1966	8.00
❑ 32123	All the Time/Wanting You But Never Having You	1967	8.00
❑ 32190	What Locks the Door/ Left Over Feelings	1967	8.00
❑ 32261	You Are My Treasure/If God Can Forgive You, So Can I	1968	8.00
❑ 32352	Love Takes Care of Me/ Your Favorite Fool	1968	8.00
❑ 32423	Until My Dreams Come True/ We'll Try a Little Bit Harder	1968	8.00
❑ 32490	Statue of a Fool/There's More to Love	1969	8.00
❑ 32558	Back in the Arms of Love/ The Key That Fits Her Door	1969	8.00
❑ 32631	Lord Is That Me/Just a Little While Ago	1970	7.00
❑ 32699	The Whole World Comes to Me/ If This Is Love	1970	7.00
❑ 32755	Something Unseen/ What's the Use	1970	7.00
❑ 32823	There's a Whole Lot About a Woman (A Man Don't Know)/ Makin' Up His Mind	1971	7.00
❑ 32863	Hanging Over Me/The Birth of Our Love	1971	7.00
❑ 32939	If You Ever Need My Love/ Ask Me to Stay	1972	7.00
❑ 33008	Satisfaction/From Here On Out	1972	7.00
EMH			
❑ 0015	I'd Be Home On Christmas Day/ (B-side unknown)	1982	6.00
❑ 0016	The Jukebox Never Plays Home Sweet Home/I Don't Want to Be Alone Tonight	1983	5.00
❑ 0019	From Cotton to Satin/I'd Be Home on Christmas Day	1983	5.00
❑ 0025	Midnight Tennessee Woman/ Goin' Through Hell for an Angel	1983	5.00
❑ 0028	I'd Do As Much for You/Singing My Heart Out for You	1984	5.00
❑ 0031	Dying to Believe/There Goes My Everything	1984	5.00
❑ 0035	If It's Love (Then Bet It All)/ Statue of a Fool	1984	5.00
FIRSTLINE			
❑ 709	Devil's Den/It's Not the End of the World	1980	5.00
FRONTLINE			
❑ 704	Yours for the Taking/Sixty Days	1979	5.00
❑ 706	The Rock I'm Leaning On/ I'll Do It Better Next Time	1980	5.00
MCA			
❑ 40035	The Fool I've Been Today/ You Left Me	1973	5.00
❑ 40108	I Need Somebody Bad/Joyride	1973	5.00
❑ 40179	It's Time to Cross That Bridge/ Half That Much	1974	5.00
❑ 40263	Sing for the Good Times/ Something Seems to Fall Apart Inside	1974	5.00
❑ 40354	This Time The Hurtin's On Me/ Sawmill Depot	1974	5.00
❑ 40415	Cheatin' River/On the Way Home	1975	5.00
❑ 40481	He Little Thing'd Her Out of His Arms/Let Me Love You Back Together Again	1975	5.00
❑ 40526	Birmingham/My Long Gone Reason	1976	5.00
STEP ONE			
❑ 456	I'd Be Home on Christmas Day/ My Favorite Time of Year	199?	5.00
—B-side by Jack Robertson; red vinyl			
Albums			
DECCA			
❑ DL 4845 [M]	There Goes My Everything	1967	20.00
❑ DL 4904 [M]	All the Time	1967	20.00
❑ DL 4939 [M]	What Locks the Door	1968	25.00
❑ DL 4979 [M]	You Are My Treasure	1968	30.00
❑ DL 74845 [S]	There Goes My Everything	1967	15.00
❑ DL 74904 [S]	All the Time	1967	15.00
❑ DL 74939 [S]	What Locks the Door	1968	15.00
❑ DL 74979 [S]	You Are My Treasure	1968	15.00
❑ DL 75080	I Am Not Alone	1969	15.00
❑ DL 75124	Statue of a Fool	1969	15.00
❑ DL 75156	Back in the Arms of Love	1969	15.00
❑ DL 75188	Lord Is That Me	1970	15.00
❑ DL 75208	Greatest Hits	1970	15.00
❑ DL 75283	There's a Whole Lot About a Woman	1971	15.00
❑ DL 75308	Greene Country	1972	15.00
❑ ST-91433 [S]	What Locks the Door	1968	20.00
—Capitol Record Club edition			
❑ T-91433 [M]	What Locks the Door	1968	40.00
—Capitol Record Club edition			
MCA			
❑ 291	Greatest Hits	1973	12.00
—Reissue of Decca 75208			
❑ 295	Greene Country	1973	12.00
—Reissue of Decca 75308			
PICKWICK			
❑ SPC-6173	I Never Had It So Good	197?	10.00

GREENE, JACK, AND JEANNIE SEELY

Number	Title (A Side/B Side)	Yr	NM
45s			
DECCA			
❑ 32580	Wish I Didn't Have to Miss You/ My Tears Don't Show	1969	7.00
❑ 32898	Much Oblige/First Day	1971	7.00
❑ 32991	What in the World Has Gone Wrong with Our Love/Willingly	1972	6.00
Albums			
DECCA			
❑ DL 75171	Jack Greene and Jeannie Seely	1970	15.00
❑ DL 75392	Two for the Show	1972	15.00
MCA			
❑ 77	Two for the Show	1973	12.00
—Reissue of Decca 75392			

GREENE, RUDY

Number	Title (A Side/B Side)	Yr	NM
45s			
CHANCE			
❑ 1139	Love Is a Pain/No Need of Your Crying	1953	150.00
❑ 1146	The Letter/It's You I Love	1953	150.00
❑ 1151	I Had a Feeling/Meet Me Baby	1954	150.00
—Black vinyl			
❑ 1151	I Had a Feeling/Meet Me Baby	1954	400.00
—Red vinyl			
CLUB 51			
❑ 103	Highway No. 1/You Mean Everything to Me	1956	200.00
—With the Four Buddies			
EMBER			
❑ 1012	Juicy Fruit/You're the One for Me	1957	40.00
❑ 1020	Lonesome/Wild Life	1957	40.00
EXCELLO			
❑ 2074	Cool Lovin' Mama/ My Mumblin' Baby	1955	50.00
❑ 2090	Teeny Weeny Baby/ Queer Feeling	1956	50.00

Except when noted otherwise, VG = 25% of NM, and VG+ = 50% of NM. (Example: VG = $2.00, VG+ = $4.00 and NM = $8.00.)

GREENSLADE

Number	Title (A Side/B Side)	Yr	NM
Albums			
MERCURY			
❑ SRM-1-1015	Spy Guest	1974	16.00
❑ SRM-1-1025	Time and Tide	1975	16.00
WARNER BROS.			
❑ BS 2698	Greenslade	1973	16.00

GREENWICH, ELLIE

Also see THE RAINDROPS.

Number	Title (A Side/B Side)	Yr	NM
45s			
BELL			
❑ 855	Ain't That Peculiar/I Don't Want to Be Left Outside	1970	10.00
❑ 933	That Certain Someone/It's Like a Sad Old Kind of Movie	1970	10.00
MADISON			
❑ 160	Red Corvette/I Go, You Go	1961	30.00
—As "Ellie Gee"			
RED BIRD			
❑ 10-034	You Don't Know/Baby	1965	150.00
UNITED ARTISTS			
❑ 50151	I Want You to Be My Baby/Goodnight, Goodnight	1967	30.00
❑ 50278	A Long Time Comin'/Niki-Hoeky	1968	15.00
VERVE			
❑ 10719	Today I Met the Boy I'm Gonna Marry/Maybe I Know	1973	10.00
❑ 10724	Chapel of Love/River Deep, Mountain High	1973	10.00
Albums			
UNITED ARTISTS			
❑ UAS-6648	Ellie Greenwich Composes, Produces and Sings	1968	50.00
VERVE			
❑ V6-5091	Let It Be Written, Let It Be Sung	1973	25.00

GREENWOOD COUNTY SINGERS, THE

Includes "The Greenwood Singers" and "The Greenwoods," though we're not sure if "The Greenwoods" on Decca were the same group. VAN DYKE PARKS was a member of this group on the Kapp records.

Number	Title (A Side/B Side)	Yr	NM
45s			
KAPP			
❑ KJB-47	Seven Daffodils/Old Home Place	1965	8.00
❑ 591	Frankie and Johnny/Climb Up Sunshine Mountain	1964	8.00
❑ 591	The New Frankie and Johnny Song/Climb Up Sunshine Mountain	1964	10.00
❑ 623	Anne/Cake Walking Babies from Home	1964	8.00
❑ 660	Easter Rebellion/Trombone Cholly	1965	8.00
❑ 675	The Bridge Washed Out/Nobody Waved Goodbye	1965	8.00
❑ 688	Ballad of Cat Ballou/Blue Is the Wind	1965	8.00
❑ 742	Please Don't Sell My Daddy No More Wine/Southbound	1966	8.00
—As "The Greenwoods"			
❑ 760	Tear Down the Walls/Friends I Used to Know	1966	8.00
—As "The Greenwood Singers"			
❑ 774	The Eagle and Me/Eternal Love, Eternal Spring	1966	8.00
—As "The Greenwood Singers"			
Albums			
KAPP			
❑ KL 1362 [M]	The New Frankie and Johnny Song	1964	12.00
❑ KL 1362 [M]	The First Recordings by the Joyful Greenwood County Singers	1964	15.00
—Original title			
❑ KL 1422 [M]	Have You Heard	1965	12.00
❑ KL 1448 [M]	Ballad of Cat Ballou	1965	12.00
❑ KL 1487 [M]	Tear Down the Walls	1966	12.00
—As "The Greenwood Singers"			
❑ KS 3362 [S]	The New Frankie and Johnny Song	1964	15.00
❑ KS 3362 [S]	The First Recordings by the Joyful Greenwood County Singers	1964	20.00
—Original title			
❑ KS 3422 [S]	Have You Heard	1965	15.00
❑ KS 3448 [S]	Ballad of Cat Ballou	1965	15.00
❑ KS 3487 [S]	Tear Down the Walls	1966	15.00
—As "The Greenwood Singers"			
RCA VICTOR			
❑ LSP-4384	Return to Greenwood County	1970	15.00

GREENWOODS, THE

Probably not the same group as THE GREENWOOD COUNTY SINGERS.

Number	Title (A Side/B Side)	Yr	NM
45s			
DECCA			
❑ 31651	The Riddle/All My Trials	1964	8.00
❑ 31953	Silver Dagger/Harlan Breakdown	1965	8.00
Albums			
DECCA			
❑ DL 4496 [M]	Folk Instrumentals	1964	12.00
❑ DL 74496 [S]	Folk Instrumentals	1964	15.00

GREER, BIG JOHN

Number	Title (A Side/B Side)	Yr	NM
45s			
GROOVE			
❑ 0002	Bottle It Up and Go/You'll Never Be Mine	1954	40.00
❑ 0016	When the Roses Bloom in Lover's Lane/Too Long	1954	40.00
❑ 0038	We Wanna See Santa Do the Mambo/Wait Till After Christmas	1954	40.00
❑ 0108	Soon, Soon, Soon/I'm Glad for Your Sake	1955	40.00
❑ 0119	Come Back Maybellene/Night Crawlin'	1955	50.00
❑ 0131	A Man and a Woman/Blam	1955	60.00
—With the Four Students			
KING			
❑ 4878	Record Hop/Keep On Loving Me	1956	20.00
❑ 4941	Let Me Come Home/Come Back, Uncle John	1956	20.00
❑ 5006	Midnight Ramble/Sweet Slumber	1957	20.00
❑ 5057	Duck Walk/I Still Love You So	1957	20.00
RCA VICTOR			
❑ 47-4293	Have Another Drink/I'm Savin' All My Lovin'	1951	40.00
❑ 47-4348	Got You on My Mind/Woman Is a Five-Letter Word	1951	40.00
❑ 47-4484	Strong Red Whiskey/If You Let Me	1952	40.00
❑ 47-5037	I'm the Fat Man/Since You Went Away from Me	1952	40.00
❑ 47-5170	I'll Never Let You Go/You Played on My Piano	1953	40.00
❑ 47-5259	Ride Pretty Baby/Don't Worry 'Bout Me	1953	40.00
❑ 47-5531	Drinkin' Fool/Gettin' Mighty Lonesome for You	1953	40.00
❑ 50-0007	Drinkin' Wine Spo-Dee-O-Dee/Long Tall Gal	1949	70.00
—Orange vinyl			
❑ 50-0029	If I Told You Once/I Found a Dream	1949	70.00
—Orange vinyl			
❑ 50-0051	Rockin' Jenny Jones/I've Just Found Love	1950	70.00
—Orange vinyl			
❑ 50-0076	I'll Never Do That Again/A Fool Hasn't Got a Chance	1950	60.00
—Orange vinyl			
❑ 50-0096	Cheatin'/It's Better to Have Been Taken for Granted	1950	60.00
—Orange vinyl			
❑ 50-0104	Red Juice/Big John's a-Blowin'	1950	60.00
—Orange vinyl			
❑ 50-0108	Once There Lived a Fool/I Want Ya, I Need Ya	1951	50.00
❑ 50-0113	Why Did You Go/Our Wedding Time	1951	50.00
❑ 50-0125	Clambake Boogie/When You Love	1951	50.00
❑ 50-0137	Big Rock/How Can You Forget?	1951	50.00

GREER, DAN

Number	Title (A Side/B Side)	Yr	NM
45s			
BIG BEAT			
❑ 149	My Baby's Got a New Way/Wait for Me	196?	40.00
MGM			
❑ 14653	Hell Paso (Part I)/(Part II)	1973	10.00
❑ 14653 [PS]	Hell Paso (Part I)/(Part II)	1973	15.00
ODE			
❑ 66002	Curiosity Killed the Cat/I Remember Mama	1970	50.00
SOUNDS OF MEMPHIS			
❑ 702	Masquerade/Thanks to You	1972	12.00

GREGG, BOBBY

Number	Title (A Side/B Side)	Yr	NM
45s			
COTTON			
❑ 1003	The Jam Part 1/Part 2	1962	15.00
❑ 1006	Potato Peeler/Sweet Georgia Brown	1962	15.00
EPIC			
❑ 5-9541	Let's Jam Again Part 1/Part 2	1962	12.00
❑ 5-9579	Drummer Man/Walk On	1963	12.00
❑ 5-9601	Scarlet O'Hara/Take Me Out to the Ball Game	1963	12.00
❑ 5-9616	Kootanda/Kangaroo Part 2 (Tie Me Kangaroo Down, Sport)	1963	12.00
LAURIE			
❑ 3358	Theme from The Other Side/If You Wanna Be Happy	1966	10.00
VEEP			
❑ 1207	Hullabaloo/Charly Ba-Ba	1965	10.00

GREGORY, DICK

Number	Title (A Side/B Side)	Yr	NM
45s			
VEE JAY			
❑ 469	They Won't Hire Me/Benefit	1962	12.00
Albums			
COLPIX			
❑ CP 417 [M]	In Living Black and White	1961	25.00
❑ CP 420 [M]	East and West	1961	25.00
❑ CP 480 [M]	We All Have Problems	1964	25.00
GATEWAY			
❑ GLP 9007 [M]	My Brother's Keeper	1963	40.00
POPPY			
❑ PP-LA176-G2 [(2)]	Caught in the Act	1973	15.00
❑ PYS 40008	Dick Gregory On...	1970	15.00
❑ PYS 40011	Dick Gregory at the Village Gate	1972	15.00
❑ PYS 60001 [(2)]	The Light Side: The Dark Side	1969	20.00
❑ PYS 60004 [(2)]	Frankenstein	1970	15.00
❑ PYS 60005 [(2)]	Dick Gregory at Kent State	1971	15.00
TOMATO			
❑ 9001 [(3)]	The Best of Dick Gregory	1978	20.00
VEE JAY			
❑ LP 1093 [M]	Running for President	1964	25.00
❑ LP 4001 [M]	Dick Gregory Talks Turkey	1962	25.00
❑ LP 4005 [M]	Two Sides of Dick Gregory	1963	25.00

GREGORY, IVAN, AND THE BLUE NOTES

Number	Title (A Side/B Side)	Yr	NM
45s			
G&G			
❑ 110	Elvis Presley Blues/Kathy	1956	250.00

GRENFELL, JOYCE

Number	Title (A Side/B Side)	Yr	NM
Albums			
ELEKTRA			
❑ EKL-184 [M]	Presenting Joyce Grenfell	1960	30.00

GRIER, FRANKIE, QUARTET

Number	Title (A Side/B Side)	Yr	NM
45s			
SWAN			
❑ 4019	Oh, Gloria/Lonesome for You	1958	400.00

GRIER, ROOSEVELT

Most of his 1970s records, and scattered earlier ones, were as "Rosey Grier."

Number	Title (A Side/B Side)	Yr	NM
45s			
A			
❑ 105	Sincerely/Why Don't You Do Me Right	1959	25.00
❑ 110	Moonlight in Vermont/Smoky Morning	1960	25.00
A&M			
❑ 1457	Beautiful People/I'll Be Back Tomorrow	1973	150.00
❑ 1500	If You Hit a Good Lick, Lay On It/You're the Violin	1974	5.00
ABC			
❑ 11275	Rat Race/I Don't Want Nobody (To Lead Me On)	1970	30.00
AGP			
❑ 109	Bad News/Ring Around the World	1969	8.00
AMY			
❑ 11004	Who's Got the Ball (Y'All)/Halftime	1967	30.00
❑ 11015	High Society Woman/C'mon Cupid	1968	30.00
❑ 11029	Hard to Forget/People Make the World	1968	15.00
BATTLE			
❑ 45911	Why/Lover Set Me Free	1963	40.00
BELL			
❑ 45459	It's All Right to Cry/(B-side unknown)	1974	8.00
D-TOWN			
❑ 1058	Pizza Pie Man/Welcome to the Club	1965	200.00

G

Number	Title (A Side/B Side)	Yr	NM
LIBERTY			
❑ 55413	Struttin' 'n Twistin'/Let the Cool Wind Blow	1962	15.00
❑ 55453	The Mail Must Go Thru/ Your Has Been	1962	15.00
MGM			
❑ 13698	Slow Drag/Yesterday	1967	30.00
❑ 13840	Spanish Harlem/I'm Living Good	1967	12.00
RIC			
❑ 102	Fool, Fool, Fool/Since You've Been Gone	1964	20.00
❑ 112	Down So Long/In My Tenement	1964	300.00
SPINDLE TOP			
❑ 102	I'm Going Home/Jinny	1961	20.00
20TH CENTURY			
❑ 2212	Take the Time to Love Somebody/Your Love Is Right Up My Alley	1975	8.00
UNITED ARTISTS			
❑ 50893	Bring Back the Time/ Oh How I Miss You Baby	1972	40.00
YOUNGSTOWN			
❑ 609	Deputy Dog/(B-side unknown)	1966	30.00
Albums			
RIC			
❑ M-1008 [M]	Soul City	1964	20.00
❑ S-1008 [S]	Soul City	1964	25.00
WORD			
❑ WR-8342	Committed	1986	12.00

GRIEVES, GRANT

Number	Title (A Side/B Side)	Yr	NM
45s			
BIG K			
❑ 1002	Four in the Floor/Married Woman	196?	60.00

GRIFFIN, BUCK

Number	Title (A Side/B Side)	Yr	NM
45s			
HOLIDAY INN			
❑ 109	Pretty Lou/The Girl in Room 1209	1963	40.00
LIN			
❑ 1005	Meadowlark Boogie/It Don't Make No Never Mind	1954	60.00
❑ 1007	Rollin' Tears/One Day After Pay Day	1955	60.00
❑ 1008	Going Home, All Alone/ Lookin' for the Green	1955	60.00
❑ 1014	Next to Mine/Lord, Give Me Strength	1955	60.00
❑ 1015	Bawlin' and Squallin'/ Let's Elope, Baby	1955	75.00
❑ 1016	Go-Stop-O/Cochise	1955	100.00
❑ 1018	Little Dan/Neither Do I	1956	60.00
METRO			
❑ 20007	The Party/Every Night	1958	30.00
MGM			
❑ 12284	Stutterin' Papa/Watchin' the 7:10 Roll By	1956	100.00
❑ 12439	Bow My Back/Old Bee Tree	1957	80.00
❑ 12597	Jessie Lee/You'll Never Come Back	1957	80.00

GRIFFIN, JIMMY

Some of these were credited to "James Griffin." Also see BREAD.

Number	Title (A Side/B Side)	Yr	NM
45s			
IMPERIAL			
❑ 66108	These Are the Times/Walking to New Orleans	1965	12.00
❑ 66152	He Will Break Your Heart/Hard Row to Hoe	1965	12.00
POLYDOR			
❑ 14213	Breakin' Up Is Easy/ Melody Maker	1973	5.00
❑ 14236	She Knows/Beachwood Band	1974	5.00
❑ 14282	Treat Her Right/How Do You Say Goodbye	1975	5.00
REPRISE			
❑ 0268	All My Loving/My Baby Made Me Cry	1964	15.00
❑ 0280	Gotta Lotta Love/Running to You	1964	15.00
❑ 0304	You're Nobody Till Somebody Loves You/Try	1964	15.00
❑ 20114	Girls Grow Up Faster Than Boys/It's a Free Country	1962	20.00
❑ 20161	What Kind of Girl Are You/ A Little Like Lovin' You	1963	20.00
❑ 20178	Love Letters in the Sand/ Summer Holiday	1963	20.00
❑ 20221	Little Miss Cool/Marie Is Moving	1963	20.00
VIVA			
❑ 611	Miracle Worker/Looking So Much Better	1967	10.00
❑ 627	Thank You Love/ Light of Your Mind	1968	10.00
❑ 642	Miracle Worker/Thank You Love	1970	10.00
Albums			
POLYDOR			
❑ PD 6018	James Griffin and Co.	1973	15.00
REPRISE			
❑ R-6091 [M]	Summer Holiday	1963	50.00
❑ R9-6091 [S]	Summer Holiday	1963	60.00

GRIFFINS, THE

Number	Title (A Side/B Side)	Yr	NM
45s			
MERCURY			
❑ 70558	I Swear By All the Stars Above/ Sing to Me	1955	120.00
❑ 70650	Bad Little Girl/Scheming	1955	120.00
❑ 70913	My Baby's Gone/Why Must You Go	1956	40.00
WING			
❑ 90067	Forever More/Leave It to Me	1956	200.00

GRIFFITH, ANDY

Number	Title (A Side/B Side)	Yr	NM
45s			
CAPITOL			
❑ 2571	Romeo and Juliet (Part 1)/ Romeo and Juliet (Part 2)	1969	8.00
❑ F2693	What It Was, Was Football (Part 1)/What It Was, Was Football (Part 2)	195?	25.00
—Later pressings (purple Capitol label, large logo at top) as "Andy Griffith"			
❑ F2693	What It Was, Was Football (Part 1)/What It Was, Was Football (Part 2)	1953	30.00
—Original pressings as "Deacon Andy Griffith"			
❑ F2696	Romeo and Juliet (Part 1)/ Romeo and Juliet (Part 2)	195?	25.00
—Later pressings (purple label, large Capitol logo at top) as "Andy Griffith"			
❑ F2696	Romeo and Juliet (Part 1)/ Romeo and Juliet (Part 2)	1954	30.00
—Original pressings as "Deacon Andy Griffith"			
❑ F2855	Swan Lake (Part 1)/ Swan Lake (Part 2)	1954	25.00
❑ F3057	Make Yourself Comfortable/ Ko Ko Mo (I Love You So)	1955	20.00
❑ F3402	Opera Carmen (Part 1)/ Opera Carmen (Part 2)	1956	25.00
❑ F3498	Standing on the Corner/ No Time for Sergeants	1956	20.00
❑ F3705	Mama Guitar/A Face in the Crowd	1957	20.00
❑ F3706	Free Man in the Morning/Just a Closer Walk with Thee	1957	20.00
❑ F3872	Silhouettes/Conversation with a Mule	1958	20.00
❑ F3938	Andy's Lament/Thank Heaven for Little Girls	1958	20.00
❑ F3990	Love Poems: To the Lovely Juanita Beasley/ Togetherness	1958	20.00
❑ F4052	Midnight Special/She's Bad, Bad Business	1958	20.00
❑ F4157	Hamlet (Part 1)/Hamlet (Part 2)	1959	20.00
❑ F4204	Once Knew a Fella/ Don't Look Back	1959	15.00
❑ 4236	Look at the Son-Shine/ My Dog Underdog	1976	6.00
❑ 4539	New River Train/ (B-side unknown)	1961	15.00
❑ 4684	Flop Eared Mule/A Good Man Is Hard to Find	1962	15.00
❑ 4848	The Pool Table/Whistling Ping Pong Game	1962	15.00
❑ 5073	Andy and Cleopatra (Part 1)/ Andy and Cleopatra (Part 2)	1963	15.00
COLONIAL			
❑ E3	What It Was, Was Football (Part 1)/What It Was, Was Football (Part 2)	1953	60.00
COLUMBIA			
❑ 4-45711	Lead Me to That Rock/ Somebody Bigger Than You and I	1972	8.00
7-Inch Extended Plays			
CAPITOL			
❑ EAP 1-498	What It Was, Was Football/ Romeo and Juliet	1954	40.00
❑ EAP 1-498 [PS]	What It Was, Was Football!	1954	40.00
❑ EAP 1-630	Make Yourself Comfortable/ Ko Ko Mo//Swan Lake	1955	30.00
❑ EAP 1-630 [PS]	Make Yourself Comfortable	1955	30.00
Albums			
CAPITOL			
❑ T 962 [M]	Just for Laughs	1958	40.00
❑ ST 1105 [S]	Andy Griffith Shouts the Blues and Old Timey Songs	1959	50.00
❑ T 1105 [M]	Andy Griffith Shouts the Blues and Old Timey Songs	1959	40.00
❑ ST 1215 [S]	This Here Andy Griffith	1959	40.00
❑ T 1215 [M]	This Here Andy Griffith	1959	30.00
❑ ST 1611 [S]	Songs, Themes and Laughs from The Andy Griffith Show	1961	120.00
❑ T 1611 [M]	Songs, Themes and Laughs from The Andy Griffith Show	1961	80.00
❑ ST 2066 [S]	Andy and Cleopatra	1964	25.00
❑ T 2066 [M]	Andy and Cleopatra	1964	20.00

GRIFFITH, NANCI

Number	Title (A Side/B Side)	Yr	NM
45s			
MCA			
❑ 53009	Lone Star State of Mind/ There's a Light Beyond the Woods (Mary Margaret)	1987	4.00
❑ 53082	Trouble in the Fields/ Love in a Memory	1987	4.00
❑ 53147	Cold Heart, Closed Minds/ Ford Econoline	1987	4.00
❑ 53184	Never Mind/From a Distance	1987	5.00
❑ 53306	I Knew Love/So Long Ago	1988	4.00
❑ 53374	Anyone Can Be Someone's Fool/Love Wore a Halo (Back Before the War)	1988	4.00
❑ 53700	It's a Hard Life Wherever You Go/From a Distance	1989	4.00
❑ 53761	I Don't Want to Talk About Love/ Drive-In Movies and Dashboard Lights	1989	4.00
PHILO			
❑ 1096	Once in a Very Blue Moon/ (B-side unknown)	1986	6.00
Albums			
B.F. DEAL			
❑ BFD 9	There's a Light Beyond These Woods	1978	50.00
ELEKTRA			
❑ 62015	Blue Roses from the Moons	1997	12.00
FEATHERBED			
❑ FB 902	Poet in My Window	1982	20.00
❑ FB 903	There's a Light Beyond These Woods	1982	20.00
MCA			
❑ 5927	Lone Star State of Mind	1987	8.00
❑ 6319	Storms	1989	10.00
❑ 42102	Little Love Affairs	1988	8.00
❑ 42255	One Fair Summer Evening	1988	8.00
PHILO			
❑ PH-1096	Once in a Very Blue Moon	1984	12.00
❑ PH-1097	There's a Light Beyond These Woods	1986	12.00
❑ PH-1098	Poet in My Window	1986	12.00
❑ PH-1109	Last of the True Believers	1986	12.00

GRIFFITH, PEGGI

Number	Title (A Side/B Side)	Yr	NM
45s			
DOLTON			
❑ 35	Lovely Girl/You're In My Dreams to Stay	1961	20.00

GRIN

Features NILS LOFGREN.

Number	Title (A Side/B Side)	Yr	NM
45s			
A&M			
❑ 1502	Beggar's Day/You're the Weight	1974	4.00
SPINDIZZY			
❑ ZS7 4001	If I Were a Song/See What a Love Can Do	1971	6.00
❑ ZS7 4002	Everybody's Missing the Sun/ Eighteen-Faced Lover	1971	6.00
❑ ZS7 4005	White Lies/Just to Have You	1972	6.00
❑ ZS7 4006	End Unkind/Slippery Fingers	1972	6.00
THUNDER			
❑ 4000	We All Sung Together/ See What a Love Can Do	1970	8.00
Albums			
A&M			
❑ SP-4415	Gone Crazy	1973	10.00
COLUMBIA LIMITED EDITION			
❑ LE 10265	All Out	197?	10.00
—Remixed version on Columbia's brown-label "Limited Edition" series			
EPIC			
❑ PE 34247	The Best of Grin	1976	10.00
—Without bar code on back			
❑ PE 34247	The Best of Grin	198?	8.00
—With bar code on back			

Except when noted otherwise, VG = 25% of NM, and VG+ = 50% of NM. (Example: VG = $2.00, VG+ = $4.00 and NM = $8.00.)

Number | Title (A Side/B Side) | Yr | NM

SPINDIZZY
❑ Z 30321 | Grin | 1971 | 12.00
❑ Z 31038 | 1 + 1 | 1972 | 12.00
❑ KZ 31701 | All Out | 1973 | 12.00

GRINER, LINDA
45s
MOTOWN
❑ 1037 | Good-By Cruel Love/Envious | 1963 | 400.00
—With corrected A-side title
❑ 1037 | Good-By Cruel World/Envious | 1963 | 600.00
—With incorrect A-side title

GRISMAN, DAVID
Albums
HORIZON
❑ SP-731 | Hot Dawg | 1979 | 16.00
ROUNDER
❑ 0069 | The Rounder Album | 1976 | 16.00
❑ 0169 | Here Today | 198? | 10.00
❑ 0190 | Acoustic Christmas | 1983 | 12.00
❑ 0251/2 [(2)] | Home Is Where the Heart Is | 1988 | 12.00
SUGAR HILL
❑ SH-3713 | Early Dawg | 1980 | 10.00
WARNER BROS.
❑ BSK 3469 | David Grisman Quintet '80 | 1980 | 10.00
❑ BSK 3618 | Mondo Mando | 1982 | 10.00
❑ 23804 | Dawg Jazz | 1983 | 10.00
ZEBRA/ACOUSTIC
❑ ZEA-6153 | Acousticity | 1986 | 10.00

GRODECK WHIPPERJENNY
Albums
PEOPLE
❑ 3000 | Grodeck Whipperjenny | 1969 | 200.00

GROGAN, TOBY
45s
VEE JAY
❑ 560 | Angel/Just a Friend | 1963 | 30.00
—The Four Seasons sing on this record.

GROOTNA
45s
COLUMBIA
❑ 45461 | Full Time Woman/Is It All Over | 1971 | 8.00
❑ 45538 | Waitin' for My Ship/That's What You Get | 1972 | 8.00
Albums
COLUMBIA
❑ C 31033 | Grootna | 1971 | 20.00

GROOV-U
Albums
GATEWAY
❑ GLP-3010 | Groov-U On Campus | 196? | 40.00

GROOVIE GOOLIES, THE
45s
RCA VICTOR
❑ 74-0383 | The First Annual Semi-Formal Combination Celebration Meet-the-Monster Population Party/Save Your Good Lovin' for Me | 1970 | 10.00
Albums
RCA VICTOR
❑ LSP-4420 | The Groovie Goolies | 1970 | 25.00

GROSS, HENRY
45s
A&M
❑ 1494 | Fly Away/Simone | 1974 | 4.00
❑ 1534 | Come On Say It/Ever Lovin' Days | 1974 | 4.00
❑ 1613 | Meet Me on the Corner/With the Sleep in My Eyes | 1974 | 4.00
❑ 1682 | One More Tomorrow/Evergreen | 1975 | 4.00
❑ 1701 | Travelin' Time/All My Love | 1975 | 4.00
ABC
❑ 11322 | New York City/My Sunshine | 1972 | 6.00
❑ 11334 | Close My Eyes/Prayer for All | 1972 | 6.00
CAPITOL
❑ 4946 | Better Now We're Friends/You're My Ride Home | 1980 | 4.00
❑ 4980 | How Long Is Forever/I Love You Now | 1981 | 4.00
LIFESONG
❑ 1761 | Only the Beautiful/Creepin' Jenny | 1978 | 4.00
❑ 1769 | Love Is the Stuff/Shake Down Your Love | 1978 | 4.00
❑ 45002 | Shannon/Pokey | 1976 | 5.00
❑ 45008 | Springtime Mama/Overton Square | 1976 | 4.00
❑ 45014 | Someday (I Didn't Want to Have to Be the One)/Lincoln Road | 1976 | 4.00
❑ 45023 | String of Hearts/Painting My Love Song | 1977 | 4.00
❑ 45024 | What a Sound/Painting My Love Song | 1977 | 4.00
Albums
A&M
❑ SP-4416 | Henry Gross | 1973 | 12.00
❑ SP-4502 | Plug Me Into Something | 1974 | 12.00
ABC
❑ X-747 | Henry Gross | 1971 | 15.00
CAPITOL
❑ ST 12113 | What's in a Name | 1980 | 10.00
LIFESONG
❑ LS 6002 | Release | 1976 | 10.00
❑ LS 6010 | Show Me to the Stage | 1977 | 10.00
❑ PZ 34995 | Release | 1978 | 8.00
—Reissue of 6002
❑ PZ 35002 | Show Me to the Stage | 1978 | 8.00
—Reissue of 6010
❑ JZ 35280 | Love Is the Stuff | 1978 | 10.00

GROSS SISTERS, THE
45s
CHECKER
❑ 932 | Oom Baby!/My Baby Ain't Nothin' But Bad | 1959 | 40.00

GROUNDHOGS, THE
Featuring Tony McPhee.
45s
INTERPHON
❑ 7715 | Rock Me/Shake It | 1965 | 12.00
LIBERTY
❑ 56205 | Ship on the Ocean/Sailor | 1970 | 8.00
Albums
CLEVE
❑ CH-82871 | The Groundhogs with John Lee Hooker and John Mayall | 196? | 100.00
IMPERIAL
❑ LP-12452 | Blues Obituary | 1969 | 40.00
LIBERTY
❑ LST-7644 | Thank Christ for the Bomb | 1970 | 30.00
UNITED ARTISTS
❑ UA-LA008-F | Hogwash | 1973 | 20.00
❑ UA-LA603-G | Crosscut Saw | 1976 | 20.00
❑ UA-LA680-G | Black Diamond | 1976 | 20.00
❑ UAS-5513 | The Groundhogs Split | 1971 | 20.00
❑ UAS-5570 | Who Will Save the World | 1972 | 20.00
WORLD PACIFIC
❑ WPS-21892 | Scratching the Surface | 1968 | 40.00

GROUNDSPEED
45s
DECCA
❑ 32344 | In a Dream/L-12 East | 1968 | 25.00

GROUP, THE
Probably more than one group.
45s
WARNER BROS.
❑ 5840 | Baby, Baby It's You/Can't Get Enough of Your Love | 1966 | 12.00
Albums
BELL
❑ 6038 | The Group | 1970 | 20.00
RCA VICTOR
❑ LPM-2663 [M] | The Group | 1963 | 20.00
❑ LSP-2663 [S] | The Group | 1963 | 25.00

GROUP "B"
Early incarnation of BLUE CHEER.
45s
SCORPIO
❑ 402 | Stop Calling Me/She's Gone | 1967 | 25.00
❑ 406 | I Know Your Name Girl/I Never Really Knew | 1967 | 25.00

GROUP IMAGE, THE
Albums
COMMUNITY
❑ A-101 | A Mouth in the Clouds | 1968 | 30.00

GROUP ONE
Albums
RCA VICTOR
❑ LPM-3524 [M] | Brothers Go to Mothers and Others | 1966 | 15.00
❑ LSP-3524 [S] | Brothers Go to Mothers and Others | 1966 | 20.00

GROUP THERAPY
45s
CANTERBURY
❑ 517 | Magic in the Air/Bad News | 1967 | 12.00
MERCURY
❑ 72702 | Thoughts/Come On | 1967 | 12.00
PHILIPS
❑ 40598 | Can't Stop Lovin' You Baby/I Must Go | 1969 | 8.00
RCA VICTOR
❑ 47-9527 | People Get Ready/Who'll Be Next | 1968 | 8.00
Albums
PHILIPS
❑ PHS 600303 | 37 Minutes of Group Therapy | 1969 | 15.00
RCA VICTOR
❑ LPM-3976 [M] | People Get Ready for Group Therapy | 1968 | 40.00
❑ LSP-3976 [S] | People Get Ready for Group Therapy | 1968 | 20.00

GROUPIES, THE
45s
ATCO
❑ 6393 | I'm a Hog for You/Primitive | 1966 | 30.00

GROWING CONCERN, THE
45s
MAINSTREAM
❑ 685 | Tomorrow Has Been Canceled/A Boy I Once Knew Well | 1968 | 30.00
Albums
MAINSTREAM
❑ S-6108 [S] | The Growing Concern | 1968 | 250.00
❑ 56108 [M] | The Growing Concern | 1968 | 80.00

GROWL
Albums
DISCREET
❑ DS 2209 | Growl | 1974 | 200.00

GRUNDY, DAVE, COMBO
45s
HIT
❑ 32 | Green Onions/I Remember You | 1962 | 8.00
—B-side by Ed Mendel

GRUNION HUNTERS, THE
45s
HIGHLAND
❑ 1035 | The Four-Eyed, Tongue-Tied, Swimmin' Surfer Biter/Sing Along to the Swimmin' Surfer Biter | 1963 | 40.00

GRUNIONS, THE
45s
JOCKO
❑ 505 | Surfin' Psycho/Big Noise from Winnetka | 1963 | 50.00

GRYPHON
Albums
(NO LABEL)
❑ 12497 | Gryphon | 1973 | 80.00
BELL
❑ 1316 | Red Queen to Gryphon Three | 1974 | 18.00

GTR
Also see YES; GENESIS.
45s
ARISTA
❑ 9470 | When the Heart Rules the Mind/Reach Out (Never Say No) | 1986 | 3.00
❑ 9470 [PS] | When the Heart Rules the Mind/Reach Out (Never Say No) | 1986 | 3.00
❑ 9512 | The Hunter/Sketches in the Sun | 1986 | 3.00
❑ 9512 [PS] | The Hunter/Sketches in the Sun | 1986 | 3.00
Albums
ARISTA
❑ AL8-8400 | GTR | 1986 | 8.00

GUADALCANAL DIARY

12-Inch Singles

ELEKTRA

Number	Title (A Side/B Side)	Yr	NM
❑ ED 5071 [DJ]	Trail of Tears (same on both sides)	1985	6.00
❑ ED5071 [DJ]	Trail of Tears (same on both sides)	1985	6.00
❑ ED 5107 [DJ]	Watusi Rodeo (same on both sides)	1985	6.00
❑ ED5155 [DJ]	Lonely Street (same on both sides)	1986	5.00
❑ ED 5155 [DJ]	Lonely Street (same on both sides)	1986	6.00
❑ ED5172 [DJ]	Spirit Train (same on both sides)	1986	5.00
❑ ED 5172 [DJ]	Cattle Prod/Spirit Train	1986	6.00
❑ ED5256 [DJ]	Litany (same on both sides)	1987	5.00
❑ ED 5256 [DJ]	Litany (same on both sides)	1987	8.00
❑ ED5272 [DJ]	Lips of Steel (same on both sides)	1987	5.00
❑ ED 5272 [DJ]	Lips of Steel (same on both sides)	1987	6.00
❑ ED 5291 [DJ]	Get Over It (same on both sides)	1987	5.00
❑ ED5291 [DJ]	Get Over It (same on both sides)	1987	5.00
❑ ED5359 [DJ]	Always Saturday (Edit)/Always Saturday (LP Version)	1989	5.00
❑ ED 5359 [DJ]	Always Saturday (Edit) (LP Version)	1989	8.00
❑ ED5379 [DJ]	Pretty Is As Pretty Does (same on both sides)	1989	5.00
❑ ED 5379 [DJ]	Pretty Is As Pretty Does (same on both sides)	1989	6.00

45s

ELEKTRA

Number	Title (A Side/B Side)	Yr	NM
❑ 69316	Always Saturday/Kiss of Fire	1989	4.00
❑ 69316 [PS]	Always Saturday/Kiss of Fire	1989	6.00

Albums

DB

Number	Title (A Side/B Side)	Yr	NM
❑ 73	Walking in the Shadow of the Big Man	1984	15.00

ELEKTRA

Number	Title (A Side/B Side)	Yr	NM
❑ 60429	Walking in the Shadow of the Big Man	1985	10.00
❑ 60478	Jamboree	1986	10.00
❑ 60752	2X4	1987	10.00
❑ 60848 [DJ]	Flip-Flop	1989	10.00

—Promo-only white label audiophile vinyl

Number	Title (A Side/B Side)	Yr	NM
❑ 60848	Flip-Flop	1989	10.00
❑ 60848 [DJ]	Flip-Flop	1989	12.00

—Promo-only white label audiophile vinyl

ENTERTAINMENT ON DISC

Number	Title (A Side/B Side)	Yr	NM
❑ EOD 102 [EP]	Watusi Rodeo	1983	25.00

GUARD, DAVE, AND THE WHISKEYHILL SINGERS

Dave Guard had split from THE KINGSTON TRIO.

45s

CAPITOL

Number	Title (A Side/B Side)	Yr	NM
❑ 4787	Plane Wreck at Los Gatos/ Ride On, Railroad Bill	1962	10.00

Albums

CAPITOL

Number	Title (A Side/B Side)	Yr	NM
❑ ST 1728 [S]	Dave Guard and the Whiskeyhill Singers	1962	25.00
❑ T 1728 [M]	Dave Guard and the Whiskeyhill Singers	1962	20.00

GUESS WHO, THE

Also see CHAD ALLAN; RANDY BACHMAN; BURTON CUMMINGS.

45s

AMY

Number	Title (A Side/B Side)	Yr	NM
❑ 967	And She's Mine/All Right	1966	20.00

—The existence of stock copies of this record has been questioned

Number	Title (A Side/B Side)	Yr	NM
❑ 976	His Girl/It's My Pride	1967	30.00

—Price is for stock copy; promos go for less

FONTANA

Number	Title (A Side/B Side)	Yr	NM
❑ 1597	This Time Long Ago/There's No Getting Away from It	1967	30.00

HILLTAK

Number	Title (A Side/B Side)	Yr	NM
❑ 7803	C'mon Little Mama/Moon Wave Maker	1979	6.00
❑ 7807	Sweet Young Thing/It's Getting Pretty Bad	1979	6.00

RCA VICTOR

Number	Title (A Side/B Side)	Yr	NM
❑ 74-0102	These Eyes/Lightfoot	1969	6.00
❑ 74-0195	Laughing/Undun	1969	6.00
❑ 74-0300	No Time/Proper Stranger	1969	6.00
❑ 74-0325	American Woman/ No Sugar Tonight	1970	5.00
❑ 74-0367	Hand Me Down World/ Runnin' Down the Street	1970	5.00
❑ 74-0388	Share the Land/Bus Rider	1970	5.00
❑ 74-0388 [PS]	Share the Land/Bus Rider	1970	10.00
❑ 74-0414	Hang On to Your Life/ Do You Miss Me, Darlin'?	1970	5.00
❑ 74-0414 [PS]	Hang On to Your Life/ Do You Miss Me, Darlin'?	1970	25.00
❑ 74-0458	Albert Flasher/Broken	1971	5.00
❑ 74-0522	Rain Dance/One Divided	1971	5.00
❑ 74-0578	Sour Suite/Life in the Bloodstream	1971	5.00
❑ 74-0659	Heartbroken Bopper/ Arrividerci Girl	1972	5.00
❑ 74-0708	Guns, Guns, Guns/Heaven Only Moved Once Yesterday	1972	5.00
❑ 74-0803	Runnin' Back to Saskatoon/ New Mother Nature	1972	5.00
❑ 74-0880	Follow Your Daughter Home/ Bye Bye Babe	1973	5.00
❑ 74-0926	The Watcher/Orly	1973	5.00
❑ 74-0977	Lie Down/Glamour Boy	1973	5.00
❑ APBO-0217	Star Baby/Musicione	1974	5.00
❑ SPS-45-223 [DJ]	Friends of Mine (Part 1)/ Friends of Mine (Part 2)	1969	12.00
❑ APBO-0324	Clap for the Wolfman/Road Food	1974	5.00
❑ PB-10075	Dancin' Fool/Seems Like I Can't Live With You, But I Can't Live Without You	1974	5.00
❑ GB-10161	Clap for the Wolfman/Star Baby	1975	4.00

—Gold Standard Series

Number	Title (A Side/B Side)	Yr	NM
❑ PB-10216	Loves Me Like a Brother/ Hoe Down Time	1975	5.00
❑ PB-10360	Dreams/Rosanne	1975	5.00
❑ PB-10410	When the Band Was Singin' (Shakin' All Over)/Women	1975	6.00
❑ PB-10716	Silver Bird/Runnin' Down the Street	1976	12.00

SCEPTER

Number	Title (A Side/B Side)	Yr	NM
❑ 1295	Shakin' All Over/Till We Kissed	1965	15.00
❑ 1295	Shakin' All Over/ Monkey in a Cage	1965	30.00

—B-side by the Discotays

Number	Title (A Side/B Side)	Yr	NM
❑ 12108	Hey Ho What You Do to Me/ Goodnight Goodnight	1965	15.00
❑ 12118	Hurting Each Other/ Baby's Birthday	1965	20.00
❑ 12131	Believe Me/Baby Feelin'	1966	20.00
❑ 12144	One Day/Clock on the Wall	1966	20.00

Albums

COMPLEAT

Number	Title (A Side/B Side)	Yr	NM
❑ 672012-1 [(2)]	The Best of the Gues Who, Live	1986	20.00

HILLTAK

Number	Title (A Side/B Side)	Yr	NM
❑ HT 19227	All This for a Song	1979	12.00

MGM

Number	Title (A Side/B Side)	Yr	NM
❑ SE-4645	The Guess Who	1969	15.00

—Compilation of pre-RCA Victor recordings

P.I.P.

Number	Title (A Side/B Side)	Yr	NM
❑ 6806	The Guess Who Play Pure Guess Who	197?	12.00

PICKWICK

Number	Title (A Side/B Side)	Yr	NM
❑ SPC-3246	Wild One	1970	12.00

—Available in two different covers - "bike" cover and "girl on car" cover; both same price

PRIDE

Number	Title (A Side/B Side)	Yr	NM
❑ PRD 0012	The History of the Guess Who	197?	12.00

RCA

Number	Title (A Side/B Side)	Yr	NM
❑ 7622-1-R	The Greatest of the Guess Who	1987	10.00

—Late reissue

RCA VICTOR

Number	Title (A Side/B Side)	Yr	NM
❑ APD1-0130 [Q]	#10	1974	25.00
❑ APL1-0130	#10	1973	15.00
❑ AFL1-0269	The Best of the Guess Who, Vol. II	1977	10.00

—Reissue with new prefix

Number	Title (A Side/B Side)	Yr	NM
❑ APD1-0269 [Q]	The Best of the Guess Who, Vol. II	1974	25.00
❑ APL1-0269	The Best of the Guess Who, Vol. II	1973	15.00
❑ APD1-0405 [Q]	Road Food	1974	25.00
❑ APL1-0405	Road Food	1974	15.00
❑ CPD1-0636 [Q]	Flavours	1975	25.00
❑ CPL1-0636	Flavours	1975	15.00
❑ ANL1-0983	Canned Wheat Packed By the Guess Who	1975	10.00

—Reissue of LSP-4157

Number	Title (A Side/B Side)	Yr	NM
❑ APD1-0995 [Q]	Power in the Music	1975	25.00
❑ APL1-0995	Power in the Music	1975	15.00
❑ LSPX-1004	The Best of the Guess Who	1971	15.00
❑ ANL1-1117	Wheatfield Soul	1975	10.00

—Reissue of LSP-4141

Number	Title (A Side/B Side)	Yr	NM
❑ APL1-1778	The Way They Were	1976	15.00
❑ APL1-2253	The Greatest of the Guess Who	1977	15.00
❑ AFL1-2594	The Best of the Guess Who	1978	10.00

—Reissue of LSPX-1004

Number	Title (A Side/B Side)	Yr	NM
❑ AYL1-3662	The Best of the Guess Who	1979	8.00

—"Best Buy Series" reissue

Number	Title (A Side/B Side)	Yr	NM
❑ AYL1-3673	American Woman	1979	8.00

—"Best Buy Series" reissue

Number	Title (A Side/B Side)	Yr	NM
❑ AYL1-3746	The Greatest of the Guess Who	1980	8.00

—"Best Buy Series" reissue

Number	Title (A Side/B Side)	Yr	NM
❑ LSP-4141	Wheatfield Soul	1969	20.00

—Orange label, non-flexible vinyl

Number	Title (A Side/B Side)	Yr	NM
❑ LSP-4141	Wheatfield Soul	1971	12.00

—Orange label, flexible vinyl

Number	Title (A Side/B Side)	Yr	NM
❑ LSP-4157	Canned Wheat Packed By the Guess Who	1969	20.00

—Orange label, non-flexible vinyl

Number	Title (A Side/B Side)	Yr	NM
❑ LSP-4157	Canned Wheat Packed By the Guess Who	1971	12.00

—Orange label, flexible vinyl

Number	Title (A Side/B Side)	Yr	NM
❑ AFL1-4266	American Woman	1977	10.00

—Reissue with new prefix

Number	Title (A Side/B Side)	Yr	NM
❑ LSP-4266	American Woman	1970	20.00

—Orange label, non-flexible vinyl

Number	Title (A Side/B Side)	Yr	NM
❑ LSP-4266	American Woman	1971	12.00

—Orange label, flexible vinyl

Number	Title (A Side/B Side)	Yr	NM
❑ LSP-4359	Share the Land	1970	20.00

—Orange label, non-flexible vinyl

Number	Title (A Side/B Side)	Yr	NM
❑ LSP-4359	Share the Land	1971	12.00

—Orange label, flexible vinyl

Number	Title (A Side/B Side)	Yr	NM
❑ LSP-4574	So Long, Bannatyne	1971	15.00
❑ LSP-4602	Rockin'	1972	15.00
❑ LSP-4779	Live at the Paramount (Seattle)	1972	25.00
❑ LSP-4830	Artificial Paradise	1973	15.00

—Add 1/3 if paper bag is with package

SCEPTER

Number	Title (A Side/B Side)	Yr	NM
❑ SP-533 [M]	Shakin' All Over	1966	40.00
❑ SPS-533 [P]	Shakin' All Over	1966	25.00

—The above lists the artist as "The Guess Who's Chad Allan & The Expressions" on the cover

SPRINGBOARD

Number	Title (A Side/B Side)	Yr	NM
❑ SPB-4022	Shakin' All Over	1972	10.00

SUNDAZED

Number	Title (A Side/B Side)	Yr	NM
❑ LP 5113 [(2)]	Shakin' All Over	2001	15.00

WAND

Number	Title (A Side/B Side)	Yr	NM
❑ WDS-691 [P]	Born in Canada	1969	15.00

—Reissue of Scepter LP; three tracks are rechanneled

GUIDED BY VOICES

Albums

E RECORDS

Number	Title (A Side/B Side)	Yr	NM
❑ GBV 0001	Devil Between My Toes	1987	300.00

HALO

Number	Title (A Side/B Side)	Yr	NM
❑ 1	Sandbox	1987	75.00
❑ 2	Self Inflicted Aerial Nostalgia	1989	150.00

I WANNA

Number	Title (A Side/B Side)	Yr	NM
❑ (no #) [EP]	Forever Since Breakfast	1986	150.00

MATADOR

Number	Title (A Side/B Side)	Yr	NM
❑ OLE-123	Alien Lanes	1995	10.00
❑ OLE-161 [(2)]	Under the Bushes, Under the Stars	1996	12.00

—One side of Record 2 is blank

Number	Title (A Side/B Side)	Yr	NM
❑ OLE-185 [EP]	Sunfish Holy Breakfast	1996	10.00
❑ OLE-241	Mag Earwhig!	1997	10.00

ROCKATHON

Number	Title (A Side/B Side)	Yr	NM
❑ (no #)	Propeller	1992	1000.

—Hand-colored cover with nature-book paste-on; signed and numbered

Number	Title (A Side/B Side)	Yr	NM
❑ 02	Tonics & Twisted Chasers	1997	12.00

—1,000 copies were pressed on various colors of vinyl

ROCKATHON/FADING CAPTAIN SERIES

Number	Title (A Side/B Side)	Yr	NM
❑ 7	Suitcase Abridged: Drinks and Deliveries	2000	12.00

—500 copies were pressed

Number	Title (A Side/B Side)	Yr	NM
❑ 10	Daredevil Stamp Collector: Do the Collapse B-Sides	2001	12.00

—1,000 copies were pressed

ROCKET #9

Number	Title (A Side/B Side)	Yr	NM
❑ (no #)	Same Place the Fly Got Smashed	1990	40.00

SCAT

Number	Title (A Side/B Side)	Yr	NM
❑ 31	Vampire on Titus	1993	15.00
❑ 35	Bee Thousand	1994	12.00
❑ 40 [(6)]	Box	1994	60.00

TVT

Number	Title (A Side/B Side)	Yr	NM
❑ 1980	Do the Collapse	1999	10.00
❑ 2160	Isolation Drills	2001	10.00

GUIDES, THE

45s

GUYDEN

Number	Title (A Side/B Side)	Yr	NM
❑ 2023	How Long Must a Fool Go On/ You Must Try	1959	30.00

—Originally released under the name "The Swallows"

G

Except when noted otherwise, VG = 25% of NM, and VG+ = 50% of NM. (Example: VG = $2.00, VG+ = $4.00 and NM = $8.00.)

Number	Title (A Side/B Side)	Yr	NM
GUILLOTEENS, THE			
45s			
COLUMBIA			
❑ 43852	Wild Child/You Think You're Happy	1966	15.00
❑ 43852 [PS]	Wild Child/You Think You're Happy	1966	40.00
—Sleeve is promo only			
❑ 44089	I Love That Girl/ Dear Mrs. Applebee	1967	12.00
HANNA-BARBERA			
❑ 446	I Don't Believe/Hey You	1965	15.00
❑ 451	Don't Let the Rain Get You Down/For My Own	1965	15.00
❑ 451 [PS]	Don't Let the Rain Get You Down/For My Own	1965	30.00
❑ 486	I Sit and Cry/Crying All Over My Time	1966	20.00
GUITAR, BILLY			
45s			
DECCA			
❑ 30634	Here Comes the Night/You Should Have Loved Her More	1958	70.00
GUITAR SLIM			
45s			
ATCO			
❑ 6072	Oh Yeah/Down Through the Years	1956	40.00
❑ 6097	It Hurts to Love Someone/ If I Should Lose You	1957	30.00
❑ 6108	I Won't Mind at All/Hello, How Ya' Been, Goodbye	1958	30.00
❑ 6120	If I Had My Life to Live Over/ When There's No Way Out	1958	30.00
IMPERIAL			
❑ 5278	Woman Troubles/Cryin' in the Mornin'	1954	60.00
❑ 5310	New Arrival/Standing at the Station	1954	60.00
SPECIALTY			
❑ 482	The Things That I Used to Do/ Well, I Done Get Over It	1954	50.00
❑ 490	Story of My Life/A Letter to My Girl Friend	1954	40.00
❑ 527	Later for You Baby/ Troubles Don't Last	1954	25.00
❑ 536	Sufferin' Mind/Twenty-Five Lies	1955	25.00
❑ 542	Stand By Me/Our Only Child	1955	25.00
❑ 551	You're Gonna Miss Me/ I Got Sumpin' for You	1955	25.00
❑ 557	Think It Over/Quicksand	1955	25.00
❑ 569	Sumthin' to Remember Me By/ You Give Me Nothin' But the Blues	1956	25.00
Albums			
ATLANTIC			
❑ 81760	The Atco Sessions	1987	10.00
SPECIALTY			
❑ SP-2130	Things That I Used to Do	1969	20.00
GUITARS, INC. Pseudonym for THE FIREBALLS.			
45s			
HAMILTON			
❑ 50035	Little Toy/Holiday Love	1960	25.00
GULLIVER With Daryl Hall. John Oates joined later, but is not on these records.			
45s			
ELEKTRA			
❑ 45689	Angelina/Every Day's a Lovely Day	1970	8.00
❑ 45698	A Truly Good Song/Every Day's a Lovely Day	1970	8.00
Albums			
ELEKTRA			
❑ EKS-74070	Gulliver	1970	20.00
GUM DROPS, THE			
45s			
CORAL			
❑ 62003	My Own True Love/On the Wings of the Wind	1958	15.00
❑ 62102	I Spoke Too Soon/Sie Tu (It's You, It's You)	1959	15.00
❑ 62138	It Happens Every Day/ They Wake Me	1959	15.00
DECCA			
❑ 30584	You're the One/Gum Drop Shoes and Bells in Her Hair	1958	20.00

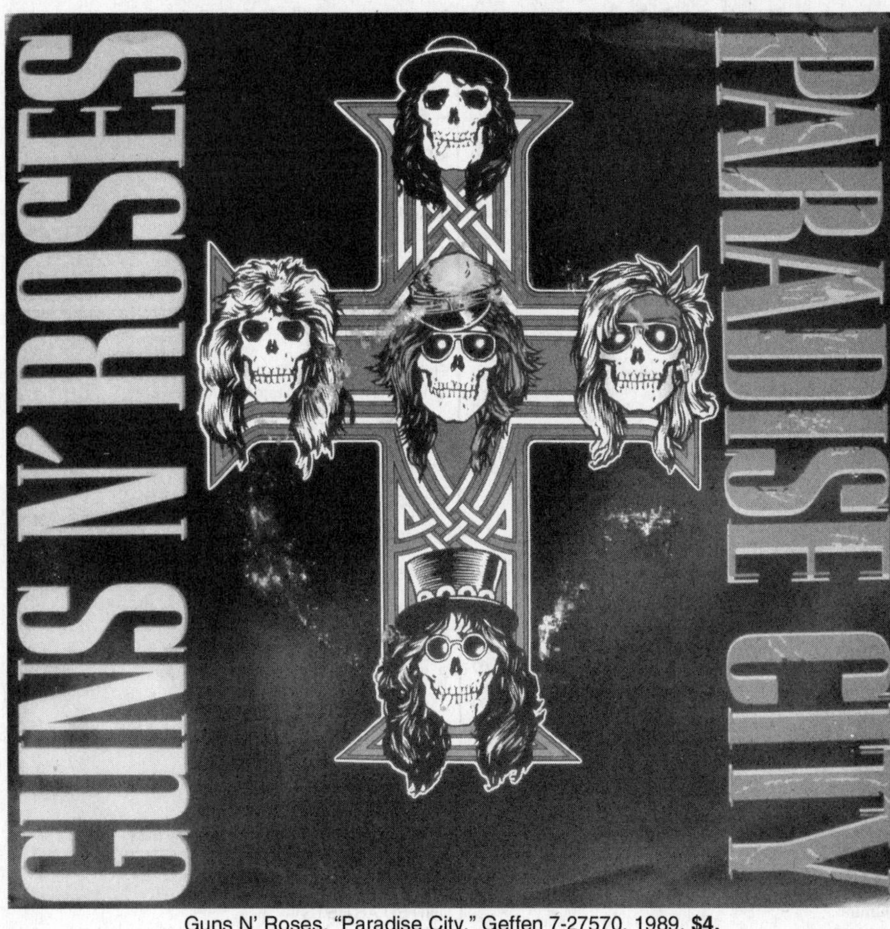

Guns N' Roses, "Paradise City," Geffen 7-27570, 1989, $4.

Number	Title (A Side/B Side)	Yr	NM
KING			
❑ 1496	Gum Drop/Don't Take It So Hard	1955	20.00
❑ 1499	I'll Wait for One More Train/ Don't Take It So Hard	1955	20.00
❑ 4913	I Wonder and Wonder/ I'll Follow You	1956	25.00
❑ 4963	Natural Born Lover/ Chapel of Hearts	1956	25.00
❑ 5051	Ba-Bee Da Boat Is Leaving/ Pigeon	1957	20.00
GUN			
45s			
EPIC			
❑ 10413	Race with the Devil/Sunshine	1968	10.00
❑ 10537	Don't Look Back/Hobo	1969	10.00
❑ 10593	Drown Yourself in the River/ Long Hair Wildman	1970	10.00
Albums			
EPIC			
❑ BN 26468	Gun	1969	20.00
❑ BN 26551	Gunsight	1970	25.00
GUNHILL ROAD			
45s			
KAMA SUTRA			
❑ 562	Ford, De Soto, Cadillac/ (B-side unknown)	1972	5.00
❑ 569	Back When My Hair Was Short/ We Can't Ride the Roller Coaster Anymore	1973	6.00
❑ 582	Ford, De Soto, Cadillac/Sailing	1973	5.00
❑ 591	She Made a Man Out of Me/ (B-side unknown)	1974	5.00
MERCURY			
❑ 73232	42nd Street/(B-side unknown)	1971	6.00
Albums			
KAMA SUTRA			
❑ KLS-2061	Gunhill Road	1972	12.00

Number	Title (A Side/B Side)	Yr	NM
MERCURY			
❑ SR-61341	Gun Hill Road	1971	12.00
GUNS & BUTTER			
Albums			
COTILLION			
❑ SD 9901	Guns & Butter	1972	20.00
GUNS N' ROSES Also see VELVET REVOLVER.			
45s			
GEFFEN			
❑ PRO-S-3094 [DJ]	Welcome to the Jungle (same on both sides)	1987	10.00
❑ PRO-S-3094 [PS]	Welcome to the Jungle (same on both sides)	1987	20.00
—Promo-only "Don't Report This Record" sleeve			
❑ 19027	Don't Cry/Don't Cry (Alt. Lyrics)	1991	5.00
❑ 19039	You Could Be Mine/Civil War	1991	5.00
❑ 19067	November Rain/ Sweet Child O' Mine	1992	5.00
—The longest 45 version of a Top 10 hit in chart history (8:53)			
❑ 19114	Live and Let Die/(Live)	1991	5.00
❑ 19142	Yesterdays/Yesterdays (Live in Las Vegas)	1992	5.00
❑ 19266	Since I Don't Have You/ You Can't Put Your Arms Around a Memory	1993	5.00
❑ 19381	Sympathy for the Devil/ Escape to Paris	1994	5.00
—B-side by Elliott Goldenthal			
❑ 7-21901	Sweet Child O' Mine/ Welcome to the Jungle	1989	3.00
—"Back to Back Hits" series			
❑ 7-22869	Nightrain/Reckless Life	1989	5.00
❑ 7-22996	Patience/Rocket Queen	1989	4.00
❑ 7-22996 [PS]	Patience/Rocket Queen	1989	4.00
❑ 7-27570	Paradise City/Move to the City	1989	4.00
❑ 7-27570 [PS]	Paradise City/Move to the City	1989	4.00
❑ 7-27759	Welcome to the Jungle/ Mr. Brownstone	1988	4.00
❑ 7-27759 [PS]	Welcome to the Jungle/ Mr. Brownstone	1988	4.00

Number	Title (A Side/B Side)	Yr	NM
❑ 7-27963	Sweet Child O' Mine/It's So Easy	1988	4.00
❑ 7-27963 [PS]	Sweet Child O' Mine/It's So Easy	1988	4.00

Albums

GEFFEN

Number	Title (A Side/B Side)	Yr	NM
❑ GHS 24148	Appetite for Destruction	1987	15.00
❑ GHS 24148	Appetite for Destruction	2008	20.00
❑ XXXG 24148	Appetite for Destruction	1987	40.00
—Original "rape cover"; the XXXG prefix is on the cover only; all copies of the record use the GHS prefix			
❑ GHS 24198	G N' R Lies	1988	12.00
❑ GEF 24415 [(2)]	Use Your Illusion I	1991	30.00
❑ GEF 24420 [(2)]	Use Your Illusion II	1991	30.00
❑ GEF 24617	The Spaghetti Incident?	1993	20.00
—Orange vinyl			
❑ R 100805	G N' R Lies	1988	12.00
—BMG Direct Marketing edition			
❑ R 170348	Appetite for Destruction	1987	12.00
—BMG Direct Marketing edition			
❑ 490514-1 [(4)]	Live Era '87-'93	1999	120.00

UZI SUICIDE

Number	Title (A Side/B Side)	Yr	NM
❑ USR 001 [EP]	Live ?!*@ Like a Suicide	1986	200.00

GUNTER, ARTHUR

45s

EXCELLO

Number	Title (A Side/B Side)	Yr	NM
❑ 2047	Baby Let's Play House/Blues After Hours	1954	120.00
❑ 2053	She's Mine, All Mine/You Are Doin' Me Wrong	1955	60.00
❑ 2058	Honey Babe/No Happy Home	1955	60.00
❑ 2073	Baby You Better Listen/Trouble with My Baby	1955	30.00
❑ 2084	Hear My Plea Baby/Love Has Got Me	1956	30.00
❑ 2125	Baby Can't You See/You're Always on My Mind	1958	25.00
❑ 2137	Ludella/We're Gonna Shake	1959	25.00
❑ 2147	Crazy Me/Don't Leave Me Now	1959	25.00
❑ 2164	No Naggin' No Draggin'/I Want Her Back	1959	25.00
❑ 2191	Little Blue Jeans/Mind Your Own Business Babe	1960	20.00
❑ 2201	My Heart's Always Lonesome/I'm Fallin', Love's Got Me	1961	20.00

Albums

EXCELLO

Number	Title (A Side/B Side)	Yr	NM
❑ LPS-8017	Black and Blues	1971	25.00

GUNTER, CORNEL

45s

ABC-PARAMOUNT

Number	Title (A Side/B Side)	Yr	NM
❑ 9698	She Loves to Rock/In Self Defense	1956	40.00
—As "Cornel Gunter and the Flairs"			

CHALLENGE

Number	Title (A Side/B Side)	Yr	NM
❑ 59281	If I Had the Key to Your Heart/Wishful	1965	10.00

DOT

Number	Title (A Side/B Side)	Yr	NM
❑ 15654	You Send Me/Call Me a Fool	1957	20.00

EAGLE

Number	Title (A Side/B Side)	Yr	NM
❑ 301	Baby Come Home/I Want You Madly	1957	30.00

LIBERTY

Number	Title (A Side/B Side)	Yr	NM
❑ 55096	If We Should Meet Again/Neighborhood Dance	1957	20.00

LOMA

Number	Title (A Side/B Side)	Yr	NM
❑ 701	True Love/Peek, Peek-a-Boo	1955	100.00
❑ 703	You Broke My Heart/(Pretty Baby) I'm Used to You Now	1956	150.00
❑ 704	Keep Me Alive/Muchacha, Muchacha	1956	80.00
❑ 705	I'm Sad/One Thing	1956	100.00
—The Loma singles credit "The Ermines," and may or may not mention Gunter.			

WARNER BROS.

Number	Title (A Side/B Side)	Yr	NM
❑ 5266	Lieft Me Up Angel/Hope of Sand	1962	12.00
❑ 5292	It Ain't No Use/In a Dream of Love	1962	12.00

GUNTER, HARDROCK

45s

DECCA

Number	Title (A Side/B Side)	Yr	NM
❑ 9-46300	Boogie Woogie on a Saturday Night/Honky Tonk	1951	40.00
❑ 9-46350	I've Done Gone Hog Wild/I Believe That Mountain Music	1951	25.00
❑ 9-46363	Sixty Minute Man/Tennessee Blues	1951	25.00
❑ 9-46367	Dixieland Boogie/If I Could Only Live My Dreams	1951	25.00
❑ 9-46383	Hesitation Boogie/Don't You Agree	1951	25.00
❑ 9-46401	Silver and Gold/Senator from Tennessee	1952	25.00

KING

Number	Title (A Side/B Side)	Yr	NM
❑ 4858	Turn the Other Cheek/Before My Time	1955	20.00

MGM

Number	Title (A Side/B Side)	Yr	NM
❑ K-11520	Like the Lovers Do/Naptown, Indiana	1953	25.00
❑ K-11596	Sunday Angel/Where Have You Been	1953	25.00

SUN

Number	Title (A Side/B Side)	Yr	NM
❑ 201	Fallen Angel/Gonna Dance All Night	1954	2000.

GUNTER, SHIRLEY

45s

FLAIR

Number	Title (A Side/B Side)	Yr	NM
❑ 1020	Send Him Back/Since I Fell for You	1953	40.00
❑ 1027	Found Some Good Lovin'/Strange Romance	1954	30.00
❑ 1050	Oop Shoop/It's You	1955	30.00
❑ 1060	You're Mine/Why	1955	30.00
❑ 1065	What Difference Does It Make/Baby I Love You So	1955	30.00
❑ 1070	That's the Way I Like It/Gimme, Gimme, Gimme	1955	30.00
❑ 1076	How Can I Tell You/Ipsy Gypsy Ooh	1955	60.00
—With the Flairs			

MODERN

Number	Title (A Side/B Side)	Yr	NM
❑ 979	Please Tell Me/Come On	1956	25.00
❑ 1001	Fortune in Love/Just Got Rid of a Heartache	1956	25.00
—With the Flairs			
❑ 1011	I'm So Sorry/I've Been Searching	1956	25.00

TANGERINE

Number	Title (A Side/B Side)	Yr	NM
❑ 949	Stuck Up/You Let My Love Grow Cold	1965	50.00

TENDER

Number	Title (A Side/B Side)	Yr	NM
❑ 503	Believe Me/Crazy Little Baby	1958	40.00

GURUS, THE

45s

UNITED ARTISTS

Number	Title (A Side/B Side)	Yr	NM
❑ 50089	Come Girl/Blue Snow Night	1966	12.00
❑ 50089 [PS]	Come Girl/Blue Snow Night	1966	25.00
❑ 50140	It Just Won't Be That Way/Everybody's Got to Be Alone Sometime	1967	12.00

GUTHRIE, ARLO

45s

REPRISE

Number	Title (A Side/B Side)	Yr	NM
❑ PRO 304 [DJ]	Motorcycle Song/The Pause of Mr. Claus	1970	20.00
❑ 0644	Motorcycle Song/Now and Then	1967	12.00
❑ 0793	Motorcycle Song (Part 1)/Motorcycle Song (Part 2)	1968	12.00
❑ 0877	Alice's Rock & Roll Restaurant/Coming Into Los Angeles	1969	12.00
❑ 0951	Gabriel's Mother's Hiway/Ballad #16 Blues	1970	8.00
❑ 0994	The Ballad of Tricky Fred/Shackles and Chains	1971	6.00
❑ 1103	The City of New Orleans/Days Are Short	1972	6.00
❑ 1137	Ukulele Lady/Cooper's Lament	1972	5.00
❑ 1158	A Week on the Rag/Gypsy Dave	1973	5.00
❑ 1211	Nostalgia Rag/Presidential Rag	1974	4.00
❑ 1363	Patriot's Dream/Ocean Crossing	1976	4.00
❑ 1376	Grocery Blues/Guabi, Guabi	1976	4.00
❑ 1388	Massachusetts/My Love	1977	4.00

WARNER BROS.

Number	Title (A Side/B Side)	Yr	NM
❑ 49037	Wedding Song/Prologue	1979	4.00
❑ 49796	Slow Boat/If I Could Only Touch Your Life	1981	4.00
❑ 49889	Oklahoma Nights/Power of Love	1981	4.00

Albums

REPRISE

Number	Title (A Side/B Side)	Yr	NM
❑ MS 2060	Hobo's Lullabye	1972	12.00
❑ MS 2142	Last of the Brooklyn Cowboys	1973	12.00
❑ MS4 2142 [Q]	Last of the Brooklyn Cowboys	1973	20.00
❑ MS 2183	Arlo Guthrie	1974	12.00
❑ MS 2239	Amigo	1976	12.00
❑ R 6267 [M]	Alice's Restaurant	1967	20.00
❑ RS 6267 [S]	Alice's Restaurant	1967	15.00
—Pink, green and gold label			
❑ RS 6267 [S]	Alice's Restaurant	1968	12.00
—With "W7" and "r:" logos on two-tone orange label			
❑ RS 6267 [S]	Alice's Restaurant	1970	10.00
—With only "r:" logo on all-orange (tan) label			
❑ RS 6299	Arlo	1968	15.00
—With "W7" and "r:" logos on two-tone orange label			
❑ RS 6299	Arlo	1970	10.00
—With only "r:" logo on all-orange (tan) label			
❑ RS 6346	Running Down the Road	1969	15.00
—With "W7" and "r:" logos on two-tone orange label			
❑ RS 6346	Running Down the Road	1970	10.00
—With only "r:" logo on all-orange (tan) label			
❑ RS 6411	Washington County	1970	12.00

WARNER BROS.

Number	Title (A Side/B Side)	Yr	NM
❑ BSK 3117	The Best of Arlo Guthrie	1977	10.00
—"Burbank" palm trees label			
❑ BSK 3117	The Best of Arlo Guthrie	1979	8.00
—White or tan label			
❑ BSK 3232	One Night	1978	10.00
❑ BSK 3336	Outlasting the Blues	1979	10.00
❑ BSK 3558	Power of Love	1981	10.00

GUTHRIE, WOODY

Albums

COLLECTABLES

Number	Title (A Side/B Side)	Yr	NM
❑ COL-5095	Golden Classics Vol. 1: Worried Man Blues	198?	12.00
❑ COL-5098	Golden Classics Vol. 2: Immortal	198?	12.00

ELEKTRA

Number	Title (A Side/B Side)	Yr	NM
❑ EKL-271/2 [(3)M]	The Library of Congress Recordings	1964	40.00
—Original pressing has "guitar player" labels			

EVEREST ARCHIVE OF FOLK & JAZZ

Number	Title (A Side/B Side)	Yr	NM
❑ 204	Woody Guthrie	1966	12.00

FOLKWAYS

Number	Title (A Side/B Side)	Yr	NM
❑ FP-11 [10]	Dust Bowl Ballads	1950	150.00
❑ FP-715 [10]	Songs to Grow On For Mother and Child	195?	150.00
❑ FA-2011 [10]	Dust Bowl Ballads	195?	75.00
—Reissue of FP-11			
❑ FA-2481 [M]	Bound for Glory: Songs and Stories of Woody Guthrie	1956	50.00
❑ FA-2483 [M]	Woody Guthrie Sings Folk Songs	1964	50.00
❑ FA-2484 [M]	Woody Guthrie Sings Folk Songs, Vol. 2	1964	50.00
❑ FA-2485 [M]	Struggle	1964	50.00
❑ FH-5212 [M]	Dust Bowl Ballads	1964	30.00
❑ FH-5485 [M]	Ballds of Sacco and Vanzetti	196?	30.00
❑ FC-7005 [10]	Songs to Grow On	1950	500.00
❑ FC-7015 [10]	Songs to Grow On For Mother and Child	1953	150.00
—Reissue of FP-715			
❑ FC-7027 [10]	Songs to Grow On Vol. 3	1951	150.00
❑ 31001 [R]	This Land Is Your Land	196?	12.00

RCA VICTOR

Number	Title (A Side/B Side)	Yr	NM
❑ LPV-502 [M]	Dust Bowl Ballads	1964	25.00

ROUNDER

Number	Title (A Side/B Side)	Yr	NM
❑ 1036	Columbia River Collection	1987	10.00
❑ 1040	Dust Bowl Ballads	1988	10.00
❑ 1041/2/3 [(3)]	The Library of Congress Recordings	1988	20.00

SMITHSONIAN FOLKWAYS

Number	Title (A Side/B Side)	Yr	NM
❑ SF-40007	Woody Guthrie Sings Folk Songs	1989	12.00
❑ SF-40025	Struggle	1989	12.00

VERVE FOLKWAYS

Number	Title (A Side/B Side)	Yr	NM
❑ FV-9007 [M]	Bed on the Floor	1965	30.00
❑ FVS-9007 [R]	Bed on the Floor	1965	20.00
❑ FV-9036 [M]	Bonneville Dam & Other Columbia River Songs	1965	30.00
❑ FVS-9036 [R]	Bonneville Dam & Other Columbia River Songs	1965	20.00

GUTHRIE, WOODY, AND CISCO HOUSTON

Albums

STINSON

Number	Title (A Side/B Side)	Yr	NM
❑ SLP-32 [10]	Cowboy Songs	1951	200.00
❑ SLP-44 [10]	Folk Songs, Vol. 1	1952	200.00
—Red vinyl			
❑ SLP-53 [10]	More Songs	1953	200.00

GUTHRIE, WOODY; SONNY TERRY; ALEX STEWART

Albums

STINSON

Number	Title (A Side/B Side)	Yr	NM
❑ SLP-7 [10]	Chain Gang, Vol. 1	1950	200.00
❑ SLP-8 [10]	Chain Gang, Vol. 2	1950	200.00

GUY, ART

45s

VALIANT

Number	Title (A Side/B Side)	Yr	NM
❑ 762	Where You Gonna Go/Teenage Millionaire	1967	30.00

GUY, BOB
Pseudonym for FRANK ZAPPA.

45s

DONNA

Number	Title (A Side/B Side)	Yr	NM
❑ 1380	Letter from Jeepers/Dear Jeepers	1963	100.00

GUY, BOBBY

45s

APT

Number	Title (A Side/B Side)	Yr	NM
❑ 25052	A Vow/Good Enough	1960	400.00

GUY, BROWLEY, AND THE SKYSCRAPERS

45s

CHECKER

Number	Title (A Side/B Side)	Yr	NM
❑ 779	Watermelon Man/You Look Good to Me	1954	300.00
—Black vinyl			
❑ 779	Watermelon Man/You Look Good to Me	1954	750.00
—Red vinyl			

GUY, BUDDY

45s

ARTISTIC

Number	Title (A Side/B Side)	Yr	NM
❑ 1501	Sit and Cry/Try to Quit You Baby	1958	40.00
❑ 1503	You Sure Can't Do/This Is the End	1958	40.00

CHESS

Number	Title (A Side/B Side)	Yr	NM
❑ 1753	I Got My Eyes on You/The First Time I Met the Blues	1960	30.00
❑ 1759	Stop Around/Broken Hearted Blues	1960	25.00
❑ 1784	Let Me Love You Baby/Ten Years Ago	1961	25.00
❑ 1812	Stone Crazy/Skippin'	1962	25.00
❑ 1838	When My Left Eye Jumps/My Treasure Untold	1962	25.00
❑ 1878	No Lie/Hard But It's Fair	1963	20.00
❑ 1899	My Time After a While/I Dig Your Wig	1964	20.00
❑ 1936	Leave My Girl Alone/Crazy Music	1965	20.00
❑ 1974	My Mother/Mother-in-Law Blues	1966	20.00
❑ 2022	Gonna Keep It to Myself/Suffer	1967	15.00
❑ 2067	She Suits Me to a Tee/Buddy's Groove	1969	15.00

VANGUARD

Number	Title (A Side/B Side)	Yr	NM
❑ 35060	Sweet Little Angel/Mary Had a Little Lamb	1968	12.00

Albums

BLUE THUMB

Number	Title (A Side/B Side)	Yr	NM
❑ BTS 20	Buddy and the Juniors	1970	25.00

CHESS

Number	Title (A Side/B Side)	Yr	NM
❑ LP-409	I Was Walking Through the Woods	1970	20.00
❑ LP-1527 [M]	I Left My Blues in San Francisco	1968	30.00
❑ CH-9115	Buddy Guy	1984	8.00

MCA

Number	Title (A Side/B Side)	Yr	NM
❑ 11165	I Was Walking Through the Woods	1995	25.00
—"Heavy Vinyl" audiophile reissue			

VANGUARD

Number	Title (A Side/B Side)	Yr	NM
❑ VSD-79272	A Man and the Blues	1968	25.00
❑ VSD-79290	This Is Buddy Guy	1969	25.00
❑ VSD-79323	Hold That Plane!	1972	20.00

GUYTON, HOWARD

45s

VERVE

Number	Title (A Side/B Side)	Yr	NM
❑ 10386	I Watched You Slowly Slip Away/I Got My Own Thing Going	1966	100.00

GUYTONES, THE

45s

DELUXE

Number	Title (A Side/B Side)	Yr	NM
❑ 6144	You Won't Let Me Go/Ooh Bop Sha Boo (Give All Your Love to Me)	1957	80.00
❑ 6152	She's Mine/Not Wanted	1957	80.00
❑ 6159	Hunky Dory/This Is Love	1958	80.00
❑ 6163	Baby, I Don't Care/Young Dreamer	1958	60.00
❑ 6169	Tell Me (How Was I to Know)/Your Heart's Bigger Than Mine	1958	60.00

GYPSIES, THE

45s

ATLAS

Number	Title (A Side/B Side)	Yr	NM
❑ 1073	Why/Young Girl to Calypso	1957	80.00

GROOVE

Number	Title (A Side/B Side)	Yr	NM
❑ 0117	One, Two, Three, Go/I'm Good to You Baby	1955	20.00
❑ 0129	Rock Around the Christmas Tree/You've Been Away Too Long	1955	20.00

OLD TOWN

Number	Title (A Side/B Side)	Yr	NM
❑ 1168	Blue Bird/Hey There Hey There	1964	50.00
❑ 1180	Jerk It/Diamonds, Rubies, Gold and Fame	1965	30.00
❑ 1184	It's a Woman's World/They're Having a Party	1965	300.00
❑ 1193	Oh I Wonder Why/Diamonds, Rubies, Gold and Fame	1966	40.00

GYPSY

45s

METROMEDIA

Number	Title (A Side/B Side)	Yr	NM
❑ 202	Gypsy Queen/Dead and Gone	1970	6.00

RCA VICTOR

Number	Title (A Side/B Side)	Yr	NM
❑ 74-0862	Lean On Me/Day After Day	1973	5.00
❑ 74-0933	Make Peace with Jesus/Don't Bother Me	1973	5.00
❑ APBO-0036	Need You Baby/Precious One	1973	5.00

Albums

METROMEDIA

Number	Title (A Side/B Side)	Yr	NM
❑ MD-1031 [(2)]	Gypsy	1970	20.00
❑ MD 1044	In the Garden	1971	15.00

RCA VICTOR

Number	Title (A Side/B Side)	Yr	NM
❑ APL1-0093	Unlock the Gates	1973	15.00
❑ LSP-4775	Antithesis	1972	15.00

GYPSY TRIPS, THE

45s

WORLD PACIFIC

Number	Title (A Side/B Side)	Yr	NM
❑ 77809	Rock 'n Roll Gypsies/Ain't It Hard	1966	30.00

H

H.P. LOVECRAFT

45s

MERCURY

Number	Title (A Side/B Side)	Yr	NM
❑ 73698	Flight/I Feel Better	1975	6.00
—As "Lovecraft"			
❑ 73707	We Love You (Whoever You Are)/Ain't Gettin' Home	1975	6.00
—As "Lovecraft"			

PHILIPS

Number	Title (A Side/B Side)	Yr	NM
❑ 40464	Anyway That You Want Me/It's All Over for You	1967	12.00
❑ 40491	Wayfaring Stranger/The Time Machine	1967	12.00
❑ 40491 [PS]	Wayfaring Stranger/The Time Machine	1967	25.00
❑ 40506	The White Ship (Part 1)/The White Ship (Part 2)	1967	12.00
❑ 40578	Blue Jack of Diamonds/Keeper of the Keys	1968	12.00

REPRISE

Number	Title (A Side/B Side)	Yr	NM
❑ 0996	We Can All Have It Together/Will I Know When My Time Comes	1971	8.00
—As "Lovecraft"			

Albums

MERCURY

Number	Title (A Side/B Side)	Yr	NM
❑ SRM-1-1041	We Love You	1975	18.00

PHILIPS

Number	Title (A Side/B Side)	Yr	NM
❑ PHM 200252 [M]	H.P. Lovecraft	1967	20.00
❑ PHS 600252 [S]	H.P. Lovecraft	1967	25.00
❑ PHS 600279	Lovecraft II	1968	25.00

REPRISE

Number	Title (A Side/B Side)	Yr	NM
❑ RS 6419	Valley of the Moon	1970	25.00

SUNDAZED

Number	Title (A Side/B Side)	Yr	NM
❑ LP-5004	Live May 11, 1968	1991	20.00

H.Y. SLEDGE

Albums

SSS INTERNATIONAL

Number	Title (A Side/B Side)	Yr	NM
❑ 22	Bootleg Music	1971	20.00

HA'PENNYS, THE

Albums

FERSCH

Number	Title (A Side/B Side)	Yr	NM
❑ FL-1110	Love Is Not the Same	1968	200.00

HACKAMORE BRICK

45s

KAMA SUTRA

Number	Title (A Side/B Side)	Yr	NM
❑ 521	Searchin'/Radio	1971	6.00

Albums

KAMA SUTRA

Number	Title (A Side/B Side)	Yr	NM
❑ KSBS-2025	One Kiss Leads to Another	1971	12.00

HACKERT, VALINE

45s

BRUNSWICK

Number	Title (A Side/B Side)	Yr	NM
❑ 55151	Billy Boy/Show Me How	1959	200.00

HADLEY, RED

45s

METEOR

Number	Title (A Side/B Side)	Yr	NM
❑ 5017	Ring Out Those Bells/Brother, That's All	1955	150.00

HAGAN, SAMMY, AND THE VISCOUNTS

45s

CAPITOL

Number	Title (A Side/B Side)	Yr	NM
❑ F-3772	Out of Your Heart/Shoochie Poochie	1957	40.00
❑ F-3818	Wild Bird/Don't Cry	1957	40.00
❑ F-3885	Tail Light/Snuggle Bunny	1958	30.00

HAGAR, SAMMY
Also see MONTROSE; VAN HALEN; CHICKENFOOT.

45s

CAPITOL

Number	Title (A Side/B Side)	Yr	NM
❑ 4261	Urban Guerilla/Flamingos Fly	1976	5.00
❑ 4388	Catch the Wind/Red	1977	5.00
❑ 4411	Cruisin' and Boozin'/Love Has Found Me	1977	5.00
❑ 4502	Reckless/You Made Me Crazy	1977	5.00
❑ 4550	Turn Up the Music/Hey Boys	1978	5.00
❑ 4596	I've Done Everything for You/Someone Out There	1978	5.00
❑ 4699	(Sittin' On) The Dock of the Bay/I've Done Everything for You	1979	5.00
❑ 4757	Plain Jane/Wounded in Love	1979	5.00
❑ 4825	Growing Pains/Straight to the Top	1980	4.00
❑ 4893	Heartbeat/Miles from Boredom	1980	4.00

COLUMBIA

Number	Title (A Side/B Side)	Yr	NM
❑ 06647	Winner Takes It All/The Fight	1987	3.00
—B-side by Giorgio Moroder			
❑ 06647 [PS]	Winner Takes It All/The Fight	1987	4.00

GEFFEN

Number	Title (A Side/B Side)	Yr	NM
❑ 28185	Eagles Fly/Hands and Knees	1987	3.00
❑ 28185 [PS]	Eagles Fly/Hands and Knees	1987	4.00
❑ 28314	Give to Live/When the Hammer Falls	1987	3.00
❑ 28314 [PS]	Give to Live/When the Hammer Falls	1987	3.00
❑ 29090	I'll Only Fall in Love Again/Only the Young	1985	4.00
—B-side by Journey			
❑ 29173	I Can't Drive 55/Dick in the Dirt	1984	3.00
❑ 29173 [PS]	I Can't Drive 55/Dick in the Dirt	1984	4.00
❑ 29173 [PS]	I Can't Drive 55	1984	7.00
—Promo-only version contains facsimile speeding ticket			
❑ 29246	Two Sides of Love/Burnin' Down the City	1984	5.00
—Red vinyl			
❑ 29246 [PS]	Two Sides of Love/Burnin' Down the City	1984	5.00
❑ 29718	Fast Times At Ridgemont High/Never Give Up	1983	3.00
❑ 29816	Your Love Is Driving Me Crazy/I Don't Need Love	1982	3.00
❑ 49881	I'll Fall in Love Again/Satisfied	1981	3.00
❑ 50059	Piece of My Heart/Sweet Hitchhiker	1982	3.00

MCA

Number	Title (A Side/B Side)	Yr	NM
❑ 55574	Mas Tequila/Little White Lie	1999	3.00

Albums

CAPITOL

Number	Title (A Side/B Side)	Yr	NM
❑ ST-11489	Nine on a Ten Scale	1976	12.00
❑ ST-11599	Sammy Hagar	1977	12.00
❑ ST-11706	Musical Chairs	1977	12.00
❑ SMAS-11812	All Night Long	1978	12.00
❑ ST-11983	Street Machine	1979	12.00
❑ ST-12069	Danger Zone	1980	12.00
—With poster (deduct if missing)			
❑ ST-12238	Rematch	1982	10.00
❑ SK-12299	Live 1980	1983	10.00
❑ SN-16049	Nine on a Ten Scale	1979	8.00
—Budget-line reissue of 11489			
❑ SN-16050	Sammy Hagar	1979	8.00
—Budget-line reissue of 11599			
❑ SN-16051	Musical Chairs	1979	8.00
—Budget-line reissue of 11706			
❑ SN-16326	All Night Long	198?	8.00
—Budget-line reissue of 11812			
❑ SN-16336	Rematch	198?	8.00
—Budget-line reissue of 12238			
❑ SN-16340	Street Machine	198?	8.00
—Budget-line reissue of 11983			
❑ SN-16376	Live 1980	1986	8.00
—Budget-line reissue of 12299			

Number	Title (A Side/B Side)	Yr	NM
GEFFEN			
❑ GHS 2006	Standing Hampton	1982	10.00
❑ GHS 2021	Three Lock Box	1982	10.00
❑ GHS 24043	VOA	1984	10.00
❑ GHS 24144	Sammy Hagar	1987	10.00
HAGGARD, MERLE Also see PAYCHECK AND HAGGARD.			
45s			
CAPITOL			
❑ 2017	Sing Me Back Home/Good Times	1967	8.00
❑ 2017 [PS]	Sing Me Back Home/Good Times	1967	8.00
❑ 2123	The Legend of Bonnie and Clyde/I Started Loving You Again	1968	8.00
❑ 2219	Mama Tried/You'll Never Love Me Now	1968	8.00
❑ 2219 [PS]	Mama Tried/You'll Never Love Me Now	1968	8.00
❑ 2289	I Take a Lot of Pride in What I Am/Keep Me from Cryin' Today	1968	8.00
❑ 2289 [PS]	I Take a Lot of Pride in What I Am/Keep Me from Cryin' Today	1968	8.00
❑ 2383	Hungry Eyes/California Blues	1969	8.00
❑ 2383 [PS]	Hungry Eyes/California Blues	1969	8.00
❑ 2503	Workin' Man Blues/Silver Wings	1969	8.00
❑ 2503 [PS]	Workin' Man Blues/Silver Wings	1969	8.00
❑ 2626	Okie from Muskogee/If I Had Left It Up to You	1969	8.00
❑ 2626 [PS]	Okie from Muskogee/If I Had Left It Up to You	1969	8.00
❑ 2719	The Fightin' Side of Me/Every Fool Has a Rainbow	1970	8.00
❑ 2719 [PS]	The Fightin' Side of Me/Every Fool Has a Rainbow	1970	8.00
❑ 2778	Street Singer/Mexican Rose	1970	8.00
❑ 2838	Jesus, Take a Hold/No Reason to Quit	1970	8.00
❑ 2891	I Can't Be Myself/Sidewalks of Chicago	1970	8.00
❑ 2891 [PS]	I Can't Be Myself/Sidewalks of Chicago	1970	8.00
❑ 3024	Soldier's Last Letter/The Farmer's Daughter	1971	6.00
❑ 3024 [PS]	Soldier's Last Letter/The Farmer's Daughter	1971	8.00
❑ 3112	Someday We'll Look Back/It's Great to Be Alive	1971	6.00
❑ 3198	Daddy Frank (The Guitar Man)/My Heart Would Know	1971	6.00
❑ 3222	Carolyn/When the Feelin' Goes Away	1971	6.00
❑ 3294	Grandma Harp/Turnin' Off a Memory	1972	6.00
❑ 3419	It's Not Love (But It's Not Bad)/My Woman Keeps Lovin' Her Man	1972	6.00
❑ 3488	I Wonder If They Ever Think of Me/I Forget You Every Day	1972	6.00
❑ 3552	The Emptiest Arms in the World/Radiator Man from Waco	1973	5.00
❑ 3641	Everybody's Had the Blues/Nobody Knows I'm Hurtin'	1973	5.00
❑ 3746	If We Make It Through December/Bobby Wants a Puppy Dog for Christmas	1973	5.00
❑ 3830	Things Aren't Funny Anymore/Honky Tonk Night Time Man	1974	5.00
❑ 3900	Old Man from the Mountain/Holding Things Together	1974	5.00
❑ 3974	Kentucky Gambler/I've Got a Darlin' (For a Wife)	1974	5.00
❑ 3989	Santa Claus and Popcorn/If We Make It Through December	1974	5.00
❑ 4027	Always Wanting You/I've Got a Yearning	1975	5.00
❑ 4085	Movin' On/Here in Frisco	1975	5.00
❑ 4141	It's All in the Movies/Living with the Shades Pulled Down	1975	5.00
❑ 4204	The Roots of My Raising/The Way It Was in '51	1975	5.00
❑ 4267	Here Comes the Freedom Train/I Won't Give Up My Train	1976	5.00
❑ 4326	Cherokee Maiden/What Have You Got Planned Tonight Diana	1976	5.00
❑ 4477	A Workin' Man Can't Get Nowhere Today/Blues Stay Away from Me	1977	5.00
❑ 4525	Running Kind/Making Believe	1978	5.00
❑ 4636	The Way It Was in '51/Moanin' the Blues	1978	5.00
❑ 5460	I'm Gonna Break Every Heart I Can/Falling for You	1965	10.00
❑ 5523	This Town's Not Big Enough/Shade Tree	1965	10.00
❑ 5600	Swinging Doors/The Girl Turned Ripe	1966	10.00
❑ 5704	The Bottle Let Me Down/The Longer You Wait	1966	10.00
❑ 5803	The Fugitive/Someone Told My Story	1966	12.00
❑ 5803	I'm a Lonesome Fugitive/Someone Told My Story	1967	8.00
—Retitled A-side			
❑ 5844	I Threw Away the Rose/Loneliness Is Eating Me Alive	1967	8.00
❑ 5844 [PS]	I Threw Away the Rose/Loneliness Is Eating Me Alive	1967	8.00
❑ 5931	Branded Man/You Don't Have Very Far to Go	1967	8.00
❑ 5931 [PS]	Branded Man/You Don't Have Very Far to Go	1967	8.00
CAPITOL NASHVILLE			
❑ S7-19346	White Christmas/Silver Bells	1996	4.00
CURB			
❑ 76832	When It Rains It Pours/Me and Crippled Soldiers	1990	4.00
❑ 76846	Blue Jungle/Me and Crippled Soldiers	1990	4.00
❑ 76854	A Bar in Bakersfield/Lucky Old Colorado	1991	4.00
ELEKTRA			
❑ 46634	Bar Room Buddies/The Not So Great Train Robbery	1980	4.00
—With Clint Eastwood			
❑ 46634 [PS]	Bar Room Buddies/The Not So Great Train Robbery	1980	5.00
EPIC			
❑ AE7 1777 [DJ]	Santa Claus and Popcorn/Grandma's Homemade Christmas Card	1982	5.00
❑ 02504	My Favorite Memory/Texas Fiddle Song	1981	3.00
❑ 02686	Big City/I Think I'm Gonna Live Forever	1981	3.00
❑ 02894	Are the Good Times Really Over (I Wish a Buck Was Still Silver)/I Always Get Lucky with You	1982	3.00
❑ 03315	Going Where the Lonely Go/Someday You're Gonna Need Your Friends Again	1982	3.00
❑ 03365	Going Where the Lonely Go	1982	8.00
—One-sided budget release			
❑ 03406	Goin' Home for Christmas/If We Make It Through December	1982	4.00
❑ 03723	You Take Me for Granted/I Won't Give Up My Train	1983	3.00
❑ 04006	What Am I Gonna Do (With the Rest of My Life)/I Think I'll Stay	1983	3.00
❑ 04226	That's the Way Love Goes/Don't Seem Like We've Been Together All Our Lives	1983	3.00
❑ 04402	Someday When Things Are Good/If You Hated Me	1984	3.00
❑ 04512	Let's Chase Each Other Around the Room/All I Want to Do Is Sing My Song	1984	3.00
❑ 04830	Natural High/I Never Go Home Anymore	1985	3.00
❑ 05426	Kern River/The Old Water Mill	1985	3.00
❑ 05659	Amber Waves of Grain/I Wish Things Were Simple Again	1985	3.00
❑ 05734	American Waltz/The Farmer's Daughter	1985	3.00
❑ 05782	I Had a Beautiful Time/This Time I Really Do	1986	3.00
❑ 06097	A Friend in California/Mama's Prayers	1986	3.00
❑ 06344	Out Among the Stars/Suzie	1986	3.00
❑ 07036	Almost Persuaded/Love Don't Hurt Everytime	1987	3.00
❑ 07631	Twinkle, Twinkle, Lucky Star/I Don't Have Any Love Around	1987	3.00
❑ 07754	Chill Factor/Thanking the Good Lord	1988	3.00
❑ 07944	We Never Touch at All/Man from Another Time	1988	3.00
❑ 08111	You Babe/Thirty Again	1988	3.00
❑ 68598	5:01 Blues/Man from Another Time	1989	3.00
❑ 68979	A Better Love Next Time/Losin' in Las Vegas	1989	3.00
❑ 73076	If You Want to Be My Woman/Someday We'll Know	1989	3.00
❑ 73303	Broken Friend/Wouldn't That Be Something	1990	4.00
MCA			
❑ 40700	If We're Not Back in Love By Monday/I Think It's Gone Forever	1977	4.00
❑ 40743	Ramblin' Fever/When My Blue Moon Turns to Gold Again	1977	4.00
❑ 40804	From Graceland to the Promised Land/Are You Lonesome Tonight	1977	6.00
❑ 40869	I'm Always on a Mountain When I Fall/The Life of a Rodeo Cowboy	1978	4.00
❑ 40936	It's Been a Great Afternoon/Love Me When You Can	1978	4.00
❑ 41007	Red Bandana/I Must Have Done Something Bad	1979	4.00
❑ 41112	My Own Kind of Hat/Heaven Was a Drink of Wine	1979	4.00
❑ 41168	If We Make It Through December/The Fightin' Side of Me	1979	5.00
❑ 41200	The Way I Am/Wake Up	1980	4.00
❑ 41255	Misery and Gin/No One to Sing For	1980	4.00
❑ 41255 [PS]	Misery and Gin/No One to Sing For	1980	5.00
❑ 51014	I Think I'll Just Stay Here and Drink/Back to the Barrooms	1980	4.00
❑ 51048	Leonard/Our Paths May Never Cross	1981	4.00
❑ 51120	Rainbow Stew/Blue Yodel No. 9	1981	4.00
❑ 52020	Dealing with the Devil/Fiddle Breakdown	1982	4.00
❑ 52276	It's All in the Game/New Cocaine Blues	1983	3.00
❑ 52595	Make-Up and Faded Blue Jeans/Love Me When You Can	1985	3.00
TALLY			
❑ 152	Singin' My Heart Out/Skid Row	1963	20.00
❑ 155	Sing a Sad Song/You Don't Even Try	1963	15.00
❑ 178	Sam Hill/You Don't Have Far to Go	1964	15.00
❑ 179	(My Friends Are Gonna Be) Strangers/Please Mr. D.J.	1964	15.00
7-Inch Extended Plays			
CAPITOL			
❑ SU-384	Hobo Bill's Last Ride/No Hard Times/Silver Wings//Billy Overcame His Size/Blue Rock/White Line Fever	1970	15.00
—Jukebox issue; small hole, plays at 33 1/3 rpm			
❑ SU-384 [PS]	Okie from Muskogee	1970	15.00
❑ SU-2702	I'm a Lonesome Fugitive/Skid Row/If You Want to Be My Woman//Someone Told My Story/My Rough and Rowdy Ways/Mixed Up Mess of a Heart	1967	20.00
—Jukebox issue; small hole, plays at 33 1/3 rpm			
❑ SU-2702 [PS]	I'm a Lonesome Fugitive	1967	20.00
Albums			
CAPITOL			
❑ SKAO-168	Pride In What I Am	1969	25.00
❑ SM-168	Pride In What I Am	197?	10.00
—Reissue with new prefix			
❑ SWBB-223 [(2)]	Same Train, A Different Time	1969	30.00
❑ SWBB-259 [(2)]	Close-Up	1969	30.00
—Reissue in one package of "Strangers" and "Swinging Doors"			
❑ ST-319	A Portrait of Merle Haggard	1969	20.00
❑ ST-384	Okie from Muskogee	1970	20.00
❑ ST-451	The Fightin' Side of Me	1970	20.00
❑ ST-638	A Tribute to the Best Damn Fiddle Player in the World (Or, My Salute to Bob Wills)	1970	25.00
❑ STBB-707 [(2)]	Sing a Sad Song/High on a Hilltop	1971	30.00
❑ ST-735	Hag	1971	15.00
❑ SWBO-803 [(2)]	The Land of Many Churches	1971	60.00
❑ ST-823	Truly the Best of Merle Haggard	1971	40.00
❑ ST-835	Someday We'll Look Back	1971	20.00
❑ ST-882	Let Me Tell You About a Song	1972	20.00
❑ ST 2373 [S]	Strangers	1965	30.00
❑ T 2373 [M]	Strangers	1965	25.00
❑ SM-2585	Swinging Doors	197?	10.00
—Reissue with new prefix			
❑ ST 2585 [S]	Swinging Doors	1966	30.00
❑ T 2585 [M]	Swinging Doors	1966	25.00
❑ SM-2702	I'm a Lonesome Fugitive	197?	10.00
—Reissue with new prefix			
❑ ST 2702 [S]	I'm a Lonesome Fugitive	1967	30.00
❑ T 2702 [M]	I'm a Lonesome Fugitive	1967	25.00
❑ ST 2789 [S]	Branded Man	1967	30.00
❑ T 2789 [M]	Branded Man	1967	25.00
❑ ST 2848 [S]	Sing Me Back Home	1968	25.00
❑ T 2848 [M]	Sing Me Back Home	1968	30.00
❑ ST 2912	The Legend of Bonnie and Clyde	1968	25.00
❑ SKAO 2951	The Best of Merle Haggard	1968	25.00
❑ ST 2972	Mama Tried	1968	25.00
❑ ST-11082	The Best of the Best of Merle Haggard	1972	15.00
❑ ST-11127	It's Not Love	1972	12.00
❑ ST-11141	Totally Instrumental with One Exception	1973	15.00

Except when noted otherwise, VG = 25% of NM, and VG+ = 50% of NM. (Example: VG = $2.00, VG+ = $4.00 and NM = $8.00.)

Number	Title (A Side/B Side)	Yr	NM
❑ ST-11200	I Love Dixie Blues...So I Recorded "Live" in New Orleans	1973	12.00
❑ ST-11230	Merle Haggard's Christmas Present (Something Old, Something New)	1973	12.00
❑ ST-11276	If We Make It Through December	1974	12.00
❑ ST-11331	Merle Haggard Presents His 30th Album	1974	12.00
❑ ST-11365	Keep Movin' On	1975	12.00
❑ ST-11483	It's All in the Movies	1975	12.00
❑ SABB-11531 [(2)]	Songs I'll Always Sing	1976	15.00
❑ ST-11544	My Love Affair with Trains	1976	12.00
❑ ST-11586	The Roots of My Raising	1976	12.00
❑ ST-11693	A Working Man Can't Get Nowhere Today	1977	12.00
❑ ST-11745	Eleven Winners	1977	12.00
❑ SM-11823	My Love Affair with Trains	1978	10.00
—Reissue			
❑ SW-11839	The Way It Was	1978	12.00
❑ SM-12036	It's All in the Movies	1979	10.00
—Reissue			
❑ SN-16052	Sing a Sad Song	1979	8.00
—Budget-line reissue			
❑ SN-16053	High on a Hilltop	1979	8.00
—Budget-line reissue			
❑ SN-16054	The Best of Merle Haggard	1979	8.00
—Budget-line reissue			
❑ SN-16277	Okie from Muskogee	1982	8.00
—Budget-line reissue			
❑ SN-16278	The Fightin' Side of Me	1982	8.00
—Budget-line reissue			
❑ SN-16279	A Tribute to the Best Damn Fiddle Player in the World (Or, My Salute to Bob Wills)	1982	8.00
—Budget-line reissue			
❑ SN-16303	Eleven Winners	1984	8.00
—Budget-line reissue			
CAPITOL SPECIAL MARKETS			
❑ SL-8086 [(2)]	Songs I'll Always Sing	1977	20.00
❑ SLB-8137 [(2)]	Merle Haggard Salutes the Greats	1980	15.00
EPIC			
❑ FE 37593	Big City	1981	10.00
❑ PE 37593	Big City	1985	8.00
—Budget-line reissue			
❑ FE 38092	Going Where the Lonely Go	1982	10.00
❑ PE 38092	Going Where the Lonely Go	1985	8.00
—Budget-line reissue			
❑ PE 38307	Goin' Home for Christmas	1982	10.00
❑ FE 38815	That's the Way Love Goes	1983	10.00
❑ FE 39159	The Epic Collection	1983	10.00
❑ PE 39159	The Epic Collection	1985	8.00
—Budget-line reissue			
❑ FE 39364	It's All in the Game	1984	10.00
❑ FE 39545	His Epic Hits: The First 11	1985	10.00
❑ FE 39602	Kern River	1985	10.00
❑ FE 40107	Out Among the Stars	1986	10.00
❑ PE 40107	Out Among the Stars	1986	8.00
—Budget-line reissue			
❑ FE 40224	Amber Waves of Grain	1985	10.00
❑ FE 40286	A Friend in California	1986	10.00
❑ FE 40986	Chill Factor	1988	10.00
❑ FE 44283	5:01 Blues	1989	10.00
MCA			
❑ 2267	Ramblin' Fever	1977	12.00
❑ 2314	My Farewell to Elvis	1977	15.00
❑ 2375	I'm Always on a Mountain	1978	12.00
❑ 3089	Serving 190 Proof	1979	12.00
❑ 3229	The Way I Am	1980	12.00
❑ 5139	Back to the Barrooms	1980	12.00
❑ 5250	Songs for the Mamma	1981	12.00
❑ 5386	Greatest Hits	1982	12.00
❑ 5573	His Best	1985	10.00
❑ 37138	Ramblin' Fever	1980	8.00
—Budget-line reissue			
❑ 37139	My Farewell to Elvis	1980	8.00
—Budget-line reissue			
❑ 37140	I'm Always on a Mountain	1980	8.00
—Budget-line reissue			
❑ 37141	Serving 190 Proof	1980	8.00
—Budget-line reissue			
❑ 37207	The Way I Am	1982	8.00
—Budget-line reissue			

HAGGARD, MERLE, AND JANIE FRICKE

45s

Number	Title (A Side/B Side)	Yr	NM
EPIC			
❑ 04663	A Place to Fall Apart/All I Want to Do Is Sing My Song	1984	3.00

HAGGARD, MERLE, AND JEWEL

45s

Number	Title (A Side/B Side)	Yr	NM
BNA			
❑ 65895	That's the Way Love Goes/Silver Wings	1999	3.00

HAGGARD, MERLE, AND GEORGE JONES

Also see each artist's individual listings.

45s

Number	Title (A Side/B Side)	Yr	NM
EPIC			
❑ 03072	Yesterday's Wine/I Haven't Found Her Yet	1982	3.00
❑ 03405	C.C. Waterback/After I Sing All My Songs	1982	3.00

Albums

Number	Title (A Side/B Side)	Yr	NM
EPIC			
❑ FE 38203	A Taste of Yesterday's Wine	1982	10.00

HAGGARD, MERLE, AND WILLIE NELSON

Also see each artist's individual listings.

45s

Number	Title (A Side/B Side)	Yr	NM
EPIC			
❑ 03494	Reasons to Quit/Half a Man	1983	4.00
❑ ENR-03495	Reasons to Quit	1983	8.00
—One-sided budget release			
❑ 03842	Pancho and Lefty/Opportunity to Cry	1983	4.00
—As "Willie Nelson and Merle Haggard"			
❑ 34-07400	If I Could Only Fly/Without You on My Side	1987	3.00

Albums

Number	Title (A Side/B Side)	Yr	NM
EPIC			
❑ FE 37958	Pancho and Lefty	1983	10.00
—Reissue corrects spelling of LP title			
❑ FE 37958	Poncho and Lefty	1983	15.00
—Note misspelled LP title			
❑ FE 40293	Seashores of Old Mexico	1987	10.00

HAGGARD, MERLE, AND BONNIE OWENS

Also see each artist's individual listings.

45s

Number	Title (A Side/B Side)	Yr	NM
TALLY			
❑ 181	Just Between the Two of Us/Slowly But Sure	1964	20.00

Albums

Number	Title (A Side/B Side)	Yr	NM
CAPITOL			
❑ ST 2453 [S]	Just Between the Two of Us	1966	30.00
❑ T 2453 [M]	Just Between the Two of Us	1966	25.00

HAGGARD, MERLE, AND LEONA WILLIAMS

Also see each artist's individual listings.

45s

Number	Title (A Side/B Side)	Yr	NM
MCA			
❑ 40962	The Bull and the Beaver/I'm Gettin' High	1978	4.00
MERCURY			
❑ 812214-7	We're Strangers Again/Sally Let Your Bangs Hang Down	1983	3.00
❑ 814359-7	Waltz Across Texas/Waitin' on the Good Life to Come	1983	3.00
❑ 880139-7	Don't Ever Let Your Lover Sleep Alone/It's Cold in California	1984	4.00

Albums

Number	Title (A Side/B Side)	Yr	NM
MERCURY			
❑ 812183-1	Heart to Heart	1983	10.00

HAGGETT, JIMMY

45s

Number	Title (A Side/B Side)	Yr	NM
CAPROCK			
❑ 107	All I Have Is You/Without You	1958	40.00
METEOR			
❑ 5043	Gonna Shut You Off Baby/Tell Her True	1957	200.00
SUN			
❑ 236	No More/They Call Our Love a Sin	1956	600.00

HAIG, RONNIE

45s

Number	Title (A Side/B Side)	Yr	NM
ABC-PARAMOUNT			
❑ 9912	Don't You Hear Me Calling, Baby/Traveler of Love	1958	30.00
❑ 10209	Don't You Hear Me Calling, Baby/Traveler of Love	1961	80.00
NOTE			
❑ 10010	Don't You Hear Me Calling, Baby/Traveler of Love	1958	30.00
❑ 10014	Rockin' with Rhythm and Blues/Money Is a Thing of the Past	1958	100.00

HAINES, CONNIE

45s

Number	Title (A Side/B Side)	Yr	NM
MOTOWN			
❑ 1092	What's Easy for Two Is Hard for One/Walk in Silence	1966	40.00

HAIRCUTS, THE

45s

Number	Title (A Side/B Side)	Yr	NM
PARKWAY			
❑ 899	She Loves You/Love Me Do	1964	20.00
❑ 899 [PS]	She Loves You/Love Me Do	1964	40.00

HAIRSTON, BROTHER WILL

45s

Number	Title (A Side/B Side)	Yr	NM
JVB			
❑ 44	The Alabama Bus (Part 1)/The Alabama Bus (Part 2)	1956	300.00

HAIRSTON, JACKIE

45s

Number	Title (A Side/B Side)	Yr	NM
ATCO			
❑ 6464	Monkey on My Back/Hijack	1967	20.00

HALE AND THE HUSHABYES

All-star group including BRIAN WILSON, JACKIE DeSHANNON, and SONNY AND CHER.

45s

Number	Title (A Side/B Side)	Yr	NM
APOGEE			
❑ 104	Yes Sir, That's My Baby/900 Quetzals	1964	300.00
REPRISE			
❑ 0299	Yes Sir, That's My Baby/Jack's Theme	1964	200.00
—Reissued in 1967 by "A Date With Soul"			
YORK			
❑ 408	Yes Sir, That's My Baby/Bee Side Soul	1967	50.00
—As "A Date with Soul"			

HALEE'S COMET

Roy Halee, later producer for SIMON AND GARFUNKEL.

45s

Number	Title (A Side/B Side)	Yr	NM
EPIC			
❑ 10207	All I Want Is What's Real/From a Parachute	1967	12.00

HALEY, BILL, AND HIS COMETS

45s

Number	Title (A Side/B Side)	Yr	NM
APT			
❑ 25081	Stop, Look, and Listen/Burn That Candle	1965	20.00
❑ 25087	Haley A-Go-Go/Tongue Tied Tony	1965	25.00
ARZEE			
❑ 4677	Yodel Your Blues Away/Within This Broken Heart of Mine	1978	25.00
❑ 4677 [PS]	Yodel Your Blues Away/Within This Broken Heart of Mine	1978	25.00
BUDDAH			
❑ 169	Rock Around the Clock/Framed	1970	15.00
DECCA			
❑ 29124	(We're Gonna) Rock Around the Clock/Thirteen Women (And Only One Man in Town)	196?	10.00
—Black label with color bars			
❑ 9-29124	(We're Gonna) Rock Around the Clock/Thirteen Women (And Only One Man in Town)	1954	60.00
—With lines on either side of "Decca"			
❑ 9-29124	(We're Gonna) Rock Around the Clock/Thirteen Women (And Only One Man in Town)	1955	20.00
—With star under "Decca"			
❑ 29204	Shake, Rattle and Roll/A.B.C. Boogie	1954	20.00
—With star under "Decca"			
❑ 29204	Shake, Rattle and Roll/A.B.C. Boogie	1954	40.00
—With lines on either side of "Decca"			
❑ 29317	Dim, Dim the Lights (I Want Some Atmosphere)/Happy Baby	1954	20.00
—With star under "Decca"			
❑ 29317	Dim, Dim the Lights (I Want Some Atmosphere)/Happy Baby	1954	40.00
—With lines on either side of "Decca"			
❑ 29418	Mambo Rock/Birth of the Boogie	1955	25.00
❑ 29552	Razzle-Dazzle/Two Hound Dogs	1955	25.00
❑ 29713	Burn That Candle/Rock-a-Beatin' Boogie	1955	25.00
❑ 29791	See You Later, Alligator/The Paper Boy (On Main Street, U.S.A.)	1956	25.00
❑ 29870	R-O-C-K/The Saints Rock 'N' Roll	1956	25.00
❑ 29948	Hot Dog Buddy Buddy/Rockin' Through the Rye	1956	25.00

Bill Haley and His Comets, *Shake, Rattle and Roll,* Decca ED 2168, 1954, **$60.**

Number	Title (A Side/B Side)	Yr	NM
❑ 30028	Rip It Up/Teenager's Mother (Are You Right?)	1956	25.00
❑ 30085	Rudy's Rock/Blue Comet Blues	1956	25.00
❑ 30148	Don't Knock the Rock/ Choo Choo Ch'Boogie	1956	25.00
❑ 30214	Forty Cups of Coffeee/Hook, Line and Sinker	1957	25.00
❑ 30314	(You Hit the Wrong Note) Billy Goat/Rockin' Rollin' Rover	1957	25.00
❑ 30314 [PS]	(You Hit the Wrong Note) Billy Goat/Rockin' Rollin' Rover	1957	120.00
❑ 30394	The Dipsy Doodle/Miss You	1957	25.00
❑ 30461	Rock the Joint/How Many	1957	25.00
❑ 30530	It's a Sin/Mary, Mary Lou	1957	25.00
❑ 30530 [PS]	It's a Sin/Mary, Mary Lou	1957	80.00
❑ 30592	Skinny Minnie/Sway with Me	1958	30.00
❑ 30681	Lean Jean/Don't Nobody Move	1958	25.00
❑ 30741	Chiquita Linda/Whoa Mabel	1958	25.00
❑ 30781	Corrine, Corrina/B.B. Betty	1958	25.00
❑ 30844	Charmaine/I Got a Woman	1959	25.00
❑ 30873	(Now and Then, There's) A Fool Such As I/Where Did You Go Last Night	1959	25.00
❑ 30926	Caldonia/Shakey	1959	25.00
❑ 30956	Joey's Song/Ooh, Look-a-There, Ain't She Pretty	1959	25.00
❑ 31030	Skokiaan (South African Song)/ Puerto Rican Peddler	1959	25.00
❑ 31080	Music, Music, Music/ Strictly Instrumental	1960	25.00
❑ 31649	The Green Door/ Yeah, She's Evil	1964	12.00
ESSEX			
❑ 102	Rock Around the Clock/Crazy Man, Crazy	1955	50.00
—Actually a bootleg, but highly sought-after nonetheless			
❑ 303	Rock the Joint/Icy Heart	1952	60.00
—Black vinyl, script logo ("Essex" not in all caps)			
❑ 303	Rock the Joint/Icy Heart	1952	100.00
—Black vinyl, block logo ("ESSEX" in all caps)			
❑ 303	Rock the Joint/Icy Heart	1952	1800.
—Red vinyl			
❑ 305	Rocking Chair on the Moon/ Dance with a Dolly (With a Hole in Her Stocking)	1952	100.00
—Essex 303 and 305 credit "Bill Haley and the Saddlemen"			
❑ 310	Real Rock Drive/Stop Beatin' Round the Mulberry Bush	1952	80.00
—Orange label			
❑ 310	Real Rock Drive/Stop Beatin' Round the Mulberry Bush	1952	150.00
—Blue label			
❑ 321	Crazy Man, Crazy/ Whatcha Gonna Do	1953	60.00
❑ 327	Pat-a-Cake/Fractured	1953	40.00
❑ 332	Live It Up/Farewell, So Long, Goodbye	1953	40.00
❑ 340	Ten Little Indians/I'll Be True	1953	40.00
❑ 348	Chattanooga Choo Choo/ Straight Jacket	1954	40.00
❑ 374	Sundown Boogie/ Jukebox Cannonball	1954	75.00
❑ 381	Rocket 88/Green Tree Boogie	1955	125.00
❑ 399	Rock the Joint/Farewell, So Long, Goodbye	1955	75.00
GNP CRESCENDO			
❑ 475	I'm Walkin'/Crazy Man, Crazy	1974	12.00
GONE			
❑ 5111	Spanish Twist/My Kind of Woman	1961	25.00
❑ 5116	Riviera/War Paint	1961	25.00
HOLIDAY			
❑ 113	Sundown Boogie/ Jukebox Cannonball	1951	500.00
—As "Bill Haley and the Saddlemen"; the only Holiday single known to exist on a 45. Earlier Holiday singles only exist on 78s.			
JANUS			
❑ 162	Travelin' Band/A Little Piece at a Time	1971	12.00
KAMA SUTRA			
❑ 508	Rock Around the Clock/Framed	1970	20.00
KASEY			
❑ 7006	A.B.C. Boogie/Rock Around the Clock	1961	20.00
—B-side by Phil Flowers			
MCA			
❑ 60025	(We're Gonna) Rock Around the Clock/Thirteen Women (And Only One Man in Town)	1973	5.00
—Reissue on black label with rainbow; made the Top 40 in 1974			
NEWTOWN			
❑ 5013	Tenor Man/Up Goes My Love	1962	20.00
❑ 5024	Dance Around the Clock/What Can I Say After I Say I'm Sorry	1963	20.00
NICETOWN			
❑ 5025	You Call Everybody Darling/ Tandy	1963	20.00
TRANS WORLD			
❑ 718	Real Rock Drive/Yes, Indeed	1954	200.00
UNITED ARTISTS			
❑ 50483	Ain't Love Funny, Ha Ha Ha/ That's How I Got to Memphis	1969	12.00
WARNER BROS.			
❑ 5145	Candy Kisses/Tamiami	1960	25.00
❑ 5145 [DJ]	Candy Kisses/Tamiami	1960	50.00
—Promo only on yellow vinyl			
❑ 5154	Hawk/Chick Safari	1960	25.00
❑ 5171	Let the Good Times Roll, Creole/So Right Tonight	1960	25.00
❑ 5228	Flip, Flop and Fly/Honky Tonk	1961	25.00
❑ 7124	Rock Around the Clock/Shake, Rattle and Roll	1969	15.00

7-Inch Extended Plays

Number	Title (A Side/B Side)	Yr	NM
CLAIRE			
❑ 4779	*All I Need Is Some More Lovin'/ Trouble in Mind/Life of the Party/I Should Write a Song About You	1978	15.00
❑ 4779 [PS]	Bill Haley and the Comets	1978	15.00
DECCA			
❑ ED 2168	Shake, Rattle and Roll/A.B.C. Boogie//(We're Gonna) Rock Around the Clock/Thirteen Women (And Only One Man in Town)	1954	60.00
❑ ED 2168 [PS]	Shake, Rattle and Roll	1954	60.00
❑ ED 2209	Dim, Dim the Lights/Happy Baby//Birth of the Boogie/ Mambo Rock	1955	60.00
❑ ED 2209 [PS]	Dim, Dim the Lights	1955	60.00
❑ ED 2322	Razzle-Dazzle/Two Hound Dogs//Burn That Candle/ Rock-a-Beatin' Boogie	1956	60.00
❑ ED 2322 [PS]	Rock and Roll	1956	60.00
❑ ED 2398	See You Later Alligator/R-O-C-K//The Saints Rock 'n Roll/ Burn That Candle	1956	50.00
❑ ED 2398 [PS]	He Digs RnR (Music for the Boyfriend)	1956	50.00
❑ ED 2416	Calling All Comets/Rockin' Through the Rye//Hook, Line and Sinker/Rudy's Rock	1956	50.00
❑ ED 2416 [PS]	Rock 'n' Roll Stage Show, Part 1	1956	50.00
❑ ED 2417	A Rockin' Little Tune/Hide and Seek//Choo Choo Ch' Boogie/Blue Comet Blues	1956	50.00
❑ ED 2417 [PS]	Rock 'n' Roll Stage Show, Part 2	1956	50.00
❑ ED 2418	Hey Then, There Now/Goofin' Around//Hot Dog Buddy Buddy/Tonight's the Night	1956	50.00
❑ ED 2418 [PS]	Rock 'n' Roll Stage Show, Part 3	1956	50.00
❑ ED 2532	The Dipsy Doodle/Miss You//Is It True What They Say About Dixie?/Carolina in the Morning	1957	50.00
❑ ED 2532 [PS]	Rockin' the Oldies	1957	50.00
❑ ED 2533	*One Sweet Letter from You/ Please Don't Talk About Me When I'm Gone/Apple Blossom Time/Somebody Else Is Taking My Place	1957	50.00
❑ ED 2533 [PS]	Rock 'n' Roll Party	1957	50.00
❑ ED 2534	*Moon Over Miami/Ain't Misbehavin'/You Can't Stop Me from Dreaming/I'm Gonna Sit Right Down and Write Myself a Letter	1957	50.00
❑ ED 2534 [PS]	Rockin' & Rollin'	1957	50.00
❑ ED 2564	*Me Rock-a-Hula/Wooden Shoe Rock/Oriental Rock/ Rockin' Matilda	1957	50.00
❑ ED 2564 [PS]	Rockin' Around the World	1957	50.00
❑ ED 2576	*Piccadilly Rock/Vive La Rock & Roll/Rockin' Rollin' Schnitzlebank/Come Rock with Me	1957	50.00
❑ ED 2576 [PS]	Rockin' Around Europe	1957	50.00

Number	Title (A Side/B Side)	Yr	NM
❑ ED 2577	*Pretty Alouette/El Rocko/ Rockin' Rita/Jamaican DJ	1957	50.00
❑ ED 2577 [PS]	Rockin' Around the Americas	1957	50.00
❑ ED 2615	Rock Lomond/It's a Sin//Move It On Over/New Rock the Joint	1958	40.00
❑ ED 2615 [PS]	Rockin' the Joint, Part 1	1958	40.00
❑ ED 2616	Rip It Up/The Beak (Speaks)// Sway with Me/Forty Cups of Coffee	1958	40.00
❑ ED 2616 [PS]	Rockin' the Joint, Part 2	1958	40.00
❑ ED 2638 [M]	*Whoa Mabel!/Ida Sweet as Apple Cider/Eloise/Dinah	1958	40.00
❑ ED 2638 [PS]	Bill Haley's Chicks	1958	40.00
❑ ED 7-2638 [PS]	Bill Haley's Chicks	1959	80.00
❑ ED 7-2638 [S]	*Whoa Mabel!/Ida Sweet as Apple Cider/Eloise/Dinah	1959	80.00
❑ ED 2670 [M]	Joe's Song/Ooh Look-a There Ain't She Pretty//Shakey/ Caledonia	1959	40.00
❑ ED 2670 [PS]	Bill Haley and His Comets	1959	40.00
❑ ED 7-2670 [PS]	Bill Haley and His Comets	1959	80.00
❑ ED 7-2670 [S]	Joe's Song/Ooh Look-a There Ain't She Pretty//Shakey/ Caledonia	1959	80.00
❑ ED 2671 [M]	Strictly Instrumental/South Africa Song//Mack the Knife/ In a Little Spanish Town	1959	40.00
❑ ED 2671 [PS]	Strictly Instrumental	1959	40.00
❑ ED 7-2671 [PS]	Strictly Instrumental	1959	80.00
❑ ED 7-2671 [S]	Strictly Instrumental/South Africa Song//Mack the Knife/ In a Little Spanish Town	1959	80.00
ESSEX			
❑ TWEP-102	Rock the Joint/Rockin' Chair on the Moon//Crazy Man, Crazy/ Pat-a-Cake	1954	100.00
❑ TWEP-102 [PS]	For Your Dance Party	1954	120.00
❑ EP-117	*Live It Up/Farewell, So Long, Goodbye/Real Rock Drive/ Fractured	1954	100.00
❑ EP-117 [PS]	Rock with Bill Haley and His Comets, Vol. 1	1954	120.00
❑ EP-118	*Stop Beatin' Round the Mulberry Bush/Watcha Gonna Do/I'll Be True/Juke Box Cannon Ball	1954	100.00
❑ EP-118 [PS]	Rock with Bill Haley and His Comets, Vol. 2	1954	120.00
❑ EP-119	(contents unknown)	1954	100.00
❑ EP-119 [PS]	Rock with Bill Haley and His Comets, Vol. 3	1954	120.00
SOMERSET			
❑ 460	(contents unknown)	1955	80.00
❑ 460 [PS]	Rock with Bill Haley and His Comets	1955	80.00
TRANS WORLD			
❑ TWEP-117	(contents unknown)	1955	80.00
❑ TWEP-117 [PS]	Rock with Bill Haley and His Comets, Vol. 1	1955	80.00
❑ TWEP-118	(contents unknown)	1955	80.00
❑ TWEP-118 [PS]	Rock with Bill Haley and His Comets, Vol. 2	1955	80.00
❑ TWEP-119	(contents unknown)	1955	80.00
❑ TWEP-119 [PS]	Rock with Bill Haley and His Comets, Vol. 3	1955	80.00
Albums			
ACCORD			
❑ SN-7125	Rockin' and Rollin'	1981	10.00
DECCA			
❑ DL 5560 [10]	Shake, Rattle and Roll	1955	800.00
❑ DXSE-7211 [(2)]	Bill Haley's Golden Hits	1972	15.00
❑ DL 8225 [M]	Rock Around the Clock	1955	150.00
—All-black label with silver print			
❑ DL 8225 [M]	Rock Around the Clock	1960	50.00
—Black label with colorband, no mention of MCA on label			
❑ DL 8225 [M]	Rock Around the Clock	1967	30.00
—Black label with colorband, "A Division of MCA" on label			
❑ DL 8315 [M]	Music for the Boyfriend	1956	150.00
❑ DL 8345 [M]	Rock 'n Roll Stage Show	1956	150.00
❑ DL 8569 [M]	Rockin' the Oldies	1957	150.00
❑ DL 8692 [M]	Rockin' Around the World	1958	150.00
❑ DL 8775 [M]	Rockin' the Joint	1958	150.00
❑ DL 8821 [M]	Bill Haley's Chicks	1959	100.00
❑ DL 8964 [M]	Strictly Instrumental	1960	100.00
❑ DL 75027	Bill Haley's Greatest Hits	1968	15.00
❑ DL 78225 [R]	Rock Around the Clock	1959	75.00
—All-black label with silver print			
❑ DL 78225 [R]	Rock Around the Clock	1960	25.00
—Black label with colorband, no mention of MCA on label			
❑ DL 78225 [R]	Rock Around the Clock	1967	15.00
—Black label with colorband, "A Division of MCA" on label			
❑ DL 78821 [S]	Bill Haley's Chicks	1959	150.00
❑ DL 78964 [S]	Strictly Instrumental	1960	150.00
ESSEX			
❑ LP 202 [M]	Rock with Bill Haley and the Comets	1955	500.00

Daryl Hall, "Dreamtime," RCA 14387, 1986, $3.

Number	Title (A Side/B Side)	Yr	NM
51 WEST			
❑ Q 16120	Live in New York/Greatest Hits	1981	10.00
—"All selections under license from Buddah Records"			
GNP CRESCENDO			
❑ GNPS-2077	Rock 'N' Roll	1973	12.00
❑ GNPS-2097	Rock Around the Country	1976	12.00
GREAT NORTHWEST			
❑ GNW 4015	Interviewed by Red Robinson	1981	12.00
JANUS			
❑ 3035	Travelin' Band	1972	25.00
❑ 7003 [(2)]	Razzle-Dazzle	1972	15.00
KAMA SUTRA			
❑ KLPS-2014	Scrapbook	1970	30.00
MCA			
❑ 161	Bill Haley's Greatest Hits	1973	10.00
—Reissue of Decca 75027			
❑ 4010 [(2)]	Bill Haley's Golden Hits	1973	12.00
—Reissue of Decca 7211			
❑ 5539 [(2)]	From the Original Master Tapes	1987	12.00
PAIR			
❑ MSM2-35069 [(2)]	Rock and Roll Giant	1986	12.00
PICCADILLY			
❑ PIC-3408	Greatest Hits	1980	10.00
PICKWICK			
❑ PTP-2077 [(2)]	Rock 'N' Roll	197?	12.00
❑ SPC-3256	Bill Haley and the Comets	1970	10.00
❑ SPC-3280	Rock 'N' Roll Revival	197?	10.00
ROULETTE			
❑ R 25174 [M]	Twistin' Knights at the Roundtable	1962	80.00
❑ SR 25174 [S]	Twistin' Knights at the Roundtable	1962	100.00
SOMERSET			
❑ P-4600 [M]	Rock with Bill Haley and the Comets	1958	150.00
TRANS WORLD			
❑ LP 202 [M]	Rock with Bill Haley and the Comets	1956	300.00
VOCALION			
❑ VL 3696 [M]	Bill Haley and the Comets	1963	25.00
WARNER BROS.			
❑ W 1378 [M]	Bill Haley and His Comets	1959	50.00
❑ WS 1378 [S]	Bill Haley and His Comets	1959	70.00
❑ W 1391 [M]	Bill Haley's Jukebox	1960	50.00
❑ WS 1391 [S]	Bill Haley's Jukebox	1960	70.00
❑ WS 1831	Rock 'N' Roll Revival	1970	15.00
❑ ST-93103	Rock 'N' Roll Revival	1970	25.00
—Capitol Record Club edition			

HALFNELSON See SPARKS.

HALIFAX THREE, THE

Number	Title (A Side/B Side)	Yr	NM
45s			
EPIC			
❑ 5-9560	Bull Train/Come On By	1962	10.00
❑ 5-9572	The Man Who Wouldn't Sing Along with Mitch/Come Down the Mountain Katie Daly	1963	10.00
❑ 5-9572 [PS]	The Man Who Wouldn't Sing Along with Mitch/Come Down the Mountain Katie Daly	1963	20.00
❑ 5-9637	All the Good Times/ San Francisco Bay Blues	1963	8.00
Albums			
COLUMBIA SPECIAL PRODUCTS			
❑ CSRP 26038 [S]	The Halifax Three	196?	10.00
—"Special Archive Series" sticker on cover			
EPIC			
❑ LN 24038 [M]	The Halifax Three	1962	12.00
❑ LN 24060 [M]	San Francisco Bay Blues	1963	12.00
❑ BN 26038 [S]	The Halifax Three	1962	15.00
❑ BN 26060 [S]	San Francisco Bay Blues	1963	15.00

HALL, DARYL Also see GULLIVER; DARYL HALL AND JOHN OATES; THE TEMPTONES.

Number	Title (A Side/B Side)	Yr	NM
12-Inch Singles			
RCA			
❑ 5714-1-RD	Dreamtime (Extended)/(Dub)	1986	8.00

H

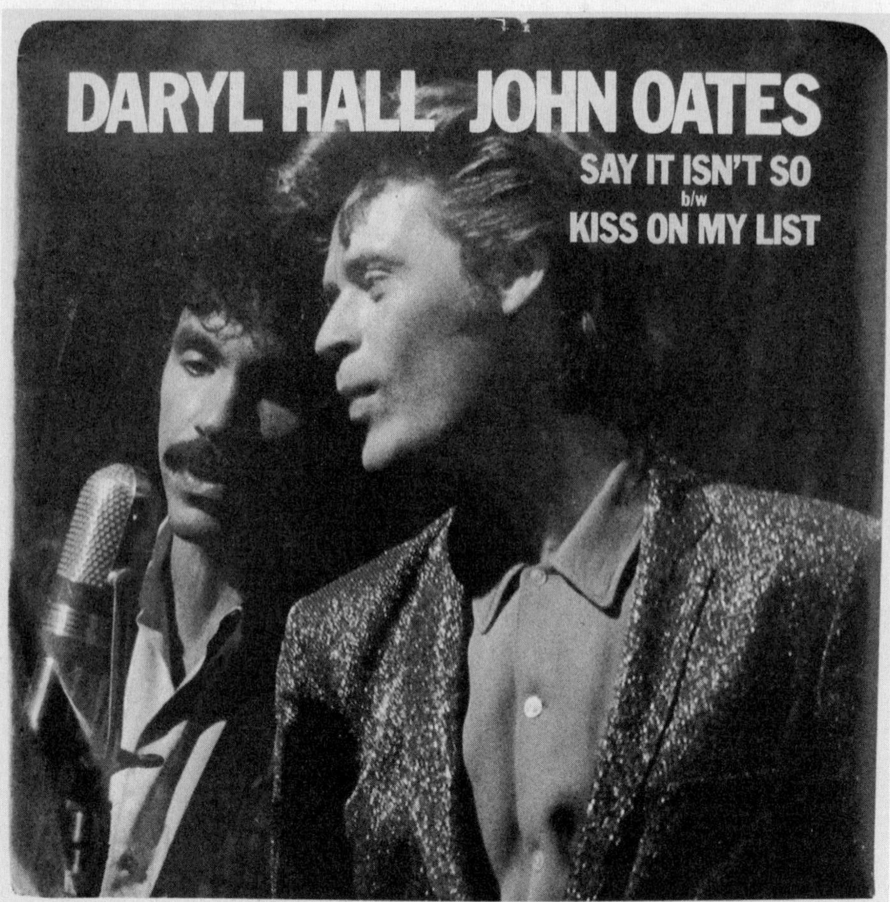

Daryl Hall and John Oates, "Say It Isn't So," RCA 13654, 1983, **$4.**

Number	Title (A Side/B Side)	Yr	NM
❑ 5745-1-RD	Foolish Pride/Let It Out	1986	8.00
❑ 5748-1-RD	Foolish Pride (Extended Version) (Edit Remix) (Dub)/ What's Gonna Happen to Us	1986	8.00
❑ PD-14386 [DJ]	Dreamtime (same on both sides)	1986	8.00
45s			
AMY			
❑ 11049	The Princess and the Soldier (Part 1)/The Princess and the Soldier (Part 2)	1969	6.00
EPIC			
❑ 34-77139	I'm in a Philly Mood/Money Changes Everything	1993	3.00
❑ 34-77258	Stop Lovin' Me, Stop Lovin' You/(Churban Remix)	1993	3.00
PARALLAX			
❑ 404	A Lonely Girl/Vicky - Vicky	196?	30.00
RCA			
❑ 5038-7-R	Foolish Pride/What's Gonna Happen to Us	1986	3.00
❑ 5038-7-R [PS]	Foolish Pride/What's Gonna Happen to Us	1986	3.00
❑ 5105-7-R	Someone Like You (The Guitar Solo)/Someone Like You (The Sax Solo)	1987	3.00
❑ 5105-7-R [PS]	Someone Like You (The Guitar Solo)/Someone Like You (The Sax Solo)	1987	3.00
❑ PB-12001	Something in 4/4 Time/ Sacred Songs	1980	4.00
❑ PB-12001 [PS]	Something in 4/4 Time/ Sacred Songs	1980	5.00
❑ PB-14387	Dreamtime/Let It Out	1986	3.00
❑ PB-14387 [PS]	Dreamtime/Let It Out	1986	3.00
Albums			
RCA VICTOR			
❑ AFL1-3573	Sacred Songs	1980	10.00
❑ AJL1-7196	Three Hearts in the Happy Ending Machine	1986	8.00

Number	Title (A Side/B Side)	Yr	NM
HALL, DARYL, AND JOHN OATES			
12-Inch Singles			
ARISTA			
❑ AD1-9685	Everything Your Heart Desires (If You Want the World Mix 7:53) (54th Street Remix 9:12) (No Words Can Help Dub Mix 5:57) (7th Avenue Remix 4:26)/Realove	1988	10.00
❑ AD1-9728	Missed Opportunity (Unlimited Mix 6:58) (Smooth Mix 8:57) (Radio Mix 4:39)/Soul Love	1988	8.00
❑ AD1-9768	Downtown Life (5 versions)	1989	8.00
❑ ADP-9779 [DJ]	Talking All Night (Extended Remix 6:08) (Dub Mix) (A Cappella) (LP Version) (Radio Remix)	1989	15.00
PUSH			
❑ 90405-1 [(2)DJ]	Hold On to Yourself (Tommy Musto's Club Mix 5:54) (Rachid Wehbi's Extended Mix 6:07) (Tribal Path Mix 4:37) (Naughty G's Rubber Mix 6:10) (Tommy Musto's Dub Mix 5:21) (Tommy Musto's Club Instrumental 5:57) (Tribal Path Hip-Hop Mix 4:39) (Tommy Musto's Radio Mix 4:18)	1998	40.00
RCA			
❑ JT-11022 [DJ]	Back Together Again/Kerry	1977	20.00
—B-side by Stephen Dees			
❑ JD-11302 [DJ]	Do What You Want, Be What You Are (Long Version) (Short Version)	1977	20.00
❑ JD-11431 [DJ]	I Don't Wanna Lose You/ August Day	1977	20.00
❑ JD-11770 [DJ]	Running from Paradise (6:29)/ Portable Radio	1979	15.00
❑ JD-12053 [DJ]	How Does It Feel to Be Back (same on both sides)	1980	20.00

Number	Title (A Side/B Side)	Yr	NM
❑ PD-12297	Private Eyes/Tell Me What You Want	1981	12.00
❑ PD-12358	I Can't Go for That (No Can Do)/ Unguarded Minute	1981	12.00
❑ PD-13080	Did It in a Minute/Head Above Water	1982	12.00
❑ PD-13253	Your Imagination (Extended Remix 5:41)/Sara Smile (3:07)	1982	12.00
❑ JD-13403 [DJ]	Maneater (Special Extended Club Mix)/I Can't Go for That (Club Mix)	1982	15.00
❑ PD-13428	One on One (Club Mix 5:30)/ I Can't Go for That (Long)	1983	12.00
❑ PD-13508	Family Man (Extended Dance Remix)/Maneater	1983	10.00
❑ JD-13659 [DJ]	Say It Isn't So/Wait for Me (Live)	1983	12.00
❑ PW-13679	Say It Isn't So (Special Extended Dance Mix 6:49)// (Dub Version 4:47)/ Kiss on My List	1983	10.00
❑ JM-13705 [DJ]	Jingle Bell Rock from Daryl/ Jingle Bell Rock from John	1983	30.00
—Promo-only picture disc in plastic sleeve			
❑ PD-13715	Adult Edudation (Special Club Mix 6:04)/Maneater	1984	8.00
❑ JD-13736 [DJ]	Adult Education (Special Extended Mix Long) (Special Extended Mix Short)	1984	12.00
❑ PW-13917	Out of Touch (Extended Remix 7:37)//(Dub Version 7:24)/ Cold, Dark and Yesterday	1984	10.00
❑ JR-13927 [DJ]	Out of Touch (4:24) (same on both sides)	1984	12.00
❑ PW-13971	Method of Modern Love (7:50)/ /(Dub)/Bank On Your Love	1984	10.00
❑ JD-13972 [DJ]	Method of Modern Love (5:27)/ Bank On Your Love	1984	12.00
❑ JD-13983 [DJ]	Jingle Bell Rock from Daryl/ Jingle Bell Rock from John	1984	12.00
—Promo-only reissue, not a picture disc			
❑ PW-14036	Some Things Are Better Left Unsaid (Special New Mix 5:24)//All American Girl/ Some Things Are Better Left Unsaid (Instrumental 5:25)	1985	8.00
❑ JD-14038 [DJ]	Some Things Are Better Left Unsaid (Special New Mix 5:24) (same on both sides)	1985	12.00
❑ PW-14099	Possession Obsession//Dance on Your Knees/Everytime You Go Away	1985	8.00
❑ JR-14100 [DJ]	Possession Obsession (Special New Mix) (same on both sides)	1985	10.00
❑ PW-14179	A Nite at the Apollo Live! The Way You Do the Things You Do-My Girl//Everytime You Go Away/Adult Education	1985	8.00
❑ JR-14180 [DJ]	A Nite at the Apollo Live! The Way You Do the Things You Do-My Girl (same on both sides)	1985	10.00
❑ PD-14250	Jingle Bell Rock from Daryl/ Jingle Bell Rock from John// Everytime You Go Away/ When Something Is Wrong with My Baby	1985	—
—Canceled			
45s			
ARISTA			
❑ 2085	So Close/So Close (Unplugged)	1990	3.00
❑ 2157	Don't Hold Back Your Love/ Change of Season	1990	3.00
❑ 9684	Everything Your Heart Desires/ Real Love	1988	3.00
❑ 9684 [PS]	Everything Your Heart Desires/ Real Love	1988	3.00
❑ 9727	Missed Opportunity/Soul Love	1988	3.00
❑ 9727 [PS]	Missed Opportunity/Soul Love	1988	3.00
❑ 9753	Downtown Life (LP Version)/ Downtown Life (Urban Mix)	1988	3.00
❑ 9753 [PS]	Downtown Life (LP Version)/ Downtown Life (Urban Mix)	1988	3.00
ATLANTIC			
❑ 2922	Goodnight & Good Morning/ All Our Love	1972	10.00
—As "Whole Oats"			
❑ 2939	Lilly (Are You Happy)/I'm Sorry	1973	8.00
❑ 2993	She's Gone/I'm Just a Kid (Don't Make Me Feel Like a Man)	1973	8.00
❑ 3026	Lady Rain/When the Morning Comes	1974	5.00
❑ 3239	Can't Stop the Music/ 70's Scenario	1975	5.00
❑ 3332	She's Gone/I'm Just a Kid (Don't Make Me Feel Like a Man)	1976	4.00
❑ 3332 [DJ]	She's Gone (Long Version)/ She's Gone	1976	6.00

Except when noted otherwise, VG = 25% of NM, and VG+ = 50% of NM. (Example: VG = $2.00, VG+ = $4.00 and NM = $8.00.)

Number	Title (A Side/B Side)	Yr	NM
❑ 3397	It's Uncanny/Lilly (Are You Happy)	1977	4.00

CHELSEA

Number	Title (A Side/B Side)	Yr	NM
❑ 3063	If That's What Makes You Happy/The Reason Why	1977	5.00

—B-side by "Daryl Hall and Gulliver"

Number	Title (A Side/B Side)	Yr	NM
❑ 3065	Red River Blues/ (B-side unknown)	1977	5.00
❑ 3069	Perkiomen/The Provider	1977	5.00

RCA

Number	Title (A Side/B Side)	Yr	NM
❑ PB-10808	Do What You Want, Be What You Are/You'll Never Learn	1976	4.00
❑ PB-10860	Rich Girl/London Luck, & Love	1976	4.00
❑ PB-10860 [PS]	Rich Girl/London Luck, & Love	1976	8.00
❑ GB-10942	Sara Smile/Do What You Want, Be What You Are	1977	3.00

—Gold Standard Series

Number	Title (A Side/B Side)	Yr	NM
❑ PB-10970	Back Together Again/ Room to Breathe	1977	4.00
❑ PB-11132	Why Do Lovers (Break Each Other's Heart?)/A Girl Who Used to Be	1977	4.00
❑ PB-11181	Don't Change/The Emptiness	1977	4.00
❑ GB-11324	Rich Girl/Back Together Again	1978	3.00

—Gold Standard Series

Number	Title (A Side/B Side)	Yr	NM
❑ PB-11371	It's a Laugh/Serious Music	1978	4.00
❑ PB-11424	I Don't Wanna Lose You/ August Day	1978	4.00
❑ PB-11747	Wait for Me/No Brain No Pain	1979	4.00
❑ PB-11920	All You Want Is Heaven/Who Said the World Was Fair	1980	4.00
❑ GB-11970	It's a Laugh/I Don't Wanna Lose You	1980	3.00

—Gold Standard Series

Number	Title (A Side/B Side)	Yr	NM
❑ PB-12048	How Does It Feel to Be Back/ United State	1980	4.00
❑ PB-12103	You've Lost That Lovin' Feeling/Diddy Doo Wap (I Hear the Voices)	1980	4.00
❑ PB-12142	Kiss on My List/Africa	1981	4.00
❑ PB-12217	You Make My Dreams/ Gotta Lotta Love	1981	4.00
❑ PB-12296	Private Eyes/Tell Me What You Want	1981	4.00
❑ GB-12318	Kiss on My List/You've Lost That Lovin' Feeling	1981	3.00

—Gold Standard Series

Number	Title (A Side/B Side)	Yr	NM
❑ PB-12357	I Can't Go for That (No Can Do)/ Unguarded Minute	1981	4.00
❑ JB-12361 [DJ]	I Can't Go for That (No Can Do)/ (Club Mix)	1981	10.00

—Promo only

Number	Title (A Side/B Side)	Yr	NM
❑ PB-13065	Did It in a Minute/ Head Above Water	1982	4.00
❑ PB-13252	Your Imagination/Sara Smile	1982	4.00
❑ PB-13354	Maneater/Delayed Reaction	1982	3.00
❑ PB-13354 [PS]	Maneater/Delayed Reaction	1982	4.00
❑ PB-13421	One on One/Art of Heartbreak	1983	3.00
❑ PB-13421 [PS]	One on One/Art of Heartbreak	1983	4.00
❑ GB-13480	Private Eyes/I Can't Go for That (No Can Do)	1983	3.00

—Gold Standard Series

Number	Title (A Side/B Side)	Yr	NM
❑ GB-13481	You Make My Dreams/ Did It in a Minute	1983	3.00

—Gold Standard Series

Number	Title (A Side/B Side)	Yr	NM
❑ PB-13507	Family Man/Open All Night	1983	3.00
❑ PB-13654	Say It Isn't So/Kiss on My List	1983	3.00
❑ PB-13654 [PS]	Say It Isn't So/Kiss on My List	1983	4.00
❑ PB-13714	Adult Education/Maneater	1984	3.00
❑ PB-13714 [PS]	Adult Education/Maneater	1984	4.00
❑ GB-13796	Maneater/One on One	1984	3.00

—Gold Standard Series

Number	Title (A Side/B Side)	Yr	NM
❑ GB-13797	Family Man/Say It Isn't So	1984	3.00

—Gold Standard Series

Number	Title (A Side/B Side)	Yr	NM
❑ PB-13916	Out of Touch/Cold, Dark, and Yesterday	1984	3.00
❑ PB-13916 [PS]	Out of Touch/Cold, Dark, and Yesterday	1984	3.00
❑ PB-13970	Method of Modern Love (Remix Edit)/Method of Modern Love	1984	3.00
❑ PB-13970 [PS]	Method of Modern Love (Remix Edit)/Method of Modern Love	1984	3.00
❑ PB-14035	Some Things Are Better Left Unsaid/All American Girl	1985	3.00
❑ PB-14035 [PS]	Some Things Are Better Left Unsaid/All American Girl	1985	3.00
❑ GB-14064	Out of Touch/Adult Education	1985	3.00

—Gold Standard Series

Number	Title (A Side/B Side)	Yr	NM
❑ PB-14098	Possession Obsession/ Dance on Your Knees	1985	3.00
❑ PB-14098 [PS]	Possession Obsession/ Dance on Your Knees	1985	3.00
❑ PB-14178	A Nite at the Apollo Live! The Way You Do the Things You Do-My Girl/Everytime You Go Away	1985	3.00

—A-side: With David Ruffin and Eddie Kendrick (sic)

Number	Title (A Side/B Side)	Yr	NM
❑ PB-14178 [PS]	A Nite at the Apollo Live! The Way You Do the Things You Do-My Girl/Everytime You Go Away	1985	3.00

—A-side: With David Ruffin and Eddie Kendrick (sic)

Number	Title (A Side/B Side)	Yr	NM
❑ JR-14259 [DJ]	Jingle Bell Rock from Daryl/ Jingle Bell Rock from John	1985	10.00

—Promo only on green vinyl

Number	Title (A Side/B Side)	Yr	NM
❑ JR-14259 [DJ]	Jingle Bell Rock from Daryl/ Jingle Bell Rock from John	1985	10.00

—Promo only on red vinyl

Number	Title (A Side/B Side)	Yr	NM
❑ JR-14259 [PS]	Jingle Bell Rock from Daryl/ Jingle Bell Rock from John	1985	10.00
❑ GB-14340	Method of Modern Love/ Possession Obsession	1986	3.00

—Gold Standard Series

Number	Title (A Side/B Side)	Yr	NM
❑ GB-14341	Some Things Are Better Left Unsaid/A Nite at the Apollo Live! The Way You Do the Things You Do-My Girl	1986	3.00

—Gold Standard Series

RCA VICTOR

Number	Title (A Side/B Side)	Yr	NM
❑ PB-10373	Camellia/Ennui on the Mountain	1975	5.00
❑ PB-10436	Nothing at All/Alone Too Long	1975	5.00
❑ PB-10530	Sara Smile/Soldering	1975	5.00

SIRE

Number	Title (A Side/B Side)	Yr	NM
❑ 22967	Love Train/"Earth Girls Are Easy" Theme	1989	3.00
❑ 22967 [PS]	Love Train/"Earth Girls Are Easy" Theme	1989	3.00

Albums

ALLEGIANCE

Number	Title (A Side/B Side)	Yr	NM
❑ AV-5014	Nucleus	198?	8.00

ARISTA

Number	Title (A Side/B Side)	Yr	NM
❑ AL-8539	Ooh Yeah!	1988	10.00
❑ AL-8614	Change of Season	1989	12.00

ATLANTIC

Number	Title (A Side/B Side)	Yr	NM
❑ 7242 [M]	Whole Oats	1972	60.00

—White label promo only with "d/j copy monaural" sticker on cover

Number	Title (A Side/B Side)	Yr	NM
❑ SD 7242	Whole Oats	1972	12.00
❑ SD 7269	Abandoned Luncheonette	1973	12.00
❑ SD 18109	War Babies	1974	12.00
❑ SD 18213	No Goodbyes	1977	10.00
❑ SD 19139	Abandoned Luncheonette	1977	8.00

CHELSEA

Number	Title (A Side/B Side)	Yr	NM
❑ CHL-547	Past Times Behind	1976	12.00

INTERMEDIA

Number	Title (A Side/B Side)	Yr	NM
❑ QS-5040	The Early Years	198?	8.00

JEM

Number	Title (A Side/B Side)	Yr	NM
❑ 55002	Early Years	198?	8.00

MOBILE FIDELITY

Number	Title (A Side/B Side)	Yr	NM
❑ 1-069	Abandoned Luncheonette	1982	20.00

—Audiophile vinyl

RCA VICTOR

Number	Title (A Side/B Side)	Yr	NM
❑ APL1-1144	Daryl Hall & John Oates	1976	10.00
❑ APL1-1467	Bigger Than Both of Us	1976	10.00
❑ AFL1-2300	Beauty on a Back Street	1977	10.00
❑ AFL1-2802	Livetime!	1978	10.00
❑ AFL1-2804	Along the Red Ledge	1978	10.00
❑ AFL1-2804	Along the Red Ledge	1978	15.00

—Red vinyl

Number	Title (A Side/B Side)	Yr	NM
❑ ANL1-3463	Daryl Hall & John Oates	1979	8.00
❑ AFL1-3494	X-Static	1979	10.00
❑ DJL1-3512 [DJ]	Post Static	1979	20.00

—Promo-only one-sided 4-song sampler

Number	Title (A Side/B Side)	Yr	NM
❑ AQL1-3646	Voices	1980	8.00

—"RE 4" on back cover. Color photo of Hall and Oates on each side

Number	Title (A Side/B Side)	Yr	NM
❑ AQL1-3646	Voices	1980	10.00

—"RE 2" on back cover. Cover not embossed; Hall's head 3 inches-plus below "Voices" on front cover

Number	Title (A Side/B Side)	Yr	NM
❑ AQL1-3646	Voices	1980	12.00

—No "RE" of any type on back cover. Embossed lettering and sound waves, Hall's head almost touches the word "Voices" on front

Number	Title (A Side/B Side)	Yr	NM
❑ AQL1-3646	Voices	1980	12.00

—"RE 3" on back cover. Cover lettering in black

Number	Title (A Side/B Side)	Yr	NM
❑ AQL1-3646	Voices	1980	12.00

—"RE" on back cover. Variation unknown

Number	Title (A Side/B Side)	Yr	NM
❑ AQL1-3646	Voices	1981	8.00

—"RE 5" on back cover. Variation unknown

Number	Title (A Side/B Side)	Yr	NM
❑ AQL1-3646	Voices	1981	8.00

—"RE 6" on back cover. Bar code on upper left back cover

Number	Title (A Side/B Side)	Yr	NM
❑ DJL1-3832	RCA Radio Special Interview Series	1980	15.00
❑ AYL1-3836	Daryl Hall & John Oates	1980	8.00
❑ AYL1-3866	Bigger Than Both of Us	1980	8.00
❑ AFL1-4028	Private Eyes	1981	10.00
❑ DJL1-4179	Special Radio Series	1981	15.00
❑ AYL1-4230	Beauty on a Back Street	1981	8.00
❑ AYL1-4231	Along the Red Ledge	1981	8.00
❑ AYL1-4303	X-Static	1982	8.00
❑ AFL1-4383	H2O	1982	10.00
❑ AYL1-4722	Livetime!	1983	8.00
❑ CPL1-4858	Rock 'n Soul Part 1	1983	8.00

—"RE 2" on lower left back. Variation unknown

Number	Title (A Side/B Side)	Yr	NM
❑ CPL1-4858	Rock 'n Soul Part 1	1983	10.00

—"RE" on lower left back: back cover says "Plus Two New Songs (Recorded September 1983)," then mentions "Say It Isn't So" and "Adult Education"

Number	Title (A Side/B Side)	Yr	NM
❑ CPL1-4858	Rock 'n Soul Part 1	1983	12.00

—Original cover: back cover says "Plus Two New Songs (Recorded September 1983)" WITHOUT mentioning what the songs are

Number	Title (A Side/B Side)	Yr	NM
❑ AFL1-5309	Big Bam Boom	1984	12.00
❑ AJL1-5336	Big Bam Boom	1984	10.00
❑ AFL1-7035	Live at the Apollo	1985	10.00

HALL, DICKSON

45s

EPIC

Number	Title (A Side/B Side)	Yr	NM
❑ 9262	Cowboy/It's a Long Walk Home	1958	15.00
❑ 9262 [PS]	Cowboy/It's a Long Walk Home	1958	25.00

Albums

EPIC

Number	Title (A Side/B Side)	Yr	NM
❑ LN 3427 [M]	25 All-Time Country and Western Hits	1958	25.00

KAPP

Number	Title (A Side/B Side)	Yr	NM
❑ KL-1067 [M]	Fabulous Country Hits Way Out West	1957	30.00
❑ KL-1464 [M]	24 Fabulous Country Hits	1966	20.00
❑ KS-3464 [S]	24 Fabulous Country Hits	1966	25.00

MGM

Number	Title (A Side/B Side)	Yr	NM
❑ E-329 [10]	Outlaws of the Old West	1954	60.00
❑ E-3263 [M]	Outlaws of the Old West	1956	40.00

PERFECT

Number	Title (A Side/B Side)	Yr	NM
❑ P-14016 [M]	Country & Western Million Sellers	1960	20.00
❑ PS-14016 [S]	Country & Western Million Sellers	1960	25.00

HALL, LARRY

45s

HOT

Number	Title (A Side/B Side)	Yr	NM
❑ 1	Sandy/Lovin' Tree	1959	50.00

STRAND

Number	Title (A Side/B Side)	Yr	NM
❑ 25007	Sandy/Lovin' Tree	1959	25.00
❑ 25013	A Girl Like You/Rosemary	1960	20.00
❑ 25016	For Every Boy/I'll Stay Single	1960	20.00
❑ 25025	The Girl I Left Behind/Kool Love	1961	20.00
❑ 25029	Lips of Wine/Rebel Heart	1961	20.00
❑ 25048	Ladder of Love/The One You Left Behind	1961	20.00

Albums

STRAND

Number	Title (A Side/B Side)	Yr	NM
❑ SL-1005 [M]	Sandy	1960	150.00
❑ SLS-1005 [S]	Sandy	1960	200.00

HALL, ROY (1)

Rockabilly and country singer-pianist; wrote "Whole Lot of Shakin' Goin' On." Not to be confused with the pre-World War II country singer of the same name.

45s

DECCA

Number	Title (A Side/B Side)	Yr	NM
❑ 29697	Whole Lotta Shakin' Goin' On/ All By Myself	1955	80.00
❑ 29786	See You Later, Alligator/ Don't Stop Now	1956	50.00
❑ 29880	Blue Suede Shoes/Luscious	1956	50.00
❑ 30060	Three Alley Cats/ Diggin' the Boogie	1956	50.00

FORTUNE

Number	Title (A Side/B Side)	Yr	NM
❑ 170	Going Down the Road/ Jealous Love	1952	40.00

—B-side by the Davis Sisters

Number	Title (A Side/B Side)	Yr	NM
❑ 521	Corrine, Corrina/Don't Ask Me No Questions	1956	50.00

HI-Q

Number	Title (A Side/B Side)	Yr	NM
❑ 5045	Three Alley Cats/ Bedspring Motel	196?	60.00
❑ 5050	Go Go Little Queenie/ Everybody Dig That Boogie	196?	60.00

HALL, SIDNEY

45s

SHRINE

Number	Title (A Side/B Side)	Yr	NM
❑ 109	The Weekend/I'm a Lover	1966	1000.

HALLMARKS, THE

45s

DOT

Number	Title (A Side/B Side)	Yr	NM
❑ 16418	My Little Sailor Boy/ Congratulations	1963	20.00

EPIC

Number	Title (A Side/B Side)	Yr	NM
❑ 9681	Let There Be You/Royal King	1964	12.00

SMASH

Number	Title (A Side/B Side)	Yr	NM
❑ 2115	Soul Shakin' Psychedelic Sally/ Girl of My Dreams	1967	30.00

HALLOWAY, LARRY

45s

PARKWAY

Number	Title (A Side/B Side)	Yr	NM
❑ 903	Beatle Teen Beat/Going Up	1964	20.00

HALLYDAY, JOHNNY

45s

PHILIPS

Number	Title (A Side/B Side)	Yr	NM
❑ 40024	I Got a Woman/Be-Bop-a-Lula	1962	25.00
❑ 40043	Hey Little Girl/Caravan of Lonely Men	1962	25.00

Albums

PHILIPS

Number	Title (A Side/B Side)	Yr	NM
❑ PHM 200019 [M]	America's Rockin' Hits	1962	80.00
❑ PHS 600019 [S]	America's Rockin' Hits	1962	100.00

HALOS, THE

45s

CONGRESS

Number	Title (A Side/B Side)	Yr	NM
❑ 244	Do I/Just Keep On Loving Me	1965	12.00
❑ 249	Since I Fell for You/You're Never Gonna Find	1965	12.00
❑ 253	Baby What You Want Me to Do/Hey, Hey, Love Me	1965	12.00
❑ 262 [DJ]	Come Softly to Me/(B-side unknown)	1966	12.00

—May be promo-only

7 ARTS

Number	Title (A Side/B Side)	Yr	NM
❑ 709	Nag/Copy Cat	1961	20.00
❑ 720	Come On/What'd I Say	1962	20.00

Albums

WARWICK

Number	Title (A Side/B Side)	Yr	NM
❑ W-2046 [M]	The Halos	1962	400.00

HAMILTON, CHICO

45s

COLUMBIA

Number	Title (A Side/B Side)	Yr	NM
❑ 42045	Afternoon of a Breeze (Part 1)/Afternoon of a Breeze (Part 2)	1961	12.00

ENTERPRISE

Number	Title (A Side/B Side)	Yr	NM
❑ 9102	Conquistadores '74/Fancy	1974	5.00

IMPULSE!

Number	Title (A Side/B Side)	Yr	NM
❑ 238	Forest Flower (Part 1)/Forest Flower (Part 2)	1965	10.00
❑ 241	Conquistadores (Part 1)/Conquistadores (Part 2)	1966	10.00
❑ 249	Monday, Monday/Evil Eye	1967	8.00
❑ 258	For Mods Only/The Dealer	1968	8.00

PACIFIC JAZZ

Number	Title (A Side/B Side)	Yr	NM
❑ 628	Blue Sands/The Morning After	1955	20.00
❑ 631	The Squimp/Mr. Jo Jones	1955	20.00

WORLD PACIFIC

Number	Title (A Side/B Side)	Yr	NM
❑ 88134	Siete Quatro/Satin Doll	1966	8.00

Albums

ABC IMPULSE!

Number	Title (A Side/B Side)	Yr	NM
❑ AS-29 [S]	Passin' Thru	1968	15.00
❑ AS-59 [S]	Man from Two Worlds	1968	15.00
❑ AS-82 [S]	Chi Chi Chico	1968	15.00
❑ AS-9102 [S]	El Chico	1968	15.00
❑ AS-9114 [S]	The Further Adventures of El Chico	1968	15.00
❑ AS-9130 [S]	The Dealer	1968	15.00
❑ AS-9174	The Best of Chico Hamilton	1969	15.00
❑ AS-9213 [(2)]	His Great Hits	1971	20.00

BLUE NOTE

Number	Title (A Side/B Side)	Yr	NM
❑ BN-LA520-G	Peregrinations	1975	12.00
❑ BN-LA622-G	Chico Hamilton & Players	1976	12.00

COLUMBIA

Number	Title (A Side/B Side)	Yr	NM
❑ CL 1590 [M]	Selections from "Bye Bye Birdie"	1961	20.00
❑ CL 1619 [M]	Chico Hamilton Special	1961	20.00
❑ CL 1807 [M]	Drumfusion	1962	20.00
❑ CS 8390 [S]	Selections from "Bye Bye Birdie"	1961	25.00
❑ CS 8419 [S]	Chico Hamilton Special	1961	25.00
❑ CS 8607 [S]	Drumfusion	1962	25.00

DECCA

Number	Title (A Side/B Side)	Yr	NM
❑ DL 8614 [M]	Jazz from the Sweet Smell of Success	1957	50.00

DISCOVERY

Number	Title (A Side/B Side)	Yr	NM
❑ 831	Gongs East	1981	10.00

—Reissue of Warner Bros. 1271

ELEKTRA

Number	Title (A Side/B Side)	Yr	NM
❑ 6E-257	Nomad	1980	10.00

ENTERPRISE

Number	Title (A Side/B Side)	Yr	NM
❑ SD 7501	The Master	1974	12.00

FLYING DUTCHMAN

Number	Title (A Side/B Side)	Yr	NM
❑ 10135	Exigente	1971	15.00

IMPULSE!

Number	Title (A Side/B Side)	Yr	NM
❑ A-29 [M]	Passin' Thru	1963	25.00
❑ AS-29 [S]	Passin' Thru	1963	30.00
❑ A-59 [M]	Man from Two Worlds	1964	25.00
❑ AS-59 [S]	Man from Two Worlds	1964	30.00
❑ A-82 [M]	Chi Chi Chico	1965	20.00
❑ AS-82 [S]	Chi Chi Chico	1965	25.00
❑ A-9102 [M]	El Chico	1965	20.00
❑ AS-9102 [S]	El Chico	1965	25.00
❑ A-9114 [M]	The Further Adventures of El Chico	1966	20.00
❑ AS-9114 [S]	The Further Adventures of El Chico	1966	25.00
❑ A-9130 [M]	The Dealer	1966	20.00
❑ SMAS-91138 [S]	The Dealer	1966	30.00

—Capitol Record Club edition

JAZZTONE

Number	Title (A Side/B Side)	Yr	NM
❑ J-1264 [M]	Delightfully Modern	1957	40.00

MCA

Number	Title (A Side/B Side)	Yr	NM
❑ 637	Man from Two Worlds	198?	8.00

—Reissue of Impulse! 59

Number	Title (A Side/B Side)	Yr	NM
❑ 638	El Chico	198?	8.00

—Reissue of Impulse! 9102

Number	Title (A Side/B Side)	Yr	NM
❑ 29037	Passin' Thru	198?	10.00

—Reissue of Impulse! 29

Number	Title (A Side/B Side)	Yr	NM
❑ 29038	The Best of Chico Hamilton	198?	10.00

—Reissue of Impulse! 9174

MERCURY

Number	Title (A Side/B Side)	Yr	NM
❑ SRM-1-1163	Catwalk	1977	12.00

NAUTILUS

Number	Title (A Side/B Side)	Yr	NM
❑ NR-13	Reaching for the Top	1981	30.00

—Audiophile vinyl

PACIFIC JAZZ

Number	Title (A Side/B Side)	Yr	NM
❑ PJLP-17 [10]	Chico Hamilton Trio	1955	100.00
❑ PJ-39 [M]	Spectacular	1962	25.00

—Reissue of 1209

Number	Title (A Side/B Side)	Yr	NM
❑ PJ-1209 [M]	Chico Hamilton Quintet	1955	75.00
❑ PJ-1216 [M]	Chico Hamilton Quintet In Hi-Fi	1956	75.00
❑ PJ-1220 [M]	Chico Hamilton Trio	1956	75.00
❑ PJ-1225 [M]	Chico Hamilton Quintet	1957	75.00
❑ PJ-1231 [M]	Chico Hamilton Plays the Music of Fred Katz	1957	75.00

REPRISE

Number	Title (A Side/B Side)	Yr	NM
❑ R-6078 [M]	A Different Journey	1963	30.00
❑ R9-6078 [S]	A Different Journey	1963	40.00

SOLID STATE

Number	Title (A Side/B Side)	Yr	NM
❑ SS-18043	The Gamut	1969	15.00
❑ SS-18050	Headhunters	1969	15.00

SOUL NOTE

Number	Title (A Side/B Side)	Yr	NM
❑ 121191	Reunion	1989	12.00

SUNSET

Number	Title (A Side/B Side)	Yr	NM
❑ SUS-5215	Easy Livin'	196?	12.00

WARNER BROS.

Number	Title (A Side/B Side)	Yr	NM
❑ W 1245 [M]	Chico Hamilton Quintet with Strings Attached	1958	50.00
❑ WS 1245 [S]	Chico Hamilton Quintet with Strings Attached	1958	60.00
❑ W 1271 [M]	Gongs East	1958	50.00
❑ WS 1271 [S]	Gongs East	1958	60.00
❑ W 1344 [M]	The Three Faces of Chico	1959	50.00
❑ WS 1344 [S]	The Three Faces of Chico	1959	60.00

WORLD PACIFIC

Number	Title (A Side/B Side)	Yr	NM
❑ ST-1003 [S]	South Pacific in Hi-Fi	1958	40.00
❑ ST-1005 [S]	Chico Hamilton Quintet	1958	40.00
❑ ST-1008 [S]	The Chico Hamilton Trio Featuring Freddie Gambrell	1958	40.00
❑ ST-1016 [S]	Ellington Suite	1959	40.00
❑ WP-1216 [M]	Chico Hamilton Quintet In Hi-Fi	1958	50.00
❑ WP-1225 [M]	Chico Hamilton Quintet	1958	50.00
❑ WP-1231 [M]	Chico Hamilton Plays the Music of Fred Katz	1958	50.00
❑ PJ-1238 [M]	South Pacific in Hi-Fi	1957	50.00
❑ WP-1238 [M]	South Pacific in Hi-Fi	1958	40.00
❑ PJ-1242 [M]	The Chico Hamilton Trio Featuring Freddie Gambrell	1957	50.00
❑ WP-1242 [M]	The Chico Hamilton Trio Featuring Freddie Gambrell	1958	40.00
❑ WP-1258 [M]	Ellington Suite	1959	50.00
❑ WP-1287 [M]	The Original Hamilton Quintet	1960	50.00

HAMILTON, JUDD

45s

AMERICAN INT'L.

Number	Title (A Side/B Side)	Yr	NM
❑ 151	Rules/Someday Morning	1970	8.00
❑ 163	Baltimore/Sunshine Man	1970	8.00

DOLTON

Number	Title (A Side/B Side)	Yr	NM
❑ 80	Dream/Your Only Boy	1963	30.00

HAMILTON, LITTLE JOHNNY

45s

DORE

Number	Title (A Side/B Side)	Yr	NM
❑ 754	Oh How I Love You/Go	1966	500.00
❑ 760	Keep On Movin'/Mudpie	1966	3000.

HAMILTON, ROY

45s

AGP

Number	Title (A Side/B Side)	Yr	NM
❑ 113	The Dark End of the Street/100 Years	1969	20.00
❑ 116	Angelica/Hang Ups	1969	30.00
❑ 125	It's Only Make Believe/100 Years	1969	20.00

CAPITOL

Number	Title (A Side/B Side)	Yr	NM
❑ 2057	Let This World Be Free/Wait Until Dark	1967	20.00

EPIC

Number	Title (A Side/B Side)	Yr	NM
❑ 9015	You'll Never Walk Alone/I'm Gonna Sit Right Down and Cry	1954	25.00
❑ 9047	So Let There Be Love/If You Loved Me	1954	25.00
❑ 9068	Ebb Tide/Beware	1954	25.00
❑ 9086	Hurt/Star of Love	1954	25.00
❑ 9092	I Believe/If You Are But a Dream	1955	20.00
❑ 9102	Unchained Melody/From Here to Eternity	1955	25.00
❑ 9111	Forgive This Fool/You Wanted to Change Me	1955	20.00
❑ 9118	A Little Voice/All This Is Mine	1955	20.00
❑ 9125	Without a Song/Cuban Love Song	1955	20.00
❑ 9132	Everybody's Got a Home/Take Me with You	1955	20.00
❑ 9147	There Goes My Heart/Walk Along with Kings	1956	20.00
❑ 9160	Somebody, Somewhere/Since I Fell for You	1956	20.00
❑ 9180	I Took My Grief to Him/Chained	1956	20.00
❑ 9203	The Simple Prayer/A Mother's Love	1957	20.00
❑ 9212	My Faith, My Hope, My Love/So Long	1957	20.00
❑ 9224	The Aisle/That Old Feeling	1957	20.00
❑ 9232	(All of a Sudden) My Heart Sings/I'm Gonna Lock You in My Heart	1957	20.00
❑ 9257	Don't Let Go/The Night to Love	1957	20.00
❑ 9268	Crazy Feelin'/In a Dream	1958	30.00
❑ 9274	Lips/Jungle Fever	1958	15.00
❑ 9282	Wait for Me/Everything	1958	15.00
❑ 9294	Pledging My Love/My One and Only Love	1958	15.00
❑ 9301	It's Never Too Late/Somewhere Along the Way	1959	15.00
❑ 9307	I Need Your Lovin'/Blue Prelude	1959	20.00
❑ 9323	Time Marches On/Take It Easy, Joe	1959	15.00
❑ 9342	Great Romance/On My Way Back Home	1959	15.00
❑ 9354	The Ten Commandments/Down by the Riverside	1959	15.00
❑ 9354	The Ten Commandments/Nobody Knows the Trouble I've Seen	1959	20.00
❑ 9372	Down by the Riverside/Nobody Knows the Trouble I've Seen	1960	15.00
❑ 9373	I Let a Song Go Out of My Heart/I Get the Blues When It Rains	1960	15.00
❑ 9374	My Story/Please Send Me Someone to Love	1960	15.00
❑ 9375	Something's Gotta Give/Cheek to Cheek	1960	—

—Unreleased?

Number	Title (A Side/B Side)	Yr	NM
❑ 9376	Sing You Sinners/Blow, Gabriel, Blow	1960	15.00
❑ 9386	Having Myself a Ball/Slowly	1960	15.00

—B-side by Bobby Sykes

Number	Title (A Side/B Side)	Yr	NM
❑ 9388	Never Let Me Go/I Get the Blues When It Rains	1960	—

—Unreleased?

Number	Title (A Side/B Side)	Yr	NM
❑ 9390	The Clock/I Get the Blues When It Rains	1960	30.00
❑ 9398	A Lover's Prayer/Never Let Me Go	1960	15.00
❑ 9407	Lonely Hands/Your Love	1960	15.00
❑ 9434	You Can Have Her/Abide With Me	1961	15.00
❑ 9434 [PS]	You Can Have Her/Abide With Me	1961	30.00
❑ 9443 [PS]	You're Gonna Need Magic/To the One I Love	1961	30.00
❑ 9443	You're Gonna Need Magic/To the One I Love	1961	20.00
❑ 9449	No Substitute for Love/Please Louise	1961	15.00
❑ 9449 [PS]	No Substitute for Love/Please Louise	1961	30.00
❑ 9460	Excerpts from "You Can Have Her"	1961	15.00
❑ 9461	Excerpts from "You Can Have Her"	1961	15.00
❑ 9462	Excerpts from "You Can Have Her"	1961	15.00

Number	Title (A Side/B Side)	Yr	NM
❑ 9463	Excerpts from "You Can Have Her"	1961	15.00
❑ 9464	Excerpts from "You Can Have Her"	1961	15.00
❑ 9466	There We Were/If	1961	12.00
❑ 9492	Don't Come Cryin' to Me/ If Only I Had Known	1962	30.00
❑ 9520	Climb Ev'ry Mountain/I'll Come Running Back to You	1962	20.00
❑ 9538	I Am/Earthquake	1962	150.00
❑ 10559	You'll Never Walk Alone/The Golden Boy	1969	8.00
MGM			
❑ 13138	Let Go/You Still Love Him	1963	30.00
❑ 13157	Midnight Town-Daybreak City/ Intermezzo	1963	15.00
❑ 13175	Theme from "The V.I.P.'s" (The Willow)/The Sinner	1963	40.00
❑ 13217	The Panic Is On/There She Is	1964	200.00
❑ 13247	Answer Me, My Love/ Unchained Melody	1964	10.00
❑ 13291	You Can Count on Me/She Makes Me Wanna Dance	1964	150.00
❑ 13315	Sweet Violets/A Thousand Years Ago	1965	10.00
RCA VICTOR			
❑ 47-8641	Heartache/Ain't It the Truth	1965	75.00
❑ 47-8705	And I Love Her/Tore Up Over You	1965	20.00
❑ 47-8813	The Impossible Dream/ She's Got a Heart	1966	60.00
❑ 47-8960	Walk Hand in Hand/Crackin' Up Over You	1966	300.00
❑ 47-9061	I Taught Her Everything She Knows/Lament	1967	30.00
❑ 47-9171	So High My Love/ You Shook Me Up	1967	400.00
❑ 48-1034	Walk Hand in Hand/ Crackin' Up Over You	1972	50.00
7-Inch Extended Plays			
EPIC			
❑ EG-7065	You'll Never Walk Alone/I'm Gonna Sit Right Down and Cry (Over You)//If I Loved You/So Let There Be Love	195?	20.00
❑ EG-7065 [PS]	You'll Never Walk Alone	195?	20.00
❑ EG-7079	Ebb Tide/Beware//If You Are But a Dream/From Here to Eternity	195?	20.00
❑ EG-7079 [PS]	Ebb Tide	195?	20.00
❑ EG-7080	(contents unknown)	195?	20.00
❑ EG-7080 [PS]	Faith, Hope and Hamilton	195?	20.00
❑ EG-7133	Unchained Melody/Star of God/ /Hurt/One God	195?	20.00
❑ EG-7133 [PS]	Roy Hamilton Sings Unchained Melodies	195?	20.00
❑ EG-7158	(contents unknown)	195?	15.00
❑ EG-7158 [PS]	Roy Hamilton	195?	15.00
❑ EG-7159	(contents unknown)	195?	15.00
❑ EG-7159 [PS]	Roy Hamilton	195?	15.00
❑ EG-7200	(contents unknown)	1958	15.00
❑ EG-7200 [PS]	Don't Let Go	1958	15.00
❑ EG-7205	(contents unknown)	1958	15.00
❑ EG-7205 [PS]	Lips	1958	15.00
❑ EG-7210	(contents unknown)	195?	15.00
❑ EG-7210 [PS]	With All My Love	195?	15.00
❑ EG-7214	(contents unknown)	195?	15.00
❑ EG-7214 [PS]	You Belong to My Heart	195?	15.00
Albums			
EPIC			
❑ BN 518 [S]	With All My Love	1958	40.00
❑ BN 525 [S]	Why Fight The Feeling?	1959	30.00
❑ BN 530 [S]	Come Out Swingin'	1959	30.00
❑ BN 535 [S]	Have Blues, Must Travel	1959	30.00
❑ BN 551 [S]	Spirituals	1960	30.00
❑ BN 578 [S]	Soft 'n Warm	1960	30.00
❑ BN 595 [S]	You Can Have Her	1961	40.00
❑ BN 610 [S]	Only You	1961	30.00
❑ BN 632 [R]	You'll Never Walk Alone	1962	20.00
❑ LN 1023 [10]	You'll Never Walk Alone	1954	200.00
❑ LN 1103 [10]	The Voice of Roy Hamilton	1954	200.00
❑ LN 3176 [M]	Roy Hamilton	1955	60.00
❑ LN 3294 [M]	You'll Never Walk Alone	1956	70.00
❑ LN 3364 [M]	Golden Boy	1957	50.00
❑ LN 3519 [M]	With All My Love	1958	30.00
❑ LN 3545 [M]	Why Fight The Feeling?	1959	25.00
❑ LN 3561 [M]	Come Out Swingin'	1959	25.00
❑ LN 3580 [M]	Have Blues, Must Travel	1959	25.00
❑ LN 3628 [M]	Roy Hamilton At His Best	1960	40.00
❑ LN 3654 [M]	Spirituals	1960	25.00
❑ LN 3717 [M]	Soft 'n Warm	1960	25.00
❑ LN 3775 [M]	You Can Have Her	1961	30.00
❑ LN 3807 [M]	Only You	1961	25.00
❑ LN 24000 [M]	Mr. Rock and Soul	1962	25.00
❑ LN 24009 [M]	Roy Hamilton's Greatest Hits	1962	20.00
❑ LN 24316 [M]	Roy Hamilton's Greatest Hits, Vol. 2	1967	20.00
❑ BN 26000 [S]	Mr. Rock and Soul	1962	30.00
❑ BN 26009 [S]	Roy Hamilton's Greatest Hits	1962	25.00
❑ BN 26316 [S]	Roy Hamilton's Greatest Hits, Vol. 2	1967	25.00
MGM			
❑ E-4139 [M]	Warm and Soul	1963	15.00
❑ SE-4139 [S]	Warm and Soul	1963	20.00
❑ E-4233 [M]	Sentimental, Lonely & Blue	1964	15.00
❑ SE-4233 [S]	Sentimental, Lonely & Blue	1964	20.00
RCA VICTOR			
❑ LPM-3552 [M]	The Impossible Dream	1966	15.00
❑ LSP-3552 [S]	The Impossible Dream	1966	20.00

HAMILTON, RUSS

Number	Title (A Side/B Side)	Yr	NM
45s			
KAPP			
❑ 184	Rainbow/We Will Make Love	1957	15.00
❑ 194	Wedding Ring/I Still Belong to You	1957	12.00
❑ 204	My Mother's Eyes/I Had a Dream	1957	12.00
❑ 219	Drifting and Dreaming/ Tip Toe Through the Tulips	1958	12.00
❑ 250	All Alone/The Things I Didn't Say	1958	12.00
❑ 281	I Found Out/My Unbreakable Heart	1959	12.00
❑ 612	Valley of Love/The Loneliest Boy in Town	1964	10.00
MGM			
❑ 12947	Gonna Find Me a Bluebird/ Choir Girl	1960	12.00
Albums			
KAPP			
❑ KL-1076 [M]	Rainbow	1957	80.00

HAMILTON, JOE FRANK & DENNISON

See HAMILTON, JOE FRANK & REYNOLDS.

HAMILTON, JOE FRANK & REYNOLDS

Includes records as "Hamilton, Joe Frank & Dennison." Also see THE T-BONES.

Number	Title (A Side/B Side)	Yr	NM
45s			
ABC DUNHILL			
❑ 4276	Don't Pull Your Love/ Funk-In-Wagnall	1971	6.00
❑ 4287	Annabelle/Goin' Down	1971	5.00
❑ 4296	Daisy Mae/It Takes the Best	1971	5.00
❑ 4305	Don't Refuse My Love/ One Good Woman	1972	5.00
PLAYBOY			
❑ 5801	Now That I've Got You/ Get On the Bus	1977	4.00
	—As "Hamilton, Joe Frank & Dennison"		
❑ 6024	Fallin' in Love/So Good at Lovin' You	1975	5.00
❑ 6054	Winners and Losers/ Barroom Blues	1975	4.00
❑ 6068	Everyday Without You/Badman	1976	4.00
❑ 6077	Light Up the World with Sunshine/Houdini	1976	4.00
	—As "Hamilton, Joe Frank & Dennison"		
❑ 6077 [PS]	Light Up the World with Sunshine/Houdini	1976	5.00
	—As "Hamilton, Joe Frank & Dennison"		
❑ 6088	Don't Fight the Hands (That Need You)/Get On the Bus	1976	4.00
	—As "Hamilton, Joe Frank & Dennison"		
❑ 6088 [PS]	Don't Fight the Hands (That Need You)/Get On the Bus	1976	5.00
	—As "Hamilton, Joe Frank & Dennison"		
Albums			
ABC DUNHILL			
❑ DS-50103	Hamilton, Joe Frank & Reynolds	1971	10.00
❑ DSX-50113	Hallway Symphony	1972	10.00
❑ SKAO-93823	Hamilton, Joe Frank & Reynolds	1971	15.00
	—Capitol Record Club edition; label has the old-style "Dunhill" label without the "ABC" in the logo		
PLAYBOY			
❑ PB-407	Fallin' in Love	1975	10.00
❑ PZ 34741	Fallin' in Love	1977	8.00
	—Reissue of 107		

HAMILTON STREETCAR

Number	Title (A Side/B Side)	Yr	NM
45s			
DOT			
❑ 17253	Silver Wings/I See I Am	1969	12.00
❑ 17279	Brother Speed/Wasn't It You	1969	12.00
❑ 17306	Honey and Wine/ Now I Taste the Tears	1969	12.00
LHI			
❑ 1206	Confusion/Your Own Come Down	1968	15.00
❑ 17016	Invisible People/Flash	1967	15.00
Albums			
DOT			
❑ DLP-25939	Hamilton Streetcar	1969	15.00

HAMLISCH, MARVIN

Number	Title (A Side/B Side)	Yr	NM
45s			
A&M			
❑ 1775	All I Needed Was the Laughter/ If You Hadn't Left Me Crying	1975	4.00
ARISTA			
❑ 0392	Theme from "Ice Castles"/Touch	1979	4.00
MCA			
❑ 40174	The Entertainer/Solace	1974	5.00
❑ 40307	Maple Leaf Rag/ Mexican Dreams	1974	4.00
❑ 52175	The Entertainer/ Heliotrope Bouquet	1983	4.00
	—B-side by Lalo Schifrin		
PLANET			
❑ 45922 [DJ]	Theme from "Ordinary People" (same on both sides)	1980	4.00
UNITED ARTISTS			
❑ XW1082	Bond '77 — James Bond Theme (Part 1)/Bond '77 — James Bond Theme (Part 2)	1977	4.00
❑ 50798	Bananas/'Cause I Believe in Loving	1971	5.00
Albums			
MCA			
❑ 390	The Sting	1973	10.00
❑ 2115	The Entertainer	1974	10.00
❑ 37091	The Sting	198?	8.00
	—Budget-line reissue		

HAMMER

Number	Title (A Side/B Side)	Yr	NM
Albums			
SAN FRANCISCO			
❑ SD 203	Hammer	1970	15.00

HAMMILL, PETER

Also see VAN DER GRAAF GENERATOR.

Number	Title (A Side/B Side)	Yr	NM
Albums			
CHARISMA			
❑ CAS-1037	Fool's Mate	1972	15.00
❑ CH-1-2202	The Future Now	1978	12.00
❑ CH-1-2205	PH 7	1979	12.00
ENIGMA			
❑ ST-73206	Skin	1986	10.00
❑ ST-73246	And Close As This	1987	10.00
PVC			
❑ 8902	Sitting Targets	1981	12.00

HAMMOND, ALBERT

Number	Title (A Side/B Side)	Yr	NM
45s			
COLUMBIA			
❑ 02470	Memories/I Want You Back with Me	1981	4.00
❑ 03412	Before You Change the World/ Somewhere in America	1982	4.00
❑ 60510	When I'm Gone/World of Love	1981	4.00
EPIC			
❑ 50277	Moonlight Lady/Cry Baby	1976	4.00
MUMS			
❑ 6009	Down by the River/ The Last One to Know	1972	4.00
❑ 6011	It Never Rains in Southern California/Anyone Here in the Audience	1972	5.00
	—Bizarrely, the stock copy is in rechanneled stereo		
❑ 6015	If You Gotta Break Another Heart/ That Old American Dream	1973	4.00
❑ 6018	The Free Electric Band/You Taught Me to Sing the Blues	1973	4.00
❑ 6021	The Peacemaker/Who's for Lunch Today	1973	4.00
❑ 6024	Half a Million Miles from Home/ I Think I'll Go That Way	1973	4.00
❑ 6026	I'm a Train/Brand New Day	1974	4.00
❑ 6030	Air Disaster/Candlelight, Sweet Candlelight	1974	4.00
❑ 6032	Fountain Avenue/Names, Tags, Numbers, Labels	1974	4.00
❑ 6037	99 Miles from L.A./ Rivers Are for Boats	1975	4.00
Albums			
COLUMBIA			
❑ JC 36964	Your World and My World	1981	10.00
❑ FC 38181	Somewhere in America	1982	10.00
EPIC			
❑ JE 35049	When I Need You	1977	10.00

H

Number	Title (A Side/B Side)	Yr	NM
MUMS			
❑ KZ 31905	It Never Rains in Southern California	1972	10.00
❑ KZ 32267	The Free Electric Band	1973	10.00
❑ KZ 32834	Albert Hammond	1974	10.00

HAMMOND, JOHN

45s

Number	Title (A Side/B Side)	Yr	NM
ATLANTIC			
❑ 2696	I'm Tore Down/Shake for Me	1969	8.00
COLUMBIA			
❑ 45372	As the Years Go Passing By/Mellow Down Easy	1971	6.00
POINTBLANK/VIRGIN			
❑ 38775	Heartattack and Vine/2:19	2001	4.00
RED BIRD			
❑ 10-047	I Wish You Would/I Can Tell	1966	20.00

Albums

Number	Title (A Side/B Side)	Yr	NM
ATLANTIC			
❑ 8152 [M]	I Can Tell	1967	20.00
❑ SD 8152 [S]	I Can Tell	1967	20.00
❑ SD 8206	Sooner or Later	1968	15.00
❑ SD 8251	Southern Fried	1969	15.00
CAPRICORN			
❑ CP 0153	Can't Beat the Kid	1975	12.00
COLUMBIA			
❑ C 30458	Source Point	1971	12.00
❑ KC 31318	I'm Satisfied	1972	12.00
FLYING FISH			
❑ FF-502	Nobody But You	1988	10.00
ROUNDER			
❑ 3042	Mileage	1980	10.00
❑ 3060	Frogs for Snakes	1982	10.00
❑ 3074	John Hammond Live	1984	10.00
VANGUARD			
❑ VSD 11/12 [(2)]	The Best of John Hammond	1970	15.00
❑ VSD-2148 [S]	John Hammond	1964	25.00
❑ VRS-9132 [M]	John Hammond	1964	24.00
❑ VRS-9153 [M]	Big City Blues	1964	24.00
❑ VRS-9178 [M]	So Many Roads	1965	24.00
❑ VRS-9198 [M]	Country Blues	1966	24.00
❑ VRS-9245 [M]	Mirrors	1967	24.00
❑ VSD-79153 [S]	Big City Blues	1964	28.00
❑ VSD-79178 [S]	So Many Roads	1965	28.00
❑ VSD-79198 [S]	Country Blues	1966	28.00
❑ VSD-79245 [S]	Mirrors	1967	24.00
❑ VSD-79380	Solo	1976	10.00
❑ VSD-79400	Footwork	1978	10.00
❑ VSD-79424	Hot Tracks	1979	10.00

HAMMOND, JOHNNY

Originally recorded as Johnny "Hammond" Smith; those records are included below.

45s

Number	Title (A Side/B Side)	Yr	NM
KUDU			
❑ 900	It's Too Late/Workin' on a Groovy Thing	1971	6.00
❑ 907	Rock Steady (Part 1)/Rock Steady (Part 2)	1972	6.00
❑ 914	Thunder and Lightning (Part 1)/Thunder and Lightning (Part 2)	1973	6.00
MILESTONE			
❑ 302	Los Conquistadores Chocolates/Shifting Gears	1975	5.00
NEW JAZZ			
❑ 45-501	Sweet Cookies/Secret Love	196?	10.00
❑ 45-502	All Soul/The Masquerade Is Over	196?	10.00
❑ 45-509	I'll Remember April/That Good Feeling	196?	10.00
PRESTIGE			
❑ 193	End of a Love Affair/Sticks An' Stones	196?	10.00
❑ 209	Swanee River (Part 1)/Swanee River (Part 2)	196?	10.00
❑ 386	Brother John/Cleopatra and the African Knight	196?	8.00
❑ 407	Sad Eyes/Opus de Funk	196?	8.00
❑ 422	Golden Thrush/Stormy Monday Blues	196?	8.00
❑ 449	Ebb Tide/Stand By Me	196?	8.00
❑ 455	N.Y.P.D./Dirty Apple	196?	8.00
❑ 725	Soul Talk (Part 1)/Soul Talk (Part 2)	1970	6.00
❑ 748	I'll Be Yours/Smokin' Kool	197?	6.00

Albums

Number	Title (A Side/B Side)	Yr	NM
KUDU			
❑ 01	Breakout	1971	12.00
❑ 04	Wild Horses/Rock Steady	1972	12.00
❑ 10	The Prophet	1973	12.00
❑ 16	Higher Ground	1974	12.00
❑ KSQX-16 [Q]	Higher Ground	1974	20.00
MILESTONE			
❑ 9062	Gears	1975	15.00
❑ 9068	Forever Taurus	1976	15.00
❑ 9076	Storm Warning	1977	15.00
❑ 9083	Don't Let the System Get You	1978	15.00
NEW JAZZ			
❑ NJLP-8221 [M]	All Soul	1959	50.00
—Purple label			
❑ NJLP-8221 [M]	All Soul	1965	25.00
—Blue label with trident logo			
❑ NJLP-8229 [M]	That Good Feelin'	1959	50.00
—Purple label			
❑ NJLP-8229 [M]	That Good Feelin'	1965	25.00
—Blue label with trident logo			
❑ NJLP-8241 [M]	Talk That Talk	1960	50.00
—Purple label			
❑ NJLP-8241 [M]	Talk That Talk	1965	25.00
—Blue label with trident logo			
❑ NJLP-8288 [M]	Look Out!	1962	50.00
—Purple label			
❑ NJLP-8288 [M]	Look Out!	1965	25.00
—Blue label with trident logo			
PRESTIGE			
❑ PRLP-7203 [M]	Stimulation	1961	40.00
—Yellow label			
❑ PRLP-7203 [M]	Stimulation	1965	25.00
—Blue label with trident logo			
❑ PRLP-7217 [M]	Gettin' the Message	1961	40.00
—Yellow label			
❑ PRLP-7217 [M]	Gettin' the Message	1965	25.00
—Blue label with trident logo			
❑ PRLP-7408 [M]	The Stinger	1965	20.00
❑ PRST-7408 [S]	The Stinger	1965	25.00
❑ PRLP-7420 [M]	Opus de Funk	1966	20.00
❑ PRST-7420 [S]	Opus de Funk	1966	25.00
❑ PRLP-7464 [M]	The Stinger Meets the Golden Thrush	1966	20.00
❑ PRST-7464 [S]	The Stinger Meets the Golden Thrush	1966	25.00
❑ PRLP-7482 [M]	Love Potion #9	1967	25.00
❑ PRST-7482 [S]	Love Potion #9	1967	20.00
❑ PRLP-7494 [M]	Ebb Tide	1967	25.00
❑ PRST-7494 [S]	Ebb Tide	1967	20.00
❑ PRST-7549	Soul Flowers	1968	20.00
❑ PRST-7564	Dirty Grape	1968	20.00
❑ PRST-7588	Nasty	1968	20.00
❑ PRST-7681	Soul Talk	1969	20.00
❑ PRST-7705	The Best of Johnny "Hammond" Smith	1969	15.00
❑ PRST-7736	Black Feeling	1969	15.00
❑ PRST-7777	Best for Lovers	1970	15.00
❑ PRST-7786	Stimulation	1970	15.00
❑ PRST-7846	Good 'Nuff	1970	15.00
❑ 10002	Here It 'Tis	1971	15.00
❑ 10015	What's Going On	1971	15.00
RIVERSIDE			
❑ RLP-442 [M]	Black Coffee	1963	25.00
❑ RLP-466 [M]	Mr. Wonderful	1963	25.00
❑ RLP-482 [M]	Open House!	1965	20.00
❑ RLP-496 [M]	A Little Taste	1965	20.00
❑ RS-9442 [S]	Black Coffee	1963	30.00
❑ RS-9466 [S]	Mr. Wonderful	1963	30.00
❑ RS-9482 [S]	Open House!	1965	25.00
❑ RS-9496 [S]	A Little Taste	1965	25.00
SALVATION			
❑ 702	A Gambler's Life	1974	12.00

HAMMOND-HAZLEWOOD

Also see ALBERT HAMMOND.

45s

Number	Title (A Side/B Side)	Yr	NM
CAPITOL			
❑ 2616	Wendy, Wendy/Broken Hearts Brigade	1969	10.00

HAMPTON, JOHN

45s

Number	Title (A Side/B Side)	Yr	NM
UNITED			
❑ 210	Honey Hush/Shadow Blues	1958	120.00

HANCOCK, HERBIE

12-Inch Singles

Number	Title (A Side/B Side)	Yr	NM
COLUMBIA			
❑ AS 751 [DJ]	Go For It (6:58)/Go For It (7:32)	1980	8.00
❑ AS751 [DJ]	Go For It (6:58)/Go For It (7:32)	1980	8.00
❑ AS 814 [DJ]	Saturday Night/Making Love	1980	8.00
❑ AS814 [DJ]	Saturday Night/Making Love	1980	8.00
❑ AS 1251 [DJ]	Everybody's Broke (3:53)/Everybody's Broke (7:05)	1981	8.00
❑ AS 1262 [DJ]	Magic Number/Everybody's Broke	1981	8.00
❑ AS1262 [DJ]	Magic Number/Everybody's Broke	1981	8.00
❑ AS 1333 [DJ]	Magic Number (Remix)/Magic Number (Edit)	1981	8.00
❑ AS1333 [DJ]	Magic Number (Remix)/Magic Number (Edit)	1981	8.00
❑ AS 1413 [DJ]	Lite Me Up (long)/Lite Me Up (short)	1982	8.00
❑ AS1413 [DJ]	Lite Me Up (long)/Lite Me Up (short)	1982	8.00
❑ AS 1504 [DJ]	Gettin' to the Good Part/The Fun Tracks	1982	8.00
❑ AS1504 [DJ]	Gettin' to the Good Part/The Fun Tracks	1982	8.00
❑ 03978	Rockit (2 versions)	1983	10.00
❑ 04200	Autodrive/Chameleon	1983	6.00
❑ 04637	Metal Beat (extended)/Metal Beat (edit)	1984	6.00
❑ 04960	Mega-Mix (same on both sides)	1984	8.00
❑ 05027	Hardrock (long)/Hardrock (short)	1984	6.00
❑ 07804	Vibe Alive (extended) (edit) (bonus beats)	1988	6.00
❑ 07896	Beat Wise (4 versions)	1988	6.00
❑ 10906	Ready or Not (6:43)/You Bet Your Love (8:12)	1979	8.00
❑ 11019	Tell Everybody (7:48)/Honey from the Jar (5:36)	1979	8.00
❑ 11310	Stars in Your Eyes/Go For It	1980	8.00

45s

Number	Title (A Side/B Side)	Yr	NM
BLUE NOTE			
❑ 1862	Watermelon Man/Three Bags Full	1962	8.00
❑ 1863	Driftin'/Alone Am I	1962	8.00
❑ 1887	Blind Man (Part 1)/Blind Man (Part 2)	196?	8.00
COLUMBIA			
❑ 02404	Everybody's Broke/Help Yourself	1981	4.00
❑ 02615	Magic Number/Help Yourself	1981	4.00
❑ 02824	Lite Me Up/Satisfied with Love	1982	4.00
❑ 03004	Gettin' to the Good Part/The Fun Tracks	1982	4.00
❑ 03318	Paradise/The Fun Tracks	1982	4.00
❑ 04054	Rockit (2 versions)	1983	5.00
❑ 04054	Rockit (2 versions)	1984	4.00
—Gold-label "Instant Classic" early reissue			
❑ 04268	Autodrive/Chameleon	1983	4.00
❑ 04473	Mega-Mix/TFS	1984	4.00
❑ 04565	Hardrock (2 versions)	1984	4.00
❑ 04565 [PS]	Hardrock (2 versions)	1984	4.00
❑ 04633	Metal Beat/Karabali	1984	4.00
❑ 07718	Vibe Alive/P. Bop	1988	3.00
❑ 07718 [PS]	Vibe Alive/P. Bop	1988	3.00
❑ 07987	Beat Wise/Chemical Residue	1988	3.00
❑ 10050	Palm Grease/Butterfly	1974	5.00
❑ 10094	Spank-a-Lee/Actual Proof	1975	5.00
❑ 10239	Suntouch/Hang Up Your Hang-Ups	1975	5.00
❑ 10408	Doin' It/People Music	1976	5.00
❑ 10563	Maiden Voyage/Spider	1977	5.00
❑ 10781	I Thought It Was You/No Means Yes	1978	5.00
❑ 10835	Sunlight/Come Running to Me	1978	5.00
❑ 10894	Knee Deep/You Get Your Love	1979	5.00
❑ 10936	Ready or Not/Trust Me	1979	5.00
❑ 11021	Tell Everybody/Honey from the Jar	1979	5.00
❑ 11122	Doin' It/Honey from the Jar	1979	4.00
❑ 11227	Go For It/Trust Me	1980	—
—Canceled?			
❑ 11236	Stars in Your Eyes/Go For It	1980	4.00
❑ 11323	Making Love/It All Comes Around	1980	4.00
❑ 46002	Chameleon/Vein Melter	1974	5.00
❑ 46073	Watermelon Man/Sly	1974	5.00
WARNER BROS.			
❑ 7358	Fat Mama/Wiggle-Waggle	1969	6.00
❑ 7598	Water Torture/Crossings	1972	6.00

Albums

Number	Title (A Side/B Side)	Yr	NM
BLUE NOTE			
❑ BN-LA152-F	Succotash	1974	12.00
❑ BN-LA399-H2 [(2)]	Herbie Hancock	1975	15.00
❑ BLP-4109 [M]	Takin' Off	1962	50.00
❑ BLP-4126 [M]	My Point of View	1963	35.00
❑ BLP-4147 [M]	Inventions and Dimensions	1963	35.00
❑ BLP-4175 [M]	Empyrean Isles	1964	35.00
❑ BLP-4195 [M]	Maiden Voyage	1965	35.00
❑ B1-46339	Maiden Voyage	1997	20.00
—Audiophile reissue			
❑ BST-84109	Takin' Off	1987	10.00
—"The Finest in Jazz Since 1939" reissue			
❑ BST-84109 [S]	Takin' Off	1962	40.00
—With New York, USA address on label			
❑ BST-84109 [S]	Takin' Off	1967	15.00
—With "A Division of Liberty Records" on label			
❑ BST-84126	My Point of View	1987	10.00
—"The Finest in Jazz Since 1939" reissue			
❑ BST-84126 [S]	My Point of View	1963	35.00
—With New York, USA address on label			
❑ BST-84126 [S]	My Point of View	1967	15.00
—With "A Division of Liberty Records" on label			
❑ BST-84147	Inventions and Dimensions	1987	10.00
—"The Finest in Jazz Since 1939" reissue			

Except when noted otherwise, VG = 25% of NM, and VG+ = 50% of NM. (Example: VG = $2.00, VG+ = $4.00 and NM = $8.00.)

Number	Title (A Side/B Side)	Yr	NM
❑ BST-84147 [S]	Inventions and Dimensions	1963	35.00
—With New York, USA address on label			
❑ BST-84147 [S]	Inventions and Dimensions	1967	15.00
—With "A Division of Liberty Records" on label			
❑ BST-84175	Empyrean Isles	1985	10.00
—"The Finest in Jazz Since 1939" reissue			
❑ BST-84175 [S]	Empyrean Isles	1964	35.00
—With New York, USA address on label			
❑ BST-84175 [S]	Empyrean Isles	1967	15.00
—With "A Division of Liberty Records" on label			
❑ BST-84195 [S]	Maiden Voyage	1965	35.00
—With New York, USA address on label			
❑ BST-84195 [S]	Maiden Voyage	1967	15.00
—With "A Division of Liberty Records" on label			
❑ BST-84195 [S]	Maiden Voyage	197?	12.00
—"A Division of United Artists" on label			
❑ BST-84195 [S]	Maiden Voyage	1985	10.00
—"The Finest in Jazz Since 1939" reissue			
❑ BST-84279	Speak Like a Child	1968	15.00
❑ BST-84279	Speak Like a Child	1986	10.00
—"The Finest in Jazz Since 1939" reissue			
❑ BST-84321	The Prisoner	1969	15.00
❑ BST-84321	The Prisoner	1987	10.00
—"The Finest in Jazz Since 1939" reissue			
❑ BST-84407	The Best of Herbie Hancock	1971	15.00
❑ B1-91142	The Best of Herbie Hancock	1988	10.00
COLUMBIA			
❑ KC 32212	Sextant	1973	12.00
❑ PC 32212	Sextant	198?	8.00
—Budget-line reissue			
❑ PCQ 32212 [Q]	Sextant	197?	20.00
❑ CQ 32371 [Q]	Head Hunters	1973	25.00
❑ KC 32371	Head Hunters	1973	12.00
❑ PC 32371	Head Hunters	197?	8.00
—Reissue (with or without bar code)			
❑ PC 32965	Thrust	1974	12.00
—No bar code on cover			
❑ PC 32965	Thrust	198?	8.00
—Budget-line reissue with bar code			
❑ PCQ 32965 [Q]	Thrust	1974	25.00
❑ PC 33812	Man-Child	1975	12.00
—No bar code on cover			
❑ PC 33812	Man-Child	198?	8.00
—Budget-line reissue with bar code			
❑ PC 34280	Secrets	1976	12.00
—No bar code on cover			
❑ PC 34280	Secrets	198?	8.00
—Budget-line reissue with bar code			
❑ PCQ 34280 [Q]	Secrets	1976	25.00
❑ PG 34688 [(2)]	V.S.O.P.	1977	15.00
❑ JC 34907	Sunlight	1978	12.00
❑ C2 34976 [(2)]	V.S.O.P. Quintet	1978	15.00
❑ JC 35764	Feets Don't Fail Me Now	1979	12.00
❑ PC 35764	Feets Don't Fail Me Now	198?	8.00
—Budget-line reissue			
❑ JC 36309	The Best of Herbie Hancock	1979	12.00
❑ JC 36415	Monster	1980	10.00
❑ PC 36415	Monster	198?	8.00
—Budget-line reissue			
❑ JC 36578	Mr. Hands	1980	10.00
❑ PC 36578	Mr. Hands	198?	8.00
—Budget-line reissue			
❑ FC 37387	Magic Windows	1981	10.00
❑ PC 37387	Magic Windows	198?	8.00
—Budget-line reissue			
❑ FC 37928	Lite Me Up	1982	10.00
❑ PC 37928	Lite Me Up	198?	8.00
—Budget-line reissue			
❑ FC 38814	Future Shock	1983	10.00
❑ FC 39478	Sound-System	1984	10.00
❑ PC 39478	Sound-System	1985	8.00
—Budget-line reissue			
❑ FC 39870	Village Life	1985	10.00
❑ 8C8 39913 [EP]	Hardrock	1984	12.00
—Picture disc			
❑ FC 40025	Perfect Machine	1988	10.00
❑ SC 40464	'Round Midnight	1986	10.00
MGM			
❑ E-4447 [M]	Blow-Up	1967	40.00
❑ SE-4447 [S]	Blow-Up	1967	50.00
—Also includes one track by the Yardbirds			
PAUSA			
❑ 9002	Succotash	198?	10.00
TRIP			
❑ UPF-194	Traces	197?	12.00
WARNER BROS.			
❑ WS 1834	Fat Albert Rotunda	1970	15.00
❑ WS 1898	Mwandishi	1971	15.00
❑ BS 2617	Crossings	1972	15.00
❑ 2WS 2807 [(2)]	Treasure Chest	1974	15.00

HANCOCK, HERBIE, AND CHICK COREA

Number	Title (A Side/B Side)	Yr	NM
Albums			
COLUMBIA			
❑ PC2 35663 [(2)]	An Evening with Herbie Hancock and Chick Corea	1979	12.00
POLYDOR			
❑ PD-2-6238 [(2)]	An Evening with Chick Corea and Herbie Hancock	1979	15.00

HANDS OF TIME, THE

Number	Title (A Side/B Side)	Yr	NM
45s			
SIDEWALK			
❑ 903	Got to Get You Into My Life/ Midnight Rider	1966	30.00

HANDY, JOHN

Number	Title (A Side/B Side)	Yr	NM
45s			
ABC IMPULSE!			
❑ 31005	Hard Work/Young Enough to Dream	1976	4.00
❑ 31012	Make Her Mine/Watch Your Money Go	1977	4.00
COLUMBIA			
❑ 4-43706	If Only We Knew/Spanish Lady	1966	8.00
❑ 4-44977	Lay Lady Lay/Spinning Wheel	1969	7.00
Albums			
ABC IMPULSE!			
❑ ASD-9314	Hard Work	1976	15.00
❑ AS-9324	Carnival	1977	10.00
COLUMBIA			
❑ CL 2462 [M]	Recorded Live at the Monterey Jazz Festival	1966	15.00
❑ CL 2567 [M]	The Second John Handy Album	1966	20.00
❑ CL 2697 [M]	New View	1967	25.00
❑ CS 9262 [S]	Recorded Live at the Monterey Jazz Festival	1966	20.00
❑ CS 9367 [S]	The Second John Handy Album	1966	30.00
❑ CS 9497 [S]	New View	1967	25.00
❑ CS 9689	Projections	1968	25.00
MILESTONE			
❑ M-9173	Centerpiece: John Handy with Class	1989	12.00
QUARTET			
❑ Q-1005	Excursion in Blue	1988	25.00
ROULETTE			
❑ RE-132 [(2)]	In the Vernacular	197?	20.00
—Compilation of earlier material			
❑ R 52042 [M]	In the Ver-nac'-u-lar	1960	20.00
❑ SR 52042 [S]	In the Ver-nac'-u-lar	1960	22.00
❑ R 52088 [M]	No Coast Jazz	1962	24.00
❑ SR 52088 [S]	No Coast Jazz	1962	30.00
❑ R 52121 [M]	John Handy Jazz	1964	24.00
❑ SR 52121 [S]	John Handy Jazz	1964	30.00
❑ R 52124 [M]	Quote, Unquote	1964	24.00
❑ SR 52124 [S]	Quote, Unquote	1964	30.00
WARNER BROS.			
❑ BSK 3170	Where Go the Boats	1978	12.00
❑ BSK 3242	Handy Dandy Man	1978	12.00

HANDY, WAYNE

Number	Title (A Side/B Side)	Yr	NM
45s			
DIAL			
❑ 3002	Conscience Let Me Go/ Pain Reliever	1961	12.00
RENOWN			
❑ 102	Say Yeah/Could It Be	195?	20.00
❑ 104	Betcha Didn't Know/ Don't Be Unfair	195?	20.00
❑ 107	Problem Child/I'll Never Be the Same	195?	20.00
TREND			
❑ 30006	Betcha Didn't Know/ Don't Be Unfair	195?	25.00
❑ 30015	Seminole Rock 'n' Roll/I Think You Oughta Love Again	195?	25.00

HANEY, JACK, AND NIKITER ARMSTRONG

Number	Title (A Side/B Side)	Yr	NM
45s			
MEL-O-DY			
❑ 107	The Interview/Peaceful	1963	20.00

HANGMEN, THE

Number	Title (A Side/B Side)	Yr	NM
45s			
MONUMENT			
❑ 910	What a Girl Can't Do/ The Girl Who Faded Away	1965	20.00
❑ 951	Faces/Bad Goodbye	1966	20.00
Albums			
MONUMENT			
❑ MLP-8077 [M]	Bitter Sweet	1967	30.00
❑ SLP-18077 [S]	Bitter Sweet	1967	40.00

HANK AND CAROLEE

Number	Title (A Side/B Side)	Yr	NM
45s			
MALA			
❑ 424	Go On and Go/I've Never Known	1960	40.00

HANK'S HOUNDS

Number	Title (A Side/B Side)	Yr	NM
45s			
HIT			
❑ 223	Just a Little Bit Better/ Catch Us If You Can	1965	12.00
—B-side by the Jalopy Five			

HANNAN, JIMMY

Number	Title (A Side/B Side)	Yr	NM
45s			
ATLANTIC			
❑ 2247	Beach Ball/You Gotta Have Love	1964	150.00
—Backing Hannan on this record are THE BEE GEES, three years before their first American release!			

HANS CHRISTIAN

With Jon Anderson, pre-YES.

Number	Title (A Side/B Side)	Yr	NM
45s			
TOWER			
❑ 409	Never My Love/All of the Time	1968	100.00

HANSON

Number	Title (A Side/B Side)	Yr	NM
45s			
MANTICORE			
❑ 2001	Love Knows Everything/ (B-side unknown)	1973	6.00
❑ 2004	Boy Meets Girl/Modern Day Religion	1973	6.00
Albums			
MANTICORE			
❑ MC 66670	Now Hear This	1973	12.00
❑ MC 66672	Magic Dragon	1974	10.00

HANSSON, BO

Number	Title (A Side/B Side)	Yr	NM
45s			
CHARISMA			
❑ 104	The Black Riders/Flight to the Ford//(B-side unknown)	1973	10.00
Albums			
CHARISMA			
❑ CAS-1059	Lord of the Rings	1973	12.00
❑ FC 6062	Magician's Hat	1974	12.00
SIRE			
❑ SR 6044	Music Inspired by Watership Down	1977	10.00
❑ SASD-7525	Attic Thoughts	1976	10.00

HAPPENINGS, THE

Also see BOB MIRANDA; THE TOKENS.

Number	Title (A Side/B Side)	Yr	NM
45s			
B.T. PUPPY			
❑ 181 [DJ]	Have Yourself a Merry Little Christmas (same on both sides)	1966	30.00
—Stock copies do not exist			
❑ 517	Girls on the Go/Go-Go	1966	10.00
❑ 520	See You in September/ He Thinks He's a Hero	1966	10.00
❑ 522	Go Away Little Girl/Tea Time	1966	8.00
❑ 523	Goodnight My Love/ Lillies By Money	1966	8.00
❑ 527	I Got Rhythm/You're in a Bad Way	1967	8.00
❑ 530	My Mammy/I Believe in Nothing	1967	8.00
❑ 530 [PS]	My Mammy/I Believe in Nothing	1967	15.00
❑ 532	Why Do Fools Fall in Love/When the Summer Is Through	1967	8.00
❑ 532 [PS]	Why Do Fools Fall in Love/When the Summer Is Through	1967	15.00
❑ 538	Music, Music, Music/ When I Lock My Door	1968	8.00
❑ 538 [PS]	Music, Music, Music/ When I Lock My Door	1968	15.00
❑ 540	Randy/Love Song of Mommy and Daddy	1968	8.00
❑ 542	Sealed with a Kiss/Anyway	1968	8.00
❑ 543	Breaking Up Is Hard to Do/ Anyway	1968	8.00
❑ 545	Crazy Rhythm/Love Song of Mommy and Daddy	1968	8.00
❑ 549	That's All I Want from You/ He Thinks He's a Hero	1968	8.00
BIG TREE			
❑ 146	Strawberry Morning/ Workin' My Way Back to You	1972	4.00
❑ 153	Me Without You/ God Bless Joanna	1972	4.00
JUBILEE			
❑ 5666	Where Do I Go and Be In/ New Day Comin'	1969	6.00
❑ 5677	El Paso County Jail/ Won't Anybody Listen	1969	6.00
❑ 5686	Answer Me, My Love/ I Need a Woman	1970	6.00

Number	Title (A Side/B Side)	Yr	NM
❑ 5698	Tomorrow, Today Will Be Yesterday/Chain of Hands	1970	6.00
❑ 5702	Crazy Love/Chain of Hands	1970	6.00
❑ 5703	Condition Red/Sweet September	1970	10.00

—As "The Honor Society"

Number	Title (A Side/B Side)	Yr	NM
❑ 5712	Lullaby in the Rain/I Wish You Could Know Me (Naomi)	1971	6.00
❑ 5721 [DJ]	Make Your Own Kind of Music (mono/stereo)	1971	6.00

—Stock copies may not exist

MIDLAND INT'L.

Number	Title (A Side/B Side)	Yr	NM
❑ MB-10897	That's Why I Love You/Beyond the Hurt	1977	4.00
❑ MB-11127	Let Me Stay/Someone Special	1977	4.00

PHILCO-FORD

Number	Title (A Side/B Side)	Yr	NM
❑ HP-7	Go Away Little Girl/See You in September	1967	20.00

—4-inch plastic "Hip Pocket Record" with color sleeve

Albums

B.T. PUPPY

Number	Title (A Side/B Side)	Yr	NM
❑ BTP-1001 [M]	The Happenings (Bye-Bye, So Long, Farewell...See You in September)	1966	25.00
❑ BTS-1001 [S]	The Happenings (Bye-Bye, So Long, Farewell...See You in September)	1966	30.00
❑ BTP-1003 [M]	Psycle	1967	25.00
❑ BTPS-1003 [S]	Psycle	1967	30.00
❑ BTS-1004	The Happenings Golden Hits!	1968	40.00

JUBILEE

Number	Title (A Side/B Side)	Yr	NM
❑ JGS-8028	Piece of Mind	1969	25.00
❑ JGS-8030	The Happenings' Greatest Hits	1969	25.00

HAPPY OTTO See CRAZY OTTO.

HAPSHASH AND THE COLOURED COAT

Albums

IMPERIAL

Number	Title (A Side/B Side)	Yr	NM
❑ LP-9377 [M]	Hapshash and the Coloured Coat	1968	50.00
❑ LP-12377 [S]	Hapshash and the Coloured Coat	1968	40.00
❑ LP-12430	Western Flyer	1969	40.00

HARBOR LIGHTS, THE Early JAY AND THE AMERICANS.

45s

JARO

Number	Title (A Side/B Side)	Yr	NM
❑ 77020	Is That Too Much to Ask/What Would I Do Without You	1960	40.00

MALA

Number	Title (A Side/B Side)	Yr	NM
❑ 422	Angel of Love/Tick-a-Tick-a-Tock	1960	50.00

HARBOUR LITES, THE

45s

FONTANA

Number	Title (A Side/B Side)	Yr	NM
❑ 1544	Run for Your Life/Lonely Journey	1966	10.00

HARD, RANDY

45s

NRC

Number	Title (A Side/B Side)	Yr	NM
❑ 013	Honey Doll/May It Be My Fortune	1959	60.00
❑ 044	Let Her Go/Make Me a Dreamer	1959	50.00

HARD MEAT

Albums

WARNER BROS.

Number	Title (A Side/B Side)	Yr	NM
❑ WS 1852	Hard Meat	1969	15.00
❑ WS 1879	Through a Window	1970	15.00

HARD TIMES, THE

45s

WORLD PACIFIC

Number	Title (A Side/B Side)	Yr	NM
❑ 77816	There'll Be a Time/You're Bound to Cry	1966	10.00
❑ 77826	Come To Your Window/That's All I'll Do	1966	10.00
❑ 77851	Fortune Teller/Good-By	1966	10.00
❑ 77873	Blew Mind/Colours	1967	10.00

Albums

WORLD PACIFIC

Number	Title (A Side/B Side)	Yr	NM
❑ WP-1867 [M]	Blew Mind	1968	25.00
❑ WPS-21867 [S]	Blew Mind	1968	30.00

HARDEN TRIO, THE

45s

COLUMBIA

Number	Title (A Side/B Side)	Yr	NM
❑ 43229	Poor Boy/Let It Be Me	1965	8.00
❑ 43463	Tippy Toeing/Don't Remind Me	1965	8.00
❑ 43710	Little Boy Walk Like a Man/Dear Brother	1966	6.00
❑ 43844	Seven Days of Crying (Makes One Weak)/Husbands and Wives	1966	6.00
❑ 44059	Sneaking 'Cross the Border/Childhood Place	1967	6.00
❑ 44249	Forbidden/Manana (Is Soon Enough for Me)	1967	6.00
❑ 44420	He Looks a Lot Like You/My Friend Mr. Echo	1968	5.00
❑ 44552	Everybody Wants to Be Somebody Else/Diddle Diddle Dumplin'	1968	5.00

Albums

COLUMBIA

Number	Title (A Side/B Side)	Yr	NM
❑ CL 2506 [M]	Tippy Toeing	1966	20.00
❑ CS 9306 [S]	Tippy Toeing	1966	25.00

HARDIE, CELEST

45s

LOADSTONE

Number	Title (A Side/B Side)	Yr	NM
❑ 3955	Thank You Love/(Instrumental)	196?	20.00
❑ 3961	You Touched the Inner Part of Me/(Instrumental)	197?	30.00

REYNOLDS

Number	Title (A Side/B Side)	Yr	NM
❑ R-200	You're Gone/That's Why I Cried	196?	500.00

HARDIN, ED

45s

HIT

Number	Title (A Side/B Side)	Yr	NM
❑ 02	Good Luck Charm/Slow Twistin'	1962	8.00
—B-side by Herbert Hunter			
❑ 03	Young World/Lover Please	1962	8.00
—B-side by Herbert Hunter			
❑ 13	Follow That Dream/Lovers Who Wander	1962	8.00
❑ 33	Only Love Can Break a Heart/Do You Love Me	1962	8.00
—B-side by Leroy Jones			
❑ 35	Return to Sender/Don't Go Near the Indians	1962	8.00
—B-side by Sandy Carmichael			
❑ 44	Love Came to Me/Everybody Loves a Lover	1962	8.00
—B-side by Alpha Zoe			
❑ 54	One Broken Heart for Sale/Let's Turkey Trot	1963	8.00
—B-side by Alpha Zoe			
❑ 87	Donna the Prima Donna/Washington Square	1963	8.00
—B-side by the Music City Five & Ten			
❑ 98	Drip Drop/Midnight Mary	1963	8.00
—B-side by Ricky Dickens			
❑ 103	For You/Um, Um, Um, Um, Um, Um	1964	8.00
—B-side by Thomas Henry			
❑ 112	Suspicion/Don't Let the Rain Come Down	1964	8.00
—B-side by the Music City Singers			
❑ 117	Little Children/My Guy	1964	8.00
—B-side by Clara Wilson			
❑ 130	Memphis/Bad to Me	1964	8.00
❑ 138	Such a Night/And I Love Her	1964	10.00
—B-side by the Jalopy Five			
❑ 142	Oh Pretty Woman/Broken Hearted, Sad and Blue	1964	8.00
❑ 149	That's All That's Important Now/From a Window	1964	8.00
❑ 157	Ask Me/Pay It No Mind	1964	8.00
—B-side by Fred York			
❑ 175	My World's a Blue World/Don't Forget I Still Love You	1965	8.00
—B-side by Shari Baker			
❑ 190	True Love You Can't Buy/You've Lost That Lovin' Feelin'	1965	8.00
—B-side by Wayne Harris			
❑ 199	Goodnight/Hearts Are Funny Things	1965	8.00
—B-side by Bobby Brooks			
❑ 211	Game of Love/One Fine Day	1965	8.00
❑ 219	Down in the Boondocks/What's New Pussycat?	1965	8.00
—B-side by Bobby Brooks			
❑ 245	It's Too Late/Nowhere Man	1966	12.00
—B-side by the Jalopy Five			
❑ 247	Sure Gonna Miss Her/The Cheater	1966	8.00
—B-side by the Chellows			
❑ 256	Green Grass/A Groovy Kind of Love	1966	8.00
—B-side by the Chords (2)			
❑ 261	Love Letters/Sweet Pea	1966	8.00
❑ 268	See See Rider/Psychotic Reaction	1966	8.00
—As "Ed Hardin and the Cadets"; B-side by the Jalopy Five			
❑ 279	Good Thing/Tell It Like It Is	1967	8.00
—As "Ed Hardin and the Cadets"; B-side by Leroy Jones			
❑ 280	Green, Green Grass of Home/Mercy, Mercy, Mercy	1967	8.00
—B-side by the New Society Group			
❑ 282	Baby I Need Your Lovin'/Pretty Ballerina	1967	8.00
—B-side by the Chords (2)			
❑ 285	Detroit City/A Little Bit Me, A Little Bit You	1967	8.00
—B-side by the Jalopy Five			
❑ 294	Release Me/Mirage	1967	8.00
—B-side by the Chords (2)			
❑ 315	By the Time I Get to Phoenix/Daydream Believer	1967	8.00
—B-side by the Jalopy Five			
❑ 320	The Ballad of Bonnie and Clyde/Honey	1968	8.00
—B-side by Bobby Sims			
❑ 329	I Wanna Live/Mony Mony	1968	8.00
—B-side by the Fantastics			
❑ 349	Hold Me Tight/Abraham, Martin and John	1968	8.00
—B-side by Joe Smith			

HARDIN, RETT

45s

HIT

Number	Title (A Side/B Side)	Yr	NM
❑ 52	You're the Reason I'm Living/Ruby Baby	1963	8.00

—B-side by Larry Dexter

HARDIN, TIM

45s

COLUMBIA

Number	Title (A Side/B Side)	Yr	NM
❑ 44879	Once-Touched by Flame/A Question of Birth	1969	6.00
❑ 44920	Simple Song of Freedom/A Question of Birth	1969	6.00
❑ 45426	Bird on the Wire/Soft Summer Breeze	1971	5.00
❑ 45695	Do the Do/Sweet Lady	1972	5.00

VERVE FOLKWAYS

Number	Title (A Side/B Side)	Yr	NM
❑ 5008	Hang On to a Dream/It'll Never Happen Again	1966	10.00
❑ 5017	Misty Roses/Don't Make Promises	1966	10.00
❑ 5031	If I Were a Carpenter/Hang On to a Dream	1966	10.00
❑ 5042	Green Rocky Road/Never Too Far	1967	8.00
❑ 5048	Black Sheep Boy/Misty Roses	1967	8.00

VERVE FORECAST

Number	Title (A Side/B Side)	Yr	NM
❑ 5059	Tribute to Hank Williams/You Upset the Grace of Living When You Die	1967	6.00
❑ 5097	Reason to Believe/Smugglin' Man	1968	6.00
❑ 5116	Reason to Believe/Smugglin' Man	1971	5.00

Albums

ANTILLES

Number	Title (A Side/B Side)	Yr	NM
❑ 7023	Nine	1974	10.00

ATCO

Number	Title (A Side/B Side)	Yr	NM
❑ 33-210 [M]	This Is Tim Hardin	1967	25.00
❑ SD 33-210 [R]	This Is Tim Hardin	1967	15.00

COLUMBIA

Number	Title (A Side/B Side)	Yr	NM
❑ CS 9787	Suite for Susan Moore and Damion — We Are — One, One, All in One	1969	25.00
—"360 Sound" label			
❑ C 30551	Bird on a Wire	1971	20.00
❑ KC 31764	Painted Head	1972	20.00
❑ PC 37164	The Shock of Grace	1981	12.00

MGM

Number	Title (A Side/B Side)	Yr	NM
❑ GAS-104	Tim Hardin (Golden Archive Series)	1970	12.00
❑ M3G-4952	Archetypes	1974	10.00

POLYDOR

Number	Title (A Side/B Side)	Yr	NM
❑ PD-1-6333	Memorial Album	1981	12.00

VERVE FOLKWAYS

Number	Title (A Side/B Side)	Yr	NM
❑ FT-3004 [M]	Tim Hardin/1	1966	25.00
❑ FTS-3004 [S]	Tim Hardin/1	1966	30.00

VERVE FORECAST

Number	Title (A Side/B Side)	Yr	NM
❑ FT-3004 [M]	Tim Hardin/1	1967	15.00
❑ FTS-3004 [S]	Tim Hardin/1	1967	20.00
❑ FTS-3022	Tim Hardin/2	1967	25.00
❑ FTS-3049	Tim Hardin/3 — Live in Concert	1968	25.00
❑ FTS-3064	Tim Hardin/4	1969	25.00
❑ FTS-3078	The Best of Tim Hardin	1970	20.00

HARDLY WORTHIT PLAYERS, THE See SENATOR BOBBY.

HARDWATER

45s

CAPITOL

Number	Title (A Side/B Side)	Yr	NM
❑ 2230	Not So Hard/City Sidewalks	1968	12.00

Albums

CAPITOL

Number	Title (A Side/B Side)	Yr	NM
❑ ST-2954	Hardwater	1968	40.00

HARDY, FRANCOISE

Number	Title (A Side/B Side)	Yr	NM
45s			
4 CORNERS OF THE WORLD			
❑ 103	Catch a Falling Star/Find Me a Boy	196?	10.00
❑ 123	How Ever Much/Only You Can Do It	196?	10.00
❑ 125	All Over the World/Another Place	196?	10.00
❑ 132	The Love of a Boy/Just Call and I'll Be There	196?	10.00
REPRISE			
❑ 0808	Loving You/Hang On to a Dream	1969	8.00
Albums			
4 CORNERS OF THE WORLD			
❑ FCL-4208 [M]	The "Yeh Yeh" Girl from Paris!	1965	28.00
❑ FCS-4208 [S]	The "Yeh Yeh" Girl from Paris!	1965	32.00
❑ FCL-4219 [M]	Maid in Paris	1967	28.00
❑ FCS-4219 [S]	Maid in Paris	1967	32.00
❑ FCL-4231 [M]	Francoise...	1968	28.00
❑ FCS-4231 [S]	Francoise...	1968	32.00
❑ FCL-4238 [M]	Je Vous Aime	1969	28.00
❑ FCS-4238 [S]	Je Vous Aime	1969	32.00
❑ FCS-4255 [S]	The Best of Francoise Hardy	1969	28.00
REPRISE			
❑ RS 6290	Francoise Hardy	1968	30.00
❑ RS 6318	Loving	1969	30.00
❑ RS 6345	Mon Amour, Adieu	1969	30.00

HARDY, HAGOOD

Number	Title (A Side/B Side)	Yr	NM
45s			
CAPITOL			
❑ 4156	The Homecoming/The Queen	1975	4.00
❑ 4292	The Missouri Breaks/Afternoon in Venice	1976	4.00
HERITAGE			
❑ 833	I'll Take Love/Just a Little Lovin'	1971	5.00
Albums			
CAPITOL			
❑ ST-11488	The Homecoming	1975	10.00
❑ ST-11552	Maybe Tomorrow	1976	10.00
❑ SN-16300	The Homecoming	198?	8.00
—Budget-line reissue			

HARDY BOYS, THE

Number	Title (A Side/B Side)	Yr	NM
45s			
RCA VICTOR			
❑ 47-9795	Wheels/Sha-La-La	1969	8.00
❑ 47-9831	Good, Good Lovin'/Love Train	1970	8.00
❑ 74-0228	Love and Let Love/Sink or Swim	1969	8.00
Albums			
RCA VICTOR			
❑ LSP-4217	Here Come the Hardy Boys	1969	20.00
❑ LSP-4315	Wheels	1970	20.00

HARGETT, JOHNNIE

Number	Title (A Side/B Side)	Yr	NM
45s			
CHERRY			
❑ 1016	Rock This Town Tonight/God's Gift to Men	1960	100.00

HARGRAVE, RON

Number	Title (A Side/B Side)	Yr	NM
45s			
CUB			
❑ 9025	Drive-In Movie/Buttercup	1959	12.00
MGM			
❑ 12344	A Fool Am I/Too Late	1956	20.00
❑ 12422	Latch On/Only a Daydream	1957	40.00
❑ 12475	Hold Me/Song of the Moonlight	1957	20.00
❑ 12571	If You Should Go/Heartbreaker	1957	20.00
❑ 12644	Young Romance/Should Have Been Home in Bed	1958	20.00

HARLAN, BILLY

Number	Title (A Side/B Side)	Yr	NM
45s			
BRUNSWICK			
❑ 55066	I Wanna Bop/School House Rock	1958	200.00

HARMONAIRES, THE

Number	Title (A Side/B Side)	Yr	NM
45s			
HOLIDAY			
❑ 2602	Come Back/Lorraine	1957	300.00
—Black label			
❑ 2602	Come Back/Lorraine	196?	25.00
—Red label, single horizontal line			
❑ 2602	Come Back/Lorraine	1960	60.00
—Red label, double horizontal lines			
LOST-NITE			
❑ 181	Come Back/Lorraine	196?	6.00
—Reissue			

HARMONICA FRANK

Number	Title (A Side/B Side)	Yr	NM
45s			
SUN			
❑ 205	Rockin' Chair Daddy/The Great Musical Menagerist	1954	4500.
—VG 1500; VG+ 3000			

HARMONY GRITS, THE

Members of the original DRIFTERS formed this group after their firing.

Number	Title (A Side/B Side)	Yr	NM
45s			
END			
❑ 1051	Am I to Be the One/I Could Have Told You	1959	25.00
❑ 1063	Gee/I Could Have Told You	1959	25.00
❑ 1063	Gee/Santa Claus Is Coming to Town	1959	40.00

HARNELL, JOE

Number	Title (A Side/B Side)	Yr	NM
45s			
COLUMBIA			
❑ 43549	Autumn Leaves/Near You	1966	5.00
❑ 43756	Our Concerto/Meeskeit	1966	5.00
❑ 43756 [DJ]	Our Concerto (same on both sides)	1966	15.00
—Promo only on red vinyl			
❑ 43902	Nature Boy/Bermuda Concerto	1966	5.00
❑ 44148	Un Poco Rio/Sunrise Serenade	1967	5.00
❑ 44244	Guantanamera/Seranata	1967	5.00
❑ 44365	Blame It on the Bossa Nova/So Soon	1967	5.00
❑ 44407	Theme to Candice/Spanish Eyes	1967	5.00
❑ 44571	The Mighty Quinn/Simon Says	1968	5.00
❑ 44670	Sky Hawk/Work Sunny Work	1968	5.00
EPIC			
❑ 9304	The Way of Love/You Are the Song	1959	10.00
❑ 9328	What Is This Thing Called Love/My Little Grass Shack in Kealakekua, Hawaii	1959	10.00
❑ 9406	Time on My Hands/Without a Song	1960	8.00
KAPP			
❑ 497	Fly Me to the Moon Bossa Nova/Harlem Nocturne	1962	8.00
❑ 521	Diane/Walking Song	1963	6.00
❑ 528	Our Day Will Come/My One and Only Love	1963	6.00
❑ 541	Hud/Come Away with Me	1963	6.00
❑ 562	Dawn of Love/Who Am I Kiddin'	1963	6.00
❑ 579	You're Nobody Till Somebody Loves You/When the World Was Young	1964	6.00
❑ 604	Sonata Portuguese/I'll Set My Love to Music	1964	6.00
❑ 633	St. Thomas/Ill Wind	1964	6.00
MCA			
❑ 40953	Theme from "The Incredible Hulk"/Love Theme from "The Incredible Hulk"	1978	5.00
MOTOWN			
❑ 1154	Midnight Cowboy/Green Grow the Lilacs	1969	6.00
❑ 1161	My Cherie Amour/Green Grow the Lilacs	1970	6.00
Albums			
CAPITOL			
❑ ST-11657	Harnell	1977	12.00
COLUMBIA			
❑ CL 2466 [M]	Golden Piano Hits	1966	12.00
❑ CL 2699 [M]	Bossa Now	1967	15.00
❑ CS 9266 [S]	Golden Piano Hits	1966	15.00
❑ CS 9499 [S]	Bossa Now	1967	12.00
EPIC			
❑ LN (# unknown) [M]	I Want to Be Happy	1960	15.00
❑ BN 573 [S]	I Want to Be Happy	1960	20.00
JUBILEE			
❑ JLP-1015 [M]	Piano Inventions of Jo Harnell	1956	50.00
❑ JGM-5020 [M]	Joe Harnell and His Trio	1963	15.00
—Reissue of 1015			
KAPP			
❑ KL 1318 [M]	Fly Me to the Moon and the Bossa Nova Pops	1962	15.00
❑ KL 1325 [M]	More Joe Harnell, More Bossa Nova Pops	1963	15.00
❑ KL 1339 [M]	Joe Harnell	1963	15.00
❑ KL 1416 [M]	The Rhythm and the Fire	1965	12.00
❑ KL 1480 [M]	The Best of Joe Harnell	1966	12.00
❑ KS 3318 [S]	Fly Me to the Moon and the Bossa Nova Pops	1962	20.00
❑ KS 3325 [S]	More Joe Harnell, More Bossa Nova Pops	1963	20.00
❑ KS 3339 [S]	Joe Harnell	1963	20.00
❑ KS 3416 [S]	The Rhythm and the Fire	1965	15.00
❑ KS 3480 [S]	The Best of Joe Harnell	1966	15.00
MOTOWN			
❑ MS-698	Moving On!!	1969	40.00

HARNER, BILLY

Number	Title (A Side/B Side)	Yr	NM
45s			
ATLANTIC			
❑ 2351	A Message to My Babe/Everything's Hunky-Dory	1966	12.00
KAMA SUTRA			
❑ 226	Sally Sayin' Somethin'/Don't Want My Lovin'	1967	12.00
❑ 238	Homicide Dresser/Lavender Room	1967	12.00
❑ 242	What About the Music/Please Spare Me This Time	1968	12.00
KENT			
❑ 493	Irresistible You/Honky Dory	1968	12.00
LAWN			
❑ 239	Anymore/Whatcha Gonna Do	1964	40.00
❑ 244	Coney Island Wild Child/Feel Good	1964	70.00
MIDLAND INT'L.			
❑ MB-10783	Two Lonely People/Whenever I'm Away from You	1976	10.00
OPEN			
❑ 1253	She's Almost You/Fool Me	1969	15.00
OR			
❑ 1253	She's Almost You/Fool Me	1969	12.00
❑ 1255	I Struck It Rich/Watch Your Step	1969	25.00
PARKWAY			
❑ 950	Let's Get in Line/All Through the Night	1965	20.00
SOUND GEMS			
❑ (# unknown)	I Got It from Heaven/(B-side unknown)	197?	600.00
V-TONE			
❑ 1001	A Message to My Babe/Everything's Hunky-Dory	196?	40.00
❑ 1003	All in My Mind/Fool Me	196?	25.00

HAROLD AND THE CASUALS

Number	Title (A Side/B Side)	Yr	NM
45s			
SCOTTY			
❑ 628	Darling Do You Love Me/You Can Shake a Tail Feather	1959	300.00

HARPER, BEN

Number	Title (A Side/B Side)	Yr	NM
45s			
CENCO			
❑ 120	Red Dress Woman/Drop In to See Me	196?	12.00
TALENT			
❑ 106	Drive Away Blues/Here Comes My Girl	196?	10.00

HARPER, CHUCK

As "Chuck Fassert," he recorded with THE REGENTS.

Number	Title (A Side/B Side)	Yr	NM
45s			
FELSTED			
❑ 8658	Summer Is Thru/Call on Me	1962	30.00

HARPER, ROY

Number	Title (A Side/B Side)	Yr	NM
45s			
EPIC			
❑ 10268	Midspring Dithering/Zengfm	1967	15.00
Albums			
CHRYSALIS			
❑ PRO-620 [DJ]	Introduction to Roy Harper	1976	30.00
❑ CHR 1105	When An Old Cricketer Leaves the Crease	1976	15.00
❑ CHR 1139	One of Those Days in England	1977	15.00
❑ CHR 1160	Flat Baroque and Berserk	1978	15.00
—Reissue of Harvest LP			
❑ CHR 1161	Stormcock	1978	12.00
—Released in the UK in 1971			
❑ CHR 1162	Lifemask	1978	12.00
—Released in the UK in 1973			
❑ CHR 1163	Valentine	1978	12.00
—Released in the UK in 1974			
❑ CH2 1164 [(2)]	Flashes from the Archives of Oblivion	1978	15.00
—Released in the UK in 1974			
HARVEST			
❑ SKAO-418	Flat Baroque and Berserk	1970	30.00
PVC			
❑ 8937	Whatever Happened to Jugula	198?	12.00
WORLD PACIFIC			
❑ WPS-21888	Folkjokeopus	1969	30.00

HARPERS BIZARRE

45s

WARNER BROS.

Number	Title (A Side/B Side)	Yr	NM
❑ 5890	The 59th Street Bridge Song (Feelin' Groovy)/Lost My Love Today	1967	10.00
❑ 7028	Come to the Sunshine/Debutante's Ball	1967	8.00
❑ 7063	Anything Goes/Malibu U.	1967	8.00
❑ 7090	Chattanooga Choo Choo/Hey, You in the Crowd	1967	8.00
❑ 7106	The 59th Street Bridge Song (Feelin' Groovy)/Come to the Sunshine	1968	6.00
—"Back to Back Hits" series — originals have green labels with "W7" logo			
❑ 7123	Anything Goes/Chattanooga Choo Choo	1969	6.00
—"Back to Back Hits" series — originals have green labels with "W7" logo			
❑ 7172	Virginia City/Cotton Candy Sandman	1968	6.00
❑ 7200	Both Sides Now/Small Talk	1968	6.00
❑ 7223	Battle of New Orleans/Green Apple Tree	1968	6.00
❑ 7238	I Love You, Alice B. Toklas/Look to the Rainbow	1968	6.00
❑ 7296	Knock on Wood/Witchi-Tai-Yo	1969	5.00
❑ 7377	Poly High/Soft Soundin' Music	1970	5.00
❑ 7388	Anything Goes/Virginia City	1970	5.00
❑ 7399	If We Ever Needed the Lord Before/Mad	1970	5.00
❑ 7647	Knock on Wood/Poly High	1972	4.00

7-Inch Extended Plays

WARNER BROS.

Number	Title (A Side/B Side)	Yr	NM
❑ S 1739	Battle of New Orleans/Las Mananitas/Sentimental Journey//I'll Build a Stairway to Paradise/Sit Down, You're Rocking the Boat/Green Apple Tree	1968	15.00
—Jukebox issue; small hole, plays at 33 1/3 rpm			
❑ S 1739 [PS]	The Secret Life of Harpers Bizarre	1968	15.00

Albums

FOREST BAY

Number	Title (A Side/B Side)	Yr	NM
❑ 7545	As Time Goes By	1976	15.00

WARNER BROS.

Number	Title (A Side/B Side)	Yr	NM
❑ W 1693 [M]	Feelin' Groovy	1967	18.00
❑ WS 1693 [S]	Feelin' Groovy	1967	14.00
—Gold label			
❑ WS 1693 [S]	Feelin' Groovy	1968	15.00
—Green "W7" label			
❑ WS 1716	Anything Goes	1967	18.00
❑ WS 1739	The Secret Life of Harpers Bizarre	1968	16.00
❑ WS 1784	Harpers Bizarre Four	1969	16.00
❑ ST-91351	Anything Goes	1968	18.00
—Capitol Record Club edition			

HARPO, SLIM

45s

EXCELLO

Number	Title (A Side/B Side)	Yr	NM
❑ 2113	I'm a King Bee/I Got Love If You Want It	1957	60.00
❑ 2138	Wonderin' and Worryin'/Strange Love	1958	30.00
❑ 2162	One More Day/You'll Be Sorry One Day	1959	30.00
❑ 2171	Buzz Me Babe/Late Last Night	1960	30.00
❑ 2184	Blues Hangover/What a Dream	1960	30.00
❑ 2194	Rainin' in My Heart/Don't Start Cryin' Now	1961	20.00
❑ 2239	Buzzin'/I Love the Life I'm Livin'	1963	15.00
❑ 2246	Little Queen Bee (Got a Brand New King)/I Need Money (Keep Your Alibis)	1964	12.00
❑ 2253	Still Rainin' in My Heart/We're Two of a Kind	1964	12.00
❑ 2261	Sittin' Here Wondering/What's Goin' On Baby	1964	12.00
❑ 2265	Please Don't Turn Me Down/Harpo's Blues	1965	12.00
❑ 2273	Baby Scratch My Back/I'm Gonna Miss You (Like the Devil)	1965	12.00
❑ 2276	Goin' Away Blues/Just a Lonely Stranger	1966	10.00
❑ 2278	Midnight Blues/Shake Your Hips	1966	10.00
❑ 2282	I'm Your Bread-Maker, Baby/Loving You (The Way I Do)	1966	10.00
❑ 2285	Tip On In (Part 1)/Tip On In (Part 2)	1967	10.00
❑ 2289	I'm Gonna Keep What I've Got/I've Got to Be with You Tonight	1967	10.00
❑ 2294	Te-Ni-Lee-Ni-Nu/Mailbox Bues	1968	30.00
❑ 2301	Mohair Sam/I Just Can't Leave You	1969	25.00
❑ 2305	Just for You/That's Why I Love You	1969	10.00
❑ 2306	Folsom Prison Blues/Mututal Friend	1969	15.00
❑ 2309	I've Got My Finger on Your Trigger/The Price Is Too High	1969	20.00
❑ 2316	Rainin' in My Heart/Jody Man	1970	8.00

Albums

EXCELLO

Number	Title (A Side/B Side)	Yr	NM
❑ LP-8003 [M]	Raining in My Heart	1961	250.00
—Orange and blue label			
❑ LPS-8003 [M]	Raining in My Heart	196?	100.00
—All-blue label			
❑ LP-8005 [M]	Baby Scratch My Back	1966	200.00
—Orange and blue label			
❑ LPS-8005 [M]	Baby Scratch My Back	196?	100.00
—All-blue label			
❑ LPS-8008 [M]	Tip On In	1968	50.00
❑ LPS-8010 [M]	The Best of Slim Harpo	1969	50.00
❑ LPS-8013 [M]	Slim Harpo Knew the Blues	1970	50.00

RHINO

Number	Title (A Side/B Side)	Yr	NM
❑ RNLP-106	The Best of Slim Harpo	198?	15.00
❑ R1-70169	Scratch My Back: The Best of Slim Harpo	1989	12.00

HARPS, THE See THE CAMELOTS.

HARPTONES, THE

45s

AMBIENT SOUND

Number	Title (A Side/B Side)	Yr	NM
❑ 02807	Love Needs a Heart/It's You	1982	6.00

ANDREA

Number	Title (A Side/B Side)	Yr	NM
❑ 100	What Is Your Decision/Gimme Some	1956	40.00

BRUCE

Number	Title (A Side/B Side)	Yr	NM
❑ 101	A Sunday Kind of Love/I'll Never Tell	1953	80.00
—"Bruce" in block lettering			
❑ 101	A Sunday Kind of Love/I'll Never Tell	1953	3000.
—"Bruce" in script lettering. VG 1000; VG+ 2000			
❑ 102	My Memories of You/The Laughs on You	1954	120.00
—Same B-side with different title (and missing the apostrophe)			
❑ 102	My Memories of You/It Was Just for Laughs	1954	200.00
❑ 104	I Depended on You/Mambo Boogie	1954	80.00
❑ 109	Forever Mine/Why Should I Love You	1954	80.00
❑ 113	Since I Fell for You/Oobidee-Oobidee-Oo	1954	80.00
❑ 123	High Flying Baby/Loving a Girl Like You	1955	60.00
❑ 128	I Almost Lost My Mind/Oh Wee Baby	1955	60.00

COED

Number	Title (A Side/B Side)	Yr	NM
❑ 540	Answer Me My Love/Rain Down Kisses	1960	20.00

COMPANION

Number	Title (A Side/B Side)	Yr	NM
❑ 102	All in Your Mind/The Last Dance	1961	30.00
❑ 103	What Will I Tell My Heart/Foolish Me	1961	80.00

CUB

Number	Title (A Side/B Side)	Yr	NM
❑ 9097	Devil in Velvet/Your Love Is a Good Love	1961	20.00

GEE

Number	Title (A Side/B Side)	Yr	NM
❑ 1045	Cry Like I Cried/So Good, So Fine, You're Mine	1957	60.00
—Red label			

KT

Number	Title (A Side/B Side)	Yr	NM
❑ 201	Sunset/I Gotta Have Your Love	1963	50.00

LOST-NITE

Number	Title (A Side/B Side)	Yr	NM
❑ 395	A Sunday Kind of Love/I'll Never Tell	197?	5.00
—Reissue			
❑ 397	My Memories of You/The Laughs on You	197?	5.00
—Reissue			
❑ 399	I Almost Lost My Mind/Oh Wee Baby	197?	5.00
—Reissue			
❑ 401	Forever Mine/Why Should I Love You	197?	5.00
—Reissue			
❑ 403	Since I Fell for You/Oobidee-Oobidee-Oo	197?	5.00
—Reissue			
❑ 405	I Depended on You/Mambo Boogie	197?	5.00
—Reissue			
❑ 407	What Is Your Decision/Gimme Some	197?	5.00
—Reissue			
❑ 409	High Flying Baby/Loving a Girl Like You	197?	5.00
—Reissue			

PARADISE

Number	Title (A Side/B Side)	Yr	NM
❑ 101	Life Is But a Dream/You Know You're Doing Me Wrong	1954	60.00
—Purple label			
❑ 101	Life Is But a Dream/You Know You're Doing Me Wrong	1954	150.00
—Maroon label			
❑ 103	My Success/I've Got a Notion	1955	300.00
❑ 105	It All Depends on You/Guitar Shuffle	1955	60.00
—Purple label			
❑ 105	It All Depends on You/Guitar Shuffle	1955	150.00
—Maroon label			

RAMA

Number	Title (A Side/B Side)	Yr	NM
❑ 203	Three Wishes/That's the Way It Goes	1956	80.00
❑ 214	The Masquerade Is Over/On Sunday Afternoon	1956	80.00
❑ 221	The Shrine of St. Cecelia/Oo Wee Baby	1957	80.00

RAVEN

Number	Title (A Side/B Side)	Yr	NM
❑ 8001	A Sunday Kind of Love/Mambo Boogie	1962	15.00

TIP TOP

Number	Title (A Side/B Side)	Yr	NM
❑ 401	My Memories of You/High Flyin' Baby	1956	40.00

WARWICK

Number	Title (A Side/B Side)	Yr	NM
❑ 500	I Remember/Laughing on the Outside	1959	25.00
❑ 512	Love Me Completely/Hep Teenager	1959	25.00
❑ 551	No Greater Miracle/What Kind of a Fool	1960	25.00

7-Inch Extended Plays

BRUCE

Number	Title (A Side/B Side)	Yr	NM
❑ BEP 201	A Sunday Kind of Love/Ou Wee Baby//Forever Mine/I Almost Lost My Mind	1954	5000.
—VG 2500; VG+ 3750			
❑ BEP 201 [PS]	The Sensational Harptones	1954	5000.
—VG 2500; VG+ 3750			

Albums

AMBIENT SOUND

Number	Title (A Side/B Side)	Yr	NM
❑ FZ 37718	Love Needs	1982	12.00

HARLEM HIT PARADE

Number	Title (A Side/B Side)	Yr	NM
❑ 5006	The Harptones	197?	15.00

RELIC

Number	Title (A Side/B Side)	Yr	NM
❑ LP-5001	The Greatest Hits of the Harptones, Vol. 1	197?	12.00
❑ LP-5003	The Greatest Hits of the Harptones, Vol. 2	197?	12.00

HARRIS, ANITA

45s

BRUT

Number	Title (A Side/B Side)	Yr	NM
❑ 1345	I Just Need a Lover/Music	197?	6.00

COLUMBIA

Number	Title (A Side/B Side)	Yr	NM
❑ 44236	Just Loving You/Butterfly with Coloured Wings	1967	8.00
❑ 44438	Anniversary Waltz/Comes the Night	1968	8.00

LONDON

Number	Title (A Side/B Side)	Yr	NM
❑ 9720	Lies/Don't Think About Love	1964	12.00

WARNER BROS.

Number	Title (A Side/B Side)	Yr	NM
❑ 5638	Trains and Boats and Planes/Upside Down	1965	10.00

HARRIS, EDDIE

45s

ATLANTIC

Number	Title (A Side/B Side)	Yr	NM
❑ 2404	When a Man Loves a Woman/The Tender Storm	1967	8.00
❑ 2447	Sham Time (Part 1)/Sham Time (Part 2)	1967	8.00
❑ 2487	Listen Here/A Theme in Search of a Movie	1968	20.00
❑ 2561	Live Right Now/It's Crazy	1968	15.00
❑ 2607	1974 Blues/Free at Last	1969	15.00
❑ 2667	Movin' On Out/Funky Doo	1969	15.00
❑ 3216	Is It In/Funkaroma	1974	15.00
❑ 3245	I Don't Want Nobody/I Need Some Money	1975	8.00
❑ 3256	Get On Down/Time to Do Your Thing	1975	8.00

Except when noted otherwise, VG = 25% of NM, and VG+ = 50% of NM. (Example: VG = $2.00, VG+ = $4.00 and NM = $8.00.)

Number	Title (A Side/B Side)	Yr	NM
❑ 3288	Get Up and Dance/Why Must We Part	1975	8.00
❑ 3347	That Is Why You're Overweight/It's All Right Now	1976	8.00
❑ 5052	Love Theme from "The Sandpiper"/Cryin' Blues	1966	8.00
❑ 5072	Listen Here/Mean Greens	1968	6.00
❑ 5101	Foolish/Why Don't You Quit	1971	6.00
❑ 5105	Really/Live Right Now	1971	6.00
❑ 5106	Boogie Woogie Bossa Nova/Wait Please	1971	6.00
❑ 5112	Carry On Brother/Children's Song	1972	6.00
❑ 5115	Instant Death/Was	1972	6.00
❑ 5116	Ten Minutes to Four/Please Let Me Go	1973	6.00
❑ 5117	Baby/I've Tried Everything	1973	6.00
❑ 5118	Drunk Man/Here Goes Funky	1973	10.00
❑ 5120	Is It In/Funkaroma	1974	6.00
COLUMBIA			
❑ 43075	Chicago Serenade/More Soul Than Soulful	1964	8.00
❑ 43188	People/Groovy Movies	1964	8.00
VEE JAY			
❑ 378	Exodus/Alicia	1961	10.00
❑ 407	God Bless the Child/My Buddy	1961	8.00
❑ 410	Spartacus/Willow Weep for Me	1961	8.00
❑ 420	Moon River/Mr. Yunioshi	1962	8.00
❑ 447	Just Friends/Olifant Gesang	1962	8.00
❑ 464	Tonight/Be My Love	1962	8.00
❑ 496	Mima/Lolita Marie	1963	8.00
❑ 518	Theme from Lawrence of Arabia/Yea! Yea! Yea!	1963	8.00
❑ 543	Half and Half/K.C. Blues	1963	8.00
WARNER BROS.			
❑ 49890	Sharkey's Theme/Theme from "Sharkey's Machine"	1980	4.00
—B-side by Sarah Vaughan			
Albums			
ANGELACO			
❑ AN 3002	Sounds Incredible	1980	12.00
ATLANTIC			
❑ SD 2-311 [(2)]	Excursions	1973	15.00
❑ 1448 [M]	The In Sound	1966	12.00
❑ SD 1448 [S]	The In Sound	1966	15.00
❑ 1453 [M]	Mean Greens	1966	12.00
❑ SD 1453 [S]	Mean Greens	1966	15.00
❑ 1478 [M]	The Tender Storm	1967	15.00
❑ SD 1478 [S]	The Tender Storm	1967	15.00
❑ SD 1495	The Electrifying Eddie Harris	1968	15.00
❑ SD 1506	Plug Me In	1968	15.00
❑ SD 1517	Silver Cycles	1969	15.00
❑ SD 1529	High Voltage	1969	15.00
❑ 1545 [M]	The Best of Eddie Harris	1970	25.00
—Promo-only white label mono pressing			
❑ SD 1545	The Best of Eddie Harris	1970	15.00
❑ SD 1554	Come On Down!	1970	15.00
❑ SD 1573	Free Speech	1971	15.00
❑ SD 1595	Eddie Harris Live at Newport	1971	12.00
❑ SD 1611	Instant Death	1972	12.00
❑ SD 1625	Eddie Harris Sings the Blues	1973	12.00
❑ SD 1647	E.H. in the U.K.	1974	12.00
❑ SD 1659	Is It In	1974	12.00
❑ SD 1669	I Need Some Money	1975	12.00
❑ SD 1675	Bad Luck Is All I Have	1975	12.00
❑ SD 1683	Why You're Overweight	1976	12.00
❑ SD 1698	How Can You Live Like That	1977	12.00
❑ SD 8807	The Versatile Eddie Harris	1982	10.00
❑ SW-94771	Instant Death	1972	15.00
—Capitol Record Club edition			
BUDDAH			
❑ BDS 4004	Sculpture	1969	12.00
COLUMBIA			
❑ CL 2168 [M]	Cool Sax, Warm Heart	1964	15.00
❑ CL 2295 [M]	Cool Sax from Hollywood to Broadway	1965	15.00
❑ CS 8968 [S]	Cool Sax, Warm Heart	1964	20.00
❑ CS 9095 [S]	Cool Sax from Hollywood to Broadway	1965	20.00
❑ CS 9681 [M]	Here Comes the Judge	1968	25.00
—Mono copies are promo only			
❑ CS 9681 [S]	Here Comes the Judge	1968	15.00
EXODUS			
❑ EX-6002 [M]	For Bird and Bags	1966	15.00
GNP CRESCENDO			
❑ GNPS-2073 [(2)]	Black Sax	1973	15.00
JANUS			
❑ 3020	Smokin'	1970	12.00
MUTT & JEFF			
❑ 5018	The Real Electrifying Eddie Harris	1982	12.00
RCA VICTOR			
❑ APL1-2942	I'm Tired	1978	10.00
❑ AFL1-3402	Playin' With Myself	1980	10.00
STEEPLECHASE			
❑ 1151	Eddie Harris Steps Up	1981	10.00
SUNSET			
❑ SUS-5234	The Explosive Eddie Harris	1969	12.00
TRADITION			
❑ 2067	Genius	1969	12.00
TRIP			
❑ 5005 [(2)]	Shades of Eddie Harris	1974	12.00
UPFRONT			
❑ UPF-106	The Soul of Eddie Harris	197?	10.00
VEE JAY			
❑ VJLP 1081 [M]	The Theme from Exodus and Other Film Spectaculars	1964	15.00
❑ VJLPS 1081 [S]	The Theme from Exodus and Other Film Spectaculars	1964	20.00
❑ LP 3016 [M]	Exodus to Jazz	1961	30.00
❑ SR 3016 [S]	Exodus to Jazz	1961	40.00
❑ VJS-3016	Exodus to Jazz	198?	10.00
—Reissue with thinner vinyl			
❑ LP 3025 [M]	Mighty Like a Rose	1961	30.00
❑ SR 3025 [S]	Mighty Like a Rose	1961	40.00
❑ LP 3027 [M]	Jazz for "Breakfast at Tiffany's"	1961	30.00
❑ SR 3027 [S]	Jazz for "Breakfast at Tiffany's"	1961	40.00
❑ LP 3028 [M]	A Study in Jazz	1962	20.00
❑ SR 3028 [S]	A Study in Jazz	1962	30.00
❑ LP 3031 [M]	Eddie Harris Goes to the Movies	1962	20.00
❑ SR 3031 [S]	Eddie Harris Goes to the Movies	1962	30.00
❑ LP 3034 [M]	Bossa Nova	1963	20.00
❑ SR 3034 [S]	Bossa Nova	1963	30.00
❑ LP 3037 [M]	Half and Half	1963	25.00
❑ SR 3037 [S]	Half and Half	1963	30.00
❑ VJS-3058	For Bird and Bags	198?	10.00

HARRIS, EMMYLOU

Number	Title (A Side/B Side)	Yr	NM
45s			
ASYLUM			
❑ 64570	Thanks to You/Lovin' You Again	1993	3.00
❑ 64610	High Powered Love/Ballad of a Runaway Horse	1992	3.00
JUBILEE			
❑ 5679	I'll Be Your Baby Tonight/I'll Never Fall in Love Again	1969	20.00
❑ 5697	Paddy/Fugue for the Ox	1970	20.00
MCA			
❑ 53236	I Still Dream of You/Back in Baby's Arms	1988	3.00
REPRISE			
❑ 1326	Too Far Gone/Boulder to Birmingham	1975	5.00
❑ 1332	If I Could Only Win Your Love/Boulder to Birmingham	1975	5.00
❑ 1341	Light of the Stable/Bluebird Wine	1975	10.00
—A-side is a longer version than later releases			
❑ 1341 [PS]	Light of the Stable/Bluebird Wine	1975	12.00
❑ 1346	Together Again/Here, There and Everywhere	1976	5.00
❑ 1353	Till I Gain Control Again/One of These Days	1976	5.00
❑ 1371	Sweet Dreams/Amarillo	1976	5.00
❑ 1379	Light of the Stable/Boulder to Birmingham	1976	5.00
❑ 19281	Rollin' and Ramblin'/Sweet Dreams Of You	1991	3.00
❑ 19510	Wheels of Love/Better Off Without You	1991	3.00
❑ 19707	Never Be Anyone Else But You/Red, Red Rose	1990	3.00
❑ 19870	Gulf Coast Highway/Evangeline	1990	3.00
—A-side with Willie Nelson			
❑ 22850	I Still Miss Someone/No Regrets	1989	3.00
❑ 22999	Heaven Only Knows/A River for Him	1989	3.00
❑ 27635	Heartbreak Hill/Icy Blue Heart	1989	3.00
WARNER BROS.			
❑ PRO-S-2872 [DJ]	Light of the Stable/It Came Upon a Midnight Clear	1987	10.00
—B-side by Highway 101			
❑ 8329	C'est La Vie (You Never Can Tell)/You're Supposed to Be Feeling Good	1977	5.00
❑ 8388	Making Believe/I'll Be Your San Antone Rose	1977	5.00
❑ 8498	To Daddy/Tulsa Queen	1977	5.00
❑ 8553	Two More Bottles of Wine/I Ain't Living Long Like This	1978	5.00
❑ 8623	Easy from Now On/You're Supposed to Be Feeling Good	1978	5.00
❑ 8732	Too Far Gone/Tulsa Queen	1979	4.00
❑ 8815	Save the Last Dance for Me/Even Cowgirls Get the Blues	1979	5.00
❑ 28302	Someday My Ship Will Sail/When He Calls	1987	3.00
❑ 28714	Today I Started Loving You Again/When I Was Young	1986	3.00
❑ 28770	I Had My Heart Set on You/Your Long Journey	1986	3.00
❑ 28852	Timberline/Sweet Chariot	1985	4.00
❑ 28952	Rhythm Guitar/Diamond in My Crown	1985	3.00
❑ 29041	White Line/Long Tall Sally Rose	1985	4.00
❑ 29138	Someone Like You/Light of the Stable	1984	4.00
❑ 29218	Pledging My Love/Baby, Better Start Turnin' 'Em Down	1984	4.00
❑ 29329	In My Dreams/Like an Old Fashioned World	1984	4.00
❑ 29443	Drivin' Wheel/Good News	1983	4.00
❑ 29583	So Sad (To Watch Good Love Go Bad)/Amarillo	1983	4.00
❑ 29729	I'm Movin' On/Maybe Tonight	1983	4.00
❑ 29898	(Lost His Love) On Our Last Date/Another Pot O' Tea	1982	4.00
❑ 29993	Born to Run/Colors of My Heart	1982	4.00
❑ 49056	Blue Kentucky Girl/Leaving Louisiana in the Broad Daylight	1979	4.00
❑ 49164	Beneath Still Waters/'Til I Gain Control Again	1980	4.00
❑ 49239	Wayfaring Stranger/Green Pastures	1980	4.00
❑ 49262	That Lovin' You Feeling Again/Lola	1980	5.00
—A-side with Roy Orbison; B-side by Craig Hundley			
❑ 49551	The Boxer/Precious Love	1980	4.00
❑ 49633	Beautiful Star of Bethlehem/The Little Drummer Boy	1980	4.00
❑ 49645	Little Drummer Boy/Light of the Stable	1980	4.00
❑ 49684	Mister Sandman/Fools' Thin Air	1981	4.00
❑ 49739	I Don't Have to Crawl/Colors of Your Heart	1981	4.00
❑ 49809	If I Needed You/Ashes By Now	1981	4.00
—A-side with Don Williams			
❑ 49892	Tennessee Rose/Mama Help	1982	4.00
Albums			
JUBILEE			
❑ JGS-8031	Gliding Bird	1969	120.00
—Originals have color covers; counterfeit covers are black and white			
MOBILE FIDELITY			
❑ 1-015	Quarter Moon in a Ten Cent Town	1979	40.00
—Audiophile vinyl			
REPRISE			
❑ MS 2213	Pieces of the Sky	1975	10.00
❑ MS 2236	Elite Hotel	1976	10.00
❑ MSK 2284	Pieces of the Sky	1977	8.00
—Reissue of 2213			
❑ MSK 2286	Elite Hotel	1977	8.00
—Reissue of 2236			
❑ 25776	Bluebird	1989	12.00
WARNER BROS.			
❑ BS 2998	Luxury Liner	1977	12.00
❑ BSK 3115	Luxury Liner	1977	10.00
—Reissue of 2998			
❑ BSK 3141	Quarter Moon in a Ten Cent Town	1978	10.00
❑ BSK 3258	Profile/Best of Emmylou Harris	1978	10.00
❑ BSK 3318	Blue Kentucky Girl	1979	10.00
❑ BSK 3422	Roses in the Snow	1980	10.00
❑ BSK 3484	Light of the Stable: The Christmas Album	1980	10.00
❑ BSK 3508	Evangeline	1981	10.00
❑ BSK 3603	Cimarron	1981	10.00
❑ 23740	Last Date	1982	10.00
❑ 23961	White Shoes	1983	10.00
❑ 25161	Profile II — The Best of Emmylou Harris	1984	10.00
❑ 25205	The Ballad of Sally Rose	1985	10.00
❑ 25352	Thirteen	1986	10.00
❑ 25585	Angel Band	1987	10.00

HARRIS, GENEE

Number	Title (A Side/B Side)	Yr	NM
45s			
ABC-PARAMOUNT			
❑ 9900	Bye Bye Elvis/You're Like a Jumping Jack	1958	50.00

HARRIS, GEORGIA, AND THE LYRICS

Number	Title (A Side/B Side)	Yr	NM
45s			
HY-TONE			
❑ 111	Let's Exchange Hearts for Christmas/It's Time to Rock	1958	500.00
❑ 117	Let's Exchange Hearts for Christmas/Kiss, Kiss, Kiss	1958	500.00

HARRIS, JACKIE

Number	Title (A Side/B Side)	Yr	NM
45s			
HIT			
194	Can't You Hear My Heartbeat/You Were Gone	1965	8.00
—B-side by John Preston			

HARRIS, JET, AND TONY MEECHAN

Also see THE SHADOWS.

Number	Title (A Side/B Side)	Yr	NM
45s			
LONDON			
9589	Diamonds/Footstomp	1963	15.00
9608	Scarlet O'Hara/(Doin' the) Hully Gully	1963	15.00
9622	Applejack/Tall Texan	1963	15.00

HARRIS, KURT

Number	Title (A Side/B Side)	Yr	NM
45s			
DIAMOND			
158	Go On/Emperor of My Baby's Heart	1964	500.00
JOSIE			
898	Let Her Dance/I Can't Love Nobody Else	1962	20.00
902	Uh-Uh/You Better Shut Your Mouth	1962	20.00

HARRIS, MAJOR

Also see THE DELFONICS.

Number	Title (A Side/B Side)	Yr	NM
12-Inch Singles			
POP ART			
1401	All My Life/(B-side unknown)	1983	6.00
45s			
ATLANTIC			
3217	Each Morning I Wake Up/Just a Thing I Do	1974	5.00
3248	Love Won't Let Me Wait/After Loving You	1975	15.00
3299 [DJ]	Loving You Is Mellow (mono/stereo)	1975	5.00
—May be promo-only			
3303	I Got Over Love/Loving You Is Mellow	1975	30.00
3321	Jealousy/Tynisa (What's Your Hurry)	1976	4.00
3336	It's Got to Be Magic/Just a Thing That I Do	1976	4.00
OKEH			
7314	Just Love Me/Loving You More	1968	100.00
7327	Like a Rolling Stone/Call Me Tomorrow	1969	500.00
WMOT			
02091	Here We Are/Living's Easy Now	1981	4.00
4002	Laid Back Love/This Is What You Mean to Me	1976	4.00
Albums			
ATLANTIC			
SD 18119	My Way	1974	15.00
SD 18160	Jealousy	1976	15.00
RCA VICTOR			
APL1-2803	How Do You Take Your Love	1978	12.00
WMOT			
627	Mellow Major	1977	12.00
PW 37067	The Best of Major Harris, Now and Then	1981	10.00

HARRIS, PEPPERMINT

Number	Title (A Side/B Side)	Yr	NM
45s			
ALADDIN			
3097	I Got Loaded/It's You, Yes It's You	1951	100.00
—Black vinyl			
3097	I Got Loaded/It's You, Yes It's You	1951	250.00
—Green vinyl			
3107	Have Another Drink and Talk to Me/Middle of Winter	1951	80.00
3108	Let the Back Door Hit You/P.H. Blues	1951	80.00
3130	Right Back On It/Maggie's Boogie	1952	80.00
3141	I Cry for My Baby/There's a Dead Cat on the Line	1952	80.00
3154	I Sure Do Miss My Baby/Hey Little Schoolgirl	1952	80.00
3177	Wasted Love/Goodbye Blues	1953	80.00
3183	Don't Leave Me Alone/Wet Rat	1953	80.00
3206	I Never Get Enough of You/Three Sheets in the Wind	1953	80.00
CASH			
1003	Cadillac Funeral/Treat Me Like I Treat You	1954	150.00
COMBO			
114	Love at First Sight/I Don't Care	1956	60.00
DART			
103	You Get Me Wondering/Messing Around with the Blues	1959	25.00
DUKE			
319	Ain't No Business/Angel Child	1960	30.00
JEWEL			
742	Marking Time/Bad, Mad Woman	1965	40.00
747	Ma Ma/Anything You Can Do	1965	10.00
762	Raining in My Heart/My Time After Awhile	1966	10.00
772	Anytime Is the Right Time/Wait Until It Happens to You	1966	200.00
789	Bad Bad Whiskey/Lonesome As Can Be	1967	10.00
795	24 Hours/Little Girl	1968	30.00
MODERN			
936	Bye Bye, Fare Thee Well/Black Cat Bone	1951	100.00
SITTIN' IN WITH			
543	Raining in My Heart/My Blues Have Rolled Away	1950	150.00
—Other Peppermint Harris 45s on this label may exist.			
"X"			
0142	Need Your Lovin'/Just Me and You	1955	100.00
Albums			
TIME			
5 [M]	Peppermint Harris	1962	200.00

HARRIS, PHIL

Number	Title (A Side/B Side)	Yr	NM
45s			
BUENA VISTA			
F-461	The Bare Necessities/I Wanna Be Like You	1967	15.00
—B-side by Louis Prima			
F-464	The Bare Necessities/The Bare Necessities	1968	15.00
—B-side by the Jungle V.I.P.'s			
F-477	What! No Mickey Mouse (What Kind of Party Is This)/Minnie's Yoo Hoo	1970	8.00
F-477 [PS]	What! No Mickey Mouse (What Kind of Party Is This)/Minnie's Yoo Hoo	1970	12.00
F-478	Everybody Wants to Be a Cat/Thomas O'Malley Cat	1970	15.00
COLISEUM			
2711	But I Loved You/This Is All I Ask	1968	8.00
MEGA			
0111	Dark Town Poker Club/That's What I Like About the South	1973	8.00
RCA VICTOR			
47-2770	Woodman, Spare That Tree/Ain't Nobody Here But Us Chickens	1949	25.00
47-2771	Pappy's Little Jug/Minnie the Mermaid	1949	—
—Unreleased?			
47-2846	Look Out Stranger, I'm a Texas Ranger/That's What I Like About the South	1949	15.00
47-2847	44 Sycamore/Darktown Poker Club	1949	15.00
47-2848	Pappy's Little Jug/Minnie the Mermaid	1949	15.00
—The above three comprise box set WP 199			
47-2909	Shadrach/The General's House	1949	20.00
47-2938	Thank the Man Upstairs/I Wish I Were a Goldfish	1949	20.00
47-3003	Silas Lee/Is It True What They Say About Dixie?	1949	20.00
47-3064	I Ain't Gonna Give Nobody None of This Jelly Roll/Row, Row, Row	1949	20.00
47-3066	Is It True What They Say About Dixie?/After You've Gone	1949	20.00
47-3114	The Old Master Painter/St. James Infirmary	1949	20.00
47-3216	Chattanoogie Shoe Shine Boy/That's a Plenty	1950	20.00
47-3260	Smoke, Smoke, Smoke (That Cigarette)/Crawdad Song	1950	20.00
—78 originally released in 1947 with a different number			
47-3723	Muskrat Ramble/Walk with a Wiggle	1950	20.00
47-3781	Simple Melody/On the Mississippi	1950	20.00
47-3825	Dig-Dig-Dig for Your Dinner/I've Been Floating Down Green River	1950	20.00
47-3968	The Thing/Goofus	1950	20.00
47-4070	Oh What a Face/Southern Fried Boogie	1951	20.00
47-4124	The Letter/Possibilities	1951	20.00
—With Alice Faye			
47-4224	Golden Train/Tennessee Hillbilly Ghost	1951	20.00
47-4225	The Musicians/How D'Ya Do and Shake Hands	1951	20.00
—With Dinah Shore, Betty Hutton and Tony Martin			
47-4342	Where the Blues Were Born in New Orleans/Ragged But Right	1951	20.00
47-4450	Wine, Women, Song/8th Street Association	1952	20.00
47-4584	Hambone/Mama's on the Warpath	1952	20.00
47-4750	Under the Lamp Post/Potato Chips	1952	20.00
47-5615	I Know an Old Lady/Take Your Girlie to the Movies	1954	15.00
47-5730	Persian Kitty/I Guess I'll Have to Change My Plan	1954	15.00
47-5873	Muskrat Ramble/Stars Fell on Alabama	1954	15.00
47-5945	I Wouldn't Touch You with a Ten-Foot Pole/There's a Lot More Layin' Down	1954	15.00
WP 199 [PS]	On the Record by Phil Harris	1949	15.00
—Box for three 45s (47-2846, 47-2847, 47-2848)			
REPRISE			
20117	Run Red Run/Old Man Time	1962	10.00
7-Inch Extended Plays			
RCA VICTOR			
547-0188	That's What I Like About the South/The Dark Town Poker Club//Ain't Nobody Here But Us Chickens/Pappy's Little Jug	1952	20.00
—Part of 2-EP set EPB 3037			
547-0189	Minnie the Mermaid (A Love Song in Fish Time)/Woodman, Spare That Tree//44 Sycamore/Look Out Stranger I'm a Texas Ranger	1952	20.00
—Part of 2-EP set EPB 3037			
EPB 3037 [PS]	On the Record by Phil Harris	1952	20.00
—Cover for 2-EP set (547-0188, 547-0189)			
EPA-5127	(contents unknown)	1958	12.00
EPA-5127 [PS]	That's What I Like About the South	1958	12.00
Albums			
MEGA			
MLPS-608	Southern Comfort ... The Best of Phil Harris	1974	15.00
RCA CAMDEN			
CAL-456 [M]	That's What I Like About the South	1963	15.00
CAS-456(e) [R]	That's What I Like About the South	1963	10.00
RCA VICTOR			
LPM-1985 [M]	The South Shall Rise Again	1959	25.00
LSP-1985 [S]	The South Shall Rise Again	1959	30.00
LPM-3037 [10]	Phil Harris On the Record	1952	40.00
SUNBEAM			
HB 302	Broadcasts from the Cocoanut Grove, L.A., 1932	198?	10.00

HARRIS, RAY

Number	Title (A Side/B Side)	Yr	NM
45s			
SUN			
254	Come On Little Mama/Where'd You Stay Last Night	1956	150.00
272	Greenback Dollar Watch and Chain/Foolish Hearts	1957	100.00

HARRIS, RICHARD

Number	Title (A Side/B Side)	Yr	NM
45s			
ABC DUNHILL			
4134	MacArthur Park/Didn't We	1968	6.00
—With both ABC and Dunhill logos at top of label			
4134 [PS]	MacArthur Park/Didn't We	1968	8.00
—Regular stock sleeve			
4170	The Yard Went On Forever/Lucky Me	1968	5.00
4185	Watermark/One of the Nicer Things	1969	5.00
4194	Didn't We/Paper Chase	1969	5.00
4218	Fill the World with Love/What a Lot of Flowers	1969	5.00
4218 [PS]	Fill the World with Love/What a Lot of Flowers	1969	6.00
4241	Ballad of a Man Called Horse/Morning of the Mourning for Another	1970	5.00
4293	My Boy/Why Did You Leave Me	1971	5.00

Number	Title (A Side/B Side)	Yr	NM
❑ 4310	Half of Every Dream/ Turning Back the Pages	1972	5.00
❑ 4322	There Are Too Many Saviours on My Cross/All the Broken Children	1972	5.00
❑ 4322 [PS]	There Are Too Many Saviours on My Cross/All the Broken Children	1972	6.00
❑ 4336	How I Spent My Summer/ I Don't Have to Tell You	1973	5.00

ATLANTIC

Number	Title (A Side/B Side)	Yr	NM
❑ 3238	On Crime and Punishment/ Theme from "The Prophet"	1975	4.00
❑ 3238 [PS]	On Crime and Punishment/ Theme from "The Prophet"	1975	5.00

DUNHILL

Number	Title (A Side/B Side)	Yr	NM
❑ 4134	MacArthur Park/Didn't We	1968	8.00

—First pressings have Dunhill standing alone at top of label

Number	Title (A Side/B Side)	Yr	NM
❑ 4134 [PS]	MacArthur Park/Didn't We	1968	15.00

—Special promotional issue, so marked on sleeve

7-Inch Extended Plays

ABC DUNHILL

Number	Title (A Side/B Side)	Yr	NM
❑ LP-DS-50032	MacArthur Park//Didn't We/ If You Must Leave My Life	1968	15.00

—Stereo jukebox issue; small hole, plays at 33 1/3 rpm

Number	Title (A Side/B Side)	Yr	NM
❑ LP-DS-50032 [PS]	A Tramp Shining	1968	15.00

Albums

ABC DUNHILL

Number	Title (A Side/B Side)	Yr	NM
❑ DS-50032	A Tramp Shining	1968	10.00
❑ DS-50042	The Yard Went On Forever	1968	10.00
❑ DS-50074	The Love Album	1970	10.00
❑ DSX-50116	My Boy	1971	8.00
❑ DSX-50133	Slides	1972	8.00
❑ DSX-50139	The Great Performances	1973	8.00
❑ DSX-50159	I, In the Membership	1974	8.00
❑ DSX-50160	Jonathan Livingston Seagull	1973	8.00

—Spoken-word recording

ATLANTIC

Number	Title (A Side/B Side)	Yr	NM
❑ QD 18120 [Q]	The Prophet by Kahlil Gibran	1974	15.00

—Spoken-word recording

Number	Title (A Side/B Side)	Yr	NM
❑ SD 18120	The Prophet by Kahlil Gibran	1974	8.00

—Spoken-word recording

MCA

Number	Title (A Side/B Side)	Yr	NM
❑ 27016	A Tramp Shining	198?	8.00

—Budget-line reissue

PICKWICK

Number	Title (A Side/B Side)	Yr	NM
❑ SPC-3626	A Tramp Shining	1978	10.00

HARRIS, ROLF

45s

EPIC

Number	Title (A Side/B Side)	Yr	NM
❑ 9567	Sun Arise/Someone's Pinched My Winkles	1963	12.00
❑ 9596	Tie Me Kangaroo Down, Sport/ The Big Black Hat	1963	15.00
❑ 9596 [PS]	Tie Me Kangaroo Down, Sport/ The Big Black Hat	1963	20.00
❑ 9615	Nick Teen & Al K. Hall/ I Know a Man	1963	12.00
❑ 9615 [PS]	Nick Teen & Al K. Hall/ I Know a Man	1963	20.00
❑ 9641	Lost Little Boy/Six White Boomers	1963	10.00
❑ 9641 [PS]	Lost Little Boy/Six White Boomers	1963	20.00
❑ 9682	The Court of King Caractacus/ Two Buffalos	1964	10.00
❑ 9721	Ringo for President/ Click Go the Shears	1964	15.00
❑ 9756	The Thing/Wild Colonial Boy	1965	10.00
❑ 9780	Tie My Hunting Dog Down, Jed/ Five Young Apprentices	1965	10.00
❑ 10037	Jake the Peg/Big Dog	1966	10.00

MGM

Number	Title (A Side/B Side)	Yr	NM
❑ 14103	Two Little Boys/I Love My Love	1970	10.00

20TH FOX

Number	Title (A Side/B Side)	Yr	NM
❑ 207	Tie Me Kangaroo Down, Sport/ Nick Teen & Al K. Hall	1960	20.00

—Different versions than the Epic recordings

Number	Title (A Side/B Side)	Yr	NM
❑ 230	Lost Little Boy/The Big Black Hat	1960	15.00
❑ 295	Six White Boomers/Tame Eagle	1962	15.00
❑ 414	Lost Little Boy/The Big Black Hat	1963	12.00

Albums

EPIC

Number	Title (A Side/B Side)	Yr	NM
❑ LN 24053 [M]	Tie Me Kangaroo Down, Sport & Sun Arise	1963	10.00
❑ LN 24110 [M]	Join Rolf Harris Singing The Count of King Caractacus (And Other Fun Songs)	1964	10.00
❑ BN 26053 [S]	Tie Me Kangaroo Down, Sport & Sun Arise	1963	12.00
❑ BN 26110 [S]	Join Rolf Harris Singing The Count of King Caractacus (And Other Fun Songs)	1964	12.00

HARRIS, TED

45s

RCA VICTOR

Number	Title (A Side/B Side)	Yr	NM
❑ 47-7422	Just Thought I'd Set You Straight/Please Don't Say Take Me Home	1958	30.00

HARRIS, THURSTON

45s

ALADDIN

Number	Title (A Side/B Side)	Yr	NM
❑ 3398	Little Bitty Pretty One/I Hope You Won't Hold It Against Me	1957	40.00
❑ 3399	Do What You Did/I'm Asking Forgiveness	1957	30.00
❑ 3415	Be Baby Leba/I'm Out to Getcha	1958	30.00
❑ 3428	Only One Love Is Blessed/ Smokey Joe's	1958	30.00
❑ 3430	Over and Over/You're Gonna Miss Me	1958	20.00
❑ 3435	Over Someone Else's Shoulder/ Tears from My Heart	1958	20.00
❑ 3440	Purple Stew/I Heard a Rhapsody	1958	20.00
❑ 3447	From the Bottom of My Heart/ You Don't Know How Much I Love You	1959	20.00
❑ 3448	Don't You Know/From the Bottom of My Heart	1959	20.00
❑ 3450	Hey Little Girl/My Love Will Last	1959	20.00
❑ 3452	Runk Bunk/Bless Your Heart	1959	20.00
❑ 3456	Slip Slop/Paradise Hill	1959	20.00
❑ 3462	Moonlight Cocktail/ Recess in Heaven	1960	20.00
❑ 3468	One Scotch, One Bourbon, One Beer/Send Me Some Loving	1960	20.00

CUB

Number	Title (A Side/B Side)	Yr	NM
❑ 9108	I'd Like to Start Over Again/ Mr. Satan	1962	12.00

DOT

Number	Title (A Side/B Side)	Yr	NM
❑ 16415	Quiet As It's Kept/Goddess of Angels	1963	10.00
❑ 16427	Poop-A-Loop/She's the One	1963	10.00

IMPERIAL

Number	Title (A Side/B Side)	Yr	NM
❑ 5928	Got You on My Mind/Tears from My Heart	1963	10.00
❑ 5971	You're Gonna Need Me/ I'm Asking Forgiveness	1963	10.00

REPRISE

Number	Title (A Side/B Side)	Yr	NM
❑ 0255	Dance On Little Girl/ Dancing Silhouettes	1964	30.00

UNITED ARTISTS

Number	Title (A Side/B Side)	Yr	NM
❑ 0152	Little Bitty Pretty One/Over and Over	1973	4.00

—"Silver Spotlight Series" reissue

HARRIS, TONY

45s

DEE GEE

Number	Title (A Side/B Side)	Yr	NM
❑ 3014	Super Man/How Much Do I Love You	1966	16.00

EBB

Number	Title (A Side/B Side)	Yr	NM
❑ 104	Chicken Baby Chicken/ I'll Forever Love You	1957	50.00
❑ 120	Try This Little Ol' Heart/ When I Get You Back	1957	30.00
❑ 128	You Fascinate Me/ Swing, Swing, Swing	1957	30.00

TRIUMPH

Number	Title (A Side/B Side)	Yr	NM
❑ 60	Go, Go, Little Scrambler/ Poor Boy	1964	30.00

HARRIS, WAYNE

45s

HIT

Number	Title (A Side/B Side)	Yr	NM
❑ 75	(You're the) Devil in Diguise/ Blowin' in the Wind	1963	8.00

—B-side by Jimmy, Wayne and Betty

Number	Title (A Side/B Side)	Yr	NM
❑ 86	Wonderful! Wonderful!/ I Can't Stay Mad at You	1963	8.00

—B-side by Kathy Taylor

Number	Title (A Side/B Side)	Yr	NM
❑ 100	Forget Him/Drag City	1964	8.00

—B-side by the Jalopy Five

Number	Title (A Side/B Side)	Yr	NM
❑ 190	You've Lost That Lovin' Feelin'/ True Love You Can't Buy	1965	8.00

—B-side by Ed Hardin

Number	Title (A Side/B Side)	Yr	NM
❑ 193	For Me/Tell Her No	1965	12.00

—B-side by the Mummies

HARRIS, WEE WILLIE

45s

CHARLIE PARKER

Number	Title (A Side/B Side)	Yr	NM
❑ 217	I Go Ape/Trouble in Mind	1963	10.00

HARRIS, WYNONIE

45s

ATCO

Number	Title (A Side/B Side)	Yr	NM
❑ 6081	Destination Love/Tell a Whale of a Tale	1956	30.00

KING

Number	Title (A Side/B Side)	Yr	NM
❑ 4210	Good Rockin' Tonight/ Good Morning Mister Blues	1952	150.00

—78 originally released in 1948; the only known Wynonie Harris 45 on King before 4461

Number	Title (A Side/B Side)	Yr	NM
❑ 4461	Bloodshot Eyes/Confessin' the Blues	1951	120.00
❑ 4468	I'll Never Give Up/Man Have I Got Troubles	1951	120.00
❑ 4485	Lovin' Machine/ Luscious Woman	1951	120.00

—Black vinyl

Number	Title (A Side/B Side)	Yr	NM
❑ 4485	Lovin' Machine/ Luscious Woman	1951	400.00

—Blue vinyl

Number	Title (A Side/B Side)	Yr	NM
❑ 4507	My Playful Baby's Gone/ Here Comes the Night	1952	100.00
❑ 4526	Keep On Churnin'/Married Women Stay Married	1952	100.00
❑ 4555	Do it Again Please/Night Train	1952	100.00
❑ 4565	Drinking Blues/Adam Come and Get Your Rib	1952	100.00
❑ 4592	Greyhound/Rot Gut	1953	100.00
❑ 4593	Bad News Baby (There'll Be Rockin' Tonight)/Bring It Back	1953	100.00
❑ 4620	Mama Your Daughter Done Lied on Me/Wasn't That Good	1953	100.00
❑ 4635	Song of the Bayou/The Deacon Doesn't Like It	1953	100.00
❑ 4662	Tremblin'/Rot Gut	1953	80.00
❑ 4668	Please Louise/Nearer My Love to Thee	1953	80.00
❑ 4685	Down Boy Down/ Quiet Whiskey	1953	80.00
❑ 4716	Shake That Thing/ Keep A-Talking	1954	80.00
❑ 4724	I Get a Thrill/Don't Take My Whiskey Away from Me	1954	80.00
❑ 4763	All She Wants to Do Is Mambo/ Christina	1955	60.00
❑ 4774	Good Mambo Tonight/ Git to Gittin' Baby	1955	60.00
❑ 4789	Fishtail Blues/Mr. Dollar	1955	60.00
❑ 4814	Drinkin' Sherry Wine/ Get With the Guts	1955	50.00
❑ 4826	Wine, Wine, Sweet Wine/ Man's Best Friend	1955	50.00
❑ 4839	Shot Gun Wedding/I Don't Know Where to Go	1955	50.00
❑ 4852	Good Morning Judge/ Bloodshot Eyes	1955	50.00
❑ 5050	Big Ole Country Fool/ That's Me Right Now	1957	30.00
❑ 5073	There's No Substitute for Love/ A Tale of Woe	1957	30.00
❑ 5416	Good Rockin' Tonight/ Bloodshot Eyes	1960	15.00
❑ 6011	Big Old Country Fool/ Bloodshot Eyes	1965	10.00
❑ 6304	Good Rockin' Tonight/Good Morning Judge	1970	6.00

ROULETTE

Number	Title (A Side/B Side)	Yr	NM
❑ 4291	Bloodshot Eyes/Sweet Lucy Brown	1960	12.00

7-Inch Extended Plays

KING

Number	Title (A Side/B Side)	Yr	NM
❑ EP-260	*Good Rockin' Tonight/ Bloodshot Eyes/All She Wants to Do Is Rock/Good Morning Judge	1954	500.00
❑ EP-260 [PS]	Wynonie Harris	1954	500.00

Albums

KING

Number	Title (A Side/B Side)	Yr	NM
❑ KS-1086	Good Rockin' Blues	1970	25.00

HARRIS BROTHERS, THE

45s

HIT

Number	Title (A Side/B Side)	Yr	NM
❑ 258	The Sun Ain't Gonna Shine Anymore/Paint It Black	1966	12.00

—B-side by the Jalopy Five

Except when noted otherwise, VG = 25% of NM, and VG+ = 50% of NM. (Example: VG = $2.00, VG+ = $4.00 and NM = $8.00.)

George Harrison, "You," Apple 1884, 1975, **$15.**

Number	Title (A Side/B Side)	Yr	NM
HARRISON, GEORGE Also see THE BEATLES.			
12-Inch Singles			
COLUMBIA			
❑ CAS 2085 [DJ]	I Don't Want to Do It (same on both sides)	1985	20.00
DARK HORSE			
❑ PRO-A-949 [DJ]	All Those Years Ago (same on both sides)	1981	25.00
❑ PRO-A-1075 [DJ]	Wake Up My Love (same on both sides)	1982	25.00
❑ PRO-A-2845 [DJ]	Got My Mind Set on You (same on both sides)	1987	25.00
❑ PRO-A-2885 [DJ]	When We Was Fab (same on both sides)	1987	25.00
❑ PRO-A-2889 [DJ]	Devil's Radio (Gossip) (same on both sides)	1987	30.00
45s			
APPLE			
❑ 1828	What Is Life/Apple Scruffs	1971	8.00
—Without star on A-side label			
❑ 1828	What Is Life/Apple Scruffs	1971	15.00
—With star on A-side label			
❑ 1828 [PS]	What Is Life/Apple Scruffs	1971	40.00
❑ 1836	Bangla-Desh/Deep Blue	1971	8.00
—Without star on A-side label			
❑ 1836	Bangla-Desh/Deep Blue	1971	25.00
—With star on A-side label			
❑ 1836 [PS]	Bangla-Desh/Deep Blue	1971	20.00
❑ 1862	Give Me Love (Give Me Peace on Earth)/Miss O'Dell (2:20)	1973	8.00
—B-side playing time corrected			
❑ 1862	Give Me Love (Give Me Peace on Earth)/Miss O'Dell (2:30)	1973	8.00
—With incorrect time for B-side listed			
❑ P-1862 [DJ]	Give Me Love (Give Me Peace on Earth) (mono/stereo)	1973	50.00
❑ 1877	Dark Horse/I Don't Care Anymore	1974	8.00
—Light blue and white custom photo label			
❑ 1877	Dark Horse/I Don't Care Anymore	1974	10.00
—White label; NOT a promo			
❑ 1877 [PS]	Dark Horse/I Don't Care Anymore	1974	80.00
❑ P-1877 [DJ]	Dark Horse (full length mono/stereo)	1974	40.00
❑ P-1877 [DJ]	Dark Horse (edited mono/stereo)	1974	60.00
❑ 1879	Ding Dong, Ding Dong/Hari's on Tour (Express)	1974	20.00
—Black and white custom photo label			
❑ 1879	Ding Dong, Ding Dong/Hari's on Tour (Express)	1974	250.00
—Blue and white custon photo label			
❑ 1879 [PS]	Ding Dong, Ding Dong/Hari's on Tour (Express)	1974	20.00
❑ P-1879 [DJ]	Ding Dong, Ding Dong (remixed mono/edited stereo)	1974	40.00
❑ 1884	You/World of Stone	1975	6.00
❑ 1884 [PS]	You/World of Stone	1975	15.00
❑ P-1884 [DJ]	You (mono/stereo)	1975	40.00
❑ 1885	This Guitar (Can't Keep from Crying)/Maya Love	1975	25.00
—The last Apple 45 until 1995			
❑ P-1885 [DJ]	This Guitar (Can't Keep from Crying) (mono/stereo)	1975	50.00
❑ 2995	My Sweet Lord/Isn't It a Pity	1970	8.00
—With "Mfd. by Apple" on label			
❑ 2995	My Sweet Lord/Isn't It a Pity	1970	40.00
—With black star on label			
❑ 2995	My Sweet Lord/Isn't It a Pity	1975	25.00
—With "All Rights Reserved" disclaimer			
❑ 2995 [PS]	My Sweet Lord/Isn't It a Pity	1970	40.00
CAPITOL			
❑ 1828	What Is Life/Apple Scruffs	1976	30.00
—Orange label			
❑ 1828	What Is Life/Apple Scruffs	1978	6.00
—Purple late-1970s label			
❑ 1836	Bangla-Desh/Deep Blue	1976	30.00
—Orange label			
❑ 1836	Bangla-Desh/Deep Blue	1978	6.00
—Purple late-1970s label			
❑ 1836	Bangla-Desh/Deep Blue	1983	15.00
—Black colorband label			
❑ 1862	Give Me Love (Give Me Peace on Earth)/Miss O'Dell	1978	8.00
—Purple late-1970s label			
❑ 1862	Give Me Love (Give Me Peace on Earth)/Miss O'Dell	1978	15.00
—Black colorband label			
❑ 1879	Ding Dong, Ding Dong/Hari's on Tour (Express)	1978	8.00
—Purple late-1970s label			
❑ 2995	My Sweet Lord/Isn't It a Pity	1976	20.00
—Orange label with "Capitol" at bottom			
❑ 2995	My Sweet Lord/Isn't It a Pity	1978	6.00
—Purple label; label has reeded edge			
❑ 2995	My Sweet Lord/Isn't It a Pity	1983	6.00
—Black label with colorband			
❑ 2995	My Sweet Lord/Isn't It a Pity	1988	5.00
—Purple label; label has smooth edge			
❑ 15930 [DJ]	My Sweet Lord/My Sweet Lord 2000	2001	10.00
—White label, small hole			
❑ 15930 [PS]	My Sweet Lord/My Sweet Lord 2000	2001	15.00
—Promo item for the re-release of the All Things Must Pass CD			
❑ 58983	My Sweet Lord (2000)/All Things Must Pass	2001	5.00
—Green vinyl			
COLUMBIA			
❑ 04887	I Don't Want to Do It/Queen of the Hop	1985	25.00
—B-side by Dave Edmunds			
DARK HORSE			
❑ 8294	This Song/Learning How to Love You	1976	8.00
—White label, NOT a promo			
❑ 8294	This Song/Learning How to Love You	1976	10.00
—Tan label			
❑ 8294 [DJ]	This Song (mono/stereo)	1976	25.00
❑ 8294 [PS]	This Song/Learning How to Love You	1976	30.00
❑ 8294 [PS]	This Song (mono/stereo)	1976	40.00
—Flyer with "The Story Behind This Song"			
❑ 8294 [PS]	This Song (mono/stereo)	1976	40.00
—Promotional only sleeve, different from stock sleeve			
❑ 8313	Crackerbox Palace/Learning How to Love You	1977	5.00
❑ 8763	Blow Away/Soft-Hearted Hana	1979	5.00
—With "RE-1" on label			
❑ 8763	Blow Away/Soft-Hearted Hana	1979	20.00
—Without "RE-1" on label (no "Loka Productions S.A." on label)			
❑ 8763 [PS]	Blow Away/Soft-Hearted Hana	1979	5.00
❑ 8844	Love Comes to Everyone/Soft Touch	1979	10.00
❑ 8844 [PS]	Love Comes to Everyone/Soft Touch	1979	750.00
❑ 21891	Got My Mind Set on You/When We Was Fab	198?	4.00
—"Back to Back Hits" series			
❑ 27913	This Is Love/Breath Away from Heaven	1988	5.00
❑ 27913 [PS]	This Is Love/Breath Away from Heaven	1988	5.00
❑ 28131	When We Was Fab/Zig Zag	1988	5.00
❑ 28131 [PS]	When We Was Fab/Zig Zag	1988	5.00
❑ 28178	Got My Mind Set on You/Lay His Head	1987	4.00
❑ 28178 [PS]	Got My Mind Set on You/Lay His Head	1987	4.00
❑ 29744	I Really Love You/Circles	1983	25.00
❑ 29864	Wake Up My Love/Greece	1982	10.00
❑ 49725	All Those Years Ago/Writing's on the Wall	1981	5.00
❑ 49725 [PS]	All Those Years Ago/Writing's on the Wall	1981	5.00
❑ 49785	Teardrops/Save the World	1981	10.00
WARNER BROS.			
❑ 22807	Cheer Down/That's What It Takes	1989	15.00
❑ 22807 [DJ]	Cheer Down (same on both sides)	1989	200.00
❑ 22807 [PS]	Cheer Down/That's What It Takes	1989	15.00
Albums			
APPLE			
❑ STCH-639 [(3)]	All Things Must Pass	1970	40.00
—Apple labels on first two records and "Apple Jam" labels on third; includes poster and lyric innersleeves			
❑ ST-3350	Wonderwall Music Bonus Photo	1968	5.00
❑ ST-3350	Wonderwall Music	1968	25.00
—With "Mfd. by Apple" on label			
❑ ST-3350	Wonderwall Music	1968	150.00
—With Capitol logo on Side 2 bottom			
❑ SMAS-3410	Living in the Material World	1973	15.00

Except when noted otherwise, VG = 25% of NM, and VG+ = 50% of NM. (Example: VG = $2.00, VG+ = $4.00 and NM = $8.00.)

Number	Title (A Side/B Side)	Yr	NM
❑ SMAS-3418	Dark Horse	1974	15.00
❑ SW-3420	Extra Texture (Read All About It)	1975	15.00
CAPITOL			
❑ STCH-639 [(3)]	All Things Must Pass	1976	30.00
—Orange labels with poster and lyric innersleeves			
❑ STCH-639 [(3)]	All Things Must Pass	1978	25.00
—Purple labels with poster and lyric innersleeves			
❑ STCH-639 [(3)]	All Things Must Pass	1983	100.00
—Black labels, print in colorband, with poster and lyric innersleeves			
❑ ST-11578	The Best of George Harrison	1976	15.00
—Custom label, no bar code on back			
❑ ST-11578	The Best of George Harrison	1976	180.00
—Orange label			
❑ ST-11578	The Best of George Harrison	1978	10.00
—Purple label, large Capitol logo			
❑ ST-11578	The Best of George Harrison	1983	25.00
—Black label, print in colorband			
❑ ST-11578	The Best of George Harrison	1988	25.00
—Odd reissue with custom label; large stand-alone "S" in trail-off area; bar code on cover			
❑ ST-11578	The Best of George Harrison	1989	80.00
—Purple label, small Capitol logo			
❑ SN-16055	Dark Horse	1980	15.00
—Budget-line reissue; reverses front and back covers			
❑ SN-16216	Living in the Material World	1980	20.00
—Budget-line reissue			
❑ SN-16217	Extra Texture (Read All About It)	1980	25.00
—Budget-line reissue			
CAPITOL/APPLE			
❑ STCH-639 [(3)]	All Things Must Pass	1988	80.00
—Odd pressing with Apple labels and Capitol cover (look for stand-alone "S" in trail-off wax); with large sticker on back cover			
DARK HORSE			
❑ (no #) [DJ]	Dark Horse Radio Special	1974	400.00
—Promo-only; George Harrison introduces his new record label and artists			
❑ PRO 649 [DJ]	A Personal Music Dialogue at Thirty Three and 1/3	1976	40.00
❑ DH 3005	Thirty Three and 1/3	1976	10.00
—Deduct 30% for cut-outs			
❑ DHK 3255	George Harrison	1979	10.00
—Deduct 30% for cut-outs			
❑ DHK 3255	George Harrison	1979	40.00
—Columbia House edition (back cover says "Manufactured by Columbia House Under License")			
❑ DHK 3492	Somewhere in England	1981	10.00
—Deduct 30% for cut-outs			
❑ 23724	Gone Troppo	1982	10.00
—Deduct 30% for cut-outs			
❑ 23724 [DJ]	Gone Troppo	1982	25.00
—Promo on Quiex II vinyl			
❑ 25643	Cloud Nine	1987	10.00
❑ W1-25643	Cloud Nine	1987	12.00
—Columbia House edition			
❑ 25726	Best of Dark Horse 1976-1989	1989	25.00
❑ W1-25726	Best of Dark Horse 1976-1989	1989	15.00
—Columbia House edition			
❑ R 174328	Cloud Nine	1987	15.00
—BMG Direct Marketing edition			
❑ R 180307	Best of Dark Horse 1976-1989	1989	15.00
—BMG Direct Marketing edition			
ZAPPLE			
❑ ST-3358	Electronic Sound	1969	50.00

HARRISON, GEORGE, AND FRIENDS The "Friends" include BADFINGER; ERIC CLAPTON; BOB DYLAN; BILLY PRESTON; LEON RUSSELL; RAVI SHANKAR; RINGO STARR.

Albums

Number	Title (A Side/B Side)	Yr	NM
APPLE			
❑ STCX-3385 [(3)]	The Concert for Bangla Desh	1971	40.00
—With 64-page booklet and custom innersleeves			
❑ STCX-3385 [(3)]	The Concert for Bangla Desh	1975	50.00
—As above, but with "All Rights Reserved" on labels			
CAPITOL			
❑ SABB-12248 [(2)]	The Concert for Bangla Desh	1982	300.00
—Scheduled reissue that was never officially released, though a few copies got out by mistake			

HARRISON, GEORGE/JEFF BECK/DAVE EDMUNDS

12-Inch Singles

Number	Title (A Side/B Side)	Yr	NM
COLUMBIA			
❑ CAS 2034 [DJ]	I Don't Want to Do It/Sleepwalk/ Queen of the Hop	1985	20.00
—Promo sampler from movie "Porky's Revenge"			

HARRISON, NOEL

45s

Number	Title (A Side/B Side)	Yr	NM
LONDON			
❑ 9755	One Too Many Mornings/ Barbara Allen	1965	8.00
❑ 9795	A Young Girl/The Future Mrs. 'Awkins	1965	10.00
❑ 9815	It's All Over Now, Baby Blue/ Much As I Love You	1966	8.00
❑ 20011	The Man Behind the Red Balloon/Marlene	1966	8.00
❑ 20017	Cheryl's Going Home/ In a Dusty Old Room	1966	8.00
❑ 20017 [PS]	Cheryl's Going Home/ In a Dusty Old Room	1966	12.00
❑ 20021	Out for the Day/Fly Sing Song	1967	8.00
REPRISE			
❑ 0599	Sign of the Queen/ Mrs. Williams' Rose	1967	6.00
❑ 0615	Life Is a Dream/Suzanne	1967	6.00
❑ 0682	Santa Monica Pier/ In Your Chidren	1968	6.00
❑ 0758	The Windmills of Your Mind/ Leitch on the Beach	1968	8.00
❑ 0795	I'll Be Your Baby Tonight/The Greatest Experiment Is Over	1968	6.00
❑ 0914	Another Virgin Spring/ Tin Wedding	1970	6.00

Albums

Number	Title (A Side/B Side)	Yr	NM
LONDON			
❑ PS 459 [S]	Noel Harrison	1966	25.00
❑ LL 3459 [M]	Noel Harrison	1966	20.00
REPRISE			
❑ R-6263 [M]	Collage	1967	15.00
❑ RS-6263 [S]	Collage	1967	20.00
❑ R-6295 [M]	Santa Monica Pier	1968	40.00
—White label promo only			
❑ RS-6295 [S]	Santa Monica Pier	1968	15.00
❑ RS-6321	The Great Electric Experiment Is Over	1969	15.00

HARRISON, WILBERT

45s

Number	Title (A Side/B Side)	Yr	NM
BELL			
❑ 869	C.C. Rider/Since I Fell for You	1970	6.00
BRUNSWICK			
❑ 55511	Lovin' Operator/Love You	1974	6.00
❑ 55519	I'm Going to the River/I Need Some (Honey Honey)	1975	6.00
CHART			
❑ 626	Cool Water/Calypso Man	1956	25.00
CONSTELLATION			
❑ 122	New York World's Fair/ Mama, Mama, Mama	1964	10.00
DELUXE			
❑ 6002	This Woman of Mine/The Letter	1953	60.00
❑ 6031	Nobody Knows My Trouble/ Gin and Coconut Milk	1954	60.00
FURY			
❑ 1023	Kansas City/Listen, My Darling	1959	15.00
❑ 1027	Cheating Baby/Don't Wreck My Life	1959	20.00
❑ 1028	Goodbye Kansas City/1960	1960	15.00
❑ 1031	C.C. Rider/Why Did You Leave	1960	15.00
❑ 1037	Since I Fell for You/ Little School Girl	1960	15.00
❑ 1041	The Horse/Da-De-Ya-Da (I'd Do Anything for You)	1961	30.00
❑ 1047	Happy in Love/Calypso Dance	1961	15.00
❑ 1055	Drafted/My Heart Is Yours	1961	20.00
❑ 1059	Let's Stick Together/ Kansas City Twist	1962	10.00
❑ 1063	Let's Stick Together/ My Heart Is Yours	1962	15.00
GLADES			
❑ 603	Gonna Tell You a Story/Letter Edged in Black	1959	12.00
LOST-NITE			
❑ 365	Kansas City/Listen, My Darling	197?	5.00
—Reissue			
PORT			
❑ 3003	Baby Move On/You're Still My Baby	1965	30.00
❑ 3009	Don't Take It So Hard/ Sugar Lump	1965	30.00
ROCKIN'			
❑ 526	This Woman of Mine/The Letter	1952	100.00
ROULETTE			
❑ 4752	No One's Love But Yours/ Mini-Parade	1967	20.00
SAVOY			
❑ 1138	Don't Drop It/The Ways of a Woman	1954	40.00
❑ 1149	Women and Whiskey/Da-De-Ya-Da (I'd Do Anything for You)	1955	30.00
❑ 1164	Florida Special/Darling, Listen to This Song	1955	30.00
❑ 1198	Confessin' My Dream/ The Way I Feel	1956	30.00
❑ 1517	My Love Is True/I Know My Baby Loves Me	1957	25.00
❑ 1531	Baby Don't You Know/ My Love for You Lingers On	1958	20.00
❑ 1571	Don't Drop It/Baby Don't You Know	1959	15.00
SEA HORN			
❑ 502	Say It Again/Near to You	1963	20.00
SSS INTERNATIONAL			
❑ 830	My Heart Is Yours/ Pretty Little Woman	1971	6.00
❑ 830 [DJ]	My Heart Is Yours (mono/stereo)	1971	10.00
—Promo only on blue vinyl			
SUE			
❑ 11	Let's Work Together (Part 1)/ Let's Work Together (Part 2)	1969	20.00
WET SOUL			
❑ 4	My Heart Is Yours/ Pretty Little Woman	1970	20.00

Albums

Number	Title (A Side/B Side)	Yr	NM
BUDDAH			
❑ BDS-5002	Wilbert Harrison	1971	30.00
CHELSEA			
❑ CH 523	Wilbert Harrison	1977	20.00
JUGGERNAUT			
❑ ST-8803	Shoot You Full of Love	1971	50.00
SAVOY JAZZ			
❑ SJL-1182	Listen to My Song	1987	12.00
SPHERE SOUND			
❑ SSR-7000 [M]	Kansas City	1965	250.00
❑ SSSR-7000 [R]	Kansas City	1965	200.00
SUE			
❑ SSLP-8801	Let's Work Together	1970	50.00
WET SOUL			
❑ 1001	Anything You Want	197?	50.00

HARRY, DEBBIE

12-Inch Singles

Number	Title (A Side/B Side)	Yr	NM
CHRYSALIS			
❑ CHS-32PDJ [DJ]	Chrome (4:16)/ Under Arrest (2:56)	1981	15.00
❑ CHS-33PDJ [DJ]	Backfired (Long) (Short)	1981	8.00
❑ CDS-2547	Backfired (Special Long Version 6:19)/ Military Rap (3:48)	1981	8.00
❑ 4V9 42741	Rush Rush (Extended Version) (Dub Mix)	1983	10.00
GEFFEN			
❑ PRO2594 [DJ]	French Kissin' (Remix)/French Kissin' (LP Version)	1986	7.00
❑ PRO-A-2594 [DJ]	French Kissin' (Dance Mix) (LP Version)	1986	10.00
❑ 20575	French Kissin' (Dance Mix 7:25) (Edit 4:09) (Dub Version 8:02)/ Rockbird (LP Version 3:09)	1986	8.00
❑ 20654	In Love with Love (Heart of Fire Mix) (The Passionate Dub) (Debapella Version)	1987	8.00
❑ 20687	In Love with Love (London Extended Mix) (London Mix Edit) (Heart of Fire Mix)/ Secret Life	1987	8.00
SIRE			
❑ 21322	I Want That Man (12" Remix) (Instrumental) (Remix Edit)/ Bike Boy (CD Version)	1989	8.00
❑ 21446	Sweet and Low (Sweet House Mix) (Sweet House Dub)/ Lamplight (LP Version)/ Sweet and Low (Swing Low Mix) (Swing Low Dub) (Sweet Chariot Mix)	1989	10.00
❑ 21492	Sweet and Low (Phil Harding 12" Mix) (Phil Harding Dub)/ Lovelight (LP Version)/Sweet and Low (Sweet House Mix) (Sweet House Dub) (Swing Low Mix)	1989	8.00
❑ 41000	I Can See Clearly (The Club Mix) (NYC Dub) (Blonde Rave) (Dub-a-mental) (Boriqua Tribal Mix)	1993	8.00
WARNER BROS.			
❑ 20391	Feel the Spin (Dance Version 6:50) (Dub 4:34)	1985	8.00

45s

Number	Title (A Side/B Side)	Yr	NM
CHRYSALIS			
❑ 2526	Backfired/Military Rap	1981	3.00
❑ 2526 [PS]	Backfired/Military Rap	1981	3.00
❑ 2554	The Jam Was Moving/ Inner City Spillover	1981	4.00

H

Number	Title (A Side/B Side)	Yr	NM
❑ VS4 42745	Rush Rush/Dance, Dance, Dance	1983	3.00
❑ VS4 42745 [PS]	Rush Rush/Dance, Dance, Dance	1983	3.00
❑ VS4 43328	Denis (The '88 Remix)/ Rapture (Teddy Riley Remix)	1988	3.00
❑ VS4 43328 [PS]	Denis (The '88 Remix)/ Rapture (Teddy Riley Remix)	1988	3.00
GEFFEN			
❑ 7-28476	In Love with Love/Secret Life	1987	3.00
❑ 7-28476 [PS]	In Love with Love/Secret Life	1987	3.00
❑ 7-28546	French Kissin'/Rockbird	1986	3.00
❑ 7-28546 [PS]	French Kissin'/Rockbird	1986	3.00
REPRISE			
❑ 7-27792	Liar, Liar/Queen of Voodoo	1988	3.00
—B-side by Voodooist Corporation			
❑ 7-27792 [PS]	Liar, Liar/Queen of Voodoo	1988	3.00
SIRE			
❑ 7-22816	I Want That Man/Bike Boy	1989	3.00
❑ 7-22816 [PS]	I Want That Man/Bike Boy	1989	4.00
Albums			
CHRYSALIS			
❑ CHR 1347	Koo Koo	1981	10.00
❑ FV 41347	Koo Koo	1983	10.00
—Reissue			
GEFFEN			
❑ GHS 24123	Rockbird	1986	10.00
❑ R 124347	Rockbird	1986	12.00
—RCA Music Service edition			
SIRE			
❑ 25938	Def, Dumb & Blonde	1989	12.00

HARSHMAN, ROBERT LUKE See BOBBY HART.

HART, BILLY AND DON

Number	Title (A Side/B Side)	Yr	NM
45s			
ROULETTE			
❑ 4133	Rock-a-Bop-a-Lena/ More and More	1959	60.00
❑ 4172	Check-Mated and Bingoed/ Blabbermouth	1959	30.00

HART, BOBBY

Number	Title (A Side/B Side)	Yr	NM
45s			
ARIOLA AMERICA			
❑ 809	Lovers for the Night/You Get Smoke in Your Eyes	1980	5.00
BAMBOO			
❑ 507	The Girl I Used to Know/ The Spider and the Fly	1961	30.00
CHELSEA			
❑ BCBO-0026	Easy Evil/California	1973	5.00
DCP			
❑ 1113	That'll Be the Day/Turn On Your Lovelight	1964	15.00
❑ 1142	Baby Let Your Hair Down/ Jealous Feeling	1965	30.00
❑ 1152	Around the Corner/ Cry My Eyes Out	1966	40.00
ERA			
❑ 3039	Girl in the Window/ Journey of Love	1961	20.00
GUYDEN			
❑ 2022	Is You Is Or Is You Ain't My Baby/Girl of My Dreams	1959	30.00
—As "Robert Luke Harshman"			
INFINITY			
❑ 017	Too Many Teardrops/ The People Next Door	1963	20.00
❑ 022	Lovesick Blues/I Think It's Called a Heartache	1963	20.00
RADIO			
❑ 122	Stop Talkin', Start Lovin'/ Love Whatcha Doin' to Me	1959	40.00
—As "Robert Luke Harshman"			
REEL			
❑ 100	Girl in the Window/Journey of Love	1961	40.00
WARNER BROS.			
❑ 8058	Hard Core Man/To Keep from Crying	1974	5.00
❑ 8058 [PS]	Hard Core Man/To Keep from Crying	1974	8.00
❑ 49079	The Loneliest Night/ Sometimes Love	1979	5.00

HART, MICKEY

Also see THE GRATEFUL DEAD.

Number	Title (A Side/B Side)	Yr	NM
45s			
WARNER BROS.			
❑ 7644	Blind John/Pump Man	1972	10.00
Albums			
RELIX			
❑ 2026	Rolling Thunder	1987	12.00
WARNER BROS.			
❑ BS 2635	Rolling Thunder	1972	20.00

HART, MICKEY, AIRTO, FLORA PURIM, BATUCAJE

Number	Title (A Side/B Side)	Yr	NM
Albums			
REFERENCE RECORDINGS			
❑ RR-12	Dafos	1985	15.00

HART, ROCKY

Number	Title (A Side/B Side)	Yr	NM
45s			
BIG TOP			
❑ 3069	Crying/Baby You've Got It Made	1961	30.00
CUB			
❑ 9052	Every Day/Come with Me	1959	30.00
GLO			
❑ 216	I Play the Part of a Fool/ Someone Stole My Baby While Doing the Twist	1961	200.00

HARTFORD, JOHN

Number	Title (A Side/B Side)	Yr	NM
45s			
AMPEX			
❑ 11019	One Too Many Mornings/ (B-side unknown)	1971	5.00
FLYING FISH			
❑ 4013	Piece of My Heart/ (B-side unknown)	1984	4.00
MCA DOT			
❑ 53104	Ohio River Rag/Love Wrote This Song	1987	4.00
RCA VICTOR			
❑ 47-8987	Tall Tall Grass/Jack's in the Sack	1966	8.00
❑ 47-9175	Gentle on My Mind/ Electric Washing Machine	1967	8.00
❑ 47-9345	A Simple Thing As Love/ Landscape Grown Cold	1967	8.00
❑ 47-9451	Big Blue Balloon/Six O'Clock Train and a Girl with Green Eyes	1968	8.00
❑ 47-9507	Shiny Rails of Steel/Natural to Be Gone	1968	8.00
❑ 47-9611	I Didn't Know the World Would Last This Long/The Category Stomp	1968	6.00
❑ 47-9668	California Earthquake/Mouth to Mouth Resuscitation	1968	6.00
❑ 47-9753	I Didn't Know the World Would Last This Long/Orphan of World War II	1969	6.00
❑ 47-9772	Like Unto a Mockingbird/ Natural to Be Gone	1969	6.00
Albums			
FLYING FISH			
❑ FF-020	Mark Twang	1976	10.00
❑ FF-028	Nobody Knows What You Do	1977	10.00
❑ FF-044	All in the Name of Love	1983	10.00
❑ FF-063	Headin' Down Into the Mystery Below	1978	10.00
❑ FF-095	Slumberin' on the Cumberland	1979	10.00
—With Pat Burton and Benny Martin			
❑ FF-228	You and Me at Home	1980	10.00
❑ FF-259	Catalogue	1982	10.00
❑ FF-289	Gum Tree Canoe	1984	10.00
❑ FF-440	Me Oh My, How Time Flies	1987	10.00
MCA			
❑ 5861	Annual Waltz	1987	8.00
RCA VICTOR			
❑ LPM-3687 [M]	John Hartford Looks at Life	1966	20.00
❑ LSP-3687 [S]	John Hartford Looks at Life	1966	15.00
❑ LPM-3796 [M]	Earthwords and Music	1967	25.00
❑ LSP-3796 [S]	Earthwords and Music	1967	15.00
❑ LPM-3884 [M]	The Love Album	1967	25.00
❑ LSP-3884 [S]	The Love Album	1967	15.00
❑ LPM-3998 [M]	Housing Project	1968	50.00
❑ LSP-3998 [S]	Housing Project	1968	15.00
❑ LSP-4068	Gentle on My Mind and Other Originals	1968	15.00
❑ LSP-4156	John Hartford	1969	15.00
❑ LSP-4337	Iron Mountain Depot	1970	15.00
WARNER BROS.			
❑ WS 1916	Aereo-Plain	1971	12.00
❑ BS 2651	Morning Bugle	1972	12.00

HARTFORD, KEN

Number	Title (A Side/B Side)	Yr	NM
45s			
SOUTHERN SOUND			
❑ 119	Jay Walker/Little Joe, Go Lightly	1963	25.00
—With Frankie Valli			

HARTLEY, KEEF

Number	Title (A Side/B Side)	Yr	NM
45s			
DERAM			
❑ 85060	Don't Be Afraid/Don't Give Up	1970	6.00
❑ 85069	Roundabout (Part 1)/ Roundabout (Part 2)	1971	6.00
Albums			
DERAM			
❑ DES 18024	Halfbreed	1969	15.00
❑ DES 18035	The Battle of North West Six	1970	15.00
❑ DES 18047	The Time Is Near	1970	15.00
❑ DES 18057	Overdog	1971	15.00
❑ XDES 18065	The 72nd Brave	1972	15.00
❑ XDES 18070	Lancashire Hustler	1973	15.00

HARTMAN, LISA

Number	Title (A Side/B Side)	Yr	NM
Albums			
KIRSHNER			
❑ PZ 34109	Lisa Hartman	1976	30.00
❑ JZ 35609	Hold On	1978	25.00

HARUMI

Number	Title (A Side/B Side)	Yr	NM
45s			
VERVE FORECAST			
❑ 5086	First Impressions/Talk About It	1968	12.00
Albums			
VERVE FORECAST			
❑ FTS-3030	Harumi	1968	30.00

HARVEY

Also see ETTA AND HARVEY; THE MOONGLOWS.

Number	Title (A Side/B Side)	Yr	NM
45s			
CHESS			
❑ 1713	I Want Somebody/ Da Da Goo Goo	1959	40.00
❑ 1725	Twelve Months of the Year/ Don't Be Afraid of Love	1959	40.00
❑ 1749	Blue Skies/Ooh, Ouch, Stop!	1960	25.00
❑ 1760	If I Can't Have You/ My Heart Cries	1960	25.00
—As "Etta and Harvey" (Etta is Etta James)			
❑ 1771	Spoonful/It's a Crying Shame	1960	25.00
—As "Etta and Harvey" (Etta is Etta James)			
❑ 1781	The First Time/Mama	1961	25.00
—As "Harvey Fuqua"			
HARVEY			
❑ 121	What Can You Do Now/Will I Do	1962	40.00
—As "Harvey and Ann"			
TRI-PHI			
❑ 1017	She Loves Me So/Any Way You Wanta	1962	100.00
❑ 1024	Memories of You/Come On and Answer Me	1963	30.00

HARVEY, ALEX (1)

British; fronted the Sensational Alex Harvey Band.

Number	Title (A Side/B Side)	Yr	NM
45s			
ATLANTIC			
❑ 3293	Delilah/Soul in Chains	1975	5.00
DECCA			
❑ 31649	New Orleans/I Just Wanna Make Love to You	1964	75.00
VERTIGO			
❑ 113	Swamp Snake/Gang Bang	1974	5.00
❑ 200	Tomahawk Kid/Sergeant Fury	1974	5.00
Albums			
ATLANTIC			
❑ SD 18248	Live	1975	12.00
VERTIGO			
❑ VEL-1017	Next	1973	12.00
❑ VEL-2000	The Impossible Dream	1974	12.00
❑ VEL-2004	Tomorrow Belongs to Me	1975	12.00

HARVEY, ALEX (2)

American country singer.

Number	Title (A Side/B Side)	Yr	NM
45s			
CAPITOL			
❑ 3172	To Make My Life Beautiful/Lady	1971	4.00
❑ 3336	Delta Dawn/Momma's Waiting	1972	4.00
❑ 3469	Angeline/Devil on My Shoulder	1972	4.00
❑ 3493	Good Time Christmas/ Someone Who Cares	1972	4.00
—With Son Lex			
❑ 3649	Right On/Summer Days	1973	4.00
❑ 3703	You Don't Need a Reason/ Goodbye Miss Carolina	1973	4.00
❑ 3847	Tangerine/Jody's Face	1974	4.00
METROMEDIA			
❑ 143	Louisiana River Bay/ King of Oak Street	1969	6.00
❑ 173	Tell It All Brother/Mama Tried	1970	6.00

Except when noted otherwise, VG = 25% of NM, and VG+ = 50% of NM. (Example: VG = $2.00, VG+ = $4.00 and NM = $8.00.)

Number	Title (A Side/B Side)	Yr	NM
UNITED ARTISTS			
❑ 50494	It Takes a Lot of Tenderness/I'll Be Your Tomorrow	1969	8.00
Albums			
CAPITOL			
❑ ST-789	Alex Harvey	1972	12.00
❑ ST-11128	Souvenirs	1973	12.00

HARVEY, PHIL Actually PHIL SPECTOR.

Number	Title (A Side/B Side)	Yr	NM
45s			
IMPERIAL			
❑ 5583	Willy Boy/Bumbershoot	1959	150.00

HARVEY AND DOC WITH THE DWELLERS

Number	Title (A Side/B Side)	Yr	NM
45s			
ANNETTE			
❑ 1002	Oh, Baby/Uncle Kev	1964	250.00
—Phil Spector appeared on and produced this			

HARVEY AND THE MOONGLOWS
See THE MOONGLOWS.

HASSAN, ALI Also see B. BUMBLE AND THE STINGERS.

Number	Title (A Side/B Side)	Yr	NM
45s			
PHILLES			
❑ 103	Malaguena/Chop Sticks	1962	30.00

HASSELL, JON

Number	Title (A Side/B Side)	Yr	NM
Albums			
ECM			
❑ 1327	Power Spot	1987	12.00
INTUITION			
❑ C1-46880	The Surgeon of the Nightsky Restores Dead Things by the Power of Sound	1988	12.00
❑ C1-91186	Flash of the Spirit	1989	12.00
LOVELY			
❑ 1021	Vernal Equinox	1978	15.00
OPAL/WARNER BROS.			
❑ 26153	City: Works of Fiction	1990	15.00
TOMATO			
❑ TOM-7019	Earthquake Island	1979	15.00

HASSLES, THE BILLY JOEL was in this group.

Number	Title (A Side/B Side)	Yr	NM
45s			
UNITED ARTISTS			
❑ 50215	You've Got Me Hummin'/I'm Thinkin'	1967	12.00
❑ 50215 [PS]	You've Got Me Hummin'/I'm Thinkin'	1967	20.00
❑ 50258	I Hear Voices/Every Step I Take	1968	12.00
❑ 50450	4 O'Clock in the Morning/Let Me Bring You to the Sunshine	1968	12.00
❑ 50513	Night After Day/Country Boy	1969	12.00
❑ 50586	Traveling Band/Great Balls of Fire	1969	12.00
Albums			
LIBERTY			
❑ LN-10138	The Hassles	1981	12.00
❑ LN-10139	Hour of the Wolf	1981	12.00
UNITED ARTISTS			
❑ UAS-6631	The Hassles	1968	25.00
❑ UAS-6699	Hour of the Wolf	1969	25.00

HATCH, TONY

Number	Title (A Side/B Side)	Yr	NM
45s			
LONDON			
❑ 10505	Ghost Squad/What's All That About	1962	12.00
❑ 10523	Cyril's Tune/Out of This World	1963	12.00
❑ 10524	Theme from Dick Powell Theatre/Sharon	1963	12.00
REPRISE			
❑ 0356	Crossroads/The Marie Celeste	1965	10.00
WARNER BROS.			
❑ 5887	I Didn't Know What Time It Was/Working in the Coal Mine	1967	8.00
❑ 7023	Beautiful Rain/While the City Sleeps	1967	8.00

HATCHER, ROGER

Number	Title (A Side/B Side)	Yr	NM
45s			
BROWN DOG			
❑ 9009	We Gonna Make It/High Blood Pressure	1976	20.00
COLUMBIA			
❑ 4-45993	Caught Making Love (mono/stereo)	1974	40.00
❑ 4-45993	Caught Making Love/Do Not Disturb	1974	—
—Stock copy may not exist			
EXCELLO			
❑ 2297	Sweetest Girl in the World/I'm Gonna Dedicate My Song to You	1968	500.00
VOLT			
❑ 4084	I'm Gonna Make Love to Someone's Old Lady/I Dedicate My Love to You	1972	25.00

HATCHER, WILLIE

Number	Title (A Side/B Side)	Yr	NM
45s			
COLUMBIA			
❑ 44259	Good Things Come to Those Who Wait/Searching	1968	150.00
COTILLION			
❑ 44014	Have a Heart, Girl/You Got Quality	1968	60.00
EXCELLO			
❑ 2310	Tell Me So/Who's Got a Woman Like Mine	1970	40.00
KING			
❑ 6360	Head Over Heels/Who's Gotta Woman Like Mine	1971	75.00

HATFIELD, BOBBY Also see THE RIGHTEOUS BROTHERS.

Number	Title (A Side/B Side)	Yr	NM
45s			
MOONGLOW			
❑ 220	I Need a Girl/Hot Tamale	1963	30.00
VERVE			
❑ 10598	Hang-Ups/Soul Cafe	1968	8.00
❑ 10621	Brothers/What's the Matter Baby	1968	8.00
❑ 10634	Only You/The Wonder of You	1969	8.00
❑ 10639	My Prayer/I Wish I Didn't Love You So	1969	8.00
❑ 10641	Answer Me My Love/I Only Have Eyes for You	1969	8.00
WARNER BROS.			
❑ 7566	Rock 'N Roll Woman/Oo Wee Baby, I Love You	1972	5.00
❑ 7649	Stay with Me/Rock 'N Roll Woman	1972	5.00
Albums			
MGM			
❑ SE-4727	Messin' in Muscle Shoals	1971	12.00

HATFIELD, JEANNE

Number	Title (A Side/B Side)	Yr	NM
45s			
ATCO			
❑ 6653	Stop/Busy Signal	1969	40.00
CAMEO			
❑ 386	Time/Unprejudice Girl	1965	20.00
JOX			
❑ 047	Time/Wonderin'	1965	25.00
—Black vinyl			
❑ 047 [DJ]	Time/Wonderin'	1965	40.00
—Promo only on green vinyl			
PHAROAH			
❑ 120	My Babe/Summertime	196?	15.00

HATHAWAY, DONNY Also see ROBERTA FLACK.

Number	Title (A Side/B Side)	Yr	NM
45s			
ATCO			
❑ 6719	The Ghetto (Part 1)/The Ghetto (Part 2)	1969	15.00
❑ 6759	Thank You Master/Je Vous Aime	1970	5.00
❑ 6768	Tryin' Times/Voices Inside	1970	5.00
❑ 6799	This Christmas/Be There	1970	8.00
❑ 6817	Take a Love Song/Magnificent Sanctuary Band	1971	5.00
❑ 6828	A Song for You/Put Your Hand in the Hand	1971	10.00
❑ 6880	Little Ghetto Boy/We're Still Friends	1972	5.00
❑ 6884	Giving Up/Jealous Love	1972	5.00
❑ 6899	Bossa Nova/Come Back Charleston Blue	1972	5.00
—With Margie Joseph			
❑ 6903	I Love You More Than You'll Ever Know/Lord Help Me	1972	5.00
❑ 6928	Love, Love, Love/Someday We'll All Be Free	1973	5.00
❑ 6951	Come Little Children/The Slums	1973	5.00
❑ 7066	This Christmas/Be There	1975	5.00
❑ 7092	You Were Meant for Me/Valdez in the Country	1978	4.00
❑ 7320	This Christmas/Be There	1980	4.00
❑ 99956	This Christmas/Be There	1982	4.00
CURTOM			
❑ 1935	I Thank You Baby/What's This I See	1969	30.00
—By "June and Donnie"			
❑ 1971	I Thank You/Just Another Reason	1972	5.00
—By "June Conquest and Donnie Hathaway"; same A-side as 1935 but with revised title			
7-Inch Extended Plays			
ATCO			
❑ SD 7-7029	I Know It's You/Flying Easy//The Slums/Valdez in the Country	1973	8.00
—Jukebox issue; small hole, plays at 33 1/3 rpm			
❑ SD 7-7029 [PS]	Extension of a Man	1973	8.00
Albums			
ATCO			
❑ SD 38-107	The Best of Donny Hathaway	1978	10.00
❑ SD 33-332	Everything Is Everything	1970	12.00
❑ SD 33-360	Donny Hathaway	1971	12.00
❑ SD 33-386	Donny Hathaway Live	1972	12.00
❑ QD 7029 [Q]	Extension of a Man	1974	18.00
❑ SD 7029	Extension of a Man	1973	10.00
ATLANTIC			
❑ SD 19278	In Performance	1980	10.00

H

HAVEN, SHIRLEY

Number	Title (A Side/B Side)	Yr	NM
45s			
FEDERAL			
❑ 12092	Troubles of My Own/Stop Foolin' Around	1952	300.00
—With the Four Jacks			

HAVENS, RICHIE

Number	Title (A Side/B Side)	Yr	NM
45s			
A&M			
❑ 1869	We Can't Hide It Anymore/Dreaming as One	1976	4.00
❑ 1882	I'm Not in Love/Dreaming as One	1976	4.00
❑ 1901	You Can Close Your Eyes/We Can't Hide It Anymore	1976	4.00
❑ 1984	We All Wanna Boogie/Nobody Left to Crown	1977	4.00
ELEKTRA			
❑ 46619	Every Night/Here's a Song	1980	4.00
❑ 46657	The Girl, the Gold Watch and Everything/Two Hearts in Perfect Time	1980	4.00
MGM			
❑ 14141	Sandy/Handsome Johnny	1970	5.00
ODE			
❑ 66032	Eyesight to the Blind/Underture	1973	8.00
STORMY FOREST			
❑ 650	Rocky Raccoon/Stop Pulling and Pushing Me	1970	6.00
❑ 651	Minstrel from Gault/There's a Hole in My Future	1970	5.00
❑ 653	Give All My Love Away/Nobody Knows	1970	5.00
❑ 656	Here Comes the Sun/Younger Men Get Older	1971	6.00
—Second (hit) pressing has full-length version of A-side and "REV" on label			
❑ 656	Here Comes the Sun/Younger Men Get Older	1971	8.00
—First pressing has an edited version of A-side			
❑ 658	Missing Train/I've Got to Get to Know Myself	1971	5.00
❑ 660	Fire and Rain/Think About the Children	1971	5.00
❑ 664	Where You Gonna Run To/I've Got to Get to Know Myself	1972	5.00
❑ 666	Freedom/Handsome Johnny	1972	5.00
❑ 671	It Was a Very Good Year/I Know I Won't Be There	1973	5.00
❑ 672	Tight Rope/Woman	1973	5.00
VERVE FOLKWAYS			
❑ 5022	I Can't Make It Anymore/Morning Morning	1966	8.00
❑ 5039	I've Gotta Go/Morning Morning	1967	15.00
VERVE FORECAST			
❑ 5068	Three Day Eternity/No Opportunity Necessary, No Experience Needed	1968	10.00
❑ 5092	Indian Rope Man/Just Above My Hobby Horse's Head	1968	30.00
Albums			
A&M			
❑ SP-4598	The End of the Beginning	1976	10.00
❑ SP-4641	Mirage	1977	10.00
DOUGLAS			
❑ D-779 [M]	Richie Havens' Record	1966	15.00
❑ SD-779 [S]	Richie Havens' Record	1966	16.00

Number	Title (A Side/B Side)	Yr	NM
❑ D-780 [M]	Electric Havens	1966	18.00
❑ SD-780 [S]	Electric Havens	1966	15.00
ELEKTRA			
❑ 6E-242	Connections	1980	10.00
MGM			
❑ SE-4698	Mixed Bag	1970	15.00
—Reissue of Verve Forecast 3006			
❑ SE-4699	Something Else Again	1970	15.00
—Reissue of Verve Forecast 3034			
❑ SE-4700 [(2)]	Richard P. Havens, 1963	1970	20.00
—Reissue of Verve Forecast 3047			
RBI			
❑ 400	Simple Things	1987	10.00
STORMY FOREST			
❑ SFS-6001	Stonehenge	1969	15.00
❑ SFS-6005	Alarm Clock	1970	12.00
❑ SFS-6010	The Great Blind Degree	1971	12.00
❑ SFS-6012 [(2)]	Richie Havens On Stage	1972	15.00
❑ SFS-6013	Portfolio	1973	12.00
❑ SFS-6201	Mixed Bag II	1974	12.00
VERVE FOLKWAYS			
❑ FT-3006 [M]	Mixed Bag	1967	25.00
❑ FTS-3006 [S]	Mixed Bag	1967	20.00
VERVE FORECAST			
❑ FTS-3006	Mixed Bag	1968	15.00
❑ FT-3034 [M]	Something Else Again	1968	40.00
❑ FTS-3034 [S]	Something Else Again	1968	20.00
❑ FTS-3047 [(2)]	Richard P. Havens, 1983	1968	25.00
❑ FTS-3061	Richie Havens	1969	—
—Canceled			

HAWK, THE
See JERRY LEE LEWIS.

HAWKETTS, THE

Number	Title (A Side/B Side)	Yr	NM
45s			
CHESS			
❑ 1591	Mardi Gras Mambo/ Your Time Is Up	1955	100.00

HAWKINS, DALE

Number	Title (A Side/B Side)	Yr	NM
45s			
ABC-PARAMOUNT			
❑ 10668	I'll Fly High/La La Song	1965	10.00
ABNAK			
❑ 110	The Flag/And I Believed You	1965	12.00
ATLANTIC			
❑ 2126	Stay at Home, Lulu/ I Can't Erase You	1961	20.00
❑ 2150	What a Feeling/Women, That's What's Happening	1962	20.00
BELL			
❑ 807	Back Street/Little Rain Cloud	1969	8.00
❑ 827	Heavy on My Mind/Joe	1969	8.00
CHECKER			
❑ 843	See You Soon, Baboon/ Four Letter Word	1956	30.00
❑ 863	Susie-Q/Don't Treat Me This Way	1957	50.00
❑ 876	Baby, Baby/Mrs. Merguitory's Daughter	1957	30.00
❑ 892	Little Pig/Tornado	1958	25.00
❑ 900	La-Do-Dada/Cross Ties	1958	25.00
❑ 906	My Babe/A House, a Car, and a Wedding Ring	1958	25.00
❑ 913	Someday, One Day/ Take My Heart	1959	25.00
❑ 916	Class Cutter (Yeah Yeah)/ Lonely Nights	1959	25.00
❑ 923	Ain't That Lovin' You Baby/ My Dream	1959	25.00
❑ 929	Our Turn/Lifeguard Man	1959	25.00
❑ 934	Liza Jane/Back to School Blues	1959	25.00
❑ 940	Hot Dog/Don't Break Your Promise to Me	1960	20.00
❑ 944	Poor Little Rhode Island/ Every Little Girl	1960	20.00
❑ 944 [PS]	Poor Little Rhode Island/ Every Little Girl	1960	300.00
❑ 962	Linda/Who	1960	20.00
❑ 970	Grandma's House/ I Want to Love You	1961	20.00
LINCOLN			
❑ 002	Johnny B. Goode/ Baby We Had It	196?	8.00
NORTON			
❑ 45-055	Number Nine Train/ On Account of You	1997	2.00
❑ 45-055 [PS]	Number Nine Train/ On Account of You	1997	2.00
PAULA			
❑ 424	First Cut Is the Deepest/ Nothing Left to Do But Say Goodbye	1977	5.00
TILT			
❑ 781	Money Honey/The Same Old Way	1962	20.00
❑ 783	Forbidden Love/Wish I Hadn't Called Home	1962	20.00
❑ 785	Hawk Blows, Band Plays (Part 1)/Hawk Blows, Band Plays (Part 2)	1962	20.00
ZONK			
❑ 1002	Gotta Dance/Peaches	1973	5.00
Albums			
BELL			
❑ 6036	L.A., Memphis and Tyler, Texas	1969	40.00
CHESS			
❑ ACRR-706	Dale Hawkins	1976	15.00
❑ LP-1429 [M]	Oh! Susie-Q	1958	1500.
—VG value 500; VG+ value 1000			
ROULETTE			
❑ R 25175 [M]	Let's All Twist at the Miami Beach Peppermint Lounge	1962	200.00
❑ SR 25175 [S]	Let's All Twist at the Miami Beach Peppermint Lounge	1962	300.00

HAWKINS, EDWIN

Number	Title (A Side/B Side)	Yr	NM
45s			
BUDDAH			
❑ 145	Blowin' in the Wind/ Pray for Peace	1970	5.00
❑ 155	I Believe/He's a Friend of Mine	1970	5.00
❑ 200	Try the Real Thing/Praise Him	1971	5.00
❑ 251	Children Get Together/ There's a Place for Me	1971	5.00
❑ 271	Give Me a Star/Jesus	1971	5.00
❑ 324	Jesu, Joy of Man's Desiring/ (B-side unknown)	1972	5.00
❑ 360	Jubilation/Do My Thing	1973	5.00
PAVILION			
❑ 20001	Oh Happy Day/Jesus, Lover of My Soul	1969	6.00
❑ 20002	Ain't It Like Him/Lord Don't Move That Mountain	1969	6.00
Albums			
ACCORD			
❑ SN-7120	The Genius of Edwin Hawkins	1981	10.00
BIRTHRIGHT			
❑ 4020	The Comforter	197?	12.00
❑ LS 5904	The Edwin Hawkins Christmas Album	1985	15.00
❑ WR-8119	Edwin Hawkins Live	198?	10.00
❑ ST-70200	The Edwin Hawkins Christmas Album	1987	8.00
—Reissue			
❑ ST-70201	Have Mercy	1987	8.00
❑ ST-70202	Angels Will Be Singing	1987	8.00
❑ D1-70208	Live with the Oakland Symphony, Vol. 1	1988	8.00
—Reissue of Myrrh 6691			
❑ D1-70210	Live with the Oakland Symphony, Vol. 2	1988	8.00
—Reissue of Myrrh 6700			
❑ ST-70300	Give Us Peace	1987	8.00
❑ D1-70315	The Name	1988	10.00
BUDDAH			
❑ BDS-5054	Peace Is Blowin' in the Wind	1969	15.00
❑ BDS-5064	More Happy Days	1970	15.00
❑ BDS-5070	Oh Happy Day	1970	12.00
—Reissue of Pavilion LP			
❑ BDS-5086	Children (Get Together)	1971	15.00
❑ BDS-5101	I'd Like to Teach the World to Sing	1972	15.00
❑ BDS-5606	The Edwin Hawkins Singers — Live	1974	15.00
LECTION			
❑ 501	Imagine Heaven	1982	10.00
❑ 810639-1	The Edwin Hawkins Mass Choir	198?	10.00
MYRRH			
❑ 6691	Live with the Oakland Symphony, Vol. 1	198?	10.00
❑ 6700	Live with the Oakland Symphony, Vol. 2	198?	10.00
PAVILION			
❑ BPS-10001	Let Us Go Into the House of the Lord	1969	15.00
❑ BPS-10002	He's a Friend of Mine	1969	15.00
SAVOY			
❑ 7077 [(2)]	The Best of the Edwin Hawkins Singers	198?	12.00

HAWKINS, HAWKSHAW

Number	Title (A Side/B Side)	Yr	NM
45s			
COLUMBIA			
❑ 4-41419	Soldier's Joy/Big Red Benson	1959	20.00
❑ 4-41574	Alaska Lil and Texas Bill/Patanio	1960	20.00
❑ 4-41714	Put a Nickel in the Jukebox/ Your Conscience	1960	20.00
❑ 4-41811	You Know Me Too Well/My Story	1960	20.00
❑ 4-42002	No Love for Me/The Love I Have for You	1961	15.00
❑ 4-42223	Twenty Miles from Shore/ Big Ole Heartache	1961	15.00
❑ 4-42441	I Can't Seem to Say Goodbye/ Darkness on the Face of the Earth	1962	15.00
KING			
❑ 969	I'm Waiting Just for You/ A Heartache to Recall	1951	40.00
❑ 997	Sunny Side of the Mountain/ Blue Skies in Your Eyes	1951	40.00
❑ 998	Slow Poke/Two Roads	1951	40.00
❑ 1039	Be My Life's Companion/ Everybody's Got a Girl But Me	1952	30.00
❑ 1047	Over the Hill/I Am Slowly Dying of a Broken Heart	1952	30.00
❑ 1062	Unwanted/Got You on My Mind	1952	30.00
❑ 1081	Loaded with Love/I Love the Way You Say Goodnight	1952	30.00
❑ 1133	Heavenly Road/ An Empty Mansion	1952	30.00
❑ 1134	I'm a Lone Wolf/I Hope You're Cryin' Too	1952	30.00
❑ 1154	Tangled Heart/Betty Lorraine	1953	30.00
❑ 1174	The Life Story of Hank Williams/ Picking Sweethearts	1953	40.00
❑ 1175	Kaw-Liga/If I Ever Get Rich Mom	1953	30.00
❑ 1190	Barbara Allen/The Life Story of Hank Williams	1953	30.00
❑ 5404	Nothing More to Say/ Between the Lines	1960	15.00
❑ 5692	Silver Threads and Golden Needles/Girl Without a Name	1962	15.00
❑ 5695	Bad News Travels Fast/ Let Them Talk	1962	15.00
❑ 5712	Lonesome 7-7203/ Everything Has Changed	1963	15.00
❑ 5765	Love Died Tonight/Sunny Side of the Mountain	1963	15.00
❑ 5810	Caught in the Middle of Two Hearts/If I Ever Get Rich Mom	1963	15.00
❑ 5871	I'm Beginning to Forget/ Teardrops on Your Letter	1964	15.00
❑ 5909	This Particular Baby/ The Shadows	1964	15.00
❑ 6047	The Last Letter/Never Mind the Tears	1967	12.00
❑ 6074	Jealous Fate/It's Easy to Remember	1967	12.00
RCA VICTOR			
❑ 47-5333	I'll Trade Yours for Mine/ Long Way	1953	25.00
❑ 47-5444	A Heap of Lovin'/Mark Round My Finger	1953	25.00
❑ 47-5549	I'll Never Close My Heart to You/When You Say Yes	1953	25.00
❑ 47-5623	Flashing Lights/Waitin' for My Baby	1954	25.00
❑ 47-5702	Rebound/Why Didn't I Hear It from You	1954	25.00
❑ 47-5808	One White Rose/I Wanna Be Hugged to Death	1954	25.00
❑ 47-5890	I'll Take a Chance with You/Why Don't You Leave This Town	1954	25.00
❑ 47-6022	Ling Ting Tong/Ko Ko Mo, I Love You So	1955	25.00
—With Rita Robbins			
❑ 47-6103	How Can Anything So Pretty Be So Doggone Mean/Pedro Gonzalez Tennessee Lopez	1955	25.00
❑ 47-6211	Car Hoppin' Mama/ The Love You Steal	1955	25.00
❑ 47-6298	I Gotta Have You/Standing at the End of My World	1955	25.00
❑ 47-6396	If It Ain't on the Menu/Borrowing	1956	25.00
❑ 47-6509	It Would Be a Doggone Lie/ Sunny Side of the Mountain	1956	25.00
❑ 47-6716	I'll Be Gone/My Fate Is In Your Hands	1956	25.00
❑ 47-6794	Action/Oh How I Cried	1957	20.00
❑ 47-6910	Dark Moon/With This Pen	1957	20.00
❑ 47-7054	Is My Ring on Your Finger/ Sensation	1957	20.00
❑ 47-7145	Guilty of Dreaming/It's Easier Said Than Done	1958	20.00
❑ 47-7222	I Don't Apologize/I'll Get Even with You	1958	20.00
❑ 47-7389	I've Got It Again/Freedom	1958	20.00

Except when noted otherwise, VG = 25% of NM, and VG+ = 50% of NM. (Example: VG = $2.00, VG+ = $4.00 and NM = $8.00.)

Number	Title (A Side/B Side)	Yr	NM
❑ 47-7486	Are You Happy/She Was Here	1959	20.00
Albums			
GLADWYNNE			
❑ G-2006 [M]	Country Western Cavalcade with Hawkshaw Hawkins	195?	120.00
HARMONY			
❑ HL 7301 [M]	The Great Hawkshaw Hawkins	1963	20.00
❑ HS 11044 [R]	The Great Hawkshaw Hawkins	1963	15.00
KING			
❑ 587 [M]	Hawkshaw Hawkins	1958	100.00
❑ 592 [M]	Grand Ole Opry Favorites	1958	100.00
❑ 599 [M]	Hawkshaw Hawkins	1959	100.00
❑ 808 [M]	The All New Hawkshaw Hawkins	1963	80.00
❑ KS-808 [S]	The All New Hawkshaw Hawkins	1963	100.00
❑ 858 [M]	Taken From Our Vaults, Vol. 1	1963	40.00
❑ 870 [M]	Taken From Our Vaults, Vol. 2	1963	40.00
❑ 873 [M]	Taken From Our Vaults, Vol. 3	1964	40.00
LABREA			
❑ 8020 [M]	Hawkshaw Hawkins	195?	100.00
RCA CAMDEN			
❑ CAL-808 [M]	Hawkshaw Hawkins Sings	1964	20.00
❑ CAS-808 [R]	Hawkshaw Hawkins Sings	1964	15.00
❑ CAL-931 [M]	The Country Gentleman	1966	20.00
❑ CAS-931 [R]	The Country Gentleman	1966	15.00

HAWKINS, JALACY

See SCREAMIN' JAY HAWKINS.

HAWKINS, RONNIE

His backing band, The Hawks, evolved into THE BAND.

Number	Title (A Side/B Side)	Yr	NM
45s			
COTILLION			
❑ 44060	Matchbox/Down in the Alley	1970	6.00
❑ 44067	Forty Days/Bitter Green	1970	6.00
❑ 44076	Little Bird/One More Night	1970	6.00
MONUMENT			
❑ 8548	Lawdy Miss Clawdy/Cora Mae	1972	5.00
❑ 8561	Lonesome Town/Kinky	1973	5.00
❑ 8573	Diddley Daddy/Cora Mae	1973	5.00
❑ 8583	Bo Diddley/Lonely Hours	1973	5.00
ROULETTE			
❑ 4154 [M]	Forty Days/One of These Days	1959	25.00
❑ SSR-4154 [S]	Forty Days/One of These Days	1959	50.00
❑ 4177 [M]	Mary Lou/Need Your Lovin'	1959	30.00
❑ SSR-4177 [S]	Mary Lou/Need Your Lovin'	1959	50.00
❑ 4209	Southern Love/Love Me Like You Can	1959	75.00
❑ 4228	Lonely Hours/Clara	1960	20.00
❑ 4231	The Ballad of Caryl Chessman/ The Tale of Floyd Collins	1960	20.00
❑ 4249	Ruby Baby/Hayride	1960	20.00
❑ 4267	Sumemrtime/Mister and Mississippi	1960	20.00
❑ 4311	Cold, Cold Heart/Nobody's Lonesome for Me	1960	20.00
❑ 4400	Come Love/I Feel Good	1961	20.00
❑ 4483	Bo Diddley/Who Do You Love	1963	20.00
❑ 4502	High Blood Pressure/ There's a Screw Loose	1963	20.00
Albums			
ACCORD			
❑ SN-7213	Premonition	1983	10.00
COTILLION			
❑ SD 9019	Ronnie Hawkins	1970	15.00
❑ SD 9039	The Hawk	1971	15.00
MONUMENT			
❑ KZ 31330	Rock and Roll Resurrection	1972	12.00
❑ KZ 32940	The Giant of Rock 'n' Roll	1974	12.00
❑ ZG 33855 [(2)]	Rock and Roll Resurrection/ The Ghost of Rock and Roll	1976	15.00
ROULETTE			
❑ R 25078 [M]	Ronnie Hawkins	1959	150.00
—White label with spokes			
❑ R 25078 [M]	Ronnie Hawkins	1964	50.00
—Orange/yellow label			
❑ SR 25078 [S]	Ronnie Hawkins	1959	200.00
—White label with spokes; black vinyl			
❑ SR 25078 [S]	Ronnie Hawkins	1959	600.00
—White label with spokes; red vinyl			
❑ SR 25078 [S]	Ronnie Hawkins	1964	60.00
—Orange/yellow label			
❑ R 25102 [M]	Mr. Dynamo	1960	150.00
❑ SR 25102 [S]	Mr. Dynamo	1960	200.00
—Black vinyl			
❑ SR 25102 [S]	Mr. Dynamo	1960	600.00
—Red vinyl			
❑ R 25120 [M]	The Folk Ballads of Ronnie Hawkins	1960	100.00
❑ SR 25120 [S]	The Folk Ballads of Ronnie Hawkins	1960	150.00
❑ R 25137 [M]	Ronnie Hawkins Sings the Songs of Hank Williams	1960	100.00
❑ SR 25137 [S]	Ronnie Hawkins Sings the Songs of Hank Williams	1960	150.00
❑ SR 42045	The Best of Ronnie Hawkins and His Band	1970	25.00
UNITED ARTISTS			
❑ UA-LA968-H	The Hawk	1979	10.00

HAWKINS, SCREAMIN' JAY

Number	Title (A Side/B Side)	Yr	NM
45s			
APOLLO			
❑ 506	Please Try to Understand/Not Anymore	1957	25.00
❑ 528	Baptize Me in Wine/Not Anymore	1958	25.00
CHANCELLOR			
❑ 1117	Ashes/Nitty Gritty	1962	15.00
DECCA			
❑ 32019	All Night/I'm Not Made of Clay	1966	15.00
❑ 32100	I Put a Spell on You/You're an Exception to the Rule	1967	100.00
ENRICA			
❑ 1010	I Hear Voices/I Just Don't Care	1962	25.00
GRAND			
❑ 135	Take Me Back/I Is	1957	25.00
MERCURY			
❑ 70549	This Is All/She Put the Whammee on Me	1955	80.00
OKEH			
❑ 7072	I Put a Spell on You/Little Demon	1956	50.00
❑ 7084	You Made Me Love You/ Darling, Please Forgive Me	1957	30.00
❑ 7087	Person to Person/Frenzy	1957	30.00
❑ 7101	Alligator Wine/There's Something Wrong with You	1958	30.00
PHILIPS			
❑ 40606	Stone Crazy/I'm Lonely	1969	6.00
❑ 40636	Too Many Teardrops/ Makaka Ways	1969	6.00
❑ 40645	Constipation Blues/ Do You Really Love Me	1969	6.00
❑ 40668	Moanin'/Do You Really Love Me	1970	30.00
❑ 40674	Our Love Is Not for Three/ Take Me Back	1970	6.00
PROVIDENCE			
❑ 411	My Kind of Love/Po' Folks	1965	12.00
QUEEN BEE			
❑ 1314	Monkberry Moon Delight/ Sweet Ginny	1973	6.00
RCA VICTOR			
❑ PB-10127	You Put the Spell on Me/Voodoo	1974	5.00
ROULETTE			
❑ 4579	The Whammy/Strange	1964	15.00
TIMELY			
❑ 1004	Baptize Me in Wine/Not Anymore	1954	80.00
❑ 1005	I Found My Way to Wine/ Please Try to Understand	1954	80.00
WING			
❑ 90005	Well, I Tried/You're All of Life to Me	1955	40.00
❑ 90055	Even Though/Talk About Me	1956	30.00
Albums			
EPIC			
❑ LN 3448 [M]	At Home with Screamin' Jay Hawkins	1958	800.00
❑ LN 3457 [M]	I Put a Spell on You	1958	500.00
❑ BN 26457 [R]	I Put a Spell on You	1969	60.00
PHILIPS			
❑ PHS 600319	What That Is	1969	40.00
❑ PHS 600336	Screamin' Jay Hawkins	1970	40.00
SOUNDS OF HAWAII			
❑ 5015	A Night at Forbidden City	196?	50.00

HAWKS, COLBY

Number	Title (A Side/B Side)	Yr	NM
45s			
CAMEO			
❑ 411	I'm Gonna Jump Right Off (The Brooklyn Bridge)/A Little Love Goes a Long, Long Way	1966	15.00

HAWKS, THE (1)

Number	Title (A Side/B Side)	Yr	NM
45s			
IMPERIAL			
❑ 5266	Joe the Grinder/Candy Girl	1954	250.00
❑ 5281	She's All Right/Good News	1954	200.00
❑ 5292	It Ain't That Way/I-Yi	1954	100.00
❑ 5306	Nobody But You/Give It Up	1954	100.00
❑ 5317	All Women Are the Same/ That's What You Are	1954	100.00
❑ 5332	It's Too Late Now/I Can't See for Lookin'	1955	100.00
MODERN			
❑ 990	It's All Over/Ever Since You Been Gone	1956	250.00
POST			
❑ 2004	These Blues/Why Oh Why	1955	300.00

HAWKS, THE (U)

None of these are group (1), but we don't know how many groups are represented below.

Number	Title (A Side/B Side)	Yr	NM
45s			
ABC-PARAMOUNT			
❑ 10116	Grasshopper/The Grissle	1960	25.00
DEL-FI			
❑ 4108	A Little More Wine, My Dear?/ Fussy	1958	40.00
MALA			
❑ 401	Cupcake/Lupp!!	1959	20.00

HAWKWIND

Also see HIGH TIDE; MOTORHEAD.

Number	Title (A Side/B Side)	Yr	NM
45s			
ATCO			
❑ 7017	Kings of Speed/Motor Head	1975	5.00
UNITED ARTISTS			
❑ XW314	Urban Guerrilla/Brainbox Position	1973	5.00
❑ 50949	Seven by Seven/Silver Necklace	1972	5.00
Albums			
ATCO			
❑ SD 36-115	Warrior on the Edge of Time	1975	25.00
GWR			
❑ 1237 [(2)]	Live Chronicles	1986	12.00
LIBERTY			
❑ LWB-120 [(2)]	Space Ritual/Alive in Liverpool and London	1981	12.00
—Reissue of United Artists 120			
❑ LW-5567	In Search of Space	1981	10.00
—Reissue of United Artists 5567			
SIRE			
❑ SRK 6047	Quark Strangeness and Charm	1978	12.00
UNITED ARTISTS			
❑ UA-LA001-F	Doremi Fasol Latido	1973	20.00
❑ UA-LA120-H [(2)]	Space Ritual/Alive in Liverpool and London	1973	30.00
❑ UA-LA328-G	Hall of the Mountain Grill	1974	20.00
❑ UAS-5519	Hawkwind	1971	20.00
❑ UAS-5567	In Search of Space	1972	25.00

HAWLEY, DEANE

Number	Title (A Side/B Side)	Yr	NM
45s			
DORE			
❑ 524	New Fad/Pretty Little Mary	1959	15.00
❑ 536	Good Morning, Mr. Sun/ Bossman	1959	15.00
❑ 543	Where Is My Angel/I'll Never Be a Fool Again	1960	15.00
❑ 554	Look for a Star/Bossman	1960	15.00
❑ 569	Like a Fool/Stay at Home Blues	1960	15.00
❑ 577	Hey There/Rainbow	1960	15.00
LIBERTY			
❑ 55359	Pocketful of Rainbows/That Dream Could Never Be	1961	20.00
❑ 55446	Queen of the Angels/ You Conquered Me	1962	25.00
SUNDOWN			
❑ 111	I Hate to See Me Go/Love of the Common People	196?	10.00
❑ 113	That's the Name of the Game/ Canterbury Station	196?	10.00
VALOR			
❑ 2003	Mummy's Bracelet/ Don't Keep Me Guessin'	1961	30.00
WARNER BROS.			
❑ 5484	I Know She'll Be There/You'll Never Have to Cry Again	1964	12.00

HAWN, GOLDIE

Number	Title (A Side/B Side)	Yr	NM
45s			
REPRISE			
❑ 1089	Butterfly/Uncle Pen	1972	8.00
❑ 1126	Pitta Patta/(Instrumental)	1972	8.00
❑ 1126 [PS]	Pitta Patta/(Instrumental)	1972	10.00
Albums			
REPRISE			
❑ MS 2061	Goldie	1972	15.00

HAYES, ISAAC

Number	Title (A Side/B Side)	Yr	NM
45s			
ABC/HBS			
❑ 12118	Chocolate Chip/(Instrumental)	1975	4.00
❑ 12138	Come Live with Me/ Body Language	1975	4.00

H

Number	Title (A Side/B Side)	Yr	NM
❑ 12171	Disco Connection/St. Thomas Square	1976	4.00
—By the "Isaac Hayes Movement"			
❑ 12176	Rock Me Easy Baby (Pt. 1)/Rock Me Easy Baby (Pt. 2)	1976	4.00
❑ 12206	Juicy Fruit (Disco Freak) (Pt. 1)/Juicy Fruit (Disco Freak) (Pt. 2)	1976	4.00
BRUNSWICK			
❑ 55258	Sweet Temptation/Laura	1964	10.00
CAPITOL			
❑ S7-18869	Walk On By/Tired of Being Alone	1995	3.00
—B-side by Al Green			
COLUMBIA			
❑ 06363	Ike's Rap/Hey Girl (Edited)	1986	3.00
❑ 06363 [PS]	Ike's Rap/Hey Girl (Edited)	1986	4.00
❑ 06655	Thing for You/Thank God for Love	1987	3.00
❑ 07104	If You Want My Lovin' (Do Me Right)/(Instrumental)	1987	3.00
❑ 07978	Showdown/(Instrumental)	1988	3.00
❑ 08116	Let Me Be Your Everything/Curious	1988	3.00
ENTERPRISE			
❑ 002	Precious Precious/Going to Chicago Blues	1969	8.00
❑ 9003	By the Time I Get to Phoenix/Walk On By	1969	6.00
❑ 9006	The Mistletoe and Me/Winter Snow	1969	6.00
❑ 9017	I Stand Accused/I Just Don't Know What to Do with Myself	1970	5.00
❑ 9028	The Look of Love/Ike's Mood	1970	5.00
❑ 9031	Never Can Say Goodbye/I Can't Help It If I'm Still in Love with You	1971	5.00
❑ 9038	Theme from Shaft/Cafe Regio's	1971	5.00
❑ 9042	Do Your Thing/Ellie's Love Theme	1972	5.00
❑ 9045	Let's Stay Together/Soulville	1972	5.00
❑ 9049	Ain't That Loving You (For More Reasons Than One)/Baby I'm-a Want You	1972	5.00
—With David Porter			
❑ 9058	Theme from The Men/Type Thang	1972	5.00
❑ 9065	(If Loving You Is Wrong) I Don't Want to Be Right/Rolling Down a Mountainside	1973	30.00
❑ 9085	Joy (Part 1)/Joy (Part 2)	1973	5.00
❑ 9095	Wonderful/Someone Made You for Me	1974	30.00
❑ 9104	Title Theme/Hung Up on My Baby	1974	5.00
POLYDOR			
❑ 2011	Don't Let Go/You Can't Hold Your Woman	1979	4.00
❑ 2068	A Few More Kisses to Go/What Does It Take	1980	4.00
❑ 2090	I Ain't Never/Love Has Been Good to Us	1980	4.00
❑ 2102	It's All in the Game/Wherever You Are	1980	4.00
❑ 2182	I'm So Proud/I'm Gonna Make Me Love You	1981	4.00
❑ 2192	Fugitive/Lifetime Thing	1981	4.00
❑ 14446	Out of the Ghetto/It's Heaven to Me	1977	4.00
❑ 14464	Moonlight Lovin' (Menage a Trois)/It's Heaven to Me	1978	4.00
❑ 14521	Zeke the Freak/If We Ever Needed Peace	1978	4.00
❑ 14534	Just the Way You Are (Part 1)/Just the Way You Are (Part 2)	1979	4.00
STAX			
❑ 3209	Feel Like Makin' Love (Part 1)/Feel Like Makin' Love (Part 2)	1978	5.00
VIRGIN			
❑ S7-18950	Fragile/Thanks to the Fool	1995	4.00
❑ 38759	Only If You Were Here/Oh Come All Ye Faithful	2000	4.00
—B-side by Ideal			
Albums			
ABC/HBS			
❑ D-874	Chocolate Chip	1975	15.00
❑ D-923	Disco Connection	1975	12.00
❑ D-925	Groove-a-Thon	1976	12.00
❑ D-953	Juicy Fruit (Disco Freak)	1976	12.00
ATLANTIC			
❑ SD 1599	In the Beginning	1972	15.00
—Reissue of Enterprise 100			
COLUMBIA			
❑ FC 40316	U-Turn	1986	10.00
❑ FC 40941	Love Attack	1988	10.00

Number	Title (A Side/B Side)	Yr	NM
ENTERPRISE			
❑ E-100 [M]	Presenting Isaac Hayes	1968	40.00
❑ ES-100 [S]	Presenting Isaac Hayes	1968	30.00
❑ ENS-1001	Hot Buttered Soul	1969	20.00
❑ ENS-1010	The Isaac Hayes Movement	1970	20.00
❑ ENS-1014	To Be Continued	1970	20.00
❑ ENS-5002 [(2)]	Shaft	1971	20.00
❑ EQS-2-5002 [(2)Q]	Shaft	1971	40.00
❑ ENS-5003 [(2)]	Black Moses	1971	20.00
❑ ENS-5005 [(2)]	Live at the Sahara Tahoe	1973	15.00
❑ XQS-5005 [(2)Q]	Live at the Sahara Tahoe	1973	30.00
❑ ENS-5007	Joy	1973	12.00
❑ EQS-5007 [Q]	Joy	1973	20.00
❑ ENS-7504	Tough Guys	1974	12.00
❑ EQS-7504 [Q]	Tough Guys	1974	20.00
❑ ENS-7507 [(2)]	Truck Turner	1974	15.00
❑ ENS-7510	The Best of Isaac Hayes	1975	12.00
MOBILE FIDELITY			
❑ MFSL 1-273	Hot Buttered Soul	2003	50.00
—"Original Master Recording" at top of front cover			
POINTBLANK			
❑ SPRO-12787 [DJ]	Funky Junky	1995	15.00
—Vinyl is promo only			
POLYDOR			
❑ PD-1-6120	New Horizon	1977	10.00
❑ PD-1-6164	For the Sake of Love	1978	10.00
❑ PD-1-6224	Don't Let Go	1979	10.00
❑ PD-1-6269	And Once Again	1980	10.00
STAX			
❑ STX-4102	Hotbed	197?	10.00
❑ STX-4114	Hot Buttered Soul	1978	10.00
—Reissue of Enterprise 1001			
❑ STX-4129	The Isaac Hayes Movement	197?	10.00
—Reissue of Enterprise 1010			
❑ STX-4133	To Be Continued	197?	10.00
—Reissue of Enterprise 1014			
❑ MPS-8509	Excerpts from Black Moses	1981	10.00
❑ MPS-8515	His Greatest Hit Singles	1982	10.00
❑ MPS-8530	Joy	1984	10.00
—Reissue of Enterprise 5007			
❑ STX-88002 [(2)]	Shaft	1979	12.00
—Reissue of Enterprise 5002			
❑ STX-88003 [(2)]	Enterprise: His Greatest Hits	1980	12.00
❑ STX-88004 [(2)]	Live at the Sahara Tahoe	198?	12.00
—Reissue of Enterprise 5005			

HAYES, ISAAC, AND DIONNE WARWICK

Also see each artist's individual listings.

Number	Title (A Side/B Side)	Yr	NM
45s			
ABC/HBS			
❑ 12253	By the Time I Get to Phoenix—I Say a Little Prayer/That's the Way I Like It—Cry Down	1977	4.00
Albums			
ABC/HBS			
❑ D-996 [(2)]	A Man and a Woman	1977	15.00
MCA			
❑ 10012 [(2)]	A Man and a Woman	198?	12.00
—Reissue of ABC/HBS 996			

HAYES, JIMMY, AND THE SOUL SURFERS

Number	Title (A Side/B Side)	Yr	NM
45s			
IMPERIAL			
❑ 5986	Summer Surfin'/Down on the Beach	1963	25.00

HAYES, LINDA

Number	Title (A Side/B Side)	Yr	NM
45s			
ANTLER			
❑ 4000	I Had a Dream/You Ain't Movin' Me	1956	30.00
DECCA			
❑ 29644	Our Love's Forever Blessed/You're the Only One for Me	1955	30.00
HOLLYWOOD			
❑ 1003	Take Me Back/Yours for the Asking	1953	50.00
❑ 1009	No Next Time/Don't Do Nothin' Baby	1954	40.00
❑ 1016	Play It Right/Your Back's Out	1954	40.00
❑ 1019	Non-Cooperation/Grrr! Mambo	1954	40.00
❑ 1027	Change of Heart/Darling Angel	1954	40.00
❑ 1031	Johnny Ace's Last Letter/Why Johnny Why	1955	50.00
—With Johnny Moore			
❑ 1032	Our Love's Forever Blessed/You're the Only One for Me	1955	60.00
KING			
❑ 4752	My Name Ain't Annie/Let's Babalu	1954	75.00
❑ 4773	Please Have Mercy/Oochi Poochi	1955	50.00
RECORDED IN HOLLYWOOD			
❑ 244	Yes! I Know (What You're Putting Down)/Sister Ann	1953	50.00
❑ 246	Big City (Part 1)/Big City (Part 2)	1953	50.00

HAYES, TOMMY

Number	Title (A Side/B Side)	Yr	NM
45s			
PHILIPS			
❑ 40259	Trance/Glistening Lights	1965	100.00
—The Four Seasons sing backup			

HAYMARKET SQUARE

Number	Title (A Side/B Side)	Yr	NM
Albums			
CHAPARRAL			
❑ 201	Magic Lantern	1968	1500.

HAYMES, DICK

Number	Title (A Side/B Side)	Yr	NM
45s			
CAPITOL			
❑ F3531	Love Is a Great Big Nothin'/I Never Get Enough of You	1956	12.00
❑ F3565	Two Different Worlds/Never Leave Me	1956	12.00
❑ F3662	C'est La Vie/Now at Last	1957	12.00
CONGRESS			
❑ 105	Down the Road/A Woman Knows	1962	10.00
DECCA			
❑ 9-23751	They Didn't Believe Me/Where or When	1950	15.00
—78 originally issued in 1947			
❑ 9-23753	Let the Rest of the World Go By/Indiana	1950	15.00
—78 originally issued in 1947			
❑ 9-24169	Christmas Dreaming/The Christmas Song	1950	15.00
—Sides 5 and 6 of "Album No. 9-70"; 78 originally issued in 1947			
❑ 9-24305	Serenade of the Bells/Some Hearts Sing	1950	20.00
—78 originally issued in 1948			
❑ 9-24480	Little White Lies/I'll Never Smile Again	1950	20.00
—78 originally issued in 1948			
❑ 9-25484	Our Waltz/Some Hearts Sing	195?	15.00
❑ 9-27008	Roses/I Still Get a Thrill	1950	20.00
❑ 9-27020	Is There Anything Wrong with That/A Little Bit Independent	1950	20.00
❑ 9-27042	Count Every Star/If You Were Only Mine	1950	20.00
—With Artie Shaw			
❑ 9-27076	Blind Date/Say When	1950	20.00
—With Evelyn Knight			
❑ 9-27161	Can Anyone Explain? (No, No, No!)/If I Had a Magic Carpet	1950	20.00
❑ 9-27175	My Silent Love/Don't Be Afraid	1950	20.00
❑ 9-27195	Boulevard of Broken Dreams/Your Eyes Have Told Me So	1950	20.00
❑ 9-27217	Home/Could Be	1950	20.00
❑ 9-27234	Till the End of Time/Love Letters	1950	20.00
—Originally issued on 78 on Decca 18699 in 1945			
❑ 9-27235	You'll Never Know/It Can't Be Wrong	1950	20.00
—Originally issued on 78s as the A-sides of Decca 18556 and 18557 in 1943			
❑ 9-27312	I Guess I'll Have to Dream the Rest/Everything Happens to Me	1951	15.00
—With Tommy Dorsey and His Orchestra			
❑ 9-27317	You're Just in Love/Something to Dance About	1951	15.00
—With Ethel Merman			
❑ 9-27318	Once Upon a Time Today/It's a Lovely Day Today	1951	15.00
❑ 9-27392	The Night Is Young and You're So Beautiful/I Don't Want to Love You	1951	15.00
❑ 9-27448	What'll I Do/Our Waltz	1951	15.00
❑ 9-27472	There's More Pretty Girls Than One/No One But You	1951	15.00
❑ 9-27473	Operetta/Little Child	1951	15.00
❑ 9-27497	It Might As Well Be Spring/It's a Grand Night for Singing.	1951	15.00
❑ 9-27498	It's Magic/Searching Wind	1951	15.00
—With Gordon Jenkins and His Orchestra			
❑ 9-27499	When I'm Not Near the Girl I Love/My Future Just Passed	1951	15.00
❑ 9-27517	Nora, the Darlin'/I Only Have Eyes for You	1951	15.00
❑ 9-27518	Laura/The Girl That I Marry	1951	15.00
❑ 9-27533	Naughty Angeline/And Mimi	1951	15.00
❑ 9-27545	I'll Never Know Why/How Thoughtful of You	1951	15.00
❑ 9-27565	My Prayer/Too Late Now	1951	15.00
❑ 9-27598	Tahiti, My Island/At the Bay of Rainbows	1951	15.00

Number	Title (A Side/B Side)	Yr	NM
❑ 9-27644	There's a Big Blue Cloud/ These Things I Offer You	1951	15.00
❑ 9-27646	Who'll Take My Place/Tell Me	1951	15.00
❑ 9-27682	I Believe/When the Lights Are Low	1951	15.00
❑ 9-27731	And So to Sleep Again/Long Ago	1951	15.00
❑ 9-27737	Who Can I Turn To/Just One of Those Things	1951	15.00
❑ 9-27811	Such Is My Love/My Beloved	1951	15.00
❑ 9-27841	Never Before/Here's to My Lady	1951	15.00
❑ 9-27885	Anytime/Bouquet of Roses	1951	15.00
❑ 9-27953	No Other Love But Yours/When You're in Love	1952	15.00
❑ 9-27980	Darlene/Dreamer's Cloth	1952	15.00
❑ 9-28087	I Am a Heart/And So I Waited Around	1952	15.00
❑ 9-28213	I'm Sorry/Here in My Heart	1952	15.00

—With the Andrews Sisters

Number	Title (A Side/B Side)	Yr	NM
❑ 9-28239	Never Let the Sun Set on a Quarrel/Are We in Love	1952	15.00

—With Three Hits and a Miss

Number	Title (A Side/B Side)	Yr	NM
❑ 9-28361	That's the Last Tear/ Tinsel and Gold	1952	15.00
❑ 9-28540	All I Need to Know/ Let's Fall in Love	1953	15.00

—With Gordon Jenkins and His Orchestra

Number	Title (A Side/B Side)	Yr	NM
❑ 9-28636	Your Home Is In My Arms/ Gone with the Wind	1953	15.00

—With Gordon Jenkins and His Orchestra

GNP CRESCENDO

Number	Title (A Side/B Side)	Yr	NM
❑ 494	Bein' Green/Feel Like Makin' Love	1975	6.00

JUBILEE

Number	Title (A Side/B Side)	Yr	NM
❑ 5299	Lonesome and Sorry/ I'll Still Be True	1957	15.00

SUNBEAM

Number	Title (A Side/B Side)	Yr	NM
❑ 113	As Young As You Feel/Suffer	1958	12.00
❑ 120	She Is Beautiful/C'est Fini	1958	12.00

WARWICK

Number	Title (A Side/B Side)	Yr	NM
❑ 568	Blue Champagne/ Playboy's Theme	1960	10.00
❑ 571	Anything Goes/Pick Yourself Up	1960	10.00

Albums

AUDIOPHILE

Number	Title (A Side/B Side)	Yr	NM
❑ AP-79	Imagination	1978	12.00
❑ AP-130	For You, For Me, Forevermore	197?	12.00
❑ AP-200	Keep It Simple	198?	12.00

BALLAD

Number	Title (A Side/B Side)	Yr	NM
❑ DHS-6	As Time Goes By	1978	15.00
❑ DHS-7	Last Goodbye	1980	15.00
❑ DHS-8	Rare Dick Haymes	198?	15.00

DAYBREAK

Number	Title (A Side/B Side)	Yr	NM
❑ DR 2016	Dick Haymes Comes Home	1973	15.00

MCA CORAL

Number	Title (A Side/B Side)	Yr	NM
❑ CB-20016	Easy	1973	10.00

VOCALION

Number	Title (A Side/B Side)	Yr	NM
❑ VL 3616 [M]	Dick Haymes	196?	15.00

HAYWARD, JUSTIN

Also see THE MOODY BLUES.

45s

COLUMBIA

Number	Title (A Side/B Side)	Yr	NM
❑ 10799	Forever Autumn/The Fighting Machine	1978	8.00

DERAM

Number	Title (A Side/B Side)	Yr	NM
❑ 401	Night Flight/Suitcase	1980	4.00
❑ 402	A Face in the Crowd/It's Not On	1980	4.00
❑ 7541	Lay It On Me/Songwriter Part 2	1977	4.00
❑ 7542	Country Girl/Songwriter Part 2	1977	4.00

RED BIRD

Number	Title (A Side/B Side)	Yr	NM
❑ 10-049	London Is Behind Me/ Day Must Come	1966	20.00

Albums

DERAM

Number	Title (A Side/B Side)	Yr	NM
❑ DRL 4801	Night Flight	1980	12.00
❑ DES 18073	Songwriter	1977	15.00

HAYWARD, JUSTIN, AND JOHN LODGE

Also see JUSTIN HAYWARD; THE MOODY BLUES.

45s

THRESHOLD

Number	Title (A Side/B Side)	Yr	NM
❑ 67019	I Dreamed Last Night/Remember Me, My Friend	1975	4.00
❑ 67021	Blue Guitar/When You Wake Up	1975	4.00
❑ 67021 [PS]	Blue Guitar/When You Wake Up	1975	5.00

Albums

THRESHOLD

Number	Title (A Side/B Side)	Yr	NM
❑ THS 14	Blue Jays	1975	15.00
❑ THSX 101 [DJ]	Blue Jays	1975	30.00

—Open-end interview with script; used to promote the LP of the same name

HAYWOOD, LEON

12-Inch Singles

CASABLANCA

Number	Title (A Side/B Side)	Yr	NM
❑ 812164-1	I'm Out to Catch (LP version)/ (Dub Version)	1983	6.00

MCA

Number	Title (A Side/B Side)	Yr	NM
❑ 13911	Disco Fever/Party	1978	12.00

45s

ATLANTIC

Number	Title (A Side/B Side)	Yr	NM
❑ 2799	You and Your Moody Ways/ You Know What	1971	6.00
❑ 2858	Clean Up Your Own Back Yard/ String Bean	1972	6.00

CAPITOL

Number	Title (A Side/B Side)	Yr	NM
❑ 2584	Just Your Fool/Consider the Source	1969	150.00
❑ 2752	I Wanna Thank You/I Was Sent to Love You	1970	30.00

CASABLANCA

Number	Title (A Side/B Side)	Yr	NM
❑ 812164-7	I'm Out to Catch/Keep It in the Family	1983	3.00

—With Karen Roberts

Number	Title (A Side/B Side)	Yr	NM
❑ 814217-7	T.V. Mama/Steppin' Out	1983	3.00

COLUMBIA

Number	Title (A Side/B Side)	Yr	NM
❑ 10413	The Streets Will Love You to Death - Part 1/The Streets Will Love You to Death - Part 2	1976	4.00
❑ 10477	Dream Dream/Let Me Make It Good	1977	4.00

DECCA

Number	Title (A Side/B Side)	Yr	NM
❑ 32164	It's Got to Be Mellow/ Cornbread & Buttermilk	1967	30.00
❑ 32230	Mellow Moonlight/Tennessee Waltz	1967	20.00
❑ 32310	Mercy, Mercy, Mercy/It's the Last Time	1968	20.00
❑ 32348	I Want to Talk About My Baby/ You Don't Have to See Me Cry	1968	25.00
❑ 32414	Blues Get Off My Shoulder/ Everyday Will Be Like a Holiday	1968	15.00

FANTASY

Number	Title (A Side/B Side)	Yr	NM
❑ 581	The Truth About Money/Would I	1964	75.00

FAT FISH

Number	Title (A Side/B Side)	Yr	NM
❑ 8005	Soul Cargo/Spice of the Blues	1966	30.00

IMPERIAL

Number	Title (A Side/B Side)	Yr	NM
❑ 66123	She's With Her Other Love/ Pain in My Heart	1965	30.00

—As "Leon Hayward"

Number	Title (A Side/B Side)	Yr	NM
❑ 66149	Soul-On/1-2-3	1965	30.00

MCA

Number	Title (A Side/B Side)	Yr	NM
❑ 40793	Super Sexy/Life Goes On	1977	4.00
❑ 40849	Double My Pleasure/It's Gonna Be Alright	1978	4.00
❑ 40889	Fine and Healthy Thing/She's Built, She's Stacked	1978	4.00
❑ 40941	Party/Life Goes On	1978	4.00
❑ 40989	Disco Fever/Self Respect	1979	4.00
❑ 41035	Energy/You Bring Out the Freak in Me	1979	4.00

MODERN

Number	Title (A Side/B Side)	Yr	NM
❑ 99708	Tenderoni/(Instrumental)	1984	3.00

20TH CENTURY

Number	Title (A Side/B Side)	Yr	NM
❑ 2003	One Way Ticket to Loveland/ There Ain't Enough Love Around	1972	6.00
❑ 2022	La La Song/Sweet Loving Fair	1973	6.00
❑ 2065	Keep It in the Family/Long As There's You (I Got Love)	1974	5.00
❑ 2103	Sugar Lump/That Sweet Woman of Mine	1974	5.00
❑ 2146	Believe Half of What You See (And None of What You Hear)/ The Day I Laid Eyes on You	1974	15.00
❑ 2191	Come an' Get Yourself Some/ Who You Been Givin' It Up To	1975	5.00
❑ 2191	Come an' Get Yourself Some/ B.M.F. Beautiful	1975	6.00
❑ 2228	I Want'a Do Something Freaky to You/I Know What Love Is	1975	5.00
❑ 2264	Just Your Fool/Consider the Source	1975	15.00
❑ 2285	Strokin' (Part 1)/Strokin' (Part 2)	1976	5.00
❑ 2443	Don't Push It Don't Force It/ Who You Been Givin' It Up To	1980	4.00
❑ 2454	If You're Lookin' for a Night of Fun (Look Past Me, I'm Not the One)/That's What Time It Is	1980	4.00
❑ 2469	Daydream/Love Is What We Came Here For	1980	4.00

Albums

COLUMBIA

Number	Title (A Side/B Side)	Yr	NM
❑ PC 34363	Intimate	1976	10.00

DECCA

Number	Title (A Side/B Side)	Yr	NM
❑ DL 74949	It's Got to Be Mellow	1969	20.00

FAT FISH

Number	Title (A Side/B Side)	Yr	NM
❑ LP 2525	Soul Cargo	1966	60.00

GALAXY

Number	Title (A Side/B Side)	Yr	NM
❑ 8206	Mellow, Mellow	196?	20.00

MCA

Number	Title (A Side/B Side)	Yr	NM
❑ 2322	Double My Pleasure	1978	10.00
❑ 3090	Energy	1979	10.00

20TH CENTURY

Number	Title (A Side/B Side)	Yr	NM
❑ T-411	Back to Stay	1973	12.00
❑ T-440	Keep It in the Family	1974	12.00
❑ T-476	Come and Get Yourself Some	1975	10.00
❑ T-613	Naturally	1980	10.00

HAZEL, EDDIE

Albums

WARNER BROS.

Number	Title (A Side/B Side)	Yr	NM
❑ BSK 3058	Games, Dames and Guitar Thangs	1977	50.00

HAZLEWOOD, LEE

Also see ANN-MARGRET; SUZI JANE HOKUM; NANCY SINATRA.

45s

CAPITOL

Number	Title (A Side/B Side)	Yr	NM
❑ 3611	Kari/Nancy and Me	1973	8.00
❑ 3737	Feathers/The Performer	1973	8.00

JAMIE

Number	Title (A Side/B Side)	Yr	NM
❑ 1158	The Girl on Death Row/ Words Mean Nothing	1960	15.00

—With Duane Eddy

LHI

Number	Title (A Side/B Side)	Yr	NM
❑ 7	Greyhound Bus Depot/ No Regrets	1969	10.00
❑ 17	The Bed/(B-side unknown)	1969	10.00
❑ 20	Trouble Maker/Greyhound Bus Depot	1970	10.00
❑ 28	No Train to Stockholm/What's More, I Don't Need Her	1970	10.00

MCA

Number	Title (A Side/B Side)	Yr	NM
❑ 41003	Dolly Parton's Guitar/ A Taste of You	1979	5.00
❑ 41188	Hollywood (Just Ain't No Place)/Willie John	1980	4.00

MGM

Number	Title (A Side/B Side)	Yr	NM
❑ K13434	I Move Around/Bugles in the Afternoon	1965	15.00
❑ K13490	My Autumn's Done Come/Sand	1966	15.00
❑ K13605	The Old Man and His Guitar/ Suzie Jane Is Back in Town	1966	10.00
❑ K13664	Summer Wine/After Six	1967	10.00
❑ K13716	Girls in Paris/Them Girls	1967	8.00

REPRISE

Number	Title (A Side/B Side)	Yr	NM
❑ 0613	Charlie Bill Nelson/ Ode to Billie Joe	1967	10.00
❑ 0667	Rainbow Woman/I Am, You Are	1968	10.00
❑ 0699	The House Song/Morning Dew	1968	10.00

SMASH

Number	Title (A Side/B Side)	Yr	NM
❑ 1734	Don't Cry No More/Della	1961	15.00

Albums

CAPITOL

Number	Title (A Side/B Side)	Yr	NM
❑ ST-11171	Poet, Fool or Bum	1973	40.00

HARMONY

Number	Title (A Side/B Side)	Yr	NM
❑ HS 11290 [S]	Houston	196?	20.00

—Reissue of Reprise 6163

LHI

Number	Title (A Side/B Side)	Yr	NM
❑ S-12006	Trouble Is a Lonesome Town	1969	20.00

—Reissue of Mercury 60860

Number	Title (A Side/B Side)	Yr	NM
❑ S-12009	Forty	1969	40.00

MERCURY

Number	Title (A Side/B Side)	Yr	NM
❑ MG-20860 [M]	Trouble Is a Lonesome Town	1964	25.00
❑ SR-60860 [S]	Trouble Is a Lonesome Town	1964	30.00

MGM

Number	Title (A Side/B Side)	Yr	NM
❑ E-4362 [M]	The Very Special World of Lee Hazlewood	1966	25.00
❑ SE-4362 [S]	The Very Special World of Lee Hazlewood	1966	30.00
❑ E-4403 [M]	Lee Hazlewoodism - Its Cause and Cure	1966	30.00
❑ SE-4403 [S]	Lee Hazlewoodism - Its Cause and Cure	1966	40.00

REPRISE

Number	Title (A Side/B Side)	Yr	NM
❑ R-6133 [M]	The N.S.V.I.P.'s	1965	30.00
❑ RS-6133 [S]	The N.S.V.I.P.'s	1965	40.00
❑ R-6163 [M]	Friday's Child	1965	25.00
❑ RS-6163 [S]	Friday's Child	1965	30.00
❑ RS-6297	Love and Other Crimes	1968	40.00

Number	Title (A Side/B Side)	Yr	NM
SMELLS LIKE			
❑ SLR-30	Cowboy in Sweden	1999	15.00
❑ SLR-37	Trouble Is a Lonesome Town	1999	15.00
❑ SLR-38	Requiem for an Almost Lady	1999	15.00
❑ SLR-40	13	2000	15.00

HEE

Albums

Number	Title (A Side/B Side)	Yr	NM
BUDDAH			
❑ BDS-5062	Head	1970	30.00
—With coloring book (deduct 1/3 if missing)			

HEAD, JIM, AND HIS DEL RAYS

Albums

Number	Title (A Side/B Side)	Yr	NM
HP			
❑ 22893 [M]	Jim Head and His Del Rays	1963	300.00

HEAD, MURRAY

45s

Number	Title (A Side/B Side)	Yr	NM
A&M			
❑ 1796	Say It Ain't So, Joe/She's Such a Drag	1976	4.00
❑ 1836	Somebody's Rockin' My Dreamboat/She's Such a Drag	1976	4.00
DECCA			
❑ 32603	Superstar/John Nineteen Forty-One	1969	6.00
—First pressings use this reference on the A-side: "Superstar (From JESUS CHRIST)"			
❑ 32603	Superstar/John Nineteen Forty-One	1970	5.00
—Reissues have the word "Superstar" without a subtitle, and small print mentions the LP "Jesus Christ Superstar"			
❑ 32603 [PS]	Superstar/John Nineteen Forty-One	1970	8.00
—Picture sleeve accompanies second pressings			
❑ 32709	Heaven on Their Minds/Strange Thing (Mystifying)	1970	5.00
❑ 32709 [PS]	Heaven on Their Minds/Strange Thing (Mystifying)	1970	8.00
RCA			
❑ PB-13988	One Night in Bangkok/Merano	1985	4.00
❑ PB-13988 [PS]	One Night in Bangkok/Merano	1985	4.00
❑ PB-14152	Pity the Child/The Deal (No Deal)	1985	4.00
❑ GB-14339	One Night in Bangkok/Pity the Child	1986	3.00
—Gold Standard Series			

Albums

Number	Title (A Side/B Side)	Yr	NM
A&M			
❑ SP-4558	Say It Ain't So	1976	12.00

HEAD, ROY

45s

Number	Title (A Side/B Side)	Yr	NM
ABC			
❑ 12346	How You See 'Em, Now You Don't/Smooth Whiskey	1978	4.00
❑ 12383	Tonight's the Night/A Lady in My Room	1978	4.00
❑ 12418	Dixie/Love Survived	1978	4.00
❑ 12462	Kiss You and Make It Better/You Do It	1979	4.00
ABC DOT			
❑ 17608	Lady Luck and Mother Nature/The Door I Used to Close	1976	4.00
❑ 17629	Ain't It Funny (How Times Haven't Changed)/A Bridge for Crawling Back	1976	4.00
❑ 17650	One Night/Deep Elem Blues	1976	4.00
❑ 17669	Just Because/Angel with a Broken Wing	1976	4.00
❑ 17706	Julianne/Velvet Strings	1977	4.00
❑ 17722	Come to Me/Georgia on My Mind	1977	4.00
ABC DUNHILL			
❑ 4240	I'm Not a Fool Anymore/Mama Mama	1970	6.00
ATLANTIC AMERICA			
❑ 99529	There's Something on Your Mind/Everything A Man Can Do (And I Love You)	1986	3.00
AVION			
❑ 105	Where Did He Go Right/(B-side unknown)	1983	7.00
BACK BEAT			
❑ 543	Teenage Letter/Pain	1965	20.00
❑ 546	Treat Her Right/So Long, My Love	1965	20.00
❑ 555	Apple of My Eye/I Pass the Day	1965	20.00
❑ 560	My Babe/Pain	1966	10.00
❑ 563	Driving Wheel/Wigglin' and Gigglin'	1966	20.00
❑ 571	Don't Cry No More/To Make a Big Man Cry	1966	20.00
❑ 576	You're (Almost) Tough/Tush Hog	1966	10.00
❑ 582	Nobody But Me/A Good Man Is Hard to Find	1967	15.00
CHURCHILL			
❑ 7778	After Texas/California Day	1981	5.00
ELEKTRA			
❑ 46549	In Our Room/Things I Never Could Have Left Behind	1979	4.00
❑ 46582	The Fire of Two Old Flames/Under Suspicion	1980	4.00
❑ 46653	Long Drop/Gonna Save It for My Baby	1980	4.00
❑ 47029	Drinking Them Long Necks/Baby's Found Another Way to Love Me	1980	4.00
❑ 47081	I've Never Gone to Bed With an Ugly Woman/All Night Long Is Gone	1981	4.00
MEGA			
❑ 1219	Baby's Not Home/Do What You Can Do	1974	5.00
MERCURY			
❑ 72750	Got Down on Saturday (Sunday in the Rain)/The Grass Was Green	1967	8.00
❑ 72799	Broadway Walk/Turn Out the Lights	1968	20.00
❑ 72848	Ain't Goin' Down Right/Lovin' Man on Your Hands	1968	8.00
❑ 72922	I Miss You Baby/I Want Some Action	1969	25.00
NSD			
❑ 129	Play Another Gettin' Drunk and Take Somebody Home Song/Your Next One and Only	1982	5.00
❑ 146	The Trouble with Hearts/Naughty Smile	1982	5.00
❑ 156	Your Mama Don't Dance/Party Time	1982	5.00
SCEPTER			
❑ 12116	Just a Little Bit/Treat Me Right	1965	30.00
❑ 12117	Won't Be Blue/One More Time	1965	10.00
❑ 12124	Get Back — Part 1/Get Back — Part 2	1965	15.00
❑ 12138	Convicted/One More Time	1966	10.00
SHANNON			
❑ 829	The Most Wanted Woman in Town/Gingerbread Man	1975	5.00
❑ 833	Help Yourself to Me/To Make a Big Man Cry	1975	5.00
❑ 838	I'll Take It/The One That Got Away	1975	5.00
TEXAS CRUDE			
❑ 614	Break Out the Good Stuff/She Needs Time	1985	8.00
TMI			
❑ 75-0103	Rock and Roll Mood/You Got the Power	1972	5.00
❑ 75-0106	Why Don't We Go Somewhere and Love/Smell-A-Woman	1972	5.00
❑ BTBO-0111	Small Town Girl/Chug All Night	1973	5.00
❑ 75-0113	Carol/Clyde O'Riley	1973	5.00
❑ 9000	Puff of Smoke/Lord Take a Bow	1971	6.00
❑ 9010	Bit By Bit/Wait Till I Arrive	1972	6.00
TNT			
❑ 194	Don't Be Blue/One More Time	1965	15.00

Albums

Number	Title (A Side/B Side)	Yr	NM
ABC			
❑ AB-1054	Tonight's the Night	1978	10.00
ABC DOT			
❑ DO-2051	Head First	1976	12.00
❑ DO-2066	A Head of His Time	1977	12.00
ABC DUNHILL			
❑ DS-50080	Same People	1970	20.00
ELEKTRA			
❑ 6E-234	In Our Room	1979	10.00
❑ 6E-298	The Many Sides of Roy Head	1980	10.00
MCA			
❑ 796	Tonight's the Night	1980	8.00
—Reissue of ABC album			
SCEPTER			
❑ S-532 [M]	Treat Me Right	1965	30.00
❑ SS-532 [S]	Treat Me Right	1965	40.00
TMI			
❑ 1000	Dismal Prisoner	1972	15.00
TNT			
❑ 101 [M]	Roy Head and the Traits	1965	150.00
—Counterfeit alert: Authentics do NOT contain the hit "Treat Her Right."			

HEAD EAST

45s

Number	Title (A Side/B Side)	Yr	NM
A&M			
❑ 1718	Never Been Any Reason/One Against the Other	1975	4.00
❑ 1784	Love Me Tonight/Brother Jacob	1976	4.00
❑ 1930	Gettin' Lucky/Sands of Time	1977	4.00
❑ 2026	Since You Been Gone/Pictures	1978	4.00
❑ 2026 [PS]	Since You Been Gone/Pictures	1978	8.00
❑ 2122	Never Been Any Reason/I'm Feelin' Fine	1979	4.00
❑ 2208	Got to Be Real/Morning	1979	4.00
❑ 2222	Specialty/Morning	1980	4.00
❑ 2278	I Surrender/Out of the Blue	1980	4.00

Albums

Number	Title (A Side/B Side)	Yr	NM
A&M			
❑ SP-3162	Get Yourself Up	198?	8.00
—Budget-line reissue			
❑ SP-3196	Flat as a Pancake	198?	8.00
—Budget-line reissue			
❑ SP-4537	Flat as a Pancake	1975	10.00
❑ SP-4579	Get Yourself Up	1976	10.00
❑ SP-4624	Gettin' Lucky	1977	10.00
❑ SP-4680	Head East	1978	10.00
❑ SP-4795	A Different Kind of Crazy	1979	10.00
❑ SP-4826	U.S. 1	1980	10.00
❑ SP-6007 [(2)]	Head East Live!	1979	12.00
ALLEGIANCE			
❑ AV-432	Onward and Upward	1986	8.00
PYRAMID			
❑ (no #)	Flat as a Pancake	1974	200.00
—Original issue; 5,000 were pressed; has a different cover than the A&M version of the same album, plus the A and B sides are opposite the reissue			

HEAD OVER HEELS

Albums

Number	Title (A Side/B Side)	Yr	NM
CAPITOL			
❑ ST-797	Head Over Heels	1971	30.00

HEAD SHOP, THE

Albums

Number	Title (A Side/B Side)	Yr	NM
EPIC			
❑ BN 26476	The Head Shop	1969	60.00

HEADHUNTERS Also see HERBIE HANCOCK.

45s

Number	Title (A Side/B Side)	Yr	NM
ARISTA			
❑ 0115	God Made Me Funky/Daffy's Dance	1975	4.00
❑ 0137	If You've Got It, You'll Get It/(B-side unknown)	1975	4.00

Albums

Number	Title (A Side/B Side)	Yr	NM
ARISTA			
❑ AL 4038	Survival of the Fittest	1975	60.00
—Reproductions exist			
❑ AB 4146	Straight from the Gate	1978	40.00

HEADS, THE

45s

Number	Title (A Side/B Side)	Yr	NM
LIBERTY			
❑ 56025	Are You Lonely for Me, Baby/You	1968	10.00

Albums

Number	Title (A Side/B Side)	Yr	NM
LIBERTY			
❑ LST-7581	Heads Up	1968	25.00

HEADS, HANDS AND FEET

45s

Number	Title (A Side/B Side)	Yr	NM
ATCO			
❑ 6923	One Woman/Dirty, Heavy Weather Road	1973	6.00

Albums

Number	Title (A Side/B Side)	Yr	NM
ATCO			
❑ SD 7025	Old Soldiers Never Die	1973	15.00
CAPITOL			
❑ SVBB-680 [(2)]	Heads, Hands and Feet	1971	20.00
❑ ST-11051	Tracks	1972	15.00

HEADSTONE

Albums

Number	Title (A Side/B Side)	Yr	NM
STARR			
❑ (# unknown)	Still Looking	1974	150.00

Except when noted otherwise, VG = 25% of NM, and VG+ = 50% of NM. (Example: VG = $2.00, VG+ = $4.00 and NM = $8.00.)

HEART Featuring Ann and Nancy Wilson. Featuring Ann and Nancy Wilson. Records on EMI, Look, Natural Resources and Reprise are not by this Heart, thus are outside the scope of this book. Records on EMI, Look, Natural Resources and Reprise are not by this Heart, thus are outside the scope of this book.

12-Inch Singles

CAPITOL

Number	Title (A Side/B Side)	Yr	NM
❑ SPRO-9403 [DJ]	What About Love (same on both sides)	1985	12.00
—With heart-shaped sticker on cover			
❑ SPRO-9427/8 [DJ]	What About Love (Extended Version 5:27) (3:41)	1985	15.00
❑ SPRO-9460/1 [DJ]	Never (Extended Remix 5:10) (Remix Edit 4:05)	1985	15.00
❑ SPRO-9566/7 [DJ]	If Looks Could Kill (LP Version) (Live Version)	1985	15.00
❑ SPRO-9578 [DJ]	These Dreams (Edit 3:46) (LP Version 4:12)	1985	20.00
❑ SPRO-9659 [DJ]	Nothin' at All (Remix) (same on both sides)	1986	12.00
❑ SPRO-9742 [DJ]	If Looks Could Kill (same on both sides)	1986	10.00
❑ SPRO-79174 [DJ]	There's The Girl (Remix) (same on both sides)	1987	12.00
❑ SPRO-79175 [DJ]	Wait For An Answer (same on both side)	1986	10.00
❑ SPRO-79262 [DJ]	I Want You So Bad (Remixed for Rock Radio 4:15) (same on both sides)	1988	10.00

EPIC

Number	Title (A Side/B Side)	Yr	NM
❑ AS 733 [DJ]	Even It Up (5:10) (same on both sides)	1980	15.00
❑ AS 1720 [DJ]	How Can I Refuse (same on both sides)	1983	15.00

MUSHROOM

Number	Title (A Side/B Side)	Yr	NM
❑ MRS 7023DJ [DJ]	Dreamboat Annie (stereo) (mono)	1977	20.00
—With custom picture labels and custom die-cut title sleeve			
❑ M 7035SP [DJ]	Without You (stereo) (mono)	1978	40.00
—Red vinyl			

PORTRAIT

Number	Title (A Side/B Side)	Yr	NM
❑ ASF 377 [DJ]	Little Queen (Long Version 5:10) (Short Version 3:29)	1977	20.00
❑ AS 498 [DJ]	Straight On (Special FM Version) (same on both sides)	1978	15.00

45s

CAPITOL

Number	Title (A Side/B Side)	Yr	NM
❑ B-5481	What About Love/Heart of Darkness	1985	3.00
❑ B-5481 [PS]	What About Love/Heart of Darkness	1985	3.00
❑ B-5512	Never (Remix)/Shell Shock	1985	3.00
—A-side eventually replaced original mix on "Heart" LP			
❑ B-5512 [PS]	Never (Remix)/Shell Shock	1985	3.00
❑ B-5541	These Dreams/Shell Shock	1985	3.00
❑ B-5541 [PS]	These Dreams/Shell Shock	1985	3.00
❑ B-5572	Nothin' at All/The Wolf	1986	3.00
❑ B-5572 [PS]	Nothin' at All/The Wolf	1986	3.00
❑ B-5605	If Looks Could Kill/What He Don't Know	1986	3.00
❑ B-5605 [PS]	If Looks Could Kill/What He Don't Know	1986	3.00
❑ S7-17799	Will You Be There (In the Morning)/Back to Avalon	1994	3.00
❑ S7-17904	The Woman in Me/Risin' Suspicion	1994	3.00
❑ B-44002	Alone/Barracuda (Live)	1987	3.00
❑ B-44002 [PS]	Alone/Barracuda (Live)	1987	3.00
❑ B-44040	Who Will You Run To/Magic Man (Live)	1987	3.00
❑ B-44040 [PS]	Who Will You Run To/Magic Man (Live)	1987	3.00
❑ B-44089	There's the Girl/Bad Animals	1987	3.00
❑ B-44089 [PS]	There's the Girl/Bad Animals	1987	3.00
❑ B-44116	I Want You So Bad/Easy Target	1988	3.00
❑ NR-44507	All I Wanna Do Is Make Love to You/Call of the Wild	1990	3.00
❑ NR-44507 [PS]	All I Wanna Do Is Make Love to You/Call of the Wild	1990	4.00
❑ NR-44553	I Didn't Want to Need You/The Night	1990	3.00
❑ 7PRO-79311 [DJ]	I Want You So Bad (7" Remix) (same on both sides)	1988	8.00

Heart, "All I Wanna Do is Make Love to You," Capitol NR-44507, 1990, **$4.**

CAPITOL STARLINE

Number	Title (A Side/B Side)	Yr	NM
❑ X-6342	What About Love/Never	1986	3.00
—Reissue			

COLLECTABLES

Number	Title (A Side/B Side)	Yr	NM
❑ 4694	Magic Man/Crazy on You	199?	3.00
—Reissue			
❑ 6063	Alone/Who Will You Run To	1992	3.00
—Reissue			
❑ 6292	These Dreams/All I Wanna Do Is Make Love to You	1993	3.00
—Reissue			
❑ 6293	Never'/Nothin' at All	1993	3.00
—Reissue			
❑ 6294	What About Love/There's the Girl	1993	3.00
—Reissue			
❑ 6295	Stranded/I Didn't Want to Need You	1993	3.00
—Reissue; "Stranded" made its first U.S. 45 appearance on this record			

EPIC

Number	Title (A Side/B Side)	Yr	NM
❑ 14-02925	This Man Is Mine/America	1982	3.00
❑ 14-02925 [PS]	This Man Is Mine/America	1982	3.00
❑ 14-03071	Private Audition/Bright Light Girl	1982	3.00
❑ 34-04047	How Can I Refuse/Johnny Moon	1983	3.00
❑ 34-04047 [PS]	How Can I Refuse/Johnny Moon	1983	3.00
❑ 34-04184	Allies/Together Now	1983	5.00
❑ 34-04184 [PS]	Allies/Together Now	1983	5.00
❑ 15-08101	Barracuda/Straight On	1988	3.00
—Reissue			
❑ 9-50847	Even It Up/Pilot	1980	4.00
❑ 9-50874	Raised on You/Down on Me	1980	4.00
❑ 9-50892	Bebe Le Strange/Silver Wheels	1980	4.00
❑ 19-50950	Tell It Like It Is/Strange Euphoria	1980	4.00
❑ 19-51010	Unchained Melody/Mistral Wind	1981	4.00

MUSHROOM

Number	Title (A Side/B Side)	Yr	NM
❑ 7011	Magic Man/How Deep It Goes	1976	5.00
❑ 7011 [DJ]	Magic Man (2:45) (5:35)	1976	10.00
❑ 7021	Crazy on You/Dreamboat Annie	1976	6.00
❑ 7023	Dreamboat Annie/Sing Child	1976	5.00
—Bizarre version of A-side with part of the intro to "Crazy on You" grafted on.			
❑ 7031	Heartless/Just the Wine	1978	4.00
❑ 7035	Without You/Here Song	1978	4.00
❑ 7043	Magazine/Devil Delight	1978	4.00

PORTRAIT

Number	Title (A Side/B Side)	Yr	NM
❑ AE7 1168 [DJ]	Straight On (Edit) (same on both sides)	1978	8.00
❑ 17-8101	Barracuda/Straight On	1981	4.00
—Reissue			
❑ 6-70004	Barracuda/Cry to Me	1977	4.00
❑ 6-70008	Little Queen/Treat Me Well	1977	5.00
❑ 6-70010	Kick It Out/Go On, Cry	1977	5.00
❑ 6-70020	Straight On/Lighter Touch	1978	4.00
—Custom label			
❑ 6-70025	Dog and Butterfly/Mistral Wind	1979	5.00

Albums

CAPITOL

Number	Title (A Side/B Side)	Yr	NM
❑ ST-12410	Heart	1985	10.00
—With remix of "Never." Side one trail-off wax has an "RE-1"			
❑ ST-12410	Heart	1985	15.00
—With original mix of "Never"			
❑ SQ-12500	Dreamboat Annie	1986	8.00
❑ SQ-12501	Magazine	1986	8.00
❑ PJ-12546	Bad Animals	1987	8.00
❑ 72435-21184-1	Dreamboat Annie	1999	15.00
—180-gram audiophile reissue			
❑ C1-91820	Brigade	1990	12.00
❑ R 153552	Bad Animals	1987	10.00
—BMG Direct Marketing edition			
❑ ST-512410	Heart	1985	15.00
—Columbia House edition; has original mix of "Never"			
❑ PJ-512546	Bad Animals	1987	10.00
—Columbia House edition			
❑ C1-591820	Brigade	1990	12.00
—Columbia House edition			

EPIC

Number	Title (A Side/B Side)	Yr	NM
❑ AS 884 [DJ]	Heart	1980	20.00
—Promo-only sampler from "Greatest Hits/Live"			
❑ AS884 [DJ]	Heart	1980	20.00
—Promo-only sampler from "Greatest Hits/Live"			
❑ FE 36371	Bebe Le Strange	1980	10.00
❑ KE2 36888 [(2)]	Greatest Hits/Live	1980	12.00
❑ FE 38049	Private Audition	1982	10.00
❑ PE 38049	Private Audition	1985	8.00
❑ PE 38800	Passionworks	1985	8.00

Number	Title (A Side/B Side)	Yr	NM
❑ QE 38800	Passionworks	1983	10.00

MUSHROOM

Number	Title (A Side/B Side)	Yr	NM
❑ MRS-1-SP [PD]	Magazine	1978	20.00
❑ MRS-2-SP [PD]	Dreamboat Annie	1978	25.00
❑ MRS-5005	Dreamboat Annie	1976	10.00
❑ MRS-5008	Magazine	1977	60.00

—Original issue, quickly recalled; "Magazine" is the last song on side 1; Side 2, Track 3 is "Blues Medley (Mother Earth) (You Shook Me Babe)"; at the bottom of the back cover is "Mushroom Records regrets that a contractual dispute has made it necessary to complete this record without the cooperation or endorsement of the group Heart, who have expressly disclaimed artistic involvement in completing this record."

Number	Title (A Side/B Side)	Yr	NM
❑ MRS-5008	Magazine	1978	10.00

—Authorized edition; Side 2, Track 3 is "Mother Earth Blues"

NAUTILUS

Number	Title (A Side/B Side)	Yr	NM
❑ NR-3	Dreamboat Annie	1980	40.00

—Audiophile pressing

PORTRAIT

Number	Title (A Side/B Side)	Yr	NM
❑ JR 34799	Little Queen	1977	10.00
❑ PR 34799	Little Queen	1984	8.00
❑ FR 35555	Dog and Butterfly	1978	10.00
❑ PR 35555	Dog and Butterfly	1981	8.00
❑ HR 44799	Little Queen	1981	50.00

—Half-speed mastered edition

HEART (2)

45s

EMI

Number	Title (A Side/B Side)	Yr	NM
❑ 4008	Beautiful Woman/Lovemaker	1974	4.00

HEART (3)

45s

LOOK

Number	Title (A Side/B Side)	Yr	NM
❑ 5023	Give Me a Happy Heart/ Now	1969	6.00
❑ 5029	I Love You/Love	1970	6.00

Albums

LOOK

Number	Title (A Side/B Side)	Yr	NM
❑ LLP-11000	Heart	1969	12.00

HEART (U)

Some of these could be group (3), but others probably are not. None of these, by the way, are the Seattle-based group featuring Ann and Nancy Wilson. That group's first record did not come out in the U.S. until 1976, thus it is not in this book.

45s

REPRISE

Number	Title (A Side/B Side)	Yr	NM
❑ 0772	Heartbeat/The Train	1968	6.00

Albums

KING

Number	Title (A Side/B Side)	Yr	NM
❑ KS-1119	Have a Heart	1970	12.00

NATURAL RESOURCES

Number	Title (A Side/B Side)	Yr	NM
❑ NR-102	Heart	1972	12.00

HEARTBEATS, THE

Also see SHEP AND THE LIMELITES.

45s

GEE

Number	Title (A Side/B Side)	Yr	NM
❑ 1043	When I Found You/ Hands Off My Baby	1957	50.00
❑ 1047	500 Miles to Go/After New Year's Eve	1958	20.00

—Gray label

Number	Title (A Side/B Side)	Yr	NM
❑ 1047	500 Miles to Go/After New Year's Eve	1958	40.00

—Red label

Number	Title (A Side/B Side)	Yr	NM
❑ 1061	People Are Talking/Your Way	1960	20.00
❑ 1062	Darling How Long/ Hurry Home Baby	1960	20.00

GUYDEN

Number	Title (A Side/B Side)	Yr	NM
❑ 2011	One Million Years/Darling, I Want to Get Married	1959	30.00

—Purple label

Number	Title (A Side/B Side)	Yr	NM
❑ 2011	One Million Years/Darling, I Want to Get Married	1959	40.00

—Yellow label

HULL

Number	Title (A Side/B Side)	Yr	NM
❑ 711	Crazy for You/Rockin-N-Rollin-N-Rhythm-N-Blues-N	1955	100.00

—Black label

Number	Title (A Side/B Side)	Yr	NM
❑ 711	Crazy for You/Rockin-N-Rollin-N-Rhythm-N-Blues-N	1955	200.00

—Pink label, "Miller" as A-side composer

Number	Title (A Side/B Side)	Yr	NM
❑ 711	Crazy for You/Rockin-N-Rollin-N-Rhythm-N-Blues-N	1955	300.00

—Pink label, "Sheppard-Miller" as A-side composers

Number	Title (A Side/B Side)	Yr	NM
❑ 711 [DJ]	Crazy for You/Rockin-N-Rollin-N-Rhythm-N-Blues-N	1955	600.00

—White label

Number	Title (A Side/B Side)	Yr	NM
❑ 713	Darling How Long/ Hurry Home Baby	1956	200.00
❑ 716	People Are Talking/Your Way	1956	200.00
❑ 720	A Thousand Miles Away/ Oh Baby Don't	1957	80.00

—Red label

Number	Title (A Side/B Side)	Yr	NM
❑ 720	A Thousand Miles Away/ Oh Baby Don't	1957	250.00

—Black label

JUBILEE

Number	Title (A Side/B Side)	Yr	NM
❑ 5202	Finally/Boil and Bubble	1955	30.00

NETWORK

Number	Title (A Side/B Side)	Yr	NM
❑ 71200	Tormented/After Everybody's Gone	195?	25.00

—Red vinyl The Network release as "The Heart Beats Quintet"

Number	Title (A Side/B Side)	Yr	NM
❑ 71200	Tormented/After Everybody's Gone	195?	120.00

—Yellow label, black vinyl

Number	Title (A Side/B Side)	Yr	NM
❑ 71200	Tormented/After Everybody's Gone	1955	300.00

—Cream label, black vinyl

RAMA

Number	Title (A Side/B Side)	Yr	NM
❑ 216	A Thousand Miles Away/ Oh Baby Don't	1956	80.00
❑ 222	Wedding Bells/I Won't Be the Fool Anymore	1957	100.00
❑ 231	I Want to Know/Everybody's Somebody's Fool	1957	100.00

ROULETTE

Number	Title (A Side/B Side)	Yr	NM
❑ 4054	I Found a Job/Down on My Knees	1958	30.00
❑ 4091	One Day Next Year/ Sometimes I Wonder	1958	30.00
❑ 4194	Crazy for You/Down on My Knees	1959	30.00

Albums

EMUS

Number	Title (A Side/B Side)	Yr	NM
❑ ES-12033	A Thousand Miles Away	1979	25.00

ROULETTE

Number	Title (A Side/B Side)	Yr	NM
❑ R 25107 [M]	A Thousand Miles Away	1960	400.00

HEARTBEATS, THE /SHEP AND THE LIMELITES

Also see each artist's individual listings.

Albums

ROULETTE

Number	Title (A Side/B Side)	Yr	NM
❑ RE-115 [(2)]	Echoes of a Rock Era: The Groups	1972	15.00

HEARTBREAKERS, THE

Several different groups.

45s

ATCO

Number	Title (A Side/B Side)	Yr	NM
❑ 6258	The Willow Wept/You Had Time	1963	60.00

BRENT

Number	Title (A Side/B Side)	Yr	NM
❑ 7037	I'm Leaving It All Up to You/ Corrido Mash	1962	30.00

DONNA

Number	Title (A Side/B Side)	Yr	NM
❑ 1381	Everytime I See You/Cradle Rock	1963	120.00

—Frank Zappa plays guitar on this record

LINDA

Number	Title (A Side/B Side)	Yr	NM
❑ 114	Please Answer/She Is My Baby	1964	15.00

MARKAY

Number	Title (A Side/B Side)	Yr	NM
❑ 106	Since You've Been Gone/ John Law	1962	80.00

MGM

Number	Title (A Side/B Side)	Yr	NM
❑ 13129	It's Hard Being a Girl/ Special Occasions	1963	15.00

RCA VICTOR

Number	Title (A Side/B Side)	Yr	NM
❑ 47-4327	Heartbreaker/Wanda	1951	600.00
❑ 47-4508	You're So Necessary to Me/ I'm Only Following My Heart	1952	600.00
❑ 47-4662	Why Don't I/Rockin' Daddy-O	1952	500.00
❑ 47-4849	There Is Time/It's OK With Me	1952	500.00

SWAN

Number	Title (A Side/B Side)	Yr	NM
❑ 4242	Baby Baby/I Told You So	1966	15.00

VIK

Number	Title (A Side/B Side)	Yr	NM
❑ 0261	Without a Cause/One, Two, I Love You	1957	150.00
❑ 0299	My Love/Love You Till the Day I Die	1957	250.00

HEARTS, THE

45s

BATON

Number	Title (A Side/B Side)	Yr	NM
❑ 208	Lonely Nights/Oo-Wee	1955	50.00
❑ 211	All My Love Belongs to You/ Talk About Him Girlie	1955	50.00
❑ 215	Gone, Gone, Gone/Until the Real Thing Comes Along	1955	50.00
❑ 222	Disappointed Bride/ Going Home to Stay	1956	30.00
❑ 228	He Drives Me Crazy/ I Had a Guy	1956	25.00

J&S

Number	Title (A Side/B Side)	Yr	NM
❑ 425/6	My Love Has Gone/You or Me Have Got to Go	1959	50.00
❑ 995	A Thousand Years from Today/ I Feel So Good	1960	40.00
❑ 1180/1	You Weren't Home/I Couldn't Let You See Me Crying	1961	50.00
❑ 1626/7	I Want Your Love Tonight/ Like Later Baby	1958	50.00
❑ 1657	Dancing in a Dream World/ You Needn't Tell, I Know	1957	60.00
❑ 1660	So Long, Baby/You Say You Love Me	1957	60.00
❑ 4571/2	Goodbye Baby/There Is No Love at All	1959	40.00
❑ 10002/3	If I Had Known/There Are So Many Ways	1958	50.00

TUFF

Number	Title (A Side/B Side)	Yr	NM
❑ 370	Dear Abby/(Instrumental)	1963	15.00

HEARTS AND FLOWERS

45s

CAPITOL

Number	Title (A Side/B Side)	Yr	NM
❑ 2167	She Sang Hymns Out of Tune/ Tin Angel (Will You Ever Come Down)	1968	10.00
❑ 5897	View from Ward 3/Please	1967	10.00

Albums

CAPITOL

Number	Title (A Side/B Side)	Yr	NM
❑ ST 2762 [S]	Now Is the Time for Hearts and Flowers	1967	40.00
❑ T 2762 [M]	Now Is the Time for Hearts and Flowers	1967	40.00
❑ ST 2868	Of Horses, Kids and Forgotten Women	1968	50.00

HEARTS OF STONE

45s

V.I.P.

Number	Title (A Side/B Side)	Yr	NM
❑ 25058	It's a Lonesome Road/ Yesterday's Love Is Over	1970	10.00
❑ 25064	If I Could Give You the World/ You Gotta Sacrifice	1970	10.00

Albums

V.I.P.

Number	Title (A Side/B Side)	Yr	NM
❑ VIPS-404	Stop the World... We Wanna Get On	1970	40.00

HEARTSFIELD

45s

MERCURY

Number	Title (A Side/B Side)	Yr	NM
❑ 73449	Music Eyes/Gypsy Rider	1974	5.00
❑ 73600	Shine On/Eight Hours at a Time	1974	5.00
❑ 73628	Racin' the Sun/Pass Me By	1974	5.00
❑ 73706	Nashville/As I Look Into the Fire	1975	5.00
❑ 73742	Magic Mood/Rocking Chair	1975	5.00

Albums

COLUMBIA

Number	Title (A Side/B Side)	Yr	NM
❑ PC 34456	Collector's Item	1976	10.00

MERCURY

Number	Title (A Side/B Side)	Yr	NM
❑ SRM-1-688	Heartsfield	1973	10.00
❑ SRM-1-1003	The Wonder of It All	1974	10.00
❑ SRM-1-1034	Foolish Pleasures	1975	10.00

HEAT BROTHERS '84

See CANNED HEAT.

HEATH, TED

45s

LONDON

Number	Title (A Side/B Side)	Yr	NM
❑ 1006	Sixty Seconds/The Girl in the Little Green Hat	1951	12.00
❑ 1014	Saxophone Mambo/ Take a Letter Miss Smith	1951	12.00
❑ 1015	This Is the Time/In a Little Spanish Town	1951	12.00
❑ 1026	London Fog/Romanian Roundabout	1951	12.00
❑ 1056	The Nearness of You/Lyonia	1951	12.00
❑ 1057	Button Up Your Overcoat/ You're Nearer	1951	12.00
❑ 1181	Turkey in the Straw/Entry of the Gladiators	1952	12.00
❑ 1182	L'Heure Bleu/A Kiss in the Dark	1952	12.00
❑ 1183	Live House Blues/ The Black Bottom	1952	12.00
❑ 1184	Casey Jones/I Want to Be Happy	1952	12.00
❑ 1198	Obsession/Hawaiian Mambo	1952	12.00
❑ 1256	Vanessa/Early Autumn	1952	12.00
❑ 1259	Jungle Fantasy/ The Piper's Patrol	1952	12.00
❑ 1290	Alpine Boogie/Floreintine	1952	12.00
❑ 1305	Beyond the Sea/On the Bridge	1953	12.00
❑ 1324	Phantom Regiment/ Strike Up the Band	1953	12.00
❑ 1344	Alouette/Yours Is My Heart	1953	12.00
❑ 1379	Dragnet/Sloppy Joe	1953	12.00
❑ 1390	Lullaby of Birdland/ Seven-Eleven	1953	12.00
❑ 1404	Slim Jim/The Original Creep	1954	12.00

Except when noted otherwise, VG = 25% of NM, and VG+ = 50% of NM. (Example: VG = $2.00, VG+ = $4.00 and NM = $8.00.)

Number	Title (A Side/B Side)	Yr	NM
❑ 1418	Jitterbug Waltz/Alligator Crawl	1954	12.00
❑ 1421	The Champ/Pick Yourself Up	1954	12.00
❑ 1495	Stomp and Whistle/ Bernie's Tune	1954	12.00
❑ 1500	Skokiaan/Skokiaan	1954	12.00

—B-side by the Johnston Brothers

Number	Title (A Side/B Side)	Yr	NM
❑ 1531	Asia Minor/Dig Deep	1955	10.00
❑ 1534	Peg o' My Heart Mambo/ In the Mood	1955	10.00
❑ 1621	Malaguena/Barber Shop Jump	1955	10.00
❑ 1644	Main Title — The Man with the Golden Arm/Siboney	1956	10.00
❑ 1647	Cloudburst/The Trouble with Harry	1956	10.00
❑ 1675	The Faithful Hussar/ Have You Met Miss Jones	1956	10.00
❑ 1690	Autumn Concerto/Lost	1956	10.00

—B-side by Bobbie Britton

Number	Title (A Side/B Side)	Yr	NM
❑ 1692	Canadian Sunset/ Oriental Holiday	1956	10.00
❑ 1712	Madagascar/Jungle Drums	1957	10.00
❑ 1762	Witch Doctor/Headin' North	1957	10.00
❑ 1800	Little Serenade/I've Got the World on a String	1958	10.00
❑ 1809	Cha Cha Baby/Tom Hark	1958	10.00
❑ 1836	Bullfighters Patrol/Strolling Along with the Blues	1958	10.00
❑ 1867	Frogmarch/9:20 Special	1959	8.00
❑ 1887	Honky Tonk Train Blues/ Bluest Kind of Blue	1959	8.00
❑ 1893	Swinging Ghosts/ Indian Love Call	1959	8.00
❑ 1920	Slaughter on Tenth Avenue/ Sleepy Lagoon	1960	8.00
❑ 1975	Man from Madrid/Theme from "Dangerman"	1961	8.00
❑ 2014	Peanut Vendor/Daddy	1961	8.00
❑ 9503	Charmaine Cha Cha/Sucu Sucu	1962	6.00
❑ 9602	Theme from Cleopatra/Mirage	1963	6.00
❑ 9629	Theme from "Lord of the Flies"/ Paris Mist	1963	6.00
❑ 9680	Theme from "The Carpetbaggers"/Wigwam	1964	6.00

7-Inch Extended Plays

LONDON

Number	Title (A Side/B Side)	Yr	NM
❑ BEP 6091	Twilight Boogie/Clair de Lune// Alouette/La Mer	195?	10.00
❑ BEP 6091 [PS]	Ted Heath and His Music	195?	10.00
❑ BEP.6270	The Man I Love/Love Walked In//Nice Work If You Can Get It/Love Is Here to Stay	195?	10.00
❑ BEP.6270 [PS]	Love Is Here to Stay	195?	10.00

Albums

EVEREST ARCHIVE OF FOLK & JAZZ

Number	Title (A Side/B Side)	Yr	NM
❑ 215	Ted Heath's Big Band	1970	10.00

LONDON

Number	Title (A Side/B Side)	Yr	NM
❑ PS 116 [S]	Hits I Missed	1958	25.00
❑ PS 117 [S]	All Time Top Twelve	1958	25.00

—Re-recorded version of LL 1716

Number	Title (A Side/B Side)	Yr	NM
❑ PS 138 [S]	Swing Session	1958	25.00

—New stereo recordings of the same material as appears on LL 802

Number	Title (A Side/B Side)	Yr	NM
❑ PS 140 [S]	Ted Heath Swings in High Stereo	1958	25.00
❑ PS 148 [S]	Shall We Dance	1959	25.00
❑ PS 159 [S]	Great Film Hits	1959	25.00
❑ PS 171 [S]	Pop Hits from the Classics	1959	25.00
❑ PS 172 [S]	Big Band Blues	1959	25.00
❑ PS 174 [S]	My Very Good Friends The Bandleaders	1959	25.00
❑ PS 175 [S]	The Hits of the Twenties	1960	20.00
❑ PS 184 [S]	The Big Band Dixie Sound	1960	20.00
❑ PS 187 [S]	Ted Heath in Concert	1960	20.00
❑ PS 190 [S]	Songs for the Young at Heart	1960	20.00
❑ PS 216 [S]	The Hits of the Thirties	1961	20.00
❑ PS 219 [S]	Latin Swingers	1961	20.00
❑ LPB-340 [10]	Tempo for Dancing	195?	40.00
❑ LPB-374 [10]	Ted Heath and His Orchestra	195?	40.00
❑ LB-511 [10]	Listen to My Music	195?	40.00
❑ PS 535	21st Anniversary Album	1968	12.00
❑ LB-732 [10]	Black and White Magic	195?	40.00
❑ LL 750 [M]	Ted Heath Strikes Up the Band	1953	20.00
❑ LL 802 [M]	Ted Heath at the London Palladium	1953	20.00
❑ LL 978 [M]	Ted Heath Plays the Music of Fats Waller	1954	20.00
❑ LL 1000 [M]	The 100th London Palladium Concert	1955	20.00
❑ LL 1211 [M]	Jazz Concert at the London Palladium, Vol. 3	1955	20.00
❑ LL 1217 [M]	Gershwin for Moderns	1956	20.00
❑ LL 1279 [M]	Kern for Moderns	1956	20.00
❑ LL 1379 [M]	Jazz Concert at the London Palladium, Vol. 4	1956	20.00
❑ LL 1475 [M]	Ted Heath Swings in Hi-Fi	1956	20.00
❑ LL 1500 [M]	Rodgers for Moderns	1956	20.00
❑ LL 1564 [M]	Ted Heath's First American Tour	1956	20.00
❑ LL 1566 [M]	Ted Heath at Carnegie Hall	1956	20.00
❑ LL 1676 [M]	A Yank in Europe	1956	20.00
❑ LL 1716 [M]	All Time Top Twelve	1957	20.00
❑ LL 1721 [M]	Spotlight on Sidemen	1957	20.00
❑ LL 1737 [M]	Showcase	1957	20.00
❑ LL 1743 [M]	Tribute to the Fabulous Dorseys	1957	20.00
❑ LL 1749 [M]	Rhapsody in Blue	1957	20.00
❑ LL 3047 [M]	Things to Come	1958	20.00
❑ LL 3057 [M]	Hits I Missed	1958	20.00
❑ LL 3058 [M]	Old English	1958	20.00
❑ LL 3062 [M]	Shall We Dance	1959	20.00
❑ LL 3106 [M]	Great Film Hits	1959	20.00
❑ LL 3124 [M]	Pop Hits from the Classics	1959	20.00
❑ LL 3125 [M]	Big Band Blues	1959	20.00
❑ LL 3127 [M]	My Very Good Friends The Bandleaders	1959	20.00
❑ LL 3128 [M]	The Hits of the Twenties	1960	15.00
❑ LL 3138 [M]	The Big Band Dixie Sound	1960	15.00
❑ LL 3143 [M]	Ted Heath in Concert	1960	15.00
❑ LL 3146 [M]	Songs for the Young at Heart	1960	15.00
❑ LL 3192 [M]	The Hits of the Thirties	1961	15.00
❑ LL 3195 [M]	Latin Swingers	1961	15.00
❑ LL 3325 [M]	Big Band Spirituals	1963	12.00
❑ LL 3367 [M]	New Palladium Performances	1964	12.00

LONDON PHASE 4

Number	Title (A Side/B Side)	Yr	NM
❑ SP 44002 [S]	Big Band Percussion	1961	15.00
❑ SP 44017	Big Band Bash	1962	15.00
❑ SP 44023	Satin Strings and Bouncing Brass	1963	15.00
❑ SP 44036 [S]	Big Band Spirituals	1963	15.00
❑ SP 44038	Swing vs. Latin	1964	15.00
❑ SP 44046 [S]	New Palladium Performances	1964	12.00
❑ SP 44063	The Sound of Music	1965	12.00
❑ SP 44074	Chartbusters	1966	12.00
❑ SP 44079	Pow!	1966	12.00
❑ P 54002 [M]	Big Band Percussion	1961	12.00

RICHMOND

Number	Title (A Side/B Side)	Yr	NM
❑ B 20034 [M]	Big Band Beat	196?	12.00
❑ B 20037 [M]	Ted Heath Plays Gershwin	196?	12.00
❑ B 20082 [M]	Ted Heath Plays the Music of Fats Waller	196?	12.00
❑ B 20096 [M]	Big Band Gershwin	196?	12.00
❑ B 20097 [M]	Big Band Kern	196?	12.00
❑ B 20098 [M]	Big Band Rodgers	196?	12.00

HEATHER BLACK

Albums

AMERICAN PLAYBOY

Number	Title (A Side/B Side)	Yr	NM
❑ 1001	Heather Black Live	197?	60.00
❑ 1001 [(2)]	Heather Black Live	197?	150.00

—Evidently, some copies of this were 2-record sets

DOUBLE BAYOU

Number	Title (A Side/B Side)	Yr	NM
❑ 2000	Heather Black	197?	30.00

HEATHERTON, JOEY

45s

CORAL

Number	Title (A Side/B Side)	Yr	NM
❑ 62422	That's How It Goes/ I'll Be Seeing You	1964	30.00
❑ 62422 [PS]	That's How It Goes/ I'll Be Seeing You	1964	40.00
❑ 62451	Hullabaloo/My Blood Runs Cold	1965	100.00
❑ 62459	Tomorrow Is Another Day/ But He's Not Mine	1965	25.00

DECCA

Number	Title (A Side/B Side)	Yr	NM
❑ 31962 [PS]	Live and Learn/When You Call Me Baby	1966	80.00
❑ 31962	Live and Learn/When You Call Me Baby	1966	300.00

MGM

Number	Title (A Side/B Side)	Yr	NM
❑ 14387	Gone/The Road I Took to You	1972	5.00
❑ 14387 [PS]	Gone/The Road I Took to You	1972	10.00
❑ 14434	I'm Sorry/Someone to Watch Over Me	1972	5.00
❑ 14434	I'm Sorry/Crazy	1972	6.00
❑ 14499	Crazy/God Only Knows	1973	5.00

Albums

MGM

Number	Title (A Side/B Side)	Yr	NM
❑ SE-4858	The Joey Heatherton Album	1972	15.00

HEAVEN & HELL

Albums

WARNER BROS./RHINO

Number	Title (A Side/B Side)	Yr	NM
❑ 519252 [(2)]	The Devil You Know	2009	20.00

HEAVY BALLOON, THE

Albums

ELEPHANT

Number	Title (A Side/B Side)	Yr	NM
❑ EVS-104	32,000 Lbs.	1969	70.00

HEBB, BOBBY

45s

BOOM

Number	Title (A Side/B Side)	Yr	NM
❑ 60017	Betty Jo from Ohio/Sam Hall Jr.	1966	8.00

CADET

Number	Title (A Side/B Side)	Yr	NM
❑ 5690	I Was a Boy When You Needed a Man/Woman in the Window	1972	20.00

LAURIE

Number	Title (A Side/B Side)	Yr	NM
❑ 3632	True, I Love You/Proud Soul Heritage	1975	40.00
❑ 3638	Sunny '76/Sunny Disco	1976	10.00

PHILIPS

Number	Title (A Side/B Side)	Yr	NM
❑ 40365	Sunny/Bread	1966	10.00
❑ 40400	A Satisfied Mind/ Love, Love, Love	1966	8.00
❑ 40400 [PS]	A Satisfied Mind/ Love, Love, Love	1966	12.00
❑ 40421	Love Me/Crazy Baby	1966	15.00
❑ 40431	My Pretty Sunshine/Ooh La La	1967	8.00
❑ 40448	I Love Everything About You/ Some Kind of Magic	1967	15.00
❑ 40482	Everything Is Coming Up Roses/Bound by Love	1967	20.00
❑ 40551	Dreamy/You Want to Change Me	1968	60.00

RICH

Number	Title (A Side/B Side)	Yr	NM
❑ 1006	Cherry/Feel So Good	1960	15.00
❑ 1740	Just a Little Bit More/ Walk Me On Alone	1962	15.00

SCEPTER

Number	Title (A Side/B Side)	Yr	NM
❑ 12166	I Love Mary (Part 1)/ I Love Mary (Part 2)	1966	8.00

Albums

EPIC

Number	Title (A Side/B Side)	Yr	NM
❑ BN 26523	Love Games	1970	12.00

PHILIPS

Number	Title (A Side/B Side)	Yr	NM
❑ PHM 200212 [M]	Sunny	1966	25.00

—With "200-212" in trail-off; this record is mono

Number	Title (A Side/B Side)	Yr	NM
❑ PHM 200212 [S]	Sunny	1966	25.00

—With "2/600-212" in trail-off; this record plays stereo, though labeled mono

Number	Title (A Side/B Side)	Yr	NM
❑ PHS 600212 [S]	Sunny	1966	30.00

HEDGE & DONNA

45s

CAPITOL

Number	Title (A Side/B Side)	Yr	NM
❑ 2695	Black Betty/Tomorrow Is the First Day of the Rest of Your Life	1969	8.00
❑ 2840	My God and I/Sunshine	1970	8.00

JANUS

Number	Title (A Side/B Side)	Yr	NM
❑ 216	Guava Jelly/Well I Never	1973	7.00

—As "Capers & Carson"

Number	Title (A Side/B Side)	Yr	NM
❑ 229	Mirror, Mirror/(B-side unknown)	1973	8.00

—As "Capers & Carson"

POLYDOR

Number	Title (A Side/B Side)	Yr	NM
❑ 14090	Touch Caste on the Water/ She Said She Said	1971	8.00

Albums

CAPITOL

Number	Title (A Side/B Side)	Yr	NM
❑ ST-107	2	1969	15.00

—Black label with rainbow ring

Number	Title (A Side/B Side)	Yr	NM
❑ ST-279	All the Friendly Colours	1969	15.00

—Lime green label

Number	Title (A Side/B Side)	Yr	NM
❑ ST-447	Special Circumstances	1970	15.00
❑ ST-2869	Hedge & Donna	1968	15.00

—The label calls this LP "Love"

JANUS

Number	Title (A Side/B Side)	Yr	NM
❑ JLS-3045	Capers & Carson	1973	12.00

POLYDOR

Number	Title (A Side/B Side)	Yr	NM
❑ 24-4063	Revolution	1971	12.00

HEDGEHOPPERS ANONYMOUS

45s

PARROT

Number	Title (A Side/B Side)	Yr	NM
❑ 3002	Remember/Baby (You're My Everything)	1966	10.00
❑ 9800	It's Good News Week/ Afraid of Love	1965	12.00
❑ 9817	Don't Push Me/Please Don't Hurt Your Heart for Me	1966	10.00

HEIGHT, RONNIE

45s

BAMBOO

Number	Title (A Side/B Side)	Yr	NM
❑ 500	Dolores/I'm Confessin'	1961	12.00

DORE

Number	Title (A Side/B Side)	Yr	NM
❑ 516	Come Softly to Me/ So Young, So Wise	1959	20.00

ERA

Number	Title (A Side/B Side)	Yr	NM
❑ 3000	Portrait of Linda/It's Not That Easy	1959	15.00
❑ 3005	Mr. Blue, I Presume/Juvenile	1959	15.00

Number	Title (A Side/B Side)	Yr	NM
❑ 3009	Maybe Tomorrow/A Kiss to Build a Dream On	1959	15.00
❑ 3017	Mem'ries and Habits/One Finger Symphony	1960	15.00
❑ 3031	No Date/Mr. Blue, I Presume	1960	15.00

HEINTJE

Number	Title (A Side/B Side)	Yr	NM
45s			
MGM			
❑ 14183	Mama/Mother's Tears	1970	4.00
❑ 14272	When the Summer Comes/You Are the Best of All	1971	4.00
Albums			
MGM			
❑ SE-4739	Mama	1970	12.00
❑ SE-4772	Best of All	1971	12.00

HEINZ

Also see FREDDIE AND THE DREAMERS.

Number	Title (A Side/B Side)	Yr	NM
45s			
LONDON			
❑ 9619	Just Like Eddie/Don't You Knock on My Door	1963	15.00
TOWER			
❑ 110	Questions I Can't Answer/The Beating of My Heart	1964	20.00
❑ 172	Digging My Potatoes/Don't Think Twice, It's All Right	1965	20.00
❑ 195	Don't Worry Baby/Heart Full of Sorrow	1966	30.00
❑ 253	I'm Not a Bad Boy/Movin' In	1966	20.00

HELL, RICHARD, AND THE VOIDOIDS

Early member of TELEVISION.

Number	Title (A Side/B Side)	Yr	NM
45s			
ORK			
❑ 81976 [PS]	I Could Live With You in Another World/Blank Generation/You Gotta Lose	1977	15.00
❑ 81976	I Could Live With You in Another World/Blank Generation/You Gotta Lose	1977	15.00
SIRE			
❑ 1003	Blank Generation/Love Comes in Spurts	1977	10.00
❑ 1003 [PS]	Blank Generation/Love Comes in Spurts	1977	10.00
7-Inch Extended Plays			
SHAKE			
❑ SHK 101	Don't Die/Time//That's All I Know (Right Now)/Love Comes in Spurts	1980	14.00
—B-side tracks by Neon Boys			
❑ SHK 101 [PS]	Don't Die/Time//That's All I Know (Right Now)/Love Comes in Spurts	1980	14.00
Albums			
RED STAR			
❑ RED 801	Destiny Street	1982	18.00
—Richard Hell solo			
SIRE			
❑ SRK 6037	Blank Generation	1977	30.00

HELLBORG, JONAS

Number	Title (A Side/B Side)	Yr	NM
Albums			
DAY EIGHT			
❑ DEM (# unknown)	Jonas Hellborg Group	1988	12.00
❑ DEM 001	The Bassic Thing	1982	20.00
❑ DEM 002	All Our Steps	1983	15.00
❑ DEM 004	Elegant Punk	1984	12.00
❑ DEM 006	Axis	1986	12.00
❑ DEM 009	Bass	1988	12.00

HELLERS, THE

Number	Title (A Side/B Side)	Yr	NM
Albums			
COMMAND			
❑ RS 934 SD	Singers, Talkers, Players, Swingers and Doers	1968	20.00

HELLO PEOPLE, THE

Number	Title (A Side/B Side)	Yr	NM
45s			
ABC			
❑ 12160	Book of Love/How High Is the Moon	1976	5.00
ABC DUNHILL			
❑ 15023	Future Shock/Destiny	1974	5.00
❑ 15031	Just One Victory/Take the Love in Your Body	1975	5.00
MEDIARTS			
❑ 109	Pass Me By/Maybe We Should Have Had Rain	1971	10.00
PHILIPS			
❑ 40481	Let's Go Hide in the Forest/Disparity Waterfront Blues	1967	8.00
❑ 40522	A Stranger at Her Door/Paisley Teddy Bear	1968	8.00
❑ 40531	(As I Went Down to) Jerusalem/It's a Monday Kind of Tuesday	1968	8.00
❑ 40572	If I Should Sing Too Softly/Pray for Rain	1968	8.00
❑ 40585	Anthem/Jelly Jam	1969	8.00
UNITED ARTISTS			
❑ 50797	Pass Me By/Maybe We Should Have Had Rain	1971	6.00
Albums			
ABC			
❑ D-882	Bricks	1975	10.00
ABC DUNHILL			
❑ DS-50184	The Handsome Devils	1974	10.00
MEDIARTS			
❑ 41-8	Have You Seen the Light	1970	12.00
PHILIPS			
❑ PHS 200265 [M]	The Hello People	1968	15.00
—Possibly white label promo only			
❑ PHS 600265 [S]	The Hello People	1968	15.00
❑ PHS 600276	Fusion	1969	15.00
UNITED ARTISTS			
❑ UAS 5524	Have You Seen the Light	1971	10.00
—Reissue of Mediarts LP			

HELMET

Number	Title (A Side/B Side)	Yr	NM
45s			
AMPHETAMINE REPTILE			
❑ Scale 22	Born Annoying/Rumble	1989	25.00
❑ Scale 22 [PS]	Born Annoying/Rumble	1989	25.00
❑ Scale 41	Unsung/Your Head	1990	10.00
—Red vinyl			
❑ Scale 41	Unsung/Your Head	1990	10.00
—White vinyl			
❑ Scale 41 [PS]	Unsung/Your Head	1990	10.00
❑ Scale 55	Primitive/Born Annoying	1992	3.00
❑ Scale 55 [PS]	Primitive/Born Annoying	1992	3.00

HELMS, BOBBY

Number	Title (A Side/B Side)	Yr	NM
45s			
CERTRON			
❑ 10002	Mary Goes 'Round/Cold Winds Blow on Me	1970	8.00
❑ 10021	Jingle Bell Rock/The Old Year Is Gone	1970	8.00
❑ 10021 [PS]	Jingle Bell Rock/The Old Year Is Gone	1970	15.00
❑ 10023	I Wouldn't Take the World for You/Look What You've Done	1970	8.00
COLUMBIA			
❑ 4-42801	Fraulein/My Special Angel	1963	10.00
❑ 4-43031	It's a Girl/Put Your Arms Around Him	1964	10.00
DECCA			
❑ 9-29947	Tennessee Rock 'N' Roll/I Don't Owe You Nothing	1956	50.00
❑ 9-30194	Fraulein/(Got a) Heartsick Feeling	1957	20.00
❑ 9-30194 [PS]	Fraulein/(Got a) Heartsick Feeling	1957	50.00
❑ 9-30423	My Special Angel/Standing at the End of My World	1957	25.00
❑ 9-30513	Jingle Bell Rock/Captain Santa Claus	1957	25.00
—Black label, star under "Decca"			
❑ 9-30513	Jingle Bell Rock/Captain Santa Claus	1957	40.00
—Black label, lines on either side of "Decca"			
❑ 9-30513	Jingle Bell Rock/Captain Santa Claus	1960	12.00
—Black label with color bars			
❑ 9-30513 [PS]	Jingle Bell Rock/Captain Santa Claus	1957	50.00
❑ 9-30557	Just a Little Lonesome/Love My Baby	1958	20.00
❑ 9-30619	Jacqueline/Living in the Shadow of the Past	1958	20.00
❑ 9-30682	Schoolboy Crush/Borrowed Dreams	1958	20.00
❑ 9-30749	A Hundred Hearts/The Fool and the Angel	1958	20.00
❑ 9-30831	New River Train/Miss Memory	1959	15.00
❑ 9-30886	Soon It Can Be Told/I Guess I'll Miss the Prom	1959	15.00
❑ 9-30928	No Other Baby/You're No Longer Mine	1959	15.00
❑ 9-30976	My Lucky Day/Hurry Baby	1959	15.00
❑ 9-31041	To My Sorrow/Someone Was Already There	1960	15.00
❑ 31103	Let Me Be the One/I Wanna Be with You	1960	15.00
❑ 31148	Lonely River Rhine/Guess We Thought the World Would End	1960	15.00
❑ 31230	Sad-Eyed Baby/You're the One	1961	12.00
❑ 31287	How Can You Divide a Little Child/My Greatest Weakness	1961	12.00
❑ 31356	One Deep Love/Once in a Lifetime	1962	12.00
❑ 31403	Then Came You/Yesterday's Champagne	1962	12.00
GUSTO			
❑ 116	That Heart Belongs to Me/With Jenny on My Mind	1974	6.00
❑ 119	Work Things Out with Annie/With Jenny on My Mind	1974	6.00
KAPP			
❑ 708	I'm the Man/Have This Love on Me	1965	10.00
❑ 719	Jingle Bell Rock/The Bell That Couldn't Jingle	1965	12.00
❑ 732	Those Snowy Glowy Blowy Days of Winter/Sailor	1965	10.00
❑ 777	The Things I Remember Most/Sorry, My Name Isn't Fred	1966	10.00
❑ 876	I Miss My Fraulein/Where Does a Shadow Go	1967	8.00
LITTLE DARLIN'			
❑ 0030	He Thought He'd Die Laughing/You'd Better Make Up Your Mind	1967	10.00
❑ 0034	The Day You Stop Loving Me/You Can Tell the World	1967	10.00
❑ 0038	Jingle Bell Rock/I Wanta Go to Santa Claus Land	1967	12.00
❑ 0041	I Feel You, I Love You/The Day You Stop Loving Me	1968	10.00
❑ 0049	Or Is It Love/Touch My Heart	1968	10.00
❑ 0054	My Special Angel/Expressing My Love	1968	10.00
❑ 0062	So Long/Just Do the Best You Can	1969	10.00
❑ 0073	Echoes and Shadows/Step Into My Soul	1969	10.00
❑ 7801	I'm Gonna Love the Devil Out of You/I Can't Promise You	1978	6.00
❑ 7807	The Things I Remember Most/I'm Not Sorry	1978	6.00
❑ 7809	Jingle Bell Rock/I Wanta Go to Santa Claus Land	1978	6.00
❑ 7916	One More Dollar for the Band/Touch My Heart	1979	6.00
MCA			
❑ 65026	Jingle Bell Rock/Captain Santa Claus	1973	5.00
—Black label with rainbow			
❑ 65026	Jingle Bell Rock/Captain Santa Claus	1980	3.00
—Blue label with rainbow			
❑ 65029	Jingle Bell Rock/The Bell That Couldn't Jingle	1973	5.00
—Black label with rainbow; this contains the 1965 Kapp re-recording of the A-side			
❑ 65029	Jingle Bell Rock/The Bell That Couldn't Jingle	1980	3.00
—Blue label with rainbow			
MILLION			
❑ 5	It's the Little Things/Love's Sweet Mystery	1972	7.00
❑ 22	It's Starting to Rain Again/Wouldn't Give Up on You	1972	7.00
MISTLETOE			
❑ 802	Jingle Bell Rock/Jingle Bells	197?	5.00
❑ 802 [PS]	Jingle Bell Rock/Jingle Bells	197?	8.00
PLAYBACK			
❑ 1305	Lay Me Down Look/Dance with Me	1988	6.00
❑ 1322	Somebody Wrong Is Looking Right/This Song for You	1988	6.00
❑ 1328	Southern Belle/Troubles Wall to Wall	1989	6.00
❑ 75709	Southern Belle/Troubles Wall to Wall	1989	5.00
SPEED			
❑ 45-114	Yesterday's Lovin'/Hanging Around	1957	30.00
❑ 45-117	Freedom Lovin' Guy/I've Never Seen Anyone	1957	30.00
7-Inch Extended Plays			
DECCA			
❑ ED 2555	If Only I Knew/Far Away Heart//My Shoes Keep Walking Back to You/Sugar Moon	1957	20.00

Number	Title (A Side/B Side)	Yr	NM
❑ ED 2555 [PS]	(title unknown)	1957	20.00
❑ ED 2586	Plaything/Magic Song// Tonight's the Night/Just a Little Lonesome	1957	20.00
❑ ED 2586 [PS]	Tonight's the Night	1957	20.00
❑ ED 2629	Jacqueline/My Special Angel// Borrowed Dreams/ Schoolboy Crush	1957	20.00
❑ ED 2629 [PS]	Bobby Helms	1957	20.00
Albums			
COLUMBIA			
❑ CL 2060 [M]	The Best of Bobby Helms	1963	25.00
❑ CS 8860 [S]	The Best of Bobby Helms	1963	30.00
DECCA			
❑ DL 8638 [M]	Bobby Helms Sings to My Special Angel	1957	120.00
HARMONY			
❑ HL 7409 [M]	Fraulein	1967	12.00
❑ HS 11209 [S]	Fraulein	1967	12.00
KAPP			
❑ KL 1463 [M]	I'm the Man	1966	15.00
❑ KL 1505 [M]	Sorry My Name Isn't Fred	1966	15.00
❑ KS 3463 [S]	I'm the Man	1966	20.00
❑ KS 3505 [S]	Sorry My Name Isn't Fred	1966	20.00
LITTLE DARLIN'			
❑ 8088	All New Just for You	1968	25.00
MISTLETOE			
❑ MLP-1206	Jingle Bell Rock	197?	12.00
POWER PAK			
❑ 283	Greatest Hits	197?	10.00
VOCALION			
❑ VL 3743 [M]	Someone Already There	1965	15.00
❑ VL 73743 [R]	Someone Already There	1965	12.00
❑ VL 73874	My Special Angel	1969	12.00

HELMS, DON

Number	Title (A Side/B Side)	Yr	NM
45s			
SMASH			
❑ 1781	Fire Ball Mail/I Can't Help It (If I'm Still in Love with You)	1962	20.00
Albums			
SMASH			
❑ MGS-27001 [M]	The Steel Guitar Sounds of Hank Williams	1962	20.00
❑ MGS-27019 [M]	Don Helms' Steel Guitar	1962	20.00
❑ SRS-67001 [S]	The Steel Guitar Sounds of Hank Williams	1962	25.00
❑ SRS-67019 [S]	Don Helms' Steel Guitar	1962	25.00

HELMS, JIMMY

Number	Title (A Side/B Side)	Yr	NM
45s			
CAPITOL			
❑ 3003	The Only Thing That Matters/ Just Hold My Hand and Sing	1970	20.00

HELP

Number	Title (A Side/B Side)	Yr	NM
45s			
DECCA			
❑ 32879	Good Time Music/Hold On Child	1971	12.00
Albums			
DECCA			
❑ DL 75257	Help	1970	30.00
❑ DL 75304	Second Coming	1971	30.00

HEMLOCKS, THE

Number	Title (A Side/B Side)	Yr	NM
45s			
FURY			
❑ 1004	Cora Lee/Joys of Love	1957	100.00
LOST-NITE			
❑ 361	Cora Lee/Joys of Love	197?	5.00
—Reissue			

HENDERSON, JOE

Number	Title (A Side/B Side)	Yr	NM
45s			
FONTANA			
❑ 1638	Help Yourself/A Man Without Love	1969	6.00
❑ 1658	Don't Forget to Catch Me/ Please Don't Go	1969	6.00
KAPP			
❑ 590	If We Could Start All Over/You Take One Step, I'll Take Two	1964	10.00
RIC			
❑ 141	I Ain't Never/The River or the Railroad Track	1964	15.00
❑ 149	Honey on My Lips/Like a Child	1965	8.00
❑ 181	Sweet Lovin' Baby/Too Much to Lose	1966	8.00
TODD			
❑ 1066	Baby Don't Leave Me/Right Now	1961	15.00
❑ 1072	Snap Your Fingers/ If You See Me Cry	1962	15.00
❑ 1077	Big Love/After Loving You	1962	12.00
❑ 1079	Three Steps/The Searching Is Over	1962	20.00
❑ 1082	Cause We're in Love/ Sad Teardrops at Dawn	1963	12.00
❑ 1083	You Can't Lose/All Day Every Day	1963	12.00
❑ 1085	Love Me Sweet/My Hands Are Tied	1963	12.00
❑ 1091	Lovin' Part Time/Blues for a Four-String Guitar	1963	12.00
❑ 1096	If We Could Start All Over/You Take One Step, I'll Take Two	1964	12.00
Albums			
FONTANA			
❑ SRF-67590	Hits, Hits, Hits!	1969	30.00
TODD			
❑ MT-2701 [M]	Snap Your Fingers	1962	50.00
❑ ST-2701 [S]	Snap Your Fingers	1962	70.00

Jimi Hendrix, "...and a Happy New Year," Reprise PRO 595, 1974, **$80.**

HENDRICKS, BOBBY

Number	Title (A Side/B Side)	Yr	NM
45s			
MERCURY			
❑ 71788	Happy Hearts/Pleasing You	1961	12.00
❑ 71810	Good Lovin'/Honey Crisp	1961	12.00
❑ 71881	I'm Comin' Home/ Every Other Night	1961	12.00
MGM			
❑ 13179	Let's Get It Over/Love in My Heart	1963	100.00
SUE			
❑ 706	Itchy Twitchy Feeling/ A Thousand Dreams	1958	30.00
❑ 708	Dreamy Eyes/Molly Be Good	1958	20.00
❑ 710	Cast Your Vote/It's Misery	1959	20.00
❑ 712	I'm a Big Boy Now/Good Things Will Come	1959	20.00
❑ 717	Little John Green/Sincerely, Your Lover	1959	20.00
❑ 727	City of Angels/If I Just Had Your Love	1960	20.00
❑ 732	Psycho/Too Good to Be True	1960	20.00
UNITED ARTISTS			
❑ 0142	Itchy Twitchy Feeling/Psycho	1973	4.00
—"Silver Spotlight Series" reissue			

HENDRIX, AL

Number	Title (A Side/B Side)	Yr	NM
45s			
ABC-PARAMOUNT			
❑ 9901	Rhonda Lee/Go, Daddy. Rock	1958	25.00
LEGREE			
❑ 701	Young and Wild/I Need You	1960	120.00
TALLY			
❑ 119	Rhonda Lee/Go, Daddy Rock	1957	80.00

HENDRIX, JIMI The albums list includes many posthumous "cash-in" records of early material.

Number	Title (A Side/B Side)	Yr	NM
12-Inch Singles			
CAPITOL			
❑ SPRO 11284 [DJ]	Star Spangled Banner (same on both sides)	199?	100.00
—Promo only, blue vinyl with eight star-shaped holes in outer part of record			
45s			
AUDIO FIDELITY			
❑ 167	No Such Animal (Part 1)/ No Such Animal (Part 2)	1970	15.00
❑ 167 [PS]	No Such Animal (Part 1)/ No Such Animal (Part 2)	1970	40.00
EXPERIENCE HENDRIX			
❑ RTH-1007	The Jimi Hendrix Classic Singles Collection	1998	60.00
—Boxed set of 10 45s, each with picture sleeves and white sleeve, with booklet			
❑ 5651-7	Little Drummer Boy-Auld Lang Syne/Three Little Bears	1999	15.00
—Red vinyl, small hole			

Number	Title (A Side/B Side)	Yr	NM
❑ 5651-7	Little Drummer Boy-Auld Lang Syne/Three Little Bears	2001	5.00
—Green vinyl, small hole; reissue			
❑ 5651-7 [PS]	Little Drummer Boy-Auld Lang Syne/Three Little Bears	1999	5.00
—The same sleeve appears on both pressings of the single			
❑ 13487 [DJ]	Star Spangled Banner/ Purple Haze	1999	15.00
—Promo-only picture disc			

MCA

Number	Title (A Side/B Side)	Yr	NM
❑ 55336 [DJ]	Dolly Dagger/Night Bird Flying	1997	10.00
—Promo only on purple vinyl			
❑ 55336 [PS]	Dolly Dagger/Night Bird Flying	1997	10.00
❑ 55454 [DJ]	Can You Please Crawl Out Your Window?/Burning of the Midnight Lamp	1998	5.00
—Promo only on orange vinyl			
❑ 55454 [PS]	Can You Please Crawl Out Your Window?/Burning of the Midnight Lamp	1998	5.00
—Cardboard sleeve			

H

REPRISE

Number	Title (A Side/B Side)	Yr	NM
❑ 0572	Hey Joe/51st Anniversary	1967	100.00
❑ 0572 [PS]	Hey Joe/51st Anniversary	1967	1000.
❑ PRO 595 [DJ]	Medley: The Little Drummer Boy-Silent Night/Auld Lang Syne	1974	150.00
❑ PRO 595 [PS]	...And a Happy New Year	1974	80.00
❑ 0597	Purple Haze/The Wind Cries Mary	1967	25.00
❑ 0641	Foxey Lady/Hey Joe	1967	25.00
❑ 0665	Up from the Skies/ One Rainy Wish	1968	30.00
❑ 0728	Purple Haze/Foxey Lady	1968	15.00
—"Back to Back Hits" series — originals have both "r:" and "W7" logos			
❑ 0742	All Along the Watchtower/ Crosstown Traffic	1971	6.00
—"Back to Back Hits" series			
❑ 0767	All Along the Watchtower/ Burning of the Midnight Lamp	1968	30.00
❑ 0792	Crosstown Traffic/Gypsy Eyes	1968	30.00
❑ 0853	If 6 Was 9/Stone Free	1969	40.00
❑ 0905	Stepping Stone/Izabella	1970	100.00
—As "Hendrix Band of Gypsys"			
❑ 1000	Freedom/Angel	1971	15.00
❑ 1044	Dolly Dagger/Star Spangled Banner	1971	15.00
❑ 1082	Johnny B. Goode/Lover Man	1972	15.00
❑ 1118	The Wind Cries Mary/Little Wing	1972	15.00
❑ EP 2239	Gloria (B-side blank)	1979	5.00
❑ EP 2239 [PS]	Gloria (B-side blank)	1979	5.00
—Above was a bonus record in "The Essential Jimi Hendrix, Vol. 2"			
❑ 29845	Fire/Little Wing	1982	6.00

TRIP

Number	Title (A Side/B Side)	Yr	NM
❑ 3002	Hot Trigger/Suspicious	1972	5.00

Albums

ACCORD

Number	Title	Yr	NM
❑ SN-7101	Kaleidoscope	1981	10.00
❑ SN-7112	Before London	1981	10.00
❑ SN-7139	Cosmic Feeling	1981	10.00

CAPITOL

Number	Title	Yr	NM
❑ STAO-472	Band of Gypsys	1970	20.00
❑ SWBB-659 [(2)]	Get That Feeling/Flashing	1971	25.00
❑ ST 2856 [S]	Get That Feeling	1967	40.00
❑ T 2856 [M]	Get That Feeling	1967	80.00
❑ ST 2894 [S]	Flashing	1968	40.00
❑ T 2894 [M]	Flashing	1968	100.00
❑ SJ-12416	Band of Gypsys 2	1986	10.00
—Side 2 lists, and plays, three songs			
❑ SJ-12416	Band of Gypsys 2	1986	15.00
—Side 2 lists three songs, but plays four completely different songs. Four bands are visible on the record.			
❑ MLP-15022 [EP]	Johnny B. Goode	1986	8.00
❑ SN-16319	Band of Gypsys	1985	10.00
—Budget-line reissue			
❑ C1-96414	Band of Gypsys	1995	15.00
—Numbered reissue			

EXPERIENCE HENDRIX/CAPITOL

Number	Title	Yr	NM
❑ ST-472	Band of Gypsys	1997	25.00
—Limited edition on "heavy vinyl" with booklet; distributed by Classic Records			

EXPERIENCE HENDRIX/CLASSIC

Number	Title	Yr	NM
❑ B0000698-01 [(2)]	Martin Scorsese Presents the Blues: Jimi Hendrix	2004	40.00
—Regular edition on black vinyl			
❑ B0000698-01 [(2)]	Martin Scorsese Presents the Blues: Jimi Hendrix	2004	50.00
—Limited edition of 1,000 on blue vinyl			
❑ RTH 2006 [(2)]	Blues	2002	60.00
—Limited edition on 200-gram blue vinyl			
❑ RTH 2006 [(2)]	Blues	2003	40.00
—Limited edition on 200-gram black vinyl			
❑ RTH-2016 [(4)]	Voodoo Child: The Jimi Hendrix Collection	2005	40.00
—Box set; red vinyl			
❑ RTH-2016 [(4)]	Voodoo Child: The Jimi Hendrix Collection	2005	80.00
—Black 200-gram vinyl			

EXPERIENCE HENDRIX/MCA

Number	Title	Yr	NM
❑ B0001159-01 [(2)]	Live at Berkeley	2003	25.00
❑ 11599 [(2)]	First Rays of the New Rising Sun	1997	50.00
—Limited edition on "heavy vinyl" with booklet			
❑ 11600 [(2)]	Electric Ladyland	1997	40.00
—Limited edition on "heavy vinyl" with booklet			
❑ 11601	Axis: Bold As Love	1997	50.00
—Limited edition on "heavy vinyl" with booklet			
❑ 11602 [(2)]	Are You Experienced?	1997	50.00
—Limited edition on "heavy vinyl" with booklet			
❑ 11607	Band of Gypsys	1997	25.00
—Limited edition on "heavy vinyl" with booklet; pressed in U.S. for export to Europe			
❑ 11608	Are You Experienced?	1997	40.00
—Limited edition on "heavy vinyl" with booklet; pressed in U.S. for export to Europe; has different cover than US version			
❑ 11671 [(2)]	Experience Hendrix: The Best of Jimi Hendrix	1998	25.00
—Despite lower number, was released after South Saturn Delta			
❑ 11684 [(2)]	South Saturn Delta	1997	25.00
—Numbered, limited edition on "heavy vinyl"			
❑ 11742 [(3)]	BBC Sessions	1998	30.00
❑ 11931 [(3)]	Live at the Fillmore East	1999	30.00
❑ 11987 [(3)]	Live at Woodstock	1999	40.00
❑ 112316 [(8)]	The Jimi Hendrix Experience	2000	100.00
—Limited edition of 5,000 in purple felt box			
❑ 112984	Smash Hits	2002	15.00
—Limited edition on "heavy vinyl"			
❑ 113086-1 [(3)]	Blue Wild Angel: Jimi Hendrix Live at the Isle of Wight	2002	40.00
❑ 311987 [(3)]	Live at Woodstock	2009	40.00

EXPERIENCE HENDRIX/UME

Number	Title	Yr	NM
❑ B0009845-01	The Jimi Hendrix Experience Live at Monterey	2007	15.00

NUTMEG

Number	Title	Yr	NM
❑ 1001	High, Live 'N' Dirty	1978	25.00
—Black vinyl			
❑ 1001	High, Live 'N' Dirty	1978	25.00
—Red vinyl			
❑ 1002	Cosmic Turnaround	1981	12.00

PHOENIX 10

Number	Title	Yr	NM
❑ PHX 320	Rare Hendrix	1981	8.00
❑ PHX 324	Roots of Hendrix	1981	8.00

PICKWICK

Number	Title	Yr	NM
❑ SPC-3528	Jimi	197?	10.00

REPRISE

Number	Title	Yr	NM
❑ MS 2025	Smash Hits	1969	40.00
—With "W7" and "r:" logos on two-tone orange label			
❑ MS 2025	Smash Hits Bonus Poster	1969	40.00
❑ MS 2025	Smash Hits	1970	12.00
—With only "r:" logo on all-orange (tan) label			
❑ MS 2025	Smash Hits	198?	8.00
—Red and black label or gold and light blue label			
❑ MS 2029	Historic Performances As Recorded at the Monterey International Pop Festival	1970	20.00
—Side 1: Jimi Hendrix; Side 2: Otis Redding; with only "r:" logo on all-orange (tan) label			
❑ MS 2029	Historic Performances As Recorded at the Monterey International Pop Festival	1970	200.00
—Side 1: Jimi Hendrix; Side 2: Otis Redding; with "W7" and "r:" logos on two-tone orange label			
❑ MS 2034	The Cry of Love	1971	15.00
—With only "r:" logo on all-orange (tan) label			
❑ MS 2034	The Cry of Love	1971	500.00
—With "W7" and "r:" logos on two-tone orange label			
❑ MS 2040	Rainbow Bridge	1971	20.00
❑ MS 2049	Hendrix in the West	1972	20.00
❑ MS 2103	War Heroes	1972	20.00
❑ MS 2204	Crash Landing	1975	15.00
❑ MS 2229	Midnight Lightning	1975	15.00
❑ 2RS 2245 [(2)]	The Essential Jimi Hendrix	1978	20.00
❑ MSK 2276	Smash Hits	1977	10.00
—Reissue			
❑ HS 2293	The Essential Jimi Hendrix Vol. Two	1979	15.00
—Add 100% if bonus single of "Gloria" with picture sleeve is enclosed			
❑ HS 2299	Nine to the Universe	1980	10.00
❑ R 6261 [M]	Are You Experienced?	1967	200.00
❑ RS 6261 [S]	Are You Experienced?	1967	50.00
—Pink, gold and green label			
❑ RS 6261 [S]	Are You Experienced?	1968	25.00
—With "W7" and "r:" logos on two-tone orange label			
❑ RS 6261 [S]	Are You Experienced?	1970	12.00
—With only "r:" logo on all-orange (tan) label			
❑ RS 6261 [S]	Are You Experienced?	198?	8.00
—Red and black label or gold and light blue label			
❑ R 6281 [M]	Axis: Bold As Love	1968	2500.
❑ RS 6281 [S]	Axis: Bold As Love	1968	25.00
—With "W7" and "r:" logos on two-tone orange label			
❑ RS 6281 [S]	Axis: Bold As Love	1968	80.00
—Pink, gold and green label			
❑ RS 6281 [S]	Axis: Bold As Love	1970	12.00
—With only "r:" logo on all-orange (tan) label			
❑ RS 6281 [S]	Axis: Bold As Love	198?	8.00
—Red and black label or gold and light blue label			
❑ 2R 6307 [(2)M]	Electric Ladyland	1968	4000.
—Mono is promo only; VG value 2000; VG+ value 3000			
❑ 2RS 6307 [(2)S]	Electric Ladyland	1968	100.00
—With "W7" and "r:" logos on two-tone orange label			
❑ 2RS 6307 [(2)S]	Electric Ladyland	1970	15.00
—With only "r:" logo on all-orange (tan) label			
❑ 2RS 6307 [(2)S]	Electric Ladyland	198?	12.00
—Red and black label or gold and light blue label			
❑ 2RS 6481 [(2)]	Soundtrack Recordings from the Film Jimi Hendrix	1973	25.00
❑ 22306 [(2)]	The Jimi Hendrix Concerts	1982	12.00
❑ 25119	Kiss the Sky	1984	10.00
❑ 25358	Jimi Plays Monterey	1986	10.00
❑ SKAO-91441	Axis: Bold As Love	1968	40.00
—Capitol Record Club edition; two-tone orange label with "W7" and "r:" at top			
❑ STBO-91568 [(2)]	Electric Ladyland	1968	150.00
—Capitol Record Club edition			
❑ SMAS-93467	The Cry of Love	1971	60.00
—Capitol Record Club edition			
❑ SMAS-93972	Rainbow Bridge	1971	50.00
—Capitol Record Club edition			

RHINO

Number	Title	Yr	NM
❑ RNDF-254 [PD]	The Jimi Hendrix Interview	1982	25.00

RYKO ANALOGUE

Number	Title	Yr	NM
❑ RALP-0038 [(2)]	Live at Winterland	1988	25.00
❑ RALP-0078 [(2)]	Radio One	1988	25.00
—Clear vinyl			

SPRINGBOARD

Number	Title	Yr	NM
❑ SPB-4010	Jimi Hendrix	197?	10.00

TRACK

Number	Title	Yr	NM
❑ 612003 [M]	Axis: Bold As Love	2000	25.00
—Classic Records issue of the original U.K. mono mix, on a reproduction of the original British label			

TRIP

Number	Title	Yr	NM
❑ 3509 [(2)]	Superpak	197?	15.00
❑ TLP-9500	Rare Hendrix	1972	15.00
❑ TLP-9501	Roots of Hendrix	1972	12.00
❑ TLP-9512	Moods	1973	12.00
❑ TLP-9523	The Genius of Jimi Hendrix	1973	12.00

UNITED ARTISTS

Number	Title	Yr	NM
❑ UA-LA505-E	The Very Best of Jimi Hendrix	1975	12.00

WARNER BROS.

Number	Title	Yr	NM
❑ HS 2299	Nine to the Universe	1980	15.00
—Reprise cover, Warner Bros. tan "pinstripe" label; possibly Columbia House edition?			

HENDRIX, JIMI, AND LITTLE RICHARD

Also see each artist's individual listings.

45s

ALA

Number	Title (A Side/B Side)	Yr	NM
❑ 1175	Goodnight Irene/Why Don't You Love Me	1972	8.00

Albums

EVEREST ARCHIVE OF FOLK & JAZZ

Number	Title	Yr	NM
❑ 296	Roots of Rock	1974	12.00

PICKWICK

Number	Title	Yr	NM
❑ SPC-3347	Jimi Hendrix and Little Richard Together	1973	12.00

HENDRIX, JIMI, AND LONNIE YOUNGBLOOD

Albums

MAPLE

Number	Title	Yr	NM
❑ 6004	Two Great Experiences Together	1971	50.00

HENRY, CLARENCE

45s

ARGO

Number	Title (A Side/B Side)	Yr	NM
❑ 5259	Ain't Got No Home/ Troubles, Troubles	1956	20.00
❑ 5266	I'm a Country Boy/Lonely Tramp	1957	16.00
❑ 5273	I Found a Home/ It Won't Be Long	1957	16.00
❑ 5305	I'm in Love/Baby Baby Please	1958	16.00
❑ 5378	But I Do/Just My Baby and Me	1960	16.00
—A-side: Same song, new title			
❑ 5378	I Don't Know Why/Just My Baby and Me	1960	20.00
❑ 5388	You Always Hurt the One You Love/Little Suzy	1961	16.00
❑ 5395	Lonely Street/Why Can't You	1961	15.00
❑ 5401	On Bended Knees/Standing in the Need of Love	1961	15.00
❑ 5408	A Little Too Much/I Wish I Could Stay the Same	1962	12.00

Except when noted otherwise, VG = 25% of NM, and VG+ = 50% of NM. (Example: VG = $2.00, VG+ = $4.00 and NM = $8.00.)

Number	Title (A Side/B Side)	Yr	NM
❑ 5414	Dream Myself a Sweetheart/ Lost Without You	1962	12.00
❑ 5426	Jealous Kind/Come On and Dance	1962	12.00
❑ 5448	If I Didn't Care/It Takes Two to Tango	1963	12.00
❑ 5480	Looking Back/Long Lost and Worried	1964	10.00
CADET			
❑ 5259	Ain't Got No Home/ Troubles, Troubles	1966	8.00
DIAL			
❑ 4057	This Time/Hummin' a Heartache	1967	6.00
❑ 4072	Shake Your Money Maker/ That's When I Guessed	1968	6.00
PARROT			
❑ 45004	Have You Ever Been Lonely/ Little Green Frog	1964	10.00
❑ 45009	I Told My Pillow/Can't Hide My Tear	1964	10.00
❑ 45015	I Might As Well/Tore Up Over You	1965	10.00
Albums			
ARGO			
❑ LP-4009 [M]	You Always Hurt the One You Love	1961	150.00
CADET			
❑ LP-4009 [M]	You Always Hurt the One You Love	1966	50.00
—Includes copies of Cadet LP in Argo sleeves			
ROULETTE			
❑ SR 42039	Alive and Well and Living in New Orleans	1969	25.00

HENRY, EARL

Number	Title (A Side/B Side)	Yr	NM
45s			
DOT			
❑ 15756	Whatcha Gonna Do?/ I Am the Man	1958	50.00
❑ 15875	My Suzanne/Believe a Traveler	1958	30.00

HENRY, THOMAS

Number	Title (A Side/B Side)	Yr	NM
45s			
HIT			
❑ 73	So Much in Love/No One	1963	8.00
—B-side by Leroy Jones			
❑ 103	Um, Um, Um, Um, Um, Um/ For You	1964	8.00
—B-side by Ed Hardin			

HENRY TREE

Number	Title (A Side/B Side)	Yr	NM
45s			
MAINSTREAM			
❑ 729	Penfield Town/(B-side unknown)	1970	12.00
Albums			
MAINSTREAM			
❑ S-6129	Electric Holy Man	1968	30.00

HENSLEE, GENE

Number	Title (A Side/B Side)	Yr	NM
45s			
IMPERIAL			
❑ 8227	Diggin' and Datin'/A Girl Named Haertbreak	1954	70.00
❑ 8260	Naughty and Nice/Try As I May	1954	60.00
❑ 8277	Rockin' Baby/What Will I Do	1954	60.00
MEL-O-DY			
❑ 110	Beautiful Women/Shambles	1963	20.00
UNITED ARTISTS			
❑ 946	I Don't Wanna Go Home/ Shambles	1964	15.00

HENSLEY, KEN

Also see URIAH HEEP; BLACKFOOT.

Number	Title (A Side/B Side)	Yr	NM
45s			
MERCURY			
❑ 73410	When Evening Comes/Fortune	1973	5.00
Albums			
MERCURY			
❑ SRM-1-661	Proud Words on a Dusty Shelf	1973	12.00
WARNER BROS.			
❑ BS 2863	Eager to Please	1975	10.00

HENSON, JIM

Number	Title (A Side/B Side)	Yr	NM
45s			
ATLANTIC			
❑ 3610	Rainbow Connection/I Hope That Somethin' Better Comes Along	1979	6.00
—As "Kermit (Jim Henson)"; B-side by "Kermit and Fozzie"			
❑ 3642	Movin' Right Along/Never Before, Never Again	1980	6.00
—As "Kermit and Fozzie Bear (Jim Henson)"			
COLUMBIA			
❑ 4-45207	Rubber Duckie/Sesame Street	1970	8.00
—As "Ernie (Jim Henson)"; B-side by "The Kids"			
❑ 4-45247	Up and Down/I Love Trash	1970	8.00
—As "Two Monsters (Jim Henson, Frank Oz)"; B-side by Carroll Spinney as "Oscar"			
SIGNATURE			
❑ 12023	Tick-Tock Sick/The Countryside	1960	50.00

HEP STARS, THE

With Benny Andersson, later of BJORN & BENNY and ABBA. Also see SVEN & CHARLOTTE.

Number	Title (A Side/B Side)	Yr	NM
45s			
CAMEO			
❑ 376	Cadillac/Farmer John	1965	40.00
CHARTMAKER			
❑ 414	It's Now Winter's Day/ Musty Dusty	1969	40.00
DUNHILL			
❑ 4040	Sunny Girl/No Response	1966	40.00

HEPSTERS, THE

Number	Title (A Side/B Side)	Yr	NM
45s			
RONEL			
❑ 107	Rockin' N' Rollin' with Santa Claus/I Hate To Let You Go	1955	400.00
❑ 110	I Gotta Sing the Blues/ This-a-Way	1956	300.00
XMAS			
❑ 3711	Rockin' & Rollin' With Santa Claus/Sleigh Bell Rock	19??	8.00
—B-side by Three Aces and a Joker; reissue of rare R&B sides			

HERALDS, THE

Number	Title (A Side/B Side)	Yr	NM
45s			
HERALD			
❑ 435	Eternal Love/Gonna Love You	1954	250.00

HERD, THE

PETER FRAMPTON was in this group.

Number	Title (A Side/B Side)	Yr	NM
45s			
FONTANA			
❑ 1588	I Can Fly/Understand Me	1967	10.00
❑ 1602	Sweet William/From the Underworld	1967	10.00
❑ 1610	Paradise Lost/Come On, Believe Me	1968	10.00
❑ 1618	I Don't Want Our Loving to Die/ Our Fairy Tale	1968	10.00
❑ 1646	The Game/Beauty Queen	1969	10.00
Albums			
FONTANA			
❑ SRF-67579	Lookin' Thru You	1968	25.00

HERMAN, WOODY

Number	Title (A Side/B Side)	Yr	NM
45s			
CADET			
❑ 5635	Light My Fire/Hush	1969	5.00
❑ 5643	Pontico/Keep On Keeping On	1969	5.00
❑ 5659	I Can't Get Next to You/ It's Your Thing	1969	5.00
❑ 5669	My Cherie Amour/The Hut	1970	5.00
CAPITOL			
❑ F1126	Music to Dance To/ I Want a Little Girl	1950	20.00
❑ F1170	Sonny Speaks/Pennies from Heaven	1950	20.00
❑ F1215	When It Rains It Pours/ Starlight Souvenirs	1950	15.00
❑ F1272	Johannesburg/Nearness	1950	15.00
❑ F1637	Lemon Drop/Early Autumn	1951	12.00
❑ F2942	Muskrat Ramble/ Woodchopper Mambo	1954	12.00
❑ F2960	Mexican Hat Trick/ Sleepy Serenade	1954	12.00
❑ F3042	Have It Your Way/My Sin Is You	1955	12.00
❑ F3087	Kiss the Baby/Long Long Night	1955	12.00
❑ F3173	You're Here My Love/ The Girl Upstairs	1955	12.00
❑ F3202	Love Is a Many-Splendored Thing/House of Bamboo	1955	12.00
❑ F3269	Skinned/Skinned Again	1955	12.00
❑ F3488	I Don't Want Nobody (To Have My Love But You)/ To Love Again	1956	12.00
COLUMBIA			
❑ 39409	Caldonia/(B-side unknown)	1951	12.00
❑ 39410	Happiness Is a Thing Called Joe/Bijou	1951	12.00
❑ 39411	Apple Honey/Wild Root	1951	12.00
❑ 39412	Northwest Passage/ (B-side unknown)	1951	12.00
—The above four comprise a box set			
❑ 43262	My Favorite Things/Do Anything You Wanna	1965	6.00
❑ 43449	Mardi Gras/Sting Ray	1965	6.00
❑ 43750	Sidewinder/Greasy Sack Blues	1966	6.00
❑ 44124	The Duck/Hallelujah, Baby!	1967	6.00
DECCA			
❑ 9-25079	Woodchopper's Ball/Indian Boogie Woogie	195?	20.00
—Black label, lines on either side of "Decca"			
FANTASY			
❑ 672	After Hours/(B-side unknown)	1972	4.00
❑ 695	Fat Mama/The Raven Speaks	1973	4.00
❑ 699	The First Thing I Do/ Freedom Jazz Dance	1973	4.00
❑ 723	Corazon/America Drinks and Goes Home	1974	4.00
MGM			
❑ 11661	Prelude to a Kiss/Cuban Holiday	1954	15.00
PHILIPS			
❑ 40003	Swing Low, Sweet Chariot/ Rose Room	1962	8.00
❑ 40064	Ramblin' Rose/What Kind of Fool Am I	1962	8.00
❑ 40125	Days of Wine and Roses/ Jazz Me Blues	1963	8.00
❑ 40187	Taste of Honey/Hallelujah Time	1964	8.00
❑ 40213	C'mon and Ska/Theme from Golden Boy	1964	8.00
VERVE			
❑ 10053	I Wonder/Like a House Built on a Strong Foundation	1957	10.00
❑ 10069	Makin' Whoopee/Comes Love	1957	10.00
7-Inch Extended Plays			
CAPITOL			
❑ EAP 2-658	Gina/I Remember Dixie// Captain Ahab	195?	15.00
❑ EAP 2-658 [PS]	Road Band! Part 2	195?	15.00
❑ EAP 2-748	Bass Face/Junior//Jumpin' at the Woodside	195?	12.00
❑ EAP 2-748 [PS]	Jackpot! Part 2	195?	12.00
COLUMBIA			
❑ B-2521	Caledonia/Bijou// Woodchopper's Ball/ Northwest Passage	195?	12.00
❑ B-2521 [PS]	Woody Herman (Hall of Fame Series)	195?	12.00
MARS			
❑ MREP-A3	Men from Mars/Mambo the Most	195?	25.00
❑ MREP-A3 [PS]	The Third Herd	195?	25.00
MGM			
❑ X1010	(contents unknown)	195?	15.00
❑ X1010 [PS]	New Golden Wedding	195?	15.00
❑ X1046	(contents unknown)	195?	15.00
❑ X1046 [PS]	Woody Herman and the Third Herd	195?	15.00
Albums			
ACCORD			
❑ SN-7185	All Star Session	1981	10.00
AMERICAN RECORDING SOCIETY			
❑ G-410 [M]	The Progressive Big Band Sound	1956	40.00
ATLANTIC			
❑ 1328 [M]	Woody Herman at the Monterey Jazz Festival	1960	40.00
❑ SD 1328 [S]	Woody Herman at the Monterey Jazz Festival	1960	30.00
❑ 90044	Woody Herman at the Monterey Jazz Festival	1982	10.00
—Reissue of 1328			
BRUNSWICK			
❑ BL 54024 [M]	The Swinging Herman Herd	1957	40.00
BULLDOG			
❑ 2005	20 Golden Pieces of Woody Herman	198?	10.00
CADET			
❑ LPS-819	Light My Fire	1969	12.00
❑ LPS-835	Heavy Exposure	1969	12.00
❑ LPS-845	Woody	1970	12.00
CAPITOL			
❑ H 324 [10]	Classics in Jazz	1952	70.00
❑ T 324 [M]	Classics in Jazz	1955	40.00
❑ T 560 [M]	The Woody Herman Band	1955	40.00
❑ T 658 [M]	Road Band	1955	40.00
❑ T 748 [M]	Jackpot!	1956	40.00
❑ T 784 [M]	Blues Groove	1956	40.00
❑ DT 1554 [R]	The Hits of Woody Herman	1961	12.00
❑ SM-1554	The Hits of Woody Herman	197?	8.00
❑ T 1554 [M]	The Hits of Woody Herman	1961	20.00
❑ M-11034	Early Autumn	1972	10.00
CENTURY			
❑ CRDD-1080	Road Father	1979	25.00
—Direct-to-disc recording			

H

Number	Title (A Side/B Side)	Yr	NM
❑ CR-1110	Chick, Donald, Walter and Woodrow	1978	12.00
CHESS			
❑ 402 [(2)]	Double Exposure	197?	15.00
CLEF			
❑ MGC-745 [M]	Jazz, the Utmost!	1956	80.00
COLUMBIA			
❑ C3L 25 [(3)M]	The Thundering Herds	1963	50.00
❑ CL 592 [M]	The Three Herds	1955	50.00
—Maroon label with gold print			
❑ CL 592 [M]	The Three Herds	1956	30.00
—Red and black label with six "eye" logos			
❑ CL 651 [M]	Music for Tired Lovers	1955	40.00
❑ CL 683 [M]	Twelve Shades of Blue	1956	30.00
❑ CL 2357 [M]	My Kind of Broadway	1965	12.00
❑ CL 2436 [M]	Woody's Winners	1965	12.00
❑ CL 2491 [M]	Woody Herman's Greatest Hits	1966	12.00
❑ CL 2509 [10]	Ridin' Herd	1955	60.00
❑ CL 2552 [M]	The Jazz S(w)inger	1966	12.00
❑ CL 2563 [10]	Woody!	1955	60.00
❑ CL 2693 [M]	Woody Live — East & West	1967	15.00
❑ CL 6026 [10]	Sequence in Jazz	1949	70.00
❑ CL 6049 [10]	Dance Parade	1949	70.00
❑ CL 6092 [10]	Woody Herman and His Woodchoppers	1950	70.00
❑ CS 9157 [S]	My Kind of Broadway	1965	15.00
❑ CS 9236 [S]	Woody's Winners	1965	15.00
❑ CS 9291 [S]	Woody Herman's Greatest Hits	1966	15.00
❑ PC 9291	Woody Herman's Greatest Hits	198?	8.00
—Reissue with new prefix			
❑ CS 9352 [S]	The Jazz S(w)inger	1966	15.00
❑ CS 9493 [S]	Woody Live — East & West	1967	12.00
❑ C 32530	Jazz Hoot	1974	12.00
CONCORD JAZZ			
❑ CJ-170	Woody Herman and Friends at the Monterey Jazz Festival 1979	198?	12.00
❑ CJ-191	Live at the Concord Jazz Festival	1982	12.00
❑ CJ-240	World Class	1983	12.00
❑ CJ-302	50th Anniversary Tour	1986	12.00
❑ CJ-330	Woody's Gold Star	1987	12.00
CORAL			
❑ CRL 56005 [10]	Blue Prelude	1950	70.00
❑ CRL 56010 [10]	Woody Herman Souvenirs	1950	70.00
❑ CRL 56090 [10]	Woody's Best	1953	70.00
CROWN			
❑ CST 205 [S]	The New Swingin' Herman Herd	1960	20.00
❑ CLP 5180 [M]	The New Swingin' Herman Band	1960	20.00
DECCA			
❑ DL 4484 [M]	Woody Herman's Golden Hits	1964	15.00
❑ DL 8133 [M]	Woodchopper's Ball	1955	40.00
❑ DL 9229 [M]	The Turning Point — 1943-44	1967	15.00
❑ DL 74484 [R]	Woody Herman's Golden Hits	1964	10.00
❑ DL 79229 [R]	The Turning Point — 1943-44	1967	10.00
DIAL			
❑ LP-210 [10]	Swinging with the Woodchoppers	1950	150.00
DISCOVERY			
❑ 815	The Third Herd	198?	10.00
❑ 845	The Third Herd, Vol. 2	198?	10.00
EVEREST			
❑ SDBR-1003 [S]	The Herd Rides Again… In Stereo	1958	40.00
❑ SDBR-1032 [S]	Moody Woody	1958	40.00
❑ EV-1222 [M]	The Best of Woody Herman	1963	15.00
❑ LPBR-5003 [M]	The Herd Rides Again	1958	30.00
❑ LPBR-5032 [M]	Moody Woody	1958	30.00
❑ EV-5222 [S]	The Best of Woody Herman	1963	20.00
EVEREST ARCHIVE OF FOLK & JAZZ			
❑ 281	Woody Herman	197?	10.00
❑ 316	Woody Herman, Vol. 2	197?	10.00
❑ 338	Woody Herman, Vol. 3	197?	10.00
FANTASY			
❑ OJC-344	Giant Steps	198?	10.00
—Reissue of 9432			
❑ FPM-4003 [Q]	Children of Lima	1975	20.00
❑ 8414	Brand New	1971	12.00
❑ 9416	The Raven Speaks	1972	12.00
❑ F-9432	Giant Steps	1973	12.00
❑ F-9452	The Thundering Herd	1973	12.00
❑ F-9470	The Herd at Montreux	1974	12.00
❑ F-9477	Children of Lima	1975	12.00
❑ F-9499	King Cobra	1976	12.00
❑ F-9609	Feelin' So Blue	1982	10.00
FORUM			
❑ F-9016 [M]	Woody Herman Sextet at the Round Table	196?	20.00
❑ FS-9016 [S]	Woody Herman Sextet at the Round Table	196?	25.00

Number	Title (A Side/B Side)	Yr	NM
HARMONY			
❑ HL 7013 [M]	Bijou	1957	20.00
❑ HL 7093 [M]	Summer Sequence	1957	20.00
HINDSIGHT			
❑ HSR-116	Woody Herman and His Orchestra 1937	198?	10.00
❑ HSR-134	Woody Herman and His Orchestra 1944	198?	10.00
INSIGHT			
❑ 208	Woody Herman and His Orchestra 1937-44	198?	10.00
JAZZLAND			
❑ JLP-17 [M]	The Fourth Herd	1960	25.00
❑ JLP-917 [S]	The Fourth Herd	1960	25.00
LION			
❑ L-70059 [M]	The Herman Herd at Carnegie Hall	1958	25.00
MARS			
❑ MRX-1 [10]	Dance Date on Mars	1952	250.00
❑ MRX-2 [10]	Woody Herman Goes Native	1953	250.00
MCA			
❑ 219	Golden Favorites	1973	10.00
❑ 4077 [(2)]	The Best of Woody Herman	197?	15.00
METRO			
❑ M-514 [M]	Woody Herman	1966	15.00
❑ MS-514 [R]	Woody Herman	1966	10.00
MGM			
❑ E-158 [10]	Woody Herman at Carnegie Hall, 1946, Vol. 1	1952	70.00
❑ E-159 [10]	Woody Herman at Carnegie Hall, 1946, Vol. 2	1952	70.00
❑ E-192 [10]	The Third Herd	1953	70.00
❑ E-284 [10]	Blue Flame	1955	70.00
❑ E-3043 [M]	Carnegie Hall 1946	1953	50.00
—Compiles 158 and 159 on one 12-inch LP			
❑ E-3385 [M]	Hi-Fi-ing Herd	1956	40.00
MOBILE FIDELITY			
❑ 1-219	The Fourth Herd	1994	30.00
—Audiophile vinyl			
PHILIPS			
❑ PHM 200004 [M]	Swing Low, Sweet Chariot	1962	15.00
❑ PHM 200065 [M]	Woody Herman 1963	1963	15.00
❑ PHM 200092 [M]	Encore: Woody Herman 1963	1963	15.00
❑ PHM 200118 [M]	Woody Herman: 1964	1964	15.00
❑ PHM 200131 [M]	The Swinging Herman Herd Recorded Live	1964	15.00
❑ PHM 200171 [M]	Woody's Big Band Goodies	1965	15.00
❑ PHS 600004 [S]	Swing Low, Sweet Chariot	1962	20.00
❑ PHS 600065 [S]	Woody Herman 1963	1963	20.00
❑ PHS 600092 [S]	Encore: Woody Herman 1963	1963	20.00
❑ PHS 600118 [S]	Woody Herman: 1964	1964	20.00
❑ PHS 600131 [S]	The Swinging Herman Herd Recorded Live	1964	20.00
❑ PHS 600171 [S]	Woody's Big Band Goodies	1965	20.00
PICCADILLY			
❑ 3333	It's Coolin' Time	198?	10.00
PICKWICK			
❑ SPC-3591	Blowin' Up a Storm	1978	10.00
RCA VICTOR			
❑ BGL2-2203 [(2)]	40th Anniversary Carnegie Hall Concert	1977	15.00
ROULETTE			
❑ R 25067 [M]	Woody Herman Sextet at the Round Table	1959	30.00
❑ SR 25067 [S]	Woody Herman Sextet at the Round Table	1959	40.00
SUNBEAM			
❑ 206	Woody Herman and His Orchestra 1936	198?	10.00
SUNSET			
❑ SUM-1139 [M]	Blowin' Up a Storm	1966	10.00
❑ SUS-5139 [S]	Blowin' Up a Storm	1966	12.00
TIME-LIFE			
❑ STBB-09 [(2)]	Big Bands: Woody Herman	1984	15.00
TRIP			
❑ 5547	Woody 1963	1974	10.00
VERVE			
❑ VSP-1 [M]	The First Herd at Carnegie Hall	1966	15.00
❑ VSPS-1 [R]	The First Herd at Carnegie Hall	1966	10.00
❑ VSP-26 [M]	Woody Herman's Woodchoppers & The First Herd Live at Carnegie Hall	1966	15.00
❑ VSPS-26 [R]	Woody Herman's Woodchoppers & The First Herd Live at Carnegie Hall	1966	10.00
❑ MGV-2030 [M]	Early Autumn	1957	40.00
❑ V-2030 [M]	Early Autumn	1963	15.00
❑ MGV-2069 [M]	Songs for Hip Lovers	1957	40.00
❑ V-2069 [M]	Songs for Hip Lovers	1963	15.00

Number	Title (A Side/B Side)	Yr	NM
❑ MGV-2096 [M]	Love Is the Sweetest Thing — Sometimes	1958	40.00
❑ V-2096 [M]	Love Is the Sweetest Thing — Sometimes	1963	15.00
❑ MGV-8014 [M]	Jazz, the Utmost!	1957	40.00
—Reissue of Clef LP			
❑ V-8014 [M]	Jazz, the Utmost!	1963	15.00
❑ MGV-8216 [M]	Men from Mars	1958	40.00
❑ MGV-8255 [M]	Woody Herman '58	1958	40.00
❑ V-8255 [M]	Woody Herman '58	1963	15.00
❑ V-8558 [M]	Hey! Heard the Herd?	1963	20.00
—Reissue of Verve 8216			
❑ V6-8558 [S]	Hey! Heard the Herd?	1963	15.00
❑ V6-8764	Concerto for Herd	1968	20.00
WHO'S WHO IN JAZZ			
❑ 21013	Lionel Hampton Presents Woody Herman	1979	12.00
WING			
❑ MGW-12329 [M]	Woody's Big Band Goodies	1966	10.00
❑ SRW-16329 [S]	Woody's Big Band Goodies	1966	12.00

HERMAN, WOODY/TITO PUENTE

Albums

Number	Title (A Side/B Side)	Yr	NM
EVEREST			
❑ SDBR-1010 [S]	Herman's Beat of Puente	1958	40.00
❑ LPBR-5010 [M]	Herman's Beat of Puente	1958	40.00

HERMAN'S HERMITS Also see PETER NOONE.

45s

Number	Title (A Side/B Side)	Yr	NM
ABKCO			
❑ 4021	Mrs. Brown You've Got a Lovely Daughter/I'm Henry VIII, I Am	1972	5.00
❑ 4022	I'm Into Something Good/Can't You Hear My Heartbeat	1972	5.00
❑ 4023	There's a Kind of Hush (All Over the World)/Wonderful World	1972	5.00
❑ 4024	Listen People/Dandy	1972	5.00
❑ 4042	Silhouettes/Just a Little Bit Better	1973	5.00
❑ 4043	A Must to Avoid/Leaning on the Lamp Post	1973	5.00
BUDDAH			
❑ 516	Lonely Situation (Love Is All I Need)/Blond Haired Blue Eyed Boy	1976	8.00
MGM			
❑ (no #) [PS]	Hold On	1966	250.00
—Promo-only sleeve similar to the LP cover of the same name; rear of sleeve has "The Mod Shirts Are Here" advertisement; this may have come with some promos of MGM 13500			
❑ 13280	I'm Into Something Good/Your Hand in Mine	1964	10.00
❑ 13310	Can't You Hear My Heartbeat/I Know Why	1964	10.00
❑ 13310 [PS]	Can't You Hear My Heartbeat/I Know Why	1964	15.00
❑ 13332	Silhouettes/Walkin' With My Angel	1965	10.00
❑ 13341	Mrs. Brown You've Got a Lovely Daughter/I Gotta Dream On	1965	10.00
❑ 13341 [PS]	Mrs. Brown You've Got a Lovely Daughter/I Gotta Dream On	1965	15.00
❑ 13354	Wonderful World/Traveling Light	1965	10.00
❑ 13354 [PS]	Wonderful World/Traveling Light	1965	15.00
❑ 13367	I'm Henry VIII, I Am/The End of the World	1965	10.00
❑ 13367 [PS]	I'm Henry VIII, I Am/The End of the World	1965	20.00
❑ 13398	Just a Little Bit Better/Sea Cruise	1965	10.00
❑ 13398 [PS]	Just a Little Bit Better/Sea Cruise	1965	15.00
❑ 13437	A Must to Avoid/The Man with the Cigar	1966	8.00
❑ 13462	Listen People/Got a Feeling	1966	8.00
❑ 13500	Leaning on the Lamp Post/Hold On	1966	8.00
❑ 13548	This Door Swings Both Ways/For Love	1966	8.00
❑ 13603	Dandy/My Reservation's Been Confirmed	1966	8.00
❑ 13603 [PS]	Dandy/My Reservation's Been Confirmed	1966	15.00
❑ 13639	East West/What Is Wrong What Is Right	1966	8.00
❑ 13681	There's a Kind of Hush/No Milk Today	1967	8.00
❑ 13681	There's a Kind of Hush (All Over the World)/No Milk Today	1967	10.00
❑ 13681 [PS]	There's a Kind of Hush/No Milk Today	1967	15.00
❑ 13761	Don't Go Out Into the Rain (You're Going to Melt)/Moonshine Man	1967	8.00
❑ 13761 [PS]	Don't Go Out Into the Rain (You're Going to Melt)/Moonshine Man	1967	15.00
❑ 13787	Museum/Last Bus Home	1967	8.00
❑ 13787 [PS]	Museum/Last Bus Home	1967	15.00

Except when noted otherwise, VG = 25% of NM, and VG+ = 50% of NM. (Example: VG = $2.00, VG+ = $4.00 and NM = $8.00.)

Number	Title (A Side/B Side)	Yr	NM
❑ 13885	I Can Take or Leave Your Loving/Marcel's	1967	8.00
❑ 13934	Sleepy Joe/Just One Girl	1968	8.00

—Blue and gold label

Number	Title (A Side/B Side)	Yr	NM
❑ 13934	Sleepy Joe/Just One Girl	1968	10.00

—Black label

Number	Title (A Side/B Side)	Yr	NM
❑ 13973	Sunshine Girl/Nobody Needs to Know	1968	10.00
❑ 13994	Ooh, She's Done It Again/The Most Beautiful Thing in My Life	1968	10.00
❑ 14035	Something's Happening/Little Miss Sorrow, Child of Tomorrow	1969	10.00
❑ 14060	My Lady/My Sentimental Friend	1969	10.00
❑ 14100	It's Alright Now/(Here Comes) The Star	1969	10.00

PRIVATE STOCK

Number	Title (A Side/B Side)	Yr	NM
❑ 45,019	Ginny Go Softly/Blond Haired, Blue Eyed Boy	1975	8.00

ROULETTE

Number	Title (A Side/B Side)	Yr	NM
❑ 7213	Truck Stop Mama/Heart Get Ready for Love	1977	15.00

Albums

ABKCO

Number	Title (A Side/B Side)	Yr	NM
❑ 4227-1	Their Greatest Hits	1988	8.00

—Abridged version of AB 4227

Number	Title (A Side/B Side)	Yr	NM
❑ AB-4227 [(2)]	XX (Greatest Hits)	1973	12.00

MGM

Number	Title (A Side/B Side)	Yr	NM
❑ E-4282 [M]	Introducing Herman's Hermits	1965	15.00

—Version 3: With "Including 'Mrs. Brown You've Got a Lovely Daughter'" on front cover

Number	Title (A Side/B Side)	Yr	NM
❑ E-4282 [M]	Introducing Herman's Hermits	1965	20.00

—Version 2: Same as above, but with a sticker that says "Featuring 'Mrs. Brown You Have a Lovely Daughter'."

Number	Title (A Side/B Side)	Yr	NM
❑ E-4282 [M]	Introducing Herman's Hermits	1965	25.00

—Version 1: With "Including Their Hit Single I'm Into Something Good'" on front cover

Number	Title (A Side/B Side)	Yr	NM
❑ SE-4282 [R]	Introducing Herman's Hermits	1965	10.00

—Version 3: With "Including 'Mrs. Brown You've Got a Lovely Daughter'" on front cover

Number	Title (A Side/B Side)	Yr	NM
❑ SE-4282 [R]	Introducing Herman's Hermits	1965	15.00

—Version 2: Same as above, but with a sticker that says "Featuring 'Mrs. Brown You Have a Lovely Daughter'."

Number	Title (A Side/B Side)	Yr	NM
❑ SE-4282 [R]	Introducing Herman's Hermits	1965	20.00

—Version 1: With "Including Their Hit Single 'I'm Into Something Good'" on front cover

Number	Title (A Side/B Side)	Yr	NM
❑ E-4295 [M]	Herman's Hermits On Tour	1965	12.00
❑ SE-4295 [R]	Herman's Hermits On Tour	1965	10.00
❑ E-4315 [M]	The Best of Herman's Hermits	1965	12.00
❑ SE-4315 [R]	The Best of Herman's Hermits	1965	10.00
❑ E-4342 [M]	Hold On!	1966	10.00
❑ SE-4342 [P]	Hold On!	1966	12.00
❑ E-4386 [M]	Both Sides of Herman's Hermits	1966	10.00
❑ SE-4386 [R]	Both Sides of Herman's Hermits	1966	8.00
❑ E-4416 [M]	The Best of Herman's Hermits, Vol. 2	1966	12.00

—Add 50% if bonus photo of Herman is included

Number	Title (A Side/B Side)	Yr	NM
❑ SE-4416 [P]	The Best of Herman's Hermits, Vol. 2	1966	10.00

—Add 50% if bonus photo of Herman is included. "Hold On" and "Leaning on the Lamp Post" are in true stereo.

Number	Title (A Side/B Side)	Yr	NM
❑ E-4438 [M]	There's a Kind of Hush All Over the World	1967	10.00
❑ SE-4438 [R]	There's a Kind of Hush All Over the World	1967	8.00
❑ E-4478 [M]	Blaze	1967	10.00
❑ SE-4478 [S]	Blaze	1967	10.00
❑ E-4505 [M]	The Best of Herman's Hermits, Vol. 3	1967	10.00
❑ SE-4505 [P]	The Best of Herman's Hermits, Vol. 3	1967	10.00

—"Don't Go Out Into the Rain," "Museum," "Last Bus Home" and "Mum and Dad" are in true stereo.

Number	Title (A Side/B Side)	Yr	NM
❑ SE-4548 [P]	Mrs. Brown You've Got a Lovely Daughter	1968	10.00

—"Mrs. Brown You've Got a Lovely Daughter" and "There's a Kind of Hush" are rechanneled

Number	Title (A Side/B Side)	Yr	NM
❑ ST-90416 [R]	Introducing Herman's Hermits	1965	20.00

—Capitol Record Club edition

Number	Title (A Side/B Side)	Yr	NM
❑ T-90416 [M]	Introducing Herman's Hermits	1965	25.00

—Capitol Record Club edition

Number	Title (A Side/B Side)	Yr	NM
❑ ST-90421 [R]	Herman's Hermits On Tour	1965	20.00

—Capitol Record Club edition

Number	Title (A Side/B Side)	Yr	NM
❑ T-90421 [M]	Herman's Hermits On Tour	1965	25.00

—Capitol Record Club edition

Number	Title (A Side/B Side)	Yr	NM
❑ KAO-90613 [M]	The Best of Herman's Hermits	1966	15.00

—Capitol Record Club edition

Number	Title (A Side/B Side)	Yr	NM
❑ ST-90646 [R]	Hold On!	1966	20.00

—Capitol Record Club edition

Number	Title (A Side/B Side)	Yr	NM
❑ T-90646 [M]	Hold On!	1966	25.00

—Capitol Record Club edition

Number	Title (A Side/B Side)	Yr	NM
❑ ST-91286 [S]	Blaze	1967	20.00

—Capitol Record Club edition

Number	Title (A Side/B Side)	Yr	NM
❑ T-91286 [M]	Blaze	1967	30.00

—Capitol Record Club edition

HERON, MIKE

45s

ELEKTRA

Number	Title (A Side/B Side)	Yr	NM
❑ 45739	Call Me Diamond/Brindaban	1971	8.00

Albums

ELEKTRA

Number	Title (A Side/B Side)	Yr	NM
❑ EKS-74093	Smiling Men with Bad Reputations	1971	20.00

HERROLD, DENNIS

45s

IMPERIAL

Number	Title (A Side/B Side)	Yr	NM
❑ 5482	Hip Hip Baby/Make with the Lovin'	1957	80.00

HESITATIONS, THE

45s

GWP

Number	Title (A Side/B Side)	Yr	NM
❑ 504	Is This the Way to Treat a Girl/Yes I'm Ready	1969	50.00

KAPP

Number	Title (A Side/B Side)	Yr	NM
❑ 790	Soul Superman/I'm Not Built That Way	1966	150.00
❑ 810	Soul Kind of Love/Wait a Minute	1967	100.00
❑ 822	I'll Be Right There/She Won't Come Back	1967	100.00
❑ 848	You Can't Bypass Love/You'll Never Know	1967	75.00
❑ 878	Born Free/Love Is Everywhere	1967	20.00
❑ 899	The Impossible Dream/Nobody Knows You When You're Down and Out	1968	10.00
❑ 911	Climb Every Mountain/My World	1968	15.00
❑ 926	Who Will Answer/If You Ever Need a Hand	1968	20.00
❑ 948	A Whiter Shade of Pale/With Pen in Hand	1968	10.00

Albums

KAPP

Number	Title (A Side/B Side)	Yr	NM
❑ KL-1525 [M]	Soul Superman	1967	30.00
❑ KS-3525 [S]	Soul Superman	1967	25.00
❑ KS-3548	The New Born Free	1968	25.00
❑ KS-3561	Where We're At	1968	25.00
❑ KS-3574	Solid Gold	1969	25.00

HESS, FRED

45s

HIT

Number	Title (A Side/B Side)	Yr	NM
❑ 206	Something's Happened/Goldfinger	1965	8.00

—B-side by Sherry Young

Number	Title (A Side/B Side)	Yr	NM
❑ 213	Count Me In/You're Not the Same Now	1965	8.00

HESTER, CAROLYN

45s

CAPITOL

Number	Title (A Side/B Side)	Yr	NM
❑ 4101	Come On Home and Sing the Blues to Mama/Don't Touch Me	1975	6.00

DOT

Number	Title (A Side/B Side)	Yr	NM
❑ 16660	Stay Not Late/That's My Song	1964	10.00
❑ 16717	Amapola/Momma's Tough Little Soldier	1965	10.00
❑ 16800	High Flyin' Bird/What Does It Get You	1965	10.00

METROMEDIA

Number	Title (A Side/B Side)	Yr	NM
❑ 120	Magic, Man/Big City Streets	1969	8.00

RCA VICTOR

Number	Title (A Side/B Side)	Yr	NM
❑ APBO-0008	You Made My Life a Song/Comin' On Back to You	1973	6.00

Albums

COLUMBIA

Number	Title (A Side/B Side)	Yr	NM
❑ CL 1796 [M]	Carolyn Hester	1962	60.00

—With Bob Dylan on harmonica on three tracks; black and red label with six "eye" logos

Number	Title (A Side/B Side)	Yr	NM
❑ CL 1796 [M]	Carolyn Hester	1963	20.00

—Red label with "Guaranteed High Fidelity"

Number	Title (A Side/B Side)	Yr	NM
❑ CL 2032 [M]	This Life I'm Living	1963	20.00
❑ CS 8596 [S]	Carolyn Hester	1962	80.00

—With Bob Dylan on harmonica on three tracks; black and red label with six "eye" logos

Number	Title (A Side/B Side)	Yr	NM
❑ CS 8596 [S]	Carolyn Hester	1963	25.00

—Red label, "360 Sound Stereo" in black

Number	Title (A Side/B Side)	Yr	NM
❑ CS 8832 [S]	This Life I'm Living	1963	25.00

CORAL

Number	Title (A Side/B Side)	Yr	NM
❑ CRL 57143 [M]	Scarlet Ribbons	1957	50.00

DOT

Number	Title (A Side/B Side)	Yr	NM
❑ DLP-3604 [M]	That's My Song	1964	15.00
❑ DLP-3638 [M]	Carolyn Hester at Town Hall One	1965	15.00
❑ DLP-3649 [M]	Carolyn Hester at Town Hall Two	1965	15.00
❑ DLP-25604 [S]	That's My Song	1964	20.00
❑ DLP-25638 [S]	Carolyn Hester at Town Hall One	1965	20.00
❑ DLP-25649 [S]	Carolyn Hester at Town Hall Two	1965	20.00

FOLK ODYSSEY

Number	Title (A Side/B Side)	Yr	NM
❑ 32160264	Simply Carolyn Hester	196?	20.00

METROMEDIA

Number	Title (A Side/B Side)	Yr	NM
❑ MD-1001	The Carolyn Hester Coalition	1969	20.00
❑ MD-1022	Magazine	1970	60.00

RCA VICTOR

Number	Title (A Side/B Side)	Yr	NM
❑ APD1-0086 [Q]	Carolyn Hester	1973	20.00

—Only released in quadraphonic

TRADITION

Number	Title (A Side/B Side)	Yr	NM
❑ TLP-1043 [M]	Carolyn Hester	1961	40.00

HESTER, DOT

45s

HIT

Number	Title (A Side/B Side)	Yr	NM
❑ 80	My Boyfriend's Back/The Monkey Time	1963	8.00

—B-side by Sammy Fox

HEWITT, BEN

45s

MERCURY

Number	Title (A Side/B Side)	Yr	NM
❑ 71413	You Break Me Up/I Ain't Givin' Up Nothin'	1959	100.00
❑ 71472	Patricia June/For Quite a While	1959	50.00
❑ 71577	My Search/I Want a New Girl Now	1960	40.00
❑ 71612	The Queen in the Kingdom/Whirlwind Blues	1960	40.00

HEYWOOD, EDDIE

Pianist on the Hugo Winterhalter hit single "Canadian Sunset."

45s

COLUMBIA

Number	Title (A Side/B Side)	Yr	NM
❑ 39316	Without a Song/A Pretty Girl Is Like a Melody	1951	10.00
❑ 39317	All the Things You Are/St. Louis Blues	1951	10.00
❑ 39318	Mighty Like a Rose/When Your Lover Has Gone	1951	10.00
❑ 39319	Try a Little Tenderness/The Birth of the Blues	1951	10.00

—The above four comprise a box set

DECCA

Number	Title (A Side/B Side)	Yr	NM
❑ 28549	Begin the Beguine/On the Sunny Side of the Street	1953	12.00
❑ 28893	The Moon Was Yellow/You Too, You Too	1953	12.00
❑ 30007	Jasmine/The Continental	1956	10.00

LIBERTY

Number	Title (A Side/B Side)	Yr	NM
❑ 55396	The Good Earth/Dream of Olwen	1961	8.00
❑ 55539	Harlem Blues/The Sidewalks of New York	1963	8.00
❑ 55575	Canadian Sunset Bossa Nova/The Good Life	1963	8.00

MERCURY

Number	Title (A Side/B Side)	Yr	NM
❑ 70645	Land of Dreams/Summer Holiday	1955	10.00
❑ 70677	Love for Love/Sunny Sunday	1955	10.00
❑ 70863	Soft Summer Breeze/Heywood's Bounce	1956	10.00
❑ 70950	Secret Love/Let's Fall in Love	1956	10.00
❑ 71014	Lover/If It's Sunny Sunday	1956	10.00
❑ 71462	Soft Summer Breeze/Castillian Rhapsody	1959	8.00
❑ 71504	High on a Windy Hill/Wings in Autumn	1959	8.00
❑ 71603	Out of Bounds/There You Are	1960	8.00
❑ 71650	(Love Theme) Rat Race/Everything in Manhattan	1960	8.00
❑ 71685	Jalousie/Cheek to Cheek	1960	8.00
❑ 71781	Velvet Rock/Mountains on the Moon	1961	8.00

RCA VICTOR

Number	Title (A Side/B Side)	Yr	NM
❑ 47-6674	Lost Love/Mozambique	1956	12.00
❑ 47-6816	Begin the Beguine/No Miracle Needed	1957	10.00
❑ 47-6956	Love Is All/Virgin Isle Vamp	1957	10.00
❑ 47-7058	Lies/All About You	1957	10.00
❑ 47-7262	Haiti Lady/It's Really Nothing	1957	10.00
❑ 47-7385	St. Louis Blues/Rendezvous	1958	10.00

20TH CENTURY FOX

Number	Title (A Side/B Side)	Yr	NM
❑ 453	Theme from "The Prize"/Li'l Darlin'	1963	8.00

7-Inch Extended Plays

DECCA

Number	Title (A Side/B Side)	Yr	NM
❑ ED 2032	Begin the Beguine/Laura//I Don't Know Why/Please Don't Talk About Me When I'm Gone	195?	12.00

H

Number	Title (A Side/B Side)	Yr	NM
❑ ED 2032 [PS]	Eddie Heywood, Vol. 1	195?	12.00
Albums			
BRUNSWICK			
❑ BL 58036 [10]	Eddie Heywood '45	1953	50.00
CAPITOL			
❑ ST-163	Soft Summer Breeze	1969	12.00
❑ ST 2833	With Love and Strings	1968	12.00
COLUMBIA			
❑ CL 6157 [10]	Piano Moods	1951	50.00
COMMODORE			
❑ XFL-15876	The Biggest Little Band of the Forties	198?	12.00
❑ FL-20007 [10]	Eight Selections	1950	75.00
CORAL			
❑ CRL 57095 [M]	Featuring Eddie Heywood	1957	40.00
DECCA			
❑ DL 8202 [M]	Lightly and Politely	1956	30.00
❑ DL 8270 [M]	Swing Low Sweet Heywood	1956	30.00
EMARCY			
❑ MG-36042 [M]	Eddie Heywood	1955	40.00
EPIC			
❑ LN 3327 [M]	Eddie Heywood at Twilight	1956	30.00
LIBERTY			
❑ LRP-3250 [M]	Eddie Heywood's Golden Encores	1962	12.00
❑ LRP-3279 [M]	Manhattan Beat	1963	12.00
❑ LRP-3313 [M]	Canadian Sunset Bossa Nova	1963	12.00
❑ LST-7250 [S]	Eddie Heywood's Golden Encores	1962	15.00
❑ LST-7279 [S]	Manhattan Beat	1963	15.00
❑ LST-7313 [S]	Canadian Sunset Bossa Nova	1963	15.00
MAINSTREAM			
❑ S-6001 [S]	Begin the Beguine	1964	15.00
❑ 96001 [M]	Begin the Beguine	1964	12.00
MERCURY			
❑ MG-20445 [M]	Breezin' Along with the Breeze	1959	20.00
❑ MG-20590 [M]	Eddie Heywood at the Piano	1960	20.00
❑ MG-20632 [M]	One for My Baby	1960	20.00
❑ SR-60115 [S]	Breezin' Along with the Breeze	1959	25.00
❑ SR-60248 [S]	Eddie Heywood at the Piano	1960	25.00
❑ SR-60632 [S]	One for My Baby	1960	25.00
MGM			
❑ E-135 [10]	It's Easy to Remember	1952	50.00
❑ E-3093 [M]	Pianorama	1955	40.00
❑ E-3260 [M]	Eddie Heywood	1956	40.00
RCA VICTOR			
❑ LPM-1466 [M]	The Touch of Eddie Heywood	1957	30.00
❑ LPM-1529 [M]	Canadian Sunset	1957	30.00
❑ LSP-1529 [S]	Canadian Sunset	1958	40.00
❑ LPM-1900 [M]	The Keys and I	1958	30.00
SUNSET			
❑ SUM-1121 [M]	An Affair to Remember	196?	12.00
❑ SUS-5121 [S]	An Affair to Remember	196?	12.00
VOCALION			
❑ VL 3748 [M]	The Piano Stylings of Eddie Heywood	1966	15.00
❑ VL 73748 [R]	The Piano Stylings of Eddie Heywood	1966	12.00
WING			
❑ MGW-12137 [M]	Eddie Heywood	196?	15.00
❑ MGW-12287 [M]	Breezin' Along	196?	15.00
❑ SRW-16137 [S]	Eddie Heywood	196?	12.00
❑ SRW-16287 [S]	Breezin' Along	196?	12.00

HI-FI'S, THE

Number	Title (A Side/B Side)	Yr	NM
45s			
CAMEO			
❑ 349	I Keep Forgettin'/Why Can't I Stop Loving You	1965	12.00
INTERPHON			
❑ 7701	Will Yer or Won't Yer/She's the One	1964	12.00
UNITED ARTISTS			
❑ 50160	I'm a Box/No Two Ways	1967	8.00

HI-FI-DELS, THE

Number	Title (A Side/B Side)	Yr	NM
45s			
ATLANTIC			
❑ 2121	Did I Cry/Tricky Tricky	1961	15.00

HI-FIVES, THE (1)

Number	Title (A Side/B Side)	Yr	NM
45s			
BELL			
❑ 634	Julie/Son of Raunchy	1965	40.00
JERDEN			
❑ 730	Goin' Away/Tort	1964	15.00

HI-FIVES, THE (2)

Number	Title (A Side/B Side)	Yr	NM
45s			
BINGO			
❑ 1006	Felicia/Windy City Special	1960	30.00
DECCA			
❑ 30576	My Friend/How Can I Win?	1958	40.00
❑ 30657	Dorothy/Just a Shoulder to Cry On	1958	50.00
❑ 30744	Lonely/What's New	1958	40.00

HI-LITERS, THE (1)

With King Bassie and His Three Aces...Ben Vereen was a member.

Number	Title (A Side/B Side)	Yr	NM
45s			
HICO			
❑ 2432	Let Me Be True to You/In the Night	1958	100.00
❑ 2433	Over the Rainbow/(B-side unknown)	1958	150.00

HI-LITERS, THE (U)

Probably not group (1), but we don't know if these are the same group or two different groups.

Number	Title (A Side/B Side)	Yr	NM
45s			
VEE JAY			
❑ 184	Bobby Sox Baby/Hello Dear	1956	1000.
WEN-DEE			
❑ 1927	Baby Don't Treat Me This Way/Route 66	1955	60.00

HI-LITES, THE (1)

For records on Daran, see THE CHI-LITES.

HI-LITES, THE (2)

Number	Title (A Side/B Side)	Yr	NM
45s			
JULIA			
❑ 1105	Gloria/For Your Precious Love	1962	120.00
MONOGRAM			
❑ 119	Everybody's Somebody's Fool/Moonlight	1976	8.00
❑ 120	Zoom Zoom Zoom/To the Aisle	1976	8.00
❑ 121	Pretty Face/Maybe You'll Be There	1976	8.00
RECORD FAIR			
❑ 500	I'm Falling in Love/Walking My Baby Back Home	1961	50.00
❑ 501	For Sentimental Reasons/For Your Precious Love	1962	50.00
Albums			
DANDEE			
❑ DLP-206 [M]	For Your Precious Love	1961	2000.

HI-LITES, THE (U)

None of these are group (1). Some could be group (2). The rest could be several more groups.

Number	Title (A Side/B Side)	Yr	NM
45s			
BRUNSWICK			
❑ 55102	Friday Night Go Go/Chicka-Rocka-Chee-Chi-Cho (Cha Cha)	1958	20.00
JET			
❑ 501	The Pony (Part 1)/The Pony (Part 2)	1961	20.00
❑ 502	4000 Miles Away/Woke Up This Morning	1961	30.00
KING			
❑ 5730	Death of an Angel/Our Winter Love	1963	20.00
MERCURY			
❑ 70987	The Next Four Years/The Girls with the Bells	1956	25.00
OKEH			
❑ 7046	I Found a Love/Zanzee	1954	500.00
RENO			
❑ 1030	Please Believe Me I Love You/Sweet and Lovely	1958	250.00
TWIST TIME			
❑ 12	Twistin' Time/Twistin' Pony	1962	15.00
WASSEL			
❑ 701	Groovy/Hey Baby	1965	10.00

HI-LO'S, THE

Number	Title (A Side/B Side)	Yr	NM
45s			
COLUMBIA			
❑ 40915	A Face in the Crowd/Autumn Rain	1957	10.00
❑ 41050	A Very Special Love/My Sugar Is So Refined	1957	10.00
❑ 41197	Whistlin' Down the Lane/When I Remember	1958	10.00
❑ 41465	Goody Goody/Indiana	1959	10.00
❑ 41647	Cindy's Prayer/A Lot of Livin' to Do	1960	10.00
❑ 41867	The Trolley Song/Five Foot Two, Eyes of Blue	1960	10.00
7-Inch Extended Plays			
COLUMBIA			
❑ B-10231	Sunnyside Up/Laura//A Shine on Your Shoes/The Heather on the Hill	195?	12.00
❑ B-10231 [PS]	Sunnyside Up	195?	12.00
STARLITE			
❑ ST 455	Rockin' Chair/Jeepers Creepers//Nice Work If You Can Get It/Button Up Your Overcoat	195?	15.00
❑ ST 455 [PS]	The Hi-Lo's, I Presume	195?	15.00
❑ ST 456	Stars Fell on Alabama/Speak Low//I Thought About You/Put Your Dreams Away	195?	15.00
❑ ST 456 [PS]	The Hi-Lo's, I Presume	195?	15.00
❑ ST 457	Summertime/Through the Years//Skylark/Shadow Waltz	195?	15.00
❑ ST 457 [PS]	Under Glass, Part 1	195?	15.00
Albums			
COLUMBIA			
❑ CL 952 [M]	Suddenly It's the Hi-Lo's	1957	30.00
❑ CL 1023 [M]	Now Hear This	1957	30.00
❑ CL 1259 [M]	The Hi-Lo's and All That Jazz	1958	30.00
❑ CL 1416 [M]	Broadway Playbill	1959	30.00
❑ CL 1509 [M]	All Over the Place	1960	25.00
❑ CL 1723 [M]	This Time It's Love	1962	25.00
❑ CS 8057 [S]	Love Nest	1958	40.00
❑ CS 8077 [S]	The Hi-Lo's and All That Jazz	1958	40.00
❑ CS 8213 [S]	Broadway Playbill	1959	40.00
❑ CS 8300 [S]	All Over the Place	1960	30.00
❑ CS 8523 [S]	This Time It's Love	1962	30.00
COLUMBIA SPECIAL PRODUCTS			
❑ P 14387	Harmony in Jazz	1978	12.00
DRG			
❑ SL 5184	Clap Yo' Hands	198?	12.00
KAPP			
❑ KL 1027 [M]	The Hi-Lo's and the Jerry Fielding Band	1956	30.00
❑ KL 1184 [M]	Under Glass *—Reissue of Starlite 7005*	1959	25.00
❑ KL 1194 [M]	On Hand *—Reissue of Starlite 7008*	1960	25.00
MCA			
❑ 4171 [(2)]	The Hi-Lo's Collection	197?	15.00
OMEGA			
❑ OSL-11 [S]	The Hi-Lo's in Stereo	195?	30.00
PAUSA			
❑ 7040	Back Again	198?	12.00
❑ 7093	Now	198?	12.00
REPRISE			
❑ R-6066 [M]	The Hi-Lo's Happen to Bossa Nova	1963	20.00
❑ R9-6066 [S]	The Hi-Lo's Happen to Bossa Nova	1963	25.00
STARLITE			
❑ 6004 [10]	Listen!	1955	60.00
❑ 6005 [10]	The Hi-Lo's, I Presume	1955	60.00
❑ 7005 [M]	Under Glass	1956	40.00
❑ 7006 [M]	Listen! *—Reissue of 6004*	1956	40.00
❑ 7007 [M]	The Hi-Lo's. I Presume *—Reissue of 6005*	1956	40.00
❑ 7008 [M]	On Hand	1956	40.00

HIATT, JOHN

Number	Title (A Side/B Side)	Yr	NM
45s			
A&M			
❑ 1245	Slow Turning/Your Dad Did (Live)	1988	3.00
❑ 2950	Lipstick Sunset/Thank You Girl	1987	3.00
❑ 2970	Have a Little Faith in Me/Thank You Girl	1987	3.00
ATLANTIC			
❑ 89461	Snakecharmer/This Is Your Day	1985	4.00
CAPITOL			
❑ S7-19626	Little Head/Runaway	1997	3.00
EPIC			
❑ 10990	The Boulevard Ain't So Bad/We Make Spirit	1973	6.00
❑ 11095	Sure As I'm Sittin' Here/Ocean	1974	5.00
❑ 50022	Hangin' Around the Observatory/Full Moon	1974	5.00
❑ 50115	Down Home (Keep On Fallin')/Motorboat to Heaven	1975	5.00
GEFFEN			
❑ 29045	Living a Little, Laughing a Little/I'm a Real Man	1985	4.00

Except when noted otherwise, VG = 25% of NM, and VG+ = 50% of NM. (Example: VG = $2.00, VG+ = $4.00 and NM = $8.00.)

Number	Title (A Side/B Side)	Yr	NM
❑ 29945	I Look for Love/Take Time to Know Her	1982	4.00
MCA			
❑ 41019	Radio Girl/Sharon's Got a Drugstore	1979	4.00
❑ 41132	Madonna Road/Slug Line	1979	4.00
❑ 41300	I Spy (For the FBI)/It Hasn't Happened Yet	1980	4.00
THE RIGHT STUFF			
❑ S7-19856	Johnny 99/I Wish I Were Blind	1998	3.00
—B-side by the Yell Leaders			
Albums			
A&M			
❑ SP-5158	Bring the Family	1987	10.00
❑ SP-5206	Slow Turning	1988	10.00
❑ 75021 5310 1	Stolen Moments	1990	12.00
EPIC			
❑ KE 32688	Hangin' Around the Observatory	1974	10.00
❑ KE 33190	Overcoats	1975	10.00
❑ PE 33190	Overcoats	198?	8.00
—Budget-line reissue			
GEFFEN			
❑ GHS 2009	All of a Sudden	1982	10.00
❑ GHS 4017	Riding with the King	1983	10.00
❑ GHS 24055	Warming Up to the Ice Age	1984	10.00
MCA			
❑ 741	Two-Bit Monster	198?	8.00
—Reissue			
❑ 747	Slug Line	198?	8.00
—Reissue			
❑ 3088	Slug Line	1979	12.00
❑ 5123	Two-Bit Monster	1980	12.00
MOBILE FIDEILTY			
❑ 1-210	Bring the Family	1994	50.00
—Audiophile vinyl			

HICKEY, ERSEL

Number	Title (A Side/B Side)	Yr	NM
45s			
APOLLO			
❑ 761	Upside Down Love/The Millionaire	1949	50.00
EPIC			
❑ 9263	Bluebirds Over the Mountain/Hangin' Around	1958	30.00
❑ 9278	Goin' Down That Road/Lovers' Land	1958	25.00
❑ 9298	You Never Can Tell/Wedding Day	1958	25.00
❑ 9309	Don't Be Afraid of Love/You Threw a Dart	1959	25.00
❑ 9320	I Can't Love Another/People Gotta Talk	1959	25.00
❑ 9357	Love in Bloom/What Do You Want	1960	25.00
❑ 9395	Another Wasted Day/Money Brought Me You	1960	25.00
JANUS			
❑ 151	Bluebirds Over the Mountain/Self Made Man	1971	5.00
KAPP			
❑ 372	Teardrops at Dawn/I Guess You Can Call It Love	1961	20.00
LAURIE			
❑ 3165	Some Enchanted Evening/Put Your Mind at Ease	1963	20.00
RAMESES II			
❑ 2003	Waitin' for Baby/In Spite of the Fool That I Am	1976	6.00
TOOT			
❑ 602	Tryin' to Get to You/Blue Skies	196?	10.00
UNIFAX			
❑ 100	How Unlucky Can You Get/Put It to Your Heart	1972	8.00
7-Inch Extended Plays			
EPIC			
❑ EG-7206	(contents unknown)	1958	100.00
❑ EG-7206 [PS]	Ersel Hickey in Lover's Land	1958	100.00
Albums			
BACK-TRAC			
❑ P 18750	The Rockin' Bluebird	1985	60.00
—Allegedly, only 200 copies of this were pressed			

HICKMAN, DWAYNE

Starred as Dobie Gillis on TV.

Number	Title (A Side/B Side)	Yr	NM
45s			
ABC-PARAMOUNT			
❑ 9908	School Dance/Pretty Baby	1958	25.00
❑ 9908 [PS]	School Dance/Pretty Baby	1958	40.00
CAPITOL			
❑ 4445	I'm a Lover, Not a Fighter/I Pass Your House	1960	20.00
Albums			
CAPITOL			
❑ ST 1441 [S]	Dobie!	1960	50.00
❑ T 1441 [M]	Dobie!	1960	40.00

HICKS, DAN, AND HIS HOT LICKS

Number	Title (A Side/B Side)	Yr	NM
45s			
BLUE THUMB			
❑ 211	Moody Richard/Walkin' One and Only	1972	5.00
❑ 213	I'm an Old Cowhand/Woe the Luck	1972	5.00
❑ 235	My Old Timey Baby/Cheaters Don't Win	1973	5.00
EPIC			
❑ 10511	How Can I Miss You When You Won't Go/Canned Music	1969	6.00
Albums			
BLUE THUMB			
❑ BTS-29	Where's the Money?	1971	12.00
❑ BTS-36	Striking It Rich!	1972	12.00
❑ BTS-51	Last Train to Hicksville... The Home of Happy Feet	1973	12.00
EPIC			
❑ BN 26464	Original Recordings	1969	15.00
—Yellow label			
❑ BN 26464	Original Recordings	1973	10.00
—Orange label			
❑ PE 26464	Original Recordings	198?	8.00
—Reissue with new prefix			
MCA			
❑ 670	Striking It Rich!	198?	8.00
—Reissue			
❑ 671	Last Train to Hicksville... The Home of Happy Feet	198?	8.00
—Reissue			
WARNER BROS.			
❑ BSK 3158	It Happened One Bite	1978	10.00

HICKS, JEANETTE

Number	Title (A Side/B Side)	Yr	NM
45s			
COLUMBIA			
❑ 4-21374	Just Like in the Movies/Such a Wonderful Feeling	1955	25.00
OKEH			
❑ 18008	I Think of You/Still I Lost You	195?	25.00
❑ 18021	He Knows Why/All I Care About	195?	25.00
❑ 18055	Lipstick on a Glass/Kingless Hand	195?	25.00
STARDAY			
❑ 271	Extra Extra/Cry, Cry, It's Good for You	1956	20.00

HICKS, JEANETTE, AND BILLY WALKER

Number	Title (A Side/B Side)	Yr	NM
45s			
COLUMBIA			
❑ 4-21392	Which One of Us Is to Blame/Let's Make Memories Tonight	1955	20.00
❑ 4-21471	Blue Mountain Waltz/Why Does It Have to Be	1955	20.00

HIDE-A-WAYS, THE

Number	Title (A Side/B Side)	Yr	NM
45s			
LOST-NITE			
❑ 119	Can't Help Loving That Girl of Mine/I'm Coming Home	196?	8.00
—Reissue label			
MGM			
❑ 55004	Cherie/Me Make Em Powwow	1955	500.00
RONNI			
❑ 1000	Can't Help Lovin' That Girl of Mine/I'm Coming Home	1954	6000.
—VG 2000; VG+ 4000			

HIGH, BOBBY

Number	Title (A Side/B Side)	Yr	NM
45s			
KAMA SUTRA			
❑ 261	Turn On the Oven/Two Apartments	1969	10.00
—B-side by "The Gang on 29th Street"			

HIGH NUMBERS, THE

See THE WHO.

HIGH SOCIETY

British band with Graham Gouldman, later of 10CC, and JOHN PAUL JONES, later of LED ZEPPELIN.

Number	Title (A Side/B Side)	Yr	NM
45s			
CAMEO			
❑ 452	People Passing By/Star of Eastern Street	1967	60.00
—Red and orange label with "CP" logo at top			

HIGH TIDE

Includes Simon House of HAWKWIND.

Number	Title (A Side/B Side)	Yr	NM
Albums			
LIBERTY			
❑ LST-7638	Sea Shanties	1969	60.00

HIGH TREASON

Number	Title (A Side/B Side)	Yr	NM
Albums			
ABBOTT			
❑ ABS-1209	High Treason	1968	60.00

HIGHLIGHTS, THE

Number	Title (A Side/B Side)	Yr	NM
45s			
BALLY			
❑ 1016	City of Angels/Listen, My Love	1956	30.00
❑ 1027	To Be with You/Will I Ever Know	1957	30.00
❑ 1044	Indian Style/Turn Around Shoes	1957	25.00

HIGHTOWER, WILLIE

Number	Title (A Side/B Side)	Yr	NM
45s			
ADVENTURE ONE			
❑ 8502	Tell Me What You Want/Too Many Irons in the Fire	197?	20.00
CAPITOL			
❑ 2226	It's a Miracle/Nobody But You	1968	40.00
❑ 2547	Ooh Baby How I Love You/It's Wonderful to Be in Love with You	1969	20.00
❑ 2651	If I Had a Hammer/It's Too Late	1969	15.00
❑ 5916	Because I Love You/For Sentimental Reasons-You Send Me	1967	200.00
ENJOY			
❑ 2019	Too Late/What Am I Living For	196?	30.00
FAME			
❑ 1465	Walk a Mile in My Shoes/You Used Me Baby	1970	30.00
❑ 1474	I Can't Love Without You/Time Has Brought About a Change	1970	30.00
❑ 1477	Back Road Into Town/Poor Man	1971	40.00
FURY			
❑ 5002	If I Had a Hammer/So Tired (Of Running Away from Love)	196?	20.00
❑ 5004	Let's Walk Together/I Love You	196?	20.00
MERCURY			
❑ 73338	I Love You So/Easy Lovin'	1972	15.00
❑ 73390	Don't Blame Me/Hungry for Your Love	1973	30.00
SOUND STAGE 7			
❑ 2503	Chicago, Send Her Home/Ain't Nothing Wrong	1977	75.00
Albums			
CAPITOL			
❑ ST-367	If I Had a Hammer	1969	100.00
COLLECTABLES			
❑ COL-5170	Golden Classics	198?	10.00

HIGHWAYMEN, THE

Number	Title (A Side/B Side)	Yr	NM
45s			
ABC			
❑ 10801	She's Not There/Little Bird, Little Bird	1966	8.00
❑ 10824	Fling/My Foolish Pride	1966	8.00
ABC-PARAMOUNT			
❑ 10688	Should I Go, Should I Stay/Permit to Be a Hermit	1965	8.00
❑ 10716	I'll Show You the Way/Never a Thought for Tomorrow	1965	8.00
UNITED ARTISTS			
❑ 258	Michael/Santiano	1960	15.00
❑ 370	Cotton Fields/Gypsy Rover	1961	12.00
❑ 439	Whiskey in the Jar/I'm On My Way	1962	12.00
❑ 475	Cindy, Oh Cindy/The Birdman	1962	12.00
❑ 540	I Know Where I'm Going/Well, Well, Well	1963	12.00
❑ 568	I Never Will Marry/Pretoria	1963	12.00
❑ 602	All My Trials/Midnight Train	1963	12.00
❑ 647	Universal Soldier/I'll Fly Away	1963	12.00
❑ 679	Roll On Columbia, Roll On/The Tale of Michael Flynn	1963	12.00
❑ 695	The Sinking of the Reuben James/Bon Soir	1964	10.00
❑ 752	Nellie/Sweet Mama Tree Top Tall	1964	10.00
❑ 788	Puttin' On the Style/Michael	1964	10.00
❑ 801	Michael '65/Puttin' On the Style	1964	10.00
Albums			
ABC-PARAMOUNT			
❑ 522 [M]	On a New Road	1965	10.00
❑ S-522 [S]	On a New Road	1965	12.00

Number	Title (A Side/B Side)	Yr	NM
UNITED ARTISTS			
❑ UAL 3125 [M]	The Highwaymen	1961	10.00
❑ UAL 3168 [M]	Standing Room Only!	1962	10.00
❑ UAL 3225 [M]	Encore!	1962	10.00
❑ UAL 3245 [M]	March On, Brothers	1963	10.00
❑ UAL 3294 [M]	Hootenanny with the Highwaymen	1963	10.00
❑ UAL 3323 [M]	One More Time	1964	10.00
❑ UAL 3348 [M]	Homecoming	1964	10.00
❑ UAS 6125 [S]	The Highwaymen	1961	15.00
❑ UAS 6168 [S]	Standing Room Only!	1962	15.00
❑ UAS 6225 [S]	Encore!	1962	15.00
❑ UAS 6245 [S]	March On, Brothers	1963	15.00
❑ UAS 6294 [S]	Hootenanny with the Highwaymen	1963	15.00
❑ UAS 6323 [S]	One More Time	1964	15.00
❑ UAS 6348 [S]	Homecoming	1964	15.00

HIGHWAYMEN, THE (2)
See JOHNNY CASH; WAYLON JENNINGS; KRIS KRISTOFFERSON; WILLIE NELSON.

HILDEBRAND, RAY
See PAUL AND PAULA.

45s

Number	Title (A Side/B Side)	Yr	NM
PHILIPS			
❑ 40174	It's All Over, Paula/Snow Girl	1964	10.00
—As "Paul"			
❑ 40318	Hey Little Julie/The Way of the DJ	1965	8.00
❑ 40339	Hello Viet Nam (Goodbye My Love)/You, Wonderful You	1965	8.00
TOWER			
❑ 304	Paper Clown/Patsy	1966	8.00
—As "Paul (Paul and Paula)"			

Albums

Number	Title (A Side/B Side)	Yr	NM
WORD			
❑ WST-8411	He's Everything to Me	196?	12.00
❑ WST-8465	I Need You Every Hour	1971	12.00

HILL, BUNKER

45s

Number	Title (A Side/B Side)	Yr	NM
MALA			
❑ 451	Hide and Go Seek (Part 1)/Hide and Go Seek (Part 2)	1962	20.00
❑ 457	Red Ridin' Hood and the Wolf/Nobody Knows	1962	20.00
❑ 464	The Girl Can't Dance/You Can't Make Me Doubt My Baby	1963	25.00

HILL, JESSIE

45s

Number	Title (A Side/B Side)	Yr	NM
BLUE THUMB			
❑ 204	Naturally/Livin' a Lie	1971	6.00
DOWNEY			
❑ 115	Chip Chop/Woodshed	1964	15.00
❑ 117	Understanding/Down the Street	1964	15.00
❑ 124	Never Thought/TV Guide	1964	15.00
MINIT			
❑ 607	Ooh Poo Pah Doo — Part 1/Ooh Poo Pah Doo — Part 2	1960	15.00
❑ 611	Whip It On Me/I Need Your Love	1960	12.00
❑ 616	Scoop Scoobie Doobie/Highland Blues	1960	12.00
❑ 622	Oh My Oh My/I Got Mine	1961	12.00
❑ 628	Oogsey Moo/My Love	1961	12.00
❑ 638	Sweet Jelly Roll/It's My Fault	1961	15.00
❑ 646	Can't Get Enough of That Ooh Pah Doo/Pot's on a Strike	1962	15.00
UNITED ARTISTS			
❑ 0081	Ooh Poo Pah Doo — Part 1/Ooh Poo Pah Doo — Part 2	1973	4.00
—"Silver Spotlight Series" reissue			

HILL, LAINIE

45s

Number	Title (A Side/B Side)	Yr	NM
NEW VOICE			
❑ 809	Time Marches On/Ain't I Worth a Dime	1966	400.00

HILL, RAYMOND

45s

Number	Title (A Side/B Side)	Yr	NM
SUN			
❑ 204	Bourbon Street Jump/The Snuggle	1954	750.00

HILL, VERNELL

45s

Number	Title (A Side/B Side)	Yr	NM
TUFF			
❑ 381	Long Haired Daddy/Sometimes Love	1964	8.00

HILL, VINCE

45s

Number	Title (A Side/B Side)	Yr	NM
LONDON INT'L.			
❑ 10514	The River's Run Dry/Not Any More	1962	12.00
PARAMOUNT			
❑ 0132	(Love Story) Look Around/In Every Corner of the World	1971	5.00
TOWER			
❑ 173	Yesterday's Hero/Unexpectedly	1965	8.00
❑ 207	Push Push/Take Me to Your Heart Again	1966	8.00
❑ 223	Looking at Me/Love Me True	1966	8.00
❑ 254	Heartaches/Merci Cherie	1966	8.00
❑ 323	Edelweiss/A Woman Needs Love	1967	8.00
❑ 358	When You Go/When the World Is Ready	1967	8.00
❑ 389	Why or When or Where/Why Can't I Remember	1968	6.00

HILL, Z.Z.

45s

Number	Title (A Side/B Side)	Yr	NM
ATLANTIC			
❑ 2659	It's a Hang-Up Baby/(Home Just Ain't Home at) Suppertime	1969	8.00
COLUMBIA			
❑ 10552	Love Is So Good When You're Stealing It/Need You By My Side	1977	5.00
❑ 10680	This Time They Told the Truth/Near But Yet So Far	1978	5.00
❑ 10748	Universal Love/That's All That's Left	1978	5.00
HILL			
❑ 222	Don't Make Me Pay for His Mistakes/Think People	1971	6.00
KENT			
❑ 404	I Could Do It All Over/You Don't Love Me	1964	10.00
❑ 416	I Need Someone (To Love Me)/Have Mercy Someone	1965	10.00
❑ 427	Hey Little Girl/Oh Darlin'	1965	10.00
❑ 432	That's It/What's More	1965	10.00
❑ 439	Everybody Has to Cry/Happiness Is All I Need	1965	10.00
❑ 444	No More Doggin'/The Kind of Love I Want	1966	10.00
❑ 449	I Found Love/Set Your Sights Higher	1966	10.00
❑ 453	You Can't Hide a Heartache/Gimme Gimme	1966	10.00
❑ 460	Oh Darling/Greatest Love	1967	10.00
❑ 464	Baby I'm Sorry/Where She At	1967	10.00
❑ 469	You Just Cheat and Lie/Everybody Needs Somebody	1967	10.00
❑ 478	What Am I Living For/You're Gonna Need My Lovin'	1967	10.00
❑ 481	Steal Away/Nothing Can Change the Love I Have for You	1967	10.00
❑ 494	You Got What I Need/Have Mercy Someone	1968	10.00
❑ 502	Don't Make Promises (You Can't Keep)/Set Your Sights Higher	1968	10.00
❑ 4547	I Need Someone (To Love Me)/Oh Darling	1971	8.00
❑ 4550	You Don't Love Me/Have Mercy Someone	1971	8.00
❑ 4560	If I Could Do It All Over/You Won't Hurt No More	1971	8.00
❑ 4577	Nothing Can Change This Love/Eveyrbody Has to Cry	1972	8.00
M.H.			
❑ 200	You Were Wrong/(B-side unknown)	1964	10.00
MALACO			
❑ 2069	Please Don't Make Me (Do Something Bad to You)/Blue Monday	1981	4.00
❑ 2074	Separate Ways/Chained to Your Love	1981	4.00
❑ 2076	Bump and Grind/Somethin' Goin' On	1981	4.00
❑ 2079	Cheating in the Next Room/Right Arm for Your Love	1982	4.00
❑ 2082	When It Rains It Pours/When Can We Do This Again	1982	4.00
❑ 2085	What Am I Gonna Tell Her/Get You Some Business	1982	4.00
❑ 2090	Open House at My House/Who You Been Givin' It To	1983	4.00
❑ 2094	Get a Little, Give a Little/Blind Side	1983	4.00
❑ 2097	Steal Away/Three Into Two Won't Go	1984	4.00
❑ 2103	Someone Else Is Steppin' In/Shade Tree Mechanic	1984	4.00
❑ 2109	I'm Gonna Stop You from Givin' Me the Blues/Personally	1984	4.00
❑ 2141	Down Home Blues/Please Don't Let Our Good Thing End	1988	4.00
MANKIND			
❑ 12003	Faithful and True/I Think I'd Do It	1971	8.00
❑ 12007	The Chokin' Kind/Hold Back	1971	8.00
❑ 12012	Second Chance/It Ain't No Use	1972	7.00
❑ 12015	It Ain't No Use/Ha Ha	1972	7.00
❑ 12017	The Chokin' Kind/A Man Needs a Woman	197?	7.00
UNITED ARTISTS			
❑ XW225	Ain't Nothing You Can Do/Love in the Street	1973	6.00
❑ XW307	I Don't Need Half a Love/Friendship Only Goes So Far	1973	6.00
❑ XW365	Let Them Talk/Red Rooster	1973	6.00
❑ XW412	Am I Groovin' You/Bad Mouth and Gossip	1974	6.00
❑ XW536	I Keep On Lovin' You/Whatever's Thrilling You Is Killing Me	1974	6.00
❑ XW631	I Created a Monster/Steppin' in the Shoes of a Fool	1975	6.00
❑ 50977	Your Love Makes Me Feel Good/I've Got to Get You Back	1972	7.00

Albums

Number	Title (A Side/B Side)	Yr	NM
COLUMBIA			
❑ JC 35030	Let's Make a Deal	1978	12.00
❑ JC 36125	The Mark of Z.Z.	1979	12.00
KENT			
❑ KST-528	A Whole Lot of Soul	1969	15.00
❑ KST-560	Dues Paid in Full	1971	15.00
MALACO			
❑ 7411	The Rhyhtm & The Blues	1983	10.00
❑ 7415	I'm a Blues Man	1984	10.00
MANKIND			
❑ 201	The Brand New Z.Z. Hill	1971	15.00
UNITED ARTISTS			
❑ UA-LA417-G	Keep On Lovin' You	1975	12.00
❑ UAS 5589	The Best Thing That's Ever Happened to Me	1972	12.00

HILL SISTERS, THE

45s

Number	Title (A Side/B Side)	Yr	NM
ANNA			
❑ 103	Hit and Run Away Love/Advertising for Love	1959	500.00
❑ 1103	Hit and Run Away Love/Advertising for Love	1959	50.00

HILLMAN, CHRIS

45s

Number	Title (A Side/B Side)	Yr	NM
ASYLUM			
❑ 45330	Step On Out/Take It on the Run	1976	4.00
❑ 45350	Falling Again/Love Is the Sweetest Amnesty	1976	4.00
❑ 45428	Heartbreaker/Lucky in Love	1977	4.00
SUGAR HILL			
❑ 4105	Somebody's Back in Town/Desert Rose	1984	5.00
❑ 4106	Running the Roadblocks/Turn Your Radio On	1985	5.00

Albums

Number	Title (A Side/B Side)	Yr	NM
ASYLUM			
❑ 7E-1062	Slippin' Away	1976	12.00
❑ 7E-1104	Clear Sailin'	1977	12.00
SUGAR HILL			
❑ SH 3729	Morning Sky	1982	12.00
❑ SH 3743	Desert Rose	1984	12.00

HILLMEN, THE

Albums

Number	Title (A Side/B Side)	Yr	NM
TOGETHER			
❑ STT-1012	The Hillmen	1970	80.00

HILLOW HAMMET

Albums

Number	Title (A Side/B Side)	Yr	NM
HOUSE OF FOX			
❑ 2	Hammer	1968	150.00

HILLSIDE SINGERS, THE

45s

Number	Title (A Side/B Side)	Yr	NM
METROMEDIA			
❑ 231	I'd Like to Teach the World to Sing (In Perfect Harmony)/I Believe It All	1971	5.00
❑ 241	We're Together/Day by Day	1972	5.00
❑ 246	Kum Ba Yah/Tomorrow Belongs to Me	1972	5.00
❑ 255	The Last Happy Song/Ah Man, See What You've Done	1972	5.00

Except when noted otherwise, VG = 25% of NM, and VG+ = 50% of NM. (Example: VG = $2.00, VG+ = $4.00 and NM = $8.00.)

Number	Title (A Side/B Side)	Yr	NM

Albums

METROMEDIA

Number	Title (A Side/B Side)	Yr	NM
❑ MD 1051	I'd Like to Teach the World to Sing	1971	12.00

HILLSIDERS, THE

45s

MEL-O-DY

Number	Title (A Side/B Side)	Yr	NM
❑ 120	You Only Pass This Way One Time/Rain Is a Lonesome Thing	1964	30.00

HIM See DOUG SAHM.

HINSON, DON, AND THE RIGAMORTICIANS

45s

CAPITOL

Number	Title (A Side/B Side)	Yr	NM
❑ 5314	Riboflavin Flavored, Non-Carbonated, Polyunsaturated Blood/ Monster Jerk	1964	12.00

Albums

CAPITOL

Number	Title (A Side/B Side)	Yr	NM
❑ ST 2219 [S]	Monster Dance Party	1964	40.00
❑ T 2219 [M]	Monster Dance Party	1964	30.00

HINTON, JOE

45s

ARVEE

Number	Title (A Side/B Side)	Yr	NM
❑ 5028	My Love Is Real/I Won't Be Your Fool	1961	60.00

—Arvee titles as "Little Joe Hinton"

Number	Title (A Side/B Side)	Yr	NM
❑ 5029	Your Kind of Love/Let's Start a Romance	1961	40.00

BACK BEAT

Number	Title (A Side/B Side)	Yr	NM
❑ 519	I Know/Ladder of Prayer	1958	15.00
❑ 526	Pretty Little Mama/Will You	1959	15.00
❑ 526 [PS]	Pretty Little Mama/Will You	1959	30.00
❑ 532	If You Love Me/A Thousand Cups of Happiness	1960	20.00
❑ 535	The Girls in My Life/ Come On Baby	1961	20.00
❑ 537	You Know It Ain't Right/ Lovre Sick Blues	1963	20.00
❑ 539	Better to Give Than Receive/ There Is No In Between	1963	15.00
❑ 540	There Oughta Be a Law/ You're My Girl	1964	20.00
❑ 541	Funny/You Gotta Have Love	1964	20.00
❑ 545	I Want a Little Girl/True Love	1965	15.00
❑ 547	Darling Come and Talk to Me/ Everything	1965	10.00
❑ 550	Pledging My Love/ Just a Kid Named Joe	1965	15.00
❑ 565	I'm Waiting/How Long Can I Last	1966	10.00
❑ 574	If I Had Only Known/ Lots of Love	1966	25.00
❑ 581	Close to MyHeart/ You've Been Good to Me	1967	20.00
❑ 589	I'm Satisfied/Be Ever Wonderful	1968	30.00
❑ 594	Got You on My Mind/Please	1968	75.00

SOUL

Number	Title (A Side/B Side)	Yr	NM
❑ 35080	Let's Save the Children/ You Are Blue	1971	20.00

Albums

BACK BEAT

Number	Title (A Side/B Side)	Yr	NM
❑ B-60 [M]	Funny (How Time Slips Away)	1965	50.00
❑ BS-60 [S]	Funny (How Time Slips Away)	1965	70.00

DUKE

Number	Title (A Side/B Side)	Yr	NM
❑ DLPS-91	Duke-Peacock Remembers Joe Hinton	1969	20.00

HIPPIES, THE

45s

PARKWAY

Number	Title (A Side/B Side)	Yr	NM
❑ 863	Memory Lane/A Lonely Piano	1963	20.00

—Originally released as "The Tams"; B-side by Reggie Harrison

HIPPY DIPPYS, THE

45s

UNI

Number	Title (A Side/B Side)	Yr	NM
❑ 55004	Thoroughly Modem Millie/Jimmy	1967	12.00

HIT COMBO, THE

45s

HIT

Number	Title (A Side/B Side)	Yr	NM
❑ 08	Stranger on the Shore/ Twist Twist Senora	1962	8.00

—B-side by Herbert Hunter

Number	Title (A Side/B Side)	Yr	NM
❑ 09	Soul Twist/What'd I Say	1962	8.00

—B-side by Ray Fowler

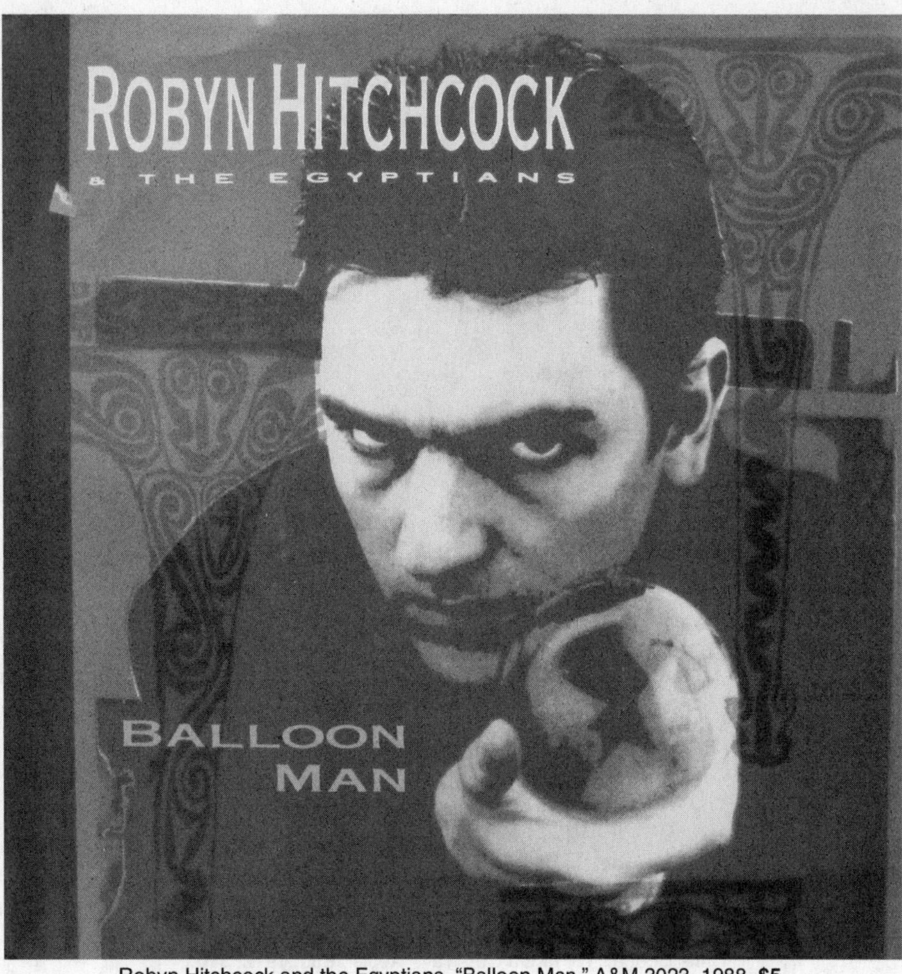

Robyn Hitchcock and the Egyptians, "Balloon Man," A&M 3023, 1988, **$5.**

HIT PACK, THE

45s

SOUL

Number	Title (A Side/B Side)	Yr	NM
❑ 35010	Never Say No to Your Baby/ Let's Dance	1965	50.00

HITCHCOCK, ROBYN, AND THE EGYPTIANS

12-Inch Singles

A&M

Number	Title (A Side/B Side)	Yr	NM
❑ 75021 7271 1 [DJ]	So You Think You're in Love/ Watch Your Intelligence	1991	12.00
❑ 75021 7277 1 [DJ]	Dark Green Energy (3:13)/ Unbelievable Love (3:48)/ Ride (Demo Version 5:04)	1991	15.00
❑ 75021 7300 1 [DJ]	Oceanside/Fair Play/Linden Arden/One Long Pair of Eyes	1991	15.00
❑ SP-17530 [DJ]	Balloon Man/A Globe of Frogs (Electric)/The Ghost Ship	1988	15.00

—Green vinyl

Number	Title (A Side/B Side)	Yr	NM
❑ SP-17537 [DJ]	Balloon Man (same on both sides)	1988	10.00
❑ SP-17549 [DJ]	Flesh Number One/ Legalized Murder	1988	15.00

—Blue vinyl

Number	Title (A Side/B Side)	Yr	NM
❑ SP-17697 [DJ]	Madonna of the Wasps/One Long Pair of Eyes (Acoustic)/ More Than This	1989	12.00

—Purple vinyl

Number	Title (A Side/B Side)	Yr	NM
❑ SP-17729 [DJ]	One Long Pair of Eyes (Edit)/ The Ghost in You (Live)/ Freeze (Sunset Mix)	1989	15.00

—Red vinyl

Number	Title (A Side/B Side)	Yr	NM
❑ SP-17765 [DJ]	Interview with Deidre O'Donoghue	1989	20.00

RELATIVITY

Number	Title (A Side/B Side)	Yr	NM
❑ 88561-8130 [DJ]	Somewhere Apart/ If You Were a Priest	1987	12.00

45s

A&M

Number	Title (A Side/B Side)	Yr	NM
❑ 1409	Madonna of the Wasps/ Ruling Class	1989	20.00
❑ 3023	Balloon Man/A Globe of Frogs (Electric)	1988	5.00
❑ 3023 [PS]	Balloon Man/A Globe of Frogs (Electric)	1988	5.00

K

Number	Title (A Side/B Side)	Yr	NM
❑ IPU-55	I Something You/Zipper in My Spine/Man with a Woman's Shadow	1995	4.00
❑ IPU-55 [PS]	I Something You/Zipper in My Spine/Man with a Woman's Shadow	1995	4.00

RELATIVITY

Number	Title (A Side/B Side)	Yr	NM
❑ 8076 [DJ]	Heaven/Listening to the Higsons	1985	20.00

THE BOB

Number	Title (A Side/B Side)	Yr	NM
❑ 54	Alright Yeah/All Good Creatures	1996	4.00

—Flexi-disc with The Bob magazine; both songs on one side; second song by Jason Falkner

Albums

A&M

Number	Title (A Side/B Side)	Yr	NM
❑ SP-5182	Globe of Frogs	1988	12.00
❑ SP-5241	Queen Elvis	1989	12.00
❑ 75021 5368 1	Perspex Island	1991	20.00

RELATIVITY

Number	Title (A Side/B Side)	Yr	NM
❑ EMC 8056	Gotta Let This Hen Out	1985	12.00
❑ 8074 [EP]	Exploding in Silence	1986	25.00

—Picture disc

Number	Title (A Side/B Side)	Yr	NM
❑ 88561-8082-1	I Often Dream of Trains	1986	12.00

—First U.S. issue of U.K. album

Number	Title (A Side/B Side)	Yr	NM
❑ 88561-8083-1	Groovy Decoy	1986	12.00

—First U.S. issue of U.K. album

Number	Title (A Side/B Side)	Yr	NM
❑ 88561-8088-1	Black Snake Diamond Role	1986	12.00

—First U.S. issue of U.K. album

Number	Title (A Side/B Side)	Yr	NM
❑ 88561-8089-1	Invisible Hitchcock	1986	12.00
❑ 88561-8130-1	Element of Light	1987	12.00

SLASH

Number	Title (A Side/B Side)	Yr	NM
❑ 25316	Fegmania!	1985	12.00

Chris Hodge, "We're On Our Way," Apple 1850, 1972, **$10.**

Number	Title (A Side/B Side)	Yr	NM
TWIN/TONE			
❑ TTR 89175	Eye	1990	12.00
WARNER BROS.			
❑ 46399	Mossy Liquor	1996	30.00
—Collection of demos; released only on vinyl			
❑ 47147 [(2)]	Storefront Hitchcock	1998	20.00

HIVES, THE

Number	Title (A Side/B Side)	Yr	NM
Albums			
GEARHEAD			
❑ RPM 30	Barely Legal	2000	15.00

HJERPE, BILL

Number	Title (A Side/B Side)	Yr	NM
45s			
EPIC			
❑ 5-9897	Navigation Blues/Not for Sale	1966	30.00
❑ 5-9897 [PS]	Navigation Blues/Not for Sale	1966	50.00
❑ 5-10026	Behind the Times/Mrs. Frost	1966	30.00

HO, DON

Number	Title (A Side/B Side)	Yr	NM
45s			
HEL			
❑ 149	Christmas Is for Everyone/ Christmas Is You and Me	1977	4.00
❑ 149 [PS]	Christmas Is for Everyone/ Christmas Is You and Me	1977	4.00
MEGA			
❑ 1215	Watch Out Woman/ A New Love Song	1974	4.00
❑ 1225	Today I Started Loving You Again/Take a Walk in the Country	1975	4.00
REPRISE			
❑ 0388	I'll Remember You/ E Lei Ka Lei Lei	1965	8.00
❑ 0441	Suck 'Em Up/La Haina Luna	1965	8.00
❑ 0451	Sweet Someone/La Haina Luna	1966	8.00
❑ 0507	Tiny Bubbles/Born Free	1966	8.00
❑ 0573	I Love You/All That's Left Is the Lemon Tree	1967	8.00
❑ 0590	Tiny Bubbles/Macao	1967	10.00
❑ 0591	What Now My Love/ One Paddle, Two Paddle	1967	8.00
❑ 0600	Tomorrow/ This Sacred Hour	1967	8.00
❑ 0609	Forbidden Fruit/ Sleepy Summer Days	1967	8.00
❑ 0643	The Windward Side (Of the Island)/Tu Tu Kane	1967	8.00
❑ 0669	Instant Happy/ White Silver Sands	1968	6.00
❑ 0705	Tiny Bubbles/Do I Love You	1968	4.00
—"Back to Back Hits" series			
❑ 0754	Remembering/ Sunny Days, Starry Nights	1968	6.00
❑ 0800	Galveston/Has Anybody Lost a Love	1968	6.00
❑ 0871	Honey Come Back/ Sands of Waikiki	1969	6.00
❑ 0896	It Must Have Been the Wine/ Questions	1970	5.00
❑ 0936	Melody Fair/Only Foolish People	1970	5.00
❑ 0950	Gotta Move Along/Home	1970	5.00
❑ 0960	This Is America/United We Stand	1970	5.00
❑ 1016	My God and I/What Do I Need to Be Free	1971	4.00
❑ 1059	Waikiki/Chotto Matte Kidasi	1971	4.00
Albums			
REPRISE			
❑ R-6161 [M]	The Don Ho Show	1965	12.00
❑ RS-6161 [S]	The Don Ho Show	1965	15.00
❑ R-6186 [M]	Don Ho...Again!	1966	10.00
❑ RS-6186 [S]	Don Ho...Again!	1966	12.00
❑ R-6219 [M]	You're Gonna Hear From Me	1966	10.00
❑ RS-6219 [S]	You're Gonna Hear From Me	1966	12.00
❑ R-6232 [M]	Tiny Bubbles	1966	10.00
❑ RS-6232 [S]	Tiny Bubbles	1966	12.00
❑ R-6244 [M]	East Coast/West Coast	1967	12.00
❑ RS-6244 [S]	East Coast/West Coast	1967	12.00
❑ RS-6283	Instant Happy	1968	12.00
❑ RS-6303	Hawaii-Ho!	1968	12.00
❑ RS-6331	Suck 'Em Up	1969	12.00
❑ RS-6357	Don Ho — Greatest Hits!	1969	12.00
❑ RS-6367	The Don Ho TV Show	1969	12.00
❑ RS-6418	Hawaii's Greatest Hits	1970	10.00
❑ RS-6461	Don Ho at the Polynesian Palace	1970	10.00

HO-DADS, THE

Number	Title (A Side/B Side)	Yr	NM
45s			
IMPERIAL			
❑ 66001	Legends/Honey	1963	30.00
❑ 66023	After Dark/Space Race	1964	30.00

HOBBITS, THE

Number	Title (A Side/B Side)	Yr	NM
45s			
DECCA			
❑ 32226	Sunny Day Girl/Daffodil Days	1967	12.00
❑ 32270	Pretty Young Thing/ Strawberry Children	1968	12.00
ZAR			
❑ 25	Frodo Lives/Jolly Good Fellow	1967	20.00
Albums			
DECCA			
❑ DL 4920 [M]	Down to Middle-Earth	1967	40.00
❑ DL 5009 [M]	Men and Doors	1968	80.00
❑ DL 74920 [S]	Down to Middle-Earth	1967	50.00
❑ DL 75009 [S]	Men and Doors	1968	30.00

HODGE, CHRIS

Number	Title (A Side/B Side)	Yr	NM
45s			
APPLE			
❑ 1850	We're On Our Way/Supersoul	1972	8.00
❑ 1850 [PS]	We're On Our Way/Supersoul	1972	10.00
❑ 1858	Goodnight Sweet Lorraine/ Contact Love	1973	8.00
RCA VICTOR			
❑ APBO-0289	Beautiful Love/Sweet Lady from the Sky	1974	5.00

HODGES, EDDIE

Number	Title (A Side/B Side)	Yr	NM
45s			
AURORA			
❑ 150	Across the Street (Is a Million Miles Away)/She Doesn't Love Me	1965	10.00
❑ 153	New Orleans/Hard Times for Young Lovers	1965	10.00
❑ 156	Love Minus Zero (No Limit)/ The Water Is Over My Head	1965	10.00
❑ 161	Hitch Hike/Old Man Rag	1966	10.00
CADENCE			
❑ 1397	I'm Gonna Knock on Your Door/ Ain't Gonna Wash for a Week	1961	15.00
—Red and black label with "Cadence Records" along edge three times			
❑ 1397	I'm Gonna Knock on Your Door/ Ain't Gonna Wash for a Week	1961	25.00
—Maroon and silver label with metronome at top			
❑ 1397 [PS]	I'm Gonna Knock on Your Door/ Ain't Gonna Wash for a Week	1961	25.00
❑ 1410	Bandit of My Dreams/ Mugmates	1962	20.00
❑ 1421	(Girls, Girls, Girls) Made to Love/I Make Believe It's You	1962	15.00
COLUMBIA			
❑ 42649	Seein' Is Believin'/Secret	1962	12.00
❑ 42649 [PS]	Seein' Is Believin'/Secret	1962	16.00
❑ 42697	Would You Come Back?/ Too Soon to Know	1962	12.00
❑ 42811	Rainin' in My Heart/Halfway	1963	12.00
DECCA			
❑ 30675	That Funny Little Dog/What Would It Be Like in Heaven	1958	15.00
❑ 30903	High Hopes/Don't Dance on Momma's Rug	1959	15.00
MGM			
❑ 13219	Avalanche/Just a Kid in Love	1964	10.00

HOFFMAN, ABBIE

Number	Title (A Side/B Side)	Yr	NM
Albums			
BIG TOE			
❑ 1	Wake Up, America!	196?	30.00

HOG HEAVEN

The Shondells after Tommy James went solo.

Number	Title (A Side/B Side)	Yr	NM
45s			
ROULETTE			
❑ 7091	Theme from a Thought/ (B-side unknown)	1970	8.00
❑ 7101	Happy/Prayer	1971	8.00
❑ 7106	If It Feels Good/(B-side unknown)	1971	8.00
Albums			
ROULETTE			
❑ SR 42057	Hog Heaven	1971	20.00

Except when noted otherwise, VG = 25% of NM, and VG+ = 50% of NM. (Example: VG = $2.00, VG+ = $4.00 and NM = $8.00.)

HOGG, SMOKEY

Number	Title (A Side/B Side)	Yr	NM
45s			
COMBO			
❑ 11	Where Have You Been/Believe I'll Change My Towns	1952	200.00
—Also had releases on Combo 4 and 9, but these are unknown on 45			
EBB			
❑ 127	Good Morning Baby/Sure 'Nuff	1958	25.00
FEDERAL			
❑ 12109	Keep a-Walkin'/Do It No More	1953	100.00
❑ 12117	Your Little Wagon/Penny Pinching Mama	1953	100.00
❑ 12127	Gone, Gone, Gone/I Ain't Got Over It Yet	1953	100.00
IMPERIAL			
❑ 5269	When I've Been Drinkin'/Tear Me Down	1954	100.00
❑ 5290	My Baby's Gone/Train Whistle	1954	100.00
METEOR			
❑ 5021	I Declare/Dark Clouds	1955	100.00
SPECIALTY			
❑ 753	I Want My Baby for Christmas/I Want My Baby for Christmas	197?	10.00
—B-side by Jimmy Liggins			
Albums			
CROWN			
❑ CLP-5226 [M]	Smokey Hogg Sings the Blues	1962	50.00
TIME			
❑ 6 [M]	Smokey Hogg	1962	80.00
UNITED			
❑ US-7745	Smokey Hogg	1970	12.00

HOGS, THE

Early version of THE CHOCOLATE WATCH BAND.

Number	Title (A Side/B Side)	Yr	NM
45s			
HANNA-BARBERA			
❑ 511	Loose Lip Sync Ships/Blues Theme	1967	150.00
—Contrary to previous reports, Frank Zappa was NOT involved with this record in any way			

HOLDEN, RANDY

Also see BLUE CHEER.

Number	Title (A Side/B Side)	Yr	NM
Albums			
HOBBIT			
❑ 5002	Population II	1968	200.00

HOLDEN, RON

Number	Title (A Side/B Side)	Yr	NM
45s			
CHALLENGE			
❑ 59360	I Tried/I'll Forgive and Forget	1967	300.00
DONNA			
❑ 1315	Love You So/My Babe	1959	30.00
❑ 1324	Gee, But I'm Lonesome/Susie Jane	1960	25.00
❑ 1328	True Love Can Be/Everything's Gonna Be Alright	1960	25.00
❑ 1331	Who Says There Ain't No Santa Claus/Your Line Is Busy	1960	25.00
❑ 1335	The Big Shoe/Rock and Roll Call	1961	20.00
ELDO			
❑ 117	I'll Be Happy/I'll Always Have You	1961	20.00
LANA			
❑ 154	Love You So/My Babe	196?	8.00
—Oldies reissue			
LOST-NITE			
❑ 199	Love You So/My Babe	196?	5.00
—Reissue			
❑ 207	Gee, But I'm Lonesome/Susie Jane	196?	5.00
—Reissue			
NITE OWL			
❑ 10	Love You So/My Babe	1959	800.00
NOW			
❑ 6	Can You Talk?/I Need Ya	1974	20.00
RAMPART			
❑ 645	Girl I Love You/Nothing I Wouldn't Do	1965	40.00
Albums			
DONNA			
❑ DLP-2111 [M]	I Love You So	1960	250.00
❑ DLPS-2111 [M]	I Love You So	1960	300.00
—Stereo records not known to exist; this is for a mono record in a stereo cover			

HOLIDAY, BILLIE

Number	Title (A Side/B Side)	Yr	NM
45s			
ATLANTIC			
❑ 2923	Strange Fruit/I Love My Man	1973	6.00
CLEF			
❑ 89089	My Man/He's Funny That Way	1954	15.00
❑ 89096	Remember/I Can't Face the Music	1954	15.00
❑ 89108	If the Moon Turns Green/Autumn in New York	1954	15.00
❑ 89132	How Deep Is the Ocean/What a Little Moonlight Can Do	1955	15.00
❑ 89150	Love Me or Leave Me/I Thought About You	1955	15.00
COLUMBIA			
❑ 1-613	Am I Blue/God Bless the Child	1950	50.00
—Microgroove 33 1/3 rpm 7-inch record, small hole			
❑ S7 31706 [S]	(titles unknown)	1963	15.00
❑ S7 31707 [S]	(titles unknown)	1963	15.00
❑ S7 31708 [S]	(titles unknown)	1963	15.00
❑ S7 31709 [S]	You've Changed/It's Easy to Remember	1963	15.00
❑ S7 31710 [S]	But Beautiful/I'll Be Around	1963	15.00
—The above five are "Stereo Seven" 33 1/3 rpm jukebox singles from set "JS 7-71" entitled "Lady in Satin"			
DECCA			
❑ 27145	Them There Eyes/Keeps On Rainin'	1950	25.00
❑ 48259	Do Your Duty/The Blues Are Brewin'	1951	25.00
KENT GOSPEL			
❑ 3003	God Bless the Child/(Instrumental)	197?	8.00
MAINSTREAM			
❑ 614	Strange Fruit/Fine and Mellow	1964	8.00
MERCURY			
❑ 89002	These Foolish Things/I Only Have Eyes for You	1952	20.00
❑ 89003	You Turned the Tables on Me/Easy to Love	1952	20.00
❑ 89004	You Go to My Head/Blue Moon	1952	20.00
❑ 89005	East o' the Sun/Solitude	1952	20.00
❑ 89037	Lover Come Back to Me/Yesterdays	1953	20.00
❑ 89064	Stormy Weather/Tenderly	1953	20.00
MGM			
❑ 12813	Don't Worry 'Bout Me/Just One More Chance	1959	12.00
UNITED ARTISTS			
❑ 50999	My Man/Them There Eyes	1973	6.00
❑ 50999 [PS]	My Man/Them There Eyes	1973	10.00
VERVE			
❑ 10181	Strange Fruit/The Foolish Things	1959	12.00
7-Inch Extended Plays			
COLUMBIA			
❑ 7-00021	When a Woman Loves a Man/The Man I Love//I'll Never Be the Same//Back in Your Own Backyard/God Bless the Child/All of Me	1972	15.00
—Jukebox issue; small hole, plays at 33 1/3 rpm			
❑ 7-00021 [PS]	The Golden Years	1972	15.00
❑ B-2534	*Gloomy Sunday/Am I Blue/Body and Soul/Long Gone Blues	195?	20.00
❑ B-2534 [PS]	Billie Holiday (Hall of Fame Series)	195?	20.00
DECCA			
❑ ED 2031	Easy Living/What Is This Thing Called Love//There Eyes/God Bless the Child	195?	20.00
❑ ED 2031 [PS]	Billie Holiday, Vol. 1	195?	20.00
❑ 34900	Good Morning Heartache/Crazy He Calls Me/Solitude//Ain't Nobody's Business If I Do/Lower Man/Them There Eyes	197?	15.00
—Jukebox issue; small hole, plays at 33 1/3 rpm			
❑ 34900 [PS]	Billie Holiday's Greatest Hits!	197?	15.00
—Part of iLittle LPi series (#203)			
Albums			
AMERICAN RECORDING SOCIETY			
❑ G-409 [M]	Billie Holiday Sings	1956	60.00
—Reissue of Clef 713			
❑ G-431 [M]	Lady Sings the Blues	1957	60.00
—Reissue of Clef 721			
ATLANTIC			
❑ 1614	Strange Fruit	1972	15.00
BLACKHAWK			
❑ BKH-50701	Billie Holiday at Monterey	1986	10.00
BOOK-OF-THE-MONTH CLUB			
❑ 90-5652 [(4)]	Ain't Nobody's Business If I Do	1975	25.00
—Box set with booklet; pressed on CSP labels; alternate number is "P4 12969"			
BULLDOG			
❑ 1007	Billie's Blues	198?	10.00
CLEF			
❑ MGC-118 [10]	Billie Holiday Sings	1953	180.00
❑ MGC-144 [10]	An Evening with Billie Holiday	1954	180.00
❑ MGC-161 [10]	Billie Holiday Favorites	1954	180.00
❑ MGC-169 [10]	Billie Holiday at Jazz at the Philharmonic	1955	180.00
❑ MGC-669 [M]	Music for Torching	1955	100.00
❑ MGC-686 [M]	A Recital by Billie Holiday	1956	120.00
—Reissue of 144 and 161 as one 12-inch LP			
❑ MGC-690 [M]	Solitude — Songs by Billie Holiday	1956	120.00
—Reissue of 118			
❑ MGC-713 [M]	Velvet Moods	1956	120.00
❑ MGC-721 [M]	Lady Sings the Blues	1956	120.00
COLLECTABLES			
❑ COL-5142	Fine and Mellow	198?	12.00
COLUMBIA			
❑ C3L 21 [(3)M]	The Golden Years	1962	50.00
—Red and black label with six "eye" logos			
❑ C3L 21 [(3)M]	The Golden Years	1963	25.00
—Red "Guaranteed High Fidelity" or "360 Sound" label			
❑ C3L 40 [(3)M]	The Golden Years, Vol. 2	1966	30.00
—Red label, "Mono" at bottom			
❑ C3L 40 [(3)M]	The Golden Years, Vol. 2	197?	20.00
—Orange labels			
❑ CL 637 [M]	Lady Day	1954	70.00
—Maroon label, gold print			
❑ CL 637 [M]	Lady Day	1956	40.00
—Red and black label with six "eye" logos			
❑ CL 637 [M]	Lady Day	1962	15.00
—Red "Guaranteed High Fidelity" or "360 Sound" label			
❑ CL 637 [M]	Lady Day	197?	12.00
—Orange label			
❑ CL 1157 [M]	Lady in Satin	1958	40.00
—Red and black label with six "eye" logos			
❑ CL 1157 [M]	Lady in Satin	1962	15.00
—Red "Guaranteed High Fidelity" or "360 Sound" label			
❑ CL 2666 [M]	Billie Holiday's Greatest Hits	1967	15.00
❑ CL 6129 [10]	Billie Holiday Sings	1950	200.00
❑ CL 6163 [10]	Billie Holiday Favorites	1951	200.00
❑ CS 8048 [S]	Lady in Satin	1958	40.00
—Red and black label with six "eye" logos			
❑ CS 8048 [S]	Lady in Satin	1962	15.00
—Red "Guaranteed High Fidelity" or "360 Sound" label			
❑ CS 8048 [S]	Lady in Satin	1999	25.00
—Classic Records reissue on audiophile vinyl			
❑ G 30782 [(2)]	God Bless the Child	1972	20.00
❑ C 32080	Billie's Blues/The Original Recordings by Billie Holiday	1973	15.00
❑ PC 32080	Billie's Blues/The Original Recordings by Billie Holiday	198?	8.00
—Reissue of Harmony LP			
❑ CG 32121 [(2)]	The Billie Holiday Story, Vol. 1	1973	15.00
❑ CG 32124 [(2)]	The Billie Holiday Story, Vol. 2	1973	15.00
❑ CG 32127 [(2)]	The Billie Holiday Story, Vol. 3	1973	15.00
COLUMBIA JAZZ MASTERPIECES			
❑ CJ 40247	Lady in Satin	1987	10.00
❑ CJ 40646	The Quintessential Billie Holiday, Vol. 1	1987	10.00
❑ CJ 40790	The Quintessential Billie Holiday, Vol. 2	1987	10.00
❑ CJ 44048	The Quintessential Billie Holiday, Vol. 3	1988	10.00
❑ CJ 44252	The Quintessential Billie Holiday, Vol. 4	1988	10.00
❑ CJ 44423	The Quintessential Billie Holiday, Vol. 5	1989	10.00
❑ C 45449	The Quintessential Billie Holiday, Vol. 6	1990	10.00
❑ C 46180	The Quintessential Billie Holiday, Vol. 7	1990	10.00
COLUMBIA MUSICAL TREASURY			
❑ P3M 5869 [(3)]	The Golden Years	197?	20.00
COLUMBIA SPECIAL PRODUCTS			
❑ P 14338	Swing, Brother, Swing	198?	10.00
COMMODORE			
❑ FL-20005 [10]	Billie Holiday, Vol. 1	1950	250.00
❑ FL-20006 [10]	Billie Holiday, Vol. 2	1950	250.00
❑ FL-30008 [M]	Billie Holiday	1959	50.00
—Reissue of 20006			
❑ FL-30011 [M]	Billie Holiday with Eddie Heywood and His Orchestra	1959	50.00
—Reissue of 20005			
CROWN			
❑ CST-380 [R]	Billie Holiday & Vivian Fears	196?	12.00
❑ CLP-5380 [M]	Billie Holiday & Vivian Fears	196?	20.00
DECCA			
❑ DXB-161 [(2)M]	The Billie Holiday Story	1959	20.00
❑ DL 5040 [M]	Billie Holiday's Greatest Hits	1968	30.00
—Mono is white label promo only; "Monaural" sticker covers the word "Stereo" on cover			
❑ DL 5345 [10]	Lover Man	1951	200.00
❑ DXSB-7161 [(2)R]	The Billie Holiday Story	1959	15.00
❑ DL 8215 [M]	The Lady Sings	1956	60.00
❑ DL 8701 [M]	The Blues Are Brewin'	1958	60.00

Number	Title (A Side/B Side)	Yr	NM
❑ DL 8702 [M]	Lover Man	1958	60.00
❑ DL 75040 [R]	Billie Holiday's Greatest Hits	1968	12.00
ESP-DISK'			
❑ 3002	The Lady Lives, Vol. 1	1973	12.00
❑ 3003	The Lady Lives, Vol. 2	1973	12.00
EVEREST ARCHIVE OF FOLK & JAZZ			
❑ 265	Billie Holiday	197?	12.00
❑ FS-310	Billie Holiday, Vol. 2	1976	12.00
HALL			
❑ 622	I've Gotta Right to Sing	197?	12.00
HARMONY			
❑ KH 32080	Billie's Blues	1973	10.00
INTERMEDIA			
❑ QS-5076	Billie Holiday Talks and Sings	198?	10.00
JAZZ MAN			
❑ 5005	Billie Holiday at Storyville	198?	10.00
JAZZTONE			
❑ J-1209 [M]	Billie Holiday Sings	1955	50.00
—Reissue of Commodore 20005			
JOLLY ROGER			
❑ 5020 [10]	Billie Holiday, Vol. 1	1954	100.00
❑ 5021 [10]	Billie Holiday, Vol. 2	1954	100.00
❑ 5022 [10]	Billie Holiday, Vol. 3	1954	100.00
KENT GOSPEL			
❑ KST 600	Billie Holiday Sings	197?	15.00
MAINSTREAM			
❑ S-6000 [R]	The Commodore Recordings	1965	12.00
❑ S-6022 [R]	Once Upon a Time	1965	12.00
❑ 56000 [M]	The Commodore Recordings	1965	25.00
❑ 56022 [M]	Once Upon a Time	1965	25.00
MCA			
❑ 275	Billie Holiday's Greatest Hits	1973	10.00
—Reissue of Decca 75040			
❑ 4006 [(2)]	The Billie Holiday Story	1973	12.00
—Reissue of Decca 7161			
METRO			
❑ M-515 [M]	Billie Holiday	1965	15.00
❑ MS-515 [R]	Billie Holiday	1965	12.00
MGM			
❑ GAS-122	Billie Holiday (Golden Archive Series)	1970	12.00
❑ E-3764 [M]	Billie Holiday	1959	40.00
❑ SE-3764 [S]	Billie Holiday	1959	50.00
❑ M3G-4948	Archetypes	1974	12.00
MOBILE FIDELITY			
❑ 1-247	Body and Soul	1996	120.00
—Audiophile vinyl			
MONMOUTH/EVERGREEN			
❑ 7046	Gallant Lady	1973	12.00
PARAMOUNT			
❑ PA-6059	Songs and Conversations	1973	12.00
PHOENIX 10			
❑ PHX-312	Billie Holiday Live	1981	8.00
PICKWICK			
❑ PC-3335	Billie Holiday Sings the Blues	197?	10.00
RIC			
❑ M-2001 [M]	Rare Live Recording	1964	25.00
SCORE			
❑ SLP-4014 [M]	Billie Holiday Sings the Blues	1957	120.00
SOLID STATE			
❑ SS-18040	Lady Love	1969	12.00
SUNSET			
❑ SUM-1147 [M]	Shades of Blue	1967	12.00
❑ SUS-5147 [R]	Shades of Blue	1967	10.00
TIME-LIFE			
❑ STL-J-03 [(3)]	Giants of Jazz	1979	30.00
—Alternate number is Columbia Special Products P3 14786			
TOTEM			
❑ 1037	Billie Holiday On the Air	198?	10.00
TRIP			
❑ 5024	Billie Holiday Live	1974	10.00
UNITED ARTISTS			
❑ UAS-5625	Lady Love	1972	10.00
—Reissue of 15014			
❑ UAJ-14014 [M]	Lady Love	1962	40.00
❑ UASJ-15014 [S]	Lady Love	1962	50.00
VERVE			
❑ VSP-5 [M]	Lady	1966	15.00
❑ VSPS-5 [R]	Lady	1966	12.00
❑ VE-2-2503 [(2)]	The First Verve Sessions	1976	15.00
❑ VE-2-2515 [(2)]	Stormy Blues	1976	15.00
❑ VE-2-2529 [(2)]	All or Nothing at All	198?	15.00
❑ MGVS-6021 [S]	Songs for Distingue Lovers	1960	60.00
❑ MGVS-6021 [S]	Songs for Distingue Lovers	199?	25.00
—Classic Records reissue on audiophile vinyl			
❑ MGVS-6021-45 [(2)S]	Songs for Distingue Lovers	1999	20.00
—Classic Records reissue on two 12-inch 45-rpm records			
❑ MGV-8026 [M]	Music for Torching	1957	40.00
—Reissue of Clef 669			
❑ V-8026 [M]	Music for Torching	1961	20.00
❑ MGV-8027 [M]	A Recital by Billie Holiday	1957	40.00
—Reissue of Clef 686			
❑ V-8027 [M]	A Recital by Billie Holiday	1961	20.00
❑ MGV-8074 [M]	Solitude — Songs by Billie Holiday	1957	40.00
—Reissue of Clef 690			
❑ V-8074 [M]	Solitude — Songs by Billie Holiday	1961	20.00
❑ V6-8074 [R]	Solitude — Songs by Billie Holiday	196?	12.00
❑ MGV-8096 [M]	Velvet Moods	1957	40.00
—Reissue of Clef 713			
❑ V-8096 [M]	Velvet Moods	1961	20.00
❑ MGV-8099 [M]	Lady Sings the Blues	1957	40.00
—Reissue of Clef 721			
❑ V-8099 [M]	Lady Sings the Blues	1957	20.00
❑ MGV-8197 [M]	Body and Soul	1957	60.00
❑ V-8197 [M]	Body and Soul	1961	20.00
❑ MGV-8257 [M]	Songs for Distingue Lovers	1958	60.00
❑ V-8257 [M]	Songs for Distingue Lovers	1961	20.00
❑ V6-8257 [S]	Songs for Distingue Lovers	1961	25.00
❑ MGV-8302 [M]	Stay with Me	1959	50.00
❑ V-8302 [M]	Stay with Me	1961	20.00
❑ MGV-8329 [M]	All or Nothing at All	1959	50.00
❑ V-8329 [M]	All or Nothing at All	1959	20.00
❑ V6-8329 [R]	All or Nothing at All	196?	12.00
❑ MGV-8338-2 [(2)M]	The Unforgettable Lady Day	1959	80.00
❑ V-8338-2 [(2)M]	The Unforgettable Lady Day	1961	25.00
❑ V-8410 [M]	The Essential Billie Holiday	1961	20.00
❑ V6-8410 [R]	The Essential Billie Holiday	1961	12.00
❑ V-8505 [M]	The Essential Jazz Vocals	1963	20.00
❑ V6-8505 [R]	The Essential Jazz Vocals	1963	12.00
❑ V6-8808 [R]	The Best of Billie Holiday	1973	10.00
❑ 2V6S-8816 [(2)]	History of the Real Billie Holiday	1973	15.00
❑ 817359-1 [(2)]	Embraceable You	198?	12.00
❑ 823230-1 [(2)]	Stormy Blues	198?	12.00
❑ 823233-1 [(2)]	History of the Real Billie Holiday	198?	12.00
❑ 823246-1	The Billie Holiday Songbook	198?	10.00
❑ 827160-1	All or Nothing at All	1987	10.00

HOLIDAY, BILLIE, AND STAN GETZ

Number	Title (A Side/B Side)	Yr	NM
Albums			
DALE			
❑ 25 [10]	Billie and Stan	1951	400.00

HOLIDAY, BILLIE/AL HIBBLER

Number	Title (A Side/B Side)	Yr	NM
Albums			
IMPERIAL			
❑ LP-9185 [M]	Billie Holiday, Al Hibbler and the Blues	1962	50.00
❑ LP-12185 [R]	Billie Holiday, Al Hibbler and the Blues	196?	30.00

HOLIDAY, GEORGIE

Number	Title (A Side/B Side)	Yr	NM
45s			
DATE			
❑ 1541	Have a Gluey Christmas/Clarence the Cross-Eyed Bear	1966	12.00
—As "'Little' Georgie Holiday"			
MAP CITY			
❑ 302	Have a Gluey Christmas/A Little Boy's Christmas Prayer	1969	10.00

HOLIDAY, JIMMY

Number	Title (A Side/B Side)	Yr	NM
45s			
DIAL			
❑ 1004	Save Me/Sing a Song of Love	1971	8.00
DIPLOMACY			
❑ 20	The New Breed/Love Me One More Time	1965	12.00
❑ 23	I Can't Stand It/I've Been Done Wrong	1965	12.00
EVEREST			
❑ 2022	How Can I Forget/Janet	1963	15.00
❑ 2027	Don't Laugh/Poor Boy	1963	12.00
❑ 2034	Country Girl/I've Got a Woman	1963	12.00
❑ 2038	I Lied/Alison	1964	12.00
❑ 2049	I Believe in Love/One More Thing	1964	12.00
❑ 2056	Ol' Man River/Hollywood	1965	12.00
KENT			
❑ 482	I Can't Stand It/The New Breed	1968	10.00
MINIT			
❑ 32002	Baby I Love You/You Won't Get Away	1966	12.00
❑ 32011	Turning Point/I'm Gonna Move to the City	1966	10.00
❑ 32021	Ready, Willing and Able/We Got a Good Thing Goin'	1967	10.00
—With Clydie King			
❑ 32023	We Forgot About Love/I'm Gonna Help Hurry My Brothers Home	1967	10.00
❑ 32028	The Beauty of a Girl in Love/Everything Is Love	1967	10.00
❑ 32040	Spread Your Love/We Got a Good Thing Goin'	1968	10.00
❑ 32053	I Don't Want to Hear It/I'm Gonna Use What I Got	1968	10.00
❑ 32058	If You've Got the Money, I've Got the Time/Baby Boy's in Love with You	1969	10.00
❑ 32079	Yesterday Died/Would You Like to Love Me	1969	10.00
❑ 32097	Man Ain't Nothin' Without a Woman/I'm in Love with You	1970	10.00
OLDIES 45			
❑ 138	How Can I Forget/Janet	1964	10.00
—Reissue of Everest 2022			
Albums			
MINIT			
❑ LP-24005 [M]	Turning Point	1966	30.00
❑ LP-40005 [S]	Turning Point	1966	40.00

HOLIDAY, JOHN E.

Number	Title (A Side/B Side)	Yr	NM
45s			
ATLANTIC			
❑ 2091	Yes I Will Love You Tomorrow/Till the End of Time	1961	20.00

HOLIDAY TRIO, THE

Number	Title (A Side/B Side)	Yr	NM
45s			
SANTO			
❑ 500	Desperate/Dark Valley	196?	15.00

HOLIDAYS, THE (1)

Detroit-based R&B group.

Number	Title (A Side/B Side)	Yr	NM
45s			
GOLDEN WORLD			
❑ 36	Makin' Up Time/I'll Love You Forever	1966	20.00
❑ 47	No Greater Love/Watch Out Girl	1966	20.00
GROOVE CITY			
❑ 206	Easy Living/I've Lost You	196?	100.00
—As "The New Holidays"			
REVILOT			
❑ 205	Love's Creeping Up on Me/Never Alone	1967	40.00
❑ 210	I Know She Cares/I Keep Holding On	1967	20.00
❑ 226	I'll Keep Coming Back/All That Is Required of You	1968	50.00

HOLIDAYS, THE (U)

None of these are group (1), but exactly how many groups are represented here is not known.

Number	Title (A Side/B Side)	Yr	NM
45s			
ANDIE			
❑ 5019	The Stars Will Remember/Who Knows, Who Cares	1960	60.00
BRENT			
❑ 7018	Come Back to Me/No Other Love	1961	20.00
BRUNSWICK			
❑ 55084	Sands of Gold/French Riviera	1958	15.00
CORAL			
❑ 62430	Love and Learn/I Want You to Love Me	1964	20.00
DIXIE			
❑ 1156	Little Miss Hurt/I Got News for You	196?	30.00
GALAXY			
❑ 714	Send Back My Love/Deacon Brown	1962	20.00
❑ 714 [DJ]	Send Back My Love/Deacon Brown	1962	30.00
—Promo on colored vinyl			
KING			
❑ 1217	I'm a-Like a-You (Pizza Pie)/Rolling River	1953	30.00
❑ 1246	Just Out of Reach/Let the Dice Decide	1953	30.00
MELBA			
❑ 112	The Robin/Desperately	1957	300.00
MONUMENT			
❑ 431	Merry Christmas Song/A Very Merry Christmas	1960	15.00
NIX			
❑ 537	One Little Kiss/My Girl	1961	30.00

Except when noted otherwise, VG = 25% of NM, and VG+ = 50% of NM. (Example: VG = $2.00, VG+ = $4.00 and NM = $8.00.)

Number	Title (A Side/B Side)	Yr	NM
PAM			
❑ 111	Refreshing/Crazy Discharge	1959	200.00
ROBBEE			
❑ 103	Them There Eyes/The Kiss Cha Cha	1960	60.00
❑ 107	Lonely Summer/Then I'll Be Tired of You	1960	50.00
SPECIALTY			
❑ 533	Irene/Aw-Aw Baby	1954	40.00
TRACK			
❑ 101	Patty Ann/Big Brown Eyes	1962	15.00

HOLLAND, BRIAN

Number	Title (A Side/B Side)	Yr	NM
45s			
INVICTUS			
❑ 1265	I'm So Glad (Part 1)/I'm So Glad (Part 2)	1974	5.00
❑ 1272	Super Woman/Let's Get Together	1974	5.00
KUDO			
❑ 667	(Where's the Joy?) In Nature Boy/Shock	1958	600.00
—First name as "Briant"			

HOLLAND, EDDIE Also see HOLLAND-DOZIER.

Number	Title (A Side/B Side)	Yr	NM
45s			
MERCURY			
❑ 71290	You/Little Miss Ruby	1958	200.00
MOTOWN			
❑ 1021	Jamie/Take a Chance on Me	1961	25.00
❑ 1026	You Deserve What You Got/Last Night I Had a Vision	1962	500.00
❑ 1030 [PS]	If Cleopatra Took a Chance/What About Me	1962	100.00
❑ 1030	If Cleopatra Took a Chance/What About Me	1962	20.00
❑ 1031	If It's Love (It's All Right)/It's Not Too Late	1962	40.00
❑ 1036	Darling I Hum Our Song/Just a Few Memories	1963	60.00
❑ 1043	Brenda/Baby Shake	1963	40.00
❑ 1049	I'm On the Outside Looking In/I Couldn't Cry If I Wanted To	1963	300.00
❑ 1052	Leaving Here/Brenda	1964	60.00
❑ 1058	Just Ain't Enough Love/Last Night I Had a Vision	1964	40.00
❑ 1063	Candy to Me/If You Don't Want My Love	1964	30.00
TAMLA			
❑ 102	Merry-Go-Round/It Moves Me	1959	400.00
UNITED ARTISTS			
❑ 172	Merry-Go-Round/It Moves Me	1959	30.00
❑ 191	Because I Love Her/Everybody's Going	1959	30.00
❑ 207	Magic Mirror/Will You Love Me	1960	30.00
❑ 280	The Last Laugh/Why Do You Want to Let Me Go	1960	50.00
Albums			
MOTOWN			
❑ 604 [M]	Eddie Holland	1963	400.00

HOLLAND-DOZIER Also see LAMONT DOZIER; EDDIE HOLLAND.

Number	Title (A Side/B Side)	Yr	NM
45s			
INVICTUS			
❑ 1253	Slipping Away/Can't Get Enough	1973	15.00
❑ 1254	If You Don't Wanta Be in My Life/New Breed Kinda Woman	1973	100.00
❑ 1258	You Took Me from a World Outside/I'm Gonna Hijack Ya, Kidnap Ya, Take What I Want	1973	8.00
❑ 9110	Don't Leave Me (Part 1)/Don't Leave Me (Part 2)	1972	15.00
❑ 9125	Why Can't We Be Lovers/Don't Leave Me	1972	8.00
❑ 9133	Don't Leave Me Starvin' for Your Love (Part 1)/Don't Leave Me Starvin' for Your Love (Part 2)	1972	8.00
MOTOWN			
❑ 1045	What Goes Up Must Come Down/Come On Home	1963	50.00

HOLLIDAY, MICHAEL

Number	Title (A Side/B Side)	Yr	NM
45s			
CAPITOL			
❑ F3720	Good Luck, Good Health, God Bless You/John and Julie	1957	12.00
❑ F4018	Rooney/Keep Your Heart	1958	12.00

The Hollies, "King Midas in Reverse," Epic 5-10234, 1967, **$15.**

HOLLIES, THE Also see ALLAN CLARKE; GRAHAM NASH; TERRY SYLVESTER; THE TREMELOES/THE HOLLIES.

Number	Title (A Side/B Side)	Yr	NM
12-Inch Singles			
ATLANTIC			
❑ PR 502 [DJ]	Stop in the Name of Love/If the Lights Go Out	1983	8.00
45s			
ATLANTIC			
❑ 89768 [DJ]	Casualty (same on both sides)	1983	5.00
—May be promo only			
❑ 89784	If the Lights Go Out/Someone Else's Eyes	1983	3.00
❑ 89819	Stop in the Name of Love/Musical Pictures	1983	3.00
❑ 89819 [PS]	Stop in the Name of Love/Musical Pictures	1983	5.00
EPIC			
❑ 10180	Carrie-Anne/Signs That Will Never Change	1967	8.00
❑ 10180 [PS]	Carrie-Anne/Signs That Will Never Change	1967	15.00
❑ 10234	King Midas in Reverse/Water on the Brain	1967	8.00
❑ 10234 [PS]	King Midas in Reverse/Water on the Brain	1967	15.00
❑ 10251	Dear Eloise/When Your Light's Turned On	1967	8.00
❑ 10251 [PS]	Dear Eloise/When Your Light's Turned On	1967	15.00
❑ 10298	Jennifer Eccles/Try It	1968	8.00
❑ 10361	Do the Best You Can/Elevated Observations	1968	8.00
❑ 10400	Listen to Me/Everything Is Sunshine	1968	8.00
❑ 10454	Sorry Suzanne/Not That Way at All	1969	8.00
❑ 10532	He Ain't Heavy, He's My Brother/Cos You Like to Love Me	1969	6.00
—A-side: Elton John on piano			
❑ 10613	I Can't Tell the Bottom from the Top/Mad Professor Blythe	1970	6.00
❑ 10677	Gasoline Alley Bred/Dandelion Wine	1970	10.00
❑ 10716	Survival of the Fittest/Man Without a Heart	1971	12.00
❑ 10754	Hey Willy/Row the Boat Together	1971	10.00
❑ 10842	The Baby/Oh Granny	1972	10.00
❑ 10842 [PS]	The Baby/Oh Granny	1972	100.00
❑ 10871	Long Cool Woman (In a Black Dress)/Look What We've Got	1972	5.00
❑ 10920	Long Dark Road/Indian Girl	1972	5.00
❑ 10951	Magic Woman Touch/Blue in the Morning	1973	5.00
❑ 10989	Jesus Was a Crossmaker/I Had a Dream	1973	5.00
❑ 11025	Won't We Feel Good/Slow Down	1973	5.00
❑ 11051	The Day That Curley Billy Shot Down Crazy Sam McGee/Born a Man	1973	5.00
❑ 11100	The Air That I Breathe/No More Riders	1974	5.00
❑ 50029	Don't Let Me Down/Layin' to the Music	1974	5.00
❑ 50086	Sandy/Second Hand Hangups	1975	5.00
❑ 50110	Another Night/Time Machine Jive	1975	4.00
❑ 50144	Look Out Johnny/I'm Down	1975	4.00
❑ 50204	Crocodile Woman (She Bites)/Write On	1976	4.00
❑ 50359	Sandy/Second Hand Hangups	1977	4.00
❑ 50422	Draggin' My Heels/I Won't Move Over	1977	4.00
❑ 50522	Burn Out/Writing on the Wall	1978	4.00
IMPERIAL			
❑ 54050	Look Through My Window/I'm Alive	196?	15.00
—"The Golden Series" gold label reissue with incorrect A-side title			
❑ 66026	Just One Look/Keep Off That Friend of Mine	1964	20.00
❑ 66044	Here I Go Again/Lucille	1964	15.00
❑ 66070	Come On Back/We're Through	1964	15.00
❑ 66099	Yes I Will/Nobody	1965	40.00
❑ 66119	I'm Alive/You Know He Did	1965	15.00
❑ 66134	Look Through Any Window/So Lonely	1965	12.00

Number	Title (A Side/B Side)	Yr	NM
❑ 66158	I Can't Let Go/I've Got a Way of My Own	1966	15.00
❑ 66186	Bus Stop/Don't Run and Hide	1966	12.00
❑ 66214	Stop Stop Stop/It's You	1966	12.00
❑ 66231	On a Carousel/All the World Is Love	1967	12.00
❑ 66231 [PS]	On a Carousel/All the World Is Love	1967	30.00
❑ 66240	Pay You Back With Interest/ Whatcha Gonna Do 'Bout It	1967	12.00
❑ 66258	Just One Look/Running Through the Night	1967	12.00
❑ 66271	If I Needed Someone/I'll Be True to You (Yes I Will)	1968	40.00
LIBERTY			
❑ 55674	Stay/Now's the Time	1964	60.00
UNITED ARTISTS			
❑ 50079	After the Fox/The Fox Trot	1966	20.00
—With Peter Sellers			
Albums			
ATLANTIC			
❑ 80076	What Goes Around	1983	10.00
CAPITOL			
❑ N-16056	Hollies' Greatest	1980	8.00
COLUMBIA LIMITED EDITION			
❑ LE 10178	He Ain't Heavy, He's My Brother	1976	12.00
EMI AMERICA			
❑ SN-16397	More Great Hits (1963-1968)	1986	8.00
EPIC			
❑ AS 138 [DJ]	Everything You Always Wanted to Hear by the Hollies But Were Afraid to Ask For	1976	20.00
—Promo-only sampler album			
❑ LN 24315 [M]	Evolution	1967	30.00
❑ LN 24344 [M]	Dear Eloise/King Midas in Reverse	1967	30.00
❑ BN 26315 [S]	Evolution	1967	25.00
❑ BN 26344 [S]	Dear Eloise/King Midas in Reverse	1967	25.00
❑ BN 26447	Words and Music by Bob Dylan	1969	15.00
—Yellow label			
❑ BN 26447	Words and Music by Bob Dylan	1973	10.00
—Orange label			
❑ BN 26538	He Ain't Heavy, He's My Brother	1970	20.00
❑ E 30255	Moving Finger	1971	20.00
❑ KE 30958	Distant Light	1972	15.00
—Yellow label			
❑ KE 30958	Distant Light	1974	10.00
—Orange label			
❑ PE 30958	Distant Light	1986	8.00
—Blue label			
❑ KE 31992	Romany	1972	12.00
—Yellow label			
❑ KE 31992	Romany	1974	10.00
—Orange label			
❑ KE 32061	The Hollies' Greatest Hits	1973	12.00
—Yellow label			
❑ KE 32061	The Hollies' Greatest Hits	1974	10.00
—Orange label			
❑ PE 32061	The Hollies' Greatest Hits	1979	8.00
—Blue label			
❑ KE 32574	Hollies	1974	10.00
❑ PE 33387	Another Night	1975	10.00
❑ PE 34714	Clarke, Hicks, Sylvester, Calvert & Elliot	1977	10.00
❑ JE 35334	A Crazy Steal	1978	10.00
IMPERIAL			
❑ LP-9265 [M]	Here I Go Again	1964	50.00
—Black and pink label			
❑ LP-9265 [M]	Here I Go Again	1964	150.00
—Black label with stars			
❑ LP-9299 [M]	Hear! Here!	1965	50.00
❑ LP-9312 [M]	The Hollies — Beat Group	1966	30.00
❑ LP-9330 [M]	Bus Stop	1966	25.00
—Black and green label			
❑ LP-9330 [M]	Bus Stop	1966	30.00
—Black and pink label			
❑ LP-9339 [M]	Stop! Stop! Stop!	1966	25.00
❑ LP-9350 [M]	The Hollies' Greatest Hits	1967	20.00
❑ LP-12265 [R]	Here I Go Again	1964	30.00
—Black and pink label			
❑ LP-12265 [R]	Here I Go Again	1964	100.00
—Black label with silver print			
❑ LP-12299 [R]	Hear! Here!	1965	30.00
❑ LP-12312 [S]	The Hollies — Beat Group	1966	40.00
❑ LP-12330 [R]	Bus Stop	1966	20.00
—Black and green label			
❑ LP-12330 [R]	Bus Stop	1966	25.00
—Black and pink label			
❑ LP-12339 [S]	Stop! Stop! Stop!	1966	30.00
❑ LP-12350 [P]	The Hollies' Greatest Hits	1967	25.00
LIBERTY			
❑ LN-10216	Pay You Back with Interest	1982	8.00
PAIR			
❑ PDL2-1041 [(2)]	Hottest Hits	1986	15.00
REALM			
❑ 2V-8026 [(2)]	The Hollies, Vol. 1	1976	15.00
—Two-record TV package			
❑ 1V-8027	The Hollies, Vol. 2	1976	12.00
—TV package sold with Realm 8026			
UNITED ARTISTS			
❑ UA-LA329-E	The Very Best of the Hollies	1975	10.00

HOLLISTER, BOBBY

Number	Title (A Side/B Side)	Yr	NM
45s			
PIKE			
❑ 5910	Ring Around Your Neck/ Love's Gamble	1961	15.00
❑ 5910 [PS]	Ring Around Your Neck/ Love's Gamble	1961	40.00

HOLLOWAY, BRENDA

Number	Title (A Side/B Side)	Yr	NM
45s			
DONNA			
❑ 1358	Echo/Hey Fool	1962	40.00
❑ 1366	Game of Love/Echo-Echo-Echo	1962	50.00
❑ 1370	I'll Give My Life/More Echo	1962	50.00
TAMLA			
❑ 54094	Every Little Bit Hurts/ Land of 1,000 Boys	1964	12.00
❑ 54099	I'll Always Love You/Sad Song	1964	15.00
❑ 54111	When I'm Gone/I've Been Good to You	1965	15.00
❑ 54111 [PS]	When I'm Gone/I've Been Good to You	1965	100.00
❑ 54115	Operator/I'll Be Available	1965	15.00
❑ 54121	You Can Cry on My Shoulder/ How Many Times Did You Mean It	1965	20.00
❑ 54125	Sad Song/Together 'Til the End of Time	1965	20.00
❑ 54137	Hurt a Little Every Day/ Where Were You	1966	30.00
❑ 54144	'Til Johnny Comes/ Where Were You	1967	200.00
❑ 54148	Just Look What You've Done/ Starting the Hurt All Over Again	1967	25.00
❑ 54155	You've Made Me So Very Happy/I've Got to Find It	1967	20.00
❑ 206312 [DJ]	Play It Cool, Stay in School	1966	1000.
—Promo for Women's Ad Club of Detroit			
Albums			
MOTOWN			
❑ 5242 ML	Every Little Bit Hurts	1982	12.00
TAMLA			
❑ T 257 [M]	Every Little Bit Hurts	1964	200.00
❑ TS 257 [R]	Every Little Bit Hurts	1964	150.00

HOLLOWAY, LOLEATTA

Number	Title (A Side/B Side)	Yr	NM
12-Inch Singles			
GOLD MIND			
❑ 402	Catch Me on the Rebound (10:51)/(7:22)	1978	15.00
❑ 4006	Hit and Run/It's Getting Stronger	1977	20.00
SELECT			
❑ 5585	Strong Enough (5 versions)	1991	8.00
STREETWISE			
❑ 2230	Crash Goes Love/Sweet Thing	1984	10.00
45s			
AWARE			
❑ 033	Our Love/Mother of Shame	1973	6.00
❑ 039	H-E-L-P Me My Love/ (B-side unknown)	1974	6.00
❑ 047	Cry to Me/So Can I	1974	6.00
❑ 050	The Show Must Go On/I Know Where You're Coming From	1975	6.00
❑ 054	Casanova/Only a Fool	1975	6.00
GALAXY			
❑ 780	Rainbow '71/Bring It On Up	1971	8.00
GOLD MIND			
❑ 4000	Dreamin'/Worn Out Broken Heart	1976	6.00
❑ 4001	Hit and Run/Is It Just a Man's Way	1977	6.00
❑ 4007	It's Getting Stronger/How Heartaches Are Made	1977	6.00
❑ 4012	Only You/Good Good Feeling	1978	6.00
—A-side with Bunny Sigler			
❑ 4016	Catch Me on the Rebound/ Mama Don't, Papa Won't	1978	6.00
❑ 4021	That's What You Said/ There'll Come a Time	1979	6.00
❑ 4024	Love Sensation/Short End of the Stick	1980	10.00
❑ 4025	I've Been Loving You Too Long/ Two Became a Crowd	1980	6.00
SALSOUL			
❑ 2045	Run Away/Run Away (Part 2)	1977	6.00
—With the Salsoul Orchestra			
❑ 7034	Seconds/Columbia: The Space Shuttle	1981	6.00
—With the Salsoul Orchestra			
STREETWISE			
❑ 1130	Crash Goes Love/Sweet Thing	1984	6.00
Albums			
GOLD MIND			
❑ 7500	Loleatta	1977	20.00
❑ A-9501	Queen of the Night	1978	20.00
❑ GA-9506	Love Sensation	1979	20.00

HOLLOWAY, PATRICE

Also see JOSIE AND THE PUSSYCATS.

Number	Title (A Side/B Side)	Yr	NM
45s			
CAPITOL			
❑ 3176	Evidence/That's the Chance You Gotta Take	1971	40.00
❑ 3265	Black Mother Goose/That's the Chance You Gotta Take	1972	30.00
❑ 5680	Stolen Hours/Lucky My Boy	1966	500.00
❑ 5778	Love and Desire/Ecstasy	1967	300.00
❑ 5985	Stay with Your Own Kind/ That's All You Got to Do	1967	40.00
TASTE			
❑ 125	Do the Del Viking (Pt. 1)/ Do the Del Viking (Pt. 2)	1963	80.00
V.I.P.			
❑ 25001	(He Is) The Boy of My Dreams/ Stevie	1964	5000.
—VG 2500; VG+ 3750			

HOLLY, BUDDY

Also see THE CRICKETS (1).

Number	Title (A Side/B Side)	Yr	NM
45s			
CORAL			
❑ 61852	Words of Love/Mailman, Bring Me No More Blues	1957	400.00
—Promos for any Coral title valued at $50 or under Near Mint are worth 2-4 times the stock copy value.			
❑ 61885	Peggy Sue/Everyday	1957	50.00
—Orange label			
❑ 61885	Peggy Sue/Everyday	196?	25.00
—Black color bars label			
❑ 61947	I'm Gonna Love You Too/ Listen to Me	1958	50.00
❑ 61985	Rave On/Take Your Time	1958	50.00
❑ 62006	Early in the Morning/ Now We're One	1958	50.00
❑ 62051	Heartbeat/Well...All Right	1958	50.00
❑ 62074	It Doesn't Matter Anymore/ Raining in My Heart	1959	40.00
❑ 62134	Peggy Sue Got Married/ Crying, Waiting, Hoping	1959	60.00
❑ 62210	True Love Ways/That Makes It Tough	1960	50.00
❑ 62283	You're So Square (Baby I Don't Care)/Valley of Tears	1961	160.00
—Evidently only released in Canada			
❑ 62329	Reminiscing/Wait Till the Sun Shines, Nellie	1962	30.00
❑ 62352	True Love Ways/Bo Diddley	1963	60.00
❑ 62369	Brown Eyed Handsome Man/ Wishing	1963	40.00
❑ 62390	Rock Around with Ollie Vee/ I'm Gonna Love You Too	1963	40.00
❑ 62448	Slippin' and Slidin'/What to Do	1965	100.00
❑ 62554	Rave On/Early in the Morning	1968	30.00
❑ 62558	Love Is Strange/You're the One	1969	20.00
❑ 62558 [PS]	Love Is Strange/You're the One	1969	30.00
DECCA			
❑ 29854	Blue Days, Black Nights/Love Me	1956	300.00
—With star under "Decca"			
❑ 29854	Blue Days, Black Nights/Love Me	1956	600.00
—With lines on either side of "Decca"			
❑ 29854 [DJ]	Blue Days, Black Nights/Love Me	1956	400.00
—Promos have pink labels			
❑ 30166	Modern Don Juan/You Are My One Desire	1956	250.00
—With star under "Decca"			
❑ 30166	Modern Don Juan/You Are My One Desire	1956	500.00
—With lines on either side of "Decca"			
❑ 30166 [DJ]	Modern Don Juan/You Are My One Desire	1956	300.00
—Promos have pink labels			
❑ 30434	That'll Be the Day/Rock Around with Ollie Vee	1957	250.00
—With star under "Decca"			
❑ 30434	That'll Be the Day/Rock Around with Ollie Vee	1957	400.00
—With lines on either side of "Decca"			
❑ 30434 [DJ]	That'll Be the Day/Rock Around with Ollie Vee	1957	250.00
—Pink label promo			

Except when noted otherwise, VG = 25% of NM, and VG+ = 50% of NM. (Example: VG = $2.00, VG+ = $4.00 and NM = $8.00.)

Number	Title (A Side/B Side)	Yr	NM
❑ 30543	Love Me/You Are My One Desire	1958	300.00
❑ 30543 [DJ]	Love Me/You Are My One Desire	1958	200.00
—Pink label promos			
❑ 30543 [DJ]	Love Me/You Are My One Desire	1958	300.00
—Green label promos			
❑ 30650	Ting-a-Ling/Girl on My Mind	1958	300.00
❑ 30650 [DJ]	Ting-a-Ling/Girl on My Mind	1958	200.00
—Promos have pink labels			
MCA			
❑ 40905	It Doesn't Matter Anymore/ Peggy Sue	1978	5.00
❑ 40905 [PS]	It Doesn't Matter Anymore/ Peggy Sue	1978	5.00
7-Inch Extended Plays			
CORAL			
❑ EC 81169	Listen to Me/Peggy Sue// I'm Gonna Love You Too/ Everyday	1958	300.00
❑ EC 81169 [PS]	Listen to Me	1958	300.00
❑ EC 81182	It Doesn't Matter Anymore/ Heartbeat//Raining in My Heart/Early in the Morning	1959	300.00
❑ EC 81182 [PS]	The Buddy Holly Story	1959	300.00
❑ EC 81191	Peggy Sue Got Married/Crying, Waiting, Hoping//Learning the Game/That Makes It Tough	1961	250.00
❑ EC 81191 [PS]	Buddy Holly	1961	250.00
❑ EC 81193	Brown Eyed Handsome Man/ Wishing//Bo Diddley/ True Love Ways	1961	250.00
❑ EC 81193 [PS]	Brown Eyed Handsome Man	1961	250.00
DECCA			
❑ ED 2575	*That'll Be the Day/Blue Days — Black Nights/Ting-a-Ling/ You Are My One Desire	1958	600.00
❑ ED 2575 [PS]	That'll Be the Day	1958	600.00
—Sleeve has other EP ads on back			
❑ ED 2575 [PS]	That'll Be the Day	1958	2000.
—Sleeve has liner notes on back			
Albums			
CORAL			
❑ CXB 8 [(2)M]	The Best of Buddy Holly	1966	80.00
❑ CXSB 8 [(2)R]	The Best of Buddy Holly	1966	50.00
❑ CRL 57210 [M]	Buddy Holly	1958	400.00
—Maroon label			
❑ CRL 57210 [M]	Buddy Holly	1964	100.00
—Black label with color bars			
❑ CRL 57279 [M]	The Buddy Holly Story	1959	150.00
—Maroon label; back color print in all black			
❑ CRL 57279 [M]	The Buddy Holly Story	1959	300.00
—Maroon label; back color print in black and red			
❑ CRL 57279 [M]	The Buddy Holly Story	1963	80.00
—Black label with color bars			
❑ CRL 57326 [M]	The Buddy Holly Story, Vol. 2	1959	200.00
—Maroon label			
❑ CRL 57326 [M]	The Buddy Holly Story, Vol. 2	1963	80.00
—Black label with color bars			
❑ CRL 57405 [M]	Buddy Holly and the Crickets	1962	150.00
—Reissue of the Crickets LP on Brunswick 54038			
❑ CRL 57426 [M]	Reminiscing	1963	200.00
—Maroon label			
❑ CRL 57426 [M]	Reminiscing	1964	80.00
—Black label with color bars			
❑ CRL 57450 [M]	Buddy Holly Showcase	1964	100.00
❑ CRL 57463 [M]	Holly in the Hills	1965	120.00
❑ CRL 57492 [M]	Buddy Holly's Greatest Hits	1967	80.00
❑ CRL 757279 [R]	The Buddy Holly Story	1963	40.00
❑ CRL 757326 [R]	The Buddy Holly Story, Vol. 2	1963	40.00
❑ CRL 757405 [R]	Buddy Holly and the Crickets	1963	40.00
❑ CRL 757426 [R]	Reminiscing	1964	40.00
❑ CRL 757450 [R]	Buddy Holly Showcase	1964	80.00
❑ CRL 757463 [R]	Holly in the Hills	1965	100.00
❑ CRL 757492 [P]	Buddy Holly's Greatest Hits	1967	50.00
❑ CRL 757504 [S]	Giant	1969	50.00
CRICKET			
❑ C001000	Buddy Holly Live — Vol. 1	197?	20.00
❑ C001001	Buddy Holly Live — Vol. 1	197?	20.00
DECCA			
❑ DXSE 7207 [(2)]	A Rock 'n' Roll Collection	1972	40.00
❑ DL 8707 [M]	That'll Be the Day	1958	1500.
—Black label with silver print			
❑ DL 8707 [M]	That'll Be the Day	1961	300.00
—Black label with color bars			
GREAT NORTHWEST			
❑ GNW-4014	Visions of Buddy	197?	10.00
—Interview album			
MCA			
❑ 737	The Great Buddy Holly	197?	10.00
—Reissue of MCA Coral LP			
❑ 1484	Buddy Holly/The Crickets 20 Golden Greats	198?	8.00
—Reissue of 3040			
❑ 3040	Buddy Holly/The Crickets 20 Golden Greats	1978	15.00
❑ 4009 [(2)]	A Rock 'n' Roll Collection	1973	20.00
—Black labels with rainbow			
❑ 4009 [(2)]	A Rock 'n' Roll Collection	1978	12.00
—Later pressings on tan or blue/rainbow labels			
❑ 4184 [(2)]	Legend	1985	20.00
❑ 5540 [(2)]	From the Original Master Tapes	1986	25.00
❑ 11161	Buddy Holly	1995	40.00
—Audiophile "Heavy Vinyl" reissue with gatefold cover			
❑ 25239	Buddy Holly	1989	12.00
—Reissue of Coral 57210			
❑ 27059	For the First Time Anywhere	1983	10.00
❑ 80000 [(6)]	The Complete Buddy Holly	1981	80.00
—Box set with booklet and custom innersleeves			
MCA CORAL			
❑ CD-20101	The Great Buddy Holly	1973	12.00
VOCALION			
❑ VL 3811 [M]	The Great Buddy Holly	1967	80.00
❑ VL 73811 [R]	The Great Buddy Holly	1967	50.00
❑ VL 73923	Good Rockin'	1971	120.00

HOLLY TWINS, THE

Number	Title (A Side/B Side)	Yr	NM
45s			
LIBERTY			
❑ 55015	Take Me Back/It's Easy	1956	25.00
❑ 55048	I Want Elvis for Christmas/ The Tender Age	1956	50.00
RENDEZVOUS			
❑ 180	Okee-Feenokee/Potato Chips	1962	12.00
❑ 180 [PS]	Okee-Feenokee/Potato Chips	1962	30.00

HOLLYHAWKS, THE With Niki Sullivan, ex-CRICKETS (1).

Number	Title (A Side/B Side)	Yr	NM
45s			
JUBILEE			
❑ 5441	I Cry All the Time/When Came the Fall	1962	80.00

HOLLYRIDGE STRINGS, THE

Number	Title (A Side/B Side)	Yr	NM
45s			
CAPITOL			
❑ 4557	Lucy's Theme/Hippodrome	1961	10.00
❑ 4600	The Thunder of Drums/The Guns of Navarone	1961	10.00
❑ 4631	Moon River/Something Big	1961	10.00
❑ 4664	The Comancheros/Theme from "The Devil at 4 O'Clock"	1961	10.00
❑ 4687	My Melancholy Baby/ Light in the Piazza	1962	8.00
❑ 4720	It Happened in Athens/ Song of Greece	1962	8.00
❑ 5165	The Seven Faces of Dr. Lao/ The Fall of Love	1964	8.00
❑ 5207	Love Me Do/All My Loving	1964	12.00
❑ 5432	L-O-V-E/Those Lazy-Hazy-Crazy Days of Summer	1965	8.00
❑ 5533	Santa's Got a Brand New Bag/ Have Yourself a Merry Little Christmas	1965	10.00
❑ 5551	Skyscraper/Gaiety	1965	8.00
7-Inch Extended Plays			
CAPITOL			
❑ SXA-2221	Don't Be Cruel/Teddy Bear/ Return to Sender//Bossa Nova, Baby/Good Luck Charm/Are You Lonesome Tonight?	1964	20.00
—Jukebox issue; small hole, plays at 33 1/3 rpm			
❑ SXA-2221 [PS]	The Hollyridge Strings Play Instrumental Versions of Hits Made Famous by Elvis Presley	1964	20.00
—Title as listed on cover; title on label is "The Hollyridge Strings Play Hit Songs Made Famous by Elvis Presley"			
Albums			
CAPITOL			
❑ ST-883	Hits of the 70's	1971	12.00
❑ SM-2116	The Beatles Song Book	197?	10.00
❑ ST 2116 [S]	The Beatles Song Book	1964	20.00
❑ T 2116 [M]	The Beatles Song Book	1964	15.00
❑ SM-2156	The Beach Boys Song Book	197?	10.00
❑ ST 2156 [S]	The Beach Boys Song Book	1964	20.00
❑ T 2156 [M]	The Beach Boys Song Book	1964	15.00
❑ ST 2199 [S]	Hits Made Famous by the Four Seasons	1965	20.00
❑ T 2199 [M]	Hits Made Famous by the Four Seasons	1965	15.00
❑ ST 2202 [S]	The Beatles Song Book, Vol. 2	1965	20.00
❑ T 2202 [M]	The Beatles Song Book, Vol. 2	1965	15.00
❑ ST 2221 [S]	Hits Made Famous by Elvis Presley	1965	20.00
❑ T 2221 [M]	Hits Made Famous by Elvis Presley	1965	15.00
❑ ST 2310 [S]	The Nat King Cole Song Book	1965	20.00
❑ T 2310 [M]	The Nat King Cole Song Book	1965	15.00
❑ ST 2404 [S]	Christmas Favorites by the Hollyridge Strings	1965	15.00
❑ T 2404 [M]	Christmas Favorites by the Hollyridge Strings	1965	12.00
❑ SM-2429	The New Beatles Song Book	197?	10.00
❑ ST 2429 [S]	The New Beatles Song Book	1966	20.00
❑ T 2429 [M]	The New Beatles Song Book	1966	15.00
❑ ST 2564 [S]	Oldies But Goldies	1966	20.00
❑ T 2564 [M]	Oldies But Goldies	1966	15.00
❑ ST 2611 [S]	Skyscraper	1966	20.00
❑ T 2611 [M]	Skyscraper	1966	15.00
❑ ST 2656 [S]	The Beatles Song Book, Vol. 4	1967	15.00
❑ T 2656 [M]	The Beatles Song Book, Vol. 4	1967	20.00
❑ ST 2749 [S]	The Beach Boys Song Book, Vol. 2	1967	15.00
❑ T 2749 [M]	The Beach Boys Song Book, Vol. 2	1967	20.00
❑ ST 2998	Hits Made Famous by Simon and Garfunkel	1968	15.00
❑ SM-11830	Christmas Favorites by the Hollyridge Strings	1978	10.00
—Abridged reissue of ST 2404			

H

HOLLYWOOD ARGYLES, THE Also see FLESH GORDON AND THE NUDE HOLLYWOOD ARGYLES; GARY PAXTON.

Number	Title (A Side/B Side)	Yr	NM
45s			
BRENT			
❑ 7004	Vacation Days Are Over/ It Takes Time	1959	30.00
—As "The Argyles"			
CHATTAHOOCHIE			
❑ 691	Long Hair, Unsquare Dude Called Jack/Ole	1965	15.00
FELSTED			
❑ 8674	Bossy Nover/Find Another Way	1963	20.00
FINER ARTS			
❑ 1002	The Morning After/See You in the Morning	1961	20.00
KAMMY			
❑ 105	Alley-Oop '65/Do the Funky Foot	1965	20.00
—As "The New Hollywood Argyles"			
LUTE			
❑ 5905	Alley Oop/Sho' Know a Lot About Love	1960	25.00
❑ 5908	Gun Totin' Critter Called Jack/ Bug-Eye	1960	20.00
❑ 6002	Hully Gully/So Fine	1960	20.00
PAXLEY			
❑ 200	Unemployment (same on both sides)	196?	10.00
❑ 752	You've Been Torturing Me/ The Grubble	1960	20.00
TRILL			
❑ 6311	The Watermelon Song/ Short Fat Outlaw	196?	25.00
Albums			
LUTE			
❑ L-9001 [M]	The Hollywood Argyles (Alley Oop)	1960	700.00

HOLLYWOOD FLAMES, THE Also see BOBBY DAY.

Number	Title (A Side/B Side)	Yr	NM
45s			
ATCO			
❑ 6155	Every Day, Every Way/ If I Thought I Needed You	1959	15.00
❑ 6164	Ball and Chain/I Found a Boy	1960	15.00
❑ 6171	Devil or Angel/Do You Ever Think of Me	1960	15.00
❑ 6180	Money Honey/My Heart's On Fire	1960	15.00
CHESS			
❑ 1787	Gee/Yes They Do	1961	12.00
DECCA			
❑ 29285	Peggy/Ooh La La	1954	75.00
❑ 48331	Let's Talk It Over/I Know	1955	75.00
EBB			
❑ 119	Buzz-Buzz-Buzz/Crazy	1957	30.00
❑ 131	Give Me Back My Heart/ A Little Bird	1958	25.00
❑ 144	Frankenstein's Den/ Strollin' on the Beach	1958	25.00
❑ 146	Chains of Love/Let's Talk It Over	1958	25.00
❑ 149	A Star Fell/I'll Get By	1958	25.00
❑ 153	I'll Be Seeing You/Just for You	1959	30.00
❑ 158	So Good/There Is Something on Your Mind	1959	25.00
❑ 162	Now That You're Gone/ Hawaiian Dream	1959	25.00
❑ 163	Much Too Much/In the Dark	1959	25.00
LUCKY			
❑ 001	One Night with a Fool/ Ride, Helen, Ride	1954	600.00
❑ 006	Peggy/Ooh-La-La	1954	600.00

Number	Title (A Side/B Side)	Yr	NM
❑ 009	Let's Talk It Over/I Know	1954	400.00
MONA-LEE			
❑ 135	Buzz-Buzz-Buzz/Crazy	1958	25.00
MONEY			
❑ 202	Fare Thee Well/I'm Leaving	1954	400.00
SWING TIME			
❑ 345	Let's Talk It Over/I Know	1953	500.00
❑ 346	Go and Get Some More/Another Soldier Gone	1953	500.00
—B-side by the Question Marks			
SYMBOL			
❑ 211	Dance Senorita/Annie Don't Love Me Anymore	1965	150.00
❑ 215	I'm Coming Home/I'm Gonna Stand By You	1966	50.00
VEE JAY			
❑ 515	Drop Me a Line/Letter to My Love	1963	75.00

HOLLYWOOD PERSUADERS, THE

45s

Number	Title (A Side/B Side)	Yr	NM
ORIGINAL SOUND			
❑ 39	Tijuana Surf/Grunion Run	1964	50.00
❑ 39	Tijuana/Grunion Run	1964	50.00
❑ 44	Persuasion/Juarez	1964	25.00
❑ 50	Drums-A-Go-Go/Agua Caliente	1965	25.00
❑ 58	Hollywood A-Go-Go/Eve of Destruction	1965	50.00

Albums

Number	Title (A Side/B Side)	Yr	NM
ORIGINAL SOUND			
❑ LPM-5013 [M]	Drums a-Go-Go	1965	50.00
❑ LPS-8874 [S]	Drums a-Go-Go	1965	60.00

HOLLYWOOD PLAYBOYS, THE

With Nick Massi, later of THE FOUR SEASONS.

45s

Number	Title (A Side/B Side)	Yr	NM
SURE			
❑ 105	Ding Dong School Is Out/Talk to Audrey	1960	30.00

HOLLYWOOD PRODUCERS, THE

45s

Number	Title (A Side/B Side)	Yr	NM
PARKWAY			
❑ 993	Whits Silk Glove/You're Not Welcome	1966	30.00

HOLMAN, EDDIE

45s

Number	Title (A Side/B Side)	Yr	NM
ABC			
❑ 11149	I Love You/I Surrender	1968	50.00
❑ 11240	Hey There Lonely Girl/It's All in the Game	1969	15.00
❑ 11261	Don't Stop Now/Since I Don't Have You	1970	6.00
❑ 11265	I'll Be There/Cause You're Mine Little Girl	1970	6.00
❑ 11276	Cathy Called/I Need Somebody	1970	30.00
❑ 11292	Love Story/Four Walls	1971	6.00
ASCOT			
❑ 2142	Go Get Your Own/Laughing at Me	1963	150.00
BELL			
❑ 712	I'm Not Gonna Give Up/I'll Cry 1,000 Tears	1968	30.00
GSF			
❑ 6873	My Mind Keeps Telling Me (That I Really Love You, Girl)/Stranded in a Dream	1972	10.00
❑ 6885	Young Girl/I'll Call You Joy	1972	15.00
LEOPARD			
❑ 45-5001	What You Don't Know (Won't Hurt You)/I'm Counting Every Tear	196?	30.00
PARKWAY			
❑ 106	Am I a Loser/You Know That I Will	1966	20.00
❑ 133	Somewhere Waits a Lonely Girl/Stay Mine for Heaven's Sake	1967	40.00
❑ 157	Why Do Fools Fall in Love/Never Let Me Go	1967	50.00
❑ 960	This Can't Be True/A Free Country	1965	20.00
❑ 981	Don't Stop Now/Eddie's My Name	1966	75.00
❑ 994	Return to Me/Stay Mine for Heaven's Sake	1966	30.00
SALSOUL			
❑ 2026	This Will Be a Night to Remember/Time Will Tell	1977	30.00
❑ 2043	You Make My Life Complete/Somehow You Make Me Feel	1977	20.00
SILVER BLUE			
❑ 807	You're My Lady (Right Or Wrong)/(Instrumental)	1974	15.00
❑ 815	Just Say I Love Her/Darling Take Me Back	1974	10.00
UNITED ARTISTS			
❑ 609	Go Get Your Own/Laughing at Me	1963	—
—Unreleased			

Albums

Number	Title (A Side/B Side)	Yr	NM
ABC			
❑ S-701	I Love You	1970	30.00
SALSOUL			
❑ 5511	A Night to Remember	1977	10.00

HOLMES, CARL, AND THE COMMANDERS

45s

Number	Title (A Side/B Side)	Yr	NM
ATLANTIC			
❑ 2140	Mashed Potatoes (Part 1)/(Part 2)	1962	20.00
C.R.S.			
❑ 000005	The Pot's Hot/Your Game	196?	100.00
—As "Sherlock Holmes Investigation"			
PARKWAY			
❑ 900	I Want My Ya Ya/I'm At My Best (When I'm Down)	1964	20.00
VERVE			
❑ 10510	Telegram/My Lonely Sad Eyes	1967	15.00

Albums

Number	Title (A Side/B Side)	Yr	NM
ATLANTIC			
❑ 8060 [M]	Twist Party at the Roundtable	1962	40.00
❑ SD 8060 [S]	Twist Party at the Roundtable	1962	50.00

HOLMES, CECIL'S, SOULFUL SOUNDS

45s

Number	Title (A Side/B Side)	Yr	NM
BUDDAH			
❑ 354	Superfly/Soulful Sounds	1973	5.00
❑ 391	Kung Fu/Soulful Love	1973	5.00

Albums

Number	Title (A Side/B Side)	Yr	NM
BUDDAH			
❑ BDS-5129	The Black Motion Picture Experience	1973	12.00
❑ BDS-5139	Music for Soulful Lovers	1973	12.00

HOLMES, CLINT

45s

Number	Title (A Side/B Side)	Yr	NM
ATCO			
❑ 6958	Playground in My Mind/Goodbye Maria	1974	5.00
❑ 7000	Let Me Hear It Out There/When You're No. 1	1974	5.00
❑ 7005	Bad Can Be Good/Hang In There Josie	1974	5.00
EPIC			
❑ 10891	Playground in My Mind/There's No Future in My Future	1972	5.00
—Originals have yellow labels			
❑ 10891	Playground in My Mind/There's No Future in My Future	1973	4.00
—Reissue have orange labels			
❑ 11033	Shiddle-Ee-Dee/Like the Fellow Once Said	1973	4.00
PRIVATE STOCK			
❑ 45,126	I Can Count on You	1976	4.00
❑ 45,186	It Wouldn't Have Made Any Difference/Got to Give In to Love	1978	4.00
❑ 45,201	No Walls, No Ceilings, No Floors	1979	4.00

Albums

Number	Title (A Side/B Side)	Yr	NM
EPIC			
❑ KE 32269	Playground in My Mind	1973	10.00

HOLMES, JAKE

45s

Number	Title (A Side/B Side)	Yr	NM
COLUMBIA			
❑ 45517	Trust Me/Just as Lost as Me	1971	5.00
❑ 45570	How Much Time/Silence	1972	5.00
POLYDOR			
❑ 14006	How Are You/(B-side unknown)	1969	5.00
❑ 14011	The Very First Time/Suitcase Room	1969	5.00
❑ 14023	A Little Later/Beautiful Girl Goodbye	1970	5.00
❑ 14041	So Close/Django and Friend	1970	5.00
TOWER			
❑ 392	Genuine Imitation Life/Hard to Keep My Mind on You	1968	6.00
❑ 393	Dazed and Confused/Penny's	1968	6.00
❑ 451	Saturday Night/Late Sleeping Day	1968	6.00
❑ 458	Sleeping Woman/Leaves Never Break	1969	6.00
❑ 459	High School Hero/The Diner Song	1969	6.00

Albums

Number	Title (A Side/B Side)	Yr	NM
COLUMBIA			
❑ C 30996	Jake Holmes	1972	12.00
POLYDOR			
❑ 24-4007	Jake Holmes	1969	12.00
❑ 24-4034	So Close, So Very Far to Go	1970	12.00
TOWER			
❑ DT 5079 [R]	Above Ground	1967	15.00
❑ T 5079 [M]	Above Ground	1967	20.00
❑ ST 5127	Letter to Katherine December	1968	15.00

HOLMES, MARVIN

12-Inch Singles

Number	Title (A Side/B Side)	Yr	NM
MCA			
❑ 23619	Feel So Good (Vocal 5:30)/(Instrumental 5:30)	1986	12.00

45s

Number	Title (A Side/B Side)	Yr	NM
BROWN DOOR			
❑ 6576	You Better Keep Her/Kwami	1974	40.00
KIMBERLY			
❑ 104	Find Yourself - Part 1/Part 2	196?	40.00
REVUE			
❑ 11026	Ride Your Mule (Pt. 1)/(Pt. 2)	1969	25.00
UNI			
❑ 55111	Ooh, Ooh, The Dragon (Part 1)/Ooh, Ooh, The Dragon (Part 2)	1969	25.00
❑ 55233	Sweet Talk/Thang	1970	25.00

Albums

Number	Title (A Side/B Side)	Yr	NM
BROWN DOOR			
❑ MH-6573	Summer of '73	1973	50.00
❑ MH-6581	Honor Thy Father	1975	50.00
UNI			
❑ 73046	Ooh, Ooh, The Dragon And Other Monsters	1969	100.00
—Reproductions exist			

HOLMES, RICHARD "GROOVE"

45s

Number	Title (A Side/B Side)	Yr	NM
BLUE NOTE			
❑ 1967	Theme from "Love Story"/Don't Mess with Me	1971	5.00
FLYING DUTCHMAN			
❑ DB-10671	Morning Children/This Is the Me Me (Not the You You)	1976	4.00
—With Brenda Jones			
❑ DB-10735	Caravan/I've Got Love for You	1976	4.00
GROOVE MERCHANT			
❑ 1012	Night Glider/Flapjack	1972	5.00
❑ 1020	Finger Lickin' Good/The Squirrel	1973	5.00
PACIFIC JAZZ			
❑ 321	Harmonica Boogie Shuffle/Them That's Got	1961	10.00
❑ 330	Groovin' with Jug/Morris the Minor	1961	10.00
❑ 347	Comin' Through the Apple/Something Special	1962	10.00
❑ 88130	Secret Love/Hallelujah I Love Her So	1966	8.00
❑ 88137	It Might As Well Be Spring/This Here	1967	8.00
❑ 88147	The Odd Couple/Madison Time	1968	8.00
❑ 88149	I Can't Stop Dancing/Listen Here	1969	6.00
PRESTIGE			
❑ 380	Soul Message/Song for My Father	1965	10.00
❑ 401	Misty/Groove's Groove	1966	8.00
❑ 427	What Now My Love/Living Soul	1966	8.00
❑ 428	The More I See You/On the Street Where You Live	1967	8.00
❑ 431	Never on Sunday/Boo-D-Doo	1967	8.00
❑ 442	1-2-3/If I Had a Hammer	1967	8.00
❑ 451	Ain't That Peculiar/Super Soul	1967	8.00
❑ 460	Gimme Little Sign/Soul Power	1968	8.00
❑ 718	See See Rider (Part 1)/See See Rider (Part 2)	1968	6.00
❑ 723	Misty/What Now My Love	1969	6.00

7-Inch Extended Plays

Number	Title (A Side/B Side)	Yr	NM
PACIFIC JAZZ			
❑ ST-4-0105	Secret Love/Hittin' the Jug	196?	12.00
—Jukebox issue; small hole, plays at 33 1/3 rpm			
❑ ST-4-0105 [PS]	Tell It Like It Tis	196?	12.00

Albums

Number	Title (A Side/B Side)	Yr	NM
BLUE NOTE			
❑ BST-84372	Comin' On Home	1971	12.00

Number	Title (A Side/B Side)	Yr	NM
FANTASY			
❑ OJC-329	Soul Message	1988	10.00
—Reissue of Prestige 7435			
FLYING DUTCHMAN			
❑ BDL1-1537	I'm in the Mood for Love	1976	12.00
GROOVE MERCHANT			
❑ 505	American Pie	1972	12.00
❑ 512	Night Glider	1972	12.00
❑ 527	New Groove	1973	12.00
❑ 4402 [(2)]	Hunk-A-Funk	1975	15.00
MUSE			
❑ 5134	Shippin' Out	1978	10.00
❑ 5167	Good Vibrations	1979	10.00
❑ 5239	Broadway	1981	10.00
❑ 5358	Blues All Day Long	1989	10.00
PACIFIC JAZZ			
❑ PJ-23 [M]	Richard "Groove" Holmes	1961	25.00
❑ ST-23 [S]	Richard "Groove" Holmes	1961	30.00
❑ PJ-32 [M]	Groovin' with Jug	1961	30.00
❑ ST-32 [S]	Groovin' with Jug	1961	40.00
❑ PJ-51 [M]	Somethin' Special	1962	20.00
❑ ST-51 [S]	Somethin' Special	1962	25.00
❑ PJ-59 [M]	After Hours	1962	20.00
❑ ST-59 [S]	After Hours	1962	25.00
❑ PJ-10105 [M]	Tell It Like It Tis	1966	15.00
❑ LN-10130	Groovin' with Jug	198?	8.00
—Busget-line reissue			
❑ ST-20105 [S]	Tell It Like It Tis	1966	20.00
❑ ST-20153	Workin' on a Groovy Thing	1969	15.00
❑ ST-20163	X-77	1969	15.00
❑ ST-20171	Come Together	1970	15.00
PRESTIGE			
❑ PRLP-7435 [M]	Soul Message	1966	15.00
❑ PRST-7435 [S]	Soul Message	1966	20.00
❑ PRLP-7468 [M]	Living Soul	1966	15.00
❑ PRST-7468 [S]	Living Soul	1966	20.00
❑ PRLP-7485 [M]	Misty	1966	15.00
❑ PRST-7485 [S]	Misty	1966	20.00
❑ PRLP-7493 [M]	Spicy	1967	20.00
❑ PRST-7493 [S]	Spicy	1967	15.00
❑ PRLP-7497 [M]	Super Cool	1967	20.00
❑ PRST-7497 [S]	Super Cool	1967	15.00
❑ PRLP-7514 [M]	Get Up and Get It	1967	20.00
❑ PRST-7514 [S]	Get Up and Get It	1967	15.00
❑ PRST-7543	Soul Power	1968	15.00
❑ PRST-7570	The Groover	1968	15.00
❑ PRST-7601	That Healin' Feelin'	1969	15.00
❑ PRST-7700	The Best of Richard "Groove" Holmes	1969	15.00
❑ PRST-7741	Soul Mist	1970	15.00
❑ PRST-7768	The Best for Beautiful People	1971	15.00
❑ PRST-7778	The Best of Soul Organ Giants	1972	12.00
VERSATILE			
❑ MSG 6003	Dancing in the Sun	1977	15.00
WARNER BROS.			
❑ W 1553 [M]	Book of the Blues	1964	20.00
❑ WS 1553 [S]	Book of the Blues	1964	25.00
WORLD PACIFIC			
❑ ST-20147	Welcome Home	1968	20.00

HOLMES, RUPERT

Number	Title (A Side/B Side)	Yr	NM
45s			
EPIC			
❑ 11014	Philly/Talk	1973	6.00
❑ 11117	Our National Pastime/Phantom of the Opera	1974	6.00
❑ 50013	Terminal/Bagdad	1974	6.00
❑ 50096	I Don't Wanna Hold Your Hand/The Man Behind the Woman	1975	6.00
❑ 50096 [PS]	I Don't Wanna Hold Your Hand	1975	10.00
—Promo-only sleeve			
❑ 50161	Terminal/Deco Lady	1975	6.00
❑ 50161 [PS]	Terminal/Deco Lady	1975	10.00
❑ 50223	Weekend Lover/Weekend Lover	1976	5.00
❑ 50295	You Make Me Real/Who, What, When, Where, How	1976	5.00
INFINITY			
❑ 50035	Escape (The Pina Colada Song)/Drop It	1979	5.00
❑ 50051	Him/Get Outta Yourself	1980	—
—Canceled			
MCA			
❑ 41173	Him/Get Outta Yourself	1980	4.00
❑ 41235	Answering Machine/Lunch Hour	1980	4.00
❑ 50035	Escape (The Pina Colada Song)/Drop It	1980	4.00
❑ 51019	Morning Man/The Mask	1980	4.00
❑ 51045	Blackjack/Crowd Pleaser	1981	4.00
❑ 51092	I Don't Need You/Cold	1981	4.00
PRIVATE STOCK			
❑ 45,183	Bedside Companions/So Beautiful It Hurts	1978	5.00
❑ 45,199	Let's Get Crazy Tonight/The Long Way Home	1978	5.00
Albums			
ELEKTRA			
❑ 5E-560	Full Circle	1982	10.00
EPIC			
❑ KE 32864	Widescreen	1974	12.00
❑ KE 33443	Rupert Holmes	1975	12.00
❑ PE 34288	Singles	1976	12.00
EXCELSIOR			
❑ XMP-6000	Rupert Holmes	1980	10.00
❑ XMP-6022	She Lets Her Hair Down	1981	10.00
INFINITY			
❑ 9020	Partners in Crime	1979	10.00
MCA			
❑ 5129	Adventure	1980	10.00
❑ 9020	Partners in Crime	1980	8.00
—Reissue of Infinity LP			
❑ 37166	Pursuit of Happiness	198?	8.00
—Reissue of Private Stock LP			
PRIVATE STOCK			
❑ PS-7006	Pursuit of Happiness	1978	12.00

HOLMES, SHERLOCK, INVESTIGATION

See CARL HOLMES AND THE COMMANDERS.

HOLY MACKEREL, THE

Number	Title (A Side/B Side)	Yr	NM
Albums			
REPRISE			
❑ RS-6311	The Holy Mackerel	1968	25.00

HOLY MODAL ROUNDERS, THE

Number	Title (A Side/B Side)	Yr	NM
45s			
ELEKTRA			
❑ 45644	Bird Song/Dame Fortune	1968	15.00
METROMEDIA			
❑ 223	Boobs a Lot/Love Is the Closest Thing	1971	10.00
Albums			
ADELPHIA			
❑ 1030	Last Round	198?	10.00
ELEKTRA			
❑ EKS-74026	The Moray Eels Eat the Holy Modal Rounders	1968	30.00
ESP-DISK'			
❑ 1068 [M]	Indian War Whoop	1967	40.00
❑ 1068-S [S]	Indian War Whoop	1967	40.00
FANTASY			
❑ F-24711	Stampfel and Weber	1972	20.00
FOLKLORE			
❑ FRLP-14031 [M]	The Holy Modal Rounders	1964	80.00
METROMEDIA			
❑ MD-1039	Good Taste Is Timeless	1970	30.00
PRESTIGE			
❑ PRLP-7410 [M]	The Holy Modal Rounders 2	1965	40.00
❑ PRLP-7451 [M]	The Holy Modal Rounders	1966	40.00
—Reissue of Folklore LP			
❑ PR-7720	The Holy Modal Rounders	1969	25.00
ROUNDER			
❑ 3004	Alleged in Their Own Time	198?	10.00
SUNDAZED			
❑ LP 5126	The Moray Eels Eat the Holy Modal Rounders	2002	12.00
—Reissue on 180-gram vinyl			

HOMBRES, THE

Number	Title (A Side/B Side)	Yr	NM
45s			
SUN			
❑ 1104	If This Ain't Loving You Baby/You Made Me What I Am	1969	10.00
VERVE			
❑ 5058	Let It Out (Let It All Hang Out)/Go Girl, Go	196?	15.00
—Blue label; may be later than the Verve Forecast edition			
VERVE FORECAST			
❑ 5058	Let It Out (Let It All Hang Out)/Go Girl, Go	1967	12.00
❑ 5058	Let It All Hang Out/Go Girl, Go	1967	15.00
❑ 5076	It's a Gas/Am I High	1967	10.00
❑ 5083	The Prodigal/Mau, Mau, Mau	1968	10.00
❑ 5093	Take My Overwhelming Love (And Cram It Up Your Heart)/Pumpkin Man	1968	10.00
Albums			
VERVE FORECAST			
❑ FT-3036 [M]	Let It Out (Let It All Hang Out)	1967	30.00
❑ FTS-3036 [S]	Let It Out (Let It All Hang Out)	1967	25.00
❑ FTS-3068	The Hombres	1968	—
—Canceled			

HOMEMADE THEATER

Number	Title (A Side/B Side)	Yr	NM
45s			
A&M			
❑ 1776	Santa Jaws (Part 1)/Santa Jaws (Part 2)	1975	15.00
❑ 1887	C.B. Santa/Soup of the Day	1976	15.00

HOMER

Number	Title (A Side/B Side)	Yr	NM
45s			
UNITED			
❑ 123-6/7	I Never Cared for You/Dandilion Wine	1969	25.00
❑ 123-8	Texas Lights/(B-side unknown)	1970	20.00
❑ 123-10	Dandelion Wine/(B-side unknown)	1970	20.00
Albums			
UNITED			
❑ HS-101	Grown in U.S.A.	1970	250.00

HOMER AND JETHRO

Number	Title (A Side/B Side)	Yr	NM
45s			
KING			
❑ 1216	Don't Let Your Sweet Love Die/Long Handle Line	1953	30.00
❑ 5747	Five Minutes More/Tell a Woman	1963	12.00
RCA VICTOR			
❑ 47-4239	Sound Off #2/I Love You 1,000 Ways	1951	25.00
❑ 47-4290	Too Young/Too Old to Cut the Mustard	1951	30.00
❑ 47-4397	Cold, Cold Heart #2/Alabama Jubilee	1951	25.00
❑ 47-4557	Slow Poke #2/When It's Tooth Pickin' Time in False Teeth Valley	1952	25.00
❑ 47-4770	Li'l Ole Kiss of Fire/I'm Torn	1952	25.00
❑ 47-4936	The Billboard Song/Child Psychology	1952	25.00
❑ 47-5043	Jam Bowl Liar/You Belong to Me No. 2	1952	25.00
❑ 47-5099	A Screwball's Love Song/Settin' the Woods on Fire No. 2	1952	25.00
❑ 47-5214	Don't Let the Stars Get In Your Eyeballs/Unhappy Day	1953	25.00
❑ 47-5280	(How Much Is) That Hound Dog in the Window/Pore Ol' Koo-Liger	1953	30.00
❑ 47-5372	I'm Walking Behind You-All/Mexican Joe #6 7/8	1953	25.00
❑ 47-5429	Your Clobbered Heart/Gamblers Git Box	1953	25.00
❑ 47-5456	I Saw Mommy Smoochin' Santa Claus/(All I Want for Christmas Is) My Upper Plate	1953	20.00
❑ 47-5456 [PS]	I Saw Mommy Smoochin' Santa Claus/(All I Want for Christmas Is) My Upper Plate	1953	30.00
❑ 47-5555	You-Ewe-U/Hey Shmo!	1953	25.00
❑ 47-5633	Oh My Pappy/Swappin' Partners	1954	20.00
❑ 47-5708	Crazy Mixed Up Song/That Tired Run Down Feeling	1954	20.00
❑ 47-5788	Hernando's Hideaway/Wanted	1954	20.00
❑ 47-5903	The Night After Christmas/Santy Baby	1954	20.00
❑ 47-6029	Mister Sandman/The Nutty Lady of Shady Lane	1955	20.00
❑ 47-6053	Let Me Go, Blubber/Over the Rainbow	1955	20.00
❑ 47-6178	The Ballad of Davy Crew-Cut/Pickin' and Singin' (Medley)	1955	25.00
❑ 47-6241	The Yellow Rose of Texas, You All/Listen to the Gooney Bird	1955	20.00
❑ 47-6322	Nuttin' for Christmas/Santy's Movin' On	1955	20.00
❑ 47-6342	The Sifting, Whimpering Sands/They Laid Him in the Ground	1955	20.00
❑ 47-6374	Love and Marriage/This Is a Wife?	1955	20.00
❑ 47-6542	Two Tone Shoes/Hart Brake Motel	1956	25.00
❑ 47-6651	Where Is That Doggone Gal of Mine/Just Be Here	1956	20.00
❑ 47-6706	Houn' Dawg/Screen Door (Green Door)	1956	25.00
❑ 47-6765	I'm My Own Grand Paw/Mama from the Train	1956	20.00
❑ 47-6954	Gone/Ramblin' Rose	1957	15.00
❑ 47-7030	My Dog Likes Your Dog/Kentucky	1957	15.00
❑ 47-7162	At the Flop/My Special Angel	1958	15.00
❑ 47-7342	Lullaby of Bird Dog/I Guess Things Happen That Way	1958	15.00

H

Number	Title (A Side/B Side)	Yr	NM
❑ 47-7493	Don't Sing Along (On Top of Old Smoky)/Middle Aged Teenager	1959	15.00
❑ 47-7585	The Battle of Kookamonga/Waterloo	1959	15.00
❑ 47-7704	El Paso (Numero Dos)/That's Good, That's Bad	1960	15.00
❑ 47-7744	Sink the Bismarck/He'll Have to Go	1960	15.00
❑ 47-7790	Itsy Bitsy Teenie Weenie Yellow Polka Dot Bikini/Please Help Me, I'm Falling	1960	15.00
❑ 47-7852	Are You Lonesome Tonight/I Love Your Pizza	1961	15.00
❑ 47-8075	She Thinks I Don't Care/Are You Kissing More Now (But Enjoying It Less)	1962	12.00
❑ 47-8305	Joe Bean/Freda on the Freeway	1963	12.00
❑ 47-8345	I Want to Hold Your Hand/She Loves You	1964	15.00
❑ 47-8345 [PS]	I Want to Hold Your Hand/She Loves You	1964	30.00
❑ 47-8604	Misty/Tenderly	1965	12.00
❑ 47-8664	King of the Camp/Camp Runamuck	1965	12.00
❑ 47-8874	Act Naturally/Finished Musicians	1966	10.00
❑ 47-9130	Nashville Cats/Winchester Cathedral	1967	10.00
❑ 47-9299	Somethin' Stupid/The Ballad of Roger Miller	1967	10.00
❑ 47-9581	Hill Billy Boogie/I Crept Into the Crypt and Cried	1968	10.00
❑ 47-9674	The Gal from Possum Holler/There Ain't a Chicken Safe in Tennessee	1968	10.00
❑ 47-9866	Daddy Played First Base/You Smell Like Turtles	1970	8.00
❑ 47-9922	Hello Darlin' No. 2/Funny Farm	1970	8.00
❑ 48-0075	Baby, It's Cold Outside/Country Girl	1949	50.00
—With June Carter; originals on green vinyl			
❑ 48-0086	Waltz with Me/Roll Along Kentucky Moon	1949	40.00
—Originals on green vinyl			
❑ 48-0113	Tennessee Border — No. 2/I'm Gettin' Older Every Day	1949	40.00
—Originals on green vinyl			
❑ 48-0144	The Wedding of Hillbilly Lilli Marlene/The Hucklebuck	1950	40.00
—With June Carter; originals on green vinyl			
❑ 48-0170	She Made Toothpicks Out of the Timber of My Heart/I've Got Tears in My Ears	1950	40.00
—Originals on green vinyl			
❑ 48-0181	I Said My Nightshirt (And Put On My Prayers)/Music, Music, Music	1950	40.00
—Originals on green vinyl			
❑ 48-0308	You Tell Her I Stutter/Does the Spearmint Lose Its Flavor	1950	40.00
—Originals on green vinyl			
❑ 48-0349	Pistol Pete/Put That Knife Away Nellie	1950	40.00
—Originals on green vinyl			
❑ 48-0404	Oh Babe/Disc Jockey Nightmare	1951	30.00
❑ 48-0446	So Long — No. 2/I'm Movin' On — No. 2	1951	30.00
❑ 48-0468	King Sized Baby/That Texas Land	1951	30.00
❑ 48-0484	Knock-Kneed Susy/She Loves to Cry	1951	30.00
—With June Carter			
❑ 74-0566	We Didn't Make It Through the Night/Fer the Good Times	1971	8.00

7-Inch Extended Plays

RCA VICTOR

Number	Title (A Side/B Side)	Yr	NM
❑ EPA 424	Jam-Bowl-Liar/Settin' the Woods on Fire No. 2//Li'l Ole Kiss of Fire/Hey, Good Lookin' No. 2	1952	20.00
❑ EPA 424 [PS]	Homer & Jethro Kid the Top Pops	1952	20.00
❑ EPA 534	Randolph the Flat-Nosed Reindeer/(All I Want for Christmas Is) My Upper Plate//I Saw Mommy Smoochin' Santa Claus/Frosty the De-Frosted Snow Man	195?	15.00
❑ EPA 534 [PS]	Seasoned Greetings	195?	15.00
❑ EPA 1-1412	Cigareetes, Whusky and Wild Wild Women/The West Virginny Hills//Keep Them Cold Icy Fingers Off of Me/Ground Hog	1956	20.00
❑ EPA 1-1412 [PS]	Barefoot Ballads, Vol. I	1956	20.00

Albums

AUDIO LAB

Number	Title (A Side/B Side)	Yr	NM
❑ AL-1513 [M]	Musical Madness	1958	100.00

KING

Number	Title (A Side/B Side)	Yr	NM
❑ 639 [M]	They Sure Are Corny	1959	100.00
❑ 848 [M]	Cornier Than Corn	1963	70.00
❑ KS-1005	24 Great Songs in the Homer & Jethro Style	1967	20.00

RCA CAMDEN

Number	Title (A Side/B Side)	Yr	NM
❑ CAL-707 [M]	Homer and Jethro Strike Back	1961	15.00

RCA VICTOR

Number	Title (A Side/B Side)	Yr	NM
❑ LPM-1412 [M]	Barefoot Ballads	1957	50.00
❑ LPM-1560 [M]	The Worst of Homer & Jethro	1958	50.00
❑ LPM-1880 [M]	Life Can Be Miserable	1958	30.00
❑ LSP-1880 [S]	Life Can Be Miserable	1958	50.00
❑ LPM-2181 [M]	Homer and Jethro at the Country Club	1960	25.00
❑ LSP-2181 [S]	Homer and Jethro at the Country Club	1960	40.00
❑ LPM-2286 [M]	Songs My Mother Never Sang	1961	25.00
❑ LSP-2286 [S]	Songs My Mother Never Sang	1961	30.00
❑ LPM-2455 [M]	Zany Songs of the '30s	1962	25.00
❑ LSP-2455 [S]	Zany Songs of the '30s	1962	30.00
❑ LPM-2459 [M]	Playing It Straight	1962	25.00
❑ LSP-2459 [S]	Playing It Straight	1962	30.00
❑ LPM-2492 [M]	Homer and Jethro at the Convention	1962	25.00
❑ LSP-2492 [S]	Homer and Jethro at the Convention	1962	30.00
❑ LPM-2674 [M]	Homer and Jethro Go West	1963	25.00
❑ LSP-2674 [S]	Homer and Jethro Go West	1963	30.00
❑ LPM-2743 [M]	Ooh, That's Corny	1963	25.00
❑ LSP-2743 [S]	Ooh, That's Corny	1963	30.00
❑ LPM-2928 [M]	Cornfucius Say	1964	25.00
❑ LSP-2928 [S]	Cornfucius Say	1964	30.00
❑ LPM-2954 [M]	Fractured Folk Songs	1964	25.00
❑ LSP-2954 [S]	Fractured Folk Songs	1964	30.00
❑ LPM-3112 [10]	Homer & Jethro Fracture Frank Loesser	1953	150.00
❑ LPM-3357 [M]	Homer and Jethro Sing Tenderly	1965	25.00
❑ LSP-3357 [S]	Homer and Jethro Sing Tenderly	1965	30.00
❑ LPM-3462 [M]	The Old Crusty Minstrels	1965	25.00
❑ LSP-3462 [S]	The Old Crusty Minstrels	1965	30.00
❑ LPM-3474 [M]	The Best of Homer and Jethro	1966	25.00
❑ LSP-3474 [S]	The Best of Homer and Jethro	1966	30.00
❑ LPM-3538 [M]	Any News from Nashville?	1966	25.00
❑ LSP-3538 [S]	Any News from Nashville?	1966	30.00
❑ LPM-3673 [M]	Wanted for Murder	1966	25.00
❑ LSP-3673 [S]	Wanted for Murder	1966	30.00
❑ LPM-3701 [M]	It Ain't Necessarily Square	1967	30.00
❑ LSP-3701 [S]	It Ain't Necessarily Square	1967	25.00
❑ LPM-3822 [M]	Nashville Cats	1967	40.00
❑ LSP-3822 [S]	Nashville Cats	1967	25.00
❑ LPM-3877 [M]	Somethin' Stupid	1967	50.00
❑ LSP-3877 [S]	Somethin' Stupid	1967	25.00
❑ LPM-3973 [M]	There's Nothing Like an Old Hippie	1968	100.00
❑ LSP-3973 [S]	There's Nothing Like an Old Hippie	1968	25.00
❑ LSP-4001	Cool, Crazy Christmas	1968	20.00
❑ LSP-4024	Homer and Jethro at Vanderbilt U.	1969	20.00
❑ LSP-4148	Homer and Jethro's Next Album	1969	20.00

HONDELLS, THE

45s

AMOS

Number	Title (A Side/B Side)	Yr	NM
❑ 131	Follow the Bouncing Ball/The Legend of Frankie and Johnny	1969	12.00
❑ 150	Shine On Ruby Mountain/The Legend of Frankie and Johnny	1970	12.00

COLUMBIA

Number	Title (A Side/B Side)	Yr	NM
❑ 44361	Just One More Chance/Yes to You	1967	20.00
❑ 44557	Another Woman/Atlanta Georgia Stray	1968	20.00

MERCURY

Number	Title (A Side/B Side)	Yr	NM
❑ 72324	Little Honda/Hot Rod High	1964	20.00
❑ 72366	My Buddy Seat/You're Gonna Ride with Me	1964	20.00
❑ 72366 [PS]	My Buddy Seat/You're Gonna Ride with Me	1964	25.00
❑ 72405	Little Sidewalk Surfer Girl/Come On Baby (Pack It In)	1965	20.00
❑ 72443	Sea of Love/Do As I Say	1965	20.00
❑ 72479	You Meet the Nicest People on a Honda/Sea Cruise	1965	20.00
❑ 72479 [PS]	You Meet the Nicest People on a Honda/Sea Cruise	1965	30.00
❑ 72523	Endless Sleep/Follow Your Heart	1966	15.00
❑ 72563	Younger Girl/All American Girl	1966	15.00
❑ 72605	Country Love/Kissin' My Life Away	1966	15.00
❑ 72626	Cheryl's Goin' Home/Show Me	1966	15.00

Albums

MERCURY

Number	Title (A Side/B Side)	Yr	NM
❑ MG-20940 [M]	Go Little Honda	1964	40.00
❑ MG-20982 [M]	The Hondells	1965	50.00
❑ SR-60940 [S]	Go Little Honda	1964	60.00
❑ SR-60982 [S]	The Hondells	1965	80.00

HONEY BEES, THE (1)

45s

FONTANA

Number	Title (A Side/B Side)	Yr	NM
❑ 1505	You Turn Me On Boy/Some of Your Lovin'	1965	60.00
❑ 1939	One Wonderful Night/She Don't Deserve You	1964	60.00

GARRISON

Number	Title (A Side/B Side)	Yr	NM
❑ 3005	Never in a Million Years/Let's Get Back Together	1966	1500.

VEE JAY

Number	Title (A Side/B Side)	Yr	NM
❑ 611	One Girl, One Boy/No Guy	1964	25.00

WAND

Number	Title (A Side/B Side)	Yr	NM
❑ 1141	Never in a Million Years/Let's Get Back Together	1966	12.00

HONEY BEES, THE (2)

45s

IMPERIAL

Number	Title (A Side/B Side)	Yr	NM
❑ 5400	Endless/Let's See What's Happening	1956	40.00
❑ 5436	Just to Live Again/What's to Become of Me	1957	40.00

HONEY CONE, THE

45s

HOT WAX

Number	Title (A Side/B Side)	Yr	NM
❑ 6901	While You're Out Looking for Sugar?/The Feeling's Gone	1969	15.00
❑ 6903	Girls It Ain't Easy/The Feeling's Gone	1969	20.00
❑ 7001	Take Me With You/Take My Love	1970	6.00
❑ 7005	When Will It End/Take Me With You	1970	6.00
❑ 7011	Want Ads/We Belong Together	1970	5.00
—Mostly orange label			
❑ 7011	Want Ads/We Belong Together	1970	6.00
—Mostly white label			
❑ 7106	Stick-Up/V.I.P.	1971	6.00
❑ 7110	One Monkey Don't Stop No Show Part I/One Monkey Don't Stop No Show Part II	1971	15.00
❑ 7113	The Day I Found Myself/When Will It End	1971	6.00
❑ 7205	Sittin' on a Time Bomb (Waitin' for the Hurt to Come)/It's Better to Have Loved and Lost	1972	6.00
❑ 7208	Innocent Till Proven Guilty/Don't Send Me an Invitation	1972	20.00
❑ 7212	Ace in the Hole/Ooo Baby Baby	1972	6.00
❑ 7301	If I Can't Fly/Woman Can't Live by Bread Alone	1973	30.00
❑ 9255	The Truth Will Come Out/Somebody Is Always Messing Up a Good Thing	1974	40.00

Albums

HOT WAX

Number	Title (A Side/B Side)	Yr	NM
❑ HA-701	Take Me With You	1970	12.00
❑ HA-706	Sweet Replies	1971	12.00
❑ HA-707	Soulful Tapestry	1971	12.00
❑ HA-713	Love, Peace & Soul	1972	12.00

HONEYCOMBS, THE

45s

INTERPHON

Number	Title (A Side/B Side)	Yr	NM
❑ 7707	Have I the Right?/Please Don't Pretend Again	1964	12.00
❑ 7713	I Can't Stop/I'll Cry Tomorrow	1964	10.00
❑ 7713 [PS]	I Can't Stop/I'll Cry Tomorrow	1964	25.00
❑ 7716	Color Slide/That's the Way	1965	10.00
❑ 7716 [PS]	Colour Slide/That's the Way	1965	25.00
—Yes, the American sleeve spells the A-side the British way			

WARNER BROS.

Number	Title (A Side/B Side)	Yr	NM
❑ 5634	I'll See You Tomorrow/Something Better Beginning	1965	10.00
❑ 5655	I Can't Get Through to You/That's the Way	1965	10.00
❑ 5803	How Will I Know/Who Is Sylvia	1966	10.00

Albums

INTERPHON

Number	Title (A Side/B Side)	Yr	NM
❑ IN-88001 [M]	Here Are the Honeycombs	1964	40.00
❑ IN-88001 [R]	Here Are the Honeycombs	1964	30.00

VEE JAY

Number	Title (A Side/B Side)	Yr	NM
❑ IN-88001 [M]	Here Are the Honeycombs	1964	50.00
❑ IN-88001 [R]	Here Are the Honeycombs	1964	40.00

Number	Title (A Side/B Side)	Yr	NM

HONEYCONES, THE

45s

EMBER

Number	Title (A Side/B Side)	Yr	NM
❑ 1033	Betty Moretti/Cool It Baby	1958	20.00
❑ 1036	Op/Vision of You	1958	25.00
❑ 1042	Gee Whiz/Rockin' in the Knees	1958	20.00
❑ 1049	Tell Me Baby/Your Face	1959	20.00

HONEYCUTT, GLENN

45s

FERNWOOD

Number	Title (A Side/B Side)	Yr	NM
❑ 142	Campus Love/ Tombigbee Queen	1964	100.00

SUN

Number	Title (A Side/B Side)	Yr	NM
❑ 264	I'll Be Around/I'll Wait Forever	1957	30.00

HONEYCUTT, JOHNNY

45s

TRIODE

Number	Title (A Side/B Side)	Yr	NM
❑ 111	I'm Coming Over/ (B-side unknown)	196?	1200.

HONEYDRIPPERS, THE

45s

ES PARANZA

Number	Title (A Side/B Side)	Yr	NM
❑ 99686	Rockin' at Midnight/ Young Boy Blues	1984	3.00
❑ 99686 [PS]	Rockin' at Midnight/ Young Boy Blues	1984	4.00
❑ 99701	Sea of Love/I Get a Thrill	1984	3.00
❑ 99701	Sea of Love/Rockin' at Midnight	1984	5.00
❑ 99701 [PS]	Sea of Love/I Get a Thrill	1984	4.00
❑ 99701 [PS]	Sea of Love/Rockin' at Midnight	1984	6.00

Albums

ES PARANZA

Number	Title (A Side/B Side)	Yr	NM
❑ 90220 [EP]	The Honeydrippers, Vol. One	1984	6.00

HONEYS, THE

45s

CAPITOL

Number	Title (A Side/B Side)	Yr	NM
❑ 2454	Goodnight My Love/ Tonight You Belong to Me	1969	80.00
❑ 4952	Surfin' Down the Swanee River/ Shoot the Curl	1963	150.00
❑ 4952 [PS]	Surfin' Down the Swanee River/ Shoot the Curl	1963	800.00
❑ 5034	Hide Go Seek/Pray for Surf	1963	200.00
❑ 5093	The One You Can't Have/ From Jimmy With Tears	1963	200.00

WARNER BROS.

Number	Title (A Side/B Side)	Yr	NM
❑ 5430	He's a Doll/The Love of a Boy and Girl	1964	600.00
—Stock copy; red label			
❑ 5430 [DJ]	He's a Doll/The Love of a Boy and Girl	1964	200.00
—Promotional copy; white label			

HONEYTONES, THE

45s

BIG TOP

Number	Title (A Side/B Side)	Yr	NM
❑ 3002	Don't Look Now, But/ I Know, I Know	1958	20.00

MERCURY

Number	Title (A Side/B Side)	Yr	NM
❑ 70557	Too Bad/Somewhere, Sometime, Someday	1955	25.00

WING

Number	Title (A Side/B Side)	Yr	NM
❑ 90013	False Alarm/Honeybun Cha Cha	1955	30.00

HONK

45s

AMARET

Number	Title (A Side/B Side)	Yr	NM
❑ 123	Don't Take Anything/Love Machine	1970	8.00

EPIC

Number	Title (A Side/B Side)	Yr	NM
❑ 8-50056	Hesitation/Dog at Your Dog	1974	5.00

GRANITE

Number	Title (A Side/B Side)	Yr	NM
❑ 101	Made My Statement/ Pipeline Sequence	1972	8.00

20TH CENTURY

Number	Title (A Side/B Side)	Yr	NM
❑ 2007	Made My Statement/ Pipeline Sequence	1973	6.00
❑ 2029	I Wanna Do for You/Another Light	1973	6.00

Albums

EPIC

Number	Title (A Side/B Side)	Yr	NM
❑ KE 33094	Honk	1974	12.00

GRANITE

Number	Title (A Side/B Side)	Yr	NM
❑ GR 7720	Five Summer Stories	1972	15.00

20TH CENTURY

Number	Title (A Side/B Side)	Yr	NM
❑ T-406	Honk	1973	12.00

The Honeydrippers, "Sea of Love," Warner 7-99701, 1984, $6.

HONOR SOCIETY, THE

See THE HAPPENINGS.

HOODOO GURUS

12-Inch Singles

A&M

Number	Title (A Side/B Side)	Yr	NM
❑ 17286 [DJ]	I Want You Back (Edit) (same on both sides)	1984	6.00

BIG TIME

Number	Title (A Side/B Side)	Yr	NM
❑ 1001 [DJ]	Bittersweet (same on both sides)	1985	6.00
❑ 1002 [DJ]	Poison Pen (same on both sides)	1985	5.00

ELEKTRA

Number	Title (A Side/B Side)	Yr	NM
❑ 5151 [DJ]	Death Defying (Remix) (same on both sides)	1985	6.00
❑ 5215 [DJ]	Good Time (same on both sides)	1987	6.00
❑ 5235 [DJ]	Out That Door (same on both sides)	1987	5.00
❑ 5255 [DJ]	What's My Scene (same on both sides)	1987	5.00
❑ 5255 [DJ]	What's My Scene (same on both sides)	1987	5.00

RCA

Number	Title (A Side/B Side)	Yr	NM
❑ 8998-1	Come Anytime/Hallucination/ Where's the Hit?	1989	5.00

45s

A&M

Number	Title (A Side/B Side)	Yr	NM
❑ 2670	I Want You Back/Death Ship	1984	6.00

BIG TIME

Number	Title (A Side/B Side)	Yr	NM
❑ BTS 1503	Bittersweet/Mars Needs Guitars	1985	5.00
❑ BTS 1503 [PS]	Bittersweet/Mars Needs Guitars	1985	5.00
❑ BTS 1588	Like Wow — Wipeout/ Bring the Hoodoo Down	1985	5.00
❑ BTS 1588 [PS]	Like Wow — Wipeout/ Bring the Hoodoo Down	1985	5.00

ELEKTRA

Number	Title (A Side/B Side)	Yr	NM
❑ 69440	What's My Scene/ Heart of Darkness	1987	3.00
❑ 69481	Good Times/Heart of Darkness	1987	3.00
❑ 69481 [PS]	Good Times/Heart of Darkness	1987	3.00
❑ 69536	Death Defying (Ooh-Wee)/ Turkey Dinner	1986	3.00
❑ 69544	Bittersweet/Bring the Hoodoo Down	1986	3.00

Albums

A&M

Number	Title (A Side/B Side)	Yr	NM
❑ SP 5012	Stone Age Romeos	1983	12.00

BIG TIME

Number	Title (A Side/B Side)	Yr	NM
❑ 009	Mars Needs Guitars	1985	12.00

ELEKTRA

Number	Title (A Side/B Side)	Yr	NM
❑ 60485	Mars Needs Guitars	1986	10.00
—Reissue of Big Time LP			
❑ 60728	Blow Your Cool	1987	10.00

RCA

Number	Title (A Side/B Side)	Yr	NM
❑ 9781-1-R	Magnum Cum Louder	1989	10.00

HOOK, THE

45s

UNI

Number	Title (A Side/B Side)	Yr	NM
❑ 55057	Son of Fantasy/ Plug Your Head In	1968	10.00
❑ 55077	Love Theme in E Major/Homes	1968	10.00
❑ 55149	In the Beginning/ Show You the Way	1969	10.00

Albums

UNI

Number	Title (A Side/B Side)	Yr	NM
❑ 73023	The Hook Will Grab You	1968	15.00
❑ 73038	Hooked	1969	15.00

HOOKER, JOHN LEE

45s

ABC

Number	Title (A Side/B Side)	Yr	NM
❑ 11298	Doin' the Shout/Kick Hit 4 Hit Kix U	1971	6.00
❑ 11320	Never Get Out of These Blues Alive/Boogie with the Hook	1972	6.00

BATTLE

Number	Title (A Side/B Side)	Yr	NM
❑ 45901	No More Doggin'/ I Need Some Money	1962	10.00

Number	Title (A Side/B Side)	Yr	NM
BLUESWAY			
❑ 61010	Motor City Is Burning/ Want Ad Blues	1967	8.00
❑ 61014	Mr. Lucky/Cry Before I Go	1968	6.00
❑ 61017	Back Biters and Syndicators/ Think Twice Before You Go	1968	6.00
❑ 61023	I Don't Wanna Go to Vietnam/ Simply the Truth	1969	6.00
CHANCE			
❑ 1108	Miss Lorraine/Talkin' Boogie	1951	3000.
—As "John Lee Booker"			
❑ 1110	Graveyard Blues/ I Love to Boogie	1952	3000.
—As "John Lee Booker"			
❑ 1122	609 Boogie/Road Trouble	1952	2000.
—As "John L. Booker"			
CHART			
❑ 609	Going South/Wobbling Baby	1955	50.00
❑ 614	Blue Monday/My Baby Put Me Down	1955	50.00
CHESS			
❑ 1505	High Priced Woman/ Union Station Blues	1952	1200.
❑ 1513	Sugar Mama/Walkin' the Boogie	1952	1000.
❑ 1562	It's My Own Fault/ Women and Money	1954	250.00
❑ 1965	Let's Go Out Tonight/In the Mood	1966	10.00
DELUXE			
❑ 6004	Blue Monday/Lovin' Guitar Man	1953	500.00
—As "John Lee Booker"			
❑ 6009	I Came to See You Baby/ I'm a Boogie Man	1953	800.00
—As "Johnny Lee"			
❑ 6032	Stuttering Blues/Pouring Down Rain	1954	400.00
—As "John Lee Booker"			
❑ 6046	My Baby Don't Love Me/ Real, Real Gone	1954	400.00
—As "John Lee Booker"			
ELMOR			
❑ 303	Blues for Christmas/ Big Fine Woman	1959	20.00
FEDERAL			
❑ 12377	Late Last Night/Don't You Remember Me	1960	15.00
FORTUNE			
❑ 846	609 Boogie/Curl My Baby's Hair	1959	20.00
❑ 853	Cry Baby/Love You Baby	1960	20.00
❑ 855	Crazy About That Walk/ We're All God's Chillun	1960	20.00
GALAXY			
❑ 716	I Lost My Job/You Gotta Shake It Up and Go	1963	10.00
HI-Q			
❑ 5018	Blues for Christmas/ Big Fine Woman	1960	20.00
❑ 5018X	609 Blues/Blues for Christmas	1961	20.00
IMPULSE			
❑ 242	Honey/Bottle Up and Go	1966	40.00
JEWEL			
❑ 824	I Feel Good (Part 1)/ I Feel Good (Part 2)	1971	5.00
❑ 852	Stand By (Part 1)/Stand By (Part 2)	1977	4.00
JVB			
❑ 30	Boogie Rambler/ No More Doggin'	1953	1500.
KENT			
❑ 332	Boogie Chillen/I'm in the Mood	1960	20.00
KING			
❑ 45-4504	Moaning Blues/Stomp Boogie	1952	1000.
—As "John Lee Cooker"			
❑ 6298	Don't Go Baby/Moanin' and Stompin' Blues	1970	6.00
LAUREN			
❑ 361	Ballad to Abraham Lincoln (He Got Assassinated)/Mojo Hand (Louisiana Voodoo)	1961	20.00
❑ 362	I Lost My Job/You Gotta Shake It Up and Go	1961	20.00
MODERN			
❑ 45x835	How Can You Do It/ I'm in the Mood	1951	400.00
❑ 45x847	Anybody Seen My Baby? (Johnny Says Come Back)/ Turn Over a New Leaf	1951	300.00
❑ 45x852	Ground Hog Blues/Louise	1951	120.00
❑ 45x862	Cold Chills All Over Me/ Rock Me, Mama	1952	80.00
❑ 45x876	It Hurts Me So/I Got Eyes for You	1952	80.00
—With Little Eddie Kirkland			

Number	Title (A Side/B Side)	Yr	NM
❑ 45x886	Key to the Highway/ Bluebird Blues	1952	80.00
❑ 45x893	New Boogie Chillen/I Tried	1952	80.00
❑ 45x897	It's Been a Long Time Baby/ Rock House Boogie	1952	80.00
❑ 45x901	Ride Till I Die/It's Stormin' and Rainin'	1953	60.00
❑ 45x908	Please Take Me Back/ Love Money Can't Buy	1953	60.00
❑ 45x916	Too Much Boogie/ Need Somebody	1953	60.00
❑ 45x923	Gotta Boogie/Down Child	1953	60.00
❑ 45x931	Jump Me/I Wonder Little Darling	1954	60.00
❑ 45x935	I Tried Hard/Let's Talk It Over	1954	50.00
❑ 45x942	Cool Little Car/Bad Boy	1954	50.00
❑ 45x948	Half a Stranger/ Shake, Holler and Run	1954	50.00
❑ 45x958	Taxi Driver/You Receive Me	1955	50.00
❑ 45x966	Hug and Squeeze/ The Syndicator	1955	50.00
❑ 45x978	Looking for a Woman/I'm Ready	1955	60.00
POINTBLANK			
❑ S7-19518	Dimples/Don't Look Back	1997	4.00
❑ 38664	Burnin' Hell/Boogie at Russian Hill	1999	3.00
RIVERSIDE			
❑ 438	I Need Some Money/ No More Diggin'	1960	25.00
ROCKIN'			
❑ 524	Blue Monday/Lovin' Guitar Man	1953	1000.
—As "John Lee Booker"			
❑ 525	Stuttering Blues/Pouring Down Rain	1953	1000.
—As "John Lee Booker"			
SPECIALTY			
❑ 528	Everybody's Blues/I'm Mad	1954	40.00
STAX			
❑ 0053	Slow and Easy/Grinder Man	1969	6.00
VEE JAY			
❑ 164	Mambo Chillen/Time Is Marching	1955	30.00
❑ 188	Every Night/Trouble Blues	1956	30.00
❑ 205	Dimples/Baby Lee	1956	30.00
❑ 233	The Road Is So Rough/ I'm So Worried Baby	1957	25.00
❑ 245	I'm So Excited/I See You When You're Weak	1957	25.00
❑ 255	Little Wheel/Rosie Mae	1957	25.00
❑ 265	You Can Lead Me, Baby/ Unfriendly Baby	1958	25.00
❑ 293	I Love You Honey/ You've Taken My Woman	1958	25.00
❑ 308	Maudie/I'm In the Mood	1959	25.00
❑ 319	Tennessee Blues/Boogie Chillun	1959	25.00
❑ 331	Hobo Blues/Crawlin' King Snake	1959	25.00
❑ 349	No Shoes/Solid Sender	1960	25.00
❑ 366	Dusty Road/Tupelo	1960	25.00
❑ 379	I'm Mad Again/I'm Going Upstairs	1961	25.00
❑ 397	Want Ad Blues/Take Me As I Am	1961	25.00
❑ 438	Boom Boom/Drug Store Woman	1962	25.00
❑ 453	She's Mine/A New Leaf	1962	25.00
❑ 493	Take a Look at Yourself/ Frisco Blues	1963	20.00
❑ 493	Take a Look at Yourself/ I Love Her	1963	50.00
❑ 538	I'm Leaving/Birmingham Blues	1963	15.00
❑ 575	Send Me Your Pillow/ Don't Look Back	1964	15.00
❑ 670	Big Legs, Tight Skirt/Your Baby Ain't Sweet Like Mine	1965	12.00
❑ 708	It Serves Me Right/ Flowers on the Hour	1966	10.00

Albums

Number	Title	Yr	NM
ABC			
❑ S-720 [(2)]	Endless Boogie	1971	20.00
❑ X-736	Never Get Out of These Blues Alive	1972	20.00
❑ XQ-736 [Q]	Never Get Out of These Blues Alive	1974	25.00
❑ X-761	Live at Soledad Prison	1972	20.00
❑ XQ-761 [Q]	Live at Soledad Prison	1974	25.00
❑ X-768	Born in Mississippi, Raised Up in Tennessee	1973	20.00
❑ XQ-768 [Q]	Born in Mississippi, Raised Up in Tennessee	1974	25.00
❑ X-838	Free Beer and Chicken	1974	15.00
❑ XQ-838 [Q]	Free Beer and Chicken	1974	25.00
ATCO			
❑ 33-151 [M]	Don't Turn Me From Your Door	1963	100.00
❑ SD 33-151 [R]	Don't Turn Me From Your Door	1967	50.00
ATLANTIC			
❑ SD 7228	Detroit Special	1972	20.00
BATTLE			
❑ BLP-6113 [M]	John Lee Hooker	196?	150.00
❑ BLP-6114 [M]	How Long Blues	196?	150.00

Number	Title (A Side/B Side)	Yr	NM
BLUESWAY			
❑ BL-6002 [M]	Live at Café A-Go-Go	1967	25.00
❑ BLS-6002 [S]	Live at Café A-Go-Go	1967	20.00
❑ BL-6012 [M]	Urban Blues	1967	25.00
❑ BLS-6012 [S]	Urban Blues	1967	20.00
❑ BLS-6023	Simply the Truth	1968	20.00
❑ BLS-6038	If You Miss 'Em	1969	20.00
❑ BLQ-6052 [Q]	Live at Kabuki-Wuki	1974	25.00
❑ BLS-6052	Live at Kabuki-Wuki	1973	15.00
BUDDAH			
❑ BDS-4002	The Very Best of John Lee Hooker	1970	15.00
❑ BDS-7506	Big Band Blues	1970	15.00
CHAMELEON			
❑ D1-74794	The Hook	1989	10.00
❑ D1-74808	The Healer	1989	10.00
CHESS			
❑ LP-1438 [M]	House of the Blues	1960	300.00
—Black label			
❑ LP-1438 [M]	House of the Blues	1966	50.00
—Blue and white label			
❑ LP-1454 [M]	John Lee Hooker Plays and Sings the Blues	1961	300.00
—Black label			
❑ LP-1454 [M]	John Lee Hooker Plays and Sings the Blues	1966	50.00
—Blue and white label			
❑ LP-1508 [M]	Real Folk Blues	1966	50.00
❑ LPS-1508 [R]	Real Folk Blues	1966	30.00
❑ CH-9199	John Lee Hooker Plays and Sings the Blues	1986	8.00
—Reissue			
❑ CH-9258	House of the Blues	1987	8.00
❑ CH-9271	The Real Folk Blues	1988	8.00
❑ 60011 [(2)]	Mad Man Blues	1973	20.00
❑ CH2-92507 [(2)]	Mad Man Blues	198?	12.00
COLLECTABLES			
❑ COL-5151	Golden Classics	198?	12.00
CROWN			
❑ CLP-5157 [M]	The Blues	196?	12.00
—Black label with multi-color "Crown"			
❑ CLP-5157 [M]	The Blues	1960	100.00
—Black label with silver "Crown"			
❑ CLP-5157 [M]	The Blues	1962	30.00
—Gray label			
❑ CLP-5232 [M]	John Lee Hooker Sings the Blues	196?	12.00
—Black label with multi-color "Crown"			
❑ CLP-5232 [M]	John Lee Hooker Sings the Blues	1962	30.00
—Gray label			
❑ CLP-5232 [M]	John Lee Hooker Sings the Blues	1962	100.00
—Black label with silver "Crown"			
❑ CLP-5295 [M]	Folk Blues	1962	12.00
—Black label with multi-color "Crown"			
❑ CLP-5295 [M]	Folk Blues	1962	30.00
—Gray label			
❑ CLP-5353 [M]	The Great John Lee Hooker	1963	12.00
—Black label with multi-color "Crown"			
❑ CLP-5353 [M]	The Great John Lee Hooker	1963	30.00
—Gray label			
EVEREST ARCHIVE OF FOLK & JAZZ			
❑ 222	John Lee Hooker	1968	12.00
❑ 347	Hooked On Blues	1980	12.00
EXODUS			
❑ 325 [M]	Is He the World's Greatest Blues Singer?	1966	25.00
FANTASY			
❑ 24706 [(2)]	Boogie Chillun	1972	15.00
❑ 24722 [(2)]	Black Snake	197?	15.00
GALAXY			
❑ 201 [M]	I'm John Lee Hooker	1961	250.00
❑ 205 [M]	Live at Sugar Hill	1962	250.00
❑ 8205 [S]	Live at Sugar Hill	1962	250.00
GNP CRESCENDO			
❑ GNPS-10007 [(2)]	The Best of John Lee Hooker	1974	15.00
GREENE BOTTLE			
❑ 3130 [(2)]	Johnny Lee	1972	15.00
IMPULSE!			
❑ A-9103 [M]	It Serves You Right to Suffer	1966	30.00
❑ AS-9103 [S]	It Serves You Right to Suffer	1966	40.00
JEWEL			
❑ 5005	I Feel Good	1971	15.00
KING			
❑ 727 [M]	John Lee Hooker Sings the Blues	1960	500.00
❑ KLP-727	John Lee Hooker Sings the Blues	1988	8.00
—Reissue of earlier 727			
❑ KS-1085	Moanin' and Stompin' Blues	1970	25.00
LABOR			
❑ 4	Alone	1982	10.00
MUSE			
❑ 5205	Sittin' Here Thinkin'	1980	12.00

Except when noted otherwise, VG = 25% of NM, and VG+ = 50% of NM. (Example: VG = $2.00, VG+ = $4.00 and NM = $8.00.)

Number	Title (A Side/B Side)	Yr	NM
PAUSA			
❑ PR-7197	Jealous	1986	10.00
RIVERSIDE			
❑ RLP 12-321 [M]	That's My Story	1960	100.00
❑ RLP 12-838 [M]	The Country Blues of John Lee Hooker	1959	100.00
SPECIALTY			
❑ SPS-2125	Alone	1970	30.00
❑ SPS-2127	Going Down Highway 51	1970	30.00
STAX			
❑ STS-2013	That's Where It's At	1970	15.00
❑ STX-4134	That's Where It's At	1979	10.00
—Reissue of 2013			
TOMATO			
❑ 7009 [(2)]	The Cream	1978	15.00
TRADITION			
❑ 2089	Real Blues	1970	15.00
UNITED ARTISTS			
❑ UA-LA127-J [(3)]	John Lee Hooker's Detroit	1974	25.00
❑ UAS-5512	Coast to Coast Blues Band	1971	15.00
VEE JAY			
❑ LP-1007 [M]	I'm John Lee Hooker	1959	300.00
—Maroon label			
❑ LP-1007 [M]	I'm John Lee Hooker	1960	80.00
—Black label with colorband			
❑ VJLP-1007	I'm John Lee Hooker	1986	8.00
—Reissue of original on flimsier vinyl			
❑ LP-1023 [M]	Travelin'	1960	80.00
❑ LP-1033 [M]	The Folk Lore of John Lee Hooker	1961	50.00
❑ SR-1033 [S]	The Folk Lore of John Lee Hooker	1961	80.00
❑ LP-1043 [M]	Burnin'	1962	50.00
❑ SR-1043 [S]	Burnin'	1962	150.00
❑ LP-1049 [M]	The Best of John Lee Hooker	1962	50.00
❑ SR-1049 [P]	The Best of John Lee Hooker	1962	80.00
❑ VJLP-1049	The Best of John Lee Hooker	1986	8.00
—Reissue of original on flimsier vinyl			
❑ LP-1058 [M]	The Big Soul of John Lee Hooker	1963	50.00
❑ SR-1058 [S]	The Big Soul of John Lee Hooker	1963	150.00
❑ VJLP-1058	The Big Soul of John Lee Hooker	1986	8.00
—Reissue of original on flimsier vinyl			
❑ LP-1066 [M]	John Lee Hooker On Campus	1963	50.00
❑ SR-1066 [S]	John Lee Hooker On Campus	1963	150.00
❑ LP-1078 [M]	John Lee Hooker at Newport	1964	50.00
❑ SR-1078 [S]	John Lee Hooker at Newport	1964	150.00
❑ VJLP-1078	John Lee Hooker at Newport	1986	8.00
—Reissue of original on flimsier vinyl			
❑ DY-7301	John Lee Hooker In Person	198?	8.00
❑ LP-8502 [M]	Is He the World's Greatest Blues Singer?	1965	40.00
—This is the title on the cover; the label calls it "Is He Really the World's Greatest Blues Singer?"			
❑ VJLP-8502	Is He the World's Greatest Blues Singer?	1986	8.00
—Reissue of original on flimsier vinyl; this is the title on the cover; the label calls it "Is He Really the World's Greatest Blues Singer?"			
VERVE FOLKWAYS			
❑ FT-3003 [M]	John Lee Hooker and Seven Nights	1965	25.00
❑ FTS-3003 [S]	John Lee Hooker and Seven Nights	1965	40.00
WAND			
❑ WDS-689	On the Waterfront	1972	15.00

HOOKER, JOHN LEE, AND CANNED HEAT

Also see each artist's individual listings.

45s

Number	Title (A Side/B Side)	Yr	NM
UNITED ARTISTS			
❑ 50779	Whiskey and Wimmen/Let's Make It	1971	5.00
Albums			
LIBERTY			
❑ 35002	Hooker 'n' Heat	1971	20.00
RHINO			
❑ RNLP-801	Recorded Live at the Fox Venice Theatre	1985	12.00
❑ RNDA-71105	Infinite Boogie	1987	12.00

HOOTCH

Albums

Number	Title (A Side/B Side)	Yr	NM
PROGRESS			
❑ PRS-4844	Hootch	1974	600.00

HOOTERS

12-Inch Singles

Number	Title (A Side/B Side)	Yr	NM
COLUMBIA			
❑ AS 2043 [DJ]	All You Zombies (long & short)	1985	15.00
❑ AS2043 [DJ]	All You Zombies (long & short)	1985	15.00
❑ CAS 2232 [DJ]	Day by Day (same on both sides)	1985	6.00
❑ CAS2232 [DJ]	Day by Day (same on both sides)	1985	6.00
❑ CAS 2734 [DJ]	Johnny B (same on both sides)	1987	6.00
❑ CAS2734 [DJ]	Johnny B (same on both sides)	1987	6.00

45s

Number	Title (A Side/B Side)	Yr	NM
ANTENNA			
❑ HOO 84	Hangin' on a Heartbeat/Concubine	1984	10.00
❑ HOO 84 [PS]	Hangin' on a Heartbeat/Concubine	1984	10.00
COLUMBIA			
❑ 04854	All You Zombies/Nervous Night	1985	4.00
—Not issued with picture sleeve in U.S.			
❑ 05568	And We Danced/Blood from a Stone	1985	3.00
❑ 05568 [PS]	And We Danced/Blood from a Stone	1985	3.00
❑ 05730	Day By Day/South Ferry Road	1985	3.00
❑ 05730 [PS]	Day By Day/South Ferry Road	1985	3.00
❑ 05854	Where Do the Children Go/Nervous Night	1986	3.00
❑ 05854 [PS]	Where Do the Children Go/Nervous Night	1986	3.00
❑ 07241	Johnny B/Lucy in the Sky with Diamonds	1987	3.00
❑ 07241 [PS]	Johnny B/Lucy in the Sky with Diamonds	1987	3.00
❑ 07607	Satellite/One Way Home	1987	3.00
❑ 07607 [PS]	Satellite/One Way Home	1987	3.00
❑ 07666	Karla with a K/Washington's Day	1988	3.00
❑ 08384	And We Danced/All You Zombies	1988	3.00
—Reissue			
❑ 73013	500 Miles/The House of Wolfgang	1989	3.00
—Backing vocals on A-side: Peter, Paul and Mary			
❑ 73235	Brother, Don't You Walk Away/A Man Understands	1990	—
—Cassette only			
❑ 73320	Heaven Laughs/Mr. Big Baboon	1990	—
—Cassette only			
EIGHTY PERCENT			
❑ HOO 80	Fightin' on the Same Side/Wireless	1980	10.00
❑ HOO 80 [PS]	Fightin' on the Same Side/Wireless	1980	10.00
❑ HOO 82	All You Zombies (Live)/Rescue Me	1982	10.00
❑ HOO 82 [PS]	All You Zombies (Live)/Rescue Me	1982	10.00

Albums

Number	Title (A Side/B Side)	Yr	NM
ANTENNA			
❑ HOO 83	Amore	1983	20.00
COLUMBIA			
❑ BFC 39912	Nervous Night	1985	12.00
❑ FC 39912	Nervous Night	1985	10.00
—Reissue with new prefix			
❑ OC 40659	One Way Home	1987	10.00
❑ C 45058	Zig Zag	1989	10.00

HOPE, EDDIE

45s

Number	Title (A Side/B Side)	Yr	NM
MARLIN			
❑ 804	A Fool No More/Lost Child	1956	200.00

HOPE, LYNN

45s

Number	Title (A Side/B Side)	Yr	NM
ALADDIN			
❑ 3095	Blue Moon/Blow, Lynn, Blow	1951	40.00
❑ 3103	Too Young/Free and Easy	1951	40.00
❑ 3109	She's Funny That Way/Eleven Till Two	1951	40.00
❑ 3134	Driftin'/Sentimental Journey	1952	30.00
❑ 3155	Move It/Don't Worry 'Bout Me	1952	30.00
❑ 3165	September Song/Blues for Anna Bocoa	1953	25.00
❑ 3178	Broken Heart/Morocco	1953	25.00
❑ 3185	Jet/Tenderly	1953	25.00
❑ 3208	Swing Train/Rose Room	1953	25.00
❑ 3229	Brazil/C. Jam Blues	1954	25.00
❑ 3297	All of Me/Summertime	1955	25.00
❑ 3322	Cherry/Blues in F	1956	25.00
KING			
❑ 5336	Tenderly/Full Moon	1960	12.00
❑ 5352	Body and Soul/Sands of Sahara	1960	12.00
❑ 5378	A Ghost of a Chance/Little Landslide	1960	12.00
❑ 5431	Shockin'/Blue and Sentimental	1960	12.00

HOPEFUL, THE

45s

Number	Title (A Side/B Side)	Yr	NM
MERCURY			
❑ 72637	7 O'Clock News (Silent Night)/6 O'Clock News (America The Beautiful)	1966	12.00

HOPKIN, MARY

45s

Number	Title (A Side/B Side)	Yr	NM
APPLE			
❑ 1801	Those Were the Days/Turn, Turn, Turn	1968	10.00
❑ 1806	Goodbye/Sparrow	1969	8.00
❑ 1806 [PS]	Goodbye/Sparrow	1969	12.00
❑ 1816	Temma Harbour/Lantano Dagli Occhi	1970	8.00
❑ 1816 [PS]	Temma Harbour/Lantano Dagli Occhi	1970	12.00
❑ 1823	Que Sera, Sera (Whatever Will Be, Will Be)/Fields of St. Etienne	1970	8.00
❑ 1825	Think About Your Children/Heritage	1970	8.00
❑ 1825	Think About Your Children/Heritage	1970	12.00
—With star on A-side label			
❑ 1825 [PS]	Think About Your Children/Heritage	1970	12.00
❑ 1843	Water, Paper and Clay/Streets of London	1972	8.00
❑ 1843	Water, Paper and Clay/Streets of London	1972	12.00
—With star on A-side label			
❑ 1855	Knock Knock Who's There/International	1972	8.00
APPLE/AMERICOM			
❑ 1801P/M-238	Those Were the Days/Turn, Turn, Turn	1969	600.00
—Four-inch flexi-disc sold from vending machines			
RCA VICTOR			
❑ PB-10694	Tell Me Now/If You Love Me	1976	4.00

Albums

Number	Title (A Side/B Side)	Yr	NM
APPLE			
❑ ST-3351	Post Card	1969	15.00
❑ ST-5-3351	Post Card	1969	20.00
—Capitol Record Club edition			
❑ SMAS-3381	Earth Song/Ocean Song	1970	15.00
❑ SW-3395	Those Were the Days	1972	25.00

HOPKINS, LIGHTNIN'

45s

Number	Title (A Side/B Side)	Yr	NM
ACE			
❑ 516	Bad Boogie/Wonder What Is Wrong with Me	1956	40.00
ALADDIN			
❑ 3063	Shotgun Blues/Rolling Blues	1950	700.00
❑ 3077	Moonrise Blues/Honey, Honey Blues	1951	200.00
❑ 3096	Miss Me Blues/Abilene	1951	200.00
❑ 3117	You Are Not Going to Worry About My Life Anymore/Daddy Will Be Home Someday	1951	200.00
❑ 3262	So Long/My California	1954	100.00
ARHOOLIE			
❑ 508	My Woman/Lousiana Blues	1965	12.00
❑ 513	Come On Baby/Money Taker	1965	12.00
BLUESVILLE			
❑ 813	So Sorry to Leave You/Got to Move Your Baby	1960	20.00
❑ 814	Death Bells/Sail On	1961	20.00
❑ 817	Back to New Orleans/Hard to Love a Woman	1961	20.00
❑ 820	Happy Blues for John Glenn (Part 1)/Happy Blues for John Glenn (Part 2)	1962	20.00
❑ 821	Last Night Blues/Walkin' Blues	1962	20.00
❑ 822	Sinner's Prayer/Angel Child	1962	20.00
❑ 823	The Business You're Doing/Wake Up Old Lady	1963	20.00
❑ 824	Going Away/Better Stop Her	1963	20.00
❑ 825	Katie Mae/My Babe	1963	20.00
CHART			
❑ 636	Walkin' the Streets/Mussy Haired Woman	1957	30.00
DART			
❑ 123	Grievance Blues/Unsuccessful Blues	1959	20.00
❑ 152	Mary Lou/Wait to Go Home	1960	20.00
DECCA			
❑ 9-28841	The War Is Over/Policy Game	1953	80.00
❑ 9-48306	Merry Christmas/Happy New Year	1953	80.00
❑ 9-48312	Highway Blues/Cemetery Blues	1954	80.00
❑ 9-48321	I'm Wild About You Baby/Bad Things on My Mind	1954	100.00
FIRE			
❑ 1034	Mojo Hand/Glory Be	1961	20.00
HARLEM			
❑ 2321	Contrary Mary/I'm Begging You	1954	200.00

Number	Title (A Side/B Side)	Yr	NM
❑ 2324	Mad Man's Boogie/Nobody Cares for Me	1954	200.00
❑ 2331	Fast Life/The Jackstropper	1955	200.00
❑ 2336	Good Old Woman/Untrue	1955	200.00
HERALD			
❑ 425	Lightnin's Boogie/Don't Think 'Cause You're Pretty	1954	30.00
❑ 428	Lightnin's Special/Life Is Used to Live	1954	30.00
❑ 436	Movin' On Out Boogie/Sick Feelin' Blues	1954	30.00
❑ 443	Nothin' But the Blues/Early Morning Boogie	1954	30.00
❑ 449	Evil Hearted Woman/They Wonder Who I Am	1955	30.00
❑ 456	My Baby's Gone/Don't Need No Job	1955	25.00
❑ 465	I Had a Gal Named Sal/Blues for My Cookie	1955	25.00
❑ 471	Hopkins Sky Hop/Lonesome in Your Home	1956	25.00
❑ 476	Grandma's Boogie/I Love You Baby	1956	25.00
❑ 483	Finally Met My Baby/That's Alright Baby	1956	25.00
❑ 490	Shine On Moon/Sitting and Thinking	1956	25.00
❑ 497	Remember Me/Please Don't Go Baby	1957	25.00
❑ 504	Boogie Woogie Dance/The Blues Is a Mighty Bad Feeling	1957	20.00
❑ 520	Little Kewpie Doll/Lightnin' Don't Feel Well	1958	20.00
❑ 531	Hear Me Talkin'/Lightnin's Stomp	1958	20.00
❑ 542	Let's Move/I'm Achin'	1959	20.00
❑ 547	Flash Lightnin'/Gonna Change My Ways	1960	20.00
IMPERIAL			
❑ 5834	Feel So Bad/Shotgun	1962	15.00
❑ 5852	Picture on the Wall/Lightnin's Boogie	1962	15.00
IVORY			
❑ 91272	Got Me a Lousiana Woman/War Is Starting Again	196?	15.00
JAX			
❑ 315	No Good Woman/Been a Bad Man	1953	300.00
—Red vinyl			
❑ 318	Automobile/Organ Blues	1953	300.00
—Red vinyl			
❑ 321	Contrary Mary/I'm Begging You	1953	300.00
—Red vinyl			
❑ 635	Coffee Blues/New Short Haired Woman	1954	250.00
—Reissue of Sittin' In With 635			
❑ 642	You Caused My Heart to Weep/Tap Dance Boogie	1954	250.00
—Reissue of Sittin' In With 642			
❑ 649	New Worried Life Blues/One Kind of Favor	1954	250.00
—Reissue of Sittin' In With 649; this may be its first issue on 45 rpm			
❑ 660	Mad Blues/I've Been a Bad Man	1954	250.00
—Reissue of Sittin' In With 660			
❑ 661	Gone Again/Down to the River	1954	250.00
—Reissue of Sittin' In With 661			
JEWEL			
❑ 788	Back Door Friends/Fishing Clothes	1968	6.00
❑ 796	Wig Wearin' Woman/Move On Out, Part 2	1968	6.00
❑ 803	Lovin' Arms/Ride in Your New Auto	1969	6.00
❑ 807	Play with Your Poodle/Breakfast Time	1970	30.00
❑ 809	I'm Comin' Home/You're Too Fast	1970	30.00
❑ 816	My Charlie (Part 1)/My Charlie (Part 2)	1970	6.00
❑ 819	Rock Me Mama/Love Me This Morning	1971	6.00
❑ 825	Uncle Sam the Hip Hit Record Man/Found My Baby Crying	1971	6.00
LIGHTNING			
❑ 104	Unsuccessful Blues/Grieving Blues	1955	500.00
MERCURY			
❑ 8252x45	Everybody's Down on Me/You Do Too	1952	120.00
❑ 8274x45	Sad News from Korea/Let Me Fly Your Kite	1952	100.00
❑ 8293x45	Gone with the Wind/She's Almost Dead	1952	100.00
❑ 70081x45	Ain't It a Shame/Crazy About My Baby	1953	100.00

Number	Title (A Side/B Side)	Yr	NM
❑ 70191x45	My Mama Told Me/What's the Matter Now	1953	100.00
PRESTIGE			
❑ 326	I Like to Boogie/Let's Go Sit on the Lawn	1964	10.00
❑ 343	Mojo Hand/Automobile Blues	1964	10.00
❑ 374	T Model Blues/You Cook Alright	1965	10.00
❑ 391	Sinner's Prayer/Got to Move Your Baby	1965	10.00
❑ 405	I'm Gonna Build Me a Heaven (Part 1)/I'm Gonna Build Me a Heaven (Part 2)	1966	10.00
❑ 452	Mama Blues/Pneumonia Blues	1968	8.00
RPM			
❑ 45x337	Beggin' You to Stay/Bad Luck and Trouble	1951	600.00
❑ 45x346	Lonesome Dog Blues/Jake Head	1952	800.00
❑ 45x351	Don't Keep My Baby Long/Last Affair	1952	400.00
❑ 45x359	Needed Time/One Kind Favor	1952	400.00
❑ 45x378	Another Fool in Town/Candy Kitchen	1953	300.00
❑ 45x388	Black Cat/Mistreated Blues	1953	300.00
❑ 45x398	Santa Fe Blues/Some Day Baby	1954	200.00
SHAD			
❑ 5011	Hello Central/Mad As I Can Be	1959	15.00
SITTIN' IN WITH			
❑ 621	Give Me Central 209/New York Boogie	1951	500.00
❑ 621	Hello Central/New York Boogie	1952	400.00
❑ 635	Coffee Blues/New Short Haired Woman	1952	500.00
❑ 642	You Caused My Heart to Weep/Tap Dance Boogie	1952	500.00
❑ 644	Jail House Blues/"T" Model Blues	1952	500.00
❑ 647	Bald Headed Woman/Dirty House	1952	500.00
❑ 649	New Worried Life Blues/One Kind of Favor	1952	—
—Unreleased on 45 rpm?			
❑ 652	Papa Bones Boogie/Everything Happens to Me	1953	500.00
❑ 658	Freight Train Blues (When I Started Hoboing)/Broken Hearted Blues	1953	500.00
❑ 660	Mad Blues/I've Been a Bad Man	1953	500.00
❑ 661	Gone Again/Down to the River	1953	500.00
SPHERE SOUND			
❑ 710	Santa/Black Mare Trot	196?	10.00
TNT			
❑ 8002	Lightnin' Jump/Late in the Evening	1954	700.00
❑ 8003	Moanin' Blues/Leavin' Blues	1954	700.00
VAULT			
❑ 965	Easy on Your Heels/No Education	1970	40.00

Albums

Number	Title	Yr	NM
ANALOGUE PRODUCTIONS			
❑ AAPB-014	Goin' Away	199?	40.00
—Audiophile reissue			
ARHOOLIE			
❑ 1011	Lightnin' Hopkins and His Guitar	196?	20.00
❑ 1022	Lightnin' Hopkins, His Brother and Barbara Dane	196?	20.00
❑ 1030	Blues Festival	196?	15.00
❑ 1034	Texas Blues Man	1968	15.00
❑ 1063	Lightnin' Hopkins in Berkeley	1969	15.00
❑ 1087	Poor Lightnin'	1970	15.00
❑ 2007	Early Recordings	197?	15.00
❑ 2010	Early Recordings Vol. 2	197?	15.00
BARNABY			
❑ Z 30247	Lightnin' Hopkins in New York	1970	15.00
BLUES CLASSICS			
❑ 30	Historic Recordings 1952-1953	1986	12.00
BLUESVILLE			
❑ BVLP-1019 [M]	Lightnin'	1961	100.00
—Blue label, silver print			
❑ BVLP-1019 [M]	Lightnin'	1964	30.00
—Blue label, trident logo on right			
❑ BVLP-1029 [M]	Last Night Blues	1961	100.00
—Blue label, silver print			
❑ BVLP-1045 [M]	Blues in My Bottle	1962	100.00
—Blue label, silver print			
❑ BVLP-1045 [M]	Blues in My Bottle	1964	30.00
—Blue label, trident logo on right			
❑ BVLP-1057 [M]	Walkin' This Street	1962	100.00
—Blue label, silver print			
❑ BVLP-1057 [M]	Walkin' This Street	1964	30.00
—Blue label, trident logo on right			
❑ BVLP-1061 [M]	Lightnin' & Co.	1963	100.00
—Blue label, silver print			
❑ BVLP-1061 [M]	Lightnin' & Co.	1964	30.00
—Blue label, trident logo on right			
❑ BVLP-1070 [M]	Smokes Like Lightnin'	1963	100.00
—Blue label, silver print			
❑ BVLP-1070 [M]	Smokes Like Lightnin'	1964	30.00
—Blue label, trident logo on right			
❑ BVLP-1073 [M]	Goin' Away	1963	100.00
—Blue label, silver print			
❑ BVLP-1073 [M]	Goin' Away	1964	30.00
—Blue label, trident logo on right			
❑ BVLP-1081 [M]	Gotta Move Your Baby	1964	30.00
—Blue label, trident logo on right			
❑ BVLP-1084 [M]	Lightnin' Hopkins' Greatest Hits	1964	40.00
❑ BVLP-1086 [M]	Down Home Blues	1964	25.00
BLUESWAY			
❑ S-6039	If You Miss 'Im	1969	20.00
BULLDOG			
❑ 1010	The Texas Bluesman	1965	15.00
CANDID			
❑ CM-8010 [M]	Lightnin' in New York	1961	120.00
❑ CS-9010 [S]	Lightnin' in New York	1961	150.00
COLLECTABLES			
❑ COL-5111	Golden Classics — Mojo Hand	198?	10.00
❑ COL-5121	The Herald Recordings/1954	198?	10.00
❑ COL-5143	Golden Classics, Part 1: Drinkin' the Blues	198?	10.00
❑ COL-5144	Golden Classics, Part 2: Prison Blues	198?	10.00
❑ COL-5145	Golden Classics, Part 3: Mama and Papa Hopkins	198?	10.00
❑ COL-5146	Golden Classics, Part 4: Nothin' But the Blues	198?	10.00
❑ COL-5203	The Lost Texas Tapes, Vol. 1	198?	10.00
❑ COL-5204	The Lost Texas Tapes, Vol. 2	198?	10.00
❑ COL-5205	The Lost Texas Tapes, Vol. 3	198?	10.00
❑ COL-5206	The Lost Texas Tapes, Vol. 4	198?	10.00
❑ COL-5207	The Lost Texas Tapes, Vol. 5	198?	10.00
CROWN			
❑ CLP-5224 [M]	Lightnin' Hopkins Sings the Blues	196?	25.00
—Black label, multi-color logo			
❑ CLP-5224 [M]	Lightnin' Hopkins Sings the Blues	1962	50.00
—Gray label			
❑ CLP-5224 [M]	Lightnin' Hopkins Sings the Blues	1962	100.00
—Black label, silver "Crown"			
DART			
❑ D-8000 [M]	Blues Underground	196?	200.00
—Retitled version of above			
❑ D-8000 [M]	Lightning Strikes Again	1960	400.00
DCC COMPACT CLASSICS			
❑ LPZ-2007	Blues Hoot	1996	50.00
—Audiophile vinyl			
EVEREST ARCHIVE OF FOLK & JAZZ			
❑ 241	Lightnin' Hopkins	1969	15.00
❑ 313	Lightnin' Hopkins, Vol. 2	197?	15.00
❑ 342	Autobiography in Blues	1979	12.00
FANTASY			
❑ OBC-506	Blues in My Bottle	198?	12.00
❑ OBC-522	Goin' Away	1988	12.00
❑ OBC-532	Lightnin'	1990	12.00
❑ 24702 [(2)]	Double Blues	1972	20.00
❑ 24725 [(2)]	How Many More Years	1981	15.00
FIRE			
❑ FLP 104 [M]	Mojo Hand	1960	1500.
FOLKLORE			
❑ FRLP-14021 [M]	Hootin' the Blues	1964	60.00
❑ FRST-14021 [S]	Hootin' the Blues	1964	70.00
FOLKWAYS			
❑ FS-3822 [M]	Lightnin' Hopkins	1962	40.00
❑ 31011	Roots	196?	15.00
GNP CRESCENDO			
❑ 10022	Legacy of the Blues, Vol. 12	1978	12.00
GUEST STAR			
❑ G-1459 [M]	"Live" at the Bird Lounge, Houston, Texas	1964	30.00
❑ GS-1459 [R]	"Live" at the Bird Lounge, Houston, Texas	1964	20.00
HERALD			
❑ LP 1012 [M]	Lightnin' and the Blues	1959	800.00
—Yellow label			
❑ LP 1012 [M]	Lightnin' and the Blues	1959	1500.
—Black label; VG value 750; VG+ value 1125			
❑ LP 1012 [M]	Lightnin' and the Blues	196?	500.00
—Multi-color label			
IMPERIAL			
❑ LP-9180 [M]	Lightnin' Hopkins On Stage	1962	300.00
❑ LP-9186 [M]	Lightnin' Hopkins Sings the Blues	1962	300.00
❑ LP-9211 [M]	Lightnin' Hopkins and the Blues	1963	200.00
❑ LP-12211 [R]	Lightnin' Hopkins and the Blues	1963	100.00
INTERNATIONAL ARTISTS			
❑ IA-6	Free Form Patterns	1968	50.00
—With psychedelic art on cover			

Except when noted otherwise, VG = 25% of NM, and VG+ = 50% of NM. (Example: VG = $2.00, VG+ = $4.00 and NM = $8.00.)

Number	Title (A Side/B Side)	Yr	NM
❑ IA-6	Free Form Patterns	1968	200.00
—With photo on cover			
JAZZ MAN			
❑ BLZ-5502	Lightnin' in New York	1982	10.00
JEWEL			
❑ 5000	Blue Lightnin'	1967	15.00
❑ 5001	Talkin' Some Sense	1968	15.00
❑ 5015	Great Electric Show and Dance	1970	15.00
KING			
❑ KS-1085	Moanin' Blues	1969	15.00
MAINSTREAM			
❑ 311	The Blues	1971	15.00
❑ 326	Dirty Blues	197?	15.00
❑ 405	Low Down Dirty Blues	1974	15.00
❑ S-6040 [S]	Blues	196?	30.00
❑ 56040 [M]	Blues	196?	25.00
MOUNT VERNON			
❑ 104 [M]	Nothin' But the Blues	196?	25.00
OLYMPIC GOLD MEDAL			
❑ 7110	Blues Giant	1974	12.00
POPPY			
❑ 60002 [(2)]	Lightnin'!	1969	25.00
PRESTIGE			
❑ PRLPT-7370 [(2)M]	My Life with the Blues	1965	60.00
❑ PRST-7370 [(2)S]	My Life with the Blues	1965	70.00
❑ PRLP-7377 [M]	Soul Blues	1966	50.00
❑ PRST-7377 [S]	Soul Blues	1966	60.00
❑ PRST-7592	Lightnin' Hopkins' Greatest Hits	1969	15.00
❑ PRST-7714	The Best of Lightnin' Hopkins & His Texas Blues Band	1969	15.00
❑ PRST-7806	Hootin' the Blues	1969	15.00
❑ PRST-7811	The Blues of Lightnin' Hopkins	1969	15.00
❑ PRST-7831	Gotta Move Your Baby	1970	15.00
RHINO			
❑ RNLP 103	Los Angeles Blues	1982	10.00
SCORE			
❑ SLP-4022 [M]	Lightnin' Hopkins Strums the Blues	1958	1200.
SMITHSONIAN FOLKWAYS			
❑ SF-40019	Lightnin' Hopkins	1990	12.00
SPHERE SOUND			
❑ SSR-7001 [M]	Lightnin' Hopkins	1964	400.00
❑ SSSR-7001 [R]	Lightnin' Hopkins	1964	300.00
TIME			
❑ 1 [M]	Blues/Folk	1960	120.00
❑ 2 [M]	Blues/Folk Vol. 2	1960	120.00
❑ ST-70004 [S]	Last of the Great Blues Singers	1962	120.00
❑ T-70004 [M]	Last of the Great Blues Singers	1962	120.00
TOMATO			
❑ 7004 [(2)]	Lightnin'!	1977	15.00
TRADITION			
❑ TLP-1035 [M]	Country Blues	1960	30.00
❑ TLP-1040 [M]	Autobiography in Blues	1961	30.00
❑ TLP-2056 [M]	The Best of Lightnin' Hopkins	1967	20.00
❑ TLP-2103 [M]	Lightnin' Strikes	1972	15.00
TRIP			
❑ TLP-8015	Lightnin' Hopkins	1971	12.00
UNITED			
❑ US-7713	Lightnin' Hopkins Sings the Blues	196?	15.00
❑ US-7744	Original Folk Blues	196?	15.00
❑ US-7785	A Legend in His Time	196?	15.00
UNITED ARTISTS			
❑ UAS-5512	Coast to Coast Blues Band	197?	15.00
UP FRONT			
❑ 158	Lightnin' Blues	1973	12.00
VAULT			
❑ 129	California Mudslide	1969	25.00
VEE JAY			
❑ LP 1044 [M]	Lightnin' Strikes	1962	50.00
VERVE			
❑ V-8453 [M]	Fast Life Woman	1962	40.00
VERVE FOLKWAYS			
❑ FV-9000 [M]	The Roots of Lightnin' Hopkins	1965	25.00
❑ FVS-9000 [S]	The Roots of Lightnin' Hopkins	1965	30.00
❑ FV-9022 [M]	Lightnin' Strikes	1965	25.00
❑ FVS-9022 [S]	Lightnin' Strikes	1965	30.00
VERVE FORECAST			
❑ FT-3013 [M]	Something Blue	1967	20.00
❑ FTS-3013 [S]	Something Blue	1967	25.00
❑ FTS-3031	Lightnin' Strikes	1968	20.00
WORLD PACIFIC			
❑ ST-1817 [S]	First Meetin'	1963	40.00
—Black vinyl			
❑ ST-1817 [S]	First Meetin'	1963	80.00
—Red vinyl			
❑ WP-1817 [M]	First Meetin'	1963	30.00

HOPKINS, NICKY Prominent session keyboardist who played on BEATLES and ROLLING STONES sessions, among dozens of others.

Number	Title (A Side/B Side)	Yr	NM
45s			
COLUMBIA			
❑ 45869	Speed On/Sundown in Mexico	1973	5.00
DECCA			
❑ 32139	Mister Pleasant/Nothing As Yet	1967	12.00
Albums			
COLUMBIA			
❑ KC 32074	The Tin Man Was a Dreamer	1973	20.00
MERCURY			
❑ SRM-1-1028	No More Changes	1975	20.00

HOPNEY

Number	Title (A Side/B Side)	Yr	NM
Albums			
ILLUSION			
❑ CM-1032	Ends and Means	1979	250.00
❑ CM-1033	Perils of Love	1978	250.00
❑ CM-1034	Cosmic Rockout	1977	500.00

HOPSON, JOYCE

Number	Title (A Side/B Side)	Yr	NM
45s			
REVUE			
❑ 11034	I Surrender to You/This Time	1969	150.00

HORNE, JIMMY "BO"

Number	Title (A Side/B Side)	Yr	NM
12-Inch Singles			
EDGE			
❑ 12011	Show Me How Much (You Want My Love) (2 versions)	1987	12.00
RHYTHM DRIVE			
❑ RD-504	What You Do (Club Remix) (Dub) (Radio Mix) (Instrumental)	1994	10.00
SUNNYVIEW			
❑ SUN 409	You're So Good to Me (Vocal 5:52) (Dub 6:15) (Instrumental 7:55)	1983	12.00
❑ SUN 423	Let's Do It (5:45) (Dub 8:10)	1985	15.00
❑ SUN 33002	Spank (Long Version 6:23) (one other version)	1986	20.00
SUNSHINE SOUND			
❑ SSD-200	Dance Across the Floor/Let Me (Let Me Be Your Lover)	1978	100.00
❑ SSD-205	Spank (6:10)/I Wanna Go Home with You (3:35)	1978	50.00
❑ SSD-206	Spank (6:10) (Paarty Remix)	1978	50.00
❑ SSD-4215	You Get Me Hot (6:50)/ They Long to Be Close to You (4:50)	1979	30.00
❑ SSD-4218	Is It In (5:20)/I Wanna Go Home with You	1979	25.00
T.K. DISCO			
❑ TKD-25	Gimme Some/Get Happy (4:23)	1977	80.00
❑ TKD-33	Get Happy (4:23)/It's Your Sweet Love (3:14)	1977	50.00
45s			
ALSTON			
❑ 3712	Don't Worry About It/ Music to Make Love By	1975	10.00
❑ 3714	Gimme Some (Part 1)/(Part 2)	1975	6.00
❑ 3724	It's Your Sweet Love/ Don't Worry About It	1976	10.00
❑ 3729	Get Happy/It's Your Sweet Love	1977	6.00
❑ 4606	Clean Up Man/Down the Road of Love	1972	30.00
—Reissue of Dade 2031			
❑ 4612	On the Street Corner/ If You Want My Love	1972	30.00
❑ 4618	If We Were Still Together/ Two People in Love	1973	30.00
DADE			
❑ 2025	I Can't Speak/Street Corners	1969	2000.
—Reproductions exist as double A-sides on Dade JBH-001; these usually sell in the $20-$25 range			
❑ 2031	Clean Up Man/Down the Road of Love	1972	100.00
—Original issue			
EDGE			
❑ 7011	Show Me How Much (You Want My Love)/(Extended Version)	1987	8.00
SUNSHINE SOUND			
❑ 1003	Dance Across the Floor/ It's Your Sweet Love	1978	8.00
❑ 1005	Let Me (Let Me Be Your Lover)/ Ask the Birds and the Bees	1978	8.00
❑ 1007	Spank/I Wanna Go Home with You	1978	8.00
❑ 1014	You Get Me Hot/They Long to Be Close to You	1979	8.00
—Light brown label			
❑ 1014	You Get Me Hot/They Long to Be Close to You	1979	10.00
—Black label			
❑ 1015	Without You/Goin' Home for Love	1980	7.00
❑ 1016	They Long to Be Close to You/ (B-side unknown)	1980	8.00
❑ 1018	Is It In/I Wanna Go Home with You	1980	7.00
Albums			
SUNSHINE SOUND			
❑ SSE-7801	Dance Across the Floor	1978	20.00
❑ SSE-7805	Goin' Home for Love	1979	15.00

HORNE, LENA

Number	Title (A Side/B Side)	Yr	NM
45s			
BUDDAH			
❑ 215	Watch What Happens/Rocky Raccoon	1971	6.00
❑ 233	Feels So Good/Nature's Baby	1971	6.00
CAPITOL			
❑ S7-57888	Let It Snow! Let It Snow! Let It Snow!/Jingle Bells	1992	4.00
—B-side by Count Basie			
MCA			
❑ 40979	Believe in Yourself/Main Title Overture (Part 1)	1978	5.00
MGM			
❑ K30396	Can't Help Lovin' Dat Man/ Where or When	1951	12.00
❑ K30397	Is It Always Like This/ Love of My Life	1951	12.00
—One record of box set K-72			
RCA VICTOR			
❑ 47-6073	Love Me or Leave Me/ I Love to Love	1955	12.00
❑ 47-6175	It's All Right with Me/It's Love	1955	12.00
❑ 47-6431	If You Can Dream/ What's Right for You	1956	12.00
❑ 47-7037	Push De Button/Coconut Street	1957	12.00
❑ 47-7332	When Johnny Comes Marching Home/You'd Better	1957	12.00
❑ 47-8092	Where Is Love/Come On Strong	1962	10.00
❑ 47-8092 [PS]	Where Is Love/Come On Strong	1962	15.00
SKYE			
❑ 4523	Watch What Happens/ Rocky Raccoon	1970	8.00
THREE CHERRIES			
❑ 7301	I Wish I'd Met You/ When I Fall in Love	1989	4.00
—A-side with Sammy Davis Jr.			
❑ 7301 [PS]	I Wish I'd Met You/ When I Fall in Love	1989	4.00
20TH CENTURY FOX			
❑ 449	Now!/Silent Spring	1963	10.00
❑ 460	Blowin' in the Wind/ The Eagle and Me	1964	10.00
UNITED ARTISTS			
❑ 851	Pleasures and Palaces/ Feeling Good	1965	8.00
❑ 911	The Sand and the Sea/ Softly, As I Leave You	1965	8.00
❑ 1661	Let It Snow! Let It Snow! Let It Snow!/What Are You Doing New Year's Eve	1966	10.00
—Silver Spotlight Series			
❑ 1661 [DJ]	Let It Snow! Let It Snow! Let It Snow! (same on both sides)	1966	8.00
—Silver Spotlight Series promo			
❑ 50051	Love Bug/Wonder What I'm Gonna Do	1966	8.00
7-Inch Extended Plays			
RCA CAMDEN			
❑ CAE 380	St. Louis Blues/Beale Street Blues//Aunt Hagar's Blues/ Careless Love Blues	1956	12.00
❑ CAE 380 [PS]	Lena Horne Sings the Blues	1956	12.00
RCA VICTOR			
❑ 947-0164	Moanin' Low/I Gotta Right to Sing the Blues//The Man I Love/Where or When	1954	20.00
—Silver label, red print; part of 2-EP set EPBT-3061			
❑ 947-0165	Stormy Weather/Ill Wind//Mad About the Boy/What Is This Thing Called Love?	1954	20.00
—Silver label, red print; part of 2-EP set EPBT-3061			
❑ VLP 2587	I've Grown Accustomed to His Face/I Concentrate on You/ I Found a New Baby//		

H

Number	Title (A Side/B Side)	Yr	NM
	I Surrender, Dear/I Let a Song Go Out of My Heart/I Want to Be Happy	1963	12.00
—Jukebox issue; small hole, plays at 33 1/3 rpm			
❑ VLP 2587 [PS]	Lena...Lovely and Alive	1963	12.00
❑ EPA-4038	Ain't It De Truth?/Take It Slow, Joe//Cocoanut Sweet/Push De Button	1957	15.00
❑ EPA-4038 [PS]	Jamaica	1957	15.00
Albums			
ACCORD			
❑ SN-7190	Standing Room Only	198?	10.00
BLUEBIRD			
❑ 9985-1-RB	Stormy Weather: The Legendary Lena	1990	12.00
BUDDAH			
❑ BDS-5084	Nature's Baby	1971	12.00
❑ BDS-5669 [(2)]	The Essential Lena Horne	197?	12.00
BULLDOG			
❑ BDL-2000	20 Golden Pieces of Lena Horne	198?	10.00
CHARTER			
❑ CLP-101 [M]	Lena Sings Your Requests	1963	15.00
❑ CLS-101 [S]	Lena Sings Your Requests	1963	20.00
❑ CLP-106 [M]	Like Latin	1964	15.00
❑ CLS-106 [S]	Like Latin	1964	20.00
DRG			
❑ MRS-501	Lena Horne With Lennie Hayton & the Marty Paich Orchestra	1985	10.00
❑ MRS-510	Lena Goes Latin	1986	10.00
JAZZTONE			
❑ J-1262 [M]	Lena and Ivie	1957	50.00
LIBERTY			
❑ LN-10194	Lena in Hollywood	198?	8.00
LION			
❑ L-70050 [M]	I Feel So Smoochie	1959	20.00
MGM			
❑ E-545 [10]	Lena Horne Sings	1952	50.00
❑ M3G-5409	The One and Only	197?	10.00
MOBILE FIDELITY			
❑ 2-094 [(2)]	Lena Horne: The Lady and Her Music	1982	40.00
—Audiophile vinyl			
MOVIETONE			
❑ MTM 71005 [M]	Once in a Lifetime	196?	15.00
❑ MTS 72005 [S]	Once in a Lifetime	196?	20.00
PAIR			
❑ PDL2-1055 [(2)]	Lena	1986	12.00
QWEST			
❑ 2QW 3597 [(2)]	Lena Horne: The Lady and Her Music	1981	12.00
RCA VICTOR			
❑ BGL1-1026	Lena and Michel	1975	12.00
—With Michel Legrand			
❑ LOC-1028 [M]	Lena Horne at the Waldorf Astoria	1957	30.00
❑ LSO-1028 [S]	Lena Horne at the Waldorf Astoria	1957	40.00
❑ LPM-1148 [M]	It's Love	1955	50.00
❑ LPM-1375 [M]	Stormy Weather	1956	50.00
❑ BGL1-1799	Lena	1976	12.00
❑ LPM-1879 [M]	Give the Lady What She Wants	1958	30.00
❑ LSP-1879 [S]	Give the Lady What She Wants	1958	40.00
❑ LPM-1895 [M]	Songs of Burke and Van Heusen	1959	30.00
❑ LSP-1895 [S]	Songs of Burke and Van Heusen	1959	40.00
❑ LPM-2364 [M]	Lena Horne at the Sands	1961	25.00
❑ LSP-2364 [S]	Lena Horne at the Sands	1961	30.00
❑ LPM-2465 [M]	Lena on the Blue Side	1962	25.00
❑ LSP-2465 [S]	Lena on the Blue Side	1962	30.00
❑ LPM-2587 [M]	Lena...Lovely and Alive	1963	25.00
❑ LSP-2587 [S]	Lena...Lovely and Alive	1963	30.00
❑ LPT-3061 [10]	This Is Lena Horne	1952	50.00
❑ AYL1-4389	Lena, A New Album	1983	8.00
—"Best Buy Series" reissue			
SKYE			
❑ 15	Lena & Gabor	1970	15.00
—With Gabor Szabo			
STANYAN			
❑ POW-3006	Stormy Weather	198?	10.00
—Reissue of 10126			
❑ 10126	Stormy Weather	197?	12.00
SUNBEAM			
❑ 212	A Date with Lena Horne	198?	10.00
—With Fletcher Henderson and His Orchestra			
THREE CHERRIES			
❑ TC-44411	The Men in My Life	1989	10.00
TIME-LIFE			
❑ SLGD-05 [(2)]	Legendary Singers: Lena Horne	1985	15.00
TOPS			
❑ L-910 [10]	Moanin' Low	195?	40.00
❑ L-931 [10]	Lena Horne Sings	195?	40.00
❑ L-1502 [M]	Lena Horne	1958	20.00
20TH CENTURY FOX			
❑ TF-4115 [M]	Here's Lena Now	1964	15.00
❑ TFS-4115 [S]	Here's Lena Now	1964	20.00
UNITED ARTISTS			
❑ UAL 3433 [M]	Feelin' Good	1965	15.00
❑ UAL 3470 [M]	Lena in Hollywood	1966	15.00
❑ UAL 3496 [M]	Soul	1966	15.00
❑ UAL 3546 [M]	Merry from Lena	1966	15.00
❑ UAS 6433 [S]	Feelin' Good	1965	20.00
❑ UAS 6470 [S]	Lena in Hollywood	1966	20.00
❑ UAS 6496 [S]	Soul	1966	20.00
❑ UAS 6546 [S]	Merry from Lena	1966	20.00
—Black label, "United Artists" in rounded box at top			
❑ UAS 6546 [S]	Merry from Lena	1972	12.00
—Tan label			

HORNE, LENA, AND HARRY BELAFONTE

Also see each artist's individual listings.

Number	Title (A Side/B Side)	Yr	NM
Albums			
RCA VICTOR			
❑ LOC-1507 [M]	Porgy and Bess	1959	25.00
❑ LSO-1507 [S]	Porgy and Bess	1959	40.00

HORNETS, THE

More than one group.

Number	Title (A Side/B Side)	Yr	NM
45s			
COLUMBIA			
❑ 42999	Fruit Cake/Seven Days to Tahiti	1964	60.00
EMERALD			
❑ 501	Runt/Breakfast in Bed	196?	30.00
FLASH			
❑ 125	Crying Over You/Tango Moon	1957	250.00
LIBERTY			
❑ 55688	Motorcycle U.S.A./On the Track	1964	30.00
REV			
❑ 3515	Slow Dance/Strollin'	1958	25.00
STATES			
❑ 127	I Can't Believe/Lonesome Baby	1953	8000.
—Black vinyl. VG 4000; VG+ 6000			
❑ 127	I Can't Believe/Lonesome Baby	1953	15000.
—Red vinyl. VG 7500; VG+ 10000			
V.I.P.			
❑ 25004	She's My Baby/Give Me a Kiss	1964	60.00
Albums			
LIBERTY			
❑ LRP-3348 [M]	Motorcycles U.S.A.	1963	40.00
❑ LRP-3364 [M]	Big Drag Boats U.S.A.	1964	50.00
❑ LST-7348 [S]	Motorcycles U.S.A.	1963	50.00
❑ LST-7364 [S]	Big Drag Boats U.S.A.	1964	60.00

HORSES

Don Johnson of "Miami Vice" and "Nash Bridges" fame was supposedly in this band.

Number	Title (A Side/B Side)	Yr	NM
45s			
WHITE WHALE			
❑ 301	Class of '69/Country Boy	1969	8.00
❑ 320	Freight Train/(B-side unknown)	1969	10.00
Albums			
WHITE WHALE			
❑ WWS-7121	Horses	1970	40.00

HORSLIPS

Number	Title (A Side/B Side)	Yr	NM
45s			
ATCO			
❑ 6935	High Reel/Furniture	1973	8.00
DJM			
❑ 1026	Warm Sweet Breath of Love/(B-side unknown)	1977	5.00
❑ 1032	Trouble (With a Capital T)/(B-side unknown)	1978	5.00
❑ 1036	Sure the Boy Was Green/Exiles	1978	10.00
—Green vinyl			
❑ 1105	Loneliness/Homesick	1979	5.00
MERCURY			
❑ 76030	Rescue Me/Soap Opera	1979	5.00
❑ 76072 [DJ]	Shakin' All Over (mono/stereo)	1979	6.00
—May be promo only			
RCA VICTOR			
❑ PB-10123	Nighttown Boys/We Bring the Summer With Me	1974	6.00
Albums			
ATCO			
❑ SD 7030	Happy to Meet, Sorry to Part	1973	12.00
❑ SD 7039	The Tain	1974	12.00
DJM			
❑ 10	Book of Invasions	1977	10.00
❑ 16	Aliens	1978	10.00
❑ 20	The Man Who Built America	1979	10.00
MERCURY			
❑ SRM-1-3809	Short Stories/Tall Tales	1979	10.00
❑ SRM-1-3842	Belfast Gigs	1980	10.00
RCA VICTOR			
❑ CPL1-0709	Dancehall Sweethearts	1974	12.00

HOSEA, DON

Number	Title (A Side/B Side)	Yr	NM
45s			
SUN			
❑ 368	Since I Met You/Uh Huh Unh	1961	20.00

HOT BUTTER

Number	Title (A Side/B Side)	Yr	NM
45s			
MUSICOR			
❑ 1458	Popcorn/At the Movies	1972	6.00
❑ 1466	Apache/Hot Butter	1972	5.00
❑ 1468	Tequila/Hot Butter	1972	5.00
❑ 1473	Percolator/Tristana	1973	5.00
❑ 1481	Slay Solution/Kappi Maki	1973	5.00
❑ 1491	Pipeline/Apache	1974	5.00
Albums			
MUSICOR			
❑ MS-3242	Popcorn	1972	12.00
—Regular cover			
❑ MS-3242	Popcorn	1972	20.00
—Die-cut cover			

HOT CHOCOLATE

Number	Title (A Side/B Side)	Yr	NM
45s			
APPLE			
❑ 1812	Give Peace a Chance/Living Without Tomorrow	1969	10.00
—As "Hot Chocolate Band"			
BELL			
❑ 45390	Rumors/(B-side unknown)	1973	5.00
❑ 45466	Emma/(B-side unknown)	1974	7.00
BIG TREE			
❑ 16031	Emma/A Love Like Yours	1975	5.00
❑ 16038	Disco Queen/Makin' Music	1975	5.00
❑ 16047	You Sexy Thing/Amazing Skin Song	1975	5.00
❑ 16060	Don't Stop It Now/Beautiful Lady	1976	5.00
❑ 16078	Heaven Is in the Back Seat of My Cadillac/(B-side unknown)	1976	5.00
❑ 16096	So You Win Again/Part of Being with You	1977	5.00
❑ 16101	Man to Man/Brother Louie	1977	5.00
EMI AMERICA			
❑ 8143	Are You Getting Enough Happiness/One Night's Not Enough	1982	4.00
❑ 8157	Bed Games/It Started with a Kiss	1983	4.00
EMI-CAPITOL			
❑ S7-19894	You Sexy Thing/So You Win Again	1998	3.00
INFINITY			
❑ 50002	Every 1's a Winner/Power of Love	1978	4.00
❑ 50016	Going Through the Motions/Don't Turn It Off	1979	4.00
❑ 50033	I Just Love What You're Doing/Congas Man	1979	4.00
❑ 50048	Mindless Boogie/Dance (Get Down To It)	1979	4.00
RAK			
❑ 4503	You Could Have Been a Lady/Everybody's Laughing	1972	6.00
❑ 4506	I Believe in Love/Caveman Billy	1972	6.00
❑ 4508	Mary Anne/Ruth	1972	6.00
❑ 4515	Brother Louie/I Want to Be Free	1973	6.00
Albums			
BIG TREE			
❑ BT 76002	10 Greatest Hits	1977	10.00
❑ BT 89503	Cicero Park	1975	10.00
❑ BT 89512	Hot Chocolate	1975	10.00
❑ BT 89519	Man to Man	1976	10.00
EMI AMERICA			
❑ ST-17077	Mystery	1982	10.00
INFINITY			
❑ INF-9002	Every 1's a Winner	1978	10.00
❑ INF-9010	Going Through the Motions	1979	10.00

HOT DOGGERS, THE

BRUCE JOHNSTON was in this group.

Number	Title (A Side/B Side)	Yr	NM
Albums			
EPIC			
❑ LN 24054 [M]	Surfin' U.S.A.	1963	150.00
❑ BN 26054 [S]	Surfin' U.S.A.	1963	200.00

Except when noted otherwise, VG = 25% of NM, and VG+ = 50% of NM. (Example: VG = $2.00, VG+ = $4.00 and NM = $8.00.)

HOT POOP

Albums

Number	Title (A Side/B Side)	Yr	NM
HOT POOP			
❑ 3072	Hot Poop Does Their Own Thing	1971	300.00

HOT RODDERS, THE

Albums

Number	Title (A Side/B Side)	Yr	NM
CROWN			
❑ CST-378 [S]	Big Hot Rod	1963	25.00
❑ CLP-5378 [M]	Big Hot Rod	1963	20.00

HOT-TODDYS, THE

See ROCKIN' REBELS.

HOT TUNA

Offshoot of JEFFERSON AIRPLANE.

45s

Number	Title (A Side/B Side)	Yr	NM
GRUNT			
❑ 65-0502	Water Song/Keep On Truckin'	1972	6.00
❑ 65-0502 [PS]	Water Song/Keep On Truckin'	1972	12.00
❑ PB-10443	Hot Jellyroll Blues/Surphase Tension	1975	5.00
❑ PB-10776	It's So Easy/I Can't Be Satisfied	1976	5.00
RCA VICTOR			
❑ 74-0528	Candy Man/Been So Long	1971	6.00
❑ 74-0528 [PS]	Candy Man/Been So Long	1971	20.00

Albums

Number	Title (A Side/B Side)	Yr	NM
GRUNT			
❑ BFL1-0348	The Phosphorescent Rat	1974	15.00
❑ BFD1-0820 [Q]	America's Choice	1975	25.00
❑ BFL1-0820	America's Choice	1975	15.00
❑ FTR-1004	Burgers	1972	15.00
❑ BFD1-1238 [Q]	Yellow Fever	1975	25.00
❑ BFL1-1238	Yellow Fever	1975	15.00
❑ BFL1-1920	Hoppkorv	1976	15.00
❑ CYL2-2545 [(2)]	Double Dose	1978	20.00
❑ BXL1-2591	Burgers	1978	12.00
—Reissue of 1004			
❑ DJL1-2852 [DJ]	The Last Interview? A Live Hot Tuna Radio Classic	1978	30.00
❑ BXL1-3357	Final Vinyl	1979	12.00
RCA VICTOR			
❑ AYL1-3864	Hot Tuna	1981	8.00
—"Best Buy Series" reissue			
❑ AYL1-3865	First Pull Up Then Pull Down	1981	8.00
—"Best Buy Series" reissue			
❑ AYL1-3951	Burgers	1981	8.00
—"Best Buy Series" reissue			
❑ LSP-4353	Hot Tuna	1970	15.00
❑ LSP-4550	First Pull Up Then Pull Down	1971	15.00

HOTLEGS

Early incarnation of 10CC. Also see GRAHAM GOULDMAN.

45s

Number	Title (A Side/B Side)	Yr	NM
CAPITOL			
❑ 2886	Neanderthal Man/You Didn't Like It, Because You Didn't Think of It	1970	8.00
❑ 3043	Run Baby Run/How Many Times	1971	12.00

Albums

Number	Title (A Side/B Side)	Yr	NM
CAPITOL			
❑ ST-587	Hotlegs Thinks: School Stinks	1970	25.00

HOUK, RALPH

Albums

Number	Title (A Side/B Side)	Yr	NM
CARLTON			
❑ HH-16 [M]	Hear How to Play Better Baseball	1961	40.00

HOUND DOG CLOWNS

45s

Number	Title (A Side/B Side)	Yr	NM
UNI			
❑ 55047	Superfox/Wicked Witch	1968	20.00

HOUR GLASS, THE

Also see DUANE ALLMAN; DUANE AND GREGG ALLMAN; GREGG ALLMAN.

45s

Number	Title (A Side/B Side)	Yr	NM
LIBERTY			
❑ 56002	Heartbeat/Nothing But Tears	1967	12.00
❑ 56029	Power of Love/I Still Want Your Love	1968	12.00
❑ 56053	D-I-V-O-R-C-E/Changing of the Guard	1968	12.00
❑ 56065	She Is My Woman/Going Nowhere	1968	12.00
❑ 56072	Now Is the Time/She Is My Woman	1968	12.00
❑ 56091	I've Been Trying/Silently	1969	12.00

Albums

Number	Title (A Side/B Side)	Yr	NM
LIBERTY			
❑ LRP-3536 [M]	The Hour Glass	1967	25.00
❑ LST-7536 [S]	The Hour Glass	1967	30.00
❑ LST-7555	The Power of Love	1968	30.00
SPRINGBOARD			
❑ SPB-4016	Duane and Gregg Allman with the Hour Glass	1976	10.00
UNITED ARTISTS			
❑ UA-LA013-G2 [(2)]	The Hour Glass	1973	15.00

HOUSTON, CISSY

12-Inch Singles

Number	Title (A Side/B Side)	Yr	NM
PRIVATE STOCK			
❑ PS 5108	Think It Over (6:00)/An Umbrella Song	1978	10.00

45s

Number	Title (A Side/B Side)	Yr	NM
COLUMBIA			
❑ 11058	Warning-Danger (This Love Affair May Be Hazardous to You)/An Umbrella Song	1979	4.00
❑ 11208	Break It To Me Gently/Gonna Take the Easy Way Out	1980	4.00
COMMONWEALTH UNITED			
❑ 3010	I'll Be There/Me — I Believe	1970	6.00
CONGRESS			
❑ 268	Bring Him Back/World of Broken Hearts	1966	60.00
—As "Susie Houston"			
JANUS			
❑ 131	I Just Don't Know What to Do with Myself/Empty Place	1970	40.00
❑ 145	Be My Baby/I'll Be There	1971	6.00
❑ 159	Hang On to a Dream/Darling Take Me Back	1971	15.00
❑ 177	I Love You/Making Love	1971	6.00
❑ 190	Didn't We/It's Not Easy	1972	6.00
❑ 206	Midnight Train to Georgia/Will You Still Love Me Tomorrow	1972	6.00
❑ 230	I'm So Glad I Can Love Again/One Time You Say You Love Me	1973	6.00
❑ 255	I Believe/Nothing Can Stop Me	1975	6.00
KAPP			
❑ 814	Don't Come Running to Me/One Broken Heart for Sale	1967	30.00
—As "Sissie Houston"			
PRIVATE STOCK			
❑ 45,137	Love Is Something That Leads You/If I Ever Lose This Heaven	1977	5.00
❑ 45,137	Love Is Something That Leads You/It Never Really Ended	1977	5.00
❑ 45,153	Tomorrow/Love Is Holding On	1977	5.00
❑ 45,171	Things to Do/It Never Really Ended	1977	5.00
❑ 45,204	Think It Over/The Umbrella Song	1978	5.00

Albums

Number	Title (A Side/B Side)	Yr	NM
COLUMBIA			
❑ JC 36112	Warning Danger	1979	10.00
❑ JC 36193	Step Aside for a Lady	1980	10.00
COMMONWEALTH UNITED			
❑ 6008	Cissy Houston	1970	—
—Canceled?			
JANUS			
❑ 3001	Cissy Houston	1970	15.00
PRIVATE STOCK			
❑ PS 2031	Cissy Houston	1977	12.00
❑ PS 7015	Think It Over	1978	12.00

HOUSTON, JOHNNY

45s

Number	Title (A Side/B Side)	Yr	NM
EVENT			
❑ 4277	Slick Chick/Playboy	1959	30.00
❑ 4280	Torrid Tessie Lee/Our Very First Kiss	1959	30.00

HOUSTON, SOLDIER BOY

45s

Number	Title (A Side/B Side)	Yr	NM
ATLANTIC			
❑ 971	Western Rider Blues/Hug Me Baby	1952	250.00

HOUSTON, THELMA

12-Inch Singles

Number	Title (A Side/B Side)	Yr	NM
CENTURY 2000			
❑ 1001	Hold On (4 versions)/Athens Grooves/Olympus Thunder	1990	6.00
MCA			
❑ L33-1253 [DJ]	I'd Rather Spend the Bad Times with You (3 versions)	1984	8.00
❑ L33-1795 [DJ]	Working Girl (3:45)/(5:00)	1983	8.00
❑ 13963	Working Girl/Running in Circles	1983	6.00
❑ 23520	You Used to Hold Me So Tight (12" Version)/(Dub) (LP)	1984	6.00
❑ 23552	Fantasy and Heartbreak (Dance Version)/(LP Version)	1985	6.00
MOTOWN			
❑ 00053	Ride to the Rainbow/Love Machine	1979	8.00
RCA VICTOR			
❑ PD-12293	96 Tears/There's No Runnin' Away from Love	1981	7.00
REPRISE			
❑ PRO-A-4475 [DJ]	High (4 versions)	1990	8.00
❑ PRO-A-4487 [DJ]	Out of My Hands (Remix) (same on both sides)	1990	8.00
❑ 21765	High (5 versions)	1990	6.00
❑ 21769	Our of My Hands (5 versions)	1990	6.00
❑ 40080	Throw You Down (4 version)/What He Has (2 versions)	1990	6.00

45s

Number	Title (A Side/B Side)	Yr	NM
ABC DUNHILL			
❑ 11 [DJ]	Everybody Gets to Go to the Moon (same on both sides)	1969	15.00
—Special Apollo 11 promotional item			
❑ 11 [PS]	Everybody Gets to Go to the Moon (same on both sides)	1969	20.00
—Special Apollo 11 promotional item			
❑ 4197	Sunshower/If This Was the Last Song	1969	10.00
❑ 4212	Jumpin' Jack Flash/This Is Your Life	1969	10.00
❑ 4222	Save the Country/I Just Can't Stay Away	1970	8.00
❑ 4260	The Good Earth/Ride, Louie, Ride	1970	8.00
CAPITOL			
❑ 5767	Baby Mine/Woman Behind Her Man	1966	200.00
❑ 5882	Don't Cry, My Soldier Boy/Let's Try to Make It	1967	50.00
MCA			
❑ 52196	Working Girl/Running in Circles	1983	3.00
❑ 52239	Make It Last/Just Like All the Rest	1983	3.00
❑ 52489	(I Guess) It Must Be Love/Running in Circles	1984	3.00
❑ 52491	Love Is a Dangerous Game/You Used to Hold Me So Tight	1984	3.00
❑ 52574	Keep It Light/My Lucille	1985	3.00
—B-side by B.B. King			
❑ 52582	What a Woman Feels Inside/Fantasy and Heartbreak	1985	3.00
MOTOWN			
❑ 1245	I'm Just a Part of Yesterday/Piano Man	1973	5.00
❑ 1260	Do You Know Where You're Going/Together	1973	5.00
❑ 1316	You've Been Doing Wrong for So Long/Pick Up the Week	1974	5.00
❑ 1385	The Bingo Long Song/Razzle Dazzle	1976	5.00
—B-side by William Goldstein			
❑ 1385 [PS]	The Bingo Long Song/Razzle Dazzle	1976	12.00
—B-side by William Goldstein			
MOWEST			
❑ 5008	I Want to Go Back There Again/Pick Up the Week	1972	6.00
❑ 5013	Me and Bobby McGee/No One's Gonna Be a Fool Forever	1972	6.00
❑ 5023	Piano Man/Me and Bobby McGee	1972	6.00
❑ 5027	What If/There Is a Fool	1972	6.00
❑ 5046	If It's the Last Thing I Do/And I Never Did	1973	—
—Unreleased			
❑ 5050	I'm Just a Part of Yesterday/Piano Man	1973	6.00
RCA			
❑ PB-11913	Suspicious Minds/Gone	1980	5.00
❑ PB-12215	If You Feel It/Hollywood	1981	4.00
❑ PB-12285	96 Tears/There's No Runnin' Away from Love	1981	4.00
TAMLA			
❑ 54275	One Out of Every Six (Censored)/Pick of the Week	1976	10.00
❑ 54278	Don't Leave Me This Way (Short Version)/Today Will Soon Be Yesterday	1977	4.00
❑ 54278 [DJ]	Don't Leave Me This Way (Long Version)/Don't Leave Me This Way (Short Version)	1977	6.00
❑ 54283	If It's the Last Thing I Do/If You Won't Let Me Walk on the Water	1977	4.00

Number	Title (A Side/B Side)	Yr	NM
❑ 54287	I'm Here Again/Sharin' Something Perfect	1977	4.00
❑ 54292	I Can't Go On Living Without Your Love/Any Way You Like It	1978	4.00
❑ 54295	I'm Not Strong Enough to Love You/Triplin'	1978	4.00
❑ 54297	Saturday Night, Sunday Morning/Come to Me	1979	20.00

Albums

ABC DUNHILL

Number	Title (A Side/B Side)	Yr	NM
❑ DS-50054	Sun Shower	1969	25.00

MCA

Number	Title (A Side/B Side)	Yr	NM
❑ 5395	Thelma Houston	1983	10.00
❑ 5527	Qualifying Heat	1984	10.00

MOTOWN

Number	Title (A Side/B Side)	Yr	NM
❑ M5-120V1	Superstar Series, Vol. 20	1981	10.00
❑ M5-127V1	Sunshower	1981	8.00
❑ M5-226V1	Any Way You Like It	1982	10.00

MOWEST

Number	Title (A Side/B Side)	Yr	NM
❑ MW-102	Thelma Houston	1972	20.00

RCA VICTOR

Number	Title (A Side/B Side)	Yr	NM
❑ AFL1-3500	Breakwater Cat	1980	10.00
❑ AFL1-3842	Never Gonna Be Another One	1981	10.00

REPRISE

Number	Title (A Side/B Side)	Yr	NM
❑ 26234	Throw You Down	1990	15.00

SHEFFIELD LABS

Number	Title (A Side/B Side)	Yr	NM
❑ 2	I've Got the Music In Me	1975	40.00

SHEFFIELD TREASURY

Number	Title (A Side/B Side)	Yr	NM
❑ ST-200	I've Got the Music In Me	1983	20.00

—Reissue of Sheffield Labs 2

TAMLA

Number	Title (A Side/B Side)	Yr	NM
❑ T6-345R1	Any Way You Like It	1976	12.00
❑ T7-358R1	The Devil in Me	1977	10.00
❑ T7-361R1	Ready to Roll	1978	10.00

HOUSTON, THELMA, AND JERRY BUTLER

Also see each artist's individual listings.

45s

MOTOWN

Number	Title (A Side/B Side)	Yr	NM
❑ 1422	It's a Lifetime Thing/Kiss Me Now	1977	5.00

Albums

MOTOWN

Number	Title (A Side/B Side)	Yr	NM
❑ M6-887	Thelma and Jerry	1977	10.00
❑ M7-903	Two to One	1978	10.00

HOUSTON, WHITNEY

12-Inch Singles

ARISTA

Number	Title (A Side/B Side)	Yr	NM
❑ AD-2120	I'm Your Baby Tonight (Extended Remix)/I'm Knocking/Feels So Good	1990	12.00
❑ ADP 2123 [DJ]	I'm Your Baby Tonight (4 versions)	1990	15.00
❑ ADP 2370 [DJ]	I Belong to You (U.K. Mix 8:55) (U.K. Dub 8:45)/(69th St. Mix 9:27) (69th St. Dub 4:16)	1991	12.00
❑ ADP 2530 [DJ]	I'm Every Woman (2 versions)	1993	10.00
❑ ADP 2650 [DJ]	Queen of the Night (5 versions)	1993	10.00
❑ ADP 3214 [DJ]	Why Does It Hurt So Bad (LP Version) (Live Version)/I Wanna Dance with Somebody (Who Loves Me) Remix 1996 (Junior's Happy Hand Bag Mix) (Junior's X Beat Dub)	1996	15.00
❑ ADP 3287 [DJ]	Somebody Bigger Than You and I (4 versions)	1996	10.00
❑ ADP 3299 [(2)DJ]	Step by Step (7 versions)	1997	25.00
❑ ADP 3337 [DJ]	Step by Step (Tony Moran Diva x Diva Mix) (Junior Tribal x Tribal Beats) (Junior Deep Dub)	1997	15.00
❑ ADP 3578 [DJ]	It's Not Right But It's Okay (Vocal) (Instrumental) (Acappella)	1999	10.00
❑ ADP 3600 [DJ]	It's Not Right But It's Okay — Thunderpuss 2000 Remixes (Dub) (Beats) (Club) (Radio)	1999	12.00
❑ ADP 3612 [DJ]	It's Not Right But It's Okay (Johnny Vicious Momentous Mix 13:03) (Johnny Vicious Dub 8:31) (Johnny Vicious Radio Mix 4:11)	1999	12.00
❑ ADP 3618 [DJ]	Heartbreak Hotel (Hex Hector Club Mix) (Hex Hector NYC Rough Mix) (Hex Hector Radio Mix)	1998	12.00
❑ ADP 3641 [DJ]	It's Not Right But It's Okay (Album Version) (Album Version Instrumental) (Album Version Acapella) (Smooth Mix) (Smooth Instrumental) (Smooth Acapella)	1999	15.00
❑ ADP 3688 [DJ]	It's Not Right But It's Okay (KCC's Release the Love Groove Mix Bootleg 7:05) (Club 69 Future Mix 8;02) (Club 69 Future Dub 7:49)	1999	10.00
❑ ARDP 3715 [(2)DJ]	My Love Is Your Love (Thunderpuss Club) (Thunderpuss Radio) (Jonathan Peters Vocal) (Thunderpuss Severe Dub) (Acapella) (Jonathan Peters Tight Mix) (Jonathan Peters Mixshow)	1999	15.00
❑ ARDP 3727 [DJ]	My Love Is Your Love (Wyclef Remix Featuring Dyme 4:22) (LP Version 4:18) (Salaam Remix 5:33) (Wyclef Remix Instrumental 4:23) (LP Version Instrumental 4:24) (Salaam Remix Instrumental 5:36)	1999	10.00
❑ ARDP 3793 [(2)DJ]	I Learned from the Best (6 versions)	1999	20.00
❑ ARDP 3796 [DJ]	Learned from the Best — HQ2 Mixes (Vocal 10:25) (Dub 8:25)	1999	10.00
❑ ARDP 3845 [DJ]	Fine (3 versions)	2000	10.00
❑ ARDP 3872 [(2)DJ]	Same Script, Different Cast (Joe Smooth Slang Club Mix 5:49) (Jonathan Peters Vocal Club Mix 9:35) (Jonathan Peters Goes There Dub 11:07) (Victor Romeo Slang Vocal Mix 6:19)	2000	15.00
❑ ARDP 3873 [DJ]	Same Script, Different Cast (Friburn & Urik Uncover Your Ears Mix 10:49) (Mel Hammond Beautiful Slang Dub 6:41) (Jonathan Peters Radio Edit 4:21)	2000	12.00
❑ AD1-9413	Thinking About You (Extended Dance Mix 7:19) (Dub Version 8:04) (Single Version 4:03)	1985	15.00
❑ AD1-9449	How Will I Know (Dance Remix) (Instrumental) (LP Version)	1985	8.00
❑ AD1-9599	I Wanna Dance with Somebody (Who Loves Me) (12" Remix) (Single Version)/(12" Remix Radio Edit) (Dub Mix) (Acappella Mix)	1987	8.00
❑ AD1-9632	Didn't We Almost Have It All/For the Love of You (2 versions)/Shock Me	1987	8.00
❑ AD1-9641	So Emotional (6 versions)	1987	10.00
❑ AD1-9721	Love Will Save the Day (Extended Version) (Acappella Version) (Single Version)/Dub Will Save the Day	1988	8.00
❑ 12260	My Name Is Not Susan (Extended Mix 5:56) (Dub Mix 4:28) (Extended U.K. Mix 6:16) (Alternate U.K. Mix 7:40)	1991	10.00
❑ 12520 [(2)]	I'm Every Woman (Every Woman's House Club Mix) (Every Woman's Beat)/(Clivilles & Cole House Mix I)/(Clivilles & Cole House Mix II)/(The C&C Dub) (A Cappella Mix)	1992	15.00
❑ 12916	Exhale (Shoop Shoop)/Dancing on the Smooth Edge/Moment of Truth/Do You Hear What I Hear/It Isn't, It Wasn't, It Ain't Never Gonna Be	1995	8.00

—Last track with Aretha Franklin

Number	Title (A Side/B Side)	Yr	NM
❑ 12977	Count on Me/One Moment in Time/Jesus Loves Me/I Know Him So Well/Hold Up the Light	1996	12.00

—First track with CeCe Winans; last track by BeBe and CeCe Winans

Number	Title (A Side/B Side)	Yr	NM
❑ 13214	Why Does It Hurt So Bad (LP Version) (Live Version)/I Wanna Dance with Somebody (Who Loves Me) Remix 1996 (Junior's Happy Hand Bag Mix) (Junior's X Beat Dub)	1996	10.00
❑ 13313 [(2)]	Step by Step (8 versions)	1997	15.00
❑ 13613 [(3)]	Heartbreak Hotel (3 versions)/It's Not Right But It's Okay (5 versions)	1998	15.00
❑ 13680	It's Not Right But It's Okay (3 versions)	1999	8.00
❑ 13823 [(2)]	I Learned from the Best (HQ2 Club Mix)/(Junior Vasquez USA Millennium Mix)//(HQ2 Dub)/(Junior Vasquez Disco Club Mix)	1999	10.00
❑ 13860	Same Script, Different Cast (unknown versions)	2000	10.00

45s

ARISTA

Number	Title (A Side/B Side)	Yr	NM
❑ 2108	I'm Your Baby Tonight/I'm Knockin'	1990	3.00
❑ 2156	All the Man That I Need/Dancin' on the Smooth Edge	1990	3.00
❑ 2207	The Star Spangled Banner/America the Beautiful	1991	3.00
❑ 2222	Miracle/After We Make Love	1991	3.00
❑ 9274	You Give Good Love/Greatest Love of All	1985	3.00
❑ 9274 [PS]	You Give Good Love/Greatest Love of All	1985	3.00
❑ 9381	Saving All My Love for You/All at Once	1985	3.00
❑ 9381 [PS]	Saving All My Love for You/All at Once	1985	3.00
❑ 9412	Thinking About You/Someone for Me	1985	4.00
❑ 9412 [PS]	Thinking About You/Someone for Me	1985	4.00
❑ 9434	How Will I Know/Someone for Me	1985	3.00
❑ 9434 [PS]	How Will I Know/Someone for Me	1985	3.00
❑ 9466	Greatest Love of All/Thinking About You	1986	3.00
❑ 9466 [PS]	Greatest Love of All/Thinking About You	1986	3.00
❑ 9598	I Wanna Dance with Somebody (Who Loves Me)/Moment of Truth	1987	3.00
❑ 9598 [PS]	I Wanna Dance with Somebody (Who Loves Me)/Moment of Truth	1987	3.00
❑ 9616	Didn't We Almost Have It All/Shock Me	1987	3.00
❑ 9616 [PS]	Didn't We Almost Have It All/Shock Me	1987	3.00
❑ 9642	So Emotional/For the Love of You	1987	3.00
❑ 9642 [PS]	So Emotional/For the Love of You	1987	3.00
❑ 9674	Where Do Broken Hearts Go/Where Are You	1988	3.00
❑ 9674 [PS]	Where Do Broken Hearts Go/Where Are You	1988	3.00
❑ 9690	Just the Lonely Talking Again/If You Say My Eyes Are Beautiful	1988	5.00

—B-side with Jermaine Jackson

Number	Title (A Side/B Side)	Yr	NM
❑ 9720	Love Will Save the Day/How Will I Know	1988	3.00
❑ 9720 [PS]	Love Will Save the Day/How Will I Know	1988	3.00
❑ 9743	One Moment in Time/Love Is a Contact Sport	1988	3.00
❑ 9743 [PS]	One Moment in Time/Love Is a Contact Sport	1988	3.00
❑ 12259	My Name Is Not Susan/(U.K. Mix)	1991	3.00
❑ 12369	I Belong to You/(International Mix)	1991	3.00
❑ 12490	I Will Always Love You/Jesus Loves Me	1992	3.00
❑ 12519	I'm Every Woman/Who Do You Love	1993	3.00
❑ 12527	I Have Nothing/Where Are You	1993	3.00
❑ 12570	Run to You/After We Make Love	1993	3.00
❑ 12885	Exhale (Shoop Shoop)/Dancin' on the Smooth Edge	1995	3.00
❑ 12976	Count on Me/One Moment in Time	1996	3.00

—A-side: Whitney Houston & Cece Winans

Number	Title (A Side/B Side)	Yr	NM
❑ 13213	Why Does It Hurt So Bad/(Live Version)	1996	3.00
❑ 13293	I Believe in You and Me/Step By Step	1996	3.00
❑ 13312	Step by Step/(Teddy Riley Remix)	1997	3.00
❑ 50971	Try It on My Own/(Thunderpuss Mix)	2003	4.00
❑ 50978	One of Those Days/My Love	2003	4.00

—B-side featuring Bobby Brown

Albums

ARISTA

Number	Title (A Side/B Side)	Yr	NM
❑ AL 8212	Whitney Houston	1985	8.00
❑ AL 8405	Whitney	1987	8.00
❑ 14652 [(4)]	The Unreleased Mixes	2000	20.00

—Box set of 12-inch single remixes

Number	Title (A Side/B Side)	Yr	NM
❑ AL 18616	I'm Your Baby Tonight	1990	10.00
❑ 19037 [(2)]	My Love Is Your Love	1998	12.00

Except when noted otherwise, VG = 25% of NM, and VG+ = 50% of NM. (Example: VG = $2.00, VG+ = $4.00 and NM = $8.00.)

HOUSTON FEARLESS

45s

IMPERIAL

Number	Title (A Side/B Side)	Yr	NM
❑ 66354	Race with the Devil/Someone Else's Blues	1969	—

—Canceled

Albums

IMPERIAL

Number	Title (A Side/B Side)	Yr	NM
❑ LP-12421	Houston Fearless	1969	20.00

HOUSTONS, THE

45s

HIT

Number	Title (A Side/B Side)	Yr	NM
❑ 133	Where Did Our Love Go/Steal Away	1964	8.00

—B-side by Leroy Jones

HOWARD, EDDY

45s

MERCURY

Number	Title (A Side/B Side)	Yr	NM
❑ 5433	American Beauty Rose/Seems Like Only Yesterday	1950	15.00
—Note: Earlier Eddy Howard releases on Mercury may exist on 45.			
❑ 5439	Put Your Arms Around Me Honey/Lassus Trombone	1950	15.00
❑ 5453	My Heart Isn't In It/I Do Better in the Mountains	1950	15.00
❑ 5475	Daddy's Little Boy/They Put the Lights Out	1950	15.00
❑ 5490	I'm Forever Blowing Bubbles/Red We Want	1950	15.00
❑ 5491	Patricia/So Long, Sally	1950	15.00
❑ 5516	I'll Be Home for Christmas/Dearest Santa	1950	15.00
❑ 5517	To Think You've Chosen Me/The One Rose	1950	15.00
❑ 5567	A Penny a Kiss — A Penny a Hug/I Still Feel the Same About You	1951	15.00
❑ 5576	When You Return/Little Small Town Girl	1951	15.00
❑ 5578	Daddy's Little Girl/Daddy's Little Boy	1951	15.00
❑ 5590	Around the World/That's All That's Left	1951	15.00
❑ 5623	One Kind Word/How Thoughtful of You	1951	15.00
❑ 5630	What Will I Tell My Heart/The Strange Little Girl	1951	15.00
❑ 5663	(A Woman Is a) Deadly Weapon/I'm in Love Again	1951	15.00
❑ 5678	Hello Young Lovers/We Kiss in a Shadow	1951	15.00
❑ 5697	I'm Cryin'/Put All Your Kisses in an Envelope	1951	15.00
❑ 5711	Sin/My Wife and I	1951	15.00
—Revised A-side title			
❑ 5711	It's No Sin/My Wife and I	1951	20.00
❑ 5722	Uncle Mistletoe/When Christmas Rolls Around	1951	15.00
❑ 5748	It's All Over But the Memories/Chances Are	1951	15.00
❑ 5752	There's a Christmas Tree/Auld Lang Syne	1951	15.00
❑ 5771	Stolen Love/I'll See You in My Dreams	1952	15.00
❑ 5791	My Adobe Hacienda/Wishin'	1952	15.00
❑ 5815	Be Anything (But Be Mine)/She Took	1952	15.00
❑ 5832	Singing in the Rain/All I Do Is Dream of You	1952	15.00
❑ 5837	The Family That Prays Together/(B-side unknown)	1952	15.00
❑ 5871	Auf Wiederseh'n Sweetheart/I Don't Want to Take a Chance	1952	15.00
❑ 5898	Mademoiselle/I Don't Know Any Better	1952	15.00
❑ 70015	It's Worth Any Price You Pay/Kentucky Babe	1952	12.00
❑ 70071	Your Mother and Mine/You've Got Me Crying	1953	12.00
❑ 70107	Gomen Nasai (Forgive Me)/Someone to Kiss Your Tears Away	1953	12.00
❑ 70134	Say You're Mine Again/Broken Wings	1953	12.00
❑ 70135	Am I Loving You/Almost Always	1953	12.00
❑ 70176	Love Every Moment That You Live/The Right Way	1953	12.00
❑ 70225	That's the Price I Paid for You/Skirts	1953	12.00
❑ 70272	Ebenezer Scrooge/Bimbo	1953	15.00
❑ 70293	Little Miss One/Till We Two Are One	1954	12.00
❑ 70301	Bimbo/Call Me Darling	1954	12.00
❑ 70304	Melancholy Me/I Wonder What's Become of Sally	1954	12.00
❑ 70388	Vieni Su/Don't Worry Baby	1954	12.00
❑ 70467	Love Me Tonight/You're Always Welcome Home	1954	12.00
❑ 70475	Happy Birthday/Anniversary Waltz	1954	15.00
❑ 70513	All of You/I'll Wrap You in My Arms	1954	12.00
❑ 70533	Old Memories/Finger of Suspicion	1955	12.00
❑ 70566	Words of Love/Forevermore	1955	12.00
❑ 70639	The Man from Laramie/The Three of Us	1955	12.00
❑ 70700	The Teen-Agers' Waltz/Choo Choo Cha Cha	1955	12.00
❑ 70763	Round, Round the Christmas Tree/Silver Bells	1955	12.00
❑ 70800	Why Is Your Dog Following Me/Rustic Old Cathedral	1956	10.00
❑ 70881	Whatever Will Be, Will Be/You Can't Keep Running	1956	10.00
❑ 70946	Never, Never, Never/Thank You Lord	1956	10.00
❑ 70989	Confidential/Tiger Lily	1956	10.00
❑ 71002	Uncle Mistletoe/Silver Bells	1956	12.00
❑ 71008	Driftwood/The Hour of Love	1956	10.00
❑ 71072	Delia's Gone/Love Me a Little Bit	1957	10.00
❑ 71300	Just Foolin'/My Last Goodbye	1958	10.00
❑ 71773	I Want You to Want Me to Want You/Just a Year Ago Tonight	1961	10.00

7-Inch Extended Plays

MERCURY

Number	Title (A Side/B Side)	Yr	NM
❑ EP 1-3213	I Wonder What's Become of Sally/Little Miss One//Call Me Darling/Yellow Roses	195?	15.00
❑ EP 1-3213 [PS]	Yellow Roses	195?	15.00

Albums

CIRCLE

Number	Title (A Side/B Side)	Yr	NM
❑ 29	Eddy Howard 1949-1952	198?	10.00
❑ 79	Eddy Howard 1949-1953	1985	10.00

COLUMBIA

Number	Title (A Side/B Side)	Yr	NM
❑ CL 6067 [10]	Eddy Howard	1949	60.00

HINDSIGHT

Number	Title (A Side/B Side)	Yr	NM
❑ HSR-119	Eddy Howard 1946-1951	198?	10.00
❑ HSR-156	Eddy Howard 1945-1948	198?	10.00
❑ HSR-405 [(2)]	Eddy Howard and His Orchestra Play 22 Original Big Band Favorites	198?	12.00

INSIGHT

Number	Title (A Side/B Side)	Yr	NM
❑ 205	Eddy Howard and His Orchestra 1945-1951	198?	10.00

MERCURY

Number	Title (A Side/B Side)	Yr	NM
❑ MG-20112 [M]	Singing in the Rain	195?	25.00
❑ MG-20312 [M]	Paradise Isle	195?	25.00
❑ MG-20432 [M]	Great for Dancing	1958	20.00
❑ MG-20562 [M]	Eddy Howard's Golden Hits	1961	15.00
❑ MG-20593 [M]	More Eddy Howard's Golden Hits	1962	15.00
❑ MG-20665 [M]	Eddy Howard Sings and Plays the Great Old Waltzes	1962	15.00
❑ MG-20817 [M]	Eddy Howard Sings and Plays the Great Band Hits	196?	15.00
❑ MG-20910 [M]	Intimately Yours	1965	15.00
❑ MG-21014 [M]	Softly and Sincerely	196?	15.00
❑ MG-25011 [10]	Selected Song Favorites	1949	50.00
—Title appears only on label; cover simply states "Eddy Howard and His Orchestra"			
❑ SR-60104 [S]	Great for Dancing	1959	25.00
❑ SR-60562 [S]	Eddy Howard's Golden Hits	1961	20.00
❑ SR-60593 [S]	More Eddy Howard's Golden Hits	1962	20.00
❑ SR-60665 [S]	Eddy Howard Sings and Plays the Great Old Waltzes	1962	20.00
❑ SR-60817 [S]	Eddy Howard Sings and Plays the Great Band Hits	196?	20.00
❑ SR-60910 [S]	Intimately Yours	1965	20.00
❑ SR-61014 [S]	Softly and Sincerely	196?	20.00

WING

Number	Title (A Side/B Side)	Yr	NM
❑ MGW-12104 [M]	Saturday Night Dance Date	196?	12.00
❑ MGW-12171 [M]	Eddy Howard Sings Words of Love	196?	12.00
❑ MGW-12171 [M]	Words of Love	196?	12.00
❑ MGW-12194 [M]	Sleepy Serenade	196?	12.00
❑ MGW-12249 [M]	The Velvet Voice	196?	12.00
❑ SRW-16104 [S]	Saturday Night Dance Date	196?	12.00
❑ SRW-16171 [S]	Eddy Howard Sings Words of Love	196?	12.00
❑ SRW-16171 [S]	Words of Love	196?	12.00
❑ SRW-16194 [S]	Sleepy Serenade	196?	12.00
❑ SRW-16249 [S]	The Velvet Voice	196?	12.00

HOWARD, RONNIE

45s

BIG TOP

Number	Title (A Side/B Side)	Yr	NM
❑ 3093	If Santa Fell/Give My Toy to the Boy Next Door	1961	15.00

HOWE, STEVE

Also see ANDERSON BRUFORD WAKEMAN HOWE; YES; ASIA; GTR. Also see YES.

Albums

ATLANTIC

Number	Title (A Side/B Side)	Yr	NM
❑ SD 18154	Beginnings	1975	12.00
❑ SD 19243	The Steve Howe Album	1980	12.00

HOWELL, BILL

45s

PALLADIUM

Number	Title (A Side/B Side)	Yr	NM
❑ 513	Rocket Rollin' Blues/Bayou City Blues	195?	50.00

HOWELL, REUBEN

45s

MOTOWN

Number	Title (A Side/B Side)	Yr	NM
❑ 1274	When You Take Another Chance on Love/You Can't Stop a Man in Love	1973	20.00
❑ 1274 [PS]	When You Take Another Chance on Love/You Can't Stop a Man in Love	1973	30.00
❑ 1305	Rings/I'll Be Your Brother	1974	10.00
❑ 1325	Constant Disappointment/I Believe	1974	10.00

Albums

MOTOWN

Number	Title (A Side/B Side)	Yr	NM
❑ M 771L	Reuben Howell	1973	20.00
❑ M6-799S1	Rings	1974	15.00

HOWL THE GOOD

45s

RARE EARTH

Number	Title (A Side/B Side)	Yr	NM
❑ 5045	Long Way from Home/Why Do You Cry	1972	8.00

Albums

RARE EARTH

Number	Title (A Side/B Side)	Yr	NM
❑ RS-537	Howl the Good	1972	25.00

HOWLIN' WOLF

45s

CADET CONCEPT

Number	Title (A Side/B Side)	Yr	NM
❑ 7013	Evil/Tail Dragger	1969	8.00

CHESS

Number	Title (A Side/B Side)	Yr	NM
❑ 1528	Oh! Red/My Last Affair	1952	700.00
—Note: Howlin' Wolf releases on Chess before 1528 are unknown on 45 rpm			
❑ 1557	All Night Boogie/I Love My Baby	1953	300.00
❑ 1566	No Place to Go/Rockin' Daddy	1954	100.00
❑ 1575	How Long/Evil Is Going On	1954	100.00
❑ 1584	I'll Be Around/Forty Four	1955	50.00
❑ 1593	Who Will Be Next/I Have a Little Girl	1955	40.00
❑ 1607	Come to Me Baby/Don't Mess with My Baby	1955	40.00
❑ 1618	Smoke Stack Lightning/You Can't Be Beat	1956	40.00
❑ 1632	I Asked for Water/So Glad	1956	40.00
❑ 1648	Goin' Back Home/My Life	1957	40.00
❑ 1668	Somebody in My Home/Nature	1957	40.00
❑ 1679	Sittin' On Top of the World/Poor Boy	1958	40.00
❑ 1695	Moaning for My Baby/I Didn't Know	1958	40.00
❑ 1712	I'm Leaving You/Change My Way	1959	40.00
❑ 1726	Howlin' Blues/I Better Go Now	1959	40.00
❑ 1735	Mr. Airplane Man/I've Been Abused	1959	40.00
❑ 1744	The Natchez Burning/You Gonna Wreck My Life	1959	40.00
❑ 1762	Spoonful/Howlin' for My Baby	1960	30.00
❑ 1777	Wang Dang Doodle/Back Door Man	1961	30.00
❑ 1793	Little Baby/Down in the Bottom	1961	30.00
❑ 1804	The Red Rooster/Shake for Me	1961	25.00
❑ 1813	You'll Be Mine/Goin' Down Slow	1962	25.00
❑ 1823	Just Like I Treat You/I Ain't Superstitious	1962	25.00
❑ 1844	Do the Do/Mama's Baby	1962	25.00
❑ 1870	300 Pounds of Joy/Built for Comfort	1963	20.00
❑ 1890	Tail Dragger/Hidden Charms	1964	20.00
❑ 1911	Love Me Darlin'/My Country Sugar Mama	1964	20.00
❑ 1923	Killin' Floor/Louise	1965	20.00
❑ 1928	Tell Me What I've Done/Ooh Baby	1965	15.00
❑ 1945	I Walked from Dallas/Don't Laugh at Me	1965	15.00
❑ 1968	New Crawlin' King Snake/Wild Ramblin'	1966	15.00
❑ 2009	I Had a Dream/Pop It to Me	1967	15.00
❑ 2081	Mary Sue/Hard Luck	1970	8.00
❑ 2108	I Smell a Rat/Just As Long	1971	8.00

H

Number	Title (A Side/B Side)	Yr	NM
❑ 2118	Do the Do/Red Rooster	1971	8.00
❑ 2145	Back Door Wolf/ Coon on the Moon	1973	8.00
RPM			
❑ 340	Passing By Blues/ Crying at Daybreak	1952	3000.
—Note: Howlin' Wolf releases on RPM before 340 are unknown on 45 rpm. VG 1000; VG+ 2000			
❑ 347	My Baby Stole Off/ I Want Your Picture	1952	2400.
—VG 800; VG+ 1600			
7-Inch Extended Plays			
CHESS			
❑ 7-LPS-1469	Tell Me/Who's Been Talkin'/ Spoonfull//Shake for Me/ Goin' Down Slow/Down in the Bottom	1963	100.00
—Stereo jukebox issue; small hole, plays at 33 1/3 rpm; we don't know if these tracks are true stereo or rechanneled stereo			
❑ 7-LPS-1469 [PS]	Howlin' Wolf	1963	200.00
Albums			
CADET			
❑ LPS-319	This Is Howlin' Wolf's New Album	1969	25.00
CHESS			
❑ 201 [(2)]	Howlin' Wolf	1976	15.00
❑ LP-1434 [M]	Moanin' in the Moonlight	1958	600.00
❑ LP-1469 [M]	Howlin' Wolf	1962	600.00
❑ LP-1502 [M]	The Real Folk Blues	1966	50.00
❑ LP-1512 [M]	More Real Folk Blues	1966	50.00
❑ LP-1540	Evil	1969	25.00
❑ CH-9107	His Greatest Sides, Vol. 1	1985	10.00
❑ CH-9182	Chicago — 26 Golden Years	1985	10.00
❑ CH-9195	Moanin' in the Moonlight	1986	8.00
—Reissue of 1434			
❑ CH-9273	The Real Folk Blues	1988	10.00
—Reissue of 1502			
❑ CH-9279	More Real Folk Blues	1988	10.00
—Reissue of 1512			
❑ CH-9297	The London Howlin' Wolf Sessions	1989	10.00
—Reissue of 60008			
❑ CH5-9332 [(5)]	The Chess Box	1991	40.00
❑ CH-50002	Message to the Young	1971	20.00
❑ CH-50015	Live and Cookin'	1972	20.00
❑ CH-50045	Back Door Wolf	1974	20.00
❑ CH-60008	The London Howlin' Wolf Sessions	1971	20.00
❑ CH-60016 [(2)]	Howlin' Wolk, AKA Chester Burnett	1972	25.00
❑ CH-93001	Change My Way	198?	10.00
CROWN			
❑ CLP-5240 [M]	Howlin' Wolf Sings the Blues	1962	25.00
CUSTOM			
❑ CM-2055 [M]	Big City Blues	196?	40.00
❑ CS-2055 [R]	Big City Blues	196?	20.00
KENT			
❑ KLP-526 [M]	Original Folk Blues	1967	15.00
❑ KST-526 [R]	Original Folk Blues	1967	12.00
❑ KST-527	Howlin' Wolf's 20 Greatest R&B Hits	1968	12.00
❑ KST-535	Underground Blues	1968	12.00
ROUNDER			
❑ SS-28	Cadillac Daddy: Memphis Recordings, 1952	1989	12.00

HUBBARD, FREDDIE

Number	Title (A Side/B Side)	Yr	NM
12-Inch Singles			
FANTASY			
❑ F 204	Splash (5:05)/You're Gonna Lose Me (5:28)	1981	8.00
45s			
ATLANTIC			
❑ 2677	Wichita Lineman/Lonely Soul	1969	8.00
BLUE NOTE			
❑ 1779	One Mint Julep/Gypsy Blues	196?	10.00
❑ 1809	Changing Scene/I Wish I Knew	196?	10.00
❑ 1810	Cry Me Not/Osie Mae	196?	10.00
❑ 1908	Blue Frenzy/Mirrors	196?	10.00
COLUMBIA			
❑ 10060	Baraka Sasa/Crisis	1974	5.00
❑ 10434	Neo Terra (New Land)/ Rock Me Arms	1976	5.00
CTI			
❑ 6	Red Clay (Part 1)/ Red Clay (Part 2)	1970	6.00
❑ 514	Here's That Rainy Day (Part 1)/ Here's That Rainy Day (Part 2)	197?	6.00
❑ 519	Red Clay (Part 1) /Red Clay (Part 2)	197?	6.00
Albums			
ABC IMPULSE!			
❑ AS-27 [S]	The Artistry of Freddie Hubbard	1968	12.00
❑ AS-38 [S]	The Body and Soul of Freddie Hubbard	1968	12.00
❑ AS-9237 [(2)]	Re-Evaluation: The Impulse Years	1973	15.00
ATLANTIC			
❑ SD 2-314 [(2)]	The Art of Freddie Hubbard	1974	15.00
❑ 1477 [M]	Backlash	1967	25.00
❑ SD 1477 [S]	Backlash	1967	15.00
❑ SD 1501	High Pressure Blues	1969	15.00
❑ SD 1526	Soul Experiment	1970	12.00
❑ SD 1549	Black Angel	1971	12.00
❑ 80108	Sweet Return	1983	10.00
❑ 90466	Backlash	1986	8.00
—Reissue of SD 1477			
BASF			
❑ 10726	The Hub of Hubbard	1972	12.00
BLUE NOTE			
❑ BN-LA356-H [(2)]	Freddie Hubbard	1975	15.00
❑ BLP-4040 [M]	Open Sesame	1960	80.00
—Regular version with W. 63rd St. address on label			
❑ BLP-4040 [M]	Open Sesame	1960	120.00
—"Deep groove" version (deep indentation under label on both sides)			
❑ BLP-4040 [M]	Open Sesame	1963	20.00
—With New York, USA address on label			
❑ BLP-4056 [M]	Goin' Up	1960	80.00
—With W. 63rd St. address on label			
❑ BLP-4056 [M]	Goin' Up	1963	20.00
—With New York, USA address on label			
❑ BLP-4073 [M]	Hub Cap	1961	80.00
—With W. 63rd St. address on label			
❑ BLP-4073 [M]	Hub Cap	1963	20.00
—With New York, USA address on label			
❑ BLP-4085 [M]	Ready for Freddie	1961	80.00
—With 61st St. address on label			
❑ BLP-4085 [M]	Ready for Freddie	1963	20.00
—With New York, USA address on label			
❑ BLP-4115 [M]	Hub Tones	1962	25.00
❑ 4135/84135	Here to Stay	1963	—
—Scheduled, but unreleased until 1985			
❑ BLP-4172 [M]	Breaking Point	1964	25.00
❑ BLP-4196 [M]	Blue Spirits	1965	25.00
❑ BLP-4207 [M]	The Night of the Cookers — Live at Club Le Marchal, Vol. 1	1965	25.00
❑ BLP-4208 [M]	The Night of the Cookers — Live at Club Le Marchal, Vol. 2	1965	25.00
❑ B1-32094	Ready for Freddie	1995	12.00
—"The Finest in Jazz Since 1939" reissue			
❑ BJT-48017	The Eternal Triangle	1988	12.00
❑ BST-84040	Open Sesame	1989	10.00
—"The Finest in Jazz Since 1939" reissue			
❑ BST-84040 [S]	Open Sesame	1960	60.00
—With W. 63rd St. addresss on label			
❑ BST-84040 [S]	Open Sesame	1963	25.00
—With New York, USA address on label			
❑ BST-84040 [S]	Open Sesame	1967	15.00
—With "A Division of Liberty Records" on label			
❑ BST-84040 [S]	Open Sesame	199?	25.00
—Classic Records reissue on audiophile vinyl			
❑ BST-84056 [S]	Goin' Up	1960	60.00
—With W. 63rd St. addresss on label			
❑ BST-84056 [S]	Goin' Up	1963	25.00
—With New York, USA address on label			
❑ BST-84056 [S]	Goin' Up	1967	15.00
—With "A Division of Liberty Records" on label			
❑ BST-84073	Hub Cap	198?	10.00
—"The Finest in Jazz Since 1939" reissue			
❑ BST-84073 [S]	Hub Cap	1961	60.00
—With W. 63rd St. addresss on label			
❑ BST-84073 [S]	Hub Cap	1963	25.00
—With New York, USA address on label			
❑ BST-84073 [S]	Hub Cap	1967	15.00
—With "A Division of Liberty Records" on label			
❑ BST-84085 [S]	Ready for Freddie	1961	60.00
—With 61st St. address on label			
❑ BST-84085 [S]	Ready for Freddie	1963	25.00
—With New York, USA address on label			
❑ BST-84085 [S]	Ready for Freddie	1967	15.00
—With "A Division of Liberty Records" on label			
❑ BST-84115	Hub-Tones	1985	10.00
—"The Finest in Jazz Since 1939" reissue			
❑ BST-84115 [S]	Hub-Tones	1962	30.00
—With New York, USA address on label			
❑ BST-84115 [S]	Hub-Tones	1967	15.00
—With "A Division of Liberty Records" on label			
❑ BST-84135	Here to Stay	1985	12.00
❑ BST-84172 [S]	Breaking Point	1964	30.00
—With New York, USA address on label			
❑ BST-84172 [S]	Breaking Point	1967	15.00
—With "A Division of Liberty Records" on label			
❑ BST-84196	Blue Spirits	1987	10.00
—"The Finest in Jazz Since 1939" reissue			
❑ BST-84196 [S]	Blue Spirits	1965	30.00
—With New York, USA address on label			
❑ BST-84196 [S]	Blue Spirits	1967	15.00
—With "A Division of Liberty Records" on label			
❑ BST-84207 [S]	The Night of the Cookers — Live at Club Le Marchal, Vol. 1	1965	30.00
—With New York, USA address on label			
❑ BST-84207 [S]	The Night of the Cookers — Live at Club Le Marchal, Vol. 1	1967	15.00
—With "A Division of Liberty Records" on label			
❑ BST-84208 [S]	The Night of the Cookers — Live at Club Le Marchal, Vol. 2	1965	30.00
—With New York, USA address on label			
❑ BST-84208 [S]	The Night of the Cookers — Live at Club Le Marchal, Vol. 2	1967	15.00
—With "A Division of Liberty Records" on label			
❑ B1-85121	Doubletake	1987	10.00
❑ B1-85139	Life-Flight	1987	10.00
❑ B1-90905	Times 'R Changin'	1989	12.00
❑ B1-93202	The Best of Freddie Hubbard	1989	12.00
COLUMBIA			
❑ KC 33048	High Energy	1974	10.00
❑ PC 33556	Liquid Love	1975	10.00
❑ PC 34166	Windjammer	1976	10.00
❑ PC 34902	Bundle of Joy	1977	10.00
❑ JC 35386	Super Blue	1978	10.00
❑ JC 36015	Love Connection	1979	10.00
❑ JC 36358	The Best of Freddie Hubbard	1979	10.00
❑ FC 36418	Skagly	1980	10.00
CTI			
❑ CTS-6001	Red Clay	1970	12.00
❑ CTS-6007	The Straight Life	1971	12.00
❑ CTS-6013	First Light	1972	12.00
❑ CTS-6018	Sky Dive	1973	10.00
❑ CTS-6036	Keep Your Soul Together	1974	10.00
❑ CTS-6044	Freddie Hubbard In Concert	1974	10.00
❑ CTS-6047	The Baddest Hubbard	1974	10.00
❑ CTS-6056	Polar AC	1975	10.00
❑ 8016	Red Clay	198?	8.00
—Reissue of 6001			
❑ 8017	First Light	198?	8.00
—Reissue of 6013			
❑ 8022	The Straight Life	198?	8.00
—Reissue of 6007			
CTI/CBS ASSOCIATED			
❑ FZ 40687	First Light	1987	10.00
ELEKTRA/MUSICIAN			
❑ 60029	Ride Like the Wind	1982	10.00
ENJA			
❑ 3095	Outpost	1981	10.00
FANTASY			
❑ 9610	Splash	1981	10.00
❑ 9615	Keystone Bop	1982	10.00
❑ 9626	A Little Night Music	1983	10.00
❑ 9635	Classics	1984	10.00
IMPULSE!			
❑ A-27 [M]	The Artistry of Freddie Hubbard	1962	25.00
❑ AS-27 [S]	The Artistry of Freddie Hubbard	1962	30.00
❑ A-38 [M]	The Body and Soul of Freddie Hubbard	1963	25.00
❑ AS-38 [S]	The Body and Soul of Freddie Hubbard	1963	30.00
LIBERTY			
❑ LT-1110	Mistral	1981	10.00
PABLO			
❑ 2310884	The Best of Freddie Hubbard	1983	10.00
❑ 2312134	Born to Be Blue	1982	10.00
PABLO LIVE			
❑ 2620113 [(2)]	Live at the Northsea Jazz Festival, The Hague, 1980	1983	12.00
PABLO TODAY			
❑ 2312134	Born to Be Blue	198?	10.00
PAUSA			
❑ 7122	Rollin'	1982	10.00
PHOENIX 10			
❑ PHX 318	Extended	1981	8.00
PICCADILLY			
❑ 3467	Intrepid Fox	198?	10.00
QUINTESSENCE			
❑ 25161	Skylark	1978	10.00
REAL TIME			
❑ 305	Back to Birdland	198?	10.00

HUBBARD, FREDDIE, AND OSCAR PETERSON

Number	Title (A Side/B Side)	Yr	NM
Albums			
PABLO			
❑ 2310876	Face to Face	198?	10.00

HUBBARD, FREDDIE, AND STANLEY TURRENTINE

Number	Title (A Side/B Side)	Yr	NM
Albums			
CTI			
❑ CTS-6044	In Concert, Vol. 1	1974	10.00
❑ CTS-6049	In Concert, Vol. 2	1975	10.00

Number	Title (A Side/B Side)	Yr	NM

HUBCAPS, THE
ERNIE MARESCA is in this group.

45s

Number	Title (A Side/B Side)	Yr	NM
LAURIE			
❑ 3219	Hot Rod City (Vocal)/ Hot Rod City (Instrumental)	1964	15.00

HUDDLE, JACK

45s

Number	Title (A Side/B Side)	Yr	NM
KAPP			
❑ 207	Starlight/Believe Me	1959	200.00
—Buddy Holly plays guitar on these tracks			
PETSY			
❑ 1002	Starlight/Believe Me	1958	500.00

HUDSON, POOKIE
Lead singer with THE SPANIELS.

45s

Number	Title (A Side/B Side)	Yr	NM
DOUBLE L			
❑ 711	Jealous Heart/I Know, I Know	1963	20.00
❑ 720	I Love You For Sentimental Reasons/Miracles	1963	20.00
JAMIE			
❑ 1319	This Gets To Me/ All the Places I've Been	1966	60.00
PARKWAY			
❑ 839	John Brown/Turn Out the Lights	1962	20.00

HUDSON, ROCK

45s

Number	Title (A Side/B Side)	Yr	NM
DECCA			
❑ 30966	Pillow Talk/Roly Poly	1959	15.00
❑ 30966 [PS]	Pillow Talk/Roly Poly	1959	25.00

Albums

Number	Title (A Side/B Side)	Yr	NM
STANYAN			
❑ SR-10014	Rock Gently	1971	25.00

HUDSON AND LANDRY

45s

Number	Title (A Side/B Side)	Yr	NM
DORE			
❑ 852	The Hippie and the Redneck/ Top 40 DJ's	1971	10.00
❑ 855	Ajax Liquor Store/The Hippie and the Redneck	1971	10.00
❑ 868	Ajax Airlines/Bruiser La Rue	1972	10.00
❑ 874	Obscene Phone Bust/ The Prospectors	1972	10.00
❑ 879	Soul Bowl/Friar Shuck	1972	10.00
❑ 880	Frontier Christmas (Harlowe and The Mrs.)/The Soul Bowl	1972	10.00
❑ 881	Ajax Mortuary/Ajax Pet Store	1973	10.00
❑ 891	The Chocolate Freak/The Fate of the Mightiest Nation	1973	10.00
❑ 895	The Gas Man/Sir Basil	1974	10.00
❑ 898	The Weird Kingdom/Montague for President	1974	10.00

Albums

Number	Title (A Side/B Side)	Yr	NM
DORE			
❑ 324	Hanging In There	1971	20.00
❑ 326	Losing Their Heads	1971	20.00
❑ 329	Right-Off!	1972	20.00
❑ 331	Weird Kingdom	1973	20.00
❑ 333	The Best of Hudson and Landry	1974	15.00
❑ 334	The Best of Hudson and Landry 2	1975	15.00

HUDSON BROTHERS, THE

45s

Number	Title (A Side/B Side)	Yr	NM
ARISTA			
❑ 0208	Help Wanted/Last Time I Looked	1976	5.00
❑ 0286	I Don't Wanna Be Lonely/Pauline	1977	5.00
❑ 0371	The Runaway/You Can't Make Me Cry	1978	5.00
CASABLANCA			
❑ 0108	So You Are a Star/ Ma Ma Ma Baby	1974	6.00
—With long version of A-side			
❑ 801	So You Are a Star/ Ma Ma Ma Baby	1974	5.00
—With short version of A-side			
❑ 816	Me and My Guitar/ Coochie Coochie Coo	1975	5.00
COLUMBIA			
❑ 03976	Don't Try to Fight It/ You Keep Me Up	1983	4.00
—As "The Hudsons"			
DECCA			
❑ 32634	Love Is a Word/ Laugh, Funny, Funny	1970	6.00
—As "Everyday Hudson"			
ELEKTRA			
❑ 46648	Annie/Joni	1980	4.00
—As "Hudson"			
❑ 47049	Afraid to Love/Sidewalk	1980	4.00
—As "Hudson"			
LIONEL			
❑ 3211	Love Nobody/The World Would Be a Little Bit Better	1971	6.00
—As "Hudson"			
PLAYBOY			
❑ 50001	Someday/Leavin' It's Over	1972	6.00
ROCKET			
❑ 40141	America — Fight Back/If You Really Need Me	1973	6.00
—As "Hudson"			
❑ 40141 [PS]	America — Fight Back/If You Really Need Me	1973	10.00
❑ 40317	Sunday Driver/Be a Man	1974	6.00
❑ 40417	Rendezvous/Medley	1975	5.00
❑ 40464	Lonely School Year/If You Really Need Me	1975	5.00
❑ 40464 [PS]	Lonely School Year/If You Really Need Me	1975	8.00
❑ 40508	Spinning the Wheel (With the Girl You Love)/Bernie Was a Friend of Ours	1976	5.00

Albums

Number	Title (A Side/B Side)	Yr	NM
ARISTA			
❑ AB 4199	The Truth About Us	1978	10.00
CASABLANCA			
❑ NBLP-7004	Hollywood Situation	1974	10.00
ELEKTRA			
❑ 6E-299	Damn Those Kids	1980	10.00
—As "Hudson"			
FIRST AMERICAN			
❑ 7708	The Hudson Brothers	1980	10.00
PLAYBOY			
❑ 102	Hudson	1972	15.00
ROCKET			
❑ PIG-460	Totally Out of Control	1974	10.00
❑ PIG-2169	Ba-Fa	1975	10.00

HUES CORPORATION, THE

45s

Number	Title (A Side/B Side)	Yr	NM
LIBERTY			
❑ 56204	Goodfootin'/We're Keepin' Our Business Together	1970	6.00
—As "The Hughes Corporation"			
RCA VICTOR			
❑ 74-0813	There He Is Again/Main Chance	1972	5.00
❑ 74-0900	Freedom for the Stallion/ Off My Cloud	1973	5.00
❑ APBO-0139	Go to the Poet/Miracle Maker	1973	5.00
❑ APBO-0232	Rock the Boat/All Goin' Down Together	1974	5.00
❑ PB-10066	Rockin' Soul/Go to the Poet	1974	5.00
❑ PB-10200	Love Corporation/ He's My Home	1975	5.00
❑ PB-10311	One Good Night Together/When You Look Down the Road	1975	5.00
❑ PB-10390	You Showed Me What Love Is/ When You Look Down the Road	1975	5.00
❑ GB-10480	Rockin' Soul/Go to the Poet	1975	3.00
—Gold Standard Series			
❑ GB-10481	Rock the Boat/All Goin' Down Together	1975	3.00
—Gold Standard Series			
WARNER BROS.			
❑ 8400	I Caught Your Act/Natural Find	1977	4.00
❑ 8454	Telegram of Love/ Dancing Together Again	1977	4.00
❑ 8454 [PS]	Telegram of Love/ Dancing Together Again	1977	8.00
❑ 8559	Give Me Everything/Needed	1978	4.00
❑ 8638	Love Dance/With All My Love and Affection	1978	4.00

Albums

Number	Title (A Side/B Side)	Yr	NM
RCA VICTOR			
❑ APL1-0323	Freedom for the Stallion	1973	10.00
❑ APD1-0755 [Q]	Rockin' Soul	1974	15.00
❑ APL1-0755	Rockin' Soul	1974	10.00
❑ APD1-0938 [Q]	Love Corporation	1975	15.00
❑ APL1-0938	Love Corporation	1975	10.00
❑ ANL1-2147	Rock the Boat	1976	8.00
❑ APL1-2408	The Best of the Hues Corporation	1977	10.00
WARNER BROS.			
❑ BS 3043	I Caught Your Act	1977	10.00
❑ BSK 3196	Your Place or Mine	1978	10.00

HUGHES, CAROL

45s

Number	Title (A Side/B Side)	Yr	NM
CARLTON			
❑ 571	Hello Heartbreak/If She's Right for You	1962	10.00
DOT			
❑ 15863	Don't Forget I Love You/ The Bass	1958	12.00
❑ 15923	Bobby/Sholem Aleichem	1959	12.00
MERCURY			
❑ 70986	Mine All Mine/Fancy Dance	1956	15.00
❑ 71095x45	My Big Brother's Friend/ Lover Boy	1957	15.00
RCA VICTOR			
❑ 47-7605	Goin' to the Dogs/ Staying Young	1959	20.00
❑ 47-7617	It's Me, It's Me, It's Me/ I Must Have Done Something Wonderful	1959	20.00
❑ 47-7665	Let Me Go Lover/When Did I Fall in Love	1960	12.00
❑ 47-7726	Creation/Love, Kisses and Heartaches	1960	12.00
❑ 47-7763	Congratulations/I Can Tell	1960	12.00
ROULETTE			
❑ 4032	Pick Another Baby/ Never Go 'Way	1957	15.00
❑ 4041	Lend Me Your Comb/First Date	1958	15.00

HUGHES, FRED

45s

Number	Title (A Side/B Side)	Yr	NM
BRUNSWICK			
❑ 55419	Baby Boy/Who You Really Are	1969	8.00
❑ 55439	Oo Wee Baby, I Love You/ I Understand	1970	8.00
❑ 55446	Don't Let This Happen to Me/ In My Time of Need	1971	8.00
CADET			
❑ 5616	Baby Don't Go/Love Is Ending	1968	10.00
VEE JAY			
❑ 684	Oo Wee Baby, I Love You/ Love Me Baby	1965	15.00
❑ 703	You Can't Take It Away/ My Heart Cries On	1965	15.00
❑ 718	Don't Let Me Down/ My Heart Cries On	1965	15.00

Albums

Number	Title (A Side/B Side)	Yr	NM
BRUNSWICK			
❑ BL 754147	Baby Boy	1970	15.00

HUGHES, FREDDY
We're not sure if this is the same artist as the Fred Hughes above.

45s

Number	Title (A Side/B Side)	Yr	NM
WAND			
❑ 1182	Send My Baby Back/Where's My Baby	1968	10.00
❑ 1192	A Natural Man/I Gotta Keep My Bluff In	1968	10.00
❑ 1197	He's No Good/I Gotta Keep My Bluff In	1969	10.00

HUGHES, JIMMY

45s

Number	Title (A Side/B Side)	Yr	NM
ATLANTIC			
❑ 2454	Uncle Sam/It Ain't What You've Got	1967	60.00
FAME			
❑ 1000	Midnight Affair/When It Comes to Dancing	1965	20.00
❑ 1003	Neighbor, Neighbor/ It's a Good Thing	1966	30.00
❑ 1006	I Worship the Ground You Walk On/A Shot of Rhythm and Blues	1966	20.00
❑ 1011	Why Not Tonight/ I'm a Man of Action	1967	20.00
❑ 1014	Don't Lose Your Good Thing/ You Can't Believe Everything That You Hear	1967	10.00
❑ 1015	Hi-Heel Sneakers/Time Will Bring You Back	1967	20.00
❑ 6401	Steal Away/Lollipops, Lace and Lipstick	1964	12.00
—Red label			
❑ 6401	Steal Away/Lollipops, Lace and Lipstick	1964	10.00
—Black label			
❑ 6403	Try Me/Lovely Ladies	1964	10.00
❑ 6404	I Want Justice/I'm Getting Better	1964	10.00
❑ 6407	Goodbye My Lover, Goodbye/ It Was Nice	1965	20.00
❑ 6410	You Really Know How to Hurt a Guy/The Loving Physician	1965	30.00
GUYDEN			
❑ 2075	I'm Qualified/My Loving Time	1962	40.00
JAMIE			
❑ 1280	I'm Qualified/My Loving Time	1964	20.00

VOLT

Number	Title (A Side/B Side)	Yr	NM
❑ 4002	I Like Everything About You/What Side of the Door	1968	8.00
❑ 4008	Let 'Em Down Baby/The Sweet Things You Do	1969	8.00
❑ 4017	Chains of Love/I'm Not Ashamed to Beg or Plead	1969	15.00
❑ 4024	I'm So Glad/Lay It on the Line	1969	8.00

Albums

ATCO

Number	Title (A Side/B Side)	Yr	NM
❑ 33-209 [M]	Why Not Tonight	1967	20.00
❑ SD 33-209 [S]	Why Not Tonight	1967	20.00

VEE JAY

Number	Title (A Side/B Side)	Yr	NM
❑ VJ-1102 [M]	Steal Away	1965	25.00
❑ VJS-1102 [R]	Steal Away	1965	25.00

VOLT

Number	Title (A Side/B Side)	Yr	NM
❑ VOS-6003	Something Special	1969	20.00

HUGO AND LUIGI

45s

MERCURY

Number	Title (A Side/B Side)	Yr	NM
❑ 70563	Medley: Nobody's Sweetheart-Somebody Stole My Gal/The Crazy Otto Rag	1955	12.00
❑ 70676	A Satisfied Mind/The Goodbye Song	1955	12.00
❑ 70721	Young Abe Lincoln/Two-Thirds of the Tennessee River	1955	12.00
❑ 70803	Our Melody/Anywhere Is Home with You	1956	12.00

RCA VICTOR

Number	Title (A Side/B Side)	Yr	NM
❑ 47-7518	La Plume de Ma Tante/Honolulu Lu	1959	8.00
❑ 47-7569	Watusi Wedding/Yalaloo	1959	8.00
❑ 47-7639	Just Come Home/Lonesome Stranger	1959	8.00
❑ 47-7808	Smile/Tweedle Dee	1960	8.00
❑ 47-7868	La Pachange/Bimbombey	1961	8.00
❑ 47-7955	Brotherhood of Man/Love from a Heart of Gold	1961	8.00
❑ SP-45-101 [DJ]	RCA Victor Special DJ Spots	1959	10.00

ROULETTE

Number	Title (A Side/B Side)	Yr	NM
❑ 4012	Rockabilly Party/Shenandoah Rose	1957	15.00
❑ 4050	76 Trombones/Twilight in Tennessee	1958	12.00
❑ 4074	Cha-Hua-Hua/Something's Always Happening on the River	1958	12.00
❑ 4074 [PS]	Cha-Hua-Hua/Something's Always Happening on the River	1958	12.00

Albums

RCA VICTOR

Number	Title (A Side/B Side)	Yr	NM
❑ LPM-2254 [M]	The Sound of Children at Christmas	1960	15.00
❑ LSP-2254 [S]	The Sound of Children at Christmas	1960	20.00
❑ LPM-2641 [M]	The Cascading Voices of the Hugo & Luigi Chorus	1963	10.00
❑ LSP-2641 [S]	The Cascading Voices of the Hugo & Luigi Chorus	1963	12.00
❑ LPM-2717 [M]	Let's Fall in Love	1963	10.00
❑ LSP-2717 [S]	Let's Fall in Love	1963	12.00
❑ LPM-2789 [M]	The Cascading Voices of the Hugo & Luigi Chorus — With Brass	1964	10.00
❑ LSP-2789 [S]	The Cascading Voices of the Hugo & Luigi Chorus — With Brass	1964	12.00
❑ LPM-2863 [M]	The Cascading Voices of the Hugo & Luigi Chorus — With Strings	1964	10.00
❑ LSP-2863 [S]	The Cascading Voices of the Hugo & Luigi Chorus — With Strings	1964	12.00
❑ LSP-4083	Maggie Flynn	1968	10.00

ROULETTE

Number	Title (A Side/B Side)	Yr	NM
❑ R-25044 [M]	When Good Fellows Get Together	1959	20.00
❑ R-25283 [M]	Cascading Voices	1965	12.00
❑ SR-25283 [S]	Cascading Voices	1965	15.00

WING

Number	Title (A Side/B Side)	Yr	NM
❑ MGW 12207 [M]	Sing Along by the Fireside	195?	12.00

HULLABALLOOS, THE

45s

ROULETTE

Number	Title (A Side/B Side)	Yr	NM
❑ 4587	I'm Gonna Love You Too/Party Doll	1964	20.00
❑ 4587 [PS]	I'm Gonna Love You Too/Party Doll	1964	40.00
❑ 4593	Beware/Did You Ever	1965	20.00
❑ 4593 [PS]	Beware/Did You Ever	1965	40.00
❑ 4612	Learning the Game/Don't Stop	1965	20.00
❑ 4612 [PS]	Learning the Game/Don't Stop	1965	40.00
❑ 4622	I Won't Turn Around Now/My Heart Keeps Telling Me	1965	20.00
❑ 4622 [PS]	I Won't Turn Around Now/My Heart Keeps Telling Me	1965	40.00

Albums

ROULETTE

Number	Title (A Side/B Side)	Yr	NM
❑ R-25297 [M]	England's Newest Singing Sensations	1965	50.00
❑ SR-25297 [P]	England's Newest Singing Sensations	1965	75.00
❑ R-25310 [M]	The Hullabaloos on Hullabaloo	1965	50.00
❑ SR-25310 [P]	The Hullabaloos on Hullabaloo	1965	75.00

HULLABALOO SINGERS AND ORCHESTRA, THE

Albums

COLUMBIA

Number	Title (A Side/B Side)	Yr	NM
❑ CL 2410 [M]	The Hullabaloo Show	1965	20.00
❑ CS 9210 [S]	The Hullabaloo Show	1965	25.00

HUMAN BEINZ, THE

45s

CAPITOL

Number	Title (A Side/B Side)	Yr	NM
❑ 2119	Turn On Your Love Light/It's Fun to Be Clean	1968	10.00
❑ 2119 [PS]	Turn On Your Love Light/It's Fun to Be Clean	1968	20.00
❑ 2198	Every Time Woman/The Face	1968	10.00
❑ 2431	I've Got to Keep On Pushin'/This Little Girl of Mine	1969	10.00
❑ 5990	Nobody But Me/Sueno	1967	15.00

GATEWAY

Number	Title (A Side/B Side)	Yr	NM
❑ 828	Gloria/The Times They Are a-Changin'	1967	15.00
❑ 838	You Can't Make Me Cry/The Pied Piper	1967	15.00

Albums

CAPITOL

Number	Title (A Side/B Side)	Yr	NM
❑ ST 2906	Nobody But Me	1968	30.00
❑ ST 2926	Evolutions	1968	40.00

GATEWAY

Number	Title (A Side/B Side)	Yr	NM
❑ GLP-3012	Nobody But Me	1968	40.00

—With added tracks by The Mammals

HUMAN EXPRESSION, THE

45s

ACCENT

Number	Title (A Side/B Side)	Yr	NM
❑ 1214	Every Night/Love at Psychedelic Velocity	1967	200.00
❑ 1226	Calm Me Down/Optical Sound	1967	100.00
❑ 1252	I Don't Need Nobody/Sweet Child of Nothingness	1967	100.00

HUMBLE PIE

Also see PETER FRAMPTON; STEVE MARRIOTT.

45s

A&M

Number	Title (A Side/B Side)	Yr	NM
❑ 1282	I Don't Need No Doctor/Song for Jenny	1971	4.00
❑ 1282 [PS]	I Don't Need No Doctor/Song for Jenny	1971	6.00
❑ 1349	Hot and Nasty/You're So Good for Me	1972	4.00
❑ 1349 [PS]	Hot and Nasty/You're So Good for Me	1972	6.00
❑ 1366	Sweet Peace and Time/30 Days in the Hole	1972	4.00
❑ 1406	Black Coffee/Say No More	1973	4.00
❑ 1406 [PS]	Black Coffee/Say No More	1973	12.00
❑ 1440	Honky Tonk Woman/Get Down to It	1973	4.00
❑ 1484	Oh La De Da/The Out Crowd	1974	4.00
❑ 1530	Rally with Ali/Ninety-Nine Pounds	1974	4.00
❑ 1711	Road Hog/Rock and Roll Music	1975	4.00

ATCO

Number	Title (A Side/B Side)	Yr	NM
❑ 7216	Fool for a Pretty Face/You Soppy Pratt	1980	5.00

IMMEDIATE

Number	Title (A Side/B Side)	Yr	NM
❑ 001	Natural Born Woman/I'll Go Alone	1969	8.00

Albums

A&M

Number	Title (A Side/B Side)	Yr	NM
❑ SP-3127	Humble Pie	1981	8.00
—Budget-line reissue			
❑ SP-3132	Smokin'	1981	8.00
—Budget-line reissue			
❑ SP-3208	The Best of Humble Pie	1982	10.00
❑ SP-3506 [(2)]	Performance — Rockin' the Fillmore	1971	15.00
❑ SP-3513 [(2)]	Lost and Found	1972	15.00
❑ SP-3611	Thunderbox	1974	12.00
❑ SP-3701 [(2)]	Eat It	1973	15.00
❑ SP-4270	Humble Pie	1970	12.00
❑ SP-4301	Rock On	1971	12.00
❑ SP-4342	Smokin'	1972	12.00
❑ SP-4514	Street Rats	1975	12.00
❑ SP-6008 [(2)]	Performance — Rockin' the Fillmore	1981	10.00
—Budget-line reissue			
❑ SP-6009 [(2)]	Lost and Found	1981	10.00
—Budget-line reissue			
❑ SP-6503 [(2)]	Eat It	1981	10.00
—Budget-line reissue			

ACCORD

Number	Title (A Side/B Side)	Yr	NM
❑ SN-7192	Recaptured	1981	10.00

ATCO

Number	Title (A Side/B Side)	Yr	NM
❑ SD 38-122	On to Victory	1980	10.00
❑ SD 38-131	Go for the Throat	1981	10.00

COMPLEAT

Number	Title (A Side/B Side)	Yr	NM
❑ 672009-1 [(2)]	A Slice of Humble Pie	1985	12.00

IMMEDIATE

Number	Title (A Side/B Side)	Yr	NM
❑ IMOCS-101	As Safe As Yesterday Is	1969	25.00

HUMBLEBUMS, THE

GERRY RAFFERTY was in this group.

45s

UNITED ARTISTS

Number	Title (A Side/B Side)	Yr	NM
❑ 50771	All the Best People Do It/Cruisin'	1971	10.00

Albums

LIBERTY

Number	Title (A Side/B Side)	Yr	NM
❑ LST-7636	The Humblebums	1969	20.00
❑ LST-7656	Open Up the Door	1970	25.00

HUMES, ANITA

45s

ROULETTE

Number	Title (A Side/B Side)	Yr	NM
❑ 4564	Don't Fight It Baby/When Somethin's Hard to Get	1964	15.00
❑ 4575	I'm Making It Over/Just for the Boy	1964	15.00
❑ 4750	Are You Going My Way/Everybody's Got You	1967	20.00

HUMOROUS DIAN

45s

VELTONE

Number	Title (A Side/B Side)	Yr	NM
❑ 712	Interview with Mr-K/The Three Hep Piggies	1961	30.00

HUMPERDINCK, ENGELBERT

45s

EPIC

Number	Title (A Side/B Side)	Yr	NM
❑ AE7 1170 [DJ]	Christmas Song/Silent Night	1978	4.00
❑ AE7 1170 [PS]	Christmas Song/Silent Night	1978	4.00
❑ 02060	Don't You Love Me Anymore/Till I Get It Right	1981	3.00
❑ 02245	Maybe This Time/When the Night Ends	1981	3.00
❑ 03817	Till You and Your Lover Are Lovers Again/What Will I Write	1983	3.00
❑ 50270	After the Lovin'/Let's Remember the Good Times	1976	5.00
❑ 50365	I Believe in Miracles/Goodbye My Friend	1977	4.00
❑ 50447	A Lover's Holiday/Look at Me	1977	4.00
❑ 50488	A Night to Remember/Silent Night	1977	4.00
❑ 50526	The Last of the Romantics/I Have Paid the Toll	1978	4.00
❑ 50566	Love Me Tender/This Time One Year Ago	1978	4.00
❑ 50579	Love's In Need of Love Today/Sweet Marjorene	1978	4.00
❑ 50632	This Moment in Time/And the Day Begins	1978	4.00
❑ 50692	Can't Help Falling in Love/You Know Me	1979	4.00
❑ 50732	Lovin' Too Well/Much, Much Greater Love	1979	4.00
❑ 50844	Love's Only Love/Burning Ember	1980	3.00
❑ 50899	A Chance to Be a Hero/Any Kind of Love at All	1980	3.00
❑ 50933	Don't Cry Out Loud/Don't Touch That Dial	1980	3.00
❑ 50958	It's Not Easy to Live Together/Royal Affair	1980	3.00

HICKORY

Number	Title (A Side/B Side)	Yr	NM
❑ 1337	Baby Turn Around/If I Could Do the Things I Want to Do	1965	16.00

—As "Gerry Dorsey"

PARROT

Number	Title (A Side/B Side)	Yr	NM
❑ 40011 [M]	Release Me (And Let Me Love Again)/Ten Guitars	1967	8.00
❑ 40011 [S]	Release Me (And Let Me Love Again)/Ten Guitars	1967	20.00

—Both sides in true stereo. Letters "XDR" are stamped in run-off area before the matrix number

Except when noted otherwise, VG = 25% of NM, and VG+ = 50% of NM. (Example: VG = $2.00, VG+ = $4.00 and NM = $8.00.)

Number	Title (A Side/B Side)	Yr	NM
❑ 40015	There Goes My Everything/ You Love	1967	8.00
❑ 40019	The Last Waltz/That Promise	1967	8.00
❑ 40019 [PS]	The Last Waltz/That Promise	1967	12.00
❑ 40023	Am I That Easy to Forget/ Pretty Ribbons	1967	8.00
❑ 40023 [PS]	Am I That Easy to Forget/ Pretty Ribbons	1967	12.00
❑ 40027	A Man Without Love/Call on Me	1968	8.00
❑ 40032	Les Bicyclettes De Belsize/ Three Little Words	1968	8.00
❑ 40032 [PS]	Les Bicyclettes De Belsize/ Three Little Words	1968	12.00
❑ 40036	The Way It Used to Be/ A Good Thing Going	1969	6.00
❑ 40036 [PS]	The Way It Used to Be/ A Good Thing Going	1969	10.00
❑ 40040	I'm a Better Man/Cafe	1969	6.00
❑ 40044	Winter World of Love/ Take My Heart	1969	6.00
❑ 40044 [PS]	Winter World of Love/ Take My Heart	1969	10.00
❑ 40049	My Marie/Our Song (La Paloma)	1970	6.00
❑ 40049 [PS]	My Marie/Our Song (La Paloma)	1970	8.00
❑ 40054	Sweetheart/Born to Be Wanted	1970	6.00
❑ 40054 [PS]	Sweetheart/Born to Be Wanted	1970	8.00
❑ 40059	When There's No You/ Stranger, Step In My World	1971	6.00
❑ 40059 [PS]	When There's No You/ Stranger, Step In My World	1971	8.00
❑ 40065	Another Time, Another Place/ You're the Window of My World	1971	6.00
❑ 40069	Too Beautiful to Last/ A Hundred Times a Day	1972	5.00
❑ 40071	In Time/How Does It Feel	1972	5.00
❑ 40072	I Never Said Goodbye/ Time After Time	1972	5.00
❑ 40073	I'm Leavin' You/ My Summer Song	1973	4.00
❑ 40076	Love Is All/Lady of the Night	1973	4.00
❑ 40077	Free as the Wind/ My Friend the Wind	1974	4.00
❑ 40079	Catch Me I'm Falling/ Love, Oh Precious Love	1974	4.00
❑ 40082	Forever and Ever/Precious Love	1974	4.00
❑ 40085	This Is What You Mean to Me/ A World Without Music	1975	4.00

7-Inch Extended Plays

PARROT

Number	Title (A Side/B Side)	Yr	NM
❑ SBG 73	Love Can Fly/Let Me Into Your Life/Through the Eyes of Love//Marry Me/To Get to You/You're Easy to Love	1969	8.00
—Stereo jukebox issue; small hole, plays at 33 1/3 rpm			
❑ SBG 73 [PS]	Engelbert	1969	8.00
❑ SBG 77	Café/A Time for Us/Didn't We// Aquarius-Let the Sunshine In/ The Signs of Love/Love Letters	1969	8.00
—Stereo jukebox issue; small hole, plays at 33 1/3 rpm			
❑ SBG 77 [PS]	Engelbert Humperdinck	1969	8.00
❑ SBG 80	Raindrops Keep Fallin' on My Head/My Cherie Amour/ Something//(B-side unknown)	1970	8.00
—Jukebox issue; small hole, plays at 33 1/3 rpm			
❑ SBG 80 [PS]	We Made It Happen	1970	8.00
❑ SBG 82	Help Me Make It Through the Night/My Prayer/You'll Never Walk Alone//My Wife the Dancer/Just a Little Bit of You/It's Impossible	1971	8.00
—Jukebox issue; small hole, plays at 33 1/3 rpm			
❑ SBG 82 [PS]	Live at the Riviera, Las Vegas	1971	8.00

Albums

EPIC

Number	Title (A Side/B Side)	Yr	NM
❑ (no #) [PD]	Last of the Romantics	1978	25.00
❑ PE 34381	After the Lovin'	1976	10.00
—Orange label			
❑ PE 34381	After the Lovin'	1979	8.00
—Dark blue label; back cover does not yet have bar code			
❑ PE 34381	After the Lovin'	198?	6.00
—Dark blue label; back cover has bar code			
❑ E 34436	The Ultimate	1977	10.00
—Orange label			
❑ PE 34436	The Ultimate	198?	8.00
—Reissue with bar code; dark blue label			
❑ E 34719	Golden Love Songs	1977	10.00
—Orange label			
❑ PE 34719	Golden Love Songs	198?	8.00
—Reissue with bar code; dark blue label			
❑ PE 34730	Miracles	1977	10.00
—Orange label			
❑ PE 34730	Miracles	198?	8.00
—Reissue with bar code; dark blue label			
❑ JE 35020	Last of the Romantics	1978	10.00
—Orange label			
❑ PE 35020	Last of the Romantics	198?	8.00
—Reissue with bar code; dark blue label			
❑ PE 35031	Christmas Tyme	1977	12.00
❑ JE 35791	This Moment in Time	1979	10.00
❑ PE 35791	This Moment in Time	198?	8.00
—Budget-line reissue			
❑ JE 36431	Love's Only Love	1980	10.00
❑ PE 36765	A Merry Christmas with Engelbert Humperdinck	1980	10.00
—Some copies of the record have a "JE" prefix			
❑ E2X 36782 [(2)]	All of Me/Live in Concert	1980	12.00
❑ FE 37128	Don't You Love Me Anymore	1981	10.00
❑ PE 37128	Don't You Love Me Anymore	1983	8.00
—Budget-line reissue			
❑ FE 38087	You and Your Lover	1983	10.00
❑ PE 39469	White Christmas	1984	10.00

LONDON

Number	Title (A Side/B Side)	Yr	NM
❑ BP 688/9 [(2)]	Engelbert Humperdinck Sings for You	1977	15.00
❑ PS 709	Love Letters	1978	10.00

PARROT

Number	Title (A Side/B Side)	Yr	NM
❑ PA 61012 [M]	Release Me	1967	20.00
❑ PA 61015 [M]	The Last Waltz	1967	20.00
❑ PAS 71012 [S]	Release Me	1967	15.00
❑ PAS 71015 [S]	The Last Waltz	1967	15.00
❑ PAS 71022	A Man Without Love	1968	15.00
❑ PAS 71026	Engelbert	1969	15.00
❑ XPAS 71030	Engelbert Humperdinck	1969	15.00
❑ XPAS 71038	We Made It Happen	1970	15.00
❑ XPAS 71043	Sweetheart	1971	15.00
❑ XPAS 71048	Another Time, Another Place	1971	15.00
❑ XPAS 71051	Live at the Riviera, Las Vegas	1971	15.00
❑ XPAS 71056	In Time	1972	15.00
❑ XPAS 71061	King of Hearts	1973	15.00
❑ APAS 71065	My Love	1974	15.00
❑ PAS 71067	His Greatest Hits	1974	15.00
❑ SW-93216	We Made It Happen	1970	20.00
—Capitol Record Club edition			

SILVER EAGLE

Number	Title (A Side/B Side)	Yr	NM
❑ SE 1034 [(2)]	A Lovely Way to Spend an Evening	1985	15.00
—Mail-order offer			

HUMPHREY, BOBBI

12-Inch Singles

EPIC

Number	Title (A Side/B Side)	Yr	NM
❑ 50537	Home-Made Jam/ Sunset Burgundy	1978	10.00
❑ 50746	Love When I'm In Your Arms/ Sweet and Low	1979	10.00

WARNER BROS.

Number	Title (A Side/B Side)	Yr	NM
❑ 21716	Let's Get Started (2 versions)/ Rainbows	1990	6.00

45s

BLUE NOTE

Number	Title (A Side/B Side)	Yr	NM
❑ XW395	Chicago, Damn/Just a Love Child	1974	5.00
❑ XW455	Harlem River Drive/ Black and Blues	1974	5.00
❑ XW592	Fun House/San Francisco Lights	1975	5.00
❑ XW785	Uno Esta/Sweeter Than Sugar	1976	5.00
❑ 1971	Spanish Harlem/Sad Bag	1971	8.00
❑ 1974	Ain't No Sunchine/Sad Bag	1972	8.00
❑ 1980	Is This All/Lonely Town, Lonely Street	1972	8.00

EPIC

Number	Title (A Side/B Side)	Yr	NM
❑ 50448	Dancin' to Keep From Cryin'/ Theme I	1977	5.00
❑ 50529	Home-Made Jam/ Sunset Burgundy	1978	5.00
❑ 50745	Love When I'm In Your Arms/ Sweet and Low	1979	5.00

Albums

BLUE NOTE

Number	Title (A Side/B Side)	Yr	NM
❑ BN-LA142-G	Blacks and Blues	1974	10.00
❑ BN-LA344-G	Satin Doll	1974	10.00
❑ BN-LA550-G	Fancy Dancer	1975	10.00
❑ BN-LA699-G	The Best of Bobbi Humphrey	1976	10.00
❑ BST-84379	Flute-In	1971	12.00
❑ BST-84421	Dig This	1972	12.00

EPIC

Number	Title (A Side/B Side)	Yr	NM
❑ PE 34704	Tailor Made	1977	10.00
❑ JE 35338	Freestyle	1978	10.00
❑ JE 35607	The Good Life	1979	10.00
❑ JE 36368	The Best of Bobbi Humphrey	1980	10.00

HUMPHREY, PAUL

45s

LIZARD

Number	Title (A Side/B Side)	Yr	NM
❑ 1009	Funky L.A./Baby Rice	1971	6.00
❑ 21006	Cool Aid/Detroit	1971	6.00

Albums

BLUE THUMB

Number	Title (A Side/B Side)	Yr	NM
❑ BTS 47	Supermellow	1973	12.00
❑ BTS 66	America, Wake Up!	1974	12.00

DISCOVERY

Number	Title (A Side/B Side)	Yr	NM
❑ DS-850	Paul Humphrey Sextet	1981	10.00

LIZARD

Number	Title (A Side/B Side)	Yr	NM
❑ 20106	Paul Humphrey & the Cool Aid Chemists	1971	15.00

HUNDLEY, CRAIG

Albums

WORLD PACIFIC

Number	Title (A Side/B Side)	Yr	NM
❑ WPS-21880	Arrival of a Young Giant	1968	15.00

HUNG JURY, THE

45s

COLGEMS

Number	Title (A Side/B Side)	Yr	NM
❑ 66-1010	Roses/Let the Good Times In	1967	15.00

HUNGER

45s

PUBLIC

Number	Title (A Side/B Side)	Yr	NM
❑ 101	Mind Machine/(B-side unknown)	1968	25.00
❑ 103	No Shame/(B-side unknown)	1968	25.00
❑ 1001	Colors/(B-side unknown)	1969	30.00

Albums

PUBLIC

Number	Title (A Side/B Side)	Yr	NM
❑ 1006	Strictly from Hunger	1969	600.00

HUNT, GERALDINE

45s

ABC

Number	Title (A Side/B Side)	Yr	NM
❑ 10859	Winner Take All/For Lovers Only	1966	500.00

BOMBAY

Number	Title (A Side/B Side)	Yr	NM
❑ 4501	(Two Can Live) Cheaper Than One/He's for Real	1964	200.00
—Black label			
❑ 4501	(Two Can Live) Cheaper Than One/He's for Real	1964	300.00
—Yellow label			

CHECKER

Number	Title (A Side/B Side)	Yr	NM
❑ 1028	I Let Myself Go/I Wished I Had Listened	1962	40.00

PRISM

Number	Title (A Side/B Side)	Yr	NM
❑ 315	Can't Fake the Feeling/ (B-side unknown)	1980	4.00
❑ 323	Heart Heart/(B-side unknown)	1981	4.00

ROULETTE

Number	Title (A Side/B Side)	Yr	NM
❑ 7068	Never, Never Leave Me/ Push, Sweet	1970	30.00
❑ 7109	Now That There's You/ Shades of Blue	1971	15.00
❑ 7129	Baby, I Need Your Loving/ (B-side unknown)	1972	10.00
❑ 7132	Cold Blood/Just Believe in Me	1972	30.00
❑ 7149	You Brought Joy/Shades of Blue	1973	15.00

U.S.A.

Number	Title (A Side/B Side)	Yr	NM
❑ 732	Sneak Around/It Never Happened Before	1962	30.00
❑ 737	Sneak Around/It Never Happened Before	1963	25.00

HUNTER, CHRISTINE

45s

ROULETTE

Number	Title (A Side/B Side)	Yr	NM
❑ 4589	Santa Bring Me Ringo/ Where Were You Daddy	1964	15.00

HUNTER, HERBERT

45s

HIT

Number	Title (A Side/B Side)	Yr	NM
❑ 01	The Twist/Twistin' the Night Away	1962	8.00
❑ 02	Slow Twistin'/Good Luck Charm	1962	8.00
—B-side by Ed Hardin			
❑ 03	Lover Please/Young World	1962	8.00
—B-side by Ed Hardin			
❑ 08	Twist Twist Senora/ Stranger on the Shore	1962	8.00
—B-side by the Hit Combo			
❑ 11	Hide 'Nor Hair/Shout! Shout! (Knock Yourself Out)	1962	8.00
—B-side by Bill Austin			
❑ 14	I Can't Stop Loving You/ Second Hand Love	1962	8.00
—B-side by Connie Dee			
❑ 22	Dancin' Party/Ahab the Arab	1962	8.00
—B-side by John Dunn			
❑ 24	Bring It On Home to Me/ The Loco-Motion	1962	8.00
—B-side by Peggy Gaines			
❑ 25	The Right String But the Wrong Yo-Yo/You Don't Know Me	1962	8.00
❑ 47	Loop-De-Loop/The Night Has a Thousand Eyes	1963	8.00
—B-side by Joe Cash			
❑ 61	Take These Chains from My Heart/I Will Follow Him	1963	8.00
—B-side by Connie and Clara			

Number	Title (A Side/B Side)	Yr	NM
❑ 78	Twist It Up/My Whole World Is Falling Down	1963	8.00
—B-side by Betty Scott			

HUNTER, IAN

Also see MOTT THE HOOPLE.

45s

Number	Title (A Side/B Side)	Yr	NM
CHRYSALIS			
❑ 2324	When the Daylight Comes/Life After Death	1979	5.00
❑ 2352	Cleveland Rocks/Just Another Night	1979	5.00
❑ 2405	We Gotta Get Out of Here/Sons and Daughters	1980	4.00
❑ 2542	I Need Your Love/(B-side unknown)	1981	4.00
❑ 2569	Central Park 'N' West/(B-side unknown)	1981	4.00
COLUMBIA			
❑ 03929	All of the Good Ones Are Taken/Death 'N' Glory Boys	1983	4.00
❑ 04166	Seeing Double/That Girl Is Rock 'N' Roll	1983	4.00
❑ 10161	Once Bitten Twice Shy/3000 Miles from Here	1975	6.00

Albums

Number	Title (A Side/B Side)	Yr	NM
CHRYSALIS			
❑ CHR 1214	You're Never Alone with a Schizophrenic	1979	10.00
❑ 2CHS 1269 [(2)]	Ian Hunter Live/Welcome to the Club	1980	12.00
❑ CHS 1326	Short Back N' Sides	1981	10.00
❑ PV 41214	You're Never Alone with a Schizophrenic	1982	8.00
—Budget-line reissue			
❑ PV 41326	Short Back N' Sides	1982	8.00
—Budget-line reissue			
COLUMBIA			
❑ PC 33480	Ian Hunter	1975	10.00
—No bar code on cover			
❑ PC 33480	Ian Hunter	198?	8.00
—Budget-line reissue with bar code			
❑ PC 34142	All American Alien Boy	1976	10.00
—No bar code on cover			
❑ PC 34142	All American Alien Boy	198?	8.00
—Budget-line reissue with bar code			
❑ PC 34721	Overnight Angels	1977	10.00
—No bar code on cover			
❑ C2 36251 [(2)]	Shades of Ian Hunter	1980	12.00
❑ FC 38628	All of the Good Ones Are Taken	1983	10.00

HUNTER, IVORY JOE

45s

Number	Title (A Side/B Side)	Yr	NM
ATLANTIC			
❑ 1049	It May Sound Silly/I Got to Learn to Do the Mambo	1954	25.00
❑ 1066	I Want Somebody/Heven Came Down to Earth	1955	25.00
❑ 1086	A Tear Fell/I Need You By My Side	1956	25.00
❑ 1095	You Mean Everything to Me/That's Why I Dream	1956	25.00
❑ 1111	Since I Met You Baby/You Can't Stop This Rocking and Rolling	1956	30.00
❑ 1128	Empty Arms/Love's a Hurting Game	1957	20.00
❑ 1151	She's Gone/Everytime I Hear That Song	1957	20.00
❑ 1164	All About the Blues/If Only You Were Here with Me	1957	20.00
❑ 1173	You're On My Mind/Baby, Count on Me	1958	20.00
❑ 1183	I'm So Glad I Found You/Shooty Booty	1958	20.00
❑ 1191	You Flip Me Baby/Yes, I Want You	1958	20.00
❑ 2020	I Just Want to Love You/Now I Don't Worry No More	1959	15.00
CAPITOL			
❑ 4587	I'm Hooked/Because I Love You	1961	12.00
❑ 4648	May the Best Man Win/You Better Believe It Baby	1961	12.00
❑ 4688	The Life I Live/A Great Big Heart Full of Love	1962	12.00
DOT			
❑ 15880	City Lights/Stolen Moments	1958	15.00
❑ 15930	Old Fashioned Love/Cottage for Sale	1959	15.00
❑ 15957	I Love You So Much/Welcome Home Baby	1959	15.00
❑ 15986	My Search Was Ended/Did You Mean It	1959	15.00
EPIC			
❑ 10725	Heartbreak and Misery/I'm Coming Down with the Blues	1971	6.00
❑ 10725	Heartbreak and Misery/We All Like That Groovy Feeling	1971	6.00
4 STAR			
❑ 1634	Foolish Pride/Did You Mean It	1953	40.00
GOLDISC			
❑ 3010	It's Love, It's Love, It's Love/You Satisfy Me Baby	1960	15.00
GOLDWAX			
❑ 307	Every Little Bit Helped Me/I Can Make You Happy	1966	20.00
KING			
❑ 4424	False Friend Blues/Send Me Pretty Mama	1951	40.00
—Ivory Joe Hunter records on King before 4422 are unconfirmed on 45 rpm			
❑ 4443	She's Gone Blues/Stop Rockin' That Train	1951	40.00
❑ 4455	Old Gal and New Gal Blues/Woo Wee Blues	1951	40.00
❑ 5166	Jealous Heart/I Like It	1958	15.00
❑ 5271	Guess Who/Don't Fall in Love with Me	1959	—
—Unreleased			
❑ 5280	Guess Who/Don't Fall in Love with Me	1959	15.00
MGM			
❑ 8011	I Almost Lost My Mind/If I Give You My Love	1949	50.00
—Original 45 issue of this record			
❑ K10578	I Almost Lost My Mind/If I Give You My Love	1949	40.00
❑ K10618	S.P. Blues/Why Fool Yourself	1950	30.00
❑ K10663	I Need You So/Leave Her Alone	1950	30.00
❑ K10733	Let Me Dream/Gimme a Pound of Round Ground	1950	30.00
❑ K10761	Old Man's Boogie/Living a Lie	1950	30.00
❑ K10818	It's A Sin/Don't You Believe Me	1950	30.00
❑ K10899	I Found My Baby/I Ain't Got No Gal	1951	30.00
❑ K10951	I Can't Get You Off My Mind/I Can't Resist You	1951	30.00
❑ K10995	You Lied/When I Lost You	1951	30.00
❑ K11052	I'm Yours/Wrong Woman Blues	1951	30.00
❑ K11132	Blue Moon/U Name It	1952	30.00
❑ K11165	Laugh/Where Shall I Go	1952	30.00
❑ K11195	I'm Sorry for You My Friend/I Will Be	1952	30.00
❑ K11263	I Get That Lonesome Feeling/I Thought I Had Loved	1952	30.00
❑ K11325	Big Bounce/Tell Her for Me	1952	30.00
❑ K11378	Rockin' Chair Boogie/Music Before Dawn	1952	30.00
❑ K11459	I Had a Girl/If You See My Baby	1953	30.00
❑ K11549	I'm Afraid/Don't Make Me Cry	1953	30.00
❑ K11599	I Must Be Talking to Myself/My Best Wishes	1953	30.00
❑ K11702	I Have a Secret/I Feel So Good	1954	25.00
❑ K11818	Do You Miss Me/Whose Arms Are You Missing	1954	25.00
PARAMOUNT			
❑ 0253	He'll Never Love You/San Antonio Rose	1973	6.00
SMASH			
❑ 1825	My Arms Are Waiting/Congratulations	1963	12.00
❑ 1860	There's No Forgetting You/My Lover's Prayer	1963	12.00
SOUND STAGE 7			
❑ 2623	Ivory Tower/I'll Give You All Night to Stop	1968	8.00
❑ 2635	Until the Day I Die/I Built a Wall Around Me	1969	8.00
❑ 2643	Straighten Up Baby/Baby Me Baby	1969	8.00
STAX			
❑ 155	This Kind of Woman/Can't Explain Why It Happened	1964	12.00
TEARDROP			
❑ 3058	I've Asked You for the Last Time/Heart	196?	10.00
VEE JAY			
❑ 452	Somebody's Stealing My Love/You Only Want Me When You Need Me	1962	12.00
VEEP			
❑ 1258	What's the Matter Baby/Don't You Believe Me	1967	8.00
❑ 1270	Did She Ask About Me/From the First Time We Met	1967	8.00

7-Inch Extended Plays

Number	Title (A Side/B Side)	Yr	NM
ATLANTIC			
❑ EP 589	*Since I Met You Baby/I Got to Learn to Do the Mambo/It May Sound Silly/A Tear Fell	1958	50.00
❑ EP 589 [PS]	Ivory Joe Hunter (Since I Met You Baby)	1958	50.00
❑ EP 608	*Empty Arms/Love's a Hurting Game/She's Gone/Everytime I Hear That Song	1958	60.00
❑ EP 608 [PS]	Rock with Ivory Joe Hunter	1958	60.00
KING			
❑ 265	(contents unknown)	1954	80.00
❑ 265 [PS]	Ivory Joe Hunter	1954	80.00
MGM			
❑ X-1376	(contents unknown)	1957	50.00
❑ X-1376 [PS]	I Get That Lonesome Feeling, Vol. 1	1957	50.00
❑ X-1377	I Get That Lonesome Feeling/I Found a New Baby//I Need You So/If You See My Baby	1957	50.00
❑ X-1377 [PS]	I Get That Lonesome Feeling, Vol. 2	1957	50.00
❑ X-1378	(contents unknown)	1957	50.00
❑ X-1378 [PS]	I Get That Lonesome Feeling, Vol. 3	1957	50.00

Albums

Number	Title (A Side/B Side)	Yr	NM
ATLANTIC			
❑ 8008 [M]	Ivory Joe Hunter	1957	200.00
—Black label			
❑ 8008 [M]	Ivory Joe Hunter	1960	100.00
—Purple and red label			
❑ 8015 [M]	The Old and the New	1958	200.00
—Black label			
❑ 8015 [M]	The Old and the New	1960	100.00
—Purple and red label			
DOT			
❑ DLP-3569 [M]	This Is Ivory Joe Hunter	1964	40.00
❑ DLP-25569 [S]	This Is Ivory Joe Hunter	1964	50.00
EPIC			
❑ E 30348	The Return of Ivory Joe Hunter	1971	20.00
EVEREST ARCHIVE OF FOLK & JAZZ			
❑ 289	Ivory Joe Hunter	1974	12.00
GOLDISC			
❑ 403 [M]	The Fabulous Ivory Joe Hunter	1961	60.00
HOME COOKING			
❑ 112	I'm Coming Down with the Blues	1989	12.00
KING			
❑ 605 [M]	16 of His Greatest Hits	1958	400.00
LION			
❑ L-70068 [M]	I Need You So	1959	60.00
MGM			
❑ E-3488 [M]	I Get That Lonesome Feeling	1957	300.00
PARAMOUNT			
❑ PAS-6080	I've Always Been Country	1974	12.00
POLYDOR			
❑ 830897-1	Since I Met You Baby	1987	12.00
SMASH			
❑ MGS-27037 [M]	Ivory Joe Hunter's Golden Hits	1963	40.00
❑ SRS-67037 [S]	Ivory Joe Hunter's Golden Hits	1963	50.00
SOUND			
❑ M-603 [M]	Ivory Joe Hunter	1959	150.00
STRAND			
❑ SL-1123 [M]	The Artistry of Ivory Joe Hunter	196?	40.00
❑ SLS-1123 [S]	The Artistry of Ivory Joe Hunter	196?	50.00

HUNTER, ROBERT

GRATEFUL DEAD lyricist.

Albums

Number	Title (A Side/B Side)	Yr	NM
RELIX			
❑ 2002 [PD]	Promontory Rider	1982	20.00
—Limited edition of 1,000 picture discs			
ROUND			
❑ RX-101	Tales of the Great Rum Runners	1974	20.00
❑ RX-105	Tiger Rose	1975	20.00

HUNTER, TAB

45s

Number	Title (A Side/B Side)	Yr	NM
DOT			
❑ 15533	Young Love/Red Sails in the Sunset	1957	25.00
❑ 15548	Ninety-Nine Ways/Don't Get Around Much Anymore	1957	25.00
❑ 15657	Don't Let It Get Around/I'm Alone Because I Love You	1957	20.00
❑ 15767	I'm a Runaway/It's All Over Town	1958	20.00
❑ 16036	Young Love/Ninety-Nine Ways	1960	20.00
❑ 16187	My Devotion/You Cheated	1961	15.00
❑ 16205	Wild Side of Life/My Devotion	1961	15.00

Except when noted otherwise, VG = 25% of NM, and VG+ = 50% of NM. (Example: VG = $2.00, VG+ = $4.00 and NM = $8.00.)

Number	Title (A Side/B Side)	Yr	NM
❑ 16264	The Way You Look Tonight/You Cheated	1961	15.00
❑ 16355	I Can't Stop Loving You/Born to Lose	1962	15.00
WARNER BROS.			
❑ 5008	Jealous Heart/Lonesome Road	1958	20.00
❑ 5021	Candy/My Baby Just Cares for Me	1958	20.00
❑ 5032 [M]	I'll Be With You in Apple Blossom Time/What Can I Give My Only Love	1959	20.00
❑ S-5032 [S]	I'll Be With You in Apple Blossom Time/What Can I Give My Only Love	1959	25.00
❑ 5051 [M]	There's No Fool Like a Young Fool/I'll Never Smile Again	1959	20.00
❑ 5051 [PS]	There's No Fool Like a Young Fool/I'll Never Smile Again	1959	20.00
❑ S-5051 [S]	There's No Fool Like a Young Fool/I'll Never Smile Again	1959	25.00
❑ 5093	Our Love/Waitin' for Fall	1959	20.00
❑ 5093 [PS]	Our Love/Waitin' for Fall	1959	25.00
❑ 5160	Again/Love Is Just Around the Corner	1960	20.00
❑ 5160 [PS]	Again/Love Is Just Around the Corner	1960	25.00
7-Inch Extended Plays			
WARNER BROS.			
❑ EA 1221 [M]	(contents unknown)	1958	20.00
❑ EA 1221 [PS]	Tab Hunter	1958	20.00
❑ ESB 1221 [PS]	Tab Hunter	1959	25.00
❑ ESB 1221 [S]	(contents unknown)	1959	25.00
Albums			
DOT			
❑ DLP-3370 [M]	Young Love	1961	20.00
❑ DLP-25370 [S]	Young Love	1961	20.00
WARNER BROS.			
❑ W 1221 [M]	Tab Hunter	1958	20.00
❑ WS 1221 [S]	Tab Hunter	1958	25.00
❑ W 1292 [M]	When I Fall in Love	1959	20.00
❑ WS 1292 [S]	When I Fall in Love	1959	25.00
❑ W 1367 [M]	R.F.D. Tab Hunter	1960	20.00
❑ WS 1367 [S]	R.F.D. Tab Hunter	1960	25.00

HUNTER, TOMMY

Number	Title (A Side/B Side)	Yr	NM
45s			
COLUMBIA			
❑ 4-44104	In a Way/Cup of Disgrace	1967	8.00
❑ 4-44234	Mary in the Morning/The Battle of the Little Big Horn	1967	8.00
❑ 4-44367	Half a World Away/Charlie's Side	1967	7.00
❑ 4-44541	Are You Sad/Tyin' Me Down	1968	7.00
❑ 4-44684	I Couldn't Find a Space/Nowhere Bound with Greyhound	1968	7.00

HUNTER, TY

Number	Title (A Side/B Side)	Yr	NM
45s			
ANNA			
❑ 1114	Everything About You/Orphan Boy	1960	25.00
❑ 1123	Every Time/I'm Free	1960	30.00
CHECK MATE			
❑ 1002	Memories/The Envy of Every Man	1961	25.00
❑ 1015	Gladness to Sadness/Lonely Baby	1961	25.00
CHESS			
❑ 1857	Darling, My Babe/In Time	1963	20.00
❑ 1881	Am I Losing You/Love Walked Right Out on Me	1964	15.00
❑ 1893	Bad Loser/Something Like a Storm	1964	15.00
INVICTUS			
❑ 9120	Hey There Lonely Girl/I Don't See Me in Your Eyes Anymore	1972	15.00

HUNTER MUSKETT

Number	Title (A Side/B Side)	Yr	NM
Albums			
BRADLEY			
❑ 1003	Hunter Muskett	1973	80.00

HURRICANES, THE

Number	Title (A Side/B Side)	Yr	NM
45s			
KING			
❑ 4817	Poor Little Dancin' Girl/Pistol Packin' Mama	1955	200.00
❑ 4867	Maybe It's All for the Best/Yours	1956	200.00
❑ 4898	Raining in My Heart/Tell Me Baby	1956	200.00
❑ 4926	Little Girl of Mine/Your Promise to Me	1956	150.00
❑ 4947	Dear Mother/You May Not Know	1956	120.00
❑ 5018	Fallen Angel/I'll Always Be in Love with You	1957	100.00
❑ 5042	Priceless/Now That I Need You	1957	100.00

HURT, MISSISSIPPI JOHN

Number	Title (A Side/B Side)	Yr	NM
Albums			
BIOGRAPH			
❑ C-4 [M]	1928: His First Recordings	1972	20.00
PIEDMONT			
❑ PLP-13157 [M]	Folk Songs and Blues	1963	80.00
❑ PLP-13181 [M]	Worried Blues	1964	80.00
VANGUARD			
❑ VSD-19/20 [(2)]	The Best of Missisippi John Hurt	197?	25.00
❑ VRS-9145 [M]	Blues at Newport	1965	25.00
❑ VRS-9220 [M]	Mississippi John Hurt/Today	1966	25.00
❑ VRS-9248 [M]	The Immortal Mississippi John Hurt	1967	25.00
❑ VSD-79145 [S]	Blues at Newport	1965	30.00
❑ VSD-79220 [S]	Mississippi John Hurt/Today	1966	30.00
❑ VSD-79248 [S]	The Immortal Mississippi John Hurt	1967	30.00
❑ VSD-79327	The Last Session	1972	20.00

HURVITZ, SANDY

Number	Title (A Side/B Side)	Yr	NM
Albums			
VERVE			
❑ V6-5064	Sandy's Album Is Here at Last	1968	30.00
	—Produced by FRANK ZAPPA		

HUSKER DU

Also see BOB MOULD; SUGAR. Also see BOB MOULD; SUGAR.

Number	Title (A Side/B Side)	Yr	NM
12-Inch Singles			
WARNER BROS.			
❑ PRO-A-2524 [DJ]	Sorry Somehow (same on both sides)	1986	8.00
❑ PRO-A-2654 [DJ]	Could You Be the One (same on both sides)	1987	7.00
45s			
NEW ALLIANCE			
❑ 010	In a Free Land/What Do I Want/M.I.C.	1982	70.00
❑ 010 [PS]	In a Free Land/What Do I Want/M.I.C.	1982	50.00
REFLEX			
❑ A	Statues/Amusement (Live)	1980	40.00
❑ A [PS]	Statues/Amusement (Live)	1980	60.00
SST			
❑ 025	Eight Miles High/Masochism World (Live)	1984	2.00
❑ 025	Eight Miles High/Masochism World (Live)	199?	3.00
	—Reissue on purple vinyl		
❑ 025	Eight Miles High/Masochism World (Live)	199?	4.00
	—Reissue on blue vinyl		
❑ 025 [PS]	Eight Miles High/Masochism World (Live)	1984	2.00
❑ PSST 031 [DJ]	Celebrated Summer/New Day Rising	1984	15.00
❑ PSST 031 [PS]	Celebrated Summer/New Day Rising	1984	15.00
	—Rubber-stamped sleeve with sticker and enclosed press release		
❑ 051	Makes No Sense at All/Love Is All Around	1985	2.00
❑ 051	Makes No Sense at All/Love Is All Around	199?	3.00
	—Reissue on white vinyl		
❑ 051 [PS]	Makes No Sense at All/Love Is All Around	1985	2.00
Albums			
NEW ALLIANCE			
❑ 007	Land Speed Record	1982	12.00
	—Second pressing, "Marketed by SST" on cover		
❑ 007	Land Speed Record	1982	25.00
	—No reference to SST on cover		
REFLEX			
❑ #D	Everything Falls Apart	1982	40.00
SST			
❑ 020 [EP]	Metal Circus	1983	12.00
❑ 027 [(2)]	Zen Arcade	1984	15.00
❑ PSST E-27 [DJ]	Eight Miles High/6 from Zen Arcade	1984	30.00
	—Promo sampler, etched design on side 1, sticker cover		
❑ 031	New Day Rising	1985	15.00
❑ 055	Flip Your Wig	1985	15.00
❑ 195	Land Speed Record	198?	12.00
	—Reissue of New Alliance 007		
❑ 908 [10]	Metal Circus	199?	8.00
❑ 915 [10]	Eight Miles High/Makes No Sense at All	199?	10.00
WARNER BROS.			
❑ PRO2719 [DJ]	Warehouse: Songs and Stories	1987	8.00
	—Promo-only four-song sampler		
❑ WBMS-145 [DJ]	The Warehouse Interview	1987	25.00
	—Promo only, part of the Warner Bros. Music Show series		
❑ PRO-A-2719 [DJ]	Warehouse: Songs and Stories	1987	15.00
	—Promo-only four-song sampler		
❑ 25385	Candy Apple Grey	1986	12.00
❑ 25544 [(2)]	Warehouse: Songs and Stories	1987	15.00

HUSTLER

Number	Title (A Side/B Side)	Yr	NM
Albums			
A&M			
❑ SP 4504	High Street	1974	15.00
❑ SP 4556	Play Loud	1975	15.00

HUTCH, WILLIE

Number	Title (A Side/B Side)	Yr	NM
45s			
DUNHILL			
❑ 4012	The Duck/Love Runs Out	1965	1500.
MAVERICK			
❑ 1003	Use What You Got (Part 1)/Use What You Got (Part 2)	1968	20.00
MODERN			
❑ 1021	I Can't Get Enough/Your Love Has Made Me a Man	1966	75.00
MOTOWN			
❑ 1222	Brother's Gonna Work It Out/I Choose You	1973	15.00
❑ 1252	Slick/Mother's Theme	1973	5.00
❑ 1252 [PS]	Slick/Mother's Theme	1973	6.00
❑ 1282	Sunshine Lady/I Just Wanted to Make Her Happy	1973	5.00
❑ 1287	If You Ain't Got No Money (You Can't Get No Honey) Pt. 1/Pt. 2	1974	5.00
❑ 1292	Theme of Foxy Brown/Give Me Some of That Good Old Love	1974	5.00
❑ 1331	I'm Gonna Stay/Woman You Touched Me	1975	5.00
❑ 1339	Get Ready for the Get Down/Don't Let Nobody Tell You How to Do Your Thing	1975	5.00
❑ 1360	Love Power/Talk to Me	1975	15.00
❑ 1371	Party Down/Just Another Day	1976	15.00
❑ 1406	Let Me Be the One, Baby/She's Just Doing Her Thing	1976	4.00
❑ 1411	Shake It, Shake It/I Feel Like We Can Make It	1976	4.00
❑ 1416	We Gonna Have a House Party/Never Had It So Good	1977	4.00
❑ 1424	We Gonna Party Tonight/Precious Pearl	1977	4.00
❑ 1433	What You Gonna Do After the Party/I Feel Like We Can Make It	1977	4.00
❑ 1637	In and Out/Girl	1982	4.00
❑ 1797	Keep On Jammin'/The Glow	1985	4.00
RCA VICTOR			
❑ 74-0189	Ain't Gonna Stop/Do What You Wanna Do	1969	30.00
❑ 74-0294	When a Boy Falls in Love (Part 1)/When a Boy Falls in Love (Part 2)	1969	60.00
❑ 74-0327	Magic of Love/Walking on My Love	1970	30.00
WHITFIELD			
❑ 8615	All American Funkathon/And All Hell Broke Loose	1978	4.00
❑ 8689	Paradise/Hip Shakin' Sexy Lady	1978	4.00
❑ 49015	Deep in Your Love/Everybody Needs Money	1979	20.00
❑ 49102	Down Here on Disco Street/Kelly Green	1979	4.00
Albums			
MOTOWN			
❑ M 766	The Mack	1973	12.00
❑ M 784	Fully Exposed	1973	12.00
❑ M6-811	Foxy Brown	1974	12.00
❑ M6-815	Mark of the Beast	1974	12.00
❑ M6-838	Ode to My Lady	1975	12.00
❑ M6-854	Concert in Blues	1976	12.00
❑ M6-871	Color Her...	1977	12.00
❑ M6-874	Havin' a House Party	1977	12.00
❑ 5281 ML	The Mack	1983	8.00
	—Reissue of 766		
RCA VICTOR			
❑ LSP-4213	Soul Portrait: Willie Hutch	1969	15.00
WHITFIELD			
❑ BSK 3226	In Tune	1978	10.00
❑ BSK 3352	Midnight Dancer	1979	10.00

HUTTO, J.B.

Number	Title (A Side/B Side)	Yr	NM
45s			
CHANCE			
❑ 1155	Now She's Gone/Combination Boogie	1954	1000.

Number	Title (A Side/B Side)	Yr	NM
1160	Lovin' You/Pet Cream Man	1954	4000.
—The above two may be listed on the label as "J.B. and the Hawks"			
1165	Dim Lights/Things Are So Slow	1955	3000.

HUTTON, DANNY

Also see THREE DOG NIGHT.

Number	Title (A Side/B Side)	Yr	NM
45s			
ALMO			
213	Why Don't You Love Me Anymore/Home in Pasadena	1964	20.00
—As "Daring Dan Hutton"			
HANNA-BARBERA			
447	Roses and Rainbows/Monster Shindig	1965	15.00
447 [PS]	Roses and Rainbows/Monster Shindig	1965	30.00
453	Big Bright Eyes/Monester Shindig (Part 2)	1965	15.00
MGM			
13502	Funny How Love Can Be/Dreamin' Isn't Good for You	1966	10.00
13502 [PS]	Funny How Love Can Be/Dreamin' Isn't Good for You	1966	20.00
13613	Hang On to a Dream/Hit the Wall	1966	10.00
Albums			
MGM			
SE-4664	Pre-Dog Night	1970	20.00

HYLAND, BRIAN

Number	Title (A Side/B Side)	Yr	NM
45s			
ABC-PARAMOUNT			
10236	Let Me Belong to You/Let It Die	1961	10.00
10262	I'll Never Stop Wanting You/The Night I Cried	1961	10.00
10262 [PS]	I'll Never Stop Wanting You/The Night I Cried	1961	20.00
10294	Ginny Come Lately/I Should Be Gettin' Better	1962	10.00
10294 [PS]	Ginny Come Lately/I Should Be Gettin' Better	1962	20.00
10336	Sealed with a Kiss/Summer Job	1962	12.00
10336 [PS]	Sealed with a Kiss/Summer Job	1962	20.00
10359	Warmed Over Kisses (Left Over Love)/Walk a Lonely Mile	1962	10.00
10359 [PS]	Warmed Over Kisses (Left Over Love)/Walk a Lonely Mile	1962	20.00
10374	I May Not Live to See Tomorrow/It Ain't That Way at All	1962	10.00
10374 [PS]	I May Not Live to See Tomorrow/It Ain't That Way at All	1962	20.00
10400	If Mary's There/Remember Me	1963	10.00
10400 [PS]	If Mary's There/Remember Me	1963	20.00
10427	Somewhere in the Night/I Wish Today Was Yesterday	1963	10.00
10452	I'm Afraid to Go Home/Save Your Heart for Me	1963	10.00
10494	Nothing Matters But You/Let Us Make Our Own Mistakes	1963	10.00
10549	Act Naturally/Out of Sight, Out of Mind	1964	10.00
DOT			
17050	Apologize/Words on Paper	1967	6.00
17061	It's Christmas Time Once Again/Words on Paper	1967	12.00
17078	Come with Me/Delilah	1968	6.00
17109	The Lover/Springfield, Illinois	1968	6.00
17176	Tragedy/You'd Better Stop and Think It Over	1968	6.00
17222	A Million to One/It Could All Begin Again	1969	6.00
17258	Early April Morning/Stay and Love Me All Summer	1969	6.00
17291	Dreamy Eyes/Gonna Make a Woman Out of You	1970	6.00
KAPP			
342	Itsy Bitsy Teeny Weeny Yellow Polka Dot Bikini/Don't Dilly Dally, Sally	1960	15.00
342 [PS]	Itsy Bitsy Teeny Weeny Yellow Polka Dot Bikini/Don't Dilly Dally, Sally	1960	30.00
352	Four Little Heels (The Clickety Clack Song)/That's How Much	1960	12.00
352 [PS]	Four Little Heels (The Clickety Clack Song)/That's How Much	1960	25.00
363	I Gotta Go/Lopsided, Over Loaded	1960	12.00
363 [PS]	I Gotta Go/Lopsided, Over Loaded	1960	25.00
401	Lipstick on Your Lips/When Will I Know	1961	12.00
LEADER			
801	Library Love Affair/Rosemary	1960	20.00
805	Itsy Bitsy Teeny Weeny Yellow Polka Dot Bikini/Don't Dilly Dally, Sally	1960	30.00
PHILIPS			
40179	Here's to Our Love/Two Kinds of Girls	1964	8.00
40179 [PS]	Here's to Our Love/Two Kinds of Girls	1964	12.00
40203	Devoted to You/Pledging My Love	1964	8.00
40203 [PS]	Devoted to You/Pledging My Love	1964	12.00
40221	Now I Belong to You/One Step Forward, Two Steps Back	1964	8.00
40263	He Don't Understand You/Love Will Find a Way	1965	8.00
40263 [PS]	He Don't Understand You/Love Will Find a Way	1965	12.00
40306	Stay Away from Her/I Can't Keep a Secret	1965	8.00
40354	3000 Miles/Sometimes They Do, Sometimes They Don't	1966	8.00
40377	The Joker Went Wild/I Can Hear the Rain	1966	15.00
40405	Why Did You Do It/Run, Run, Look and See	1966	8.00
40424	Hung Up in Your Eyes/Why Mine	1967	8.00
40424 [PS]	Hung Up in Your Eyes/Why Mine	1967	12.00
40444	Holiday for Clowns/Yesterday I Had a Girl	1967	8.00
40472	Get the Message/Kinda Groovy	1967	6.00
UNI			
55193	You and Me/Could You Dig It	1970	6.00
55240	Gypsy Woman/You and Me (#2)	1970	15.00
55272	Lonely Teardrops/Lorraine	1971	15.00
55287	So Long, Marianne/No Place to Run	1971	5.00
55306	Out of the Blue/If You Came Back	1971	5.00
55323	I Love Every Little Thing About You/With My Eyes Wide Open	1972	5.00
55334	Only Wanna Make You Happy/When You're Lovin' Me	1972	5.00
Albums			
ABC-PARAMOUNT			
400 [M]	Let Me Belong to You	1961	30.00
S-400 [S]	Let Me Belong to You	1961	40.00
431 [M]	Sealed with a Kiss	1962	30.00
S-431 [S]	Sealed with a Kiss	1962	40.00
463 [M]	Country Meets Folk	1964	30.00
S-463 [S]	Country Meets Folk	1964	40.00
DOT			
DLP 25926	Tragedy/A Million to One	1969	15.00
DLP 25954	Stay and Love Me All Summer	1969	15.00
KAPP			
KL 1202 [M]	The Bashful Blonde	1960	50.00
KS 3202 [S]	The Bashful Blonde	1960	80.00
PHILIPS			
PHM 200136 [M]	Here's to Our Love	1964	20.00
PHM 200158 [M]	Rockin' Folk	1965	20.00
PHM 200217 [M]	Run, Run, Look and See/The Joker Went Wild	1966	20.00
—With "200-217" in trail-off; this record plays mono			
PHM 200217 [S]	Run, Run, Look and See/The Joker Went Wild	1966	20.00
—With "2/600-217" in trail-off; this record plays stereo, though labeled mono			
PHS 600136 [S]	Here's to Our Love	1964	25.00
PHS 600158 [S]	Rockin' Folk	1965	25.00
PHS 600217 [S]	Run, Run, Look and See/The Joker Went Wild	1966	25.00
PICKWICK			
SPC-3261	Young Years	197?	10.00
PRIVATE STOCK			
PS-7003	In a State of Bayou	1977	12.00
RHINO			
RNLP-70226	Greatest Hits	1987	10.00
UNI			
73097	Brian Hyland	1970	15.00
—The album is listed as "stereo," but "Gypsy Woman" is rechanneled			
WING			
MGW-12341 [M]	Here's to Our Love	1967	12.00
SRW-16341 [S]	Here's to Our Love	1967	12.00

HYMAN, DICK

Number	Title (A Side/B Side)	Yr	NM
45s			
COLUMBIA			
3-10003	Grandpa's Spells/The Pearls	1974	6.00
COMMAND			
4015	Boogie Woogie/Mack the Knife	196?	8.00
4018	Love for Sale/Down Home Melody	196?	8.00
4036	Side by Side/Satin Doll	196?	8.00
4066	Alabama Song/Kurt Weill's Melody	1965	8.00
4077	The Man from O.R.G.A.N./Mister Kiss Kiss Bang Bang	196?	8.00
4078	Agent Double-O-Soul/The Liquidator	196?	8.00
4088	England Swings/Take Oh Take Those Lips Away	196?	8.00
4100	Samba de Duas Notas/Sugarloaf	196?	8.00
4114	In the Heat of the Night/Respect	1968	7.00
4119	Since You've Been Gone/Watch It	1968	7.00
4126	The Minotaur/Topless Dancers of Corfu	1969	7.00
4126 [DJ]	The Minotaur (Short Version 3:15)/(Full Length Version 7:30)	1969	10.00
4129	Green Onions/Aquarius	1969	8.00
4132	Dick Hyman Piano Concerto Excerpts from Movement I/Dick Hyman Piano Concerto Excerpts from Movement II	1970	7.00
4136	Lay Lady Lay/Strobo	1970	8.00
EVEREST			
19356	Glow-Worm/Symphony	1960	10.00
MGM			
K11743	Unforgettable/Out of Nowhere	1954	12.00
K11811	Cecilia/East of the Sun (And West of the Moon)	1954	12.00
K11889	Jealous/I've Got My Love to Keep Me Warm	1954	12.00
K11916	Panama/Stardust	1955	12.00
K11951	Besame Mucho (Kiss Me Much)/The Old Professor	1955	12.00
K12005	The Very Thought of You/When Day Is Done	1955	12.00
K12076	Sleep/Pleasure	1955	12.00
K12125	Honky Tonk Train/Rockin' the Boogie	1955	12.00
K12149	Moritat — A Theme from "The Three Penny Opera"/Baubles, Bangles and Beads	1955	12.00
—With the entire A-side title in large bold print			
K12149	Moritat — A Theme from "The Three Penny Opera"/Baubles, Bangles and Beads	1955	15.00
—With "Moritat" in larger letters than the rest of the title			
K12207	Hi-Lili, Hi-Lo/Junglero	1956	12.00
K12258	When You're Smiling/Rollin' the Boogie	1956	12.00
K12296	One Finger Piano/The Blue Whistler	1956	12.00
K12325	Chlo-E/Blues in My Heart	1956	12.00
—With Sam "The Man" Taylor			
K12343	Blue Danube Bounce/Yancey Special	1956	12.00
K12404	I'll Get By/Congo Mambo	1957	10.00
—With Sam "The Man" Taylor			
K12415	Threepenny Tango/The Red Cat	1957	12.00
K12441	Drummer Boy Blues/Look Up	1957	10.00
—With Sam "The Man" Taylor			
K12476	Tokyo Alley/Sweet Georgia Brown	1957	12.00
K12516	The Redhead/Band of Angels	1957	12.00
K12568	Walk with Me/The Peanut Vendor	1957	10.00
—With Sam "The Man" Taylor			
K12600	Good Times/Mandolins of Venice	1957	12.00
K12646	My Goodness/Ya Ya	1958	12.00
—With the Pepper Sisters			
K12698	Chichy-Cha/Not So Cold in Alaska	1958	10.00
K12730	John and Mary Sittin' in a Tree/Gimme a Little Kiss, Will Ya, Huh?	1958	10.00
K12772	Look Up/Show Me the Way to Go Home	1959	10.00
PROJECT 3			
1403	A Letter from My Brother in Brazil/Losing My Mind	197?	7.00
RCA VICTOR			
47-8125	Tell the Story/Liy Aduma	1963	10.00
7-Inch Extended Plays			
MGM			
X1168	Pleasure/The Way You Look Tonight//(Lookie Lookie Lookie) Here Comes Cookie/Marv	1955	10.00
X1168 [PS]	The Dick Hyman Trio Swings	1955	10.00
Albums			
ATLANTIC			
SD 1671	Satchmo Remembered	1975	10.00
CHIAROSCURO			
198	Themes and Variations on "A Child Is Born"	1978	10.00
COLUMBIA MASTERWORKS			
M 32587	Ferdinand "Jelly Roll" Morton — Transcriptions for Orchestra	1974	12.00

Except when noted otherwise, VG = 25% of NM, and VG+ = 50% of NM. (Example: VG = $2.00, VG+ = $4.00 and NM = $8.00.)

Number	Title (A Side/B Side)	Yr	NM
COMMAND			
❑ RS 811 SD [S]	Provocative Piano	1960	20.00
❑ RS 33-811 [M]	Provocative Piano	1960	15.00
❑ RS 824 SD [S]	Provocative Piano Vol. 2	1961	20.00
❑ RS 33-824 [M]	Provocative Piano Vol. 2	1961	15.00
❑ RS 832 SD [S]	The Dick Hyman Trio	1961	20.00
❑ RS 33-832 [M]	The Dick Hyman Trio	1961	15.00
❑ RS 856 SD [S]	Electrodynamics	1963	20.00
❑ RS 33-856 [M]	Electrodynamics	1963	15.00
❑ RS 862 SD [S]	Fabulous	1963	20.00
❑ RS 33-862 [M]	Fabulous	1963	15.00
❑ RS 875 SD [S]	Keyboard Kaleidoscope	1964	20.00
❑ RS 33-875 [M]	Keyboard Kaleidoscope	1964	15.00
❑ RS 891 SD [S]	The Man from O.R.G.A.N.	1965	50.00
❑ RS 33-891 [M]	The Man from O.R.G.A.N.	1965	40.00
❑ RS 899 SD [S]	Happening!	1966	20.00
❑ RS 33-899 [M]	Happening!	1966	15.00
❑ RS 911 SD [S]	Brazilian Impressions	1966	20.00
❑ RS 33-911 [M]	Brazilian Impressions	1966	15.00
❑ RS 924 SD	Mirrors	1967	20.00
❑ RS 933 SD	Sweet Sweet Soul	1968	25.00
❑ RS 938 SD	Moog — The Electric Eclectics of Dick Hyman	1968	30.00
❑ RS 946 SD	The Age of Electronicus	1969	40.00
❑ RS 951 SD	Concerto Electro	1970	30.00
❑ RSSD 968/2 [(2)]	The Synthesizer	1973	40.00
—Reissue of "Electric Eclectics" and "Age of Electronicus"			
❑ RSSD 973/2 [(2)]	The Kaleidoscopic Keyboard	1974	20.00
❑ RSSD 980/2 [(2)]	Organ Antics	1974	20.00
GRAPEVINE			
❑ 3309	Waltz Dressed in Blue	1978	12.00
LION			
❑ L-70067 [M]	Swingin' Double Date	1958	15.00
MGM			
❑ E-289 [10]	The "Unforgettable" Sound of the Dick Hyman Trio	1955	40.00
❑ E-3280 [M]	The Dick Hyman Trio Swings	1954	25.00
—Yellow label			
❑ E-3329 [M]	The "Unforgettable" Sound of the Dick Hyman Trio	1955	25.00
—Yellow label			
❑ E-3379 [M]	Behind a Shady Nook	1956	25.00
—Yellow label			
❑ E-3483 [M]	Red Sails in the Sunset	1957	25.00
—Yellow label			
❑ E-3494 [M]	Hi-Fi Suite	1957	25.00
—Yellow label			
❑ E-3535 [M]	60 Great All-Time Songs, Vol. 1	1957	20.00
—Yellow label			
❑ E-3536 [M]	60 Great All-Time Songs, Vol. 2	1957	20.00
—Yellow label			
❑ E-3537 [M]	60 Great All-Time Songs, Vol. 3	1957	20.00
—Yellow label			
❑ E-3553 [M]	Rockin' Sax and Rollin' Organ	1958	25.00
—Yellow label			
❑ E-3586 [M]	60 Great All-Time Songs, Vol. 4	1958	20.00
—Yellow label			
❑ E-3587 [M]	60 Great All-Time Songs, Vol. 5	1958	20.00
—Yellow label			
❑ E-3588 [M]	60 Great All-Time Songs, Vol. 6	1958	20.00
—Yellow label			
❑ E-3606 [M]	Dick Hyman and Harpsichord in Hi-Fi	1958	20.00
—Yellow label			
❑ E-3642 [M]	Gigi	1958	20.00
—Yellow label			
❑ E-3724 [M]	60 Great Songs That Say "I Love You"	1959	20.00
—Yellow label			
❑ E-3725 [M]	60 Great Songs from Broadway Musicals	1959	20.00
—Yellow label			
❑ E-3726 [M]	60 Great Continental and Classical Favorites	1959	20.00
❑ E-3747 [M]	Whoop-Up!	1959	20.00
—Yellow label			
❑ SE-3747 [S]	Whoop-Up!	1959	30.00
❑ E-3808 [M]	Strictly Organic	1960	20.00
❑ SE-3808 [S]	Strictly Organic	1960	30.00
❑ E-3821 [M]	After Six	1960	20.00
❑ SE-3821 [S]	After Six	1960	25.00
❑ E-4119 [M]	Moon Gas	1963	20.00
❑ SE-4119 [S]	Moon Gas	1963	30.00
❑ SE-4649	Space Reflex	1969	15.00
MONMOUTH-EVERGREEN			
❑ MES 7065	Genius at Play	1974	15.00
MUSICAL HERITAGE SOCIETY			
❑ MHS 912213K	Face the Music: Irving Berlin	198?	10.00
PROJECT 3			
❑ PR 5054 SD	The Sensuous Piano of "D"	1970	15.00
❑ PR 5057 SD	Fantomfingers	1971	25.00
❑ PR 5070 SD	Piano Solos	1972	15.00
❑ PR 5080 SD	Traditional Jazz Piano	1973	15.00

Janis Ian, "At Seventeen," Columbia 3-10154, 1975, **$8.**

Number	Title (A Side/B Side)	Yr	NM
RCA VICTOR GOLD SEAL			
❑ AGL1-3651	Scott Joplin: 16 Classic Rags	1980	8.00
—Reissue			
RCA VICTOR RED SEAL			
❑ ARL1-1257	Scott Joplin: 16 Classic Rags	1976	10.00
❑ XRL1-4746	Kitten on the Keys: Music of Zez Confrey	1983	10.00
REFERENCE RECORDINGS			
❑ RR-33	Dick Hyman Plays Fats Waller	1991	25.00
SEAGULL			
❑ LG-8209	Love Story	198?	10.00
STOMP OFF			
❑ SOS-1141	Gulf Coast Blues: The Music of Clarence Williams	1987	10.00
SUNSET			
❑ SUM-1140 [M]	I'll Never Be the Same	1966	12.00
❑ SUS-5140 [S]	I'll Never Be the Same	1966	15.00

I

Number	Title (A Side/B Side)	Yr	NM
I KADEZ			
45s			
HIT			
❑ 95	Louie Louie/Popsicles and Icicles	1963	8.00
—B-side by the Scotties			
I.V. LEAGUERS, THE			
45s			
DOT			
❑ 15677	Ring Chimes/The Story	1957	20.00
NAU-VOO			
❑ 803	Told by the Stars/Jim Jam	1959	400.00
PORTER			
❑ 1004	Ring Chimes/The Story	1957	50.00

Number	Title (A Side/B Side)	Yr	NM
IAN, JANIS			
45s			
CAPITOL			
❑ 3107	He's a Rainbow/Here in Spain	1971	8.00
CASABLANCA			
❑ 2245	Night Rains/Fly Too High	1980	5.00
COLUMBIA			
❑ 02176	Sugar Mountain/Under the Covers	1981	4.00
❑ 02546	Restless Eyes/I Remember Yesterday	1981	4.00
❑ 10119	When the Party's Over/Bright Lights and Promises	1975	5.00
❑ 10154	At Seventeen/Stars	1975	5.00
❑ 10154 [PS]	At Seventeen/Stars	1975	8.00
❑ 10228	In the Winter/Thankyouse	1975	5.00
❑ 10297	Aftertones/Boy, I Really Tied One On	1976	5.00
❑ 10331	I Would Like to Dance/Goodbye to Morning	1976	5.00
❑ 10391	Roses/Love Is Blind	1976	5.00
❑ 10484	Miracle Row/Take It to the Sky	1977	5.00
❑ 10526	Candlelight/I Want to Make You Love Me	1977	5.00
❑ 10813	That Grand Illusion/Hopper Paining	1978	5.00
❑ 10864	The Bridge/Do You Wanna Dance	1978	5.00
❑ 10979	Here Comes the Night/Tonight Will Last Forever	1979	4.00
❑ 11111	Night Rains/Fly Too High	1979	4.00
❑ 11327	The Other Side of the Sun/Memories	1980	4.00
❑ 46034	Jesse/The Man You Are in Me	1974	5.00
POLYDOR			
❑ 14299	Society's Child (Baby I've Been Thinking)/I'll Give You a Stone If You Throw It	1975	6.00

Number	Title (A Side/B Side)	Yr	NM
VERVE			
5027	Society's Child (Baby I've Been Thinking)/Letter to Jon	1967	10.00
VERVE FOLKWAYS			
5027	Society's Child (Baby I've Been Thinking)/Letter to Jon	1966	12.00
VERVE FORECAST			
5027	Society's Child (Baby I've Been Thinking)/Letter to Jon	1967	8.00
5041	I'll Give You a Stone If You'll Throw It/Younger Generation Blues	1967	8.00
5072	Insanity Comes Quietly to the Structured Mind/Snowflakes Fall, Snowrays Call	1967	8.00
5079	Song for All the Seasons of Your Mind/Lonely One	1968	8.00
5090	Lady of the Night/Friends Again	1968	8.00
5099	Everybody Knows/Janey's Blues	1968	8.00
5113	Month of May/Calling Your Name	1969	8.00
Albums			
ANALOGUE PRODUCTIONS			
AAP 027	Breaking Silence	1995	25.00
—Audiophile vinyl			
CAPITOL			
SKAO-683	Present Company	1971	15.00
SN-683	Present Company	1975	10.00
COLUMBIA			
KC 32857	Stars	1974	10.00
PC 32857	Stars	197?	8.00
PC 33394	Between the Lines	1975	10.00
—No bar code on cover			
PC 33394	Between the Lines	1979	8.00
—With bar code on cover			
PCQ 33394 [Q]	Between the Lines	1975	15.00
PC 33919	Aftertones	1976	10.00
—No bar code on cover			
PC 33919	Aftertones	1979	8.00
—With bar code on cover			
PCQ 33919 [Q]	Aftertones	1976	15.00
JC 34440	Miracle Row	1977	10.00
JC 35325	Janis Ian	1978	10.00
JC 36139	Night Rains	1979	10.00
PC 36139	Night Rains	198?	8.00
FC 37360	Restless Eyes	1981	10.00
MGM			
GAS-121	Janis Ian (Golden Archive Series)	1970	25.00
POLYDOR			
PD-6058	Janis Ian	1976	10.00
VERVE			
V/VS-5027	Janis Ian	1967	—
—Scheduled, possibly not released; same LP is Verve Forecast 3017			
VERVE FOLKWAYS			
FT-3017 [M]	Janis Ian	1967	20.00
FTS-3017 [S]	Janis Ian	1967	20.00
VERVE FORECAST			
FT-3017 [M]	Janis Ian	1967	20.00
FTS-3017 [S]	Janis Ian	1967	15.00
FT-3024 [M]	For All the Seasons of Your Mind	1967	20.00
FTS-3024 [S]	For All the Seasons of Your Mind	1967	15.00
FTS-3048	The Secret Life of J. Eddy Fink	1968	15.00
FTS-3063	Who Really Cares?	1969	15.00

IAN AND SYLVIA

Number	Title (A Side/B Side)	Yr	NM
45s			
COLUMBIA			
45430	Creatures of Rain/Summer Wages	1971	6.00
45475	More Often Than Not/Some Kind of Fool	1971	6.00
45680	You Were On My Mind/Salmon in the Sea	1972	6.00
MGM			
13686	Lovin' Sound/Pilgrimage to Paradise	1967	8.00
14082	Give It to the World/Shinbone Alley	1969	8.00
VANGUARD			
35021	Four Strong Winds/C.C. Rider	1963	10.00
35025	You Were On My Mind/Someday Soon	1964	10.00
35035	Play One More/The French Girl	1964	10.00
35062	House of Cards/90" By 90"	1968	8.00
Albums			
AMPEX			
A-10103	Great Speckled Bird	1970	20.00
COLUMBIA			
C 30736	Ian and Sylvia	1971	12.00
KC 31337	You Were On My Mind	1972	12.00
G 32516 [(2)]	The Best of Ian and Sylvia	1973	15.00
MGM			
GAS-115	Ian and Sylvia (Golden Archive Series)	1970	15.00
E-4388 [M]	Lovin' Sound	1967	20.00
SE-4388 [S]	Lovin' Sound	1967	15.00
E-4550 [M]	Full Circle	1968	40.00
—Mono is yellow label promo only; cover has "DJ Monaural" sticker on front			
SE-4550 [S]	Full Circle	1968	20.00
VANGUARD			
VSD-5/6 [(2)]	Ian and Sylvia's Greatest Hits	1969	15.00
VSD-23/24 [(2)]	Ian and Sylvia's Greatest Hits, Vol. 2	1970	15.00
VSD-2113 [S]	Ian and Sylvia	1963	30.00
VSD-2149 [S]	Four Strong Winds	1963	25.00
VRS-9109 [M]	Ian and Sylvia	1963	25.00
VRS-9133 [M]	Four Strong Winds	1963	20.00
VRS-9154 [M]	Northern Journey	1964	20.00
VRS-9175 [M]	Early Morning Rain	1965	20.00
VRS-9215 [M]	Play One More	1966	20.00
VRS-9241 [M]	So Much for Dreaming	1967	20.00
VSD-73114	Greatest Hits	1985	10.00
VSD-79154 [S]	Northern Journey	1964	25.00
VSD-79175 [S]	Early Morning Rain	1965	25.00
VSD-79215 [S]	Play One More	1966	25.00
VSD-79241 [S]	So Much for Dreaming	1967	25.00
VSD-79269	The Best of Ian & Sylvia	1968	15.00
VSD-79284	Nashville	1968	15.00

IAN AND THE ZODIACS

Number	Title (A Side/B Side)	Yr	NM
45s			
PHILIPS			
40244	The Cryin' Game/Livin' Lovin' Wreck	1964	10.00
40277	Good Morning Little Schoolgirl/Message to Martha	1965	10.00
40291	So Much in Love with You/This Empty Place	1965	10.00
40291 [PS]	So Much in Love with You/This Empty Place	1965	25.00
40343	Why Can't It Be Me/Leave It to Me	1965	10.00
40369	No Money, No Honey/Where Were You	1966	10.00
7-Inch Extended Plays			
PHILIPS			
PHS-807-C	Good Morning, Little Schoolgirl/The Crying Game/Jump Back//So Much in Love with You/Clarabella/Baby, I Need Your Loving	1965	40.00
—Jukebox issue; small hole, plays at 33 1/3 rpm			
PHS-807-C [PS]	Ian and the Zodiacs	1965	40.00
Albums			
PHILIPS			
PHM 200176 [M]	Ian and the Zodiacs	1965	40.00
PHS 600176 [S]	Ian and the Zodiacs	1965	50.00

ICE-T

Number	Title (A Side/B Side)	Yr	NM
12-Inch Singles			
ATOMIC POP			
APPRO-5003	Exodus (Clean Version Featuring Top Gunz) (Instrumental) (A Cappella - Clean)/Always Wanted Ta Be a Ho (Clean Featuring Ice's Ho) (Instrumental)/Fuck It (LP Version Featuring Elsadiq and Powerlord Jel) (Instrumental)	1999	20.00
ELECTROBEAT			
EB 002	Killers (Vocal Mix 4:30) (Instrumental Dub 4:37)/Body Rock (Vocal Mix 6:04) (Bonus Beats 2:55)	198?	30.00
GIANT			
PRO-A-4643 [DJ]	New Jack Hustler (3 versions)	1991	12.00
21845	New Jack Hustler (4 versions)	1991	10.00
RHINO			
393	Ice-A Mix (7:00)/Ice-O-Tek (5:00)	1993	8.00
RHYME SYNDICATE			
7023	That's How I'm Livin' (4 versions)/99 Problems (2 versions)	1993	6.00
SPRO-30046 [DJ]	I Must Stand (Clean) (Instrumental)/Where It Goes Down (Clean)/Where the Shit Goes Down (LP Version)	1996	10.00
SPRO-50897 [DJ]	Where It Goes Down (Radio)/Where the Shit Goes Down (LP Version)//Pimp Anthem	1996	12.00
53210	I Must Stand (2 versions)/Where the Shit Goes Down (2 versions)	1996	10.00
53821	Gotta Lotta Love (3 versions)	199?	7.00
—Reissue of Sire 40737			
SIRE			
PRO-A-3686 [DJ]	Lethal Weapon (Radio Version) (same on both sides?)	1989	8.00
PRO-A-5143 [DJ]	Mind Over Matter (4 versions)/Ricochet (3 versions)	1991	8.00
PRO-A-5367 [DJ]	Mind Over Matter (4 versions)	1991	8.00
20711	Make It Funky (3 versions)/Sex (2 versions)	1987	10.00
20805	Somebody Gotta Do It (Pimpin' Ain't Easy) (12" Mix) (Dub)/Our Most Requested Record (Short Version) (Long Version)	1987	15.00
20936	Colors (5 versions)/Squeeze the Trigger	1993	8.00
21026	I'm Your Pusher (3 versions)/Girls L.G.B.N.A.F. (3 versions)	1988	8.00
21149	High Rollers/The Hunted Child (3 versions)/Power (Remix) (Instrumental)	1989	8.00
21325	Lethal Weapon (2 versions)/This One's for Me/Heartbeat	1989	8.00
21426	You Played Yourself (3 versions)/Freedom of Speech	1990	10.00
21445	What Ya Wanna Do (Edit) (LP Version) (Instrumental)/The Girl Tried to Kill Me (Radio Remix)	1990	10.00
21704	Dick Tracy (4 versions)	1990	8.00
40104	Original Gangster (3 versions)/Bitches 2 (2 versions)	1991	8.00
40131	Lifestyles of the Rich and Infamous (3 versions)/The Tower (2 versions)	1991	6.00
40210	Ricochet (2 versions)/Mind Over Matter (Remix)	1991	10.00
40737	Gotta Lotta Love (3 versions)	1992	10.00
TECHNOHOP			
10	Ya Don't Quit (3 versions)	1986	12.00
13	Dog'n the Wax (3 versions)/6 in the Morning	1986	15.00
45s			
SIRE			
PRO-S-2751 [DJ]	Make It Funky (same on both sides)	1987	6.00
19994	You Played Yourself/Freedom of Speech	1990	6.00
22810	Lethal Weapon/Heartbeat	1989	4.00
27574	High Rollers/The Hunted Child	1989	4.00
27768	I'm Your Pusher/Girls L.G.B.N.A.F.	1988	4.00
27768 [PS]	I'm Your Pusher/Girls L.G.B.N.A.F.	1988	4.00
27902	Colors/Squeeze the Trigger	1988	5.00
27902 [PS]	Colors/Squeeze the Trigger	1988	5.00
28126	Somebody Gotta Do It/Our Most Requested Record	1988	5.00
Albums			
ATOMIC POP			
AP 0011 [(2)]	Greatest Hits: The Evidence	2000	20.00
RHYME SYNDICATE			
53858	Home Invasion	1993	20.00
SIRE			
PRO-A-4959 [(2)DJ]	O.G. Original Gangster	1991	25.00
—Promo-only radio-ready version of album otherwise unavailable on U.S. vinyl			
25602	Rhyme Pays	1987	15.00
25765	Power	1988	15.00
26028	The Iceberg/Freedom of Speech...Just Watch What You Say	1989	15.00

ID, THE

Number	Title (A Side/B Side)	Yr	NM
45s			
RCA VICTOR			
47-9136	Short Circuit/Boil the Kettle, Mother	1967	12.00
47-9195	Wild Times/The Take	1967	12.00
Albums			
AURA			
1000	Where Are We Going?	1976	50.00
RCA VICTOR			
LPM-3805 [M]	The Inner Sounds of the Id	1967	40.00
LSP-3805 [S]	The Inner Sounds of the Id	1967	40.00

IDEALS, THE (1)

Chicago-based group that, at one time, featured MAJOR LANCE. He is not on the Satellite singles, however.

45s

PASO

Number	Title (A Side/B Side)	Yr	NM
❑ 6401	Together/What's the Matter with You Sam	1961	50.00
❑ 6402	Magic/Teens	1961	50.00

SATELLITE

Number	Title (A Side/B Side)	Yr	NM
❑ 2007	You Lost and I Won/You Hurt Me	1965	30.00
❑ 2009	Kissing/I Had a Dream	1966	50.00
❑ 2011	Go Go Gorilla/Kissing Won't Go Out of Style	1966	200.00

IDEALS, THE (2)

45s

CHECKER

Number	Title (A Side/B Side)	Yr	NM
❑ 920	Knee Socks/Mary's Lamb	1959	25.00
❑ 979	Knee Socks/Mary's Lamb	1961	15.00
—As "Johnny Brantley and the Ideals"			

IDEALS, THE (U)

Some of these could be groups (1) or (2), but others are likely other groups.

45s

COOL

Number	Title (A Side/B Side)	Yr	NM
❑ 108	Do I Have the Right/ You Won't Like It	1958	300.00

CORTLAND

Number	Title (A Side/B Side)	Yr	NM
❑ 110	Don Juan/Gorilla	1963	60.00
❑ 113	Mo Joe Hanna/Simple Simon	1964	15.00
❑ 115	Feeling of a Kiss/You Came a Long Way from St. Louis	1964	40.00
❑ 117	Local Boy/L.A.	1964	15.00

DECCA

Number	Title (A Side/B Side)	Yr	NM
❑ 30720	Annie Has a Stroller/My Girl	1959	40.00
❑ 30800	Ivy League Lover/Don't Be a Baby, Baby	1959	25.00

FARGO

Number	Title (A Side/B Side)	Yr	NM
❑ 1024	The Duchess/Trans Zizstor	1962	20.00

ST. LAWRENCE

Number	Title (A Side/B Side)	Yr	NM
❑ 1001	Cathy's Clown/Go Get a Wig	1965	12.00
❑ 1020	I Got Lucky (When I Found You)/Tell Her I Apologize	1966	30.00

STARS OF HOLLYWOOD

Number	Title (A Side/B Side)	Yr	NM
❑ 1001	Please, Jan/Always Yours	1959	40.00

IDENTITIES, THE

45s

HOUSE OF THE FOX

Number	Title (A Side/B Side)	Yr	NM
❑ HOF-6	Hey Brother/When Love Slips Away	1971	40.00

TOGETHERNESS

Number	Title (A Side/B Side)	Yr	NM
❑ 300	When You Find Love Slipping Away/(B-side unknown)	1971	40.00

IDES OF MARCH, THE

45s

KAPP

Number	Title (A Side/B Side)	Yr	NM
❑ 992	Nobody Loves Me/ Strawberry Sunday	1969	10.00

PARROT

Number	Title (A Side/B Side)	Yr	NM
❑ 304	I'll Keep Searching/ You Wouldn't Listen	1966	10.00
❑ 310	Roller Coaster/Things Aren't Always What They Seem	1966	10.00
❑ 312	You Need Love/Sha-La-La-La-Lee	1966	10.00
❑ 321	My Foolish Pride/Give Your Mind Wings	1967	10.00
❑ 326	Hole in My Soul/Girls Don't Grow on Trees	1967	10.00

RCA VICTOR

Number	Title (A Side/B Side)	Yr	NM
❑ 74-0850	Mother America/Ladyland	1972	5.00
❑ APBO-0052	Hot Water/Heavy on the Country	1973	5.00

SUNDAZED

Number	Title (A Side/B Side)	Yr	NM
❑ 142	I'm Gonna Say My Prayers/ The Sun Ain't Gonna Shine Anymore	1999	2.00
❑ 142 [PS]	I'm Gonna Say My Prayers/ The Sun Ain't Gonna Shine Anymore	1999	2.00

WARNER BROS.

Number	Title (A Side/B Side)	Yr	NM
❑ 7140	Vehicle/L.A. Goodbye	1972	4.00
—"Back to Back Hits" series — originals have green labels			
❑ 7334	High on a Hillside/One Woman Man	1969	6.00
❑ 7378	Vehicle/Lead Me Home, Gently	1970	8.00
❑ 7403	Superman/Home	1970	6.00
❑ 7426	Melody/The Sky Is Falling	1970	6.00
❑ 7466	L.A. Goodbye/Mrs. Grayson's Farm	1971	6.00
❑ 7507	Tie-Dye Princess/Friends of Feeling	1971	6.00
❑ 7526	Giddy-Up, Ride Me/ Freedom Sweet	1971	6.00

Albums

RCA VICTOR

Number	Title	Yr	NM
❑ APL1-0143	Midnight Oil	1973	15.00
❑ LSP-4812	World Woven	1972	15.00

SUNDAZED

Number	Title	Yr	NM
❑ LP-5032	Ideology	199?	12.00

WARNER BROS.

Number	Title	Yr	NM
❑ WS 1863	Vehicle	1970	15.00
—Green "WB" label			
❑ WS 1863	Vehicle	1970	20.00
—Green "W7" label			
❑ WS 1896	Common Bond	1971	15.00

IDLE RACE, THE

Jeff Lynne, later of THE MOVE and ELECTRIC LIGHT ORCHESTRA, was in this group.

45s

LIBERTY

Number	Title (A Side/B Side)	Yr	NM
❑ 55997	Here We Go 'Round the Lemon Tree/My Father's Son	1967	80.00
—Stock copy on black label			
❑ 55997 [DJ]	Here We Go 'Round the Lemon Tree/My Father's Son	1967	25.00
—"Audition Copy" on cream label			
❑ 56064	The End of the Road/ The Morning Sunshine	1968	—
—May not exist			

Albums

LIBERTY

Number	Title	Yr	NM
❑ LST-7603	Birthday Party	1969	50.00

IDOL, BILLY

12-Inch Singles

CHRYSALIS

Number	Title (A Side/B Side)	Yr	NM
❑ CHS-27PDJ [DJ]	Dancing with Myself/ Happy People	1981	25.00
❑ CHS-38PDJ [DJ]	Mony Mony (5:00) (same on both sides)	1981	25.00
❑ CHS-43PDJ [DJ]	Hot in the City (5:08)/ White Wedding Part 2	1982	15.00
❑ AS 1699 [DJ]	White Wedding (Live 6:59) (Live with Intro 7:40)	1983	15.00
❑ AS 1761 [DJ]	Rebel Yell (same on both sides)	1983	15.00
❑ AS 1831 [DJ]	Blue Highway (same on both sides)	1983	6.00
❑ AS 1856 [DJ]	Eyes Without a Face (LP Version) (Single Version)	1984	10.00
❑ AS 1894 [DJ]	Flesh for Fantasy (Below the Belt Mix) (Regular Mix)	1984	12.00
❑ AS 1901 [DJ]	Flesh for Fantasy (Below the Belt Mix) (Standard Mix)	1984	10.00
❑ AS 1956 [DJ]	Catch My Fall (Special Radio Remix) (same on both sides)	1984	15.00
❑ VAS 2449 [DJ]	To Be a Lover (same on both sides)	1986	12.00
❑ VAS 2587 [DJ]	Don't Need a Gun (same on both sides)	1986	8.00
❑ VAS 2672 [DJ]	Sweet Sixteen (same on both sides)	1987	12.00
❑ VAS 2865 [DJ]	Hot in the City (Edit) (Exterminator Mix)	1988	8.00
❑ EPC 5002	White Wedding Part 2 (4:27)/ White Wedding Part 1 & 2 (8:20)	1982	15.00
—White vinyl			
❑ SPRO-24826 [DJ]	Heroin (V.R. Heroin 6:17) (Original Mix 6:59) (Needle Park Mix 5:12)/(Overlords Mix 7:20) (Nosebleed Mix 8:04)	1994	25.00
—White vinyl; contains only one of the two records and has the "SPRO" prefix			
❑ VV-24826 [(2)]	Heroin (V.R. Heroin 6:17) (Original Mix 6:59) (Needle Park Mix 5:12)/(Overlords Mix 7:20) (Nosebleed Mix 8:04)// (Durga Trance Dub 5:10) (Durga Death Dub 5:10)/(Don't Touch That Needle Mix 5:10) (Smack Attak 7:15)	1994	15.00
—White vinyl			
❑ 4V9 42685	White Wedding Part 2 (4:27)/ White Wedding Part 1 & 2 (8:20)	1983	10.00
—Reissue of white vinyl version			
❑ 8V8 42791	Eyes Without a Face/ Blue Highway/Do Not Stand in the Shadows	1982	15.00
—Picture disc in plastic sleeve			
❑ 4V9 42810	Flesh for Fantasy (Below the Belt Mix) (LP Version)	1984	10.00
❑ 4V9 43025	To Be a Lover (Mother of Mercy Mix 6:45) (Original Version 4:07)/All Summer Single (4:33)	1986	10.00
❑ 4V9 43090	Don't Need a Gun (Melt Down Mix 7:05) (Acappella 3:02)/ Fatal Charm	1986	10.00
❑ 4V9 43159	Mony Mony (Hung Like a Pony Remix 6:59) (Steel Toe Dub 6:50) (Live Mix 4:00) (Single Mix 5:01)	1987	12.00

45s

CHRYSALIS

Number	Title (A Side/B Side)	Yr	NM
❑ 2488	Dancing with Myself/ Happy People	1981	15.00
—Label credit: "Billy Idol and Gen X"			
❑ 2543	Mony Mony/Baby Talk	1981	12.00
❑ 2605	Hot in the City/Hole in the Wall	1982	5.00
❑ 2605 [PS]	Hot in the City/Hole in the Wall	1982	5.00
❑ 2648	White Wedding/Dead on Arrival	1982	5.00
❑ S7-17403	Shock to the System/Heroin	1993	4.00
❑ S7-17516	Wasteland/Neuromancer	1993	4.00
❑ S7-19027	Dancing with Myself/ Catch My Fall	1996	3.00
—Reissue			
❑ B-23509	Cradle of Love/311 Man	1990	5.00
❑ B-23509 [PS]	Cradle of Love/311 Man	1990	5.00
❑ NR-23571	L.A. Woman/License to Thrill	1990	6.00
❑ VS4 42697	White Wedding/Dead on Arrival	1983	4.00
❑ VS4 42723	Dancing with Myself/Love Calling (Rub a Dub Dub Mix)	1983	5.00
—Label credit: "Billy Idol and Gen X"			
❑ VS4 42723 [PS]	Dancing with Myself/Love Calling (Rub a Dub Dub Mix)	1983	5.00
❑ VS4 42762	Rebel Yell/Crank Call	1983	3.00
❑ VS4 42762 [PS]	Rebel Yell/Crank Call	1983	3.00
❑ VS4 42786	Eyes Without a Face/ Blue Highway	1984	3.00
❑ VS4 42786 [PS]	Eyes Without a Face/ Blue Highway	1984	3.00
❑ VS4 42809	Flesh for Fantasy/ The Dead Next Door	1984	3.00
❑ VS4 42809 [PS]	Flesh for Fantasy/ The Dead Next Door	1984	3.00
❑ VS4 42840	Catch My Fall/Daytime Drama	1984	5.00
❑ VS8 42953	Hot in the City/Mony Mony	1985	3.00
—Silver label reissue			
❑ VS8 42954	White Wedding/Dancing with Myself	1985	3.00
—Silver-label reissue			
❑ VS8 42955	Rebel Yell/Blue Highway	1985	3.00
—Silver label reissue			
❑ VS8 42956	Eyes Without a Face/ Flesh for Fantasy	1985	3.00
—Silver label reissue			
❑ VS4 43024	To Be a Lover/All Summer Single	1986	3.00
❑ VS4 43024 [PS]	To Be a Lover/All Summer Single	1986	3.00
❑ VS4 43087	Don't Need a Gun/Fatal Charm	1986	3.00
❑ VS4 43087 [PS]	Don't Need a Gun/Fatal Charm	1986	3.00
❑ VS4 43114	Sweet Sixteen/Beyond Belief	1987	3.00
❑ VS4 43114 [PS]	Sweet Sixteen/Beyond Belief	1987	3.00
❑ VS4 43161	Mony Mony "Live"/Shakin' All Over "Live"	1987	4.00
❑ VS4 43161 [PS]	Mony Mony "Live"/Shakin' All Over "Live"	1987	4.00
—Non-LP tracks (both sides!)			
❑ VS4 43203	Hot in the City/Catch My Fall (Remix Fix)	1988	3.00
❑ VS4 43203 [PS]	Hot in the City/Catch My Fall (Remix Fix)	1988	3.00
❑ 58984	Eyes Without a Face/Rebel Yell	2001	4.00
—Reissue			
❑ 58985	Mony Mony (Live)/Hot in the City	2001	4.00
—Reissue			

Albums

CHRYSALIS

Number	Title	Yr	NM
❑ CHR 1377	Billy Idol	1982	12.00
❑ VAS 2610 [DJ]	Billy Idol Interview	1983	25.00
❑ CEP 4000 [EP]	Don't Stop	1981	12.00
❑ F1-21735	Charmed Life	1990	12.00
❑ FV 41377	Billy Idol	1983	10.00
—Reissue of Chrysalis CHR 1377			
❑ FV 41450	Rebel Yell	1983	10.00
❑ OV 41514	Whiplash Smile	1986	10.00
❑ OV 41620	Vital Idol	1987	10.00
❑ 5V 44000 [EP]	Don't Stop	1983	8.00
—Reissue of CEP 4000			
❑ PV 44000 [EP]	Don't Stop	198?	6.00
—Reissue with new prefix			
❑ R 104806	Billy Idol	1982	12.00
—RCA Music Service edition			
❑ R 124674	Rebel Yell	1984	12.00
—RCA Music Service edition			
❑ R 153899 [EP]	Don't Stop	1981	12.00
—RCA Music Service edition			
❑ R 154038	Vital Idol	1987	12.00
—BMG Direct Marketing edition			

The Illusion, *Together (As a Way of Life)*, Steed ST 37005, 1969, **$15.**

Number	Title (A Side/B Side)	Yr	NM
❑ R 154108	Whiplash Smile	1986	12.00
—RCA Music Service edition			
❑ R 162264	Charmed Life	1990	14.00
—BMG Direct Marketing edition			

IDOLS, THE Probably more than one group.

45s

DOT

Number	Title (A Side/B Side)	Yr	NM
❑ 16210	Just a Little Bit More/ Why Must I Cry	1961	15.00
—B-side by the Swans			

E-Z

Number	Title (A Side/B Side)	Yr	NM
❑ 1	Jeannine/Can't Tag Along	1961	40.00

RCA VICTOR

Number	Title (A Side/B Side)	Yr	NM
❑ 47-7339	30 Days/The Prowler	1958	20.00
❑ 47-7417	Here in My Heart/The Counterfeiter	1958	20.00

REVEILLE

Number	Title (A Side/B Side)	Yr	NM
❑ 1002	Just a Little Bit More/ Why Must I Cry	1961	30.00
—B-side by the Swans			

IF

45s

CAPITOL

Number	Title (A Side/B Side)	Yr	NM
❑ 2909	The Promised Land/I'm Reaching Out on All Sides	1970	8.00
❑ 2990	Raise the Level of Your Conscious Mind/What Did I Say About the Box, Jack	1970	8.00
❑ 3068	Your City Is Falling/Woman Can't You See	1971	8.00
❑ 3932	I Believe in Rock and Roll/ Still Alive	1974	6.00

METROMEDIA

Number	Title (A Side/B Side)	Yr	NM
❑ 258	Waterfall/(B-side unknown)	1972	6.00

Albums

CAPITOL

Number	Title (A Side/B Side)	Yr	NM
❑ ST-539	If	1970	15.00
❑ SW-676	If2	1971	15.00
❑ SMAS-820	If3	1971	15.00
❑ ST-11299	Not Just Another Bunch of Pretty Faces	1974	12.00
❑ ST-11344	Tea Break Over — Back On Your 'Eads!	1974	12.00

METROMEDIA

Number	Title (A Side/B Side)	Yr	NM
❑ BML1-0174	Double Diamond	1973	12.00
❑ KMD-1057	Waterfall	1972	12.00

IGGY AND THE STOOGES

12-Inch Singles

BOMP!

Number	Title (A Side/B Side)	Yr	NM
❑ 12139	I Got a Right/Gimme Some Skin	1991	5.00

45s

BOMP!

Number	Title (A Side/B Side)	Yr	NM
❑ 139	I Got a Right/Gimme Some Skin	1991	5.00
❑ 139 [PS]	I Got a Right/Gimme Some Skin	1991	8.00

COLUMBIA

Number	Title (A Side/B Side)	Yr	NM
❑ 45877	Search and Destroy/Penetration	1973	15.00

ELEKTRA

Number	Title (A Side/B Side)	Yr	NM
❑ 45664	I Wanna Be Your Dog (Part 1)/ I Wanna Be Your Dog (Part 2)	1970	30.00
—As "The Stooges"			
❑ 45695	Down on the Street/I Feel Alright	1970	30.00
—As "The Stooges"			

SIAMESE

Number	Title (A Side/B Side)	Yr	NM
❑ 001	I Got a Right/Gimme Some Skin	1977	10.00
—Second pressing: "Siamese" in fake Asian lettering with iguana logo			
❑ 001	I Got a Right/Gimme Some Skin	1977	25.00
❑ 001 [PS]	I Got a Right/Gimme Some Skin	1977	8.00
—Only issued with Bomp!-distributed copies; has "Iggy & & The Stooges" on cover			

7-Inch Extended Plays

BOMP!

Number	Title (A Side/B Side)	Yr	NM
❑ 114	Jesus Loves the Stooges	1977	7.50
❑ 114 [PS]	Jesus Loves the Stooges	1977	7.50

Albums

BOMP!

Number	Title (A Side/B Side)	Yr	NM
❑ 1018	Kill City	1978	15.00
—By "Iggy Pop and James Williamson"			

COLUMBIA

Number	Title (A Side/B Side)	Yr	NM
❑ KC 32111	Raw Power	1973	50.00

ELEKTRA

Number	Title (A Side/B Side)	Yr	NM
❑ EKS 74051	The Stooges	1969	60.00
—By "The Stooges"; red label with large stylized "E" (butterfly label, deduct 60%)			
❑ EKS 74101	Fun House	1970	60.00
—By "The Stooges"; red label with large stylized "E" (butterfly label, deduct 60%)			

IMPORT/BOMP!

Number	Title (A Side/B Side)	Yr	NM
❑ 1015	Metallic K.O.	1977	18.00
❑ 1018	Kill City	1978	20.00
—By "Iggy Pop and James Williamson"; original issue on green vinyl			

SUNDAZED

Number	Title (A Side/B Side)	Yr	NM
❑ LP 5149	The Stooges	2002	15.00
—By "The Stooges"; reissue on 180-gram vinyl			
❑ LP 5150	Fun House	2002	15.00
—By "The Stooges"; reissue on 180-gram vinyl			

IKETTES, THE Also see THE MIRETTES.

45s

ATCO

Number	Title (A Side/B Side)	Yr	NM
❑ 6212	I'm Blue (The Gong-Gong Song)/Find My Baby	1961	20.00
❑ 6223	Troubles on My Mind/ Come On and Truck	1962	15.00
❑ 6232	Zizzy Zee Zum Zum/ Heavenly Love	1962	15.00
❑ 6243	I Do Love You/I Had a Dream the Other Night	1962	15.00

MODERN

Number	Title (A Side/B Side)	Yr	NM
❑ 1005	Peaches 'N' Cream/ The Biggest Players	1965	10.00
❑ 1008	(He's Gonna Be) Fine, Fine, Fine/How Come	1965	10.00
❑ 1011	I'm So Thankful/Don't Feel Sorry for Me	1965	8.00
❑ 1015	Sally Go Round the Roses/ Lonely for You	1965	8.00
❑ 1024	Da Doo Ron Ron/Not That I Recall	1966	8.00

PHI-DAN

Number	Title (A Side/B Side)	Yr	NM
❑ 5009	Down Down/What'cha Gonna Do	1966	10.00

POMPEII

Number	Title (A Side/B Side)	Yr	NM
❑ 66683	Beauty Is Just Skin Deep/ Make Them Wait	1968	6.00

TEENA

Number	Title (A Side/B Side)	Yr	NM
❑ 1702	Prisoner in Love/Those Words	1963	20.00

UNITED ARTISTS

Number	Title (A Side/B Side)	Yr	NM
❑ 50866	If You Take a Close Look/ Got What It Takes	1971	5.00
❑ 51103	I'm Just Not Ready for Love/ Two Timin' Double Dealin'	1973	5.00

Albums

MODERN

Number	Title (A Side/B Side)	Yr	NM
❑ M-102 [M]	Soul Hits	1965	30.00
❑ MST-102 [S]	Soul Hits	1965	40.00

UNITED ARTISTS

Number	Title (A Side/B Side)	Yr	NM
❑ UA-LA190-F	(G)Old and New	1973	12.00

ILL WIND, THE

45s

ABC

Number	Title (A Side/B Side)	Yr	NM
❑ 11107	In My Dark World/ Walkin' and Singin'	1968	25.00

Albums

ABC

Number	Title (A Side/B Side)	Yr	NM
❑ S-641	Flashes	1968	100.00

ILL WINDS, THE Later incarnation of CHANTAY'S.

45s

REPRISE

Number	Title (A Side/B Side)	Yr	NM
❑ 0423	So Be On Your Way (I Won't Cry)/ Fear of the Rain	1965	15.00
❑ 0492	I Idolize You/A Letter	1966	15.00

ILLINOIS SPEED PRESS, THE

45s

COLUMBIA

Number	Title (A Side/B Side)	Yr	NM
❑ 44564	Get In the Wind (Part 1)/ Get In the Wind (Part 2)	1968	10.00
❑ 45166	Country Dumplin'/Sadly Out of Place	1970	10.00

Albums

COLUMBIA

Number	Title (A Side/B Side)	Yr	NM
❑ CS 9792	The Illinois Speed Press	1969	15.00

Except when noted otherwise, VG = 25% of NM, and VG+ = 50% of NM. (Example: VG = $2.00, VG+ = $4.00 and NM = $8.00.)

Number	Title (A Side/B Side)	Yr	NM
❑ CS 9976	Duet	1970	15.00

ILLUSION, THE

Number	Title (A Side/B Side)	Yr	NM
45s			
DYNO VOICE			
❑ 914	It's Groovy Time/My Party	1968	10.00
STEED			
❑ 712	Did You See Her Eyes/ Falling in Love	1969	10.00
❑ 717	Run Run Run/I Love You Yes I Do	1969	8.00
❑ 718	Did You See Her Eyes/ Falling in Love	1969	6.00
❑ 721	How Does It Feel/Once in a Lifetime	1969	6.00
❑ 722	Together/Don't Push It	1969	6.00
❑ 726	Let's Make Each Other Happy/ Beside You	1970	6.00
❑ 732	Collection/Wait a Minute	1970	6.00
Albums			
STEED			
❑ ST-37003	The Illusion	1969	20.00
❑ ST-37005	Together (As a Way of Life)	1969	15.00
❑ ST-37006	If It's So	1970	15.00

ILLUSIONS, THE

More than one group.

Number	Title (A Side/B Side)	Yr	NM
45s			
COLUMBIA			
❑ 43700	I Know/Take My Heart	1966	10.00
CORAL			
❑ 62173	The Letter/Henry and Henrietta	1960	40.00
DIAL			
❑ 4004	I Don't Believe It/The World Outside	1965	10.00
DOT			
❑ 16752	Secrets of Love/Don't Put Me Down	1965	20.00
EMBER			
❑ 1071	How High Is the Mountain/ Can't We Fall in Love	1961	40.00
KAPE			
❑ 1001	The Closer You Are/ For Sentimental Reasons	196?	10.00
LAURIE			
❑ 3245	Maybe/In the Beginning	1964	20.00
LITTLE DEBBIE			
❑ 105	Story of My Life/Walking Boy	1964	600.00
MALI			
❑ 104	Hey Boy/Lonely Soldier	1962	50.00
NORTHEAST			
❑ 801	Hey Boy/Lonely Soldier	1962	15.00
RELIC			
❑ 512	Hey Boy/Lonely Soldier	1964	10.00
ROUND			
❑ 1018	Jezebel/Nightmare	1963	80.00
SHERATON			
❑ 104	Hey Boy/Lonely Soldier	1962	25.00

ILLUSTRATION

Number	Title (A Side/B Side)	Yr	NM
Albums			
JANUS			
❑ JLP-3010	Illustration	1969	20.00

ILMO SMOKEHOUSE

Number	Title (A Side/B Side)	Yr	NM
Albums			
BEAUTIFUL SOUND			
❑ 3002	Ilmo Smokehouse	1971	40.00
ROULETTE			
❑ RS-3002	Ilmo Smokehouse	1971	20.00

IMAGINATIONS, THE (1)

Number	Title (A Side/B Side)	Yr	NM
45s			
BALLAD			
❑ 500	Wait a Little Longer Son/ Mama's Little Baby	1962	200.00
BO MARC			
❑ 301	Guardian Angel/Hey You	1961	40.00
DUEL			
❑ 507	Guardian Angel/Hey You	1961	20.00
MUSIC MAKERS			
❑ 103	Goodnight Baby/ The Search Is Over	1961	50.00
❑ 108	Guardian Angel/Hey You	1961	50.00
Albums			
RELIC			
❑ LP-5058	The Imaginations (1961-1962)	198?	10.00

IMAGINATIONS, THE (2)

Another concoction of STEVE BARRI and P.F. SLOAN.

Number	Title (A Side/B Side)	Yr	NM
45s			
DUNHILL			
❑ 4092	I Love You When You're Mad/ Summer in New York	1967	20.00

IMAGINATIONS, THE (3)

Number	Title (A Side/B Side)	Yr	NM
45s			
FRATERNITY			
❑ 1001	I Just Can't Get Over Losing You/Strange Neighborhood	1967	600.00
❑ 1006	No One Ever Lost More/ Strange Voice	1968	25.00

IMPACS, THE

Number	Title (A Side/B Side)	Yr	NM
45s			
KING			
❑ 5851	Jo-Ann/Two Strangers	1964	10.00
❑ 5863	Shimmy, Shimmy/Zot	1964	10.00
❑ 5891	She Didn't Even Say Hello/Kool It	1964	10.00
❑ 5910	Ain't That the Way Life Is/ Don't Cry Baby	1964	10.00
❑ 5965	Your Mama Put the Hurt on Me/ Cape Kennedy, Florida	1964	10.00
PARKWAY			
❑ 865	I'm Gonna Make You Cry/ Tears in My Heart	1963	12.00
Albums			
KING			
❑ 886 [M]	Impact!	1964	200.00
❑ KS-886 [S]	Impact!	1964	300.00
❑ 916 [M]	A Weekend with the Impacs	1964	200.00
❑ KS-916 [S]	A Weekend with the Impacs	1964	300.00

IMPACTS, THE

Several different groups.

Number	Title (A Side/B Side)	Yr	NM
45s			
ANDERSON			
❑ 104	Summer/Linda	1964	50.00
CARLTON			
❑ 548	Darling, Now You're Mine/ Help Me Somebody	1961	30.00
❑ 548	Darling, No You're Mine/ Help Me Somebody	1961	50.00
—With incorrect A-side title			
DCP			
❑ 1147	Wishing Well/Heartaches	1965	50.00
—As "Kenny and the Impacts"			
❑ 1150	Just Because/Pigtails	1965	100.00
KIP			
❑ 1890	Burnt Valves/Chrome Reverse	1963	50.00
RCA VICTOR			
❑ 47-7583	Bobby Sox Squaw/Croc-O-Doll	1959	20.00
❑ 47-7609	Canadian Sunset/They Say	1959	50.00
WATTS			
❑ 5599	Now Is the Time/Soup	1959	80.00
Albums			
DEL-FI			
❑ DFLP-1234 [M]	Wipe Out	1963	60.00
❑ DFS-1234 [S]	Wipe Out	1963	80.00
❑ DLF-1234	Wipe Out	199?	12.00
—Reissue with bar code			

IMPALA SYNDROME, THE

Number	Title (A Side/B Side)	Yr	NM
Albums			
PARALLAX			
❑ 4002	The Impala Syndrome	1970	100.00

IMPALAS, THE

Number	Title (A Side/B Side)	Yr	NM
45s			
BUNKY			
❑ 7760	Whay Should He Do/ I Still Love You	1969	15.00
❑ 7762	Whip it On Me/I Still Love You	1969	20.00
CAPITOL			
❑ 2709	Speed Up/Soul	1969	75.00
CHECKER			
❑ 999	For the Love of Mike/ I Need You So Much	1961	12.00
CUB			
❑ 9022	Sorry (I Ran All the Way Home)/ Fool, Fool, Fool	1959	20.00
❑ 9022	I Ran All the Way Home/ Fool, Fool, Fool	1959	60.00
—Original A-side title			
❑ 9033	Oh What a Fool/ Sandy Went Away	1959	20.00
❑ 9053	Peggy Darling/Bye Everybody	1959	20.00
❑ 9066	All Alone/When My Heart Does All the Talking	1960	20.00
—As "Speedo and the Impalas"			
HAMILTON			
❑ 50026	I Was a Fool/First Date	1960	20.00
RED BOY			
❑ 113	When You Dance/I Can't See Me Without You	1966	25.00
RITE-ON			
❑ 101	I Can't See Me Without You/ Old Man Mose	196?	20.00
STEADY			
❑ 044	When You Dance/I Can't See Me Without You	1967	20.00
SUNDOWN			
❑ 115	The Lonely One/Lost Boogie	1959	15.00
20TH FOX			
❑ 428	Last Night I Saw a Girl/There Is Nothin' Like a Dame	1963	12.00
7-Inch Extended Plays			
CUB			
❑ 5000	(contents unknown)	1959	400.00
❑ 5000 [PS]	Sorry (I Ran All the Way Home)	1959	400.00
Albums			
CUB			
❑ 8003 [M]	Sorry (I Ran All the Way Home)	1959	400.00
❑ S-8003 [S]	Sorry (I Ran All the Way Home)	1959	600.00

IMPERIALITES, THE

Number	Title (A Side/B Side)	Yr	NM
45s			
IMPERIAL			
❑ 66015	Have Love, Will Travel/ Let's Get One	1964	20.00

IMPERIALS, THE (1)

See LITTLE ANTHONY AND THE IMPERIALS.

IMPERIALS, THE (2)

Number	Title (A Side/B Side)	Yr	NM
45s			
BUZZY			
❑ 1	My Darling/You Should Have Told Me	1962	20.00
—Red vinyl			
SAVOY			
❑ 1104	My Darling/You Should Have Told Me	1954	200.00

IMPERIALS, THE (3)

Number	Title (A Side/B Side)	Yr	NM
45s			
NEWTIME			
❑ 503	A Short Prayer/Where Will You Be	1962	15.00
❑ 505	The Letter/Go and Get Your Heart Broken	1962	150.00

IMPERIALS, THE (4)

Number	Title (A Side/B Side)	Yr	NM
45s			
OMNI			
❑ 5501	Who's Gonna Love Me/ You Better Take Time to Love	1978	5.00

IMPERIALS, THE (U)

We're not sure which group these are.

Number	Title (A Side/B Side)	Yr	NM
45s			
CAPITOL			
❑ 4921	I'm Still Dancing/ Bermuda Wonderful	1963	40.00
CARLTON			
❑ 566	Faithfully Yours/Vut Vut	1961	20.00

IMPERIALS MINUS TWO, THE

Number	Title (A Side/B Side)	Yr	NM
45s			
IMPERIAL			
❑ 5787	A Swingin' Dream/ In Any Language	1961	20.00

IMPOSSIBLES, THE

More than one group.

Number	Title (A Side/B Side)	Yr	NM
45s			
BLANCHE			
❑ 029	Chapel Bells/Little by Little	1960	400.00
REPRISE			
❑ 0305	Lonely Bluebird/Paint Me a Pretty Picture	1964	25.00
RMP			
❑ 501	Everywhere I Go/ Well, It's Alright	1966	25.00
❑ 1030	Mr. Maestro/Well, It's Alright	1964	25.00
ROULETTE			
❑ 4745	I Wanna Know/It's All Right	1967	100.00

IMPRESSIONS, THE

Also see JERRY BUTLER; CURTIS MAYFIELD.

45s

ABC

Number	Title (A Side/B Side)	Yr	NM
❑ 10831	Can't Satisfy/This Must End	1966	8.00
❑ 10869	Love's a-Comin'/Wade in the Water	1966	8.00
❑ 10900	You Always Hurt Me/Little Girl	1967	8.00
❑ 10932	It's Hard to Believe/You've Got Me Runnin'	1967	8.00
❑ 10964	I Can't Stay Away from You/You Ought to Be in Heaven	1967	8.00
❑ 11022	We're a Winner/It's All Over	1967	8.00
❑ 11071	We're Rolling On (Part 1)/We're Rolling On (Part 2)	1968	8.00
❑ 11103	I Loved and I Lost/Up, Up and Away	1968	8.00
❑ 11135	Don't Cry My Love/Sometimes I Wonder	1968	8.00
❑ 11188	East of Java/Just Before Sunrise	1969	8.00

ABC-PARAMOUNT

Number	Title (A Side/B Side)	Yr	NM
❑ 10241	Gypsy Woman/As Long As You Love Me	1961	15.00
❑ 10289	Grow Closer Together/Can't You See	1962	15.00
❑ 10328	Little Young Lover/Never Let Me Go	1962	15.00
❑ 10357	You've Come Home/Minstrel and Queen	1962	15.00
❑ 10386	I'm the One Who Loves You/I Need Your Love	1962	50.00
❑ 10431	Sad, Sad Girl and Boy/Twist and Limbo	1963	15.00
❑ 10487	It's All Right/You'll Want Me Back	1963	15.00
❑ 10511	Talking About My Baby/Never Too Much Love	1963	15.00
❑ 10537	Girl You Don't Know Me/A Woman Who Loves Me	1964	15.00
❑ 10544	I'm So Proud/I Made a Mistake	1964	15.00
❑ 10554	Keep On Pushing/I Love You (Yeah)	1964	15.00
❑ 10581	You Must Believe Me/See the Real Me	1964	15.00
❑ 10602	Amen/Long, Long Winter	1964	15.00
❑ 10622	People Get Ready/I've Been Trying	1965	15.00
❑ 10647	Woman's Got Soul/Get Up and Move	1965	12.00
❑ 10670	Meeting Over Yonder/I've Found That I've Lost	1965	12.00
❑ 10710	I Need You/Never Could You Be	1965	12.00
❑ 10725	Just One Kiss from You/Twilight Time	1965	12.00
❑ 10750	You've Been Cheatin'/Man, Oh Man	1965	30.00
❑ 10761	Since I Lost the One I Love/Falling in Love with You	1966	10.00
❑ 10789	Too Slow/No One Else	1966	10.00

ABNER

Number	Title (A Side/B Side)	Yr	NM
❑ 1013	For Your Precious Love/Sweet Was the Wine	1958	40.00
—As "Jerry Butler and the Impressions"			
❑ 1017	Come Back My Love/Love Me	1958	30.00
❑ 1023	The Gift of Love/At the County Fair	1959	30.00
❑ 1025	Lonely One/Senorita I Love You	1959	30.00
❑ 1034	Say That You Love Me/A New Love	1960	30.00

BANDERA

Number	Title (A Side/B Side)	Yr	NM
❑ 2504	Listen/Shorty's Got to Go	1959	30.00

CHI-SOUND

Number	Title (A Side/B Side)	Yr	NM
❑ 2418	Sorry/All I Wanna Do Is Make Love to You	1979	5.00
❑ 2438	Maybe I'm Mistaken/All I Wanna Do Is Make Love to You	1980	5.00
❑ 2491	For Your Precious Love/You're Mine	1981	5.00
❑ 2499	Love, Love, Love/Fan the Fire	1981	5.00

COTILLION

Number	Title (A Side/B Side)	Yr	NM
❑ 44210	This Time/I'm a Fool for Love	1976	5.00
❑ 44211	Silent Night/I Saw Mommy Kissing Santa Claus	1976	6.00
❑ 44214	You'll Never Find/Stardust	1977	5.00
❑ 44222	Can't Get Along/You're So Right for Me	1977	5.00

CURTOM

Number	Title (A Side/B Side)	Yr	NM
❑ SP-3 [DJ]	Merry Christmas Happy New Year	197?	12.00
❑ 0103	Sooner or Later/Miracle Woman	1975	5.00
❑ 0106	Same Thing It Took/I'm So Glad	1975	5.00
❑ 0110	Loving Power/First Impressions	1975	5.00
❑ 0116	Sunshine/I Wish I'd Stayed in Bed	1976	5.00
❑ 1932	Fool for You/I'm Loving Nothing	1968	6.00
❑ 1932 [PS]	Fool for You/I'm Loving Nothing	1968	15.00
❑ 1934	This Is My Country/My Woman's Love	1968	6.00
❑ 1937	My Deceiving Heart/You Want Somebody Else	1969	6.00
❑ 1940	Seven Years/The Girl I Find	1969	6.00
❑ 1943	Choice of Colors/Mighty Mighty Spade and Whitey	1969	6.00
❑ 1946	Say You Love Me/You'll Be Always Mine	1969	6.00
❑ 1948	Wherever She Leadeth Me/Amen (1970)	1970	6.00
❑ 1951	Check Out Your Mind/Can't You See	1970	6.00
❑ 1954	(Baby) Turn On to Me/Soulful Love	1970	6.00
❑ 1957	Ain't Got Time/I'm So Proud	1971	6.00
❑ 1959	Love Me/Do You Wanna Win	1971	6.00
❑ 1966	Inner City Blues/We Must Be in Love	1971	6.00
❑ 1970	This Loves for Real/Times Have Changed	1972	6.00
❑ 1973	I Need to Belong to Someone/Love Me	1972	6.00
❑ 1982	Preacher Man/Times Have Changed	1973	6.00
❑ 1985	Thin Line/I'm Loving You	1973	6.00
❑ 1994	If It's In You to Do Wrong/Times Have Changed	1973	6.00
❑ 1997	Finally Got Myself Together (I'm a Changed Man)/I'll Always Be Here	1974	6.00
❑ 2003	Something's Mighty, Mighty Wrong/Three the Hard Way	1974	6.00

FALCON

Number	Title (A Side/B Side)	Yr	NM
❑ 1013	For Your Precious Love/Sweet Was the Wine	1958	60.00
—As "Jerry Butler and the Impressions"			

LOST-NITE

Number	Title (A Side/B Side)	Yr	NM
❑ 266	For Your Precious Love/Sweet Was the Wine	197?	5.00
—As "Jerry Butler and the Impressions"; reissue			

MCA

Number	Title (A Side/B Side)	Yr	NM
❑ 52995	Can't Wait 'Til Tomorrow/Love Workin' On Me	1987	10.00

PORT

Number	Title (A Side/B Side)	Yr	NM
❑ 70031	Listen/Shorty's Got to Go	1962	15.00

SWIRL

Number	Title (A Side/B Side)	Yr	NM
❑ 107	I Need Your Love/Don't Leave Me	1962	40.00

20TH FOX

Number	Title (A Side/B Side)	Yr	NM
❑ 172	All Through the Night/Meanwhile, Back in My Heart	1959	40.00

VEE JAY

Number	Title (A Side/B Side)	Yr	NM
❑ 280	For Your Precious Love/Sweet Was the Wine	1958	8000.
—As "Jerry Butler and the Impressions." VG 4000; VG+ 6000			
❑ 424	Say That You Love Me/Senorita I Love You	1962	20.00
❑ 574	The Gift of Love/At the County Fair	1963	15.00
❑ 621	Say That You Love Me/Senorita I Love You	1964	15.00

7-Inch Extended Plays

ABC-PARAMOUNT

Number	Title (A Side/B Side)	Yr	NM
❑ LP-ABCS-505	Woman's Got Soul/Emotions/We're in Love//People Get Ready/See the Real Me/You Must Believe Me	1965	30.00
—Stereo jukebox issue; small hole, plays at 33 1/3 rpm			
❑ LP-ABCS-505 [PS]	People Get Ready	1965	30.00

Albums

ABC

Number	Title (A Side/B Side)	Yr	NM
❑ 606 [M]	The Fabulous Impressions	1967	25.00
❑ S-606 [S]	The Fabulous Impressions	1967	20.00
❑ S-635	We're a Winner	1968	15.00
❑ S-654	The Best of the Impressions	1968	15.00
❑ S-668	The Versatile Impressions	1969	15.00
❑ S-727	16 Greatest Hits	1971	12.00
❑ D-780 [(2)]	Curtis Mayfield/His Early Years with the Impressions	1973	20.00
❑ ST-91540	The Best of the Impressions	1968	20.00
—Capitol Record Club edition			

ABC-PARAMOUNT

Number	Title (A Side/B Side)	Yr	NM
❑ 450 [M]	The Impressions	1963	30.00
❑ S-450 [S]	The Impressions	1963	40.00
❑ 468 [M]	The Never Ending Impressions	1964	30.00
❑ S-468 [S]	The Never Ending Impressions	1964	40.00
❑ 493 [M]	Keep On Pushing	1964	30.00
❑ S-493 [S]	Keep On Pushing	1964	40.00
❑ 505 [M]	People Get Ready	1965	30.00
❑ S-505 [S]	People Get Ready	1965	40.00
❑ 515 [M]	The Impressions' Greatest Hits	1965	20.00
❑ S-515 [S]	The Impressions' Greatest Hits	1965	25.00
❑ 523 [M]	One By One	1965	20.00
❑ S-523 [S]	One By One	1965	25.00
❑ 545 [M]	Ridin' High	1966	20.00
❑ S-545 [S]	Ridin' High	1966	25.00
❑ ST-90097 [S]	People Get Ready	1965	50.00
—Capitol Record Club edition			
❑ ST-90106 [S]	Keep On Pushing	1965	50.00
—Capitol Record Club edition			
❑ T-90472 [M]	The Impressions	1965	40.00
—Capitol Record Club edition			
❑ ST-90492 [S]	The Never Ending Impressions	1965	50.00
—Capitol Record Club edition			
❑ ST-90520 [S]	One By One	1965	30.00
—Capitol Record Club edition			
❑ T-90520 [M]	One By One	1965	25.00
—Capitol Record Club edition			

CHI-SOUND

Number	Title (A Side/B Side)	Yr	NM
❑ T-596	Come to My Party	1979	10.00
❑ T-624	Fan the Fire	1981	10.00

COTILLION

Number	Title (A Side/B Side)	Yr	NM
❑ SD 9912	It's About Time	1976	12.00

CURTOM

Number	Title (A Side/B Side)	Yr	NM
❑ CUR-2006	Lasting Impressions	198?	10.00
❑ CU 5003	First Impressions	1975	12.00
❑ CU 5009	Loving Power	1976	12.00
❑ CRS-8001	This Is My Country	1968	15.00
❑ CRS-8003	The Young Mods' Forgotten Story	1969	15.00
❑ CRS-8004	Best Impressions — Curtis, Sam, Dave	1969	15.00
❑ CRS-8006	Check Out Your Mind	1970	15.00
❑ CRS-8012	Times Have Changed	1972	15.00
❑ CRS-8016	Preacher Man	1973	15.00
❑ CRS-8019	Finally Got Myself Together	1974	15.00

LOST-NITE

Number	Title (A Side/B Side)	Yr	NM
❑ LLP-22 [10]	Jerry Butler and the Impressions	1981	15.00
—Red vinyl			

MCA

Number	Title (A Side/B Side)	Yr	NM
❑ 1500	The Impressions Greatest Hits	1982	8.00
❑ 5373	In the Heat of the Night	1982	10.00

PICKWICK

Number	Title (A Side/B Side)	Yr	NM
❑ SPC-3602	The Impressions	1978	8.00

SCEPTER CITATION

Number	Title (A Side/B Side)	Yr	NM
❑ CTN-18018	The Best of Curtis Mayfield and the Impressions	1972	10.00

SIRE

Number	Title (A Side/B Side)	Yr	NM
❑ SASH-3717 [(2)]	The Vintage Years	1977	15.00
—Includes solo hits by Jerry Butler and Curtis Mayfield			

IMUS, DON

45s

HAPPY TIGER

Number	Title (A Side/B Side)	Yr	NM
❑ 576	From Adam's Rib to Women's Lib/The Ballad of Rick Nelson	1971	8.00
—As "Imus in the Morning"			

RCA VICTOR

Number	Title (A Side/B Side)	Yr	NM
❑ 48-1031	Rev. Billy Sol Hargus/1200 Hamburgers to Go	1972	8.00
—As "Imus in the Morning"			
❑ 74-0789	Holy Land Record Package/Rent-A-Car Phone Call	1972	8.00
—As "Imus in the Morning"			
❑ 74-0982	Son of Checkers (The Watergate Case)/Oh, Billy Sol, Please Heal Us All	1973	8.00
❑ PB-10170	Everybody Needs Milk/Play That Country Juke Box	1975	8.00

Albums

BANG

Number	Title (A Side/B Side)	Yr	NM
❑ 407	This Honky's Nuts	1974	25.00

RCA VICTOR

Number	Title (A Side/B Side)	Yr	NM
❑ LSP-4699	1200 Hamburgers to Go	1972	25.00
—As "Imus in the Morning"			
❑ LSP-4819	One Sacred Chicken to Go	1973	25.00

IN CROWD, THE (1)

Also see JON AND ROBIN & THE IN CROWD.

45s

ABNAK

Number	Title (A Side/B Side)	Yr	NM
❑ 121	Inside Out/Big Cities	1967	8.00
❑ 121 [DJ]	Inside Out/Big Cities	1967	12.00
—Promo only on yellow vinyl			
❑ 129	Let's Take a Walk/Hangin' From Your Lovin' Tree	1968	8.00
❑ 129 [DJ]	Let's Take a Walk/Hangin' From Your Lovin' Tree	1968	12.00
—Promo only on yellow vinyl			

Except when noted otherwise, VG = 25% of NM, and VG+ = 50% of NM. (Example: VG = $2.00, VG+ = $4.00 and NM = $8.00.)

IN CROWD, THE (2) Includes two members of THE ELIGIBLES.

45s

VIVA

Number	Title (A Side/B Side)	Yr	NM
❑ 604	Questions and Answers/Happiness in My Heart	1966	30.00
❑ 610	If I Knew a Magic Word/Never Ending Symphony	1967	15.00

IN CROWD, THE (3) British group.

45s

TOWER

Number	Title (A Side/B Side)	Yr	NM
❑ 147	That's How Strong My Love Is/Things She Says	1965	25.00
❑ 196	Why Must They Criticize/I Don't Mind	1966	25.00

IN CROWD, THE (U) It's doubtful that any of these are group (1) or (3). Some may be group (2), though.

45s

BRENT

Number	Title (A Side/B Side)	Yr	NM
❑ 7046	Grapevine/Cat Dance	1965	40.00

HICKORY

Number	Title (A Side/B Side)	Yr	NM
❑ 1378	Speed Queen/Cry, Boy, Cry	1966	15.00
❑ 1413	In the Midnight Hour/Just Give Me Time	1966	12.00

MUSICOR

Number	Title (A Side/B Side)	Yr	NM
❑ 1111	Do the Surfer Jerk/Girl in the Black Bikini	1965	20.00

RONN

Number	Title (A Side/B Side)	Yr	NM
❑ 1	In the Midnight Hour/Nothing You Do	1967	10.00

SWAN

Number	Title (A Side/B Side)	Yr	NM
❑ 4204	Let's Shindig/Klink	1965	15.00

IN GROUP, THE

Albums

IN

Number	Title (A Side/B Side)	Yr	NM
❑ I-1002 [M]	Swinging 12 String	1964	20.00
❑ IS-1002 [S]	Swinging 12 String	1964	25.00

IN-SECT, THE

Albums

RCA CAMDEN

Number	Title (A Side/B Side)	Yr	NM
❑ CAL-909 [M]	Introducing the In-Sect Direct from England	1964	40.00
❑ CAS-909 [S]	Introducing the In-Sect Direct from England	1964	50.00

IN-BETWEENS, THE Early incarnation of SLADE.

45s

HIGHLAND

Number	Title (A Side/B Side)	Yr	NM
❑ 1173	Girl Child, I Am An Evil Witchman/Security	1966	300.00

INCREDIBLE BONGO BAND, THE

45s

MGM

Number	Title (A Side/B Side)	Yr	NM
❑ 14588	Bongo Rock/Bongolia	1973	6.00
❑ 14635	Let There Be Drums/Dueling Bongos	1973	8.00

PRIDE

Number	Title (A Side/B Side)	Yr	NM
❑ 1015	Bongo Rock/Bongolia	1972	12.00
❑ 7601	Kirburi/When the Bed Breaks Down, I'll Meet You in the Spring	1974	10.00

Albums

PRIDE

Number	Title (A Side/B Side)	Yr	NM
❑ 0028	Bongo Rock *—Note: This album has been reissued to look like the original*	1973	80.00
❑ 6010	The Return of the Incredible Bongo Band	1974	20.00

INCREDIBLE STRING BAND, THE

45s

ELEKTRA

Number	Title (A Side/B Side)	Yr	NM
❑ 45696	This Moment/Big Ted	1970	8.00

Albums

CARTHAGE

Number	Title (A Side/B Side)	Yr	NM
❑ CGLP-4421	The Hangman's Beautiful Daughter	198?	12.00

ELEKTRA

Number	Title (A Side/B Side)	Yr	NM
❑ EKM-322 [M]	The Incredible String Band	1967	30.00
❑ 7E-2002 [(2)]	'U' *—Butterfly label*	1971	25.00
❑ 7E-2004 [(2)]	Relics of the Incredible String Band *—Butterfly label*	1971	20.00
❑ EKM-4010 [M]	The 5,000 Spirits	1967	30.00
❑ EKS-7322	The Incredible String Band *—Red label, large stylized "E"*	1969	15.00
❑ EKS-7322	The Incredible String Band *—Butterfly label*	1971	12.00
❑ EKS-7322 [S]	The Incredible String Band *—Brown label*	1967	20.00
❑ EKS-74010	The 5,000 Spirits *—Red label, large stylized "E"*	1969	15.00
❑ EKS-74010	The 5,000 Spirits *—Butterfly label*	1971	12.00
❑ EKS-74010 [S]	The 5,000 Spirits *—Brown label*	1967	20.00
❑ EKS-74021	The Hangman's Beautiful Daughter *—Brown label*	1968	20.00
❑ EKS-74021	The Hangman's Beautiful Daughter *—Red label, large stylized "E"*	1969	15.00
❑ EKS-74021	The Hangman's Beautiful Daughter *—Butterfly label*	1971	12.00
❑ EKS-74036	Wee Tam *—Red label, large stylized "E"*	1969	15.00
❑ EKS-74036	Wee Tam *—Brown label*	1969	20.00
❑ EKS-74036	Wee Tam *—Butterfly label*	1971	12.00
❑ EKS-74037	The Big Huge *—Red label, large stylized "E"*	1969	15.00
❑ EKS-74037	The Big Huge *—Brown label*	1969	20.00
❑ EKS-74037	The Big Huge *—Butterfly label*	1971	12.00
❑ EKS-74057	Changing Horses *—Red label, large stylized "E"*	1969	15.00
❑ EKS-74057	Changing Horses *—Butterfly label*	1971	12.00
❑ EKS-74061	I Looked Up *—Red label, large stylized "E"*	1970	15.00
❑ EKS-74061	I Looked Up *—Butterfly label*	1971	12.00
❑ EKS-74112	Liquid Acrobat As Regards the Air *—Butterfly label*	1972	15.00

REPRISE

Number	Title (A Side/B Side)	Yr	NM
❑ MS 2122	Earthspan	1973	12.00
❑ MS 2139	No Ruinous Feud	1973	12.00
❑ MS 2198	Hard Rope and Silver Twine	1974	12.00

SUNDAZED

Number	Title (A Side/B Side)	Yr	NM
❑ LP 5127 [S]	The Incredible String Band *—Reissue on 180-gram vinyl*	2003	12.00
❑ LP 5128 [S]	The 5,000 Spirits *—Reissue on 180-gram vinyl*	2003	12.00
❑ LP 5129 [S]	The Hangman's Beautiful Daughter *—Reissue on 180-gram vinyl*	2003	12.00

INCREDIBLES, THE

45s

AUDIO ARTS

Number	Title (A Side/B Side)	Yr	NM
❑ 60001	I'll Make It Easy (If You Come On Home)/Crying Heart	1966	12.00
❑ 60006	There's Nothing Else to Say/Another Dirty Deal	1967	10.00
❑ 60007	Heart and Soul/I Found Another Love	1967	10.00
❑ 60009	Without a Word/Standing Here Crying	1967	10.00
❑ 60014	Fool, Fool, Fool/Lost Without You	1968	10.00
❑ 60016	Miss Treatment/All of a Sudden	1968	10.00
❑ 60017	Standing Here Crying/All of a Sudden	1968	10.00
❑ 60018	Stop the Raindrops/Fool, Fool, Fool	1968	10.00

TETRAGRAMMATON

Number	Title (A Side/B Side)	Yr	NM
❑ 1515	All of a Sudden/Standing Here Crying	1969	8.00

Albums

AUDIO ARTS

Number	Title (A Side/B Side)	Yr	NM
❑ AAS-7000	Heart and Soul	1970	20.00

INDEPENDENTS, THE

45s

WAND

Number	Title (A Side/B Side)	Yr	NM
❑ 11245	Just As Long As You Need Me, Part 1/Part 2	1972	6.00
❑ 11249	I Just Want to Be There/Can't Understand It	1972	6.00
❑ 11252	Leaving Me/I Love You Yes I Do	1973	6.00
❑ 11258	Baby I've Been Missing You/Couldn't Hear Nobody Say	1973	6.00
❑ 11263	It's All Over/Sara Lee	1973	6.00
❑ 11267	The First Time We Met/Show Me How	1973	6.00
❑ 11273	Arise and Shine (Let's Get It On)/I Found Love	1974	6.00
❑ 11279	Let This Be a Lesson to You/No Wind, No Rain	1974	6.00

Albums

WAND

Number	Title (A Side/B Side)	Yr	NM
❑ WDS-694	The First Time We Met	1973	20.00
❑ WDS-696	The Independents	1973	20.00
❑ WDS-699	Discs of Gold	1974	20.00

INDEX

Albums

DC

Number	Title (A Side/B Side)	Yr	NM
❑ 71	The Index *—Black label; issued with black and white jacket; number is from deal wax; VG value 1500; VG+ value 2250*	1968	3000.
❑ 4736	The Index *—Red label; issued with generic white jacket, though sometimes found in first LP's jacket; number in dead wax; VG value 1000; VG+ value 1500*	1968	2000.

INDIAN SUMMER

Albums

RCA/NEON

Number	Title (A Side/B Side)	Yr	NM
❑ NE-3	Indian Summer	1971	30.00

INDIGO GIRLS

12-Inch Singles

EPIC

Number	Title (A Side/B Side)	Yr	NM
❑ EAS 41374 [DJ]	Shed Your Skin (Stephen Nikolas Club Mix) (A.D.S. Skinless Mix) (Stephen Nikolas Dub Mix) (A.D.S. Ascension Mix)	1998	10.00

45s

EPIC

Number	Title (A Side/B Side)	Yr	NM
❑ 34-68912	Closer to Fine/Cold As Ice	1989	15.00
❑ 73003	Land of Canaan/Never Stop	1989	10.00
❑ 74326	Galileo/Ghost/Joking/Love Will Come to You/Jonas & Ezekiel *—Cassette only*	1992	—

J ELLIS

Number	Title (A Side/B Side)	Yr	NM
❑ A 1264	Crazy Game/Everybody's Waiting (For Someone to Come Home) *—A-side is credited to Emily Saliers; B-side credited to Amy Ray*	1985	120.00
❑ A 1264 [PS]	Crazy Game/Everybody's Waiting (For Someone to Come Home)	1985	150.00

Albums

DRAGON PATH

Number	Title (A Side/B Side)	Yr	NM
❑ LMM-I [EP]	Indigo Girls *—Black vinyl*	1986	150.00
❑ LMM-I [EP]	Indigo Girls *—Blue or clear vinyl (each of equal value)*	1986	200.00

EPIC

Number	Title (A Side/B Side)	Yr	NM
❑ EAS 1481 [EP]	Indigo Girls Sampler *—Promo-only with tour-dates sticker on white cardboard cover; includes Kid Fears/Closer to Fine/Center Stage/Prince of Darkness*	1989	15.00
❑ EAS 1861 [EP]	Land of Canaan Plus Five Live *—Promo-only item with five live tracks on B-side*	1989	30.00
❑ EAS 2201 [DJ]	Shades of Indigo: An Interview by Shawn Colvin	1990	70.00
❑ EAS 4020 [DJ]	Indigo Girls Live *—Promo-only version of "Back on the Bus Y'All"*	1991	40.00
❑ FE 45044	Indigo Girls	1989	15.00
❑ FE 45427	Strange Fire *—Reissue of Indigo release*	1989	15.00
❑ E 46820	Nomads*Indians*Saints	1990	20.00
❑ E 57621	Swamp Ophelia *—Black vinyl; all copies autographed on the label by the Indigo Girls*	1994	40.00
❑ E 57621	Swamp Ophelia *—Green vinyl; all copies autographed on the label by the Indigo Girls*	1994	40.00

INDIGO

Number	Title (A Side/B Side)	Yr	NM
❑ LMM-II	Strange Fire *—Blue, clear or red vinyl (each of equal value)*	1987	200.00
❑ LMM-II	Strange Fire *—Black vinyl*	1987	150.00

INFLUENCE

Albums

ABC

Number	Title (A Side/B Side)	Yr	NM
❑ ABCS-630	Influence	1968	30.00

INGMANN, JORGEN

45s

ATCO

Number	Title (A Side/B Side)	Yr	NM
❑ 6184	Apache/Echo Boogie	1960	15.00
❑ 6195	Anna/Cherokee	1961	12.00
❑ 6205	Milord/Oceans of Love	1961	10.00
❑ 6216	Violetta/Pinetop's Boogie Woogie	1962	10.00
❑ 6235	Africa/Johnny's Tune	1962	10.00
❑ 6277	Fourth Man Theme/Drina	1963	8.00
❑ 6305	Tovarisch/Desert March	1964	8.00
❑ 6370	Theme from "Zorba the Greek"/Gorilla	1965	8.00

Jorgen Ingmann, *Apache*, Atco 33-130, 1961, **$40.**

Number	Title (A Side/B Side)	Yr	NM
❑ 6403	Corfu/Seven Roses	1966	8.00
PARROT			
❑ 45006	Sunrise Serenade/Tokyo Melody	1964	10.00
Albums			
ATCO			
❑ 33-130 [M]	Apache	1961	40.00
❑ 33-139 [M]	The Many Guitars of Jorgen Ingmann	1962	40.00
MERCURY			
❑ MG-20200 [M]	Swinging Guitar	1956	60.00
❑ MG-20292 [M]	Swing Softly	1956	60.00
UNITED ARTISTS			
❑ UAS-6785	El Condor Pasa	1970	20.00

INGRAM, JAMES

Number	Title (A Side/B Side)	Yr	NM
12-Inch Singles			
MAW			
❑ 056-V	Lean On Me (MAW Mix 9:52) (MT's Remix 9:49)	2001	7.00
MCA			
❑ L33-17338 [DJ]	Better Way (same on both sides)	1987	15.00
❑ 23768	Better Way (4 versions)	1987	7.00
QWEST			
❑ PRO-A-2073 [DJ]	Party Animal (4:55) (Instrumental 4:55)	1983	10.00
❑ PRO-A-2506 [DJ]	Always (Edit) (Album Version)	1986	10.00
❑ 20270	It's Your Night (Jellybean Remix 7:02) (Jellybean Instrumental Remix 5:26)/Yah Mo B There	1984	10.00
—"Yah Mo B There" with Michael McDonald			
WARNER BROS.			
❑ PRO-A-3493 [DJ]	It's Real (2 versions)	1989	10.00
❑ PRO-A-3637 [DJ]	I Wanna Come Back (LP Version) (Fade)	1989	25.00
❑ PRO-A-3638 [DJ]	(You Make Me Feel Like) A Natural Man (2 versions)	1989	25.00
❑ PRO-A-3939 [DJ]	I Don't Have the Heart (Fade) (LP Version)	1990	8.00
❑ PRO-A-4311 [DJ]	When Was the Last Time Music Made You Cry (Fade) (LP Version)	1990	8.00
❑ PRO-A-5132 [DJ]	Get Ready (Edit 4:09) (LP Version 4:33)	1991	8.00
❑ PRO-A-5363 [DJ]	Remember the Dream (LP Version 4:22) (Edit 4:07)	1991	8.00
❑ PRO-A-6133 [DJ]	Someone Like You (unknown versions)	1993	10.00
❑ PRO-A-6505 [DJ]	Treat Her Right (unknown versions)	1993	10.00
❑ 21208	It's Real (12" Extended Version) (Smooth Dub Mix) (7" Instrumental Smooth Dub Moaner Mix) (7" Edit)/Aren't You Tired	1989	8.00
❑ 21311	I Wanna Come Back (12" Extended Version 6:39) (Instrumental 4:48) (7" Edit 5:03)/Ooo	1989	8.00
45s			
MAW			
❑ 056-7	Lean On Me (Acapella)/(Bonus Beats)	2001	4.00
—Green vinyl			
MCA			
❑ 53125	Better Way/Bad Guys	1987	3.00
—B-side by The Heat			
❑ 53125 [PS]	Better Way/Bad Guys	1987	3.00
QWEST			
❑ 28537	Never Felt So Good/(Instrumental)	1986	5.00
❑ 28669	Always/(Instrumental)	1986	3.00
❑ 28669 [PS]	Always/(Instrumental)	1986	3.00
❑ 29132	Whatever We Imagine/It's Your Night	1984	4.00
❑ 29235	She Loves Me (The Best That I Can Be)/Come A Da Machine (To Take A My Place)	1984	4.00
❑ 29316	There's No Easy Way/Come A Da Machine (To Take A My Place)	1984	4.00
❑ 29316 [PS]	There's No Easy Way/Come A Da Machine (To Take A My Place)	1984	4.00
❑ 29394	Yah Mo B There/Come A Da Machine (To Take A My Place)	1983	4.00
—A-side with Michael McDonald			
❑ 29493	Party Animal/Come A Da Machine (To Take A My Place)	1983	4.00
WARNER BROS.			
❑ 19911	I Don't Have the Heart/Baby Be Mine	1991	4.00
❑ 22862	(You Make Me Feel Like) A Natural Man/Aren't You Tired	1989	3.00
❑ 22863	I Wanna Come Back/Ooo	1989	3.00
❑ 22975	It's Real/Aren't You Tired	1989	3.00
❑ 22975 [PS]	It's Real/Aren't You Tired	1989	5.00
Albums			
QWEST			
❑ 23970	It's Your Night	1983	8.00
❑ 23970 [DJ]	It's Your Night	1983	15.00
—Promo version on "Quiex II" vinyl			
❑ 25424	Never Felt So Good	1986	8.00
WARNER BROS.			
❑ 25924	It's Real	1989	12.00

INGRAM, LUTHER

Number	Title (A Side/B Side)	Yr	NM
45s			
DECCA			
❑ 31794	Ain't That Nice/You Never Miss Your Water	1965	300.00
HIB			
❑ 698	If It's All the Same To You Babe/Exus Trek	1967	75.00
—Orange label (with "Wylia" credit)			
❑ 698	If It's All the Same To You Babe/Exus Trek	1967	750.00
—Light green label			
❑ 698	If It's All the Same To You Babe/Exus Trek	1967	1000.
—Orange label (with "Wylie" credit)			
KOKO			
❑ 101	I Can't Stop/You Got to Give Love to Get Love	1968	30.00
❑ 103	Missing You/Since You Don't Want Me	1968	50.00
❑ 721	Ain't Good for Nothing/These Are the Things	1976	6.00
❑ 724	Let's Steal Away to the Hideaway/I've Got Your Love in My Life	1977	6.00
❑ 725	I Like the Feeling/Gonna Be the Next Time	1977	6.00
❑ 728	Do You Love Somebody/How I Miss My Baby	1977	6.00
❑ 731	Get to Me/Trying to Find My Love	1978	40.00
❑ 2101	You Can Depend on Me/Looking for a New Love	1969	8.00
❑ 2102	Pity for the Lonely/Looking for a New Love	1969	8.00
❑ 2103	Puttin' Game Down/Since You Don't Want Me	1969	8.00
❑ 2104	My Honey and Me/I Can't Stop	1969	15.00
❑ 2105	Ain't That Loving You (For More Reasons Than One)/Home Don't Seem Like Home	1970	8.00
❑ 2106	To the Other Man/I'll Just Call You Honey	1970	15.00
❑ 2107	Be Good to Me Baby/Since You Don't Want Me	1971	8.00
❑ 2108	I'll Love You Until the End/Ghetto Train	1971	8.00
❑ 2110	You Were Made for Me/Missing You	1972	8.00
❑ 2111	(If Loving You Is Wrong) I Don't Want to Be Right/Puttin' Game Down	1972	8.00
❑ 2113	I'll Be Your Shelter (In Time of Storm)/I Can't Stop	1972	8.00
❑ 2115	Always/Help Me Love	1973	8.00
❑ 2116	Love Ain't Gonna Run Me Away/To the Other Man	1973	8.00

Except when noted otherwise, VG = 25% of NM, and VG+ = 50% of NM. (Example: VG = \$2.00, VG+ = \$4.00 and NM = \$8.00.)

Number	Title (A Side/B Side)	Yr	NM
PROFILE			
❑ 5125	Baby Don't Go Too Far/ How Sweet It Would Be	1986	3.00
❑ 5132	Don't Turn Around/ (B-side unknown)	1987	3.00
❑ 5143	Gotta Serve Somebody/ All in the Name of Love	1987	3.00
SMASH			
❑ 2019	(I Spy) For the F.B.I./Foxey Devil	1966	50.00
Albums			
KOKO			
❑ KOS-2201	I've Been Here All the Time	1971	15.00
❑ KOS-2202	If Loving You Is Wrong I Don't Want to Be Right	1972	15.00
INITIALS, THE (1)			
45s			
CONGRESS			
❑ 207	School Day/The Song Is Number One	1964	12.00
❑ 219	Dancing on the Sand/ Seventeen Guys on a Blanket at the Beach	1964	12.00
❑ 229	Someday She'll Love Me/ I Should Have Listened	1964	12.00
—As "Angelo and the Initials"			
INITIALS, THE (2)			
45s			
DEE			
❑ 1001	You/Bells of Joy	1959	200.00
SHERRY			
❑ 667	You/Bells of Joy	1959	50.00
INK SPOTS			
45s			
DECCA			
❑ 9-5 [PS]	Ink Spots, Vol. 2	1950	15.00
—Box for 25238, 25239 and 25240			
❑ 23615	To Each His Own/I Never Had a Dream Come True	1960	8.00
—Black label, color bars at right			
❑ 9-23615	To Each His Own/I Never Had a Dream Come True	1950	25.00
—Black label, lines on either side of "Decca"; reissue of 78 from 1946			
❑ 9-23615	To Each His Own/I Never Had a Dream Come True	1955	12.00
—Black label, star under "Decca"			
❑ 23632	If I Didn't Care/Whispering Grass (Don't Tell the Trees)	1961	10.00
—Black label, color bars at right			
❑ 9-23632	If I Didn't Care/Whispering Grass (Don't Tell the Trees)	1950	25.00
—Black label, lines on either side of "Decca"			
❑ 9-23632	If I Didn't Care/Whispering Grass (Don't Tell the Trees)	1955	12.00
—Black label, star under "Decca"			
❑ 9-23633	Java Jive/Do I Worry?	1950	25.00
—Black label, lines on either side of "Decca"			
❑ 9-25238	I'll Get By (As Long As I Have You)/Just for a Thrill	1950	20.00
—Side 1 and 6 of "Album No. 9-5"			
❑ 9-25239	I'd Climb the Highest Mountain/ I'm Gettin' Sentimental Over You	1950	20.00
—From "Album No. 9-5"			
❑ 9-25240	Coquette/When the Swallows Come Back to Capistrano	1950	20.00
—From "Album No. 9-5"			
❑ 25505	It's a Sin to Tell a Lie/That's When Your Heartaches Begin	1961	10.00
❑ 25533	All My Life/You Were Only Fooling	1961	12.00
❑ 9-27102	Sometime/I Was Dancing with Someone	1950	25.00
❑ 9-27214	The Way It Used to Be/ Right About Now	1950	25.00
❑ 9-27256	Our Lady of Fatima/ Stranger in the City	1950	25.00
❑ 9-27259	Dream Awhile/Time Out for Tears	1950	25.00
❑ 9-27391	If/A Friend of Johnny's	1951	20.00
❑ 9-27464	Tell Me You Love Me/ Castles in the Sand	1951	20.00
❑ 9-27493	Do Something for Me/ A Fool Grows Wise	1951	20.00
❑ 9-27632	More of the Same Sweet You/ What Can You Do	1951	20.00
❑ 9-27742	I Don't Stand a Ghost of a Chance/I'm Lucky I Have You	1951	20.00
❑ 9-27996	Honest and Truly/All My Life	1952	20.00
❑ 9-29750	Memories of You/It's Funny to Everyone But Me	1955	20.00
❑ 9-29991	My Prayer/Bewildered	1956	20.00
❑ 9-30058	The Best Things in Life Are Free/I Don't Stand a Ghost of a Chance	1956	15.00
GRAND AWARD			
❑ 1001	Rock and Roll Rag/Do I Worry	1956	20.00
KING			
❑ 1297	Ebb Tide/If You Should Say Goodbye	1953	60.00
❑ 1304	Changing Partners/ Stranger in Paradise	1954	70.00
❑ 1336	Melody of Love/Am I Too Late	1954	70.00
❑ 1378	Yesterdays/Planting Rice	1954	60.00
❑ 1425	When You Come to the End of the Day/Someone's Rocking My Dreamboat	1955	50.00
❑ 1429	Melody of Love/There Is Something Missing	1955	40.00
❑ 1512	Don't Laugh at Me/Keep It Movin'	1955	40.00
❑ 4670	Here in My Lonely Room/ A Fool in Love	1953	150.00
❑ 4857	Command Me/I'll Walk a Country Mile	1955	40.00
SWIFT			
❑ 1001	If I Didn't Care//Into Each Life Some Rain Must Fall/We Three	195?	15.00
VERVE			
❑ 10198	Secret Love/A Little Bird Told Me	1960	12.00
7-Inch Extended Plays			
DECCA			
❑ ED 2008	The Gypsy/To Each His Own// Bless You/With My Eyes Wide Open, I'm Dreaming	195?	25.00
❑ ED 2008 [PS]	The Ink Spots, Vol. 1	195?	25.00
❑ ED 2047	*It's Funny to Everyone But Me/ It's a Sin to Tell a Lie/Don't Get Around Much Anymore/ My Prayer	195?	25.00
❑ ED 2047 [PS]	The Ink Spots, Vol. 2	195?	25.00
KING			
❑ EP-376	*Melody of Love/Ebb Tide/ Stranger in Paradise/ Yesterdays	195?	30.00
❑ EP-376 [PS]	Great Songs of Our Times	195?	30.00
WALDORF MUSIC HALL			
❑ MH 45-186	Do I Worry?/Paper Doll// Maybe/We Three	195?	25.00
❑ MH 45-186 [PS]	The Ink Spots	195?	25.00
—Label calls this "The Ink Spots Quartet"			
Albums			
COLORTONE			
❑ 4901 [M]	The Ink Spots	1958	60.00
❑ 4947 [M]	The Ink Spots, Vol. 2	1959	60.00
CROWN			
❑ CST-144 [S]	The Ink Spots' Greatest Hits	1959	25.00
—Black vinyl			
❑ CST-144 [S]	The Ink Spots' Greatest Hits	1959	50.00
—Red vinyl			
❑ CST-175 [S]	The Ink Spots	1961	25.00
—Black vinyl			
❑ CST-175 [S]	The Ink Spots	1961	50.00
—Red vinyl			
❑ CST-217 [S]	The Sensational Ink Spots	1962	25.00
—Black vinyl			
❑ CST-217 [S]	The Sensational Ink Spots	1962	50.00
—Red vinyl			
❑ CLP-5112 [M]	The Ink Spots' Greatest Hits	1959	20.00
❑ CLP-5142 [M]	The Ink Spots	1961	20.00
❑ CLP-5187 [M]	The Sensational Ink Spots	1962	20.00
❑ CLP 5221 [M]	More Ink Spots	196?	15.00
DECCA			
❑ DXB 182 [(2)M]	The Best of the Ink Spots	1965	30.00
❑ DL 4297 [M]	Our Golden Favorites	1962	25.00
❑ DL 5056 [10]	The Ink Spots	1950	50.00
❑ DL 5071 [10]	The Ink Spots, Vol. 2	1950	50.00
❑ DL 5333 [10]	Precious Memories	1951	50.00
❑ DL 5541 [10]	Street of Dreams	1954	50.00
❑ DXSB 7182 [(2)P]	The Best of the Ink Spots	1965	20.00
❑ DL 8154 [M]	The Best of the Ink Spots	1955	40.00
—Black label, silver print			
❑ DL 8232 [M]	Time Our for Tears	1956	40.00
—Black label, silver print			
❑ DL 8768 [M]	Torch Time	1958	40.00
—Black label, silver print			
❑ DL 74297 [S]	Our Golden Favorites	1962	20.00
EVEREST ARCHIVE OF FOLK & JAZZ			
❑ 350	The Ink Spots in London	197?	10.00
GOLDEN TONE			
❑ C4024	The Fabulous Ink Spots	195?	12.00
❑ C4037	Ink Spots Vol. II	195?	12.00
GRAND AWARD			
❑ GA 232 SD [S]	The Ink Spots' Greatest, Vol. 3	1959	40.00
❑ GA 33-328 [M]	The Ink Spots' Greatest, Vol. 1	1958	25.00
❑ GA 33-354 [M]	The Ink Spots' Greatest, Vol. 2	1958	25.00
❑ GA 33-396 [M]	The Ink Spots' Greatest, Vol. 3	1959	25.00
KING			
❑ 535 [M]	Something Old, Something New	1956	400.00
❑ 642 [M]	Songs That Will Live Forever	1959	300.00
—Reissue of 535			
❑ 5001	18 Hits by the Ink Spots	197?	10.00
LONGINES SYMPHONETTE			
❑ SYS 5830	10 of the Best Ink Spots Hits	197?	10.00
—Label calls this "The Best of the Ink Spots"; also on label is "New Premium for Mills Bros. V&R Offer"			
MCA			
❑ 4005 [(2)]	The Best of the Ink Spots	197?	12.00
❑ MSM2-35253 [(2)]	The Beautiful Music Company Presents the Ink Spots	1991	20.00
OPEN SKY			
❑ 3125	Just Like Old Times	198?	10.00
PAULA			
❑ 2212	The Ink Spots Sing Country	1972	10.00
RONDO			
❑ R-2010 [M]	The Ink Spots in the Spotlite	1963	12.00
❑ RS-2010 [S]	The Ink Spots in the Spotlite	1963	15.00
—Title on label is "The Ink Spots"			
TOPS			
❑ L-1561 [M]	The Ink Spots	1957	40.00
❑ L-1668 [M]	The Ink Spots, Vol. 2	1959	40.00
VERVE			
❑ MGV-2124 [M]	The Ink Spots' Favorites	1959	25.00
❑ MGVS-6096 [S]	The Ink Spots' Favorites	1959	40.00
VOCALION			
❑ VL 3606 [M]	Sincerely Yours	196?	12.00
❑ VL 3725 [M]	Lost in a Dream	1965	12.00
❑ VL 73606 [R]	Sincerely Yours	196?	10.00
❑ VL 73725 [R]	Lost in a Dream	1965	10.00
WALDORF MUSIC HALL			
❑ MH 33-144 [10]	Songs of the South Seas	195?	80.00
❑ MH 33-152 [10]	The Ink Spots Quartet	195?	80.00
INMAN, AUTRY			
45s			
DECCA			
❑ 28290	Who Do You Love/Just Smile As You Go By	1952	20.00
❑ 28495	Does Your Sweetheart Seem Different Lately/All of a Sudden	1952	20.00
❑ 28592	I'll Miss My Heart/Stop Stallin'	1953	20.00
❑ 28629	That's All Right/Uh Huh Honey	1953	25.00
❑ 28778	Pucker Up/That's When I Need You the Most	1953	20.00
❑ 28798	A Dear John Letter/ Brown Eyed Baby	1953	20.00
❑ 28960	It Hurts Too Much to Cry/ Happy Go Lucky	1953	20.00
❑ 29060	Just Reminiscing/ Under the Moon	1954	20.00
❑ 29170	Little One/Once More	1954	20.00
❑ 29362	Finally I'm Free/Don't Put It Off	1954	20.00
❑ 29447	You Said Goodbye/It's a Shame	1955	20.00
❑ 29635	Tell Me Now/A Friend	1955	20.00
❑ 29690	Blue Monday/Look Over Your Shoulder	1955	25.00
❑ 29936	Be-Bop Baby/It Would Be a Doggone Lie	1956	100.00
❑ 46407	Let's Take the Long Way Home Tonight/I Hope Tomorrow Never Comes	1952	20.00
EPIC			
❑ 10232	Don't Call Me (I'll Call You)/ Love Has to Die (All By Itself)	1967	8.00
❑ 10276	There Stands the Glass/This Heart Was Made for Lovin'	1968	8.00
❑ 10327	I Can See an Angel/Wish in One Hand (Cry in the Other)	1968	8.00
❑ 10389	Ballad of Two Brothers/Don't Call Me (I'll Call You)	1968	8.00
❑ 10452	Home Is Heavy on My Mind/ You're the Only One in My Heart	1969	8.00
❑ 10494	I'll Be Waiting/ Traveling Salesman	1969	8.00
GLAD			
❑ 1002	I'm Still in Love with Mary/ Please Cut Me Down	1960	15.00
JUBILEE			
❑ 9001	The Drinks Are On Me/You Don't Live There Anymore	1964	8.00
❑ 9010	Keep Her Out of Sight/ Blue Is Next in Line	1965	8.00
❑ 9016	Hurtache/Mr. Love Passed Away	1965	8.00
❑ 9023	You Don't Live There Anymore/ The Drinks Are on Me	1965	8.00

Number	Title (A Side/B Side)	Yr	NM
KOALA			
❑ 325	That's Why You're Being Paid/ (B-side unknown)	1980	5.00
MERCURY			
❑ 71983	Living with One and Loving Two/I Guess I'm Crazy	1962	12.00
MILLION			
❑ 4	Please Let Me Love You/ Maybe This Is the Day	1972	6.00
❑ 24	If You Were Mine/Please Let Me Love You	1972	6.00
RCA VICTOR			
❑ 47-7173	Dream Boat/Remember the Night	1958	30.00
❑ 47-7260	Mary Nell/The Hard Way	1958	30.00
SIMS			
❑ 131	The Volunteer/Unlucky Am I	1963	10.00
❑ 140	Big Sam/My Word	1963	10.00
❑ 170	The Ballad of John F. Kennedy/ The World's Worst Lover	1964	10.00
❑ 188	My Past/You're Welcome Dear	1964	10.00
❑ 219	Give Me 40 Acres (To Turn This Rig Around)/Six Rounds of Love and Hate	1964	10.00
UNITED ARTISTS			
❑ 278	That's All Right/Farther to Go Than I've Been	1960	15.00
❑ 303	Let's Take the Long Way Home/ Too Blue to Cry	1961	15.00

Albums

Number	Title	Yr	NM
EPIC			
❑ BN 26428	Ballad of Two Brothers	1968	20.00
JUBILEE			
❑ JGM-2055 [M]	Riscotheque Saturday Night	1964	20.00
❑ JGS-2055 [S]	Riscotheque Saturday Night	1964	25.00
❑ JGM-2056 [M]	New Year's Eve with Autry Inman	1964	20.00
❑ JGS-2056 [S]	New Year's Eve with Autry Inman	1964	25.00
MOUNTAIN DEW			
❑ 7022 [M]	Autry Inman	1963	20.00
❑ S-7022 [S]	Autry Inman	1963	25.00
SIMS			
❑ 107 [M]	Autry Inman at the Frontier Club	1964	20.00
❑ S-107 [S]	Autry Inman at the Frontier Club	1964	25.00

INNER CIRCLE, THE
Another STEVE BARRI and P.F. SLOAN creation.

45s

Number	Title (A Side/B Side)	Yr	NM
DUNHILL			
❑ 4128	So Long Mary Ann/Goes to Show	1968	20.00
IMPACT			
❑ 1019	Sally Go Round the Roses/Sugar	1967	40.00

INNOCENCE, THE

45s

Number	Title (A Side/B Side)	Yr	NM
KAMA SUTRA			
❑ 214	There's Got to Be a Word!/ I Don't Wanna Be Around You	1966	8.00
❑ 222	Mairzy Doats/Lifetime Lovin' You	1967	10.00
❑ 228	All I Do Is Think About You/ Whence, I Make Thee Mine	1967	8.00
❑ 232	Someone Got Caught in My Eye/Your Show Is Over	1967	8.00
❑ 237	Day Turns Me On (The Bufferin Song)/It's Not Gonna Take Too Long	1967	8.00

Albums

Number	Title	Yr	NM
KAMA SUTRA			
❑ KLP-8059 [M]	The Innocence	1967	20.00
❑ KLPS-8059 [S]	The Innocence	1967	30.00

INNOCENTS, THE
Also see KATHY YOUNG AND THE INNOCENTS.

45s

Number	Title (A Side/B Side)	Yr	NM
DECCA			
❑ 31519	Don't Cry/Come On Lover	1963	20.00
INDIGO			
❑ 105	Honest I Do/My Baby Hully Gullys	1960	20.00
❑ 111	Gee Whiz/Please Mr. Sun	1960	20.00
❑ 116	Kathy/In the Beginning	1961	20.00
❑ 124	Beware/Because I Love You	1961	20.00
❑ 128	Donna/You Got Me Goin'	1961	20.00
❑ 132	Pains in My Heart/When I Become a Man	1961	20.00
PORT			
❑ 3026	Gee Whiz/Please Mr. Sun	196?	8.00
REPRISE			
❑ 20112	Be Mine/Oh How I Miss My Baby	1962	25.00
❑ 20122	Be Mine/Oh How I Miss My Baby	1962	—
—Unreleased			
❑ 20125	You're Never Satisfied/ Oh How I Miss My Baby	1962	20.00
TRANS WORLD			
❑ 7001	Tick Tock/The Rut	196?	20.00
WARNER BROS.			
❑ 5450	My Heart Stood Still/Don't Call Me Lonely Anymore	1964	30.00

Albums

Number	Title	Yr	NM
INDIGO			
❑ 503 [M]	Inocently Yours	1961	80.00
❑ 503 [M]	Inocently Yours	1961	500.00
—Plain white cover; promo only			

INSECT TRUST, THE

45s

Number	Title (A Side/B Side)	Yr	NM
ATCO			
❑ 6764	Reciprocity/Reincarnations	1970	10.00
CAPITOL			
❑ 2386	Miss Fun City/Special Rider Blues	1969	15.00

Albums

Number	Title	Yr	NM
ATCO			
❑ SD 33-313	Hoboken Saturday Night	1970	50.00
CAPITOL			
❑ SKAO-109	The Insect Trust	1968	50.00

INSECTS, THE

45s

Number	Title (A Side/B Side)	Yr	NM
APPLAUSE			
❑ 1002	Let's Bug the Beatles/ Dear Beatles	1964	25.00
—B-side by the Little Lady Beatles			

INSIDE OUT

Albums

Number	Title	Yr	NM
FREDLO			
❑ 6834	Bringing It All Back	1968	200.00

INSIDERS, THE

45s

Number	Title (A Side/B Side)	Yr	NM
RCA VICTOR			
❑ 47-9225	I'm Just a Man/I'm Better Off Without You	1967	100.00
❑ 47-9325	If You Had a Heart/Movin' On	1967	75.00
RED BIRD			
❑ 10-055	Chapel Bells Are Calling/ I'm Stuck on You	1966	75.00

INSIGHT, THE

45s

Number	Title (A Side/B Side)	Yr	NM
CASCADE			
❑ 364	Please Come Home For Christmas/Out Of Sight	1964	30.00

INSPIRATIONS, THE
More than one group.

45s

Number	Title (A Side/B Side)	Yr	NM
AL-BRITE			
❑ 1651	Angel in Disguise/Stool Pigeon	1960	80.00
APOLLO			
❑ 494	Raindrops/Maggie	1956	250.00
BELTONE			
❑ 2037	The Girl By My Side/Neckin'	1963	60.00
BLACK PEARL			
❑ 100	Touch Me, Kiss Me, Hold Me/ Funny Situation	196?	40.00
—Second issue			
❑ 711	Touch Me, Kiss Me, Hold Me/ What Am I Gonna Do with You Hey Baby	196?	75.00
—Original issue			
BREAKTHROUGH			
❑ 1001 [DJ]	No One Else Can Take Your Place/(B-side blank)	196?	7500.
FEATURE			
❑ 110	Baby Please Come Back/ That Girl	1966	50.00
GONE			
❑ 5097	Angel in Disguise/Stool Pigeon	1961	25.00
JAMIE			
❑ 1034	Dry Your Eyes/Good-Bye	1956	75.00
❑ 1212	Dry Your Eyes/Good-Bye	1962	20.00
LAMP			
❑ 2019	Don't Cry/Indian Jane	1958	150.00
MIDAS			
❑ 9003	Your Wish Is My Command/ I'll Take a Chance on You	196?	750.00
RONDAK			
❑ 9787	Ring Those Bells/ The Cumberland and the Merrimac	1961	800.00
SPARKLE			
❑ 102	Angel in Disguise/Stool Pigeon	1960	150.00
SULTAN			
❑ 1	The Genie/The Feeling of Her Kiss	1959	30.00
❑ 1 [PS]	The Genie/The Feeling of Her Kiss	1959	50.00
WAND			
❑ 182	Kiss and Make Up/Love Can Be So Wonderful	1965	40.00

INTENTIONS, THE
Probably more than one group.

45s

Number	Title (A Side/B Side)	Yr	NM
JAMIE			
❑ 1253	Summertime Angel/Mr. Misery	1963	1500.
KENT			
❑ 455	Dancing Fast, Dancing Slow/ My Love She's Gone	1966	50.00
MELRON			
❑ 5014	I'm in Love with a Go-Go Girl/ Wonderful Girl	1965	200.00
PHILIPS			
❑ 40428	Don't Forget That I Love You/ Night Rider	1967	25.00
UPTOWN			
❑ 710	Time/Cool Summer Night	1965	150.00

INTERLUDES, THE
Probably more than one group.

45s

Number	Title (A Side/B Side)	Yr	NM
ABC-PARAMOUNT			
❑ 10213	Number 1 in the Nation/Beautiful, Wonderful, Heavenly You	1961	15.00
KING			
❑ 5633	Darling I'll Be True/ Wilted Rose Bud	1962	30.00
RCA VICTOR			
❑ 47-7281	I Shed a Million Tears/Oo-Wee	1958	25.00
STAR-HI			
❑ 103	I Want You to Know/Split a Kiss	1959	15.00
VALLEY			
❑ 105	Heartbreaker/Scandalous	1959	15.00
❑ 106	No One for Me/Fort Lauderdale	1960	15.00
❑ 107	White Sailor Hat/Evil	1960	15.00

INTERNATIONAL POP ORCHESTRA

45s

Number	Title (A Side/B Side)	Yr	NM
CAMEO			
❑ 188	If You Love Me (Really Love Me)/Theme from Carmen	1961	8.00
❑ 191	La Strada/Summer Day	1961	8.00
❑ 200	Old Man River/You'll Never Walk Alone	1961	8.00
❑ 263	Slaughter on Tenth Avenue/ Blue Tango	1963	8.00
❑ 323	(Love Theme from) Carpetbagger/If You Love Me (Really Love Me)	1964	8.00

7-Inch Extended Plays

Number	Title	Yr	NM
CAMEO			
❑ C-2003 [M]	The 12 Greatest Songs Ever Written	1962	12.00

Albums

Number	Title	Yr	NM
CAMEO			
❑ C-1037 [M]	Songs That Will Live Forever	1963	12.00
❑ SC-1037 [S]	Songs That Will Live Forever	1963	15.00
❑ C-1039 [M]	Musical Jewels	1963	12.00
❑ SC-1039 [S]	Musical Jewels	1963	15.00
❑ C-2001 [M]	International Pop Orchestra — 110 Men	1962	12.00
❑ SC-2001 [S]	International Pop Orchestra — 110 Men	1962	15.00
❑ SC-2003 [S]	The 12 Greatest Songs Ever Written	1962	15.00
❑ C-4001 [M]	An Exciting Evening at Home	1962	12.00
❑ SC-4001 [S]	An Exciting Evening at Home	1962	15.00
WYNCOTE			
❑ SW-9005 [S]	110 Musicians (Fascination)	1964	15.00
❑ W-9005 [M]	110 Musicians (Fascination)	1964	12.00
❑ SW-9014 [S]	The International Pop Orchestra Visits the World's Fair	1964	15.00
❑ W-9014 [M]	The International Pop Orchestra Visits the World's Fair	1964	12.00
❑ SW-9021 [S]	The International Pop Orchestra Plays for Lovers Only	1964	15.00
❑ W-9021 [M]	The International Pop Orchestra Plays for Lovers Only	1964	12.00

Number	Title (A Side/B Side)	Yr	NM
❑ SW-9040 [S]	Love Themes from the Classics	1964	15.00
❑ W-9040 [M]	Love Themes from the Classics	1964	12.00
❑ SW-9059 [S]	Stardust	1964	15.00
❑ W-9059 [M]	Stardust	1964	12.00
❑ SW-9063 [S]	Cole Porter Favorites	1964	15.00
❑ W-9063 [M]	Cole Porter Favorites	1964	12.00
❑ SW-9071 [S]	Richard Rodgers Favorites	1964	15.00
❑ W-9071 [M]	Richard Rodgers Favorites	1964	12.00
❑ SW-9076 [S]	The Sound of Music	1965	15.00
❑ W-9076 [M]	The Sound of Music	1965	12.00
❑ SW-9084 [S]	Rhapsody in Blue/Slaughter on Tenth Avenue	1965	15.00
❑ W-9084 [M]	Rhapsody in Blue/Slaughter on Tenth Avenue	1965	12.00
❑ SW-9090 [S]	Lerner and Loewe Favorites	1965	15.00
❑ W-9090 [M]	Lerner and Loewe Favorites	1965	12.00
❑ SW-9102 [S]	George Gershwin Favorites	1965	15.00
❑ W-9102 [M]	George Gershwin Favorites	1965	12.00
❑ SW-9117 [S]	Christmas Favorites	1965	15.00
❑ W-9117 [M]	Christmas Favorites	1965	12.00
❑ SW-9120 [S]	Musical Jewels	1965	15.00
❑ W-9120 [M]	Musical Jewels	1965	12.00
❑ SW-9123 [S]	Reminiscing	1966	15.00
❑ W-9123 [M]	Reminiscing	1966	12.00
❑ SW-9124 [S]	When Lights Are Low	1966	15.00
❑ W-9124 [M]	When Lights Are Low	1966	12.00
❑ SW-9135 [S]	Fascination and Other All-Time Favorites	1966	15.00
❑ W-9135 [M]	Fascination and Other All-Time Favorites	1966	12.00
❑ SW-9165 [S]	For Lovers Everywhere	1967	12.00
❑ W-9165 [M]	For Lovers Everywhere	1967	15.00
❑ SW-9185 [S]	110 Musicians Play "That's Life"	1967	12.00
❑ W-9185 [M]	110 Musicians Play "That's Life"	1967	15.00
❑ SW-9193 [S]	Let's Fall in Love	1967	12.00
❑ W-9193 [M]	Let's Fall in Love	1967	15.00

INTERNATIONAL SUBMARINE BAND, THE

Also see GRAM PARSONS.

45s

ASCOT

Number	Title (A Side/B Side)	Yr	NM
❑ 2218	The Russians Are Coming/Truck Driving Man	1966	15.00
❑ 2218 [PS]	The Russians Are Coming/Truck Driving Man	1966	50.00

—Counterfeit identification: Fake copies are missing the Ascot logo and catalog number.

COLUMBIA

Number	Title (A Side/B Side)	Yr	NM
❑ 43935	Sum Up Broke/One Day Week	1966	30.00

LHI

Number	Title (A Side/B Side)	Yr	NM
❑ 1205	Luxury Liner/Blue Eyes	1968	15.00
❑ 1217	Miller's Cave/I Must Be Somebody Else	1968	15.00

Albums

LHI

Number	Title (A Side/B Side)	Yr	NM
❑ 12001	Safe at Home	1968	100.00

—Counterfeits have white labels, legitimate copies have multi-color labels

RHINO

Number	Title (A Side/B Side)	Yr	NM
❑ RNLP 069	Safe at Home	1985	25.00

SUNDAZED

Number	Title (A Side/B Side)	Yr	NM
❑ LP 5112	Safe at Home	2001	12.00

—Reissue on 180-gram vinyl

INTERNS, THE

45s

CAPITOL

Number	Title (A Side/B Side)	Yr	NM
❑ 5747	Is It Really What You Want/Just Like Me	1966	12.00

UPTOWN

Number	Title (A Side/B Side)	Yr	NM
❑ 730	Hard to Get/And I'm Glad	1966	12.00

INTIMATES, THE

45s

EPIC

Number	Title (A Side/B Side)	Yr	NM
❑ 9743	I've Got a Tiger in My Tank/Smart, Too Late	1964	15.00

INTRIGUES, THE

45s

TOOT

Number	Title (A Side/B Side)	Yr	NM
❑ 609	Soul Brother (Part 1)/Soul Brother (Part 2)	1968	10.00

YEW

Number	Title (A Side/B Side)	Yr	NM
❑ 1001	In a Moment/Scotchman Rock	1969	12.00
❑ 1002	I'm Gonna Love You/I Gotta Find Out for Myself	1969	10.00
❑ 1007	Just a Little Bit More/Let's Dance	1970	10.00
❑ 1010	Tuck a Little Love Away/I Know There's Love	1970	10.00
❑ 1012	The Language of Love/I Got Love	1971	10.00
❑ 1013	Mojo Hannah/To Make a World	1971	10.00

Albums

YEW

Number	Title (A Side/B Side)	Yr	NM
❑ YS-777	In a Moment	1970	30.00

INTRUDERS, THE (1)

Early Philly Soul group.

45s

GAMBLE

Number	Title (A Side/B Side)	Yr	NM
❑ 201	(We'll Be) United/Up and Down the Ladder	1966	10.00
❑ 203	Devil with an Angel's Smile/A Book for the Broken Hearted	1966	10.00
❑ 203 [PS]	Devil with an Angel's Smile/A Book for the Broken Hearted	1966	15.00
❑ 204	It Must Be Love/Check Yourself	1966	10.00
❑ 205	Together/Up and Down the Ladder	1967	10.00
❑ 209	Baby I'm Lonely/A Love That's Real	1967	10.00
❑ 214	Cowboys to Girls/Turn the Hands of Time	1968	10.00
❑ 217	(Love Is Like a) Baseball Game/Friends No More	1968	10.00
❑ 221	Slow Drag/So Glad I'm Yours	1968	10.00
❑ 223	Give Her a Transplant/Girls, Girls, Girls	1969	10.00
❑ 225	Me Tarzan You Jane/Favorite Candidate	1969	10.00
❑ 231	Lollipop (I Like You)/Don't Give It Away	1969	10.00
❑ 235	Sad Girl/Let's Go Downtown	1969	10.00
❑ 240	Old Love/Every Day Is a Holiday	1969	10.00
❑ 2501	(Win, Place or Show) She's a Winner/Memories Are Here to Stay	1972	8.00
❑ 2506	I'll Always Love My Mama (Part 1)/I'll Always Love My Mama (Part 2)	1973	8.00
❑ 2508	I Wanna Know Your Name/Hang On In There	1973	8.00
❑ 4001	Tender (Was the Love We Knew)/By the Time I Get to Phoenix	1970	8.00
❑ 4004	When We Get Married/Doctor Doctor	1970	8.00
❑ 4007	This Is My Love Song/Let Me in Your Mind	1970	8.00
❑ 4009	I'm Girl Scoutin'/Wonder What Kind of Bag She's In	1971	8.00
❑ 4014	Pray for Me/Best Days of My Life	1971	15.00
❑ 4016	I Bet He Don't Love You (Like I Love You)/Do You Remember Yesterday	1971	20.00
❑ 4019	(Win, Place or Show) She's a Winner/Memories Are Here to Stay	1972	10.00

GOWEN

Number	Title (A Side/B Side)	Yr	NM
❑ 1401	I'm Sold on You/Come Home Soon	1961	40.00

LOST-NITE

Number	Title (A Side/B Side)	Yr	NM
❑ 195	I'm Sold on You/Come Home Soon	196?	6.00

—Reissue

PHILADELPHIA INT'L.

Number	Title (A Side/B Side)	Yr	NM
❑ 3624	I'll Always Love My Mama (Part 1)/I'll Always Love My Mama (Part 2)	1977	5.00
❑ 3689	I'll Always Love My Mama/Save the Children	1979	5.00

TSOP

Number	Title (A Side/B Side)	Yr	NM
❑ 4758	A Nice Girl Like You/To Be Happy Is the Real Thing	1974	6.00
❑ 4766	Rainy Days and Mondays/Be on Time	1975	6.00
❑ 4771	Plain Old Fashioned Girl/Energy of Love	1975	6.00

Albums

GAMBLE

Number	Title (A Side/B Side)	Yr	NM
❑ G-5001 [M]	The Intruders Are Together	1967	40.00
❑ GS-5001 [S]	The Intruders Are Together	1967	50.00
❑ GS-5004	Cowboys to Girls	1968	50.00
❑ GS-5005	The Intruders Greatest Hits	1969	40.00
❑ GS-5008	When We Get Married	1970	50.00
❑ KZ 31991	Save the Children	1973	20.00
❑ KZ 32131	Super Hits	1973	20.00

PHILADELPHIA INT'L.

Number	Title (A Side/B Side)	Yr	NM
❑ PZ 32131	Super Hits	198?	8.00

—Reissue of Gamble 32131

TSOP

Number	Title (A Side/B Side)	Yr	NM
❑ KZ 33149	Energy of Love	1974	15.00

INTRUDERS, THE (2)

Instrumental group from New Jersey.

45s

BELTONE

Number	Title (A Side/B Side)	Yr	NM
❑ 1009	Camptown Rock/Morse Code	1961	15.00

FAME

Number	Title (A Side/B Side)	Yr	NM
❑ 101	Fried Eggs/Jeffrie's Rock	1959	25.00
❑ 313	Creepin'/Frankfurters and Sauerkraut	1959	25.00
❑ 616	Rock-A-Ma-Roll/Era-Rock-A	1959	25.00

INVISIBLE MAN'S BAND, THE

Albums

BOARDWALK

Number	Title (A Side/B Side)	Yr	NM
❑ NB1-33238	Really Wanna See Ya	1981	20.00

INVITATIONS, THE

45s

DIAMOND

Number	Title (A Side/B Side)	Yr	NM
❑ 253	Got to Have It Now/Swingin' on the Love Vine	1968	30.00

DYNO VOICE

Number	Title (A Side/B Side)	Yr	NM
❑ 206	Written on the Wall/Hallelujah	1965	60.00
❑ 210	What's Wrong with Me Baby/Why Did My Baby Turn Bad	1965	300.00
❑ 215	Skiing in the Snow/Why Did My Baby Turn Bad	1966	400.00

MGM

Number	Title (A Side/B Side)	Yr	NM
❑ 13574	The Skate/Girl I'm Leavin' You	1966	40.00
❑ 13666	Watch Out Little Girl/You're Like a Mystery	1967	100.00

SILVER BLUE

Number	Title (A Side/B Side)	Yr	NM
❑ 801	They Say the Girl's Crazy/For Your Precious Love	1973	40.00
❑ 804	Let's Love/Love Has to Grow	1973	60.00
❑ 809	Living Together Is Keeping Us Apart/I Didn't Know	1974	30.00
❑ 818	Look on the Good Side/Look on the Good Side (Part 2)	1974	40.00

INXS

12-Inch Singles

ATCO

Number	Title (A Side/B Side)	Yr	NM
❑ PR 481 [DJ]	The One Thing (Extended) (Edit)	1983	8.00
❑ PR 499 [DJ]	Don't Change (same on both sides)	1982	12.00
❑ PR 527 [DJ]	To Look at You (long & short)	1983	15.00
❑ PR 586 [DJ]	Original Sin (Edit) (LP Version) (Dance Mix)	1984	20.00
❑ PR 618 [DJ]	I Send a Message (Remix)/(LP Version)	1984	12.00
❑ PR 639 [DJ]	Burn for You (3:38) (4:58) (6:09)	1984	12.00
❑ 96957	Original Sin (2 versions)/Stay Young/Just Keep Walking	1984	12.00

ATLANTIC

Number	Title (A Side/B Side)	Yr	NM
❑ PR 788 [DJ]	This Time (same on both sides)	1985	7.00
❑ PR 824 [DJ]	What You Need (3:33) (same on both sides)	1985	8.00
❑ PR 865 [DJ]	Listen Like Thieves (same on both sides)	1985	8.00
❑ PR 885 [DJ]	Kiss the Dirt (Falling Down the Mountain) (same on both sides)	1985	12.00
❑ PR 888 [DJ]	Kiss the Dirt (Falling Down the Mountain) (Live)/Listen Like Thieves (Live)	1986	15.00
❑ DMD 910 [DJ]	What You Need (LP Version) (Extended)	1985	12.00
❑ DMD 936 [DJ]	Listen Like Thieves (3 versions)	1985	8.00
❑ DMD 1137 [DJ]	Devil Inside (Remix) (Edit)/On the Rocks	1987	6.00
❑ DMD 1172 [DJ]	New Sensation (Nick's 12" Mix) (Radio Remix Edit) (LP Version)	1988	8.00
❑ DMD 1550 [DJ]	Suicide Blonde (4 versions)	1990	8.00
❑ DMD 1616 [DJ]	Bitter Tears (Lorimer Remix) (Instrumental)	1990	8.00
❑ DMD 1933 [DJ]	Taste It (3 versions)	1992	15.00
❑ PR 2050 [DJ]	Good Times (same on both sides)	1986	8.00

—With Jimmy Barnes

Number	Title (A Side/B Side)	Yr	NM
❑ DMD 2078 [DJ]	Please (You Got That...) (E-Smoove's Club Mix) (E-Smoove's Needful Dub) (Downtown Dub)/Freedom Deep (Extended Version)	1993	15.00
❑ PR 2116 [DJ]	Need You Tonight (same on both sides)	1987	8.00
❑ PR 2191 [DJ]	Devil Inside (LP version)/Devil Inside (edit)	1987	8.00
❑ PR 2276 [(2)DJ]	New Sensation: Music and Interview	1988	20.00

—Contains two versions of the title song, a third side of Q&A and a fourth side of the answers with no questions; includes cue sheet

Number	Title (A Side/B Side)	Yr	NM
❑ 85942	Shining Star/Send a Message (Live)/Faith in Each Other (Live)/Bitter Tears (Live)	1991	8.00
❑ 86080	Bitter Tears (Lorimer Remix) (Instrumental)/The Other Side	1990	8.00

I

Iron Maiden, "Flight of Icarus," Capitol B-5248, 1983, $15.

Number	Title (A Side/B Side)	Yr	NM
❑ 86093	Disappear (Extended 12" Mix)/ Middle Beast/What You Need (Coldcut Force Mix)	1990	10.00
❑ 86139	Suicide Blonde (7" Mix) (Earth Mix) (Devastation Mix) (Milk Mix) (Demolition Mix)/ Everybody Wants U Tonight	1990	10.00
❑ 86538	Never Tear Us Apart/Different World (12" Mix)/Move On	1988	8.00
❑ 86563 [PD]	New Sensation (Nick's 12" Mix)/ Guns in the Sky (Kick Ass Mix)	1988	20.00
—Picture disc			
❑ 86572	New Sensation (Nick's 12" Mix)/ Guns in the Sky (Kick Ass Mix)	1988	8.00
—Black vinyl			
❑ 86622	Devil Inside (Remix) (7" Edit)/ On the Rocks	1987	10.00
❑ 86645	Need You Tonight/Mediate/ I'm Coming (Home)	1987	8.00
❑ 86818	Listen Like Thieves (Extended) (Instrumental) (Live)/Begotten	1985	12.00
❑ 86832	What You Need (2 versions)/ Melting in the Sun/Burn for You	1985	10.00
45s			
ATCO			
❑ 99703	Burn for You/Johnson's Aeroplane	1984	4.00
❑ 99703 [PS]	Burn for You/Johnson's Aeroplane	1984	4.00
❑ 99731	I Send a Message/Mechanical	1984	4.00
❑ 99731 [PS]	I Send a Message/Mechanical	1984	4.00
❑ 99766	Original Sin/Stay Young	1984	4.00
❑ 99766 [PS]	Original Sin/Stay Young	1984	4.00
❑ 99833	To Look at You/Sax Thing	1983	4.00
❑ 99833 [PS]	To Look at You/Sax Thing	1983	4.00
❑ 99874	Don't Change/Long in Tooth	1983	4.00
❑ 99874 [PS]	Don't Change/Long in Tooth	1983	4.00
❑ 99905	The One Thing/Phantim of the Opera	1983	4.00
❑ 99905 [PS]	The One Thing/Phantim of the Opera	1983	4.00

Number	Title (A Side/B Side)	Yr	NM
ATLANTIC			
❑ 87784	Disappear/Middle Beast	1990	3.00
❑ 87784 [PS]	Disappear/Middle Beast	1990	3.00
❑ 87860	Suicide Blonde/Everyboidy Wants U Tonight	1990	3.00
—Not issued with picture sleeve in U.S.			
❑ 89038	Never Tear Us Apart/ Different World	1988	3.00
❑ 89038 [PS]	Never Tear Us Apart/ Different World	1988	3.00
❑ 89080	New Sensation/Guns in the Sky	1988	3.00
❑ 89080 [PS]	New Sensation/Guns in the Sky	1988	3.00
❑ 89144	Devil Inside/On the Rocks	1988	3.00
❑ 89144 [PS]	Devil Inside/On the Rocks	1988	3.00
❑ 89188	Need You Tonight/ I'm Comin' Home	1987	3.00
❑ 89188 [PS]	Need You Tonight/ I'm Comin' Home	1987	3.00
❑ 89237	Good Times/Laying Down the Law	1987	3.00
—With Jimmy Barnes			
❑ 89237 [PS]	Good Times/Laying Down the Law	1987	3.00
—With Jimmy Barnes			
❑ 89418	Kiss the Dirt (Falling Down the Mountain)//Six Knots/The One Thing (Live)	1986	3.00
❑ 89429	Listen Like Thieves/Begotten	1986	3.00
❑ 89429 [PS]	Listen Like Thieves/Begotten	1986	3.00
❑ 89460	What You Need/Sweet as Sin	1986	3.00
❑ 89460 [PS]	What You Need/Sweet as Sin	1986	3.00
❑ 89497	This Time/I'm Over You	1985	3.00
❑ 89497 [PS]	This Time/I'm Over You	1985	3.00
ATLANTIC OLDIES SERIES			
❑ 84876	Suicide Blonde/The One Thing	1993	3.00
❑ 84877	Disappear/Good Times	1993	3.00
—B-side with Jimmy Barnes			
❑ 84926	New Sensation/Never Tear Us Apart	199?	3.00
❑ 84927	Need You Tonight/Devil Inside	199?	3.00
❑ 84967	What You Need/This Time	198?	3.00

Number	Title (A Side/B Side)	Yr	NM
Albums			
ATCO			
❑ 90072	Shabooh Shoobah	1983	10.00
❑ 90115 [EP]	Dekadance	1983	12.00
❑ 90160	The Swing	1984	10.00
❑ 90184	INXS	1984	10.00
—U.S. issue of 1980 Australian album			
❑ 90185	Underneath the Colours	1984	12.00
—U.S. issue of 1981 Australian album			
ATLANTIC			
❑ 81277	Listen Like Thieves	1985	10.00
❑ 81796	Kick	1987	10.00
❑ 82140	X	1990	10.00
❑ A1-82294	Live Baby Live	1991	25.00
—Columbia House version (only U.S. vinyl pressing)			
❑ R 114468	Listen Like Thieves	1985	12.00
—RCA Music Service edition			
❑ R 153606	Kick	1987	12.00
—BMG Direct Marketing edition			
❑ R 164378	X	1990	12.00
—BMG Direct Marketing edition			

IRIDESCENTS, THE

Number	Title (A Side/B Side)	Yr	NM
45s			
HUDSON			
❑ 8102	Three Coins in the Fountain/ Strong Love	1963	25.00
❑ 8102	Three Coins in the Fountain/ Strong Love	1963	100.00
—Blue vinyl			
ULTRASONIC			
❑ 109	I Know/The Angels Sang	1960	400.00

IRISH ROVERS, THE

Number	Title (A Side/B Side)	Yr	NM
45s			
DECCA			
❑ 32254	The Unicorn/Black Velvet Band	1968	10.00
❑ 32333	(The Puppet Song) Whiskey on a Sunday/The Orange and the Green	1968	8.00
❑ 32371	Liverpool Lou/The Bi-Plane, Ever More	1968	8.00
❑ 32444	Lily the Pink/Mrs. Crandall's Boardinghouse	1969	8.00
❑ 32529	Peter Knight/Did She Mention My Name	1969	8.00
❑ 32575	Fifi O'Toole/Winkin', Blinkin', and Nod	1969	8.00
❑ 32616	Rhymes and Reasons/ Penny Whistler Peddler	1970	6.00
❑ 32616 [PS]	Rhymes and Reasons/ Penny Whistler Peddler	1970	10.00
❑ 32723	Two Little Boys/Years May Come, Years May Go	1970	6.00
❑ 32775	The Marvelous Toy/ Marika's Lullaby	1970	6.00
Albums			
DECCA			
❑ DL 4835 [M]	First	1967	20.00
❑ DL 4951 [M]	The Unicorn	1968	25.00
❑ DL 74835 [S]	First	1967	15.00
❑ DL 74951 [S]	The Unicorn	1968	15.00
❑ DL 75037	All Hung Up	1968	15.00
❑ DL 75081	Tales to Warm Your Mind	1969	15.00
❑ DL 75157	Life of the Rover	1969	15.00
❑ DL 75302	On the Shores of Americay	1971	15.00
MCA			
❑ 15	The Unicorn	1973	10.00
—Reissue of Decca 74951			
❑ 175	On the Shores of Americay	1973	10.00
—Reissue of Decca 75302			
❑ 249	First	1973	10.00
—Reissue of Decca 74835			
❑ 284	Life of the Rover	1973	10.00
—Reissue of Decca 75157			
❑ 4066 [(2)]	Greatest Hits	1976	15.00

IRMA AND THE LARKS

Number	Title (A Side/B Side)	Yr	NM
45s			
FAIRMOUNT			
❑ 1003	Without You Baby/Don't Cry	1966	100.00
PRIORITY			
❑ 322	Without You Baby/Don't Cry	1966	200.00

IRON BUTTERFLY

Also see CAPTAIN BEYOND.

Number	Title (A Side/B Side)	Yr	NM
45s			
ATCO			
❑ 6573	Possession/Unconscious Power	1968	8.00
❑ 6606	In-A-Gadda-Da-Vida/ Iron Butterfly Theme	1968	10.00
❑ 6647	Soul Experience/In the Crowds	1969	8.00
❑ 6676	In the Times of Our Lives/ It Must Be Love	1969	8.00
❑ 6712	To Be Alone/I Can't Help But Deceive You Little Girl	1969	8.00

Except when noted otherwise, VG = 25% of NM, and VG+ = 50% of NM. (Example: VG = $2.00, VG+ = $4.00 and NM = $8.00.)

Number	Title (A Side/B Side)	Yr	NM
❑ 6782	Easy Rider (Let the Wind Pay the Way)/Soldier in Town	1970	8.00
❑ 6818	Silly Sally/Stone Believer	1971	6.00

MCA

Number	Title (A Side/B Side)	Yr	NM
❑ 40379	Pearly Gates/Searchin' Circles	1975	4.00
❑ 40493	Beyond the Milky Way/Get It Out	1975	4.00

Albums

ATCO

Number	Title (A Side/B Side)	Yr	NM
❑ 33-227 [M]	Heavy	1967	30.00
❑ SD 33-227 [S]	Heavy	1967	25.00
—Brown and purple label			
❑ SD 33-227 [S]	Heavy	1969	15.00
—Yellow label			
❑ 33-250 [M]	In-A-Gadda-Da-Vida	1968	50.00
❑ SD 33-250 [S]	In-A-Gadda-Da-Vida	1968	25.00
—Brown and purple label			
❑ SD 33-250 [S]	In-A-Gadda-Da-Vida	1969	15.00
—Yellow label			
❑ SD 33-250 [S]	In-A-Gadda-Da-Vida	197?	10.00
—Any later Atco label; LP was in print into the late 1980s			
❑ SD 33-280	Ball	1969	15.00
❑ SD 33-318	Iron Butterfly Live	197?	10.00
—Any later Atco label; LP was in print into the late 1980s			
❑ SD 33-318	Iron Butterfly Live	1970	15.00
—Yellow label			
❑ SD 33-339	Metamorphosis	1970	15.00
❑ SD 33-369	The Best of Iron Butterfly/ Evolution	1971	15.00

MCA

Number	Title (A Side/B Side)	Yr	NM
❑ 465	Scorching Beauty	1975	12.00
❑ 2164	Sun and Steel	1976	12.00

PAIR

Number	Title (A Side/B Side)	Yr	NM
❑ PDL2-1065 [(2)]	Rare Flight	1986	15.00

IRON MAIDEN

45s

CAPITOL

Number	Title (A Side/B Side)	Yr	NM
❑ B-5248	Flight of Icarus/I've the Fire	1983	10.00
❑ B-5248 [PS]	Flight of Icarus/I've the Fire	1983	15.00
❑ B-44154	Can I Play with Madness/ Black Bart Blues	1988	8.00

Albums

CAPITOL

Number	Title (A Side/B Side)	Yr	NM
❑ ST-12094	Iron Maiden	198?	12.00
—Reissue of Harvest 12094			
❑ ST-12141	Killers	198?	12.00
—Reissue of Harvest 12141			
❑ ST-12202	The Number of the Beast	1982	12.00
❑ SEAX-12219 [PD]	The Number of the Beast	1982	50.00
❑ ST-12274	Piece of Mind	1983	12.00
❑ SEAX-12306 [PD]	Piece of Mind	1983	60.00
❑ SJ-12321	Powerslave	1984	12.00
❑ SABB-12441 [(2)]	Live After Death	1985	18.00
❑ SJ-12524	Somewhere in Time	1986	12.00
❑ SQ-15017 [EP]	Maiden Japan	198?	10.00
—Reissue of Harvest 15000			
❑ 53185 [(4)]	Best of the Beast	1996	80.00
—Box set with booklet; probably a UK pressing stickered with US bar code			
❑ C1-90258	Seventh Son of a Seventh Son	1988	10.00

EPIC

Number	Title (A Side/B Side)	Yr	NM
❑ E 46905	No Prayer for the Dying	1990	25.00
—Red vinyl			

HARVEST

Number	Title (A Side/B Side)	Yr	NM
❑ ST-12094	Iron Maiden	1980	15.00
❑ ST-12141	Killers	1981	15.00
❑ MLP-15000 [EP]	Maiden Japan	1981	10.00

IRRIDESCENTS, THE

45s

HAWK

Number	Title (A Side/B Side)	Yr	NM
❑ 4001	Bali Ha'i/Swamp Surfer	1963	50.00

INFINITY

Number	Title (A Side/B Side)	Yr	NM
❑ 037	Bali Ha'i/Swamp Surfer	1963	25.00

OLDIES 45

Number	Title (A Side/B Side)	Yr	NM
❑ 183	Bali Ha'i/Swamp Surfer	1964	12.00

IRWIN, BIG DEE

45s

CUB

Number	Title (A Side/B Side)	Yr	NM
❑ 9155	I Only Got This Feeling/ Wrong Direction	1968	8.00
—As "Dee Erwin"			

DIMENSION

Number	Title (A Side/B Side)	Yr	NM
❑ 1001	Everybody's Gotta Dance But Me/And Heaven Was There	1962	60.00
❑ 1010	Swinging on a Star/Another Night with the Boys	1963	20.00
❑ 1015	Soul Waltzin'/Happy Being Fat	1963	15.00
❑ 1018	You're My Inspiration/Skeeter	1963	15.00
❑ 1021	The Christmas Song/I Wish You a Merry Christmas	1963	15.00
—With Little Eva			
❑ 1028	Heigh Ho/I Want So Much to Know You	1964	50.00

FAIRMOUNT

Number	Title (A Side/B Side)	Yr	NM
❑ 1005	You Really Are Together/A Sweet Young Thing Like You	1966	50.00

IMPERIAL

Number	Title (A Side/B Side)	Yr	NM
❑ 66295	Wrong Direction/I Only Get This Feeling	1968	40.00
—As "Dee Irwin"			
❑ 66320	I Can't Stand the Pain/ My Hope to Die Girl	1968	20.00
❑ 66334	All I Want for Christmas Is Your Love//By the Time I Get to Phoenix/I Say a Little Prayer	1968	12.00
—With Mamie Galore			
❑ 66359	Day Tripper/I Didn't Wanna Do It, But I Did	1969	8.00
—With Mamie Galore			
❑ 66420	Ain't No Way/Cherish	1969	20.00

PHIL-LA OF SOUL

Number	Title (A Side/B Side)	Yr	NM
❑ 303	Better to Have Loved and Lost/ Linda	1967	40.00
—As "Dee Erwin"			

ROULETTE

Number	Title (A Side/B Side)	Yr	NM
❑ 4596	Discotheque/The Sun's Gonna Shine Tomorrow	1965	10.00
—As "Big Dee Erwin"			

ISAAK, CHRIS

12-Inch Singles

WARNER BROS.

Number	Title (A Side/B Side)	Yr	NM
❑ PRO-A-2265 [DJ]	Dancin'/Gone Ridin'	1985	10.00
❑ PRO-A-2332 [DJ]	Livin' for Your Lover (same on both sides)	1985	10.00
❑ PRO-A-2359 [DJ]	Gone Ridin' (same on both sides)	1985	8.00
❑ PRO-A-2682 [DJ]	You Owe Me Some Kind of Love (same on both sides)	1987	10.00
❑ PRO-A-2736 [DJ]	Heart Full of Soul (same on both sides)	1987	12.00
❑ PRO-A-2768 [DJ]	Blue Hotel (same on both sides)	1987	8.00

45s

REPRISE

Number	Title (A Side/B Side)	Yr	NM
❑ 7-17781	Go Walking Down There/ Things Go Wrong	1995	4.00
❑ 7-17872	Somebody's Crying/ Changed Your Mind	1995	4.00
❑ 7-18263	Dark Moon/Except the New Girl	1993	4.00
❑ 7-18462	Solitary Man/5:15	1993	4.00
❑ 7-18604	Can't Do a Thing (To Stop Me)/ Lonely with a Broken Heart	1993	5.00
❑ 7-19704	Wicked Game/(instrumental)	1990	5.00

WARNER BROS.

Number	Title (A Side/B Side)	Yr	NM
❑ 7-28374	Blue Hotel/Waiting for the Rain to Fall	1987	8.00
❑ 7-28374 [DJ]	Blue Hotel (same on both sides)	1987	4.00
❑ 7-28374 [PS]	Blue Hotel/Waiting for the Rain to Fall	1987	8.00
❑ 7-28907	Gone Ridin' (Theme from American Flyers)/Tears	1985	6.00
❑ 7-28907 [DJ]	Gone Ridin' (Theme from American Flyers) (same on both sides)	1985	3.00
❑ 7-28907 [PS]	Gone Ridin' (Theme from American Flyers)/Tears	1985	6.00
❑ 7-28971	Livin' for Your Lover/Talk to Me	1985	6.00
❑ 7-28971 [DJ]	Livin' for Your Lover (same on both sides)	1985	3.00
❑ 7-28971 [PS]	Livin' for Your Lover/Talk to Me	1985	6.00
❑ 7-29073	Dancin'/Unhappiness	1985	6.00
❑ 7-29073 [DJ]	Dancin' (same on both sides)	1985	3.00
❑ 7-29073 [PS]	Dancin'/Unhappiness	1985	6.00

Albums

REPRISE

Number	Title (A Side/B Side)	Yr	NM
❑ 25837	Heart Shaped World	1989	12.00

WARNER BROS.

Number	Title (A Side/B Side)	Yr	NM
❑ 25156	Silvertone	1985	10.00
❑ 25336	Chris Isaak	1987	10.00

ISLE, JIMMY

45s

BALLY

Number	Title (A Side/B Side)	Yr	NM
❑ 1034	Baby-O/Hssle	1957	25.00

EVEREST

Number	Title (A Side/B Side)	Yr	NM
❑ 19320	Oh Judy/Billy Boy	1959	25.00

MALA

Number	Title (A Side/B Side)	Yr	NM
❑ 459	Our Town/Everybody Gotta Little Girl But Me	1963	20.00

ROULETTE

Number	Title (A Side/B Side)	Yr	NM
❑ 4065	Goin' Wild/You and Johnny Smith	1958	30.00

SUN

Number	Title (A Side/B Side)	Yr	NM
❑ 306	Diamond Ring/I've Been Waiting	1958	25.00
❑ 318	Time Will Tell/Without a Love	1959	25.00
❑ 332	What a Life/Together	1959	25.00

ISLEY BROTHERS, THE

12-Inch Singles

T-NECK

Number	Title (A Side/B Side)	Yr	NM
❑ AS 947 [DJ]	Hurry Up and Wait (3:54) (4:09)	1981	8.00
❑ 2267	Livin' in the Life/Go for Your Guns	1977	15.00
❑ 2276	Tell Me When You Need It Again/ Take Me to the Next Phase	1977	15.00
❑ 2283	I Wanna Be with You (6:20)/ Rockin' with Fire (5:57)	1978	12.00
❑ 2289	It's a Disco Night (Rock Don't Stop)/Ain't Givin' Up on Love	1979	12.00
❑ 03282	It's Alright with Me (Vocal) (Instrumental)	1982	10.00
❑ 04148	I Need Your Body/(Instrumental)	1983	8.00

WARNER BROS.

Number	Title (A Side/B Side)	Yr	NM
❑ PRO-A-2378 [DJ]	Colder Are My Night (Edit Version) (LP Version)	1985	8.00
❑ PRO-A-4511 [DJ]	Spend the Night (Edit)/Colder Are My Nights (Edit)/Smooth Sailin' Tonight (Edit)	1989	8.00
❑ PRO-A-5417 [DJ]	Sensitive Lover (4 versions)	1992	8.00
❑ 20827	I Wish (Vocal) (Instrumental)	1987	8.00
❑ 21415	You'll Never Walk Alone (4 versions)/One of a Kind	1989	8.00

45s

ATLANTIC

Number	Title (A Side/B Side)	Yr	NM
❑ 2092	Jeepers Creepers/Teach Me How to Shimmy	1961	15.00
❑ 2100	Shine On Harvest Moon/ Standing on the Dance Floor	1961	15.00
❑ 2110	Your Old Lady/Write to Me	1961	30.00
❑ 2122	A Fool for You/Just One More Time	1961	15.00
❑ 2263	Looking for a Love/The Last Girl	1964	30.00
❑ 2277	Simon Says/Wild As a Tiger	1965	30.00
❑ 2303	Move Over and Let Me Dance/ Have You Ever Been Disappointed	1965	20.00

CINDY

Number	Title (A Side/B Side)	Yr	NM
❑ 3009	Don't Be Jealous/This Is the End	1958	75.00
—"Cindy" in regular print			
❑ 3009	Don't Be Jealous/This Is the End	1958	150.00
—"Cindy" in shadow print			

GONE

Number	Title (A Side/B Side)	Yr	NM
❑ 5022	I Wanna Know/Everybody's Gonna Rock and Roll	1958	80.00
❑ 5048	My Love/The Drag	1958	80.00

MARK-X

Number	Title (A Side/B Side)	Yr	NM
❑ 7003	The Drag/Rockin' MacDonald	1957	100.00
❑ 8000	The Drag/Rockin' MacDonald	1959	30.00

PHILCO-FORD

Number	Title (A Side/B Side)	Yr	NM
❑ HP-41	Twist and Shout/Rubberleg Twist	1969	25.00
—4-inch plastic "Hip Pocket Record" with color sleeve			

RCA

Number	Title (A Side/B Side)	Yr	NM
❑ 447-0589	Shout (Part 1)/Shout (Part 2)	1976	4.00
—Gold Standard Series; black label, dog near top			

RCA VICTOR

Number	Title (A Side/B Side)	Yr	NM
❑ 47-7537	I'm Gonna Knock on Your Door/ Turn to Me	1959	25.00
❑ 47-7588	Shout (Part 1)/Shout (Part 2)	1959	30.00
❑ 47-7657	Respectable/Without a Song	1959	25.00
❑ 47-7718	He's Got the Whole World in His Hands/How Deep Is the Ocean	1960	25.00
❑ 47-7746	Gypsy Love Song/Open Up Your Heart	1960	25.00
❑ 47-7787	Say You Love Me Too/ Tell Me Who	1960	25.00
❑ 61-7588 [S]	Shout (Part 1)/Shout (Part 2)	1959	60.00
—"Living Stereo" (large hole, plays at 45 rpm)			
❑ 447-0589	Shout (Part 1)/Shout (Part 2)	1962	12.00
—Gold Standard Series; black label, dog on top (this charted with this number in 1962)			
❑ 447-0589	Shout (Part 1)/Shout (Part 2)	1965	8.00
—Gold Standard Series; black label, dog on side			
❑ 447-0589	Shout (Part 1)/Shout (Part 2)	1969	5.00
—Gold Standard Series; red label			

T-NECK

Number	Title (A Side/B Side)	Yr	NM
❑ 501	Testify (Part 1)/Testify (Part 2)	1964	30.00
❑ 901	It's Your Thing/Don't Give It Away	1969	6.00

I

Number	Title (A Side/B Side)	Yr	NM
❑ 902	I Turned You On/I Know Who You Been Socking It To	1969	6.00
❑ 906	Black Berries — Pt. 1/Black Berries — Pt. 2	1969	6.00
❑ 908	Was It Good to You/I Got to Get Myself Together	1969	6.00
❑ 912	Bless Your Heart/Give the Women What They Want	1969	6.00
❑ 914	Keep On Doin'/Save Me	1970	6.00
❑ 919	If He Can, You Can/Holdin' On	1970	6.00
❑ 921	Girls Will Be Girls, Boys Will Be Boys/Get Down Off of the Train	1970	6.00
❑ 924	Get Into Something/Get Into Something (Part 2)	1970	15.00
❑ 927	Freedom/I Need You So	1970	6.00
❑ 929	Warpath/I Got to Find Me One	1971	6.00
❑ 930	Love the One You're With/He's Got Your Love	1971	6.00
❑ 932	Spill the Wine/Take Inventory	1971	15.00
❑ 933	Lay Lady Lay/Vacuum Cleaner	1971	15.00
❑ 934	Lay-Away/Feel Like the World	1972	6.00
❑ 935	Pop That Thang/I Got to Find Me One	1972	6.00
❑ 936	Work to Do/Beautiful	1972	20.00
❑ 937	It's Too Late/Nothing to Do But Today	1973	6.00
❑ 02033	Hurry Up and Wait/(Instrumental)	1981	5.00
❑ 02151	Don't Say Goodnight (It's Time for Love) (Parts 1 & 2)	1981	4.00
—Reissue			
❑ 02179	I Once Had Your Love (And I Can't Let Go)/(Instrumental)	1981	5.00
❑ 2251	That Lady (Part 1)/That Lady (Part 2)	1973	5.00
❑ 2252	What It Comes Down To/Highways of My Life	1973	5.00
❑ 2253	Summer Breeze (Part 1)/Summer Breeze (Part 2)	1974	5.00
❑ 2254	Live It Up (Part 1)/Live It Up (Part 2)	1974	5.00
❑ 2255	Midnight Sky (Part 1)/Midnight Sky (Part 2)	1974	5.00
❑ 2256	Fight the Power Part 1/Fight the Power Part 2	1975	5.00
❑ 2259	For the Love of You (Part 1&2)/You Walk Your Way	1975	5.00
❑ 2260	Who Loves You Better-Part 1/Who Loves You Better-Part 2	1976	5.00
❑ 2261	Harvest for the World/Harvest for the World (Part 2)	1976	5.00
❑ 2262	The Pride (Part 1)/The Pride (Part 2)	1977	5.00
❑ 2264	Livin' in the Life/Go for Your Guns	1977	5.00
❑ 2270	Voyage to Atlantis/Do You Wanna Stay Down	1977	5.00
❑ 02270	Voyage to Atlantis/Do You Wanna Stay Down	1981	4.00
—Reissue			
❑ 2272	Take Me to the Next Phase (Part 1)/Take Me to the Next Phase (Part 2)	1978	5.00
❑ 2277	Groove with You/Footsteps in the Dark	1978	5.00
❑ 2278	Showdown (Part 1)/Showdown (Part 2)	1978	5.00
❑ 2279	I Wanna Be with You (Part 1)/I Wanna Be with You (Part 2)	1979	5.00
❑ 2284	Winner Takes All/Fun and Games	1979	5.00
❑ 2287	It's a Disco Night (Rock Don't Stop)/Ain't Givin' Up on Love	1979	5.00
❑ 2290	Don't Say Goodnight (It's Time for Love) (Part 1)/Don't Say Goodnight (It's Time for Love) (Part 2)	1980	5.00
❑ 2291	Here We Go Again (Part 1)/Here We Go Again (Part 2)	1980	5.00
❑ 2292	Say You Will (Part 1)/Say You Will (Part 2)	1980	5.00
❑ 2293	Who Said?/(Can't You See) What You've Done to Me	1980	5.00
❑ 02293	Who Said?/(Can't You See) What You Do to Me	1981	4.00
—Reissue			
❑ 02531	Inside You (Part 1)/Inside You (Part 2)	1981	5.00
❑ 02705	Party Night/Welcome Into My Night	1982	5.00
❑ 02985	The Real Deal/(Instrumental)	1982	5.00
❑ 03281	It's Alright with Me/(Instrumental)	1982	5.00
❑ 03797	Between the Sheets/(Instrumental)	1983	5.00
❑ 03994	Choosey Lover/(Instrumental)	1983	5.00
❑ 04320	Let's Make Love Tonight/(Instrumental)	1984	5.00
TAMLA			
❑ 54128	This Old Heart of Mine (Is Weak for You)/There's No Love Left	1966	15.00
❑ 54133	Take Some Time Out for Love/Who Could Ever Doubt My Love	1966	15.00
❑ 54135	I Guess I'll Always Love You/I Hear a Symphony	1966	20.00
❑ 54146	Got to Have You Back/Just Ain't Enough Love	1967	15.00
❑ 54154	One Too Many Heartaches/That's the Way Love Is	1967	15.00
❑ 54164	Take Me in Your Arms (Rock Me a Little While)/Why When Love Is Gone	1968	15.00
❑ 54175	Behind a Painted Smile/All Because I Love You	1968	25.00
❑ 54182	Take Some Time Out for Love/Just Ain't Enough Love	1969	20.00
TEENAGE			
❑ 1004	Angels Cried/The Cow Jumped Over the Moon	1957	800.00
UNITED ARTISTS			
❑ 605	She's Gone/Tango	1963	20.00
❑ 638	Surf and Shout/Whatcha Gonna Do	1963	20.00
❑ 659	Please, Please, Please/You'll Never Leave Him	1963	20.00
❑ 714	Who's That Lady/My Little Girl	1964	50.00
❑ 798	Love Is a Wonderful Thing/Open Up Her Eyes	1964	—
—Unreleased			
❑ 923	Love Is a Wonderful Thing/Open Up Her Eyes	1965	—
—Unreleased			
V.I.P.			
❑ 25020	I Hear a Symphony/Who Could Ever Doubt My Love	1965	400.00
VEEP			
❑ 1230	Love Is a Wonderful Thing/Open Up Her Eyes	1966	10.00
WAND			
❑ 118	Right Now/The Snake	1962	10.00
❑ 124	Twist and Shout/Spanish Twist	1962	10.00
❑ 127	Twistin' with Linda/You Better Come Home	1962	15.00
❑ 131	Nobody But Me/I'm Laughing to Keep from Crying	1963	12.00
❑ 137	I Say Love/Hold On Baby	1963	15.00
WARNER BROS.			
❑ 22748	One of a Kind/You'll Never Walk Alone	1989	3.00
❑ 22900	Spend the Night (Ce Soir)/(Instrumental)	1989	3.00
❑ 22900 [PS]	Spend the Night (Ce Soir)/(Instrumental)	1989	3.00
❑ 27954	It Takes a Good Woman/(Instrumental)	1988	4.00
❑ 28129	I Wish/(Instrumental)	1988	4.00
❑ 28129 [PS]	I Wish/(Instrumental)	1988	4.00
❑ 28241	Come My Way/(Instrumental)	1987	4.00
❑ 28385	Smooth Sailin' Tonight/(Instrumental)	1987	4.00
❑ 28385 [PS]	Smooth Sailin' Tonight/(Instrumental)	1987	4.00
❑ 28764	May I?/(Instrumental)	1986	4.00
❑ 28860	Colder Are My Nights/(Instrumental)	1985	4.00
Albums			
BUDDAH			
❑ BDS-5652 [(2)]	The Best of the Isley Brothers	1976	15.00
COLLECTABLES			
❑ COL-5103	Shout!	198?	10.00
DEF SOUL			
❑ B0004812-01 [(2)]	Baby Makin' Music	2006	15.00
ISLAND			
❑ 7243 [(2)DJ]	Mission to Please	1996	20.00
—Promo-only vinyl in generic cover			
MOTOWN			
❑ M5-106V1	Motown Superstar Series, Vol. 6	1981	8.00
❑ M5-128V1	This Old Heart of Mine	1981	8.00
—Reissue of Tamla 269			
❑ M5-143V1	Doin' Their Thing (Best of the Isley Brothers)	1981	8.00
—Reissue of Tamla 287			
PICKWICK			
❑ SPC-3331	Soul Shout!	197?	10.00
RCA CAMDEN			
❑ ACL1-0126	Rock On Brother	1973	12.00
❑ ACL1-0861	Rock Around the Clock	1975	12.00
RCA VICTOR			
❑ LPM-2156 [M]	Shout!	1959	120.00
—"Long Play" label			
❑ LSP-2156 [S]	Shout!	1959	200.00
—"Living Stereo" label			
SCEPTER			
❑ SC-552 [M]	Take Some Time Out for the Isley Brothers	1966	30.00
❑ SCS-552 [S]	Take Some Time Out for the Isley Brothers	1966	40.00
SUNSET			
❑ SUS-5257	The Isley Brothers Do Their Thing	1969	15.00
T-NECK			
❑ ASZ 137 [DJ]	Everything You Always Wanted to Hear by the Isley Brothers But Were Afraid to Ask For	1976	20.00
—Promo-only compilation			
❑ TNS-3001	It's Our Thing	1969	20.00
❑ TNS-3002	The Brothers: Isley	1969	20.00
❑ TNS-3006	Get Into Something	1970	15.00
❑ TNS-3007	In the Beginning (With Jimi Hendrix)	1970	20.00
❑ TNS-3008	Givin' It Back	1971	15.00
❑ TNS-3009	Brother, Brother, Brother	1972	15.00
❑ TNS-3010 [(2)]	The Isleys Live	1973	20.00
❑ TNS-3011	Isleys' Greatest Hits	1973	15.00
❑ KZ 32453	3 + 3	1973	12.00
❑ PZ 32453	3 + 3	197?	8.00
—Reissue with new prefix			
❑ ZQ 32453 [Q]	3 + 3	1974	20.00
❑ PZ 33070	Live It Up	1974	12.00
—No bar code on cover			
❑ PZQ 33070 [Q]	Live It Up	1974	20.00
❑ PZ 33536	The Heat Is On	1975	12.00
—No bar code on cover			
❑ PZ 33536	The Heat Is On	198?	8.00
—Budget-line reissue with bar code			
❑ PZ 33809	Harvest for the World	1976	12.00
—No bar code on cover			
❑ PZQ 33809 [Q]	Harvest for the World	1976	20.00
❑ PZ 34432	Go for Your Guns	1977	12.00
—No bar code on cover			
❑ PZ 34432	Go for Your Guns	198?	8.00
—Budget-line reissue with bar code			
❑ PZQ 34432 [Q]	Go for Your Guns	1977	20.00
❑ PZ 34452	Forever Gold	1977	10.00
❑ JZ 34930	Showdown	1978	10.00
❑ PZ 34930	Showdown	198?	8.00
—Budget-line reissue			
❑ KZ2 35650 [(2)]	Timeless	1978	12.00
❑ PZ2 36077 [(2)]	Winner Takes All	1979	12.00
❑ FZ 36305	Go All the Way	1980	10.00
❑ PZ 36305	Go All the Way	198?	8.00
—Budget-line reissue			
❑ FZ 37080	Grand Slam	1981	10.00
❑ PZ 37080	Grand Slam	198?	8.00
—Budget-line reissue			
❑ FZ 37533	Inside You	1981	10.00
❑ FZ 38047	The Real Deal	1982	10.00
❑ FZ 38674	Between the Sheets	1983	10.00
❑ PZ 38674	Between the Sheets	1985	8.00
—Budget-line reissue			
❑ FZ 39240	Greatest Hits, Vol. 1	1984	10.00
❑ PZ 39240	Greatest Hits, Vol. 1	1985	8.00
—Budget-line reissue			
TAMLA			
❑ T-269 [M]	This Old Heart of Mine	1966	25.00
❑ TS-269 [S]	This Old Heart of Mine	1966	30.00
❑ T-275 [M]	Soul on the Rocks	1967	25.00
❑ TS-275 [S]	Soul on the Rocks	1967	30.00
❑ TS-287	Doin' Their Thing (Best of the Isley Brothers)	1969	20.00
UNITED ARTISTS			
❑ UA-LA500-E	The Very Best of the Isley Brothers	1975	10.00
❑ UAL-3313 [M]	The Famous Isley Brothers	1963	50.00
❑ UAS-6313 [S]	The Famous Isley Brothers	1963	60.00
WAND			
❑ WD-653 [M]	Twist & Shout	1962	80.00
❑ WDS-653 [S]	Twist & Shout	1962	100.00
WARNER BROS.			
❑ 25347	Masterpiece	1985	10.00
❑ 25586	Smooth Sailin'	1987	10.00
❑ 25940	Spend the Night	1989	10.00

IT'S A BEAUTIFUL DAY

45s

Number	Title (A Side/B Side)	Yr	NM
COLUMBIA			
❑ 44928	White Bird/Wasted Union Blues	1969	8.00
❑ 45152	Good Lovin'/Soapstone Mountain	1970	6.00
❑ 45309	Do You Remember the Sun/Dolphin	1971	5.00
❑ 45536	Anytime/Apples and Oranges	1972	5.00
❑ 45788	White Bird/Wasted Union Blues	1973	5.00
❑ 45853	Ain't That Lovin' You Baby/Time	1973	6.00
SAN FRANCISCO SOUND			
❑ 11680	Aquarian Dream/Bulgaria	198?	10.00

Albums

COLUMBIA

Number	Title (A Side/B Side)	Yr	NM
CS 1058	Marrying Maiden	1970	15.00
—Orange label			
CS 1058	Marrying Maiden	1970	30.00
—Red "360 Sound" label			
CS 9768	It's A Beautiful Day	1969	30.00
—Red "360 Sound" label			
CS 9768	It's A Beautiful Day	1970	20.00
—Orange label			
C 30734	Choice Quality Stuff/Anytime	1971	15.00
KC 31338	It's a Beautiful Day at Carnegie Hall	1972	15.00
KC 32181	It's a Beautiful Day...Today	1973	15.00
KC 32660 [DJ]	A Thousand and One Nights	1973	50.00
—Canceled before commercial release?			

SAN FRANCISCO SOUND

Number	Title (A Side/B Side)	Yr	NM
11790	It's A Beautiful Day	1985	25.00
—Limited reissue			

ITALIAN ASPHALT AND PAVEMENT COMPANY, THE

See THE DUPREES.

IVAN

45s

CORAL

Number	Title (A Side/B Side)	Yr	NM
62017	Real Wild Child/Oh You Beautiful Doll	1958	200.00
—With Buddy Holly on guitar			
62081	That'll Be Alright/Frankie Frankenstein	1959	400.00
65607	Real Wild Child/That'll Be Alright	1967	50.00

IVERS, PETER

Albums

EPIC

Number	Title (A Side/B Side)	Yr	NM
BN 26500	Knight of the Blue Communion	1970	40.00

WARNER BROS.

Number	Title (A Side/B Side)	Yr	NM
BS 2804	Terminal Love	1974	12.00
BS 2930	Peter Ivers	1976	12.00

IVES, BURL

45s

BELL

Number	Title (A Side/B Side)	Yr	NM
930	Real Roses/Roll Up Some Inspiration	1970	5.00
943	Time/Galisteo	1970	5.00

BIG TREE

Number	Title (A Side/B Side)	Yr	NM
130	Gingerbread House/Tumbleweed Snowman	1971	5.00

BUENA VISTA

Number	Title (A Side/B Side)	Yr	NM
419	On the Front Porch/Ugly Bug Ball	1963	8.00
419 [PS]	On the Front Porch/Ugly Bug Ball	1963	12.00

COLUMBIA

Number	Title (A Side/B Side)	Yr	NM
4-124	Grandfather Kringle/The 12 Days Of Christmas	1951	12.00
—Yellow-label "Chidren's Series" record; alternate number is 90138			
4-124 [PS]	Grandfather Kringle/The 12 Days Of Christmas	1951	15.00
1-173	Riders in the Sky (Cowboy Legend)/Wayfaring Stranger-Woolie Boogie Bee	1949	40.00
—Microgroove 33 1/3 rpm 7-inch single			
1-418	Mule Train/Greer County Bachelor	1950	30.00
—Microgroove 33 1/3 rpm 7-inch single			
1-550 (?)	John Henry/Mah Lindy Lou	1950	30.00
—Microgroove 33 1/3 rpm 7-inch single			
1-580 (?)	The Doughnut Song/I Got a Fever in My Bones	1950	30.00
—Microgroove 33 1/3 rpm 7-inch single			
1-630 (?)	Got the World by the Tail/My Momma Told Me	1950	30.00
—Microgroove 33 1/3 rpm 7-inch single			
1-780 (?)	Pig Pig/Last Night the Nightingale Woke Me	1950	30.00
—Microgroove 33 1/3 rpm 7-inch single			
6-780 (?)	Pig Pig/Last Night the Nightingale Woke Me	1950	25.00
1-910 (?)	There's a Little White House/Little White Duck	1950	30.00
—Microgroove 33 1/3 rpm 7-inch single			
6-910 (?)	There's a Little White House/Little White Duck	1950	25.00
39328	On Top of Old Smoky/The Syncopated Clock	1951	15.00
—With Percy Faith co-credited			
44508	I'll Be Your Baby Tonight/Maria	1968	6.00
44606	Little Green Apples/One Too Many Mornings	1968	6.00
44711	Santa Mouse/Oh What a Lucky Boy Am I	1968	6.00
44711 [PS]	Santa Mouse/Oh What a Lucky Boy Am I	1968	10.00
44974	Montego Bay/Tessie's Bar Mystery	1969	6.00

CYCLONE

Number	Title (A Side/B Side)	Yr	NM
75014	One More Time Billy Brown/Tied Down Here at Home	1970	7.00

DECCA

Number	Title (A Side/B Side)	Yr	NM
25524	Mockin' Bird Hill/Royal Telephone (Telephone to Glory)	196?	8.00
25585	Twelve Days of Christmas/The Indian Christmas Carol	1962	10.00
25691	You Know You Belong to Someone Else/Jealous	196?	8.00
25754	I Talk to the Trees/They Call the Wind Maria	1970	6.00
27079	This Time Tomorrow/One Hour Ahead of the Posse	1950	20.00
28055	Wild Side of Life/It's So Long and Goodbye to You	1952	15.00
28079	This Time Tomorrow/One Hour Ahead of the Posse	1952	15.00
28161	Diesel Smoke, Dangerous Curves/The Little Green Valley	1952	15.00
—With Grady Martin			
28299	There's a Mule Up in Tombstone, Arizona/Lonesome, So Lonesome	1952	15.00
28347	The Friendly Beasts/There Were Three Ships	1952	12.00
28348	Jesous Anatonia/What Child Is This	1952	12.00
28349	The Seven Joys of Mary (Part 1)/The Seven Joys of Mary (Part 2)	1952	12.00
28350	King Herod and the Clock/Down in Yon Forest	1952	12.00
—The above four comprise a box set			
28708	Close the Door Richard/Left My Gal in the Mountains	1953	15.00
28849	Great White Bird/Brighten the Corner Where You Are	1953	15.00
28935	The Crawdad Song/Hound Dog	1953	15.00
29039	There's Plenty of Fish in the Ocean/The Old Red Barn	1954	15.00
29088	True Love Goes On and On/Brave Man	1954	15.00
29129	Wait for Me Darling/Casey Jones	1954	12.00
29282	The Mission San Miguel/Tangled Web	1954	15.00
29423	The Ballad of Davy Crockett/Goober Peas	1955	15.00
29533	I Wonder What's Become of Sally/Wabash Cannonball	1955	12.00
29549	Be Sure You're Right (Then Go Ahead)/Ol' Betsy	1955	15.00
29910	Jack Was Every Inch a Sailor/Harlem Man	1956	12.00
30046	The Bus Stop Song/That's My Heart Strings	1956	12.00
30217	Marianne/Pretty Girl	1957	12.00
30855	We Love Ye, Jimmy/I Never See Maggie Alone	1959	12.00
31248	Long Black Veil/Forty Hour Week	1961	10.00
31330	A Little Bitty Tear/Shanghaid	1961	10.00
31371	Funny Way of Laughin'/Mother Wouldn't Do That	1962	10.00
31405	Call Me Mr. In-Between/What You Gonna Do, Leroy	1962	10.00
31433	Mary Ann Regrets/How Do You Fall Out of Love	1962	10.00
31453	The Same Old Hurt/Curry Road	1963	10.00
31479	Roses and Orchids/Baby Come Home to Me	1963	10.00
31504	I'm the Boss/The Moon Is High	1963	10.00
31518	This Is All I Ask/There Goes Another Pal of Mine	1963	10.00
31543	It Comes and Goes/I Found My Best Friend in the Dog Pound	1963	10.00
31571	True Love Goes On and On/I Wonder What's Become of Sally	1963	10.00
31610	Four Initials on a Tree/This Is Your Day	1964	8.00
31659	Pearly Shells/What Little Tears Are Made Of	1964	8.00
31695	A Holly Jolly Christmas/Snow for Johnny	1964	10.00
31729	Call My Name/My Gal Sal	1965	8.00
31772	On the Beach at Waikiki/Some Hangin' Round You All the Time	1965	8.00
31811	Salt Water Guitar/The Story of Bobby Lee Trent	1965	8.00
31857	Frangipani/A Girl Sittin' Up in a Tree	1965	8.00
31918	The Sixties/Don't Forget Your Paddle	1966	8.00
31981	Here She Comes (There She Goes)/Atlantic Coastal Line	1966	8.00
31997	Evil Off My Mind/Taste of Heaven	1966	8.00
32078	Lonesone 7-7203/Hollow Words	1967	8.00
32165	Funny Little Show/Holding Hands for Joe	1967	8.00
32282	Bury the Bottle/That's Where My Baby Used to Be	1968	8.00
32990	Stayin' Song/The Best Is Yet to Come	1972	6.00
33049	Miss Johnson's Happiness Emporium/Anytime You Say	1972	6.00

DISNEYLAND

Number	Title (A Side/B Side)	Yr	NM
F-130	Chim Chim Chiree/Lavender Blue	1964	8.00
F-130 [PS]	Chim Chim Chiree/Lavender Blue	1964	12.00

MCA

Number	Title (A Side/B Side)	Yr	NM
31695	A Holly Jolly Christmas/Snow for Johnny	1989	5.00
—Double the NM value if insert is enclosed			
40082	Payin' My Dues Again/All Around	1973	5.00
40175	Tale of the Comet Kohoutek/A Very Fine Lady	1974	5.00

MONKEY JOE

Number	Title (A Side/B Side)	Yr	NM
MJ-1 [DJ]	The Christmas Legend of Monkey Joe/It's Gonna Be A Mixed Up Xmas	1978	10.00

UNITED ARTISTS

Number	Title (A Side/B Side)	Yr	NM
293	Alexander's Ragtime Band/Say It Isn't So	1961	8.00
429	All Alone/Always	1962	8.00
1568	Go 'Way from My House/Two Maidens Went Milking	196?	8.00
1569	Willie Boy/Irish Rover	196?	8.00
1570	Alexander's Ragtime Band/What'll I Do	196?	8.00
1571	All Alone/Always	196?	8.00
—The above four all are "Silver Spotlight Series" releases			

7-Inch Extended Plays

DECCA

Number	Title (A Side/B Side)	Yr	NM
ED 2103	*Dublin City/Cockle Shells/Old Dan Tucker/The Erie Canal/The Eddystone Light/Hullabaloo-Belay/Venezuela	195?	12.00
ED 2103 [PS]	Burl Ives, Vol. 1	195?	12.00
ED 2235	*The Locktender's Lament/Ox Driver's Song/The Bold Soldier/The Young Married Man (Cod Liver Oil)/Sad Man's Song (Fare Thee Well, O Honey)/The Harlem Man	195?	12.00
ED 2235 [PS]	Songs For and About Men, Part 1	195?	12.00
ED 2236	The Western Settler/Waltzing Matilda (The Jolly Swagman's Song)//The Wild Rover/Frankie and Johnny/The Deceiver	195?	12.00
ED 2236 [PS]	Songs For and About Men, Part 2	195?	12.00
ED 2714	(contents unknown)	1961	10.00
ED 2714 [PS]	Burl Ives	1961	10.00
ED 2720	Funny Way of Laughin'/Mother Wouldn't Do That//What You Gonna Do Leroy/I Ain't Comin' Home Tonight	1962	10.00
ED 2720 [PS]	It's Just My Funny Way of Laughin'	1962	10.00
ED 2726	Call Me Mr. In-Between/Poor Little Jimmie//In Foggy Old London/Thumbin' Johnny Brown	1962	10.00
ED 2726 [PS]	Call Me Mr. In-Between	1962	10.00
ED 2741	(contents unknown)	1962	10.00
ED 2741 [PS]	Mary Ann Regrets	1962	10.00
ED 2771	True Love Goes On and On/This Is All I Ask//It Comes and Goes/I'm the Boss	1963	10.00
ED 2771 [PS]	True Love Goes On and On	1963	10.00

Albums

BELL

Number	Title (A Side/B Side)	Yr	NM
6055	Time	1971	10.00

COLUMBIA

Number	Title (A Side/B Side)	Yr	NM
CL 628 [M]	The Wayfaring Stranger	1955	30.00
CL 980 [M]	Burl Ives Sings Songs for All Ages	1956	30.00
CL 1459 [M]	Return of the Wayfaring Stranger	1960	30.00
CL 2570 [10]	Children's Favorites	1955	40.00
—"House Party Series" issue			
CL 6058 [10]	The Return of the Wayfaring Stranger	1949	50.00
CL 6109 [10]	The Wayfaring Stranger	1950	50.00
CL 6144 [10]	More Folk Songs	1950	50.00
CS 9041 [R]	The Wayfaring Stranger	1964	12.00
CS 9675	The Times They Are a-Changin'	1969	12.00
CS 9728	Burl Ives Christmas Album	1968	12.00
CS 9925	Softly and Tenderly	1969	12.00

Number	Title (A Side/B Side)	Yr	NM
DECCA			
❑ DXB 167 [(2)M]	The Best of Burl Ives	1961	25.00
❑ DL 4152 [M]	The Versatile Burl Ives	1961	15.00
❑ DL 4179 [M]	Songs of the West	1961	15.00
❑ DL 4279 [M]	It's Just My Funny Way of Laughin'	1962	15.00
❑ DL 4304 [M]	Sing Out, Sweet Land	1962	15.00
❑ DL 4320 [M]	Sunshine in My Soul	1962	15.00
❑ DL 4361 [M]	Burl	1963	15.00
❑ DL 4390 [M]	The Best of Burl's for Boys and Girls	1963	15.00
❑ DL 4433 [M]	Singin' Easy	1964	15.00
❑ DL 4533 [M]	True Love	1964	15.00
❑ DL 4578 [M]	Pearly Shells	1964	15.00
❑ DL 4606 [M]	My Gal Sal	1965	12.00
❑ DL 4668 [M]	On the Beach at Waikiki	1965	12.00
❑ DL 4689 [M]	Have a Holly Jolly Christmas	1965	12.00
❑ DL 4734 [M]	Burl's Choice	1966	12.00
❑ DL 4789 [M]	Something Special	1966	12.00
❑ DL 4850 [M]	Burl Ives' Greatest Hits	1967	15.00
❑ DL 4876 [M]	Broadway	1967	15.00
❑ DL 4972 [M]	Big Country Hits	1968	15.00
❑ DL 5013 [10]	Ballads and Folk Songs, Vol. II	1949	50.00
❑ DL 5080 [10]	A Collection of Ballads and Folk Songs, Vol. One	1949	50.00
❑ DL 5093 [10]	Ballads, Folk and Country Songs	1949	50.00
❑ DL 5428 [10]	Christmas Day in the Morning	1952	50.00
❑ DL 5467 [10]	Folk Songs Dramatic and Dangerous	1953	50.00
❑ DL 5490 [10]	Women: Folk Songs About the Fair Sex	1954	50.00
❑ DXSB 7167 [(2)S]	The Best of Burl Ives	1961	30.00
❑ DL 8080 [M]	Coronation Concert	1953	40.00
❑ DL 8107 [M]	The Wild Side of Life	1955	25.00
❑ DL 8125 [M]	Men	1956	25.00
❑ DL 8245 [M]	Down to the Sea in Ships	1956	25.00
❑ DL 8246 [M]	Women	1956	25.00
❑ DL 8247 [M]	In the Quiet of Night	1956	25.00
❑ DL 8248 [M]	Burl Ives Sings for Fun	1956	25.00
❑ DL 8391 [M]	Christmas Eve	1957	25.00
❑ DL 8444 [M]	Songs of Ireland	1958	25.00
❑ DL 8587 [M]	Captain Burl Ives' Ark	1958	25.00
❑ DL 8637 [M]	Old Time Varieties	1958	25.00
❑ DL 8749 [M]	Australian Folk Songs	1959	25.00
❑ DL 8886 [M]	Cheers	1959	25.00
❑ DL 74152 [S]	The Versatile Burl Ives	1961	20.00
❑ DL 74179 [S]	Songs of the West	1961	20.00
❑ DL 74279 [S]	It's Just My Funny Way of Laughin'	1962	20.00
❑ DL 74304 [S]	Sing Out, Sweet Land	1962	20.00
❑ DL 74320 [S]	Sunshine in My Soul	1962	20.00
❑ DL 74361 [S]	Burl	1963	20.00
❑ DL 74390 [S]	The Best of Burl's for Boys and Girls	1963	20.00
❑ DL 74433 [S]	Singin' Easy	1964	20.00
❑ DL 74533 [S]	True Love	1964	20.00
❑ DL 74578 [S]	Pearly Shells	1964	20.00
❑ DL 74606 [S]	My Gal Sal	1965	15.00
❑ DL 74668 [S]	On the Beach at Waikiki	1965	15.00
❑ DL 74689 [S]	Have a Holly Jolly Christmas	1965	15.00
❑ DL 74734 [S]	Burl's Choice	1966	15.00
❑ DL 74789 [S]	Something Special	1966	15.00
❑ DL 74850 [S]	Burl Ives' Greatest Hits	1967	12.00
❑ DL 74876 [S]	Broadway	1967	12.00
❑ DL 74972 [S]	Big Country Hits	1968	12.00
❑ DL 78391 [R]	Christmas Eve	196?	10.00
❑ DL 78886 [S]	Cheers	1959	30.00
DISNEYLAND			
❑ ST-3927 [M]	Chim Chim Chiree and Other Children's Choices	1964	15.00
❑ STER-3927 [S]	Chim Chim Chiree and Other Children's Choices	1964	20.00
EVEREST ARCHIVE OF FOLK & JAZZ			
❑ 340	Burl Ives Live	1978	10.00
HARMONY			
❑ HL 9507 [M]	The Little White Duck	196?	15.00
❑ HL 9551 [M]	The Lollipop Tree	196?	15.00
❑ HS 11275	Got the World by the Tail	196?	10.00
MCA			
❑ 114	Burl Ives' Greatest Hits	1973	10.00
—Reissue of Decca 74850			
❑ 318	Paying My Dues Again	1973	10.00
❑ 4034 [(2)]	The Best of Burl Ives	197?	12.00
❑ 4089 [(2)]	The Best of Burl Ives Vol. 2	197?	12.00
❑ 15002	Have a Holly Jolly Christmas	1973	12.00
—Reissue of Decca 74689; black label with rainbow			
❑ 15002	Have a Holly Jolly Christmas	1980	8.00
—Blue label with rainbow			
❑ 15030	Santa Claus Is Coming to Town	198?	10.00
NATIONAL GEOGRAPHIC			
❑ 07806	We Americans	1978	12.00
PICKWICK			
❑ SPC-1018	Twelve Days of Christmas	197?	10.00
STINSON			
❑ SLP-1 [10]	The Wayfaring Stranger	1949	60.00
SUNSET			
❑ SUS-5280	Favorites	1970	10.00
UNITED ARTISTS			
❑ UAL 3060 [M]	Ballads	1959	15.00
❑ UAS 6060 [S]	Ballads	1959	20.00
WORD			
❑ 3259 [M]	Faith and Joy	196?	15.00
❑ 3339 [M]	Shall We Gather at the River	1966	12.00
❑ 3391 [M]	I Do Believe	1967	12.00
❑ 8140 [S]	Faith and Joy	196?	20.00
❑ 8339 [S]	Shall We Gather at the River	1966	15.00
❑ 8391 [S]	I Do Believe	1967	15.00
❑ 8537	How Great Thou Art	1971	12.00

IVEYS, THE See BADFINGER.

IVIES, THE

Number	Title (A Side/B Side)	Yr	NM
45s			
BRUNSWICK			
❑ 9-55112	Sunshine/Come On	1959	30.00
IVY			
❑ 110	Sunshine/Come On	1958	100.00
ROULETTE			
❑ 4183	I Really Want You to Know/ Voodoo	1959	12.00

IVOLEERS, THE

Number	Title (A Side/B Side)	Yr	NM
45s			
BUZZ			
❑ 101	Lover's Quarrel/Come with Me	1959	400.00

IVORY

Number	Title (A Side/B Side)	Yr	NM
Albums			
PLAYBOY			
❑ 115	Ivory	1973	12.00
TETRAGRAMMATON			
❑ T-104	Ivory	1968	20.00

IVORY, JACKIE

Number	Title (A Side/B Side)	Yr	NM
45s			
ATCO			
❑ 6398	Hi-Heel Sneakers/Three Tickets to Georgia	1966	10.00
Albums			
ATCO			
❑ 33-178 [M]	Soul Discovery	1965	20.00
❑ SD 33-178 [S]	Soul Discovery	1965	25.00

IVORYS, THE

Number	Title (A Side/B Side)	Yr	NM
45s			
DARLA			
❑ 1000	Wishing Well/Deep Freeze	1962	400.00
SPARTA			
❑ 001	Why Don't You Write Me/ Deep Freeze	1962	80.00

IVY LEAGUE, THE

Number	Title (A Side/B Side)	Yr	NM
45s			
CAMEO			
❑ 343	Wait a Minute/What More Do You Want	1965	15.00
❑ 356	Lonely Room/Funny How Love Can Be	1965	15.00
❑ 365	A Girl Like You/That's Why I'm Crying	1965	15.00
❑ 377	Tossing & Turning/ Graduation Day	1965	15.00
❑ 377 [PS]	Tossing & Turning/ Graduation Day	1965	30.00
❑ 388	Our Love Is Slipping Away/ I Could Make You Fall in Love	1966	15.00
❑ 388 [PS]	Our Love Is Slipping Away/ I Could Make You Fall in Love	1966	25.00
❑ 402	Rain Rain Go Away/ Running Around in Circles	1966	15.00
❑ 449	When You're Young/ My World Fell Down	1966	15.00
Albums			
CAMEO			
❑ C 2000 [M]	Tossing and Turning	1965	30.00
❑ CS 2000 [R]	Tossing and Turning	1965	30.00

IVY LEAGUE TRIO, THE

Number	Title (A Side/B Side)	Yr	NM
45s			
CORAL			
❑ 62204	Sailors' Women/Watcha	1960	10.00
❑ 62229	If You Go Across the Sea/ I'm Just a Country Boy	1960	10.00
❑ 62301	Take Me for a Ride in the Car Car (Riding in My Car)/Bury Me Beneath the Willows	1962	—
❑ 62327	Winken, Blinken and Nod/ The Deep Blue Sea	1962	—
—Original pressings have blue or white labels			
Albums			
CORAL			
❑ CRL 57399 [M]	On and Off Campus	1962	15.00
❑ CRL 57404 [M]	Rare and Well Done	1962	15.00
❑ CRL 757399 [S]	On and Off Campus	1962	20.00
❑ CRL 757404 [S]	Rare and Well Done	1962	20.00
REPRISE			
❑ R-6087 [M]	Folk Ballads from the World of Edgar Allan Poe	1963	20.00
❑ R9-6087 [R]	Folk Ballads from the World of Edgar Allan Poe	1963	30.00

IVY THREE, THE

Number	Title (A Side/B Side)	Yr	NM
45s			
SHELL			
❑ 302	Nine Out of Ten/I've Cried Enough for Two	1961	20.00
—Multicolored label			
❑ 302	Nine Out of Ten/I've Cried Enough for Two	1961	30.00
—Gold label			
❑ 306	Bagoo/Suicide	1961	15.00
❑ 720	Yogi/Was Judy There	1960	20.00
—Originals have blue labels			
❑ 720	Yogi/Was Judy There	1961	15.00
—Reissues have multicolored labels			
❑ 723	Alone in the Chapel/ Hush Little Baby	1960	25.00

IVY-TONES, THE

Number	Title (A Side/B Side)	Yr	NM
45s			
RED TOP			
❑ 105	Oo-Wee Baby/Each Time	1958	15.00
—Red label			
❑ 105	Oo-Wee Baby/Each Time	1958	20.00
—Blue label			

J

J.B. AND THE HAWKS See J.B. HUTTO.

J.B.'S, THE See FRED WESLEY.

J.K. AND COMPANY

Number	Title (A Side/B Side)	Yr	NM
Albums			
BEAT ROCKET			
❑ BR-126	Suddenly One Summer	2000	12.00
—Reissue on 180-gram vinyl			
WHITE WHALE			
❑ WWS-7117	Suddenly One Summer	1969	75.00

J'S WITH JAMIE, THE

Number	Title (A Side/B Side)	Yr	NM
45s			
COLUMBIA			
❑ 4-42422	Momma, Momma, Momma/ The Sound of Money	1962	10.00
❑ 4-42488	One Little World Apart/Let's Not Be Sensible	1962	10.00
❑ 4-42595	Laugh It Up/Nowhere to Go But Up	1962	10.00
❑ 4-42635	Little Me/Come On Strong	1962	10.00
❑ 4-42855	Your Dog/For the Last Time	1963	10.00
❑ 4-42903	Here's Love/Au Revoir	1963	10.00
❑ 4-42939	London (Is a Little Bit of All Right)/This Ole House	1964	10.00
❑ 4-43017	Everybody Says Don't/Yoshiko	1984	10.00
❑ 4-43068	Theme from "A Summer Place"/ Popsicles in Paris	1964	10.00
Albums			
COLUMBIA			
❑ CL 2005 [M]	Hey, Look Us Over!	1963	30.00
❑ CL 2149 [M]	The Remarkable J's with Jamie	1964	30.00
❑ CS 8805 [S]	Hey, Look Us Over!	1963	40.00
❑ CS 8949 [S]	The Remarkable J's with Jamie	1964	40.00

JACK AND JILL May be two different groups.

Number	Title (A Side/B Side)	Yr	NM
45s			
ARLEN			
❑ 726	Very Few Heartaches (Very Few Tears)/Laurie's Love	1963	15.00
CADDY			
❑ 110	Party Time/No One to Talk To (But the Blues)	1957	40.00
IMPERIAL			
❑ 5464	Record Hop/No One to Talk To	1957	30.00
JOSIE			
❑ 943	Something Special/The Chase	1965	20.00

Except when noted otherwise, VG = 25% of NM, and VG+ = 50% of NM. (Example: VG = $2.00, VG+ = $4.00 and NM = $8.00.)

Number	Title (A Side/B Side)	Yr	NM
LIBERTY			
❑ 55170	Young Marriage/Dear Hearts and Gentle People	1958	15.00
MAXX			
❑ 330	Two of a Kind/Just As You Are	1964	30.00
SMASH			
❑ 1824	Very Few Heartaches (Very Few Tears)/Laurie's Love	1963	10.00

JACKIE AND JILL

45s

Number	Title (A Side/B Side)	Yr	NM
U.S.A.			
❑ 791	I Want a Beatle for Christmas/Jingle Bells	1964	20.00

JACKIE AND THE GIANTS

45s

Number	Title (A Side/B Side)	Yr	NM
HIT			
❑ 185	I Go to Pieces/Ford G.T.	1965	10.00
❑ 209	I'm Telling You Now/Come On In	1965	10.00
❑ 230	Turn! Turn! Turn!/May the Bird of Paradise Fly Up Your Nose	1965	10.00
—B-side by Buddy Scott			

JACKIE AND THE RAINDROPS

45s

Number	Title (A Side/B Side)	Yr	NM
COLPIX			
❑ 738	Down Our Street/My Heart Is Your Heart	1964	10.00

JACKIE AND THE STARLITES

45s

Number	Title (A Side/B Side)	Yr	NM
EVERLAST			
❑ 5027	Valarie/Way Up in the Sky	1964	15.00
—As "The Starlites"			
FIRE & FURY			
❑ 1000	They Laughed at Me/You Put One Over on Me	1959	2000.
FURY			
❑ 1034	Valarie/Way Up in the Sky	1960	80.00
—As "The Starlites"			
❑ 1045	Silver Lining/Ain't Cha' Ever Coming Home	1961	50.00
—As "The Starlites"			
❑ 1057	I Found Out Too Late/I'm Coming Home	1962	30.00
HULL			
❑ 760	I Cried My Heart Out/I Still Remember	1964	50.00
LANA			
❑ 120	Valarie/Lonesome Boy	196?	8.00
LOST-NITE			
❑ 185	Valarie/Way Up in the Sky	196?	6.00
—As "The Starlites"; reissue			
❑ 444	I Found Out Too Late/I'm Coming Home	197?	6.00
—Reissue			
MASCOT			
❑ 128	For All We Know/I Heard You	1962	40.00
—With horseshoe on label			
❑ 128	For All We Know/I Heard You	1962	60.00
—No horseshoe on label			
❑ 130	You Keep Telling Me/Sha Pobo Baby	1962	50.00
❑ 131	I'll Burn Your Letter/Walking from School	1963	50.00
SPHERE SOUND			
❑ 705	Seven Day Fool/Don't Be Afraid	1966	80.00
—As "The Starlites"			

JACKS, TERRY

Also see THE POPPY FAMILY.

45s

Number	Title (A Side/B Side)	Yr	NM
BELL			
❑ 45432	Seasons in the Sun/Put the Bone In	1974	5.00
❑ 45467	If You Go Away/Me and You	1974	4.00
❑ 45606	Love Game/Rock and Roll	1974	4.00
LONDON			
❑ 181	Concrete Sea/She Even Took the Cat	1972	5.00
❑ 188	I'm Gonna Love You, Too/Something Good Was Over Before It Ever Got to Start	1972	5.00
PARROT			
❑ 347	A Good Thing Lost/I'm Gonna Capture You	1970	6.00
PRIVATE STOCK			
❑ 45,023	Christina/The Feeling That We've Lost	1975	4.00
❑ 45,094	In My Father's Footsteps/Until You're Down	1976	4.00

Albums

Number	Title (A Side/B Side)	Yr	NM
BELL			
❑ 1307	Seasons in the Sun	1974	10.00

JACKS, THE

Also see THE CADETS.

45s

Number	Title (A Side/B Side)	Yr	NM
KENT			
❑ 344	Why Don't You Write Me/This Empty Heart	1960	15.00
RPM			
❑ 428	Why Don't You Write Me/My Darling	1955	60.00
❑ 428	Why Don't You Write Me/Smack Dab in the Middle	1955	200.00
❑ 433	I'm Confessin'/Since My Baby's Been Gone	1955	60.00
❑ 444	This Empty Heart/My Clumsy Heart	1955	50.00
❑ 454	So Wrong/How Soon	1956	50.00
❑ 458	Sugar Baby/Why Did I Fall in Love	1956	60.00
❑ 467	Let's Make Up/Dream a Little Longer	1956	60.00

Albums

Number	Title (A Side/B Side)	Yr	NM
CROWN			
❑ CST-372 [R]	Jumpin' with the Jacks	1962	50.00
❑ CLP-5021 [M]	Jumpin' with the Jacks	1960	200.00
❑ CLP-5372 [M]	Jumpin' with the Jacks	1962	100.00
RELIC			
❑ 5023	The Jacks' Greatest Hits	198?	10.00
RPM			
❑ LRP-3006 [M]	Jumpin' with the Jacks	1956	2000.
—VG value 1000; VG+ value 1500			
UNITED			
❑ US-7797	Rock 'n' Roll Hits of the 50's	197?	15.00

JACKSON, BULL MOOSE

45s

Number	Title (A Side/B Side)	Yr	NM
BOGUS			
❑ 12-042684	Get Off the Table, Mable (The Two Dollars Is For the Beer)/I've Got a Gal Who Lives Up on a Hill	1984	5.00
❑ 12-042684 [PS]	Get Off the Table, Mable (The Two Dollars Is For the Beer)/I've Got a Gal Who Lives Up on a Hill	1984	5.00
ENCINO			
❑ 1005	Understanding/(B-side unknown)	1957	60.00
KING			
❑ 4181	I Love You Yes I Do/Sneaky Pete	1951	60.00
—78 originally released in 1947			
❑ 4189	I Want a Bowlegged Woman/All My Love Belongs to You	1951	80.00
—78 originally released in 1948 -- 5191 and 5198 are the only legitimate 45s known before 4451			
❑ 4451	Trust in Me/Wonder When My Baby's Coming Home	1951	60.00
❑ 4462	Unless/End This Misery	1951	60.00
❑ 4472	Cherokee Boogie/I'm Lucky I Have You	1951	60.00
❑ 4493	I'll Be Home for Christmas/I Never Loved Anyone But You	1951	60.00
❑ 4524	Nosey Joe/Sad	1952	80.00
❑ 4535	(Let Me Love You) All Night Long/Bootsie	1952	60.00
❑ 4551	Bearcat Blues/There Is No Greater Love	1952	60.00
❑ 4580	Big Ten Inch Record/I Needed You	1952	200.00
❑ 4634	Meet Me with Your Black Dress On/Try to Forget Him	1953	40.00
❑ 4655	If You'll Let Me/Hodge Podge	1953	40.00
❑ 4775	If You Ain't Lovin'/I Wanna Hug Ya, Kiss Ya	1955	25.00
❑ 4802	I'm Glad for Your Sake/Must You Keep On Pretending	1955	25.00
SEVEN ARTS			
❑ 705	I Love You Yes I Do/Aw Shucks Baby	1961	20.00
WARWICK			
❑ 575	I Found My Love/More of the Same	1960	20.00

7-Inch Extended Plays

Number	Title (A Side/B Side)	Yr	NM
KING			
❑ EP-211	*I Love You, Yes I Do/I Want a Bowlegged Woman/All My Love Belongs to You/Little Girl Don't Cry	1953	150.00
❑ EP-211 [PS]	Bull Moose Jackson Sings His All Time Hits	1953	150.00

Albums

Number	Title (A Side/B Side)	Yr	NM
AUDIO LAB			
❑ AL-1524 [M]	Bull Moose Jackson	1959	600.00
BOGUS			
❑ 6-0214851	Moosemania!	1985	10.00

JACKSON, CHUCK

45s

Number	Title (A Side/B Side)	Yr	NM
ABC			
❑ 11368	I Only Get This Feeling/Slowly But Surely	1973	20.00
❑ 11398	I Can't Break Away/Just a Little Tear	1973	50.00
❑ 11423	If Only You Believe/Maybe This Will Be the Morning	1974	20.00
❑ 12024	Take Off Your Make-Up/Talk a Little Less	1974	20.00
ALL PLATINUM			
❑ 2357	Love Lights/(Instrumental)	1975	5.00
❑ 2360	I'm Needing You, Wanting You/We Can't Hide It Anymore	1975	5.00
❑ 2363	If You Were My Woman (Part 1)/If You Were My Woman (Part 2)	1976	5.00
❑ 2370	One of Those Yesterdays/Love Lights	1976	15.00
❑ 2373	I Fell Asleep/One of Those Yesterdays	1976	5.00
AMY			
❑ 849	Come On and Love Me/Ooh Baby	1962	20.00
❑ 868	I'm Yours/Hula Lula	1962	15.00
ATCO			
❑ 6197	Never Let Me Go/Baby I Want to Marry You	1961	12.00
BELTONE			
❑ 1005	Mr. Price/Hula Lula	1961	20.00
CLOCK			
❑ 1015	Come On and Love Me/Ooh Baby	1959	25.00
—Clock sides as "Charles Jackson"			
❑ 1022	Hula Lula/I'm Yours	1960	25.00
❑ 1027	This Is It/Mr. Pride	1960	25.00
DAKAR			
❑ 4512	I Forgot to Tell You/The Man and the Woman	1972	20.00
DOT			
❑ 15673	Woke Up This Morning/Wilette	1957	30.00
—With Kripp Johnson			
EMI AMERICA			
❑ 8042	I Wanna Give You Some Love/Waiting in Vain	1980	4.00
❑ 8056	After You/Let's Get Together	1980	4.00
MOTOWN			
❑ 1118	(Don't Let the Boy Overpower) The Man in You/Girls, Girls, Girls	1968	20.00
❑ 1144	Are You Lonely for Me Baby/Your Wonderful Love	1969	15.00
❑ 1152	Honey Come Back/What Am I Gonna Do Without You	1969	20.00
❑ 1160	The Day My World Stood Still/Baby, I'll Get It	1970	500.00
SUGARHILL			
❑ 764	Sometimes When We Touch/(B-side unknown)	1981	4.00
V.I.P.			
❑ 25052	The Day My World Stood Still/Baby, I'll Get It	1970	20.00
❑ 25056	Let Somebody Love Me/Two Feet from Happiness	1970	20.00
❑ 25059	Is There Anything Love Can't Do/Pet Names	1971	30.00
❑ 25067	Who You Gonna Run To/Forgive My Jealousy	1971	400.00
VIBRATION			
❑ 569	We Can't Hide It Anymore/I'm Needing You, Wanting You	1977	5.00
—With Sylvia			
WAND			
❑ 106	I Don't Want to Cry/Just Once	1961	15.00
❑ 108	(It Never Happens) In Real Life/The Same Old Story	1961	30.00
❑ 110	I Wake Up Crying/Everybody Needs Love	1961	20.00
❑ 115	The Breaking Point/My Willow Tree	1961	15.00
❑ 119	What'cha Gonna Say Tomorrow/Angel of Angels	1962	20.00
❑ 122	Any Day Now (My Wild Beautiful Bird)/The Prophet	1962	20.00

Number	Title (A Side/B Side)	Yr	NM
❑ 126	I Keep Forgetting/Who's Gonna Pick Up the Pieces	1962	20.00
❑ 128	Gettin' Ready for the Heartbreak/ In Between Tears	1962	30.00
❑ 132	Tell Him I'm Not Home/ Lonely Am I	1963	20.00
❑ 132 [PS]	Tell Him I'm Not Home/ Lonely Am I	1963	40.00
❑ 138	I Will Never Turn My Back on You/Tears of Joy	1963	10.00
❑ 141	Any Other Way/Big New York	1963	20.00
❑ 149	Hand It Over/Look Over Your Shoulder	1964	50.00
❑ 154	Beg Me/This Broken Heart	1964	20.00
❑ 161	Somebody New/Stand By Me	1964	20.00
❑ 169	Since I Don't Have You/Hand It Over	1964	40.00
❑ 179	I Need You/Soul Brother Twist	1965	20.00
❑ 188	If I Didn't Love You/Just a Little Bit of Your Soul	1965	20.00
❑ 1105	Good Things Come to Those Who Wait/Yah	1965	20.00
❑ 1119	All in My Mind/And That's Saying a Lot	1966	20.00
❑ 1129	These Chains of Love/ Theme to the Blues	1966	8.00
❑ 1142	I've Got to Be Strong/ Where Did She Stay	1967	20.00
❑ 1151	Every Man Needs a Down Home Girl/Need You There	1967	8.00
❑ 1159	Hound Dog/Love Me Tender	1967	8.00
❑ 1166	Shame on Me/Candy	1967	15.00
❑ 1178	My Child's Child/ Theme to the Blues	1968	8.00

Albums

Number	Title	Yr	NM
ABC			
❑ X-798	Through All Times	1973	15.00
ALL PLATINUM			
❑ 3014	Needing You, Wanting You	1976	15.00
COLLECTABLES			
❑ COL-5115	Golden Classics	198?	10.00
EMI AMERICA			
❑ SW-17031	I Wanna Give You Some Love	1980	10.00
GUEST STAR			
❑ GS-1912 [M]	Chuck Jackson	196?	20.00
❑ GSS-1912 [R]	Chuck Jackson	196?	12.00
MOTOWN			
❑ M-667 [M]	Chuck Jackson Arrives!	1967	40.00
❑ MS-667 [S]	Chuck Jackson Arrives!	1967	25.00
❑ MS-687	Goin' Back to Chuck Jackson	1969	25.00
SCEPTER			
❑ 5100	A Tribute to Burt Bacharach	1972	15.00
SPIN-O-RAMA			
❑ 123 [M]	Starring Chuck Jackson	196?	20.00
❑ S-123 [R]	Starring Chuck Jackson	196?	12.00
STRAND			
❑ SL-1125 [M]	The Great Chuck Jackson	196?	25.00
❑ SLS-1125 [S]	The Great Chuck Jackson	196?	30.00
UNITED ARTISTS			
❑ UA-LA499-E	The Very Best of Chuck Jackson	1974	10.00
V.I.P.			
❑ 403	Teardrops Keep Fallin' on My Heart	1970	40.00
WAND			
❑ LP-650 [M]	I Don't Want to Cry	1961	40.00
❑ LP-654 [M]	Any Day Now	1962	40.00
❑ WD-655 [M]	Encore	1963	40.00
❑ WD-658 [M]	Chuck Jackson On Tour	1964	40.00
❑ WDM-667 [M]	Mr. Everything	1965	30.00
❑ WDS-667 [S]	Mr. Everything	1965	40.00
❑ WD-673 [M]	A Tribute to Rhythm and Blues	1966	30.00
❑ WDS-673 [S]	A Tribute to Rhythm and Blues	1966	40.00
❑ WD-676 [M]	A Tribute to Rhythm and Blues, Vol. 2	1966	30.00
❑ WDS-676 [S]	A Tribute to Rhythm and Blues, Vol. 2	1966	40.00
❑ WD-680 [M]	Dedicated to the King!!	1966	40.00
❑ WDS-680 [S]	Dedicated to the King!!	1966	50.00
❑ WD-683 [M]	Chuck Jackson's Greatest Hits	1967	20.00
❑ WDS-683 [S]	Chuck Jackson's Greatest Hits	1967	25.00

JACKSON, CHUCK, AND MAXINE BROWN

Also see each artist's individual listings.

45s

Number	Title	Yr	NM
WAND			
❑ 181	Something You Got/ Baby Take Me	1965	15.00
❑ 191	Don't Go/Can't Let You Out of My Sight	1965	15.00
❑ 198	I Need You So/Cause We're in Love	1965	15.00
❑ 1109	Plerase Don't Hurt Me/ I'm Satisfied	1966	15.00
❑ 1148	Hold On I'm Comin'/ Never Had It So Good	1967	15.00
❑ 1155	Daddy's Home/Don't Go	1967	15.00
❑ 1162	See See Rider/Tennesee Waltz	1967	15.00

Albums

Number	Title	Yr	NM
WAND			
❑ WD-669 [M]	Say Something	1965	30.00
❑ WDS-669 [S]	Say Something	1965	40.00
❑ WD-678 [M]	Hold On, We're Coming	1966	30.00
❑ WDS-678 [S]	Hold On, We're Coming	1966	40.00

JACKSON, CHUCK, AND TAMMI TERRELL

Also see each artist's individual listings.

Albums

Number	Title	Yr	NM
WAND			
❑ WD-682 [M]	The Early Show	1967	30.00
❑ WDS-682 [S]	The Early Show	1967	30.00

JACKSON, DEON

45s

Number	Title	Yr	NM
ATLANTIC			
❑ 2213	Hush Little Baby/You Said You Loved Me	1963	10.00
❑ 2252	Come Back Home/ Nursery Rhymes	1964	10.00
CARLA			
❑ 1900	I Can't Go On/I Need a Love Like Yours	1968	8.00
❑ 1903	You'll Wake Up Wiser Baby/ You Gotta Love	1968	8.00
❑ 2526	Love Makes the World Go Round/You Said You Loved Me	1966	10.00
❑ 2527	Love Takes a Long Time Growing/Hush Little Baby	1966	8.00
❑ 2530	I Can't Do Without You/ That's What You Do to Me	1966	8.00
❑ 2533	When Your Love Has Gone/ Hard to Get Thing Called Love	1967	8.00
❑ 2537	Ooh Baby/All on a Sunny Day	1967	8.00
SHOUT			
❑ 254	I'll Always Love You/Life Can Be That Way	1969	25.00

Albums

Number	Title	Yr	NM
ATCO			
❑ 33-188 [M]	Love Makes the World Go Round	1966	30.00
❑ SD 33-188 [S]	Love Makes the World Go Round	1966	40.00
COLLECTABLES			
❑ COL-5106	Golden Classics	198?	10.00

JACKSON, EARL

45s

Number	Title	Yr	NM
ABC			
❑ 11142	Self Soul Satisfaction/Looking Through the Eyes of Love	1968	30.00

JACKSON, GEORGE

45s

Number	Title	Yr	NM
ATLANTIC			
❑ 1024	Uh Huh/I'm Sorry	1954	50.00
CAMEO			
❑ 460	When I Stop Lovin' You/ That Lonely Night	1967	60.00
CHESS			
❑ 2167	Things Are Gettin' Better/ Mackin' on You	1975	150.00
DOT			
❑ 16724	Blinkety Blink/There Goes My Pride	1965	100.00
FAME			
❑ 1457	Find 'Em, Fool 'Em, and Forget 'Em/My Desires Are Getting the Best of Me	1969	25.00
❑ 1468	That's How Much You Mean to Me/I'm Gonna Hold On	1970	20.00
HI			
❑ 2130	I'm Gonna Wait/So Good to Me	1967	40.00
❑ 2212	Aretha, Sing One for Me/ I'm Gonna Wait	1972	15.00
❑ 2236	Let Them Know You Care/ Patricia	1973	30.00
MERCURY			
❑ 72736	Kiss Me/Tossin' and Turnin'	1967	40.00
❑ 72782	I Don't Have the Time to Love You/Don't Use Me	1968	400.00
MGM			
❑ 14680	We've Only Just Begun/You Can't Run Away from Love	1973	6.00
❑ 14732	Willie Lump Lump/How Can I Get Next to You	1974	20.00
❑ 14767	Soul Train/Smoking and Drinking	1974	6.00
RPM			
❑ 441	Hold Me Up/Heaven on Earth	1955	25.00
VERVE			
❑ 10658	Love Highjacker/I Found What I Wanted	1970	100.00

JACKSON, GEORGE, AND DAN GREER

See GEORGE AND GREER.

JACKSON, J.J.

45s

Number	Title	Yr	NM
CALLA			
❑ 119	But It's Alright/Boogaloo Baby	1966	40.00
❑ 125	I Dig Girls/That Ain't Right	1966	15.00
❑ 130	Til Love Goes Out of Style/ Seems Like I've Been Here Before	1967	50.00
❑ 133	Four Walls (Three Windows and Two Doors)/Here We Go Again	1967	20.00
CONGRESS			
❑ 6008	Fat, Black and Together/ That Woman Loving	1969	8.00
EVEREST			
❑ 2012	False Face/Ring Telephone	1963	50.00
LOMA			
❑ 2082	Try Me/Sho Nuff (Gotta Good Thing Goin')	1967	20.00
❑ 2090	Down But Not Out/Why Does It Take So Long	1968	20.00
❑ 2096	Come See Me (I'm Your Man)/ I Don't Want to Live My Life Alone	1968	20.00
❑ 2102	Too Late/You Do It Cause You Wanna	1968	15.00
❑ 2104	That Ain't Right/Courage Ain't Strength	1968	15.00
MAGNA GLIDE			
❑ 5N-325	Let Me Try Again/ (B-side unknown)	1975	15.00
PERCEPTION			
❑ 7	Nobody's Gonna Help You/ Help Me Get to My Grits	1970	8.00
WARNER BROS.			
❑ 7130	But It's Alright/Four Walls (Three Windows and Two Doors)	1970	6.00
—"Back to Back Hits" series			
❑ 7278	But It's Alright/Ain't Too Proud to Beg	1969	8.00
❑ 7321	Four Walls (Three Windows and Two Doors)/ That Ain't Right	1969	8.00

Albums

Number	Title	Yr	NM
CALLA			
❑ C-1101 [M]	But It's Alright/I Dig Girls	1967	20.00
❑ CS-1101 [S]	But It's Alright/I Dig Girls	1967	25.00
CONGRESS			
❑ CS-7000	The Greatest Little Soul Band in the World	1968	25.00
PERCEPTION			
❑ 3	J.J. Jackson's Dilemma	1970	15.00
WARNER BROS.			
❑ WS 1797	The Great J.J. Jackson	1969	20.00

JACKSON, JACKIE

12-Inch Singles

Number	Title	Yr	NM
POLYDOR			
❑ 871549-1	Stay (4 versions)/ Who's Loving You Now	1989	8.00
❑ 889035-1	Cruzin' (12" Remix) (7" Remix) (7" Edit) (House Mix) (House Dub)	1989	8.00

45s

Number	Title	Yr	NM
POLYDOR			
❑ 871548-7	Stay/Who's Loving You Now	1989	3.00
❑ 871548-7 [PS]	Stay/Who's Loving You Now	1989	3.00
❑ 889034-7	Cruzin/(another mix)	1989	3.00
❑ 889034-7 [PS]	Cruzin/(another mix)	1989	3.00

Albums

Number	Title	Yr	NM
MOTOWN			
❑ M 785V1	Jackie Jackson	1973	15.00
POLYDOR			
❑ 837766-1	Be the One	1989	10.00

Except when noted otherwise, VG = 25% of NM, and VG+ = 50% of NM. (Example: VG = $2.00, VG+ = $4.00 and NM = $8.00.)

JACKSON, JERMAINE

12-Inch Singles

ARISTA

Number	Title (A Side/B Side)	Yr	NM
❑ ADP 9189 [DJ]	Tell Me I'm Not Dreamin' (Too Good to Be True)/ Do What You Do/Escape from the Planet	1984	12.00
❑ AD1-9222	Dynamite/(Instrumental)/ Tell Me I'm Not Dreaming (Instrumental)	1984	8.00
❑ AD1-9317	When the Rain Begins to Fall/ Come to Me	1985	8.00
—A-side with Pia Zadora			
❑ AD1-9357	(Closest Thing to) Perfect/ (Instrumental)	1985	8.00
❑ AD1-9445	I Think It's Love (4 versions)	1986	8.00
❑ AD1-9501	Do You Remember Me (6 versions)	1986	8.00
❑ ADP 9876 [DJ]	Don't Take It Personal (same on both sides)	1989	8.00
❑ AD1-9878	Don't Take It Personal (3 versions)	1989	8.00
❑ AD1-9934	Two Ships (In the Night) (4 versions)	1990	8.00

LAFACE

Number	Title (A Side/B Side)	Yr	NM
❑ 24004	You Said, You Said (5 versions)	1991	8.00
❑ 24012	Word to the Badd!! (5 versions)	1991	12.00
❑ 24017	I Dream, I Dream (5 versions)	1992	10.00

MOTOWN

Number	Title (A Side/B Side)	Yr	NM
❑ M 00001D1	Let's Be Young Tonight (5:07)/ Down to Love Town (5:55)	1976	20.00
—B-side by the Originals on Soul			
❑ PR-66 [DJ]	Let's Get Serious (Short Version 3:33) (Long Version 7:55)	1980	20.00
❑ PR-73 [DJ]	Burnin' Hot (7:44)/Feelin' Free (6:32)	1980	25.00
—No label name on label			
❑ PR-101 [DJ]	Let Me Tickle Your Fancy (Vocal) (Instrumental)/Hard to Get (Vocal) (Instrumental)	1982	15.00
—No label name on label; B-side by Rick James			
❑ PR-108 [DJ]	Very Special Part (6:32)/ (Instrumental)	1982	12.00

45s

ARISTA

Number	Title (A Side/B Side)	Yr	NM
❑ 2029	I'd Like to Get to Know You/ Spare the Rod, Love the Child	1990	3.00
❑ 9190	Dynamite/Tell Me I'm Not Dreaming (Too Good to Be True) (Instrumental)	1984	3.00
❑ 9190 [DJ]	Dynamite (same on both sides)	1984	8.00
—Promo only on red vinyl			
❑ 9190 [PS]	Dynamite/Tell Me I'm Not Dreaming (Too Good to Be True) (Instrumental)	1984	3.00
❑ 9275	Take Good Care of My Heart/ Tell Me I'm Not Dreaming (Too Good to Be True) (Instrumental)	1984	5.00
—A-side with Whitney Houston			
❑ 9279	Do What You Do/ Tell Me I'm Not Dreaming (Too Good to Be True)	1984	3.00
❑ 9356	(Closest Thing to) Perfect/ (Instrumental)	1985	3.00
❑ 9356 [PS]	(Closest Thing to) Perfect/ (Instrumental)	1985	3.00
❑ 9444	I Think It's Love/ Voices in the Dark	1985	3.00
❑ 9444 [PS]	I Think It's Love/ Voices in the Dark	1985	3.00
❑ 9495	Words Into Action/Our Love Story	1986	3.00
❑ 9495 [PS]	Words Into Action/Our Love Story	1986	3.00
❑ 9502	Do You Remember Me/ Whatcha' Doin'	1986	3.00
❑ 9502 [PS]	Do You Remember Me/ Whatcha' Doin'	1986	3.00
❑ 9788	Clean Up Your Act/ I'm Gonna Git Ya Sucka	1988	3.00
—B-side by the Gap Band			
❑ 9788 [PS]	Clean Up Your Act/ I'm Gonna Git Ya Sucka	1988	3.00
❑ 9875	Don't Take It Personal/ Clean Up Your Act	1989	3.00
❑ 9875 [PS]	Don't Take It Personal/ Clean Up Your Act	1989	3.00
❑ 9933	Two Ships (In the Night)/ Next to You	1990	3.00
❑ 9933 [PS]	Two Ships (In the Night)/ Next to You	1990	3.00

LAFACE

Number	Title (A Side/B Side)	Yr	NM
❑ 24003	You Said, You Said/ (Instrumental)	1991	4.00

MOTOWN

Number	Title (A Side/B Side)	Yr	NM
❑ 1201	That's How Love Goes/I Lost My Love in the Big City	1972	5.00
❑ 1216	Daddy's Home/Take Me in Your Arms (Rock Me for a Little While)	1972	5.00
❑ 1244	You're in Good Hands/Does Your Mama Know About Me	1973	5.00
❑ 1386	She's the Ideal Girl/I'm So Glad You Chose Me	1976	—
—Unreleased			
❑ 1401	Let's Be Young Tonight/ Boss Odyssey	1976	5.00
❑ 1409	You Need to Be Loved/My Touch of Madness	1977	5.00
❑ 1441	Castles of Sand/I Love Every Little Thing About You	1978	5.00
❑ 1469	Let's Get Serious/Je Vous Aime Beaucoups	1980	4.00
❑ 1490	You're Supposed to Keep Your Love for Me/Let It Ride	1980	4.00
❑ 1499	Little Girl Don't You Worry/We Can Put It Back Together	1980	4.00
❑ 1503	You Like Me Don't You/ (Instrumental)	1981	4.00
❑ 1525	I'm Just Too Shy/ All Because of You	1981	4.00
❑ 1600	Paradise in Your Eyes/I'm My Brother's Keeper	1982	4.00
❑ 1628	Let Me Tickle Your Fancy/ Maybe Next Time	1982	4.00
—Devo is the backing group			
❑ 1649	Very Special Part/You're Givin' Me the Runaround	1982	4.00

Albums

ARISTA

Number	Title (A Side/B Side)	Yr	NM
❑ AL8-8203	Jermaine Jackson	1984	10.00
❑ AL8-8277	Precious Moments	1986	10.00
❑ AL-8421	Jermaine Jackson	1986	8.00
—Budget-line reissue			
❑ AL-8493	Don't Take It Personal	1989	10.00

MOTOWN

Number	Title (A Side/B Side)	Yr	NM
❑ M5-117V1	Motown Superstar Series, Vol. 17	1981	10.00
❑ M-752L	Jermaine	1972	10.00
❑ M-775L	Come Into My Life	1973	10.00
❑ M6-842S1	My Name Is Jermaine	1976	10.00
❑ M6-888S1	Feel the Fire	1977	10.00
❑ M7-898R1	Frontiers	1978	10.00
❑ M7-928R1	Let's Get Serious	1980	10.00
❑ M8-948M1	Jermaine	1980	10.00
❑ M8-952M1	I Like Your Style	1981	10.00
❑ 6017 ML	Let Me Tickle Your Fancy	1982	10.00

JACKSON, JERRY

45s

CAPITOL

Number	Title (A Side/B Side)	Yr	NM
❑ 2112	Miss You/Take Over Now	1968	40.00

COLUMBIA

Number	Title (A Side/B Side)	Yr	NM
❑ 43056	Shrimp Boats/Always	1964	12.00
❑ 43158	Tell Her Johnny Said Goodbye/ Are You Glad When We're Apart	1964	60.00
❑ 43231	You're Mine (And I Love You)/ Hey, Sugarfoot	1965	30.00

KAPP

Number	Title (A Side/B Side)	Yr	NM
❑ 387	Time/Se Habla Espanol	1961	20.00
❑ 420	I Don't Play Games/You Might Be There With Him	1961	30.00
❑ 438	If I Only Had Known How to Keep Her (She Would Never Have Gone to You)/Till the End of Time	1961	20.00
❑ 448	La-Dee-Dah (Ha-Ha-Ha)/ You Don't Wanna Hurt Me	1962	15.00
❑ 464	They Really Don't Know You/ Blues in the Night	1962	15.00
❑ 496	She Lied/Wide Awake in a Dream	1962	300.00
❑ 511	Gypsy Eyes/Turn Back	1963	100.00
❑ 543	Blowin' in the Wind (Part 1)/ Blowin' in the Wind (Part 2)	1963	25.00

PARKWAY

Number	Title (A Side/B Side)	Yr	NM
❑ 100	It's Rough Out There/ I'm Gonna Paint a Picture	1966	300.00

TOP RANK

Number	Title (A Side/B Side)	Yr	NM
❑ 2042	A Chance to Prove My Love/For Every One There's Someone	1960	20.00
❑ 2072	Every Time You Kiss Me/ Meaning of My Love	1960	20.00

JACKSON, JILL Also see PAUL AND PAULA.

45s

REPRISE

Number	Title (A Side/B Side)	Yr	NM
❑ 0297	Hey Handsome Boy/ All Over Again	1964	15.00
❑ 0323	Pixie Girl/I Just Don't Know What to Do With Myself	1964	15.00
❑ 0362	Born Too Late/Here Comes the Night	1965	15.00
❑ 0411	Treasure of Love/I'll Love You for a While	1965	15.00

JACKSON, JOE

12-Inch Singles

A&M

Number	Title (A Side/B Side)	Yr	NM
❑ SP-12098	You Can't Get What You Want (Till You Know What You Want) (Special Remixed Version) (Dub Version)/ Cha Cha Loco	1984	7.00
❑ SP-17201 [DJ]	Steppin' Out (LP Version 4:27) (Edit 3:43)	1982	12.00
❑ SP-17273 [DJ]	You Can't Get What You Want (Till You Know What You Want)/The Verdict/Go For It	1984	10.00
❑ SP-17374 [DJ]	Right and Wrong (4:35) (4:11)	1986	12.00
❑ SP-17375 [DJ]	Wild West/Right and Wrong/ Home Town/Tonight	1986	15.00
❑ SP-17395 [DJ]	Home Town (same on both sides)	1986	15.00

45s

A&M

Number	Title (A Side/B Side)	Yr	NM
❑ 1207	Look Sharp (Live)/ Memphis (Live)	1988	5.00
❑ 1228	(He's a) Shape in a Drape/ Speedway	1988	4.00
❑ 1404	Nineteen Forever/Acropolis Now	1989	5.00
❑ 2132	Is She Really Going Out with Him?/(Do the) Instant Mash	1979	4.00
❑ 2132 [PS]	Is She Really Going Out with Him?/(Do the) Instant Mash	1979	5.00
❑ 2186	It's Different for Girls/Come On	1979	5.00
❑ 2186 [PS]	It's Different for Girls/Come On	1979	5.00
❑ 2209	I'm the Man/Come On	1979	5.00
❑ 2276	One to One/Enough Is Not Enough	1980	5.00
❑ 2365	Jumpin' Jive/Knock Me a Kiss	1981	8.00
❑ 2428	Steppin' Out/Chinatown	1982	3.00
❑ 2428 [PS]	Steppin' Out/Chinatown	1982	5.00
❑ 2510	Breaking Us in Two/Target	1982	3.00
❑ 2510 [PS]	Breaking Us in Two/Target	1982	3.00
❑ 2510 [DJ]	Breaking Us in Two (3:48)/(4:57)	1982	6.00
—The shorter version does not appear on the stock copy			
❑ 2548	Another World/Otro Mundo	1983	5.00
❑ 2601	Memphis/Breakdown	1983	4.00
❑ 2601 [PS]	Memphis/Breakdown	1983	5.00
❑ 2628	You Can't Get What You Want (Till You Know What You Want)/Cha Cha Loco	1984	3.00
❑ 2628 [PS]	You Can't Get What You Want (Till You Know What You Want)/Cha Cha Loco	1984	3.00
❑ 2635	Happy Ending/Loisaida	1984	4.00
❑ 2635 [PS]	Happy Ending/Loisaida	1984	4.00
❑ 2673	Be My Number Two/Heart of Ice	1984	5.00
❑ 2829 [PS]	Right and Wrong/Breaking Us in Two	1986	3.00
❑ 2829	Right and Wrong/Breaking Us in Two (Live)	1986	4.00
❑ 2847	Home Town/I'm the Man (Live)	1986	5.00
❑ 2847 [PS]	Home Town/I'm the Man (Live)	1986	7.00
❑ 2944	Nocturne/Will Power	1987	5.00
❑ SP-18000 [(5)]	I'm the Man	1979	20.00
—Boxed set of five 7" singles with small holes and picture sleeves, comprising the album of the same name			

Albums

A&M

Number	Title (A Side/B Side)	Yr	NM
❑ SP-3187	Look Sharp!	198?	8.00
—Reissue of SP-4743			
❑ SP-3221	I'm the Man	198?	8.00
—Reissue of SP-4794			
❑ SP-3241	Beat Crazy	198?	8.00
—Reissue of SP-4837			
❑ SP-3271	Joe Jackson's Jumpin' Jive	198?	8.00
—Reissue of SP-4871			
❑ SP-3286	Body and Soul	1986	8.00
—Reissue of SP-5000			
❑ SP-3666 [(2)]	Look Sharp!	1979	20.00
—Two 10-inch records in gatefold sleeve with button			
❑ SP-3908	Will Power	1987	12.00
❑ SP-4743	Look Sharp!	1979	12.00
❑ SP-4794	I'm the Man	1979	10.00
❑ SP-4837	Beat Crazy	1980	10.00
❑ SP-4871	Joe Jackson's Jumpin' Jive	1981	10.00
❑ SP-4906	Night and Day	1982	10.00
❑ SP-4931	Mike's Murder [Soundtrack]	1983	12.00
❑ SP-5000	Body and Soul	1984	10.00
❑ SP-5249	Blaze of Glory	1989	10.00
❑ SP-6021 [(2)]	Big World	1986	15.00
❑ SP-6706 [(2)]	Live: 1980-1986	1988	15.00
❑ R 101141	Blaze of Glory	1989	12.00
—BMG Direct Marketing edition			

J

Except when noted otherwise, VG = 25% of NM, and VG+ = 50% of NM. (Example: VG = $2.00, VG+ = $4.00 and NM = $8.00.)

Number	Title (A Side/B Side)	Yr	NM
R 209597 [(2)]	Live 1980-1986	1987	15.00
—BMG Direct Marketing edition			
R 244331 [(2)]	Big World	1986	15.00
—RCA Music Service edition			
MOBILE FIDELITY			
1-080	Night and Day	1982	50.00
—Audiophile vinyl			
RYKODISC			
310921	Rain	2008	15.00

JACKSON, JUNE

Number	Title (A Side/B Side)	Yr	NM
45s			
BELL			
45173	Little Dog Heaven/Tenderly with Feeling	1972	40.00
IMPERIAL			
66185	It's What's Up Front That Counts/Fifty Per Cent Won't Do	1966	200.00
MUSETTE			
112	You're Welcome/(B-side unknown)	196?	1500.

JACKSON, LIL' SON

Number	Title (A Side/B Side)	Yr	NM
45s			
IMPERIAL			
5204	Journey Back Home/Rockin' and Rollin' #2	1952	100.00
—Note: Lil' Son Jackson records on Imperial before 5204 are unconfirmed on 45 rpm			
5218	Black and Brown/Sad Letter Blues	1953	100.00
5229	Lonely Blues/Freight Train Blues	1953	100.00
5237	Spending Money Blues/All Alone	1953	100.00
5248	Movin' to the Country/Confession	1953	100.00
5259	Dirty Work/Little Girl	1953	100.00
5267	Thrill Me, Baby/Doctor, Doctor	1954	80.00
5276	Big Rat/Piggly Wiggly	1954	80.00
5286	Trouble Don't Last Always/Blues by the Hour	1954	80.00
5300	Get High Everybody/Let Me Down Easy	1954	80.00
5312	How Long/Good Ole Wagon	1954	80.00
5319	My Younger Days/I Wish to Go Home	1954	80.00
5339	Sugar Mama/Messin' Up	1955	80.00
5703	Rockin' and Rollin'/Peace Breaking People	1960	15.00
5851	Everybody's Blues/Travelin' Woman	1962	15.00
5963	Prison Bound/Rolling Mill	1963	12.00
POST			
2014	No Money/Lonely Blues	1955	40.00
Albums			
ARHOOLIE			
1004 [M]	Lil' Son Jackson	1960	25.00
IMPERIAL			
LP-9142 [M]	Rockin' and Rollin'	1961	400.00

JACKSON, MAHALIA

Number	Title (A Side/B Side)	Yr	NM
45s			
APOLLO			
235	Silent Night, Holy Night/Go Tell It On The Mountain	1951	20.00
—Note: Earlier Mahalia Jackson 45s on Apollo may exist			
240	Get Away Jordan/I Gave Up Everything	1951	20.00
245	Bless This House/The Lord's Prayer	1951	20.00
246	His Eyes Are On the Sparrow/It Is No Secret (What God Can Do)	1951	20.00
248	How I Got Over/Just As I Am	1951	20.00
258	He's the One/I'm Getting Nearer My Home	1952	20.00
262	In the Upper Room (Part 1)/In the Upper Room (Part 2)	1952	20.00
269	He Said He Would/God Spoke to Me	1953	20.00
273	I'm Going Down the River/Do You Know Him	1953	20.00
278	I Wonder If I Will Ever Rest/Coming to Jesus	1953	20.00
282	Hands of God/It's Real	1954	20.00
286	I'm On My Way/My Story	1954	20.00
289	Walking to Jerusalem/What Then	1954	20.00
291	I Walked Into the Garden/I'm Going to Tell God	1955	20.00
298	Nobody Knows/Run All the Way	1955	20.00
304	He's My Light/If You Just Keep Still	1956	18.00
311	His Eyes Are On the Sparrow/I Can Put My Trust in Jesus	1956	18.00
313	Didn't It Rain/Nobody Knows	1956	18.00
314	I'm On My Way/My Story	1956	18.00
539	Silent Night/The Lord's Prayer	1959	15.00
750	Silent Night/The Lord's Prayer	1962	12.00
750 [PS]	Silent Night/The Lord's Prayer	1962	20.00
COLUMBIA			
40411	A Rusty Old Halo/The Treasure of Love	1955	15.00
40412	Walk Over God's Heaven/Jesus Met the Woman	1955	15.00
40473	You'll Never Walk Alone/One God	1955	15.00
40529	His Hands/I See God	1955	15.00
40554	The Bible Tells Me So/Satisfied Mind	1955	15.00
40610	The Lord Is a Busy Man/You're Not Living in Vain	1955	15.00
40712	Round the Rainbow/An Evening Star	1956	15.00
40721	I Ask the Lord/I'm Going to Live	1956	15.00
40753	The Lord's Prayer/Precious Lord	1956	15.00
40777	Silent Night, Holy Night/Mary's Little Boy Chile	1956	15.00
40854	God Is So Good/I Complained	1957	15.00
41000	Trouble/He's a Light Unto My Pathway	1957	15.00
41055	Sweet Little Jesus Boy/A Star Stood Still	1957	12.00
41150	He's Got the Whole World In His Hands/Didn't It Rain	1958	12.00
41258	For My Good Fortune/Have You Any Rivers	1958	12.00
41322	Elijah Rock/Hold Me	1959	12.00
41382	Tell the World About This/Trouble of the World	1959	12.00
41779	My Country 'Tis of Thee (America)/Onward, Christian Soldiers	1960	12.00
42633	Joy To The World!/Go Tell It On The Mountain	1962	10.00
42910	We Shall Overcome/Let's Pray Together	1963	10.00
42946	In the Summer of His Years/Song for My Brother	1964	10.00
43474	Sunrise, Sunset/Like the Breeze Blows	1965	10.00
44529	Take My Hand, Precious Lord/We Shall Overcome	1968	8.00
45068	Abraham, Martin and John/Day Is Done	1970	6.00
JZSP 137705/6 [DJ]	Happy Birthday To You, Our Lord/Silver Bells	1968	5.00
GRAND AWARD			
1025	Dig a Little Deeper/I'm On My Way	1959	15.00
KENWOOD			
300	In the Upper Room (Part 1)/In the Upper Room (Part 2)	1964	8.00
301	His Eyes Are On the Sparrow/Walking to Jerusalem	196?	8.00
302	How I Got Over/Didn't It Rain	196?	8.00
303	Go Tell It On the Mountain/Bless This House	196?	8.00
304	Move On Up a Little Higher (Part 1)/Move On Up a Little Higher (Part 2)	196?	8.00
305	These Are They/Get Away Jordan	196?	8.00
750	Silent Night/The Lord's Prayer	1964	10.00
NASHBORO			
750 [DJ]	Silent Night/The Lord's Prayer	197?	4.00
—Reissue of Kenwood 750			
U.S.A.			
109	The Holy Bible (Part 1)/The Holy Bible (Part 2)	196?	10.00
7-Inch Extended Plays			
COLUMBIA			
B-2072	*Trouble in My Way/Down by the Riverside/Joshua Fit the Battle of Jericho/You'll Never Walk Alone	195?	20.00
B-2072 [PS]	You'll Never Walk Alone	195?	20.00
Albums			
APOLLO			
201/202 [M]	Spirituals	1954	30.00
482 [M]	No Matter How You Pray	1959	25.00
499 [M]	Mahalia Jackson	1962	25.00
1001/2 [M]	Command Performance	1961	25.00
COLUMBIA			
CL 644 [M]	Mahalia Jackson	1955	40.00
CL 702 [M]	Sweet Little Jesus Boy	1955	40.00
CL 899 [M]	Bless This House	1956	30.00
CL 1244 [M]	Newport 1958	1959	20.00
CL 1343 [M]	That Great Gettin' Up Morning	1959	20.00
CL 1428 [M]	Come On Children, Let's Sing	1960	20.00
CL 1473 [M]	The Power and the Glory	1960	20.00
CL 1549 [M]	I Believe	1960	15.00
CL 1643 [M]	Every Time I Feel the Spirit	1961	15.00
CL 1726 [M]	Recorded in Europe During Her Latest Concert Tour	1962	15.00
CL 1824 [M]	Great Songs of Love and Faith	1962	15.00
CL 1903 [M]	Silent Night	1962	15.00
CL 1936 [M]	Make a Joyful Noise Unto the Lord	1962	15.00
CL 2004 [M]	Mahalia Jackson's Greatest Hits	1963	12.00
CL 2130 [M]	Let's Pray Together	1964	12.00
CL 2452 [M]	Mahalia Sings	1966	12.00
CL 2546 [M]	Garden of Prayer	1967	15.00
CL 2552 [10]	You'll Never Walk Alone	1955	50.00
CL 2605 [M]	My Faith	1967	15.00
CL 2690 [M]	Mahalia Jackson In Concert, Easter Sunday 1967	1967	15.00
CS 8071 [S]	Newport 1958	1959	30.00
CS 8153 [S]	That Great Gettin' Up Morning	1959	25.00
CS 8225 [S]	Come On Children, Let's Sing	1960	25.00
CS 8264 [S]	The Power and the Glory	1960	25.00
CS 8349 [S]	I Believe	1960	20.00
CS 8443 [S]	Every Time I Feel the Spirit	1961	20.00
CS 8526 [S]	Recorded in Europe During Her Latest Concert Tour	1962	20.00
CS 8624 [S]	Great Songs of Love and Faith	1962	20.00
CS 8703 [S]	Silent Night	1962	20.00
CS 8736 [S]	Make a Joyful Noise Unto the Lord	1962	20.00
CS 8759 [R]	Mahalia Jackson	1963	12.00
CS 8761 [R]	Bless This House	1963	12.00
PC 8761	Bless This House	198?	8.00
—Budget-line reissue			
CS 8804 [S]	Mahalia Jackson's Greatest Hits	1963	15.00
CS 8930 [S]	Let's Pray Together	1964	15.00
CS 9252 [S]	Mahalia Sings	1966	15.00
CS 9346 [S]	Garden of Prayer	1967	12.00
CS 9405 [S]	My Faith	1967	12.00
CS 9490 [S]	Mahalia Jackson In Concert, Easter Sunday 1967	1967	12.00
CS 9659	A Mighty Fortress	1968	12.00
CS 9686	The Best-Loved Hymns of Dr. Martin Luther King Jr.	1968	15.00
PC 9686	The Best-Loved Hymns of Dr. Martin Luther King Jr.	198?	8.00
—Budget-line reissue			
CS 9727	Christmas with Mahalia	1968	12.00
CS 9813	Right Out of the Church	1969	12.00
CS 9950	What the World Needs Now	1970	12.00
CG 30744 [(2)]	America's Favorite Hymns	1971	15.00
KG 31379 [(2)]	The Great Mahalia Jackson	1972	15.00
KC 34073	How I Got Over	1976	10.00
PC 37710	Mahalia Jackson's Greatest Hits	198?	8.00
3C 38304	Silent Night	1982	8.00
—Reissue			
COLUMBIA SPECIAL PRODUCTS			
P2 13200 [(2)]	(HRB Music Proudly Presents) The Best of Mahalia Jackson: Hymns, Spirituals & Songs of Inspiration	1976	15.00
FOLKWAYS			
31101	I Sing Because I'm Happy, Vol. 1	198?	10.00
31102	I Sing Because I'm Happy, Vol. 2	198?	10.00
GRAND AWARD			
GA 265 SD	I Believe	1966	15.00
—Reissue of 326			
GA 33-326 [M]	Mahalia Jackson	1955	30.00
GA 33-390 [M]	Mahalia Jackson	195?	30.00
HARMONY			
HS 11279	You'll Never Walk Alone	196?	10.00
HS 11372	Abide with Me	1970	10.00
H 30019	Sunrise, Sunset	1970	10.00
KH 31111	Lord Don't Let Me Fall	1972	10.00
KENWOOD			
474	In the Upper Room	196?	15.00
479	Just As I Am	196?	15.00
482	No Matter How You Pray	196?	15.00
486	Mahalia	196?	15.00
489	Mahalia Jackson With the Greatest Spiritual Singers	196?	15.00
500	The Best of Mahalia Jackson	196?	15.00
501	I Lift My Voice	196?	15.00
502	Sing Out	196?	15.00
1001/2 [(2)]	Command Performance	196?	20.00
PICKWICK			
SPC-3510	I Believe	197?	10.00
PRIORITY			
PU 37710	Mahalia Jackson's Greatest Hits	1981	10.00

Except when noted otherwise, VG = 25% of NM, and VG+ = 50% of NM. (Example: VG = $2.00, VG+ = $4.00 and NM = $8.00.)

JACKSON, MICHAEL Also see THE JACKSONS or JACKSON 5; MICHAEL JACKSON AND PAUL McCARTNEY.

12-Inch Singles

CBS INTERNATIONAL

Number	Title (A Side/B Side)	Yr	NM
❑ EPSL-69007	Todo Mi Amor Eres Tu/I Just Can't Stop Loving You	1988	80.00

—Spanish version of "I Just Can't Stop Loving You," pressed in U.S. for Hispanic markets in the U.S. and elsewhere

EPIC

Number	Title (A Side/B Side)	Yr	NM
❑ AS 654 [DJ]	Don't Stop 'Til You Get Enough (5:45) (same on both sides?)	1979	25.00
❑ AS 687 [DJ]	Rock with You (3:39) (same on both sides)	1979	25.00
❑ EAS 0781 [DJ]	Blood on the Dance Floor — The Dubs (T&G Pool of Blood Dub) (Refugee Camp Dub) (Fire Island Dub) (A Cappella)	1997	20.00
❑ AS 1624 [DJ]	Beat It (same on both sides)	1983	20.00
❑ 49-03557	Billie Jean (Extended Version 6:20) (Instrumental 6:20)	1983	25.00
❑ 49-03915	Wanna Be Startin' Somethin' (6:30)/(Instrumental)	1983	12.00
❑ EAS 4363 [DJ]	Black or White (Club Mix) (Dub Mix) (Underground House Mix) (House Radio Mix with Guitars) (Tribal Beats)	1991	20.00
❑ EAS 4454 [DJ]	Remember the Time (unknown versions)	1992	20.00
❑ E2S 4467 [(2)DJ]	In the Closet (11 versions)	1991	30.00
❑ E2S 4533 [(2)DJ]	In the Closet (11 versions)	1991	30.00
❑ E2S 4580 [(2)DJ]	Jam (13 versions)	1991	30.00
❑ E2S 4582 [(2)DJ]	Jam (Atlanta Techno Dub 5:11) (Roger's Slam Jam Mix 4:51) (Silky Dub 4:22) (Acapella Mix 4:31) (More Than Enuff Dub 5:56) (Maurice's Jammin' Dub Mix 7:18) (Roger's Club Dub 6:14) (Roger's Club Mix 6:20) (More Than Enuff Mix 5:56) (E-Smoove's Jazzy Jam 6:44) (Atlanta Techno Mix 6:06) (Roger's Underground Mix 6:02) (Silky 12" 6:20)	1991	30.00
❑ EAS 4656 [DJ]	Jam (Roger's Jeep Mix) (Teddy's 12" Mix) (Percapella) (Teddy's Jam) (Roger's Jeep Dub) (MJ's Raw Mix)	1992	20.00
❑ E2S 4686 [(2)DJ]	Who Is It (11 versions)	1993	30.00
❑ 49-04961	Thriller/(Instrumental)	1983	10.00
❑ 49-06911	Don't Stop 'Til You Get Enough/Wanna Be Startin' Somethin'	1987	12.00

—"Mixed Masters" series

Number	Title (A Side/B Side)	Yr	NM
❑ E2S 7125 [(2)DJ]	Scream (12 versions)	1995	30.00
❑ E2S 7127 [(2)DJ]	Scream (unknown versions)	1995	30.00
❑ AED 7192 [DJ]	The Megamixes (10:33) (4:58) (MJ Urban Megamix)/Scream (Jam & Lewis Remix) (Jam & Lewis Instrumental)	1995	30.00
❑ AED 7298 [DJ]	You Are Not Alone (Franctified Club Mix) (Album Version) (Knuckluv Dub Version) (Classic Club Mix)	1995	20.00
❑ 49-07462	Bad (Dance Extended Mix) (7" Single Version) (Dance Remix Radio Edit) (Dub Version) (Acappella)	1987	10.00
❑ 49-07487	The Way You Make Me Feel (Dance Extended Mix) (Dance Remix Radio Edit) (Dub Version) (A Cappella)	1987	10.00
❑ 49-07510	Man in the Mirror (Single Mix) (Album Mix1)	1988	10.00
❑ 49-07583	Dirty Diana/(Instrumental)	1988	10.00
❑ E2S 7603 [DJ]	This Time Around (DM Mad Club) (DM Radio) (Maurice's Club) (Georgie's House 'n Around Mix) (Timeland Dub) (Neverland Dub) (Don's Control This Dub) (UBQ's Opera Vibe) (DM Bang Da Drums Mix)	1995	100.00
❑ EAS 7605 [DJ]	Earth Song (Hani's Around the World Experience) (Hani's Club Experience) (Hani's Extended Radio Experience)	1995	30.00
❑ EAS 7606 [DJ]	This Time Around (unknown versions)	1995	50.00
❑ EAS 7607 [DJ]	This Time Around (4 versions)	1995	50.00

Michael Jackson, "Man in the Mirror," Epic 07668, 1988, **$3.**

Number	Title (A Side/B Side)	Yr	NM
❑ E2S 7770 [(2)DJ]	They Don't Care About Us (10 versions)	1996	30.00
❑ 49-07855	Another Part of Me (Extended Dance Mix) (Radio Edit) (Dub Mix) (Acappella)	1988	8.00
❑ EAS 8337 [DJ]	Stranger in Moscow (Tee's In-House Club Mix) (Basement Boys 12" Club Mix) (Hani's Num Club Mix) (Charlie Roane's Full R&B Mix)	1996	15.00
❑ EAS 8338 [DJ]	Stranger in Moscow (Tee's Freeze Mix) (Tee's Mission Mix) (Tee'sq Cappella) (Bonus Beats) (Hani's Extended Chili Hop Mix) (Basement Boys Danger Dub)	1996	15.00
❑ EAS 9961 [DJ]	Blood on the Dance Floor (TM's Switchblade Mix) (Refugee Camp Mix) (Fire Island Vocal Mix) (TM's O-Positive Dub)	1997	12.00
❑ 28-50658	You Can't Win (Part 1 7:14)/(Part 2 2:58)	1978	25.00
❑ EAS 54863 [DJ]	Butterflies (same on both sides)	2001	15.00
❑ EAS 54911 [DJ]	You Rock My World (Track Masters Remix with Jay-Z) (same on both sides)	2001	20.00
❑ EAS 56719 [DJ]	Butterflies (Master Mix Featuring Eve) (Michael A Cappella) (Eve A Cappella) (Instrumental)	2002	20.00
❑ 49-74099	Black or White (The Clivilles & Cole House/Club Mix) (The Clivilles and Core House/Dub Mix) (House with Guitar Radio Mix) (Single Version) (Instrumental) (Tribal Beats)	1991	10.00
❑ 49-74201	Remember the Time (4 versions)/Black or White (The Underground Club Mix)	1991	12.00
❑ 49-74267	In the Closet (Club Mix) (The Underground Mix) (Touch Me Dub) (Kl's 12" Mix)	1992	12.00
❑ 49-74304	In the Closet (The Mission 9:20) (Freestyle Mix 6:20)/(The Mix of Life 7:38) (The Underground Dub 6:24)	1992	12.00
❑ 49-74334	Jam (Roger's Club Mix) (Atlanta Techno Mix) (Teddy's Jam) (Roger's Jeep Mix) (E-Smoove's Jazzy Jam)/Don't Stop 'Til You Get Enough (Roger's Underground Solution Mix)	1992	12.00
❑ 49-74420	Who Is It (4 versions)/Beat It (Moby's Sub Mix)	1993	12.00
❑ 49-78001	Scream (5 versions)/Childhood	1995	14.00
❑ 49-78003	You Are Not Alone (Franctified Club Mix) (Album Version)/MJ Megaremix (10:33)/Scream Louder (Flyte Tyme Remix)	1995	12.00
❑ 49-78008	Blood on the Dance Floor (2 versions?)/Dangerous (Roger's Dangerous Mix)	1997	12.00
❑ 49-78013	Stranger in Moscow (Hani's Num Club Mix) (TNT Danger Dub) (Basement Boys 12" Club Mix)/Blood on the Dance Floor	1997	12.00
❑ 49X-78212 [(2)]	They Don't Care About Us (7 versions)/Earth Song/Rock with You (Club Mix)/This Time Around	1996	15.00
❑ 49-78581	Beat It/Working Day and Night	1997	12.00

—"Mixed Masters" series

Number	Title (A Side/B Side)	Yr	NM
❑ 49-78582	Billie Jean/Off the Wall	1997	12.00

—"Mixed Masters" series

MOTOWN

Number	Title (A Side/B Side)	Yr	NM
❑ PR-153 [DJ]	Farewell My Summer Love (4:21)/Call on Me (3:38)//The Jackson 5 Motown Medley (6:49)	1984	12.00

45s

EPIC

Number	Title (A Side/B Side)	Yr	NM
❑ 15-02156	Rock with You/Off the Wall	1981	6.00

—"Memory Lane" reissue

Except when noted otherwise, VG = 25% of NM, and VG+ = 50% of NM. (Example: VG = $2.00, VG+ = $4.00 and NM = $8.00.)

Number	Title (A Side/B Side)	Yr	NM
❑ 15-02157	She's Out of My Life/Lovely One	1981	6.00
—"Memory Lane" reissue; B-side by The Jacksons			
❑ 34-03509	Billie Jean/Can't Get Outta the Rain	1983	6.00
❑ ENR-03575	Billie Jean/(B-side blank)	1983	15.00
—One-sided budget release			
❑ 34-03759	Beat It/Get On the Floor	1983	6.00
❑ 34-03914	Wanna Be Startin' Somethin'/(Instrumental)	1983	8.00
❑ 34-03914 [PS]	Wanna Be Startin' Somethin'/(Instrumental)	1983	5.00
❑ 34-04026	Human Nature/Baby Be Mine	1983	6.00
❑ 34-04026 [PS]	Human Nature/Baby Be Mine	1983	5.00
❑ 34-04026 [PS]	Human Nature	1983	10.00
—"Demonstration — Not for Sale" on sleeve			
❑ 34-04165	P.Y.T. (Pretty Young Thing)/Working Day and Night	1983	6.00
❑ 34-04165 [PS]	P.Y.T. (Pretty Young Thing)/Working Day and Night	1983	5.00
❑ 34-04364	Thriller/Can't Get Outta the Rain	1984	6.00
❑ 34-07253	I Just Can't Stop Loving You/Baby Be Mine	1987	3.00
❑ 34-07253 [PS]	I Just Can't Stop Loving You/Baby Be Mine	1987	3.00
❑ 34-07418	Bad/I Can't Help It	1987	3.00
❑ 34-07418 [PS]	Bad/I Can't Help It	1987	3.00
❑ 34-07645	The Way You Make Me Feel/(Instrumental)	1987	5.00
❑ 34-07645 [PS]	The Way You Make Me Feel/(Instrumental)	1987	3.00
❑ 34-07668	Man in the Mirror/(Instrumental)	1988	3.00
❑ 34-07668 [PS]	Man in the Mirror/(Instrumental)	1988	3.00
❑ 34-07739	Dirty Diana/(Instrumental)	1988	3.00
❑ 34-07739 [PS]	Dirty Diana/(Instrumental)	1988	3.00
❑ 34-07962	Another Part of Me/(Instrumental)	1988	3.00
❑ 34-07962 [PS]	Another Part of Me/(Instrumental)	1988	3.00
❑ 34-08044	Smooth Criminal/(Instrumental)	1988	3.00
❑ 34-08044 [PS]	Smooth Criminal/(Instrumental)	1988	3.00
❑ 8-50654	You Can't Win (Part 1)/You Can't Win (Part 2)	1979	6.00
❑ 9-50742	Don't Stop 'Til You Get Enough/I Can't Help It	1979	4.00
❑ 9-50797	Rock with You/Working Day and Night	1979	4.00
❑ 9-50838	Off the Wall/Get On the Floor	1980	4.00
❑ 9-50871	She's Out of My Life/Get On the Floor	1980	4.00
❑ 34-74100	Black or White/(Instrumental)	1991	6.00
❑ 34-74200	Remember the Time/Black or White (The Underground Club Mix)	1992	8.00
❑ 34-74266	In the Closet (7" Edit)/(The Mission Radio Edit)	1992	7.00
❑ 34-74333	Jam/Rock with You (Masters At Work Remix)	1992	7.00
❑ 34-74406	Who Is It/Wanna Be Startin' Somethin'	1992	7.00
❑ 34-74708	Heal the World/She Drives Me Wild	1992	7.00
❑ 34-77060	Will You Be There/(Instrumental)	1993	7.00
❑ 34-77312	Gone Too Soon/(Instrumental)	1993	7.00
❑ 34-78000	Scream/Childhood	1995	7.00
—A-side: With Janet Jackson			
❑ 34-78002	You Are Not Alone/Scream Louder	1995	7.00
❑ 38-78007	Blood on the Dance Floor/Dangerous (Roger's Dangerous Edit)	1997	7.00
❑ 34-78012	Stranger in Moscow (Radio Edit)/(Tee's Radio Mix)	1997	7.00
❑ 34-78264	They Don't Care About Us/Rock with You (Frankie Knuckles Mix)	1996	7.00
❑ 34 79656	You Rock My World (same on both sides)	2001	6.00
❑ 34 79656 [PS]	You Rock My World (same on both sides)	2001	2.00
❑ 34 79660	Cry (same on both sides)	2001	6.00

MCA

Number	Title (A Side/B Side)	Yr	NM
❑ S45-1786 [DJ]	Someone in the Dark (same on both sides)	1982	50.00
❑ S45-1786 [PS]	Someone in the Dark (same on both sides)	1982	50.00
❑ 40947	Ease On Down the Road/Poppy Girls	1978	5.00
—With Diana Ross			
❑ 40947 [PS]	Ease On Down the Road/Poppy Girls	1978	8.00

MOTOWN

Number	Title (A Side/B Side)	Yr	NM
❑ 1191	Got to Be There/Maria (You Were the Only One)	1971	7.00
❑ 1197	Rockin' Robin/Love Is Here and Now You're Gone	1972	7.00
❑ 1202 [PS]	I Wanna Be Where You Are/We Got a Good Thing Going	1972	10.00
❑ 1202	I Wanna Be Where You Are/We Got a Good Thing Going	1972	7.00
❑ 1207	Ben/You Can Cry on My Shoulder	1972	5.00
❑ 1218	With a Child's Heart/Morning Glow	1973	7.00
❑ 1270	Doggin' Around/Up Again	1974	—
—Unreleased			
❑ 1341	We're Almost There/Take Me Back	1975	5.00
❑ 1349	Just a Little Bit of You/Dear Michael	1975	7.00
❑ 1512	One Day in Your Life/Take Me Back	1981	5.00
❑ 1739 [PS]	Farewell My Summer Love/Call On Me	1984	5.00
❑ 1739	Farewell My Summer Love/Call On Me	1984	5.00
❑ 1757	Girl You're So Together/Touch the One You Love	1984	5.00
❑ 1914 [PS]	Twenty-Five Miles/Up on the House Top	1987	8.00
❑ 1914	Twenty-Five Miles/Up on the House Top	1987	8.00

Albums

EPIC

Number	Title	Yr	NM
❑ FE 35745	Off the Wall	1979	12.00
❑ QE 38112	Thriller	1982	15.00
❑ 8E8 38867 [PD]	Thriller	1983	20.00
❑ OE 40600	Bad	1987	8.00
❑ 9E9 44043 [PD]	Bad	1987	12.00
❑ E2 45400 [(2)]	Dangerous	1991	15.00
❑ HE 47545	Off the Wall	1982	40.00
—Half-speed mastered edition			
❑ HE 48112	Thriller	1982	40.00
—Half-speed mastered edition			
❑ E3 59000 [(3)]	HIStory: Past, Present and Future — Book I	1995	30.00
—Box set with 12x12 booklet			
❑ E2 68000 [(2)]	Blood on the Dance Floor: HIStory in the Mix	1997	25.00
❑ E2 69400 [(2)]	Invincible	2001	30.00

MOTOWN

Number	Title	Yr	NM
❑ M5-107V1	Motown Superstar Series, Vol. 7	1981	10.00
❑ M5-130V1	Got to Be There	1981	12.00
—Reissue of Motown 747			
❑ M5-153V1	Ben	1981	14.00
—Reissue of Motown 755			
❑ M5-194V1	The Best of Michael Jackson	1981	10.00
—Reissue of Motown 851			
❑ M 747	Got to Be There	1972	18.00
❑ M 755	Ben	1972	18.00
—With only Michael Jackson on front cover			
❑ M 755	Ben	1972	60.00
—With Michael Jackson on top half of cover, rats on the bottom half			
❑ M 767	Music and Me	1973	18.00
❑ M6-825S	Forever, Michael	1975	12.00
❑ M6-851S	The Best of Michael Jackson	1975	12.00
❑ M8-956M1	One Day in Your Life	1981	12.00
❑ 6099 ML	Michael Jackson and The Jackson 5 — 14 Greatest Hits	1984	12.00
—Picture disc packaged with one glove			
❑ 6101 ML	Farewell My Summer Love 1984	1984	12.00

JACKSON, MICHAEL, AND PAUL MCCARTNEY

Also see each artist's individual listings.

12-Inch Singles

COLUMBIA

Number	Title (A Side/B Side)	Yr	NM
❑ AS 1758 [DJ]	Say Say Say (same on both sides)	1983	12.00
—As "Paul McCartney and Michael Jackson"			
❑ 44-04169	Say, Say, Say//(Instrumental)/Ode to a Koala Bear	1983	12.00
—As "Paul McCartney and Michael Jackson"			

45s

COLUMBIA

Number	Title (A Side/B Side)	Yr	NM
❑ 38-04168	Say, Say, Say/Ode to a Koala Bear	1983	5.00
—As "Paul McCartney and Michael Jackson"; B-side by Paul McCartney			
❑ 38-04168 [PS]	Say, Say, Say/Ode to a Koala Bear	1983	4.00

EPIC

Number	Title (A Side/B Side)	Yr	NM
❑ 34-03288	The Girl Is Mine/Can't Get Outta the Rain	1982	5.00
—B-side by Michael Jackson			
❑ 34-03288 [PS]	The Girl Is Mine/Can't Get Outta the Rain	1982	7.00
❑ ENR-03372	The Girl Is Mine/(B-side blank)	1982	12.00
—One-sided budget release			

JACKSON, MILLIE

12-Inch Singles

JIVE

Number	Title (A Side/B Side)	Yr	NM
❑ 1015	Hot! Wild! Unrestricted! Crazy Love (4 versions)	1986	6.00
❑ 1022	Love Is a Dangerous Game/(Instrumental)	1986	6.00
❑ 1057	It's a Thang (4 versions)	1987	6.00
❑ 1109	Something You Can Fee I (3 versions)	1988	6.00
❑ 1194	You Knocked the Love (Right Out of My Heart) (3 versions)/Let Me Show You	1989	6.00
❑ 1247	Will You Love Me Tomorrow (same on both sides)	1989	6.00

SPRING

Number	Title (A Side/B Side)	Yr	NM
❑ 028 [DJ]	All the Way Lover/You Created a Monster	1977	10.00
❑ 099	We Got to Hit It Off (same on both sides)	1979	10.00
❑ 195	Mess on Your Hands-Finger Rap (censored & uncensored)	1982	12.00

45s

JIVE

Number	Title (A Side/B Side)	Yr	NM
❑ 1007-7-J	Hot! Wild! Unrestricted! Crazy Love (long & short version)	1986	3.00
❑ 1007-7-J [PS]	Hot! Wild! Unrestricted! Crazy Love (long & short version)	1986	3.00
❑ 1009-7-J	Love Is a Dangerous Game/(Instrumental)	1986	3.00
❑ 1009-7-J [PS]	Love Is a Dangerous Game/(Instrumental)	1986	3.00
❑ 1040-7-J	An Imitation of Love/Mind Over Matter	1987	3.00
❑ 1040-7-J [PS]	An Imitation of Love/Mind Over Matter	1987	3.00
❑ 1056-7-J	It's a Thang/(Instrumental)	1987	3.00
❑ 1108-7-J	The Tide Is Turning/Cover Me (Wall to Wall)	1988	3.00
❑ 1111-7-J	Something You Can Feel/(Instrumental)	1988	3.00
❑ 1111-7-J [PS]	Something You Can Feel/(Instrumental)	1988	3.00
❑ 1246-7-J	Will You Love Me Tomorrow/Muffle That Fart	1989	4.00

MGM

Number	Title (A Side/B Side)	Yr	NM
❑ 14050	Little Bit of Something/My Heart Took a Licking	1969	8.00

SPRING

Number	Title (A Side/B Side)	Yr	NM
❑ 119	A Child of God (It's Hard to Believe)/You're the Joy of My Life	1971	5.00
❑ 123	Ask Me What You Want/I Just Can't Stand It	1972	5.00
❑ 127	My Man, a Sweet Man/I Gotta Get Away	1972	5.00
❑ 131	I Miss You Baby/I Ain't Giving Up	1972	5.00
❑ 134	Breakaway/Strange Things	1973	5.00
❑ 139	Hurts So Good/Love Doctor	1973	5.00
❑ 144	I Got to Try It One Time/Get Your Love Right	1974	5.00
❑ 147	How Do You Feel the Morning After/In the Wash	1974	5.00
❑ 155	The Rap/If Loving You Is Wrong I Don't Want to Be Right	1974	5.00
❑ 157	I'm Through Trying to Prove My Love to You/All I Want Is a Fighting Chance	1975	5.00
❑ 161	Leftovers/Loving Arms	1975	5.00
❑ 164	Bad Risk/There You Are	1976	5.00
❑ 167	Feel Like Making Love/I'm in Love Again	1976	5.00
❑ 170	I Can't Say Goodbye/Help Me Finish My Song	1977	5.00
❑ 173	A Love of Your Own/Live My Love for You	1977	5.00
❑ 175	If You're Not Back in Love by Monday/A Taste of Outside Love	1977	5.00
❑ 179	All the Way Lover/Cheatin' Is	1978	5.00
❑ 185	Sweet Music Man/Go Out and Get Some	1978	5.00
❑ 189	Keep the Home Fire Burnin'/Logs and Thangs	1978	5.00
❑ 192	Never Change Lovers in the Middle of the Night/Seeing You Again	1979	5.00
❑ 197	A Moment's Pleasure/Once You've Had It	1979	5.00
❑ 3002	We Got to Hit It Off/What Went Wrong Last Night	1979	4.00
❑ 3007	Didn't I Blow Your Mind/Be a Sweetheart	1980	4.00

Except when noted otherwise, VG = 25% of NM, and VG+ = 50% of NM. (Example: VG = $2.00, VG+ = $4.00 and NM = $8.00.)

Number	Title (A Side/B Side)	Yr	NM
❑ 3011	Despair/Wish That I Could Have Hurt That Way Again	1980	4.00
❑ 3013	This Is It (Part 1)/This Is It (Part 2)	1980	4.00
❑ 3017	I Had to Say It/It's Going to Take Some Time This Time	1981	4.00
❑ 3019	I Can't Stop Loving You/Loving You	1981	4.00
❑ 3021	Anybody That Don't Like Millie Jackson/Rose Colored Glasses	1981	5.00
❑ 3024	Passion/Lovers and Girlfriends	1982	4.00
❑ 3028	Special Occasion/Blues Don't Get Tired of Me	1982	4.00
❑ 3034	I Feel Like Walking in the Rain/(B-side unknown)	1983	4.00
❑ 3036	E.S.P./(B-side unknown)	1984	4.00
❑ 3040	Sister in the System/(B-side unknown)	1984	4.00

Albums

JIVE

Number	Title (A Side/B Side)	Yr	NM
❑ 1016-1-J	An Imitation of Love	1986	8.00
❑ 1103-1-J	The Tide Is Turning	1988	8.00
❑ 1186-1-J	Back to the Shit	1989	10.00
❑ 1447-1-J	Young Man, Older Woman	1991	12.00

SPRING

Number	Title (A Side/B Side)	Yr	NM
❑ SPR-5703	Millie Jackson	1972	12.00
❑ SPR-5706	It Hurts So Good	1973	12.00
❑ SPR-6701	Millie	1974	10.00
❑ SPR-6703	Caught Up	1974	10.00
❑ SPR-6708	Still Caught Up	1975	10.00
❑ SP-6712	Lovingly Yours	1976	10.00
❑ SP-6715	Feelin' Bitchy	1977	10.00
❑ SP-1-6719	Get It Out'cha System	1978	10.00
❑ SP-1-6722	A Moment's Pleasure	1979	10.00
❑ SP-2-6725 [(2)]	Live & Uncensored	1979	12.00
❑ SP-1-6727	For Men Only	1980	10.00
❑ SP-1-6730	I Had to Say It	1981	10.00
❑ SP-1-6735	Live and Outrageous (Rated XXX)	1982	10.00
❑ SP-1-6737	Hard Times	1983	10.00

JACKSON, MILLIE, AND ISAAC HAYES

45s

POLYDOR

Number	Title (A Side/B Side)	Yr	NM
❑ 2036	Do You Wanna Make Love/I Changed My Mind	1979	4.00
❑ 2063	You Never Cross My Mind/Feels Like the First Time	1980	4.00

Albums

POLYDOR

Number	Title (A Side/B Side)	Yr	NM
❑ PD-1-6229	Royal Rappin's	1979	10.00

JACKSON, RUDY

45s

IMPERIAL

Number	Title (A Side/B Side)	Yr	NM
❑ 5425	Teasing Me/Give Me Your Hand	1957	40.00
❑ 5945	Go On Lover, Go On/Who Do You Think You Are	1963	12.00

R & B

Number	Title (A Side/B Side)	Yr	NM
❑ 1310	I'm Crying/Enfold Me	1955	80.00

JACKSON, SHIRLEY

45s

METRO

Number	Title (A Side/B Side)	Yr	NM
❑ 20031	The Wedding/Wait for Me	1960	12.00

JACKSON, STONEWALL

45s

COLUMBIA

Number	Title (A Side/B Side)	Yr	NM
❑ 4-40883	Don't Be Angry/Knock Off Your Naggin'	1957	25.00
❑ 4-40997	I Need You Real Bad/A Broken Heart, A Wedding Band	1957	25.00
❑ 4-41114	Tears on Her Brodal Bouquet/Gettin' Older	1958	20.00
❑ 4-41199	Grieving in My Heart/I Can't Go On Living This Way	1958	20.00
❑ 4-41257	Life to Go/Misery Known As Heartache	1958	20.00
❑ 4-41393	Waterloo/Smoke Along the Track	1959	15.00
❑ 4-41393 [PS]	Waterloo/Smoke Along the Track	1959	30.00
❑ 4-41488	Igmoo (The Pride of South Central High)/Uncle Sam and Big John Bull	1959	15.00
❑ 4-41533	Mary Don't You Weep/Run	1959	15.00
❑ 4-41591	Why I'm Walkin'/Life of a Poor Boy	1960	15.00
❑ 4-41695	Thirty Links of Chain/Sixteen Fathoms	1960	15.00
❑ 4-41785	A Little Guy Called Joe/I'm Gonna Find You	1960	15.00
❑ 4-41932	Greener Pastures/Wedding Bells for You and Me	1961	15.00
❑ 4-42028	Hungry for Love/For the Last Time	1961	15.00
❑ 4-42229	A Wound Time Can't Erase/Second Choice	1961	15.00
❑ 4-42426	Leona/One Look at Heaven	1962	12.00
❑ 4-42628	Can't Hang Up the Phone/Slowly	1962	12.00
❑ 4-42765	Old Showboat/A Toast to the Bride	1963	12.00
❑ 4-42846	Wild Wind Wind/The Water's So Cold	1963	12.00
❑ 4-42889	B.J. the D.J./Big House on the Corner	1963	12.00
❑ 4-43011	Not My Kind of People/Give It Back to the Indians	1964	12.00
❑ 4-43076	Don't Be Angry/It's Not Me	1964	12.00
❑ 4-43197	I Washed My Hands in Muddy Water/I've Got to Change	1964	12.00
❑ 4-43304	Lost in the Shuffle/Trouble and Me	1965	10.00
❑ 4-43411	If This House Could Talk/Poor Red Georgia Dirt	1965	10.00
❑ 4-43552	The Minute Men (Are Turning in Their Graves)/I Wish I Had a Girl	1966	10.00
❑ 4-43552 [PS]	The Minute Men (Are Turning in Their Graves)/I Wish I Had a Girl	1966	20.00
❑ 4-43718	Blues Plus Booze (Means I Lose)/Still Awake	1966	10.00
❑ 4-43917	Mommy Look, Santa Is Crying/Blue Christmas	1966	12.00
❑ 4-43966	Stamp Out Loneliness/Road to Recovery	1967	10.00
❑ 4-44121	Promises and Hearts (Were Made to Break)/While the Daisies Go Free	1967	10.00
❑ 4-44283	This World Means Nothing (Since You're Gone)/Almsot Hear the Blues	1967	10.00
❑ 4-44416	Nothing Takes the Place of Loving You/If Heartaches Were Wine	1968	10.00
❑ 4-44501	I Believe in Love/Drinking and Driving	1968	10.00
❑ 4-44501 [PS]	I Believe in Love/Drinking and Driving	1968	15.00
❑ 4-44625	Angry Words/Red Roses Blooming Back Home	1968	10.00
❑ 4-44726	Somebody's Always Leaving/Recess Time	1969	10.00
❑ 4-44863	"Never More" Quoth the Raven/How Many Lies Can I Tell	1969	10.00
❑ 4-44976	Ship in the Bottle/Thoughts of a Lonely Man	1969	10.00
❑ 4-45075	Better Days for Mama/The Harm You've Done	1970	8.00
❑ 4-45151	Born That Way/Blue Field	1970	8.00
❑ 4-45217	Oh, Lonesome Me/When He Was Nine	1970	8.00
❑ 4-45291	Save a Little Place for Me/Wings of a Dove	1970	8.00
❑ 4-45381	Me and You and a Dog Named Boo/Here's to Hank	1971	8.00
❑ 4-45465	Push the Panic Button/Waitin' for Dawn 'Til Dawn	1971	8.00
❑ 4-45546	That's All This Old World Needs/Big Busy World	1972	8.00
❑ 4-45632	Torn from the Pages of Life/Waterloo	1972	8.00
❑ 4-45738	I'm Not Strong Enough (To Build Another Dream)/I've Run Out of Reasons	1972	8.00
❑ 4-45831	True Love Is the Thing/House of Bottles and Cans	1973	8.00

GRT

Number	Title (A Side/B Side)	Yr	NM
❑ 013	Read Between the Lines/Don't Be Late	1974	6.00
❑ 023	Waterloo/I Washed My Hands in Muddy Water	1975	6.00

LITTLE DARLIN'

Number	Title (A Side/B Side)	Yr	NM
❑ 7800	Spirits of St. Louis/Alcohol of Fame	1978	6.00
❑ 7802	Walk Out on Me Before I Walk Out on You/Burned On Low	1978	6.00
❑ 7806	I Can't Sing a Love Song/My Favorite Sin	1978	6.00
❑ 7915	Come On Home/Point of No Return	1979	6.00
❑ 7927	Listening to Johnny Paycheck/Here's to the Ripoff	1979	6.00

MGM

Number	Title (A Side/B Side)	Yr	NM
❑ 14569	Herman Schwartz/Lovin' the Fool Out of Me	1973	7.00

Albums

COLUMBIA

Number	Title (A Side/B Side)	Yr	NM
❑ CL 1391 [M]	The Dynamic Stonewall Jackson	1959	25.00
❑ CL 1770 [M]	Sadness in a Song	1962	20.00
❑ CL 2059 [M]	I Love a Song	1963	20.00
❑ CL 2278 [M]	Trouble & Me	1964	15.00
❑ CL 2377 [M]	Stonewall Jackson's Greatest Hits	1965	15.00
❑ CL 2509 [M]	All's Fair in Love 'n' War	1966	15.00
❑ CL 2674 [M]	Help Stamp Out Loneliness	1967	25.00
❑ CL 2762 [M]	Stonewall Jackson Country	1967	25.00
❑ CS 8186 [S]	The Dynamic Stonewall Jackson	1959	30.00
❑ CS 8570 [S]	Sadness in a Song	1962	25.00
❑ CS 8859 [S]	I Love a Song	1963	25.00
❑ CS 9078 [S]	Trouble & Me	1964	20.00
❑ CS 9177 [S]	Stonewall Jackson's Greatest Hits	1965	20.00
❑ CS 9309 [S]	All's Fair in Love 'n' War	1966	20.00
❑ CS 9474 [S]	Help Stamp Out Loneliness	1967	20.00
❑ CS 9562 [S]	Stonewall Jackson Country	1967	20.00
❑ CS 9669	Nothing Takes the Place of Loving You	1968	20.00
❑ CS 9708	The Great Old Songs	1968	20.00
❑ CS 9754	The Old Country Church	1969	25.00
❑ CS 9880	Tribute to Hank Williams	1969	20.00
❑ C 30254	The Real Thing	1971	15.00

HARMONY

Number	Title (A Side/B Side)	Yr	NM
❑ HS 11187	The Exciting Stonewall Jackson	196?	12.00

JACKSON, TONY, AND THE VIBRATIONS

45s

KAPP

Number	Title (A Side/B Side)	Yr	NM
❑ 639	This Little Girl of Mine/You Beat Me to the Punch	1965	15.00

RED BIRD

Number	Title (A Side/B Side)	Yr	NM
❑ 10-038	That's What I Want/Stage Door	1965	15.00

JACKSON, WALTER

45s

BRUNSWICK

Number	Title (A Side/B Side)	Yr	NM
❑ 55502	It Doesn't Take Much/Let Me Come Back	1973	150.00

CHI-SOUND

Number	Title (A Side/B Side)	Yr	NM
❑ XW908	Feelings/Words (Are Impossible)	1976	5.00
❑ XW964	Baby, I Love Your Way/What Would You Do	1977	5.00
❑ XW1044	It's All Over/Gonna Find Me an Angel	1977	5.00
❑ XW1140	If I Had My Way/We Could Fly	1978	15.00
❑ XW1216	Manhattan Skyline/I Won't Remember Ever Loving You	1978	5.00
❑ 2426	Magic Man/Golden Rays	1979	4.00

COLUMBIA

Number	Title (A Side/B Side)	Yr	NM
❑ 02037	Tell Me Where It Hurts/When I See You	1981	4.00
❑ 02294	What If I Walked Out on You/Come to Me	1981	4.00
❑ 42528	This World of Mine/I Don't Want to Suffer	1962	100.00
❑ 42659	Starting Tomorrow/Then, Only Then	1963	150.00
❑ 42823	Opportunity/It Will Be the Last Time	1963	100.00

COTILLION

Number	Title (A Side/B Side)	Yr	NM
❑ 44053	Anyway That You Want Me/Life Has Its Ups and Downs	1969	15.00

EPIC

Number	Title (A Side/B Side)	Yr	NM
❑ 10408	Ad Lib/No Butterflies	1968	8.00

KELLI-ARTS

Number	Title (A Side/B Side)	Yr	NM
❑ 1006	If I Had a Chance/(B-side unknown)	1982	20.00

OKEH

Number	Title (A Side/B Side)	Yr	NM
❑ 7189	That's What Mama Say/What Would You Do	1964	40.00
❑ 7204	It's All Over/Lee Cross	1964	20.00
❑ 7215	Suddenly I'm All Alone/Special Love	1965	20.00
❑ 7219	Welcome Home/Blowin' in the Wind	1965	30.00
❑ 7229	I'll Keep On Trying/Where Have All the Flowers Gone	1965	40.00
❑ 7236	Funny (Not Much)/One Heart Lonely	1965	50.00
❑ 7247	It's an Uphill Climb to the Bottom/Tear for Tear	1966	60.00
❑ 7247 [PS]	It's an Uphill Climb to the Bottom/Tear for Tear	1966	100.00
❑ 7256	After You There Can Be Nothing/My Funny Valentine	1966	30.00
❑ 7260	A Corner in the Sun/Not You	1966	20.00
❑ 7272	Speak Her Name/They Don't Give Medals (To Yesterday's Heroes)	1967	20.00
❑ 7272 [PS]	Speak Her Name/They Don't Give Medals (To Yesterday's Heroes)	1967	50.00
❑ 7285	Deep in the Heart of Harlem/My One Chance to Make It	1967	20.00
❑ 7285 [PS]	Deep in the Heart of Harlem/My One Chance to Make It	1967	50.00

Number	Title (A Side/B Side)	Yr	NM
7295	Cold, Cold Winter/My Ship Is Comin' In	1967	30.00
7305	Everything/Road to Ruin	1968	20.00

U.S.A.

Number	Title (A Side/B Side)	Yr	NM
104	Fool for You/Walls That Separate	196?	15.00

Albums

CHI-SOUND

Number	Title (A Side/B Side)	Yr	NM
CS-LA656-G	Feeling Good	1976	12.00
CS-LA733-G	I Want to Come Back As A Song	1977	12.00
CS-LA844-G	Good to See You	1978	12.00

COLUMBIA

Number	Title (A Side/B Side)	Yr	NM
FC 37132	Tell Me Where It Hurts	1981	10.00

EPIC

Number	Title (A Side/B Side)	Yr	NM
E 34657	Greatest Hits	1977	10.00
PE 40434	Greatest Hits	1987	8.00

OKEH

Number	Title (A Side/B Side)	Yr	NM
OKM 12107 [M]	It's All Over	1965	25.00
OKM 12108 [M]	Welcome Home	1966	25.00
OKM 12120 [M]	Speak Her Name	1967	25.00
OKS 14107 [S]	It's All Over	1965	30.00
OKS 14108 [S]	Welcome Home	1966	30.00
OKS 14120 [S]	Speak Her Name	1967	30.00
OKS 14128	Walter Jackson's Greatest Hits	1969	15.00

JACKSON, WANDA

45s

ABC

Number	Title (A Side/B Side)	Yr	NM
12116	Take a Look/I Can't Stand to Hear You Say Goodbye	1975	5.00

CAPITOL

Number	Title (A Side/B Side)	Yr	NM
2021	A Girl Don't Have to Drink to Have Fun/My Days Are Darker Than Your Nights	1967	10.00
2085	By the Time You Get to Phoenix/Wishing Well	1968	8.00
2151	My Baby Walked Right Out on Me/No Place to Go But Home	1968	8.00
2245	Little Boy Soldier/I Talk a Pretty Story	1968	8.00
2315	I Wish I Was Your Friend/Poor Old Me	1968	8.00
2379	If I Had a Hammer/The Pain of It All	1969	8.00
2472	Your Tender Love/As the Day Wears On	1969	8.00
2524	Everything's Leaving/You Cheated Me	1969	8.00
2614	My Big Iron Skillet/The Hunter	1969	8.00
2693	Two Separate Bar Stools/Two Wrongs Don't Make a Right	1969	8.00
2761	A Woman Lives for Love/What Have We Done	1970	6.00
2872	Who Shot John/Stop the World	1970	6.00
2986	Fancy Satin Pillows/Why Don't We Love Like That Anymore	1970	6.00
3070	People Gotta Be Loving/Glory Hallelujah	1971	6.00
3143	Back Then/I'm Gonna Walk Out of Your Life	1971	6.00
3218	I Already Know (What I'm Gettin' for My Birthday)/The Man You Could Have Been	1971	6.00
3293	I'll Be Whatever You Say/The More You See Me Less	1972	6.00
3385	I Wouldn't Want You Any Other Way/Song of the Wind	1972	6.00
F3485	I Gotta Know/Half As Good a Girl	1956	40.00
3498	Roll with the Tide/Tennessee Women's Prison	1972	6.00
F3575	Hot Dog! That Made Him Mad/Silver Threads and Golden Needles	1956	40.00
3599	I Don't Know How to Tell Him/Your Memory Comes and Gets Me	1973	6.00
F3637	Cryin' Through the Night/Baby Loves Him	1957	50.00
F3683	Don'a Wan'a/Let Me Explain	1957	30.00
F3764	Cool Love/Did You Miss Me	1957	30.00
F3843	Fujiyama Mama/No Wedding Bells for Joe	1957	30.00
F3941	Just a Queen for a Day/Honey Bop	1958	30.00
F4026	(Every Time They Play) Our Song/Mean, Mean Man	1958	30.00
F4081	Sinful Heart/Rock Your Baby	1958	30.00
F4142	Savin' My Love/I Wanna Waltz	1959	25.00
F4207	A Date with Jerry/You're the One for Me	1959	25.00
F4286	Reaching/I'd Rather Have You	1959	25.00
4354	My Destiny/Please Call Today	1960	25.00
4397	Let's Have a Party/Cool Love	1960	40.00
4469	Mean, Mean Man/Happy, Happy Birthday	1960	25.00
4520	Riot in Cell Black #9/Little Charm Bracelet	1961	25.00
4553	Right or Wrong/Funnel of Love	1961	25.00
4635	In the Middle of a Heartache/I'd Be Ashamed	1961	25.00
4681	A Little Bitty Tear/I Don't Wanta Go	1962	20.00
4723	If I Cried Every Time You Hurt Me/Let My Love Walk In	1962	20.00
4723 [PS]	If I Cried Every Time You Hurt Me/Let My Love Walk In	1962	30.00
4785	I Misunderstood/Between the Window and the Phone	1962	15.00
4833	The Greatest Actor/You Bug Me Bad	1962	15.00
4884	Whirlpool/One Teardrop at a Time	1962	100.00
4917	But I Was Lying/Sympathy	1963	15.00
4973	This Should Go On Forever/We Haven't a Moment to Lose	1963	15.00
5015	Memory Mountain/Let Me Talk to You	1963	15.00
5072	Slippin'/Just for You	1963	15.00
5142	The Violet and a Rose/To Tell You the Truth	1964	12.00
5228	Leave My Baby Alone/I'm Mad at Me	1964	12.00
5287	Candy Man/Weary Blues From Waitin'	1964	12.00
5364	My Baby's Gone/If I Were You	1965	12.00
5433	Have I Grown Used to Missing You/Take Me Home	1965	12.00
5491	My First Day Without You/Send Me No Roses	1965	12.00
5559	The Box It Came In/Look Out Heart	1965	12.00
5645	Because It's You/Long As I Have You	1966	10.00
5712	This Gun Don't Care/I Wonder If She Knows	1966	10.00
5789	Tears Will Be the Chaser for Your Wine/Reckless Love Affair	1967	10.00
5863	Both Sides of the Line/Famous Last Words	1967	10.00
5960	My Heart Gets All the Breaks/You'll Always Have My Love	1967	10.00

DECCA

Number	Title (A Side/B Side)	Yr	NM
29140	You Can't Have My Love/Lovin' Country Style	1954	60.00
—With Billy Gray			
29253	The Right to Love/If You Knew What I Know	1954	60.00
29267	If You Don't, Somebody Else Will/You'd Be the First One to Know	1954	50.00
—With Billy Gray			
29514	Tears at the Grand Ole Opry/Nobody's Darlin' But Mine	1955	50.00
29677	Don't Do the Things He'd Do/It's the Same World	1955	30.00
29803	Wasted/I Cried Again	1956	50.00
30153	You Won't Forget (About Me)/A Heart You Could Have Had	1956	30.00

JIN

Number	Title (A Side/B Side)	Yr	NM
300	Lonely Days, Lonely Nights/My Memories	197?	5.00

MYRRH

Number	Title (A Side/B Side)	Yr	NM
122	When It's Time to Fall in Love Again/Say "I Do"	1973	5.00
126	Come On Home (To This Lonely Heart)/It's a Long, Long Time to Cry	1973	5.00
143	Jesus Put a Yodel in My Soul/(B-side unknown)	1974	5.00
152	Where Do I Put His Memory/Take a Look	1975	5.00

7-Inch Extended Plays

CAPITOL

Number	Title (A Side/B Side)	Yr	NM
SXA-1776	In the Middle of a Heartache/Is It Wrong/Don't Ask Me Why//If I Cried Every Time You Hurt Me/You Don't Know/A Little Bitty Tear	196?	30.00
—Stereo jukebox issue; small hole, plays at 33 1/3 rpm			
SXA-1776 [PS]	Wonderful Wanda	196?	30.00

Albums

CAPITOL

Number	Title (A Side/B Side)	Yr	NM
ST-129	The Many Moods of Wanda Jackson	1969	15.00
ST-238	The Happy Side of Wanda Jackson	1969	15.00
ST 8-0345	Wanda Jackson In Person	1970	20.00
—Capitol Record Club edition			
ST-345	Wanda Jackson In Person	1970	15.00
ST-434	Wanda Jackson Country!	1970	15.00
ST-554	A Woman Lives for Love	1970	15.00
ST-669	I've Gotta Sing!	1971	15.00
T 1041 [M]	Wanda Jackson	1958	300.00
—Black colorband label, Capitol logo at left			
T 1041 [M]	Wanda Jackson	1962	100.00
—Black colorband label, Capitol logo at top			
T 1384 [M]	Rockin' with Wanda	1960	400.00
—Black colorband label, Capitol logo at left			
T 1384 [M]	Rockin' with Wanda	1962	250.00
—Gold "Star Line" label			
T 1384 [M]	Rockin' with Wanda	1963	150.00
—Black "Star Line" label			
ST 1511 [S]	There's a Party Goin' On	1961	400.00
—Black colorband label, Capitol logo at left			
T 1511 [M]	There's a Party Goin' On	1961	250.00
—Black colorband label, Capitol logo at left			
ST 1596 [S]	Right or Wrong	1961	50.00
—Black colorband label, Capitol logo at left			
ST 1596 [S]	Right or Wrong	1962	25.00
—Black colorband label, Capitol logo at top			
T 1596 [M]	Right or Wrong	1961	40.00
—Black colorband label, Capitol logo at left			
T 1596 [M]	Right or Wrong	1962	20.00
—Black colorband label, Capitol logo at top			
ST 1776 [S]	Wonderful Wanda	1962	30.00
T 1776 [M]	Wonderful Wanda	1962	25.00
ST 1911 [S]	Love Me Forever	1963	30.00
T 1911 [M]	Love Me Forever	1963	25.00
ST 2030 [S]	Two Sides of Wanda	1964	30.00
T 2030 [M]	Two Sides of Wanda	1964	25.00
ST 2306 [S]	Blues in My Heart	1965	30.00
T 2306 [M]	Blues in My Heart	1965	25.00
ST 2438 [S]	Wanda Jackson Sings Country Songs	1965	30.00
T 2438 [M]	Wanda Jackson Sings Country Songs	1965	25.00
ST 2606 [S]	Wanda Jackson Salutes the Country Music Hall of Fame	1966	20.00
T 2606 [M]	Wanda Jackson Salutes the Country Music Hall of Fame	1966	15.00
ST 2704 [S]	Reckless Love Affair	1967	15.00
T 2704 [M]	Reckless Love Affair	1967	20.00
ST 2812 [S]	You'll Always Have My Love	1967	15.00
T 2812 [M]	You'll Always Have My Love	1967	20.00
ST 2883 [S]	The Best of Wanda Jackson	1968	15.00
T 2883 [M]	The Best of Wanda Jackson	1968	40.00
—Red and white "Starline" label			
ST 2976	Cream of the Crop	1968	15.00
ST-11023	Praise the Lord	1972	15.00
ST-11096	I Wouldn't Want You Any Other Way	1972	15.00
ST-11161	Country Keepsakes	1973	15.00

DECCA

Number	Title (A Side/B Side)	Yr	NM
DL 4224 [M]	Lovin' Country Style	1962	50.00

GUSTO

Number	Title (A Side/B Side)	Yr	NM
GT 0057	Greatest Hits	1980	10.00

HILLTOP

Number	Title (A Side/B Side)	Yr	NM
6058	Please Help Me I'm Falling	1968	10.00
6074	Leave My Baby Alone	1969	12.00
6116	We'll Sing in the Sunshine	1972	12.00
6123	By the Time I Get to Phoenix	1973	10.00
6182	Tears at the Grand Ole Opry	1974	10.00

MYRRH

Number	Title (A Side/B Side)	Yr	NM
MSB-6513	When It's Time to Fall in Love Again	1974	12.00
MSB-6533	Now I Have Everything	1975	12.00
MSB-6556	Make Me Like a Child Again	1976	12.00

PICKWICK

Number	Title (A Side/B Side)	Yr	NM
PTP-2053 [(2)]	Wanda Jackson	1974	12.00

SYMPATHY FOR THE RECORD INDUSTRY

Number	Title (A Side/B Side)	Yr	NM
SFTRI-724	Heart Trouble	2003	12.00

VARRICK

Number	Title (A Side/B Side)	Yr	NM
VR-025	Rock 'n' Roll Away Your Blues	1987	12.00

VOCALION

Number	Title (A Side/B Side)	Yr	NM
VL 73861 [R]	Nobody's Darlin'	1968	12.00

WORD

Number	Title (A Side/B Side)	Yr	NM
WST-8614	Country Gospel	1973	12.00
WST-8781	Closer to Jesus	1977	12.00

JACKSON, WILLIS

45s

ATCO

Number	Title (A Side/B Side)	Yr	NM
6089	Later 'Gator/Back Door	1957	50.00

ATLANTIC

Number	Title (A Side/B Side)	Yr	NM
946	Harlem Nocturne/Street Scene	1951	150.00
957	Wine-O-Wine/Good Gliding	1952	150.00
967	Here in My Heart/Rock, Rock, Rock	1952	100.00
975	Gator's Groove/Estralita	1952	80.00
998	Walkin' Home/Shake Dance	1953	80.00
3294	Brown Eyed Girl/The Way We Were	1975	8.00

BIG CHANCE

Number	Title (A Side/B Side)	Yr	NM
205	Love Story/Heavy Makes You Happy (Sha-Na-Boom-Boom)	197?	8.00

Number	Title (A Side/B Side)	Yr	NM
CADET			
❑ 5529	Goose Pimples/Who Can I Turn To (When Nobody Wants Me)	1966	20.00
COTILLION			
❑ 44204	Feelings/Do It, Do It	1976	6.00
DELUXE			
❑ 6060	The Cracker Jack/Try a Little Tenderness	1954	40.00
❑ 6073	Howling at Midnight/We'll Be Together Again	1955	30.00
FIRE			
❑ 1003	Good to the Bone/Making It	1959	15.00
PAUL WINLEY			
❑ 1101	Bow Legged Daddy/(Instrumental)	196?	20.00
—With Ann Winley on A-side			
PRESTIGE			
❑ 159	Cool Grits (Part 1)/(Part 2)	196?	15.00
❑ 170	Come Back to Sorrento/Sunny Side of the Street	196?	15.00
❑ 178	Keep On a-Blowin' (Part 1)/(Part 2)	196?	15.00
❑ 187	Blue Gator (Part 1)/(Part 2)	196?	15.00
❑ 194	Careless Love/He Said, She Said, I Said	196?	15.00
❑ 207	Cookin' Sherry (Part 1)/(Part 2)	1961	12.00
❑ 221	Thunderbird/Jambalaya	1962	12.00
❑ 234	I Left My Heart in San Francisco/What Kind of Fool Am I	1962	12.00
❑ 243	Neapolitan Nights/Mama	1963	10.00
❑ 258	Secret Love (Part 1)/(Part 2)	1963	10.00
❑ 277	Arrivederci Roma/Y'All	1963	10.00
❑ 293	Gra-a-avy/Brother Elijah	1963	10.00
❑ 303	As Long As She Needs Me/Troubled Times	1963	10.00
❑ 327	Nightingale/People	1964	10.00
❑ 339	Pool Shark/More Gravy	196?	10.00
❑ 372	Jive Samba (Part 1)/(Part 2)	196?	10.00
❑ 393	This'll Get To Ya (Part 1)/(Part 2)	196?	10.00
❑ 411	Tu'gether (Part 1)/(Part 2)	196?	10.00
❑ 457	Song of Ossanha/Soul Grabber	1968	12.00
❑ 719	Swivel Hips (Part 1)/(Part 2)	1969	8.00
❑ 724	This'll Get To Ya (Part 1)/(Part 2)	197?	8.00
TRU-SOUND			
❑ 410	Backtrack/Without a Song	196?	15.00
❑ 410	That Twistin' Train/Without a Song	1962	12.00
—A-side is the same recording as "Backtrack" with a new title			
VERVE			
❑ 10332	I Almost Lost My Mind/Swimmin' Home Babe	1964	10.00
Albums			
ATLANTIC			
❑ SD 18145	The Way We Were	1975	12.00
CADET			
❑ LP-763 [M]	Smoking with Willis	1966	15.00
❑ LPS-763 [S]	Smoking with Willis	1966	20.00
COTILLION			
❑ SD 9908	Willis Jackson Plays with Feeling	1977	15.00
CTI			
❑ 6024	Sunflower	1972	15.00
FANTASY			
❑ OJC-220	Cool Gator	198?	10.00
❑ OJC-321	Please, Mr. Jackson	1988	10.00
MOODSVILLE			
❑ MVLP-17 [M]	In My Solitude	1961	50.00
—Green label			
❑ MVLP-17 [M]	In My Solitude	1965	25.00
—Blue label, trident logo at right			
MUSE			
❑ MR-5036	West Africa	1974	12.00
❑ MR-5048	Headed and Gutted	1975	12.00
❑ MR-5100	In the Valley	1976	12.00
❑ MR-5146	The Gator Horn	1978	12.00
❑ MR-5162	Bar Wars	1978	12.00
❑ MR-5200	Lockin' Horns	1979	12.00
❑ MR-5294	Nothing Butt	198?	10.00
❑ MR-5316	Ya Understand Me?	198?	10.00
PRESTIGE			
❑ 2516	Gatorade	198?	12.00
❑ PRLP-7162 [M]	Please, Mr. Jackson	1959	50.00
❑ PRLP-7172 [M]	Cool Gator	1959	50.00
❑ PRLP-7183 [M]	Blue Gator	1960	50.00
❑ PRLP-7196 [M]	Really Groovin'	1961	50.00
❑ PRLP-7211 [M]	Cookin' Sherry	1961	30.00
❑ PRST-7211 [S]	Cookin' Sherry	1961	40.00
❑ PRLP-7232 [M]	Thunderbird	1962	30.00
❑ PRST-7232 [S]	Thunderbird	1962	40.00
❑ PRLP-7260 [M]	Bossa Nova Plus	1962	30.00
❑ PRST-7260 [S]	Bossa Nova Plus	1962	40.00
❑ PRLP-7264 [M]	Neapolitan Nights	1963	30.00
❑ PRST-7264 [S]	Neapolitan Nights	1963	40.00
❑ PRLP-7273 [M]	Loose...	1963	30.00
❑ PRST-7273 [S]	Loose...	1963	40.00
❑ PRLP-7285 [M]	Grease 'n' Gravy	1963	30.00
❑ PRST-7285 [S]	Grease 'n' Gravy	1963	40.00
❑ PRLP-7296 [M]	The Good Life	1964	30.00
❑ PRST-7296 [S]	The Good Life	1964	40.00
❑ PRLP-7317 [M]	More Gravy	1964	30.00
❑ PRST-7317 [S]	More Gravy	1964	40.00
❑ PRLP-7329 [M]	Boss Shoutin'	1964	25.00
❑ PRST-7329 [S]	Boss Shoutin'	1964	30.00
❑ PRLP-7348 [M]	Live! Jackson's Action	1965	25.00
❑ PRST-7348 [S]	Live! Jackson's Action	1965	30.00
❑ PRLP-7364 [M]	Together Again	1965	25.00
❑ PRST-7364 [S]	Together Again	1965	30.00
❑ PRLP-7380 [M]	Live! Action	1965	25.00
❑ PRST-7380 [S]	Live! Action	1965	30.00
❑ PRLP-7396 [M]	Soul Night — Live!	1965	25.00
❑ PRST-7396 [S]	Soul Night — Live!	1965	30.00
❑ PRLP-7412 [M]	Tell It...	1966	20.00
❑ PRST-7412 [S]	Tell It...	1966	25.00
❑ PRLP-7428 [M]	Together Again...Again	1966	20.00
❑ PRST-7428 [S]	Together Again...Again	1966	25.00
❑ PRST-7551	Soul Grabber	1968	20.00
❑ PRST-7571	Star Bag	1968	20.00
❑ PRST-7602	Swivel Hips	1969	20.00
❑ PRST-7648	Gator's Groove	1969	20.00
❑ PRST-7702	The Best of Willis Jackson with Brother Jack McDuff	1969	15.00
❑ PRST-7770	The Best — Soul Stompin'	1971	15.00
❑ PRST-7783	Please Mr. Jackson	1970	20.00
❑ PRST-7830	Keep On a-Blowing	1971	20.00
❑ PRST-7850	Blue Gator	197?	15.00
TRIP			
❑ 5007 [(2)]	Mellow Blues	197?	12.00
❑ 5028	Funky Reggae	197?	10.00
❑ 5030	Willis Jackson Plays Around with the Hits	197?	10.00
VERVE			
❑ V-8589 [M]	'Gator Tails	1964	15.00
❑ V6-8589 [S]	'Gator Tails	1964	20.00
❑ V6-8782	Willis Jackson	1969	15.00

JACKSON FIVE, THE

See THE JACKSONS.

JACKSON HEIGHTS

Number	Title (A Side/B Side)	Yr	NM
45s			
VERVE			
❑ 10706	Long Time Dying/Maureen	1973	8.00
Albums			
MERCURY			
❑ SR-61331	King Progress	1970	25.00
VERVE			
❑ V6-5089	Jackson Heights	1973	20.00

JACKSON JILLS, THE

Number	Title (A Side/B Side)	Yr	NM
45s			
DOT			
❑ 16541	Mommie's Little Baby/Pretty Little Dutch Girl	1963	15.00

JACKSONS, THE

Includes records as "The Jackson Five." Also see JACKIE JACKSON; JERMAINE JACKSON; MICHAEL JACKSON.

Number	Title (A Side/B Side)	Yr	NM
12-Inch Singles			
EPIC			
❑ ASD 523 [DJ]	Blame It on the Boogie (Extended Disco Mix 7:00) (same on both sides)	1978	70.00
❑ AS 551 [DJ]	Shake Your Body (Down to the Ground) (7:58)/Things I Do for You	1978	30.00
❑ AS 858 [DJ]	Lovely One (same on both sides?)	1980	15.00
❑ AS 894 [DJ]	Heartbreak Hotel (same on both sides)	1980	15.00
❑ AS 936 [DJ]	Can You Feel It (same on both sides)	1981	20.00
❑ AS 1244 [DJ]	Walk Right Now/(Instrumental)	1981	10.00
❑ AS 1351 [DJ]	Heartbreak Hotel/She's Out of My Life/Jacksons Medley	1982	20.00
❑ AS 1387 [DJ]	Working Day and Night/Things I Do for You	1982	15.00
❑ EAS 1724 [DJ]	2300 Jackson Street (Short Version 4:12) (LP Version 5:06)	1989	12.00
❑ AS 1910 [DJ]	Torture/(Instrumental)	1984	12.00
❑ AS 1954 [DJ]	Body/(Instrumental)	1984	12.00
❑ 49-02403	Walk Right Now (Vocal 7:35) (Instrumental 6:55)	1981	15.00
❑ 49-05022	State of Shock (Dance Mix)/(Instrumental)	1984	10.00
—A-side vocal shared by Mick Jagger			
❑ 49-05075	Torture (Dance Mix)/(Instrumental)	1984	10.00
❑ 49H-07548	Lovely One/Can You Feel It	198?	10.00
—"Mixed Masters" reissue			
❑ 49H-08142	Blame It on the Boogie/Heartbreak Hotel	1988	10.00
—"Mixed Masters" reissue			
❑ 28-50721	Shake Your Body (Down to the Ground) (European Version 7:59)/That's What You Get (For Being Polite) (4:56)	1978	20.00
❑ 49-68233	Nothin' (That Compares 2 U) (5 versions)	1989	8.00
❑ 49-78583	Enjoy Yourself/Blame It on the Boogie/Walk Right Now	1997	10.00
—"Mixed Masters" reissue			
❑ 49-78584	Shake Your Body (Down to the Ground)/Can You Feel It	1997	10.00
—"Mixed Masters" reissue			
MCA			
❑ 23729	Time Out for the Burglar (Extended Version 7:52) (Radio Edit 5:37) (Bonus Beats 7:44) (Instrumental 7:52)	1987	10.00
MOTOWN			
❑ 37463 1066 1 [DJ]	Who's Lovin' You (Live LP Version 5:40) (Live Radio Edit 4:02) (Original Version 3:42)	1992	15.00
❑ 37463 3004 1	I Want You Back '98 (6 versions)	1998	20.00
45s			
DYNAMO			
❑ 146	You Don't Have to Be Over Twenty-One to Fall in Love/Some Girls Want Me for Their Love	1971	40.00
EPIC			
❑ 19-01032	Can You Feel It/Everybody	1981	4.00
❑ 19-02132	Walk Right Now/Your Ways	1981	4.00
❑ 15-02157	Lovely One/She's Out of My Life	1981	3.00
—Reissue; B-side by Michael Jackson			
❑ 14-02720	The Things I Do for You/Working Day and Night	1982	4.00
❑ 34-04503	State of Shock/Your Ways	1984	4.00
—A-side with Mick Jagger			
❑ 34-04503 [PS]	State of Shock/Your Ways	1984	4.00
❑ 34-04575	Torture/(Instrumental)	1984	4.00
❑ 34-04575 [PS]	Torture/(Instrumental)	1984	4.00
❑ 34-04673	Body/(Instrumental)	1984	4.00
❑ 34-04673 [PS]	Body/(Instrumental)	1984	4.00
❑ 8-50595	Blame It on the Boogie/Do What You Wanna	1978	4.00
❑ 8-50656	Shake Your Body (Down to the Ground)/That's What You Get (For Being Polite)	1979	4.00
—Second issue has dark blue label			
❑ 8-50656	Shake Your Body (Down to the Ground)/That's What You Get (For Being Polite)	1979	5.00
—Original issue has orange label			
❑ 9-50938	Lovely One/Bless His Soul	1980	4.00
❑ 19-50959	Heartbreak Hotel/The Things I Do for You	1980	4.00
❑ 34-68688	Nothin' (That Compares 2 U)/Alright with Me	1989	3.00
❑ 34-69022	2300 Jackson Street/When I Look at You	1989	3.00
EPIC/PHILADELPHIA INT'L.			
❑ 8-50289	Enjoy Yourself/Style of Life	1976	5.00
❑ 8-50350	Show You the Way to Go/Blues Away	1977	5.00
❑ 8-50454	Goin' Places/Do What You Wanna	1977	5.00
❑ 8-50496	Find Me a Girl/Different Kind of Lady	1977	5.00
MCA			
❑ 53032	Time Out for the Burglar/News at Eleven	1987	3.00
—B-side by the Distants			
❑ 53032 [PS]	Time Out for the Burglar/News at Eleven	1987	3.00
MOTOWN			
❑ 1157	I Want You Back/Who's Lovin' You	1969	8.00
❑ 1163	ABC/The Young Folks	1970	8.00
❑ 1166	The Love You Save/I Found That Girl	1970	8.00
❑ 1166 [DJ]	I Found That Girl (same on both sides)	1970	20.00
—Red vinyl			
❑ 1166 [DJ]	The Love You Save	1970	30.00
—Blank back promo			
❑ 1171	I'll Be There/One More Chance	1970	8.00
❑ 1174	Santa Claus Is Coming to Town/Christmas Won't Be the Same This Year	1970	12.00
❑ 1177	Mama's Pearl/Darling Dear	1971	6.00
❑ 1177 [PS]	Mama's Pearl/Darling Dear	1971	15.00

J

Number | Title (A Side/B Side) | Yr | NM

❑ 1179 Never Can Say Goodbye/She's Good 1971 6.00
❑ 1186 Maybe Tomorrow/I Will Find a Way 1971 6.00
❑ 1194 Sugar Daddy/I'm So Happy 1971 6.00
❑ 1199 Little Bitty Pretty One/If I Had to Move a Mountain 1972 6.00
❑ 1205 Looking Through the Windows/Love Song 1972 6.00
❑ 1214 Corner of the Sky/To Know 1972 6.00
❑ 1224 Hallelujah Day/You Made Me What I Am 1973 6.00
❑ 1230 Boogie Man/Don't Let Your Baby Catch You 1973 —
—Unreleased
❑ 1277 Get It Together/Touch 1973 6.00
❑ 1277 [DJ] Get It Together (same on both sides) 1973 20.00
—Promo only on red vinyl
❑ 1286 Dancing Machine/It's Too Late to Change the Time 1974 6.00
❑ 1308 Whatever You Got, I Want/I Can't Quit Your Love 1974 6.00
❑ 1310 I Am Love (Parts 1 & 2)/I Am Love (Part 2) 1975 6.00
❑ 1310 I Am Love (Part 1)/I Am Love (Part 2) 1975 8.00
❑ 1356 Forever Came Today/All I Do Is Think of You 1975 6.00
❑ 1365 Body Language/Call of the Wild 1975 —
—Unreleased
❑ 2193 Who's Lovin' You/In the Still of the Night (I'll Remember) 1992 4.00
—B-side by Boyz II Men

STEELTOWN
❑ 681 Big Boy/You've Changed 1968 50.00
❑ 684 You Don't Have to Be Over Twenty-One to Fall in Love/Some Girls Want Me for Their Love 1968 50.00

7-Inch Extended Plays

MOTOWN
❑ M 60718 Ready or Not Here I Come/Goin' Back to Indiana/Darling Dear//Oh How Happy/Reach In/Can I See You in the Morning 1970 15.00
—Jukebox issue; small hole, plays at 33 1/3 rpm
❑ M 60718 [PS] Third Album 1970 15.00
—Part of "Little LP" series (LLP #132)

Albums

EPIC
❑ PE 34229 The Jacksons 1976 14.00
—Orange label
❑ PE 34229 The Jacksons 198? 6.00
—Budget-line reissue with bar code and dark blue label
❑ JE 34835 Goin' Places 1977 14.00
—Orange label
❑ PE 34835 Goin' Places 198? 6.00
—Budget-line reissue
❑ JE 35552 Destiny 1978 12.00
—Orange label
❑ JE 35552 Destiny 1979 8.00
—Dark blue label
❑ FE 36424 Triumph 1980 8.00
❑ KE2 37545 [(2)] Jacksons Live 1981 12.00
❑ QE 38946 Victory 1984 8.00
❑ 8E8 39576 [PD] Victory 1984 15.00
❑ OE 40911 2300 Jackson Street 1989 8.00
❑ HE 46424 Triumph 1982 60.00
—Half-speed mastered edition

MOTOWN
❑ M5-112V1 Motown Superstar Series, Vol. 12 1981 12.00
❑ M5-129V1 Diana Ross Presents the Jackson Five 1981 10.00
❑ M5-152V1 ABC 1981 10.00
❑ M5-157V1 Third Album 1981 10.00
❑ M5-201V1 Jackson 5 Greatest Hits 1981 10.00
❑ MS 700 Diana Ross Presents the Jackson 5 1969 25.00
❑ MS 709 ABC 1970 25.00
❑ MS 713 Christmas Album 1970 25.00
❑ MS 718 Third Album 1970 15.00
❑ M-735 Maybe Tomorrow 1971 20.00
❑ M-741 Jackson 5 Greatest Hits 1971 18.00
❑ M-742 Goin' Back to Indiana 1971 18.00
❑ M-750 Lookin' Through the Windows 1972 18.00
❑ M-761 Skywriter 1973 15.00
❑ M6-780 Dancing Machine 1974 15.00
❑ M6-783 Get It Together 1973 15.00
❑ M6-829 Moving Violation 1975 15.00
❑ M6-865 Joyful Jukebox Music 1976 15.00
❑ M7-868 [(3)] Anthology 1976 20.00
❑ 37463 1294-1 [DJ] Soulsation! 1995 20.00
—Vinyl is promo only; 4-song sampler from box set
❑ 5228 ML Maybe Tomorrow 1982 10.00
❑ 5250 ML Christmas Album 1982 8.00
—Reissue of Motown 713

UNIVERSAL MOTOWN
❑ 5316421 ABC 2009 22.00

JACOBI, LOU

Albums

CAPITOL
❑ ST 2596 [S] Al Tijuana and His Jewish Brass 1966 20.00
❑ T 2596 [M] Al Tijuana and His Jewish Brass 1966 15.00

JACOBS, HANK

45s

IMPERIAL
❑ 5894 Sting Ray/Sheryl Ann 1962 15.00

SUE
❑ 102 Bacon Fat/Out of Sight 1964 10.00
❑ 113 Heide/Playboy's Penthouse 1964 10.00
❑ 795 So Far Away/Monkey Hips & Rice 1963 12.00

Albums

SUE
❑ LP-1023 [M] So Far Away 1964 80.00

JACQUET, RUSSELL

45s

IMPERIAL
❑ 5722 Sail On/You're Gonna Be Paid 1961 30.00

Albums

KING
❑ 295-81 [10] Russell Jacquet and His All Stars 1954 250.00

JADE WARRIOR

45s

VERTIGO
❑ 106 We Have Reason to Believe/Barazinbar 1972 8.00
❑ 108 A Winter's Tale/The Demon Trucker 1972 8.00

Albums

ANTILLES
❑ AN-7045 Floating World 198? 8.00
—Reissue of Island 9290
❑ AN-7048 Waves 198? 8.00
—Reissue of Island 9318
❑ AN-7056 Kites 198? 8.00
—Reissue of Island 9393
❑ AN-7068 Way of the Sun 1978 10.00

ISLAND
❑ ILPS 9290 Floating World 1974 10.00
❑ ILPS 9318 Waves 1975 10.00
❑ ILPS 9393 Kites 1976 10.00

VERTIGO
❑ VEL-1007 Jade Warrior 1971 12.00
❑ VEL-1009 Released 1972 12.00
❑ VEL-1012 Last Autumn's Dream 1972 12.00

JADES, THE

Many different groups.

45s

ADONA
❑ 1445 Hey Senorita/(B-side unknown) 1962 30.00

CAPITOL
❑ 2281 Ain't It Funny What Love Can Do/Baby I Need Your Love 1968 30.00

CHRISTY
❑ 110 Oh Why/Big Beach Party 1959 500.00
❑ 111 Tell Me Pretty Baby/Applesauce 1959 250.00
❑ 113 Don't Be a Fool/Friday Night with My Baby 1959 500.00
❑ 114 Look for a Lie/Blue Memories 1959 1500.

DORE
❑ 687 Hold Back the Dawn/When They Ask About You 1963 20.00

DOT
❑ 15822 I'm Pretending/Beverly 1958 80.00

GAITY
❑ 2-23-64 Surfin' Crow/Blue Black Hair 1964 180.00

IMPERIAL
❑ 66383 Wheel of Fortune/Gotta Find Somebody to Love 1969 6.00
❑ 66425 L-O-V-E I Love You/Don't Give What's Mine Away 1969 75.00

LIBERTY
❑ 56192 All's Quiet on West 23rd/Love of a Woman 1970 5.00

MGM
❑ 13399 There's a Kinder Way to Say Goodbye/You're So Right for Me 1965 30.00

NAU VOO
❑ 807 Walking All Alone/Hey Little Girl 1959 150.00

OXBORO
❑ 2002 Surfin' Crow/Blue Black Hair 1964 120.00
❑ 2005 Little Marlene/Shake Baby Shake 1965 120.00

PORT
❑ 70042 He's My Guy/There Will Come a Day 1964 25.00

TIME
❑ 1002 Leave Her For Me/So Blue 1957 200.00
—Lou Reed is alleged to have been in this group, but he would have been 15 at the time.

UNI
❑ 55019 The Glide/Flower Power 1967 15.00
❑ 55032 [DJ] Privilege (same on both sides) 1967 8.00

VERVE
❑ 10385 For Just Another Day/I'm By Your Side (Baby) 1966 30.00

Albums

JARRETT
❑ 21517 [M] Live at the Disco a-Go-Go 1965 120.00

JAG PANZER

Albums

AZRA IRON WORKS
❑ 1001 [PD] Ample Destruction 1985 25.00
—Allegedly, 250 were pressed as picture discs

JAGGED EDGE, THE

45s

RCA VICTOR
❑ 47-8880 Baby You Don't Know/Deep Inside 1966 40.00

TWIRL
❑ 2024 How Many Times/Midnight to Six Man 1966 30.00

JAGGER, CHRIS

45s

ASYLUM
❑ 11028 Riddle Song/Handful of Dust 1973 6.00

Albums

ASYLUM
❑ 7E-1009 The Adventures of Valentine Vox the Ventriloquist 1974 12.00
❑ SD 5069 Chris Jagger 1973 12.00

JAGGER, MICK

12-Inch Singles

ATLANTIC
❑ DMD 1960 [DJ] Sweet Thing (6 versions) 1993 30.00
—Promo only on red vinyl
❑ 85775 Sweet Thing (6 versions) 1993 60.00

COLUMBIA
❑ AS 1991 [DJ] Just Another Night (LP Version 5:13) (Edited Version 4:39) 1985 10.00
❑ CAS 2060 [DJ] Lucky in Love (3:57) (same on both sides) 1985 20.00
❑ CAS 2771 [DJ] Let's Work (4 versions) 1987 20.00
❑ 44-05181 Just Another Night (Extended) (Album Version) (Dub) 1985 15.00
❑ 44-05214 Lucky in Love (Dance Mix 6:19) (Dub Mix) (Single Mix 4:45) 1985 15.00
❑ 44-06926 Let's Work (Dance Mix) (Edit)/Catch as Catch Can 1987 15.00
❑ 44-07492 Throwaway (Remix) (Vocal Dub Version)/Peace for the Wicked 1987 15.00
❑ 44-07570 Say You Will (2 versions)/Shoot Off Your Mouth 1988 15.00

EPIC
❑ 49-05931 Ruthless People/I'm Ringing 1986 12.00
—With generic cover
❑ 49-05931 Ruthless People/I'm Ringing 1986 80.00
—With "Ruthless People" picture cover

45s

ATLANTIC
❑ 87410 Sweet Thing/Whispering Spirit 1992 4.00

COLUMBIA
❑ 38-04743 Just Another Night/Turn the Girl Loose 1985 3.00
❑ 38-04743 [PS] Just Another Night/Turn the Girl Loose 1985 4.00
❑ 38-04893 Lucky in Love/Running Out of Luck 1985 3.00
❑ 38-04893 [PS] Lucky in Love/Running Out of Luck 1985 4.00
❑ 38-07306 Let's Work/Catch as Catch Can 1987 3.00
❑ 38-07306 [PS] Let's Work/Catch as Catch Can 1987 3.00

Number	Title (A Side/B Side)	Yr	NM
❑ 38-07653	Throwaway/Peace for the Wicked	1987	3.00
❑ 38-07653 [PS]	Throwaway/Peace for the Wicked	1987	3.00
❑ 38-07703	Say You Will/Shoot Off Your Mouth	1988	3.00
❑ 38-07703 [PS]	Say You Will/Shoot Off Your Mouth	1988	5.00

EPIC

Number	Title (A Side/B Side)	Yr	NM
❑ 34-06211	Ruthless People/I'm Ringing	1986	4.00
❑ 34-06211 [PS]	Ruthless People/I'm Ringing	1986	5.00

VIRGIN

Number	Title (A Side/B Side)	Yr	NM
❑ 38823	God Gave Me Everything/ Visions of Paradise	2002	4.00

Albums

COLUMBIA

Number	Title (A Side/B Side)	Yr	NM
❑ FC 39940	She's the Boss	1985	10.00
❑ OC 40919	Primitive Cool	1987	8.00

JAGGERZ, THE

45s

GAMBLE

Number	Title (A Side/B Side)	Yr	NM
❑ 218	(That's Why) Baby I Love You/ Bring It Back	1968	20.00
❑ 226	Gotta Find My Way Back Home/Forever Together, Together Forever	1968	40.00
❑ 238	Together/Let Me Be the One	1969	30.00
❑ 4008	Higher and Higher/Ain't No Sun	1970	30.00
❑ 4012	Need Your Love/Here's a Heart	1970	10.00

KAMA SUTRA

Number	Title (A Side/B Side)	Yr	NM
❑ 502	The Rapper/Born Poor	1970	8.00
❑ 509	I Call My Baby Candy/ Will She Believe Me	1970	6.00
❑ 513	What a Bummer/Memories of the Traveller	1970	6.00
❑ 517	Let's Talk About Love/ I'll Never Forget You	1971	5.00
❑ 583	Let's Talk About Love/ Ain't That Sad	1973	4.00

WOODEN NICKEL

Number	Title (A Side/B Side)	Yr	NM
❑ PB-10194	Don't It Make You Want to Dance/ 2 Plus 2	1975	4.00

Albums

GAMBLE

Number	Title (A Side/B Side)	Yr	NM
❑ GS-5006	Introducing the Jaggerz	1969	20.00

KAMA SUTRA

Number	Title (A Side/B Side)	Yr	NM
❑ KSBS-2017	We Went to Different Schools Together	1970	15.00

WOODEN NICKEL

Number	Title (A Side/B Side)	Yr	NM
❑ BWL1-0772	Come Again	1975	12.00

JAGUARS, THE (1)

45s

AARDELL

Number	Title (A Side/B Side)	Yr	NM
❑ 0003	Rock It Davy, Rock It/ I Wanted You	1955	50.00
❑ 0006	Be My Sweetie/Why Don't You Believe Me	1956	50.00

BARONET

Number	Title (A Side/B Side)	Yr	NM
❑ 1	The Way You Look Tonight/ Baby, Baby, Baby	1962	25.00

CLASSIC ARTISTS

Number	Title (A Side/B Side)	Yr	NM
❑ 117	Happy Holiday/More Than Enough for Me	1989	6.00
—B-side by Johnny Staton and the Feathers			
❑ 136	Merry Christmas, Darling/ Lost and Found	1990	6.00

ORIGINAL SOUND

Number	Title (A Side/B Side)	Yr	NM
❑ 6	Thinking of You/Look Into My Eyes	1959	80.00
❑ 20	Thinking of You/Look Into My Eyes	1962	40.00
❑ 59	The Way You Look Tonight/ Baby, Baby, Baby	1966	20.00

R-DELL

Number	Title (A Side/B Side)	Yr	NM
❑ 11	The Way You Look Tonight/ Baby, Baby, Baby	1956	50.00
❑ 11	The Way You Look Tonight/ Moonlight and You	1956	250.00
—Black vinyl			
❑ 11	The Way You Look Tonight/ Moonlight and You	1956	600.00
—Red vinyl			
❑ 16	I Love You Baby/ Baby, Baby, Baby	1957	120.00
❑ 45	Rock It Davy, Rock It/ I Wanted You	1958	40.00
❑ 107	Rock It Davy, Rock It/ The Big Bear	1958	40.00
❑ 117	Girl of My Dreams/ Don't Go Home	1960	60.00

JAGUARS, THE (2)

45s

DOT

Number	Title (A Side/B Side)	Yr	NM
❑ 16723	Dead Sea/Supersonic	1965	10.00
❑ 16931	The Gorilla/He'll Turn Away	1966	10.00

JAGUARS, THE (3)

45s

EPIC

Number	Title (A Side/B Side)	Yr	NM
❑ 9325	Drive-In/Exit 6	1959	20.00

JAGUARS, THE (4)

45s

FARO

Number	Title (A Side/B Side)	Yr	NM
❑ 618	Where Lovers Go/ Discover a Lover	1965	12.00

JAGUARS, THE (U)

Some of these could be the above groups.

45s

EBB

Number	Title (A Side/B Side)	Yr	NM
❑ 129	Hold Me Tight/Piccadilly	1958	100.00

RENDEZVOUS

Number	Title (A Side/B Side)	Yr	NM
❑ 159	Fine, Fine, Fine/ It Finally Happened	1961	20.00
❑ 216	Fine, Fine, Fine/ It Finally Happened	1963	12.00

SKOOP

Number	Title (A Side/B Side)	Yr	NM
❑ 1067	It's Gonna Be Alright/ (B-side unknown)	1966	25.00

SPAY

Number	Title (A Side/B Side)	Yr	NM
❑ 121	Rendezvous/(B-side unknown)	196?	60.00

JAIM

Albums

ETHEREAL

Number	Title (A Side/B Side)	Yr	NM
❑ 1001	Prophecy Fulfilled	1970	50.00

JALOPY FIVE, THE

45s

HIT

Number	Title (A Side/B Side)	Yr	NM
❑ 81	Surfer Girl/Then He Kissed Me	1963	8.00
—B-side by the Dacrons			
❑ 100	Drag City/Forget Him	1964	8.00
—B-side by Wayne Harris			
❑ 110	Fun, Fun, Fun/Glad All Over	1964	8.00
❑ 132	Can't You See That She's Mine/ The Little Old Lady from Pasadena	1964	10.00
—B-side by the Roamers			
❑ 134	A Hard Day's Night/Rag Doll	1964	8.00
—B-side by the Chellows			
❑ 138	And I Love Her/Such a Night	1964	10.00
—B-side by Ed Hardin			
❑ 145	(I've Got a) Tiger in My Tank/ Dancing in the Street	1964	10.00
—B-side by Mary Sue and the Trams			
❑ 147	Matchbox/When I Grow Up (To Be a Man)	1964	10.00
—B-side by the Roamers			
❑ 150	Little Honda/Making a Fool of Myself	1964	8.00
❑ 156	Be Yourself/Mountain of Love	1964	10.00
—B-side by Bobby Brooks			
❑ 161	Sidewalk Surfin'/ Any Way You Want It	1964	12.00
—B-side by the Bugs			
❑ 171	I Feel Fine/She's a Woman	1965	12.00
❑ 183	Let's Lock the Door/ California Street	1965	10.00
—As "Johnny and the Jalopy Five"			
❑ 192	Eight Days a Week/ She's Come of Age	1965	12.00
—B-side by Bobby Brooks			
❑ 215	Wooly Bully/First Impressions	1965	10.00
❑ 217	(I Can't Get No) Satisfaction/ I Want Candy	1965	12.00
—B-side by the Roamers			
❑ 218	I Like It Like That/I Want Candy	1965	12.00
—B-side by the Roamers			
❑ 220	Help!/California Girls	1965	12.00
—B-side by the Chellows			
❑ 223	Catch Us If You Can/ Just a Little Bit Better	1965	12.00
—B-side by Hank's Hounds			
❑ 225	Yesterday/Kansas City Star	1965	12.00
—B-side by Richard Phillips			
❑ 228	Get Off of My Cloud/ One, Two, Three	1965	12.00
—B-side by Henry Bary			
❑ 232	We Can Work It Out/ Over and Over	1965	12.00
—B-side by the Chords (2)			
❑ 240	California Dreamin'/Uptight (Everything's Alright)	1966	10.00
—B-side by Ritchie Brown			
❑ 245	Nowhere Man/It's Too Late	1966	12.00
—B-side by Ed Hardin			
❑ 252	Monday, Monday/Gloria	1966	12.00
—B-side by the Chellows			
❑ 253	Sloop John B/Rhapsody in the Rain	1966	12.00
—B-side by Fred York			
❑ 258	Paint It Black/The Sun Ain't Gonna Shine Anymore	1966	12.00
—B-side by the Harris Brothers			
❑ 259	Did You Ever Have to Make Up Your Mind/I Am a Rock	1966	8.00
—B-side by Sammy and Theodore			
❑ 262	Wild Thing/Little Red Riding Hood	1966	8.00
—B-side by the Chellows			
❑ 263	Mother's Little Helper/ This Door Swings Both Ways	1966	10.00
—B-side by the Chords (2)			
❑ 266	Last Train to Clarksville/ Yellow Submarine	1966	10.00
❑ 268	Psychotic Reaction/ See See Rider	1966	8.00
—B-side by Ed Hardin and the Cadets			
❑ 271	The Hair on My Chinny Chin Chin/Have You Seen Your Mother, Baby	1966	10.00
—B-side by the Chords (2)			
❑ 273	I'm a Believer/Mellow Yellow	1966	8.00
—B-side by Joe King			
❑ 276	Music to Watch Girls By/ Wild Thing	1967	8.00
—B-side by Bobby Sims			
❑ 277	98.6/Kind of a Drag	1967	8.00
—B-side by the Buchanans			
❑ 281	Sock It To Me Baby/ The Beat Goes On	1967	8.00
—B-side by Bobby and Connie			
❑ 283	Then You Can Tell Me Goodbye/Ruby Tuesday	1967	8.00
—B-side by the Chellows			
❑ 285	A Little Bit Me, A Little Bit You/ Detroit City	1967	8.00
—B-side by Ed Hardin			
❑ 287	Penny Lane/I Think We're Alone Now	1967	10.00
—B-side by Bobby Sims			
❑ 293	I Got Rhythm/Here Comes My Baby	1967	8.00
—B-side by the Fantastics			
❑ 295	Groovin'/Somebody to Love	1967	8.00
—B-side by the Chellows			
❑ 299	Windy/Up, Up and Away	1967	8.00
—B-side by the Chords (2)			
❑ 300	Pleasant Valley Sunday/ Carrie-Anne	1967	8.00
—B-side by the Chords (2)			
❑ 307	Dandelion/The Letter	1967	10.00
—B-side by the Chords (2)			
❑ 311	Even the Bad Times Are Good/ To Sir with Love	1967	8.00
—B-side by the Jalopy Five			
❑ 315	Daydream Believer/By the Time I Get to Phoenix	1967	8.00
—B-side by Ed Hardin			
❑ 317	We Can Fly/Judy in Disguise (With Glasses)	1967	8.00
—B-side by Jack Jones and the Jet Set Band			
❑ 325	Young Girl/The Unicorn	1968	8.00
—B-side by the Chords (2)			
❑ 327	Cry Like a Baby/Do You Know the Way to San Jose	1968	8.00
—B-side by Kathy Shannon			
❑ 332	D.W. Washburn/Reach Out of the Darkness	1968	8.00
—B-side by the Chords (2)			
❑ 334	Jumpin' Jack Flash/ Angel of the Morning	1968	8.00
—B-side by Kathy Shannon			
❑ 336	Hurdy Gurdy Man/ Stoned Soul Picnic	1968	8.00
—B-side by the Fantastics			
❑ 342	Revolution/Born to Be Wild	1968	10.00
—B-side by the Chords (2)			
❑ 343	Hey Jude/Harper Valley P.T.A.	1968	8.00
—B-side by Kathy Shannon			
❑ 345	Midnight Confessions/Suzie-Q	1968	8.00
—B-side by the Classmates			
❑ 347	Elenore/Little Green Apples	1968	8.00
—B-side by Leroy Jones			
❑ 352	Everyday People/Touch Me	1969	8.00
—B-side by the Fantastics			

JAM, THE

Paul Weller next's band was THE STYLE COUNCIL.

12-Inch Singles

POLYDOR

Number	Title (A Side/B Side)	Yr	NM
❑ 180 [DJ]	Town Called Malice (same on both sides)	1982	10.00

J

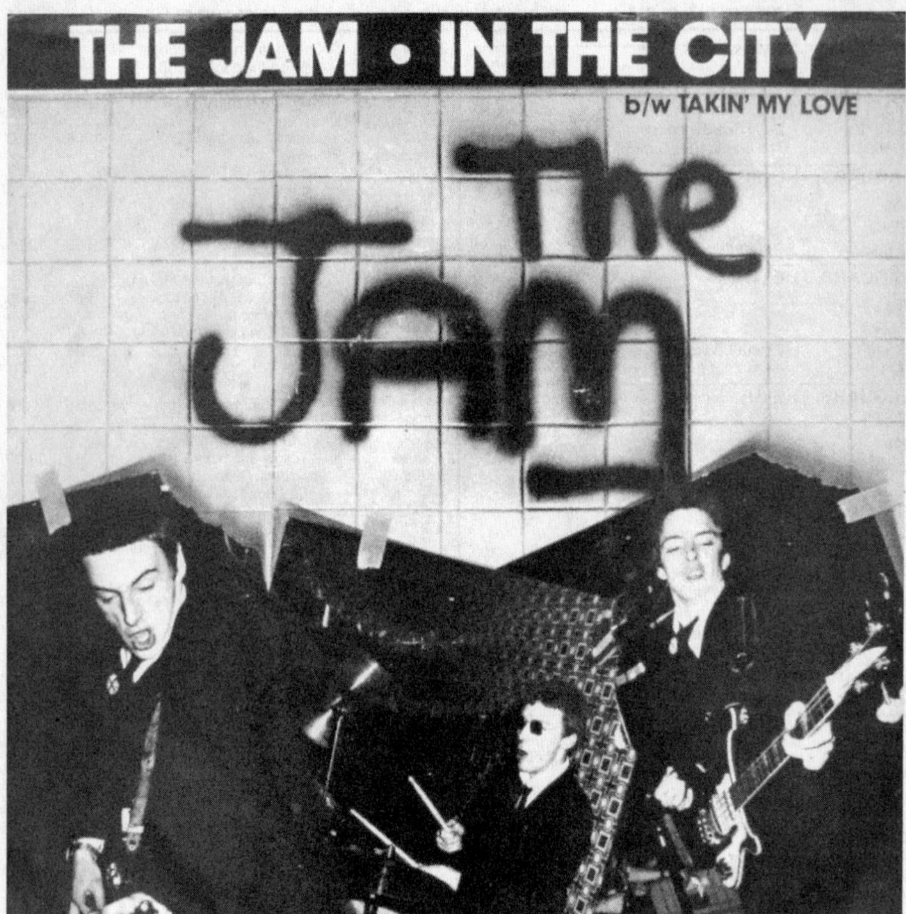

The Jam, "In the City," Polydor 14442, 1977, **$10.**

Number	Title (A Side/B Side)	Yr	NM
45s			
POLYDOR			
❑ PRO 145 [DJ]	Going Underground/ Dreams of Children	1980	8.00
❑ 2051	Eton Rifles/Smithers-Jones	1980	6.00
❑ 2074	(Love Is Like a) Heat Wave/ Saturday's Kids	1980	6.00
❑ 2155	Start/When You're Young	1980	6.00
❑ 2155 [PS]	Start/When You're Young	1980	8.00
❑ 2206	Town Called Malice/Precious	1982	6.00
❑ 14442	In the City/Takin' My Love	1977	10.00
❑ 14462	I Need You (For Someone)/ In the City	1978	8.00
❑ 14553	The Butterfly Collector/ Strange Town	1979	10.00
—Yellow vinyl stock copy			
❑ 14553 [DJ]	The Butterfly Collector (same on both sides)	1979	8.00
—Yellow vinyl promo			
❑ 14566	Down in the Tube Station at Midnight/Mr. Clean	1979	6.00
Albums			
POLYDOR			
❑ PX1-503 [EP]	The Jam	1982	10.00
❑ PX1-506 [EP]	The Bitterest Pill	1982	10.00
❑ PD1-6110	In the City	1977	20.00
❑ PD1-6129	This Is the Modern World	1978	20.00
❑ PD1-6188	All Mod Cons	1979	18.00
❑ PD1-6249	Setting Sons	1980	12.00
❑ PD1-6315	Sound Affects	1981	12.00
❑ PD1-6349	The Gift	1982	12.00
❑ PD1-6365	Dig the New Breed	1982	10.00
❑ 810751-1 [EP]	Beat Surrender	1982	10.00
❑ 815537-1 [(2)]	Snap!	1983	15.00
❑ 817124-1	In the City	198?	10.00
—Reissue			
❑ 823281-1	This Is the Modern World	198?	10.00
—Reissue			

JAM FACTORY

Number	Title (A Side/B Side)	Yr	NM
45s			
EPIC			
❑ 5-10766	Talk Is Cheap/Together	1971	12.00
Albums			
EPIC			
❑ BN 26521	Sittin' in the Trap	1970	25.00

JAMAL, AHMAD

Number	Title (A Side/B Side)	Yr	NM
45s			
ARGO			
❑ 5294	But Not for Me/Music, Music, Music	1958	10.00
❑ 5306	Poinciana/Soft Winds	1958	10.00
❑ 5317	Secret Love/Taking a Chance on Love	1958	10.00
❑ 5337	Tangerine/Seleritus	1959	10.00
❑ 5354	Should I/I Like to Recognize the Tune	1959	10.00
❑ 5370	Billy Boy/Poor Butterfly	1960	10.00
❑ 5379	It's a Wonderful World/ Valentina	1960	10.00
❑ 5397	The Breeze and I/We Kiss in a Shadow	1961	8.00
❑ 5416	All of You/You're Blase	1962	8.00
❑ 5419	April in Paris/Like Someone in Love	1962	8.00
❑ 5429	Night Mist Blues/We Live in Two Different Worlds	1962	8.00
❑ 5434	Haitian Market Place/ Montevidas Has Macanudo	1963	8.00
❑ 5441	Bossa Nova Do Marilia (Part 1)/ Bossa Nova Do Marilia (Part 2)	1963	8.00
❑ 5487	Naked City Theme/ Haitian Market Place	1965	8.00
❑ 5504	Feeling Good/A Wonderful Day Like Today	1965	8.00
❑ 5508	Who Can I Turn To/ Look at the Face	1965	8.00
❑ 5512	This Terrible Planet/ Dance to the Lady	1965	8.00
❑ 5513	Extensions (Part 1)/ Extensions (Part 2)	1965	8.00
ATLANTIC			
❑ 89476 [DJ]	It's That Time Of Year Again (same on both sides)	1985	5.00
—With Larry Goshorn; may be promo only			
CADET			
❑ 5527	Love Theme from "The Sandpiper"/This Could Be the Start of Something Big	1966	6.00
❑ 5569	Nature Boy/Little Ditty	1967	6.00
❑ 5581	Minor Moods/Beautiful Friendship	1967	6.00
❑ 5605	Wild Is the Wind/I Wish I Knew (How It Would Feel to Be Free)	1968	6.00
OKEH			
❑ 6855	The Surrey with the Fringe on Top/Rica Pulpa	1952	20.00
❑ 6889	Billy Boy/Perfidia	1952	20.00
❑ 6921	A Gal in Calico/Aki And Ukthay	1952	20.00
❑ 6945	Will You Still Be Mine/ Ahmad's Blues	1953	20.00
PARROT			
❑ 810	But Not for Me/Seleritus	1955	25.00
❑ 818	It Could Happen to You/ Excerpts from the Blues	1955	25.00
20TH CENTURY			
❑ 2026	Peace at Last/The World Is a Ghetto	1973	5.00
❑ 2053	M*A*S*H Theme/Keep On Trucking	1973	8.00
❑ 2260	Pablo Sierra/(B-side unknown)	1975	5.00
❑ 2448	Don't Ask My Neighbors/Chaser	1980	5.00
Albums			
ABC			
❑ S-660	Tranquility	1968	12.00
ABC IMPULSE!			
❑ AS-9176	At the Top — Poinciana Revisited	1969	15.00
❑ AS-9194	The Awakening	1970	15.00
❑ AS-9217	Freeflight	1971	12.00
❑ AS-9226	Outertimeinnerspace	1972	12.00
❑ AS-9238	Tranquility	1973	12.00
❑ AS-9260 [(2)]	Re-evaluations: The Impulse Years	1975	12.00
❑ SMAS-92005	At the Top — Poinciana Revisited	1969	20.00
—Capitol Record Club edition			
ARGO			
❑ LP-602 [M]	Chamber Music of the New Jazz	1956	30.00
—Dark green label, gold or silver print			
❑ LP-602 [M]	Chamber Music of the New Jazz	1956	50.00
—With "Creative Hi-Fidelity Modern Music" on cover; "ship" label; reissue of Parrot LP			
❑ LP-610 [M]	Count 'Em 88	1957	30.00
❑ LP-628 [M]	But Not for Me/Ahmad Jamal at the Pershing	1958	30.00
❑ LPS-628 [S]	But Not for Me/Ahmad Jamal at the Pershing	1958	40.00
❑ LP-636 [M]	Ahmad Jamal, Vol. IV	1958	30.00
❑ LPS-636 [S]	Ahmad Jamal, Vol. IV	1958	40.00
❑ LP-646 [M]	Jamal at the Penthouse	1959	30.00
❑ LPS-646 [S]	Jamal at the Penthouse	1959	40.00
❑ LP-662 [M]	Happy Moods	1960	20.00
❑ LPS-662 [S]	Happy Moods	1960	25.00
❑ LP-667 [M]	Ahmad Jamal at the Pershing Vol. 2	1961	20.00
❑ LPS-667 [S]	Ahmad Jamal at the Pershing Vol. 2	1961	25.00
❑ LP-673 [M]	Listen to Ahmad Jamal	1961	20.00
❑ LPS-673 [S]	Listen to Ahmad Jamal	1961	25.00
❑ LP-685 [M]	Alhambra	1961	20.00
❑ LPS-685 [S]	Alhambra	1961	25.00
❑ LP-691 [M]	All of You	1962	20.00
❑ LPS-691 [S]	All of You	1962	25.00
❑ LP-703 [M]	Ahmad Jamal at the Blackhawk	1962	20.00
❑ LPS-703 [S]	Ahmad Jamal at the Blackhawk	1962	25.00
❑ LP-712 [M]	Macanudo	1963	20.00
❑ LPS-712 [S]	Macanudo	1963	25.00
❑ LP-719 [M]	Poin'-ci-an'a	1963	20.00
❑ LPS-719 [S]	Poin'-ci-an'a	1963	25.00
❑ LP-733 [M]	"Naked City" Theme	1964	20.00
❑ LPS-733 [S]	"Naked City" Theme	1964	25.00
❑ LP-751 [M]	The Roar of the Greasepaint	1965	20.00
❑ LPS-751 [S]	The Roar of the Greasepaint	1965	25.00
❑ LP-758 [M]	Extensions	1965	20.00
❑ LPS-758 [S]	Extensions	1965	25.00
❑ LP-2638 [(2)M]	Portfolio of Ahmad Jamal	1959	40.00
—Textured cover with raised image of Jamal; limited, numbered edition			
❑ LPS-2638 [(2)S]	Portfolio of Ahmad Jamal	1959	50.00
ATLANTIC			
❑ 81258 [(2)]	Digital Works	1985	12.00
❑ 81645	Rossiter Road	1986	10.00
❑ 81699 [(2)]	Live at the Montreal Jazz Festival 1985	1986	12.00
❑ 81793	Crystal	1987	10.00

Except when noted otherwise, VG = 25% of NM, and VG+ = 50% of NM. (Example: VG = $2.00, VG+ = $4.00 and NM = $8.00.)

Number	Title (A Side/B Side)	Yr	NM
CADET			
❑ LP-628 [M]	But Not for Me/Ahmad Jamal at the Pershing	1966	12.00
❑ LPS-628 [S]	But Not for Me/Ahmad Jamal at the Pershing	1966	15.00
❑ LP-636 [M]	Ahmad Jamal, Vol. IV	1966	12.00
❑ LPS-636 [S]	Ahmad Jamal, Vol. IV	1966	15.00
❑ LP-646 [M]	Jamal at the Penthouse	1966	12.00
❑ LPS-646 [S]	Jamal at the Penthouse	1966	15.00
❑ LP-662 [M]	Happy Moods	1966	12.00
❑ LPS-662 [S]	Happy Moods	1966	15.00
❑ LP-667 [M]	Ahmad Jamal at the Pershing Vol. 2	1966	12.00
❑ LPS-667 [S]	Ahmad Jamal at the Pershing Vol. 2	1966	15.00
❑ LP-673 [M]	Listen to Ahmad Jamal	1966	12.00
❑ LPS-673 [S]	Listen to Ahmad Jamal	1966	15.00
❑ LP-685 [M]	Alhambra	1966	12.00
❑ LPS-685 [S]	Alhambra	1966	15.00
❑ LP-691 [M]	All of You	1966	12.00
❑ LPS-691 [S]	All of You	1966	15.00
❑ LP-703 [M]	Ahmad Jamal at the Blackhawk	1966	12.00
❑ LPS-703 [S]	Ahmad Jamal at the Blackhawk	1966	15.00
❑ LP-712 [M]	Macanudo	1966	12.00
❑ LPS-712 [S]	Macanudo	1966	15.00
❑ LP-719 [M]	Poin'-ci-an'a	1966	12.00
❑ LPS-719 [S]	Poin'-ci-an'a	1966	15.00
❑ LP-733 [M]	"Naked City" Theme	1966	12.00
❑ LPS-733 [S]	"Naked City" Theme	1966	15.00
❑ LP-751 [M]	The Roar of the Greasepaint	1966	12.00
❑ LPS-751 [S]	The Roar of the Greasepaint	1966	15.00
❑ CA-758 [S]	Extensions	197?	12.00
—Reissue; yellow and red label with "A Division of All Platinum Record Group" on label			
❑ LP-758 [M]	Extensions	1966	12.00
❑ LPS-758 [S]	Extensions	1965	15.00
❑ LP-764 [M]	Rhapsody	1966	15.00
❑ LPS-764 [S]	Rhapsody	1966	20.00
❑ LP-777 [M]	Heat Wave	1966	15.00
❑ LPS-777 [S]	Heat Wave	1966	20.00
—Original with fading blue label			
❑ LPS-777 [S]	Heat Wave	1977	12.00
—Reissue, "a division of All Platinum Record Group" on back cover			
❑ LP-786 [M]	Standard Eyes	1967	15.00
❑ LPS-786 [S]	Standard Eyes	1967	20.00
❑ LP-792 [M]	Cry Young	1967	20.00
❑ LPS-792 [S]	Cry Young	1967	15.00
❑ LPS-807	The Bright, the Blue and the Beautiful	1968	15.00
❑ LP-2638 [(2)M]	Portfolio of Ahmad Jamal	1966	15.00
—Cadet issues generally did not have embossed covers			
❑ LPS-2638 [(2)S]	Portfolio of Ahmad Jamal	1966	20.00
—Cadet issues generally did not have embossed covers			
❑ 50035 [(2)]	Inspiration	1974	15.00
CATALYST			
❑ 7606	Live at Oil Can Harry's	1978	12.00
CHESS			
❑ CH-2-9223 [(2)]	Sun Set	1984	12.00
❑ CH-91553	Poinciana	198?	10.00
EPIC			
❑ BN 627 [R]	Ahmad Jamal Trio	196?	20.00
❑ BN 634 [S]	The Piano Scene of Ahmad Jamal	1959	20.00
❑ LN 3212 [M]	Ahmad Jamal Trio	1956	50.00
—Yellow label with lines around rim			
❑ LN 3212 [M]	Ahmad Jamal Trio	1963	25.00
—Yellow label, no lines around rim			
❑ LN 3631 [M]	The Piano Scene of Ahmad Jamal	1959	30.00
GRP/IMPULSE!			
❑ 226	The Awakening	199?	15.00
—Reissue on audiophile vinyl			
MCA			
❑ 29041	At the Top—Poinciana Revisited	198?	8.00
—Reissue of Impulse! 9178			
❑ 29042	The Awakening	198?	8.00
—Reissue of Impulse! 9194			
❑ 29043	Freelight	198?	8.00
—Reissue of Impulse! 9217			
MCA/IMPULSE!			
❑ 5644	The Awakening	1986	10.00
—Another reissue of Impulse! 9194			
MOTOWN			
❑ M8-945	Night Song	1981	10.00
PARROT			
❑ 55-245/6 [M]	Ahmad Jamal Plays	1955	1500.
—VG value 500; VG+ value 1000			
20TH CENTURY			
❑ T-417	Ahmad Jamal '73	1973	10.00
❑ T-432	Jamaica	1974	10.00
❑ T-459	Jamal Plays Jamal	1975	10.00
❑ T-515	Steppin' Out with a Dream	1977	10.00
❑ T-555	One	1978	10.00
❑ T-600	Genetic Walk	1980	10.00
❑ T-622	Intervals	1980	10.00
❑ T-631	Greatest Hits	1981	10.00

JAMES, BOB

Number	Title (A Side/B Side)	Yr	NM
45s			
CTI			
❑ 22	In the Garden/Soulero	1974	5.00
❑ 23	Night on Bald Mountain/In the Garden	1974	5.00
❑ 24	Feel Like Makin' Love/Soulero	1974	5.00
❑ 26	I Feel a Song (In My Heart)/Golden Apple	1975	5.00
❑ 31	Westchester Lady (Part 1)/Westchester Lady (Part 2)	1976	5.00
❑ 37	Where the Wind Blows Free/El Verano	1977	5.00
TAPPAN ZEE			
❑ 02530	Sign of the Times/Enchanted Forest	1981	4.00
❑ 02672	Steamin' Feelin'/Enchanted Forest	1982	4.00
❑ 03191	Janus/Spunky	1982	4.00
❑ 04532	Courtship (Basketball Theme)/Marco Polo	1984	4.00
❑ 10668	We're All Alone/Heads	1978	4.00
❑ 10715	You Are So Beautiful/Night Crawler	1978	4.00
❑ 3-10896	Angela (Theme from "Taxi")/Caribbean Nights	1979	6.00
❑ 10969	Touchdown/Sun Runner	1979	4.00
❑ 11096	Friends/Blue Lick	1979	4.00
❑ 1-11171	Main Theme from Star Trek—The Motion Picture/I Want to Thank You (Very Much)	1980	6.00
❑ 1-11171 [PS]	Main Theme from Star Trek—The Motion Picture/I Want to Thank You (Very Much)	1980	8.00
Albums			
CBS MASTERWORKS			
❑ IM 39540	Rameau	1985	12.00
COLUMBIA			
❑ FC 38678	The Genie (Themes & Variations from the TV Series "Taxi")	1983	10.00
CTI			
❑ CTS-6043	One	1974	20.00
❑ CTS-6057	Two	1975	25.00
❑ CTS-6063	Three	1976	15.00
❑ 7074	BJ4	1977	15.00
ESP-DISK'			
❑ 1009 [M]	Explosions	1965	40.00
❑ S-1009 [S]	Explosions	1965	50.00
MERCURY			
❑ MG-20768 [M]	Bold Conceptions	1963	40.00
❑ SR-60768 [S]	Bold Conceptions	1963	50.00
TAPPAN ZEE			
❑ AS 699 [DJ]	Lucky Seven/One on One Sampler	1979	30.00
—Edited selections from both of the above albums; promo only			
❑ AS 1299 [DJ]	Bob James/Dave Herman Interview	1981	15.00
—Promo-only radio program			
❑ JC 34896	Heads	1977	10.00
❑ PC 34896	Heads	1985	6.00
—Budget-line reissue			
❑ JC 35594	Touchdown	1978	10.00
❑ PC 35594	Touchdown	1985	6.00
—Budget-line reissue			
❑ JC 36056	Lucky Seven	1979	10.00
❑ PC 36056	Lucky Seven	1985	6.00
—Budget-line reissue			
❑ JC 36422	"H"	1980	10.00
❑ C2X 36786 [(2)]	All Around the Town	1981	12.00
❑ FC 36835	One	1981	10.00
—Reissue of CTI 6043			
❑ PC 36835	One	1985	6.00
—Budget-line reissue			
❑ FC 36836	Two	1981	12.00
—Reissue of CTI 6057			
❑ PC 36836	Two	1985	8.00
—Budget-line reissue			
❑ FC 36837	Three	1981	12.00
—Reissue of CTI 6063			
❑ PC 36837	Three	1985	6.00
—Budget-line reissue			
❑ FC 36838	BJ4	1981	10.00
—Reissue of CTI 7074			
❑ PC 36838	BJ4	1985	6.00
—Budget-line reissue			
❑ FC 37495	Sign of the Times	1981	10.00
❑ FC 38067	Hands Down	1982	10.00
❑ FC 38801	Foxie	1983	10.00
❑ FC 39580	12	1985	10.00
❑ HC 45594	Touchdown	1982	30.00
—Half-speed mastered edition			
❑ HC 47495	Sign of the Times	1982	30.00
—Half-speed mastered edition			
WARNER BROS.			
❑ 25495	Obsession	1986	10.00
❑ 25757	Ivory Coast	1988	10.00
❑ 26256	Grand Piano Canyon	1990	15.00

JAMES, BOB, AND EARL KLUGH

Number	Title (A Side/B Side)	Yr	NM
Albums			
CAPITOL			
❑ SMAS-12244	Two of a Kind	1982	12.00
MOBILE FIDELITY			
❑ 1-124	Two of a Kind	1984	40.00
—"Original Master Recording" banner across top of front cover			
TAPPAN ZEE			
❑ FC 36241	One on One	1979	10.00
❑ HC 46241	One on One	198?	30.00
—Half-speed mastered edition			

JAMES, BOB, AND DAVID SANBORN

Number	Title (A Side/B Side)	Yr	NM
Albums			
WARNER BROS.			
❑ 25393	Double Vision	1986	10.00

JAMES, BOBBY

Number	Title (A Side/B Side)	Yr	NM
45s			
INDIGO			
❑ 145	Memories Linger/5000 Years Ago	1962	15.00
KAROL			
❑ 3727	I Really Love You/(B-side unknown)	196?	3000.
LANOR			
❑ 530	Fortune Teller/Get Out of My Life Woman	1967	10.00
❑ 533	Going Back to Philly/That's What People Say	1967	10.00

JAMES, CHARLES

Number	Title (A Side/B Side)	Yr	NM
45s			
ABC-PARAMOUNT			
❑ 10254	Rockin' Chair/Thief in the Night	1961	12.00
ZAB			
❑ 102	Rockin' Chair/Thief in the Night	1961	20.00
❑ 103	One Mint Julep/Please Wait	1961	15.00

JAMES, DICK

Number	Title (A Side/B Side)	Yr	NM
45s			
LONDON			
❑ 1002	Eleanor/Mary Rose	1950	15.00
❑ 1013	Theater/My Life's Desire	1950	15.00
❑ 1027	Unless/Now That You've Left Me	1950	15.00
❑ 1044	We'll Keep a Welcome/The Minute Waltz	1951	15.00
❑ 1050	Happy Valley/My Truly Truly Fair	1951	15.00
❑ 1053	Tell Me Again/With All My Heart and Soul	1951	15.00
❑ 1139	Unforgettable/My Love for You	1951	15.00
❑ 1162	Pretending/It Would Break My Heart	1951	15.00

JAMES, ELMORE

Some of the below were as "Elmo James."

Number	Title (A Side/B Side)	Yr	NM
45s			
ACE			
❑ 508	I Believe My Time Ain't Long/I Wish I Was a Catfish	1955	250.00
CHECKER			
❑ 777	Country Boogie/She Just Won't Do Right	1953	1000.
CHESS			
❑ 1756	I Can't Hold Out/The Sun Is Shining	1960	15.00
CHIEF			
❑ 7001	The Twelve Year Old Boy/Coming Home	1957	80.00
❑ 7004	It Hurts Me Too/Elmore's Contribution to Jazz	1957	80.00
❑ 7006	Cry for Me Baby/Take Me Where You Go	1957	60.00
❑ 7020	Knocking at Your Door/Calling All Blues	1960	40.00
ENJOY			
❑ 2015	It Hurts Me Too/Pickin' the Blues	1965	15.00
❑ 2015	It Hurts Me Too/Bleeding Heart	1965	20.00
❑ 2020	Mean Mistreatin' Mama/Bleeding Heart	1965	20.00
❑ 2027	Dust My Broom/Everyday I Have the Blues	1965	15.00
FIRE			
❑ 504	Shake Your Moneymaker/Look on Yonder Wall	1962	40.00
❑ 1011	Make My Dreams Come True/Bobby's Rock	1960	30.00
❑ 1016	The Sky Is Crying/Held My Baby Last Night	1960	40.00

Number	Title (A Side/B Side)	Yr	NM
❑ 1024	I'm Worried/Rollin' and Tumblin'	1960	20.00
❑ 1031	Fine Little Mama/Done Somebody Wrong	1961	20.00
❑ 1503	Stranger Blues/Anna Lee	1963	15.00
❑ 2020	It Hurts Me Too/Pickin' the Blues	196?	15.00

—Red vinyl

FLAIR

Number	Title (A Side/B Side)	Yr	NM
❑ 1011	Early in the Morning/ Hawaiian Boogie	1953	500.00
❑ 1014	Can't Stop Lovin'/ Make a Little Love	1953	200.00
❑ 1022	Strange Kinda Feeling/ Please Find My Baby	1953	200.00
❑ 1031	Make My Dreams Come True/ Hand in Hand	1954	300.00
❑ 1039	Sho'nuff, I Do/1839 Blues	1954	300.00
❑ 1048	Dark and Dreary/ Rock My Baby Right	1954	300.00
❑ 1057	Standing at the Cross Roads/ Sunny Land	1955	250.00
❑ 1062	Late Hours at Midnight/ The Way You Treat Me	1955	150.00
❑ 1069	Happy Home/No Love in My Heart	1955	150.00
❑ 1074	Dust My Blues/I Was a Fool	1955	250.00
❑ 1079	Blues Before Sunrise/ Goodbye Baby	1955	200.00

JEWEL

Number	Title (A Side/B Side)	Yr	NM
❑ 764	Dust My Broom/Gotta Find My Baby	1966	10.00
❑ 783	Catfish Blues/Make a Little Love	1967	10.00

KENT

Number	Title (A Side/B Side)	Yr	NM
❑ 331	Dust My Blues/Happy Home	1960	12.00
❑ 394	Dust My Blues/Happy Home	1964	30.00
❑ 465	Sunnyland/Goodbye Baby	1967	8.00
❑ 508	I Believe/1839 Blues	1969	6.00

M-PAC

Number	Title (A Side/B Side)	Yr	NM
❑ 7231	Cry for Me/Take Me Where You Go	1966	10.00

MEL

Number	Title (A Side/B Side)	Yr	NM
❑ 7011	Cry for Me Baby/ (B-side unknown)	197?	6.00

METEOR

Number	Title (A Side/B Side)	Yr	NM
❑ 5000	I Believe/I Held My Baby Last Night	1953	800.00
❑ 5003	Baby What's Wrong/ Sinful Woman	1953	500.00
❑ 5016	Saxony Boogie/ Dumb Woman Blues	1954	300.00
❑ 5024	San Symphonic Boogie/ Flaming Blues	1955	250.00

MODERN

Number	Title (A Side/B Side)	Yr	NM
❑ 983	Wild About You/Long Tall Woman	1956	300.00

VEE JAY

Number	Title (A Side/B Side)	Yr	NM
❑ 249	Coming Home/The 12-Year-Old Boy	1957	25.00
❑ 259	It Hurts Me Too/Elmore's Contribution to Jazz	1957	25.00
❑ 269	Cry for Me Baby/Take Me Where You Go	1958	25.00

Albums

BELL

Number	Title (A Side/B Side)	Yr	NM
❑ 6037	Elmore James	1969	25.00

CHESS

Number	Title (A Side/B Side)	Yr	NM
❑ LP-1537	Whose Muddy Shoes	1969	25.00

COLLECTABLES

Number	Title (A Side/B Side)	Yr	NM
❑ COL-5112	Golden Classics	198?	12.00
❑ COL-5184	The Complete Fire and Enjoy Sessions, Part 1	198?	10.00
❑ COL-5185	The Complete Fire and Enjoy Sessions, Part 2	198?	10.00
❑ COL-5186	The Complete Fire and Enjoy Sessions, Part 3	198?	10.00
❑ COL-5187	The Complete Fire and Enjoy Sessions, Part 4	198?	10.00

CROWN

Number	Title (A Side/B Side)	Yr	NM
❑ CLP-5168 [M]	Blues After Hours	1961	250.00

—Black label, silver "Crown"

Number	Title (A Side/B Side)	Yr	NM
❑ CLP-5168 [M]	Blues After Hours	1962	50.00

—Gray label

INTERMEDIA

Number	Title (A Side/B Side)	Yr	NM
❑ QS-5034	Red Hot Blues	198?	10.00

KENT

Number	Title (A Side/B Side)	Yr	NM
❑ KST-522 [R]	Original Folk Blues	1964	25.00
❑ KLP-5022 [M]	Original Folk Blues	1964	40.00
❑ KLP-9001	Anthology of the Blues Legend	196?	25.00
❑ KLP-9010	The Resurrection of Elmore James	196?	25.00

SPHERE SOUND

Number	Title (A Side/B Side)	Yr	NM
❑ SR-7002 [M]	The Sky Is Crying	1965	180.00
❑ SSR-7002 [R]	The Sky Is Crying	1965	120.00
❑ SR-7008 [M]	I Need You	1966	150.00
❑ SSR-7008 [R]	I Need You	1966	120.00

UP FRONT

Number	Title (A Side/B Side)	Yr	NM
❑ UP-122	The Great Elmore James	1970	12.00

JAMES, ETTA

45s

ARGO

Number	Title (A Side/B Side)	Yr	NM
❑ 5359	All I Could Do Was Cry/ Girl of My Dreams	1960	12.00
❑ 5368	My Dearest Darling/Tough Mary	1960	12.00
❑ 5380	At Last/I Just Want to Make Love to You	1961	15.00
❑ 5385	Trust in Me/Anything to Say You're Mine	1961	10.00
❑ 5390	Dream/Fool That I Am	1961	10.00
❑ 5393	Sunday Kind of Love/ Don't Cry, Baby	1961	10.00
❑ 5402	It's Too Soon to Know/ Seven Day Fool	1961	75.00

—Brown label

Number	Title (A Side/B Side)	Yr	NM
❑ 5402	It's Too Soon to Know/ Seven Day Fool	1961	100.00

—Black label

Number	Title (A Side/B Side)	Yr	NM
❑ 5409	Something's Got a Hold on Me/ Waiting for Charlie to Come Home	1962	20.00
❑ 5418	Stop the Wedding/Street of Tears	1962	20.00
❑ 5424	Next Door to the Blues/ Fools Rush In	1962	20.00
❑ 5430	How Do You Speak to An Angel/Would It Make Any Difference to You	1962	10.00
❑ 5437	Pushover/I Can't Hold It In Anymore	1963	20.00
❑ 5445	Be Honest with Me/Pay Back	1963	20.00
❑ 5452	Two Sides (To Every Story)/ I Worry Bout You	1963	20.00
❑ 5459	Baby What You Want Me to Do/ What I Say	1964	15.00
❑ 5465	Look Who's Blue/Loving You More Every Day	1964	10.00
❑ 5477	Breaking Point/That Man Belongs Back Here with Me	1964	20.00
❑ 5485	Mellow Fellow/Bobby Is His Name	1964	75.00

—Brown label

Number	Title (A Side/B Side)	Yr	NM
❑ 5485	Mellow Fellow/Bobby Is His Name	1964	100.00

—Black label

CADET

Number	Title (A Side/B Side)	Yr	NM
❑ 5519	Somewhere Down the Line/ Do I Make Myself Clear	1966	8.00

—With Sugar Pie DeSanto

Number	Title (A Side/B Side)	Yr	NM
❑ 5526	Only Time Will Tell/ I'm Sorry for You	1966	8.00
❑ 5539	In the Basement — Part 1/ In the Basement — Part 2	1966	8.00

—With Sugar Pie DeSanto

Number	Title (A Side/B Side)	Yr	NM
❑ 5552	I Prefer You/I'm So Glad	1966	15.00
❑ 5564	Don't Take Me for Your Fool/ It Must Be Your Love	1967	15.00
❑ 5568	Happiness/842-3089 (Call My Name)	1967	8.00
❑ 5578	Tell Mama/I'd Rather Go Blind	1967	15.00
❑ 5594	Security/I'm Gonna Take What He's Got	1968	20.00
❑ 5606	I Got You Babe/I Worship the Ground You Walk On	1968	8.00
❑ 5620	Fire/You Got It	1968	15.00
❑ 5630	Almost Persuaded/Steal Away	1968	8.00
❑ 5655	Miss Pitiful/Bobby Is His Name	1969	15.00
❑ 5664	Tighten Up Your Own Thing/ What Fools We Mortals Be	1970	20.00
❑ 5671	The Sound of Love/ When I Stop Dreaming	1970	15.00
❑ 5676	Losers Weepers — Part I/ Weepers	1970	8.00

CAPITOL

Number	Title (A Side/B Side)	Yr	NM
❑ B-44333	Avenue D/My Head Is a City	1989	4.00

—With David A. Stewart

CHESS

Number	Title (A Side/B Side)	Yr	NM
❑ 2100	The Love of My Man/Nothing from Nothing Leaves Nothing	1971	6.00
❑ 2112	I Think It's You/Take Out Some Insurance	1971	6.00
❑ 2125	I Found a Love/Nothing from Nothing Leaves Nothing	1972	6.00
❑ 2144	All the Way Down/ Lay Back Daddy	1973	6.00
❑ 2148	Leave Your Hat On/Only a Fool	1974	6.00
❑ 2153	Out on the Street Again/ Feeling Uneasy	1974	6.00
❑ 2171	Lovin' Arms/Take Out Some Insurance	1975	6.00
❑ 9007	At Last/All I Could Do Was Cry	197?	5.00

—"Blue Chip Series" reissue

Number	Title (A Side/B Side)	Yr	NM
❑ 9029	My Dearest Darling/Tell Mama	197?	5.00

—"Blue Chip Series" reissue

Number	Title (A Side/B Side)	Yr	NM
❑ 31001	Jump Into Love/ (B-side unknown)	1976	5.00

EPIC

Number	Title (A Side/B Side)	Yr	NM
❑ 68593	Baby What You Want Me to Do/ Max's Theme (Instrumental)	1989	4.00

KENT

Number	Title (A Side/B Side)	Yr	NM
❑ 304	Baby, Baby, Every Night/ Sunshine of Love	1958	30.00
❑ 345	Roll with Me Henry/ Good Rockin' Daddy	1960	25.00
❑ 352	How Big a Fool/Good Rockin' Daddy	1961	25.00
❑ 370	Do Something Crazy/ Good Rockin' Daddy	1962	25.00

MODERN

Number	Title (A Side/B Side)	Yr	NM
❑ 947	The Wallflower (Dance With Me Henry)/Hold Me, Squeeze Me	1955	25.00
❑ 947	The Wallflower (Roll With Me Henry)/Hold Me, Squeeze Me	1955	40.00
❑ 957	Hey Henry (Doin' Fine, Henry)/ Be Mine	1955	25.00
❑ 962	Good Rockin' Daddy/ Crazy Feeling	1955	30.00
❑ 972	That's All/W-O-M-A-N	1955	25.00
❑ 984	I'm a Fool/Number One (My One and Only)	1956	25.00
❑ 988	Shortnin' Bread Rock/ Tears of Joy	1956	25.00
❑ 998	Fools We Mortals Be/ Tough Lover	1956	30.00
❑ 1007	Good Lookin'/Then I'll Care	1957	25.00
❑ 1016	The Pick-Up/Market Place	1957	25.00
❑ 1022	By the Light of the Silvery Moon/ Come What May	1957	25.00

PHILCO-FORD

Number	Title (A Side/B Side)	Yr	NM
❑ HP-31	Tell Mama/Security	1968	20.00

—4-inch plastic "Hip Pocket Record" with color sleeve

T-ELECTRIC

Number	Title (A Side/B Side)	Yr	NM
❑ 41264	It Takes Love to Keep a Woman/Mean Mother	1980	5.00

WARNER BROS.

Number	Title (A Side/B Side)	Yr	NM
❑ 8545	Piece of My Heart/ Lovesick Blues	1978	5.00
❑ 8611	Sugar on the Floor/ Lovesick Blues	1978	5.00

Albums

ARGO

Number	Title (A Side/B Side)	Yr	NM
❑ LP-4003 [M]	At Last!	1961	40.00
❑ LPS-4003 [S]	At Last!	1961	60.00
❑ LP-4011 [M]	The Second Time Around	1961	30.00
❑ LPS-4011 [S]	The Second Time Around	1961	40.00
❑ LP-4013 [M]	Etta James	1962	30.00
❑ LPS-4013 [P]	Etta James	1962	40.00

—Two duets with Harvey Fuqua are rechanneled

Number	Title (A Side/B Side)	Yr	NM
❑ LP-4018 [M]	Etta James Sings for Lovers	1962	30.00
❑ LPS-4018 [S]	Etta James Sings for Lovers	1962	40.00
❑ LP-4025 [M]	Etta James Top Ten	1963	30.00
❑ LPS-4025 [S]	Etta James Top Ten	1963	40.00
❑ LP-4032 [M]	Etta James Rocks the House	1964	100.00
❑ LPS-4032 [S]	Etta James Rocks the House	1964	150.00
❑ LP-4040 [M]	The Queen of Soul	1965	30.00
❑ LPS-4040 [S]	The Queen of Soul	1965	40.00

CADET

Number	Title (A Side/B Side)	Yr	NM
❑ LP-802 [M]	Tell Mama	1968	25.00
❑ LPS-802 [S]	Tell Mama	1968	20.00
❑ LPS-832	Etta James Sings Funk	1969	20.00
❑ LPS-847	Losers Weepers	1970	15.00
❑ LP-4003 [M]	At Last!	1966	12.00
❑ LPS-4003 [S]	At Last!	1966	15.00
❑ LP-4011 [M]	The Second Time Around	1966	12.00
❑ LPS-4011 [S]	The Second Time Around	1966	15.00
❑ LP-4013 [M]	Etta James	1966	12.00
❑ LPS-4013 [S]	Etta James	1966	15.00
❑ LP-4018 [M]	Etta James Sings for Lovers	1966	12.00
❑ LPS-4018 [S]	Etta James Sings for Lovers	1966	15.00
❑ LP-4025 [M]	Etta James Top Ten	1966	12.00
❑ LPS-4025 [S]	Etta James Top Ten	1966	15.00
❑ LP-4040 [M]	The Queen of Soul	1966	12.00
❑ LPS-4040 [S]	The Queen of Soul	1966	15.00
❑ LP-4055 [M]	Call My Name	1967	15.00
❑ LPS-4055 [S]	Call My Name	1967	20.00

CHESS

Number	Title (A Side/B Side)	Yr	NM
❑ CH2-6028 [(2)]	The Sweetest Peaches	1989	12.00
❑ CH-9110	Her Greatest Sides, Vol. 1	1984	10.00
❑ CH-9184	Etta James Rocks the House	1986	8.00

—Reissue

Number	Title (A Side/B Side)	Yr	NM
❑ CH-9266	At Last!	1987	8.00

—Reissue

Number	Title (A Side/B Side)	Yr	NM
❑ CH-9269	Tell Mama	1987	8.00

—Reissue

Number	Title (A Side/B Side)	Yr	NM
❑ CH-9287	The Second Time Around	1989	8.00

—Reissue

Number	Title (A Side/B Side)	Yr	NM
❑ ACH-19003	Etta Is Betta Than Evvah!	1976	15.00

J

Except when noted otherwise, VG = 25% of NM, and VG+ = 50% of NM. (Example: VG = $2.00, VG+ = $4.00 and NM = $8.00.)

Number	Title (A Side/B Side)	Yr	NM
❑ CH-50042	Etta James	1973	15.00
❑ 2CH-60004 [(2)]	Peaches	1971	20.00
❑ CH-60029	Come a Little Closer	1974	15.00
❑ CH-91509	Come a Little Closer	198?	8.00
—Reissue			
CROWN			
❑ CST-360 [R]	Etta James	1963	20.00
—With Etta smiling on cover			
❑ CST-360 [R]	Etta James	1963	20.00
—With Etta somber on cover			
❑ CLP-5209 [M]	Miss Etta James	1961	100.00
—First edition, with framed picture on cover			
❑ CLP-5209 [M]	Miss Etta James	1962	60.00
—Second edition, all-white cover with "Miss Etta James"			
❑ CLP-5234 [M]	The Best of Etta James	1962	60.00
—Black label			
❑ CLP-5234 [M]	The Best of Etta James	1963	30.00
—Gray label			
❑ CLP-5250 [M]	Twist with Etta James	1962	60.00
—Black label			
❑ CLP-5250 [M]	Twist with Etta James	1963	30.00
—Gray label			
❑ CLP-5360 [M]	Etta James	1963	30.00
—With Etta smiling on cover			
❑ CLP-5360 [M]	Etta James	1963	30.00
—With Etta somber on cover			
INTERMEDIA			
❑ QS-5014	Etta, Red Hot 'N' Live!	198?	10.00
ISLAND			
❑ 91018	Seven Year Itch	1988	10.00
❑ 842926-1	Sticking to My Guns	1990	12.00
KENT			
❑ KST-500 [R]	Miss Etta James	1964	25.00
—Black vinyl			
❑ KST-500 [R]	Miss Etta James	1964	80.00
—Red vinyl			
❑ KLP-5000 [M]	Miss Etta James	1964	30.00
UNITED			
❑ US 7712	Etta James Sings	197?	10.00
WARNER BROS.			
❑ BSK 3156	Deep in the Night	1978	12.00

JAMES, JESSE

Probably more than one performer using the same name; also, some of these may have been issued as "Jessie James."

Number	Title (A Side/B Side)	Yr	NM
12-Inch Singles			
T.T.E.D.			
❑ TDE-3026	I Can Do Bad by Myself (5:05)/(Dub Version) (Instrumental)	1987	15.00
45s			
HIT			
❑ 6120	Believe in Me Baby - Part I/Part II	1967	50.00
KENT			
❑ 314	Red Hot Rockin' Blues/The South's Gonna Rise Again	1958	200.00
MIDTOWN			
❑ 008	At Last/I Can Feel Your Love Vibes	1984	10.00
MUSICOR			
❑ 1008	Dreams Never Hurt Nobody/Somebody Really Mine	1961	25.00
SHIRLEY			
❑ 103	I Will Go/Cha Cha Minnie	196?	150.00
❑ 106	Baby Please Come Home/I Gotta Little Girl	196?	100.00
❑ 109	Open Up Your Heart/The Gamble	196?	100.00
❑ 110	A Sad, Sad Situation/My Future	196?	100.00
❑ 112	I Got a Little Girl/I Wanna Full Time Love	196?	40.00
T.T.E.D.			
❑ 3026	I Can Do Bad by Myself/(Dub Version)	1987	6.00
❑ 3031	I'm Gonna Be Rich and Famous/Don't Get Amnesia on Me Baby	1987	6.00
20TH CENTURY			
❑ 2201	If You Want a Love Affair/I Never Meant to Love Her	1975	150.00
20TH CENTURY FOX			
❑ 6684	Believe in Me Baby - Part I/Part II	1967	15.00
❑ 6700	Thank You Darlin'/Bring My Baby Back	1967	15.00
❑ 6704	If You're Lonely (Take My Hand)/Green Power	1968	30.00
UNI			
❑ 55171	Ain't Much of a Home/Don't Fight It	1969	15.00
ZAY			
❑ 30002	At Last/I Know I'll Never Find Another One	1971	50.00
❑ 30003	I Know I'll Never Find Another One/I Need Your Love So Bad	1971	40.00
ZEA			
❑ 50000	Don't Nobody Want to Get Married (Part I)/(Part II)	1970	20.00
❑ 50003	I Need You, Baby/Home at Last	1971	15.00

JAMES, JIMMY, AND THE VAGABONDS

Number	Title (A Side/B Side)	Yr	NM
12-Inch Singles			
PYE			
❑ 121	I Am Somebody (same on both sides)	1976	15.00
❑ 125	Now Is the Time/I Go Where the Music Takes Me	1976	15.00
45s			
ATCO			
❑ 6551	Come to Me Softly/Hi-Diddley Dee Dum Dum	1968	8.00
❑ 6608	Red Red Wine/No Good to Cry	1968	8.00
PYE			
❑ 71017	You Don't Stand a Chance If You Can't Dance (Part 1 & 2)	1975	6.00
❑ 71019	Lay Some Lovin' on Me/You Don't Stand a Chance If You Can't Dance	1975	5.00
❑ 71057	I Am Somebody/Chains of Love	1975	5.00
❑ 71068	I Go Where the Music Takes Me/Let's Love Together	1976	5.00
❑ 71075	Now Is the Time/Never Had This Dream Before	1976	5.00
Albums			
ATCO			
❑ 33-222 [M]	The New Religion	1967	20.00
❑ SD 33-222 [S]	The New Religion	1967	20.00
PYE			
❑ 12111	You Don't Stand a Chance If You Can't Dance	1975	10.00

JAMES, LEONARD

Number	Title (A Side/B Side)	Yr	NM
Albums			
DECCA			
❑ DL 8772 [M]	Boppin' and a-Strollin'	1958	50.00

JAMES, MARK

Number	Title (A Side/B Side)	Yr	NM
45s			
BELL			
❑ 45323	Flyin' to Memphis/(B-side unknown)	1973	6.00
❑ 45355	Roller Coaster/I'd Get Enthused	1973	6.00
JAMIE			
❑ 1261	Running Back/Free Me My Darling	1963	12.00
LIBERTY			
❑ 55953	I Can't Let You Go/Bimbo Knows	1967	8.00
MERCURY			
❑ 73718	Moody Blue/Wrong Kind of Love	1975	8.00
NEW DESIGN			
❑ ZS7 1002	It's No Laughing Matter/Restless Mood	1971	7.00
PRIVATE STOCK			
❑ 45,190	Who's Loving You/(B-side unknown)	1978	5.00
SCEPTER			
❑ 12221	Suspicious Minds/Taste of Heaven	1968	10.00

JAMES, MILTON

Number	Title (A Side/B Side)	Yr	NM
45s			
DORE			
❑ 767	My Lonely Feeling/(B-side unknown)	1966	1500.

JAMES, RICK

Number	Title (A Side/B Side)	Yr	NM
12-Inch Singles			
GORDY			
❑ PR 72 [DJ]	Big Time (6:27)/Upside Down (4:05)	1980	50.00
—No label name on label; B-side by Diana Ross			
❑ PR-101 [DJ]	Hard to Get (Vocal) (Instrumental)/Let Me Tickle Your Fancy (Vocal) (Instrumental)	1982	15.00
—No label name on label; B-side by Jermaine Jackson			
MOTOWN			
❑ 00012	High on Your Love Suite (7:20)/You and I (8:04)	1978	12.00
❑ PR-60 [DJ]	Love Gun (10:03) (3:45)	1979	12.00
❑ PR-81 [DJ]	Give It To Me Baby (3 versions)	1981	12.00
❑ 144	17 (6:40 vocal) (5:38 instrumental)	1984	6.00
❑ 981 [DJ]	You and I (8:04) (same on both sides)	1978	10.00
❑ 4511	Cold Blooded/(Instrumental)	1983	6.00
❑ 4528	Can't Stop/Oh What a Night	1985	6.00
❑ 4561	Sweet and Sexy Thing (3 versions)	1986	6.00
❑ 4565	Forever and a Day/(Instrumental)	1986	6.00
REPRISE			
❑ PRO-A-3376 [DJ]	Sexual Love Affair (Club) (Remix Edit) (LP)	1988	8.00
❑ 20941	Loosey's Rap (5 versions)	1988	6.00
❑ 21035	This Magic Moment (3 versions)	1988	6.00
❑ 21036	Sexual Luv Affair (4 versions)/In the Girls Room	1988	6.00
45s			
A&M			
❑ 1615	Funkin' Around/My Mama	1974	25.00
GORDY			
❑ 1619	Dance Wit' Me — Part 1/Dance Wit' Me — Part 2	1982	4.00
❑ 1619 [PS]	Dance Wit' Me — Part 1/Dance Wit' Me — Part 2	1982	5.00
❑ 1634	Hard to Get/My Love	1982	4.00
❑ 1646	She Blew My Mind (69 Times)/(B-side unknown)	1982	4.00
❑ 1658	Teardrops/Throwdown	1983	4.00
❑ 1687	Cold Blooded/(Instrumental)	1983	4.00
❑ 1703	U Bring the Freak Out/He Talks	1983	4.00
❑ 1714	Ebony Eyes/1,2,3	1983	4.00
—As "Rick James and Smokey Robinson"			
❑ 1714	Ebony Eyes/1,2,3	1983	5.00
—As "Rick James and Friend"			
❑ 1730	17/(Instrumental)	1984	4.00
❑ 1763	You Turn Me On/Fire and Desire	1984	4.00
❑ 1776	Can't Stop/Oh What a Night	1985	4.00
❑ 1776 [PS]	Can't Stop/Oh What a Night	1985	5.00
❑ 1796	Glow/(Instrumental)	1985	4.00
❑ 1806	Spend the Night with Me/(Instrumental)	1985	4.00
❑ 1844	Sweet and Sexy Thing/(Instrumental)	1986	3.00
❑ 1844 [PS]	Sweet and Sexy Thing/(Instrumental)	1986	8.00
—Sleeve may be promo only			
❑ 1862	Forever and a Day/(Instrumental)	1986	3.00
❑ 7156	You & I/Hollywood	1978	5.00
❑ 7162	Mary Jane/Dream Maker	1978	5.00
❑ 7164	High on Your Love Suite/Stone City Band High	1979	5.00
❑ 7164 [PS]	High on Your Love Suite/Stone City Band High	1979	6.00
❑ 7167	Bustin' Out/Sexy Lady	1979	5.00
❑ 7171	Fool on the Street/Jefferson Hall	1979	5.00
❑ 7176	Love Gun/Stormy Love	1979	5.00
❑ 7177	Come Into My Life (Part 1)/Come Into My Life (Part 2)	1980	5.00
❑ 7185	Big Time/Island Lady	1980	5.00
❑ 7191	Gettin' it On (In the Summertime)/Summer Love	1980	5.00
❑ 7197	Give It to Me Baby/Don't Give Up on Love	1981	4.00
❑ 7205	Super Freak (Part 1)/Super Freak (Part 2)	1981	4.00
❑ 7215	Ghetto Life/Below the Funk (Pass the J)	1981	4.00
REPRISE			
❑ 27764	Sexual Love Affair/In the Girls' Room	1988	3.00
❑ 27828	Wonderful/(Instrumental)	1988	3.00
❑ 27828 [PS]	Wonderful/(Instrumental)	1988	3.00
❑ 27885	Loosey's Rap/(Instrumental)	1988	3.00
—With Roxanne Shante			
❑ 27885 [PS]	Loosey's Rap/(Instrumental)	1988	3.00
WARNER BROS.			
❑ 27763	This Magic Moment-Dance with Me/(Instrumental)	1989	3.00
❑ 27763 [PS]	This Magic Moment-Dance with Me/(Instrumental)	1989	3.00
Albums			
GORDY			
❑ G7-981	Come Get It!	1978	10.00
❑ G7-984	Bustin' Out of L. Seven	1979	10.00
❑ G8-990	Fire It Up	1979	10.00
❑ G8-995	Garden of Love	1980	10.00
❑ G8-1002	Street Songs	1981	8.00
❑ 6005 GL	Throwin' Down	1982	8.00
❑ 6043 GL	Cold Blooded	1983	8.00
❑ 6095 GL	Reflections	1984	8.00
❑ 6135 GL	Glow	1985	8.00
MOTOWN			
❑ 5263 ML	Come Get It!	198?	8.00
❑ 5382 ML	Greatest Hits	1986	8.00

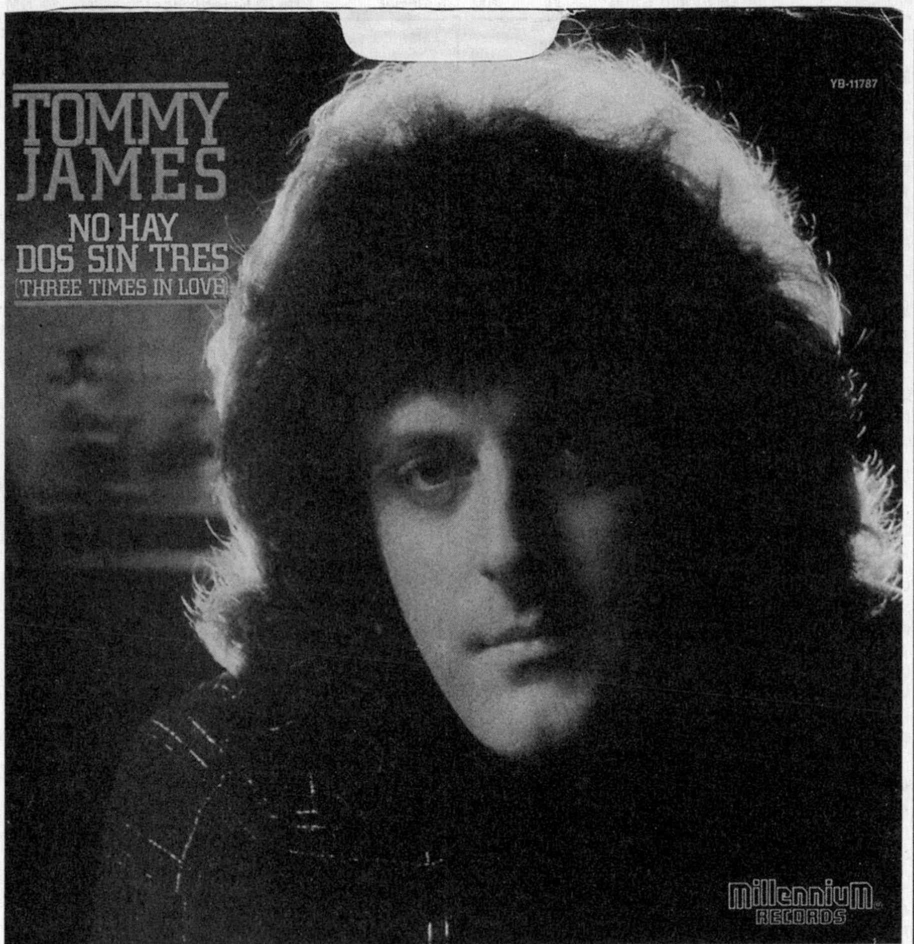

Tommy James, "No Hay Dos Sin Tres (Three Times in Love)," Millennium YB-11787, 1980, **$10.**

Number	Title (A Side/B Side)	Yr	NM
❑ MOT-5405	Street Songs	1987	6.00
REPRISE			
❑ 25659	Wonderful	1988	10.00
UNIVERSAL MOTOWN			
❑ 5316010	Street Songs	2009	20.00

JAMES, TOMMY

45s

Number	Title (A Side/B Side)	Yr	NM
FANTASY			
❑ 761	I Love You Love Me Love/ Devil Gate Drive	1976	4.00
❑ 761 [PS]	I Love You Love Me Love/ Devil Gate Drive	1976	5.00
❑ 776	Tighter, Tighter/Comin' Down	1976	5.00
❑ 811	Love Is Gonna Find a Way/ I Don't Love You Anymore	1977	5.00
❑ 886	Tighter, Tighter/Comin' Down	1980	4.00
MCA			
❑ 40289	Glory, Glory/Comin' Down	1974	5.00
MILLENNIUM			
❑ YB-11785	Three Times in Love/I Just Wanna Play the Music	1980	4.00
❑ YB-11787	No Hay Dos Sin Tres (Three Times in Love)/ I Just Wanna Play the Music	1980	5.00
❑ YB-11787 [PS]	No Hay Dos Sin Tres (Three Times in Love)/ I Just Wanna Play the Music	1980	10.00
❑ YB-11788	It's Alright (For Now)/You Got Me	1980	4.00
❑ YB-11802	You're So Easy to Love/ Halfway to Heaven	1981	4.00
❑ YB-11814	The Lady in White/Payin' for My Lover's Mistake	1981	4.00
ROULETTE			
❑ 7084	Ball and Chain/Candy Maker	1970	6.00
❑ 7093	Church Street Soul Revival/ Draggin' the Line	1970	8.00
❑ 7100	Adrienne/Light of Day	1971	6.00
❑ 7103	Draggin' the Line/Bits & Pieces	1971	6.00
❑ 7110	I'm Coming Home/ Sing, Sing, Sing	1971	5.00
❑ 7114	Nothing to Hide/ Walk a Country Mile	1971	5.00
❑ 7119	Tell 'Em Willie Boy's A-Comin'/ Forty Days and Dorty Nights	1972	5.00
❑ 7126	Cat's Eye in the Window/ Dark Is the Night	1972	5.00
❑ 7130	Love Song/Kingston Highway	1972	5.00
❑ 7135	Celebration/The Last One to Know	1972	5.00
❑ 7140	Boo, Boo, Don't Cha Be Blue/ Rings and Things	1973	5.00
❑ 7147	Calico/Hey, My Lady	1973	5.00
21 RECORDS			
❑ 105	Two-Time Lover/Say Please	1983	3.00
❑ 105 [PS]	Two-Time Lover/Say Please	1983	4.00

Albums

Number	Title	Yr	NM
FANTASY			
❑ 9509	In Touch	1976	12.00
❑ 9532	Midnight Rider	1977	12.00
MILLENNIUM			
❑ BXL1-7748	Three Times in Love	1980	10.00
❑ BXL1-7758	Easy to Love	1981	10.00
ROULETTE			
❑ SR-3001	Christian of the World	1971	15.00
❑ SR-3007	My Head, My Bed, My Red Guitar	1972	15.00
❑ SR-42061	Tommy James	1970	15.00

JAMES, TOMMY, AND THE SHONDELLS Also see HOG HEAVEN; TOMMY JAMES.

45s

Number	Title (A Side/B Side)	Yr	NM
PHILCO-FORD			
❑ HP-1	Mirage/I Think We're Alone Now	1967	15.00
—4-inch plastic "Hip Pocket Record" with color sleeve			
❑ HP-2	Hanky Panky/Gettin' Together	1967	15.00
—4-inch plastic "Hip Pocket Record" with color sleeve			
RED FOX			
❑ 110	Hanky Panky/Thunderbolt	1966	40.00
—As "The Shondells"			
ROULETTE			
❑ 4686	Hanky Panky/Thunderbolt	1966	10.00
❑ 4695	Say I Am (What I Am)/ Lots of Pretty Girls	1966	8.00
❑ 4695 [PS]	Say I Am (What I Am)/ Lots of Pretty Girls	1966	15.00
❑ 4710	It's Only Love/Don't Let My Love Pass You By	1966	8.00
❑ 4710	It's Only Love/Ya Ya	1966	12.00
❑ 4720	I Think We're Alone Now/ Gone, Gone, Gone	1967	10.00
❑ 4720 [PS]	I Think We're Alone Now/ Gone, Gone, Gone	1967	15.00
❑ 4736	Mirage/Run, Run, Baby, Run	1967	8.00
❑ 4736 [PS]	Mirage/Run, Run, Baby, Run	1967	15.00
❑ 4756	I Like the Way/(Baby) Baby I Can't Take It No More	1967	8.00
❑ 4762	Gettin' Together/Real Girl	1967	8.00
❑ 4762 [PS]	Gettin' Together/Real Girl	1967	15.00
❑ 4775	Out of the Blue/Love's Closin' In on Me	1967	8.00
❑ 7000	Get Out Now/Wish It Were True	1968	8.00
❑ 7008	Mony Mony/One Two Three and I Fell	1968	10.00
❑ 7016	Somebody Cares/Do Unto Me	1968	8.00
❑ 7024	Do Something to Me/ Ginger Bread Man	1968	8.00
❑ 7028	Crimson and Clover/ Some Kind of Love	1968	10.00
❑ 7028	Crimson and Clover/(I'm) Taken	1968	15.00
❑ 7039	Sweet Cherry Wine/Breakaway	1969	8.00
❑ 7050	Crystal Blue Persuasion/ I'm Alive	1969	10.00
❑ 7060	Ball of Fire/Makin' Good Time	1969	8.00
❑ 7066	She/Loved One	1969	8.00
❑ 7071	Gotta Get Back to You/ Red Rover	1970	8.00
❑ 7076	Come to Me/Talkin' and Signifyin'	1970	8.00
SNAP			
❑ 102	Hanky-Panky/Thunderbolt	1964	150.00
—As "The Shondells"; A-side title is hyphenated, which is true only on the 1964 pressings			
❑ 102	Hanky Panky/Thunderbolt	1966	20.00
—As "The Shondells"; with "Dist. by Red Fox Records, Pgh, Pa." on label			
❑ 102	Hanky Panky/Thunderbolt	1966	40.00
—As "The Shondells"; with A-side title NOT hyphenated; no mention of Red Fox on the label			

Albums

Number	Title	Yr	NM
RHINO			
❑ R1-70920 [(2)]	Anthology	1989	15.00
ROULETTE			
❑ R 25336 [M]	Hanky Panky	1966	20.00
❑ SR 25336 [P]	Hanky Panky	1966	25.00
—"Hanky Panky" is rechanneled			
❑ R 25344 [M]	It's Only Love	1967	30.00
❑ SR 25344 [S]	It's Only Love	1967	25.00
❑ R 25353 [M]	I Think We're Alone Now	1967	30.00
❑ SR 25353 [P]	I Think We're Alone Now	1967	15.00
—Photo cover			
❑ SR 25353 [P]	I Think We're Alone Now	1967	25.00
—Footprints cover; "I Think We're Alone Now" is rechanneled			
❑ R 25355 [M]	Something Special! The Best of Tommy James & The Shondells	1968	50.00
❑ SR 25355 [S]	Something Special! The Best of Tommy James & The Shondells	1968	25.00
❑ R 25357 [M]	Gettin' Together	1968	40.00
❑ SR 25357 [S]	Gettin' Together	1968	25.00
❑ SR 42005	Something Special! The Best of Tommy James & The Shondells	1968	15.00
❑ SR 42012	Mony Mony	1968	20.00
❑ SR 42023	Crimson and Clover	1969	20.00
❑ SR 42030	Cellophane Symphony	1969	20.00
❑ SR 42040	The Best of Tommy James & The Shondells	1969	20.00
—Original versions are in a Unipak (gatefold must be opened to remove record)			
❑ SR 42040	The Best of Tommy James & The Shondells	197?	15.00
—Later versions have gatefold covers, but record can be removed without opening it			
❑ SR 42044	Travelin'	1970	15.00
SCEPTER CITATION			
❑ CTN-18025	The Best of Tommy James and the Shondells	1973	10.00

JAMES GANG, THE (1) Also see TOMMY BOLIN; JOE WALSH; THE EAGLES.

45s

Number	Title (A Side/B Side)	Yr	NM
ABC			
❑ 11272	Funk #49/Thanks	1970	6.00
❑ 11301	Walk Away/Yadig?	1971	6.00
❑ 11312	White Man—Black Man/Midnight	1971	6.00
❑ 11325	Looking for My Lady/ Hairy Hypochondriac	1972	6.00
❑ 11336	Had Enough/Kick Back Man	1972	6.00

Except when noted otherwise, VG = 25% of NM, and VG+ = 50% of NM. (Example: VG = $2.00, VG+ = $4.00 and NM = $8.00.)

Number	Title (A Side/B Side)	Yr	NM
ATCO			
❑ 6953	Must Be Love/Got No Time for Trouble	1974	5.00
❑ 6966	Standing in the Rain/From Another Time	1974	5.00
❑ 7006	Cruisin' Down the Highway/Miami Two-Step	1974	5.00
❑ 7021	Merry Go Round/Red Satin Lover	1975	5.00
❑ 7067	I Need Love/Feelin' Alright	1975	5.00
BLUESWAY			
❑ 61027	I Don't Have the Time/Fred	1969	8.00
❑ 61030	Funk #48/Collage	1969	10.00
❑ 61033	Take a Look Around/Stop	1970	8.00

Albums

Number	Title (A Side/B Side)	Yr	NM
ABC			
❑ S-688	Yer' Album	1970	12.00
❑ S-711	James Gang Rides Again	1970	12.00

—Standard pressing without "Bolero" as part of "The Bomber"; "RE-1" in trail-off wax

Number	Title (A Side/B Side)	Yr	NM
❑ S-711	James Gang Rides Again	1970	25.00

—First pressing with a short version of Ravel's "Bolero" as part of the song "The Bomber"; exists on both promos and early stock copies; no "RE-1" in trail-off wax

Number	Title (A Side/B Side)	Yr	NM
❑ X-721	Thirds	1971	12.00
❑ X-733	James Gang Live in Concert	1971	12.00
❑ X-741	Straight Shooter	1972	12.00
❑ X-760	Passin' Thru	1972	12.00
❑ ABCX-774	The Best of the James Gang Featuring Joe Walsh	1973	12.00

—Most copies of this LP contain the edited version of "The Bomber." The full title of the LP is on the spine, and the record's trail-off wax has the number "ABCX-774-A-RE-1".

Number	Title (A Side/B Side)	Yr	NM
❑ ABCX-774	The Best of the James Gang Featuring Joe Walsh	1973	20.00

—A few copies of this LP contain the full version of "The Bomber" with the "Bolero" excerpt. The words "The Best Of" do NOT appear on the spine, and the record's trail-off wax has the number "ABCX-774-A".

Number	Title (A Side/B Side)	Yr	NM
❑ X-801 [(2)]	16 Greatest Hits	1973	15.00
ATCO			
❑ SD 36-102	Miami	1974	10.00
❑ SD 36-112	Newborn	1975	10.00
❑ SD 36-141	Jesse Come Home	1976	10.00
❑ SD 7037	Bang	1973	10.00
BLUESWAY			
❑ BLS-6034	Yer' Album	1969	15.00
MCA			
❑ 6012 [(2)]	16 Greatest Hits	1980	10.00
—Reissue			
❑ 37111	James Gang Rides Again	1980	8.00
—Reissue			
❑ 37112	The Best of the James Gang Featuring Joe Walsh	1980	8.00
—Reissue			

JAMES GANG, THE (2)

45s

Number	Title (A Side/B Side)	Yr	NM
ASCOT			
❑ 2168	Everybody Knows/Ladies' Man	1965	12.00
❑ 2196	Georgia Pines/Baby Take Me Back	1965	12.00
❑ 2205	Right String But the Wrong Yo-Yo/Satin and Lace	1966	12.00

JAMESON, BOBBY

45s

Number	Title (A Side/B Side)	Yr	NM
CURRENT			
❑ 103	All Alone/Your Sweet Lovin'	1964	12.00
LONDON			
❑ 9730	All I Want Is My Baby/Each and Everyday	1965	40.00
TALAMO			
❑ 1934	I'm So Lonely/I Wanna Love You	1964	10.00

JAMESTOWN MASSACRE

45s

Number	Title (A Side/B Side)	Yr	NM
DESTINATION			
❑ (no #)	Comin' Home to You/The Next Road	1971	15.00
LUV			
❑ 104	Summer Sun/Words and Rhymes	1972	15.00
WARNER BROS.			
❑ 7603	Summer Sun/Words and Rhymes	1972	8.00
❑ 7787	Saturday Night/Valley	1974	8.00

JAMIE AND JANE

"Jamie" is GENE PITNEY.

45s

Number	Title (A Side/B Side)	Yr	NM
DECCA			
❑ 30862	Snuggle Up Baby/Strollin' Thru the Park	1959	30.00
❑ 30934	Faithful Our Love/Classical Rock and Roll	1959	30.00

James Gang, *Passin' Thru*, ABC X-760, 1972, **$12.**

JAMIES, THE

45s

Number	Title (A Side/B Side)	Yr	NM
EPIC			
❑ 9281	Summertime, Summertime/Searching for You	1958	12.00

—Reissued in 1962 with the same catalog number and label design

Number	Title (A Side/B Side)	Yr	NM
❑ 9281 [PS]	Summertime, Summertime/Searching for You	1958	20.00
❑ 9299	When the Sun Goes Down/Snow Train	1958	20.00
❑ 9565	When the Sun Goes Down/Snow Train	1963	12.00
❑ 11129	Summertime, Summertime/Searching for You	1974	5.00
UNITED ARTISTS			
❑ 193	The Evening Star/Don't Darken My Door	1959	20.00

JAMME

45s

Number	Title (A Side/B Side)	Yr	NM
ABC DUNHILL			
❑ 4231	Poor Widow/She Sits There	1970	8.00

Albums

Number	Title (A Side/B Side)	Yr	NM
ABC DUNHILL			
❑ DS-50072	Jamme	1970	20.00

JAN AND ARNIE

Also see JAN AND DEAN.

45s

Number	Title (A Side/B Side)	Yr	NM
ARWIN			
❑ 108	Jennie Lee/Gotta Getta Date	1958	40.00
❑ 111	Gas Money/Bonnie Lou	1958	40.00
❑ 113	I Love Linda/The Beat That Can't Be Beat	1958	60.00
DORE			
❑ 522	Baby Talk/Jeannette Get Your Hair Done	1959	600.00

—Actually by Jan and Dean, but incorrectly credited

Number	Title (A Side/B Side)	Yr	NM
DOT			
❑ 16116	Gas Money/Gotta Getta Date	1960	50.00

7-Inch Extended Plays

Number	Title (A Side/B Side)	Yr	NM
DOT			
❑ DEP-1097	Jennie Lee/Gas Money//Gotta Getta Date/The Beat That Can't Be Beat	1960	500.00
❑ DEP-1097 [PS]	Jan and Arnie	1960	500.00

JAN AND DEAN

Also see JAN BERRY; THE LEGENDARY MASKED SURFERS; THE RALLY PACKS.

45s

Number	Title (A Side/B Side)	Yr	NM
CHALLENGE			
❑ 9111	Heart and Soul/A Midsummer Night's Dream	1961	20.00
❑ 9111	Heart and Soul/Those Words	1961	40.00
❑ 9120	Wanted: One Girl/Something a Little Bit Different	1961	30.00
COLUMBIA			
❑ 44036	Yellow Balloon/Taste of Rain	1967	30.00
DORE			
❑ 522	Baby Talk/Jeannette Get Your Hair Done	1959	30.00
❑ 531	There's a Girl/My Heart Sings	1959	25.00
❑ 539	Clementine/You're On My Mind	1960	25.00
❑ 548	Cindy/Whiter Tennis Sneakers	1960	25.00
❑ 555	We Go Together/Rosie Lane	1960	25.00

—B-side title was altered after the record no longer was issued with picture sleeve

Number	Title (A Side/B Side)	Yr	NM
❑ 555	We Go Together/Rosilane	1960	25.00
❑ 555 [PS]	We Go Together/Rosilane	1960	120.00
❑ 576	Gee/Such a Good Night to Be Together	1960	25.00
❑ 576 [PS]	Gee/Such a Good Night to Be Together	1960	300.00
❑ 583	Baggy Pants/Judy's an Angel	1961	30.00
❑ 610	Julie/Don't Fly Away	1961	30.00
EVATONE			
❑ 7801X	Surf Bunkey	1980	8.00

—6-inch red flexi-disc; Dutch version of "Surf City"

Number	Title (A Side/B Side)	Yr	NM
J&D			
❑ 001	California Lullabye/Summertime	1966	30.00
❑ 402	Like a Summer Rain/Louisiana Man	1966	30.00
❑ 1271 [DJ]	Ocean Park Angel/Wipe Out	1981	10.00
—B-side by the Surfaris			
JAN & DEAN			
❑ 10	Hawaii/Tijuana	1966	75.00
❑ 11	Fan Tan/Love and Hate	1966	120.00
LIBERTY			
❑ S7-19770	Frosty (The Snow Man)/Rudolph the Red-Nosed Reindeer	1997	3.00
—B-side by the Ventures on Dolton			
❑ 55397	A Sunday Kind of Love/Poor Little Puppet	1961	25.00
❑ 55454	Tennessee/Your Heart Has Changed Its Mind	1962	25.00
❑ 55496	Who Put the Bomp/My Favorite Dream	1962	50.00
❑ 55522	Frosty (The Snow Man)/(She's Still Talking) Baby Talk	1962	150.00
—Promos worth about half this value			
❑ 55531	Linda/When I Learn How to Cry	1963	25.00
❑ 55580	Surf City/She's My Summer Girl	1963	15.00
❑ 55580 [PS]	Surf City/She's My Summer Girl	1963	40.00
❑ 55613	Honolulu Lulu/Someday	1963	15.00
❑ 55613 [PS]	Honolulu Lulu/Someday	1963	40.00
❑ 55641	Drag City/Schlock Rod (Part 1)	1963	15.00
❑ 55641 [PS]	Drag City/Schlock Rod (Part 1)	1963	40.00
❑ 55672	Dead Man's Curve/The New Girl in School	1964	15.00
❑ 55672 [PS]	Dead Man's Curve/The New Girl in School	1964	40.00
❑ 55704	The Little Old Lady (From Pasadena)/My Mighty G.T.O.	1964	15.00
❑ 55704 [PS]	The Little Old Lady (From Pasadena)/My Mighty G.T.O.	1964	40.00
❑ 55724	Ride the Wild Surf/The Anaheim, Azusa and Cucamonga Sewing Circle, Book Review and Timing Association	1964	15.00
❑ 55724 [PS]	Ride the Wild Surf/The Anaheim, Azusa and Cucamonga Sewing Circle, Book Review and Timing Association	1964	40.00
❑ 55727	Sidewalk Surfin'/When It's Over	1964	15.00
❑ 55727 [PS]	Sidewalk Surfin'/When It's Over	1964	40.00
❑ 55766	(Here They Come) From All Over the World/Freeway Flyer	1965	12.00
❑ 55766 [PS]	(Here They Come) From All Over the World/Freeway Flyer	1965	200.00
❑ 55792	You Really Know How to Hurt a Guy/It's As Easy As 1-2-3	1965	12.00
❑ 55792 [PS]	You Really Know How to Hurt a Guy/It's As Easy As 1-2-3	1965	30.00
❑ 55816	It's a Shame to Say Goodbye/The Submarine Races	1965	—
—Unreleased			
❑ 55833	I Found a Girl/It's a Shame to Say Goodbye	1965	12.00
❑ 55849	Folk City/A Beginning from an End	1965	12.00
❑ 55849 [PS]	Folk City/A Beginning from an End	1965	30.00
❑ 55856	Norwegian Wood/I Can't Wait to Love You	1966	—
—Unreleased			
❑ 55860	Batman/Bucket "T"	1966	25.00
❑ 55886	Popsicle/Norwegian Wood	1966	12.00
❑ 55905	Fiddle Around/Surfer's Dream	1966	12.00
❑ 55923	The New Girl in School/School Days	1966	12.00
MAGIC LAMP			
❑ 401	California Lullabye/Summertime	1966	30.00
ODE			
❑ 66111	Fun City/Totally Wild	1975	25.00
UNITED ARTISTS			
❑ 0089	Jennie Lee/Baby Talk	1973	15.00
❑ 0090	Linda/The New Girl in School	1973	15.00
❑ 0091	Surf City/Ride the Wild Surf	1973	15.00
❑ 0092	Dead Man's Curve/Drag City	1973	15.00
❑ 0093	Honolulu Lulu/Sidewalk Surfin'	1973	15.00
❑ 0094	The Little Old Lady (From Pasadena)/Popsicle	1973	15.00
—0089 through 0094 are "Silver Spotlight Series" reissues			
❑ XW670	Sidewalk Surfin'/Gonna Hustle You	1975	15.00
❑ 50859	Jennie Lee/Vegetables	1971	15.00
❑ 50859 [PS]	Jennie Lee/Vegetables	1971	25.00
WARNER BROS.			
❑ 7151	Only a Boy/Love and Hate	1967	40.00
❑ 7219	Laurel and Hardy/I Know My Mind	1968	50.00
❑ 7240 [DJ]	In the Still of the Night/Girl, You're Blowing My Mind	1968	80.00
—Stock copy may not exist			

7-Inch Extended Plays

Number	Title (A Side/B Side)	Yr	NM
SUNDAZED			
❑ SEP 125	Yellow Balloon/Raindrops//California Lullaby/Here Comes the Rain	1996	2.50
—Light blue marbled vinyl; instrumental versions of songs on the reissue of the "Save for a Rainy Day" LP			
❑ SEP 125 [PS]	Sounds for a Rainy Day	1996	2.50

Albums

Number	Title (A Side/B Side)	Yr	NM
COLUMBIA			
❑ CL 2661 [M]	Save for a Rainy Day	1967	—
—Canceled			
❑ CS 9461 [S]	Save for a Rainy Day	1967	4000.
—LP not known to exist, but an acetate does, and possibly an import on this label and number; VG value 2000; VG+ value 3000			
DEADMAN'S CURVE			
❑ (no #)	Live at the Keystone Berkeley	1981	25.00
—With front and back covers pasted on			
❑ (no #)	Live at the Keystone Berkeley	1981	50.00
—Plain jacket with front and back cover inserts			
DORE			
❑ LP-101	Jan and Dean Bonus Photo	1960	120.00
❑ LP-101	Jan and Dean	197?	15.00
—Reissue with black label			
❑ LP-101 [M]	Jan and Dean	1960	400.00
—Original with blue label			
J&D			
❑ 101 [M]	Save for a Rainy Day	1967	300.00
—Private pressing by Dean Torrence of unreleased Columbia album			
LIBERTY			
❑ LRP-3248 [M]	Jan and Dean's Golden Hits	1962	30.00
❑ LRP-3294 [M]	Jan and Dean Take Linda Surfin'	1963	50.00
—With correct title on LP spine			
❑ LRP-3294 [M]	Jan and Dean Take Linda Surfin'	1963	60.00
—With title on spine "Mr. Bass Man Takes Linda Surfin'"			
❑ LRP-3314 [M]	Surf City and Other Swingin' Cities	1963	40.00
❑ LRP-3339 [M]	Drag City	1963	40.00
❑ LRP-3361 [M]	The New Girl in School/Dead Man's Curve	1964	20.00
—Reissue with reversed title			
❑ LRP-3361 [M]	Dead Man's Curve/The New Girl in School	1964	30.00
—Full-color cover			
❑ LRP-3361 [M]	Dead Man's Curve/The New Girl in School	1964	40.00
—Black and white cover with pink tint			
❑ LRP-3368 [M]	Ride the Wild Surf	1964	30.00
❑ LRP-3377 [M]	The Little Old Lady from Pasadena	1964	30.00
❑ LRP-3403 [M]	Command Performance/Live in Person	1965	30.00
❑ LRP-3417 [M]	Jan and Dean's Golden Hits, Vol. 2	1965	25.00
❑ LRP-3431 [M]	Folk 'N' Roll	1965	30.00
❑ LRP-3441 [M]	Filet of Soul	1966	30.00
❑ LRP-3444 [M]	Jan and Dean Meet Batman	1966	50.00
❑ LRP-3458 [M]	Popsicle	1966	30.00
❑ LRP-3460 [M]	Jan and Dean's Golden Hits, Vol. 3	1966	25.00
❑ LST-7248 [S]	Jan and Dean's Golden Hits	1962	40.00
❑ LST-7294 [S]	Jan and Dean Take Linda Surfin'	1963	80.00
—With correct title on LP spine			
❑ LST-7294 [S]	Jan and Dean Take Linda Surfin'	1963	100.00
—With title on spine "Mr. Bass Man Takes Linda Surfin'"			
❑ LST-7314 [S]	Surf City and Other Swingin' Cities	1963	50.00
❑ LST-7339 [S]	Drag City	1963	50.00
❑ LST-7361 [S]	The New Girl in School/Dead Man's Curve	1964	30.00
—Reissue with reversed title			
❑ LST-7361 [S]	Dead Man's Curve/The New Girl in School	1964	40.00
—Full-color cover			
❑ LST-7361 [S]	Dead Man's Curve/The New Girl in School	1964	50.00
—Black and white cover with pink tint			
❑ LST-7368 [S]	Ride the Wild Surf	1964	40.00
❑ LST-7377 [S]	The Little Old Lady from Pasadena	1964	40.00
❑ LST-7403 [S]	Command Performance/Live in Person	1965	40.00
❑ LST-7417 [S]	Jan and Dean's Golden Hits, Vol. 2	1965	30.00
❑ LST-7431 [S]	Folk 'N' Roll	1965	40.00
❑ LST-7441 [S]	Filet of Soul	1966	40.00
❑ LST-7444 [S]	Jan and Dean Meet Batman	1966	70.00
❑ LST-7458 [S]	Popsicle	1966	40.00
❑ LST-7460 [S]	Jan and Dean's Golden Hits, Vol. 3	1966	30.00
❑ LN-10011	Dead Man's Curve	1980	8.00
—Budget-line reissue			
❑ LN-10115	The Best of Jan and Dean	1981	8.00
❑ LN-10151	The Little Old Lady from Pasadena	1982	8.00
—Budget-line reissue			
PAIR			
❑ PDL2-1071 [(2)]	California Gold	1986	12.00
RHINO			
❑ RNDA 1498 [(2)]	One Summer Night — Live	1982	20.00
SUNDAZED			
❑ LP 5022 [(2)]	Save for a Rainy Day	1996	15.00
—First release to the general public; colored vinyl			
❑ LP 5040	Jan and Dean (The Dore Album)	1996	10.00
—Reissue of Dore LP on colored vinyl with extra tracks and poster			
SUNSET			
❑ SUM-1156 [M]	Jan and Dean	1967	15.00
❑ SUS-5156 [S]	Jan and Dean	1967	15.00
UNITED ARTISTS			
❑ UA-LA341-H2 [(2)]	Gotta Take That One Last Ride	1974	15.00
❑ UA-LA443-E	The Very Best of Jan and Dean	1975	10.00
❑ UA-LA515-E	The Very Best of Jan and Dean, Vol. 2	1975	10.00
❑ UAS-9961 [(2)]	Anthology (Legendary Masters Series, Vol. 3)	1971	25.00

JAN AND KJELD

45s

Number	Title (A Side/B Side)	Yr	NM
IMPERIAL			
❑ 5568	Tiger Rag/Buona Sera	1959	10.00
JARO			
❑ 77032	Ting-a-Ling My Banjo Sings/Penny Melody	1960	10.00
KAPP			
❑ 335	Banjo Boy/Don't Raise a Storm	1960	10.00
❑ 346	Yes Sir, That's My Baby/When Irish Eyes Are Smiling	19601	10.00
❑ 373	Carry Me Back to Old Virginny/Oh, Mein Papa	1961	15.00

Albums

Number	Title (A Side/B Side)	Yr	NM
KAPP			
❑ KL-1190 [M]	Banjo Boy	1960	30.00

JAN AND LORRAINE

Albums

Number	Title (A Side/B Side)	Yr	NM
ABC			
❑ S-691	Gypsy People	1969	25.00

JANE'S ADDICTION

PORNO FOR PYROS and RED HOT CHILI PEPPERS related.

12-Inch Singles

Number	Title (A Side/B Side)	Yr	NM
WARNER BROS.			
❑ 21559	Stop/I Would For You (Demo)/Three Days	1990	10.00
❑ 21736	Been Caught Stealing (2 versions)/Had a Dad (Demo)	1990	6.00

45s

Number	Title (A Side/B Side)	Yr	NM
WARNER BROS.			
❑ 19574	Been Caught Stealing/Had a Dad	1991	—
—Cassette only			
❑ 27520	Mountain Song/Standing in the Shower...Thinking	1989	10.00
❑ 27520 [PS]	Mountain Song/Standing in the Shower...Thinking	1989	10.00

Albums

Number	Title (A Side/B Side)	Yr	NM
TRIPLE X			
❑ 51004	Jane's Addiction	1987	25.00
WARNER BROS.			
❑ PRO-A-3369 [DJ]	Words and Music	1988	40.00
—Promo-only interview album			
❑ 25727	Nothing's Shocking	1988	12.00
❑ 25993	Ritual de lo Habitual	1990	15.00
—First cover, with drawing			
❑ 26223	Ritual de lo Habitual	1990	12.00
—Second cover, all white with text of First Amendment			

JANET, JOANNA

45s

Number	Title (A Side/B Side)	Yr	NM
DREAMWORKS			
❑ 0044-50812-7	7 Little Steps/Since I've Seen You Last	2002	3.00

JANIS, JOHNNY

45s

Number	Title (A Side/B Side)	Yr	NM
ABC-PARAMOUNT			
❑ 45-9800	Pledge of Love/I Played the Field	1957	20.00
❑ 45-9840	All the Time/Later Baby	1957	20.00
BOMARC			
❑ 304	I Never Believed/Willing to Learn	1959	15.00

Except when noted otherwise, VG = 25% of NM, and VG+ = 50% of NM. (Example: VG = $2.00, VG+ = $4.00 and NM = $8.00.)

Number	Title (A Side/B Side)	Yr	NM
❑ 307	Living in a Candy Store/ I Said You	1960	15.00
CARLTON			
❑ 463	The Better to Love You/ Can This Be Love	1958	25.00
COLUMBIA			
❑ 4-41797	Gina/If the Lord's Willin'	1960	15.00
❑ 4-41933	Catch a Falling Star/ As I Was Walkin'	1961	12.00
❑ 4-42040	I Get Ideas/Save a Thought for Me	1961	12.00
CORAL			
❑ 9-61552	Move It or Lose It/I'm Throwing Rice (At the Girl That I Love)	1956	25.00
MONUMENT			
❑ 977	You're Free to Go/Ninety Miles an Hour (Down a Dead End Street)	1966	10.00
❑ 1042	I Hear It Now/A Rose Is a Rose	1967	10.00
❑ 1117	Anything's the Part of You/ One of These Days	1968	10.00
❑ 1177	Walk Through This World with Me/All This World and the Seven Seas	1969	8.00
❑ 1205	Distant Dreams/Ride Me Donkey	1970	8.00
❑ ZS7 8532	I'll Need You Forever/No	1972	7.00

JANKOWSKI, HORST

45s

Number	Title (A Side/B Side)	Yr	NM
MERCURY			
❑ 72425	A Walk in the Black Forest/Nola	1965	8.00
❑ 72465	Simple Gimple/Charming Vienna	1965	6.00
❑ 72465 [PS]	Simple Gimple/Charming Vienna	1965	8.00
❑ 72492	Heide/Happy Frankfurt	1965	6.00
❑ 72520	Cruisin' Down the River/ Play a Simple Melody	1966	6.00
❑ 72567	Black Forest Holiday/ Elmer's Tune	1966	6.00
❑ 72615	A Place in the Sun/ So What's New	1966	6.00
❑ 72647	Spy with a Cold Nose/ Big, Big River	1966	6.00
❑ 72740	A Man and a Woman/ A Lover's Concerto	1967	6.00
❑ 72766	Glory of Love/Lazy	1968	5.00
❑ 72809	And We Got Love/Zabadak	1968	5.00
❑ 72851	Chitty Chitty Bang Bang/ This Guy's in Love with You	1968	5.00
❑ 72948	Dream Flight/Pink Balloon	1969	5.00

Albums

Number	Title (A Side/B Side)	Yr	NM
MERCURY			
❑ MG-20993 [M]	The Genius of Jankowski	1965	12.00
❑ MG-21054 [M]	More Genius of Jankowski	1965	12.00
❑ MG-21076 [M]	Still More Genius of Jankowski	1966	12.00
❑ MG-21093 [M]	So What's New?	1966	12.00
❑ MG-21106 [M]	Baby But Grand	1967	12.00
❑ MG-21125 [M]	With Love	1967	12.00
❑ SR-60993 [S]	The Genius of Jankowski	1965	15.00
❑ SR-61054 [S]	More Genius of Jankowski	1965	15.00
❑ SR-61076 [S]	Still More Genius of Jankowski	1966	15.00
❑ SR-61093 [S]	So What's New?	1966	15.00
❑ SR-61106 [S]	Baby But Grand	1967	15.00
❑ SR-61125 [S]	With Love	1967	15.00
❑ SR-61160	And We Got Love	1968	12.00
❑ SR-61195	Piano Affairs	1968	12.00
❑ SR-61219	Jankowski Plays Jankowski	1969	12.00
❑ SR-61232	A Walk in the Evergreens	1970	12.00

JANSSEN, DAVID

Albums

Number	Title (A Side/B Side)	Yr	NM
EPIC			
❑ LN 24150 [M]	Hidden Island	1965	20.00
❑ BN 26150 [S]	Hidden Island	1965	25.00

JAPAN

12-Inch Singles

Number	Title (A Side/B Side)	Yr	NM
ARIOLA AMERICA			
❑ PRO 7727 [DJ]	Sometimes I Feel So Low (same on both sides)	1978	20.00
❑ PRO 7756 [DJ]	Life in Japan (Long)/ Life in Japan (Short)	1979	10.00
VIRGIN/EPIC			
❑ 02756	Canton/Visions of China	1981	8.00

45s

Number	Title (A Side/B Side)	Yr	NM
ARIOLA AMERICA			
❑ 7727	Sometimes I Feel So Low/ Love Is Infectious	1979	8.00
❑ 7756	Life in Tokyo/Love Is Infectious	1979	8.00

Albums

Number	Title (A Side/B Side)	Yr	NM
ARIOLA AMERICA			
❑ SW-50037	Adolescent Sex	1978	20.00
❑ SW-50047 [EP]	Obscure Alternatives	1979	15.00
VIRGIN/EPIC			
❑ ARE 37914	Japan	1982	10.00

JAPANESE BEATLES, THE

45s

Number	Title (A Side/B Side)	Yr	NM
GOLDEN CREST			
❑ 584	The Beatle Song (Japanese Style) (Part 1)/The Beatle Song (Japanese Style) (Part 2)	1964	20.00

JARMELS, THE

45s

Number	Title (A Side/B Side)	Yr	NM
LAURIE			
❑ 3085	Little Lonely One/She Loves to Dance	1961	15.00
❑ 3098	A Little Bit of Soap/The Way You Look Tonight	1961	20.00
❑ 3116	I'll Follow You/Gee Oh Gosh	1962	15.00
❑ 3124	Red Sails in the Sunset/ Loneliness	1962	15.00
❑ 3142	Little Bug/One By One	1962	15.00
❑ 3174	Come On Girl/Keep Your Mind on Me	1963	15.00

Albums

Number	Title (A Side/B Side)	Yr	NM
COLLECTABLES			
❑ COL-5044	Golden Classics	198?	10.00

JARRETT, CHARLIE

45s

Number	Title (A Side/B Side)	Yr	NM
HIT			
❑ 12	Old Rivers/Everybody Loves Me But You	1962	8.00
—B-side by Connie Dee			

JARRETT, KEITH

12-Inch Singles

Number	Title (A Side/B Side)	Yr	NM
ECM			
❑ PRO-A-768 [DJ]	Country/My Song	1978	10.00
❑ PRO-A-1088 [DJ]	Mon Coeur Est Rouge (2 versions)/Heartland	1982	8.00
❑ PRO-A-2072 [DJ]	God Bless the Child (Edit)/ The Masquerade Is Over	1983	6.00
❑ PRO-A-2186 [DJ]	Flying Part 1 and 2/Prism	1984	6.00

45s

Number	Title (A Side/B Side)	Yr	NM
ABC IMPULSE!			
❑ 31001	Treasure Island/Sister Fortune	1975	5.00
ATLANTIC			
❑ 5110	All I Want/Standing Outside	1971	6.00
ECM			
❑ 29483	God Bless the Child/ Meaning of the Blues	1983	4.00

Albums

Number	Title (A Side/B Side)	Yr	NM
ABC IMPULSE!			
❑ AS-9240	Fort Yawuh	1973	15.00
❑ AS-9274	Treasure Island	1974	15.00
❑ ASD-9301	Death and the Flower	1974	15.00
❑ ASH-9305	Backhand	1975	20.00
❑ ASD-9315	Mysteries	1976	12.00
❑ ASD-9322	Shades	1976	12.00
❑ AS-9331	Byablue	1977	12.00
❑ IA-9334	Bop-Be	1977	12.00
❑ IA-9348	The Best of Keith Jarrett	1978	10.00
ATLANTIC			
❑ SD 1596	Mourning of a Star	1971	20.00
❑ SD 1612	Birth	1972	15.00
❑ SD 1673	El Juicio (The Judgment)	1975	12.00
❑ SD 8808	Somewhere Before	1981	12.00
—Reissue of Vortex 2012			
COLUMBIA			
❑ KG 31580 [(2)]	Expectations	1972	20.00
—Original edition			
❑ PG 31580 [(2)]	Expectations	198?	12.00
—Reissue with new prefix; some with bar code on cover			
ECM			
❑ 1017 ST	Facing You	1973	15.00
—Original edition, made in Germany?			
❑ ECM 1-1017	Facing You	197?	12.00
—U.S. pressing, distributed by Polydor			
❑ 1033/4 ST [(2)]	In the Light	1976	20.00
—Original edition			
❑ ECM 2-1033 [(2)]	In the Light	197?	15.00
—Reissue with new prefix, distributed by Polydor			
❑ 1035/6/7 ST [(3)]	Solo Concerts	1974	25.00
—Original issue, made in Germany?			
❑ ECM-3-1035 [(3)]	Solo Concerts	197?	20.00
—Distributed by Polydor			
❑ 1049 ST	Luminessence	1974	15.00
—Original, made in Germany			
❑ ECM1-1049	Luminessence	197?	12.00
—Distributed by Warner Bros.			
❑ 1050 ST	Belonging	1974	15.00
—Original, made in Germany?			
❑ ECM-2-1064 [(2)]	The Koln Concert	1976	15.00
—Distributed by Polydor			
❑ ECM-1-1070	Arbour Zena	1976	12.00
—Distribuited by Polydor			
❑ ECM1-1070	Arbour Zena	197?	10.00
—Distributed by Warner Bros. (reissue)			
❑ ECM-1-1085	Survivors' Suite	1977	12.00
—Distributed by Polydor			
❑ ECM-2-1086 [(2)]	Hymns/Spheres	1977	15.00
—Distributed by Polydor			
❑ ECM-2-1090 [(2)]	Staircase	1977	15.00
—Distributed by Polydor			
❑ 1100 [(10)]	The Sun Bear Concerts	1977	150.00
—Made in Germany			
❑ ECM1-1115	My Song	1978	12.00
—Distributed by Warner Bros.			
❑ ECM-T-1150 [(2)]	Eyes of the Heart	1979	15.00
—Distributed by Warner Bros.			
❑ ECM2-1171 [(2)]	Nude Ants	1980	15.00
—Distributed by Warner Bros.			
❑ ECM1-1174	G.I. Gurdjieff Sacred Hymns	1981	10.00
—Distributed by Warner Bros.			
❑ ECM1-1175	Celestial Hawk	1981	10.00
—Distributed by Warner Bros.			
❑ ECM-D-1201 [(2)]	Invocations/The Moth and the Flame	1981	12.00
—Distributed by Warner Bros.			
❑ ECM3-1227 [(3)]	Concerts	1982	20.00
—Distributed by Warner Bros.; box set			
❑ ECM1-1228	Concerts	1982	10.00
—Abridged version of 1227; distributed by Warner Bros.			
❑ 1255	Standards, Vol. 1	1983	15.00
—Made in Germany			
❑ 1276	Changes	1984	15.00
—Made in Germany (U.S. version issued on 25007)			
❑ 1289	Standards, Vol. 2	1985	15.00
—Made in Germany			
❑ 1317	Standards Live	1986	15.00
—Made in Germany			
❑ 1333/4 [(2)]	Spirits	1986	20.00
—Made in Germany			
❑ 1344/5 [(2)]	Book of Ways	1986	12.00
—Made in Germany			
❑ 1360/1 [(2)]	Still Live	1988	25.00
—Made in Germany			
❑ 1379	Dark Intervals	1988	15.00
—Made in Germany			
❑ 1382	Personal Mountains	1989	15.00
—Made in Germany			
❑ 1392	Changeless	1990	25.00
—Made in Germany			
❑ 23793	Standards, Vol. 1	1983	12.00
—Distributed by Warner Bros.			
❑ 25007	Changes	1984	10.00
—Distributed by Warner Bros.			
❑ 25023	Standards, Vol. 2	1985	12.00
—Distributed by Warner Bros.			
❑ 25041	Standards Live	1986	12.00
—Distributed by Warner Bros.			
MCA			
❑ 2-4125 [(2)]	Great Moments with Keith Jarrett	1981	20.00
❑ 29044	Fort Yawuh	1980	10.00
—Reissue of Impulse 9240			
❑ 29045	Treasure Island	1980	10.00
—Reissue of Impulse 9274			
❑ 29046	Death and the Flower	1980	10.00
—Reissue of Impulse 9301			
❑ 29047	Byablue	1980	10.00
—Reissue of Impulse 9331			
❑ 29048	Bop-Be	1980	10.00
—Reissue of Impulse 9334			
❑ 39106	Treasure Island	198?	25.00
—Another reissue of Impulse 9274			
VORTEX			
❑ 2006	Life Between the Exit Signs	1969	30.00
❑ 2008	Restoration Ruin	1969	30.00
❑ 2012	Somewhere Before	1970	30.00

JARRETT, KEITH, AND JACK DEJOHNETTE

Albums

Number	Title (A Side/B Side)	Yr	NM
ECM			
❑ 1021 ST	Ruta & Daitya	1973	15.00
—Original issue; made in Germany?			
❑ ECM-1-1021	Ruta & Daitya	197?	12.00
—Manufactured by Polydor			

J

JARRETT, KEITH/MCCOY TYNER

Albums

AT EASE

Number	Title (A Side/B Side)	Yr	NM
❑ MD-11119	Masters of the Piano	1978	20.00

—Record made for sale at military bases

JARVIS, FELTON

45s

ABC-PARAMOUNT

Number	Title (A Side/B Side)	Yr	NM
❑ 10570	Be-I-Bye/Ski King	1964	15.00
❑ 10610	Honky Tonk Song/Everybody's Going to the Party	1964	15.00
❑ 10641	Too Many Tigers/Knuckie, Knuckie	1965	15.00

MGM

Number	Title (A Side/B Side)	Yr	NM
❑ 12982	Indian Love Call/Goin' Downtown	1961	20.00

THUNDER INT'L.

Number	Title (A Side/B Side)	Yr	NM
❑ 1023	Swingin' Cat/Honest John the Workin' Man's Friend	1960	100.00

VIVA

Number	Title (A Side/B Side)	Yr	NM
❑ 1001	Don't Knock Elvis/Honest John	1959	40.00

JARVIS, JOHN

Albums

CRYSTAL CLEAR

Number	Title (A Side/B Side)	Yr	NM
❑ 8004	Evolutions	1980	20.00

—Direct-to-disc recording

MCA

Number	Title (A Side/B Side)	Yr	NM
❑ 5690	So Far So Good	1986	10.00
❑ 5963	Something Constructive	1987	10.00
❑ 6263	Whatever Works	1988	10.00

JASPER WRATH

45s

SUNFLOWER

Number	Title (A Side/B Side)	Yr	NM
❑ 107	It's Up to You/Did You Know That	1971	10.00

Albums

SUNFLOWER

Number	Title (A Side/B Side)	Yr	NM
❑ SNF-5003	Jasper Wrath	1971	40.00

JAUME, ANDRE

Albums

HAT ART

Number	Title (A Side/B Side)	Yr	NM
❑ 2003 [(2)]	Musique Pour 3 & 8: Errance	1986	15.00

HAT HUT

Number	Title (A Side/B Side)	Yr	NM
❑ R	Saxanimalier	1979	12.00
❑ 1989/90 [(2)]	Musique Pour 8: L'oc	1981	20.00

JAUME, ANDRE, AND JOE MCPHEE

Albums

HAT HUT

Number	Title (A Side/B Side)	Yr	NM
❑ 12 [(2)]	Tales and Prophecies	1980	20.00

JAXON, BOB

45s

ABC-PARAMOUNT

Number	Title (A Side/B Side)	Yr	NM
❑ 10364	It's a Cruel, Cruel Thing/One Way to Love Me	1962	12.00

CADENCE

Number	Title (A Side/B Side)	Yr	NM
❑ 1264	Ali Baba/Why Does a Woman Cry	1955	15.00

RCA VICTOR

Number	Title (A Side/B Side)	Yr	NM
❑ 47-6945	Beach Party/I'm Hangin' Around	1957	15.00
❑ 47-7006	(Gotta Have Something in the) Bank Frank/Come On Down	1957	20.00
❑ 47-7106	Declaration of Love/I'm Hurtin' Inside	1957	15.00
❑ 47-7168	Me! Please! Me!/All About Me	1958	15.00
❑ 47-7232	For the Love of You/(Well It's) No Lie	1958	15.00

20TH CENTURY FOX

Number	Title (A Side/B Side)	Yr	NM
❑ 441	Weep, Mary, Weep/Do the People	1963	10.00

JAY

See JAY TRAYNOR.

JAY, IRA

45s

SUN

Number	Title (A Side/B Side)	Yr	NM
❑ 351	You Don't Love Me/More Than Anything	1960	20.00

JAY, JERRY

California DJ, better known as Jerry Osborne.

45s

QUALITY

Number	Title (A Side/B Side)	Yr	NM
❑ 201	The King's Country/Merry Christmas To You	1966	200.00

JAY, MORTY

45s

KAYDEN

Number	Title (A Side/B Side)	Yr	NM
❑ 404	Beef-Eater/I Don't Care If the Sun Don't Shine	196?	12.00

LEGEND

Number	Title (A Side/B Side)	Yr	NM
❑ 124	Saltwater Taffy/What Is Surfin' All About	1963	25.00

—B-side by Jerry Norell and the Beach Girls

20TH CENTURY FOX

Number	Title (A Side/B Side)	Yr	NM
❑ 402	The Longest Day/(B-side unknown)	1963	10.00

—With a severely truncated version of the A-side

JAY, PETER, AND THE JAYWALKERS

45s

WAND

Number	Title (A Side/B Side)	Yr	NM
❑ 180	What's Easy/Parchment Farm	1965	10.00

JAY, SAMMY

45s

PRINCESS

Number	Title (A Side/B Side)	Yr	NM
❑ 4021	Candy Kisses/(B-side unknown)	196?	15.00
❑ 4031	Blue Tears/Let Them Talk	196?	15.00

TRIBE

Number	Title (A Side/B Side)	Yr	NM
❑ 8311	Never Let Me Go/You're Driving Me Insane	1965	12.00

JAY, VALERIE

45s

EPIC

Number	Title (A Side/B Side)	Yr	NM
❑ 5-10573	Kiss Away/One More Nightly Cry	1970	7.00

JAY AND THE AMERICANS

Also see JAY BLACK; JAY TRAYNOR.

45s

EEOC

Number	Title (A Side/B Side)	Yr	NM
❑ 1140	Things Are Changing/Things Are Changing	1965	150.00
❑ 1140 [PS]	Things Are Changing/Things Are Changing	1965	150.00

—Promotional item for the Equal Employment Opportunity Commission

UNITED ARTISTS

Number	Title (A Side/B Side)	Yr	NM
❑ 0026	She Cried/Come a Little Bit Closer	1973	5.00
❑ 0027	Cara Mia/Let's Lock the Door (And Throw Away the Key)	1973	5.00
❑ 0028	This Magic Moment/Walking in the Rain	1973	5.00

—0026, 0027, 0028 are "Silver Spotlight Series" reissues

Number	Title (A Side/B Side)	Yr	NM
❑ 353	Tonight/The Other Girls	1961	12.00
❑ 415	She Cried/Dawning	1962	15.00
❑ 479	It's My Turn to Cry/This Is It	1962	12.00
❑ 504	Tomorrow/Yes	1962	12.00
❑ 566	What's the Use/Strangers Tomorrow	1963	10.00
❑ 626	Only in America/My Clair De Lune	1963	10.00
❑ 669	Come Dance with Me/Look in My Eyes Maria	1963	10.00
❑ 693	To Wait for Love/Friday	1964	10.00
❑ 759	Come a Little Bit Closer/Goodbye Boys, Goodbye	1964	10.00
❑ 805	Let's Lock the Door (And Throw Away the Key)/I'll Remember You	1965	10.00
❑ 845	Think of the Good Times/If You Were Mine, Girl	1965	10.00
❑ 881	Cara Mia/When It's All Over	1965	10.00
❑ 919	Some Enchanted Evening/Girl	1965	10.00
❑ 919 [PS]	Some Enchanted Evening/Girl	1965	15.00
❑ 948	Sunday and Me/Through This Doorway	1965	10.00
❑ 948 [PS]	Sunday and Me/Through This Doorway	1965	50.00
❑ 992	Why Can't You Bring Me Home/Baby Stop Your Cryin'	1966	8.00
❑ 50016	Crying/I Don't Need a Friend	1966	8.00
❑ 50016 [PS]	Crying/I Don't Need a Friend	1966	12.00
❑ 50046	Livin' Above Your Head/Look at Me, What Do You See	1966	8.00
❑ 50046 [PS]	Livin' Above Your Head/Look at Me, What Do You See	1966	40.00
❑ 50086	Baby Come Home/Stop the Clock	1966	8.00
❑ 50094	(He's) Raining in My Sunshine/The Reason for Living (For You My Darling)	1966	8.00
❑ 50139	Nature Boy/You Ain't As Hip As All That, Baby	1967	8.00
❑ 50196	(We'll Meet in the) Yellow Forest/Got Hung Up Along the Way	1967	50.00
❑ 50222	Shanghai Noodle Factory/French Provincial	1967	8.00
❑ 50282	No Other Love/No, I Don't Know Her	1968	8.00
❑ 50448	You Ain't Gonna Wake Up Cryin'/Gemini	1968	8.00
❑ 50475	This Magic Moment/Since I Don't Have You	1969	12.00
❑ 50510	When You Dance/No, I Don't Know Her	1969	6.00
❑ 50535	Hushabye/Gypsy Woman	1969	6.00
❑ 50567	(I'd Kill) For the Love of a Lady/Learnin' How to Fly	1969	6.00
❑ 50605	Walkin' in the Rain/(I'd Kill) For the Love of a Lady	1969	8.00
❑ 50654	Do You Ever Think of Me/Capture the Moment	1970	6.00
❑ 50683	Do I Love You?/Tricia (Tell Your Daddy)	1970	6.00
❑ 50858	There Goes My Baby/Solitary Man	1971	6.00

Albums

LIBERTY

Number	Title (A Side/B Side)	Yr	NM
❑ LM-1010	Jay and the Americans Greatest Hits	1981	8.00

—Another reissue

RHINO

Number	Title (A Side/B Side)	Yr	NM
❑ RNLP 70224	All-Time Greatest Hits	1986	12.00

SUNSET

Number	Title (A Side/B Side)	Yr	NM
❑ SUS-5252	Jay and the Americans!!	1968	12.00
❑ SUS-5278	Early American Hits	1969	15.00

UNART

Number	Title (A Side/B Side)	Yr	NM
❑ M-20018 [M]	Jay and the Americans!!	196?	12.00
❑ MS-21018 [S]	Jay and the Americans!!	196?	12.00

UNITED ARTISTS

Number	Title (A Side/B Side)	Yr	NM
❑ UA-LA357-E	The Very Best of Jay and the Americans	1975	12.00
❑ LM-1010	Jay and the Americans Greatest Hits	1980	10.00

—Reissue

Number	Title (A Side/B Side)	Yr	NM
❑ UAL-3222 [M]	She Cried	1962	50.00
❑ UAL-3300 [M]	At the Café Wha?	1963	50.00
❑ UAL-3407 [M]	Come a Little Bit Closer	1964	25.00
❑ UAL-3417 [M]	Blockbusters	1965	25.00
❑ UAL-3453 [M]	Jay and the Americans Greatest Hits	1965	20.00
❑ UAL-3474 [M]	Sunday and Me	1966	20.00
❑ UAL-3534 [M]	Livin' Above Your Head	1966	20.00
❑ UAL-3555 [M]	Jay and the Americans Greatest Hits, Vol. 2	1966	20.00
❑ UAL-3562 [M]	Try Some of This!	1967	20.00
❑ UAS-6222 [S]	She Cried	1962	100.00
❑ UAS-6300 [S]	At the Café Wha?	1963	100.00
❑ UAS-6407 [S]	Come a Little Bit Closer	1964	30.00
❑ UAS-6417 [S]	Blockbusters	1965	30.00
❑ UAS-6453 [S]	Jay and the Americans Greatest Hits	1965	25.00
❑ UAS-6474 [S]	Sunday and Me	1966	25.00
❑ UAS-6534 [S]	Livin' Above Your Head	1966	25.00
❑ UAS-6555 [S]	Jay and the Americans Greatest Hits, Vol. 2	1966	20.00
❑ UAS-6562 [S]	Try Some of This!	1967	20.00
❑ UAS-6671	Sands of Time	1969	20.00
❑ UAS-6719	Wax Museum	1970	20.00
❑ UAS-6751	Wax Museum, Vol. 2	1970	20.00
❑ UAS-6762	Capture the Moment	1970	20.00
❑ ST-90814 [S]	Jay and the Americans Greatest Hits	1966	30.00

—Capitol Record Club edition

Number	Title (A Side/B Side)	Yr	NM
❑ ST-90815 [S]	Jay and the Americans Greatest Hits, Vol. 2	1966	30.00

—Capitol Record Club edition

JAY AND THE DELTAS

45s

WARNER BROS.

Number	Title (A Side/B Side)	Yr	NM
❑ 5404	Bells Are Ringing/Super Hawk	1964	50.00

JAY AND THE TECHNIQUES

45s

EVENT

Number	Title (A Side/B Side)	Yr	NM
❑ 222	I Feel Love Coming On/World of Mine	1975	5.00
❑ 228	Number Onederful/Don't Forget to Ask	1975	30.00

GORDY

Number	Title (A Side/B Side)	Yr	NM
❑ 7123	I'll Be Here/Robot Man	1973	40.00

PHILCO-FORD

Number	Title (A Side/B Side)	Yr	NM
❑ HP-22	Apples Peaches Pumpkin Pie/Loving for Money	1968	15.00

—4-inch plastic "Hip Pocket Record" with color sleeve

SMASH

Number	Title (A Side/B Side)	Yr	NM
❑ 2086	Apples, Peaches, Pumpkin Pie/Stronger Than Dirt	1967	15.00

Except when noted otherwise, VG = 25% of NM, and VG+ = 50% of NM. (Example: VG = $2.00, VG+ = $4.00 and NM = $8.00.)

Number	Title (A Side/B Side)	Yr	NM
❑ 2124	Keep the Ball Rollin'/ Here We Go Again	1967	15.00
❑ 2124 [PS]	Keep the Ball Rollin'/ Here We Go Again	1967	20.00
❑ 2142	Strawberry Shortcake/ Still (In Love with You)	1967	15.00
❑ 2142 [PS]	Strawberry Shortcake/ Still (In Love with You)	1967	20.00
❑ 2154	Baby Make Your Own Sweet Music/Help Yourself to All My Lovin'	1968	15.00
❑ 2154 [PS]	Baby Make Your Own Sweet Music/Help Yourself to All My Lovin'	1968	20.00
❑ 2171	The Singles Game/Baby How Easy Your Heart Forgets Me	1968	15.00
❑ 2171 [PS]	The Singles Game/Baby How Easy Your Heart Forgets Me	1968	20.00
❑ 2185	Hey Diddle Diddle/If I Should Lose You	1968	15.00
❑ 2217	Change Your Mind/ Are You Ready for This	1969	30.00
❑ 2237	Dancin' Mood/If I Should Lose You	1969	20.00
Albums			
SMASH			
❑ MGS-27095 [M]	Apples, Peaches, Pumpkin Pie	1967	30.00
❑ MGS-27102 [M]	Love Lost and Found	1968	60.00
—Mono may be white-label promo only			
❑ SRS-67095 [S]	Apples, Peaches, Pumpkin Pie	1967	30.00
—First cover with "live" photo of the band			
❑ SRS-67095 [S]	Apples, Peaches, Pumpkin Pie	1968	20.00
—Second cover with "posed" photo of the band			
❑ SRS-67102 [S]	Love Lost and Found	1968	30.00

JAY FIVE, THE

45s

Number	Title (A Side/B Side)	Yr	NM
RCA VICTOR			
❑ 47-9449	My Angel/Platform Ticket	1968	12.00

JAY WALKERS, THE

45s

Number	Title (A Side/B Side)	Yr	NM
CAMEO			
❑ 300	Restless People/Sleep Sleep	1964	20.00
LAURIE			
❑ 3363	Oh Babe/Love at First Sight	1966	40.00
SWAN			
❑ 4266	Nuts & Bolts/Can't Live Without You	1966	80.00

JAYBEES, THE

45s

Number	Title (A Side/B Side)	Yr	NM
RCA VICTOR			
❑ 47-8904	Do You Think I'm in Love/ I'm a Lover	1966	20.00

JAYE, JERRY

45s

Number	Title (A Side/B Side)	Yr	NM
COLUMBIA			
❑ 10170	It's All in the Game/Love Me 'Til the Morning Comes	1975	4.00
❑ 10269	Maybellene/Because It's Love	1975	4.00
HI			
❑ 2120	My Girl Josephine/ Five Miles from Home	1967	8.00
❑ 2128	Let the Four Winds Blow/ Singin' the Blues	1967	8.00
❑ 2139	Brown-Eyed Handsome Man/ In the Middle of Nowhere	1968	6.00
❑ 2150	Long Black Veil/(Today) I Started Loving You Again	1968	6.00
❑ 2171	Never Going Back/ You've Got to Go	1969	6.00
❑ 2310	Honky Tonk Women Love Redneck Men/What's Left	1976	4.00
❑ 2318	Hot and Still Heatin'/Crazy	1976	4.00
❑ 2323	When Morning Comes to Memphis/(B-side unknown)	1977	4.00
MEGA			
❑ 0033	I Didn't Hear a Thing/ Love Is a Job	1971	5.00
❑ 0045	Don't Bring the Rain Back Again/Tiny Praying Hands	1971	5.00
❑ 0066	Share Your Love with Me/ When My Ship Comes In	1972	5.00
❑ 0116	Honky Tonk Livin'/I'm Gonna Spend My Whole Life Lovin' You	1973	5.00
❑ 209	Walkin' My Baby Back Home/ I Slipped But I Didn't Fall	1974	4.00
❑ 1218	Poor Side of Town/Lay Down	1974	4.00
STEPHENY			
❑ 1820	Sugar Dumplin'/How Could You Lose Your Trust in Me	1958	40.00

Jay and the Techniques, "Strawberry Shortcake," Smash 2142, 1967, **$12.**

Number	Title (A Side/B Side)	Yr	NM
Albums			
HI			
❑ HL-12038 [M]	My Girl Josephine	1967	20.00
❑ SHL-32038 [S]	My Girl Josephine	1967	20.00
❑ SHL-32102	Honky Tonk Women Love Redneck Men	1976	12.00

JAYHAWKS, THE (1)

45s

Number	Title (A Side/B Side)	Yr	NM
ALADDIN			
❑ 3393	Everyone Should Know/ The Creature	1957	80.00
ARGYLE			
❑ 1005	Lonely Highway/La Macerena	1961	25.00
EASTMAN			
❑ 792	Start the Fire/I Wish the World Owed Me a Living	1958	150.00
❑ 798	New Love/Betty Brown	1958	150.00
FLASH			
❑ 105	Counting Teardrops/ The Devil's Cousin	1955	200.00
❑ 109	Stranded in the Jungle/ My Only Darling	1956	50.00
❑ 111	Love Train/Don't Mind Dyin'	1956	30.00

JAYHAWKS, THE (2) This is the alt-country group, not the '50s vocal group.

Albums

Number	Title (A Side/B Side)	Yr	NM
AMERICAN			
❑ 43006	Tomorrow the Green Grass	1995	20.00
❑ 43114	Sound of Lies	1997	20.00
BUNKHOUSE			
❑ 7001	The Jayhawks	1986	80.00
TWIN/TONE			
❑ TTR 89151	Blue Earth	1989	15.00

JAYNELLS, THE

45s

Number	Title (A Side/B Side)	Yr	NM
CAMEO			
❑ 286	I'll Stay Home New Year's Eve/ Down Home	1963	20.00
DIAMOND			
❑ 153	I'll Stay Home (New Year's Eve)/ Down Home	1963	40.00

JAYNETTS, THE

45s

Number	Title (A Side/B Side)	Yr	NM
J&S			
❑ 1177	Out Behind the Daisies/ Is It My Imagination	196?	8.00
❑ 1468/9	Chicken, Chicken, Crance or Crow/Winky Dinky	196?	8.00
❑ 1473	Peepin' In and Out the Window/ Extra, Extra, Read All About It	196?	8.00
❑ 1477	Who Stole the Cookie/ That's My Boy	196?	10.00
❑ 1686	Looking for Wonderland, My Lover/Make It an Extra	1965	8.00
❑ 1765/6	I Wanted to Be Free/Where Are You Tonight	196?	10.00
❑ 4418/9	Vangie Don't You Cry/My Guy Is As Sweet As Can Be	196?	8.00
TUFF			
❑ 369	Sally, Go 'Round the Roses/ (Instrumental)	1963	15.00
❑ 371	Keep an Eye on Her/ (Instrumental)	1963	10.00
❑ 374	Snowman, Snowman, Sweet Potato Nose/(Instrumental)	1963	15.00
❑ 377	No Love at All/Tonight You Belong to Me	1964	12.00
Albums			
TUFF			
❑ LP 13 [M]	Sally Go 'Round the Roses	1963	300.00

JAYTONES, THE

45s

BRUNSWICK

Number	Title (A Side/B Side)	Yr	NM
❑ 55087	The Clock/Gasoline	1958	120.00

CUB

Number	Title (A Side/B Side)	Yr	NM
❑ 9057	My Only Love/Absolutely Right	1960	60.00

TIMELY

Number	Title (A Side/B Side)	Yr	NM
❑ 1003/4	My Darling/The Bells	1958	1500.

JAZZ CRUSADERS, THE
See THE CRUSADERS.

JEFFERSON
Also see ROCKIN' BERRIES.

45s

DECCA

Number	Title (A Side/B Side)	Yr	NM
❑ 32501	The Colour of My Love/ Look No Further	1969	8.00

JANUS

Number	Title (A Side/B Side)	Yr	NM
❑ 106	Baby Take Me in Your Arms/ I Fell Flat on My Face	1969	8.00
❑ 117	You Know How It Is with a Woman/Are You Growing Tired of My Love	1970	8.00

Albums

JANUS

Number	Title (A Side/B Side)	Yr	NM
❑ JLS-3006	Jefferson	1969	15.00

JEFFERSON, BLIND LEMON

Albums

MILESTONE

Number	Title (A Side/B Side)	Yr	NM
❑ MLP-2004 [M]	The Immortal Blind Lemon Jefferson	1968	25.00
❑ MLP-2007 [M]	The Immortal Blind Lemon Jefferson, Vol. 2	1969	25.00
❑ MLP-2013 [M]	Black Snake Moan	1970	25.00

RIVERSIDE

Number	Title (A Side/B Side)	Yr	NM
❑ RLP 12-125 [M]	Blind Lemon Jefferson — Classic Folk Blues	1957	120.00
❑ RLP 12-136 [M]	Blind Lemon Jefferson, Vol. 2	1958	120.00
❑ 1014 [10]	The Folk Blues of Blind Lemon Jefferson	1953	250.00
❑ 1053 [10]	Penitentiary Blues	1955	250.00

JEFFERSON AIRPLANE
Also see MARTY BALIN; PAPA JOHN CREACH; HOT TUNA; JEFFERSON STARSHIP; PAUL KANTNER; JORMA KAUKONEN; GRACE SLICK.

45s

EPIC

Number	Title (A Side/B Side)	Yr	NM
❑ 73044	Summer of Love/Panda	1989	5.00

GRUNT

Number	Title (A Side/B Side)	Yr	NM
❑ 65-0500	Pretty As You Feel/Wild Turkey	1971	5.00
❑ 65-0500 [PS]	Pretty As You Feel/Wild Turkey	1971	10.00
❑ 65-0506	Long John Silver/Milk Train	1972	5.00
❑ 65-0506 [PS]	Long John Silver/Milk Train	1972	15.00
❑ 65-0511	Trial by Fire/Twilight Double Leader	1972	5.00
❑ JB-10988 [DJ]	White Rabbit (mono/stereo)	1978	30.00

—White vinyl

RCA

Number	Title (A Side/B Side)	Yr	NM
❑ 5156-7-R	White Rabbit/Plastic Fantastic Lover	1987	5.00

—White vinyl

Number	Title (A Side/B Side)	Yr	NM
❑ 5156-7-R [PS]	White Rabbit/Plastic Fantastic Lover	1987	5.00

RCA VICTOR

Number	Title (A Side/B Side)	Yr	NM
❑ 47-8769	It's No Secret/Runnin' 'Round This World	1966	15.00
❑ 47-8848	Come Up the Years/ Blues from an Airplane	1966	15.00
❑ 47-8967	Bringing Me Down/Let Me In	1966	15.00
❑ 47-9063	My Best Friend/ How Do You Feel	1967	15.00
❑ 47-9140	Somebody to Love/ She Has Funny Cars	1967	15.00
❑ 47-9248	White Rabbit/ Plastic Fantastic Lover	1967	15.00
❑ 47-9297	Ballad of You & Me & Pooneil/ Two Heads	1967	10.00
❑ 47-9389	Watch Her Ride/Martha	1967	10.00
❑ 47-9496	Greasy Heart/Share a Little Joke (With the World)	1968	8.00
❑ 47-9644	Crown of Creation/Lather	1968	8.00
❑ 47-9644 [PS]	Crown of Creation/Lather	1968	20.00
❑ 74-0150	Plastic Fantastic Lover/ Other Side of This Life	1969	6.00
❑ 74-0150 [PS]	Plastic Fantastic Lover/ Other Side of This Life	1969	20.00
❑ 74-0245	Volunteers/We Can Be Together	1969	6.00
❑ 74-0245 [PS]	Volunteers/We Can Be Together	1969	15.00
❑ 74-0343	Have You Seen the Saucers/ Mexico	1970	6.00
❑ 74-0343 [PS]	Have You Seen the Saucers/ Mexico	1970	15.00

Albums

DCC COMPACT CLASSICS

Number	Title (A Side/B Side)	Yr	NM
❑ LPZ-2033	Surrealistic Pillow	1997	75.00

—Audiophile vinyl

EPIC

Number	Title (A Side/B Side)	Yr	NM
❑ OE 45271	Jefferson Airplane	1989	15.00

GRUNT

Number	Title (A Side/B Side)	Yr	NM
❑ BFL1-0147	Thirty Seconds Over Winterland	1973	12.00
❑ APL1-0437	Early Flight	1974	12.00
❑ FTR-1001	Bark	1971	10.00

—Without brown paper bag

Number	Title (A Side/B Side)	Yr	NM
❑ FTR-1001	Bark	1971	15.00

—With brown paper bag

Number	Title (A Side/B Side)	Yr	NM
❑ FTR-1007	Long John Silver	1972	12.00
❑ CYL2-1255 [(2)]	Flight Log 1966-1976	1977	12.00
❑ AYL1-4386	Bark	1981	8.00
❑ AYL1-4391	Thirty Seconds Over Winterland	1981	8.00

MOBILE FIDELITY

Number	Title (A Side/B Side)	Yr	NM
❑ 1-148	Crown of Creation	1984	40.00

—Audiophile vinyl

PAIR

Number	Title (A Side/B Side)	Yr	NM
❑ PDL2-1090 [(2)]	Time Machine	1986	12.00

RCA

Number	Title (A Side/B Side)	Yr	NM
❑ 5724-1-R [(2)]	2400 Fulton Street: An Anthology	1987	15.00

RCA VICTOR

Number	Title (A Side/B Side)	Yr	NM
❑ APD1-0320 [Q]	Volunteers	1973	80.00

—Yellow/orange label

Number	Title (A Side/B Side)	Yr	NM
❑ APD1-0320 [Q]	Volunteers	1975	50.00

—Tan label

Number	Title (A Side/B Side)	Yr	NM
❑ LOP-1511 [M]	After Bathing at Baxter's	1967	50.00
❑ LSO-1511 [S]	After Bathing at Baxter's	1967	20.00

—Black label, dog on top

Number	Title (A Side/B Side)	Yr	NM
❑ LSO-1511 [S]	After Bathing at Baxter's	1969	12.00

—Orange label

Number	Title (A Side/B Side)	Yr	NM
❑ LSO-1511 [S]	After Bathing at Baxter's	1975	10.00

—Tan label

Number	Title (A Side/B Side)	Yr	NM
❑ LPM-3584 [M]	Jefferson Airplane Takes Off!	1966	25.00

—Version 3: No "Runnin' 'Round This World", altered lyrics to "Let Me In" ("Don't tell me it's so funny") and "Run Around" ("That sway as you stay here by me"). All later versions confirm to Version 3.

Number	Title (A Side/B Side)	Yr	NM
❑ LPM-3584 [M]	Jefferson Airplane Takes Off!	1966	1000.

—Version 2: No "Runnin' 'Round This World", but "questionable" lyrics remain in "Let Me In" ("Don't tell me you want money") and "Run Around" ("That sway as you lay under me"). Until the exact matrix numbers are known, it must be heard to confirm.

Number	Title (A Side/B Side)	Yr	NM
❑ LPM-3584 [M]	Jefferson Airplane Takes Off!	1966	3000.

—Version 1: With "Runnin' 'Round This World" as last song on side 1. Count the number of bands on Side 1 of the record; don't rely on the cover listing, as some jackets list the title when it's not on the record; VG value 1500; VG+ value 2250

Number	Title (A Side/B Side)	Yr	NM
❑ LSP-3584 [S]	Jefferson Airplane Takes Off!	1966	25.00

—Version 3: See Version 3 note under mono version

Number	Title (A Side/B Side)	Yr	NM
❑ LSP-3584 [S]	Jefferson Airplane Takes Off!	1966	1800.

—Version 2: See Version 2 note under mono version

Number	Title (A Side/B Side)	Yr	NM
❑ LSP-3584 [S]	Jefferson Airplane Takes Off!	1966	5000.

—Version 1: See Version 1 note under mono version; VG value 2000; VG+ value 3500

Number	Title (A Side/B Side)	Yr	NM
❑ LSP-3584 [S]	Jefferson Airplane Takes Off!	1969	12.00

—Orange label

Number	Title (A Side/B Side)	Yr	NM
❑ LSP-3584 [S]	Jefferson Airplane Takes Off!	1975	10.00

—Tan label

Number	Title (A Side/B Side)	Yr	NM
❑ AYL1-3661	The Worst of Jefferson Airplane	1980	8.00
❑ AYL1-3738	Surrealistic Pillow	1980	8.00
❑ AYL1-3739	Jefferson Airplane Takes Off!	1980	8.00
❑ LPM-3766 [M]	Surrealistic Pillow	1967	60.00
❑ LSP-3766 [S]	Surrealistic Pillow	1967	30.00

—Black label, dog on top

Number	Title (A Side/B Side)	Yr	NM
❑ LSP-3766 [S]	Surrealistic Pillow	1969	12.00

—Orange label

Number	Title (A Side/B Side)	Yr	NM
❑ LSP-3766 [S]	Surrealistic Pillow	1975	10.00

—Tan label

Number	Title (A Side/B Side)	Yr	NM
❑ AYL1-3797	Crown of Creation	1980	8.00
❑ AYL1-3798	Bless Its Pointed Little Head	1980	8.00
❑ AYL1-3867	Volunteers	1980	8.00
❑ LSP-4058	Crown of Creation	1968	30.00

—Black label, dog on top

Number	Title (A Side/B Side)	Yr	NM
❑ LSP-4058	Crown of Creation	1969	12.00

—Orange label

Number	Title (A Side/B Side)	Yr	NM
❑ LSP-4058	Crown of Creation	1975	10.00

—Tan label

Number	Title (A Side/B Side)	Yr	NM
❑ LSP-4133	Bless Its Pointed Little Head	1969	12.00

—Orange label

Number	Title (A Side/B Side)	Yr	NM
❑ LSP-4133	Bless Its Pointed Little Head	1975	10.00

—Tan label

Number	Title (A Side/B Side)	Yr	NM
❑ LSP-4238	Volunteers	1969	12.00

—Orange label

Number	Title (A Side/B Side)	Yr	NM
❑ LSP-4238	Volunteers	1975	10.00

—Tan label

Number	Title (A Side/B Side)	Yr	NM
❑ LSP-4459	The Worst of Jefferson Airplane	1970	12.00
❑ AFL1-4545	After Bathing at Baxter's	1981	8.00
❑ AYL1-4718	After Bathing at Baxter's	1983	8.00

SUNDAZED

Number	Title (A Side/B Side)	Yr	NM
❑ LP 5186 [M]	Jefferson Airplane Takes Off	2005	15.00

—Reissue on 180-gram vinyl

Number	Title (A Side/B Side)	Yr	NM
❑ LP 5187 [M]	After Bathing at Baxter's	2005	15.00

—Reissue on 180-gram vinyl

JEFFERSON STARSHIP
See cross-references under JEFFERSON AIRPLANE.

12-Inch Singles

GRUNT

Number	Title (A Side/B Side)	Yr	NM
❑ JD-11438 [DJ]	Light the Sky on Fire (LP Version 5:08) (3:56)	1978	15.00
❑ JD-11469 [DJ]	Light the Sky on Fire (same on both sides?)	1978	15.00
❑ JD-13409 [DJ]	Black Widow (stereo) (mono)	1982	10.00

45s

GRUNT

Number	Title (A Side/B Side)	Yr	NM
❑ FB-10080	Ride the Tiger/Devil's Den	1974	4.00
❑ FB-10206	Caroline/Be Young You	1975	4.00
❑ FB-10367	Miracles/Al Garimaso (There Is Love)	1975	5.00
❑ FB-10456	Play on Love/I Want to See Another World	1975	4.00
❑ FB-10746	With Your Love/Switchblade	1976	5.00
❑ FB-10791	St. Charles/Love Lovely Day	1976	4.00
❑ GB-10941	Miracles/With Your Love	1977	3.00

—Gold Standard Series

Number	Title (A Side/B Side)	Yr	NM
❑ FB-11196	Count on Me/Show Yourself	1978	4.00
❑ FB-11196 [PS]	Count on Me/Show Yourself	1978	5.00
❑ FB-11274	Runaway/Hot Water	1978	4.00
❑ FB-11274 [PS]	Runaway/Hot Water	1978	5.00
❑ JB-11274 [DJ]	Runaway (Long)/Runaway (Short)	1978	5.00
❑ JB-11274 [PS]	Runaway (Long)/Runaway (Short)	1978	6.00

—Promo-only sleeve (one song listed on jacket)

Number	Title (A Side/B Side)	Yr	NM
❑ FB-11374	Crazy Feelin'/Love Too Good	1978	4.00
❑ FB-11374 [PS]	Crazy Feelin'/Love Too Good	1978	5.00
❑ FB-11426	Light the Sky On Fire/Hyperdrive	1978	4.00
❑ FB-11426 [PS]	Light the Sky On Fire/Hyperdrive	1978	5.00
❑ GB-11506	Count on Me/Runaway	1979	3.00

—Gold Standard Series

Number	Title (A Side/B Side)	Yr	NM
❑ FB-11750	Jane/Freedom at Point Zero	1979	4.00
❑ FB-11750 [PS]	Jane/Freedom at Point Zero	1979	5.00
❑ FB-11921	Girl with the Hungry Eyes/ Just the Same	1980	4.00
❑ FB-11921 [PS]	Girl with the Hungry Eyes/ Just the Same	1980	5.00
❑ FB-11961	Rock Music/Lightning Rose	1980	4.00
❑ FB-12211	Find Your Way Back/ Modern Times	1981	3.00
❑ FB-12212	Mary/Modern Times	1981	—

—Unreleased

Number	Title (A Side/B Side)	Yr	NM
❑ FB-12275	Stranger/Free	1981	3.00
❑ FB-12332	Save Your Love/Wild Eyes	1981	3.00
❑ FB-13350	Be My Lady/Out of Control	1982	3.00
❑ FB-13439	Winds of Change/Black Widow	1983	3.00
❑ FB-13531	Can't Find Love/I Will Stay	1983	3.00
❑ FB-13811	No Way Out/Rose Goes to Yale	1984	3.00
❑ FB-13872	Layin' It on the Line/Showdown	1984	3.00
❑ FB-13872 [PS]	Layin' It on the Line/Showdown	1984	4.00

Albums

DCC COMPACT CLASSICS

Number	Title (A Side/B Side)	Yr	NM
❑ LPZ-2036	Red Octopus	1997	40.00

—Audiophile vinyl

GRUNT

Number	Title (A Side/B Side)	Yr	NM
❑ BFD1-0717 [Q]	Dragon Fly	1974	15.00
❑ BFL1-0717	Dragon Fly	1974	10.00
❑ BFD1-0999 [Q]	Red Octopus	1975	15.00
❑ BFL1-0999	Red Octopus	1975	10.00
❑ BFD1-1557 [Q]	Spitfire	1976	15.00
❑ BFL1-1557	Spitfire	1976	10.00
❑ BXL1-2515	Earth	1978	10.00
❑ BZL1-3247	Gold	1978	10.00
❑ DJL1-3363 [PD]	Gold	1978	15.00

—Promo-only picture disc

Number	Title (A Side/B Side)	Yr	NM
❑ BZL1-3452	Freedom at Point Zero	1979	10.00
❑ AYL1-3660	Red Octopus	1980	8.00
❑ AYL1-3796	Dragon Fly	1980	8.00
❑ BZL1-3848	Modern Times	1981	10.00
❑ AYL1-3953	Spitfire	1981	8.00
❑ AYL1-4172	Earth	1981	8.00
❑ BXL1-4372	Winds of Change	1982	10.00
❑ BXL1-4921	Nuclear Furniture	1984	10.00
❑ AYL1-5161	Freedom at Point Zero	1984	8.00

JEFFREY, JOE, GROUP

45s

WAND

Number	Title (A Side/B Side)	Yr	NM
❑ 11200	My Pledge of Love/Margie	1969	8.00
❑ 11207	The Train/Dreamin' Till Then	1969	6.00
❑ 11213	Chance of Loving You/ Hey Hey Woman	1969	6.00
❑ 11219	My Baby Loves Lovin'/ Chance of Loving You	1970	6.00
❑ 11235	A Hundred Pounds of Clay/ Power of Love	1971	6.00

Albums

WAND

Number	Title (A Side/B Side)	Yr	NM
❑ WDS-686	My Pledge of Love	1969	30.00

Except when noted otherwise, VG = 25% of NM, and VG+ = 50% of NM. (Example: VG = $2.00, VG+ = $4.00 and NM = $8.00.)

JEFFREYS, GARLAND

Number	Title (A Side/B Side)	Yr	NM
12-Inch Singles			
EPIC			
❑ AS 962 [DJ]	Modern Lovers/R.O.C.K./Ghost of a Chance	1981	10.00
RCA			
❑ 62175	Hail Hail Rock 'N' Roll (5 versions)	1992	8.00
❑ 62295	The Answer (6 versions)	1992	10.00
45s			
A&M			
❑ 1934	Wild in the Streets/Ghost Writer	1977	4.00
❑ 1952	New York Skyline/Cool Down Boy	1977	4.00
❑ 2030	One-Eyed Jack/Reelin'	1978	4.00
❑ 2074	She Didn't Lie/Scream in the Night	1979	4.00
❑ 2178	American Boy and Girl/Livin' for Me	1979	4.00
❑ 2244	American Boy and Girl/Matador	1980	4.00
ARISTA			
❑ 0119	The Disco Kid Part 1/The Disco Kid Part 2	1975	5.00
ATLANTIC			
❑ 2948	She Didn't Lie/Lon Chaney	1973	5.00
❑ 2981	Wild in the Streets/Lon Chaney	1973	5.00
EPIC			
❑ AE7 1225 [DJ]	Interview with Garland Jeffreys	1981	8.00
❑ AE7 1225 [PS]	Interview with Garland Jeffreys	1981	8.00
❑ 02073	Modern Lovers/Spanish Manners	1981	3.00
❑ 02173	R.O.C.K./Miami Beach	1981	3.00
❑ 03189	Surrender/Rebel Love	1982	3.00
❑ 03687	Rebel Love/What Does It Take (To Win Your Love)	1983	3.00
❑ 51008	96 Tears/Escape Goat Dab	1981	3.00
7-Inch Extended Plays			
EPIC			
❑ AE7 1223 [DJ]	(contents unknown)	1981	8.00
❑ AE7 1223 [PS]	Escapades	1981	8.00
Albums			
A&M			
❑ SP-4629	Ghost Writer	1977	12.00
❑ SP-4681	One-Eyed Jack	1978	10.00
❑ SP-4778	American Boy and Girl	1979	10.00
ATLANTIC			
❑ SD 7253	Garland Jeffreys	1973	15.00
EPIC			
❑ PE 36983	Escape Artist	1981	10.00
❑ FE 37436	Rock 'N' Roll Adult	1981	10.00
❑ ARE 38190	Guts for Love	1983	10.00

JEFFRIES, HERB

Number	Title (A Side/B Side)	Yr	NM
45s			
ALGER			
❑ 85	Los Angeles 1/Los Angeles 2	1983	5.00
❑ 85 [PS]	Los Angeles 1/Los Angeles 2	1983	5.00
COLUMBIA			
❑ 1-138 (?)	Girls Were Made to Take Care of Boys/Bewildered	1949	30.00
—Microgroove 33 1/3 rpm 7-inch single, small hole			
❑ 1-140 (?)	It's Easy to Remember/A Dreamer with a Penny	1949	30.00
—Microgroove 33 1/3 rpm 7-inch single, small hole			
❑ 1-256	The Four Winds and the Seven Seas/Never Be It Said	1949	30.00
—Microgroove 33 1/3 rpm 7-inch single, small hole			
❑ 1-287	Pagan Love Song/Twilight	1949	40.00
—Microgroove 33 1/3 rpm 7-inch single, small hole			
❑ 1-399 (?)	A Man Wrote a Song/The Shepherd	1949	30.00
—Microgroove 33 1/3 rpm 7-inch single, small hole			
❑ 1-430	Sunday Isn't Sunday Anymore/Flamingo Sand	1950	30.00
—Microgroove 33 1/3 rpm 7-inch single, small hole			
❑ 1-488 (?)	Just for Old Times/Monday. Tuesday, Wednesday	1950	30.00
—Microgroove 33 1/3 rpm 7-inch single, small hole			
❑ 1-555 (?)	Count Every Star/Our Love Story	1950	30.00
—Microgroove 33 1/3 rpm 7-inch single, small hole			
❑ 1-561 (?)	The Flying Dutchman/Baby, Won't You Say You Love Me	1950	30.00
—Microgroove 33 1/3 rpm 7-inch single, small hole			
❑ 1-589 (?)	There Goes My Heart/Swamp Girl	1950	30.00
—Microgroove 33 1/3 rpm 7-inch single, small hole			
❑ 1-672 (?)	My Mother Singing/Dancing with You	1950	30.00
—Microgroove 33 1/3 rpm 7-inch single, small hole			
❑ 1-748 (?)	If I Should Lose You/Love Me Long	1950	30.00
—Microgroove 33 1/3 rpm 7-inch single, small hole			
❑ 1-820 (?)	Wanderlust/Manon	1950	30.00
—Microgroove 33 1/3 rpm 7-inch single, small hole			
❑ 6-820 (?)	Wanderlust/Manon	1950	20.00
CORAL			
❑ 9-60403	Was It a Dream/You Know You Belong to Somebody Else	1951	15.00
❑ 9-60425	I'm Yours to Command/Love Me	1951	15.00
❑ 9-60456	A Beggar in Love/I'll Never Know Why	1951	15.00
❑ 9-60478	Old Soldiers Never Die/Unless	1951	15.00
❑ 9-60505	Wonder Why/Dark Is the Night	1951	15.00
❑ 9-60527	All Alone/Time on My Hands	1951	12.00
❑ 9-60528	All By Myself/I Didn't Know What Time It Was	1951	12.00
❑ 9-60529	Just a Memory/Among My Souvenirs	1951	12.00
❑ 9-60530	As Time Goes By/Once In Awhile	1951	12.00
—The above four comprise a box set			
❑ 9-60552	A Fool Grows Wise/Love Comes Along	1951	15.00
HERB JEFFRIES			
❑ RRE-101	The Conqueror (The Mightiest of Them All)/The Heart of a Woman	196?	10.00
MGM			
❑ K12767	A Picture No Artist Can Paint/Buenas Noches, Mi Amor	1959	10.00
RCA VICTOR			
❑ 47-6950	Mailman, Bring Me No More Blues/So Shy	1957	15.00
❑ 47-7008	Sing to Me/Sweet Leilani	1957	12.00
Albums			
BETHLEHEM			
❑ BCP-72 [M]	Say It Isn't So	1957	60.00
CORAL			
❑ CRL 56044 [10]	Time on My Hands	1951	100.00
❑ CRL 56066 [10]	Herb Jeffries Sings Flamingo and Other Songs in a Mellow Mood	1952	120.00
DOBRE			
❑ DR-1047	I Remember the Bing	1978	15.00
GOLDEN TONE			
❑ C-4066 [M]	The Devil Is a Woman	196?	12.00
❑ 14066 [S]	The Devil Is a Woman	196?	12.00
HARMONY			
❑ HL 7048 [M]	Herb Jeffries	195?	15.00
MERCURY			
❑ MG-25089 [10]	Magenta Moods	1950	100.00
❑ MG-25090 [10]	Herb Jeffries Sings	1950	100.00
❑ MG-25091 [10]	Just Jeffries	1950	100.00
RCA VICTOR			
❑ LPM-1608 [M]	Senor Flamingo	1957	40.00
RKO UNIQUE			
❑ ULP-128 [M]	Jamaica	1956	30.00

JELLY BEAN BANDITS, THE

Number	Title (A Side/B Side)	Yr	NM
45s			
MAINSTREAM			
❑ 674	Country Woman/Generation	1967	30.00
Albums			
MAINSTREAM			
❑ S-6103 [S]	The Jelly Bean Bandits	1967	150.00
❑ 56103 [M]	The Jelly Bean Bandits	1967	100.00

JELLY BEANS, THE

Number	Title (A Side/B Side)	Yr	NM
45s			
ESKEE			
❑ 001	I'm Hip to You/You Don't Mean No Good to Me	1965	200.00
RED BIRD			
❑ 10-003	I Wanna Love Him So Bad/So Long	1964	20.00
❑ 10-011	The Kind of Boy You Can't Forget/Baby Be Mine	1964	20.00

JELLYBREAD

Number	Title (A Side/B Side)	Yr	NM
Albums			
BLUE HORIZON			
❑ BH-4801	First Slice	1970	50.00

JENKINS, FLORENCE FOSTER

One of the worst singers ever to be recorded — and unlike MRS. MILLER, Jenkins sang arias!

Number	Title (A Side/B Side)	Yr	NM
Albums			
RCA VICTOR			
❑ LM-2597 [M]	The Glory (????) of the Human Voice	1961	20.00
❑ LRT-7001 [10]	A Florence! Foster!! Jenkins!!! Recital!!!!	195?	50.00

JENKINS, GORDON

Only includes records on which Gordon Jenkins has the sole or primary credit. Also see THE WEAVERS.

Number	Title (A Side/B Side)	Yr	NM
45s			
CAPITOL			
❑ F1263	White Christmas/I'm Always Chasing Rainbows	1950	15.00
❑ F3556	Married I Can Always Get/Repeat After Me	1956	12.00
❑ F3751	Theme from Saint Joan/Fire Down Below	1957	12.00
COLUMBIA			
❑ 4-42608	I Left My Heart in San Francisco/This Is All I Ask	1962	10.00
❑ 4-42981	Blues for Beverly/I'm Forever Blowing Bubbles	1963	10.00
DECCA			
❑ 9-24403	Maybe You'll Be There/Dark Eyes	1950	20.00
—78 originally issued in 1948 with the same number			
❑ 9-24478	For You/On the Painted Desert	1950	20.00
❑ 9-24523	Temptation/My Funny Valentine	1950	20.00
—78 originally issued in 1948			
❑ 9-24602	Again/Skip to My Lou	1950	20.00
—78 originally issued in 1949			
❑ 9-24830	My Foolish Heart/Don't Do Something to Someone Else (That You Wouldn't Want Done to You)	1950	20.00
❑ 9-24983	Bewitched/Where in the World	1950	20.00
❑ 9-27031	Santa Catalina/Blue Sails	1950	20.00
❑ 9-27165	The Way You Look Tonight/Long Ago (And Far Away)	1950	15.00
❑ 9-27166	Smoke Gets In Your Eyes/Yesterdays	1950	15.00
❑ 9-27167	They Didn't Believe Me/Till the Clouds Roll By	1950	15.00
❑ 9-27168	All the Things You Are/The Touch of Your Hand	1950	15.00
❑ 9-27169	Blue Prelude/You Have Taken My Heart	1950	15.00
❑ 9-27170	With You So Far Away/When a Woman Loves a Man	1950	15.00
❑ 9-27171	P.S. I Love You/Homesick, That's All	1950	15.00
❑ 9-27172	Blue Evening/Goodbye	1950	15.00
❑ 9-27319	It's a Lovely Day/Just in Love//The Ocarina	1950	20.00
❑ 9-27358	They Like Ike/Lichtenburg	1951	20.00
❑ 9-27394	More Than I Care to Remember/I Wish Someone Knew	1951	20.00
❑ 9-27433	Sally Doesn't Care/More Than I Care to Remember	1951	20.00
❑ 9-27490	I Love You Much Too Much/Would I Love You	1951	20.00
❑ 9-27585	Whsipering/Song of the Bayou	1951	20.00
❑ 9-27594	Rose, Rose, I Love You/Unless	1951	20.00
❑ 9-27681	Tell the Truth/I Wish Someone Knew I Was Lonesome	1951	20.00
❑ 9-27859	Charmaine/When a Man Is Free	1951	15.00
❑ 9-27886	Charmaine/When I Grow Too Old to Dream	1951	15.00
❑ 9-27912	Anna Maria/Somebody	1951	15.00
❑ 9-27933	Mother, Mother/Every Hour	1952	15.00
❑ 9-28148	If They Ask Me/It Only Takes a Moment	1952	15.00
❑ 9-28450	Leave Me Just a Little Bit of Love/I'll Know My Love	1952	15.00
❑ 9-28580	Are You Teasing Me?/Midnight	1953	15.00
❑ 9-28612	The Ties That Bind/Gomen Nasai	1953	15.00
❑ 9-28632	Daniel in the Lions' Den/The Masquerade Is Over	1953	15.00
❑ 9-28657	One Wild Oat/When They Speak of You	1953	15.00
❑ 9-28750	P.S. I Love You/I Thought About Marie	1953	15.00
❑ 9-28876	Secret Love/Theme from "Seven Dreams"	1953	15.00
❑ 9-29244	In an Inn in Indiana/Slowly But Surely	1954	12.00
❑ 9-29365	My Own True Love (Tara's Theme)/Vera Cruz	1954	12.00
❑ 9-29562	I Love You So/My Love Came Back to Me	1955	12.00
❑ 9-29879	Angel's Lullaby — Mama Darling/Through the Night	1956	12.00
KAPP			
❑ 326	Clock Song/Romantica	1960	10.00
❑ 339	April Moon-Lover's Moon/If She Should Come to You	1960	10.00
❑ 572	Ciumachella (Tender Flower)/What Can I Say Afer I Say I'm Sorry	1964	8.00
TIME			
❑ 1049	Theme from Lolita/Hava Nagila	1962	10.00
❑ 1051	I Wish You Love/Fascination	1962	10.00

Number	Title (A Side/B Side)	Yr	NM
VIK			
❑ 0190	How Do I Love You?/You're Not Alone	1956	12.00
"X"			
❑ 0097	My Own/Tired of Waiting	1955	12.00
❑ 0127	Theme for Lovers/Last Love	1955	12.00
❑ 0159	Goodnight, Sweet Dreams/Young Ideas	1955	12.00
❑ 0175	Follow Me, Baby/Wish I Could Say the Same	1955	12.00
7-Inch Extended Plays			
CAPITOL			
❑ EAP 1-766	Magical City//New York's My Home/Closing	195?	10.00
❑ EAP 2-766	Happiness Cocktail//The Statue of Liberty/The Party	195?	10.00
❑ EAP 3-766	Once Upon a Dream//Never Leave Me//Married I Can Always Get	195?	10.00
❑ EAP 4-766	This Close to the Dawn/Repeat After Me//The Magic Fire	195?	10.00
❑ EDM 766 [PS]	Gordon Jenkins' Complete Manhattan Tower	195?	12.00
—Box for above 4 records (no separate cardboard sleeves)			
DECCA			
❑ ED 2005	*Bewitched/Charmaine//Don't Cry Joe/Perhaps, Perhaps, Perhaps	195?	10.00
❑ ED 2005 [PS]	Gordon Jenkins and His Chorus and Orchestra, Vol. 1	195?	10.00
Albums			
BAINBRIDGE			
❑ BT-1022 [S]	Soul of a People	1980	10.00
CAPITOL			
❑ DT 766 [R]	The Complete Manhattan Tower	196?	12.00
❑ T 766 [M]	The Complete Manhattan Tower	1956	30.00
—Turquoise label			
❑ T 781 [M]	Night Dreams	1956	30.00
—Turquoise label			
❑ ST 884 [S]	Stolen Hours	1959	30.00
❑ T 884 [M]	Stolen Hours	1956	30.00
—Turquoise label			
❑ T 1023 [M]	Dream Dust	1958	25.00
❑ ST 1048 [S]	Tropicana Holiday	1958	30.00
❑ T 1048 [M]	Tropicana Holiday	1958	25.00
COLUMBIA			
❑ CL 1764 [M]	Hawaiian Wedding Songs	1962	12.00
❑ CL 1882 [M]	The Magic World of Gordon Jenkins	1962	12.00
❑ CL 2009 [M]	In a Tender Mood	1963	12.00
❑ CS 8564 [S]	Hawaiian Wedding Songs	1962	15.00
❑ CS 8682 [S]	The Magic World of Gordon Jenkins	1962	15.00
❑ CS 8809 [S]	In a Tender Mood	1963	15.00
DECCA			
❑ DL 4714 [M]	My Heart Sings	1966	12.00
❑ DL 5275 [10]	Playing His Compositions	195?	40.00
❑ DL 5307 [10]	For You	195?	40.00
❑ DL 5469 [10]	Me and Juliet/Can-Can	1953	40.00
❑ DL 8011 [M]	Manhattan Tower/California (The Golden State)	1951	30.00
—Black label, gold print			
❑ DL 8077 [M]	In the Still of the Night	195?	25.00
❑ DL 8109 [M]	P.S. I Love You	195?	25.00
❑ DL 8116 [M]	Heartbeats	195?	25.00
❑ DL 8313 [M]	He Likes to Go Dancing: Music for the Boy Friend	195?	25.00
❑ DL 74714 [S]	My Heart Sings	1966	15.00
❑ DL 78011 [R]	Manhattan Tower/California (The Golden State)	196?	12.00
DOT			
❑ DLP-3752 [M]	Soft Soul	1966	12.00
❑ DLP-25752 [S]	Soft Soul	1966	15.00
GWP			
❑ 2035	Way Back Now	1971	10.00
KAPP			
❑ KL 1361 [M]	I Live Alone	196?	12.00
❑ KS 3361 [S]	I Live Alone	196?	15.00
MAINSTREAM			
❑ S-6093 [S]	Soul of a People	196?	12.00
—Reissue of Time S-2050			
❑ 56093 [M]	Soul of a People	196?	10.00
—Reissue of Time 52050			
MCA			
❑ 166	Manhattan Tower/California (The Golden State)	1973	10.00
—Black label with rainbow			
MCA CORAL			
❑ CB-20030	Romance	1973	10.00
PICKWICK			
❑ PC-3005 [M]	Yours — The Magic of Gordon Jenkins	196?	12.00
❑ SPC-3005 [S]	Yours — The Magic of Gordon Jenkins	196?	12.00
SEARS			
❑ SPS-403 [S]	The Romantic Moods of Gordon Jenkins	196?	15.00
SUNSET			
❑ SUM-1149 [M]	Blue Prelude	196?	15.00
❑ SUS-5149 [S]	Blue Prelude	196?	12.00
TIME			
❑ S-2050 [S]	Soul of a People	196?	15.00
❑ S-2061 [S]	France	196?	15.00
❑ S-2130 [S]	Paris, I Wish You Love	196?	15.00
❑ 52050 [M]	Soul of a People	196?	12.00
❑ 52061 [M]	France	196?	12.00
❑ 52130 [M]	Paris, I Wish You Love	196?	12.00
VEE JAY			
❑ VJLP-1089 [M]	The Great Movie Themes of the 30s, 40s and 50s	1964	12.00
❑ VJLPS-1089 [S]	The Great Movie Themes of the 30s, 40s and 50s	1964	20.00
VOCALION			
❑ VL 3615 [M]	Dreamer's Holiday	196?	15.00
WARNER BROS.			
❑ W 1464 [M]	Let's Duet	1963	12.00
❑ WS 1464 [S]	Let's Duet	1963	15.00

JENKINS, NORMA See THE DOLLS.

JENNIFER See JENNIFER WARNES.

JENNINGS, WAYLON Also see JOHNNY CASH; WAYLON AND JESSI; WAYLON AND WILLIE.

Number	Title (A Side/B Side)	Yr	NM
12-Inch Singles			
RCA			
❑ WJ-01 [DJ]	Don't You Think This Outlaw Bit's Done Got Out of Hand/Medley of Buddy Holly Hits	1979	15.00
❑ WJ-0283 [DJ]	Medley of Hits (7:14) (same on both sides)	1983	15.00
45s			
A&M			
❑ 722	Rave On/Love, Denise	1963	20.00
❑ 739	Four Strong Winds/Just to Satisfy You	1964	15.00
❑ 753	The Race Is On/Sing the Girls a Song	1964	15.00
ARK 21			
❑ S7-58711	I Know About Me, Don't Know About You/Closing In on the Fire	1998	3.00
BAT			
❑ 121636	White Lightning/(B-side unknown)	1962	50.00
❑ 121639	Dream Baby/Crying	1962	40.00
BRUNSWICK			
❑ 55130	Jole Blon/When Sin Stops	1959	300.00
COLUMBIA			
❑ 04881	Highwayman/The Human Condition	1985	3.00
—A-side: Willie Nelson/Waylon Jennings/Johnny Cash/Kris Kristofferson; B-side: Nelson, Cash			
❑ 04881 [PS]	Highwayman/The Human Condition	1985	4.00
—A-side: Willie Nelson/Waylon Jennings/Johnny Cash/Kris Kristofferson; B-side: Nelson, Cash			
❑ 05594	Desperadoes Waiting for a Train/The Twentieth Century Is Almost Over	1985	3.00
—A-side: Willie Nelson/Waylon Jennings/Johnny Cash/Kris Kristofferson; B-side: Nelson, Cash			
❑ 08406	Highwayman/Desperadoes Waiting for a Train	1988	3.00
—Waylon Jennings/Willie Nelson/Johnny Cash/Kris Kristofferson; reissue			
❑ 73233	Silver Stallion/America Remains	1990	3.00
—Waylon Jennings/Willie Nelson/Johnny Cash/Kris Kristofferson			
❑ 73381	Born and Raised in Black and White/Texas	1990	3.00
—The Highwaymen (Waylon Jennings/Willie Nelson/Johnny Cash/Kris Kristofferson)			
❑ 73572	American Remains/Texas	1990	3.00
—The Highwaymen (Waylon Jennings/Willie Nelson/Johnny Cash/Kris Kristofferson)			
EPIC			
❑ 73352	Wrong/Waking Up with You	1990	3.00
❑ 73519	Where Corn Don't Grow/Waking Up with You	1990	3.00
❑ 73647	What Bothers Me Most/Wrong	1990	3.00
❑ 73718	The Eagle/What Bothers Me Most	1991	3.00
❑ 74403	Just Talkin'/I've Got My Faults	1992	3.00
❑ 74705	Too Dumb for New York City, Too Smart for L.A./I've Got My Faults	1992	3.00
LIBERTY			
❑ S7-18486	It Is What It Is/The Devil's Right Hand	1995	3.00
—By The Highwaymen			
MCA			
❑ 52776	Working Without a Net/They Ain't Got 'Em All	1986	3.00
❑ 52830	Will the Wolf Survive/I've Got Me a Woman	1986	3.00
❑ 52915	What You'll Do When I'm Gone/That Dog Won't Hurt	1986	3.00
❑ 53009	Rose in Paradise/Crying Don't Even Come Close	1987	3.00
❑ 53088	Fallin' Out/Deep in the West	1987	3.00
❑ 53158	My Rough and Rowdy Days/Love Song (I Can't Sing Anymore)	1987	3.00
❑ 53243	If Ole Hank Could Only See Us Now (Chapter Five...Nashville)/You Went Out with Rock 'n' Roll	1988	3.00
❑ 53314	How Much Is It Worth to Live in L.A./G.I. Joe	1988	3.00
❑ 53476	Which Way Do I Go (Now That I'm Gone)/Hey Willie	1988	3.00
❑ 53634	Trouble Man/Yoyos, Bozos, Bimbos and Heroes	1989	3.00
❑ 53710	You Put the Soul in the Song/Woman I Hate It	1989	3.00
RAMCO			
❑ 1997	My World/Another Blue Day	1968	12.00
RCA			
❑ 5034-7-R	The Broken Promise Land/I Don't Have Any More Love Songs	1986	4.00
❑ PB-10842	Are You Ready for the Country/So Good Woman	1976	5.00
❑ PB-10924	Luckenbach, Texas (Back to the Basics of Love)/Belle of the Ball	1977	5.00
❑ GB-10927	Dreaming My Dreams with You/Can't You See	1977	3.00
—Gold Standard Series			
❑ PB-11118	The Wurlitzer Prize (I Don't Want to Get Over You)/Lookin' for a Feeling	1977	5.00
❑ PB-11344	I've Always Been Crazy/I Never Said It Would Be Easy	1978	4.00
❑ PB-11390	Don't You Think This Outlaw Bit's Done Got Out of Hand/Girl I Can Tell (You're Trying to Work It Out)	1978	4.00
❑ GB-11500	Are You Ready for the Country/The Wurlitzer Prize (I Don't Want to Get Over You)	1978	3.00
—Gold Standard Series			
❑ PB-11596	Amanda/Lonesome, On'ry and Mean	1979	4.00
❑ PB-11596 [PS]	Amanda/Lonesome, On'ry and Mean	1979	5.00
❑ PB-11723	Come with Me/Mes'kin	1979	4.00
❑ GB-11757	Luckenbach, Texas (Back to the Basics of Love)/Belle of the Ball	1979	3.00
—Gold Standard Series			
❑ PB-11898	I Ain't Living Long Like This/The World's Crazy	1979	4.00
❑ GB-11991	I've Always Been Crazy/Don't You Think This Outlaw Bit's Done Got Out of Hand	1980	3.00
—Gold Standard Series			
❑ PB-12007	Clyde/I Came Here to Party	1980	4.00
❑ PB-12067	Theme from "The Dukes of Hazzard" (Good Ol' Boys)/It's Alright	1980	4.00
❑ PB-12067 [PS]	Theme from "The Dukes of Hazzard" (Good Ol' Boys)/It's Alright	1980	5.00
❑ GB-12187	Theme from "The Dukes of Hazzard" (Good Ol' Boys)/Come with Me	1981	3.00
—Gold Standard Series			
❑ GB-12313	Amanda/I Ain't Living Long Like This	1981	3.00
—"Gold Standard Series" reissue			
❑ PB-12367	Shine/White Water	1981	4.00
❑ PB-13257	Women Do Know How to Carry On/Honky Tonk Blues	1982	4.00
❑ PB-13465	Lucille (You Won't Do Your Daddy's Will)/Medley of Hits	1983	4.00
❑ PB-13543	Breakin' Down/Livin' Legends (A Dyin' Breed)	1983	4.00
❑ PB-13631	The Conversation/Fancy Free	1983	4.00
—A-side with Hank Williams, Jr.			
❑ PB-13729	I May Be Used (But Baby I Ain't Used Up)/So You Want to Be a Cowboy Singer	1984	4.00
❑ PB-13827	Never Could Toe the Mark/Talk Good Boogie	1984	4.00

Except when noted otherwise, VG = 25% of NM, and VG+ = 50% of NM. (Example: VG = $2.00, VG+ = $4.00 and NM = $8.00.)

Number	Title (A Side/B Side)	Yr	NM
❑ PB-13903	Silent Night, Holy Night/Precious Memories	1984	4.00
—A-side with Jessi Colter			
❑ PB-13908	America/People Up in Texas	1984	4.00
❑ PB-13984	Waltz Me to Heaven/Dream On	1984	4.00
❑ PB-14094	Drinkin' and Dreamin'/Prophets Show Up in Strange Places	1985	4.00
❑ PB-14215	The Devil's on the Loose/Good Morning John	1985	4.00
❑ PB-14291	Sweet Mother Texas/Hanging On	1985	4.00
RCA VICTOR			
❑ 47-8572	That's the Chance I'll Have to Take/I Wonder Just Where I Went Wrong	1965	10.00
❑ 47-8652	Stop the World (And Let Me Off)/The Dark Side of Fame	1965	10.00
❑ 47-8729	Anita, You're Dreaming/Look Into My Teardrops	1965	10.00
❑ 47-8822	Time to Bum Again/Norwegian Wood	1966	10.00
❑ 47-8917	(That's What You Get) For Lovin' Me/Time Will Tell the Story	1966	10.00
❑ 47-9025	Green River/Silver Ribbons	1966	10.00
❑ 47-9146	Mental Revenge/Born to Love You	1967	10.00
❑ 47-9259	The Chokin' Kind/Love of the Common People	1967	10.00
❑ 47-9414	Walk On Out of My Mind/Julie	1967	10.00
❑ 47-9480	I Got You/No One's Gonna Miss Me	1968	10.00
—A-side with Anita Carter			
❑ 47-9561	Only Daddy That'll Walk the Line/Right Before My Eyes	1968	10.00
❑ 47-9642	Yours Love/Six Strings Away	1968	10.00
❑ 47-9819	Singer of Sad Songs/Lila	1970	8.00
❑ 47-9885	The Taker/Shadows of the Gallows	1970	8.00
❑ 47-9925	(Don't Let the Sun Set on You) Tulsa/You'll Look for Me	1970	8.00
❑ 47-9967	Mississippi Woman/Life Goes On	1971	8.00
❑ 48-1003	Cedartown, Georgia/I Think It's Time She Learned	1971	8.00
❑ 74-0105	Something's Wrong in California/Farewell Party	1969	8.00
❑ 74-0157	The Days of Sand and Shovels/Delia's Gone	1969	8.00
❑ 74-0210	MacArthur Park/But You Know I Love You	1969	8.00
❑ 74-0281	Brown Eyed Handsome Man/Sorrow (Breaks a Good Man Down)	1969	8.00
❑ 74-0615	Good Hearted Woman/It's All Over Now	1971	8.00
❑ 74-0716	Sweet Dream Woman/Sure Didn't Take Him Long	1972	8.00
❑ 74-0808	Pretend I Never Happened/Nothin' Worth Takin' or Leavin'	1972	8.00
❑ 74-0886	You Can Have Her/Gone to Denver	1973	8.00
❑ 74-0961	We Had It All/Do No Good Woman	1973	8.00
❑ APBO-0086	You Asked Me To/Willy, the Wandering Gypsy and Me	1973	8.00
❑ AMAO-0122	MacArthur Park/The Taker	1973	5.00
❑ APBO-0251	This Time/Mona	1974	6.00
❑ PB-10020	I'm a Ramblin' Man/Got a Lot Going for Me	1974	6.00
❑ PB-10142	Rainy Day Woman/Let's All Help the Cowboys (Sing the Blues)	1974	6.00
❑ GB-10169	This Time/You Asked Me To	1975	4.00
—Gold Standard Series			
❑ PB-10270	Dreaming My Dreams with You/Waymore's Blues	1975	6.00
❑ PB-10379	Are You Sure Hank Done It This Way/Bob Wills Is Still the King	1975	6.00
❑ GB-10498	I'm a Ramblin' Man/Got a Lot Going for Me	1975	4.00
—Gold Standard Series			
❑ GB-10499	Rainy Day Woman/Let's All Help the Cowboys (Sing the Blues)	1975	4.00
—Gold Standard Series			
❑ GB-10673	Are You Sure Hank Done It This Way/Bob Wills Is Still the King	1976	4.00
—Gold Standard Series			
❑ PB-10721	Can't You See/I'll Go Back to Her	1976	5.00
TREND			
❑ 102	Another Blue Day/Never Again	1962	30.00
❑ 106	The Stage/My Baby Walks All Over Me	1963	100.00
Albums			
A&M			
❑ SP-4238	Don't Think Twice	1969	40.00
BAT			
❑ 1001 [M]	Waylon Jennings at JD's	1964	700.00
—Approximately 500 copies pressed			
COLUMBIA			
❑ 1P-8030	The Eagle	1990	25.00
—Vinyl released only through Columbia House			
❑ FC 40056	Highwayman	1985	10.00
—Waylon Jennings/Willie Nelson/Johnny Cash/Kris Kristofferson			
❑ C 45240	Highwayman 2	1990	15.00
—Waylon Jennings/Willie Nelson/Johnny Cash/Kris Kristofferson			
MCA			
❑ 731	Waylon Jennings	198?	12.00
—Reissue of Vocalion LP			
❑ 5688	Will the Wolf Survive	1986	10.00
❑ 5911	Hangin' Tough	1987	10.00
❑ 42038	A Man Called Hoss	1987	10.00
❑ 42038 [DJ]	A Man Called Hoss	1987	60.00
—Promo-only edition with letter and 48-page book			
❑ 42222	Full Circle	1988	10.00
❑ 42287	New Classic Waylon	1989	10.00
MCA CORAL			
❑ VL 73873	Waylon Jennings	197?	12.00
—Reissue of Vocalion 73873; cover still says "Vocalion" but label is "MCA Coral"			
PAIR			
❑ PDL1-1005 [(2)]	Waylon!	1986	12.00
❑ PDL1-1033 [(2)]	A Couple More Years	1986	12.00
❑ PDL1-1110 [(2)]	Honly Tonk Hero	1986	12.00
PICKWICK			
❑ ACL-0306	Only Daddy That'll Walk the Line	197?	8.00
—Reissue of RCA Camden LP			
❑ CAS-2556	Heartaches by the Number	197?	8.00
—Reissue of RCA Camden CAS-2556			
❑ ACL-7019 [S]	The Dark Side of Fame	1976	10.00
—Reissue of RCA Camden CAS-2183			
RCA			
❑ 5620-1-RB	The Best of Waylon	1987	10.00
❑ 9561-1-R	The Early Years (1965-1969)	1989	10.00
RCA CAMDEN			
❑ ACL1-0306	Only Daddy That'll Walk the Line	1973	10.00
❑ CAL-2183 [M]	The One and Only Waylon Jennings	1967	15.00
❑ CAS-2183 [S]	The One and Only Waylon Jennings	1967	12.00
❑ CAS-2556	Heartaches by the Number	1972	12.00
❑ CAS-2608	Ruby, Don't Take Your Love to Town	1972	12.00
RCA VICTOR			
❑ APL1-0240	Honky Tonk Heroes	1973	15.00
❑ APL1-0539	This Time	1974	12.00
❑ AFL1-0734	The Ramblin' Man	197?	10.00
—Reissue with new prefix			
❑ APL1-0734	The Ramblin' Man	1974	12.00
—Original issue; tan label			
❑ APL1-1062	Dreaming My Dreams	1975	10.00
❑ APL1-1108	Waylon Live	1976	10.00
❑ AFL1-1816	Are You Ready for the Country	1977	8.00
—Black label, dog near side; new prefix			
❑ APL1-1816	Are You Ready for the Country	1976	10.00
❑ AAL1-2317	Ol' Waylon	198?	8.00
—Reissue			
❑ APL1-2317	Ol' Waylon	1977	10.00
❑ AFL1-2979	I've Always Been Crazy	1978	10.00
❑ AHL1-3378	Greatest Hits	1979	10.00
❑ AHL1-3493	What Goes Around Comes Around	1979	10.00
❑ LPM-3523 [M]	Folk-Country	1966	30.00
❑ LSP-3523 [S]	Folk-Country	1966	40.00
❑ AHL1-3602	Music Man	1980	10.00
❑ LPM-3620 [M]	Leavin' Town	1966	30.00
❑ LSP-3620 [S]	Leavin' Town	1966	40.00
❑ LPM-3660 [M]	Waylon Sings Ol' Harlan	1967	30.00
❑ LSP-3660 [S]	Waylon Sings Ol' Harlan	1967	40.00
❑ AYL1-3663	Are You Ready for the Country	1980	8.00
—Budget-line reissue			
❑ LPM-3736 [M]	Nashville Rebel	1967	40.00
❑ LSP-3736 [S]	Nashville Rebel	1967	50.00
❑ LPM-3825 [M]	Love of the Common People	1967	30.00
❑ LSP-3825 [S]	Love of the Common People	1967	25.00
❑ AYL1-3897	Honky Tonk Heroes	1980	8.00
—Budget-line reissue			
❑ LPM-3918 [M]	Hangin' On	1968	100.00
❑ LSP-3918 [S]	Hangin' On	1968	25.00
❑ LPM-4023 [M]	Only the Greatest	1968	150.00
❑ LSP-4023 [S]	Only the Greatest	1968	25.00
❑ AYL1-4072	Dreaming My Dreams	1981	8.00
—Budget-line reissue			
❑ AYL1-4073	The Ramblin' Man	1981	8.00
—Budget-line reissue			
❑ LSP-4085	Jewels	1968	25.00
❑ LSP-4137	Just to Satisfy You	1969	25.00
❑ AYL1-4163	Waylon Live	1981	8.00
—Budget-line reissue			
❑ AYL1-4164	I've Always Been Crazy	1981	8.00
—Budget-line reissue			
❑ LSP-4180	Country-Folk	1969	25.00
❑ AHL1-4247	Black On Black	1982	10.00
❑ AYL1-4250	Music Man	1982	8.00
—Budget-line reissue			
❑ LSP-4260	Waylon	1970	20.00
❑ LSP-4341	The Best of Waylon Jennings	1970	20.00
❑ LSP-4418	Singer of Sad Songs	1970	20.00
❑ LSP-4487	The Taker/Tulsa	1971	20.00
❑ LSP-4567	Cedartown, Georgia	1971	20.00
❑ LSP-4647	Good Hearted Woman	1972	20.00
❑ AHL1-4673	It's Only Rock & Roll	1983	10.00
❑ LSP-4751	Ladies Love Outlaws	1972	20.00
❑ AHL1-4826	Waylon and Company	1983	10.00
❑ AYL1-4828	The Best of Waylon Jennings	1983	8.00
—Budget-line reissue			
❑ AFL1-4854	Lonesome, On'ry and Mean	197?	10.00
—Reissue with new prefix			
❑ LSP-4854	Lonesome, On'ry and Mean	1973	15.00
—Original issue; orange label			
❑ AHL1-5017	Never Could Toe the Mark	1984	10.00
❑ AYL1-5126	Ol' Waylon	1984	8.00
—Budget-line reissue			
❑ AHL1-5325	Waylon's Greatest Hits, Vol. 2	1984	10.00
❑ AHL1-5428	Turn the Page	1985	10.00
❑ AYL1-5433	Waylon and Company	1985	8.00
—Budget-line reissue			
❑ AHL1-5473	Collector's Series	1985	10.00
❑ AYL1-7046	Never Could Toe the Mark	1985	8.00
—Budget-line reissue			
❑ AHL1-7184	Sweet Mother Texas	1986	10.00
SOUNDS			
❑ 1001 [M]	Waylon Jennings at JD's	1964	500.00
—Approximately 500 copies pressed; reissue of Bat 1001			
TIME-LIFE			
❑ STW-102	Country Music	1981	10.00

JENNINGS, WAYLON; WILLIE NELSON; JESSI COLTER; TOMPALL GLASER

Also see JESSI COLTER; WAYLON JENNINGS; WILLIE NELSON; WAYLON AND JESSI; WAYLON AND WILLIE.

Albums

Number	Title (A Side/B Side)	Yr	NM
RCA VICTOR			
❑ AAL1-1321	Wanted! The Outlaws	198?	8.00
—Reissue			
❑ APL1-1321	Wanted! The Outlaws	1976	10.00
—Black label, dog near top			
❑ APL1-1321	Wanted! The Outlaws	1976	12.00
—Tan label			

JENNINGS, WAYLON, AND JERRY REED

Also see each artist's individual listings.

45s

Number	Title (A Side/B Side)	Yr	NM
RCA			
❑ PB-13580	Hold On, I'm Comin'/Waiting On Down the Line	1983	4.00
❑ GB-13789	Hold On, I'm Comin'/The Conversation	1984	3.00
—Gold Standard Series; B-side by Waylon and Hank Williams, Jr.			

JENNY AND THE JEWELS

45s

Number	Title (A Side/B Side)	Yr	NM
HIT			
❑ 153	Baby Love/Baby Don't You Do It	1964	8.00
—B-side by Leroy Jones			
❑ 257	Love Is Like an Itching in My Heart/It's a Man's Man's Man's World	1966	8.00
—B-side by Leroy Jones			
❑ 313	In and Out of Love/Everlasting Love	1967	8.00
—B-side by Steve Miller			

JENSEN, KRIS

45s

Number	Title (A Side/B Side)	Yr	NM
A&M			
❑ 1204	Dead End Street/Me and Bobby McGee	1970	5.00
COLPIX			
❑ 118	Bonnie Baby/Staying Up Late	1959	12.00
HICKORY			
❑ 1173	Torture/Let's Sit Down	1962	12.00
❑ 1195	Claudette/Don't Take Her from Me	1962	8.00
❑ 1203	Poor Unlucky Me/Cut Me Down (From Your Whipping Post)	1963	8.00
❑ 1224	Big As I Can Dream/Donna, Donna	1963	8.00
❑ 1224 [PS]	Big As I Can Dream/Donna, Donna	1963	20.00
❑ 1243	In Time/Lookin' for Love	1964	8.00
❑ 1256	Come Back to Me (My Love)/You've Only Got Me to Lose	1964	8.00
❑ 1285	Little Wind-Up Doll/Somebody's Smilin'	1964	8.00
❑ 1311	That's a Whole Lotta Love/What Should I Do	1965	8.00

J

Number	Title (A Side/B Side)	Yr	NM
KAPP			
393	The Jackie Look/Tender Hearted Baby	1961	10.00
410	Danny'd Dream/3 Vanilla, 2 Chocolate, 1 Pistachio Ice Cream Cones	1961	10.00
433	Busy Signal/Mary, Mary	1961	10.00
493	Busy Signal/Mary, Mary	1962	8.00
LEADER			
808	Perfect Love/School Bus	1960	12.00
813	Please Let Me Love You Tonight/Your Daddy Don't Like Me	1961	12.00
WHITE WHALE			
229	I Got You/I Can't Get Nowhere with You	1966	6.00
240	I Love to Call You Sweetheart/Good Pop Music	1966	6.00
Albums			
HICKORY			
LP 110 [M]	Torture	1963	80.00

JEREMY AND THE SATYRS

Number	Title (A Side/B Side)	Yr	NM
45s			
REPRISE			
0664	Let's Go to the Movie Show/Lonely Child of Tears	1968	10.00
Albums			
REPRISE			
R-6282 [M]	Jeremy and the Satyrs	1968	40.00
—Mono is white label promo only			
RS-6282 [S]	Jeremy and the Satyrs	1968	20.00

JEREMY'S FRIENDS

Alan Arkin was a member of this group.

Number	Title (A Side/B Side)	Yr	NM
Albums			
WARWICK			
W-2019 [M]	Jeremy's Friends	1960	50.00

JERICHO

Number	Title (A Side/B Side)	Yr	NM
45s			
BEARSVILLE			
31003	Cheater Man/Make It Better	1971	8.00
Albums			
AMPEX			
A-10112	Jericho	1971	25.00

JERRY AND WAYNE

Number	Title (A Side/B Side)	Yr	NM
45s			
ABC-PARAMOUNT			
9806	Baby Baby Baby/I'm Sad, Blue and Lonesome	1957	20.00
9808	Baby Baby Baby, Be Mine/I'm Sad, Blue and Lonesome	1957	25.00

JESSE AND MARVIN

"Jesse" is JESSE BELVIN. "Marvin" later was with MARVIN AND JOHNNY.

Number	Title (A Side/B Side)	Yr	NM
45s			
SPECIALTY			
447	Dream Girl/Daddy Loves Baby	1952	75.00
—Black vinyl			
447	Dream Girl/Daddy Loves Baby	1952	200.00
—Red vinyl			

JESSIE MAE

Number	Title (A Side/B Side)	Yr	NM
45s			
DRA			
319	Don't Freeze on Me/It Might As Well Be Spring	1962	12.00

JESTERS, THE

Also see THE PARAGONS/THE JESTERS.

Number	Title (A Side/B Side)	Yr	NM
45s			
AMY			
859	Alexander Graham Bell/Buffalo	1962	8.00
CYCLONE			
5011	I Laughed/Now That You're Gone	1958	50.00
FEATURE			
101	Panther Pounce/Tiger Tail	1964	50.00
LOST-NITE			
117	The Wind/Sally Green	196?	8.00
—Reissue			
122	The Plea/Oh! Baby	196?	8.00
—Reissue			
124	Love No One But You/Oh! Baby	196?	8.00
126	So Strange/Oh! Baby	196?	8.00
129	I Laughed/Now That You're Gone	196?	8.00
—Reissue			
131	I'm Falling in Love/Please Let Me Love You	196?	8.00
—Reissue			
SIDEWALK			
910	Leave Me Alone/Don't Try to Crawl Back	1967	10.00
916	Hands of Time/If You Love Her, Tell Her So	1967	10.00
SUN			
400	Cadillac Man/My Babe	1966	30.00
ULTIMA			
705	Drag Like Boogie/A-Rab	1964	30.00
WINLEY			
218	So Strange/Love No One But You	1957	50.00
221	I'm Falling in Love/Please Let Me Love You	1957	50.00
225	The Plea/Oh Baby	1958	40.00
242	The Wind/Sally Green	1959	40.00
248	That's How It Goes/Tutti Frutti	1961	30.00
—Black vinyl			
248	That's How It Goes/Tutti Frutti	1961	50.00
—Red vinyl			
252	Come Let Me Show You/Uncle Henry's Basement	1961	30.00
Albums			
COLLECTABLES			
COL-5036	The Best of the Jesters	198?	10.00

JESUS AND MARY CHAIN, THE

Number	Title (A Side/B Side)	Yr	NM
12-Inch Singles			
DEF AMERICAN			
PRO-A-5340 [DJ]	Reverence (4 versions)	1992	15.00
REPRISE			
20714	April Skies (Long Version)/Kill Surf City	1987	8.00
WARNER BROS.			
PRO-A-2857 [DJ]	Happy When It Rains (same on both sides)	1987	8.00
PRO-A-3750 [DJ]	Blues from a Gun (same on both sides)	1989	12.00
20931	Sidewalking (2 versions)/Taste of Candy (Live)/April Skies (Live)	1988	15.00
45s			
ROUGH TRADE			
RTUS 006	Upside Down/Vegetable Man	1984	8.00
RTUS 006 [PS]	Upside Down/Vegetable Man	1984	8.00
SUB POP			
SP 434	The Birthday/Hide Myself	1998	8.00
—Blue vinyl			
SP 434 [PS]	The Birthday/Hide Myself	1998	9.00
—Sub Pop Singles Club, Apr 1998 (first of the new series)			
WARNER BROS.			
19891	Head On/Penetration	1990	5.00
27754	Surfin' USA (Summer Mix)/Kill Surf City	1988	4.00
27754 [PS]	Surfin' USA (Summer Mix)/Kill Surf City	1988	7.00
Albums			
REPRISE			
25383	Psychocandy	1985	12.00
WARNER BROS.			
25656	Darklands	1987	12.00
25729	Barbed Wire Kisses	1988	12.00
26015	Automatic	1989	14.00

JET SET, THE

Number	Title (A Side/B Side)	Yr	NM
45s			
CAPITOL			
5358	True to You/You Got Me Hooked	1965	25.00
5421	How Can I Know/Dancing Yet	1965	25.00
—As "Liza and the Jet Set"			

JETHRO TULL

Featuring flutist Ian Anderson. Also BLODWYN PIG related.

Number	Title (A Side/B Side)	Yr	NM
12-Inch Singles			
CHRYSALIS			
CHS 3 PDJ [DJ]	Ring Out, Solstice Bells/March, The Mad Scientist//Christmas Song/Pan Dance	1976	25.00
45s			
CHRYSALIS			
2006	Living in the Past/Christmas Song	1972	6.00
2012	A Passion Play (Edit #9)/A Passion Play (Edit #8)	1973	6.00
2017	A Passion Play (Edit #6)/A Passion Play (Edit #10)	1973	5.00
2101	Bungle in the Jungle/Back Door Angels	1974	5.00
2101 [PS]	Bungle in the Jungle/Back Door Angels	1974	10.00
2103	Skating Away (On the Thin Ice of a New Day)/Sealion	1975	5.00
2106	Minstrel in the Gallery/Sumer Day Sand	1975	5.00
2110	Locomotive Breath/Fat Man	1975	5.00
2114	Too Old to Rock and Roll, Too Young to Die/Bad Eyed and Loveless	1976	5.00
2135	The Whistler/Strip Cartoon	1977	5.00
2387	Home/Warm Sporran	1979	5.00
2613	Fallen on Hard Times/Pussy Willow	1982	4.00
S7-18211	Christmas Song/Skating Away on the Thin Ice of a New Day	1994	5.00
—Green vinyl			
43172	Steel Monkey/Down at the End of Your Road	1987	4.00
REPRISE			
0815 [DJ]	Love Story/Song for Jeffrey	1969	15.00
—May be promo-only			
0845 [DJ]	Living in the Past/Driving Song	1969	20.00
—May be promo-only			
0886	Reasons for Waiting/Sweet Dream	1970	15.00
0899	Teacher/Witch's Promise	1970	15.00
0927	Inside/Time for Everything	1970	5.00
1024	Hymn 43/Mother Goose	1971	5.00
1054	Locomotive Breath/Wind-Up	1971	5.00
1153	Thick as a Brick (Edit)/Hymn 43	1972	5.00
—"Back to Back Hits" series			
Albums			
CHRYSALIS			
PRO 623 [DJ]	The Jethro Tull Radio Show	1975	50.00
CHR 1003	Thick as a Brick	1973	12.00
—Green label, "3300 Warner Blvd." address			
CHR 1003	Thick as a Brick	1977	10.00
—Blue label, New York address			
2CH 1035 [(2)]	Living in the Past	1972	20.00
—Two-record set with booklet; green labels			
CHR 1035 [(2)]	Living in the Past	1977	15.00
—Blue label, New York address			
CHR 1040	A Passion Play	1973	12.00
—Green label, "3300 Warner Blvd." address			
CHR 1040	A Passion Play	1977	10.00
—Blue label, New York address			
CHR 1041	This Was	1973	12.00
—Green label, "3300 Warner Blvd." address			
CHR 1041	This Was	1977	10.00
—Blue label, New York address			
CHR 1042	Stand Up	1973	12.00
—Green label, "3300 Warner Blvd." address			
CHR 1042	Stand Up	1977	10.00
—Blue label, New York address			
CHR 1043	Benefit	1973	12.00
—Green label, "3300 Warner Blvd." address			
CHR 1043	Benefit	1977	10.00
—Blue label, New York address			
CH4 1044 [Q]	Aqualung	1974	40.00
CHR 1044	Aqualung	1973	12.00
—Green label, "3300 Warner Blvd." address			
CHR 1044	Aqualung	1977	10.00
—Blue label, New York address			
CH4 1067 [Q]	War Child	1974	40.00
CHR 1067	War Child	1974	10.00
—Blue label, New York address			
CHR 1067	War Child	1974	12.00
—Green label, "3300 Warner Blvd." address			
CHR 1078	M.U. — The Best of Jethro Tull	1975	12.00
—Green label, "3300 Warner Blvd." address			
CHR 1078	M.U. — The Best of Jethro Tull	1977	10.00
—Blue label, New York address			
CHR 1082	Minstrel in the Gallery	1975	12.00
—Green label, "3300 Warner Blvd." address			
CHR 1082	Minstrel in the Gallery	1977	10.00
—Blue label, New York address			
CHR 1111	Too Old to Rock 'N' Roll; Too Young to Die!	1976	12.00
—Green label, "3300 Warner Blvd." address			
CHR 1111	Too Old to Rock 'N' Roll; Too Young to Die!	1977	10.00
—Blue label, New York address			
CHR 1132	Songs from the Wood	1977	10.00
CHR 1135	Repeat — The Best of Jethro Tull, Vol. II	1977	10.00
CHR 1175	Heavy Horses	1978	10.00
CHR2 1201 [(2)]	Jethro Tull Live — Bursting Out	1978	12.00
CHR 1238	Stormwatch	1979	10.00
CHR 1301	"A"	1980	10.00
CHR 1380	The Broadsword and the Beast	1982	10.00
F1-21708	Rock Island	1989	10.00
FV 41003	Thick as a Brick	1983	8.00
PV 41003	Thick as a Brick	1986	8.00
KV2 41035 [(2)]	Living in the Past	1983	12.00
PV 41040	A Passion Play	1983	8.00
PV 41041	This Was	1983	8.00
PV 41042	Stand Up	1983	8.00

Except when noted otherwise, VG = 25% of NM, and VG+ = 50% of NM. (Example: VG = $2.00, VG+ = $4.00 and NM = $8.00.)

Number | Title (A Side/B Side) | Yr | NM

❑ PV 41043 Benefit 1983 8.00
❑ FV 41044 Aqualung 1983 8.00
❑ PV 41067 War Child 1983 8.00
❑ FV 41078 M.U. — The Best of Jethro Tull 1983 8.00
❑ PV 41082 Minstrel in the Gallery 1983 8.00
❑ PV 41111 Too Old to Rock 'N' Roll; Too Young to Die! 1983 8.00
❑ PV 41132 Songs from the Wood 1983 8.00
❑ FV 41135 Repeat — The Best of Jethro Tull, Vol. II 1983 8.00
❑ PV 41135 Repeat — The Best of Jethro Tull, Vol. II 1986 8.00
❑ PV 41175 Heavy Horses 1983 8.00
❑ V2X 41201 [(2)] Jethro Tull Live — Bursting Out 1983 12.00
❑ PV 41238 Stormwatch 1983 8.00
❑ PV 41301 "A" 1983 8.00
❑ FV 41380 The Broadsword and the Beast 1983 8.00
❑ PV 41380 The Broadsword and the Beast 1986 8.00
❑ FV 41461 Under Wraps 1984 10.00
❑ PV 41461 Under Wraps 1986 8.00
❑ FV 41515 Original Masters 1985 10.00
❑ FV 41590 Crest of a Knave 1987 10.00
❑ V5X 41653 [(5)] 20 Years of Jethro Tull 1988 80.00
❑ VX2 41655 [(2)] 20 Years of Jethro Tull 1989 25.00
—Abridged version of Chrysalis 41653

DCC COMPACT CLASSICS
❑ LPZ 2033 Aqualung 1997 100.00
—Audiophile vinyl
❑ LPZ-2059 Original Masters 1998 40.00
—Audiophile vinyl

MOBILE FIDELITY
❑ 1-061 Aqualung 1980 70.00
—Audiophile vinyl
❑ 1-092 The Broadsword and the Beast 1982 50.00
—Audiophile vinyl
❑ 1-187 Thick as a Brick 1985 50.00
—Audiophile vinyl

REPRISE
❑ MS 2035 Aqualung 1971 15.00
❑ MS 2072 Thick as a Brick 1972 15.00
❑ 2MS 2106 [(2)] Living in the Past 1972 25.00
—Two-record set with booklet; original edition, rather than using cardboard outer sleeve for the records, has record sleeves attached to enclosed booklet, and thus is difficult to find intact
❑ RS 6336 This Was 1969 20.00
—Two-tone orange label with "r:" and "W7" logos on label
❑ RS 6336 This Was 1970 15.00
—All-one-color (orange/brown) label with no "W7" on label
❑ RS 6360 Stand Up 1969 20.00
—Two-tone orange label with "r:" and "W7" logos on label; band "stands up" when gatefold is opened
❑ RS 6360 Stand Up 1970 15.00
—All-one-color (orange/brown) label with no "W7" on label
❑ RS 6400 Benefit 1970 15.00
—All-one-color (orange/brown) label with no "W7" on label
❑ RS 6400 Benefit 1970 20.00
—Two-tone orange label with "r:" and "W7" logos on label

JETT, JOAN, AND THE BLACKHEARTS

12-Inch Singles

BLACKHEART
❑ BH 007 [DJ] Light of Day/Roadrunner 1987 20.00
❑ ZAS 1094 [DJ] I Hate Myself for Loving You (same on both sides) 1988 12.00
❑ ZAS 2517 [DJ] Good Music (3:29)/Good Music (5:45) 1985 12.00
❑ ZAS 2559 [DJ] Roadrunner/You Got Me Floatin'/This Means War 1986 20.00
❑ ZAS 4256 [DJ] Don't Surrender (6:42)/Don't Surrender (4:04) 1991 12.00

BOARDWALK
❑ 005 [DJ] Little Drummer Boy/Victim of Circumstance 1981 20.00
❑ 012 [DJ] Crimson and Clover (AOR Remix) (same on both sides) 1982 15.00
❑ 019 [DJ] Do You Wanna Touch Me (Oh Yeah)/Summertime Blues 1982 15.00

MCA
❑ L33-1117 [DJ] Fake Friends (same on both sides) 1983 10.00
❑ L33-1121 [DJ] Everyday People (Short)/Everyday People (Long) 1983 8.00
❑ L33-1247 [DJ] I Love You Love/New Orleans/Little Drummer Boy 1984 15.00
❑ 13973 Everyday People/Star Star 1983 20.00

45s

BLACKHEART
❑ F-15 Spinster//Go Home/Hostility 1994 5.00
—Blue vinyl, small center hole
❑ F-15 [PS] Spinster//Go Home/Hostility 1994 3.00
—Both versions have the same picture sleeve
❑ FR-15 Spinster//Go Home/Hostility 1994 3.00
—Blue vinyl, large center hole
❑ 06336 Good Music/Fantasy 1986 3.00
❑ 06336 [PS] Good Music/Fantasy 1986 3.00
❑ 06692 Light of Day/Roadrunner (Radio On) 1987 3.00
—As "The Barbusters"
❑ 06692 [PS] Light of Day/Roadrunner (Radio On) 1987 3.00
—As "The Barbusters"
❑ 07919 I Hate Myself for Loving You/Love Is Pain (Live) 1988 3.00
❑ 07919 [PS] I Hate Myself for Loving You/Love Is Pain (Live) 1988 3.00
❑ 08095 Little Liar/What Can I Do for You 1988 3.00
❑ 08095 [PS] Little Liar/What Can I Do for You 1988 3.00
❑ 73267 Dirty Deeds/Let It Bleed 1990 8.00
—Credited solely to Joan Jett
❑ 73314 Love Hurts/Handiman 1990 —
—Cassette only

BOARDWALK
❑ NBS-7-006 [DJ] Little Drummer Boy (same on both sides) 1981 15.00
❑ NB7-11-135 I Love Rock 'N Roll/You Don't Know What You've Got 1982 3.00
❑ NB7-11-135 [PS] I Love Rock 'N Roll/You Don't Know What You've Got 1982 10.00
❑ NB7-11-144 Crimson and Clover/Oh Woe Is Me 1982 3.00
❑ NB7-11-144 [PS] Crimson and Clover/Oh Woe Is Me 1982 3.00
❑ NB 11-150-7 Do You Wanna Touch Me (Oh Yeah)/Victim of Circumstance 1982 3.00
❑ NB 11-150-7 [PS] Do You Wanna Touch Me (Oh Yeah)/Victim of Circumstance 1982 3.00
❑ 5706 You Don't Own Me/Jezebel 1981 8.00

DEF JAM
❑ 07630 She's Lost You/Hazy Shade of Winter 1987 3.00
—B-side by Bangles
❑ 07630 [PS] She's Lost You/Hazy Shade of Winter 1987 3.00
—B-side by Bangles

EPIC ASSOCIATED
❑ 74067 Don't Surrender/Don't Surrender (The Most Excellent Mix) 1991 —
—Cassette only

MCA
❑ 52240 Fake Friends/Nite Time 1983 3.00
❑ 52240 [PS] Fake Friends/Nite Time 1983 3.00
—"Nite Time" has a locked groove. In other words, if left on an automatic turntable, it'll just keep playing...
❑ 52254 Fake Friends/Handy Man 1983 4.00
—Evidently a jukebox single with a different flip side so the needle wouldn't get stuck!
❑ 52272 Everyday People/Why Can't We Be Happy 1983 3.00
❑ 52272 [PS] Everyday People/Why Can't We Be Happy 1983 3.00
❑ 52472 I Love You Love/Talkin' 'Bout My Baby 1984 3.00
❑ 52472 [PS] I Love You Love/Talkin' 'Bout My Baby 1984 3.00

REPRISE
❑ 18245 I Love Rock 'N Roll/Activity Grrrl 1994 3.00

WARNER BROS.
❑ 17637 Love Is All Around/Rubber & Glue 1996 3.00

Albums

BLACKHEART
❑ JJ 707 Joan Jett 1980 60.00
❑ BFZ 40544 Good Music 1986 12.00
❑ FZ 44146 Up Your Alley 1988 10.00
❑ Z 45473 The Hit List 1990 15.00
❑ Z 47488 Notorious 1991 30.00

BOARDWALK
❑ NB1-33243 I Love Rock-n-Roll 1982 10.00
—First pressing contains "Little Drummer Boy," which was replaced on second pressings
❑ NB1-33243 I Love Rock-n-Roll 1982 12.00
—Second pressing, with "Oh Woe Is Me"
❑ NB1-33251 Bad Reputation 1982 10.00
—Reissue of FW 37065
❑ FW 37065 Bad Reputation 1981 12.00
—Essentially a reissue of Blackheart JJ 707

MCA
❑ 5437 Album 1983 12.00
❑ 5476 Glorious Results of a Misspent Youth 1984 12.00
❑ R 163731 Glorious Results of a Misspent Youth 1984 16.00
—RCA Music Service edition

REPRISE
❑ 45567 Pure and Simple 1994 20.00

JEWEL AND EDDIE
JEWEL AKENS and Eddie Daniels; EDDIE COCHRAN plays guitar.

45s

SILVER
❑ 1004 Opportunity/Strollin' Guitar 1960 30.00
❑ 1004 Opportunity/Doin' the Hully Gully 1960 40.00
❑ 1008 My Eyes Are Cryin' for You/Sixteen Tons 1960 30.00

JEWELL, LEN

45s

TERI DE
❑ 004 Bettin' on Love/(B-side unknown) 196? 4000.

JEWELL AND THE RUBIES

45s

ABC-PARAMOUNT
❑ 10485 The Kidnapper/A Thrill 1963 12.00

LA LOUISIANNE
❑ 8041 The Kidnapper/A Thrill 1963 30.00

JEWELS, THE (1)
Female vocal group.

45s

DIMENSION
❑ 1034 Opportunity/Gotta Find a Way 1964 20.00
❑ 1048 Smokey Joe/But I Do 1965 15.00

JEWELS, THE (2)
Male vocal group, did the original version of the hit "Hearts of Stone."

45s

ANTLER
❑ 1102 The Wind/Pearlie Mae 1959 40.00

IMPERIAL
❑ 5351 Angel in My Life/Hearts Can Be Broken 1955 100.00
❑ 5362 Natural, Natural Ditty/Please Return 1955 100.00
❑ 5377 How/Rickety Rock 1956 100.00
❑ 5387 My Baby/Goin', Goin', Goin' 1956 100.00

ORIGINAL SOUND
❑ 38 Hearts of Stone/Oh Yes I Know 1964 20.00

R&B
❑ 1301 Hearts of Stone/Runnin' 1954 200.00
❑ 1303 Oh Yes I Know/A Fool in Paradise 1954 300.00

RPM
❑ 474 She's a Flirt/Be-Bomp Baby 1956 70.00

JEWELS, THE (3)

45s

DYNAMITE
❑ 2000 Papa Left Mama Holdin' the Bag/This Is My Story 1966 15.00

FEDERAL
❑ 12541 My Song/This Is My Story 1966 20.00

KING
❑ 6068 Smokie Joe's/Lookie Lookie 1967 12.00

JEWELS, THE (4)
Probably an instrumental group.

45s

FERN
❑ 806 Jewel Rock/Space Guitar 1961 20.00

JEWELS, THE (5)
For recordings on Rama, see THE CROWS.

JEWELS, THE (U)
We can't definitely put these with any of the above groups. This could be as many as three more groups!

45s

MGM
❑ 13577 We Got Togetherness/I'm Forever Blowing Bubbles 1966 20.00

OLIMPIC
❑ 244 Jimmy Lee/The Hash 1964 30.00

SHASTA
❑ 115 I Worry 'Bout You/Are You Coming to the Party 1959 20.00

JIANTS, THE

45s

CLAUDRA
❑ 112 Tornado/She's My Woman 1959 200.00

JILL AND RAY
See PAUL AND PAULA.

JIMENEZ, JOSE
Also includes records under his real name, Bill Dana.

45s

A&M
❑ 773 Jose's Dream/Cry 1965 8.00
—As "Bill Dana"

Except when noted otherwise, VG = 25% of NM, and VG+ = 50% of NM. (Example: VG = $2.00, VG+ = $4.00 and NM = $8.00.)

Number	Title (A Side/B Side)	Yr	NM
❑ 779	All I Need Is You/Make Nice	1965	8.00
—As "Bill Dana"			
❑ 811	Jose Jimenezchevitz/ Childhood Scenes	1966	8.00
—As "Bill Dana"			
KAPP			
❑ 409	The Astronaut (Part 1)/ The Astronaut (Part 2)	1961	8.00
❑ 409 [PS]	The Astronaut (Part 1)/ The Astronaut (Part 2)	1961	12.00
❑ 434	Christmas Sing Along with Jose: Jingle Bells/Sing Along with Jose: Shine On Harvest Moon	1961	15.00
❑ 443	Jose Jimenez in Orbit/Press Conference with Jose Jimenez in Orbit	1962	10.00
❑ 540	Jose and Cleopatra (Part 1)/ Jose and Cleopatra (Part 2)	1963	10.00
❑ 552	King of the Surf (Part 1)/ King of the Surf (Part 2)	1963	15.00
SIGNATURE			
❑ 12041	My Name — Jose Jimenez/ In the Wee Small Hours	1960	12.00
❑ 12046	Bob Sled Racer/U.S. Senator	1960	12.00
—As "Bill Dana"			
Albums			
A&M			
❑ SP-4144	Mashuganishi Yogi	1968	15.00
CAPITOL			
❑ ST-464	Hoo Ha! Direct from Noshville	1970	15.00
KAPP			
❑ KL 1215 [M]	More Jose Jimenez	1961	20.00
❑ KL 1215 [M]	Jose Jimenez the Submarine Officer	1961	25.00
—Original title			
❑ KL 1238 [M]	Jose Jimenez at the Hungry I	196?	15.00
—Reissue with new title			
❑ KL 1238 [M]	Jose Jimenez — The Astronaut (The First Man in Space)	1961	20.00
❑ KL-1257 [M]	Jose Jimenez in Orbit — Bill Dana on Earth	1961	20.00
❑ KL 1304 [M]	Jose Jimenez Talks to Teenagers of All Ages	1962	20.00
❑ KL-1320 [M]	Jose Jimenez — Our Secret Weapon	1963	20.00
❑ KL-1332 [M]	Jose Jimenez in Jollywood	1963	20.00
❑ KL-1402 [M]	Bill Dana in Las Vegas	1964	20.00
❑ KS 3238 [S]	Jose Jimenez at the Hungry I	196?	15.00
—Reissue with new title			
❑ KS 3238 [S]	Jose Jimenez — The Astronaut (The First Man in Space)	1961	25.00
❑ KS-3257 [S]	Jose Jimenez in Orbit — Bill Dana on Earth	1961	25.00
❑ KS 3304 [S]	Jose Jimenez Talks to Teenagers of All Ages	1962	25.00
❑ KS-3332 [S]	Jose Jimenez in Jollywood	1963	25.00
ROULETTE			
❑ R 25161 [M]	My Name...Jose Jimenez	1961	20.00
—Reissue of Signature LP			
SIGNATURE			
❑ SM 1013 [M]	My Name...Jose Jimenez	1960	25.00

JIMMIE DALE AND THE FLATLANDERS

Number	Title (A Side/B Side)	Yr	NM
45s			
PLANTATION			
❑ 92	Dallas/Tonight I'm Gonna Go Downtown	1972	50.00
❑ 106	Jole Blon/You've Never Seen Me Cry	1972	50.00
Albums			
PLANTATION			
❑ 22	One Road More	1972	—
—May exist only as an 8-track tape. Should an LP exist, its value would be in the hundreds.			
ROUNDER			
❑ SS-34	More a Legend Than a Band	1990	12.00
—As "The Flatlanders"; reissue of Plantation material			

JIMMY AND DUANE

"Duane" is DUANE EDDY.

Number	Title (A Side/B Side)	Yr	NM
45s			
EB X. PRESTON			
❑ 212	I Want Some Lovin' Baby/ Soda Fountain Girl	1955	300.00

JIMMY AND JOE

Number	Title (A Side/B Side)	Yr	NM
45s			
HIT			
❑ 71	Surf City/Easier Said Than Done	1963	8.00
—B-side by Clara Wilson			

JIMMY AND PAT

Number	Title (A Side/B Side)	Yr	NM
45s			
HIT			
❑ 224	Baby Don't Go/You Were On My Mind	1965	10.00
—B-side by the Roamers			

JIMMY AND WALTER

Number	Title (A Side/B Side)	Yr	NM
45s			
SUN			
❑ 180	Easy/Before Long	1953	2000.
—The earliest known 45 on Sun			

JIMMY, JOE AND BETTY

Number	Title (A Side/B Side)	Yr	NM
45s			
HIT			
❑ 59	Puff the Magic Dragon/Don't Be Afraid Little Darling	1963	8.00
—B-side by Fred York			

JIMMY, WAYNE AND BETTY

Number	Title (A Side/B Side)	Yr	NM
45s			
HIT			
❑ 75	Blowin' in the Wind/(You're the) Devil in Diguise	1963	8.00
—B-side by Wayne Harris			
❑ 88	Don't Think Twice, It's All Right/ That Sunday, That Summer	1963	8.00
—B-side by Berry Bradley			

JIVE BOMBERS, THE

Number	Title (A Side/B Side)	Yr	NM
45s			
SAVOY			
❑ 1508	Bad Boy/When Your Hair Has Turned to Silver	1957	25.00
❑ 1513	If I Had a Talking Picture of You/ The Blues Don't Mean a Thing	1957	20.00
❑ 1515	You Took My Love/Cherry	1957	20.00
❑ 1535	Just Around the Corner/ Is This the End	1958	20.00
❑ 1560	Star Dust/You Give Your Love to Me	1959	20.00
Albums			
SAVOY JAZZ			
❑ SJL-1150	Bad Boy	1986	10.00

JIVE FIVE, THE

Number	Title (A Side/B Side)	Yr	NM
45s			
AMBIENT SOUND			
❑ 452	Are You Lonesome Tonight/ Happier Than Before	1985	6.00
❑ 02742	Magic Maker, Music Maker/ Oh Baby	1982	5.00
❑ 03053	Hey Sam/Don't Believe Him Donna	1982	5.00
AVCO			
❑ 4568	Come Down in Time/Love Is Pain	1971	6.00
❑ 4589	Follow the Lamb/Lady Lady Lay	1972	6.00
❑ 4589	Follow the Lamb/Let the Feeling Belong	1972	6.00
BELTONE			
❑ 1006	My True Story/When I Was Single	1961	30.00
❑ 1014	Never, Never/People from Another World	1961	20.00
❑ 2019	Hully Gully Calling Time/ No, Not Again	1962	20.00
❑ 2024	What Time Is It?/ Beggin' You Please	1962	20.00
❑ 2029	These Golden Rings/Do You Hear Wedding Bells	1962	20.00
❑ 2030	Lily Marlene/Johnny Never Knew	1963	20.00
❑ 2034	She's My Girl/Rain	1963	20.00
BRUT			
❑ 814	All I Ever Do Is Dream About You/Super Woman (Part 2)	1973	6.00
DECCA			
❑ 32671	(If You Let Me Make Love to You) Why Can't I Touch You/You Showed Me the Light of Love	1970	8.00
❑ 32736	I Want You to Be My Baby/ Give Me Just a Chance	1970	8.00
LANA			
❑ 105	My True Story/When I Was Single	196?	8.00
—Oldies reissue			
LOST-NITE			
❑ 144	My True Story/When I Was Single	196?	6.00
—Reissue			
❑ 147	What Time Is It?/Beggin' You Please	196?	6.00
—Reissue			
MUSICOR			
❑ 1250	Crying Like a Baby/ You'll Fall in Love	1967	40.00
❑ 1270	No More Tears/You'll Fall in Love	1967	12.00
❑ 1305	Sugar (Don't Take Away My Candy)/Blues in the Ghetto	1968	12.00
SKETCH			
❑ 219	United/Prove Every Word You Say	1964	15.00
UNITED ARTISTS			
❑ 0100	I'm a Happy Man/It Will Stand	1973	5.00
—"Silver Spotlight Series" reissue; B-side by The Showmen			
❑ 807	United/Prove Every Word You Say	1965	20.00
❑ 853	I'm a Happy Man/Kiss Kiss Kiss	1965	20.00
❑ 936	Please Baby Please/ A Bench in the Park	1965	20.00
❑ 50004	Goin' Wild/Main Street	1966	20.00
❑ 50033	In My Neighborhood/ Then Came Heartbreak	1966	50.00
❑ 50069	You're a Puzzle/Ha Ha	1966	100.00
❑ 50107	You/You Promised Me Great Things	1966	75.00
Albums			
AMBIENT SOUND			
❑ FZ 37717	Here We Are	1982	15.00
AMBIENT SOUND/ROUNDER			
❑ ASR-801	Way Back	1985	12.00
COLLECTABLES			
❑ COL-5022	Greatest Hits	198?	10.00
RELIC			
❑ 5020	The Jive Five's Greatest Hits (1961-1963)	198?	10.00
UNITED ARTISTS			
❑ UAL-3455 [M]	The Jive Five	1965	50.00
❑ UAS-6455 [S]	The Jive Five	1965	75.00

JIVERS, THE

Number	Title (A Side/B Side)	Yr	NM
45s			
ALADDIN			
❑ 3329	Cherie/Little Mama	1956	160.00
❑ 3347	Ray Pearl/Dear Little One	1956	120.00

JO JO GUNNE

Featuring Jay Ferguson.

Number	Title (A Side/B Side)	Yr	NM
45s			
ASYLUM			
❑ 11003	Run Run Run/Take It Easy	1972	5.00
❑ 11007	Shake That Fat/I Make Love	1972	5.00
❑ 11018	Ready Freddie/Wait a Lifetime	1973	5.00
❑ 11020	Take Me Down Easy/ Rock Around the Symbol	1973	5.00
❑ 11031	I Wanna Love You/New City	1974	5.00
❑ 45225	Where Is the Show/Into My Life	1975	5.00
Albums			
ASYLUM			
❑ 7E-1022	So...Where's the Show?	1974	10.00
❑ SD 5053	Jo Jo Gunne	1972	15.00
❑ SD 5065	Bite Down Hard	1973	15.00
❑ SD 5071	Jumpin' the Gunne	1973	15.00
—Gatefold cover			
❑ SD 5071	Jumpin' the Gunne	1974	10.00
—Regular cover			

JODIMARS, THE

Contains ex-members of BILL HALEY AND HIS COMETS.

Number	Title (A Side/B Side)	Yr	NM
45s			
CAPITOL			
❑ F3285	Well Now — Dig This/ Let's All Rock Together	1955	25.00
❑ F3360	Dancin' the Bop/Boom Boom My Bayou Baby	1956	25.00
❑ F3436	Lotsa Love/Rattle My Bones	1956	25.00
❑ F3512	Rattle Shakin' Daddy/ Eat Your Heart Out, Annie	1956	25.00
❑ F3588	Clarabella/Midnight	1956	25.00
❑ F3633	Cloud 99/Later	1957	25.00
PRESIDENT			
❑ 1017	Shoo-Sue/Story-Telling Baby	1957	20.00

JOE & ANN

Number	Title (A Side/B Side)	Yr	NM
45s			
ACE			
❑ 577	Gee Baby/Wherever You May Be	1959	12.00

JOE & EDDIE

Number	Title (A Side/B Side)	Yr	NM
45s			
CAPITOL			
❑ F4149	The Fox/Lonesome Road	1959	10.00
❑ F4209	Green Grass/And I Believe	1959	10.00

Number	Title (A Side/B Side)	Yr	NM
❑ F4288	Take My Hand/Remember Me	1959	10.00

GNP CRESCENDO

Number	Title (A Side/B Side)	Yr	NM
❑ 185	I Got Shoes/Water Boy	1962	8.00
❑ 195	Lonesome Traveler/There's a Meetin' Here Tonight	1963	8.00
❑ 305	Children Go/I Laid Around	1963	8.00
❑ 306	What's That I Hear/Farewell My Cindy Jane	1963	8.00
❑ 316	Wild Is the Wind/Swing Down Chariot	1964	6.00
❑ 321	Frankie and Johnny Blues/Gonna Build a Mountain	1964	6.00
❑ 324	Goodnight Irene/Pearly Shells	1964	6.00
❑ 333	Lonesome Road/Tear Down the Walls	1964	6.00
❑ 338	He's Got the Whole World in His Hands/Gabrielle	1965	6.00
❑ 344	Depend On Yourself/With You in Mind	1965	6.00
❑ 353	It Ain't Me Babe/Walkin' Down the Line	1965	6.00
❑ 355	I Got You (I've Got Everything)/Petticoat White (Summer Blue Sky)	1965	6.00
❑ 366	Michael, Row the Boat Ashore/That Was the Last Thing on My Mind	1965	6.00

Albums

GNP CRESCENDO

Number	Title	Yr	NM
❑ GNP-75 [M]	Joe & Eddie	1963	20.00
❑ GNP-86 [M]	There's a Meetin' Here Tonite	1963	20.00
❑ GNP-96 [M]	Coast to Coast	1964	20.00
❑ GNPS-96 [S]	Coast to Coast	1964	25.00
❑ GNP-99 [M]	Joe & Eddie, Vol. 4	1964	20.00
❑ GNPS-99 [S]	Joe & Eddie, Vol. 4	1964	25.00
❑ GNP-2005 [M]	Tear Down the Walls	1965	15.00
❑ GNPS-2005 [S]	Tear Down the Walls	1965	20.00
❑ GNP-2007 [M]	Joe & Eddie Live in Hollywood	1965	15.00
❑ GNPS-2007 [S]	Joe & Eddie Live in Hollywood	1965	20.00
❑ GNP-2014 [M]	Walkin' Down the Line	1965	15.00
❑ GNPS-2014 [S]	Walkin' Down the Line	1965	20.00
❑ GNP-2021 [M]	The Magic of Their Singing	1966	15.00
❑ GNPS-2021 [S]	The Magic of Their Singing	1966	20.00
❑ GNP-2032 [M]	The Best of Joe & Eddie	1966	15.00
❑ GNPS-2032 [S]	The Best of Joe & Eddie	1966	20.00

JOEL, BILLY

12-Inch Singles

COLUMBIA

Number	Title (A Side/B Side)	Yr	NM
❑ AS 1718 [DJ]	Tell Her About It/Easy Money/Keeping the Faith	1983	12.00
❑ AS 1738 [DJ]	Tell Her About It (12" Version) (same on both sides)	1983	10.00
❑ AS 1982 [DJ]	Keeping the Faith (Special Mix) (same on both sides)	1984	10.00
❑ CAS 2109 [DJ]	You're Only Human (Second Wind) (LP Version) (Short Version)	1985	8.00
❑ CAS 2321 [DJ]	Back in the U.S.S.R./The Times They Are a-Changin'	1987	15.00
❑ CAS 2367 [DJ]	A Matter of Trust (same on both sides?)	1986	8.00
❑ 44-04138	Tell Her About It (Special 12" Version 5:35)//Easy Money/You Got Me Hummin' (Live)	1983	12.00

45s

COLUMBIA

Number	Title (A Side/B Side)	Yr	NM
❑ AE7 1338 [DJ]	Nobody Knows But Me/Root Beer Rag	1981	15.00
—Promo-only release of song from the "In Harmony 2" album			
❑ 18-02518	Say Goodbye to Hollywood/Summer, Highland Falls	1981	4.00
❑ 18-02518 [PS]	Say Goodbye to Hollywood/Summer, Highland Falls	1981	4.00
❑ 18-02628	She's Got a Way/The Ballad of Billy the Kid	1981	4.00
❑ 18-02628 [PS]	She's Got a Way/The Ballad of Billy the Kid	1981	4.00
❑ 13-03238	It's Still Rock and Roll to Me/Don't Ask Me Why	1982	3.00
—Reissue			
❑ 13-03239	You May Be Right/She's Got a Way	1982	3.00
—Reissue			
❑ 13-03241	Honesty/Sometimes a Fantasy	1982	3.00
—Reissue			
❑ 38-03244	Pressure/Laura	1982	4.00
❑ 38-03244 [PS]	Pressure/Laura	1982	4.00
❑ CNR-03321	Pressure/(B-side blank)	1982	8.00
—One-sided budget release (large hole)			
❑ 38-03413	Allentown/Elvis Presley Blvd.	1982	4.00
❑ 38-03413 [PS]	Allentown/Elvis Presley Blvd.	1982	4.00
❑ CNR-03426	Allentown/(B-side blank)	1982	8.00
—One-sided budget release			
❑ 38-03780	Goodnight Saigon/A Room of Our Own	1983	4.00
❑ 38-03780 [PS]	Goodnight Saigon/A Room of Our Own	1983	4.00
❑ 38-04012	Tell Her About It/Easy Money	1983	3.00
❑ 38-04012 [PS]	Tell Her About It/Easy Money	1983	4.00
❑ 38-04012 [PS]	Tell Her About It	1983	8.00
—"Demonstration — Not for Sale" on sleeve			
❑ 38-04149	Uptown Girl/Careless Talk	1983	3.00
❑ 38-04149 [PS]	Uptown Girl/Careless Talk	1983	4.00
❑ 38-04149 [PS]	Uptown Girl	1983	8.00
—"Demonstration — Not for Sale" on sleeve			
❑ 53-04149	Uptown Girl/Careless Talk	1984	3.00
—Gold "Instant Classics" reissue label			
❑ 38-04259	An Innocent Man/I'll Cry Instead	1983	3.00
❑ 38-04259 [PS]	An Innocent Man/I'll Cry Instead	1983	4.00
❑ 38-04400	The Longest Time/Christie Lee	1984	3.00
❑ 38-04400 [PS]	The Longest Time/Christie Lee	1984	4.00
❑ 38-04514	Leave a Tender Moment Alone/This Night	1984	3.00
❑ 38-04514 [PS]	Leave a Tender Moment Alone/This Night	1984	4.00
❑ 38-04681	Keeping the Faith (Special Mix)/She's Right On Time	1984	3.00
❑ 38-04681 [PS]	Keeping the Faith (Special Mix)/She's Right On Time	1984	4.00
❑ 38-05417	You're Only Human (Second Wind)/Surprises	1985	3.00
❑ 38-05417 [PS]	You're Only Human (Second Wind)/Surprises	1985	3.00
❑ 38-05657	The Night Is Still Young/Summer, Highland Falls	1985	3.00
❑ 38-05657 [PS]	The Night Is Still Young/Summer, Highland Falls	1985	4.00
❑ 38-05657 [PS]	The Night Is Still Young	1985	10.00
—Promotional black & white sleeve, different from stock sleeve			
❑ 38-06108	A Matter of Trust/Getting Closer	1986	3.00
❑ 38-06526	This Is the Time/Code of Silence	1986	3.00
❑ 38-06526 [PS]	This Is the Time/Code of Silence	1986	3.00
❑ 38-06994	Baby Grand/Big Man on Mulberry Street	1987	3.00
—A-side with Ray Charles			
❑ 38-06994 [PS]	Baby Grand/Big Man on Mulberry Street	1987	3.00
❑ 38-07626	Back in the U.S.S.R./Big Shot	1987	3.00
❑ 38-07626 [DJ]	Back in the U.S.S.R.//Back in the U.S.S.R./The Times They Are a-Changin'	1987	10.00
—Promo-only coupling; white label			
❑ 38-07626 [PS]	Back in the U.S.S.R./Big Shot	1987	4.00
❑ 38-07626 [PS]	Back in the U.S.S.R.//Back in the U.S.S.R/The Times They Are a-Changin'	1987	15.00
—Promo-only picture sleeve for promo-only coupling; "Demonstration--Not for Sale" on upper right rear corner of sleeve			
❑ 38-07664	The Times They Are a-Changin'/Back in the U.S.S.R.	1987	4.00
❑ 13-08415	Tell Her About It/Easy Money	1988	3.00
—Reissue			
❑ 13-08416	An Innocent Man/I'll Cry Instead	1988	3.00
—Reissue			
❑ 13-08417	The Longest Time/Christie Lee	1988	3.00
—Reissue			
❑ 13-08418	Leave a Tender Moment Alone/This Night	1988	3.00
—Reissue			
❑ 13-08419	Keeping the Faith/She's Right on Time	1988	3.00
—Reissue			
❑ 13-08420	You're Only Human (Second Wind)/Surprises	1988	3.00
—Reissue			
❑ 3-10015	Travelin' Prayer/Ain't No Crime	1974	10.00
❑ 3-10064	The Entertainer/The Mexican Connection	1974	8.00
❑ 3-10412	James/Summer, Highland Falls	1976	10.00
❑ 3-10562	Say Goodbye to Hollywood/I've Loved These Days	1977	10.00
❑ 3-10624	Movin' Out (Anthony's Song)/She's Always a Woman	1977	12.00
❑ 3-10646	Just the Way You Are/Get It Right the First Time	1977	4.00
❑ 3-10708	Movin' Out (Anthony's Song)/Everybody Has a Dream	1978	4.00
❑ 3-10750	Only the Good Die Young/Get It Right the First Time	1978	5.00
❑ 3-10788	She's Always a Woman/Vienna	1978	4.00
❑ 3-10853	My Life/52nd Street	1978	4.00
❑ 3-10913	Big Shot/Root Beer Rag	1979	4.00
❑ 3-10959	Honesty/The Mexican Connection	1979	4.00
❑ 1-11229	All for Leyna/Souvenir	1980	—
—Canceled			
❑ 1-11231	You May Be Right/Close to the Borderline	1980	3.00
❑ 1-11231 [PS]	You May Be Right/Close to the Borderline	1980	6.00
❑ 1-11276	It's Still Rock and Roll to Me/Through the Long Night	1980	4.00
❑ 1-11276 [PS]	It's Still Rock and Roll to Me/Through the Long Night	1980	6.00
❑ 1-11331	Don't Ask Me Why/C'etait Toi (You Were the One)	1980	3.00
❑ 1-11331 [PS]	Don't Ask Me Why/C'etait Toi (You Were the One)	1980	6.00
❑ 1-11379	Sometimes a Fantasy/All for Leyna	1980	5.00
❑ 1-11379 [PS]	Sometimes a Fantasy/All for Leyna	1980	8.00
❑ 4-45963	Piano Man/You're My Home	1973	8.00
❑ 4-46055	Worse Comes to Worst/Somewhere Along the Line	1974	10.00
❑ 38-73021	We Didn't Start the Fire/House of Blue Light	1989	3.00
❑ 38-73091	I Go to Extremes/When in Rome	1989	3.00
❑ 38-73442	That's Not Her Style/And So It Goes	1990	3.00
❑ 38-77086	The River of Dreams/No Man's Land	1993	3.00
❑ 38-77254	All About Soul/Picked a Real Bad Time	1993	3.00
❑ 38-77363	Lullabye (Goodnight, My Angel)/Two Thousand Years	1994	3.00
❑ 38-78641	To Make You Feel My Love//Intro/Summer, Highland Falls/Summer, Highland Falls	1997	3.00

EPIC

Number	Title (A Side/B Side)	Yr	NM
❑ 34-06118	Modern Woman/Sleeping with the Television On	1986	3.00
❑ 34-06118 [PS]	Modern Woman/Sleeping with the Television On	1986	4.00
❑ 34-74422	All Shook Up/Wear My Ring Around Your Neck	1992	4.00
—B-side is instrumental track of Ricky Van Shelton's recording			

FAMILY PRODUCTIONS

Number	Title (A Side/B Side)	Yr	NM
❑ 0900	She's Got a Way/Everybody Loves You Now	1971	30.00
❑ 0906	Tomorrow Is Today/Everybody Loves You Now	1971	30.00

Albums

COLUMBIA

Number	Title	Yr	NM
❑ AS 326 [DJ]	Souvenir	1976	20.00
—Promo-only LP with one side live, one side a compilation of studio tracks			
❑ AS 402 [DJ]	Inter Chords/Billy Joel Interview	1977	20.00
—Promo-only interview album			
❑ AS 1343 [DJ]	Billy Joel Interview	1982	20.00
❑ CQ 32544 [Q]	Piano Man	1974	20.00
❑ KC 32544	Piano Man	1973	12.00
—Some copies have the first song spelled "Travelin' Prayer," others have it "Travellin' Prayer." No difference in value.			
❑ PC 32544	Piano Man	1976	10.00
—No bar code on back cover			
❑ PC 32544	Piano Man	1979	8.00
—With bar code on back cover			
❑ PC 33146	Streetlife Serenade	1975	10.00
—No bar code on back cover			
❑ PC 33146	Streetlife Serenade	1979	8.00
—With bar code on back cover			
❑ PCQ 33146 [Q]	Streetlife Serenade	1975	20.00
❑ PC 33848	Turnstiles	1976	8.00
—With bar code on back cover			
❑ PC 33848	Turnstiles	1976	10.00
—No bar code on back cover			
❑ PCQ 33848 [Q]	Turnstiles	1976	20.00
❑ HC 34987	The Stranger	1981	30.00
—Original pressing of half-speed mastered edition			
❑ JC 34987	The Stranger	1977	10.00
❑ PC 34987	The Stranger	1979	8.00
❑ FC 35609	52nd Street	1978	10.00
❑ PC 35609	52nd Street	1985	8.00
❑ FC 36384	Glass Houses	1980	10.00
❑ PC 36384	Glass Houses	1986	8.00
❑ PC 37461	Songs in the Attic	1984	8.00
❑ TC 37461	Songs in the Attic	1981	10.00
❑ QC 38200	The Nylon Curtain	1982	10.00
❑ QC 38837	An Innocent Man	1983	10.00
❑ PC 38984	Cold Spring Harbor	1983	8.00
—Remixed, remastered version of Family Productions album			
❑ C2 40121 [(2)]	Greatest Hits, Vol.s 1 and 2	1985	12.00
❑ OC 40402	The Bridge	1986	10.00
❑ C2 40996 [(2)]	KOHUEPT	1987	15.00
❑ OC 44366	Storm Front	1989	12.00
❑ HC 44987	The Stranger	1982	25.00
—Half-speed mastered edition (reissue)			
❑ HC 45609	52nd Street	1982	25.00
—Half-speed mastered edition			
❑ HC 47461	Songs in the Attic	1982	70.00
—Half-speed mastered edition			
❑ HC 48837	An Innocent Man	1983	30.00
—Half-speed mastered edition			

FAMILY PRODUCTIONS

Number	Title (A Side/B Side)	Yr	NM
❑ FPS-2700	Cold Spring Harbor	1971	40.00

—Authentic copies have mostly dark blue labels; when reissued on Columbia, the entire LP was remixed and remastered, and "You Can Make Me Free" was shortened by three minutes

JOEY AND DANNY

45s

SWAN

Number	Title (A Side/B Side)	Yr	NM
❑ 4276	Santa's Got a Brand New Bag/Rats in My Room	1967	20.00

JOEY AND THE CONTINENTALS

45s

CLARIDGE

Number	Title (A Side/B Side)	Yr	NM
❑ 304	She Rides with Me/Rudy Vahoo	1966	25.00

—Reissued on Claridge 312 as "The G.T.O.'s"

KOMET

Number	Title (A Side/B Side)	Yr	NM
❑ 1001	Linda/Will Love Ever Come My Way	196?	15.00

LAURIE

Number	Title (A Side/B Side)	Yr	NM
❑ 3294	Sad Girl/Baby	1965	25.00

JOEY AND THE FLIPS See LITTLE JOEY AND THE FLIPS.

JOEY AND THE LEXINGTONS

45s

COMET

Number	Title (A Side/B Side)	Yr	NM
❑ 2154	Heaven/The Girl I Love	1962	150.00

DUNES

Number	Title (A Side/B Side)	Yr	NM
❑ 2029	Bobbie/Tears from My Eyes	1963	100.00

JOEY AND THE TEENAGERS

45s

COLUMBIA

Number	Title (A Side/B Side)	Yr	NM
❑ 42054	What's On Your Mind/The Draw	1961	80.00

JOHANSEN, DAVID Also see NEW YORK DOLLS.

12-Inch Singles

BLUE SKY

Number	Title (A Side/B Side)	Yr	NM
❑ AS 740 [DJ]	Swaheto Woman (Long)/Swaheto Woman (Short)	1979	15.00
❑ AS 972 [DJ]	Here Comes the Night/You Fool You/ + 2	1981	6.00

PASSPORT

Number	Title (A Side/B Side)	Yr	NM
❑ 4112	King of Babylon (Extended)/Stinkin' Rich + 1	1985	8.00

45s

BLUE SKY

Number	Title (A Side/B Side)	Yr	NM
❑ 02584	She Loves Strangers/Here Comes the Night	1981	3.00
❑ 2771	Funky But Chic/The Rope	1978	4.00
❑ 2781	Melody/Reckless Crazy	1979	4.00
❑ 2789	Swaheto Woman/She Knew She Was Falling in Love	1980	4.00
❑ 03003	Medley: We Gotta Get Out of This Place-Don't Bring Me Down/Bohemian Love Dad	1982	3.00
❑ 03382	Melody/Here Comes the Night	1982	3.00

—Reissue

Albums

BLUE SKY

Number	Title (A Side/B Side)	Yr	NM
❑ AS 519 [DJ]	The David Johansen Group Live	1978	30.00
❑ AS 1281 [DJ]	Live and Sampler	1981	12.00

—Promo-only four-song sampler

Number	Title (A Side/B Side)	Yr	NM
❑ JZ 34926	David Johansen	1978	10.00
❑ JZ 36082	In Style	1979	10.00
❑ FZ 36589	Here Comes the Night	1981	10.00
❑ ARZ 38004	Live It Up	1982	10.00

PASSPORT

Number	Title (A Side/B Side)	Yr	NM
❑ PB-6043	Sweet Revenge	1984	10.00

JOHN, ELTON

12-Inch Singles

GEFFEN

Number	Title (A Side/B Side)	Yr	NM
❑ PRO-A-948 [DJ]	Nobody Wins (5:20)/Nobody Wins (French Version) (5:09)	1981	15.00
❑ PRO-A-1018 [DJ]	Empty Garden (Hey Hey Johnny) (Long)/(Short)	1981	50.00
❑ PRO-A-2025 [DJ]	I'm Still Standing (same on both sides)	1983	12.00
❑ PRO-A-2066 [DJ]	Kiss the Bride (LP Version) (Edit)	1983	12.00
❑ PRO-A-2160 [DJ]	Sad Songs (Say So Much) (same on both sides)	1984	12.00
❑ PRO-A-2188 [DJ]	Who Wears These Shoes? (same on both sides)	1984	10.00
❑ PRO-A-2374 [DJ]	Wrap Her Up (same on both sides)	1985	10.00
❑ PRO-A-2440 [DJ]	Nikita (LP Version 5:42) (Edit 4:54)	1985	10.00
❑ PRO-A-2569 [DJ]	Heartache All Over the World (Edit) (Shorter Edit)	1986	12.00
❑ 20563	Heartache All Over the World (2 versions)/Highlander	1986	8.00

MCA

Number	Title (A Side/B Side)	Yr	NM
❑ L33-1850 [DJ]	Victim of Love (same on both sides)	1979	10.00
❑ L33-1854 [DJ]	Johnny B. Goode (same on both sides)	1979	12.00
❑ L33-1979 [DJ]	Ego (same on both sides)	1978	50.00
❑ L33-17458 [DJ]	Candle in the Wind (Live) (same on both sides)	1987	10.00
❑ L33-17475 [DJ]	Take Me to the Pilot (Live) (same on both sides)	1987	10.00
❑ L33-17539 [DJ]	I Don't Wanna Go On with You Like That (4:34) (3:57)	1988	15.00
❑ 23870	I Don't Wanna Go On with You Like That (The Shep Pettibone Mix 7:29) (The Pub Dub 5:18) (Just for Radio Mix 4:00) (Just Elton and His Piano Mix 4:50)	1988	8.00
❑ 23917	Mona Lisas and Mad Hatters (Renaissance Mix) (Da Vinci Mix) (Slef Portrait Instrumental Mix)/A Word in Spanish	1988	12.00

ROCKET

Number	Title (A Side/B Side)	Yr	NM
❑ L33-1172 [DJ]	Bite Your Lip (Get Up and Dance) (6:39) (same on both sides)	1977	25.00
❑ 852093-1	Made in England (Junior's Sound Factory Mix 10:59) (Junior's Sound Factory Dub 8:34) (Junior's Joyous Mix 4:21) / Believe (Hardkiss Mix 10:27)	1995	10.00

45s

CONGRESS

Number	Title (A Side/B Side)	Yr	NM
❑ 6017	Lady Samantha/It's Me That You Need	1970	50.00
❑ 6017 [DJ]	Lady Samantha/It's Me That You Need	1970	30.00
❑ 6022	Border Song/Bad Side of the Moon	1970	50.00
❑ 6022 [DJ]	Border Song/Bad Side of the Moon	1970	30.00

DJM

Number	Title (A Side/B Side)	Yr	NM
❑ 70008	Lady Samantha/All Across the Havens	1969	300.00
❑ 70008 [DJ]	Lady Samantha/All Across the Havens	1969	100.00

GEFFEN

Number	Title (A Side/B Side)	Yr	NM
❑ 28578	Heartache All Over the World/Highlander	1986	3.00
❑ 28578 [PS]	Heartache All Over the World/Highlander	1986	3.00
❑ 28800	Nikita/Restless	1985	3.00
❑ 28800 [PS]	Nikita/Restless	1985	3.00
❑ 28800DJ [DJ]	Nikita (U.S. Edit)/(U.K. Edit)	1985	6.00
❑ 28873	Wrap Her Up/The Man Who Never Died	1985	3.00
❑ 28873 [PS]	Wrap Her Up/The Man Who Never Died	1985	3.00
❑ 29111	In Neon/Tactics	1984	3.00
❑ 29189	Who Wears These Shoes?/Lonely Boy	1984	3.00
❑ 29189 [PS]	Who Wears These Shoes?/Lonely Boy	1984	3.00
❑ 29292	Sad Songs (Say So Much)/A Simple Man	1984	3.00
❑ 7-29292 [DJ]	Sad Songs (Say So Much) (Special Radio Mix) (same on both sides)	1984	10.00

—Contains a 4:05 mix unavailable elsewhere; label has "RE-1" on both sides

Number	Title (A Side/B Side)	Yr	NM
❑ 29402	Cold As Christmas (In the Middle of the Year)/(B-side unassigned)	1983	—

—Unreleased

Number	Title (A Side/B Side)	Yr	NM
❑ 29460	I Guess That's Why They Call It the Blues/The Retreat	1983	3.00
❑ 29460 [PS]	I Guess That's Why They Call It the Blues/The Retreat	1983	3.00
❑ 29568	Kiss the Bride/Choc Ice Goes Mental	1983	3.00
❑ 29568 [PS]	Kiss the Bride/Choc Ice Goes Mental	1983	3.00
❑ 29639	I'm Still Standing/Love So Cold	1983	3.00
❑ 29639 [PS]	I'm Still Standing/Love So Cold	1983	3.00
❑ 29846	Ball & Chain/Where Have All the Good Times Gone?	1982	4.00
❑ 29954	Blue Eyes/Hey Papa Legba	1982	4.00
❑ 29954 [PS]	Blue Eyes/Hey Papa Legba	1982	5.00
❑ 49722	Nobody Wins/Fools in Fashion	1981	4.00
❑ 49722 [PS]	Nobody Wins/Fools in Fashion	1981	5.00
❑ 49788	Chloe/Tortured	1981	4.00
❑ 49788 [DJ]	Chloe//Fanfare/Chloe	1981	8.00

—B-side of this promo-only single is full-length version

Number	Title (A Side/B Side)	Yr	NM
❑ 50049	Empty Garden (Hey Hey Johnny)/Take Me Down to the Ocean	1982	4.00
❑ 50049 [DJ]	Empty Garden (LP version)/Empty Garden (Edit)	1982	8.00
❑ 50049 [PS]	Empty Garden (Hey Hey Johnny)/Take Me Down to the Ocean	1982	5.00

MCA

Number	Title (A Side/B Side)	Yr	NM
❑ S45-1938 [DJ]	Love Song (Long)/(Short)	1976	20.00

—Promo-only release from the Here And There live album

Number	Title (A Side/B Side)	Yr	NM
❑ 40000	Crocodile Rock/Elderberry Wine	1972	6.00

—Original pressings have a solid black label

Number	Title (A Side/B Side)	Yr	NM
❑ 40046	Daniel/Skyline Pigeon	1973	5.00
❑ 40105	Saturday Night's Alright for Fighting//Jack Rabbit/Whenever You're Ready	1973	5.00
❑ 40148	Goodbye Yellow Brick Road/Young Man's Blues	1973	5.00
❑ 40198	Bennie and the Jets/Harmony	1974	5.00
❑ 40259	Don't Let the Sun Go Down on Me/Sick City	1974	5.00
❑ 40297	The Bitch Is Back/Cold Highway	1974	5.00
❑ 40344	Lucy in the Sky with Diamonds/One Day at a Time	1974	5.00

—Both sides feature "Dr. Winston O'Boogie" (John Lennon)

Number	Title (A Side/B Side)	Yr	NM
❑ 40344 [PS]	Lucy in the Sky with Diamonds/One Day at a Time	1974	10.00
❑ 40364	Philadelphia Freedom/I Saw Her Standing There	1975	5.00

—B-side features John Lennon

Number	Title (A Side/B Side)	Yr	NM
❑ 40364 [PS]	Philadelphia Freedom/I Saw Her Standing There	1975	6.00
❑ 40364 [PS]	Philadelphia Freedom/I Saw Her Standing There	1975	40.00

—Promo-only sleeve from WFIL radio in Philadelphia

Number	Title (A Side/B Side)	Yr	NM
❑ 40421	Someone Saved My Life Tonight/House of Cards	1975	4.00

—With MCA black/rainbow label

Number	Title (A Side/B Side)	Yr	NM
❑ 40421	Someone Saved My Life Tonight/House of Cards	1975	5.00

—Original copies have "Captain Fantastic" label

Number	Title (A Side/B Side)	Yr	NM
❑ 40461	Island Girl/Sugar on the Floor	1975	4.00
❑ 40505	Grow Some Funk of Your Own/I Feel Like a Bullet (in the Gun of Robert Ford)	1976	4.00
❑ 40892	Ego/Flinstone Boy	1978	4.00
❑ 40892 [PS]	Ego/Flinstone Boy	1978	10.00
❑ 40973	Part-Time Love/I Cry at Night	1978	4.00
❑ 40973 [PS]	Part-Time Love/I Cry at Night	1978	4.00
❑ 40993	Song for Guy/Lovesick	1979	10.00

—The stock copy is much scarcer than the promo, the only Elton John MCA single where this is the case.

Number	Title (A Side/B Side)	Yr	NM
❑ 40993 [DJ]	Song for Guy/Lovesick	1979	5.00
❑ 40993 [PS]	Song for Guy/Lovesick	1979	5.00
❑ 41042	Mama Can't Buy You Love/Three Way Love Affair	1979	4.00
❑ 41042 [PS]	Mama Can't Buy You Love/Three Way Love Affair	1979	4.00
❑ 41126	Victim of Love/Strangers	1979	4.00

—Label correctly says "From the MCA LP...'Victim of Love'"

Number	Title (A Side/B Side)	Yr	NM
❑ 41126	Victim of Love/Strangers	1979	8.00

—Label incorrectly says "From the MCA LP...'Thunder in the Night'"

Number	Title (A Side/B Side)	Yr	NM
❑ 41159	Johnny B. Goode/Georgia	1980	5.00
❑ 41236	Little Jeannie/Conquer the Sun	1980	4.00

—Originals have a colorful custom label

Number	Title (A Side/B Side)	Yr	NM
❑ 41236 [PS]	Little Jeannie/Conquer the Sun	1980	5.00
❑ 41293	(Sartorial Eloquence) Don't Ya Wanna Play This Game No More?//Cartier/White Man Danger	1980	4.00
❑ 53196	Candle in the Wind/Sorry Seems to Be the Hardest Word	1987	3.00
❑ 53196 [PS]	Candle in the Wind/Sorry Seems to Be the Hardest Word	1987	3.00

—Yellow sleeve with album jackets pictured on back

Number	Title (A Side/B Side)	Yr	NM
❑ 53196 [PS]	Candle in the Wind/Sorry Seems to Be the Hardest Word	1987	4.00

—White sleeve

Number	Title (A Side/B Side)	Yr	NM
❑ 53260	Take Me to the Pilot/Tonight	1988	4.00
❑ 53260 [PS]	Take Me to the Pilot/Tonight	1988	4.00
❑ 53345	I Don't Wanna Go On with You Like That/Rope Around a Fool	1988	3.00
❑ 53345 [PS]	I Don't Wanna Go On with You Like That/Rope Around a Fool	1988	3.00
❑ 53408	A Word in Spanish/Heavy Traffic	1988	3.00
❑ 53408 [PS]	A Word in Spanish/Heavy Traffic	1988	3.00
❑ 53692	Healing Hands/Dancing in the End Zone	1989	3.00
❑ 53750	Sacrifice/Love Is a Cannibal	1989	3.00
❑ 54423	The One/Suit of Wolves	1992	3.00

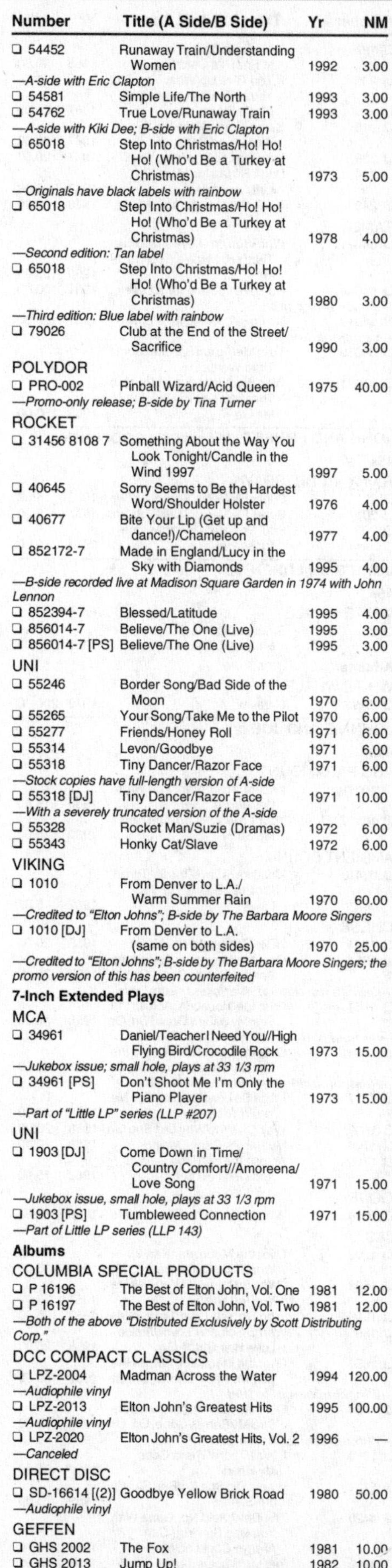

Number	Title (A Side/B Side)	Yr	NM
❑ 54452	Runaway Train/Understanding Women	1992	3.00
—A-side with Eric Clapton			
❑ 54581	Simple Life/The North	1993	3.00
❑ 54762	True Love/Runaway Train	1993	3.00
—A-side with Kiki Dee; B-side with Eric Clapton			
❑ 65018	Step Into Christmas/Ho! Ho! Ho! (Who'd Be a Turkey at Christmas)	1973	5.00
—Originals have black labels with rainbow			
❑ 65018	Step Into Christmas/Ho! Ho! Ho! (Who'd Be a Turkey at Christmas)	1978	4.00
—Second edition: Tan label			
❑ 65018	Step Into Christmas/Ho! Ho! Ho! (Who'd Be a Turkey at Christmas)	1980	3.00
—Third edition: Blue label with rainbow			
❑ 79026	Club at the End of the Street/ Sacrifice	1990	3.00
POLYDOR			
❑ PRO-002	Pinball Wizard/Acid Queen	1975	40.00
—Promo-only release; B-side by Tina Turner			
ROCKET			
❑ 31456 8108 7	Something About the Way You Look Tonight/Candle in the Wind 1997	1997	5.00
❑ 40645	Sorry Seems to Be the Hardest Word/Shoulder Holster	1976	4.00
❑ 40677	Bite Your Lip (Get up and dance!)/Chameleon	1977	4.00
❑ 852172-7	Made in England/Lucy in the Sky with Diamonds	1995	4.00
—B-side recorded live at Madison Square Garden in 1974 with John Lennon			
❑ 852394-7	Blessed/Latitude	1995	4.00
❑ 856014-7	Believe/The One (Live)	1995	3.00
❑ 856014-7 [PS]	Believe/The One (Live)	1995	3.00
UNI			
❑ 55246	Border Song/Bad Side of the Moon	1970	6.00
❑ 55265	Your Song/Take Me to the Pilot	1970	6.00
❑ 55277	Friends/Honey Roll	1971	6.00
❑ 55314	Levon/Goodbye	1971	6.00
❑ 55318	Tiny Dancer/Razor Face	1971	6.00
—Stock copies have full-length version of A-side			
❑ 55318 [DJ]	Tiny Dancer/Razor Face	1971	10.00
—With a severely truncated version of the A-side			
❑ 55328	Rocket Man/Suzie (Dramas)	1972	6.00
❑ 55343	Honky Cat/Slave	1972	6.00
VIKING			
❑ 1010	From Denver to L.A./ Warm Summer Rain	1970	60.00
—Credited to "Elton Johns"; B-side by The Barbara Moore Singers			
❑ 1010 [DJ]	From Denver to L.A. (same on both sides)	1970	25.00
—Credited to "Elton Johns"; B-side by The Barbara Moore Singers; the promo version of this has been counterfeited			

7-Inch Extended Plays

Number	Title (A Side/B Side)	Yr	NM
MCA			
❑ 34961	Daniel/Teacher I Need You//High Flying Bird/Crocodile Rock	1973	15.00
—Jukebox issue; small hole, plays at 33 1/3 rpm			
❑ 34961 [PS]	Don't Shoot Me I'm Only the Piano Player	1973	15.00
—Part of "Little LP" series (LLP #207)			
UNI			
❑ 1903 [DJ]	Come Down in Time/ Country Comfort//Amoreena/ Love Song	1971	15.00
—Jukebox issue, small hole, plays at 33 1/3 rpm			
❑ 1903 [PS]	Tumbleweed Connection	1971	15.00
—Part of Little LP series (LLP 143)			

Albums

Number	Title (A Side/B Side)	Yr	NM
COLUMBIA SPECIAL PRODUCTS			
❑ P 16196	The Best of Elton John, Vol. One	1981	12.00
❑ P 16197	The Best of Elton John, Vol. Two	1981	12.00
—Both of the above "Distributed Exclusively by Scott Distributing Corp."			
DCC COMPACT CLASSICS			
❑ LPZ-2004	Madman Across the Water	1994	120.00
—Audiophile vinyl			
❑ LPZ-2013	Elton John's Greatest Hits	1995	100.00
—Audiophile vinyl			
❑ LPZ-2020	Elton John's Greatest Hits, Vol. 2	1996	—
—Canceled			
DIRECT DISC			
❑ SD-16614 [(2)]	Goodbye Yellow Brick Road	1980	50.00
—Audiophile vinyl			
GEFFEN			
❑ GHS 2002	The Fox	1981	10.00
❑ GHS 2013	Jump Up!	1982	10.00

Elton John, "Nobody Wins," Geffen 49722, 1981, **$5.**

Number	Title (A Side/B Side)	Yr	NM
❑ PRO-A-2176 [DJ]	Sasson Presents Elton John	1983	30.00
—One-sided promo with four tracks on A-side and an etched facsimile autograph on B-side			
❑ GHS 4006	Too Low for Zero	1983	10.00
❑ GHS 24031	Breaking Hearts	1984	10.00
❑ GHS 24031 [DJ]	Breaking Hearts	1984	20.00
—Promo pressing on Quiex II vinyl			
❑ GHS 24077	Ice on Fire	1985	10.00
❑ GHS 24114	Leather Jackets	1986	10.00
❑ GHS 24153	Elton John's Greatest Hits, Vol. 3, 1979-1987	1987	10.00
MCA			
❑ 619	11-17-70	1979	8.00
❑ 620	Empty Sky	1979	8.00
❑ 621	Rock of the Westies	1979	8.00
❑ 622	Here and There	1979	8.00
❑ 771	Victim of Love	1981	8.00
❑ 772	21 at 33	1981	8.00
❑ 1689	Elton John's Greatest Hits	198?	8.00
❑ 4L33-1848 [(4)DJ]	Victim of Love	1979	100.00
—Promo-only collection of the entire album as four 12-inch singles			
❑ L33-1995 [PD]	A Single Man	1978	40.00
—Promo picture disc			
❑ 2012	Elton John	1973	10.00
❑ 2014	Tumbleweed Connection	1973	10.00
—With booklet			
❑ 2015	11-17-70	1973	10.00
❑ 2016	Madman Across the Water	1973	10.00
—With booklet			
❑ 2017	Honky Chateau	1973	10.00
❑ 2100	Don't Shoot Me, I'm Only the Piano Player	1973	10.00
—With black rainbow label and booklet			
❑ 2100	Don't Shoot Me, I'm Only the Piano Player	1973	20.00
—With all-black label (no rainbow) and booklet			
❑ 2116	Caribou	1974	10.00
❑ 2128	Elton John's Greatest Hits	1974	10.00
❑ 2130	Empty Sky	1975	10.00
—First American issue of his 1969 debut			

Number	Title (A Side/B Side)	Yr	NM
❑ 2142	Captain Fantastic and the Brown Dirt Cowboy	1975	12.00
—With custom label, two booklets and poster			
❑ 2142 [DJ]	Captain Fantastic and the Brown Dirt Cowboy	1975	300.00
—Brown vinyl promo, autographed by Elton John and Bernie Taupin			
❑ 2163	Rock of the Westies	1975	10.00
❑ 2197	Here and There	1976	10.00
❑ 3001	Tumbleweed Connection	1977	8.00
❑ 3003	Madman Across the Water	1977	8.00
❑ 3027	Elton John's Greatest Hits, Vol. 2	1977	10.00
❑ 3065	A Single Man	1978	10.00
❑ 5104	Victim of Love	1979	10.00
❑ 5121	21 at 33	1980	10.00
—Originals have custom labels			
❑ 5224	Elton John's Greatest Hits	1981	8.00
❑ 5225	Elton John's Greatest Hits, Vol. 2	1981	8.00
❑ 6011 [(2)]	Blue Moves	1979	10.00
❑ 6240	Reg Strikes Back	1988	10.00
❑ 6321	Sleeping with the Past	1989	10.00
❑ 6894 [(2)]	Goodbye Yellow Brick Road	1980	10.00
❑ 8022 [(2)]	Live in Australia with the Melbourne Symphony Orchestra	1987	15.00
❑ 2-10003 [(2)]	Goodbye Yellow Brick Road	1973	15.00
❑ 13921 [EP]	The Thom Bell Sessions	1979	8.00
❑ 14951 [PD]	A Single Man	1978	20.00
—Stock picture disc			
❑ 37064	Honky Chateau	1979	8.00
❑ 37065	Caribou	1979	8.00
❑ 37066	Captain Fantastic and the Brown Dirt Cowboy	1979	8.00
❑ 37067	Elton John	1979	8.00
❑ 37068	A Single Man	1979	8.00
❑ 37113	Don't Shoot Me, I'm Only the Piano Player	1979	8.00
❑ 37199	Tumbleweed Connection	1982	8.00
❑ 37200	Madman Across the Water	1982	8.00
❑ 37215	Elton John's Greatest Hits	1983	8.00
❑ 37216	Elton John's Greatest Hits	1983	8.00
❑ 37266	Your Songs	1986	10.00
❑ 39115	The Complete Thom Bell Sessions	1989	30.00

Number	Title (A Side/B Side)	Yr	NM
❏ R231711 [(2)]	Greatest Hits Vol.s One and Two	198?	15.00
—RCA Music Service exclusive; combines both MCA greatest-hits sets			
MERCURY			
❏ 5310374 [(2)]	Goodbye Yellow Brick Road	2008	30.00
MOBILE FIDELITY			
❏ 2-160 [(2)]	Goodbye Yellow Brick Road	1984	60.00
—Audiophile vinyl			
NAUTILUS			
❏ NR-42	Elton John's Greatest Hits	198?	100.00
—Audiophile vinyl			
PARAMOUNT			
❏ PAS 6004	Friends (Soundtrack)	1971	20.00
—Whitish gray label original			
❏ PAS 6004	Friends (Soundtrack)	1975	25.00
—Dark blue label with "Paramount" logo at top and ABC Records reference along edge; much rarer than the original			
ROCKET			
❏ L33-1173/4 [DJ]	Get Up and Dance	1977	100.00
—Promo-only sampler from "Blue Moves" LP; blue vinyl			
❏ 2-11004 [(2)]	Blue Moves	1976	15.00
—Originals have light blue labels with a train at the top of the label			
❏ 526915-1	Made in England	1995	20.00
—U.S. version is on 180-gram vinyl, distributed by Classic Records			
UNI			
❏ 73090	Elton John	1970	15.00
❏ 73096	Tumbleweed Connection	1971	15.00
—With booklet			
❏ 93090	Elton John	1971	12.00
❏ 93096	Tumbleweed Connection	1971	12.00
—With booklet			
❏ 93105	11-17-70	1971	15.00
❏ 93120	Madman Across the Water	1971	15.00
—With booklet			
❏ 93135	Honky Chateau	1972	15.00
—With "(P) 1972 This Record Co., Ltd." on label			
❏ 93135	Honky Chateau	1972	20.00
—With "(P) 1972 MCA Records, Inc." on label			

JOHN, ELTON, AND KIKI DEE

Also see each artist's individual listings.

45s

Number	Title (A Side/B Side)	Yr	NM
ROCKET			
❏ 40585	Don't Go Breakin' My Heart/ Snow Queen	1976	4.00
❏ 40585 [PS]	Don't Go Breakin' My Heart/ Snow Queen	1976	5.00

JOHN, ELTON, AND MILLIE JACKSON

Also see each artist's individual listings.

12-Inch Singles

Number	Title (A Side/B Side)	Yr	NM
GEFFEN			
❏ PRO-A-2324 [DJ]	Act of War (Edit)/(Instrumental)	1985	8.00
❏ 20347	Act of War (8:32)/(5:04)	1985	8.00

45s

Number	Title (A Side/B Side)	Yr	NM
GEFFEN			
❏ 28956	Act of War, Part 1/ Act of War, Part 2	1985	4.00
❏ 28956 [PS]	Act of War, Part 1/ Act of War, Part 2	1985	4.00

JOHN, LITTLE WILLIE

45s

Number	Title (A Side/B Side)	Yr	NM
ATLANTIC			
❏ 89189	Fever/Ruby Baby	1987	3.00
—B-side by the Drifters			
❏ 89189 [PS]	Fever/Ruby Baby	1987	3.00
—From the movie "Big Town"			
KING			
❏ 4818	All Around the World/ Don't Leave Me Dear	1955	25.00
❏ 4841	Need Your Love So Bad/ Home at Last	1955	25.00
❏ 4893	Are You Ever Coming Back/ I'm Stickin' with You Baby	1956	25.00
❏ 4935	Fever/Letter from My Darling	1956	30.00
❏ 4960	Do Something for Me/My Nerves	1956	25.00
❏ 4989	I've Been Around/Suffering with the Blues	1956	25.00
❏ 5003	Will the Sun Shine Tomorrow/ A Little Bit of Loving	1956	25.00
❏ 5023	Love, Life and Money/You Got to Get Up Early in the Morning	1957	25.00
❏ 5045	I've Got to Go Cry/Look What You've Done to Me	1957	25.00
❏ 5066	Young Girl/If I Thought You Needed Me	1957	25.00
❏ 5083	Uh Uh Baby/Summer Date	1957	25.00
❏ 5091	Person to Person/Until You Do	1957	25.00
❏ 5108	Talk to Me, Talk to Me/Spasms	1958	25.00
❏ 5142	Let's Rock While the Rockin's Good/You're a Sweetheart	1958	25.00
❏ 5147	Tell It Like It Is/Don't Be Ashamed to Call My Name	1958	25.00
❏ 5154	All My Love Belongs to You/ Why Don't You Haul Off and Love Me	1958	25.00
❏ 5170	No Regrets/I'll Carry Your Love Wherever I Go	1959	20.00
❏ 5179	Made for Me/Do More in Life	1959	20.00
❏ 5219	Leave My Kitten Alone/ Let Nobody Love You	1959	20.00
❏ 5274	Let Them Talk/Right There	1959	20.00
❏ 5318	Loving Care/My Love Is	1960	20.00
❏ 5342	I'm Shakin'/Cottage for Sale	1960	100.00
❏ 5356	Heartbreak (It's Hurtin' Me)/ Do You Love Me	1960	20.00
❏ 5394	Sleep/There's a Difference	1960	20.00
❏ 5428	Walk Slow/You Hurt Me	1960	15.00
❏ 5428/30 [DJ]	Walk Slow/The Hoochi Coochi Coo	1960	25.00
—White label; B-side by Hank Ballard and the Midnighters			
❏ 5452	Leave My Kitten Alone/I'll Never Go Back on My Word	1961	15.00
❏ 5458	I'm Sorry/The Very Thought of You	1961	15.00
❏ 5503	(I've Got) Spring Fever/Flamingo	1961	15.00
❏ 5516	Take My Love (I Want to Give It All to You)/Now You Know	1961	15.00
❏ 5539	Need Your Love So Bad/ Drive Me Home	1961	15.00
❏ 5577	There Is Someone in This World for Me/Autumn Leaves	1961	15.00
❏ 5591	Fever/Bo-Da-Ley Dino-Ley	1962	15.00
❏ 5602	The Masquerade Is Over/ Katanga	1962	15.00
❏ 5628	Until Again My Love/Mister Glenn	1962	15.00
❏ 5641	Every Beat of My Heart/ I Wish I Could Cry	1962	15.00
❏ 5667	She Thinks I Still Care/ Come Back to Me	1962	15.00
❏ 5681	Doll Face/Big Blue Diamonds	1962	15.00
❏ 5694	Without a Friend/Half a Love	1962	15.00
❏ 5717	Don't Play with Love/ Heaven All Around Me	1963	12.00
❏ 5744	My Baby's in Love with Another Guy/Come On Sugar	1963	12.00
❏ 5799	Let Them Talk/Talk to Me	1963	12.00
❏ 5818	So Lovely/Inside Information	1963	12.00
❏ 5823	Person to Person/I'm Shakin'	1963	40.00
❏ 5850	Bill Bailey/My Love Will Never Change	1964	12.00
❏ 5870	Rock Love/It Only Hurts for a Little While	1964	40.00
❏ 5886	All Around the World/All My Love Belongs to You	1964	12.00
❏ 5949	Do Something for Me/ Don't You Know I'm in Love	1964	12.00
❏ 6003	Talk to Me/Take My Love	1965	10.00
❏ 6170	Fever/Let Them Talk	1968	10.00
❏ 6302	All Around the World/ Need Your Love So Bad	1970	8.00

7-Inch Extended Plays

Number	Title (A Side/B Side)	Yr	NM
KING			
❏ EP-423	*Talk to Me, Talk to Me/ You're a Sweetheart/Fever/ Tell It Like It Is	1958	250.00
❏ EP-423 [PS]	Talk to Me	1958	250.00

Albums

Number	Title (A Side/B Side)	Yr	NM
BLUESWAY			
❏ BLS-6069	Free at Last	1973	25.00
KING			
❏ 564 [M]	Fever	1957	600.00
—White cover with "Fever" in large colorful letters			
❏ 395-564 [M]	Fever	1956	1000.
—"Nurse with thermometer" cover			
❏ 596 [M]	Talk to Me	1958	300.00
❏ 603 [M]	Mister Little Willie John	1958	250.00
❏ 691 [M]	Little Willie John In Action	1960	250.00
❏ 739 [M]	Sure Things	1961	150.00
❏ 767 [M]	The Sweet, the Hot, the Teenage Beat	1961	150.00
❏ 802 [M]	Come On and Join Little Willie John	1962	120.00
❏ 895 [M]	These Are My Favorite Songs	1964	100.00
❏ 949 [M]	Little Willie Sings All Originals	1966	100.00
❏ KS-949 [S]	Little Willie Sings All Originals	1966	150.00
❏ KS-1081	Free at Last	1970	40.00

JOHN, MABLE

45s

Number	Title (A Side/B Side)	Yr	NM
MOTOWN			
❏ 54031	Who Wouldn't Love a Man Like That/You Made a Fool Out of Me	1960	500.00
—Mispress with wrong label; may have been promo only			
STAX			
❏ 0016	Running Out/Shouldn't I Love Him	1968	20.00
❏ 192	Your Good Thing (Is About to End)/It's Catching	1966	20.00
❏ 205	If You Give Up What You Got/ You're Taking Up Another Man's Place	1967	20.00
❏ 215	Same Time, Same Place/ Bigger and Better	1967	20.00
❏ 225	I'm a Big Girl Now/Wait You Dog	1967	20.00
❏ 234	Don't Hit Me No More/ Left Over Love	1967	20.00
❏ 249	Don't Get Caught/Able Mable	1968	20.00
TAMLA			
❏ 54031	Who Wouldn't Love a Man Like That/You Made a Fool Out of Me	1960	150.00
❏ 54040	No Love/Looking for a Love	1961	100.00
—Version with no intro			
❏ 54040	No Love/Looking for a Love	1961	120.00
—Version with long intro			
❏ 54050	Take Me/Action Speaks Louder Than Words	1962	500.00
❏ 54081	Who Wouldn't Love a Man Like That/Say You'll Never Let Me Go	1963	150.00

JOHN AND ERNEST

Also see DICKIE GOODMAN.

45s

Number	Title (A Side/B Side)	Yr	NM
RAINY WEDNESDAY			
❏ 201	Super Fly Meets Shaft/Part Two	1973	5.00
❏ 201	Super Fly Meets Shaft/Problems	1973	5.00
❏ 203	Soul President Number One/ Crossover	1973	5.00

JOHN'S CHILDREN

45s

Number	Title (A Side/B Side)	Yr	NM
WHITE WHALE			
❏ 239	Strange Affair/ Smashed, Blocked	1966	20.00

Albums

Number	Title (A Side/B Side)	Yr	NM
WHITE WHALE			
❏ WWS 7128	Orgasm	1970	200.00

JOHNNIE AND JOE

45s

Number	Title (A Side/B Side)	Yr	NM
ABC-PARAMOUNT			
❏ 10079	I Adore You/I Want You Here Beside Me	1960	15.00
❏ 10117	Your Love/Why Do You Hurt Me So	1960	15.00
AMBIENT SOUND			
❏ 03410	Kingdom of Love/Tossin' Turnin' (Yeamin' Burnin' For Your Love)	1982	5.00
CHESS			
❏ 1641	I'll Be Spinning/Feel Alright	1956	20.00
❏ 1654	Over the Mountain; Across the Sea/My Baby's Gone, On, On	1957	25.00
—Originals with blue and silver "chess pieces" label			
❏ 1654	Over the Mountain; Across the Sea/My Baby's Gone, On, On	1958	12.00
—Reissues on blue labels with vertical "CHESS"			
❏ 1654	Over the Mountain; Across the Sea/My Baby's Gone, On, On	1963	10.00
—Reissues on other labels (multicolor, black)			
❏ 1677	I Was So Lonely/If You Tell Me You're Mine	1957	20.00
❏ 1693	Why Oh Why/Why Did She Go	1958	20.00
❏ 1706	My Baby's Gone/Darling	1958	20.00
❏ 1769	Across the Sea/You Said It, And Don't Forget It	1960	15.00
GONE			
❏ 5024	Who Do You Love/Trust in Me	1958	30.00
J&S			
❏ 1008	Over the Mountain (Part 2)/ Won't You Come Back to Me	1959	25.00
❏ 1603	I Was So Lonely/If You Tell Me You're Mine	1957	25.00
❏ 1605/6	Who Do You Love/Trust in Me	1958	25.00
❏ 1630/1	Warm, Soft and Lovely/False Love Has Got to Go	1958	25.00
❏ 1654	Over the Mountain; Across the Sea/My Baby's Gone, On, On	1957	150.00
—With horizontal lines on label			
❏ 1654	Over the Mountain; Across the Sea/My Baby's Gone, On, On	1962	20.00
—Without horizontal lines on label			
❏ 1659	It Was There/There Goes My Heart	1957	25.00
❏ 1701	Where Did She Go/Red Sails in the Sunset	1959	25.00
❏ 4420	The Devil Said No, Gone With You Bad Self/You Can Always Count on Me	196?	15.00
❏ 8719	Tell Me/Sincere Love	196?	15.00

Except when noted otherwise, VG = 25% of NM, and VG+ = 50% of NM. (Example: VG = $2.00, VG+ = $4.00 and NM = $8.00.)

Number	Title (A Side/B Side)	Yr	NM
❑ 42832	You're the Loveliest Song/Let Your Mind Do the Walking	196?	15.00
❑ 87187	False Love Has Got to Go/ Jamaica — Our Thing	196?	15.00
LANA			
❑ 121	Over the Mountain; Across the Sea/Shortening Bread	196?	10.00
TUFF			
❑ 379	Here We Go Baby/That's the Way You Go	1964	12.00
Albums			
AMBIENT SOUND			
❑ FZ 38345	Kingdom of Love	1982	12.00

JOHNNY AND JACKEY
Also see JACKEY BEAVERS; JOHNNY BRISTOL.

Number	Title (A Side/B Side)	Yr	NM
45s			
ANNA			
❑ 1108	Let's Go to a Movie Baby/ Lonely and Blue	1960	25.00
❑ 1120	Hoy Boy/No One Else But You	1960	25.00
TRI-PHI			
❑ 1002	Carry Your Own Load/ So Disappointing	1961	25.00
❑ 1005	Someday We'll Be Together/ She Don't Play	1961	30.00
❑ 1016	Do You See My Love for You Growing/Carry Your Own Load	1962	25.00
❑ 1019	Baby Don'tcha Worry/Stop What You're Saying	1963	25.00

JOHNNY AND JON

Number	Title (A Side/B Side)	Yr	NM
45s			
JEWEL			
❑ 776	Christmas in Viet Nam/Why Did You Leave Me Crawl	1966	30.00

JOHNNY AND THE BLUE BEATS

Number	Title (A Side/B Side)	Yr	NM
Albums			
WINSOR			
❑ 1001	Smile	196?	40.00

JOHNNY AND THE DREAMS

Number	Title (A Side/B Side)	Yr	NM
45s			
RICHIE			
❑ 457	You're Too Young/Are You for Me	1961	250.00
—Black vinyl			
❑ 457	You're Too Young/Are You for Me	1961	500.00
—Red vinyl			

JOHNNY AND THE HURRICANES

Number	Title (A Side/B Side)	Yr	NM
45s			
ATILA			
❑ 211	Saga of the Beatles/Rene	1967	10.00
❑ 214	Judy's Moody/I Love You	1967	10.00
❑ 215	Because I Love You/ Wisdom's 5th Take	1967	10.00
❑ 216	Red River Rock '67/The Psychedlic Woman	1967	10.00
BIG TOP			
❑ 3036	Down Yonder/Sheba	1960	20.00
❑ 3036 [PS]	Down Yonder/Sheba	1960	40.00
❑ 3051	Revival/Rocking Goose	1960	20.00
❑ 3051 [PS]	Revival/Rocking Goose	1960	40.00
❑ 3056	You Are My Sunshine/Molly-O	1960	20.00
❑ 3056 [PS]	You Are My Sunshine/Molly-O	1960	40.00
❑ 3063	Ja-Da/Mr. Lonely	1961	20.00
❑ 3063 [PS]	Ja-Da/Mr. Lonely	1961	40.00
❑ 3076	Old Smokie/High Voltage	1961	20.00
❑ 3076 [PS]	Old Smokie/High Voltage	1961	40.00
❑ 3090	Traffic Jam/Farewell, Farewell	1961	20.00
❑ 3103	Misirlou/Salvation	1962	20.00
❑ 3113	San Antonio Rose/ Come On Train	1962	20.00
❑ 3125	Shiek of Araby/Minnesota Fats	1962	20.00
❑ 3132	Whatever Happened to Baby Jane/Greens and Beans	1963	20.00
❑ 3146	James Bond Theme/Hungry Eye	1963	20.00
❑ 3159	Rough Road/Kaw-Liga	1963	20.00
JEFF			
❑ 211	Saga of the Beatles/Rene	1964	15.00
LOST-NITE			
❑ 221	Reveille Rock/Sheba	196?	5.00
—Reissue			
MALA			
❑ 470	It's a Mad, Mad, Mad, Mad World/ Shadows	1963	10.00
❑ 483	That's All/Honey, Honey	1964	10.00
TWIRL			
❑ 1001	Crossfire/Lazy	1958	50.00
WARWICK			
❑ 502	Crossfire/Lazy	1959	25.00
❑ 509 [M]	Red River Rock/Buckeye	1959	25.00
❑ 509 ST [S]	Red River Rock/Buckeye	1959	50.00
❑ 513 [M]	Reveille Rock/Time Bomb	1959	25.00
❑ 513 ST [S]	Reveille Rock/Time Bomb	1959	50.00
❑ 520	Beatnik Fly/Sand Storm	1960	20.00
❑ 520 [PS]	Beatnik Fly/Sand Storm	1960	60.00
7-Inch Extended Plays			
WARWICK			
❑ EX-700	Red River Rock/Storm Warning//Joy Ride/Bam Boo	1959	80.00
❑ EX-700 [PS]	Johnny and the Hurricanes	1959	120.00
—Came with paper sleeve rather than cardboard sleeve			
Albums			
ATILA			
❑ 1030 [M]	Live at the Star-Club	1964	300.00
BIG TOP			
❑ 12-1302 [M]	The Big Sound of Johnny and the Hurricanes	1960	250.00
❑ ST 12-1302 [S]	The Big Sound of Johnny and the Hurricanes	1960	300.00
WARWICK			
❑ W-2007 [M]	Johnny and the Hurricanes	1959	150.00
❑ W-2007ST [S]	Johnny and the Hurricanes	1959	300.00
❑ W-2010 [M]	Stormsville	1960	150.00
❑ W-2010ST [S]	Stormsville	1960	250.00

JOHNNY AND THE JAMMERS
"Johnny" is JOHNNY WINTER. His debut single.

Number	Title (A Side/B Side)	Yr	NM
45s			
DART			
❑ 131	School Day Blues/You Know I Love You	1959	300.00

JOHNNY AND THE TOKENS
Also see THE TOKENS.

Number	Title (A Side/B Side)	Yr	NM
45s			
WARWICK			
❑ 658	The Taste of a Tear/ Never Till Now	1961	20.00

JOHNS, LUCILLE

Number	Title (A Side/B Side)	Yr	NM
45s			
HIT			
❑ 39	Release Me/Desafinado	1962	8.00
—B-side by the Boots Purcell Combo			

JOHNS, SAMMY

Number	Title (A Side/B Side)	Yr	NM
45s			
ELEKTRA			
❑ 47189	Common Man/Easy to Be with You	1981	4.00
❑ 47248	Love Me Off the Road/This Time	1981	4.00
GRC			
❑ 1001	Shake a Hand/(B-side unknown)	1973	4.00
❑ 1007	America/(B-side unknown)	1973	4.00
❑ 2021	Early Morning Love/Holy Mother, Aging Father	1974	4.00
❑ 2046	Chevy Van/Hang My Head and Moan	1975	5.00
❑ 2062	Rag Doll/Friends of Mine	1975	4.00
MCA			
❑ 53398	Chevy Van/Love Me Off the Road	1988	3.00
REAL WORLD			
❑ 7307	Falling Over You/Six Feet Tall and Handsome	1980	4.00
SOUTHERN TRACKS			
❑ 1010	There! I've Said It Again/All Wrapped Up in Your Love	1982	5.00
❑ 1031	I'd Rather Be Hurt by You/All Wrapped Up in Your Love	1984	5.00
❑ 1036	Desperado Love/All Wrapped Up in Your Love	1985	5.00
❑ 1046	You Just Made Me Up in Your Mind/Lifetime Thing	1985	5.00
❑ 1075	Rock You Like a Baby/ Tennessee Valley Girl	1987	5.00
❑ 1086	Early Morning Love/ (B-side unknown)	1988	5.00
❑ 1096	Sam's Song/Tennessee Valley Girl	1988	5.00
WARNER BROS.			
❑ 8224	Peas in a Pod/Friends of Mine	1976	4.00
❑ 8270	America/Bless Our Soul	1976	4.00
❑ 8335	Hey Mr. Dreamer/Female Chauvinist Sow	1977	4.00
❑ 8441	Chevy Van/Music of the Band	1977	4.00
Albums			
GRC			
❑ 5003	Sammy Johns	1975	12.00

JOHNSON, BETTY

Number	Title (A Side/B Side)	Yr	NM
45s			
ATLANTIC			
❑ 1169	The Little Blue Man/ Winter in Miami	1958	15.00
❑ 1186	Dream/How Much	1958	12.00
❑ 2002	Hoopa Hoola/One More Time	1958	12.00
❑ 2009	You Can't Get to Heaven on Roller Skates/I Want a Good Home for My Cat	1958	12.00
❑ 2019	Does Your Heart Beat for Me?/ You and Only You	1959	12.00
❑ 2039	The Lonely Willow Tree/ Waltz Me Around	1959	12.00
❑ 2056	Fantastic/You Don't Care a Rowboat	1960	12.00
BALLY			
❑ 1000	I'll Wait/Please Tell Me Why	1956	12.00
❑ 1005	Honky Tonk Rock/ Say It Ain't So, Joe	1956	15.00
❑ 1013	Clay Idol/Why Do You Cry?	1956	12.00
❑ 1020	I Dreamed/If It's Wrong to Love You	1956	12.00
❑ 1033	Little White Lies/1492	1957	12.00
❑ 1041	The Song You Heard When You Fell in Love/I'm Beginning to Wonder	1957	12.00
BELL			
❑ 1074	Make Yourself Comfortable/ All of You	1955	15.00
—May or may not be the same Betty Johnson as the others			
COED			
❑ 532	There's a Star Spangled Banner Waving Somewhere/Take a Little Look (In the Good Book)	1960	10.00
DOT			
❑ 16127	Slipping Around/One Has My Name, The Other Has My Heart	1960	10.00
NEW-DISC			
❑ 10013	I Want Eddie Fisher For Christmas/Show Me	1954	25.00
RCA VICTOR			
❑ 47-6034	Seven Pretty Dreams/Be a Lover	1955	12.00
❑ 47-6158	That's Happiness/Give Me Something I Can Dream About	1955	12.00
❑ 47-6268	I'm a Sinner/Beginner's Luck	1955	12.00
❑ 47-8143	Betty's Bossa Nova/ Ginny's Got a Phone	1963	8.00
REPUBLIC			
❑ 2011	Depend on Me/I Don't Want to Go to Sleep Tonight	1961	10.00
❑ 2017	Let Me Be the One/ Only When I Dream	1961	10.00
❑ 2021	My Kind of Guy/A Gal's Best Friend Is Her Makeup	1961	10.00
❑ 2025	How Do You Tell Your Heart/ Why, Why	1961	10.00
❑ 2026	I Dreamed/Luna Caprese	1962	10.00
WORLD ARTISTS			
❑ 1014	Wednesday's Child/ What's the Matter	1963	8.00
Albums			
ATLANTIC			
❑ 8017 [M]	Betty Johnson	1958	50.00
❑ 8027 [M]	The Song You Heard When You Fell in Love	1959	50.00
—Black label			
❑ 8027 [M]	The Song You Heard When You Fell in Love	1960	20.00
—White "fan" logo on right			
❑ SD 8027 [S]	The Song You Heard When You Fell in Love	1959	80.00
—Green label			
❑ SD 8027 [S]	The Song You Heard When You Fell in Love	1960	25.00
—White "fan" logo on right			

JOHNSON, BILL

Number	Title (A Side/B Side)	Yr	NM
45s			
SUN			
❑ 340	Bobaloo/Bad Times Ahead	1960	20.00

JOHNSON, BLIND WILLIE

Number	Title (A Side/B Side)	Yr	NM
Albums			
FOLKWAYS			
❑ FG-3585 [M]	Blind Willie Johnson: His Story	1957	100.00
RBF			
❑ 10 [M]	Blind Willie Johnson 1927-1930	1965	70.00

JOHNSON, BUBBER

45s

Number	Title (A Side/B Side)	Yr	NM
KING			
4793	Drop Me a Line/Ding Dang Doo	1955	20.00
4822	Come Home/There'll Be No One	1955	20.00
4855	It's Christmas Time/Let's Make Everyday a Christmas Day	1955	20.00
4872	Wonderful Things Happen/Keep a Light in the Window	1956	20.00
4924	My One Desire/I Lost Track of Everything	1956	20.00
4939	My Lonely Heart/Have a Little Faith in Me	1956	20.00
4988	Confidential/Let's Take a Walk	1956	20.00
5014	Butterfly/Too Many Hearts	1957	20.00
5034	Little Girls Don't Cry/The Search	1957	20.00
5068	Crazy Afternoon/So Much Tonight	1957	20.00
5089	Muddy Water/The Whisperers	1957	20.00
5117	Dedicated to the One I Love/Prince of Players	1958	15.00
5132	Finger Tips/I'm Confessin'	1958	15.00
5143	I Surrender Dear/Everybody's With You When You're Winning	1958	15.00
5148	I Can't See Why/As Long As I Live	1958	15.00
5174	One Good Reason/Time Was	1959	15.00
5193	House of Love/Until Sunrise	1959	15.00
5232	I Do (Love You)/Come On	1959	15.00
5267	Tell Me Who/I Know My Way	1959	15.00
5298	Those Who Dream/Atlanta	1959	15.00
MERCURY			
8285	I've Got an Invitation/Forget It If You Can	1952	60.00

Albums

Number	Title (A Side/B Side)	Yr	NM
KING			
569 [M]	Come Home	1957	200.00
624 [M]	Bubber Johnson Sings Sweet Love Songs	1959	150.00

JOHNSON, BUDDY

45s

Number	Title (A Side/B Side)	Yr	NM
ATLANTIC			
1013	Don't Take Your Love from Me/Off Shore	1953	25.00
DECCA			
28907	Talkin' About Another Man's Wife/Jeannette	1953	25.00
29058	A Handful of Stars/Two Cigarettes in the Dark	1954	25.00
MERCURY			
70173	Jit Jit/That's What I Feel About You	1953	20.00
70488	I Never Had It So Good/There's No One Like You	1954	15.00
70656	Send Out for a Bottle of Beer/Bitter Sweet	1955	15.00
70695	It's Obdacious/Save Your Love for Me	1955	15.00
71017	Why Don't Cha Stop It/Kool Kitty	1956	12.00
71159	I've Surrendered/Slide's Mambo	1957	12.00
71262	Minglin'/I Wonder Where Our Love Has Gone	1958	12.00
71799	The Last Laugh's on You (Ha, Ha, Baby)/Good Time Man	1961	10.00
WING			
90064	Doot Doot Dow/I Don't Want Nobody	1956	15.00
90074	Buddy's Boogie/I'll Dearly Love You	1956	15.00
90084	Goodbye Baby/I Still Love You	1956	15.00

Albums

Number	Title (A Side/B Side)	Yr	NM
MCA			
1356	Fine Brown Frame	198?	10.00
MERCURY			
MG-20209 [M]	Rock 'N' Roll	195?	80.00
MG-20322 [M]	Walkin'	195?	80.00
MG-20330 [M]	Buddy Johnson Wails	195?	80.00
MG-20347 [M]	Swing Me	195?	80.00
SR-60072 [S]	Buddy Johnson Wails	195?	100.00
WING			
MGW-12005 [M]	Rock 'N' Roll	1956	150.00
MGW-12111 [M]	Rock 'n' Roll Stage Show	1963	40.00
MGW-12234 [M]	Buddy Johnson Wails	196?	30.00

JOHNSON, BUDDY & ELLA

Also see BUDDY JOHNSON.

45s

Number	Title (A Side/B Side)	Yr	NM
MERCURY			
70251	I'm Just Your Fool/A-12	1953	20.00
70321	One More Time/Mush Mouth	1954	20.00
70377	Ain't Cha Got Me/Let's Start All Over Again	1954	20.00
70421	Any Day Now/A Pretty Girl, a Cadillac and Money	1954	20.00
70459	We'll Do It/It Used to Hurt Me	1954	20.00
70523	Crazy 'Bout a Saxophone/Gotta Go Upside Your Head	1955	15.00
70775	Doot Doot Dow/I Don't Want Nobody	1956	12.00
70912	Bring It Home to Me/You Got It Made	1956	12.00
71723	I Don't Want Nobody (To Have My Love But You)/I'm Just Your Fool	1960	10.00
ROULETTE			
4134	Tune No. 1/Don't Fail Me Baby	1959	12.00
4188	Keep My Love for You/A Woman, a Lover, a Friend	1959	12.00

Albums

Number	Title (A Side/B Side)	Yr	NM
MERCURY			
MG-20347 [M]	Swing Me	195?	80.00
ROULETTE			
R 25085 [M]	Go Ahead and Rock and Roll	1959	80.00
SR 25085 [S]	Go Ahead and Rock and Roll	1959	120.00

JOHNSON, CLIFF

45s

Number	Title (A Side/B Side)	Yr	NM
COLUMBIA			
40865	Go 'Way Hound Dog/Twenty Four Hours a Day	1957	80.00

JOHNSON, ERNIE

Also see EDDIE AND ERNIE.

45s

Number	Title (A Side/B Side)	Yr	NM
ARTCO			
45-104	I Can't Stand the Pain/These Very Tender Moments	1967	1500.
ASNES			
104	Tell Her For Me/You Need Love	1961	25.00
ROLO			
8800	You're Unforgettable (same on both sides)	198?	5.00
RONN			
102	Mouth to Mouth Resuscitation/You're Gonna Miss Me	1984	6.00
104	You're About to Succeed/Give Me a Little Bit of Your Lovin'	1984	10.00
109	Cold Woman/Party All Night	1984	10.00
113	Forever/Just in Time	198?	15.00
115	It's Party Time/Final Notice	198?	10.00
117	Dreams to Remember/Hard Times	198?	20.00
121	Honey I Love You/I'm Doing Alright	198?	6.00
124	I'm Doin' Alright/That Thang	198?	6.00
126	In My Dreams/Forever	198?	6.00
STEPH & LEE			
8667	Big Man Cry/Drowning in Misery	197?	60.00
WALDOXY			
109	Cold This Winter/I'm in the Mood for the Blues	1995	10.00

Albums

Number	Title (A Side/B Side)	Yr	NM
RONN			
LPS-8001	Just in Time	1985	15.00

JOHNSON, HOYT

45s

Number	Title (A Side/B Side)	Yr	NM
ERWIN			
555	Eeny Meany Minie Mo/(B-side unknown)	1957	200.00
RCA VICTOR			
47-7522	Sylvia/Bella Renee	1959	40.00
47-7607	Little Boy Blue/My Special Girl	1959	150.00
47-7731	Too Shy/Eca-La	1960	40.00
SATELLITE			
110	Cindy/I Just Can't Learn	1961	25.00

JOHNSON, J.J.

Albums

Number	Title (A Side/B Side)	Yr	NM
SAVOY			
MG-12205 [M]	Jazz South Pacific	196?	20.00
—Reissue of Regent 6001			

JOHNSON, JIMMY

45s

Number	Title (A Side/B Side)	Yr	NM
ALLIGATOR			
792	Serves Me Right to Suffer/Your Turn to Cry	1979	4.00
CLASS			
237	Cool, Cool School/Lone Ranger Gonna Get Married	1958	60.00
MID WEST			
1002	Mean Woman Blues/(B-side unknown)	195?	250.00
RENDEZVOUS			
145	Cool, Cool School/Lone Ranger Gonna Get Married	1961	25.00
VIV			
3001	How About Me? Pretty Baby/Cat Daddy	1956	200.00

JOHNSON, JOHNNY, AND THE BANDWAGON

See THE BANDWAGON.

JOHNSON, LEN

45s

Number	Title (A Side/B Side)	Yr	NM
RAY-CO			
503	Sweet Thing/One Day	1963	15.00

JOHNSON, LONNIE

45s

Number	Title (A Side/B Side)	Yr	NM
BLUESVILLE			
806	Don't Ever Love/You Don't Move Me	196?	12.00
812	I'll Get Along Somehow/Memories of You	196?	12.00
FEDERAL			
12376	Friendless Blues/What a Real Woman	1960	15.00
KING			
4201	Tomorrow Night/What a Woman	1951	60.00
—78 released in 1948			
4459	Take Me I'm Yours/Why Should I Cry	1951	40.00
4473	It Was All in Vain/You Only Want Me When You're Lonely	1951	40.00
4492	Happy New Year, Darling/Christmas Blues	1951	50.00
—B-side by Gatemouth Moore			
4503	Seven Long Days/Darlin'	1951	40.00
4510	My Mother's Eyes/My Crazy Self	1951	40.00
4553	I'm Guilty/Can't Sleep Anymore	1952	40.00
4572	You Can't Buy Love/Just Another Day	1952	40.00
4758	Tomorrow Night/Pleasing You	1954	40.00
5293	Tomorrow Night/Pleasing You	1959	15.00
5907	Love Me Tonight/Brenda	1964	10.00
6303	Tomorrow Night/Blues Stay Away from Me	1970	6.00
PRESTIGE			
310	Mr. Jelly Roll Baker/I'll Get Along Somehow	1964	10.00
RAMA			
9	My Woman Is Gone/Don't Make Me Cry Baby	1953	60.00
—Black vinyl			
9	My Woman Is Gone/Don't Make Me Cry Baby	1953	150.00
—Red vinyl			
14	Stick With It Baby/Will You Remember	1953	60.00
19	It's Been So Long/Vaya Con Dios	1953	60.00
20	This Love of Mine/I Love a Dream	1953	60.00

Albums

Number	Title (A Side/B Side)	Yr	NM
BLUESVILLE			
BVLP-1007 [M]	Blues by Lonnie	1960	200.00
—Blue label, silver print			
BVLP-1007 [M]	Blues by Lonnie	1964	60.00
—Blue label with trident logo at right			
BVLP-1011 [M]	Blues and Ballads	1960	200.00
—Blue label, silver print			
BVLP-1011 [M]	Blues and Ballads	1964	60.00
—Blue label with trident logo at right			
BVLP-1024 [M]	Losing Game	1961	200.00
—Blue label, silver print			
BVLP-1024 [M]	Losing Game	1964	60.00
—Blue label with trident logo at right			
BVLP-1062 [M]	Another Night to Cry	1963	200.00
—Blue label, silver print			
BVLP-1062 [M]	Another Night to Cry	1964	60.00
—Blue label with trident logo at right			
COLUMBIA			
C 46221	Steppin' On the Blues	1990	20.00
FANTASY			
OBC-502	Blues by Lonnie	198?	12.00
OBC-531	Blues and Ballads	1990	12.00
KING			
520 [M]	Lonesome Road	1958	2000.
—VG value 750; VG+ value 1375			
958 [M]	Lonnie Johnson 24 Twelve-Bar Blues	1966	60.00
KS-958 [R]	Lonnie Johnson 24 Twelve-Bar Blues	1966	60.00
KS-1083	Tomorrow Night	1970	25.00

Except when noted otherwise, VG = 25% of NM, and VG+ = 50% of NM. (Example: VG = $2.00, VG+ = $4.00 and NM = $8.00.)

Number | Title (A Side/B Side) | Yr | NM

PRESTIGE
❑ PRST-7724 The Blues of Lonnie Johnson 1970 20.00

JOHNSON, LONNIE, AND VICTORIA SPIVEY

Albums

BLUESVILLE
❑ BVLP-1044 [M] Idle Hours 1962 150.00
—Blue label, silver print
❑ BVLP-1044 [M] Idle Hours 1964 50.00
—Blue label with trident logo at right
❑ BVLP-1054 [M] Woman Blues 1962 150.00
—Blue label, silver print
❑ BVLP-1054 [M] Woman Blues 1964 50.00
—Blue label with trident logo at right

FANTASY
❑ OBC-518 Idle Hours 198? 12.00

JOHNSON, MARV

45s

GORDY
❑ 7042 Why Do You Want to Let Me Go/I'm Not a Plaything 1965 15.00
❑ 7051 Just the Way You Are/Miss You Baby 1966 15.00
❑ 7077 I'll Pick a Rose for My Rose/You Got the Love I Love 1968 15.00

KUDO
❑ 663 My Baby-O/Once Upon a Time 1958 600.00

TAMLA
❑ 101 Come to Me/Whisper 1959 150.00
—With Gladstone St., Detroit, address on label
❑ 101 Come to Me/Whisper 1959 200.00
—No address on label

UNITED ARTISTS
❑ 0030 You've Got What It Takes/I Love the Way You Love 1973 5.00
—"Silver Spotlight Series" reissue
❑ 0031 Move Two Mountains/Come to Me 1973 5.00
—"Silver Spotlight Series" reissue
❑ 160 Come to Me/Whisper 1959 25.00
❑ 175 River of Tears/I'm Coming Home 1959 20.00
❑ 185 You Got What It Takes/Don't Leave Me 1959 20.00
❑ 208 I Love the Way You Love/Let Me Love You 1960 20.00
❑ 226 Ain't Gonna Be That Way/All the Love I've Got 1960 20.00
❑ 241 (You've Got to) Move Two Mountains/I Need You 1960 15.00
❑ 273 Happy Days/Baby, Baby 1960 15.00
❑ 294 Merry-Go-Round/Tell Me That You Love Me 1961 15.00
❑ 322 How Can We Tell Him/I've Got a Notion 1961 20.00
❑ 359 Show Me/Oh Mary 1961 20.00
❑ 386 Easier Said Than Done/Johnny One Stop 1961 20.00
❑ 423 Magic Mirror/With All That's In Me 1962 20.00
❑ 454 He Gave Me You/That's How Bad 1962 20.00
❑ 483 Let Yourself Go/That's Where I Lost My Baby 1962 20.00
❑ 556 Keep Tellin' Yourself/Everyone Who's Been in Love with You 1963 20.00
❑ 590 He's Got the Whole World In His Hands/Another Tear Falls 1963 20.00
❑ 617 Come On and Stop/Not Available 1963 150.00
❑ 643 Congratulations, You've Hurt Me Again/Crying on My Pillow 1963 20.00
❑ 691 Unbreakable Love/A Man Who Don't Believe in Love 1964 25.00

7-Inch Extended Plays

UNITED ARTISTS
❑ 10,007 I Love the Way You Love/Let Me Love You/You Got What It Takes/Don't Leave Me 1960 100.00
❑ 10,007 [PS] Marv Johnson 1960 100.00
❑ 10,009 Ain't Gonna Be That Way/All the Love I've Got/Come to Me/Whisper 1960 100.00
❑ 10,009 [PS] Marv Johnson 1960 100.00

Albums

UNITED ARTISTS
❑ UAL 3081 [M] Marvelous Marv Johnson 1960 150.00
❑ UAL 3118 [M] More Marv Johnson 1961 150.00
❑ UAL 3187 [M] I Believe 1962 150.00
❑ UAS 6081 [S] Marvelous Marv Johnson 1960 200.00
❑ UAS 6118 [S] More Marv Johnson 1961 200.00
❑ UAS 6187 [S] I Believe 1962 200.00

JOHNSON, MIRRIAM See JESSI COLTER.

JOHNSON, ROBERT

Albums

COLUMBIA
❑ CL 1654 [M] King of the Delta Blues Singers 1961 500.00
—Red and black label with six "eye" logos
❑ CL 1654 [M] King of the Delta Blues Singers 1963 50.00
—"Guaranteed High Fidelity" label
❑ CL 1654 [M] King of the Delta Blues Singers 1965 25.00
—"360 Sound Mono" label
❑ CL 1654 [M] King of the Delta Blues Singers 1970 12.00
—Orange label with "Columbia" circling the edge
❑ CL 1654 [M] King of the Delta Blues Singers 1998 10.00
—Red label, "Columbia" in white at top, "Sony Music" under side numbers
❑ CL 1654 [M] King of the Delta Blues Singers 2001 15.00
—Reissue on 180-gram vinyl (sealed copies have a sticker indicating this)
❑ C 30034 [M] King of the Delta Blues Singers, Vol. 2 1970 20.00
❑ PC 30034 [M] King of the Delta Blues Singers, Vol. 2 1979 10.00
❑ C3 46222 [(3)] Robert Johnson — The Complete Recordings 1990 50.00

JOHNSON, ROZETTA

45s

ATLANTIC
❑ 2297 That Hurts/It's Nice to Know 1965 150.00
—As "Rosetta Johnson"

CLINTONE
❑ 001 A Woman's Way/Mine Was Real 1970 50.00
❑ 003 Who Are You Gonna Love (Your Woman or Your Wife)/I Can Feel My Love Comin' Down 1971 30.00
❑ 006 Chained and Bound/Holding the Losing Hand 1971 60.00
❑ 007 To Love Somebody/Can't You Just See Me 1971 12.00
❑ 008 How Can You Lose Something You Never Had/Personal Woman 1971 300.00

JOHNSON, TERRY

45s

GORDY
❑ 7091 My Springtime/Suzie 1969 120.00
❑ 7095 Whatcha Gonna Do/Suzie 1970 25.00

JOHNSON BROTHERS, THE

45s

IMPERIAL
❑ 5550 Love Ain't Got a Thing/Find Another Heart 1958 20.00

VALOR
❑ 2006 Zombie Lou/Castin' My Spell 1958 100.00

JOHNSTON, BRUCE Also see THE BEACH BOYS; BRUCE AND TERRY; THE GAMBLERS; THE KUSTOM KINGS; PAPA DOO RUN RUN; THE REVERES (3); THE VETTES.

45s

COLUMBIA
❑ 10568 Pipeline/Disney Girls 1977 10.00
—Promos (with "Pipeline" on both sides) worth 50% less

DEL-FI
❑ 4202 The Original Surfer Stomp/Pajama Party 1963 30.00
❑ 4202 The Original Surfer Stomp/Pajama Party 1963 60.00
—Originals credit "The Surf Stompers"

DONNA
❑ 1354 Do the Surfer Stomp (Part 1)/Do the Surfer Stomp (Part 2) 1962 30.00
❑ 1354 Do the Surfer Stomp (Part 1)/Do the Surfer Stomp (Part 2) 1962 50.00
—Originals credit "The Surf Stompers"
❑ 1354 [PS] Do the Surfer Stomp (Part 1)/Do the Surfer Stomp (Part 2) 1962 100.00
❑ 1364 Soupy Shuffle Stomp (SSS)/Moon Shot 1962 30.00
❑ 1374 The Original Surfer Stomp (Part 1)/The Original Surfer Stomp (Part 2) 1962 30.00

RONDA
❑ 1003 Do the Surfer Stomp (Part 1)/Do the Surfer Stomp (Part 2) 1962 40.00

Albums

COLUMBIA
❑ CL 2057 [M] Surfin' 'Round the World 1963 150.00
❑ CS 8857 [S] Surfin' 'Round the World 1963 300.00
❑ PC 34459 Going Public 1976 15.00

DEL-FI
❑ DFLP-1228 [M] Surfers' Pajama Party 1963 100.00
❑ DFST-1228 [S] Surfers' Pajama Party 1963 200.00

JOHNSTON, COLONEL JUBILATION B., AND THE MYSTIC KNIGHTS BAND AND STREET SINGERS

Albums

COLUMBIA
❑ CL 2532 [M] Moldy Goldies 1966 25.00
❑ CS 9332 [S] Moldy Goldies 1966 30.00

JOINER, ARKANSAS, JUNIOR HIGH SCHOOL BAND

45s

LIBERTY
❑ 55244 National City/Big Ben 1959 10.00
❑ 55276 Arkansas Traveler/Hot Time in the Old Town 1960 10.00
❑ 55341 Highland Rock/Hop-Scotch 1960 10.00
—This one by the "Joiner, Arkansas, State College Band"

JOLLY, PETE

45s

A&M
❑ 934 Dancing in the Streets/A Love So Fine 1968 6.00
❑ 963 Like a Lover/Serenta 1968 6.00
❑ 1032 Give a Damn/A Love So Fine 1969 6.00
❑ 1089 Little Green Apples/What the World Needs Now Is Love 1969 6.00

AVA
❑ 116 Falling in Love with Love/Little Bird 1963 8.00
❑ 149 Sweet September/Kiss Me Baby 1963 8.00
❑ 167 A Hard Day's Night/Three, Four, Five 1964 8.00
❑ 169 Moment of Truth/Sweet September 1964 8.00

MAINSTREAM
❑ 699 Sweet September/Little Bird 1969 6.00

Albums

A&M
❑ SP-3033 Seasons 1969 12.00
❑ SP-4145 Herb Alpert Presents Pete Jolly 1968 12.00
❑ SP-4184 Give a Damn 1970 12.00

AVA
❑ A-22 [M] Little Bird 1963 20.00
❑ AS-22 [S] Little Bird 1963 25.00
❑ A-39 [M] Sweet September 1963 20.00
❑ AS-39 [S] Sweet September 1963 25.00
❑ A-51 [M] Hello Jolly 1964 20.00
❑ AS-51 [S] Hello Jolly 1964 25.00

CHARLIE PARKER
❑ PLP-825 [M] Pete Jolly Gasses Everybody 1962 20.00
❑ PLP-825S [S] Pete Jolly Gasses Everybody 1962 25.00

COLUMBIA
❑ CL 2397 [M] Too Much, Baby 1965 20.00
❑ CS 9197 [S] Too Much, Baby 1965 25.00

MAINSTREAM
❑ S-6114 The Best of Pete Jolly 196? 15.00

METROJAZZ
❑ E-1014 [M] Impossible 1958 35.00
❑ SE-1014 [S] Impossible 1958 35.00

MGM
❑ E-4127 [M] 5 O'Clock Shadows 1963 20.00
❑ SE-4127 [S] 5 O'Clock Shadows 1963 25.00

RCA VICTOR
❑ LPM-1105 [M] Jolly Jumps In 1955 50.00
❑ LPM-1125 [M] Duo, Trio, Quartet 1955 50.00
❑ LPM-1367 [M] When Lights Are Low 1957 50.00

STEREO FIDELITY
❑ SFS-11000 [S] Continental Jazz 1960 25.00

TRIP
❑ TLP-5817 A Touch of Jazz 197? 10.00

JOLSON, AL Almost his entire recording career predates the 45 and the LP. It's likely that other Decca 78s from the 23000 and 24000 series were reissued onto 45s, but we list only those for which we have confirmation.

45s

DECCA
❑ 9-4 [PS] Jolson Sings Again 1950 20.00
—Box for set of four 45s (24681, 24682, 24683, 24684)
❑ 9-8 [PS] Souvenir Album, Vol. 2 1950 20.00
—Box for set of four records (24106, 24107, 24108, 24109)
❑ 9-23612 Rock-a-Bye Your Baby with a Dixie Melody/California Here I Come 1950 20.00
—Reissue of 78 from 1947
❑ 9-23614 Sonny Boy/My Mammy 1950 20.00
❑ 9-23714 Avalon/Anniversary Song 1950 20.00
—Reissue of 78 from 1947

Number	Title (A Side/B Side)	Yr	NM
❑ 9-24106	Waiting for the Robert E. Lee/When You Were Sweet Sixteen	1950	20.00
—Side 1 and Side 2 of "Album No. 9-8"; reissue of 78 rpm material			
❑ 9-24107	Golden Gate/I'm Sitting on Top of the World (Just Rolling Along — Just Rolling Along)	1950	20.00
—Side 3 and Side 4 of "Album No. 9-8"; reissue of 78 rpm material			
❑ 9-24108	Toot, Toot, Tootsie! (Goo'Bye)/Back in Your Own Back Yard	1950	20.00
—Side 5 and Side 6 of "Album No. 9-8"; reissue of 78 rpm material			
❑ 9-24109	Carolina in the Morning/Liza	1950	20.00
—Side 7 and Side 8 of "Album No. 9-8"; reissue of 78 rpm material			
❑ 9-24681	Pretty Baby//I'm Looking Over a Four Leaf Clover/Baby Face	1950	20.00
—Side 1 and Side 2 of "Album No. 9-4"; reissue of 78 rpm material			
❑ 9-24682	Give My Regards to Broadway/I'm Just Wild About Harry	1950	20.00
—Side 3 and Side 4 of "Album No. 9-4"; reissue of 78 rpm material			
❑ 9-24683	After You've Gone/Chinatown, My Chinatown	1950	20.00
—Side 5 and Side 6 of "Album No. 9-4"; reissue of 78 rpm material			
❑ 9-24684	I Only Have Eyes for You/Is It True What They Say About Dixie?	1950	20.00
—Side 7 and Side 8 of "Album No. 9-4"; reissue of 78 rpm material			
❑ 9-27024	The Old Piano Roll Blues/Way Down Yonder in New Orleans	1950	20.00
❑ 9-27043	Are You Lonesome Tonight/No Sad Songs for Me	1950	20.00
❑ 9-27181	De Camptown Races/Oh Susannah	1950	20.00
❑ 9-27363	Beautiful Dreamer/Old Folks at Home	1951	15.00
❑ 9-27364	I Dream of Jeannie with the Light Brown Hair/Old Black Joe	1951	15.00
❑ 9-27365	Massa's in De Cold, Cold Ground/My Old Kentucky Home	1951	15.00
—The above four comprise a box set			
❑ 9-27410	In Our House/I'm Crying Just for You	1951	15.00
❑ 9-28697	I'm Sitting on Top of the World/When the Red, Red Robin Comes Bob, Bob, Bobbin' Along	1953	12.00

MCA

Number	Title (A Side/B Side)	Yr	NM
❑ 60037	Swanee/April Showers	1973	5.00
—Black label with rainbow			
❑ 60038	Avalon/Anniversary Song	1973	5.00
—Black label with rainbow			
❑ 60048	You Made Me Love You/Ma Blushin' Rosie	1973	5.00
—Black label with rainbow			
❑ 60096	My Mammy/Sonny Boy	197?	5.00
—Black label with rainbow			
❑ 60136	California Here I Come/Rock-a-Bye Your Baby with a Dixie Melody	197?	5.00
—Black label with rainbow			

7-Inch Extended Plays

DECCA

Number	Title (A Side/B Side)	Yr	NM
❑ 7-34378	Way Down Yonder in New Orleans/California, Here I Come/I'm Sitting on Top of the World//I'm Looking Over a Four-Leaf Clover/Are You Lonesome Tonight/There's a Rainbow 'Round My Shoulder	196?	15.00
—Jukebox issue; small hole, plays at 33 1/3 rpm			
❑ 7-34378 [PS]	Rainbow 'Round My Shoulder	196?	15.00
❑ 7-34440	Margie/When the Red, Red Robin Comes Bob, Bob, Bobbin' Along/Baby Face//Dinah/My Melancholy Baby/I'm Always Chasing Rainbows	196?	15.00
—Jukebox issue; small hole, plays at 33 1/3 rpm			
❑ 7-34440 [PS]	The Best of Al Jolson, Vol. 2	196?	15.00

Albums

DECCA

Number	Title (A Side/B Side)	Yr	NM
❑ DXA 169 [(2)M]	The Best of Jolson	196?	25.00
❑ DLP 5006 [10]	Jolson Sings Again	1949	30.00
❑ DLP 5026 [10]	Al Jolson In Songs He Made Famous	1949	30.00
❑ DLP 5029 [10]	Souvenir Album, Vol. II	1949	30.00
❑ DLP 5030 [10]	Al Jolson, Vol. III	1949	30.00
❑ DLP 5031 [10]	Souvenir Album, Vol. IV	1949	30.00
❑ DL 5308 [10]	Stephen Foster Songs	1950	100.00
❑ DL 5314 [10]	Souvenir Album, Vol. V	1951	30.00
❑ DL 5315 [10]	Souvenir Album, Vol. VI	1951	30.00
❑ DXSA 7169 [(2)R]	The Best of Jolson	196?	15.00
❑ DL 9034 [M]	You Made Me Love You	1957	25.00
—Black label, silver print			
❑ DL 9034 [M]	You Made Me Love You	196?	15.00
—Black label with color bars			
❑ DL 9035 [M]	Rock-a-Bye Your Baby	1957	25.00
—Black label, silver print			
❑ DL 9035 [M]	Rock-a-Bye Your Baby	196?	15.00
—Black label with color bars			
❑ DL 9036 [M]	Rainbow 'Round My Shoulder	1957	25.00
—Black label, silver print			
❑ DL 9036 [M]	Rainbow 'Round My Shoulder	196?	15.00
—Black label with color bars			
❑ DL 9037 [M]	You Ain't Heard Nothin' Yet!	1957	15.00
—Black label with color bars			
❑ DL 9037 [M]	You Ain't Heard Nothin' Yet!	1957	25.00
—Black label, silver print			
❑ DL 9038 [M]	Memories	1957	15.00
—Black label with color bars			
❑ DL 9038 [M]	Memories	1957	25.00
—Black label, silver print			
❑ DL 9050 [M]	Among My Souvenirs	1957	25.00
—Black label, silver print			
❑ DL 9050 [M]	Among My Souvenirs	196?	15.00
—Black label with color bars			
❑ DL 9063 [M]	The Immortal Al Jolson	1958	25.00
—Maroon label, silver print			
❑ DL 9063 [M]	The Immortal Al Jolson	196?	15.00
—Black label with color bars			
❑ DL 9070 [M]	Overseas	1959	30.00
—Black label, silver print			
❑ DL 9070 [M]	Overseas	196?	15.00
—Black label with color bars			
❑ DL 9074 [M]	The World's Greatest Entertainer	1959	25.00
—Black label, silver print			
❑ DL 9074 [M]	The World's Greatest Entertainer	196?	15.00
—Black label with color bars			
❑ DL 9095 [M]	Al Jolson with Oscar Levant at the Piano	1961	30.00
❑ DL 9099 [M]	Jolie	196?	25.00
—Black label, silver print			
❑ DL 79034 [R]	You Made Me Love You	196?	12.00
❑ DL 79035 [R]	Rock-a-Bye Your Baby	196?	12.00
❑ DL 79036 [R]	Rainbow 'Round My Shoulder	196?	12.00
❑ DL 79037 [R]	You Ain't Heard Nothin' Yet!	196?	12.00
❑ DL 79038 [R]	Memories	196?	12.00
❑ DL 79050 [R]	Among My Souvenirs	196?	12.00
❑ DL 79070 [R]	Overseas	196?	12.00
❑ DL 79074 [R]	The World's Greatest Entertainer	196?	12.00
❑ DL 79095 [R]	Al Jolson with Oscar Levant at the Piano	196?	12.00

MCA

Number	Title (A Side/B Side)	Yr	NM
❑ 2057	You Made Me Love You	197?	10.00
❑ 2058	Rock-a-Bye Your Baby	197?	10.00
❑ 2059	Rainbow 'Round My Shoulder	197?	10.00
❑ 2060	You Ain't Heard Nothin' Yet!	197?	10.00
❑ 2061	Memories	197?	10.00
❑ 2064	Among My Souvenirs	197?	10.00
❑ 2066	The Immortal Al Jolson	197?	10.00
❑ 2067	The World's Greatest Entertainer	197?	10.00
❑ 10002 [(2)]	The Best of Jolson	1973	12.00
❑ 27051	You Made Me Love You	198?	8.00
❑ 27052	Rock-a-Bye Your Baby	198?	8.00
❑ 27053	Rainbow 'Round My Shoulder	198?	8.00
❑ 27054	You Ain't Heard Nothin' Yet!	198?	8.00
❑ 27055	Memories	198?	8.00
❑ 27057	The Immortal Al Jolson	198?	8.00
❑ 27058	The World's Greatest Entertainer	198?	8.00

SUNBEAM

Number	Title (A Side/B Side)	Yr	NM
❑ 503	Steppin' Out	197?	10.00
❑ 505	California, Here I Come	197?	10.00

TOTEM

Number	Title (A Side/B Side)	Yr	NM
❑ 1006	Al Jolson On the Air, Vol. 1	197?	10.00
❑ 1012	Al Jolson On the Air, Vol. 2	197?	10.00
❑ 1019	Al Jolson On the Air, Vol. 3	197?	10.00
❑ 1030	Al Jolson On the Air, Vol. 4	197?	10.00
❑ 1040	Al Jolson On the Air, Vol. 5	197?	10.00

JON AND ROBIN AND THE IN CROWD
Also see THE IN CROWD (1).

45s

ABNAK

Number	Title (A Side/B Side)	Yr	NM
❑ 111	Lonely One/How Come	1965	10.00
❑ 111 [DJ]	Lonely One/How Come	1965	15.00
—Promo only on yellow vinyl			
❑ 113	Can't Make It With You/If I Need Someone	1966	10.00
❑ 113 [DJ]	Can't Make It With You/If I Need Someone	1966	15.00
—Promo only on yellow vinyl			
❑ 115	Hey Girl/If I Need Someone	1966	10.00
❑ 115 [DJ]	Hey Girl/If I Need Someone	1966	15.00
—Promo only on yellow vinyl			
❑ 119	Do It Again A Little Bit Slower/If I Need Someone — It's You	1967	12.00
❑ 119 [DJ]	Do It Again A Little Bit Slower/If I Need Someone — It's You	1967	16.00
—Promo only on yellow vinyl			
❑ 122	Drums/You Don't Care	1967	10.00
❑ 122 [DJ]	Drums/You Don't Care	1967	15.00
—Promo only on yellow vinyl			
❑ 124	I Want Some More/Love Me Baby	1967	10.00
❑ 124 [DJ]	I Want Some More/Love Me Baby	1967	15.00
—Promo only on yellow vinyl			
❑ 127	Dr. Jon (The Medicine Man)/Love Me Baby	1968	8.00
❑ 127 [DJ]	Dr. Jon (The Medicine Man)/Love Me Baby	1968	12.00
—Promo only on yellow vinyl			
❑ 130	You Got Style/Thursday Morning	1968	8.00
❑ 130 [DJ]	You Got Style/Thursday Morning	1968	12.00
—Promo only on yellow vinyl			
❑ 133	Save Me, Save Me/Thursday Morning	1968	8.00
—As "Jon and the In Crowd"			
❑ 133 [DJ]	Save Me, Save Me/Thursday Morning	1968	12.00
—Promo only on yellow vinyl			
❑ 135	Gift of Love/Gift of Love (Country Style)	1969	8.00
❑ 135 [DJ]	Gift of Love/Gift of Love (Country Style)	1969	12.00
—Promo only on yellow vinyl			
❑ 138	Give Me Your Love/Lonely One	1969	8.00
❑ 138 [DJ]	Give Me Your Love/Lonely One	1969	12.00
—Promo only on yellow vinyl			
❑ 140	There's An American Flag on the Moon (Part 1)/There's An American Flag on the Moon (Part 2)	1969	8.00
❑ 140 [DJ]	There's An American Flag on the Moon (Part 1)/There's An American Flag on the Moon (Part 2)	1969	12.00
—Promo only on yellow vinyl			
❑ 141	If You Got It, Flaunt It/I'll Come Running to You	1969	8.00
❑ 141 [DJ]	If You Got It, Flaunt It/I'll Come Running to You	1969	12.00
—Promo only on yellow vinyl			

Albums

ABNAK

Number	Title (A Side/B Side)	Yr	NM
❑ ABM-2068 [M]	Soul of a Boy and Girl	1967	20.00
❑ ABST-2068 [S]	Soul of a Boy and Girl	1967	20.00
❑ ABST-2070	Elastic Event	1968	20.00

JON AND VANGELIS

45s

POLYDOR

Number	Title (A Side/B Side)	Yr	NM
❑ 2098	Thunder/I Hear You Now	1980	5.00
❑ 2130	One More Time/The Road	1980	5.00
❑ 2181	The Friends of Mr. Cairo/Beside	1981	5.00
❑ 2203	I'll Find My Way Home/I Hear You Now	1982	5.00

JONES, BRIAN Also see THE ROLLING STONES.

Albums

ROLLING STONES

Number	Title (A Side/B Side)	Yr	NM
❑ COC 49100	Brian Jones Presents the Pipes of Pan at Joujouka	1971	60.00

JONES, CORKY See BUCK OWENS.

JONES, DAVY Also see DOLENZ, JONES & TORK; DOLENZ, JONES, BOYCE & HART; THE MONKEES.

45s

BELL

Number	Title (A Side/B Side)	Yr	NM
❑ 45111	Rainy Jane/Welcome to My Love	1971	10.00
❑ 45136	I Really Love You/Sitting in the Apple Tree	1971	10.00
❑ 45159	Girl/Take My Love	1971	50.00
❑ 45178	I'll Believe in You/The Road to Love	1972	20.00

COLPIX

Number	Title (A Side/B Side)	Yr	NM
❑ 764	Dream Girl/Take Me to Paradise	1965	20.00
—Colpix sides as "David Jones"			
❑ 764 [PS]	Dream Girl/Take Me to Paradise	1965	30.00
❑ 784	What Are We Going to Do/This Bouquet	1965	20.00
❑ 784 [PS]	What Are We Going to Do/This Bouquet	1965	30.00
❑ 789	The Girl from Chelsea/Theme for a New Love	1965	20.00
❑ 789 [PS]	The Girl from Chelsea/Theme for a New Love	1965	40.00

MGM

Number	Title (A Side/B Side)	Yr	NM
❑ 14458	Who Was It/You're a Lady	1972	30.00
❑ 14524	Rubberene/Who Was It	1973	30.00

Albums

BELL

Number	Title (A Side/B Side)	Yr	NM
❑ 6067	Davy Jones	1971	20.00

COLPIX

Number	Title (A Side/B Side)	Yr	NM
❑ CP 493 [M]	David Jones	1965	25.00
❑ CPS 493 [S]	David Jones	1965	40.00
—This album charted in 1967 thanks to the singer's membership in The Monkees			

Except when noted otherwise, VG = 25% of NM, and VG+ = 50% of NM. (Example: VG = \$2.00, VG+ = \$4.00 and NM = \$8.00.)

JONES, DOROTHY

45s

COLUMBIA

Number	Title (A Side/B Side)	Yr	NM
❑ 4-42062	Take That Long Walk Home/It's Unbelievable	1961	10.00

JONES, EDDIE

45s

FAIRMOUNT

Number	Title (A Side/B Side)	Yr	NM
❑ 1009	Let's Stop Fooling Ourselves/Give Me Good Lovin'	1966	100.00

JONES, GEORGE Also see GENE PITNEY.

45s

D

Number	Title (A Side/B Side)	Yr	NM
❑ 1226	New Baby for Christmas/Maybe Next Christmas	1961	12.00

EPIC

Number	Title (A Side/B Side)	Yr	NM
❑ 02526	Still Doin' Time/Good Ones and Bad Ones	1981	3.00
❑ 02696	Same Ol' Me/Together Alone	1982	3.00
❑ 03489	Shine On (Shine All Your Sweet Love on Me)/Memories of Mama	1982	3.00
❑ 03883	I Always Get Lucky with You/I'd Rather Have What We Had	1983	3.00
❑ 04082	Tennessee Whiskey/Almost Persuaded	1983	3.00
❑ 04413	You've Still Got a Place in My Heart/I'm Ragged But Right	1984	3.00
❑ 04609	She's My Rock/(What Love Can Do) The Second Time Around	1984	3.00
❑ 04876	Size Seven Round (Made of Gold)/All I Want to Do in Life	1985	3.00
—A-side with Lacy J. Dalton; B-side with Janie Frickie			
❑ 05439	Who's Gonna Fill Their Shoes/A Whole Lot of Trouble for You	1985	3.00
❑ 05698	The One I Loved Back Then (The Corvette Song)/If Only You'd Love Me Again	1985	3.00
❑ 05862	Somebody Wants Me Out of the Way/Call the Wrecker for My Heart	1986	3.00
❑ 06296	Wine Colored Roses/These Old Eyes Have Seen It All	1986	3.00
❑ 06593	The Right Left Hand/The Very Best on Me	1986	3.00
❑ 07107	I Turn to You/Don't Leave Without Taking Your Silver	1987	3.00
❑ 07655	The Bird/I'm Goin' Home Like I Never Did Before	1987	3.00
❑ 07748	I'm a Survivor/The Real McCoy	1988	3.00
❑ 07913	The Old Man No One Loves/One Hell of a Song	1988	3.00
❑ 08011	If I Could Bottle This Up/I Always Get It Right with You	1988	3.00
—With Shelby Lynne			
❑ 08509	I'm a One Woman Man/Pretty Little Lady from Beaumont, Texas	1988	3.00
❑ 10831	We Can Make It/One of These Days	1972	5.00
❑ 10858	Loving You Could Never Be Better/Try It, You'll Like It	1972	5.00
❑ 10917	A Picture of Me (Without You)/The Man Worth Loving You	1972	5.00
❑ 10959	What My Woman Can't Do/My Loving Wife	1973	5.00
❑ 11006	Nothing Ever Hurt Me (Half As Bad As Losing You)/Wine	1973	5.00
❑ 11053	Once You've Had the Best/Mary Don't Go Round	1973	5.00
❑ 11122	The Grand Tour/Our Private Life	1974	5.00
❑ 50038	The Door/Wean Me	1974	5.00
❑ 50088	These Days (I Barely Get By)/Baby, There's Nothing Like You	1975	5.00
❑ 50127	Memories of Us/I Just Don't Give a Damn	1975	5.00
❑ 50187	The Battle/I'll Come Back	1976	5.00
❑ 50227	You Always Look Your Best (Here in My Arms)/Have You Seen My Chicken	1976	5.00
❑ 50271	Her Name Is.../Diary of My Mind	1976	5.00
❑ 50385	Old King Kong/It's a 10-33 (Let's Get Jesus on the Line)	1977	4.00
❑ 50423	If I Could Put Them All Together (I'd Have You)/You've Got the Best of Me Again	1977	4.00
❑ 50495	Bartender's Blues/Rest in Peace	1977	4.00
❑ 50564	I'll Just Take It Out in Love/Leaving Love All Over the Place	1978	4.00
❑ 50684	Someday My Day Will Come/We Oughta Be Ashamed	1979	4.00
❑ 50867	He Stopped Loving Her Today/A Hard Act to Follow	1980	6.00
❑ 50922	I'm Not Ready Yet/Garage Sale Today	1980	4.00
❑ 50968	If Drinkin' Don't Kill Me (Her Memory Will)/Brother to the Blues	1980	4.00
❑ 68743	The King Is Gone (So Are You)/Don't You Ever Get Tired (Of Hurting Me)	1989	3.00
—Same song, different title (changed for legal reasons)			
❑ 68743	Ya Ba Da Ba Do (So Are You)/Don't You Ever Get Tired (Of Hurting Me)	1989	5.00
❑ 68743 [PS]	Ya Ba Da Ba Do (So Are You)/Don't You Ever Get Tired (Of Hurting Me)	1989	5.00
❑ 68991	Writing on the Wall/Burning Bridges	1989	3.00
❑ 73070	Radio Lover/Burning Bridges	1989	3.00
❑ 73424	Six Foot Deep, Six Foot Down/He Never Got the Picture at All	1990	4.00

MCA

Number	Title (A Side/B Side)	Yr	NM
❑ 54187	You Couldn't Get the Picture/Heckle and Jeckle	1991	4.00
❑ 54272	She Loved a Lot in Her Time/Come Home to Me	1991	4.00
❑ 54370	Honky Tonk Myself to Death/Where the Tall Grass Grows	1992	4.00
❑ 54470	I Don't Need Your Rockin' Chair/Finally Friday	1992	5.00
❑ 54604	Wrong's What I Do Best/The Bottle Let Me Down	1993	4.00
❑ 54687	Walls Can Fall/You Must Have Walked Across My Mind Again	1993	3.00
❑ 54749	High-Tech Redneck/Forever's Here to Stay	1993	4.00
❑ 54969	A Good Year for the Roses/I've Still Got Some Hurtin' Left to Do	1994	4.00
—A-side with Alan Jackson			
❑ 55228	Honky Tonk Song/The Lone Ranger	1996	4.00
❑ 55287	Billy B. Bad/Back Down to Hung Up on You	1996	4.00
❑ 72038	Wild Irish Rose/No Future for Me in Our Past	1998	3.00

MERCURY

Number	Title (A Side/B Side)	Yr	NM
❑ 7045 [S]	White Lightning/Treasure of Love	196?	40.00
❑ 7046 [S]	Why Baby Why/Hearts in My Dream	196?	40.00
❑ 7047 [S]	The Window Up Above/Color of the Blues	196?	40.00
❑ 7048 [S]	Tall, Tall Trees/Don't Stop the Music	196?	40.00
❑ 7049 [S]	Who Shot Sam/Accidentally on Purpose	196?	40.00
❑ 71049	Just One More/Gonna Come Get You	1957	25.00
❑ 71096	Too Much Water/All I Want to Do	1957	25.00
❑ 71139	Nothing Can Stop Me/I'm With the Wrong One	1957	25.00
❑ 71176	Tall, Tall Trees/Hearts in My Dream	1957	20.00
❑ 71224	Take the Devil Out of Me/A Cup of Loneliness	1957	20.00
❑ 71225	New Baby for Christmas/Maybe Next Christmas	1957	20.00
❑ 71257	Color of the Blues/Eskimo Pie	1958	20.00
❑ 71340	Wandering Soul/Jesus Wants Me	1958	20.00
❑ 71373	Treasure of Love/If I Don't Love You (Grits Ain't Groceries)	1958	20.00
❑ 71406	White Lightning/Long Time to Forget	1959	15.00
❑ 71464	Who Shot Sam/Into My Arms Again	1959	15.00
❑ 71506	My Lord Has Called Me/If You Want to Wear a Crown	1959	20.00
❑ 71514	Money to Burn/Big Harlan Taylor	1959	15.00
❑ 71583	Accidently on Purpose/Sparkling Blue Eyes	1960	15.00
❑ 71615	Have Mercy on Me/If You Believe	1960	20.00
❑ 71636	Family Bible/Your Old Standby	1960	20.00
❑ 71641	Out of Control/Just Little Boy Blue	1960	15.00
❑ 71700	The Window Up Above/Candy Hearts	1960	15.00
❑ 71721	Family Bible/Taggin' Along	1961	15.00
❑ 71804	Tender Years/Battle of Love	1961	12.00
❑ 71804 [PS]	Tender Years/Battle of Love	1961	15.00
❑ 71910	Aching, Breaking Heart/When My Heart Hurts No More	1962	12.00
❑ 71910 [PS]	Aching, Breaking Heart/When My Heart Hurts No More	1962	15.00
❑ 72010	You're Still on My Mind/Cold, Cold Heart	1962	12.00
❑ 72010 [PS]	You're Still on My Mind/Cold, Cold Heart	1962	15.00
❑ 72087	I Love You Because/Revenoor Man	1963	12.00
❑ 72087 [PS]	I Love You Because/Revenoor Man	1963	15.00
❑ 72200	Mr. Fool/One Is a Lonely Number	1963	12.00
❑ 72233	The Last Town I Painted/Tarnished Angel	1964	12.00
❑ 72233 [PS]	The Last Town I Painted/Tarnished Angel	1964	15.00
❑ 72293	Oh Lonesome Me/Life to Go	1964	12.00
❑ 72293 [PS]	Oh Lonesome Me/Life to Go	1964	15.00
❑ 72362	I Wouldn't Know About That/You Better Treat Your Man Right	1964	12.00

MUSICOR

Number	Title (A Side/B Side)	Yr	NM
❑ 1067	Things Have Gone to Pieces/Wearing My Heart Away	1965	8.00
❑ 1067 [PS]	Things Have Gone to Pieces/Wearing My Heart Away	1965	15.00
❑ 1098	Love Bug/I Can't Get Used to Being Lonely	1965	8.00
❑ 1117	Take Me/Ship of Love	1965	8.00
❑ 1143	I'm a People/I Woke Up from Dreaming	1966	8.00
❑ 1174	Old Brush Arbors/Flowers for Mama	1966	8.00
❑ 1181	Four-O-Thirty Three/Don't Think I Don't	1966	8.00
❑ 1226	Walk Through This World with Me/Developing My Pictures	1967	8.00
❑ 1243	I Can't Get There from Here/A Poor Man's Riches	1967	8.00
❑ 1244	A Cup of Loneliness/That the World But Give Me Jesus	1967	12.00
❑ 1267	If My Heart Had Windows/Honky Tonk Downstairs	1967	8.00
❑ 1289	Say It's Not You/Poor Chinee	1968	8.00
❑ 1297	Small Time Laboring Man/Well It's Alright	1968	8.00
❑ 1298	As Long As I Live/Your Angel Steps Out of Heaven	1968	8.00
❑ 1333	When the Grass Grows Over Me/Heartaches and Hangovers	1968	8.00
❑ 1339	Lonely Christmas Call/My Mom and Santa Claus	1968	8.00
❑ 1351	I'll Share My World with You/I'll See You a While Ago	1969	8.00
❑ 1366	If Not for You/When the Wife Runs Off	1969	8.00
❑ 1381	She's Mine/No Blues Is Good News	1969	8.00
❑ 1392	Where Grass Won't Grow/Shoulder to Shoulder	1970	6.00
❑ 1404	Going Life's Way/Uncloudy Day	1970	6.00
❑ 1408	Tell Me My Lying Eyes Are Wrong/You've Become My Everything	1970	6.00
❑ 1425	A Good Year for the Roses/Let a Little Loving Come In	1970	8.00
❑ 1432	Sometimes You Just Can't Win/Brothers of a Bottle	1971	6.00
❑ 1440	Right Won't Touch a Hand/Someone Sweet to Love	1971	6.00
❑ 1446	I'll Follow You (Up to Our Cloud)/Getting Over the Storm	1971	6.00

RCA VICTOR

Number	Title (A Side/B Side)	Yr	NM
❑ 74-0625	A Day in the Life of a Fool/Old, Old House	1971	6.00
❑ 74-0700	I Made Leaving (Easy for You)/How Proud I Would Have Been	1972	6.00
❑ 74-0792	Wrapped Around Her Finger/With Half a Heart	1972	6.00
❑ 74-0878	I Can Still See Him in Your Eyes/She's Mine	1973	6.00
❑ AMBO-0123	Tender Years/White Lightnin'	1973	5.00
❑ APBO-0218	My Favorite Lies/You Gotta Be My Baby	1974	5.00
❑ PB-10052	I Can Love You Enough/Talk to Me Lonesome Heart	1974	5.00

STARDAY

Number	Title (A Side/B Side)	Yr	NM
❑ 130	No Money in This Deal/You're in My Heart	1954	100.00
❑ 146	Play It Cool, Man/Wrong About You	1954	60.00
—B-side with Sonny Burns			
❑ 160	Let Him Know/Let Me Catch My Breath	1954	60.00
❑ 162	You All Goodnight/Let Him Know	1954	60.00
❑ 165	Tell Her/Heartbroken Me	1954	60.00
—B-side with Sonny Burns			
❑ 188	Hold Everything/What's Wrong with You	1955	50.00
❑ 202	Why Baby Why/Season of My Heart	1955	50.00
❑ 216	What Am I Worth/Still Hurtin'	1955	40.00
❑ 234	I'm Ragged But I'm Right/Your Heart	1956	40.00
❑ 240	Rock It/How Come It	1956	200.00
—As "Thumper Jones"			

Number	Title (A Side/B Side)	Yr	NM
❑ 247	You Gotta Be My Baby/It's OK	1956	40.00
❑ 256	Boat of Life/Taggin' Along	1956	40.00
❑ 264	Just One More/Gonna Come Get You	1956	40.00
❑ 7003	Seasons of My Heart/I'm Ragged But I'm Right	197?	5.00
❑ 7020	Wasted Words/Any Old Time	197?	5.00
❑ 7036	Why Baby Why/You Gotta Be My Baby	197?	5.00
❑ 8012	Why Baby Why/Seasons of My Heart	197?	5.00
UNITED ARTISTS			
❑ 424	She Thinks I Still Care/Sometimes You Just Can't Win	1962	10.00
❑ 424 [PS]	She Thinks I Still Care/Sometimes You Just Can't Win	1962	15.00
❑ 442	Beacon in the Night/He Made Me Free	1962	12.00
❑ 462	Open Pit Mine/Geronimo	1962	10.00
❑ 463	He Is So Good to Me/Magic Valley	1962	12.00
❑ 500	A Girl I Used to Know/Big Fool of the Year	1962	10.00
❑ 528	Not What I Had in Mind/I Saw Me	1962	10.00
❑ 530	Lonely Christmas Call/My Mom and Santa Claus	1962	15.00
❑ 578	You Comb Her Hair/Ain't It Funny What a Fool Will Do	1963	10.00
❑ 578 [PS]	You Comb Her Hair/Ain't It Funny What a Fool Will Do	1963	15.00
❑ 683	Your Heart Turned Left (And I Was On the Right)/My Tears Are Overdue	1964	10.00
❑ 724	Where Does a Little Tear Come From/Something I Dreamed	1964	10.00
❑ 751	The Race Is On/She's Lonesome Again	1964	10.00
❑ 804	Least of All/Brown to Blue	1965	10.00
❑ 858	Wrong Number/Old Old House	1965	10.00
❑ 901	What's Money/I Get Lonely in a Hurry	1965	10.00
❑ 965	World's Worse Loser/I Can't Change Overnight	1965	10.00
❑ 50014	Best Guitar Picker/A Good Old Fashioned Cry	1966	10.00
7-Inch Extended Plays			
MERCURY			
❑ SR-638-C	Tarnished Angel/The Last Town I Painted/The First One//Into My Arms Again/Mr. Fool/Glad to Let Her Go	196?	25.00
—Stereo jukebox issue; small hole, plays at 33 1/3 rpm			
❑ SR-638-C [PS]	The Ballad Side of George Jones	196?	25.00
Albums			
ACCORD			
❑ SN-7201	Tender Years	1982	10.00
ALLEGIANCE			
❑ AV-5015	Cold Cold Heart	198?	10.00
BULLDOG			
❑ BDL-2009	20 Golden Pieces of George Jones	198?	10.00
EPIC			
❑ KE 31321	George Jones	1972	15.00
—Yellow label			
❑ KE 31321	George Jones	1973	12.00
—Orange label			
❑ KE 31718	A Picture of Me (Without You)	1972	15.00
—Yellow label			
❑ KE 31718	A Picture of Me (Without You)	1973	12.00
—Orange label			
❑ KE 32412	Nothing Ever Hurt Me (Half As Bad As Losing You)	1973	15.00
❑ KE 32563	In a Gospel Way	1974	15.00
❑ KE 33083	The Grand Tour	1974	15.00
❑ KE 33352	The Best of George Jones	1975	15.00
❑ PE 33352	The Best of George Jones	1981	8.00
—Budget-line reissue			
❑ KE 33547	Memories of Us	1975	15.00
❑ BG 33749 [(2)]	George Jones/A Picture of Me (Without You)	1976	15.00
❑ KE 34034	The Battle	1976	12.00
❑ KE 34290	Alone Again	1976	12.00
❑ PE 34692	All-Time Greatest Hits Vol. 1	1977	12.00
—Orange label			
❑ PE 34692	All-Time Greatest Hits Vol. 1	198?	8.00
—Dark blue label			
❑ PE 34717	I Wanta Sing	1977	12.00
—Orange label			
❑ PE 34717	I Wanta Sing	198?	8.00
—Dark blue label			
❑ KE 35414	Bartender's Blues	1978	12.00
❑ PE 35414	Bartender's Blues	198?	8.00
—Budget-line reissue			
❑ JE 35544	My Very Special Guests	1979	12.00
❑ PE 35544	My Very Special Guests	198?	8.00
—Budget-line reissue			
❑ JE 36586	I Am What I Am	1980	12.00
❑ FE 37106	Still the Same Old Me	1981	10.00
❑ PE 37106	Still the Same Ole Me	198?	8.00
—Budget-line reissue			
❑ FE 37346	Encore	1981	10.00
❑ KE2 38323 [(2)]	Anniversary — 10 Years of Hits	1982	12.00
❑ FE 38406	Shine On	1983	10.00
❑ PE 38406	Shine On	198?	8.00
—Budget-line reissue			
❑ FE 38978	Jones Country	1983	10.00
❑ PE 38978	Jones Country	1985	8.00
—Budget-line reissue			
❑ FE 39002	You've Still Got a Place in My Heart	1984	10.00
❑ FE 39272	Ladies' Choice	1984	10.00
❑ FE 39546	By Request	1984	10.00
❑ FE 39598	Who's Gonna Fill Their Shoes	1985	10.00
❑ FE 39899	First Time Live!	1985	10.00
❑ FE 40413	Wine Colored Roses	1986	10.00
❑ FE 40776	Super Hits	1987	10.00
❑ FE 40781	Too Wild Too Long	1988	10.00
❑ FE 44078	One Woman Man	1989	10.00
EVEREST ARCHIVE OF FOLK & JAZZ			
❑ 353	George Jones Sings Country Hits	198?	10.00
HILLTOP			
❑ 6048	You're In My Heart	1968	15.00
❑ 6092	Heartaches by the Number	1969	15.00
❑ 6133	Oh Lonesome Me	1970	15.00
INTERMEDIA			
❑ QS-5044	I Can't Change Overnight	198?	10.00
❑ QS-5061	How I Love These Old Songs	198?	10.00
LIBERTY			
❑ LN-10167	Trouble in Mind	1981	8.00
❑ LN-10168	I Get Lonely in a Hurry	1981	8.00
MCA			
❑ 10398	And Along Came Jones	1991	20.00
—Vinyl issued only through Columbia House			
MERCURY			
❑ ML-8014	Greatest Hits	1980	12.00
❑ MG-20282 [M]	Hillbilly Hit Parade, Vol. 1	1957	150.00
—Five tracks by George Jones, one by George Jones with Benny Barnes, and four by other artists			
❑ MG-20306 [M]	14 Country Favorites	1957	150.00
❑ MG-20462 [M]	Country Church Time	1959	200.00
❑ MG-20477 [M]	George Jones Sings White Lightning and Other Favorites	1959	150.00
❑ MG-20596 [M]	George Jones Salutes Hank Williams	1960	80.00
❑ MG-20621 [M]	George Jones' Greatest Hits	1961	40.00
❑ MG-20624 [M]	Country and Western Hits	1961	40.00
❑ MG-20694 [M]	George Jones Sings From the Heart	1962	40.00
❑ MG-20793 [M]	The Novelty Side of George Jones	1963	80.00
❑ MG-20836 [M]	The Ballad Side of George Jones	1963	40.00
❑ MG-20906 [M]	Blue and Lonesome	1964	25.00
❑ MG-20937 [M]	Country and Western No. 1 Male Singer	1964	25.00
❑ MG-20990 [M]	Heartaches and Tears	1965	25.00
❑ MG-21029 [M]	Singing the Blues	1965	25.00
❑ MG-21048 [M]	George Jones' Greatest Hits Vol. 2	1965	25.00
❑ SR-60257 [S]	George Jones Salutes Hank Williams	1960	100.00
❑ SR-60621 [P]	George Jones' Greatest Hits	1961	50.00
❑ SR-60624 [P]	Country and Western Hits	1961	50.00
❑ SR-60694 [S]	George Jones Sings From the Heart	1962	50.00
❑ SR-60793 [S]	The Novelty Side of George Jones	1963	100.00
❑ SR-60836 [S]	The Ballad Side of George Jones	1963	50.00
❑ SR-60906 [S]	Blue and Lonesome	1964	30.00
❑ SR-60937 [S]	Country and Western No. 1 Male Singer	1964	30.00
❑ SR-60990 [S]	Heartaches and Tears	1965	30.00
❑ SR-61029 [S]	Singing the Blues	1965	30.00
❑ SR-61048 [S]	George Jones' Greatest Hits Vol. 2	1965	30.00
❑ 822646-1	George Jones Salutes Hank Williams	1985	10.00
❑ 826095-1	Rockin' the Country	1985	10.00
❑ 826248-1	Greatest Hits	1986	10.00
MUSICOR			
❑ MM-2046 [M]	Mr. Country and Western Music	1965	30.00
❑ MM-2060 [M]	New Country Hits	1965	30.00
❑ MM-2061 [M]	Old Brush Arbors	1966	30.00
❑ MM-2088 [M]	Love Bug	1966	30.00
❑ MM-2099 [M]	I'm a People	1966	25.00
❑ MM-2106 [M]	We Found Heaven Right Here on Earth	1966	25.00
❑ MM-2116 [M]	George Jones' Greatest Hits	1967	25.00
❑ MM-2119 [M]	Walk Through This World with Me	1967	30.00
❑ MM-2124 [M]	Cup of Loneliness	1967	30.00
❑ MM-2128 [M]	Hits by George	1967	30.00
❑ MS-3046 [S]	Mr. Country and Western Music	1965	40.00
❑ MS-3060 [S]	New Country Hits	1965	40.00
❑ MS-3061 [S]	Old Brush Arbors	1966	40.00
❑ MS-3088 [S]	Love Bug	1966	40.00
❑ MS-3099 [S]	I'm a People	1966	30.00
❑ MS-3106 [S]	We Found Heaven Right Here on Earth	1966	30.00
❑ MS-3116 [S]	George Jones' Greatest Hits	1967	25.00
❑ MS-3119 [S]	Walk Through This World with Me	1967	20.00
❑ MS-3124 [S]	Cup of Loneliness	1967	20.00
❑ MS-3128 [S]	Hits by George	1967	20.00
❑ MS-3149	The Songs of Dallas Frazier	1968	20.00
❑ MS-3158	If My Heart Had Windows	1968	20.00
❑ M2S-3159 [(2)]	The George Jones Story: The Musical Loves, Life and Sorrows of America's Great Country Star	1968	30.00
❑ M2S-3169 [(2)]	My Country	1969	30.00
❑ MS-3177	I'll Share My World with You	1969	20.00
❑ MS-3181	Where Grass Won't Grow	1969	20.00
❑ MS-3188	Will You Visit Me on Sunday?	1970	20.00
❑ MS-3191	The Best of George Jones	1970	20.00
❑ MS-3194	George Jones With Love	1971	20.00
❑ MS-3203	The Best of Sacred Music	1971	20.00
❑ MS-3204	The Great Songs of Leon Payne	1971	20.00
NASHVILLE			
❑ 2076	Seasons of My Heart	1970	15.00
PAIR			
❑ PDL2-1074 [(2)]	The Best of George Jones	1986	12.00
❑ PDL2-1080 [(2)]	Country, By George!	1986	12.00
POWER PAK			
❑ 271	The Crown Prince of Country Music	197?	10.00
QUICKSILVER			
❑ QS-1011	Frozen in Time	198?	10.00
❑ QS-1012	If My Heart Had Windows	198?	10.00
RCA CAMDEN			
❑ ACL1-0377	The Race Is On	1973	12.00
❑ CAS-2591	Flowers for Mama	1973	12.00
RCA VICTOR			
❑ APL1-0316	Best of George Jones Vol. II	1973	15.00
❑ APL1-0486	You Gotta Be My Baby	1974	15.00
❑ APL1-0612	His Songs	1974	15.00
❑ APL1-0815	I Can Love You Enough	1974	15.00
❑ APL1-1113	The Best of the Best	1975	15.00
❑ LSP-4672	First in the Hearts of Country Music Lovers	1972	15.00
❑ LSP-4716	Best of George Jones Vol. I	1972	15.00
❑ LSP-4725	Poor Man's Riches	1972	15.00
❑ LSP-4726	I Made Leaving (Easy for You)	1972	15.00
❑ LSP-4727	Country Singer	1972	15.00
❑ LSP-4733	George Jones And Friends	1972	15.00
❑ LSP-4785	Four-O Thirty-Three	1972	15.00
❑ LSP-4786	Tender Years	1972	15.00
❑ LSP-4787	Take Me	1972	15.00
❑ LSP-4801	Wrapped Around Her Finger	1973	15.00
❑ LSP-4847	I Can Still See Him	1973	15.00
ROUNDER			
❑ SS-15	Burn the Honky Tonk Down	198?	10.00
❑ SS-17	Heartaches & Hangovers	198?	10.00
SEARS			
❑ SPS-125	Maybe, Little Baby	196?	20.00
STARDAY			
❑ SLP 101 [M]	The Grand Ole Opry's New Star	1958	1200.
❑ SLP 125 [M]	The Crown Prince of Country Music	1960	160.00
❑ SLP 150 [M]	George Jones Sings His Greatest Hits	1962	50.00
❑ SLP 151 [M]	The Fabulous Country Music Sound of George Jones	1962	50.00
❑ SLP 335 [M]	George Jones	1965	40.00
❑ SLP 344 [M]	Long Live King George	1965	40.00
❑ SLP 366	The George Jones Story Bonus Photo	1966	20.00
❑ SLP 366 [(2)M]	The George Jones Story	1966	30.00
❑ SLP 401	The George Jones Song Book & Picture Album	1967	50.00
—With book			
❑ SLP 401 [M]	The George Jones Song Book & Picture Album	1967	30.00
—Without book			
❑ SLP 440 [M]	The Golden Country Hits of George Jones	1969	30.00
❑ 3021	16 Greatest Hits	197?	10.00
❑ DT-90080 [R]	George Jones Sings His Greatest Hits	1964	80.00
—Capitol Record Club edition			
❑ DT-90611 [R]	The Crown Prince of Country Music	196?	40.00
—Capitol Record Club edition			
TIME-LIFE			
❑ STW-103	Country Music	1981	10.00
UNITED ARTISTS			
❑ UXS-85 [(2)]	George Jones Superpak	1972	20.00
❑ UAL-3193 [M]	The New Favorites of George Jones	1962	30.00

Number	Title (A Side/B Side)	Yr	NM
❑ UAL-3218 [M]	George Jones Sings the Hits of His Country Cousins	1962	30.00
❑ UAL-3219 [M]	Homecoming in Heaven	1962	30.00
❑ UAL-3220 [M]	My Favorites of Hank Williams	1962	30.00
❑ UAL-3221 [M]	George Jones Sings Bob Wills	1962	40.00
❑ UAL-3270 [M]	I Wish the Night Would Never End	1963	25.00
❑ UAL-3291 [M]	The Best of George Jones	1963	25.00
❑ UAL-3338 [M]	More New Favorites	1964	25.00
❑ UAL-3364 [M]	George Jones Sings Like the Dickens	1964	40.00
❑ UAL-3388 [M]	I Get Lonely in a Hurry	1964	30.00
❑ UAL-3408 [M]	Trouble in Mind	1965	30.00
❑ UAL-3422 [M]	The Race Is On	1965	20.00
—With cartoon on front			
❑ UAL-3422 [M]	The Race Is On	1965	30.00
—With photo of George Jones on front			
❑ UAL-3442 [M]	King of Broken Hearts	1965	30.00
❑ UAL-3457 [M]	The Great George Jones	1966	30.00
❑ UAL-3532 [M]	George Jones' Golden Hits, Vol. 1	1966	20.00
❑ UAL-3558 [M]	The Young George Jones	1967	30.00
❑ UAL-3566 [M]	George Jones' Golden Hits, Vol. 2	1967	30.00
❑ UAS-6193 [S]	The New Favorites of George Jones	1962	40.00
❑ UAS-6218 [S]	George Jones Sings the Hits of His Country Cousins	1962	40.00
❑ UAS-6219 [S]	Homecoming in Heaven	1962	40.00
❑ UAS-6220 [S]	My Favorites of Hank Williams	1962	40.00
❑ UAS-6221 [S]	George Jones Sings Bob Wills	1962	50.00
❑ UAS-6270 [S]	I Wish the Night Would Never End	1963	30.00
❑ UAS-6291 [S]	The Best of George Jones	1963	30.00
❑ UAS-6328 [S]	More New Favorites	1964	30.00
❑ UAS-6364 [S]	George Jones Sings Like the Dickens	1964	50.00
❑ UAS-6388 [S]	I Get Lonely in a Hurry	1964	40.00
❑ UAS-6408 [S]	Trouble in Mind	1965	40.00
❑ UAS-6422 [S]	The Race Is On	1965	25.00
—With cartoon on front			
❑ UAS-6422 [S]	The Race Is On	1965	40.00
—With photo of George Jones on front			
❑ UAS-6442 [S]	King of Broken Hearts	1965	40.00
❑ UAS-6457 [S]	The Great George Jones	1966	40.00
❑ UAS-6532 [S]	George Jones' Golden Hits, Vol. 1	1966	25.00
❑ UAS-6558 [S]	The Young George Jones	1967	20.00
❑ UAS-6566 [S]	George Jones' Golden Hits, Vol. 2	1967	20.00
❑ UAS-6696	George Jones' Golden Hits, Vol. 3	1968	20.00
❑ ST-90829 [S]	The Race Is On	1965	40.00
—Capitol Record Club edition; photo on front			
❑ T-90829 [M]	The Race Is On	1965	30.00
—Capitol Record Club edition; photo on front			

WING

Number	Title (A Side/B Side)	Yr	NM
❑ MGW-12266 [M]	The Great George Jones	196?	15.00
❑ SRW-16266 [S]	The Great George Jones	196?	15.00

JONES, GEORGE, AND BRENDA CARTER

Also see each artist's individual listings.

45s

MUSICOR

Number	Title (A Side/B Side)	Yr	NM
❑ 1325	Milwaukee, Here I Come/Great Big Spirit of Love	1968	8.00
❑ 1375	Lonesome End of the Line/Just Your Average Couple	1969	8.00

JONES, GEORGE, AND JEANETTE HICKS

Also see each artist's individual listings.

45s

MERCURY

Number	Title (A Side/B Side)	Yr	NM
❑ 71029	Don't Stop the Music/Uh, Huh, No	1957	25.00
❑ 71061	Yearning/Cry, Cry	1957	25.00
❑ 71339	I'm with the Wrong One/Nothing Can Stop Me	1958	25.00

STARDAY

Number	Title (A Side/B Side)	Yr	NM
❑ 279	Yearning/So Near Yet So Far Away	1956	30.00

JONES, GEORGE, AND BRENDA LEE

Also see each artist's individual listings.

45s

EPIC

Number	Title (A Side/B Side)	Yr	NM
❑ 04723	Hallelujah I Love Her So/(What Love Can Do) The Second Time Around	1984	4.00

JONES, GEORGE, AND MELBA MONTGOMERY

Also see each artist's individual listings.

45s

MUSICOR

Number	Title (A Side/B Side)	Yr	NM
❑ 1204	Close Together (As You and Me)/Long As We're Dreaming	1966	8.00
❑ 1238	Party Pickin'/Simply Divine	1967	8.00

UNITED ARTISTS

Number	Title (A Side/B Side)	Yr	NM
❑ 575	We Must Have Been Out of Our Minds/Until Then	1963	10.00
❑ 635	Let's Invite Them Over/What's In Our Hearts	1963	10.00
❑ 704	There's a Friend in the Way/Suppose Tonight Would Be Our Last	1964	10.00
❑ 732	Please Be My Love/Will There Ever Be Another	1964	10.00
❑ 784	Multiply the Heartaches/Once More	1964	10.00
❑ 828	House of Gold/I Dreamed My Baby Came Home	1965	10.00
❑ 899	Don't Go/I Let You Go	1965	10.00
❑ 941	Blue Moon of Kentucky/I Can't Get Over You	1965	10.00
❑ 50015	Afraid/Now Tell Me	1966	10.00

Albums

GUEST STAR

Number	Title (A Side/B Side)	Yr	NM
❑ GS 1465 [M]	George Jones and Melba Montgomery	196?	12.00
—Contains two solo records by each artist (no duets!) and assorted stuff by others			

LIBERTY

Number	Title (A Side/B Side)	Yr	NM
❑ LN-10169	Singing What's In Our Hearts	1981	8.00

MUSICOR

Number	Title (A Side/B Side)	Yr	NM
❑ MM-2109 [M]	Close Together (As You and Me)	1966	20.00
❑ MM-2127 [M]	Let's Get Together/Boy Meets Girl	1967	30.00
❑ MM-2127 [M]	Party Pickin'	1967	30.00
—Alternate title			
❑ MS-3109 [S]	Close Together (As You and Me)	1966	25.00
❑ MS-3127 [S]	Let's Get Together/Boy Meets Girl	1967	20.00
❑ MS-3127 [S]	Party Pickin'	1967	20.00
—Alternate title			

UNITED ARTISTS

Number	Title (A Side/B Side)	Yr	NM
❑ UAL-3301 [M]	Singing What's In Our Hearts	1963	25.00
❑ UAL-3352 [M]	Bluegrass Hootenanny	1964	25.00
❑ UAL-3472 [M]	Blue Moon of Kentucky	1966	20.00
❑ UAS-6301 [S]	Singing What's In Our Hearts	1963	30.00
❑ UAS-6352 [S]	Bluegrass Hootenanny	1964	30.00
❑ UAS-6472 [S]	Blue Moon of Kentucky	1966	25.00
❑ T-90832 [M]	Blue Moon of Kentucky	1966	25.00
—Capitol Record Club edition			

JONES, GEORGE; MELBA MONTGOMERY; JUDY LYNN

Albums

UNITED ARTISTS

Number	Title (A Side/B Side)	Yr	NM
❑ UAL-3367 [M]	A King and Two Queens	1964	20.00
❑ UAS-6367 [S]	A King and Two Queens	1964	25.00

JONES, GEORGE; MELBA MONTGOMERY; GENE PITNEY

Albums

MUSICOR

Number	Title (A Side/B Side)	Yr	NM
❑ MM-2079 [M]	Famous Country Duets	1965	20.00

JONES, GEORGE, AND JOHNNY PAYCHECK

Also see each artist's individual listings.

45s

EPIC

Number	Title (A Side/B Side)	Yr	NM
❑ 50647	Mabellene/Don't Want No Stranger Sleepin' in My Bed	1978	4.00
❑ 50708	You Can Have Her/Along Came Jones	1979	4.00
❑ 50891	When You're Ugly Like Us (You Just Naturally Got to Be Cool)/Kansas City	1980	4.00
❑ 50949	You Better Move On/Smack Dab in the Middle	1980	4.00

Albums

EPIC

Number	Title (A Side/B Side)	Yr	NM
❑ JE 35783	Double Trouble	1980	10.00

JONES, GEORGE, AND MARGIE SINGLETON

45s

MERCURY

Number	Title (A Side/B Side)	Yr	NM
❑ 71856	Did I Ever Tell You/Not Even Friends	1961	12.00
❑ 71955	Waltz of the Angels/Talk About Lovin'	1962	12.00
❑ 72159	Are You Mine/I Didn't Hear You	1963	12.00

Albums

MERCURY

Number	Title (A Side/B Side)	Yr	NM
❑ MG-20747 [M]	Duets Country Style	1962	30.00
❑ SR-60747 [S]	Duets Country Style	1962	40.00

JONES, GEORGE, AND TAMMY WYNETTE

Also see each artist's individual listings; TINA WITH DADDY AND MOMMY.

45s

EPIC

Number	Title (A Side/B Side)	Yr	NM
❑ 10815	Take Me/We Go Together	1971	5.00
❑ 10881	The Ceremony/The Great Divide	1972	5.00
❑ 10923	Old Fashioned Singing/We Love to Sing About Jesus	1972	5.00
❑ 10963	Let's Build a World Together/Touching Shoulders	1973	5.00
❑ 11031	We're Gonna Hold On/My Elusive Dreams	1973	5.00
❑ 11077	Mr. and Mrs. Santa Claus/The Greatest Christmas Gift	1973	5.00
❑ 11083	(We're Not) The Jet Set/The Crawdad Song	1974	5.00
❑ 11151	We Loved It Away/Ain't It Been Good	1974	5.00
❑ 50099	God's Gonna Getcha (For That)/Those Were the Good Times	1975	5.00
❑ 50235	Golden Ring/We're Putting It Back Together	1976	5.00
❑ 50314	Near You/Tattletale Eyes	1976	5.00
❑ 50418	Southern California/Keep the Change	1977	4.00
❑ 50849	Two Story House/It Sure Was Good	1980	4.00
❑ 50930	A Pair of Old Sneakers/We'll Talk About It Later	1980	4.00

MCA

Number	Title (A Side/B Side)	Yr	NM
❑ 55048	One/Golden Ring	1995	4.00

Albums

EPIC

Number	Title (A Side/B Side)	Yr	NM
❑ EQ 30802 [Q]	We Go Together	1971	25.00
❑ KE 30802	We Go Together	1971	15.00
❑ KE 31554	Me and the First Lady	1972	15.00
—Yellow label			
❑ KE 31554	Me and the First Lady	1973	12.00
—Orange label			
❑ KE 31719	We Love to Sing About Jesus	1972	15.00
—Yellow label			
❑ KE 31719	We Love to Sing About Jesus	1973	12.00
—Orange label			
❑ KE 32113	Let's Build a World Together	1973	15.00
❑ KE 32757	We're Gonna Hold On	1973	15.00
❑ KE 33351	George & Tammy & Tina	1975	15.00
❑ BG 33752 [(2)]	We Go Together/Me and the First Lady	1976	15.00
❑ KE 34291	Golden Ring	1976	12.00
—Orange label			
❑ PE 34291	Golden Ring	198?	8.00
—Dark blue label			
❑ KE 34716	Greatest Hits	1977	12.00
❑ PE 34716	Greatest Hits	198?	8.00
—Budget-line reissue			
❑ JE 36764	Together Again	1980	10.00
❑ PE 36764	Together Again	198?	8.00
—Budget-line reissue			
❑ FE 37348	Encore	1981	10.00
❑ PE 37348	Encore	198?	8.00
—Budget-line reissue			

JONES, JACK

45s

CAPITOL

Number	Title (A Side/B Side)	Yr	NM
❑ F3808	Good Luck Good Buddy/Baby Come Home	1957	12.00
❑ F3844	For Crying Out Loud/Born to Be Lucky	1957	12.00
❑ F3929	A Very Precious Love/What's the Use	1958	10.00
❑ F3991	Come On Baby Let's Go/You Laugh	1958	10.00
❑ F4089	Laffin' at Me/Deeply Devoted	1958	10.00
❑ F4161	Make Room for the Joy/When I Love I'll Love Forever	1959	10.00
❑ F4161 [PS]	Make Room for the Joy/When I Love I'll Love Forever	1959	15.00

KAPP

Number	Title (A Side/B Side)	Yr	NM
❑ 341	It's a Lonesome Town/A Lot of Livin' to Do	1960	10.00
❑ 380	Big Time/She's My Darling, She's My Heart	1961	10.00
❑ 435	Lollipops and Roses/This Was My Love	1961	8.00
❑ 461	Gift of Love/Pick Up the Pieces	1962	8.00
❑ 477	Poetry/Dreamin' All the Time	1962	8.00
❑ 495	I've Got My Pride/That's Her Little Way	1962	8.00
❑ 507	La Paloma/The Lonely Bull	1963	8.00
❑ 516	Call Me Irresponsible/Mutiny on the Bounty	1963	8.00
❑ 534	Love Is a Ticklish Affair/That's the Way I Come to You	1963	8.00
❑ 551	Wives and Lovers/Toys in the Attic	1963	6.00

J

Number	Title (A Side/B Side)	Yr	NM
551 [PS]	Wives and Lovers/Toys in the Attic	1963	8.00
571	Love with the Proper Stranger/The Mood I'm In	1964	6.00
571 [PS]	Love with the Proper Stranger/The Mood I'm In	1964	8.00
589	The First Night of the Full Moon/Far Away	1964	6.00
589 [PS]	The First Night of the Full Moon/Far Away	1964	8.00
608	Where Love Has Gone/The Lorelei	1964	6.00
608 [PS]	Where Love Has Gone/The Lorelei	1964	8.00
629	Lullaby for Christmas Eve/The Village of St. Bernadette	1964	8.00
635	Dear Heart/Emily	1964	6.00
635 [PS]	Dear Heart/Emily	1964	8.00
651	The Race Is On/I Can't Believe I'm Losing You	1965	6.00
651 [PS]	The Race Is On/I Can't Believe I'm Losing You	1965	8.00
672	Seein' the Right Love Go Wrong/Travelin' On	1965	6.00
699	The True Picture/Just Yesterday	1965	6.00
722	Love Bug/And I Love Her	1965	6.00
722 [PS]	Love Bug/And I Love Her	1965	8.00
736	The Weekend/Wildflower	1966	6.00
755	The Impossible Dream (The Quest)/Strangers in the Night	1966	6.00
781	A Day in the Life of a Fool/Shining Sea	1966	6.00
781 [PS]	A Day in the Life of a Fool/Shining Sea	1966	—

—Rumored to exist, but without conclusive evidence, we will delete this from future editions

Number	Title (A Side/B Side)	Yr	NM
800	Lady/Afraid to Love	1966	6.00
818	I'm Indestructible/Afterthoughts	1967	6.00
833	Now I Know/More and More	1967	6.00
847	Our Song/Michelle	1967	6.00
860	Open for Business As Usual/The Mood I'm In	1967	6.00
880	Don't Give Your Love Away/Oh How Much I Love You	1967	6.00
900	Brother, Where Are You/Gypsies, Jugglers and Clowns	1968	6.00
937	People/Don't Rain on My Parade	1968	6.00
964	Far Away/Meditation	1968	6.00
2022	Mathilda/Far Away	1969	5.00
2063	It Only Takes a Moment/Once Upon a Time	1969	5.00
2138	Mirrored Door/Feather Bed	1971	5.00
2143	Breathe Deep/Trippin' on a Country Road	1971	5.00
2154	I'll See You Through/No Concern	1971	5.00

MGM

Number	Title (A Side/B Side)	Yr	NM
14851	The Love Boat Theme/Ready to Take a Chance Again	197?	8.00
14852	Love Theme from "A Star Is Born" (Evergreen)/I Could Have Been a Sailor	197?	4.00

POLYDOR

Number	Title (A Side/B Side)	Yr	NM
815096-7	The Love Boat Theme/The Rockford Files	1983	4.00

—Reissue; B-side by Mike Post

RCA VICTOR

Number	Title (A Side/B Side)	Yr	NM
47-9365	Live for Life/That Tiny World	1967	5.00
47-9441	If You Ever Leave Me/Pretty	1968	5.00
47-9510	Without Her/Follow Me	1968	5.00
47-9564	I Really Want You to Know/This World Is Yours	1968	5.00
47-9639	The Way That I Live/Dirty Word	1968	5.00
47-9687	Love Story/L.A. Breakdown (And Take Me In)	1968	5.00
74-0185	Sweet Child/The Last Seven Days	1969	5.00
74-0278	Little Altar Boy/What's Out There for Me	1969	5.00
74-0350	Sweet Changes/I Wish We'd All Been Ready	1970	5.00
74-0425	Pieces of Dreams/Years of My Youth	1971	5.00
74-0475	Let Me Be the One/Talk It Over in the Morning	1971	5.00
74-0573	The Kind of Girl She Is/What Have They Done to the Moon	1971	5.00
74-0683	The Mountain/How Can We Run Away	1972	5.00
74-0734	Coming Apart/A Game of Magic	1972	5.00
APBO-0220	Do Me Wrong, But Do Me/Fools in Love	1974	4.00
PB-10025	She Doesn't Live Here Anymore/Write Me a Love Song Charlie	1974	4.00
PB-10317	What I Did for Love/Don't Mention Love	1975	4.00
PB-10845	Send In the Clowns/You Need a Man	1976	4.00
PB-10955	Try It Again/With One More Look at You	1977	4.00
PB-11076	Dixie Chicken/Perfect Strangers	1977	4.00

Albums

CAPITOL

Number	Title	Yr	NM
ST 1274 [S]	This Love of Mine	1959	30.00
T 1274 [M]	This Love of Mine	1959	25.00
ST 2100 [S]	In Love	1964	20.00

—Reissue of 1274

Number	Title	Yr	NM
T 2100 [M]	In Love	1964	15.00

KAPP

Number	Title	Yr	NM
KL-1228 [M]	Shall We Dance	1961	12.00
KL-1259 [M]	Lollipops and Roses	196?	12.00

—Revised title

Number	Title	Yr	NM
KL-1259 [M]	This Was My Love	1962	20.00

—Original title

Number	Title	Yr	NM
KL-1265 [M]	I've Got a Lot of Livin' to Do	1962	12.00
KL-1328 [M]	Call Me Irresponsible	1963	12.00
KL-1337 [M]	She Loves Me	1963	12.00
KL-1352 [M]	Wives and Lovers	1963	12.00
KL-1365 [M]	Bewitched	1964	12.00
KL-1396 [M]	Where Love Has Gone	1964	12.00
KL 1399 [M]	The Jack Jones Christmas Album	1964	12.00
KL-1415 [M]	Dear Heart	1964	12.00
KL-1433 [M]	My Kind of Town	1965	12.00
KL-1435 [M]	There's Love & There's Love & There's Love	1965	12.00
KL-1465 [M]	For the "In" Crowd	1966	12.00
KL-1486 [M]	The Impossible Dream	1966	12.00
KL-1500 [M]	Jack Jones Sings	1966	12.00
KL-1511 [M]	Lady	1967	15.00
KL-1531 [M]	Our Song	1967	15.00
KL-1551 [M]	What the World Needs Now Is Love!	1968	20.00

—May only exist as a white label promo; covers are stereo with "Mono" sticker

Number	Title	Yr	NM
KL-1559 [M]	Greatest Hits	1968	20.00

—May exist only as a white label promo; covers are stereo with a "Mono" sticker

Number	Title	Yr	NM
KS-3228 [S]	Shall We Dance	1961	15.00
KS-3259 [S]	Lollipops and Roses	196?	15.00

—Revised title

Number	Title	Yr	NM
KS-3259 [S]	This Was My Love	1962	25.00

—Original title

Number	Title	Yr	NM
KS-3265 [S]	I've Got a Lot of Livin' to Do	1962	15.00
KS-3328 [S]	Call Me Irresponsible	1963	15.00
KS-3337 [S]	She Loves Me	1963	15.00
KS-3352 [S]	Wives and Lovers	1963	15.00
KS-3365 [S]	Bewitched	1964	15.00
KS-3396 [S]	Where Love Has Gone	1964	15.00
KS 3399 [S]	The Jack Jones Christmas Album	1964	15.00
KS-3415 [S]	Dear Heart	1964	15.00
KS-3433 [S]	My Kind of Town	1965	15.00
KS-3435 [S]	There's Love & There's Love & There's Love	1965	15.00
KS-3465 [S]	For the "In" Crowd	1966	15.00
KS-3486 [S]	The Impossible Dream	1966	15.00
KS-3500 [S]	Jack Jones Sings	1966	15.00
KS-3511 [S]	Lady	1967	12.00
KS-3531 [S]	Our Song	1967	12.00
KS-3551 [S]	What the World Needs Now Is Love!	1968	12.00
KS-3559	Greatest Hits	1968	12.00
KS-3566	Curtain Time	1968	12.00
KS-3590	Jack Jones in Hollywood	1969	12.00
KS-3602	Greatest Hits Vol. 2	1970	12.00
KXS-5009 [(2)]	The Best of Jack Jones	196?	15.00

MCA

Number	Title	Yr	NM
4115 [(2)]	The Best of Jack Jones	197?	12.00

—Reissue of Kapp KXS-5009

Number	Title	Yr	NM
15014	The Jack Jones Christmas Album	197?	10.00

—Reissue

Number	Title	Yr	NM
15036	White Christmas	198?	8.00

MGM

Number	Title	Yr	NM
MG-1-5023	Nobody Does It Better	1979	10.00
MG-1-5024	Don't Stop Now	1980	10.00

PICKWICK

Number	Title	Yr	NM
PC-3001 [M]	This Love of Mine	196?	12.00
SPC-3001 [S]	This Love of Mine	196?	12.00
SPC-3041	A Very Precious Love	196?	10.00

RCA CAMDEN

Number	Title	Yr	NM
ACL1-0255	Christmas with Jack Jones	1973	12.00

—Reissue of RCA Victor LSP-4234

RCA VICTOR

Number	Title	Yr	NM
APL1-0139	Together	1973	10.00
APL1-0408	Harbour	1974	10.00
APL1-0773	Write Me a Love Song, Charlie	1975	10.00
ANL1-1081	Jack Jones Sings Michel Legrand	1975	8.00

—Reissue

Number	Title	Yr	NM
APL1-1111	What I Did for Love	1975	10.00
APL1-2067	The Full Life	1976	10.00
APL1-2361	With One More Look at You	1977	10.00
LPM-3911 [M]	Without Her	1967	20.00
LSP-3911 [S]	Without Her	1967	12.00
LPM-3969 [M]	If You Ever Leave Me	1968	20.00
LSP-3969 [S]	If You Ever Leave Me	1968	12.00
LSP-4048	Where Is Love	1968	12.00
LSP-4108	L.A. Break Down	1969	12.00
LSP-4209	A Time for Us	1969	12.00
LSP-4234	A Jack Jones Christmas	1969	15.00
LSP-4413	In Person at the Sands, Las Vegas	1970	12.00
LSP-4480	Jack Jones Sings Michel Legrand	1970	12.00
LSP-4613	A Song for You	1971	12.00
LSP-4692	Bread Winners	1972	10.00

VOCALION

Number	Title	Yr	NM
VL 73913	Jack Jones Showcase	1970	10.00

JONES, JACK, AND THE JET SET BAND

45s

HIT

Number	Title (A Side/B Side)	Yr	NM
317	Judy in Disguise (With Glasses)/We Can Fly	1967	8.00

—B-side by the Jalopy Five

JONES, JIMMY

Also see THE PRETENDERS (2).

45s

ABC-PARAMOUNT

Number	Title (A Side/B Side)	Yr	NM
10094	Blue and Lonely/Daddy Needs Baby	1960	150.00

—As "Jimmy Jones and the Pretenders"

ARROW

Number	Title (A Side/B Side)	Yr	NM
717	Heaven in Your Eyes/The Whistlin' Man	1957	180.00

—As "Jimmy Jones and the Jones Boys"

BELL

Number	Title (A Side/B Side)	Yr	NM
682	Personal Property/39-21-40	1967	8.00
689	True Love Ways/Snap My Fingers	1967	8.00

CAPITOL

Number	Title (A Side/B Side)	Yr	NM
3849	If I Knew Then (What I Know Now)/Everything's Gonna Be All Right	1974	5.00

CONCHILLO

Number	Title (A Side/B Side)	Yr	NM
1	Ain't Nothing Wrong Makin' Love the First Night/Time and Changes	1976	6.00

CUB

Number	Title (A Side/B Side)	Yr	NM
9049	Handy Man/The Search Is Over	1959	25.00
9067	Good Timin'/My Precious Angel	1960	25.00
9072	That's When I Cried/I Just Go for You	1960	20.00
9072 [PS]	That's When I Cried/I Just Go for You	1960	50.00
9076	Itchin'/Ee-I-Ee-I-Oh	1960	20.00
9082	Ready for Love/For You	1960	20.00
9085	I Told You So/You Got It	1961	15.00
9093	Dear One/I Say Love	1961	15.00
9102	Mr. Music Man/Holler Hey	1961	15.00
9110	You're Much Too Young/Nights of Mexico	1962	15.00

EPIC

Number	Title (A Side/B Side)	Yr	NM
9339	Whenever You Need Me/You for Me to Love	1959	120.00

PARKWAY

Number	Title (A Side/B Side)	Yr	NM
988	Don't You Just Know It/Dynamite	1966	10.00

RAMA

Number	Title (A Side/B Side)	Yr	NM
210	Lover/Plain Old Love	1956	120.00

—As "Jimmy Jones and the Pretenders"

ROULETTE

Number	Title (A Side/B Side)	Yr	NM
4232	Lover/Plain Old Love	1960	30.00

—As "Jimmy 'Handyman' Jones"

VEE JAY

Number	Title (A Side/B Side)	Yr	NM
505	No Insurance (For a Broken Heart)/Mr. Fix-It	1963	15.00

Albums

JEN JILLUS

Number	Title	Yr	NM
1001	The Handy Man's Back in Town	1977	12.00

MGM

Number	Title	Yr	NM
E-3847 [M]	Good Timin'	1960	120.00
SE-3847 [S]	Good Timin'	1960	160.00

JONES, JOE

45s

CAPITOL

Number	Title (A Side/B Side)	Yr	NM
F2951	Adam Bit the Apple/Will Call	1954	40.00

HERALD

Number	Title (A Side/B Side)	Yr	NM
488	You Done Me Wrong/When Your Hair Has Turned to Silver	1956	40.00

RIC

Number	Title (A Side/B Side)	Yr	NM
972	You Talk Too Much/I Love You Still	1960	25.00

Number	Title (A Side/B Side)	Yr	NM
ROULETTE			
❑ 4304	You Talk Too Much/I Love You Still	1960	15.00
❑ 4316	One Big Mouth/Here's What You Gotta Do	1960	12.00
❑ 4344	California Sun/Please Don't Talk About Me When I'm Gone	1961	12.00
❑ 4377	The Big Mule/I've Got a Uh Uh Wife	1961	12.00
Albums			
ROULETTE			
❑ R 25143 [M]	You Talk Too Much	1961	150.00
❑ SR 25143 [R]	You Talk Too Much	1961	100.00

JONES, JOHN PAUL

Number	Title (A Side/B Side)	Yr	NM
45s			
COTILLION			
❑ 44102	Got to Get Together Now/Man from Nazareth	1971	25.00
JERDEN			
❑ 761	Sound City/Broken Promises	1965	30.00
—B-side by Rosemary and Howard			
PARKWAY			
❑ 915	Baja/A Foggy Day in Vietnam	1964	40.00
Albums			
COLUMBIA			
❑ KC 32047	John Paul Jones	1973	20.00

JONES, JONAH

Number	Title (A Side/B Side)	Yr	NM
45s			
BETHLEHEM			
❑ 11014	You're the Cream in My Coffee/The Sheik of Araby	1959	12.00
CAPITOL			
❑ F3747	On the Street Where You Live/Rose Room	1957	10.00
❑ F3893	76 Trombones/Baubles, Bangles and Beads	1958	10.00
❑ F3999	Ballin' the Jack/Slowly But Surely	1958	10.00
❑ F4057	Night Train/Lots of Luck, Charlie	1958	10.00
❑ F4199	Cherry/I Dig Chicks	1959	10.00
❑ F4238	High Hopes/Hit Me Again	1959	10.00
❑ F4297	Where Did We Go? Out/Gentleman Jimmy	1959	10.00
❑ 4375	Blueberry Hill/Shanghai	1960	10.00
❑ 4497	I Ain't Down Yet/Blue Champagne	1961	8.00
❑ 4878	The Bells of St. Mary's/Brotherhood of Man	1962	8.00
❑ 4944	The Work Song/Jonah's Sermon	1963	8.00
❑ 4993	Doodles/Pink Shutters	1963	8.00
DECCA			
❑ 25672	People/Who Can I Turn To	196?	6.00
❑ 31765	Think Beautiful/Don't Forget 127th Street (127th Street March)	1965	6.00
GROOVE			
❑ 0140	Come Sit By Me/God Loves You Child	1956	15.00
MOTOWN			
❑ 1145	For Better or Worse/Don't Mess with Bill	1969	120.00
7-Inch Extended Plays			
CAPITOL			
❑ EAP 1-839	Rose Room/Mack the Knife//My Blue Heaven/Royal Garden Blues	1958	12.00
❑ EAP 1-839 [PS]	Muted Jazz, Part 1	1958	12.00
❑ EAP 2-839	(contents unknown)	1958	12.00
❑ EAP 2-839 [PS]	Muted Jazz, Part 2	1958	12.00
❑ EAP 3-839	(contents unknown)	1958	12.00
❑ EAP 3-839 [PS]	Muted Jazz, Part 3	1958	12.00
❑ EAP 1-963	*Baubles, Bangles and Beads/The Party's Over/Till There Was You/Seventy Six Trombones	1958	12.00
❑ EAP 1-963 [PS]	Swingin' on Broadway, Part 1	1958	12.00
❑ EAP 2-963	You're So Right for Me/Just My Luck//I Could Have Danced All Night/Whatever Lola Wants	195?	12.00
❑ EAP 2-963 [PS]	Swingin' on Broadway, Part 2	195?	12.00
❑ EAP 3-963	(contents unknown)	1958	12.00
❑ EAP 3-963 [PS]	Swingin' on Broadway, Part 3	1958	12.00
❑ EAP 1-1014	On the Street Where You Live/Rose Room//Baubles, Bangles and Beads/Seventy Six Trombones	195?	12.00
❑ EAP 1-1014 [PS]	On the Street Where You Live	195?	12.00
❑ EAP 1-1039	No Moon at All/Baby, Won't You Please Come Home//A Kiss to Build a Dream On/That's a Plenty	195?	12.00
❑ EAP 1-1039 [PS]	Jumpin' with Jonah, Part 1	195?	12.00
❑ EAP 2-1039	Bill Bailey, Won't You Please Come Home?/The Blues Don't Care (Who's Gort 'Em)//Dance Only with Me/Lots of Luck Charley	195?	12.00
❑ EAP 2-1039 [PS]	Jumpin' with Jonah, Part 2	195?	12.00
❑ EAP 3-1039	Night Train/Jumpin' with Jonah//Just a Gigolo/It's a Good Day	195?	12.00
❑ EAP 3-1039 [PS]	Jumpin' with Jonah, Part 3	195?	12.00
Albums			
ANGEL			
❑ ANG.60005 [10]	Jonah Wails — 1st Blast	1954	75.00
❑ ANG.60006 [10]	Jonah Wails — 2nd Blast	1954	75.00
BETHLEHEM			
❑ BCP-1014 [10]	Jonah Jones Sextet	1954	80.00
CAPITOL			
❑ T 839 [M]	Muted Jazz	1957	40.00
❑ T 963 [M]	Swingin' On Broadway	1958	40.00
❑ ST 1039 [S]	Jumpin' with Jonah	1958	30.00
❑ T 1039 [M]	Jumpin' with Jonah	1958	25.00
❑ ST 1083 [S]	Swingin' at the Cinema	1958	30.00
❑ T 1083 [M]	Swingin' at the Cinema	1958	25.00
❑ ST 1115 [S]	Jonah Jumps Again	1959	30.00
❑ T 1115 [M]	Jonah Jumps Again	1959	25.00
❑ ST 1193 [S]	I Dig Chicks	1959	25.00
❑ T 1193 [M]	I Dig Chicks	1959	20.00
❑ ST 1237 [S]	Swingin' 'Round the World	1959	25.00
❑ T 1237 [M]	Swingin' 'Round the World	1959	20.00
❑ ST 1375 [S]	Hit Me Again!	1960	25.00
❑ T 1375 [M]	Hit Me Again!	1960	20.00
❑ ST 1404 [S]	Jumpin' with a Shuffle	1960	25.00
❑ T 1404 [M]	Jumpin' with a Shuffle	1960	20.00
❑ ST 1405 [S]	A Touch of Blue	1960	25.00
❑ T 1405 [M]	A Touch of Blue	1960	20.00
❑ ST 1532 [S]	The Unsinkable Molly Brown	1961	25.00
❑ T 1532 [M]	The Unsinkable Molly Brown	1961	20.00
❑ ST 1557 [S]	Great Instrumental Hits Styled by Jonah Jones	1961	25.00
❑ T 1557 [M]	Great Instrumental Hits Styled by Jonah Jones	1961	20.00
❑ ST 1641 [S]	Broadway Swings Again	1961	25.00
❑ T 1641 [M]	Broadway Swings Again	1961	20.00
❑ SM-1660	Jonah Jones/Glenn Gray	197?	10.00
❑ ST 1660 [S]	Jonah Jones/Glenn Gray	1961	25.00
❑ T 1660 [M]	Jonah Jones/Glenn Gray	1961	20.00
❑ ST 1773 [S]	Jazz Bonus	1962	20.00
❑ T 1773 [M]	Jazz Bonus	1962	15.00
❑ ST 1948 [S]	And Now, In Person — Jonah Jones	1963	20.00
❑ T 1948 [M]	And Now, In Person — Jonah Jones	1963	15.00
❑ ST 2087 [S]	Blowin' Up a Storm	1964	20.00
❑ T 2087 [M]	Blowin' Up a Storm	1964	15.00
❑ ST 2594 [S]	The Best of Jonah Jones	1966	12.00
❑ T 2594 [M]	The Best of Jonah Jones	1966	15.00
CIRCLE			
❑ CLP-83	1944: Butterflies in the Rain	198?	10.00
DECCA			
❑ DL 4638 [M]	Hello Broadway	1965	12.00
❑ DL 4688 [M]	On the Sunny Side of the Street	1966	12.00
❑ DL 4765 [M]	Tijuana Taxi	1966	12.00
❑ DL 4800 [M]	Sweet with a Beat	1967	15.00
❑ DL 74638 [S]	Hello Broadway	1965	15.00
❑ DL 74688 [S]	On the Sunny Side of the Street	1966	15.00
❑ DL 74765 [S]	Tijuana Taxi	1966	15.00
❑ DL 74800 [S]	Sweet with a Beat	1967	12.00
❑ DL 74918	Jazz Tropical!	1968	12.00
GROOVE			
❑ LG-1001 [M]	Jonah Jones at the Embers	1956	50.00
HALL OF FAME			
❑ 613	After Hours Jazz	198?	10.00
JAZZ MAN			
❑ 5009	Confessin'	1981	10.00
MOTOWN			
❑ M-683	Along Came Jonah	1969	40.00
❑ M-690	Little Dis, Little Dat	1970	40.00
PICKWICK			
❑ SPC-3008	Swing Along	196?	12.00
RCA CAMDEN			
❑ CAS-2328	Jonah Jones Quartet	1969	12.00
RCA VICTOR			
❑ LPM-2004 [M]	Jonah Jones at the Embers	1959	40.00
—Reissue of Groove and Vik LP			
SWING			
❑ 8408	Paris 1954	198?	10.00
VIK			
❑ LXA-1135 [M]	Jonah Jones at the Embers	1958	40.00
—Reissue of Groove LP			

JONES, LEROY

Number	Title (A Side/B Side)	Yr	NM
45s			
HIT			
❑ 33	Do You Love Me/Only Love Can Break a Heart	1962	8.00
—B-side by Ed Hardin			
❑ 51	Send Me Some Lovin'/Walk Like a Man	1963	8.00
—B-side by the Chellows			
❑ 53	Let's Limbo Some More/Blame It on the Bossa Nova	1963	8.00
—B-side by Sylvia Richards			
❑ 60	Baby Workout/Can't Get Used to Losing You	1963	8.00
—B-side by Fred Brown			
❑ 68	Another Saturday Night/It's My Party	1963	8.00
—B-side by Connie Landers			
❑ 73	No One/So Much in Love	1963	8.00
—B-side by Thomas Henry			
❑ 79	Hey Girl/If I Had a Hammer	1963	8.00
—B-side by Ricky Dickens			
❑ 90	It's All Right/She's a Fool	1963	8.00
—B-side by Connie Dee			
❑ 97	Loddy Lo/Quicksand	1963	8.00
—B-side by Gerry and the Georgettes			
❑ 122	I Don't Want to Be Hurt Anymore/People	1964	8.00
—B-side by Morti Webb			
❑ 133	Steal Away/Where Did Our Love Go	1964	8.00
—B-side by the Houstons			
❑ 136	C'Mon and Swim/People Say	1964	8.00
—B-side by the Flower Sisters			
❑ 153	Baby Don't You Do It/Baby Love	1964	8.00
—B-side by Jenny and the Jewels			
❑ 176	Hold What You've Got/Wise Like Solomon	1965	8.00
—B-side by Bobby Brooks			
❑ 181	You Don't Want My Love/The Name Game	1965	8.00
—B-side by Lisa French			
❑ 184	Someday/Shake	1965	8.00
❑ 239	Crying Time/Lightnin' Strikes	1966	8.00
—B-side by Fred York			
❑ 249	I'm So Lonesome I Could Cry/A Sign of the Times	1966	8.00
—B-side by Fred York			
❑ 255	When a Man Loves a Woman/Rainy Day Women #12 and 35	1966	8.00
—B-side by Bobby Brooks			
❑ 257	It's a Man's Man's Man's World/Love Is Like an Itching in My Heart	1966	8.00
—B-side by Jenny and the Jewels			
❑ 267	Almost Persuaded/My Uncle Used to Love Me But She Died	1966	8.00
—B-side by Roger Frolic			
❑ 270	Satisfied Mind/Reach Out I'll Be There	1966	8.00
—B-side by the Chellows			
❑ 279	Tell It Like It Is/Good Thing	1967	8.00
—B-side by Ed Hardin and the Cadets			
❑ 337	You Keep Me Hangin' On/Sunshine of Your Love	1968	8.00
—B-side by the Chords (2)			
❑ 347	Little Green Apples/Elenore	1968	8.00
—B-side by the Jalopy Five			

JONES, LEROY, AND LUCILLE JOHNS

Also see each artist's individual listings.

Number	Title (A Side/B Side)	Yr	NM
45s			
HIT			
❑ 41	You Are My Sunshine/Keep Your Hands Off My Baby	1962	8.00
—B-side by Alpha Zoe			

JONES, LITTLE ANTHONY

Not the same Little Anthony who was with the Imperials.

Number	Title (A Side/B Side)	Yr	NM
45s			
EMBER			
❑ 1090	Dear Gesu Bambino (Part 1)/Dear Gesu Bambino (Part 2)	1962	15.00

JONES, LITTLE JOHNNY

Number	Title (A Side/B Side)	Yr	NM
45s			
ATLANTIC			
❑ 1045	Hoy, Hoy/Doin' the Best I Can	1954	80.00
FLAIR			
❑ 1010	Sweet Little Woman/I May Be Wrong	1953	800.00

Number	Title (A Side/B Side)	Yr	NM
JONES, LITTLE SONNY			
45s			
IMPERIAL			
❑ 5275	I Got Booted/Tend to Your Business Blues	1954	100.00
❑ 5287	Winehead Baby/Going to the Country	1954	100.00
SPECIALTY			
❑ 443	Is Everything All Right/Do You Really Love Me	1952	80.00
JONES, MARY			
45s			
HIT			
❑ 121	Walk On By/Diane	1964	8.00
—B-side by the Concords			
JONES, PAUL Original lead singer for MANFRED MANN.			
45s			
BELL			
❑ 805	It's Getting Better/Not Before Time	1969	8.00
CAPITOL			
❑ 5745	I Can't Hold On Much Longer/Baby Tomorrow	1966	8.00
❑ 5800	High Time/It Is Coming Closer	1966	8.00
❑ 5857	Sonny Boy Williamson/I've Been a Bad, Bad Boy	1967	8.00
❑ 5970	Privilege/Free Me	1967	8.00
LONDON			
❑ 168	Mighty Ship/Who Are the Masters	1972	5.00
❑ 178	The Pod That Came Back/Construction Worker's Song	1972	5.00
PRIVATE STOCK			
❑ 45,004	Love Enough	1974	5.00
Albums			
CAPITOL			
❑ ST 2795 [S]	Paul Jones Sings Songs from the Film "Privilege" and Others	1967	30.00
❑ T 2795 [M]	Paul Jones Sings Songs from the Film "Privilege" and Others	1967	30.00
LONDON			
❑ XPS 605	Crucifix in a Horseshoe	1971	12.00
JONES, QUINCY			
45s			
A&M			
❑ 1115	Oh Happy Day/Love and Peace	1969	6.00
❑ 1139	Oh Happy Day/Love and Peace	1969	5.00
❑ 1163	Killer Joe/Maybe Tomorrow	1970	5.00
❑ 1184	Bridge Over Troubled Water (Part 1)/Bridge Over Troubled Water (Part 2)	1970	5.00
❑ 1316	What's Going On (Part 1)/What's Going On (Part 2)	1971	5.00
❑ 1323	Ironside/Cast Your Fate to the Wind	1972	5.00
❑ 1404	Love Theme from "The Getaway" (Part 1)/Love Theme from "The Getaway" (Part 2)	1973	4.00
❑ 1455	Sanford & Son Theme/Summer in the City	1973	4.00
❑ 1606	If I Ever Lose This Heaven/Along Came Betty	1974	4.00
❑ 1606 [PS]	If I Ever Lose This Heaven/Along Came Betty	1974	6.00
❑ 1638	Soul Saga/Boogie Joe, The Grinder	1974	4.00
❑ 1663	Body Heat/One Track Mind	1975	4.00
❑ 1743	Is It Love That We're Missing/Cry Baby	1975	4.00
❑ 1743 [PS]	Is It Love That We're Missing/Cry Baby	1975	6.00
❑ 1791	Mellow Madness/Paranoid	1976	4.00
❑ 1878	Midnight Soul Patrol/Brown Soft Shoe	1976	4.00
❑ 1909	"Roots" Medley/Many Rains Ago (Oluwu)	1977	4.00
❑ 1909 [PS]	"Roots" Medley/Many Rains Ago (Oluwu)	1977	6.00
❑ 1923	What Shall I Do (Hush, Hush, Somebody's Calling My Name)/Oh, Lord, Come By Here	1977	4.00
❑ 2043	Stuff Like That/There's a Train Leavin'	1978	4.00
❑ 2043 [PS]	Stuff Like That/There's a Train Leavin'	1978	6.00
❑ 2080	Love, I Never Had It So Good/I Heard That	1978	4.00
❑ 2309	Ai No Corrida/Lenta Letina	1981	4.00
❑ 2334	Razzamatazz/Velas	1981	4.00
—Featuring Patti Austin			
❑ 2357	Just Once/The Dude	1981	4.00
—Featuring James Ingram			
❑ 2387	One Hundred Ways/Velas	1981	4.00
—Featuring James Ingram			
❑ 2417	There's a Train Leavin'/Something Special	1981	4.00
—Featuring Patti Austin			
ABC			
❑ 11086	For Love of Ivy/The Pussyfoot	1968	8.00
BELL			
❑ 832	I'm a Believer/The Time for Love Is Anytime	1969	6.00
❑ 833	Cactus Flower Theme/The Time for Love Is Anytime	1969	6.00
❑ 838	Bob & Carol & Ted & Alice/Giggle Grass	1969	6.00
COLGEMS			
❑ 66-1016	Hangin' Paper/Lonely Bottles	1968	8.00
IMPULSE			
❑ 206	Quintessence/For Lena and Lennie	1962	12.00
MERCURY			
❑ 71425	The Syncopated Clock/Tuxedo Junction	1959	12.00
❑ 71460	Choo Choo Ch-Boogie/Marchin' the Blues	1959	12.00
❑ 71489	Moanin'/The Preacher	1959	12.00
❑ 71546	Birth of a Band/Change of Pace	1959	12.00
❑ 71665	Love Is Here to Stay/Moonglow	1960	12.00
❑ 71737	G-Man Train/Pleasingly Plump	1960	12.00
❑ 71825	Mack the Knife/Hot Saki	1961	12.00
❑ 71940	St. Louis Blues/Twistin' Chicken	1962	12.00
❑ 72012	A Taste of Honey/Shagnasty	1962	12.00
❑ 72105	Boogie Bossa Nova/Morning of the Carnival	1963	10.00
❑ 72160	Jive Samba/Comin' Home Baby	1963	10.00
❑ 72289	Baby Elephant Walk/Mr. Lucky	1964	10.00
❑ 72306	Theme from "Golden Boy"/Sea Weed	1964	10.00
❑ 72348	A Hard Day's Night/Soul Serenade	1964	10.00
❑ 72423	Non-Stop to Brazil/Gentle Rain	1965	10.00
❑ 72436	The Pawnbroker/Harlem Drive	1965	10.00
❑ 72460	Mirage/Pack It Up	1965	10.00
❑ 72496	(I Can't Get No) Satisfaction/What's New Pussycat	1965	10.00
❑ 72533	Baby Cakes/Mohair Sam	1966	10.00
QWEST			
❑ 17528	Stomp (Frankie Knuckles Mix)/Stomp (Mousse T.'s Radio Mix)	1996	3.00
❑ 17673	Slow Jams (New Edit)/Slow Jams (Remix)	1996	3.00
—Featuring Babyface and Tamia with Portrait and Barry White			
❑ 19881	Tomorrow (A Better You, A Better Me)/(Instrumental)	1990	3.00
—Featuring Tevin Campbell			
❑ 19992	The Secret Garden (Sweet Seduction Suite)/(Instrumental)	1990	3.00
—With Al B. Sure!, James Ingram, El DeBarge and Barry White			
❑ 19992 [PS]	The Secret Garden (Sweet Seduction Suite)/(Instrumental)	1990	3.00
❑ 22697	I'll Be Good to You/(Instrumental)	1990	3.00
—With Ray Charles and Chaka Khan			
❑ 22697 [PS]	I'll Be Good to You/(Instrumental)	1990	3.00
RCA VICTOR			
❑ 74-0221	Ole Turkey Buzzard/Soul Full of Gold	1969	6.00
REPRISE			
❑ 1072	Passin' the Buck/Money Runner	1972	5.00
UNI			
❑ 55142	The Lost Man/Main Squeeze	1969	6.00
UNITED ARTISTS			
❑ 50706	Call Me Mister Tibbs/Soul Flower	1970	5.00
Albums			
A&M			
❑ SP-3023	Walking in Space	1969	12.00
❑ SP-3030	Gula Matari	1970	12.00
❑ SP-3037	Smackwater Jack	1971	12.00
❑ SP-3041	You've Got It Bad Girl	1973	12.00
❑ SP-3191	Body Heat	1982	8.00
—Budget-line reissue			
❑ SP-3200	The Best	1982	8.00
❑ SP-3248	The Dude	198?	8.00
—Budget-line reissue			
❑ SP-3249	Sounds…And Stuff Like That!	198?	8.00
—Budget-line reissue			
❑ SP-3278	The Best, Vol. 2	1985	8.00
❑ SP-3617	Body Heat	1974	10.00
❑ SP-3705 [(2)]	I Heard That!!	1976	12.00
❑ SP-3721	The Dude	1981	10.00
❑ SP-4526	Mellow Madness	1975	10.00
❑ SP-4626	Roots	1977	10.00
❑ SP-4685	Sounds…And Stuff Like That!	1978	10.00
❑ SP-6507 [(2)]	I Heard That!!	198?	10.00
—Budget-line reissue			
❑ QU-53041 [Q]	You've Got It Bad Girl	1974	10.00
❑ QU-53617 [Q]	Body Heat	1974	10.00
❑ QU-54526 [Q]	Mellow Madness	1975	10.00
ABC			
❑ D-782 [(2)]	Mode	1973	12.00
ABC IMPULSE!			
❑ AS-11 [S]	The Quintessence	1968	15.00
❑ IA-9342 [(2)]	Quintessential Charts	1978	12.00
ABC-PARAMOUNT			
❑ 149 [M]	This Is How I Feel About Jazz	1956	100.00
❑ 186 [M]	Go West, Man!	1957	100.00
CHESS			
❑ CH-91562	The Music of Quincy Jones	198?	10.00
COLGEMS			
❑ COM-107 [M]	In Cold Blood	1967	20.00
❑ COS-107 [S]	In Cold Blood	1967	25.00
EMARCY			
❑ MG-36083 [M]	Jazz Abroad	1956	100.00
❑ 818177-1 [(2)]	The Birth of a Band	1984	12.00
GRP/IMPULSE!			
❑ 222	The Quintessence	199?	15.00
—Reissue on audiophile vinyl			
IMPULSE!			
❑ A-11 [M]	The Quintessence	1962	20.00
❑ AS-11 [S]	The Quintessence	1962	25.00
LIBERTY			
❑ LOM-16004 [M]	Enter Laughing	1967	25.00
❑ LOS-17004 [S]	Enter Laughing	1967	30.00
MCA			
❑ 4145 [(2)]	Quintessential Charts	198?	10.00
—Reissue of ABC Impulse 9342			
❑ 5578	The Slugger's Wife	1985	12.00
MCA/IMPULSE!			
❑ 5728	The Quintessence	1986	8.00
MERCURY			
❑ SRM-2-623 [(2)]	Ndeda	1972	15.00
❑ PPS-2014 [M]	Around the World	1961	30.00
❑ PPS-6014 [S]	Around the World	1961	40.00
❑ MG-20444 [M]	Birth of a Band	1959	50.00
❑ MG-20561 [M]	The Great, Wide World of Quincy Jones	1960	50.00
❑ MG-20612 [M]	I Dig Dancers	1960	40.00
❑ MG-20653 [M]	Quincy Jones at Newport '61	1961	30.00
❑ MG-20751 [M]	Big Band Bossa Nova	1962	30.00
❑ MG-20799 [M]	Quincy Jones Plays Hip Hits	1963	30.00
❑ MG-20863 [M]	Quincy Jones Explores the Music of Henry Mancini	1964	20.00
❑ MG-20938 [M]	Golden Boy	1964	20.00
❑ MG-21011 [M]	The Pawnbroker	1964	20.00
❑ MG-21025 [M]	Mirage	1965	20.00
❑ MG-21050 [M]	Quincy Jones Plays for Pussycats	1965	20.00
❑ MG-21063 [M]	Quincy's Got a Brand New Bag	1965	20.00
❑ MG-21070 [M]	Slender Thread	1966	20.00
❑ SR-60129 [S]	Birth of a Band	1959	60.00
❑ SR-60221 [S]	The Great, Wide World of Quincy Jones	1960	60.00
❑ SR-60612 [S]	I Dig Dancers	1960	50.00
❑ SR-60653 [S]	Quincy Jones at Newport '61	1961	40.00
❑ SR-60751 [S]	Big Band Bossa Nova	1962	40.00
❑ SR-60799 [S]	Quincy Jones Plays Hip Hits	1963	40.00
❑ SR-60863 [S]	Quincy Jones Explores the Music of Henry Mancini	1964	25.00
❑ SR-60938 [S]	Golden Boy	1964	25.00
❑ SR-61011 [S]	The Pawnbroker	1964	25.00
❑ SR-61025 [S]	Mirage	1965	25.00
❑ SR-61050 [S]	Quincy Jones Plays for Pussycats	1965	25.00
❑ SR-61063 [S]	Quincy's Got a Brand New Bag	1965	25.00
❑ SR-61070 [S]	Slender Thread	1966	25.00
MOBILE FIDELITY			
❑ 1-078	You've Got It Bad Girl	1981	25.00
—Audiophile vinyl			
NAUTILUS			
❑ NR-52	The Dude	198?	40.00
—Audiophile vinyl			
PRESTIGE			
❑ PRLP-172 [10]	Quincy Jones with the Swedish-American All Stars	1953	200.00
QWEST			
❑ 25356 [(2)]	The Color Purple	1985	20.00
—Boxed set on purple vinyl			
❑ 25389 [(2)]	The Color Purple	1985	15.00
—Gatefold package on purple vinyl			
❑ 26020	Back on the Block	1989	12.00
TRIP			
❑ 5514	The Great Wide World of Quincy Jones	1974	8.00

Except when noted otherwise, VG = 25% of NM, and VG+ = 50% of NM. (Example: VG = $2.00, VG+ = $4.00 and NM = $8.00.)

Number	Title (A Side/B Side)	Yr	NM
❑ 5554	Live at Newport '61	197?	8.00

UNITED ARTISTS

Number	Title (A Side/B Side)	Yr	NM
❑ UAS-5214	They Call Me Mister Tibbs	1970	25.00

WING

Number	Title (A Side/B Side)	Yr	NM
❑ SRW-16398	Around the World	1969	12.00

JONES, RONNIE, AND THE CLASSMATES

45s

END

Number	Title (A Side/B Side)	Yr	NM
❑ 1002	Teenage Rock/Little Girl Next Door	1957	120.00
❑ 1014	Lonely Boy/Baby Cries	1958	120.00
❑ 1125	Teenage Rock/Little Girl Next Door	1963	25.00

JONES, SPIKE, AND THE CITY SLICKERS

45s

KAPP

Number	Title (A Side/B Side)	Yr	NM
❑ 314	I Want the South to Win the War for Christmas/Let's All Sing a Song for Christmas	1959	40.00
—B-side by the Happy Harts			
❑ 314 [PS]	I Want the South to Win the War for Christmas/Let's All Sing a Song for Christmas	1959	60.00

LIBERTY

Number	Title (A Side/B Side)	Yr	NM
❑ 55191	The Late Late Late Movies (Part 1)/The Late Late Late Movies (Part 2)	1959	12.00
❑ 55253	Ah-1, Ah-2, Ah-Sunset Strip (Part 1)/Ah-1, Ah-2, Ah-Sunset Strip (Part 2)	1960	12.00
❑ 55317	Keystone Kapers/Silence Please	1961	12.00
❑ 55649	The Ballad of Jed Clampett/Green, Green	1963	10.00
❑ 55684	Dominique/Sweet and Lovely	1964	10.00
❑ 55718	I'm in the Mood for Love/Paradise	1964	10.00
❑ 55788	Let's Kiss, Kiss, Kiss/Star Jenka	1965	10.00

RCA VICTOR

Number	Title (A Side/B Side)	Yr	NM
❑ 27-0030	Cocktails for Two/Chloe	195?	20.00
❑ 47-2795	Nutcracker Suite—1 (The Little Girl's Dream)/Nutcracker Suite—6 (End of the Little Girl's Dream)	1949	20.00
—Originals with aqua labels and gold print			
❑ 47-2795	Nutcracker Suite—1 (The Little Girl's Dream)/Nutcracker Suite—6 (End of the Little Girl's Dream)	1951	15.00
—Reissue on black label with white print, outline of dog on right			
❑ 47-2796	Nutcracker Suite—2 (Land of the Sugar Plum Fairy)/Nutcracker Suite—5 (Back to the Fairy Ball)	1949	20.00
—Originals with aqua labels and gold print			
❑ 47-2796	Nutcracker Suite—2 (Land of the Sugar Plum Fairy)/Nutcracker Suite—5 (Back to the Fairy Ball)	1951	15.00
—Reissue on black label with white print, outline of dog on right			
❑ 47-2797	Nutcracker Suite—3 (The Fairy Ball)/Nutcracker Suite—4 (The Mysterious Room)	1949	20.00
—Originals with aqua labels and gold print			
❑ 47-2797	Nutcracker Suite—3 (The Fairy Ball)/Nutcracker Suite—4 (The Mysterious Room)	1951	15.00
—Reissue on black label with white print, outline of dog on right			
❑ 47-2894	Ya Wanna Buy a Bunny/Knock Knock	1949	20.00
❑ 47-2963	(All I Want for Christmas Is) My Two Front Teeth/Happy New Year	1949	30.00
❑ 47-2992	Dance of the Hours/None But the Lonely Heart	1949	20.00
❑ 47-3126	Wild Bill Hiccup/Morpheus	1949	20.00
❑ 47-3198	The Charleston/Charlestone-Mio	1949	20.00
❑ 47-3199	Black Bottom/Doin' the New Raccoon	1949	20.00
❑ 47-3200	I Wonder Where My Baby Is Tonight/The Varsity Drag	1949	20.00
—The above three comprise a box set			
❑ 47-3287	That Old Black Magic/Liebestraum	1949	20.00
❑ 47-3288	Love in Bloom/My Old Flame	1949	20.00
❑ 47-3289	William Tell Overture/I Kiss Your Hand Madame	1949	20.00
—The above three comprise a box set			
❑ 47-3741	Chinese Mule Train/Riders in the Sky	1950	20.00
❑ 47-3827	I Know a Secret/Charlestone-Mio	1950	20.00
❑ 47-3912	Yaaha Hula Hickey Dula/Yes! We Have No Bananas	1950	20.00
❑ 47-3934	Rudolph the Red-Nosed Reindeer/Mommy, Won't You Buy a Baby Brother	1950	20.00
❑ 47-4011	Tennessee Waltz/I Haven't Been Home for Three Whole Nights	1950	20.00
❑ 47-4055	Peter Cottontail/Rhapsody from Hungary	1951	20.00
❑ 47-4125	My Daddy Is a General to Me/Ill Barkio	1951	20.00
❑ 47-4209	Too Young/So 'Elp Me	1951	20.00
❑ 47-4315	Rudolph the Red-Nosed Reindeer/(All I Want for Christmas Is) My Two Front Teeth	1951	20.00
❑ 47-4546	Deep Purple/It Never Rains in Sunny California	1952	20.00
❑ 47-4568	Down South/I've Turned a Gadabout	1952	20.00
❑ 47-4669	There's a Blue Sky Way Out Yonder/Stop Your Gamblin'	1952	20.00
❑ 47-4731	A Din Skal, A Min Skal (Swedish Polka)	1952	—
—Canceled?			
❑ 47-4831	(All of a Sudden) My Heart Sings/I'll Never Work There Anymore	1952	20.00
❑ 47-4875	Hotter Than a Pistol/Hot Lips	1952	20.00
❑ 47-5015	Barnyard Christmas/Socko the Smallest Snowball	1952	20.00
—With the Bell Sisters			
❑ 47-5067	I Saw Mommy Kissing Santa Claus/Winter	1952	20.00
❑ 47-5067 [PS]	I Saw Mommy Kissing Santa Claus/Winter	1952	40.00
❑ 47-5107	I Went to Your Wedding/I'll Never Work There Anymore	1952	20.00
❑ 47-5320	Three Little Fishes/A Din Skal, A Min Skal (Swedish Polka)	1953	20.00
❑ 47-5392	Captain of the Spaceship/Are My Ears On Straight	1953	—
—Canceled			
❑ 47-5472	Pal-Yat-Chee/Dragnet	1953	20.00
❑ 47-5497	Where Did My Snowman Go/Santa Brought Me Choo Choo Trains	1953	20.00
❑ 47-5602	Ricketshaw/My Heart Went Boom Boom	1954	—
—Canceled			
❑ 47-5742	Secret Love/I'm in the Mood for Love	1954	20.00
❑ 47-5917	Japanese Skokiaan/My Heart Went Boom Boom	1954	20.00
❑ 47-5920	I Want Eddie Fisher for Christmas/Japanese Skokiaan	1954	20.00
❑ 47-6064	This Song Is For the Birds/Hi Mister	1955	20.00
❑ 47-5413	I Just Love My Mommy/God Bless Us All	1953	20.00
❑ 447-0172	(All I Want for Christmas Is) My Two Front Teeth/Rudolph the Red-Nosed Reindeer	195?	15.00
—Reissue (Gold Standard Series); black label, dog on top			
❑ WP 143 [(3)]	The Nutcracker Suite	1949	80.00
—Includes aqua label records 47-2795, 47-2796 and 47-2797 plus box			
❑ WP 143 [(3)]	The Nutcracker Suite	1951	60.00
—Includes black label records 47-2795, 47-2796 and 47-2797 plus box			
❑ WY-461	Barnyard Christmas/Socko the Smallest Snowball	1952	20.00
—With the Bell Sisters; "Little Nipper" children's series			

VERVE

Number	Title (A Side/B Side)	Yr	NM
❑ 2026	My Birthday Comes on Christmas/Wouldn't It Be Fun	1956	15.00
❑ 10037	I'm Popeye the Sailor Man/My Heart Went Boom Boom	1957	15.00

WARNER BROS.

Number	Title (A Side/B Side)	Yr	NM
❑ 5116	Monster Movie Babe/Teenage Brain Surgeon	1959	15.00

7-Inch Extended Plays

RCA VICTOR

Number	Title (A Side/B Side)	Yr	NM
❑ EPA 288	That Old Black Magic/Liebestraum//Love in Bloom/My Old Flame	1952	30.00
❑ EPA 288 [PS]	Spike Jones Favorites	1952	30.00
❑ EPA-5058	*Cocktails for Two/Chloe/William Tell Overture/Hawaiian War Chant	1958	30.00
❑ EPA-5058 [PS]	Spike Jones (Gold Standard Series)	1958	30.00

VERVE

Number	Title (A Side/B Side)	Yr	NM
❑ 2003	Love and Marriage/Memories Are Made of This//16 Tacos/The Trouble with Pascual	1956	15.00

Albums

CORNOGRAPHIC

Number	Title (A Side/B Side)	Yr	NM
❑ 1001	King of Corn	197?	10.00

GOLDBERG & O'REILY

Number	Title (A Side/B Side)	Yr	NM
❑ MF 205/4 [(3)]	The Craziest Show on Earth	1977	20.00
—Collection of radio show performances			

HINDSIGHT

Number	Title (A Side/B Side)	Yr	NM
❑ HSR-185	The Uncollected Spike Jones 1946	198?	10.00

LIBERTY

Number	Title (A Side/B Side)	Yr	NM
❑ LRP-3140 [M]	Omnibust	1959	50.00
❑ LRP-3154 [M]	60 Years of Music America Hates Best	1960	50.00
❑ LRP-3338 [M]	Washington Square	1963	20.00
❑ LRP-3349 [M]	Spike Jones' New Band	1964	30.00
❑ LRP-3370 [M]	My Man	1964	20.00
❑ LRP-3401 [M]	Spike Jones Plays Hank Williams Hits	1965	20.00
❑ LST-7140 [S]	Omnibust	1959	75.00
—Black vinyl			
❑ LST-7140 [S]	Omnibust	1959	150.00
—Red vinyl			
❑ LST-7154 [S]	60 Years of Music America Hates Best	1960	75.00
❑ LST-7338 [S]	Washington Square	1963	25.00
❑ LST-7349 [S]	Spike Jones' New Band	1964	40.00
❑ LST-7370 [S]	My Man	1964	25.00
❑ LST-7401 [S]	Spike Jones Plays Hank Williams Hits	1965	25.00

RCA GOLD SEAL

Number	Title (A Side/B Side)	Yr	NM
❑ AGL1-4142	Spike Jones Is Murdering the Classics!	1982	8.00
—Reissue			

RCA RED SEAL

Number	Title (A Side/B Side)	Yr	NM
❑ LSC-3235 [R]	Spike Jones Is Murdering the Classics!	1971	20.00

RCA VICTOR

Number	Title (A Side/B Side)	Yr	NM
❑ LPT-18 [10]	Spike Jones Plays the Charleston	1952	200.00
❑ ANL1-1035	The Best of Spike Jones	1975	10.00
—Reissue			
❑ LPM-2224 [M]	Thank You Music Lovers	1960	50.00
—"RCA Victor" in silver above dog, "Long 33 1/3 Play" at bottom of label			
❑ LPM-2224 [M]	Thank You Music Lovers	1965	25.00
—"RCA Victor" in white above dog, "Monaural" at bottom of label			
❑ ANL1-2312	The Best of Spike Jones, Vol. 2	1977	10.00
—Reissue			
❑ LPM-3054 [10]	Bottoms Up	1952	200.00
❑ LPM-3128 [10]	Spike Jones Murders Carmen and Kids the Classics	1953	200.00
❑ AYL1-3748	The Best of Spike Jones, Vol. 1	1980	8.00
—"Best Buy Series" reissue			
❑ LPM-3849 [M]	The Best of Spike Jones	1967	25.00
❑ LSP-3849 [R]	The Best of Spike Jones	1967	20.00
❑ AYL1-3870	The Best of Spike Jones, Vol. 2	1981	8.00
—"Best Buy Series" reissue			

RHINO

Number	Title (A Side/B Side)	Yr	NM
❑ R1 70196	It's a Spike Jones Christmas	1988	12.00
❑ R1 70261	Dinner Music...For People Who Aren't Very Hungry	1988	12.00

UNITED ARTISTS

Number	Title (A Side/B Side)	Yr	NM
❑ UA-LA439-E	The Very Best of Spike Jones	1975	12.00

VERVE

Number	Title (A Side/B Side)	Yr	NM
❑ MGV-2021 [M]	Let's Sing a Song for Christmas	1956	50.00
❑ V-2021 [M]	Let's Sing a Song for Christmas	1961	30.00
❑ MGV-4005 [M]	Dinner Music...For People Who Aren't Very Hungry	1957	50.00
❑ V-4005 [M]	Dinner Music...For People Who Aren't Very Hungry	1961	25.00

WARNER BROS.

Number	Title (A Side/B Side)	Yr	NM
❑ W 1332 [M]	Spike Jones in Hi-Fi	1959	40.00
❑ WS 1332 [S]	Spike Jones in Hi-Fi	1959	50.00
—This is the title on the front of the LP cover, but the spine says "Spike Jones in Stereo"			

JONES, TAMIKO

12-Inch Singles

POLYDOR

Number	Title (A Side/B Side)	Yr	NM
❑ PDD-513	Can't Live Without Your Love/Let It Flow	1979	80.00

SUTRA

Number	Title (A Side/B Side)	Yr	NM
❑ SUD 051	I Want You/Tamiko's Groove	1986	50.00

T.K. DISCO

Number	Title (A Side/B Side)	Yr	NM
❑ TKD-6	Let It Flow/Let It Flow Tamiko	1976	60.00

45s

A&M

Number	Title (A Side/B Side)	Yr	NM
❑ 956	Ya Ya/Goodnight My Love	1968	8.00
❑ 1016	Please Return Your Love to Me/Goodnight My Love	1969	12.00

ARISTA

Number	Title (A Side/B Side)	Yr	NM
❑ 0110	Touch Me Baby (Reaching Out for Your Love)/Creepin' (In My Dreams)	1975	6.00
❑ 0134	Just You and Me/Read Me Right	1975	8.00

ATLANTIC

Number	Title (A Side/B Side)	Yr	NM
❑ 2362	A Man and a Woman/Sidewinder	1966	20.00

J

Number	Title (A Side/B Side)	Yr	NM
ATLANTIS			
❑ 157	Boy, You're Growing on Me/Ohh Baby Baby	197?	20.00
❑ 715	Touch Me Baby (Reaching Out for Your Love)/Creepin' (In My Dreams)	1974	8.00
❑ 716	Cloudy/Let It Flow	1977	8.00
CONTEMPO			
❑ 7001	Let It Flow/(Instrumental)	1976	8.00
DECEMBER			
❑ 881	Pearl/Don't Go Breaking My Heart	1968	50.00
❑ 882	Someone to Light Up My Life/Where Do I Go from Here	1968	10.00
GOLDEN WORLD			
❑ 40	I'm Spellbound/Am I Glad Now	1966	300.00
—Yellow label stock copy			
❑ 40 [DJ]	I'm Spellbound/Am I Glad Now	1966	100.00
—White label promo			
METROMEDIA			
❑ 197	Please Don't Tell Me/Blossom	1970	10.00
❑ 205	Cross My Heart/Since I Don't Have You	1970	40.00
POLYDOR			
❑ 14580	Can't Live Without Your Love/Let It Flow	1979	5.00
SUTRA			
❑ 157	I Want You/(B-side unknown)	1986	8.00
Albums			
A&M			
❑ SP-3011	I'll Be Anything for You	1969	25.00
ARISTA			
❑ AL-4040	Love Trip	1975	25.00
DECEMBER			
❑ DR-8500	Tamiko	1968	30.00
METROMEDIA			
❑ MD 1030	Tamiko Jones in Muscle Shoals	1970	25.00

J

JONES, TOM

Number	Title (A Side/B Side)	Yr	NM
12-Inch Singles			
INTERSCOPE			
❑ 2172 [DJ]	If I Only Knew (4 versions)	1994	10.00
❑ 2194 [DJ]	Situation (5 versions)	1994	10.00
MCA			
❑ 55144	She's a Lady (3 versions)	1995	10.00
45s			
CHINA			
❑ 871038-7	Kiss/E.F.L.	1989	3.00
—A-side: The Art of Noise with Tom Jones; B-side by Art of Noise			
❑ 871038-7 [PS]	Kiss/E.F.L.	1989	3.00
EPIC			
❑ 50308	Say You'll Stay Until Tomorrow/Lady Lay	1976	4.00
❑ 50382	Take Me Tonight/I Hope You'll Understand	1977	4.00
❑ 50468	What a Night/That's Where I Belong	1977	4.00
❑ 50506	There's Nothing Stronger Than Our Love/No One Gave Me Love	1978	4.00
❑ 50636	Hey Love/Baby, As You Turn Away	1978	4.00
MCA			
❑ 41127	Dancing Endlessly/Never Had a Lady Before	1979	4.00
MERCURY			
❑ 76100	Darlin'/I Don't Want to Know You That Way	1981	4.00
❑ 76115	What in the World's Come Over You/The Things That Matter Most to Me	1981	4.00
❑ 76125	Lady Lay Down/A Daughter's Question	1981	4.00
❑ 76172	A Woman's Touch/I'll Never Get Over You	1982	4.00
❑ 810445-7	Touch Me (I'll Be Your Fool Once More)/We're Wasting Our Time	1983	3.00
❑ 812631-7	It'll Be Me/If I Ever Had to Say Goodbye to You	1983	3.00
❑ 814820-7	I've Been Rained On Too/That Old Piano	1983	3.00
❑ 818801-7	This Time/Memphis, Tennessee	1984	3.00
❑ 870233-7	Things That Matter Most to Me/Green, Green Grass of Home	1988	3.00
❑ 880173-7	All the Love Is On the Radio/(B-side unknown)	1984	3.00
❑ 880402-7	I'm an Old Rock and Roller (Dancin' to a Different Beat)/My Kind of Girl	1984	3.00
❑ 880569-7	Give Her All the Roses (Don't Wait Until Tomorrow)/A Picture of You	1985	3.00
❑ 884039-7	Not Another Heart Song/Only My Heart Knows	1985	3.00
❑ 884252-7	It's Four in the Morning/I'll Never Get Over You	1985	3.00
❑ 888911-7	Lover to Lover/A Daughter's Question	1987	3.00
PARROT			
❑ 9737	It's Not Unusual/To Wait for Love (Is to Waste Your Life Away)	1965	10.00
❑ 9765	What's New Pussycat/Once Upon a Time	1965	10.00
❑ 9765 [PS]	What's New Pussycat/Once Upon a Time	1965	15.00
❑ 9787	With These Hands/Some Other Guy	1965	8.00
❑ 9787 [PS]	With These Hands/Some Other Guy	1965	12.00
❑ 9801	Thunderball/Key to My Heart	1965	8.00
❑ 9801 [PS]	Thunderball/Key to My Heart	1965	12.00
—Version 2: without the above elements on sleeve			
❑ 9801 [PS]	Thunderball/Key to My Heart	1965	20.00
—Version 1: with a dead female and a spear gun			
❑ 9809	Promise Her Anything/Little You	1966	8.00
❑ 40006	Not Responsible/Once There Was a Time	1966	8.00
❑ 40008	City Girl/What a Party	1966	8.00
❑ 40009	Green, Green Grass of Home/If I Had You	1966	8.00
❑ 40012	Detroit City/Ten Guitars	1967	8.00
❑ 40014	Funny Familiar Forgotten Feelings/I'll Never Let You Go	1967	8.00
❑ 40016	Sixteen Tons/Things I Wanna Do	1967	8.00
❑ 40018	I'll Never Fall in Love Again/Once Upon a Time	1967	8.00
—Later pressings delete a verse from the A-side; time is listed at 2:55			
❑ 40018	I'll Never Fall in Love Again/Once Upon a Time	1967	12.00
—First pressings contain the full-length version of the A-side; time is listed at over four minutes			
❑ 40020	Land of a Thousand Dances/I Can't Stop Loving You	1967	20.00
—May be promo only			
❑ 40024	I'm Coming Home/Lonely One	1967	8.00
❑ 40025	Delilah/Smile Away Your Blues	1968	8.00
❑ 40029	Help Yourself/Day by Day	1968	8.00
❑ 40035	A Minute of Your Time/Looking Out My Window	1968	8.00
❑ 40038	Love Me Tonight/Hide and Seek	1969	6.00
❑ 40038 [PS]	Love Me Tonight/Hide and Seek	1969	8.00
❑ 40045	Without Love (There Is Nothing)/The Man Who Knows Too Much	1969	6.00
❑ 40045 [PS]	Without Love (There Is Nothing)/The Man Who Knows Too Much	1969	8.00
❑ 40048	Daughter of Darkness/Tupelo Mississippi Flash	1970	6.00
❑ 40048 [PS]	Daughter of Darkness/Tupelo Mississippi Flash	1970	8.00
❑ 40051	I (Who Have Nothing)/Stop Breaking My Heart	1970	6.00
❑ 40051 [PS]	I (Who Have Nothing)/Stop Breaking My Heart	1970	8.00
❑ 40056	Can't Stop Loving You/Never Give Away Love	1970	6.00
❑ 40056 [PS]	Can't Stop Loving You/Never Give Away Love	1970	8.00
❑ 40058	She's a Lady/My Way	1971	6.00
❑ 40058 [PS]	She's a Lady/My Way	1971	8.00
❑ 40062	Puppet Man/Every Mile	1971	6.00
❑ 40062 [PS]	Puppet Man/Every Mile	1971	15.00
❑ 40064	Puppet Man/Resurrection Shuffle	1971	5.00
❑ 40067	Till/One Day Soon	1971	5.00
❑ 40070	The Young New Mexican Puppeteer/All That I Need Is Time	1972	5.00
❑ 40074	Letter to Lucille/Thank the Lord	1973	5.00
❑ 40078	La, La, La (Just Having You Here)/Love, Love, Love	1973	5.00
❑ 40080	Somethin' 'Bout You Baby I Like/Keep a-Talkin' 'Bout Love	1973	5.00
❑ 40081	Pledging My Love/I'm Too Far Gone	1974	5.00
❑ 40083	Ain't No Love/When the Band Goes Home	1974	5.00
❑ 40084	I Got Your Number/The Pain of Love	1974	5.00
❑ 40086	Memories Don't Leave Like People Do/Helping Hand	1975	5.00
TOWER			
❑ 126	Little Lonely One/That's What We'll All Do	1965	12.00
❑ 126 [PS]	Little Lonely One/That's What We'll All Do	1965	20.00
❑ 176	Lonely One/I Was a Fool	1965	12.00
❑ 176 [PS]	Lonely One/I Was a Fool	1965	20.00
❑ 190	Baby I'm in Love/Chills and Fever	1966	10.00
7-Inch Extended Plays			
PARROT			
❑ SBG 35	It's Not Unusual/I Need Your Loving/Watcha Gonna Do//Memphis, Tennessee/Skye Boat Song/Worried Man	1965	12.00
—Jukebox issue; small hole, plays at 33 1/3 rpm			
❑ SBG 35 [PS]	It's Not Unusual	1965	12.00
❑ SBG 62	Delilah/I Wake Up Crying/It's a Man's Man's World//Danny Boy/Don't Fight It/Get Ready	1968	10.00
—Jukebox issue; small hole, plays at 33 1/3 rpm			
❑ SBG 62 [PS]	The Tom Jones Fever Zone	1968	10.00
❑ SBG 70	Help Yourself/I Can't Break the News to Myself/The Bed//I Get Carried Away/If I Promise/All I Can Say Is Goodbye	1969	10.00
—Jukebox issue; small hole, plays at 33 1/3 rpm			
❑ SBG 70 [PS]	Help Yourself	1969	10.00
❑ SBG 75	Wichita Lineman/Fly Me to the Moon/Dance of Love//Hey Jude/I'm a Fool to Want You/Let It Be Me	1969	10.00
—Jukebox issue; small hole, plays at 33 1/3 rpm			
❑ SBG 75 [PS]	This Is Tom Jones	1969	10.00
❑ SBG 76	Turn On Your Love Light/Bright Lights and You Girl/I Can't Stop Loving You/Help Yourself//Hard to Handle/Twist and Shout	1969	10.00
—Jukebox issue; small hole, plays at 33 1/3 rpm			
❑ SBG 76 [PS]	Live in Las Vegas	1969	10.00
❑ SBG 78	You've Lost That Lovin' Feelin'/I Can't Turn You Loose/If I Ruled the World//The Impossible Dream/Proud Mary/Let There Be Love	1970	10.00
—Jukebox issue; small hole, plays at 33 1/3 rpm			
❑ SBG 78 [PS]	Tom	1970	10.00
❑ SBG 83	Bridge Over Troubled Water/My Way//Dance of Love/Cabaret/Soul Man	1971	10.00
—Jukebox issue; small hole, plays at 33 1/3 rpm			
❑ SBG 83 [PS]	Live at Caesar's Palace	1971	10.00
Albums			
EPIC			
❑ PE 34383	Classic Tom Jones	1976	12.00
❑ PE 34468	Say You'll Stay Until Tomorrow	1977	12.00
❑ PE 34720	Tom Is Love	1977	10.00
❑ JE 35023	What a Night	1978	10.00
JIVE			
❑ 1214-1-J	Move Closer	1989	12.00
LONDON			
❑ PS 717	The Country Side of Tom Jones	1978	10.00
❑ LC-50002	Tom Jones' Greatest Hits	1977	12.00
❑ 820234-1	This Is Tom Jones	1985	8.00
❑ 820319-1	Tom Jones' Greatest Hits	1985	10.00
MCA			
❑ 3182	Tom Jones	1979	10.00
❑ 37114	Rescue Me	1980	8.00
MERCURY			
❑ SRM-1-4010	Darlin'	1981	10.00
❑ SRM-1-4062	Tom Jones Country	1982	10.00
❑ 814448-1	Don't Let Our Dreams Die Young	1983	10.00
❑ 822701-1	Love Is on the Radio	1984	10.00
❑ 826140-1	Tender Loving Care	1985	10.00
❑ 830409-1	Things That Matter Most to Me	1987	10.00
PARROT			
❑ XPAS-1 [DJ]	Special Tom Jones Interview	1970	100.00
—Promo-only open-end interview with gatefold cover and script			
❑ PA 61004 [M]	It's Not Unusual	1965	15.00
❑ PA 61006 [M]	What's New Pussycat?	1965	15.00
❑ PA 61007 [M]	A-Tom-Ic Jones	1966	15.00
❑ PA 61009 [M]	Green, Green Grass of Home	1967	15.00
❑ PA 61011 [M]	Funny Familiar Forgotten Feelings	1967	15.00
❑ PA 61014 [M]	Tom Jones Live	1967	15.00
❑ PAS 71004 [S]	It's Not Unusual	1965	15.00
❑ PAS 71006 [S]	What's New Pussycat?	1965	15.00
❑ PAS 71007 [S]	A-Tom-Ic Jones	1966	15.00
❑ PAS 71009 [S]	Green, Green Grass of Home	1967	15.00
❑ PAS 71011 [S]	Funny Familiar Forgotten Feelings	1967	15.00
❑ PAS 71014 [S]	Tom Jones Live	1967	15.00
❑ PAS 71019	The Tom Jones Fever Zone	1968	12.00
❑ PAS 71025	Help Yourself	1969	12.00
❑ PAS 71028	This Is Tom Jones	1969	12.00
❑ PAS 71031	Live in Las Vegas	1969	12.00
❑ PAS 71037	Tom	1970	12.00
❑ PAS 71039	I (Who Have Nothing)	1970	12.00
❑ PAS 71046	She's a Lady	1971	12.00

Except when noted otherwise, VG = 25% of NM, and VG+ = 50% of NM. (Example: VG = $2.00, VG+ = $4.00 and NM = $8.00.)

Number | Title (A Side/B Side) | Yr | NM

❑ 2XPAS 71049/50 [(2)] Live at Caesar's Palace 1971 12.00
❑ XPAS 71055 Close Up 1972 12.00
❑ XPAS 71060 The Body and Soul of Tom Jones 197? 12.00
❑ XPAS 71062 Tom Jones' Greatest Hits 1973 12.00
❑ PAS 71066 Somethin' 'Bout You Baby I Like 1974 12.00
❑ PAS 71068 Memories Don't Leave Like People Do 197? 12.00
❑ ST-92025 This Is Tom Jones 1969 15.00
—Capitol Record Club edition
❑ SW-93186 Tom 197? 15.00
—Capitol Record Club edition

JONES, TOM (2)

45s

SYMBOL
❑ 205 Nothing But Fine/Trying to Get to My Grits 1965 12.00

JONES, TONI

45s

SMASH
❑ 1814 Love Is Strange/Dear (Here Comes My Baby) 1963 10.00

JONES BROTHERS, THE

45s

SUN
❑ 213 Every Night/Look to Jesus 1954 800.00

JOPLIN, JANIS Also see BIG BROTHER AND THE HOLDING COMPANY.

45s

COLUMBIA
❑ 45023 Kozmik Blues/Little Girl Blue 1969 6.00
❑ 45080 One Good Man/Try (Just a Little Bit Harder) 1970 6.00
❑ 45128 Wake Me, Lord/Maybe 1970 6.00
❑ 45314 Me and Bobby McGee/Half Moon 1971 5.00
❑ 45379 Mercedez Benz/Cry Baby 1971 5.00
❑ 45433 Get It While You Can/Move Over 1971 5.00
❑ 45630 Bye Bye Baby/Down on Me 1972 5.00

Albums

COLUMBIA
❑ AS 1377 [DJ] A Collection 1982 20.00
❑ KCS 9913 I Got Dem Ol' Kozmik Blues Again Mama! 1969 20.00
—"360 Sound Stereo" on label
❑ KCS 9913 I Got Dem Ol' Kozmik Blues Again Mama! 1970 12.00
—Orange label
❑ PC 9913 I Got Dem Ol' Kozmik Blues Again Mama! 198? 8.00
—Budget-line reissue
❑ CQ 30322 [Q] Pearl 1974 20.00
❑ KC 30322 Pearl 1971 15.00
❑ PC 30322 Pearl 1975 12.00
—Reissue without bar code
❑ PC 30322 Pearl 198? 8.00
—Reissue with bar code
❑ C2X 31160 [(2)] Joplin in Concert 1972 20.00
❑ CG 31160 Joplin in Concert 198? 12.00
❑ KC 32168 Janis Joplin's Greatest Hits 1973 15.00
❑ PC 32168 Janis Joplin's Greatest Hits 197? 8.00
❑ CG 33345 [(2)] Janis 198? 12.00
❑ PG 33345 [(2)] Janis 1975 15.00
❑ PC 37569 Farewell Song 1982 10.00

COLUMBIA SPECIAL PRODUCTS
❑ 2P 13792 [(2)] The Greatest Hits of Janis Joplin 1977 20.00

JORDAN, JERRY

45s

MCA
❑ 40639 What It Was, Was Football/Phone Call from God 1976 4.00

Albums

MCA
❑ 473 Phone Call from God 1975 10.00
❑ 2174 Don't Call Me... I'll Call You 1976 10.00

JORDAN BROTHERS, THE

45s

CAMEO
❑ 370 Good Love Goes Bad/Break Down and Cry 1965 15.00

CHELTENHAM
❑ 1006 What's Wrong With You Baby/The Jordan Theme 196? 50.00

GOLDEN CHARIOT
❑ 7002 It's Your Girl/Sugar Lady 196? 50.00
❑ 73134 Do You Know What It's Like/Gimme Some Lovin' 196? 15.00

JAMIE
❑ 1112 Send Me Your Picture/Oh Lolly 1958 30.00
❑ 1125 Never, Never/Don't Tell Me How 1959 25.00
❑ 1133 Be Mine/Dream Romance 1959 25.00
❑ 1169 Things I Didn't Say/Polly Plays Her Kettle Drum 1960 25.00
❑ 1176 No Wings on My Angel/Living for the Day 1961 25.00
❑ 1205 Love's Made a Fool of You/Whispering Wind 1961 25.00
❑ 1390 It's You Girl/Dream Romance 1970 60.00

JORDAN
❑ J-100/101 Send Me Your Picture/Oh Lolly 1958 50.00
❑ J-102/103 Sloe Gin/Basin Street Rumble 1963 30.00

PARKWAY
❑ 945 What's Wrong With You Baby/The Jordan Theme 1965 15.00

PHILIPS
❑ 40415 Gimme Some Lovin'/When I'm With Her 1966 10.00

RUBY
❑ 475 Revenge/(B-side unknown) 196? 20.00
❑ 476 Gee Whiz/Ya Ya 196? 20.00

SSS INTERNATIONAL
❑ 723 Good Time/I Want to Be Hers 1967 15.00

TURBO
❑ 002 We'll Make It/Charlotte 1968 12.00

VIM
❑ 523 It's a Shame/Here I Go Again 196? 15.00

Albums

JBP
❑ ASM-416 Today's Yesterdays Vol. 1 1980 30.00

JORDANAIRES, THE

45s

CAPITOL
❑ F1254 Working on the Building/I Want to Rest 1950 30.00
❑ F1363 David and Goliath/Journey to the Sky 1951 25.00
❑ F1407 One Day/Something Within 1951 25.00
❑ F1499 He Bought My Soul/Read That Book 1951 25.00
❑ F2725 Tattler's Wagon/In My Saviour's Loving Arms 1954 20.00
❑ F2815 Bugle Call from Heaven/Oh Lord Stand By Me 1954 20.00
❑ F2915 This Ole House/Be Prepared 1954 20.00
❑ F3022 When the Saints Go Marching In/All the Way 1955 20.00
❑ F3158 Let's Make a Joyful Noise/Will You Be Ready 1955 20.00
❑ F3265 Shaking Bridges/What Will the Verdict Be 1955 20.00
❑ F3356 A House of Gold/Blow, Whistle, Blow 1956 20.00
❑ F3420 Rock 'n Roll Religion/Do Unto Others 1956 20.00
❑ F3492 Hands of God/Fighting for the Lord 1956 20.00
❑ F3610 Sugaree/Baby Won't You Please Come Home 1957 20.00
❑ F3684 Walk Away/Ridin' for a Fall 1957 20.00
❑ F3750 Summer Vacation/Each Day 1957 20.00
❑ F3807 Any Which-a-Way/Mood for the Blues 1957 20.00
❑ F3940 Little Miss Ruby/All I Need Is You 1958 15.00
❑ F4025 Wella Wella Honey/Where Many Go 1958 15.00
❑ 4431 Sit Down/Girl in the Valley 1960 12.00

COLUMBIA
❑ 4-43283 Malibu Run/Who Does He Think He Is 1965 10.00
—Said to be a different group than the rest.

DECCA
❑ 9-46242 Dig a Little Deeper/I'm Free Again 1950 40.00
❑ 9-46366 Loafin' on a Lazy River/Sweet Roses of Morn 1951 25.00

DECCA FAITH SERIES
❑ 9-14530 Peace in the Valley/(B-side unknown) 1950 30.00

RCA VICTOR
❑ 47-4378 The Four Horsemen (Of the Apocalypse)/Mansion Over the Hilltop 1951 25.00
❑ 47-4607 Who Can He Be/Gonna Walk Those Golden Stairs 1952 25.00
❑ 47-4645 Goodbye Pharaoh/Roll, Jordan, Roll 1952 25.00
❑ 47-4943 Rag Mama/I Never Will Marry 1952 25.00
❑ 47-4948 My Rock/I'll Tell It Wherever I Go 1952 25.00
❑ 47-5021 He'll Understand and Say Well Done/I'm Moving On to Glory 1952 25.00
❑ 47-5076 Beautiful City/Stand by Me 1952 20.00
❑ 47-5077 By the River of Life/Noah 1952 20.00
❑ 47-5078 You Better Run/Dry Bones 1952 20.00
❑ 47-5079 When Dey Ring Dem Golden Bells/Didn't They Crucify My Lord 1952 20.00
❑ 47-5373 On the Jericho Road/The Lord Will Make a Way Somehow 1953 25.00
❑ 47-5458 Is He Satisfied/I Am So Glad Jesus Lifted Me 1953 25.00

STOP
❑ 259 You're Wasting Your Time Girl/A Hundred Years of Real Estate 1969 8.00

"X"
❑ 0034 Say It Again/I Can't Smoke You Out of My Heart 1954 20.00

7-Inch Extended Plays

RCA VICTOR
❑ 547-0246 The Beautiful City/Stand By Me//Noah/By the River of Life 195? 15.00
—Record 1 of 2-EP set EPB-3081
❑ 547-0247 Dry Bones/You Better Run//When They Ring Dem Golden Bells/Didn't They Crucify My Lord 195? 15.00
—Record 2 of 2-EP set EPB-3081
❑ EPB-3081 [PS] Beautiful City 195? 15.00
—Two-pocket jacket for two-EP set (547-0246, 547-0247)

SESAC
❑ AD 46 Wanderin'/John Henry//Honey Baby Mine/Twenty-One Froggies 195? 20.00
❑ AD 46 [PS] Songs of the Plains 195? 20.00

Albums

CAPITOL
❑ T 1011 [M] Heavenly Spirit 1958 40.00
❑ T 1167 [M] Gloryland 1959 40.00
❑ ST 1311 [S] Land of Jordan 1960 40.00
❑ T 1311 [M] Land of Jordan 1960 30.00
❑ ST 1559 [S] To God Be the Glory 1961 25.00
❑ T 1559 [M] To God Be the Glory 1961 20.00
❑ ST 1742 [S] Spotlight on the Jordanaires 1962 30.00
❑ T 1742 [M] Spotlight on the Jordanaires 1962 25.00

CLASSIC
❑ CCR 1935 Christmas to Elvis from the Jordanaires 1978 12.00

COLUMBIA
❑ CL 2214 [M] This Land 1964 20.00
❑ CL 2458 [M] The Big Country Hits 1966 20.00
❑ CS 9014 [S] This Land 1964 25.00
❑ CS 9258 [S] The Big Country Hits 1966 25.00

DECCA
❑ DL 8681 [M] Peace in the Valley 1957 50.00

RCA VICTOR
❑ LPM-3081 [10] Beautiful City 1953 100.00

SESAC
❑ 1401/2 [M] Of Rivers and Plains 195? 80.00

JORGENSON, CHRISTINE

Albums

J RECORDS
❑ J-1 [M] Christine Jorgenson Reveals 1958 50.00

JOSEFUS

45s

MAINSTREAM
❑ 725 Jimmy Jimmy/Sephus Blues 1970 15.00

Albums

HOOKAH
❑ 330 Dead Man 1969 300.00

MAINSTREAM
❑ S-6127 Josefus 1970 100.00

JOSEPH

Albums

SCEPTER
❑ SRS-674 Stoned Age Man 1970 80.00

JOSEPH, MARGIE

12-Inch Singles

COTILLION
❑ DMD 724 [DJ] Ready for the Night (5:14) (same on both sides) 1984 12.00
❑ DMD 754 [DJ] Big Strong Man/I Want Mo' Stuff 1984 12.00

H.C.R.C.
❑ 4W9 03338 Knockout (Part 1)/Knockout (Part 2) 1982 8.00
❑ HCS 10090 Knockout (Special Mix 6:18)/(Special Mix Part II 4:46) 1982 8.00

Journey, "Who's Crying Now," Columbia 02241, 1981, $4.

Number	Title (A Side/B Side)	Yr	NM
❑ HCS-10120	Move to the Groove (Special Mix) (Instrumental)	1983	10.00

ICHIBAN

Number	Title (A Side/B Side)	Yr	NM
❑ 12PO-12 [DJ]	I've Got to Have Your Love (6:22) (Persapella Version 4:07) (Bonus Beats Version 2:10)	1988	15.00

45s

ATLANTIC

Number	Title (A Side/B Side)	Yr	NM
❑ 2907	Born to Wander/Let's Go Somewhere and Love	1972	10.00
❑ 2933	Touch Your Woman/I'm So Glad I'm Your Woman	1973	6.00
❑ 2954	Let's Stay Together/ I'd Rather Go Blind	1973	10.00
❑ 2988	Come Lay Some Lovin' on Me/ Ridin' High	1973	30.00
❑ 3032	My Love/Sweet Surrender	1974	8.00
❑ 3220	Words (Are Impossible)/ I Still Love You	1974	8.00
❑ 3269	I Can't Move No Mountains/Just As Soon As the Feeling's Over	1975	10.00
❑ 3290	Stay Still/Just As Soon As the Feeling's Over	1975	10.00
❑ 3445	Come On Back to Me Lover/ He Came Into My Life	1978	50.00
❑ 3509	I Feel His Love Getting Stronger/How Will I Know	1978	15.00
❑ 3525	Love Takes Tears/I Don't Want to Get Over You	1978	20.00

COTILLION

Number	Title (A Side/B Side)	Yr	NM
❑ 44201	Hear the Words, Feel the Feeling/I Get Carried Away	1976	10.00
❑ 44207	Don't Turn the Lights Off/ All Cried Out	1976	8.00
❑ 99737	Big Strong Man/ (B-side unknown)	1984	5.00
❑ 99771	Ready for the Night/ (B-side unknown)	1984	5.00

H.C.R.C.

Number	Title (A Side/B Side)	Yr	NM
❑ WS4 03337	Knockout/(Part 2)	1982	5.00
❑ HC7-31200	Knockout/(Part 2)	1982	6.00
❑ HC7-31500	Move to the Groove/ (Instrumental)	1983	6.00
❑ HC7-31900	Give It to Me/(B-side unknown)	1983	8.00

OKEH

Number	Title (A Side/B Side)	Yr	NM
❑ 4-7304	Why Does a Man Have to Lie/ Show Me	1967	50.00
❑ 4-7313	A Matter of Life or Death/ Show Me	1968	60.00

VOLT

Number	Title (A Side/B Side)	Yr	NM
❑ 4012	One More Chance/ Never Can You Be	1969	12.00
❑ 4023	What You Gonna Do/Nobody	1969	100.00
❑ 4037	Your Sweet Lovin'/ What's Wrong Baby	1970	12.00
❑ 4046	Punish Me/A Sweeter Tomorrow	1970	40.00
❑ 4056	Stop! In the Name of Love/ Make Me Believe You'll Stay	1971	10.00
❑ 4061	The Other Woman Got My Man and Gone/I'll Always Love You	1971	80.00

Albums

ATLANTIC

Number	Title (A Side/B Side)	Yr	NM
❑ SD 7248	Margie Joseph	1973	25.00
❑ SD 7277	Sweet Surrender	1974	20.00
❑ SD 18126	Margie	1975	20.00
❑ SD 19182	Feeling My Way	1978	22.00

COTILLION

Number	Title (A Side/B Side)	Yr	NM
❑ SD 9906	Hear the Words, Feel the Feeling	1976	25.00
❑ 90158	Ready for the Night	1984	15.00

H.C.R.C.

Number	Title (A Side/B Side)	Yr	NM
❑ HLP-20009	Knockout	1983	12.00

ICHIBAN

Number	Title (A Side/B Side)	Yr	NM
❑ 1027	Stay	1988	15.00

VOLT

Number	Title (A Side/B Side)	Yr	NM
❑ VOS-6012	Margie Joseph Makes a New Impression	1971	25.00
❑ VOS-6016	Phase II	1971	30.00

JOSEPH, MARGIE, AND BLUE MAGIC Also see each artist's individual listings.

45s

ATCO/WMOT

Number	Title (A Side/B Side)	Yr	NM
❑ 7030	What's Come Over Me/You and Me (Got a Good Thing Goin')	1975	10.00

JOSEPHINE XIII

45s

CAMEO

Number	Title (A Side/B Side)	Yr	NM
❑ 427	Down on the Funny Farm (Oy Vey)/Break the Drums	1966	20.00

JOSHUA FOX

45s

TETRAGRAMMATON

Number	Title (A Side/B Side)	Yr	NM
❑ 1527	Goin' Down for Big Numbers/ Moontime Bore	1969	12.00
❑ 1532	Don't Tell Me a Story/ It's Just Meant to Be	1969	12.00

Albums

TETRAGRAMMATON

Number	Title (A Side/B Side)	Yr	NM
❑ T-125	Joshua Fox	1969	30.00

JOSIE AND THE PUSSYCATS Also see PATRICE HOLLOWAY; CHERYL LADD.

45s

CAPITOL

Number	Title (A Side/B Side)	Yr	NM
❑ CP 58-1	Letter to Mama/Inside, Outside, Upside Down	1970	20.00
❑ CP 58-1 [PS]	Letter to Mama/Inside, Outside, Upside Down	1970	30.00
❑ CP 59-2	With Every Beat of My Heart/ Josie	1970	20.00
❑ CP 59-2 [PS]	With Every Beat of My Heart/ Josie	1970	30.00
❑ CP 60-3	Voodoo/If That Isn't Love	1970	20.00
❑ CP 60-3 [PS]	Voodoo/If That Isn't Love	1970	30.00
❑ CP 61-4	I Wanna Make You Happy/ It's Gotta Be Him	1970	20.00
❑ CP 61-4 [PS]	I Wanna Make You Happy/ It's Gotta Be Him	1970	30.00
❑ 2967	Every Beat of My Heart/ It's All Right with Me	1970	20.00
—Same song as CP 59, but a slightly different title and a mono mix			
❑ 3045	Stop, Look and Listen/You've Come a Long Way, Baby	1971	20.00

Albums

CAPITOL

Number	Title (A Side/B Side)	Yr	NM
❑ ST-665	Josie and the Pussycats	1970	200.00

JOURNEY Original lead singer Gregg Rolie was also the original lead singer of SANTANA.

12-Inch Singles

COLUMBIA

Number	Title (A Side/B Side)	Yr	NM
❑ AS 568 [DJ]	Just the Same Way (3:14) (stereo/mono)	1979	10.00
❑ AS 738 [DJ]	Any Way You Want It (same on both sides)	1980	10.00
❑ AS 999 [DJ]	Who's Crying Now (5:01)/ Stone in Love (4:25)	1981	25.00
❑ AS 1487 [DJ]	Still They Ride/La Raza Del Sol	1982	10.00
❑ CAS 2312 [DJ]	Be Good to Yourself (same on both sides)	1986	15.00
❑ CAS 2374 [DJ]	Suzanne (same on both sides)	1986	12.00
❑ CAS 2478 [DJ]	Girl Can't Help It (3:50) (same on both sides)	1986	10.00
❑ CAS 2512 [DJ]	Girl Can't Help It (Live Version 3:53) (Live Version with Intro 4:00) (Original Version 3:50)	1986	20.00

GEFFEN

Number	Title (A Side/B Side)	Yr	NM
❑ PRO-A-2240 [DJ]	Only the Young (same on both sides)	1985	8.00

45s

COLUMBIA

Number	Title (A Side/B Side)	Yr	NM
❑ AS 128 [DJ]	Kohoutek/Topaz	1974	10.00
—Small hole, plays at 33 1/3 rpm			
❑ 18-02241	Who's Crying Now/ Mother, Father	1981	3.00
❑ 18-02241 [PS]	Who's Crying Now/ Mother, Father	1981	4.00
❑ 18-02567	Don't Stop Believin'/ Natural Thing	1981	3.00
❑ 18-02567 [PS]	Don't Stop Believin'/ Natural Thing	1981	4.00
❑ 18-02687	Open Arms/Little Girl	1982	3.00
❑ 18-02687 [PS]	Open Arms/Little Girl	1982	4.00
❑ 18-02883	Still They Ride/La Raza Del Sol	1982	3.00
❑ 18-02883 [PS]	Still They Ride/La Raza Del Sol	1982	4.00
❑ 13-03133	Open Arms/The Party's Over	1982	3.00
—Reissue			

Except when noted otherwise, VG = 25% of NM, and VG+ = 50% of NM. (Example: VG = $2.00, VG+ = $4.00 and NM = $8.00.)

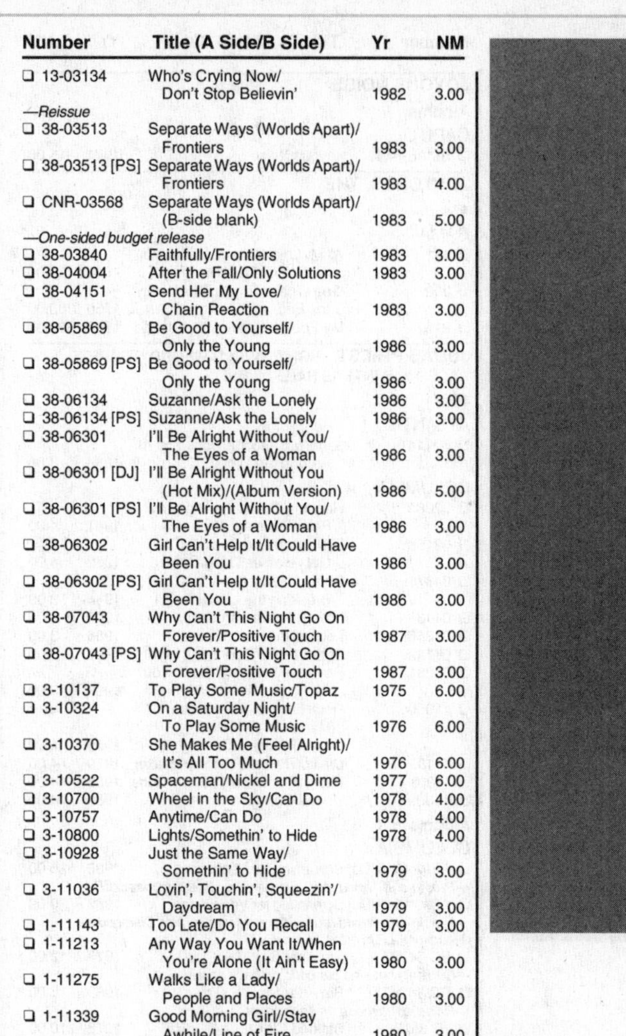

Number	Title (A Side/B Side)	Yr	NM
❑ 13-03134	Who's Crying Now/ Don't Stop Believin'	1982	3.00
—Reissue			
❑ 38-03513	Separate Ways (Worlds Apart)/ Frontiers	1983	3.00
❑ 38-03513 [PS]	Separate Ways (Worlds Apart)/ Frontiers	1983	4.00
❑ CNR-03568	Separate Ways (Worlds Apart)/ (B-side blank)	1983	5.00
—One-sided budget release			
❑ 38-03840	Faithfully/Frontiers	1983	3.00
❑ 38-04004	After the Fall/Only Solutions	1983	3.00
❑ 38-04151	Send Her My Love/ Chain Reaction	1983	3.00
❑ 38-05869	Be Good to Yourself/ Only the Young	1986	3.00
❑ 38-05869 [PS]	Be Good to Yourself/ Only the Young	1986	3.00
❑ 38-06134	Suzanne/Ask the Lonely	1986	3.00
❑ 38-06134 [PS]	Suzanne/Ask the Lonely	1986	3.00
❑ 38-06301	I'll Be Alright Without You/ The Eyes of a Woman	1986	3.00
❑ 38-06301 [DJ]	I'll Be Alright Without You (Hot Mix)/(Album Version)	1986	5.00
❑ 38-06301 [PS]	I'll Be Alright Without You/ The Eyes of a Woman	1986	3.00
❑ 38-06302	Girl Can't Help It/It Could Have Been You	1986	3.00
❑ 38-06302 [PS]	Girl Can't Help It/It Could Have Been You	1986	3.00
❑ 38-07043	Why Can't This Night Go On Forever/Positive Touch	1987	3.00
❑ 38-07043 [PS]	Why Can't This Night Go On Forever/Positive Touch	1987	3.00
❑ 3-10137	To Play Some Music/Topaz	1975	6.00
❑ 3-10324	On a Saturday Night/ To Play Some Music	1976	6.00
❑ 3-10370	She Makes Me (Feel Alright)/ It's All Too Much	1976	6.00
❑ 3-10522	Spaceman/Nickel and Dime	1977	6.00
❑ 3-10700	Wheel in the Sky/Can Do	1978	4.00
❑ 3-10757	Anytime/Can Do	1978	4.00
❑ 3-10800	Lights/Somethin' to Hide	1978	4.00
❑ 3-10928	Just the Same Way/ Somethin' to Hide	1979	3.00
❑ 3-11036	Lovin', Touchin', Squeezin'/ Daydream	1979	3.00
❑ 1-11143	Too Late/Do You Recall	1979	3.00
❑ 1-11213	Any Way You Want It/When You're Alone (It Ain't Easy)	1980	3.00
❑ 1-11275	Walks Like a Lady/ People and Places	1980	3.00
❑ 1-11339	Good Morning Girl//Stay Awhile/Line of Fire	1980	3.00
❑ 11-60505	The Party's Over (Hopelessly in Love)/Just the Same Way	1981	3.00
❑ 38-78428	When You Love a Woman/ Message of Love	1996	3.00

GEFFEN

Number	Title (A Side/B Side)	Yr	NM
❑ 7-29090	Only the Young/I'll Only Fall in Love Again	1985	4.00
—B-side by Sammy Hagar			
❑ 7-29090 [PS]	Only the Young/I'll Only Fall in Love Again	1985	4.00

Albums

COLUMBIA

Number	Title (A Side/B Side)	Yr	NM
❑ AS 914 [DJ]	Journey	1981	15.00
—Promo-only four-song sampler			
❑ AS 1606 [DJ]	A Candid Conversation with Journey	1983	20.00
—Promo-only interview and songs LP			
❑ PC 33388	Journey	1975	10.00
—No bar code on cover			
❑ PC 33388	Journey	198?	6.00
—With bar code on cover			
❑ PC 33904	Look Into the Future	1976	10.00
—No bar code on cover			
❑ PC 33904	Look Into the Future	198?	6.00
—With bar code on cover			
❑ PCQ 33904 [Q]	Look Into the Future	1976	—
—Not released			
❑ PC 34311	Next	1977	10.00
—No bar code on cover			
❑ PC 34311	Next	198?	6.00
—With bar code on cover			
❑ JC 34912	Infinity	1978	10.00
—No bar code on cover			
❑ JC 34912	Infinity	1979	6.00
—With bar code on cover			
❑ FC 35797	Evolution	1979	8.00
❑ PC 35797	Evolution	1985	6.00
—Budget-line reissue			
❑ C2 36324 [(2)]	In the Beginning	1979	10.00
❑ FC 36339	Departure	1980	8.00
❑ KC2 37016 [(2)]	Captured	1981	10.00
❑ TC 37408	Escape	1981	8.00
❑ FC 37998	Dream After Dream	1982	12.00
❑ PC 37998	Dream After Dream	1986	8.00
—Budget-line reissue			

Joy Division, *Substance*, Qwest 25747, 1988, **$30.**

Number	Title (A Side/B Side)	Yr	NM
❑ QC 38504	Frontiers	1983	8.00
❑ OC 39936	Raised on Radio	1986	8.00
❑ OC 44493	Greatest Hits	1988	10.00
❑ HC 44912	Infinity	1982	30.00
—Half-speed mastered edition			
❑ HC 46339	Departure	1980	20.00
—Half-speed mastered edition			
❑ HC 47408	Escape	1982	20.00
—Half-speed mastered edition			
❑ HC 47998	Dream After Dream	1982	30.00
—Half-speed mastered edition			
❑ HC 48504	Frontiers	1983	30.00
—Half-speed mastered edition			

MOBILE FIDELITY

Number	Title (A Side/B Side)	Yr	NM
❑ 1-144	Escape	1984	200.00
—Audiophile vinyl			

JOURNEYMEN, THE (1)

Also see SCOTT McKENZIE; JOHN PHILLIPS.

45s

AMY

Number	Title (A Side/B Side)	Yr	NM
❑ 821	Cup-E-Co/Hush Storm	1961	12.00

CAPITOL

Number	Title (A Side/B Side)	Yr	NM
❑ 4625	500 Miles/The River She Comes Down	1961	10.00
❑ 4678	Soft Blow the Summer Winds/ Kumbaya	1962	10.00
❑ 4737	Don't Turn Around/ Hush Now Sally	1962	10.00
❑ 4829	What'll I Do/Loadin' Coal	1962	10.00
❑ 4943	Rag Mama/I Never Will Marry	1963	10.00
❑ 4943 [PS]	Rag Mama/I Never Will Marry	1963	40.00
❑ 5031	Kumbaya/Ja Da	1963	10.00

Albums

CAPITOL

Number	Title (A Side/B Side)	Yr	NM
❑ ST 1629 [S]	The Journeymen	1961	30.00
❑ T 1629 [M]	The Journeymen	1961	25.00
❑ ST 1770 [S]	Coming Attraction — Live!	1962	30.00
❑ T 1770 [M]	Coming Attraction — Live!	1962	25.00
❑ ST 1951 [S]	New Directions in Folk Music	1963	30.00
❑ T 1951 [M]	New Directions in Folk Music	1963	25.00

JOURNEYMEN, THE (2)

45s

IONA

Number	Title (A Side/B Side)	Yr	NM
❑ 1111	Work Out/Bag's Groove	1961	50.00
❑ 1115	Surfer's Blues/Surfer's Rule	1963	40.00
—Rerelease as "The Baylanders"			
❑ 1115	Surfer's Blues/Surfer's Rule	1963	50.00

JOY, BENNY

45s

ANTLER

Number	Title (A Side/B Side)	Yr	NM
❑ 4011	Crash the Party/Little Red Book	1959	500.00

DECCA

Number	Title (A Side/B Side)	Yr	NM
❑ 31199	New York, Hey Hey/Sincerely, Your Friend	1961	15.00
❑ 31280	Birds of a Feather Fly Together/ You Go Your Way (And I'll Go Mine)	1961	15.00

DIXIE

Number	Title (A Side/B Side)	Yr	NM
❑ 2001	Steady with Betty/Spin the Bottle	1958	500.00

DOT

Number	Title (A Side/B Side)	Yr	NM
❑ 16445	I'm of No More Use to You Old Earth/Harry's Harem	1963	15.00

RAM

Number	Title (A Side/B Side)	Yr	NM
❑ 1107	Ittie Bittie Everything/ (B-side unknown)	1959	500.00

TRI-DEC

Number	Title (A Side/B Side)	Yr	NM
❑ 8667	Steady with Betty/Spin the Bottle	1958	600.00

JOY, RODDIE

45s

PARKWAY

Number	Title (A Side/B Side)	Yr	NM
❑ 101	Something Strange Is Going On/Stop	1966	12.00
❑ 134	Every Breath I Take/Walkin' Back	1967	12.00
❑ 151	I Want You Back/ Let's Start All Over	1967	12.00
❑ 991	A Boy Is Just a Toy/Stop	1966	15.00

Except when noted otherwise, VG = 25% of NM, and VG+ = 50% of NM. (Example: VG = $2.00, VG+ = $4.00 and NM = $8.00.)

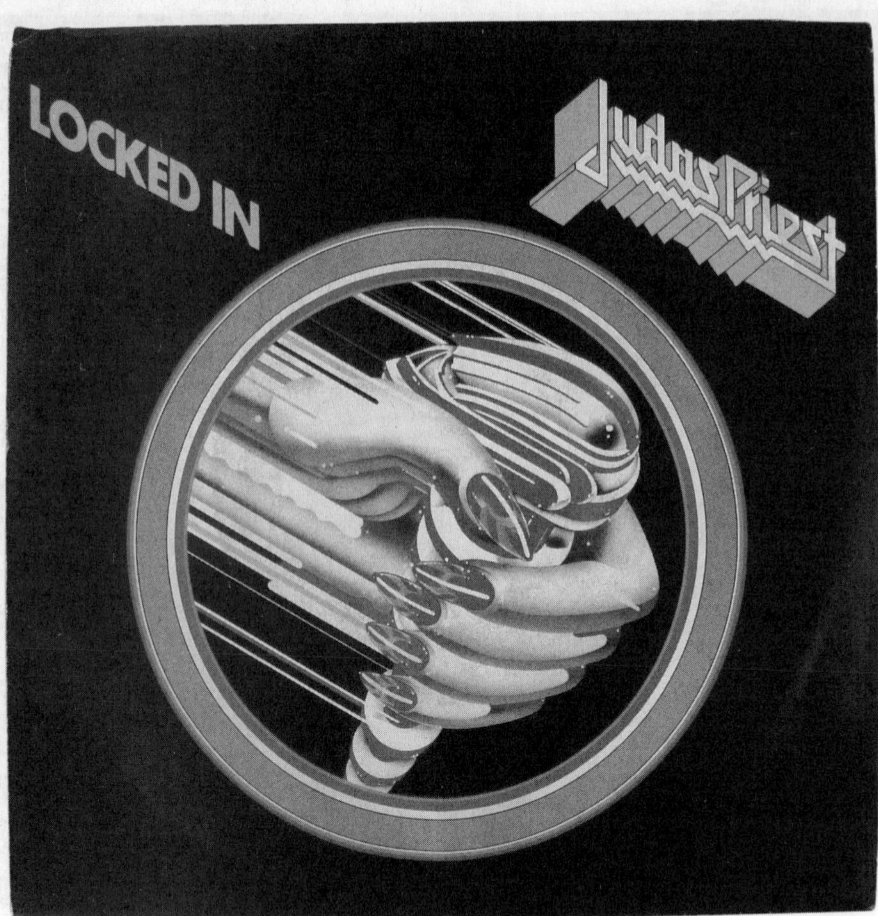

Judas Priest, "Locked in," Columbia 05856, 1986, $3.

Number	Title (A Side/B Side)	Yr	NM
RED BIRD			
❑ 10-021	Love Hit Me with a Wallop/ Come Back Baby	1965	20.00
❑ 10-031	The La La Song/ He's So Easy to Love	1965	25.00
❑ 10-037	If There's Anything Else You Want (Let Me Know)/Stop	1965	40.00

JOY DIVISION

Also see NEW ORDER.

Number	Title (A Side/B Side)	Yr	NM
12-Inch Singles			
FACTORY			
❑ FACUS 2	She's Lost Control/Atmosphere	1979	10.00
45s			
FACTORY			
❑ FACTUS 23	Love Will Tear Us Apart/ These Days	1980	15.00
❑ FACTUS 23 [PS]	Love Will Tear Us Apart/ These Days	1980	15.00
❑ FACUS 23 [DJ]	Love Will Tear Us Apart/ These Days	1980	100.00
—White label promo			
❑ FAC 28	Komakino/Incubation/Dub	1980	12.00
—Flexi-disc, with below picture sleeve			
❑ FAC 28	Komakino/Incubation/Dub	1980	15.00
—Flexi-disc with no picture sleeve, "Evatone" on label			
❑ FAC 28 [PS]	Komakino/Incubation/Dub	1980	25.00
—Numbered sleeve from fanzine "The Other Sound"			
Albums			
FACTORY			
❑ FACT US 1	Unknown Pleasures	1979	25.00
❑ FACT US 6	Closer	1980	30.00
—Red tint vinyl			
❑ FACT US 6	Closer	1980	50.00
—Purple tint vinyl			
QWEST			
❑ 25747	Substance	1988	30.00
❑ 25840	Unknown Pleasures	1989	15.00
—Reissue of FACT US 1			
❑ 25841	Closer	1989	15.00
—Reissue of FACT US 6			

JOY OF COOKING

Number	Title (A Side/B Side)	Yr	NM
45s			
CAPITOL			
❑ 3075	Brownsville/Only Time Will Tell Me	1971	6.00
❑ 3224	Closer to the Ground/Pilot	1971	5.00
❑ 3330	Let Love Carry You Along/ Home Town Man	1972	5.00
❑ 3396	Don't the Moon Look Fat and Round/All Around the Sun and the Moon	1972	5.00
Albums			
CAPITOL			
❑ ST-661	Joy of Cooking	1971	15.00
❑ SMAS-828	Closer to the Ground	1971	15.00
❑ ST-11050	Castles	1972	12.00

JOY TONES, THE

Number	Title (A Side/B Side)	Yr	NM
45s			
COED			
❑ 600	This Love (That I'm Giving You)/I Wanna Party Some More	1965	12.00

JOYE, COL, AND THE JOY BOYS

Number	Title (A Side/B Side)	Yr	NM
45s			
DECCA			
❑ 30933	(Rockin' Rollin') Clementine/ Bye Bye Baby Goodbye	1959	30.00

JOYETTES, THE

Number	Title (A Side/B Side)	Yr	NM
45s			
ONYX			
❑ 502	Story of Love/The Boy Next Door	1956	100.00

JOYOUS NOISE

Number	Title (A Side/B Side)	Yr	NM
Albums			
CAPITOL			
❑ SMAS-844	Joyous Noise	1971	15.00

JOYTONES, THE

Number	Title (A Side/B Side)	Yr	NM
45s			
RAMA			
❑ 191	All My Love Belongs to You/You Just Won't Treat Me Right	1956	150.00
❑ 202	Gee What a Boy/Is This Really the End	1956	300.00
❑ 215	My Foolish Heart/Jimbo Jango	1956	500.00

JUDAS PRIEST

FIGHT, TWO, HALFORD, TRAPEZE, RACER X, WINTERS BANE related.

Number	Title (A Side/B Side)	Yr	NM
45s			
ATLANTIC			
❑ 89114	Johnny B. Goode/Rock You All Around the World	1988	3.00
COLUMBIA			
❑ 02083	Heading Out to the Highway/ Rock Forever	1981	4.00
❑ 03168	Diamonds and Rust/You've Got Another Thing Comin'	1982	4.00
❑ 04371	Some Heads Are Gona Roll/ Breaking the Law (Live)	1984	3.00
❑ 04436	Love Bites/Jawbreaker	1984	3.00
❑ 05856	Locked In/Hot for Love	1986	3.00
❑ 06142	Turbo Lover/Reckless	1986	3.00
❑ 06281	Parental Guidance/Rock You All Around the World	1986	3.00
❑ 11000	Rock Forever/The Green Manalishi (With the Two-Pronged Crown)	1979	4.00
❑ 11135	Diamonds and Rust/Starbreaker	1979	4.00
❑ 11308	Living After Midnight/Metal Gods	1980	4.00
❑ 11396	United/Grinder	1980	4.00
Albums			
COLUMBIA			
❑ AS99 1543 [DJ]	Screaming for Vengeance	1982	25.00
—Promo-only "world tour" picture disc; plays the correct LP			
❑ AS99 1543 [DJ]	Screaming for Vengeance	1982	30.00
—Promo-only "world tour" picture disc; plays Neil Diamond's "Heartlight" LP in error			
❑ PC 34787	Sin After Sin	1977	12.00
—Originals have no bar code on back cover			
❑ PC 34787	Sin After Sin	198?	6.00
—Reissue; bar code on back cover			
❑ JC 35296	Stained Class	1978	10.00
❑ PC 35296	Stained Class	198?	6.00
—Budget-line reissue			
❑ JC 35706	Hell Bent for Leather	1979	10.00
❑ JC 36179	Unleashed in the East (Live in Japan)	1979	8.00
❑ PC 36179	Unleashed in the East (Live in Japan)	1985	6.00
—Budget-line reissue with new prefix			
❑ JC 36443	British Steel	1980	10.00
❑ FC 37052	Point of Entry	1981	8.00
❑ FC 38160	Screaming for Vengeance	1982	8.00
❑ FC 38219	Defenders of the Faith	1984	8.00
❑ 9C9 39926 [PD]	Great Vinyl and Concert Hits	1984	60.00
❑ OC 40158	Turbo	1986	8.00
❑ C2 40794 [(2)]	Priest ... Live!	1987	10.00
❑ FC 44244	Ram It Down	1988	8.00
GULL			
❑ GU6-403S1	Rocka-Rolla	1975	—
—Canceled			
JANUS			
❑ JXS-7019	Sad Wings of Destiny	1976	20.00
❑ JXS-7019 [DJ]	Sad Wings of Destiny	1976	30.00
—Promo version, with "Specially faded for easier programming" sticker on cover			
OVATION			
❑ OV-1751	Sad Wings of Destiny	1980	15.00
RCA VICTOR			
❑ AYL1-4747	Sad Wings of Destiny	1983	10.00
—Reissue of Ovation LP			
❑ AYL1-4933	The Best of Judas Priest	1984	8.00
❑ AYL1-5041	Rocka-Rolla	1984	10.00
—Reissue of Visa 7001 with new cover			
❑ CYL1-5399 [(2)]	Hero, Hero	1985	18.00
VISA			
❑ IMP-7001	Rocka Rolla	1979	15.00
—First U.S. issue of unreleased Gull LP; front cover has a bottle-cap motif			

JULIAN, DON, AND THE MEADOWLARKS

Also see THE LARKS.

Number	Title (A Side/B Side)	Yr	NM
45s			
CLASSIC ARTISTS			
❑ 101	Quickie Wedding/Our Love	1988	4.00

Except when noted otherwise, VG = 25% of NM, and VG+ = 50% of NM. (Example: VG = $2.00, VG+ = $4.00 and NM = $8.00.)

Number	Title (A Side/B Side)	Yr	NM
❑ 105	White Christmas/ Marry Christmas, Baby	1988	6.00
DOOTO			
❑ 424	Blue Moon/Big Mama Wants to Rock	1957	50.00
DOOTONE			
❑ 359	Heaven and Paradise/ Embarrassing Moments	1955	300.00
❑ 367	Always and Always/I Got Tore Up	1955	50.00
—Maroon label			
❑ 367	Always and Always/I Got Tore Up	1955	75.00
—Red label			
❑ 372	This Must Be Paradise/ Mine All Mine	1955	60.00
❑ 394	Please Love a Fool/ Oop Boopy Oop	1956	50.00
❑ 405	I Am a Believer/Boogie Woogie Teenager	1956	80.00
DYNAMITE			
❑ 1112	Heaven Only Knows/Popeye	1962	30.00
ORIGINAL SOUND			
❑ 3	Please Say You Want Me/ Doin' the Cha Cha Cha	1959	40.00
❑ 12	There's a Girl/Blue Moon	1960	30.00
RPM			
❑ 399	Love Only You/Real Pretty Mama	1954	300.00
—As "The Meadow Larks"			
❑ 406	LSMFT Blues (Lord Find My Sweet Theresa)/Pass the Gin	1954	3000.
—As "The Meadow Larks"			
7-Inch Extended Plays			
DOOTO			
❑ 203	(contents unknown)	1958	200.00
❑ 203 [PS]	Don Julian and the Meadowlarks	1958	200.00
—Reissue of Dootone 203			
DOOTONE			
❑ 203	(contents unknown)	1956	400.00
❑ 203 [PS]	Don Julian and the Meadowlarks	1956	400.00

JULIAN'S TREATMENT

Number	Title (A Side/B Side)	Yr	NM
Albums			
DECCA			
❑ DL 75224	A Time Before This	1970	25.00

JULIANA

Number	Title (A Side/B Side)	Yr	NM
45s			
RCA VICTOR			
❑ 47-7906	You Can Have Any Boy/ You're Saying Goodnight	1961	60.00

JULY

Number	Title (A Side/B Side)	Yr	NM
Albums			
EPIC			
❑ BN 26416	July	1969	200.00

JULY FOUR, THE

Number	Title (A Side/B Side)	Yr	NM
45s			
CAMEO			
❑ 480	Mr. Miff/Frightened Little Girl	1967	20.00

JUMPIN' JACKS, THE

Number	Title (A Side/B Side)	Yr	NM
45s			
DECCA			
❑ 29973	You'll Wonder Where the Yellow Went/A Frantic Antic	1956	30.00
❑ 29973 [PS]	You'll Wonder Where the Yellow Went/A Frantic Antic	1956	40.00

JUNIOR AND HIS FRIENDS

Number	Title (A Side/B Side)	Yr	NM
45s			
ABC-PARAMOUNT			
❑ 10089	Who's Our Pet, Annette!/ A.B.C. Love	1960	30.00

JUNIOR'S EYES

Number	Title (A Side/B Side)	Yr	NM
Albums			
A&M			
❑ SP-4189	Junior's Eyes	1970	20.00

JURY, THE
See BILL JUSTIS.

JUST THREE

Number	Title (A Side/B Side)	Yr	NM
45s			
HIT			
❑ 222	The "In" Crowd/Hang On Sloopy	1965	12.00
—B-side by the Roamers			

JUSTICE, BERGEN

Number	Title (A Side/B Side)	Yr	NM
45s			
HIT			
❑ 305	Gimme Little Sign/Never My Love	1967	8.00
—B-side by the Chellows			

JUSTICE, JIMMY

Number	Title (A Side/B Side)	Yr	NM
45s			
BLUE CAT			
❑ 101	Don't Let the Stars Get In Your Eyes/Guitar Player (Her and Him)	1964	10.00
KAPP			
❑ 469	Ain't That Funny/One	1962	12.00
❑ 482	When My Little Girl Is Smiling/ If I Lost Your Love	1962	12.00
❑ 514	I Wake Up Crying/ World of Lonely People	1963	12.00
Albums			
KAPP			
❑ KL-1308 [M]	Justice for All	1963	25.00
❑ KS-3308 [S]	Justice for All	1963	40.00

K

K.C. AND THE SUNSHINE BAND
Includes K.C. as a solo performer.

Number	Title (A Side/B Side)	Yr	NM
12-Inch Singles			
EPIC			
❑ 49-03187	(You Said) You'd Gimme Some More (7:33) (Instrumental 5:37)	1982	8.00
MECA			
❑ D-5000	Give It Up (Vocal 5:18) (Instrumental 3:30)/ Are You Ready	1983	8.00
❑ D-5001	Don't Break My Heart (8:42)/ Are You Ready (6:20)	1984	8.00
—K.C. solo			
SISAPA/CURB			
❑ V-77201	Game of Love (Hot Radio Edit) (Radio Regular Edit) (Extended Edit) (D.I.Y. Beats)	1990	8.00
SUNSHINE SOUND			
❑ SSD-202	Do You Feel All Right/I Will Love You Tomorrow	1978	10.00
❑ SSD-207	Do You Wanna Go Party (7:27) (10:00)	1979	12.00
45s			
CASABLANCA			
❑ 2227	Yes I'm Ready/With Your Love	1979	4.00
—As "Teri DeSario with K.C."			
❑ 2278	Dancin' in the Streets/ Moonlight Madness	1980	4.00
—As "Teri DeSario with K.C."			
❑ 812991-7	Yes I'm Ready/ Dancin' in the Streets	1983	4.00
—As "Teri DeSario with K.C."; reissue			
EPIC			
❑ 14-02545	Love Me/Don't Say No	1981	4.00
❑ 14-02652	It Happens Every Night/Stand Up	1981	4.00
❑ 34-03286	(You Said) You'd Gimme Some More/When You Dance to the Music	1982	4.00
❑ 34-03556	Don't Run (Come Back to Me)/ On the One	1983	4.00
MECA			
❑ 1001	Give It Up/Uptight	1983	4.00
—K.C. solo			
❑ 1003	On the Top/(B-side unknown)	1984	6.00
T.K.			
❑ 1001	Blow Your Whistle/I'm Going to Do Something Good to You	1973	5.00
—As "K.C. and the Sunshine Junkanoo Band"			
❑ 1003	Sound Your Funky Horn/Why Don't We Get Together	1974	5.00
❑ 1005	Queen of Clubs/Do It Good	1974	5.00
❑ 1008	I'm a Pushover/You Don't Know	1974	5.00
❑ 1009	Get Down Tonight/ You Don't Know	1975	4.00
❑ 1010	Shotgun Shuffle/Hey J	1975	4.00
—As "The Sunshine Band"			
❑ 1015	That's the Way (I Like It)/ What Makes You Happy	1975	4.00
❑ 1018	Rock Your Baby/S.O.S.	1976	4.00
—As "The Sunshine Band"			
❑ 1019	(Shake, Shake, Shake) Shake Your Booty/Boogie Shoes	1976	4.00
❑ 1020	I Like to Do It/Come On In	1976	4.00
❑ 1022	I'm Your Boogie Man/Wrap Your Arms Around Me	1977	4.00
❑ 1023	Keep It Comin' Love/ Baby I Love You	1977	4.00
❑ 1023 [PS]	Keep It Comin' Love/ Baby I Love You	1977	5.00
❑ 1025	Boogie Shoes/I Get Lifted	1978	4.00
❑ 1025 [PS]	Boogie Shoes/I Get Lifted	1978	8.00
❑ 1026	Black Water Gold (Part 1)/ Black Water Gold (Part 2)	1978	4.00
—As "The Sunshine Band"			
❑ 1028	It's the Same Old Song/ Let's Go Party	1978	4.00
❑ 1028 [PS]	It's the Same Old Song/ Let's Go Party	1978	4.00
❑ 1030	Do You Feel All Right/ I Will Love You Tomorrow	1978	4.00
❑ 1030 [PS]	Do You Feel All Right/I Will Love You Tomorrow	1978	4.00
❑ 1031	Who Do Ya Love/Sho-Nuff	1978	4.00
❑ 1031 [PS]	Who Do Ya Love/Sho-Nuff	1978	4.00
❑ 1033	Do You Wanna Go Party/ Come to My Island	1979	4.00
❑ 1035	Please Don't Go/I Betcha Didn't Know That	1979	4.00
❑ 1036	Let's Go Rock and Roll /I've Got the Feeling	1980	4.00
❑ 1037	Que Pasa?/Por Favor No Te Vayas	1980	4.00
❑ 1038	Make Me a Star/Do Me	1980	4.00
—K.C. solo			
❑ 1044	Space Cadet/Do Me	1981	4.00
—K.C. solo			
❑ 1048	Redlight/I Don't Wanna Make Love	1982	4.00
—K.C. solo			
Albums			
EPIC			
❑ FE 37490	The Painter	1981	10.00
❑ PE 37490	The Painter	1982	8.00
—Budget-line reissue			
❑ FE 38073	All in a Night's Work	1982	10.00
❑ PE 38073	All in a Night's Work	1984	8.00
—Budget-line reissue			
MECA			
❑ 8301	KC Ten	1984	10.00
SUNSHINE SOUND			
❑ 614	Space Cadet/Solo Flight	1981	10.00
T.K.			
❑ 500	Do It Good	1974	12.00
❑ 603	K.C. and the Sunshine Band	1975	10.00
❑ 604	The Sound of Sunshine	1975	10.00
—By "The Sunshine Band" (all instrumental)			
❑ 605	Part 3	1976	10.00
❑ 607	Who Do Ya (Love)	1978	10.00
❑ 611	Do You Wanna Go Party	1979	10.00
❑ 612	Greatest Hits	1980	10.00

K.C. AND THE SUNSHINE BAND AND KOOL & THE GANG FEATURING JT TAYLOR

Number	Title (A Side/B Side)	Yr	NM
45s			
EMI-CAPITOL			
❑ S7-19725	Casper, the Friendly Ghost/ Delicious	1997	3.00
—B-side by Shampoo			

K-DOE, ERNIE

Number	Title (A Side/B Side)	Yr	NM
45s			
DUKE			
❑ 378	My Mother-in-Law (Is In My Hair Again)/Looking Into the Future	1964	8.00
❑ 387	Little Bit of Everything/Someone	1965	8.00
❑ 400	Please Don't Stop/Boomerang	1966	8.00
❑ 404	Little Marie/Somebody Told Me	1966	8.00
❑ 411	Later for Tomorrow/Dancin' Man	1966	8.00
❑ 420	Love Me Like I Wanna/ Don't Kill My Groove	1967	8.00
❑ 423	(It Will Have to Do) Until the Real Thing Comes Along/ Little Marie	1967	8.00
❑ 437	Gotta Pack My Bag/ How Sweet You Are	1968	8.00
❑ 450	I'm Sorry/Trying to Make You Love Me	1969	8.00
❑ 456	I'll Make Everything Be Alright/ Wishing in Vain	1969	8.00
EMBER			
❑ 1050	My Love for You/Tuff-Enuff	1959	25.00
❑ 1075	My Love for You/Shirley's Tuff	1961	15.00
INSTANT			
❑ 3260	Baby, Since I Met You/ Sufferin' So	1963	10.00
❑ 3264	Reaping What I Sow/ Talking Out of My Head	1964	10.00
ISLAND			
❑ 031	Let Me Love You/So Good	1975	6.00

K

Number	Title (A Side/B Side)	Yr	NM
JANUS			
❑ 167	Here Come the Girls/ Long Way Home	1971	6.00
MINIT			
❑ 604	Make You Love Me/There's a Will, There's a Way	1959	30.00
❑ 614	'Tain't It the Truth/Hello My Lover	1960	20.00
❑ 623	Mother-in-Law/Wanted, $10,000 Reward	1961	25.00
—Side 1 is at the correct speed. Trail-off number is "SO-738-2"			
❑ 623	Mother-in-Law/Wanted, $10,000 Reward	1961	200.00
—Side 1 was accidentally mis-mastered at 33 1/3 rpm. Trail-off number is "45-SO-738"			
❑ 627	Te-Ta-Te-Ta-Ta/Real Man	1961	15.00
❑ 634	A Certain Girl/I Cried My Last Tear	1961	15.00
❑ 641	Popeye Joe/Come On Home	1962	15.00
❑ 645	Hey Hey Hey/Love You the Best	1962	15.00
❑ 651	Beating Like a Tom-Tom/ I Got to Find Somebody	1962	15.00
❑ 656	Loving You/Get Out of My House	1962	15.00
❑ 661	Easier Said Than Done/ Be Sweet	1963	15.00
❑ 665	I'm the Boss/Pennies Worth o' Happiness	1963	15.00
❑ 32042	Real Man/Te Ta Te Ta Ta	1968	10.00
SANSU			
❑ 1006	Stoop Down/(B-side unknown)	197?	20.00
❑ 1016	Hotcha Mama/She Gave It All to Me	197?	20.00
SPECIALTY			
❑ 563	Eternity/Do Baby Do	1955	40.00
—As "Ernest Kador"			
UNITED ARTISTS			
❑ 0110	Mother-in-Law/A Wonderful Dream	1973	5.00
—"Silver Spotlight Series" reissue; B-side by the Majors			

Albums

Number	Title	Yr	NM
JANUS			
❑ JLS-3030	Ernie K-Doe	1971	25.00
MINIT			
❑ LP-0002 [M]	Mother-in-Law	1961	200.00
—Orange label			
❑ LP-24002 [R]	Mother-in-Law	196?	150.00
—Black label, not issued until after Imperial bought Minit			

KACT-TIES, THE

45s

Number	Title (A Side/B Side)	Yr	NM
ATCO			
❑ 6299	Oh What a Night/Let Me In Your Life	1964	15.00
—As "The Kac-Ties"			
KAPE			
❑ 501	Happy Birthday/Girl in My Heart	1965	15.00
—As "The Kac-Ties"			
❑ 502	Walkin' in the Rain/Smile	1965	15.00
—As "The Kac-Ties"			
❑ 503	Let Your Love Light Shine/ Were-Wolf	1965	15.00
—As "The Kac-Ties"			
SHELLEY			
❑ 163	Let Your Love Light Shine/ Were-Wolf	1963	25.00
❑ 165	Oh What a Night/Let Me In Your Life	1963	25.00
TRANS ATLAS			
❑ 695	Walkin' in the Rain/Smile	1962	150.00
—Without thunderstorm sound effects			
❑ 695	Walkin' in the Rain/Smile	1962	300.00
—With thunderstorm sound effects			

KAK

Gary Yoder of BLUE CHEER was in this group.

45s

Number	Title (A Side/B Side)	Yr	NM
EPIC			
❑ 10383 [DJ]	Everything's Changing (Long Version)/Everything's Changing (Edited Version)	1968	20.00
—May be promo only			
❑ 10446	I've Got Time/Disbelievin'	1969	20.00

Albums

Number	Title	Yr	NM
EPIC			
❑ BN 26429	Kak	1969	250.00
—Beware — a reissue that looks almost identical to the original and sells for around $12 appeared in stores in 2000-2001			

KALABASH CORP., THE

Albums

Number	Title	Yr	NM
UNCLE BILL			
❑ KB-3114	The Kalabash Corp.	1970	80.00

KALEIDOSCOPE, THE

45s

Number	Title (A Side/B Side)	Yr	NM
EPIC			
❑ 10117	Elevator Man/Please	1967	30.00
❑ 10219	Little Orphan Annie/Why Try	1967	30.00
❑ 10239	I Found Out/Rampe Rampe	1967	30.00
❑ 10332	Just a Taste/Hello Trouble	1968	30.00
❑ 10481	Lie to Me/Let the Good Love Flow	1969	30.00
❑ 10500	Killing Floor/Lie to Me	1969	30.00
FONTANA			
❑ 1633	Jimmy Artichoke/Just How Much You Are	1968	—
—Unreleased			

Albums

Number	Title	Yr	NM
EPIC			
❑ LN 24304 [M]	Side Trips	1967	30.00
❑ LN 24333 [M]	Beacon from Mars	1967	60.00
❑ BN 26304 [S]	Side Trips	1967	40.00
❑ BN 26333 [S]	Beacon from Mars	1967	100.00
❑ BN 26467	Incredible Kaleidoscope	1969	30.00
❑ BN 26508	Bernice	1970	30.00
PACIFIC ARTS			
❑ 102	When Scopes Collide	1978	12.00

KALIN TWINS, THE

45s

Number	Title (A Side/B Side)	Yr	NM
AMY			
❑ 969	Thinkin' About You Baby/ Sometimes It Comes	1966	8.00
DECCA			
❑ 30552	Jumpin' Jack/Walkin' to School	1958	20.00
❑ 30642	When/Three O'Clock Thrill	1958	25.00
❑ 30745	Forget Me Not/Dream of Me	1958	25.00
❑ 30807	It's Only the Beginning/ Oh My Goodness	1959	20.00
❑ 30868	Cool/When I Look in the Mirror	1959	20.00
❑ 30911	Sweet Sugar Lips/Moody	1959	20.00
❑ 30977	Why Don't You Believe Me/ The Meaning of the Blues	1959	20.00
❑ 30977 [PS]	Why Don't You Believe Me/ The Meaning of the Blues	1959	30.00
❑ 31064	Loneliness/Chicken Thief	1960	15.00
❑ 31111	True to You/Blue, Blue Town	1960	15.00
❑ 31169	Zing! Went the Strings of My Heart/No Money Can Buy	1960	15.00
❑ 31220	Momma-Poppa/You Mean the World to Me	1961	15.00
❑ 31286	Bubbles (I'm Forever Blowing Bubbles)/One More Time	1961	15.00
❑ 31410	Trouble/A Picture of You	1962	15.00

7-Inch Extended Plays

Number	Title	Yr	NM
DECCA			
❑ ED 2623	When/Three O'Clock Thrill// Jumpin' Jack/Walkin' to School	1958	60.00
❑ ED 2623 [PS]	When	1958	80.00
❑ ED 2641	Forget Me Not/Cool// Clickety Clack/Tag-A-Long	1958	50.00
❑ ED 2641 [PS]	Forget Me Not	1958	60.00

Albums

Number	Title	Yr	NM
DECCA			
❑ DL 8812 [M]	The Kalin Twins	1959	100.00
VOCALION			
❑ VL 3771 [M]	When	1966	15.00
❑ VL 73771 [R]	When	1966	12.00

KALLMANN, GUNTER, CHORUS

45s

Number	Title (A Side/B Side)	Yr	NM
4 CORNERS OF THE WORLD			
❑ 119	Music for Falling in Love/ Serenade	1965	6.00
❑ 138	Wish Me a Rainbow/ The Day the Rains Came	1966	6.00
❑ 139	Morning, Noon and Night/ Chanson d'Amour	1967	6.00
❑ 144	Paint Yourself a Rainbow/ This Is My Song	1967	6.00
❑ 146	Tammy/You Know What to Do	1967	6.00
❑ 148	Counting the Days/ Our Day Will Come	1968	6.00
❑ 150	Talk to the Animals/ In the Heat of the Night	1968	6.00
POLYDOR			
❑ 15008	Where's the Playground Susie/ Once in Each Life	1969	5.00

Albums

Number	Title	Yr	NM
4 CORNERS OF THE WORLD			
❑ FCL-4209 [M]	Serenade for Elisabeth	1965	12.00
❑ FCS-4209 [S]	Serenade for Elisabeth	1965	15.00
❑ FCL-4218 [M]	Serenade for a Lady in Love	1965	12.00
❑ FCS-4218 [S]	Serenade for a Lady in Love	1965	15.00
❑ FCL-4226 [M]	Songs for My Love	1966	12.00
❑ FCS-4226 [S]	Songs for My Love	1966	15.00
❑ FCL-4235 [M]	Wish Me a Rainbow	1966	12.00
❑ FCS-4235 [S]	Wish Me a Rainbow	1966	15.00
❑ FCL-4237 [M]	With All My Heart	1967	12.00
❑ FCS-4237 [S]	With All My Heart	1967	15.00
❑ FCS-4248	Live for Love	1968	12.00
❑ FCS-4256	Love Is Blue	1968	12.00
POLYDOR			
❑ 24-4506	Early in the Morning	1970	10.00
❑ 24-6003	Once in Each Life	1969	10.00

KANE, BIG DADDY

12-Inch Singles

Number	Title (A Side/B Side)	Yr	NM
COLD CHILLIN'			
❑ PRO-A-4570 [DJ]	All of Me (Radio Remix 4:09). (Single Remix 4:33)/ (Extended Remix 6:20)	1991	8.00
❑ PRO-A-4706 [DJ]	Mr. Pitiful (Album Version 3:27) (same on both sides)	1991	10.00
❑ PRO-A-4897 [DJ]	It's Hard Being the Kane (Remix Radio Version With Fade) (Remix Radio Version Without Fade)	1991	8.00
❑ PRO-A-4974 [DJ]	Ooh, Aah, Nah-Nah-Nah (Master Mix) (Instrumental)	1991	10.00
❑ PRO-A-5092 [DJ]	Groove With It (LP Version) (Instrumental)	1991	8.00
❑ PRO-A-6116 [DJ]	How U Get a Record Deal (Album Version) (Instrumental)/(Clean Radio Edit) (A Cappella)	1993	20.00
❑ PRO-A-6350 [DJ]	Stop Shammin' (Album Version)/ Brother Man Brother Man (Album Version)	1993	25.00
❑ PRO-A-6610 [DJ]	Looks Like a Job for Big Daddy Kane (Album Version) (Instrumental)/Rest in Peace (Intro Edit) (Album Version) (Instrumental)	1993	20.00
❑ 21235	Rap Summary (Lean On Me) (Remix 5:10) (LP Version 4:24)/Long Live the Kane (LP Version 4:55)	1989	20.00
❑ 21389	I Get the Job Done (LP Version) (Edit) (Dub Version)/Big Daddy Theme (LP Version)	1989	8.00
❑ 21528	To Be Your Man (Remix Edit) (Remix)/Ain't No Stoppin' Us Now (Brixton Bass Mix) (LP Version)	1989	15.00
❑ 21763	Cause I Can Do It Right (LP Version) (Instrumental)/ Dance with the Devil (LP Version) (Instrumental)	1990	8.00
❑ 40129	It's Hard Being the Kane (unknown versions)	1991	8.00
❑ 40149	Ooh, Aah, Nah-Nah-Nah (Master Mix) (Instrumental)/ Raw '91/It's Hard Being the Kane (Remix Radio Edit)/ Taste of Chocolate (Remix)	1991	12.00
❑ 40343	The Lover in You (Album Version 4:19) (Mr. Cee's Remix 4:07) (Mr. Cee's Remix Instrumental 4:08)/ Git Bizzy (Album Version 3:33)/Get Down (Remix 4:16) (Remix Instrumental 4:16)	1992	8.00
❑ 40830	How U Get a Record Deal (Album Version) (Clean Radio Edit) (A Cappella) (Instrumental)/Here Comes Kane Scoob and Scrap (Album Version) (Instrumental)	1993	25.00
❑ 40940	Very Special (unknown versions)/Stop Shammin' (unknown versions)	1993	15.00
LABEL			
❑ 371700-1	Uncut, Pure (LP Version) (Underground Version) (Radio Version) (Instrumental)/Earth, Wind & Fire (Radio Version) (LP Version)	1998	8.00
MCA			
❑ MCA8P-2942 [DJ]	Gunman (Remix Master Version) (Remix Instrumental)/ (same on both sides)	1994	8.00
❑ MCA8P-3070 [DJ]	In the PJ's/Show and Prove	1994	20.00

Except when noted otherwise, VG = 25% of NM, and VG+ = 50% of NM. (Example: VG = $2.00, VG+ = $4.00 and NM = $8.00.)

Number	Title (A Side/B Side)	Yr	NM
PRISM			
❑ PS 2016	Raw (Main) (Dubapella)/ Word to the Mother (Land)	1987	80.00
45s			
COLD CHILLIN'			
❑ 19429	Smooth Operator/I Get the Job Done	1991	3.00
—"Back to Back Hits" series; first appearance of B-side on U.S. 45			
❑ 22867	Smooth Operator/ Warm It Up, Kane	1989	4.00
❑ 22867 [PS]	Smooth Operator/ Warm It Up, Kane	1989	4.00
❑ 22906	Rap Summary (Lean On Me)/ Long Live the Kane	1989	8.00
❑ 27708	I'll Take You There/Wrath of Kane	1989	5.00
❑ 27708 [PS]	I'll Take You There/Wrath of Kane	1989	5.00
❑ 27834	Ain't No Half Steppin'/Get Into It	1988	5.00
❑ 27834 [PS]	Ain't No Half Steppin'/Get Into It	1988	5.00
Albums			
COLD CHILLIN'			
❑ PRO-A-5205 [(2)DJ]	Prince of Darkness	1991	30.00
—Vinyl is promo only			
❑ 25731	Long Live the Kane	1988	40.00
❑ 25941	It's a Big Daddy Thing	1989	30.00
❑ 26303	Taste of Chocolate	1990	20.00
LABEL			
❑ 371801-1	Veteranz Day	1998	15.00
MCA			
❑ 11102 [(2)DJ]	Daddy's Home	1994	15.00

KANE, EDEN

Number	Title (A Side/B Side)	Yr	NM
45s			
FONTANA			
❑ 1891	Boys Cry/Don't Come Crying to Me	1964	12.00
❑ 1961	Hangin' Around/Do Something About You	1964	12.00
LONDON			
❑ 1993	Well, I Ask You/Before I Lose My Mind	1961	15.00
❑ 9508	Get Lost/I'm Telling You	1961	15.00
❑ 9516	Forget Me Not/New Kind of Lovin'	1962	15.00
❑ 9532	I Don't Know Why/ Music for Strings	1962	15.00
T-A			
❑ 193	Reason to Believe/ (B-side unknown)	1970	6.00

KANE, PAUL See PAUL SIMON.

KANE'S COUSINS

Number	Title (A Side/B Side)	Yr	NM
Albums			
SHOVE LOVE			
❑ 9827	Undergum Bubbleground	1969	40.00

KANGAROO

Number	Title (A Side/B Side)	Yr	NM
45s			
MGM			
❑ 13960	I Never Tell Me Twice/ Such a Long Long Time	1968	12.00
❑ 13961	Daydream Stallion/ The Only Thing I Had	1968	12.00
—As "Barbara Keith and Kangaroo"			
❑ 13962	Frogg Giggin'/Maybe Tomorrow	1968	12.00
—As "N.D. Smart and Kangaroo"			
Albums			
MGM			
❑ SE-4586	Kangaroo	1968	25.00

KANNIBAL KOMIX

Number	Title (A Side/B Side)	Yr	NM
45s			
COLOSSUS			
❑ 118	Little Little/Neurotic Reaction	1970	8.00
Albums			
COLOSSUS			
❑ 1004	Kannibal Komix	1970	20.00

KANSAS Vocalist Steve Walsh was also in STREETS. Chief writer Kerry Livgren's solo album included a Ronnie James Dio cameo.

Number	Title (A Side/B Side)	Yr	NM
12-Inch Singles			
CBS ASSOCIATED			
❑ AS 1747 [DJ]	Mainstream/Everybody's My Friend	1983	6.00
KIRSHNER			
❑ AS 1451 [DJ]	Play the Game Tonight/ Confessions Pre-Release Montage	1982	8.00
❑ AS 1534 [DJ]	Right Away/Diamonds and Pearls	1982	8.00

Kansas, *Leftoverture,* Kirshner JZ 34224, 1976, **$10.**

Number	Title (A Side/B Side)	Yr	NM
MCA			
❑ L33-17209 [DJ]	All I Wanted (same on both sides?)	1986	8.00
❑ L33-17306 [DJ]	Can't Cry Anymore (same on both sides)	1987	6.00
45s			
CBS ASSOCIATED			
❑ ZS4-04057	Fight Fire with Fire/ Incident on a Bridge	1983	3.00
❑ ZS4-04057 [PS]	Fight Fire with Fire/ Incident on a Bridge	1983	4.00
❑ ZS4-04057 [PS]	Fight Fire with Fire/ Incident on a Bridge	1983	8.00
—"Demonstration Only — Not for Sale" on sleeve (sleeve lists both tracks, though the enclosed promo record only has the A-side on both sides)			
❑ ZS4-04213	Everybody's My Friend/ End of the Age	1983	3.00
❑ ZS4-04213 [PS]	Everybody's My Friend/ End of the Age	1983	4.00
❑ ZS4-04213 [PS]	Everybody's My Friend	1983	8.00
—"Demonstration Only — Not for Sale" on sleeve			
KIRSHNER			
❑ ZS5-02903	Play the Game Tonight/Play On	1982	4.00
❑ ZS5-03084	Right Away/Windows	1982	4.00
❑ ZS5-03084 [PS]	Right Away/Windows	1982	5.00
❑ ZS7 4253	Can I Tell You/The Pilgrimage	1974	6.00
❑ ZS8 4256	Lonely Wind/Bringing It Back	1974	6.00
❑ ZS8 4258	Song for America (Part 1)/(Part 2)	1975	6.00
❑ ZS8 4259	It's You/It Takes a Woman's Love to Make a Man	1975	6.00
❑ ZS8 4267	Carry On Wayward Son/ Questions of My Childhood	1976	5.00
❑ ZS8 4270	What's On My Mind/Lonely Street	1977	4.00
❑ ZS8 4273	Point of Know Return/ Closet Chronicles	1977	4.00
❑ ZS8 4274	Dust in the Wind/Paradox	1978	5.00
❑ ZS8 4276	Portrait (He Knew)/ Lightning's Hand	1978	4.00
❑ ZS8 4280	Lonely Wind/Song for America	1979	4.00
❑ ZS8 4284	People of the South Wind/ Stay Out of Trouble	1979	4.00
❑ ZS9 4285	Reason to Be/How My Soul Cries Out for You	1979	4.00
❑ ZS9 4291	Hold On/Don't Open Your Eyes	1980	4.00
❑ ZS6 4292	Got to Rock On/No Room for a Stranger	1980	4.00
MCA			
❑ S45-17290 [DJ]	Power (same on both sides)	1987	4.00
❑ S45-17290 [PS]	Power (same on both sides)	1987	4.00
❑ 52958	All I Wanted/We're Not Alone Anymore	1986	3.00
❑ 52958 [PS]	All I Wanted/We're Not Alone Anymore	1986	3.00
❑ 53027	Power/Tomb 19	1987	3.00
❑ 53027 [PS]	Power/Tomb 19	1987	3.00
❑ 53070	Can't Cry Anymore/ Three Pretenders	1987	3.00
❑ 53070 [PS]	Can't Cry Anymore/ Three Pretenders	1987	3.00
❑ 53425	Stand Beside Me/House on Fire	1988	3.00
❑ 53425 [PS]	Stand Beside Me/House on Fire	1988	4.00
Albums			
CBS ASSOCIATED			
❑ QZ 38733	Drastic Measures	1983	8.00
❑ QZ 39283	The Best of Kansas	1984	8.00
KIRSHNER			
❑ AS 555 [DJ]	Two for the Show (Sampler)	1978	20.00
—Promo-only single disc of selections from 35660			
❑ KZ 32817	Kansas	1974	12.00
❑ PZ 32817	Kansas	197?	8.00
—Reissue			
❑ PZ 33385	Song for America	1975	12.00
—Without bar code on cover			
❑ PZ 33385	Song for America	198?	8.00
—With bar code on cover			
❑ PZ 33806	Masque	1975	12.00
—Without bar code on cover			
❑ PZ 33806	Masque	198?	8.00
—With bar code on cover			
❑ JZ 34224	Leftoverture	1976	10.00
❑ PZ 34224	Leftoverture	198?	8.00
—Budget-line reissue			
❑ JZ 34929	Point of Know Return	1977	10.00

Number	Title (A Side/B Side)	Yr	NM
❑ PZ2 35660 [(2)]	Two for the Show	1978	15.00
❑ FZ 36008	Monolith	1979	10.00
❑ PZ 36008	Monolith	198?	8.00
—Budget-line reissue			
❑ FZ 36588	Audio-Visions	1980	10.00
❑ PZ 36588	Audio-Visions	198?	8.00
—Budget-line reissue			
❑ FZ 38002	Vinyl Confessions	1982	10.00
❑ PZ 38002	Vinyl Confessions	198?	8.00
—Budget-line reissue			
❑ HZ 44224	Leftoverture	1982	40.00
—Half-speed mastered edition			
❑ HZ 44929	Point of Know Return	1982	40.00
—Half-speed mastered edition			
❑ HZ 46008	Monolith	1982	50.00
—Half-speed mastered edition			
❑ HZ 48002	Vinyl Confessions	1982	100.00
—Half-speed mastered edition			
MCA			
❑ 5838	Power	1986	8.00
❑ 6254	In the Spirit of Things	1988	8.00

KANTNER, PAUL/JEFFERSON STARSHIP

Also see JEFFERSON STARSHIP.

45s

Number	Title (A Side/B Side)	Yr	NM
RCA VICTOR			
❑ 74-0426	Let's Go Together/A Child Is Coming	1971	5.00
❑ 74-0426 [PS]	Let's Go Together/A Child Is Coming	1971	8.00

Albums

Number	Title (A Side/B Side)	Yr	NM
RCA VICTOR			
❑ AYL1-3868	Blows Against the Empire	1981	8.00
—Budget-line reissue			
❑ LSP-4448	Blows Against the Empire	1970	15.00
❑ LSP-4448 [DJ]	Blows Against the Empire	1970	100.00
—Clear vinyl promo			

KANTNER, PAUL, AND GRACE SLICK

Also see JEFFERSON AIRPLANE; JEFFERSON STARSHIP; GRACE SLICK.

45s

Number	Title (A Side/B Side)	Yr	NM
GRUNT			
❑ BFBO-0094	Sketches of China/Ballad of Chrome Men	1973	5.00
—With David Freiberg			
❑ 65-0503	Sunfighter/China	1971	5.00
❑ 65-0503 [PS]	Sunfighter/China	1971	6.00

Albums

Number	Title (A Side/B Side)	Yr	NM
GRUNT			
❑ BFL1-0148	Baron Von Tollbooth and the Chrome Nun	1977	10.00
—Reissue with new prefix			
❑ BXL1-0148	Baron Von Tollbooth and the Chrome Nun	1973	12.00
—Original prefix			
❑ FTR-1002	Sunfighter	1971	15.00
—With booklet (deduct 33% if missing)			
❑ AYL1-3799	Baron Von Tollbooth and the Chrome Nun	1980	8.00
—Budget-line reissue			

KAPLAN, GABRIEL

45s

Number	Title (A Side/B Side)	Yr	NM
ABC			
❑ 12027	De Amerikans/Ed Sullivan, Ed Sullivan	1974	8.00
ELEKTRA			
❑ 45369	Up Your Nose/Bye Centennial Minutes	1976	6.00
❑ 45369 [PS]	Up Your Nose/Bye Centennial Minutes	1976	8.00

Albums

Number	Title (A Side/B Side)	Yr	NM
ABC			
❑ ABC-102 [10]	Holes and Mellow Rolls	1974	15.00
—Promo-only 10-inch sampler			
❑ ABCD-815	Holes and Mellow Rolls	1974	15.00
—Original release with painting of ice-cream bars on cover			
❑ ABCD-905	Holes and Mello-Rolls	1976	12.00
—Reissue with photo of the "Welcome Back, Kotter" cast on cover			

KAPTIONS, THE

45s

Number	Title (A Side/B Side)	Yr	NM
HAM-MIL			
❑ 1520	Dreaming of You/I Know Somewhere	196?	20.00

KARAS, ANTON

45s

Number	Title (A Side/B Side)	Yr	NM
LONDON			
❑ 11015	"The Third Man" Theme/The Cafe Mozart Waltz	196?	8.00
—"Demand Performance" reissue			
❑ 30005	"The Third Man" Theme/The Cafe Mozart Waltz	1950	25.00

Albums

Number	Title (A Side/B Side)	Yr	NM
COLUMBIA			
❑ CL 2576 [M]	Rendezvous in Vienna	1967	12.00
❑ CS 9376 [S]	Rendezvous in Vienna	1967	15.00
DESIGN			
❑ DLP-120 [M]	The Viennese Strings of Anton Karas	1959	15.00
LONDON			
❑ PS 319 [S]	Vienna, City of Dreams	1963	15.00
❑ LL 1560 [M]	"The Third Man" Theme	1959	25.00
❑ LL 3319 [M]	Vienna, City of Dreams	1963	12.00
PERIOD			
❑ SPL-1917	Viennese Bonbons	196?	10.00
❑ SPL-1918	Viennese Bonbons Vol. II	196?	10.00
SURREY			
❑ S-1001 [M]	Zither Magic	196?	12.00
❑ SS-1001 [S]	Zither Magic	196?	12.00
VOX			
❑ VX-25180 [10]	Movie Cocktails	1954	30.00

KAREN, KENNY

45s

Number	Title (A Side/B Side)	Yr	NM
BIG TREE			
❑ 16007	That's Why You Remember/A Nice Place to Live	1973	12.00
COLUMBIA			
❑ 4-42264	Oh Susie Forgive Me/The Light in Your Window	1962	30.00
❑ 4-42452	To Sandy with Love/A Face in the Crowd	1962	30.00
❑ 4-42638	Sixteen Years Ago Tonight/Take Me Back	1962	30.00
STRAND			
❑ 25008	Little Boy/Nature Boy	1959	20.00
❑ 25017	Broken Dreams/You're the Only One I Love	1960	20.00

KARIM, TY

45s

Number	Title (A Side/B Side)	Yr	NM
CAR-A-MEL			
❑ 1677	Lighten Up Baby/All in Vain	196?	1000.
—Orange label			
❑ 1677	Lighten Up Baby/All in Vain	196?	1200.
—Pink label			
ROACH			
❑ 101/102	I Ain't Lying/Only a Fool	197?	100.00
ROMARK			
❑ 73-101	You Reallly Made It Good to Me/All at Once	1973	1200.
❑ 73-104	Lightin' Up/Don't Let Me Be Lonely Tonight	1973	1200.
❑ 113	You Just Don't Know/All in Vain	197?	5000.
—VG 2500; VG+ 3750			

KARL, FRANKIE

45s

Number	Title (A Side/B Side)	Yr	NM
CONGRESS			
❑ 255	You Should 'O Held On/The Boy Next Door	1965	800.00
—Reissue; as "The 7th Avenue Aviators"			
DC			
❑ 180	Don't Be Afraid (Do As I Say)/I'm So Glad	1968	20.00
LIBERTY			
❑ 56164	Don't Sleep Too Long/Put a Little Love in Your Heart	1970	30.00
PHILTOWN			
❑ 105	You Should 'O Held On/The Boy Next Door	1965	1000.
—Original issue; as "Frankie Karl and the Chevrons"			

KARMEN, STEVE

45s

Number	Title (A Side/B Side)	Yr	NM
AUDIO FIDELITY			
❑ 171	You've Said It All (Four Feeling)/(Tuba Version)	1971	12.00
❑ 179	Everybody Likes It/The Easy Way	1971	12.00
❑ 190	I've Never Had the Time/37-21	1972	10.00
CUB			
❑ 9059	Free Passes/Lost	1960	40.00
EL DORADO			
❑ 510	Freight Train/Mama Look a Boo Boo	1957	30.00
JUBILEE			
❑ 5486	Jazz Waltz from "The Candidate"/No One Has Ever Cried for Me Before	1964	10.00
MERCURY			
❑ 71164X45	We Belong Together/Wild Eyes and Tender Lips	1957	25.00
❑ 71208X45	Didja Mean Watcha Said?/How Soon	1957	25.00
❑ 71301X45	River in My Blood/Night Time	1958	50.00
❑ 71386X45	Watchin' and Waitin'/Oh! Oh!	1958	25.00
STRUTTIN'			
❑ 103	I Love New York/(B-side unknown)	1977	12.00
UNITED ARTISTS			
❑ 50451	Breakaway Part 1/Part 2	1968	50.00
—Featuring Jimmy Radcliffe			
❑ 50534	Moments (Vocal)/(Instrumental)	1969	30.00
❑ 50636	What Do You Say to a Naked Lady?/Too Bad You Can't Read My Mind	1970	12.00

Albums

Number	Title (A Side/B Side)	Yr	NM
JUBILEE			
❑ JGM-2048 [M]	This Is a City?	1963	20.00
STRUTTIN'			
❑ STR-104	Reconnecting	1977	12.00

KARTUNES, THE

45s

Number	Title (A Side/B Side)	Yr	NM
MGM			
❑ 12598	Raindrops/Will You Marry Me	1957	30.00
❑ 12680	Dedicated to Love/Willie the Weeper	1958	25.00

KASANDRA

Also recorded as "John KaSandra," though his only hits were under the abbreviated name.

45s

Number	Title (A Side/B Side)	Yr	NM
CAPITOL			
❑ 2342	Don't Pat Me On the Back and Call Me Brother/Just Look in My Face	1968	8.00
RESPECT			
❑ 2501	(What's Under) The Natural Do/Tired Old Subject	1972	7.00
❑ 2502	Ain't I Good/Down Home Ups-Good Whiskey and Bad Women	1972	7.00
❑ 2504	Mose Part III/Tired Old Subject	1972	7.00

Albums

Number	Title (A Side/B Side)	Yr	NM
CAPITOL			
❑ ST-157	A Higher Plateau	1969	15.00
❑ ST-2957	John W. Anderson Presents KaSandra	1968	15.00
RESPECT			
❑ TAS-2602	Color Me Human	1972	15.00
❑ TAS-2603	Beautiful New World	1972	15.00
❑ TAS-2604	True Genius	1972	15.00
❑ TAS-2605	The Mod Messiah	1974	15.00

KASENETZ-KATZ SINGING ORCHESTRAL CIRCUS

45s

Number	Title (A Side/B Side)	Yr	NM
BELL			
❑ 966	When He Come/Ah-La	1970	10.00
—As "Kasenetz-Katz Fighter Squadron"			
BUDDAH			
❑ 52	Down in Tennessee/Mrs. Green	1968	8.00
❑ 64	Quick Joey Small (Run Joey Run)/Mr. Jensen	1968	8.00
❑ 82	I'm in Love with You/To You, With Love	1969	8.00
❑ 90	Embrasez-Moi/Mrs. Green	1969	8.00
EPIC			
❑ 50443	Heart Get Ready for Love/Jungle Junk	1977	5.00
—As "K&K Super Cirkus"			
SUPER K			
❑ 109	Bubblegum March/Dong-Dong-Diki-Di-Ki-Dong	1970	8.00

Albums

Number	Title (A Side/B Side)	Yr	NM
BUDDAH			
❑ BDM-1020 [M]	Kasenetz-Katz Singing Orchestral Circus	1968	40.00
—Mono is promo only; in stereo cover with "Mono" sticker			
❑ BDS-5020 [S]	Kasenetz-Katz Singing Orchestral Circus	1968	15.00
❑ BDS-5028	Kasenetz-Katz Super Circus	1969	15.00

KAT MANDU

12-Inch Singles

Number	Title (A Side/B Side)	Yr	NM
T.K. DISCO			
❑ TKD-155	The Break (8:44)/There's Only Been a Few (7:37)	1979	30.00

Except when noted otherwise, VG = 25% of NM, and VG+ = 50% of NM. (Example: VG = $2.00, VG+ = $4.00 and NM = $8.00.)

Number	Title (A Side/B Side)	Yr	NM
45s			
MARLIN			
❑ 3338	The Break (Short Version)/(Long Version)	1979	10.00
Albums			
MARLIN			
❑ 2233	Kat Mandu	1979	20.00

KATFISH

Number	Title (A Side/B Side)	Yr	NM
45s			
BIG TREE			
❑ 16045	Dear Prudence/Street Walkin'	1975	8.00

KATMANDU

Number	Title (A Side/B Side)	Yr	NM
Albums			
MAINSTREAM			
❑ S-6131	Katmandu	1971	40.00

KAUKONEN, JORMA

Also see HOT TUNA; JEFFERSON AIRPLANE.

Number	Title (A Side/B Side)	Yr	NM
Albums			
GRUNT			
❑ BFL1-0209	Quah	1973	12.00
❑ BXL1-0209	Quah	197?	10.00
—Reissue with new prefix			
❑ AYL1-3747	Quah	1981	8.00
—"Best Buy Series" reissue			
RCA VICTOR			
❑ AFL1-3446	Jorma	1979	10.00
❑ AFL1-3725	Barbecue King	1981	10.00

KAY, JOANNE

Number	Title (A Side/B Side)	Yr	NM
45s			
HIT			
❑ 94	Wonderful Summer/Be True to Your School	1963	8.00
—B-side by the Roamers			
❑ 148	Lonesome Fool/Chug-a-Lug	1964	8.00
—B-side by Harvey Frolic			
❑ 250	Wonderful Summer/Be True to Your School	1966	8.00
—B-side by the Roamers			

KAY, JOHN

Also see SPARROW; STEPPENWOLF.

Number	Title (A Side/B Side)	Yr	NM
45s			
ABC DUNHILL			
❑ 4309	I'm Movin' On/Walk Beside Me	1972	4.00
❑ 4319	You Win Again/Somebody	1972	4.00
❑ 4351	Moonshine/Nobody Lives Here Anymore	1973	4.00
❑ 4360	Dance to My Song/Easy Evil	1973	4.00
COLUMBIA			
❑ 4-44769	Twistin'/Square-Headed People	1969	8.00
MERCURY			
❑ 74004	Say You Will/Give Me Some News I Can Use	1978	4.00
Albums			
ABC DUNHILL			
❑ DSX-50120	Forgotten Songs & Unsung Heroes	1972	10.00
❑ DSX-50147	My Sportin' Life	1973	10.00
MERCURY			
❑ SRM-1-3715	All in Good Time	1978	10.00

KAY, JOHN, AND SPARROW

See SPARROW.

KAY, JOHN, AND STEPPENWOLF

See STEPPENWOLF.

KAY-GEES, THE

Number	Title (A Side/B Side)	Yr	NM
45s			
DELITE			
❑ 903	Kilowatt/Kilowatt Invasion	1978	4.00
❑ 906	Cheek to Cheek/Tango Hustle	1978	4.00
❑ 913	Heavenly Love/Burn Me Up	1979	4.00
GANG			
❑ 321	You've Got to Keep On Bumpin' (Pt 1)/You've Got to Keep On Bumpin' (Pt 2)	1974	5.00
❑ 1322	Master Plan/(B-side unknown)	1974	5.00
❑ 1323	Get Down/My Favorite Song	1975	5.00
❑ 1325	Hustle Wit Every Muscle (Theme from "Party" TV Show)/(Instrumental)	1975	5.00
❑ 1326	Waiting at the Bus Stop (Part 1)/Waiting at the Bus Stop (Part 2)	1976	5.00
Albums			
DE-LITE			
❑ 9505	Kilowatt	1978	10.00
❑ 9510	Burn Me Up	1979	10.00
GANG			
❑ 101	Keep On Bumpin' & Masterplan	1975	10.00
❑ 102	Find a Friend	1975	10.00

KAYAK

Number	Title (A Side/B Side)	Yr	NM
45s			
JANUS			
❑ 274	I Want You to Be Mine/Irene	1978	5.00
❑ 278	Keep the Change/Ivory Dance	1979	5.00
MERCURY			
❑ 76059	Periscope Life/Stop That Song	1980	4.00
Albums			
HARVEST			
❑ ST-11305	See See the Sun	1973	15.00
JANUS			
❑ (no #) [PD]	Phantom of the Night	1979	25.00
—Numbered limited edition of 3,000			
❑ NXS-7023	Royal Bed Bouncer	1975	10.00
❑ NXS-7034	Starlight Dancer	1978	10.00
❑ NXS-7039	Phantom of the Night	1979	10.00
MERCURY			
❑ SRM-1-3824	Periscope Life	1980	10.00

KAYE, DEBBIE LORI

Number	Title (A Side/B Side)	Yr	NM
45s			
COLUMBIA			
❑ 4-43295	What Makes You Do Me Like You Do/Pick Up My Hat	1965	10.00
❑ 4-43454	Soldier Boy/Could That Be	1965	10.00
❑ 4-43591	Every Song You Sing/You're Not There	1966	8.00
❑ 4-43730	The Iron Cross/Baby What I Mean	1966	8.00
❑ 4-43999	Lonely Clown/The Playground	1967	8.00
❑ 4-44142	Legend in My Time/Sweet Georgia Brown	1967	8.00
❑ 4-44311	Break My Mind/Ride, Ride, Ride	1967	8.00
❑ 4-44538	Come On Home/Help Me Love You	1968	8.00
❑ 4-44815	Baby's Come Home/It's Only a Daydream	1969	8.00
POLYDOR			
❑ 15061	God Bless the Child/Gloomy Sunday	1973	8.00
SSS INTERNATIONAL			
❑ 810	Taste of Tears/No Brass Band	197?	7.00

KAYE, MARY, TRIO

Number	Title (A Side/B Side)	Yr	NM
45s			
CAMELOT			
❑ 132	Can't Get You Off My Mind/Writing on the Wall	1967	8.00
COLUMBIA			
❑ 1-230 (?)	I'm in the Mood for Love/The Monkey Song	1949	40.00
—Microgroove 33 1/3 rpm 7-inch single, small hole			
DECCA			
❑ 9-29622	Mad About the Boy/My Funny Valentine	1955	12.00
❑ 9-29761	Lonesome Road/Get Out of Town	1955	12.00
❑ 9-30145	Fools Rush In/Add Another Leaf	1956	12.00
❑ 9-30241	Almost Like Being in Love/Spring Reunion	1957	12.00
❑ 9-30344	Calypso Rock/Boy on a Dolphin	1957	15.00
❑ 9-30596	Another Time, Another Place/With a Love That's True	1958	12.00
RCA VICTOR			
❑ 47-5586	Do You Believe in Dreams?/Toreador	1954	15.00
❑ 47-5751	Almost/Don't Laugh at Me	1954	15.00
❑ 47-5784	Anyone Can Dream/The Cuddlin' Song	1954	15.00
20TH CENTURY FOX			
❑ 457	Man's Favourite Sport/What's Yours?	1964	8.00
VERVE			
❑ 10228	Kiss Me Again/When My Sugar Walks Down the Street	1960	10.00
WARNER BROS.			
❑ 5020	Home Before Dark/Belong to Me	1958	10.00
❑ 5041	Believe in Me/Wonder Why	1959	10.00
❑ 5050	You Can't Be True Dear/Because of You	1959	10.00
❑ 5095	My Isle of Golden Dreams/That Wasn't Me	1959	10.00
Albums			
COLUMBIA			
❑ CL 1910 [M]	Our Hawaii	1962	15.00
❑ CS 8710 [S]	Our Hawaii	1962	20.00
DECCA			
❑ DL 8238 [M]	The Mary Kaye Trio	1956	30.00
❑ DL 8434 [M]	Music on a Silver Platter	1957	30.00
❑ DL 8650 [M]	You Don't Know What Love Is	1958	30.00
MOVIETONE			
❑ 71027 [M]	Just Us	1967	12.00
❑ S 72027 [S]	Just Us	1967	12.00
20TH CENTURY FOX			
❑ TFM-3117 [M]	Night Life	1964	12.00
❑ TFS-4117 [S]	Night Life	1964	15.00
VERVE			
❑ MGV-2142 [M]	Up Front!	1960	40.00
❑ V-8446 [M]	For the Record	1962	20.00
❑ V6-8446 [S]	For the Record	1962	25.00
WARNER BROS.			
❑ B 1222 [M]	Too Much!	1958	20.00
❑ W 1263 [M]	Jackpot	1959	20.00
❑ WS 1263 [S]	Jackpot	1959	25.00
❑ W 1342 [M]	The Mary Kaye Trio on the Sunset Strip	1959	20.00
❑ WS 1342 [S]	The Mary Kaye Trio on the Sunset Strip	1959	25.00

KAYE, SAMMY

Number	Title (A Side/B Side)	Yr	NM
45s			
COLUMBIA			
❑ 1-740 (?)	Guilty/Checky-Checky Hoopla	1950	30.00
—Microgroove 33 1/3 rpm 7-inch single			
❑ 6-740 (?)	Guilty/Checky-Checky Hoopla	1950	20.00
❑ 38963	Harbor Lights/Sugar Sweet	1950	15.00
❑ 39030	Patricia/Petite Waltz	1950	15.00
❑ 39036	To Think You've Chosen Me/You Oughta Be in Pictures	1950	15.00
❑ 39113	Tennessee Waltz/Get Out Those Old Records	1950	15.00
❑ 39140	Tell Me You Love Me/Dear Little Girl of Theta Chi	1950	15.00
❑ 39156	You and Beautiful You/Tonda Wonda Hoy	1951	15.00
❑ 39186	Peter Cottontail/Easter Parade	1951	15.00
❑ 39270	I Love You Because/Pretty Little Bells	1951	15.00
❑ 3-39270	I Love You Because/Pretty Little Bells	1951	20.00
—Microgroove 33 1/3 rpm 7-inch single (note prefix)			
❑ 39325	I'm Yours to Command/Shenandoah Waltz	1951	15.00
❑ 39360	My Prayer/Down the Trail of Aching Hearts	1951	15.00
❑ 39376	Come Back to Angeuleme/Please Don't Talk About Me	1951	15.00
❑ 39421	Del Rio/Would Mind	1951	15.00
❑ 39492	Dixie/Tennessee Tears	1951	15.00
❑ 39499	Longing for You/Mary Rose	1951	15.00
❑ 39531	It's All in the Game/Be Mine Tonight	1951	15.00
❑ 39567	(It's No) Sin/Jealous Eyes	1951	15.00
❑ 39572	Silent Night-O Little Town Of Bethlehem/Joy To The World-Hark the Herald Angels Sing-O Come All Ye Faithful	1951	12.00
❑ 39573	White Christmas/Jingle Bells	1951	12.00
❑ 39574	Winter Wonderland/Rudolph the Red-Nosed Reindeer	1951	12.00
❑ 39575	Frosty the Snow Man/Santa Claus Is Coming to Town	1951	12.00
—The above four comprise a box set			
❑ 39583	Daddy/Bouquet of Roses	1951	15.00
❑ 39602	The Three Bells/I Only Have One Life	1951	15.00
❑ 39633	You Know You Belong to Someone Else/My Lei-Ee-Yana	1952	15.00
❑ 39667	Wheel of Fortune/Goodbye Sweetheart	1952	15.00
❑ 39688	Winnipesaukee/I Ain't Lazy	1952	15.00
❑ 39724	You/Oh How I Miss You	1952	15.00
❑ 39731	You/Pittsburgh, Pennsylvania	1952	12.00
—B-side by Guy Mitchell; part of a 4-record box set			
❑ 39769	Walkin' to Missouri/One for the Wonder	1952	15.00
❑ 39771	Girl of My Dreams/My Extraordinary Girl	1952	12.00
❑ 39772	All the Things You Are/Who	1952	12.00
❑ 39773	Josephine/Would You Like to Take a Walk	1952	12.00
❑ 39774	Little Girl/We'll Meet Again	1952	12.00
—The above four comprise a box set			
❑ 39816	I Don't Know Any Better/God's Little Candles	1952	15.00
❑ 39856	It Wasn't God Who Made Honky Tonk Angels/I Went to Your Wedding	1952	15.00
❑ 39883	Forget Me Not/Sailin' Along the Ohio	1952	15.00

Number	Title (A Side/B Side)	Yr	NM
❑ 39894	All Around the Christmas Tree/ Santa, Santa, Santa Claus	1952	15.00
❑ 39917	Hurry, Hurry, Hurry/ Dance of Mexico	1953	12.00
❑ 39936	Lighthouse in the Harbor/ Angel Made of Ice	1953	12.00
❑ 39957	Gomen-Sasai (Forgive Me)/ Until Tomorrow	1953	12.00
❑ 39977	Sweet Sue-Just You/I Couldn't Keep from Crying	1953	12.00
❑ 39999	Orange Blossom Serenade/ The Tattle-Tale Duck	1953	12.00
❑ 40025	The Midnight Ride/The One in Your Heart	1953	12.00
❑ 40061	In the Mission of St. Augustine/ No Stone Unturned	1953	12.00
❑ 40151	Bella Bella Donna Mis/Y (That's Why)	1954	12.00
❑ 40205	Godspeed to You/Till You Kiss Me at the Altar	1954	12.00
❑ 40248	Dream for Sale/Sittin' 'n' Waitin'	1954	12.00
❑ 40269	Friends and Neighbors/Through	1954	12.00
❑ 40299	Sentimental/If We Should Ever Meet Again	1954	12.00
❑ 40417	Melody of Love/You Are the One	1955	12.00
❑ 40431	Hindustan/She Went That-a-Way	1955	12.00
❑ 40485	Impossible/Jim, Johnny and Jonas	1955	12.00
❑ 40517	The Banjo's Back in Town/ Joe, Joe, Joe	1955	12.00
❑ 40518	Sweet and Lovely/Yearning	1955	12.00
❑ 40556	Queen of My Lonesome Heart/I'll Never Learn Cha-Cha-Cha	1955	12.00
❑ 40574	The Lucky Little Bell/ Don't Cry Baby	1955	12.00
❑ 40621	Hey Pretty Girl/In the Valley of the Moon	1955	12.00
❑ 40645	We All Need Love/Try Another Cherry Tree	1956	12.00
❑ 40698	Once Again/Every Sunday Morning	1956	12.00
❑ 40707	I Could Have Danced All Night/ I've Grown Accustomed to Your Face	1956	12.00
❑ 40752	The Rich People of Brooklyn/ Dreamy River	1956	12.00
❑ 40795	Faded Roses/I'm Through with Love	1956	12.00
❑ 40839	I Met a Girl/Mountain of Kisses	1957	10.00
❑ 40869	Money/The Ship That Never Sailed	1957	10.00
❑ 40909	What a Saturday Night/ A Young Lover's Dream	1957	10.00
❑ 40936	Past My Prime/Charm Bracelet	1957	10.00
❑ 40966	Charleston/Posin'	1957	10.00
❑ 40988	Mary Lou/Moonlight Swim	1957	10.00
❑ 41028	Ha, Ha, Ha/You'd Be Surprised	1957	10.00
❑ 41084	Garden of Allah/Well, Anyway	1957	10.00
❑ 41140	That Girl Next Door/ Our First Formal Dance	1958	10.00
❑ 41178	That Daffodil Feelin'/Spain	1958	10.00
❑ 41206	Why Can't This Night Go On Forever/Yearning	1958	10.00
❑ 41255	Roses Remind Me of You/ At the High School Prom	1958	10.00
❑ 41293	Sweet Leilani/How Good Can a Good Girl Be	1958	10.00
❑ 41348	Leave the Door Wide Open/ Dah Dee (Daddy)	1959	10.00
❑ 41398	Until Tomorrow/Sammy Kaye's Theme Song	1959	10.00
❑ 41508	Deep Purple/Till Tomorrow	1959	10.00
❑ 41552	My Happiness/Melody of Love	1960	10.00
❑ 41656	Chopsticks Boogie/ Harvey's Melody	1960	10.00

DECCA

Number	Title (A Side/B Side)	Yr	NM
❑ 25511	Oh Johnny, Oh Johnny, Oh!/ Got a Date with an Angel	1962	8.00
❑ 25555	After You've Gone/ Who's Sorry Now	1962	8.00
❑ 25604	Roses Are Red/Ramblin' Rose	1963	8.00
❑ 25722	The Whiffenpoof Song/There Is a Tavern in the Town	1967	6.00
❑ 25752	Charley, My Boy/Hot Lips	1969	5.00
❑ 31174	Merry Merry Christmas (To You)/Silver Bells	1960	10.00
❑ 31175	Christmas Child (Loo, Loo, Loo)/Let It Snow, Let It Snow, Let It Snow	1960	10.00
❑ 31204	Welcome Home/What's New at the Zoo	1961	8.00
❑ 31264	I'm a Big Girl Now/ Strange Interlude	1961	8.00
❑ 31294	Lydia, the Tattooed Lady/ I'm Married to a Strip Tease Dancer	1961	8.00
❑ 31336	Swing and Sway Twist/ Mama and Papa Twist	1961	12.00
❑ 31448	Big Deal/Shoot the Piano Player	1962	8.00
❑ 31589	Charade/Maria Elena	1964	6.00
❑ 31642	Night Train/Bedtime Story	1964	6.00
❑ 31700	House of the Rising Sun/ Theme from Golden Boy	1964	6.00
❑ 31738	Night Walker/Sophia	1965	6.00
❑ 31773	Goldfinger/Blue Prelude	1965	6.00
❑ 31854	Hush…Hush, Sweet Charlotte/ The Hucklebuck	1965	6.00
❑ 31935	Lara's Theme (from Dr. Zhivago)/Swedish Rhapsody (Madame X Love Theme)	1966	6.00
❑ 32034	Smile/In the Arms of Love	1966	6.00
❑ 32071	Oh, How I Miss You Tonight/ Gambit	1966	6.00
❑ 32258	Talk to the Animals/Glory of Love	1968	5.00
❑ 32442	I Love to Cry at Weddings/ I'm a Brass Band	1969	5.00
❑ 32624	Something/Juanita (Love Theme from "Topaz")	1970	5.00

PROJECT 3

Number	Title (A Side/B Side)	Yr	NM
❑ 1421	For the Good Times/ If You've Got the Time	1972	4.00

RCA VICTOR

Number	Title (A Side/B Side)	Yr	NM
❑ 47-2810	Cuddle Up a Little Closer, Lovey Mine/I Want a Girl (Just Like the Girl That Married Dear Old Dad)	1949	15.00
❑ 47-2811	Down Among the Sheltering Palms/The World Is Waiting for the Sunrise	1949	15.00
❑ 47-2812	There But For You Go I/My Son	1949	15.00
❑ 47-2813	I Still Love You/We Just Couldn't Say Goodbye	1949	15.00
❑ 47-2862	April Showers/June Is Bustin' Out All Over	1949	15.00
❑ 47-2863	Indian Summer/September Song	1949	15.00
❑ 47-2864	White Christmas/ Winter Wonderland	1949	15.00
❑ 47-2901	Careless Hands/Powder Your Face with Sunshine	1949	15.00
❑ 47-2908	Room Full of Roses/It's Springtime Again	1949	15.00
❑ 47-2923	The Four Winds and the Seven Seas/Out of Love	1949	15.00
❑ 47-2936	Belmont Boogie/Hollywood Square Dance	1949	15.00
❑ 47-2942	Fiddle Dee Dee/ It's a Great Feeling	1949	15.00
❑ 47-3010	Dime a Dozen/Everything They Said Came True	1949	15.00
❑ 47-3038	The Last Mile Home/ Hawaiian Sunset	1949	15.00
❑ 47-3048	Let's Harmonize/Makin' Love Ukulele Style	1949	15.00
❑ 47-3067	Funny Face/Toot Toot Tootsie	1949	15.00
❑ 47-3071	Here Comes Santa Claus/ I Want to Wish You a Merry Christmas	1949	15.00
❑ 47-3075	My Little Grass Shack in Kaelakekua, Hawaii/My Tan	1949	15.00
❑ 47-3076	My Isle of Golden Dreams/ Sweet Leilani	1949	15.00
❑ 47-3077	Hawaiian War Chant/ Hawaiian Sunset	1949	15.00
❑ 47-3101	Careless Kisses/Echoes	1949	15.00
❑ 47-3115	It Isn't Fair/My Lily and My Rose	1950	15.00
❑ 47-3168	Always/Blue Skies	1950	15.00
❑ 47-3169	How Deep Is the Ocean/ Say It Isn't So	1950	15.00
❑ 47-3170	Alexander's Ragtime Band/ A Pretty Girl Is Like a Melody	1950	15.00
❑ 47-3203	Wanderin'/The Bicycle Song	1950	15.00
❑ 47-3754	Roses/Tiddley Winkle Woe	1950	15.00
❑ 47-3828	The Object of My Affection/ I Thought She Was a Local	1950	15.00
❑ 47-3891	Miss You/There's No Use	1950	15.00

7-Inch Extended Plays

COLUMBIA

Number	Title (A Side/B Side)	Yr	NM
❑ B-2546	Daddy/Harbor Lights// Walkin' to Missouri/In the Mission of St. Augustine	195?	15.00
❑ B-2546 [PS]	Sammy Kaye (Hall of Fame Series)	195?	15.00

RCA CAMDEN

Number	Title (A Side/B Side)	Yr	NM
❑ CAE-264	You Always Hurt the One You Love/Taking a Chance on Love//Amapola/Taboo	195?	10.00
❑ CAE-264 [PS]	Sammy Kaye and His Orchestra Play	195?	10.00
❑ CAE-271	Easter Parade/Baby Face//Begin the Beguine/Pretty Baby	195?	10.00
❑ CAE-271	Sammy Kaye and His Orchestra	195?	10.00

RCA VICTOR

Number	Title (A Side/B Side)	Yr	NM
❑ EPA 258	Sweet Leilani/My Isle of Golden Dreams//Hawaiian War Chant/Hawaiian Sunset	1952	12.00
❑ EPA 258 [PS]	The Heart of the Islands in Song	1952	12.00

Albums

COLUMBIA

Number	Title (A Side/B Side)	Yr	NM
❑ CL 561 [M]	Swing and Sway with Sammy Kaye	195?	30.00
❑ CL 668 [M]	Music, Maestro, Please!	195?	30.00
❑ CL 885 [M]	My Fair Lady (For Dancing)	1956	20.00
❑ CL 891 [M]	What Makes Sammy Swing and Sway	1956	20.00
❑ CL 964 [M]	Sunday Serenade	1957	20.00
❑ CL 1018 [M]	Popular American Waltzes	1957	20.00
❑ CL 1236 [M]	Strauss Waltzes for Dancing	1959	15.00
❑ CL 1571 [M]	Dancing on a Silken Cloud	1960	15.00
❑ CL 2541 [10]	Christmas Serenade	1955	40.00
	—"House Party Series" issue		
❑ CL 6155 [10]	Sunday Serenade	1953	40.00
❑ CS 8371 [S]	Dancing on a Silken Cloud	1960	20.00

DECCA

Number	Title (A Side/B Side)	Yr	NM
❑ DL 4070 [M]	Christmas Day with Sammy Kaye	1960	12.00
❑ DL 4071 [M]	Sing and Sway with Sammy Kaye	1960	12.00
❑ DL 4121 [M]	Dance to My Golden Favorites	1961	12.00
❑ DL 4154 [M]	Songs I Wish I Had Played… The First Time Around	1961	12.00
❑ DL 4215 [M]	Sexy Strings and Subtle Saxes	1962	12.00
❑ DL 4247 [M]	New Twists on Old Favorites	1962	12.00
❑ DL 4306 [M]	For Your Dancing Pleasure	1962	12.00
❑ DL 4357 [M]	Come Dance with Me	1963	12.00
❑ DL 4424 [M]	Dreamy Serenades	1963	12.00
❑ DL 4502 [M]	Come Dance to the Hits	1964	12.00
❑ DL 4590 [M]	Come Dance with Me (Vol. 2)	1965	12.00
❑ DL 4655 [M]	Dancetime	1965	12.00
❑ DL 4687 [M]	Swing and Sway Au-Go-Go	1965	12.00
❑ DL 4754 [M]	Shall We Dance	1966	12.00
❑ DL 4823 [M]	Let's Face the Music	1967	12.00
❑ DL 4862 [M]	Swing & Sway in Hawaii	1967	15.00
❑ DL 4924 [M]	Dance and Be Happy	1967	15.00
❑ DL 4970 [M]	Glory of Love	1967	15.00
❑ DL 74070 [S]	Christmas Day with Sammy Kaye	1960	15.00
❑ DL 74071 [S]	Sing and Sway with Sammy Kaye	1960	15.00
❑ DL 74121 [S]	Dance to My Golden Favorites	1961	15.00
❑ DL 74154 [S]	Songs I Wish I Had Played… The First Time Around	1961	15.00
❑ DL 74215 [S]	Sexy Strings and Subtle Saxes	1962	15.00
❑ DL 74247 [S]	New Twists on Old Favorites	1962	15.00
❑ DL 74306 [S]	For Your Dancing Pleasure	1962	15.00
❑ DL 74357 [S]	Come Dance with Me	1963	15.00
❑ DL 74424 [S]	Dreamy Serenades	1963	15.00
❑ DL 74502 [S]	Come Dance to the Hits	1964	15.00
❑ DL 74590 [S]	Come Dance with Me (Vol. 2)	1965	15.00
❑ DL 74655 [S]	Dancetime	1965	15.00
❑ DL 74687 [S]	Swing and Sway Au-Go-Go	1965	15.00
❑ DL 74754 [S]	Shall We Dance	1966	15.00
❑ DL 74823 [S]	Let's Face the Music	1967	15.00
❑ DL 74862 [S]	Swing & Sway in Hawaii	1967	12.00
❑ DL 74924 [S]	Dance and Be Happy	1967	12.00
❑ DL 74970 [S]	Glory of Love	1967	12.00
❑ DL 75106	The 30's Are Here to Stay	1968	12.00

HARMONY

Number	Title (A Side/B Side)	Yr	NM
❑ HL 7187 [M]	Dancing with Sammy Kaye in Hi-Fi	196?	15.00
❑ HL 7230 [M]	In a Dancing Mood	196?	15.00
❑ HL 7321 [M]	My Fair Lady	1964	15.00
❑ HL 7357 [M]	Beautiful Waltzes for Dancing	196?	15.00
❑ HS 11087 [R]	Dancing with Sammy Kaye in Hi-Fi	196?	12.00
❑ HS 11121 [R]	My Fair Lady	1964	12.00
❑ HS 11157 [R]	Beautiful Waltzes for Dancing	196?	12.00
❑ HS 11261	All-Time Waltz Favorites	1968	12.00
❑ HS 11377	Harbor Lights	1970	10.00
❑ KH 32013	Best of the Big Bands	1971	10.00

HINDSIGHT

Number	Title (A Side/B Side)	Yr	NM
❑ HSR-158	1940-41	198?	10.00
❑ HSR-163	1942-43	198?	10.00
❑ HSR-207	1944-46	198?	10.00
❑ HSR-402 [(2)]	22 Original Big Band Recordings	198?	12.00

MCA

Number	Title (A Side/B Side)	Yr	NM
❑ 191	Dance to My Golden Favorites	1973	10.00
	—Reissue of Decca 74121		
❑ 205	Plays Swing & Sway	1973	10.00
	—Reissue of Decca 74306		
❑ 278	The 30's Are Here to Stay	197?	10.00
	—Reissue of Decca material		
❑ 4027 [(2)]	The Best of Sammy Kaye	197?	12.00

PROJECT 3

Number	Title (A Side/B Side)	Yr	NM
❑ PR-5065 QD [Q]	If You've Got the Time	1972	15.00
❑ PR-5065 SD	If You've Got the Time	1972	10.00

RCA CAMDEN

Number	Title (A Side/B Side)	Yr	NM
❑ CAL-261 [M]	Music for Dancing	1956	20.00

Except when noted otherwise, VG = 25% of NM, and VG+ = 50% of NM. (Example: VG = $2.00, VG+ = $4.00 and NM = $8.00.)

Number	Title (A Side/B Side)	Yr	NM
❑ CAL-355 [M]	Swing and Sway with Sammy Kaye	1957	20.00
RCA VICTOR			
❑ LPM 15 [10]	Sammy Kaye Plays Irving Berlin for Dancing	1950	50.00
❑ LPM-3966 [M]	The Best of Sammy Kaye	1967	20.00
❑ LSP-3966 [R]	The Best of Sammy Kaye	1967	12.00
❑ VPM-6070 [(2)]	This Is Sammy Kaye	1972	12.00
VOCALION			
❑ VL 73919	Theme from "Love Story"	1971	10.00

KAYLI, BOB

45s

Number	Title (A Side/B Side)	Yr	NM
ANNA			
❑ 1104	Never More/Peppermint (You Know What to Do)	1959	40.00
CARLTON			
❑ 482	Everyone Was There/ I Took a Dare	1958	20.00
GORDY			
❑ 7004	Toodle Loo/Everyone Was There	1962	400.00
❑ 7008	Toodle Loo/Hold On Pearl	1962	75.00
TAMLA			
❑ 54051	Small Sad Sam/Tie Me Tight	1962	75.00

KAZAN, LAINIE

45s

Number	Title (A Side/B Side)	Yr	NM
COLPIX			
❑ 768	Color of Love/Ouzo	1965	10.00
MGM			
❑ 13479	I'm Shooting High/ No More Songs for Me	1966	8.00
❑ 13526	Can I Trust You/I Can't Remember (Ever Loving You)	1966	8.00
❑ 13657	Kiss Tomorrow Goodbye/ Sweet Talk	1967	8.00
❑ 13777	Road to Ruin/What Did I Lose by Loving You	1967	8.00
❑ 13877	Sunny/When I Look in Your Eyes	1967	8.00
❑ 13943	Night Song/They Don't Give Medals	1968	8.00
POMPEII			
❑ 7001	Window on My Mind/It's You	1971	6.00

Albums

Number	Title (A Side/B Side)	Yr	NM
MGM			
❑ E-4340 [M]	Right Now	1966	20.00
❑ SE-4340 [S]	Right Now	1966	25.00
❑ E-4385 [M]	Lainie Kazan	1966	20.00
❑ SE-4385 [S]	Lainie Kazan	1966	25.00
❑ E-4451 [M]	The Love Album	1967	25.00
❑ SE-4451 [S]	The Love Album	1967	20.00
❑ SE-4496	Love Is	1968	20.00
❑ SE-4631	The Best of Lainie Kazan	1969	20.00

KEATON, JOHNNY

45s

Number	Title (A Side/B Side)	Yr	NM
HIT			
❑ 10	PT 109/Funny Way of Laughin'	1962	8.00

—B-side by Tom Walls

KEGGS, THE

45s

Number	Title (A Side/B Side)	Yr	NM
ORBIT			
❑ 20959	To Find Out/(B-side unknown)	1967	4000.

—Counterfeit identification: The producer's first name, "Yolanda," is misspelled "Yalanda" on fakes.

KEITH

45s

Number	Title (A Side/B Side)	Yr	NM
COLUMBIA			
❑ 43268	Dream/Caravan of Lonely Men	1965	15.00

—As "Keith and the Admirations"

Number	Title (A Side/B Side)	Yr	NM
DISCREET			
❑ 1193	What Did You Do in the Revolution, Dad/In and Out of Love	1974	5.00
MERCURY			
❑ 72596	Ain't Gonna Lie/Our Love Started All Over Again	1966	8.00
❑ 72639	98.6/The Teenie Bopper Song	1966	10.00
❑ 72639 [PS]	98.6/The Teenie Bopper Song	1966	15.00
❑ 72652	Tell Me To My Face/ Pretty Little Shy One	1967	8.00
❑ 72652 [PS]	Tell Me To My Face/ Pretty Little Shy One	1967	15.00
❑ 72695	Daylight Savin' Time/ Happy Walking Around	1967	8.00
❑ 72695 [PS]	Daylight Savin' Time/ Happy Walking Around	1967	12.00
❑ 72715	Easy-As-Pie/Sugar Man	1967	8.00
❑ 72715 [PS]	Easy-As-Pie/Sugar Man	1967	12.00
❑ 72746	I'm So Proud/Candy Candy	1967	8.00

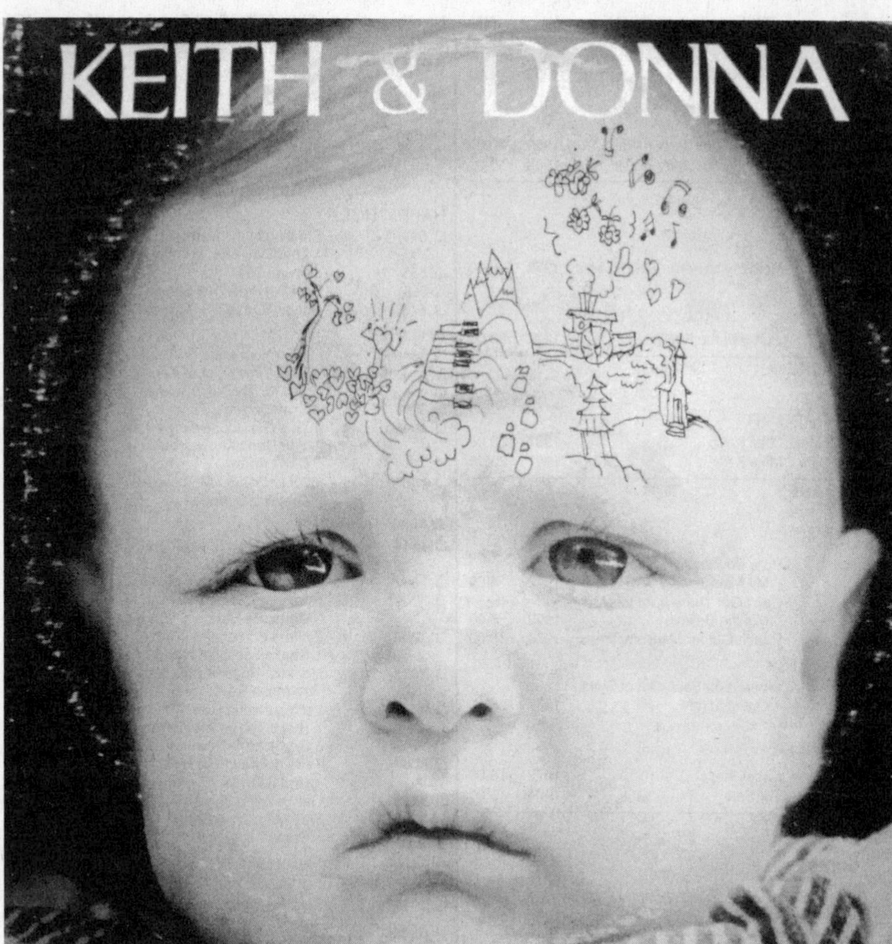

Keith and Donna, *Keith and Donna*, Round RX-104, 1975, **$25.**

Number	Title (A Side/B Side)	Yr	NM
❑ 72746 [PS]	I'm So Proud/Candy Candy	1967	20.00
❑ 72794	Hurry/Pleasure of Your Company	1968	8.00
❑ 72824	Always Tomorrow/ I Can't Go Wrong	1968	8.00
PHILCO-FORD			
❑ HP-20	98.6/Ain't Gonna Lie	1968	15.00

—4-inch plastic "Hip Pocket Record" with color sleeve

Number	Title (A Side/B Side)	Yr	NM
RCA VICTOR			
❑ 74-0140	Marstrand/The Problem	1969	6.00
❑ 74-0222	Trixin's Election/A Fairy Tale or Two	1969	6.00

Albums

Number	Title (A Side/B Side)	Yr	NM
MERCURY			
❑ MG-21102 [M]	98.6/Ain't Gonna Lie	1967	15.00
❑ MG-21129 [M]	Out of Crank	1967	15.00
❑ SR-61102 [S]	98.6/Ain't Gonna Lie	1967	20.00
❑ SR-61129 [S]	Out of Crank	1967	20.00
RCA VICTOR			
❑ LSP-4143	The Adventures of Keith	1969	20.00

KEITH AND DONNA

Also see THE GRATEFUL DEAD.

Albums

Number	Title (A Side/B Side)	Yr	NM
ROUND			
❑ RX-104	Keith and Donna	1975	25.00

KELLEM, MANNY

45s

Number	Title (A Side/B Side)	Yr	NM
EPIC			
❑ 10282	Love Is Blue/Claudine	1968	6.00
❑ 10308	Trains and Boats and Planes/ Free Again	1968	6.00
METROMEDIA			
❑ 104	Red White and Maddox/ Jubilee Joe	1969	6.00

Albums

Number	Title (A Side/B Side)	Yr	NM
EPIC			
❑ BN 26367	Love Is Blue	1968	10.00

KELLER, JERRY

45s

Number	Title (A Side/B Side)	Yr	NM
CAPITOL			
❑ 4630	Never Wake Up/Be Careful How You Drive, Young Joey	1961	12.00
❑ 4668	I'll Get By/My Year of Love	1961	12.00
CORAL			
❑ 62348	It's Too Late/What Will I Tell My Darling	1963	10.00
❑ 62361	Sume Summer/ Goodnight Pretty Girl	1963	10.00
❑ 62378	Sea Shell Sherry/What Happens When He Comes Home	1963	10.00
❑ 62409	Small Wonder/The Tears Keep Falling Down	1964	10.00
KAPP			
❑ 277 [M]	Here Comes Summer/ Time Has a Way	1959	15.00
❑ 277 [PS]	Here Comes Summer/ Time Has a Way	1959	25.00
❑ KS-277 [S]	Here Comes Summer/ Time Has a Way	1959	30.00
❑ 295	If I Had a Girl/Lovable	1959	12.00
❑ 295 [PS]	If I Had a Girl/Lovable	1959	25.00
❑ 310	Now, Now, Now/There Are Such Things	1959	12.00
❑ 322	American Beauty Rose/ Lonesome Lullaby	1960	12.00
❑ 337	My Name Ain't Joe/White for You and Bless for Me	1960	12.00
❑ 353	What More Can I Say/ Whole-Heartedly	1960	12.00
RCA VICTOR			
❑ 47-9221	You're Leanin' On My Mind/ My Heart Loves the Samba (Best of All)	1967	8.00
REPRISE			
❑ 0351	Fickle Finger of Fate/ Glory of Love	1965	8.00

Number	Title (A Side/B Side)	Yr	NM
0397	Ma (She's Such a Quiet Girl)/The Mack	1965	8.00

Albums

KAPP

Number	Title (A Side/B Side)	Yr	NM
KL-1178 [M]	Here Comes Jerry Keller	1959	40.00
KS-3178 [S]	Here Comes Jerry Keller	1959	50.00

KELLERMAN, SALLY

45s

DECCA

Number	Title (A Side/B Side)	Yr	NM
33024	Roll with the Feelin'/Child of Mine	1972	6.00

Albums

DECCA

Number	Title (A Side/B Side)	Yr	NM
DL 75359	Roll with the Feelin'	1972	20.00

KELLIN, MIKE

Albums

VERVE FORECAST

Number	Title (A Side/B Side)	Yr	NM
FT-3028 [M]	Mike Kellin	1967	25.00
FTS-3028 [S]	Mike Kellin	1967	25.00

KELLY, CASEY

45s

ELEKTRA

Number	Title (A Side/B Side)	Yr	NM
45804	Poor Boy/You'll Never Leave My Mind	1972	8.00
45826	Can't Get There from Here/Making Believe	1972	8.00
45885	Reach Out for Me/Sometimes	1974	8.00

PRIVATE STOCK

Number	Title (A Side/B Side)	Yr	NM
45,145	Where You Been/Out of Sight, Out of Mind	1977	8.00

Albums

ELEKTRA

Number	Title (A Side/B Side)	Yr	NM
EKS-75040	Casey Kelly	1972	15.00
EKS-75072	For Sale	1974	15.00

KELLY, EMMETT

Albums

ROULETTE

Number	Title (A Side/B Side)	Yr	NM
R-25130 [M]	Sing Along with Emmett Kelly	1962	25.00
SR-25130 [S]	Sing Along with Emmett Kelly	1962	30.00

KELLY, MONTY

45s

CARLTON

Number	Title (A Side/B Side)	Yr	NM
495	Willingly/The Blue Cha Cha	1959	10.00
517	I Loves You Porgy/Tango Bongo	1959	10.00
527	Summer Set/Amalia	1960	10.00

ESSEX

Number	Title (A Side/B Side)	Yr	NM
325 [S]	Tropicana/Life in New York	1953	12.00
328	Three O'Clock in the Morning/Doreen	1953	12.00
341	Granada/Snow, Snow	1953	12.00
351	Cubamba/Cross Winds	1954	12.00
373	Shangri-La/Monte Carlo	1954	12.00
375	Neapolitan Nights/Majorca	1954	12.00
386	Blue Mirage/That Sweetheart of Mine	1955	12.00
404	Bali Ha'i/To You with Love	1955	12.00

OLYMPIA

Number	Title (A Side/B Side)	Yr	NM
815	Ski Song/The Clicking of the Skis	196?	8.00

Albums

ALSHIRE

Number	Title (A Side/B Side)	Yr	NM
SAS 610	Passport to Romance	196?	10.00

ESSEX

Number	Title (A Side/B Side)	Yr	NM
ESLP-106 [10]	I Love	1954	30.00
ESLP-108 [10]	Monty Kelly Takes Me to Far Away Places	1954	30.00
ESLP-203 [M]	Tropicana	1955	25.00

SOMERSET

Number	Title (A Side/B Side)	Yr	NM
P 7300 [M]	Tropicana	196?	10.00
—Reissue of Trans World 203			

TRANS WORLD

Number	Title (A Side/B Side)	Yr	NM
TWLP-203 [M]	Tropicana	1956	20.00
—Reissue of Essex 203			

KELLY, PAT

45s

CHIC

Number	Title (A Side/B Side)	Yr	NM
1009	She's a Devil/The Stranger Dressed in Black	1957	30.00

JUBILEE

Number	Title (A Side/B Side)	Yr	NM
5315	Hey Doll Baby/Cloud 13	1958	60.00
5333	Patsy/That Is Where My Money Goes	1958	25.00

KELLY, PAUL

45s

DIAL

Number	Title (A Side/B Side)	Yr	NM
4021	Chills and Fever/Only Your Love	1965	40.00
4025	Since I Found You/Can't Help It	1966	60.00
4088	Call Another Doctor/We're Gonna Make It	1968	10.00

HAPPY TIGER

Number	Title (A Side/B Side)	Yr	NM
541	Stealing in the Name of the Lord/Day After Forever	1970	20.00
555	Sailing/509	1970	6.00
568	Poor But Proud/Hot Runnin' Soul	1971	6.00
573	Hangin' On In There/Soul Flow	1971	15.00

PHILIPS

Number	Title (A Side/B Side)	Yr	NM
40409	I Need Your Love So Bad/Nine Times Out of Ten	1966	30.00
40457	Cryin' for My Baby/Sweet Sweet Lovin'	1967	30.00
40480	If This Old House Could Talk/You Don't Know, You Just Don't Know	1967	75.00
40513	Glad to Be Sad/My Love Is Growing Stronger	1968	20.00

WARNER BROS.

Number	Title (A Side/B Side)	Yr	NM
7614	Travelin' Man/Here Comes Old Jezebel	1972	5.00
7657	Don't Burn Me/Love Me Now	1972	5.00
7707	Come Lay Some Lovin' on Me/Come By Here	1973	5.00
7765	I'm Into Something I Can't Shake Loose/Joy	1974	5.00
7823	Hooked, Hogtied & Collared/I Wanna Be Close to You	1974	5.00
8040	Let Your Love Come Down (Let It Fall on Me)/I Wanna Be Close to You	1974	5.00
8067	Take It Away from Him (Put It On Me)/Try My Love	1975	5.00
8120	Get Sexy/I Believe I Can	1975	5.00
8187	Play Me a Love Song/Stealin' Love on the Side	1976	5.00

Albums

HAPPY TIGER

Number	Title (A Side/B Side)	Yr	NM
1015	Stealing in the Name of the Lord	1970	15.00

WARNER BROS.

Number	Title (A Side/B Side)	Yr	NM
BS 2605	Dirt	1972	12.00
BS 2689	Don't Burn Me	1973	12.00
BS 2812	Hooked, Hogtied & Collared	1974	12.00
BS 3026	Stand on the Positive Side	1976	12.00

KELLY FOUR, THE

45s

CANDIX

Number	Title (A Side/B Side)	Yr	NM
325	Annie Had a Party/Sweet Angelina	1961	25.00
—A-side is an alternate take of Silver 1006			
325	Annie Had a Party/Sweet Angelina	1961	25.00
—As "Big Daddy Greenfield"; same recordings as above			

SILVER

Number	Title (A Side/B Side)	Yr	NM
1001	Strollin' Guitar/Guybo	1959	40.00
—A-side was reissued on Silver 1004 by "Jewel and Eddie"			
1006	Annie Had a Party/So Fine, Be Mine	1960	40.00
—A-side was reissued on Crest 1088 by "The Gee Cees"			

KEMPER, JIMMY, AND THE TIERS

45s

LE MANS

Number	Title (A Side/B Side)	Yr	NM
002	Lonely for Kathy/I'm Free to Choose	1964	150.00

KENDALL SISTERS, THE

45s

ARGO

Number	Title (A Side/B Side)	Yr	NM
5278	I'm Available/Don't Bother Me	1957	15.00
5291	Yea, Yea/Won't You Be My Baby	1958	15.00
5310	Billy, Billy, Billy/Let's Wait	1958	15.00

CHECKER

Number	Title (A Side/B Side)	Yr	NM
884	Make It Soon/Three Wishes	1958	15.00
889	Yea, Yea/Won't You Be My Baby	1958	25.00

KENDRICK, NAT, AND THE SWANS

James Brown's backing band, later known as the J.B.'s. Also see FRED WESLEY.

45s

DADE

Number	Title (A Side/B Side)	Yr	NM
1804	(Do the) Mashed Potatoes (Part 1)/(Do the) Mashed Potatoes (Part 2)	1959	15.00
1808	Dish Rag (Part 1)/Dish Rag (Part 2)	1960	15.00
1812	Hot Chili/Slow Down	1960	15.00
5003	Wobble Wobble (Part 1)/Wobble Wobble (Part 2)	1961	15.00
5004	(Do the) Mashed Potatoes (Part 1)/(Do the) Mashed Potatoes (Part 2)	1961	12.00

KENDRICK, WILLIE

45s

GOLDEN WORLD

Number	Title (A Side/B Side)	Yr	NM
1	Fine As Wine/Stop This Train	1963	75.00

RCA VICTOR

Number	Title (A Side/B Side)	Yr	NM
47-8947	Give Me Lots of Lovin'/You Can't Bypass Love	1966	200.00
47-9212	What's That on Your Finger/Change Your Ways	1967	1000.

KENDRICKS, EDDIE

Also see DARYL HALL AND JOHN OATES; THE TEMPTATIONS.

12-Inch Singles

ARISTA

Number	Title (A Side/B Side)	Yr	NM
SP-15 [DJ]	Ain't No Smoke Without Fire (5:58)/Whip (5:05)	1978	12.00

CORNER STONE

Number	Title (A Side/B Side)	Yr	NM
3001	Surprise Attack (3 versions)	1984	8.00

45s

ARISTA

Number	Title (A Side/B Side)	Yr	NM
0325	Ain't No Smoke Without Fire/Love, Love, Love	1978	4.00
0346	The Best of Strangers Now/Don't Underestimate the Power of Love	1978	4.00
0466	I Just Want to Be the One in Your Life/I Can't Let You Walk Away	1979	4.00
0500	Your Love Has Been So Good/I Never Used to Dance	1980	4.00

ATLANTIC

Number	Title (A Side/B Side)	Yr	NM
3796	Looking for Love/Need Your Lovin'	1981	4.00
3874 [DJ]	I Don't Need Nobody Else (same on both sides)	1981	5.00
—May be promo only			

CORNER STONE

Number	Title (A Side/B Side)	Yr	NM
1001	Surprise Attack/(B-side unknown)	1984	4.00

TAMLA

Number	Title (A Side/B Side)	Yr	NM
54203	It's So Hard for Me to Say Good-Bye/This Used to Be the Home of Johnnie Mae	1971	5.00
54210	Can I/I Did It All for You	1971	5.00
54218	Eddie's Love/Let Me Run Into Your Lonely Heart	1972	5.00
54222	If You Let Me/Just Memories	1972	5.00
54230	Girl You Need a Change of Mind (Part 1)/Girl You Need a Change of Mind (Part 2)	1973	5.00
54236	Darling Come Back Home/Loving You the Second Time Around	1973	5.00
54238	Keep On Truckin' (Part 1)/Keep On Truckin' (Part 2)	1973	5.00
54243	Boogie Down/Can't Help What I Am	1974	5.00
54247	Son of Sagittarius/Trust Your Heart	1974	5.00
54249	Tell Her Love Has Felt the Need/Loving You the Second Time Around	1974	5.00
54255	One Tear/The Thin Man	1974	5.00
54257	Shoeshine Boy/Hooked on Your Love	1975	5.00
54260	Get the Cream Off the Top/Honey Brown	1975	5.00
54263	Happy/Deep and Quiet Love	1975	5.00
54266	He's a Friend/All of My Life	1976	5.00
54266 [DJ]	He's a Friend (stereo/mono)	1976	15.00
—Promo only on red vinyl			
54270	Get It While It's Hot/Never Gonna Leave You	1976	5.00
54277	Goin' Up in Smoke/Thanks for the Memories	1976	20.00
54285	Date with the Rain/Born Again	1977	60.00
54289	Baby/I Want to Live (My Life with You)	1977	—
—Unreleased			
54290	Baby/Intimate Friends	1977	5.00

Albums

ARISTA

Number	Title (A Side/B Side)	Yr	NM
AB 4170	Vintage '78	1978	10.00
AB 4250	Something More	1979	10.00

ATLANTIC

Number	Title (A Side/B Side)	Yr	NM
SD 19294	Love Keys	1981	10.00

Except when noted otherwise, VG = 25% of NM, and VG+ = 50% of NM. (Example: VG = $2.00, VG+ = $4.00 and NM = $8.00.)

Number	Title (A Side/B Side)	Yr	NM
MOTOWN			
❑ M5-151V1	Eddie Kendricks	1981	8.00
—Reissue of Tamla 327			
❑ M5-196V1	He's a Friend	1981	8.00
—Reissue of Tamla 343			
TAMLA			
❑ T-309	All By Myself	1971	10.00
❑ T 315L	People...Hold On	1972	10.00
❑ T 327L	Eddie Kendricks	1973	10.00
❑ T 330V1	Boogie Down!	1974	10.00
❑ T6-335	For You	1974	10.00
❑ T6-338	The Hit Man	1975	10.00
❑ T6-343	He's a Friend	1976	10.00
❑ T6-346	Goin' Up in Smoke	1976	10.00
❑ T7-354	Eddie Kendricks at His Best	1977	10.00
❑ T8-356	Slick	1978	10.00

KENNEDY, JOHN FITZGERALD Various tribute records, most of which were released in the immediate aftermath of his assassination in 1963.

Number	Title (A Side/B Side)	Yr	NM
Albums			
CAEDMON			
❑ TC-2021 [(2)]	Self-Portrait	196?	20.00
CAPITOL			
❑ ST 2486 [S]	Years of Lightning, Day of Drums	1966	30.00
❑ T 2486 [M]	Years of Lightning, Day of Drums	1966	20.00
—Narrated by Gregory Peck; U.S. Information Agency movie soundtrack			
COLPIX			
❑ CP 2500 [M]	Four Days That Shocked the World	1964	50.00
—Narrated by Reid Collins; covers Nov. 22-25, 1963			
DECCA			
❑ DL 9116 [M]	That Was The Week That Was	1963	20.00
—BBC show's tribute to JFK, broadcast Nov. 23, 1963			
DIPLOMAT			
❑ 10000 [M]	John F. Kennedy — A Memorial Album	1963	15.00
DOCUMENTARIES UNLIMITED			
❑ (no #) [M]	JFK The Man, The President	1963	20.00
—Narrated by Barry Gray			
HARMONICA			
❑ HLP-3005 [M]	Kennedy Speaks	1963	20.00
LEGACY			
❑ L2L 1017 [(2)M]	John Fitzgerald Kennedy... As We Remember Him	1965	25.00
—Narrated by Charles Kuralt; with 240-page book			
PICKWICK			
❑ 169 [M]	The Presidential Years (1960-1963)	1963	15.00
PREMIER			
❑ 2099 [M]	A Memorial Album	1963	20.00
—From WMCA Radio, New York, Nov. 22, 1963			
RCA VICTOR			
❑ VDM-101 [M]	The Kennedy Wit	1964	15.00
—Narrated by David Brinkley with introduction by Adlai E. Stevenson			
SOMERSET			
❑ 16100 [M]	Actual Speeches of Franklin D. Roosevelt and John F. Kennedy	1963	15.00
—One side has FDR speeches, the other, JFK speeches			
20TH CENTURY			
❑ TCF 3127 [M]	The Presidential Years 1960-1963	1963	20.00
—Narrated by David Teig			

KENNEDY, JOYCE

Number	Title (A Side/B Side)	Yr	NM
12-Inch Singles			
A&M			
❑ SP-12117	Tailor Made (Specially Remixed Version 6:27) (Instrumental 5:30)/Stronger Than Before (4:04)	1984	8.00
❑ SP-12127	Didn't I Tell You (Album Version) (Single Version)	1985	8.00
❑ SP-12158	Hold On (For Love's Sake) (Specially Remixed Version 5:20) (Instrumental 5:44)	1985	8.00
❑ SP-17319 [DJ]	Didn't I Tell You/Fire in the Twilight	1985	10.00
—B-side by Wang Chung			
45s			
A&M			
❑ 2656	The Last Time I Made Love/Different Now	1984	4.00
—A-side with Jeffrey Osborne			
❑ 2665 [DJ]	Tailor Made (same on both sides?)	1984	8.00
—45 is promo only			
❑ 2685	Stronger Than Before/Chain Reaction	1984	4.00
❑ 2685 [PS]	Stronger Than Before/Chain Reaction	1984	4.00
❑ 2710	Tailor Made/Watch My Body	1985	8.00
❑ 2727	Didn't I Tell You/Different Now	1985	4.00
❑ 2790	Hold On (For Love's Sake)/Oh	1985	4.00
❑ 2809	Do Me Right/Too Much Smoke (Not Enough Fire)	1986	4.00
BLUE ROCK			
❑ 4016	I'm a Good Girl/Does Anybody Love Me	1965	100.00
❑ 4023	Does Anybody Love Me/Hi Fi Albums and I	1965	30.00
FONTANA			
❑ 1924	Paddle My Own Canoe/Could This Be Love	1964	20.00
RAN-DEE			
❑ 110	I Still Love You (Darling)/Misunderstood	1963	30.00
Albums			
A&M			
❑ SP-4996	Lookin' for Trouble	1984	10.00
❑ SP-5073	Wanna Play Your Game!	1985	10.00

KENNEDY, MIKE Also see LOS BRAVOS.

Number	Title (A Side/B Side)	Yr	NM
45s			
ABC			
❑ 11309	Louisianna/The Lover (Of the Lost Face of the Moon)	1972	6.00
❑ 11326	Livin' I'm Doin'/Forgive and Forget	1972	10.00
❑ 11333	Mother America/Naked in the Cradle	1972	12.00
Albums			
ABC			
❑ ABCX-754	Louisianna	1972	20.00

KENNEDY, RAY (1) Pop-rock singer; not to be confused with the country singer-songwriter of the same name, who is outside the scope of this book.

Number	Title (A Side/B Side)	Yr	NM
45s			
ARC			
❑ 1-11298	Starlight/Let Me Sing You a Love Letter	1980	4.00
CREAM			
❑ 1001	She's a Lady/Try Acting Like a Woman, Woman	1972	6.00
Albums			
ARC			
❑ NJC 36395	Ray Kennedy	1980	12.00
CREAM			
❑ CR 9001	Raymond Louis Kennedy	1972	15.00

KENNEDY, ROBERT FRANCIS Tribute album released shortly after his death.

Number	Title (A Side/B Side)	Yr	NM
Albums			
COLUMBIA			
❑ C2S 792 [(2)]	A Memorial	1968	20.00

KENNER, CHRIS

Number	Title (A Side/B Side)	Yr	NM
45s			
BATON			
❑ 220	Grandma's House/Don't Let Her Pin That Charge	1956	40.00
IMPERIAL			
❑ 5448	Sick and Tired/Nothing Will Keep Me from You	1957	25.00
❑ 5488	Will You Be Mine/I Have News for You	1958	25.00
❑ 5767	Sick and Tired/Nothing Will Keep Me from You	1961	12.00
INSTANT			
❑ 3229	I Like It Like That, Part 1/I Like It Like That, Part 2	1961	15.00
❑ 3234	A Very True Story/Packin' Up	1961	12.00
❑ 3237	Something You Got/Come See About Me	1961	12.00
❑ 3244	How Far/Time	1962	12.00
❑ 3247	Let Me Show You How (To Twist)/Johnny Little	1962	12.00
❑ 3252	Land of 1000 Dances/That's My Girl	1962	12.00
❑ 3257	Come Back and See/Go Thru Life	1963	12.00
❑ 3263	What's Wrong with Life/Never Reach Perfection	1963	12.00
❑ 3265	She Can Dance/Anybody Here See My Baby	1964	12.00
❑ 3277	I'm Lonely, Take Me/Cinderella	1966	10.00
❑ 3280	All Night Rambler, Part 1/All Night Rambler, Part 2	1966	10.00
❑ 3283	Shoo Rah/Stretch My Hands to You	1967	10.00
❑ 3286	Fumigate Funky Broadway/Wind the Clock	1967	10.00
❑ 3290	Memories of a King (Let Freedom Ring), Part 1/Memories of a King (Let Freedom Ring), Part 2	1968	12.00
❑ 3293	Mini-Skirts and Soul/Sad Mistake	1968	10.00
PRIGAN			
❑ 2002	Don't Make No Noise/Right Kind of Girl	196?	20.00
RON			
❑ 335	Rocket to the Moon/Life's Just a Struggle	1961	12.00
UPTOWN			
❑ 708	Life of My Baby/They Took My Money	1965	10.00
❑ 716	I'm the Greatest/Get On This Train	1965	10.00
VALIANT			
❑ 3229	I Like It Like That, Part 1/I Like It Like That, Part 2	1960	40.00
Albums			
ATLANTIC			
❑ 8117 [M]	Land of 1,000 Dances	1965	50.00
COLLECTABLES			
❑ COL-5116	Golden Classics: I Like It Like That	198?	12.00

KENNY AND THE CADETS Also see THE BEACH BOYS.

Number	Title (A Side/B Side)	Yr	NM
45s			
RANDY			
❑ 422	Barbie/What Is a Young Man Made Of	1962	400.00
—Pink label original (white labels are counterfeits)			
❑ 422	Barbie/What Is a Young Man Made Of	1962	1000.
—Red and gold vinyl			

KENNY AND THE FIENDS

Number	Title (A Side/B Side)	Yr	NM
45s			
DOT			
❑ 16568	House on Haunted Hill (Part 1)/House on Haunted Hill (Part 2)	1963	20.00
❑ 16596	Moon Shot/One-Two-Three-Four	1964	20.00
POSEA			
❑ 80	The Raven (Part 1)/The Raven (Part 2)	1963	30.00
❑ 87	House on Haunted Hill/Green Door	1963	40.00
—As "Kenny and the Beach Fiends"			
PRINCESS			
❑ 51	House on Haunted Hill (Part 1)/House on Haunted Hill (Part 2)	1963	30.00

KENNY AND THE KASUALS

Number	Title (A Side/B Side)	Yr	NM
45s			
MARK IV			
❑ 911	Nothin' Better to Do/Floatin'	1965	30.00
❑ 1002	Don't Let Your Baby Go/(B-side unknown)	1966	30.00
❑ 1003	It's All Right/You Make Me Feel So Good	1966	30.00
❑ 1004	Strings of Time/(B-side unknown)	1966	30.00
❑ 1006	I'm Gonna Make It/Journey to Tyme	1966	40.00
❑ 1008	See-Saw Ride/As I Knew	1967	30.00
UNITED ARTISTS			
❑ 50085	I'm Gonna Make It/Journey to Tyme	1966	20.00
Albums			
MARK			
❑ 5000 [M]	The Impact Sound of Kenny and the Kasuals Live at the Studio Club	1966	1000.
❑ 5000 [M]	The Impact Sound of Kenny and the Kasuals Live at the Studio Club	1977	25.00
—"Reissue, 1977" appears on cover			
❑ 6000 [M]	Teen Dreams	1978	250.00
—Red vinyl; numbered, signed limited edition			
❑ 7000 [S]	Garage Kings	1979	25.00

KENNY AND THE SOCIALITES

Number	Title (A Side/B Side)	Yr	NM
45s			
CROSSTOWN			
❑ 001	I'll Have to Decide/King Tut Rock	1958	150.00

K

KENSINGTON MARKET

45s

WARNER BROS.

Number	Title (A Side/B Side)	Yr	NM
❑ 7221	I Would Be the One/Speaking of Dreams	1968	8.00

Albums

WARNER BROS.

Number	Title (A Side/B Side)	Yr	NM
❑ WS 1754	Avenue Road	1968	20.00
❑ WS 1780	Aardvark	1969	20.00

KENT, AL

45s

BARITONE

Number	Title (A Side/B Side)	Yr	NM
❑ 942	Hold Me/Tell Me Why	1960	75.00

CHECKER

Number	Title (A Side/B Side)	Yr	NM
❑ 881	Dat's Why (I Love You So)/Am I the Man	1958	150.00

RIC-TIC

Number	Title (A Side/B Side)	Yr	NM
❑ 123	The Way You Been Acting Lately/(Instrumental)	1967	40.00
❑ 127	You've Got to Pay the Price/Where Do I Go from Here	1967	20.00
❑ 133	Finders Keepers/Ooh! Pretty Lady	1967	20.00
❑ 140	Bless You (My Love)/(Instrumental)	1968	15.00

WINGATE

Number	Title (A Side/B Side)	Yr	NM
❑ 004	You Know I Love You/Country Boy	1965	15.00

WIZARD

Number	Title (A Side/B Side)	Yr	NM
❑ 100	Hold Me/You Know Me	1959	100.00

KENT, BILLY, AND THE ANDANTES

45s

MAH'S

Number	Title (A Side/B Side)	Yr	NM
❑ 000.2	Your Love/Take All of Me	1960	60.00
—Second pressing, without address and with Roulette distribution mentioned on label			
❑ 000.2	Your Love/Take All of Me	1960	120.00
—First pressing, with Detroit address on label			

KENTON, STAN

45s

CAPITOL

Number	Title (A Side/B Side)	Yr	NM
❑ F899	Intermission Riff/Minor Riff	1950	20.00
—Note: Earlier Stan Kenton 45s on Capitol may exist			
❑ F900	Artistry in Boogie/Machito	1950	20.00
❑ F901	Concerto to End All Concertos, Part 1/Part 2	1950	20.00
❑ F902	Painted Rhythm/Southern Scandal	1950	20.00
❑ F903	Eager Beaver/Harlem Folk Dance	1950	20.00
❑ F904	The Peanut Vendor/Lover	1950	20.00
❑ F905	Theme to the West/Collaboration	1950	20.00
❑ F906	Harlem Holiday/Ricka Jicka Jack	1950	20.00
❑ F907	Unison Riff/Bongo Riff	1950	20.00
❑ F908	Interlude/Thermopolae	1950	20.00
❑ F909	Peg o' My Heart/How Am I to Know	1950	20.00
❑ F910	Tampico/And Her Tears Flowed Like Wine	1950	20.00
❑ F911	Willow Weep for Me/How High the Moon	1950	20.00
❑ F912	Just a-Sittin' a-Rockin'/Soothe Me	1950	20.00
❑ F913	His Feets Too Big for De Bed/Down in Chihuahua	1950	20.00
❑ F1043	Evening in Pakistan/Jolly Rogers	1950	20.00
❑ F1191	Easy Go/But Then You Kissed Me	1950	20.00
❑ F1236	Love for Sale/Be Easy, Be Tender	1950	20.00
❑ F1279	Viva Prado/I'm So in the Mood	1950	20.00
❑ F1306	Pagliacci/Santa Lucia	1950	15.00
❑ F1480	September Song/Artistry in Tango1	1951	15.00
❑ F1535	Tortillas and Beans/Dynaflow	1951	15.00
❑ F1616	The Spider and the Fly/Are You Livin' Old Man	1951	12.00
—Reissue of 78 rpm material			
❑ F1625	Love for Sale/Opus in Pastels	1951	12.00
❑ F1636	Artistry in Rhythm/Artistry Jumps	1951	12.00
—Reissue of 78 rpm material			
❑ F1661	Across the Alley from the Alamo/After You	1951	12.00
—Reissue of 78 rpm material			
❑ F1680	September Song/Laura	195?	12.00
—Reissue			
❑ F1704	Laura/Jump for Joe	1951	15.00
❑ F1774	Francesca/Night Watch	1951	15.00
❑ F1823	Daddy/Street of Dreams	1951	15.00
—A-side with June Christy, vocals			
❑ F1874	Blues in Burlesque (Part 1)/Blues in Burlesque (Part 2)	1951	15.00
❑ F2020	Yes/Mambo Rhapsody	1952	15.00
❑ F2040	Delicado/Bag and Baggage	1952	15.00
❑ F2064	Cool Eyes/She's a Comely Wench	1952	15.00
❑ F2214	Stardust/Beehive	1952	15.00
❑ F2250	Taboo/Lonesome Train	1952	15.00
❑ 2278	The Odd Couple/MacArthur Park	1968	10.00
❑ F2373	Hushabye/Harlem Nocturne	1953	15.00
❑ F2388	Jeepers Creepers/And the Bull Walked Around Olay	1953	15.00
❑ F2409	Do Nothing Till You Hear from Me/How Many Hearts Have You Broken	1953	12.00
❑ F2410	Sweet Dreams Sweetheart/Gotta Be Gettin'	1953	12.00
❑ F2411	Don't Let Me Dream/It's Been a Long, Long Time	1953	12.00
❑ F2412	Every Time We Say Goodbye/Four Months, Three Weeks, Two Days	1953	12.00
❑ F2413	Shoo Fly Pie and Apple Pie Down/I Been Down in Texas	1953	12.00
❑ F2414	It's a Pity to Say Goodnight/There Is No Greater Love	1953	12.00
❑ F2415	Curiosity/Theme to the West	1953	12.00
❑ F2416	Unison Riff/I Told Ya I Love Ya Now Get Out	1953	12.00
❑ F2418	Harlem Holiday/Don't Want That Man Around	1953	12.00
❑ F2419	How Am I to Know/He Was a Good Man	1953	12.00
❑ F2446	Sophisticated Lady/Begin the Beguine	1953	12.00
❑ F2447	There's a Small Hotel/Shadow Waltz	1953	12.00
❑ F2449	Fascinating Rhythm/Over the Rainbow	1953	12.00
❑ F2511	Baja/All About Ronnie	1953	12.00
❑ F2685	Tenderly/The Creep	1953	12.00
❑ F2789	Alone Too Long/Don't Take Your Love from Me	1954	12.00
❑ F2822	The Lady in Red/Under a Blanket of Blue	1954	12.00
❑ F2871	More Love Than Your Love/Skoot	1954	12.00
❑ F2879	Sambo Mambo/Mambo Riff	1954	12.00
❑ F3046	A-Ting-a-Ling/Malaguena	1955	12.00
❑ F3110	Casanova/Dark Eyes	1955	12.00
❑ F3134	23 Degrees N — 82 Degrees W/Falling	1955	12.00
❑ F3151	Freddy/Handwriting on the Wall	1955	12.00
❑ F3243	Sunset Tower/Opus in Chartreuse	1955	12.00
❑ F3345	Baa Too Kee/Winter in Madrid	1956	12.00
❑ F3836	Lemon Twist/Baby You're Through	1957	10.00
❑ F3928	Tequila/Cuban Mumble	1958	10.00
❑ F4196	Whistle Walk/Tamer Lane	1959	10.00
❑ 4370	Opus in Chartreuse Cha Cha Cha/Chocolate Caliente	1960	10.00
❑ 4500	Carnival/Malibu Moonlight	1961	8.00
❑ 4629	Theme from "Splendor in the Grass"/Officer Krupke	1961	8.00
❑ 4666	Maria/Tonight	1961	8.00
❑ 4707	Magic Moment/Waltz of the Prophet	1962	8.00
❑ 4764	Come On Back/Warm Blue Stream	1962	8.00
❑ 4847	Mama Sang a Song/Whispering Hope	1962	8.00
❑ 5085	O Tannenbaum/What Is a Santa Claus	1963	10.00
❑ 5480	Peyton Place Theme/007	1965	8.00
❑ 5572	Patch of Blue/Make Me Love You	1966	8.00
❑ 5828	Dragnet/Spanish Eyes	1967	10.00
❑ F15530	Artistry in Bolero/Come Back to Sorrento	1950	15.00
❑ F15531	Willow Weep for Me/Fantasy	1950	15.00
❑ F15532	Safranski (Artistry in Bass)/Opus in Pastels	1950	15.00
❑ F15533	Artistry in Percussion/Ain't No Misery in Me	1950	15.00
—The above four comprise a box set			

CREATIVE WORLD

Number	Title (A Side/B Side)	Yr	NM
❑ 1001 [DJ]	The Twelve Days of Christmas//O Tannenbaum/We Three Kings Of Orient Are	197?	4.00

7-Inch Extended Plays

CAPITOL

Number	Title (A Side/B Side)	Yr	NM
❑ EAP 1-358	Tampico/Artistry in Boogie//Across the Valley from the Alamo/Unison Riff	1954	15.00
❑ EAP 1-358 [PS]	A Collection of Stan Kenton Classics, Part 1	1954	15.00
❑ EAP 2-358	Southern Scandal/Machito//And Her Tears Flowed Like Wine/Minor Riff	1954	15.00
❑ EAP 2-358 [PS]	A Collection of Stan Kenton Classics, Part 2	1954	15.00
❑ EBF 358 [PS]	A Collection of Stan Kenton Classics	1954	20.00
—Gatefold sleeve for some editions of 1-358 and 2-358			
❑ 1-383	23 degrees N — 82 degrees W/Portrait of a Count//Young Blood/Frank Speaking	195?	12.00
❑ 2-383	Improvisation//Invention for Guitar and Trumpet/My Lady	195?	12.00
❑ EBF 383 [PS]	New Concepts of Artistry in Rhythm	195?	12.00
—Cover for 2-EP set			
❑ EAP 1-421	September Song/Delicado//Laura/Stardust	195?	15.00
❑ EAP 1-421 [PS]	Popular Favorites by Stan Kenton	195?	15.00
❑ EAP 1-426	Sophisticated Lady/Begin the Beguine//There's a Small Hotel/Shadow Waltz	195?	15.00
❑ EAP 1-426 [PS]	Sketches on Standards, Part 1	195?	15.00
❑ EAP 2-426	Lover Man, Oh Where Can You Be?/Pennies from Heaven//Over the Rainbow/Fascinating Rhythm	195?	15.00
❑ EAP 2-426 [PS]	Sketches on Standards, Part 2	195?	15.00
❑ EAP 1-462	You and the Night and the Music/Reverie//Crazy Rhythm/I Got It Bad and That Ain't Good	195?	15.00
❑ EAP 1-462 [PS]	Portraits on Standards, Part 1	195?	15.00
❑ EAP 2-462	I've Got You Under My Skin/Autumn in New York//April in Paris/How High the Moon	195?	15.00
❑ EAP 2-462 [PS]	Portraits on Standards, Part 2	195?	15.00
❑ EBF 462 [PS]	Portraits on Standards	195?	25.00
—Both of above EPs in gatefold sleeve			
❑ EAP 1-508	(contents unknown)	195?	15.00
❑ EAP 1-508 [PS]	Stan Kenton Plays the Compositions of Pete Rugolo	195?	15.00
❑ EAP 1-610	(contents unknown)	195?	12.00
❑ EAP 1-610 [PS]	Kenton with Voices, Part 1	195?	12.00
❑ EAP 2-610	(contents unknown)	195?	12.00
❑ EAP 2-610 [PS]	Kenton with Voices, Part 2	195?	12.00
❑ EAP 3-610	Temptation/Opus in Chartreuse//All About Ronnie/Interlude	195?	12.00
❑ EAP 3-610 [PS]	Kenton with Voices, Part 3	195?	12.00
❑ EAP 1-666	What's New/Stella by Starlight	195?	12.00
❑ EAP 1-666 [PS]	Contemporary Concepts, Part 1	195?	12.00
❑ EAP 1-666 [PS]	Contemporary Concepts, Part 3	195?	12.00
❑ EAP 2-666	Cherokee/Limelight//Yesterdays	195?	12.00
❑ EAP 2-666 [PS]	Contemporary Concepts, Part 2	195?	12.00
❑ EAP 3-666	I've Got You Under My Skin/Stompin' at the Savoy	195?	12.00
❑ EAP 1-731	(contents unknown)	195?	12.00
❑ EAP 1-731 [PS]	Cuban Fire, Part 1	195?	12.00
❑ EAP 2-731	El Congo Valiente/La Guera Baila	195?	12.00
❑ EAP 2-731 [PS]	Cuban Fire, Part 2	195?	12.00
❑ EAP 3-731	Recuerdos/Quien Sabe	195?	12.00
❑ EAP 3-731 [PS]	Cuban Fire, Part 3	195?	12.00
❑ SXA-1796	Lime House Blues/Misty//Waltz of the Prophets	196?	10.00
—Jukebox issue; small hole, plays at 33 1/3 rpm			
❑ SXA-1796 [PS]	Adventures in Jazz	196?	10.00

Albums

CAPITOL

Number	Title (A Side/B Side)	Yr	NM
❑ H 155 [10]	Encores	1950	60.00
❑ T 155 [M]	Encores	195?	40.00
—Turquoise label			
❑ DT 167 [R]	Artistry in Rhythm	1969	10.00
❑ H 167 [10]	Artistry in Rhythm	1950	60.00
❑ SM-167 [R]	Artistry in Rhythm	1975	8.00
—Reissue with new prefix			
❑ T 167 [M]	Artistry in Rhythm	195?	40.00
—Turquoise label			
❑ T 167 [M]	Artistry in Rhythm	1959	15.00
—Black label with colorband, Capitol logo at left			
❑ T 167 [M]	Artistry in Rhythm	1962	12.00
—Black label with colorband, Capitol logo at top			
❑ H 172 [10]	A Presentation of Progressive Jazz	1950	60.00
❑ T 172 [M]	A Presentation of Progressive Jazz	195?	40.00
❑ P 189 [10]	Innovations in Modern Music	1950	60.00
❑ H 190 [10]	Milestones	1950	60.00
❑ T 190 [M]	Milestones	195?	40.00
—Turquoise label			
❑ T 190 [M]	Milestones	196?	25.00
—Black colorband label, logo at left			
❑ PRO-206/7 [DJ]	The Kenton Era (Excerpts)	1955	40.00
❑ L 248 [10]	Stan Kenton Presents	1951	60.00
❑ T 248 [M]	Stan Kenton Presents	195?	40.00
—Turquoise label			

Number	Title (A Side/B Side)	Yr	NM
❑ T 248 [M]	Stan Kenton Presents	196?	15.00
—Black colorband label, logo at top			
❑ T 248 [M]	Stan Kenton Presents	196?	25.00
—Black colorband label, logo at left			
❑ ST-305	Music from "Hair"	1969	15.00
❑ H 353 [10]	City of Glass	1952	60.00
❑ H 358 [10]	Classics	1952	60.00
❑ T 358 [M]	Classics	195?	40.00
—Turquoise label			
❑ H 383 [10]	New Concepts of Artistry in Rhythm	1953	60.00
❑ T 383 [M]	New Concepts of Artistry in Rhythm	195?	40.00
—Turquoise label			
❑ H 386 [10]	Prologue: This Is an Orchestra	1953	60.00
❑ H 421 [10]	Popular Favorites	1953	60.00
❑ T 421 [M]	Popular Favorites	195?	40.00
—Turquoise label			
❑ H 426 [10]	Sketches on Standards	1953	60.00
❑ T 426 [M]	Sketches on Standards	195?	40.00
—Turquoise label			
❑ H 460 [10]	This Modern World	1953	60.00
❑ H 462 [10]	Portraits on Standards	1953	60.00
❑ T 462 [M]	Portraits on Standards	195?	40.00
—Turquoise label			
❑ T 462 [M]	Portraits on Standards	196?	25.00
—Black colorband label, logo at left			
❑ W 524 [M]	Kenton Showcase	1954	40.00
❑ H 525 [10]	Kenton Showcase — The Music of Bill Russo	1954	60.00
❑ H 526 [10]	Kenton Showcase — The Music of Bill Holman	1954	60.00
❑ TDB 569 [(4)M]	The Kenton Era	1955	100.00
—Box set with 44-page book			
❑ WDX 569 [(4)M]	The Kenton Era	196?	70.00
—Box set with 44-page book; limited edition reissue with black label, Capitol logo at left			
❑ STCL-575 [(3)]	Stan Kenton	1970	20.00
❑ T 656 [M]	Duet	1955	40.00
—With June Christy; turquoise label			
❑ T 666 [M]	Contemporary Concepts	1955	40.00
—Turquoise label			
❑ SW 724 [S]	Kenton in Hi-Fi	1959	50.00
—Black label with colorband, logo at left; one fewer track than mono version			
❑ SW 724 [S]	Kenton in Hi-Fi	1962	30.00
—Black label with colorband, logo at top; one fewer track than mono version			
❑ W 724 [M]	Kenton in Hi-Fi	1956	40.00
—Gray label			
❑ W 724 [M]	Kenton in Hi-Fi	1959	20.00
—Black label with colorband, logo at left			
❑ T 731 [M]	Cuban Fire!	1956	40.00
—Turquoise label			
❑ T 731 [M]	Cuban Fire!	1959	20.00
—Black label with colorband, Capitol logo at left			
❑ T 731 [M]	Cuban Fire!	1962	15.00
—Black label with colorband, Capitol logo at top			
❑ T 736 [M]	City of Glass/This Modern World	1956	40.00
—Combination of 353 and 460 onto one 12-inch LP, turquoise label			
❑ T 810 [M]	Kenton with Voices	1957	40.00
—Turquoise label			
❑ T 932 [M]	Rendezvous with Kenton	1957	40.00
—Turquoise label			
❑ T 995 [M]	Back to Balboa	1958	40.00
—Turquoise label			
❑ ST 1068 [S]	The Ballad Style of Stan Kenton	1959	20.00
—Black label with colorband, Capitol logo at left			
❑ ST 1068 [S]	The Ballad Style of Stan Kenton	1962	12.00
—Black label with colorband, Capitol logo at top			
❑ T 1068 [M]	The Ballad Style of Stan Kenton	1959	25.00
—Black label with colorband, Capitol logo at left			
❑ T 1068 [M]	The Ballad Style of Stan Kenton	1962	15.00
—Black label with colorband, Capitol logo at top			
❑ ST 1130 [S]	Lush Interlude	1959	20.00
—Black label with colorband, Capitol logo at left			
❑ T 1130 [M]	Lush Interlude	1959	25.00
—Black label with colorband, Capitol logo at left			
❑ ST 1166 [S]	The Stage Door Swings	1959	20.00
—Black label with colorband, Capitol logo at left			
❑ T 1166 [M]	The Stage Door Swings	1959	25.00
—Black label with colorband, Capitol logo at left			
❑ ST 1276 [S]	The Kenton Touch	1960	20.00
—Black label with colorband, Capitol logo at left			
❑ T 1276 [M]	The Kenton Touch	1960	25.00
—Black label with colorband, Capitol logo at left			
❑ SW 1305 [S]	Viva Kenton!	1960	20.00
—Black label with colorband, Capitol logo at left			
❑ W 1305 [M]	Viva Kenton!	1960	25.00
—Black label with colorband, Capitol logo at left			
❑ STBO 1327 [(2)S]	Road Show	1960	30.00
—Black label with colorband, Capitol logo at left			
❑ STBO 1327 [(2)S]	Road Show	1962	15.00
—Black label with colorband, Capitol logo at top			
❑ TBO 1327 [(2)M]	Road Show	1960	40.00
—Black label with colorband, Capitol logo at left			
❑ TBO 1327 [(2)M]	Road Show	1962	20.00
—Black label with colorband, Capitol logo at top			
❑ ST 1394 [S]	Standards in Silhouette	1960	20.00
—Black label with colorband, Capitol logo at left			
❑ ST 1394 [S]	Standards in Silhouette	1962	12.00
—Black label with colorband, Capitol logo at top			
❑ T 1394 [M]	Standards in Silhouette	1960	25.00
—Black label with colorband, Capitol logo at left			
❑ T 1394 [M]	Standards in Silhouette	1962	15.00
—Black label with colorband, Capitol logo at top			
❑ ST 1460 [S]	Kenton at the Las Vegas Tropicana	1961	20.00
—Black label with colorband, Capitol logo at left			
❑ T 1460 [M]	Kenton at the Las Vegas Tropicana	1961	25.00
—Black label with colorband, Capitol logo at left			
❑ ST 1533 [S]	The Romantic Approach	1961	12.00
—Black label with colorband, Capitol logo at top			
❑ ST 1533 [S]	The Romantic Approach	1961	20.00
—Black label with colorband, Capitol logo at left			
❑ T 1533 [M]	The Romantic Approach	1961	15.00
—Black label with colorband, Capitol logo at top			
❑ T 1533 [M]	The Romantic Approach	1961	25.00
—Black label with colorband, Capitol logo at left			
❑ ST 1609 [S]	Kenton's West Side Story	1961	12.00
—Black label with colorband, Capitol logo at top			
❑ ST 1609 [S]	Kenton's West Side Story	1961	20.00
—Black label with colorband, Capitol logo at left			
❑ T 1609 [M]	Kenton's West Side Story	1961	15.00
—Black label with colorband, Capitol logo at top			
❑ T 1609 [M]	Kenton's West Side Story	1961	25.00
—Black label with colorband, Capitol logo at left			
❑ ST 1621 [S]	A Merry Christmas	1961	20.00
❑ T 1621 [M]	A Merry Christmas	1961	15.00
❑ ST 1674 [S]	The Sophisticated Approach	1962	15.00
—Black label with colorband, Capitol logo at top			
❑ T 1674 [M]	The Sophisticated Approach	1962	12.00
—Black label with colorband, Capitol logo at top			
❑ ST 1796 [S]	Adventures in Jazz	1962	15.00
—Black label with colorband, Capitol logo at top			
❑ T 1796 [M]	Adventures in Jazz	1962	12.00
—Black label with colorband, Capitol logo at top			
❑ ST 1844 [S]	Adventures in Time	1963	15.00
—Black label with colorband, Capitol logo at top			
❑ T 1844 [M]	Adventures in Time	1963	12.00
—Black label with colorband, Capitol logo at top			
❑ ST 1931 [S]	Artistry in Bossa Nova	1963	15.00
❑ T 1931 [M]	Artistry in Bossa Nova	1963	12.00
❑ ST 1985 [S]	Adventures in Blues	1963	15.00
—Black label with colorband, Capitol logo at top			
❑ T 1985 [M]	Adventures in Blues	1963	12.00
—Black label with colorband, Capitol logo at top			
❑ ST 2132 [S]	Artistry in Voices and Brass	1964	15.00
—Black label with colorband, Capitol logo at top			
❑ T 2132 [M]	Artistry in Voices and Brass	1964	12.00
—Black label with colorband, Capitol logo at top			
❑ STAO 2217 [S]	Kenton Plays Wagner	1964	15.00
—Black label with colorband, Capitol logo at top			
❑ TAO 2217 [M]	Kenton Plays Wagner	1964	12.00
—Black label with colorband, Capitol logo at top			
❑ DT 2327 [R]	Stan Kenton's Greatest Hits	1965	10.00
—Black label with colorband, Capitol logo at top			
❑ SM-2327	Stan Kenton's Greatest Hits	197?	8.00
—Reissue with new prefix			
❑ T 2327 [M]	Stan Kenton's Greatest Hits	1965	12.00
—Black label with colorband, Capitol logo at top			
❑ MAS 2424 [M]	Stan Kenton Conducts the Los Angeles Neophonic Orchestra	1966	12.00
—Black label with colorband, Capitol logo at top			
❑ SMAS 2424 [S]	Stan Kenton Conducts the Los Angeles Neophonic Orchestra	1966	15.00
—Black label with colorband, Capitol logo at top			
❑ ST 2655 [S]	Kenton Plays for Today	1966	15.00
—Black label with colorband, Capitol logo at top			
❑ T 2655 [M]	Kenton Plays for Today	1966	12.00
—Black label with colorband, Capitol logo at top			
❑ ST 2810	The World We Know	1968	12.00
❑ ST 2932	Jazz Compositions of Dee Barton	1968	12.00
❑ ST 2974	Finian's Rainbow	1968	12.00
❑ STCL 2989 [(3)]	The Stan Kenton Deluxe Set	1968	20.00
❑ M-11027	Artistry in Jazz	1972	10.00
❑ SM-11794 [M]	Cuban Fire!	1978	10.00
—Reissue of Capitol T 731			
❑ STB-12016 [(2)]	The Comprehensive Kenton	1979	15.00
❑ SM-12037	Kenton's West Side Story	1979	10.00
—Reissue of Capitol ST 1609			
❑ N-16182	Stan Kenton's Greatest Hits	1984	8.00
—Budget-line reissue			

CREATIVE WORLD

Number	Title (A Side/B Side)	Yr	NM
❑ ST 1001	Kenton's Christmas	1970	12.00
❑ ST 1002 [R]	New Concepts of Artistry in Rhythm	197?	10.00
—Reissue of Capitol T 383			
❑ ST 1003 [R]	Contemporary Concepts	197?	8.00
—Reissue of Capitol T 666			
❑ ST 1004 [R]	Kenton in Stereo	197?	10.00
—Reissue of Capitol W 724			
❑ ST 1005	Lush Interlude	197?	10.00
—Reissue of Capitol ST 1130			
❑ ST 1006 [R]	City of Glass/This Modern World	197?	8.00
—Reissue of Capitol T 736			
❑ ST 1007	Kenton's West Side Story	197?	10.00
—Reissue of Capitol ST 1609			
❑ ST 1008 [R]	Cuban Fire!	197?	8.00
—Reissue of Capitol T 731			
❑ ST 1009 [R]	Innovations in Modern Music	197?	8.00
—Reissue of Capitol P 189			
❑ ST 1010	Adventures in Jazz	197?	10.00
—Reissue of Capitol ST 1796			
❑ ST 1011	Adventures in Time	197?	10.00
—Reissue of Capitol ST 1844			
❑ ST 1012	Adventures in Blues	197?	10.00
—Reissue of Capitol ST 1985			
❑ ST 1013	Stan Kenton Conducts the Los Angeles Neophonic Orchestra	197?	10.00
—Reissue of Capitol SMAS 2424			
❑ ST 1015 [(2)]	Live at Redlands University	1971	10.00
❑ ST 1017	The Romantic Approach	197?	8.00
—Reissue of Capitol ST 1533			
❑ ST 1018	The Sophisticated Approach	197?	10.00
—Reissue of Capitol ST 1674			
❑ ST 1019	Road Show, Vol. 1	197?	10.00
—Partial reissue of Capitol STBO 1327			
❑ ST 1020	Road Show, Vol. 2	197?	10.00
—Partial reissue of Capitol STBO 1327			
❑ ST 1022	Jazz Compositions of Dee Barton	197?	10.00
—Reissue of Capitol ST 2932			
❑ ST 1023 [R]	Stan Kenton Presents	197?	8.00
—Reissue of Capitol T 248			
❑ ST 1024	Kenton Plays Wagner	197?	10.00
—Reissue of Capitol STAO 2217			
❑ ST 1025	Adventures in Standards	197?	10.00
❑ ST 1026 [R]	Kenton Showcase	197?	8.00
—Reissue of Capitol W 524			
❑ ST 1027 [R]	Collector's Choice	197?	8.00
❑ ST 1028 [R]	The Fabulous Alumni of Stan Kenton	197?	8.00
❑ ST 1029 [R]	Some Women I've Known	197?	8.00
❑ ST 1030 [(4)R]	The Kenton Era	197?	20.00
—Reissue of Capitol TDB 569			
❑ ST 1031	Back to Balboa	197?	10.00
—Reissue of Capitol T 995			
❑ ST 1032	Kenton at the Las Vegas Tropicana	197?	10.00
—Reissue of Capitol ST 1460			
❑ ST 1033	The Kenton Touch	197?	10.00
—Reissue of Capitol ST 1276			
❑ ST 1034 [R]	Encores	197?	8.00
—Reissue of Capitol T 155			
❑ ST 1035 [R]	The Christy Years	197?	8.00
❑ ST 1036 [R]	Kenton By Request, Vol. I	197?	8.00
❑ ST 1037 [R]	A Concert in Progessive Jazz	197?	8.00
—Reissue of Capitol T 172			
❑ ST 1038	Artistry in Voices and Brass	197?	10.00
—Reissue of Capitol ST 2132			
❑ ST 1039 [Q]	Live at Brigham Young	1971	15.00
❑ ST 1040 [R]	Kenton By Request, Vol. II	197?	8.00
❑ ST 1041 [R]	Sketches on Standards	197?	8.00
—Reissue of Capitol T 426			
❑ ST 1042 [R]	Portraits on Standards	197?	8.00
—Reissue of Capitol T 462			
❑ ST 1043 [R]	Artistry in Rhythm	197?	8.00
—Reissue of Capitol DT 167			
❑ ST 1044	The Stage Door Swings	197?	10.00
—Reissue of Capitol ST 1166			
❑ ST 1045	Artistry in Bossa Nova	197?	10.00
❑ ST 1046	Stan Kenton with Jean Turner	197?	10.00
❑ ST 1047 [R]	Milestones	197?	8.00
—Reissue of Capitol T 190			
❑ ST 1048 [R]	Duet	197?	8.00
—Reissue of Capitol T 656			
❑ ST 1049	Standards in Silhouette	197?	10.00
—Reissue of Capitol ST 1394			
❑ ST 1050 [R]	The Lighter Side of Stan Kenton	197?	8.00
❑ ST 1057	Rendezvous with Kenton	197?	10.00
—Reissue of Capitol T 932			
❑ ST 1058 [(2)Q]	Live at Butler University	1972	20.00
❑ ST 1059 [(2)Q]	Stan Kenton with the Four Freshmen at Butler University	1972	20.00
❑ ST 1060 [(2)Q]	National Anthems of the World	1972	20.00
❑ ST 1061 [R]	Stan Kenton — Formative Years	197?	8.00
—Reissue of Decca DL 8259			
❑ ST 1062 [R]	Kenton By Request, Vol. III	197?	8.00
❑ ST 1063	Viva Kenton!	197?	10.00
—Reissue of Capitol SW 1305			
❑ ST 1064 [R]	Kenton By Request, Vol. IV	197?	8.00
❑ ST 1065	Birthday in Britain	1973	10.00
❑ ST 1066 [R]	Kenton By Request, Vol. V	197?	8.00
❑ ST 1067	Too Much	197?	10.00
❑ ST 1068	The Ballad Style of Stan Kenton	197?	8.00
—Reissue of Capitol ST 1068			
❑ ST 1069	Kenton By Request, Vol. VI	197?	10.00
❑ ST 1070	7.5 on the Richter Scale	1973	10.00
❑ ST 1071	Solo	1973	10.00
❑ ST 1072	Kenton Plays Chicago	1974	10.00
❑ ST 1073	Fire, Fury and Fun	1974	10.00
❑ ST 1074	Hits in Concert	197?	10.00
❑ ST 1076	Kenton '76	1976	10.00

K

Number	Title (A Side/B Side)	Yr	NM
❑ ST 1077	Journey Into Capricorn	1977	10.00
❑ ST 1078 [R]	The Jazz Compositions of Stan Kenton	197?	8.00
❑ ST 1079	Street of Dreams	197?	10.00
❑ ST 1080	The Exciting Stan Kenton	197?	10.00
❑ CW-3005	Stan Kenton Presents Gabe Baltazar	1979	10.00

DECCA

Number	Title (A Side/B Side)	Yr	NM
❑ DL 8259 [M]	Stan Kenton — Formative Years	195?	25.00
—All-black label with silver print			
❑ DL 8259 [M]	Stan Kenton — Formative Years	1960	15.00
—Black label with color bars			

HINDSIGHT

Number	Title (A Side/B Side)	Yr	NM
❑ HSR-118	Stan Kenton 1941	1984	8.00
❑ HSR-124	Stan Kenton 1941, Vol. 2	1984	8.00
❑ HSR-136	Stan Kenton 1943-44	1984	8.00
❑ HSR-147	Stan Kenton 1944-45	1984	8.00
❑ HSR-157	Stan Kenton 1945-47	1984	8.00
❑ HSR-195	Stan Kenton 1962	1984	8.00

INSIGHT

Number	Title (A Side/B Side)	Yr	NM
❑ 206	Stan Kenton and His Orchestra, Vol. 1	197?	10.00
❑ 217	Stan Kenton and His Orchestra, Vol. 2	197?	10.00

LONDON PHASE 4

Number	Title (A Side/B Side)	Yr	NM
❑ BP 44179/80 [(2)]	Stan Kenton Today	1972	40.00
❑ ST-44276	Live in Europe	1976	10.00

MOBILE FIDELITY

Number	Title (A Side/B Side)	Yr	NM
❑ 1-091	Kenton Plays Wagner	1982	25.00
—Audiophile vinyl			

MOSAIC

Number	Title (A Side/B Side)	Yr	NM
❑ MR6-136 [(6)]	The Complete Capitol Recordings of the Holmanand Russo Charts	199?	120.00
❑ MQ10-163 [(10)]	The Complete Capitol Studio Recordings of Stan Kenton 1943-47	199?	200.00

SUNBEAM

Number	Title (A Side/B Side)	Yr	NM
❑ 213	Artistry in Rhythm, 1944-45	197?	10.00

TIME-LIFE

Number	Title (A Side/B Side)	Yr	NM
❑ STBB-13 [(2)]	Big Bands: Stan Kenton	1984	15.00

KENTON, STAN/JUNE CHRISTY/THE FOUR FRESHMEN

Albums

CAPITOL

Number	Title (A Side/B Side)	Yr	NM
❑ STCL-575 [(3)]	Stan Kenton/June Christy/ The Four Freshmen	1970	25.00

—Reissue of an album by each artist in a 3-LP box — ST 1796 (Kenton), ST 516 (Christy), ST 1008 (Four Freshmen)

KENTON, STAN, AND TEX RITTER

Also see each artist's individual listings.

Albums

CAPITOL

Number	Title (A Side/B Side)	Yr	NM
❑ ST 1757 [S]	Stan Kenton/Tex Ritter	1962	80.00
❑ T 1757 [M]	Stan Kenton/Tex Ritter	1962	60.00

KENTS, THE

45s

ARGO

Number	Title (A Side/B Side)	Yr	NM
❑ 5299	I Found My Girl/With All My Heart and Soul	1958	30.00

DOME

Number	Title (A Side/B Side)	Yr	NM
❑ 501	I Love You So/Happy Beat	1958	500.00

KERMIT; KERMIT AND FOZZIE BEAR; TWO MONSTERS

See JIM HENSON.

KEROUAC, JACK

Albums

DOT

Number	Title (A Side/B Side)	Yr	NM
❑ DLP-3154 [M]	Poetry for the Beat Generation	1959	10000.

—Acknowledged to be extremely rare; approximately 130 copies were distributed and only a small handful are known to exist today; the same performance is on Hanover 5000; VG value 5000; VG+ value 7500

HANOVER

Number	Title (A Side/B Side)	Yr	NM
❑ HML-5000 [M]	Poetry for the Beat Generation	1959	400.00
—Reissue of Dot LP with new cover; STEVE ALLEN plays piano on this record			
❑ HML-5006 [M]	Blues and Haikus	1959	250.00
—AL COHN and ZOOT SIMS play saxophones behind Kerouac on this album			

RHINO

Number	Title (A Side/B Side)	Yr	NM
❑ R1-70939 [(4)]	The Jack Kerouac Collection	1990	60.00

—Box set compiling the Hanover and Verve LPs plus an LP of unreleased material

VERVE

Number	Title (A Side/B Side)	Yr	NM
❑ MGV-15005 [M]	Readings on the Beat Generation	1960	250.00

KERSHAW, RUSTY AND DOUG

45s

FEATURE

Number	Title (A Side/B Side)	Yr	NM
❑ 2003	It's Better to Be a Has Been (Than Be a Never Was)/ No, No, It's Not So	1954	100.00

HICKORY

Number	Title (A Side/B Side)	Yr	NM
❑ 1027	So Lovely, Baby/Why Cry for You	1955	30.00
❑ 1036	Can I Be Dreaming/Look Around	1955	30.00
❑ 1042	Honey Honey/ Let's Stay Together	1956	30.00
❑ 1048	Hey You There/Your Crazy, Crazy Heart	1956	30.00
❑ 1055	I'll Understand/Mister Love	1956	30.00
❑ 1061	If I Win, I Win/Money	1957	30.00
—B-side by Al Terry			
❑ 1063	Going Down the Road/ You'll See	1957	40.00
❑ 1068	Love Me to Pieces/ I Never Had the Blues	1957	40.00
❑ 1072	Dream Queen/Take My Love	1957	30.00
❑ 1077	Hey Mae/Why Don't You Love Me	1958	30.00
❑ 1083	Hey Sheriff/Sweet Thing	1958	30.00
❑ 1091	It's Too Late/We'll Do It Anyway	1958	30.00
❑ 1095	Kaw-Liga/Never Love Again	1959	60.00
❑ 1101	Dancing Shoes/I Love You Like This	1959	60.00
❑ 1110	The Love I Want/Oh Love	1959	30.00
❑ 1137	Louisiana Man/Make Me Realize	1960	50.00
❑ 1151	Diggy Liggy Lo/Hey Mae	1961	60.00
❑ 1163	Cheated Too/So Lovely Baby	1961	30.00
❑ 1177	Cajun Joe (Bully of the Bayou)/ Sweet Sweet to Me	1962	30.00
❑ 1575	Louisiana Man/(Our Own) Jole Blon	1970	10.00

RCA VICTOR

Number	Title (A Side/B Side)	Yr	NM
❑ 47-8266	Cajun Stripper/Half the Time	1963	15.00
❑ 47-8362	Cleopatra/Malinda	1964	15.00
❑ 47-8415	St. Louis Blues/I Can't See Myself	1964	15.00

Albums

HICKORY

Number	Title (A Side/B Side)	Yr	NM
❑ LPM-103 [M]	Rusty and Doug Sing Louisiana Man	1960	120.00

HICKORY/MGM

Number	Title (A Side/B Side)	Yr	NM
❑ H3G-4506	Louisiana Man	1974	20.00

KESEY, KEN

Albums

SOUND CITY

Number	Title (A Side/B Side)	Yr	NM
❑ 27690 [M]	The Acid Test	1967	300.00

—THE GRATEFUL DEAD appear on this LP

KESNER, DICK

Albums

BRUNSWICK

Number	Title (A Side/B Side)	Yr	NM
❑ BL 54044 [M]	Lawrence Welk Presents Dick Kesner	1958	20.00
❑ BL 54051 [M]	Dick Kesner and His Magic Stradivarius	1959	15.00
❑ BL 54054 [M]	Intermezzo	1960	15.00
❑ BL 754044 [S]	Lawrence Welk Presents Dick Kesner	1959	25.00
❑ BL 754051 [S]	Dick Kesner and His Magic Stradivarius	1959	20.00
❑ BL 754054 [S]	Intermezzo	1960	20.00

CORAL

Number	Title (A Side/B Side)	Yr	NM
❑ CRL 57352 [M]	Music of Hawaii	1960	12.00
❑ CRL 57360 [M]	A "New" Old Refrain	1961	12.00
❑ CRL 57376 [M]	The Sound of Gypsy Music	1961	12.00
❑ CRL 57393 [M]	Amor Latino	1962	12.00
❑ CRL 57435 [M]	Golden Favorites	1964	12.00
❑ CRL 757352 [S]	Music of Hawaii	1960	15.00
❑ CRL 757360 [S]	A "New" Old Refrain	1961	15.00
❑ CRL 757376 [S]	The Sound of Gypsy Music	1961	15.00
❑ CRL 757393 [S]	Amor Latino	1962	15.00
❑ CRL 757435 [S]	Golden Favorites	1964	15.00

VOCALION

Number	Title (A Side/B Side)	Yr	NM
❑ VL 3777 [M]	Latin Favorites	196?	12.00
❑ VL 73777 [S]	Latin Favorites	196?	15.00

KESTRELS, THE

45s

LAURIE

Number	Title (A Side/B Side)	Yr	NM
❑ 3053	There Comes a Time/In the Chapel in the Moonlight	1960	25.00

KEY, JOANIE

45s

HIT

Number	Title (A Side/B Side)	Yr	NM
❑ 179	Anything/My Love, Forgive Me	1965	8.00

—B-side by Fred York

KEYES, TROY

45s

ABC

Number	Title (A Side/B Side)	Yr	NM
❑ 11027	Love Explosion/ I'm Crying (Inside)	1967	10.00
❑ 11060	No Sad Songs/You Told Your Story (Now Let Me Tell Mine)	1968	15.00
❑ 11116	A Good Love Gone Bad/ I Can Wait My Turn	1968	20.00

—With Norma Jenkins

KEYMEN, THE

45s

ABC-PARAMOUNT

Number	Title (A Side/B Side)	Yr	NM
❑ 9976	Sentimental Journey/ Like Help, Man	1958	15.00
❑ 9977 [M]	Miss You/Isle of Capri	1958	15.00
❑ S-9977 [S]	Miss You/Isle of Capri	1958	25.00
❑ 9991 [M]	Gazachstahagen/Miss You	1959	15.00
❑ S-9991 [S]	Gazachstahagen/Miss You	1959	25.00
❑ 10016	Dream/Nancy Lee	1959	12.00
❑ 10039	Camilia/Cha Cha Marcha Congo	1959	12.00

Albums

ABC-PARAMOUNT

Number	Title (A Side/B Side)	Yr	NM
❑ 258 [M]	Dance with Dick Clark	1958	30.00
❑ S-258 [S]	Dance with Dick Clark	1958	50.00
❑ 288 [M]	Dance with Dick Clark, Vol. 2	1959	30.00
❑ S-288 [S]	Dance with Dick Clark, Vol. 2	1959	50.00

CORAL

Number	Title (A Side/B Side)	Yr	NM
❑ CRL 57112 [M]	Vocal Sounds of the Keymen	1957	30.00

GOLDUST

Number	Title (A Side/B Side)	Yr	NM
❑ LPS-153 [M]	The Keymen Live	196?	50.00

KEYNOTES, THE

Possibly all the same group.

45s

APOLLO

Number	Title (A Side/B Side)	Yr	NM
❑ 478	Suddenly/Zenda	1955	150.00
❑ 484	I Don't Know/A Star	1955	80.00
❑ 493	Really Wish You Were Here/ Bye Bye Baby	1956	120.00
❑ 498	Now I Know/Zup Zup	1956	100.00
❑ 503	In the Evening/O Yeah Hm-m-m	1956	80.00
❑ 513	One Little Kiss/Now I Know	1957	80.00

DOT

Number	Title (A Side/B Side)	Yr	NM
❑ 15225	Who/They Say	1954	30.00

INDEX

Number	Title (A Side/B Side)	Yr	NM
❑ 101	Open the Door (To Your Heart)/ Dum-De, Dum-Dum	1958	100.00

POP

Number	Title (A Side/B Side)	Yr	NM
❑ 111	Carelessly/Congratulations Baby	1957	80.00

TOP RANK

Number	Title (A Side/B Side)	Yr	NM
❑ 2005	With These Rings/We're Not Getting Along	1959	15.00

KEYSTONERS, THE

45s

EPIC

Number	Title (A Side/B Side)	Yr	NM
❑ 9187	The Magic Kiss/After I Propose	1956	60.00

G&M

Number	Title (A Side/B Side)	Yr	NM
❑ 102	The Magic Kiss/I'd Write About the Blues	1956	300.00

OKEH

Number	Title (A Side/B Side)	Yr	NM
❑ 7210	The Magic Kiss/After I Propose	1964	20.00

RIFF

Number	Title (A Side/B Side)	Yr	NM
❑ 202	Sleep and Dream/T.V. Gal	1961	200.00

KEYTONES, THE

45s

CHELSEA

Number	Title (A Side/B Side)	Yr	NM
❑ 101	I Don't Care/La-Do-Da Da	1962	30.00
❑ 1013	Sweet Chariot/One, Two, Three	1963	15.00

OLD TOWN

Number	Title (A Side/B Side)	Yr	NM
❑ 1041	Seven Wonders of the World/ A Fool in Love	1957	100.00
❑ 1041	Wonders of the World/ A Fool in Love	1957	300.00

KHAN, CHAKA

12-Inch Singles

FOX

Number	Title (A Side/B Side)	Yr	NM
❑ 62974 [DJ]	Miles Blowin' (Vinyl Republic Dub) (Disco 9000 Mix) (Afro Cube Mix)	1994	15.00

MCA

Number	Title (A Side/B Side)	Yr	NM
❑ MCA8P-3494 [DJ]	Love Me Still (LP Version) (Instrumental)/ (same on both sides)	1995	10.00
❑ 23604	Own the Night (3 versions)	1985	6.00

Except when noted otherwise, VG = 25% of NM, and VG+ = 50% of NM. (Example: VG = \$2.00, VG+ = \$4.00 and NM = \$8.00.)

Number	Title (A Side/B Side)	Yr	NM
REPRISE			
❑ PRO-A-8454 [DJ]	Never Miss the Water (Album Version) (Radio Edit) (Stylus Remix) (Stylus Street Mix) (A Cappella)	1996	12.00
❑ PRO-A-8638 [DJ]	Never Miss the Water (Deeper Mix) (Lewis and Rich Remix) (Deeper Dub) (Addis-Polvere Remix)	1996	10.00
❑ 43787	Never Miss the Water (unknown versions)	1996	10.00
WARNER BROS.			
❑ PRO-A-787 [DJ]	Life Is a Dance/Some Love	1979	15.00
❑ PRO-A-883 [DJ]	Papillon (AKA Hot Butterfly)/Too Much Love	1980	20.00
❑ PRO-A-909 [DJ]	Get Ready, Get Set (Stereo) (Mono)	1980	10.00
❑ PRO-A-3316 [DJ]	It's My Party (Edit) (LP Version)	1988	6.00
❑ PRO-A-3451 [DJ]	Baby Me (3 CK's and a Baby Mix) (Big Baby Mix Radio Edit) (Instrumental Mix) (Midget Mix)	1989	10.00
❑ PRO-A-3481 [DJ]	Baby Me (Babysitting Mix) (same on both sides)	1988	6.00
❑ PRO-A-3571 [DJ]	Soul Talkin' (Edit) (Serious Soul Edit)	1988	10.00
❑ PRO-A-5783 [DJ]	I Want (unknown versions)	1992	8.00
❑ 20249	I Feel for You (Remix 7:12)/Chinatown (LP Version 4:33)	1984	6.00
❑ 20296	This Is My Night (6:11)/Caught in the Act	1984	6.00
❑ 20367	(Krush Groove) Can't Stop the Street (Vocal) (Instrumental)	1985	6.00
❑ 20487	Love of a Lifetime (Extended)/Coltrane Dreams (Long)	1986	6.00
❑ 20561	Tight Fit (Extended Version)/Who's It Gonna Be	1986	6.00
❑ 21097	It's My Party (New Party Mix 8:40) (Club Instrumental 5:05) (LP Version 5:10) (Club Edit 5:10) (Dance Dub 5:18)/Where Are You Tonite	1988	6.00
❑ 21179	Baby Me/Everybody Needs Some Love	1989	7.00
❑ 21250	Soul Talkin' (Soul Mix) (Soul Edit)/I'm Every Woman (Remix) (Remix Edit)/Ain't Nobody	1988	8.00
❑ 29721	Tearin' It Up (Long Version Remix 7:21) (Instrumental Version 8:07)	1983	12.00
45s			
ARISTA			
❑ 12957	My Funny Valentine/Not Gon' Cry	1996	3.00
—B-side by Mary J. Blige			
ATLANTIC			
❑ 89449	The Other Side of the World/(Instrumental)	1986	3.00
MCA			
❑ 52730	Own the Night/(Instrumental)	1985	3.00
❑ 52730 [PS]	Own the Night/(Instrumental)	1985	3.00
REPRISE			
❑ 17503	Never Miss the Water/Papillon (AKA Hot Butterfly)	1996	3.00
—A-side with Me'Shell NdegeOcello			
WARNER BROS.			
❑ 8683	I'm Every Woman/Woman in a Man's World	1978	5.00
—Tan label			
❑ 8683	I'm Every Woman/Woman in a Man's World	1978	8.00
—"Burbank" palm trees label			
❑ 8683 [PS]	I'm Every Woman/Woman in a Man's World	1978	5.00
❑ 8740	Life Is a Dance/Some Love	1979	4.00
❑ 22913	Soul Talkin'/I'm Every Woman	1989	3.00
❑ 27541	Baby Me/Everybody Needs Some Love	1989	3.00
❑ 27678	It's My Party/Where Are You Tonite	1988	3.00
❑ 27678 [PS]	It's My Party/Where Are You Tonite	1988	3.00
❑ 28459	Earth to Mickey/My Destiny	1987	3.00
❑ 28576	Tight Fit/Who's It Gonna Be	1986	3.00
❑ 28576 [PS]	Tight Fit/Who's It Gonna Be	1986	3.00
❑ 28671	Love of a Lifetime/Coltrane Dreams	1986	3.00
❑ 28671 [PS]	Love of a Lifetime/Coltrane Dreams	1986	3.00
❑ 28923	(Krush Groove) Can't Stop the Street/(Instrumental)	1985	3.00
❑ 28923 [PS]	(Krush Groove) Can't Stop the Street/(Instrumental)	1985	3.00
❑ 29025	Through the Fire/La Flamme	1985	3.00
❑ 29097	This Is My Night/Caught in the Act	1985	3.00
❑ 29097 [PS]	This Is My Night/Caught in the Act	1985	3.00
❑ 29195	I Feel for You/Chinatown	1984	4.00
❑ 29195 [PS]	I Feel for You/Chinatown	1984	4.00
❑ 29745	Tearin' It Up/So Not to Worry	1983	4.00
❑ 29881	Got to Be There/Pass It On, A Sure Thing	1982	4.00
❑ 49216	Clouds/What You Did	1980	4.00
❑ 49256	Papillon (AKA Hot Butterfly)/Too Much Love	1980	4.00
❑ 49571	Get Ready, Get Set/So Naughty	1980	4.00
❑ 49692	What Cha' Gonna Do for Me/Lover's Touch	1981	4.00
❑ 49759	We Can Work It Out/Only Once	1981	4.00
❑ 49804	Any Old Sunday/Heed the Warning	1981	4.00
❑ 49847	And the Melody Still Lingers On/I Know You, I Live You	1981	4.00
Albums			
REPRISE			
❑ PRO-A-8478 [DJ]	Epiphany: The Best of Chaka Khan Sampler	1996	15.00
—Promo-only six-song sampler			
WARNER BROS.			
❑ BSK 3245	Chaka	1978	10.00
❑ BSK 3385	Naughty	1980	10.00
❑ HS 3526	What Cha' Gonna Do for Me	1981	10.00
❑ 23729	Chaka Khan	1982	10.00
❑ 25162	I Feel for You	1984	10.00
❑ 25425	Destiny	1986	10.00
❑ 25707	C.K.	1988	10.00
❑ 25946 [(2)]	Life Is a Dance: The Remix Project	1989	15.00

KHAZAD DOOM

Number	Title (A Side/B Side)	Yr	NM
Albums			
LPL			
❑ 892	Level 6 1/2	1970	1000.

KICKSTANDS, THE

Number	Title (A Side/B Side)	Yr	NM
Albums			
CAPITOL			
❑ ST 2078 [S]	Black Boots and Bikes	1964	150.00
❑ T 2078 [M]	Black Boots and Bikes	1964	120.00
❑ T/ST 2078	Black Boots and Bikes Bonus Fold-Out	1964	50.00

KID, THE

Number	Title (A Side/B Side)	Yr	NM
45s			
RUMBLE			
❑ 1347	Sleep Tight/True Love	1959	180.00

KID ROCK

Number	Title (A Side/B Side)	Yr	NM
12-Inch Singles			
ATLANTIC			
❑ DMD 2550 [DJ]	Cowboy (Neptune's Remix Radio Edit 4:41) (Neptune's Remix Instrumental 4:35) (Neptune's Remix Acapella 4:41)	1999	12.00
CONTINUUM			
❑ 12205	U Don't Know Me (Funk Mix) (Beyond the Door Mix) (Cali Boy Mix) (Cali Boy Instrumental)	1993	15.00
❑ 19255	Back from the Dead (Radio Edit) (Instrumental) (Acappella) (Extended Mix)	1992	20.00
JIVE			
❑ 1349-1-JD	Yo-Da-Lin in the Valley (Time 2 Lick Mix)/Wax the Booty (Wax On Mix)//Pimp The Nation/Yo-Da-Lin in the Valley (Instrumuffled Mix)	1990	15.00
—Title on sleeve is "Triple Maxi Pad"			
45s			
ATLANTIC			
❑ 84705	Bawitdaba/Cowboy	2000	3.00
❑ 84708	Only God Knows Why/American Bad Ass	2000	3.00
❑ 85300	Forever/Lonely Road of Faith	2002	3.00
CONTINUUM			
❑ 15205	Fire It Up//I Am the Bullgod/My Oedipus Complex	1992	15.00
—Orange vinyl			
❑ 15205 [PS]	Fire It Up//I Am the Bullgod/My Oedipus Complex	1992	15.00
Albums			
ATLANTIC			
❑ 83119 [(2)]	Devil Without a Cause	1999	20.00
❑ 83314 [(2)]	The History of Rock	2000	20.00
❑ 83482 [(2)]	Cocky	2001	20.00
❑ 83685 [(2)]	Kid Rock	2003	15.00
JIVE			
❑ 1409-1	Grits Sandwiches for Breakfast	1990	20.00

KIDD, JOHNNY, AND THE PIRATES

Number	Title (A Side/B Side)	Yr	NM
45s			
APT			
❑ 25040	Shakin' All Over/Yes Sir, That's My Baby	1960	25.00
CAPITOL			
❑ 5065	I'll Never Get Over You/Then I Got Everything	1963	15.00

KIDDS, THE

Number	Title (A Side/B Side)	Yr	NM
45s			
IMPERIAL			
❑ 5335	Are You Forgetting Me/Drunk, Drunk, Drunk	1955	500.00
POST			
❑ 2003	You Broke My Heart/I Won't Be Back	1955	300.00

KIDS NEXT DOOR, THE

Number	Title (A Side/B Side)	Yr	NM
45s			
DECCA			
❑ 32157	The Devil Rides in Jericho/Hold Me, Now and Forever	1967	8.00
4 CORNERS OF THE WORLD			
❑ 129	Inky Dinky Spider (The Spider Song)/Goodbye, Don't Cry (Fare Thee Well)	1965	8.00
❑ 129 [PS]	Inky Dinky Spider (The Spider Song)/Goodbye, Don't Cry (Fare Thee Well)	1965	12.00

KILGORE, MERLE

Number	Title (A Side/B Side)	Yr	NM
45s			
ASHLEY			
❑ 6000	Packing an Unpacking/Beyond My Conscience and the Door	1968	10.00
❑ 35007	That's Alright/God Bless the Working Man	197?	7.00
COLUMBIA			
❑ 4-44279	Fast Talking Louisiana Man/Avenue of Tears	1967	10.00
❑ 4-44463	Patches (Made the Change)/Wild Rose	1968	10.00
D			
❑ 1042	It'll Be My First Time/I Take a Trip to the Moon	1959	20.00
ELEKTRA			
❑ 47252	Mister Garfield/I'm a One Woman Man	1981	5.00
❑ 69895	The Night They Drove Old Dixie Down/She Went a Little Bit Farther	1982	5.00
EPIC			
❑ 5-9762	Every Day's a Holiday/It's All Over Now	1965	12.00
❑ 5-9816	Dig, Dig, Dig, Dig (There's No More)/Help Me Up Darling (All Fools Fall Down)	1965	12.00
❑ 5-9873	Baby, I Got It/Mama's Killing Daddy	1965	12.00
❑ 5-10049	Nevada Smith/Too Many Mountains	1966	12.00
❑ 5-10146	I Just Don't Care Anymore/I'd Cry Like a Baby	1967	12.00
IMPERIAL			
❑ 5379	Please, Please, Please/Teen-Ager's Holiday	1956	30.00
❑ 5409	Ernie/Trying to Find (Someone Like You)	1956	60.00
❑ 5555	Tom Dooley, Jr./Hang Doll	1958	20.00
❑ 5584	Start All Over Again/Static	1959	20.00
❑ 8256	More and More/What Makes Me Love You	1954	40.00
❑ 8266	Seeing Double, Feeling Single/It Can't Rain	1954	40.00
❑ 8300	Everybody Needs a Little Lovin'/Funny Feelin'	1955	50.00
MERCURY			
❑ 71839	Wicked City/I'll Take Ginger and Run Away	1961	20.00
❑ 71918	42 in Chicago/Lover's Hell	1962	20.00
❑ 71978	A Girl Named Liz/Trouble at the Towers	1962	20.00
❑ 72048	Ain't Nothin' but a Man/Somethin' Goin' On	1962	20.00
MGM			
❑ 13168	Five Miles Down the Road/Whiskey Road	1963	15.00
❑ 13277	The Bell Witch/Slow Hard Way	1964	15.00

K

Number	Title (A Side/B Side)	Yr	NM
PARKWAY			
❑ 864	I Am/When It Rains the Blues on You	1963	15.00
STARDAY			
❑ 469	Dear Mama/Jimmie Brings Sunshine	1959	20.00
❑ 497	Love Has Made You Beautiful/ Gettin' Old Before My Time	1960	20.00
❑ 533	Daddy's Place/Just Another Song Now	1961	20.00
❑ 644	Pinball Machine/Old Smokey	1963	15.00
❑ 964	Different Kind of Pretty/ My Side of Life	1973	8.00
WARNER BROS.			
❑ 7831	Montgomery Mable/Old Home Filler-Up An' Keep On-a Truckin' Cafe	1974	5.00
❑ 8039	Love o' Love/Baby's Comin' Home to Stay	1974	5.00
❑ 8081	I'm Not Responsible/Tied	1975	5.00
❑ 29062	Guilty/When You Leave That Way You Can Never Go Back	1985	4.00
❑ 29267	Just Out of Reach/Road Women	1984	4.00
Albums			
STARDAY			
❑ SLP-251 [M]	There's Gold in Them Thar Hills	1963	30.00
WING			
❑ MGW-12316 [M]	Tall Texan	196?	15.00
❑ SRW-16316 [S]	Tall Texan	196?	12.00
KILGORE, THEOLA			
45s			
CANDIX			
❑ 311	The Sound of My Man/ Later I'll Cry	1960	25.00
KT			
❑ 501	I'll Keep Trying/He's Coming Back to Me	1964	15.00
MERCURY			
❑ 72564	I Can't Stand It/It's Gonna Be Alright	1966	12.00
SCEPTER			
❑ 12170	The Love of My Man/ As Long As You Need Me	1966	12.00
SEROCK			
❑ 2004	The Love of My Man/ I Know That He Loves Me	1963	15.00
❑ 2006	This Is My Prayer/As Long As You Need Me (Want Me, Love Me)	1963	15.00
KILLEBREW, GEORGE			
45s			
HIT			
❑ 27	She's Not You/Sheila	1962	8.00
—B-side by Sandy Gold			
❑ 46	Half Heaven Half Heartache/I'm Gonna Be Warm This Winter	1962	8.00
—B-side by Connie Landers			
KILLING FLOOR			
Albums			
SIRE			
❑ SES-97019	Killing Floor	1970	60.00
KIM, ANDY			
45s			
CAPITOL			
❑ 3895	Rock Me Gently/Rock Me Gently (Part 2)	1974	5.00
❑ 3962	Fire, Baby, I'm on Fire/ Here Comes the Mornin'	1974	4.00
❑ 3962 [PS]	Fire, Baby, I'm on Fire/ Here Comes the Mornin'	1974	6.00
❑ 4032	Hang Up Those Rock 'N' Roll Shoes/Essence of Joan	1975	4.00
❑ 4086	Mary Ann/You Are My Everything	1975	4.00
❑ 4130	(She Got Me) Dancin'/Baby, You're All I Got	1975	4.00
❑ 4234	Oh, Pretty Woman/ Baby You're All I Got	1976	4.00
RED BIRD			
❑ 10-040	I Hear You Say (I Love You Baby)/Falling in Love	1965	15.00
STEED			
❑ 707	How'd We Ever Get This Way/ Are You Ever Coming Home	1968	8.00
❑ 710	Shoot 'Em Up Baby/ Ordinary Kind of Girl	1968	8.00
❑ 711	Rainbow Ride/Resurrection	1968	8.00
❑ 715	Foundation of My Soul/Tricia Tell Your Daddy	1969	8.00
❑ 716	Baby I Love You/Gee Girl	1969	8.00
❑ 720	So Good Together/I Got to Know	1969	6.00
❑ 720 [PS]	So Good Together/I Got to Know	1969	12.00
❑ 723	A Friend in the City/You	1970	6.00
❑ 723 [PS]	A Friend in the City/You	1970	12.00
❑ 727	It's Your Life/ To Be Continued	1970	6.00
❑ 729	Be My Baby/Love That Little Woman	1970	6.00
❑ 731	I Wish I Were/ Walking My La De La	1971	6.00
❑ 734	I Been Moved/If I Had You Here	1971	6.00
❑ 734 [PS]	I Been Moved/If I Had You Here	1971	12.00
TCF			
❑ 5	Give Me Your Love/Li'l Liz (I Love You)	1964	15.00
20TH CENTURY FOX			
❑ 6709	Give Me Your Love/That Girl	1968	8.00
UNI			
❑ 55332	Who Has the Answers?/ Shady Hollow Dreamers	1972	5.00
❑ 55353	Love Song/Love the Poor Boy	1972	5.00
❑ 55356	Oh What a Day/Sunshine	1972	5.00
UNITED ARTISTS			
❑ 591	Love Me, Love Me/ I Loved You Once	1963	15.00
Albums			
ABC DUNHILL			
❑ DSDP-50193	Andy Kim's Greatest Hits	1974	12.00
—Reissue of Steed 37008			
CAPITOL			
❑ ST-11318	Andy Kim	1974	12.00
❑ ST-11368	The Pilot	1975	12.00
STEED			
❑ ST-7001 [M]	How Did We Ever Get This Way?	1968	40.00
—In stereo cover with "Monaural" sticker			
❑ STS-37001 [S]	How Did We Ever Get This Way?	1968	15.00
❑ STS-37002	Rainbow Ride	1969	15.00
❑ ST 37004	Baby I Love You	1969	15.00
❑ ST 37008	Andy Kim's Greatest Hits	1970	15.00
UNI			
❑ 73137	Andy Kim	1972	12.00
KIMBERLY, ADRIAN Actually DON EVERLY.			
45s			
CALLIOPE			
❑ 6501	The Graduation Song...Pomp and Circumstance/ Black Mountain Stomp	1961	40.00
❑ 6503	Greensleeves/God Bless America	1961	40.00
❑ 6504	When You Wish Upon a Star/ Draggin' Dragon	1961	40.00
KIMBERLYS, THE			
45s			
CANADIAN AMERICAN			
❑ 138	Kimberly/Once	1962	10.00
❑ 147	Save Me a Kiss at Your Wedding/You Just Smiled	1962	10.00
❑ 154	Since the Word Got Around/ One Room Flat	1963	10.00
❑ 160	Forever/I Won't Be Back This Year	1963	10.00
COLUMBIA			
❑ 4-43287	You Can't Roller Skate in a Buffalo Herd/Four Long Seasons	1965	10.00
❑ 4-43399	Denver/Pretty Little Children	1965	10.00
❑ 4-43601	Soldiers and Lilies/ Don't Send Me Away	1965	10.00
❑ 4-44403	I Never Will Marry/ Early Morning Sun	1967	8.00
HAPPY TIGER			
❑ 535	Elusive Butterfly/ Take Me with You	1970	7.00
❑ 547	Family/Leavin' California	1970	7.00
❑ 548	Let It Be/Hello and Happy Birthday	1970	7.00
—As "Verna and the Kimberlys"			
❑ 561	And I Love Her/Sal's Got a Sugar Lip	1970	7.00
❑ 572	I Don't Know How to Love Him-Everything's Alright/ Hello and Happy Birthday	1971	7.00
❑ 577	Any Way That You Want Me/ Sunny Day Blues	1971	7.00
RCA VICTOR			
❑ 47-9782	Drivin' Nails in the Wall/ These New Changing Times	1969	8.00
Albums			
HAPPY TIGER			
❑ HT-1006	The Kimberlys	1970	15.00
❑ HT-1014	New Horizon	1970	15.00
KIME, WARREN, AND HIS BRASS IMPACT ORCHESTRA			
45s			
COMMAND			
❑ 4093	The Breeze and I/Mas Que Nada	1967	5.00
❑ 4106	Feeling Good/No Moon at All	1967	5.00
❑ 4118	Let's Get Away From It All/On My Mind	1968	5.00
Albums			
COMMAND			
❑ 33-910 [M]	Brass Impact	1967	10.00
❑ SD-910 [S]	Brass Impact	1967	12.00
❑ 33-919 [M]	Explosive Brass Impact	1967	10.00
❑ SD-919 [S]	Explosive Brass Impact	1967	12.00
KING, ALBERT			
45s			
ATLANTIC			
❑ 2604	The Hunter/As the Years Go Passing By	1969	8.00
BOBBIN			
❑ 114	Why Are You So Mean to Me/ Ooh-Ee Baby	1959	25.00
❑ 119	Need You By My Side/ The Time Has Come	1960	25.00
❑ 126	Blues at Sunrise/Let's Have a Natural Ball	1960	25.00
❑ 129	I Walked All Night Long/ I've Made Nights By Myself	1961	25.00
❑ 130	Travelin' to California/Dyna-Flow	1961	25.00
❑ 131	Don't Thow Your Love on Me So Strong/This Morning	1961	25.00
❑ 135	I Get Evil/What Can I Do to Change Your Mind	1962	25.00
❑ 141	I'll Do Anything for You/Got to Be Some Changes Made	1963	25.00
❑ 143	Old Blue Ribbon/I've Made Nights By Myself	1963	25.00
KING			
❑ 5575	Don't Throw Your Love on Me So Strong/This Morning	1961	12.00
❑ 5588	Travelin' to California/Dyna-Flow	1961	12.00
❑ 5751	This Funny Feeling/Had You Told It Like It Was	1963	12.00
❑ 6265	Travelin' to California/ Don't Throw Your Love on Me So Strong	1969	8.00
PARROT			
❑ 798	Bad Luck Blues/Be On Your Merry Way	1954	1200.
STAX			
❑ 0020	Night Stomp/Blues Power	1968	8.00
❑ 0034	Drowning on Dry Land (Vocal)/ (Instrumental)	1969	8.00
❑ 0058	Wrapped Up in Love Again/ Cockroach	1969	8.00
❑ 0069	Can't You See What You're Doing to Me/Cold Sweat	1970	8.00
❑ 0101	Everybody Wants to Go to Heaven/Lovejoy, Ill.	1971	7.00
❑ 0121	Angel of Mercy/Funky London	1972	7.00
❑ 0135	I'll Play the Blues for You (Part 1)/ I'll Play the Blues for You (Part 2)	1972	7.00
❑ 0147	Breaking Up Somebody's Home/Little Brother	1972	7.00
❑ 0166	The High Cost of Loving/ Playing on Me	1973	7.00
❑ 0189	That's What the Blues Is All About/I Wanna Get Funky	1973	7.00
❑ 190	Laundromat Blues/ Overall Junction	1966	10.00
❑ 197	Funk-Shun/Pretty Woman (Can't Make You Love Me)	1966	10.00
❑ 201	Crosscut Saw/Down Don't Bother Me	1966	10.00
❑ 217	Born Under a Bad Sign/ Personal Manager	1967	10.00
❑ 0217	I Can Hear Nothing But the Blues/Flat Tire	1974	7.00
❑ 0228	Crosscut Saw/Don't Burn Down the Bridge	1974	7.00
❑ 0234	Santa Claus Wants Some Lovin'/ Don't Burn Down the Bridges	1974	7.00
❑ 241	Cold Feet/Drive a Hard Bargain	1967	10.00
❑ 252	(I Love) Lucy/You're Gonna Need Me	1968	10.00

Except when noted otherwise, VG = 25% of NM, and VG+ = 50% of NM. (Example: VG = $2.00, VG+ = $4.00 and NM = $8.00.)

Number	Title (A Side/B Side)	Yr	NM
❑ 1056	Santa Claus Wants Some Lovin'/What Do The Lonely Do At Christmas?	197?	6.00
—B-side by Emotions; reissue			
❑ 1073	Christmas Comes Once A Year/I'll Be Your Santa Claus	197?	5.00
—B-side by Rufus Thomas; reissue			
❑ 3203	The Pinch Paid Off (Part 1)/ The Pinch Paid Off (Part 2)	1978	5.00
❑ 3225	Santa Claus Wants Some Lovin'/ Don't Burn Down the Bridges	1979	6.00

TOMATO

Number	Title (A Side/B Side)	Yr	NM
❑ 10001	Call My Job/Love Shack	1978	5.00
❑ 10002	Chump Change/ Good Time Charlie	1978	5.00
❑ 10009	The Very Thought of You/ I Get Evil	1979	5.00
❑ 10012	Born Under a Bad Sign/ I've Got the Blues	1979	5.00

UTOPIA

Number	Title (A Side/B Side)	Yr	NM
❑ PB-10544	Cadillac Assembly Line/ Nobody Wants a Loser	1976	5.00
❑ PB-10682	Sensation, Communication Together/Gonna Make It Somehow	1976	5.00
❑ PB-10770	Guitar Man/Rub My Back	1976	5.00
❑ PB-10879	Ain't Nothing You Can Do/I Don't Care What My Baby Do	1977	5.00

Albums

ATLANTIC

Number	Title (A Side/B Side)	Yr	NM
❑ SD 8213	King of the Blues Guitar	1969	25.00

FANTASY

Number	Title (A Side/B Side)	Yr	NM
❑ 9627	San Francisco '83	1983	10.00
❑ 9633	I'm in a Phone Booth, Baby	1984	10.00

KING

Number	Title (A Side/B Side)	Yr	NM
❑ 852 [M]	Big Blues	1963	500.00
❑ KS-1060	Travelin' to California	1969	25.00

MODERN BLUES

Number	Title (A Side/B Side)	Yr	NM
❑ MBLP-723	Let's Have a Natural Ball	198?	10.00

STAX

Number	Title (A Side/B Side)	Yr	NM
❑ ST-723 [M]	Born Under a Bad Sign	1967	80.00
❑ STS-723 [S]	Born Under a Bad Sign	1967	120.00
❑ STS-2003	Live Wire/Blues Power	1968	50.00
❑ STS-2010	Years Gone By	1969	25.00
❑ STS-2015	King Does the King's Thing	1969	25.00
❑ STS-2040	Lovejoy	1971	20.00
❑ STS-3009	I'll Play the Blues for You	1972	20.00
❑ STX-4101	The Pinch	1977	12.00
❑ STX-4128	Live Wire/Blues Power	1979	10.00
—Reissue of 2003			
❑ STX-4132	Montreux Festival	1980	10.00
—Retitled reissue of 5520			
❑ STS-5505	I Wanna Get Funky	1974	15.00
❑ STS-5520	Montreux Festival	1975	15.00
❑ MPS-8504	Blues for Elvis	1981	10.00
—Retitled reissue of 2015			
❑ MPS-8513	I'll Play the Blues for You	1981	10.00
—Reissue of 3309			
❑ MPS-8517	Lovejoy	1981	10.00
—Reissue of 2040			
❑ MPS-8522	Years Gone By	1982	10.00
—Reissue of 2010			
❑ MPS-8534	The Lost Session	1986	10.00
❑ MPS-8536	I Wanna Get Funky	1987	10.00
—Reissue of 5505			
❑ MPS-8546	Blues at Sunrise	1988	10.00
❑ MPS-8556	Wednesday Night in San Francisco	1990	10.00
❑ MPS-8557	Tuesday Night in San Francisco	1990	10.00

SUNDAZED

Number	Title (A Side/B Side)	Yr	NM
❑ LP 5031	Born Under a Bad Sign	1999	15.00
—Reissue on 180-gram vinyl			

TOMATO

Number	Title (A Side/B Side)	Yr	NM
❑ TOM-6002	King Albert	1978	12.00
❑ TOM-7022	New Orleans Heat	1979	12.00

UTOPIA

Number	Title (A Side/B Side)	Yr	NM
❑ BUL1-1387	Truckload of Lovin'	1976	12.00
❑ BUL1-1731	Albert	1976	12.00
❑ CUL2-2205 [(2)]	Albert Live	1977	15.00

KING, ALBERT/STEVE CROPPER/POP STAPLES

45s

STAX

Number	Title (A Side/B Side)	Yr	NM
❑ 0047	Tupelo (Part 1)/Tupelo (Part 2)	1969	8.00
❑ 0048	Water/Opus de Soul	1969	8.00

Albums

STAX

Number	Title (A Side/B Side)	Yr	NM
❑ STS-2020	Jammed Together	1969	25.00
❑ MPS-8544	Jammed Together	1988	10.00
—Reissue			

KING, ALBERT/LITTLE MILTON

Albums

STAX

Number	Title (A Side/B Side)	Yr	NM
❑ STX-4123	Chronicle	1979	12.00
—One side devoted to each artist			

KING, ALBERT/OTIS RUSH

Albums

CHESS

Number	Title (A Side/B Side)	Yr	NM
❑ LPS 1538	Door to Door	1969	25.00
❑ CH-9322	Door to Door	1990	10.00
—Reissue			

KING, ANNA

45s

END

Number	Title (A Side/B Side)	Yr	NM
❑ 1126	Mama's Got a Bag of Her Own/ Sally	1963	30.00

LUDIX

Number	Title (A Side/B Side)	Yr	NM
❑ 103	You Don't Love Me Anymore/ Big Change	1963	40.00

SMASH

Number	Title (A Side/B Side)	Yr	NM
❑ 1858	If Somebody Told You/Come and Get These Memories	1963	20.00
❑ 1884	Baby, Baby, Baby/(Instrumental)	1964	20.00
—With Bobby Byrd			
❑ 1904	If You Don't Think/ Make Up Your Mind	1964	20.00
❑ 1942	Come On Home/ Sittin' in the Dark	1964	20.00
❑ 1970	That's When I Cry/ Tennessee Waltz	1965	15.00

Albums

SMASH

Number	Title (A Side/B Side)	Yr	NM
❑ MGS-27059 [M]	Back to Soul	1964	100.00
❑ SRS-67059 [S]	Back to Soul	1964	120.00

KING, B.B. Also see BOBBY BLAND AND B.B. KING.

12-Inch Singles

MCA

Number	Title (A Side/B Side)	Yr	NM
❑ L33-1284 [DJ]	My Lucille (Extended)/ Into the Night	1985	8.00
❑ 2118 [DJ]	The Blues Come Over Me (6 versions)	1991	6.00
❑ L33-17810 [DJ]	Lay Another Log on the Fire/ Go On	1989	6.00
❑ 23831	Habit to Me (LP Version) (TV Mix)	1988	6.00

45s

ABC

Number	Title (A Side/B Side)	Yr	NM
❑ 10856	Don't Answer the Door (Part 1)/ Don't Answer the Door (Part 2)	1966	15.00
❑ 10889	Waitin' on You/Night Life	1966	15.00
❑ 11268	Hummingbird/Ask Me No Questions	1970	8.00
❑ 11280	Chains and Things/ King's Special	1970	8.00
❑ 11290	Ask Me No Questions/Nobody Loves Me But My Mother	1971	8.00
❑ 11302	Help the Poor/Lucille's Granny	1971	8.00
❑ 11310	Ghetto Woman/Seven Minutes	1971	8.00
❑ 11316	Ain't Nobody Home/ Alexi's Boogie	1971	8.00
❑ 11319	Sweet Sixteen/I've Been Blue Too Long	1972	6.00
❑ 11321	I Got Some Help I Don't Need/ Lucille's Granny	1972	6.00
❑ 11330	Guess Who/Better Lovin' Man	1972	6.00
❑ 11339	Summer in the City/ Five Long Years	1972	6.00
❑ 11373	To Know You Is to Love You/ I Can't Leave	1973	6.00
❑ 11406	I Like to Live the Love/Love	1973	6.00
❑ 11433	Who Are You/On to Me	1974	6.00
❑ 12029	Philadelphia/Up at 5 A.M.	1974	6.00
❑ 12053	Friends/My Song	1974	6.00
❑ 12158	When I'm Wrong/Have Faith	1976	6.00
❑ 12247	Slow and Easy/I Wonder Why	1977	6.00
❑ 12380	Never Make a Move Too Soon/ Let Me Make You Cry a Little Longer	1978	6.00
❑ 12412	I Just Can't Leave Your Love Alone/Midnight Believer	1978	6.00

ABC-PARAMOUNT

Number	Title (A Side/B Side)	Yr	NM
❑ 10316	I'm Gonna Sit In Till You Give In/You Ask Me	1962	15.00
❑ 10334	Blues at Midnight/My Baby's Coming Home	1962	15.00
❑ 10361	Chains of Love/Sneakin' Around	1962	15.00
❑ 10367	Tomorrow Night/Mother's Love	1962	15.00
❑ 10390	Guess Who/By Myself	1962	15.00
❑ 10455	On My Word of Honor/ Young Dreamers	1963	15.00
❑ 10486	How Do I Love You/ Slowly Losing My Mind	1963	15.00
❑ 10527	How Blue Can You Get/ Please Accept My Love	1964	15.00
❑ 10552	Help the Poor/I Wouldn't Have It Any Other Way	1964	15.00
❑ 10576	Whole Lotta Lovin'/The Hurt	1964	15.00
❑ 10597	Never Trust a Woman/ Worryin' Blues	1964	15.00
❑ 10616	Please Send Me Someone to Love/The Worst Thing in My Life	1965	15.00
❑ 10634	Everyday I Have the Blues/ It's My Own Fault	1965	15.00
❑ 10675	Tired of Your Jive/Night Owl	1965	15.00
❑ 10724	All Over Again/The Things You Put Me Through	1965	15.00
❑ 10754	Goin' to Chicago Blues/I'd Rather Drink Muddy Water	1965	15.00
❑ 10766	Tormented/You're Still a Square	1966	15.00

BLUESWAY

Number	Title (A Side/B Side)	Yr	NM
❑ 61004	Think It Over/I Don't Want You Cutting Off Your Hair	1967	10.00
❑ 61007	Worried Dream/That's Wrong, Little Mama	1967	10.00
❑ 61011	Raining in My Heart/ Heartbreaker	1967	10.00
❑ 61012	Sweet Sixteen (Part 1)/ Sweet Sixteen (Part 2)	1968	10.00
❑ 61015	Paying the Cost to Be the Boss/ Having My Say	1968	10.00
❑ 61018	I'm Gonna Do What They Do to Me/Losing Faith in You	1968	10.00
❑ 61019	You Put It On Me/B.B. Jones	1968	10.00
❑ 61021	Dance with Me/Please Send Me Someone to Love	1968	10.00
❑ 61022	Don't Waste My Time/Get Myself Somebody	1969	10.00
❑ 61024	Why I Sing the Blues/Friends	1969	10.00
❑ 61026	Get Off My Back Woman/ I Want You So Bad	1969	10.00
❑ 61029	Just a Little Love/My Mood	1969	10.00
❑ 61032	The Thrill Is Gone/You're Mean	1969	12.00
❑ 61032 [PS]	The Thrill Is Gone/You're Mean	1969	20.00
❑ 61035	So Excited/Confessin' the Blues	1970	8.00

KENT

Number	Title (A Side/B Side)	Yr	NM
❑ BB 100-1 [S]	I've Got Papers on You Baby / We Can't Make It	196?	25.00
—Small hole, plays at 33 1/3 rpm			
❑ BB 100-2 [S]	Treat Me Right/I Love You So	196?	25.00
—Small hole, plays at 33 1/3 rpm			
❑ BB 100-3 [S]	You're on the Top/ What Way To Go	196?	25.00
—Small hole, plays at 33 1/3 rpm			
❑ BB 100-4 [S]	Long Nights/ I'll Survive	196?	25.00
—Small hole, plays at 33 1/3 rpm			
❑ BB 100-5 [S]	If I Love You/I'm the King	196?	25.00
—Small hole, plays at 33 1/3 rpm			
❑ 301	You Know I Go for You/Why Do Everything Happen to Me	1958	20.00
❑ 307	Days of Old/Don't Look Now, But You Got the Blues	1958	20.00
❑ 315	Please Accept My Love/ You've Been an Angel	1958	25.00
—With the Vocal Chords			
❑ 317	Worry Worry/I Am	1959	20.00
❑ 319	The Fool/Come By Here	1959	20.00
❑ 325	A Lonely Lover's Plea/ Woman in Love	1959	20.00
❑ 327	Everyday I Have the Blues/ Time to Say Goodbye	1959	20.00
❑ 329	Sugar Mama/Mean Old Friend	1959	20.00
❑ 330	Sweet Sixteen, Pt. 1/ Sweet Sixteen, Pt. 2	1960	20.00
❑ 333	Got a Right to Love My Baby/ My Own Fault	1960	15.00
❑ 336	Please Love Me/Crying Won't Help You	1960	15.00
❑ 337	Blind Love/You Upset Me Baby	1960	15.00
❑ 338	Ten Long Years/Everyday I Have the Blues	1960	15.00
❑ 339	Did You Ever Love a Woman/ Three O'Clock Blues	1960	15.00
❑ 340	Sweet Little Angel/You Done Lost Your Good Thing Now	1960	15.00
❑ 346	Partin' Time/Good Man Gone Bad	1960	15.00
❑ 350	Waking Dr. Bill/You Done Lost Your Good Thing Now	1960	15.00
❑ 351	Things Are Not the Same/ Fishin' After Me	1961	15.00
❑ 353	Bad Luck Soul/Get Out of Here	1961	15.00
❑ 358	Hold That Train/Understand	1961	15.00
❑ 360	Peace of Mind/Someday	1961	15.00
❑ 362	You're Breaking My Heart/ Bad Case of Love	1961	15.00
❑ 365	My Sometime Baby/Lonely	1962	12.00
❑ 372	Gonna Miss You Around Here/ Hully Gully Twist	1962	12.00

K

Number	Title (A Side/B Side)	Yr	NM
❑ 373	3 O'Clock Stomp/ Mashed Potato Twist	1962	12.00
❑ 381	Tell Me Baby/ Mashing the Popeye	1962	12.00
❑ 383	Going Down Slow/When My Heart Beats Like a Hammer	1962	12.00
❑ 386	Your Letter/Blues for Me	1962	12.00
❑ 387	Christmas Celebration/ Easy Listening	1962	12.00
❑ 388	Whole Lot of Loving/Down Now	1963	10.00
❑ 389	Trouble in Mind/Long Nights	1963	10.00
❑ 390	My Reward/The Road I Travel	1963	10.00
❑ 391	The Letter/You Never Know	1963	10.00
❑ 392	Army of the Lord/Precious Lord	1964	15.00
❑ 393	Rock Me Baby/I Can't Lose	1964	10.00
❑ 396	Let Me Love You/You're Gonna Miss Me	1964	10.00
❑ 403	Beautician Blues/I Can Hear My Name	1964	10.00
❑ 412	Christmas Celebration/ Easy Listening	1964	12.00
❑ 415	Got 'Em Bad/The Worst Thing in My Life	1965	12.00
❑ 421	Please Love Me/Baby Look at You	1965	12.00
❑ 426	Blue Shadows/And Like That	1965	12.00
❑ 429	Just a Dream/Why Do Everything Happen to Me	1965	12.00
❑ 435	Mercy, Mercy, Mercy/ Broken Promise	1965	12.00
❑ 441	Eyesight to the Blind/ Just Like a Woman	1966	12.00
❑ 445	Five Long Years/ Love, Honor and Obey	1966	12.00
❑ 447	Ain't Nobody's Business /I Wonder Why	1966	12.00
❑ 450	I Stay in the Mood/ Early Every Morning	1966	12.00
❑ 458	It's a Mean World/ Blues Stay Away	1966	8.00
❑ 462	The Jungle/Long Gone Baby	1967	8.00
❑ 467	Treat Me Right/Who Can Your Good Man Be	1967	8.00
❑ 470	Bad Breaks/Growing Old	1967	8.00
❑ 475	Sweet Thing/Soul Beat	1967	8.00
❑ 484	Worry, Worry, Worry/Why Do Everything Happen to Me	1968	6.00
❑ 492	The Woman I Love/Blues for Me	1968	6.00
❑ 499	Slow Burn/3 O'Clock Blues	1968	6.00
❑ 510	Your Fool/Shoutin' the Blues	1969	6.00
❑ 4513	I'm Cracking Up Over You/ Powerhouse	1969	10.00
❑ 4515	Dreams/House Rocker	1970	10.00
❑ 4526	Worried Life/Walkin' Dr. Bill	1970	10.00
❑ 4542	That Evil Child/Tell Me Baby	1971	8.00
❑ 4549	I'll Survive/Long Nights	1971	8.00
❑ 4562	Precious Lord/Swing Low, Sweet Chariot	1972	8.00
❑ 4566	Don't Get Around Much Anymore/Poontangling	1972	8.00
❑ 4572	Recession Blues/Walkin' Dr. Bill	1972	8.00

MCA

Number	Title (A Side/B Side)	Yr	NM
❑ 41062	Happy Birthday Blues/ Better Not Look Down	1979	4.00
❑ 51101	There Must Be a Better World Somewhere/You're Going with Me	1981	4.00
❑ 52057	Since I Met You Baby/ One of Those Nights	1982	3.00
❑ 52098	Street Life/Overture	1982	3.00
—With the Crusaders and the London Symphony Orchestra			
❑ 52125	Love Me Tender/The World I Never Made	1982	3.00
❑ 52218	Sell My Monkey/Inflation Blues	1983	3.00
❑ 52530	Into the Night/Century City Chase of J.B. in Teheran	1985	3.00
❑ 52530 [PS]	Into the Night/Century City Chase of J.B. in Teheran	1985	3.00
❑ 52574	My Lucille/Keep It Light	1985	3.00
—B-side by Thelma Houston			
❑ 52675	Big Boss Man/My Guitar Sings the Blues	1985	3.00
❑ 52751	Memory Lane/Six Silver Strings	1985	3.00
❑ 53269	(You've Become a) Habit to Me/ (You've Become a) Habit to Me (Long)	1988	3.00
❑ 53644	Lay Another Log on the Fire/ Go On	1989	3.00
❑ 54339	The Blues Come Over Me (Wild & Bluesy Club Mix Edit)/ The Blues Come Over Me (Integrity Mix)	1992	4.00

POINTBLANK

Number	Title (A Side/B Side)	Yr	NM
❑ 58820	Christmas Celebration/ White Christmas	1999	3.00
—B-side by Hadda Brooks			

RPM

Number	Title (A Side/B Side)	Yr	NM
❑ 339	3 O'Clock Blues/That Ain't the Way to Do It	1951	900.00
—B.B. King singles on RPM before 339 are unconfirmed on 45 rpm			
❑ 348	Fine Lookin' Woman/She Don't Move Me No More	1952	300.00
❑ 355	Shake It Up and Go/ My Own Fault, Darling	1952	150.00
❑ 360	Gotta Find My Baby/ Someday Somewhere	1952	100.00
❑ 363	You Know I Love You/ You Didn't Want Me	1952	80.00
❑ 374	Story from My Heart and Soul/ Boogie Woogie Woman	1952	150.00
❑ 380	Woke Up This Morning (My Baby She Was Gone)/ Don't Have to Cry	1953	100.00
❑ 386	Please Love Me/Highway Bound	1953	150.00
❑ 391	Please Hurry Home/ Neighborhood Affair	1953	80.00
❑ 395	Why Did You Leave Me/ Blind Love	1953	80.00
❑ 403	Praying to the Lord/ Please Help Me	1954	30.00
❑ 408	Love Me Baby/The Woman I Love	1954	30.00
❑ 411	Everything I Do Is Wrong/Don't You Want a Man Like Me	1954	30.00
❑ 412	When My Heart Beats Like a Hammer/Bye Bye Baby	1954	30.00
❑ 416	You Upset Me Baby/Whole Lotta' Love	1954	30.00
❑ 421	Every Day I Have the Blues/ Sneakin' Around	1955	30.00
❑ 425	Lonely and Blue/Jump with You Baby	1955	30.00
❑ 430	I'm in Love/Shut Your Mouth	1955	30.00
❑ 435	Talkin' the Blues/Boogie Rock	1955	30.00
❑ 437	Ten Long Years/What Can I Do	1955	30.00
❑ 450	I'm Cracking Up Over You/ Ruby Lee	1956	25.00
❑ 451	Crying Won't Help You/ Can't We Talk It Over	1956	25.00
❑ 451	Crying Won't Help You/ Sixteen Tons	1956	25.00
❑ 457	Did You Ever Love a Woman/ Let's Do the Boogie	1956	25.00
❑ 459	Dark Is the Night (Part 1)/ Dark Is the Night (Part 2)	1956	25.00
❑ 468	Bad Luck/Sweet Little Angel	1956	25.00
❑ 479	On My Word of Honor/Bim Bam	1956	25.00
❑ 486	You Don't Know/ Early in the Morning	1957	25.00
❑ 490	How Do I Love You/ You Can't Fool My Heart	1957	25.00
❑ 492	Troubles, Troubles, Troubles/ I Want to Get Married	1957	25.00
❑ 494	Quit My Baby/Be Careful with a Fool	1957	25.00
❑ 498	I Wonder/I Need You So Bad	1957	25.00
❑ 501	The Key to My Kingdom/My Heart Belongs to Only You	1957	25.00

7-Inch Extended Plays

ABC

Number	Title (A Side/B Side)	Yr	NM
❑ LP-ABCS-528	See See Rider/I'd Rather Drink Muddy Water/Confessin' the Blues//Goin' to Chicago Blues/I'm Gonna Move to the Outskirts of Town/How Long, How Long Blues	1966	25.00
—Jukebox issue; small hole, plays at 33 1/3 rpm			
❑ LP-ABCS-528 [PS]	Confessin' the Blues	1966	25.00

ABC-PARAMOUNT

Number	Title (A Side/B Side)	Yr	NM
❑ LP-ABCS-456	Young Dreamers/By My Self/ Chains of Love//On My Word of Honor/Tomorrow Night/My Baby's Comin' Home	1963	25.00
—Jukebox issue; small hole, plays at 33 1/3 rpm			
❑ LP-ABCS-456 [PS]	Mr. Blues	1963	25.00

BLUESWAY

Number	Title (A Side/B Side)	Yr	NM
❑ LP-BLS-6016	You Move Me So/No Money No Luck/I Need Your Love//Rainin' All the Time/I'm with You/Stop Putting the Hurt on Me	1968	25.00
—Jukebox issue; small hole, plays at 33 1/3 rpm			
❑ LP-BLS-6016 [PS]	Lucille	1968	25.00

Albums

ABC

Number	Title (A Side/B Side)	Yr	NM
❑ D-704	Blues Is King	1970	12.00
—Reissue of BluesWay 6001			
❑ D-709	Blues on Top of Blues	1970	12.00
—Reissue of BluesWay 6011			
❑ D-712	Lucille	1970	12.00
—Reissue of BluesWay 6016			
❑ D-713	Indianola Mississippi Seeds	1970	12.00
❑ D-723	Live in Cook County Jail	1971	12.00
❑ D-724	Live at the Regal	1971	12.00
—Reissue of ABC-Paramount 509			
❑ D-730	B.B. King in London	1971	12.00
❑ D-743	L.A. Midnight	1972	12.00
❑ X-759	Guess Who	1972	12.00
❑ X-767	The Best of B.B. King	1973	12.00
❑ X-794	To Know You Is to Love You	1973	12.00
❑ D-813	His Best/The Electric B.B. King	1974	12.00
—Reissue of BluesWay 6022			
❑ D-819	Live and Well	1974	12.00
—Reissue of BluesWay 6031			
❑ D-825	Friends	1974	12.00
❑ D-868	Completely Well	1975	12.00
—Reissue of BluesWay 6037			
❑ D-878	Back in the Alley	1975	12.00
—Reissue of BluesWay 6050			
❑ D-898	Lucille Talks Back	1975	12.00
❑ AB-977	King Size	1977	12.00
❑ AA-1061	Midnight Believer	1978	12.00

ABC-PARAMOUNT

Number	Title (A Side/B Side)	Yr	NM
❑ 456 [M]	Mr. Blues	1963	30.00
❑ S-456 [S]	Mr. Blues	1963	40.00
❑ 509 [M]	Live at the Regal	1965	40.00
❑ S-509 [S]	Live at the Regal	1965	50.00
❑ 528 [M]	Confessin' the Blues	1965	30.00
❑ S-528 [S]	Confessin' the Blues	1965	40.00

BLUESWAY

Number	Title (A Side/B Side)	Yr	NM
❑ BL-6001 [M]	Blues Is King	1967	40.00
❑ BLS-6001 [S]	Blues Is King	1967	25.00
❑ BL-6011 [M]	Blues on Top of Blues	1968	50.00
—Mono is white label promo only			
❑ BLS-6011 [S]	Blues on Top of Blues	1968	25.00
❑ BLS-6016	Lucille	1968	25.00
❑ BLS-6022	His Best/The Electric B.B. King	1969	20.00
❑ BLS-6031	Live and Well	1969	20.00
❑ BLS-6037	Completely Well	1969	20.00
❑ BLS-6050	Back in the Alley	1970	20.00

COMMAND

Number	Title (A Side/B Side)	Yr	NM
❑ CQD-40022 [Q]	Friends	1974	20.00

CROWN

Number	Title (A Side/B Side)	Yr	NM
❑ CST-147 [R]	B.B. King Wails	1960	12.00
—Black vinyl			
❑ CST-147 [R]	B.B. King Wails	1960	100.00
—Red vinyl			
❑ CST-152 [R]	B.B. King Sings Spirituals	1960	12.00
—Black vinyl			
❑ CST-152 [R]	B.B. King Sings Spirituals	1960	100.00
—Red vinyl			
❑ CST-195 [S]	King of the Blues	1961	20.00
—Black vinyl; this album is in true stereo, contrary to prior reports			
❑ CST-195 [S]	King of the Blues	1961	120.00
—Red vinyl; this album is in true stereo, contrary to prior reports			
❑ CST-309 [R]	Blues in My Heart	1963	12.00
❑ CST-359 [P]	B.B. King	1963	12.00
—Half of the album is in stereo, half is rechanneled			
❑ CLP-5020 [M]	Singin' the Blues	1957	100.00
—Black label, silver "Crown"			
❑ CLP-5020 [M]	Singin' the Blues	196?	12.00
—Black label, multi-color "Crown"			
❑ CLP-5020 [M]	Singin' the Blues	1963	20.00
—Gray label, black "Crown"			
❑ CLP-5063 [M]	The Blues	1958	80.00
—Black label, silver "Crown"			
❑ CLP-5063 [M]	The Blues	196?	12.00
—Black label, multi-color "Crown"			
❑ CLP-5063 [M]	The Blues	1963	20.00
—Gray label, black "Crown"			
❑ CLP-5115 [M]	B.B. King Wails	1959	80.00
—Black label, silver "Crown"			
❑ CLP-5115 [M]	B.B. King Wails	196?	12.00
—Black label, multi-color "Crown"			
❑ CLP-5115 [M]	B.B. King Wails	1963	20.00
—Gray label, black "Crown"			
❑ CLP-5119 [M]	B.B. King Sings Spirituals	196?	12.00
—Black label, multi-color "Crown"			
❑ CLP-5119 [M]	B.B. King Sings Spirituals	1960	60.00
—Gray label, black "Crown"			
❑ CLP-5143 [M]	The Great B.B. King	196?	12.00
—Black label, multi-color "Crown"			
❑ CLP-5143 [M]	The Great B.B. King	1961	60.00
—Gray label, black "Crown"			
❑ CLP-5167 [M]	King of the Blues	196?	12.00
—Black label, multi-color "Crown"			
❑ CLP-5167 [M]	King of the Blues	1961	60.00
—Gray label, black "Crown"			
❑ CLP-5188 [M]	My Kind of Blues	196?	12.00
—Black label, multi-color "Crown"			
❑ CLP-5188 [M]	My Kind of Blues	1961	60.00
—Gray label, black "Crown"			
❑ CLP-5230 [M]	More B.B. King	196?	12.00
—Black label, multi-color "Crown"			
❑ CLP-5230 [M]	More B.B. King	1962	60.00
—Gray label, black "Crown"			
❑ CLP-5248 [M]	Twist with B.B. King	196?	12.00
—Black label, multi-color "Crown"			
❑ CLP-5248 [M]	Twist with B.B. King	1962	60.00
—Gray label, black "Crown"			

Number	Title (A Side/B Side)	Yr	NM
❑ CLP-5286 [M]	Easy Listening Blues	196?	12.00
—Black label, multi-color "Crown"			
❑ CLP-5286 [M]	Easy Listening Blues	1962	60.00
—Gray label, black "Crown"			
❑ CLP-5309 [M]	Blues in My Heart	196?	12.00
—Black label, multi-color "Crown"			
❑ CLP-5309 [M]	Blues in My Heart	1963	40.00
—Gray label, black "Crown"			
❑ CLP-5359 [M]	B.B. King	196?	12.00
—Black label, multi-color "Crown"			
❑ CLP-5359 [M]	B.B. King	1963	40.00
—Gray label, black "Crown"			
CRUSADERS			
❑ 16013	Live in London	1982	25.00
—Part of MCA's "Audiophile Series"			
CUSTOM			
❑ CM-2046 [M]	Blues for Me	196?	12.00
❑ CM-2049 [M]	I Love You So	196?	12.00
❑ CM-2052 [M]	The Soul of B.B. King	196?	12.00
DIRECT DISK			
❑ SD-16616	Midnight Believer	1980	50.00
—Audiophile vinyl			
GALAXY			
❑ 202 [M]	16 Greatest Hits	1963	60.00
❑ 8202 [S]	16 Greatest Hits	1963	80.00
GRP			
❑ GR-9637	Live at the Apollo	1991	15.00
KENT			
❑ KST-512 [R]	Rock Me Baby	1964	15.00
❑ KST-513 [R]	Let Me Love You	1965	15.00
❑ KST-515 [R]	B.B. King Live on Stage	1965	15.00
❑ KST-516 [R]	The Soul of B.B. King	1966	15.00
❑ KST-517 [R]	Pure Soul	1966	15.00
❑ KST-521 [R]	The Jungle	1967	15.00
❑ KST-529 [R]	Boss of the Blues	1968	15.00
❑ KST-533 [(2)]	From the Beginning	1969	20.00
❑ KST-535	Underground Blues	1969	15.00
❑ KST-539	The Incredible Soul of B.B. King	1970	15.00
❑ KST-548	Turn On to B.B. King	1970	15.00
❑ KST-552	Greatest Hits, Vol. 1	1971	15.00
❑ KST-561	Better Than Ever	1971	15.00
❑ KST-563	Doing My Thing, Lord	1971	15.00
❑ KST-565	B.B. King Live	1972	15.00
❑ KST-568	The Original Sweet Sixteen	1972	15.00
❑ KLP-2008	Incredible Soul of B.B. King	1987	12.00
❑ KLP-5012 [M]	Rock Me Baby	1964	20.00
❑ KLP-5013 [M]	Let Me Love You	1965	20.00
❑ KLP-5015 [M]	B.B. King Live on Stage	1965	20.00
❑ KLP-5016 [M]	The Soul of B.B. King	1966	20.00
❑ KLP-5017 [M]	Pure Soul	1966	20.00
❑ KLP-5021 [M]	The Jungle	1967	20.00
❑ KLP-5029 [M]	Boss of the Blues	1968	20.00
MCA			
❑ 3151	Take It Home	1979	10.00
❑ 5162	There Must Be a Better World Somewhere	1981	10.00
❑ 5307	Love Me Tender	1982	10.00
❑ 5413	Blues 'N' Jazz	1983	10.00
❑ 5616	Six Silver Strings	1985	10.00
❑ 6455	Live at San Quentin	1990	12.00
❑ 2-8016 [(2)]	"Now Appearing" at Ole Miss	1980	12.00
❑ 27005	Live in Cook County Jail	1980	8.00
—Reissue of ABC 723			
❑ 27006	Live at the Regal	1980	8.00
—Reissue of ABC 724			
❑ 27007	His Best/The Electric B.B. King	1980	8.00
—Reissue of ABC 813			
❑ 27008	Live and Well	1980	8.00
—Reissue of ABC 819			
❑ 27009	Completely Well	1980	8.00
—Reissue of ABC 868			
❑ 27010	Back in the Alley	1980	8.00
—Reissue of ABC 878			
❑ 27011	Midnight Believer	1980	8.00
—Reissue of ABC 1061			
❑ 27028	Take It Home	1981	8.00
—Reissue of MCA 3151			
❑ 27034	There Must Be a Better World Somewhere	1983	8.00
—Reissue of MCA 5162			
❑ 27074	The Best of B.B. King	1984	8.00
—Reissue of ABC 767			
❑ 42183	The King of the Blues: 1989	1989	10.00
MCA IMPULSE!			
❑ MCA2-4124 [(2)]	Great Moments with B.B. King	1981	12.00
MOBILE FIDELITY			
❑ 1-235	Lucille	1995	50.00
—Audiophile vinyl			
PICKWICK			
❑ SPC-3593	Live at the Regal	197?	8.00
❑ SPC-3654	Live in Cook County Jail	197?	8.00
STAX			
❑ ORS-4508	16 Original Big Hits	198?	8.00

Number	Title (A Side/B Side)	Yr	NM
UNITED			
❑ US-7703	Heart Full of Blues	197?	8.00
❑ US-7705	Easy Listening Blues	197?	8.00
—Reissue of Crown 5286			
❑ US-7708	Blues for Me	197?	8.00
—Reissue of Custom 2046			
❑ US-7711	I Love You So	197?	8.00
—Reissue of Custom 2049			
❑ US-7714	The Soul of B.B. King	197?	8.00
—Reissue of Custom 2052			
❑ US-7721	Swing Low	197?	8.00
❑ US-7724	My Kind of Blues	197?	8.00
—Reissue of Crown 5188			
❑ US-7726	Singin' the Blues	197?	8.00
—Reissue of Crown 5020			
❑ US-7728	The Great B.B. King	197?	8.00
—Reissue of Crown 5143			
❑ US-7732	The Blues	197?	8.00
—Reissue of Crown 5063			
❑ US-7733	Rock Me, Baby	197?	8.00
—Reissue of Kent 5012			
❑ US-7734	Let Me Love You	197?	8.00
—Reissue of Kent 513			
❑ US-7736	B.B. King Live on Stage	197?	8.00
—Reissue of Kent 515			
❑ US-7742	The Jungle	197?	8.00
—Reissue of Kent 521			
❑ US-7750	Boss of the Blues	197?	8.00
—Reissue of Kent 529			
❑ US-7756	The Incredible Soul of B.B. King	197?	8.00
—Reissue of Kent 539			
❑ US-7763	Turn On with B.B. King	197?	8.00
—Reissue of Kent 548			
❑ US-7766	Greatest Hits, Vol. 1	197?	8.00
—Reissue of Kent 552			
❑ US-7773	The Original Sweet Sixteen	197?	8.00
—Reissue of Kent 568			
❑ US-7788	9 x 9	197?	8.00

KING, B.B./ERIC CLAPTON Also see each artist's individual listings.

45s

Number	Title (A Side/B Side)	Yr	NM
REPRISE			
❑ 7-16831	Riding with the King/Key to the Highway	2000	3.00
❑ 7-16832	Worried Life Blues/Days of Old	2000	3.00
❑ 7-16833	Marry You/Three O'Clock Blues (Edit)	2000	3.00
❑ 7-16834	When My Heart Beats Like a Hammer (Edit)/I Wanna Be	2000	3.00
❑ 7-16835	Help the Poor/Hold On I'm Coming	2000	3.00
❑ 7-16836	Come Rain or Come Shine/Ten Long Years	2000	3.00

KING, BEN E. Also see AVERAGE WHITE BAND; THE DRIFTERS.

45s

Number	Title (A Side/B Side)	Yr	NM
ATCO			
❑ 6166	Show Me the Way/Brace Yourself	1960	16.00
❑ 6185	Spanish Harlem/First Taste of Love	1960	20.00
❑ 6194	Stand By Me/On the Horizon	1961	20.00
❑ 6203	Amor/Souvenir of Mexico	1961	16.00
❑ 6207	Young Boy Blues/Here Comes the Night	1961	16.00
❑ 6215	Ecstasy/Yes	1962	16.00
❑ 6222	Don't Play That Song (You Lied)/Hermit of Misty Mountain	1962	16.00
❑ 6231	Too Bad/My Heart Cries for You	1962	12.00
❑ 6237	I'm Standing By/Walking in the Footsteps of a Fool	1962	12.00
❑ 6246	Tell Daddy/Auf Weidersehn, My Dear	1962	12.00
❑ 6256	How Can I Forget/Gloria Gloria	1963	12.00
❑ 6267	I (Who Have Nothing)/The Beginning of Time	1963	12.00
❑ 6275	I Could Have Danced All Night/Gypsy	1963	12.00
❑ 6284	What Now My Love/Groovin'	1964	10.00
❑ 6288	That's When It Hurts/Around the Corner	1964	10.00
❑ 6303	What Can a Man Do/Si, Senor	1964	10.00
❑ 6315	It's All Over/Let the Water Run Down	1964	10.00
❑ 6328	Seven Letters/River of Tears	1964	10.00
❑ 6343	The Record (Baby I Love You)/The Way You Shake It	1965	10.00
❑ 6357	She's Gone Again/Not Now (I'll Tell You When)	1965	10.00
❑ 6371	Cry No More/There's No Place to Hide	1965	10.00
❑ 6390	Goodnight My Love/I Can't Break the News to Myself	1965	10.00
❑ 6413	So Much Love/Don't Drive Me Away	1966	8.00
❑ 6431	Get in a Hurry/I Swear by Stars Above	1966	8.00
❑ 6454	They Don't Give Medals to Yesterday's Heroes/What Is Soul	1966	8.00
❑ 6472	A Man Without a Dream/Tears, Tears, Tears	1967	8.00
❑ 6493	Katherine/Teeny Weeny Little Bit	1967	8.00
❑ 6527	Don't Take Your Sweet Love Away/She Knows What to Do for Me	1967	10.00
❑ 6557	We Got a Thing Goin' On/What 'Cha Gonna Do About It	1968	8.00
—With Dee Dee Sharp			
❑ 6571	Don't Take Your Love from Me/Forgive This Soul	1968	8.00
❑ 6596	Where's the Girl/It's Amazing	1968	8.00
❑ 6637	It Ain't Fair/Till I Can't Take It Anymore	1968	8.00
❑ 6666	Hey Little One/When You Love Someone	1969	10.00
ATLANTIC			
❑ 3241	Supernatural Thing — Part 1/Supernatural Thing — Part 2	1975	5.00
❑ 3274	Do It in the Name of Love/Imagination	1975	5.00
❑ 3308	We Got Love/I Had a Love	1975	5.00
❑ 3337	I Betch'a You Didn't Know/Smooth Sailing	1976	5.00
❑ 3359	One More Time/Somebody's Knocking	1976	5.00
❑ 3402	Get It Up/Keepin' It To Myself	1977	5.00
—With the Average White Band			
❑ 3427	A Star in the Ghetto/What Is Soul?	1977	5.00
—With the Average White Band			
❑ 3444	Fool for You Anyway/The Message	1977	5.00
—With the Average White Band			
❑ 3494	I See the Light/Tippin'	1978	5.00
❑ 3535	Fly Away to My Wonderland/Spoiled	1978	5.00
❑ 3635	Music Trance/And This Is Love	1979	4.00
❑ 3808	Street Tough/Why Is the Question	1981	4.00
❑ 3839	You Made the Difference in My Life/Souvenirs of Love	1981	4.00
❑ 89234	Spanish Harlem/First Taste of Love	1987	3.00
❑ 89361	Stand By Me/Yakety Yak	1986	3.00
—B-side by the Coasters			
❑ 89361 [DJ]	Stand By Me Medley (same on both sides)	1986	8.00
—Contains excerpts from all 10 songs on the "Stand By Me" soundtrack album. It is listed here because it uses the same number as the stock release of "Stand By Me."			
❑ 89361 [PS]	Stand By Me/Yakety Yak	1986	3.00
❑ 89361 [PS]	Stand By Me Medley	1986	8.00
—Promo-only sleeve accompanying above medley. Stock and promo sleeves are identical in front but different on back.			
ICHIBAN			
❑ 254	You've Got All of Me/It's All Right	1992	3.00
❑ 257	You Still Move Me/I'm Gonna Be Somebody	1992	3.00
MANDALA			
❑ 2512	Take Me to the Pilot/I Guess It's Goodbye	1972	5.00
❑ 2513	Into the Mystic/White Moon	1972	5.00
❑ 2518	Spread Myself Around/Travellin' Woman	1973	5.00
MANHATTAN			
❑ 50078	Save the Last Dance for Me/Wheel of Love	1987	3.00
❑ 50078 [PS]	Save the Last Dance for Me/Wheel of Love	1987	3.00
MAXWELL			
❑ 800	I Can't Take It Like a Man/(B-side unknown)	1969	8.00
THE RIGHT STUFF			
❑ S7-19728	4th of July, Asbury Park (Sandy)/Janey, Don't You Lose Heart	1997	3.00
—B-side by Mrs. Fun/Tina & The B-Side Movement			

Albums

Number	Title (A Side/B Side)	Yr	NM
ATCO			
❑ 33-133 [M]	Spanish Harlem	1961	100.00
—Yellow label with harp			
❑ 33-133 [M]	Spanish Harlem	1962	40.00
—Gold and gray label			
❑ SD 33-133 [S]	Spanish Harlem	1961	150.00
—Yellow label with harp			
❑ SD 33-133 [S]	Spanish Harlem	1962	50.00
—Purple and brown label			
❑ 33-137 [M]	Ben E. King Sings for Soulful Lovers	1962	40.00
❑ SD 33-137 [S]	Ben E. King Sings for Soulful Lovers	1962	60.00
❑ 33-142 [M]	Don't Play That Song	1962	40.00
❑ SD 33-142 [S]	Don't Play That Song	1962	60.00

K

Except when noted otherwise, VG = 25% of NM, and VG+ = 50% of NM. (Example: VG = $2.00, VG+ = $4.00 and NM = $8.00.)

Carole King, "Music," Ode LLP 77013, 1971, **$8.**

Number	Title (A Side/B Side)	Yr	NM
❑ 33-165 [M]	Ben E. King's Greatest Hits	1964	30.00
❑ SD 33-165 [S]	Ben E. King's Greatest Hits	1964	40.00
—Purple and brown label			
❑ SD 33-165 [S]	Ben E. King's Greatest Hits	1969	12.00
—Yellow label			
❑ SD 33-165 [S]	Ben E. King's Greatest Hits	197?	8.00
—Any other color label			
❑ 33-174 [M]	Seven Letters	1965	40.00
❑ SD 33-174 [S]	Seven Letters	1965	50.00
ATLANTIC			
❑ SD 18132	Supernatural	1975	12.00
❑ SD 18169	I Have a Love	1976	12.00
❑ SD 18191	Rhapsody	1976	12.00
❑ SD 19200	Let Me Live in Your Life	1978	12.00
❑ SD 19269	Music Trance	1980	10.00
❑ SD 19300	Street Tough	1981	10.00
❑ 81716	Stand By Me: The Best of Ben E. King	1987	8.00
—Includes seven Ben E. King tracks and three by the Drifters			
CLARION			
❑ 606 [M]	Young Boy Blues	1966	25.00
❑ SD 606 [S]	Young Boy Blues	1966	30.00
MANDALA			
❑ MLP 3007	The Beginning of It All for Ben E. King	1972	20.00
❑ MLP-3008 [DJ]	Audio Biography	1972	30.00
—Promo-only interview by Richard Robinson			
MAXWELL			
❑ ML-88001	Rough Edges	1969	20.00

KING, CAROLE Also see THE CITY; BERTELL DACHE.

12-Inch Singles

Number	Title (A Side/B Side)	Yr	NM
ATLANTIC			
❑ PR 427 [DJ]	One to One (same on both sides)	1982	8.00
CAPITOL			
❑ SPRO-8863/4 [DJ]	Main Street Saturday Night/ Disco Tech	1978	12.00

45s

Number	Title (A Side/B Side)	Yr	NM
ABC-PARAMOUNT			
❑ 9921	Goin' Wild/The Right Girl	1958	150.00
❑ 9986	Baby Sittin'/Under the Stars	1958	150.00
ALPINE			
❑ 57	Oh, Neil/A Very Special Boy	1959	700.00
ATLANTIC			
❑ 4026	One to One/Goat Annie	1982	4.00
❑ 4026 [PS]	One to One/Goat Annie	1982	5.00
❑ 4062	Read Between the Lines/ Life Without Love	1982	4.00
❑ 89694 [DJ]	Speeding Time (same on both sides)	1984	4.00
—May be promo only			
❑ 89756	Crying in the Rain/ Sacred Heart of Stone	1983	4.00
CAPITOL			
❑ 4455	Hard Rock Cafe/To Know That I Love You	1977	4.00
❑ 4455 [PS]	Hard Rock Cafe/To Know That I Love You	1977	5.00
❑ 4497	Simple Things/Hold On	1977	4.00
❑ 4593	Main Street Saturday Night/ Changes	1978	4.00
❑ 4649	Sunbird/Morning Sun	1978	4.00
❑ 4718	Move Lightly/Whiskey	1979	4.00
❑ 4718 [PS]	Move Lightly/Whiskey	1979	5.00
❑ 4766	Time Gone By/ Dreamlike I Wander	1979	4.00
❑ 4864	One Fine Day/Rulers of This World	1980	4.00
❑ 4864 [PS]	One Fine Day/Rulers of This World	1980	4.00
—Second pressing sleeves don't list a B-side at all			
❑ 4864 [PS]	One Fine Day/Recipients of History	1980	8.00
—First pressing sleeves list the wrong title for the B-side (no records are known to exist with this title)			
❑ 4911	The Locomotion/ Oh No Not My Baby	1980	4.00
❑ 4941	Chains/Bad Girl	1980	4.00
❑ B-44336	City Streets/Time Heals All Wounds	1989	3.00
❑ B-44336 [PS]	City Streets/Time Heals All Wounds	1989	3.00
❑ 7PRO-79520 [DJ]	City Streets (same on both sides)	1989	4.00
❑ 7PRO-79520 [PS]	City Streets (same on both sides)	1989	4.00
❑ 7PRO-79873 [DJ]	Lovelight (same on both sides)	1989	5.00
—Vinyl is promo only			
COMPANION			
❑ 2000	It Might As Well Rain Until September/Nobody's Perfect	1962	300.00
DIMENSION			
❑ 1004	School Bells Are Ringing/I Didn't Have Any Summer Romance	1962	20.00
❑ 1009	He's a Bad Boy/We Grew Up Together	1963	20.00
❑ 2000	It Might As Well Rain Until September/Nobody's Perfect	1962	12.00
—Blue label			
❑ 2000	It Might As Well Rain Until September/Nobody's Perfect	1962	15.00
—Purple label			
ODE			
❑ 66006	Eventually/Up On the Roof	1970	8.00
❑ 66015	It's Too Late/I Feel the Earth Move	1971	4.00
❑ 66015 [PS]	It's Too Late/I Feel the Earth Move	1971	5.00
❑ 66019	So Far Away/Smackwater Jack	1971	4.00
❑ 66019 [PS]	So Far Away/Smackwater Jack	1971	5.00
❑ 66022	Sweet Seasons/Pocket Money	1971	4.00
❑ 66022 [PS]	Sweet Seasons/Pocket Money	1971	5.00
❑ 66026	It's Going to Take Some Time/ Brother Brother	1972	6.00
❑ 66031	Been to Canaan/ Bitter with the Sweet	1972	4.00
❑ 66031 [PS]	Been to Canaan/ Bitter with the Sweet	1972	5.00
❑ 66035	Believe in Humanity/ You Light Up My Life	1973	4.00
❑ 66035 [PS]	Believe in Humanity/ You Light Up My Life	1973	5.00
❑ 66039	Corazon/That's How Things Go Down	1973	4.00
❑ 66047	Jazzman/You Go Your Way, I'll Go Mine	1974	5.00
❑ 66047 [PS]	Jazzman/You Go Your Way, I'll Go Mine	1974	6.00
❑ 66101	Jazzman/You Go Your Way, I'll Go Mine	1974	4.00
❑ 66101 [PS]	Jazzman/You Go Your Way, I'll Go Mine	1974	5.00
❑ 66106	Nightingale/You're Something New	1975	4.00
❑ 66112 SP	Chicken Soup with Rice/Pierre	1975	8.00
—33 1/3 rpm 7-inch record			
❑ 66112 SP [PS]	Chicken Soup with Rice/Pierre	1975	10.00
❑ 66119	Only Love Is Real/Still Here Thinking of You	1976	4.00
❑ 66123	High Out of Time/I'd Like to Know You Better	1976	4.00
RCA VICTOR			
❑ 47-7560	Short Mort/Queen of the Beach	1959	100.00
TOMORROW			
❑ 7502	A Road to Nowhere/ Some of Your Lovin'	1966	40.00

7-Inch Extended Plays

Number	Title (A Side/B Side)	Yr	NM
ODE			
❑ LLP 77013	Brother, Brother/Song of Long Ago/Brighter//Some Kind of Wonderful/Sweet Seasons	1971	8.00
—Jukebox issue; small hole, plays at 33 1/3 rpm			
❑ LLP 77013 [PS]	Music	1971	8.00
—Part of "Little LP" series (LLP #180)			

Albums

Number	Title (A Side/B Side)	Yr	NM
ATLANTIC			
❑ SD 19344	One to One	1982	10.00
❑ 80118	Speeding Time	1983	10.00
CAPITOL			
❑ SPRO-9103/4 [EP]	Touch the Sky Sampler	1979	15.00
—Promo-only four-song excerpt from "Touch the Sky"			
❑ SMAS-11667	Simple Things	1977	10.00
❑ SW-11785	Welcome Home	1978	10.00
❑ SW-11785	Welcome Home	1978	10.00
❑ ST-11953	Touch the Sky	1979	10.00
❑ SWAK-11963	Touch the Sky	1979	10.00
❑ SOO-12073	Pearls — Songs of Goffin and King	1980	10.00

Except when noted otherwise, VG = 25% of NM, and VG+ = 50% of NM. (Example: VG = $2.00, VG+ = $4.00 and NM = $8.00.)

Number	Title (A Side/B Side)	Yr	NM
❑ SN-16057	Simple Things	1980	8.00
—Budget-line reissue			
❑ SN-16058	Welcome Home	1980	8.00
—Budget-line reissue			
❑ SN-16059	Touch the Sky	1980	8.00
—Budget-line reissue			
❑ C1-90885	City Streets	1989	12.00
ODE			
❑ PE 34944	Carole King: Writer	1977	10.00
—Reissue of 77006			
❑ FE 34946	Tapestry	1979	10.00
—Reissue with new prefix			
❑ PE 34946	Tapestry	1977	10.00
—Reissue of 77009			
❑ PE 34949	Music	1977	10.00
—Reissue of 77013			
❑ PE 34950	Rhymes and Reasons	1977	10.00
—Reissue of 77016			
❑ PE 34953	Wrap Around Joy	1977	10.00
—Reissue of 77024			
❑ PE 34955	Really Rosie	1977	10.00
—Reissue of 77027			
❑ PE 34962	Fantasy	1977	10.00
—Reissue of 77018			
❑ PE 34963	Thoroughbred	1977	10.00
—Reissue of 77034			
❑ JE 34967	Her Greatest Hits	1978	10.00
❑ HE 44946	Tapestry	1980	50.00
—Half-speed mastered edition			
❑ SP-77006	Writer: Carole King	1970	12.00
❑ SP-77009	Tapestry	1971	12.00
❑ SP-77013	Music	1971	12.00
❑ SP-77016	Rhymes and Reasons	1972	12.00
❑ SP-77018	Fantasy	1973	12.00
❑ SP-77024	Wrap Around Joy	1974	12.00
❑ SP-77027	Really Rosie	1975	12.00
❑ SP-77034	Thoroughbred	1976	12.00
❑ QU-88013 [Q]	Music	1974	20.00

KING, CLAUDE

45s

Number	Title (A Side/B Side)	Yr	NM
CINNAMON			
❑ 808	Don't Do Me Mad/It's Such a Perfect Day for Making Love	1974	5.00
COLUMBIA			
❑ 42043	Big River, Big Man/Sweet Lovin'	1961	10.00
❑ 42196	The Comancheros/I Can't Get Over the Way You Got Over Me	1961	10.00
❑ 42196 [PS]	The Comancheros/I Can't Get Over the Way You Got Over Me	1961	15.00
❑ 42352	Wolverton Mountain/Little Bitty Heart	1962	12.00
❑ 42352 [PS]	Wolverton Mountain/Little Bitty Heart	1962	15.00
❑ 42581	The Burning of Atlanta/Don't That Moon Look Lonesome	1962	10.00
❑ 42581 [PS]	The Burning of Atlanta/Don't That Moon Look Lonesome	1962	15.00
❑ 42630	I've Got the World by the Tail/Shopping Center	1962	10.00
❑ 42630 [PS]	I've Got the World by the Tail/Shopping Center	1962	15.00
❑ 42688	Sheepskin Valley/I Backed Out	1963	10.00
❑ 42688 [PS]	Sheepskin Valley/I Backed Out	1963	15.00
❑ 42782	Building a Bridge/What Will I Do	1963	10.00
❑ 42782 [PS]	Building a Bridge/What Will I Do	1963	15.00
❑ 42833	Hey Lucille!/Scarlet O'Hara	1963	10.00
❑ 42833 [PS]	Hey Lucille!/Scarlet O'Hara	1963	15.00
❑ 42959	That's What Makes the World Go Around/A Lace Mantilla and a Rose of Red	1964	8.00
❑ 43083	Sam Hill/Big Ole Shoulder	1964	8.00
❑ 43157	Whirlpool (Of Your Love)/This Land of Yours and Mine	1964	8.00
❑ 43298	Tiger Woman/When You Gotta Go	1965	8.00
❑ 43416	Little Buddy/Come On Home	1965	8.00
❑ 43510	Catch a Little Raindrop/Hold That Tiger	1966	8.00
❑ 43714	The Juggler/I Won't Be Long in Your Town	1966	10.00
❑ 43867	Little Things That Every Girl Should Know/The Right Place	1966	8.00
❑ 44035	The Watchman/That's the Way the Wind Blows	1967	8.00
❑ 44237	Laura (What's He Got That I Ain't Got)/Good-By My Love	1967	8.00
❑ 44340	Yellow Haired Woman/Ninety-Nine Years	1967	8.00
❑ 44504	Parchman Farm Blues/Birmingham Bus Station	1968	8.00
❑ 44642	The Power of Your Sweet Love/Beertops and Teardrops	1968	8.00
❑ 44749	Sweet Love on My Mind/Four Roses	1969	8.00
❑ 44833	All for the Love of a Girl/I Remember Johnny	1969	8.00
❑ 44833 [PS]	All for the Love of a Girl/I Remember Johnny	1969	12.00
❑ 45015	Friend, Lover, Woman, Wife/The House of the Rising Sun	1969	8.00
❑ 45142	I'll Be Your Baby Tonight/It's Good to Have My Baby Home	1970	6.00
❑ 45248	Mary's Vineyard/Johnny Valentine	1970	6.00
❑ 45340	Chip 'n' Dale's Place/Highway Lonely	1971	6.00
❑ 45441	When You're Twenty-One/Heart	1971	6.00
❑ 45515	Darlin' Raise the Shade (Let the Sun Shine In)/Sweet Mary Ann	1971	6.00
❑ 45614	The Lady of Our Town/Just As Soon As I Get Over Loving You	1972	6.00
❑ 45704	He Ain't Country/This Time I'm Through	1972	6.00
TRUE			
❑ 103	Cotton Dan/I'll Spend My Lifetime Loving You	1977	6.00
❑ 106	Sugar Baby, Candy Girl/(B-side unknown)	1977	6.00
❑ 124	Wobble Water/(B-side unknown)	197?	6.00

Albums

Number	Title (A Side/B Side)	Yr	NM
COLUMBIA			
❑ CS 1024	Friend, Lover, Woman, Wife	1970	15.00
❑ CL 1810 [M]	Meet Claude King	1962	25.00
—Six "eye" logos on label			
❑ CL 1810 [M]	Meet Claude King	1963	15.00
—"Guaranteed High Fidelity" or "Mono" on red label			
❑ CL 2415 [M]	Tiger Woman	1965	20.00
❑ CS 8610 [S]	Meet Claude King	1962	40.00
—Six "eye" logos on label			
❑ CS 8610 [S]	Meet Claude King	1963	20.00
—"360 Sound Stereo" on red label			
❑ CS 9215 [S]	Tiger Woman	1965	25.00
—"360 Sound Stereo" on red label			
❑ CS 9789	I Remember Johnny Horton	1968	15.00
—"360 Sound Stereo" on red label			
❑ C 30804	Chip 'n' Dale's Place	1971	15.00
HARMONY			
❑ HS 11300	The Best of Claude King	1969	12.00

KING, CLYDIE

45s

Number	Title (A Side/B Side)	Yr	NM
IMPERIAL			
❑ 66109	The Thrill Is Gone/If You Were a Man	1965	20.00
❑ 66139	My Love Grows Deeper/Missin' My Baby	1965	20.00
❑ 66172	He Always Comes Back to Me/Soft and Gentle Ways	1966	20.00
LIZARD			
❑ 21007	'Bout Love/(B-side unknown)	1971	6.00
MINIT			
❑ 32025	Good for Cryin' Over You Days/Mistakes of Yesterday	1967	12.00
❑ 32054	Love Now, Pay Later/One Part, Two Part	1969	8.00
PHILIPS			
❑ 40001	Boys in My Life/Promises	1962	20.00
❑ 40051	Turn Around/Don't Hang Up the Phone	1962	20.00
❑ 40107	Only the Guilty Cry/By Noro	1963	20.00
SPECIALTY			
❑ 605	Our Romance/Written on the Wall	1957	30.00

Albums

Number	Title (A Side/B Side)	Yr	NM
LIZARD			
❑ A-20104	Direct Me	1971	12.00

KING, CURTIS No, not King Curtis.

45s

Number	Title (A Side/B Side)	Yr	NM
COLUMBIA			
❑ 44096	Bad Habits/So Nice While It Lasted	1967	20.00

KING, EARL

45s

Number	Title (A Side/B Side)	Yr	NM
ACE			
❑ 509	Those Lonely, Lonely Nights/Baby You Can Get Your Gun	1955	60.00
❑ 514	My Love Is Strong/Little Girl	1956	50.00
❑ 517	It Must Have Been Love/I'll Take You Back Home	1956	50.00
❑ 520	Is Everything Alright/Mother Told Me Not to Go	1956	50.00
❑ 529	Those Lonely, Lonely Feelings/You Can Fly High	1957	50.00
❑ 543	I'll Never Get Tired/Well'o, Well'o, Well'o Baby	1958	50.00
❑ 564	Weary Silent Night/Everybody's Carried Away	1959	40.00
❑ 598	Don't You Know You're Wrong/Buddy It's Time to Go	1960	40.00
IMPERIAL			
❑ 5713	Come On — Part 1/Come On — Part 2	1960	25.00
❑ 5730	Love Me Now/The Things That I Used to Do	1961	25.00
❑ 5750	Come Along with Me/You're More to Me Than Gold	1961	25.00
❑ 5774	You Better Know/Mama and Papa	1961	25.00
❑ 5811	Trick Bag/Always a First Time	1962	25.00
❑ 5858	We Are Just Friends/You're More to Me That Gold	1962	25.00
❑ 5891	Come Along with Me/Case of Love	1962	25.00
REX			
❑ 1015	I Can't Help Myself/Darling Honey, Angel Child	1961	20.00
SPECIALTY			
❑ 495	A Mother's Love/I'm Your Best Bet Baby	1954	60.00
❑ 531	No One But Me/Eating and Sleeping	1954	60.00
❑ 558	Funny Face/Sittin' and Wonderin'	1955	60.00

KING, FREDDIE

45s

Number	Title (A Side/B Side)	Yr	NM
COTILLION			
❑ 44015	Funky/Play It Cool	1968	8.00
❑ 44058	I Wonder Why/Yonder Wall	1970	8.00
EL-BEE			
❑ 157	Country Boy/That's What You Think	1956	400.00
FEDERAL			
❑ 12384	Have You Ever Loved a Woman/You've Got to Love Her with a Feeling	1960	40.00
❑ 12401	Hideaway/I Love the Woman	1961	30.00
❑ 12415	Lonesome Whistle Blues/It's Too Bad Things Are Going So Tough	1961	30.00
❑ 12428	San-Ho-Zay/See See Baby	1961	30.00
❑ 12432	I'm Tore Down/Sen-Say-Shun	1961	30.00
❑ 12439	Christmas Tears/I Hear Jingle Bells	1961	30.00
❑ 12443	If You Believe in What You Do/Heads Up	1961	20.00
❑ 12450	Takin' Care of Business/The Stumble	1962	20.00
❑ 12456	Side Tracked/Sittin' on the Boat Dock	1962	20.00
❑ 12462	What About Love/Texas Oil	1962	20.00
❑ 12470	Come On/Just Pickin'	1962	20.00
❑ 12475	In the Open/I'm On My Way to Atlanta	1962	20.00
❑ 12482	The Bossa Nova Watusi Twist/Look Ma, I'm Crying	1963	15.00
❑ 12491	(I'd Love To) Make Love to You/One Hundred Years	1963	15.00
❑ 12499	(The Welfare) Turns Its Back on You/You're Barkin' Up the Wrong Tree	1963	15.00
❑ 12509	Surf Monkey/Monkey Donkey	1963	20.00
❑ 12515	Meet Me at the Station/Ting-a-Ling	1964	15.00
❑ 12518	Driving Sideways/Someday After Awhile (You'll Be Gone)	1964	12.00
❑ 12521	She Put the Whammy on Me/High Rise	1964	12.00
❑ 12529	Now I've Got a Woman/Onion Rings	1964	12.00
❑ 12532	Some Other Day, Some Other Time/Manhole	1965	12.00
❑ 12535	If You Have It/I Love You More Every Day	1965	12.00
❑ 12537	Full Time Love/She's the One	1965	12.00
KING			
❑ 6057	Use What You've Got/Double Eyed Whammy	1966	12.00
❑ 6080	You've Got Me Licked/The Girl from Kookamunga	1967	12.00
❑ 6264	Have You Ever Loved a Woman/Hideaway	1969	8.00
RSO			
❑ 505	My Credit Didn't Go Through/Texas Flyer	1975	5.00
❑ 516	Boogie Bump/It's Your Love	1975	5.00
SHELTER			
❑ 7303	Going Down/Toke Down	1971	6.00
❑ 7320	Me and My Guitar/Downtown in Lodi	1972	6.00
❑ 7333	Woman Across the River/Help Me Through the Day	1973	6.00
❑ 40410	Going Down/Me and My Guitar	1975	5.00

Number	Title (A Side/B Side)	Yr	NM
Albums			
COTILLION			
❑ SD 9004	Freddie King Is a Blues Master	1969	25.00
❑ SD 9016	My Feeling for the Blues	1970	25.00
KING			
❑ 762 [M]	Freddie King Sings the Blues	1961	250.00
❑ 773 [M]	Let's Hide Away and Dance Away	1961	250.00
❑ 821 [M]	Bossa Nova and Blues	1962	150.00
❑ 856 [M]	Freddie King Goes Surfin'	1963	80.00
❑ KS-856 [S]	Freddie King Goes Surfin'	1963	120.00
❑ 928 [M]	A Bonanza of Instrumentals	1965	50.00
❑ KS-928 [S]	A Bonanza of Instrumentals	1965	60.00
❑ 964 [M]	24 Vocals and Instrumentals	1966	25.00
❑ KS-1059	Hide Away	1969	15.00
MCA			
❑ 690	The Best of Freddie King	1979	8.00
—Reissue of Shelter 52021			
MODERN BLUES			
❑ MB2LP-721	[(2)]Just Pickin'	198?	15.00
❑ MBLP-722	Freddie King Sings	198?	10.00
RSO			
❑ RS-1-3025	Freddie King 1934-1976	1977	12.00
❑ SD 4803	Burglar	1974	12.00
❑ SD 4811	Larger Than Life	1975	12.00
SHELTER			
❑ 2140	The Best of Freddie King	1975	15.00
—Original with MCA distribution			
❑ SW-8905	Getting Ready	1971	15.00
❑ SW-8913	Texas Cannonball	1972	15.00
❑ SW-8919	Woman Across the River	1973	15.00
❑ SRL 52021	The Best of Freddie King	1977	12.00
—Second edition with ABC distribution			
STARDAY/GUSTO			
❑ 5012	17 Original Hits	1977	10.00
❑ 5033	Hide Away	1978	10.00

KING, FREDDIE/LULA REED/BOBBY THOMPSON

Number	Title (A Side/B Side)	Yr	NM
Albums			
KING			
❑ 777 [M]	Boy-Girl-Boy	1962	250.00

KING, JEAN

Number	Title (A Side/B Side)	Yr	NM
45s			
HANNA-BARBERA			
❑ 497	Don't Say Goodbye/It's Good Enough for Me	1966	10.00
Albums			
HANNA-BARBERA			
❑ HLP-8505 [M]	Jean King Sings for the In Crowd	1966	20.00

KING, JO ANN

Number	Title (A Side/B Side)	Yr	NM
45s			
FAIRMOUNT			
❑ 1008	Let Them Love and Be Loved/Don't Play with Fire	1966	250.00
PHIL-L.A. OF SOUL			
❑ 344	Hey Lancelot/This Lovin' Way (Let's Leave It)	1970	40.00

KING, JOE

Number	Title (A Side/B Side)	Yr	NM
45s			
HIT			
❑ 265	Sunshine Superman/Dandy	1966	8.00
—B-side by the Chords (2)			
❑ 273	Mellow Yellow/I'm a Believer	1966	8.00
—B-side by the Jalopy Five			

KING, JONATHAN

Also see HEDGEHOPPERS ANONYMOUS.

Number	Title (A Side/B Side)	Yr	NM
45s			
PARROT			
❑ 3005	Just Like a Woman/Land of the Golden Tree	1966	8.00
❑ 3008	Icicles (Fell from the Heart of a Bluebird)/In a Hundred Years from Now	1966	8.00
❑ 3011	Round, Round/Time and Motion	1967	8.00
❑ 3021	1968 (Message to the Presidential Candidates)/Colloquial Sex	1968	8.00
❑ 3027	Lazy Bones/Just Want to Say Thank You	1968	8.00
❑ 3029	Hooked on a Feeling/I Don't Want to Be Gay	1969	6.00
❑ 3030	Flirt/Hey Jim	1969	6.00
❑ 9774	Everyone's Gone to the Moon/Summer's Coming	1965	10.00
❑ 9804	Green Is the Grass/Where the Sun Has Never Shown	1965	8.00
❑ 40047	Let It All Hang Out/Colloquial Sex	1970	6.00
❑ 40055	Cherry Cherry/Gay Girl	1970	6.00
UK			
❑ 49002	It's a Tall Order for a Short Guy/Learned Tax Counsel	1972	5.00
❑ 49014	Mary, My Love/A Little Bit Left of Right	1973	5.00
❑ 49018	The Kung Fu Anthem/A Little Bit Left of Right	1973	5.00
❑ 49034	The Way You Look Tonight/The True Story of Molly Malone	1974	5.00
Albums			
PARROT			
❑ PA 61013 [M]	Jonathan King Or Then Again....	1967	40.00
❑ PAS 71013 [P]	Jonathan King Or Then Again....	1967	50.00
—Only "Where the Sun Has Never Shown" is rechanneled.			
U.K.			
❑ 53101	Bubble Rock Is Here to Stay	1972	25.00
❑ 53104	Pandora's Box	1973	25.00

KING, MORGANA

Number	Title (A Side/B Side)	Yr	NM
45s			
MAINSTREAM			
❑ 600	A Taste of Honey/Corcavado	1964	10.00
❑ 602	When the World Was Young/Lazy Afternoon	1964	10.00
❑ 623	Try to Remember/Cuore di Mama	1964	10.00
MERCURY			
❑ 70927	Homesick in Paris/For You and Me	1956	15.00
❑ 70967	Four Walls, Two Windows, One Broken Heart/Mine for the Taking	1956	15.00
PARAMOUNT			
❑ 0245	A Song for You/You Are the Sunshine of My Life	1973	5.00
❑ 0275	Jennifer Had/Like a Seed	1974	5.00
REPRISE			
❑ 0481	If You Should Leave Me (E Se Domani)/Mountain High, Valley Low	1966	8.00
❑ 0604	The Look of Love/I Have Loved Me a Man	1967	8.00
20TH FOX			
❑ 142	Give Me Love/Lost, Lonely and Looking for Love	1959	12.00
VERVE			
❑ 10615	I Know How It Feels to Be Lonely/I Only Know I Loved You	1968	6.00
❑ 10630	Didn't We/Eleanor Rigby	1968	6.00
WING			
❑ 90073	In the Wee Small Hours of the Morning/It's De-Lovely	1956	15.00
Albums			
ASCOT			
❑ AM 13014 [M]	The Winter of My Discontent	1964	25.00
❑ AM 13019 [M]	The End of a Love Affair	1965	25.00
—Reissue of United Artists 30020			
❑ AM 13020 [M]	Everybody Loves Saturday Night	1965	25.00
❑ AM 13025 [M]	More Morgana	1965	25.00
❑ AS 16014 [S]	The Winter of My Discontent	1964	30.00
❑ AS 16019 [S]	The End of a Love Affair	1965	30.00
—Reissue of United Artists 40020			
❑ AS 16020 [S]	Everybody Loves Saturday Night	1965	30.00
❑ AS 16025 [S]	More Morgana	1965	30.00
EMARCY			
❑ MG-36079 [M]	For You, For Me, For Evermore	1956	120.00
MAINSTREAM			
❑ MRL-321	Taste of Honey	1972	15.00
❑ MRL-355	Cuore di Mama	1974	15.00
❑ S-6015 [S]	With a Taste of Honey	1964	25.00
❑ S-6052 [S]	Miss Morgana King	1965	25.00
❑ 56015 [M]	With a Taste of Honey	1964	20.00
❑ 56052 [M]	Miss Morgana King	1965	20.00
MERCURY			
❑ MG-20231 [M]	Morgana King Sings the Blues	1958	80.00
MUSE			
❑ MR-5166	Stretchin' Out	1977	10.00
❑ MR-5190	Everything Must Change	1978	10.00
❑ MR-5224	Higher Ground	1979	10.00
❑ MR-5257	Looking Through the Eyes of Love	1981	10.00
❑ MR-5301	Portraits	1983	10.00
❑ MR-5326	Simply Eloquent	1986	10.00
❑ MR-5339	Another Time, Another Space	1988	10.00
PARAMOUNT			
❑ PAS-6067	New Beginnings	1973	12.00
RCA CAMDEN			
❑ CAL-543 [M]	The Greatest Songs Ever Swung	1959	20.00
❑ CAS-543 [S]	The Greatest Songs Ever Swung	1959	30.00
REPRISE			
❑ R 6192 [M]	It's a Quiet Thing	1966	20.00
❑ RS 6192 [S]	It's a Quiet Thing	1966	25.00
❑ R 6205 [M]	Wild Is Love	1966	20.00
❑ RS 6205 [S]	Wild Is Love	1966	25.00
❑ R 6257 [M]	Gemini Changes	1967	20.00
❑ RS 6257 [S]	Gemini Changes	1967	25.00
TRIP			
❑ 5533	Morgana King Sings	197?	10.00
UNITED ARTISTS			
❑ UAL 3028 [M]	Folk Songs A La King	1960	80.00
❑ UAS 6028 [S]	Folk Songs A La King	1960	100.00
❑ UAL 30020 [M]	Let Me Love You	1960	100.00
❑ UAS 30020-S [S]	Let Me Love You	1960	120.00
VERVE			
❑ V-5061 [M]	I Know How It Feels	1968	25.00
❑ V6-5061 [S]	I Know How It Feels	1968	25.00
WING			
❑ MGW-12307 [M]	More Morgana King	1965	15.00
❑ SRW-16307 [S]	More Morgana King	1965	20.00

KING, PEE WEE

Number	Title (A Side/B Side)	Yr	NM
45s			
BRIAR			
❑ 120	Tennessee Waltz/Wooden Heart Polka	196?	12.00
CUCA			
❑ 1207	Guitar Polka/Wings of a Dove	1965	10.00
❑ 1247	Danny Boy/I Am Praying for the Day Peace Will Come	1965	10.00
❑ 1275	History Repeats Itself/Hope, Faith and Love	1966	10.00
❑ 1315	Too Many Years/I Want to Light a Candle	1966	10.00
❑ 1316	Night Friends/Alone in San Antone	1966	10.00
❑ 1420	I'm in Love with the Bridesmaid/(No One) Unless It's You	1966	10.00
JARO			
❑ 77025	Hi Diddle Diddle/Vagabond Waltz	1960	12.00
LANDA			
❑ 668	Looking Back to Sea/Slow Poke	1961	12.00
❑ 673	Bumming Around/When, When, When	1961	12.00
RCA VICTOR			
❑ 47-4238	Two Roads/Makin' Like a Train	1951	25.00
❑ 47-4458	Silver and Gold/Ragtime Annie Lee	1952	20.00
❑ 47-4601	Tennessee Waltz/Bullfiddle Boogie	1952	15.00
❑ 47-4602	Silver and Gold/Texas Toni Lee	1952	15.00
❑ 47-4603	Slow Poke/Ten Gallon Boogie	1952	15.00
❑ 47-4604	Kentucky Waltz/Bonaparte's Retreat	1952	15.00
—The above four comprise a box set			
❑ 47-4655	Busybody/I Don't Mind	1952	20.00
❑ 47-4883	Two Faced Clock/Mighty Pretty Waltz	1952	20.00
❑ 47-4969	My Adobe Hacienda/Spanish Two-Step	1952	15.00
❑ 47-4970	Steel Guitar Rag/Over the Waves	1952	15.00
❑ 47-4971	San Antonio Rose/Varsouviana	1952	15.00
❑ 47-4972	The One Rose/Under the Double Eagle	1952	15.00
—The above four comprise a box set			
❑ 47-5009	Tennessee Tango/Crazy Waltz	1952	20.00
❑ 47-5144	Railroad Boogie/The Crying Steel Guitar Waltz	1953	20.00
❑ 47-5260	Screwball/Last Night on the Back Porch	1953	20.00
❑ 47-5344	Your Kisses Aren't Kisses Anymore/If and When	1953	20.00
❑ 47-5454	Ricochet/Oh Mis'rable Love	1953	20.00
❑ 47-5537	Changing Partners/Bimbo	1953	20.00
❑ 47-5587	Red Deck of Cards/Deck of Cards	1954	25.00
❑ 47-5632	Why Don't Y'All Go Home/Huggin' My Pillow	1954	20.00
❑ 47-5694	Backward, Turn Backward/Indian Giver	1954	20.00
❑ 47-5782	In a Garden of Roses/How Long	1954	20.00
❑ 47-5847	Keep Your Eye on My Darling/Here Lies My Heart	1954	20.00
❑ 47-5889	Peaches and Cream/I Can't Tell a Waltz from a Tango	1954	20.00
❑ 47-6005	Tweedlee Dee/You Can't Hardly Get Them No More	1955	15.00
❑ 47-6070	Plantation Boogie/Jim, Johnny and Jonas	1955	15.00
❑ 47-6162	Nevermind/Beauty Is As Beauty Gets	1955	15.00

Number	Title (A Side/B Side)	Yr	NM
❑ 47-6233	Seven Come Eleven/ Farewell Blues	1955	15.00
❑ 47-6302	Peek-a-Boo Waltz/You Won't Need My Love Anymore	1955	15.00
❑ 47-6450	Blue Suede Shoes/ Tennessee Dancin' Doll	1956	25.00
❑ 47-6666	Ballroom Baby/ Absolutely Positive	1956	15.00
❑ 47-6793	Sugar Beet/I'll Be Walking Alone in a Crowd	1957	15.00
❑ 47-7090	Congratulations Joe/ Prelude to a Broken Heart	1957	15.00
❑ 47-7375	Janie/Unbreakable Heart	1958	15.00
❑ 48-0003	Tennessee Waltz/Rootie Tootie	1949	30.00
—Green vinyl original			
❑ 48-0037	Bull Fiddle Boogie/ Chattanooga Bus	1949	30.00
—Green vinyl original			
❑ 48-0085	Tennessee Polka/ The Nashville Waltz	1949	30.00
—Green vinyl original			
❑ 48-0114	Bonaparte's Retreat/ The Waltz of Regret	1949	30.00
—Green vinyl original			
❑ 48-0118	You Call Everybody Darlin'/ Shocking Rye Straw	1950	25.00
—Green vinyl original			
❑ 48-0119	The Battle Hymn of the Republic/ Blackeyed Susie	1950	25.00
—Green vinyl original			
❑ 48-0120	Cornbread, Lasses and Sassafras Tea/Fire on the Mountain	1950	25.00
—Green vinyl original; the above three comprise a box set			
❑ 48-0122	Fisher's Hornpipe/Devil's Dream	1950	25.00
—Green vinyl original			
❑ 48-0123	Sally Goodin/Arkansas Traveler	1950	25.00
—Green vinyl original			
❑ 48-0124	Billy in the Low Ground/ Whistling Rufus	1950	25.00
—Green vinyl original; the above three comprise a box set			
❑ 48-0179	Rag Mop/When They Played That Old Missouri Waltz	1950	30.00
—Green vinyl original			
❑ 48-0223	Kentucky Waltz/Keep Them Cold Icy Fingers Off Me	1950	30.00
—Green vinyl original			
❑ 48-0307	Blame It All on Nashville/ The Kissing Dance	1950	25.00
—Green vinyl original			
❑ 48-0332	Birmingham Bounce/ What, Where and When	1950	25.00
—Green vinyl original			
❑ 48-0354	Blue Grass Waltz/ Get Together Polka	1950	25.00
—Green vinyl original			
❑ 48-0379	Cincinnati Dancing Pig/ We're Gonna Go Fishin'	1950	25.00
—Green vinyl original			
❑ 48-0393	Mop Rag Boogie/River Road Two-Step	1950	30.00
—Green vinyl original			
❑ 48-0407	Tennessee Waltz/ Hilegged, Hilegged	1951	25.00
❑ 48-0429	No One But You/ Within My Heart	1951	25.00
❑ 48-0451	The Strange Little Girl/ Chew Tobacco Rag	1951	25.00
❑ 48-0489	Slow Poke/Whisper Waltz	1951	25.00
❑ 47-2736	Tennessee Waltz/Rootie Tootie	1949	—
—Assigned this number, but released on 48-0003			

STARDAY

Number	Title (A Side/B Side)	Yr	NM
❑ 668	Goodbye New Orleans/Waitin'	1964	10.00
❑ 682	When the Lights Go Dim Downtown/Stay Away from Me	1964	10.00
❑ 698	Ten Thousand Crying Towels/ The Urge	1964	10.00

TODD

Number	Title (A Side/B Side)	Yr	NM
❑ 1009	Slow Poke Cha Cha/I Got a Wife	1959	12.00
❑ 1020	Too Tall/Slow Poke Cha Cha	1959	12.00

TOP RANK

Number	Title (A Side/B Side)	Yr	NM
❑ 2087	Do You Remember/ (B-side unknown)	1960	12.00

7-Inch Extended Plays

RCA VICTOR

Number	Title (A Side/B Side)	Yr	NM
❑ EPA 256	You Call Everybody Darlin'/ Shocking Rye Straw//Fire on the Mountain/Cornbread, 'Lasses and Sassafras Tea	195?	15.00
—Calls by Lee Bedford, Jr.			
❑ EPA 256 [PS]	Square Dances	195?	15.00
❑ EPA 797	Flying Home/Over the Waves// Tippin' In/San Antonio Rose	1956	15.00
❑ EPA 797 [PS]	Swing West	1956	15.00

Albums

BRIAR

Number	Title (A Side/B Side)	Yr	NM
❑ 102	Golden Olde Tyme Dances	1975	60.00

LONGHORN

Number	Title (A Side/B Side)	Yr	NM
❑ 1236 [M]	The Legendary Pee Wee King	1967	25.00

RCA CAMDEN

Number	Title (A Side/B Side)	Yr	NM
❑ CAL-876 [M]	Country Barn Dance	1965	20.00
❑ CAS-876 [R]	Country Barn Dance	1965	12.00

RCA VICTOR

Number	Title (A Side/B Side)	Yr	NM
❑ LPM-1237 [M]	Swing West	1956	40.00
❑ LPM-3028 [10]	Pee Wee King	195?	80.00
❑ LPM-3071 [10]	Western Hits	195?	80.00
❑ LPM-3109 [10]	Waltzes	195?	80.00
❑ LPM-3280 [10]	Swing West	195?	80.00

STARDAY

Number	Title (A Side/B Side)	Yr	NM
❑ SLP-284 [M]	Back Again with the Songs That Made Them Famous	1964	30.00

KING, PEGGY

45s

BUENA VISTA

Number	Title (A Side/B Side)	Yr	NM
❑ 397	Bon Voyage/I Get a Kick Out of Kissin'	1962	10.00

BULLET

Number	Title (A Side/B Side)	Yr	NM
❑ 77	I Can't Make It on My Own/ I Can't Get Over Gettin'	1971	6.00

COLUMBIA

Number	Title (A Side/B Side)	Yr	NM
❑ 4-40273	Burn 'Em Up/The Hottentot	1954	15.00
❑ 4-40362	I'm Gonna Put Some Glue 'Round The Christmas Tree/ Counting Sheep	1954	15.00
❑ 4-40363	Make Yourself Comfortable/ The Gentleman in the Next Apartment	1954	12.00
❑ 4-40437	Any Questions/You Never Gave It a Try	1955	12.00
❑ 4-40524	Please Wait for Me/ You Did, You Did	1955	12.00
❑ 4-40562	Learning to Love/Song of Seventeen	1955	12.00
❑ 4-40614	You Better Go Now/ Learning to Love	1955	12.00
❑ 4-40638	Kiss and Run/Angel Pie (Postillon!)	1956	12.00
❑ 4-40744	Tall Boy/The Test of Time	1956	12.00
❑ 4-40773	Love Sick/He Never Looks My Way	1956	12.00
❑ 4-40863	Mircle Man/In My Own Little Corner	1957	12.00
❑ 4-40996	If You Don't Love Me/ C'mon Over	1957	12.00
❑ 4-41054	Zero Hour/No Sleep Till Dawn	1957	12.00

MGM

Number	Title (A Side/B Side)	Yr	NM
❑ K11260	There's Doubt in My Mind/ I Cried for You	1952	15.00

ROULETTE

Number	Title (A Side/B Side)	Yr	NM
❑ 4327	I'll Be Around/Up, Up, Up (Flying High)	1961	10.00

Albums

COLUMBIA

Number	Title (A Side/B Side)	Yr	NM
❑ CL 2549 [10]	Wish Upon a Star	1955	50.00

IMPERIAL

Number	Title (A Side/B Side)	Yr	NM
❑ LP-9078 [M]	Lazy Afternoon	1959	20.00
❑ LP-12026 [S]	Lazy Afternoon	1959	30.00

STASH

Number	Title (A Side/B Side)	Yr	NM
❑ 246	Peggy King Sings Jerome Kern: Till the Clouds Roll By	198?	8.00

KING, REV. MARTIN LUTHER

The 1968 releases are posthumous tributes.

45s

GORDY

Number	Title (A Side/B Side)	Yr	NM
❑ 7023	I Have a Dream/ We Shall Overcome	1963	30.00
❑ 7023	I Have a Dream/ We Shall Overcome	1968	8.00
—B-side by Liz Lands; "Gordy" on side of label			

MERCURY

Number	Title (A Side/B Side)	Yr	NM
❑ 72814	I Have a Dream/I've Been to the Mountain Top-Eulogy	1968	8.00

Albums

BUDDAH

Number	Title (A Side/B Side)	Yr	NM
❑ BDS-2002	Man of Love	1968	20.00

CREED

Number	Title (A Side/B Side)	Yr	NM
❑ 3201 [M]	I Have a Dream	1968	20.00

DOOTO

Number	Title (A Side/B Side)	Yr	NM
❑ DTL-831 [M]	Martin Luther King at Zion Hill	1962	30.00
❑ DTL-841	The American Dream	1968	20.00

GORDY

Number	Title (A Side/B Side)	Yr	NM
❑ G-906 [M]	The Great March to Freedom	1963	40.00
—"Gordy" in script at top of label			
❑ G-906 [M]	The Great March to Freedom	1968	15.00
—Later pressings			
❑ G-908 [M]	The Great March on Washington	1963	40.00
—"Gordy" in script at top of label			
❑ G-908 [M]	The Great March on Washington	1968	15.00
—Later pressings			
❑ G-929	...Free at Last	1968	30.00
—Original with gatefold cover			

MERCURY

Number	Title (A Side/B Side)	Yr	NM
❑ SR-61170	In Search of Freedom	1968	20.00

MR. MAESTRO

Number	Title (A Side/B Side)	Yr	NM
❑ 1000 [M]	The March on Washington	1963	30.00

SUNSET

Number	Title (A Side/B Side)	Yr	NM
❑ 21033	The Struggle for Freedom	1968	15.00

20TH CENTURY

Number	Title (A Side/B Side)	Yr	NM
❑ TCF-3110 [M]	Freedom March on Washington	1963	30.00
❑ S-3201	The Rev. Dr. Martin Luther King, Jr.	1968	20.00

UNART

Number	Title (A Side/B Side)	Yr	NM
❑ S 21033	In the Struggle for Freedom and Human Dignity	1968	20.00

KING, SLEEPY

45s

AWAKE

Number	Title (A Side/B Side)	Yr	NM
❑ 852	Rock Rock/Still in My Heart	196?	50.00
❑ 909	Lost Man/The Pillow	196?	60.00

JOY

Number	Title (A Side/B Side)	Yr	NM
❑ 257	Pushin' Your Luck/ The King Steps Out	1961	15.00
❑ 261	It's Written All Over Your Face/ Happy Music	1962	15.00
❑ 263	Lovin' Time/Slowly But Surely	1962	15.00

SYMBOL

Number	Title (A Side/B Side)	Yr	NM
❑ 904	Begging/My Time Ain't Long	1959	30.00

VEEP

Number	Title (A Side/B Side)	Yr	NM
❑ 1236	Hello Martha/Please Let a Fool In Out of the Rain	1966	12.00

KING, TEDDI

45s

CORAL

Number	Title (A Side/B Side)	Yr	NM
❑ 9-62094	BLue Tango/River of Regret	1959	10.00

RCA VICTOR

Number	Title (A Side/B Side)	Yr	NM
❑ 47-6392	Mr. Wonderful/Are You Slipping Through My Fingers	1956	12.00
❑ 47-6392 [PS]	Mr. Wonderful/Are You Slipping Through My Fingers	1956	25.00
—Promo-only "This Is Her Life" cartoon sleeve			
❑ 47-6575	Impossible/I Can Honestly Say It's a Lie	1956	12.00
❑ 47-6660	Married I Can Always Get/ Traveling Down a Lonely Road	1956	12.00
❑ 47-6866	Say It Isn't So/There's So Much More	1956	12.00
❑ 47-7026	I Was a Child Till Tonight/ Then It Starts Again	1956	12.00
❑ 47-7074	Every Woman/A Lot in Common	1957	12.00
❑ 47-7297	Say a Prayer/Baisez-Moi (Kiss Me)	1958	12.00

Albums

AUDIOPHILE

Number	Title (A Side/B Side)	Yr	NM
❑ AP-117	Lovers and Losers	1976	15.00
❑ AP-150	Someone to Light Up Your Life	1979	12.00

CORAL

Number	Title (A Side/B Side)	Yr	NM
❑ CRL 57278 [M]	All the King's Songs	1959	60.00
❑ CRL 757278 [S]	All the King's Songs	1959	80.00

RCA VICTOR

Number	Title (A Side/B Side)	Yr	NM
❑ LPM-1147 [M]	Bidin' My Time	1956	80.00
❑ LPM-1313 [M]	To You from Teddi King	1957	100.00
❑ LPM-1454 [M]	A Girl and Her Songs	1957	80.00

STORYVILLE

Number	Title (A Side/B Side)	Yr	NM
❑ STLP-302 [10]	'Round Midnight	1954	250.00
❑ STLP-314 [10]	Storyville Presents Teddi King	1954	200.00
❑ STLP-903 [M]	Now In Vogue	1956	150.00

KING, TEDDI, AND DAVE MCKENNA

Albums

INNER CITY

Number	Title (A Side/B Side)	Yr	NM
❑ IC-1044	This Is New	1977	20.00

KING BEES, THE

More than one group.

45s

CHECKER

Number	Title (A Side/B Side)	Yr	NM
❑ 909	Buzzin'/Good Rockin' Tonight	1958	80.00

FLIP

Number	Title (A Side/B Side)	Yr	NM
❑ 323	Puppy Love/Give Me Your Number	1957	40.00

KRC

Number	Title (A Side/B Side)	Yr	NM
❑ 302	Lovely Love/Can't You Understand?	1957	40.00

King Crimson, *In the Wake of Poseidon*, Atlantic SD 8266, 1970, **$20.**

Number	Title (A Side/B Side)	Yr	NM
NOBLE			
❑ 715	Tender Love/What Could Have Been Can't Be	1959	250.00
RCA VICTOR			
❑ 47-8688	What She Does to Me/ That Ain't Love	1965	12.00
❑ 47-8787	On Your Way Down the Drain/ Rhythm and Blues	1966	12.00
❑ 47-8979	Lost in the Shuffle/Hardly (Part 3)	1966	12.00

KING BISCUIT BOY

Number	Title (A Side/B Side)	Yr	NM
45s			
EPIC			
❑ 50129	New Orleans/I'm Writing You a Letter	1975	5.00
PARAMOUNT			
❑ 0052	Corrina, Corrina/ Cookin' Little Baby	1970	5.00
❑ 0076	King Biscuit's Boogie/Badly Bent	1971	5.00
Albums			
EPIC			
❑ KE 32891	King Biscuit Boy	1974	12.00
PARAMOUNT			
❑ PAS-5030	Official Music	1970	15.00
—As "King Biscuit Boy with Crowbar"			
❑ PAS-6023	Gooduns	1972	15.00

KING CRIMSON

Also see YES; ADRIAN BELEW; PETER GABRIEL; URIAH HEEP.

Number	Title (A Side/B Side)	Yr	NM
12-Inch Singles			
WARNER BROS.			
❑ PRO-A-2131 [DJ]	Sleepless (Long Version)/ Sleepless (Short Version)	1984	8.00
❑ PRO-A-2148 [DJ]	3 of a Perfect Pair/Man with an Open Heart	1984	8.00
❑ 20193	Sleepless (Dance Mix)/ (Instrumental)	1984	6.00
45s			
ATLANTIC			
❑ 2702	The Court of the Crimson King - Part 1/Part 2	1970	12.00
❑ 3016	Night Watch/The Great Deceiver	1974	8.00
WARNER BROS.			
❑ 29309	Sleepless/Nuages (That Which Passes, Passes Like Clouds)	1984	5.00
❑ 29964	Heartbeat/Requiem	1982	5.00
Albums			
ATLANTIC			
❑ SD 7212	Islands	1972	20.00
❑ SD 7263	Larks' Tongues in Aspic	1973	20.00
❑ SD 7298	Starless and Bible Black	1974	20.00
❑ 8245 [M]	In the Court of the Crimson King — An Observation by King Crimson	1969	50.00
—Mono is white label promo only; comes in stereo cover with "DJ Copy Monaural" sticker on front			
❑ SD 8245	In the Court of the Crimson King — An Observation by King Crimson	1969	20.00
❑ SD 8266	In the Wake of Poseidon	1970	20.00
❑ SD 8278	Lizard	1971	20.00
❑ SD 18110	Red	1974	15.00
❑ SD 18136	USA	1975	15.00
❑ SD 19155	In the Court of the Crimson King — An Observation by King Crimson	1978	12.00
—Reissue of Atlantic 8245			
EDITIONS EG			
❑ EGKC-1	In the Court of the Crimson King — An Observation by King Crimson	1985	12.00
—Reissue of Atlantic 19155			
❑ EGKC-2	In the Wake of Poseidon	1985	12.00
—Reissue of Atlantic 8266			
❑ EGKC-3	Lizard	1985	12.00
—Reissue of Atlantic 8278			
❑ EGKC-4	Islands	1985	12.00
—Reissue of Atlantic 7212			
❑ EGKC-6	Lark's Tongue in Aspic	1985	12.00
—Reissue of Atlantic 7263			
❑ EGKC-7	Starless and Bible Black	1985	12.00
—Reissue of Atlantic 7298			
❑ EGKC-8	Red	1985	12.00
—Reissue of Atlantic 18110			
❑ EGKC-9	USA	1985	12.00
—Reissue of Atlantic 18135			
❑ EGKC-10 [(2)]	The Young Person's Guide to King Crimson	1985	22.00
MOBILE FIDELITY			
❑ 1-075	In the Court of the Crimson King — An Observation by King Crimson	1981	120.00
—Audiophile vinyl			
WARNER BROS.			
❑ WBMS-119 [DJ]	The Return of King Crimson	1981	35.00
—Promo-only interview and music show			
❑ BSK 3629	Discipline	1981	10.00
❑ 23692	Beat	1982	10.00
❑ 25071	Three of a Perfect Pair	1984	10.00

KING CROONERS, THE

Number	Title (A Side/B Side)	Yr	NM
45s			
EXCELLO			
❑ 2168	Won't You Let Me Know/ Now That She's Gone	1959	40.00
❑ 2187	Memoirs/School Daze	1960	60.00
HART			
❑ 1002	She's Mine All Mine/ Lonely Nights	1959	400.00

KING CURTIS

Number	Title (A Side/B Side)	Yr	NM
45s			
ABC-PARAMOUNT			
❑ 10133	Beatnick Hoedown/ King Neptune's Guitar	1960	15.00
ALCOR			
❑ 1016	Jay Walk/The Lone Prairie	1961	20.00
APOLLO			
❑ 507	King's Rock/Dynamite at Midnight	1957	30.00
ATCO			
❑ 6114	The Birth of the Blues/ Just Smoochin'	1958	20.00
❑ 6124	You Made Me Love You/Ific	1958	20.00
❑ 6135	Castle Rock/Chili	1959	20.00
❑ 6143	Honey Dripper (Part 1)/ Honey Dripper (Part 2)	1959	20.00
❑ 6152	Heavenly Blues/Restless Guitar	1959	20.00
❑ 6387	Spanish Harlem/The Boss	1965	10.00
❑ 6406	On Broadway/Quicksand	1966	8.00
❑ 6419	Make the World Go Away/You've Lost That Lovin' Feeling	1966	8.00
❑ 6429	Dancing in the Streets/ He'll Have to Go	1966	8.00
❑ 6447	Pots and Pans (Part 1)/ Pots and Pans (Part 2)	1966	8.00
❑ 6457	Something on Your Mind/ Soul Theme	1966	8.00
❑ 6476	Jump Back/When Something Is Wrong with My Baby	1967	8.00
❑ 6496	You Don't Miss Your Water/ Green Onions	1967	8.00
❑ 6511	Memphis Soul Stew/ Blue Nocturne	1967	8.00
❑ 6516	Ode to Billie Joe/In the Pocket	1967	8.00
—As :The Kingpins:			
❑ 6534	For What It's Worth/Cook Out	1968	8.00
❑ 6547	I Never Loved a Man (The Way I Love You)/I Was Made to Love Her	1968	8.00
❑ 6562	(Sittin' On) The Dock of the Bay/ This Is Soul	1968	8.00
❑ 6582	(Theme from) Valley of the Dolls/Eighth Wonder	1968	8.00
❑ 6598	I Heard It Through the Grapevine/ Whiter Shade of Pale	1968	8.00
❑ 6613	Harper Valley P.T.A./Makin' Hey	1968	8.00
❑ 6630	The Christmas Song/What Are You Doing New Year's Eve?	1968	12.00
❑ 6664	Games People Play/ Foot Pattin' (Part 2)	1969	8.00
❑ 6680	Instant Groove/Sweet Inspiration	1969	8.00
❑ 6695	Little Green Apples/La Jeanne	1969	8.00
❑ 6711	C.C. Rider/Rocky Roll	1969	8.00
❑ 6720	Pop Corn Willie/Patty Cake	1969	8.00
❑ 6738	Soulin'/Teasin'	1970	6.00
❑ 6762	Get Ready/Bridge Over Troubled Water	1970	6.00
❑ 6779	Whole Lotta Love/Floatin'	1970	6.00
❑ 6785	Changes (Part 1)/ Changes (Part 2)	1970	6.00
❑ 6834	Changes (Part 1)/ Changes (Part 2)	1971	6.00

Except when noted otherwise, VG = 25% of NM, and VG+ = 50% of NM. (Example: VG = $2.00, VG+ = $4.00 and NM = $8.00.)

Number	Title (A Side/B Side)	Yr	NM
❑ 6908	Ridin' Thumb (Part 1)/ Ridin' Thumb (Part 2)	1972	6.00
CAPITOL			
❑ 4788	Beach Party/Turn 'Em On	1962	10.00
❑ 4841	Beautiful Brown Eyes/ Your Cheatin' Heart	1962	10.00
❑ 4891	Strollin' Home/Mess Around	1962	10.00
❑ 4998	Do the Monkey/Feel All Right	1963	10.00
❑ 5061	Theme from "Lilies of the Field" (Part 1)/Theme from "Lilies of the Field" (Part 2)	1963	10.00
❑ 5109	Soul Serenade/More Soul	1964	10.00
❑ 5212	Summer Dream/ Melancholy Serenade	1964	10.00
❑ 5270	Stranger on the Shore/Hide Away	1964	10.00
❑ 5324	Sister Sadie/Tanya	1964	10.00
❑ 5377	Bill Bailey/Soul Twine	1965	10.00
❑ 5490	The Prance/Slow Drag	1965	10.00
DELUXE			
❑ 6142	The Stranger/Steel Guitar Rag	1957	25.00
❑ 6157	Wicky Wacky (Part 1)/ Wicky Wacky (Part 2)	1958	25.00
ENJOY			
❑ 1000	Soul Twist/Twisting Time	1962	15.00
❑ 1001	Twisting with the King/ Wobble Twist	1962	15.00
EVEREST			
❑ 19406	Jay Walk/The Lone Prairie	1961	15.00
EVERLAST			
❑ 5030	Soul Twist/Twisting Time	1965	10.00
GEM			
❑ 208	Tenor in the Sky/No More Crying on My Pillow	1954	40.00
GROOVE			
❑ 1060	Movin' On/Rockabye Baby	1956	25.00
KING			
❑ 5647	King Curtis Stomp/ Steel Guitar Rag	1962	12.00
MONARCH			
❑ 702	Wine Head/I've Got News for You Baby	1953	60.00
NEW JAZZ			
❑ 45-510	Soul Meeting/All the Way	1961	15.00
SEG-WAY			
❑ 1006	Hot Rod/Bonaparte's Retreat	1962	15.00
SKY ROCKET			
❑ 106	Madisonville (Part 1)/ Madisonville (Part 2)	1960	20.00
TRU SOUND			
❑ 401	Trouble in Mind/But That's Alright	1961	15.00
❑ 406	Twistin' and Jivin'/I Have to Worry	1961	15.00
❑ 412	So Rare/Hucklebuck Twist	1961	15.00
❑ 415	Free for All/When the Saints Go Marching In	1962	15.00
❑ 422	Low Down/I'll Wait for You	1962	15.00
7-Inch Extended Plays			
ATCO			
❑ SD 37-189	Spanish Harlem/I Left My Heart in San Francisco/Cryin' Time/ /You've Lost That Lovin' Feeling/And I Love Her/ Make the World Go Away	1966	20.00
—Jukebox issue; small hole, plays at 33 1/3 rpm			
❑ SD 37-189 [PS]	That Lovin' Feeling	1966	20.00
❑ SD 37-266	Harper Valley P.T.A./Ode to Billy Joe/I Was Made to Love Her//Soul Serenade/The Dock of the Bay/Jump Back	1968	20.00
—Jukebox issue; small hole, plays at 33 1/3 rpm			
❑ SD 37-266 [PS]	The Best of King Curtis	1968	20.00
ATLANTIC			
❑ SD 7-33-338	Let It Be/Get Ready/Something// Sugar Foot/Soulin'/Someday We'll Be Together	197?	15.00
—Stereo jukebox issue; small hole, plays at 33 1/3 rpm			
❑ SD 7-33-338 [PS]	Get Ready	197?	15.00
—Part of "Little LP" series (#217)			
CAPITOL			
❑ SXA-1756	Home on the Range/Wagon Wheels/Walkin' the Floor Over You//Brown Eyes/Tennessee Waltz/Night Train to Memphis	1963	30.00
—Jukebox issue; small hole, plays at 33 1/3 rpm			
❑ SXA-1756 [PS]	Country Soul	1963	30.00

King Curtis, *Arthur Murray's Music for Dancing: The Twist*, RCA Victor LSP-2494, 1962, stereo, **$30.**

Number	Title (A Side/B Side)	Yr	NM
EVEREST			
❑ 196121	Close Your Eyes/Unchained Melody/Off Shore//It Ain't Necessarily So/Our Love Is Here to Stay/My Love Is Your Love	1961	50.00
—Jukebox issue; small hole, plays at 33 1/3 rpm			
❑ 196121 [PS]	Azure	1961	50.00
Albums			
ATCO			
❑ 33-113 [M]	Have Tenor Sax, Will Blow	1959	40.00
❑ SD 33-113 [S]	Have Tenor Sax, Will Blow	1959	60.00
❑ 33-189 [M]	That Lovin' Feeling	1966	20.00
❑ SD 33-189 [S]	That Lovin' Feeling	1966	25.00
❑ 33-198 [M]	Live at Small's Paradise	1966	20.00
❑ SD 33-198 [S]	Live at Small's Paradise	1966	25.00
❑ 33-211 [M]	The Great Memphis Hits	1967	20.00
❑ SD 33-211 [S]	The Great Memphis Hits	1967	25.00
❑ 33-231 [M]	King Size Soul	1967	25.00
❑ SD 33-231 [S]	King Size Soul	1967	20.00
❑ 33-247 [M]	Sweet Soul	1968	30.00
❑ SD 33-247 [S]	Sweet Soul	1968	20.00
❑ SD 33-266	The Best of King Curtis	1968	20.00
❑ SD 33-293	Instant Groove	1969	20.00
❑ SD 33-338	Get Ready	1970	20.00
❑ SD 33-359	Live at Fillmore West	1971	20.00
❑ SD 33-385	Everybody's Talkin'	1972	20.00
ATLANTIC			
❑ SD 1637	Blues Montreux	1973	12.00
CAPITOL			
❑ ST 1756 [S]	Country Soul	1963	40.00
❑ T 1756 [M]	Country Soul	1963	30.00
❑ ST 2095 [S]	Soul Serenade	1964	30.00
❑ T 2095 [M]	Soul Serenade	1964	25.00
❑ ST 2341 [S]	King Curtis Plays the Hits Made Famous by Sam Cooke	1965	30.00
❑ T 2341 [M]	King Curtis Plays the Hits Made Famous by Sam Cooke	1965	25.00
❑ ST 2858 [S]	The Best of King Curtis	1968	25.00
❑ T 2858 [M]	The Best of King Curtis	1968	50.00
—Red and white "Starline" label; may be promo only			

Number	Title (A Side/B Side)	Yr	NM
❑ SM-11798	Soul Serenade	1978	10.00
—Reissue			
❑ SM-11963	The Best of King Curtis	1979	10.00
—Reissue			
CLARION			
❑ 615 [M]	The Great "K" Curtis	1966	20.00
❑ SD 615 [S]	The Great "K" Curtis	1966	25.00
COLLECTABLES			
❑ COL-5119	Soul Twist	198?	10.00
❑ COL-5156	Golden Classics: Enjoy... The Best of King Curtis	198?	10.00
ENJOY			
❑ ENLP-2001 [M]	Soul Twist	1962	50.00
EVEREST			
❑ SDBR-1121 [S]	Azure	1961	75.00
❑ LPBR-5121 [M]	Azure	1961	50.00
FANTASY			
❑ OJC-198	The New Scene of King Curtis	1985	10.00
—Reissue of New Jazz 8237			
❑ OBC-512	Trouble in Mind	1988	10.00
—Reissue of Tru-Sound 15001			
NEW JAZZ			
❑ NJLP-8237 [M]	The New Scene of King Curtis	1960	60.00
—Purple label			
❑ NJLP-8237 [M]	The New Scene of King Curtis	1965	30.00
—Blue label with trident logo on right			
PRESTIGE			
❑ PRLP-7222 [M]	Soul Meeting	1962	50.00
❑ PRST-7222 [S]	Soul Meeting	1962	75.00
❑ PRST-7709	The Best of King Curtis	1969	15.00
❑ PRST-7775	The Best of King Curtis — One More Time	1970	15.00
❑ PRST-7789	King Soul	1970	15.00
❑ PRST-7833	Soul Meeting	1971	15.00
—Reissue of 7222			
❑ 24033 [(2)]	Jazz Groove	198?	15.00
RCA CAMDEN			
❑ CAS-2242	Sax in Motion	1968	15.00

K

Number	Title (A Side/B Side)	Yr	NM
RCA VICTOR			
❑ LPM-2494 [M]	Arthur Murray's Music for Dancing: The Twist!	1962	25.00
❑ LSP-2494 [S]	Arthur Murray's Music for Dancing: The Twist!	1962	30.00
TRU-SOUND			
❑ TS-15001 [M]	Trouble in Mind	1961	50.00
❑ TS-15008 [M]	It's Party Time	1962	50.00
❑ TS-15009 [M]	Doin' the Dixie Twist	1962	50.00

KING FAMILY, THE

Number	Title (A Side/B Side)	Yr	NM
45s			
WARNER BROS.			
❑ PRO 216 [DJ]	Go Tell It on the Mountain/Here the Sledges with the Bells	1965	10.00
❑ 5647	The Sweetheart Tree/Amen	1965	6.00
❑ 5678	Just One Smile/Today I'm in Love	1965	6.00
❑ 5869	The Men in My Little Girl's Life/Bill Bailey (Won't You Please Come Home)	1966	6.00
Albums			
CAPITOL			
❑ DT 2352 [R]	Love at Home	1965	12.00
❑ T 2352 [M]	Love at Home	1965	15.00
FANNY FARMER/FLEETWOOD			
❑ FCLP 3039	Fanny Farmer Presents The King Family Christmas Album	196?	12.00
HARMONY			
❑ HS 11293	The Wonderful King Family	196?	10.00
WARNER BROS.			
❑ W 1601 [M]	The King Family Show!	1965	12.00
❑ WS 1601 [S]	The King Family Show!	1965	15.00
❑ W 1613 [M]	The King Family Album	1965	12.00
❑ WS 1613 [S]	The King Family Album	1965	15.00
❑ W 1627 [M]	Christmas with the King Family	1965	12.00
❑ WS 1627 [S]	Christmas with the King Family	1965	15.00
❑ W 1633 [M]	Sunday with the King Family	1966	12.00
❑ WS 1633 [S]	Sunday with the King Family	1966	15.00

KING FLOYD

Because this is a male singer whose first name is 'King" and last name is "Floyd," he can be found in the letter F under "Floyd."

KING HARVEST

Number	Title (A Side/B Side)	Yr	NM
45s			
A&M			
❑ 1726	Little Bit Like Magic/Vaea	1975	4.00
❑ 1761	Lovestruck/Hickory	1975	4.00
PERCEPTION			
❑ 515	Dancing in the Moonlight/Marty and the Captain	1972	5.00
❑ 527	A Little Bit Like Magic/Elmore Bacon	1973	4.00
❑ 534	Take It Slow/Idaho	1973	4.00
❑ 556	Celestial Navigator/Angels of Mercy	1974	4.00
Albums			
A&M			
❑ SP-4540	King Harvest	1975	10.00
PERCEPTION			
❑ 36	Dancing in the Moonlight	1973	12.00

KING PINS, THE (1)

Number	Title (A Side/B Side)	Yr	NM
45s			
FEDERAL			
❑ 12480	Believe in Me/Don't Wait Pretty Baby	1963	20.00
❑ 12484	It Won't Be This Way (Always)/How Long Will It Last	1963	20.00
❑ 12505	The Monkey One More Time/With the Other Guy	1963	15.00
❑ 12512	Hop Scotch/Wonderful One	1964	15.00
❑ 12517	Two Hearts/I Won't Have It	1964	15.00
❑ 12519	I Got the Monkey Off My Back/You're Using Me	1964	15.00
Albums			
KING			
❑ 865 [M]	It Won't Be This Way Always	1963	300.00

KING PINS, THE (2)

Number	Title (A Side/B Side)	Yr	NM
45s			
LARSE			
❑ 101	94 Second Turf/Rod Hot Rod	1966	40.00
MGM			
❑ 13535	Rod Hot Rod/Door Banger	1966	30.00

KING RICHARD'S FLUEGEL KNIGHTS

Number	Title (A Side/B Side)	Yr	NM
45s			
MTA			
❑ 101	Milord/Happiness Is	1966	6.00
❑ 107	A Sign of the Times/England Swings	1966	6.00
❑ 110	The Crusades/Castle Holiday	1966	6.00
❑ 115	Cabaret/Sing, Sing, Sing	1966	6.00
❑ 120	Two Different Worlds/Everybody Loves My Baby	1967	6.00
❑ 131	Miniskirt Waltz/Horn Duey	1967	6.00
❑ 138	Camelot/Bye Bye Blues	1967	6.00
❑ 151	Feelin' Good/To Life	1968	5.00
❑ 154	Mrs. Robinson/Dessert	1968	5.00
❑ 161	Gentle on My Mind/Something Classic	1968	5.00
❑ 166	Memories Are Made of This/One of Those Songs	1969	5.00
❑ 187	Everybody Loves My Baby/Horn Duey	1970	5.00
Albums			
MTA			
❑ 5001	A Sign of the Times	1966	12.00
❑ 5005	Something Super	1967	12.00
❑ 5005	Something Super!	1968	12.00
❑ 5014	One of Those Songs	1969	12.00

KINGDOM

Number	Title (A Side/B Side)	Yr	NM
45s			
SPECIALTY			
❑ 722	Seven Fathoms Deep/If I Never Was to See Her Again	1970	12.00
Albums			
SPECIALTY			
❑ SPS-2135	Kingdom	1970	60.00

KINGFISH

Number	Title (A Side/B Side)	Yr	NM
Albums			
ROUND			
❑ RX-108	Kingfish	1976	16.00

KINGS, THE

Several different groups.

Number	Title (A Side/B Side)	Yr	NM
45s			
BATON			
❑ 245	Long Lonely Nights/Let Me Know	1957	40.00
EPIC			
❑ 9370	I Want to Know/Bomp-I-Ty Bump	1960	30.00
GONE			
❑ 5013	Don't Go/Love Is Something from Within	1957	100.00
GOTHAM			
❑ 316	God Made You Mine/The Good Book	1956	100.00
HARLEM			
❑ 2322	Fire in My Heart/You Never Know	1954	150.00
JALO			
❑ 203	Angel/Come On Little Baby	1958	40.00
JAY-WING			
❑ 5805	Surrender/Hold Me	1959	150.00
JOX			
❑ 052	I've Got a License/Just a Little Bit of You	1965	40.00
LOOKIE			
❑ 18	I Want to Know/Bomp-I-Ty Bump	1960	40.00
RCA VICTOR			
❑ 47-7419	Till You/Elephant Walk	1958	25.00
❑ 47-7544	Troubles Don't Last/Your Sweet Love	1959	25.00
SPECIALTY			
❑ 497	What Can I Do/Till I Say Well Done	1954	120.00

KINGSMEN, THE (1)

Northwest garage band. Northwest garage band. Also see JACK EELY.

Number	Title (A Side/B Side)	Yr	NM
45s			
FOREVER OLDIES			
❑ 21011	Louie Louie/Haunted Castle	197?	4.00
—Later issue of Scepter-Wand Forever 21011, "a product of Springboard International" at bottom			
JERDEN			
❑ 712	Louie Louie/Haunted Castle	1963	60.00
SCEPTER-WAND FOREVER			
❑ 21011	Louie Louie/Haunted Castle	197?	5.00
—Reissue			
WAND			
❑ 143	Louie Louie/Little Green Thing	196?	15.00
❑ 143	Louie, Louie/Haunted Castle	1963	20.00
❑ 143	Louie Louie 64-65-66.../Haunted Castle	1966	15.00
❑ 150	Money/Bent Scepter	1964	12.00
❑ 157	Little Latin Lupe Lu/David's Mood	1964	10.00
❑ 164	Death of an Angel/Searching for Love	1964	10.00
❑ 172	The Jolly Green Giant/Long Green	1965	12.00
❑ 183	The Climb/I'm Waiting	1965	10.00
❑ 189	Annie Fanny/Give Her Lovin'	1965	10.00
❑ 1107	(You Got) Gamma Goochie/It's Only the Dog	1965	15.00
❑ 1115	Killer Joe/Little Green Thing	1966	15.00
❑ 1118	The Krunch/The Climb	1966	15.00
❑ 1118 [PS]	The Krunch/The Climb	1966	25.00
❑ 1127	My Wife Can't Dance/Little Sally Tease	1966	10.00
❑ 1137	If I Need Someone/The Grass Is Green	1966	10.00
❑ 1147	Trouble/Daytime Shadows	1967	8.00
❑ 1154	The Wolf of Manhattan/Children's Caretaker	1967	8.00
❑ 1157	(I Have Found) Another Girl/Don't Say No	1967	8.00
❑ 1164	Bo Diddley Bach/Just Before the Break of Day	1968	8.00
❑ 1174	Get Out of My Life Woman/Since You've Been Gone	1968	8.00
❑ 1180	I Guess I Was Dreamin'/Oh Love	1968	8.00
Albums			
RHINO			
❑ RNLP-126	The Best of the Kingsmen	1985	10.00
SCEPTER			
❑ CTN-18002	The Best of the Kingsmen	1972	10.00
WAND			
❑ WDM-657 [M]	The Kingsmen In Person	1964	30.00
❑ WDS-657 [P]	The Kingsmen In Person	1964	40.00
❑ WDM-659 [M]	The Kingsmen, Vol. II	1964	30.00
—With "Death of an Angel"			
❑ WDM-659 [M]	The Kingsmen, Vol. II	1964	40.00
—Without "Death of an Angel" (replaced by untitled instrumental)			
❑ WDS-659 [S]	The Kingsmen, Vol. II	1964	40.00
—With "Death of an Angel"			
❑ WDS-659 [S]	The Kingsmen, Vol. II	1964	50.00
—Without "Death of an Angel" (replaced by untitled instrumental)			
❑ WDM-662 [M]	The Kingsmen, Vol. 3	1965	25.00
❑ WDS-662 [S]	The Kingsmen, Vol. 3	1965	30.00
❑ WDM-670 [M]	The Kingsmen On Campus	1965	25.00
❑ WDS-670 [S]	The Kingsmen On Campus	1965	30.00
❑ WDM-674 [M]	15 Great Hits	1966	20.00
❑ WDS-674 [P]	15 Great Hits	1966	25.00
❑ WDM-675 [M]	Up and Away	1966	20.00
❑ WDS-675 [S]	Up and Away	1966	25.00
❑ WDM-681 [M]	The Kingsmen's Greatest Hits	1967	15.00
❑ WDS-681 [S]	The Kingsmen's Greatest Hits	1967	20.00
❑ ST-91011 [S]	Up and Away	1966	30.00
—Capitol Record Club edition			

KINGSMEN, THE (2)

Instrumental group composed of former members of BILL HALEY AND HIS COMETS.

Number	Title (A Side/B Side)	Yr	NM
45s			
EASTWEST			
❑ 115	Week End/Better Believe It	1958	40.00
❑ 120	Conga Rock/The Cat Walk	1958	40.00

KINGSMEN, THE (3)

Number	Title (A Side/B Side)	Yr	NM
45s			
ALL STAR			
❑ 500	Guardian Angel/I'm Your Lover Man	1957	80.00

KINGSMEN, THE (U)

Some of these could have been by groups (1), (2) or (3).

Number	Title (A Side/B Side)	Yr	NM
45s			
ARNOLD			
❑ 2106	Goodnight Sweetheart/Humpty Dumpty	196?	120.00
CAPITOL			
❑ 3576	You Better Do Right/Today	1973	5.00
JALYNNE			
❑ 108	Ladies Choice/Dig This	1960	20.00
NEIL			
❑ 102	One Foolish Mistake/Stranded Love	1956	60.00

KINKS, THE

Also see DAVE DAVIES.

Number	Title (A Side/B Side)	Yr	NM
12-Inch Singles			
ARISTA			
❑ SP-34 [DJ]	Father Christmas/A Rock 'n' Roll Fantasy	1978	25.00
❑ SP-45 [DJ]	(Wish I Could Fly Like) Superman (3:45) (5:58)	1979	15.00
❑ SP-152 [DJ]	Come Dancing (same on both sides)	1983	15.00
❑ CP 700	(Wish I Could Fly Like) Superman/Low Budget	1979	8.00
❑ ADP 9095 [DJ]	Don't Forget to Dance (same on both sides)	1983	6.00
❑ ADP 9297 [DJ]	Do It Again (same on both sides)	1984	6.00

Except when noted otherwise, VG = 25% of NM, and VG+ = 50% of NM. (Example: VG = $2.00, VG+ = $4.00 and NM = $8.00.)

Number	Title (A Side/B Side)	Yr	NM
❑ ADP 9337 [DJ]	Summer's Gone (same on both sides)	1983	6.00

MCA

Number	Title (A Side/B Side)	Yr	NM
❑ L33-17207 [DJ]	Rock 'n' Roll Cities (same on both sides)	1987	6.00
❑ L33-17260 [DJ]	Lost and Found (same on both sides)	1987	6.00
❑ L33-17345 [DJ]	How Are You (same on both sides)	1987	6.00
❑ L33-17460 [DJ]	The Road (same on both sides)	1988	8.00
❑ L33-17498 [DJ]	The Road (Edit) (same on both sides)	1988	6.00
❑ L33-17531 [DJ]	Art Lover (Live)/Destroyer (Live)	1988	6.00

45s

ARISTA

Number	Title (A Side/B Side)	Yr	NM
❑ SP-5 [DJ]	Sleepwalker/All the Kids on the Street	1977	10.00

—Gold vinyl; B-side by the Hollywood Stars

Number	Title (A Side/B Side)	Yr	NM
❑ SP-5 [PS]	Sleepwalker/All the Kids on the Street	1977	10.00
❑ 0240	Sleepwalker/Full Moon	1977	4.00
❑ 0247	Life Goes On/Juke Box Music	1977	4.00
❑ 0296	Father Christmas/Prince of the Punks	1977	5.00
❑ 0296 [PS]	Father Christmas/Prince of the Punks	1977	5.00
❑ 0342	A Rock and Roll Fantasy/Live Life	1978	4.00
❑ 0372	Black Messiah/Live Life	1978	4.00
❑ 0409	(Wish I Could Fly Like) Superman/Party Line	1979	4.00
❑ 0409	Superman/Low Budget	1979	5.00
❑ 0448	Low Budget/A Gallon of Gas	1979	4.00
❑ 0458	Catch Me Now I'm Falling/Low Budget	1979	4.00
❑ 0541	Lola/Celluloid Heroes	1980	4.00
❑ 0541 [PS]	Lola/Celluloid Heroes	1980	5.00
❑ 0577	You Really Got Me/Attitude	1980	4.00
❑ 0619	Destroyer/Back to Back	1981	4.00
❑ 0649	Better Things/Yo-Yo	1981	4.00
❑ 1054	Come Dancing/Noise	1983	4.00
❑ 1054 [PS]	Come Dancing/Noise	1983	4.00
❑ 9016	Come Dancing/Noise	1983	3.00
❑ 9016 [PS]	Come Dancing/Noise	1983	3.00
❑ 9075	Don't Forget to Dance/Young Conservatives	1983	3.00
❑ 9309	Do It Again/Guilty	1984	3.00
❑ 9309 [PS]	Do It Again/Guilty	1984	3.00
❑ 9334	Summer's Gone/Going Solo	1985	3.00

CAMEO

Number	Title (A Side/B Side)	Yr	NM
❑ 308	Long Tall Sally/I Took My Baby Home	1964	600.00
❑ 345	Long Tall Sally/I Took My Baby Home	1965	300.00
❑ 348	You Still Want Me/You Do Something to Me	1965	—

—Canceled. NOTE: An EP on Cameo, which contains the four songs assigned to Cameo in the U.S., is a bootleg with little collector value.

MCA

Number	Title (A Side/B Side)	Yr	NM
❑ 52960	Rock 'N' Roll Cities/Sleazy Town	1986	3.00
❑ 52960 [PS]	Rock 'N' Roll Cities/Sleazy Town	1986	3.00
❑ 53015	Lost and Found/Killing Time	1987	3.00
❑ 53015 [PS]	Lost and Found/Killing Time	1987	3.00
❑ 53093	Working at the Factory/How Are You	1987	10.00
❑ 53699	How Do I Get Close/War Is Over	1989	10.00

RCA VICTOR

Number	Title (A Side/B Side)	Yr	NM
❑ 74-0620	20th Century Man/Skin and Bones	1971	8.00
❑ 74-0807	Supersonic Rocket Ship/You Don't Know My Name	1972	8.00
❑ 74-0852	Celluloid Heroes/Hot Potatoes	1972	8.00
❑ 74-0940	One of the Survivors/Scrap Heap City	1973	200.00

—Released with acoustic versions of the two songs rather than the LP versions and quickly deleted

Number	Title (A Side/B Side)	Yr	NM
❑ APBO-0275	Money Talks/Here Comes Flash	1974	10.00
❑ DJBO-0275 [DJ]	Money Talks (short/long versions)	1974	8.00
❑ LPBO-5001	Sitting in the Midday Sun/Sweet Lady Genevieve	1973	10.00
❑ PB-10019	Mirror of Love/It's Evil	1974	6.00
❑ PB-10121	Preservation/Salvation Road	1974	6.00
❑ PB-10251	Everybody's a Star (Starmaker)/Ordinary People	1975	6.00
❑ PB-10551	I'm in Disgrace/The Hard Way	1976	6.00

REPRISE

Number	Title (A Side/B Side)	Yr	NM
❑ 0306	You Really Got Me/It's All Right	1964	15.00

—Second pressings have orange and brown labels

Number	Title (A Side/B Side)	Yr	NM
❑ 0306	You Really Got Me/It's All Right	1964	25.00

—Originals have peach labels

Number	Title (A Side/B Side)	Yr	NM
❑ 0334	All Day and All of the Night/I Gotta Move	1964	20.00
❑ 0347	Tired of Waiting for You/Come On Now	1965	20.00
❑ 0366	Who'll Be the Next in Line/Everybody's Gonna Be Happy	1965	20.00

The Kinks, *Kinks-Size*, Reprise R 6158, 1965, mono, **$50.**

Number	Title (A Side/B Side)	Yr	NM
❑ 0379	Set Me Free/I Need You	1965	20.00
❑ 0409	See My Friends/Never Met a Girl Like You Before	1965	15.00
❑ 0420	A Well Repected Man/Such a Shame	1965	15.00
❑ 0454	Till the End of the Day/Where Have All the Good Times Gone	1966	15.00
❑ 0471	Dedicated Follower of Fashion/Sittin' on My Sofa	1966	15.00
❑ 0497	Sunny Afternoon/I'm Not Like Everybody Else	1966	15.00
❑ 0540	Dead End Street/Big Black Smoke	1966	40.00
❑ 0587	Mr. Pleasant/Harry Rag	1967	40.00
❑ 0612	Waterloo Sunset/Two Sisters	1967	40.00
❑ 0647	Autumn Almanac/David Watts	1967	40.00
❑ 0691	Wonderboy/Polly	1968	40.00
❑ 0708	Sunny Afternoon/Dead End Street	1968	10.00
❑ 0712	Dedicated Follower of Fashion/Who'll Be the Next in Line	1968	10.00
❑ 0715	A Well Respected Man/Set Me Free	1968	10.00
❑ 0719	Tired of Waiting for You/All Day and All of the Night	1968	10.00
❑ 0722	You Really Got Me/It's All Right	1968	10.00

—0708 through 0722 are "Back to Back Hits" series — originals have both "r:" and "W7" on label

Number	Title (A Side/B Side)	Yr	NM
❑ 0743	Lola/Apeman	1972	5.00

—"Back to Back Hits" series

Number	Title (A Side/B Side)	Yr	NM
❑ 0762	Days/She's Got Everything	1968	40.00
❑ 0806	Starstruck/Picture Book	1969	40.00
❑ 0847	The Village Green Preservation Society/Do You Remember Walter	1969	40.00
❑ 0863	Victoria/Brainwashed	1969	15.00
❑ 0930	Lola/Mindless Child of Motherhood	1970	10.00
❑ 0979	Apeman/Rats	1970	10.00
❑ 1017	God's Children/The Way Love Used to Be	1971	20.00
❑ 1094	King Kong/Waterloo Sunset	1972	15.00

7-Inch Extended Plays

ARISTA

Number	Title (A Side/B Side)	Yr	NM
❑ SP-22 [DJ]	A Rock 'n' Roll Fantasy/Black Messiah//Misfits/Permanent Waves	1978	10.00

—Promo-only square record; small hole, plays at 33 1/3 rpm

Number	Title (A Side/B Side)	Yr	NM
❑ SP-22 [PS]	The Kinks Misfit Record	1978	15.00

—Cardboard sleeve is round with slgithly squared-off sides and slits in all four corners and the top

CAMEO

Number	Title (A Side/B Side)	Yr	NM
❑ 315	Long Tall Sally/I Took My Baby Home//You Still Want Me/You Do Something To Me	196?	—

—This is a fake with little collector value; also comes with title sleeve; no such item was ever issued by Cameo

Albums

ARISTA

Number	Title	Yr	NM
❑ SP-69 [DJ]	Low Budget Radio Interview	1979	30.00

—Promo-only radio show featuring Ray Davies

Number	Title	Yr	NM
❑ SP-85 [EP]	A Fistful of Kinks	1980	18.00

—Promo-only four-song sampler from "One for the Road"

Number	Title	Yr	NM
❑ AL 4106	Sleepwalker	1977	10.00
❑ AL 4106 [DJ]	Sleepwalker	1977	30.00

—White label promo

Number	Title	Yr	NM
❑ AL 4167	Misfits	1978	10.00
❑ AL 4167 [DJ]	Misfits	1978	30.00

—White label promo

Number	Title	Yr	NM
❑ AB 4240	Low Budget	1979	10.00
❑ AL 8-8018	State of Confusion	1983	10.00
❑ AL13 8041 [(2)]	One for the Road	1983	10.00

—Reissue of 8609

Number	Title	Yr	NM
❑ AL 8264	Word of Mouth	1984	10.00
❑ ALB6 8300	Low Budget	1985	8.00

—Budget-line reissue

Number	Title	Yr	NM
❑ ALB6 8328	Give the People What They Want	1985	8.00

—Budget-line reissue

Number	Title	Yr	NM
❑ ALB6 8375	Sleepwalker	1985	8.00

—Budget-line reissue

Number	Title	Yr	NM
❑ ALB6 8377	Misfits	1985	8.00

—Budget-line reissue

Number	Title	Yr	NM
❑ A2L 8401 [(2)]	One for the Road	1980	15.00

—Original edition has this number

Number	Title (A Side/B Side)	Yr	NM
❑ AL11 8428 [(2)]	Come Dancing with the Kinks	1986	12.00
❑ A2L 8609 [(2)]	One for the Road	198?	12.00
—Second edition of 8401			
❑ AL 9567	Give the People What They Want	1981	10.00
COMPLEAT			
❑ CPL2-2001 [(2)]	A Compleat Collection	1984	12.00
❑ CPL2-2003 [(2)]	20th Anniversary Edition	1984	12.00
MCA			
❑ 5822	Think Visual	1987	10.00
❑ 6337	UK Jive	1989	12.00
❑ L33-17281 [DJ]	A Look at "Think Visual"	1987	30.00
—Promo only in white jacket			
❑ 42107	Live: The Road	1988	10.00
MOBILE FIDELITY			
❑ 1-070	Misfits	1981	40.00
—Audiophile vinyl			
PICKWICK			
❑ ACL-7072	Preservation Act 1	197?	12.00
—Reissue of RCA Victor LPL1-5002			
PYE			
❑ 505	The Kinks	1975	12.00
❑ 509	The Kinks, Vol. 2	1976	12.00
RCA VICTOR			
❑ APL1-1743	Celluloid Heroes (The Kinks' Greatest)	1976	10.00
❑ APL1-3520	Second Time Around	1980	10.00
❑ AYL1-3749	Schoolboys in Disgrace	1980	8.00
—Budget-line reissue			
❑ AYL1-3750	Soap Opera	1980	8.00
—Budget-line reissue			
❑ AYL1-3869	Celluloid Heroes (The Kinks' Greatest)	1981	8.00
—Budget-line reissue			
❑ AYL1-4558	Muswell Hillbillies	1982	8.00
—Budget-line reissue			
❑ LSP-4644	Muswell Hillbillies	1971	30.00
❑ AYL1-4719	Second Time Around	1983	8.00
—Budget-line reissue			
❑ LPL1-5002	Preservation Act 1	1973	15.00
❑ CPL2-5040 [(2)]	Preservation Act 2	1974	20.00
❑ LPL1-5081	Soap Opera	1975	10.00
—Brown label			
❑ LPL1-5081	Soap Opera	1975	15.00
—Orange label			
❑ LPL1-5102	Schoolboys in Disgrace	1975	10.00
❑ VPS-6065 [(2)]	Everybody's in Showbiz	1972	20.00
—Orange label			
❑ VPS-6065 [(2)]	Everybody's in Showbiz	1975	12.00
—Brown label			
REPRISE			
❑ PRO 328 [P]	Then Now and In Between	1969	50.00
—Album that came with above box is sometimes found by itself without all the other goodies.			
❑ PRO 328 [P]	God Save the Kinks	1969	500.00
—Mail-order box with decal, postcard, bag of grass, two pins, letter, Kinks consumer guide and "Then Now and In Between" LP. Price is for complete package.			
❑ MS-2127	The Great Lost Kinks Album	1973	50.00
❑ R-6143 [M]	You Really Got Me	1965	60.00
❑ R-6143 [M]	You Really Got Me	1965	400.00
—White label promo			
❑ RS-6143 [P]	You Really Got Me	1965	80.00
—Pink, gold and green label			
❑ RS-6143 [P]	You Really Got Me	1971	10.00
—Orange label with "r:" and steamboat at top			
❑ R-6158 [M]	Kinks-Size	1965	50.00
❑ R-6158 [M]	Kinks-Size	1965	200.00
—White label promo			
❑ RS-6158 [R]	Kinks-Size	1965	30.00
❑ R-6173 [M]	Kinda Kinks	1965	50.00
❑ R-6173 [M]	Kinda Kinks	1965	200.00
—White label promo			
❑ RS-6173 [R]	Kinda Kinks	1965	30.00
❑ R-6184 [M]	Kinks Kinkdom	1965	50.00
❑ R-6184 [M]	Kinks Kinkdom	1965	200.00
—White label promo			
❑ RS-6184 [R]	Kinks Kinkdom	1965	30.00
❑ R-6197 [M]	The Kink Kontroversy	1966	50.00
❑ R-6197 [M]	The Kink Kontroversy	1966	200.00
—White label promo			
❑ RS-6197 [R]	The Kink Kontroversy	1966	30.00
❑ R-6217 [M]	The Kinks Greatest Hits!	1966	40.00
❑ RS-6217 [R]	The Kinks Greatest Hits!	1966	25.00
—Pink, gold and green label			
❑ RS-6217 [R]	The Kinks Greatest Hits!	1971	10.00
—Orange label with "r:" and steamboat at top			
❑ R-6228 [M]	Face to Face	1967	40.00
❑ RS-6228 [P]	Face to Face	1967	30.00
—Pink, gold and green label			
❑ RS-6228 [P]	Face to Face	1971	10.00
—Orange label with "r:" and steamboat at top			
❑ R-6260 [M]	The Live Kinks	1967	35.00
❑ RS-6260 [S]	The Live Kinks	1967	25.00
—Pink, gold and green label			
❑ RS-6260 [S]	The Live Kinks	1971	10.00
—Orange label with "r:" and steamboat at top			
❑ R-6279 [M]	Something Else by the Kinks	1968	300.00
—White label promo; no stock copies were issued in mono			
❑ RS-6279 [S]	Something Else by the Kinks	1968	20.00
—Two-tone orange label with "r:" and "W7" logos with steamboat			
❑ RS-6279 [S]	Something Else by the Kinks	1968	30.00
—Pink, gold and green label			
❑ RS-6279 [S]	Something Else by the Kinks	1971	10.00
—Orange label with "r:" and steamboat at top			
❑ RS-6327	The Kinks Are the Village Green Preservation Society	1969	30.00
—Two-tone orange label with "r:" and "W7" logos with steamboat			
❑ RS-6327	The Kinks Are the Village Green Preservation Society	1971	10.00
—Orange label with "r:" and steamboat at top			
❑ RS-6366	Arthur (Or The Decline and Fall of the British Empire)	1969	25.00
—Two-tone orange label with "r:" and "W7" logos with steamboat			
❑ RS-6366	Arthur (Or The Decline and Fall of the British Empire)	1971	10.00
—Orange label with "r:" and steamboat at top			
❑ RS-6423	Lola Versus Powerman and the Moneygoround, Part One	1970	15.00
—Original pressings have blue printing on a white cover			
❑ RS-6423	Lola Versus Powerman and the Moneygoround, Part One	1971	10.00
—Later pressings have black printing on a white cover			
❑ 2XS-6454 [(2)]	The Kink Kronicles	1972	15.00
❑ SMAS-93034	Arthur (Or The Decline and Fall of the British Empire)	1970	40.00
—Capitol Record Club edition			
RHINO			
❑ R1 70086	The Kinks Greatest Hits! Vol. 1	1989	12.00
❑ R1 70315	You Really Got Me	1988	12.00
❑ R1 70316	Kinda Kinks	1988	12.00
❑ R1 70317	Kinks-Size	1988	12.00
❑ R1 70318	Kinks Kinkdom	1988	12.00

KIPPINGTON LODGE With Nick Lowe.

45s

Number	Title (A Side/B Side)	Yr	NM
CAPITOL			
❑ 2236	And She Cried/Rumors	1968	30.00

KIRBY, BUZZ

45s

Number	Title (A Side/B Side)	Yr	NM
PARKWAY			
❑ 906	Speedo/She's My Girl	1964	12.00

KIRBY, DAVE

45s

Number	Title (A Side/B Side)	Yr	NM
BOONE			
❑ 1078	Marie St. John/My Faults Will Fade Away	1969	8.00
❑ 1083	A Walk on the Outside/Mary and Jane	1969	8.00
CAPITOL			
❑ 4119	Colorado/Good to Be Back on the Road	1975	6.00
DIMENSION			
❑ 1013	Great All American Good Timin' Honky Tonk Man/Ain't Nothing Older Than That	1980	5.00
❑ 1019	North Alabama/How Can I Tell You Goodbye	1981	5.00
❑ 1022	Moccasin Man/When Will Forgetting Begin	1981	5.00
❑ 1030	Something New to Love/Cowboy Connection	1982	5.00
DOT			
❑ 17437	Lila Is My Kind of Woman/So Long Train Whistle	1972	6.00
MONUMENT			
❑ 1168	Her and the Car and the Mobile Home/Don't It Make You Want to Go Home	1969	6.00
❑ 1215	I Came Out Smelling Like a Rose/The Hobo	1970	6.00
RED FEATHER			
❑ 18174	The Old Old House/Cantaloupe Jones	196?	20.00
—Red vinyl			
SOMA			
❑ 1416	The Old, Old House/Cantalope Jones	1964	12.00
ZODIAC			
❑ 1007	What Kind of Bird Is That/Gonna Ride the Santa Fe to Santa Fe	1976	6.00

Albums

Number	Title (A Side/B Side)	Yr	NM
DOT			
❑ DLP-26014	Singer, Picker, Writer	1973	12.00

KIRBY, GEORGE

45s

Number	Title (A Side/B Side)	Yr	NM
ARGO			
❑ 5498	Feeling Good/No More	1965	15.00
❑ 5498 [PS]	Feeling Good/No More	1965	20.00
CADET			
❑ 5523	What Can I Do/Goodnight Irene	1966	500.00
CAMEO			
❑ 317	(I Want Some) Meat on My Tomatoes/No Communication	1964	50.00

7-Inch Extended Plays

Number	Title (A Side/B Side)	Yr	NM
DOOTO			
❑ DTE-257	(contents unknown)	196?	10.00
❑ DTE-257 [PS]	A Night in Hollywood, Part 1	196?	10.00
❑ DTE-258	(contents unknown)	196?	10.00
❑ DTE-258 [PS]	A Night in Hollywood, Part 2	196?	10.00

Albums

Number	Title (A Side/B Side)	Yr	NM
ARGO			
❑ LP-4045 [M]	The Real George Kirby	1965	30.00
❑ LPS-4045 [S]	The Real George Kirby	1965	40.00
DOOTO			
❑ DTL-250 [M]	A Night in Hollywood	196?	20.00

KIRBY, KATHY

45s

Number	Title (A Side/B Side)	Yr	NM
ASCOT			
❑ 2232	In All the World/Time	1967	8.00
LONDON			
❑ 9572	(He's a) Big Man/Slowly	1963	15.00
❑ 9621	Dance On/Playboy	1963	15.00
❑ 9628	Secret Love/Too Bad for Johnny	1964	15.00
❑ 9645	Let Me Go Lover/Sweetest Sounds	1964	15.00
❑ 9677	Love Me Baby/You're the One	1964	15.00
❑ 9750	I Belong/I'll Try Not to Cry	1965	15.00
PARROT			
❑ 9767	Secret Love/Soon I'll Wed My Love	1965	12.00
❑ 9775	The Way of Love/Oh Darling How I Miss You	1965	12.00
❑ 9805	Where in the World/Wonderful Feeling of Love	1965	12.00
❑ 9827	Till the End of Time/Spanish Flea	1966	10.00

KIRK, DAVE

45s

Number	Title (A Side/B Side)	Yr	NM
HI-Q			
❑ 5024	Oh! Baby/Those Lonely Blue Nights	1962	50.00

KISS Also see PETER CRISS; ACE FREHLEY; GENE SIMMONS; PAUL STANLEY (and their simultaneously released solo albums from 1978).

12-Inch Singles

Number	Title (A Side/B Side)	Yr	NM
CASABLANCA			
❑ 20169	I Was Made for Lovin' You/Charisma	1979	25.00
MERCURY			
❑ PRO 229-1 [DJ]	Lick It Up (same on both sides)	1983	15.00
❑ PRO 244-1 [DJ]	All Hell's Breaking Loose (same on both sides)	1983	15.00
❑ PRO 311-1 [DJ]	Heaven's on Fire (same on both sides)	1984	15.00
❑ PRO 326-1 [DJ]	Thrills in the Night (same on both sides)	1984	15.00
❑ PRO 377-1 [DJ]	Tears Are Falling (3:55) (same on both sides)	1985	15.00
❑ PRO 395-1 [DJ]	Uh! All Night (3:43) (same on both sides)	1985	15.00
❑ PRO 531-1 [DJ]	Crazy Crazy Nights (same on both sides)	1987	12.00
❑ PRO 559-1 [DJ]	Reason to Live (same on both sides)	1987	12.00
❑ PRO 572-1 [DJ]	Turn On the Night (same on both sides)	1987	12.00
❑ PRO 693-1 [DJ]	Let's Put the X in Sex (X-Cessive Mix 7:33)/(Hot Urban Mix 3:58) (Sex-A-Pella Mix 4:37)/Calling Dr. Love	1989	40.00

45s

Number	Title (A Side/B Side)	Yr	NM
CASABLANCA			
❑ 0004	Love Theme from Kiss/Nothin' to Lose	1974	15.00
❑ 0011	Kissin' Time/Nothin' to Lose	1974	15.00
❑ 0015	Strutter/100,000 Years	1974	15.00
❑ 823	Let Me Go, Rock and Roll/Hotter Than Hell	1975	20.00
—Blue label			
❑ 823	Let Me Go, Rock and Roll/Hotter Than Hell	1977	12.00
—"Casablanca Record and FilmWorks" label			

Except when noted otherwise, VG = 25% of NM, and VG+ = 50% of NM. (Example: VG = $2.00, VG+ = $4.00 and NM = $8.00.)

Number	Title (A Side/B Side)	Yr	NM
❑ 829	Rock and Roll All Nite/Getaway	1975	20.00
❑ 841	C'mon and Love Me/Getaway	1975	20.00
—Blue label			
❑ 841	C'mon and Love Me/Getaway	1977	12.00
—"Casablanca Record and FilmWorks" label			
❑ 850	Rock and Roll All Nite (Live)/Rock and Roll All Nite (Studio)	1975	10.00
—Blue label			
❑ 850	Rock and Roll All Nite (Live)/Rock and Roll All Nite (Studio)	1977	12.00
—"Casablanca Record and FilmWorks" label			
❑ 854	Shout It Out Loud/Sweet Pain	1976	10.00
—Blue label			
❑ 854	Shout It Out Loud/Sweet Pain	1977	8.00
—"Casablanca Record and FilmWorks" label			
❑ 858	Flaming Youth/God of Thunder	1976	10.00
❑ 858 [PS]	Flaming Youth/God of Thunder	1976	60.00
❑ 863	Beth/Detroit Rock City	1976	6.00
—With "Beth" listed as "Side A"; brown label with camel			
❑ 863	Detroit Rock City/Beth	1976	10.00
—With "Detroit Rock City" listed as "Side A"			
❑ 863	Beth/Detroit Rock City	1977	5.00
—With "Beth" listed as "Side A"; "Casablanca Record and FilmWorks" label			
❑ 873	Hard Luck Woman/Mr. Speed	1976	6.00
❑ 880	Calling Dr. Love/Take Me	1977	5.00
—"Casablanca Record and FilmWorks" label			
❑ 880	Calling Dr. Love/Take Me	1977	6.00
—Brown label with camel			
❑ 889	Christine Sixteen/Shock Me	1977	5.00
—A-side time listed as 2:52, B-side time listed as 4:17; "Casablanca Record and FilmWorks" label			
❑ 889	Christine Sixteen/Shock Me	1977	5.00
—A-side time listed as 3:10, B-side time listed as 3:45; "Casablanca Record and FilmWorks" label			
❑ 889	Christine Sixteen/Shock Me	1977	6.00
—A-side time listed as 2:52, B-side time listed as 4:17; brown label with camel			
❑ 889	Christine Sixteen/Shock Me	1977	6.00
—A-side time listed as 3:10, B-side time listed as 3:45; brown label with camel			
❑ 895	Love Gun/Hooligan	1977	6.00
❑ 906	Shout It Out Loud (Live)/ Nothin' to Lose	1977	6.00
❑ 915	Rocket Ride/Tomorrow and Tonight	1978	6.00
❑ 928	Strutter '78/Shock Me	1978	6.00
❑ 983	I Was Made for Lovin' You/ Hard Times	1979	5.00
❑ 2205	Sure Know Something/ Dirty Livin'	1979	5.00
❑ 2282	Shandi/She's So European	1980	5.00
❑ 2299	Tomorrow/Naked City	1980	5.00
❑ 2343	A World Without Heroes/ Dark Light	1981	5.00
❑ 2365	I Love It Loud/Danger	1982	5.00
❑ 2365 [PS]	I Love It Loud/Danger	1982	20.00

LOOKOUT!

Number	Title (A Side/B Side)	Yr	NM
❑ LK-238	Detroit Rock City/Strutter	1999	8.00
—B-side by The Donnas; small hole, clear vinyl			
❑ LK-238 [PS]	Detroit Rock City/Strutter	1999	8.00

MERCURY

Number	Title (A Side/B Side)	Yr	NM
❑ PRO 694-7 [DJ]	Let's Put the X in Sex (Hot Urban Mix)/(Hot Rock Mix)	1989	25.00
❑ PRO 1086-7 [DJ]	Rock and Roll All Nite	1993	30.00
—White label; small hole; B-side blank; comes in white sleeve that says "It's the Music Stupid" (included in above value)			
❑ 814671-7	Lick It Up/Dance All Over Your Face	1983	4.00
❑ 818216-7	All Hell's Breaking Loose/ Young and Wasted	1984	4.00
❑ 858894-7	Detroit Rock City/ Detroit Rock City	1994	4.00
—B-side by Mighty Mighty Bosstones; small center hole; green vinyl			
❑ 858894-7 [PS]	Detroit Rock City/ Detroit Rock City	1994	5.00
❑ 870022-7	Reason to Live/Thief in the Night	1987	4.00
❑ 870022-7 [PS]	Reason to Live/Thief in the Night	1987	6.00
❑ 870215-7	Turn On the Night/ Hell or High Water	1988	4.00
❑ 870215-7 [PS]	Turn On the Night/ Hell or High Water	1988	5.00
❑ 872244-7	Let's Put the X in Sex/ Calling Dr. Love	1989	5.00
❑ 872244-7 [PS]	Let's Put the X in Sex/ Calling Dr. Love	1989	6.00
❑ 876146-7	Hide Your Heart/Betrayed	1989	5.00
❑ 876716-7	Forever/The Street Giveth and the Street Taketh Away	1990	5.00
❑ 880205-7	Heaven's on Fire/ Lonely Is the Hunter	1984	4.00
❑ 880535-7	Thrills in the Night/ Burn Bitch Burn	1985	4.00
❑ 884141-7	Tears Are Falling/Any Way You Slice It	1985	4.00
❑ 884141-7 [PS]	Tears Are Falling/Any Way You Slice It	1985	5.00
❑ 888796-7	Crazy Crazy Nights/No, No, No	1987	4.00
❑ 888796-7 [PS]	Crazy Crazy Nights/No, No, No	1987	5.00

Kiss, *Hotter Than Hell*, Casablanca NBLP 7006, 1974, blue label, **$30.**

Albums

CASABLANCA

Number	Title (A Side/B Side)	Yr	NM
❑ Kiss '76 [DJ]	Special Kiss Tour Album	1976	80.00
—Special four-track sampler			
❑ NBLP 737 [DJ]	Rock and Roll Over Special Edition	1977	120.00
—Five-track sampler from the LP			
❑ NBLP 7001	Kiss	1974	30.00
—All renumbered versions have "Kissin' Time"; dark blue label			
❑ NBLP 7001	Kiss	1976	15.00
—Tan label with desert scene, "Casablanca" label			
❑ NBLP 7001	Kiss	1977	12.00
—Tan label with desert scene, "Casablanca Record and FilmWorks" label			
❑ NBLP 7006	Hotter Than Hell	1974	30.00
—Dark blue label			
❑ NBLP 7006	Hotter Than Hell	1976	15.00
—Tan label with desert scene, "Casablanca" label			
❑ NBLP 7006	Hotter Than Hell	1977	12.00
—Tan label with desert scene, "Casablanca Record and FilmWorks" label			
❑ NBLP 7016	Dressed to Kill	1975	30.00
—Dark blue label			
❑ NBLP 7016	Dressed to Kill	1976	15.00
—Tan label with desert scene, "Casablanca" label			
❑ NBLP 7016	Dressed to Kill	1977	12.00
—Tan label with desert scene, "Casablanca Record and FilmWorks" label			
❑ NBLP 7020 [(2)]	Alive!	1975	40.00
—Dark blue labels; with booklet			
❑ NBLP 7020 [(2)]	Alive!	1976	20.00
—Tan labels with desert scene, "Casablanca" label			
❑ NBLP 7020 [(2)]	Alive!	1977	15.00
—Tan labels with desert scene, "Casablanca Record and FilmWorks" label			
❑ NBLP 7025	Destroyer	1976	15.00
—Tan label with desert scene, "Casablanca" label			
❑ NBLP 7025	Destroyer	1976	30.00
—Dark blue label			
❑ NBLP 7025	Destroyer	1977	12.00
—Tan label with desert scene, "Casablanca Record and FilmWorks" label			
❑ NBLP 7032 [(3)]	The Originals	1976	100.00
—Tan label with desert scene, "Casablanca" label; without extras			
❑ NBLP 7032 [(3)]	The Originals	1976	150.00
—Tan label with desert scene, "Casablanca" label; with booklet, six Kiss cards, a Kiss Army sticker			
❑ NBLP 7032 [(3)]	The Originals	1977	50.00
—Tan label with desert scene, "Casablanca Record and FilmWorks" label; "Second Printing" on cover; without extras			
❑ NBLP 7032 [(3)]	The Originals	1977	100.00
—Tan label with desert scene, "Casablanca Record and FilmWorks" label; "Second Printing" on cover; with extras listed above			
❑ NBLP 7037	Rock and Roll Over	1976	20.00
—Tan label with desert scene, "Casablanca" label; comes with sticker and Kiss Army paraphenalia order form			
❑ NBLP 7037	Rock and Roll Over	1977	12.00
—Tan label with desert scene, "Casablanca Record and FilmWorks" label, with inserts			
❑ NBLP 7057	Love Gun	1977	12.00
—Without inserts			
❑ NBLP 7057	Love Gun	1977	40.00
—with "Hot Goods from the Supply Depot" order form, unpunched-out cardboard gun and "Bang!" sticker. All items must be intact to get top dollar for this.			
❑ NBLP 7076 [(2)]	Alive II	1977	15.00
—Without inserts			
❑ NBLP 7076 [(2)]	Alive II	1977	40.00
—With 8-page booklet, tattoo insert and "Combat Gear" order form; back cover contents are correct			
❑ NBLP 7076 [(2)]	Alive II	1977	400.00
—With 8-page booklet, tattoo insert and "Combat Gear" order form; back cover lists three tracks — "Take Me," "Hooligan" and "Do You Love Me" — that were not included on the record; no records with these tracks were made; perhaps as few as 50 copies of this cover were made			
❑ NBLP 7100 [(2)]	Double Platinum	1978	15.00
—Without inserts			
❑ NBLP 7100 [(2)]	Double Platinum	1978	40.00
—With "platinum award" cardboard insert and "Double Platinum Kiss Gear" order form			
❑ NBLP 7152	Dynasty	1979	10.00
—With neither poster nor order form			
❑ NBLP 7152	Dynasty	1979	15.00
—With poster and merchandise order form			
❑ NBLP 7225	Kiss Unmasked	1980	10.00
—With neither poster nor order form			
❑ NBLP 7225	Kiss Unmasked	1980	15.00
—With poster and "Kiss Essential Gear" order form			

Kiss, "Let's Put the X in Sex," Mercury 872244-7, 1989, **$6.**

Number	Title (A Side/B Side)	Yr	NM
❑ NBLP 7261	Music from The Elder	1981	30.00
—Various editions have paper or plastic innersleeves, lyric sheets, even incorrect track listings on the back cover; no difference in value is noted between variations			
❑ NBLP 7270	Creatures of the Night	1982	40.00
—Original version has band with makeup			
❑ NB 9001	Kiss	1974	50.00
—Second Warner Bros.-distributed version DOES have "Kissin' Time" on Side 2 (RE-1 on label)			
❑ NB 9001	Kiss	1974	80.00
—First Warner Bros.-distributed version does NOT have "Kissin' Time"			
❑ NB 20128 [DJ]	A Taste of Platinum	1978	50.00
—Promo-only sampler from Double Platinum			
❑ NB 20137 [DJ]	Peter Criss, Ace Frehley, Gene Simmons, Paul Stanley	1978	40.00
—Promo-only sampler from the band's solo albums			
❑ 812770-1	Dynasty	1983	8.00
—Reissue			
❑ 822780-1 [(2)]	Alive!	1984	10.00
—Reissue			
❑ 822781-1 [(2)]	Alive II	1984	10.00
—Reissue			
❑ 824146-1	Kiss	1984	8.00
—Reissue			
❑ 824147-1	Hotter Than Hell	1984	8.00
—Reissue			
❑ 824148-1	Dressed to Kill	1984	8.00
—Reissue			
❑ 824149-1	Destroyer	1984	8.00
—Reissue			
❑ 824150-1	Rock and Roll Over	1984	8.00
—Reissue			
❑ 824151-1	Love Gun	1984	8.00
—Reissue			
❑ 824153-1	Music from The Elder	1984	8.00
—Reissue			
❑ 824154-1	Creatures of the Night	1984	8.00
—Reissue; features band without its makeup on cover			
❑ 824154-1	Creatures of the Night	1994	25.00
—Reissue; glow-in-the-dark vinyl; gatefold edition; makeup cover restored			
❑ 824155-1 [(2)]	Double Platinum	1984	10.00
—Reissue			
❑ 826242-1	Unmasked	1985	8.00
—Reissue			

Number	Title (A Side/B Side)	Yr	NM
MERCURY			
❑ 792-1 [DJ]	First Kiss, Last Licks	1990	100.00
—Promo-only sampler			
❑ 522647-1 [(2)]	Alive III	1994	25.00
—Limited edition black vinyl			
❑ 522647-1 [(2)]	Alive III	1994	25.00
—Limited edition blue vinyl			
❑ 522647-1 [(2)]	Alive III	1994	25.00
—Limited edition red vinyl			
❑ 522647-1 [(2)]	Alive III	1994	25.00
—Limited edition white vinyl			
❑ 528674-1 [PD]	Creatures of the Night	1995	25.00
—Reissue; picture disc of makeup cover			
❑ 528950-1 [(2)]	MTV Unplugged	1996	20.00
—First editions are on black vinyl			
❑ 528950-1 [(2)]	MTV Unplugged	1996	20.00
—Second editions are on yellow marbled vinyl			
❑ 532741-1 [(2)]	You Wanted the Best, You Got the Best!!	1996	20.00
❑ 814297-1	Lick It Up	1983	12.00
❑ 822495-1	Animalize	1984	12.00
❑ 826099-1	Asylum	1985	10.00
❑ 832632-1	Crazy Nights	1987	10.00
❑ 832903-1 [PD]	Crazy Nights	1987	25.00
❑ 836427-1	Smashes, Thrashes and Hits	1988	10.00
❑ 836887-1 [PD]	Smashes, Thrashes and Hits	1988	25.00
❑ 838913-1	Hot in the Shade	1989	10.00
❑ 8227801 [(2)]	Alive!	2008	30.00

KISSOON, MAC AND KATIE

45s

Number	Title (A Side/B Side)	Yr	NM
ABC			
❑ 11306	Chirpy Chirpy Cheep Cheep/ Walking Around	1971	6.00
BELL			
❑ 45198	I Found My Freedom/ Love Game Today	1972	5.00
❑ 45436	Love Will Keep Us Together/ I'm Up in Heaven	1974	5.00
MCA			
❑ 40409	Black Rose/Sugar Candy Kisses	1975	4.00
❑ 40482	Like a Butterfly/Beautiful Day	1975	4.00
❑ 40550	Two of Us/Dream of Me	1976	4.00
❑ 40609	Fly Away/Where Would Our Love Be	1976	4.00

Albums

Number	Title (A Side/B Side)	Yr	NM
STATE/MCA			
❑ 2192	The Two of Us	1976	12.00

KIT AND THE OUTLAWS

45s

Number	Title (A Side/B Side)	Yr	NM
BLACK KNIGHT			
❑ 902	Midnight Hour/Don't Tread on Me	1966	30.00
PHILIPS			
❑ 40420	Midnight Hour/Don't Tread on Me	1966	12.00

KIT KATS, THE

45s

Number	Title (A Side/B Side)	Yr	NM
JAMIE			
❑ 1321	That's the Way/Won't Find Better Than Me	1966	12.00
❑ 1326	Let's Get Lost on a Country Road/Find Someone (Who'll Make You Happy)	1966	12.00
❑ 1331	You've Got to Know/Cold Walls	1967	12.00
❑ 1337	Breezy/Won't Find Better Than Me	1967	12.00
❑ 1343	Sea of Love/Cold Walls	1967	12.00
❑ 1345	Distance/Find Someone	1968	10.00
❑ 1346	I Got the Feeling/That's the Way	1968	10.00
❑ 1353	I Want to Be/Need You	1968	10.00
❑ 1354	You're So Good to Me/Need You	1968	10.00
❑ 1362	Hey Saturday Noon/ That's the Way	1968	10.00
❑ 1381	Won't Find Better (Than Me)/ (They Call It) Love	1969	8.00
—As "New Hope"			
❑ 1385	Rain/Let's Get Lost on a Country Road	1970	8.00
—As "New Hope"			
❑ 1388	Look Away/The Money Game	1970	8.00
—As "New Hope"			
❑ 1422	Find Someone/Breezy	1974	6.00
—As "New Hope"			
LAURIE			
❑ 3186	Good Luck Charlie/ Aba Daba Honeymoon	1963	20.00
LAWN			
❑ 249	You're No Angel/Cold Walls	1964	15.00
PARAMOUNT			
❑ 0110	That You Love/Taking My Time	1971	8.00

Albums

Number	Title (A Side/B Side)	Yr	NM
JAMIE			
❑ LPM-3029 [M]	It's Just a Matter of Time	1966	25.00
❑ LPS-3029 [S]	It's Just a Matter of Time	1966	30.00
❑ LPM-3032 [M]	The Kit Kats Do Their Thing — Live!	1967	30.00
❑ LPS-3032 [S]	The Kit Kats Do Their Thing — Live!	1967	40.00
❑ JLPS-3034	To Understand Is to Love	1970	30.00
—As "New Hope"			

KITCHEN CINQ, THE

45s

Number	Title (A Side/B Side)	Yr	NM
DECCA			
❑ 32262	Good Lovin'/For Never We Met	1968	10.00
❑ 32374	She's So Fine/The Minstrel	1968	10.00
LHI			
❑ 17000	You'll Be Sorry Someday/ Determination	1966	12.00
❑ 17005	If You Think/Ride the Wind	1967	12.00
❑ 17010	Still in Love with You Baby/ Ride the Wind	1967	12.00
❑ 17015	Street Song/When the Rain Disappears	1967	12.00

Albums

Number	Title (A Side/B Side)	Yr	NM
LHI			
❑ E-12000 [M]	Everything But the Kitchen Cinq	1967	30.00
❑ E7-12000 [S]	Everything But the Kitchen Cinq	1967	40.00

KITT, EARTHA

12-Inch Singles

Number	Title (A Side/B Side)	Yr	NM
STREETWISE			
❑ SWRL-2217	Where Is My Man (Vocal Version 6:24) (Instrumental 5:10)	1983	6.00
SUNNYVIEW			
❑ SUN 417	I Love Men (Vocal Dance) (Dub) (Instrumental)	1984	20.00
❑ SUN 437	This Is My Life (Vocal 5:35) (Dub Mix 5:21)	1986	10.00

45s

Number	Title (A Side/B Side)	Yr	NM
DECCA			
❑ 31807	The Art of Love/Nikki	1965	20.00

Except when noted otherwise, VG = 25% of NM, and VG+ = 50% of NM. (Example: VG = $2.00, VG+ = $4.00 and NM = $8.00.)

Number	Title (A Side/B Side)	Yr	NM
KAPP			
❑ 294	Love Is a Gamble/Sholem	1959	12.00
❑ 333	I Wantcha Around/Johnny with the Gentle Hands	1960	12.00
MUSICOR			
❑ 1203	Anyway You Want It Baby/ The Little Gold Screw	1966	50.00
❑ 1220	There Comes a Time/ Anyway You Want It, Baby	1966	200.00
RCA VICTOR			
❑ 47-4952	Monotonous/Boston Beguine	1952	20.00
❑ 47-5358	C'est Si Bon (It's So Good)/ African Lullaby	1953	20.00
❑ 47-5447	I Want to Be Evil/Annie Doesn't Live Here Anymore	1953	20.00
❑ 47-5502	Santa Baby/Under the Bridges of Paris	1953	25.00
❑ 47-5502 [PS]	Santa Baby/Under the Bridges of Paris	1953	40.00
❑ 47-5610	Somebody Bad Stole De Wedding Bell/Lovin' Spree	1954	15.00
❑ 47-5737	Let's Do It/Senor	1954	15.00
❑ 47-5756	Mink Schmink/Easy Does It	1954	15.00
❑ 47-5882	If I Was a Boy/Tea in Chicago	1954	15.00
❑ 47-5914	(This Year's) Santa Baby/ Hey Jacque	1954	20.00
❑ 47-6009	The Heel/My Heart's Delight	1955	15.00
❑ 47-6138	Fredy/Sweet and Gentle	1955	15.00
❑ 47-6197	Do You Remember/ Mambo de Paree	1955	15.00
❑ 47-6319	Nothin' for Christmas/Je Cherche Un Homme (I Want a Man)	1955	15.00
❑ 47-6521	Honolulu Rock and Roll/There Is No Cure for L'Amour	1956	15.00
❑ 47-6727	I'm a Funny Dame/Put More Wood on the Fire	1956	15.00
❑ 47-6928	A Woman Wouldn't Be a Woman/Toujour Gai	1957	12.00
❑ 47-7013	Take My Love, Take My Love/ Yomme Yomme	1957	12.00
❑ 47-7118	If I Can't Take It With Me/ Proceed with Caution	1957	12.00
STREETWISE			
❑ 1117	Where Is My Man/(Instrumental)	1983	6.00
Albums			
CAEDMON			
❑ TC-1267	Folk Tales of the Tribes of Africa	1969	20.00
DECCA			
❑ DL 4635 [M]	Eartha Kitt Sings in Spanish	1965	30.00
❑ DL 74635 [S]	Eartha Kitt Sings in Spanish	1965	40.00
GNP CRESCENDO			
❑ GNP-2008 [M]	At the Plaza	1965	15.00
❑ GNPS-2008 [S]	At the Plaza	1965	20.00
KAPP			
❑ KL-1162 [M]	The Fabulous Eartha Kitt	1959	25.00
❑ KL-1192 [M]	Eartha Kitt Revisited	1960	25.00
❑ KS-3046 [S]	The Fabulous Eartha Kitt	1959	30.00
❑ KS-3192 [S]	Eartha Kitt Revisited	1960	30.00
MCA			
❑ 1554	The Best of Eartha Kitt	1983	12.00
MGM			
❑ E-4009 [M]	Bad But Beautiful	1962	25.00
❑ SE-4009 [S]	Bad But Beautiful	1962	30.00
RCA VICTOR			
❑ LPM-1109 [M]	Down to Eartha	1955	50.00
❑ LPM-1153 [M]	That Bad Eartha	1955	50.00
❑ LPM-1300 [M]	Thursday's Child	1956	50.00
❑ LPM-1661 [M]	St. Louis Blues	1958	40.00
❑ LSP-1661 [S]	St. Louis Blues	1958	50.00
❑ LPM-3062 [10]	RCA Victor Presents Eartha Kitt	1953	80.00
❑ LPM-3187 [10]	That Bad Eartha	1953	80.00
STANYAN			
❑ SR-10037	Best of All Possible Worlds	1972	15.00
❑ SR-10040	For Always	1975	15.00
SUNNYVIEW			
❑ SUN-4902	I Love Men	1984	10.00

KITTENS, THE Probably more than one group.

Number	Title (A Side/B Side)	Yr	NM
45s			
ABC			
❑ 10835	The Masquerade Is Over/ It's Gotta Be Love	1966	10.00
ABC-PARAMOUNT			
❑ 10619	Shindig/I Got to Know Him	1965	75.00
❑ 10730	Lookie Lookie/We Find Him Guilty	1965	100.00
❑ 10783	Is It Our Baby/Undecided You	1966	150.00
ALPINE			
❑ 64	Dark, Dark Sunglasses/ Itsy Bitsy Teeny Weeny Yellow Polka Dot Bikini	1960	30.00
❑ 67	A Letter on His Sweater/ Broken Dreams	1960	30.00
CHESS			
❑ 2027	Hey Operator/Ain't No More Room	1967	40.00
❑ 2055	How Long Can I Go On/ I've Got to Get Over You	1968	40.00
CHESTNUT			
❑ 203	Count Every Star/I'm Worried	1963	50.00
DON-EL			
❑ 122	Walter/Lite Bulb	1963	15.00
❑ 205	I Need Your Love Tonight/ Johnny's Place	1963	15.00
MURBO			
❑ 1015	Joey Has a New Love/ Lonely Summer	1967	10.00
UNART			
❑ 2010	It's All Over Now/Letter to Donna	1959	50.00

Klark Kent, "Away from Home," I.R.S. 0-9012, 1980, **$6.**

KLAATU Subject of extensive BEATLES hoax.

Number	Title (A Side/B Side)	Yr	NM
45s			
CAPITOL			
❑ 4377	Calling Occupants/ Doctor Marvello	1976	8.00
❑ 4412	Calling Occupants/ Sub-Rosa Subway	1977	5.00
❑ 4516	Around the Universe in 80 Days/We're Off You Know	1977	5.00
❑ 4627	Dear Christine/Older	1978	5.00
❑ 4866	Knee Deep in Love/Dog Star	1980	5.00
ISLAND			
❑ 011	California Jam/Doctor Marvello	1975	10.00
Albums			
CAPITOL			
❑ ST-11542	Klaatu	1976	15.00
❑ ST-11633	Hope	1977	12.00
❑ SW-11836	Sir Army Suit	1978	12.00
❑ ST-12080	Endangered Species	1980	12.00
❑ SN-16060	Klaatu	1980	8.00
—Budget-line reissue			
❑ SN-16061	Hope	1980	8.00
—Budget-line reissue			
❑ SN-16062	Sir Army Suit	1980	8.00
—Budget-line reissue			

KLARK KENT

Number	Title (A Side/B Side)	Yr	NM
45s			
KRYPTONE/I.R.S.			
❑ 9012	Away from Home/Office Talk	1980	5.00
—Green vinyl, custom label, small hole			
❑ 9012 [PS]	Away from Home/Office Talk	1980	6.00
Albums			
KRYPTONE/I.R.S.			
❑ SP 70600 [EP]	Music Madness from the Kinetic Kid	1980	20.00
—Green vinyl 10" in die-cut 12" sleeve			

KLEIN, GEORGE

Number	Title (A Side/B Side)	Yr	NM
45s			
SUN			
❑ 358	U.T. Party (Part 1)/ U.T. Party (Part 2)	1961	20.00

KLEIN, ROBERT

Number	Title (A Side/B Side)	Yr	NM
45s			
BRUT			
❑ 802	The Fabulous Fifties/ (B-side unknown)	1973	6.00
CASABLANCA			
❑ 972	Fallin'/Fill In the Words	1979	4.00
Albums			
BRUT			
❑ 6001	Child of the 50's	1973	12.00
❑ 6600	Mind Over Matter	1974	12.00
CAEDMON			
❑ TC 9100	The Unauthorized Biography of Howard Who	1969	12.00

Klark Kent, *Music Madness from the Kinetic Kid*, Kryptone/I.R.S. SP 70600, 1980, **$20.**

Number	Title (A Side/B Side)	Yr	NM
EPIC			
❑ PE 33535	New Teeth	1975	10.00

KLEMMER, JOHN

45s

Number	Title (A Side/B Side)	Yr	NM
ABC			
❑ 12172	Touch/Glass Dolphins	1976	5.00
❑ 12228	Forest Child/At Seventeen	1976	5.00
❑ 12301	Caress/Quiet Afternoon	1977	4.00
CADET			
❑ 5603	And We Were Lovers/ Look to the Sky	1968	8.00
CADET CONCEPT			
❑ 7023	Here Comes the Child/ Soliloquy for Tenor and Voice	197?	6.00
ELEKTRA			
❑ 47050	Magnificent Madness/Heart	1980	4.00
❑ 47170	Let's Make Love/Hush	1981	4.00

Albums

Number	Title (A Side/B Side)	Yr	NM
ABC			
❑ ABCD-836	Fresh Feathers	1974	15.00
❑ ABCD-922	Touch	1975	10.00
❑ ABCD-950	Barefoot Ballet	1976	10.00
❑ AB-1007	LifeStyle (Living & Loving)	1977	10.00
❑ AA-1068	Arabesque	1978	10.00
❑ AA-1106	Cry	1978	10.00
❑ AA-1116	Brazilia	1979	10.00
ABC IMPULSE!			
❑ AS-9214	Constant Throb	1973	15.00
❑ AS-9220	Waterfalls	1973	15.00
❑ AS-9244	Intensity	1974	20.00
❑ AS-9269	Magic and Movement	1974	20.00
ARISTA/NOVUS			
❑ AN2-3500 [(2)]	Nexus	1979	15.00
BLUEBIRD			
❑ 6577-1-RB	Nexus One	1987	10.00
CADET			
❑ CA-797 [S]	Involvement	197?	15.00
—Pink and yellow label reissue			
❑ LP 797 [M]	Involvement	1967	40.00
❑ LPS 797 [S]	Involvement	1967	20.00
—Fading blue label			
❑ LPS 808	And We Were Lovers	1968	20.00
CADET CONCEPT			
❑ LPS 321	Blowin' Gold	1969	30.00
❑ LPS 326	All the Children Cried	1970	20.00
❑ LPS 330	Eruptions	1971	20.00
CHESS			
❑ 2ACMJ-401 [(2)]	Magic Moments	1976	15.00
❑ CH-8300 [(2)]	Blowin' Gold	1982	12.00
—Compilation of tracks from three Cadet Concept LPs			
❑ CH2-92501 [(2)]	Blowin' Gold	1984	12.00
—Reissue of CH-8300			
ELEKTRA			
❑ 6E-284	Magnificent Madness	1980	10.00
❑ 5E-527	Hush	1981	10.00
❑ 5E-566	Solo Saxophone II: Life	1982	10.00
ELEKTRA/MUSICIAN			
❑ 60197	Finesse	1983	10.00
MCA			
❑ AA-1116	Brazilia	1979	8.00
—Reissue of ABC 1116			
❑ 1585	Arabesque	198?	8.00
—Reissue of MCA 37015			
❑ 1639	Brazilia	198?	8.00
—Reissue of MCA 37115			
❑ 1654	Touch	198?	8.00
—Reissue of MCA 37152			
❑ 6007 [(2)]	The Best of John Klemmer, Vol. One/Mosaic	198?	10.00
—Reissue of MCA 8014			
❑ 6017 [(2)]	The Best of John Klemmer, Vol. Two/The Impulse Years	1982	12.00
❑ 6246	Music	1989	12.00
❑ 8014 [(2)]	The Best of John Klemmer, Vol. One/Mosaic	1979	12.00
❑ 37012	Fresh Feathers	1980	10.00
—Reissue of ABC 836			
❑ 37013	Barefoot Ballet	1980	8.00
—Reissue of ABC 950			
❑ 37014	LifeStyle (Living & Loving)	1980	8.00
—Reissue of ABC 1007			
❑ 37015	Arabesque	1980	8.00
—Reissue of ABC 1068			
❑ 37016	Cry	1980	8.00
—Reissue of ABC 1106			
❑ 37017	Constant Throb	1980	8.00
—Reissue of ABC Impulse 9214			
❑ 37018	Waterfalls	1980	10.00
—Reissue of ABC Impulse 9220			
❑ 37019	Intensity	1980	10.00
—Reissue of ABC Impulse 9244			
❑ 37020	Magic and Movement	1980	10.00
—Reissue of ABC Impulse 9269			
❑ 37115	Brazilia	1980	8.00
—Reissue of MCA 1116			
❑ 37152	Touch	198?	8.00
—Reissue of ABC 922			
MOBILE FIDELITY			
❑ 1-006	Touch	1979	30.00
—"Original Master Recording" at top of front cover; audiophile vinyl			
NAUTILUS			
❑ NR-4	Straight from the Heart	1980	80.00
—"Super Disc" audiophile vinyl			
❑ NR-22	Finesse	1981	80.00
—"SuperDisc" audiophile vinyl			

KLEMMER, JOHN, AND EDDIE HARRIS

Albums

Number	Title (A Side/B Side)	Yr	NM
CRUSADERS			
❑ 16015	Two Tone	1982	30.00
—Part of MCA's "Audiophile Series"			

KLF, THE

12-Inch Singles

Number	Title (A Side/B Side)	Yr	NM
ARISTA			
❑ AD-2231	3 A.M. Eternal (Live at the S.S.L.) (Guns of Mu Mu) (Klonk Blip Every Trip) (Wayward Dub)	1991	10.00
❑ 12366	America: What Time Is Love/ What Time Is Love (Live at Trancentral) (Moody Boys vs. the KLF)	1991	15.00
❑ 12383	Last Train to Transcentral (Iron Horse Mix 4:12) (Live from the Lost Continent 5:35) (Mu D Vari-Speed Version 6:59)	1991	10.00
❑ 12403	Justified and Ancient (All Bound For Mu Mu Land [Lead Vocals: Maxine Harvey] 7:47) (Make Mine a 99 5:53) (Stand By The Jams [Lead Vocals: The First Lady of Country Miss Tammy Wynette] 3:36) (Let Them Eat Ice Cream 6:31)	1991	12.00
TVT			
❑ 4020	Doctorin' the Tardis (Radio 3:37) (Minimal 4:28) (Club Mix 8:25)	1988	12.00
—As "The Timelords"			
❑ 4041	Burn the Beat (JAMS Have a Party) (Mu Mu Mix) (Club Mix) (LP Version)	1988	12.00
—As "The JAMS, AKA The Timelords"			
❑ 4071	What Time Is Love?/Pure Trance	1989	15.00
WAX TRAX!			
❑ 9157	What Time Is Love (Live at Trancentral) (Techno Gate Mix)	1990	15.00

45s

Number	Title (A Side/B Side)	Yr	NM
ARISTA			
❑ 2230	3 A.M. Eternal (Live at the S.S.L.)/(Guns of Mu Mu)	1991	4.00
❑ 12365	What Time Is Love (Live at Trancentral)/Build a Fire	1991	8.00
❑ 12401	Justified and Ancient (Stand By the Jams)/ (The White Room Version)	1991	5.00
—A-side guest vocalist is Tammy Wynette (uncredited)			
TVT			
❑ 4025	Doctorin' the Tardis/ Gary in the Tardis Remix	1988	5.00
—As "The Timelords"			
❑ 4025 [PS]	Doctorin' the Tardis/ Gary in the Tardis Remix	1988	5.00
—As "The Timelords"			

Albums

Number	Title (A Side/B Side)	Yr	NM
TVT			
❑ 4040	History of the JAMS a.k.a. The Timelords	1988	20.00
—As "The JAMs"			
WAX TRAX!			
❑ 7155	Chill Out	1990	20.00

Number	Title (A Side/B Side)	Yr	NM

KLINT, PETE, QUINTET

45s

ATLANTIC

Number	Title (A Side/B Side)	Yr	NM
❑ 2533	Just Holding On/Hey Diddle Diddle	1968	12.00

MERCURY

Number	Title (A Side/B Side)	Yr	NM
❑ 72709	Walkin' Proud/Shake	1967	10.00

KLOWNS, THE

45s

RCA VICTOR

Number	Title (A Side/B Side)	Yr	NM
❑ 74-0393	Lady Love/If You Can't Be a Clown	1970	5.00
❑ 74-0393 [PS]	Lady Love/If You Can't Be a Clown	1970	8.00
❑ 74-0485	Flower in My Garden/ I Don't Believe in Magic	1971	5.00

Albums

RCA VICTOR

Number	Title (A Side/B Side)	Yr	NM
❑ LSP-4438	The Klowns	1970	10.00

KLUGH, EARL

Albums

BLUE NOTE

Number	Title (A Side/B Side)	Yr	NM
❑ BN-LA596-G	Earl Klugh	1976	10.00
❑ BN-LA667-G	Living Inside Your Love	1976	10.00
❑ LO-667	Living Inside Your Love	198?	8.00
—Reissue with new prefix			
❑ BN-LA737-H	Finger Paintings	1977	10.00
❑ LO-737	Finger Paintings	198?	8.00
—Reissue with new prefix			
❑ LN-10163	Earl Klugh	198?	8.00
—Budget-line reissue			

CAPITOL

Number	Title (A Side/B Side)	Yr	NM
❑ ST-12253	Low Ride	1983	10.00
❑ ST-12323	Wishful Thinking	1984	10.00
❑ ST-12372	Nightsongs	1984	10.00
❑ ST-12405	Key Notes (Greatest Hits)	1985	10.00

LIBERTY

Number	Title (A Side/B Side)	Yr	NM
❑ LMAS-877	Magic in Your Eyes	198?	8.00
—Reissue of United Artists 877			
❑ LO-942	Heart String	198?	8.00
—Reissue of United Artists 942			
❑ LT-1079	Late Night Guitar	1980	10.00
❑ LN-10231	Heart String	198?	8.00
—Budget-line reissue			
❑ LN-10233	Living Inside Your Love	198?	8.00
—Budget-line reissue			
❑ LN-10257	Finger Paintings	198?	8.00
—Budget-line reissue			
❑ LN-10308	Crazy for You	1986	8.00
—Budget-line reissue			
❑ LT-51113	Crazy for You	1981	10.00

MOBILE FIDELITY

Number	Title (A Side/B Side)	Yr	NM
❑ 1-025	Finger Paintings	1979	30.00
—Audiophile vinyl			
❑ UHQR 1-025	Finger Paintings	1982	120.00
—"Ultra High Quality" audiophile vinyl in box			
❑ 1-076	Late Night Guitar	1981	50.00
—Audiophile vinyl			

NAUTILUS

Number	Title (A Side/B Side)	Yr	NM
❑ NR-46	Crazy for You	198?	40.00
—Audiophile vinyl			

UNITED ARTISTS

Number	Title (A Side/B Side)	Yr	NM
❑ UA-LA877-H	Magic in Your Eyes	1978	10.00
❑ UA-LA942-H	Heart String	1979	10.00
❑ LT-1026	Dream Come True	1980	10.00

WARNER BROS.

Number	Title (A Side/B Side)	Yr	NM
❑ 25262	Soda Fountain Shuffle	1985	10.00
❑ 25478	Life Stories	1986	10.00
❑ 25902	Whispers and Promises	1989	12.00
❑ 26018	Solo Guitar	1989	12.00

KNACK, THE No relation to the late-1970s pop group.

12-Inch Singles

CAPITOL

Number	Title (A Side/B Side)	Yr	NM
❑ SPRO-9199 [DJ]	My Sharona (same on both sides)	1979	150.00
❑ SPRO-9712/3 [DJ]	Art War//Africa/Pay the Devil	1981	7.00

45s

ATCO

Number	Title (A Side/B Side)	Yr	NM
❑ 7051	Pick It Up/Always	1976	8.00
—Probably not the same as The "My Sharona" Knack; also probably not The Knack that were on Capitol in the 1960s			

CAPITOL

Number	Title (A Side/B Side)	Yr	NM
❑ 2075	Freedom Now/Lady in the Window	1968	10.00
❑ 4731	My Sharona/Let Me Out	1979	4.00
❑ 4731 [PS]	My Sharona/Let Me Out	1979	6.00
❑ 4771	Good Girls Don't/Frustrated	1979	4.00
—A-side contains different lyrics from LP version in three places			

The Knack, "My Sharona," Capitol 07863-62800-7, 1994, $5.

Number	Title (A Side/B Side)	Yr	NM
❑ 4771 [PS]	Good Girls Don't/Frustrated	1979	6.00
❑ 4822	Baby Talks Dirty/ End of the Game	1980	4.00
❑ 4822 [PS]	Baby Talks Dirty/ End of the Game	1980	10.00
❑ 4853	Can't Put a Price on Love/ Rave Up	1980	4.00
❑ A-5054	Pay the Devil (Ooo, Baby, Ooo)/Lil' Cal's Big Mistake	1981	4.00
❑ A-5054 [PS]	Pay the Devil (Ooo, Baby, Ooo)/Lil' Cal's Big Mistake	1981	4.00
❑ A-5078	Boys Go Crazy/We Are Waiting	1981	6.00
❑ 5774	Time Waits for No One/I'm Aware	1966	10.00
❑ 5889	The Spell/Softly, Softly	1967	10.00
❑ 5940	Banana Man/Pretty Daisy	1967	10.00
❑ S7-17905	My Sharona/Locked Out	1994	4.00
—B-side by Crowded House			

RCA

Number	Title (A Side/B Side)	Yr	NM
❑ 62800	My Sharona/Tempted	1994	5.00
—B-side by Squeeze			
❑ 62800 [PS]	My Sharona/Tempted	1994	5.00
—B-side by Squeeze			

THE RIGHT STUFF

Number	Title (A Side/B Side)	Yr	NM
❑ S7-19729	Don't Look Back/ All or Nothin' at All	1997	3.00
—B-side by Marshall Crenshaw			

Albums

CAPITOL

Number	Title (A Side/B Side)	Yr	NM
❑ SO-11948	Get the Knack	1979	5.00
❑ SOO-12045	...But the Little Girls Understand	1980	5.00
❑ ST-12168	Round Trip	1981	6.00
❑ R 142110	Get the Knack	1979	5.00
—RCA Music Service edition			
❑ SO-511948	Get the Knack	1979	5.00
—Columbia House edition			
❑ SOO-512045	...But the Little Girls Understand	1980	5.00
—Columbia House edition			

KNICKERBOCKERS, THE

45s

CHALLENGE

Number	Title (A Side/B Side)	Yr	NM
❑ 59268	All I Need Is You/ Bite, Bite Barracuda	1965	40.00
❑ 59293	Jerktown/Room for One More	1965	15.00
❑ 59321	Lies/The Coming Generation	1965	16.00
❑ 59326	One Track Mind/I Must Be Doing Something Right	1966	15.00
❑ 59332	High on Love/Stick with Me	1966	15.00
❑ 59335	Just One Girl/Chapel in the Fields	1966	15.00
❑ 59341	Love Is a Bird/Rumors, Gossip, Words Untrue	1966	15.00
❑ 59348	Can You Help Me/Please Don't Love Him	1966	15.00
❑ 59359	What Does That Make You/ Sweet Green Fields	1967	15.00
❑ 59366	Come and Get It/ Wishful Thinking	1967	50.00
❑ 59380	You'll Never Walk Alone/ I Can Do It Better	1967	15.00
❑ 59384	As a Matter of Fact/They Ran for Their Lives	1968	15.00

LANA

Number	Title (A Side/B Side)	Yr	NM
❑ 156	Lies/The Coming Generation	196?	8.00
—Oldies reissue			

SUNDAZED

Number	Title (A Side/B Side)	Yr	NM
❑ S 186	Gotta Stop This Dreaming/ I Want a Girl for Christmas	2006	3.00
—White replica "Challenge" label			
❑ S 186 [PS]	Gotta Stop This Dreaming/ I Want a Girl for Christmas	2006	3.00
—Cardboard sleeve			

Albums

CHALLENGE

Number	Title (A Side/B Side)	Yr	NM
❑ CH-621 [M]	Jerk and Twine Time	1965	400.00
❑ CH-622 [M]	Lies	1966	100.00
❑ CHS-622 [S]	Lies	1966	200.00
❑ LP-12664 [M]	Llyod Thaxton Presents the Knickerbockers	1965	200.00

Number	Title (A Side/B Side)	Yr	NM
SUNDAZED			
❑ LP-5000	The Great Lost Knickerbockers Album	1990	12.00
—Blue vinyl			
❑ LP-5154	Rockin' with the Knickerbockers	2003	12.00

KNIGHT, CHRIS
"Peter Brady" of THE BRADY BUNCH.

Number	Title (A Side/B Side)	Yr	NM
45s			
PARAMOUNT			
❑ 0177	Good for Each Other/Over and Over	1972	15.00
❑ 0177 [PS]	Good for Each Other/Over and Over	1972	15.00

KNIGHT, CHRIS, AND MAUREEN MCCORMICK
Also see each artist's individual listings; THE BRADY BUNCH.

Number	Title (A Side/B Side)	Yr	NM
45s			
PARAMOUNT			
❑ 0246	Little Bird/Just a-Singin' Along	1973	15.00
Albums			
PARAMOUNT			
❑ PAS-6062	Chris Knight and Maureen McCormick	1973	120.00

KNIGHT, FREDERICK

Number	Title (A Side/B Side)	Yr	NM
45s			
JUANA			
❑ 1948	Let Me Ring Your Bell Again/When It Ain't Right	1980	5.00
❑ 3402	I'm Falling in Love Again/Done Got Over Lover	1976	5.00
❑ 3404	Sugar/I'm Falling in Love	1976	5.00
❑ 3408	High Society/(Instrumental)	1976	5.00
❑ 3411	Staying Power/Wrapped in Your Love	1977	5.00
❑ 3415	Sit Down on Your Love/Staying Power	1977	5.00
❑ 3418	You and Me/When It Ain't Right with My Baby	1978	5.00
❑ 3420	My Music Makes Me Feel Good/When It Ain't Right with My Baby	1978	5.00
❑ 3423	You Can't Deny Me/If You Love Your Baby	1979	5.00
❑ 3700	The Old Songs/Bundle of Love	1981	5.00
❑ 3702	You're the Best Thing in My Life/(B-side unknown)	1981	5.00
1-2-3			
❑ 1724	Have a Little Mercy/Sauerkraut	1970	15.00
STAX			
❑ 0117	I've Been Lonely for So Long/Lean on Me	1972	8.00
❑ 0139	Trouble/A Friend	1972	7.00
❑ 0167	Take Me On Home Witcha/This Is My Song of Love to You	1973	7.00
❑ 0201	I Let My Chance Go By/Suzy	1974	7.00
TRUTH			
❑ 3202	Passing Through/Sometimes Storm	1974	6.00
❑ 3216	I Betcha Didn't Know That/Let's Make a Deal	1974	6.00
❑ 3228	I Wanna Play with You/I Miss You	1975	6.00
Albums			
STAX			
❑ STS-3011	I've Been Lonely So Long	1973	20.00

KNIGHT, GLADYS, AND THE PIPS
Includes Gladys Knight solo and the Pips without Gladys.

Number	Title (A Side/B Side)	Yr	NM
12-Inch Singles			
BUDDAH			
❑ DSC 115	Love Is Always On Your Mind/(Instrumental)	1977	12.00
❑ DSC 126	It's a Better Than Good Time/(Instrumental)	1978	12.00
COLUMBIA			
❑ AS 803 [DJ]	Taste of Bitter Love/Bourgie, Bourgie	1980	12.00
❑ AS 1307 [DJ]	I Will Fight (4:10)/God Is (3:48)	1981	10.00
❑ AS 1643 [DJ]	Save the Overtime (For Me) (5:07) (same on both sides)	1983	12.00
❑ CAS 2052 [DJ]	Keep Givin' Me Love (same on both sides)	1985	8.00
❑ 44-03969	Save the Overtime (For Me)/(Instrumental)	1983	8.00
❑ 44-04965	When You're Far Away/(Instrumental)	1983	6.00
❑ 44-05161	My Time (2 versions)	1984	10.00
❑ 23-10996	You Bring Out the Best in Me (8:20)/You Loved Away the Pain	1979	15.00
MCA			
❑ L33-1456 [DJ]	Men (5 versions)	1990	8.00
❑ L33-1621 [DJ]	Where Would I Be (Vocal) (Instrumental) (Suite)	1991	8.00
❑ L33-1653 [DJ]	Meet Me in the Middle (LP Version) (Instrumental) (7" Version) (Suite)	1991	15.00
❑ L33-1694 [DJ]	Superwoman (LP Mix 6:19) (Radio Edit 5:37) (Instrumental Mix 6:15) (Single Version 4:29)	1991	8.00
❑ L33-2080 [DJ]	Meet Me in the Middle (6 versions)	1991	8.00
❑ MCA8P-3311 [DJ]	This Time (Spike Club Mix 8:48) (Spike Beats Mix) (Radio Mix) (Spike Next Dub 9:35)	1994	8.00
❑ L33-17429 [DJ]	Lovin' On Next to Nothin' (Extended) (Radio Edit) (Instrumental) (Percussapella)	1987	8.00
❑ L33-17431 [DJ]	Love Overboard (4 versions)	1987	8.00
❑ L33-17444 [DJ]	Love Overboard (6:10) (5:44)	1987	8.00
❑ L33-17546 [DJ]	Lovin' on Next to Nothin' (5 versions)	1988	10.00
❑ L33-17561 [DJ]	It's Gonna Take All Our Love (same on both sides)	1988	8.00
❑ 23713	Send It To Me (Extended Version 7:34)/When You Love Somebody (It's Christmas Everyday) (6:12)	1986	12.00
❑ 23803	Love Overboard (Extended Version 6:00)/(Instrumental)	1987	6.00
❑ 23804	Lovin' On Next to Nothin' (Extended Version) (Instrumental)	1987	6.00
❑ 23871	It's Gonna Take All Our Love/(Instrumental)	1988	8.00
❑ 25371 [DJ]	If I Were Your Woman II (LP Version) (Instrumental) (Acappella)/(same on both sides)	2001	12.00
❑ 54130	Men (Extended Club Version 7:13) (Instrumental)	1990	6.00
45s			
BRUNSWICK			
❑ 55048	Whistle My Love/Ching Ching	1958	120.00
BUDDAH			
❑ 363	Where Peaceful Waters Flow/Perfect Love	1973	5.00
❑ 363 [PS]	Where Peaceful Waters Flow/Perfect Love	1973	8.00
❑ 383	Midnight Train to Georgia/Window Raising Granny	1973	5.00
❑ 383	Midnight Train to Georgia/(Instrumental)	1973	6.00
❑ 393	I've Got to Use My Imagination/I Can See Clearly Now	1973	5.00
❑ 403	Best Thing That Ever Happened to Me/Once in a Lifetime	1974	5.00
❑ 423	On and On/The Makings of You	1974	5.00
❑ 423 [PS]	On and On/The Makings of You	1974	8.00
❑ 433	I Feel a Song (In My Heart)/Don't Burn Down the Bridge	1974	5.00
❑ 453	Love FInds It's Own Way/Better You Go Your Way	1975	5.00
—Some copies have a grammatically incorrect A-side title as above			
❑ 453-N	Love FInds Its Own Way/Better You Go Your Way	1975	6.00
—Some copies have the grammatically correct A-side title as above			
❑ 463	The Way We Were-Try to Remember/The Need to Be	1975	5.00
❑ 487	Money/Street Brothers	1975	5.00
❑ 513	Part Time Love/Where Did I Put His Memory	1975	5.00
❑ 523	Make Yours a Happy Home/The Going Up and the Coming Down	1976	5.00
❑ 544	So Sad the Song/(Instrumental)	1976	5.00
❑ 569	Baby Don't Change Your Mind/I Love to Feel That Feeling	1977	5.00
❑ 584	Sorry Doesn't Always Make It Right/You Put a New Life in My Body	1977	5.00
❑ 592	The One and Only/Pipe Dreams	1978	5.00
❑ 598	It's a Better Than Good Time/Everybody's Got to Find a Way	1978	5.00
❑ 601	I'm Coming Home Again/Love Gives You the Power	1978	5.00
❑ 605	Sail Away/I'm Still Caught Up with You	1979	5.00
❑ 1974 [DJ]	Do You Hear What I Hear/Silent Night	1974	6.00
❑ 1974 [PS]	Do You Hear What I Hear/Silent Night	1974	6.00
CASABLANCA			
❑ 912	If I Could Bring Back Yesterday/Since I Found Love	1978	4.00
—As "The Pips"			
❑ 949	Baby I'm Your Fool/Lights of the City	1978	4.00
—As "The Pips"			
COLUMBIA			
❑ 11-02113	Forever Yesterday (For the Children)/(Instrumental)	1981	4.00
❑ 11-02113 [PS]	Forever Yesterday (For the Children)/(Instrumental)	1981	5.00
❑ 18-02413	If That'll Make You Happy/Love Was Made for Two	1981	4.00
❑ 18-02549	I Will Fight/God Is	1981	4.00
❑ 18-02706	Friend of Mine/Reach High	1982	4.00
❑ 38-03418	That Special Time of Year/Santa Claus Is Comin' to Town	1982	5.00
❑ 38-03761	Save the Overtime (For Me)/Ain't No Greater Love	1983	4.00
❑ 38-04033	You're Number 1 in My Book/Oh La De Dah	1983	4.00
❑ 38-04219	Hero (The Wind Beneath My Wings)/Seconds	1983	5.00
❑ 38-04333	Here's That Sunny Day/Oh La De Da	1984	4.00
❑ 38-04369	When You're Far Away/Seconds	1984	4.00
❑ 38-04761	My Time/(Instrumental)	1985	4.00
❑ 38-04761 [PS]	My Time/(Instrumental)	1985	5.00
❑ 38-04873	Keep Givin' Me Love/Do You Wanna Have Some Fun	1985	4.00
❑ 38-05679	Till I See You Again/Strivin'	1985	4.00
❑ 3-10922	Am I Too Late/It's the Same Old Song	1979	4.00
❑ 3-10997	You Bring Out the Best in Me/You Loved Away the Pain	1979	4.00
❑ 3-11088	The Best Thing We Can Do Is Say Goodbye/You Don't Have to Say I Love You	1979	4.00
❑ 1-11239	Landlord/We Need Hearts	1980	4.00
❑ 1-11330	Taste of Bitter Love/Add It Up	1980	4.00
❑ 1-11375	Bourgie', Bourgie'/Get the Love	1980	4.00
❑ 11-11409	When a Child Is Born/The Lord's Prayer	1980	5.00
—With Johnny Mathis			
ENJOY			
❑ 2012	What Shall I Do/Love Call	1964	15.00
EVERLAST			
❑ 5025	Happiness/I Had a Dream Last Night	1963	25.00
—As "The Pips"			
FURY			
❑ 1050	Every Beat of My Heart/Room in Your Heart	1961	25.00
—Re-recordings of the same songs on Huntom and Vee Jay			
❑ 1052	Guess Who/Stop Running Around	1961	15.00
❑ 1054	Letter Full of Tears/You Broke Your Promise	1961	15.00
❑ 1064	Operator/I'll Trust in You	1962	15.00
❑ 1067	Darling/Linda	1962	20.00
—As "The Pips"			
❑ 1073	Come See About Me/I Want That Kind of Love	1963	30.00
HUNTOM			
❑ 2510	Every Beat of My Heart/Room in Your Heart	1961	500.00
—As "The Pips"			
LOST-NITE			
❑ 261	Giving Up/Lovers Always Forgive	196?	5.00
—Reissue			
❑ 382	Every Beat of My Heart/Room in Your Heart	197?	6.00
—Reissue of Fury versions			
❑ 386	Letter Full of Tears/You Broke Your Promise	197?	5.00
—Reissue			
❑ 389	Darling/Linda	197?	5.00
—As "The Pips"; reissue			
MAXX			
❑ 326	Giving Up/Maybe, Maybe Baby	1964	15.00
❑ 329	Lovers Always Forget/Another Love	1964	15.00
❑ 331	Either Way I Lose/Go Away, Stay Away	1964	15.00
❑ 334	Who Knows/Stop and Get a Hold of Myself	1965	15.00
❑ 335	Tell Her You're Mine/If I Should Ever Be in Love	1965	15.00
MCA			
❑ 53002	Send It to Me/When You Love Somebody (It's Christmas Every Day)	1987	3.00
❑ 53002 [PS]	Send It to Me/When You Love Somebody (It's Christmas Every Day)	1987	3.00

Except when noted otherwise, VG = 25% of NM, and VG+ = 50% of NM. (Example: VG = $2.00, VG+ = $4.00 and NM = $8.00.)

Number	Title (A Side/B Side)	Yr	NM
❑ 53210	Love Overboard/(Instrumental)	1987	3.00
❑ 53210 [PS]	Love Overboard/(Instrumental)	1987	3.00
❑ 53211	Lovin' on Next to Nothin'/ (Instrumental)	1988	3.00
❑ 53211 [PS]	Lovin' on Next to Nothin'/ (Instrumental)	1988	3.00
❑ 53351	It's Gonna Take All Our Love/ (Instrumental)	1988	3.00
❑ 53657	Licence to Kill/You	1989	3.00
❑ 53676	Licence to Kill/Pam	1989	3.00
—B-side by National Philharmonic Orchestra			
❑ 54117	Men/(Instrumental)	1991	3.00
SCOTTI BROS.			
❑ ZS4-06267	Loving on Borrowed Time (Love Theme from Cobra)/ Angel of the City	1986	3.00
—A-side: Gladys Knight and Bill Medley; B-side: Robert Tepper			
SOUL			
❑ 35023	Just Walk in My Shoes/Stepping Closer to Your Heart	1966	8.00
❑ 35033	Take Me in Your Arms and Love Me/Do You Love Me Just a Little More?	1967	8.00
❑ 35034	Everybody Needs Love/ Since I've Lost You	1967	8.00
❑ 35039	I Heard It Through the Grapevine/ It's Time to Go Now	1967	10.00
❑ 35042	The End of Our Road/Don't Let Her Take Your Love from Me	1968	8.00
❑ 35045	It Should Have Been Me/ You Don't Love Me No More	1968	8.00
❑ 35047	I Wish It Would Rain/ It's Summer	1968	8.00
❑ 35057	Didn't You Know (You'd Have to Cry Sometime)/Keep an Eye	1969	8.00
❑ 35063	The Nitty Gritty/Got Myself a Good Man	1969	8.00
❑ 35068	Friendship Train/Cloud Nine	1969	8.00
❑ 35071	You Need Love Like I Do (Don't You)/You're My Everything	1970	8.00
❑ 35078	If I Were Your Woman/ The Tracks of My Tears	1970	7.00
❑ 35083	I Don't Want to Do Wrong/ Is There a Place In His Heart for Me	1971	6.00
❑ 35091	Make Me the Woman You Come Home To/If You're Gonna Leave (Just Leave)	1972	6.00
❑ 35094	Help Me Make It Through the Night/If You're Gonna Leave (Just Leave)	1972	6.00
❑ 35098	Neither One of Us (Wants to Be the First to Say Goodbye)/ Can't Give It Up No More	1972	6.00
❑ 35105	Daddy Could Swear I Declare/ For Once in My Life	1973	6.00
❑ 35107	All I Need Is Time/The Only Time You Love Me (Is When You're Losing Me)	1973	6.00
❑ 35111	Betwen Her Goodbye and My Hello/This Child Needs Its Father	1974	6.00
TRIP			
❑ 3004	It Hurt Me So Bad/What Will Become of Me	1973	6.00
❑ 3004 [PS]	It Hurt Me So Bad/What Will Become of Me	1973	12.00
VEE JAY			
❑ 386	Every Beat of My Heart/ Ain'tcha Got Some Room (In Your Heart for Me)	1961	20.00
—By "The Pips"; same B-side, different title			
❑ 386	Every Beat of My Heart/ Room in Your Heart	1961	20.00
—By "The Pips"			
❑ 545	A Love Like Mine/Queen of Tears	1963	20.00
Albums			
ACCORD			
❑ SN-7103	Every Beat of My Heart	1981	10.00
❑ SN-7105	Letter Full of Tears	1981	10.00
❑ SN-7131	I Feel a Song	1981	10.00
❑ SN-7188	It's Showtime	1982	10.00
ALLEGIANCE			
❑ AV-5002	Glad to Be...	198?	10.00
BELL			
❑ 1323	In the Beginning	1975	12.00
❑ 6013	Tastiest Hits	1968	20.00
BUDDAH			
❑ BDS-5141	Imagination	1973	12.00
❑ BDS-5602	Claudine	1974	30.00
❑ BDS-5612	I Feel a Song	1974	12.00
❑ BDS-5639	2nd Anniversary	1975	12.00
❑ BDS-5653	The Best of Gladys Knight & The Pips	1976	12.00
❑ BDS-5676	Pipe Dreams	1976	12.00

Number	Title (A Side/B Side)	Yr	NM
❑ BDS-5689	Still Together	1977	12.00
❑ BDS-5701	The One and Only	1978	12.00
❑ BDS-5714	Miss Gladys Knight	1978	12.00
CASABLANCA			
❑ NBLP 7081	At Last…The Pips	1977	10.00
—As "The Pips"			
❑ NBLP 7113	Callin'	1978	10.00
—As "The Pips"			
COLLECTABLES			
❑ COL-5154	Golden Classics: Letter Full of Tears	198?	10.00
COLUMBIA			
❑ JC 35704	Gladys Knight	1979	10.00
❑ PC 35704	Gladys Knight	198?	8.00
—Budget-line reissue			
❑ JC 36387	About Love	1980	10.00
❑ PC 36387	About Love	198?	8.00
—Budget-line reissue			
❑ FC 37086	Touch	1981	10.00
❑ PC 37086	Touch	198?	8.00
—Budget-line reissue			
❑ FC 38114	That Special Time of Year	1982	10.00
❑ PC 38114	That Special Time of Year	1983	8.00
—Same as above with new prefix			
❑ FC 38205	Visions	1983	10.00
❑ PC 38205	Visions	198?	8.00
—Budget-line reissue			
❑ FC 39423	Life	1985	10.00
❑ PC 39423	Life	198?	8.00
—Budget-line reissue			
❑ FC 40376	Greatest Hits	1986	10.00
❑ FC 40878	The Best of Gladys Knight and the Pips/The Columbia Years	1988	10.00
FURY			
❑ 1003 [M]	Letter Full of Tears	1962	500.00
LOST-NITE			
❑ LLP-17 [10]	The Best of Gladys Knight and the Pips	1981	12.00
—Red vinyl			
MAXX			
❑ 3000 [M]	Gladys Knight and the Pips	1964	150.00
MCA			
❑ 10329	Good Woman	1991	15.00
❑ 42004	All Our Love	1987	10.00
MOTOWN			
❑ M5-113V1	Motown Superstar Series, Vol. 13	1981	10.00
❑ M5-126V1	Everybody Needs Love	1981	12.00
—Reissue of Soul 706			
❑ M5-148V1	Nitty Gritty	1981	12.00
—Reissue of Soul 713			
❑ M5-193V1	Neither One of Us	1981	12.00
—Reissue of Soul 737			
❑ M 792S2 [(2)]	Anthology	1974	15.00
❑ MOT 5303	All the Great Hits of Gladys Knight and the Pips	198?	8.00
NATURAL RESOURCES			
❑ NR 4004T1	Silk N' Soul	1978	10.00
—Reissue of Soul 711			
PAIR			
❑ PDL2-1198	The Best of Gladys Knight and the Pips	1987	12.00
PICKWICK			
❑ SPC-3349	Every Beat of My Heart	197?	10.00
SOUL			
❑ S 706 [M]	Everybody Needs Love	1967	20.00
❑ SS 706 [S]	Everybody Needs Love	1967	25.00
❑ S 707 [M]	Feelin' Bluesy	1968	40.00
—Mono copies are white label promo only; cover has "Monaural Record DJ Copy" sticker			
❑ SS 707 [S]	Feelin' Bluesy	1968	25.00
❑ SS 711	Silk N' Soul	1968	25.00
❑ SS 713	Nitty Gritty	1969	25.00
❑ SS 723	Gladys Knight and the Pips Greatest Hits	1970	15.00
❑ SS 730	All in a Knight's Work	1970	15.00
❑ SS 731	If I Were Your Woman	1971	15.00
❑ S 736L	Standing Ovation	1971	15.00
❑ S 737L	Neither One of Us	1973	15.00
❑ S 739L	All I Need Is Time	1973	15.00
❑ S 741	Knight Time	1974	12.00
❑ S 744	A Little Knight Music	1975	12.00
SPHERE SOUND			
❑ SR-7006 [M]	Gladys Knight and the Pips	196?	200.00
❑ SSR-7006 [R]	Gladys Knight and the Pips	196?	120.00
SPRINGBOARD			
❑ SPB-4035	Early Hits	1972	10.00
❑ SPB-4050	How Do You Say Goodbye	1973	10.00
TRIP			
❑ TLP-9509	It Hurt Me So Bad	1973	10.00
UNITED ARTISTS			
❑ UA-LA503-E	The Very Best of Gladys Knight and the Pips	1975	12.00

Number	Title (A Side/B Side)	Yr	NM
UPFRONT			
❑ UPF 130	Gladys Knight and the Pips	197?	10.00
❑ UPF 185	Gladys Knight and the Pips	197?	10.00
VEE JAY			
❑ D1-74796	Every Beat of My Heart: The Greatest Hits of the Early Years	1989	15.00

KNIGHT, JEAN

Number	Title (A Side/B Side)	Yr	NM
45s			
CHELSEA			
❑ 3020	Don't Ask for 24 Hours/ Hold Back the Night	1975	5.00
❑ 3035	Jesse James Is an Outlaw/ Hold Back the Night	1975	5.00
COTILLION			
❑ 46020	You Got the Papers (But I Got the Man)/Anything You Can Do (I Can Do As Well)	1981	4.00
❑ 46027	Keep It Comin'/One on One	1981	4.00
❑ 47002	You Show Me Yours, I'll Show You Mine/(B-side unknown)	1982	4.00
—All of the above with Premium			
DIAL			
❑ 1026	Dirt/Jesse Joe	1974	5.00
ICHIBAN			
❑ 97-422	Bill/Bus Stop	1997	3.00
JETSTREAM			
❑ 706	Doggin' Around/The Man That Left Me	1965	10.00
MIRAGE			
❑ 99606	Let the Good Times Roll/Magic	1985	3.00
❑ 99643	My Toot Toot/My Heart Is Willing (And My Body Is Too)	1985	3.00
❑ 99643 [PS]	My Toot Toot/My Heart Is Willing (And My Body Is Too)	1985	3.00
STAX			
❑ 0088	Mr. Big Stuff/Why I Keep Living These Memories	1971	6.00
❑ 0105	You Think You're Hot Stuff/ Don't Talk About Jody	1971	5.00
❑ 0116	Carry On/Call Me Your Fool	1972	5.00
❑ 0136	Helping Man/Pick Up the Pieces	1972	5.00
❑ 0150	Do Me/Save the Last Kiss for Me	1972	5.00
TRIBE			
❑ 8304	Lonesome Tonight/Love	1964	12.00
❑ 8306	T'Ain't It the Truth/I'm So Glad for Your Sake	1965	12.00
❑ 8313	Anyone Can Love Him/A Tear	1966	12.00
Albums			
COTILLION			
❑ SD 5230	Jean Knight and Premium	1981	15.00
MIRAGE			
❑ 90282	My Toot Toot	1985	10.00
STAX			
❑ STS-2045	Mr. Big Stuff	1971	40.00
❑ MPS-8554	Mr. Big Stuff	198?	10.00

KNIGHT, LARRY, AND THE UPSETTERS

Number	Title (A Side/B Side)	Yr	NM
45s			
GOLDEN WORLD			
❑ 37	Hurt Me/Everything's Gone Wrong	1966	40.00

KNIGHT, ROBERT

Also see THE PARAMOUNTS (3).

Number	Title (A Side/B Side)	Yr	NM
45s			
DOT			
❑ 16256	Because/Dance Only with Me	1961	30.00
❑ 16303	Free Me/The Other Half of Man	1962	40.00
ELF			
❑ 90019	Isn't It Lonely Together/ We'd Better Stop	1968	6.00
❑ 90030	Smokey/If I Had My Way	1969	6.00
❑ 90037	I Only Have Eyes for You/I'm Sticking with You	1969	30.00
MONUMENT			
❑ 8612	Better Get Ready for Love/ Somebody's Baby	1974	15.00
❑ 8629	Dynamite/The Outsider	1974	15.00
PRIVATE STOCK			
❑ 45,038	I'm Coming Home to You/ (B-side unknown)	1975	10.00
❑ 45,069	Second Chance/Glitter Lady	1976	5.00
❑ 45,118	I've Got News for You/ (B-side unknown)	1976	5.00
RISING SONS			
❑ 705	Everlasting Love/ Somebody's Baby	1967	15.00
❑ 707	Blessed Are the Lonely/ It's Been Worth It All	1967	20.00

K

Except when noted otherwise, VG = 25% of NM, and VG+ = 50% of NM. (Example: VG = $2.00, VG+ = $4.00 and NM = $8.00.)

Number	Title (A Side/B Side)	Yr	NM
❑ 708	Power of Love/Love on a Mountain Top	1968	15.00
Albums			
RISING SONS			
❑ RSM-7000 [M]	Everlasting Love	1967	30.00
❑ RSS-17000 [S]	Everlasting Love	1967	40.00

KNIGHT, SONNY

Number	Title (A Side/B Side)	Yr	NM
45s			
A&M			
❑ 718	Evil Minded Woman/Georgia Town	1963	10.00
❑ 728	Be True to Your Dog/State Street	1964	10.00
ALADDIN			
❑ 3357	But Officer/Dear Wonderful God	1957	30.00
AURA			
❑ 403	If You Want This Love/I Just Called to Say Hello	1964	8.00
❑ 4505	Love Me As Though There Were No Tomorrow/Fool Like Me	1964	8.00
❑ 4505 [PS]	Love Me As Though There Were No Tomorrow/Fool Like Me	1964	20.00
❑ 4508	Rose Mary/(B-side unknown)	1965	8.00
DOT			
❑ 15507	Confidential/Jailbird	1956	15.00
—Second pressings have black labels			
❑ 15507	Confidential/Jailbird	1956	20.00
—Originals have maroon labels			
❑ 15542	End of a Dream/Worthless and Lowdown	1957	15.00
❑ 15597	Lovesick Blues/Insha Allot	1957	15.00
❑ 15635	Dedicated to You/Short Walk	1957	15.00
EASTMAN			
❑ 787	Lipstick Kisses/East Your Mush and Hush	1959	50.00
FIFO			
❑ 102	Cold, Cold Night/Saving My Love	1961	15.00
❑ 105	A Swingin' Door/(B-side unknown)	1961	15.00
MERCURY			
❑ 72033	Just One More Chance/Lost Child	1962	10.00
ORIGINAL SOUND			
❑ 2	Once in Awhile/School's Out	1959	20.00
❑ 18	Those Oldies But Goodies Are Dedicated to You/She Had Me Reelin'	1961	15.00
SPECIALTY			
❑ 594	Keep a-Walkin'/My Baby Don't Want Me	1957	15.00
STARLA			
❑ 1	Dedicated to You/Short Walk	1957	30.00
❑ 10	Once in a While/School's Out	1958	15.00
VITA			
❑ 137	Confidential/Jailbird	1956	40.00
WORLD PACIFIC			
❑ 403	If You Want This Love/I Just Called to Say Hello	1964	12.00
❑ 77811	If I May/Need Your Love So Bad	1966	8.00
❑ 77832	Angel Love/If I Ruled the World	1966	8.00
❑ 77858	A Quiet Man/I Can't Let You Go	1966	25.00
—This record exists as a promo at least (we have listed it as "Unreleased" in the past)			
Albums			
AURA			
❑ AR-3001 [M]	If You Want This Love	1964	25.00
❑ AS-3001 [S]	If You Want This Love	1964	30.00

KNIGHT, TED

Number	Title (A Side/B Side)	Yr	NM
Albums			
RANWOOD			
❑ R-8149	Hi Guys!	1976	20.00

KNIGHT, TERRY, AND THE PACK Group evloved into GRAND FUNK RAILROAD.

Number	Title (A Side/B Side)	Yr	NM
45s			
A&M			
❑ 769	Kids Will Be the Same/You Lie	1965	15.00
CAMEO			
❑ 482	Forever and a Day/Lizbeth Peach	1967	10.00
❑ 495	Come Home Baby/Dirty Lady	1967	10.00
CAPITOL			
❑ 2174	Without a Woman/Let Me Stand Next to Your Fire	1968	12.00
—As "The Pack"			
❑ 2409	Such a Lonely Life/Lullaby	1969	10.00
❑ 2506	St. Paul/(Legend of) William and Mary	1969	10.00
❑ 2737	I'll Keep Waiting Patiently/Lullaby	1970	10.00
LUCKY ELEVEN			
❑ 003	Harlem Shuffle/I've Got News for You	1965	16.00
—As "The Pack"			
❑ 007	Does It Matter to You Girl/Wide Trackin'	1965	16.00
—As "The Fabulous Pack"			
❑ 007 [PS]	Does It Matter to You Girl/Wide Trackin'	1965	25.00
—As "The Fabulous Pack"			
❑ 225	How Much More/I've Been Told	1966	15.00
❑ 226	I Got Love/Better Man Than I	1966	15.00
❑ 228	Lady Jane/Lovin' Kind	1966	15.00
❑ 229	What's On Your Mind/A Change on the Way	1966	15.00
❑ 230	I (Who Have Nothing)/Numbers	1966	15.00
❑ 235	This Precious Time/Love, Love, Love, Love	1967	15.00
❑ 236	One Monkey Don't Stop No Show/The Train	1967	15.00
WINGATE			
❑ 007	The Tears Come Rollin'/The Colour of My Love	1965	25.00
—As "The Pack"			
Albums			
ABKCO			
❑ AB-4217 [(2)]	Mark, Don and Terry 1966-67	1972	20.00
CAMEO			
❑ C 2007 [M]	Reflections	1967	20.00
—Reissue of Lucky Eleven LE-8001			
❑ CS 2007 [S]	Reflections	1967	25.00
—Reissue of Lucky Eleven LES-8001			
LUCKY ELEVEN			
❑ LE-8000 [M]	Terry Knight and the Pack	1966	40.00
❑ LES-8000 [R]	Terry Knight and the Pack	1966	25.00
❑ LE-8001 [M]	Reflections	1967	25.00
❑ LES-8001 [S]	Reflections	1967	40.00

KNIGHT BROS., THE

Number	Title (A Side/B Side)	Yr	NM
45s			
CHECKER			
❑ 1064	I Really Love You/Second Hand Lover	1963	25.00
❑ 1076	Come On Girl/City Life	1964	25.00
❑ 1107	Temptation 'Bout to Get Me/Sinking Low	1965	25.00
❑ 1124	I Owe Her My Life/I'm Never Gonna Live It Down	1965	25.00
❑ 1146	All I Have to Do Is Dream/Hand of Faith	1966	20.00
❑ 1153	That'll Get It/She's A-1	1966	20.00
MERCURY			
❑ 72718	Nobody's Fault/You're My Love	1967	20.00
❑ 72829	Ghetto Joe/Tried So Hard to Please Her	1968	20.00

KNIGHT OWLS, THE

Number	Title (A Side/B Side)	Yr	NM
45s			
CAMEO			
❑ 379	Goody Galum-Shus/What	1965	15.00

KNIGHT RIDERS, THE Featuring BILLY VERA.

Number	Title (A Side/B Side)	Yr	NM
45s			
UNITED ARTISTS			
❑ 366	Annie's Place/Unchained Melody	1961	25.00

KNIGHTS, THE At least three, and perhaps four, different groups.

Number	Title (A Side/B Side)	Yr	NM
45s			
CAPITOL			
❑ 5302	Hot Rod High/Theme for Teen Love	1964	50.00
FELSTED			
❑ 8640	White Fang/Night Train	1962	12.00
Albums			
ACE			
❑ 4763	Cold Days, Hot Knights	196?	400.00
❑ 200854	Across the Board	1966	400.00
❑ 201302	The Knights 1967	1967	400.00
CAPITOL			
❑ DT 2189 [R]	Hot Rod High	1964	400.00
❑ T 2189 [M]	Hot Rod High	1964	400.00
JUSTICE			
❑ JLP-156	On the Move	196?	300.00

KNIGHTSBRIDGE STRINGS, THE

Number	Title (A Side/B Side)	Yr	NM
45s			
TOP RANK			
❑ 2006	Cry/My Prayer	1959	10.00
❑ 2014	Wheel of Fortune/Cow Cow Boogie	1959	10.00
❑ 2031	Blues from "An American in Paris"/Fiddler's Boogie	1959	10.00
❑ 2082	If I Didn't Care/I Hear a Rhapsody	1960	10.00
❑ 3000	The Singer Not the Song/Anacleto's Theme	1961	10.00
Albums			
MONUMENT			
❑ MAM-3000 [M]	Espana	1966	10.00
❑ MAM-3001 [M]	3/4 Time	1966	10.00
❑ MAM-3002 [M]	Cinema	1966	10.00
❑ MAM-3003 [M]	The Knightsbridge Strings Go Pop	1966	10.00
❑ MAM-3004 [M]	Reverie	1966	10.00
❑ MAM-3005 [M]	Hawaii	1967	12.00
❑ MAM-3006 [M]	Gilbert and Sullivan	1967	12.00
❑ MAS-13000 [S]	Espana	1966	12.00
❑ MAS-13001 [S]	3/4 Time	1966	12.00
❑ MAS-13002 [S]	Cinema	1966	12.00
❑ MAS-13003 [S]	The Knightsbridge Strings Go Pop	1966	12.00
❑ MAS-13004 [S]	Reverie	1966	12.00
❑ MAS-13005 [S]	Hawaii	1967	12.00
❑ MAS-13006 [S]	Gilbert and Sullivan	1967	12.00
❑ MAS-13007	Marching Strings	1969	10.00
❑ MAS-13008	Nashville	1969	10.00
PURIST			
❑ SR-3	Spanish Mood	196?	12.00
❑ SR-9	Nostalgic Swing Mood	196?	12.00
RIVERSIDE			
❑ RM-7518 [M]	Strings on the March	196?	10.00
❑ RM-7532 [M]	Waltzing Strings	196?	10.00
❑ RM-7533 [M]	Big Beat	196?	10.00
❑ RS-97518 [S]	Strings on the March	196?	12.00
❑ RS-97532 [S]	Waltzing Strings	196?	12.00
❑ RS-97533 [S]	Big Beat	196?	12.00
SESAC			
❑ C-1701/2 [M]	Songs of America Vol. 1	195?	15.00
❑ C-1703/4 [M]	Songs of America Vol. 2	195?	15.00
TOP RANK			
❑ RM-303 [M]	The Strings Sing	1959	12.00
❑ RM-308 [M]	The Strings Swing	1959	12.00
❑ RM-315 [M]	Latin Cameos	1960	12.00
❑ RM-325 [M]	More Swinging Strings	1960	12.00
❑ RM-341 [M]	Soft Swaying Strings	1960	12.00
—Title on label is "More Swaying Strings"			
❑ RS-603 [S]	The Strings Sing	1959	15.00
❑ RS-608 [S]	The Strings Swing	1959	15.00
❑ RS-615 [S]	Latin Cameos	1960	15.00
❑ RS-625 [S]	More Swinging Strings	1960	15.00
❑ RS-641 [S]	Soft Swaying Strings	1960	15.00
—Title on label is "More Swaying Strings"			

KNOCKOUTS, THE (1)

Number	Title (A Side/B Side)	Yr	NM
45s			
SCEPTER			
❑ 1269	Got My Mojo Workin'/Every Day of the Week	1964	12.00
SHAD			
❑ 5013	Darling Lorraine/Riot in Room 3C	1959	25.00
—With short ending on A-side			
❑ 5013	Darling Lorraine/Riot in Room 3C	1959	50.00
—With long ending on A-side			
❑ 5018	Please Be Mine/Rich Boy, Poor Boy	1960	25.00
TRIBUTE			
❑ 199	Got My Mojo Working (Part 1)/Got My Mojo Working (Part 2)	1964	15.00
❑ 201	Tweet-Tweet/What's On Your Mind	1964	16.00
Albums			
TRIBUTE			
❑ 1202 [M]	Go Ape with the Knockouts	1964	200.00

KNOCKOUTS, THE (U) May be different or the same group as above, but we're not sure.

Number	Title (A Side/B Side)	Yr	NM
45s			
MGM			
❑ 13010	Fever/You Can Take My Girl	1961	20.00

KNOTT SISTERS, THE

Number	Title (A Side/B Side)	Yr	NM
45s			
BIG TOP			
❑ 3003	Undivided Attention/Sun Glasses	1958	100.00

KNOX, BUDDY

Number	Title (A Side/B Side)	Yr	NM
45s			
LIBERTY			
❑ 55290	Lovey Dovey/I Got You	1960	12.00
❑ 55305	Ling, Ting, Tong/The Kisses	1961	12.00
❑ 55305 [PS]	Ling, Ting, Tong/The Kisses	1961	30.00
❑ 55366	All By Myself/Three Eyed Man	1961	12.00
❑ 55411	Cha-Hua-Hua/Open	1962	12.00
❑ 55473	She's Gone/There's Only Me	1962	12.00

Except when noted otherwise, VG = 25% of NM, and VG+ = 50% of NM. (Example: VG = $2.00, VG+ = $4.00 and NM = $8.00.)

Number	Title (A Side/B Side)	Yr	NM
❑ 55503	Dear Abby/Three Way Love Affair	1962	12.00
❑ 55592	Shadaroom/Tomorrow Is a-Comin'	1963	10.00
❑ 55650	Thanks a Lot/Hitchhike Back to Georgia	1963	10.00
❑ 55694	Good Lovin'/All Time Loser	1964	10.00
REPRISE			
❑ 0395	Livin' in a House Full of Love/Good Time Girl	1965	10.00
❑ 0431	A Lover's Question/You Said Goodbye	1965	10.00
❑ 0463	A White Sport Coat/That Don't Do Me No Good	1966	10.00
❑ 0501	Love Has Many Ways/Sixteen Feet of Patio	1966	10.00
ROULETTE			
❑ 4002	Party Doll/My Baby's Gone	1957	25.00
—Red label, no roulette wheel			
❑ 4002	Party Doll/My Baby's Gone	1957	30.00
—Red label, roulette wheel on top half of label			
❑ 4002	Party Doll/My Baby's Gone	1957	40.00
—Red label, black print, with roulette wheel around outside			
❑ 4002	Party Doll/My Baby's Gone	1957	50.00
—Maroon label, silver print, with roulette wheel around outside			
❑ 4002	Party Doll/My Baby's Gone	1958	15.00
—White label with color spokes			
❑ 4009	Rock Your Little Baby to Sleep/Don't Make Me Cry	1957	20.00
—Red label, no roulette wheel			
❑ 4009	Rock Your Little Baby to Sleep/Don't Make Me Cry	1957	25.00
—Red label, roulette wheel on top half of label			
❑ 4009	Rock Your Little Baby to Sleep/Don't Make Me Cry	1957	40.00
—Red label with roulette wheel around outside			
❑ 4018	Hula Love/Devil Woman	1957	25.00
❑ 4042	Swingin' Daddy/Whenever I'm Lonely	1958	25.00
❑ 4082	Somebody Touched Me/C'mon Baby	1958	25.00
❑ 4120	That's Why I Cry/Teaseable, Pleaseable You	1958	25.00
❑ 4140	I Think I'm Gonna Kill Myself/To Be with You	1959	25.00
❑ 4179	Taste of the Blues/I Ain't Sharin' Sharon	1959	25.00
❑ 4262	Long Lonely Nights/Storm Clouds	1960	25.00
RUFF			
❑ 1001	Jo-Ann/Don't Make a Ripple	1965	10.00
TRIPLE D			
❑ 798	Party Doll/I'm Stickin' With You	1956	1000.
—B-side by Jimmy Bowen			
UNITED ARTISTS			
❑ 50301	This Time Tomorrow/Gypsy Man	1968	8.00
❑ 50463	Today My Sleepless Nights Came Back to Town/A Million Years or So	1968	8.00
❑ 50526	God Knows I Love You/Night Runners	1969	8.00
❑ 50596	Salt Lake City/I'm Only Rockin'	1969	8.00
❑ 50644	Yesterday Is Gone/Back to New Orleans	1970	6.00
❑ 50722	White Dove/Glory Train	1970	6.00
❑ 50789	Come Softly to Me/Travelin' Light	1971	6.00
7-Inch Extended Plays			
ROULETTE			
❑ EPR-1-301	Party Doll/Rock Your Little Baby to Sleep//Hula Love/Rock Around the Clock	1957	80.00
❑ EPR-1-301 [PS]	Buddy Knox	1957	80.00
Albums			
ACCORD			
❑ SN-7218	Party Doll and Other Hits	1981	10.00
LIBERTY			
❑ LRP-3251 [M]	Buddy Knox's Golden Hits	1962	30.00
❑ LST-7251 [S]	Buddy Knox's Golden Hits	1962	40.00
ROULETTE			
❑ R 25003 [M]	Buddy Knox	1957	150.00
—Black label, red and silver print			
❑ R 25003 [M]	Buddy Knox	1957	200.00
—Black label, all silver print (original)			
❑ R 25003 [M]	Buddy Knox	1959	100.00
—White label with colored spokes			
❑ R 25048 [M]	Buddy Knox and Jimmy Bowen	1959	100.00
—White label with colored spokes			
❑ R 25048 [M]	Buddy Knox and Jimmy Bowen	1959	200.00
—Black label, red and silver print			
UNITED ARTISTS			
❑ UAS 6689	Gypsy Man	1969	25.00

KOALA, THE

Number	Title (A Side/B Side)	Yr	NM
45s			
CAPITOL			
❑ 2365	Don't You Know What I Mean/Scattered Children's Toys	1968	15.00
Albums			
CAPITOL			
❑ SKAO-176	The Koala	1969	60.00

KODAKS, THE

Number	Title (A Side/B Side)	Yr	NM
45s			
LOST-NITE			
❑ 355	Oh Gee Oh Gosh/Make Believe World	197?	5.00
—Reissue			
❑ 358	Runaround Baby/Guardian Angel	197?	5.00
—Reissue			
❑ 362	Teenager's Dream/Little Boy and Girl	197?	5.00
—Reissue			

KOFFMAN, MOE

Number	Title (A Side/B Side)	Yr	NM
45s			
ASCOT			
❑ 2100	Swingin' Shepherd Blues Twist/Train Whistle Twist	1962	8.00
❑ 2111	Bumpin'/The Pretzel	1962	8.00
❑ 2118	Growing Up/Jazz Merengue	1963	8.00
ATCO			
❑ 6382	Bulldog Walk/Big Bad Irving	1965	8.00
GOLD EAGLE			
❑ 1804	Wishbone/Keep Walkin', Little Flock	196?	8.00
❑ 1811	Theme from Rocco and His Brothers/Hi-Fiver	196?	8.00
JUBILEE			
❑ 5311	The Swingin' Shepherd Blues/Hamburg Bound	1958	10.00
❑ 5324	Little Pixie/Koko-Mamey	1958	10.00
❑ 5352	Shepherd's Cha Cha/The Great Healer	1958	10.00
❑ 5367	Shepherd's Hoedown/Stroll Along with the Blues	1959	10.00
❑ 5471	Coffee House/Flootenanny	1964	8.00
❑ 5485	I Want to Hold Your Hand/Soul Brothers	1964	10.00
❑ 5615	Norwegian Wood/Trains and Boats and Planes	1968	7.00
❑ 5632	Do You Know the Way to San Jose/Funky Monkey	1968	7.00
PALETTE			
❑ 5045	Black Eyed Peas/Sapphire	1959	10.00
❑ 5106	Cool Ghoul/Sapphire	1963	8.00
Albums			
ASCOT			
❑ AM 13001 [M]	Moe Koffman Plays for the Teens	1962	20.00
❑ AS 16001 [S]	Moe Koffman Plays for the Teens	1962	25.00
JANUS			
❑ 7037	Museum Pieces	1978	10.00
JUBILEE			
❑ JLP-1037 [M]	Cool and Hot Sax	1957	40.00
❑ JLP-1074 [M]	The Shepherd Swings Again	1958	40.00
❑ JGS-8009	Moe Koffman Goes Electric	1968	30.00
❑ JGS-8016	Turned On	1968	25.00
KAMA SUTRA			
❑ KSBS-2018	Moe's Curried Soul	1970	10.00
SOUNDWINGS/DUKE STREET			
❑ SW 2108	Oop-Pop-A-Da	1988	12.00
—With Dizzy Gillespie			
UNITED ARTISTS			
❑ UAJ-14029 [M]	Tales of Koffman	1963	25.00
❑ UAJS-15029 [S]	Tales of Koffman	1963	30.00

KOKOMO (1)

Pseudonym for producer JIMMY WISNER.

Number	Title (A Side/B Side)	Yr	NM
45s			
FELSTED			
❑ 8612	Asia Minor/Roy's Tune	1961	10.00
❑ 8612 [PS]	Asia Minor/Roy's Tune	1961	15.00
❑ 8622	Humorous/Theme from a Silent Movie	1961	8.00
❑ 8628	Piano Rhapsody/Sweet Memories	1961	8.00
❑ 8635	Journey Home/Like Teen	1961	8.00
❑ 8641	Poinciana/The Good Earth	1962	8.00
Albums			
FELSTED			
❑ FL 7513 [M]	Asia Minor	1961	40.00
❑ FS 17513 [S]	Asia Minor	1961	50.00

KOKOMO (2)

Number	Title (A Side/B Side)	Yr	NM
45s			
COLUMBIA			
❑ 3-10207	Kitty Sittin' Pretty/It Ain't Cool (To Be Cool No More)	1975	5.00
❑ 3-10213	Kitty Sittin' Pretty/Anytime	1975	5.00
❑ 3-10283	Rise and Shine/Do It Right	1976	5.00
❑ 3-10380	Use Your Imagination/That's Enough	1976	5.00
Albums			
COLUMBIA			
❑ PC 33442	Kokomo	1975	10.00
❑ PC 34031	Rise and Shine!	1976	10.00

KOKOMOS, THE

Number	Title (A Side/B Side)	Yr	NM
45s			
GONE			
❑ 5134	Mama's Boy/Yours Truly	1962	15.00
JOSIE			
❑ 906	Open House Party/No Lies	1963	12.00

KOLBY, DIANE

Number	Title (A Side/B Side)	Yr	NM
45s			
COLUMBIA			
❑ 4-45169	Holy Man/Hallelujah Baby	1970	6.00
❑ 4-45290	Juju Woman/Nivey Klaine	1970	6.00
❑ 4-45712	Death of the Sun/Reincarnation	1972	8.00
❑ 4-45844	Once Around the Park/Bessie Kimble	1973	8.00
Albums			
COLUMBIA			
❑ KC 31386	Diane Kolby	1972	15.00

KOLE, JERRY, AND THE STRINGERS

Number	Title (A Side/B Side)	Yr	NM
Albums			
CROWN			
❑ CST-385 [S]	Hot Rod Alley	1963	40.00
❑ CLP-5385 [M]	Hot Rod Alley	1963	30.00

KONGOS, JOHN

Number	Title (A Side/B Side)	Yr	NM
45s			
ELEKTRA			
❑ 45729	He's Gonna Step on You Again/Sometimes It's Not Enough	1971	6.00
❑ 45760	Tokoloshe Man/Can Someone Please Direct Me Back to Earth	1972	5.00
❑ 45779	Jubilee Cloud/I Would Have Had a Good Time	1972	5.00
❑ 45809	He's Gonna Step on You Again/Tokoloshe Man	1972	5.00
GROOVE			
❑ 58-0009	Johnny and the Mermaid/Raunchy Twist	1963	12.00
KAPP			
❑ 799	I Love Mary/Good Time Party Companion	1966	10.00
RCA VICTOR			
❑ 47-8226	The Enchanted Sea/Tulips for 'Toinette	1963	12.00
Albums			
ELEKTRA			
❑ EKS-75019	Kongos	1971	12.00
JANUS			
❑ JLS 3032	Confusions About a Goldfish	1970	15.00

KONRADS, THE

Number	Title (A Side/B Side)	Yr	NM
45s			
DECCA			
❑ 32060	I Didn't Know How Much/I Thought of You Last Night	1966	8.00

KOOBAS, THE

Number	Title (A Side/B Side)	Yr	NM
45s			
CAPITOL			
❑ 2416	First Cut Is the Deepest/Walking Out	1969	8.00
KAPP			
❑ 737	Take Me for a Little While/Give a Little Bit	1965	15.00
❑ 737 [PS]	Take Me for a Little While/Give a Little Bit	1965	20.00

KOOL, D., AND THE KASUALS

Number	Title (A Side/B Side)	Yr	NM
45s			
CAMEO			
❑ 360	She's Good to Me/Broken Glass	1965	15.00

KOOL AND THE GANG Also see K.C. AND THE SUNSHINE BAND.

12-Inch Singles

DE-LITE

Number	Title (A Side/B Side)	Yr	NM
❑ MK 179-1 [DJ]	Take My Heart (same on both sides)	1983	6.00
❑ MK 208-1 [DJ]	Big Fun (same on both sides)	1982	15.00
❑ PRO 245-1 [DJ]	Home Is Where the Heart Is (same on both sides)	1983	8.00
❑ PRO 261-1 [DJ]	Tonight (Dance Mix) (same on both sides)	1983	8.00
❑ PRO 274-1 [DJ]	Tonight (AOR Mix) (same on both sides)	1984	10.00
❑ PRO 278-1 [DJ]	Straight Ahead (same on both sides)	1983	6.00
❑ DDS 503 [DJ]	Celebremos (5:25)/Morning Star	1981	30.00
❑ DDS 507	Tonight/Celebration	1984	12.00
❑ 880623-1	Fresh (Remix) (Dance Mix)	1985	8.00
❑ 880947-1	Cherish (Remix 5:40) Fresh-Misled (Remix 6:10)	1985	8.00
❑ 884199-1	Emergency (Remix) (Dub Mix) (Special Mix)/You Are the One	1985	12.00

MERCURY

Number	Title (A Side/B Side)	Yr	NM
❑ PRO 478-1 [DJ]	Stone Love (Club Mix) (House Mix)/Dance Champion	1986	8.00
❑ PRO 739-1 [DJ]	Raindrops (3 versions)	1989	8.00
❑ 870513-1	Rags to Riches (5 versions)	1988	8.00
❑ 870572-1	Rags to Riches (4 versions)	1988	8.00
❑ 874403-1	Raindrops (3 versions)/ Amor, Amore	1989	8.00
❑ 888074-1	Victory (12" Version) (7" Version)/Bad Woman	1986	8.00
❑ 888292-1	Stone Love (Club Version) (House Mix)/Dance Champion	1986	8.00
❑ 888712-1	Holiday (12" Club Remix 5:48) (Dub Version 5:45) (7" Version 3:35) (Jam Mix 5:20)	1988	8.00

45s

DE-LITE

Number	Title (A Side/B Side)	Yr	NM
❑ 519	Kool and the Gang/ Raw Hamburger	1969	6.00
❑ 523	The Gangs Back Again/ Kools Back Again	1969	6.00
❑ 525	Kool It (Here Comes the Fuzz)/ Can't Stop	1970	6.00
❑ 529	Let the Music Take Your Mind/ Chocolate Buttermilk	1970	6.00
❑ 534	Funky Man/1,2,3,4,5,6,7,8	1970	6.00
❑ 538	Who's Gonna Take the Weight (Part One)/Who's Gonna Take the Weight (Part Two)	1970	6.00
❑ 540	I Want to Take You Higher/ Pneumonia	1971	6.00
❑ 543	The Penguin/Lucky for Me	1971	6.00
❑ 544	N.T. (Part One)/N.T. (Part Two)	1971	6.00
❑ 546	Love the Life You Live, Part I/ Love the Life You Live, Part II	1972	6.00
❑ 547	You've Lost That Lovin' Feeling/Ike's Mood	1972	6.00
❑ 550	Music Is the Messenger, Part I/ Music Is the Messenger, Part II	1972	6.00
❑ 552	Good Times/The Frog	1972	6.00
❑ 553	Funky Granny/ Blowing with the Wind	1973	6.00
❑ 555	Country Junkie/I Remember John W. Coltrane	1973	6.00
❑ 557	Funky Stuff/More Funky Stuff	1973	6.00
❑ 559	Jungle Boogie/North, East, South, West	1973	5.00
❑ 561	Hollywood Swinging/Dujii	1974	5.00
❑ 801	Ladies Night/If You Feel Like Dancin'	1979	4.00
❑ 802	Too Hot/Tonight's the Night	1979	4.00
❑ 804	Hangin' Out/Got You Into My Life	1980	4.00
❑ 807	Celebration/Morning Star	1980	4.00
❑ 810	Take It to the Top/Love Affair	1981	4.00
❑ 813	Jones Vs. Jones/Night People	1981	4.00
❑ 815	Take My Heart (You Can Have It If You Want It)/Just Friends	1981	4.00
❑ 815	Take My Heart/Just Friends	1981	5.00
—First pressings have no subtitle			
❑ 816	Steppin' Out/Love Festival	1982	4.00
❑ 818	Get Down On It/Steppin' Out	1982	4.00
❑ 822	Big Fun/No Show	1982	4.00
❑ 824	Let's Go Dancin' (Ooh, La, La, La)/Be My Lady	1982	4.00
❑ 825	Street Kids/As One	1983	4.00
❑ 829	Joanna/A Place for Us	1983	3.00
❑ 830	Tonight/Home Is Where the Heart Is	1984	3.00
❑ 831	Straight Ahead/September Love	1984	3.00
❑ 901	Slick Superchick/Life's a Song	1978	5.00
❑ 905	A Place in Space/The Force	1978	5.00
❑ 909	I Like Music/It's All You Need	1978	5.00
❑ 910	Everybody's Dancin'/Stay Awhile	1978	5.00
❑ 1562	Higher Plane/Wild Is Love	1974	5.00
❑ 1563	Rhyme Tyme People/ Father, Father	1974	5.00
❑ 1567	Spirit of the Boogie/ Summer Madness	1975	5.00
❑ 1573	Caribbean Festival/Caribbean Festival (Disco Version)	1975	5.00
❑ 1577	Winter Sadness/Father, Father	1975	5.00
❑ 1579	Love and Understanding (Come Together)/ Sunshine and Love	1976	5.00
❑ 1583	Universal Sound/ Ancestral Ceremony	1976	5.00
❑ 1586	Open Sesame — Part 1/ Open Sesame — Part 2	1976	5.00
❑ 1590	Super Band/Sunshine	1977	5.00
❑ 880431-7	Misled/Rollin'	1984	3.00
❑ 880623-7	Fresh/In the Heart	1985	3.00
❑ 880623-7 [PS]	Fresh/In the Heart	1985	4.00
❑ 880869-7	Cherish/(Instrumental)	1985	3.00
❑ 880869-7 [PS]	Cherish/(Instrumental)	1985	4.00
❑ 884199-7	Emergency/You Are the One	1985	3.00

MERCURY

Number	Title (A Side/B Side)	Yr	NM
❑ PRO 621-7 [DJ]	Rags to Riches (Lightnin' Licks Remix) (same on both sides)	1988	6.00
❑ PRO 621-7 [PS]	Rags to Riches (Lightnin' Licks Remix) (same on both sides)	1988	6.00
❑ 870513-7	Rags to Riches/Rags to Riches (Remix)	1988	3.00
❑ 870513-7 [PS]	Rags to Riches/Rags to Riches (Remix)	1988	3.00
❑ 872038-7	Strong/Funky Stuff	1988	3.00
❑ 874402-7	Raindrops/Amor Amore	1989	3.00
❑ 876072-7	Never Give Up/Amor Amore	1989	3.00
❑ 888074-7	Victory/Bad Woman	1986	3.00
❑ 888074-7 [PS]	Victory/Bad Woman	1986	3.00
❑ 888292-7	Stone Love/Dance Champion	1987	3.00
❑ 888292-7 [PS]	Stone Love/Dance Champion	1987	3.00
❑ 888712-7	Holiday/(Jam Mix)	1987	3.00
❑ 888712-7 [PS]	Holiday/(Jam Mix)	1987	3.00
❑ 888867-7	In a Special Way/God's Country	1987	3.00
❑ 888867-7 [PS]	In a Special Way/God's Country	1987	3.00

Albums

DE-LITE

Number	Title (A Side/B Side)	Yr	NM
❑ MK-48 [DJ]	History of Kool and the Gang	1979	15.00
❑ 2003	Kool and the Gang	1969	25.00
❑ 2008	Live at the Sex Machine	1971	15.00
❑ 2009	The Best of Kool and the Gang	1971	15.00
❑ 2010	Live at PJ's	1971	15.00
❑ 2011	Music Is the Message	1972	12.00
❑ 2012	Good Times	1973	12.00
❑ 2013	Wild and Peaceful	1973	10.00
❑ 2014	Light of Worlds	1974	10.00
❑ 2015	Kool & The Gang Greatest Hits!	1975	10.00
❑ 2016	Spirit of the Boogie	1975	10.00
❑ 2018	Love and Understanding	1976	10.00
❑ 2023	Open Sesame	1976	10.00
❑ 4001	Kool Jazz	1973	10.00
❑ 8502	Something Special	1981	10.00
❑ 8505	As One	1982	10.00
❑ 8508	In the Heart	1983	10.00
❑ 9501	The Force	1978	10.00
❑ 9507	Kool & The Gang Spin Their Top Ten Hits	1978	10.00
❑ 9509	Everybody's Dancin'	1979	10.00
❑ 9513	Ladies Night	1979	10.00
❑ 9518	Celebrate!	1980	10.00
❑ 814351-1	In the Heart	1984	8.00
—Reissue			
❑ 822534-1	Something Special	1984	8.00
—Reissue			
❑ 822535-1	As One	1984	8.00
—Reissue			
❑ 822536-1	Kool & The Gang Spin Their Top Ten Hits	1984	8.00
—Reissue			
❑ 822537-1	Ladies Night	1984	8.00
—Reissue			
❑ 822538-1	Celebrate!	1984	8.00
—Reissue			
❑ 822943-1	Emergency	1984	8.00

MERCURY

Number	Title (A Side/B Side)	Yr	NM
❑ 830398-1	Forever	1986	8.00
❑ 834780-1	Everything's Kool & the Gang: Greatest Hits & More	1988	8.00
❑ 838233-1	Sweat	1989	8.00

KOOL GENTS DEE CLARK was a member of this group.

45s

VEE JAY

Number	Title (A Side/B Side)	Yr	NM
❑ 173	This Is the Night/Do Ya Do	1956	200.00
❑ 207	You Know/I Can't Help Myself	1956	200.00

KOOPER, AL Also see BLOOD, SWEAT AND TEARS; MIKE BLOOMFIELD; THE BLUES PROJECT.

45s

AURORA

Number	Title (A Side/B Side)	Yr	NM
❑ 164	New York's My Town/ My Voice, My Piano	1967	12.00

COLUMBIA

Number	Title (A Side/B Side)	Yr	NM
❑ 03312	Two Sides (To Every Situation)/ Snowblind	1982	4.00
❑ 44748	You Never Know Who Your Friends Are/Soft Landing on the Moon	1969	5.00
❑ 44811	I Stand Alone/Hey, Western Union Man	1969	5.00
❑ 45093	One Room Country Shack/ Bury My Body	1970	5.00
❑ 45148	She Gets Me Where I Live/God Sheds His Grace on Thee	1970	5.00
❑ 45179	Love Theme from "The Landlord"/Brand New Day	1970	5.00
❑ 4-45243	I Got a Woman/Easy Does It	1970	5.00
❑ 45412	John the Baptist/Back on My Feet	1971	5.00
❑ 45566	The Monkey Time/Bended Knees (Please Don't Let Me Down)	1972	5.00
❑ 45691	Sam Stone/Be Real	1972	5.00
❑ 45735	Jolie/Be Real	1972	5.00

UNITED ARTISTS

Number	Title (A Side/B Side)	Yr	NM
❑ XW879	This Diamond Ring/ Hollywood Vampire	1976	4.00

VERVE FOLKWAYS

Number	Title (A Side/B Side)	Yr	NM
❑ 5026	Changes/Pack Up Your Sorrows	1966	12.00

Albums

COLUMBIA

Number	Title (A Side/B Side)	Yr	NM
❑ CS 9718	I Stand Alone	1969	15.00
—"360 Sound" label			
❑ CS 9718	I Stand Alone	1970	10.00
—Orange label			
❑ CS 9855	You Never Know Who Your Friends Are	1969	15.00
—"360 Sound" label			
❑ CS 9855	You Never Know Who Your Friends Are	1970	10.00
—Orange label			
❑ CS 9951	Kooper Session	1970	10.00
—With Shuggie Otis; orange label			
❑ CS 9951	Kooper Session	1970	15.00
—With Shuggie Otis; "360 Sound" label			
❑ G 30031 [(2)]	Easy Does It	1970	20.00
❑ KC 30506	New York City (You're a Woman)	1971	15.00
❑ KC 31159	A Possible Projection of the Future/Childhood's End	1972	15.00
❑ KC 31723	Naked Songs	1973	15.00
❑ PG 33169 [(2)]	Unclaimed Freight (Al's Big Deal)	1975	15.00
❑ FC 38137	Championship Wrestling	1982	10.00

UNITED ARTISTS

Number	Title (A Side/B Side)	Yr	NM
❑ UA-LA702-G	Act Like Nothing's Wrong	1976	12.00

KORNER, ALEXIS

45s

COLUMBIA

Number	Title (A Side/B Side)	Yr	NM
❑ 10166	Get Off My Cloud/ Strange N' Deranged	1975	8.00

Albums

COLUMBIA

Number	Title (A Side/B Side)	Yr	NM
❑ PC 33427	Get Off of My Cloud	1975	15.00

JUST SUNSHINE

Number	Title (A Side/B Side)	Yr	NM
❑ 13	All Star Blues Incorporated	1974	12.00

MOBILE FIDELITY

Number	Title (A Side/B Side)	Yr	NM
❑ 1-265	Blues at the Marquee	1996	40.00
—Audiophile vinyl			

WARNER BROS.

Number	Title (A Side/B Side)	Yr	NM
❑ 2XS 1966 [(2)]	Bootleg Him	1972	25.00
❑ BS 2647	Accidentally Borne in New Orleans	1972	15.00

KOSSOFF, PAUL Also see FREE.

Albums

DJM

Number	Title (A Side/B Side)	Yr	NM
❑ 2300 [(2)]	Koss	1977	15.00

ISLAND

Number	Title (A Side/B Side)	Yr	NM
❑ ILPS 9264	Back Street Crawler	1975	10.00

KOSTELANETZ, ANDRE

45s

COLUMBIA

Number	Title (A Side/B Side)	Yr	NM
❑ 40044	Playing Around/Time on My Hands	1953	10.00
❑ 40350	Sweet Surrender/ April in Paradise	1954	10.00
❑ 41534	Sabre Dance/Gypsy Fiddler	1959	8.00

Except when noted otherwise, VG = 25% of NM, and VG+ = 50% of NM. (Example: VG = $2.00, VG+ = $4.00 and NM = $8.00.)

Number	Title (A Side/B Side)	Yr	NM
❑ 42604	Washington Twist/ Secret Service	1962	8.00
❑ 43034	Bluesette/Fall in Love	1964	6.00
❑ 44147	The Impossible Dream/ Born Free	1967	6.00
❑ 44255	You Are There/One of These Songs	1967	6.00
❑ 45061	Come Saturday Morning/ Leaving on a Jet Plane	1970	5.00
❑ 45244	Things of Life/ Valse de Rothschild	1970	5.00
❑ 45357	Theme from "Love Story"/ Mr. Bojangles	1971	4.00
❑ JZSP 76389/90 [DJ]	Medley: Santa Claus Is Coming To Town & Have Yourself A Merry Little Christmas/ Christmas Chopsticks	1963	10.00
❑ JZSP 111905/6 [DJ]	O Come All Ye Faithful/ Oh Tannenbaum	1965	8.00

—Black vinyl

Number	Title (A Side/B Side)	Yr	NM
❑ JZSP 111905/6 [DJ]	O Come All Ye Faithful/ Oh Tannenbaum	1965	12.00

—Green vinyl

Number	Title (A Side/B Side)	Yr	NM
❑ JZSP 116040/1 [DJ]	Galop from "Moscow, Cheremushki"/Galop from "Ballet Suite No. 2"	1966	8.00

—White label promo only

Number	Title (A Side/B Side)	Yr	NM
❑ JZSP 116040/1 [PS]	Galop from "Moscow, Cheremushki"/Galop from "Ballet Suite No. 2"	1966	12.00

—Title on sleeve: "Kosty Plays Shosty"

COLUMBIA MASTERWORKS

Number	Title (A Side/B Side)	Yr	NM
❑ A-753 [(4)]	Carnival Tropicana	195?	10.00

—Box for 4-record set

Number	Title (A Side/B Side)	Yr	NM
❑ A-925 [(5)]	Swan Lake	195?	10.00

—Box for five-record set

Number	Title (A Side/B Side)	Yr	NM
❑ 4-7603-M	Malaguena/No Taboleiro De Bahiana	195?	8.00
❑ 4-7604-M	La Cumparasita/Adios	195?	8.00
❑ 4-7605-M	Mexicana/Caminito	195?	8.00
❑ 4-7606-M	Yours/Siboney	195?	8.00

—The above four comprise box set A-753

Number	Title (A Side/B Side)	Yr	NM
❑ 4-7648-M	Swan Lake (Part 1)/ Swan Lake (Part 10)	195?	8.00
❑ 4-7649-M	Swan Lake (Part 2)/ Swan Lake (Part 9)	195?	8.00
❑ 4-7650-M	Swan Lake (Part 3)/ Swan Lake (Part 8)	195?	8.00
❑ 4-7651-M	Swan Lake (Part 4)/ Swan Lake (Part 7)	195?	8.00
❑ 4-7652-M	Swan Lake (Part 5)/ Swan Lake (Part 6)	195?	8.00

—The above five comprise box set A-925

7-Inch Extended Plays

COLUMBIA

Number	Title (A Side/B Side)	Yr	NM
❑ KZP-1	Where or When/Celeste Aida// Tales from the Vienna Woods/The Love for Three Oranges - March	195?	10.00
❑ KZP-1 [PS]	Meet Andre Kostelanetz, Music's Leading Man	195?	10.00
❑ B-7722	You and the Night and the Music/Poeme//I Could Write a Book/To a Wild Rose	195?	8.00
❑ B-7722 [PS]	You and the Night and the Music	195?	8.00

COLUMBIA MASTERWORKS

Number	Title (A Side/B Side)	Yr	NM
❑ A-502 [PS]	Musical Comedy Favorites, Vol. II	195?	10.00

—Cover for 2-EP set (1429 and 1430)

Number	Title (A Side/B Side)	Yr	NM
❑ 7-1155	Begin the Beguine/Blow, Gabriel, Blow//Night and Day/Just One of Those Things	195?	10.00

—Alternate number is "A 1506"

Number	Title (A Side/B Side)	Yr	NM
❑ 7-1266	Schumann: Traumerei, Op. 15, No. 7/Brahms: Lullaby, Op. 49, No. 4//Francois Schubert: The Bee (L'abeille)/Londonderry Air	195?	10.00

—Alternate number is "A 1571"

Number	Title (A Side/B Side)	Yr	NM
❑ 7-1429	Night and Day/Time on My Hands//I'll See You Again/ Dancing in the Dark	195?	10.00

—Alternate numbers are "A 502-1" and "A 502-4"

Number	Title (A Side/B Side)	Yr	NM
❑ 7-1430	The Touch of Your Hand/ Somebody Loves Me//With a Song in My Heart/Easter Parade	195?	10.00

—Alternate numbers are "A 502-2" and "A 502-3"

Number	Title (A Side/B Side)	Yr	NM
❑ A 1506 [PS]	(title unknown)	195?	10.00
❑ A 1571 [PS]	(title unknown)	195?	10.00

Albums

COLUMBIA

Number	Title (A Side/B Side)	Yr	NM
❑ AK 1 [M]	Musical Tour of the World	195?	20.00
❑ KZ 1 [M]	Meet Andre Kostelanetz	1955	20.00

—Red and black label with six "eye" logos

Number	Title (A Side/B Side)	Yr	NM
❑ GP 10 [(2)]	Sounds of Love	1969	12.00
❑ C2L 11 [M]	The Romantic Music of Tchaikovsky	195?	25.00

—Red and black label with six "eye" logos

Number	Title (A Side/B Side)	Yr	NM
❑ CL 704 [M]	Mood for Love	1956	20.00

—Red and black label with six "eye" logos

Number	Title (A Side/B Side)	Yr	NM
❑ CL 720 [M]	Peter and the Wolf; Carnival of the Animals	1956	20.00

—Red and black label with six "eye" logos

Number	Title (A Side/B Side)	Yr	NM
❑ CL 734 [M]	The Music of Victor Youmans	1956	20.00

—Red and black label with six "eye" logos

Number	Title (A Side/B Side)	Yr	NM
❑ CL 758 [M]	Bravo!	1956	20.00

—Red and black label with six "eye" logos

Number	Title (A Side/B Side)	Yr	NM
❑ CL 765 [M]	The Music of Victor Herbert	1956	20.00

—Red and black label with six "eye" logos

Number	Title (A Side/B Side)	Yr	NM
❑ CL 768 [M]	Music of Irving Berlin	1956	20.00

—Red and black label with six "eye" logos

Number	Title (A Side/B Side)	Yr	NM
❑ CL 780 [M]	Lure of the Tropics	1956	20.00

—Red and black label with six "eye" logos

Number	Title (A Side/B Side)	Yr	NM
❑ CL 781 [M]	Stardust	1956	20.00

—Red and black label with six "eye" logos

Number	Title (A Side/B Side)	Yr	NM
❑ CL 797 [M]	La Boheme for Orchestra	1956	20.00

—Red and black label with six "eye" logos

Number	Title (A Side/B Side)	Yr	NM
❑ CL 806 [M]	Show Boat/South Pacific/ Slaughter on 10th Avenue	1956	20.00

—Red and black label with six "eye" logos

Number	Title (A Side/B Side)	Yr	NM
❑ CL 811 [M]	Calendar Girl	1956	20.00

—Red and black label with six "eye" logos

Number	Title (A Side/B Side)	Yr	NM
❑ CL 843 [M]	The Very Thought of You	1956	20.00

—Red and black label with six "eye" logos

Number	Title (A Side/B Side)	Yr	NM
❑ CL 863 [M]	Café Continental	1956	20.00

—Red and black label with six "eye" logos

Number	Title (A Side/B Side)	Yr	NM
❑ CL 864 [M]	Beautiful Dreamer	1956	20.00

—Red and black label with six "eye" logos

Number	Title (A Side/B Side)	Yr	NM
❑ CL 1199 [M]	Theatre Party	1958	15.00
❑ CL 1220 [M]	Romantic Music of...	1958	15.00
❑ CL 1335 [M]	The Lure of Paradise	1959	12.00
❑ CL 1354 [M]	Strauss Waltzes	1959	12.00
❑ CL 1431 [M]	Gypsy Passion	1960	12.00
❑ CL 1495 [M]	Gershwin: Rhapsody in Blue; Previn: Concerto in F	1960	12.00
❑ CL 1528 [M]	Joy to the World: Music for Christmas	1959	15.00
❑ CL 1657 [M]	Wonderland of Sound	1961	12.00
❑ CL 1718 [M]	Star-Spangled Marches	1962	12.00
❑ CL 1827 [M]	Wonderland of Sound (Broadway's Greatest Hits)	1962	12.00
❑ CL 1898 [M]	Wonderland of Sound (Fire and Jealousy)	1962	12.00
❑ CL 1938 [M]	Wonderland of Sound (The World's Greatest Waltzes)	1963	10.00
❑ CL 1995 [M]	Wonderland of Opera	1963	10.00
❑ CL 2039 [M]	Wonderland of Golden Hits	1963	10.00
❑ CL 2068 [M]	Wonderland of Christmas	1963	12.00
❑ CL 2078 [M]	Kostelanetz in Wonderland	1964	10.00
❑ CL 2133 [M]	Gershwin Wonderland	1964	10.00
❑ CL 2138 [M]	New York Wonderland	1964	10.00
❑ CL 2185 [M]	I Wish You Love	1964	10.00
❑ CL 2250 [M]	New Orleans Wonderland	1965	10.00
❑ CL 2359 [M]	Thunder (The Spectacular Sound of John Philip Sousa)	1965	10.00
❑ CL 2467 [M]	The Shadow of Your Smile and Other Great Movie Themes	1966	10.00
❑ CL 2534 [M]	Today's Golden Hits	1966	10.00
❑ CL 2581 [M]	Exotic Nights	1966	10.00
❑ CL 2609 [M]	The Kostelanetz Sound of Today	1967	10.00
❑ CL 2688 [M]	Concert in the Park	1967	10.00
❑ CL 2756 [M]	Today's Greatest Movie Hits	1967	12.00
❑ CL 2823 [M]	Scarborough Fair	1968	15.00
❑ CL 2891 [M]	For the Young at Heart	1968	15.00
❑ CS 8144 [S]	The Lure of Paradise	1959	15.00
❑ CS 8162 [S]	Strauss Waltzes	1959	15.00
❑ CS 8228 [S]	Gypsy Passion	1960	15.00
❑ CS 8286 [S]	Gershwin: Rhapsody in Blue; Previn: Concerto in F	1960	15.00
❑ CS 8328 [S]	Joy to the World: Music for Christmas	1959	20.00

—Red and black label with six "eye" logos

Number	Title (A Side/B Side)	Yr	NM
❑ CS 8457 [S]	Wonderland of Sound	1961	15.00
❑ CS 8518 [S]	Star-Spangled Marches	1962	15.00
❑ CS 8627 [S]	Wonderland of Sound (Broadway's Greatest Hits)	1962	15.00
❑ CS 8698 [S]	Wonderland of Sound (Fire and Jealousy)	1962	15.00
❑ CS 8738 [S]	Wonderland of Sound (The World's Greatest Waltzes)	1963	12.00
❑ CS 8795 [S]	Wonderland of Opera	1963	12.00
❑ CS 8839 [S]	Wonderland of Golden Hits	1963	12.00
❑ CS 8868 [S]	Wonderland of Christmas	1963	15.00
❑ CS 8878 [S]	Kostelanetz in Wonderland	1964	12.00
❑ CS 8933 [S]	Gershwin Wonderland	1964	12.00
❑ CS 8938 [S]	New York Wonderland	1964	12.00
❑ CS 8985 [S]	I Wish You Love	1964	12.00
❑ CS 9050 [S]	New Orleans Wonderland	1965	12.00
❑ CS 9159 [S]	Thunder (The Spectacular Sound of John Philip Sousa)	1965	12.00
❑ CS 9267 [S]	The Shadow of Your Smile and Other Great Movie Themes	1966	10.00
❑ CS 9334 [S]	Today's Golden Hits	1966	12.00
❑ CS 9381 [S]	Exotic Nights	1966	10.00
❑ CS 9409 [S]	The Kostelanetz Sound of Today	1967	10.00
❑ CS 9488 [S]	Concert in the Park	1967	10.00
❑ CS 9556 [S]	Today's Greatest Movie Hits	1967	10.00
❑ CS 9623 [S]	Scarborough Fair	1968	10.00
❑ CS 9691 [S]	For the Young at Heart	1968	10.00
❑ CS 9724	Hits from Funny Girl, Finian's Rainbow, and Star!	1968	10.00
❑ CS 9740	Andre Kostelanetz' Greatest Hits	1969	10.00
❑ CS 9823	Traces	1969	10.00
❑ CS 9973	Greatest Hits of the 60's	1970	10.00
❑ CS 9998	I'll Never Fall in Love Again	1970	10.00
❑ C 30037	Everything Is Beautiful	1970	10.00
❑ C 30501	Love Story	1971	10.00
❑ C 30672	For All We Know	1971	10.00
❑ C 31002	Kostelanetz Plays Chicago	1971	10.00
❑ KG 31491 [(2)]	Andre Kostelanetz Plays Cole Porter	1972	15.00
❑ KG 32002 [(2)]	The World's Greatest Love Songs	1973	12.00
❑ CQ 32147 [Q]	A Quadraphonic Concert	1972	15.00
❑ KC 32187	Last Tango in Paris	1973	10.00
❑ KC 32451	Kostelanetz Plays Great Hits of Today	1973	10.00
❑ KC 32580	Andre Kostelanetz Plays Legrand's Greatest Hits	1974	10.00
❑ KG 32825 [(2)]	Andre Kostelanetz Plays Gershwin	1974	12.00
❑ CQ 32856 [Q]	Quadraphonic Pop Concert	1973	15.00
❑ KC 33061	Musical Reflections of Broadway and Hollywood	1974	10.00
❑ KG 33065 [(2)]	Strike Up the Band	1974	12.00
❑ KC 33437	Orient Express	1975	10.00
❑ C 33550	Never Can Say Goodbye	1975	8.00
❑ KC 33550	Never Can Say Goodbye	1975	10.00
❑ KC 33954	Music from A Chorus Line and Treemonisha	1975	10.00
❑ KC 34157	I'm Easy and Other Themes	1976	10.00
❑ PC 34352	Dance with Me	1977	10.00
❑ PC 34660	Music of Charlie Chaplin and Duke Ellington	1977	10.00
❑ JC 35328	You Light Up My Life	1978	10.00
❑ JC 35788	Superman	1979	8.00
❑ JC 36382	Various Themes	1980	8.00

COLUMBIA LIMITED EDITION

Number	Title (A Side/B Side)	Yr	NM
❑ LE 10083	Joy to the World: Music for Christmas	197?	10.00

—Reissue of CS 8328

Number	Title (A Side/B Side)	Yr	NM
❑ LE 10086	Wonderland of Christmas	197?	10.00

—Reissue of CS 8868

COLUMBIA MASTERWORKS

Number	Title (A Side/B Side)	Yr	NM
❑ ML 2007 [10]	Music of Stephen Foster	195?	25.00
❑ ML 2011 [10]	Waltzes of Johann Strauss	195?	25.00
❑ ML 2014 [10]	Songs of Cole Porter	195?	30.00
❑ ML 2022 [10]	Motion Picture Favorites	195?	25.00
❑ ML 2056 [10]	Chopin-Kostelanetz	195?	25.00
❑ ML 4065 [M]	Favorites	195?	20.00
❑ ML 4066 [M]	Clair de Lune	195?	20.00
❑ ML 4082 [M]	Carnival Tropicana	195?	20.00
❑ ML 4253 [M]	Music of Fritz Kreisler and Sigmund Romberg	195?	20.00
❑ ML 4308 [M]	Swan Lake (Highlights)	195?	20.00
❑ ML 4409 [M]	Bizet: L'arlesienne Suites 1 & 2	195?	20.00
❑ ML 4455 [M]	An American in Paris	195?	20.00
❑ ML 4822 [M]	Lure of the Tropics	1956	20.00
❑ MS 6106 [S]	Offenbach: Gaite Parisienne; Bizet: Carmen (Highlights)	195?	20.00
❑ ML 6111 [M]	Romantic Strings	1960	12.00
❑ ML 6129 [M]	Showstoppers	1960	12.00
❑ ML 6179 [M]	Wishing You a Merry Christmas	1960	12.00
❑ ML 6206 [M]	Promenade Favorites	1966	12.00
❑ ML 6224 [M]	Romantic Waltzes of Tchaikovsky	1961	12.00
❑ ML 6226 [M]	Favorite Romantic Concertos	1961	12.00
❑ MS 6711 [S]	Romantic Strings	1960	15.00
❑ MS 6729 [S]	Showstoppers	1960	15.00
❑ MS 6779 [S]	Wishing You a Merry Christmas	1960	15.00
❑ MS 6806 [S]	Promenade Favorites	1966	15.00
❑ MS 6824 [S]	Romantic Waltzes of Tchaikovsky	1961	15.00
❑ MS 6826 [S]	Favorite Romantic Concertos	1961	15.00
❑ MS 7087	Vienna, City of Dreams	1968	12.00
❑ MS 7108 [S]	Andre Kostelanetz Conducts Great Romantic Ballads	196?	10.00
❑ MS 7319	Musical Evenings	1969	10.00
❑ MS 7427	Extravaganza	1970	10.00
❑ M 30075	Music for Strings	1970	10.00
❑ M 35114	Festive Overtures	1978	8.00

COLUMBIA SPECIAL PRODUCTS

Number	Title (A Side/B Side)	Yr	NM
❑ C 10975	Wishing You a Merry Christmas	1972	10.00

—Reissue of Columbia Masterworks MS 6779

Number	Title (A Side/B Side)	Yr	NM
❑ P 13286	Scarborough Fair	197?	8.00

HARMONY

Number	Title (A Side/B Side)	Yr	NM
❑ HL 7368 [M]	You and the Night and the Music	196?	10.00
❑ HL 7371 [M]	Broadway Theatre Party	196?	10.00
❑ HL 7395 [M]	Grand Canyon Suite	196?	10.00

Number	Title (A Side/B Side)	Yr	NM
❑ HL 7432 [M]	Joy to the World: Music for Christmas	1967	12.00
—Reissue of Columbia 1528			
❑ HS 11168 [S]	You and the Night and the Music	196?	10.00
❑ HS 11171 [S]	Broadway Theatre Party	196?	10.00
❑ HS 11195 [S]	Grand Canyon Suite	196?	10.00
❑ HS 11232 [S]	Joy to the World: Music for Christmas	1967	12.00
—Reissue of Columbia 8328			
❑ HS 11281	The Magic of Music	1968	10.00
❑ H 30014	Be My Love	1970	10.00
❑ KH 31414	Greatest Hits of Broadway and Hollywood	1972	10.00
❑ KH 31500	Love Theme from "The Godfather"	1972	10.00
❑ KH 31571	Andre Kostelanetz Plays Richard Rogers	1973	10.00
❑ KH 32170	Strike Up the Band	1973	10.00
READER'S DIGEST			
❑ RD-120-A [(8)]	The Best of Andre Kostelanetz	197?	30.00

KOTTKE, LEO

Number	Title (A Side/B Side)	Yr	NM
45s			
CAPITOL			
❑ 3854	Pamela Brown/A Child Should Be a Fish	1974	6.00
❑ 4177	Can't Quite Put It Into Words/ Power Failure	1975	5.00
Albums			
CAPITOL			
❑ ST-682	Mudlark	1971	12.00
❑ ST-11000	Greenhouse	1972	10.00
❑ ST-11164	My Feet Are Smiling	1973	10.00
❑ ST-11262	Ice Water	1974	10.00
❑ ST-11335	Dreams and All That Stuff	1974	10.00
❑ ST-11446	Chewing Pine	1975	10.00
❑ ST-11576	Leo Kottke 1971-1976 — Did You Hear Me?	1976	10.00
❑ SWBC-11867 [(2)]	The Best of Leo Kottke	1979	12.00
❑ SN-16063	Mudlark	1979	8.00
—Budget-line reissue			
❑ SN-16064	Ice Water	1979	8.00
—Budget-line reissue			
❑ SN-16065	Greenhouse	1979	8.00
—Budget-line reissue			
❑ SN-16187	Dreams and All That Stuff	1980	8.00
—Budget-line reissue			
❑ SN-16188	Chewing Pine	1980	8.00
—Budget-line reissue			
❑ SN-16189	Leo Kottke 1971-1976 — Did You Hear Me?	1980	8.00
—Budget-line reissue			
CHRYSALIS			
❑ CHR 1106	Leo Kottke	1977	10.00
❑ CHR 1191	Burnt Lips	1978	10.00
❑ CHR 1234	Balance	1979	10.00
❑ CHR 1328	Guitar Music	1981	10.00
❑ PV 41106	Leo Kottke	1985	8.00
—Budget-line reissue			
❑ PV 41191	Burnt Lips	1985	8.00
—Budget-line reissue			
❑ PV 41234	Balance	1985	8.00
—Budget-line reissue			
❑ PV 41328	Guitar Music	1983	8.00
—Budget-line reissue			
❑ FV 41411	Time Step	1983	10.00
❑ PV 41411	Time Step	1986	8.00
—Budget-line reissue			
OBLIVION			
❑ S-1	12-String Blues/Live at the Scholar Coffee House	1969	25.00
PRIVATE MUSIC			
❑ 2007-1-P	A Shout Toward Noon	1986	10.00
❑ 2025-1-P	Regards from Chuck Pink	1988	10.00
❑ 2050-1-P	My Father's Face	1989	10.00
SYMPOSIUM			
❑ 2001	Circle Round the Sun	1970	12.00
TAKOMA			
❑ 1024	6 and 12 String Guitar	1969	12.00

KOTTKE, LEO/PETER LANG/JOHN FAHEY

Also see JOHN FAHEY; LEO KOTTKE.

Number	Title (A Side/B Side)	Yr	NM
Albums			
TAKOMA			
❑ 1040	Leo Kottke/Peter Lang/ John Fahey	1974	12.00

KRAFTWERK

Number	Title (A Side/B Side)	Yr	NM
12-Inch Singles			
CAPITOL			
❑ 8502	Showroom Dummies (6:00)/ Les Mannequins (6:02)	1977	20.00
❑ 8526	Neon Lights (9:03)/The Model	1978	25.00
ELEKTRA			
❑ ED 5551 [DJ]	Robotnik/The Robots/ Robotronik	1991	12.00
WARNER BROS.			
❑ PRO-A-951 [DJ]	Pocket Calculator/Dentaku	1981	12.00
❑ 20549	Musique Nonstop (LP Version)/ Musique Nonstop (7" Version)	1986	8.00
45s			
CAPITOL			
❑ 4211	Radioactivity/Antenna	1976	7.00
❑ 4211 [PS]	Radioactivity/Antenna	1976	10.00
❑ 4460	Trans-Europe Express/ Franz Schubert	1977	5.00
❑ 4620	Neon Lights/The Robots	1978	5.00
VERTIGO			
❑ 203	Autobahn/Morgan Spaziergance	1975	8.00
❑ 204	Mitternacht (Midnight)/Kometen Melodie (Comet Melody 2)	1975	8.00
WARNER BROS.			
❑ 28441	The Telephone Call/ Der Telefon Anruf	1987	3.00
❑ 28441 [PS]	The Telephone Call/ Der Telefon Anruf	1987	6.00
❑ 28532	Musique Non-Stop (Long)/ Musique Non-Stop (Short)	1986	2.00
❑ 28532 [PS]	Musique Non-Stop (Long)/ Musique Non-Stop (Short)	1986	6.00
❑ 29342	Tour de France (Remix)/ Tour de France (French)	1984	3.00
❑ 49723	Pocket Calculator/Dentaku	1981	5.00
—Yellow vinyl			
❑ 49723	Pocket Calculator/Dentaku	1981	4.00
❑ 49723 [PS]	Pocket Calculator/Dentaku	1981	7.00
—Plastic sleeve that goes with yellow vinyl pressing			
❑ 49795	Numbers/Computer Love	1981	3.00
Albums			
ASTRALWERKS			
❑ ASW 60611 [(4)]	Minimum-Maximum	2005	50.00
—Box set; each LP is in a cardboard inner sleeve and paper sleeve			
CAPITOL			
❑ ST-11457	Radio-Activity	1975	20.00
❑ SW 11603	Trans-Europe Express	1977	20.00
❑ SW-11728	The Man-Machine	1978	20.00
❑ SN-16301	Trans-Europe Express	198?	15.00
—Reissue			
❑ SN-16302	The Man-Machine	198?	10.00
—Reissue			
❑ SN-16380	Radio-Activity	1986	10.00
—Reissue			
ELEKTRA			
❑ 60789	Computer World	1988	15.00
—Reissue			
❑ 60797	Autobahn	1988	15.00
—Still another reissue of this album			
❑ 60798	Electric Cafe	1988	15.00
—Reissue			
❑ 60869 [(2)]	The Mix	1991	18.00
MERCURY			
❑ SRM-1-3704	Autobahn	1977	15.00
—Reissue of Vertigo VEL-2003			
VERTIGO			
❑ VEL-2003	Autobahn	1974	30.00
❑ VEL-2006	Ralf & Florian	1976	30.00
—Recorded in 1973			
WARNER BROS.			
❑ HS 3549	Computer World	1981	10.00
❑ 25326	Autobahn	1985	12.00
—Another reissue of Vertigo VEL-2003			
❑ 25525	Electric Cafe	1986	12.00

KRAMER, BILLY J., AND THE DAKOTAS

Number	Title (A Side/B Side)	Yr	NM
45s			
EPIC			
❑ 10331	1941/His Love Is Just a Lie	1968	10.00
IMPERIAL			
❑ 66027	Little Children/Bad to Me	1964	12.00
❑ 66048	I'll Keep You Satisfied/I Know	1964	12.00
❑ 66051	From a Window/ I'll Be On My Way	1964	12.00
❑ 66051 [PS]	From a Window/ I'll Be On My Way	1964	25.00
❑ 66085	It's Gotta Last Forever/ They Remind Me of You	1965	12.00
❑ 66115	Trains and Boats and Planes/ That's the Way I Feel	1965	10.00
❑ 66115	Trains and Boats and Planes/ I'll Be On My Way	1965	12.00
❑ 66135	Irresistible You/Twilight Time	1965	10.00
❑ 66143	I'll Be Doggone/Neon City	1965	10.00
❑ 66210	You Make Me Feel Like Someone/Take My Hand	1966	10.00
LIBERTY			
❑ 55586	Do You Want to Know a Secret/ I'll Be On My Way	1963	30.00
❑ 55618	The Cruel Surf/The Millionaire	1963	40.00
❑ 55626	Bad to Me/I Call Your Name	1963	30.00
❑ 55643	I'll Keep You Satisfied/I Know	1963	30.00
❑ 55667	Bad to Me/Do You Want to Know a Secret	1964	25.00
❑ 55687	Little Children/They Remind Me of You	1964	—
—Unreleased			
Albums			
CAPITOL			
❑ SM-11897 [P]	The Best of Billy J. Kramer and the Dakotas	1979	10.00
IMPERIAL			
❑ LP 9267 [M]	Little Children	1964	30.00
—Black and pink label			
❑ LP 9267 [M]	Little Children	1964	50.00
—Black label with stars			
❑ LP 9273 [M]	I'll Keep You Satisfied/ From a Window	1964	30.00
❑ LP 9291 [M]	Trains and Boats and Planes	1965	30.00
❑ LP 12267 [P]	Little Children	1964	40.00
—Black and pink label			
❑ LP 12267 [P]	Little Children	1964	80.00
—Black label with silver print			
❑ LP 12273 [P]	I'll Keep You Satisfied/ From a Window	1964	40.00
❑ LP 12921 [R]	Trains and Boats and Planes	1965	25.00

KRAUSS, ALISON, AND UNION STATION

Number	Title (A Side/B Side)	Yr	NM
45s			
BNA			
❑ 64277	When You Say Nothing at All/ Charlotte's in North Carolina	1995	4.00
—B-side by Keith Whitley			
ROUNDER			
❑ 4585	New Fool/Steel Rails	1992	6.00
Albums			
MOBILE FIDELITY			
❑ MFSL 2-276 [(2)]	So Long, So Wrong	2004	40.00
—"Original Master Recording" at top of cover			
ROUNDER			
❑ 0235	Too Late to Cry	1987	15.00
❑ 0265	Two Highways	1989	15.00
❑ 0275	I've Got That Old Feeling	1990	15.00
❑ 0325	Now That I've Found You: A Collection	1995	15.00

KRAVITZ, LENNY

Number	Title (A Side/B Side)	Yr	NM
45s			
VIRGIN			
❑ S7-17445	Believe/For the First Time	1993	3.00
❑ S7-17711	Heaven Help/Spinning Around Over You	1994	3.00
❑ 38668	American Woman/Fly Away	1999	3.00
❑ 38782	Again/Black Velveteen	2001	4.00
❑ 38816	Dig In/Stillness of Heart	2001	4.00
Albums			
VIRGIN			
❑ 39169	Are You Gonna Go My Way	1993	25.00
—Clear-vinyl LP plus bonus CD with 8 unreleased tracks			
❑ 91290	Let Love Rule	1989	12.00

KREED

Number	Title (A Side/B Side)	Yr	NM
Albums			
VISION OF SOUND			
❑ 71-56	Kreed	1971	1200.

KRISTOFFERSON, KRIS

Also see WILLIE NELSON.

Number	Title (A Side/B Side)	Yr	NM
45s			
COLUMBIA			
❑ 04881	Highwayman/The Human Condition	1985	3.00
—A-side: Willie Nelson/Waylon Jennings/Johnny Cash/Kris Kristofferson; B-side: Nelson, Cash			
❑ 04881 [PS]	Highwayman/The Human Condition	1985	4.00
—A-side: Willie Nelson/Waylon Jennings/Johnny Cash/Kris Kristofferson; B-side: Nelson, Cash			
❑ 05594	Desperadoes Waiting for a Train/The Twentieth Century Is Almost Over	1985	3.00
—A-side: Willie Nelson/Waylon Jennings/Johnny Cash/Kris Kristofferson; B-side: Nelson, Cash			
❑ 08406	Highwayman/Desperadoes Waiting for a Train	1988	3.00
—Waylon Jennings/Willie Nelson/Johnny Cash/Kris Kristofferson; reissue			
❑ 10525	Watch Closely Now/ Crippled Crow	1977	4.00
❑ 10731	The Fighter/Forever in Your Love	1978	4.00

Except when noted otherwise, VG = 25% of NM, and VG+ = 50% of NM. (Example: VG = $2.00, VG+ = $4.00 and NM = $8.00.)

Number	Title (A Side/B Side)	Yr	NM
❑ 11160	Prove It to You One More Time Again/Fallen Angel	1979	4.00
❑ 11383	I'll Take Any Chance I Can with You/Maybe You Heard	1980	4.00
❑ 60507	Nobody Loves Anybody Anymore/Maybe You Heard	1981	4.00
❑ 73381	Born and Raised in Black and White/Texas	1990	3.00
—The Highwaymen (Waylon Jennings/Willie Nelson/Johnny Cash/Kris Kristofferson)			
❑ 73572	American Remains/Texas	1990	3.00
—The Highwaymen (Waylon Jennings/Willie Nelson/Johnny Cash/Kris Kristofferson)			
EPIC			
❑ 10225	Golden Idol/Killing Time	1967	15.00
LIBERTY			
❑ S7-18486	It Is What It Is/The Devil's Right Hand	1995	3.00
—By The Highwaymen			
MERCURY			
❑ 888345-7	They Killed Him/Anthem '84	1987	3.00
❑ 888554-7	Love Is the Way/This Old Road	1987	3.00
❑ 888723-7	El Coyote/They Killed Him	1987	3.00
MONUMENT			
❑ 1210	Sunday Morning Comin' Down/To Beat the Devil	1970	8.00
❑ 8525	Loving Her Was Easier (Than Anything I'll Ever Do Again)/Epitaph	1971	6.00
❑ 8531	The Taker/Pilgrim: Chapter 33	1971	6.00
❑ 8536	Josie/Border Lord	1972	6.00
❑ 8558	Jesus Was a Capricorn/Enough for You	1972	6.00
❑ 8564	Jesse Younger/Give It Time to Be Tender	1973	6.00
❑ 8571	Why Me/Help Me	1973	5.00
❑ 8618	I May Smoke Too Much/Lights of Magdala	1974	5.00
❑ 8658	Easy, Come On/Rocket to Star	1975	4.00
❑ 8679	If It's All the Same to You/The Year 2000 Minus 25	1975	4.00
❑ 8707	The Prisoner/It's Never Gonna Be the Same Again	1976	4.00
❑ 21000	Here Comes That Rainbow Again/(B-side unknown)	1981	4.00
7-Inch Extended Plays			
MONUMENT			
❑ SSP-532	To Beat the Devil/Blame It on the Stones//Casey's Last Ride/Sunday Morning Coming Down	1971	12.00
—Stereo jukebox issue; small hole, plays at 33 1/3 rpm			
❑ SSP-532 [PS]	Kristofferson	1971	12.00
❑ Z7-31909	Jesus Was a Capricorn/Out of Mind, Out of Sight/Give It Time to Be Tender// It Sure Was (Love)/Nobody Wins/Enough for You	1973	8.00
—Jukebox issue; small hole, plays at 33 1/3 rpm			
❑ Z7-31909 [PS]	Jesus Was a Capricorn	1973	8.00
Albums			
COLUMBIA			
❑ PZ 30679	The Silver Tongued Devil and I	1976	8.00
—Reissue			
❑ PZ 30817	Me and Bobby McGee	1976	8.00
—Reissue			
❑ PZ 31302	Border Lord	1976	8.00
—Reissue			
❑ PZ 31909	Jesus Was a Capricorn	1976	8.00
—Reissue			
❑ PZ 32914	Spooky Lady's Sideshow	1976	8.00
—Reissue			
❑ PZ 33379	Who's to Bless... And Who's to Blame	1976	8.00
—Reissue			
❑ PZ 34687	Songs of Kristofferson	1977	12.00
❑ JZ 35310	Easter Island	1978	12.00
❑ JZ 36135	Shake Hands with the Devil	1979	12.00
❑ JZ 36885	To the Bone	1980	12.00
❑ FC 40056	Highwayman	1985	10.00
—Waylon Jennings/Willie Nelson/Johnny Cash/Kris Kristofferson			
❑ C 45240	Highwayman 2	1990	15.00
—Waylon Jennings/Willie Nelson/Johnny Cash/Kris Kristofferson			
MERCURY			
❑ 830406-1	Repossessed	1987	10.00
MONUMENT			
❑ SLP-18139	Kristofferson	1970	25.00
—Original label is light green with a yellow ring			
❑ Z 30679	The Silver Tongued Devil and I	1971	12.00
❑ ZQ 30679 [Q]	The Silver Tongued Devil and I	1972	20.00
❑ Z 30817	Me and Bobby McGee	1971	12.00
—Reissue of 18139 with new title			
❑ KZ 31302	Border Lord	1972	12.00
❑ ZQ 31302 [Q]	Border Lord	1972	20.00
❑ KZ 31909	Jesus Was a Capricorn	1972	12.00
❑ ZQ 31909 [Q]	Jesus Was a Capricorn	1973	20.00
❑ PZ 32914	Spooky Lady's Sideshow	1974	12.00
❑ PZQ 32914 [Q]	Spooky Lady's Sideshow	1974	20.00
❑ PZ 33379	Who's to Bless...And Who's to Blame	1975	12.00
❑ PZ 34254	Surreal Thing	1976	12.00
❑ PW 38392	Songs of Kristofferson	1982	8.00
—Reissue of 34687			
PAIR			
❑ PDL2-1078 [(2)]	My Songs	1986	12.00

KRISTOFFERSON, KRIS, AND RITA COOLIDGE Also see each artist's individual listings.

Number	Title (A Side/B Side)	Yr	NM
45s			
A&M			
❑ 1475	A Song I'd Like to Sing/From the Bottle to the Bottom	1973	4.00
❑ 1475 [PS]	A Song I'd Like to Sing/From the Bottle to the Bottom	1973	6.00
❑ 1498	Loving Arms/I'm Down	1974	4.00
❑ 2121	Not Everyone Knows/Blue As I Do	1979	4.00
MONUMENT			
❑ 8630	Rain/What'cha Gonna Do	1974	4.00
❑ 8636	Lover Please/Slow Down	1975	4.00
❑ 8646	We Must Have Been Out of Our Minds/Sweet Susannah	1975	4.00
Albums			
A&M			
❑ SP-4403	Full Moon	1973	12.00
❑ PR-4690	Natural Act	1979	15.00
—Picture disc			
❑ SP-4690	Natural Act	1979	10.00
MONUMENT			
❑ PZ 33278	Breakaway	1974	12.00

KRISTYL

Number	Title (A Side/B Side)	Yr	NM
Albums			
(NO LABEL)			
❑ (no #)	Kristyl	1975	200.00

KUBAN, BOB, AND THE IN-MEN

Number	Title (A Side/B Side)	Yr	NM
45s			
MUSICLAND U.S.A.			
❑ 20001	The Cheater/Try Me Baby	1966	10.00
—With no mention of "Vocal by Walter Scott"			
❑ 20001	The Cheater/Try Me Baby	1966	12.00
—With "Vocal by Walter Scott" on only B-side label			
❑ 20001	The Cheater/Try Me Baby	1966	20.00
—With "Vocal by Walter Scott" on both sides' labels			
❑ 20006	The Teaser/All I Want	1966	10.00
❑ 20007	Drive My Car/The Pretzel	1966	10.00
❑ 20013	Harlem Shuffle/Theme from "Virginia Wolff"	1967	8.00
❑ 20017	Batman Theme/You Better Run, You Better Hide	1967	8.00
NORMAN			
❑ 558	Jerkin' Time/Turn On Your Lovelight	1965	12.00
❑ 567	Little Girl/I Don't Want to Know	1965	12.00
REPRISE			
❑ 0937	Soul Man/Hard to Handle	1970	8.00
Albums			
MUSICLAND U.S.A.			
❑ LP-3500 [M]	Look Out for the Cheater	1966	30.00
❑ SLP-3500 [S]	Look Out for the Cheater	1966	40.00

KUF-LINX, THE

Number	Title (A Side/B Side)	Yr	NM
45s			
CHALLENGE			
❑ 1013	So Tough/What'cha Gonna Do	1957	40.00
❑ 1013	So Tough/What'cha Gonna Do	1958	25.00
❑ 59004	Eyeballin'/Service with a Smile	1958	15.00
❑ 59015	Climb Love Mountain/All That's Good	1958	15.00
❑ 59102	So Tough/What'cha Gonna Do	1961	12.00

KULIS, CHARLIE

Number	Title (A Side/B Side)	Yr	NM
45s			
PLAYBOY			
❑ 6023	Runaway/When I See Her	1975	5.00
❑ 6044	Save a Rose for Me/Somebody Help Me Now	1975	5.00

KUSTOM KINGS, THE BRUCE JOHNSTON appears on the below.

Number	Title (A Side/B Side)	Yr	NM
45s			
SMASH			
❑ 1883	In My '40 Ford/Clutch Rider	1964	50.00
Albums			
SMASH			
❑ MGS-27051 [M]	Kustom City, U.S.A.	1964	120.00
❑ SRS-67051 [S]	Kustom City, U.S.A.	1964	200.00

KWESKIN, JIM

Number	Title (A Side/B Side)	Yr	NM
45s			
REPRISE			
❑ 0624	The Sheik of Araby/Minglewood	1967	8.00
VANGUARD			
❑ 35027	Rag Momma/Don't You Leave Me Here	1964	10.00
Albums			
MOUNTAIN RAILROAD			
❑ MR-52672	Jug Band Blues	198?	10.00
❑ MR-52782	Jim Kweskin Lives Again	198?	10.00
❑ MR-52790	Side by Side	198?	10.00
❑ MR-52793	Swing on a Star	198?	10.00
REPRISE			
❑ R 6266 [M]	Garden of Joy	1967	20.00
❑ RS 6266 [S]	Garden of Joy	1967	15.00
❑ RS 6464	America	1971	15.00
VANGUARD			
❑ VSD 13/14 [(2)]	Greatest Hits	1970	15.00
❑ VSD-2158 [S]	Jim Kweskin and the Jug Band	1963	25.00
❑ VRS-9139 [M]	Jim Kweskin and the Jug Band	1963	20.00
❑ VRS-9163 [M]	Jug Band Music	1965	20.00
❑ VRS-9188 [M]	Relax Your Mind	1966	20.00
❑ VRS-9234 [M]	See Reverse Side for Title	1967	20.00
❑ VRS-9243 [M]	Jump for Joy	1967	20.00
❑ VRS-9270 [M]	The Best of Jim Kweskin and the Jug Band	1968	40.00
❑ VSD-79163 [S]	Jug Band Music	1965	25.00
❑ VSD-79188 [S]	Relax Your Mind	1966	25.00
❑ VSD-79234 [S]	See Reverse Side for Title	1967	25.00
❑ VSD-79243 [S]	Jump for Joy	1967	20.00
❑ VSD-79270 [S]	The Best of Jim Kweskin and the Jug Band	1968	15.00

L

L.A. JAZZ CHOIR, THE

Number	Title (A Side/B Side)	Yr	NM
Albums			
MOBILE FIDELITY			
❑ 1-096	Listen	1982	80.00
—Audiophile vinyl			
PAUSA			
❑ 7184	From All Sides	1986	12.00

L.A. JAZZ ENSEMBLE, THE

Number	Title (A Side/B Side)	Yr	NM
Albums			
PBR			
❑ 8	Urantia	197?	12.00

L.A. JAZZ WORKSHOP, THE

Number	Title (A Side/B Side)	Yr	NM
Albums			
AM-PM			
❑ 16	The Shopwork Shuffle	1986	10.00
SEA BREEZE			
❑ SB-2021	Stan's Donuts	198?	10.00

L7

Number	Title (A Side/B Side)	Yr	NM
45s			
REPRISE			
❑ 17403	Off the Wagon/Guera	1997	3.00
SLASH			
❑ PRO-S-7783 [DJ]	Can I Run/Baggage (Live)	1995	5.00
SUB POP			
❑ 58	Shove/Packin' a Rod	1990	10.00
—Black vinyl pressing of 1,800			
❑ 58	Shove/Packin' a Rod	1990	20.00
—Green vinyl pressing of 1,200			
❑ 58 [PS]	Shove/Packin' a Rod	1990	10.00
—#15 in Sub Pop Singles Club series			
Albums			
EPITAPH			
❑ 86401	L7	1988	50.00
—Original press with Donita Sparks' head cut off			
SLASH			
❑ 45624	Hungry for Stink	1994	12.00
SUB POP			
❑ 79 [EP]	Smell the Magic	1990	12.00
❑ 79 [EP]	Smell the Magic	1990	40.00
—First 1,000 on purple vinyl			

L.T.D.

Number	Title (A Side/B Side)	Yr	NM
45s			
A&M			
❑ 1514	Elegant Love/Success	1974	5.00
❑ 1537	What Goes Around/To the Bone	1974	5.00

Number	Title (A Side/B Side)	Yr	NM
❑ 1665	Don't Lose Your Cool/ Thank You Mother	1975	5.00
❑ 1681	Trying to Find a Way/ I Told You I'd Be Back	1975	5.00
❑ 1731	Rated X/Ain't No Way	1975	5.00
❑ 1847	Love Ballad/Let the Music Keep Playing	1976	5.00
❑ 1847 [PS]	Love Ballad/Let the Music Keep Playing	1976	6.00
❑ 1897	Love to the World/ Get Your It Together	1976	5.00
❑ 1974	(Every Time I Turn Around) Back in Love Again/ Material Things	1977	5.00
❑ 1974 [PS]	(Every Time I Turn Around) Back in Love Again/ Material Things	1977	8.00
❑ 2005	Never Get Enough of Your Love/ Make Someone Smile Today	1978	5.00
❑ 2005 [PS]	Never Get Enough of Your Love/ Make Someone Smile Today	1978	6.00
❑ 2057	Holding On (When Love Is Gone)/Together Forever	1978	5.00
❑ 2095	We Both Deserve Each Other's Love/It's Time to Be Real	1978	5.00
❑ 2142	Dance "N" Sing "N"/Give It All	1979	5.00
❑ 2142 [PS]	Dance "N" Sing "N"/Give It All	1979	6.00
❑ 2176	Share My Love/Sometimes	1979	5.00
❑ 2192	Stranger/Sometimes	1979	5.00
❑ 2250	Where Did We Go Wrong/ Stand Up L.T.D.	1980	5.00
❑ 2283	Shine On/Love Is What You Need	1980	5.00
❑ 2346	Shine On (Spanish Version)/ Where Did We Go Wrong	1981	5.00
❑ 2382	Kickin' Back/Now	1981	5.00
❑ 2395	April Love/Stay on the One	1982	5.00
❑ 2414	Cuttin' It Up/Love Magic	1982	4.00

MONTAGE

Number	Title (A Side/B Side)	Yr	NM
❑ 908	For You/Party with You (All Night)	1983	4.00

Albums

A&M

Number	Title (A Side/B Side)	Yr	NM
❑ SP-3119	L.T.D.	198?	8.00
—Budget-line reissue			
❑ SP-3146	Love to the World	198?	8.00
—Budget-line reissue			
❑ SP-3148	Something to Love	198?	8.00
—Budget-line reissue			
❑ SP-3602	L.T.D.	1974	12.00
❑ SP-3660	Gittin' Down	1975	12.00
❑ SP-4589	Love to the World	1976	10.00
❑ SP-4646	Something to Love	1977	10.00
❑ SP-4705	Togetherness	1978	10.00
❑ SP-4771	Devotion	1979	10.00
❑ SP-4819	Shine On	1980	10.00
❑ SP-4881	Love Magic	1981	10.00

LA LUPE

45s

ROULETTE

Number	Title (A Side/B Side)	Yr	NM
❑ 7043	Down on Me/Touch Me	1969	8.00
❑ 7054	Don't Ever Leave Me/ (B-side unknown)	1969	8.00
❑ 7141	Unchained Melody/ Carlos Dominguez	1973	6.00

Albums

ROULETTE

Number	Title (A Side/B Side)	Yr	NM
❑ SR-42024	The Queen Does Her Thing	1969	30.00

LABEEF, SLEEPY

45s

COLUMBIA

Number	Title (A Side/B Side)	Yr	NM
❑ 43452	Everybody's Got to Have Somebody (To Love)/ You Can't Catch Me	1965	12.00
❑ 43875	I Feel a Lot More Like I Do Now/ I'm Too Broke	1966	12.00
❑ 44068	Sure Beats the Heck Out of Settlin' Down/Schneider	1967	10.00
❑ 44261	Completely Destroyed/ Go Ahead On Baby	1967	10.00
❑ 44455	Every Day/If I'm Right I'm Wrong	1968	10.00

CRESCENT

Number	Title (A Side/B Side)	Yr	NM
❑ 102	Turn Me Loose/ (B-side unknown)	195?	200.00

MERCURY

Number	Title (A Side/B Side)	Yr	NM
❑ 71112	I'm Through/All Alone	1957	100.00
❑ 71179	All the Time/Lonely	1957	100.00

PICTURE

Number	Title (A Side/B Side)	Yr	NM
❑ 1937	Ride On Josephine/ (B-side unknown)	1959	150.00

PLANTATION

Number	Title (A Side/B Side)	Yr	NM
❑ 55	Too Much Monkey Business/ Got You on My Mind	1970	25.00
❑ 66	Asphalt Cowboy/ Got You on My Mind	1971	10.00
❑ 74	Blackland Farmer/ Got You on My Mind	1971	10.00
❑ 74 [DJ]	Blackland Farmer (mono/stereo)	1971	12.00
—Promo only on green vinyl			

STARDAY

Number	Title (A Side/B Side)	Yr	NM
❑ 292	I'm Through/All Alone	1957	150.00

SUN

Number	Title (A Side/B Side)	Yr	NM
❑ 1132	Thunder Road/A Hundred Pounds of Lovin'	1974	4.00
❑ 1133 [DJ]	Ghost Riders in the Sky (same on both sides)	1975	4.00
—Promo only			
❑ 1134	There Ain't Much After Taxes/ A Hundred Pounds of Lovin'	1976	4.00
❑ 1137	Good Rockin' Boogie (Part 1)/ Good rockin' Boogie (Part 2)	1978	4.00
❑ 1145	Flying Saucers Rock and Roll/ Boogie Woogie Country Girl	1979	4.00

WAYSIDE

Number	Title (A Side/B Side)	Yr	NM
❑ 1651	Ride On Josephine/ (B-side unknown)	1959	200.00
—Wayside titles as "Tommy LaBeef"			
❑ 1652	Walkin' Slowly/(B-side unknown)	1959	250.00
❑ 1654	Tore Up/Lonely	1959	300.00

Albums

ROUNDER

Number	Title (A Side/B Side)	Yr	NM
❑ 3052	It Ain't What You Eat...	198?	10.00
❑ 3070	Electricity	198?	10.00
❑ 3072	Nothin' But the Truth	198?	10.00

SUN

Number	Title (A Side/B Side)	Yr	NM
❑ 130	Bull's Night Out	1974	12.00
❑ 138	Western Gold	197?	12.00
❑ 1004	Rockabilly 1977	1977	12.00
❑ 1018	Downtown Rockabilly	1978	12.00

LABELLE

Also see PATTI LaBELLE; PATTI LaBELLE AND THE BLUE BELLES.

45s

EPIC

Number	Title (A Side/B Side)	Yr	NM
❑ 50048	Lady Marmalade/Space Children	1974	6.00
❑ 50097	Night Bird/What Can I Do for You	1975	6.00
❑ 50140	Messin' My Mind/ Take the Night Off	1975	6.00
❑ 50168	Slow Burn/Far As We Felt Like Going	1975	6.00
❑ 8-50262	Get You Somebody New/ Who's Watching the Watcher	1976	8.00
❑ 50315	Isn't It a Shame/Gypsy Moths	1976	6.00

RCA VICTOR

Number	Title (A Side/B Side)	Yr	NM
❑ 74-0965	Open Up Your Heart/ Going Up a Holiday	1973	8.00
❑ APBO-0157	Mr. Sunshine Man/Sunshine	1973	8.00

WARNER BROS.

Number	Title (A Side/B Side)	Yr	NM
❑ 7512	Morning Much Better/ Shades of Difference	1971	8.00
❑ 7579	Moonshadow/If I Can't Have You	1972	8.00
❑ 7624	Touch Me All Over/Ain't It Sad It's All Over	1972	8.00

Albums

EPIC

Number	Title (A Side/B Side)	Yr	NM
❑ KE 33075	Nightbirds	1974	12.00
❑ PE 33075	Nightbirds	197?	8.00
—Reissue with new prefix			
❑ PEQ 33075 [Q]	Nightbirds	1975	20.00
❑ PE 33579	Phoenix	1975	10.00
❑ PEQ 33579 [Q]	Phoenix	1975	15.00
❑ PE 34189	Chameleon	1976	10.00
—Original with no bar code and orange label			
❑ PE 34189	Chameleon	198?	8.00
—Reissue with bar code and dark blue label			

RCA VICTOR

Number	Title (A Side/B Side)	Yr	NM
❑ APL1-0205	Pressure Cookin'	1973	12.00
❑ AYL1-4176	Pressure Cookin'	1982	8.00
—"Best Buy Series" reissue			

WARNER BROS.

Number	Title (A Side/B Side)	Yr	NM
❑ WS 1943	LaBelle	1971	15.00
❑ BS 2618	Moonshadow	1972	15.00

LABELLE, PATTI

Also see LaBELLE; PATTI LaBELLE AND THE BLUE BELLES.

12-Inch Singles

DEF SOUL

Number	Title (A Side/B Side)	Yr	NM
❑ B0002821 [(2)]	New Day (Louis Vega Dance Ritual Club Mix) (Quentin Harris West 30th Vocal Twist) (Kryia vs. Velez Club Mix) (Darryl James Full Vocal) (Louie Vega Dance Ritual Dub)	2004	15.00
❑ DEFR 16040 [DJ]	New Day (Radio) (Instrumental) (A Cappella)	2004	8.00

EPIC

Number	Title (A Side/B Side)	Yr	NM
❑ 28-50573	Eyes in the Back of My Head (8:02)/Save the Last Dance for Me (7:15)	1978	20.00
❑ 28-50664	Music Is My Way of Life (8:28) (Instrumental)	1979	15.00

MCA

Number	Title (A Side/B Side)	Yr	NM
❑ L33-1131 [DJ]	'Twas Love/Reason for the Season	1990	10.00
❑ L33-1263 [DJ]	New Attitude (Extended Version 6:14) (Single Version 3:59) (Club Version 8:06)	1985	12.00
❑ L33-1667 [DJ]	Feels Like Another One (Club Version 7:15) (Percussion 5:30) (Radio Edit 5:28) (Dub Instrumental 5:28) (Dub 5:28)	1991	10.00
❑ L33-2022 [DJ]	Feels Like Another One (7" Version) (LP Version)	1991	8.00
❑ L33-2074 [DJ]	Somebody Loves You Baby (You Know Who It Is) (LP Version) (Single Edit) (Instrumental) (Suite)	1991	8.00
❑ MCA8P-2155 [DJ]	When You've Been Blessed (Feels Like Heaven) (4 versions)	1992	10.00
❑ MCA8P-2357 [DJ]	When You Love Somebody (I'm Saving My Love for You) (3:59) (4:20)/ (same on both sides)	1992	8.00
❑ MCA8P-2433 [DJ]	All Right Now (Extended Album Version 5:51) (Radio Edit 4:01) (Album Version 4:38) Remix 5:15) (Remix Dub 4:58) (Remix Instrumental 5:15)	1992	10.00
❑ MCA8P-2520 [DJ]	All Right Now (7 versions)	1992	10.00
❑ MCA8P-2554 [DJ]	I Don't Like Goodbyes/Over the Rainbow (medley)// If Only You Knew/ Wind Beneath My Wings	1992	8.00
❑ MCA8P-2717 [DJ]	The Right Kinda Lover (Album Version) (Radio Edit) (Instrumental)/ (same on both sides)	1994	10.00
❑ MCA8P-3049 [DJ]	The Right Kinda Lover (Fusion Remix Edit 4:31) (Def Jef Remix 4:36) (Bass Fusion Instrumental 5:10) (Club Remix 7:39) (Tribal Club Remix 6:52)	1994	8.00
❑ MCA8P-3140 [DJ]	All This Love (Radio Edit) (LP Version) (Instrumental)	1994	8.00
❑ MCA8P-3160 [DJ]	All This Love (4 versions)	1994	8.00
❑ MCA8P-3198 [DJ]	I Never Stopped Loving You (4 versions)	1995	7.00
❑ MCA8P-3986 [DJ]	When You Talk About Love (unknown versions)	1997	10.00
❑ MCA8P-3992 [DJ]	When You Talk About Love (DJ Extended) (Midnight Mix) (Instrumental) (A Cappella)	1997	10.00
❑ MCA8P-4089 [DJ]	Someone Like You (Radio Edit) (LP Version) (Instrumental) (A Cappella)	1997	10.00
❑ MCA8P-4091 [DJ]	Shoe Was On the Other Foot (Moran's Miss Patti's Anthem 10:59) (Moran's Underground Vocal 6:06) (TBG's Shoe Stompin' Dub 6:40)	1997	12.00
❑ L33-17339 [DJ]	Just the Facts (same on both sides)	1987	7.00
❑ L33-17571 [DJ]	If You Asked Me To (3:56) (Dub 4:08) (Instrumental Suite 4:14)	1988	12.00
❑ L33-18014 [DJ]	Yo Mister (same on both sides)	1989	8.00
❑ L33-18108 [DJ]	I Can't Complain (Vocal) (Instrumental)	1989	8.00
❑ 23534	New Attitude (Extended Mix 6:14)/Axel F (Extended Mix 7:09)	1985	8.00
—B-side by Harold Faltermeyer			
❑ 23567	Stir It Up (Extended Mix 7:13) (Radio Mix 5:25) (Percapella Mix 5:25)	1985	8.00

Except when noted otherwise, VG = 25% of NM, and VG+ = 50% of NM. (Example: VG = $2.00, VG+ = $4.00 and NM = $8.00.)

Number	Title (A Side/B Side)	Yr	NM
❑ 23607	On My Own (4:30)/ Stir It Up (7:13)	1986	8.00

—A-side with Michael McDonald

Number	Title (A Side/B Side)	Yr	NM
❑ 23649	Something Special (Is Gonna Happen Tonight) (Extended Version) (Radio Edit) (Instrumental) (A Cappella) (Bonus Beats)	1986	8.00
❑ 23651	Oh, People (Extended Remix Version 5:04) (Instrumental 5:26)/Love Attack (4:12)	1986	8.00
❑ 23679	Kiss Away the Pain (4:28) (Instrumental)	1986	7.00
❑ 23773	Just the Facts (Cabbage Patch Version) (Slammin' Radio Version) (Slammin' Flyte Tyme Edit) (Slammin' Dubappella)	1987	8.00
❑ 23984	Yo Mister (Extended Version 6:32) (Radio Edit 5:20) (Instrumental 4:05)	1989	8.00
❑ 54238	Feels Like Another One (Club Version) (Dub)	1991	8.00
❑ 54541	All Right Now (Extended) (Remix) (Dub)	1992	8.00
❑ 54851	The Right Kinda Lover (Fusion Extended Remix) (Def Jam Remix) (Club Remix)	1994	10.00
❑ 54933	All This Love (Hip Hop Mix) (Patti's Buttah Mix)/Our World	1994	10.00
❑ 55113	Turn It Out (4 versions)	1995	10.00
❑ 55358	When You Talk About Love (Main Club Pass) (Instrumental)	1997	8.00
❑ 155740	Too Many Tears, Too Many Times/Time Will/Shoe on the Other Foot (Remix — Moran's Underground Vocals)/Too Many Tears, Too Many Times (Instrumental) (Acapella)/Time Will (Instrumental) (Acapella)	2000	7.00

PHILADELPHIA INT'L.

Number	Title (A Side/B Side)	Yr	NM
❑ 4Z9 04176	If Only You Knew (4:45)/I'll Never, Never Give Up (5:10)	1983	12.00
❑ 4Z9 05296	Shy (Special Remix 6:07) (Dub Mix 5:02)	1985	8.00

45s

ARISTA

Number	Title (A Side/B Side)	Yr	NM
❑ 12929	My Love, Sweet Love/ Sittin' Up in My Room	1996	3.00

—B-side by Brandy

BEVERLY GLEN

Number	Title (A Side/B Side)	Yr	NM
❑ 2012	Love Has Finally Come at Last/ American Dream	1984	4.00

—With Bobby Womack

Number	Title (A Side/B Side)	Yr	NM
❑ 2018	It Takes a Lot of Strength to Say Goodbye/Who's Foolin' Who	1984	4.00

—With Bobby Womack

COLLECTABLES

Number	Title (A Side/B Side)	Yr	NM
❑ 90169	New Attitude/Stir It Up	199?	3.00

—Reissue

Number	Title (A Side/B Side)	Yr	NM
❑ 90170	Feels Like Another One/ Somebody Loves You Baby (You Know Who It Is)	199?	3.00

—First issue of both of these songs on U.S. 45

Number	Title (A Side/B Side)	Yr	NM
❑ 90171	Oh, People/If You Asked Me To	199?	3.00

—Reissue

Number	Title (A Side/B Side)	Yr	NM
❑ 90206	I Don't Like Goodbyes/ Over the Rainbow (medley)// The Right Kinda Lover	199?	3.00

—First appearance of A-side on a 45

ELEKTRA

Number	Title (A Side/B Side)	Yr	NM
❑ 69887	The Best Is Yet to Come/ Bye Bye Love	1982	4.00

—With Grover Washington Jr.

EPIC

Number	Title (A Side/B Side)	Yr	NM
❑ 8-50445	Joy to Have Your Love/ Do I Stand a Chance	1977	6.00
❑ 8-50487	You Are My Friend/ I Think About You	1977	6.00
❑ 8-50510	Dan Swit Me/Since I Don't Have You	1978	8.00
❑ 8-50550	Teach Me Tonight (Me Gusta Tu Baile)/Quiet Time	1978	6.00
❑ 8-50583	Little Girls/You Make It So Hard (To Say No)	1978	6.00
❑ 8-50659	It's Alright with Me/ Music Is My Way of Life	1979	12.00
❑ 8-50718	Music Is My Way of Life/ Eyes in the Back of My Head	1979	7.00
❑ 9-50763	Love and Learn/Love Is Just a Touch Away	1979	8.00
❑ 9-50852	Release (The Tension)/ Come and Dance with Me	1980	6.00
❑ 9-50872	I Don't Go Shopping/Come and Dance with Me	1980	6.00
❑ 9-50910	Don't Make Your Angel Cry/ Ain't That Enough	1980	6.00

MCA

Number	Title (A Side/B Side)	Yr	NM
❑ S45-17357 [DJ]	Just the Facts (same on both sides)	1987	5.00
❑ 52517	New Attitude/Shoot Out	1984	4.00

—B-side by Harold Faltermeyer

Number	Title (A Side/B Side)	Yr	NM
❑ 52517 [PS]	New Attitude/Shoot Out	1984	4.00
❑ 52610	Stir It Up/The Discovery	1985	4.00

—B-side by Harold Faltermeyer

Number	Title (A Side/B Side)	Yr	NM
❑ 52610 [PS]	Stir It Up/The Discovery	1985	4.00
❑ 52770	On My Own/Stir It Up	1986	3.00

—A-side with Michael McDonald

Number	Title (A Side/B Side)	Yr	NM
❑ 52770 [PS]	On My Own/Stir It Up	1986	4.00
❑ 52876	Something Special (Is Gonna Happen Tonight)/ (Instrumental)	1986	4.00
❑ 52877	Oh, People/Love Attack	1986	3.00
❑ 52877 [PS]	Oh, People/Love Attack	1986	4.00
❑ 52945	Kiss Away the Pain/ (Instrumental)	1986	4.00
❑ 52945 [PS]	Kiss Away the Pain/ (Instrumental)	1986	4.00
❑ 53064	The Last Unbroken Heart/ Miami Vice: New York Theme	1987	3.00

—A-side with Bill Champlin; B-side by Harold Faltermeyer

Number	Title (A Side/B Side)	Yr	NM
❑ 53064 [PS]	The Last Unbroken Heart/ Miami Vice: New York Theme	1987	3.00
❑ 53100	Just the Facts/(Instrumental)	1987	3.00
❑ 53100 [PS]	Just the Facts/(Instrumental)	1987	5.00
❑ 53358	If You Asked Me To/ (Instrumental)	1988	4.00
❑ 53728	Yo Mister/I Can Fly	1989	3.00
❑ 53774	I Can't Complain/I Can Fly	1989	4.00
❑ 54376	When You've Been Blessed (Feels Like Heaven)/ (Instrumental)	1992	5.00
❑ 54481	When You Love Somebody (I'm Saving My Love for You)/ Temptation	1992	5.00
❑ 54513	All Right Now/(Remix Dub)	1992	5.00
❑ 54673	The Right Kinda Lover/ (Instrumental)	1993	5.00

PHILADELPHIA INT'L.

Number	Title (A Side/B Side)	Yr	NM
❑ AE7 1816 [DJ]	If Only You Knew (same on both sides?)	1983	8.00
❑ ZS5 02309	Rocking Pneumonia and the Boogie Woogie Flu/ Over the Rainbow	1981	5.00
❑ ZS5 02655	The Spirit's In It/The Family	1981	6.00
❑ ZS4 04248	If Only You Knew/I'll Never, Never Give Up	1983	5.00
❑ ZS4 04399	Love, Need and Want You/ I'm in Love Again	1984	6.00
❑ ZS4 05436	I Can't Forget You/Living Double	1985	5.00
❑ ZS4 05658	Shy/Love Symphony	1985	5.00
❑ ZS4 05755	If You Don't Know Me By Now - Part 1/Part 2	1986	5.00
❑ ZS4 05877	Look to the Rainbow/ What Can I Do for You	1986	6.00

Albums

EPIC

Number	Title (A Side/B Side)	Yr	NM
❑ PE 34847	Patti LaBelle	1977	15.00

—Original with no bar code and orange label

Number	Title (A Side/B Side)	Yr	NM
❑ PE 34847	Patti LaBelle	1986	8.00

—Reissue with bar code and dark blue label

Number	Title (A Side/B Side)	Yr	NM
❑ JE 35335	Tasty	1978	15.00
❑ JE 35772	It's Alright with Me	1979	12.00
❑ JE 36381	Released	1980	12.00
❑ FE 36997	Best of Patti LaBelle	1981	10.00
❑ PE 36997	Best of Patti LaBelle	198?	8.00

—Budget-line reissue

MCA

Number	Title (A Side/B Side)	Yr	NM
❑ 5737	Winner in You	1986	10.00
❑ 6292	Be Yourself	1989	10.00
❑ 10439	Burnin'	1991	12.00

PHILADELPHIA INT'L.

Number	Title (A Side/B Side)	Yr	NM
❑ FZ 37380	The Spirit's In It	1981	12.00
❑ PZ 37380	The Spirit's In It	198?	8.00

—Budget-line reissue

Number	Title (A Side/B Side)	Yr	NM
❑ FZ 38539	I'm in Love Again	1983	12.00
❑ FZ 40020	Patti	1985	12.00

LABELLE, PATTI, AND THE BLUE BELLES

Also see THE BLUE BELLES; LaBELLE.

45s

ATLANTIC

Number	Title (A Side/B Side)	Yr	NM
❑ 2311	All or Nothing/You Forgot How to Love	1965	12.00
❑ 2318	A Groovy Kind of Love Over the Rainbow	1966	10.00
❑ 2333	Ebb Tide/Patti's Prayer	1966	10.00
❑ 2347	I'm Still Waiting/Family Man	1966	10.00
❑ 2373	Take Me for a Little While/ I Don't Want to Go On Without You	1967	10.00
❑ 2390	(There's) Always Something There to Remind Me/ Tender Words	1967	10.00
❑ 2408	Unchained Melody/Dreamer	1967	10.00
❑ 2446	Oh My Love/I Need Your Love	1967	10.00
❑ 2548	He's My Man/Wonderful	1968	10.00
❑ 2610	Dance to the Rhythm of Love/ He's Gone	1969	10.00
❑ 2629	Loving Blues/Pride's No Match for Love	1969	75.00
❑ 2712	Suffer/Trustin' in You	1970	60.00

KING

Number	Title (A Side/B Side)	Yr	NM
❑ 5777	Down the Aisle (Wedding Song)/ C'est La Vie	1963	15.00

LOST-NITE

Number	Title (A Side/B Side)	Yr	NM
❑ 250	You'll Never Walk Alone/ Decatur Street	196?	5.00

—Reissue

Number	Title (A Side/B Side)	Yr	NM
❑ 251	Down the Aisle (Wedding Song)/ C'est La Vie	196?	5.00

—Reissue

Number	Title (A Side/B Side)	Yr	NM
❑ 252	I Sold My Heart to the Junkman/ Itty Bitty Twist	196?	5.00

—Reissue

NEWTIME

Number	Title (A Side/B Side)	Yr	NM
❑ 510	Love Me Just a Little/The Joke's On You	1962	20.00

NEWTOWN

Number	Title (A Side/B Side)	Yr	NM
❑ 5000	I Sold My Heart to the Junkman/ Itty Bitty Twist	1962	20.00

—Credited to "The Blue-Belles" but actually recorded by The Starlets

Number	Title (A Side/B Side)	Yr	NM
❑ 5006	I Found a New Love/Pitter Patter	1962	20.00

—Most of the Newtown sides credit "The Blue-Belles"

Number	Title (A Side/B Side)	Yr	NM
❑ 5007	Tear After Tear/Go On, This Is Goodbye	1962	20.00
❑ 5009	Cool Water/When Johnny Comes Marching Home	1962	20.00
❑ 5019	Academy Award/Decatur Street	1963	20.00
❑ 5777	Down the Aisle (Wedding Song)/ C'est La Vie	1963	15.00

NICETOWN

Number	Title (A Side/B Side)	Yr	NM
❑ 5020	You'll Never Walk Alone/ Where Are You	1963	15.00

PARKWAY

Number	Title (A Side/B Side)	Yr	NM
❑ 896	You'll Never Walk Alone/ Decatur Street	1964	12.00
❑ 896 [PS]	You'll Never Walk Alone/ Decatur Street	1964	80.00
❑ 913	One Phone Call/You Will Fill My Eyes No More	1964	12.00
❑ 935	Danny Boy/I Believe	1964	12.00

PEAK

Number	Title (A Side/B Side)	Yr	NM
❑ 7042	I've Got to Let Him Know/I Sold My Heart to the Junkman	1962	25.00

—Credited to "The Blue-Belles" but actually recorded by The Starlets

Number	Title (A Side/B Side)	Yr	NM
❑ 7042 [PS]	I've Got to Let Him Know/I Sold My Heart to the Junkman	1962	80.00

Albums

ATLANTIC

Number	Title (A Side/B Side)	Yr	NM
❑ 8119 [M]	Over the Rainbow	1966	30.00
❑ SD 8119 [S]	Over the Rainbow	1966	40.00
❑ 8147 [M]	Dreamer	1967	30.00
❑ SD 8147 [S]	Dreamer	1967	40.00

MISTLETOE

Number	Title (A Side/B Side)	Yr	NM
❑ MLP-1204	Merry Christmas from LaBelle	1976	20.00

NEWTOWN

Number	Title (A Side/B Side)	Yr	NM
❑ 631 [M]	Sweethearts of the Apollo	1963	400.00
❑ 632 [M]	Sleigh Bells, Jingle Bells and Blue Bells	1963	300.00

PARKWAY

Number	Title (A Side/B Side)	Yr	NM
❑ P-7043 [M]	The Bluebelles On Stage	1965	120.00

—Without bonus single

Number	Title (A Side/B Side)	Yr	NM
❑ P-7043 [M]	The Bluebelles On Stage	1965	150.00

—With bonus single

TRIP

Number	Title (A Side/B Side)	Yr	NM
❑ 3508	Patti LaBelle and the Bluebelles	197?	10.00
❑ 8000	Patti LaBelle and the Bluebelles' Greatest Hits	1971	10.00
❑ 9525	Early Hits	197?	10.00

UNITED ARTISTS

Number	Title (A Side/B Side)	Yr	NM
❑ UA-LA504-E	The Very Best of Patti LaBelle and the Bluebelles	1975	10.00

LACEWING

45s

MAINSTREAM

Number	Title (A Side/B Side)	Yr	NM
❑ 731	Paradox/(B-side unknown)	1971	12.00

Albums

MAINSTREAM

Number	Title (A Side/B Side)	Yr	NM
❑ S-6132	Lacewing	1971	50.00

Greg Lake, *Greg Lake*, Chrysalis CHR 1357, 1981, **$8.**

Number	Title (A Side/B Side)	Yr	NM
LADD, CHERYL Also see JOSIE AND THE PUSSYCATS.			
45s			
CAPITOL			
❑ 4215	Country Love/He's Lookin' More Everyday Like the Man Who Broke My Heart	1976	5.00
❑ 4599	Think It Over/Here Is a Song	1978	4.00
❑ 4599 [PS]	Think It Over/Here Is a Song	1978	6.00
❑ 4650	Good Good Lovin'/Skinnydippin'	1978	4.00
❑ 4650 [PS]	Good Good Lovin'/Skinnydippin'	1978	6.00
❑ 4698	Missing You/Thunder in the Distance	1979	4.00
❑ B-5115	Can't Say No to You/ You Make It Beautiful	1982	4.00
—With Frankie Valli			
❑ B-5115 [PS]	Can't Say No to You/ You Make It Beautiful	1982	4.00
WARNER BROS.			
❑ 7821	Mama Don't Be Blue/The Family	1974	6.00
❑ 7821 [PS]	Mama Don't Be Blue/The Family	1974	10.00
Albums			
CAPITOL			
❑ SW-11808	Cheryl Ladd	1978	12.00
❑ ST-11927	Dance Forever	1979	12.00
LADDERS, THE			
45s			
HOLIDAY			
❑ 2611	Counting the Stars/ I Want to Know	1957	300.00
—Red label, double lines			
❑ 2611	Counting the Stars/ I Want to Know	196?	80.00
—Red label, single line			
LOST-NITE			
❑ 178	My Love Is Gone/ Hey, Pretty Baby	196?	6.00
—Reissue			
❑ 191	Counting the Stars/ I Want to Know	196?	6.00
—Reissue			
VEST			
❑ 826	My Love Is Gone/ Hey, Pretty Baby	1959	150.00
—No stars around "Vest" logo			
❑ 826	My Love Is Gone/ Hey, Pretty Baby	1960	50.00
—With stars around "Vest" logo			
LADY BUGS, THE May be three different groups, two different groups, or all the same group.			
45s			
CHATTAHOOCHIE			
❑ 637	How Do You Do It/Liverpool	1964	15.00
DEL-FI			
❑ 4233	Sooner or Later/It's the Last Time	1964	20.00
LEGRAND			
❑ 1033	Who Sends the Love Note/ Fraternity U.S.A.	1964	20.00
LADYBIRDS, THE			
45s			
ATCO			
❑ 6329	Memories/Lady Bird	1964	12.00
LAWN			
❑ 231	Handsome Boy/Yes I Know	1964	10.00
LAFLORE, JOHNNY			
45s			
HIT			
❑ 195	Ferry Cross the Mersey/ Berlin Melody	1965	8.00
—B-side by the Music City Orchestra			
LAINE, DENNY Also see THE MOODY BLUES; WINGS.			
45s			
ARISTA			
❑ 0511	Japanese Tears/Guess I'm Only Fooling	1980	4.00
CAPITOL			
❑ 4340	It's So Easy-Listen to Me/I'm Lookin' for Someone to Love	1976	6.00
❑ 4425	Heartbeat/Moondreams	1977	6.00
DERAM			
❑ 7509	Ask the People/Say You Don't Mind	1967	15.00
Albums			
CAPITOL			
❑ ST-11588	Holly Days	1977	15.00
REPRISE			
❑ MS 2190	Ah, Laine!	1972	12.00
TAKOMA			
❑ 7034	Japanese Tears	1983	10.00
LAINE, LINDA, AND THE SINNERS Also see FREDDIE AND THE DREAMERS.			
45s			
TOWER			
❑ 108	Low Grades and High Fever/ After Today	1964	12.00
LAKE, GREG			
45s			
ATLANTIC			
❑ 3305	I Believe in Father Christmas/ Humbug	1975	6.00
❑ 3305 [PS]	I Believe in Father Christmas/ Humbug	1975	10.00
❑ 3405	C'est La Vie/Jeremy Bender	1977	5.00
CHRYSALIS			
❑ 2517	Let Me Love You Once/ (B-side unknown)	1981	4.00
❑ 2571	Retribution Drive/ Let Me Love You Once	1981	4.00
Albums			
CHRYSALIS			
❑ CHR 1357	Greg Lake	1981	8.00
LAKE, KAREN			
45s			
ABC-PARAMOUNT			
❑ 10050	Nine O'Clock/Will I Know	1959	20.00
❑ 10087	Kiss Me Quick and Go/When I'm Not Teen Age Anymore	1960	20.00
BIG TOP			
❑ 3077	Air Mail Special Delivery/I'd Like to Miss My Graduation	1961	30.00
—Produced by Phil Spector			
LALA AND THE LALARETTES			
45s			
ELPECO			
❑ 2922	This Day of Ours/ Getting Ready for Freddy	1963	60.00
LAMARR, GENE			
45s			
SPRY			
❑ 113	Crazy Little House on the Hill/ You Don't Love Me Anymore	1959	150.00
❑ 114	You Can Count on Me/ Just a Little Bit Longer	1959	150.00
❑ 115	Close to Me/Moon Eyes	1959	100.00
LAMAS, FERNANDO			
Albums			
ROULETTE			
❑ R-25041 [M]	With Love, Fernando Lamas	1958	40.00
LAMB			
Albums			
FILLMORE			
❑ F 30003	Sign of Change	1970	20.00
WARNER BROS.			
❑ WS 1920	Cross Between	1971	20.00
❑ WS 1952	Bring Out the Sun	1972	20.00
LAMB, BECKY			
45s			
WARNER BROS.			
❑ 7154	Little Becky's Christmas Wish/ Go to Sleep, Little Lambs	1967	12.00
—B-side by Bill Lamb			

Except when noted otherwise, VG = 25% of NM, and VG+ = 50% of NM. (Example: VG = $2.00, VG+ = $4.00 and NM = $8.00.)

Number	Title (A Side/B Side)	Yr	NM

LAMBERT, RUDY See THE MONDELLOS.

LAMM, ROBERT Of CHICAGO.

45s

COLUMBIA

❑ 10068	Skinny Boy/Temporary Jones	1974	5.00

Albums

COLUMBIA

❑ PC 33095	Skinny Boy	1974	12.00

LAMONT, BILLY

45s

KING			
❑ 5403	Come On Right Now/ Hear Me Now	1960	12.00
OKEH			
❑ 7125	Country Boy/Can't Make It By Myself	1959	25.00
❑ 7131	I'm Gonna Try/Now Darling	1960	25.00
SAVOY			
❑ 1522	I'm So Lonely/I Got a Rock 'n' Roll Gal	1957	15.00
THREE-D			
❑ 850	Country Boy/Can't Make It By Myself	1959	150.00

LAMONT, CHARLES

45s

REVUE			
❑ 11047	Before It's Over/Hog Blues	1969	12.00
❑ 11061	Two Thousand Years Ago/Lefty	1970	15.00

Albums

UNI			
❑ 73076	A Legend in His Own Mind	1970	25.00

—As "Lamont"

LAMP, BUDDY

45s

ABC-PARAMOUNT			
❑ 10398	I'm Comin' Home/Promised Land	1963	150.00
D-TOWN			
❑ 1064	Next Best Thing/Just a Little Bit of Lovin'	1966	100.00
DOUBLE L			
❑ 716	Thank You Love/My Tears	1963	75.00
DUKE			
❑ 438	I'm Coming Home/ Where Have You Been	1968	20.00
❑ 461	Devil's Gonna Get You/ Wall Around Your Heart	1970	20.00
❑ 468	Hen Pecked/If You See Kate	1971	20.00
GONE			
❑ 5104	Good News/What Here Can I Do	1961	15.00
WHEELSVILLE			
❑ 113	You've Got the Lovin' Touch/ I Wanna Go Home	196?	100.00
❑ 120	Confusion/I Wanna Go Home	196?	30.00
❑ 122	Save Your Love/I Wanna Go Home	196?	400.00

LAMP OF CHILDHOOD, THE

45s

DUNHILL			
❑ 4051	Season of the Witch/ You Can't Blame Me	1966	8.00
❑ 4063	First Time Last Time/ 2 O'Clock Morning	1967	8.00
❑ 4063 [PS]	First Time Last Time/ 2 O'Clock Morning	1967	12.00
❑ 4089	No More Running Around/2 O'Clock Morning	1967	8.00

LAMPLIGHTERS, THE

45s

FEDERAL			
❑ 12149	Part of Me/Turn Me Loose	1953	300.00
❑ 12152	Give Me/Be-Bop Wino	1953	150.00
❑ 12166	Smootchie/I Can't Stand It	1954	150.00
❑ 12176	Tell Me You Came/I Used to Cry Mercy, Mercy	1954	150.00
❑ 12182	Salty Dog/Ride, Jockey, Ride	1954	150.00
❑ 12192	Five Minutes Longer/You Hear	1954	150.00
❑ 12197	Yum! Yum!/Goody Good Times	1954	150.00
❑ 12206	I Wanna Know/Believe in Me	1955	150.00
❑ 12212	Roll On/Love, Rock and Thrill	1955	150.00
❑ 12242	Don't Make It So Good/ Hug a Little, Kiss a Little	1955	150.00
❑ 12255	You Were Sent Down from Heaven/Bo-Peep	1956	100.00
❑ 12261	It Ain't Right/Everything's All Right	1956	100.00
KING			
❑ 5890	Be-Bop Wino/Thunderbird	1964	15.00

—B-side by Dossie Terry

LANCASTRIANS, THE

45s

CAPITOL			
❑ 5501	Never Gonna Come On Home/ There'll Be No More Goodbyes	1965	10.00
JERDEN			
❑ 798	The World Keeps Going Round/ Not the Same Anymore	1966	10.00

LANCE, HERB

45s

DELUXE			
❑ 6150	You Can't Be Sure of Anything/ By the Candleglow	1957	50.00
MALA			
❑ 404	Like a Baby/My Good Mind	1959	20.00
❑ 405	Some Love/Until the Real Thing	1959	20.00
❑ 426	Deep in My Heart/Prayer in My Heart	1961	20.00

Albums

CHESS			
❑ LP-1506 [M]	The Comeback	1966	25.00
❑ LPS-1506 [S]	The Comeback	1966	30.00

LANCE, MAJOR

45s

COLUMBIA			
❑ 10488	Come On, Have Yourself a Good Time/Come What May	1977	5.00
CURTOM			
❑ 1953	Stay Away from Me (I Love You Too Much)/Gypsy Woman	1970	6.00
❑ 1956	Must Be Love Coming Down/ Little Young Lover	1970	6.00
DAKAR			
❑ 608	Follow the Leader/Since You've Been Gone	1969	8.00
❑ 612	Shadows of a Memory/ Sweeter As the Days Go By	1969	8.00
KAT FAMILY			
❑ 03024	I Wanna Go Home/(Instrumental)	1982	4.00
❑ 04185	Are You Leaving Me/ I Wanna Go Home	1983	4.00
MERCURY			
❑ 71582	I've Got a Girl/Phyllis	1960	150.00
OKEH			
❑ 7175	The Monkey Time/ Mama Didn't Know	1963	15.00
❑ 7181	Hey Little Girl/Crying in the Rain	1963	12.00
❑ 7187	Um, Um, Um, Um, Um, Um/ Sweet Music	1964	15.00
❑ 7187 [PS]	Um, Um, Um, Um, Um, Um/ Sweet Music	1964	30.00
❑ 7191	The Matador/Gonna Get Married	1964	10.00
❑ 7197	It Ain't No Use/Girls	1964	10.00
❑ 7200	Think Nothing About It/ It's Alright	1964	50.00
❑ 7203	Rhythm/Please Don't Say No More	1964	10.00
❑ 7203 [PS]	Rhythm/Please Don't Say No More	1964	15.00
❑ 7209	Sometimes I Wonder/ I'm So Lost	1965	10.00
❑ 7216	Come See/You Belong to Me My Love	1965	10.00
❑ 7216 [PS]	Come See/You Belong to Me My Love	1965	15.00
❑ 7223	Ain't It a Shame/Gotta Get Away	1965	10.00
❑ 7226	Too Hot to Hold/Dark and Lovely	1965	75.00
❑ 7233	Everybody Loves a Good Time/ I Just Can't Help It	1965	15.00
❑ 7250	Little Young Lover/Investigate	1966	15.00
❑ 7250 [PS]	Little Young Lover/Investigate	1966	50.00
❑ 7255	It's the Beat/You'll Want Me Back	1966	10.00
❑ 7266	Ain't No Soul (In These Shoes)/I	1966	15.00
❑ 7284	You Don't Want Me No More/ Wait Till I Get You in Your Arms	1967	400.00
❑ 7298	Without a Doubt/Forever	1967	10.00
OSIRIS			
❑ 001	You're Everything I Need/ (Instrumental)	1975	40.00
PLAYBOY			
❑ 6017	Um, Um, Um, Um, Um, Um/ Last of the Red Hot Lovers	1974	20.00
❑ 6020	Sweeter/Wild and Free	1975	20.00
SOUL			
❑ 35123	I Never Thought I'd Be Losing You/Chicago Disco	1977	5.00
VOLT			
❑ 4079	I Wanna Make Up/That's the Story of My Life	1972	30.00
❑ 4085	Ain't No Sweat/Since I Lost "My Baby's Love	1972	20.00

Albums

KAT FAMILY			
❑ FZ 38898	The Major's Back	1983	12.00
OKEH			
❑ OKM-12105 [M]	The Monkey Time	1963	40.00
❑ OKM-12106 [M]	Um, Um, Um, Um, Um, Um	1964	40.00
❑ OKM-12110 [M]	Major's Greatest Hits	1965	30.00
❑ OKS-14105 [S]	The Monkey Time	1963	50.00
❑ OKS-14106 [S]	Um, Um, Um, Um, Um, Um	1964	50.00
❑ OKS-14110 [S]	Major's Greatest Hits	1965	40.00
SOUL			
❑ S7-751	Now Arriving	1978	12.00

LANCELOT LINK AND THE EVOLUTION REVOLUTION

45s

ABC			
❑ 11278	Sha La Love You/Blind Date	1970	10.00
❑ 11285	Daydreams/Magic Feelings	1970	10.00

Albums

ABC			
❑ S-715	Lancelot Link and the Evolution Revolution	1970	40.00

LANDERS, CONNIE

45s

HIT

❑ 23	Heart in Hand/Things	1962	8.00
—B-side by Harvey Frolic			
❑ 26	Vacation/Rinky Dink	1962	8.00
—B-side by the Boots Purcell Combo			
❑ 34	He Thinks I Still Care/ All Alone Am I	1962	8.00
—B-side by Katy Richards			
❑ 40	Bobby's Girl/Ride!	1962	8.00
—B-side by Peggy Gaines			
❑ 43	My Coloring Book/ Go Away Little Girl	1962	8.00
—B-side by Fred York			
❑ 46	I'm Gonna Be Warm This Winter/ Half Heaven Half Heartache	1962	8.00
—B-side by George Killebrew			
❑ 48	Shake Me I Rattle/My Dad	1962	8.00
—B-side by Woody Martin			
❑ 57	Follow the Boys/He's So Fine	1963	8.00
—B-side by the Dacrons			
❑ 68	It's My Party/Another Saturday Night	1963	8.00
—B-side by Leroy Jones			

LANDIS, JERRY See PAUL SIMON.

LANDS, HOAGY

45s

ABC-PARAMOUNT			
❑ 10171	(I'm Gonna) Cry Some Tears/ Lighted Windows	1960	25.00
❑ 10392	Tender Years/I'm Yours	1963	15.00
ATLANTIC			
❑ 2217	Baby Come On Home/ Baby Let Me Hold Your Hand	1964	15.00
JUDI			
❑ 054	(I'm Gonna) Cry Some Tears/ Lighted Windows	1960	80.00
LAURIE			
❑ 3349	Theme from The Other Side/ Friends and Lovers Don't Go Together	1966	20.00
❑ 3372	Yesterday/Forever	1967	20.00
❑ 3381	The Next in Line/Please Don't Talk About Me When I'm Gone	1967	50.00
—Backing group: THE CHIFFONS.			
MGM			
❑ K-13041	My Tears Are Dry/It's Gonna Be Morning	1961	20.00
❑ K-13062	Goodnight Irene/It Ain't As Easy As That	1962	20.00

LANDS, LIZ

45s

GORDY			
❑ 7023	We Shall Overcome/ I Have a Dream	1963	25.00
—B-side by Rev. Martin Luther King			
❑ 7026	May What He Lived For Live/ He's Got the Whole World in His Hands	1963	30.00
❑ 7030	Midnight Journey/Keep Me	1964	150.00
—The Temptations sing backup			

L

Number	Title (A Side/B Side)	Yr	NM
ONE-DERFUL			
❑ 4847	One Man's Poison/ Don't Shut Me Out	1967	40.00
T&L			
❑ 201	Silent Night (Part 1)/ Silent Night (Part 2)	19??	15.00

LANDSLIDE

Albums

Number	Title (A Side/B Side)	Yr	NM
CAPITOL			
❑ ST-11006	Two-Sided Fantasy	1972	40.00

LANE, BILLY

45s

Number	Title (A Side/B Side)	Yr	NM
TABA			
❑ 201	Beginner in Love/ Space Ship Blues	196?	160.00

LANE, MICKEY

45s

Number	Title (A Side/B Side)	Yr	NM
BRUNSWICK			
❑ 55098	Daddy's Little Baby/ Toasted Love	1958	20.00
LAURIE			
❑ 3071	Dum Dee Dee Dum/Night Cap	1960	25.00

LANE, MICKEY LEE

45s

Number	Title (A Side/B Side)	Yr	NM
MALA			
❑ 12032	Tutti Frutti/With Your Love	1968	8.00
SWAN			
❑ 4183	Shaggy Dog/Oo-Oo	1964	12.00
❑ 4199	The Zoo/(They're All in the) Senior Class	1965	10.00
❑ 4210	Little Girl (I Was Wrong)/ When You're in Love	1965	10.00
❑ 4222	Hey Sah-Lo-Ney/Of Yesterday	1965	10.00
❑ 4252	The Only Thing to Do/ She Don't Want To	1966	10.00

LANE, ROCKI, AND THE GROSS GROUP

45s

Number	Title (A Side/B Side)	Yr	NM
EPIC			
❑ 10556	Happy Hairy Hippy Harry Claus/Santa Soul	1969	25.00

LANEGAN, MARK Also see SCREAMING TREES.

Albums

Number	Title (A Side/B Side)	Yr	NM
SUB POP			
❑ SP 61	The Winding Sheet	1990	10.00
—Black vinyl. Among the backing musicians are Kurt Cobain and Krist Novoselic of NIRVANA.			
❑ SP 61	The Winding Sheet	1990	25.00
—First 1,000 on red vinyl			
❑ SP 132	Whisky for the Holy Ghost	1994	20.00
❑ SP 419	Scraps at Midnight	1998	20.00

LANG, K.D.

12-Inch Singles

Number	Title (A Side/B Side)	Yr	NM
SIRE			
❑ PRO-A-2697 [DJ]	Turn Me Round (same on both sides)	1987	15.00
❑ PRO-A-6052 [DJ]	Miss Chatelaine (St. Tropez Mix) (St. Tropez Edit) (Paris 92 Mix) (Single Mix)	1992	12.00
❑ PRO-A-6079 [DJ]	Miss Chatelaine (St. Tropez Mix) (St. Tropez Edit) (Paris 92 Mix) (Single Mix)	1992	20.00
❑ PRO-A-6994 [DJ]	Lifted by Love (Elevate Your Love Mix 6:20) (Radio Remix Edit 3:14) (Vocal Tribal Dub 5:32) (Lifted by Dub 9:04)	1994	15.00
❑ 41197	Just Keep Me Moving (Movin' Mix 6:41) (Movin' Dub 6:40) (Radio Remix 4:10) (Wild Planet Mix 6:16) (Wild Planet Instrumental 6:19)/In Perfect Dreams (Album Version)	1993	10.00
—			
❑ 41379	Lifted by Love (Elevate Your Love Mix 6:20) (Vocal Tribal Dub 5:22) (Lifted by Dub 9:04) (Radio Remix Edit 3:14)/No More Tears (Enough Is Enough) (Classic Club Mix 6:04) (Tribalism Mix 6:11) (Boriqua Beats 2:46)	1994	10.00
—			
WARNER BROS.			
❑ PRO-A-7932 [DJ]	If I Were You (Main Mix) (Junior's X-Beat Mix) (Junior's X-Beat Miss Queen Dub) (Main Mix Dub)	1995	15.00
—Orange vinyl			
❑ PRO-A-8089 [DJ]	Sexuality (D.J. Krush Full Mix 3:30) (D.J. Crush Instrumental 3:29) (Angel Moraes A Cappella 2:21) (Angel Moraes Main Mix 7:14) (Angel Moraes Dub 10:51)	1996	12.00
❑ PRO-A-8147 [DJ]	Sexuality (Teri Bristol Remix Edit) (Teri Britsol Dub Mix) (Perc-A-Pella Mix) (Teri Bristol Vocal House Mix) (Tony Maserati Final Radio Mix) (Main Mix)	1996	12.00
❑ PRO-A-9044 [DJ]	Theme from the Valley of the Dolls (Junior's Arena Anthem 13:20) (Junior Vasquez 7' Mix 3:37) (Junior's Arena Dub 8:17) (Junior's Tribal Beats 5:32)	1997	12.00
❑ 43624	If I Were You (Main Mix) (Junior's X-Beat Mix) (Junior's X-Beat Miss Queen Dub) (Main Mix Dub)	1995	8.00
❑ 43952	Theme from the Valley of the Dolls (Junior's Arena Anthem 13:15) (Junior Vasquez 7' Mix 3:38) (Junior's Arena Dub [Without Slow Part] 8:20) (Junior's Tribal Beats 5:35) (Album Version 3:02)	1997	12.00
—			
❑ 44895	Summerfling (Victor Calderone Extended Vocal Remix) (Victor Calderone Dub Version) (Wamdue's Summer Bliss Extended Mix) (Wamdue's Makin' Me High Dub)	2000	6.00
❑ PRO-A-100219 [DJ]	Summerfling (Victor Calderone Extended Vocal Remix 9:00) (Victor Calderone Club Edit 6:30) (Victor Calderone Dub Version 6:00) (Victor Calderone Instrumental 6:30)	2000	10.00
❑ PRO-A-100272 [(2)DJ]	Summerfling (Wamdue's Summer Bliss Extended Mix 6:25) (Wamdue's Summer Bliss Single Edit 4:27) (Ananda's Sweet Bird of Summer Extended Mix 6:25) (Ananda's Sweet Bird of Summer Single Edit 4:27) (Wamdue's Makin' Me High Dub 5:25) (Wamdue's Summer Bliss Acapella 5:40) (Wamdue's Summer Bliss Instrumental 6:25) (Ananda's Sweet Dub of Summer 7:13) (Ananda's Sweet Bird of Summer Instrumental 8:40)	2000	15.00
—			

45s

Number	Title (A Side/B Side)	Yr	NM
SIRE			
❑ 7-18289	Just Keep Me Moving/ In Perfect Dreams	1994	5.00
❑ 7-18608	Miss Chatelaine/Outside Myself	1993	4.00
❑ 7-18942	Constant Craving/Season of Hollow Soul	1992	5.00
❑ 7-19793	Seven Lonely Days/ Ridin' the Rails	1990	5.00
❑ 7-22734	Three Days/Trail of Broken Hearts	1989	6.00
❑ 7-22734 [PS]	Three Days/Trail of Broken Hearts	1989	10.00
❑ 7-22932	Full Moon Full of Love/ Wallflower Waltz	1989	5.00
❑ 7-22932 [PS]	Full Moon Full of Love/ Wallflower Waltz	1989	8.00
❑ 7-27813	Lock, Stock and Teardrops/Don't Let the Stars Get In Your Eyes	1988	8.00
❑ 7-27813 [PS]	Lock, Stock and Teardrops/Don't Let the Stars Get In Your Eyes	1988	8.00
❑ 7-27919	I'm Down to My Last Cigarette/ Western Stars	1988	4.00
❑ 7-27919 [PS]	I'm Down to My Last Cigarette/ Western Stars	1988	5.00
❑ 7-28338	Turn Me Round/Diet of Strange Places	1987	6.00
❑ 7-28338 [PS]	Turn Me Round/Diet of Strange Places	1987	25.00
❑ 7-28465	Rose Garden/High Time for a Detour	1987	8.00
WARNER BROS.			
❑ 7-17747	If I Were You/Get Some	1995	5.00

Albums

Number	Title (A Side/B Side)	Yr	NM
BUMSTEAD			
❑ BUM-86	A Truly Western Experience	1984	25.00
—Canadian import; reissue of Bumstead 842			
❑ BUM-842	A Truly Western Experience	1984	35.00
—Canadian import; first issue			
SIRE			
❑ PRO-A-3120 [DJ]	The Making of Shadowland	1988	20.00
—Interview album			
❑ 25441	Angel with a Lariat	1987	10.00
❑ 25724	Shadowland	1988	10.00
❑ 25877	Absolute Torch and Twang	1989	12.00
❑ R 134567	Shadowland	1988	12.00
—BMG Direct Marketing edition			
❑ R 160100	Angel with a Lariat	1987	12.00
—BMG Direct Marketing edition			
WARNER BROS.			
❑ 46034	All You Can Eat	1995	20.00

LANI & BONI See DELANEY AND BONNIE.

LANIN, LESTER

45s

Number	Title (A Side/B Side)	Yr	NM
AUDIO FIDELITY			
❑ 134	All You Need Is Love/ The Windows of the World	1968	5.00
❑ 135	Mame/Cabaret	1968	5.00
❑ 148	Up-Up and Away/The Windows of the World	1968	5.00
EPIC			
❑ 9279	Lester Lanin Cha-Cha-Cha (And Medley)/Toreador Song	1958	10.00
❑ 9296	Over the Rainbow Cha-Cha-Cha/I Want My Mama	1958	10.00
❑ 9349	Winter Wonderland/Dance of the Sugar-Plum Fairies	1959	12.00
❑ 9350	Sleigh Ride/Christmas Carol Medley	1959	12.00
❑ 9396	Glow-Worm Cha Cha/Yellow Rose of Texas Meringue	1960	8.00
❑ 9426	Blue Tango Rock/This Could Be the Start of Something Big	1960	8.00
❑ 9444	The Bells/Bow and Arrow	1961	8.00
❑ 9482	Organ Twist/Sweet Georgia Brown	1961	8.00
❑ 9501	Russian Roulette/ Twelfth Street Rag	1962	8.00
❑ 9514	Give Me a Song/You Can't Be True, Dear	1962	8.00
❑ 9571	Ballad of the Red River Valley/ Tumbling Tumbleweeds	1963	8.00
❑ 9618	Theme from "The Seven Capital Sins"/Hora (Happiness)	1963	8.00
❑ 9624	Tamoure Shake/Theme from "The Seven Capital Sins"	1963	8.00
❑ JZSP 123255/6 [DJ]	Winter Wonderland/Sleigh Ride	1967	8.00
❑ JZSP 123257/8 [DJ]	Dance of the Sugar-Plum Fairies/Ring In the New	1967	8.00
❑ JZSP 123259/60 [DJ]	Christmas Medley/Jingle Bells	1967	8.00
METROMEDIA			
❑ 118	Love Theme from Romeo and Juliet/Aquarius	1969	4.00
❑ 135	Ob-La-Di, Ob-La-Da/Dizzy	1969	4.00
PHILIPS			
❑ 40217	Down by the Riverside/ West Indies Ska	1964	6.00
❑ 40344	Theme from "The Yearling"/ Dancing Tambourines	1965	6.00

7-Inch Extended Plays

Number	Title (A Side/B Side)	Yr	NM
EPIC			
❑ EG 7184	*September Song/Marianne/ Ballin' the Jack/Waltz from 'Eugen Onegin"/Anything Goes/Love for Sale/Sunny/ Greensleeves/At the Darktown Strutters' Ball	195?	10.00
❑ EG 7184 [PS]	Dance to the Music of Lester Lanin, Vol. 1	195?	10.00
❑ EG 7203	*Laura/Deep Purple/Tin Roof Blues/After You've Gone/Do I Love You Because You're Beautiful/Hawaiian War Chant/It's Delovely/You're		

Except when noted otherwise, VG = 25% of NM, and VG+ = 50% of NM. (Example: VG = $2.00, VG+ = $4.00 and NM = $8.00.)

Number	Title (A Side/B Side)	Yr	NM
	Sensational/Everything I've Got/Love Walked In/ Charleston/Alexander's Ragtime Band	195?	10.00
❑ EG 7203 [PS]	Lester Lanin Goes to College	195?	10.00

Albums

AUDIO FIDELITY

Number	Title (A Side/B Side)	Yr	NM
❑ AFLP-2180 [M]	Thoroughly Modern	1968	15.00
❑ AFSD-6180 [S]	Thoroughly Modern	1968	12.00

EPIC

Number	Title (A Side/B Side)	Yr	NM
❑ BSN 146 [(2)S]	The Dance Album	1964	20.00
❑ BN 501 [S]	Lester Lanin Goes to College	1959	20.00
❑ BN 505 [S]	Lester Lanin at the Tiffany Ball	1959	20.00
❑ BN 516 [S]	Cocktail Dancing	1959	20.00
❑ BN 517 [S]	Have Band, Will Travel	1959	20.00
❑ BN 547 [S]	Christmas Dance Party (Vol. 9)	1959	20.00
❑ BN 556 [S]	Dance to the Lester Lanin Beat	1960	20.00
❑ BN 570 [S]	High Society	1961	15.00
❑ BN 620 [S]	Twistin' in High Society!	1961	15.00
❑ BN 628 [R]	Lester Lanin and His Orchestra	1962	12.00
❑ BN 633 [R]	Dance to the Music of Lester Lanin	1962	12.00
❑ LN 3242 [M]	Lester Lanin and His Orchestra	1956	15.00
❑ LN 3340 [M]	Dance to the Music of Lester Lanin	1957	15.00
❑ LN 3410 [M]	Lester Lanin at the Tiffany Ball	1957	15.00
❑ LN 3474 [M]	Lester Lanin Goes to College	1958	15.00
❑ LN 3525 [M]	Have Band, Will Travel	1958	15.00
❑ LN 3531 [M]	Cocktail Dancing	1959	15.00
❑ LN 3617 [M]	Christmas Dance Party (Vol. 9)	1959	15.00
❑ LN 3656 [M]	Dance to the Lester Lanin Beat	1960	15.00
❑ LN 3699 [M]	High Society	1961	12.00
❑ LN 3825 [M]	Twistin' in High Society!	1961	12.00
❑ SN 6046 [(2)M]	The Dance Album	1964	15.00
❑ LN 24016 [M]	Dancing Theatre Party	1962	12.00
❑ LN 24105 [M]	Richard Rogers Hits	1964	12.00
❑ LN 24317 [M]	Cole Porter's Greatest Hits	1967	12.00
❑ BN 26016 [S]	Dancing Theatre Party	1962	15.00
❑ BN 26105 [S]	Richard Rogers Hits	1964	15.00
❑ BN 26317 [S]	Cole Porter's Greatest Hits	1967	12.00

HARMONY

Number	Title (A Side/B Side)	Yr	NM
❑ HS 11262	Everybody Dance	1968	10.00

HINDSIGHT

Number	Title (A Side/B Side)	Yr	NM
❑ HSR-210	Dance Instrumentals: 1960-1962	198?	8.00

METROMEDIA

Number	Title (A Side/B Side)	Yr	NM
❑ MD-1006	Narrowing the Generation Gap	1969	12.00

PHILIPS

Number	Title (A Side/B Side)	Yr	NM
❑ PHM 200132 [M]	Lester Lanin Plays for Dancing	1964	10.00
❑ PHM 200145 [M]	Dancing at the Discotheque	1964	10.00
❑ PHM 200165 [M]	I Had a Ball	1965	10.00
❑ PHM 200181 [M]	Hits for Dancing	1965	10.00
❑ PHM 200192 [M]	Lester Lanin at the Country Club	1966	10.00
❑ PHM 200211 [M]	Forty Beatles Hits	1966	12.00
❑ PHS 600132 [S]	Lester Lanin Plays for Dancing	1964	12.00
❑ PHS 600145 [S]	Dancing at the Discotheque	1964	12.00
❑ PHS 600165 [S]	I Had a Ball	1965	12.00
❑ PHS 600181 [S]	Hits for Dancing	1965	12.00
❑ PHS 600192 [S]	Lester Lanin at the Country Club	1966	12.00
❑ PHS 600211 [S]	Forty Beatles Hits	1966	15.00

LAPELS, THE

45s

DOT

Number	Title (A Side/B Side)	Yr	NM
❑ 16129	Sneakin' Around/Sneakin' Blues	1960	12.00

MELKER

Number	Title (A Side/B Side)	Yr	NM
❑ 103	Sneakin' Around/Sneakin' Blues	1960	40.00

LARADOS, THE Members of this group were later in THE REFLECTIONS.

45s

FOX

Number	Title (A Side/B Side)	Yr	NM
❑ 962/3	Now the Parting Begins/ Bad Guitar Man	1958	200.00

MADOG

Number	Title (A Side/B Side)	Yr	NM
❑ 801	Will You Love Me Tomorrow/ You Didn't Care	1980	15.00

LARKS, THE (1) Also see DON JULIAN AND THE MEADOWLARKS.

45s

MONEY

Number	Title (A Side/B Side)	Yr	NM
❑ 106	The Jerk/Forget Me	1964	20.00
❑ 109	Mickey's East Coast Jerk/ Soul Jerk	1965	12.00
❑ 110	The Slauson Shuffle/Soul Jerk	1965	12.00
❑ 112	The Roman/Heavenly Father	1965	12.00

Nicolette Larson, *Radioland*, Warner Bros. BSK 3502, 1980, **$10.**

Number	Title (A Side/B Side)	Yr	NM
❑ 115	Can You Do the Duck/ Sad Sad Boy	1965	12.00
❑ 119	Lost My Love Yesterday/ The Answer Came Too Late	1966	12.00
❑ 122	Philly Dog/Heaven Only Knows	1966	12.00
❑ 127	The Skate/Come Back Baby	1967	12.00
❑ 601	I Love You/I Want You Back	1973	6.00
❑ 604	My Favorite Beer Joint/ (Instrumental)	1973	6.00
❑ 607	Shorty the Pimp (Part 1)/ Shorty the Pimp (Part 2)	1974	6.00

—Money 604 and 607 as "Don Julian and the Larks"

Albums

COLLECTABLES

Number	Title (A Side/B Side)	Yr	NM
❑ COL-5176	Golden Classics: The Jerk	198?	10.00

MONEY

Number	Title (A Side/B Side)	Yr	NM
❑ LP-1102 [M]	The Jerk	1965	40.00
❑ ST-1102 [S]	The Jerk	1965	50.00
❑ LP-1107 [M]	Soul Kaleidoscope	1966	40.00
❑ ST-1107 [S]	Soul Kaleidoscope	1966	50.00
❑ LP-1110 [M]	Superslick	1967	40.00
❑ ST-1110 [S]	Superslick	1967	50.00

LARKS, THE (2)

45s

SHERYL

Number	Title (A Side/B Side)	Yr	NM
❑ 334	It's Unbelievable/I Can't Believe It	1961	30.00
❑ 338	There Is a Girl/Let's Drink a Toast	1961	25.00

LARKS, THE (3)

45s

APOLLO

Number	Title (A Side/B Side)	Yr	NM
❑ 429	Little Side Car/Hey Little Girl	1951	4000.
❑ 430	Ooh, It Feels So Good/ I Don't Believe in Tomorrow	1951	4000.
❑ 435	My Lost Love/How Long Must I Wait for You	1952	1000.
❑ 437	Darlin'/Lucy Brown	1952	1000.
❑ 475	No Mama No/Honey from the Bee	1955	400.00
❑ 1180	Hopefully Yours/When I Leave These Prison Walls	1951	4000.
❑ 1184	My Reverie/Let's Say a Prayer	1951	2000.
—Black vinyl			
❑ 1184	My Reverie/Let's Say a Prayer	1951	8000.
—Red vinyl. VG 4000; VG+ 6000			
❑ 1189	Shadrack/Honey in the Rock	1952	2000.
❑ 1190	Stolen Love/In My Lonely Room	1952	2500.
—Black vinyl			
❑ 1190	Stolen Love/In My Lonely Room	1952	5000.
—Red vinyl. VG 2500; VG+ 3750			
❑ 1194	I Live True to You/Hold Me	1952	1000.

LLOYDS

Number	Title (A Side/B Side)	Yr	NM
❑ 108	Margie/Rockin' in the Rockin' Room	1954	800.00
❑ 110	Tippin' In/If It's a Crime	1954	800.00
❑ 112	No Other Girl/The World Is Waiting for the Sunrise	1954	800.00
❑ 114	Forget It/I Live True to You	1954	600.00

LARKS, THE (U) It's doubtful that any of these are groups (1) or (3). Some could be by group (2).

45s

CROSS FIRE

Number	Title (A Side/B Side)	Yr	NM
❑ 74-49/50	Fabulous Cars and Diamond Rings/Life Is Sweeter Now	1961	20.00

GUYDEN

Number	Title (A Side/B Side)	Yr	NM
❑ 2098	I Want Her to Love Me/ (Instrumental)	1963	12.00
❑ 2103	Fabulous Cars and Diamond Rings/Life Is Sweeter Now	1964	12.00

JETT

Number	Title (A Side/B Side)	Yr	NM
❑ 3001	Love You So/Love Me True	1965	60.00

NASCO

Number	Title (A Side/B Side)	Yr	NM
❑ 028	I Love You/I Want You Back	1972	8.00

STACY

Number	Title (A Side/B Side)	Yr	NM
❑ 969	Food Sticks/Scavenger	1963	12.00

VIOLET

Number	Title (A Side/B Side)	Yr	NM
❑ 1051	I Want Her to Love Me/ (Instrumental)	1962	20.00

LARKTONES, THE

45s

ABC-PARAMOUNT

Number	Title (A Side/B Side)	Yr	NM
❑ 9909	The Letter/Rockin' Swingin' Man	1958	30.00

RIKI

Number	Title (A Side/B Side)	Yr	NM
❑ 140	Why Are You Tearing Us Apart/ Nosy Neighbor	1960	60.00

LARRY AND THE CROSSFIRES

45s

SEARCY

Number	Title (A Side/B Side)	Yr	NM
❑ 711	Torquay '65/Wee Wee Hours	1965	50.00

LARRY AND THE LEGENDS

45s

ATLANTIC

Number	Title (A Side/B Side)	Yr	NM
❑ 2220	Don't Pick On My Baby/ The Creep	1964	25.00

—With the Four Seasons

LARSON, NICOLETTE

45s

MCA

Number	Title (A Side/B Side)	Yr	NM
❑ 52528	Only Love Will Make It Right/ Blow On Chilly Wind	1985	4.00
❑ 52571	When You Get a Little Lonely/ I Just Keep Falling in Love	1985	4.00
❑ 52653	Building Bridges/You Were the One	1985	4.00
❑ 52797	Let Me Be the First/If I Didn't Love You	1986	4.00
❑ 52839	That's How You Know When Love's Right/As an Eagle Stirreth Her Nest	1986	4.00
❑ 52937	That's More About Love (Than I Wanted to Know)/ Captured by Love	1986	4.00

WARNER BROS.

Number	Title (A Side/B Side)	Yr	NM
❑ 8664	Lotta Love/Angels Rejoiced	1978	5.00
❑ 8795	Rhumba Girl/Last in Love	1979	5.00
❑ 8851	Mexican Divorce/Give a Little	1979	5.00
❑ 29948	I Only Want to Be with You/Now We Can Go Home	1982	4.00
❑ 49130	Let Me Go, Love/Trouble	1979	4.00
❑ 49130 [PS]	Let Me Go, Love/Trouble	1979	6.00
❑ 49520	Back in My Arms/Just in the Nick of Time	1980	4.00
❑ 49666	Ooo-Eee/Straight from the Heart	1981	4.00
❑ 49710	When You Come Around/How Can We Go On	1981	4.00
❑ 49763	Radioland/How Can We Go On	1981	4.00
❑ 49820	Fool Me Again/Arthur's Theme (Instrumental)	1981	4.00

Albums

MCA

Number	Title (A Side/B Side)	Yr	NM
❑ 5556	... Say When	1985	8.00
❑ 5719	Rose of My Heart	1986	8.00

WARNER BROS.

Number	Title (A Side/B Side)	Yr	NM
❑ BSK 3243	Nicolette	1978	10.00
❑ HS 3370	In the Nick of Time	1979	10.00
❑ BSK 3502	Radioland	1980	10.00
❑ BSK 3678	All Dressed Up & No Place to Go	1982	10.00

LASALLE, DENISE

45s

ABC

Number	Title (A Side/B Side)	Yr	NM
❑ 12225	Hellfire Loving/I Get What I Want	1976	20.00
❑ 12238	Freedom to Express Yourself/ Second Breath	1977	4.00
❑ 12312	Love Me Right/Fool Me Good	1977	4.00
❑ 12353	One Life to Live/Before You Take It to the Streets	1978	4.00
❑ 12419	Workin' Overtime/No Matter What They Say	1978	30.00
❑ 12443	P.A.R.T.Y. (Where It Is)/ Under the Influence	1979	4.00

CHESS

Number	Title (A Side/B Side)	Yr	NM
❑ 2005	A Love Reputation/ One Little Thing	1967	100.00
❑ 2044	Private Property/I've Been Waiting	1968	10.00
❑ 2058	Count Down (And Fly Me to the Moon)/A Promise Is a Promise	1968	20.00

MALACO

Number	Title (A Side/B Side)	Yr	NM
❑ 2089	Lady in the Street/I Was Not the Best Woman	198?	4.00
❑ 2092	Lay Me Down/I Was Telling Him About You	198?	4.00
❑ 2095	Down Home Blues/Down Home Blues (X-Rated)	198?	4.00
❑ 2098	Right Place, Right Time/ He's Not Available	1984	4.00

—With Latimore

Number	Title (A Side/B Side)	Yr	NM
❑ 2105	Treat Your Man Like a Baby/ Come to Bed	1985	4.00
❑ 2112	My Tu-Tu/Give Me Yo' Strongest Whiskey	1985	4.00
❑ 2124	Santa Claus Got the Blues/ Love Is a Five Letter Word	1985	5.00
❑ 2131	What's Going On in My House/ He's That Way Sometime	1986	4.00
❑ 2138	Hold What You Got/ Footsteps of a Fool	1986	4.00
❑ 2152	Bring It On Home to Me/Write This One Off (As Actors)	1987	4.00
❑ 2156	Caught in Your Mess/ I Forgot to Remember	1987	4.00
❑ 2167	Drop That Zero/Chain Letter	1988	4.00

MCA

Number	Title (A Side/B Side)	Yr	NM
❑ 41222	I'm So Hot/Miracle, You and Me	1980	4.00
❑ 51046	I'm Trippin' on You/ I'll Get You Some Help	1981	4.00
❑ 51098	Sharing Your Love/ I'll Get You Some Help	1981	4.00

TARPEN

Number	Title (A Side/B Side)	Yr	NM
❑ 6603	A Love Reputation/ One Little Thing	1967	25.00

WESTBOUND

Number	Title (A Side/B Side)	Yr	NM
❑ 162	Heartbreaker of the Year/ Hung Up, Strung Out	1971	20.00
❑ 182	Trapped by a Thing Called Love/Keep It Coming	1971	15.00
❑ 201	Now Run and Tell That/ The Deeper I Go	1972	15.00
❑ 206	Man Sized Job/I'm Over You	1972	6.00
❑ 215	What It Takes to Get a Good Woman (That's What It's Gonna Take to Keep Her)/ Making a Good Thing Better	1973	6.00
❑ 219	Your Man and Your Best Friend/ What Am I Doing Wrong	1973	6.00
❑ 221	Don't Nobody Live Here (By the Name of Fool)/ Goody Goody Getter	1973	6.00
❑ 223	Get Up Off My Mind/The Best Thing I Ever Had	1974	6.00
❑ 229	Trying to Forget/We've Got Love	1974	6.00
❑ 5004	My Brand on You/Anytime Is the Right Time	1975	5.00
❑ 5008	Here I Am Again/Hung Up, Strung Out	1975	60.00
❑ 5019	Married, But Not to Each Other/ Who's the Fool	1976	5.00

Albums

ABC

Number	Title (A Side/B Side)	Yr	NM
❑ D-966	Second Breath	1976	12.00
❑ D-1027	The Bitch Is Bad	1977	12.00
❑ AA-1087	Under the Influence	1978	12.00

MALACO

Number	Title (A Side/B Side)	Yr	NM
❑ 7412	A Lady in the Street	198?	10.00
❑ 7417	Right Place, Right Time	1984	10.00
❑ 7422	Love Talkin'	198?	10.00
❑ 7434	Rain and Fire	198?	10.00
❑ 7441	It's Lying Time Again	198?	10.00
❑ 7447	Hittin' Where It Hurts	198?	10.00
❑ 7454	Still Trapped	198?	10.00
❑ 7464	Love Me Right	198?	10.00

MCA

Number	Title (A Side/B Side)	Yr	NM
❑ 759	Unwrapped	198?	8.00
—Reissue of 3089			
❑ 760	I'm So Hot	198?	8.00
—Reissue of 3239			
❑ 3089	Unwrapped	1979	10.00
❑ 3239	I'm So Hot	1980	10.00

WESTBOUND

Number	Title (A Side/B Side)	Yr	NM
❑ 209	Here I Am Again	1975	12.00
❑ 2012	Trapped by a Thing Called Love	1972	15.00
❑ 2016	On the Loose	1973	15.00

LAST, JAMES

45s

MGM

Number	Title (A Side/B Side)	Yr	NM
❑ 13599	Lara's Theme/Games That Lovers Play	1966	10.00

POLYDOR

Number	Title (A Side/B Side)	Yr	NM
❑ 2071	The Seduction (Love Theme)/ Night Drive	1980	3.00
❑ 2108	Fantasy/Last Glow	1980	3.00
❑ 2119	So Excited/Last Glow	1980	3.00
❑ 15004	Happy Heart/A Man and a Woman	1969	4.00
❑ 15017	Proud Mary/Washington Square	1970	4.00
❑ 15024	Girl of the North Country/The Party Is Over	1971	4.00
❑ 15028	Music from Across the Way/ Endless Journey	1971	4.00
❑ 15045	Wedding Song (There Is Love)/ Love Must Be the Reason	1972	4.00
❑ 15050	Heart of Gold/It's Going to Take Some Time	1972	4.00
❑ 15082	Jenny Jenny/But I Can Sleep in a Park	1973	4.00
❑ 15108	Summertime/Love for Sale	1975	4.00
❑ 15115	Theme from Prisoner of Second Avenue/Jubilation	197?	4.00

Albums

POLYDOR

Number	Title (A Side/B Side)	Yr	NM
❑ 24-4505	Classics Up to Date	1970	12.00
❑ 24-4507	Soft Rock	1970	12.00
❑ 24-4509	El Condor Pasa	1971	12.00
❑ 24-4512	Good Times	1971	12.00
❑ PD-5505	Music from Across the Way	1972	10.00
❑ PD-5506	The Love Album	197?	10.00
❑ PD-5512	Love Must Be the Reason	1972	10.00
❑ PD-5534	Non Stop Dancing	1973	10.00
❑ PD-5538	M.O.R.	1973	10.00
❑ 24-6004	Hair	1969	12.00
❑ PD-6040	Well Kept Secret	1975	10.00
❑ PD-1-6283	Seduction	1980	10.00

LAST CALL OF SHILOH, THE

Albums

LAST CALL

Number	Title (A Side/B Side)	Yr	NM
❑ 5136	The Last Call	196?	200.00

LAST POETS, THE

45s

BLUE THUMB

Number	Title (A Side/B Side)	Yr	NM
❑ 216	Tribute to Orabi/Bird's Word	1972	12.00

DOUGLAS

Number	Title (A Side/B Side)	Yr	NM
❑ ADS 8	O.D./Black Thighs	1971	15.00
❑ ADS 8 [PS]	O.D./Black Thighs	1971	30.00
❑ ZS7 6500	True Blues/Black Is	1971	12.00

Albums

BLUE THUMB

Number	Title (A Side/B Side)	Yr	NM
❑ BT-39	Chastisement	1972	30.00
❑ BT-52	At Last	1973	30.00

CASABLANCA

Number	Title (A Side/B Side)	Yr	NM
❑ NBLP 7051	Delights of the Garden	1977	25.00

CELLULOID

Number	Title (A Side/B Side)	Yr	NM
❑ 6101	The Last Poets	198?	10.00
❑ 6105	This Is Madness	198?	10.00
❑ 6108	Oh My People	198?	10.00
❑ 6136	Delights of the Garden	198?	10.00

COLLECTABLES

Number	Title (A Side/B Side)	Yr	NM
❑ COL-6500	Right On!	198?	10.00

DOUGLAS

Number	Title (A Side/B Side)	Yr	NM
❑ 3	The Last Poets	1970	50.00
❑ Z 30583	This Is Madness	1971	50.00
❑ Z 30811	The Last Poets	1971	40.00

JUGGERNAUT

Number	Title (A Side/B Side)	Yr	NM
❑ 8802	Right On!	1971	50.00

—As "The Original Last Poets"

LATEEF, YUSEF

45s

ARGO

Number	Title (A Side/B Side)	Yr	NM
❑ 5292	Cookin'/Marching Piper Blues	1958	12.00

ATLANTIC

Number	Title (A Side/B Side)	Yr	NM
❑ 2562	Othelia/Stay with Me	1968	6.00
❑ 2641	Raymond Winchester/ Bishop's School	1969	6.00
❑ 2997	Superfine/Down in Atlanta	1973	5.00
❑ 5104	Buddy and Lou/Russel and Eliot	1971	5.00
❑ 5114	Nubian Lady/Below Yellow Bell	1972	5.00

IMPULSE!

Number	Title (A Side/B Side)	Yr	NM
❑ 223	Theme from "The Prize"/Megeve	1963	8.00
❑ 225	Trouble in Mind/Yusef's French Brother	196?	8.00
❑ 233	Sister Mamie (Part 1)/ Sister Mamie (Part 2)	196?	8.00

NEW JAZZ

Number	Title (A Side/B Side)	Yr	NM
❑ 45-506	Yesterdays/Dopolous	196?	8.00

PRESTIGE

Number	Title (A Side/B Side)	Yr	NM
❑ 127	Love and Humor/Meditation	1957	12.00
❑ 254	Love Theme from "Spartacus"/ Snafu	1960	10.00
❑ 332	Blues for the Orient/I'll Remember April	1964	8.00
❑ 419	Love Theme from "Spartacus"/ Sea Breeze	196?	8.00

RIVERSIDE

Number	Title (A Side/B Side)	Yr	NM
❑ 445	Goin' Home/Salt Water Blues	1960	10.00
❑ 4504	Jungle Fantasy/Titoro	1961	10.00

Except when noted otherwise, VG = 25% of NM, and VG+ = 50% of NM. (Example: VG = \$2.00, VG+ = \$4.00 and NM = \$8.00.)

Number	Title (A Side/B Side)	Yr	NM
Albums			
ABC IMPULSE!			
❑ AS-56 [S]	Jazz Around the World	1968	20.00
❑ AS-69 [S]	Live at Pep's	1968	25.00
❑ AS-84 [S]	1984	1968	20.00
❑ AS-92 [S]	Psychicemotus	1968	20.00
❑ AS-9117 [S]	A Flat, G Flat and C	1968	20.00
❑ AS-9125 [S]	The Golden Flute	1968	20.00
❑ AS-9259 [(2)]	Re-evaluations: The Impulse Years	1974	25.00
❑ ASD-9310	Club Date	1976	40.00
❑ IA-9353 [(2)]	The Live Session	1978	30.00
ALA			
❑ AJ-502	Archives of Jazz, Vol. 2	198?	10.00
ARGO			
❑ LP-634 [M]	Live at Cranbrook	1959	80.00
ATLANTIC			
❑ SD 2-1000 [(2)]	10 Years Hence	1977	30.00
❑ SD 1499	The Complete Lateef	1968	40.00
—Blue and green label			
❑ SD 1499	The Complete Lateef	1969	20.00
—Red and green label			
❑ SD 1508	The Blue Lateef	1968	30.00
—Blue and green label			
❑ SD 1508	The Blue Lateef	1969	20.00
—Red and green label			
❑ SD 1525	Yusef Lateef's Detroit	1969	100.00
—Reproductions exist			
❑ SD 1548	The Diverse Lateef	1970	25.00
❑ SD 1563	Suite 16	1970	30.00
❑ SD 1591	The Best of Yusef Lateef	1971	20.00
—"1841 Broadway" address on label			
❑ SD 1591	The Best of Yusef Lateef	1976	12.00
—"75 Rockefeller Plaza" address on label			
❑ SD 1602	The Gentle Giant	1972	30.00
❑ SD 1635	Hush 'n' Thunder	1973	20.00
❑ SD 1650	Part of the Search	1974	15.00
❑ SD 1685	The Doctor Is In... And Out	1976	20.00
❑ 81663	Concerto for Yusef Lateef	1988	12.00
❑ 81717	Yusef Lateef's Little Symphony	1987	15.00
❑ 81977	Nocturnes	1989	15.00
CADET			
❑ LP-634 [M]	Live at Cranbrook	1966	40.00
❑ LPS-816	Live at Cranbrook	1969	25.00
CHARLIE PARKER			
❑ PLP-814 [M]	Lost in Sound	1962	50.00
❑ PLP-814S [S]	Lost in Sound	1962	60.00
CTI			
❑ 7082	Autophysiopsychic	1977	20.00
❑ 7088	In a Temple Garden	1979	20.00
DELMARK			
❑ DL-407 [M]	Yusef!	1965	40.00
❑ DS-407 [S]	Yusef!	1965	50.00
EVEREST ARCHIVE OF FOLK & JAZZ			
❑ FS-285	Yusef Lateef	197?	10.00
FANTASY			
❑ OJC-399	Other Sounds	1989	10.00
❑ OJC-482	Cry! Tender	1991	12.00
—Reissue of Prestige 7748			
❑ OJC-612	Eastern Sounds	1991	15.00
—Reissue of Prestige 7139			
IMPULSE!			
❑ A-56 [M]	Jazz Around the World	1963	40.00
❑ AS-56 [S]	Jazz Around the World	1963	50.00
❑ A-69 [M]	Live at Pep's	1964	50.00
❑ AS-69 [S]	Live at Pep's	1964	60.00
❑ A-84 [M]	1984	1965	30.00
❑ AS-84 [S]	1984	1965	40.00
❑ A-92 [M]	Psychicemotus	1966	50.00
❑ AS-92 [S]	Psychicemotus	1966	60.00
❑ A-9117 [M]	A Flat, G Flat and C	1966	50.00
❑ AS-9117 [S]	A Flat, G Flat and C	1966	60.00
❑ A-9125 [M]	The Golden Flute	1966	50.00
❑ AS-9125 [S]	The Golden Flute	1966	60.00
❑ MAS-90216 [M]	Live at Pep's	1964	60.00
—Capitol Record Club edition			
LANDMARK			
❑ LLP-502	Yusef Lateef in Nigeria	1985	20.00
MCA			
❑ 4146 [(2)]	Live Session	198?	15.00
—Reissue of ABC Impulse! 9353			
MILESTONE			
❑ M-47009 [(2)]	The Many Faces of Yusef Lateef	1973	25.00
MOODSVILLE			
❑ MVLP-22 [M]	Eastern Sounds	1961	100.00
—Green label, silver print			
❑ MVST-22 [S]	Eastern Sounds	1961	120.00
—Green label, silver print			
NEW JAZZ			
❑ NJLP-8218 [M]	Other Sounds	1959	200.00
—Purple label			

Number	Title (A Side/B Side)	Yr	NM
❑ NJLP-8218 [M]	Other Sounds	1965	80.00
—Blue label, trident logo at right			
❑ NJLP-8234 [M]	Cry! Tender	1960	200.00
—Purple label			
❑ NJLP-8234 [M]	Cry! Tender	1965	80.00
—Blue label, trident logo at right			
❑ NJLP-8261 [M]	The Sounds of Yusef	1961	100.00
—Reissue of Prestige 7122; purple label			
❑ NJLP-8261 [M]	The Sounds of Yusef	1965	50.00
—Blue label, trident logo at right			
❑ NJLP-8272 [M]	Into Something	1962	200.00
—Purple label			
❑ NJLP-8272 [M]	Into Something	1965	80.00
—Blue label, trident logo at right			
PRESTIGE			
❑ PRLP-7122 [M]	The Sounds of Yusef	1957	200.00
—Yellow label			
❑ PRLP-7319 [M]	Eastern Sounds	1964	60.00
❑ PRST-7319 [S]	Eastern Sounds	1964	70.00
—Reissue of Moodsville 22			
❑ PRLP-7398 [M]	The Sounds of Yusef	1966	30.00
❑ PRST-7398 [S]	The Sounds of Yusef Lateef	1966	40.00
❑ PRLP-7447 [M]	Yusef Lateef Plays for Lovers	1967	30.00
❑ PRST-7447 [S]	Yusef Lateef Plays for Lovers	1967	30.00
❑ PRST-7637	Into Something	1968	15.00
❑ PRST-7653	Expressions	1969	40.00
❑ PRST-7748	Cry! Tender	1970	20.00
❑ PRST-7832	Imagination	1971	30.00
❑ PR-24007 [(2)]	Lateef	1972	30.00
❑ P-24035 [(2)]	Blues for the Orient	1974	15.00
❑ P-24105 [(2)]	Yusef's Bag	1981	25.00
RIVERSIDE			
❑ RLP 12-325 [M]	Three Faces of Yusef Lateef	1960	200.00
❑ RLP-337 [M]	The Centaur and the Phoenix	1960	80.00
❑ RLP-1176 [S]	Three Faces of Yusef Lateef	1960	150.00
❑ RS-3011	This Is Yusef Lateef	1968	40.00
❑ RLP-9337 [S]	The Centaur and the Phoenix	1960	60.00
SAVOY			
❑ MG-12103 [M]	Jazz Mood	1957	100.00
❑ MG-12109 [M]	Jazz for the Thinker	1957	100.00
❑ MG-12117 [M]	Prayer to the East	1957	100.00
❑ MG-12120 [M]	Jazz and the Sounds of Nature	1958	100.00
❑ MG-12139 [M]	The Dreamer	1958	100.00
❑ MG-12140 [M]	The Fabric of Jazz	1958	100.00
❑ SR-13007 [S]	The Dreamer	1959	100.00
❑ SR-13008 [S]	The Fabric of Jazz	1959	100.00
SAVOY JAZZ			
❑ SJL-2205 [(2)]	Morning: The Savoy Sessions	1976	20.00
❑ SJL-2226 [(2)]	Gong!	1978	25.00
❑ SJL-2238 [(2)]	Angel Eyes	1979	25.00
TRIP			
❑ 5018	Outside Blues	1973	12.00
UPFRONT			
❑ UPF-183	Dexterity	197?	10.00
VERVE			
❑ MGV-8217 [M]	Before Dawn	1958	200.00
❑ V-8217 [M]	Before Dawn	1961	40.00
VJ INTERNATIONAL			
❑ VJS-3052 [M]	Contemplation	1974	50.00
—Reissue of Vee-Jay 3010, which was originally credited to LOUIS HAYES.			

LATIMORE

Number	Title (A Side/B Side)	Yr	NM
12-Inch Singles			
T.K. DISCO			
❑ TKD-400	Goodbye Heartache/We Got to Hit It Off	1979	15.00
45s			
ATLANTIC			
❑ 2639	I Pity the Fool/I'm Just an Ordinary Man	1969	8.00
DADE			
❑ 2013	Girl, I Got News for You/Ain't Gonna Cry No More	1967	10.00
❑ 2014	There She Is/It Was So Nice While It Lasted	1967	10.00
❑ 2015	It's Just a Matter of Time/Let's Move and Groove Together	1967	10.00
❑ 2017	The Power and the Glory/Love Don't Love Me	1968	10.00
❑ 2020	Have a Little Faith/I'm a Believer	1968	10.00
❑ 2022	I Pity the Fool/I'm Just an Ordinary Man	1968	10.00
❑ 2026	I'll Be Good to You/Life's Little Ups and Downs	1969	10.00
GLADES			
❑ 1714	Jolie/There's No End	1973	8.00
❑ 1716	Stormy Monday/There's No End	1973	6.00
❑ 1720	If You Were My Woman/Put Pride Aside	1974	6.00
❑ 1722	Let's Straighten It Out/Ain't Nobody Gonna Make Me Change My Mind	1974	6.00
❑ 1726	Keep the Home Fires Burnin'/That's How It Is	1975	6.00
❑ 1729	There's a Red-Neck in the Soul Band/Just One Step	1975	6.00
❑ 1733	Qualified Man/She Don't Ever Lose Her Groove	1976	6.00
❑ 1739	Somethin' 'Bout 'Cha/Sweet Vibrations	1976	6.00
❑ 1742	I Get Lifted/All the Way Lover	1977	6.00
❑ 1744	Let Me Live the Life I Love/It Ain't Where You Been	1977	6.00
❑ 1750	Dig a Little Deeper/Let Me Go	1978	6.00
❑ 1752	Long Distance Love/Out to Get 'Cha	1979	6.00
❑ 1755	Goodbye Heartache/We Got to Hit It Off	1979	6.00
❑ 1756	Discoed to Death/Just One Step	1979	6.00
❑ 1761	Take Me to the Mountaintop/Joy	1980	6.00
MALACO			
❑ 2083	Let the Doorknob Hit'cha/Do That To Me One More Time	1982	4.00
❑ 2084	Ain't Nothing You Can Do/Bad Risk	198?	4.00
❑ 2093	I'll Do Anything for You/Hell Fire Lovin'	198?	4.00
❑ 2098	Right Place, Right Time/He's Not Available	1984	4.00
—With Denise LaSalle			
❑ 2099	One Shirt, Soulless Shoes/You	1984	4.00
❑ 2119	Good Time Man/You Crowed in My Bed	198?	4.00
❑ 2130	Sunshine Lady/There's No Limit to My Love	1986	4.00
Albums			
GLADES			
❑ 6502	Latimore	1973	12.00
❑ 6503	More, More, More	1974	12.00
❑ 7505	Latimore 3	1975	12.00
❑ 7509	It Ain't Where You Been	1976	10.00
❑ 7515	Dig a Little Deeper	1978	10.00
MALACO			
❑ 7409	Singing in the Key of Love	198?	10.00
❑ 7414	I'll Do Anything for You	198?	10.00
❑ 7423	Good Time Man	198?	10.00
❑ 7436	Every Way But Wrong	198?	10.00
❑ 7443	Slow Down	198?	10.00
❑ 7456	The Only Way Is Up	198?	10.00
❑ 7468	Catchin' Up	1993	12.00

LATIN SOULS, THE

Number	Title (A Side/B Side)	Yr	NM
45s			
KAPP			
❑ 844	La Bamba/The Party Is Over	1967	8.00
❑ 898	I've Got You/Look But Don't Touch	1968	8.00
Albums			
KAPP			
❑ KL-1524 [M]	Boo-Ga-Loo and Shing-a-Ling	1967	25.00
❑ KS-3524 [S]	Boo-Ga-Loo and Shing-a-Ling	1967	20.00
❑ KS-3553	Tigar Boo-Ga-Loo	1968	20.00

LATTIMORE, BENNY

Number	Title (A Side/B Side)	Yr	NM
45s			
HIT			
❑ 15	Snap Your Fingers/I Sold My Heart to the Junkman	1962	8.00
—B-side by Peggy Thompson			

LAUGHING GRAVY

Number	Title (A Side/B Side)	Yr	NM
45s			
WHITE WHALE			
❑ 261	Vegetables/Snow Flakes on Laughing Gravy's Whiskers	1968	200.00

LAUPER, CYNDI

Number	Title (A Side/B Side)	Yr	NM
12-Inch Singles			
EPIC			
❑ EAS 1197 [DJ]	Hole in My Heart (All the Way to China)/Boy Blue (Live)	1988	12.00
❑ E2S 5093 [(2)DJ]	That's What I Think (Urban Dance Mix 6:03) (Urban 7" 4:09) (Urban Dub Mix 6:14) (Hip Hop Vocal Mix 6:14) (Hip Hop Dub 5:46) (Bonus Beats 4:41) (LP Version 4:40) (Club Mix 5:31) (Club Dub 5:26) (Early Morning Mix 5:19) (Deep Mix 5:18) (Factory Mix 5:24) (Tribal Mix 5:24)	1993	50.00
❑ EAD 7286 [DJ]	Hey Now (Girls Just Want to Have Fun) (Junior's Sound Factory Mix 7:40) (Techno		

L

Cyndi Lauper, "I Drove All Night," Epic 68759, 68759, 1989, **$3.**

Number	Title (A Side/B Side)	Yr	NM
	Main Mix 8:23) (Straight Up Pass 7:13) (Factory Dub 6:50) (Techno Dub 3:55)	1995	15.00
❑ 49H-08145	Girls Just Want to Have Fun/ She Bop	1988	10.00

—*"Mixed Masters" reissue*

Number	Title (A Side/B Side)	Yr	NM
❑ EAS 9366 [DJ]	You Don't Know (TM's Know It All Mix 10:00) (TM's Know You're in the Hole Dub 5:30) (Prince Quick Mix's Amped Up Pass 6:35) (Junior's Riff Dub 6:09)	1997	10.00
❑ 49-77234	That's What I Think (Musto Club Mix 7:10) (Musto Dub Mix 7:22) (Musto Radio Mix 3:55) (Vasquez Club Mix 5:31) (Vasquez Deep Mix 5:18) (Vasquez Factory Mix 5:24)	1993	10.00
❑ 49-77941	Come On Home (Techno Vox 9:03) (Techno Dub 4:35) (Jungle Vox 6:20) (Junior's Soundfactory Mix 11:44) (Factory Dub Short Version 2:34) (Extended Club Mix: 5:35)	1995	8.00
❑ 49-78548	You Don't Know (TM's Know It All Mix 10:00) (TM's Know You're in the Hole Dub 5:30) (Prince Quick Mix's Amped Up Pass 6:35) (Junior's Riff Dub 6:09)	1997	12.00

JELLYBEAN

Number	Title (A Side/B Side)	Yr	NM
❑ JEL-2554	Disco Inferno (Soul Solution Mix 7:52) (Soul Solution A Cappella 6:58) (Boris & Beck Roxy Dub 7:16) (Rescue Me Mix 8:04)	1999	8.00

PORTRAIT

Number	Title (A Side/B Side)	Yr	NM
❑ AS 1961 [DJ]	Money Changes Everything (Recorded Live) (That Version 6:23) (This Version 5:48)	1984	15.00
❑ AS 2084 [DJ]	The Goonies 'R' Good Enough (same on both sides)	1985	8.00
❑ AS 2450 [DJ]	True Colors (same on both sides)	1986	12.00
❑ AS 2560 [DJ]	Change of Heart (AOR Mix) (same on both sides)	1986	10.00
❑ 4R9-04121	Girls Just Want to Have Fun/ Money Changes Everything	1983	15.00
❑ 4R9-04971	Girls Just Want to Have Fun// Fun With V. Knutsn/Xtra Fun	1984	8.00
❑ 4R9-05011	She Bop (Special Dance Mix)/ (Instrumental)	1984	10.00
❑ 4R9-05246	The Goonies 'R' Good Enough (Dance Version) (Dub)	1985	8.00
❑ 4R9-05974	Change of Heart (Extended Version) (Instrumental)// Heartbeats/Witness	1986	8.00
❑ 4R9-06740	What's Going On (Club Mix 6:30) (Long Mix 6:22) (Instrumental 6:35)/One Track Mind (3:39)	1986	8.00

45s

EPIC

Number	Title (A Side/B Side)	Yr	NM
❑ 34-07940	Hole in My Heart (All the Way to China)/Boy Blue (Live)	1988	3.00
❑ 34-07940 [PS]	Hole in My Heart (All the Way to China)/Boy Blue (Live)	1988	3.00
❑ 15-08443	True Colors/What's Going On	1988	3.00

—*Reissue*

Number	Title (A Side/B Side)	Yr	NM
❑ 34-68759	I Drove All Night/ Maybe He'll Know	1989	3.00
❑ 34-68945	My First Night Without You/ Unabbreviated Love	1989	4.00
❑ 34-74942	Who Let In the Rain/Cold	1993	4.00
❑ 34-77233	That's What I Think/(Live)	1993	4.00

PORTRAIT

Number	Title (A Side/B Side)	Yr	NM
❑ 37-04120	Girls Just Want to Have Fun/ Right Track Wrong Train	1983	3.00
❑ 37-04120 [PS]	Girls Just Want to Have Fun	1983	8.00

—*"Demonstration — Not for Sale" on back*

Number	Title (A Side/B Side)	Yr	NM
❑ 37-04120 [PS]	Girls Just Want to Have Fun/ Right Track Wrong Train	1983	8.00
❑ 37-04432	Time After Time/I'll Kiss You	1984	3.00
❑ 37-04516	She Bop/Witness	1984	3.00
❑ 37-04516 [PS]	She Bop/Witness	1984	3.00
❑ 37-04639	All Through the Night/Witness	1984	3.00
❑ 37-04639 [PS]	All Through the Night/Witness	1984	3.00
❑ 37-04737	Money Changes Everything (Studio)/(Live)	1984	3.00
❑ 37-04737 [PS]	Money Changes Everything (Studio)/(Live)	1984	3.00
❑ 34-04918	The Goonies 'R' Good Enough/ What a Thrill	1985	3.00
❑ 34-04918 [PS]	The Goonies 'R' Good Enough/ What a Thrill	1985	3.00

—*Picture sleeve claims to be on "Epic" but the record is on Portrait*

Number	Title (A Side/B Side)	Yr	NM
❑ 17-05480	Girls Just Want to Have Fun/ Time After Time	198?	3.00

—*Reissue*

Number	Title (A Side/B Side)	Yr	NM
❑ 17-05537	She Bop/All Through the Night	198?	3.00

—*Reissue*

Number	Title (A Side/B Side)	Yr	NM
❑ 37-06247	True Colors/Heading for the Moon	1986	3.00
❑ 37-06247 [PS]	True Colors/Heading for the Moon	1986	3.00
❑ 37-06431	Change of Heart/Witness	1986	3.00
❑ 37-06431 [DJ]	Change of Heart (3:58)/(4:24)	1986	6.00
❑ 37-06431 [PS]	Change of Heart/Witness	1986	3.00
❑ 37-06970	What's Going On/ One Track Mind	1987	3.00
❑ 37-06970 [PS]	What's Going On/ One Track Mind	1987	3.00
❑ 37-07181	Boy Blue/The Faraway Nearby	1987	3.00
❑ 37-07181 [PS]	Boy Blue/The Faraway Nearby	1987	15.00

Albums

EPIC

Number	Title (A Side/B Side)	Yr	NM
❑ OE 44318	A Night to Remember	1989	10.00

PORTRAIT

Number	Title (A Side/B Side)	Yr	NM
❑ BFR 38930	She's So Unusual	1983	12.00
❑ FR 38930	She's So Unusual	1984	8.00

—*Reissue with new prefix*

Number	Title (A Side/B Side)	Yr	NM
❑ 9R9 39610	She's So Unusual	1984	20.00

—*Picture disc in plastic sleeve with sticker*

Number	Title (A Side/B Side)	Yr	NM
❑ OR 40313	True Colors	1986	10.00

LAURELS, THE (1)

45s

ABC-PARAMOUNT

Number	Title (A Side/B Side)	Yr	NM
❑ 10048	Hand in Hand/Picture of Love	1959	50.00

LAURELS, THE (2)

45s

"X"

Number	Title (A Side/B Side)	Yr	NM
❑ 0143	Truly, Truly/'Tis Night	1955	250.00

LAURELS, THE (U)

May also be by group (2), but we're not sure.

45s

SPRING

Number	Title (A Side/B Side)	Yr	NM
❑ 1112	Baby Talk/You Left Me	1959	60.00

LAUREN, ROD

45s

CHANCELLOR

Number	Title (A Side/B Side)	Yr	NM
❑ 1126	I Ain't Got You/Mexicali Rose	1962	12.00
❑ 1132	Oh How I Miss You Tonight/ Blame Your Friends	1963	12.00
❑ 1136	Yesterday's Lovers/I Know	1963	12.00
❑ 1141	I Wanna Know/Searcher for Love	1963	12.00
❑ 1146	Let Me Tell You 'Bout My Baby/I can't Get You Out of My Heart	1963	12.00

RCA VICTOR

Number	Title (A Side/B Side)	Yr	NM
❑ 47-7645	If I Had a Girl/No Wonder	1959	15.00
❑ 47-7645 [PS]	If I Had a Girl/No Wonder	1959	20.00
❑ 47-7720	Listen My Love/This I Know	1960	15.00
❑ 47-7786	A Wild Imagination/The One Finger Symphony	1960	15.00
❑ 47-8020	I Dreamed/A Wondrous Place	1962	12.00

Albums

RCA VICTOR

Number	Title (A Side/B Side)	Yr	NM
❑ LPM-2176 [M]	I'm Rod Lauren	1961	40.00
❑ LSP-2176 [S]	I'm Rod Lauren	1961	50.00

LAURIE, ANNIE

45s

DELUXE

Number	Title (A Side/B Side)	Yr	NM
❑ 6107	It Hurts to Be in Love/ Hand in Hand	1957	20.00
❑ 6135	It Must Be You/Please Honey Don't Go	1957	15.00
❑ 6140	You're the Only One for Me/ Out of My Mind	1957	15.00
❑ 6151	Love Is a Funny Thing/Nobody's Gonna Hurt You Baby	1957	15.00
❑ 6173	Someday Someway/ Hold On to What You Got	1958	15.00
❑ 6182	Since I Fell for You/Lost Love	1959	15.00
❑ 6189	If You're Lonely/It's Gonna Come Out in the Wash Someday	1960	15.00

Except when noted otherwise, VG = 25% of NM, and VG+ = 50% of NM. (Example: VG = $2.00, VG+ = $4.00 and NM = $8.00.)

Number	Title (A Side/B Side)	Yr	NM
OKEH			
❑ 6915	You Belong to Me/I Feel So Right Tonight	1952	25.00
❑ 6933	Stop Talkin' and Start Walkin'/ Give Me Half a Chance	1953	25.00
❑ 6973	It's Been a Long, Long Time/ I Ain't Got It Bad No More	1953	25.00
❑ 7025	I'm in the Mood for You/Feeling the Need	1954	20.00
SAVOY			
❑ 1197	You Promised Love/ Rockin' and Rollin' Again	1956	20.00
Albums			
AUDIO LAB			
❑ AL-1510 [M]	It Hurts to Be in Love	1959	300.00

LAVELLE, RONNIE

Number	Title (A Side/B Side)	Yr	NM
45s			
PARKWAY			
❑ 831	Cartoons/The Crazy Way of Love	1961	12.00
❑ 837	Let Her Go/A Dog's Life	1962	12.00

LAVETTE, BETTY

Number	Title (A Side/B Side)	Yr	NM
45s			
ATCO			
❑ 6891	Heart of Gold/You'll Wake Up Wisely	1972	40.00
❑ 6913	Your Turn to Cry/ Soul Tambourine	1973	6.00
ATLANTIC			
❑ 2160	My Man — He's a Lovin' Man/ Shut Your Mouth	1962	30.00
—As "Betty LaVett"			
❑ 2198	You'll Never Change/Here I Am	1963	50.00
—As "Betty LaVett"			
CALLA			
❑ 102	Let Me Down Easy/What I Don't Know (Won't Hurt Me)	1965	30.00
❑ 104	I Feel Good (All Over)/Only Your Love Can Save Me	1965	75.00
❑ 106	Stand Up Like a Man/ I'm Just a Fool for You	1965	40.00
EPIC			
❑ 8-50143	You Made a Believer Out of Me/ Thank You for Loving Me	1975	200.00
KAREN			
❑ 1540	Love Makes the World Go Round/Almost	1968	40.00
❑ 1544	Get Away/What Condition My Condition Is In	1968	150.00
❑ 1545	With a Little Help from My Friends/Hey Love	1969	20.00
❑ 1548	Ticket to the Moon/Let Me Down Easy	1969	8.00
LUPINE			
❑ 123	Witch Craft in the Air/ You Killed the Love	1964	40.00
—As "Betty LaVett"			
❑ 1021	Witch Craft in the Air/ You Killed the Love	1964	25.00
—As "Betty LaVett"			
MOTOWN			
❑ 1532	Right in the Middle (Of Falling in Love)/You Seen One, You Seen 'Em All	1981	5.00
—As "Bettye LaVette"			
❑ 1614	Either Way, We Lose/I Can't Stop	1982	5.00
—As "Bettye LaVette"			
SILVER FOX			
❑ 17	He Made a Woman Out of Me/ Nearer to You	1969	6.00
❑ 21	Do Your Duty/Love's Made a Fool Out of Me	1970	6.00
❑ 24	Games People Play/My Train's Comin' In	1970	6.00
SSS INTERNATIONAL			
❑ 839	Take Another Piece of My Heart/At the Mercy of a Man	1971	6.00
WEST END			
❑ 1213	Doin' the Best That I Can/ (Instrumental)	1983	15.00
—As "Bettye LaVette"			
Albums			
ANTI			
❑ 86873-1	Scene of the Crime	2007	15.00
—As "Bettye LaVette"; comes with a certificate for a free MP3 download of the album			
DBK WORKS			
❑ DBK 116	I've Got My Own Hell to Raise	2005	15.00
—As "Bettye LaVette"			
MOTOWN			
❑ 6000 ML	Tell Me a Lie	1982	12.00
—As "Bettye LaVette"			
SUNDAZED			
❑ LP 5208	Do Your Duty	2006	15.00
—As "Bettye LaVette"; compilation of recordings for Silver Fox and SSS International			

LAVOIE, KENT

See LOBO.

LAWRENCE, BILL

Number	Title (A Side/B Side)	Yr	NM
45s			
BERTRAM INT'L.			
❑ 207	Hey Baby!/Caribbean	1959	100.00
❑ 227	Please Don't Leave Me/Billy Boy	1960	60.00
FREEDOM			
❑ 44004	Hey Baby!/Caribbean	1958	150.00
MOOD			
❑ 1013	Little Girl/(B-side unknown)	195?	70.00
Albums			
TOPS			
❑ L-1576 [M]	Bill Lawrence Sings I'm in the Mood for Love	1957	20.00

LAWRENCE, EDDIE

Number	Title (A Side/B Side)	Yr	NM
45s			
CORAL			
❑ 61168	Old, Old Vienna (Part 1)/ Old, Old Vienna (Part 2)	1954	12.00
❑ 61671	The Old Philosopher/ King Arthur's Mine	1956	15.00
❑ 61713	The New Philosopher/ Loco Baseball	1956	12.00
❑ 61799	German Baseball/ Golden Baskos	1957	12.00
❑ 61821	Abner the Baseball (Part 1)/ Abner the Baseball (Part 2)	1957	12.00
❑ 61863	The Old Philosopher on the Range/Memories of Louise	1957	12.00
❑ 61915	The Merry Old Philosopher/ That Holiday Spirit	1957	20.00
❑ 61940	The Visitor/Fix Your Watch	1958	12.00
❑ 61978	The Philosopher Strikes Back/ Frankensteiner Polka	1958	12.00
❑ 62005	The Good Old Days/Hi-Fi Blues	1958	12.00
❑ 62049	The Space Philosopher/Outta This World	1958	12.00
❑ 62070	The Mother Philosopher/ The Salesman's Philosopher	1959	10.00
❑ 62267	The Suburban Philosopher/ We Sure Had Fun	1961	10.00
❑ 62298	The Philosopher Twist/The D.J. Philosopher Returns	1961	10.00
❑ 62367	The Mets' Philosopher/ We Love the Mets	1963	15.00
EPIC			
❑ 9804	The World's Fair Philosopher/ The Old Philosopher and the Single Girl	1965	12.00
SHASTA			
❑ 139	Stardust/Harlem Nocturne	196?	8.00
❑ 144	Cattle Call/Cielito Lindo	196?	8.00
SIGNATURE			
❑ 12010	The Doctor's Philosopher/ Blackouts of 1984	1960	10.00
❑ 12031	Anyone for President/Unequal	1960	10.00
Albums			
CORAL			
❑ CRL 57103 [M]	The Old Philosopher	1956	30.00
❑ CRL 57155 [M]	Eddie "The Old Philosopher" Lawrence	1957	30.00
❑ CRL 57203 [M]	The Kingdom of Eddie Lawrence	1958	30.00
❑ CRL 57371 [M]	The Side Splitting Personality of Eddie Lawrence	1961	30.00
❑ CRL 57411 [M]	Seven Characters In Search of Eddie Lawrence	1962	30.00
❑ CRL 757411 [S]	Seven Characters In Search of Eddie Lawrence	1962	40.00
EPIC			
❑ LN 24149 [M]	Is That What's Bothering You Bunkie?	1965	30.00
❑ BN 26149 [S]	Is That What's Bothering You Bunkie?	1965	40.00
SIGNATURE			
❑ SM-1003 [M]	The Garden of Eddie Lawrence	1960	40.00

LAWRENCE, MARK

Number	Title (A Side/B Side)	Yr	NM
45s			
GNP CRESCENDO			
❑ 419	Is There A Santa Claus?/ The Heavenly Forest	1968	6.00
JERDEN			
❑ 110	Is There A Santa Claus/ Santa Claus Square Dance	196?	8.00

LAWRENCE, SYD

Number	Title (A Side/B Side)	Yr	NM
45s			
COSMIC			
❑ 1001	The Answer to the Flying Saucer/Haunted Guitar	1956	40.00
—B-side by Billy Mure			

LAWRENCE, VICKI

Number	Title (A Side/B Side)	Yr	NM
45s			
BELL			
❑ 45303	The Night the Lights Went Out in Georgia/Dime a Dance	1973	5.00
❑ 45362	He Did with Me/Mr. Allison	1973	4.00
❑ 45409	Sensual Man/Ships in the Night	1973	4.00
❑ 45437	Mama's Gonna Make It Better/ Cameo	1974	4.00
ELF			
❑ 90035	And I'll Go/The Whole State of Alabama	1970	6.00
PRIVATE STOCK			
❑ 45,036	The Other Woman/Cameo	1975	4.00
❑ 45,067	There's a Gun Still Smokin' in Nashville	1976	4.00
❑ 45,121	Love in the Hot Afternoon/ (B-side unknown)	1976	4.00
SOMA			
❑ 5248	The Night the Lights Went Out in Georgia/He Did with Me	197?	5.00
—Original, reissue or bootleg? Please advise.			
UNITED ARTISTS			
❑ 50748	No, No/Lincoln Street Chapel	1971	6.00
Albums			
BELL			
❑ 1120	The Night the Lights Went Out in Georgia	1973	12.00

LAWRENCE, WALT

Number	Title (A Side/B Side)	Yr	NM
45s			
HOLLYWOOD INT'L.			
❑ 2	Cascade/Twilight Adrift	195?	40.00

LAWS, HUBERT

Number	Title (A Side/B Side)	Yr	NM
45s			
ATLANTIC			
❑ 5046	Miss Thing/Blue Eyed Peas and Rice	1965	8.00
COLUMBIA			
❑ 02694	Goodbye for Now (Theme from "Reds")/(Instrumental)	1982	4.00
❑ 10736	False Faces/The Baron	1978	4.00
❑ 10811	It Happens Every Day/ Love Gets Better	1978	4.00
❑ 11022	Land of Passion/Heartbeats	1979	4.00
❑ 11368	Wildfire/Family	1980	4.00
CTI			
❑ 3	Fire and Rain/Theme from Love Story	1971	5.00
❑ 13	Amazing Grace (Part 1)/ Amazing Grace (Part 2)	1973	5.00
❑ 21	Mean Lene/Come All Ye Disconsolate	1974	5.00
❑ 27	The Chicago Theme (Love Loop)/I Had a Dream	1975	5.00
❑ 501	La Jean/Let It Be	197?	4.00
❑ 505	Feelin' Alright/Let It Be	197?	4.00
Albums			
ATLANTIC			
❑ 1432 [M]	The Laws of Jazz	1965	20.00
❑ SD 1432 [S]	The Laws of Jazz	1965	25.00
—Red and purple label			
❑ SD 1432 [S]	The Laws of Jazz	1969	15.00
—Red and green label			
❑ 1452 [M]	Flute By-Laws	1966	20.00
❑ SD 1452 [S]	Flute By-Laws	1966	20.00
❑ SD 1509	Laws Cause	1970	25.00
❑ SD 1624	Wild Flower	1973	15.00
❑ SD 8813	The Laws of Jazz	1981	8.00
—Reissue of 1432			
CBS			
❑ M 39858	Blanchard: New Earth Sonata; Telemann: Suite in A; Amazing Grace	1985	10.00
COLUMBIA			
❑ PC 34330	Romeo and Juliet	1976	12.00
❑ JC 35022	Say It with Silence	1978	10.00
❑ JC 35708	Land of Passion	1979	10.00
❑ FC 36365	The Best of Hubert Laws	1981	10.00
❑ JC 36396	Family	1980	15.00

L

Number	Title (A Side/B Side)	Yr	NM
FC 38850	Make It Last	1983	10.00
CTI			
CTX-3 + 3 [(2)]	In the Beginning	1974	20.00
1002	Crying Song	1970	30.00
—Original issue			
6000	Crying Song	1970	15.00
—Reissue of 1002			
6006	Afro-Classic	1971	20.00
6012	Rite of Spring	1972	15.00
6022	Morning Star	1972	15.00
6025	Carnegie Hall	1973	15.00
6058	The Chicago Theme	1975	15.00
6065	Then There Was Light, Vol. 1	1976	12.00
—Half of "In the Beginning," originally issued as part of CTX 3+3			
6066	Then There Was Light, Vol. 2	1976	12.00
—Half of "In the Beginning," originally issued as part of CTX 3+3			
7071	The San Francisco Concert	1977	15.00
8015	The Chicago Theme	198?	10.00
—Reissue of 6058			
8019	Afro-Classic	198?	10.00
—Reissue of 6006			
8020	Rite of Spring	198?	10.00
—Reissue of 6012			

LAWS, RONNIE

Number	Title (A Side/B Side)	Yr	NM
45s			
BLUE NOTE			
XW738	Always There/Tidal Wave	1975	5.00
XW848	Carmen/All the Time	1976	5.00
XW1007	Just Love/Nuthin' But Nuthin'	1977	5.00
XW1036	Friends and Strangers/ Goodtime Ride	1977	5.00
CAPITOL			
B-5241	In the Groove/Summer Fool	1983	3.00
B-5241 [PS]	In the Groove/Summer Fool	1983	4.00
B-5274	Mr. Nice Guy/Off and On Again	1983	3.00
B-5421	City Girl/Rolling	1984	3.00
B-5465	(You Are) Paradise/Stay Awake	1985	3.00
COLUMBIA			
06240	Come to Me/Take a Chance	1986	3.00
06574	Mirror Town/Midnight Side	1986	3.00
07629	Rhythm of Romance/Nite Life	1987	3.00
07787	Smoke House/All Day Rhythm	1988	3.00
LIBERTY			
1424	Stay Awake/Summer Fool	1981	4.00
1442	There's a Way/Just As You Are	1981	4.00
1459	Heavy On Easy/Just As You Are	1982	4.00
UNITED ARTISTS			
1264	Love Is Here/Grace	1978	4.00
1278	All for You/These Days	1979	4.00
1334	Every Generation/Every Generation (Part 2)	1980	4.00
1334 [PS]	Every Generation/Every Generation (Part 2)	1980	5.00
1354	Love's Victory/It's One	1980	4.00
1376	Young Child/(B-side unknown)	1980	4.00
Albums			
BLUE NOTE			
BN-LA452-G	Pressure Sensitive	1975	15.00
BN-LA628-G	Fever	1976	12.00
BN-LA730-H	Friends and Strangers	1977	10.00
CAPITOL			
ST-12261	Mr. Nice Guy	1983	10.00
ST-12375	Classic Masters	1984	10.00
ST-512375	Classic Masters	1984	12.00
—Columbia House edition			
COLUMBIA			
BFC 40089	Mirror Town	1986	10.00
FC 40902	All Day Rhythm	1987	10.00
LIBERTY			
LO-628	Fever	198?	8.00
—Reissue of Blue Note 628			
LW-730	Friends and Strangers	198?	8.00
—Reissue of Blue Note 730			
LO-881	Flame	198?	8.00
—Reissue of United Artists 881			
LT-1001	Every Generation	1981	8.00
—Reissue of United Artists 1001			
LN-10164	Pressure Sensitive	198?	8.00
—Reissue of Blue Note 452			
LN-10232	Flame	198?	8.00
—Budget-line reissue			
LN-10255	Fever	198?	8.00
—Budget-line reissue			
LN-10307	Solid Ground	1986	8.00
—Budget-line reissue			
LO-51087	Solid Ground	1981	10.00
UNITED ARTISTS			
UA-LA881-H	Flame	1978	10.00
LT-1001	Every Generation	1980	12.00

LAWSON, LINDA

Number	Title (A Side/B Side)	Yr	NM
Albums			
CHANCELLOR			
CHL-5010 [M]	Introducing Linda Lawson	1960	20.00

LAWSON, ROBBY

Number	Title (A Side/B Side)	Yr	NM
45s			
KYSER			
2122	Burning Sensation/ (B-side unknown)	196?	1200.

LAY, SAM

Number	Title (A Side/B Side)	Yr	NM
Albums			
BLUE THUMB			
BTS 14	Sam Lay in Bluesland	1970	25.00

LEADBELLY

Number	Title (A Side/B Side)	Yr	NM
7-Inch Extended Plays			
CAPITOL			
EAP 1-369	Back Water Blues/Take This Hammer//On a Christmas Day/Irene	1954	100.00
EAP 1-369 [PS]	Classics in Jazz, Part 1	1954	100.00
EAP 2-369	Sweet Mary Blues/Ella Speed// Tell Me Baby/Western Plain	1954	100.00
EAP 2-369 [PS]	Classics in Jazz, Part 2	1954	100.00
Albums			
ALLEGRO			
L-4027 [10]	Sinful Songs	195?	250.00
CAPITOL			
H 369 [10]	Classics in Jazz	1953	250.00
T 1821 [M]	Leadbelly: Huddie Ledbetter's Best	1962	40.00
ELEKTRA			
EKL-301/2 [(2)]	The Library of Congress Recordings	1966	25.00
FOLKWAYS			
FP-4 [10]	Lead Belly's Legacy, Vol. 1: Take This Hammer	1950	120.00
FP-14 [10]	Lead Belly's Legacy, Vol. 2: Rock Island Line	1951	120.00
FP-24 [10]	Lead Belly's Legacy, Vol. 3: Early Recordings	1951	120.00
FP-34 [10]	Lead Belly's Legacy, Vol. 4: Easy Rider	1951	120.00
FP-241 [(2)M]	Leadbelly's Last Sessions, Vol. 1	196?	40.00
FP-242 [(2)M]	Leadbelly's Last Sessions, Vol. 2	196?	40.00
FA-2004 [10]	Lead Belly's Legacy, Vol. 1: Take This Hammer	195?	50.00
—Reissue of FP-4			
FA-2014 [10]	Lead Belly's Legacy, Vol. 2: Rock Island Line	195?	50.00
—Reissue of FP-14			
FA-2024 [10]	Lead Belly's Legacy, Vol. 3: Early Recordings	195?	50.00
—Reissue of FP-24			
FA-2034 [10]	Lead Belly's Legacy, Vol. 4: Easy Rider	195?	50.00
—Reissue of FP-34			
FA-2941 [M]	Leadbelly's Last Sessions, Vol. 3	196?	25.00
FA-2942 [M]	Leadbelly's Last Sessions, Vol. 4	196?	25.00
FA-3106 [M]	Leadbelly Sings Folk Songs	196?	25.00
RCA VICTOR			
LPV-505 [M]	Midnight Special	1964	40.00
ROYALE			
18131 [10]	Blues Songs	1954	120.00
—As "The Lonesome Blues Singer"			
VERVE FOLKWAYS			
FT-3019 [M]	From the Last Sessions	1967	25.00
FTS-3019 [R]	From the Last Sessions	1967	15.00
FV-9001 [M]	Take This Hammer	1965	25.00
FVS-9001 [R]	Take This Hammer	1965	15.00
FV-9021 [M]	Keep Your Hands Off Her	1965	25.00
FVS-9021 [R]	Keep Your Hands Off Her	1965	15.00

LEADERS, THE

Number	Title (A Side/B Side)	Yr	NM
45s			
GLORY			
239	Nobody Loves Me/Dearest Beloved Darling	1956	80.00
243	Can't Help Lovin' That Girl of Mine/Lovers	1956	80.00

LEAPER, BOB

Number	Title (A Side/B Side)	Yr	NM
45s			
REPRISE			
0274	Sunday Morning/ Come and Join Us	1964	10.00
Albums			
LONDON			
LL 3391 [M]	Big Band Beatle Songs	1964	30.00
SP 44056 [S]	Big Band Beatle Songs	1964	40.00

LEAPING FERNS, THE
Also recorded as CHANTAY'S.

Number	Title (A Side/B Side)	Yr	NM
45s			
X-PANDED SOUND			
103	It Never Works Out for Me/ Maybe Baby	1964	30.00

LEARY, DR. TIMOTHY

Number	Title (A Side/B Side)	Yr	NM
45s			
MERCURY			
72713	Turn On, Tune In, Drop Out (Part 1)/Turn On, Tune In, Drop Out (Part 2)	1967	30.00
Albums			
DOUGLAS			
1	You Can Be Anyone This Time Around	1969	100.00
ESP-DISK'			
1027 [M]	Turn On, Tune In, Drop Out	1966	150.00
MERCURY			
MG-21131 [M]	Turn On, Tune In, Drop Out	1967	40.00
SR-61131 [S]	Turn On, Tune In, Drop Out	1967	50.00
PIXIE			
CA-1069 [M]	L.S.D.	1966	80.00

LEATHER BOY

Number	Title (A Side/B Side)	Yr	NM
45s			
FLOWER			
100	My Prayer/You Gotta Have Soul	1968	30.00
MGM			
13724	I'm a Leather Boy/Shadows	1967	30.00
13724 [PS]	I'm a Leather Boy/Shadows	1967	60.00
13790	On the Go/Soulin'	1967	30.00
PARKWAY			
125	Jersey Thursday/Black Friday	1966	30.00

LEATHERCOATED MINDS, THE

Number	Title (A Side/B Side)	Yr	NM
Albums			
VIVA			
V-6003 [M]	Trip Down Sunset Strip	1967	60.00
V-36003 [S]	Trip Down Sunset Strip	1967	80.00

LEAVES, THE

Number	Title (A Side/B Side)	Yr	NM
45s			
CAPITOL			
5799	Lemon Princess/ Twilight Sanctuary	1966	12.00
LOST-NITE			
314	Hey Joe/Girl from the East	197?	6.00
—Reissue			
MIRA			
202	Love Minus Zero-No Limit/ Too Many People	1965	50.00
207	Hey Joe, Where You Gonna Go/Be with You	1965	100.00
213	You Better Move On/ A Different Story	1966	50.00
220	Be with You/Funny Little World	1966	50.00
222	Hey Joe/Girl from the East	1966	40.00
222	Hey Joe/Funny Little World	1966	50.00
227	Too Many People/ Girl from the East	1966	40.00
231	Get Out of My Life Woman/ Girl from the East	1966	40.00
234	Be with You/You Better Move On	1966	40.00
Albums			
CAPITOL			
ST 2638 [S]	All the Good That's Happening	1967	30.00
T 2638 [M]	All the Good That's Happening	1967	25.00
MIRA			
LP-3005 [M]	Hey Joe	1966	40.00
LPS-3005 [S]	Hey Joe	1966	50.00
SURREY			
LPS-3005	Hey Joe	196?	150.00
—Issued in Mira jackets			

LED ZEPPELIN
Also see JOHN PAUL JONES; JIMMY PAGE; ROBERT PLANT; THE FIRM.

Number	Title (A Side/B Side)	Yr	NM
45s			
ATLANTIC			
PR 157 [DJ]	Gallows Pole (mono/stereo)	1971	200.00
PR 175 [DJ]	Stairway to Heaven (mono/stereo)	1972	100.00
PR 175 [PS]	Stairway to Heaven (mono/stereo)	1972	250.00

Except when noted otherwise, VG = 25% of NM, and VG+ = 50% of NM. (Example: VG = $2.00, VG+ = $4.00 and NM = $8.00.)

Number	Title (A Side/B Side)	Yr	NM
❑ PR 269 [DJ]	Stairway to Heaven (stereo/stereo)	1973	50.00
❑ 2613	Communication Breakdown/ Good Times Bad Times	1969	25.00
❑ 2613	Communication Breakdown/ Good Times Bad Times	198?	8.00
—Later edition with Warner Communcations logo in perimeter print and a reference to "From Atlantic LP 19126 — 'Led Zeppelin'" at bottom, plus a "(P) 1969 Atlantic Recording Corp." underneath			
❑ 2690	Whole Lotta Love/Living Loving Maid (She's Just a Woman)	1969	15.00
—With A-side time of 3:12			
❑ 2690	Whole Lotta Love/Living Loving Maid (She's Just a Woman)	1969	20.00
—With A-side time of 5:33; no Warner Communications logo in perimeter print			
❑ 2690	Whole Lotta Love/Living Loving Maid (She's Just a Woman)	198?	8.00
—Later edition with Warner Communcations logo in perimeter print, "(P) 1969 Atlantic Recording Corp." at right and a reference to "From Atlantic LP 19127 — 'Led Zeppelin II'" at bottom			
❑ 2777 [DJ]	Immigrant Song	1970	120.00
—One-sided promo			
❑ 2777	Immigrant Song/Hey, Hey, What Can I Do	1970	25.00
—First pressings with "Do What Thou Wilt Shalt Be the Whole of the Law" in trail-off			
❑ 2777	Immigrant Song/Hey, Hey, What Can I Do	1971	15.00
—Second pressings without "Do What Thou Wilt Shalt Be the Whole of the Law" in trail-off; no Warner Commuications logo in perimeter print			
❑ 2777	Immigrant Song/Hey, Hey, What Can I Do	1977	8.00
—Third pressings with smaller, bolder type and Warner Communications logo in perimeter print; available well into the late 1980s			
❑ 2849	Black Dog/Misty Mountain Hop	1971	10.00
❑ 2865	Rock and Roll/Four Sticks	1972	10.00
—Label has "From Atlantc LP 7208" on label; no Warner Commuications logo in perimeter print			
❑ 2865	Rock and Roll/Four Sticks	198?	8.00
—Label has smaller, bolder type, "From Atlantic LP 19129 — 'Led Zeppelin'," and Warner Commuications logo in perimeter print			
❑ 2970	Over the Hills & Far Away/ Dancing Days	1973	10.00
❑ 2986	D'yer Mak'er/The Crunge	1973	6.00
—Defective pressing — the left channel starts to fade out midway through the A-side, making it sound like rechanneled stereo. The number "3" follows the matrix number in the trail-off wax of those copies we've encountered.			
❑ 2986	D'yer Mak'er/The Crunge	1973	10.00
—Normal pressing in true stereo throughout			

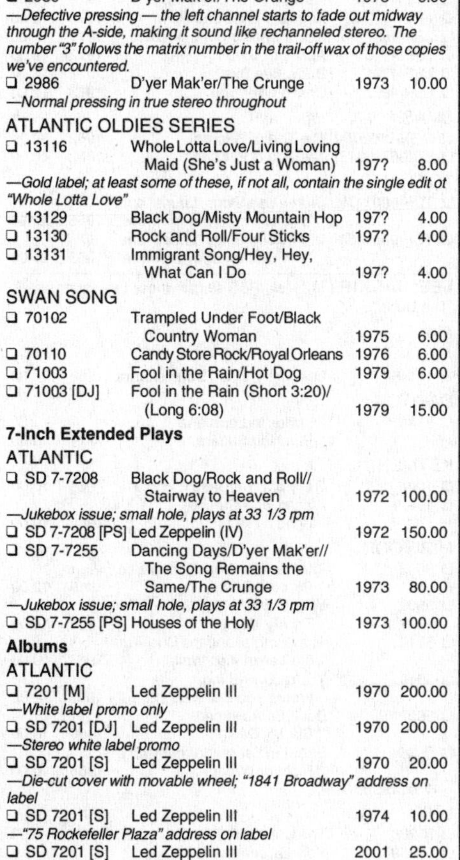

ATLANTIC OLDIES SERIES

Number	Title (A Side/B Side)	Yr	NM
❑ 13116	Whole Lotta Love/Living Loving Maid (She's Just a Woman)	197?	8.00
—Gold label; at least some of these, if not all, contain the single edit of "Whole Lotta Love"			
❑ 13129	Black Dog/Misty Mountain Hop	197?	4.00
❑ 13130	Rock and Roll/Four Sticks	197?	4.00
❑ 13131	Immigrant Song/Hey, Hey, What Can I Do	197?	4.00

SWAN SONG

Number	Title (A Side/B Side)	Yr	NM
❑ 70102	Trampled Under Foot/Black Country Woman	1975	6.00
❑ 70110	Candy Store Rock/Royal Orleans	1976	6.00
❑ 71003	Fool in the Rain/Hot Dog	1979	6.00
❑ 71003 [DJ]	Fool in the Rain (Short 3:20)/ (Long 6:08)	1979	15.00

7-Inch Extended Plays

ATLANTIC

Number	Title (A Side/B Side)	Yr	NM
❑ SD 7-7208	Black Dog/Rock and Roll// Stairway to Heaven	1972	100.00
—Jukebox issue; small hole, plays at 33 1/3 rpm			
❑ SD 7-7208 [PS]	Led Zeppelin (IV)	1972	150.00
❑ SD 7-7255	Dancing Days/D'yer Mak'er// The Song Remains the Same/The Crunge	1973	80.00
—Jukebox issue; small hole, plays at 33 1/3 rpm			
❑ SD 7-7255 [PS]	Houses of the Holy	1973	100.00

Albums

ATLANTIC

Number	Title (A Side/B Side)	Yr	NM
❑ 7201 [M]	Led Zeppelin III	1970	200.00
—White label promo only			
❑ SD 7201 [DJ]	Led Zeppelin III	1970	200.00
—Stereo white label promo			
❑ SD 7201 [S]	Led Zeppelin III	1970	20.00
—Die-cut cover with movable wheel; "1841 Broadway" address on label			
❑ SD 7201 [S]	Led Zeppelin III	1974	10.00
—"75 Rockefeller Plaza" address on label			
❑ SD 7201 [S]	Led Zeppelin III	2001	25.00
—Classic Records reissue on audioiphile vinyl			
❑ 7208 [M]	Led Zeppelin (IV) (Runes)	1971	300.00
—White label promo only			
❑ SD 7208 [DJ]	Led Zeppelin (IV) (Runes)	1971	150.00
—Stereo white label promo			
❑ SD 7208 [S]	Led Zeppelin (IV) (Runes)	1971	15.00
—"1841 Broadway" address on label			

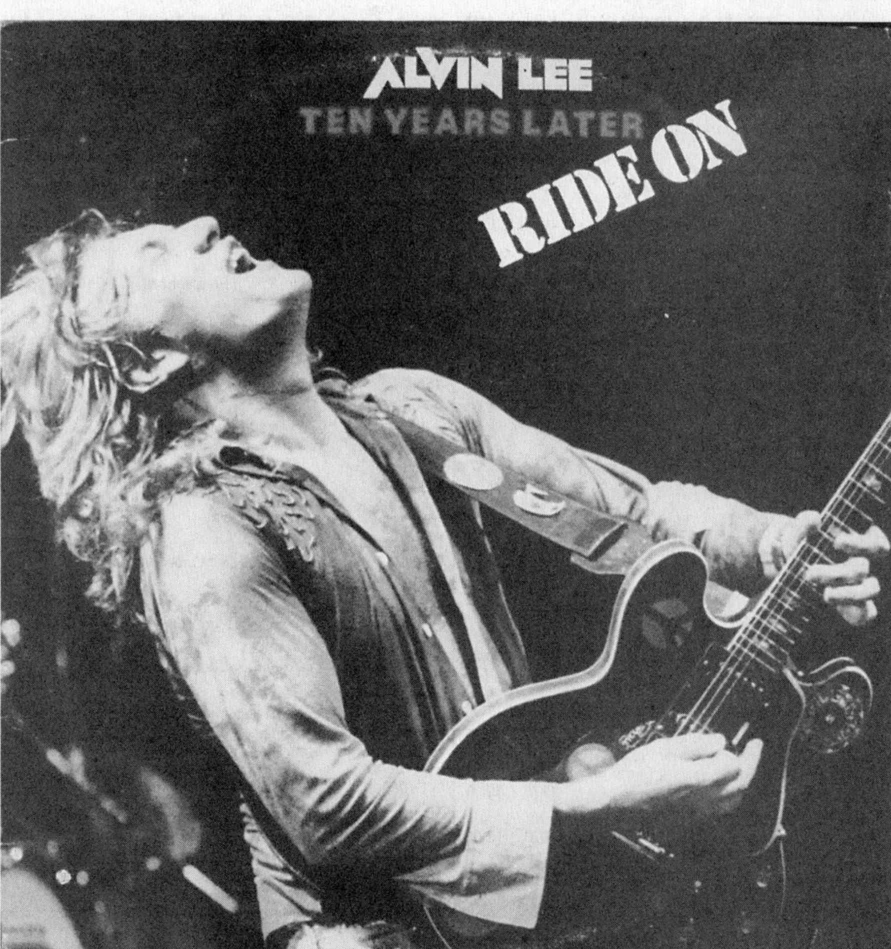

Alvin Lee, *Ride On*, RSO RS-1-3049, 1979, **$12.**

Number	Title (A Side/B Side)	Yr	NM
❑ SD 7208 [S]	Led Zeppelin (IV) (Runes)	1974	10.00
—"75 Rockefeller Plaza" address on label			
❑ SD 7208 [S]	Led Zeppelin (IV) (Runes)	2001	25.00
—Classic Records reissue on audioiphile vinyl			
❑ 7255 [M]	Houses of the Holy	1973	1000.
—White label promo only			
❑ SD 7255 [S]	Houses of the Holy	1973	15.00
—"1841 Broadway" address on label			
❑ SD 7255 [S]	Houses of the Holy	1974	10.00
—"75 Rockefeller Plaza" address on label			
❑ SD 7255 [S]	Houses of the Holy	2001	25.00
—Classic Records reissue on audiophile vinyl			
❑ 8216 [M]	Led Zeppelin	1969	400.00
—White label promo only			
❑ SD 8216 [DJ]	Led Zeppelin	1969	200.00
—Stereo white label promo			
❑ SD 8216 [S]	Led Zeppelin	1969	20.00
—"1841 Broadway" address on label			
❑ SD 8216 [S]	Led Zeppelin	1969	250.00
—Possible mispress with purple and brown labels			
❑ SD 8216 [S]	Led Zeppelin	1974	10.00
—"75 Rockefeller Plaza" address on label			
❑ SD 8216 [S]	Led Zeppelin	2000	25.00
—Classic Records reissue on audioiphile vinyl			
❑ 8236 [M]	Led Zeppelin II	1969	200.00
—White label promo only			
❑ SD 8236 [DJ]	Led Zeppelin II	1969	300.00
—Stereo white label promo			
❑ SD 8236 [S]	Led Zeppelin II	1969	20.00
—"1841 Broadway" address on label			
❑ SD 8236 [S]	Led Zeppelin II	1974	10.00
—"75 Rockefeller Plaza" address on label			
❑ SD 8236 [S]	Led Zeppelin II	2000	25.00
—Classic Records reissue on audioiphile vinyl			
❑ SD 19126	Led Zeppelin	1977	8.00
❑ SD 19127	Led Zeppelin II	1977	8.00
❑ SD 19128	Led Zeppelin III	1977	8.00
❑ SD 19129	Led Zeppelin (IV) (Runes)	1977	8.00
❑ SD 19130	Houses of the Holy	1977	8.00
❑ 82144 [(6)]	Led Zeppelin (Box Set)	1990	100.00
❑ 83061 [(4)]	BBC Sessions	2000	60.00
—Classic Records limited edition; each LP is in its own cardboard sleeve inside a box with a sheet of liner notes			
❑ 83268 [(2)]	Early Days: The Best of Led Zeppelin Vol. 1	1999	15.00
❑ 83278 [(2)]	Latter Days: The Best of Led Zeppelin Vol. 2	2000	15.00
❑ SMAS-94019	Led Zeppelin (IV) (Runes)	1972	40.00
—Capitol Record Club edition			

ATLANTIC CATALOGUE GROUP

Number	Title (A Side/B Side)	Yr	NM
❑ 344700	Mothership	2008	60.00
❑ 371900	The Song Remains the Same	2008	60.00

MOBILE FIDELITY

Number	Title (A Side/B Side)	Yr	NM
❑ 1-065	Led Zeppelin II	1981	100.00
—Audiophile vinyl			

SWAN SONG

Number	Title (A Side/B Side)	Yr	NM
❑ SS 2-200 [(2)]	Physical Graffiti	1975	20.00
❑ SS 2-200 [(2)]	Physical Graffiti	2002	40.00
—Classic Records reissue on audiophile vinyl			
❑ SS 2-201 [(2)]	The Song Remains the Same	1976	20.00
❑ SS 2-201 [(2)]	The Song Remains the Same	2003	40.00
—Classic Records edition on 200-gram vinyl			
❑ SS 8416	Presence	1976	15.00
❑ SS 8416	Presence	2002	25.00
—Classic Records reissue on audiophile vinyl			
❑ SS 16002	In Through the Out Door	1979	12.00
—Letter "B" on spine; add 50% if brown paper bag is still with jacket			
❑ SS 16002	In Through the Out Door	1979	12.00
—Letter "C" on spine; add 50% if brown paper bag is still with jacket			
❑ SS 16002	In Through the Out Door	1979	12.00
—Letter "D" on spine; add 50% if brown paper bag is still with jacket			
❑ SS 16002	In Through the Out Door	1979	12.00
—Letter "E" on spine; add 50% if brown paper bag is still with jacket			
❑ SS 16002	In Through the Out Door	1979	12.00
—Letter "F" on spine; add 50% if brown paper bag is still with jacket			
❑ SS 16002	In Through the Out Door	1979	12.00
—Letter "A" on spine; add 50% if brown paper bag is still with jacket			
❑ SS 16002	In Through the Out Door	2003	30.00
—Classic Records reissue on 200-gram vinyl; contains a 12-page insert with all six covers; we don't know if the label actually pressed these with six different covers			
❑ 90051	Coda	1982	14.00

LEE See LEE MARENO.

LEE, ALVIN Also see TEN YEARS AFTER.

12-Inch Singles

21 RECORDS

Number	Title (A Side/B Side)	Yr	NM
❑ PR 918 [DJ]	Detroit Diesel (same on both sides)	1986	6.00
❑ PR 956 [DJ]	Shot in the Dark (same on both sides)	1986	6.00

45s

ATLANTIC

Number	Title (A Side/B Side)	Yr	NM
❑ 3792 [DJ]	Ridin' Truckin' (same on both sides)	1981	4.00
—May be promo only			
❑ 4004 [DJ]	Can't Stop (same on both sides)	1982	4.00
—May be promo only			

COLUMBIA

Number	Title (A Side/B Side)	Yr	NM
❑ 45987	So Sad/Riffin'	1974	4.00
—With Mylon LeFevre			

RSO

Number	Title (A Side/B Side)	Yr	NM
❑ 936	Ride On Cowboy/Can't Sleep at Night	1979	4.00
—With "Ten Years Later"			

21 RECORDS

Number	Title (A Side/B Side)	Yr	NM
❑ 99501	Heart of Stone/She's So Cute	1986	3.00
❑ 99527	Detroit Diesel/Let's Go	1986	3.00

Albums

ATLANTIC

Number	Title (A Side/B Side)	Yr	NM
❑ SD 19287	Free Fall	1980	10.00
❑ SD 19306	RX5	1981	10.00

COLUMBIA

Number	Title (A Side/B Side)	Yr	NM
❑ KC 32729	On the Road to Freedom	1973	12.00
—With Mylon LeFevre			
❑ PC 32729	On the Road to Freedom	197?	8.00
—With Mylon LeFevre; reissue with new prefix			
❑ PG 33187 [(2)]	In Flight	1974	15.00
❑ PC 33796	Pump Iron!	1975	12.00

RSO

Number	Title (A Side/B Side)	Yr	NM
❑ RS-1-3033	Rocket Fuel	1978	12.00
—With "Ten Years Later"			
❑ RS-1-3049	Ride On	1979	12.00
—With "Ten Years Later"			

21 RECORDS

Number	Title (A Side/B Side)	Yr	NM
❑ 90517	Detroit Diesel	1986	10.00

LEE, ARTHUR Also see LOVE.

45s

A&M

Number	Title (A Side/B Side)	Yr	NM
❑ 1361	Everybody's Gotta Live/Love Jumped Through My Window	1972	4.00
❑ 1381	Sad Song/You Want Change for Your Re-Run	1972	4.00

CAPITOL

Number	Title (A Side/B Side)	Yr	NM
❑ 4980	Ninth Wave/Rumble Still Skins	1963	30.00

Albums

A&M

Number	Title (A Side/B Side)	Yr	NM
❑ SP-4356	Vindicator	1972	30.00

RHINO

Number	Title (A Side/B Side)	Yr	NM
❑ RNLP 020	Arthur Lee	1981	10.00

LEE, BILLY, AND THE RIVIERAS Early version of MITCH RYDER AND THE DETROIT WHEELS.

45s

HYLAND

Number	Title (A Side/B Side)	Yr	NM
❑ 3016	Won't You Dance with Me/You Know	1964	25.00

LEE, CURTIS Also see C.L. AND THE PICTURES.

45s

DUNES

Number	Title (A Side/B Side)	Yr	NM
❑ 801	California GH-903/Then I'll Know	1960	20.00
❑ 2001	Special Love/"D" in Love	1960	20.00
❑ 2003	Pledge of Love/Then I'll Know	1961	20.00
❑ 2003 [PS]	Pledge of Love/Then I'll Know	1961	25.00
❑ 2007	Pretty Little Angel Eyes/Gee, How I Wish You Were Here	1961	25.00
❑ 2008	Under the Moon of Love/Beverly Jean	1961	25.00
—2007 and 2008 were Phil Spector productions			
❑ 2012	Just Another Fool/A Night at Daddy Gee's	1962	20.00
❑ 2015	Does He Mean That Much to You/The Wobble	1962	20.00
❑ 2020	Lonely Weekends/Better Him Than Me	1963	20.00
❑ 2021	Pickin' Up the Pieces of My Heart/Mr. Mistaker	1963	20.00

HOT

Number	Title (A Side/B Side)	Yr	NM
❑ 7	I Never Knew What Love Could Do/Gotta Have You	1960	75.00

LOST-NITE

Number	Title (A Side/B Side)	Yr	NM
❑ 217	Pretty Little Angel Eyes/Gee, How I Wish You Were Here	196?	5.00
—Reissue			

MIRA

Number	Title (A Side/B Side)	Yr	NM
❑ 240	Sweet Baby/Is She In Your Town	1967	20.00

ROJAC

Number	Title (A Side/B Side)	Yr	NM
❑ 114	Get In My Bag/Everybody's Going Wild	1967	12.00

SABRA

Number	Title (A Side/B Side)	Yr	NM
❑ 517	Let's Take a Ride/I'm Asking Forgiveness	1960	25.00

WARRIOR

Number	Title (A Side/B Side)	Yr	NM
❑ 1555	With All My Heart/Pure Love	1959	30.00

LEE, DICKEY

45s

ATCO

Number	Title (A Side/B Side)	Yr	NM
❑ 6546	Run Right Back/Red, Green, Yellow, Blue	1968	8.00
❑ 6580	All My Life/Hang-Ups	1968	8.00
❑ 6609	You're Young and You'll Forget/Waitin' for Love to Come My Way	1968	8.00

DIAMOND

Number	Title (A Side/B Side)	Yr	NM
❑ 266	Ruby Baby/I Remember Barbara	1969	8.00

DOT

Number	Title (A Side/B Side)	Yr	NM
❑ 16087	Life in a Teenage World/Why Don't You Write On	1960	15.00

HALLWAY

Number	Title (A Side/B Side)	Yr	NM
❑ 1924	Big Brother/She's Walking Away	1964	10.00

MERCURY

Number	Title (A Side/B Side)	Yr	NM
❑ 55068	I'm Just a Heartache Away/Midnight Flyer	1979	4.00
❑ 57005	He's an Old Rock 'N' Roller/It Hurts to Be in Love	1979	4.00
❑ 57017	Don't Look Back/I'm Trustin' a Feelin'	1980	4.00
❑ 57027	Workin' My Way to Your Heart/If You Want Me	1980	4.00
❑ 57036	Lost in Love/Again	1980	4.00
—A-side with Kathy Burdick			
❑ 57052	Honky Tonk Hearts/Best I Hit the Road	1981	4.00
❑ 57056	I Wonder If I Care As Much/Further Than a Country Mile	1981	4.00
❑ 76129	Everybody Loves a Winner/You Won't Be Here Tonight	1982	4.00

RCA

Number	Title (A Side/B Side)	Yr	NM
❑ PB-10764	9,999,999 Tears/I Never Will Get Over You	1976	4.00
❑ PB-10914	If You Gotta Make a Fool of Somebody/My Love Shows Thru	1977	4.00
❑ GB-10929	Rocky/9,999,999 Tears	1977	3.00
—Gold Standard Series			
❑ PB-11009	Virginia, How Far Will You Go/My Love Shows Thru	1977	4.00
❑ PB-11125	Peanut Butter/Breezy Was Her Name	1977	4.00
❑ PB-11191	Love Is a Word/I'll Be Leaving Alone	1978	4.00
❑ PB-11294	My Heart Won't Cry Anymore/Danna	1978	4.00
❑ PB-11389	It's Not Easy/I've Been Honky-Tonkin' Too Long	1978	4.00

RCA VICTOR

Number	Title (A Side/B Side)	Yr	NM
❑ 47-9862	All Too Soon/Charlie	1970	6.00
❑ 47-9941	Home To/Special	1971	6.00
❑ 47-9988	The Mahogany Pulpit/Everybody's Reaching Out for Someone	1971	6.00
❑ 48-1013	Never Ending Song of Love/On the Southbound	1971	6.00
❑ 74-0623	I Saw My Lady/What We Used to Hang On To	1971	6.00
❑ 74-0710	Ashes of Love/The Kingdom I Call Home	1972	5.00
❑ 74-0798	Baby, Bye Bye/She Thinks I Still Care	1972	5.00
❑ 74-0892	Crying Over You/My World Around You	1973	5.00
❑ 74-0980	Put Me Down Softly/If She Turns Up in Atlanta	1973	5.00
❑ APBO-0082	Sparklin' Brown Eyes/Country Song	1973	5.00
❑ APBO-0227	I Use the Soap/Strawberry Women	1974	5.00
❑ PB-10014	Give Me One Good Reason/Sweet Fever	1974	5.00
❑ PB-10091	The Busiest Memory in Town/Way to Go On	1974	5.00
❑ PB-10289	You Make It Look So Easy/The Door's Always Open	1975	4.00
❑ PB-10361	Rocky/The Closest Thing to You	1975	4.00
❑ PB-10543	Angels, Roses and Rain/Danna	1976	4.00
❑ PB-10684	Makin' Love Don't Always Make Love Grow/I Never Will Get Over You	1976	4.00

RENDEZVOUS

Number	Title (A Side/B Side)	Yr	NM
❑ 188	Dream Boy/Stay True Baby	1962	25.00

SMASH

Number	Title (A Side/B Side)	Yr	NM
❑ 1758	Patches/More or Less	1962	15.00
❑ 1791	I Saw Linda Yesterday/The Girl I Can't Forget	1962	12.00
❑ 1808	Don't Wanna Talk About Paula/Just a Friend	1963	12.00
❑ 1822	I Go Lonely/Ten Million Faces	1963	12.00
❑ 1844	She Wants to Be Bobby's Girl/The Day the Sawmill Closed Down	1963	12.00
❑ 1871	To the Aisle/Mother Nature	1964	12.00
❑ 1913	Me and My Teardrops/Only Trust in Me	1964	12.00

SUN

Number	Title (A Side/B Side)	Yr	NM
❑ 280	Good Lovin'/Memories Never Grow Old	1957	30.00
❑ 297	Dreamy Nights/Fool, Fool, Fool	1958	80.00

TAMPA

Number	Title (A Side/B Side)	Yr	NM
❑ 131	Dream Boy/Stay True Baby	1957	30.00

TCF HALL

Number	Title (A Side/B Side)	Yr	NM
❑ 102	Laurie (Strange Things Happen)/Party Doll	1965	10.00
❑ 111	The Girl from Peyton Place/The Girl I Used to Know	1965	10.00
❑ 118	Good Girl Goin' Bad/Pretty White Dress	1965	10.00
❑ 128	Good Guy/Annie	1966	10.00

Albums

MERCURY

Number	Title (A Side/B Side)	Yr	NM
❑ SRM-1-5020	Dickey Lee	1979	10.00
❑ SRM-1-5026	Dickey Lee Again	1980	10.00

RCA VICTOR

Number	Title (A Side/B Side)	Yr	NM
❑ APL1-0311	Sparklin' Brown Eyes	1974	12.00
❑ APL1-1243	Rocky	1975	12.00
❑ APL1-1725	Angels, Roses and Rain	1976	12.00
❑ LSP-4637	Never Ending Song of Love	1971	12.00
❑ LSP-4715	Ashes of Love	1972	12.00
❑ LSP-4791	Baby, Bye Bye	1972	12.00
❑ LSP-4857	Crying Over You	1973	12.00

SMASH

Number	Title (A Side/B Side)	Yr	NM
❑ MGS-27020 [M]	The Tale of Patches	1962	30.00
❑ SRS-67020 [S]	The Tale of Patches	1962	40.00

TCF HALL

Number	Title (A Side/B Side)	Yr	NM
❑ TCF-8001 [M]	Dickey Lee Sings "Laurie" and "The Girl from Peyton Place"	1965	20.00
❑ TCF-9001 [S]	Dickey Lee Sings "Laurie" and "The Girl from Peyton Place"	1965	25.00

LEE, JACKIE (1) Male R&B singer whose biggest hit was "The Duck."

45s

ABC

Number	Title (A Side/B Side)	Yr	NM
❑ 11146	One for the Road/Darkest Days	1968	20.00

CAPITOL

Number	Title (A Side/B Side)	Yr	NM
❑ 3145	25 Miles to Louisiana/Pershing Square	1971	6.00

KEYMEN

Number	Title (A Side/B Side)	Yr	NM
❑ 109	Glory of Love/Bring It Home	1968	10.00
❑ 114	African Boo-Ga-Loo/Bring It Home	1968	10.00

MIRWOOD

Number	Title (A Side/B Side)	Yr	NM
❑ 5502	The Duck/Let Your Conscience Be Your Guide	1965	12.00
❑ 5509	Your P-E-R-S-O-N-A-L-I-T-Y/Try My Method	1966	10.00
❑ 5510	The Shotgun and the Duck/Do the Temptation Walk	1966	10.00
❑ 5519	You're Everything/Would You Believe	1966	10.00
❑ 5527	Don't Be Ashamed/Oh, My Darlin'	1966	10.00
❑ 5528	Baby I'm Satisfied/Whether It's Right or Wrong	1966	10.00
—With Dolores Hall			

UNI

Number	Title (A Side/B Side)	Yr	NM
❑ 55206	The Chicken/I Love You	1970	8.00
❑ 55259	Your Sweetness Is My Weakness/You Were Searching for a Love	1970	8.00

Albums

MIRWOOD

Number	Title (A Side/B Side)	Yr	NM
❑ MW-7000 [M]	The Duck	1966	20.00
❑ SW-7000 [S]	The Duck	1966	25.00

Except when noted otherwise, VG = 25% of NM, and VG+ = 50% of NM. (Example: VG = $2.00, VG+ = $4.00 and NM = $8.00.)

LEE, JACKIE (2) Phialdelphia-based keyboard player.

45s

Number	Title (A Side/B Side)	Yr	NM
ABC-PARAMOUNT			
❑ 9892	The Storm/Bye Bye Blues	1958	10.00
CORAL			
❑ 61214	The Donkey Serenade/Mr. Hot Piano	1954	12.00
❑ 61259	Bei Mir Bist Du Schoen/Missouri Waltz	1954	12.00
❑ 61304	I Can't Give You Anything But Love/Blue Boogie	1954	12.00
❑ 61400	Chop Sticks/Luigi's Wedding	1955	12.00
❑ 61461	Cannibal King/The Spoon Song	1955	12.00
❑ 61534	Aloha Oe/More, More, More	1955	12.00
❑ 61579	A String of Pearls/Always Love Me	1956	10.00
❑ 61638	Crazy Polka/Elmer's Tune	1956	10.00
❑ 61734	Chatterbox/Dardanella	1956	10.00
❑ 61827	Baby Buggy Boogie/Sippin' Soda	1957	10.00
SURE			
❑ 1005	Bongo Shuffle Boogie/Isle of Capri Boogie	196?	12.00
❑ 1738	Do the New Hully Gully/Patricia	1962	10.00
❑ 1767	Hungarian Rhapsody Boogie/Bumpy	1962	10.00
SWAN			
❑ 4034	Happy Vacation/The Hucklebuck	1959	12.00
❑ 4039	Like Sunset/Rancho	1959	12.00

LEE, JACKIE (3) Female singer.

45s

Number	Title (A Side/B Side)	Yr	NM
EPIC			
❑ 9807	I Cry Alone/'Cause I Love Him	1965	10.00
❑ 10183	Love Is Gone/The Lonely Clown	1967	8.00

LEE, JACKIE, AND THE RAINDROPS

45s

Number	Title (A Side/B Side)	Yr	NM
LONDON INT'L.			
❑ 10602	The Last One to Know/There's No One in the Whole Wide World	1962	12.00

LEE, JENNY, AND THE STARLETS

45s

Number	Title (A Side/B Side)	Yr	NM
CONGRESS			
❑ 107	What I Gotta Do/Show Me a Man	1962	75.00

LEE, JOHNNY For records on DeLuxe, see JOHN LEE HOOKER.

LEE, JULIA

45s

Number	Title (A Side/B Side)	Yr	NM
CAPITOL			
❑ F838	Ain't It a Crime/Don't Save It Too Long	1950	40.00
—Note: Julia Lee singles before 838 are unknown on 45 rpm			
❑ F956	Do You Want It/Decent Woman Blues	1950	40.00
❑ F1009	There Goes My Heart/Nobody Knows You When You're Down and Out	1950	40.00
❑ F1111	My Man Stands Out/Don't Come Too Soon	1950	50.00
❑ F1149	Pagan Love Song/I'm Forever Blowing Bubbles	1950	50.00
❑ F1252	It Won't Be Long/Bleeding Hearted Blues	1950	40.00
❑ F1376	Lotus Blossom/Pipe Dreams	1951	30.00
❑ F1432	Ugly Papa/I Know It's Wrong	1951	30.00
❑ F1589	Mama Don't Allow It/The Breeze	1951	30.00
❑ F1798	Scream in the Night/If You Hadn't Gone Away	1951	30.00
❑ F1896	Charmaine/Out in the Cold Again	1951	30.00
Albums			
CAPITOL			
❑ H 228 [10]	Party Time	1950	120.00
❑ T 228 [M]	Party Time	195?	80.00

LEE, LAURA

12-Inch Singles

Number	Title (A Side/B Side)	Yr	NM
FANTASY			
❑ D-133	Sat-Is-Fac-Tion (6:20)/Your Song	1979	12.00
45s			
ARIOLA AMERICA			
❑ 7652	Love's Got Me Tired (But I Ain't Tired of Love)/You're Barking Up the Wrong Tree	1976	5.00
CHESS			
❑ 1989	Stop Giving Your Man Away/You Need Me	1967	12.00
❑ 2013	Dirty Man/It's Mighty Hard	1967	10.00
❑ 2030	Wanted: Lover, No Experience Necessary/Up Tight, Good Man	1967	10.00
❑ 2041	As Long As I Got You/A Man with Some Backbone	1968	10.00
❑ 2052	Need to Belong/He Will Break Your Heart	1968	10.00
❑ 2062	Hang It Up/It's How You Make It Good	1968	10.00
❑ 2068	Mama's Got a Good Thing/Love More Than Pride	1969	10.00
COTILLION			
❑ 44054	What a Man/Separation Line	1970	8.00
❑ 44073	Together/But You Know I Love You	1970	8.00
FANTASY			
❑ 865	Sat-Is-Fac-Tion/Your Song	1979	5.00
HOT WAX			
❑ 7007	Wedlock Is a Padlock/Her Picture Matches Mine	1970	8.00
❑ 7105	Women's Love Rights/Her Picture Matches Mine	1971	8.00
❑ 7111	Love and Liberty/I Don't Want Nothing Old But Money	1971	8.00
❑ 7201	Since I Fell for You/I Don't Want Nothing Old But Money	1972	7.00
❑ 7204	Rip Off/Two Lovely Pillows	1972	7.00
❑ 7207	If You Can Beat Me Rockin' (You Can Have My Chair)/If I'm Good Enough to Love	1972	7.00
❑ 7210	Crumbs Off the Table/You've Got to Save Me	1972	7.00
❑ 7302	(If You Want to Try Love Again) Remember Me/If I'm Good Enough to Love	1973	7.00
❑ 7305	I'll Catch You When You Fall/I Can't Hold On Much Longer	1973	7.00
INVICTUS			
❑ 1264	I Need It Just As Bad As You/If I'm Good Enough to Love	1974	6.00
❑ 1273	Don't Leave Me Starving for Your Love/Remember Me	1974	6.00
RIC-TIC			
❑ 111	To Win Your Heart/So Will I	1966	15.00
Albums			
CHESS			
❑ CH-50031	Love More Than Pride	1972	20.00
HOT WAX			
❑ HA-708	Women's Love Rights	1971	15.00
❑ HA-714	Laura Lee	1972	15.00
❑ HA-715	The Best of Laura Lee	1973	15.00
INVICTUS			
❑ KZ 33133	Laura Lee	1974	10.00

LEE, LES

LEE, LONDON

45s

Number	Title (A Side/B Side)	Yr	NM
AMERAMA			
❑ 5009	Roots of Glory/You're So Ugly	1978	6.00
MR. G			
❑ 802	Junkyard in the Sky/I Love You	1967	10.00
PHILIPS			
❑ PEP-1 [DJ]	Monologue 1/Monologue 2	1969	8.00
UNITED ARTISTS			
❑ 877	Who Is London Lee/Mutiny	1965	12.00
Albums			
PHILIPS			
❑ PHS 600322	The Rich Kid	1969	15.00

LEE, MICHELE

45s

Number	Title (A Side/B Side)	Yr	NM
ABC-PARAMOUNT			
❑ 10365	I'm Sorry Missus Murray (But I Cannot Baby-Sit for You Tonight)/Havin' a Party for One	1962	15.00
❑ 10365 [PS]	I'm Sorry Missus Murray (But I Cannot Baby-Sit for You Tonight)/Havin' a Party for One	1962	30.00
❑ 10411	He's Not Good Enough for You/I See It All Now	1963	15.00
COLUMBIA			
❑ 4-43288	Pretty Lies, Pretty Make Believe/Somewhere in the World	1965	8.00
❑ 4-43376	Call Me/You Were There	1965	8.00
❑ 4-43476	Feeling Good/Steady, Steady	1965	8.00
❑ 4-43575	Laugh, Clown, Laugh/I'll Never Go There Anymore	1966	8.00
❑ 4-43923	If You Go Away/Wednesday's Child	1966	8.00
❑ 4-44165	Being Good Isn't Good Enough/I Believe in You	1967	8.00
❑ 4-44413	L. David Sloane/Everybody Loves My Baby (But My Baby Don't Love Nobody But Me)	1967	8.00
❑ 4-44554	I Can't Believe I'm Losing You/I Didn't Come to New York to Meet a Guy from My Home Town	1968	8.00
❑ 4-44698	Knowing When to Leave/The Look of Love	1968	8.00
❑ 4-44835	It's a Long Way to Fall/You'll Remember Me	1969	6.00
Albums			
COLUMBIA			
❑ CL 2486 [M]	A Taste of the Fantastic	1966	15.00
❑ CS 9286 [S]	A Taste of the Fantastic	1966	20.00
❑ CS 9682	L. David Sloane and Other Hits of Today	1968	20.00

LEE AND THE LEOPARDS

45s

Number	Title (A Side/B Side)	Yr	NM
FORTUNE			
❑ 867	What About Me/Don't Press Your Luck	1964	50.00
GORDY			
❑ 7002	Come Into My Palace/Trying to Make It	1962	60.00
LAURIE			
❑ 3197	Come Into My Palace/Trying to Make It	1963	25.00

LEFEVRE, RAYMOND

45s

Number	Title (A Side/B Side)	Yr	NM
ATLANTIC			
❑ 2093	Come Softly to Me/Havah Nagilah	1961	10.00
BUDDAH			
❑ 269	Mammy Blue/What Have They Done to My Song, Ma	1971	5.00
4 CORNERS OF THE WORLD			
❑ 142	When a Man Loves a Woman/Black Is Black	1967	5.00
❑ 145	Groovin'/A Whiter Shade of Pale	1967	5.00
❑ 147	Ame Caline (Soul Coaxing)/If I Were a Carpenter	1968	5.00
❑ 149	La, La, La (He Gives Me Love)/C'est La Rose	1968	5.00
❑ 151	Delilah/If I Only Had Time	1968	5.00
JAMIE			
❑ 1161	Never on Sunday/Sleepy Time	1960	10.00
❑ 1171	Rendezvous/The Right Girl on the Left Bank	1960	10.00
KAPP			
❑ 231	The Day the Rains Came/Butterfingers	1958	10.00
❑ 279	You Are My Destiny/Le Belle Helene	1959	10.00
❑ 766	You Don't Have to Say You Love Me/La Boheme	1966	6.00
❑ 809	Spanish Eyes/Stars of the Way	1967	6.00
❑ AS-949 [DJ]	Silver Bells (mono/stereo)	196?	8.00
MERCURY			
❑ 71599	What Good Does It Do Me/(Instrumental)	1960	10.00
VERVE			
❑ 10263	Come Une Symphonie/Un Voms Vivo	1962	8.00
Albums			
ATLANTIC			
❑ 8044 [M]	Romantica	1961	20.00
❑ SD 8044 [S]	Romantica	1961	25.00
BUDDAH			
❑ BDS-5095	Raymond Lefevre	1971	10.00
❑ BDS-5109	Oh Happy Day	1972	10.00
4 CORNERS OF THE WORLD			
❑ FCL-4239 [M]	Love Me, Please Love Me	1967	12.00
❑ FCS-4239 [S]	Love Me, Please Love Me	1967	12.00
❑ FCS-4244	Soal Coaxing (Ame Caline)	1968	12.00
❑ FCS-4250	La La La (He Gives Me Love)	1968	12.00
❑ FCS-4257	Merry Christmas	1968	12.00
KAPP			
❑ KL-1510 [M]	You Don't Have to Stay	1967	15.00
❑ KS-3510 [S]	You Don't Have to Stay	1967	12.00
MONUMENT			
❑ MLP-8067 [M]	Paris Cancan	1967	15.00
❑ SLP-18067 [S]	Paris Cancan	1967	12.00

L

LEFT BANKE, THE

45s

Number	Title (A Side/B Side)	Yr	NM
CAMERICA			
❑ 005	Queen of Paradise/And One Day	1978	5.00
SMASH			
❑ 2041	Walk Away Renee/ I Haven't Got the Nerve	1966	15.00
❑ 2074	Pretty Ballerina/Lazy Day	1966	15.00
❑ 2089	Ivy, Ivy/And Suddenly	1967	12.00
❑ 2097	She May Call You Up Tonight/ Barterers and Their Wives	1967	12.00
❑ 2119	Desiree/I've Got Something on My Mind	1967	12.00
❑ 2119 [PS]	Desiree/I've Got Something on My Mind	1967	25.00
❑ 2165	Dark Is the Bark/My Friend Today	1968	12.00
❑ 2198	Goodbye Holly/Sing, Little Bird, Sing	1968	12.00
❑ 2209	Bryant Hotel/Give the Man a Hand	1969	12.00
❑ 2243	Myrah/Pedestal	1969	40.00
—Picture sleeves are bootlegs			

Albums

Number	Title (A Side/B Side)	Yr	NM
RHINO			
❑ RNLP-123	History of the Left Banke	1985	10.00
SMASH			
❑ MGS-27088 [M]	Walk Away Renee/ Pretty Ballerina	1967	40.00
❑ SRS-67088	Walk Away Renee/ Pretty Ballerina	198?	10.00
—Reissue with thinner vinyl			
❑ SRS-67088 [S]	Walk Away Renee/Pretty Ballerina	1967	40.00
❑ SRS-67113	The Left Banke, Too	1968	50.00

LEGENDARY MASKED SURFERS, THE

45s

Number	Title (A Side/B Side)	Yr	NM
UNITED ARTISTS			
❑ XW270	Summer Means Fun/ Gonna Hustle You	1973	20.00
—Original pressings have a Jan & Dean recording on them by mistake			
❑ XW270	Summer Means Fun/ Gonna Hustle You	1973	120.00
—With the intended recording, a newly-recorded vocal track			
❑ XW270 [PS]	Summer Means Fun/ Gonna Hustle You	1973	30.00
❑ 50958	Summertime, Summertime/ Gonna Hustle You	1972	30.00

LEGENDARY STARDUST COWBOY, THE

45s

Number	Title (A Side/B Side)	Yr	NM
MERCURY			
❑ 72862	Paralyzed/Who's Knocking on My Door	1968	20.00
❑ 72891	Down in the Wrecking Yard/ I Took a Trip on a Gemini Spaceship	1969	20.00
❑ 72912	Everything's Getting Bigger But Our Love/Kiss and Run	1969	20.00
NORTON			
❑ 012	I Hate CD's/Linda	199?	2.00
❑ 012 [PS]	I Hate CD's/Linda	199?	2.00
PSYCHO-SUAVE			
❑ 1033	Paralyzed/Who's Knocking on My Door	1968	30.00

LEGENDS, THE

Several different groups.

45s

Number	Title (A Side/B Side)	Yr	NM
BRIDGE SOCIETY			
❑ 2204	Keep On Running/Cheating	1968	40.00
CALDWELL			
❑ 410	Go Away with Me/Jungle Lullaby	1962	25.00
CAPITOL			
❑ 5014	Summertime Blues/ Run to the Movies	1963	20.00
COLUMBIA			
❑ 41949	Theme from "Exodus"/Later	1961	12.00
DOC HOLLIDAY			
❑ 107	Surf's Up/Dance with the Drummer Man	1963	40.00
❑ 107 [PS]	Surf's Up/Dance with the Drummer Man	1963	50.00
EPIC			
❑ 10937	Rock and Roll Woman/Problems	1973	8.00
ERMINE			
❑ 39	My Love for You/Say Mama	1962	50.00
❑ 41	Lariat/Late Train	1962	40.00
❑ 43	Bop-A-Lena/I Wish I Knew	1962	50.00
❑ 45	Temptation/Marionette	1962	40.00
HART-VAN			
❑ 18003	Traction/As Long As I Live	1962	30.00
HEART			
❑ 7672	Rock and Roll Woman/Problems	1972	20.00
HULL			
❑ 727	The Legend of Love/ Now I'm Telling You	1958	100.00
—Red label			
❑ 727	The Legend of Love/ Now I'm Telling You	1962	30.00
—Multicolor label			
JAMIE			
❑ 1228	Tell the Truth/You'll Never See the Forest	1962	20.00
KEY			
❑ 1002	Lariat/Gail	1961	40.00
❑ 1002	Lariat/Late Train	1961	40.00
MELBA			
❑ 109	I'll Never Fall in Love Again/ Eyes of an Angel	1957	150.00
—Label with double horizontal lines			
❑ 109	I'll Never Fall in Love Again/ Eyes of an Angel	1961	40.00
—Label with no horizontal lines			
PARROT			
❑ 45010	Just in Case/If I Only Had Her Back	1965	12.00
❑ 45011	Alright/How Can I Find Her	1965	12.00
RAILROAD HOUSE			
❑ 12003	High Towers/Fever Games	1969	20.00
❑ 12003 [PS]	High Towers/Fever Games	1969	30.00
THAMES			
❑ 104	Raining in My Heart/ (B-side unknown)	1964	30.00
UP			
❑ 2202	Baby, Get Your Head Screwed On/Why	1968	50.00
WARNER BROS.			
❑ 5457	Here Comes the Rain/ Don't Be Ashamed	1964	15.00

Albums

Number	Title (A Side/B Side)	Yr	NM
CAPITOL			
❑ ST 1925 [S]	The Legends Let Loose	1963	80.00
❑ T 1925 [M]	The Legends Let Loose	1963	60.00
COLUMBIA			
❑ CL 1707 [M]	Hit Sounds of Today's Smash Hit Combos	1961	30.00
❑ CS 8507 [S]	Hit Sounds of Today's Smash Hit Combos	1961	40.00
ERMINE			
❑ LP-101 [M]	The Legends Let Loose	1963	200.00

LEGRAND, MICHEL

45s

Number	Title (A Side/B Side)	Yr	NM
BELL			
❑ 45118	The Summer Knows/I Will Say Goodbye	1971	5.00
❑ 45171	Brian's Song/Theme from "The Go-Between"	1972	5.00
❑ 45215	Jesus Christ Superstar-Day by Day/Amy's Theme	1972	5.00
COLUMBIA			
❑ 40661	Under Paris Skies/ Merry-Go-Round	1956	12.00
❑ 40692	Smile/Bon Jour, Paris	1956	12.00
❑ 40732	Love Theme from "La Strada"/ Paris Canaille	1956	12.00
❑ 40751	Friendly Persuasion/ Lovers and Lollipops	1956	12.00
❑ 41312	Cheek to Cheek/Only You	1958	10.00
DECCA			
❑ 32287	Pretty Polly/The Race Is to the Swift	1968	6.00
MCA			
❑ 40160	Walking on the Beach/ Breezy's Song	1973	4.00
❑ 40523	Gable and Lombard Love Theme/I Can't Give You Anything But Love, Baby	1976	4.00
MGM			
❑ 13816	Tara's Theme (Part 1)/ Tara's Theme (Part 2)	1967	6.00
❑ 13816	Tara's Theme (Part 1)/ Theme from Orfell Negro	1967	6.00
❑ 13894	Love Theme from "Elvira Madigan"/Melange	1968	6.00
PHILIPS			
❑ 40098	Love Is a Ball/Millie's Theme	1963	8.00
❑ 40188	Monkey Business/Come Ray or Come Charles	1964	8.00
❑ 40257	Love Theme from Parapailies de Cherbourg/Garage Scene	1965	8.00
❑ 40357	I Will Wait for You/Melody from the Stars	1966	8.00
RCA VICTOR			
❑ PB-10234	Blue, Green, Gray and Gone/ Brian's Song	1975	4.00
20TH CENTURY			
❑ 2346	The Other Side of Midnight (Noelle's Theme)/ Drive to Demeris	1977	4.00
UNITED ARTISTS			
❑ 50618	What Are You Doing the Rest of Your Life/Floating Time	1969	7.00
❑ 50662	What Are You Doing the Rest of Your Life (English)/What Are You Doing the Rest of Your Life (French)	1970	6.00
WARNER BROS.			
❑ 7486	Theme from "Summer of '42"/ Summer Song	1971	5.00

7-Inch Extended Plays

Number	Title (A Side/B Side)	Yr	NM
COLUMBIA			
❑ B-441 [PS]	I Love Paris, Vol. I	195?	12.00
—Cover for 2-EP set (5-1944, 5-1945)			
❑ 5-1944	I Love Paris/Mademoiselle de Paris//Paris in the Spring/ Paris Canaille	195?	10.00
—Alternate numbers are "B-441-1" and "B-441-4"			
❑ 5-1945	Paris/Autumn Leaves//Under the Bridges of Paris (Sous les ponts de Paris)/La Seine	195?	10.00
—Alternate numbers are "B-441-2" and "B-441-3"			
❑ B-2554	*I Love Paris/April in Paris/ La Vie En Rose/The Last Time I Saw Paris	195?	10.00
❑ B-2554 [PS]	Michel Legrand (Hall of Fame Series)	195?	10.00

Albums

Number	Title (A Side/B Side)	Yr	NM
BELL			
❑ 4200 [(2)]	Twenty Songs of the Century	1974	12.00
❑ 6071	Brian's Song Themes & Variations	1972	10.00
COLUMBIA			
❑ CL 555 [M]	I Love Paris	1954	40.00
❑ CL 647 [M]	Holiday in Rome	1955	25.00
❑ CL 706 [M]	Vienna Holiday	1955	25.00
❑ CL 888 [M]	Castles in Spain	1956	25.00
❑ CL 1115 [M]	Michel Legrand Plays Cole Porter	1957	25.00
❑ CL 1139 [M]	Legrand in Rio	1957	25.00
❑ CL 1250 [M]	Legrand Jazz	1958	40.00
—Miles Davis appears on this record			
❑ CL 1437 [M]	I Love Paris	1960	25.00
❑ CS 8079 [S]	Legrand Jazz	1959	40.00
—Miles Davis appears on this record			
❑ CS 8237 [S]	I Love Paris	1960	20.00
❑ PC 9237	I Love Paris	1987	8.00
—Reissue with new prefix			
GRYPHON			
❑ 786	Jazz Grand	1978	10.00
HARMONY			
❑ HL 7331 [M]	I Love Paris	196?	12.00
❑ HS 11131 [S]	I Love Paris	196?	12.00
❑ KH 31540	Cole Porter, Vol. II	1972	10.00
❑ KH 31549	Cole Porter, Vol. I	1972	10.00
MERCURY			
❑ MG 20342 [M]	C'est Magnifique	1958	20.00
MGM			
❑ SE-4491	Cinema La Grand	1967	15.00
MOBILE FIDELITY			
❑ 1-504	Jazz Grand	198?	50.00
—Audiophile vinyl			
PABLO TODAY			
❑ 2312139	After the Rain	198?	10.00
PHILIPS			
❑ PHM 200074 [M]	The Michel Legrand Big Band Plays Richard Rogers	1963	20.00
❑ PHM 200143 [M]	Michel Legrand Sings	1964	25.00
❑ PHS 600074 [S]	The Michel Legrand Big Band Plays Richard Rogers	1963	25.00
❑ PHS 600143 [S]	Michel Legrand Sings	1964	30.00
RCA VICTOR			
❑ BGL1-0850	Jimmy's	1975	10.00
❑ BXL1-0850	Jimmy's	1978	8.00
—Reissue with new prefix			
❑ BGL1-1028	Concert	1976	10.00
❑ BXL1-1028	Concert	1978	8.00
—Reissue with new prefix			
❑ BGL1-1392	Michel Legrand and Friends	1976	10.00
❑ BXL1-1392	Michel Legrand and Friends	1978	8.00
—Reissue with new prefix			

Except when noted otherwise, VG = 25% of NM, and VG+ = 50% of NM. (Example: VG = $2.00, VG+ = $4.00 and NM = $8.00.)

Number	Title (A Side/B Side)	Yr	NM
VERVE			
❑ V6-8760	Michel Legrand at Shelly's Mann-Hole	1969	12.00

LEGS DIAMOND

Albums

Number	Title (A Side/B Side)	Yr	NM
CREAM			
❑ CR 1010	Fire Power	1979	25.00
MERCURY			
❑ SRM-1-1136	Legs Diamond	1977	30.00
❑ SRM-1-1191	A Diamond Is a Hard Rock	1977	30.00

LEIBER, JERRY

Albums

Number	Title (A Side/B Side)	Yr	NM
KAPP			
❑ KL-1127 [M]	Scooby-Doo	1959	50.00

LEIBER AND STOLLER BIG BAND, THE

45s

Number	Title (A Side/B Side)	Yr	NM
UNITED ARTISTS			
❑ 441	Blue Baion/Café Espresso	1962	12.00

Albums

Number	Title (A Side/B Side)	Yr	NM
ATLANTIC			
❑ 8047 [M]	Yakety Yak	1960	40.00
—White "fan" logo on right side of label			
❑ 8047 [M]	Yakety Yak	1962	20.00
—Black "fan" logo on right side of label			
❑ SD 8047 [S]	Yakety Yak	1960	50.00
—White "fan" logo on right side of label			
❑ SD 8047 [S]	Yakety Yak	1962	25.00
—Black "fan" logo on right side of label			

LEMMON, JACK

45s

Number	Title (A Side/B Side)	Yr	NM
EPIC			
❑ 9318	Daphne/Sleepy Lagoon	1959	10.00
❑ 9364	I Cover the Waterfront/ I'm Forever Blowing Bubbles	1960	10.00
❑ 9399	Theme from The Apartment/ Lemmon Flavored Blues	1960	10.00
❑ 9399 [PS]	Theme from The Apartment/ Lemmon Flavored Blues	1960	20.00

Albums

Number	Title (A Side/B Side)	Yr	NM
CAPITOL			
❑ ST 1943 [S]	Jack Lemmon Plays Piano Selections from Irma La Douce	1963	35.00
❑ T 1943 [M]	Jack Lemmon Plays Piano Selections from Irma La Douce	1963	30.00
EPIC			
❑ BN 523 [S]	A Twist of Lemmon	1959	30.00
❑ BN 528 [S]	Jack Lemmon Sings and Plays Music from Some Like It Hot	1959	30.00
❑ LN 3491 [M]	A Twist of Lemmon	1959	25.00
❑ LN 3559 [M]	Jack Lemmon Sings and Plays Music from Some Like It Hot	1959	25.00

LEMON PIPERS, THE

45s

Number	Title (A Side/B Side)	Yr	NM
BUDDAH			
❑ 11	Turn Around and Take a Look/ Danger	1967	10.00
❑ 23	Green Tambourine/ No Help from Me	1967	12.00
❑ 31	Rice Is Nice/Blueberry Blue	1968	10.00
❑ 31 [PS]	Rice Is Nice/Blueberry Blue	1968	15.00
❑ 41	Jelly Jungle (Of Orange Marmalade)/Shoe Shine Boy	1968	10.00
❑ 63	Wine and Violet/ Lonely Atmosphere	1968	10.00
❑ 136	I Was Not Born to Follow/ Rainbow Tree	1969	8.00
CAROL			
❑ 107	Quiet Please/Monaural 78	1966	15.00

Albums

Number	Title (A Side/B Side)	Yr	NM
BUDDAH			
❑ BDM-1009 [M]	Green Tambourine	1968	25.00
❑ BDM-1016 [M]	Jungle Marmalade	1968	40.00
—Mono is promo only; in stereo cover with "Mono" sticker			
❑ BDS-5009 [S]	Green Tambourine	1968	25.00
❑ BDS-5016 [S]	Jungle Marmalade	1968	25.00

LEMONHEADS, THE

Featuring Evan Dando. Featuring Evan Dando.

12-Inch Singles

Number	Title (A Side/B Side)	Yr	NM
ATLANTIC			
❑ PR 3499 [DJ]	Half the Time/Left for Dead/Li'l Seed/(same on both sides)	1990	10.00

45s

Number	Title (A Side/B Side)	Yr	NM
ATLANTIC			
❑ PR 5336 [DJ]	Style/Acoustic Rick James Style	1993	6.00
—White label promo with small hole			
❑ PR 5336 [PS]	Style/Acoustic Rick James Style	1993	6.00
TAANG!			
❑ 31	Luka//Strange/Mad	1989	3.00
—Black vinyl			
❑ 31	Luka//Strange/Mad	1989	4.00
—White vinyl			
❑ 31	Luka//Strange/Mad	1989	6.00
—Blue vinyl			
❑ 31	Luka//Strange/Mad	1989	8.00
—Blue/yellow vinyl			
❑ 31	Luka//Strange/Mad	1989	12.00
—Red vinyl			
❑ 31 [PS]	Luka//Strange/Mad	1989	3.00
—With "Colored Vinyl Limited Edition" sticker			
THE BOB			
❑ 44	Confetti (acoustic demo)	1993	12.00
—Yellow flexi-disc included with The Bob magazine			

Legs Diamond, *Fire Power*, Cream CR 1010, 1979, **$25.**

7-Inch Extended Plays

Number	Title (A Side/B Side)	Yr	NM
ARMORY ARMS/HUH-BAG			
❑ 1/2	Glad I Don't Know/I Like To//I Am a Rabbit/So I Fucked Up...	1986	60.00
—Original pressing on black vinyl; any copy on colored vinyl (usually blue) is a reproduction			
❑ 1/2 [PS]	Laughing All the Way to the Cleaners	1986	60.00
—Also has lyric insert; both record and sleeve have been counterfeited			

Albums

Number	Title (A Side/B Side)	Yr	NM
ATLANTIC			
❑ SAM1267 [DJ]	Come On Feel the Lemonheads	1993	20.00
—Promo-only four-song sampler			
❑ 82137	Lovey	1990	20.00
—U.S. edition; imports with a similar number go for less			
❑ 82537	Come On Feel the Lemonheads	1993	25.00
—5,000 copies pressed, all on green vinyl; imports sell for less			
TAANG!			
❑ 15	Hate Your Friends	1987	12.00
—Any edition not listed among the first five pressings above			
❑ 15	Hate Your Friends	1987	20.00
—Fifth pressing: Yellow vinyl, yellow lettering on sleeve, yellow label			
❑ 15	Hate Your Friends	1987	25.00
—Fourth pressing: Black vinyl, red lettering on sleeve, blue and green label			
❑ 15	Hate Your Friends	1987	25.00
—Third pressing: Black vinyl, red lettering on sleeve, red label			
❑ 15	Hate Your Friends	1987	30.00
—The second 2,000 are on black vinyl, red lettering on sleeve, yellow label			
❑ 15	Hate Your Friends	1987	40.00
—The first 3,000 were on black vinyl, yellow lettering on sleeve, yellow label			
❑ 23	Creator	1988	15.00
❑ 32	Lick	1989	15.00
TAG/ATLANTIC			
❑ 92726	Car Button Cloth	1996	20.00
TPM/RHINO EXCLUSIVE			
❑ 138	It's a Shame About Ray	2008	15.00

LENNON, FREDDIE

45s

Number	Title (A Side/B Side)	Yr	NM
JERDEN			
❑ 792	That's My Life (My Love and My Home)/Next Time You Feel Important	1966	80.00

LENNON, JOHN

Includes records as "Plastic Ono Band," "John Ono Lennon," "John Lennon/Plastic Ono Band" and other records he made with Yoko Ono. Also see THE BEATLES.

12-Inch Singles

Number	Title (A Side/B Side)	Yr	NM
CAPITOL			
❑ SPRO-9585/6 [DJ]	Imagine/Come Together	1986	40.00
❑ SPRO-9894 [DJ]	Happy Xmas (War Is Over) (same on both sides)	1986	200.00
—Limited edition for the Central Virginia Food Bank			
❑ SPRO-9917 [DJ]	Rock and Roll People (same on both sides)	1986	60.00
❑ SPRO-9929 [DJ]	Happy Xmas (War Is Over)/ Listen, the Snow Is Falling	1986	50.00
—Custom silver label, plastic sleeve with sticker			

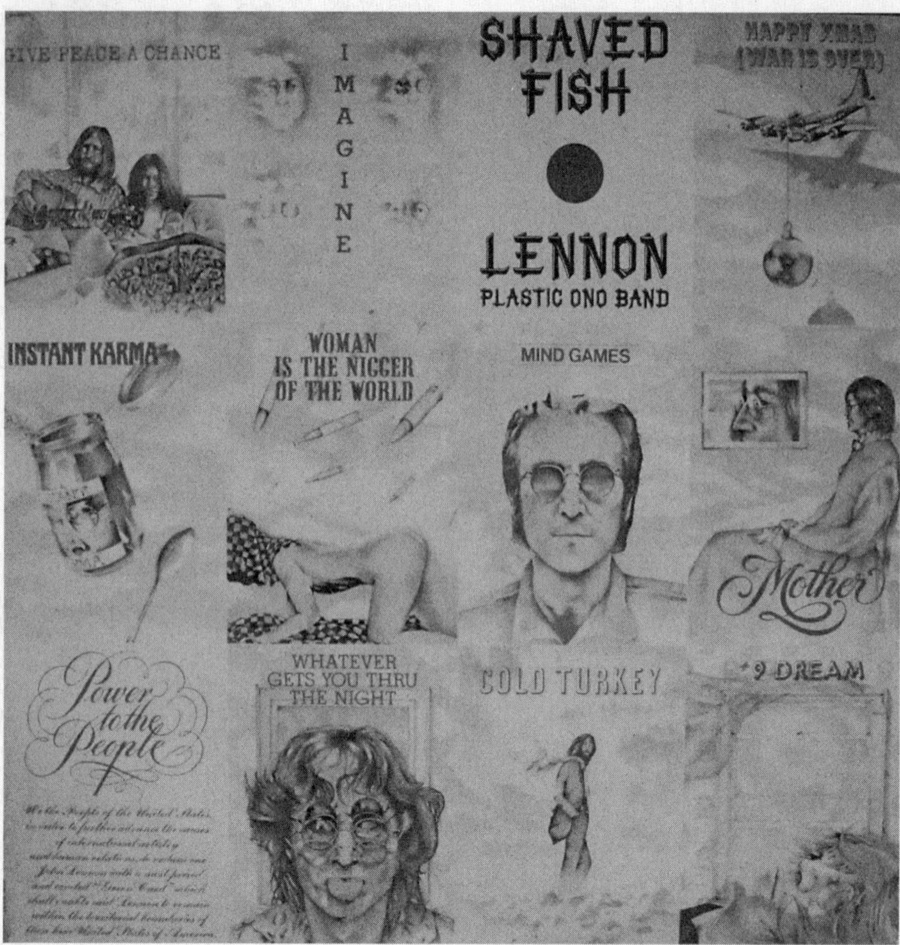

John Lennon, *Shaved Fish*, Capitol SW-3421, 1978, **$12.**

Number	Title (A Side/B Side)	Yr	NM
❑ SPRO-79463 [DJ]	Stand By Me (same on both sides)	1988	40.00

GEFFEN

Number	Title (A Side/B Side)	Yr	NM
❑ PRO-A-919 [DJ]	(Just Like) Starting Over/ Kiss Kiss Kiss	1980	80.00
—A-side is slightly longer (4:17) than any other release of this song			
❑ PRO-A-1079 [DJ]	Happy Xmas (War Is Over)/ Beautiful Boy (Darling Boy)	1982	30.00

POLYDOR

Number	Title (A Side/B Side)	Yr	NM
❑ PRO 250-1 [DJ]	Nobody Told Me/O' Sanity	1983	30.00

45s

APPLE

Number	Title (A Side/B Side)	Yr	NM
❑ 1809	Give Peace a Chance/ Remember Love	1969	5.00
—As "Plastic Ono Band"			
❑ 1809 [PS]	Give Peace a Chance/ Remember Love	1969	15.00
—As "Plastic Ono Band"			
❑ 1813	Cold Turkey/Don't Worry Kyoko (Mummy's Only Looking for a Hand in the Snow)	1969	5.00
—As "Plastic Ono Band"; most copies skip on A-side on the third chorus because of a pressing defect			
❑ 1813	Cold Turkey/Don't Worry Kyoko (Mummy's Only Looking for a Hand in the Snow)	1969	10.00
—As "Plastic Ono Band"; some copies don't skip on A-side. They tend to have wider, bolder print than those that do.			
❑ 1813 [PS]	Cold Turkey/Don't Worry Kyoko (Mummy's Only Looking for a Hand in the Snow)	1969	40.00
—As "Plastic Ono Band"			
❑ 1818	Instant Karma! (We All Shine On)/ Who Has Seen the Wind?	1970	4.00
—As "John Ono Lennon"; B-side by "Yoko Ono Lennon"			
❑ 1818 [DJ]	Instant Karma! (We All Shine On)	1970	200.00
—As "John Ono Lennon"; one-sided promo			
❑ 1818 [PS]	Instant Karma! (We All Shine On)/ Who Has Seen the Wind?	1970	15.00
—As "John Ono Lennon"; B-side by "Yoko Ono Lennon"			
❑ 1827	Mother/Why	1970	8.00
—As "John Lennon/Plastic Ono Band"; B-side by "Yoko Ono/Plastic Ono Band"			
❑ 1827	Mother/Why	1970	12.00
—As "John Lennon/Plastic Ono Band"; star on A-side label			
❑ 1827	Mother/Why	1970	40.00
—As "John Lennon/Plastic Ono Band"; "MONO" on A-side label			
❑ 1827 [PS]	Mother/Why	1970	120.00
—As "John Lennon/Plastic Ono Band"; B-side by "Yoko Ono/Plastic Ono Band"			
❑ 1830	Power to the People/Touch Me	1971	8.00
—As "John Lennon/Plastic Ono Band"; with star on A-side label			
❑ 1830	Power to the People/Touch Me	1971	8.00
—As "John Lennon/Plastic Ono Band"; B-side by "Yoko Ono/Plastic Ono Band"			
❑ 1830 [PS]	Power to the People/Touch Me	1971	30.00
—As "John Lennon/Plastic Ono Band"; B-side by "Yoko Ono/Plastic Ono Band"			
❑ 1840	Imagine/It's So Hard	1971	8.00
—As "John Lennon Plastic Ono Band"; tan label			
❑ 1840	Imagine/It's So Hard	1975	12.00
—As "John Lennon Plastic Ono Band"; green label with "All Rights Reserved"			
❑ 1842	Happy Xmas (War Is Over)/ Listen, the Snow Is Falling	1971	10.00
—As "John & Yoko/Plastic Ono Band with the Harlem Community Choir"; green vinyl, Apple label			
❑ 1842	Happy Xmas (War Is Over)/ Listen, the Snow Is Falling	1971	15.00
—As "John & Yoko/Plastic Ono Band with the Harlem Community Choir"; green vinyl, faces label			
❑ 1842 [PS]	Happy Xmas (War Is Over)/ Listen, the Snow Is Falling	1971	20.00
—As "John & Yoko/Plastic Ono Band with the Harlem Community Choir"			
❑ 1848	Woman Is the Nigger of the World/Sisters O Sisters	1972	8.00
—As "John Lennon/Plastic Ono Band..."; B-side by "Yoko Ono/Plastic Ono Band..."			
❑ 1848 [PS]	Woman Is the Nigger of the World/Sisters O Sisters	1972	25.00
—As "John Lennon/Plastic Ono Band..."; B-side by "Yoko Ono/Plastic Ono Band..."			
❑ 1868	Mind Games/Meat City	1973	6.00
❑ 1868 [PS]	Mind Games/Meat City	1973	15.00
❑ P-1868 [DJ]	Mind Games (mono/stereo)	1973	50.00
❑ 1874	Whatever Gets You Thru the Night/Beef Jerky	1974	6.00
—As "John Lennon and the Plastic Ono Nuclear Band"			
❑ P-1874 [DJ]	Whatever Gets You Thru the Night (mono/stereo)	1974	50.00
—As "John Lennon and the Plastic Ono Nuclear Band"			
❑ 1878	#9 Dream/What You Got	1974	8.00
❑ P-1878 [DJ]	#9 Dream (edited mono/stereo)	1974	50.00
❑ P-1878 [DJ]	What You Got (mono/stereo)	1974	100.00
❑ 1881	Stand By Me/Move Over Ms. L.	1975	8.00
❑ P-1881 [DJ]	Stand By Me (mono/stereo)	1975	50.00
❑ P-1883 [DJ]	Ain't That a Shame (mono/stereo)	1975	200.00
—No stock copies issued			
❑ P-1883 [DJ]	Slippin' and Slidin' (mono/stereo)	1975	200.00
—No stock copies issued			
❑ S45X-47663/4 [DJ]	Happy Xmas (War Is Over)/ Listen, the Snow Is Falling	1971	800.00
—As "John & Yoko/Plastic Ono Band with the Harlem Community Choir"; white label on styrene			

APPLE/AMERICOM

Number	Title (A Side/B Side)	Yr	NM
❑ 1809P/M-435	Give Peace a Chance/ Remember Love	1969	750.00
—As "Plastic Ono Band"; four-inch flexi-disc sold in vending machines			

ATLANTIC

Number	Title (A Side/B Side)	Yr	NM
❑ PR-104/5 [DJ]	John Lennon on Ronnie Hawkins: The Short Rap/ The Long Rap	1970	100.00

CAPITOL

Number	Title (A Side/B Side)	Yr	NM
❑ 1840	Imagine/It's So Hard	1978	6.00
—As "John Lennon Plastic Ono Band"; purple late 1970s label			
❑ 1840	Imagine/It's So Hard	1983	6.00
—As "John Lennon Plastic Ono Band"; black colorband label			
❑ 1840	Imagine/It's So Hard	1988	5.00
—As "John Lennon Plastic Ono Band"; purple late-1980s label (wider)			
❑ 1842	Happy Xmas (War Is Over)/ Listen, the Snow Is Falling	1976	50.00
—As "John & Yoko/Plastic Ono Band with the Harlem Community Choir"; orange label			
❑ 1842	Happy Xmas (War Is Over)/ Listen, the Snow Is Falling	1978	6.00
—As "John & Yoko/Plastic Ono Band with the Harlem Community Choir"; purple late-1970s label			
❑ 1842	Happy Xmas (War Is Over)/ Listen, the Snow Is Falling	1983	6.00
—As "John & Yoko/Plastic Ono Band with the Harlem Community Choir"; black colorband label			
❑ 1842	Happy Xmas (War Is Over)/ Listen, the Snow Is Falling	1988	20.00
—As "John & Yoko/Plastic Ono Band with the Harlem Community Choir"; purple late-1980s label (wider)			
❑ 1868	Mind Games/Meat City	1978	6.00
—Purple late-1970s label			
❑ 1868	Mind Games/Meat City	1983	12.00
—Black colorband label			
❑ 1874	Whatever Gets You Thru the Night/Beef Jerky	1978	6.00
—Purple late-1970s label			
❑ 1874	Whatever Gets You Thru the Night/Beef Jerky	1983	6.00
—Black colorband label			
❑ 1874	Whatever Gets You Thru the Night/Beef Jerky	1988	6.00
—Purple late-1980s label			
❑ 1878	#9 Dream/What You Got	1976	40.00
—Orange label			
❑ 1878	#9 Dream/What You Got	1978	6.00
—Purple late-1970s label			
❑ 1878	#9 Dream/What You Got	1983	10.00
—Black colorband label			
❑ 7PRO 6 15998 7 [DJ]	Every Man Has a Woman Who Loves Him (Lennon Version)/ (Ono Version)	2001	15.00
—White label promo, small hole; B-side has Yoko Ono's version of the song with Lennon backing her			
❑ 7PRO 6 15998 7 [PS]	Every Man Has a Woman Who Loves Him (Lennon Version)/(Ono Version)	2001	15.00
❑ S7-17644	Happy Xmas (War Is Over)/ Listen, the Snow Is Falling	1993	4.00
—John & Yoko/The Plastic Ono Band; green vinyl			
❑ S7-17783	Give Peace a Chance/ Remember Love	1994	100.00
—CEMA Special Markets issue; meant for gold-plating in a special plaque. About 100 were not.			
❑ B-44230	Jealous Guy/Give Peace a Chance	1988	5.00
❑ B-44230 [PS]	Jealous Guy/Give Peace a Chance	1988	5.00

Except when noted otherwise, VG = 25% of NM, and VG+ = 50% of NM. (Example: VG = $2.00, VG+ = $4.00 and NM = $8.00.)

Number	Title (A Side/B Side)	Yr	NM
❑ S7-57849	Imagine/It's So Hard	1992	50.00
—CEMA Special Markets issue; meant for gold-plating in a special plaque. About 1,000 were not.			
❑ 58894	(Just Like) Starting Over/ Watching the Wheels	2000	5.00
—Blue vinyl			
❑ 58895	Woman/Walking on Thin Ice	2000	5.00
—Clear vinyl; B-side as "John Lennon and Yoko Ono" though originally issued as a Yoko Ono solo single			
COTILLION			
❑ PR-104/5 [DJ]	John Lennon on Ronnie Hawkins: The Short Rap/The Long Rap	1970	80.00
—White label with promo markings			
❑ PR-104/5 [DJ]	John Lennon on Ronnie Hawkins: The Short Rap/The Long Rap	1970	90.00
—No promo markings on white label			
GEFFEN			
❑ 29855	Happy Xmas (War Is Over)/ Beautiful Boy (Darling Boy)	1982	5.00
❑ 29855 [PS]	Happy Xmas (War Is Over)/ Beautiful Boy (Darling Boy)	1982	5.00
❑ 49604	(Just Like) Starting Over/Kiss Kiss Kiss	1980	4.00
—B-side by Yoko Ono			
❑ 49604 [PS]	(Just Like) Starting Over/Kiss Kiss Kiss	1980	4.00
—B-side by Yoko Ono			
❑ 49644	Woman/Beautiful Boys	1980	4.00
—B-side by Yoko Ono			
❑ 49644 [PS]	Woman/Beautiful Boys	1980	4.00
—B-side by Yoko Ono			
❑ 49695	Watching the Wheels/ Yes, I'm Your Angel	1981	4.00
—B-side by Yoko Ono			
❑ 49695 [PS]	Watching the Wheels/ Yes, I'm Your Angel	1981	4.00
—B-side by Yoko Ono			
KYA			
❑ 1260 [DJ]	The KYA 1969 Peace Talk	1969	200.00
—Blue vinyl copies are counterfeits			
NOISEVILLE			
❑ 43	John Lennon Talks About David Peel	199?	10.00
—Black vinyl			
❑ 43	John Lennon Talks About David Peel	199?	40.00
—Red vinyl, signed by David Peel			
❑ 43 [PS]	John Lennon Talks About David Peel	199?	10.00
POLYDOR			
❑ 817254-7	Nobody Told Me/O' Sanity	1983	5.00
—With "Manufactured and Marketed by Polygram..." on label; B-side by Yoko Ono			
❑ 817254-7	Nobody Told Me/O' Sanity	1983	10.00
—With "Manufactured by Polydor Incorporated..." on label; B-side by Yoko Ono			
❑ 817254-7 [PS]	Nobody Told Me/O' Sanity	1983	5.00
❑ 821107-7	I'm Stepping Out/Sleepless Night	1984	4.00
—B-side by Yoko Ono			
❑ 821107-7 [PS]	I'm Stepping Out/Sleepless Night	1984	4.00
❑ 821204-7	Borrowed Time/Your Hands	1984	5.00
—B-side by Yoko Ono			
❑ 821204-7 [PS]	Borrowed Time/Your Hands	1984	5.00
❑ 881378-7	Every Man Has a Woman Who Loves Him/It's Alright	1984	8.00
—B-side by Sean Ono Lennon			
❑ 881378-7 [PS]	Every Man Has a Woman Who Loves Him/It's Alright	1984	8.00
QUAKER GRANOLA DIPPS			
❑ (no #)	A Tribute to John Lennon	1986	15.00
—Cardboard record included in specially marked boxes of Quaker Granola Dipps			
QUAYE/TRIDENT			
❑ SK 3419 [DJ]	Rock 'N' Roll	1975	500.00
—Radio spot to promote the album Rock 'N' Roll			

Albums

Number	Title	Yr	NM
ADAM VIII			
❑ A-8018	John Lennon Sings the Great Rock & Roll Hits (Roots)	1975	1000.
—Counterfeits abound. On authentic copies, cover is posterboard (not slicks); labels are normal size (not overly large); printing on cover is sharp, not blurry; the word "Greatest" does NOT appear on the spine. Authentic copies usually have ad sleeve also.			
APPLE			
❑ SMAX-3361	Wedding Album	1969	150.00
—With photo strip, postcard, poster of wedding photos, poster of lithographs, "Bagism" bag, booklet, photo of slice of wedding cake. Missing inserts reduce the value.			
❑ SW-3362	Live Peace in Toronto 1969	1970	15.00
—By "The Plastic Ono Band" — without calendar			
❑ SW-3362	Live Peace in Toronto 1969	1970	20.00
—By "The Plastic Ono Band"; with calendar			

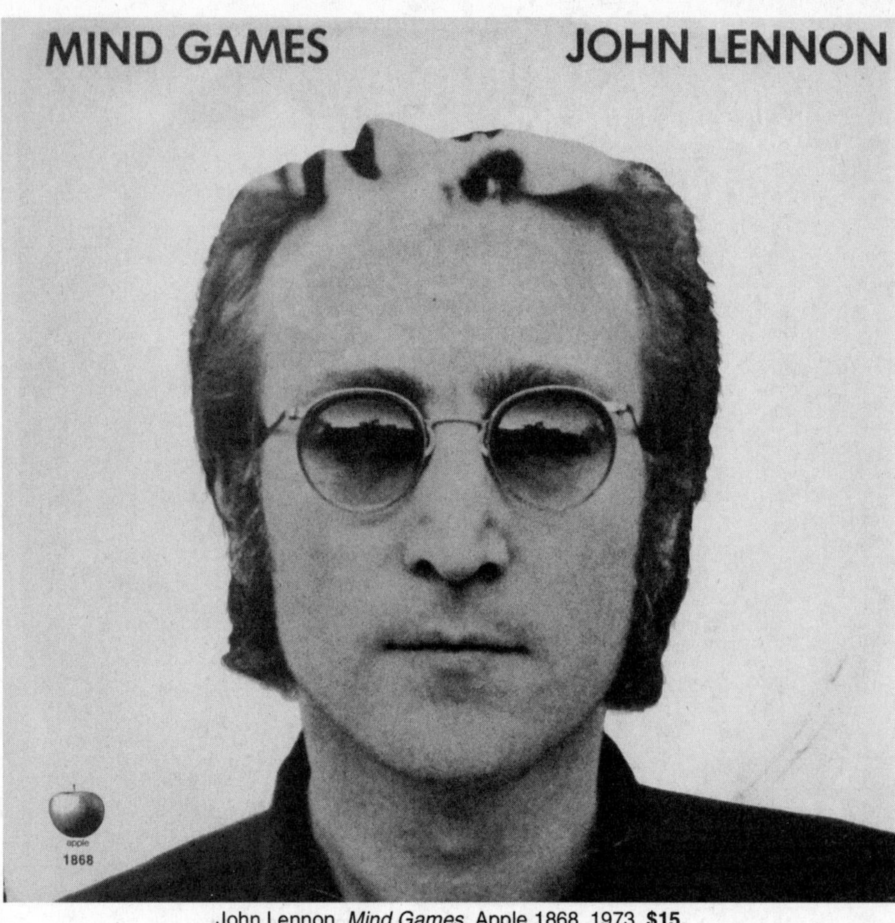

John Lennon, *Mind Games*, Apple 1868, 1973, **$15.**

Number	Title (A Side/B Side)	Yr	NM
❑ SW-3372	John Lennon Plastic Ono Band	1970	20.00
❑ SW-3379	Imagine	1971	20.00
—With either of two postcard inserts, lyric sleeve, poster			
❑ SW-3379	Imagine	1975	20.00
—"All Rights Reserved" label			
❑ SVBB-3392 [(2)]	Some Time in New York City	1972	30.00
—By John and Yoko; with photo card and petition			
❑ SVBB-3392 [(2)DJ]	Some Time in New York City	1972	1000.
—White label promo			
❑ SW-3414	Mind Games	1973	20.00
❑ SW-3416	Walls and Bridges	1974	20.00
—With fold-open segmented front cover			
❑ SK-3419	Rock 'N' Roll	1975	20.00
❑ SW-3421	Shaved Fish	1975	20.00
❑ T-5001	Two Virgins — Unfinished Music No. 1	1968	50.00
—With Yoko Ono; without brown bag			
❑ T-5001	Two Virgins — Unfinished Music No. 1	1968	150.00
—With Yoko Ono; with die-cut bag			
❑ T-5001	Two Virgins — Unfinished Music No. 1	1968	150.00
—With Yoko Ono; price with brown bag			
❑ T-5001	Two Virgins — Unfinished Music No. 1	1985	15.00
—With Yoko Ono; reissue, flat label			
CAPITOL			
❑ SW-3372	John Lennon Plastic Ono Band	1978	12.00
—Purple label, large Capitol logo			
❑ SW-3372	John Lennon Plastic Ono Band	1982	20.00
—Black label, print in colorband			
❑ SW-3372	John Lennon Plastic Ono Band	1988	30.00
—Purple label, small Capitol logo			
❑ SW-3379	Imagine	1978	10.00
—Purple label, large Capitol logo			
❑ SW-3379	Imagine	1986	30.00
—Black label, print in colorband			
❑ SW-3379	Imagine	1987	25.00
—Black label, print in colorband; "Digitally Re-Mastered" at top of front cover			
❑ SW-3379	Imagine	1988	30.00
—Purple label, small Capitol logo			
❑ SVBB-3392 [(2)]	Some Time in New York City	197?	25.00
—By John and Yoko; purple label, large Capitol logo			
❑ SVBB-3392 [(2)]	Some Time in New York City	197?	100.00
—Both discs in single-pocket gatefold (the other pocket is glued shut)			
❑ SW-3414	Mind Games	1978	40.00
—Purple label, large Capitol logo			
❑ SW-3416	Walls and Bridges	1978	15.00
—Purple label, large Capitol logo; standard front cover			
❑ SW-3416	Walls and Bridges	1982	30.00
—Black label, print in colorband			
❑ SW-3416	Walls and Bridges	1989	30.00
—Purple label, small Capitol logo			
❑ SK-3419	Rock 'N' Roll	1978	40.00
—Purple label, large Capitol logo			
❑ SW-3421	Shaved Fish	1978	12.00
—Purple Capitol label with Apple logo on cover			
❑ SW-3421	Shaved Fish	1978	40.00
—Purple Capitol label with Capitol logo on cover			
❑ SW-3421	Shaved Fish	1983	20.00
—Black Capitol label with Apple logo on cover			
❑ SW-3421	Shaved Fish	1983	40.00
—Black Capitol label with Capitol logo on cover			
❑ SW-3421	Shaved Fish	1989	40.00
—Purple Capitol label (small logo) with Capitol logo on cover			
❑ ST-12239	Live Peace in Toronto 1969	1982	10.00
—By "The Plastic Ono Band"; reissue, purple Capitol label			
❑ ST-12239	Live Peace in Toronto 1969	1983	50.00
—By "The Plastic Ono Band"; reissue, black Capitol label			
❑ SV-12451	Live in New York City	1986	12.00
❑ SJ-12533	Menlove Ave.	1986	15.00
❑ SN-16068	Mind Games	1980	12.00
—Budget-line reissue			
❑ SN-16069	Rock 'N' Roll	1980	12.00
—Budget-line reissue			
❑ C1-90803 [(2)]	Imagine: Music from the Motion Picture	1988	20.00
❑ C1-91425	Double Fantasy	1989	20.00
—Very briefly available reissue			
❑ R 144136	Menlove Ave.	198?	50.00
—BMG Direct Marketing edition			
❑ R 144136	Menlove Ave.	1986	50.00
—RCA Music Service edition			

Julian Lennon, "Stick Around," Atlantic 89437, 1986, **$4.**

Number	Title (A Side/B Side)	Yr	NM
R 144497	Live in New York City	1986	15.00
—RCA Music Service edition			
SV-512451	Live in New York City	1986	15.00
—Columbia House edition			
C1-591425	Double Fantasy	1989	60.00
—Columbia House edition of reissue			
GEFFEN			
GHS 2001	Double Fantasy	1980	10.00
—Seven tracks by John, seven by Yoko; off-white label; titles on back cover out of order			
GHS 2001	Double Fantasy	1981	12.00
—Columbia House edition (all have corrected back cover) without "CH" on label			
GHS 2001	Double Fantasy	1981	12.00
—Off-white label, titles in order on the back cover			
GHS 2001	Double Fantasy	1981	75.00
—Columbia House edition (all have corrected back cover) with "CH" on label			
GHS 2001	Double Fantasy	1986	50.00
—Same as above, but with black Geffen label			
GHSP 2023	The John Lennon Collection	1982	20.00
GHSP 2023 [DJ]	The John Lennon Collection	1982	50.00
—Promo only on Quiex II audiophile vinyl			
R 104689	Double Fantasy	1981	40.00
—RCA Music Service edition			
MOBILE FIDELITY			
1-153	Imagine	1984	75.00
—Audiophile vinyl			
MFSL 1-277	Imagine	2004	25.00
—"Original Master Recording" at top of front cover			
MFSL 1-280	John Lennon Plastic Ono Band	2004	25.00
—"Original Master Recording" at top of front cover			
NAUTILUS			
NR-47	Double Fantasy	1982	80.00
—Half-speed master			
NR-47	Double Fantasy	1982	2000.
—Half-speed master; alternate experimental cover with yellow and red added to black and white front			
PARLOPHONE			
21954 [(2)]	Lennon Legend	1998	20.00
—"Made in U.S.A." on back cover			

Number	Title (A Side/B Side)	Yr	NM
POLYDOR			
817160-1	Milk and Honey	1983	10.00
—Six tracks by John, six by Yoko			
817160-1	Milk and Honey	1984	150.00
—Yellow or green vinyl; unauthorized "inside jobs"			
817238-1	Heart Play (Unfinished Dialogue)	1983	12.00
—Interviews with John Lennon and Yoko Ono			
SILHOUETTE			
SM-10012 [(2)]	Reflections and Poetry	1984	25.00
ZAPPLE			
ST-3357	Life with the Lions — Unfinished Music No. 2	1969	20.00
—With Yoko Ono			

LENNON, JULIAN

45s

Number	Title (A Side/B Side)	Yr	NM
ATLANTIC			
88890	You're the One/ (B-side unknown)	1989	4.00
88925	Now You're in Heaven/ Second Time	1989	4.00
88925 [PS]	Now You're in Heaven/ Second Time	1989	4.00
89385	This Is My Day/Everyday	1986	4.00
89405	Want Your Body/Everyday	1986	4.00
89437	Stick Around/Always Think Twice	1986	4.00
89437 [PS]	Stick Around/Always Think Twice	1986	4.00
89529	Jesse/Bebop	1985	4.00
89529 [PS]	Jesse/Bebop	1985	4.00
89567	Say You're Wrong/Big Mama	1985	4.00
89567 [PS]	Say You're Wrong/Big Mama	1985	4.00
89589	Too Late for Goodbyes/ Let Me Go	1985	4.00
89589 [PS]	Too Late for Goodbyes/ Let Me Go	1985	4.00
89609	Valotte/Well I Don't Know	1984	4.00
89609 [PS]	Valotte/Well I Don't Know	1984	4.00
CAPITOL			
B-5618	Time Will Teach Us All/ (Instrumental)	1986	4.00

Albums

Number	Title (A Side/B Side)	Yr	NM
ATLANTIC			
PR 2693 [DJ]	Mr. Jordan According to Mr. Lennon	1989	15.00
—Promo-only interview album			
81084	Valotte	1984	10.00
81640	The Secret Value of Daydreaming	1986	10.00
81928	Mr. Jordan	1989	10.00

LENNON SISTERS, THE

Also see LAWRENCE WELK.

45s

Number	Title (A Side/B Side)	Yr	NM
BRUNSWICK			
55000	Young and In Love/ Teenage Waltz	1957	10.00
55013	White Silver Sands/ One Day a Little Girl	1957	10.00
55028	Shake Me I Rattle/Pocahontas	1957	10.00
55044	Let's Light the Christmas Tree/ Merry, Merry Christmas	1957	12.00
55051	To Know You Is to Love You/Hide Your Troubles Behind a Smile	1958	10.00
55058	Dear One/Mr. Clarinet Man	1958	10.00
55063	How Will I Know My Love/ Graduation Dance	1958	10.00
55075	Bubble Gum/Have You Ever Been Lonely	1958	10.00
—With Larry Dean			
55082	Walk with Me/Goodnight God	1958	10.00
55113	The Children's Marching Song/ Slumber Party	1959	10.00
DOT			
15965	A Hundred and One in the Sun/ Vacation Waltz	1959	8.00
16131	Freckles/I Wakled with the Wind	1960	8.00
16184	Did'Ja Know/What a Sky	1961	8.00
16215	Darlin' Meggie/On the Double	1961	8.00
16255	Sad Movies (Make Me Cry)/ I Don't Know Why	1961	8.00
16277	Kaw-Liga/We Live in Two Different Worlds	1961	8.00
16423	Bei Mir Bist Du Schoen/Lida Rose	1963	8.00
16489	The Heartstrings/Speak, Sugar, Speak	1963	8.00
16681	Little Stranger/Little Lady Make Believe	1964	6.00
16748	Chim Chim Cheree/ A Step in Time	1965	6.00
17010	He's Got a Lotta Lovin'/ I'm Coming Back to You	1967	6.00
17046	I Love/Gypsy, What Can I Do	1967	6.00
MERCURY			
72830	As Long As There's an Apple Tree/I'm So Glad That You've Found Me	1968	6.00
72883	The Christmas Waltz/Lullaby for Christmas	1968	6.00

Albums

Number	Title (A Side/B Side)	Yr	NM
BRUNSWICK			
BL 54031 [M]	Let's Get Acquainted	1957	25.00
BL 54039 [M]	Lawrence Welk Presents the Lennon Sisters	1958	25.00
DOT			
DLP-3250 [M]	Best-Loved Catholic Hymns	1959	15.00
DLP-3292 [M]	The Lennon Sisters Sing 12 Great Hits	1960	15.00
DLP 3343 [M]	Christmas with the Lennon Sisters	1961	15.00
DLP-3398 [M]	Sad Movies (Make Me Cry)	1961	15.00
DLP-3417 [M]	Can't Help Falling in Love	1962	12.00
DLP-3481 [M]	The Lennon Sisters' Favorites	1963	12.00
DLP-3557 [M]	Dominique and Other Great Folk Songs	1964	12.00
DLP-3589 [M]	No. 1 Hits of the 1960s	1964	12.00
DLP-3622 [M]	Twelve Great Hits, Vol. 2	1965	12.00
DLP-3659 [M]	Solos	1965	12.00
DLP-3797 [M]	Somethin' Stupid	1967	15.00
DLP-25250 [S]	Best-Loved Catholic Hymns	1959	20.00
DLP-25292 [S]	The Lennon Sisters Sing 12 Great Hits	1960	20.00
DLP 25343 [S]	Christmas with the Lennon Sisters	1961	20.00
DLP-25398 [S]	Sad Movies (Make Me Cry)	1961	20.00
DLP-25417 [S]	Can't Help Falling in Love	1962	15.00
DLP-25481 [S]	The Lennon Sisters' Favorites	1963	15.00
DLP-25557 [S]	Dominique and Other Great Folk Songs	1964	15.00
DLP-25589 [S]	No. 1 Hits of the 1960s	1964	15.00
DLP-25622 [S]	Twelve Great Hits, Vol. 2	1965	15.00
DLP-25659 [S]	Solos	1965	15.00
DLP-25797 [S]	Somethin' Stupid	1967	12.00
HAMILTON			
HLP-119 [M]	Melody of Love	196?	12.00
HLP-12119 [S]	Melody of Love	196?	12.00

Number	Title (A Side/B Side)	Yr	NM
MERCURY			
❑ SR-61164	The Lennon Sisters Today!!	1968	12.00
❑ SR-61201	Pop Country	1969	12.00
PICKWICK			
❑ PTP-2014 [(2)]	America's Sweethearts	1973	12.00
❑ SPC-3084	Our Favorite Songs	196?	10.00
❑ SPC-3110	Goodnight Sweetheart	197?	10.00
RANWOOD			
❑ 7027 [(2)]	22 Songs of Faith and Inspiration	198?	10.00
❑ 8205	Best of the Lennon Sisters	198?	8.00
❑ 8212	How Great Thou Art	198?	8.00
VOCALION			
❑ VL 73864	Too Marvelous for Words	1969	10.00
❑ VL 73887	The Lennon Sisters with Lawrence Welk	1970	10.00

LENNY AND THE CHIMES

45s

Number	Title (A Side/B Side)	Yr	NM
VEE JAY			
❑ 605	Only Forever/Two Times Two	1964	12.00

LENNY AND THE THUNDERTONES

45s

Number	Title (A Side/B Side)	Yr	NM
DOT			
❑ 16177	The Street Beat/Happy Little Jug	1961	25.00

LENOIR, J.B.

45s

Number	Title (A Side/B Side)	Yr	NM
CHECKER			
❑ 844	Let Me Die with the One I Love/If I Give My Love to You	1956	40.00
❑ 856	Don't Touch My Head/I've Been Down So Long	1957	40.00
❑ 874	What About Your Daughter/Five Years	1957	30.00
❑ 901	Daddy Talk to Your Son/She Don't Know	1958	30.00
J.O.B.			
❑ 1012	The Mojo/How Can I Leave	1952	200.00
❑ 1102	Play a Little While/Louise	1952	120.00
PARROT			
❑ 802	Eisenhower Blues/I'm in Korea	1954	400.00
❑ 802	Tax Paying Blues/I'm in Korea	1954	1000.
—A-side is similar, though not identical, to "Eisenhower Blues"			
❑ 802	Tax Paying Blues/I'm in Korea	1954	2000.
—Red vinyl			
❑ 809	Mama Talk to Your Daughter/Man, Watch Your Woman	1955	80.00
❑ 814	Mama Your Daughter Is Going to Miss Me/What Have I Done	1955	100.00
❑ 821	Fine Girls/I Lost My Baby	1955	150.00
SHAD			
❑ 5012	Back Door/Louella	1959	20.00
U.S.A.			
❑ 744	I Feel So Good/Sing Um the Way I Feel	1963	20.00
VEE JAY			
❑ 352	Do What I Say/Oh Baby	1960	12.00
—As "J.B. Lenore"			

Albums

Number	Title (A Side/B Side)	Yr	NM
CHESS			
❑ LP-410	Natural Man	1970	40.00
❑ CH-9323	Natural Man	1990	12.00
POLYDOR			
❑ 24-4011	J.B. Lenoir	1970	15.00

LEON AND THE DREAMERS

45s

Number	Title (A Side/B Side)	Yr	NM
PARKWAY			
❑ 843	Haircut/If It Hadn't Been for You	1962	15.00

LEONARD, BILLY

45s

Number	Title (A Side/B Side)	Yr	NM
FAIRMOUNT			
❑ 1007	Tell Me Do You Love Me/Tears for Love	1966	80.00

LEONARD, JACK E.

Albums

Number	Title (A Side/B Side)	Yr	NM
VIK			
❑ LX-1080 [M]	Rock 'n Roll for People Over Sixteen	1957	40.00

LEOPARDS, THE

Albums

Number	Title (A Side/B Side)	Yr	NM
MOON			
❑ (# unknown)	Kansas City Slickers	1977	25.00

LES CHANSONETTES

45s

Number	Title (A Side/B Side)	Yr	NM
SHRINE			
❑ 114	Don't Let Him Hurt You/Deeper	1966	800.00

LESTER, BOBBY, AND THE MOONLIGHTERS

The Moonlighters are THE MOONGLOWS.

45s

Number	Title (A Side/B Side)	Yr	NM
CHECKER			
❑ 806	So All Alone/Shoo Doo-Be Do (My Loving Baby)	1954	100.00
—Maroon label with checkerboard top			
❑ 806	So All Alone/Shoo Doo-Be Do (My Loving Baby)	1958	40.00
—Maroon label, vertical logo			
❑ 813	New Gal/The Hug and a Kiss	1955	80.00

LEVERETT, CHICO

45s

Number	Title (A Side/B Side)	Yr	NM
BETHLEHEM			
❑ 3062	Baby (Don't Leave)/Work, Work	1963	40.00
TAMLA			
❑ 54024	Solid Sender/I'll Never Love Again	1959	2000.
—VG 1000; VG+ 1500			

LEVIATHAN

Albums

Number	Title (A Side/B Side)	Yr	NM
MACH			
❑ XMA-12501	Leviathan	1974	30.00

LEVINSON, MARK

Albums

Number	Title (A Side/B Side)	Yr	NM
MARK LEVINSON			
❑ 7	Jazz at Long Wharf	1979	30.00
—Audiophile edition pressed at 45 rpm			

LEVON AND THE HAWKS

Early version of THE BAND.

45s

Number	Title (A Side/B Side)	Yr	NM
ATCO			
❑ 6383	He Don't Love You (And He'll Break Your Heart)/Stones I Throw	1965	30.00
❑ 6625	He Don't Love You (And He'll Break Your Heart)/Go Go Lisa Jane	1968	30.00

LEWD

45s

Number	Title (A Side/B Side)	Yr	NM
SCRATCHED			
❑ 101	Kill Yourself/Trash Can Baby/Pay or Die	1978	37.50
❑ 101 [PS]	Kill Yourself/Trash Can Baby/Pay or Die	1978	37.50

Albums

Number	Title (A Side/B Side)	Yr	NM
ICI			
❑ CF 200	American Wino	1982	40.00

LEWIS, BARBARA

45s

Number	Title (A Side/B Side)	Yr	NM
ATLANTIC			
❑ 2141	My Heart Went Do Dat Da/The Longest Night of the Year	1962	10.00
❑ 2159	My Mama Told Me/Gonna Love You Till the Day I Die	1962	40.00
❑ 2184	Hello Stranger/Think a Little Sugar	1963	15.00
❑ 2200	Straighten Up Your Heart/If You Love Her	1963	40.00
❑ 2214	Puppy Love/Snap Your Fingers	1963	10.00
❑ 2227	Someday We're Gonna Love Again/Spend a Little Time	1964	40.00
❑ 2255	Come Home/Pushin' a Good Thing Too Far	1964	20.00
❑ 2283	Baby, I'm Yours/I Say Love	1965	15.00
❑ 2300	Make Me Your Baby/Love to Be Loved	1965	15.00
❑ 2316	Don't Forget About Me/It's Magic	1965	20.00
❑ 2346	Make Me Belong to You/Girls Need Loving Care	1966	15.00
❑ 2361	I Remember the Feeling/Baby What You Want Me to Do	1966	50.00
❑ 2400	Love Makes the World Go Round/I'll Make Him Love Me	1967	20.00
❑ 2413	Fool, Fool, Fool/Only All the Time	1967	20.00
❑ 2482	Thankful for What I Got/Sho Nuff	1968	20.00
❑ 2514	On Bended Knees/I'll Keep Believing	1968	20.00
❑ 2550	I'm All You've Got/You're a Dream Maker	1968	20.00
ENTERPRISE			
❑ 9012	You Made Me a Woman/Just the Way You Are Today	1970	40.00
❑ 9027	Ask the Lonely/Why Did It Take You So Long	1970	30.00
❑ 9029	Anyway/That's the Way I Like It	1970	10.00
KAREN			
❑ 313	My Heart Went Do Dat Da/The Longest Night of the Year	1961	40.00
REPRISE			
❑ 1146	Rock and Roll Lullaby/I'm So Thankful	1972	30.00

7-Inch Extended Plays

Number	Title (A Side/B Side)	Yr	NM
ATLANTIC			
❑ LSD 8110 [DJ]	Baby I'm Yours/Hy Heart Went Do Da Dat/Puppy Love//Hello Stranger/Someday We're Gonna Love Again/Snap Your Fingers	196?	15.00
—Jukebox mini-LP, small hole, plays at 33 1/3 rpm			
❑ LSD 8110 [PS]	Baby I'm Yours	196?	15.00

Albums

Number	Title (A Side/B Side)	Yr	NM
ATLANTIC			
❑ 8086 [M]	Hello Stranger	1963	40.00
❑ SD 8086 [S]	Hello Stranger	1963	50.00
❑ 8090 [M]	Snap Your Fingers	1964	40.00
❑ SD 8090 [S]	Snap Your Fingers	1964	50.00
❑ 8110 [M]	Baby, I'm Yours	1965	40.00
❑ SD 8110 [S]	Baby, I'm Yours	1965	50.00
❑ 8118 [M]	It's Magic	1966	30.00
❑ SD 8118 [S]	It's Magic	1966	40.00
❑ SD 8173	Workin' on a Groovy Thing	1968	25.00
❑ 8286 [M]	The Best of Barbara Lewis	1971	40.00
—Mono is white label promo only; front cover has "d/j copy monaural" sticker			
❑ SD 8286 [S]	The Best of Barbara Lewis	1971	20.00
COLLECTABLES			
❑ COL-5104	Golden Classics	198?	10.00
ENTERPRISE			
❑ ENS-1006	The Many Grooves of Barbara Lewis	1970	25.00

LEWIS, BOBBY (1)

R&B singer. R&B singer; not to be confused with the country singer of the same name, who recorded for Ace of Hearts, Capricorn, GRT, HME, RPA and United Artists.

45s

Number	Title (A Side/B Side)	Yr	NM
ABC-PARAMOUNT			
❑ 10565	That's Right/Fannie Lewis	1964	12.00
❑ 10592	Jealous Love/Stark Raving Wild	1964	12.00
BELTONE			
❑ 1002	Tossin' and Turnin'/Oh Yes I Love You	1961	25.00
❑ 1012	One Track Mind/Are You Ready	1961	25.00
❑ 1015	What a Walk/Cry No More	1961	15.00
❑ 1016	Yes, Oh Yes, It Did/Mamie in the Afternoon	1962	15.00
❑ 2018	A Man's Gotta Be a Man/Day by Day I Need Your Love	1962	15.00
❑ 2023	I'm Tossin' and Turnin' Again/Nothin' But the Blues	1962	15.00
❑ 2026	Lonely Teardrops/Boom-a-Chick-Chick	1962	15.00
❑ 2035	Nothin' But the Blues/Intermission	1963	15.00
LANA			
❑ 104	Tossin' and Turnin'/Oh Yes I Love You	196?	8.00
—Oldies reissue			
LOST-NITE			
❑ 146	Tossin' An' Turnin'/Oh Yes I Love You	196?	6.00
—Reissue; note slightly different spelling of A-side			
MERCURY			
❑ 71245	Mumbles Blues/Oh Baby	1957	25.00
PHILIPS			
❑ 40519	Soul Seekin'/Give Me Your Yesterdays	1968	20.00
ROULETTE			
❑ 4182	You Better Stop/Fire of Love	1959	15.00
❑ 4382	Solid as a Rock/Oh Mr. Somebody	1961	15.00
SPOTLIGHT			
❑ 394	Mumbles Blues/Oh Baby	1957	30.00
❑ 397	Solid as a Rock/You Even Forgot My Name	1957	30.00

Albums

Number	Title (A Side/B Side)	Yr	NM
BELTONE			
❑ 4000 [M]	Tossin' and Turnin'	1961	200.00

LEWIS, BOBBY (2) Country singer.

45s

ACE OF HEARTS

Number	Title (A Side/B Side)	Yr	NM
❑ 0463	Already Gone to My Heart/ Mr. President	1973	6.00
❑ 0466	Here with You/ Where Happiness Is	1973	6.00
❑ 0472	Too Many Memories/ With Meaning	1973	6.00
❑ 0480	I Never Get Through Missing You/Lady Lover	1974	6.00
❑ 0502	Let Me Take Care of You/ Where Happiness Is	1975	6.00
❑ 7503	It's So Nice to Be with You/ (B-side unknown)	1975	6.00

CAPRICORN

Number	Title (A Side/B Side)	Yr	NM
❑ 0318	She's Been Keeping Me Up Nights/I Keep Falling in Love with You	1979	5.00
❑ 0331	Love Won't Be Love Without You/This Is a Man and Woman Kind of Night	1979	5.00

GRT

Number	Title (A Side/B Side)	Yr	NM
❑ 007	Lady Lover/I Never Get Through Missing You	1974	6.00
❑ 008	I See Love/Your Love	1974	6.00

HME

Number	Title (A Side/B Side)	Yr	NM
❑ 04853	Love Is An Overload/Treat Her Like a Stranger	1985	4.00

RPA

Number	Title (A Side/B Side)	Yr	NM
❑ 7603	For Your Love/(B-side unknown)	1976	6.00
❑ 7613	I'm Getting High Remembering/With Meaning	1976	6.00
❑ 7622	What a Diff'rence a Day Made/ I Can Feel It	1977	6.00

UNITED ARTISTS

Number	Title (A Side/B Side)	Yr	NM
❑ 842	Everybody's Baby/Perfect Example of a Fool	1965	10.00
❑ 920	Why Me/Six Days a Week, Twice on Sunday	1965	10.00
❑ 50009	You Remind Me Of Myself/I Hope You Find in Him What You Were Looking For in Me	1966	8.00
❑ 50067	How Long Has It Been/ Easy to Say, Hard to Do	1966	8.00
❑ 50133	Two of the Usual/Your B.A.B.Y. Baby Don't Love You	1967	8.00
❑ 50161	Love Me and Make It All Better/ My Tears Don't Care (They Fall Anywhere)	1967	8.00
❑ 50208	I Doubt It/Laughing Girl, She's Not Happy	1967	8.00
❑ 50263	Ordinary Miracle/These Are Things I Miss	1968	8.00
❑ 50327	From Heaven to Heartache/ Only for Me	1968	8.00
❑ 50476	Each and Every Part of Me/ My (Is Such a Lonely Word)	1969	8.00
❑ 50528	Til Something Better Comes Along/I'm Only a Man	1969	8.00
❑ 50573	Things for You and I/ Somebody Lied to Me	1969	8.00
❑ 50620	I'm Going Home/I May Never Be Free	1969	8.00
❑ 50668	Hello Mary Lou/Love, Wonderful Love	1970	7.00
❑ 50719	Simple Days and Simple Ways/ Love's Garden	1970	7.00
❑ 50754	Come Sundown/He Gives Us All His Love	1971	7.00
❑ 50791	If I Had You/Doggone This Heartache	1971	7.00
❑ 50850	Today's Teardrops/ Love's Satisfaction	1971	7.00
❑ 50885	Only Love Can Break a Heart/ We Ran Out of Time	1972	7.00

Albums

ACE OF HEARTS

Number	Title	Yr	NM
❑ 1002	Too Many Memories	1974	15.00

RPA

Number	Title	Yr	NM
❑ 1002	Portrait in Love	1976	10.00
❑ 1013	Soul Full of Music	1977	10.00

UNITED ARTISTS

Number	Title	Yr	NM
❑ UAL-3582 [M]	How Long Has It Been	1967	25.00
❑ UAS-6582 [S]	How Long Has It Been	1967	25.00
❑ UAS-6616	A World of Love from Bobby Lewis	1967	20.00
❑ UAS-6629	An Ordinary Miracle	1968	20.00
❑ UAS-6673	From Heaven to Heartache	1968	20.00
❑ UAS-6717	Thanks for You and I	1969	20.00
❑ UAS-6760	The Best of Bobby Lewis, Vol. 1	1970	15.00

LEWIS, CLARENCE

45s

FURY

Number	Title (A Side/B Side)	Yr	NM
❑ 1032	Cupid's Little Helper/Half a Heart	1960	15.00

RED ROBIN

Number	Title (A Side/B Side)	Yr	NM
❑ 136	Lost Everything/Your Heart Must Be Made of Stone	1955	80.00

LEWIS, EARL, AND THE CHANNELS See THE CHANNELS.

LEWIS, GARY, AND THE PLAYBOYS

45s

EPIC

Number	Title (A Side/B Side)	Yr	NM
❑ 50068	One Good Woman/Ooh Baby	1975	8.00

—Gary Lewis solo

LIBERTY

Number	Title (A Side/B Side)	Yr	NM
❑ (no #) [DJ]	Way Way Out (same on both sides)	1967	500.00
❑ 65-227	Doin' the Flake//This Diamond Ring/Little Miss Go-Go	1965	25.00
—Record available by mail order from Kellogg's Corn Flakes; all copies have black labels with silver print			
❑ 65-227 [PS]	Doin' the Flake//This Diamond Ring/Little Miss Go-Go	1965	50.00
—Kellogg's Corn Flakes giveaway			
❑ 55756	This Diamond Ring/Tijuana Wedding	1964	10.00
❑ 55756	This Diamond Ring/Hard to Find	1964	12.00
❑ 55778	Count Me In/Little Miss Go-Go	1965	10.00
❑ 55809	Save Your Heart for Me/ Without a Word of Warning	1965	10.00
❑ 55818	Everybody Loves a Clown/ Time Stands Still	1965	10.00
❑ 55818 [PS]	Everybody Loves a Clown/ Time Stands Still	1965	15.00
❑ 55846	She's Just My Style/I Won't Make That Mistake Again	1965	10.00
❑ 55846 [PS]	She's Just My Style/I Won't Make That Mistake Again	1965	15.00
❑ 55865	Sure Gonna Miss Her/I Don't Wanna Say Goodnight	1966	10.00
❑ 55865 [PS]	Sure Gonna Miss Her/I Don't Wanna Say Goodnight	1966	15.00
❑ 55880	Green Grass/I Can Read Between the Lines	1966	10.00
❑ 55880 [PS]	Green Grass/I Can Read Between the Lines	1966	15.00
❑ 55898	My Heart's Symphony/Tina	1966	10.00
❑ 55898 [PS]	My Heart's Symphony/Tina	1966	15.00
❑ 55914	(You Don't Have to) Paint Me a Picture/Looking for the Stars	1966	10.00
❑ 55914 [PS]	(You Don't Have to) Paint Me a Picture/Looking for the Stars	1966	15.00
❑ 55932	Down on the Sloop John B/ Ice Melts in the Sun	1966	—
—Unreleased			
❑ 55933	Where Will the Words Come From/May the Best Man Win	1966	10.00
❑ 55949	The Loser (With a Broken Heart)/Ice Melts in the Sun	1967	10.00
❑ 55949 [PS]	The Loser (With a Broken Heart)/Ice Melts in the Sun	1967	15.00
❑ 55971	Girls in Love/Let's Be More Than Friends	1967	8.00
❑ 55985	Jill/New in Town	1967	8.00
❑ 56011	Has She Got the Nicest Eyes/ Happiness	1967	8.00
❑ 56037	Sealed with a Kiss/Sara Jane	1968	8.00
❑ 56075	C.C. Rider/Main Street	1968	6.00
❑ 56093	Every Day I Have to Cry Some/ Mister Memory	1969	6.00
❑ 56093	Rhythm of the Rain/ Mister Memory	1969	6.00
❑ 56121	Hayride/Gary's Groove	1969	6.00
❑ 56144	I Saw Elvis Presley Last Night/ Something Is Wrong	1969	12.00
❑ 56158	Great Balls of Fire/I'm On the Road Right Now	1970	6.00

SCEPTER

Number	Title (A Side/B Side)	Yr	NM
❑ 12359	Peace of Mind/ Then Again Maybe	1972	8.00

—Gary Lewis solo

UNITED ARTISTS

Number	Title (A Side/B Side)	Yr	NM
❑ 0064	This Diamond Ring/ My Heart's Symphony	1973	4.00
❑ 0065	Count Me In/Save Your Heart for Me	1973	4.00
❑ 0066	Everybody Loves a Clown/ Sure Gonna Miss Her	1973	4.00
❑ 0067	She's Just My Style/Green Grass	1973	4.00

—0064 through 0067 are "Silver Spotlight Series" reissues

Albums

LIBERTY

Number	Title	Yr	NM
❑ LM-1003	This Diamond Ring	1981	8.00
—Reissue of United Artists 1008			
❑ LRP-3408 [M]	This Diamond Ring	1965	20.00
❑ LRP-3419 [M]	A Session with Gary Lewis and the Playboys	1965	20.00
❑ LRP-3428 [M]	Everybody Loves a Clown	1965	20.00
❑ LRP-3435 [M]	She's Just My Style	1966	15.00
❑ LRP-3452 [M]	Hits Again!	1966	15.00
❑ LRP-3468 [M]	Golden Greats	1966	15.00
❑ LRP-3487 [M]	(You Don't Have to) P aint Me a Picture	1967	15.00
—Side 1 plays as listed			
❑ LRP-3487 [M]	(You Don't Have to) Paint Me a Picture	1967	20.00
—Side 1, Song 4 claims to be "Tina" but plays "Ice Melts in the Sun"			
❑ LRP-3519 [M]	New Directions	1967	15.00
❑ LRP-3524 [M]	Listen!	1967	15.00
❑ LST-7408 [S]	This Diamond Ring	1965	25.00
❑ LST-7419 [S]	A Session with Gary Lewis and the Playboys	1965	25.00
❑ LST-7428 [S]	Everybody Loves a Clown	1965	25.00
❑ LST-7435 [S]	She's Just My Style	1966	20.00
❑ LST-7452 [S]	Hits Again!	1966	20.00
❑ LST-7468 [S]	Golden Greats	1966	20.00
—Side 2 plays as listed			
❑ LST-7468 [S]	Golden Greats	1966	30.00
—Side 2, Song 2 claims to be "I Won't Make That Mistake Again" but it plays "You've Got to Hide Your Love Away"			
❑ LST-7487 [S]	(You Don't Have to) Paint Me a Picture	1967	20.00
—Side 1 plays as listed			
❑ LST-7487 [S]	(You Don't Have to) Paint Me a Picture	1967	25.00
—Side 1, Song 4 claims to be "Tina" but plays "Ice Melts in the Sun"			
❑ LST-7519 [S]	New Directions	1967	15.00
❑ LST-7524 [S]	Listen	1967	15.00
❑ LST-7568	Gary Lewis Now!	1968	15.00
❑ LST-7589	More Golden Greats	1968	15.00
❑ LST-7606	Close Cover Before Playing	1969	15.00
❑ LST-7623	Rhythm of the Rain	1969	15.00
❑ LST-7633	I'm On the Right Road Now	1970	15.00
❑ LN-10241	Golden Greats	198?	8.00
—Budget-line reissue			

RHINO

Number	Title	Yr	NM
❑ RNLP-163	Greatest Hits (1965-1968)	1985	10.00

SUNSET

Number	Title	Yr	NM
❑ SUM-1168 [M]	Gary Lewis and the Playboys	1967	12.00
❑ SUS-5168 [S]	Gary Lewis and the Playboys	1967	12.00
❑ SUS-5262	Rhythm!	1969	12.00

UNITED ARTISTS

Number	Title	Yr	NM
❑ UA-LA430-E	The Very Best of Gary Lewis and the Playboys	1975	10.00
❑ LM-1003	This Diamond Ring	1980	10.00

—Edited reissue of Liberty 7408

LEWIS, HERMAN

45s

STONE BLUE

Number	Title (A Side/B Side)	Yr	NM
❑ 101	Who's Kissing You Tonite/(B-side unknown)	196?	2500.

—VG 1000; VG+ 1750

LEWIS, HUEY, AND THE NEWS

12-Inch Singles

CHRYSALIS

Number	Title (A Side/B Side)	Yr	NM
❑ CHS 41-PDJ [DJ]	Workin' for a Livin' (Album Version) (Live)	1982	12.00
❑ VAS 1165 [DJ]	Perfect World (same on both sides)	1988	7.00
❑ VAS 1267 [DJ]	Small World (same on both sides)	1988	8.00
❑ VAS 1353 [DJ]	Give Me the Keys (And I'll Drive You Crazy) (Remix 4:39) (Live 5:27)	1988	10.00
❑ AS 1728 [DJ]	Heart and Soul (same on both sides)	1983	10.00
❑ AS 1818 [DJ]	I Want a New Drug (Vocal Dance Mix 5:32) (Instrumental 4:30)	1983	8.00
❑ AS 1925 [DJ]	Walking on a Thin Line (LP Version) (Live)	1984	10.00
❑ VAS 2032 [DJ]	Bad Is Bad (same on both sides)	1985	10.00
❑ VAS 2155 [DJ]	Back in Time (same on both sides)	1985	15.00
❑ VAS 2390 [DJ]	Stuck with You (same on both sides)	1986	10.00
❑ VAS 2488 [DJ]	Jacob's Ladder (Special Radio Remix) (same on both sides)	1986	8.00
❑ VAS 2507 [DJ]	Hip to Be Square (same on both sides)	1986	8.00
❑ VAS 2596 [DJ]	Jacob's Ladder (Live) (same on both sides)	1987	8.00
❑ 4V9 42779	I Want a New Drug (Vocal Dance Mix 5:32) (Instrumental 4:30)	1983	8.00

Except when noted otherwise, VG = 25% of NM, and VG+ = 50% of NM. (Example: VG = $2.00, VG+ = $4.00 and NM = $8.00.)

Number	Title (A Side/B Side)	Yr	NM
❑ 4V9 42889	The Power of Love (Extended Mix 7:20) (Instrumental 4:12) (LP Version 4:18)	1985	8.00
❑ 4V9 43075	Hip to Be Square (Dance Remix 6:05) (Dub Mix)	1986	8.00
❑ 4V9 43308	Small World (Extended Dance Mix 6:59) (Part 1 and 2 7:39)/Perfect World	1986	8.00
45s			
CHRYSALIS			
❑ 2446	Some of My Lies Are True/Hearts	1980	10.00
❑ 2446 [PS]	Some of My Lies Are True/Hearts	1980	15.00
—Newspaper-like sleeve with "The Bay Area's Free Daily SPECIAL EDITION" on front			
❑ 2458	Now Here's You/Hearts	1980	10.00
❑ 2589	Do You Believe in Love/Is It Me	1981	5.00
❑ 2604	Hope You Love Me Like You Say You Do/Whatever Happened to True Love	1982	5.00
❑ 2604 [PS]	Hope You Love Me Like You Say You Do/Whatever Happened to True Love	1982	5.00
❑ 2630	Workin' for a Livin'/(Live)	1982	5.00
❑ VS4 42726	Heart and Soul/You Crack Me Up	1983	3.00
❑ VS4 42726 [PS]	Heart and Soul/You Crack Me Up	1983	3.00
❑ VS4 42766	I Want a New Drug/Finally Found a Home	1983	3.00
❑ VS4 42766 [PS]	I Want a New Drug/Finally Found a Home	1983	5.00
❑ VS4 42782	The Heart of Rock and Roll/Workin' for a Livin' (Live)	1984	3.00
❑ VS4 42782 [PS]	The Heart of Rock and Roll/Workin' for a Livin' (Live)	1984	4.00
❑ VS4 42803	If This Is It/Change of Heart	1984	3.00
❑ VS4 42803 [PS]	If This Is It/Change of Heart	1984	3.00
❑ VS4 42825	Walking on a Thin Line/The Only One	1984	3.00
❑ VS4 42825 [PS]	Walking on a Thin Line/The Only One	1984	3.00
❑ VS4 42876	The Power of Love/Bad Is Bad	1985	3.00
—Later edition, with "The" added to A-side title			
❑ VS4 42876	Power of Love/Bad Is Bad	1985	5.00
—Original edition			
❑ VS4 42876 [PS]	The Power of Love/Bad Is Bad	1985	5.00
—All of the picture sleeves have this title on them			
❑ VS8 42947	Do You Believe in Love/Working for a Living	1986	4.00
—Silver label reissue			
❑ VS8 42948	Heart and Soul/I Want a New Drug	1986	4.00
—Silver label reissue			
❑ VS8 42949	The Heart of Rock and Roll/If This Is It	1986	4.00
—Silver label reissue			
❑ VS4 43019	Stuck with You/Don't Ever Tell Me That You Love Me	1986	3.00
❑ VS4 43019 [PS]	Stuck with You/Don't Ever Tell Me That You Love Me	1986	3.00
❑ VS4 43065	Hip to Be Square/Some of My Lies Are True	1986	3.00
❑ VS4 43065 [PS]	Hip to Be Square/Some of My Lies Are True	1986	3.00
❑ VS4 43097	Jacob's Ladder/The Heart of Rock and Roll	1987	3.00
❑ VS4 43097 [PS]	Jacob's Ladder/The Heart of Rock and Roll	1987	3.00
❑ VS4 43108	I Know What I Like/Forest for the Trees	1987	3.00
❑ VS4 43108 [PS]	I Know What I Like/Forest for the Trees	1987	3.00
❑ VS4 43143	Doing It All for My Baby/Naturally	1987	3.00
❑ VS4 43143 [PS]	Doing It All for My Baby/Naturally	1987	3.00
❑ VS4 43265	Perfect World/Slammin'	1988	3.00
❑ VS4 43265 [PS]	Perfect World/Slammin'	1988	3.00
❑ VS4 43306	Small World/(Instrumental)	1988	3.00
❑ VS4 43306 [PS]	Small World/(Instrumental)	1988	3.00
❑ VS4 43335	Give Me the Keys (And I'll Drive You Crazy)/It's All Right (Live)	1989	4.00
❑ VS4 43335 [PS]	Give Me the Keys (And I'll Drive You Crazy)/It's All Right (Live)	1989	3.00
COLLECTABLES			
❑ 6316	Do You Believe in Love/I Hit Me Like a Hammer	199?	4.00
—B-side's only appearance on a U.S. 45			
❑ 6317	Hip to Be Square/Heart and Soul	199?	3.00
❑ 6318	I Want a New Drug/Couple Days Off	199?	4.00
—B-side's only appearance on a U.S. 45			
❑ 6319	Jacob's Ladder/The Heart of Rock and Roll	199?	3.00
❑ 6320	The Power of Love/If This Is It	199?	3.00
❑ 6321	Stuck with You/Doing It All for My Baby	199?	3.00
ELEKTRA			
❑ 64542	(She's) Some Kind of Wonderful/Good Morning Little Schoolgirl	1994	8.00

Number	Title (A Side/B Side)	Yr	NM
Albums			
CHRYSALIS			
❑ CHR 1292	Huey Lewis and the News	1980	12.00
❑ CHR 1340	Picture This	1982	10.00
❑ FV 41292	Huey Lewis and the News	1983	8.00
—Reissue of 1292			
❑ PV 41292	Huey Lewis and the News	198?	6.00
—Reissue with new prefix			
❑ FV 41340	Picture This	1983	8.00
—Reissue of 1340			
❑ FV 41412	Sports	1983	8.00
❑ OV 41412	Sports	198?	6.00
—Reissue with new prefix			
❑ OV 41534	Fore!	1986	8.00
❑ OV 41622	Small World	1988	8.00
❑ 8V8 42795 [EP]	84 Sports Tour	1984	15.00
—Three-song picture disc numbered as if it were a single			
MOBILE FIDELITY			
❑ 1-181	Sports	1985	30.00
—"Original Master Recording" on front cover			

LEWIS, HUGH X.

Number	Title (A Side/B Side)	Yr	NM
45s			
COLUMBIA			
❑ 4-45047	Everything I Love/Mr. Policeman	1969	6.00
❑ 4-45144	My Babysitter/When Love's Gone	1970	6.00
GRT			
❑ 28	Blues Sells a Lot of Booze/Help Yourself to Me	1970	6.00
KAPP			
❑ 622	What I Need Most/Too Late	1964	8.00
❑ 673	Out Where the Ocean Meets the Sky/Talking to a Bottle	1965	7.00
❑ 717	I'd Better Call the Law on Me/Take Me Out of It	1965	7.00
❑ 757	I'm Losing You (I Can Tell)/Just Before Dawn	1966	7.00
❑ 771	Wish Me a Rainbow/You Belong to My Heart	1966	7.00
❑ 812	Tender Hearted Me (The Bug Song)/Another Day Just Slipped Away	1967	7.00
❑ 830	You're So Cold (I'm Turning Blue)/No Chance for Happiness	1967	7.00
❑ 868	Wrong Side of the World/Your Steppin' Stone	1967	7.00
❑ 895	Evolution and the Bible/Gone, Gone, Gone	1968	7.00
❑ 921	War Is Hell/With These Hands	1968	7.00
❑ 939	Country Music Fever/The World Doesn't End Here	1968	7.00
❑ 955	Tonight We're Calling It a Day/Sittin' and Thinkin'	1968	7.00
❑ 978	All Heaven Broke Loose/Some Other Time	1969	7.00
❑ 2020	Restless Melissa/Our Angels Just Aren't Singing Anymore	1969	7.00
LITTLE DARLIN'			
❑ 7803	Love Don't Hide from Me/Thinking of You Thinking of Him	1978	6.00
❑ 7913	What Can I Do (To Make You Love Me)/Once Before I Die	1979	6.00
Albums			
KAPP			
❑ KL-1462 [M]	The Hugh X. Lewis Album	1966	20.00
❑ KL-1494 [M]	Just Before Dawn	1966	20.00
❑ KL-1522 [M]	My Kind of Country	1967	30.00
❑ KS-3462 [S]	The Hugh X. Lewis Album	1966	25.00
❑ KS-3494 [S]	Just Before Dawn	1966	25.00
❑ KS-3522 [S]	My Kind of Country	1967	25.00
❑ KS-3545	Just a Prayer Away	1968	25.00
❑ KS-3563	Country Fever	1968	25.00

LEWIS, JERRY LEE

Number	Title (A Side/B Side)	Yr	NM
45s			
ELEKTRA			
❑ 46030	Rockin' My Life Away/I Wish I Was Eighteen Again	1979	4.00
❑ 46067	Who Will the Next Fool Be/Rita May	1979	4.00
❑ 46591	When Two Worlds Collide/Good News Travels Fast	1980	4.00
❑ 46642	Honky Tonk Stuff/Rockin' Jerry Lee	1980	4.00
❑ 47026	Over the Rainbow/Folsom Prison Blues	1980	4.00
❑ 47095	Thirty-Nine and Holding/Change Places with Me	1980	4.00
❑ 69962	I'd Do It All Again/Who Will Buy the Wine	1982	4.00
MCA			
❑ 52151	My Fingers Do the Talkin'/Forever Forgiving	1983	3.00
❑ 52188	Come As You Were/Circumstantial Evidence	1983	3.00
❑ 52233	She Sings Amazing Grace/Why You Been Gone So Long	1983	3.00
❑ 52369	I Am What I Am/That Was the Way It Was Then	1984	3.00
MERCURY			
❑ 55011	Middle Age Crazy/Georgia on My Mind	1977	6.00
❑ 55021	Come On In/Who's Sorry Now	1977	6.00
❑ 55028	I'll Find It Where I Can/Don't Let the Stars Get In Your Eyes	1977	6.00
❑ 73099	There Must Be More to Love Than This/Home Away from Home	1970	8.00
❑ 73155	I Can't Have a Merry Christmas, Mary (Without You)/In Loving Memories	1970	10.00
❑ 73192	Touching Home/Woman, Woman	1971	8.00
❑ 73227	When He Walks on You (Like You Have Walked on Me)/Foolish Kind of Man	1971	8.00
❑ 73248	Would You Take Another Chance on Me/Me and Bobby McGee	1971	8.00
❑ 73273	Chantilly Lace/Think About It Darlin'	1972	8.00
❑ 73296	Lonely Weekends/Turn On Your Love Light	1972	8.00
❑ 73328	Who's Gonna Play This Old Piano/No Honky Tonks in Heaven	1972	8.00
❑ 73361	No More Hanging On/Mercy of a Letter	1973	8.00
❑ 73374	Drinking Wine Spo-Dee O'Dee/Rock and Roll Medley	1973	8.00
❑ 73402	No Headstone on My Grave/Jack Daniels	1973	8.00
❑ 73423	Sometimes a Memory Ain't Enough/I Think I Need to Pray	1973	8.00
❑ 73452	I'm Left, You're Right, She's Gone/I've Fallen to the Bottom	1974	8.00
❑ 73462	Meat Man/Just a Little Bit	1974	8.00
❑ 73491	Tell Tale Signs/Cold, Cold Morning Light	1974	8.00
❑ 73618	He Can't Fill My Shoes/Tomorrow's Taking Baby Away	1974	6.00
❑ 73661	I Can Still Hear the Music in the Restroom/Remember Me	1975	6.00
❑ 73685	Boogie Woogie Country Man/I'm Still Jealous of You	1975	6.00
❑ 73729	A Damn Good Country Song/When I Take My Vacation in Heaven	1975	6.00
❑ 73763	Don't Boogie Woogie/That Kind of Fool	1976	6.00
❑ 73822	Let's Put It Back Together Again/Jerry Lee's Rock and Roll Revival Show	1976	6.00
❑ 73872	The Closest Thing to You/You Belong to Me	1976	6.00
❑ 76148	I'm So Lonesome I Could Cry/Pick Me Up on Your Way Down	1982	5.00
PHILLIPS INT'L.			
❑ 3559	In the Mood/I Get the Blues When It Rains	1960	50.00
—As "The Hawk"			
POLYDOR			
❑ 889312-7	Breathless/Great Balls of Fire	1989	4.00
❑ 889312-7 [PS]	Breathless/Great Balls of Fire	1989	4.00
❑ 889798-7	Crazy Arms/Great Balls of Fire	1989	4.00
SCR			
❑ 386	Get Out Your Big Roll, Daddy/Honky Tonkin' Rock 'N' Roll Piano Man	1985	5.00
SIRE			
❑ 19809	It Was the Whiskey Talkin' (Not Me)/same (Rock and Roll Version)	1990	3.00
❑ 64423	Goose Bumps/Crown Victoria 51	1995	5.00
SMASH			
❑ 1857	Pen and Paper/Hit the Road Jack	1963	15.00
❑ 1886	I'm on Fire/Bread and Butter Man	1964	40.00
❑ 1906	She Was My Baby (He Was My Friend)/The Hole He Said He'd Dig for Me	1964	15.00
❑ 1930	High Heel Sneakers/You Went Back on Your Word	1964	15.00
❑ 1969	Baby Hold Me Close/I Believe in You	1965	15.00

Number	Title (A Side/B Side)	Yr	NM
❑ 1992	This Must Be the Place/Rocking Pneumonia and the Boogie Woogie Flu	1965	15.00
❑ 2006	Green, Green Grass of Home/You've Got What It Takes	1965	15.00
❑ 2027	Sticks and Stones/What a Heck of a Mess	1966	12.00
❑ 2053	If I Had It All to Do Over/Memphis Beat	1966	12.00
❑ 2103	Holding On/It's a Hang-Up, Baby	1967	12.00
❑ 2122	Turn On Your Love Light/Shotgun Man	1967	12.00
❑ 2146	Another Place, Another Time/Walking the Floor Over You	1968	10.00
❑ 2164	What's Made Milwaukee Famous (Has Made a Loser Out of Me)/All the Good Is Gone	1968	10.00
❑ 2186	She Still Comes Around (To Love What's Left of Me)/Slipping Around	1968	10.00
❑ 2202	To Make Love Sweeter for You/Let's Talk About Us	1968	10.00
❑ 2224	One Has My Name (The Other Has My Heart)/I Can't Stop Loving You	1969	10.00
❑ 2244	She Even Woke Me Up to Say Goodbye/Echoes	1969	10.00
❑ 2257	Once More with Feeling/You Went Out of Your Way (To Walk on Me)	1970	10.00
❑ 884934-7	Sixteen Candles/Rock and Roll (Fais-Do-Do)	1986	4.00
—B-side with Roy Orbison, Carl Perkins and Johnny Cash			
❑ 888142-7	We Remember the King/Class of '55	1987	4.00
—With Johnny Cash, Roy Orbison and Carl Perkins; B-side by Carl Perkins solo			

SUN

Number	Title (A Side/B Side)	Yr	NM
❑ 259	Crazy Arms/End of the Road	1957	50.00
—As "Jerry Lee Lewis and His Pumping Piano"			
❑ 259	Crazy Arms/End of the Road	1957	100.00
—As "Jerry Lee Lewis"			
❑ 267	Whole Lot of Shakin' Going On/It'll Be Me	1957	40.00
❑ 281	Great Balls of Fire/You Win Again	1957	40.00
❑ 281 [PS]	Great Balls of Fire/You Win Again	1957	80.00
❑ 288	Breathless/Down the Line	1958	40.00
❑ 296	High School Confidential/Fools Like Me	1958	30.00
❑ 296 [PS]	High School Confidential/Fools Like Me	1958	80.00
❑ 301	Lewis Boogie/The Return of Jerry Lee	1958	30.00
—B-side by George and Louis			
❑ 303	I'll Make It All Up to You/Break-Up	1958	30.00
❑ 312	I'll Sail My Ship Alone/It Hurt Me So	1958	25.00
❑ 317	Lovin' Up a Storm/Big Blon' Baby	1959	25.00
❑ 324	Let's Talk About Us/Ballad of Billy Joe	1959	25.00
❑ 330	Little Queenie/I Could Never Be Ashamed of You	1959	25.00
❑ 337	Old Black Joe/Baby Baby, Bye Bye	1960	20.00
❑ 344	Hang Up My Rock and Roll Shoes/John Henry	1960	20.00
❑ 352	Love Made a Fool of Me/When I Get Paid	1960	20.00
❑ 356	What'd I Say/Livin' Lovin' Wreck	1961	20.00
❑ 364	Cold, Cold Heart/It Won't Happen with Me	1961	20.00
❑ 367	Save the Last Dance for Me/As Long As I Live	1961	20.00
❑ 371	Money/Bonnie B	1961	20.00
❑ 374	I've Been Twistin'/Ramblin' Rose	1962	20.00
❑ 379	Sweet Little Sixteen/How's My Ex Treating You	1962	20.00
❑ 382	Good Golly Miss Molly/I Can't Trust Me	1962	20.00
❑ 384	Teenage Letter/Seasons of My Heart	1963	20.00
❑ 396	Carry Me Back to Old Virginny/I Know What It Means	1965	20.00
❑ 1101	Invitation to Your Party/I Could Never Be Ashamed of You	1969	6.00
❑ 1107	One Minute Past Eternity/Frankie and Johnny	1969	6.00
❑ 1115	I Can't Seem to Say Goodbye/Goodnight Irene	1970	5.00
❑ 1119	Waiting for the Train (All Around the Watertank)/Big Legged Woman	1970	5.00
❑ 1125	Love on Broadway/Matchbox	1971	5.00
❑ 1128	Your Loving Ways/I Can't Trust Me in Your Arms Anymore	1972	5.00
❑ 1130	Good Rockin' Tonight/I Can't Trust Me in Your Arms Anymore	1973	5.00
❑ 1138	Matchbox/Am I to Be the One	1978	4.00
❑ 1139	Save the Last Dance for Me/Am I to Be the One	1978	4.00
—With uncredited "duet" partner, actually Orion (Jimmy Ellis); a shameless attempt to concoct a "lost Elvis Presley duet"			
❑ 1141	Cold, Cold Heart/Hello Josephine	1979	4.00
❑ 1151	Be-Bop-a-Lula/The Breakup	1980	4.00
—B-side by Charlie Rich; both sides are duets with Orion			

7-Inch Extended Plays

SUN

Number	Title (A Side/B Side)	Yr	NM
❑ EPA-107	Mean Woman Blues/I'm Feelin' Sorry//Whole Lot of Shakin' Goin' On/Turn Around	1958	80.00
❑ EPA-107 [PS]	The Great Ball of Fire	1958	80.00
❑ EP-108	One Minute Past Eternity/Cold, Cold Heart/Invitation to Your Party// I Can't Trust Me in Your Arms Anymore/How's My Ex Treating You/Ramblin' Rose	197?	20.00
—Jukebox issue; small hole, plays at 33 1/3 rpm			
❑ EP-108 [PS]	The Golden Cream of the Country	197?	20.00
—Part of "Little LP" series (LLP #155)			
❑ EPA-108	Don't Be Cruel/Goodnight Irene//Put Me Down/It All Depends	1958	50.00
❑ EPA-108 [PS]	Jerry Lee Lewis	1958	50.00
❑ EPA-109	Ubangi Stomp/Crazy Arms//Jambalaya/Fools Like Me	1958	50.00
❑ EPA-109 [PS]	Jerry Lee Lewis	1958	50.00
❑ EPA-110	High School Confidential/When the Saints Go Marching In//Matchbox/It'll Be Me	1958	50.00
❑ EPA-110 [PS]	Jerry Lee Lewis	1958	50.00
❑ EP-114	You Win Again/I Can't Seem to Say Goodbye/Am I to Be the One//As Long As I Live/I Love You So Much It Hurts/Night Train to Memphis	197?	20.00
—Jukebox issue; small hole, plays at 33 1/3 rpm			
❑ EP-114 [PS]	A Taste of Country	197?	20.00

Albums

ACCORD

Number	Title	Yr	NM
❑ SN-7133	I Walk the Line	1981	10.00

DESIGN

Number	Title	Yr	NM
❑ DLP-165 [M]	Rockin' with Jerry Lee Lewis	1963	25.00
❑ DST-165 [R]	Rockin' with Jerry Lee Lewis	1963	20.00

ELEKTRA

Number	Title	Yr	NM
❑ 6E-184	Jerry Lee Lewis	1979	12.00
❑ 6E-254	When Two Worlds Collide	1980	12.00
❑ 6E-291	Killer Country	1980	12.00
❑ 60191	The Best of Jerry Lee Lewis Featuring 39 and Holding	1982	10.00

HILLTOP

Number	Title	Yr	NM
❑ 6102	Sunday After Church	1971	10.00
❑ 6110	Roll Over Beethoven	1972	10.00
❑ 6120	Rural Route #1	1972	10.00

MCA

Number	Title	Yr	NM
❑ 5387	My Fingers Do the Talkin'	1983	10.00
❑ 5478	I Am What I Am	1984	10.00

MERCURY

Number	Title	Yr	NM
❑ SRM-1-637	The "Killer" Rocks On	1972	15.00
❑ SRM-1-677	Sometimes a Memory Ain't Enough	1973	15.00
❑ 690 [DJ]	A Jerry Lee Lewis Radio Special	1973	50.00
❑ SRM-1-690	Southern Roots — Back Home to Memphis	1973	15.00
❑ SRM-1-710	I-40 Country	1974	15.00
❑ SRM-2-803 [(2)]	The Session	1973	20.00
❑ SRM-1-1030	Boogie Woogie Country Man	1975	15.00
❑ SRM-1-1064	Odd Man In	1975	15.00
❑ SRM-1-1109	Country Class	1976	15.00
❑ SRM-1-5004	Country Memories	1977	15.00
❑ SRM-1-5006	The Best of Jerry Lee Lewis Vol. II	1978	15.00
❑ SRM-1-5010	Jerry Lee Lewis Keeps Rockin'	1978	15.00
❑ SR-61278	Live at the International, Las Vegas	1970	15.00
❑ SR-61318	In Loving Memories	1970	30.00
❑ SR-61323	There Must Be More to Love Than This	1971	15.00
❑ SR-61343	Touching Home	1971	15.00
—With photo of Jerry Lee in front of a brick wall			
❑ SR-61343	Touching Home	1971	20.00
—With drawing on cover and small photo of Jerry Lee			
❑ SR-61346	Would You Take Another Chance on Me?	1971	15.00
❑ SR-61366	Who's Gonna Play This Old Piano… (Think About It Darlin')	1972	15.00
❑ 822789-1	The Best of Jerry Lee Lewis Vol. II	198?	10.00
❑ 826251-1	Greatest Hits	198?	10.00
❑ 830399-1	Would You Take Another Chance on Me	1987	10.00
—Reissue of 61346			
❑ 836935-1	Killer: The Mercury Years Vol. One, 1963-1968	1989	12.00
❑ 836938-1	Killer: The Mercury Years Vol. Two, 1969-1972	1989	12.00
❑ 836941-1	Killer: The Mercury Years Vol. Three, 1973-1977	1989	12.00

PAIR

Number	Title	Yr	NM
❑ PDL2-1132 [(2)]	Solid Gold	1986	12.00

PICKWICK

Number	Title	Yr	NM
❑ PTP-2055 [(2)]	Jerry Lee Lewis	1973	12.00
❑ SPC-3224	High Heel Sneakers	1970	10.00
❑ SPC-3344	Drinking Wine Spo-Dee-O-Dee	1973	10.00

POLYDOR

Number	Title	Yr	NM
❑ 826139-1	I'm on Fire	1985	10.00
❑ 839516-1	Great Balls of Fire!	1989	12.00

POWER PAK

Number	Title	Yr	NM
❑ 247	From the Vaults of Sun	1974	10.00

RHINO

Number	Title	Yr	NM
❑ RNDF-255 [PD]	Original Sun Greatest Hits	1983	15.00
❑ RNDA-1499 [(2)]	Milestones	1985	15.00
❑ R1-70255	Original Sun Greatest Hits	1989	10.00
—Reissue of 255 on black vinyl			
❑ R1-70656	Jerry Lee Lewis	1989	12.00
—Reissue of Sun 1230			
❑ R1-70657	Jerry Lee's Greatest	1989	12.00
—Reissue of Sun 1265			
❑ R1-70899	Wild One: Rare Tracks from Jerry Lee Lewis	1989	12.00
❑ R1-71499 [(2)]	Milestones	1989	12.00
—Reissue of 1499			

SEARS

Number	Title	Yr	NM
❑ SPS-610	Hound Dog	1970	25.00

SMASH

Number	Title	Yr	NM
❑ SL-7001	Golden Hits	1980	12.00
❑ MGS-27040 [M]	The Golden Hits of Jerry Lee Lewis	1964	25.00
❑ MGS-27056 [M]	The Greatest Live Show on Earth	1964	100.00
❑ MGS-27063 [M]	The Return of Rock	1965	30.00
❑ MGS-27071 [M]	Country Songs for City Folks	1965	25.00
❑ MGS-27079 [M]	Memphis Beat	1966	25.00
❑ MGS-27086 [M]	By Request — More of the Greatest Live Show on Earth	1966	30.00
❑ MGS-27097 [M]	Soul My Way	1967	30.00
❑ SRS-67040 [S]	The Golden Hits of Jerry Lee Lewis	1964	30.00
❑ SRS-67040 [S]	The Golden Rock Hits of Jerry Lee Lewis	1969	15.00
—Retitled reissue			
❑ SRS-67056 [S]	The Greatest Live Show on Earth	1964	150.00
❑ SRS-67063 [S]	The Return of Rock	1965	40.00
❑ SRS-67071	All Country	1969	15.00
—Retitled reissue			
❑ SRS-67071 [S]	Country Songs for City Folks	1965	30.00
❑ SRS-67079 [S]	Memphis Beat	1966	30.00
❑ SRS-67086 [S]	By Request — More of the Greatest Live Show on Earth	1966	40.00
❑ SRS-67097 [S]	Soul My Way	1967	40.00
❑ SRS-67104	Another Place Another Time	1968	20.00
❑ SRS-67112	She Still Comes Around (To Love What's Left of Me)	1969	20.00
❑ SRS-67117	Jerry Lee Lewis Sings the Country Music Hall of Fame Hits, Vol. 1	1969	20.00
❑ SRS-67118	Jerry Lee Lewis Sings the Country Music Hall of Fame Hits, Vol. 2	1969	20.00
❑ SRS-67128	She Even Woke Me Up to Say Goodbye	1970	20.00
❑ SRS-67131	The Best of Jerry Lee Lewis	1970	20.00

SUN

Number	Title	Yr	NM
❑ LP-102	Original Golden Hits — Vol. 1	1969	15.00
❑ LP-103	Original Golden Hits — Vol. 2	1969	15.00
❑ LP-107	Rockin' Rhythm and Blues	1969	15.00
❑ SUN-108	The Golden Cream of the Country	1969	15.00
❑ SUN-108 [M]	The Golden Cream of the Country	1969	40.00
—Mono version is white label promo only; the word "MONO" appears at 9 o'clock on the label			
❑ LP-114	A Taste of Country	1970	15.00
❑ LP-121	Ole Tyme Country Music	1971	15.00
❑ LP-124	Monsters	1971	15.00
❑ LP-128	Original Golden Hits — Vol. 3	1972	15.00
❑ SUN-145	Roots	1982	12.00
❑ 1005	The Original	1978	12.00
❑ SUN-1011	Duets	1978	15.00
—As "Jerry Lee Lewis and Friends"; gold vinyl			
❑ 1018	Trio +	1979	12.00
—With Carl Perkins, Charlie Rich and (uncredited) Orion			
❑ SLP-1230 [M]	Jerry Lee Lewis	1958	200.00
❑ SLP-1265 [M]	Jerry Lee's Greatest	1961	250.00

Except when noted otherwise, VG = 25% of NM, and VG+ = 50% of NM. (Example: VG = $2.00, VG+ = $4.00 and NM = $8.00.)

Number	Title (A Side/B Side)	Yr	NM
SLP-1265 [M]	Jerry Lee's Greatest	1961	800.00
—	*—White label promo*		
SUNNYVALE			
905	The Sun Story, Vol. 5	1977	10.00
WING			
PKW2-125 [(2)]	The Legend of Jerry Lee Lewis	1969	25.00
MGW-12340 [M]	The Return of Rock	1967	12.00
SRW-16340	In Demand	1968	10.00
SRW-16340 [S]	The Return of Rock	1967	12.00
SRW-16406	Unlimited	1968	12.00
LEWIS, JERRY LEE, AND LINDA GAIL LEWIS			
45s			
MERCURY			
73303	Writing on the Wall/Me and Jesus	1972	7.00
SMASH			
2220	Don't Let Me Cross Over/We Live in Two Different Worlds	1969	10.00
2220 [PS]	Don't Let Me Cross Over/We Live in Two Different Worlds	1969	20.00
2254	Roll Over Beethoven/Secret Places	1969	10.00
Albums			
SMASH			
SRS-67126	Together	1969	20.00
LEWIS, JIMMY, AND THE ELFS			
45s			
HIT			
306	Come Back When You Grow Up/How Can I Be Sure	1967	8.00
—	*—B-side by the Olives*		
312	Keep the Ball Rollin'/An Open Letter to My Teenage Son	1967	8.00
—	*—B-side by Bobby Sims*		
LEWIS, JUNIOR			
45s			
ATCO			
6242	Please Send Me Someone to Love/Tumbling Down	1962	20.00
COLUMBIA			
4-42129	Hear What I Say/Where the World Begins	1961	25.00
4-42129 [PS]	Hear What I Say/Where the World Begins	1961	40.00
4-42208	Just to Make Me Cry/The Nature of Things	1961	—
—	*—Canceled*		
4-42236	Too Bad/Tears on My Face	1961	25.00
4-42361	Forty Days and Forty Nights/The Only Girl	1962	40.00
MGM			
K13728	All About Love/Why Take It Out on Me	1967	30.00
SCEPTER			
1257	Raise Your Hand/(Tell Me) Where Do I Go from Here	1963	20.00
1268	Hi Dee You All/(Tell Me) Where Do I Go from Here	1964	30.00
LEWIS, PAT			
45s			
GOLDEN WORLD			
42	Can't Shake It Loose/Let's Go Together	1966	30.00
SOLID HIT			
101	Look at What I Almost Missed/No, Baby, No	1967	40.00
105	Warning/I'll Wait	1967	100.00
109	No One to Love/(I Owe) You Something	1967	2000.
—	*—VG 1000; VG+ 1500*		
112	The Loser/Baby I Owe You Something	196?	50.00
LEWIS, RAMSEY Includes releases by "Ramsey Lewis Trio."			
12-Inch Singles			
COLUMBIA			
05311	This Ain't No Fantasy (Extended with Male)/(Extended with Female)	1985	6.00
06850	7-11 (Club Mix) (Booster Mix)	1987	6.00
10937	Aquarius-Let the Sunshine In/Just Can't Give You Up	1979	12.00
45s			
ARGO			
108-S [S]	Scarlet Ribbons/Here 'Tis	1960	20.00
110-S [S]	Solo Para Ti/These Foolish Things	1960	20.00
5303	Black Eyed Peas/Carmen	1958	12.00
5322	Tracy Blues/Delilah	1958	12.00

Number	Title (A Side/B Side)	Yr	NM
5344	C.C. Rider/Consider the Source	1959	12.00
5351	Ol' Devil Moon/Please Send Me Someone to Love	1959	12.00
5352	The Chant/Here 'Tis	1959	12.00
5362	Little Liza Jane/Put Your Little Foot Right Out	1960	12.00
5377	Santa Claus Is Coming to Town/Winter Wonderland	1960	12.00
5387	Blues for the Night Owl/Hello, Cello	1961	10.00
5398	Never on Sunday/The Ripper	1961	10.00
5407	Sound of Christmas/Merry Christmas Baby	1961	12.00
5411	I Got Plenty of Nothin'/Thanks for the Memory	1962	10.00
5413	Blue Spring/Spring Fever	1962	10.00
5423	Blueberry Hill/Memphis in June	1962	10.00
5431	Maha de Carnaval/Tangleweed 'Round My Heart	1963	8.00
5438	Look-a Here/Andaluza	1963	8.00
5454	Lonely Avenue/Come On Baby	1963	8.00
5467	Dance Mystique/For the Love of a Princess	1964	8.00
5474	Why Don't You Do It Right/Travel On	1964	8.00
5481	Something You Got/My Babe	1964	8.00
5488	Jingle Bells/Egg Nog	1964	10.00
5496	Let It Be Me/It Had Better Be Tonight	1965	8.00
5506	The "In" Crowd/Since I Fell for You	1965	10.00
CADET			
5377	Santa Claus Is Coming to Town/Winter Wonderland	1966	8.00
—	*—Reissue of Argo 5377*		
5423	Blueberry Hill/Memphis in June	1966	6.00
5431	Maha de Carnaval/Tangleweed 'Round My Heart	1966	6.00
5481	Something You Got/My Babe	1966	6.00
5496	Let It Be Me/It Had Better Be Tonight	1966	6.00
5506	The "In" Crowd/Since I Fell for You	1966	6.00
5522	Hang On Sloopy/Movin' Easy	1965	8.00
5525	A Hard Day's Night/All My Love Belongs to You	1966	8.00
5531	Hi Heel Sneakers — Pt. 1/Hi Heel Sneakers — Pt. 2	1966	8.00
5541	Wade in the Water/Ain't That Peculiar	1966	8.00
5547	Up Tight/Money in the Pocket	1966	8.00
5553	Rudolph the Red-Nosed Reindeer/Day Tripper	1966	8.00
5556	One, Two, Three/Down by the Riverside	1967	8.00
5562	Function at the Junction/Hey, Mrs. Jones	1967	8.00
5565	Saturday Night After the Movies/China Gate	1967	8.00
5573	Dancing in the Street/Girls Talk	1967	8.00
5583	Soul Man/Struttin' Lightly	1967	8.00
5593	The Look of Love/Bear Mash	1968	6.00
5596	Jade Easy/Party Time	1968	6.00
5609	Since You've Been Gone/Les Fleurs	1968	6.00
5629	Mary's Boy Child/Have Yourself a Merry Little Christmas	1968	6.00
5640	Julia/Do What You Wanna	1969	6.00
5645	If You've Got It, Flaunt It/Wanderin' Rose	1969	6.00
5662	Mary's Boy Child/My Cherie Amour	1969	6.00
5668	Everybody's Talkin'/Love I Feel for You	1970	6.00
5674	Them Changes/Unsilent Minority	1970	6.00
5678	Do Whatever Sets You Free/Close Your Eyes and Remember	1970	6.00
5681	Candida/Love Me Now	1971	6.00
5684	He Ain't Heavy, He's My Brother/Up in Yonder	1971	6.00
5695	Summertime/Look-a There	1973	6.00
COLUMBIA			
02043	So Much More/Romance Me	1981	4.00
02572	Lakeshore Cowboy/Michelle	1981	4.00
02704	You Never Know/Lynn	1982	4.00
03274	Up Where We Belong/Chance Encounter	1982	4.00
04524	The Two of Us/Song Without Words (Remembering)	1984	4.00
04655	Quiet Storm/Ram	1984	4.00
05640	This Ain't No Fantasy/The Quest	1985	3.00
05819	Ram Jam/Slow Dancin'	1986	3.00
07220	7-11/My Love Will Lead You Home	1987	3.00
10056	Hot Dawgit/R.L. Tambura	1974	5.00
—	*—A-side with Earth, Wind and Fire*		

Number	Title (A Side/B Side)	Yr	NM
10103	Sun Goddess/Jungle Strut	1975	5.00
—	*—A-side with Earth, Wind and Fire*		
10235	What's the Name of This Funk (Spider Man)/Juacklyn	1975	5.00
10293	Don't It Feel Good/Fish Bite	1976	5.00
10382	Brazilica/Salongo	1976	5.00
10571	Spring High/The Messenger	1977	5.00
10643	Skippin'/Camino El Bueno	1977	5.00
10698	Tequila Mockingbird/My Angel's Smile	1978	5.00
10827	All the Way Live/Toccata	1978	5.00
10932	Aquarius-Let the Sunshine In/Just Can't Give You Up	1979	5.00
11042	Wearin' It Out/Spanoletta	1979	5.00
45634	Slipping Into Darkness/Collage	1972	5.00
45707	Upendo Mi Pamoja/Eternal Peace	1972	5.00
45766	Kufanya Mapenzi (Making Love)/What It Is	1973	5.00
45847	Dreams/Hang On Sloopy	1973	5.00
45973	Hi-Heel Sneakers/Wade in the Water	1973	5.00
46037	Summer Breeze/Everywhere Calypso	1974	5.00
7-Inch Extended Plays			
ARGO			
EP-1084	Sleigh Ride/Christmas Blues//Sound of Christmas/The Christmas Song	1961	10.00
EP-1084 [PS]	Sound of Christmas	1961	12.00
Albums			
ARGO			
LP-611 [M]	Gentleman of Swing	1958	50.00
LPS-611 [S]	Gentleman of Swing	1959	60.00
LP-627 [M]	Gentleman of Jazz	1958	50.00
LPS-627 [S]	Gentleman of Jazz	1959	60.00
LP-642 [M]	The Ramsey Lewis Trio with Lee Winchester	1959	40.00
LPS-642 [S]	The Ramsey Lewis Trio with Lee Winchester	1959	50.00
LP-645 [M]	An Hour with the Ramsey Lewis Trio	1959	40.00
LPS-645 [S]	An Hour with the Ramsey Lewis Trio	1959	50.00
LP-665 [M]	Stretching Out	1960	40.00
LPS-665 [S]	Stretching Out	1960	50.00
LP-671 [M]	The Ramsey Lewis Trio in Chicago	1961	40.00
LPS-671 [S]	The Ramsey Lewis Trio in Chicago	1961	50.00
LP-680 [M]	More Music from the Soil	1961	40.00
LPS-680 [S]	More Music from the Soil	1961	50.00
LP-687 [M]	Sound of Christmas	1961	40.00
LPS-687 [S]	Sound of Christmas	1961	50.00
LP-693 [M]	The Sound of Spring	1962	25.00
LPS-693 [S]	The Sound of Spring	1962	30.00
LP-701 [M]	Country Meets the Blues	1962	25.00
LPS-701 [S]	Country Meets the Blues	1962	30.00
LP-705 [M]	Bossa Nova	1962	25.00
LPS-705 [S]	Bossa Nova	1962	30.00
LP-715 [M]	Pot Luck	1963	25.00
LPS-715 [S]	Pot Luck	1963	30.00
LP-723 [M]	Barefoot Sunday Blues	1963	25.00
LPS-723 [S]	Barefoot Sunday Blues	1963	30.00
LP-732 [M]	Bach to the Blues	1964	25.00
LPS-732 [S]	Bach to the Blues	1964	30.00
LP-741 [M]	The Ramsey Lewis Trio at the Bohemian Caverns	1964	25.00
LPS-741 [S]	The Ramsey Lewis Trio at the Bohemian Caverns	1964	30.00
LP-745 [M]	More Sounds of Christmas	1964	25.00
LPS-745 [S]	More Sounds of Christmas	1964	30.00
LP-755 [M]	Choice! The Best of the Ramsey Lewis Trio	1965	30.00
LPS-755 [S]	Choice! The Best of the Ramsey Lewis Trio	1965	40.00
LP-757 [M]	The In Crowd	1965	25.00
LPS-757 [S]	The In Crowd	1965	30.00
CADET			
LP-611 [M]	Gentleman of Swing	1966	12.00
LPS-611 [S]	Gentleman of Swing	1966	15.00
LP-627 [M]	Gentleman of Jazz	1966	12.00
LPS-627 [S]	Gentleman of Jazz	1966	15.00
LP-645 [M]	An Hour with the Ramsey Lewis Trio	1966	12.00
LPS-645 [S]	An Hour with the Ramsey Lewis Trio	1966	15.00
LP-665 [M]	Stretching Out	1966	12.00
LPS-665 [S]	Stretching Out	1966	15.00
LP-671 [M]	The Ramsey Lewis Trio in Chicago	1966	12.00
LPS-671 [S]	The Ramsey Lewis Trio in Chicago	1966	15.00
LP-680 [M]	More Music from the Soil	1966	12.00
LPS-680 [S]	More Music from the Soil	1966	15.00
LPS-680 [S]	More Music from the Soil	197?	12.00
—	*—Reissue with "A Division of All Platinum Record Group" on label*		

Number	Title (A Side/B Side)	Yr	NM
❑ LP-687X [M]	Sound of Christmas	1966	20.00
—Reissue of Argo 687			
❑ LPS-687X [S]	Sound of Christmas	1966	20.00
—Reissue of Argo 687-S			
❑ LP-693 [M]	The Sound of Spring	1966	12.00
❑ LPS-693 [S]	The Sound of Spring	1966	15.00
❑ LP-701 [M]	Country Meets the Blues	1966	12.00
❑ LPS-701 [S]	Country Meets the Blues	1966	15.00
❑ LP-705 [M]	Bossa Nova	1966	12.00
❑ LPS-705 [S]	Bossa Nova	1966	15.00
❑ LP-715 [M]	Pot Luck	1966	12.00
❑ LPS-715 [S]	Pot Luck	1966	15.00
❑ LP-723 [M]	Barefoot Sunday Blues	1966	12.00
❑ LPS-723 [S]	Barefoot Sunday Blues	1966	15.00
❑ LP-732 [M]	Bach to the Blues	1966	12.00
❑ LPS-732 [S]	Bach to the Blues	1966	15.00
❑ LP-741 [M]	The Ramsey Lewis Trio at the Bohemian Caverns	1966	12.00
❑ LPS-741 [S]	The Ramsey Lewis Trio at the Bohemian Caverns	1966	15.00
❑ LP-745 [M]	More Sounds of Christmas	1966	15.00
❑ LPS-745 [S]	More Sounds of Christmas	1966	20.00
❑ LP-750 [M]	You Better Believe It	1966	12.00
❑ LPS-750 [S]	You Better Believe It	1966	15.00
❑ LP-755 [M]	Choice! The Best of the Ramsey Lewis Trio	1965	15.00
❑ LPS-755 [S]	Choice! The Best of the Ramsey Lewis Trio	1965	20.00
❑ LP-757 [M]	The In Crowd	1965	12.00
❑ LPS-757 [S]	The In Crowd	1965	15.00
❑ LP-761 [M]	Hang On Ramsey!	1966	15.00
❑ LPS-761 [S]	Hang On Ramsey!	1966	20.00
❑ LP-771 [M]	Swingin'	1966	15.00
❑ LPS-771 [S]	Swingin'	1966	20.00
❑ LP-774 [M]	Wade in the Water	1966	15.00
❑ LPS-774 [S]	Wade in the Water	1966	20.00
❑ LP-782 [M]	The Movie Album	1967	20.00
❑ LPS-782 [S]	The Movie Album	1967	15.00
❑ LP-790 [M]	Goin' Latin	1967	20.00
❑ LPS-790 [S]	Goin' Latin	1967	15.00
❑ LP-794 [M]	Dancing in the Street	1967	20.00
❑ LPS-794 [S]	Dancing in the Street	1967	15.00
❑ LPS-799	Up Pops Ramsey Lewis	1968	15.00
❑ LPS-811	Maiden Voyage	1968	15.00
❑ LPS-821	Mother Nature's Son	1969	15.00
❑ LPS-827	Another Voyage	1969	15.00
❑ LPS-836	Ramsey Lewis, The Piano Player	1970	15.00
❑ LPS-839	The Best of Ramsey Lewis	1970	15.00
❑ LPS-844	Them Changes	1970	15.00
❑ 50020	Groover	1973	12.00
❑ 50058 [(2)]	Solid Ivory	1974	15.00
❑ 60001	Back to the Roots	1971	12.00
❑ 60018 [(2)]	Inside Ramsey Lewis	1972	15.00

CBS

Number	Title (A Side/B Side)	Yr	NM
❑ FM 42661	A Classic Encounter	1988	10.00

CHESS

Number	Title (A Side/B Side)	Yr	NM
❑ 9001 [(2)]	Solid Ivory	197?	12.00
—Reissue of Cadet 50058			
❑ CH 9716	Sound of Christmas	1984	10.00
—Reissue of Argo 687-S			

COLUMBIA

Number	Title (A Side/B Side)	Yr	NM
❑ CQ 31096 [Q]	Upendo Ni Pamoja	1972	18.00
❑ KC 31096	Upendo Ni Pamoja	1972	12.00
❑ KC 32030	Funky Serenity	1973	12.00
❑ KC 32490	Ramsey Lewis' Newly Recorded All-Time, Non-Stop Golden Hits	1973	12.00
❑ PC 32490	Ramsey Lewis' Newly Recorded All-Time, Non-Stop Golden Hits	197?	8.00
—Reissue with new prefix			
❑ KC 32897	Solar Wind	1974	12.00
❑ KC 33194	Sun Goddess	1974	10.00
❑ PC 33194	Sun Goddess	197?	8.00
—Reissue with new prefix			
❑ CG 33663 [(2)]	Upendo Ni Pamoja/Funky Serenity	1975	12.00
❑ PC 33800	Don't It Feel Good	1975	10.00
—Originals have no bar code			
❑ PC 33800	Don't It Feel Good	198?	8.00
—Budget-line reissue with bar code			
❑ PC 34173	Salongo	1976	10.00
—Originals have no bar code			
❑ PC 34173	Salongo	198?	8.00
—Budget-line reissue with bar code			
❑ PC 34696	Love Notes	1977	10.00
❑ JC 35018	Tequila Mockingbird	1977	10.00
❑ JC 35483	Legacy	1978	10.00
❑ PC 35483	Legacy	198?	8.00
—Budget-line reissue			
❑ JC 35815	Ramsey	1979	10.00
❑ FC 36364	The Best of Ramsey Lewis	1980	10.00
❑ JC 36423	Routes	1980	10.00
❑ PC 36423	Routes	198?	8.00
—Budget-line reissue			
❑ FC 37153	Three Piece Suite	1981	10.00
❑ FC 37687	Live at the Savoy	1982	10.00
❑ PC 37687	Live at the Savoy	198?	8.00
—Budget-line reissue			
❑ FC 38294	Chance Encounter	1983	10.00
❑ FC 38787	Les Fleurs	1983	10.00
❑ FC 39158	Reunion	1983	10.00
❑ FC 40108	Fantasy	1985	10.00
❑ FC 40677	Keys to the City	1987	10.00
❑ HC 43194	Sun Goddess	1982	50.00
—Half-speed mastered edition			
❑ FC 44190	Urban Renewal	1989	15.00
❑ HC 47687	Live at the Savoy	1982	80.00
—Half-speed mastered edition			

COLUMBIA JAZZ ODYSSEY

Number	Title (A Side/B Side)	Yr	NM
❑ PC 37019	Blues for the Night Owl	1981	10.00

EMARCY

Number	Title (A Side/B Side)	Yr	NM
❑ MG-36150 [M]	Down to Earth	1958	40.00
❑ SR-80029 [S]	Down to Earth	1958	50.00

MERCURY

Number	Title (A Side/B Side)	Yr	NM
❑ MG-20536 [M]	Down to Earth	1965	20.00
❑ SR-60536 [S]	Down to Earth	1965	25.00

LEWIS, RAMSEY, AND JEAN DUSHON

Albums

ARGO

Number	Title (A Side/B Side)	Yr	NM
❑ 750 [M]	You Better Believe Me	1965	25.00
❑ 750S [S]	You Better Believe Me	1965	30.00

LEWIS, RAMSEY, AND NANCY WILSON

Also see each artist's individual listings.

Albums

COLUMBIA

Number	Title (A Side/B Side)	Yr	NM
❑ FC 39326	The Two of Us	1984	10.00

LEWIS, RAY

45s

ATCO

Number	Title (A Side/B Side)	Yr	NM
❑ 6846	Cool Love/Sugar Toe	1971	40.00

FAIRMOUNT

Number	Title (A Side/B Side)	Yr	NM
❑ 1013	Give My Love a Try/Getting Over You	1966	300.00

SMASH

Number	Title (A Side/B Side)	Yr	NM
❑ 2134	I Still Love You/Sorry, You've Got the Wrong Number	1967	75.00

LEWIS, RUDY

Also see THE DRIFTERS.

45s

ATLANTIC

Number	Title (A Side/B Side)	Yr	NM
❑ 2193	I've Loved You So Long/Baby I Dig Love	1963	40.00

RCA VICTOR

Number	Title (A Side/B Side)	Yr	NM
❑ 47-7792	Moonbeam/Beer, Beer and More Beer	1960	20.00
—With the Sputnicks			

LEWIS, SABBY

45s

ABC-PARAMOUNT

Number	Title (A Side/B Side)	Yr	NM
❑ 9685	Ding-a-Ling/Kenny's Blues	1956	40.00
❑ 9687	Forgive Me, My Love/Regretting	1956	40.00

GONE

Number	Title (A Side/B Side)	Yr	NM
❑ 5074	Swana/Sabby	1959	25.00
—With the Uniques			

LEWIS, SAMMIE

45s

SUN

Number	Title (A Side/B Side)	Yr	NM
❑ 218	So Long Baby Goodbye/I Feel So Worried	1955	80.00

LEWIS, SMILEY

45s

DOT

Number	Title (A Side/B Side)	Yr	NM
❑ 16674	I Wonder/Lookin' for My Woman	1964	10.00

IMPERIAL

Number	Title (A Side/B Side)	Yr	NM
❑ 5194	The Bells Are Ringing/Lillie Mae	1952	120.00
—Note: Smiley Lewis records on Imperial before 5194 are unconfirmed on 45 rpm			
❑ 5208	Gumbo Blues/It's So Peaceful	1952	100.00
❑ 5224	Gypsy Blues/You're Not the One	1953	100.00
❑ 5234	Play Girl/Big Mamou	1953	80.00
❑ 5234	Play Girl/Big Mamou	1953	250.00
—Red vinyl			
❑ 5241	Caldonia's Party/Oh Baby	1953	80.00
❑ 5252	Little Fernandez/It's Music	1953	80.00
❑ 5268	Down the Road/Blue Monday	1954	80.00
❑ 5279	I Love You for Sentimental Reasons/The Rocks	1954	80.00
❑ 5296	Can't Stop Loving You/That Certain Door	1954	80.00
❑ 5316	Too Many Drivers/Ooh La La	1954	80.00
❑ 5325	Jailbird/Farewell	1955	80.00
❑ 5349	Real Gone Lover/Nobody Knows	1955	80.00
❑ 5356	I Hear You Knocking/Bumpity Bump	1955	80.00
❑ 5372	Queen of Hearts/Come On	1956	80.00
❑ 5380	One Night/Ain't Gonna Do It	1956	80.00
❑ 5389	She's Got Me (Hook, Line and Sinker)/Please Listen to Me	1956	80.00
❑ 5404	Down Yonder We Go Ballin'/Someday You'll Want Me	1956	80.00
❑ 5418	Shame, Shame, Shame/No No	1957	60.00
❑ 5431	You Are My Sunshine/Sweeter Words Have Never Been Spoken	1957	40.00
❑ 5450	Go On Fool/Goin' to Jump and Shout	1957	30.00
❑ 5470	Rootin' and Tootin'/I Can't Believe	1957	30.00
❑ 5478	Bad Luck Blues/School Days Are Back Again	1957	30.00
❑ 5531	Lil' Liza Jane/My Love Is Gone	1958	25.00
❑ 5662	Oh Red!/I Want to Be with Her	1960	15.00
❑ 5676	Last Night/Ain't Goin' There No More	1960	15.00
❑ 5719	Stormy Monday Blues/Tell Me Who	1961	15.00
❑ 5820	Gumbo Blues/Tee Nah Nah	1962	15.00

KNIGHT

Number	Title (A Side/B Side)	Yr	NM
❑ 2007	Baby Please/I Shall Not Be Moved	1959	15.00
❑ 2011	Lost Weekend/By the Water	1959	15.00

LOMA

Number	Title (A Side/B Side)	Yr	NM
❑ 2024	Bells Are Ringing/Walkin' the Girl	1965	10.00

OKEH

Number	Title (A Side/B Side)	Yr	NM
❑ 7146	I'm Coming Down with the Blues/Tune-Up	1962	12.00

Albums

IMPERIAL

Number	Title (A Side/B Side)	Yr	NM
❑ LP-9141 [M]	I Hear You Knocking	1961	600.00
—Black vinyl			
❑ LP-9141 [M]	I Hear You Knocking	1961	6000.
—Green vinyl (one copy known)			

LEWIS AND CLARKE EXPEDITION, THE

45s

CHARTMAKER

Number	Title (A Side/B Side)	Yr	NM
❑ 402	Expedition West/For Your Freedom Tonight	1966	8.00

COLGEMS

Number	Title (A Side/B Side)	Yr	NM
❑ 66-1006	I Feel Good (I Feel Bad)/Blue Revelations	1967	8.00
❑ 66-1006 [PS]	I Feel Good (I Feel Bad)/Blue Revelations	1967	15.00
❑ 66-1011	Destination Unknown/Freedom Bird	1967	8.00
❑ 66-1011 [PS]	Destination Unknown/Freedom Bird	1967	15.00
❑ 66-1022	Chain Around the Flowers/Why Need They Pretend	1968	8.00
❑ 66-1028	Daddy's Plastic Child/Gypsy Song Man	1968	8.00

Albums

COLGEMS

Number	Title (A Side/B Side)	Yr	NM
❑ COM-105 [M]	The Lewis and Clarke Expedition	1967	25.00
❑ COS-105 [S]	The Lewis and Clarke Expedition	1967	30.00

LEWIS CONNECTION, THE

Albums

(NO LABEL)

Number	Title (A Side/B Side)	Yr	NM
❑ (no #)	The Lewis Connection	1979	400.00

LEYTON, JOHN

45s

ABC-PARAMOUNT

Number	Title (A Side/B Side)	Yr	NM
❑ 10292	Son, This Is She/Six White Horses	1962	12.00

ATCO

Number	Title (A Side/B Side)	Yr	NM
❑ 6319	Make Love to Me/I'll Cut Your Tail Off	1964	12.00

LIVERPOOL SOUND

Number	Title (A Side/B Side)	Yr	NM
❑ 901	Beautiful Dreamer/I Guess You Are Always On My Mind	1964	12.00

LIBERMAN, JEFFERY

Albums

LIBRAH

Number	Title (A Side/B Side)	Yr	NM
❑ 1545	Jeffery Liberman	1975	80.00
❑ 6969	Solitude Within	1975	120.00
❑ 12157	Synergy	1976	120.00

LIEBERMAN, LORI

45s

CAPITOL

Number	Title (A Side/B Side)	Yr	NM
❑ 3370	L.A. Texas Boy/Louisiana Cock Fight	1972	5.00

Number	Title (A Side/B Side)	Yr	NM
❑ 3379	Killing Me Softly with His Song/ Back to Before	1972	6.00
❑ 3577	And the Feeling's Good/ My Lover Do You Know	1973	5.00
❑ 3709	Becoming/House Full of Women	1973	5.00
❑ 3889	Make No Mistake/ The World Is Turning	1974	5.00
❑ 4020	Raise Up Off of Me/Legacy	1974	5.00

MILLENNIUM

Number	Title (A Side/B Side)	Yr	NM
❑ 622	Let Me Down Easy/Boston	1978	4.00

Albums

CAPITOL

Number	Title (A Side/B Side)	Yr	NM
❑ ST-11081	Lori Lieberman	1972	12.00
❑ ST-11203	Becoming	1973	12.00
❑ ST-11297	A Piece of Time	1974	12.00

LIFEGUARDS, THE (1)

45s

ABC-PARAMOUNT

Number	Title (A Side/B Side)	Yr	NM
❑ 10021	Everybody Out'a the Pool/ Teenage Tango	1959	40.00

CASA BLANCA

Number	Title (A Side/B Side)	Yr	NM
❑ 5535	Everybody Out'a the Pool/ Teenage Tango	1959	50.00

DR

Number	Title (A Side/B Side)	Yr	NM
❑ 69	Everybody Out'a the Pool/ Teenage Tango	1965	15.00

LIFEGUARDS, THE (2)

Yet another production of STEVE BARRI and P.F. SLOAN.

45s

CATCH

Number	Title (A Side/B Side)	Yr	NM
❑ 104	State Beach/Big Swim	1964	30.00

REPRISE

Number	Title (A Side/B Side)	Yr	NM
❑ 0277	Swim Party/Swimtime U.S.A.	1964	25.00

LIFEGUARDS, THE (U)

May be group (1); may be group (2); may be neither.

Albums

WYNCOTE

Number	Title (A Side/B Side)	Yr	NM
❑ SW-9043 [S]	C'mon and Swim	1964	15.00
❑ W-9043 [M]	C'mon and Swim	1964	12.00

LIGHT, ENOCH

Includes records made by the same musicians under other names; examples include "Terry Snyder and the All-Stars" and "The Command All-Stars."

45s

COMMAND

Number	Title (A Side/B Side)	Yr	NM
❑ 4008	The Private Life of a Private Eye/Gum Shoe Lullaby	1960	10.00
❑ 4009	Young at Heart Cha Cha/ Travel Now, Pay Next Year, Pleasure Cruise	1960	10.00
❑ 4010	Mack the Knife Cha Cha/ (B-side unknown)	1960	10.00
❑ 4011	Rock-a-Bongo Boogie/ Blue Is the Night	1960	10.00
—By "Terry Snyder and the All-Stars"			
❑ 4013	No Rest for the Drummer Man/ American Patrol	196?	10.00
❑ 4014	Waltzing Matilda/Sunrise Over Sumatra	196?	10.00
❑ 4019	Satan Never Sleeps/The Four Horsemen of the Apocalypse	1961	8.00
❑ 4028	Perdido/Rio Junction	1962	8.00
❑ 4029	Meditation (Meditacao)/ Big Ben Bossa	1962	8.00
❑ 4031	Ching Ching Chow Chow/ Istanbul	196?	8.00
❑ 4033	Nola/Big Ben Bossa	196?	8.00
❑ 4035	Hud/Speak Not a Word	196?	8.00
❑ 4050	A Hard Day's Night/Carribe	1964	8.00
❑ 4062	Begin the Beguine/ (B-side unknown)	196?	8.00
❑ 4067	Downtown/Easy Baby, Go Easy Baby	1965	8.00
❑ 4068	Forget Domani/Love Me Now	1965	8.00
❑ 4069	Theme from "Zorba the Greek"/ Von Ryan's Express	1965	8.00
❑ 4072	Love Theme from "The Sandpiper"/Forget Domani	1966	8.00

GRAND AWARD

Number	Title (A Side/B Side)	Yr	NM
❑ 1020	I Want to Be Happy Cha Cha/ Cara Mia Cha Cha	1958	12.00
❑ 1026	Baby, It's Cold Outside Cha Cha/Chiquita Cha Cha	1958	12.00
❑ 1032	With My Eyes Wide Open I'm Dreaming/I Cried for You	1959	12.00
❑ 1035	Scarlet Ribbons/Greensleeves	1959	12.00

PROJECT 3

Number	Title (A Side/B Side)	Yr	NM
❑ 1305	Is Paris Burning/And We Were Lovers	1967	6.00
❑ 1310	Come On, Come On, Come On, Don't Be Timid/I Love, I Live, I Love	1967	6.00
❑ 1322	In the Heat of the Night/ Live for Life	1967	6.00
❑ 1330	Green Tambourine/I Wonder What She's Doing Tonight	1968	6.00
❑ 1339	Lullaby from "Rosemary's Baby"/ The Windmills of Your Mind	1968	6.00
❑ 1341	Hang 'Em High/The Windmills of Your Mind	1968	6.00
❑ 1344	A Man Without Love/Whoever You Are, I Love You	1969	6.00
❑ 1346	Interlude/Now	1969	6.00
❑ 1348	Funny Girl/Ol' Devil Moon	1969	6.00
❑ 1354	Blowin' in the Wind/ Happy Ever After	1969	6.00
❑ 1359	Hair/(B-side unknown)	1969	6.00
❑ 1367	Alice's Restaurant/Raindrops Keep Fallin' on My Head	1970	5.00
❑ 1368	My Silent Song/Little Fugue for You and Me	1970	5.00
❑ 1369	Day of Anger/Song from "The Wild Bunch"	1970	5.00
❑ 1379	A Lover's Concerto/Bond Street	197?	5.00
❑ 1385	The Out-of-Towners/ Patton Theme	197?	5.00
❑ 1389	In the Mood/Let's Dance	197?	5.00
❑ 1394	One O'Clock Jump/ Take the "A" Train	197?	5.00
❑ 1395	South Rampart Street Parade/ Woodchopper's Ball	197?	5.00
❑ 1396	Marie/I'll Never Smile Again	197?	5.00
❑ 1397	Jersey Bounce/Tuxedo Junction	197?	5.00
❑ 1398	I'm Getting Sentimental Over You/A String of Pearls	197?	5.00
❑ 1399	Cherokee/Flying Home	197?	5.00
❑ 1401	Moonlight Serenade/Snowfall	197?	5.00
❑ 1405	Chicago/Happy Days Are Here Again	197?	5.00
❑ 1406	Bye Bye Blackbird/Charleston	197?	5.00
❑ 1407	If You Knew Susie/I'm Looking Over a Four-Leaf Clover	197?	5.00
❑ 1408	Ain't She Sweet/Yes Sir, That's My Baby	197?	5.00
❑ 1409	Tea for Two/Toot, Toot, Tootsie	197?	5.00
❑ 1411	The Theme from "Shaft"/ The Night They Drove Old Dixie Down	197?	5.00
❑ 1412	Diamonds Are Forever/ Fiddler on the Roof	197?	5.00
❑ 1416	The Godfather Waltz/ The French Connection	197?	5.00
❑ 1420	Cecelia/Eglantine	197?	5.00
❑ 1427	Give Joy to the World/ (B-side unknown)	197?	5.00

7-Inch Extended Plays

COMMAND

Number	Title (A Side/B Side)	Yr	NM
❑ SE 70SD	I'm Looking Over a Four Leaf Clover/Mary Lou/If I Could Be with You One Hour Tonight// Last Night on the Back Porch (I Loved Her Best of All)/ California Here I Come/ Sunny Side Up	196?	10.00
—Stereo jukebox issue; small hole, plays at 33 1/3 rpm			
❑ SE 70SD [PS]	The Roaring '20s	196?	10.00

Albums

ABC WESTMINSTER/GRAND AWARD

Number	Title (A Side/B Side)	Yr	NM
❑ 68008	Sing Along with the Original Roaring 20's	1974	10.00
❑ 68009	The Flirty 30's	1974	10.00
❑ 68012	The Torchy Thirties	1974	10.00

COMMAND

Number	Title (A Side/B Side)	Yr	NM
❑ 800 SD [S]	Persuasive Percussion	1960	15.00
—By "Terry Snyder and the All-Stars"			
❑ 33-800 [M]	Persuasive Percussion	1960	12.00
—By "Terry Snyder and the All-Stars"			
❑ 804 SD [S]	The Sound of Strings	1960	15.00
❑ 33-804 [M]	The Sound of Strings	1960	12.00
❑ 805 SD [S]	Paperback Ballet	1960	15.00
❑ 33-805 [M]	Paperback Ballet	1960	12.00
❑ 806 SD [S]	Provocative Percussion	1960	15.00
—By "The Command All-Stars"			
❑ 33-806 [M]	Provocative Percussion	1960	12.00
—By "The Command All-Stars"			
❑ 808 SD [S]	Persuasive Percussion, Vol. 2	1960	15.00
—By "Terry Snyder and the All-Stars"			
❑ 33-808 [M]	Persuasive Percussion, Vol. 2	1960	12.00
—By "Terry Snyder and the All-Stars"			
❑ 810 SD [S]	Provocative Percussion, Vol. 2	1960	15.00
❑ 33-810 [M]	Provocative Percussion, Vol. 2	1960	12.00
❑ 814 SD [S]	Pertinent Percussion Cha-Cha's	1960	15.00
❑ 33-814 [M]	Pertinent Percussion Cha-Cha's	1960	12.00
❑ 817 SD [S]	Persuasive Percussion, Vol. 3	1961	15.00
—By "The Command All-Stars"			
❑ 33-817 [M]	Persuasive Percussion, Vol. 3	1961	12.00
—By "The Command All-Stars"			
❑ 818 SD [S]	Big Bold and Brassy	1961	15.00
❑ 33-818 [M]	Big Bold and Brassy	1961	12.00
❑ 821 SD [S]	Provocative Percussion, Vol. 3	1961	15.00
❑ 33-821 [M]	Provocative Percussion, Vol. 3	1961	12.00
❑ 822 SD [S]	Far Away Places	1961	15.00
❑ 33-822 [M]	Far Away Places	1961	12.00
❑ 826 SD [S]	Stereo 35/MM	1961	15.00
❑ 830 SD [S]	Persuasive Percussion, Vol. 4	1962	15.00
❑ 33-830 [M]	Persuasive Percussion, Vol. 4	1962	12.00
❑ 831 SD [S]	Stereo 35/MM, Vol. Two	1962	15.00
❑ 833 SD [S]	Vibrations	1962	15.00
❑ 33-833 [M]	Vibrations	1962	12.00
❑ 834 SD [S]	Provocative Percussion, Vol. 4	1962	15.00
❑ 33-834 [M]	Provocative Percussion, Vol. 4	1962	12.00
❑ 835 SD [S]	Great Themes from Hit Films	1962	15.00
❑ 33-835 [M]	Great Themes from Hit Films	1962	12.00
❑ 840 SD [S]	Enoch Light and His Orchestra At Carnegie Hall Play Irving Berlin	1962	15.00
❑ 33-840 [M]	Enoch Light and His Orchestra At Carnegie Hall Play Irving Berlin	1962	12.00
❑ 844 SD [S]	Big Band Bossa Nova	1962	15.00
❑ 33-844 [M]	Big Band Bossa Nova	1962	12.00
❑ 850 SD [S]	Far Away Places, Vol. 2	1963	15.00
❑ 33-850 [M]	Far Away Places, Vol. 2	1963	12.00
❑ 851 SD [S]	Let's Dance the Bossa Nova	1963	15.00
❑ 33-851 [M]	Let's Dance the Bossa Nova	1963	12.00
❑ 854 SD [S]	1963 — The Year's Most Popular Themes	1963	15.00
❑ 33-854 [M]	1963 — The Year's Most Popular Themes	1963	12.00
❑ 863 SD [S]	Rome 35/MM	1964	15.00
❑ 33-863 [M]	Rome 35/MM	1964	12.00
❑ 867 SD [S]	Dimension "3"	1964	15.00
❑ 33-867 [M]	Dimension "3"	1964	12.00
❑ 868 SD [S]	Command Performances	1964	15.00
❑ 33-868 [M]	Command Performances	1964	12.00
❑ 871 SD [S]	Great Themes from Hit Films	1964	15.00
❑ 33-871 [M]	Great Themes from Hit Films	1964	12.00
❑ 873 SD [S]	Discotheque Dance...Dance...Dance	1964	15.00
❑ 33-873 [M]	Discotheque Dance...Dance...Dance	1964	12.00
❑ 879 SD [S]	Great Cole Porter Songs	1965	15.00
❑ 33-879 [M]	Great Cole Porter Songs	1965	12.00
❑ 882 SD [S]	Discotheque Dance...Dance... Dance, Vol. 2	1965	15.00
❑ 33-882 [M]	Discotheque Dance...Dance... Dance, Vol. 2	1965	12.00
❑ 887 SD [S]	Magnificent Movie Themes	1965	15.00
❑ 33-887 [M]	Magnificent Movie Themes	1965	12.00
❑ 895 SD [S]	Persuasive Percussion 1966	1966	15.00
❑ 33-895 [M]	Persuasive Percussion 1966	1966	12.00
❑ 915 SD	Command Performances, Vol. 2	1969	15.00
❑ QD-40002 [Q]	A New Concept	1972	15.00

GRAND AWARD

Number	Title (A Side/B Side)	Yr	NM
❑ GA-201 SD [S]	The Roaring Twenties	1958	25.00
❑ GA-202 SD [S]	The Flirty Thirties	1958	25.00
❑ GA-203 SD [S]	Waltzes for Dancing	1958	25.00
❑ GA-206 SD [S]	Tommy Dorsey's Song Hits	1958	25.00
❑ GA-207 SD [S]	Glenn Miller's Song Hits	1958	25.00
❑ GA-211 SD [S]	The Roaring Twenties, Vol. 2	1958	25.00
❑ GA-214 SD [S]	Around the World in 80 Days	1958	25.00
❑ GA-215 SD [S]	Gigi	1958	25.00
❑ GA-216 SD [S]	My Fair Lady	1958	25.00
❑ GA-217 SD [S]	Oklahoma/South Pacific	1958	25.00
❑ GA-220 SD [S]	The Torchy Thirties	1958	25.00
❑ GA-222 SD [S]	I Want to Be Happy Cha Cha's	1959	25.00
❑ GA-224 SD [S]	New World Symphony	1958	25.00
❑ GA-225 SD [S]	The Great Themes of America's Great Bands	1958	25.00
❑ GA-227 SD [S]	Happy Cha Cha's, Vol. 2	1959	25.00
❑ GA-228 SD [S]	Show Spectacular	1959	25.00
❑ GA-229 SD [S]	The Roaring Twenties, Vol. 3	1959	25.00
❑ GA-236 SD [S]	All the Things You Are	1959	25.00
❑ GA-237 SD [S]	Come to Hawaii	1959	25.00
❑ GA-238 SD [S]	With My Eyes Wide Open I'm Dreaming	1959	25.00
❑ GA-242 SD [S]	Something to Remember You By	1959	25.00
❑ GA-246 SD [S]	Just for Kicks	1959	25.00
❑ GA-251 SD [S]	Sing Along with the Original Roaring 20's	1959	25.00
❑ GA 33-327 [M]	The Roaring Twenties	1958	20.00
❑ GA 33-353 [M]	The Roaring Twenties, Vol. 3	1959	20.00
❑ GA 33-371 [M]	The Flirty Thirties	1958	20.00
❑ GA 33-372 [M]	Waltzes for Dancing	1958	20.00
❑ GA 33-380 [M]	Paris Spectacular	1958	20.00
❑ GA 33-381 [M]	Glenn Miller's Song Hits	1958	20.00
❑ GA 33-382 [M]	Tommy Dorsey's Song Hits	1958	20.00
❑ GA 33-388 [M]	I Want to Be Happy Cha Cha's	1959	20.00
❑ GA 33-391 [M]	Happy Cha Cha's, Vol. 2	1959	20.00
❑ GA 33-392 [M]	The Great Themes of America's Great Bands	1958	20.00
❑ GA 33-399 [M]	All the Things You Are	1959	20.00
❑ GA 33-405 [M]	Come to Hawaii	1959	20.00
❑ GA 33-406 [M]	With My Eyes Wide Open I'm Dreaming	1959	20.00

L

Lighthouse, *Live!*, Evolution 3014, 1972, **$20.**

Number	Title (A Side/B Side)	Yr	NM
❑ GA 33-410 [M]	Something to Remember You By	1959	20.00
❑ GA 33-419 [M]	Sing Along with the Original Roaring 20's	1959	20.00

PROJECT 3

Number	Title (A Side/B Side)	Yr	NM
❑ PR-5000 SD	Spanish Strings	1967	12.00
❑ PR4C-5000 [Q]	Spanish Strings	1973	15.00
❑ PR-5004 SD	It's Happening	1967	12.00
❑ PR-5005 SD	Film on Film — Great Movie Themes	1967	12.00
❑ PR-5013 SD	Film Fame	1968	12.00
❑ PR-5021 SD	Twelve Smash Hits	1968	12.00
❑ PR-5027 SD	The Best of Hollywood '68-'69	1968	12.00
❑ PR-5030 SD	Whoever You Are, I Love You	1968	12.00
❑ PR-5036 SD	Enoch Light and the Brass Menagerie	1969	12.00
❑ PR4C-5036 [Q]	Enoch Light and the Brass Menagerie	1973	15.00
❑ PR-5038 SD	Glittering Guitars	1969	12.00
❑ PR-5042 SD	Enoch Light and the Brass Menagerie, Vol. 2	1969	12.00
❑ PR4C-5042 [Q]	Enoch Light and the Brass Menagerie, Vol. 2	1973	15.00
❑ PR-5043 SD	Spaced Out	1970	12.00
❑ PR4C-5043 [Q]	Spaced Out	1973	15.00
❑ PR-5046 SD	Best of the Movie Themes 1970	1970	12.00
❑ PR4C-5046 [Q]	Best of the Movie Themes 1970	1973	15.00
❑ PR-5048 SD	Permissive Polyphonics	1970	12.00
❑ PR4C-5048 [Q]	Permissive Polyphonics	1973	15.00
❑ PR-5049 SD	Big Band Hits of the 30's	1971	12.00
❑ PR4C-5049 [Q]	Big Band Hits of the 30's	1973	15.00
❑ PR-5051 SD	Hit Movie Themes	1971	12.00
❑ PR4C-5051 [Q]	Hit Movie Themes	1973	15.00
❑ PR-5056 SD	Big Band Hits of the 30's & 40's!	1971	12.00
❑ PR4C-5056 [Q]	Big Band Hits of the 30's & 40's!	1973	15.00
❑ PR-5059 SD	Big Hits of the 20's	1971	12.00
❑ PR4C-5059 [Q]	Big Hits of the 20's	1973	15.00
❑ PR-5060 SD	Enoch Light and the Brass Menagerie 1973	1972	12.00
❑ PR4C-5060 [Q]	Enoch Light and the Brass Menagerie 1973	1973	15.00
❑ PR-5063 SD	Movie Hits!	1972	12.00
❑ PR4C-5063 [Q]	Movie Hits!	1973	15.00
❑ PR4C-5068 [Q]	4 Channel Dynamite!	1973	15.00
❑ PR4C-5073 [Q]	Charge!	1973	15.00
❑ PR4C-5076 [Q]	Big Band Hits of the 40's & 50's	1973	15.00
❑ PR4C-5077 [Q]	Future Sound Shock	1973	15.00
❑ PR-5084 SD	Beatles Classics	1974	12.00
❑ PR4C-5084 [Q]	Beatles Classics	1974	15.00
❑ PR-5086 SD	Great Hits from the Gatsby Era	1974	12.00
❑ PR4C-5086 [Q]	Great Hits from the Gatsby Era	1974	15.00
❑ PR-5089 SD	Big Band Hits of the 30's, Vol. 2	1975	12.00
❑ PR4C-5089 [Q]	Big Band Hits of the 30's, Vol. 2	1975	15.00
❑ PR-5092 SD	Disco Disque	197?	12.00
❑ PR4C-5092 [Q]	Disco Disque	197?	15.00
❑ PR-5100	Let It Be	197?	12.00
❑ PR-5109	The Most Beautiful Music in the World	1981	12.00
❑ PR-6003/4 [(2)]	Big Hits of the Seventies	1974	15.00
❑ PR4C-6003/4 [(2)Q]	Big Hits of the Seventies	1974	20.00
❑ PR-6005/6 [(2)]	Big Band Hits of the 30's, 40's & 50's	1974	15.00
❑ PR4C-6005/6 [(2)Q]	Big Band Hits of the 30's, 40's & 50's	1974	20.00
❑ PR-6011/12 [(2)]	Music Maestro, Please	197?	15.00
❑ PR-6013/14 [(2)]	Big Band Hits of the 30's and 40's	197?	15.00
❑ PR4C-6013/14 [(2)Q]	Big Band Hits of the 30's and 40's	197?	20.00
❑ PR-6034 [(2)]	20 Great Movie Themes	1980	15.00

SEAGULL

Number	Title (A Side/B Side)	Yr	NM
❑ LG-8204	Blowin' in the Wind	198?	10.00
❑ LG-8207	Music from the Movies	198?	10.00

LIGHTFOOT, GORDON

45s

ABC-PARAMOUNT

Number	Title (A Side/B Side)	Yr	NM
❑ 10352	Daisy-Doo/I'm the One (Remember Me)	1962	25.00
—As "Gord Lightfoot"			
❑ 10373	It's Too Late, He Wins/ Negotiations	1962	25.00

CHATEAU

Number	Title (A Side/B Side)	Yr	NM
❑ 142	Daisy-Doo/I'm the One (Remember Me)	1962	50.00
❑ 148	It's Too Late, He Wins/ Negotiations	1962	50.00
❑ 152	I'll Meet You in Michigan/ Is My Baby Blue Tonight	1962	40.00

REPRISE

Number	Title (A Side/B Side)	Yr	NM
❑ 0744	If You Could Read My Mind/ Me and Bobby McGee	1972	4.00
—"Back to Back Hits" series			
❑ 0745	Talking in Your Sleep/ Summer Side of Life	1972	4.00
—"Back to Back Hits" series			
❑ 0926	Me and Bobby McGee/Pony Man	1970	5.00
❑ 0974	If You Could Read My Mind/ Poor Little Allison	1970	6.00
❑ 1020	Talking in Your Sleep/ Nous Vivons Ensemble	1971	5.00
❑ 1035	Summer Side of Life/ Love and Maple Syrup	1971	5.00
❑ 1088	Beautiful/Don Quixote	1972	5.00
❑ 1128	You Are What I Am/ The Same Old Obsession	1972	5.00
❑ 1145	Can't Depend on You/ It's Worth Believin'	1972	5.00
❑ 1194	Sundown/Too Late for Prayin'	1974	4.00
❑ 1309	Carefree Highway/ Seven Island Suite	1974	4.00
❑ 1328	Rainy Day People/ Cherokee Bend	1975	4.00
❑ 1369	The Wreck of the Edmund Fitzgerald/The House You Live In	1976	4.00
❑ 1380	Race Among the Ruins/Protocol	1976	4.00

UNITED ARTISTS

Number	Title (A Side/B Side)	Yr	NM
❑ 929	Just Like Tom Thumb's Blues/ Ribbon of Darkness	1965	10.00
❑ 50055	For Lovin' Me/Spin, Spin	1966	8.00
❑ 50114	I'll Be Alright/Go Go Round	1967	8.00
❑ 50152	The Way I Feel/Peaceful Waters	1967	8.00
❑ 50281	Pussywillows, Cat-Tails/ Black Day in July	1968	8.00
❑ 50447	Does Your Mother Know/ Bitter Green	1968	8.00
❑ 50765	If I Could/Softly	1971	5.00

WARNER BROS.

Number	Title (A Side/B Side)	Yr	NM
❑ 5621	For Lovin' Me/I'm Not Sayin'	1965	15.00
❑ 8518	The Circle Is Small (I Can See It In Your Eyes)/ Sweet Guinevere	1978	4.00
—Subtitle added to later pressings			
❑ 8518	The Circle Is Small/Sweet Guinevere	1978	5.00
—Without A-side subtitle			
❑ 8579	Daylight Katy/Hangdog Hotel Room	1978	4.00
❑ 8644	Dreamland/Songs the Minstrel Sang	1978	4.00
❑ 28222	Ecstasy Made Easy /Morning Glory	1987	3.00
❑ 28422	East of Midnight/I'll Tag Along	1987	3.00
❑ 28553	Stay Loose/Morning Glory	1986	3.00
❑ 28655	Anything for Love/Let It Ride	1986	3.00
❑ 28655 [PS]	Anything for Love/Let It Ride	1986	4.00
❑ 29466	Someone to Believe In/Without You	1983	4.00
❑ 29511	Knotty Pine/Salute	1983	4.00
❑ 29859	Shadows/In My Fashion	1982	4.00
❑ 29963	Blackberry Wine/ (B-side unknown)	1982	4.00
❑ 49230	Dream Street Rose/ Make Way for the Lady	1980	4.00
❑ 49516	If You Need Me/ Mister Rock of Ages	1980	4.00
❑ 50012	Baby Step Back/Thank You for the Promises	1982	4.00

Albums

LIBERTY

Number	Title (A Side/B Side)	Yr	NM
❑ LN-10038	The Best of Lightfoot	198?	8.00
—Budget-line reissue			
❑ LN-10039	Sunday Concert	198?	8.00
—Budget-line reissue			
❑ LN-10040	Back Here on Earth	198?	8.00
—Budget-line reissue			
❑ LN-10041	Did She Mention My Name	198?	8.00
—Budget-line reissue			
❑ LN-10043	The Way I Feel	198?	8.00
—Budget-line reissue			
❑ LN-10044	Lightfoot	198?	8.00
—Budget-line reissue			

MOBILE FIDELITY

Number	Title (A Side/B Side)	Yr	NM
❑ 1-018	Sundown	1979	40.00
—Audiophile vinyl			

PAIR

Number	Title (A Side/B Side)	Yr	NM
❑ PDL2-1081 [(2)]	Songbook	1986	12.00

Except when noted otherwise, VG = 25% of NM, and VG+ = 50% of NM. (Example: VG = $2.00, VG+ = $4.00 and NM = $8.00.)

REPRISE

Number	Title (A Side/B Side)	Yr	NM
❑ MS 2037	Summer Side of Life	1971	12.00
❑ MS 2056	Don Quixote	1972	12.00
❑ MS 2116	Old Dan's Records	1972	12.00
❑ MS 2177	Sundown	1974	12.00
❑ MS4-2177 [Q]	Sundown	1974	20.00
❑ MS 2206	Cold on the Shoulder	1975	12.00
❑ MS4-2206 [Q]	Cold on the Shoulder	1975	20.00
❑ 2RS 2237 [(2)]	Gord's Gold	1975	15.00
❑ MS 2246	Summertime Dream	1976	12.00
❑ RS 6392	Sit Down Young Stranger	1970	15.00
❑ RS 6392	If You Could Read My Mind	1971	10.00

—Retitled version

Number	Title (A Side/B Side)	Yr	NM
❑ ST-93228	Sit Down Young Stranger	1970	20.00

—Capitol Record Club edition

UNITED ARTISTS

Number	Title (A Side/B Side)	Yr	NM
❑ UA-LA243-G	The Very Best of Gordon Lightfoot	1974	12.00
❑ UAL-3487 [M]	Lightfoot	1966	20.00
❑ UAL-3587 [M]	The Way I Feel	1967	20.00
❑ UAS-5510	Classic Lightfoot (The Best of Lightfoot/Vol. 2)	1971	15.00
❑ UAS-6487 [S]	Lightfoot	1966	25.00
❑ UAS-6587 [S]	The Way I Feel	1967	25.00
❑ UAS-6649	Did She Mention My Name	1968	20.00
❑ UAS-6672	Back Here on Earth	1969	20.00
❑ UAS-6714	Sunday Concert	1969	15.00
❑ UAS-6754	The Best of Gordon Lightfoot	1970	15.00

WARNER BROS.

Number	Title (A Side/B Side)	Yr	NM
❑ BSK 3149	Endless Wire	1978	10.00
❑ HS 3426	Dream Street Rose	1980	10.00
❑ BSK 3633	Shadows	1982	10.00
❑ 23901	Salute	1983	10.00
❑ 25482	East of Midnight	1986	10.00
❑ 25784	Gord's Gold, Vol. II	1989	12.00

LIGHTFOOT, PAPA

45s

ALADDIN

Number	Title (A Side/B Side)	Yr	NM
❑ 3171	After a While (Blue Lights)/P.L.'s Blues	1953	200.00
❑ 3304	Blue Lights/Jumpin' with Jarvis	1955	150.00

IMPERIAL

Number	Title (A Side/B Side)	Yr	NM
❑ 5289	Wine, Women, Whiskey/Mean Old Train	1954	150.00

SAVOY

Number	Title (A Side/B Side)	Yr	NM
❑ 1161	Mean Old Train/Wild Fire	1955	30.00

Albums

VAULT

Number	Title (A Side/B Side)	Yr	NM
❑ 130	Natchez Trace	1969	15.00

—As "Papa George Lightfoot"

LIGHTHOUSE

45s

EVOLUTION

Number	Title (A Side/B Side)	Yr	NM
❑ 1041	Hats Off/Sing, Sing, Sing	1971	5.00
❑ 1048	One Fine Morning/Little Kind Words	1971	6.00
❑ 1052	Take It Slow (Out in the Country)/Sweet Lullaby	1971	5.00
❑ 1058	I Just Wanna Be Your Friend/1849	1972	5.00
❑ 1061	I'd Be So Happy/Old Man	1972	5.00
❑ 1069	Sunny Days/Lonely Places	1972	5.00
❑ 1072	You Girl/Merlin	1972	5.00
❑ 1076	Broken Guitar Blues/Merlin	1973	5.00

POLYDOR

Number	Title (A Side/B Side)	Yr	NM
❑ 14197	Can You Feel It/Bright Side	1973	4.00
❑ 14198	Pretty Lady/Bright Side	1973	4.00
❑ 14220	Magic's in the Dancing/Disagreeable man	1974	4.00
❑ 14246	Good Day/Going Downtown	1974	4.00

RCA VICTOR

Number	Title (A Side/B Side)	Yr	NM
❑ 47-9808	The Chant (Nam-Myo-Ho Renge Kyo)/Could You Be Concerned	1969	6.00
❑ 74-0224	Eight Miles High/If There Ever Was a Time	1969	6.00
❑ 74-0285	Feel So Good/Places on Faces Four Blue Carpet Traces	1969	6.00

Albums

EVOLUTION

Number	Title (A Side/B Side)	Yr	NM
❑ 3007	One Fine Morning	1971	15.00
❑ 3010	Thoughts of Movin' On	1972	15.00
❑ 3014 [(2)]	Lighthouse Live!	1972	20.00
❑ 3016	Sunny Days	1973	15.00

JANUS

Number	Title (A Side/B Side)	Yr	NM
❑ JSX-7025	The Best of Lighthouse	1976	12.00

POLYDOR

Number	Title (A Side/B Side)	Yr	NM
❑ PD-5056	Can You Feel It	1973	12.00
❑ PD-1-6028	Good Day	1974	12.00

RCA VICTOR

Number	Title (A Side/B Side)	Yr	NM
❑ LSP-4173	Lighthouse	1969	15.00
❑ LSP-4241	Suite Feeling	1969	15.00
❑ LSP-4325	Peacing It All Together	1970	15.00

LIGHTNIN' SLIM

45s

ACE

Number	Title (A Side/B Side)	Yr	NM
❑ 505	Bad Feeling Blues/Lightning Slim Boogie	1955	150.00

EXCELLO

Number	Title (A Side/B Side)	Yr	NM
❑ 2066	I Can't Be Successful/Lightnin' Blues	1955	40.00
❑ 2075	Sugar Plum/Just Made Twenty One	1956	30.00
❑ 2080	Goin' Home/Wonderin' and Goin'	1956	30.00
❑ 2096	Have Your Way/Bad Luck and Trouble	1956	30.00
❑ 2106	Mean Old Lonesome Train/I'm Grown	1957	30.00
❑ 2116	I'm a Rollin' Stone/Love Me Mama	1957	30.00
❑ 2131	Hoo-Doo Blues/It's Mighty Crazy	1958	30.00
❑ 2142	My Starter Won't Work/Long Leanie Mama	1958	30.00
❑ 2150	Feelin' Awful Blues/I'm Leavin' You Baby	1959	30.00
❑ 2160	Sweet Little Woman/Lightnin's Troubles	1959	30.00
❑ 2169	Rooster Blues/G.I. Slim	1959	30.00
❑ 2179	My Little Angel Child/Too Close Blues	1960	25.00
❑ 2186	Cool Down Baby/Nothin' But the Devil	1960	25.00
❑ 2195	Somebody Knockin'/I Just Don't Know	1961	25.00
❑ 2203	Hello Mary Lee/I'm Tired Waitin' Baby	1961	25.00
❑ 2215	Mind Your Own Business/You're Old Enough to Understand	1962	25.00
❑ 2224	Winter Time Blues/I'm Warnin' You Baby	1962	25.00
❑ 2228	If You Ever Need Me/I'm Evil	1963	25.00
❑ 2234	Loving Around the Clock/You Know You're So Fine	1963	25.00
❑ 2240	Blues at Night/Don't Mistreat Me Baby	1963	25.00
❑ 2245	You Give Me the Blues/Strangest Feelin'	1964	25.00
❑ 2252	Greyhound Blues/She's My Crazy Little Baby	1964	25.00
❑ 2258	Baby Please Come Back/You Move Me Baby	1964	25.00
❑ 2262	Have Mercy on Me Baby/I've Been a Fool for You Darlin'	1965	25.00
❑ 2267	Bad Luck Blues/Can't Live This Life No More	1965	25.00
❑ 2269	Don't Start Me Talkin'/Darlin' You're the One	1965	20.00
❑ 2272	I Hate to See You Leave/Love Is Just a Gamble	1965	20.00
❑ 2320	My Babe/Good Morning Heartaches	1971	10.00

FEATURE

Number	Title (A Side/B Side)	Yr	NM
❑ 3006	Rock Me, Mama/Bad Luck	1954	300.00
❑ 3008	I Can't Live Happy/New Orleans Bound	1954	60.00
❑ 3012	Bugger Bugger Boy/Ethel Mae	1954	60.00

Albums

EXCELLO

Number	Title (A Side/B Side)	Yr	NM
❑ LP 8000 [M]	Rooster Blues	1960	800.00
❑ LPS 8000 [M]	Rooster Blues	196?	50.00

—Thogh labeled "Electronic Stereo," this record is mono

Number	Title (A Side/B Side)	Yr	NM
❑ LP 8004 [M]	Lightnin' Slim's Bell Ringer	1965	300.00
❑ LPS 8004 [M]	Lightnin' Slim's Bell Ringer	196?	50.00

—Thogh labeled "Electronic Stereo," this record is mono

Number	Title (A Side/B Side)	Yr	NM
❑ LPS 8018	High and Low Down	1971	15.00
❑ LPS 8023	London Gumbo	1972	15.00

INTERMEDIA

Number	Title (A Side/B Side)	Yr	NM
❑ QS-5062	That's All Right	198?	10.00

LIGHTNING

45s

P.I.P.

Number	Title (A Side/B Side)	Yr	NM
❑ 8921	Hideaway/Freedom	1970	20.00

Albums

P.I.P.

Number	Title (A Side/B Side)	Yr	NM
❑ 6807	Lightning	1971	30.00

LIMELIGHTERS, THE

45s

JOSIE

Number	Title (A Side/B Side)	Yr	NM
❑ 795	Cabin Hideaway/My Sweet Norma Lee	1956	150.00

LIMELITERS, THE

Also see GLENN YARBROUGH.

45s

RCA VICTOR

Number	Title (A Side/B Side)	Yr	NM
❑ 47-7859	A Dollar Down/When Twice the Moon Has Come and Gone	1961	8.00
❑ 47-7859 [PS]	A Dollar Down/When Twice the Moon Has Come and Gone	1961	12.00
❑ 47-7913	Paco Peco/A Hundred Years Ago	1961	8.00
❑ 47-7942	Milk and Honey/Red Roses and White Wine	1961	8.00
❑ 47-7966	Jonah/Just an Honest Mistake	1961	8.00
❑ 47-8069	The Riddle Song/I Had a Mule	1962	8.00
❑ 47-8094	Who Will Buy/Funk	1962	8.00
❑ 47-8094 [PS]	Who Will Buy/Funk	1962	12.00
❑ 47-8255	Midnight Special/McClintock's Theme	1963	8.00
❑ 47-8361	No Man Is an Island/A Casinda Pequenina	1964	8.00

WARNER BROS.

Number	Title (A Side/B Side)	Yr	NM
❑ 7254	Time to Gather Seed/The Importance of the Rose	1968	6.00

7-Inch Extended Plays

RCA VICTOR

Number	Title (A Side/B Side)	Yr	NM
❑ LPC-132	Hey Li Lee Li Lee/Rumania, Rumania	1961	15.00

—"Compact Double 33" with small hole; this is an extended play record despite having only one song per side

Number	Title (A Side/B Side)	Yr	NM
❑ LPC-132 [PS]	Tonight: In Person	1961	15.00
❑ VLP 2445	A Wayfaring Stranger/Charmin' Betsy/Gotta Travel On//(B-side unknown)	196?	20.00

—Jukebox issue; small hole, plays at 33 1/3 rpm

Number	Title (A Side/B Side)	Yr	NM
❑ VLP 2445 [PS]	(title unknown)	196?	20.00

Albums

ELEKTRA

Number	Title (A Side/B Side)	Yr	NM
❑ EKM-180 [M]	The Limeliters	1960	20.00
❑ EKS-7180 [S]	The Limeliters	1960	25.00

GNP CRESCENDO

Number	Title (A Side/B Side)	Yr	NM
❑ GNPS-2188	Alive! In Concert, Vol. 1	1986	10.00
❑ GNPS-2190	Alive! In Concert, Vol. 2	1987	10.00

LEGACY

Number	Title (A Side/B Side)	Yr	NM
❑ 113	Their First Historic Album	1970	12.00

RCA CAMDEN

Number	Title (A Side/B Side)	Yr	NM
❑ ACL1-0602	This Train	1974	10.00

RCA VICTOR

Number	Title (A Side/B Side)	Yr	NM
❑ LPM-2272 [M]	Tonight: In Person	1961	20.00
❑ LSP-2272 [S]	Tonight: In Person	1961	25.00
❑ ANL1-2336	Pure Gold	1977	8.00
❑ LPM-2393 [M]	The Slightly Fabulous Limeliters	1961	20.00
❑ LSP-2393 [S]	The Slightly Fabulous Limeliters	1961	25.00
❑ LPM-2445 [M]	Sing Out!	1962	20.00
❑ LSP-2445 [S]	Sing Out!	1962	25.00
❑ LPM-2512 [M]	Through Children's Eyes	1962	20.00
❑ LSP-2512 [S]	Through Children's Eyes	1962	25.00
❑ LPM-2547 [M]	Folk Matinee	1962	20.00
❑ LSP-2547 [S]	Folk Matinee	1962	25.00
❑ LPM-2588 [M]	Makin' a Joyful Noise	1963	20.00
❑ LSP-2588 [S]	Makin' a Joyful Noise	1963	25.00
❑ LPM-2609 [M]	Our Men in San Francisco	1963	20.00
❑ LSP-2609 [S]	Our Men in San Francisco	1963	25.00
❑ LPM-2671 [M]	Fourteen 14K Folk Songs	1963	20.00
❑ LSP-2671 [S]	Fourteen 14K Folk Songs	1963	25.00
❑ LPM-2844 [M]	More of Everything!	1964	15.00
❑ LSP-2844 [S]	More of Everything!	1964	20.00
❑ LPM-2889 [M]	The Best of the Limeliters	1964	15.00
❑ LSP-2889 [S]	The Best of the Limeliters	1964	20.00
❑ LPM-2906 [M]	Leave It to the Limeliters	1964	15.00
❑ LSP-2906 [S]	Leave It to the Limeliters	1964	20.00
❑ LPM-2907 [M]	London Concert	1964	15.00
❑ LSP-2907 [S]	London Concert	1964	20.00
❑ LPM-3385 [M]	The Limeliters Look at Love…In Depth	1965	15.00
❑ LSP-3385 [S]	The Limeliters Look at Love…In Depth	1965	20.00
❑ LSP-4100	The Original "Those Were the Days"	1969	15.00

WEST KNOLL

Number	Title (A Side/B Side)	Yr	NM
❑ WK-1001	Alive! In Concert, Vol. 1	198?	10.00
❑ WK-1002	Alive! In Concert, Vol. 2	198?	10.00

LIMEYS, THE

45s

DOT

Number	Title (A Side/B Side)	Yr	NM
❑ 16725	Don't Cry/I Can't Find My Way Through	1965	15.00

SCEPTER

Number	Title (A Side/B Side)	Yr	NM
❑ 12156	Come Back/Scraped: Green and Blue	1966	15.00

Number	Title (A Side/B Side)	Yr	NM
LIMOUSINE			
Albums			
GSF			
❑ 1002	Limousine	1972	20.00
LIND, BOB			
45s			
CAPITOL			
❑ 3169	Theme from the Music Box/ She Can Get Along	1971	5.00
UNITED ARTISTS			
❑ 0032	Elusive Butterfly/Truly Julie's Blues	1973	4.00
—"Silver Spotlight Series" reissue			
VERVE FOLKWAYS			
❑ 5018	Wandering/Hey Nellie Hellie	1966	8.00
❑ 5029	Black Night/White Snow	1966	8.00
WORLD PACIFIC			
❑ 77808	Elusive Butterfly/ Cheryl's Goin' Home	1965	10.00
❑ 77822	Remember the Rain/Truly Julie's Blues (I'll Be There)	1966	8.00
❑ 77830	We've Never Spoken/ I Just Let It Take Me	1966	8.00
❑ 77839	San Francisco Woman/ Baby Take Me Home	1966	8.00
❑ 77865	Good Time Special/Just My Love	1967	8.00
❑ 77879	Goodbye Neon Lies/ We May Have Touched	1967	8.00
Albums			
CAPITOL			
❑ ST-780	Since There Were Circles	1971	15.00
VERVE FOLKWAYS			
❑ FT-3005 [M]	The Elusive Bob Lind	1966	25.00
❑ FTS-3005 [S]	The Elusive Bob Lind	1966	30.00
WORLD PACIFIC			
❑ WP-1841 [M]	Don't Be Concerned	1966	20.00
❑ WP-1851 [M]	Photographs of Feeling	1966	20.00
❑ ST-21841 [S]	Don't Be Concerned	1966	25.00
❑ ST-21851 [S]	Photographs of Feeling	1966	25.00
LINDA AND THE VISTAS			
45s			
SHRINE			
❑ 0100	Bad Apple/She Went Away	1965	400.00
LINDE, JOHN			
45s			
CADET			
❑ 5611	Accordingly/I Learned Some Things Today	1968	8.00
PARKWAY			
❑ 856	Bossa Nova Bill/Round Sound	1962	12.00
LINDEN, KATHY			
45s			
CAPITOL			
❑ 4700	Remember Me (To Jimmy)/ Beautiful Brown Eyes	1962	8.00
❑ 4770	Words/There'll Always Be Sadness	1962	8.00
❑ 4811	If You Really Love Me/Jimmy	1962	8.00
❑ 5018	People Say/There'll Always Be Sadness	1963	8.00
FELSTED			
❑ 8510	Billy/If I Could Hold You in My Arms	1958	15.00
❑ 8521	You'd Be Surprised/Why Oh Why	1958	15.00
❑ 8533	Oh Johnny Oh/Georgie	1958	15.00
❑ 8544	Kissin' Conversation/Just a Sandy Haired Boy Called Sandy	1958	15.00
❑ 8554	Somebody Loves You/ You Walked Into My Life	1959	15.00
❑ 8571	Goodbye, Jimmy, Goodbye/ Heartaches at Sweet Sixteen	1959	15.00
❑ 8587	You Don't Know Girls/ So Close to My Heart	1959	12.00
❑ 8596	Think Love/Mary Lou Wilson and Johnny Brown	1959	12.00
MONUMENT			
❑ 420	Allentown Jail/That's What Love Is	1960	10.00
❑ 423	Midnight/The Willow Weeps	1960	10.00
❑ 428	Take Me Home (To My Lover)/ We Had Words	1960	10.00
❑ 436	So in Love (With You)/ Take Me Home, Jimmy	1961	10.00
Albums			
FELSTED			
❑ 7501 [M]	That Certain Boy	1959	60.00

Number	Title (A Side/B Side)	Yr	NM
LINDISFARNE			
45s			
ATCO			
❑ 7093	Run for Home/Stick Together	1978	4.00
❑ 7095	Warm Feeling/Woman	1979	4.00
ELEKTRA			
❑ 45733	We Can Swing Together/ Float Me Down the River	1971	—
—Canceled			
❑ 45778	Fog on the Tyne/Meet Me on the Corner	1972	7.00
❑ 45799	Lady Eleanor/Down	1972	6.00
❑ 45819	Don't Ask Him/All Fall Down	1972	5.00
❑ 45835	Court in the Act/Poor Old Ireland	1973	5.00
Albums			
ATCO			
❑ SD 38-108	Back and Fourth	1978	12.00
ELEKTRA			
❑ 7E-1018	Happy Daze	1975	12.00
❑ EKS-74099	Nicely Out of Tune	1971	15.00
❑ EKS-75021	Fog on the Tyne	1972	15.00
❑ EKS-75043	Dingly Dell	1972	15.00
❑ EKS-75077	Roll On, Ruby	1974	15.00
LINDSAY, MARK Also see PAUL REVERE AND THE RAIDERS; THE UNKNOWNS.			
45s			
COLUMBIA			
❑ 10081	Mamacita/Song for a Friend	1974	5.00
❑ 10114	Photograph/Song for a Friend	1975	5.00
❑ 44875	First Hymn from Grand Terrace/ The Old Man at the Fair	1969	6.00
❑ 45037	Arizona/Man from Houston	1969	6.00
❑ 45125	Miss America/Small Town Woman	1970	6.00
❑ 45180	Silver Bird/So Hard to Leave You	1970	6.00
❑ 45229	And the Grass Won't Pay No Mind/Funny How Little Men Care	1970	6.00
❑ 45286	Problem Child/Bookends	1970	6.00
❑ 45385	Been Too Long on the Road/ All I Really See Is You	1971	5.00
❑ 45462	Are You Old Enough/ Don't You Know	1971	5.00
❑ 45506	Pretty Pretty/Something Big	1971	5.00
❑ 45895	California/Someone's Been Hiding	1973	5.00
ELKA			
❑ 310	Sing Your Own Song/Sing Your Own Song (Theme)	1976	10.00
GREEDY			
❑ 106	Sing Your Own Song/Sing Your Own Song (Theme)	1976	6.00
WARNER BROS.			
❑ 8359	Sing Me High, Sing Me Low/ Flips-Eyed	1977	4.00
❑ 8479	Little Ladies of the Night/ Flips-Eyed	1977	4.00
Albums			
COLUMBIA			
❑ CS 9986	Arizona	1970	12.00
—Orange label			
❑ CS 9986	Arizona	1970	15.00
—Red "360 Sound" label			
❑ C 30111	Silver Bird	1970	12.00
❑ C 30735	You've Got a Friend	1971	12.00
LINK-EDDY COMBO			
45s			
REPRISE			
❑ 20002	Big Mr. C./The Man with the Golden Arm	1961	15.00
❑ 20008	Katrina/The Cat's Pajamas	1961	15.00
LINKLETTER, BOB			
45s			
CHATTAHOOCHIE			
❑ 702	The Out Crowd/Final Season	1965	20.00
LINKS, THE			
45s			
TEENAGE			
❑ 1009	Ba-Bee/She's the One	1958	1000.
LINN, RAY			
Albums			
DISCOVERY			
❑ DS-823	Empty Suit Blues	1981	10.00
TREND			
❑ 515	Chicago Jazz	1980	20.00
—Direct-to-disc recording			

Number	Title (A Side/B Side)	Yr	NM
LINN, ROBERTA			
45s			
KEEN			
❑ 2013	Merry Christmas Darling/ Katie the Kangaroo	1958	15.00
LINN COUNTY			
45s			
MERCURY			
❑ 72852	Cave Song/Think	1968	8.00
❑ 72882	Fast Days/Lower Lemons	1969	8.00
❑ 72907	The Girl Can't Help It/Fever Shot	1969	8.00
PHILIPS			
❑ 40644	Let the Music Begin/ Wine Take Me Away	1969	8.00
Albums			
MERCURY			
❑ SR-61181	Proud Flesh Soothseer	1968	20.00
❑ SR-61218	Fever Shot	1969	20.00
PHILIPS			
❑ PHS 600326	Till the Break of Dawn	1970	15.00
LINNEAS, THE			
45s			
DIAMOND			
❑ 241	It's a Good Kind of Hurt/ Forever Baby	1968	12.00
❑ 248	My Baby Comes Home Today/ Born to Be Your Baby	1968	12.00
LIONS, THE			
45s			
EVEREST			
❑ 19388	No One But You/Giggles	1961	15.00
IMPERIAL			
❑ 5678	Hickory Dickory/The Yodel	1960	15.00
RENDEZVOUS			
❑ 116	The Feast of the Beasts/ Two-Timing Lovers	1960	15.00
LIPSTIQUE			
Albums			
TOM N JERRY			
❑ TJ-4701	At the Discotheque	1978	20.00
LIPTON, PEGGY			
45s			
ODE			
❑ 111	Let Me Pass By/Stoney End	1968	8.00
❑ 114	San Francisco Glide/Stoney End	1968	8.00
❑ 114 [PS]	San Francisco Glide/Stoney End	1968	12.00
❑ 118	Just a Little Lovin' (Early in the Morning)/Red Clay County Line	1969	8.00
❑ 124	Lu/Let Me Pass By	1969	8.00
❑ 124 [PS]	Lu/Let Me Pass By	1969	12.00
❑ 66001	Wear Your Love Like Heaven/ Honey Won't Let Me	1970	6.00
❑ 66001 [PS]	Wear Your Love Like Heaven/ Honey Won't Let Me	1970	12.00
Albums			
ODE			
❑ Z12 44006	Peggy Lipton	1968	25.00
LIQUID SMOKE			
45s			
AVCO EMBASSY			
❑ 4522	I Who Have Nothing/ Warm Touch	1970	8.00
❑ 4532	The Shelter of Your Arms/ Let Me Down Easy	1970	8.00
❑ 4546	Hard to Handle/ (B-side unknown)	1970	8.00
ROULETTE			
❑ 7166	Dance, Dance, Dance/ Where's Our Love	1975	6.00
Albums			
AVCO EMBASSY			
❑ AVE-33005	Liquid Smoke	1970	25.00
LISTEN (1) With Robert Plant, later of LED ZEPPELIN.			
45s			
COLUMBIA			
❑ 43967	You Better Run/Everybody's Gonna Say	1967	300.00
—Promotional copies go for about half these values			

L

Except when noted otherwise, VG = 25% of NM, and VG+ = 50% of NM. (Example: VG = $2.00, VG+ = $4.00 and NM = $8.00.)

LISTENING

Number	Title (A Side/B Side)	Yr	NM
45s			
VANGUARD			
❑ 35077	I Can Teach You/Cuando	1968	20.00
❑ 35094	Life Stories/Hello You	1968	20.00
Albums			
VANGUARD			
❑ VSD-6504	Listening	1968	60.00

LITTER

Number	Title (A Side/B Side)	Yr	NM
45s			
PROBE			
❑ 461	Silly People/Feeling	1968	25.00
❑ 467	Blue Ice/On Our Minds	1969	25.00
SCOTTY			
❑ 6710	Action Woman/A Legal Matter	1967	100.00
WARICK			
❑ 6711	Somebody Help Me/I'm a Man	1967	200.00
❑ 6712	Action Woman/Whatcha Gonna Do About It	1967	150.00
Albums			
EVA			
❑ 12013	Rare Tracks	1983	15.00
HEXAGON			
❑ 681	$100 Fine	1968	400.00
PROBE			
❑ 4504	Emerge	1969	50.00
WARICK			
❑ 671	Distortions	1967	500.00

LITTLE ANTHONY AND THE IMPERIALS

Number	Title (A Side/B Side)	Yr	NM
45s			
APOLLO			
❑ 521	The Fires Burn No More/Lift Up Your Hands	1957	60.00
—As "The Chesters"			
AVCO			
❑ 4635	I'm Falling in Love with You/What Good Am I Without You	1974	5.00
❑ 4645	I Don't Have to Worry/Loneliest House on the Block	1974	5.00
❑ 4651	Hold On (Just a Little Bit Longer)/I've Got to Let You Go (Part 1)	1975	5.00
❑ 4655	I'll Be Loving You Sooner or Later/Young Girl	1975	5.00
DCP			
❑ 1104	I'm On the Outside (Looking In)/Please Go	1964	10.00
❑ 1119	Goin' Out of My Head/Make It Easy on Yourself	1964	10.00
❑ 1128	Hurt So Bad/Reputation	1965	10.00
❑ 1128 [PS]	Hurt So Bad/Reputation	1965	40.00
❑ 1136	Take Me Back/Our Song	1965	8.00
❑ 1149	I Miss You So/Get Out of My Life	1965	8.00
❑ 1154	Hurt/Never Again	1966	8.00
END			
❑ 1027	Tears on My Pillow/Two People in the World	1958	25.00
—As "Little Anthony and the Imperials"			
❑ 1027	Tears on My Pillow/Two People in the World	1958	40.00
—As "The Imperials"			
❑ 1036	So Much/Oh Yeah	1958	25.00
❑ 1038	The Diary/Cha Cha Henry	1959	25.00
❑ 1039	When You Wish Upon a Star/Wishful Thinking	1959	25.00
❑ 1047	A Prayer and a Juke Box/River Path	1959	25.00
❑ 1053	So Near and Yet So Far/I'm Alright	1959	25.00
❑ 1060	Shimmy, Shimmy, Ko-Ko Bop/I'm Still in Love with You	1959	30.00
❑ 1067	My Empty Room/Bayou, Bayou, Baby	1960	15.00
❑ 1074	I'm Taking a Vacation from Love/Only Sympathy	1960	15.00
❑ 1080	Limbo (Part 1)/Limbo (Part 2)	1960	15.00
❑ 1083	Formula of Love/Dream	1961	15.00
❑ 1086	Please Say You Want Me/So Near Yet So Far	1961	15.00
❑ 1091	Traveling Stranger/Say Yea	1961	15.00
❑ 1104	Dream/A Lovely Way to Spend an Evening	1961	15.00
JANUS			
❑ 160	Father, Father/Each One, Teach One	1971	6.00
❑ 166	Madeline/Universe	1971	6.00
❑ 178	(Where Do I Begin) Love Story/There's an Island	1972	6.00
LIBERTY			
❑ 55119	The Glory of Love/C'mon Tiger (Gimme a Growl)	1958	30.00
—As "The Imperials"			
MCA			
❑ 41258	Daylight/Your Love	1980	4.00
—Little Anthony solo			
NEWTIME			
❑ 503	A Short Prayer/Where Will You Be	196?	12.00
—As "Anthony and the Imperials"			
PCM			
❑ 202	This Time We're Winning/Your Love	1983	4.00
PURE GOLD			
❑ 101	Nothing from Nothing/Running with the Wrong Crowd	1976	5.00
ROULETTE			
❑ 4379	That Lil' Ole Lovemaker Me/It Just Ain't Fair	1961	12.00
—Little Anthony solo			
❑ 4477	Lonesome Romeo/I've Got a Lot to Offer Darling	1963	12.00
—Little Anthony solo			
UNITED ARTISTS			
❑ 0117	Goin' Out of My Head/I'm On the Outside (Looking In)	1973	4.00
—"Silver Spotlight Series" reissue			
❑ 0118	Hurt So Bad/Take Me Back	1973	4.00
—"Silver Spotlight Series" reissue			
❑ 50552	Out of Sight, Out of Mind/Summer's Comin'	1969	6.00
❑ 50598	The Ten Commandments of Love/Let the Sunshine In	1969	6.00
❑ 50625	It'll Never Be the Same Again/Don't Get Close	1970	6.00
❑ 50677	World of Darkness/The Change	1970	6.00
❑ 50720	Help Me Find a Way (To Say I Love You)/If I Love You	1970	6.00
VEEP			
❑ 1228	Better Use Your Head/The Wonder of It All	1966	8.00
❑ 1228 [PS]	Better Use Your Head/The Wonder of It All	1966	40.00
❑ 1233	You Better Take It Easy Baby/Gonna Fix You Good (Every Time You're Bad)	1966	8.00
❑ 1239	Tears on My Pillow/Who's Sorry Now	1966	6.00
❑ 1240	I'm On the Outside (Looking In)/Please Go	1966	6.00
❑ 1241	Goin' Out of My Head/Shing-a-Ling	1966	6.00
❑ 1242	Hurt So Bad/Reputation	1966	6.00
❑ 1243	Take Me Back/Our Song	1966	6.00
❑ 1244	I Miss You So/Get Out of My Life	1966	6.00
❑ 1245	Hurt/Never Again	1966	6.00
❑ 1248	It's Not the Same/Down on Love	1966	8.00
❑ 1255	Don't Tie Me Down/Where There's a Will There's a Way	1967	8.00
❑ 1262	Hold On to Someone/Lost in Love	1967	8.00
❑ 1269	You Only Live Twice/Hungry Heart	1967	8.00
❑ 1275	Beautiful People/If I Remember to Forget	1967	8.00
❑ 1278	I'm Hypnotized/Hungry Heart	1968	8.00
❑ 1283	What Greater Love/In the Back of My Heart	1968	8.00
❑ 1285	Yesterday Has Gone/My Love Is a Rainbow	1968	8.00
❑ 1293	The Flesh Failures (Let the Sunshine In)/Gentle Rain	1969	8.00
❑ 1303	Anthem (Revelation)/Goodbye Good Times	1969	8.00
7-Inch Extended Plays			
END			
❑ 203	*The Diary/Tears on My Pillow/Traveling Stranger/So Much	1959	200.00
❑ 203 [PS]	Little Anthony and the Imperials	1959	300.00
❑ 204	When You Wish Upon a Star/Over the Rainbow//Love Is a Many-Splendored Thing/What Did I Do	1959	200.00
❑ 204 [PS]	We Are Little Anthony and the Imperials	1959	300.00
Albums			
ACCORD			
❑ SN-7216	Tears on My Pillow	1983	10.00
AVCO			
❑ AV-11012	On a New Street	1973	20.00
DCP			
❑ DCL-3801 [M]	I'm On the Outside Looking In	1964	25.00
❑ DCL-3808 [M]	Goin' Out of My Head	1965	25.00
❑ DCL-3809 [M]	The Best of Little Anthony and the Imperials	1965	20.00
❑ DCS-6801 [S]	I'm On the Outside Looking In	1964	30.00
❑ DCS-6808 [S]	Goin' Out of My Head	1965	30.00
❑ DCS-6809 [S]	The Best of Little Anthony and the Imperials	1965	25.00
END			
❑ LP 303 [M]	We Are The Imperials Featuring Little Anthony	1959	250.00
❑ LP 311 [M]	Shades of the 40's	1960	200.00
FORUM			
❑ F-9107 [M]	Little Anthony and the Imperials' Greatest Hits	196?	15.00
❑ FS-9107 [R]	Little Anthony and the Imperials' Greatest Hits	196?	12.00
LIBERTY			
❑ LM-1017	Out of Sight, Out of Mind	1981	8.00
—Reissue of United Artists 1017			
❑ LN-10133	The Best of Little Anthony and the Imperials	1981	8.00
—Budget-line reissue			
PICKWICK			
❑ SPC-3029	The Hits of Little Anthony and the Imperials	196?	12.00
RHINO			
❑ R1-70919	The Best of Little Anthony and the Imperials	1989	12.00
ROULETTE			
❑ R-25294 [M]	Little Anthony and the Imperials' Greatest Hits	1965	25.00
❑ SR-25294 [R]	Little Anthony and the Imperials' Greatest Hits	1965	20.00
❑ SR-42007	Forever Yours	1968	15.00
SONGBIRD			
❑ 3245	Daylight	1980	10.00
SUNSET			
❑ SUS-5287	Little Anthony and the Imperials	1970	15.00
UNITED ARTISTS			
❑ UA-LA026-G [(2)]	Legendary Masters Series	1972	25.00
❑ UA-LA255-G	The Very Best of Little Anthony and the Imperials	1974	10.00
❑ LM-1017	Out of Sight, Out of Mind	1980	10.00
—Reissue of United Artists 6720			
❑ UAS 6720	Out of Sight, Out of Mind	1969	20.00
VEEP			
❑ VP 13510 [M]	I'm On the Outside Looking In	1966	15.00
❑ VP 13511 [M]	Goin' Out of My Head	1966	15.00
❑ VP 13512 [M]	The Best of Little Anthony and the Imperials	1966	15.00
❑ VP 13513 [M]	Payin' Our Dues	1966	15.00
❑ VP 13514 [M]	Reflections	1967	15.00
❑ VP 13516 [M]	Movie Grabbers	1967	15.00
❑ VPS 16510 [S]	I'm On the Outside Looking In	1966	20.00
❑ VPS 16511 [S]	Goin' Out of My Head	1966	20.00
❑ VPS 16512 [S]	The Best of Little Anthony and the Imperials	1966	20.00
❑ VPS 16513 [S]	Payin' Our Dues	1966	20.00
❑ VPS 16514 [S]	Reflections	1967	20.00
❑ VPS 16516 [S]	Movie Grabbers	1967	20.00
❑ VPS 16519	The Best of Little Anthony, Vol. 2	1968	15.00
❑ ST-90840 [S]	The Best of Little Anthony and the Imperials	1966	25.00
—Capitol Record Club edition			

LITTLE BILL AND THE BLUENOTES

Number	Title (A Side/B Side)	Yr	NM
45s			
DOLTON			
❑ 4	I Love an Angel/Bye Bye Baby	1959	30.00
Albums			
CAMELOT			
❑ 102 [M]	The Fiesta Club Presents Little Bill and the Bluenotes	1960	400.00

LITTLE BILLY

Number	Title (A Side/B Side)	Yr	NM
45s			
ABC-PARAMOUNT			
❑ 9896	I Found Me a Girl/Say It Like You Mean It	1958	15.00

LITTLE BOOKER

Number	Title (A Side/B Side)	Yr	NM
45s			
ACE			
❑ 547	Open the Door/Teen-Age Rock	1958	25.00
IMPERIAL			
❑ 5293	Thinkin' 'Bout My Baby/Doing the Ham Bone	1954	100.00

LITTLE BOY BLUES

Number	Title (A Side/B Side)	Yr	NM
45s			
FONTANA			
❑ 1623	It's Only You/Is Love?	1968	15.00

Little Feat, *Little Feat,* Warner Bros. WS 1890, 1971, **$15.**

Number	Title (A Side/B Side)	Yr	NM
IRC			
❑ 6928	Look at the Sun/Love for a Day	1966	20.00
❑ 6936	I'm Ready/Little Boy Blues' Blues	1966	30.00
❑ 6939	I Can Only Give You Everything/ You Don't Love Me	1966	30.00
Albums			
FONTANA			
❑ SRF-67578	In the Woodland of Weir	1968	30.00

LITTLE BUBBER

Number	Title (A Side/B Side)	Yr	NM
45s			
IMPERIAL			
❑ 5225	High Class Woman/ Come Back Baby	1953	80.00
❑ 5238	Runnin' Around/Never Trust a Woman	1953	80.00

LITTLE CAESAR

Number	Title (A Side/B Side)	Yr	NM
45s			
BIG TOWN			
❑ 106	Can't Stand It All Alone/Big Eyes	195?	60.00
❑ 110	What Kind of Fool Is He/Wonder Why I'm Leaving (Rat Song)	195?	60.00
RCA VICTOR			
❑ 47-7270	Who Slammed the Door/ I'm Reachin'	1958	25.00
RECORDED IN HOLLYWOOD			
❑ 234	Long Time Baby/ (Going Down to) The River	1952	60.00
❑ 235	Goodbye Baby/If I Could See My Baby	1952	60.00
❑ 236	Move Me/Lying Woman	1953	60.00
❑ 237	You're Part of Me/Here Is a Letter	1953	60.00
❑ 238	Do Right/Money Ain't Long Enough	1953	60.00
❑ 239	Atomic Love/You Can't Bring Me Down	1953	60.00
RPM			
❑ 393	Chains of Love Have Disappeared/Tried to Reason with You Baby	1953	60.00

LITTLE CAESAR AND THE CONSULS

Number	Title (A Side/B Side)	Yr	NM
45s			
MALA			
❑ 512	(My Girl) Sloopy/Poison Ivy	1965	15.00
❑ 518	You've Really Got a Hold on Me/ It's So Easy	1965	12.00
❑ 523	Hey Girl/You Laugh Too Much	1966	12.00

LITTLE CAESAR AND THE EMPIRE

Number	Title (A Side/B Side)	Yr	NM
45s			
PARKWAY			
❑ 152	Everybody Dance Now/ (Instrumental)	1967	25.00

LITTLE CAESAR AND THE ROMANS

Number	Title (A Side/B Side)	Yr	NM
45s			
DEL-FI			
❑ 4158	Those Oldies But Goodies (Remind Me of You)/ She Don't Wanna Dance	1961	30.00
❑ 4164	Hully Gully Again/ Frankie and Johnny	1961	25.00
❑ 4166	Memories of Those Oldies But Goodies/Fever	1961	60.00
❑ 4170	Ten Commandments of Love/ C.C. Rider	1961	50.00
❑ 4176	Popeye One More Time/ Yoyo Yo Yoyo	1962	25.00
LANA			
❑ 152	Those Oldies But Goodies (Remind Me of You)/She Don't Wanna Dance	196?	8.00
—Oldies reissue			
LOST-NITE			
❑ 204	Those Oldies But Goodies (Remind Me of You)/ She Don't Wanna Dance	196?	5.00
—Reissue			
SCEPTER			
❑ 12237	Baby Love/When Will I Get Over You	1969	8.00
—As "Caesar and the Romans"			
❑ 12264	Jailhouse Rock/Leavin' My Past Behind	1969	8.00
—As "Caesar and the Romans"			
Albums			
DEL-FI			
❑ DFLP-1218 [M]	Memories of Those Oldies But Goodies	1961	300.00

LITTLE CHARLES AND THE SIDEWINDERS

Number	Title (A Side/B Side)	Yr	NM
45s			
DECCA			
❑ 31980	I'm Available/It's a Heartache	1966	300.00
❑ 32095	Talkin' About You, Babe/ A Taste of the Good Life	1967	300.00
❑ 32233	The Loner (Part 1)/ The Loner (Part 2)	1967	75.00
❑ 32321	Sweet Lorene/Twice as Much for My Baby	1968	30.00
JEWEL			
❑ 752	Give Me a Chance/Guess I'll Have to Take What's Left	1965	40.00

LITTLE CHERYL

Number	Title (A Side/B Side)	Yr	NM
45s			
CAMEO			
❑ 270	Heaven Only Knows/ Can't We Just Be Friends	1963	40.00
❑ 276	Mama Let the Phone Bell Ring/ Can't We Just Be Friends	1963	12.00
❑ 292	Come On Home/I Love You Conrad	1964	12.00
❑ 307	Yeh Yeh We Love 'Em All/ Nick and Joe Callin'	1964	16.00
REPRISE			
❑ 20109	Jim/Pocketful of Money	1962	15.00

LITTLE COOLBREEZERS, THE See THE COOLBREEZERS.

LITTLE DOUG See DOUG SAHM.

LITTLE ESTHER See LITTLE ESTHER PHILLIPS.

LITTLE EVA

Number	Title (A Side/B Side)	Yr	NM
45s			
AMY			
❑ 943	Stand By Me/That's My Man	1965	8.00
BELL			
❑ 45264	The Loco-Motion/Will You Love Me Tomorrow	1972	5.00
DIMENSION			
❑ 1000	The Loco-Motion/He Is the Boy	1962	15.00
❑ 1003	Keep Your Hands Off My Baby/ Where Do I Go	1962	12.00
—Most copies have longer, and correct, title			
❑ 1003	Keep Your Hands Off/Where Do I Go	1962	30.00
—Some copies have this shortened title			
❑ 1006	Let's Turkey Trot/Down Home	1963	12.00
❑ 1011	Old Smokey Locomotion/Just a Little Girl	1963	12.00
❑ 1013	The Trouble with Boys/What I Gotta Do	1963	20.00
❑ 1019	Let's Start the Party Again/ Please Hurt Me	1963	12.00
❑ 1021	The Christmas Song/I Wish You a Merry Christmas	1963	15.00
—With Big Dee Irwin			
❑ 1021 [PS]	The Christmas Song/I Wish You a Merry Christmas	1963	40.00
—With Big Dee Irwin			
❑ 1035	Makin' with the Magilla/Conga	1964	10.00
❑ 1035	Makin' with the Magilla/ Run to Her	1964	10.00
❑ 1035 [PS]	Makin' with the Magilla/ Run to Her	1964	40.00
❑ 1042	Wake Up John/Takin' Back What I Said	1964	60.00
SPRING			
❑ 101	Mama Said/Something About You Boy	1970	20.00
❑ 107	Night After Night/Something About You Boy	1970	20.00
VERVE			
❑ 10459	Bend It/Just One Word Isn't Enough	1966	30.00

Except when noted otherwise, VG = 25% of NM, and VG+ = 50% of NM. (Example: VG = $2.00, VG+ = $4.00 and NM = $8.00.)

Number	Title (A Side/B Side)	Yr	NM
❑ 10529	Everything Is Beautiful About You Boy/Take a Step in My Direction	1967	40.00

Albums

DIMENSION

❑ DLP-6000 [M] LLLLLoco-Motion 1962 150.00
—Without "Keep Your Hands Off My Baby"
❑ DLP-6000 [M] LLLLLoco-Motion 1962 200.00
—With "Keep Your Hands Off My Baby"
❑ DLPS-6000 [R] LLLLLoco-Motion 1962 150.00
—Without "Keep Your Hands Off My Baby"
❑ DLPS-6000 [R] LLLLLoco-Motion 1962 200.00
—With "Keep Your Hands Off My Baby"

LITTLE FEAT Also see LOWELL GEORGE.

45s

WARNER BROS.

❑ 7431 Strawberry Flats/Hamburger Midnight 1970 8.00
❑ 7553 Easy to Slip/Cat Fever 1972 8.00
❑ 7689 Dixie Chicken/Lafayette Railroad 1973 6.00
❑ 8054 Oh Atlanta/Down the Road 1974 5.00
❑ 8174 Long Distance Love/Romance Dance 1975 5.00
❑ 8219 All That You Dream/One Love Stand 1976 5.00
❑ 8420 Time Loves a Hero/Sailin' Shoes 1977 5.00
❑ 8566 Oh Atlanta/Willin' 1978 5.00
❑ 27684 One Clear Moment/Changin' Luck 1988 3.00
❑ 27684 [PS] One Clear Moment/Changin' Luck 1988 3.00
❑ 27728 Hate to Lose Your Lovin'/Cajun Girl 1988 3.00
❑ 27728 [PS] Hate to Lose Your Lovin'/Cajun Girl 1988 3.00
❑ 49169 Wake Up Dreaming/Front Page News 1980 5.00
❑ 49801 Front Page News/Easy to Sleep 1981 5.00
❑ 49841 Strawberry Flats/Gringo 1981 5.00

Albums

MOBILE FIDELITY

❑ 1-013 [(2)] Waiting for Columbus 1979 80.00
—Audiophile vinyl

NAUTILUS

❑ NR-24 Time Loves a Hero 198? 50.00
—Audiophile vinyl

TPM/RHINO EXCLUSIVE

❑ 299 Little Feat 2008 22.00

WARNER BROS.

❑ 307 Sailin' Shoes 2008 22.00
❑ PRO-A-984 [DJ]Hoy-Hoy! 1981 20.00
—Single-album sampler of 2-LP set
❑ WS 1890 Little Feat 1971 15.00
—Green "WB" label; without photo on back cover
❑ WS 1890 Little Feat 1971 20.00
—Green "WB" label; with photo on back cover
❑ WS 1890 Little Feat 1973 10.00
—"Burbank" palm trees label
❑ WS 1890 Little Feat 1979 8.00
—Tan or white label
❑ BS 2600 Sailin' Shoes 1972 15.00
—Green "WB" label
❑ BS 2600 Sailin' Shoes 1973 10.00
—"Burbank" palm trees label
❑ BS 2600 Sailin' Shoes 1979 8.00
—Tan or white label
❑ BS 2686 Dixie Chicken 1973 15.00
—"Burbank" palm trees label
❑ BS 2686 Dixie Chicken 1979 8.00
—Tan or white label
❑ BS 2748 Feats Don't Fail Me Now 1974 15.00
—"Burbank" palm trees label
❑ BS 2748 Feats Don't Fail Me Now 1979 8.00
—Tan or white label
❑ BS 2884 The Last Record Album 1975 15.00
—"Burbank" palm trees label
❑ BS 2884 The Last Record Album 1979 8.00
—Tan or white label
❑ BS 3015 Time Loves a Hero 1977 12.00
—"Burbank" palm trees label
❑ BS 3015 Time Loves a Hero 1979 8.00
—Tan or white label
❑ 2WS 3140 [(2)] Waiting for Columbus 1978 15.00
—"Burbank" palm trees label
❑ 2WS 3140 [(2)] Waiting for Columbus 1979 10.00
—Tan or white label
❑ HS 3345 Down on the Farm 1979 10.00
❑ 2BSK 3538 [(2)] Hoy-Hoy! 1981 12.00
❑ 25750 Let It Roll 1988 10.00
❑ 26263 Representing the Mambo 1990 15.00

ZOO/CLASSIC

❑ 11097 [(2)] Ain't Had Enough Fun 1995 18.00
—150-gram vinyl
❑ 11097 [(2)] Ain't Had Enough Fun 1995 20.00
—180-gram vinyl

LITTLE GIRLS

Albums

FTM ENTERPRISES

❑ (no #) [EP] Little Girls 1985 1985 100.00
—Promo-only three-song EP, with all songs on same side, on clear vinyl in clear plastic sleeve; also contains two black & white photos of the group and three pages of biographical notes and reviews; 100 pressed

PVC

❑ 5904 [EP] Thank Heaven! 1983 20.00

LITTLE GUY AND THE GIANTS

45s

LAWN

❑ 103 It's You/So Young 1960 200.00

LITTLE IKE

45s

CHAMPION

❑ 1011 She Can Rock/Am I Losin' You 1959 100.00

LITTLE JOE

45s

BRUNSWICK

❑ 55369 Holiday/Fool on the Hill 1968 8.00

Albums

BRUNSWICK

❑ BL 754135 Little Joe (Sure Can Sing) 1968 20.00

LITTLE JOE AND THE THRILLERS

45s

ENJOY

❑ 2011 Peanuts and Popcorn/Chicken Little Boo Boo 1964 10.00

EPIC

❑ 9293 Mine/It's Too Bad We Had to Say Goodbye 1958 15.00
❑ 9431 Run Little Girl/Public Opinion 1961 12.00

MGM

❑ 14129 Somehow, Someway/Days 'Til Morning 1970 5.00
❑ 14230 People Show/Baby I Could Be So Good at Lovin' You 1971 5.00
❑ 14290 Don't Take the Rain Away/The Children 1971 5.00
❑ 14361 Shelly Made Me Smile/Words and Music 1972 5.00
❑ 14466 Baby I Could Be So Good at Lovin' You/Cherry Pink and Apple Blossom White 1972 5.00
❑ 14662 Folks Who Live on the Hill/Baby I Could Be So Good at Lovin' You 1973 5.00

OKEH

❑ 7075 Let's Do the Slop/This I Know 1956 15.00
❑ 7088 Peanuts/Lilly Lou 1957 20.00
❑ 7094 Lonesome/The Echoes Keep Calling Me 1957 15.00
❑ 7099 Don't Leave Me Alone/What's Happened to Your Halo 1958 15.00
❑ 7107 Mine/It's Too Bad We Had to Say Goodbye 1958 15.00
❑ 7116 Cherry (Part 1)/Cherry (Part 2) 1959 12.00
❑ 7121 I'm Tryin'/Strange Dreams 1959 12.00
❑ 7127 Give Me All Your Love/I'll Never Let You Go 1959 12.00
❑ 7134 Ev'ry Now and Then/Goodnight, Little Girl 1960 12.00
❑ 7136 Stay/Please Don't Go 1960 30.00
❑ 7140 Run Little Girl/Public Opinion 1961 12.00

REPRISE

❑ 20142 Peanuts/No, No, I Can't Stop 1963 10.00

7-Inch Extended Plays

EPIC

❑ EG-7198 (contents unknown) 1958 100.00
❑ EG-7198 [PS] Little Joe and the Thrillers 1958 100.00

LITTLE JOEY AND THE FLIPS

45s

CAMEO

❑ 327 The Beachcomber/Fool, Fool, Fool 1964 40.00
—As "Joey and the Flips"

JOY

❑ 262 Bongo Stomp/Lost Love 1962 15.00
❑ 268 Bongo Gully/It Was Like Heaven 1962 12.00

LITTLE JUNIOR'S BLUE FLAMES See JUNIOR PARKER.

LITTLE LADY BEATLES, THE See THE INSECTS.

LITTLE MILTON

45s

BOBBIN

❑ 101 I'm a Lonely Man/That Will Never Do 1958 25.00
❑ 103 Long Distance Operator/I Found Me a New Love 1959 25.00
❑ 112 Strange Dreams/I'm Tryin' 1959 25.00
❑ 117 Hold Me Tight/Same Old Blues 1959 25.00
❑ 120 Dead Love/My Baby Pleases Me 1960 25.00
❑ 125 Let It Be Known/Hey Girl 1960 25.00
❑ 128 I'm in Love/Cross My Heart 1961 25.00

CHECKER

❑ 977 Saving My Love for You/Lonely No More 1961 15.00
❑ 994 So Mean to Me/I Need Somebody 1961 15.00
❑ 1012 Satisfied/Someone to Love 1962 15.00
❑ 1020 I Wonder Why/Losing Hand 1962 15.00
❑ 1048 She Put a Spell on Me/Never Too Old 1963 15.00
❑ 1063 Meddlin'/One of These Old Days 1963 15.00
❑ 1078 Sacrifice/What Kind of Love Is This 1964 15.00
❑ 1096 Blind Man/Blues in the Night 1964 15.00
❑ 1105 We're Gonna Make It/Can't Hold Back the Tears 1965 15.00
❑ 1113 Who's Cheating Who?/Ain't No Big Deal on You 1965 15.00
❑ 1118 Help Me Help You/Without My Sweet Baby 1965 15.00
❑ 1128 My Baby's Something Else/Your People 1965 15.00
❑ 1132 Sometimes/We Got the Winning Hand 1965 15.00
❑ 1138 I'm Mighty Grateful/When Does Heartache End 1966 15.00
❑ 1149 Man Loves Two/Believe in Me 1966 15.00
❑ 1162 Feel So Bad/You Colored My Blues Right 1966 20.00
❑ 1172 I'll Never Turn My Back on You/Don't Leave Her 1967 12.00
❑ 1178 I'm Shorty/Sitting Home Alone 1967 12.00
❑ 1186 A Whole Lot of Fun Before the Weekend Is Done/Real True Love 1967 12.00
❑ 1189 More and More/Cost of Living 1967 12.00
❑ 1194 I Know What I Want/You Mean Everything to Me 1968 12.00
❑ 1203 At the Dark End of the Street/I (Who Have Nothing) 1968 12.00
❑ 1208 Let Me Down Easy/Lonely Drifter 1968 12.00
❑ 1212 Grits Ain't Groceries (All Around the World)/I Can't Quit You Baby 1969 30.00
❑ 1217 Just a Little Bit/Spring 1969 12.00
❑ 1221 Poor Man/So Blue 1969 12.00
❑ 1225 Let's Get Together/I'll Always Love You 1969 12.00
❑ 1226 If Walls Could Talk/Loving You 1969 12.00
❑ 1227 Baby I Love You/Don't Talk Back 1970 12.00
❑ 1231 Somebody's Changin' My Sweet Baby's Mind/I'm Tired 1970 12.00
—As "Little Milton Campbell"
❑ 1236 Many Rivers to Cross/Mother's Love 1970 12.00
❑ 1239 I Play Dirty/Nothing Beats a Failure 1971 8.00

GLADES

❑ 1734 Friend of Mine/(Instrumental) 1976 5.00
❑ 1738 Baby It Ain't No Way/Bring It On Back 1976 5.00
❑ 1741 Just One Step/(Instrumental) 1977 5.00
❑ 1743 Loving You (Is the Best Thing to Happen to Me)/9:59 A.M. 1977 5.00
❑ 1747 Me for You, You for Me/My Thing Is You 1977 5.00

MALACO

❑ 2104 The Blues Is All Right/Come Back Kind of Loving 1985 4.00
❑ 2108 Misty Blue/Catch You on the Way Down 1985 4.00
❑ 2123 Lonesome Christmas/Come To Me 1985 4.00
❑ 2127 I Will Survive/4:59 A.M. 1986 4.00
❑ 2134 Real Good Woman/Annie Mae's Café 198? 4.00
❑ 2147 His Old Lady and My Old Lady/(B-side unknown) 198? 4.00
❑ 2162 Bad Dream/The Woman I Love 198? 4.00

Little Richard, Greatest Hits, Okeh OKS 14121, 1967, **$20.**

Number	Title (A Side/B Side)	Yr	NM
MCA			
❑ 52184	Age Ain't Nothin' But a Number/ (Instrumental)	1983	4.00
❑ 52254	Living on the Dark Side of Love/ Why Are You So Hard to Please	1983	4.00
METEOR			
❑ 5040	Love at First Sight/ Let's Boogie Baby	1957	200.00
❑ 5045	Let My Baby Be/ Oh My Little Baby	1957	800.00
STAX			
❑ 0100	If That Ain't a Reason (For Your Woman to Leave You)/Mr. Mailman	1971	6.00
❑ 0111	That's What Love Will Make You Do/I'm Livin' Off the Love You Give	1972	6.00
❑ 0124	Walking the Back Streets and Crying/Before the Honeymoon	1972	6.00
❑ 0141	I'm Gonna Cry a River/What It Is	1972	6.00
❑ 0148	Lovin' Stick/Rainy Day	1972	6.00
❑ 0174	What It Is/Who Can Handle Me Is You	1973	6.00
❑ 0191	Tin Pan Alley/Sweet Woman of Mine	1974	6.00
❑ 0210	Behind Closed Doors/ Bet You I Win	1974	6.00
❑ 0229	Let Me Back In/Let Your Loss Be Your Lesson	1974	6.00
❑ 0238	If You Talk in Your Sleep/ Sweet Woman of Mine	1975	6.00
❑ 0252	How Could You Do It to Me/ Packed Up and Took My Mind	1975	6.00
SUN			
❑ 194	Beggin' My Baby/ Somebody Told Me	1954	300.00
❑ 200	If You Love Me/Alone and Blue	1954	600.00
❑ 220	Lookin' for My Baby/ Homesick for My Baby	1955	800.00

Number	Title (A Side/B Side)	Yr	NM
Albums			
CHECKER			
❑ LP-2995 [M]	We're Gonna Make It	196?	25.00
—Blue, fading to white, label			
❑ LP-2995 [M]	We're Gonna Make It	1965	100.00
—Black label			
❑ LP-2995 [M]	We're Gonna Make It	1966	70.00
—Blue label with red and black checkers			
❑ LP-3002 [M]	Little Milton Sings Big Blues	1966	50.00
❑ LP-3011	Grits Ain't Groceries	1969	25.00
❑ LP-3012	If Walls Could Talk	1970	25.00
CHESS			
❑ 204 [(2)]	Little Milton	1976	15.00
❑ CH-9252	We're Gonna Make It	1986	10.00
—Reissue of Checker 2995			
❑ CH-9265	Little Milton Sings Big Blues	1987	10.00
—Reissue of Checker 3002			
❑ CH-9289	If Walls Could Talk	1989	10.00
—Reissue of Checker 3012			
❑ CH-50013	Little Milton's Greatest Hits	1972	15.00
GLADES			
❑ 7508	Friend of Mine	1976	12.00
❑ 7511	Me for You, You for Me	1977	12.00
MALACO			
❑ 7419	Playin' for Keeps	198?	12.00
❑ 7427	I Will Survive	198?	12.00
❑ 7435	Annie Mae's Café	198?	12.00
❑ 7445	Movin' to the Country	198?	12.00
❑ 7448	Back to Back	198?	12.00
❑ 7453	Too Much Pain	198?	12.00
MCA			
❑ 5414	Age Ain't Nothin' But a Number	1983	10.00
ROUNDER			
❑ SS-35	The Sun Masters	198?	12.00
STAX			
❑ STS-3012	Waiting for Little Milton	1973	20.00
❑ 4117	Waiting for Little Milton	1978	12.00
—Reissue of 3012			
❑ 5514	Blues 'n' Soul	1974	20.00
❑ MPS-8514	Walking the Back Streets	1981	10.00

Number	Title (A Side/B Side)	Yr	NM
❑ MPS-8518	Blues 'n' Soul	1981	10.00
—Reissue of 5514			
❑ MPS-8529	Grits Ain't Groceries	198?	10.00
—Despite the title, this is NOT a reissue of Checker 3011, but a later live recording			
❑ MPS-8550	What It Is	198?	10.00

LITTLE MISS CORNSHUCKS

Number	Title (A Side/B Side)	Yr	NM
45s			
CHESS			
❑ 1785	No Teasing Around/ It Do Me No Good	1961	15.00
Albums			
CHESS			
❑ LP-1453 [M]	The Loneliest Gal in Town	1961	200.00

LITTLE OTIS

Number	Title (A Side/B Side)	Yr	NM
45s			
TAMLA			
❑ 54058	I Out-Duked the Duke/ Baby I Need You	1962	30.00

LITTLE PEOPLE

Number	Title (A Side/B Side)	Yr	NM
45s			
ENTRANCE			
❑ ZS7 7504	I Don't Want to Go On Without You/You've Really Got a Hold on Me	1972	7.00

LITTLE RICHARD Also see THE DEUCES OF RHYTHM AND THE TEMPO TOPPERS; JIMI HENDRIX.

Number	Title (A Side/B Side)	Yr	NM
12-Inch Singles			
MCA			
❑ L33-17101 [DJ]	Great Gosh A' Mighty! (same on both sides)	1986	8.00
SPECIALTY			
❑ SPS 4000	Lucille/Heebie-Jeebies Love	198?	8.00
WTG			
❑ 08169	Twins (5 versions)	1988	6.00
—With Philip Bailey			
45s			
ATLANTIC			
❑ 2181	Crying in the Chapel/ Hole in the Wall	1963	12.00
❑ 2192	It Is No Secret (What God Can Do)/Travelin' Shoes	1963	12.00
BELL			
❑ 45385	Good Golly Miss Molly/Good Golly Miss Molly (Part 2)	1973	5.00
BRUNSWICK			
❑ 55362	She's Together/Try Some of Mine	1968	8.00
❑ 55377	Stingy Jenny/Baby Don't You Tear My Clothes	1968	8.00
❑ 55386	Soul Train/Can I Count on You	1968	8.00
CORAL			
❑ 62366	Milky White Way/Need Him	1963	10.00
CRITIQUE			
❑ 99392	Happy Endings/California Girls	1987	4.00
—A-side with the Beach Boys; B-side is The Beach Boys without Little Richard			
ELEKTRA			
❑ 69370	Tutti Frutti/Rave On	1988	3.00
—B-side by John Cougar Mellencamp			
❑ 69384	Tutti Frutti/Powerful Stuff	1988	3.00
—B-side by the Fabulous Thunderbirds			
❑ 69385	Tutti Frutti/Kokomo	1988	3.00
—B-side by the Beach Boys			
END			
❑ 1057	Troubles of the World/ Save Me Lord	1959	15.00
❑ 1058	Milky White Way/I've Just Come From the Fountain	1959	15.00
GREEN MOUNTAIN			
❑ 413	In the Middle of the Night/ Where Will I Find a Place to Sleep This Evening	1973	5.00
KENT			
❑ 4567	Mississippi/In the Name	1972	—
—Unreleased			
❑ 4568	Don't You Know I/In the Name	1972	5.00
LOST-NITE			
❑ 296	Keep a-Knockin'/She's Got It	197?	6.00
—Reissue from Vee-Jay masters (not the original versions)			
❑ 302	Lucille/Good Golly Miss Molly	197?	6.00
—Reissue from Vee-Jay masters (not the original versions)			
❑ 309	Tutti Frutti/Long Tall Sally	197?	6.00
—Reissue from Vee-Jay masters (not the original versions)			
❑ 315	The Girl Can't Help It/Rip It Up	197?	6.00
—Reissue from Vee-Jay masters (not the original versions)			

Except when noted otherwise, VG = 25% of NM, and VG+ = 50% of NM. (Example: VG = $2.00, VG+ = $4.00 and NM = $8.00.)

Number	Title (A Side/B Side)	Yr	NM
MAINSTREAM			
❑ 5572	Try to Help Your Brother/ Funk Proof	1975	5.00
MANTICORE			
❑ 7007	Call My Name/Steal Miss Liza (Miss Liza Jane)	1975	4.00
MCA			
❑ 52780	Great Gosh A-Mighty! (It's a Matter of Time)/The Ride	1986	3.00
—B-side by Charlie Midnight			
❑ 52780 [PS]	Great Gosh A-Mighty! (It's a Matter of Time)/The Ride	1986	3.00
MERCURY			
❑ 71884	He's Not Just a Soldier/ Joy, Joy, Joy	1962	15.00
❑ 71911	Do You Care/Ride On King Jesus	1962	15.00
❑ 71965	Why Don't You Change Your Ways/He Got What He Wanted	1962	15.00
MODERN			
❑ 1018	Holy Mackeral/Baby, Don't You Want a Man Like Me	1966	12.00
❑ 1018 [PS]	Holy Mackeral/Baby, Don't You Want a Man Like Me	1966	20.00
❑ 1019	Do You Feel It (Part 1)/ Do You Feel It (Part 2)	1966	12.00
❑ 1022	Directly from My Heart to You/ I'm Back	1966	12.00
❑ 1030	Slippin' and Slidin'/Bring It Back Home to Me	1967	12.00
❑ 1043	Baby What You Want Me to Do (Part 1)/Baby What You Want Me to Do (Part 2)	1967	12.00
OKEH			
❑ 7251	Poor Dog (Who Can't Wag His Own Tail)/Well	1966	15.00
❑ 7251 [PS]	Poor Dog (Who Can't Wag His Own Tail)/Well	1966	25.00
❑ 7262	I Need Love/Commandments of Love	1966	12.00
❑ 7271	Hurry Sundown/I Don't Want to Discuss It	1967	12.00
❑ 7278	Don't Deceive Me (Please Don't Go)/Never Gonna Let You Go	1967	12.00
❑ 7286	Money/Little Bit of Something	1967	12.00
❑ 7325	Lucille/Whole Lotta Shakin' Goin' On	1969	10.00
PEACOCK			
❑ 1658	Little Richard's Boogie/Directly from My Heart to You	1956	150.00
❑ 1673	Maybe I'm Right/I Love My Baby	1957	80.00
RCA VICTOR			
❑ 47-4392	Taxi Blues/Every Hour	1951	900.00
❑ 47-4582	Get Rich Quick/Thinkin' 'Bout My Mother	1952	800.00
❑ 47-4772	Why Did You Leave Me?/ Ain't Nothin' Happenin'	1952	800.00
❑ 47-5025	Please Have Mercy on Me /I Brought It All on Myself	1952	600.00
REPRISE			
❑ 0907	Freedom Blues/Dew Drop Inn	1970	10.00
❑ 0942	Greenwood Mississippi/ I Saw Her Standing There	1970	10.00
❑ 1005	Shake a Hand (If You Can)/ Somebody Saw You	1971	8.00
❑ 1043	Green Power/Dancing in the Street	1971	8.00
❑ 1062	Money Is/Money Runner	1972	8.00
—B-side by Quincy Jones			
❑ 1130	Mockingbird Sally/Nuki Suki	1972	8.00
SPECIALTY			
❑ 561	Tutti-Frutti/I'm Just a Lonely Guy	1955	50.00
❑ 572	Long Tall Sally/Slippin' and Slidin' (Peepin' and Hidin')	1956	40.00
❑ 579	Rip It Up/Ready Teddy	1956	40.00
❑ 584	Heebie-Jeebies/She's Got it	1956	40.00
❑ 591	The Girl Can't Help It/All Around the World	1956	40.00
❑ 598	Lucille/Send Me Some Lovin'	1957	40.00
❑ 606	Jenny, Jenny/Miss Ann	1957	40.00
❑ 606 [PS]	Jenny, Jenny/Miss Ann	1957	60.00
❑ 611	Keep a Knockin'/Can't Believe You Wanna Leave	1957	30.00
❑ 611 [PS]	Keep a Knockin'/Can't Believe You Wanna Leave	1957	60.00
❑ 624	Good Golly, Miss Molly/ Hey-Hey-Hey-Hey!	1958	30.00
❑ 624 [PS]	Good Golly, Miss Molly/ Hey-Hey-Hey-Hey!	1958	50.00
❑ 633	Ooh! My Soul/True, Fine Mama	1958	25.00
❑ 633 [PS]	Ooh! My Soul/True, Fine Mama	1958	50.00
❑ 633/624	Ooh! My Soul/True, Fine Mama	1958	80.00
—Some copies have the B-side misnumbered; all other information is correct, including the master number			
❑ 645	Baby Face/I'll Never Let You Go	1958	25.00
❑ 652	She Knows How to Rock/ Early One Morning	1958	25.00
❑ 660	By the Light of the Silvery Moon/ Wonderin'	1959	25.00
❑ 664	Kansas City/Lonesome and Blue	1959	25.00
❑ 670	Shake a Hand/All Night Long	1959	25.00
❑ 680	Whole Lotta Shakin' Goin' On/ Maybe I'm Right	1959	25.00
❑ 681	I Got It/Baby	1960	25.00
❑ 686	The Most I Can Offer/ Directly from My Heart	1964	15.00
❑ 692	Bama Lama Bama Loo/ Annie Is Back	1964	15.00
❑ 697	Keep a Knockin'/Bama Lama Bama Loo	1964	15.00
❑ 699	Poor Boy Paul/Wonderin'	1964	15.00
❑ 734	Chicken Little Baby/Oh Why	1974	6.00
VEE JAY			
❑ 612	Whole Lotta Shakin' Goin' On/ Goodnight Irene	1964	10.00
❑ 625	Blueberry Hill/Cherry Red	1964	10.00
❑ 652	It Ain't Whatcha Do/Cross Over	1965	10.00
❑ 665	Without Love/Dance What You Wanna	1965	10.00
❑ 698	I Don't Know What You've Got But It's Got Me — Part I/I Don't Know What You've Got But It's Got Me — Part II	1965	10.00
WARNER BROS.			
❑ 28491	Big House Reunion/ Somebody's Comin'	1987	4.00
WTG			
❑ 08492	Twins (Long)/Twins (Short)	1988	4.00
—With Philip Bailey			

7-Inch Extended Plays

Number	Title (A Side/B Side)	Yr	NM
RCA CAMDEN			
❑ CAE-416	Ain't Nothin' Happenin'/Why Did You Leave Me//Every Hour/I Brought It All on Myself	1955	150.00
❑ CAE-416 [PS]	Little Richard	1955	150.00
❑ CAE-446	Taxi Blues/Please Have Mercy on Me//Get Rich Quick/ Thinkin' 'Bout My Mother	1956	100.00
❑ CAE-446 [PS]	Little Richard Rocks	1956	100.00
SPECIALTY			
❑ SEP-400	Long Tall Sally/Miss Ann// She's Got It/Can't Believe You Wanna Leave	1957	100.00
❑ SEP-400 [PS]	Here's Little Richard	1957	100.00
❑ SEP-401	Slippin' and Slidin'/Oh Why// Ready Teddy/Baby	1957	100.00
❑ SEP-401 [PS]	Here's Little Richard	1957	100.00
❑ SEP-402	Tutti-Frutti/True, Fine Mama// Rip It Up/Jenny, Jenny	1957	100.00
❑ SEP-402 [PS]	Here's Little Richard	1957	100.00
❑ SEP-403	Keep a Knockin'/By the Light of the Silvery Moon//Lucille/ Hey-Hey-Hey-Hey	1958	80.00
❑ SEP-403 [PS]	Little Richard	1958	80.00
❑ SEP-404	Ooh! My Soul/All Around the World//Good Golly, Miss Molly/Babyface	1958	80.00
❑ SEP-404 [PS]	Little Richard	1958	80.00
❑ SEP-405	Boo Hoo Hoo Hoo/The Girl Can't Help It//Send Me Some Lovin'/Heeby-Jeebies	1958	80.00
❑ SEP-405 [PS]	Little Richard	1958	80.00

Albums

Number	Title	Yr	NM
ACCORD			
❑ SN-7123	Tutti Frutti	1981	10.00
AUDIO ENCORES			
❑ 1002	Little Richard	1980	25.00
BUDDAH			
❑ BDS-7501	Little Richard	1969	30.00
CORAL			
❑ CRL 57446 [M]	Coming Home	1963	40.00
❑ CRL 757446 [S]	Coming Home	1963	50.00
CROWN			
❑ CLP-5362 [M]	Little Richard Sings Freedom Songs	1963	20.00
CUSTOM			
❑ 2061 [M]	Little Richard Sings Spirituals	196?	12.00
EPIC			
❑ EG 30428 [(2)]	Cast a Long Shadow	1971	20.00
❑ PE 40389	Little Richard's Greatest Hits	1986	10.00
❑ PE 40390	The Explosive Little Richard	1986	10.00
EXACT			
❑ 206	The Best of Little Richard	1980	10.00
GNP CRESCENDO			
❑ GNP-9033	The Big Hits	1974	12.00
GRT			
❑ 2103	The Original Little Richard	1977	10.00
GUEST STAR			
❑ GS-1429 [M]	Little Richard with Sister Rosetta Tharpe	196?	12.00
❑ GSS-1429 [R]	Little Richard with Sister Rosetta Tharpe	196?	12.00
KAMA SUTRA			
❑ KSBS-2023	Little Richard	1970	25.00
MERCURY			
❑ MG-20656 [M]	It's Real	1961	50.00
❑ SR-60656 [S]	It's Real	1961	60.00
MODERN			
❑ 100 [M]	His Greatest Hits/Recorded Live	1966	20.00
❑ 103 [M]	The Explosive Little Richard	1966	20.00
❑ 1000 [S]	His Greatest Hits/Recorded Live	1966	25.00
❑ 1003 [S]	The Explosive Little Richard	1966	25.00
OKEH			
❑ OKM 12117 [M]	The Explosive Little Richard	1967	25.00
❑ OKM 12121 [M]	Little Richard's Greatest Hits	1967	25.00
❑ OKS 14117 [S]	The Explosive Little Richard	1967	20.00
❑ OKS 14121 [S]	Little Richard's Greatest Hits	1967	20.00
PICKWICK			
❑ SPC-3258	King of the Gospel Singers	197?	10.00
RCA CAMDEN			
❑ CAL-420 [M]	Little Richard	1956	200.00
❑ CAS-2430(e)	Every Hour with Little Richard	1970	12.00
REPRISE			
❑ MS 2107	The Second Coming	1973	20.00
❑ RS 6406	The Rill Thing	1971	20.00
❑ RS 6462	King of Rock and Roll	1972	20.00
RHINO			
❑ R1-70236	Shut Up! A Collection of Rare Tracks, 1951-1964	1988	12.00
SCEPTER CITATION			
❑ CTN-18020	The Best of Little Richard	1972	12.00
SPECIALTY			
❑ 100 [M]	Here's Little Richard	1957	700.00
❑ SP-2100 [M]	Here's Little Richard	1957	200.00
—Thick vinyl			
❑ SP-2103 [M]	Little Richard	1958	150.00
—Front cover photo occupies the entire cover			
❑ SP-2103 [M]	Little Richard	196?	100.00
—Front cover photo partially obscured by a black triangle at uper right; thick vinyl			
❑ SP-2103 [M]	Little Richard	197?	20.00
—Reissue with thinner vinyl			
❑ SP-2104 [M]	The Fabulous Little Richard	1958	150.00
—Thick vinyl			
❑ SP-2104 [M]	The Fabulous Little Richard	197?	20.00
—Reissue with thinner vinyl			
❑ SP-2111	Little Richard — His Biggest Hits	1963	50.00
—Thick vinyl			
❑ SP-2111 [M]	Little Richard — His Biggest Hits	197?	20.00
—Reissue with thinner vinyl			
❑ SP-2113	Little Richard's Grooviest 17 Original Hits	1968	25.00
—Thick vinyl			
❑ SP-2136	Well Alright!	1970	20.00
❑ SP-8508 [(5)]	The Specialty Sessions	1989	40.00
SPIN-O-RAMA			
❑ 119 [M]	Clap Your Hands	196?	12.00
TRIP			
❑ 8013 [(2)]	Greatest Hits	1972	12.00
20TH FOX			
❑ FXG-5010 [M]	Little Richard Sings Gospel	1959	100.00
❑ SGM-5010 [S]	Little Richard Sings Gospel	1959	150.00
UNITED			
❑ US-7775	His Greatest Hits/Recorded Live	197?	10.00
❑ US-7777	The Wild and Frantic Little Richard	197?	10.00
UNITED ARTISTS			
❑ UA-LA497-E	The Very Best of Little Richard	1975	10.00
UPFRONT			
❑ UPF-123	The Best of Little Richard	197?	10.00
❑ UPF-197	Little Richard Sings Gospel	197?	10.00
VEE JAY			
❑ LP-1107 [M]	Little Richard Is Back!	1964	50.00
❑ LPS-1107 [S]	Little Richard Is Back!	1964	70.00
❑ VJLP-1107	Little Richard's Back	198?	10.00
—Reissue with thin vinyl			
❑ LP-1124 [M]	Little Richard's Greatest Hits	1965	25.00
❑ LPS-1124 [S]	Little Richard's Greatest Hits	1965	40.00
❑ VJLP-1124	Little Richard's Greatest Hits	198?	10.00
—Reissue with thin vinyl			
❑ DY-7304	Talkin' 'Bout Soul	198?	12.00
VEE JAY/CHAMELEON			
❑ D1-74797	Rip It Up	1989	12.00
WARNER BROS.			
❑ 25529	Lifetime Friend	1986	12.00

Number	Title (A Side/B Side)	Yr	NM
WING			
❑ MGW-12288 [M]	King of the Gospel Singers	1964	15.00
❑ SRW-16288 [S]	King of the Gospel Singers	1964	20.00

LITTLE SAMMY AND THE TONES

45s

Number	Title (A Side/B Side)	Yr	NM
JACLYN			
❑ 1761	Christine/Over the Rainbow	1962	50.00

LITTLE SYLVIA
See SYLVIA (1).

LITTLE TOMMY AND THE ELGINS

45s

Number	Title (A Side/B Side)	Yr	NM
ABC-PARAMOUNT			
❑ 10358	Never Love Again/I Walk On	1962	150.00
ELMAR			
❑ 1084	Never Love Again/I Walk On	1962	400.00

LITTLE WALTER

45s

Number	Title (A Side/B Side)	Yr	NM
CHANCE			
❑ 1116	That's All Right/Just Keep Loving Her	1952	3000.
—As "Little Walter J." VG 1000; VG+ 2000			
CHECKER			
❑ 758	Juke/Can't Hold On Much Longer	1952	200.00
❑ 764	Mean Old World/Sad Hours	1952	120.00
❑ 767	Don't Have to Hunt No More/Tonight with a Fool	1953	80.00
❑ 770	Off the Wall/Tell Me Mama	1953	80.00
—Black vinyl			
❑ 770	Off the Wall/Tell Me Mama	1953	3000.
—Red vinyl			
❑ 780	Blues with a Feeling/Quarter to Twelve	1953	100.00
❑ 786	Lights Out/You're So Fine	1953	50.00
❑ 793	Oh Baby/Rocker	1954	40.00
❑ 799	You'd Better Watch Yourself/Blue Light	1954	40.00
—Black vinyl			
❑ 799	You'd Better Watch Yourself/Blue Light	1954	100.00
—Red vinyl			
❑ 805	Last Night/Mellow Down Easy	1954	60.00
❑ 811	My Babe/Thunder Bird	1955	40.00
❑ 817	Roller Coaster/I Got to Go	1955	40.00
❑ 825	Too Late/I Hate to See You Go	1955	40.00
❑ 833	Who/It Ain't Right	1956	40.00
❑ 838	Flying Saucer/One More Chance with You	1956	40.00
❑ 845	Teenage Beat/What a Feeling	1956	40.00
❑ 852	It's Too Late Brother/Take Me Back	1957	40.00
❑ 859	Everybody Needs Somebody/Nobody But You	1957	40.00
❑ 867	Boom, Boom — Out Goes the Light/Temperature	1957	40.00
❑ 890	The Toddle/Confessin' the Blues	1958	30.00
❑ 904	Key to the Highway/Rock Bottom	1958	30.00
❑ 919	My Baby's Sweeter/Crazy Mixed-Up World	1959	25.00
❑ 930	Everything's Gonna Be All Right/Back Track	1959	25.00
❑ 938	Break It Up/Me and Piney Brown	1960	20.00
❑ 945	Ah'w Baby/I Had My Fun	1960	20.00
❑ 955	My Babe/Blue Midnight	1960	20.00
❑ 968	I Don't Play/As Long As I Have You	1961	20.00
❑ 986	Crazy Legs/Crazy for My Baby	1961	20.00
❑ 1013	Just You Fool/I Got to Find My Baby	1962	15.00
❑ 1043	Up the Line/Southern Feeling	1963	15.00
❑ 1071	Diggin' My Potatoes/Snake Dancer	1964	15.00
❑ 1081	Dead Presidents/I'm a Business Man	1964	15.00
❑ 1117	Mean Ole Frisco/Blue and Lonesome	1965	15.00

Albums

Number	Title (A Side/B Side)	Yr	NM
CHECKER			
❑ LP-1428 [M]	The Best of Little Walter	1957	500.00
—Black or maroon label			
❑ LP-3004 [M]	The Best of Little Walter	1967	50.00
—Reissue of 1428			
CHESS			
❑ 2ACMB-202 [(2)]	Little Walter	1976	20.00
—Reissue of 60014			
❑ CHV-416 [M]	Confessin' the Blues	1974	12.00
❑ LP-1535 [M]	Hate to See You Go	1969	25.00
❑ 2CH-60014 [(2)]	Boss Blues Harmonica	1972	20.00

LITTLE WHEELS, THE
With RAY HILDEBRAND and JILL JACKSON, better known as PAUL AND PAULA.

45s

Number	Title (A Side/B Side)	Yr	NM
DOT			
❑ 16676	Four Wheeles, Ball Bearing Surfing Board/The Bumper	1964	30.00

LITTLEFIELD, LITTLE WILLIE

45s

Number	Title (A Side/B Side)	Yr	NM
BULLSEYE			
❑ 1005	Ruby-Ruby/Easy Go	1958	30.00
FEDERAL			
❑ 12101	Sticking on You Baby/Blood Is Redder Than Wine	1952	100.00
❑ 12110	K.C. Loving/Pleading at Midnight	1953	100.00
❑ 12137	The Midnight Hour Was Shining/My Best Wishes and Regards	1953	100.00
❑ 12148	Miss K.C.'s Fine/Rock-a-Bye Baby	1953	100.00
❑ 12163	Please Don't Go-o-o-o-oh/Don't Take My Heart Little Girl	1954	80.00
❑ 12174	Goofy Dust Blues/Falling Tears	1954	80.00
❑ 12221	Jim Wilson's Boogie/Sitting on the Curbstone	1955	60.00
❑ 12351	Kansas City/Midnight Hour Was Shining	1959	30.00
RHYTHM			
❑ 107	Baby Shame/Mistreated	1956	150.00
❑ 108	Ruby-Ruby/Easy Go	1956	150.00
❑ 115	I Need a Pay Day/I Want a Little Girl	195?	100.00
❑ 124	Theresa/The Day the Rains Came	195?	80.00
❑ 130	I Wanna Love You/Goodbye Baby	195?	80.00

LITTLES, HATTIE

45s

Number	Title (A Side/B Side)	Yr	NM
GORDY			
❑ 7004	Back in My Arms Again/(B-side unknown)	1962	800.00
❑ 7007	Here You Come/Your Love Is Wonderful	1962	80.00

LITTLETON, JOHN, AND THE CAPISTRANOS

45s

Number	Title (A Side/B Side)	Yr	NM
DUKE			
❑ 179	Po Mary/Now Darling	1959	80.00

LIVELY ONES, THE

45s

Number	Title (A Side/B Side)	Yr	NM
DEL-FI			
❑ 4184	Guitarget/Crying Guitar	1962	30.00
❑ 4189	Misirlou/Blue Tears	1962	30.00
❑ 4189	Misirlou/Livin'	1962	30.00
❑ 4196	Surf Rider/Surfer's Lament	1963	30.00
❑ 4205	Surfer Boogie/Ric-a-Tic	1963	25.00
❑ 4210	High Tide/Goofy Foot	1963	25.00
❑ 4217	Surf City/Telstar Surf	1963	25.00
MGM			
❑ 13691	Bugalu Movement/Take It While You Can	1967	15.00
SMASH			
❑ 1880	Night and Day/Hey Scrounge	1964	25.00

Albums

Number	Title (A Side/B Side)	Yr	NM
DEL-FI			
❑ DFLP-1226 [M]	Surf Rider	1963	100.00
❑ DFST-1226 [S]	Surf Rider	1963	150.00
❑ DFLP-1231 [M]	Surf Drums	1963	50.00
❑ DFST-1231 [S]	Surf Drums	1963	70.00
❑ DLF 1231	Surf Drums	1997	12.00
❑ DFLP-1237 [M]	Surf City	1963	40.00
❑ DFST-1237 [S]	Surf City	1963	50.00
❑ DLF 1237	Surf City	1997	12.00
❑ DFLP-1240 [M]	Surfin' South of the Border	1964	40.00
❑ DFST-1240 [S]	Surfin' South of the Border	1964	50.00
MGM			
❑ E-4449 [M]	Bugalu Party	1967	20.00
❑ SE-4449 [S]	Bugalu Party	1967	25.00

LIVERBIRDS, THE

45s

Number	Title (A Side/B Side)	Yr	NM
PHILIPS			
❑ 40276	Shop Around/It's Got to Be You	1965	10.00
❑ 40288	Why Do You Hang Around Me/Diddley Daddy	1965	10.00

LIVERPOOL BEATS, THE

Albums

Number	Title (A Side/B Side)	Yr	NM
RONDO			
❑ 2026 [M]	The New Merseyside Sound	1964	30.00

LIVERPOOL SPINNERS, THE
British group known as "The Spinners" in their homeland; because of its existence, the R&B group The Spinners was called the "Motown Spinners" or the "Detroit Spinners" in the U.K.

45s

Number	Title (A Side/B Side)	Yr	NM
FONTANA			
❑ 1574	Seth Davey/All For Me Grog	1967	10.00

LIVERPOOLS, THE

Albums

Number	Title (A Side/B Side)	Yr	NM
WYNCOTE			
❑ SW-9001 [S]	Beatle Mania! In the U.S.A.	1964	25.00
❑ W-9001 [M]	Beatle Mania! In the U.S.A.	1964	20.00
❑ SW-9061 [S]	The Hit Sounds from England	1964	20.00
❑ W-9061 [M]	The Hit Sounds from England	1964	15.00

LIVERS, THE

45s

Number	Title (A Side/B Side)	Yr	NM
CONSTELLATION			
❑ 118	Beatle Time/This Is the Night	1964	15.00

LIVIGNI, JOHN
See JOHN VALENTI.

LIVIN' BLUES

Albums

Number	Title (A Side/B Side)	Yr	NM
DWARF			
❑ 2003	Dutch Treat	1971	30.00

LIVING COLOUR

12-Inch Singles

Number	Title (A Side/B Side)	Yr	NM
EPIC			
❑ EAS 01074 [DJ]	Middleman (same on both sides)	1988	7.00
❑ EAS 01265 [DJ]	Cult of Personality + 4 live songs	1988	10.00
❑ EAS 2147 [DJ]	Type/Final Solution/Sailin' On (Live)	1990	18.00
—Promo-only on yellow vinyl with picture cover			
❑ EAS 04952 [DJ]	Leave It Alone/Hemp	1992	10.00
—Red vinyl			
❑ EAS 5140 [DJ]	Auslander (4 versions)	1993	10.00
❑ EAS 6296 [DJ]	Sunshine of Your Love/Sunshine of Your Love (Adrian Sherwood Remix)	1994	7.00
❑ 73677	Love Rears Its Ugly Head (2 mixes)/Elvis Is Dead (2 mixes)	1991	7.00

45s

Number	Title (A Side/B Side)	Yr	NM
EPIC			
❑ 68548	Glamour Boys/Cult of Personality (Live)	1989	3.00
❑ 68611	Cult of Personality/Funny Vibe	1989	3.00
❑ 68934	Open Letter (To a Landlord)/Talkin' About a Revolution	1989	3.00
❑ 73575	Type/Should I Stay Or Should I Go	1990	4.00
—Non-LP B-side			
❑ 73660	Love Rears Its Ugly Head/Love Rears Its Ugly Head (Soulpower Edit)	1991	—
—Cassette only			
❑ 73800	Solace of You/Someone Like You	1991	3.00
❑ 77046	Nothingness/Nothingness (Colour Mix)	1993	—
—Cassette only			

Albums

Number	Title (A Side/B Side)	Yr	NM
EPIC			
❑ FE 44099	Vivid	1988	6.00
❑ E 46202	Time's Up	1990	10.00
—Yellow vinyl			

LIVING SOULS

45s

Number	Title (A Side/B Side)	Yr	NM
REVUE			
❑ 11013	Drop It on Me/Soul Searchin'	196?	40.00

LLOYD, CHARLES

45s

Number	Title (A Side/B Side)	Yr	NM
A&M			
❑ 1415	Seagull/TM	1973	5.00
ATLANTIC			
❑ 2435	Love-In/Sunday Morning	1967	8.00
❑ 5071	Sombrero Sam (Part 1)/Sombrero Sam (Part 2)	1966	8.00
❑ 5078	Forest Flower Sunday (Part 1)/Forest Flower Sunday (Part 2)	1967	8.00
COLUMBIA			
❑ 43290	She's a Woman/You Know	1965	10.00

Except when noted otherwise, VG = 25% of NM, and VG+ = 50% of NM. (Example: VG = $2.00, VG+ = $4.00 and NM = $8.00.)

Number	Title (A Side/B Side)	Yr	NM
KAPP			
❑ 2118	Moonman/I Don't Care What You Tell Me	1971	6.00
Albums			
A&M			
❑ SP-3044	Waves	1973	15.00
❑ SP-3046	Geeta	1973	20.00
ATLANTIC			
❑ 1459 [M]	Dream Weaver	1966	15.00
❑ SD 1459 [S]	Dream Weaver	1966	20.00
—Blue and green label			
❑ SD 1459 [S]	Dream Weaver	1969	12.00
—Red and green label, white stripe through center hole			
❑ 1473 [M]	Forest Flower	1967	25.00
❑ SD 1473 [S]	Forest Flower	1967	25.00
❑ 1481 [M]	Love-In	1967	40.00
❑ SD 1481 [S]	Love-In	1967	40.00
❑ SD 1493	Journey Within	1968	25.00
❑ SD 1500	Charles Lloyd in Europe	1969	20.00
❑ SD 1519	Soundtrack	1970	20.00
❑ SD 1556	The Best of Charles Lloyd	1970	15.00
❑ SD 1571	Charles Lloyd in the Soviet Union	1971	20.00
❑ SD 1586	Flowering of the Original Charles Lloyd Quintet	1972	20.00
BLUE NOTE			
❑ BT-85104	A Night in Copenhagen	1985	15.00
COLUMBIA			
❑ CL 2267 [M]	Discovery!	1965	25.00
❑ CL 2412 [M]	Of Course, Of Course	1966	25.00
❑ CS 9067 [S]	Discovery!	1965	30.00
❑ CS 9212 [S]	Of Course, Of Course	1966	30.00
❑ CS 9609 [M]	Nirvana	1968	50.00
—White label promo; "Special Mono Radio Station Copy" sticker on stereo cover			
❑ CS 9609 [S]	Nirvana	1968	25.00
❑ PC 36981 [S]	Of Course, Of Course	1980	10.00
—Reissue of CS 9212			
DESTINY			
❑ 10003	Autumn in New York Vol. 1	1979	15.00
ECM			
❑ 1398	Fish Out of Water	1990	20.00
—Made in Germany			
ELEKTRA/MUSICIAN			
❑ 60220	Montreux '82	1983	12.00
4 MEN WITH BEARDS			
❑ 4M-119	Love-In	2003	15.00
—180-gram audiophile reissue			
KAPP			
❑ KS-3634	Moon Man	1971	15.00
❑ KS-3647	Warm Waters	1971	30.00
PACIFIC ARTS			
❑ 7-123	Weavings	1978	12.00
❑ 7-139	Big Sur Tapestry	1979	12.00

LLOYD, DAVID

Number	Title (A Side/B Side)	Yr	NM
Albums			
EPIC			
❑ LN 24151 [M]	Confidential (Sounds for a Secret Agent)	1965	20.00
❑ BN 26151 [S]	Confidential (Sounds for a Secret Agent)	1965	25.00

LLOYD, JIMMY

Number	Title (A Side/B Side)	Yr	NM
45s			
ROULETTE			
❑ 4062	I Got a Rocket in My Pocket/You're Gone Baby	1958	100.00
❑ 7001	Where the Rio De Rosa Flows/The Beginning of the End	1957	60.00

LOAD OF MISCHIEF

Number	Title (A Side/B Side)	Yr	NM
45s			
HOLIDAY INN			
❑ 2205	I'm a Lover/Back in My Arms Again	1967	20.00
SUN			
❑ 407	I'm a Lover/Back in My Arms Again	1967	80.00
—The last of the Sam Phillips Sun 45s			

LOBO

Number	Title (A Side/B Side)	Yr	NM
45s			
ATLANTIC			
❑ 3851 [DJ]	Caribbean Carnival (same on both sides)	1981	5.00
—May be promo only			
BIG TREE			
❑ 112	Me and You and a Dog Named Boo/Walk Away from It All	1971	6.00
❑ 116	She Didn't Do Magic/I'm the Only One	1971	5.00
❑ 119	California Kid and Reemo/A Little Different	1971	5.00
❑ 134	The Albatross/We'll Make It, I Know We Will	1972	5.00
❑ 141	A Simple Man/Don't Expect Me to Be Your Friend	1972	5.00
❑ 147	I'd Love You to Want Me/Am I True to Myself	1972	5.00
❑ 158	Don't Expect Me to Be Your Friend/A Big Red Kite	1973	4.00
❑ 15001	Standing at the End of the Line/Stoney	1974	4.00
❑ 15008	Rings/I'm Only Sleeping	1974	4.00
❑ 16001	It Sure Took a Long, Long Time/Running Deer	1973	4.00
❑ 16004	How Can I Tell Her/Hope You're Proud of Me Girl	1973	4.00
❑ 16012	There Ain't No Way/Love Me for What I Am	1973	4.00
❑ 16033	Don't Tell Me Goodnight/My Mama Had Soul	1975	4.00
❑ 16040	Would I Still Have You/Morning Sun	1975	4.00
ELEKTRA			
❑ 47099	I Can't Believe You Anymore/Fight Fire with Fire	1980	4.00
EVERGREEN			
❑ 1028	Am I Going Crazy (Or Just Out of My Mind)/I Don't Want to Want You	1985	5.00
—Stock copies have corrected title			
❑ 1028 [DJ]	Am I Gowing Crazy (Or Just Out of Her Mind) (same on both sides)	1985	6.00
—Promo copies have incorrect title			
LAURIE			
❑ 3526	Happy Days in New York City/My Friend Is Here	1969	15.00
—As "Kent LaVoie"			
LOBO			
❑ I	I Don't Want to Want You/No One Will Ever Know	1981	5.00
❑ IV	Come Looking for Me/I Don't Want to Want You	1982	5.00
❑ X	Living My Life Without You/A Simple Man	1982	5.00
MCA			
❑ 41065	Where Were You When I Was Falling in Love/I Don't Wanna Make Love Anymore	1979	4.00
❑ 41152	Holdin' On for Dear Love/Gus, the Dancing Dog	1979	4.00
WARNER BROS.			
❑ 8493	Afterglow/Our Best Time	1977	4.00
❑ 8537	You Are All I'll Ever Need/Our Best Time	1978	4.00
Albums			
BIG TREE			
❑ 2003	Introducing Lobo	1971	15.00
❑ 2013	Of a Simple Man	1972	15.00
❑ 2100	Introducing Lobo	1973	12.00
—Reissue of 2003 with new cover			
❑ 2101	Calumet	1973	15.00
❑ BT 89501	Just a Singer	1974	12.00
❑ BT 89505	A Cowboy Afraid of Horses	1975	12.00
❑ BT 89513	The Best of Lobo	1976	12.00
MCA			
❑ 3194	Lobo	1979	10.00

LOCKETS, THE

Number	Title (A Side/B Side)	Yr	NM
45s			
ARGO			
❑ 5455	Little Boy/Don'tcha Know	1963	12.00

LOCKLIN, HANK

Number	Title (A Side/B Side)	Yr	NM
45s			
DECCA			
❑ 9-28526	I Like to Play with Your Kisses/Picking Sweethearts	1953	25.00
❑ 9-28740	I Can't Run Away/Red Rose	1953	25.00
❑ 9-28826	Lessons in Love/Shadows	1953	25.00
❑ 9-29030	Queen of Hearts/Mysteries of Life	1954	25.00
❑ 9-29270	Baby You Can Count on Me/Whispering Scandal	1954	25.00
❑ 9-29599	Let Me Confess/I'll Always Be Standing By	1955	25.00
4 STAR			
❑ 1556	I Could Love You Darling/The Song of the Whispering Leaves	1951	40.00
❑ 1564	Your House of Love Won't Stand/Who Do You Think You're Fooling	1951	40.00
❑ 1574	Send Me the Pillow You Dream On, No. 2/I Always Lose	1951	40.00
❑ 1582	Stumpy Joe/I'm Going to Copyright Your Kisses	1951	40.00
❑ 1594	Tell Me You Love Me/Tomorrow's Just Another Day to Cry	1952	40.00
❑ 1605	Could You/Down Texas Way	1952	30.00
❑ 1608	Who's Knocking at My Heart/The Harvest Is Ripe	1952	30.00
❑ 1624	Alone at a Table for Two/Golden Wristwatch	1953	30.00
❑ 1632	Won't You Change Your Mind/Crazy Over You	1953	30.00
❑ 1641	Let Me Be the One/I'm Tired of Runnin' Around	1953	30.00
❑ 1688	Who Will It Be/Empty Bottle, Empty Heart	1954	30.00
❑ 1747	The Same Sweet Girl/You Burned a Hole in My Heart	1960	15.00
KING			
❑ 5283	Send Me the Pillow You Dream On/Let Me Be the One	1959	15.00
MGM			
❑ 14753	Send Me Your Coffee Cup/True Love Is Always Hard to Find	1974	5.00
❑ 14777	The Sweetest Mistake/Hang My Picture in Your Heart	1975	5.00
❑ 14802	Irish Eyes/Please Let Me Have You	1975	5.00
PLANTATION			
❑ 135	These Arms You Push Away/Baby I Need You	1976	5.00
❑ 142	Daytime Love Affair/You Never Miss the Water	1976	5.00
❑ 151	You Love Me Don't Cha/(B-side unknown)	1977	5.00
❑ 160	There Never Was a Time/(B-side unknown)	1977	5.00
RCA VICTOR			
❑ 47-6170	Your Heart Is an Island/You're Out of Step	1955	20.00
❑ 47-6242	Who Am I to Cast the First Stone/These Ruins Belong to You	1955	20.00
❑ 47-6347	Why Baby Why/Love or Spite	1955	20.00
❑ 47-6434	I'm a Fool/A Good Woman's Love	1956	20.00
❑ 47-6571	Seven or Eleven/You Can't Never Tell	1956	20.00
❑ 47-6672	How Much/She's Better Than Most	1956	20.00
❑ 47-6778	14 Karat Gold/By the Sweat of My Brow	1956	20.00
❑ 47-6867	Goin' Home All By Myself/The Rich and the Poor	1957	20.00
❑ 47-6967	Geisha Girl/Livin' Alone	1957	20.00
❑ 47-7127	Send Me the Pillow You Dream On/Why Don't You Haul Off and Love Me	1957	20.00
❑ 47-7203	It's a Little More Like Heaven/Blue Grass Skirt	1958	15.00
❑ 47-7317	That Inner Glow/The Upper Room	1958	15.00
❑ 47-7393	I Gotta Talk to Your Heart/The Other Side of the Door	1958	15.00
❑ 47-7472	Foreign Car/When the Band Plays the Blues	1959	15.00
❑ 47-7561	Hiding in My Heart/The Border of the Blues	1959	15.00
❑ 47-7612	Seven Days (The Humming Song)/Blues in Advance	1959	15.00
❑ 47-7692	Please Help Me, I'm Falling/My Old Home Town	1960	15.00
❑ 47-7813	One Step Ahead of My Past/Toujours Moi	1960	12.00
❑ 47-7871	From Here to There to You/This Song Is Just for You	1961	12.00
❑ 47-7921	You're the Reason/Happy Birthday to Me	1961	12.00
❑ 47-7965	Happy Journey/I Need You Now	1961	12.00
❑ 47-8034	We're Gonna Go Fishin'/Welcome Home, Mister Blues	1962	12.00
❑ 47-8106	Wabash Cannonball/Once More	1962	12.00
❑ 47-8156	Flyin' South/Behind the Footlights	1963	12.00
❑ 47-8248	Wooden Soldier/Kiss on the Door	1963	12.00
❑ 47-8318	Followed Closely by My Teardrops/You Never Want to Love Me	1964	12.00
❑ 47-8399	Hello Heartache/I Was Coming Home to You	1964	12.00
❑ 47-8497	I'm Blue/Give Your Wife a Kiss for Me	1965	10.00
❑ 47-8560	Forty Nine, Fifty One/Faith and Trust	1965	10.00
❑ 47-8695	The Girls Get Prettier (Every Day)/To Him	1965	10.00
❑ 47-8783	Insurance/I Feel a Cry Coming On	1966	10.00

L

Number	Title (A Side/B Side)	Yr	NM
47-8891	There's More Pretty Girls Than One/A Good Woman's Love	1966	10.00
47-8928	The Best Part of Loving You/The Last Thing on My Mind	1966	10.00
47-9092	Hasta Luego (See You Later)/Wishing on a Star	1967	10.00
47-9218	Nashville Women/Behind My Back	1967	10.00
47-9323	The Country Hall of Fame/Evergreen	1967	10.00
47-9476	Love Song for You/Little Geisha Girl	1968	10.00
47-9582	Everlasting Love/I'm Slowly Going Out of Your Mind	1968	10.00
47-9646	Lovin' You (The Way I Do)/Hot Pepper Doll	1968	10.00
47-9710	Where the Blue of the Night Meets the Gold of the Day/The Girls Who Wait	1969	8.00
47-9849	Flying South/Rosalita	1970	8.00
47-9894	Bless Her Heart...I Love Her/Morning	1970	8.00
47-9955	She's As Close As I Can Get to Loving You/I Like a Woman	1971	8.00
47-9986	My Heart Needs a Friend/Only a Fool	1971	8.00
48-1014	The Devil Out of Me/Softly	1971	8.00
74-0196	Jeannie/Cuban Girl	1969	8.00
74-0287	Please Help Me, I'm Falling/Anna	1969	8.00
74-0634	Imagination Running Wild/Love Has a Mind of Its Own	1972	6.00
74-0772	Eventually/I Forgot to Live Today	1972	6.00
74-0848	Goodbye Dear Ole Ryman/Just Call Me Darling	1972	6.00
74-0941	Before My Time/If Loving You Means Anything	1973	6.00
APBO-0031	Jonas P. Jones/Send Me the Pillow You Dream On	1973	6.00
SP-45-177 [DJ]	Hurt Me Again (same on both sides)	1968	20.00
APBO-0226	Wildwood Flower/Sweet Inspiration	1974	6.00

7-Inch Extended Plays

RCA VICTOR

Number	Title (A Side/B Side)	Yr	NM
EPA-4366	Please Help Me, I'm Falling/Seven Days (The Humming Song)//Livin' Alone/Hiding in My Heart	1960	20.00
EPA-4366 [PS]	Please Help Me, I'm Falling	1960	20.00

Albums

Number	Title (A Side/B Side)	Yr	NM
DESIGN			
DLP-603 [M]	Hank Locklin	196?	15.00
HILLTOP			
JM-6003 [M]	Born to Ramble	196?	15.00
JS-6003 [R]	Born to Ramble	196?	12.00
JM-6041 [M]	Hank Locklin Sings Hank Locklin	196?	15.00
JS-6041 [R]	Hank Locklin Sings Hank Locklin	196?	12.00
JM-6083	Queen of Hearts	196?	15.00
KING			
672 [M]	The Best of Hank Locklin	1961	60.00
738 [M]	Encores	1961	60.00
METRO			
M 541 [M]	Down Texas Way	196?	15.00
MS 541 [R]	Down Texas Way	196?	12.00
RCA CAMDEN			
CAL-705 [M]	Hank Locklin	1962	15.00
CAL-912 [M]	My Kind of Country Music	196?	15.00
CAS-912 [R]	My Kind of Country Music	196?	12.00
RCA VICTOR			
LPM-1673 [M]	Foreign Love	1958	60.00
LPM-2291 [M]	Please Help Me, I'm Falling	1960	30.00
LSP-2291 [S]	Please Help Me, I'm Falling	1960	40.00
LPM-2464 [M]	Happy Journey	1962	25.00
LSP-2464 [S]	Happy Journey	1962	30.00
LPM-2597 [M]	A Tribute to Roy Acuff, the King of Country Music	1962	25.00
LSP-2597 [S]	A Tribute to Roy Acuff, the King of Country Music	1962	30.00
LPM-2680 [M]	The Ways of Life	1963	25.00
LSP-2680 [S]	The Ways of Life	1963	30.00
LPM-2801 [M]	Irish Songs, Country Style	1964	20.00
LSP-2801 [S]	Irish Songs, Country Style	1964	25.00
LPM-2997 [M]	Hank Locklin Sings Hank Williams	1964	20.00
LSP-2997 [S]	Hank Locklin Sings Hank Williams	1964	25.00
LPM-3391 [M]	Hank Locklin Sings Eddy Arnold	1965	20.00
LSP-3391 [S]	Hank Locklin Sings Eddy Arnold	1965	25.00
LPM-3465 [M]	Once Over Lightly	1965	20.00
LSP-3465 [S]	Once Over Lightly	1965	25.00
LPM-3559 [M]	The Best of Hank Locklin	1966	20.00
LSP-3559 [S]	The Best of Hank Locklin	1966	25.00
LPM-3588 [M]	The Girls Get Prettier	1966	20.00
LSP-3588 [S]	The Girls Get Prettier	1966	25.00
LPM-3656 [M]	The Gloryland Way	1966	20.00
LSP-3656 [S]	The Gloryland Way	1966	25.00
LPM-3770 [M]	Send Me the Pillow You Dream On	1967	25.00
LSP-3770 [S]	Send Me the Pillow You Dream On	1967	20.00
LPM-3841 [M]	Nashville Women	1967	25.00
LSP-3841 [S]	Nashville Women	1967	20.00
LPM-3946 [M]	Country Hall of Fame	1968	100.00
LSP-3946 [S]	Country Hall of Fame	1968	20.00
LSP-4030	My Love Song for You	1968	20.00
LSP-4113	Softly	1969	20.00
LSP-4191	Lookin' Back	1969	15.00
SEARS			
SPS-104	Send Me the Pillow You Dream On	196?	25.00
STEREO-SPECTRUM			
SDLP-603 [R]	Hank Locklin	196?	12.00
—"Stereo" version of Design DLP-603			
WRANGLER			
1004 [M]	Hank Locklin	1962	25.00

LOCOMOTIONS, THE

45s

Number	Title (A Side/B Side)	Yr	NM
GONE			
5142	Little Eva/Adios My Love	1962	20.00
SWAN			
4237	Weekend Workout/Make It Saturday Night	1965	10.00

LODI

45s

Number	Title (A Side/B Side)	Yr	NM
MOWEST			
5003	Happiness/I Hope I See It in My Lifetime	1971	8.00

Albums

Number	Title (A Side/B Side)	Yr	NM
MOWEST			
MW 101L	Happiness	1972	25.00

LOE AND JOE

45s

Number	Title (A Side/B Side)	Yr	NM
HARVEY			
112	Little Ole Boy, Little Ole Girl/That's How I Am Without You	1962	30.00

LOFGREN, NILS

Also see GRIN. Also was a member of BRUCE SPRINGSTEEN's E Street Band in the 1980s.

12-Inch Singles

Number	Title (A Side/B Side)	Yr	NM
BACKSTREET			
L33-1127 [DJ]	Across the Tracks/Daddy Dream	1983	8.00
COLUMBIA			
CAS 2100 [DJ]	Secrets in the Street (same on both sides)	1985	6.00
CAS 2173 [DJ]	Delivery Night (same on both sides)	1985	6.00

45s

Number	Title (A Side/B Side)	Yr	NM
A&M			
1692	Back It Up/If I Say It, It's So	1975	5.00
1812	Cry Tough/Share a Little	1976	5.00
1839	It's Not a Crime/Share a Little	1976	5.00
1927	I Came to Dance/Code of the Road	1977	4.00
2173	Kool Skool/No Mercy	1979	4.00
BACKSTREET			
51191	Night Fades Away/Ancient History	1981	4.00
COLUMBIA			
05406	Secrets in the Street/From the Heart	1985	3.00
05598	Delivery Night/Flip Ya Flip	1985	3.00

Albums

Number	Title (A Side/B Side)	Yr	NM
A&M			
SP-3145	Cry Tough	198?	8.00
—Reissue of 4573			
SP-3201	The Best	1982	10.00
SP-3707 [(2)]	Night After Night	1977	12.00
SP-4509	Nils Lofgren	1975	10.00
SP-4573	Cry Tough	1976	10.00
SP-4628	I Came to Dance	1977	10.00
SP-4756	Nils	1979	10.00
SP-6509 [(2)]	Night After Night	198?	10.00
—Reissue of 3707			
SP-8362 [DJ]	Authorized Bootleg	1976	25.00
BACKSTREET			
5251	Night Fades Away	1981	10.00
5421	Wonderland	1983	10.00
COLUMBIA			
BFC 39982	Flip	1985	10.00

LOGGINS, DAVE

45s

Number	Title (A Side/B Side)	Yr	NM
EPIC			
02152	Please Come to Boston/Someday	1981	3.00
—Reissue			
11115	Please Come to Boston/Let Me Go Now	1974	5.00
50035	Someday/Girl from Knoxville	1974	4.00
50069	Second Hand Lady/So You Couldn't Get to Me	1975	4.00
50221	Saviour of My Natural Life/You've Got Me to Hold On To	1976	4.00
50246	Movin' to the Country/Wild Millie the Country Girl	1976	4.00
50326	Three Little Words (I Love You)/Don't Treat Me Like a Stranger	1976	4.00
50491	Ship in a Bottle/The Ballad of Cowboy 20	1977	4.00
50509	One-Way Ticket to Paradise/Crowd of Lonely People	1978	4.00
50578	So Much for Dreams/You Found It Now	1978	4.00
50711	Pieces of April/Color of My Mood	1979	4.00
50783	One Way Ticket to Paradise/The Fool in Me	1979	4.00
VANGUARD			
35147	Claudia/Think'n of You	1972	5.00
35167	Pieces of April/Think'n of You	1972	5.00
35177	Building Condemned/Lady in an Orange Silk Blouse	1973	5.00

Albums

Number	Title (A Side/B Side)	Yr	NM
EPIC			
KE 32833	Apprentice (In a Musical Workshop)	1974	10.00
PE 33946	Country Suite	1975	10.00
PE 34713	One Way	1977	10.00
JE 35792	David Loggins	1979	10.00
VANGUARD			
VSD-6580	Personal Belongings	1972	15.00

LOGGINS, KENNY

12-Inch Singles

Number	Title (A Side/B Side)	Yr	NM
COLUMBIA			
CAS 2452 [DJ]	Playing with the Boys (same on both sides)	1986	8.00
44-05940	Playing with the Boys (Dance Mix 6:46) (Dub Mix 5:50)	1986	8.00

45s

Number	Title (A Side/B Side)	Yr	NM
COLUMBIA			
AE7 1216 [DJ]	I'm Alright (Theme from "Caddyshack") (Soundtrack Version 3:25)/(Live Album Version 4:47)	1980	6.00
CS7-01466 [DJ]	Tell Her (Short Intro 3:11)/(3:35)	1989	6.00
13-02167	I'm Alright (Theme from "Caddyshack")/This Is It	1981	3.00
—Reissue			
18-03192	Don't Fight It/The More We Try	1982	3.00
—A-side with Steve Perry			
18-03192 [PS]	Don't Fight It/The More We Try	1982	4.00
CNR-03270	Don't Fight It/(B-side blank)	1982	6.00
—Kenny Loggins with Steve Perry; one-sided budget release			
38-03377	Heart to Heart/The More We Try	1982	3.00
CNR-03427	Heart to Heart/(B-side blank)	1982	8.00
—One-sided budget release			
38-03555	Welcome to Heartlight/Only a Miracle	1983	3.00
38-03555 [PS]	Welcome to Heartlight/Only a Miracle	1983	4.00
38-04310	Footloose/Swear Your Love	1984	3.00
38-04310 [PS]	Footloose/Swear Your Love	1984	6.00
38-04452	I'm Free (Heaven Helps the Man)/Welcome to Heartlight (Live)	1984	3.00
38-04452 [PS]	I'm Free (Heaven Helps the Man)/Welcome to Heartlight (Live)	1984	3.00
38-04849	Vox Humana/Love Will Follow	1985	3.00
38-04849 [PS]	Vox Humana/Love Will Follow	1985	3.00
38-04931	Forever/At Last	1985	3.00
38-04931 [PS]	Forever/At Last	1985	3.00
38-05625	I'll Be There/No Lookin' Back	1985	4.00
38-05893	Danger Zone/I'm Gonna Do It Right	1986	3.00
38-05893 [PS]	Danger Zone/I'm Gonna Do It Right	1986	3.00
38-05902	Playing with the Boys/Love Will Follow	1986	3.00
38-05902 [PS]	Playing with the Boys/Love Will Follow	1986	3.00
38-06690	Meet Me Half Way/Semifinal	1987	3.00
—B-side by Giorgio Moroder			
38-06690 [PS]	Meet Me Half Way/Semifinal	1987	3.00

Except when noted otherwise, VG = 25% of NM, and VG+ = 50% of NM. (Example: VG = $2.00, VG+ = $4.00 and NM = $8.00.)

Number	Title (A Side/B Side)	Yr	NM
❑ 38-07971	Nobody's Fool (Theme from Caddyshack II)/I'm Gonna Do It Right	1988	3.00
❑ 38-07971 [PS]	Nobody's Fool (Theme from Caddyshack II)/I'm Gonna Do It Right	1988	3.00
❑ 38-08091	I'm Gonna Miss You/Isabella's Eyes	1988	3.00
❑ 38-08091 [PS]	I'm Gonna Miss You/Isabella's Eyes	1988	3.00
❑ 3-10569	I Believe in Love/Enter My Dream	1977	5.00
❑ 3-10652	Celebrate Me Home/Why Do People Lie	1977	5.00
❑ 3-10794	Whenever I Call You "Friend"/Angelique	1978	5.00
—With Stevie Nicks on A-side (uncredited)			
❑ 3-10866	Easy Driver/Somebody Knows	1978	5.00
❑ 1-11109	This Is It/Will It Last	1979	5.00
❑ 1-11215	Keep the Fire/Now and Then	1980	4.00
❑ 1-11290	Love Has Come of Age/Junkanoo Holiday (Fallin', Flyin')	1980	6.00
❑ 1-11317	I'm Alright (Theme from "Caddyshack")/Lead the Way	1980	4.00
❑ 11-11417	Celebrate Me Home (Live)/Celebrate Me Home (Studio)	1980	5.00
❑ 38-68531	Tell Her/Hope for the Runaway	1989	4.00
❑ 38-74029	Conviction of the Heart/My Father's House	1991	4.00

Albums

COLUMBIA

Number	Title	Yr	NM
❑ AS 569 [DJ]	Kenny Loggins Live	1979	15.00
—One-sided promo with three otherwise unavailable live recordings			
❑ AS 946 [DJ]	For Radio Only	1980	15.00
—Promo-only four-song sampler from "Kenny Loggins Alive"			
❑ PC 34655	Celebrate Me Home	1977	10.00
—Originals have no bar code			
❑ PC 34655	Celebrate Me Home	1979	8.00
—Reissues have bar code			
❑ JC 35387	Nightwatch	1978	10.00
—Originals have no bar code			
❑ PC 35387	Nightwatch	198?	8.00
—Reissue with new prefix			
❑ JC 36172	Keep the Fire	1979	10.00
❑ PC 36172	Keep the Fire	198?	8.00
—Budget-line reissue			
❑ C2X 36738 [(2)]	Kenny Loggins Alive	1980	12.00
❑ TC 38127	High Adventure	1982	10.00
❑ FC 39174	Vox Humana	1985	8.00
❑ OC 40535	Back to Avalon	1988	10.00
❑ HC 45387	Nightwatch	198?	70.00
—Half-speed mastered edition			

LOGGINS AND MESSINA
Also see JIM MESSINA.

45s

COLUMBIA

Number	Title (A Side/B Side)	Yr	NM
❑ JBQ 507 [Q]	Your Mama Don't Dance/Thinking of You	1973	10.00
—"Special Coin Operator Release" in quadraphonic			
❑ 10077	Changes/Get a Hold	1974	5.00
❑ 10118	Growin'/Keep Me in Mind	1975	5.00
❑ 10188	I Like It Like That/Angry Eyes	1975	5.00
❑ 10222	A Lover's Question/Oh, Lonesome Me	1975	5.00
❑ 10311	When I Was a Child/Peacemaker	1976	5.00
❑ 10376	Native Son/Pretty Princess	1976	5.00
❑ 10444	Angry Eyes/Watching the River Run	1976	5.00
❑ 45550	Same Old Wine/Vahevela	1972	6.00
—As "Kenny Loggins and Jim Messina"			
❑ 45617	Nobody But You/Danny's Song	1972	6.00
—As "Kenny Loggins and Jim Messina"			
❑ 45664	Peace of Mind/House at Pooh Corner	1972	6.00
—As "Kenny Loggins and Jim Messina"			
❑ 45719	Your Mama Don't Dance/Golden Ribbons	1972	5.00
—As "Kenny Loggins and Jim Messina"; orange label			
❑ 45719	Your Mama Don't Dance/Golden Ribbons	1972	6.00
—As "Kenny Loggins and Jim Messina"; gray label			
❑ 45815	Thinking of You/Till the Ends Meet	1973	5.00
—A-side is a different version than on most LPs			
❑ 45952	My Music/A Love Song	1973	5.00
❑ 46010	Watching the River Run/Travelin' Blues	1974	5.00

Albums

COLUMBIA

Number	Title	Yr	NM
❑ C 31044	Kenny Loggins with Jim Messina Sittin' In	1972	10.00
❑ PC 31044	Kenny Loggins with Jim Messina Sittin' In	197?	8.00
—Reissue with new prefix			
❑ CQ 31748 [Q]	Loggins and Messina	1973	15.00
❑ KC 31748	Loggins and Messina	1972	10.00
❑ PC 31748	Loggins and Messina	197?	8.00
—Reissue with new prefix			
❑ CQ 32540 [Q]	Full Sail	1973	15.00
❑ KC 32540	Full Sail	1973	10.00
❑ PC 32540	Full Sail	197?	8.00
—Reissue with new prefix			
❑ PG 32848 [(2)]	On Stage	1974	12.00
—Original with no bar code			
❑ PG 32848 [(2)]	On Stage	198?	10.00
—With bar code			
❑ PC 33175	Mother Lode	1974	10.00
—Original with no bar code			
❑ PC 33175	Mother Lode	198?	8.00
—With bar code			
❑ PC 33578	Native Sons	1976	10.00
—Original with no bar code			
❑ PC 33578	Native Sons	198?	8.00
—With bar code			
❑ PCQ 33578 [Q]	Native Sons	1976	15.00
❑ PC 33810	So Fine	1975	10.00
—Original with no bar code			
❑ PC 33810	So Fine	198?	8.00
—With bar code			
❑ JG 34167 [(2)]	Finale	1977	12.00
❑ PC 34388	The Best of Friends	1976	10.00
—Original with no bar code			
❑ PC 34388	The Best of Friends	198?	8.00
—With bar code			
❑ HC 44388	The Best of Friends	1982	50.00
—Half-speed mastered edition			

DIRECT DISC

Number	Title	Yr	NM
❑ SD 16606	Full Sail	198?	30.00
—Audiophile vinyl			

EPIC

Number	Title	Yr	NM
❑ PC 34388	The Best of Friends	1976	20.00
—Mispressing with wrong label			

LOLITA

45s

4 CORNERS OF THE WORLD

Number	Title (A Side/B Side)	Yr	NM
❑ 131	Come Back/When Our Father Is Happy	1965	7.00

KAPP

Number	Title (A Side/B Side)	Yr	NM
❑ 349	Sailor (Your Home Is the Sea)/La Luna (Quando La Luna)	1960	8.00
—Black label			
❑ 349	Sailor (Your Home Is the Sea)/La Luna (Quando La Luna)	1960	12.00
—Maroon and silver label			
❑ 349 [PS]	Sailor (Your Home Is the Sea)/La Luna (Quando La Luna)	1960	20.00
❑ 370	Cowboy Jimmy Joe (Die Sterne Der Prarie)/Theme from "A Summer Place"	1961	8.00
❑ 370 [PS]	Cowboy Jimmy Joe (Die Sterne Der Prarie)/Theme from "A Summer Place"	1961	20.00
❑ 402	For the First Time (I've Fallen in Love)/Souvenir d'Amour	1961	8.00

Albums

KAPP

Number	Title	Yr	NM
❑ KL-1219 [M]	Sailor	1961	25.00
❑ KL-1229 [M]	Songs You Will Never Forget	1961	25.00
❑ KS-3219 [S]	Sailor	1961	30.00
❑ KS-3229 [S]	Songs You Will Never Forget	1961	30.00

LOLLIPOP SHOPPE, THE

45s

SHAMLEY

Number	Title (A Side/B Side)	Yr	NM
❑ 44005	Someone I Know/Through My Window	1969	12.00

UNI

Number	Title (A Side/B Side)	Yr	NM
❑ 55050	You Must Be a Witch/Don't Close the Door	1968	15.00
❑ 55050 [PS]	You Must Be a Witch/Don't Close the Door	1968	25.00

Albums

UNI

Number	Title	Yr	NM
❑ 73019	The Lollipop Shoppe	1968	80.00

LOLLIPOPS, THE (1)

45s

ATCO

Number	Title (A Side/B Side)	Yr	NM
❑ 6787	Nothing's Gonna Stop Our Love/I Believe in Love	1970	40.00

GORDY

Number	Title (A Side/B Side)	Yr	NM
❑ 7089	Cheating Is Telling On You/Need Your Love	1969	800.00

IMPACT

Number	Title (A Side/B Side)	Yr	NM
❑ 1021	Lovin' Good Feelin'/Step Aside Baby	1967	200.00

V.I.P.

Number	Title (A Side/B Side)	Yr	NM
❑ 25051	Cheating Is Telling On You/Need Your Love	1968	300.00

LOLLIPOPS, THE (2)

45s

SSS INTERNATIONAL

Number	Title (A Side/B Side)	Yr	NM
❑ 777	You Don't Know/Feel So Comfortable	1969	15.00

LOLLIPOPS, THE (3)

45s

WARNER BROS.

Number	Title (A Side/B Side)	Yr	NM
❑ 5122	Mister Santa/Little Donkey (Carry Mary Safely on Her Way)	1959	12.00

LOLLIPOPS, THE (U)
Some of these could be group (1).

45s

RCA VICTOR

Number	Title (A Side/B Side)	Yr	NM
❑ 47-8344	Peggy Got Engaged/I'll Set My Love to Music	1964	20.00
❑ 47-8430	Billy, Billy Baby/Big Brother	1964	20.00
❑ 47-8390	Don't Monkey With Me/Love Is the Only Answer	1964	75.00
❑ 47-8494	Busy Signal/I Want You Back Again	1965	100.00

SMASH

Number	Title (A Side/B Side)	Yr	NM
❑ 2057	He's the Boy/Gee Whiz Baby	1966	125.00

LOMAX, JACKIE

45s

APPLE

Number	Title (A Side/B Side)	Yr	NM
❑ 1802	Sour Milk Sea/The Eagle Laughs at You	1968	20.00
—With B-side author listed as "(George Harrison)"			
❑ 1802	Sour Milk Sea/The Eagle Laughs at You	1968	20.00
—With B-side author listed as "(Jackie Lomax)"			
❑ 1807	New Day/Thumbin' a Ride	1969	60.00
—Without star on A-side label			
❑ 1807	New Day/Thumbin' a Ride	1969	75.00
—With star on A-side label			
❑ 1819	How the Web Was Woven/I Fall Inside Your Eyes	1970	8.00
❑ 1819 [PS]	How the Web Was Woven/I Fall Inside Your Eyes	1970	10.00
❑ 1834	Sour Milk Sea/(I) Fall Inside Your Eyes	1971	8.00
❑ PRO-6240/1 [DJ]	Sour Milk Sea/(I) Fall Inside Your Eyes	1971	30.00

CAPITOL

Number	Title (A Side/B Side)	Yr	NM
❑ 4384	More (Livin' for Lovin')/I Remember (Memorabilia)	1976	5.00

EPIC

Number	Title (A Side/B Side)	Yr	NM
❑ 10270	One Minute Woman/Genuine Imitation of Life	1967	12.00

WARNER BROS.

Number	Title (A Side/B Side)	Yr	NM
❑ 7503	Helluva Woman/Higher Ground	1971	6.00
❑ 7564	Lavender Dream/Lost	1972	6.00
❑ 7589	Roll On/Hellfire, Night Crier	1972	6.00

Albums

APPLE

Number	Title	Yr	NM
❑ ST-3354	Is This What You Want?	1969	20.00

CAPITOL

Number	Title	Yr	NM
❑ ST-11558	Livin' for Lovin'	1976	10.00
❑ ST-11668	Did You Ever	1977	10.00

WARNER BROS.

Number	Title	Yr	NM
❑ PRO 520 [DJ]	An Interview with Jackie Lomax	1972	25.00
❑ WS 1914	Home Is In My Head	1971	12.00
❑ BS 2591	Three	1972	12.00

LONDON, JULIE

45s

BETHLEHEM

Number	Title (A Side/B Side)	Yr	NM
❑ 11003	Sometimes I Feel Like a Motherless Child/A Foggy Day	1958	20.00
❑ 11015	Don't Worry 'Bout Me/You're Blase	1959	12.00

LIBERTY

Number	Title (A Side/B Side)	Yr	NM
❑ 33006 [S]	Lonesome Road/Goodbye	1960	20.00
❑ 33007 [S]	When I Fall in Love/The More I See You	1960	20.00
❑ 33008 [S]	Blue Moon/I Guess I'll Have to Change My Plan	1960	20.00
❑ 33009 [S]	Bye Bye Blues/Basin Street Blues	1960	20.00
❑ 33010 [S]	Daddy/Bye Bye Blackbird	1960	20.00
—The above four are 33 1/3 rpm jukebox singles			
❑ 55006	Cry Me a River/S'Wonderful	1955	12.00
❑ 55009	Baby, Baby, All the Time/Shadow Woman	1955	10.00
❑ 55025	September in the Rain/Lonely Girl	1956	10.00

L

Number	Title (A Side/B Side)	Yr	NM
❑ 55032	Tall Boy/Now, Baby, Now	1956	10.00
❑ 55052	The Meaning of the Blues/Boy on a Dolphin	1957	10.00
❑ 55076	It Had to Be You/Dark	1957	10.00
❑ 55108	I'd Like You for Christmas/Saddle the Wind	1957	12.00
❑ 55131	Tell Me You're Home/The Freshman	1958	10.00
❑ 55139	It's Easy/Voice in the Mirror	1958	10.00
❑ 55157	Blue Moon/Man of the West	1958	10.00
❑ 55175	Come On-a My House/My Strange Affair	1959	10.00
❑ 55182	Must Be Catchin'/Something I Dreamed Last Night	1959	10.00
❑ 55216	Comin' Through the Rye/Makin' Whoopee	1959	10.00
❑ 55227	Cry Me a River/It's a Blue World	1959	10.00
❑ 55269	In the Wee Small Hours of the Morning/Time for Lovers	1960	10.00
❑ 55300	Send for Me/Evenin'	1961	8.00
❑ 55309	Sanctuary/Every Chance I Get	1961	8.00
❑ 55337	My Darling, My Darling/My Love, My Love	1961	8.00
❑ 55512	Desafinado/Where Did the Gentleman Go	1962	8.00
❑ 55605	I'm Coming Back to You/When Snowflakes Fall in the Summer	1963	8.00
❑ 55666	Guilty Heart/I Want to Find Out for Myself	1964	6.00
❑ 55702	Girl (Boy) from Ipanema/My Lover Is a Stranger	1964	6.00
❑ 55759	We Proved Them Wrong/You're Free to Go	1964	6.00
❑ 55830	Girl Talk/Won't Somebody Please Belong to Me	1965	6.00
❑ 55911	Nice Girls Don't Stay for Breakfast/Bill Bailey (Won't You Please Come Home)	1966	6.00
❑ 55966	Mickey Mouse March/Baby Won't You Please	1967	6.00
❑ 56074	Yummy, Yummy, Yummy/Come to Me Slowly	1968	5.00
❑ 56085	Louie Louie/Hushabye Mountain	1969	5.00
❑ 56112	Too Much of a Man/Sittin' Pretty	1969	—
—Unreleased			
UNITED ARTISTS			
❑ 0013	Cry Me a River/Come On-a My House	1973	4.00
—"Silver Spotlight Series" reissue			

7-Inch Extended Plays

Number	Title (A Side/B Side)	Yr	NM
LIBERTY			
❑ LSX-1001	Cry Me a River/I'll Cry Tomorrow//Baby, Baby All the Time/Shadow Woman	195?	12.00
❑ LSX-1001 [PS]	Cry Me a River	195?	12.00
❑ LEP-1-3006	Laura/S' Wonderful//I'm in the Mood for Love/Can't Help Lovin' That Man	1956	12.00
❑ LEP-1-3006 [PS]	Julie Is Her Name, Part One	1956	12.00
❑ LEP-2-3006	(contents unknown)	1956	12.00
❑ LEP-2-3006 [PS]	Julie Is Her Name, Part Two	1956	12.00
❑ LEP-3-3006	(contents unknown)	1956	12.00
❑ LEP-3-3006 [PS]	Julie Is Her Name, Part Three	1956	12.00
❑ LEP-1-3012	*Lonely Girl/Fools Rush In/How Deep Is the Ocean/Mean to Me	1956	12.00
❑ LEP-1-3012 [PS]	Lonely Girl, Part One	1956	12.00
❑ LEP-2-3012	*When Your Lover Has Gone/All Alone/Remember/Moments Like This/I Lost My Sugar in Salt Lake City	1956	12.00
❑ LEP-2-3012 [PS]	Lonely Girl, Part Two	1956	12.00
❑ LEP-3-3012	Don't Take Your Love from Me/Where or When//It's the Talk of the Town/What'll I Do	1956	12.00
❑ LEP-3-3012 [PS]	Lonely Girl, Part Three	1956	12.00
❑ LEP-1-3043	Basin Street Blues/Get Set for the Blues//Invitation to the Blues/Meaning of the Blues	195?	12.00
❑ LEP-1-3043 [PS]	About the Blues, Part One	195?	12.00
❑ LEP-1-3060	If I Could Be with You/It's Good to Want You Bad//You're My Thrill/Lover Man	195?	12.00
❑ LEP-1-3060 [PS]	Make Love to Me, Part One	195?	12.00
❑ LST-7342	Since I Fell for You/Fools Rush In/You Don't Have to Be a Baby to Cry//I Wish You Love/Charade/Wives and Lovers	1964	15.00
—Jukebox issue; small hole, plays at 33 1/3 rpm			
❑ LST-7342 [PS]	Julie London	1964	15.00
❑ LEP-1-9002	*June in January/February Brings the Rain/Melancholy March/I'll Remember April	1956	12.00
❑ LEP-1-9002 [PS]	Calendar Girl, Part One	1956	12.00
❑ LEP-2-9002	*People Who Are Born in May/Memphis in June/Sleigh Ride in July/Time for August	1956	12.00
❑ LEP-2-9002 [PS]	Calendar Girl, Part Two	1956	12.00
❑ LEP-3-9002	*September in the Rain/This October/November Twilight/Warm December	1956	12.00
❑ LEP-3-9002 [PS]	Calendar Girl, Part Three	1956	12.00

Albums

Number	Title	Yr	NM
LIBERTY			
❑ MCR-1 [M]	By Myself	196?	25.00
—Columbia Record Club exclusive			
❑ SCR-1 [S]	By Myself	196?	30.00
—Columbia Record Club exclusive			
❑ LRP-3006 [M]	Julie Is Her Name	1956	50.00
—Green label			
❑ LRP-3006 [M]	Julie Is Her Name	1960	20.00
—Black label, colorband and logo at left			
❑ LRP-3012 [M]	Lonely Girl	1956	50.00
—Green label			
❑ LRP-3012 [M]	Lonely Girl	1960	20.00
—Black label, colorband and logo at left			
❑ LRP-3043 [M]	About the Blues	1957	40.00
—Green label			
❑ LRP-3043 [M]	About the Blues	1960	20.00
—Black label, colorband and logo at left			
❑ LRP-3060 [M]	Make Love to Me	1957	40.00
—Green label			
❑ LRP-3060 [M]	Make Love to Me	1960	20.00
—Black label, colorband and logo at left			
❑ LRP-3096 [M]	Julie	1957	40.00
—Green label			
❑ LRP-3100 [M]	Julie Is Her Name, Vol. 2	1958	40.00
—Green label			
❑ LRP-3100 [M]	Julie Is Her Name, Vol. 2	1960	20.00
—Black label, colorband and logo at left			
❑ LRP-3105 [M]	London By Night	1958	30.00
—Green label			
❑ LRP-3119 [M]	Swing Me an Old Song	1959	30.00
—Green label			
❑ LRP-3130 [M]	Your Number Please	1959	30.00
—Green label			
❑ LRP-3130 [M]	Your Number Please	1960	20.00
—Black label, colorband and logo at left			
❑ LRP-3152 [M]	Julie...At Home	1960	30.00
❑ LRP-3164 [M]	Around Midnight	1960	30.00
❑ LRP-3171 [M]	Send for Me	1961	30.00
❑ LRP-3192 [M]	Whatever Julie Wants	1961	30.00
❑ LRP-3203 [M]	Sophisticated Lady	1962	25.00
❑ LRP-3231 [M]	Love Letters	1962	25.00
❑ LRP-3249 [M]	Love on the Rocks	1963	25.00
❑ LRP-3278 [M]	Latin in a Satin Mood	1963	25.00
❑ LRP-3291 [M]	Julie's Golden Greats	1963	25.00
—Black cover			
❑ LRP-3291 [M]	Julie's Golden Greats	1963	25.00
—White cover			
❑ LRP-3300 [M]	The End of the World	1963	25.00
❑ LRP-3324 [M]	The Wonderful World of Julie London	1963	25.00
❑ LRP-3342 [M]	Julie London	1964	25.00
❑ LRP-3375 [M]	Julie London In Person at the Americana	1964	25.00
❑ LRP-3392 [M]	Our Fair Lady	1965	25.00
❑ LRP-3416 [M]	Feeling Good	1965	25.00
❑ LRP-3434 [M]	All Through the Night	1965	25.00
❑ LRP-3478 [M]	For the Night People	1966	25.00
❑ LRP-3493 [M]	Nice Girls Don't Stay for Breakfast	1967	25.00
❑ LRP-3514 [M]	With Body and Soul	1967	30.00
❑ L-5501 [M]	The Best of Julie London	1962	30.00
❑ S-6601 [S]	The Best of Julie London	1962	40.00
❑ LST-7004 [S]	Julie	1958	70.00
—Black label, silver print			
❑ LST-7012 [S]	About the Blues	1958	70.00
—Black label, silver print			
❑ LST-7012 [S]	About the Blues	1960	25.00
—Black label, colorband and logo at left			
❑ LST-7027 [S]	Julie Is Her Name	1958	40.00
—Black label, silver print			
❑ LST-7027 [S]	Julie Is Her Name	1958	100.00
—Blue vinyl			
❑ LST-7027 [S]	Julie Is Her Name	1958	100.00
—Red vinyl			
❑ LST-7027 [S]	Julie Is Her Name	1960	25.00
—Black label, colorband and logo at left			
❑ LST-7029 [S]	Lonely Girl	1958	40.00
—Black label, silver print			
❑ LST-7029 [S]	Lonely Girl	1960	25.00
—Black label, colorband and logo at left			
❑ LST-7060 [S]	Make Love to Me	1958	40.00
—Black label, silver print			
❑ LST-7060 [S]	Make Love to Me	1960	25.00
—Black label, colorband and logo at left			
❑ LST-7100 [S]	Julie Is Her Name, Vol. 2	1958	40.00
—Black label, silver print			
❑ LST-7100 [S]	Julie Is Her Name, Vol. 2	1960	25.00
—Black label, colorband and logo at left			
❑ LST-7105 [S]	London By Night	1958	40.00
—Black label, silver print			
❑ LST-7119 [S]	Swing Me an Old Song	1959	40.00
—Black label, silver print			
❑ LST-7130 [S]	Your Number Please	1959	40.00
—Black label, silver print			
❑ LST-7130 [S]	Your Number Please	1960	25.00
—Black label, colorband and logo at left			
❑ LST-7152 [S]	Julie...At Home	1960	40.00
—Black vinyl			
❑ LST-7152 [S]	Julie...At Home	1960	100.00
—Blue vinyl			
❑ LST-7164 [S]	Around Midnight	1960	40.00
❑ LST-7171 [S]	Send for Me	1961	40.00
❑ LST-7192 [S]	Whatever Julie Wants	1961	40.00
❑ LST-7203 [S]	Sophisticated Lady	1962	30.00
❑ LST-7231 [S]	Love Letters	1962	30.00
❑ LST-7249 [S]	Love on the Rocks	1963	30.00
❑ LST-7278 [S]	Latin in a Satin Mood	1963	30.00
❑ LST-7291 [S]	Julie's Golden Greats	1963	30.00
—Black cover			
❑ LST-7291 [S]	Julie's Golden Greats	1963	30.00
—White cover			
❑ LST-7300 [S]	The End of the World	1963	30.00
❑ LST-7324 [S]	The Wonderful World of Julie London	1963	30.00
❑ LST-7342 [S]	Julie London	1964	30.00
❑ LST-7375 [S]	Julie London In Person at the Americana	1964	30.00
❑ LST-7392 [S]	Our Fair Lady	1965	30.00
❑ LST-7416 [S]	Feeling Good	1965	30.00
❑ LST-7434 [S]	All Through the Night	1965	30.00
❑ LST-7478 [S]	For the Night People	1966	30.00
❑ LST-7493 [S]	Nice Girls Don't Stay for Breakfast	1967	25.00
❑ LST-7514 [S]	With Body and Soul	1967	25.00
❑ LST-7546	Easy Does It	1968	20.00
❑ LST-7609	Yummy, Yummy, Yummy	1969	20.00
❑ SL-9002 [M]	Calendar Girl	1956	100.00
SUNSET			
❑ SUM-1104 [M]	Julie London	196?	12.00
❑ SUM-1161 [M]	Soft and Sweet	196?	12.00
❑ SUS-5104 [S]	Julie London	196?	15.00
❑ SUS-5161 [S]	Soft and Sweet	196?	15.00
❑ SUS-5207	Gone with the Wind	196?	12.00
UNITED ARTISTS			
❑ UA-LA437-E	The Very Best of Julie London	1975	12.00

LONDON, LAURIE

45s

Number	Title (A Side/B Side)	Yr	NM
CAPITOL			
❑ F3891	He's Got the Whole World (In His Hands)/Handed Down	1958	15.00
❑ F3973	Joshua/I Gotta Robe	1958	12.00
❑ F4133	My Mother/Three O'Clock	1959	12.00
ROULETTE			
❑ 4176	Pretty Eyed Baby/Boom Ladda Boom Boom	1959	10.00

7-Inch Extended Plays

Number	Title (A Side/B Side)	Yr	NM
CAPITOL			
❑ EAP 1-10182	He's Got the Whole World in His Hands/Handed Down//The Gospel Train/Boomerang	1958	20.00
❑ EAP 1-10182 [PS]	Laurie London!	1958	20.00

Albums

Number	Title	Yr	NM
CAPITOL			
❑ T 10169 [M]	England's 14 Year Old Singing Sensation — Laurie London	1958	50.00

LONDON, MARK

45s

Number	Title (A Side/B Side)	Yr	NM
CAMEO			
❑ 362	Moanin'/Stranger in the World	1965	15.00

LONDON SOUND 70 ORCHESTRA AND CHORUS

Albums

Number	Title	Yr	NM
DECCA			
❑ DEB 7-7 [(3)]	The Sounds of Christmas	1970	25.00

LONE TWISTER, THE

45s

Number	Title (A Side/B Side)	Yr	NM
ATLANTIC			
❑ 2130	The Lone Twister/Twistin' Up a Storm	1961	15.00

Except when noted otherwise, VG = 25% of NM, and VG+ = 50% of NM. (Example: VG = $2.00, VG+ = $4.00 and NM = $8.00.)

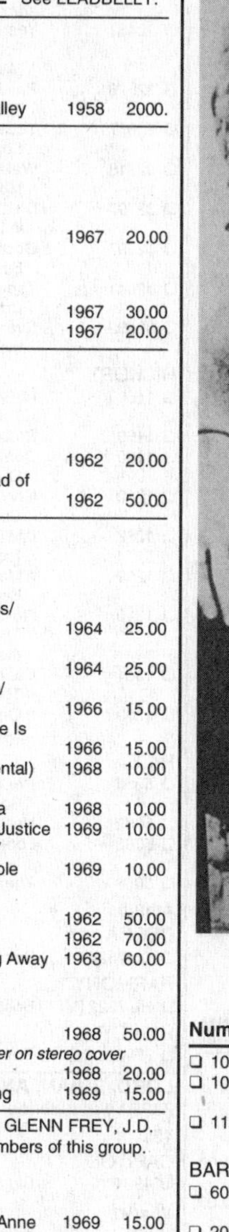

Number	Title (A Side/B Side)	Yr	NM

LONELY HEARTS CLUB BAND See BEE GEES.

LONESOME BLUES SINGER, THE See LEADBELLY.

LONESOME DRIFTER, THE

45s

K

Number	Title (A Side/B Side)	Yr	NM
❑ 5812	Eager Boy/Teardrop Valley	1958	2000.

LONESOME RHODES

45s

RCA VICTOR

Number	Title (A Side/B Side)	Yr	NM
❑ 47-9305	The Delight of My Day/ (B-side unknown)	1967	20.00

Albums

RCA VICTOR

Number	Title (A Side/B Side)	Yr	NM
❑ LPM-3759 [M]	Lonesome Rhodes	1967	30.00
❑ LSP-3759 [S]	Lonesome Rhodes	1967	20.00

LONG, HUEY

45s

FIDELITY

Number	Title (A Side/B Side)	Yr	NM
❑ 4054	How to Tell My Heart/ Waiting for a Letter	1962	20.00
❑ 4055	Elvis Stole My Gal/Ballad of John Glenn	1962	50.00

LONG, SHORTY (1) R&B singer.

45s

SOUL

Number	Title (A Side/B Side)	Yr	NM
❑ 35001	Devil with the Blue Dress/ Wind It Up	1964	25.00
❑ 35005	It's a Crying Shame/ Out to Get You	1964	25.00
❑ 35021	Function at the Junction/ Call On Me	1966	15.00
❑ 35031	Chantilly Lace/Your Love Is Amazing	1966	15.00
❑ 35040	Night Fo' Last/(Instrumental)	1968	10.00
❑ 35044	Here Comes the Judge/ Sing What You Wanna	1968	10.00
❑ 35054	I Had a Dream/Ain't No Justice	1969	10.00
❑ 35064	A Whiter Shade of Pale/ When You Are Available	1969	10.00

TRI-PHI

Number	Title (A Side/B Side)	Yr	NM
❑ 1006	I'll Be There/Bad Willie	1962	50.00
❑ 1015	Too Smart/I'll Be There	1962	70.00
❑ 1021	What's the Matter/Going Away	1963	60.00

Albums

SOUL

Number	Title (A Side/B Side)	Yr	NM
❑ SM-709 [M]	Here Comes the Judge	1968	50.00
—Mono is white label promo only; mono sticker on stereo cover			
❑ SS-709 [S]	Here Comes the Judge	1968	20.00
❑ SS-719	The Prime of Shorty Long	1969	15.00

LONGBRANCH PENNYWHISTLE GLENN FREY, J.D. SOUTHER and RY COODER all were members of this group.

45s

AMOS

Number	Title (A Side/B Side)	Yr	NM
❑ 121	Don't Talk Now/Jubilee Anne	1969	15.00
❑ 129	Lucky Love/Rebecca	1969	15.00
❑ 148	Star Spangled Bus/Bring Back Founky Women	1970	15.00

Albums

AMOS

Number	Title (A Side/B Side)	Yr	NM
❑ AAS-7007	Longbranch Pennywhistle	1969	50.00

LONGET, CLAUDINE

45s

A&M

Number	Title (A Side/B Side)	Yr	NM
❑ 817	Meditation (Meditacao)/ Sunrise, Sunset	1966	6.00
❑ 832	A Man and a Woman/Here, There and Everywhere	1967	6.00
❑ 846	Hello, Hello/Wonderlove	1967	6.00
❑ 864	Good Day Sunshine/ The Look of Love	1967	6.00
❑ 877	Small Talk/A Man in a Raincoat	1967	6.00
❑ 895	Snow/I Don't Intend to Spend My Christmas Without You	1967	8.00
❑ 897	When I'm Sixty-Four/ I Love How You Love Me	1968	5.00
❑ 909	Love Is Blue (L'amour Est Bleu)/Think of Rain	1968	5.00
❑ 936	Nothing to Lose/White Horses	1968	5.00
❑ 954	Lullaby from "Rosemary's Baby" (Sleep Safe and Warm)/ It's Hard to Say Goodbye	1968	5.00
❑ 967	A Walk in the Park/ Who Needs You	1968	5.00
❑ 1002	Am I Blue/Flea in Her Ear	1968	5.00
❑ 1024	I Think It's Gonna Rain Today/ Hurry On Down	1969	5.00

Looking Glass, *Looking Glass*, Epic KE 31320, 1972, **$15.**

Number	Title (A Side/B Side)	Yr	NM
❑ 1059	Colours/Love Can Never Die	1969	5.00
❑ 1098	Quentin's Theme/Lazy Summer Night	1969	5.00
❑ 1181	A Bushel and a Peck/ Run Wild, Run Free	1970	5.00

BARNABY

Number	Title (A Side/B Side)	Yr	NM
❑ 603	Goodbye Jimmy Goodbye/ (B-side unknown)	1974	4.00
❑ 2022	Broomstick Cowboy/ Long Long Time	1970	4.00
❑ 2028	Ain't No Mountain High Enough/Electric Moon	1971	4.00
❑ 2033	Anytime of the Year/Guess Who I Saw in Paris	1971	4.00
❑ 2060	Let's Spend the Night Together/ Wake Up to Me Gentle	1972	4.00
❑ 5001	Remember the Good/ While You're Sleeping	1972	4.00
❑ 5021	Every Beat of My Heart/Sugar Me	1973	4.00

Albums

A&M

Number	Title (A Side/B Side)	Yr	NM
❑ LP-121 [M]	Claudine	1967	15.00
❑ LP-128 [M]	The Look of Love	1967	15.00
❑ SP-4121 [S]	Claudine	1967	12.00
❑ SP-4128 [S]	The Look of Love	1967	12.00
❑ SP-4142	Love Is Blue	1968	12.00
❑ SP-4163	Colours	1969	12.00
❑ SP-4232	Run Wild, Run Free	1970	12.00

BARNABY

Number	Title (A Side/B Side)	Yr	NM
❑ Z 30377	We've Only Just Begun	1971	12.00
❑ KZ 31383	Let's Spend the Night Together	1972	12.00

LONNIE AND THE CAROLLONS

45s

MOHAWK

Number	Title (A Side/B Side)	Yr	NM
❑ 108	Chapel of Tears/My Heart	1958	150.00
—Green label			
❑ 108	Chapel of Tears/My Heart	1961	30.00
—Red label			
❑ 108	Chapel of Tears/My Heart	1965	20.00
—White label			

Number	Title (A Side/B Side)	Yr	NM
❑ 111	Hold Me Close/Trudy	1958	50.00
❑ 112	Back Yard Rock/You Say	1958	50.00
❑ 113	The Gang All Knows/Ike Hammer	1959	60.00
❑ 122	Need Your Lovin'/Beeline	1960	25.00
—As "Lonnie"			

LONNIE AND THE CRISIS

45s

RELIC

Number	Title (A Side/B Side)	Yr	NM
❑ 532	Bells in the Chapel/ Santa Town USA	196?	6.00
—Reissue of Universal 103			

TIMES SQUARE

Number	Title (A Side/B Side)	Yr	NM
❑ 25	Bells in the Chapel/ Santa Town USA	196?	8.00
—Reissue of Universal 103			

UNIVERSAL

Number	Title (A Side/B Side)	Yr	NM
❑ 103	Bells in the Chapel/ Santa Town USA	1961	200.00

LOOKING GLASS Also see ELLIOTT LURIE.

45s

EPIC

Number	Title (A Side/B Side)	Yr	NM
❑ 10834	Don't It Make You Feel Good/ Catherine Street	1972	5.00
❑ 10874	Brandy (You're a Fine Girl)/ One by One	1972	6.00
❑ 10900	Jenn-Lyne/Golden Rainbow	1972	5.00
❑ 10953	Sweet Somethin'/Rainbow Man	1973	5.00
❑ 11001	Jimmy Loves Mary-Anne/ Wooly Eyes	1973	5.00
❑ 11061	City Lady/Who's Gonna Sing My Rock 'N' Roll Song	1973	5.00
❑ 11085	Sweet Somethin'/Who's Gonna Sing My Rock 'N' Roll Song	1974	5.00
❑ 20001	Rock This Town/Highway to Hollywood	1974	5.00

Albums

EPIC

Number	Title (A Side/B Side)	Yr	NM
❑ KE 31320	Looking Glass	1972	15.00
❑ KE 32167	Subway Serenade	1973	15.00

L

Lords of the New Church, *The Method to Our Madness*, I.R.S. SP-70049, **$12.**

Number	Title (A Side/B Side)	Yr	NM

LOOKING GLASS, THE Their one hit was "Brandy."

45s

UNI

Number	Title (A Side/B Side)	Yr	NM
❑ 55034	Virginia Day's Ragtime/Cry//Memories/What Am I Doin'	1967	10.00

VALIANT

Number	Title (A Side/B Side)	Yr	NM
❑ 750	Silver and Sunshine (How Wonderful My Love)/If I Never Love Again	1966	10.00

WARNER BROS.

Number	Title (A Side/B Side)	Yr	NM
❑ 7050	Lonely Stranger/Love Is Not Everything	1967	10.00

LOOKINLAND, MIKE "Bobby Brady" of THE BRADY BUNCH.

45s

CAPITOL

Number	Title (A Side/B Side)	Yr	NM
❑ 3914	Gum Drop/Love Doesn't Care Who's In It	1974	10.00
❑ 3914 [PS]	Gum Drop/Love Doesn't Care Who's In It	1974	15.00

LOOSE

45s

NOCTURNE

Number	Title (A Side/B Side)	Yr	NM
❑ 1909	Freaky Billy the Wheelie King/It's Happenin'	1969	10.00

Albums

NOCTURNE

Number	Title (A Side/B Side)	Yr	NM
❑ 906	Freaky Billie, The Wheelie King	1970	30.00

LOOSE FUR

Albums

DRAG CITY

Number	Title (A Side/B Side)	Yr	NM
❑ DC 203	Loose Fur	2003	25.00

LORD, BOBBY

45s

COLUMBIA

Number	Title (A Side/B Side)	Yr	NM
❑ 21339	No More/Why Were You Only Fooling Me	1955	25.00
❑ 21339	No More No More/Why Were You Only Fooling Me	1955	50.00
—With longer A-side title			
❑ 21367	I'm the Devil Who Made Her That Way/Ain'tcha Ever Gonna	1955	25.00
❑ 21397	Something's Missing/Sittin' Home Prayin' for Rain	1955	20.00
❑ 21437	Hawk-Eye/I Can't Make My Dreams Understand	1955	30.00
❑ 21459	I Can't Do Without You Anymore/Don't Make Me Laugh	1955	20.00
❑ 21498	So Doggone Lonesome/Pie Peachie Pie Pie	1956	20.00
❑ 21539	Everybody's Rockin' But Me/Without Your Love	1956	80.00
—"Without Your Love" was the hit, but "Everybody's Rockin' But Me" is the collectible side			
❑ 40666	Fire of Love/Beautiful Baby	1956	30.00
❑ 40819	Your Sweet Love/My Baby's Not My Baby Anymore	1957	20.00
❑ 40927	High Voltage/Just Wonderful	1957	40.00
❑ 41030	Am I a Fool/I Know It Was You	1957	20.00
❑ 41155	Sack/Fire of Love	1958	25.00
❑ 41288	When I've Learned/Walking Alone	1958	20.00
❑ 41352	Party Pooper/What a Thrill	1959	25.00
❑ 41505	Too Many Miles/Swamp Fox	1959	25.00
❑ 41596	Give Me a Woman/Where Did My Woman Go	1960	20.00
❑ 41824	Before I Lose My Mind/When the Snow Falls	1960	20.00
❑ 42012	A Rose and a Thorn/Fascination	1961	20.00

DECCA

Number	Title (A Side/B Side)	Yr	NM
❑ 32115	Look What You're Doing/On and On Goes the Hurt	1967	8.00
❑ 32174	Shadows on the Wall/One Day Down	1967	8.00
❑ 32277	Live Your Life Out Loud/Charlotte, North Carolina	1968	6.00
❑ 32373	The True and Lasting Kind/It's My Life	1968	6.00
❑ 32431	Yesterday's Letters/Don't Forget to Smell the Flowers (Along the Way)	1969	6.00
❑ 32578	Rainbow Girl/Do You Ever Think of Me	1969	6.00
❑ 32657	You and Me Against the World/Something Real	1970	6.00
❑ 32718	Wake Me Up Early in the Morning/Violets Are Red	1970	6.00
❑ 32797	Do It to Someone You Love/So in Love with You	1970	8.00
❑ 32797	Goodbye Jukebox/Do It to Someone You Love	1971	6.00
❑ 32841	They've Got Something in the Country/Peace of Mind	1971	6.00
❑ 32932	Everybody's Here/Sweet Inspiration	1972	6.00

HICKORY

Number	Title (A Side/B Side)	Yr	NM
❑ 1158	I'll Go On Alone/My Heart Tells Me So	1961	12.00
❑ 1169	Precious Jewel/Trail of Tears	1962	12.00
❑ 1190	Don't Shed Any Tears for Me/Out Behind the Barn	1962	12.00
❑ 1210	Cry, Cry Darling/Shopping Center	1963	10.00
❑ 1232	Life Can Have Meaning/Pickin' White Gold	1963	10.00
❑ 1259	A Man Needs a Woman/Take a Bucket to the Wall	1964	10.00
❑ 1310	I'm Going Home Next Summer/That Room in the Corner of the House	1965	10.00
❑ 1361	Cash on the Barrelhead/That's Love	1965	10.00
❑ 1389	It Only Hurts When I'm Laughing/Losers Like Me	1966	8.00

RICE

Number	Title (A Side/B Side)	Yr	NM
❑ 5056	I've Had You/Got Yourself Something	1973	8.00
❑ 5062	Hello Wine/(B-side unknown)	1973	8.00
❑ 5063	Looking for a Cold, Lonely Winter/Hello Wine	1973	8.00
❑ 5068	The Look of Love/Your Song	1974	8.00

Albums

DECCA

Number	Title (A Side/B Side)	Yr	NM
❑ DL 75246	Bobby Lord	1970	12.00

HARMONY

Number	Title (A Side/B Side)	Yr	NM
❑ HL 7322 [M]	Bobby Lord's Best	1964	25.00

HICKORY

Number	Title (A Side/B Side)	Yr	NM
❑ LP-126 [M]	The Bobby Lord Show	1965	20.00

LORD, BRIAN, AND THE MIDNIGHTERS FRANK ZAPPA was a member of this group.

45s

CAPITOL

Number	Title (A Side/B Side)	Yr	NM
❑ 4981	Big Surfer/Not Another One	1963	150.00

VIGAH

Number	Title (A Side/B Side)	Yr	NM
❑ 001	Big Surfer/Not Another One	1963	300.00

LORD ROCKINGHAM'S XI

45s

LONDON

Number	Title (A Side/B Side)	Yr	NM
❑ 1810	Fried Onions/The Squelch	1958	12.00
❑ 1839	Hoots Mon/Blue Train	1958	12.00

LORD SITAR Sometimes rumored to be GEORGE HARRISON, but it's not.

45s

CAPITOL

Number	Title (A Side/B Side)	Yr	NM
❑ 5972	Black Is Black/Have You Seen Your Mother, Baby, Standing in the Shadow	1967	40.00

Albums

CAPITOL

Number	Title (A Side/B Side)	Yr	NM
❑ ST 2916	Lord Sitar	1968	30.00

LORDAN, JERRY

45s

CAPITOL

Number	Title (A Side/B Side)	Yr	NM
❑ 4389	Who Could Be Bluer/Do I Worry	1960	15.00

LORDS OF LONDON, THE

45s

DECCA

Number	Title (A Side/B Side)	Yr	NM
❑ 32196	Time Waits for No One/Cornflakes and Ice Cream	1967	20.00

MGM

Number	Title (A Side/B Side)	Yr	NM
❑ 13919	Candy Rainbow/Within Your Mind	1968	20.00

Except when noted otherwise, VG = 25% of NM, and VG+ = 50% of NM. (Example: VG = $2.00, VG+ = $4.00 and NM = $8.00.)

LORDS OF THE NEW CHURCH

12-Inch Singles

I.R.S.

Number	Title (A Side/B Side)	Yr	NM
❑ 70409	Live for Today/Opening Nightmares/Dreams and Desires	1983	10.00
❑ 70962 [DJ]	Holy War/Open Your Eyes	1982	8.00
❑ 70985 [DJ]	The Method to My Madness (same on both sides)	1985	18.00
❑ 70985 [DJ]	The Method to My Madness (same on both sides)	1985	18.00

45s

I.R.S.

Number	Title (A Side/B Side)	Yr	NM
❑ 9908	Open Your Eyes/A Question of Temperature	1982	4.00
❑ 9921	Live for Today/Girls Girls Girls	1983	4.00
❑ 9921 [PS]	Live for Today/Girls Girls Girls	1983	4.00

Albums

I.R.S.

Number	Title (A Side/B Side)	Yr	NM
❑ 5726	Killer Lords	1986	12.00
❑ SP-70029	The Lords of the New Church	1982	15.00
❑ SP-70039	Is Nothing Sacred?	1983	12.00
❑ SP-70049	The Method to Our Madness	1984	12.00

—As "The Lords"

LORELEIS, THE

45s

BRUNSWICK

Number	Title (A Side/B Side)	Yr	NM
❑ 55271	Strange Way/Why Do I Put Up with You	1964	8.00

LORRAINE AND THE SOCIALITES

45s

MERCURY

Number	Title (A Side/B Side)	Yr	NM
❑ 72163	Any Old Way/The Conqueror	1963	12.00

LORY, DICK

45s

COLUMBIA

Number	Title (A Side/B Side)	Yr	NM
❑ 41224	Wild Blooded Woman/No One But You Knows When	1958	50.00
❑ 41276	Crazy Little Daisy/Don't Be a Fool for Love	1958	40.00

DOT

Number	Title (A Side/B Side)	Yr	NM
❑ 15496	Cool It Baby/Ball Room Baby	1956	60.00

LIBERTY

Number	Title (A Side/B Side)	Yr	NM
❑ 55306	The Pain Is Here/You	1961	15.00
❑ 55319	Hello Walls/City of Love	1961	15.00
❑ 55529	I Got Over You/Welcome Home Again	1963	15.00
❑ 55600	Crazy Arms/There's Going to Be a Fight	1963	15.00
❑ 55707	I Will/I Catch Myself Crying	1964	12.00

LOS ADMIRADORES

45s

COMMAND

Number	Title (A Side/B Side)	Yr	NM
❑ LPSAM6 [S]	How High the Moon/Caravan	1960	10.00
—Small hole, plays at 33 1/3 rpm			
❑ LPSAM7 [S]	My Funny Valentine/Makin' Whoopie	1960	10.00
—Small hole, plays at 33 1/3 rpm			
❑ LPSAM8 [S]	Golden Earrings/Birth of the Blues	1960	10.00
—Small hole, plays at 33 1/3 rpm			
❑ LPSAM9 [S]	titles unknown	1960	10.00
—Small hole, plays at 33 1/3 rpm			
❑ LPSAM10 [S]	Laura/I Can Dream, Can't I	1960	10.00
—Small hole, plays at 33 1/3 rpm			

Albums

COMMAND

Number	Title (A Side/B Side)	Yr	NM
❑ 809 SD [S]	Bongos Bongos Bongos	1960	15.00
❑ 812 SD [S]	Bongos/Flutes/Guitars	1960	15.00

LOS BRAVOS

Also see MIKE KENNEDY.

45s

PARROT

Number	Title (A Side/B Side)	Yr	NM
❑ 3020	Bring a Little Lovin'/Make It Last	1968	12.00
❑ 3023	Dirty Street/Two People in Me	1968	10.00

PRESS

Number	Title (A Side/B Side)	Yr	NM
❑ 60002	Black Is Black/I Want a Name	1966	15.00
❑ 60003	Going Nowhere/Brand New Baby	1966	10.00
❑ 60004	You'll Never Get the Chance Again/I'm All Ears	1967	10.00

Albums

PARROT

Number	Title (A Side/B Side)	Yr	NM
❑ PAS 71021	Bring a Little Lovin'	1968	80.00

—Among the other tracks, "Black Is Black" in in true stereo.

PRESS

Number	Title (A Side/B Side)	Yr	NM
❑ PR 73003 [M]	Black Is Black	1966	50.00
❑ PRS 83003 [R]	Black Is Black	1966	30.00

LOS INDIOS TABAJARAS

45s

RCA VICTOR

Number	Title (A Side/B Side)	Yr	NM
❑ 47-8216	Maria Elena/Jungle Dream	1963	8.00
❑ 47-8313	Always in My Heart/Moonlight and Shadows	1964	6.00
❑ 47-8401	Marta/St. Louis Blues	1964	6.00
❑ 47-8510	Darktown Strutters' Ball/The Third Man Theme	1965	6.00
❑ 47-9094	The Petite Waltz/Sentimental Journey	1967	5.00
❑ 47-9388	Rio Antigo/Os Quindins De Ya Ya	1967	5.00

Albums

RCA CAMDEN

Number	Title (A Side/B Side)	Yr	NM
❑ CXS-9031 [(2)]	Los Indios Tabajaras	1973	15.00

RCA INTERNATIONAL

Number	Title (A Side/B Side)	Yr	NM
❑ IL5-7367	Los Grandes Exitos	198?	12.00

RCA VICTOR

Number	Title (A Side/B Side)	Yr	NM
❑ AFL1-0210	Favorite Movie Themes	1977	10.00
—Reissue with new prefix			
❑ APL1-0210	Favorite Movie Themes	1973	12.00
❑ FSP-296	Maria Elena	1971	12.00
❑ FSP-300	Siempre En Mi Corazon	1972	12.00
❑ FSP-310	Softly	1972	12.00
❑ AFL1-0668	Classical Guitars	1977	10.00
—Reissue with new prefix			
❑ CPL1-0668	Classical Guitars	1974	12.00
❑ AFL1-1033	Secret Love	1977	10.00
—Reissue with new prefix			
❑ APL1-1033	Secret Love	1975	12.00
❑ ANL1-1179	Maria Elena	1976	10.00
—Reissue			
❑ LPM-1788 [M]	Sweet and Savage	1958	40.00
❑ LSP-1788 [S]	Sweet and Savage	1958	50.00
❑ APL1-2082	Mellow Nostalgia	1977	12.00
❑ ANL1-2321	In a Sentimental Mood	1977	10.00
❑ AFL1-2526	Masterpieces	1978	12.00
❑ LPM-2822 [M]	Maria Elena	1963	20.00
—Reissue of LPM-1788			
❑ LSP-2822 [S]	Maria Elena	1963	25.00
—Reissue of LSP-1788			
❑ AFL1-2912	Always in My Heart	1977	10.00
—Reissue with new prefix			
❑ LPM-2912 [M]	Always in My Heart	1964	15.00
❑ LSP-2912 [S]	Always in My Heart	1964	20.00
❑ LPM-2959 [M]	Twin Guitar Moods	1964	15.00
❑ LSP-2959 [S]	Twin Guitar Moods	1964	20.00
❑ AFL1-3241	Two Guitars	1979	10.00
❑ LPM-3413 [M]	Many-Splendored Guitars	1965	15.00
❑ LSP-3413 [S]	Many-Splendored Guitars	1965	20.00
❑ AFL1-3505	Casually Classical	1977	10.00
—Reissue with new prefix			
❑ LPM-3505 [M]	Casually Classical	1966	15.00
❑ LSP-3505 [S]	Casually Classical	1966	20.00
❑ AFL1-3535	Rainbows	1980	10.00
❑ LPM-3611 [M]	Twin Guitars — In a Mood for Lovers	1966	15.00
❑ LSP-3611 [S]	Twin Guitars — In a Mood for Lovers	1966	20.00
❑ LPM-3723 [M]	Their Very Special Touch	1967	15.00
❑ LSP-3723 [S]	Their Very Special Touch	1967	20.00
❑ LPM-3909 [M]	Fascinating Rhythms of Their Brazil	1968	20.00
❑ LSP-3909 [S]	Fascinating Rhythms of Their Brazil	1968	15.00
❑ AFL1-3990	Beautiful Sounds	1981	10.00
❑ AFL1-4007	The Best of Los Indios Tabajaras	1977	10.00
—Reissue with new prefix			
❑ LSP-4007	The Best of Los Indios Tabajaras	1968	15.00
❑ LSP-4013	In a Sentimental Mood	1968	15.00
❑ LSP-4129	Song of the Islands	1969	15.00
❑ AFL1-4273	Music for Romance	1982	10.00
❑ LSP-4365	Dreams of Love	1970	15.00
❑ LSP-4496	The Very Thought of You	1971	15.00
❑ LSP-4615	What the World Needs Now	1971	12.00
❑ AFL1-4649	Guitars on the Go	1983	10.00

LOS LOBOS

12-Inch Singles

SLASH

Number	Title (A Side/B Side)	Yr	NM
❑ PRO2226 [DJ]	Don't Worry Baby/Will the Wolf Survive?	1984	7.00
❑ PRO2252 [DJ]	Will the Wolf Survive? (Remix Edit)/Will the Wolf Survive? (LP Version)	1984	7.00
❑ PRO2640 [DJ]	Shakin' Shakin' Shakes (same on both sides)	1986	8.00
❑ PRO2685 [DJ]	Is That All There Is (same on both sides)	1987	7.00
❑ PRO2690 [DJ]	Set Me Free (Rosa Lee) (same on both sides)	1987	5.00
❑ PRO2737 [DJ]	La Bamba/La Bamba (Fade)	1987	8.00
❑ PRO-A-2226 [DJ]	Don't Worry Baby/Will the Wolf Survive?	1984	10.00
❑ PRO-A-2252 [DJ]	Will the Wolf Survive? (Remix Edit) (LP Version)	1984	8.00
❑ PRO-A-2640 [DJ]	Shakin' Shakin' Shakes (same on both sides)	1986	10.00
❑ PRO-A-2685 [DJ]	Is This All There Is? (same on both sides)	1987	10.00
❑ PRO-A-2690 [DJ]	Set Me Free (Rosa Lee) (same on both sides)	1987	8.00
❑ PRO-A-2737 [DJ]	La Bamba (2:54) (Fade 2:13)	1987	8.00
❑ PRO-A-2829 [DJ]	Come On, Let's Go (same on both sides)	1987	10.00

45s

SLASH

Number	Title (A Side/B Side)	Yr	NM
❑ 7-21942	La Bamba/Come On, Let's Go	198?	3.00
—"Back to Back Hits" reissue			
❑ 7-28186	Come On, Let's Go/Ooh My Head	1987	3.00
❑ 7-28336	La Bamba/Charlena	1987	4.00
❑ 7-28336 [PS]	La Bamba/Charlena	1987	4.00
❑ 7-28336DJ [DJ]	La Bamba (2:54)/(Fade 2:13)	1987	8.00
❑ 7-28390	Set Me Free (Rosa Lee)/Tears of God	1987	6.00
❑ 7-28464	One Time One Night/All I Wanted to Do Was Dance	1987	4.00
❑ 7-28464 [PS]	One Time One Night/All I Wanted to Do Was Dance	1987	6.00
❑ 7-29093	Will the Wolf Survive?/The Breakdown	1985	5.00
❑ 7-29093 [PS]	Will the Wolf Survive?/The Breakdown	1985	6.00

Albums

NEW VISTAS

Number	Title (A Side/B Side)	Yr	NM
❑ 1001	Just Another Band from East L.A.	1978	250.00

SLASH

Number	Title (A Side/B Side)	Yr	NM
❑ 23963 [EP]	And a Time to Dance	1983	12.00
❑ 25177	How Will the Wolf Survive?	1984	10.00
❑ 25523	By the Light of the Moon	1987	10.00
❑ 25790	La Pistola y El Corazon	1988	15.00
❑ 26131	The Neighborhood	1990	20.00
❑ R 144507	By the Light of the Moon	1987	12.00

—RCA Music Service edition

LOS LOCOS DEL RITMO

Albums

DIMSA

Number	Title (A Side/B Side)	Yr	NM
❑ 8178	Rock!	196?	100.00

LOS SEVEN DAYS

Albums

ECO

Number	Title (A Side/B Side)	Yr	NM
❑ 314	Sha-La-La	196?	50.00

LOST, THE

45s

CAPITOL

Number	Title (A Side/B Side)	Yr	NM
❑ 5519	Back Door Blues/Maybe More Than You Do	1965	15.00
❑ 5708	Mean Motorcycle/Violet Gown	1966	15.00
❑ 5725	No Reason Why/Violet Gown	1966	15.00

JANUS

Number	Title (A Side/B Side)	Yr	NM
❑ 109	I Shall Be Released/Shame	1969	10.00

LOST & FOUND

45s

INTERNATIONAL ARTISTS

Number	Title (A Side/B Side)	Yr	NM
❑ 120	Everybody's Here/Forever Lasting Plastic Words	1968	25.00
❑ 125	When Will You Come Through/Professor Black	1968	25.00

Albums

INTERNATIONAL ARTISTS

Number	Title (A Side/B Side)	Yr	NM
❑ IA-3	Everybody's Here	1968	100.00
—Original pressing, no "Masterfonics" in dead wax			
❑ IA-3	Everybody's Here	1979	15.00
—Reissue with "Masterfonics" in trail-off wax			

LOST NATION, THE

Albums

RARE EARTH

Number	Title (A Side/B Side)	Yr	NM
❑ RS-518	Paradise Lost	1970	20.00

L

LOTHAR AND THE HAND PEOPLE

45s

CAPITOL

Number	Title (A Side/B Side)	Yr	NM
❑ 2008	Have Mercy (Mercy, Mercy, Mercy)/Let the Boy Pretend	1967	10.00
❑ 2376	Machines/Milkweed Love	1969	8.00
❑ 2556	Midnight Ranger/Yes, I Love You	1969	8.00
❑ 5874	L-O-V-E/Rose Colored Glasses	1967	10.00
❑ 5945	Comic Strip/Every Single Word	1967	10.00

Albums

CAPITOL

Number	Title (A Side/B Side)	Yr	NM
❑ ST-247	Space Hymn	1969	40.00
❑ SM-2997	Presenting Lothar and the Hand People	1977	8.00
—Reissue with new prefix			
❑ ST 2997	Presenting Lothar and the Hand People	1968	40.00

LOU, HERB B., AND THE LEGAL EAGLES

Break-in record with HERB ALPERT involvement.

45s

ARCH

Number	Title (A Side/B Side)	Yr	NM
❑ 1607	The Trial/Kiss Me	1958	40.00

LOUDERMILK, JOHN D.

45s

COLONIAL

Number	Title (A Side/B Side)	Yr	NM
❑ 430	Sittin' in the Balcony/A-Plus in Love	1957	30.00
—As "Johnny Dee"			
❑ 430 [PS]	Sittin' in the Balcony/A-Plus in Love	1957	400.00
—As "Johnny Dee"			
❑ 433	Teenage Queen/It's Gotta Be You	1957	30.00
—As "Johnny Dee"			

COLUMBIA

Number	Title (A Side/B Side)	Yr	NM
❑ 4-41165	Yearbook/Susie's House	1958	15.00
❑ 4-41165 [PS]	Yearbook/Susie's House	1958	25.00
❑ 4-41209	Lover's Lane/Yo Yo	1958	15.00
❑ 4-41247	Goin' Away to School/This Cold War with You	1958	15.00
❑ 4-41507	The Happy Wanderer/Red Headed Stranger	1959	15.00
❑ 4-41562	Tobacco Road/Midnight Bus	1960	20.00

DOT

Number	Title (A Side/B Side)	Yr	NM
❑ 15699	Somebody Sweet/They Were Right	1958	30.00
—As "Johnny Dee"			

RCA VICTOR

Number	Title (A Side/B Side)	Yr	NM
❑ 47-7938	Language of Love/Darling Jane	1961	12.00
❑ 47-7993	Thou Shalt Not Steal/Mister Jones	1962	12.00
❑ 47-8054	Callin' Doctor Casey/Oh How Sad	1962	12.00
❑ 47-8101	Road Hog/Angela Jones	1962	12.00
❑ 47-8101 [PS]	Road Hog/Angela Jones	1962	20.00
❑ 47-8154	Bad News/The Guitar Player	1963	12.00
❑ 47-8308	Blue Train (Of the Heartbreak Line)/Rhythm and Blues	1962	12.00
❑ 47-8389	Th' Wife/Nothing to Gain	1964	12.00
❑ 47-8826	Run On Home Baby Brother/Silver Cloud Talking Blues	1966	10.00
❑ 47-8973	I Hear It Now/You're the Guilty One	1966	10.00
❑ 47-9189	It's My Time/Bahama Mama	1967	10.00
❑ 47-9592	Sidewalks/The Odd Folks of Okracoke	1968	8.00
❑ 74-0121	Brown Girl/The Jones'	1969	8.00

WARNER BROS.

Number	Title (A Side/B Side)	Yr	NM
❑ 7489	When I Was Nine/Lord Have Mercy	1971	7.00

Albums

RCA VICTOR

Number	Title (A Side/B Side)	Yr	NM
❑ LPM-2434 [M]	Language of Love	1961	25.00
❑ LSP-2434 [S]	Language of Love	1961	30.00
❑ LPM-2539 [M]	Twelve Sides of Loudermilk	1962	20.00
❑ LSP-2539 [S]	Twelve Sides of Loudermilk	1962	25.00
❑ LPM-3497 [M]	A Bizarre Collection of the Most Unusual Songs	1965	20.00
❑ LSP-3497 [S]	A Bizarre Collection of the Most Unusual Songs	1965	25.00
❑ LPM-3807 [M]	Suburban Attitudes in Country Music	1967	25.00
❑ LSP-3807 [S]	Suburban Attitudes in Country Music	1967	20.00
❑ LSP-4040	Country Love Songs	1968	20.00
❑ LSP-4097	The Open Mind of John D. Loudermilk	1968	20.00

WARNER BROS.

Number	Title (A Side/B Side)	Yr	NM
❑ WS 1922	Vol. 1, Elloree	1971	15.00

LOUIE AND THE LOVERS

45s

EPIC

Number	Title (A Side/B Side)	Yr	NM
❑ 5-10616	Driver Go Slow/I Know You Know	1970	8.00
❑ 5-10678	Rise/I Don't Want to Be Seen with You	1970	8.00
❑ 5-10825	Little Georgie Baker/Tomorrows Just Might Change	1972	8.00

Albums

EPIC

Number	Title (A Side/B Side)	Yr	NM
❑ E 30026	Rise	1970	20.00

LOUIS, BOBBY

45s

CAPITOL

Number	Title (A Side/B Side)	Yr	NM
❑ F4224	Adult Western/Love at First Sight	1959	30.00
❑ F4272	I'm a Coward/Cell of Love	1959	30.00

LOUISE, TINA

Albums

CONCERT HALL

Number	Title (A Side/B Side)	Yr	NM
❑ H-1503 [M]	Her Portrait in Hi-Fi	1958	50.00
❑ H-1521 [M]	It's Time for Tina	1958	200.00

URANIA

Number	Title (A Side/B Side)	Yr	NM
❑ ULM-2005 [M]	It's Time for Tina	1959	200.00
❑ USD-2005 [S]	It's Time for Tina	1959	300.00

LOUVIN, CHARLIE

45s

CAPITOL

Number	Title (A Side/B Side)	Yr	NM
❑ 2007	The Only Way Out (Is to Walk Over Me)/Too Little and Too Late	1967	10.00
❑ 2106	Will You Visit Me on Sundays?/Tears, Wine and Flowers	1968	8.00
❑ 2231	Hey Daddy/She Will Get Lonesome	1968	8.00
❑ 2350	What Are Those Things (With Big Black Wings)/What Then	1968	8.00
❑ 2448	Let's Put Our World Back Together/Heart of Clay	1969	8.00
❑ 2612	Little Reasons/After Awhile	1969	8.00
❑ 2703	Here's a Toast to Mama/Show Me the Way Back to Your Heart	1969	8.00
❑ 2770	Tiny Wings/I Ain't Gonna Work Tomorrow	1970	8.00
❑ 2824	Come and Get It Mama/Is Home Sweet Home	1970	8.00
❑ 2972	Sittin' Bull/It Ain't No Big Thing	1970	8.00
❑ 3048	Love Has to Die All By Itself/I Wish It Had Been a Dream	1971	8.00
❑ 3243	I Placed a Call/I'm Going Home	1971	8.00
❑ 3319	Just in Time (To Watch Love Die)/She Just Wants to Be Needed	1972	8.00
❑ 3528	Bottom of the Fifth/The Roses and the Rain	1973	8.00
❑ 3607	Funny Man/Harvest Time	1973	8.00
❑ 5173	I Don't Love You Anymore/My Book of Memories	1964	10.00
❑ 5296	Less and Less/I Don't Want It	1964	10.00
❑ 5369	See the Big Man Cry/I Just Don't Understand	1965	10.00
❑ 5475	Think I'll Go Somewhere and Cry Myself to Sleep/Life Begins at Love	1965	10.00
❑ 5550	You Finally Said Something Good (When You Said Goodbye)/Something to Think About	1965	10.00
❑ 5606	To Tell the Truth (I Told a Lie)/That's What Your Leaving's Done to Me	1966	10.00
❑ 5665	Something's Wrong/I Want a Happy Life	1966	10.00
❑ 5729	The Proof Is in the Kissing/Scared of the Blues	1966	10.00
❑ 5791	Off and On/Still Loving You	1967	10.00
❑ 5872	On the Other Hand/Someone's Heartache	1967	10.00
❑ 5948	I Forgot to Cry/Drive Me Out of My Mind	1967	10.00

LITTLE DARLIN'

Number	Title (A Side/B Side)	Yr	NM
❑ 7922	Love Don't Care/Who's Gonna Love Me Now	1979	5.00
—A-side with Emmylou Harris			

UNITED ARTISTS

Number	Title (A Side/B Side)	Yr	NM
❑ XW368	You're My Wife, She's My Woman/If I Had to Build a Bridge	1973	6.00
❑ XW430	It Almost Felt Like Love/Until I'm Out of Sight	1974	6.00
❑ XW540	When Love Is Gone/I Want to See You One More Time	1974	6.00
❑ XW616	When You Have to Fly Alone/I Just Want a Happy Life	1975	6.00
❑ XW689	I Just Went Out, That's All/Is I Love You That Easy to Say	1975	6.00
❑ XW919	Sweet Texas/(B-side unknown)	1976	6.00

Albums

CAPITOL

Number	Title (A Side/B Side)	Yr	NM
❑ ST-142	Hey Daddy	1969	20.00
❑ ST-8-0142	Hey Daddy	1969	25.00
—Capitol Record Club edition			
❑ ST-248	The Kind of Man I Am	1969	20.00
❑ ST-416	Here's a Toast to Mama	1970	20.00
❑ ST-555	Ten Times Charlie	1970	20.00
❑ ST 2208 [S]	Less and Less and I Don't Love You Anymore	1965	25.00
❑ T 2208 [M]	Less and Less and I Don't Love You Anymore	1965	20.00
❑ ST 2437 [S]	The Many Moods of Charlie Louvin	1966	25.00
❑ T 2437 [M]	The Many Moods of Charlie Louvin	1966	20.00
❑ ST 2482 [S]	Lonesome Is Me	1966	25.00
❑ T 2482 [M]	Lonesome Is Me	1966	20.00
❑ ST 2689 [S]	I'll Remember Always	1967	20.00
❑ T 2689 [M]	I'll Remember Always	1967	25.00
❑ ST 2787 [S]	I Forgot to Cry	1967	20.00
❑ T 2787 [M]	I Forgot to Cry	1967	25.00
❑ ST 2958	Will You Visit Me on Sundays	1968	20.00

UNITED ARTISTS

Number	Title (A Side/B Side)	Yr	NM
❑ UA-LA248-G	It Almost Felt Like Love	1974	15.00

LOUVIN, CHARLIE, AND ROY ACUFF

Also see each artist's individual listings.

45s

HAL KAT

Number	Title (A Side/B Side)	Yr	NM
❑ 63058	The Precious Jewel/Buried Alive	1989	8.00

LOUVIN, CHARLIE, AND MELBA MONTGOMERY

Also see each artist's individual listings.

45s

CAPITOL

Number	Title (A Side/B Side)	Yr	NM
❑ 2915	Something to Brag About/Let's Help Each Other to Forget	1970	8.00
❑ 3029	Did You Ever/Don't Believe Me	1971	8.00
❑ 3111	Baby, You've Got What It Takes/If We Don't Make It	1971	8.00
❑ 3208	I'm Gonna Leave You/When I Stop Dreaming	1971	8.00
❑ 3388	Baby, What's Wrong with Us/Unmatched Wedding Bands	1972	8.00
❑ 3508	A Man Likes Things Like That/That Don't Mean I Don't Love You	1973	8.00

Albums

CAPITOL

Number	Title (A Side/B Side)	Yr	NM
❑ ST-686	Somethin' to Brag About	1971	20.00
❑ ST-808	Baby, You've Got What It Takes	1971	20.00

LOUVIN, IRA

Also see THE LOUVIN BROTHERS.

45s

CAPITOL

Number	Title (A Side/B Side)	Yr	NM
❑ 5190	Make Believe It's Me/Who Threw Dat Rock	1964	10.00
❑ 5428	Yodel, Sweet Molly/You're Looking for an Angel	1965	10.00

Albums

CAPITOL

Number	Title (A Side/B Side)	Yr	NM
❑ ST 2413 [S]	The Unforgettable Ira Louvin	1965	30.00
❑ T 2413 [M]	The Unforgettable Ira Louvin	1965	25.00

LOUVIN BROTHERS, THE

Also see CHARLIE LOUVIN; IRA LOUVIN.

45s

CAPITOL

Number	Title (A Side/B Side)	Yr	NM
❑ F2296	The Family Who Prays Together/Let Us Travel On	1952	25.00
❑ F2381	Broadminded/I Know What You're Talking About	1953	25.00
❑ F2510	Born Again/From Mother's Arms to Korea	1952	25.00
❑ F2612	Preach the Gospel/I Love God's Way of Living	1953	25.00
❑ F2753	God Bless Her/No One to Sing for Me	1954	25.00
❑ F2852	If We Forget God/Satan Lied to Me	1954	25.00
❑ F2965	Satan and the Saint/Swing Low Sweet Chariot	1954	25.00
❑ F3083	Love Thy Neighbor As Thyself/Make Him a Soldier	1955	25.00
❑ F3177	When I Stop Dreaming/Pitfall	1955	20.00
❑ F3241	Just Rehearsing/Pray for Me	1955	20.00
❑ F3300	I Don't Believe You've Met My Baby/In the Middle of Nowhere	1955	20.00

Except when noted otherwise, VG = 25% of NM, and VG+ = 50% of NM. (Example: VG = $2.00, VG+ = $4.00 and NM = $8.00.)

Number	Title (A Side/B Side)	Yr	NM
❑ F3413	Hoping That You're Hoping/ Childish Love	1956	20.00
❑ F3467	Where Will You Build/That's All He's Asking of Me	1956	20.00
❑ F3523	You're Running Wild/Cash on the Barrel Head	1956	20.00
❑ F3630	Don't Laugh/New Partner Waltz	1957	20.00
❑ F3715	Plenty of Everything But You/ The First One to Love You	1957	20.00
❑ F3770	Praying/There's No Excuse	1957	20.00
❑ F3804	Call Me/I Wish You Knew	1957	20.00
❑ F3871	Dog Sled/When I Loved You	1958	15.00
❑ F3974	My Baby Came Back/She Didn't Even Know I Was Gone	1958	15.00
❑ F4055	My Baby's Gone/Lorene	1958	15.00
❑ F4112	The River of Jordan/ He Can Be Found	1959	15.00
❑ F4117	Knoxville Girl/I Wish It Had Been a Dream	1959	15.00
❑ F4200	Blue from Now On/While You're Cheating on Me	1959	15.00
❑ F4255	You're Learning/My Curly Headed Baby	1959	15.00
❑ 4331	Nellie Moved to Town/Stagger	1960	15.00
❑ 4359	Just Suppose/I See a Bridge	1960	15.00
❑ 4395	Ruby's Song/If You Love Me, Stay Away	1960	15.00
❑ 4430	Love Is a Lonely Street/ What a Change	1960	15.00
❑ 4473	Santa Claus Parade/ It's Christmas Time	1960	15.00
❑ 4473 [PS]	Santa Claus Parade/ It's Christmas Time	1960	30.00
❑ 4506	I Love You Best of All/ Scared of the Blues	1961	15.00
❑ 4559	I Ain't Gonna Work Tomorrow/I Can't Keep You in Love with Me	1961	15.00
❑ 4628	How's the World Treating You/ It Hurts Me More	1961	15.00
❑ 4686	Weapon of Prayer/Great Atomic Power	1962	15.00
❑ 4757	Broken Engagement/Time Goes So Slow	1962	15.00
❑ 4822	Must You Throw Dirt in My Face/The First Time in Life	1962	15.00
❑ 4886	Keep Your Eyes on Jesus/Don't Let Them Take the Bible	1962	15.00
❑ 4941	Love Turns to Hate/I Cried After You Left	1963	12.00
❑ 4999	I'm Glad That I'm Not Him/ Message to Your Heart	1963	12.00
❑ 5075	Every Time You Leave/ There Is No Easy Way	1963	12.00

MGM

Number	Title (A Side/B Side)	Yr	NM
❑ K10988	Weapon of Prayer/They've Got the Church Outnumbered	1951	30.00
❑ K11065	You'll Be Rewarded Over There/Robe of White	1951	30.00
❑ K11221	Get Acquainted/My Love Song	1952	30.00
❑ K11277	Insured Before the Grave/ Great Atomic Power	1952	30.00
❑ K11392	Do You Live What You Preach/ I'll Live with God	1953	30.00

7-Inch Extended Plays

CAPITOL

Number	Title (A Side/B Side)	Yr	NM
❑ EAP 1-825	*Wait a Little Longer, Please Jesus/Last Chance to Pray/ Are You Washed in the Blood/ Thankful	1957	12.00
❑ EAP 1-825 [PS]	Nearer My God to Thee, Part 1	1957	12.00
❑ EAP 2-825	*Nearer My God to Thee/ There's No Excuse/Praying/ I Can't Say No	1957	12.00
❑ EAP 2-825 [PS]	Nearer My God to Thee, Part 2	1957	12.00
❑ EAP 3-825	*I Won't Have to Cross Jordan Alone/This Little Light of Mine/Lord, I'm Coming Home/I Steal Away and Pray	1957	12.00
❑ EAP 3-825 [PS]	Nearer My God to Thee, Part 3	1957	12.00

MGM

Number	Title (A Side/B Side)	Yr	NM
❑ X1324	(contents unknown)	1956	15.00
❑ X1324 [PS]	The Louvin Brothers (Ira and Charles), Vol. 1	1956	15.00
❑ X1325	(contents unknown)	1956	15.00
❑ X1325 [PS]	The Louvin Brothers (Ira and Charles), Vol. 2	1956	15.00
❑ X1326	(contents unknown)	1956	15.00
❑ X1326 [PS]	The Louvin Brothers (Ira and Charles), Vol. 3	1956	15.00

Albums

CAPITOL

Number	Title (A Side/B Side)	Yr	NM
❑ DT 769 [R]	Tragic Songs of Life	196?	20.00
❑ T 769 [M]	Tragic Songs of Life	1956	100.00
—Turquoise label			
❑ T 769 [M]	Tragic Songs of Life	1959	40.00
—Black colorband label, logo at left			

Love, *Four Sail*, Elektra EKS-74049, 1969, **$25.**

Number	Title (A Side/B Side)	Yr	NM
❑ T 769 [M]	Tragic Songs of Life	1962	25.00
—Black colorband label, logo at top			
❑ T 825 [M]	Nearer My God to Thee	1957	100.00
—Turquoise label			
❑ T 825 [M]	Nearer My God to Thee	1959	40.00
—Black colorband label, logo at left			
❑ T 825 [M]	Nearer My God to Thee	1962	25.00
—Black colorband label, logo at top			
❑ T 910 [M]	Ira and Charlie	1958	100.00
—Turquoise label			
❑ T 910 [M]	Ira and Charlie	1959	40.00
—Black colorband label, logo at left			
❑ T 910 [M]	Ira and Charlie	1962	25.00
—Black colorband label, logo at top			
❑ DT 1061 [R]	The Family Who Prays	196?	20.00
❑ T 1061 [M]	The Family Who Prays	1958	80.00
—Black colorband label, logo at left			
❑ T 1061 [M]	The Family Who Prays	1962	25.00
—Black colorband label, logo at top			
❑ T 1106 [M]	Country Love Ballads	1959	80.00
—Black colorband label, logo at left			
❑ T 1106 [M]	Country Love Ballads	1962	25.00
—Black colorband label, logo at top			
❑ T 1277 [M]	Satan Is Real	1960	80.00
—Black colorband label, logo at left			
❑ T 1277 [M]	Satan Is Real	1962	25.00
—Black colorband label, logo at top			
❑ T 1385 [M]	My Baby's Gone	1960	80.00
—Black colorband label, logo at left			
❑ T 1385 [M]	My Baby's Gone	1962	25.00
—Black colorband label, logo at top			
❑ T 1449 [M]	A Tribute to the Delmore Brothers	1960	80.00
—Black colorband label, logo at left			
❑ T 1449 [M]	A Tribute to the Delmore Brothers	1962	25.00
—Black colorband label, logo at top			
❑ T 1547 [M]	Encore	1961	80.00
—Black colorband label, logo at left			
❑ T 1547 [M]	Encore	1962	25.00
—Black colorband label, logo at top			
❑ ST 1616 [S]	Country Christmas	1961	80.00
—Black rainbow label with "Capitol" at left			
❑ ST 1616 [S]	Country Christmas	1962	25.00
—Black rainbow label with "Capitol" at top			
❑ T 1616 [M]	Country Christmas	1961	50.00
—Black rainbow label with "Capitol" at left			
❑ T 1616 [M]	Country Christmas	1962	20.00
—Black rainbow label with "Capitol" at top			
❑ ST 1721 [S]	Weapon of Prayer	1962	50.00
❑ T 1721 [M]	Weapon of Prayer	1962	40.00
❑ ST 1834 [S]	Keep Your Eyes on Jesus	1963	50.00
❑ T 1834 [M]	Keep Your Eyes on Jesus	1963	40.00
❑ ST 2091 [S]	The Louvin Brothers Sing and Play Their Current Hits	1964	30.00
❑ T 2091 [M]	The Louvin Brothers Sing and Play Their Current Hits	1964	25.00
❑ ST 2331 [S]	Thank God for My Christian Home	1965	30.00
❑ T 2331 [M]	Thank God for My Christian Home	1965	25.00
❑ ST 2827 [S]	The Great Roy Acuff Songs	1967	30.00
❑ T 2827 [M]	The Great Roy Acuff Songs	1967	40.00

METRO

Number	Title (A Side/B Side)	Yr	NM
❑ M-598 [M]	The Louvin Brothers	1966	25.00
❑ MS-598 [R]	The Louvin Brothers	1966	20.00

MGM

Number	Title (A Side/B Side)	Yr	NM
❑ E-3426 [M]	The Louvin Brothers	1957	200.00

SEARS

Number	Title (A Side/B Side)	Yr	NM
❑ SP-119 [M]	Ira & Charles Louvin	196?	20.00
❑ SPS-119 [R]	Ira & Charles Louvin	196?	15.00

TOWER

Number	Title (A Side/B Side)	Yr	NM
❑ DT 5038 [R]	Two Different Worlds	1966	20.00
❑ T 5038 [M]	Two Different Worlds	1966	30.00
❑ DT 5122	Country Heart and Soul	1968	20.00

LOVE

45s

BLUE THUMB

Number	Title (A Side/B Side)	Yr	NM
❑ 106	Stand Out/I'll Pray for You	1970	6.00
❑ 7116	Keep On Shining/ Everlasting First	1970	6.00

Except when noted otherwise, VG = 25% of NM, and VG+ = 50% of NM. (Example: VG = $2.00, VG+ = $4.00 and NM = $8.00.)

Love and Rockets, *Earth.Sun.Moon*, Big Time/RCA 6058-1-B8, 1987, **$10.**

Number	Title (A Side/B Side)	Yr	NM
ELEKTRA			
❑ 45603	My Little Red Book/ Message to Pretty	1966	10.00
❑ 45605	7 and 7 Is/No. Fourteen	1966	10.00
❑ 45608	She Comes in Colors/ Orange Sky	1966	10.00
❑ 45608	Stephanie Knows Who/ Orange Sky	1966	30.00
❑ 45613	Que Vida/Hey Joe	1967	50.00
❑ 45629	Alone Again Or/A House Is Not a Motel	1968	10.00
❑ 45633	Laughing Stock/You're Mine and We Belong Together	1968	15.00
❑ 45700	Alone Again Or/Good Times	1970	8.00
RSO			
❑ 502	Time Is Like a River/With a Little Energy	1974	5.00
❑ 506	Good Old Fashioned Dream/ You Said You Would	1975	5.00
Albums			
BLUE THUMB			
❑ BTS-8822	False Start	1970	20.00
❑ BTS-9000 [(2)]	Out Here	1969	25.00
ELEKTRA			
❑ EKL-4001 [M]	Love	1966	100.00
❑ EKL-4001 [M]	Love	1966	300.00
—White label promo			
❑ EKL-4005 [M]	Da Capo	1967	100.00
❑ EKL-4013 [M]	Forever Changes	1967	50.00
❑ EKL-4013 [M]	Forever Changes	1967	150.00
—White label promo			
❑ EKS-74001 [S]	Love	1966	50.00
—Brown label			
❑ EKS-74001 [S]	Love	1969	15.00
—Red label with large stylized "E"			
❑ EKS-74001 [S]	Love	1971	12.00
—Butterfly label			
❑ EKS-74005 [S]	Da Capo	1967	40.00
—Brown label			
❑ EKS-74005 [S]	Da Capo	1969	15.00
—Red label with large stylized "E"			
❑ EKS-74005 [S]	Da Capo	1971	12.00
—Butterfly label			
❑ EKS-74013 [S]	Forever Changes	1967	30.00
—Brown label			
❑ EKS-74013 [S]	Forever Changes	1969	15.00
—Red label with large stylized "E"			
❑ EKS-74013 [S]	Forever Changes	1971	12.00
—Butterfly label			
❑ EKS-74013 [S]	Forever Changes	1980	10.00
—Red label, small "E," Warner Communications logo on label			
❑ EKS-74013 [S]	Forever Changes	1984	8.00
—Red and black label			
❑ EKS-74049	Four Sail	1969	25.00
—Red label with large stylized "E"			
❑ EKS-74049	Four Sail	1971	12.00
—Butterfly label			
❑ EKS-74049 [DJ]	Four Sail	1969	80.00
—White label promo			
❑ EKS-74058	Revisited	1970	25.00
—Red label with large stylized "E"			
❑ EKS-74058	Revisited	1971	12.00
—Butterfly label			
❑ EKS-74058	Revisited	198?	10.00
—Red label, small "E," Warner Communications logo on label			
❑ EKS-74058	Revisited	1984	8.00
—Red and black label			
MCA			
❑ 27025	Studio/Live	1982	10.00
RHINO			
❑ RNDF-251 [PD]	Love Live	1981	15.00
❑ RNLP-800	Best of Love	1980	10.00
❑ RNLP-70175	The Best of Love (1966-1969) (Golden Archive Series)	1987	10.00
RSO			
❑ SO 4804	Reel to Real	1974	15.00
SUNDAZED			
❑ LP 5100	Love	2001	12.00
—Reissue on 180-gram vinyl			
❑ LP 5101	Da Capo	2001	12.00
—Reissue on 180-gram vinyl			
❑ LP 5102	Forever Changes	2001	12.00
—Reissue on 180-gram vinyl			
❑ LP 5103	Four Sail	2004	12.00
❑ LP 5104	Revisited	2001	12.00
—Reissue on 180-gram vinyl			

LOVE, DARLENE Also see THE BLOSSOMS; THE CRYSTALS.

Number	Title (A Side/B Side)	Yr	NM
45s			
COLUMBIA			
❑ 07984	He's Sure the Man I Love/ Everybody Needs	1988	5.00
ELEKTRA			
❑ 69647	River Deep, Mountain High/ Leader of the Pack	1985	4.00
—B-side by Leader of the Pack			
❑ 69647 [PS]	River Deep, Mountain High/ Leader of the Pack	1985	4.00
PASSPORT			
❑ 7926	Christmas (Baby Please Come Home)/Playing for Keeps	1983	12.00
PHILLES			
❑ 111	(Today I Met) The Boy I'm Gonna Marry/Playing for Keeps	1963	20.00
❑ 111	(Today I Met) The Boy I'm Gonna Marry/My Heart Beat a Little Bit Faster	1963	30.00
❑ 114	Wait 'Til My Bobby Gets Home/ Take It From Me	1963	20.00
❑ 117	A Fine Fine Boy/Nino & Sonny (Big Trouble)	1963	20.00
❑ 119	Christmas (Baby Please Come Home)/Harry and Milt Meet Hal B.	1963	40.00
❑ 123	Stumble and Fall/(He's a) Quiet Guy	1964	300.00
—Yellow and red label, "D.J. Copy Not for Sale" on label			
❑ 123	Stumble and Fall/(He's a) Quiet Guy	1964	800.00
—Yellow and red label stock copy; has been verified to exist			
❑ 123 [DJ]	Stumble and Fall/(He's a) Quiet Guy	1964	150.00
—White label promo			
❑ 125	Christmas (Baby Please Come Home)/X-Mas Blues	1964	400.00
❑ 125X	Christmas (Baby Please Come Home)/Winter Wonderland	1965	25.00
REPRISE			
❑ 0534	Too Late to Say You're Sorry/If	1966	200.00
WARNER/SPECTOR			
❑ 0401	Christmas (Baby Please Come Home)/Winter Wonderland	1974	20.00
❑ 0410	Lord, If You're a Woman/ Stumble and Fall	1975	10.00
Albums			
COLUMBIA			
❑ FC 40605	Paint Another Picture	1988	12.00

LOVE, HONEY, AND THE LOVE NOTES

Number	Title (A Side/B Side)	Yr	NM
45s			
CAMEO			
❑ 380	We Belong Together/Mary Ann	1965	60.00
❑ 409	Baby Baby You/Beg Me	1966	40.00
—As "The Lovenotes"			

LOVE, HOT SHOT

Number	Title (A Side/B Side)	Yr	NM
45s			
SUN			
❑ 196	Wolf Call Boogie/Harmonica Jam	1954	4000.

LOVE, JOHNNY See RONNIE LOVE.

LOVE, MICHAEL Not the Beach Boy.

Number	Title (A Side/B Side)	Yr	NM
45s			
COLUMBIA			
❑ 44253	Mrs. MacAbee/I Love Those Trees	1967	8.00

LOVE, RONNIE

Number	Title (A Side/B Side)	Yr	NM
45s			
D-TOWN			
❑ 1021	Judy/Show Me What You Got	1963	120.00
❑ 1027	'Deed I Do/Always Be Good	1964	30.00
❑ 1040	Come Dance with Me/ She's Got Love	196?	50.00
❑ 1047	Judy/Detroit, Michigan	1965	50.00
DOT			
❑ 16144	Chills and Fever/No Use Pledging My Love	1960	20.00
❑ 16186	Just to Be Loved/North to St. Louis	1961	20.00
MERCURY			
❑ 71492	Bless Your Heart/Lead Me	1959	25.00
—As "Johnny Love"			

Except when noted otherwise, VG = 25% of NM, and VG+ = 50% of NM. (Example: VG = $2.00, VG+ = $4.00 and NM = $8.00.)

Number	Title (A Side/B Side)	Yr	NM
❑ 71575	Because You Love Me/ While Our Hearts Are Young	1960	25.00
—As "Johnny Love"			
❑ 71667	There Goes My Heart/ I Love You, Yes I Do	1960	25.00
—As "Johnny Love"			
STARTIME			
❑ 5001	Chills and Fever/No Use Pledging My Love	1960	50.00
—As "Johnny Love"			
❑ 5003	Shakin' and a Breakin'/ (B-side unknown)	1961	30.00

LOVE AFFAIR, THE

45s

Number	Title (A Side/B Side)	Yr	NM
DATE			
❑ 2-1591	Everlasting Love/Gone Are the Songs of Yesterday	1968	10.00
❑ 2-1608	Rainbow Valley/ Someone Like Me	1968	10.00
❑ 2-1627	A Day Without Love/I'm Happy	1968	10.00
❑ 2-1646	Let Me Know/One Road	1969	10.00
❑ 2-1652	Bringing On Back the Good Times/Another Day	1969	10.00

LOVE AND ROCKETS

BAUHAUS related. BAUHAUS related.

12-Inch Singles

Number	Title (A Side/B Side)	Yr	NM
BIG TIME			
❑ 6018	Kundalini Express/Lucifer Sam/Holiday on the Moon	1986	10.00
❑ 6018 [DJ]	Kundalini Express (same on both sides)	1986	8.00
❑ 6023	All in My Mind (electric)/ All in My Mind (acoustic)	1986	10.00
❑ 6035 [DJ]	Ball of Confusion (same on both sides)	1986	8.00
❑ 6035 [DJ]	Ball of Confusion (same on both sides)	1986	8.00
❑ 6038	Ball of Confusion (3 mixes)/ All in My Mind	1986	10.00
❑ 6063 [DJ]	No New Tale to Tell (same on both sides)	1987	10.00
❑ 6063 [DJ]	No New Tale to Tell (same on both sides)	1987	10.00
❑ 6067 [DJ]	Mirror People (same on both sides)	1987	10.00
❑ 6067 [DJ]	Mirror People (same on both sides)	1987	10.00
❑ 6070	Mirror People (5 versions)	1987	12.00
❑ 6071 [DJ]	Waiting for the Flood (same on both sides)	1987	10.00
❑ 6071 [DJ]	Waiting for the Flood (same on both sides)	1987	10.00
RCA			
❑ 8758 [DJ]	Dog End of the Day Gone By (2 versions)/Interview	1988	15.00
❑ 9041	Rock and Roll Babylon/No New Tale to Tell (Live)/ Ball of Confusion (Live)	1989	20.00
❑ 9097	No Big Deal (2 versions)/ 1000 Watts of Your Love/ No Words No More	1989	10.00

45s

Number	Title (A Side/B Side)	Yr	NM
BIG TIME			
❑ 6069-7-B	No New Tale to Tell/ Earth, Sun, Moon	1987	5.00
❑ 8956-7-R	So Alive/Dreamtime	1989	3.00
❑ 8956-7-R [PS]	So Alive/Dreamtime	1989	3.00
❑ 9045-7-R	No Big Deal/No Words No More	1989	3.00

Albums

Number	Title	Yr	NM
BEGGARS BANQUET			
❑ 9715-1-R	Love and Rockets	1989	10.00
BIG TIME/RCA			
❑ 6011-1-B	Express	1986	12.00
❑ 6058-1-B8	Earth.Sun.Moon	1987	10.00
RCA			
❑ 8507-1-R	Seventh Dream of Teenage Heaven	1988	10.00

LOVE CHILDS AFRO CUBAN BLUES BAND

12-Inch Singles

Number	Title (A Side/B Side)	Yr	NM
MIDSONG INT'L.			
❑ MD-10983	Oye Como Va (9:56)/Medley: Spanish Harlem-Dancin' to Spandisco	1977	12.00

45s

Number	Title (A Side/B Side)	Yr	NM
ROULETTE			
❑ 7172	Life and Death in G & A/ Bang Bang	1975	5.00
❑ 7180	Black Skin Blue Eyed Boys/ Ask Me	1975	5.00

Albums

Number	Title	Yr	NM
MIDSONG INT'L.			
❑ BKL1-2292	Spandisco	1977	10.00
ROULETTE			
❑ 3016	Out Among 'Em	1975	10.00

LOVE EXCHANGE, THE

45s

Number	Title (A Side/B Side)	Yr	NM
UPTOWN			
❑ 755	Swallow the Sun/Mellow Memory	1968	25.00

Albums

Number	Title	Yr	NM
TOWER			
❑ ST 5115 [S]	The Love Exchange	1968	25.00
❑ T 5115 [M]	The Love Exchange	1968	60.00

LOVE GENERATION, THE

45s

Number	Title (A Side/B Side)	Yr	NM
IMPERIAL			
❑ 66243	Groovy Summertime/Playin' on the Strings of the Wind	1967	8.00
❑ 66254	Meet Me at the Love-In/ She Touched Me	1967	8.00
❑ 66275	Maman (Mama)/W.C. Fields	1968	8.00
❑ 66289	Love and Sunshine/Magic Land	1968	8.00
❑ 66310	Montage from "How Sweet It Is" (I Know That You Know)/ Consciousness Expansion	1968	8.00
❑ 66336	Let the Good Time In/Catching Up on Fun	1968	8.00

Albums

Number	Title	Yr	NM
IMPERIAL			
❑ LP-9351 [M]	The Love Generation	1967	20.00
❑ LP-12351 [S]	The Love Generation	1967	20.00
❑ LP-12364	A Generation of Love	1968	20.00
❑ LP-12408	Montage	1968	20.00

LOVE NOTES, THE (1)

45s

Number	Title (A Side/B Side)	Yr	NM
HOLIDAY			
❑ 2605	United/Tonight	1957	20.00
—Flat (matte) label			
❑ 2605	United/Tonight	1957	60.00
—Glossy label			
❑ 2607	If I Could Make You Mine/ Don't Go	1957	40.00
LOST-NITE			
❑ 179	United/Tonight	196?	6.00
—Reissue			

LOVE NOTES, THE (2)

45s

Number	Title (A Side/B Side)	Yr	NM
IMPERIAL			
❑ 5254	Surrender Your Heart/ Get On My Train	1953	1200.
RAINBOW			
❑ 266	I'm Sorry/Sweet Lulu	1954	300.00
RIVIERA			
❑ 970	I'm Sorry/Sweet Lulu	1954	800.00
❑ 975	Since I Fell for You/ Don't Be No Fool	1954	1000.
—Authentic copies have a lavender (light purple) label, counterfeits have a pink label			

LOVE NOTES, THE (3)

45s

Number	Title (A Side/B Side)	Yr	NM
WILSHIRE			
❑ 200	Nancy/Our Songs of Love	1963	40.00
❑ 203	Gloria/The Mathematics of Love	1963	100.00

LOVE, PEACE AND HAPPINESS

Also see THE NEW BIRTH; THE NITE-LITERS.

45s

Number	Title (A Side/B Side)	Yr	NM
RCA VICTOR			
❑ 74-0402	Don't Blame the Young Folks for the Drug Society/You've Got to Be the One for Me	1970	6.00
❑ 74-0468	Message to the Establishment/ Love Is Far Stronger Than We	1971	5.00
❑ 74-0584	Strip Me Naked/Unborn Child	1971	5.00
❑ 74-0740	I Don't Want to Do Wrong/ Lonely Room	1972	5.00

Albums

Number	Title	Yr	NM
RCA VICTOR			
❑ LSP-4535	Love Is Stronger	1971	12.00
❑ LSP-4721	Here 'Tis	1972	12.00

LOVE POTION, THE

45s

Number	Title (A Side/B Side)	Yr	NM
KAPP			
❑ 979	This Love/Moby Binks	1969	8.00
TCB			
❑ 1601	This Love/Mr. Farouk	1968	15.00

LOVE SCULPTURE

DAVE EDMUNDS was in this group.

45s

Number	Title (A Side/B Side)	Yr	NM
PARROT			
❑ 335	Sabre Dance/Think of Love	1969	15.00
❑ 362	In the Land of the Few/Farandole	1970	15.00

Albums

Number	Title	Yr	NM
EMI AMERICA			
❑ SQ-17208	Blues Helping	1986	12.00
—Reissue of Rare Earth LP			
PARROT			
❑ PAS 71035	Forms and Feelings	1970	25.00
RARE EARTH			
❑ RS-505	Blues Helping	1969	40.00

LOVE SOCIETY, THE

45s

Number	Title (A Side/B Side)	Yr	NM
MERCURY			
❑ 73130	America/Wanda	1970	15.00
RCA VICTOR			
❑ 74-0257	Don't Worry Baby/You Know How I Feel (And Why)	1969	10.00
SCEPTER			
❑ 12223	Without You/Do You Wanna Dance	1968	12.00
❑ 12236	Tobacco Road/Drops of Rain	1969	12.00

LOVE UNLIMITED

12-Inch Singles

Number	Title (A Side/B Side)	Yr	NM
UNLIMITED GOLD			
❑ 1410	High Steppin', Hip Dressin' Fella (You Got It Together)/ (Instrumental)	1979	12.00

45s

Number	Title (A Side/B Side)	Yr	NM
MCA			
❑ 40009	Fragile/I'll Be Yours Forever	1973	6.00
20TH CENTURY			
❑ 2025	Oh Love, Well We Finally Made It/Yes, We Finally Made It	1973	5.00
❑ 2062	It May Be Winter Outside (But In My Heart It's Spring)/ It's Winter Again	1973	5.00
❑ 2082	Under the Influence of Love/ (Instrumental)	1974	5.00
❑ 2110	People of Tomorrow Are the Children of Today/ So Nice to Hear	1974	5.00
❑ 2141	I Belong to You/And Only You	1974	5.00
❑ 2183	Share a Little Love in Your Heart/I Love You So, Never Gonna Let You Go	1975	5.00
UNI			
❑ 55319	Walkin' in the Rain with the One I Love/I Should Have Known	1972	6.00
❑ 55342	Is It Really True Boy — Is It Really Me?/Another Chance	1972	6.00
❑ 55349	Are You Really Sure/ Another Chance	1972	6.00
UNLIMITED GOLD			
❑ 1409	High Steppin', Hip Dressin' Fella (You Got It Together)/ (Instrumental)	1979	5.00
❑ 1412	I'm So Glad That I'm a Woman/ Gotta Be Where You Are	1980	5.00
❑ 1417	If You Want Me, Say It/ When I'm In Your Arms, Everything's Okay	1980	5.00
❑ 7001	I Did It for Love/(Instrumental)	1977	5.00

Albums

Number	Title	Yr	NM
MCA			
❑ 181	Love Unlimited	1973	12.00
—Reissue of Uni 73131			
❑ 316	Under the Influence of...	1973	—
—Canceled; issued on 20th Century 414			
20TH CENTURY			
❑ T-414	Under the Influence of...	1973	10.00
❑ T-443	In Heat	1974	10.00
UNI			
❑ 73131	Love Unlimited	1972	15.00
UNLIMITED GOLD			
❑ 101	He's All I Got	1977	10.00
❑ JZ 36130	Love Is Back	1979	10.00

LOVE UNLIMITED ORCHESTRA

12-Inch Singles

Number	Title (A Side/B Side)	Yr	NM
20TH CENTURY			
❑ TCD-61	Theme from King Kong/ Blues Concerto	1976	15.00

L

Number | Title (A Side/B Side) | Yr | NM

❑ TCD-66 Don't You Know How Much I Love You/Hey Look at Me, I'm in Love 1978 15.00

UNLIMITED GOLD
❑ 1406 Jamaican Girl/I'm in the Mood 1979 12.00
❑ 1414 Young America/Freeway Flyer 1980 12.00
❑ 02135 Lift Your Voice and Say (United We Can Live in Peace Today)/My Fantasies 1981 10.00
❑ 02479 Welcome Aboard/Strange 1981 10.00
❑ 02636 Night Life in the City/Wind 1981 10.00
❑ 03882 My Laboratory Is Ready for You/Goodbye Concerto 1983 10.00

45s

20TH CENTURY
❑ 2069 Love's Theme/Sweet Moments 1973 5.00
❑ 2090 Rhapsody in White/Barry's Theme 1974 5.00
❑ 2107 Theme from "Together Brothers"/Find the Man Brothers 1974 5.00
❑ 2145 Baby Blues/What a Groove 1974 5.00
❑ 2162 Satin Soul/Just Living It Up 1975 5.00
❑ 2197 Forever in Love/Only You Can Make Me Blue 1975 5.00
❑ 2281 Midnight Groove/It's Only What I Feel 1976 5.00
❑ 2301 My Sweet Summer Suite/Just Living It Up 1976 5.00
❑ 2325 Theme from King Kong (Pt. 1)/Theme from King Kong (Pt. 2) 1977 5.00
❑ 2348 Brazilian Love Song/My Sweet Summer Suite 1977 5.00
❑ 2364 Whisper Softly/Hey Look at Me, I'm in Love 1978 5.00
❑ 2367 Don't You Know How Much I Love You/Hey Look at Me, I'm in Love 1978 5.00
❑ 2399 Theme from "Superman"/Theme from "Shaft" 1978 5.00

UNLIMITED GOLD
❑ 1405 Jamaican Girl/I'm in the Mood 1979 5.00
❑ 1413 Young America/Freeway Flyer 1980 5.00
❑ 1421 I Wanna Boogie and Woogie with You/I'm in the Mood 1980 5.00
❑ 1423 Vieni Qua Bella Mi/Bayou 1980 5.00
❑ 02134 Lift Your Voice and Say (United We Can Live in Peace Today)/My Fantasies 1981 4.00
❑ 02478 Welcome Aboard/Strange 1981 4.00
❑ 02635 Night Life in the City/Wind 1981 4.00
❑ 03881 My Laboratory Is Ready for You/Goodbye Concerto 1983 4.00

Albums

20TH CENTURY
❑ T-101 Together Brothers 1974 12.00
❑ T-433 Rhapsody in White 1974 10.00
❑ T-458 White Gold 1974 10.00
❑ T-480 Music Maestro Please 1975 10.00
❑ T-517 My Sweet Summer Suite 1976 10.00
❑ T-554 My Musical Bouquet 1978 10.00
❑ T-582 Movie Themes 1978 10.00

UNLIMITED GOLD
❑ FZ 37425 Welcome Aboard 1981 10.00
❑ FZ 38366 Rise 1983 10.00

LOVECRAFT See H.P. LOVECRAFT.

LOVEJOYS, THE

45s

RED BIRD
❑ 10-004 Payin'/It's Mighty Nice 1964 30.00

LOVELITES, THE

45s

BANDERA
❑ 2515 I Found Me a Lover/You Better Stop It 1967 15.00

LOVENOTES, THE See HONEY LOVE AND THE LOVE NOTES.

LOVERBOY Includes members of STREETHEART and MOXY. Includes members of STREETHEART and MOXY.

12-Inch Singles

COLUMBIA
❑ CAS 2223 [DJ] Dangerous (3:36) (same on both sides) 1985 7.00
❑ CAS 2251 [DJ] This Could Be the Night (Edit 4:14) (LP Version 4:56) 1985 8.00

45s

COLUMBIA
❑ 02068 The Kid Is Hot Tonite/Teenage Overdose 1981 4.00
❑ 02068 [PS] The Kid Is Hot Tonite/Teenage Overdose 1981 4.00
❑ 02589 Working for the Weekend/Emotional 1981 4.00
❑ 02589 [PS] Working for the Weekend/Emotional 1981 4.00
❑ 02814 When It's Over/It's Your Life 1982 4.00
❑ 02814 [PS] When It's Over/It's Your Life 1982 4.00
❑ 03054 Lucky Ones/Gangs in the Streets 1982 4.00
❑ 03108 Turn Me Loose/The Kid Is Hot Tonite 1982 3.00
—Reissue
❑ 38-03346 Jump/Take Me to the Top 1982 4.00
❑ 38-03346 [PS] Jump/Take Me to the Top 1982 4.00
❑ 03866 Working for the Weekend/When It's Over 1983 3.00
—Reissue
❑ 38-03941 Hot Girls in Love/Meltdown 1983 3.00
❑ 38-03941 [PS] Hot Girls in Love/Meltdown 1983 3.00
❑ 38-04096 Queen of the Broken Hearts/Chance of a Lifetime 1983 3.00
❑ 38-04096 [PS] Queen of the Broken Hearts/Chance of a Lifetime 1983 4.00
❑ 05569 Lovin' Every Minute of It/Bullet in the Chamber 1985 3.00
❑ 05569 [PS] Lovin' Every Minute of It/Bullet in the Chamber 1985 3.00
❑ 05711 Dangerous/Too Much Too Soon 1985 3.00
❑ 05711 [PS] Dangerous/Too Much Too Soon 1985 3.00
❑ 05765 This Could Be the Night/It's Your Life 1986 3.00
❑ 05765 [PS] This Could Be the Night/It's Your Life 1986 3.00
❑ 05867 Lead a Double Life/Steal the Thunder 1986 3.00
❑ 05867 [PS] Lead a Double Life/Steal the Thunder 1986 3.00
❑ 06178 Heaven in Your Eyes/Friday Night 1986 3.00
❑ 06178 [PS] Heaven in Your Eyes/Friday Night 1986 3.00
❑ 07324 Notorious/Wildside 1987 3.00
❑ 07324 [PS] Notorious/Wildside 1987 3.00
❑ 07652 Love Will Rise Again/Read My Lips 1987 3.00
❑ 11421 Turn Me Loose/Prissy Prissy 1981 5.00
❑ 11421 [DJ] Turn Me Loose (Long)/Turn Me Loose (Short) 1981 8.00
❑ 11421 [DJ] Turn Me Loose (Long)/Turn Me Loose (Short) 1981 8.00

Albums

COLUMBIA
❑ A2S 1256 [(2)DJ] Loverboy Live from Dayton, Ohio 1981 20.00
—Promo-only release; three sides have music, the fourth side has the band's autographs etched into the record
❑ JC 36762 Loverboy 1980 8.00
❑ FC 37638 Get Lucky 1981 8.00
❑ QC 38703 Keep It Up 1983 8.00
❑ FC 39953 Lovin' Every Minute of It 1985 8.00
❑ OC 40893 Wildside 1987 8.00
❑ OC 45411 Big Ones 1989 12.00

LOVERS, THE (1) Husband-and-wife R&B duo.

45s

ALADDIN
❑ 3419 Tell Me/Love Bug Bit Me 1958 40.00

IMPERIAL
❑ 5845 Darling It's Wonderful/I Want to Be Loved 1962 20.00
❑ 5960 Tell Me/Let's Elope 1963 20.00
❑ 66055 Darling It's Wonderful/I Want to Be Loved 1964 15.00

LAMP
❑ 2005 Darling It's Wonderful/Gotta Whole Lot of Livin' to Do 1957 50.00
❑ 2013 I Wanna Be Loved/Let's Elope 1957 50.00
❑ 2018 Tell Me/Love Bug Bit Me 1958 50.00

POST
❑ 10007 Darling It's Wonderful/Gotta Whole Lot of Livin' to Do 1963 15.00

LOVERS, THE (2)

45s

AGON
❑ 1011 Caravan of Lonely Men/In My Tenement 1965 25.00

GATE
❑ 501 Someone/Do This for Me 1965 150.00

PHILIPS
❑ 40353 Someone/Do This for Me 1966 30.00

LOVERS, THE (3)

45s

CASINO
❑ 103 Let's/Big Axe 1958 20.00

LOVERS, THE (4)

45s

MARLIN
❑ 3313 Discomania (Part 1)/Discomania (Part 2) 1977 5.00

LOVERS, THE (U) These could be groups (1) or (2).

45s

CHECKER
❑ 1100 It's Too Late/Security 1965 40.00

DECCA
❑ 29862 Don't Touch Me/Let Me Be the First to Know 1956 40.00

KELLER
❑ 101 Party Line/Strange As It Seems 1961 40.00

LOVETONES, THE

45s

LOVE-TONE
❑ 101 You Can Tell Me That This Is Christmas/When I Asked My Love 1961 20.00

PLUS
❑ 108 Talk to an Angel/Take It Easy, Baby 1956 500.00

LOVETT, LEE

Albums

STRAND
❑ SL-1055 [M] Jazz Dance Party 1962 20.00
❑ SLS-1055 [S] Jazz Dance Party 1962 25.00
❑ SL-1059 [M] Misty 1962 20.00
❑ SLS-1059 [S] Misty 1962 25.00

WYNNE
❑ WLP-108 [M] Jazz Dance Party 195? 30.00

LOVETT, LYLE

45s

MCA
❑ 52818 Farther Down the Line/Why I Don't Know 1986 3.00
❑ 52818 [DJ] Farther Down the Line (same on both sides) 1986 8.00
—Green vinyl
❑ 52818 [DJ] Farther Down the Line (same on both sides) 1986 10.00
—Promo only on green vinyl
❑ 79025 Here I Am/Nobody Knows Me 1990 3.00

MCA NASHVILLE
❑ 088 172218 7 San Antonio Girl/Cowboy Man 2001 3.00

MCA/CURB
❑ 52951 Cowboy Man/The Waltzing Fool 1986 3.00
❑ 52951 [DJ] Cowboy Man (same on both sides) 1986 8.00
—Clear vinyl
❑ 52951 [DJ] Cowboy Man (same on both sides) 1986 15.00
—Promo only on clear vinyl
❑ 53030 God Will/An Acceptable Level of Ecstasy (The Wedding Song) 1987 3.00
❑ 53030 [DJ] God Will (same on both sides) 1987 10.00
—Promo only on blue vinyl
❑ 53102 Why I Don't Know/If I Were the Man You Wanted 1987 3.00
❑ 53157 Give Back My Heart/Simple Song 1987 3.00
❑ 53246 She's No Lady/Pontiac 1988 3.00
❑ 53316 I Loved You Yesterday/L.A. County 1988 3.00
❑ 53401 If I Had a Boat/Black and Blue 1988 3.00
❑ 53471 I Married Her Just Because She Looks Like You/If I Had a Boat 1988 3.00
❑ 53611 Stand By Your Man/Wallisville Road 1989 3.00
❑ 53650 Nobody Knows Me/Here I Am 1989 3.00
❑ 53703 If I Were the Man You Wanted/Cryin' Shame 1989 3.00

SBK
❑ S7-56996 Stand By Your Man/The Crying Game 1993 4.00
—B-side by Boy George; black vinyl
❑ S7-56996 Stand By Your Man/The Crying Game 1993 6.00
—B-side by Boy George; red vinyl

Albums

MCA/CURB
❑ 5748 Lyle Lovett 1986 10.00
❑ 17355 [EP] Not Exactly Mr. Showbiz 1987 15.00
—Promo-only five-song EP with special sleeve
❑ 42028 Pontiac 1988 10.00
❑ 42263 Lyle Lovett And His Large Band 1989 10.00
❑ R 100932 Lyle Lovett And His Large Band 1989 12.00
—BMG Direct Marketing edition

Except when noted otherwise, VG = 25% of NM, and VG+ = 50% of NM. (Example: VG = $2.00, VG+ = $4.00 and NM = $8.00.)

Number	Title (A Side/B Side)	Yr	NM
❑ R 133603	Lyle Lovett	1986	12.00
—RCA Music Service edition			
❑ R 153258	Pontiac	1988	12.00
—BMG Direct Marketing edition			

LOVICH, LENE

12-Inch Singles

CBS SPECIAL PRODUCTS

Number	Title (A Side/B Side)	Yr	NM
❑ P 20135	Lucky Number/New Toy	1987	12.00
PATHFINDER			
❑ PTF 8009	Wonderland (4 versions)	1989	6.00
STIFF/EPIC			
❑ 03342	It's You, Only You (Remix)/ It's You, Only You (Dub)	1982	8.00
❑ 03799	Blue Hotel (Dance Mix)/ Blue Hotel	1983	10.00

45s

STIFF/EPIC

Number	Title (A Side/B Side)	Yr	NM
❑ 03499	It's You, Only You (Mein Schmerz)/Blue	1983	5.00
❑ 03863	Blue Hotel/Savages	1983	5.00
❑ 50725	Lucky Number/Lucky Number (Slavic Dance Version)	1979	6.00
❑ 50767	Home/The Writing on the Wall	1979	6.00
❑ 50866	The Night/Monkey Talk (Live)	1980	6.00

Albums

STIFF/EPIC

Number	Title (A Side/B Side)	Yr	NM
❑ JE 36102	Stateless	1979	12.00
❑ JE 36102	Stateless	1979	20.00
—Red vinyl			
❑ JE 36308	Flex	1980	12.00
❑ 5E 37452 [EP]	New Toy	1981	15.00
❑ ARE 38399	No Man's Land	1983	10.00

LOVIN' SPOONFUL, THE Also see JOE BUTLER; JOHN SEBASTIAN; ZALMAN YANOVSKY.

45s

KAMA SUTRA

Number	Title (A Side/B Side)	Yr	NM
❑ 201	Do You Believe in Magic/ On the Road Again	1965	8.00
—Mostly yellow label with "Kama Sutra" in black			
❑ 201	Do You Believe in Magic/On the Road Again	1965	10.00
—Mostly yellow label with "Kama Sutra" in red			
❑ 201	Do You Believe in Magic/ On the Road Again	1965	15.00
—Mostly red-orange label			
❑ 205	You Didn't Have to Be So Nice/ My Gal	1965	8.00
—Mostly yellow label with "Kama Sutra" in black			
❑ 205	You Didn't Have to Be So Nice/ My Gal	1965	10.00
—Mostly yellow label with "Kama Sutra" in red			
❑ 205	You Didn't Have to Be So Nice/ My Gal	1965	12.00
—Mostly red-orange label			
❑ 205 [PS]	You Didn't Have to Be So Nice/ My Gal	1965	15.00
❑ 208	Daydream/Night Owl Blues	1966	10.00
—Mostly yellow label with "Kama Sutra" in black			
❑ 208	Daydream/Night Owl Blues	1966	12.00
—Mostly yellow label with "Kama Sutra" in red			
❑ 208	Daydream/Night Owl Blues	1966	15.00
—Mostly red-orange label			
❑ 208 [PS]	Daydream/Night Owl Blues	1966	15.00
❑ 209	Did You Ever Have to Make Up Your Mind/Didn't Want to Have to Do It	1966	10.00
❑ 209 [PS]	Did You Ever Have to Make Up Your Mind/Didn't Want to Have to Do It	1966	15.00
❑ 211	Summer in the City/ Butchie's Tune	1966	10.00
❑ 211 [PS]	Summer in the City/ Butchie's Tune	1966	15.00
❑ 216	Rain on the Roof/Pow	1966	10.00
❑ 216 [PS]	Rain on the Roof/Pow	1966	15.00
❑ 219	Nashville Cats/Full Measure	1966	10.00
❑ 219 [PS]	Nashville Cats/Full Measure	1966	15.00
❑ 220	Darling Be Home Soon/ Darlin' Companion	1967	10.00
❑ 220 [PS]	Darling Be Home Soon/ Darlin' Companion	1967	15.00
❑ 225	Six O'Clock/The Finale	1967	10.00
❑ 225 [PS]	Six O'Clock/The Finale	1967	15.00
❑ 231	Lonely (Amy's Theme)/ You're a Big Boy Now	1967	15.00
❑ 239	She Is Still a Mystery/ Only Pretty, What a Pity	1967	10.00
❑ 239 [PS]	She Is Still a Mystery/ Only Pretty, What a Pity	1967	15.00
❑ 241	Money/Close Your Eyes	1967	8.00
❑ 250	Never Going Back/Forever	1968	8.00
❑ 251	Revelation Revolution '69/ Run with You	1968	8.00
❑ 255	Me About You/Amazing Air	1968	8.00

Lene Lovich, *Stateless*, Stiff/Epic JE 36102, 1979, **$12.**

Number	Title (A Side/B Side)	Yr	NM
❑ 551	Summer in the City/You and Me and Rain on the Roof	1972	6.00
❑ 551 [PS]	Summer in the City/You and Me and Rain on the Roof	1972	15.00
—Sleeve evidently is promo only			
❑ 608 [DJ]	Daydream (mono/stereo)	1976	6.00
—Stock copy not known to exist			

7-Inch Extended Plays

KAMA SUTRA

Number	Title (A Side/B Side)	Yr	NM
❑ EK-1 [DJ]	It's Not Time Now/Nashville Cats//Henry Thomas/ Darlin' Companion	1967	20.00
❑ EK-1 [PS]	The Lovin' Spoonful	1967	50.00

Albums

ACCORD

Number	Title (A Side/B Side)	Yr	NM
❑ SN-7196	Distant Echoes	1981	10.00
BUDDAH			
❑ BDM-5706	The Best of the Lovin' Spoonful	197?	12.00
❑ BLB6-8339	The Best of the Lovin' Spoonful	198?	10.00
—Reissue of 5706			
51 WEST			
❑ Q 16023	... So Nice	1979	10.00
KAMA SUTRA			
❑ KLPS-750-2 [(2)]	24 Karat Hits	1968	20.00
❑ KSBS-2011	The John Sebastian Song Book	1970	15.00
❑ KSBS-2013	The Very Best of the Lovin' Spoonful	1970	15.00
❑ KSBS-2029	Once Upon a Time	1971	15.00
❑ KSBS-2608 [(2)]	The Best...Lovin' Spoonful	1976	20.00
❑ KLP-8050 [M]	Do You Believe in Magic	1965	20.00
❑ KLPS-8050 [S]	Do You Believe in Magic	1965	30.00
❑ KLP-8051 [M]	Daydream	1966	20.00
❑ KLPS-8051 [S]	Daydream	1966	30.00
❑ KLP-8053 [M]	What's Up, Tiger Lily?	1966	20.00
❑ KLPS-8053 [S]	What's Up, Tiger Lily?	1966	30.00
❑ KLP-8054 [M]	Hums of the Lovin' Spoonful	1966	20.00
❑ KLPS-8054 [S]	Hums of the Lovin' Spoonful	1966	30.00
❑ KLP-8056 [M]	The Best of the Lovin' Spoonful	1967	15.00
—Came with four bonus photos of the band, which are priced separately			
❑ KLP/S-8056	The Best of the Lovin' Spoonful Bonus Photos (4)	1967	10.00
❑ KLPS-8056 [S]	The Best of the Lovin' Spoonful	1967	15.00
—Came with four bonus photos of the band, which are priced separately			
❑ KLP-8058 [M]	You're a Big Boy Now	1967	20.00
❑ KLPS-8058 [S]	You're a Big Boy Now	1967	20.00
❑ KLP-8061 [M]	Everything Playing	1968	30.00
❑ KLPS-8061 [S]	Everything Playing	1968	20.00
❑ KLP-8064 [M]	The Best of the Lovin' Spoonful, Vol. 2	1968	50.00
❑ KLPS-8064 [S]	The Best of the Lovin' Spoonful, Vol. 2	1968	20.00
❑ KLPS-8073	Revelation: Revolution '69	1969	25.00
❑ ST-90597 [S]	Do You Believe in Magic	1965	40.00
—Capitol Record Club edition			
❑ T-90597 [M]	Do You Believe in Magic	1965	30.00
—Capitol Record Club edition			
❑ ST-90675 [S]	Daydream	1966	40.00
—Capitol Record Club edition			
❑ T-90675 [M]	Daydream	1966	25.00
—Capitol Record Club edition			
❑ ST-90988 [S]	Hums of the Lovin' Spoonful	1966	40.00
—Capitol Record Club edition			
❑ KAO-91102 [M]	The Best of the Lovin' Spoonful	1967	25.00
—Capitol Record Club edition			
❑ SKAO-91102 [S]	The Best of the Lovin' Spoonful	1967	20.00
—Capitol Record Club edition			
❑ ST-91198 [S]	You're a Big Boy Now	1967	25.00
—Capitol Record Club edition			
KOALA			
❑ KO 14221	Day Dream	1979	10.00
PAIR			
❑ PDL2-1200 [(2)]	The Best of the Lovin' Spoonful	1986	12.00
RHINO			
❑ RNLP-114	The Best of the Lovin' Spoonful, Vol. 2	1985	10.00

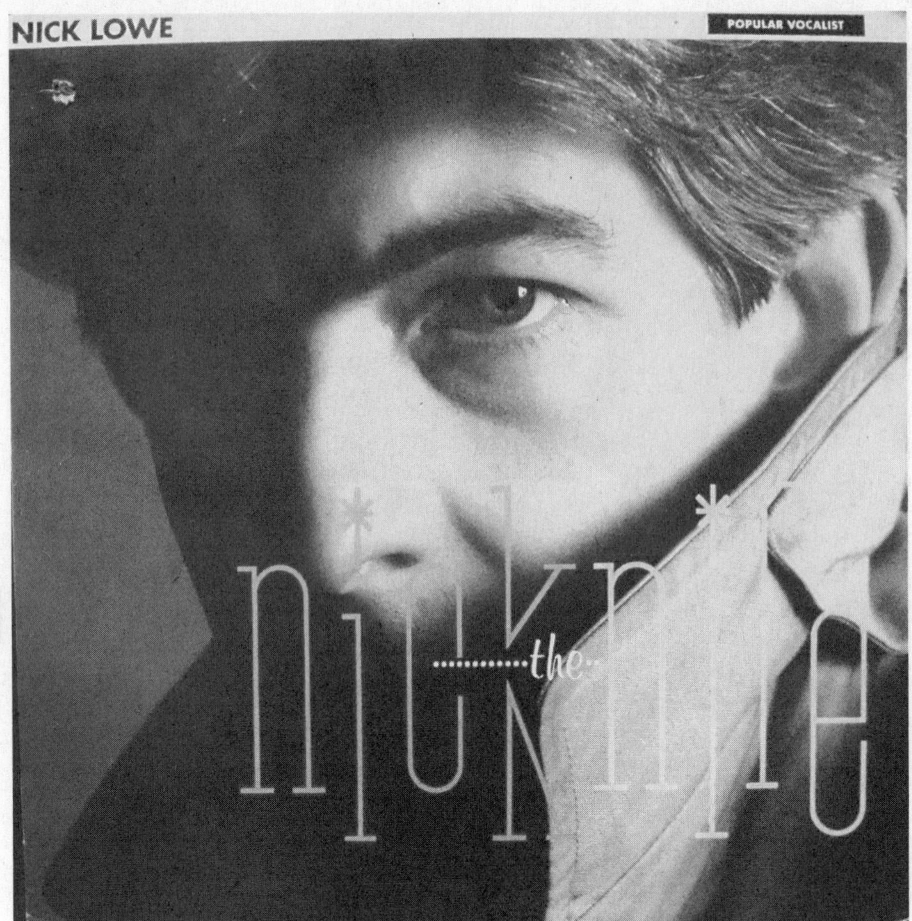

Nick Lowe, *Nick The Knife*, Columbia FC 37932, 1982, **$12.**

Number	Title (A Side/B Side)	Yr	NM
SUNDAZED			
❑ LP 5159	Do You Believe in Magic	2002	15.00
—Reissue on 180-gram vinyl			
❑ LP 5160	Daydream	2002	15.00
—Reissue on 180-gram vinyl			
❑ LP 5166	Hums of the Lovin' Spoonful	2003	15.00
—Reissue on 180-gram vinyl			

LOWE, JIM

Number	Title (A Side/B Side)	Yr	NM
45s			
BUDDAH			
❑ 44	Michael J. Polalrd for President/ The Ol' Racetrack	1968	6.00
DECCA			
❑ 31153	Someone Else's Arms/ Man of the Cloth	1960	10.00
❑ 31198	That Do Make It Nice/ Two Sides to Every Story	1961	10.00
DOT			
❑ 15381	Close the Door/Nuevo Laredo	1955	12.00
❑ 15407	Maybellene/Rene La Rue	1955	12.00
❑ 15429	John Jacob Jingleheimer Smith/St. James Avenue	1955	12.00
❑ 15456	The Sixty-Four Thousand Dollar Question/ Blue Suede Shoes	1956	12.00
❑ 15486	The Green Door/(The Story of) The Little Man in Chinatown	1956	12.00
—Second pressings have black labels			
❑ 15486	The Green Door/(The Story of) The Little Man in Chinatown	1956	15.00
—Originals have maroon labels			
❑ 15525	By You, By You, By You/ I Feel the Beat	1957	10.00
❑ 15569	Four Walls/Talkin' to the Blues	1957	12.00
❑ 15611	From a Jack to a King/Slow Train	1957	10.00
❑ 15665	Rick-a-Chickie/The Bright Light	1957	10.00
❑ 15693	Kewpie Doll/The Lady from Johannesburg	1958	10.00
❑ 15753	Take Us To Your President/ Later On Tonight	1958	10.00
❑ 15832	Chapel Bells on Chapel Hill/ Ja, Ja, Ja	1958	10.00
❑ 15869	Play Number Eleven/ Come Away from Her Arms	1958	10.00
❑ 15954	I'm Movin' On/Without You	1959	10.00
❑ 16046	He'll Have to Go/ Dress Rehearsal	1960	10.00
❑ 16074	The Midnight Ride of Paul Revere/A Tomorrow That Never Comes	1960	10.00
❑ 16636	Addis Ababa/Have You Ever Been Lonely	1964	6.00
MERCURY			
❑ 70163	Gambler's Guitar/The Martins and the Coys	1953	20.00
❑ 70265	Santa Claus Rides a Strawberry Roan/Love in Both Directions	1953	20.00
❑ 70319	Goodbye Little Sweetheart/ River Boat	1954	20.00
❑ 71016	Prince of Peace/Santa Claus Rides a Strawberry Roan	1956	15.00
SIGNATURE			
❑ 75001	Green Door/San Francisco Bay	197?	5.00
20TH CENTURY FOX			
❑ 426	Hootenanny Granny/These Bones Gonna Rise Again	1963	8.00
UNITED ARTISTS			
❑ 874	Mr. Moses/Make Your Back Strong	1965	6.00
❑ 50124	Gambler's Guitar/Blotson Bottom	1967	6.00
7-Inch Extended Plays			
DOT			
❑ DEP 1061	Rainbow/Love Ya//The Crossing/ Honky Tonk Rock	1957	15.00
❑ DEP 1061 [PS]	Rainbow	1957	15.00
Albums			
DOT			
❑ DLP-3051 [M]	The Green Door	1956	150.00
❑ DLP-3114 [M]	Wicked Women	1958	100.00
❑ DLP-3681 [M]	Songs They Sing Behind the Green Door	1965	25.00
❑ DLP-25881 [S]	Songs They Sing Behind the Green Door	1965	30.00
MERCURY			
❑ MG-20246 [M]	The Door of Fame	1957	150.00

LOWE, NICK Also see BRINSLEY SCHWARZ; DAVE EDMUNDS; KIPPINGTON LODGE; ROCKPILE. Also see BRINSLEY SCHWARZ; DAVE EDMUNDS; KIPPINGTON LODGE; ROCKPILE.

Number	Title (A Side/B Side)	Yr	NM
12-Inch Singles			
COLUMBIA			
❑ AS 921 [DJ]	Without Love (same on both sides)	198?	8.00
—Nick Lowe with Johnny Cash and Dave Edmunds			
❑ AS921 [DJ]	Without Love (same on both sides)	198?	8.00
—Nick Lowe with Johnny Cash and Dave Edmunds			
❑ AS 1626 [DJ]	Raging Eyes (same on both sides)	1983	5.00
❑ AS1626 [DJ]	Raging Eyes (same on both sides)	1983	5.00
❑ AS 1876 [DJ]	Half a Boy and Half a Man (same on both sides)	1984	5.00
❑ AS1876 [DJ]	Half a Boy and Half a Man (same on both sides)	1984	5.00
❑ CAS 2171 [DJ]	I Knew the Bride (When She Used to Rock and Roll) (same on both sides)	1985	8.00
❑ CAS2171 [DJ]	I Knew the Bride (When She Used to Rock and Roll) (same on both sides)	1985	8.00
❑ CAS 2923 [DJ]	Lover's Jamboree (same on both sides)	1988	5.00
❑ CAS2923 [DJ]	Lover's Jamboree (same on both sides)	1988	5.00
45s			
COLUMBIA			
❑ 02813	Stick It Where the Sun Don't Shine/My Heart Hurts	1982	3.00
❑ 3837 [DJ]	Cool Reaction (same on both sides)	1983	3.00
❑ 03837	Wish You Were Here/How Do You Talk to An Angel	1983	3.00
❑ 03837 [DJ]	Cool Reaction (same on both sides)	1983	3.00
❑ 04486	Half a Boy and Half a Man/ Awesome	1984	3.00
❑ 05570	I Knew the Bride (When She Used to Rock and Roll)/ Long Walk Back	1985	3.00
—Label credit: Nick Lowe And His Cowboy Outfit			
❑ 07734	Lovers Jamboree/ Crying in My Sleep	1988	3.00
❑ 10734	So It Goes/Heart of the City (Live)	1978	5.00
❑ 10844	(I Love the Sound of) Breaking Glass/Endless Sleep	1978	5.00
❑ 11018	Cruel to Be Kind/Endless Grey Ribbon	1979	5.00
❑ 11131	Switch Board Susan/Basin Street	1979	5.00
❑ 33398	Cruel to Be Kind/So It Goes	198?	3.00
—"Hall of Fame" reissue			
Albums			
COLUMBIA			
❑ AS 1400 [DJ]	An Interrogation of Nick Lowe	1990	20.00
—Promo-only interview album			
❑ AS1400 [DJ]	An Interrogation of Nick Lowe	1990	25.00
—Promo-only interview album			
❑ JC 35529	Pure Pop for Now People	1978	20.00
❑ PC 35529	Pure Pop for Now People	198?	8.00
—Budget-line reissue			
❑ JC 36087	Labour of Lust	1979	10.00
❑ PC 36087	Labour of Lust	198?	8.00
—Budget-line reissue			
❑ FC 37932	Nick the Knife	1982	12.00
❑ PC 37932	Nick the Knife	198?	8.00
—Budget-line reissue			
❑ FC 38589	The Abominable Showman	1983	12.00
❑ PC 38589	The Abominable Showman	1986	8.00
—Budget-line reissue			
❑ FC 39371	Nick Lowe and His Cowboy Outfit	1984	12.00
❑ PC 39371	Nick Lowe and His Cowboy Outfit	1986	8.00
—Budget-line reissue			
❑ FC 39958	The Rose of England	1985	12.00
❑ FC 40381	Pinker and Prouder Than Previous	1988	14.00
REPRISE			
❑ 26132	Party of One	1990	12.00

LOWE, VIRGINIA

Number	Title (A Side/B Side)	Yr	NM
45s			
MELBA			
❑ 107	I'm in Love with Elvis Presley/ Empty Feeling	1956	50.00

Except when noted otherwise, VG = 25% of NM, and VG+ = 50% of NM. (Example: VG = $2.00, VG+ = $4.00 and NM = $8.00.)

LRY

Albums

CONGRESS OF THE CROW

Number	Title (A Side/B Side)	Yr	NM
❑ 8031002	The LRY Record	1968	200.00

LUCAS, AL

45s

CHALLENGE

Number	Title (A Side/B Side)	Yr	NM
❑ 59042	She's My Baby/Got the Ring	1959	60.00
❑ 59050	Sweet Tooth for My Baby Ruth/ Always	1959	40.00

LUCAS, JIMMY

45s

HIT

Number	Title (A Side/B Side)	Yr	NM
❑ 19	Roses Are Red (My Love)/Gravy (For My Mashed Potatoes)	1962	8.00

—B-side by Peggy Gaines

LUCAS, MITCH

45s

HIT

Number	Title (A Side/B Side)	Yr	NM
❑ 31	Patches/You Beat Me to the Punch	1962	8.00

—B-side by Alpha Zoe

LUDDEN, ALLEN

Albums

RCA VICTOR

Number	Title (A Side/B Side)	Yr	NM
❑ LPM-2934 [M]	Allen Ludden Sings His Favorite Songs	1964	20.00
❑ LSP-2934 [S]	Allen Ludden Sings His Favorite Songs	1964	25.00

LUKE, ROBIN

45s

BERTRAM INTERNATIONAL

Number	Title (A Side/B Side)	Yr	NM
❑ 206	Susie Darlin'/Living's Loving You	1958	60.00
❑ 206 [PS]	Susie Darlin'/Living's Loving You	1958	100.00
❑ 208	My Girl/Chicka Chicka Honey	1958	30.00
❑ 210	Strollin' Blues/You Can't Stop Me from Dreaming	1959	30.00
❑ 212	Five Minutes More/Who's Gonna Hold Your Hand	1959	30.00

DOT

Number	Title (A Side/B Side)	Yr	NM
❑ 15781	Susie Darlin'/Living's Loving You	1958	25.00
❑ 15839	My Girl/Chicka Chicka Honey	1958	20.00
❑ 15899	Strollin' Blues/You Can't Stop Me from Dreaming	1959	20.00
❑ 15959	Five Minutes More/Who's Gonna Hold Your Hand	1959	20.00
❑ 16001	Make Me a Dreamer/ Walkin' in the Moonlight	1959	20.00
❑ 16040	Bad Boy/School Bus Love Affair	1960	20.00
❑ 16096	Everlovin'/Well Oh Well Oh	1960	20.00
❑ 16096 [PS]	Everlovin'/Well Oh Well Oh	1960	60.00
❑ 16170	So Alone/All Because of You	1960	20.00
❑ 16229	Part of a Fool/Poor Little Rich Boy	1961	15.00
❑ 16366	Foggin' Up the Windows/Time	1962	15.00

—With Roberta Shore

INTERNATIONAL

Number	Title (A Side/B Side)	Yr	NM
❑ 206	Susie Darlin'/Living's Loving You	1958	1000.

—Light blue label

7-Inch Extended Plays

DOT

Number	Title (A Side/B Side)	Yr	NM
❑ DEP-1092	Susie Darlin'/Bad Boy// Won't You Please Be Mine/ Chicka Chicka Honey	1958	400.00
❑ DEP-1092 [PS]	Susie Darlin'	1958	400.00

LUKE THE DRIFTER

See HANK WILLIAMS.

LUKE THE DRIFTER, JR.

See HANK WILLIAMS, JR.

LULU

12-Inch Singles

SBK

Number	Title (A Side/B Side)	Yr	NM
❑ 19777	Independence (5 versions)	1993	8.00

45s

ALFA

Number	Title (A Side/B Side)	Yr	NM
❑ 7006	I Could Never Miss You (More Than I Do)/ Dance to the Feeling	1981	4.00
❑ 7006 [PS]	I Could Never Miss You (More Than I Do)/ Dance to the Feeling	1981	5.00

—With Lulu wearing a spotted headband

Number	Title (A Side/B Side)	Yr	NM
❑ 7006 [PS]	I Could Never Miss You (More Than I Do)/ Dance to the Feeling	1981	6.00

—With Lulu not wearing a headband (original)

Number	Title (A Side/B Side)	Yr	NM
❑ 7011	If I Were You/You Win, I Lose	1981	4.00
❑ 7011 [PS]	If I Were You/You Win, I Lose	1981	5.00
❑ 7021	Who's Foolin' Who/ You Win, I Lose	1982	4.00

ATCO

Number	Title (A Side/B Side)	Yr	NM
❑ 6722	Oh Me Oh My (I'm a Fool for You Baby)/Sweep Around Your Own Back Door	1969	8.00
❑ 6749	Hum a Song (From Your Heart)/ Where's Eddie	1970	6.00
❑ 6761	Good Day Sunshine/ After the Feeling Is Gone	1970	6.00
❑ 6774	Melody Fair/To the Other Woman	1970	6.00
❑ 6819	Goodbye My Love, Goodbye/ Everybody's Got to Clap	1971	6.00
❑ 6885	It Takes a Real Man/You Ain't Wrong, You Just Ain't Right	1972	6.00

CHELSEA

Number	Title (A Side/B Side)	Yr	NM
❑ 78-0121	Make Believe World/ Help Me Help You	1973	8.00
❑ 3001	The Man Who Sold the World/ Watch That Man	1974	30.00

—A David Bowie song on the A-side...and produced by Bowie, too

Number	Title (A Side/B Side)	Yr	NM
❑ 3009	The Man with a Golden Gun/ Baby I Don't Care	1974	20.00
❑ 3011	Take Your Mama for a Ride (Long)/Take Your Mama for a Ride (Short)	1975	10.00
❑ 3019	Boy Meets Girl/(B-side unknown)	1975	10.00
❑ 3038	Heaven and Earth and the Stars/(B-side unknown)	1976	20.00

EPIC

Number	Title (A Side/B Side)	Yr	NM
❑ 10187	To Sir with Love/The Boat That I Row	1967	10.00
❑ 10210	Dreamy Nights and Days/ Let's Pretend	1967	8.00
❑ 10260	Best of Both Worlds/ Love Loves to Love Love	1967	8.00
❑ 10260 [PS]	Best of Both Worlds/ Love Loves to Love Love	1967	20.00
❑ 10260/65 [DJ]	Best of Both Worlds/ Everybody Knows	1968	25.00

—B-side by the Dave Clark Five; odd promo

Number	Title (A Side/B Side)	Yr	NM
❑ 10302	Me, the Peaceful Heart/Look Out	1968	8.00
❑ 10302 [PS]	Me, the Peaceful Heart/Look Out	1968	20.00
❑ 10346	Sad Memories/Boy	1968	8.00
❑ 10367	Morning Dew/You and I	1968	8.00
❑ 10403	Without Him/This Time	1968	8.00
❑ 10420	Rattler/I'm a Tiger	1968	8.00

PARROT

Number	Title (A Side/B Side)	Yr	NM
❑ 9678	Shout/Forget Me Baby	1964	20.00
❑ 9714	Here Comes the Night/ I'll Come Running	1964	20.00
❑ 9778	Leave a Little Love/He Don't Want Your Love Anymore	1965	20.00
❑ 9791	Try to Understand/Not in This Whole World	1965	20.00
❑ 40021	Shout/When He Touches Me	1967	10.00

ROCKET

Number	Title (A Side/B Side)	Yr	NM
❑ YB-11355	Don't Take Love for Granted/ Love Is the Sweetest Mistake	1978	5.00

7-Inch Extended Plays

EPIC

Number	Title (A Side/B Side)	Yr	NM
❑ 5-26339 [DJ]	To Sir With Love/Morning Dew/ Love Loves to Love Love// Best of Both Worlds/Day Tripper/Take Me in Your Arms (And Love Me)	1967	15.00

—Jukebox mini-LP, small hole, plays at 33 1/3 rpm

Number	Title (A Side/B Side)	Yr	NM
❑ 5-26339 [PS]	To Sir with Love	1967	15.00

Albums

ALFA

Number	Title (A Side/B Side)	Yr	NM
❑ 10006	Lulu	1981	12.00

ATCO

Number	Title (A Side/B Side)	Yr	NM
❑ 33-310 [M]	New Routes	1970	30.00

—White label promo; no stock copies were issued in mono

Number	Title (A Side/B Side)	Yr	NM
❑ SD 33-310 [S]	New Routes	1970	12.00
❑ 33-330 [M]	Melody Fair	1970	30.00

—White label promo, "DJ Copy Monaural" on cover; no stock copies were issued in mono

Number	Title (A Side/B Side)	Yr	NM
❑ SD 33-330 [S]	Melody Fair	1970	12.00

CHELSEA

Number	Title (A Side/B Side)	Yr	NM
❑ BCL1-0144	Lulu	1973	12.00
❑ CHL-518	Heaven and Earth and the Stars	1976	20.00

EPIC

Number	Title (A Side/B Side)	Yr	NM
❑ LN 24339 [M]	To Sir with Love	1967	25.00
❑ BN 26339 [P]	To Sir with Love	1967	30.00
❑ BN 26536	It's Lulu	1970	12.00

HARMONY

Number	Title (A Side/B Side)	Yr	NM
❑ H 30249	To Love Somebody	1970	20.00

PARROT

Number	Title (A Side/B Side)	Yr	NM
❑ PA 61016 [M]	From Lulu with Love	1967	60.00
❑ PAS 71016 [S]	From Lulu with Love	1967	80.00

PICKWICK

Number	Title (A Side/B Side)	Yr	NM
❑ SPC-3237	Lulu	1973	8.00

ROCKET

Number	Title (A Side/B Side)	Yr	NM
❑ BXL1-3073	Don't Take Love for Granted	1978	12.00

LUMAN, BOB

45s

CAPITOL

Number	Title (A Side/B Side)	Yr	NM
❑ F3972	Try Me/I Know My Baby Cares	1958	30.00
❑ F4059	Precious/Svengali	1958	30.00

EPIC

Number	Title (A Side/B Side)	Yr	NM
❑ 10312	Ain't Got Time to Be Unhappy/ I Can't Remember to Forget	1968	6.00
❑ 10381	I Like Trains/A World of Unhappiness	1968	6.00
❑ 10416	I'm In This Town for Good/ A Woman Without Love	1968	6.00
❑ 10439	Come On Home and Sing the Blues to Daddy/Big, Big World	1969	6.00
❑ 10480	Every Day I Have to Cry Some/ Livin' in a House Full of Love	1969	6.00
❑ 10535	The Gun/Cleanin' Up the Streets of Memphis	1969	6.00
❑ 10581	Gettin' Back to Norma/ Maybelline	1970	6.00
❑ 10631	Honky Tonk Man/I Ain't Built That Way	1970	6.00
❑ 10667	What About the Hurt/ The Time to Remember	1970	6.00
❑ 10699	Is It Any Wonder That I Love You?/Give Us One More Chance	1971	5.00
❑ 10755	I Got a Woman/One Hundred Songs on the Jukebox	1971	5.00
❑ 10786	A Chain Don't Take to Me/Don't Let Love Pass You By	1971	5.00
❑ 10823	When You Say Love/ Have a Little Faith	1972	5.00
❑ 10869	It Takes You/Let's Think About Livin'	1972	5.00
❑ 10905	Lonely Women Make Good Lovers/Love Ought to Be a Happy Thing	1972	5.00
❑ 10943	Neither One of Us/Anything But Lonesome	1973	4.00
❑ 10994	A Good Love Is Like a Good Song/Have I Ever Said "I Love You" to a Lady	1973	4.00
❑ 11039	Still Loving You/I'm Gonna Write a Song	1973	4.00
❑ 11087	Just Enough to Make Me Stay/ Baby Make It Good	1974	4.00
❑ 11138	Let Me Make the Bright Lights Shine for You/The Closest Thing to Heaven That I Love	1974	4.00
❑ 50065	Proud of You Baby/Tonight Your Baby's Coming Home	1975	4.00
❑ 50136	Shame on Me/How Do You Start Over	1975	4.00
❑ 50183	A Satisfied Mind/Cleanin' Up the Streets of Memphis	1975	4.00
❑ 50216	The Man from Bowling Green/ It's Only Make Believe	1976	4.00
❑ 50247	How Do You Start Over/Red Cadillac and Black Mustache	1976	4.00
❑ 50297	Labor of Love/ Blond Haired Woman	1976	4.00
❑ 50323	He's Got a Way with Women/ Here We Are Making Love Again	1976	4.00

HICKORY

Number	Title (A Side/B Side)	Yr	NM
❑ 1201	You're Welcome/Interstate 40	1963	12.00
❑ 1219	Can't Take the Country from the Boy/I'm Gonna Write a Song of Love	1963	12.00
❑ 1221	Too Hot to Dance/I Like Your Kind of Love	1963	12.00

—With Sue Thompson

Number	Title (A Side/B Side)	Yr	NM
❑ 1238	The File/Bigger Men Than I (Have Cried)	1964	12.00
❑ 1266	Lonely Room (Empty Walls)/ Run On Home Baby Brother	1964	12.00
❑ 1277	Fire Engine Red/Old George Dickel	1964	12.00
❑ 1289	Bad, Bad Day/Tears from Out of Nowhere	1965	10.00
❑ 1307	Jealous Heart/Go On Home Boy	1965	10.00
❑ 1333	I Love You Because/ Love Worked a Miracle	1965	10.00
❑ 1355	Five Miles from Home (Soon I'll See Mary)/(I Get So) Sentimental	1965	10.00
❑ 1382	Poor Boy Blues/(Can't Get You) Off My Mind	1966	10.00
❑ 1410	Come On and Sing/It's a Sin	1966	10.00

L

Number	Title (A Side/B Side)	Yr	NM
❑ 1430	Hardly Anymore/Freedom of Living	1967	8.00
❑ 1460	If You Don't Love Me (Then Why Don't You Leave Me Alone)/Throwin' Kisses	1967	8.00
❑ 1481	Running Scared/The Best Years of My Wife	1967	8.00
❑ 1536	It's All Over (But the Shouting)/ Still Loving You	1969	6.00
❑ 1564	Still Loving You/Meet Mr. Mud	1970	6.00

IMPERIAL

Number	Title (A Side/B Side)	Yr	NM
❑ 5705	A Red Cadillac and a Black Moustache/All Night Long	1960	25.00
❑ 8311	A Red Cadillac and a Black Moustache/All Night Long	1957	80.00
❑ 8313	Red Hot/Whenever You're Ready	1957	80.00
❑ 8315	Make Up Your Mind, Baby/ Your Love	1958	60.00

—The same coupling was slated for Imperial 8314 but not released.

POLYDOR

Number	Title (A Side/B Side)	Yr	NM
❑ 14408	I'm a Honky-Tonk Woman's Man/Lonely Women Make Good Lovers	1977	4.00
❑ 14431	The Pay Phone/He'll Be the One	1977	4.00
❑ 14444	A Christmas Tribute/Give Someone You Love (A Little Bit of Love This Year)	1977	4.00
❑ 14454	Proud Lady/Let Me Love Him Out of You	1978	4.00

ROLLIN' ROCK

Number	Title (A Side/B Side)	Yr	NM
❑ 028	Stranger Than Fiction/ You're the Cause of It All	1978	4.00

WARNER BROS.

Number	Title (A Side/B Side)	Yr	NM
❑ 5081	My Baby Walks All Over Me/ Class of '59	1959	25.00
❑ 5105	Dreamy Doll/Buttercup	1959	25.00
❑ 5105 [PS]	Dreamy Doll/Buttercup	1959	60.00
❑ 5172	Let's Think About Living/ You've Got Everything	1960	20.00
❑ 5172 [PS]	Let's Think About Living/ You've Got Everything	1960	40.00
❑ 5184	Why, Why, Bye, Bye/Oh Lonesome Me	1960	20.00
❑ 5184 [PS]	Why, Why, Bye, Bye/ Oh Lonesome Me	1960	40.00
❑ 5204	The Great Snow Man/ The Pig Latin Song	1961	20.00
❑ 5204 [PS]	The Great Snow Man/ The Pig Latin Song	1961	40.00
❑ 5233	Private Eyes/You've Turned Down the Lights	1961	20.00
❑ 5233 [PS]	Private Eyes/You've Turned Down the Lights	1961	40.00
❑ 5255	Louisiana Man/Rocks of Reno	1962	20.00
❑ 5272	Big River Rose/Belonging to You	1962	20.00
❑ 5299	Hey Joe/The Fool	1962	20.00
❑ 5321	You're Everything/Envy	1962	20.00
❑ 5506	Boston Rocker/Old Friends// Bad Bad Day/Let's Think About Living	1960	100.00

—Part of Warner Bros. "+2" series, with two new songs and excerpts of two prior hits

Number	Title (A Side/B Side)	Yr	NM
❑ 5506 [PS]	Boston Rocker/Old Friends// Bad Bad Day/Let's Think About Living	1960	100.00

Albums

EPIC

Number	Title (A Side/B Side)	Yr	NM
❑ BN 26393	Ain't Got Time to Be Unhappy	1968	20.00
❑ BN 26463	Come On Home and Sing the Blues	1969	20.00
❑ BN 26541	Gettin' Back	1970	20.00
❑ E 30617	Is It Any Wonder	1971	20.00
❑ E 30923	Chain Don't Take to Me	1972	20.00
❑ KE 31375	When You Say Love	1972	20.00
❑ KE 31746	Lonely Women Make Good Lovers	1972	20.00
❑ KE 32192	Neither One of Us	1973	15.00
❑ KE 32759	Bob Luman's Greatest Hits	1974	15.00
❑ KE 33942	Satisfied Mind	1975	12.00
❑ KE 34445	Alive and Well!	1976	12.00

HARMONY

Number	Title (A Side/B Side)	Yr	NM
❑ KH 32006	Bob Luman	1973	12.00

HICKORY

Number	Title (A Side/B Side)	Yr	NM
❑ LPM-124 [M]	Livin' Lovin' Sounds	1965	25.00
❑ LPS-124 [S]	Livin' Lovin' Sounds	1965	30.00

HICKORY/MGM

Number	Title (A Side/B Side)	Yr	NM
❑ H3G-4508	Still Loving You	1974	15.00

POLYDOR

Number	Title (A Side/B Side)	Yr	NM
❑ PD-1-6135	Bob Luman	1978	12.00

WARNER BROS.

Number	Title (A Side/B Side)	Yr	NM
❑ W 1396 [M]	Let's Think About Livin'	1960	50.00
❑ WS 1396 [S]	Let's Think About Livin'	1960	70.00

LUMPKIN, HENRY

45s

MOTOWN

Number	Title (A Side/B Side)	Yr	NM
❑ 1005	I've Got a Notion/We Really Love Each Other	1961	125.00
❑ 1013	What Is a Man/Don't Leave Me	1961	60.00
❑ 1029	Mo Jo Hanna/ Break Down and Sing	1962	50.00

LUNCH, LYDIA

Albums

RUBY

Number	Title (A Side/B Side)	Yr	NM
❑ JRR 806	13.13	1982	30.00

ZE/BUDDAH

Number	Title (A Side/B Side)	Yr	NM
❑ 33006	Queen of Siam	1980	30.00

LUND, GARRETT

Albums

(NO LABEL)

Number	Title (A Side/B Side)	Yr	NM
❑ (no #)	Almost Grown	1975	300.00

LUREX, LARRY See FREDDIE MERCURY.

LURIE, ELLIOTT Also see LOOKING GLASS.

45s

ARISTA

Number	Title (A Side/B Side)	Yr	NM
❑ 0219	Rich Girl/Night Ride Part 2	1976	4.00

EPIC

Number	Title (A Side/B Side)	Yr	NM
❑ 11153	Your Love Song/ (B-side unknown)	1974	4.00
❑ 50083	Disco/I Don't Wanna Lose You	1975	4.00
❑ 50101	I Think I'm Fallin'/Rainbow Girl	1975	4.00

Albums

EPIC

Number	Title (A Side/B Side)	Yr	NM
❑ PE 33337	Elliott Lurie	1975	10.00

LUVWORTH, RITCHIE

45s

DATE

Number	Title (A Side/B Side)	Yr	NM
❑ 2-1597	Girl of Mine/Hey Baby, Where You Gonna Go	1968	10.00
❑ 2-1624	Can You Dig It/Let's Dance	1968	10.00

LY-DELLS, THE

45s

LOST-NITE

Number	Title (A Side/B Side)	Yr	NM
❑ 116	There Goes the Boy/ Talking to Myself	196?	8.00

—Reissue

MASTER

Number	Title (A Side/B Side)	Yr	NM
❑ 111	Genie of the Lamp/ Teenage Tears	1961	250.00
❑ 251	Wizard of Love/Let This Night Last	1961	60.00

PAM

Number	Title (A Side/B Side)	Yr	NM
❑ 103	There Goes the Boy/ Talking to Myself	1959	200.00

PARKWAY

Number	Title (A Side/B Side)	Yr	NM
❑ 897	There Goes the Boy/ Talking to Myself	1964	20.00

ROULETTE

Number	Title (A Side/B Side)	Yr	NM
❑ 4493	Karen/Doing the Wiggle Wobble	1963	25.00

SCA

Number	Title (A Side/B Side)	Yr	NM
❑ 18001	Book of Songs/Hear That Train	1962	40.00

SOUTHERN SOUND

Number	Title (A Side/B Side)	Yr	NM
❑ 122	Three Little Monkeys/ Playing Hide and Seek	1965	60.00

LYMAN, ARTHUR

45s

GNP CRESCENDO

Number	Title (A Side/B Side)	Yr	NM
❑ 315	Shangri-La/Pearly Shells	1964	6.00
❑ 349	Cast Your Fate to the Wind/ Night Train	1965	6.00
❑ 497	Skybird/Puka Shells	1975	4.00

HIFI

Number	Title (A Side/B Side)	Yr	NM
❑ 533	76 Trombones/House on a Haunted Hill	1959	10.00
❑ 550	Taboo/Dahil Sayo	1959	10.00
❑ 564	Bahia/Jungle Jalopy	1959	10.00
❑ 591	Legend of the Rain/Vera Cruz	1960	10.00
❑ 599	Jungle Fantasy/Koni Au I Ka Wai	1960	10.00
❑ 5002	Taboo Tu/Ebb Tide	1960	10.00
❑ 5024	Yellow Bird/Havah Nagilah	1961	10.00
❑ 5040	(The Sloop) John B/ Honolulu Nites	1961	10.00
❑ 5047	Never on Sunday/ I Talk to the Trees	1961	10.00
❑ 5049	Moanin'/Aloha No Honolulu	1962	10.00
❑ 5055	Anna/(B-side unknown)	1962	10.00
❑ 5057	America (West Side Story)/ Planning Rice	1962	10.00
❑ 5058	We Three Kings/Little Drummer Boy	1962	12.00
❑ 5065	Mutiny on the Bounty/ Pagan Love Song	1963	8.00
❑ 5066	Love for Sale/Dahil Sayo	1963	8.00
❑ 5071	Cottonfields/Limbo Rock	1963	8.00
❑ 5076	Sentimental Journey/ Jungle Drums	1963	8.00
❑ 5078	Blowin' in the Wind/I've Been Workin' on the Railroad	1963	8.00
❑ 5079	He's Gone Away/Suzy's Waltz	1963	8.00
❑ 5080	Charade/Arthur's Line	1963	8.00
❑ 5081	Winter Wonderland/Rudolph, the Red-Nosed Reindeer	1963	12.00
❑ 5082	Petticoat Junction/Gently, Gently	1963	12.00
❑ 5083	We Three Kings/ Little Drummer Boy	1963	12.00
❑ 5088	Swingin' Shephard Blues/ (B-side unknown)	1964	8.00
❑ 5089	Wheel of Fortune/La Montana	1964	8.00
❑ 5091	Hello, Dolly/Get Me to the Church On Time	1964	8.00
❑ 5092	Taboo/Black Orchid	1965	8.00
❑ 5096	Afro Blues/Waltzing Matilda	1965	8.00
❑ 5100	Lemon Tree/The Car	1966	8.00
❑ 5101	The Shadow of Your Smile/ Imua Kamehameha	1966	8.00
❑ 5105	The Windmills of Your Mind/ Lonely Winds	1969	8.00

Albums

GNP CRESCENDO

Number	Title (A Side/B Side)	Yr	NM
❑ GNP-605 [M]	Exotic Sounds	1963	15.00
❑ GNPS-605 [S]	Exotic Sounds	1963	20.00
❑ GNP-606 [M]	Paradise	1964	15.00
❑ GNPS-606 [S]	Paradise	1964	20.00
❑ GNP-607 [M]	Cast Your Fate to the Wind	1965	15.00
❑ GNPS-607 [S]	Cast Your Fate to the Wind	1965	20.00
❑ GNPS-2091	Puka Shells	1975	10.00

HIFI

Number	Title (A Side/B Side)	Yr	NM
❑ R-607 [M]	Leis of Jazz	1958	20.00
❑ SR-607 [S]	Leis of Jazz	1958	30.00
❑ R-806 [M]	Taboo	1958	20.00
❑ SR-806 [S]	Taboo	1958	30.00
❑ R-807 [M]	Hawaiian Sunset	1959	20.00
❑ SR-807 [S]	Hawaiian Sunset	1959	30.00
❑ R-808 [M]	Bwan-A	1959	20.00
❑ SR-808 [S]	Bwan-A	1959	30.00
❑ R-813 [M]	The Legend of Pele	1959	20.00
❑ SR-813 [S]	The Legend of Pele	1959	30.00
❑ R-815 [M]	Bahia	1959	20.00
❑ SR-815 [S]	Bahia	1959	30.00
❑ R-818 [M]	Arthur Lyman On Broadway	1960	20.00
❑ SR-818 [S]	Arthur Lyman On Broadway	1960	30.00
❑ R-822 [M]	Taboo (Vol. 2)	1960	20.00
❑ SR-822 [S]	Taboo (Vol. 2)	1960	30.00

LIFE

Number	Title (A Side/B Side)	Yr	NM
❑ L 1004 [M]	Yellow Bird	1961	20.00
—Reissue with new title reflecting the hit single			
❑ L 1004 [M]	Percussion Spectacular	1961	30.00
❑ SL 1004 [S]	Yellow Bird	1961	25.00
—Reissue with new title reflecting the hit single			
❑ SL 1004 [S]	Percussion Spectacular	1961	40.00
❑ L 1005 [M]	The Colorful Percussions of Arthur Lyman	1962	20.00
❑ SL 1005 [S]	The Colorful Percussions of Arthur Lyman	1962	25.00
❑ L 1007 [M]	The Many Moods of Arthur Lyman	1962	20.00
❑ SL 1007 [S]	The Many Moods of Arthur Lyman	1962	25.00
❑ L 1009 [M]	I Wish You Love	1963	20.00
❑ L 1009 [M]	Love for Sale!	1963	25.00
—Alternate title			
❑ SL 1009 [S]	I Wish You Love	1963	25.00
❑ SL 1009 [S]	Love for Sale!	1963	30.00
—Alternate title			
❑ L 1010 [M]	Cotton Fields	1963	20.00
❑ SL 1010 [S]	Cotton Fields	1963	25.00
❑ L 1014 [M]	Blowin' in the Wind	1963	20.00
❑ SL 1014 [S]	Blowin' in the Wind	1963	25.00
❑ L 1018 [M]	Mele Kalikimaka (Merry Christmas)	1963	20.00
❑ SL 1018 [S]	Mele Kalikimaka (Merry Christmas)	1963	25.00
❑ L 1023 [M]	Isle of Enchantment	1964	20.00
❑ SL 1023 [S]	Isle of Enchantment	1964	25.00
❑ L 1024 [M]	Call of the Midnight Sun	1964	20.00
❑ SL 1024 [S]	Call of the Midnight Sun	1964	25.00
❑ L 1025 [M]	Hawaiian Sunset, Vol. 2	1965	15.00
❑ SL 1025 [S]	Hawaiian Sunset, Vol. 2	1965	20.00
❑ L 1027 [M]	Polynesia	1965	15.00
❑ SL 1027 [S]	Polynesia	1965	20.00
❑ L 1030 [M]	Greatest Hits	1965	12.00
❑ SL 1030 [S]	Greatest Hits	1965	15.00
❑ L 1031 [M]	Lyman '66	1965	15.00

Except when noted otherwise, VG = 25% of NM, and VG+ = 50% of NM. (Example: VG = $2.00, VG+ = $4.00 and NM = $8.00.)

Number	Title (A Side/B Side)	Yr	NM
❑ SL 1031 [S]	Lyman '66	1965	20.00
❑ L 1033 [M]	The Shadow of Your Smile	1966	15.00
❑ SL 1033 [S]	The Shadow of Your Smile	1966	20.00
❑ L 1034 [M]	Aloha, Amigo	1966	15.00
❑ SL 1034 [S]	Aloha, Amigo	1966	20.00
❑ L 1035 [M]	Ilikai	1967	15.00
❑ SL 1035 [S]	Ilikai	1967	20.00
❑ L 1036 [M]	Arthur Lyman at the Port of L.A.	1967	15.00
❑ SL 1036 [S]	Arthur Lyman at the Port of L.A.	1967	20.00
❑ SL 1037	Latitude 20	1968	15.00
❑ SL 1038	Aphrodisia	1968	15.00
❑ SL 1039	Winner's Circle	1969	15.00
❑ SL 1040	Today's Greatest Hits	1970	15.00

LYMAN, JONI

45s

REPRISE

Number	Title (A Side/B Side)	Yr	NM
❑ 0378	Happy Birthday Blue/I Just Don't Know What to Do with Myself	1965	40.00

LYME AND CYBELLE

45s

WHITE WHALE

Number	Title (A Side/B Side)	Yr	NM
❑ 228	Follow Me/Like the Seasons	1966	20.00
❑ 232	If You Gotta Go, Go Now/I'll Go On	1966	20.00
❑ 245	Song No. 7/Write If You Get Work	1967	20.00

LYMON, FRANKIE

Also see FRANKIE LYMON AND THE TEENAGERS.

45s

BIG KAT

Number	Title (A Side/B Side)	Yr	NM
❑ 7008	I Want You to Be My Girl/Portable on My Shoulder	1968	10.00
❑ 7008 [PS]	I Want You to Be My Girl/Portable on My Shoulder	1968	12.00

COLUMBIA

Number	Title (A Side/B Side)	Yr	NM
❑ 43094	Somewhere/Sweet and Lovely	1964	50.00

GEE

Number	Title (A Side/B Side)	Yr	NM
❑ 1039	Goody Goody/Creation of Love	1957	25.00
❑ 1052	I'm Not Too Young to Dream/Goody Good Girl	1959	25.00

ROULETTE

Number	Title (A Side/B Side)	Yr	NM
❑ 4026	So Goes My Love/My Girl	1957	25.00
❑ 4035	It's Christmas Once Again/Little Girl	1957	25.00
❑ 4044	Footsteps/Thumb Thumb	1958	20.00
❑ 4068	Mama Don't Allow It/Portable on My Shoulder	1958	20.00
❑ 4093	Melinda/The Only Way to Love	1958	20.00
❑ 4128	No Matter What You've Done/Up Jumped a Rabbit	1959	20.00
❑ 4150	Before I Fall Asleep/What a Little Moonlight Can Do	1959	20.00
❑ 4257	Little Bitty Pretty One/Creation of Love	1960	20.00
❑ 4283	Buzz, Buzz, Buzz/Waitin' in School	1960	20.00
❑ 4310	Jailhouse Rock/Silhouettes	1961	20.00
❑ 4348	Change Partners/So Young	1961	20.00
❑ 4391	I Put the Bomp/So Young	1962	20.00

TCF

Number	Title (A Side/B Side)	Yr	NM
❑ 11	Teacher Teacher/To Each His Own	1964	15.00

7-Inch Extended Plays

ROULETTE

Number	Title (A Side/B Side)	Yr	NM
❑ EPR-1-304	Let's Fall in Love/My Baby Just Cares for Me//Goody Goody/Somebody Loves Me	1958	200.00
❑ EPR-1-304 [PS]	Frankie Lymon at the London Palladium	1958	200.00

Albums

GUEST STAR

Number	Title (A Side/B Side)	Yr	NM
❑ GS-1406 [M]	Teen Time Tunes Starring Frankie Lymon	1959	40.00

—Various-artists compilation; color cover

Number	Title (A Side/B Side)	Yr	NM
❑ GS-1406 [M]	Rock & Roll Party Starring Frankie Lymon	196?	25.00

—Various-artists compilation; retitled, black and white cover

ROULETTE

Number	Title (A Side/B Side)	Yr	NM
❑ R-25013 [M]	Frankie Lymon at the London Palladium	1958	300.00
❑ R-25036 [M]	Rock 'N' Roll	1958	300.00
❑ R-25250 [M]	Frankie Lymon's Greatest	1964	30.00
❑ SR-25250 [R]	Frankie Lymon's Greatest	1964	25.00

LYMON, FRANKIE, AND THE TEENAGERS

Also see FRANKIE LYMON; THE TEENAGERS.

45s

GEE

Number	Title (A Side/B Side)	Yr	NM
❑ 1002	Why Do Fools Fall in Love/Please Be Mine	1956	30.00

—Red and black label; vocal solo on B-side. All of the above credit "The Teenagers featuring Frankie Lymon"

Number	Title (A Side/B Side)	Yr	NM
❑ 1002	Why Do Fools Fall in Love/Please Be Mine	1956	50.00

—Red and black label; vocal duet on B-side

Number	Title (A Side/B Side)	Yr	NM
❑ 1002	Why Do Fools Fall in Love/Please Be Mine	1956	80.00

—Red and gold label

Number	Title (A Side/B Side)	Yr	NM
❑ 1002	Why Do Fools Fall in Love/My Girl	1958	25.00

—White label, "Gee Records" at top; note different B-side

Number	Title (A Side/B Side)	Yr	NM
❑ 1002	Why Do Fools Fall in Love/Please Be Mine	1959	15.00

—Gray label, "Gee Records" at bottom; label credit is "The Teenagers featuring Frankie Lymon"

Number	Title (A Side/B Side)	Yr	NM
❑ 1012	I Want You to Be My Girl/I'm Not a Know-It-All	1956	30.00

—As "Frankie Lymon and the Teenagers"

Number	Title (A Side/B Side)	Yr	NM
❑ 1012	I Want You to Be My Girl/I'm Not a Know-It-All	1956	50.00

—As "The Teenagers featuring Frankie Lymon"

Number	Title (A Side/B Side)	Yr	NM
❑ 1018	I Promise to Remember/Who Can Explain	1956	30.00
❑ 1022	The ABC's of Love/Share	1956	30.00
❑ 1026	I'm Not a Juvenile Delinquent/Baby Baby	1957	30.00
❑ 1032	Teenage Love/Paper Castles	1957	30.00
❑ 1035	Am I Fooling Myself Again/Love Is a Clown	197?	—

—Evidently a 1970s bootleg to fill in a gap in the Gee Records discography

Number	Title (A Side/B Side)	Yr	NM
❑ 1036	Miracle of Love/Out in the Cold Again	1957	30.00
❑ 1039	Goody Goody/Creation of Love	1957	40.00

—Actually a Frankie Lymon solo recording; the first pressing credited the entire group

7-Inch Extended Plays

GEE

Number	Title (A Side/B Side)	Yr	NM
❑ GEP-601	Teenage Love/Why Do Fools Fall in Love//I Want You to Be My Girl/Love Is a Clown	1956	150.00
❑ GEP-601 [PS]	The Teenagers Go Rock'n	1956	200.00
❑ GEP-602	Paper Castles/Share//Am I Fooling Myself Again/I'm Not a Know-It-All	1957	200.00
❑ GEP-602 [PS]	The Teenagers Go Romantic	1957	200.00

Albums

ACCORD

Number	Title (A Side/B Side)	Yr	NM
❑ SN-7203	Why Do Fools Fall in Love	1982	10.00

GEE

Number	Title (A Side/B Side)	Yr	NM
❑ GLP-701 [M]	The Teenagers Featuring Frankie Lymon	1956	500.00

—Red label

Number	Title (A Side/B Side)	Yr	NM
❑ GLP-701 [M]	The Teenagers Featuring Frankie Lymon	1961	150.00

—Gray label

Number	Title (A Side/B Side)	Yr	NM
❑ GLP-701 [M]	The Teenagers Featuring Frankie Lymon	197?	12.00

—White label on thinner vinyl

MURRAY HILL

Number	Title (A Side/B Side)	Yr	NM
❑ 148 [(5)]	Frankie Lymon and the Teenagers	198?	70.00

RHINO

Number	Title (A Side/B Side)	Yr	NM
❑ R1-70918	The Best of Frankie Lymon and the Teenagers	1989	12.00

LYMON, LEWIS, AND THE TEENCHORDS

45s

END

Number	Title (A Side/B Side)	Yr	NM
❑ 1003	Too Young/Your Last Chance	1957	100.00
❑ 1007	I Found Out Why/Tell Me Love	1958	80.00
❑ 1113	Too Young/Your Last Chance	1962	20.00

FURY

Number	Title (A Side/B Side)	Yr	NM
❑ 1000	I'm So Happy (Tra-La-La-La-La-La)/Lydia	1957	200.00

—Maroon label

Number	Title (A Side/B Side)	Yr	NM
❑ 1000	I'm So Happy (Tra-La-La-La-La-La)/Lydia	1958	40.00

—Yellow label

Number	Title (A Side/B Side)	Yr	NM
❑ 1003	Honey, Honey (You Don't Know)/Please Tell the Angels	1957	80.00
❑ 1006	I'm Not Too Young to Fall in Love/Falling in Love	1957	80.00

JUANITA

Number	Title (A Side/B Side)	Yr	NM
❑ 101	Dance Girl/Them There Eyes	1958	50.00

LOST-NITE

Number	Title (A Side/B Side)	Yr	NM
❑ 357	I'm So Happy (Tra-La-La-La-La-La)/Lydia	197?	5.00

—Reissue

Number	Title (A Side/B Side)	Yr	NM
❑ 360	Honey, Honey (You Don't Know)/Please Tell the Angels	197?	5.00

—Reissue

Number	Title (A Side/B Side)	Yr	NM
❑ 364	I'm Not Too Young to Fall in Love/Falling in Love	197?	5.00

—Reissue

Albums

COLLECTABLES

Number	Title (A Side/B Side)	Yr	NM
❑ COL-5049	Lewis Lymon and the Teenchords Meet the Kodaks	198?	10.00

LOST-NITE

Number	Title (A Side/B Side)	Yr	NM
❑ LLP-13 [10]	Lewis Lymon and the Teenchords	1981	10.00

—Red vinyl

LYNN, BARBARA

45s

ATLANTIC

Number	Title (A Side/B Side)	Yr	NM
❑ 2450	This Is the Thanks I Get/Ring, Telephone, Ring	1967	8.00
❑ 2513	Why Can't You Love Me/You're Losing Me	1968	8.00
❑ 2553	Love Ain't Never Hurt Nobody/You're Gonna See a Lot More	1968	8.00
❑ 2585	People Like Me/He Ain't Gonna Do Right	1968	8.00
❑ 2812	(Until Then) I'll Suffer/Take Your Love and Run	1971	6.00
❑ 2853	Nice and Easy/I'm a One Woman Man	1972	6.00
❑ 2880	(Daddy Hotstuff) You're Too Hot to Hold/You Better Quit It	1972	6.00
❑ 2931	You Make Me So Hot/It Ain't No Good to Be Too Good	1973	6.00

JAMIE

Number	Title (A Side/B Side)	Yr	NM
❑ 1220	You'll Lose a Good Thing/Lonely Heartache	1962	20.00
❑ 1233	Second Fiddle Girl/Letter to Mommy and Daddy	1962	12.00
❑ 1240	You're Gonna Need Me/I'm Sorry I Met You	1962	12.00
❑ 1244	Don't Be Cruel/You Can't Be Satisfied	1963	12.00
❑ 1251	To Love or Not to Love/Promises	1963	12.00
❑ 1260	(I Cried at) Laura's Wedding/You Better Stop	1963	12.00
❑ 1265	Everybody Loves Somebody/Dedicate the Blues to Me	1963	12.00
❑ 1269	Money/Jealous Love	1964	12.00
❑ 1277	Oh! Baby (We Got a Good Thing Goin')/Unfair	1964	12.00
❑ 1286	Don't Spread It Around/Let Her Knock Herself Out	1964	12.00
❑ 1292	It's Better to Have It/People Gonna Talk	1964	12.00
❑ 1295	(Don't Pretend) Just Lay It on the Line/Careless Hands	1965	8.00

—With Lee Maye

Number	Title (A Side/B Side)	Yr	NM
❑ 1297	Keep On Pushing Your Luck/I've Taken All I'm Gonna Take	1965	8.00
❑ 1301	Can't Buy Me Love/That's What Friends Are For	1965	8.00
❑ 1304	All I Need Is Your Love/You're Gonna Be Sorry	1965	8.00

TRIBE

Number	Title (A Side/B Side)	Yr	NM
❑ 8316	Running Back/I'm a Good Woman	1966	80.00
❑ 8319	You Left the Water Running/Until I'm Free	1966	60.00
❑ 8322	Watch the One That Brings Bad News/AUB A-Go-Go	1967	40.00
❑ 8324	I Don't Want a Playboy/New Kind of Love	1967	125.00

Albums

ATLANTIC

Number	Title (A Side/B Side)	Yr	NM
❑ 8171 [M]	Here Is Barbara Lynn	1968	50.00
❑ SD 8171 [S]	Here Is Barbara Lynn	1968	40.00

JAMIE

Number	Title (A Side/B Side)	Yr	NM
❑ JLP-3023 [M]	You'll Lose a Good Thing	1962	50.00
❑ JLPS-3023 [R]	You'll Lose a Good Thing	1962	50.00
❑ JLP-3026 [M]	Sister of Soul	1964	—

—Canceled

Number	Title (A Side/B Side)	Yr	NM
❑ JLPS-3026 [S]	Sister of Soul	1964	—

—Canceled

LYNN, DONNA

45s

CAPITOL

Number	Title (A Side/B Side)	Yr	NM
❑ 5087	Ronnie/That's Me, I'm the Brother	1963	15.00
❑ 5127	My Boyfriend Got a Beatle Haircut/That Winter Weekend	1964	20.00
❑ 5156	Java Jones/Things That I Feel	1964	15.00
❑ 5213	Silly Girl/There Goes the Boy I Love with Mary	1964	15.00
❑ 5378	I'd Much Rather Be with the Girls/I'm Sorry More Than You Know	1965	12.00
❑ 5456	True Blue/When Your Heart Rings, Answer	1965	12.00

Number	Title (A Side/B Side)	Yr	NM
EPIC			
❑ 9580	Donna Loves Jerry/Oh, I'm in Love (With George Maharis)	1963	8.00
—The B-side is the full title of the song — George Maharis does NOT appear on this record!			
PALMER			
❑ 5016	Don't You Dare/I Was Raining	1967	25.00
Albums			
CAPITOL			
❑ ST 2085 [S]	Java Jones/My Boyfriend Got a Beatle Haircut	1964	30.00
❑ T 2085 [M]	Java Jones/My Boyfriend Got a Beatle Haircut	1964	20.00
LYNN, LORETTA Also see DOLLY PARTON; ERNEST TUBB AND LORETTA LYNN; CONWAY TWITTY AND LORETTA LYNN.			
45s			
DECCA			
❑ 31323	The Girl That I Am Now/I Walked Away from the Wreck	1961	15.00
❑ 31384	Success/Hundred Proof Heartache	1962	12.00
❑ 31435	World of Forgotten People/Get Set for a Heartache	1962	15.00
❑ 31471	The Other Woman/Who'll Help Me Get Over You	1963	10.00
❑ 31541	Before I'm Over You/Where Were You	1963	10.00
❑ 31608	Wine, Women and Song/This Haunted House	1964	10.00
❑ 31707	Happy Birthday/When Lonely Hits Your Heart	1964	10.00
❑ 31769	Blue Kentucky Girl/Two Steps Forward	1965	10.00
❑ 31836	The Home You're Tearin' Down/The Farther You Go	1965	10.00
❑ 31879	When I Hear My Children Play/Everybody Wants to Go to Heaven	1965	12.00
❑ 31893	Dear Uncle Sam/Hurtin' for Certain	1966	10.00
❑ 31966	You Ain't Woman Enough/God Gave Me a Heart to Forgive	1966	10.00
❑ 32043	It Won't Seem Like Christmas/To Heck with Santa Claus	1966	10.00
❑ 32043 [PS]	It Won't Seem Like Christmas/To Heck with Santa Claus	1966	15.00
❑ 32045	Don't Come Home a-Drinkin' (With Lovin' on Your Mind)/A Saint to a Sinner	1966	10.00
❑ 32127	If You're Not Gone Too Long/A Man I Hardly Know	1967	10.00
❑ 32184	What Kind of a Girl (Do You Think I Am?)/Bargain Basement Dress	1967	10.00
❑ 32264	Fist City/Slowly Killing Me	1968	8.00
❑ 32332	You've Just Stepped In (From Stepping Out on Me)/Taking the Place of My Man	1968	8.00
❑ 32392	Your Squaw Is On the Warpath/Let Me Go, You're Hurtin' Me	1968	8.00
❑ 32439	Woman of the World (Leave My World Alone)/Sneakin' In	1969	8.00
❑ 32513	To Make a Man (Feel Like a Man)/One Little Reason	1969	8.00
❑ 32586	Wings Upon Your Horns/Let's Get Back Down to Earth	1969	8.00
❑ 32637	I Know How/The End of My World	1970	8.00
❑ 32693	You Wanna Give Me a Lift/What's the Bottle Done Today Baby	1970	8.00
❑ 32749	Coal Miner's Daughter/Man of the House	1970	10.00
❑ 32749 [PS]	Coal Miner's Daughter/Man of the House	1970	12.00
❑ 32796	I Wanna Be Free/If I Never Love Again	1971	7.00
❑ 32851	You're Lookin' at Country/When You're Poor	1971	7.00
❑ 32900	One's On the Way/Kinfolks Holler	1971	7.00
—Retitled version of A-side			
❑ 32900	Here in Topeka/Kinfolks Holler	1971	20.00
❑ 32974	Here I Am Again/My Kind of Man	1972	7.00
❑ 33039	Rated "X"/'Til the Pain Outwears the Shame	1972	7.00
MCA			
❑ 40058	Love Is the Foundation/What Sundown Does to You	1973	5.00
❑ 40150	Hey Loretta/Turn Me Any Way But Loose	1973	5.00
❑ 40223	They Don't Make 'Em Like My Daddy/Nothin'	1974	5.00
❑ 40283	Trouble in Paradise/We've Already Tasted Love	1974	5.00
❑ 40358	The Pill/Will You Be There	1975	5.00
❑ 40438	Home/You Take Me to Heaven Every Night	1975	5.00
❑ 40484	When the Tingle Becomes a Chill/All I Want from You (Is Away)	1975	5.00
❑ 40541	Red, White and Blue/Sounds of a New Love (Being Born)	1976	5.00
❑ 40607	Somebody Somewhere (Don't Know What He's Missin' Tonight)/Sundown Tavern	1976	5.00
❑ 40679	She's Got You/The Lady That Lived Here Before	1977	5.00
❑ 40747	Why Can't He Be You/I Keep On Putting On	1977	5.00
❑ 40832	Out of My Head and Back in My Bed/Old Rooster	1977	5.00
❑ 40910	Spring Fever/God Bless the Children	1978	4.00
❑ 40954	We've Come a Long Way, Baby/I Can't Feel You Anymore	1978	4.00
❑ 40954 [PS]	We've Come a Long Way, Baby/I Can't Feel You Anymore	1978	6.00
❑ 41021	I Can't Feel You Anymore/True Love Needs to Keep in Touch	1979	4.00
❑ 41129	I've Got a Picture of Us on My Mind/I Don't Feel Like a Movie Tonight	1979	4.00
❑ 41185	Pregnant Again/You're a Cross I Can't Bear	1980	4.00
❑ 41250	Naked in the Rain/I Should Be Over You by Now	1980	4.00
❑ 51015	Cheatin' On a Cheater/Until I Met You	1980	4.00
❑ 51058	Somebody Led Me Away/Everybody's Lookin' for Somebody New	1981	4.00
❑ 51226	I Lie/If I Ain't Got It	1982	5.00
❑ 52005	I Lie/If I Ain't Got It	1982	4.00
❑ 52092	Making Love from Memory/Don't It Feel Good	1982	4.00
❑ 52158	Breakin' It/There's All Kinds of Smoke (In the Barroom)	1983	4.00
❑ 52219	Lyin', Cheatin', Woman Chasin', Honky Tonkin', Whiskey Drinkin' You/Star Light, Star Bright	1983	4.00
❑ 52289	Walking with My Memories/It's Gone	1983	4.00
❑ 52621	Heart Don't Do This to Me/Adam's Rib	1985	3.00
❑ 52621 [PS]	Heart Don't Do This to Me/Adam's Rib	1985	4.00
❑ 52706	Wouldn't It Be Great/One Man Band	1985	3.00
❑ 52766	Just a Woman/Take Me in Your Arms (And Hold Me)	1986	3.00
❑ 53320	Who Was That Stranger/Elsie Banks	1988	3.00
❑ 53397	Fly Away/Your Used to Be	1988	3.00
❑ 65034	Shadrack, the Black Reindeer/Let's Put Christ Back in Christmas	1974	4.00
—Black label with rainbow			
❑ 65034	Shadrack, the Black Reindeer/Let's Put Christ Back in Christmas	1980	3.00
—Blue label with rainbow			
ZERO			
❑ 107	I'm a Honky Tonk Girl/Whispering Sea	1960	500.00
❑ 110	New Rainbow/Heartaches Meet Mr. Blues	1960	400.00
❑ 112	The Darkest Day/Gonna Pack My Troubles	1961	400.00
7-Inch Extended Plays			
DECCA			
❑ ED 2762	The Other Woman/Where Were You//Success/Before I'm Over You	1964	20.00
❑ ED 2762 [PS]	The Other Woman	1964	20.00
❑ ED 2784	(contents unknown)	1965	20.00
❑ ED 2784 [PS]	Wine, Women and Song	1965	20.00
❑ ED 2793	(contents unknown)	1965	20.00
❑ ED 2793 [PS]	The End of the World	1965	20.00
❑ ED 2800	(contents unknown)	1965	20.00
❑ ED 2800 [PS]	Songs from the Heart	1965	20.00
❑ 7-34226	Alone with You/The Other Woman/Success//Color of the Blues/A Hundred Proof Heartache/Act Naturally	1963	30.00
—Jukebox issue; small hole, plays at 33 1/3 rpm			
❑ 7-34226 [PS]	Loretta Lynn Sings	1963	30.00
❑ 7-34318	Happy Birthday/You've Made Me What I Am/It Just Looks That Way//A Boy Like You/I Don't Believe I'll Fall in Love Today/A Wound Time Can't Erase	1965	25.00
—Jukebox issue; small hole, plays at 33 1/3 rpm			
❑ 7-34318 [PS]	Songs from My Heart...	1965	25.00
❑ 7-34333	Blue Kentucky Girl/Night Girl/Farther to Go//The Race Is On/The Beginning of the End/Send Me the Pillow You Dream On	1965	25.00
—Jukebox issue; small hole, plays at 33 1/3 rpm			
❑ 7-34333 [PS]	Blue Kentucky Girl	1965	25.00
❑ 7-34374	Your Cheatin' Heart/It's Been So Long Darling/If Teardrops Were Pennies//Jealous Heart/Cry Cry Cry/Hurtin' For Certain	1966	20.00
❑ 7-34374 [PS]	I Like 'Em Country	1966	20.00
❑ 7-34418	You Ain't Woman Enough/God Gave Me a Heart to Forgive/It's Another World//The Darkest Day of My Life/Someone Before Me/Is It Wrong (For Loving You)	1966	20.00
—Jukebox issue; small hole, plays at 33 1/3 rpm			
❑ 7-34418 [PS]	You Ain't Woman Enough	1966	20.00
❑ DL 734531	Fist City/What Kind of Girl (Do You Think I Am)/How Long Will It Take//Somebody's Back in Town/I Don't Wanna Play House/A Satisfied Mind	1968	15.00
—Jukebox issue; small hole, plays at 33 1/3 rpm			
❑ DL 734531 [PS]	Fist City	1968	15.00
❑ DL 734731	Big Ole Hurt/I'm Dynamite/When I Reach the Bottom//Wings Upon Your Horns/I'll Still Be Missing You/Let's Get Back to Earth	1970	12.00
—Jukebox issue; small hole, plays at 33 1/3 rpm			
❑ DL 734731 [PS]	Wings Upon Your Horns	1970	12.00
❑ 34877	He's All I Got/One's on the Way/I Can't See Me Without You//L-O-V-E, Love/Too Wild to Be Tamed/It's Not the Miles You Traveled	1972	12.00
—Stereo jukebox issue; small hole, plays at 33 1/3 rpm			
❑ 34877 [PS]	One's on the Way	1972	12.00
Albums			
DECCA			
❑ DL 4457 [M]	Loretta Lynn Sings	1963	60.00
❑ DL 4541 [M]	Before I'm Over You	1964	30.00
❑ DL 4620 [M]	Songs from My Heart	1965	30.00
❑ DL 4665 [M]	Blue Kentucky Girl	1965	30.00
❑ DL 4695 [M]	Hymns	1965	30.00
❑ DL 4744 [M]	I Like 'Em Country	1966	25.00
❑ DL 4783 [M]	You Ain't Woman Enough	1966	25.00
❑ DL 4817 [M]	Country Christmas	1966	25.00
❑ DL 4842 [M]	Don't Come Home a-Drinkin' (With Lovin' on Your Mind)	1967	30.00
❑ DL 4928 [M]	Who Says God Is Dead!	1967	40.00
❑ DL 4930 [M]	Singin' with Feelin'	1967	30.00
❑ DL 4997 [M]	Fist City	1968	50.00
—Mono version appears to exist only as a white label promo			
❑ DL 74457 [S]	Loretta Lynn Sings	1963	80.00
❑ DL 74541 [S]	Before I'm Over You	1964	40.00
❑ DL 74620 [S]	Songs from My Heart	1965	40.00
❑ DL 74665 [S]	Blue Kentucky Girl	1965	40.00
❑ DL 74695 [S]	Hymns	1965	40.00
❑ DL 74744 [S]	I Like 'Em Country	1966	30.00
❑ DL 74783 [S]	You Ain't Woman Enough	1966	30.00
❑ DL 74817 [S]	Country Christmas	1966	30.00
❑ DL 74842 [S]	Don't Come Home a-Drinkin' (With Lovin' on Your Mind)	1967	25.00
❑ DL 74928 [S]	Who Says God Is Dead!	1967	25.00
❑ DL 74930 [S]	Singin' with Feelin'	1967	25.00
❑ DL 74997 [S]	Fist City	1968	25.00
❑ DL 75000	Loretta Lynn's Greatest Hits	1968	25.00
❑ DL 75084	Your Squaw Is On the Warpath	1969	25.00
—Later editions delete the track "Barney"			
❑ DL 75084	Your Squaw Is On the Warpath	1969	40.00
—First editions had a track called "Barney"			
❑ DL 75113	Woman of the World/To Make a Man	1969	25.00
❑ DL 75163	Wings Upon Your Horns	1970	25.00
❑ DL 75198	Loretta Lynn Writes 'Em and Sings 'Em	1970	25.00
❑ DL 75253	Coal Miner's Daughter	1971	20.00
❑ DL 75282	I Wanna Be Free	1971	20.00
❑ DL 75310	You're Lookin' at Country	1971	20.00
❑ DL 75334	One's On the Way	1972	20.00
❑ DL 75351	God Bless America Again	1972	20.00
❑ DL 75381	Here I Am Again	1972	20.00
❑ ST-91604	Loretta Lynn's Greatest Hits	1968	30.00
—Capitol Record Club edition			
MCA			
❑ 1	Loretta Lynn's Greatest Hits	1973	15.00
—Reissue of Decca 75000			
❑ 5	Hymns	1973	15.00
—Reissue of Decca 74695			
❑ 6	You Ain't Woman Enough	1973	15.00
—Reissue of Decca 74783			
❑ 7	Who Says God Is Dead!	1973	15.00
—Reissue of Decca 74928			
❑ 58	Here I Am Again	1973	15.00
—Reissue of Decca 75381			

Number	Title (A Side/B Side)	Yr	NM
❑ 113	Don't Come Home a-Drinkin' (With Lovin' on Your Mind)	1973	15.00

—Reissue of Decca 74842

Number	Title (A Side/B Side)	Yr	NM
❑ 248	Country Christmas	1973	15.00

—First reissue of Decca LP

Number	Title (A Side/B Side)	Yr	NM
❑ 300	Entertainer of the Year — Loretta	1973	15.00
❑ 355	Love Is the Foundation	1973	15.00
❑ 420	Loretta Lynn's Greatest Hits Vol. II	1974	15.00
❑ 444	They Don't Make 'Em Like My Daddy	1974	15.00
❑ 471	Back to the Country	1975	12.00
❑ 628	When the Tingle Becomes a Chill	198?	8.00

—Budget-line reissue

Number	Title (A Side/B Side)	Yr	NM
❑ 630	Somebody Somewhere	198?	8.00

—Budget-line reissue

Number	Title (A Side/B Side)	Yr	NM
❑ 721	We've Come a Long Way, Baby	198?	8.00

—Budget-line reissue

Number	Title (A Side/B Side)	Yr	NM
❑ 735	Alone with You	198?	10.00
❑ L33-1934 [DJ]	Loretta Lynn	1974	40.00

—Promo-only compilation

Number	Title (A Side/B Side)	Yr	NM
❑ 2146	Home	1975	12.00
❑ 2179	When the Tingle Becomes a Chill	1976	12.00
❑ 2228	Somebody Somewhere	1976	12.00
❑ 2265	I Remember Patsy	1977	12.00
❑ 2330	Out of My Head and Back in My Bed	1978	12.00
❑ 2341	Loretta Lynn's Greatest Hits	1978	12.00

—Reissue of MCA 1

Number	Title (A Side/B Side)	Yr	NM
❑ 2342	Coal Miner's Daughter	1978	12.00

—Reissue

Number	Title (A Side/B Side)	Yr	NM
❑ 2353	Loretta Lynn's Greatest Hits Vol. II	1978	12.00

—Reissue of MCA 420

Number	Title (A Side/B Side)	Yr	NM
❑ 3073	We've Come a Long Way, Baby	1979	12.00
❑ 3217	Loretta	1980	10.00
❑ 5148	Lookin' Good	1980	10.00
❑ 5293	I Lie	1982	10.00
❑ 5426	Lyin', Cheatin', Woman Chasin', Honky Tonkin', Whiskey Drinkin' You	1983	10.00
❑ 5613	Just a Woman	1985	10.00
❑ 15022	Country Christmas	1974	12.00

—Second reissue of Decca LP; black rainbow label

Number	Title (A Side/B Side)	Yr	NM
❑ 15022	Country Christmas	1980	10.00

—Blue rainbow label

Number	Title (A Side/B Side)	Yr	NM
❑ 15032	Christmas Without Daddy	198?	12.00
❑ 35013	Allis-Chalmers Presents Loretta Lynn	1978	40.00

—Special products compilation

Number	Title (A Side/B Side)	Yr	NM
❑ 35018	Crisco Presents Loretta Lynn's Country Classics	1979	40.00

—Special products compilation

Number	Title (A Side/B Side)	Yr	NM
❑ 37080	I Remember Patsy Cline	198?	8.00

—Budget-line reissue

Number	Title (A Side/B Side)	Yr	NM
❑ 37165	Loretta	198?	8.00

—Budget-line reissue

Number	Title (A Side/B Side)	Yr	NM
❑ 37205	Loretta Lynn's Greatest Hits Vol. II	198?	8.00

—Budget-line reissue

Number	Title (A Side/B Side)	Yr	NM
❑ 37235	Loretta Lynn's Greatest Hits	198?	8.00

—Budget-line reissue

Number	Title (A Side/B Side)	Yr	NM
❑ 37236	Coal Miner's Daughter	198?	8.00

—Budget-line reissue

Number	Title (A Side/B Side)	Yr	NM
❑ 42174	Who Was That Stranger	1988	10.00

VOCALION

Number	Title (A Side/B Side)	Yr	NM
❑ VL 73853	Here's Loretta Lynn	1968	15.00

LYNN, LORETTA, AND ERNEST TUBB See ERNEST TUBB AND LORETTA LYNN.

LYNN, LORETTA, AND CONWAY TWITTY See CONWAY TWITTY AND LORETTA LYNN.

LYNN, MICKI

45s

CAPITOL

Number	Title (A Side/B Side)	Yr	NM
❑ 5495	I've Got the Blues/Some of This and Some of That	1965	50.00

REVUE

Number	Title (A Side/B Side)	Yr	NM
❑ 11042	In the Meantime/Sure Is Something	1969	20.00

LYNN, SANDRA

45s

CONSTELLATION

Number	Title (A Side/B Side)	Yr	NM
❑ 140	Where Would I Be/Sometime	1964	12.00

LYNN, VERA

45s

ARCO

Number	Title (A Side/B Side)	Yr	NM
❑ 6703	Useless/Where Do We Go from You	1967	8.00

DJM

Number	Title (A Side/B Side)	Yr	NM
❑ 70009	Fool on the Hill/Goodnight	1969	8.00

LONDON

Number	Title (A Side/B Side)	Yr	NM
❑ 1007	Wond'ring and Wishing/That's How I Remember	195?	15.00
❑ 1008	Till the Clouds Roll By/Auld Scotch Mother	195?	15.00
❑ 1051	My Friend the Robin/Don't Make a Memory of Me	195?	15.00
❑ 1146	Wish Me Luck/We'll Meet Again	1951	15.00
❑ 1156	Jalousie/If You Go	1951	15.00
❑ 1169	Cry/And Love Was Born	1951	15.00
❑ 1196	Blue Fool/A House Is a Home	1952	15.00
❑ 1202	Be Anything (But Be Mine)/Sleeping Beauty	1952	15.00
❑ 1208	A Little Love/Marryin' Time	1952	15.00
❑ 1227	Auf Wiederseh'n Sweetheart/From the Time We Say Goodbye (The Parting Song)	1952	15.00
❑ 1233	Padam Padam (How It Echoes the Beat of My Heart)/By the Fireside	1952	15.00
❑ 1249	Homing Waltz/When Swallows Say Goodbye	1952	15.00
❑ 1261	Yours/The Love of My Life	1952	15.00
❑ 1265	Forget Me Not/What a Day We'll Have	1952	15.00
❑ 1298	I'll Always Love You/No More	1953	15.00
❑ 1302	Waiting for You/I Lived When I Met You	1953	15.00
❑ 1317	I'll Wait for You/My Love, My Life, My Happiness	1953	15.00
❑ 1348	We'll Meet Again/Windsor Waltz	1953	15.00
❑ 1350	Queen of Ev'ryone's Heart/The Lambeth Waltz	1953	15.00
❑ 1382	You Won't Forget Me/Don't Leave Me Now	1953	15.00
❑ 1412	If You Love Me (Really Love Me)/C'est La Vie	1954	15.00
❑ 1431	Have You Ever Bought a Smile/Next Time You Feel Important	1954	15.00
❑ 1434	Du Bist Mein Liebchen/Two Easter Sunday Sweethearts	1954	15.00
❑ 1475	The Greatest Love of All/Du Bist Mein Liebschen	1954	15.00
❑ 1489	Try Again/Now and Forever	1954	15.00
❑ 1501	My Son, My Son/Our Heaven on Earth	1954	15.00
❑ 1550	I Do/Addio Amore	1955	12.00
❑ 1596	Doonaree/Tell Me What Have They Told You	1955	12.00
❑ 1642	Such a Day/Unfaithful You	1956	12.00
❑ 1688	Ev'ry Day of My Life/Come Back to Me	1956	12.00
❑ 1729	Don't Cry My Love (The Faithful Hussar)/By the Fountains of Rome	1957	12.00
❑ 1752	Travellin' Home/If I Were You	1957	12.00
❑ 1773	Across the Bridge/If I Were You	1958	10.00
❑ 1774	Tonight/I Would Love You Too	1958	10.00
❑ 1793	Seventy-Six Trombones/Another Time, Another Place	1958	10.00
❑ 1811	Ev'ry Hour, Ev'ry Day of My Life/Say	1958	10.00
❑ 1830	Almost in Your Arms/Love Song from "Houseboat"	1959	10.00
❑ 1845	Be Happy/Window	1959	10.00
❑ 1870	Have I Told You Lately That I Love You/I'm a Fool to Forgive You	1959	10.00
❑ 9635	We'll Meet Again/If You Love Me (Really Love Me)	1964	10.00
❑ 9640	Theme from "Dr. Strangelove"/We'll Meet Again	1964	10.00

MGM

Number	Title (A Side/B Side)	Yr	NM
❑ K12976	Accordion/Again	1961	10.00
❑ K13028	Adios, My Love/May Your Heart Stay Young Forever	1961	10.00

UNITED ARTISTS

Number	Title (A Side/B Side)	Yr	NM
❑ 50119	It Hurts to Say Goodbye/In the Snow	1967	10.00
❑ 50238	The Village of St. Bernadette/Santa Maria	1967	15.00

—May only exist as a promo copy

7-Inch Extended Plays

LONDON

Number	Title (A Side/B Side)	Yr	NM
❑ BEP.6042	*Auf Wiederseh'n Sweetheart/From the Time You Say Goodbye (The Parting Song)/Yours/The Love of My Life	195?	10.00
❑ BEP.6042 [PS]	Sincerely Yours	195?	10.00

Albums

LONDON

Number	Title (A Side/B Side)	Yr	NM
❑ LPB-58 [10]	Sincerely Yours	195?	60.00
❑ PS 156 [S]	Vera Lynn Sings Songs of the Twenties	196?	30.00
❑ PS 359 [S]	Wonderful Vera	1964	20.00
❑ LB-690 [10]	Sincerely Yours Vol. 2	195?	60.00
❑ LL 3142 [M]	Vera Lynn Sings Songs of the Twenties	196?	20.00
❑ LL 3294 [M]	Golden Hits	196?	20.00
❑ LL 3359 [M]	Wonderful Vera	1964	20.00

MGM

Number	Title (A Side/B Side)	Yr	NM
❑ E-3887 [M]	Yours	1961	20.00
❑ SE-3887 [S]	Yours	1961	25.00
❑ E-3889 [M]	As Time Goes By	1961	20.00
❑ SE-3889 [S]	As Time Goes By	1961	25.00

STANYAN

Number	Title (A Side/B Side)	Yr	NM
❑ 10032	When the Lights Go On Again	197?	15.00
❑ 10080	Vera Lynn Remembers the World at War	197?	15.00
❑ 10123	Among My Souvenirs	197?	15.00

SUFFOLK MARKETING

Number	Title (A Side/B Side)	Yr	NM
❑ SMI-1-28	All My Best (Her World Famous Recordings)	198?	10.00

UNITED ARTISTS

Number	Title (A Side/B Side)	Yr	NM
❑ UAL-3591 [M]	It Hurts to Say Goodbye	1967	25.00
❑ UAS-6591 [S]	It Hurts to Say Goodbye	1967	15.00

LYNNE, GLORIA

45s

ABC IMPULSE!

Number	Title (A Side/B Side)	Yr	NM
❑ 31003	Out of This World/Thank You Early Bird	1976	4.00

CANYON

Number	Title (A Side/B Side)	Yr	NM
❑ 36	Love's Finally Found Me/If You Don't Get It Yourself	1970	5.00

EVEREST

Number	Title (A Side/B Side)	Yr	NM
❑ 2023	I'll Buy You a Star/Record Company Blues	1963	8.00
❑ 2030	Stormy Monday Blues/Humming Blues	1963	8.00
❑ 2036	I Wish You Love/Through a Long and Sleepless Night	1963	8.00
❑ 2042	I Should Care/Indian Love Call	1964	8.00
❑ 2044	Don't Take Your Love from Me/You Don't Know What Love Is	1964	8.00
❑ 2047	Serenade in Blue/Without a Song	1964	8.00
❑ 2051	On Christmas Day/Wouldn't It Be Loverly	1964	8.00
❑ 2055	Fly Me to the Moon/The Night Has a Thousand Eyes	1965	8.00
❑ 2058	Out of This World/Squeeze Me	1965	8.00
❑ 2059	Lonely Street/Try a Little Tenderness	1965	8.00
❑ 2061	Folks Who Live on the Hill/That's a Joy	1965	8.00
❑ 2062	My Devotion/I'm Glad There Is You	1965	8.00
❑ 19303	June Night/Perdido	1959	12.00
❑ 19308	But Not for Me/Just in Time	1959	12.00
❑ 19326	Be My Love/My Prayer for You	1960	10.00
❑ 19337	Happiness Is Just a Thing Called Joe/My Reverie	1960	10.00
❑ 19367	Gypsy Boy/Recommend to Love	1960	10.00
❑ 19373	Condemned Without Trial/Dreamy	1960	10.00
❑ 19390	Jazz in You/Love, I've Found You	1961	8.00
❑ 19409	He Needs Me/The Lamp Is Low	1961	8.00
❑ 19418	Impossible/This Little Boy of Mine	1961	8.00
❑ 19428	You Don't Have to Be a Tower of Strength/I Will Follow You	1961	12.00
❑ 19431	I'm Glad There Is You/And This Is My Beloved	1962	8.00
❑ 20008	I Know Love/It Just Happened to Me	1962	8.00
❑ 29343 [S]	Perdido/June Night	1960	12.00

—Jukebox issue, small hole, plays at 33 1/3 rpm

Number	Title (A Side/B Side)	Yr	NM
❑ 29344 [S]	Bye Bye Blackbird/April in Paris	1960	12.00

—Jukebox issue, small hole, plays at 33 1/3 rpm

Number	Title (A Side/B Side)	Yr	NM
❑ 29345 [S]	For All We Know/'Tis Autumn	1960	12.00

—Jukebox issue, small hole, plays at 33 1/3 rpm

Number	Title (A Side/B Side)	Yr	NM
❑ 29346 [S]	Little Girl Blue/Am I Blue	1960	12.00

—Jukebox issue, small hole, plays at 33 1/3 rpm

Number	Title (A Side/B Side)	Yr	NM
❑ 29347 [S]	Without a Song/They Didn't Believe Me	1960	12.00

—Jukebox issue, small hole, plays at 33 1/3 rpm

FONTANA

Number	Title (A Side/B Side)	Yr	NM
❑ 1507	The Touch of Your Lips/Intimate Moments	1965	6.00
❑ 1511	Watermelon Man/All Alone	1965	6.00
❑ 1523	The Whisperers/I Understand	1965	6.00
❑ 1538	Speaking of Happiness/Somtimes It Be's That Way	1966	6.00
❑ 1554	Strangers in the Night/Hey, Candy Man	1966	6.00
❑ 1560	Honey Machine/I Got What You Want	1966	6.00
❑ 1567	Love Is/It's Not the Truth	1967	6.00
❑ 1594	Foolish Dreamer/I Can't Stand It	1967	6.00

L

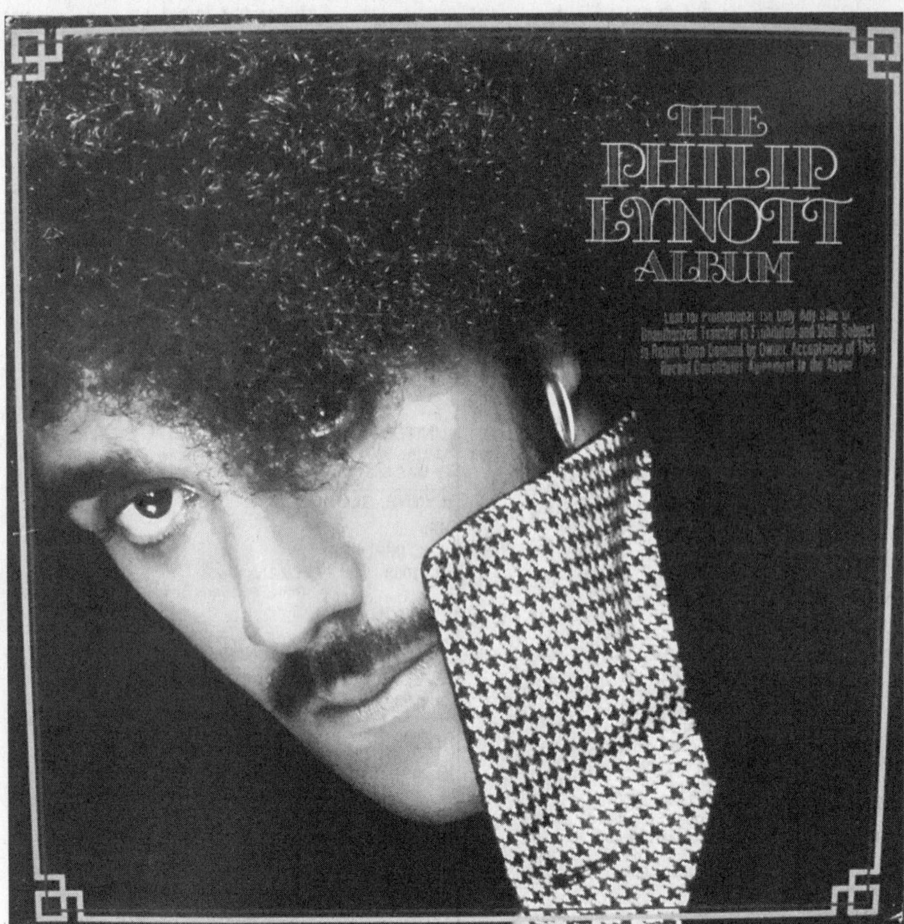

Phil Lynott, *The Philip Lynott Album*, Warner Bros. 23745, 1982, **$24.**

Number	Title (A Side/B Side)	Yr	NM
❑ 1617	I've Never Ever Loved Before/ Down Here on the Ground	1968	5.00
❑ 1627	The Guy Who Lived Up There/ Hold Back the Dawn	1968	5.00
❑ 1639	I've Got to Be Someone/ Problem Child	1969	5.00
❑ 1660	No Easy Way Down/Darlin'	1969	5.00
❑ 1674	Hold It/Untouched by Human Love	1969	5.00
❑ 1890	Be Anything (But Be Mine)/ Soul Serenade	1964	8.00
❑ 1890 [PS]	Be Anything (But Be Mine)/ Soul Serenade	1964	12.00
❑ 1966	Soul Serenade/Do Anything	1965	6.00

HIFI

Number	Title (A Side/B Side)	Yr	NM
❑ 5103	I Wish You Love/Long Long Story	1966	6.00

MERCURY

Number	Title (A Side/B Side)	Yr	NM
❑ 73267	Never My Love/ The Summer Knows	1972	5.00
❑ 73294	Just Let Me Be Me/Kickin' Life	1972	5.00

SEECO

Number	Title (A Side/B Side)	Yr	NM
❑ 6037	Little Boy Blues/Way Beyond the Hills	1959	12.00
❑ 6077	Is There Someone for Me/ I'm Not Afraid Anymore	1961	10.00

7-Inch Extended Plays

EVEREST

Number	Title (A Side/B Side)	Yr	NM
❑ SDBR-196137	And This Is My Beloved/Drinking Again/I Got Rhythm//It Just Happened to Me/Wouldn't It Be Loverly/I Get a Kick Out of You	196?	15.00

—Jukebox issue; small hole, plays at 33 1/3 rpm

Number	Title (A Side/B Side)	Yr	NM
❑ SDBR-196137 [PS]	Gloria Lynne at Basin Street East	196?	15.00

FONTANA

Number	Title (A Side/B Side)	Yr	NM
❑ SRF-751-C	It's Just a Matter of Time/Til There Was You/I Understand// A Sunday Kind of Love/The Whisperers/It May Sound Silly	196?	12.00

—Stereo jukebox issue; small hole, plays at 33 1/3 rpm

Number	Title (A Side/B Side)	Yr	NM
❑ SRF-751-C [PS]	Love and a Woman	196?	12.00

Albums

ABC IMPULSE!

Number	Title (A Side/B Side)	Yr	NM
❑ ASD-9311	I Don't Know How to Love Him	1976	12.00

CANYON

Number	Title (A Side/B Side)	Yr	NM
❑ 7709	Happy and In Love	1970	15.00

COLLECTABLES

Number	Title (A Side/B Side)	Yr	NM
❑ COL-5138	Golden Classics	198?	10.00

DESIGN

Number	Title (A Side/B Side)	Yr	NM
❑ D-177 [M]	My Funny Valentine	196?	10.00
❑ DS-177 [S]	My Funny Valentine	196?	12.00

EVEREST

Number	Title (A Side/B Side)	Yr	NM
❑ ES-1001 [S]	Gloria Lynne Live! Take 1	1959	40.00
❑ SDBR-1022 [S]	Miss Gloria Lynne	1959	30.00
❑ SDBR-1063 [S]	Lonely and Sentimental	1960	30.00
❑ SDBR-1090 [S]	Try a Little Tenderness	1960	30.00
❑ SDBR-1101 [S]	Day In, Day Out	1961	30.00
❑ SDBR-1126 [S]	I'm Glad There Is You	1961	30.00
❑ SDBR-1128 [S]	He Needs Me	1961	30.00
❑ SDBR-1131 [S]	This Little Boy of Mine	1961	30.00
❑ SDBR-1132 [S]	Gloria Lynne at Basin Street East	1962	30.00
❑ SDBR-1203 [S]	Gloria Blue	1962	30.00
❑ SDBR-1208 [S]	Gloria Lynne at the Las Vegas Thunderbird	1963	30.00
❑ EV-1220 [S]	Gloria, Marty & Strings	1963	30.00
❑ EV-1226 [S]	I Wish You Love	1964	25.00
❑ EV-1228 [S]	Glorious Gloria Lynne	1964	25.00
❑ EV-1230 [S]	After Hours	1965	25.00
❑ EV-1231 [S]	The Best of Gloria Lynne	1965	20.00
❑ EV-1237 [S]	Go! Go! Go!	1965	20.00
❑ EV-1238 [S]	Gloria Lynne '66	1966	20.00
❑ E-5001 [M]	Gloria Lynne Live! Take 1	1959	30.00
❑ LPBR-5022 [M]	Miss Gloria Lynne	1959	20.00
❑ LPBR-5063 [M]	Lonely and Sentimental	1960	20.00
❑ LPBR-5090 [M]	Try a Little Tendemess	1960	20.00
❑ LPBR-5101 [M]	Day In, Day Out	1961	20.00
❑ LPBR-5126 [M]	I'm Glad There Is You	1961	20.00
❑ LPBR-5128 [M]	He Needs Me	1961	20.00
❑ LPBR-5131 [M]	This Little Boy of Mine	1961	20.00
❑ LPBR-5132 [M]	Gloria Lynne at Basin Street East	1962	20.00
❑ LPBR-5203 [M]	Gloria Blue	1962	20.00
❑ LPBR-5208 [M]	Gloria Lynne at the Las Vegas Thunderbird	1963	20.00
❑ EV-5220 [M]	Gloria, Marty & Strings	1963	20.00
❑ EV-5226 [M]	I Wish You Love	1964	20.00
❑ EV-5228 [M]	Glorious Gloria Lynne	1964	20.00
❑ EV-5230 [M]	After Hours	1965	20.00
❑ EV-5231 [M]	The Best of Gloria Lynne	1965	15.00
❑ EV-5237 [M]	Go! Go! Go!	1965	15.00
❑ EV-5238 [M]	Gloria Lynne '66	1966	15.00
❑ ST-90057 [M]	I Wish You Love	196?	25.00

—Capitol Record Club edition

FONTANA

Number	Title (A Side/B Side)	Yr	NM
❑ MGF-27528 [M]	Intimate Moments	1964	15.00
❑ MGF-27541 [M]	Soul Serenade	1965	15.00
❑ MGF-27546 [M]	Love and a Woman	1965	15.00
❑ MGF-27555 [M]	Where It's At	1966	15.00
❑ MGF-27561 [M]	Gloria	1966	15.00
❑ MGF-27571 [M]	The Other Side of Gloria Lynne	1967	20.00
❑ SRF-67528 [S]	Intimate Moments	1964	20.00
❑ SRF-67541 [S]	Soul Serenade	1965	20.00
❑ SRF-67546 [S]	Love and a Woman	1965	20.00
❑ SRF-67555 [S]	Where It's At	1966	20.00
❑ SRF-67561 [S]	Gloria	1966	20.00
❑ SRF-67571 [S]	The Other Side of Gloria Lynne	1967	15.00
❑ SRF-67577	Here, There and Everywhere	1968	15.00

HIFI

Number	Title (A Side/B Side)	Yr	NM
❑ L-440 [M]	The Gloria Lynne Calendar	1966	15.00
❑ SL-440 [S]	The Gloria Lynne Calendar	1966	20.00
❑ SR-441	Greatest Hits	1969	15.00

INTERMEDIA

Number	Title (A Side/B Side)	Yr	NM
❑ QS-5069	Classics	198?	10.00

MERCURY

Number	Title (A Side/B Side)	Yr	NM
❑ SRM-1-633	A Very Gentle Sound	1972	15.00

MUSE

Number	Title (A Side/B Side)	Yr	NM
❑ MR-5381	A Time for Love	198?	10.00

SUNSET

Number	Title (A Side/B Side)	Yr	NM
❑ SUM-1145 [M]	Gloria Lynne	1966	12.00
❑ SUM-1171 [M]	I Wish You Love	1967	12.00
❑ SUS-5145 [S]	Gloria Lynne	1966	12.00
❑ SUS-5171 [S]	I Wish You Love	1967	12.00
❑ SUS-5221	Golden Greats	1968	12.00

UPFRONT

Number	Title (A Side/B Side)	Yr	NM
❑ 146	Gloria Lynne	197?	12.00

LYNNE, JEFF

Also see ELECTRIC LIGHT ORCHESTRA.

12-Inch Singles

JET

Number	Title (A Side/B Side)	Yr	NM
❑ JT-DW1072	Doin' That Crazy Thing (3:25)/ Going Down to Rio (3:45)	1977	20.00

45s

A&M

Number	Title (A Side/B Side)	Yr	NM
❑ 2658	Video!/Sooner or Later	1984	—

—Unreleased?

JET

Number	Title (A Side/B Side)	Yr	NM
❑ XW1060	Doin' That Crazy Thing/ Going Down to Rio	1977	6.00
❑ AE7 1220 [DJ]	Doin' That Crazy Thing/ (B-side blank)	1980	6.00

—Small hole, plays at 33 1/3 rpm; later edition than Jet 1060

VIRGIN/EPIC

Number	Title (A Side/B Side)	Yr	NM
❑ 34-04570	Video!/Sooner or Later	1984	4.00

Albums

REPRISE

Number	Title (A Side/B Side)	Yr	NM
❑ 26184	Armchair Theater	1990	15.00

LYNOTT, PHIL

Also see THIN LIZZY.

45s

WARNER BROS.

Number	Title (A Side/B Side)	Yr	NM
❑ 49272	Ode to a Black Man/King's Call	1980	12.00

Albums

WARNER BROS.

Number	Title (A Side/B Side)	Yr	NM
❑ BSK 3405	Solo in Soho	1980	20.00
❑ 23745	The Philip Lynott Album	1982	24.00

LYNYRD SKYNYRD

Also see ROSSINGTON COLLINS BAND; ROSSINGTON, BLACKFOOT, VAN ZANT, JOHNNY VAN ZANT BAND, ALLEN COLLINS, ARTIMUS PYLE BAND, OUTLAWS, DAM YANKEES.

12-Inch Singles

MCA

Number	Title (A Side/B Side)	Yr	NM
❑ L33-17385 [DJ]	Truck Drivin' Man/Simple Man	1987	8.00
❑ L33-17444 [DJ]	Georgia Peaches (same on both sides)	1987	8.00
❑ L33-17488 [DJ]	Swamp Music (same on both sides)	1987	8.00
❑ L33-17569 [DJ]	Gimme Back My Bullets/ Comin' Home	198?	8.00

45s

ATINA

Number	Title (A Side/B Side)	Yr	NM
❑ 129	Need All My Friends/Michelle	1978	15.00

Except when noted otherwise, VG = 25% of NM, and VG+ = 50% of NM. (Example: VG = $2.00, VG+ = $4.00 and NM = $8.00.)

Number	Title (A Side/B Side)	Yr	NM
COLUMBIA			
❑ 78284	White Knuckle Ride/Tearin' It Up	1996	4.00
—B-side by Joe Diffie			
MCA			
❑ L45-1966 [DJ]	Gimme Back My Bullets (same on both sides)	1976	25.00
❑ 40258	Sweet Home Alabama/ Take Your Time	1974	5.00
❑ 40328	Free Bird/Down South Jukin'	1974	5.00
❑ 40416	Saturday Night Special/Made in the Shade	1975	5.00
❑ 40532	Double Trouble/Roll Gypsy Roll	1975	5.00
❑ 40565	Gimme Back My Bullets/All I Can Do Is Write About It	1976	5.00
❑ 40647	Gimme Three Steps/ Travelin' Man	1976	5.00
❑ 40665	Free Bird/Searching	1976	5.00
❑ 40819	What's Your Name/I Know a Little	1977	5.00
—"What's Your Name" is a different mix than that on the Street Survivors LP.			
❑ 40888	You Got That Right/ Ain't No Good Life	1978	5.00
❑ 40957	Down South Jukin'/Wino	1978	5.00
❑ 53206	When You Got Good Friends/ Truck Drivin' Man	1987	4.00
❑ 60191	Sweet Home Alabama/ Saturday Night Special	1976	4.00
—Reissue			
SHADE TREE			
❑ 101	Need All My Friends/Michelle	1971	1500.
—As "Lynard Skynard"; approximately 300 copies pressed			
SOUNDS OF THE SOUTH			
❑ 40158	Gimme Three Steps/Mr. Banker	1973	8.00
❑ 40231	Don't Ask Me No Questions/ Take Your Time	1974	8.00
❑ 40258	Sweet Home Alabama/ Take Your Time	1974	8.00
Albums			
ATLANTIC			
❑ A1-82258	Lynyrd Skynyrd 1991	1991	20.00
—The only U.S. vinyl version was released through Columbia House			
GEFFEN			
❑ MCA 1686	Second Helping	2008	20.00
MCA			
❑ 363	(pronounced leh-nerd skin-nerd)	1975	12.00
—Reissue on black rainbow label			
❑ 413	Second Helping	1975	12.00
—Reissue on black rainbow label			
❑ 1448	Best of the Rest	1985	8.00
❑ L33-1946 [(2)DJ]	One More From the Road	1976	25.00
—Promo only on black vinyl			
❑ L33-1946 [(2)DJ]	One More From the Road	1976	50.00
—Promo on blue, gold, purple or red vinyl (each has the same value)			
❑ L33-1988 [DJ]	Skynyrd's First and...Last	1978	25.00
—Promo sampler			
❑ 2137	Nuthin' Fancy	1975	12.00
❑ 2170	Gimme Back My Bullets	1976	12.00
❑ 3019	(pronounced leh-nerd skin-nerd)	1976	10.00
—Second reissue with new number on black rainbow label			
❑ 3020	Second Helping	1976	10.00
—Second reissue with new number on black rainbow label			
❑ 3021	Nuthin' Fancy	1976	10.00
—Reissue with new number on black rainbow label			
❑ 3022	Gimme Back My Bullets	1977	10.00
—Reissue with new number on black rainbow label			
❑ 3029	Street Survivors	1977	10.00
—After the band's plane crash, the "flames" photo was replaced with the back cover photo; the back cover is black with only the song titles			
❑ 3029	Street Survivors	1977	25.00
—Originals with the band in flames on the front cover and a smaller band photo on the back cover			
❑ 3047	Skynyrd's First and...Last	1978	12.00
—Originals with tan labels and gatefold cover			
❑ 5221	(pronounced leh-nerd skin-nerd)	1980	8.00
❑ 5222	Second Helping	1980	8.00
❑ 5223	Street Survivors	1980	8.00
❑ 5370	Best of the Rest	1982	10.00
—Original version			
❑ 6001 [(2)]	One More From the Road	1976	15.00
—Originals with black rainbow label and gatefold cover			
❑ 6897 [(2)]	One More From the Road	1985	10.00
—Most, if not all, of these pressings have no gatefold			
❑ 6898 [(2)]	Gold & Platinum	1985	10.00
—Most, if not all, of these pressings have no gatefold			
❑ 8011 [(2)]	One More From the Road	1977	12.00
—First reissue with new number			
❑ 8027 [(2)]	Southern by the Grace of God	1988	12.00
❑ 10014 [(2)]	One More From the Road	1980	10.00
—Second reissue			
❑ 11008 [(2)]	Gold & Platinum	1979	12.00
—Originals with embossed gatefold cover			
❑ 37069	Gimme Back My Bullets	1980	8.00
❑ 37070	Nuthin' Fancy	1980	8.00
❑ 37071	Skynyrd's First and...Last	1980	8.00
❑ 37211	(pronounced leh-nerd skin-nerd)	1985	8.00

Lynyrd Skynyrd, *Gimme Back My Bullets*, MCA 2170, 1976, **$12.**

Number	Title (A Side/B Side)	Yr	NM
❑ 37212	Second Helping	1985	8.00
❑ 37213	Street Survivors	1985	8.00
❑ 42084	Legend	1987	10.00
❑ 42293	Skynyrd's Innyrds	1989	12.00
SOUNDS OF THE SOUTH			
❑ 363	(pronounced leh-nerd skin-nerd)	1973	20.00
❑ 413	Second Helping	1974	20.00
—Both of the above are original pressings with yellow labels			

LYONS, MARIE

Number	Title (A Side/B Side)	Yr	NM
45s			
DELUXE			
❑ 101	Drown in My Own Tears/Try Me	1968	12.00
—As "Queenie Lyons"			
❑ 103	Fever/Your Key Don't Fit No More	1969	10.00
—As "Marie 'Queenie' Lyons"			
❑ 123	Daddy's House/ See and Don't See	1970	10.00
Albums			
DELUXE			
❑ 12001	Soul Fever	1970	25.00

LYZER, TONY

Number	Title (A Side/B Side)	Yr	NM
45s			
LAURIE			
❑ 3019	Six Little Men/Loco	1958	150.00

M

M.H. ROYALS, THE

Number	Title (A Side/B Side)	Yr	NM
45s			
ABC			
❑ 10907	Tomorrow's Dead/ She's Gone Forever	1967	25.00
❑ 10957	Old Town/Now She's Crying	1967	25.00

M.P.D. LIMITED

Number	Title (A Side/B Side)	Yr	NM
45s			
LTD			
❑ 400	Little Boy Sad/Wendy Don't Go	1965	40.00

M-3'S, THE

Number	Title (A Side/B Side)	Yr	NM
45s			
ABC-PARAMOUNT			
❑ 10772	Funny Cafe/So Give Me Love	1966	25.00
UNITED ARTISTS			
❑ 737	When the Party's Over/ Magic Kiss	1964	12.00
❑ 889	Three Lonely Nights/ I See a Rainbow	1965	12.00

MABLEY, MOMS

Number	Title (A Side/B Side)	Yr	NM
45s			
MERCURY			
❑ 72935	Abraham, Martin and John/ Sunny	1969	6.00
❑ 72958	His Way/Yes Indeed	1969	6.00
❑ 72974	It's Your Thing/He's Got the Whole World in His Hands	1969	6.00
❑ 73240	I Surrender Dear/That's Pops	1971	5.00
Albums			
CHESS			
❑ LP-1447 [M]	Moms Mabley, Funniest Woman in the World, Onstage	1961	25.00
❑ LP-1452 [M]	Moms Mabley at the "UN"	1961	25.00
❑ LP-1460 [M]	Moms Mabley at the Playboy Club	1961	25.00
❑ LP-1463 [M]	Moms Mabley at Geneva Conference	1962	25.00
❑ LP-1472 [M]	Moms Mabley Breaks It Up	1962	25.00
❑ LP-1477 [M]	Young Men, Si — Old Men, No	1962	25.00
❑ LP-1479 [M]	I Got Somethin' to Tell You!	1963	25.00
❑ LP-1482 [M]	The Funny Sides of Moms Mabley	1963	25.00
❑ LP-1486 [M]	Moms Wows	1964	25.00
❑ LP-1487 [M]	The Best of Moms	1964	25.00

Number	Title (A Side/B Side)	Yr	NM
❑ LP-1497 [M]	The Man in My Life	1965	20.00
❑ LPS-1525	Moms Mabley Breaks Up the Network	1968	20.00
❑ LPS-1530	Moms Mabley Sings	1969	20.00

MERCURY

Number	Title (A Side/B Side)	Yr	NM
❑ MG-20889 [M]	Out on a Limb	1964	15.00
❑ MG-20907 [M]	Moms the Word	1964	15.00
❑ MG-21012 [M]	Now Hear This	1965	15.00
❑ MG-21090 [M]	Moms Mabley at the White House	1966	15.00
❑ MG-21139 [M]	The Best of Moms Mabley	1967	25.00
❑ SR-60889 [S]	Out on a Limb	1964	20.00
❑ SR-60907 [S]	Moms the Word	1964	20.00
❑ SR-61012 [S]	Now Hear This	1965	20.00
❑ SR-61090 [S]	Moms Mabley at the White House	1966	20.00
❑ SR-61139 [S]	The Best of Moms Mabley	1967	15.00
❑ SR-61205	Her Young Thing	1969	15.00
❑ SR-61229	The Youngest Teenager	1969	15.00
❑ SR-61235	Abraham, Martin and John	1969	15.00
❑ SR-61263	Live at Sing Sing	1970	15.00

MACH, LEON

45s

LAVENDER

Number	Title (A Side/B Side)	Yr	NM
❑ 1554	You Hurt Me So/It's You I Love	1960	100.00

MACK, LONNIE

45s

BUCCANEER

Number	Title (A Side/B Side)	Yr	NM
❑ 3001	Memphis/Lonnie on the Move	196?	8.00

—Reissue of Fraternity material

CAPITOL

Number	Title (A Side/B Side)	Yr	NM
❑ 4441	Running Wild/Funky Country Living	1977	5.00

ELEKTRA

Number	Title (A Side/B Side)	Yr	NM
❑ 45638	Memphis/Why	1968	10.00
❑ 45652	Save Your Money/In the Band	1969	10.00
❑ 45715	Lay It Down/She Even Woke Me Up to Say Goodbye	1971	8.00
❑ 45715 [PS]	Lay It Down/She Even Woke Me Up to Say Goodbye	1971	15.00
❑ 45761	Rings/Florida	1972	8.00

EPIC

Number	Title (A Side/B Side)	Yr	NM
❑ 07973	Too Rock for Country, Too Country for Rock and Roll/Lucille	1988	4.00
❑ 08117	Hard Life/50's-60's Man	1988	4.00

FRATERNITY

Number	Title (A Side/B Side)	Yr	NM
❑ 906	Memphis/Down in the Dumps	1963	15.00
❑ 912	Wham!/Susie-Q	1963	15.00
❑ 918	Baby, What's Wrong/Where There's a Will	1963	12.00
❑ 920	Say Something Nice to Me/Lonnie on the Move	1964	12.00
❑ 925	I've Had It/Nashville	1964	12.00
❑ 932	Chicken Pickin'/Sa-Ba-Hoola	1964	12.00
❑ 938	Don't Make My Baby Blue/Oh Boy	1964	12.00
❑ 942	Crying Over You/Coastin'	1965	12.00
❑ 946	Tonky Go Go/When I'm Alone	1965	12.00
❑ 951	Honky Tonk '65/Chicken Pickin'	1965	12.00
❑ 957	Crying Over You/Are You Guilty	1966	12.00
❑ 959	The Circus/Bucaroo	1966	12.00
❑ 967	Tension (Part 1)/Tension (Part 2)	1966	12.00
❑ 969	Wildwood Flower/Snow on the Mountain	1966	12.00
❑ 981	I Left My Heart in San Francisco/Omaha	1967	10.00
❑ 986	Save Your Money/Snow on the Mountain	1967	10.00
❑ 1004	Soul Express/Down and Out	1968	10.00
❑ 1278	Soul Express/I Found a Love	197?	6.00

ROULETTE

Number	Title (A Side/B Side)	Yr	NM
❑ 7175	All We Need Is Love, You and Me/Highway 56	1975	6.00

Albums

ALLIGATOR

Number	Title (A Side/B Side)	Yr	NM
❑ AL-3903	The Wham of That Memphis Man	1987	10.00

—Reissue of Fraternity LP

Number	Title (A Side/B Side)	Yr	NM
❑ AL-4739	Strike Like Lightning	1985	10.00
❑ AL-4750	Second Sight	1987	10.00
❑ AL-4786	Live!: Attack of the Killer V	1990	12.00

CAPITOL

Number	Title (A Side/B Side)	Yr	NM
❑ ST-11619	Home at Last	1976	12.00
❑ ST-11703	Lonnie Mack and Pismo	1977	12.00

ELEKTRA

Number	Title (A Side/B Side)	Yr	NM
❑ EKS-74040	Glad I'm In the Band	1969	25.00
❑ EKS-74050	Whatever's Right	1969	25.00
❑ EKS-74077	For Collectors Only	1970	25.00
❑ EKS-74102	The Hills of Indiana	1971	25.00

EPIC

Number	Title (A Side/B Side)	Yr	NM
❑ FE 44075	Roadhouses and Dance Halls	1989	12.00

FRATERNITY

Number	Title (A Side/B Side)	Yr	NM
❑ SF-1014 [M]	The Wham of That Memphis Man	1963	120.00
❑ SSF-1014 [S]	The Wham of That Memphis Man	1963	300.00

TRIP

Number	Title (A Side/B Side)	Yr	NM
❑ TLX-9522 [(2)]	The Memphis Sounds of Lonnie Mack	1975	12.00

MACLAINE, SHIRLEY

45s

DECCA

Number	Title (A Side/B Side)	Yr	NM
❑ 32446	My Personal Property/Where Am I Going	1969	8.00
❑ 32446 [PS]	My Personal Property/Where Am I Going	1969	12.00

RCA VICTOR

Number	Title (A Side/B Side)	Yr	NM
❑ 47-9699	The Way That I Live/Mr. Blossom Goes "Bust"	1968	8.00

—B-side by Riz Ortolani

20TH CENTURY FOX

Number	Title (A Side/B Side)	Yr	NM
❑ 558	John Goldfarb, Please Come Home/Moo Goo Gai Pan	1965	12.00

Albums

COLUMBIA

Number	Title (A Side/B Side)	Yr	NM
❑ PC 34223	Live at the Palace	1976	12.00

MACRAE, GORDON

Also see JO STAFFORD AND GORDON MacRAE.

45s

CAPITOL

Number	Title (A Side/B Side)	Yr	NM
❑ 54-628	Ting-a-Ling/Lover's Gold	1949	25.00
❑ 54-711	The Wedding of Lilli Marlene/Twenty-Four Hours of Sunshine	1949	25.00
❑ 54-755	The Prairie Is Still/Sunshine of Your Smile	1949	25.00
❑ 54-777	Mule Train/Dear Hearts and Gentle People	1949	25.00
❑ F812	I'm Yours/Just One More Chance	1950	20.00
❑ F842	Poison Ivy/Half a Heart Is All You Left Me (When You Broke My Heart in Two)	1950	20.00
❑ F924	Oh, Oh, Ophelia/Two-Faced Heart	1950	20.00
❑ F935	Kisses and Tears/As We Are Today	1950	20.00
❑ F959	River of Smoke/This Is Heaven to Me	1950	20.00
❑ F1021	The Stars and Stripes Forever/Hongi-Tongi-Goki-Poki	1950	20.00
❑ F1168	Love 'Em All/Pigskin Polka	1950	20.00
❑ F1193	Honestly, I Love You/Just the Way You Are	1950	20.00
❑ F1214	You Love Me/You're Gonna Lose Your Gal	1950	20.00
❑ F1289	Use Your Imagination/I Am Loved	1950	20.00
❑ F1317	You Did Your Hair Chartreuse/Honky Tonk 10 Cent Dance	1950	20.00
❑ F1374	O Kive Neabs Kive (Love Means Love)/Wait for Me	1951	15.00
❑ F1471	I'm Yours to Command/I'll Buy You a Star	1951	15.00
❑ F1545	Cuban Love Song/Last Night When We Were Young	1951	15.00
❑ F1684	So in Love/Ramona	1951	12.00

—Reissue

Number	Title (A Side/B Side)	Yr	NM
❑ F1705	Ol' Man River/On Sunday at Coney Island	1951	15.00
❑ F1750	Cuddle Up a Little Closer/Down Old Ox Road	1951	15.00
❑ F1836	Be My Guest/Laughing at Love	1951	15.00
❑ F1846	My Love/How Close	1951	15.00
❑ F1941	Baby Doll/Green Acres, Purple Mountains	1952	12.00
❑ F1959	My Buick, My Lover and I/Lovers' Waltz	1952	12.00

—With Gisele MacKenzie

Number	Title (A Side/B Side)	Yr	NM
❑ F1990	Call Her Sweetheart/900 Miles	1952	12.00
❑ F2010	Gentle Hands/These Things Shall Pass	1952	12.00
❑ F2047	No Other Girl/If Someone Had Told Me	1952	12.00
❑ F2115	Peace in the Valley/Mansion Over the Hilltop	1952	12.00
❑ F2196	Blame it on My Youth/There's a Lull in My Life	1952	12.00
❑ F2311	Starlight and Narrow/Brotherly Love	1952	12.00
❑ 2329	Only Love/Knowing When to Leave	1968	7.00
❑ F2352	Congratulations to Someone/How Do You Speak to an Angel	1953	12.00
❑ F2465	C'est Magnifique/Homin' Time	1953	12.00
❑ F2603	I Still Dream of You/I Don't Want to Walk Without You	1953	12.00
❑ F2652	Stranger in Paradise/Never in a Million Years	1953	12.00
❑ F2672	Soothe My Lonely Heart/High on a Windy Hill	1953	12.00
❑ F2760	Face to Face/Backward Turn Backward	1954	12.00
❑ F2784	Coney Island Boat/Open Your Arms	1954	12.00

—With June Hutton

Number	Title (A Side/B Side)	Yr	NM
❑ F2927	Count Your Blessings Instead of Sheep/Cara Mia	1954	12.00
❑ F2988	Here's What I'm Here For/Love Can Change the Stars	1954	12.00
❑ F3085	You Forgot to Tell Me/Tikatee Tikatay	1955	10.00
❑ F3122	Bella Notte/Follow Your Heart	1955	10.00
❑ F3191	Jim Bowie/Why Break the Heart That Loves You	1955	10.00
❑ F3214	People Will Say We're in Love/Surrey with the Fringe on Top	1955	10.00
❑ F3284	(Here's to) A Wonderful Christmas/A Woman in Love	1955	12.00
❑ F3315	Fate/Never Before and Never Again	1956	10.00
❑ F3384	I've Grown Accustomed to Your Face/Who Are We	1956	10.00
❑ F3438	I Asked the Lord/One Misty Morning	1956	10.00
❑ F3519	Without Love/Obey	1956	10.00
❑ F3641	Till We Meet Again/Lonely	1957	10.00
❑ F3724	When You Kiss Me/Endless Love	1957	10.00
❑ F3816	Sayonara/Never Till Now	1957	10.00
❑ F3864	If I Forget You/Now	1957	10.00
❑ F4033	The Secret/A Man Once Said	1958	10.00
❑ F4116	Fly Little Bluebird/Little Do You Know	1959	8.00
❑ F4179	Stranger/Palace of Love	1959	8.00
❑ 4323	The Sound of Music/When Did I Fall in Love	1959	8.00
❑ 4357	Our Love Story/You Were There	1960	8.00

—With Sheila MacRae

Number	Title (A Side/B Side)	Yr	NM
❑ 4483	Dolce Par Niente/If Ever I Would Leave You	1960	8.00
❑ 4613	Face to Face/Sail Away	1961	8.00
❑ 4626	Impossible/Ordinary People	1961	8.00
❑ 4736	Nobody Told Me/The Sweetest Sounds	1962	8.00
❑ 4773	Lovely/Warmer Than a Whisper	1962	8.00
❑ 5693	If She Walked Into My Life/I Want to Be with You	1966	7.00
❑ F15597	I Surrender Dear/I'm Yours	195?	15.00
❑ F15598	You Were Meant for Me/A Kiss in the Dark	195?	15.00
❑ F15599	Body and Soul/The Sunshine of Your Smile	195?	15.00

—The above three comprise a box set

Number	Title (A Side/B Side)	Yr	NM
❑ 54-90034	Merry Christmas Waltz/Adeste Fideles	1949	40.00

MGM

Number	Title (A Side/B Side)	Yr	NM
❑ K10734	They Say It's Wonderful/Prisoner of Love	1950	30.00

7-Inch Extended Plays

CAPITOL

Number	Title (A Side/B Side)	Yr	NM
❑ EAP 1-765	(contents unknown)	1956	10.00
❑ EAP 1-765 [PS]	The Best Things in Life Are Free, Part 1	1956	10.00
❑ EAP 2-765	(contents unknown)	1956	10.00
❑ EAP 2-765 [PS]	The Best Things in Life Are Free, Part 2	1956	10.00
❑ EAP 3-765	(contents unknown)	1956	10.00
❑ EAP 3-765 [PS]	The Best Things in Life Are Free, Part 3	1956	10.00
❑ EAP 3-834	*The Last Round-Up/Green Grow the Lilacs/Wagon Wheels/I Went to the City	1957	10.00
❑ EAP 3-834 [PS]	Cowboy's Lament, Part 3	1957	10.00

Albums

ALLEGRO ROYALE

Number	Title (A Side/B Side)	Yr	NM
❑ 1606 [M]	Gordon MacRae	1952	20.00

ANGEL

Number	Title (A Side/B Side)	Yr	NM
❑ S 37318	The Student Prince	1973	10.00

—Operetta with Dorothy Kirsten; reissue of Capitol SW 1841

Number	Title (A Side/B Side)	Yr	NM
❑ S 37319	The Desert Song	1973	10.00

—Operetta with Dorothy Kirsten; reissue of Capitol SW 1842

Number	Title (A Side/B Side)	Yr	NM
❑ S 37320	The New Moon	1973	10.00

—Operetta with Dorothy Kirsten; reissue of Capitol SW 1966

CAPITOL

Number	Title (A Side/B Side)	Yr	NM
❑ ST-125	Only Love	1969	12.00
❑ H 218 [10]	The Vagabond King	1951	50.00

—Operetta with Lucille Norman

Number	Title (A Side/B Side)	Yr	NM
❑ P 219 [M]	New Moon and The Vagabond King	1951	30.00

—Operettas with Lucille Norman; original

M

Except when noted otherwise, VG = 25% of NM, and VG+ = 50% of NM. (Example: VG = $2.00, VG+ = $4.00 and NM = $8.00.)

Number	Title (A Side/B Side)	Yr	NM
❑ T 219 [M]	New Moon and The Vagabond King	195?	30.00
—Operettas with Lucille Norman; turquoise label			
❑ H 231 [10]	Gordon MacRae Sings	1951	40.00
❑ L 334 [10]	Roberta	1952	40.00
—Operetta with Lucille Norman and Anne Triola			
❑ L 335 [10]	The Merry Widow	1952	40.00
—With Lucille Norman			
❑ L 351 [10]	The Desert Song	1953	40.00
—Operetta with Lucille Norman and Bob Sands			
❑ T 394 [M]	The Desert Song and Roberta	195?	30.00
—Turquoise label original			
❑ L 407 [10]	The Student Prince	1953	40.00
—Operetta with Dorothy Warenskjold and Harry Stanton			
❑ H 422 [10]	By the Light of the Silvery Moon	1953	40.00
—With June Hutton; not the soundtrack from the movie because MacRae and movie co-star Doris Day were on different labels			
❑ P 437 [M]	The Student Prince and The Merry Widow	1953	40.00
—Original			
❑ T 437 [M]	The Student Prince and The Merry Widow	195?	30.00
—Turqiouse label original			
❑ L 468 [10]	Naughty Marietta	1954	40.00
—Operetta with Marguerite Piazza			
❑ L 485 [10]	3 Sailors and a Girl	1953	60.00
—With Jane Powell and Gene Nelson			
❑ L 530 [10]	The Red Mill	1954	40.00
—Operetta with Lucille Norman			
❑ T 537 [M]	Romantic Ballads	1955	30.00
—Turquoise or gray label			
❑ T 551 [M]	Naughty Marietta and The Red Mill	1955	30.00
—Turquoise label original			
❑ T 681 [M]	Operetta Favorites	1956	30.00
—Turquoise or gray label			
❑ T 765 [M]	The Best Things in Life Are Free	1956	30.00
—Turquoise or gray label			
❑ T 834 [M]	Cowboy's Lament	1957	30.00
—Turquoise or gray label			
❑ T 875 [M]	Motion Picture Soundstage	1957	30.00
—Turquoise or gray label			
❑ ST 980 [S]	Gordon MacRae in Concert	1959	40.00
—Black colorband label, logo at left			
❑ T 980 [M]	Gordon MacRae in Concert	1957	30.00
—Turquoise or gray label			
❑ T 1050 [M]	This Is Gordon MacRae	1958	30.00
—Turquoise label			
❑ ST 1146 [S]	The Seasons of Love	1959	20.00
—Black colorband label, Capitol logo at left			
❑ T 1146 [M]	The Seasons of Love	1959	15.00
—Black colorband label, Capitol logo at left			
❑ ST 1251 [S]	Songs for an Evening at Home	1959	20.00
—Black colorband label, Capitol logo at left			
❑ T 1251 [M]	Songs for an Evening at Home	1959	15.00
—Black colorband label, Capitol logo at left			
❑ ST 1353 [S]	Our Love Story	1960	20.00
—With Sheila MacRae; black colorband label, Capitol logo at left			
❑ T 1353 [M]	Our Love Story	1960	15.00
—With Sheila MacRae; black colorband label, Capitol logo at left			
❑ ST 1466 [S]	Hallowed Be Thy Name	1960	20.00
—Black colorband label, Capitol logo at left			
❑ T 1466 [M]	Hallowed Be Thy Name	1960	15.00
—Black colorband label, Capitol logo at left			
❑ SW 1841 [S]	The Student Prince	1963	15.00
—Operetta with Dorothy Kirsten			
❑ W 1841 [M]	The Student Prince	1963	12.00
—Opertta with Dorothy Kirsten			
❑ SW 1842 [S]	The Desert Song	1963	15.00
—Operetta with Dorothy Kirsten			
❑ W 1842 [M]	The Desert Song	1963	12.00
—Operetta with Dorothy Kirsten			
❑ SW 1966 [S]	The New Moon	1963	15.00
—Operetta with Dorothy Kirsten			
❑ W 1966 [M]	The New Moon	1963	12.00
—Operetta with Dorothy Kirsten			
❑ SW 2022 [S]	Kismet	1964	15.00
—Operetta with Dorothy Kirsten			
❑ W 2022 [M]	Kismet	1964	12.00
—Operetta with Dorothy Kirsten			
❑ ST 2578 [S]	If She Walked Into My Life	1966	15.00
❑ T 2578 [M]	If She Walked Into My Life	1966	12.00
COLORTONE			
❑ 4939 [M]	Gordon MacRae Sings	1958	15.00
EVON			
❑ 320 [M]	Gordon MacRae Sings	1958	15.00
—Reissue of Allegro Royale LP			
GALAXY			
❑ 4805 [M]	Gordon MacRae	1958	15.00
—Reissue of Allegro Royale LP			
RONDO-LETTE			
❑ A5 [M]	Gordon MacRae	1958	15.00
—Reissue of Allegro Royale LP			
ROYALE			
❑ 18106 [10]	Gordon MacRae and Walter Gross Orchestra	195?	30.00
❑ 18155 [10]	Gordon MacRae and Orchestra	195?	30.00
SUTTON			
❑ SSU 292 [R]	Gordon MacRae Sings Broadway's Best!	196?	10.00
❑ SU 292 [M]	Gordon MacRae Sings Broadway's Best!	196?	10.00

MACRAE, GORDON, AND JO STAFFORD

See JO STAFFORD AND GORDON MacRAE.

MACRAE, SHEILA

Albums

Number	Title (A Side/B Side)	Yr	NM
ABC			
❑ ABCS-611	How Sweet She Is	1968	25.00

MAD HATTERS, THE

45s

Number	Title (A Side/B Side)	Yr	NM
ASCOT			
❑ 2197	I Need Love/Blowin' in the Wind	1965	25.00
FONTANA			
❑ 1582	I'll Come Running/Hello Girl	1967	20.00
IGL			
❑ 117	Her Love/Route 66	196?	15.00

MAD LADS, THE

45s

Number	Title (A Side/B Side)	Yr	NM
CAPITOL			
❑ 5284	Don't Cry at the Party/I'll Survive	1964	15.00
STAX			
❑ 160	Surf Jerk/Sidewalk Surf	1964	15.00
VOLT			
❑ 127	Don't Have to Shop Around/Tear-Maker	1965	10.00
❑ 131	I Want Someone/Nothing Can Break Through	1965	10.00
❑ 135	Come Closer to Me/Sugar Sugar	1966	10.00
❑ 137	I Want a Girl/What Will Love Tend to Make You Do	1966	10.00
❑ 139	Patch My Heart/You Mean So Much to Me	1966	10.00
❑ 143	These Simple Reasons/I Don't Want to Lose Your Love	1967	10.00
❑ 150	My Inspiration/Mr. Fix-It	1967	10.00
❑ 162	Whatever Hurts You/No Time Is Better Than Right Now	1968	10.00
❑ 4003	So Nice/Make Room	1968	8.00
❑ 4009	Love Is Here Today and Gone Tomorrow/Make This Young Lady Mine	1969	8.00
❑ 4016	By the Time I Get to Phoenix/No Strings Attached	1969	8.00
❑ 4041	Seeing Is Believing/These Old Memories	1970	8.00
❑ 4068	Gone! The Promises of Yesterday/I'm So Glad I Fell in Love with You	1971	8.00
❑ 4080	Let Me Repair Your Heart/Did My Baby Call	1972	8.00
❑ 4098	I Forgot to Be Your Lover/I'm So Glad I Fell in Love with You	1973	8.00
WAND			
❑ 11221	Let's Have Some Fun (Part 1)/Let's Have Some Fun (Part 2)	1970	10.00

Albums

Number	Title (A Side/B Side)	Yr	NM
STAX			
❑ MPS-8525	The Best of the Mad Lads	198?	10.00
VOLT			
❑ 414 [M]	The Mad Lads In Action	1966	30.00
❑ S-414 [S]	The Mad Lads In Action	1966	40.00
❑ VOS-6005	The Mad, Mad, Mad, Mad, Mad Lads	1969	30.00
❑ VOS-6020	A New Beginning	1973	20.00

MAD MILO

45s

Number	Title (A Side/B Side)	Yr	NM
COMBO			
❑ 131	Elvis on Trial/A Date with Elvis	1957	50.00
MILLION			
❑ 20018	Elvis for Christmas/New Year	1957	50.00
—B-side by Ron Tan and Combo			

MAD RIVER

45s

Number	Title (A Side/B Side)	Yr	NM
CAPITOL			
❑ 2310	A Gazelle/High All the Time	1968	12.00
❑ 2559	Copper Plates/Harfy Magnum	1969	12.00

Albums

Number	Title (A Side/B Side)	Yr	NM
CAPITOL			
❑ ST-185	Paradise Bar and Grill	1969	75.00
❑ ST 2985	Mad River	1968	75.00

MADDOX, JOHNNY

45s

Number	Title (A Side/B Side)	Yr	NM
DOT			
❑ 116	Coconut Grove/In the Mood	196?	5.00
—Reissue of 16023			
❑ 117	The Crazy Otto (Medley)/Eight Beat Boogie	196?	5.00
—Reissue of 16029			
❑ 152	San Antonio Rose/Beg Your Pardon	1966	5.00
—Reissue			
❑ 163	Crazy Bone Rag/St. Louis Tickle	1967	5.00
—Reissue of 1005			
❑ 164	Hula Blues/I Get the Blues When It Rains	1967	5.00
—Reissue of 1012			
❑ 165	Memphis Blues/Alabama Jubilee	1967	5.00
—Reissue of 1023			
❑ 166	Sweet Georgia Brown/Dill Pickles	1967	5.00
—Reissue of 1057			
❑ 167	Ida/School Days	1967	5.00
—Reissue of 15066			
❑ 168	Margie/Swanee River	1967	5.00
—Reissue of 15067			
❑ 169	Me and My Shadow/Peggy O'Neil	1967	5.00
—Reissue of 15068			
❑ 170	Angry/Shine	1967	5.00
—Reissue of 15069			
❑ 171	Blue Moon/A Shanty in Old Shanty Town	1967	5.00
—Reissue of 15070			
❑ 172	Should I/You Were Meant for Me	1967	5.00
—Reissue of 15071			
❑ 173	Baby Face/Moonlight and Roses	1967	5.00
—Reissue of 15072			
❑ 174	Jealous/Tea for Two	1967	5.00
—Reissue of 15073			
❑ 175	Hindustan/Carolina in the Morning	1967	5.00
—Reissue of 15074			
❑ 176	Avalon/Tip Toe Through the Tulips	1967	5.00
—Reissue of 15075			
❑ 177	Bye Bye Blackbird/The Sheik of Araby	1967	5.00
—Reissue of 15076			
❑ 178	Ain't She Sweet/Do You Ever Think of Me	1967	5.00
—Reissue of 15077			
❑ 179	Lady in Red/Blue Night	1967	5.00
—Reissue of 15270			
❑ 180	Oh Lady Be Good/Oh You Beautiful Doll	1967	5.00
—Reissue of 15280			
❑ 181	Camptown Races/I'm Looking Over a Four Leaf Clover	1967	5.00
—Reissue of 15281			
❑ 182	Pretty Baby/Shine On Harvest Moon	1967	5.00
—Reissue of 15282			
❑ 183	Smiles/Over the Waves	1967	5.00
—Reissue of 15283			
❑ 184	Humoresque/The Stars and Stripes Forever	1967	5.00
—Reissue of 15284			
❑ 185	Whispering/Dixie-Yankee Doodle	1967	5.00
—Reissue of 15285			
❑ 186	After the Ball/Bye Bye Blues	1967	5.00
—Reissue of 15286			
❑ 187	Golden Slippers/Washington and Lee Swing	1967	5.00
—Reissue of 15287			
❑ 188	Sidewalks of New York/Chinatown, My Chinatown	1967	5.00
—Reissue of 15288			
❑ 189	Glow-Worm/Chicken Reel	1967	5.00
—Reissue of 15289			
❑ 1005	Crazy Bone Rag/St. Louis Tickle	1950	20.00
❑ 1012	Hula Blues/I Get the Blues When It Rains	1950	20.00
❑ 1023	Memphis Blues/Alabama Jubilee	1951	20.00
❑ 1057	Sweet Georgia Brown/Dill Pickles	1951	20.00
❑ 15001	San Antonio Rose/Bully of the Town	1951	15.00
❑ 15004	Under the Double Eagle/My Mary	1951	15.00
❑ 15006	Star Dust/Piano Polka	1952	15.00
❑ 15008	Johnny Maddox Boogie/Near You	1952	15.00
❑ 15014	Why Worry/Friday Night Stomp	1952	15.00
❑ 15015	Listen to the Mocking Bird/Molly Darling	1952	15.00
❑ 15020	Little Grass Shack/Coconut Grove	1952	15.00
❑ 15021	Sioux City Sue/Johnny Maddox Special	1952	15.00

M

Number	Title (A Side/B Side)	Yr	NM
❑ 15026	At the Georgia Camp Meeting/Elite Syncopations	1952	15.00
❑ 15027	Porcupine Rag/Sunflower Slow Drag	1952	15.00
❑ 15028	Sleepy Sidney/African Pass	1952	15.00
❑ 15029	Smokey Mokes/Tickled to Death	1952	15.00
❑ 15045	In the Mood/By the Light of the Silvery Moon	1953	15.00
❑ 15056	Johnny's Boogie Blues/Blue Danube	1953	15.00
❑ 15057	12th Street Rag/Little Girl	1953	15.00
❑ 15058	Sweet Leilani/Goodbye Girls, I'm Through	1953	15.00
❑ 15059	Honey Song/Alice Blue Gown	1953	15.00
❑ 15062	Twilight Time/Alice Blue Gown	1953	15.00
❑ 15066	Ida/School Days	1953	12.00
❑ 15067	Margie/Swanee River	1953	12.00
❑ 15068	Me and My Shadow/Peggy O'Neil	1953	12.00
❑ 15069	Angry/Shine	1953	12.00
❑ 15070	Blue Moon/A Shanty in Old Shanty Town	1953	12.00
❑ 15071	Should I/You Were Meant for Me	1953	12.00
❑ 15072	Baby Face/Moonlight and Roses	1953	12.00
❑ 15073	Jealous/Tea for Two	1953	12.00
❑ 15074	Hindustan/Carolina in the Morning	1953	12.00
❑ 15075	Avalon/Tip Toe Through the Tulips	1953	12.00
❑ 15076	Bye Bye Blackbird/The Sheik of Araby	1953	12.00
❑ 15077	Ain't She Sweet/Do You Ever Think of Me	1953	12.00
❑ 15090	Eight Beat Boogie/Learning	1953	15.00
❑ 15102	Dipsy Doodle/Alexander's Ragtime Band	1953	15.00
❑ 15120	I Saw Mommy Kissing Santa Claus/Rudolph the Red-Nosed Reindeer	1953	15.00
❑ 15128	There's a Star Spangled Banner Waving Somewhere/I Don't Love Nobody	1954	15.00
❑ 15142	Josephine/Johnny's Boogie Blues	1954	15.00
❑ 15169	Peg o' My Heart/Teddy Bear Blues	1954	15.00
❑ 15226	Pattona Rag/Blue Hawaii	1954	15.00
❑ 15270	Lady in Red/Blue Night	1954	15.00
❑ 15280	Oh Lady Be Good/Oh You Beautiful Doll	1955	12.00
❑ 15281	Camptown Races/I'm Looking Over a Four Leaf Clover	1955	12.00
❑ 15282	Pretty Baby/Shine On Harvest Moon	1955	12.00
❑ 15283	Smiles/Over the Waves	1955	12.00
❑ 15284	Humoresque/The Stars and Stripes Forever	1955	12.00
❑ 15285	Whispering/Dixie-Yankee Doodle	1955	12.00
❑ 15286	After the Ball/Bye Bye Blues	1955	12.00
❑ 15287	Golden Slippers/Washington and Lee Swing	1955	12.00
❑ 15288	Sidewalks of New York/Chinatown, My Chinatown	1955	12.00
❑ 15289	Glow-Worm/Chicken Reel	1955	12.00
❑ 15325	The Crazy Otto (Medley)/Humoresque	1955	15.00
❑ 15365	Johnny's Medley/Whistlin' Piano Man	1955	15.00
❑ 15408	Do It Again/When You Were a Tulip	1955	15.00
❑ 15427	I Never Knew/Chicken Reel	1955	15.00
❑ 15432	Hop Scotch Boogie/Hands Off	1955	15.00
❑ 15452	Boppin'/Farewell to Thee	1956	12.00
❑ 15467	Honey/Where the Lazy Daisies Grow	1956	12.00
❑ 15488	Heart and Soul/Dixieland Band	1956	12.00
❑ 15509	Solitude/Nickelodeon Tango	1956	12.00
❑ 15529	Rock and Roll Medley/Mood Indigo	1957	15.00
❑ 15565	King's Rock/Hello, Aloha	1957	12.00
❑ 15619	You Can't Get Lovin'/Old Fashioned Love	1957	12.00
❑ 15683	Yellow Dog Blues/Sugar Train	1958	10.00
❑ 15730	(All That I'm Asking Is) Sympathy/Don't Get Around Much Anymore	1958	10.00
❑ 15841	San Antonio Rose/Long Gone	1958	10.00
❑ 15892	Hurdy Gurdy Song/Tempest	1959	10.00
❑ 15972	Broken Hearted/Summer Serenade	1959	10.00
❑ 15992	In the Mood/Sweet Georgia Brown	1959	10.00
❑ 16023	Coconut Grove/In the Mood	1960	8.00
—Reissue			
❑ 16029	The Crazy Otto (Medley)/Eight Beat Boogie	1960	8.00
—Reissue			
❑ 16077	The Maddox Medley (Part 1)/(Part 2)	1960	8.00
❑ 16185	Asia Minor/Shell Happy	1961	8.00
❑ 16214	Sabre Dance/Glow-Worm	1961	8.00
❑ 16267	Flip, Flop and Bop/Golden Wildwood Flowers	1961	8.00
❑ 16320	Glad Rag Doll/Frenchy	1961	8.00
❑ 16404	Ballin' the Jack/Ragtime Johnny	1962	8.00

7-Inch Extended Plays

DOT

Number	Title (A Side/B Side)	Yr	NM
❑ DEP-1018	(contents unknown)	195?	10.00
❑ DEP-1018 [PS]	Tap-Dancing Music	195?	10.00
❑ DEP-1026	*Crazy Otto Medley/Down Yonder/Eight Beat Boogie/In the Mood	195?	10.00
❑ DEP-1026 [PS]	Johnny Maddox Plays Crazy Otto	195?	10.00

Albums

DOT

Number	Title (A Side/B Side)	Yr	NM
❑ DLP-102 [10]	Authentic Ragtime	1952	40.00
❑ DLP-3000 [M]	Ragtime Melodies	1955	25.00
❑ DLP-3005 [M]	Johnny Maddox Plays	1956	25.00
❑ DLP-3008 [M]	Tap Dance Rhythms	1956	25.00
❑ DLP-3044 [M]	King of Ragtime	1957	20.00
❑ DLP-3063 [M]	The Thirties in Ragtime	1957	20.00
❑ DLP-3067 [M]	My Old Flames	1957	20.00
❑ DLP-3108 [M]	Ragtime Piano 1917-18	1958	15.00
❑ DLP-3122 [M]	Johnny Maddox Plays the Million Sellers	1958	15.00
❑ DLP-3131 [M]	Dieieland Blues	1959	15.00
❑ DLP-3198 [M]	Old Fashioned Love	1959	15.00
❑ DLP-3289 [M]	Crazy Otto Piano	1960	12.00
❑ DLP-3314 [M]	Johnny Maddox Plays More Million Sellers	1960	12.00
❑ DLP-3321 [M]	The World's Greatest Piano Rolls	1960	12.00
❑ DLP-3334 [M]	Near You	1960	12.00
❑ DLP-3378 [M]	Sabre Dance	1961	12.00
❑ DLP-3476 [M]	World's Greatest Piano Rolls, Vol. 2	1962	12.00
❑ DLP-3477 [M]	World's Greatest Piano Rolls, Vol. 3	1962	12.00
❑ DLP-3478 [M]	World's Greatest Piano Rolls, Vol. 4	1962	12.00
❑ DLP-3493 [M]	Ragtime Twenties	1963	12.00
❑ DLP-3521 [M]	Ragtime Duets	1963	12.00
—With Glenn Rowell			
❑ DLP-3539 [M]	Memphis	1963	12.00
❑ DLP-3549 [M]	Johnny Maddox Plays the Million Sellers, Vol. 3	1963	12.00
❑ DLP-3621 [M]	Raggin' the Hits	1965	12.00
❑ DLP-3633 [M]	Ragtime by Request	1965	12.00
❑ DLP-3645 [M]	More Ragtime Twenties	1965	12.00
❑ DLP-3720 [M]	World's Greatest Piano Rolls, Vol. 5	1966	12.00
❑ DLP-3721 [M]	World's Greatest Piano Rolls, Vol. 6	1966	12.00
❑ DLP-3722 [M]	World's Greatest Piano Rolls, Vol. 7	1966	12.00
❑ DLP-3724 [M]	Ragtime Memories	1966	12.00
❑ DLP-3739 [M]	Ragtime Piano Man	1966	12.00
❑ DLP-3817 [M]	Second Hand Rose	1967	15.00
❑ DLP-25122 [S]	Johnny Maddox Plays the Million Sellers	1959	20.00
❑ DLP-25131 [S]	Dieieland Blues	1959	20.00
❑ DLP-25198 [S]	Old Fashioned Love	1959	20.00
❑ DLP-25289 [S]	Crazy Otto Piano	1960	15.00
❑ DLP-25314 [S]	Johnny Maddox Plays More Million Sellers	1960	15.00
❑ DLP-25321 [S]	The World's Greatest Piano Rolls	1960	15.00
❑ DLP-25378 [S]	Sabre Dance	1961	15.00
❑ DLP-25476 [S]	World's Greatest Piano Rolls, Vol. 2	1962	15.00
❑ DLP-25477 [S]	World's Greatest Piano Rolls, Vol. 3	1962	12.00
❑ DLP-25478 [S]	World's Greatest Piano Rolls, Vol. 4	1962	15.00
❑ DLP-25493 [S]	Ragtime Twenties	1963	15.00
❑ DLP-25521 [S]	Ragtime Duets	1963	15.00
—With Glenn Rowell			
❑ DLP-25539 [S]	Memphis	1963	15.00
❑ DLP-25549 [S]	Johnny Maddox Plays the Million Sellers, Vol. 3	1963	15.00
❑ DLP-25621 [M]	Raggin' the Hits	1965	15.00
❑ DLP-25633 [S]	Ragtime by Request	1965	15.00
❑ DLP-25645 [S]	More Ragtime Twenties	1965	15.00
❑ DLP-25720 [S]	World's Greatest Piano Rolls, Vol. 5	1966	15.00
❑ DLP-25721 [S]	World's Greatest Piano Rolls, Vol. 6	1966	15.00
❑ DLP-25722 [S]	World's Greatest Piano Rolls, Vol. 7	1966	15.00
❑ DLP-25724 [S]	Ragtime Memories	1966	15.00
❑ DLP-25739 [S]	Ragtime Piano Man	1966	15.00
❑ DLP-25817 [S]	Second Hand Rose	1967	15.00

HAMILTON

Number	Title (A Side/B Side)	Yr	NM
❑ HLP-115 [M]	12 Ragtime Greats	1964	10.00
❑ HLP-150 [M]	Great Marches and Waltzes	1964	10.00
❑ HLP-12115 [S]	12 Ragtime Greats	1964	12.00
❑ HLP-12150 [S]	Great Marches and Waltzes	1964	12.00

PARAMOUNT

Number	Title (A Side/B Side)	Yr	NM
❑ PAS-2-1029 [(2)]	Piano Roll Greats	1974	12.00

PICKWICK

Number	Title (A Side/B Side)	Yr	NM
❑ PC-3097 [M]	Alley Cat and Other Piano Roll Favorites	196?	12.00
❑ SPC-3097 [S]	Alley Cat and Other Piano Roll Favorites	196?	10.00

MADHATTANS, THE

45s

ATLANTIC

Number	Title (A Side/B Side)	Yr	NM
❑ 1142	Wowie/A Basketful of Blueberries	1957	20.00

MADISONS, THE

45s

LAWN

Number	Title (A Side/B Side)	Yr	NM
❑ 240	Can You Imagine It/The Wind and the Rain	1964	40.00

LIMELIGHT

Number	Title (A Side/B Side)	Yr	NM
❑ 3018	Bad Baboon/Because I Got You	1964	20.00

MGM

Number	Title (A Side/B Side)	Yr	NM
❑ 13312	Cheryl Anne/Looking for True Love	1965	40.00

MADNESS

12-Inch Singles

GEFFEN

Number	Title (A Side/B Side)	Yr	NM
❑ PRO-A-2122 [DJ]	The Sun and the Rain/Wings of a Dove/Keep Moving	1984	6.00
❑ 29667	Our House (Extended Dance Version)/Our House (Dub Version)	1983	10.00

SIRE

Number	Title (A Side/B Side)	Yr	NM
❑ PRO-A-852 [DJ]	One Step Beyond/My Girl/Madness	1980	15.00

45s

GEFFEN

Number	Title (A Side/B Side)	Yr	NM
❑ GGEF 0466	Our House/It Must Be Love	198?	3.00
—Reissue			
❑ 29350	The Sun and the Rain/Time for Tea	1984	3.00
❑ 29350 [PS]	The Sun and the Rain/Time for Tea	1984	3.00
❑ 29562	It Must Be Love/Calling Cards	1983	3.00
❑ 29562 [PS]	It Must Be Love/Calling Cards	1983	3.00
❑ 29668	Our House/Cardiac Arrest	1983	3.00
❑ 29668 [PS]	Our House/Cardiac Arrest	1983	3.00

SIRE

Number	Title (A Side/B Side)	Yr	NM
❑ 0204	One Step Beyond/Mistakes	1979	10.00
—Canada-only single			
❑ 49205	Madness/Mistakes	1980	5.00

Albums

GEFFEN

Number	Title (A Side/B Side)	Yr	NM
❑ GHS 4003	Madness	1983	10.00
❑ GHS 4022	Keep Moving	1984	10.00
❑ GHS 24079	Mad Not Mad	1985	10.00

SIRE

Number	Title (A Side/B Side)	Yr	NM
❑ SRK 6085	One Step Beyond	1979	12.00
❑ SRK 6094	Absolutely	1980	10.00

MADONNA

12-Inch Singles

MAVERICK

Number	Title (A Side/B Side)	Yr	NM
❑ PRO-A-5665 [DJ]	Erotica (LP Version) (Radio Edit)	1992	15.00
❑ PRO-A-5860 [(2)DJ]	Erotica (Kenlou B-Boy Mix 6:23) (Kenlou B-Boy Instrumental 5:54) (Madonna's In My Jeep Mix 5:46) (Jeep Beats 5:48) (Underground Tribal Beats 3:30) (Underground Club Mix 4:53) (Masters At Work Dub 4:51) (Bass Hit Dub 4:47) (WØ 12" 6:07) (WØ Dub 4:53) (House Instrumental 4:49)	1992	50.00
—Promo-only two-record set			
❑ PRO-A-5928 [(2)DJ]	Deeper and Deeper (Shep's Deep Makeover Mix 9:07) (Shep's Deep Bass Dub 5:00) (Shep's Deeper Dub 6:08) (Shep's Classic 12" 7:26) (Shep's Fierce Deeper Dub 5:59) (Shep's Deep Beats 2:57) (David's Klub Mix 7:39) (David's Love Dub 5:37) (David's Deeper Dub		

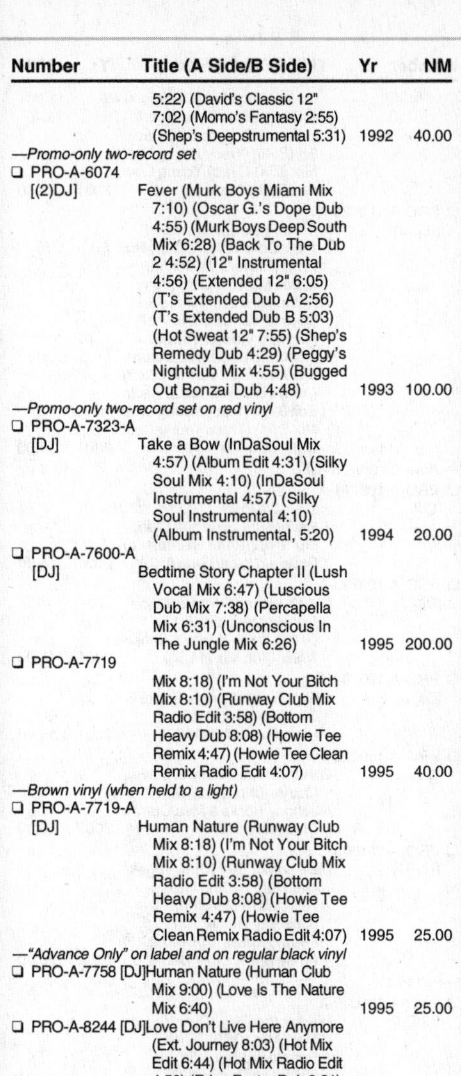

Number	Title (A Side/B Side)	Yr	NM
	5:22) (David's Classic 12" 7:02) (Momo's Fantasy 2:55) (Shep's Deepstrumental 5:31)	1992	40.00
—Promo-only two-record set			
❑ PRO-A-6074 [(2)DJ]	Fever (Murk Boys Miami Mix 7:10) (Oscar G.'s Dope Dub 4:55) (Murk Boys Deep South Mix 6:28) (Back To The Dub 2 4:52) (12" Instrumental 4:56) (Extended 12" 6:05) (T's Extended Dub A 2:56) (T's Extended Dub B 5:03) (Hot Sweat 12" 7:55) (Shep's Remedy Dub 4:29) (Peggy's Nightclub Mix 4:55) (Bugged Out Bonzai Dub 4:48)	1993	100.00
—Promo-only two-record set on red vinyl			
❑ PRO-A-7323-A [DJ]	Take a Bow (InDaSoul Mix 4:57) (Album Edit 4:31) (Silky Soul Mix 4:10) (InDaSoul Instrumental 4:57) (Silky Soul Instrumental 4:10) (Album Instrumental, 5:20)	1994	20.00
❑ PRO-A-7600-A [DJ]	Bedtime Story Chapter II (Lush Vocal Mix 6:47) (Luscious Dub Mix 7:38) (Percapella Mix 6:31) (Unconscious In The Jungle Mix 6:26)	1995	200.00
❑ PRO-A-7719	Mix 8:18) (I'm Not Your Bitch Mix 8:10) (Runway Club Mix Radio Edit 3:58) (Bottom Heavy Dub 8:08) (Howie Tee Remix 4:47) (Howie Tee Clean Remix Radio Edit 4:07)	1995	40.00
—Brown vinyl (when held to a light)			
❑ PRO-A-7719-A [DJ]	Human Nature (Runway Club Mix 8:18) (I'm Not Your Bitch Mix 8:10) (Runway Club Mix Radio Edit 3:58) (Bottom Heavy Dub 8:08) (Howie Tee Remix 4:47) (Howie Tee Clean Remix Radio Edit 4:07)	1995	25.00
—"Advance Only" on label and on regular black vinyl			
❑ PRO-A-7758 [DJ]	Human Nature (Human Club Mix 9:00) (Love Is The Nature Mix 6:40)	1995	25.00
❑ PRO-A-8244 [DJ]	Love Don't Live Here Anymore (Ext. Journey 8:03) (Hot Mix Edit 6:44) (Hot Mix Radio Edit 4:50) (Edge Factor Dub 8:31) (Early Morning Dub 10:04)	1996	50.00
—Red label			
❑ PRO-A-8244 [DJ]	Love Don't Live Here Anymore (Ext. Journey 8:03) (Hot Mix Edit 6:44) (Hot Mix Radio Edit 4:50) (Edge Factor Dub 8:31) (Early Morning Dub 10:04)	1996	50.00
—White label			
❑ PRO-A-9254 [DJ]	Frozen (William Orbit Widescreen Mix 6:34) (William Orbit Drumapella 5:15) (Victor Calderone Drumapella 5:09)	1998	50.00
❑ PRO-A-9327 [(2)DJ]	Ray of Light (Album Version 5:21) (Sasha's Ultra Violet Mix 10:45) (Victor Calderone Club Mix 9:29) (William Orbit Liquid Mix 8:05)	1998	60.00
❑ PRO-A-9333-A [(2)DJ]	Ray of Light (Album Version 5:21) (Sasha's Ultra Violet Mix 10:45) (Victor Calderone Club Mix 9:29) (William Orbit Liquid Mix 8:05)	1998	50.00
—"Advance Only" promo with less detailed labels than 9327			
❑ PRO-A-9359 [DJ]	Ray of Light: New Mixes (Sasha Twilo Mix 10:58) (Sasha Strip Down Mix 5:00) (William Orbit Ultra Violet Mix 6:59) (Victor Calderone Drum Mix 5:26)	1998	60.00
❑ PRO-A-9499 [DJ]	The Power of Good-Bye (Fabien's Good God Mix 8:25) (Slater's Filtered Mix 6:05) (Slater's Super Luper Mix 8:45) (Dallas Austin Low End Mix 4:33)	1998	40.00
❑ PRO-A-9630-A [(2)DJ]	Nothing Really Matters (Club 69 Vocal Club Mix 7:39) (Club 69 Radio Mix 3:45) (Club 69 Mix-Show Mix 5:40) (Club 69 Future Mix 8:33) (Club 69		

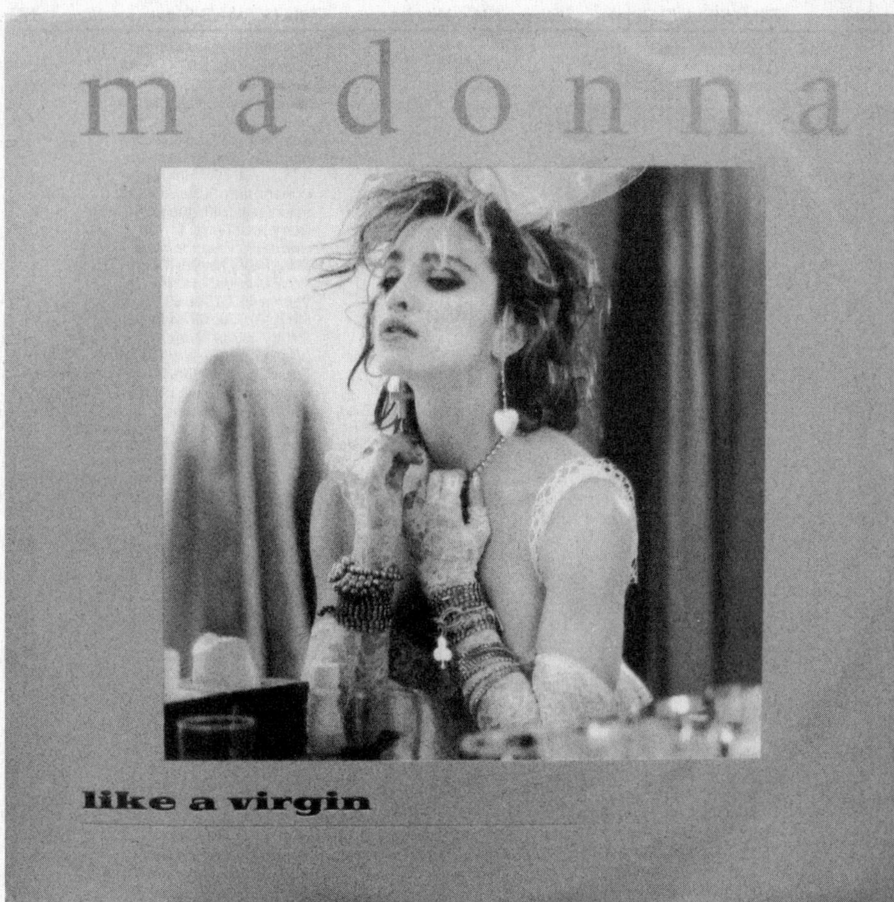

Madonna, "Like a Virgin," Sire 29210, 1984, **$3.**

Number	Title (A Side/B Side)	Yr	NM
	Phunk Mix 8:00) (Album Version 4:27) (Club 69 Future Dub 5:48) (Kruder & Dorfmeister Remix 11:10)	1999	50.00
❑ PRO-A-9647-A [(2)DJ]	Nothing Really Matters (Club 69 Vocal Club Mix 7:39) (Club 69 Radio Mix 3:45) (Club 69 Future Mix 8:33) (Club 69 Mix-Show Mix 5:40) (Club 69 Phunk Mix 8:00) (Vikram Radio Mix 7:42) (Club 69 Future Dub 5:48) (Kruder & Dorfmeister Remix 11:10)	1999	50.00
❑ PRO-A-9665-A [DJ]	Nothing Really Matters (Vikram Cybercut 13:44) (Kruder & Dorfmeister Remix 11:10)	1999	40.00
❑ PRO-A-9700-A [DJ]	Nothing Really Matters (Club 69 Speed Mix 10:35) (Club 69 Speed Dub 10:25)	1999	40.00
❑ PRO-A-9838 [DJ]	Beautiful Stranger (Calderone Club Mix 10:13) (Calderone Radio Mix 4:04) (New Club Edit 5:12) (Album Version 4:21)	1999	30.00
—Red label			
❑ PRO-A-9838-A [DJ]	Beautiful Stranger (Calderone Club Mix 10:13) (Calderone Radio Mix 4:04) (New Club Edit 5:12) (Album Version 4:21)	1999	40.00
—"Advance Only" version, white label			
❑ PRO-A-9922-A [DJ]	Beautiful Stranger (Calderone Club Mix 10:12) (Album Version 4:21) (Calderone Radio Mix 4:04) (Calderone Dub Mix 6:22)	1999	30.00

Number	Title (A Side/B Side)	Yr	NM
❑ 40585	Erotica (Kenlou B-Boy Mix 6:25) (Jeep Beats 5:51) (Madonna's In My Jeep Mix 5:50) (WØ 12" 6:09) (Underground Club Mix 4:54) (Bass Hit Dub 4:48)	1992	8.00
❑ 40722	Deeper and Deeper (Shep's Classic 12" 7:26) (Shep's Deep Makeover Mix 9:07) (Shep's Deep Beats 2:57) (David's Klub Mix 7:39) (David's Deeper Dub 5:22) (Shep's Deeper Dub 6:08)	1992	8.00
❑ 40793	Bad Girl (Extended Mix, 6:29)/ Fever (Extended 12" Mix 6:08) (Shep's Remedy Dub 4:29) (Murk Boys Miami Mix 7:10) (Murk Boys Deep South Mix 6:28) (Oscar G.'s Dope Dub 4:55)	1993	8.00
❑ 40988	Rain (Radio Remix, 4:33) (LP Version 5:30)/Up Down Suite (Dub Version 12:17)/Waiting (Remix 4:40)	1993	8.00
❑ 41355	I'll Remember (Guerilla Beach Mix 6:17) (Album Version 4:22) (Guerilla Groove Mix 6:07) (Orbit Alternative Remix 4:30)	1994	8.00
❑ 41355 [DJ]	I'll Remember (Guerilla Beach Mix 6:17) (Album Version 4:22) (Guerilla Groove Mix 6:07) (Orbit Alternative Remix 4:30)	1994	15.00
—Same as stock copy, except labels say "Advance Copy - Promotion Only"			
❑ 41772	Secret (Junior's Sound Factory Mix 10:16) (Junior's Sound Factory Dub 7:57) (Junior's Luscious Club Mix 6:19) (Junior's Luscious Club Dub 6:20) (Allstar Mix 5:11)	1994	8.00
❑ 41772 [DJ]	Secret (Junior's Sound Factory Mix 10:16) (Junior's Sound Factory Dub 7:57) (Junior's		

M

Number	Title (A Side/B Side)	Yr	NM
	Luscious Club Mix 6:19) (Junior's Luscious Club Dub 6:20) (Allstar Mix 5:11)	1994	8.00

—Same as stock copy, except labels say "Advance Copy - Promotion Only"

Number	Title (A Side/B Side)	Yr	NM
❑ 41880	Human Nature (Runway Club Mix 8:18) (I'm Not Your Bitch Mix 8:10) (Runway Club Mix Radio Edit 3:58) (Bottom Heavy Dub 7:55) (Howie Tee Remix 4:47) (Howie Tee Clean Remix 4:46) (Radio Version 4:30) (Love Is The Nature Mix 6:40)	1995	8.00
❑ 41887	Take a Bow (InDaSoul Mix 4:57) (Album Edit 4:31) (Silky Soul Mix 4:10) (InDaSoul Instrumental 4:57) (Album Instrumental 5:20)	1994	6.00
❑ 41895	Bedtime Story (Junior's Sound Factory Mix 9:15) (Junior's Sound Factory Dub 8:14) (Orbital Mix 7:42) (Junior's Wet Dream Mix 8:33) (Junior's Wet Dream Dub 7:30)	1995	6.00
❑ 42372 [(2)]	What It Feels Like for a Girl (Paul Oakenfold Perfecto Mix, 7:18) (Richard Vission Velvet Masta Mix 8:08)/(Above & Beyond 12" Club Mix 7:27) (Richard Vission Velvet Masta Edit 3:39)//(Calderone & Quayle Dark Side Mix 6:42) (Tracy Young Cool Out Radio Mix 4:45)/(Above & Beyond Club Radio Edit 3:45) (Tracy Young Club Mix 8:54)	2001	8.00
❑ 42492 [(2)]	Die Another Day (Dirty Vegas Main Mix) (Thunderpuss Club Mix) (Thee Retrolectro Mix) (Deepsky Remix) (Dirty Vegas Dub)	2002	8.00
❑ 42614 [(2)]	American Life (Missy Elliott American Dream Remix 4:49) (Oakenfold Downtempo Remix 5:32) (Felix Da Housecat's Devin Dazzle Club Mix 6:10) (Peter Rauhofer's American Anthem Part 1 10:41) (Peter Rauhofer's American Anthem Part 2 9:06)/Die Another Day (Calderone & Quayle Afterlife Mix 8:53)	2003	8.00
❑ 42638 [(2)]	Hollywood (The Micronauts Remix) (Oakenfold Full Remix) (Calderone & Quayle Glam Mix) (Jacques Lu Cont's Thin White Duck Mix) (Oakenfold 12" Dub) (Deepsky's Home Sweet Home Vocal Remix)	2003	8.00
❑ 42682 [(2)]	Nothing Fails (Peter Rauhofer's Classic House Mix 8:24) (Nevins Big Room Rock Mix 6:44) (Tracy Young's Underground Mix 7:29) (Nevins Global Dub 7:45) (Jackie's in Love in the Club Mix 7:28)/Nobody Knows Me (Peter Rauhofer's Private Life Part 1 8:07) (Above & Beyond 12" Mix 8:45) (Mount Simms Italo Kiss Mix 5:26)(	2003	8.00
❑ 42703 [(2)]	Love Profusion (The Passengerz Club Profusion 9.34) (Blow-Up Mix 6.09) (Ralphi Rosario House Vocal Extended 7.29) (Ralphi Rosario Big Room Dub 8.57) (The Passengerz Dub Profusion 8.04) (Craig J.'s "Good Vibe" Mix 7.14) (Ralphi Rosario Big Room Vox Extended 9:25)	2004	8.00
❑ 43649	You'll See (Album Version 4:39) (Instrumental 4:44) (Spanish Version 4:21)/Live To Tell (Live from the "Who's That Girl" Tour 8:14)	1995	10.00
❑ 43993	Frozen (Album Version 6:12) (Stereo MC's Remix 5:45) (Extended Club Mix 11:17) (Meltdown Mix 8:09)	1998	8.00
❑ 44523 [(2)]	Ray of Light (Sasha Untra Violet Mix 10:45) (Sasha Strip Down Mix 5:00)/(Victor Calderone Club Mix 9:29) (William Orbit Liquid Mix 8:06)//(Sasha Twilo Mix 10:58) (Victor Calderone Drum Mix 5:26)/(William Orbit Ultra Violet Mix 6:59) (Album Version 5:21)	1998	12.00
❑ 44613 [(2)]	Nothing Really Matters (Club 69 Vocal Club Mix 7:51) (Album Version 4:27)/(Club 69 Future Mix 8:19) (Club 69 Radio Mix 3:45)//(Club 69 Phunk Mix) (Vikram Radio Remix)/(Club69 Future Dub 5:48) (Kruder & Dorfmeister Remix 11:10)	1999	10.00

—Correct edition, with two different records inside

Number	Title (A Side/B Side)	Yr	NM
❑ 44613 [(2)]	Nothing Really Matters (Club 69 Vocal Club Mix 7:51) (Album Version 4:27)/(Club 69 Future Mix 8:19) (Club 69 Radio Mix 3:45)//(Club 69 Phunk Mix) (Vikram Radio Remix)/(Club69 Future Dub 5:48) (Kruder & Dorfmeister Remix 11:10)	1999	25.00

—Original edition, quickly recalled, has records labeled "Record One" and "Record Two," but both play the Record Two mixes. Holding the two records (Side 1 or especially Side 2 of each) next to each other will reveal a nearly identical groove. The dead wax of the copy we've examined has "0-44613-A-SR1" on Record 1 Side 1; "0-44613-B-SR1" on Record 1 Side 2; "PRO-A-9647-C/0-44613-C" on Record 2 Side 1; and "PRO-A-9630-D SR1" on Record 2 Side 2.

Number	Title (A Side/B Side)	Yr	NM
❑ 44909 [(2)]	Music (HQ2 Club Mix 8:46) (Groove Armada 12" Mix 5:30) (Calderone Anthem 11:55) (Album Version 3:44) (Deep Dish Dot Com Mix 11:21) (The Young Collective Club Remix 13:16)	2000	8.00
❑ 44910 [(2)]	Don't Tell Me (Timo Maas Mix 6:56) (Tracy Young Club Mix 11:00) (Vission Remix 7:52) (Thunderpuss 2001 Hands in the Air Anthem 10:20) (Victor Calderone Sensory Mix 6:48) (Vission Radio Mix 3:48) (Thunderpuss 2001 Hands in the Air Radio 4:26)	2001	8.00
❑ PRO-A-100018 [DJ]	American Pie (Victor Calderone Vocal Dub Mix 6:15) (Victor Calderone Filter Dub Mix 6:00)/(Richard "Humpty" Vission Visits Madonna 5:45) (Richard "Humpty" Vission Radio Mix 4:26)	2000	20.00
❑ PRO-A-100115 [DJ]	American Pie (Victor Calderone Vocal Club Mix 9:06) (Victor Calderone Extended Vocal Club Mix 10:30)	2000	25.00
❑ PRO-A-100303 [DJ]	Music (Album Version 3:44) (same on both sides)	2000	12.00

—In generic black sleeve with "Remixes to Come" sticker

Number	Title (A Side/B Side)	Yr	NM
❑ PRO-A-100304 [(2)DJ]	Music (Calderone Anthem Mix 11:55) (The Young Collective Club Remix 13:16) (Groove Armada's Flagship Dub 9:29) (Victor Calderone Radio Edit 4:25) (Groove Armada's 12" Revival 5:30) (Groove Armada's 7" Edit 3:38) (Groove Armada's Bonus Beats 4:50)	2000	25.00

—In generic black sleeve with "More Mixes to Come" sticker

Number	Title (A Side/B Side)	Yr	NM
❑ PRO-A-100305 [DJ]	Music (HQ2 Club Mix 8:50) (HQ2 Radio Mix 4:04)/(Deep Dish Dot Com Remix 11:21) (Deep Dish Dot Com Radio Edit 4:15)	2000	15.00

—With custom labels and picture cover

Number	Title (A Side/B Side)	Yr	NM
❑ PRO-A-100512 [DJ]	Don't Tell Me (Thunderpuss Club Mix 7:50) (Richard Humpty Vission Remix 7:51)/(Tracy Young Club Mix 11:00) (Thunderpuss Radio Mix 3:40)	2000	15.00
❑ PRO-A-100514-A [DJ]	Don't Tell Me (Timo Maas Mix) (Victor Calderone Sensory Mix) (Thunderpuss 2001 Hands in the Air Anthem)	2001	15.00
❑ PRO-A-100620 [(2)DJ]	What It Feels Like for a Girl (Paul Oakenfold Perfecto Mix 7:18) (Richard Vission Velvet Masta Mix 8:08) (Saturday Night Mix 5:22) (Above & Beyond 12" Club Mix 7:27) (Richard Vission Velvet Masta Edit 3:39) (Calderone & Quayle Dark Side Mix 6:42) (Above & Beyond Club Radio Edit 3:45) (Tracy Young Club Mix 8:54) (Tracy Young Cool Out Radio Mix 4:45)	2001	30.00
❑ PRO-A-100620-A [(2)DJ]	What It Feels Like for a Girl (Paul Oakenfold Perfecto Mix 7:18) (Richard Vission Velvet Masta Mix 8:08) (Saturday Night Mix 5:22) (Above & Beyond 12" Club Mix 7:27) (Richard Vission Velvet Masta Edit 3:39) (Calderone & Quayle Dark Side Mix 6:42) (Above & Beyond Club Radio Edit 3:45) (Tracy Young Club Mix 8:54) (Tracy Young Cool Out Radio Mix 4:45)	2001	30.00

—"Advance Only" on label

Number	Title (A Side/B Side)	Yr	NM
❑ PRO-A-100771-A [DJ]	Impressive Instant (Peter Rauhofer's Universal Club Mix 9:40) (Peter Rauhofer's Drowned World Dub 8:40)	2001	15.00
❑ PRO-A-100790-A [DJ]	GHV2 Johnny Rocks & Mac Quayle Megamix (8:17)/GHV2 Tracy Young's Shake & Stir Club Mix (11:53)	2001	15.00
❑ PRO-A-100797-A [DJ]	GHV2 Tracy Young's Shake & Stir Club Mix (11:53) (same on both sides)	2001	15.00
❑ PRO-A-100820-A [DJ]	GHV2 Johnny Rocks & Mac Quayle Dub (9:02)/GHV2 Johnny Rocks & Mac Quayle Club Mix (8:18)	2002	20.00
❑ PRO-A-101005 [(2)DJ]	Die Another Day (Dirty Vegas Main Mix 10:08) (Thee Retrolectro Mix 6:50) (Deepsky Remix 7:27) (Thunderpuss Club Mix 9:25) (Thee Die Another Dub 8:26)	2002	30.00

—Red labels

Number	Title (A Side/B Side)	Yr	NM
❑ PRO-A-101005-A [(2)DJ]	Die Another Day (Dirty Vegas Main Mix 10:08) (Thee Retrolectro Mix 6:50) (Deepsky Remix 7:27) (Thunderpuss Club Mix 9:25) (Thee Die Another Dub 8:26)	2002	50.00

—White labels

Number	Title (A Side/B Side)	Yr	NM
❑ PRO-A-101012 [DJ]	Die Another Day (Deepsky Dub 7:27) (Bond-Age Dub 7:21) (Brother Brown's Bond-Age Club 7:51)	2002	50.00
❑ PRO-A-101017 [DJ]	Die Another Day (Calderone & Quayle Afterlife Mix 8:53) (Afterlife Dub 10:06)	2002	50.00
❑ PRO-A-101097 [DJ]	American Life (Missy Elliott American Dream Remix 4:40) (American Dream Instrumental Remix 4:33) (American Dream Clean Edit 4:36)	2003	30.00
❑ PRO-A-101128 [DJ]	Hollywood (Oakenfold 12" Full Remix 7:01) (Jacques Lu Cont's Thin White Duck Mix 7:09) (Album Version 4;24) (Deepsky's Home Sweet Home Vocal Remix 7:55)	2003	25.00
❑ PRO-A-101146 [(2)DJ]	Hollywood (Calderone & Quayle Glam Mix 9:22) (The Micronauts Remix 6:25) (Oakenfold 12" Dub 7:01) (Deepsky's Home Sweet Home Dub 7:38) (Calderone & Quayle Dub 7:48) (The Micronauts Instrumental 6:23)	2003	40.00
❑ PRO-A-101204 [DJ]	Nobody Knows Me (Peter Rauhofer's Private Life Mix Pt. 1 8:07) (Mount Simms Old School Mix 4:46) (Above & Beyond 12" Mix 8:50) (Mount Simms Italo Kiss Mix 5:25)	2003	70.00

Except when noted otherwise, VG = 25% of NM, and VG+ = 50% of NM. (Example: VG = $2.00, VG+ = $4.00 and NM = $8.00.)

Number	Title (A Side/B Side)	Yr	NM
❑ PRO-A-101232 [DJ]	Nothing Fails (Peter Rauhofer's Classic House Mix 8:55) (Nevins Big Room Rock Mix 6:44) (Nevins Global Dub 7:45)	2003	25.00
❑ PRO-A-101259 [(2)DJ]	Love Profusion (The Passengerz Club Profusion 9:34) (Blow-Up Mix 6:09) (Ralphi Rosario House Vocal Mix - Extended 7:29) (Ralphi Rosario Big Room Dub 8:57) (The Passengerz Dub Profusion 8:04) (Craig J's Good Vibe Mix 7:14) (Ralphi Rosario Big Room Vox Mix - Extended 9:25)	2004	50.00

SIRE

Number	Title (A Side/B Side)	Yr	NM
❑ PRO-A-1083 [DJ]	Everybody (Extended/Dub)	1982	60.00
❑ PRO-A-2069 [DJ]	Lucky Star (5:30)/Holiday (6:08)	1983	30.00
❑ PRO-A-2120 [DJ]	Borderline (New Mix 6:54) (Instrumental 5:41)	1984	40.00
❑ PRO-A-2172 [DJ]	Like a Virgin (3:35) (same on both sides)	1984	20.00
❑ PRO-A-2223 [DJ]	Like a Virgin (Extended Remix 6:07) (same on both sides)	1984	30.00
❑ PRO-A-2257 [DJ]	Material Girl (3:56) (same on both sides)	1985	25.00
❑ PRO-A-2292 [DJ]	Angel (3:40) (Extended Dance Mix 6:15)	1985	12.00
❑ PRO-A-2353 [DJ]	Dress You Up (12" Formal Mix 6:15) (same on both sides)	1985	15.00
❑ PRO-A-2470 [DJ]	Live to Tell (Edit 4:37) (LP Version 5:49)	1986	40.00
❑ PRO-A-2517 [DJ]	Papa Don't Preach (LP Version 4:27) (Edit 3:47)	1986	25.00
❑ PRO-A-2905 [DJ]	Where's the Party (Extended Remix 7:31) (Dub 6:22)/ Spotlight (Extended Remix 6:24) (Dub 4:49)	1987	50.00
❑ PRO-A-2906 [DJ]	Into the Groove (New Remix 8:31) (Dub 6:22)/Everybody (New Remix 7:06)	1987	50.00
❑ PRO-A-2907 [DJ]	Holiday (New Remix 6:59) (Dub 6:57)/Over and Over (Extended Remix 7:11) (Dub 6:43)	1987	60.00
❑ PRO-A-3472 [DJ]	Like a Prayer (12" Dance Mix 7:50) (Instrumental Dub 6:11) (Bass Dub 5:48) (12" Club Version 6:35) (Dub Beats 4:40) (7" Remix/Edit 5:41)	1989	20.00
❑ PRO-A-3791 [DJ]	Keep It Together (12" Remix 7:50) (Dub 7:00) (12" Mix 6:48) (Bonus Beats 3:56)	1990	12.00
❑ PRO-A-4582 [DJ]	Justify My Love (Album Version 4:58) (same on both sides)	1990	12.00
❑ PRO-A-4613 [DJ]	Justify My Love (Orbit Edit 4:30) (Hip Hop Mix 6:30) (Orbit 12" Mix 7:16) (The Beast Within Mix 6:10)	1990	20.00
❑ PRO-A-4710 [(2)DJ]	Rescue Me (Titanic Vocal, 8:15) (Lifeboat Vocal 5:20) (Lifeboat Dub 6:02) (Houseboat Vocal 6:56) (Houseboat Dub 5:23) (Demanding Dub 5:20) (S.O.S. Mix 6:23) (Disaster Dub 3:20)	1990	40.00
—Promo-only two-record set			
❑ 20212	Borderline (New Mix 6:54)/ Lucky Star (New Mix 7:13)	1984	10.00
❑ 20239	Like a Virgin (Extended Dance Remix 6:07)/Stay (4:04)	1984	6.00
❑ 20304	Material Girl (Extended Dance Remix 6:06)/Pretender (4:28)	1985	8.00
❑ 20335	Angel (Extended Dance Remix 6:15)/Into the Groove (4:40)	1985	8.00
❑ 20369	Dress You Up (12" Formal Mix 6:15) (Casual Instrumental Mix 4:36)/Shoo-Be-Doo (5:14)	1985	8.00
❑ 20461	Live to Tell (LP Version 5:49) (Edit 4:37) (Instrumental 5:49)	1986	8.00
❑ 20492	Papa Don't Preach (Extended Remix 5:43)/Pretender (4:28)	1986	6.00
❑ 20533	True Blue (Color Mix 6:37) (Instrumental 6:56)/Ain't No Big Deal (4:12)/True Blue (Remix Edit 4:22)	1986	8.00
❑ 20597	Open Your Heart (Extended 10:35) (Dub 6:40)/White Heat (4:25)	1986	8.00
❑ 20633	La Isla Bonita (Extended Remix 5:20) (Extended Instrumental 5:14)	1987	6.00
❑ 20692	Who's That Girl (Extended Version 6:28) (Dub Version, 5:05)/White Heat (4:25)	1987	8.00
❑ 20762	Causing a Commotion (Silver Screen Mix 6:33) (Dub 7:04) (Movie House Mix 9:40)/ Jimmy Jimmy (3:54)	1987	10.00
❑ 21170	Like a Prayer (12" Dance Mix, 7:50) (12" Extended Remix 7:21) (Churchapella 6:14)// (12" Club Version 6:35) (7" Remix Edit 5:41)/Act of Contrition (2:18)	1989	10.00
❑ 21225	Express Yourself (Non-Stop Express Mix 7:54) (Stop & Go Dubs 10:40)//(Local Mix 6:20)/ The Look Of Love (4:03)	1989	6.00
❑ 21427	Keep It Together (12" Remix 7:44) (Dub 7:00) (12" Extended Mix 7:20) (12" Mix 6:48) (Bonus Beats 3:56) (Instrumental 5:52)	1990	6.00
❑ 21513	Vogue (12" Version 8:19) (Bette Davis Dub 7:24) (Strike-A-Pose Dub 7:37)	1990	6.00
❑ 21577	Hanky Panky (Bare Bottom 12" Mix 6:34) (Bare Bones Single Mix 3:50)/More (4:58)	1990	6.00
❑ 21813	Rescue Me (Titanic Vocal 8:15) (Lifeboat Vocal 5:20) (Houseboat Vocal 6:56) (S.O.S. Mix 6:23)	1991	8.00
❑ 21820	Justify My Love (Orbit 12" Mix 7:16) (Hip Hop Mix 6:30) (The Beast Within Mix 6:10)/Express Yourself (1990 Remix) (Long Version 9:30).	1990	8.00
❑ 29715	Burning Up (5:56)/Physical Attraction (6:35)	1983	10.00
❑ 29899	Everybody (5:56) (Dub 9:23)	1982	10.00

WARNER BROS.

Number	Title (A Side/B Side)	Yr	NM
❑ PRO-A-8544 [DJ]	Don't Cry for Me Argentina (Miami Mix Alternate Ending 7:59) (Miami Spanglish Mix 6:57) (Miami Mix Edit 4:29)/ (Miami Dub Mix 6:23) (Miami Mix Instrumental Version 6:55) (Miami Spanglish Mix Edit 4:28)	1997	20.00
❑ PRO-A-8544-A [DJ]	Don't Cry for Me Argentina (Miami Mix Alternate Ending 7:59) (Miami Spanglish Mix 6:57) (Miami Mix Edit 4:29)/ (Miami Dub Mix 6:23) (Miami Mix Instrumental Version 6:55) (Miami Spanglish Mix Edit 4:28)	1997	25.00
—"Advance Only" on label			
❑ PRO-A-8984 [DJ]	Buenos Aires (Te Amo 12" Extended Vocal Version 7:53) (Te Amo Radio Version 4:09) (Te Amo Instrumental 7:52) (Te Amo Single Edit 5:23)	1997	40.00
❑ PRO-A-8984-A [DJ]	Buenos Aires (Te Amo 12" Extended Vocal Version 7:53) (Te Amo Radio Version 4:09) (Te Amo Instrumental 7:52) (Te Amo Single Edit 5:23)	1997	40.00
—"Advance Only" on label			
❑ 42492 [(2)]	Die Another Day (Dirty Vegas Main Mix 10.08)/(Thunderpuss Mix 9.25)//(Thee RetroLectro Mix 6.59) (Deepsky Remix 7:27)/(Dirty Vegas Dub 9.10)	2002	10.00
❑ 43809	Don't Cry for Me Argentina (Miami Mix Alternate Ending 7:59) (Miami Spanglish Mix 6:57) (Miami Mix Edit 4:29)/ (Miami Dub Mix 6:23) (Miami Mix Instrumental Version 6:55) (Miami Spanglish Mix Edit 4:28)	1997	8.00
❑ PRO-A-101005 [(2)DJ]	Die Another Day (Dirty Vegas Main Mix 10:08) (Thee Retrolectro Mix 6:59) (Deepsky Remix 7:27) (Thunderpuss Club Mix 9:25) (Thee Die Another Day Dub 8:26)	2002	15.00

WEA

Number	Title (A Side/B Side)	Yr	NM
❑ 43993 [DJ]	Frozen (Album Version) (Stereo MC's Remix) (Extended Club Mix) (Meltdown Mix)	1998	400.00
—Rare test pressing with handwritten labels; fewer than 10 copies known to exist			

45s

GEFFEN

Number	Title (A Side/B Side)	Yr	NM
❑ GGEF 0540	Gambler/Crazy for You	198?	3.00
—"Back to Back Hits" series; first issue of A-side on U.S. 45			
❑ 29051	Crazy for You/No More Words	1985	3.00
—B-side by Berlin			
❑ 29051 [PS]	Crazy for You/No More Words	1985	3.00

MAVERICK

Number	Title (A Side/B Side)	Yr	NM
❑ 16658	American Life/Die Another Day (Richard Humpty Vission Radio Edit)	2003	4.00
❑ 16711	Deeper and Deeper/Secret	2001	3.00
❑ 16712	Erotica/Bedtime Story	2001	3.00
❑ 16713	Frozen/Take a Bow	2001	3.00
—Both sides are edits; the original 45s had full-length versions			
❑ 16714	The Power of Good-Bye/ Human Nature	2001	3.00
❑ 16715	Ray of Light/Beautiful Stranger	2001	3.00
❑ 16716	Don't Tell Me/What It Feels Like for a Girl	2001	3.00
❑ 16717	Music//Drowned World/ Substitute for Love	2001	3.00
❑ 16825	Don't Tell Me (Album Version)/ (Thunderpuss' 2001 Hands in the Air Radio)	2001	4.00
❑ 16826	Music/Cyberraga	2000	4.00
❑ 17102	Nothing Really Matters/ To Have and Not to Hold	1999	4.00
❑ 17160	The Power of Good-Bye/Mer Girl	1998	3.00
❑ 17206	Ray of Light/Has to Be	1998	3.00
❑ 17244	Frozen/Shanti-Ashtangi	1998	3.00
❑ 17714	Love Don't Live Here Anymore (Soulpower Radio Remix)/ (Album Remix)	1996	3.00
❑ 17719	You'll See/Live to Tell (Live Edit)	1995	3.00
❑ 17882	Human Nature/Sanctuary	1995	3.00
❑ 17924	Bedtime Story/Survival	1995	3.00
❑ 18000	Take a Bow/(InDaSoul Mix)	1994	3.00
❑ 18035	Secret/(Instrumental)	1994	3.00
❑ 18247	I'll Remember/Secret Garden	1994	3.00
❑ 18505	Rain/Waiting	1993	3.00
❑ 18639	Deeper and Deeper/ (Instrumental)	1992	3.00
❑ 18650	Bad Girl/Fever	1993	3.00
❑ 18782	Erotica/(Instrumental)	1992	3.00

SIRE

Number	Title (A Side/B Side)	Yr	NM
❑ GSRE 0494	Borderline/Holiday	198?	3.00
—"Back to Back Hits" reissue			
❑ GSRE 0506	Live a Virgin/Lucky Star	198?	3.00
—"Back to Back Hits" reissue			
❑ GSRE 0507	Material Girl/Angel	198?	3.00
—"Back to Back Hits" reissue			
❑ GSRE 0539	Into the Groove/Dress You Up	198?	3.00
—"Back to Back Hits" series; first issue of A-side on U.S. 45			
❑ PRO-S-2023 [DJ]	Physical Attraction (same on both sides)	1983	50.00
❑ 18822	This Used to Be My Playground/ (Long Version)	1992	3.00
❑ 19485	Justify My Love/Express Yourself 1990	1990	3.00
❑ 19490	Rescue Me/ (Alternate Single Mix)	1990	3.00
❑ 19789	Hanky Panky/More	1990	3.00
❑ 19863	Vogue (Single Version)/ Vogue (Bette Davis Dub)	1990	3.00
❑ 19986	Keep It Together/(Instrumental)	1990	3.00
❑ 19986 [PS]	Keep It Together/(Instrumental)	1990	80.00
❑ 21860	Express Yourself/Cherish	199?	3.00
—"Back to Back Hits" reissue			
❑ 21861	Like a Prayer/Oh Father	199?	3.00
—"Back to Back Hits" reissue			
❑ 21940	Who's That Girl/Causing a Commotion	198?	3.00
—"Back to Back Hits" reissue			
❑ 21941	La Isla Bonita/Open Your Heart	198?	3.00
—"Back to Back Hits" reissue			
❑ 21985	Live to Tell/True Blue	198?	3.00
—"Back to Back Hits" reissue			

M

Number	Title (A Side/B Side)	Yr	NM
❑ 21986	Papa Don't Preach/Everybody	198?	3.00
—"Back to Back Hits" reissue			
❑ 22723	Oh Father/Pray for Spanish Eyes	1989	3.00
❑ 22723 [PS]	Oh Father/Pray for Spanish Eyes	1989	—
—The purported sleeve appears to be a fake. Current opinion is that there is NO genuine U.S. picture sleeve.			
❑ 22883	Cherish/Supernatural	1989	3.00
❑ 22883 [PS]	Cherish/Supernatural	1989	3.00
❑ 22948	Express Yourself/ The Look of Love	1989	3.00
❑ 22948 [PS]	Express Yourself/ The Look of Love	1989	3.00
❑ 27539	Like a Prayer/Act of Contrition	1989	3.00
❑ 27539 [DJ]	Like a Prayer (7" Remix Edit)/ (7" Version with Fade)	1989	10.00
❑ 27539 [PS]	Like a Prayer/Act of Contrition	1989	3.00
❑ 28224	Causing a Commotion/ Jimmy, Jimmy	1987	3.00
❑ 28224 [PS]	Causing a Commotion/ Jimmy, Jimmy	1987	3.00
❑ 28341	Who's That Girl?/White Heat	1987	3.00
❑ 28341 [PS]	Who's That Girl?/White Heat	1987	3.00
❑ 28425	La Isla Bonita/(Instrumental)	1987	3.00
❑ 28425 [PS]	La Isla Bonita/(Instrumental)	1987	3.00
❑ 28508	Open Your Heart/White Heat	1986	3.00
❑ 28508 [PS]	Open Your Heart/White Heat	1986	3.00
❑ 28591	True Blue/Ain't No Big Deal	1986	3.00
❑ 28591	True Blue/Ain't No Big Deal	1986	5.00
—Blue vinyl			
❑ 28591 [PS]	True Blue/Ain't No Big Deal	1986	3.00
—No mention of limited edition on sleeve			
❑ 28591 [PS]	True Blue/Ain't No Big Deal	1986	5.00
—"Limited edition blue vinyl pressing" on sleeve			
❑ 28660	Papa Don't Preach/Pretender	1986	3.00
❑ 28660 [PS]	Papa Don't Preach/Pretender	1986	3.00
❑ 28717	Live to Tell/(Instrumental)	1986	3.00
❑ 28717 [PS]	Live to Tell/(Instrumental)	1986	3.00
❑ 28919	Dress You Up/Shoo-Be-Doo	1985	3.00
❑ 28919 [PS]	Dress You Up/Shoo-Be-Doo	1985	50.00
❑ 29008	Angel/(12" Remix Edit)	1985	3.00
❑ 29008 [PS]	Angel/(12" Remix Edit)	1985	3.00
❑ 29083	Material Girl/Pretender	1985	3.00
❑ 29083 [PS]	Material Girl/Pretender	1985	3.00
❑ 29177	Lucky Star/I Know It	1984	4.00
❑ 29210	Like a Virgin/Stay	1984	3.00
❑ 29210 [PS]	Like a Virgin/Stay	1984	3.00
❑ 29354	Borderline/Think of Me	1984	4.00
❑ 29354 [PS]	Borderline/Think of Me	1984	80.00
—Fold-out poster sleeve			
❑ 29478	Holiday/(Instrumental)	1983	4.00
❑ 29478	Holiday/I Know It	1983	4.00
❑ 29841	Everybody/(Instrumental)	1982	20.00
WARNER BROS.			
❑ 16684	Die Another Day (Radio Edit)/ (Album Version)	2002	3.00
❑ 17495	You Must Love Me/Rainbow High	1996	4.00
Albums			
MAVERICK			
❑ PRO-A-5904 [(2)DJ]	Erotica	1992	60.00
—Vinyl is promo only			
❑ PRO-A-7311 [(2)DJ]	Bedtime Stories	1994	100.00
—Promo only on pink vinyl			
❑ PRO-A-9378 [(2)DJ]	Ray of Light	1998	60.00
—Vinyl is promo only; generic cover with sticker			
❑ PRO-A-100500-A [(2)DJ]	Music	2000	50.00
—Vinyl is promo only; generic white die-cut sleeve			
❑ PRO-A-100871 [(3)DJ]	GHV2 Remixed — The Best of 1991-2001	2001	40.00
—Promo-only remixes of 12 songs from the "GHV2" CD; comes in generic black jacket with hole in center			
SIRE			
❑ PRO-A-2892	You Can Dance	1987	30.00
—Promo-only; contains single edits of the seven songs on the stock editions			
❑ 23867	Madonna	1983	10.00
—Second pressing with 3:49 version of "Burning Up"			
❑ 23867	Madonna	1983	20.00
—First pressing with 4:48 version of "Burning Up"; this version has only been found on copies with a gold promo stamp on the cover			
❑ W1-23867	Madonna	1984	15.00
—Columbia House edition			
❑ 25157	Like a Virgin	1984	50.00
—White vinyl with cream colored spine			
❑ 25157	Like a Virgin	1984	60.00
—White vinyl with silver colored spine			
❑ 25157	Like a Virgin	1984	10.00
❑ W1-25157	Like a Virgin	1985	15.00
—Columbia House edition			
❑ 25442	True Blue	1986	8.00
—Without poster			
❑ 25442	True Blue	1986	12.00
—With poster			
❑ W1-25442	True Blue	1986	15.00
—Columbia House edition; issued with poster			
❑ 25535	You Can Dance	1987	8.00
—Without gold obi			
❑ 25535	You Can Dance	1987	12.00
—With gold obi "Madonna and Dancing"			
❑ W1-25535	You Can Dance	1987	15.00
—Columbia House edition; not issued with obi			
❑ 25844	Like a Prayer	1989	10.00
❑ W1-25844	Like a Prayer	1989	15.00
—Columbia House edition			
❑ 26209	I'm Breathless	1990	10.00
❑ W1-26209	I'm Breathless	1990	15.00
—Columbia House edition			
❑ 26440 [(2)]	The Immaculate Collection	1990	15.00
❑ W1-26440 [(2)]	The Immaculate Collection	1990	20.00
—Columbia House edition			
❑ R 100572	I'm Breathless	1990	15.00
—BMG Direct Marketing edition			
❑ R 101029	Like a Prayer	1989	15.00
—BMG Direct Marketing edition			
❑ R 134536	You Can Dance	1987	15.00
—RCA Music Service edition; not issued with obi			
❑ R 143811	True Blue	1986	15.00
—RCA Music Service edition; issued with poster			
❑ R 161153	Like a Virgin	1985	15.00
—RCA Music Service edition			
❑ R 164288	Madonna	1984	15.00
—RCA Music Service edition			
❑ R 254164 [(2)]	The Immaculate Collection	1990	20.00
—BMG Direct Marketing edition			
WARNER BROS.			
❑ 42916-0 [(3)]	Confessions Remixed	2005	40.00
—Six remixes of five different songs from "Confessions on a Dance Floor"			
❑ 49460-1 [(2)]	Confessions on a Dance Floor	2005	40.00
—All copies on pink vinyl			

MADRIGAL

Number	Title (A Side/B Side)	Yr	NM
45s			
SSS INTERNATIONAL			
❑ 824	I Believe in Sunshine/Lady	1971	8.00
Albums			
SSS INTERNATIONAL			
❑ 18	Madrigal	1971	30.00

MADURA

Number	Title (A Side/B Side)	Yr	NM
45s			
COLUMBIA			
❑ 45483	Johnny B. Goode/ (B-side unknown)	1971	8.00
❑ 46022	Save the Miracle/Windy One	1974	8.00
Albums			
COLUMBIA			
❑ G 30794 [(2)]	Madura	1971	20.00
❑ KC 32545	Madura II	1973	15.00

MAESTRO, JOHNNY

Also see THE BROOKLYN BRIDGE; THE CRESTS.

Number	Title (A Side/B Side)	Yr	NM
45s			
APT			
❑ 25075	Phone Booth on the Highway/ She's All Mine Alone	1965	200.00
BUDDAH			
❑ 201	The Rains Came/Never Knew THis Kind of Hurt Before	1971	30.00
❑ 236	Yours Until Tomorrow/ Man in a Band	1971	10.00
❑ 289 [DJ]	Snow (mono/stereo)	1971	10.00
—May be promo only			
CAMEO			
❑ 256	Over the Weekend/I'll Be There	1963	30.00
❑ 305	Lean on Me/(It's Harder to) Make Up My Mind	1964	20.00
COED			
❑ 527	Say It Isn't So/ The Great Physician	1960	25.00
—As "Johnny Masters"			
❑ 545	Model Girl/We've Got to Tell Them	1961	25.00
—As "Johnny Mastro"			
❑ 549	What a Surprise/Warning Voice	1961	25.00
❑ 552	Mr. Happiness/Test of Love	1961	25.00
❑ 557	I.O.U./The Way You Look Tonight	1961	30.00
❑ 562	Besame Baby/It Must Be Love	1962	100.00
PARKWAY			
❑ 118	My Times/Is It You	1966	20.00
❑ 987	Heartburn/Try Me	1966	15.00
❑ 987 [DJ]	Heartburn	1966	60.00
—One-sided white label promo			
❑ 999	I Care About You/Come See Me (I'm Your Man)	1966	15.00
UNITED ARTISTS			
❑ 474	Before I Loved Her/Fifty Million Heartbeats	1962	40.00
Albums			
BUDDAH			
❑ BDS-5091	The Johnny Maestro Story	1971	40.00
—With inserts; deduct 40% if missing			

MAGAZINE

Also see BUZZCOCKS.

Number	Title (A Side/B Side)	Yr	NM
12-Inch Singles			
I.R.S.			
❑ SP-70404	About the Weather/In the Dark/ The Operative	1981	6.00
VIRGIN INTERNATIONAL			
❑ VIDJ 1 [DJ]	The Light Pours Out of Me/ Cut-Out Shapes	1979	15.00
45s			
I.R.S.			
❑ 9023	About the Weather/In the Dark	1981	5.00
Albums			
I.R.S.			
❑ SP-70015	Play	1981	12.00
❑ SP-70020	Magic, Murder and the Weather	1981	12.00
❑ SP-70030	After the Fact	1982	10.00
VIRGIN			
❑ VA 13144	The Correct Use of Soap	1980	10.00
❑ 90891	Rays & Hail 1978-1981	1987	15.00
VIRGIN INTERNATIONAL			
❑ VI-2100	Real Life	1978	15.00
❑ VI-2121	Secondhand Daylight	1979	14.00

MAGI, THE

Number	Title (A Side/B Side)	Yr	NM
Albums			
UNCLE DIRTY			
❑ 6102-N13	Win or Lose	1975	300.00

MAGIC FERN, THE

Number	Title (A Side/B Side)	Yr	NM
45s			
JERDEN			
❑ 813	Maggie/I Wonder Why	1966	20.00
PICCADILLY			
❑ 240	Nellie/Candy Day	1967	15.00
Albums			
PANORAMA			
❑ 108	The Magic Fern	1980	150.00

MAGIC LANTERNS

Contrary to some opinions, Ozzy Osbourne was never in this group. (The bass player was Michael "Oz" Osborne; notice the difference in last name spelling.) But ALBERT HAMMOND was.

Number	Title (A Side/B Side)	Yr	NM
45s			
ATLANTIC			
❑ 2560	Shame, Shame/ Baby, I Gotta Go Now	1968	10.00
❑ 2600	Give Me Love/Biding My Time	1969	8.00
❑ 2626	Melt All Your Troubles Away/ Bossa Nova 1940-Hello You Lovers	1969	8.00
❑ 2715	One Night Stand/Frisco Annie	1970	8.00
BIG TREE			
❑ 109	One Night Stand/Frisco Annie	1970	6.00
❑ 113	Let the Sunshine In/ Old Pa Bradley	1971	6.00
CHARISMA			
❑ 100	Country Woman/Pa Bradley	1972	5.00
EPIC			
❑ 10062	Excuse Me Baby/Greedy Girl	1966	8.00
❑ 10062 [PS]	Excuse Me Baby/Greedy Girl	1966	20.00
❑ 10111	Knight in Rusty Armour/ Simple Things	1966	8.00
Albums			
ATLANTIC			
❑ SD 8217	Shame, Shame	1969	20.00

MAGIC MUSHROOM, THE

Number	Title (A Side/B Side)	Yr	NM
45s			
WARNER BROS.			
❑ 5846	I'm Gone/Cry Baby	1966	25.00

MAGIC MUSHROOMS, THE

Number	Title (A Side/B Side)	Yr	NM
45s			
A&M			
❑ 815	It's a-Happening/Never More	1966	15.00
PHILIPS			
❑ 40483	Look in My Face/Never Let Go	1968	15.00

MAGIC REIGN, THE

Number	Title (A Side/B Side)	Yr	NM
45s			
JAMIE			
❑ 1364	Pop Goes the Weasel/Mirrors	1968	30.00
❑ 1374	Jefferson Street/Charcoal Sketch	1969	30.00

Except when noted otherwise, VG = 25% of NM, and VG+ = 50% of NM. (Example: VG = $2.00, VG+ = $4.00 and NM = $8.00.)

MAGIC SAND

Albums

UNI

Number	Title (A Side/B Side)	Yr	NM
❑ 73094	Magic Sand	1971	25.00

MAGIC TOUCH, THE (1) Female group.

45s

BLACK FALCON

Number	Title (A Side/B Side)	Yr	NM
❑ 19102	Step Into My World/Step Into My World (Part 2)	1971	8.00

MAGIC TOUCH, THE (2) Male group.

45s

ROULETTE

Number	Title (A Side/B Side)	Yr	NM
❑ 7143	Baby You Belong to Me/Lost and Lonely Boy	1973	12.00

MAGISTRATES, THE

45s

MGM

Number	Title (A Side/B Side)	Yr	NM
❑ 13946	Here Comes the Judge/Girl	1968	12.00
❑ 13980	After the Fox/Tear Down the Walls	1968	12.00

MAGNETICS, THE

45s

BONNIE

Number	Title (A Side/B Side)	Yr	NM
❑ (# unknown)	Lady in Green/(B-side unknown)	196?	5000.

MAGNETS, THE (1)

45s

GROOVE

Number	Title (A Side/B Side)	Yr	NM
❑ 58-0058	Surprise/You Just Say the Word	1965	60.00

MAGNETS, THE (2)

45s

LONDON INT'L.

Number	Title (A Side/B Side)	Yr	NM
❑ 10036	Drag Race/Joker	1963	25.00

MAGNETS, THE (3)

45s

RCA VICTOR

Number	Title (A Side/B Side)	Yr	NM
❑ 47-7391	When the School Bells Ring/Don't Tarry, Little Mary	1958	25.00

MAGNIFICENT FOUR, THE

45s

BLAST

Number	Title (A Side/B Side)	Yr	NM
❑ 210	The Closer You Are/Uncle Sam	1963	40.00

WHALE

Number	Title (A Side/B Side)	Yr	NM
❑ 506	The Closer You Are/Uncle Sam	1961	80.00

MAGNIFICENT MEN, THE

45s

CAPITOL

Number	Title (A Side/B Side)	Yr	NM
❑ 2062	Baby, I'm Crazy About You/Forever Together	1967	8.00
❑ 2134	By the Time I Get to Phoenix/Tired of Pushing	1968	8.00
❑ 2202	Almost Persuaded/I Found What I Wanted in You	1968	8.00
❑ 2319	Save the Country/So Much Love Waiting	1968	8.00
❑ 5608	Peace of Mind/All Your Lovin's Gone To My Head	1966	8.00
❑ 5732	I've Got News/Maybe, Maybe, Baby	1966	8.00
❑ 5812	Stormy Weather/Much, Much More of Your Love	1966	8.00
❑ 5905	I Could Be So Happy/You Changed My Life	1967	8.00
❑ 5976	Swet Soul Medley — Part 1/Sweet Soul Medley — Part 2	1967	8.00

MERCURY

Number	Title (A Side/B Side)	Yr	NM
❑ 72988	Holly Go Softly/Open Up and Get Richer	1969	6.00
❑ 73028	Lay Lady Lay/Whatever It Takes	1970	6.00

Albums

CAPITOL

Number	Title (A Side/B Side)	Yr	NM
❑ ST 2678 [S]	The Magnificent Men	1967	15.00
❑ T 2678 [M]	The Magnificent Men	1967	20.00
❑ ST 2775 [S]	The Magnificent Men "Live!"	1967	15.00
❑ T 2775 [M]	The Magnificent Men "Live!"	1967	20.00
❑ ST 2846 [S]	World of Soul	1968	15.00
❑ T 2846 [M]	World of Soul	1968	20.00

MERCURY

Number	Title (A Side/B Side)	Yr	NM
❑ SR-61252	Better Than a Ten Cent Movie	1970	15.00

MAGNIFICENT 7, THE

45s

DIAL

Number	Title (A Side/B Side)	Yr	NM
❑ 4074	Ooh, Baby Baby/Never Will I (Make My Baby Cry)	1968	50.00

DIMENSION

Number	Title (A Side/B Side)	Yr	NM
❑ 1050	Show Me/Boogidy	1965	20.00
—As "Magnificent VII"			

EASTERN

Number	Title (A Side/B Side)	Yr	NM
❑ 611	She's Called a Woman/Since You've Been Gone So Long	1966	200.00

MAGNIFICENTS, THE

45s

CHECKER

Number	Title (A Side/B Side)	Yr	NM
❑ 1016	The Dribble Twist/Do You Mind	1962	15.00

KANSOMA

Number	Title (A Side/B Side)	Yr	NM
❑ 03	The Dribble Twist/Do You Mind	1962	30.00

LOST-NITE

Number	Title (A Side/B Side)	Yr	NM
❑ 267	Up On the Mountain/Why Did She Go	197?	5.00
—Reissue			
❑ 282	Don't Leave Me/Ozeta	197?	5.00
—Reissue			

VEE JAY

Number	Title (A Side/B Side)	Yr	NM
❑ 183	Up On the Mountain/Why Did She Go	1956	75.00
❑ 208	Hiccup/Caddy Bo	1956	100.00
❑ 235	Off the Mountain/Lost Lovers	1957	75.00
❑ 281	Don't Leave Me/Ozeta	1958	100.00
❑ 367	Up On the Mountain/Let's Do the Cha Cha	1960	20.00

MAHAL, TAJ

45s

COLUMBIA

Number	Title (A Side/B Side)	Yr	NM
❑ 10055	Why Did You Have to Desert Me/Cajun Waltz	1974	4.00
❑ 10109	Salve Drive/Cajun Waltz	1975	4.00
❑ 10260	Why, And We Repeat Why, And We Repeat.../(B-side unknown)	1975	4.00
❑ 10368	Ain't Nobody's Business/Easy to Love	1976	4.00
❑ 44051	Let the Good Times Roll/Shimmy Like My Sister Kate	1967	8.00
❑ 44405	E-Z Rider/Leaving Trunk	1967	8.00
❑ 44476	Statesboro Blues/Everybody's Got to Change Sometime	1968	8.00
❑ 44696	You Don't Miss Your Water/Going Down to the Country-Paint My Mailbox Blue	1968	8.00
❑ 44767	Corinna/A Lot of Love	1969	8.00
❑ 44991	Six Days on the Road/Light Rain Blues	1969	8.00
❑ 45419	Fishin' Blues/Diving Duck Blues	1971	5.00
❑ 45455	Ain't Gwine to Whistle Dixie Anymore (Part 1/Part 2)	1971	5.00
❑ 45539	Chevrolet/Oh Susanna	1972	5.00
❑ 45990	Buck Dancer's Choice/Little Red Hen	1974	5.00
❑ 46031	Built for Comfort/Teacup's Jazzy Blues Tune	1974	5.00

WARNER BROS.

Number	Title (A Side/B Side)	Yr	NM
❑ 8528	Sing a Happy Song/Southbound with the Hammer Down	1978	4.00

Albums

COLUMBIA

Number	Title (A Side/B Side)	Yr	NM
❑ CG 18 [(2)]	Giant Step/De Ole Folks at Home	198?	10.00
—Reissue with new prefix			
❑ GP 18 [(2)]	Giant Step/De Ole Folks at Home	1969	20.00
—Red "360 Sound" label			
❑ GP 18 [(2)]	Giant Step/De Ole Folks at Home	1971	15.00
—Orange label			
❑ CL 2779 [M]	Taj Mahal	1967	30.00
❑ CS 9579 [S]	Taj Mahal	1967	15.00
—Red "360 Sound" label			
❑ CS 9579 [S]	Taj Mahal	1971	12.00
—Orange label			
❑ PC 9579 [S]	Taj Mahal	198?	8.00
—Reissue with new prefix			
❑ CS 9698	The Natch'l Blues	1968	15.00
—Red "360 Sound" label			
❑ CS 9698	The Natch'l Blues	1971	12.00
—Orange label			
❑ PC 9698	The Natch'l Blues	198?	8.00
—Reissue with new prefix			
❑ CG 30619 [(2)]	The Real Thing	198?	10.00
—Reissue with new prefix			
❑ G 30619 [(2)]	The Real Thing	1971	20.00
❑ C 30767	Happy to Be Like I Am	1971	12.00
❑ PC 30767	Happy to Be Like I Am	198?	8.00
—Budget-line reissue			
❑ KC 31605	Recycling the Blues & Other Related Stuff	1972	12.00
❑ PC 31605	Recycling the Blues & Other Related Stuff	198?	8.00
—Budget-line reissue			
❑ KC 32600	Oooh So Good 'N Blues	1973	12.00
❑ PC 32600	Oooh So Good 'N Blues	198?	8.00
—Budget-line reissue			
❑ KC 33051	Mo' Roots	1974	12.00
❑ PC 33051	Mo' Roots	198?	8.00
—Budget-line reissue			
❑ PC 33801	Music Keeps Me Together	1975	12.00
❑ PC 34103	Satisfied & Tickled Too	1976	12.00
❑ PC 34466	Anthology Vol. 1	1977	12.00
❑ FC 36528	The Best of Taj Mahal	1981	10.00
❑ PC 36528	The Best of Taj Mahal	198?	8.00
—Budget-line reissue			

CRYSTAL CLEAR

Number	Title (A Side/B Side)	Yr	NM
❑ 5011	Live and Direct	1980	25.00
—Direct-to-disc recording			

WARNER BROS.

Number	Title (A Side/B Side)	Yr	NM
❑ BS 2994	Music Fuh Ya' (Musica Para Tu)	1977	10.00
❑ BS 3024	Brothers	1977	10.00
❑ BS 3094	Evolution (Recent)	1978	10.00

MAHARIS, GEORGE

45s

EPIC

Number	Title (A Side/B Side)	Yr	NM
❑ 9504	Teach Me Tonight/After the Lights Go Down Low	1962	8.00
❑ 9504 [PS]	Teach Me Tonight/After the Lights Go Down Low	1962	10.00
❑ 9522	Love Me as I Love You/They Knew About You	1962	8.00
❑ 9522 [PS]	Love Me as I Love You/They Knew About You	1962	10.00
❑ 9555	Baby Has Gone Bye Bye/After One Kiss	1962	8.00
❑ 9555 [PS]	Baby Has Gone Bye Bye/After One Kiss	1962	10.00
❑ 9569	Don't Fence Me In/Alright, Okay, You Win	1963	8.00
❑ 9569 [PS]	Don't Fence Me In/Alright, Okay, You Win	1963	10.00
❑ 9600	Where Can You Go (For a Broken Heart)/Kiss Me	1963	8.00
❑ 9600 [PS]	Where Can You Go (For a Broken Heart)/Kiss Me	1963	10.00
❑ 9613	That's How It Goes/It Isn't There	1963	8.00
❑ 9613 [PS]	That's How It Goes/It Isn't There	1963	10.00
❑ 9653	It's a Sin to Tell a Lie/Sara Darling	1964	6.00
❑ 9696	The Object of My Affection/Tonight You Belong to Me	1964	6.00
❑ 9696 [PS]	The Object of My Affection/Tonight You Belong to Me	1964	12.00
❑ 9753	I'm Coming Back for You/Lonely People Do Foolish Things	1965	6.00
❑ 9772	More I Cannot Do/Where Does Happiness Go	1965	6.00
❑ 9844	Quien Sabe (Who Knows, Who Knows)/You Always Hurt the One You Love	1965	6.00
❑ 9858	Ivy/A World Without Sunshine	1965	6.00
❑ 10039	Never Is a Long, Long Time/Goodbye, Good Luck and God Bless You	1966	6.00

Albums

EPIC

Number	Title (A Side/B Side)	Yr	NM
❑ LN 24001 [M]	George Maharis Sings!	1962	12.00
❑ LN 24021 [M]	Portrait in Music	1962	12.00
❑ LN 24037 [M]	Just Turn Me Loose!	1963	12.00
❑ LN 24064 [M]	Where Can You Go for a Broken Heart?	1963	12.00
❑ LN 24079 [M]	Make Love to Me	1964	12.00
❑ LN 24111 [M]	Tonight You Belong to Me	1964	12.00
❑ LN 24191 [M]	A New Route: George Maharis	1966	12.00
❑ BN 26001 [S]	George Maharis Sings!	1962	15.00
❑ BN 26021 [S]	Portrait in Music	1962	15.00
❑ BN 26037 [S]	Just Turn Me Loose!	1963	15.00
❑ BN 26064 [S]	Where Can You Go for a Broken Heart?	1963	15.00
❑ BN 26079 [S]	Make Love to Me	1964	15.00
❑ BN 26111 [S]	Tonight You Belong to Me	1964	15.00
❑ BN 26191 [S]	A New Route: George Maharis	1966	15.00

MAHAVISHNU ORCHESTRA

45s

COLUMBIA

Number	Title (A Side/B Side)	Yr	NM
❑ 10134	Can't Stand Your Funk/Eternity's Breath Part 2	1975	5.00
❑ 45836	Open Country Joy/Celestial Commuters	1973	5.00

Albums

COLUMBIA

Number	Title (A Side/B Side)	Yr	NM
❑ KC 31067	The Inner Mounting Flame	1972	12.00
—As "Mahavishnu Orchestra with John McLaughlin"			

Except when noted otherwise, VG = 25% of NM, and VG+ = 50% of NM. (Example: VG = $2.00, VG+ = $4.00 and NM = $8.00.)

Number	Title (A Side/B Side)	Yr	NM
❑ PC 31067	The Inner Mounting Flame	197?	8.00
—Reissue with new prefix; with or without bar code			
❑ CQ 31996 [Q]	Birds of Fire	1973	20.00
❑ KC 31996	Birds of Fire	1973	10.00
❑ PC 31996	Birds of Fire	197?	8.00
—Reissue with new prefix; with or without bar code			
❑ CQ 32766 [Q]	Between Nothingness and Eternity	1973	25.00
❑ KC 32766	Between Nothingness and Eternity	1973	15.00
❑ PC 32766	Between Nothingness and Eternity	197?	8.00
—Reissue with new prefix; with or without bar code on cover			
❑ KC 32957	Apocalypse	1974	15.00
❑ PC 32957	Apocalypse	197?	8.00
—Reissue with new prefix			
❑ PC 33411	Visions of the Emerald Beyond	1975	10.00
—Original with no bar code			
❑ PC 33411	Visions of the Emerald Beyond	198?	8.00
—Reissue with bar code			
❑ PC 33908	Inner Worlds	1976	10.00
—Original with no bar code			
❑ PC 33908	Inner Worlds	198?	8.00
—Reissue with bar code			
❑ JC 36394	The Best of Mahavishnu Orchestra	1980	10.00

MAHOGANY RUSH
Featuring Frank Marino.

Number	Title (A Side/B Side)	Yr	NM
45s			
NINE			
❑ 369	Buddy/All in Your Mind	1973	8.00
20TH CENTURY			
❑ 2111	New Rock and Roll/Child of the Novelty	1974	5.00
❑ 2166	Buddy/Satisfy Your Soul	1975	5.00
Albums			
COLUMBIA			
❑ PC 34190	Mahogany Rush IV	1976	15.00
—Original with no bar code			
❑ PC 34190	Mahogany Rush IV	198?	8.00
—Reissue with bar code			
❑ PC 34677	World Anthem	1977	15.00
—Original with no bar code			
❑ PC 34677	World Anthem	198?	8.00
—Reissue with bar code			
❑ JC 35257	Frank Marino & Mahogany Rush Live	1978	15.00
❑ PC 35257	Frank Marino & Mahogany Rush Live	198?	8.00
—Budget-line reissue			
❑ JC 35753	Tales of the Unexpected	1979	15.00
❑ PC 35753	Tales of the Unexpected	198?	8.00
—Budget-line reissue			
❑ JC 36204	What's Next	1980	15.00
❑ PC 36204	What's Next	198?	8.00
—Budget-line reissue			
NINE			
❑ 936	Maxoom	1973	50.00
20TH CENTURY			
❑ T-451	Child of the Novelty	1974	25.00
❑ T-463	Maxoom	1975	25.00
—Reissue of Nine 936			
❑ T-482	Strange Universe	1975	20.00

MAIN ATTRACTION, THE

Number	Title (A Side/B Side)	Yr	NM
45s			
TOWER			
❑ 420	I Remember Yesterday/If I'm Wrong	1968	10.00
❑ 435	Everyday/One Must Cry	1968	10.00
❑ 464	Friends/Jonathan	1969	10.00
Albums			
TOWER			
❑ ST-5117 [S]	And Now...The Main Attraction	1968	25.00
❑ T-5117 [M]	And Now...The Main Attraction	1968	50.00

MAIN INGREDIENT, THE

Number	Title (A Side/B Side)	Yr	NM
12-Inch Singles			
RCA			
❑ PD-13046	Party People/Save Me	1981	12.00
45s			
MERCURY			
❑ 73831	Magic Touch/Very White	1976	5.00
—As "Tony Sylvester and the New Ingredient"			
❑ 73871	Puzuzu/Soca	1977	5.00
—As "Tony Sylvester and the New Ingredient"			
POLYDOR			
❑ 889910-7	I Just Wanna Love You/When We Need It Bad	1989	3.00
RCA			
❑ PB-12060	Think Positive/Spoiled	1980	4.00
—RCA 1980s titles as "Cuba Gooding and the Main Ingredient"			
❑ PB-12107	What Can a Miracle Do/Makes No Diff'rence to Me	1980	4.00
❑ PB-12320	Evening of Love/(Instrumental)	1981	—
—Unreleased			
❑ PB-12340	I Only Have Eyes for You/Only	1981	4.00
❑ PB-12340 [PS]	I Only Have Eyes for You/Only	1981	10.00
—Sleeve is not seam sealed, but folds open to promote the album from which the songs came			
❑ PB-13045	Party People/Save Me	1982	4.00
RCA VICTOR			
❑ 47-9748	I Was Born to Lose You/Psychedelic Ride	1969	6.00
❑ 74-0252	Get Back/Brotherly Love	1969	6.00
❑ 74-0313	The Girl I Left Behind/Can't Stand Your Love	1970	5.00
❑ 74-0340	You've Been My Inspiration/Life Won't Be the Same (Without You)	1970	5.00
❑ 74-0385	Need Your Love/I'm Better Off Without You	1970	5.00
❑ 74-0401	I'm So Proud/Brother Love	1970	5.00
❑ 74-0456	Spinning Around (I Must Be Falling in Love)/Magic Shoes	1971	5.00
❑ 74-0517	Black Seeds Keep On Growing/Baby Change Your Mind	1971	5.00
❑ 74-0603	I'm Leaving This Time/Another Day Has Come	1971	5.00
❑ 74-0731	Everybody Plays the Fool/Who Can I Turn To	1972	6.00
❑ 74-0856	You've Got to Take It (If You Want It)/Travelling	1973	5.00
❑ 74-0939	You Can Call Me Rover/I'm Better Off Without You	1973	5.00
❑ APBO-0046	Girl Blue/Movin' On	1973	5.00
❑ AMBO-0124	Everybody Plays the Fool/I'm So Proud	1973	4.00
—Gold Standard Series			
❑ APBO-0205	Just Don't Want to Be Lonely/Goodbye My Love	1974	5.00
❑ APBO-0305	Happiness Is Just Around the Bend/Why Can't We All Unite	1974	5.00
❑ PB-10095	California My Way/Looks Like Rain	1974	5.00
❑ PB-10224	Rolling Down a Mountainside/Family Man	1975	5.00
❑ PB-10334	The Good Old Days/I Want to Make You Glad	1975	5.00
❑ PB-10431	Shame on the World/Lillian	1975	5.00
❑ GB-10482	Why Can't We All Unite/Happiness Is Just Around the Corner	1975	4.00
—Gold Standard Series			
❑ GB-10483	Just Don't Want to Be Lonely/Goodbye My Love	1975	4.00
—Gold Standard Series			
ZAKIA			
❑ 015	Do Me Right/(B-side unknown)	1986	4.00
Albums			
COLLECTABLES			
❑ COL-5101	Golden Classics	198?	10.00
POLYDOR			
❑ 841249-1	I Just Wanna Love You	1989	12.00
RCA VICTOR			
❑ APL1-0314	Greatest Hits	1974	12.00
❑ APD1-0335 [Q]	Euphrates River	1974	20.00
❑ APL1-0335	Euphrates River	1974	12.00
❑ APL1-0644	Rolling Down a Mountainside	1975	12.00
❑ APL1-1003	Shame On the World	1975	12.00
❑ APL1-1558	Music Maximus	1977	12.00
❑ APL1-1858	Super Hits	1977	12.00
❑ ANL1-2667	Rolling Down a Mountainside	1978	10.00
—Reissue of APL1-0644			
❑ AFL1-3641	Ready for Love	1980	10.00
❑ AFL1-3963	I Only Have Eyes for You	1981	10.00
❑ LSP-4253	The Main Ingredient L.T.D.	1970	12.00
❑ LSP-4412	Tasteful Soul	1971	12.00
❑ LSP-4483	Black Seeds	1971	12.00
❑ LSP-4677	Bitter Sweet	1972	12.00
❑ LSP-4834	Afrodisiac	1973	12.00

MAJESTICS, THE (1)

Number	Title (A Side/B Side)	Yr	NM
45s			
CHESS			
❑ 1802	Oasis (Part 1)/Oasis (Part 2)	1961	20.00
V.I.P.			
❑ 25028 [DJ]	Say You/All for Someone	1965	600.00
—Promo only; stock copies credited "The Monitors"			

MAJESTICS, THE (2)

Number	Title (A Side/B Side)	Yr	NM
45s			
CHEX			
❑ 1000	Give Me a Cigarette/So I Can Forget	1962	40.00
❑ 1000	Give Me a Cigarette/Shoppin' and Hoppin'	1962	100.00
❑ 1004	Unhappy and Blue/Treat Me Like You Want	1962	50.00
❑ 1006	Lonely Heart/Gwendolyn	1962	30.00
❑ 1009	Baby/Teach Me How to Limbo	1963	25.00

MAJESTICS, THE (3)

Number	Title (A Side/B Side)	Yr	NM
45s			
CONTOUR			
❑ 501	Teen Age Gossip/Hard Times	1960	80.00
FARO			
❑ 592	TV Cowboys/So You Want to Rock	1959	25.00
FOXIE			
❑ 7004	The Lone Stranger/Sweet One	1960	20.00
NRC			
❑ 502	Please Don't Say No/Divided Heart	1958	250.00
SIOUX			
❑ 91459	The Lone Stranger/Sweet One	1959	50.00
20TH FOX			
❑ 171	The Lone Stranger/Sweet One	1959	25.00

MAJESTICS, THE (4)

Number	Title (A Side/B Side)	Yr	NM
45s			
DUNES			
❑ 2014	The Boss Walk (Part 1)/The Boss Walk (Part 2)	1962	40.00
SAM			
❑ 112	Jaguar/Blue Feeling	1962	50.00
❑ 117	Riptide/Big Noise from Makaba	1962	50.00
❑ 123	XL-3/My Little Baby	1963	50.00

MAJESTICS, THE (5)

Number	Title (A Side/B Side)	Yr	NM
45s			
JORDAN			
❑ 1057	Angel of Love/Searching for a New Love	1961	50.00
—Black vinyl			
❑ 1057	Angel of Love/Searching for a New Love	1961	300.00
—Yellow vinyl			
LINDA			
❑ 111	Strange World/Everything Is Gonna Be All Right	1963	75.00
❑ 121	Girl of My Dreams/It Hurts Me	1963	600.00
—Yellow label			
❑ 121	Girl of My Dreams/It Hurts Me	1963	750.00
—Violet label			
NU-TONE			
❑ 123	Angel of Love/Searching for a New Love	1961	70.00
PIXIE			
❑ 6901	Angel of Love/Searching for a New Love	1961	30.00

MAJESTICS, THE (6)
Sam Moore of SAM AND DAVE was in this group.

Number	Title (A Side/B Side)	Yr	NM
45s			
MARLIN			
❑ 802	Nitey Nite/Cave Man Rock	1956	1000.

MAJESTICS, THE (7)

Number	Title (A Side/B Side)	Yr	NM
45s			
MGM			
❑ 13488	Love Has Forgotten Me/Smile Through My Tears	1966	12.00

MAJOR LANCE
See listing under LANCE, MAJOR.

MAJORETTES, THE

Number	Title (A Side/B Side)	Yr	NM
45s			
TROY			
❑ 1000	White Levi's/Please Come Back	1963	20.00
❑ 1000 [PS]	White Levi's/Please Come Back	1963	40.00

MAJORS, THE (1)

Number	Title (A Side/B Side)	Yr	NM
45s			
IMPERIAL			
❑ 5855	A Wonderful Dream/Time Will Tell	1962	20.00
❑ 5879	She's a Troublemaker/A Little Bit Now, A Little Bit Later	1962	30.00
❑ 5914	What in the World/Anything You Can Do	1963	40.00
❑ 5936	Tra La La/What Have You Been Doin'	1963	12.00
❑ 5968	One Happy Ending/Get Up Now	1963	12.00
❑ 5991	Which Way Did She Go/Your Life Begins (Sweet 16)	1963	12.00
❑ 66009	I'll Be There/Ooh Wee Baby	1963	12.00
UNITED ARTISTS			
❑ 0110	A Wonderful Dream/Mother-in-Law	1973	5.00
—"Silver Spotlight Series" reissue; B-side by Ernie K-Doe			

Except when noted otherwise, VG = 25% of NM, and VG+ = 50% of NM. (Example: VG = $2.00, VG+ = $4.00 and NM = $8.00.)

Number	Title (A Side/B Side)	Yr	NM
Albums			
IMPERIAL			
❑ LP-9222 [M]	Meet the Majors	1963	100.00
❑ LP-12222 [S]	Meet the Majors	1963	200.00

MAJORS, THE (2)

Number	Title (A Side/B Side)	Yr	NM
45s			
DERBY			
❑ 763	At Last/You Ran Away from My Heart	1951	800.00
❑ 779	Laughing on the Outside/ Come On Up to My Room	1951	600.00

MAJORS, THE (3)

Number	Title (A Side/B Side)	Yr	NM
45s			
FELSTED			
❑ 8501	Blue Sunset/Rockin' the Boogie	1958	30.00
❑ 8576	Come Go with Me/Les Qua	1959	25.00
❑ 8707	Come Go with Me/Les Qua	1964	15.00

MAJORS, THE (4)

Number	Title (A Side/B Side)	Yr	NM
45s			
ORIGINAL			
❑ 1003	Big Eyes/Go 'Way	1954	400.00

MAKEBA, MIRIAM Also see HARRY BELAFONTE.

Number	Title (A Side/B Side)	Yr	NM
45s			
KAPP			
❑ 452	Carnival/Can't Cross Over	1962	12.00
LONDON			
❑ 1610	Lovely Lies/Kilimanjaro	1956	15.00
—With the Manhattan Brothers			
MERCURY			
❑ 72642	Ballad of the Sad Young Men/ Mommy, Mommy, What Is Heaven Like	1966	8.00
RCA VICTOR			
❑ 47-8326	Dubula/Forbidden Games	1964	10.00
REPRISE			
❑ 0578	Reza/When I've Passed On	1967	6.00
❑ 0606	Pata Pata/Ballad of the Sad Young Men	1967	8.00
❑ 0654	Malaysha/Ring Bell, Ring Bell	1967	6.00
❑ 0671	What Is Love/Ho Po Zamani	1968	6.00
❑ 0732	Pata Pata/Malaysha	1969	4.00
—"Back to Back Hits" series			
❑ 0755	Ibabalazie/Emavungivini (Down in the Dumps)	1968	6.00
❑ 0804	I Shall Be Released/Iphi Ndilela	1969	6.00
❑ 0921	I Shall Sing/In My Life	1970	6.00
Albums			
KAPP			
❑ KL-1274 [M]	The Many Voices of Miriam Makeba	1962	20.00
❑ KS-3274 [S]	The Many Voices of Miriam Makeba	1962	25.00
MERCURY			
❑ MG-21082 [M]	The Magnificent Miriam Makeba	1966	12.00
❑ MG-21095 [M]	All About Miriam	1967	12.00
❑ SR-61082 [S]	The Magnificent Miriam Makeba	1966	15.00
❑ SR-61095 [S]	All About Miriam	1967	15.00
MERCURY/URBAN AFRICA			
❑ 838208-1	Welela	1989	12.00
PETERS INT'L.			
❑ PLD 2082	Miriam Makeba in Concert	1977	12.00
RCA VICTOR			
❑ LPM-2267 [M]	Miriam Makeba	1960	20.00
❑ LSP-2267 [S]	Miriam Makeba	1960	25.00
❑ LPM-2750 [M]	The World of Miriam Makeba	1963	15.00
❑ LSP-2750 [S]	The World of Miriam Makeba	1963	20.00
❑ LPM-2845 [M]	The Voice of Africa	1964	15.00
❑ LSP-2845 [S]	The Voice of Africa	1964	20.00
❑ LPM-3321 [M]	Makeba Sings	1965	15.00
❑ LSP-3321 [S]	Makeba Sings	1965	20.00
❑ LPM-3512 [M]	The Magic of Makeba	1966	15.00
❑ LSP-3512 [S]	The Magic of Makeba	1966	20.00
❑ LPM-3982 [M]	The Best of Miriam Makeba	1968	25.00
❑ LSP-3982 [S]	The Best of Miriam Makeba	1968	12.00
REPRISE			
❑ R-6253 [M]	Miriam Makeba In Concert!	1967	15.00
❑ RS-6253 [S]	Miriam Makeba In Concert!	1967	12.00
❑ R-6274 [M]	Pata Pata	1967	15.00
❑ RS-6274 [S]	Pata Pata	1967	12.00
❑ RS-6310	Makeba!	1968	12.00
❑ RS-6381	Keep Me in Mind	1970	12.00
WARNER BROS.			
❑ 25673	Sangoma	1988	10.00

MAKOWICZ, ADAM

Number	Title (A Side/B Side)	Yr	NM
Albums			
CHOICE			
❑ 1028	From My Window	198?	12.00
COLUMBIA			
❑ JC 35320	Adam	1978	10.00
NOVUS			
❑ 3003-1-N	Moonray	1986	10.00
❑ 3022-1-N	Naughty Baby	1988	10.00
SHEFFIELD LABS			
❑ 21	The Name Is Makowicz (ma-ko-vitch)	1984	20.00
—Audiophile vinyl			

MAKOWICZ, ADAM, AND GEORGE MRAZ

Number	Title (A Side/B Side)	Yr	NM
Albums			
STASH			
❑ ST-216	Classic Jazz Duets	198?	10.00

MALACHI

Number	Title (A Side/B Side)	Yr	NM
Albums			
VERVE			
❑ V-5024 [M]	Holy Music	1967	30.00
❑ V6-5024 [S]	Holy Music	1967	40.00

MALCOLM X

Number	Title (A Side/B Side)	Yr	NM
Albums			
DOUGLAS			
❑ SD 795 [M]	Malcolm X Talks to Young People	1968	30.00
❑ SD 797	His Wit and Wisdom	196?	30.00
❑ Z 30743 [M]	By Any Means Necessary	1971	30.00
PAUL WINLEY			
❑ 135	The Ballot or the Bullet	197?	20.00
RCA			
❑ 66132	Words from the Frontlines: Excerpts from the Great Speeches of Malcolm X	1992	20.00
UPFRONT			
❑ UPF-152	Malcolm X Speaks to the People in Harlem	197?	15.00
WARNER BROS.			
❑ BS 2619	Malcolm X	1972	25.00
❑ PRO-A-5943 [DJ]	Malcolm X Speaks	1992	20.00
❑ PRO-A-5957 [DJ]	Music and Dialog from the Historic 1992 Documentary Film Malcolm X	1992	20.00

MALLETT, SAUNDRA, AND THE VANDELLAS

Number	Title (A Side/B Side)	Yr	NM
45s			
TAMLA			
❑ 54067	Camel Walk/It's Gonna Be Hard Times	1962	1000.

MALO

Number	Title (A Side/B Side)	Yr	NM
12-Inch Singles			
TRAQ			
❑ TR-109	Lady I Love (Dance Version 8:00) (Radio Version 3:40)	1981	8.00
45s			
TRAQ			
❑ 106	Fernando/Lady I Love	1981	6.00
WARNER BROS.			
❑ 7559	Suavecito/Nena	1972	5.00
❑ 7605	Café/Peace	1972	5.00
❑ 7651	Suavecito/Café	1973	4.00
—"Back to Back Hits" reissue			
❑ 7668	Oye Mama/I'm For Real	1972	5.00
❑ 7677	Latin Bugaloo/Midnight Thoughts	1973	5.00
❑ 7692	I Don't Know/Merengue	1973	5.00
Albums			
WARNER BROS.			
❑ BS 2584	Malo	1972	12.00
❑ BS 2652	Dos	1972	12.00
❑ BS 2702	Evolution	1973	12.00
❑ BS 2769	Ascencion	1974	12.00

MALTAIS, GENE

Number	Title (A Side/B Side)	Yr	NM
45s			
DECCA			
❑ 30387	Crazy Baby/Deep River Blues	1957	200.00
LILAC			
❑ 3159	The Raging Sea/ (B-side unknown)	1957	400.00
REGAL			
❑ 7502	Lovemakin'/The Bug	1958	150.00

MAMA CASS See CASS ELLIOT.

MAMA LION

Number	Title (A Side/B Side)	Yr	NM
45s			
FAMILY PRODUCTIONS			
❑ 0903	Ain't Too Proud to Beg/Cry	1971	8.00
❑ 0921	Sister Sister/Give It Everything I've Got	1972	8.00
Albums			
FAMILY PRODUCTIONS			
❑ FPS-2702	Mama Lion	1972	20.00
❑ FPS-2713	Give It Everything I've Got	1973	20.00

MAMAS AND THE PAPAS, THE Also see DENNY DOHERTY; CASS ELLIOT; JILL GIBSON; JOHN PHILLIPS; MICHELLE PHILLIPS.

Number	Title (A Side/B Side)	Yr	NM
45s			
ABC DUNHILL			
❑ 4125	Safe in My Garden/Too Late	1968	8.00
❑ 4150	For the Love of Ivy/ Strange Young Girls	1968	8.00
❑ 4171	Do You Wanna Dance/My Girl	1968	8.00
❑ 4301	Step Out/Shooting Star	1972	6.00
DUNHILL			
❑ 4018 [DJ]	Go Where You Wanna Go/ Somebody Groovy	1966	20.00
—Withdrawn before stock copies were released			
❑ 4018 [PS]	Go Where You Wanna Go/ Somebody Groovy	1966	400.00
—Yes, a picture sleeve has been confirmed!			
❑ 4020	California Dreamin'/ Somebody Groovy	1966	10.00
—Most of the 1966 Dunhill singles credited "The Mama's and the Papa's"			
❑ 4020 [PS]	California Dreamin'/ Somebody Groovy	1966	300.00
—Sleeve is promo only			
❑ 4026	Monday, Monday/Got a Feeling	1966	10.00
❑ 4026 [PS]	Monday, Monday/ I Call Your Name	1966	600.00
—The sleeve was printed, but after Dunhill changed the flip side of the 45 before release, most of them were destroyed			
❑ 4031	I Saw Her Again/Even If I Could	1966	10.00
❑ 4050	Look Through My Window/ Once Was a Time I Thought	1966	10.00
❑ 4057	Words of Love/ Dancing in the Street	1966	10.00
❑ 4077	Dedicated to the One I Love/ Free Advice	1967	10.00
❑ 4083	Creeque Alley/Did You Ever Want to Cry	1967	10.00
❑ 4083 [PS]	Creeque Alley/Did You Ever Want to Cry	1967	40.00
—Sleeve is promo only			
❑ 4099	Twelve Thirty (Young Girls Are Coming to the Canyon)/ Straight Shooter	1967	10.00
❑ 4107	Glad to Be Unhappy/Hey Girl	1967	10.00
❑ 4113	Dancing Bear/John's Music Box	1967	10.00
❑ 4113 [PS]	Dancing Bear/John's Music Box	1967	12.00
❑ 4125	Safe in My Garden/Too Late	1968	25.00
—Without the "ABC" logo at top of label			
7-Inch Extended Plays			
ABC DUNHILL			
❑ LP-DS-50031	Safe in My Garden/For the Love of Ivy//Mansions/Dream a Little Dream of Me	1968	15.00
—Jukebox issue; small hole, plays at 33 1/3 rpm			
❑ LP-DS-50031 [PS]	The Papas and the Mamas	1968	15.00
❑ PRO-50106	People Like Us/I Wanna Be a Star/Pearl//Pacific Coast Highway/Snowqueen of Texas/Step Out	1972	20.00
—Jukebox issue; small hole, plays at 33 1/3 rpm			
❑ PRO-50106 [PS]	People Like Us	1972	30.00
DUNHILL			
❑ LP DS-50006	Monday, Monday/I Call Your Name/Go Where You Wanna Go//California Dreamin'/You Baby/In Crowd	1966	25.00
—Jukebox issue; small hole, plays at 33 1/3 rpm			
❑ LP DS-50006 [PS]	If You Can Believe Your Eyes and Ears	1966	25.00
❑ EP-DS-50010	No Salt on Her Tail/Trip, Stumble & Fall/Dancing in the Street//I Saw Her Again/ I Can't Wait/That Kind of Girl	1966	20.00
—Stereo jukebox issue; small hole, plays at 33 1/3 rpm			
❑ EP-DS-50010 [PS]	The Mamas and the Papas	1966	20.00
Albums			
ABC			
❑ AC-30005	The ABC Collection	1976	15.00

M

ABC DUNHILL

Number	Title (A Side/B Side)	Yr	NM
❑ DS-50006	If You Can Believe Your Eyes and Ears	1968	12.00
❑ DS-50010	The Mamas and the Papas	1968	12.00
❑ DS-50014	The Mamas and the Papas Deliver	1968	12.00
❑ DS-50025	Farewell to the First Golden Era	1968	12.00
❑ DS-50031	The Papas and the Mamas	1968	15.00

—The five LPs above are reissues of records originally without the ABC logo

Number	Title (A Side/B Side)	Yr	NM
❑ DS-50038	Golden Era, Vol. 2	1968	20.00
❑ DS-50064	16 of Their Greatest Hits	1969	15.00
❑ DS-50073 [(2)]	A Gathering of Flowers	1970	25.00
❑ DSX-50100	Monterey International Pop Festival	1970	15.00
❑ DSX-50106	People Like Us	1971	12.00
❑ DSX-50145 [(2)]	20 Golden Hits	1973	20.00
❑ SMAS-93470	Monterey International Pop Festival	1970	25.00

—Capitol Record Club edition; label has the old-style "Dunhill" logo without the "ABC" as part of it

DUNHILL

Number	Title (A Side/B Side)	Yr	NM
❑ D-50006 [M]	If You Can Believe Your Eyes and Ears	1966	20.00

—With scroll over toilet

Number	Title (A Side/B Side)	Yr	NM
❑ D-50006 [M]	If You Can Believe Your Eyes and Ears	1966	40.00

—Black cover with photo cropped to render toilet invisible

Number	Title (A Side/B Side)	Yr	NM
❑ D-50006 [M]	If You Can Believe Your Eyes and Ears	1966	80.00

—With toilet completely visible in lower right

Number	Title (A Side/B Side)	Yr	NM
❑ DS-50006 [S]	If You Can Believe Your Eyes and Ears	1966	25.00

—With scroll over toilet proclaiming "Includes California Dreamin'"

Number	Title (A Side/B Side)	Yr	NM
❑ DS-50006 [S]	If You Can Believe Your Eyes and Ears	1966	25.00

—With scroll over toilet proclaiming "Includes California Dreamin'... Monday Monday... I Call Your Name"

Number	Title (A Side/B Side)	Yr	NM
❑ DS-50006 [S]	If You Can Believe Your Eyes and Ears	1966	50.00

—Black cover with photo cropped to render toilet invisible

Number	Title (A Side/B Side)	Yr	NM
❑ DS-50006 [S]	If You Can Believe Your Eyes and Ears	1966	100.00

—With toilet completely visible in lower right

Number	Title (A Side/B Side)	Yr	NM
❑ D-50010 [M]	The Mamas and the Papas	1966	20.00
❑ DS-50010 [S]	The Mamas and the Papas	1966	25.00
❑ D-50014 [M]	The Mamas and the Papas Deliver	1967	20.00
❑ DS-50014 [S]	The Mamas and the Papas Deliver	1967	25.00
❑ D-50025 [M]	Farewell to the First Golden Era	1967	20.00
❑ DS-50025 [S]	Farewell to the First Golden Era	1967	20.00
❑ DS-50031	The Papas and the Mamas	1968	25.00
❑ ST-90797 [S]	If You Can Believe Your Eyes and Ears	1966	50.00

—Capitol Record Club edition; known copies have scroll proclaiming "Includes California Dreamin'."

Number	Title (A Side/B Side)	Yr	NM
❑ T-90797 [M]	If You Can Believe Your Eyes and Ears	1966	50.00

—Capitol Record Club edition; known copies have scroll proclaiming "Includes California Dreamin'."

Number	Title (A Side/B Side)	Yr	NM
❑ ST-90924 [S]	The Mamas and the Papas	1966	40.00

—Capitol Record Club edition

Number	Title (A Side/B Side)	Yr	NM
❑ T-90924 [M]	The Mamas and the Papas	1966	30.00

—Capitol Record Club edition

MCA

Number	Title (A Side/B Side)	Yr	NM
❑ 709	Farewell to the First Golden Era	1980	8.00
❑ 710	The Papas and the Mamas	1980	8.00
❑ 6019 [(2)]	The Best of the Mamas and the Papas	1986	12.00
❑ 37145	16 of Their Greatest Hits	1980	8.00

PICKWICK

Number	Title (A Side/B Side)	Yr	NM
❑ SPC-3352	California Dreaming	1972	12.00

MANCHA, STEVE

45s

GROOVESVILLE

Number	Title (A Side/B Side)	Yr	NM
❑ 1001	You're Still in My Heart/She's So Good	1965	25.00
❑ 1002	I Don't Want to Lose You/Need to Be Needed	1966	40.00
❑ 1004	Friday Night/Monday Through Thursday	1966	500.00
❑ 1005	Don't Make Me a Storyteller/I Won't Love and Leave You	1967	60.00
❑ 1007	Just Keep On Loving Me/Sweet Baby Don't Ever Be Untrue	1967	60.00

WHEELSVILLE

Number	Title (A Side/B Side)	Yr	NM
❑ 102	Did My Baby Call/Whirlpool	1965	1000.

MANCHESTER, MELISSA

Also see NATIONAL LAMPOON.

12-Inch Singles

MCA

Number	Title (A Side/B Side)	Yr	NM
❑ 23563	Energy (Vocal)/Energy (Dub)	1985	6.00

45s

ANGEL

Number	Title (A Side/B Side)	Yr	NM
❑ S7-19771	Have Yourself a Merry Little Christmas/I've Got My Love to Keep Me Warm	1997	3.00

ARISTA

Number	Title (A Side/B Side)	Yr	NM
❑ 0116	Midnight Blue/I Got Eyes	1975	4.00
❑ 0146	Just Too Many People/This Lady's Not Home	1975	4.00
❑ 0168	Just You and I/My Sweet Thing	1976	4.00
❑ 0183	Better Days/Sing, Sing, Sing	1976	4.00
❑ 0196	Happy Endings/Rescue Me	1976	4.00
❑ 0218	Monkey See, Monkey Do/So's My Old Man	1976	4.00
❑ 0237	Dirty Work/Be Somebody	1977	4.00
❑ 0267	I Wanna Be Where You Are/No One's Ever Seen This Side of Me	1977	4.00
❑ 0373	Don't Cry Out Loud/We Had This Time	1978	4.00

—Originals have black labels

Number	Title (A Side/B Side)	Yr	NM
❑ 0373	Don't Cry Out Loud/We Had This Time	1979	3.00

—Second pressings have whitish labels

Number	Title (A Side/B Side)	Yr	NM
❑ 0405	Theme from "Ice Castles"/Such a Night	1979	4.00
❑ 0456	Pretty Girls/It's All in the Sky Above	1979	4.00
❑ 0485	Fire in the Morning/Lights of Dawn	1980	4.00
❑ 0551	If This Is Love/Talk	1980	4.00
❑ 0579	Without You/Boys in the Back Room	1980	4.00
❑ 0587	Lovers After All/Happier Than I've Ever Been	1981	4.00

—With Peabo Bryson

Number	Title (A Side/B Side)	Yr	NM
❑ 0657	Race to the End/Long Goodbyes	1982	4.00
❑ 0676	You Should Hear How She Talks About You/Long Goodbyes	1982	4.00
❑ 1028	Come In from the Rain/Hey Ricky (You're a Low Down Heel)	1982	4.00
❑ 1045	Nice Girls/Hey Ricky (You're a Low Down Heel)	1983	4.00
❑ 1057	My Boyfriend's Back/Looking for the Perfect Aah	1983	4.00
❑ 9014	My Boyfriend's Back/Looking for the Perfect Aah	1983	3.00
❑ 9087	No One Can Love You More Than Me/White Rose	1983	3.00
❑ 9162	I Don't Care What the People Say/Emergency	1984	3.00

BELL

Number	Title (A Side/B Side)	Yr	NM
❑ 45399	Never Never Land/Be Happy Now	1973	5.00
❑ 45465	Heaven/Inclined	1974	5.00

CASABLANCA

Number	Title (A Side/B Side)	Yr	NM
❑ 880308-7	Thief of Hearts/(B-side unknown)	1984	3.00

MB

Number	Title (A Side/B Side)	Yr	NM
❑ 1005	Beautiful People/A Song for You	1967	15.00

MCA

Number	Title (A Side/B Side)	Yr	NM
❑ 52575	Mathematics/So Full of Yourself	1985	3.00
❑ 52575 [PS]	Mathematics/So Full of Yourself	1985	3.00
❑ 52616	Energy/So Full of Yourself	1985	3.00
❑ 52616 [PS]	Energy/So Full of Yourself	1985	3.00
❑ 52688	Just One Lifetime/So Full of Yourself	1985	3.00
❑ 52784	Music of Goodbye (Love Theme from Out of Africa)/Have You Got a Story for Me	1986	3.00

—With Al Jarreau

Number	Title (A Side/B Side)	Yr	NM
❑ 52784 [PS]	Music of Goodbye (Love Theme from Out of Africa)/Have You Got a Story for Me	1986	3.00

—With Al Jarreau

RCA VICTOR

Number	Title (A Side/B Side)	Yr	NM
❑ 74-0366	Tellin' the World/(B-side unknown)	1970	12.00

—With Grover Kimball

Albums

ARISTA

Number	Title (A Side/B Side)	Yr	NM
❑ AL 4006	Home to Myself	1975	10.00

—Reissue of Bell 1123

Number	Title (A Side/B Side)	Yr	NM
❑ AL 4011	Bright Eyes	1975	10.00

—Reissue of Bell 1303

Number	Title (A Side/B Side)	Yr	NM
❑ AL 4031	Melissa	1975	10.00
❑ AQ 4031 [Q]	Melissa	1975	15.00
❑ AL 4067	Better Days & Happy Endings	1976	10.00
❑ AQ 4067 [Q]	Better Days & Happy Endings	1976	15.00
❑ AL 4095	Help Is On the Way	1976	10.00
❑ AL 4136	Singin'	1977	10.00
❑ AB 4186	Don't Cry Out Loud	1978	10.00
❑ AL 8055	Melissa	1983	8.00

—Budget-line reissue of 4031

Number	Title (A Side/B Side)	Yr	NM
❑ AL 8094	Emergency	1983	10.00
❑ AL 8293	Greatest Hits	198?	8.00

—Budget-line reissue of 9611

Number	Title (A Side/B Side)	Yr	NM
❑ AL 8350	Hey Ricky	198?	8.00

—Budget-line reissue of 9574

Number	Title (A Side/B Side)	Yr	NM
❑ AL 8373	Don't Cry Out Loud	198?	8.00

—Budget-line reissue of 4186

Number	Title (A Side/B Side)	Yr	NM
❑ AL 9506	Melissa Manchester	1979	10.00
❑ AL 9533	For the Working Girl	1980	10.00
❑ AL 9574	Hey Ricky	1982	10.00
❑ AL 9611	Greatest Hits	1983	10.00

BELL

Number	Title (A Side/B Side)	Yr	NM
❑ 1123	Home to Myself	1973	12.00
❑ 1303	Bright Eyes	1974	12.00

MCA

Number	Title (A Side/B Side)	Yr	NM
❑ 5587	Mathematics	1985	10.00

MIKA

Number	Title (A Side/B Side)	Yr	NM
❑ 841273-1	Tribute	1989	12.00

MOBILE FIDELITY

Number	Title (A Side/B Side)	Yr	NM
❑ 1-028	Melissa	1980	30.00

—Audiophile vinyl

NAUTILUS

Number	Title (A Side/B Side)	Yr	NM
❑ NR-33	Don't Cry Out Loud	198?	40.00

—Audiophile vinyl

PAIR

Number	Title (A Side/B Side)	Yr	NM
❑ PDL2-1086 [(2)]	The Many Moods of Melissa Manchester	1986	12.00

MANCHESTERS, THE (1)

Albums

DIPLOMAT

Number	Title (A Side/B Side)	Yr	NM
❑ D-2307 [M]	Beatlerama	1964	15.00

—No artist credited on label or cover

Number	Title (A Side/B Side)	Yr	NM
❑ D-2307 [M]	Beatlerama	1964	15.00

—With artist credited

Number	Title (A Side/B Side)	Yr	NM
❑ DS-2307 [S]	Beatlerama	1964	20.00

—No artist credited on label or cover

Number	Title (A Side/B Side)	Yr	NM
❑ DS-2307 [S]	Beatlerama	1964	20.00

—With artist credited

GUEST STAR

Number	Title (A Side/B Side)	Yr	NM
❑ G-2307 [M]	Beatlerama	1964	15.00
❑ GS-2307 [S]	Beatlerama	1964	20.00

MANCHESTERS, THE (2)

Featuring DAVID GATES.

45s

VEE JAY

Number	Title (A Side/B Side)	Yr	NM
❑ 700	I Don't Come from England/Dragonfly	1965	25.00

MANDEL, HARVEY

45s

JANUS

Number	Title (A Side/B Side)	Yr	NM
❑ 144	Midnight Sun/Baby Batter	1970	6.00
❑ 198	Pegasus/Uni Ino	1972	6.00

PHILIPS

Number	Title (A Side/B Side)	Yr	NM
❑ 40566	Cristo Redentor/Bradley's Barn	1968	8.00
❑ 40579	Wade in the Water (Part 1)/Wade in the Water (Part 2)	1968	8.00
❑ 40607	Campus Blues/Righteous	1969	8.00
❑ 40627	Moontan/Summer Sequence	1969	8.00
❑ 40643	Dry Your Eyes/Ridin' High	1969	8.00

Albums

EDITIONS EG

Number	Title (A Side/B Side)	Yr	NM
❑ CAROL-1535-1	Cristo Redentor	198?	10.00

—Reissue of Philips 600-281

JANUS

Number	Title (A Side/B Side)	Yr	NM
❑ JLS-3017	Baby Batter	1970	20.00
❑ JLS-3037	The Snake	1972	20.00
❑ JLS-3047	Shangrenade	1973	20.00
❑ JSX-3067	Feel the Sound of Harvey Mandel	1974	20.00
❑ JXS-7014	The Best of Harvey Mandel	1975	15.00

OVATION

Number	Title (A Side/B Side)	Yr	NM
❑ OV-1415	Get Off in Chicago	1971	15.00

PHILIPS

Number	Title (A Side/B Side)	Yr	NM
❑ PHS 600281	Cristo Redentor	1969	25.00
❑ PHS 600306	Righteous	1969	25.00
❑ PHS 600325	Games Guitars Play	1970	25.00

MANDEL, MIKE

Albums

VANGUARD

Number	Title (A Side/B Side)	Yr	NM
❑ VSD-79409	Sky Music	1978	12.00
❑ VSD-79437	Utopia Parkway	1979	12.00

MANDO AND THE CHILI PEPPERS

Albums

GOLDEN CREST

Number	Title (A Side/B Side)	Yr	NM
❑ CR-3023 [M]	On the Road with Rock and Roll	1957	500.00

Except when noted otherwise, VG = 25% of NM, and VG+ = 50% of NM. (Example: VG = $2.00, VG+ = $4.00 and NM = $8.00.)

MANDRAKE MEMORIAL

45s

POPPY

Number	Title (A Side/B Side)	Yr	NM
90103	Something in the Air/Musical Man	1969	10.00
90103 [PS]	Something in the Air/Musical Man	1969	25.00

Albums

POPPY

Number	Title (A Side/B Side)	Yr	NM
PYS 40002	Mandrake Memorial	1968	40.00
PYS 40003	Medium	1969	40.00
PYS 40006	Puzzle	1970	40.00

MANDRILL

45s

ARISTA

Number	Title (A Side/B Side)	Yr	NM
0274	Funky Monkey/Gilley Hines	1977	4.00
0304	Can You Get It/Holiday	1978	4.00
0326	Happy Beat/Holiday	1978	4.00
0375	Too Late/Holiday	1978	4.00
0490	My Kind of Girl/Lo Siento Mucho	1980	4.00
0507	Getting in the Mood/ (B-side unknown)	1980	4.00
0529	Dance of Love/When You Shake	1980	4.00

MONTAGE

Number	Title (A Side/B Side)	Yr	NM
1222	Put Your Money Where the Funk Is/(B-side unknown)	1982	4.00
1224	Soar Like an Eagle/Starry-Eyed	1982	4.00

POLYDOR

Number	Title (A Side/B Side)	Yr	NM
14070	Mandrill/Warning Blues	1971	5.00
14085	Rollin' On/Symphonic Revolution	1971	5.00
14127	Kofijahm/I Refuse to Smile	1972	5.00
14142	Cohelo/Git It All	1972	5.00
14156	Children of the Sun/Ace Is High	1972	5.00
14163	Fencewalk/Hagalo	1973	5.00
14187	Hang Loose/Polk Street Carnival	1973	5.00
14200	Mango Meat/ Afrikus Retrospectus	1973	5.00
14214	Love Song/Two Sisters of Mystery	1974	5.00
14235	Positive Thing/ Positive Thing Plus	1974	5.00
14257	Road to Love/Armadillo	1974	5.00

UNITED ARTISTS

Number	Title (A Side/B Side)	Yr	NM
XW673	Tee Vee/Silk	1975	4.00
XW778	Disco-Lypso/Solid	1976	4.00

Albums

ARISTA

Number	Title (A Side/B Side)	Yr	NM
AL 4144	We Are One	1977	10.00
AL 4195	New Worlds	1978	10.00
AL 9527	Getting In the Mood	1980	10.00

LIBERTY

Number	Title (A Side/B Side)	Yr	NM
LN-10196	Rebirth	1983	8.00

MONTAGE

Number	Title (A Side/B Side)	Yr	NM
ST-72008	Energize	1982	12.00

POLYDOR

Number	Title (A Side/B Side)	Yr	NM
24-4060	Mandrill	1971	12.00
PD-5025	Mandrill Is	1972	12.00
PD-5043	Composite Truth	1973	12.00
PD-5059	Just Outside of Town	1973	12.00
PD-1-6047	The Best of Mandrill	1975	12.00
PD-2-9002 [(2)]	Mandrilland	1976	15.00

UNITED ARTISTS

Number	Title (A Side/B Side)	Yr	NM
UA-LA408-G	Solid	1975	12.00
UA-LA577-G	Beast from the East	1976	12.00

MANGIONE, CHUCK

12-Inch Singles

A&M

Number	Title (A Side/B Side)	Yr	NM
8448 [DJ]	Feels So Good (4:40) (same on both sides)	1978	12.00

COLUMBIA

Number	Title (A Side/B Side)	Yr	NM
AS 1903 [DJ]	Love Wears No Disguise/ Diana "D"	1984	8.00
07827	Long Hair Soulful (Extended) (Edit)	1988	8.00

45s

A&M

Number	Title (A Side/B Side)	Yr	NM
1707	Chase the Clouds Away/Soft	1975	4.00
1773	Bellavia/Listen to the Wind	1975	4.00
1827	Soft/Can't We Do This All Night	1976	4.00
1886	Main Squeeze/Come Take a Ride with Me	1976	4.00
1886 [PS]	Main Squeeze/Come Take a Ride with Me	1976	6.00
1919	Bellavia/Doin' Everything With You	1977	4.00
2001	Feels So Good/Maui-Waui	1977	4.00
2001 [PS]	Feels So Good/Maui-Waui	1977	5.00
2088	Children of Sanchez/Doin' Everything with You	1978	4.00
2088 [PS]	Children of Sanchez/ Doin' Everything with You	1978	5.00
2118	Bellavia/Lullabye	1979	4.00
2167	Land of Make Believe/ Children of Sanchez	1979	4.00
2211	Give It All You Got/B'Bye	1980	4.00
2211 [PS]	Give It All You Got/B'Bye	1980	4.00
2236	Fun and Games/Children of Sanchez (Finale)	1980	4.00
2236 [PS]	Fun and Games/Children of Sanchez (Finale)	1980	4.00
2341	Give It All You Got, But Slowly/ Neapolitan Tarantella	1981	3.00
2354	Cannonball Run Theme/ Can't We Do This All Night	1981	3.00

COLUMBIA

Number	Title (A Side/B Side)	Yr	NM
03008	Steppin' Out/Memories of Scirocco	1982	3.00
03329	No Problem/Memories of Scirocco	1982	3.00
03986	Journey to a Rainbow/ Please Stay the Night	1983	3.00
04649	Diana "D"/Josephine	1984	3.00
05866	Save Tonight for Me/T.J.'s Gingerbread House	1986	3.00
07917	Long Hair Soulful/Do You Ever Think About Me	1988	3.00

MERCURY

Number	Title (A Side/B Side)	Yr	NM
73208	Hill Where the Lord Hides/ Friends and Lovers	1971	8.00
73238	And In the Beginning/ Feel a Vision	1972	6.00
73262	Freddie's Walkin'/ Look to the Children	1972	6.00
73371	Last Tango in Paris/Legend of the One-Eyed Sailor	1973	6.00
73453	As Long As We're Together/ Legend of the One-Eyed Sailor	1974	6.00
73635	Land of Make Believe/As Long As We're Together	1975	6.00
73920	Land of Make Believe/As Long As We're Together	1977	5.00
74016	Hill Where the Lord Hides/Land of Make Believe	1978	5.00

Albums

A&M

Number	Title (A Side/B Side)	Yr	NM
SP-3115	Chase the Clouds Away	198?	6.00
—Budget-line reissue			
SP-3172	Bellavia	198?	6.00
—Budget-line reissue			
SP-3193	Fun and Games	1983	6.00
—Budget-line reissue			
SP-3219	Feels So Good	198?	6.00
—Budget-line reissue			
SP-3220	Main Squeeze	198?	6.00
—Budget-line reissue			
SP-3237	70 Miles Young	198?	6.00
—Budget-line reissue			
SP-3282	The Best of Chuck Mangione	1985	10.00
SP-3715	Fun and Games	1980	10.00
SP-4518	Chase the Clouds Away	1975	10.00
SP-4557	Bellavia	1975	10.00
SP-4612	Main Squeeze	1976	10.00
SP-4658	Feels So Good	1977	10.00
SP-4911	70 Miles Young	1982	10.00
SP-6513 [(2)]	Tarantella	1981	12.00
SP-6700 [(2)]	Children of Sanchez	1978	12.00
SP-6701 [(2)]	An Evening of Magic — Chuck Mangione Live at the Hollywood Bowl	1979	12.00
QU-54518 [Q]	Chase the Clouds Away	1975	18.00
QU-54557 [Q]	Bellavia	1975	18.00

COLUMBIA

Number	Title (A Side/B Side)	Yr	NM
FC 38101	Love Notes	1982	10.00
PC 38101	Love Notes	198?	6.00
—Budget-line reissue			
FC 38686	Journey to a Rainbow	1983	10.00
PC 38686	Journey to a Rainbow	1986	6.00
—Budget-line reissue			
FC 39479	Disguise	1984	10.00
FC 40254	Save Tonight for Me	1986	10.00
FC 40984	Eyes of the Veiled Temptress	1988	10.00

FANTASY

Number	Title (A Side/B Side)	Yr	NM
OJC-495	Recuerdo	1991	12.00
—Reissue of Jazzland 984			

JAZZLAND

Number	Title (A Side/B Side)	Yr	NM
JLP-84 [M]	Recuerdo	1962	40.00
JLP-984 [S]	Recuerdo	1962	50.00

MERCURY

Number	Title (A Side/B Side)	Yr	NM
SRM-1-631	The Chuck Mangione Quartet	1972	12.00
SRM-1-650	Alive!	1973	12.00
SRM-1-681	Friends & Love/Highlights	1973	12.00
SRM-1-684	Land of Make Believe	1973	12.00
SRM-2-800 [(2)]	Friends & Love — A Chuck Mangione Concert	1971	15.00
SRM-1-1050	Encore/The Chuck Mangione Concerts	1975	10.00
SRM-2-7501 [(2)]	Together: A New Chuck Mangione Concert	1971	15.00
SRM-2-8601 [(2)]	The Best of Chuck Mangione	1978	12.00
824301-1	Alive!	198?	8.00
—Reissue of 650			

MILESTONE

Number	Title (A Side/B Side)	Yr	NM
47042 [(2)]	Jazz Brother	1977	12.00
—Reissue of material issued by "The Jazz Brothers"			

MOBILE FIDELITY

Number	Title (A Side/B Side)	Yr	NM
1-068	Feels So Good	1981	25.00
—Audiophile vinyl			

MANHATTAN TRANSFER

12-Inch Singles

ATLANTIC

Number	Title (A Side/B Side)	Yr	NM
PR 525 [DJ]	Spice of Life/The Night That Monk Returned to Heaven	1983	6.00
PR 560 [DJ]	American Pop/Why Not	1983	6.00
PR 2272 [DJ]	So You Say (same on both sides)	1987	6.00

45s

(NO LABEL)

Number	Title (A Side/B Side)	Yr	NM
1984 [DJ]	The Christmas Song (same on both sides)	1984	40.00
1984 [PS]	The Christmas Song (same on both sides)	1984	40.00
—Above sleeve and record are a private pressing for friends and associates of the group			

ATLANTIC

Number	Title (A Side/B Side)	Yr	NM
3277	Sweet Talking Guy/Clap Your Hands	1975	8.00
3292	Operator/Tuxedo Junction	1975	5.00
3349	Helpless/My Cat Fell in the Well	1976	5.00
3374	Chanson d'Amour/Popsicle Toes	1976	5.00
3472	Where Did Our Love Go/ Inside and Out	1978	5.00
3491	Four Brothers/It's Not the Spotlight	1978	5.00
3636	Birdland/Shaker Song	1979	5.00
3649	Twilight Zone-Twilight Tone/ Body and Soul	1980	5.00
3756 [DJ]	Nothin' You Can Do About It (same on both sides)	1980	5.00
—May be promo only			
3772	Trickle, Trickle/Foreign Affair	1980	10.00
3816	Boy from New York City/ (The World of) Confirmation	1981	4.00
3855	Smile Again/Until I Met You	1981	4.00
3877	Spies in the Night/Kafka	1981	4.00
4034	Route 66/On the Boulevard	1982	4.00
89094	So You Say/Notes from the Underground	1988	4.00
89094 [PS]	So You Say/Notes from the Underground	1988	4.00
89156	Soul Food to Go/Hear the Voices	1988	4.00
89156 [PS]	Soul Food to Go/Hear the Voices	1988	4.00
89467	That's Killer Joe/Airegin II	1985	5.00
89533	Ray's Rockhouse/Another Life in Tunisia	1985	4.00
89533 [PS]	Ray's Rockhouse/Another Life in Tunisia	1985	4.00
89594	Baby Come Back to Me (Morse Code of Love)/ That's the Way It Goes	1984	10.00
89647	This Independence/ Code of Ethics	1984	5.00
89695	Mystery/Goodbye Love	1984	4.00
89720	American Pop/Why Not!	1983	4.00
—Featuring Frankie Valli			
89720 [PS]	American Pop/Why Not!	1983	4.00
89786	Spice of Life/The Night That Monk Returned to Heaven	1983	4.00
89786 [PS]	Spice of Life/The Night That Monk Returned to Heaven	1983	5.00

CAPITOL

Number	Title (A Side/B Side)	Yr	NM
2968	Care for Me/Rosianna	1970	10.00
—With Gene Pistilli			
3036	Maybe Mexico/Winterlude	1971	10.00
—With Gene Pistilli			
3108	Java Jive/Chicken Bone Bone	1971	10.00
—With Gene Pistilli			

Albums

ATLANTIC

Number	Title (A Side/B Side)	Yr	NM
SD 16036	Mecca for Moderns	1981	10.00
SD 18133	The Manhattan Transfer	1975	10.00
SD 18183	Coming Out	1976	10.00
SD 19163	Pastiche	1978	10.00
SD 19258	Extensions	1979	10.00
SD 19319	The Best of the Manhattan Transfer	1981	10.00
80104	Bodies and Souls	1983	10.00
81233	Bop Doo-Wopp	1984	12.00
81266	Vocalese	1985	10.00
81723	Live	1987	10.00
81803	Brasil	1987	10.00

Number	Title (A Side/B Side)	Yr	NM
CAPITOL			
❑ ST-778	Jukin'	1971	15.00
—With Gene Pistilli			
❑ ST-11405	Jukin'	1975	10.00
—With Gene Pistilli; reissue of 778			
❑ SN-16223	Jukin'	198?	8.00
—With Gene Pistilli; budget-line reissue			
COLUMBIA			
❑ C 47079	The Offbeat of Avenues	1991	15.00
MOBILE FIDELITY			
❑ 1-022	Manhattan Transfer Live	1979	30.00
—Audiophile vinyl			
❑ 1-199	Extensions	1994	30.00
—Audiophile vinyl			

MANHATTANS, THE (1) Well-known male R&B vocal group.

12-Inch Singles

Number	Title (A Side/B Side)	Yr	NM
COLUMBIA			
❑ AS 1316 [DJ]	Let Your Love Come Down (same on both sides)	1981	10.00
❑ 03940	Crazy (5:00) (Instrumental)	1983	8.00
❑ 05973	Maybe Tomorrow/Where Did We Go Wrong	1986	8.00

45s

Number	Title (A Side/B Side)	Yr	NM
CARNIVAL			
❑ 504	I've Got Everything But You/For the Very First Time	1964	20.00
❑ 506	There Goes a Fool/Call Somebody Please	1964	40.00
❑ 507	I Wanna Be (Your Everything)/What's It Gonna Be	1965	15.00
❑ 509	Searchin' for My Baby/I'm the One That Love Forgot	1965	15.00
❑ 512	Follow Your Heart/The Boston Money	1965	15.00
❑ 514	Baby I Need You/Teach Me the Philly Dog	1966	15.00
❑ 517	Can I/That New Girl	1966	15.00
❑ 522	I Betcha (Couldn't Love Me)/Sweet Little Girl	1966	15.00
❑ 524	It's That Time of the Year/Alone on New Year's Eve	1966	20.00
❑ 526	All I Need Is Your Love/Our Love Will Never Die	1967	15.00
❑ 529	When We're Made As One/Baby I'm Sorry	1967	15.00
❑ 533	I Call It Love/Manhattan Stomp	1967	15.00
❑ 542	I Don't Wanna Go/Love Is Breaking Out	1968	15.00
❑ 545	Til You Come Back to Me/Call Somebody Please	1968	15.00
COLUMBIA			
❑ 02164	Shining Star/Summertime in the City	1981	3.00
—Reissue			
❑ 02191	Just One Moment Away/When I Leave Tomorrow	1981	4.00
❑ 02548	Let Your Love Come Down/I Gotta Thank You	1981	4.00
❑ 02666	Money, Money/I Wanta Thank You	1982	4.00
❑ 03939	Crazy/Gonna Find You	1983	4.00
❑ 04110	Forever By Your Side/Locked Up in Your Love	1983	4.00
❑ 04754	You Send Me/You're Gonna Love Being Loved By Me	1985	4.00
❑ 04754 [PS]	You Send Me/You're Gonna Love Being Loved By Me	1985	4.00
❑ 04930	Don't Say No/Dreamin'	1985	4.00
❑ 06376	Where Did We Go Wrong/Maybe Tomorrow	1986	4.00
—With Regina Belle			
❑ 07010	Mr. D.J./All I Need	1987	4.00
❑ 10045	Don't Take Your Love/The Day the Robins Sang to Me	1974	5.00
❑ 10140	Hurt/Nursery Rhymes	1975	5.00
❑ 10310	Kiss and Say Goodbye/Wonderful World of Love	1976	5.00
❑ 10430	I Kinda Miss You/Gypsy Man	1976	5.00
❑ 10495	It Feels So Good to Be Loved By You/On the Street (Where I Live)	1977	5.00
❑ 10586	We Never Danced to a Love Song/Let's Start It All Over Again	1977	5.00
❑ 10674	Am I Losing You/Movin'	1978	5.00
❑ 10766	Everybody Has a Dream/Happiness	1978	5.00
❑ 10921	Here Comes the Hurt Again/Don't Say Goodbye	1979	5.00
❑ 11024	The Way We Were-Memories/New York City	1979	5.00
❑ 11222	Shining Star/I'll Never Run Away from Love Again	1980	4.00
❑ 11321	Girl of My Dreams/The Closer You Are	1980	4.00
❑ 11398	I'll Never Find Another (Another Just Like You)/Rendezvous	1980	4.00
❑ 45838	There's No Me Without You/I'm Not a Run-Around	1973	6.00
❑ 45927	You'd Better Believe It/Soul Train	1973	6.00
❑ 45971	Wish That You Were Mine/It's So Hard Loving You	1973	6.00
❑ 46081	Summertime in the City/The Other Side of Me	1974	6.00
❑ 60511	Do You Really Mean Goodbye/Rendezvous	1981	4.00
DELUXE			
❑ 109	The Picture Became Quite Clear/Oh Lord, How I Wish I Could Sleep	1969	10.00
❑ 115	It's Gonna Take a Lot to Bring Me Back/Give Him Up	1970	10.00
❑ 122	If My Heart Could Speak/Loneliness	1970	10.00
❑ 129	From Atlanta to Goodbye/Fantastic Journey	1970	10.00
❑ 132	Let Them Talk/Straight to My Heart	1970	10.00
❑ 136	Do You Ever/I Can't Stand for You to Leave Me	1971	10.00
❑ 137	A Million to One/Cry If You Wanna Cry	1971	10.00
❑ 139	One Life to Live/It's the Only Way	1972	10.00
❑ 144	Back Up/Fever	1972	10.00
❑ 146	Rainbow Week/Loneliness	1973	10.00
❑ 152	Do You Ever/If My Heart Could Speak	1973	10.00
STARFIRE			
❑ 121	Alone on New Year's Eve/It's That Time of the Year	1979	5.00
VALLEY VUE			
❑ 75723	Sweet Talk/(B-side unknown)	1989	6.00
❑ 75749	Why You Wanna Love Me Like That/(B-side unknown)	1989	6.00

Albums

Number	Title	Yr	NM
CARNIVAL			
❑ CMLP-201 [M]	Dedicated to You	1966	250.00
❑ CSLP-201 [S]	Dedicated to You	1966	500.00
❑ CMLP-202 [M]	For You and Yours	1967	150.00
❑ CSLP-202 [S]	For You and Yours	1967	300.00
COLLECTABLES			
❑ COL-5135	Dedicated to You: Golden Carnival Classics, Part One	198?	10.00
❑ COL-5136	For You and Yours: Golden Carnival Classics, Part Two	198?	10.00
COLUMBIA			
❑ KC 32444	There's No Me Without You	1973	15.00
❑ PC 32444	There's No Me Without You	198?	8.00
—Budget-line reissue			
❑ KC 33064	That's How Much I Love You	1975	15.00
❑ PC 33820	The Manhattans	1976	12.00
—No bar code on back cover			
❑ PC 33820	The Manhattans	198?	8.00
—With bar code on back cover			
❑ PC 34450	It Feels So Good	1977	12.00
—No bar code on back cover			
❑ PC 34450	It Feels So Good	198?	8.00
—With bar code on back cover			
❑ PCQ 34450 [Q]	It Feels So Good	1977	20.00
❑ JC 35252	There's No Good in Goodbye	1978	12.00
❑ JC 35693	Love Talk	1979	12.00
❑ PC 35693	After Midnight	198?	8.00
—Budget-line reissue			
❑ JC 36411	After Midnight	1980	12.00
❑ JC 36861	Manhattans Greatest Hits	1980	12.00
❑ FC 37156	Black Tie	1981	10.00
❑ PC 37156	Black Tie	198?	8.00
—Budget-line reissue			
❑ FC 38600	Forever By Your Side	1983	10.00
❑ FC 39277	Too Hot to Stop It	1985	10.00
DELUXE			
❑ 12000	With These Hands	1971	25.00
❑ 12004	A Million to One	1972	25.00
SOLID SMOKE			
❑ 8007	Follow Your Heart	1981	10.00
VALLEY VUE			
❑ D1-72946	Sweet Talk	1989	12.00

MANHATTANS, THE (2)

45s

Number	Title (A Side/B Side)	Yr	NM
COLPIX			
❑ 115	Big Wheel Express/Powder Blue	1959	30.00

MANHATTANS, THE (U) Some of these are likely group (1); others could be group (2); others are probably neither.

45s

Number	Title (A Side/B Side)	Yr	NM
AVANTI			
❑ 1401	What Should I Do/Later for You	1963	75.00
BIG MACK			
❑ 3911	Why Should I Cry/The Feeling Is Mutual	196?	750.00
CAPITOL			
❑ 4591	Molly Brown Medley/I Ain't Down Yet	1961	20.00
❑ 4730	La La La/Sing All the Day	1962	20.00
ENJOY			
❑ 2008	Come On Back/Long Time No See	1964	20.00
—As "Ronnie and the Manhattans"			
GOLDEN WORLD			
❑ 14	Just a Little Loving/Beautiful Brown Eyes	1964	40.00
KING			
❑ 5228	Ebb Tide (Part 1)/Ebb Tide (Part 2)	1959	15.00
❑ 5259	Sugar Tooth/Like Saying Something	1959	15.00
PINEY			
❑ 107	Live It Up/Go Baby Go	1962	60.00
❑ 108	Crazy Love/The Hawk and the Crow	1962	50.00
WARNER			
❑ 1015	How Do I Say I'm Sorry/Love Is Where You Find It	1958	120.00

MANILLA ROAD

Albums

Number	Title	Yr	NM
ROADSTER			
❑ MR 1001	Invasion	1980	100.00
❑ MR 1002	Metal	1982	100.00
❑ MR 1003	Crystal Logic	1983	50.00

MANILOW, BARRY Also see FEATHERBED.

12-Inch Singles

Number	Title (A Side/B Side)	Yr	NM
ARISTA			
❑ (# unknown)	En El Copa (Long) (Short)	1978	30.00
❑ SP-18 [DJ]	Copacabana (At the Copa)/(B-side blank)	1978	300.00
—The B-side is banded to appear as if it has three tracks, but the groove is blank!			
❑ SP-21 [DJ]	En El Copa (same on both sides)	1978	25.00
—Spanish version of "Copacabana"			
❑ ADP 3291 [DJ]	I'd Really Love to See You Tonight (3 versions)	1997	10.00
❑ ADP 9295 [DJ]	When October Goes (same on both sides)	1984	10.00
❑ ADP 9648 [DJ]	Brooklyn Blues (same on both sides)	1987	20.00
—With Tom Scott; blue vinyl			
❑ AD1-9665	Hey Mambo (2 versions)	1988	12.00
❑ 13379	I'd Really Love to See You Tonight (2 versions)/Could It Be Magic (1993 remix)	1997	12.00
RCA			
❑ PD-14330	I'm Your Man (Club Mix)/I'm Your Man (Dub)	1986	10.00

45s

Number	Title (A Side/B Side)	Yr	NM
ARISTA			
❑ SP-11 [DJ]	It's Just Another New Year's Eve (same on both sides)	1977	8.00
❑ SP-11 [PS]	It's Just Another New Year's Eve (same on both sides)	1977	12.00
❑ SP-25 [DJ]	Ready to Take a Chance Again (same on both sides)	1978	8.00
❑ SP-25 [PS]	Ready to Take a Chance Again (same on both sides)	1978	12.00
❑ 0108	It's a Miracle/One of These Days	1975	4.00
❑ 0126	Could It Be Magic/I Am Your Child	1975	4.00
❑ 0157	I Write the Songs/A Nice Boy Like Me	1975	4.00
❑ 0172	Tryin' to Get the Feeling Again/Beautiful Music	1976	4.00
❑ 0206	This One's for You/Riders to the Stars	1976	4.00
❑ 0212	Weekend in New England/Say the Words	1976	4.00
❑ 0244	Looks Like We Made It/New York City Rhythm	1977	4.00
❑ 0273	Daybreak/Jump Shout Boogie	1977	4.00
❑ 0305	Can't Smile Without You/Sunrise	1978	4.00
❑ 0330	Even Now/I Was a Fool (To Let You Go)	1978	4.00
❑ 0330 [PS]	Even Now/I Was a Fool (To Let You Go)	1978	4.00
❑ 0339	Copacabana (Short Version)/Copacabana (Long Version)	1978	4.00
❑ 0357	Ready to Take a Chance Again/Sweet Life	1978	4.00
❑ 0382	Somewhere in the Night/Leavin' in the Morning	1978	4.00
❑ 0464	Ships/They Gave In to the Blues	1979	4.00

Except when noted otherwise, VG = 25% of NM, and VG+ = 50% of NM. (Example: VG = $2.00, VG+ = $4.00 and NM = $8.00.)

Number	Title (A Side/B Side)	Yr	NM
❑ 0481	When I Wanted You/Bobbie Lee (What's the Difference I Gotta Live)	1979	4.00
❑ 0501	I Don't Want to Walk Without You/One Voice	1980	4.00
❑ 0566	I Made It Through the Rain/ Only in Chicago	1980	4.00
❑ 0596	Lonely Together/The Last Duet	1981	4.00
—B-side with Lily Tomlin			
❑ 0633	The Old Songs/Don't Fall in Love with Me	1981	4.00
❑ 0658	Somewhere Down the Road/ Let's Take All Night to Say Goodbye	1982	4.00
❑ 0675	Let's Hang On/No Other Love	1982	4.00
❑ 0698	Oh Julie/Break Down the Door	1982	4.00
❑ 1025	Memory/Heart of Steel	1982	4.00
❑ 1046	Some Kind of Friend/Heaven	1983	4.00
❑ 2094	Jingle Bells/Because It's Christmas (For All the Children)	1990	3.00
—A-side with Expose			
❑ 9003	Some Kind of Friend/Heaven	1983	3.00
❑ 9101	Read 'Em and Weep/One Voice	1983	3.00
❑ 9185	You're Lookin' Hot Tonight/Put a Quarter in the Jukebox	1984	3.00
—B-side with Ronnie Milsap			
❑ 9666	Hey Mambo/When October Goes	1988	3.00
—With Kid Creole and the Coconuts			
❑ 9666 [PS]	Hey Mambo/When October Goes	1988	3.00
❑ 9811	Please Don't Be Scared/A Little Traveling Music, Please	1989	3.00
❑ 9838	Keep Each Other Warm/A Little Traveling Music, Please	1989	5.00
❑ 9838 [PS]	Keep Each Other Warm/A Little Traveling Music, Please	1989	5.00
❑ 9873 [DJ]	When the Good Times Come Again (same on both sides)	1989	10.00
—Record appears to be promo only			
BELL			
❑ 45357	Sweetwater Jones/ One of These Days	1973	6.00
❑ 45422	Cloudburst/Could It Be Magic	1973	6.00
❑ 45443	Let's Take Some Time to Say Goodbye/Seven More Years	1974	6.00
❑ 45613	Mandy/Something's Comin' Up	1974	5.00
RCA			
❑ PB-14223	In Search of Love/At the Dance	1985	3.00
❑ PB-14223 [PS]	In Search of Love/At the Dance	1985	4.00
❑ PB-14302	He Doesn't Care (But I Do)/It's All Behind Us Now	1986	3.00
❑ PB-14302 [PS]	He Doesn't Care (But I Do)/ It's All Behind Us Now	1986	4.00
❑ PB-14397	I'm Your Man/I'm Your Man (Dub)	1986	3.00
❑ PB-14397 [PS]	I'm Your Man/I'm Your Man (Dub)	1986	3.00
SBK			
❑ S7-17906	Let Me Be Your Wings/Follow Your Heart	1994	4.00
—A-side with Debra Byrd; B-side by Gino Conforti			
Albums			
ARISTA			
❑ AB 2500 [EP]	Oh, Julie!	1982	20.00
❑ AB 4007	Barry Manilow I	1977	8.00
—Reissue of AL 4007 with new prefix			
❑ AL 4007	Barry Manilow I	1975	10.00
—Revised version of Bell 1129 with new cover; "Could It Be Magic" especially is noticeably different between the Bell and Arista versions			
❑ AB 4016	Barry Manilow II	1977	8.00
—Reissue of AL 4016 with new prefix			
❑ AL 4016	Barry Manilow II	1975	10.00
—Reissue of Bell 1314			
❑ AQ 4016 [Q]	Barry Manilow II	1975	15.00
❑ AB 4060	Tryin' to Get the Feeling	1977	8.00
—Reissue of AL 4060 with new prefix			
❑ AL 4060	Tryin' to Get the Feeling	1975	10.00
❑ AQ 4060 [Q]	Tryin' to Get the Feeling	1975	15.00
❑ AB 4090	This One's for You	1977	8.00
—Reissue of AL 4090 with new prefix			
❑ AL 4090	This One's for You	1976	10.00
❑ AQ 4090 [Q]	This One's for You	1976	20.00
❑ AB 4164	Even Now	1978	8.00
❑ AL8-8003	Here Comes the Night	198?	6.00
—Reissue of 9610			
❑ AL13-8039 [(2)]	Greatest Hits	1983	10.00
❑ AL5-8046	One Voice	198?	6.00
—Reissue of 9505			
❑ AL13-8049 [(2)]	Barry Manilow/Live	1983	10.00
❑ AL5-8052	Even Now	198?	6.00
—Reissue of 8322			
❑ AL5-8070	Tryin' to Get the Feeling	198?	6.00
—Reissue of 8336			
❑ AL5-8085	Barry Manilow II	198?	6.00
—Reissue of 8370			
❑ AL8-8102	Barry Manilow/Greatest Hits, Vol. II	1983	8.00
❑ AL8-8117	Barry	198?	6.00
—Reissue of 9537			

Number	Title (A Side/B Side)	Yr	NM
❑ AL8-8123	If I Should Love Again	198?	6.00
—Reissue of 9573			
❑ AL5-8153	Barry Manilow I	198?	6.00
—Reissue of 8372			
❑ AL5-8160	This One's for You	198?	6.00
—Reissue of 8331			
❑ AL8-8254	2:00 A.M. Paradise Café	1984	8.00
❑ AL9-8274	The Manilow Collection — 20 Classic Hits	1985	8.00
❑ AL8-8291	Barry Manilow/Greatest Hits, Vol. II	1985	6.00
❑ AL8-8322	Even Now	1985	6.00
❑ AL8-8331	This One's for You	1985	6.00
❑ AL8-8336	Tryin' to Get the Feeling	1985	6.00
❑ AL8-8370	Barry Manilow II	1985	6.00
❑ AL8-8372	Barry Manilow I	1985	6.00
❑ AL 8500 [(2)]	Barry Manilow/Live	1977	12.00
❑ AL-8527	Swing Street	1987	8.00
❑ AL-8570	Barry Manilow	1989	8.00
❑ AL-8598	Greatest Hits, Vol. 1	1989	10.00
❑ AL-8599	Greatest Hits, Vol. 2	1989	10.00
❑ AL-8600	Greatest Hits, Vol. 3	1989	10.00
❑ A2L 8601 [(2)]	Greatest Hits	1978	12.00
❑ A2L 8601 [(2)PD]	Greatest Hits	1979	40.00
—Entire contents on two picture discs (yes, it has the same number as the regular issue)			
❑ AL-8638 [(2)]	Live on Broadway	1990	20.00
❑ AL-8644	Because It's Christmas	1990	15.00
❑ AL 9505	One Voice	1979	8.00
❑ AL 9537	Barry	1980	8.00
❑ AL 9573	If I Should Love Again	1981	8.00
❑ AL-9610	Here Comes the Night	1982	8.00
❑ NU 9740	Manilow Magic	1982	12.00
—Manufactured by K-Tel			
BELL			
❑ 1129	Barry Manilow	1973	25.00
❑ 1314	Barry Manilow II	1974	15.00
MOBILE FIDELITY			
❑ 1-097	Barry Manilow I	1981	30.00
—Audiophile vinyl			
RCA VICTOR			
❑ AFL1-7044	Manilow	1985	8.00

MANITOBA WITH JOE DOWEN

Number	Title (A Side/B Side)	Yr	NM
45s			
RCA VICTOR			
❑ 47-9908	Something in You/ You'll Never Get Back	1970	15.00
❑ 74-0417	Come On Down to My Boat/ Dead End Street	1971	25.00
❑ SP-45-234 [DJ]	Something in You/ (B-side unknown)	1970	20.00

MANN, BARRY

Number	Title (A Side/B Side)	Yr	NM
45s			
ABC-PARAMOUNT			
❑ 10143	War Paint/Counting Teardrops	1960	20.00
❑ 10180	Happy Birthday, Broken Heart/ Millionaire	1961	20.00
❑ 10237	Who Put the Bomp (In the Bomp, Bomp, Bomp)/Love, True Love	1961	25.00
❑ 10263	Little Miss U.S.A./ Find Another Fool	1961	20.00
❑ 10356	Hey Baby I'm Dancin'/ Like I Don't Love You	1962	20.00
❑ 10380	Teenage Has-Been/Bless You	1962	20.00
ARISTA			
❑ 0194	The Princess and the Punk/ Jennifer	1976	4.00
CAPITOL			
❑ 2082	Young Electric Psychedelic Hippy Flippy Folk & Funky Philosophic Turned On Groovy Twelve-String Band/ Take Your Love	1968	15.00
❑ 2217	I Just Can't Help Believin'/ Where Do I Go from Here	1968	10.00
❑ 5695	Looking at Tomorrow/Angelica	1966	10.00
❑ 5894	Where Do I Go from Here/ She Is Today	1967	10.00
CASABLANCA			
❑ 2287	Brown-Eyed Woman/ In My Own Way	1980	4.00
COLLECTABLES			
❑ 90000	Who Put the Bomp/For You	199?	3.00
—B-side by Rick Nelson			
COLPIX			
❑ 691	Graduation Time/ Johnny Surfboard	1963	20.00
JDS			
❑ 5002	I Love to Last a Lifetime/ All the Things You Are	1959	30.00
NEW DESIGN			
❑ 1000	Carry Me Home/Sundown	1971	5.00
❑ 1005	When You Get Right Down to It/Don't Give Up on Me	1972	5.00
❑ 1006	Too Many Mornings/Lay It All Out	1972	5.00
❑ 1006	Too Many Mornings/ On Broadway	1972	5.00
RCA VICTOR			
❑ PB-10104	Nobody But You/ Woman, Woman, Woman	1974	5.00
❑ PB-10230	Nothing Good Comes Easy/ Woman, Woman, Woman	1975	5.00
❑ PB-10319	Don't Seem Right/I'm a Survivor	1975	5.00
RED BIRD			
❑ 10-015	Talk to Me Baby/Amy	1964	15.00
SCEPTER			
❑ 12281	Feelings/Let Me Stay with You	1970	6.00
UNITED ARTISTS			
❑ XW1021	Best That I Know How/Lettin' Good Times Get Away	1977	4.00
WARNER BROS.			
❑ 8752	For No Reason at All/ Almost Gone	1979	4.00
❑ 8752 [PS]	For No Reason at All/ Almost Gone	1979	5.00
Albums			
ABC-PARAMOUNT			
❑ 399 [M]	Who Put the Bomp	1963	120.00
❑ S-399 [S]	Who Put the Bomp	1963	300.00
CASABLANCA			
❑ NBLP 7226	Barry Mann	1980	10.00
NEW DESIGN			
❑ Z 30876	Lay It All Out	1971	12.00
RCA VICTOR			
❑ APL1-0860	Survivor	1975	12.00
❑ DJL1-1162 [DJ]	Flo and Eddie Interview Barry Mann	1975	50.00

MANN, BOBBY

See BOBBY BLOOM.

MANN, GLORIA

Number	Title (A Side/B Side)	Yr	NM
45s			
ABC-PARAMOUNT			
❑ 9805	My Heart Has a Mind of Its Own/ Why Can't I Make You Understand	1957	12.00
DECCA			
❑ 9-29832	Why Do Fools Fall in Love?/ Partners for Life	1956	20.00
❑ 9-29886	Friendship Ring/One Heart	1956	20.00
❑ 9-29961	My Secret Sin/ Cashmere Sweater	1956	15.00
❑ 9-30069	It Happened Again/ Love, Sweet Love	1956	15.00
❑ 9-30140	Faded Photographs/ You Can't Be Mine	1956	15.00
DERBY			
❑ 841	All Dressed Up/Made Me a Present of You	1954	30.00
JUBILEE			
❑ 5142	Goodnight, Sweetheart, Goodnight/Love-Me-Boy	1954	25.00
—With the Carter Rays			
SOUND			
❑ 102	The Waltz You Saved for Me/ I'm Living My Life for You	1954	30.00
❑ 109	Earth Angel Will You Be Mine/ I Love You, Yes I Do	1955	30.00
❑ 114	I Played the Fool/Pretty Eyes	1955	30.00
❑ 121	I Can Tell/Bon Soir Cherie	1955	30.00
❑ 122	I Don't Know — I Don't Care/ My Gift from Heaven	1955	30.00
❑ 126	Teen Age Prayer/Gypsy Lady	1955	25.00

MANN, HERBIE

Number	Title (A Side/B Side)	Yr	NM
12-Inch Singles			
ATLANTIC			
❑ DSKO 172 [DJ]	Jisco Dazz/Body Oil	1979	10.00
❑ DK 4708	Superman/Etagui	1978	10.00
45s			
A&M			
❑ 896	Unchain My Heart/Glory of Love	1968	8.00
❑ 923	Upa, Neguinho/The Letter	1968	10.00
ATLANTIC			
❑ 2262	Theme from Malamondo/ Fiddler on the Roof	1964	10.00
❑ 2363	Is Paris Burning?/Happy Brass	1966	8.00
❑ 2379	The Honeydripper/The Puppet	1967	6.00
❑ 2392	Day Tripper/A Good Thing (Is Hard to Come By)	1967	50.00
—With Tamiko Jones			

M

Number	Title (A Side/B Side)	Yr	NM
❑ 2393	Uskudar/Turkish Coffee	1967	6.00
❑ 2399	The Beat Goes On/Free for All	1967	6.00
❑ 2444	To Sir with Love/Hold Back (Just a Little Longer)	1967	6.00
❑ 2451	Cottage for Sale/Live for Life	1967	6.00
—With Carmen McRae			
❑ 2498	By the Time I Get to Phoenix/Sports Car	1968	6.00
❑ 2621	Memphis Underground/New Orleans	1969	6.00
❑ 2661	Battle Hymn of the Republic/Hold On, I'm Comin'	1969	6.00
❑ 2671	It's a Funky Thing — Right On (Part 1)/It's a Funky Thing — Right On (Part 2)	1969	6.00
❑ 2882	Respect Yourself/Mississippi Gambler	1972	5.00
❑ 2960	Do It Again/Turtle Baby	1973	5.00
❑ 3009	Now I've Found a Lady/Spin Ball	1974	5.00
❑ 3037	Anata/Sound of Wood Wind	1974	5.00
❑ 3219	My Girl/Rivers of Babylon	1974	5.00
❑ 3246	Hijack/Orient Express	1975	4.00
❑ 3282	Waterbed/Body Oil	1975	4.00
❑ 3313	Stars and Stripes Forever (Part 1)/Stars and Stripes Forever (Part 2)	1976	5.00
❑ 3343	Cajun Moon/So Git It While You Can	1976	4.00
❑ 3390	Birdwalk/Aria	1977	4.00
❑ 3536	The Closer I Get to You/Watermelon Man	1978	4.00
❑ 3547	Superman/Etagui	1978	4.00
❑ 3547 [PS]	Superman/Etagui	1978	6.00
❑ 3575	Jisco Dazz/Time Is a Thief	1979	4.00
❑ 5009	Uhuru/High Life	1960	12.00
❑ 5010	Walkin'/(B-side unknown)	1961	12.00
❑ 5015	This Little Girl of Mine/Why Don't You Do Right	1961	12.00
❑ 5019	Carnival/La La La	1962	12.00
❑ 5020	Sumemrtime/Comin' Home Baby	1962	12.00
❑ 5023	Right Now/Boroquino	1962	12.00
❑ 5026	Blues Walk Bossa Nova/It Must Be Love Bossa Nova	1962	12.00
❑ 5031	Bag's Groove/New York Is a Jungle Festival	1963	10.00
❑ 5032	The Girl from Ipanema/Soft Winds	1964	10.00
❑ 5036	Love in Peace/One Note Samba	1964	10.00
❑ 5037	Harlem Nocturne/Not Now — Not Later	1964	10.00
❑ 5038	Down By the Riverside/Insensatez	1964	10.00
❑ 5044	Soul Guajira/Hushi Mushi	1965	8.00
❑ 5048	The Joker/Feeling Good	1965	8.00
❑ 5064	Today/Arrastao	1966	8.00
❑ 5065	Our Man Flint/Yesterday	1966	8.00
❑ 5070	Theme from This Is My Beloved/Scratch	1966	8.00
❑ 5074	Philly Dog/Frere Jacques	1966	8.00
❑ 89880	Theme from "Tootsie"/(B-side unknown)	1983	4.00
BETHLEHEM			
❑ 3040	Chicken Little/My Little Suede Shoes	1962	10.00
❑ 11036	Love Is a Simple Thing/Jasmine	1959	12.00
❑ 11037	Surrey with the Fringe on Top/Sorimao	1959	12.00
❑ 11038	Cuban Love Song/Scuffles	1959	12.00
PRESTIGE			
❑ 113	Let's March (Part 1)/Let's March (Part 2)	1957	20.00
❑ 318	Cherry Point/Early Morning Blues	1964	10.00
❑ 416	Tutti Flutee (Part 1)/Tutti Flutee (Part 2)	1966	8.00
Albums			
A&M			
❑ LP-2003 [M]	Glory of Love	1967	25.00
❑ SP-3003 [S]	Glory of Love	1967	15.00
❑ SP9-3003	Glory of Love	1983	20.00
—"Audio Master Plus" reissue			
ATLANTIC			
❑ 2-300 [(2)M]	The Evolution of Mann	1972	40.00
—Mono is white label promo only with "d/j copy monaural" sticker on front cover			
❑ SD 2-300 [(2)S]	The Evolution of Mann	1972	15.00
❑ 1343 [M]	The Common Ground	1960	15.00
❑ SD 1343 [S]	The Common Ground	1960	20.00
❑ 1371 [M]	The Family of Mann	1961	15.00
❑ SD 1371 [S]	The Family of Mann	1961	20.00
❑ 1380 [M]	Herbie Mann at the Village Gate	1962	15.00
❑ SD 1380 [S]	Herbie Mann at the Village Gate	1962	20.00
❑ 1384 [M]	Right Now	1962	15.00
❑ SD 1384 [S]	Right Now	1962	20.00
❑ 1397 [M]	Do the Bossa Nova with Herbie Mann	1962	15.00
❑ SD 1397 [S]	Do the Bossa Nova with Herbie Mann	1962	20.00
❑ 1407 [M]	Herbie Mann Returns to the Village Gate	1963	15.00
❑ SD 1407 [S]	Herbie Mann Returns to the Village Gate	1963	20.00
❑ 1413 [M]	Herbie Mann Live at Newport	1963	15.00
❑ SD 1413 [S]	Herbie Mann Live at Newport	1963	20.00
❑ 1422 [M]	Latin Fever	1964	15.00
❑ SD 1422 [S]	Latin Fever	1964	20.00
❑ 1426 [M]	Nirvana	1964	15.00
❑ SD 1426 [S]	Nirvana	1964	20.00
❑ 1433 [M]	My Kinda Groove	1965	15.00
❑ SD 1433 [S]	My Kinda Groove	1965	20.00
❑ 1437 [M]	The Roar of the Greasepaint, The Smell of the Crowd	1965	15.00
❑ SD 1437 [S]	The Roar of the Greasepaint, The Smell of the Crowd	1965	20.00
❑ 1445 [M]	Standing Ovation at Newport	1965	15.00
❑ SD 1445 [S]	Standing Ovation at Newport	1965	20.00
❑ 1454 [M]	Herbie Mann Today	1966	15.00
❑ SD 1454 [S]	Herbie Mann Today	1966	20.00
❑ 1462 [M]	Monday Night at the Village Gate	1966	15.00
❑ SD 1462 [S]	Monday Night at the Village Gate	1966	20.00
❑ 1464 [M]	Our Mann Flute	1966	15.00
❑ SD 1464 [S]	Our Mann Flute	1966	20.00
❑ 1471 [M]	New Mann at Newport	1967	20.00
❑ SD 1471 [S]	New Mann at Newport	1967	15.00
❑ 1475 [M]	Impressions of the Middle East	1967	20.00
❑ SD 1475 [S]	Impressions of the Middle East	1967	15.00
❑ 1483 [M]	The Beat Goes On	1967	20.00
❑ SD 1483 [S]	The Beat Goes On	1967	15.00
❑ 1490 [M]	The Herbie Mann String Album	1968	25.00
❑ SD 1490 [S]	The Herbie Mann String Album	1968	15.00
❑ SD 1497	Wailing Dervishes	1968	15.00
❑ SD 1507	Windows Open	1969	12.00
❑ 1513 [M]	The Inspiration I Feel	1969	30.00
—Mono is promo only			
❑ SD 1513 [S]	The Inspiration I Feel	1969	15.00
❑ SD 1522	Memphis Underground	1969	12.00
❑ SD 1536	Live at the Whisky A-Go-Go	1969	12.00
❑ SD 1540	Concerto Grosso in D Blues	1969	12.00
❑ SD 1544	The Best of Herbie Mann	1970	12.00
❑ SD 1610	Mississippi Gambler	1972	12.00
❑ QD 1632 [Q]	Hold On, I'm Comin'	1973	20.00
❑ SD 1632	Hold On, I'm Comin'	1973	12.00
❑ SD 1642	Turtle Bay	1973	12.00
❑ SD 1648	London Underground	1974	12.00
❑ SD 1655	Reggae	1974	12.00
❑ SD 1658	First Light	1974	12.00
❑ SD 1670	Discotheque	1975	12.00
❑ SD 1676	Waterbed	1975	12.00
❑ SD 1682	Surprises	1976	12.00
❑ 8141 [M]	Mann and a Woman	1967	20.00
❑ SD 8141 [S]	Mann and a Woman	1967	15.00
❑ SD 16046	Mellow	1981	10.00
❑ SD 18209	Bird in a Silver Cage	1977	10.00
❑ SD 19112	Herbie Mann & Fire Island	1977	10.00
❑ SD 19169	Brazil — Once Again	1978	10.00
❑ SD 19221	Super Mann	1979	10.00
❑ SD 19252	Yellow Fever	1980	10.00
❑ 80077	Astral Island	1983	10.00
❑ 81285	See Through Spirits	1986	10.00
❑ 90141	Nirvana	1984	10.00
BETHLEHEM			
❑ BCP-24 [M]	Flamingo, My Goodness — Four Flutes, Vol. 2	1955	50.00
❑ BCP-40 [M]	The Herbie Mann-Sam Most Quintet	1956	50.00
❑ BCP-58 [M]	Herbie Mann Plays	1956	50.00
❑ BCP-63 [M]	Love and the Weather	1956	50.00
❑ BCP-1018 [10]	East Coast Jazz 4	1954	120.00
❑ BCP-6011	Early Mann	1976	10.00
—Reissue of older material; distributed by Caytronics			
❑ BCP-6020 [M]	The Mann with the Most	1960	40.00
❑ BCP-6067 [M]	The Epitome of Jazz	1963	30.00
COLUMBIA			
❑ CS 1068	Big Boss	1970	12.00
❑ CL 2388 [M]	Latin Mann	1965	15.00
❑ CS 9188 [S]	Latin Mann	1965	20.00
COLUMBIA SPECIAL PRODUCTS			
❑ JCS 9188	Latin Mann	197?	12.00
—Part of "Jazz Greats" Collectors' Series			
EMBRYO			
❑ 520	Stone Flute	1970	12.00
❑ 526	Muscle Shoals Nitty Gritty	1970	12.00
❑ 531	Memphis Two-Step	1971	12.00
❑ 532	Push Push	1971	12.00
EPIC			
❑ LN 3395 [M]	Salute to the Flute	1957	60.00
❑ LN 3499 [M]	Herbie Mann with the Ilcken Trio	1958	60.00
FINNADAR			
❑ 9014	Gagaku and Beyond	197?	10.00
HERBIE MANN MUSIC			
❑ HMM-1	Herbie Mann Music	1981	25.00
—Direct-to-disc recording			
JAZZLAND			
❑ JLP-5 [M]	Herbie Mann Quintet	1960	30.00
—Reissue of Riverside 245			
MILESTONE			
❑ 47010	Let Me Tell You	1973	12.00
NEW JAZZ			
❑ NJLP-8211 [M]	Just Walkin'	1958	50.00
—Purple label			
❑ NJLP-8211 [M]	Just Walkin'	1964	25.00
—Blue label with trident logo			
PRESTIGE			
❑ PRLP-7101 [M]	Flute Souffle	1957	80.00
❑ PRLP-7124 [M]	Flute Flight	1957	80.00
❑ PRLP-7136 [M]	Mann in the Morning	1958	80.00
❑ PRLP-7432 [M]	The Best of Herbie Mann	1965	15.00
❑ PRST-7432 [R]	The Best of Herbie Mann	1965	12.00
❑ PRST-7659	Herbie Mann in Sweden	1969	12.00
RIVERSIDE			
❑ RLP 12-234 [M]	Sultry Serenade	1957	60.00
—Blue on white label			
❑ RLP 12-234 [M]	Sultry Serenade	1958	40.00
—Blue label with reel and microphone logo			
❑ RLP 12-245 [M]	Great Ideas of Western Mann	1957	40.00
❑ S-3029	Moody Mann	1969	12.00
❑ 6084	Great Ideas of Western Mann	197?	10.00
SAVOY			
❑ MG-12102 [M]	Flute Suite	1957	50.00
❑ MG-12107 [M]	Mann Alone	1957	50.00
❑ MG-12108 [M]	Yardbird Suite	1957	50.00
SAVOY JAZZ			
❑ SJL-1102	Be Bop Synthesis	197?	10.00
SOLID STATE			
❑ SS-18020	Jazz Impressions of Brazil	1968	12.00
❑ SS-18023	St. Thomas	1968	12.00
SURREY			
❑ S-1015 [M]	Big Band	1965	15.00
❑ SS-1015 [S]	Big Band	1965	20.00
TRIP			
❑ 5031	Super Mann	1974	10.00
UNITED ARTISTS			
❑ UAL-4042 [M]	African Suite	1959	30.00
❑ UAS-5042 [S]	African Suite	1959	40.00
❑ UAS-5638	Brazil Blues	1972	12.00
❑ UAJ-14009 [M]	Brasil, Bossa Nova and Blue	1962	30.00
❑ UAJ-14022 [M]	St. Thomas	1962	30.00
❑ UAJS-15009 [S]	Brasil, Bossa Nova and Blue	1962	40.00
❑ UAJS-15022 [S]	St. Thomas	1962	40.00
VERVE			
❑ VSP-8 [M]	Bongo, Conga and Flute	1966	15.00
❑ VSPS-8 [R]	Bongo, Conga and Flute	1966	12.00
❑ VSP-19 [M]	Big Band Mann	1966	15.00
❑ VSPS-19 [R]	Big Band Mann	1966	12.00
❑ MGVS-6074 [S]	Flautista! — Herbie Mann Plays Afro-Cuban Jazz	1960	30.00
❑ MGV-8247 [M]	The Magic Flute of Herbie Mann	1958	40.00
❑ V-8247 [M]	The Magic Flute of Herbie Mann	1961	20.00
❑ MGV-8336 [M]	Flautista! — Herbie Mann Plays Afro-Cuban Jazz	1959	40.00
❑ V-8336 [M]	Flautista! — Herbie Mann Plays Afro-Cuban Jazz	1961	20.00
❑ V6-8336 [S]	Flautista! — Herbie Mann Plays Afro-Cuban Jazz	1961	15.00
❑ MGV-8392 [M]	Flute, Brass, Vibes and Percussion	1960	30.00
❑ V-8392 [M]	Flute, Brass, Vibes and Percussion	1961	20.00
❑ V-8527 [M]	The Sound of Mann	1963	20.00
❑ V6-8527 [S]	The Sound of Mann	1963	15.00
❑ V6-8821 [(2)]	Et Tu Flute	1973	15.00

MANN, HERBIE, AND BUDDY COLLETTE

Number	Title (A Side/B Side)	Yr	NM
Albums			
INTERLUDE			
❑ MO-503 [M]	Flute Fraternity	1959	40.00
—Reissue of Mode 114			
❑ ST-1103 [S]	Flute Fraternity	1959	30.00
MODE			
❑ LP-114 [M]	Flute Fraternity	1957	70.00

MANN, HERBIE, AND JOAO GILBERTO

Number	Title (A Side/B Side)	Yr	NM
Albums			
ATLANTIC			
❑ 8105 [M]	Herbie Mann and Joao Gilberto with Antonio Carlos Jobim	1965	15.00
❑ SD 8105 [S]	Herbie Mann and Joao Gilberto with Antonio Carlos Jobim	1965	20.00

Except when noted otherwise, VG = 25% of NM, and VG+ = 50% of NM. (Example: VG = $2.00, VG+ = $4.00 and NM = $8.00.)

Number	Title (A Side/B Side)	Yr	NM
MANN, HERBIE, AND MACHITO			
Albums			
ROULETTE			
❑ R-52122 [M]	Afro-Jazziac	1963	15.00
❑ SR-52122 [S]	Afro-Jazziac	1963	20.00
MANN, JOHNNY, SINGERS			
45s			
EPIC			
❑ 10895	Stand Up and Cheer/America, There's So Much to Say	1972	5.00
LIBERTY			
❑ 55249	Varsity Drag/Sweet Georgia Brown	1959	10.00
❑ 55327	East of the Sun/(B-side unknown)	1961	8.00
❑ 55355	Don't/Love Me	1961	8.00
❑ 55466	Summersong/Mr. and Mrs. Millionaire	1962	8.00
❑ 55525	Cotton Fields/Shenandoah	1962	8.00
❑ 55653	African Noel/Children, Board That Train	1963	8.00
—By "The Johnny Mann Children's Choir"			
❑ 55799	The Voice of Freedom/Try to Remember	1965	6.00
❑ 55871	Cinnamint Shuffle/Rovin' Gambler	1966	6.00
❑ 55938	Whither Thou Goest/A Joyful Noise	1966	6.00
❑ 55972	Up-Up and Away/Joey Is the Name	1967	6.00
❑ 56010	Don't Look Back/Instant Happy	1967	6.00
❑ 56083	Snow/If I Only Had Time	1968	8.00
❑ 56107	Carolina on My Mind/Little Sister	1969	6.00
Albums			
EPIC			
❑ KE 31954	Stand Up and Cheer!	1973	12.00
LIBERTY			
❑ LRP-3134 [M]	Alma Mater	1959	15.00
❑ LRP-3149 [M]	Roar Along with the Singing Twenties	1960	15.00
❑ LRP-3156 [M]	Swing Along with the Singing Thirties	1960	15.00
❑ LRP-3198 [M]	Ballads of the King	1961	15.00
❑ LRP-3217 [M]	Ballads of the King, Vol. 2	1961	15.00
❑ LRP-3253 [M]	Golden Folk Song Hits	1963	12.00
❑ LRP-3296 [M]	Golden Folk Song Hits, Vol. 2	1963	12.00
❑ LRP-3355 [M]	Golden Folk Song Hits, Vol. 3	1964	12.00
❑ LRP-3387 [M]	Invisible Tears	1964	12.00
❑ LRP-3391 [M]	The Ballad Sound (Beatle Songs)	1964	15.00
❑ LRP-3411 [M]	If I Loved You	1965	12.00
❑ LRP-3436 [M]	I'll Remember You	1965	12.00
❑ LRP-3447 [M]	Daydream	1966	12.00
❑ LRP-3522 [M]	We Wish You a Merry Christmas	1967	15.00
❑ LRP-3523 [M]	We Can Fly! Up-Up and Away	1967	12.00
❑ LST-7134 [S]	Alma Mater	1959	20.00
❑ LST-7149 [S]	Roar Along with the Singing Twenties	1960	20.00
❑ LST-7156 [S]	Swing Along with the Singing Thirties	1960	20.00
❑ LST-7198 [S]	Ballads of the King	1961	20.00
❑ LST-7217 [S]	Ballads of the King, Vol. 2	1961	20.00
❑ LST-7253 [S]	Golden Folk Song Hits	1963	15.00
❑ LST-7296 [S]	Golden Folk Song Hits, Vol. 2	1963	15.00
❑ LST-7355 [S]	Golden Folk Song Hits, Vol. 3	1964	15.00
❑ LST-7387 [S]	Invisible Tears	1964	15.00
❑ LST-7391 [S]	The Ballad Sound (Beatle Songs)	1964	20.00
❑ LST-7411 [S]	If I Loved You	1965	15.00
❑ LST-7426 [S]	I'll Remember You	1965	15.00
❑ LST-7447 [S]	Daydream	1966	15.00
❑ LST-7522 [S]	We Wish You a Merry Christmas	1967	15.00
❑ LST-7523 [S]	We Can Fly! Up-Up and Away	1967	15.00
❑ LST-7629	Golden	1969	12.00
❑ LMM-13017 [M]	The Great Bands with Great Voices Swing the Great Voices of the Great Bands	1962	15.00
❑ LSS-14017 [S]	The Great Bands with Great Voices Swing the Great Voices of the Great Bands	1962	20.00
SUNSET			
❑ SUM-1115 [M]	The Flowing Voices of the Johnny Mann Singers	196?	10.00
❑ SUS-5115 [S]	The Flowing Voices of the Johnny Mann Singers	196?	12.00
❑ SUS-5196	Heart Full of Song	1968	12.00
❑ SUS-5231	Country Style	1969	12.00
❑ SUS-5288	At Our Best	1970	12.00
UNITED ARTISTS			
❑ UXS-87 [(2)]	The Johnny Mann Singers Superpak	1972	15.00

Manfred Mann, *The Manfred Mann Album*, Ascot AM 13015, 1964, mono, **$40.**

Number	Title (A Side/B Side)	Yr	NM
MANN, MANFRED Also see MIKE D'ABO; PAUL JONES; MANFRED MANN'S EARTH BAND.			
45s			
ASCOT			
❑ 2151	Hubble Bubble (Toil and Trouble)/I'm Your Kingpin	1964	200.00
❑ 2157	Do Wah Diddy Diddy/What You Gonna Do?	1964	15.00
❑ 2165	Sha La La/John Hardy	1964	10.00
❑ 2165 [PS]	Sha La La/John Hardy	1964	25.00
❑ 2170	Come Tomorrow/What Did I Do Wrong	1965	10.00
❑ 2170 [PS]	Come Tomorrow/What Did I Do Wrong	1965	25.00
❑ 2181	Poison Ivy/I Can't Believe What You Say	1965	—
—Unreleased?			
❑ 2184	My Little Red Book/What Am I Doing Wrong	1965	10.00
❑ 2194	If You Gotta Go, Go Now/The One in the Middle	1965	10.00
❑ 2210	She Needs Company/Hi Lili, Hi Lo	1966	10.00
❑ 2241	My Little Red Book/I Can't Believe What You Say	1967	10.00
MERCURY			
❑ 72607	Just Like a Woman/I Wanna Be Rich	1966	10.00
❑ 72607 [PS]	Just Like a Woman/I Wanna Be Rich	1966	25.00
❑ 72629	Semi-Detached Suburban Mr. Jones/Each and Every Day	1966	10.00
❑ 72675	Ha, Ha, Said the Clown/Feeling So Good	1967	10.00
❑ 72770	The Mighty Quinn (Quinn the Eskimo)/By Request — Edwin Garvey	1968	8.00
—Red label with white "Mercury" in a circle			
❑ 72770	Quinn the Eskimo/By Request — Edwin Garvey	1968	10.00
—Red label with white "Mercury" in a circle			
❑ 72770	The Mighty Quinn (Quinn the Eskimo)/By Request — Edwin Garvey	1968	10.00
—Orange and red swirl label			
❑ 72770	Quinn the Eskimo/By Request — Edwin Garvey	1968	12.00
—Orange and red swirl label			
❑ 72770	The Mighty Quinn (Quinn the Eskimo)/By Request — Edwin Garvey	1968	12.00
—Red label with "Mercury" in all capital letters			
❑ 72770	The Mighty Quinn (Quinn the Eskimo)/By Request — Edwin Garvey	1968	15.00
—Black label, silver print, "Mercury Records" in double oval at top; as this label was last used in 1964, this shouldn't exist, but it does			
❑ 72822	My Name Is Jack/There Is a Man	1968	8.00
❑ 72822 [PS]	My Name Is Jack/There Is a Man	1968	15.00
❑ 72879	Fox on the Run/Too Many People	1968	8.00
❑ 72921	Ragamuffin Man/A B-Side	1969	8.00
POLYDOR			
❑ 14026	Sometimes/Snakeskin Garter	1970	6.00
❑ 14074	California Coastline/Part Time	1971	—
—Unreleased			
❑ 14097	Please Mrs. Henry/Prayers	1971	5.00
PRESTIGE			
❑ 312	5-4-3-2-1/Without You	1964	40.00
❑ 314	Blue Brave/Brother Jack	1964	100.00
UNITED ARTISTS			
❑ 0048	Do Wah Diddy Diddy/Sha La La	1973	5.00
—"Silver Spotlight Series" reissue			
❑ 0049	Pretty Flamingo/Come Tomorrow	1973	5.00
—"Silver Spotlight Series" reissue			
❑ 50040	Pretty Flamingo/You're Standing By	1966	10.00
❑ 50066	When Will I Be Loved/Do You Have to Do That	1966	10.00
Albums			
ASCOT			
❑ AM-13015 [M]	The Manfred Mann Album	1964	40.00

M

Number	Title (A Side/B Side)	Yr	NM
❑ AM-13018 [M]	The Five Faces of Manfred Mann	1965	40.00
❑ AM-13021 [M]	My Little Red Book of Winners	1965	40.00
❑ AM-13024 [M]	Mann Made	1966	40.00
❑ AS-16015 [P]	The Manfred Mann Album	1964	50.00
❑ AS-16018 [P]	The Five Faces of Manfred Mann	1965	50.00
❑ AS-16021 [S]	My Little Red Book of Winners	1965	50.00
❑ AS-16024 [S]	Mann Made	1966	50.00

CAPITOL

Number	Title (A Side/B Side)	Yr	NM
❑ SM-11688	The Best of Manfred Mann	1977	10.00
❑ SN-16073	The Best of Manfred Mann	1980	8.00

JANUS

Number	Title (A Side/B Side)	Yr	NM
❑ JXS-3064	The Best of Manfred Mann	1974	12.00

MERCURY

Number	Title (A Side/B Side)	Yr	NM
❑ SR-61168	The Mighty Quinn	1968	25.00

POLYDOR

Number	Title (A Side/B Side)	Yr	NM
❑ 24-4013	Chapter Three	1970	15.00

UNITED ARTISTS

Number	Title (A Side/B Side)	Yr	NM
❑ 94 [DJ]	Manfred Mann Interview	1966	200.00
—Promotional album in plain white jacket			
❑ UAL 3549 [M]	Pretty Flamingo	1966	30.00
❑ UAL 3551 [M]	Manfred Mann's Greatest Hits	1966	30.00
❑ UAS 6549 [S]	Pretty Flamingo	1966	40.00
❑ UAS 6551 [P]	Manfred Mann's Greatest Hits	1966	40.00
—"Do Wah Diddy Diddy," "Sha La La," "I Got You Babe" and "Satisfaction" are rechanneled.			

MANN, MANFRED'S, EARTH BAND Also see MANFRED MANN.

12-Inch Singles

ARISTA

Number	Title (A Side/B Side)	Yr	NM
❑ ADP 9110 [DJ]	Demolition Man (same on both sides)	1983	8.00
❑ ADP 9147 [DJ]	Runner (same on both sides)	1983	8.00

45s

ARISTA

Number	Title (A Side/B Side)	Yr	NM
❑ 9143	Runner/Where Do They Send Them	1984	3.00
—Second pressing has black label			
❑ 9143	Runner/Where Do They Send Them	1984	4.00
—First pressing has whitish label			
❑ 9203	Rebel/Figures on a Rock	1984	3.00

POLYDOR

Number	Title (A Side/B Side)	Yr	NM
❑ 14113	Living Without You/Tribute	1972	5.00
❑ 14130	I'm Up and Leaving/Part Time Man	1972	5.00
❑ 14130 [PS]	I'm Up and Leaving/Part Time Man	1972	10.00
❑ 14160	It's All Over Now, Baby Blue/Ashes	1973	5.00
❑ 14173	Mardi Gras Day/Sad Joy	1973	5.00
❑ 14191	Get Your Rocks Off/Wind	1973	5.00
❑ 14205	Joybringer/Cloudy Eyes	1973	5.00
❑ 14225	Father of Night/Solar Fire Two	1974	5.00

WARNER BROS.

Number	Title (A Side/B Side)	Yr	NM
❑ 8152	Spirit in the Night/As Above So Below	1975	8.00
❑ 8176	Spirit in the Night/As Above So Below	1976	6.00
❑ 8176 [DJ]	Spirit in the Night (Long)/Spirit in the Night (Short)	1976	6.00
❑ 8252	Blinded by the Light/Starbird No. 2	1976	5.00
❑ 8252 [PS]	Blinded by the Light/Starbird No. 2	1976	8.00
❑ 8355	Spirit in the Night/Questions	1977	5.00
—This has newly-recorded vocal tracks by Chris Thompson			
❑ 8355 [DJ]	Spirit (same on both sides)	1977	10.00
—Newly-recorded vocal tracks by Chris Thompson; some early promos use this title in error and include a card that says "The correct title should be 'Spirit in the Night. WBS 8355"			
❑ 8574	California/Bouillabaise	1978	5.00
❑ 8620	Davy's on the Road Again/Bouillabaise	1978	5.00
❑ 8850	You Angel You/"Belle" of the Earth	1979	4.00
❑ 49678	For You/Fool I Am	1981	5.00
❑ 49762	Adolescent Dream/Lies (Through the 80's)	1981	4.00

Albums

ARISTA

Number	Title (A Side/B Side)	Yr	NM
❑ AL 8194	Somewhere in Afrika	1983	10.00

POLYDOR

Number	Title (A Side/B Side)	Yr	NM
❑ PD-5015	Manfred Mann's Earth Band	1971	15.00
❑ PD-5031	Glorified, Magnified	1972	15.00
❑ PD-5050	Get Your Rocks Off	1973	15.00
❑ PD-1-6019	Solar Fire	1974	15.00

WARNER BROS.

Number	Title (A Side/B Side)	Yr	NM
❑ BS 2826	The Good Earth	1974	12.00
❑ BS 2877	Nightingales and Bombers	1975	12.00
❑ BS 2965	The Roaring Silence	1976	12.00
—Orange cover			
❑ BSK 3055	The Roaring Silence	1977	10.00
—Blue cover; re-recording of "Spirit in the Night" is added			
❑ BSK 3157	Watch	1978	10.00
❑ BSK 3302	Angel Station	1979	10.00
❑ BSK 3498	Chance	1980	10.00

MANN, REV. COLUMBUS

45s

CYE

Number	Title (A Side/B Side)	Yr	NM
❑ 1001	Soon Very Soon (He's Coming Back)/(B-side unknown)	196?	40.00

TAMLA

Number	Title (A Side/B Side)	Yr	NM
❑ 54047	Jesus Loves/They Shall Be Mine	1961	50.00

Albums

TAMLA

Number	Title (A Side/B Side)	Yr	NM
❑ T-227 [M]	They Shall Be Mine	1962	4000.
—VG value 2000; VG+ value 3000			

WINGATE

Number	Title (A Side/B Side)	Yr	NM
❑ 701 [M]	He Satisfies Me	196?	900.00

MANN, SHADOW

Albums

TOMORROW

Number	Title (A Side/B Side)	Yr	NM
❑ TPS-69001	Come Live with Me	1974	60.00

MANNA, CHARLIE

45s

DECCA

Number	Title (A Side/B Side)	Yr	NM
❑ 31320	I Want Me Crayons (Part 1)/I Want Me Crayons (Part 2)	1961	10.00
❑ 31320 [PS]	I Want Me Crayons (Part 1)/I Want Me Crayons (Part 2)	1961	12.00
❑ 38238	The Astronaut/War at Sea	1961	10.00
❑ 38238 [PS]	The Astronaut/War at Sea	1961	20.00

JUBILEE

Number	Title (A Side/B Side)	Yr	NM
❑ 5498	Dear Sally, Mary, Lou/Give Me a Chance to Explain	1965	8.00

Albums

DECCA

Number	Title (A Side/B Side)	Yr	NM
❑ DL 4159 [M]	Manna Overboard!!	1961	25.00
❑ DL 4213 [M]	Manna Live!!	1962	25.00
❑ DL 74159 [R]	Manna Overboard!!	1961	15.00
❑ DL 74213 [R]	Manna Live!!	1962	15.00

VERVE

Number	Title (A Side/B Side)	Yr	NM
❑ V-15051 [M]	The Rise and Fall of the Great Society	1966	12.00
❑ V6-15051 [S]	The Rise and Fall of the Great Society	1966	15.00

MANNING, TERRY

Albums

ENTERPRISE

Number	Title (A Side/B Side)	Yr	NM
❑ ENS-1008	Home Sweet Home	1969	40.00

MANNO, TOMMY

45s

ATLANTIC

Number	Title (A Side/B Side)	Yr	NM
❑ 2149	Too Good to Be True/That's for Me to Know	1962	12.00

MANSON, CHARLES

Albums

AWARENESS

Number	Title (A Side/B Side)	Yr	NM
❑ 08903-1056	Lie: The Love and Terror Cult	1987	20.00
❑ LP-2144	Lie: The Love and Terror Cult	197?	40.00

ESP-DISK'

Number	Title (A Side/B Side)	Yr	NM
❑ 2003	Lie: The Love and Terror Cult	1970	200.00

MANTLE, MICKEY Also see TERESA BREWER.

Albums

RCA VICTOR

Number	Title (A Side/B Side)	Yr	NM
❑ LPM-1704 [M]	My Favorite Hits	1958	400.00

MANZAREK, RAY Also see THE DOORS; RICK AND THE RAVENS.

45s

MERCURY

Number	Title (A Side/B Side)	Yr	NM
❑ 73477	Solar Boat/Moorish Idol	1974	5.00
❑ 73601	Downbound Train/Choose Up and Choose Off	1974	5.00
❑ 73644	The Whole Thing Started with Rock and Roll (And Now It's Out of Control)/Art Deco Fandango	1974	5.00

Albums

A&M

Number	Title (A Side/B Side)	Yr	NM
❑ SP-4945	Carmina Burana	1984	10.00

MERCURY

Number	Title (A Side/B Side)	Yr	NM
❑ SRM-1-703	The Golden Scarab	1974	12.00
❑ SRM-1-1014	The Whole Thing Started with Rock & Roll Now It's Out of Control	1975	12.00

MAPHIS, JOE

45s

COLUMBIA

Number	Title (A Side/B Side)	Yr	NM
❑ 4-21427	Your Old Love Letters/You Ain't Got the Sense (You Were Borned With)	1955	20.00
❑ 4-21518	Guitar Rock and Roll/Tennessee Two-Step	1956	30.00
❑ 4-21547	Floggin' the Banjo/Bully of the Town	1956	20.00
❑ 4-40882	Town Hall Shuffle/Sweet Fern	1957	20.00
❑ 4- 41353	Moonshot/Short Recess	1959	15.00
❑ 4-41579	Del Rio/Jubilo	1959	15.00

LARIAT

Number	Title (A Side/B Side)	Yr	NM
❑ 1106	Lonesome Train Boogie/Square Dance Boogie	195?	40.00

MACGREGOR

Number	Title (A Side/B Side)	Yr	NM
❑ 8505	Green River Rag/(B-side unknown)	196?	20.00

REPUBLIC

Number	Title (A Side/B Side)	Yr	NM
❑ 2006	Water Baby Boogie/Black Combrero	1960	15.00

STARDAY

Number	Title (A Side/B Side)	Yr	NM
❑ 683	Hot Rod Guitar/Lonesome Jailhouse Blues	1964	10.00

7-Inch Extended Plays

COLUMBIA

Number	Title (A Side/B Side)	Yr	NM
❑ B-10051	*Fire on the Strings/Guitar Rock and Roll/Flying Fingers/Twin Banjo Special	1957	25.00
❑ B-10051 [PS]	Joe Maphis	1957	25.00

Albums

COLUMBIA

Number	Title (A Side/B Side)	Yr	NM
❑ CL 1005 [M]	Fire on the Strings	1957	100.00

HARMONY

Number	Title (A Side/B Side)	Yr	NM
❑ HL 7180 [M]	Hi-Fi Holiday for Banjo	1959	25.00
❑ HS 11032 [S]	Hi-Fi Holiday for Banjo	1959	30.00

KAPP

Number	Title (A Side/B Side)	Yr	NM
❑ KL-1347 [M]	Hootenanny Star	1964	20.00
❑ KS-3347 [S]	Hootenanny Star	1964	25.00

MACGREGOR

Number	Title (A Side/B Side)	Yr	NM
❑ MGR-1205 [M]	King of the Strings	196?	80.00

MOSRITE

Number	Title (A Side/B Side)	Yr	NM
❑ MA-400 [M]	The New Sound of Joe Maphis	1967	30.00
❑ MS-400 [S]	The New Sound of Joe Maphis	1967	30.00

STARDAY

Number	Title (A Side/B Side)	Yr	NM
❑ SLP-316 [M]	King of the Strings	1966	50.00
❑ SLP-373 [M]	Country Guitar Goes to the Jimmy Dean Show	1966	60.00
—Deduct 1/3 if instruction book is missing			

MAPHIS, JOE AND JODY

45s

CHART

Number	Title (A Side/B Side)	Yr	NM
❑ 5122	If I'm Gonna Have Your Lovin'/Sippin', Pickin' and Flippin'	1971	7.00

MAPHIS, JOE AND ROSE LEE

45s

CAPITOL

Number	Title (A Side/B Side)	Yr	NM
❑ 5077	Maple on the Hill/Whiskey Is the Devil in Liquid Form	1963	10.00

CHART

Number	Title (A Side/B Side)	Yr	NM
❑ 5029	Gee, Aren't We Lucky/Guitar Happy	1969	8.00
❑ 5074	Run That By Me One More Time/I Don't Care	1970	7.00

CMH

Number	Title (A Side/B Side)	Yr	NM
❑ 1520	Somewhere Between/Fiddle Pickin'	1979	6.00

COLUMBIA

Number	Title (A Side/B Side)	Yr	NM
❑ 4-21389	Honky Tonk Down Town/Parting of the Way	1955	20.00
❑ 4-21479	I Love You Deeply/Fire on the Strings	1956	20.00
❑ 4-21568	I'm Willin' to Try/Let's Pull Together	1956	20.00
❑ 4-41004	A Picture, a Ring and a Curl/I Gotta Lotta Lovin'	1957	20.00

LARIAT

Number	Title (A Side/B Side)	Yr	NM
❑ 1203	Let's Fly Away/You Can't Take the Heart Out of Me	1952	40.00

MOSRITE

Number	Title (A Side/B Side)	Yr	NM
❑ 150	Send Me Your Love A.P.O./Write Him a Letter	196?	10.00

Number	Title (A Side/B Side)	Yr	NM
❑ 290	Tunin' Up for the Blues/ Lifetime of Love	1966	10.00
❑ 310	Country Girl Courtship/ Pickin' and Guttin'	196?	10.00
OKEH			
❑ 18013	Black Mountain Rag/ Dim Lights, Thick Smoke	195?	25.00
❑ 18024	Please Mr. Mailman/I'm a Stranger in My Home	195?	25.00
❑ 18029	Henhouse Serenade/ Cold Heart of Steel	195?	25.00
❑ 18041	Dream House for Sale/ The Go'Fer Song	195?	25.00
❑ 18051	Devil's Doll/Let's Talk About Love	195?	25.00
❑ 18059	Honky Tonk Love Affair/ Quicksand	195?	25.00
STARDAY			
❑ 675	Hoot'n Annie/Remember, I'm Just As Close As the Phone	1964	10.00
❑ 710	Hot Time in Nashville/I've Come to Take You Home	1965	10.00
❑ 728	Your Little Black Book/ Don't Pass Me By	1965	10.00
❑ 745	Ridin' Down Ole 99/Turn On the Bright Lights	1965	10.00
Albums			
CAPITOL			
❑ ST 1778 [S]	Rose Lee and Joe Maphis	1962	40.00
❑ T 1778 [M]	Rose Lee and Joe Maphis	1962	30.00
STARDAY			
❑ SLP-286 [M]	Mr. and Mrs. Country Music	1964	30.00
❑ SLP-322 [M]	Golden Gospel	1966	30.00

MAPHIS, ROSE LEE

Number	Title (A Side/B Side)	Yr	NM
Albums			
COLUMBIA			
❑ CL 1598 [M]	Rose Lee Maphis	1961	30.00
❑ CS 8398 [S]	Rose Lee Maphis	1961	40.00

MAR-KEYS

Number	Title (A Side/B Side)	Yr	NM
45s			
SATELLITE			
❑ 107	Last Night/Night Before	1960	30.00
STAX			
❑ 112	Morning After/Diana	1961	12.00
❑ 114	About Noon/Sack-O-Woe	1961	12.00
❑ 115	Foxy/One Degree North	1961	12.00
❑ 121	Pop-Eye Stroll/Po-Dunk	1962	12.00
❑ 124	What's Happening/You Got It	1962	12.00
❑ 129	Sailor Man Waltz/Sack-O-Woe	1963	12.00
❑ 133	The Dribble/Bo Time	1963	12.00
❑ 156	Beach Bash/Bush Bash	1964	10.00
❑ 166	The Shovel/Banana Juice	1965	10.00
❑ 181	Grab This Thing (Part 1)/ Grab This Thing (Part 2)	1965	10.00
❑ 185	Philly Dog/Honey Pot	1966	10.00
Albums			
ATLANTIC			
❑ 8055 [M]	Last Night	1961	100.00
—White "fan" logo on right			
❑ 8055 [M]	Last Night	1962	50.00
—Black "fan" logo on right			
❑ SD 8055 [R]	Last Night	1966	40.00
❑ 8062 [M]	Do the Pop-Eye with the Mar-Keys	1962	50.00
❑ SD 8062 [R]	Do the Pop-Eye with the Mar-Keys	1966	40.00
STAX			
❑ ST-707 [M]	The Great Memphis Sound	1966	50.00
❑ STS-707 [R]	The Great Memphis Sound	1966	40.00
❑ STS-2025	Damifiknew	1969	20.00
❑ STS-2036	Memphis Experience	1971	20.00

MAR-KEYS/BOOKER T. AND THE MG'S

Also see each artist's individual listings.

Number	Title (A Side/B Side)	Yr	NM
Albums			
STAX			
❑ ST-720 [M]	Back to Back	1967	20.00
❑ STS-720 [S]	Back to Back	1967	25.00

MAR-VELS, THE

Number	Title (A Side/B Side)	Yr	NM
45s			
ANGIE			
❑ 1005	Go On and Have Yourself a Ball/ How Do I Keep the Girls Away	1963	20.00
BUTANE			
❑ 778	Go On and Have Yourself a Ball/ How Do I Keep the Girls Away	1963	15.00
IN			
❑ 102	Surfing at Makeha/ Endless Nights	1964	50.00
LOVE			
❑ 5011/2	Cherry Lips/Could Be You	1958	30.00
TAMMY			
❑ 1016	Somewhere in Life/Voo Doo Hurt	1961	300.00
❑ 1019	My Guardian Angel/ Marble Stomp	1961	300.00

MARAINEY, BIG MEMPHIS

Number	Title (A Side/B Side)	Yr	NM
45s			
SUN			
❑ 184	Call Me Anything, But Call Me/ Baby No, No	1953	4000.
—VG 2000; VG+ 3000			

MARATHONS, THE (1)

Two different groups posing as one. After the success of "Peanut Butter" on Arvee, the label hired another group to be The Marathons after losing a legal battle to keep the "real" group, which was really THE VIBRATIONS in disguise. And the Vibrations had formerly been THE JAYHAWKS. Confused yet?

Number	Title (A Side/B Side)	Yr	NM
45s			
ARGO			
❑ 5389	Peanut Butter/Down in New Orleans	1961	15.00
—As "Vibrations Named By Others As MARATHONS"			
ARVEE			
❑ 5027	Peanut Butter/Talkin' Trash	1961	20.00
❑ 5038	Tight Sweater/C. Percy Mercy of Scotland	1961	12.00
❑ 5048	Chicken Spaceman/ You Bug Me Baby	1962	12.00
CHESS			
❑ 1790	Peanut Butter/Down in New Orleans	1961	16.00
PLAZA			
❑ 507	Mashed Potatoes One More Time/Little Pancho	1962	12.00
Albums			
ARVEE			
❑ A-428 [M]	Peanut Butter	1961	180.00

MARATHONS, THE (2)

Completely unrelated to groups (1).

Number	Title (A Side/B Side)	Yr	NM
45s			
SABRINA			
❑ 334	Don't Know Why/The Stranger	1959	120.00

MARAUDERS, THE

More than one group.

Number	Title (A Side/B Side)	Yr	NM
45s			
ALMO			
❑ 221	Like You/Slippin' and Slidin'	1965	15.00
HAWK			
❑ 4002	Sand Flea/Stomp Watch	1962	50.00
LAURIE			
❑ 3356	Out of Sight, Out of Mind/ Jug Band Music	1966	20.00
LEE			
❑ 9449	Nightmare/Lovin'	1965	30.00
SKYVIEW			
❑ 001	Since I Met You/ I Don't Know How	1966	20.00
❑ 001 [PS]	Since I Met You/ I Don't Know How	1966	50.00

MARBLE PHROGG, THE

Number	Title (A Side/B Side)	Yr	NM
45s			
DERRICK			
❑ 8568	Fire/(B-side unknown)	1968	80.00
Albums			
DERRICK			
❑ 8868	The Marble Phrogg	1968	1000.

MARCEAU, MARCEL

Number	Title (A Side/B Side)	Yr	NM
Albums			
GONE			
❑ LP 1F	The Best of Marcel Marceau	196?	50.00
MGM			
❑ SE-4	The Best of Marcel Marceau	196?	40.00
—The above records are identical: 38 minutes of silence and 2 minutes of applause!			

MARCELLO

Known as "Marcello Minerbi" outside the United States.

Number	Title (A Side/B Side)	Yr	NM
45s			
PARKWAY			
❑ 962	Zorba's Dance/L'Isola Del Dole	1965	8.00

MARCELS, THE

Number	Title (A Side/B Side)	Yr	NM
45s			
ALL EARS			
❑ 810085	Blue Moon/Clap Your Hands (When I Clap My Hands)	1981	6.00
BARON			
❑ 109	Betty Lou/Take Me Back	197?	8.00
CHARTBOUND			
❑ 009	Letter Full of Tears/Tell Me	197?	8.00
COLPIX			
❑ TL-147	Blue Moon/Friendly Loans	196?	15.00
—"Torchlite Series" reissue on red label			
❑ 186	Blue Moon/Goodbye to Love	1961	30.00
❑ 186 [PS]	Blue Moon/Goodbye to Love	1961	60.00
❑ 196	Summertime/Teeter-Totter Love	1961	25.00
❑ 606	You Are My Sunshine/ Find Another Fool	1961	25.00
❑ 612	Heartaches/My Love for You	1961	25.00
❑ 612 [PS]	Heartaches/My Love for You	1961	100.00
❑ 617	Merry Twist-Mas/Don't Cry for Me This Christmas	1961	25.00
❑ 617 [PS]	Merry Twist-Mas/Don't Cry for Me This Christmas	1961	120.00
❑ 624	My Melancholy Baby/ Really Need Your Love	1962	20.00
❑ 629	Footprints in the Sand/ Twistin' Fever	1962	50.00
❑ 640	Flowerpot/Hold On	1962	30.00
❑ 651	Loved Her the Whole Week Through/Friendly Loans	1962	25.00
❑ 665	Alright, Okay, You Win/ Lollipop Baby	1962	25.00
❑ 683	That Old Black Magic/Don't Turn Your Back on Me	1963	25.00
❑ 687	Give Me Back Your Love/ I Wanna Be the Leader	1963	30.00
❑ 694	One Last Kiss/Teeter-Totter Love	1963	100.00
❑ 694	One Last Kiss/You Got to Be Sincere	1963	200.00
888			
❑ 101	How Deep Is the Ocean/ Lonely Boy	1964	15.00
KYRA			
❑ 100	Comes Love/Your Red Wagon	1964	50.00
❑ 100	Comes Love/Your Red Wagon	1964	100.00
—Red vinyl			
MONOGRAM			
❑ 112	I'll Be Forever Loving You/ A Fallen Tear	1974	12.00
❑ 113	Sweet Was the Wine/ Over the Rainbow	1974	12.00
❑ 115	Two People in the World/ Most of All	1974	12.00
OWL			
❑ 324	(You Gave Me) Peace of Mind/ Crazy Bells	197?	8.00
QUEEN BEE			
❑ 47001	In the Still of the Night/ High on a Hill	1973	15.00
ROCKY			
❑ 13711	(You Gave Me) Peace of Mind/ That Lucky Old Sun	1975	8.00
—As "The Fabulous Marcels"			
ST. CLAIR			
❑ 13711	(You Gave Me) Peace of Mind/ That Lucky Old Sun	1975	10.00
—As "The Fabulous Marcels"			
Albums			
COLPIX			
❑ CP-416 [M]	Blue Moon	1961	350.00
—Gold label			
❑ CP-416 [M]	Blue Moon	1963	120.00
—Blue label			

MARCH, LITTLE PEGGY

Number	Title (A Side/B Side)	Yr	NM
45s			
OLDE WORLD			
❑ 1105	Average People/Isn't This the Way We Are	1975	8.00
RCA VICTOR			
❑ 47-8107	Little Me/Pagan Love Song	1962	15.00
❑ 47-8139	I Will Follow Him/Wind-Up Doll	1963	20.00
❑ 47-8189	I Wish I Were a Princess/ My Teenage Castle	1963	15.00
❑ 47-8189 [PS]	I Wish I Were a Princess/ My Teenage Castle	1963	30.00
❑ 47-8221	Hello Heartache, Goodbye Love/Boy Crazy	1963	15.00
❑ 47-8221 [PS]	Hello Heartache, Goodbye Love/Boy Crazy	1963	30.00
❑ 47-8267	The Impossible Happened/ Waterfall	1963	12.00

M

Number	Title (A Side/B Side)	Yr	NM
❑ 47-8291	My Heart Keeps Telling Me/His	1963	—
—Unreleased			
❑ 47-8302	(I'm Watching) Every Little Move You Make/After You	1963	12.00
❑ 47-8357	Takin' the Long Way Home/Leave Me Alone	1964	10.00
—All records from 1964 on are as "Peggy March"			
❑ 47-8418	Oh My, What a Guy/Only You Could Do That to My Heart	1964	10.00
❑ 47-8460	Watch What You Do With My Baby/Can't Stop Thinking About Him	1964	10.00
❑ 47-8534	Why Can't He Be You/Losin' My Touch	1965	10.00
❑ 47-8605	Let Her Go/Your Girl	1965	10.00
❑ 47-8710	He Couldn't Care Less/Heaven for Lovers	1965	10.00
❑ 47-8840	Ein Boy Wie Du (A Boy Like You)/Sechs Tage Lang (Six Long Days)	1966	20.00
❑ 47-8877	Play a Simple Melody/Old Fashioned Wedding	1966	10.00
—With Gary Marshall			
❑ 47-8903	He's Back Again/Running Scared	1966	10.00
❑ 47-9033	Fool, Fool, Fool (Look in the Mirror)/Try to See It My Way	1966	10.00
❑ 47-9143	January First/How Can I Tell Him	1967	10.00
❑ 47-9223	Mama Dear, Papa Dear/Your Good Girl's Gonna Go Bad	1967	10.00
❑ 47-9283	This Heart Wasn't Made to Kick Around/Foolin' Around	1967	10.00
❑ 47-9359	Have a Good Time/Let Me Down Hard	1967	10.00
❑ 47-9494	If You Would Love Me/Thinking Through My Tears	1968	10.00
❑ 47-9566	Roses on the Sea/Time and Time Again	1968	10.00
❑ 47-9627	I've Been Here Before/Aren't You Glad	1968	10.00
❑ 47-9718	Purple Hat/Try to See It My Way	1969	10.00
❑ 74-0136	Boom Bang-a Bang/Lilac Skies	1969	10.00

Albums

RCA VICTOR

Number	Title	Yr	NM
❑ LPM-2732 [M]	I Will Follow Him	1963	60.00
❑ LSP-2732 [S]	I Will Follow Him	1963	80.00
❑ LPM-3883 [M]	No Foolin'	1968	40.00
❑ LSP-3883 [S]	No Foolin'	1968	25.00

MARCH, LITTLE PEGGY/BENNIE THOMAS

Albums

RCA VICTOR

Number	Title	Yr	NM
❑ LPM-3408 [M]	In Our Fashion	1965	40.00
❑ LSP-3408 [S]	In Our Fashion	1965	50.00

MARCHAN, BOBBY

45s

Number	Title (A Side/B Side)	Yr	NM
ACE			
❑ 523	Chickee Wah-Wah/Don't Take Your Love from Me	1956	40.00
❑ 532	I'll Never Let You Go/I Can't Stop Loving You	1957	30.00
❑ 557	Rockin' Behind the Iron Curtain/You Can't Stop Her	1959	30.00
❑ 3004	Push the Button/My Day Is Coming	1974	5.00
❑ 3008	God Bless Our Love/My Day Is Coming	1975	5.00
❑ 3016	Baby Get Your Yo-Yo/What Can I Do	1975	5.00
ALADDIN			
❑ 3189	Just a Little Walk/Have Mercy	1953	60.00
BOBBY ROBINSON			
❑ (# unknown)	There's Something on Your Mind/(B-side unknown)	1973	6.00
CAMEO			
❑ 405	There's Something About My Baby/Everything a Poor Man Needs	1966	10.00
❑ 429	Shake Your Tambourine/Just Be Yourself	1966	10.00
❑ 453	Meet Me in Church/Hooked	1967	8.00
❑ 469	You Better Hold On/Help Yourself	1967	8.00
❑ 489	Rockin' Pneumonia/Someone to Take Your Place	1967	8.00
DIAL			
❑ 1152	Bump Your Bootie/Ain't Nothing Wrong with Whitey	1975	5.00
❑ 3022	I Gotta Sit Down and Cry/I Got a Thing Going	1964	10.00
❑ 4002	Get Down to It/Half a Mind	1964	10.00
❑ 4007	Hello Happiness/Funny Style	1965	10.00
❑ 4020	I Feel It Coming/Gimme Your Love	1965	10.00
❑ 4065	I Just Want What Belongs to Me/Sad Sack	1967	8.00
FIRE			
❑ 510	Yes It's Written All Over Your Face/Look at My Heart	1962	15.00
❑ 1014	Snoopin' and Accusin'/This Is the Life	1959	15.00
❑ 1022	There's Something On Your Mind (Part 1)/There's Something On Your Mind (Part 2)	1960	25.00
❑ 1027	Booty Green/It Hurts Me to My Heart	1960	15.00
❑ 1028	You're Still My Baby (Part 1)/You're Still My Baby (Part 2)	1960	15.00
❑ 1035	All in My Mind/I Miss You So	1961	15.00
❑ 1037	What You Don't Know Don't Hurt You/I Need Someone (I Need You)	1961	15.00
GALE			
❑ 4M-101	Chickee Wah Wah/Give a Helping Hand	1957	25.00
GAMBLE			
❑ 216	(Ain't No Reason) For Girls to Be Lonely Part 1/Part 2	1968	8.00
LOST-NITE			
❑ 390	There's Something On Your Mind (Part 1)/(Part 2)	197?	5.00
—Reissue			
MERCURY			
❑ 73908	I Wanna Bump with the Big Fat Woman/Disco Rabbit	1977	5.00
VOLT			
❑ 108	What Can I Do (Part 1)/What Can I Do (Part 2)	1963	12.00

Albums

Number	Title	Yr	NM
COLLECTABLES			
❑ COL-5113	Golden Classics	198?	10.00
SPHERE SOUND			
❑ SSR-7004 [M]	There's Something on Your Mind	1964	300.00

MARCHING OTTO

See CRAZY OTTO.

MARCO, RAY

45s

THUNDERBIRD

Number	Title (A Side/B Side)	Yr	NM
❑ 503	Al Di La/If I Had a Hammer	196?	8.00
❑ 508	Sunny/Somewhere My Love	196?	8.00
❑ 513	Alfie/Moe	196?	8.00
❑ 519	Sunny/More	196?	8.00
❑ 532	Somehow We've Made the Morning/My Way	1970	8.00
❑ 535	Poor Old World/Love Rain	1970	8.00
❑ 540	Morning Song/Gypsy Girl	1971	7.00
❑ 546	The Big Hurt/Someday Soon	1971	7.00

MARENO, LEE

45s

Number	Title (A Side/B Side)	Yr	NM
NEW ART			
❑ 103	Goddess of Love/He's Gone	1961	120.00
SCEPTER			
❑ 1222	Goddess of Love/He's Gone	1961	30.00
❑ 12222	Goddess of Love/Lonely Summer	1968	12.00
—As "Lee"			

MARESCA, ERNIE

45s

Number	Title (A Side/B Side)	Yr	NM
LAURIE			
❑ 3345	The Good Life/A Bum Can't Cry	1966	10.00
❑ 3371	My Son/My Shadow and Me	1967	10.00
❑ 3447	What Is a Marine/The Night My Papa Died	1968	8.00
❑ 3496	Blind Date/People Get Jealous	1969	8.00
❑ 3519	The Spirit of Woodstock/Web of Love	1969	8.00
❑ 3671	The Night My Poppa Died/Please Don't Play Me a Seven	1978	6.00
❑ 3698	You're the Only Girl for Me/Medley	1980	6.00
—B-side by the Belmonts			
PROVIDENCE			
❑ 417	Rockin' Blvd. St./Am I Better Off Than Them	1965	50.00
RUST			
❑ 5076	The Beetle Dance/Theme from Lilly, Lilly	1964	15.00
SEVILLE			
❑ 107	Lonesome Blues/I Don't Know Why	1960	15.00
❑ 45-117	Shout! Shout! (Knock Yourself Out)/Crying Like a Baby	1962	25.00
❑ 5N-117	Shout! Shout! (Knock Yourself Out)/Crying Like a Baby	197?	6.00
—Reissue on all-black label; note different prefix			
❑ 119	Down on the Beach/Mary Jane	1962	15.00
❑ 119 [PS]	Down on the Beach/Mary Jane	1962	20.00
❑ 122	Something to Shout About/How Many Times	1962	15.00
❑ 125	Love Express/Lorelei	1963	50.00
❑ 129	The Rovin' Kind/Please Be Fair	1963	15.00
❑ 138	I Can't Dance/It's Their World	1965	15.00

Albums

SEVILLE

Number	Title	Yr	NM
❑ SV 77001 [M]	Shout! Shout! Knock Yourself Out	1962	120.00
❑ SV 87001 [S]	Shout! Shout! Knock Yourself Out	1962	200.00

MARGO AND THE MARVETTES

45s

AMERICAN ARTS

Number	Title (A Side/B Side)	Yr	NM
❑ 8	Cherry Pie/Say You Will	1965	15.00

MARGO, MARGO, MEDRESS AND SIEGEL

See THE TOKENS.

MARGOLIN, STUART

Albums

WARNER BROS.

Number	Title	Yr	NM
❑ BSK 3439	And the Angel Sings	1980	20.00

MARGULIS, CHARLIE

45s

CARLTON

Number	Title (A Side/B Side)	Yr	NM
❑ 456	Heartache for Sale/Gigi	1958	12.00
❑ 494	Malaguena/Theme from El Salon Mexico	1959	12.00

Albums

CARLTON

Number	Title	Yr	NM
❑ LP 12-103 [M]	Marvelous Margulis	1958	25.00
❑ STLP 12-103 [S]	Marvelous Margulis	1959	30.00

MARIACHI BRASS, THE

45s

WORLD PACIFIC

Number	Title (A Side/B Side)	Yr	NM
❑ 77815	Tequila/Flowers on the Wall	1966	8.00
❑ 77823	Bang Bang/Happiness Is	1966	8.00
❑ 77848	Dancing in the Street/When You're Smiling	1966	8.00
❑ 77853	La Bamba/Colonel Bogey March	1966	8.00
❑ 77857	A Man and a Woman/All	1966	8.00
❑ 77863	The Dating Game/In the Mood	1967	20.00
—Contrary to popular belief, the A-side was never done by Herb Alpert and the Tijuana Brass			

Albums

WORLD PACIFIC

Number	Title	Yr	NM
❑ WP-1839 [M]	A Taste of Tequila	1966	12.00
❑ WP-1842 [M]	Hats Off!!!	1966	12.00
❑ WP-1852 [M]	Double Shot	1966	12.00
❑ WP-1859 [M]	In the Mood	1967	12.00
❑ WPS-21839 [S]	A Taste of Tequila	1966	15.00
❑ WPS-21842 [S]	Hats Off!!!	1966	15.00
❑ WPS-21852 [S]	Double Shot	1966	15.00
❑ WPS-21859 [S]	In the Mood	1967	15.00

MARIE AND REX

45s

CARLTON

Number	Title (A Side/B Side)	Yr	NM
❑ 502	I Can't Sit Down/Miracles	1959	15.00

MARIE AND THE DECCORS

45s

CUB

Number	Title (A Side/B Side)	Yr	NM
❑ 9115	I'm the One/Queen of Fools	1962	25.00

MARIE ANN

45s

Number	Title (A Side/B Side)	Yr	NM
EPIC			
❑ 5-9465	(I Know That) Your Heart's Not Made of Wood/Dear Teddy	1961	12.00
WARWICK			
❑ 605	Dream Boy/High Heel Sneakers	1960	12.00

MARINERS, THE

45s

COLUMBIA

Number	Title (A Side/B Side)	Yr	NM
❑ 1-873	Our Lady of Fatima/The Rosary	1950	40.00
—Microgroove 7-inch, 33 1/3 rpm single			

MARINO, FRANK, AND MAHOGANY RUSH
See MAHOGANY RUSH.

MARIONETTES, THE

Number	Title (A Side/B Side)	Yr	NM
45s			
LONDON			
❑ 9738	Whirlpool of Love/Nobody But You	1965	12.00

MARIS, TOMMY

Number	Title (A Side/B Side)	Yr	NM
45s			
CAMEO			
❑ 406	Don't Come Cryin' to Me/Wait for Me My Love	1966	30.00

MARK-ALMOND

Number	Title (A Side/B Side)	Yr	NM
45s			
ABC			
❑ 12221	New York State of Mind/Return to the City	1976	4.00
BLUE THUMB			
❑ 201	The City/The Ghetto	1971	6.00
❑ 206	One Way Sunday/The Bay	1971	6.00
COLUMBIA			
❑ 45745	Organ Grinder/What Am I Living For	1972	5.00
❑ 45951	Get Yourself Together/Lonely Girl	1973	5.00
HORIZON			
❑ 118	You Look Just Like a Girl Again/The City	1978	4.00
Albums			
ABC			
❑ D-945	To the Heart	1976	10.00
BLUE THUMB			
❑ BTS 27	Mark-Almond	1971	12.00
—Reissue of 8827			
❑ BTS 32	Mark-Almond II	1971	12.00
❑ BTS 50	The Best of Mark-Almond	1973	12.00
❑ BTS-8827	Mark-Almond	1971	15.00
COLUMBIA			
❑ KC 31917	Rising	1972	12.00
❑ PC 31917	Rising	198?	8.00
—Budget-line reissue			
❑ KC 32486	Mark-Almond 73	1973	12.00
❑ CG 33648 [(2)]	Rising/Mark-Almond 73	1976	15.00
HORIZON			
❑ SP-730	Other People's Rooms	1978	10.00
MCA			
❑ 711	Mark-Almond II	198?	8.00
—Reissue of Blue Thumb 32			
❑ 792	The Best of Mark-Almond	198?	8.00
—Reissue of Blue Thumb 50			
❑ 793	To the Heart	198?	8.00
—Reissue of ABC 945			
PACIFIC ARTS			
❑ 7-142	The Best of the Mark-Almond Band...Live	1980	10.00

MARKAY, GRACE

Number	Title (A Side/B Side)	Yr	NM
45s			
CAPITOL			
❑ 2161	Sally Go 'Round the Roses/Sonny Boy	1968	20.00
❑ 5999	For Those in Love/It's a Happening World	1967	20.00
PARAMOUNT			
❑ 0137	Merry Xmas/Times Have Changed	1971	12.00
Albums			
CAPITOL			
❑ ST 2687 [S]	Grace Markay	1967	15.00
❑ T 2687 [M]	Grace Markay	1967	20.00
UNITED ARTISTS			
❑ UAS-6722	Please Come Back	1969	20.00

MARKETTS, THE

Number	Title (A Side/B Side)	Yr	NM
45s			
ARVEE			
❑ 5063	Beach Bum/Sweet Potatoes	1962	20.00
CALLIOPE			
❑ 8003	Mary Hartman, Mary Hartman/(B-side unknown)	1977	5.00
—As "The New Marketts"			
❑ 8009	City Nights/Soul Coaxing	1977	5.00
—As "The New Marketts"			
FARR			
❑ 007	Song from M.A.S.H./Song from M.A.S.H. (Disco Version)	1976	5.00
—As "The New Marketts"			
❑ 019	The Hustle/Song from M.A.S.H.	1977	5.00
—As "The New Marketts"			
❑ 021	Looking for Mr. Goodbar (Terry's Theme)/Black	1977	5.00
—As "Danny Welton and the New Marketts"			
LIBERTY			
❑ 55401	Surfer's Stomp/Start	1962	20.00
—As "The Mar-Kets"			
❑ 55443	Balboa Blue/Stompede	1962	20.00
—As "The Mar-Kets"			
❑ 55506	Stomping Room Only/Canadian Sunset	1962	20.00
—As "The Mar-Kets"			
MERCURY			
❑ 73433	Mystery Movie Theme/Sister Candy	1973	8.00
SEMINOLE			
❑ 501	Song from M.A.S.H./Song from M.A.S.H. (Disco Version)	1976	8.00
—As "The New Marketts"			
UNI			
❑ 55173	The Undefeated/They Call the Wind Maria	1969	8.00
UNION			
❑ 501	Surfer's Stomp/Start	1961	30.00
❑ 504	Balboa Blue/Stompede	1962	30.00
❑ 507	Stomping Room Only/Canadian Sunset	1962	30.00
UNITED ARTISTS			
❑ 0043	Surfer's Stomp/Balboa Blue	1973	5.00
—"Silver Spotlight Series" reissue			
WARNER BROS.			
❑ 5365	Woody Wagon/Cobra	1963	15.00
❑ 5391	Out of Limits/Bella Dalena	1963	20.00
❑ 5391	Outer Limits/Bella Dalena	1963	30.00
—Original title of A-side			
❑ 5423	Vanishing Point/Borealis	1964	12.00
❑ 5468	Come See, Come Ska/Look for a Star	1964	12.00
❑ 5641	Miami's Blue/Napoleon's Solo	1965	10.00
❑ 5670	Ready Steady Go/Lady in the Cage	1965	10.00
❑ 5696	Batman Theme/Richie's Theme	1966	12.00
❑ 5814	Theme from "The Avengers"/A Touch of Velvet, a Sting of Brass	1966	20.00
❑ 5847	Tarzan/Stirrin' Up Some Soul	1966	10.00
❑ 7116	Out of Limits/Batman Theme	1968	6.00
—"Back to Back Hits" series — originals have green labels with "W7" logo			
WORLD PACIFIC			
❑ 77874	Sunshine Girl/Sun Power	1967	10.00
❑ 77899	California Summer (People Moving West)/Groovin' Time	1968	10.00
Albums			
LIBERTY			
❑ LRP-3226 [M]	The Surfing Scene	196?	30.00
—Retitled version of above			
❑ LRP-3226 [M]	Surfer's Stomp	1962	40.00
—Add 20% if "Surfer's Stomp" instruction sheet is enclosed			
❑ LST-7226 [S]	The Surfing Scene	196?	40.00
—Retitled version of above			
❑ LST-7226 [S]	Surfer's Stomp	1962	50.00
—Add 20% if "Surfer's Stomp" instruction sheet is enclosed			
MERCURY			
❑ SRM-1-679	AM, FM, Etc.	1973	15.00
WARNER BROS.			
❑ W 1509 [M]	The Marketts Take to Wheels	1963	40.00
❑ WS 1509 [S]	The Marketts Take to Wheels	1963	50.00
❑ W 1537 [M]	Out of Limits!	1964	30.00
❑ WS 1537 [S]	Out of Limits!	1964	40.00
❑ W 1642 [M]	The Batman Theme	1966	40.00
❑ WS 1642 [S]	The Batman Theme	1966	50.00
WORLD PACIFIC			
❑ WP-1870 [M]	Sun Power	1967	25.00
❑ WPS-21870 [S]	Sun Power	1967	20.00

MARKEYS, THE No relation to THE MAR-KEYS.

Number	Title (A Side/B Side)	Yr	NM
45s			
GONE			
❑ 5028	Special Delivery/Along Came Love	1958	30.00
RCA VICTOR			
❑ 47-7256	Hot Rod/Yakkaty Yal	1958	25.00
❑ 47-7412	Time to Love/Make a Record Man	1958	25.00
20TH CENTURY			
❑ 1210	Eternal Love/You've Got Me on a String	1956	50.00

MARKHAM, PIGMEAT

Number	Title (A Side/B Side)	Yr	NM
45s			
CHESS			
❑ 1828	Hold That Ladder (Part 1)/Hold That Ladder (Part 2)	1962	10.00
❑ 1891	Open the Door, Richard (Part 1)/Open the Door, Richard (Part 2)	1964	8.00
❑ 2049	Here Comes the Judge/The Trial	1968	7.00
❑ 2059	Sock It To 'Em Judge/The Hip Judge	1968	6.00
❑ 2087	Pig's Popcorn/Who's Got the Number	1969	6.00
Albums			
CHESS			
❑ LP-1451 [M]	The Trial	1961	25.00
❑ LP-1462 [M]	Pigmeat Markham At the Party	1962	25.00
❑ LP-1467 [M]	Anything Goes	1962	25.00
❑ LP-1475 [M]	The World's Greatest Clown	1963	25.00
❑ LP-1484 [M]	Open the Door, Richard	1964	25.00
❑ LP-1493 [M]	Mr. Funny Man	1965	25.00
❑ LP-1500 [M]	This'll Kill Ya	1965	25.00
❑ LP-1505 [M]	If You Can't Be Good, Be Careful	1966	15.00
❑ LPS-1505 [S]	If You Can't Be Good, Be Careful	1966	20.00
❑ LP-1515 [M]	Mr. Vaudeville	1967	15.00
❑ LPS-1515 [S]	Mr. Vaudeville	1967	20.00
❑ LP-1517 [M]	Save Your Soul, Baby	1967	20.00
❑ LPS-1517 [S]	Save Your Soul, Baby	1967	20.00
❑ LP-1521 [M]	Backstage	1968	20.00
❑ LPS-1521 [S]	Backstage	1968	20.00
❑ LPS-1525	Here Comes the Judge	1968	20.00
❑ LPS-1526	Tune Me In	1968	15.00
❑ LPS-1529	Hustlers	1969	15.00
❑ LPS-1534	Bag	1970	15.00
❑ CH-9166	Here Comes the Judge	1985	10.00
—Reissue of 1525			
JEWEL			
❑ 5007	Crap-Shootin' Rev	1972	12.00
❑ 5012	Will the Real Pigmeat Markham Please Sit Down	1973	12.00

MARKLEY

Number	Title (A Side/B Side)	Yr	NM
Albums			
FORWARD			
❑ 1007	A Group	1969	30.00

MARKS, GUY

Number	Title (A Side/B Side)	Yr	NM
45s			
ABC			
❑ 11055	Loving You Has Made Me Bananas/Forgive Me, My Love	1968	8.00
❑ 11099	Meet Me Tonight by the Postage Machine/This Is Forever	1968	6.00
❑ 11148	How the West Was Really Won/This Is Forever	1968	6.00
ARIOLA AMERICA			
❑ 7646	The Bridge/Man in the Glass	1976	4.00
Albums			
ABC			
❑ 549 [M]	Hollywood Sings	1966	15.00
❑ S-549 [S]	Hollywood Sings	1966	15.00
❑ S-648	Loving You Has Made Me Bananas	1968	20.00

MARKSMEN, THE (1) With Don Wilson of THE VENTURES.

Number	Title (A Side/B Side)	Yr	NM
45s			
BLUE HORIZON			
❑ 6052	Night Run/Scratch	1960	150.00

MARKSMEN, THE (2)

Number	Title (A Side/B Side)	Yr	NM
45s			
ABC-PARAMOUNT			
❑ 9745	Hands/The Story of a Star	1956	15.00
CORAL			
❑ 9-61270	The Owata Song/Oh Ma Ma	1954	20.00
❑ 9-61453	Hot Rod/Red Sails in the Sunset	1955	25.00

MARKSMEN, THE (3)

Number	Title (A Side/B Side)	Yr	NM
45s			
SARA			
❑ 65128	Black Pepper/(B-side unknown)	1965	20.00

MARKSMEN, THE (U) Some of these might be by the groups above; then again, they might not be.

Number	Title (A Side/B Side)	Yr	NM
45s			
DEARBORN			
❑ 536	Castle Rock/Crawfish	196?	15.00

M

Except when noted otherwise, VG = 25% of NM, and VG+ = 50% of NM. (Example: VG = $2.00, VG+ = $4.00 and NM = $8.00.)

Number	Title (A Side/B Side)	Yr	NM
JUBILEE			
❑ 5531	Coming In on a Wing and a Prayer/Just One More Mile	1966	12.00
STARDAY			
❑ 320	Don't Gamble with My Heart/ You Hurt Me So	1957	600.00

MARLEY, BOB, AND THE WAILERS

Number	Title (A Side/B Side)	Yr	NM
12-Inch Singles			
COTILLION			
❑ PR 291 [DJ]	Reggae on Broadway (6:00) (3:15)	1981	12.00
❑ PR 414 [DJ]	Chances Are (same on both sides)	1981	15.00
ISLAND			
❑ DMD 628 [DJ]	Buffalo Soldier/Buffalo Dub	1983	10.00
❑ DMD 668 [DJ]	Mix Up, Mix Up (LP Version) (Edit Version)	1983	10.00
TUFF GONG			
❑ 864693-1	Iron Zion Lion (4 versions)/ Could You Be Loved	1992	12.00
45s			
BLACK HEART			
❑ 8042	African Herbsman/Stand Alone	1974	12.00
CLOCK TOWER			
❑ 505	Duppy Conqueror/ Duppy Version	1971	25.00
COTILLION			
❑ 46023	Reggae on Broadway/ Gonna Get You	1981	5.00
❑ 46029	Chances Are/(B-side unknown)	1981	5.00
G&C			
❑ C&G-5000	Trench Town Rock/Version	197?	20.00
ISLAND			
❑ 005	I Shot the Sheriff/Put It On	1974	6.00
❑ 027	Lively Up Yourself/So Jah Seh	1975	6.00
❑ 037	No Woman, No Cry/ Kinky Reggae	1975	6.00
❑ 060	Roots, Rock, Reggae/Cry to Me	1976	6.00
❑ 072	Who the Cap Fit/ (B-side unknown)	1976	6.00
❑ 089	Exodus/(Instrumental)	1977	6.00
❑ 092	Waiting in Vain/Roots	1977	6.00
❑ 099	Is This Love/Crisis	1978	6.00
❑ PR 670 [DJ]	Stir It Up (same on both sides)	1984	10.00
❑ 1211	Rock It Baby/Stop That Train	1972	8.00
❑ 1215	Concrete Jungle/ No More Trouble	1973	8.00
❑ 1218	Get Up, Stand Up/Slave Driver	1973	8.00
❑ 49080	Wake Up and Live/Wake Up and Live (Dub)	1979	6.00
❑ 49156	Kaya/One Drop	1980	6.00
❑ 49547	Ride Natty Ride/Could You Be Loved	1980	6.00
❑ 49636	Redemption Song/Coming In from the Cold	1980	6.00
❑ 49755	Jamming/No Woman, No Cry	1981	6.00
❑ 99740	Blackman Redemption/ Is This Love	1984	4.00
❑ 99837	Mix Up, Mix Up/French Town	1983	4.00
❑ 99882	Buffalo Soldier/Buffalo Dub	1983	4.00
❑ 99882 [PS]	Buffalo Soldier/Buffalo Dub	1983	6.00
❑ 562356-7	Kinky Reggae (Raga Mix)/ Kinky Reggae (Kinky Mix)	1999	4.00
JAD			
❑ 211	Bend Down Low/Mellow Mood	1968	100.00
—As "Bob, Rita and Peter"			
SHELTER			
❑ 7309	Doppy Conquer/Justice	1971	12.00
—B-side by the Upsetters			
TRANQUILITY			
❑ T0024	It Hurts to Be Alone/ (B-side unknown)	1965	200.00
—As "The Wailers"			
TUFF GONG			
❑ TG-5002	Ammunition/Kingston 12 Shuffle	197?	20.00
—B-side by U-Roy			
❑ TG-5004	Lick Samba/Version	197?	20.00
❑ TG-5005	Lively Up Yourself/Guava Jelly	197?	20.00
❑ TG-5007	Craven Choke Puppy/Version	197?	20.00
❑ TG-5009	Steppin' (Walking) Razor/ The Letter	197?	20.00
❑ TG-5014	Midnight Ravers/Version	197?	20.00
UPSETTER			
❑ (# unknown)	More Axe/The Axe Man	1971	25.00
❑ 007	Cross the Nation/All in One (Medley)	1970	20.00
❑ 007	Cross the Nation/Version	1970	20.00
—B-side by the Upsetters			
❑ 009	Small Axe/Version	1970	20.00
—B-side by the Upsetters			
❑ 9001	Secondhand/Secondhand Part 2	1971	20.00
Albums			
ACCORD			
❑ SN-7211	Jamaican Storm	1982	10.00
CALLA			
❑ CAS-1240 [(2)]	The Birth of a Legend	1976	15.00
❑ ZX 34759	The Birth of a Legend	1977	10.00
—Reissue of Record 1 of Calla 1240			
❑ ZX 34760	Early Music	1977	10.00
—Reissue of Record 2 of Calla 1240			
COLUMBIA			
❑ PZ 34759	The Birth of a Legend	198?	8.00
—Budget-line reissue of Calla 34759			
❑ PZ 34760	Early Music	198?	8.00
—Budget-line reissue of Calla 34760			
COTILLION			
❑ SD 5228	Chances Are	1981	10.00
ISLAND			
❑ ISLD 11 [(2)]	Babylon by Bus	1978	15.00
—Island distribution			
❑ ISLD 11 [(2)]	Babylon by Bus	1979	12.00
—Warner Bros. distribution			
❑ ILPS 9241	Catch a Fire	1978	12.00
—Reissue; Warner Bros. distribution			
❑ ILPS 9256	Burnin'	1974	15.00
—Island distribution			
❑ ILPS 9256	Burnin'	1978	12.00
—Warner Bros. distribution			
❑ ILPS 9281	Natty Dread	1974	15.00
—Island distribution			
❑ ILPS 9281	Natty Dread	1978	12.00
—Warner Bros. distribution			
❑ SW-9329	Catch a Fire	1973	100.00
—"Cigarette lighter" cover with flip-open top; Capitol distribution			
❑ SMAS-9338	Burnin'	1973	20.00
—Capitol distribution			
❑ ILPS 9376	Live!	1975	12.00
—Island distribution			
❑ ILPS 9376	Live!	1978	10.00
—Warner Bros. distribution			
❑ ILPS 9383	Rastaman Vibration	1976	12.00
—Island distribution			
❑ ILPS 9383	Rastaman Vibration	1978	10.00
—Warner Bros. distribution			
❑ ILPS 9383 [DJ]	Rastaman Vibration	1976	100.00
—Promotional package with burlap box and press kit			
❑ ILPS 9498	Exodus	1977	12.00
—Island distribution (all have multicolor labels)			
❑ ILPS 9498	Exodus	1978	10.00
—Warner Bros. distribution			
❑ ILPS 9517	Kaya	1978	12.00
—Island distribution			
❑ ILPS 9517	Kaya	1979	10.00
—Warner Bros. distribution			
❑ ILPS 9542	Survival	1979	12.00
❑ ILPS 9596	Uprising	1980	12.00
❑ 90029 [(2)]	Babylon by Bus	1983	12.00
❑ 90030	Catch a Fire	1983	8.00
❑ 90031	Burnin'	1983	8.00
❑ 90032	Live!	1983	8.00
❑ 90033	Rastaman Vibration	1983	8.00
❑ 90034	Exodus	1983	8.00
❑ 90035	Kaya	1983	8.00
❑ 90036	Uprising	1983	8.00
❑ 90037	Natty Dread	1983	8.00
—90029-90037 are reissues with Atco distribution			
❑ 90085	Confrontation	1983	10.00
❑ 90169	Legend	1984	10.00
❑ 90520	Rebel Music	1986	10.00
❑ 462011	Catch a Fire	2009	20.00
—Reissue with standard cover; Island distribution			
❑ 524419-1	Dreams of Freedom	1997	12.00
❑ 546404-1	Chant Down Babylon	1999	12.00
❑ 5303052	Legend	2009	20.00
❑ 5318419	Exodus	2009	20.00
❑ 5488941	Burnin'	2008	20.00
MOBILE FIDELITY			
❑ 1-221	Exodus	1995	100.00
—Audiophile vinyl			
❑ 1-236	Catch a Fire	1995	100.00
—Audiophile vinyl			
TUFF GONG			
❑ 524103-1	Natural Mystic	1995	15.00
❑ 846197-1 [(2)]	Babylon by Bus	1990	15.00
❑ 846200-1	Burnin'	1990	12.00
❑ 846201-1	Catch a Fire	1990	12.00
❑ 846202-1	Survival	1990	12.00
❑ 846203-1	Live!	1990	12.00
❑ 846204-1	Natty Dread	1990	12.00
❑ 846205-1	Rastaman Vibration	1990	12.00
❑ 846206-1	Rebel Music	1990	12.00
❑ 846207-1	Confrontation	1990	12.00
❑ 846208-1	Exodus	1990	12.00
❑ 846209-1	Kaya	1990	12.00
❑ 846210-1	Legend	1990	12.00
❑ 846211-1	Uprising	1990	12.00
❑ 848243-1	Talkin' Blues	1991	12.00

MARLINS, THE

Probably two different groups.

Number	Title (A Side/B Side)	Yr	NM
45s			
CAMEO			
❑ 333	(Everybody Do) The Swim (Part 1)/(Part 2)	1964	15.00
SANDY			
❑ 1002	Now I'm So Lonesome I Could Die/Tell Me Why	1957	250.00

MARLO, MICKI

Number	Title (A Side/B Side)	Yr	NM
45s			
ABC-PARAMOUNT			
❑ 9762	Little By Little/It All Started With Your Kiss	1956	25.00
❑ 9807	Ain't That Love/ The Beginning of Love	1957	15.00
❑ 9841	What You've Done to Me/ That's Right	1957	15.00
—New mix, without "Vocal assist by Paul Anka"			
❑ 9841	What You've Done to Me/ That's Right	1957	30.00
—With "Vocal assist by Paul Anka"			
CAPITOL			
❑ F2736	I'm Gonna Rock, Rock, Rock/ Love's Like That	1954	20.00
❑ F2801	I'm Going to Sit Right Down and Cry Over You/Forever Is Now	1954	20.00
❑ F2874	I'm Flying/Why Should I Cry	1954	15.00
❑ F2932	Show Me/Every Road Must Have a Turning	1954	15.00
❑ F3016	Don't Go, Don't Go, Don't Go/ Can You	1955	15.00
❑ F3062	Prize of Gold/Foolish Notion	1955	15.00
❑ F3148	I've Got Rhythm in My Nursery Rhymes/Dream Boy	1955	15.00
❑ F3266	Pet Me, Poppa/Like I Love Nobody Before	1955	15.00
❑ F3346	How Come You Love Me Like You Do/Way Down by the Cherry Tree	1956	15.00
Albums			
ABC-PARAMOUNT			
❑ 295 [M]	Married I Can Always Get	1959	20.00
❑ S-295 [S]	Married I Can Always Get	1959	25.00

MARMALADE, THE

Number	Title (A Side/B Side)	Yr	NM
45s			
ARIOLA AMERICA			
❑ 7619	Falling Apart at the Seams/ Fly, Fly, Fly	1976	4.00
❑ 7631	My Everything/Walking a Tightrope	1976	4.00
EMI			
❑ 3676	Engine Driver/Wishing Well	1973	4.00
EPIC			
❑ 10162	Can't Stop Now/There Ain't No Use in Hanging On	1967	10.00
❑ 10236	Otherwise It's Been a Perfect Day/I See the Rain	1967	10.00
❑ 10284	Cry/Man in a Shop	1968	8.00
❑ 10340	Hey Joe/Lovin' Things	1968	8.00
❑ 10404	Wait for Me Mary-Ann/ Mess Around	1968	8.00
❑ 10428	Ob-La-Di, Ob-La-Da/Chains	1969	10.00
❑ 10493	Time Is On My Side/ Baby Make It Soon	1969	8.00
LONDON			
❑ 20058	Reflections of My Life/ Rollin' My Thing	1970	6.00
❑ 20059	Rainbow/The Ballad of Cherry Flavar	1970	5.00
❑ 20066	My Little One/Is Your Life Your Own	1971	5.00
❑ 20068	Lonely Man/Cousin Norman	1971	5.00
❑ 20072	Just One Woman/Radancer	1971	5.00
Albums			
EPIC			
❑ BN 26553	The Best of the Marmalade	1970	20.00
LONDON			
❑ PS 575	Reflections of My Life	1970	20.00

MARQUEES, THE (1)

Number	Title (A Side/B Side)	Yr	NM
45s			
DAY-SEL			
❑ 1001	Ecstasy/Close to Me	1959	600.00

MARQUEES, THE (2)

Number	Title (A Side/B Side)	Yr	NM
45s			
GRAND			
❑ 141	The Bells/The Rain	195?	50.00
—With address on label			

Number	Title (A Side/B Side)	Yr	NM
❑ 141	The Bells/The Rain	1956	300.00
—With no address on label			
LOST-NITE			
❑ 330	The Bells/The Rain	197?	5.00
—Reissue			

MARQUEES, THE (3)

45s

Number	Title (A Side/B Side)	Yr	NM
JO-ANN			
❑ 128	Stay with Me/That's the Way I Feel	1960	150.00
❑ 130	I Need a Helping Hand/Don't You Do Me Like That	1961	100.00

MARQUEES, THE (4)

45s

Number	Title (A Side/B Side)	Yr	NM
LEN			
❑ 100	Say Hey/I'm in Misery	1958	100.00

MARQUEES, THE (5) MARVIN GAYE was in this group.

45s

Number	Title (A Side/B Side)	Yr	NM
OKEH			
❑ 7096	Hey Little School Girl/Wyatt Earp	1957	120.00

MARQUEES, THE (6)

45s

Number	Title (A Side/B Side)	Yr	NM
WARNER BROS.			
❑ 5072	Who Will Be the First One/Love Machine	1959	40.00
❑ 5127	Christmas in the Crowd/Sunset to Sunrise	1959	40.00
❑ 5139	Until the Day I Die/Don't Be Mean, Geraldine	1960	80.00

MARS, SYLVIA

Albums

Number	Title (A Side/B Side)	Yr	NM
LYRIC			
❑ 124	Blues Walk Right In	196?	60.00

MARSDEN, BERYL

45s

Number	Title (A Side/B Side)	Yr	NM
CAPITOL			
❑ 5552	Who You Gonna Hurt/Gonna Make Him My Baby	1965	10.00

MARSDEN, GERRY Also see GERRY AND THE PACEMAKERS.

45s

Number	Title (A Side/B Side)	Yr	NM
COLUMBIA			
❑ 44309	Gilbert Green/Please Let Them Be	1967	10.00

MARSH, RICHIE Also known as Dick Marsh, he later recorded as "Sky Saxon" in THE SEEDS.

45s

Number	Title (A Side/B Side)	Yr	NM
ACAMA			
❑ 125	Baby, Baby, Baby/Half Angel	1960	30.00
AVA			
❑ 122	Goodbye/Crying Inside My Heart	1963	20.00
ROSCO			
❑ 412	There's Only One Girl/What Chance Have I	1960	20.00
SHEPHERD			
❑ 2203	They Say Darling/I Swear That It's True	1962	25.00

MARSHALL, CHUCK

Albums

Number	Title (A Side/B Side)	Yr	NM
DECCA			
❑ DL 4267 [M]	Twist to Songs Everybody Knows	1962	15.00
❑ DL 74267 [S]	Twist to Songs Everybody Knows	1962	20.00

MARSHALL, PETER

Albums

Number	Title (A Side/B Side)	Yr	NM
DOT			
❑ DLP-25930	For the Love of Pete	1969	20.00

MARSHALL BROTHERS, THE

45s

Number	Title (A Side/B Side)	Yr	NM
SAVOY			
❑ 825	Mr. Santa's Boogie/Who'll Be the Fool from Now On	1951	500.00
❑ 833	Why Make a Fool Out of Me/Just a Poor Boy in Love	1952	400.00

MARSHALL TUCKER BAND, THE

12-Inch Singles

Number	Title (A Side/B Side)	Yr	NM
WARNER BROS.			
❑ PRO-A-816 [DJ]	Running Like the Wind (Edit)/Last of the Singing Cowboys	1979	10.00
❑ PRO-A-863 [DJ]	It Takes Time (Single Version)//Sing My Blues/Cattle Drive	1980	12.00

45s

Number	Title (A Side/B Side)	Yr	NM
CAPRICORN			
❑ 0021	Can't You See/See You Later, I'm Gone	1973	6.00
❑ 0030	Take the Highway/Jesus Told Me So	1973	6.00
❑ 0049	Another Cruel Love/Blue Ridge Mountain Sky	1974	5.00
❑ 0228	This Ol' Cowboy/Try One More Time	1975	5.00
❑ 0244	Fire on the Mountain/Bop Away My Blues	1975	5.00
❑ 0251	Searchin' for a Rainbow/Walkin' and Talkin'	1976	5.00
❑ 0258	Long Hard Ride/Windy City Blues	1976	5.00
❑ 0270	Heard It in a Love Song/Life in a Song	1977	5.00
❑ 0278	Can't You See/Fly Like an Eagle	1977	5.00
❑ 0300	Dream Lover/A Change Is Gonna Come	1978	5.00
❑ 0307	I'll Be Seeing You/Everybody Needs Somebody	1978	5.00
MERCURY			
❑ 870050-7	Once You Get the Feel of It/Slow Down	1987	3.00
❑ 870505-7	Dancin' Shoes/I'm Glad It's Gone	1988	3.00
❑ 872096-7	Still Holdin' On/Same Old Moon	1989	3.00
❑ 888774-7	Hangin' Out in Smokey Places/He Don't Know	1987	3.00
WARNER BROS.			
❑ 8841	Last of the Singing Cowboys/Pass It On	1979	5.00
❑ 8841 [PS]	Last of the Singing Cowboys/Pass It On	1979	6.00
❑ 29355	I May Be Easy But You Make It Hard/Shot Down Where You Stand	1984	4.00
❑ 29619	A Place I've Never Been/8:05	1983	4.00
❑ 29939	Reachin' for a Little Bit More/Sweet Elaine	1982	4.00
❑ 29995	Mr. President/The Sea, Dreams and Fairy Tales	1982	4.00
❑ 49068	Running Like the Wind/(B-side unknown)	1979	5.00
❑ 49215	It Takes Time/Jimi	1980	5.00
❑ 49259	Disillusioned/Without You	1980	4.00
❑ 49724	This Time I Believe/Tell the Blues to Take Off the Night	1981	4.00
❑ 49764	Time Has Come/Love Some	1981	4.00

7-Inch Extended Plays

Number	Title (A Side/B Side)	Yr	NM
CAPRICORN			
❑ SCP 0124	24 Hours at a Time/Blue Ridge Mountain Sky//A New Life	1973	10.00
—Jukebox issue; small hole, plays at 33 1/3 rpm			
❑ SCP 0124 [PS]	A New Life	1973	10.00
—Part of "Little LP" series (LLP #249)			

Albums

Number	Title (A Side/B Side)	Yr	NM
CAPRICORN			
❑ CP 0112	The Marshall Tucker Band	1973	12.00
❑ CP 0124	A New Life	1974	12.00
❑ 2CP 0145 [(2)]	Where We All Belong	1974	15.00
❑ CP 0161	Searchin' for a Rainbow	1975	12.00
❑ CP 0170	Long Hard Ride	1976	12.00
❑ CPK 0180	Carolina Dreams	1977	12.00
❑ CP 0205	Together Forever	1978	12.00
❑ CPN-0214	Greatest Hits	1978	12.00
MERCURY			
❑ 832794-1	Still Holdin' On	1988	10.00
WARNER BROS.			
❑ BSK 3317	Running Like the Wind	1979	10.00
❑ HS 3410	Tenth	1980	10.00
❑ HS 3525	Dedicated	1981	10.00
❑ BSK 3606	The Marshall Tucker Band	1982	10.00
—Reissue of Capricorn 0112			
❑ 2WS 3608 [(2)]	Where We All Belong	1982	12.00
—Reissue of Capricorn 0145			
❑ BSK 3609	Searchin' for a Rainbow	1982	10.00
—Reissue of Capricorn 0161			
❑ BSK 3610	Carolina Dreams	1982	10.00
—Reissue of Capricorn 0180			
❑ BSK 3611	Greatest Hits	1982	10.00
—Reissue of Capricorn 0214			
❑ BSK 3662	A New Life	1982	10.00
—Reissue of Capricorn 0124			
❑ BSK 3663	Long Hard Ride	1982	10.00
—Reissue of Capricorn 0170			
❑ BSK 3664	Together Forever	1982	10.00
—Reissue of Capricorn 0205			
❑ BSK 3684	Tuckerized	1982	10.00
❑ 23803	Just Us	1983	10.00

MARSHANS, THE

45s

Number	Title (A Side/B Side)	Yr	NM
ETIQUETTE			
❑ 8	I Remember/It's Almost Tomorrow	1964	20.00
JOHNSON			
❑ 736	My Letter To Santa/Main Man	1966	20.00

MARSHMALLOW WAY

45s

Number	Title (A Side/B Side)	Yr	NM
UNITED ARTISTS			
❑ 50611	Good Day/Music, Music	1969	8.00

Albums

Number	Title (A Side/B Side)	Yr	NM
UNITED ARTISTS			
❑ UAS-6708	Marshmallow Way	1969	20.00

MARTELLS, THE

45s

Number	Title (A Side/B Side)	Yr	NM
BELLA			
❑ 20	Rockin' Santa Claus/Carol Lee	1959	40.00
—B-side by Eulis Mason			
❑ 45	Forgotten Spring/Va Va Voom	1961	50.00
CESSNA			
❑ 477	Forgotten Spring/Va Va Voom	1961	80.00
RELIC			
❑ 517	Forgotten Spring/Va Va Voom	1964	10.00

MARTERIE, RALPH

45s

Number	Title (A Side/B Side)	Yr	NM
MERCURY			
❑ DJ-15-X45 [DJ]	Pennsylvania Turnpike/Melancholy Rhapsody	195?	15.00
❑ 5413-X45	Yesterdays/Vilia	1950	20.00
❑ 5428-X45	Across the Wide Missouri/Silver Moon	1950	20.00
❑ 5457-X45	It Ain't Necessarily So/Sweet and Lovely	1950	20.00
❑ 5473-X45	My Silent Love/Say It Isn't So	1950	20.00
❑ 5507-X45	I Only Have Eyes for You/I'll Never Smile Again	1950	20.00
❑ 5562-X45	Sonny Boy/Danse Arabe	1950	20.00
❑ 5570-X45	So Long (It's Been Good to Know Yuh)/Here's to Happiness	1951	15.00
❑ 5658-X45	Castle Rock/September Song	1951	15.00
❑ 5658-X45	Didn't Yer Mother Ever Tell Ya Nothin'/You Better Stop	1951	15.00
❑ 5679-X45	Beautiful Ohio/A Trumpeter's Lullaby	1951	15.00
❑ 5705-X45	Alice Blue Gown/I Only Have Eyes for You	1951	15.00
❑ 5712-X45	Alice Blue Gown/Once in a While	1951	15.00
❑ 5716-X45	It's All in the Game/Tenderly	1951	15.00
❑ 5734-X45	Christmas in Killarney/When Your Lover Has Gone	1951	15.00
❑ 5759-X45	The Object of My Affection/Lulu Had a Baby	1951	15.00
❑ 5767-X45	Tell Me Why/Perdido	1951	15.00
❑ 5782-X45	Autumn Leaves/Goodbye Sweetheart	1952	15.00
❑ 5787-X45	Perdido/Lulu (Had a Baby)	1952	15.00
❑ 5824-X45	Frenesi/What Is This Thing Called Love	1952	15.00
—With the Harmonicats			
❑ 5827-X45	Stompin' at the Savoy/Boulevard of Broken Dreams	1952	15.00
❑ 5852-X45	I'm Yours/The Music Goes Round and Round	1952	15.00
❑ 5860-X45	In a Persian Market/Street Scene	1952	15.00
❑ 5882-X45	Dark Eyes/Peanut Vendor	1952	15.00
❑ 5903-X45	Takes Two to Tango/Ol' Man Mose	1952	15.00
❑ MG-20294 [M]	Jumpin' Trumpet	1957	25.00
—Original title			
❑ 70006-X45	Running Slow/Summer Love	1952	15.00
❑ 70008-X45	The Continental/Indian Summer	1952	15.00
❑ 70045-X45	Pretend/After Midnight	1953	15.00
❑ 70097-X45	Caravan/While We Dream	1953	15.00
❑ 70153-X45	Crazy, Man, Crazy/Go Away	1953	20.00
—Vocal by Larry Ragon & the Smarty-Aires			
❑ 70199-X45	The Girl of the Golden West/The Moon Is Blue	1953	15.00
❑ 70221-X45	Warsaw Concerto/Lazy River	1953	15.00
❑ 70248-X45	All That Oil in Texas/Love for Three Oranges	1953	15.00
❑ 70281-X45	The Creep/Love Theme	1953	15.00
❑ 70328-X45	Tularosa/Big Noise from Winnetka	1954	12.00
❑ 70358-X45	Dry Marterie/Until Six	1954	12.00
❑ 70406-X45	Tantalizin' Melody/Bumble Boogie	1954	12.00
❑ 70432-X45	Skokiaan/Crazy 'Bout Lollipop	1954	12.00
❑ 70482-X45	Bongo Guitar/Kiss Crazy Baby	1954	12.00
❑ 70493-X45	Dig That Crazy Santa Claus/Rock, Rock	1954	15.00

M

Number	Title (A Side/B Side)	Yr	NM
❑ 70535-X45	Blue Mirage (Don't Go)/ Remember Me	1955	12.00
❑ 70588-X45	Silver Moon/Chicken Boogie	1955	12.00
❑ 70614-X45	Ciribiri Mambo/ O Mio Balbino Caro	1955	12.00
❑ 70655-X45	Cha-Cha-Cha/One Fine Day	1955	12.00
❑ 70682-X45	Maybellene/The Toy Tiger	1955	15.00
❑ 70692-X45	Dry Marterie with an Olive/ The Toy Tiger	1955	12.00
❑ 70720-X45	John and Julie/Ring Dang Doo	1955	12.00
❑ 70760-X45	Wondrous Love/Misirlou	1955	12.00
❑ 70771-X45	The Grass Is Green/ Where the Wind Blows	1956	12.00
❑ 70836-X45	Theme from Picnic/ Rock and Roll the Barrel	1956	12.00
❑ 70874-X45	Jamaican Rhumba/Last Call	1956	12.00
❑ 70917-X45	Yes Sir, That's My Baby/ Lola's Theme	1956	12.00
❑ 70976-X45	That Mellow Saxophone/ Do You Ever Think of Me	1956	12.00
❑ 71007-X45	Carla/Guaglione	1956	12.00
❑ 71050-X45	Tricky/Travel at Your Own Risk	1957	10.00
❑ 71092-X45	Shish-Kebab/Bop-a-Doo Bop-a-Doo	1957	10.00
❑ 71204-X45	Hesitation Hop/Driftwood	1957	10.00
❑ 71279-X45	College Man/Cinderella Tango	1958	10.00
❑ 71295-X45	Night Stroll/Trombone Blues	1958	10.00
❑ 71338-X45	Love Song from "Houseboat"/ Lou's Blues	1958	10.00
❑ 71379-X45	Pretend Cha Cha/Flighty	1958	10.00
❑ 71424-X45	Compulsion/Words of Love	1959	10.00
❑ 71473-X45	Wampum/Cleopatra's Dream	1959	10.00
❑ 71488-X45	Thin Man/When My Sugar Walks Down the Street	1959	10.00
❑ 71547-X45	B'wana/Trumpet Soliliquy	1959	10.00
❑ 71594	I Can't Give You Anything But Love/Diga Diga Doo	1960	10.00

M

UNITED ARTISTS

Number	Title (A Side/B Side)	Yr	NM
❑ 284	Moonlight Becomes You/Truly	1961	8.00
❑ 315	Bacardi/The Shuck	1961	8.00
❑ 352	Caravan/Tonight	1961	8.00
❑ 409	Lili Marlene/Schwalbenwinkel	1962	8.00
❑ 447	Caravan Twist/Dry Marterie with a Twist	1962	8.00
❑ 465	Smoke Rings/Skyliner	1962	8.00
❑ 498	Theme from Carnival/ Moonlight in Vermont	1962	8.00
❑ 524	Night River/Prociutto	1962	8.00
❑ 554	Little Girl Blue/My Romance	1963	8.00
❑ 1521	On Green Dolphin Street/ Sweet and Lovely	196?	7.00
—"Silver Spotlight Series" issue			
❑ 1522	Try a Little Tenderness/ Moonlight Becomes You	196?	7.00
—"Silver Spotlight Series" issue			
❑ 1583	At Last/Caravan	196?	7.00
—"Silver Spotlight Series" issue			
❑ 1584	You Made Me Love You/My Reverie	196?	7.00
—"Silver Spotlight Series" issue			
❑ 1585	Oh Marie/I Can't Get Started	196?	7.00
—"Silver Spotlight Series" issue			
❑ 1586	Serenade in Blue/ Sentimental Journey	196?	7.00
—"Silver Spotlight Series" issue			
❑ 1587	Smoke Rings/Skyliner	196?	7.00
—"Silver Spotlight Series" issue			
❑ 1588	Mood Indigo/Goodbye	196?	7.00
—"Silver Spotlight Series" issue			

Albums

AMBASSADOR

Number	Title (A Side/B Side)	Yr	NM
❑ S-98058	Big Band Man/On the Sunny Side of the Street	196?	10.00

MERCURY

Number	Title (A Side/B Side)	Yr	NM
❑ SRW-16238 [S]	Music for a Private Eye	196?	15.00
❑ MG-20010 [M]	Sweet and Lovely	195?	20.00
❑ MG-20054 [M]	Alone Together	195?	20.00
❑ MG-20066 [M]	Dance Band in Town	195?	20.00
❑ MG-20124 [M]	Swing Baby	195?	20.00
❑ MG-20125 [M]	On Bandstand No. 1	195?	20.00
❑ MG-20128 [M]	Salute to the Aragon Ballroom	195?	20.00
❑ MG-20174 [M]	Love Themes from the Classics	195?	20.00
❑ MG-20198 [M]	Young America Dances	195?	20.00
❑ MG-20253 [M]	Dance Date	195?	20.00
❑ MG-20294 [M]	College Dance Favorites	1959	20.00
—Revised title			
❑ MG-20336 [M]	Hits That Made Ralph Marterie and His Orchestra Famous	195?	20.00
❑ MG-20395 [M]	Dance Party	195?	15.00
❑ MG-20397 [M]	Hi-Fidelity Concert	195?	15.00
❑ MG-20437 [M]	Music for a Private Eye	1960	20.00
❑ MG-20506 [M]	Big Band Man	1960	15.00
❑ MG-25085 [10]	Ralph Marterie and His Orchestra	195?	40.00
❑ MG-25102 [10]	Moods for Dancing	195?	50.00
❑ MG-25121 [10]	Junior Prom	195?	50.00
❑ MG-25171 [10]	Dancing on the Down Beat	195?	50.00
❑ SR-60034 [S]	Dance Party	1959	25.00
❑ SR-60035 [S]	College Dance Favorites	1959	25.00
❑ SR-60036 [S]	Hi-Fidelity Concert	1959	20.00
❑ SR-60109 [S]	Music for a Private Eye	1960	25.00
❑ SR-60183 [S]	Big Band Man	1960	20.00

MUSICOR

Number	Title (A Side/B Side)	Yr	NM
❑ MS-3011	51 Discotheque Dance Favorites	196?	10.00
❑ MS-3049	Motion Picture Hits	196?	12.00

UNITED ARTISTS

Number	Title (A Side/B Side)	Yr	NM
❑ UAL-3223 [M]	Ralph Marterie Plays Again	196?	12.00
❑ UAL-3235 [M]	Dance to the Music Man	1962	12.00
❑ UAL-3285 [M]	Dancers Choice	196?	12.00
❑ UAL-3349 [M]	50 Fabulous Dance Favorites	196?	12.00
❑ WWR 3506 [M]	88 Strings	196?	12.00
❑ UAS-6223 [S]	Ralph Marterie Plays Again	196?	15.00
❑ UAS-6285 [S]	Dancers Choice	196?	15.00
❑ UAS-6325 [S]	Dance to the Music Man	1962	15.00
❑ UAS-6349 [S]	50 Fabulous Dance Favorites	196?	15.00
❑ WWS 8506 [S]	88 Strings	196?	15.00

WING

Number	Title (A Side/B Side)	Yr	NM
❑ MGW-12117 [M]	Dance Date	195?	12.00
❑ MGW-12154 [M]	Marvelous Marterie	195?	12.00
❑ MGW-12155 [M]	Trumpeters Lullaby	195?	12.00
❑ MGW-12160 [M]	Love Themes from the Classics	195?	12.00
❑ MGW-12179 [M]	Dance Album	195?	12.00
❑ MGW-12185 [M]	Soft Tender Trumpet	195?	12.00
❑ MGW-12238 [M]	Music for a Private Eye	196?	12.00
❑ MGW-12259 [M]	Dance Party	196?	12.00
❑ SRW-12511 [S]	Marvelous Marterie	1959	15.00
❑ SRW-16269 [S]	Dance Party	196?	12.00

MARTHA AND THE VANDELLAS

Also see SAUNDRA MALLETT AND THE VANDELLAS; MARTHA REEVES; THE VELLS.

45s

A&M

Number	Title (A Side/B Side)	Yr	NM
❑ 3022	Nowhere to Run/I Got You (I Feel Good)	1988	4.00
—B-side by James Brown			
❑ 3022 [PS]	Nowhere to Run/I Got You (I Feel Good)	1988	4.00
—"Good Morning Vietnam" sleeve			

GORDY

Number	Title (A Side/B Side)	Yr	NM
❑ 7011	I'll Have to Let Him Go/ My Baby Won't Come Back	1962	25.00
❑ 7014	Come and Get These Memories/Jealous Love	1963	30.00
❑ 7022	Heat Wave/A Love Like Yours	1963	20.00
❑ 7025	Quicksand/Darling, I Hum Our Song	1963	15.00
❑ 7027	Live Wire/Old Love	1964	15.00
❑ 7031	In My Lonely Room/ A Tear for the Girl	1964	15.00
❑ 7033	Dancing in the Street/ There He Is (At My Door)	1964	15.00
❑ 7033 [PS]	Dancing in the Street/ There He Is (At My Door)	1964	120.00
❑ 7036	Wild One/Dancing Slow	1964	12.00
❑ 7039	Nowhere to Run/Motoring	1965	12.00
❑ 7045	You've Been in Love Too Long/ Love (Makes You Do Foolish Things)	1965	12.00
❑ 7048	My Baby Loves Me/Never Leave Your Baby's Side	1965	12.00
❑ 7053	What Am I Gonna Do Without Your Love/Go Ahead and Laugh	1966	12.00
❑ 7056	I'm Ready for Love/He Doesn't Love Her Anymore	1966	12.00
—"Gordy" logo at left			
❑ 7056	I'm Ready for Love/He Doesn't Love Her Anymore	1966	15.00
—"Gordy" logo at top			
❑ 7058	Jimmy Mack/Third Finger, Left Hand	1967	10.00
❑ 7062	Love Bug Leave My Heart Alone/One Way Out	1967	10.00
❑ 7067	Honey Chile/Show Me the Way	1967	10.00
—Starting here, as "Martha Reeves and the Vandellas"			
❑ 7070	I Promise to Wait My Love/ Forget Me Not	1968	10.00
❑ 7075	I Can't Dance to That Music You're Playin'/I Tried	1968	10.00
❑ 7080	Sweet Darlin'/Without You	1968	10.00
❑ 7085	(We've Got) Honey Love/ I'm In Love (And I Know It)	1969	8.00
❑ 7094	Taking My Love (And Leaving Me)/Heartless	1969	8.00
❑ 7098	I Should Be Pround/ Love, Guess Who	1970	8.00
❑ 7103	I Gotta Let You Go/ You're the Loser Now	1970	8.00
❑ 7110	Bless You/Hope I Don't Get My Heart Broke	1971	8.00
❑ 7113	In and Out of My Life/Your Love Makes It All Worthwhile	1972	8.00
❑ 7118	Tear It On Down/ I Want You Back	1972	8.00
❑ 7127	Baby Don't Leave Me/I Won't Be the Fool I've Been Again	1973	8.00

TOPPS/MOTOWN

Number	Title (A Side/B Side)	Yr	NM
❑ 7	Dancing in the Street	1967	75.00
—Cardboard record			
❑ 14	Love Is Like a Heat Wave	1967	75.00
—Cardboard record			

7-Inch Extended Plays

GORDY

Number	Title (A Side/B Side)	Yr	NM
❑ G-60917	Come and Get These Memories/Love Is Like a Heat Wave/Dancing in the Street// Love (Makes Me Do Foolish Things)/A Love Like Yours (Don't Come Knocking Everyday)/Nowhere to Run	1966	50.00
—Jukebox issue; small hole, plays at 33 1/3 rpm			
❑ G-60917 [PS]	Greatest Hits	1966	50.00
❑ G-60920	I'm Ready for Love/One Way Out/ Jimmy Mack//I'll Follow You/ No More Tearstained Makeup/ Tell Me I'll Never Be Alone	1966	40.00
—Jukebox issue; small hole, plays at 33 1/3 rpm			
❑ G-60920 [PS]	Watchout!	1966	40.00

Albums

GORDY

Number	Title (A Side/B Side)	Yr	NM
❑ G-902 [M]	Come and Get These Memories	1963	400.00
❑ GS-902 [S]	Come and Get These Memories	1963	800.00
❑ G-907 [M]	Heat Wave	1963	150.00
❑ GS-907 [R]	Heat Wave	1963	150.00
—"Stereo" banner pre-printed on cover			
❑ GS-907 [S]	Heat Wave	1963	400.00
—Mono cover with "Stereo" sticker			
❑ G-915 [M]	Dance Party	1965	40.00
❑ GS-915 [S]	Dance Party	1965	60.00
❑ G-917 [M]	Greatest Hits	1966	25.00
❑ GS-917 [S]	Greatest Hits	1966	30.00
❑ G-920 [M]	Watchout!	1966	25.00
❑ GS-920 [S]	Watchout!	1966	30.00
❑ G-925 [M]	Martha and the Vandellas Live!	1967	30.00
❑ GS-925 [S]	Martha and the Vandellas Live!	1967	25.00
❑ G-926 [M]	Ridin' High	1968	40.00
—Mono is promo only			
❑ GS-926 [S]	Ridin' High	1968	20.00
❑ GS-944	Sugar 'N Spice	1969	20.00
❑ GS-952	Natural Resources	1970	20.00
❑ GS-958	Black Magic	1972	20.00

MOTOWN

Number	Title (A Side/B Side)	Yr	NM
❑ M5-111V1	Motown Superstar Series, Vol. 11	1981	10.00
❑ M5-145V1	Heat Wave	1981	10.00
—Reissue of Gordy 907			
❑ M5-204V1	Greatest Hits	1981	10.00
—Reissue of Gordy 917			
❑ M7-778 [(2)]	Anthology	1974	15.00

MARTIN, BOBBI

45s

BUDDAH

Number	Title (A Side/B Side)	Yr	NM
❑ 217	No Love at All/A Place for Me	1971	4.00
❑ 227	Devotion/A Place for Me	1971	4.00
❑ 253	Tomorrow/Sentimental Journey	1971	4.00
❑ 286	Something Tells Me (Something's Gonna Happen Tonight)/Give Me a Star to Live On	1972	4.00

CORAL

Number	Title (A Side/B Side)	Yr	NM
❑ 62263	I Need Your Love/Cry, Cry, Cry (I Never Thought I'd Make You Cry)	1961	8.00
❑ 62285	Wooden Heart/How Should I Cry	1961	8.00
❑ 62321	Forgive Me/Tired and Blue	1962	8.00
❑ 62340	Afraid/Brenda, Brenda	1962	8.00
❑ 62351	I'll Never Stop Loving You/ Why, Tell Me Why	1963	8.00
❑ 62384	"A" You're Adorable/ A Girl's Prayer	1963	8.00
❑ 62410	I'm a Fool (To Go On Loving You)/ Does Your Heart Hurt a Little	1964	6.00
❑ 62426	Don't Forget I Still Love You/ On the Outside (Looking In)	1964	6.00
❑ 62447	I Can't Stop Thinking of You/ A Million Thanks to You	1965	6.00
❑ 62452	I Love You So/When Will the Torch Go Out	1965	6.00
❑ 62452 [PS]	I Love You So/When Will the Torch Go Out	1965	10.00
❑ 62457	Holding Back the Tears/ I Don't Want to Love	1965	6.00
❑ 62466	Auf Wiedersehn Good Bye/ There Are No Rules	1965	6.00
❑ 62472	Just One Time/Trying to Get You Off My Mind	1965	6.00
❑ 62475	Don't Take It Out on Me/ Something on My Mind	1965	6.00

Number	Title (A Side/B Side)	Yr	NM
❑ 62485	I Can Give You Love/Sometimes	1966	6.00
❑ 62488	Oh, Lonesome Me/It's a Sin to Tell a Lie	1966	6.00
❑ 62503	Just As Much As Ever/You Have No Idea	1966	6.00
❑ 62512	Anytime/How Long	1967	6.00

MGM

Number	Title (A Side/B Side)	Yr	NM
❑ 14587	Smile for Me/Now Lonely Is Only a Word	1973	4.00

UNITED ARTISTS

Number	Title (A Side/B Side)	Yr	NM
❑ 0148	For the Love of Him/I Think of You	1973	4.00
—"Silver Spotlight Series" reissue			
❑ 50253	Only You (And You Alone)/Would You Believe	1968	5.00
❑ 50297	A Man and a Woman/Before You	1968	5.00
❑ 50443	Harper Valley P.T.A./He Called Me Baby	1968	5.00
❑ 50456	I Love Him/I Think of You	1968	5.00
❑ 50523	Your Cheatin' Heart/Tennessee Waltz	1969	5.00
❑ 50602	For the Love of Him/I Fall to Pieces	1969	5.00
❑ 50602	For the Love of Him/I Think of You	1969	5.00
❑ 50687	Goin' South/Give a Woman Love	1970	5.00
❑ 50728	No Love at All/What Greater Love	1970	5.00

7-Inch Extended Plays

UNITED ARTISTS

Number	Title (A Side/B Side)	Yr	NM
❑ UALP 9-6668	Harper Valley P.T.A./I Love Him/Little Green Apples//She'll Have to Go/He Called Me Baby/I Think of You	1968	10.00
—Jukebox issue; small hole, plays at 33 1/3 rpm			
❑ UALP 9-6668 [PS]	Harper Valley P.T.A.	1968	10.00

Albums

BUDDAH

Number	Title (A Side/B Side)	Yr	NM
❑ BDS-5090	Tomorrow	1971	12.00

CORAL

Number	Title (A Side/B Side)	Yr	NM
❑ CRL 57472 [M]	Don't Forget I Still Love You	1965	15.00
❑ CRL 57478 [M]	I Love You So	1965	15.00
❑ CRL 757472 [S]	Don't Forget I Still Love You	1965	20.00
❑ CRL 757478 [S]	I Love You So	1965	20.00

SUNSET

Number	Title (A Side/B Side)	Yr	NM
❑ SUS-5319	Thinking of You	197?	10.00

UNITED ARTISTS

Number	Title (A Side/B Side)	Yr	NM
❑ UAS-6668	Harper Valley P.T.A.	1968	12.00
❑ UAS-6700	For the Love of Him	1969	12.00
❑ UAS-6755	With Love	1970	12.00

VOCALION

Number	Title (A Side/B Side)	Yr	NM
❑ VL 73906	Have You Ever Been Lonely	196?	10.00

MARTIN, DEAN

45s

CAPITOL

Number	Title (A Side/B Side)	Yr	NM
❑ 54-691	Just for Fun/My One, My Only, My All	1949	20.00
—Note: Dean Martin singles on Capitol before 691 are unconfirmed on 45 rpm			
❑ 54-726	That Lucky Old Sun/Vieni Su	1949	20.00
❑ F937	Rain/Zing-a, Zing-a, Boom	1950	15.00
❑ F948	Muskrat Ramble/I'm Gonna Paper All My Walls with Love Letters	1950	15.00
❑ F981	Choo'n Gum/I Don't Care If the Sun Don't Shine	1950	15.00
❑ F1002	I Still Get a Thrill/Be Honest with Me	1950	15.00
❑ F1028	I'll Always Love You/Baby Obey Me	1950	15.00
❑ F1052	Bye Bye Blackbird/Happy Feet	1950	15.00
❑ F1139	Peddler's Serenade/Wham, Bam, Thank You, Ma'am	1950	15.00
❑ F1160	Don't Rock the Boat/I'm in Love with You	1950	15.00
—With Margaret Whiting			
❑ F1342	If/I Love the Way	1950	15.00
❑ F1358	You and Your Beautiful Eyes/Tonda Wanda Hoy	1951	15.00
❑ F1458	Beside You/Who's Sorry Now	1951	15.00
❑ F1682	Oh Marie/I'll Always Love You	1951	12.00
❑ F1703	In the Cool, Cool, Cool of the Evening/Bonne Nuit	1951	15.00
❑ F1724	Go Go Go Go/Luna Mezzo Mare	1951	15.00
❑ F1797	Hanging Around with You/Aw C'mon	1951	15.00
❑ F1811	Meanderin'/Bella Bimba	1951	15.00
❑ F1817	Solitaire/I Ran All the Way Home	1951	15.00
❑ F1885	Night Train to Memphis/Blue Smoke	1951	15.00
❑ F1901	Never Before/Sailors Polka	1951	15.00
❑ F1921	As You Are/Oh Boy	1952	15.00
❑ F1938	Until/My Heart Found Home	1952	15.00
❑ F1975	All I Have to Give/When You're Smiling	1952	15.00
❑ F2001	Pretty as a Picture/Won't You Surrender	1952	15.00
❑ F2071	Bet-i-Cha/I Passed Your House Tonight	1952	15.00
❑ F2140	Oh Marie/Come Back to Sorrento	1952	15.00
❑ F2165	You Belong to Me/Hominy Grits	1952	15.00
❑ F2240	I Know a Dream When I See One/Second Chance	1952	15.00
❑ F2319	What Could Be More Beautiful/The Kiss	1953	12.00
❑ F2378	Little Did We Know/There's My Lover	1953	12.00
❑ F2485	Love Me, Love Me/Till I Find You	1953	12.00
❑ F2555	If I Could Sing Like Bing/Don't You Remember	1953	12.00
❑ F2589	That's Amore/You're the Right One	1953	15.00
❑ F2640	The Christmas Blues/If I Should Love Again	1953	12.00
❑ F2749	Hey Brother Pour the Wine/I'd Cry Like a Baby	1954	12.00
❑ F2818	Money Burns a Hole in My Pocket/Sway	1954	12.00
❑ F2870	That's What I Like/Peddler Man	1954	12.00
❑ F2911	Try Again/One More Time	1954	12.00
❑ F2985	Open Up the Doghouse/Long, Long Ago	1954	15.00
—With Nat King Cole			
❑ F3011	Confused/Belle from Barcelona	1955	10.00
❑ F3036	Young and Foolish/Under the Bridges of Paris	1955	10.00
❑ F3133	Chee Chee Oo-Chee/Ridin' Into Love	1955	10.00
❑ F3153	Simpatico/Love Is All That Matters	1955	10.00
❑ F3196	Two Sleepy People/Relax Ay Voo	1955	10.00
—With Line Renaud			
❑ F3238	I Like Them All/In Napoli	1955	10.00
❑ F3295	Memories Are Made of This/Change of Heart	1955	12.00
❑ F3352	Innamorata/Lady with a Big Umbrella	1956	10.00
❑ F3414	Standing on the Corner/Watching the World Go By	1956	10.00
❑ F3468	Street of Love/I'm Gonna Steal You Away	1956	10.00
❑ F3521	Mississippi Dreamboat/Test of Time	1956	10.00
❑ F3577	The Look/Give Me a Sign	1956	10.00
❑ F3604	Just Kiss Me/I Know I Can't Forget	1956	10.00
❑ F3648	Captured/The Man Who Plays the Mandolino	1957	10.00
❑ F3680	Bamboozled/Only Trust Your Heart	1957	10.00
❑ F3718	I Can't Give You Anything But Love/I Never Had a Chance	1957	10.00
❑ F3752	Write to Me from Naples/Beau James	1957	10.00
❑ F3787	Promise Her Anything/Triche Trache	1957	10.00
❑ F3842	Makin' Love Ukulele Style/Good Morning Life	1957	10.00
❑ F3894	Return to Me/Forgetting You	1958	8.00
❑ F3988	Angel Baby/I'll Gladly Make the Same Mistake Again	1958	8.00
❑ F4028	Volare (Nel Blu Dipinto Di Blu)/Outa My Mind	1958	8.00
❑ F4028 [PS]	Volare (Nel Blu Dipinto Di Blu)/Outa My Mind	1958	25.00
❑ F4065	Once Upon a Time/The Magician	1958	8.00
❑ F4124	It Takes So Long/You Were Made for Love	1959	8.00
❑ F4174	Rio Bravo/My Rifle, My Pony and Me	1959	8.00
❑ F4222	On an Evening in Roma/You Can't Love 'Em All	1959	8.00
❑ F4222 [PS]	On an Evening in Roma/You Can't Love 'Em All	1959	25.00
❑ F4287	I Ain't Gonna Lead This Life No More/Career	1959	8.00
❑ 4328	Love Me, My Love/Who Was That Lady	1960	8.00
❑ 4361	Napoli/Professor, Professor	1960	8.00
❑ 4391	Just in Time/Buttercup a Golden Hair	1960	8.00
❑ 4420	Ain't That a Kick in the Head/Humdinger	1960	8.00
❑ 4472	How Sweet It Is/Sogni D'Oro	1960	8.00
❑ 4518	Sparklin' Eyes/Tu Sei Bella Signorina	1961	8.00
❑ 4551	Bella, Bella Bambina/All in a Night's Work	1961	8.00
❑ 4570	The Story of Life/Giuggiola	1961	8.00
❑ B-44153	That's Amore/It Must Be Him	1988	4.00
—B-side by Vikki Carr			
❑ B-44153 [PS]	That's Amore/It Must Be Him	1988	5.00
❑ S7-57889	Rudolph, the Red-Nosed Reindeer/White Christmas	1992	5.00
❑ 58742	The Christmas Blues/Let It Snow! Let It Snow! Let It Snow!	1998	3.00
❑ 77683	When You're Smiling/Witchcraft	2001	3.00
—B-side by Frank Sinatra			

MCA

Number	Title (A Side/B Side)	Yr	NM
❑ 52662	L.A. Is My Home/Drinking Champagne	1985	4.00

REPRISE

Number	Title (A Side/B Side)	Yr	NM
❑ PRO 248 [DJ]	White Christmas (same on both sides)	1966	10.00
❑ 0252	La Giostra (Merry-Go-Round)/Grazie, Prego, Scusi	1964	8.00
❑ 0281	Everybody Loves Somebody/A Little Voice	1964	10.00
❑ 0307	The Door Is Still Open to My Heart/Every Minute, Every Hour	1964	8.00
❑ 0333	You're Nobody Till Somebody Loves You/You'll Always Be the One I Love	1964	8.00
❑ 0344	Send Me the Pillow You Dream On/I'll Be Seeing You	1965	8.00
❑ 0369	(Remember Me) I'm the One Who Loves You/Born to Lose	1965	8.00
❑ 0393	Houston/Bumming Around	1965	8.00
❑ 0415	I Will/You're the Reason I'm in Love	1965	8.00
❑ 0443	Somewhere There's a Someone/That Old Clock on the Wall	1965	8.00
❑ 0466	Come Running Back/Bouquet of Roses	1966	6.00
❑ 0500	A Million and One/Shades	1966	6.00
❑ 0516	Nobody's Baby Again/It Just Happened That Way	1966	6.00
❑ 0538	(Open Up the Door) Let the Good Times In/I'm Not the Marrying Kind	1966	6.00
❑ 0542	Blue Christmas/A Marshmallow World	1966	6.00
❑ 0571	Lay Some Happiness on Me/Think About Me	1967	6.00
❑ 0601	In the Chapel in the Moonlight/Welcome to My World	1967	6.00
❑ 0608	Little Ole Wine Drinker, Me/I Can't Help Remembering You	1967	6.00
❑ 0640	In the Misty Moonlight/The Glory of Love	1967	6.00
❑ 0640	In the Misty Moonlight/Wallpaper Roses	1967	6.00
❑ 0672	You've Still Got a Place in My Heart/Old Yellow Line	1968	5.00
❑ 0703	Lay Some Happiness on Me/(Open Up the Door) Let the Good Times In	1968	5.00
❑ 0709	Everybody Loves Somebody/A Million and One	1968	5.00
❑ 0711	Somewhere There's a Someone/Come Running Back	1968	5.00
❑ 0714	Houston/I Will	1968	5.00
❑ 0717	You're Nobody Till Somebody Loves You/(Remember Me) I'm the One Who Loves You	1968	5.00
❑ 0718	Send Me the Pillow You Dream On/The Door Is Still Open to My Heart	1968	5.00
❑ 0730	In the Chapel in the Moonlight/Little Ole Wine Drinker, Me	1968	5.00
❑ 0735	In the Misty Moonlight/Not Enough Indians	1970	4.00
—0703 through 0735 are "Back to Back Hits" reissues			
❑ 0761	April Again/That Old Time Feelin'	1968	5.00
❑ 0765	Five Card Stud/One Lonely Boy	1968	5.00
❑ 0780	Not Enough Indians/Rainbows Are Back in Style	1968	5.00
❑ 0812	Gentle on My Mind/That's When I See the Blues	1969	5.00
❑ 0841	I Take a Lot of Pride in What I Am/Drowning in My Tears	1969	5.00
❑ 0857	Crying TIme/One Cup of Happiness	1969	5.00
❑ 0893	Down Home/Come On Down	1970	5.00
❑ 0915	For the Love of a Woman/The Tracks of My Tears	1970	5.00
❑ 0934	My Woman, My Woman, My Wife/Here We Go Again	1970	5.00
❑ 0955	Detroit City/Turn the World Around	1970	5.00
❑ 0973	For the Good Times/Georgia Sunshine	1970	5.00
❑ 1004	She's a Little Bit Country/Raining in My Heart	1971	5.00
❑ 1060	What's Yesterday/The Right Kind of Woman	1971	5.00

Number	Title (A Side/B Side)	Yr	NM
❑ 1085	I Can Give You What You Want Now/Guess Who	1972	5.00
❑ 1141	Amor Mio/You Made Me Love You	1972	5.00
❑ 1166	Smile/Get On With Your Livin'	1973	5.00
❑ 1178	You're the Best Thing That Ever Happened to Me/Free to Carry On	1973	5.00
❑ 20058	Just Close Your Eyes/ Tik-A-Tee Tik-A-Tay	1962	12.00
❑ 20082	Baby-O/Dame Su Amor	1962	10.00
❑ 20116	From the Bottom of My Heart (Dammi, Dammi, Dammi)/ Who's Got the Action	1962	10.00
❑ 20116 [PS]	From the Bottom of My Heart (Dammi, Dammi, Dammi)/ Who's Got the Action	1962	20.00
❑ 20128	Sam's Song/Me and My Shadow	1962	15.00
—A-side with Sammy Davis, Jr.; B-side: Sammy Davis Jr. and Frank Sinatra			
❑ 20128 [PS]	Sam's Song/Me and My Shadow	1962	40.00
❑ 20140	Who's Got the Action/ Send a Fine	1963	10.00
❑ 20150	Ain't Gonna Try Anymore/ A Face in the Crowd	1963	10.00
❑ 20194	Corrine, Corrina/ My Sugar's Gone	1963	10.00
❑ 20215	Via Veneto/Mama Roma	1963	10.00
❑ 20217	Fugue for Tinhorns/The Oldest Established (Permanent Floating Crap Game in New York)	1963	15.00
—By Frank Sinatra/Bing Crosby/Dean Martin			
❑ 20217 [PS]	Fugue for Tinhorns/The Oldest Established (Permanent Floating Crap Game in New York)	1963	80.00
—By Frank Sinatra/Bing Crosby/Dean Martin			

WARNER BROS.

Number	Title (A Side/B Side)	Yr	NM
❑ 29480	Drinking Champagne/ Since I Met You Baby	1983	4.00
❑ 29584	My First Country Song/ Hangin' Around	1983	4.00

7-Inch Extended Plays

CAPITOL

Number	Title (A Side/B Side)	Yr	NM
❑ EAP 1-401	(contents unknown)	195?	20.00
❑ EAP 1-401 [PS]	Dean Martin Sings	195?	20.00
❑ EAP 1-481	That's Amore/Oh Marie// Come Back to Sorrento/ Luna Mezzo Mare	1954	20.00
❑ EAP 1-481 [PS]	Sunny Italy	1954	20.00
❑ EAP 1-576	Carolina Moon/Waitin' for the Robert E. Lee//Basin Street Blues/Is It True What They Say About Dixie?	195?	15.00
❑ EAP 1-576 [PS]	Swingin' Down Yonder, Part 1	195?	15.00
❑ EAP 2-576	When It's Sleepy Time Down South/Mississippi Mud// Georgia on My Mind/Just a Little Bit South of North Carolina	195?	15.00
❑ EAP 2-576 [PS]	Swingin' Down Yonder, Part 2	195?	15.00
❑ EAP 3-576	Alabamy Bound/Dinah// Carolina in the Morning/Way Down Yonder in New Orleans	195?	15.00
❑ EAP 3-576 [PS]	Swingin' Down Yonder, Part 3	195?	15.00
❑ EAP 1-701	Memories Are Made of This/ I Like Them All//Change of Heart/Ridin' Into Love	1956	15.00
❑ EAP 1-701 [PS]	Memories Are Made of This	1956	15.00
❑ EAP 1-702	(contents unknown)	1956	15.00
❑ EAP 1-702 [PS]	Artists and Models	1956	15.00
❑ EAP 1-806	(contents unknown)	1957	15.00
❑ EAP 1-806 [PS]	Hollywood or Bust	1957	15.00
❑ EAP 1-840	(contents unknown)	1957	15.00
❑ EAP 1-840 [PS]	Ten Thousand Bedrooms	1957	15.00
❑ EAP 1-849	(contents unknown)	1957	12.00
❑ EAP 1-849 [PS]	Pretty Baby, Part 1	1957	12.00
❑ EAP 2-849	(contents unknown)	1957	12.00
❑ EAP 2-849 [PS]	Pretty Baby, Part 2	1957	12.00
❑ EAP 3-849	(contents unknown)	1957	12.00
❑ EAP 3-849 [PS]	Pretty Baby, Part 3	1957	12.00
❑ EAP 1-939	Return to Me/Don't You Remember//Forgetting You/ Buona Sera	1958	15.00
❑ EAP 1-939 [PS]	Return to Me	1958	15.00
❑ EAP 1-1285	(contents unknown)	1959	12.00
❑ EAP 1-1285 [PS]	A Winter Romance, Part 1	1959	12.00
❑ EAP 2-1285	(contents unknown)	1959	12.00
❑ EAP 2-1285 [PS]	A Winter Romance, Part 2	1959	12.00
❑ EAP 3-1285	(contents unknown)	1959	12.00
❑ EAP 3-1285 [PS]	A Winter Romance, Part 3	1959	12.00
❑ MA 1-1580	That's Amore/Memories Are Made of This//Volare/ Return to Me	1961	15.00
—Small hole, plays at 33 1/3 rpm			
❑ MA 1-1580 [PS]	Dean Martin	1961	15.00
❑ SU 1659	Just Say I Love Her/Arrivederci, Roma/Non Dimenticar//Vieni Su/Take Me in Your Arms/ I Have But One Love	196?	15.00
—Jukebox issue; small hole, plays at 33 1/3 rpm			
❑ SU 1659 [PS]	Italian Love Songs	196?	15.00
❑ DU 2601	That's Amore/Return to Me/ Volare//Memories Are Made of This/Just in Time/Come Back to Sorrento	196?	10.00
—Jukebox issue; small hole, plays at 33 1/3 rpm; red and white "Starline" label			
❑ DU 2601 [PS]	The Best of Dean Martin	196?	10.00
❑ EAP-1-9123	Let Me Go, Lover/The Naughty Lady of Shady Lane//Mambo Italiano/That's All I Want from You	1955	15.00
❑ EAP-1-9123 [PS]	Dean Martin	1955	15.00

REPRISE

Number	Title (A Side/B Side)	Yr	NM
❑ SR 2053	Guess Who/Just the Other Side of Nowhere/What's Yesterday//Blue Memories/ Party Dolls & Wine/I Can Give You What You Want	1972	10.00
—Jukebox issue; small hole, plays at 33 1/3 rpm			
❑ SR 2053 [PS]	Dino	1972	10.00
—Part of "Little LP" series (#179)			
❑ SR 2113	I Wonder Who's Kissing Her Now/At Sundown/Almost Like Being in Love//It's a Good Day/Ramblin' Rose/I'm Sittin' on Top of the World	1973	10.00
—Jukebox issue; small hole, plays at 33 1/3 rpm			
❑ SR 2113 [PS]	Sittin' on Top of the World	1973	10.00
—Part of "Little LP" series (#228)			
❑ SR 6123	I Don't Know Why (I Just Do)/ Baby Won't You Please Come Home/I'm Confessin'// "Gimme" A Little Kiss Will "Ya" Huh?/I'll Buy That Dream/Smile	1964	10.00
—Jukebox issue; small hole, plays at 33 1/3 rpm			
❑ SR 6123 [PS]	Dream with Dean	1964	10.00
❑ 6130	Everybody Loves Somebody/ Corrine Corrina/Face in the Crowd//Just Close Your Eyes/ Things/My Heart Cries for You	196?	10.00
—Jukebox issue; small hole, plays at 33 1/3 rpm; brown and orange label with white spot in middle			
❑ 6130	Everybody Loves Somebody/ Corrine Corrina/Face in the Crowd//Just Close Your Eyes/ Things/My Heart Cries for You	1964	15.00
—Jukebox issue; small hole, plays at 33 1/3 rpm; white label with "Promotion" at bottom			
❑ 6130 [PS]	Everybody Loves Somebody	1964	10.00
—Both versions have virtually identical sleeves			
❑ SR 6170	Walk On By/King of the Road/ (Remember Me) I'm the One Who Loves You//Here Comes My Baby/My Shoes Keep Walking Back to You/The Birds and the Bees	1965	10.00
—Jukebox issue; small hole, plays at 33 1/3 rpm			
❑ SR 6170 [PS]	(Remember Me) I'm the One Who Loves You	1965	10.00
❑ SR 6181	Houston/Snap Your Fingers/ Little Lovely One//I Will/The First Thing Ev'ry Morning (And the Last Thing Ev'ry Night)/Down Home	1965	10.00
—Jukebox issue; small hole, plays at 33 1/3 rpm			
❑ SR 6181 [PS]	Houston	1965	10.00
❑ SR 6201	Second Hand Rose/Bouquet of Roses/Just a Little Lovin'// Somewhere There's a Someone/I Can't Help It/ Anytime	1966	10.00
—Jukebox issue; small hole, plays at 33 1/3 rpm			
❑ SR 6201 [PS]	Somewhere There's a Someone	1966	10.00
❑ SR 6211	The Glory of Love/Empty Saddles in the Old Corral/Side by Side//On the Sunny Side of the Street/The Last Round-up/ Red Sails in the Sunset	1966	10.00
—Jukebox issue; small hole, plays at 33 1/3 rpm			
❑ SR 6211 [PS]	The Silencers	1966	10.00
❑ SR 6213	Don't Let the Blues Make You Bad/A Million and One/I'm Living in Two Worlds//Shades/ Today Is Not the Day/I Ain't Gonna Try Anymore	1966	10.00
—Jukebox issue; small hole, plays at 33 1/3 rpm			
❑ SR 6213 [PS]	The Hit Sound of Dean Martin	1966	10.00
❑ SR 6250	Little Old Wine Drinker, Me/The Green, Green Grass of Home/ Wallpaper Roses//In the Chapel in the Moonlight/ Welcome to My World/Release Me (And Let Me Love Again)	1967	10.00
—Jukebox issue; small hole, plays at 33 1/3 rpm			
❑ SR 6250 [PS]	Welcome to My World	1967	10.00
❑ SR 6301	Everybody Loves Somebody/ You're Nobody 'Til Somebody Loves You/In the Chapel in the Moonlight//Every Minute, Every Hour/Bumming Around/ You'll Always Be the One I Love	1968	10.00
—Jukebox issue; small hole, plays at 33 1/3 rpm			
❑ SR 6301 [PS]	Dean Martin's Greatest Hits! Vol. 1	1968	10.00
❑ SR 6320	In the Misty Moonlight/Send Me the Pillow That You Dream On/Little Old Wine Drinker, Me//Lay Some Happiness on Me/You've Still Got a Place in My Heart/King of the Road	1968	10.00
—Jukebox issue; small hole, plays at 33 1/3 rpm			
❑ SR 6320 [PS]	Dean Martin's Greatest Hits! Vol. 2	1968	10.00
❑ SR 6330	That Old Time Feelin'/ Welcome to My Heart/By the Time I Get to Phoenix//Gentle on My Mind/That's When I See the Blues (In Your Pretty Brown Eyes)/April Again	1968	10.00
—Jukebox issue; small hole, plays at 33 1/3 rpm			
❑ SR 6330 [PS]	Gentle on My Mind	1968	10.00
❑ 40045	Tangerine/South of the Border/ In a Little Spanish Town// What a Diff'rence a Day Made/Magic Is the Moonlight/ Besame Mucho	196?	20.00
—Jukebox issue; small hole, plays at 33 1/3 rpm			
❑ 40045 [PS]	Dino Latino	196?	20.00

Albums

CAPITOL

Number	Title	Yr	NM
❑ SKAO-140	The Best of Dean Martin, Vol. 2	1968	15.00
❑ H 401 [10]	Dean Martin Sings	1953	100.00
❑ T 401 [M]	Dean Martin Sings	1953	50.00
❑ STBB-523 [(2)]	You're Nobody 'Til Somebody Loves You/Return to Me	1970	20.00
❑ T 576 [M]	Swingin' Down Yonder	1955	30.00
❑ T 849 [M]	Pretty Baby	1957	30.00
❑ DT 1047 [R]	This Is Dean Martin	196?	12.00
❑ T 1047 [M]	This Is Dean Martin	1958	30.00
❑ ST 1150 [S]	Sleep Warm	1959	30.00
❑ T 1150 [M]	Sleep Warm	1959	25.00
❑ ST 1285 [S]	A Winter Romance	1959	30.00
❑ T 1285 [M]	A Winter Romance	1959	20.00
❑ ST 1442 [S]	This Time I'm Swingin'	1961	30.00
❑ T 1442 [M]	This Time I'm Swingin'	1961	20.00
❑ SW 1580 [S]	Dean Martin	1961	30.00
❑ W 1580 [M]	Dean Martin	1961	20.00
❑ SM-1659	Dino — Italian Love Songs	197?	10.00
—Reissue with new prefix			
❑ ST 1659 [S]	Dino — Italian Love Songs	1962	30.00
❑ T 1659 [M]	Dino — Italian Love Songs	1962	20.00
❑ ST 1702 [S]	Cha Cha De Amor	1962	30.00
❑ T 1702 [M]	Cha Cha De Amor	1962	20.00
❑ DT 2212 [R]	Hey Brother Pour the Wine	1964	12.00
❑ T 2212 [M]	Hey Brother Pour the Wine	1964	20.00
❑ ST 2297 [S]	Dean Martin Sings — Sinatra Conducts	1965	20.00
❑ T 2297 [M]	Dean Martin Sings — Sinatra Conducts	1965	15.00
❑ DT 2333 [R]	Dean Martin — Southern Style	1965	12.00
❑ T 2333 [M]	Dean Martin — Southern Style	1965	15.00
❑ STT 2343 [S]	Holiday Cheer	1965	20.00
—Some copies of this LP have labels that state the title as "Baby, It's Cold Outside."			
❑ TT 2343 [M]	Holiday Cheer	1965	15.00
—Reissue of 1285 with one fewer track			
❑ DT 2601 [R]	The Best of Dean Martin	1966	12.00
❑ SM-2601	The Best of Dean Martin	197?	10.00
—Reissue with new prefix			
❑ T 2601 [M]	The Best of Dean Martin	1966	15.00
❑ DTCL 2815 [(3)R]	The Dean Martin Deluxe Set	1967	20.00
❑ TCL 2815 [(3)M]	The Dean Martin Deluxe Set	1967	30.00

LONGINES SYMPHONETTE

Number	Title	Yr	NM
❑ LS-124A [(5)]	Memories Are Made of This	197?	25.00
—Records are individually numbered SYS 5230, 5231, 5232, 5233 and 5234			

PAIR

Number	Title	Yr	NM
❑ PDL2-1029 [(2)]	Dreams and Memories	1986	12.00

PICKWICK

Number	Title	Yr	NM
❑ PTP-2051 [(2)]	Dean Martin	197?	12.00
❑ SPC-3057	You Can't Love 'Em All	196?	10.00
❑ SPC-3089	I Can't Give You Anything But Love	196?	10.00
❑ SPC-3136	Young and Foolish	196?	10.00
❑ SPC-3175	You Were Made for Love	197?	10.00

Number	Title (A Side/B Side)	Yr	NM
❑ SPC-3283	Deluxe	197?	10.00

REPRISE

Number	Title (A Side/B Side)	Yr	NM
❑ MS 2053	Dino	1972	15.00
❑ MS 2113	Sittin' on Top of the World	1973	15.00
❑ MS 2174	You're the Best Thing That Ever Happened to Me	1973	15.00
❑ MS 2267	Once in a Lifetime	1978	12.00
❑ R-6021 [M]	French Style	1962	15.00
❑ R9-6021 [S]	French Style	1962	20.00
❑ R-6054 [M]	Dino Latino	1962	15.00
❑ R9-6054 [S]	Dino Latino	1962	20.00
❑ R-6061 [M]	Country Style	1963	15.00
❑ R9-6061 [S]	Country Style	1963	20.00
❑ R-6085 [M]	Dean "Tex" Martin Rides Again	1963	15.00
❑ R9-6085 [S]	Dean "Tex" Martin Rides Again	1963	20.00
❑ R-6123 [M]	Dream with Dean	1964	12.00
❑ RS-6123 [S]	Dream with Dean	1964	15.00
❑ R-6130 [M]	Everybody Loves Somebody	1964	12.00
❑ RS-6130 [S]	Everybody Loves Somebody	1964	15.00
❑ R-6140 [M]	The Door Is Still Open to My Heart	1964	12.00
❑ RS-6140 [S]	The Door Is Still Open to My Heart	1964	15.00
❑ R-6146 [M]	Dean Martin Hits Again	1965	12.00
❑ RS-6146 [S]	Dean Martin Hits Again	1965	15.00
❑ R-6170 [M]	(Remember Me) I'm the One Who Loves You	1965	12.00
❑ RS-6170 [S]	(Remember Me) I'm the One Who Loves You	1965	15.00
❑ R-6181 [M]	Houston	1965	12.00
❑ RS-6181 [S]	Houston	1965	15.00
❑ R-6201 [M]	Somewhere There's a Someone	1966	12.00
❑ RS-6201 [S]	Somewhere There's a Someone	1966	15.00
❑ R-6211 [M]	The Silencers	1966	20.00
❑ RS-6211 [S]	The Silencers	1966	25.00
❑ R-6213 [M]	The Hit Sound of Dean Martin	1966	12.00
❑ RS-6213 [S]	The Hit Sound of Dean Martin	1966	15.00
❑ R 6222 [M]	The Dean Martin Christmas Album	1966	15.00
❑ RS 6222 [S]	The Dean Martin Christmas Album	1966	20.00
❑ R-6233 [M]	The Dean Martin TV Show	1966	12.00
❑ RS-6233 [S]	The Dean Martin TV Show	1966	15.00
❑ R-6242 [M]	Happiness Is Dean Martin	1967	15.00
❑ RS-6242 [S]	Happiness Is Dean Martin	1967	15.00
❑ R-6250 [M]	Welcome to My World	1967	15.00
❑ RS-6250 [S]	Welcome to My World	1967	15.00
❑ RS-6301	Dean Martin's Greatest Hits! Vol. 1	1968	15.00
❑ RS-6320	Dean Martin's Greatest Hits! Vol. 2	1968	15.00
❑ R-6330 [M]	Gentle on My Mind	1968	30.00
❑ RS-6330 [S]	Gentle on My Mind	1968	15.00
❑ RS-6338	I Take a Lot of Pride in What I Am	1969	15.00
❑ RS-6403	My Woman, My Woman, My Wife	1970	15.00
❑ RS-6428	For the Good Times	1971	15.00
❑ SW-94345	Dino	1972	20.00

—Capitol Record Club edition

TOWER

Number	Title (A Side/B Side)	Yr	NM
❑ DT 5006 [R]	The Lush Years	1965	15.00
❑ T 5006 [M]	The Lush Years	1965	20.00
❑ DT 5018 [R]	Relaxin'	1966	15.00
❑ T 5018 [M]	Relaxin'	1966	20.00
❑ ST 5036 [S]	Happy in Love	1966	20.00
❑ T 5036 [M]	Happy in Love	1966	15.00

WARNER BROS.

Number	Title (A Side/B Side)	Yr	NM
❑ 23870	The Nashville Sessions	1983	12.00

MARTIN, DEAN, AND JERRY LEWIS

7-Inch Extended Plays

CAPITOL

Number	Title (A Side/B Side)	Yr	NM
❑ EAP 1-533	(contents unknown)	1954	80.00
❑ EAP 1-533 [PS]	Living It Up	1954	80.00
❑ EAP 1-733	(contents unknown)	1956	60.00
❑ EAP 1-733 [PS]	Pardners	1956	60.00

MARTIN, DEWEY, AND MEDICINE BALL

Dewey is a former member of BUFFALO SPRINGFIELD.

45s

RCA VICTOR

Number	Title (A Side/B Side)	Yr	NM
❑ 74-0489	There Must Be a Reason/Caress Me Pretty Music	1971	8.00

UNI

Number	Title (A Side/B Side)	Yr	NM
❑ 55178	Jambalaya (On the Bayou)/Ala-Bam	1969	8.00
❑ 55245	Indian Child/I Do Believe	1970	8.00

Albums

UNI

Number	Title (A Side/B Side)	Yr	NM
❑ 73088	Dewey Martin and Medicine Ball	1970	25.00

MARTIN, DICK

45s

HIT

Number	Title (A Side/B Side)	Yr	NM
❑ 77	Hello Muddah, Hello Faddah/Candy Girl	1963	8.00

—B-side by the Chellows

MARTIN, GEORGE

45s

UNITED ARTISTS

Number	Title (A Side/B Side)	Yr	NM
❑ 745	Ringo's Theme (This Boy)/And I Love Her	1964	25.00
❑ 745 [PS]	Ringo's Theme (This Boy)/And I Love Her	1964	300.00
❑ 750	A Hard Day's Night/I Should Have Known Better	1964	100.00
❑ 750 [PS]	A Hard Day's Night/I Should Have Known Better	1964	2000.
❑ 831	All Quiet on the Mersey Front/Cast Your Fate to the Wind	1965	15.00
❑ 873	I Feel Fine/Downtown	1965	15.00
❑ 50148	Love in the Open Air/Bahama Sound	1967	30.00

Albums

UNITED ARTISTS

Number	Title (A Side/B Side)	Yr	NM
❑ UAL 3377 [M]	Off the Beatle Track	1964	80.00
❑ UAL 3383 [M]	A Hard Day's Night	1964	40.00
❑ UAL 3420 [M]	George Martin	1965	40.00
❑ UAL 3448 [M]	George Martin Plays "Help"	1965	50.00
❑ UAL 3539 [M]	George Martin Salutes the Beatle Girls	1966	50.00
❑ UAL 3647 [M]	London by George	1967	30.00
❑ UAS 6377 [S]	Off the Beatle Track	1964	100.00
❑ UAS 6383 [S]	A Hard Day's Night	1964	50.00
❑ UAS 6420 [S]	George Martin	1965	50.00
❑ UAS 6448 [S]	George Martin Plays "Help"	1965	80.00
❑ UAS 6539 [S]	George Martin Salutes the Beatle Girls	1966	80.00
❑ UAS 6647 [S]	London by George	1967	40.00

MARTIN, JANIS

45s

PALETTE

Number	Title (A Side/B Side)	Yr	NM
❑ 5058	Hard Times Ahead/Here Today and Gone Tomorrow	1960	25.00
❑ 5071	Teen Street/Cry Guitar	1961	25.00

RCA VICTOR

Number	Title (A Side/B Side)	Yr	NM
❑ 47-6491	Drugstore Rock and Roll/Will You, Willyum	1956	40.00
❑ 47-6560	Ooby-Dooby/One More Year to Go	1956	40.00
❑ 47-6652	My Boy Elvis/Little Bit	1956	70.00
❑ 47-6744	Let's Elope, Baby/Barefoot Baby	1956	30.00
❑ 47-6832	Love Me to Pieces/Two Long Years	1957	30.00
❑ 47-6983	Love and Kisses/I'll Never Be Free	1957	30.00
❑ 47-7104	All Right Baby/Billy Boy, Billy Boy	1957	30.00
❑ 47-7184	Cracker Jack/Good Love	1958	30.00

7-Inch Extended Plays

RCA VICTOR

Number	Title (A Side/B Side)	Yr	NM
❑ EPA-4093	Just Squeeze Me (But Don't Tease Me)/My Confession//I Don't Hurt Anymore/Half Loved	1957	150.00
❑ EPA-4093 [PS]	Just Squeeze Me	1957	200.00

MARTIN, JIMMY

45s

DECCA

Number	Title (A Side/B Side)	Yr	NM
❑ 9-30493	I'll Drink No More Wine/Skip, Hop and Wobble	1957	15.00
❑ 9-30613	Ocean of Diamonds/Sophronic	1958	15.00
❑ 9-30703	Rock Hearts/I'll Never Take No for an Answer	1958	20.00
❑ 9-30812	The Voice of My Savior/I Like to Hear 'Em Preach It	1959	15.00
❑ 9-30877	Night/It's Not Like Home	1959	15.00
❑ 9-30965	Hold Whatcha Got/She's Left Me	1959	15.00
❑ 31073	The Joke's on You/Foggy Old London	1960	12.00
❑ 31157	Bear Tracks/You Don't Know My Mind	1960	12.00
❑ 31176	An Old-Fashioned Christmas/Hold to God's Unchanging Hand	1960	12.00
❑ 31234	Hi-De Diddle/My Walking Shoes	1961	12.00
❑ 31311	I Can, I Will, I Do Believe/There Was a Love	1961	12.00
❑ 31376	God Is Always the Same/God, Guide Our Leader's Hand	1962	12.00
❑ 31414	Don't Cry to Me/Poor Little Bullfrog	1962	12.00
❑ 31442	The Shut-In's Prayer/Prayer Bell of Heaven	1962	12.00
❑ 31461	Hey Lonesome/The Old Man's Drunk Again	1963	10.00
❑ 31558	Widow Maker/Red River Valley	1963	10.00
❑ 31629	I'd Rather Have America/Leavin' Town	1964	10.00
❑ 31680	Guitar Picking President/It Takes One to Know One	1964	10.00
❑ 31748	20-20 Vision/Sunny Side of the Mountain	1965	10.00
❑ 31846	Sweet Dixie/Last Song	1965	10.00
❑ 31921	I Can't Quit Cigarettes/Run Boy Run	1966	8.00
❑ 31987	Goodbye/Who'll Sing for Me	1966	8.00
❑ 32031	Home Run Man/You're Gonna Change (Or I'm Gonna Leave)	1966	8.00
❑ 32092	Give Me the Roses Now/Pray the Clouds Away	1967	8.00
❑ 32132	Living Like a Fool/The Big Country	1967	8.00
❑ 32201	Goin' Ape/The Wild Indian	1967	8.00
❑ 32300	Tennessee/Steal Away Somewhere and Die	1968	8.00
❑ 32378	Losing You/Free Born Man	1968	8.00
❑ 32461	Red Rooster/Moonshine Hollow	1969	8.00
❑ 32517	Give Me Your Hand/Little White Church	1969	7.00
❑ 32553	Shackles and Chains/Milwaukee Here I Come	1969	8.00
❑ 32674	Arab Bounce/Future on Ice	1970	7.00
❑ 32731	Singing All Day and Dinner on the Ground/Help Thy Brother	1970	7.00
❑ 32750	Midnight Rambler/Between Fire and Water	1970	7.00
❑ 32820	Chattanooga Dog/I Cried Again	1971	7.00
❑ 32934	Lonesome Prison Blues/I'd Like to Be Sixteen Again	1972	7.00

MCA

Number	Title (A Side/B Side)	Yr	NM
❑ 40076	Sunshine of the Mountain/You Don't Know My Mind	1973	6.00
❑ 40147	Mary Ann/Just Plain Yellow	1973	6.00
❑ 40237	Fly Me to Frisco/Theme Time	1974	6.00
❑ 40338	You Are My Sunshine/Lost to a Stranger	1974	6.00
❑ 40449	Better Times a-Comin'/I Buried My Future	1975	6.00

Albums

DECCA

Number	Title (A Side/B Side)	Yr	NM
❑ DL 4016 [M]	Good 'n Country	1960	25.00
❑ DL 4285 [M]	Country Music Time	1962	25.00
❑ DL 4360 [M]	This World Is Not My Home	1963	25.00
❑ DL 4536 [M]	Widow Maker	1964	20.00
❑ DL 4643 [M]	Sunny Side of the Mountain	1965	20.00
❑ DL 4769 [M]	Mr. Good 'n Country Music	1966	20.00
❑ DL 4891 [M]	Big and Country Instrumentals	1967	20.00
❑ DL 4996 [M]	Tennessee	1968	60.00

—Mono is white label promo only

Number	Title (A Side/B Side)	Yr	NM
❑ DL 74016 [S]	Good 'n Country	1960	30.00
❑ DL 74285 [S]	Country Music Time	1962	30.00
❑ DL 74360 [S]	This World Is Not My Home	1963	30.00
❑ DL 74536 [S]	Widow Maker	1964	25.00
❑ DL 74643 [S]	Sunny Side of the Mountain	1965	25.00
❑ DL 74769 [S]	Mr. Good 'n Country Music	1966	25.00
❑ DL 74891 [S]	Big and Country Instrumentals	1967	20.00
❑ DL 74996 [S]	Tennessee	1968	20.00

MARTIN, JOHNNY

45s

CHART

Number	Title (A Side/B Side)	Yr	NM
❑ 1015	Uncle Sam's Navy/Right on the Edge of Loneliness	1967	8.00
❑ 1035	Boobie Doo/Kiss Me	1968	8.00

MARTIN, MARTY

45s

ANVIL

Number	Title (A Side/B Side)	Yr	NM
❑ 1001	All I Got for Christmas Was a Broken Heart/Hootenanny Santa	1963	10.00

MARTIN, MILLICENT

45s

ABC-PARAMOUNT

Number	Title (A Side/B Side)	Yr	NM
❑ 10514	In the Summer of His Years/If I Can Help Somebody	1963	10.00

MARTIN, RAY

45s

CAPITOL

Number	Title (A Side/B Side)	Yr	NM
❑ F3393	Tickled Pink/If Hearts Could Talk	1956	12.00
❑ F3516	Street Symphony/Tambourine	1956	12.00
❑ F3670	Whistling Sergeant/Tango in the Rain	1957	12.00
❑ F3767	Heladero/Manhattan Tango	1957	12.00

ESSEX

Number	Title (A Side/B Side)	Yr	NM
❑ 335	Begorrah/Hi-Lilli, Hi-Lo	1953	15.00
❑ 346	Tango Waltz/Carnivalito	1954	15.00
❑ 357	Veradero/Strings on Parade	1954	15.00

RCA VICTOR

Number	Title (A Side/B Side)	Yr	NM
❑ 47-7344	Wild Gypsy/Big Dipper	1958	10.00
❑ 47-7769	Never on Sunday/Never on Sunday	1960	8.00

—B-side by Marty Gold

Number	Title (A Side/B Side)	Yr	NM
❑ 47-7920	The Boulevard of Broken Dreams/The Mime's Theme	1961	8.00
UNITED ARTISTS			
❑ 103	Song from "The Quiet American"/The Grape Stompers	1958	10.00
❑ 116	Argentina Ballerina/Spring in Spain	1958	10.00
7-Inch Extended Plays			
CAPITOL			
❑ EAP-1-10017	A Fine Romance/You Stepped Out of a Dream//Isn't It Romantic/Love Walked In	195?	15.00
❑ EAP-1-10017 [PS]	Rainy Night in London, Part 1	195?	15.00
ESSEX			
❑ EXP-110	14th Variation/Ecstasy//Veradero/Begorrah	195?	15.00
❑ EXP-110 [PS]	(title unknown)	195?	15.00
Albums			
CAPITOL			
❑ T 10017 [M]	Rainy Night in London	195?	15.00
❑ T 10056 [M]	My London	195?	15.00
❑ T 10066 [M]	International Vibrations	195?	15.00
❑ T 10067 [M]	High Barbaree	195?	15.00
❑ T 10101 [M]	Global Hop	195?	15.00
COLUMBIA			
❑ CL 529 [M]	Pop Concert	1953	25.00
ESSEX			
❑ ESLP-105 [10]	I Love	1954	30.00
IMPERIAL			
❑ LP-9083 [M]	Love of My Life	1959	12.00
❑ LP-9085 [M]	Boots and Saddle	1959	12.00
❑ LP-9087 [M]	Martin Goes Latin	1959	12.00
❑ LP-12018 [S]	Love of My Life	1959	15.00
❑ LP-12020 [S]	Boots and Saddle	1959	15.00
❑ LP-12022 [S]	Martin Goes Latin	1959	15.00
JUBILEE			
❑ JLP-1055 [M]	Witchcraft	1958	15.00
LONDON PHASE 4			
❑ SP-44040 [S]	The Sound of Sight: Music for an Experiment in Imagination	1964	20.00
MONUMENT			
❑ LP8068 [M]	Romance in Vienna	1966	10.00
❑ LP18068 [S]	Romance in Vienna	1966	12.00
RCA CAMDEN			
❑ CAL-913 [M]	Goldfinger and Other Music from James Bond Thrillers	1965	10.00
❑ CAS-913 [S]	Goldfinger and Other Music from James Bond Thrillers	1965	12.00
❑ CAL-927 [M]	Thunderball and Other Thriller Music	1965	10.00
❑ CAS-927 [S]	Thunderball and Other Thriller Music	1965	12.00
❑ CAL-976 [M]	Michelle Going for Baroque	1966	10.00
❑ CAS-976 [S]	Michelle Going for Baroque	1966	12.00
❑ CAL-2102 [M]	Comic Strip Favorites	1967	12.00
❑ CAS-2102 [S]	Comic Strip Favorites	1967	10.00
❑ CAL-2181 [M]	Up-Up and Away	1967	12.00
❑ CAS-2181 [S]	Up-Up and Away	1967	10.00
RCA VICTOR			
❑ LPM-1771 [M]	Pop Goes the Swingin' Marchin' Band	1958	12.00
❑ LSP-1771 [S]	Pop Goes the Swingin' Marchin' Band	1958	20.00
❑ LPM-2130 [M]	The Rockin' Strings of Ray Martin	1959	12.00
❑ LSP-2130 [S]	The Rockin' Strings of Ray Martin	1959	15.00
❑ LPM-2287 [M]	Dynamica	1961	12.00
❑ LSA-2287 [S]	Dynamica	1961	15.00
❑ LPM-2422 [M]	Excitement, Incorporated	1961	12.00
❑ LSA-2422 [S]	Excitement, Incorporated	1961	15.00
STRAND			
❑ SL-1037 [M]	Dancing After Dark	1962	12.00

MARTIN, TONY

Number	Title (A Side/B Side)	Yr	NM
45s			
CHART			
❑ 5059	Hills of Yesterday/Strangers	1970	6.00
❑ 5078	Coast of California/Inseparable	1970	8.00
DOT			
❑ 16361	In Other Words (Fly Me to the Moon)/The Rest of My Days	1961	8.00
❑ 16402	As Long As She Needs Me/I'll Be Seeing You	1962	8.00
❑ 16917	Alfie/Who's Afraid	1966	7.00
DUNHILL			
❑ 4073	And We Were Lovers/This Year	1967	7.00
MERCURY			
❑ 5489x45	That Old Black Magic/Tea for Two	1950	20.00
❑ 5708x45	If I Love Again/Make Believe	1951	15.00
❑ C-30022	To Each His Own/I'll See You in My Dreams	195?	8.00
—"Celebrity Series" reissue			
MOTOWN			
❑ 1071	Talkin' to Your Picture/Our Rhapsody	1964	60.00
❑ 1082	The Bigger Your Heart Is (The Harder You'll Fall)/Two of Us	1965	20.00
❑ 1088	Ask Any Man/Spanish Rose	1966	40.00
NAN			
❑ 3002	Sellisima/Winter Sun	1964	10.00
PARK AVENUE			
❑ 129	Broadway Broken Heart/Footsteps of a Fool	1963	10.00
RCA VICTOR			
❑ 47-2787	Goodnight, Sweetheart/You and the Night and the Music	1949	15.00
❑ 47-2788	Oh, How I Miss You Tonight/Deep Night	1949	15.00
❑ 47-2789	Night and Day/The Night Was Made for Love	1949	15.00
❑ 47-2790	All Through the Night/Blue Is the Night	1949	15.00
—The above four comprise a box set			
❑ 47-2918	Angels Never Leave Heaven/My Heart Beats Faster	1949	20.00
❑ 47-2947	Circus/No, No and No	1949	20.00
❑ 47-3024	Give Me Your Tired, Your Poor/If We Hadn't Broken Up on Wednesday Night, Thursday Would Have Been a Year	1949	20.00
❑ 47-3049	Toot, Toot, Tootsie, Goodbye/You Call It Madness, I Call It Love	1949	20.00
❑ 47-3054	Oh You Beautiful Doll/I Want You to Want Me (To Want You)	1949	15.00
❑ 47-3055	When I Get You Alone Tonight/Peg o' My Heart	1949	15.00
❑ 47-3056	Come, Josephine, in My Flying Machine/There's a Broken Heart for Every Light on Broadway	1949	15.00
—The above three comprise a box set			
❑ 47-3069	Remember/Speak the Word of Love	1949	20.00
—With Fran Warren			
❑ 47-3078	There's No Tomorrow/A Thousand Violins	1949	20.00
❑ 47-3119	I Said My Pajamas (And Put On My Pray'rs)/Have I Told You Lately That I Love You	1949	20.00
—With Fran Warren			
❑ 47-3219	Roulette/It's Easy for You to Say	1950	20.00
❑ 47-3228	My Sin/Begin the Beguine	1950	20.00
❑ 47-3243	Darn It Baby, That's Love/That "We" Is Me and You	1950	20.00
—With Fran Warren			
❑ 47-3254	All Through the Night/Blues in the Night	1950	20.00
❑ 47-3755	Valencia/I Don't Care If the Sun Don't Shine	1950	20.00
❑ 47-3756	The Thrill Is Gone/Spring Made a Fool of Me	1950	20.00
❑ 47-3777	An Ordinary Broom/I Theenk	1950	20.00
—With Fran Warren			
❑ 47-3799	Peace of Mind/I Still Get a Thrill	1950	20.00
❑ 47-3802	Ramona/Laura	1950	15.00
❑ 47-3803	Dolores/Rosalie	1950	15.00
❑ 47-3804	Sweet Sue/Dinah	1950	15.00
—The above three comprise a box set			
❑ 47-3819	La Vie En Rose/Tonight	1950	20.00
❑ 47-3874	Till We Meet Again/Take a Letter, Miss Smith	1950	20.00
❑ 47-3883	Music, Maestro, Please/The Big Dipper	1950	20.00
❑ 47-3941	Fascination/Johannesburg	1950	20.00
❑ 47-3972	Once Upon a Rhumba/Tambarina	1950	20.00
❑ 47-3987	Tell Me Tonight/The Sea of the Moon	1950	20.00
❑ 47-4019	A Penny a Kiss/In Your Arms	1951	20.00
—With Dinah Shore			
❑ 47-4048	Singin' in the Rain/Pagan Love Song	1951	15.00
❑ 47-4049	I Cried for You/You Are My Lucky Star	1951	15.00
❑ 47-4050	You Were Meant for Me/It Was So Beautiful	1951	15.00
—The above three comprise a box set			
❑ 47-4056	Would I Love You (Love You, Love You)/I Apologize	1951	20.00
❑ 47-4098	Faithfully Yours/No One But You	1951	20.00
❑ 47-4136	I Wish, I Wish/The Kissing Song	1951	15.00
—With Dinah Shore			
❑ 47-4141	I Get Ideas/Tahiti, My Island	1951	15.00
❑ 47-4169	Tell Me/Do You Really Love Me	1951	15.00
❑ 47-4216	Casey at the Bat/Take Me Out to the Ball Game	1951	20.00
❑ 47-4220	Over a Bottle of Wine/You'll Know	1951	15.00
❑ 47-4225	The Musicians/How D'Ya Do and Shake Hands	1951	20.00
—With Phil Harris, Dinah Shore and Betty Hutton			
❑ 47-4246	Vanity/Oh! Beauty!	1951	15.00
❑ 47-4268	Old Soft Shoe/Be Mine Tonight	1951	15.00
—With Dinah Shore			
❑ 47-4276	You Are Just a Beautiful Dream/The Closer You Are	1951	12.00
❑ 47-4277	Big Chief Hole in the Ground/Let the Worry Bird Worry for You	1951	12.00
❑ 47-4278	There's No Tomorrow/Prologue from "Pagliacci"	1951	12.00
—The above three comprise a box set			
❑ 47-4343	Domino/It's All Over But the Memories	1951	15.00
❑ 47-4345	Manhattan/If You Catch a Little Cold	1951	15.00
—With Dinah Shore			
❑ 47-4477	At Last, At Last/Make with the Magic	1952	15.00
❑ 47-4488	The Closer You Are/Prologue from "Pagliacci"	1952	15.00
❑ 47-4544	I Could Write a Book/Jump Through the Ring	1952	15.00
❑ 47-4671	Kiss of Fire/For the Very First Time	1952	15.00
❑ 47-4718	No Other Girl for Me/If Someone Had Told Me	1952	12.00
—With Dinah Shore			
❑ 47-4758	Padam, Padam/Where Did the Night Go	1952	15.00
❑ 47-4836	Some Day/Luna Rossa (Blushing Moon)	1952	15.00
❑ 47-4944	Forgive and Forget/Don't Tempt Me	1952	15.00
❑ 47-5008	Dance of Destiny/Sleepy Time Gal	1952	15.00
❑ 47-5116	You're So Dangerous/The Ghost of a Rose	1953	15.00
❑ 47-5208	Please, Please/Golden Years	1953	15.00
❑ 47-5279	April in Portugal (The Whisp'ring Serenade)/Now Hear This	1953	15.00
❑ 47-5352	Sorta on the Border/Unfair	1953	15.00
❑ 47-5414	Caribbean/Relax	1953	15.00
❑ 47-5473	There's Danger in Your Eyes, Cherie/I Just Love You	1953	15.00
❑ 47-5538	Stranger in Paradise/I Love Paris	1953	12.00
❑ 47-5596	That's What a Rainy Day Is For/Look Out, I'm Romantic	1954	12.00
❑ 47-5665	Here/Philosophy	1954	12.00
❑ 47-5757	Boulevard of Nightingales/Angels in the Sky	1954	12.00
❑ 47-5841	Uno/Let's Try Again	1954	12.00
❑ 47-5907	My Bambino/Restless Heart	1954	12.00
❑ 47-5946	All of You/Vera Cruz	1954	12.00
❑ 47-5975	Melody of Love/You're Getting to Be a Habit with Me	1955	10.00
—With Dinah Shore			
❑ 47-6039	Just a Man/Do, Do, Do What Your Heart Says	1955	10.00
❑ 47-6167	Domani/What's the Time in Nicaragua	1955	10.00
❑ 47-6209	Young Ideas/What's the Secret of Your Success	1955	10.00
❑ 47-6283	Hold Me in Your Heart/Everywhere	1955	10.00
❑ 47-6368	Just a Gigolo/Love, You Funny Thing	1955	10.00
❑ 47-6493	Walk Hand in Hand/Flamenco Love	1956	10.00
❑ 47-6597	It's Better in the Dark/Your Place in the Sun	1956	10.00
❑ 47-6682	Moderation/Since You've Been Mine	1956	10.00
❑ 47-6731	This Much I Know/Lonely Winter	1956	10.00
❑ 47-6797	My Budapest/The Rainmaker	1957	10.00
❑ 47-6863	Do I Love You (Because You're Beautiful)/Ten Minutes Ago	1957	10.00
❑ 47-6888	Mail, Mail, There Ain't No Mail/Look at 'Er	1957	10.00
❑ 47-7007	At Last/Scusami	1957	10.00
❑ 47-7099	Carioca/Souvenir d'Italie	1957	10.00
❑ 47-7170	Gigi/Noche de Amour	1958	10.00
❑ 47-7210	Say Darling/Try to Love Me Just As I Am	1958	10.00
❑ 47-7298	Walk with Me/Indiscreet	1958	10.00
❑ 47-7376	Lolita/She Serves a Nice Cup of Tea	1958	10.00
❑ 47-7494	Do You Remember As I Remember/Lilly Lu	1959	10.00
❑ 47-7633	Marina/I'll Take Romance	1959	10.00
❑ 47-7728	My Sin/Once When the World Was Mine	1960	10.00

Except when noted otherwise, VG = 25% of NM, and VG+ = 50% of NM. (Example: VG = $2.00, VG+ = $4.00 and NM = $8.00.)

Number	Title (A Side/B Side)	Yr	NM
7-Inch Extended Plays			
RCA CAMDEN			
❑ CAE-444	*I Get Ideas/I Cried for You/Kiss of Fire/Toot, Toot, Tootsie, Goodbye	195?	10.00
❑ CAE-444 [PS]	I Get Ideas	195?	10.00
Albums			
APPLAUSE			
❑ APLP-1003	I'll See You in My Dreams	1982	10.00
❑ R 134276	I'll See You in My Dreams	1982	12.00
—RCA Music Service edition			
AUDIO FIDELITY			
❑ AFSD-6200	Tony Martin	1968	15.00
CHART			
❑ CHS-1029	Tony Martin in Nashville	1970	20.00
DECCA			
❑ DL 5189 [10]	Tony Martin Sings, Vol. 1	1950	40.00
❑ DL 8286 [M]	Melody Lane	195?	25.00
—Black label, silver print			
DOT			
❑ DLP-3360 [M]	His Greatest Hits	1961	15.00
❑ DLP-25360 [S]	His Greatest Hits	1961	20.00
KOALA			
❑ KO 14140	I'm Always Chasing Rainbows	198?	12.00
MCA			
❑ 1515 [M]	Tony Martin Collectibles	198?	12.00
MCA CORAL			
❑ CB-20019	Melody	1973	12.00
MERCURY			
❑ MG-20075 [M]	Mr. Song Man	195?	25.00
❑ MG-20079 [M]	Dream Music	195?	25.00
❑ MG-20644 [M]	Golden Hits by Tony Martin	1961	15.00
❑ MG-25004 [10]	Tony Martin	1950	40.00
❑ MG-60644 [S]	Golden Hits by Tony Martin	1961	15.00
MOTOWN			
❑ MS-645 [S]	Live! At the Americana	1966	—
—Canceled			
❑ MT-645 [M]	Live! At the Americana	1966	—
—Canceled			
MOVIETONE			
❑ MTM-1007 [M]	Live at Carnegie Hall	196?	10.00
—Reissue of 20th Century Fox 3138			
❑ MTS-2007 [S]	Live at Carnegie Hall	196?	12.00
—Reissue of 20th Century Fox 4138			
RCA CAMDEN			
❑ CAL-412 [M]	I Get Ideas	195?	15.00
❑ CAL-484 [M]	Tony Martin Sings of Love	195?	15.00
❑ CAL-576 [M]	Tonight	195?	15.00
RCA SPECIAL PRODUCTS			
❑ DML2-0999 [(2)]	The Greatest Singer of Them All!	1991	15.00
RCA VICTOR			
❑ LPM-1218 [M]	The Night Was Made for Love	1956	25.00
❑ LPM-1263 [M]	Speak to Me of Love	1956	25.00
❑ LPM-1357 [M]	A Night at the Copacabana with Tony Martin	1956	25.00
❑ LPM-2107 [M]	Dream a Little Dream	1960	20.00
❑ LSP-2107 [S]	Dream a Little Dream	1960	30.00
❑ LPM-3126 [10]	World-Wide Favorites	195?	40.00
❑ LPM-3136 [10]	One for My Baby	195?	40.00
20TH CENTURY FOX			
❑ TFM-3138 [M]	Live at Carnegie Hall	1964	12.00
❑ TFS-4138 [S]	Live at Carnegie Hall	1964	15.00
VOCALION			
❑ VL 3610 [M]	Tony Martin	196?	15.00
WING			
❑ MGW-12115 [M]	It's Just Love	196?	12.00
❑ MGW-12203 [M]	Mr. Song Man	196?	12.00

MARTIN, TRADE

Number	Title (A Side/B Side)	Yr	NM
45s			
BUDDAH			
❑ 266	I Can't Do It for You/To Know the Girl	1971	10.00
COED			
❑ 570	That Stranger Used to Be My Girl/We'll Be Dancing on the Moon	1962	15.00
❑ 573	Hula Hula Dancin' Doll/Something in the Wind	1962	25.00
❑ 575	Lucky Boy, Happy Girl, Lonely Me/Strategy	1963	15.00
❑ 579	Hot Diggity/Loveability	1963	15.00
❑ 590	Send for Me/Spend Your Life with Me	1964	15.00
❑ 596	Joanne/Liverpool Baby	1964	60.00
GEE			
❑ 1053	La Mer/Loving You	1959	20.00
RCA VICTOR			
❑ 47-8926	Work Song/So This Is Love	1966	50.00
❑ 47-9112	Take Me for a Little While/Moanin'	1967	50.00
❑ 47-9210	Sixteen Tons/She's Got the Wind in Her Hair	1967	25.00
ROULETTE			
❑ 4258	My Song of Love/Pomp and Circumstance	1960	15.00
STALLION			
❑ 1003	She Put the Hurt on Me/Son of a Millionaire	196?	300.00
TOOT			
❑ 606	If I Were a Rich Man/(B-side unknown)	1968	10.00
❑ 610	I Couldn't Make You Love Me (The Way That You Loved Him)/You're the Cause of It	1968	10.00
Albums			
BUDDAH			
❑ BDS-5126	Let Me Touch You	1972	15.00

MARTIN, VINCE

Number	Title (A Side/B Side)	Yr	NM
45s			
ABC-PARAMOUNT			
❑ 9992	Goodnight Irene/The Old Grey Goose	1959	12.00
❑ 10029	Strawberry Fair/Homing Pigeon	1959	12.00
CAPITOL			
❑ 2565	Summer Wind/I Can't Escape from You	1969	6.00
GLORY			
❑ 247	Cindy, Oh Cindy/Only If You Praise the Lord	1956	20.00
—With the Tarriers			
❑ 252	Katie-O/1-2-3-4 Anyplace Road	1957	15.00
❑ 259	Big Dreams/Wait for Me	1957	15.00
❑ 262	The Midnight Special/Ginny My Joy	1957	15.00
❑ 266	Goodbye My Love/Oh My Darling, Oh	1957	15.00
❑ 283	Keep a-Movin'/Sail Me Back	1958	15.00
20TH FOX			
❑ 214	The Sea Is Green/Is There Somebody Somewhere	1960	12.00

MARTIN, VINCE, AND FRED NEIL

Number	Title (A Side/B Side)	Yr	NM
45s			
ELEKTRA			
❑ 45009	Tear Down the Walls/I Know You Rider	1964	10.00
Albums			
ELEKTRA			
❑ EKL-248 [M]	Tear Down the Walls	1964	50.00
❑ EKS-7248 [S]	Tear Down the Walls	1964	60.00

MARTIN, WOODY

Number	Title (A Side/B Side)	Yr	NM
45s			
HIT			
❑ 48	My Dad/Shake Me I Rattle	1962	8.00
—B-side by Connie Landers			

MARTINDALE, WINK

Number	Title (A Side/B Side)	Yr	NM
45s			
ABC DOT			
❑ 17606	Deck of Cards/Black Land Farmer	1976	5.00
DOT			
❑ 15728	I Don't Suppose/All Love Broke Loose	1958	12.00
❑ 15968	Deck of Cards/Now You Know How It Feels	1959	12.00
❑ 15968 [PS]	Deck of Cards/Now You Know How It Feels	1959	25.00
❑ 16020	Life Gets Tee-Jus, Don't It/I Never See Maggie Alone	1959	10.00
❑ 16051	Blue Bobby Sox/Steal Away	1960	10.00
❑ 16083	Lincoln's Gettysburg Address/Love's Old Sweet Song	1960	10.00
❑ 16138	Glory of Love/I Wanna Play House	1960	10.00
❑ 16243	Black Land Farmer/Make Him Happy	1961	10.00
❑ 16282	A Man Needs a Woman/Three Steps to the Phone	1961	10.00
❑ 16316	Melody of Love/The Thing	1961	10.00
❑ 16347	The World's Greatest Man/Sweet Little Loveable You	1961	10.00
❑ 16435	A Vision at the Peace Table/I Saw Me	1963	8.00
❑ 16491	Deck of Cards/Black Land Farmer	1963	8.00
❑ 16500	A Violet and a Rose/Next Time	1963	8.00
❑ 16531	I Heard the Bluebirds Sing/Nevertheless	1963	8.00
❑ 16555	The First Kiss/Our Love Affair	1963	8.00
❑ 16597	Why Don't They Understand/Big Buildin'	1964	8.00
❑ 16628	Bom Too Late/Hey Girl, Hey Boy	1964	8.00
❑ 16698	My True Love/A String, an Eraser, and a Blotter	1965	8.00
❑ 16821	Giddy-Up Go/Working Man's Prayer	1966	7.00
❑ 16863	To a Sleeping Beauty/A Vision at the Peace Table	1966	7.00
RANWOOD			
❑ 1005	America: An Affirmation/The People	1974	6.00
Albums			
DOT			
❑ DLP-3245 [M]	Deck of Cards	1960	20.00
❑ DLP-3293 [M]	The Bible Story	1960	15.00
❑ DLP-3403 [M]	Big Bad John	1962	15.00
❑ DLP-3571 [M]	My True Love	1964	15.00
❑ DLP-3692 [M]	Giddyup Go	1966	15.00
❑ DLP-25245 [S]	Deck of Cards	1960	25.00
❑ DLP-25293 [S]	The Bible Story	1960	20.00
❑ DLP-25403 [S]	Big Bad John	1962	20.00
❑ DLP-25571 [S]	My True Love	1964	20.00
❑ DLP-25692 [S]	Giddyup Go	1966	20.00

MARTINEZ, TONY

Number	Title (A Side/B Side)	Yr	NM
Albums			
DEL-FI			
❑ DFLP-1205 [M]	The Many Sides of Pepino	1959	30.00
❑ DFLP-1205S [S]	The Many Sides of Pepino	1959	40.00

MARTINI, LUIGI, AND THE BAY CITY 5

Number	Title (A Side/B Side)	Yr	NM
45s			
JAGUAR			
❑ 3001	Basin Street Blues/Please Don't Talk About Me	1954	300.00
❑ 3002	Oh Marie/I'm Sorry I Made You Cry	1954	300.00

M

MARTINO, AL

Number	Title (A Side/B Side)	Yr	NM
45s			
BBS			
❑ 101	Here in My Heart/I Cried Myself to Sleep	1952	30.00
—With "BBS Records" at top of label			
❑ 101	Here in My Heart/I Cried Myself to Sleep	1952	40.00
—With "BBS Record Co., Phila. 7, Pa." at top of label			
❑ 101	Here in My Heart/I Cried Myself to Sleep	1952	60.00
—Red vinyl			
CAPITOL			
❑ 2053	A Voice in the Choir/The Glory of Love	1967	6.00
❑ 2102	Love Is Blue/I'm Carrying the World on My Shoulders	1968	6.00
❑ F2122	Take My Heart/I Never Cared	1952	20.00
❑ 2158	Lili Marlene/Georgia	1968	6.00
❑ F2185	Say You'll Wait for Me/I've Never Seen	1952	20.00
❑ F2260	Now/In All This World	1952	20.00
❑ 2285	Wake Up to Me Gentle/If You Must Leave My Life	1968	6.00
❑ F2353	One Lonely Night/Rachel	1953	20.00
❑ 2355	I Can't Help It (If I'm Still in Love with You)/I Can Only See You	1968	6.00
❑ F2431	Here Are My Arms/There's Music in You	1953	20.00
❑ 2468	Sausalito/Take My Hand for Awhile	1969	6.00
❑ F2480	This Night I'll Remember/When You're Mine	1953	20.00
❑ F2535	All I Want Is a Chance/You Can't Go On Forever Breaking My Heart	1953	20.00
❑ F2649	Before/Sweetheart of Mine	1953	20.00
❑ 2674	I Started Loving You Again/Let Me Stay Awhile (With You)	1969	6.00
❑ F2737	Melancholy Serenade/Way Paesano	1954	20.00
❑ 2746	Can't Help Falling in Love/You're All the Woman That I Need	1970	5.00
❑ F2826	On and On/Give Me Something to Go with the Wine	1954	20.00
❑ 2830	Walking in the Sand/One More Mile (And Darlin' I'll Be Home)	1970	5.00
❑ F2899	Don't Go to Strangers/When	1954	20.00
❑ 2956	True Love Is Greater Than Friendship/The Call	1970	5.00
❑ F2982	Say It Again/The Story of Tina	1954	20.00
❑ 3056	Come Into My Life/One Pair of Hands	1971	5.00
❑ F3080	Love Is Eternal/Snowy, Snowy Mountains	1955	15.00

Number	Title (A Side/B Side)	Yr	NM
3120	Too Many Mornings/Losing My Mind	1971	5.00
F3171	To Please My Lady/The Man from Laramie	1955	15.00
3256	More Than Ever Now/The Summer Knows	1972	5.00
F3307	Close to Me/The Journey's End	1955	15.00
3313	Speak Softly Love/I Have But One Heart	1972	4.00
3444	Take Me Back/Canta Libre	1972	4.00
F3501	The Girl I Left in Rome/Love to Call My Own	1956	15.00
3604	If I Give My Heart to You/Hey Mama	1973	4.00
F3605	I'm Sorry/I'm a Funny Guy	1956	15.00
3748	Roses in the Sky/Daddy Let's Play	1973	4.00
3763	She/Mary Go Lightly (Como Un Nino)	1973	4.00
3771	Mary Go Lightly (Como Un Nino)/Daddy Let's Play	1973	4.00
3918	Daddy Loves You Honey/More Than Ever Now	1974	4.00
3987	To the Door of the Sun (Alle Porte Del Sol)/Mary Go Lightly	1974	4.00
4071	Charmer/Wake Up	1975	4.00
4134	Volare/You Belong to Me	1975	4.00
4241	The More I See You/My Thrill	1976	4.00
4322	May I Have the Next Dream with You/Sing My Love Song	1976	4.00
4362	Dream of Me/There's Nothing Greater Than Our Love	1976	4.00
4444	Kentucky Mornin'/Sweet Marjorene	1977	4.00
4508	The Next Hundred Years/After the Lovin'	1977	4.00
4551	One Last Time/Here I Go Again	1978	4.00
4593	Here in My Heart/Granada	1961	10.00
4643	Pardon/Another Time, Another Place	1961	10.00
4681	Torero/Now That I Found You	1979	4.00
4710	Exodus/Love, Where Are You Now	1962	10.00
4797	Make Me Believe/Because You're Mine	1962	10.00
4798	I Think About You/Only a Dream Away	1979	4.00
—With Kathy Keates			
4897	Almost Gone/Doors	1980	4.00
4930	I Love You Because/Merry-Go-Round	1963	8.00
4957	Look Around (You'll Find Me There)/More Than Ever Now	1980	4.00
5000	Painted, Tainted Rose/That's the Way It's Got to Be	1963	8.00
5060	Living a Lie/I Love You Truly	1963	8.00
A-5094	You and I/Warm Is When You Touch Me	1982	3.00
5108	I Love You More and More Every Day/I'm Living My Heaven with You	1964	8.00
5183	Tears and Roses/A Year Ago Tonight	1964	8.00
B-5191	What Your Love Did for Me/Warm Is When You Touch Me	1982	3.00
5239	Always Together/Thank You for Loving Me	1964	8.00
5293	We Could/Sunrise to Sunrise	1964	8.00
5311	Silver Bells/You're All I Want for Christmas	1964	8.00
5341	My Heart Would Know/Hush, Hush, Sweet Charlotte	1965	8.00
5341 [PS]	My Heart Would Know/Hush, Hush, Sweet Charlotte	1965	12.00
5384	Somebody Else Is Taking My Place/With All My Heart	1965	8.00
5434	My Cherie/Romana	1965	8.00
5506	Forgive Me/What Now My Love	1965	8.00
5542	Spanish Eyes/Melody of Love	1965	8.00
5598	Think I'll Go Somewhere and Cry Myself to Sleep/Hello Memory	1966	6.00
5652	Wiederseh'n/The Minute You're Gone	1966	6.00
5652 [PS]	Wiederseh'n/The Minute You're Gone	1966	10.00
5702	Just Yesterday/By the River of Roses	1966	6.00
5741	The Wheel of Hurt/Somewhere in This World	1966	6.00
5825	Daddy's Little Girl/Devotion	1967	6.00
5904	Mary in the Morning/I Love You and You Love Me	1967	6.00
5989	More Than the Eye Can See/Red Is Red	1967	6.00

20TH CENTURY FOX

Number	Title (A Side/B Side)	Yr	NM
508	My Side of the Story/It's All Over But the Shouting	1964	8.00
530	I Can't Get You Out of My Heart/Come Back to Me	1964	8.00
575	Mama/My Bella Amore	1965	8.00

20TH FOX

Number	Title (A Side/B Side)	Yr	NM
132	I Can't Get You Out of My Heart/Two Hearts Are Better Than One	1959	12.00
153	Darling, I Love You/Memory of You	1959	12.00
173	I Sold My Heart/Summertime	1960	12.00
180	Mama/And I Have You My Love	1960	12.00
184	Dearest (Cara)/Hello My Love	1960	12.00
200	Journey to Love/Only the Broken Hearted	1960	12.00
213	Heart of Hearts/Our Concerto	1960	12.00
232	Come Back to Me/It's All Over But the Shouting	1960	12.00
237	Little Boy, Little Girl/My Side of the Story	1961	12.00

7-Inch Extended Plays

CAPITOL

Number	Title (A Side/B Side)	Yr	NM
EAP 1-405	*Take My Heart/I've Never Seen/Say You'll Wait for Me/Now	195?	15.00
EAP 1-405 [PS]	Al Martino Sings	195?	15.00

Albums

CAPITOL

Number	Title (A Side/B Side)	Yr	NM
ST-180	Sausalito	1969	12.00
ST-379	Jean	1969	12.00
ST-405	Can't Help Falling in Love	1970	12.00
ST-497	My Heart Sings	1970	12.00
STBB-526 [(2)]	Here in My Heart/Yesterday	1970	15.00
STCL-572 [(3)]	Al Martino	1971	25.00
STBB-713 [(2)]	I Wish You Love/Losing You	1971	15.00
ST-793	Summer of '42	1971	12.00
ST 1774 [S]	The Exciting Voice of Al Martino	1962	20.00
T 1774 [M]	The Exciting Voice of Al Martino	1962	15.00
ST 1907 [S]	The Italian Voice of Al Martino	1963	20.00
T 1907 [M]	The Italian Voice of Al Martino	1963	15.00
ST 1914 [S]	I Love You Because	1963	15.00
T 1914 [M]	I Love You Because	1963	12.00
ST 1975 [S]	Painted, Tainted Rose	1963	15.00
T 1975 [M]	Painted, Tainted Rose	1963	12.00
ST 2040 [S]	Living a Lie	1964	15.00
T 2040 [M]	Living a Lie	1964	12.00
ST 2107 [S]	I Love You More and More Every Day/Tears and Roses	1964	15.00
T 2107 [M]	I Love You More and More Every Day/Tears and Roses	1964	12.00
ST 2165 [S]	A Merry Christmas from Al Martino	1964	15.00
T 2165 [M]	A Merry Christmas from Al Martino	1964	12.00
ST 2200 [S]	We Could	1964	15.00
T 2200 [M]	We Could	1964	12.00
ST 2312 [S]	Somebody Else Is Taking My Place	1965	15.00
T 2312 [M]	Somebody Else Is Taking My Place	1965	12.00
ST 2362 [S]	My Cherie	1965	15.00
T 2362 [M]	My Cherie	1965	12.00
ST 2435 [S]	Spanish Eyes	1966	15.00
T 2435 [M]	Spanish Eyes	1966	12.00
ST 2528 [S]	Think I'll Go Somewhere and Cry Myself to Sleep	1966	15.00
T 2528 [M]	Think I'll Go Somewhere and Cry Myself to Sleep	1966	12.00
ST 2592 [S]	This Is Love	1966	15.00
T 2592 [M]	This Is Love	1966	12.00
ST 2654 [S]	This Love for You	1967	15.00
T 2654 [M]	This Love for You	1967	15.00
ST 2733 [S]	Daddy's Little Girl	1967	15.00
T 2733 [M]	Daddy's Little Girl	1967	15.00
ST 2780 [S]	Mary in the Morning	1967	15.00
T 2780 [M]	Mary in the Morning	1967	15.00
ST 2843	This Is Al Martino	1968	15.00
ST 2908	Love Is Blue	1968	15.00
SKAO 2946	The Best of Al Martino	1968	15.00
SM-2946	The Best of Al Martino	197?	10.00
—Reissue with new prefix			
ST 2983	Wake Up to Me Gentle	1968	15.00
SM-11071	Love Theme from "The Godfather"	1977	8.00
—Reissue with new prefix			
ST-11071	Love Theme from "The Godfather"	1972	10.00
ST-11302	I Won't Last a Day Without You	1974	10.00
ST-11366	To the Door of the Sun	1975	10.00
ST-11572	Sing My Love Songs	1976	10.00
SM-11679	To the Door of the Sun	1977	8.00
—Reissue of 11366			
ST-11741	The Next Hundred Years	1978	10.00
SN-16074	The Best of Al Martino	1981	8.00
—Budget-line reissue			
SQBO-91280 [(2)]	The Romantic World of Al Martino	196?	20.00
—Capitol Record Club exclusive			

MOVIETONE

Number	Title (A Side/B Side)	Yr	NM
MTM 2002 [M]	That Old Feeling	196?	15.00
MTM 2015 [M]	All of Me	1967	20.00
MTS 72002 [S]	That Old Feeling	196?	20.00
MTS 72015 [S]	All of Me	1967	15.00

PICKWICK

Number	Title (A Side/B Side)	Yr	NM
SPC-3049	Don't Go to Strangers	196?	12.00
SPC-3276	Mary in the Morning	197?	10.00

SPRINGBOARD

Number	Title (A Side/B Side)	Yr	NM
4074	Time After Time	1978	8.00

20TH CENTURY FOX

Number	Title (A Side/B Side)	Yr	NM
SF-3025 [M]	Al Martino	1959	25.00
SFX-3025 [S]	Al Martino	1959	30.00
SF-3032 [M]	Sing Along with Al Martino	1959	25.00
SFX-3032 [S]	Sing Along with Al Martino	1959	30.00
TF-4168 [M]	Al Martino Sings	196?	20.00
TFS-4168 [S]	Al Martino Sings	196?	25.00
SXG-5009 [S]	When Your Lover Has Gone	1963	25.00
XG-5009 [M]	When Your Lover Has Gone	1963	20.00

MARTY

45s

NOVELTY

Number	Title (A Side/B Side)	Yr	NM
101	Marty on Planet Mars (Part 1)/Marty on Planet Mars (Part 2)	1956	40.00

MARTY AND THE SYMBOLS

45s

GRAPHIC ARTS

Number	Title (A Side/B Side)	Yr	NM
1000	You're the One/Rip Van Winkle	1963	80.00

MARVELETTES, THE

45s

A&M

Number	Title (A Side/B Side)	Yr	NM
1201	Danger Heartbreak Dead Ahead/Baby Please Don't Go	1988	4.00
—B-side by Them			
1201 [PS]	Danger Heartbreak Dead Ahead/Baby Please Don't Go	1988	4.00
—"Good Morning Vietnam" sleeve			

GORDY

Number	Title (A Side/B Side)	Yr	NM
7024	Too Hurt to Cry, Too Much in Love to Say Goodbye/Come On Home	1963	80.00
—As "The Darnells"			

TAMLA

Number	Title (A Side/B Side)	Yr	NM
54046	Please Mr. Postman/So Long Baby	1961	25.00
54046 [PS]	Please Mr. Postman/So Long Baby	1961	120.00
54054	Twistin' Postman/I Want a Guy	1962	20.00
54054 [PS]	Twistin' Postman/I Want a Guy	1962	100.00
54060	Playboy/All the Love I've Got	1962	20.00
54065	Beechwood 4-5789/Someday, Someway	1962	20.00
54072	Strange I Know/Too Strong to Be Strung Along	1962	15.00
54077	Forever/Locking Up My Heart	1963	15.00
54082	Tie a String Around My Finger/My Daddy Knows Best	1963	20.00
54088	As Long As I Know He's Mine/Little Girl Blue	1963	12.00
54091	He's a Good Guy (Yes He Is)/Goddess of Love	1964	12.00
54091 [DJ]	Yes He Is	1964	75.00
—One-sided promo with different title than stock copy			
54097	You're My Remedy/A Little Bit of Sympathy, A Little Bit of Love	1964	10.00
54097 [PS]	You're My Remedy/A Little Bit of Sympathy, A Little Bit of Love	1964	60.00
54105	Too Many Fish in the Sea/A Need for Love	1964	10.00
54105	Two Many Fish in the Sea/A Need for Love	1964	40.00
—Some copies feature the above incorrect A-side title			
54116	I'll Keep Holding On/No Time for Tears	1965	10.00
54120	Danger, Heartbreak Dead Ahead/Your Cheating Ways	1965	10.00
54126	Don't Mess with Bill/Anything You Wanna Do	1965	10.00
54131	You're the One/Paper Boy	1966	10.00
54143	The Hunter Gets Captured by the Game/I Think I Can Change You	1967	10.00
54150	When You're Young and In Love/The Day You Take One, You Have to Take the Other	1967	10.00
54158	My Baby Must Be a Magician/I Need Someone	1967	10.00

Number	Title (A Side/B Side)	Yr	NM
❑ 54166	Here I Am Baby/Keep Off, No Trespassing	1968	10.00
❑ 54171	Destination: Anywhere/What's So Easy for Two Is So Hard for One	1968	10.00
❑ 54177	I'm Gonna Hold On Long As I Can/Don't Make Hurting Me a Habit	1968	10.00
❑ 54186	That's How Heartaches Are Made/Rainy Mourning	1969	10.00
❑ 54198	Marionette/After All	1970	8.00
❑ 54213	A Breath Taking Guy/You're the One for Me Baby	1972	8.00

TOPPS/MOTOWN

Number	Title (A Side/B Side)	Yr	NM
❑ 12	Please Mr. Postman	1967	75.00

—Cardboard record

7-Inch Extended Plays

TAMLA

Number	Title (A Side/B Side)	Yr	NM
❑ TM-60253	Don't Mess with Bill/Locking Up My Heart/Too Many Fish in the Sea//Please Mr. Postman/Forever/Beechwood 4-5789	1967	40.00

—Stereo jukebox issue; small hole, plays at 33 1/3 rpm

Number	Title (A Side/B Side)	Yr	NM
❑ TM-60253 [PS]	Greatest Hits	1967	40.00
❑ 60274	The Hunter Gets Captured by the Game/When You're Young and In Love/I Know Better//He Was Really Sayin' Somethin'/The Day You Take One/Keep Off, No Trespassing	196?	40.00

—Jukebox issue; small hole, plays at 33 1/3 rpm

Number	Title (A Side/B Side)	Yr	NM
❑ 60274 [PS]	The Marvelettes	196?	40.00

Albums

MOTOWN

Number	Title (A Side/B Side)	Yr	NM
❑ M5-180V1	Greatest Hits	1981	10.00

—Reissue of Tamla 253

Number	Title (A Side/B Side)	Yr	NM
❑ M7-827 [(2)]	Anthology	1975	15.00
❑ 5266 ML	Please Mr. Postman	1982	10.00

—Reissue of Tamla 228

TAMLA

Number	Title (A Side/B Side)	Yr	NM
❑ T-228 [M]	Please Mr. Postman	1961	600.00

—White label

Number	Title (A Side/B Side)	Yr	NM
❑ T-228 [M]	Please Mr. Postman	1963	300.00

—Yellow label with globes logo

Number	Title (A Side/B Side)	Yr	NM
❑ T-229 [M]	The Marveletts Sing	1962	500.00

—Title as listed on front cover (misspelled); all-black cover with white circles

Number	Title (A Side/B Side)	Yr	NM
❑ T-229 [M]	Smash Hits of 62'	1962	1200.

—Title as listed on front cover; large black "M" with song titles in circles; VG value 600; VG+ value 900

Number	Title (A Side/B Side)	Yr	NM
❑ T-229 [M]	The Marveletts Sing	1963	250.00

—Yellow label with side-by-side globes logo

Number	Title (A Side/B Side)	Yr	NM
❑ T-231 [M]	Playboy	1962	500.00

—Yellow label with overlapping record and globe logo

Number	Title (A Side/B Side)	Yr	NM
❑ T-231 [M]	Playboy	1962	600.00

—White label

Number	Title (A Side/B Side)	Yr	NM
❑ T-231 [M]	Playboy	1963	250.00

—Yellow label with side-by-side globes logo

Number	Title (A Side/B Side)	Yr	NM
❑ T-237 [M]	The Marvelous Marvelettes	1963	150.00
❑ T-243 [M]	Recorded Live on Stage	1963	80.00
❑ T-253 [M]	Greatest Hits	1966	30.00

—Yellow cover

Number	Title (A Side/B Side)	Yr	NM
❑ T-253 [M]	Greatest Hits	1967	25.00

—Green cover

Number	Title (A Side/B Side)	Yr	NM
❑ TS-253 [S]	Greatest Hits	1966	40.00

—Yellow cover

Number	Title (A Side/B Side)	Yr	NM
❑ TS-253 [S]	Greatest Hits	1967	20.00

—Green cover

Number	Title (A Side/B Side)	Yr	NM
❑ T-274 [M]	The Marvelettes	1967	30.00
❑ TS-274 [S]	The Marvelettes	1967	20.00
❑ T-286 [M]	Sophisticated Soul	1968	40.00
❑ TS-286 [S]	Sophisticated Soul	1968	20.00
❑ TS-288	In Full Bloom	1969	15.00
❑ TS-305	Return of the Marvelettes	1970	15.00

MARVELLOS, THE (1)

45s

CHA CHA

Number	Title (A Side/B Side)	Yr	NM
❑ 756	Come Back My Love/Boyee Yoing	1963	30.00

STEPHENY

Number	Title (A Side/B Side)	Yr	NM
❑ 1818	Come Back My Love/Boyee Yoing	1958	200.00

MARVELLOS, THE (2)

45s

EXODUS

Number	Title (A Side/B Side)	Yr	NM
❑ 6214	Salty Sam/She Told Me Lies	1962	200.00
❑ 6216	I Ask of You/Hip Enough	1962	120.00

REPRISE

Number	Title (A Side/B Side)	Yr	NM
❑ 20088	Salty Sam/She Told Me Lies	1962	30.00

MARVELLOS, THE (3)

45s

LOMA

Number	Title (A Side/B Side)	Yr	NM
❑ 2045	Something's Burning/We Go Together	1966	150.00
❑ 2061	You're Such a Sweet Thing/Why Do You Want to Hurt the One You Love	1966	40.00

MODERN

Number	Title (A Side/B Side)	Yr	NM
❑ 1054	Down in the City/In the Sunshine	1967	30.00

WARNER BROS.

Number	Title (A Side/B Side)	Yr	NM
❑ 7011	Don't Play with My Heart/Let Me Keep You Satisfied	1967	40.00
❑ 7054	Piece of Silk/Yes I Do	1967	50.00

MARVELLOS, THE (U)

Could be group (1); it's doubtful that these could be either of the other two.

45s

MARVELLO

Number	Title (A Side/B Side)	Yr	NM
❑ 5005	Red Hot Momma/I Need a Girl	1955	300.00

THERON

Number	Title (A Side/B Side)	Yr	NM
❑ 117	You're the Dream/Calypso Mama	1957	400.00

MARVELOWS, THE

45s

ABC

Number	Title (A Side/B Side)	Yr	NM
❑ 10820	Fade Away/You've Been Going to Sally	1966	40.00
❑ 11011	In the Morning/Talkin' 'Bout Ya, Baby	1967	40.00

—As "The Mighty Marvelows"

Number	Title (A Side/B Side)	Yr	NM
❑ 11073	I'm So Confused/I'm Without a Girl	1968	40.00

—As "The Mighty Marvelows"

Number	Title (A Side/B Side)	Yr	NM
❑ 11139	Hey, Hey Girl/Wait, Be Cool	1968	30.00

—As "The Mighty Marvelows"

Number	Title (A Side/B Side)	Yr	NM
❑ 11189	You're Breaking My Heart/This Town's Too Much	1969	40.00

—As "The Mighty Marvelows"

ABC-PARAMOUNT

Number	Title (A Side/B Side)	Yr	NM
❑ 10613	A Friend/Hey, Hey Baby	1965	10.00
❑ 10629	I Do/My Heart	1965	15.00
❑ 10708	Shim Sham/Your Little Sister	1965	10.00
❑ 10756	Do It/I've Got My Eyes on You	1965	10.00

Albums

ABC

Number	Title (A Side/B Side)	Yr	NM
❑ S-643	The Mighty Marvelows	1968	30.00

MARVELS, THE (1)

Early version of THE DUBS.

45s

ABC-PARAMOUNT

Number	Title (A Side/B Side)	Yr	NM
❑ 9771	I Won't Have You Breaking My Heart/Jump Rock and Roll	1956	600.00

MARVELS, THE (2)

45s

LAURIE

Number	Title (A Side/B Side)	Yr	NM
❑ 3106	I Shed So Many Tears/So Young, So Sweet	1958	70.00

—Also released as "The Marvells"

MARVELS, THE (3)

45s

MUN-RAB

Number	Title (A Side/B Side)	Yr	NM
❑ 1008	Just Another Fool/You Crack Me Up	1959	1500.

MARVELS, THE (U)

May be group (2).

45s

WINN

Number	Title (A Side/B Side)	Yr	NM
❑ 1916	For Sentimental Reasons/Come Back	1961	200.00

MARVIN AND JOHNNY

45s

ALADDIN

Number	Title (A Side/B Side)	Yr	NM
❑ 3371	Yak Yak/Pretty Eyes	1957	30.00
❑ 3408	You're in My Heart/Smack Smack	1958	30.00
❑ 3439	It's Christmas/The Valley of Love	1958	30.00

FELSTED

Number	Title (A Side/B Side)	Yr	NM
❑ 8681	Hot Biscuits and Gravy/Tired of Being Alone	1963	12.00

JAMIE

Number	Title (A Side/B Side)	Yr	NM
❑ 1188	Once Upon a Time/Tick Tock	1961	12.00

LANA

Number	Title (A Side/B Side)	Yr	NM
❑ 127	Cherry Pie/Ain't That Right	196?	10.00

—Oldies reissue

LIBERTY

Number	Title (A Side/B Side)	Yr	NM
❑ 1394	It's Christmas/It's Christmas Time	1980	5.00

—B-side by the Five Keys

MODERN

Number	Title (A Side/B Side)	Yr	NM
❑ 933	Tick Tock/Cherry Pie	1954	75.00
❑ 941	Sugar/Kiss Me	1954	50.00
❑ 946	Little Honey/Honey Girl	1955	50.00
❑ 949	Ko Ko Mo/Sometimes I Wonder	1955	40.00
❑ 952	I Love You, Yes I Do/Baby Won't You Marry Me	1955	40.00
❑ 959	Butler Ball/Sugar Mama	1955	40.00
❑ 968	Will You Love Me/Sweet Dreams	1956	30.00
❑ 974	Ain't That Right/Let Me Know	1956	30.00

SPECIALTY

Number	Title (A Side/B Side)	Yr	NM
❑ 479	Baby Doll/I'm Not a Fool	1953	60.00
❑ 479	Baby Doll/I'm Not a Fool	1953	100.00

—Red vinyl

Number	Title (A Side/B Side)	Yr	NM
❑ 488	Jo Jo/How Long Has She Been Gone	1954	60.00
❑ 498	School of Love/Boy Loves Girl	1954	60.00
❑ 530	Day In — Day Out/Flip	1954	60.00
❑ 554	Ding Dong Baby/Mamo Mamo	1955	50.00

SWINGIN'

Number	Title (A Side/B Side)	Yr	NM
❑ 641	I'm Tired of Being Alone/Baby You Don't Know	1962	12.00
❑ 645	Pretty One/Second Helping of Cherry Pie	1963	12.00

Albums

CROWN

Number	Title (A Side/B Side)	Yr	NM
❑ CST-381 [R]	Marvin and Johnny	1963	12.00
❑ CLP-5381 [M]	Marvin and Johnny	1963	50.00

MARVIN AND THE CHIRPS

45s

TIP TOP

Number	Title (A Side/B Side)	Yr	NM
❑ 202	I'll Miss You This Christmas/Sixteen Tons	1958	200.00

MARX, THE

45s

CHANTE

Number	Title (A Side/B Side)	Yr	NM
❑ 1002	One Minute More/You Are My Love	19??	200.00

DAHLIA

Number	Title (A Side/B Side)	Yr	NM
❑ 1002	One Minute More/You Are My Love	19??	100.00

MARY BUTTERWORTH

Albums

CUSTOM FIDELITY

Number	Title (A Side/B Side)	Yr	NM
❑ 2092	Mary Butterworth	1969	300.00

MARY SUE AND THE TRAMS

45s

HIT

Number	Title (A Side/B Side)	Yr	NM
❑ 145	Dancing in the Street/(I've Got a) Tiger in My Tank	1964	10.00

—B-side by the Jalopy Five

MARYLANDERS, THE

45s

JUBILEE

Number	Title (A Side/B Side)	Yr	NM
❑ 5079	I'm a Sentimental Fool/Sittin' By the River	1952	400.00
❑ 5091	Make Me Thrill Again/Please Love Me	1952	400.00
❑ 5114	Fried Chicken/Good Old 99	1953	300.00
❑ 5114	Fried Chicken/Good Old 99	1953	400.00

—Red vinyl

MASCOTS, THE (1)

45s

ABC

Number	Title (A Side/B Side)	Yr	NM
❑ 11152	Baby, You're So Wrong/Moreen	1968	8.00

MASCOTS, THE (2)

45s

BLAST

Number	Title (A Side/B Side)	Yr	NM
❑ 206	Once Upon a Love/Hey Little Angel	1963	20.00

—White label

Number	Title (A Side/B Side)	Yr	NM
❑ 206	Once Upon a Love/Hey Little Angel	1963	40.00

—Red label

MERMAID

Number	Title (A Side/B Side)	Yr	NM
❑ 107	Bluebirds Over the Mountain/Timberlands	1962	80.00

M

MASCOTS, THE (3)
Later recorded as THE O'JAYS.

45s

Number	Title (A Side/B Side)	Yr	NM
KING			
❑ 5377	The Story of My Heart/Do the Wiggle	1960	100.00
❑ 5435	Lonely Rain/That's the Way I Feel	1960	60.00

MASCOTS, THE (4)

45s

Number	Title (A Side/B Side)	Yr	NM
MGM			
❑ 12027	Relax-Ay-Voo/The Others I Like	1955	20.00
❑ 12107	Nobody's Arms/Little Mustard Seed	1955	20.00
❑ 12236	Who Put the Devil in Evelyn's Eyes/Java Jive	1956	20.00

MASCOTS, THE (U)
If this is any of the above groups, it's most likely group (1).

45s

Number	Title (A Side/B Side)	Yr	NM
RUMBLE			
❑ 4197	I Want Love/Waited So Long	196?	20.00

MASEKELA, HUGH

12-Inch Singles

Number	Title (A Side/B Side)	Yr	NM
JIVE			
❑ 9194	Don't Go Lose It Baby (3 versions)	1984	8.00
❑ 9361	Lady (Remix)/Lady (LP Version)//Coal Train (Live 17:16)	1985	10.00
WARNER BROS.			
❑ 20634	Bring Him Back Home (Extended) (Instrumental)/Serengeti	1987	8.00
❑ 20684	Bring Him Back Home (Extended) (Live)/Stimela (Live)	1987	8.00

45s

Number	Title (A Side/B Side)	Yr	NM
A&M			
❑ 2107	Foreign Natives/Mama Way	1979	4.00
—With Herb Alpert			
BLUE THUMB			
❑ 244	Languta/Rekpete	1973	5.00
❑ 255	Been Such a Long Time Gone/Jungle Jim	1974	4.00
❑ 260	African Secret Society/Jungle Jim	1974	4.00
CASABLANCA			
❑ 848	Excuse Me Please/The Boy's Doin' It	1975	4.00
❑ 857	For the Love of You/Witch Doctor	1976	4.00
❑ 861	A Person Is a Sometime Thing/Mama	1976	4.00
❑ 862	Dance/(B-side unknown)	1976	4.00
❑ 879	Hi-Life/Toejam	1977	4.00
CHISA			
❑ 003	Chisa/What Is Wrong with Groovin'	1970	6.00
❑ 8009	You Keep Me Hangin' On/Make Me a Potion	1971	6.00
❑ 8014	Dyambo/Shebeen	1971	6.00
HORIZON			
❑ 115	Skokiaan/African Summer	1978	4.00
—With Herb Alpert			
❑ 116	Lobo/African Summer	1978	4.00
—With Herb Alpert			
JIVE			
❑ 9198	Don't Go Lose It Baby/(Instrumental)	1984	3.00
❑ 9360	Lady/Cool Train	1985	3.00
MERCURY			
❑ 72853	Emavungwani (Green Home)/U-Dwi (Smallpox)	1968	6.00
MGM			
❑ CS3-5 [DJ]	Celebrity Scene: Hugh Masekela	1966	50.00
—Box set of five singles (13643-13647). Price includes box, all 5 singles, jukebox title strips, bio. Records are sometimes found by themselves, so they are also listed separately.			
❑ 13601	Along Comes Mary/Little Star	1966	6.00
❑ 13643 [DJ]	California Dreamin'/U-Dwi	1966	8.00
❑ 13644 [DJ]	Norwegian Wood/Cantaloupe Island	1966	8.00
❑ 13645 [DJ]	She's Comin' My Way/Unhlanhla	1966	8.00
❑ 13646 [DJ]	Along Comes Mary/Little Star	1966	8.00
❑ 13647 [DJ]	If I Needed Someone/From Me to You	1966	8.00
❑ 13901	Norwegian Wood/Sound of Silence	1968	6.00
UNI			
❑ 55024	Baby, Baby, Baby/Lily the Fox	1967	6.00
❑ 55037	Up-Up and Away/Son of the Ice Bag	1967	6.00
❑ 55049	There Are Seeds to Sow/Ha Lese Le Di Khana	1968	6.00
❑ 55066	Grazing in the Grass/Bajabula Bounce	1968	6.00
❑ 55085	Puffin' On Down the Track/Do Me So Lo, So So	1968	6.00
❑ 55102	Riot/Mace and Grenades	1968	6.00
❑ 55116	A Long Ways from Home/Home Boy	1969	6.00
❑ 55130	10,000 Miles to Memphis/Gettin' It On	1969	6.00
❑ 55165	Where Has All the Grass Grown/I Haven't Slept	1969	6.00
WARNER BROS.			
❑ 28419	Bring Him Back Home/Serengeti	1987	3.00

Albums

Number	Title (A Side/B Side)	Yr	NM
ABC IMPULSE!			
❑ IA-9343 [(2)]	African Connection	1978	12.00
BLUE THUMB			
❑ BT-62	Introducing Hedzoleh Sounds	1972	10.00
❑ BT-6003	Home Is Where the Music Is	1973	10.00
❑ BT-6015	I Am Not Afraid	1974	10.00
CASABLANCA			
❑ NBLP 7017	The Boy's Doin' It	1975	10.00
❑ NBLP 7023	Colonial Man	1976	10.00
❑ NBLP 7036	Melody Maker	1977	10.00
❑ NBLP 7079	You Told Your Mama	1978	10.00
CHISA			
❑ CS-803	Reconstruction	1970	12.00
❑ CS-808	Union of South Africa	1971	12.00
JIVE			
❑ JL-8210	Techno Bush	1984	10.00
❑ JL-8382	Waiting for the Rain	1985	10.00
MERCURY			
❑ MG-20797 [M]	The Trumpet of Hugh Masekela	1963	15.00
❑ SR-60797 [S]	The Trumpet of Hugh Masekela	1963	20.00
❑ SR-61109	Grr	1969	12.00
MGM			
❑ GAS-116	Hugh Masekela (Golden Archive Series)	1970	12.00
❑ E-4372 [M]	The Americanization of Ooga Booga	1966	12.00
❑ SE-4372 [S]	The Americanization of Ooga Booga	1966	15.00
❑ E-4415 [M]	Hugh Masekela's Next Album	1966	12.00
❑ SE-4415 [S]	Hugh Masekela's Next Album	1966	15.00
❑ E-4468 [M]	The Lasting Impression of Hugh Masekela	1967	15.00
❑ SE-4468 [S]	The Lasting Impression of Hugh Masekela	1967	12.00
NOVUS			
❑ 3070-1-R	Uptownship	1990	12.00
UNI			
❑ 3010 [M]	Hugh Masekela's Latest	1967	15.00
❑ 3015 [M]	Hugh Masekela Is Alive and Well at the Whisky	1967	20.00
❑ 73010 [S]	Hugh Masekela's Latest	1967	12.00
❑ 73015 [S]	Hugh Masekela Is Alive and Well at the Whisky	1967	12.00
❑ 73028	The Promise of a Future	1968	12.00
❑ 73041	Masekela	1969	12.00
❑ 73051	Masekela — Vol. 2	1970	12.00
VERVE			
❑ V6-8651 [(2)]	24 Karat Hits	1968	15.00
WARNER BROS.			
❑ 25566	Tomorrow	1987	10.00

MASH, THE

45s

Number	Title (A Side/B Side)	Yr	NM
COLUMBIA			
❑ 45130	Song from M*A*S*H/M*A*S*H March	1970	8.00
—Alternate A-side title			
❑ 45130	Suicide Is Painless/M*A*S*H March	1970	12.00

MASHMAKHAN
Early version of APRIL WINE.

45s

Number	Title (A Side/B Side)	Yr	NM
EPIC			
❑ 10634	As the Years Go By/The Days When We Are Free	1970	6.00
JAMIE			
❑ 1418	One Night Stand/Dance a Little Step	1969	8.00

Albums

Number	Title (A Side/B Side)	Yr	NM
EPIC			
❑ E 30235	Mashmakhan	1970	16.00
❑ E 30813	The Family	1971	16.00

MASKED MARAUDERS, THE
Fictional supergroup from a Rolling Stone magazine album review, which noted the presence of Bob Dylan, Mick Jagger, John Lennon and Paul McCartney. The below, recorded using the bogus review as a guide, was actually THE CLEANLINESS AND GODLINESS SKIFFLE BAND.

45s

Number	Title (A Side/B Side)	Yr	NM
DEITY			
❑ 0870	I Can't Get No Nookie/Cow Pie	1969	15.00

Albums

Number	Title (A Side/B Side)	Yr	NM
DEITY			
❑ RS 6378	The Masked Marauders	1969	15.00

MASON, BARBARA

12-Inch Singles

Number	Title (A Side/B Side)	Yr	NM
WEST END			
❑ 22164	Another Man (Vocal) (Short Version) (Instrumental) (Rap)	1984	20.00
❑ 22171	Don't I Ever Cross Your Mind Sometime (Vocal 4:51) (Instrumental 4:29) (Radio Version 3:39)	1984	15.00
WMOT			
❑ 4W9 02237	Let Me Give You Love (Vocal 6:49) (Instrumental 4:48)	1981	8.00
❑ 4W9 02237	Let Me Give You Love (Vocal 6:49)/She Got the Papers (I Got the Man) (Vocal 7:42)	1981	15.00

45s

Number	Title (A Side/B Side)	Yr	NM
ARCTIC			
❑ 102	Girls Have Feelings Too/Come to Me	1964	40.00
❑ 105	Yes I'm Ready/Keep Him	1965	20.00
❑ 108	Sad, Sad Girl/Come to Me	1965	25.00
❑ 112	You Got What It Takes/If You Don't (Love Me, Tell Me So)	1965	15.00
❑ 116	Don't Ever Want to Lose Your Love/Is It Me	1965	40.00
❑ 120	I Need Love/Bobby Is My Baby	1966	60.00
❑ 126	Hello Baby/Poor Girl in Trouble	1966	15.00
❑ 134	You Can Depend on Me/Game of Love	1967	15.00
❑ 137	Oh, How It Hurts/Ain't Got Nobody	1967	100.00
❑ 140	I Don't Want to Lose You/Dedicated to the One I Love	1968	20.00
❑ 142	Half a Love/(I Can Feel Your Love) Slipping Away	1968	30.00
❑ 146	Don't Ever Go Away/I'm No Good for You	1968	25.00
❑ 148	Take It Easy/You Never Loved Me	1969	20.00
❑ 154	You Better Stop It/Happy Girl	1969	100.00
BUDDAH			
❑ 249	The Pow Pow Song (Sorry Sorry Baby)/Your Old Flame	1971	8.00
❑ 296	Bed and Board/Yes It's You	1972	12.00
❑ 319	Woman and Man/Who Will You Hurt Next	1972	6.00
❑ 331	Give Me Your Love/You Can Be with the One You Don't Love	1972	8.00
❑ 355	Yes I'm Ready/Who Will You Hurt Next	1973	8.00
❑ 375	Child of Tomorrow/Out of This World	1973	8.00
❑ 395	Caught in the Middle/Give Him Up	1973	8.00
❑ 405	World War III/I Miss You Gordon	1974	10.00
❑ 409	The Devil Is Busy/All in Love Is Fair	1974	8.00
❑ 424	Our Day Will Come/Half Sister, Half Brother	1974	10.00
❑ 441	From His Woman to You/When You Wake Up in Georgia	1974	8.00
❑ 459	Shackin' Up/One Man Between Us	1975	10.00
❑ 481	Make It Last/We Got Each Other	1975	50.00
—With the Futures			
❑ 481 [PS]	Make It Last/We Got Each Other	1975	60.00
CRUSADER			
❑ 111	Dedicated to You/Trouble Child	1965	40.00
NATIONAL GENERAL			
❑ 005	Raindrops Keep Fallin' on My Head/If You Knew Him Like I Do	1970	10.00
❑ 012	Just a Little Lovin'/Yes, It's You	1970	15.00
❑ 017	When You Look at Me/I Should Be Leaving You	1971	15.00
❑ 018	I Can't Help It/Jean (Gene)	1971	25.00
PRELUDE			
❑ 71103	I Am Your Woman, She Is Your Wife/Take Me Tonight	1978	6.00
❑ 71111	Darling Come Back Home Soon/It Was You Boy	1978	6.00

Number	Title (A Side/B Side)	Yr	NM
WEST END			
❑ 1264	Another Man (Vocal)/ Another Man (Rap)	1984	5.00
WMOT			
❑ WS9 02506	She's Got the Papers (But I've Got the Man)/(Instrumental)	1981	8.00
❑ 5352	I'll Never Love the Same Way Twice/(B-side unknown)	1980	5.00
❑ 70077	On and Off/You're All Inside of Me	1981	10.00
Albums			
ARCTIC			
❑ ALP-1000 [M]	Yes, I'm Ready	1965	80.00
❑ ALPS-1000 [P]	Yes, I'm Ready	1965	120.00
❑ ALPS-1004	Oh, How It Hurts	1968	80.00
BUDDAH			
❑ BDS-5117	Give Me Your Love	1972	15.00
❑ BDS-5140	Lady Love	1973	20.00
❑ BDS-5610	Transition	1974	20.00
❑ BDS-5628	Love's the Thing	1975	20.00
NATIONAL GENERAL			
❑ 2001	If You Knew Him Like I Do	1970	60.00
PRELUDE			
❑ 12159	I Am Your Woman, She Is Your Wife	1978	20.00

MASON, BARBARA, AND BUNNY SIGLER
Also see each artist's individual listings.

Number	Title (A Side/B Side)	Yr	NM
12-Inch Singles			
CURTOM			
❑ PRO-A-689 [DJ]	Locked in This Position (10:05)/ Love Song (6:14)	1977	20.00
Albums			
CURTOM			
❑ CU 5014	Locked in This Position	1977	15.00

MASON, BONNIE JO See CHER.

MASON, EULIS

Number	Title (A Side/B Side)	Yr	NM
45s			
BELLA			
❑ 20	Carol Lee/Rockin' Santa Claus	1959	40.00

—B-side by the Martels

MASON, JACKIE

Number	Title (A Side/B Side)	Yr	NM
45s			
VERVE			
❑ 10289	Don't Blame the Bossa Nova/ I Gave My Love	1963	12.00
Albums			
VERVE			
❑ V-15033 [M]	I'm the Greatest Comedian in the World Only Nobody Knows It Yet	1962	20.00
❑ V-15034 [M]	I Want to Leave You with the Words of a Great Comedian	1963	20.00
❑ V-15045 [M]	Great Moments in Comedy	1964	20.00
WARNER BROS.			
❑ 25603	The World According to Me!	1987	10.00

MASON PROFFIT

Number	Title (A Side/B Side)	Yr	NM
45s			
AMPEX			
❑ 11048	Hope/Jewel	1971	6.00
HAPPY TIGER			
❑ 545	Voice of Change/ A Rectangle Picture	1970	6.00
❑ 552	Two Hangmen/ Sweet Lady of Love	1970	6.00
❑ 570	Hard Luck Woman/ Good Friend of Mary's	1971	6.00
WARNER BROS.			
❑ 7709	I Saw the Light/Lilly	1973	5.00
Albums			
AMPEX			
❑ A-10138	Last Night I Had the Strangest Dream	1971	30.00
HAPPY TIGER			
❑ HT-1009	Wanted! Mason Proffit	1970	25.00
❑ HT-1019	Movin' Toward Happiness	1971	20.00
WARNER BROS.			
❑ BS 2657	Rockfish Crossing	1972	15.00
❑ BS 2704	Bareback Rider	1973	15.00
❑ 2WS 2746 [(2)]	Come and Gone	1974	20.00

MASONICS, THE

Number	Title (A Side/B Side)	Yr	NM
45s			
INTERPHON			
❑ 7714	Mariner II/Call It a Day	1965	10.00

MASQUERADERS, THE All of these are the same group.

Number	Title (A Side/B Side)	Yr	NM
45s			
ABC/HBS			
❑ 12141	Baby It's You/Listen	1975	10.00
❑ 12157	(Call Me) The Traveling Man/ Sweet Sweetning	1976	10.00
❑ 12190	Your Sweet Love Is a Blessing/ Please Don't Try (To Take Me Away to the Sky)	1976	15.00
AGP			
❑ 108	I'm Just an Average Guy/ I Ain't Gonna Stop	1969	30.00
❑ 114	Say It/The Grass Was Green	1969	15.00
❑ 122	Love, Peace and Understanding/Tell Me You Love Me	1969	12.00
BANG			
❑ ZS9 4806	Desire/Into Your Soul	1980	10.00
❑ ZS9 4812	Starry Love/(B-side unknown)	1980	7.00
BELL			
❑ 733	I Ain't Got to Love Nobody Else/ I Got It	1968	25.00
❑ 874	How Big Is Big/Please Take Me Back	1970	200.00
❑ 932	Brotherhood/Steamroller	1970	30.00
HI			
❑ 2251	Let the Love Bells Ring/ Now That I Found You	1973	20.00
❑ 2264	Wake Up Fool/Now That I've Found You	1974	20.00
LA BEAT			
❑ 6605	A Family (Part 1)/(Part 2)	1966	25.00
❑ 6606	I'm Gonna Make It/How	1966	1200.
❑ 6701	Be Happy for Me/(Instrumental)	1967	150.00
❑ 6702	One More Chance/Together That's the Only Way	1967	300.00
❑ 6704	I Got the Power/Together That's the Only Way	1967	300.00
MK			
❑ 101	Man's Temptation/Dancing Doll	196?	1000.
SOULTOWN			
❑ 201	That's the Same Thing/ Talk About a Woman	1965	750.00
—As "The Masquaders"			
STAIRWAY			
❑ 71A	Let Me Show the World I Love You/Masqueraders' Theme	1971	150.00
❑ 72A	The Truth Is Here/Let Me Show the World I Love You	1972	200.00
❑ 72B	The Truth Is Here/(Part 2)	1972	30.00
TOWER			
❑ 281	A Family (Part 1)/(Part 2)	1966	12.00
WAND			
❑ 1168	I Don't Want Nobody to Lead Me On/Let's Face Facts	1968	40.00
❑ 1172	Do You Love Me Baby/ Sweet Lovin' Woman	1968	600.00
Albums			
ABC/HBS			
❑ ABCD-921	Everybody Wanna Live On	1975	15.00
❑ AB-962	Love Anonymous	1976	15.00
BANG			
❑ NJZ 36321	The Masqueraders	1980	15.00

MASTER-TONES, THE

Number	Title (A Side/B Side)	Yr	NM
45s			
BRUCE			
❑ 111	What'll You Do/Tell Me	1954	300.00
—Blue vinyl			
❑ 111	What'll You Do/Tell Me	1954	500.00
—Black vinyl, "New York 19, N.Y." address			
❑ 111	What'll You Do/Tell Me	1962	50.00
—Black vinyl, "New York, N.Y." address			
LOST-NITE			
❑ 396	What'll You Do/Tell Me	197?	6.00
—Reissue			

MASTERETTES, THE

Number	Title (A Side/B Side)	Yr	NM
45s			
LE SAGE			
❑ 716	Never Ever/Follow the Leader	1961	150.00

MASTERS, JOHNNY; MASTRO, JOHNNY See JOHNNY MAESTRO.

MASTERS, KEN

Number	Title (A Side/B Side)	Yr	NM
45s			
DECCA			
❑ 31084	Too Late/Parting Hour	1960	20.00

MATADORS, THE (1)

Number	Title (A Side/B Side)	Yr	NM
45s			
CHART MAKER			
❑ 404	Let Me Dream/Wiggle Wobble	1966	150.00
FORBES			
❑ 230	Let Me Dream/Wiggle Wobble	1966	25.00

MATADORS, THE (2)

Number	Title (A Side/B Side)	Yr	NM
45s			
COLPIX			
❑ 698	Ace of Hearts/Perfidia	1963	25.00
❑ 718	I've Gotta Drive/La Corrida	1963	50.00
—A-side is a Jan and Dean track with a new spoken introduction			
❑ 741	C'mon, Let Yourself Go (Part 1)/ C'mon, Let Yourself Go (Part 2)	1964	25.00

MATADORS, THE (3)

Number	Title (A Side/B Side)	Yr	NM
45s			
KEITH			
❑ 6502	If You Left Me Today/It Ain't Nothin' But Rock 'N' Roll	1962	40.00
❑ 6504	You'd Be Crying, Too/ My Foolish Heart	1963	350.00

MATADORS, THE (4)

Number	Title (A Side/B Side)	Yr	NM
45s			
SUE			
❑ 700	Pennies from Heaven/ Vengeance	1957	120.00
❑ 701	Be Good to Me/Have Mercy Baby	1957	80.00

MATADORS, THE (U) Could be group (2) or (3).

Number	Title (A Side/B Side)	Yr	NM
45s			
JAMIE			
❑ 1226	Listen/So Near	1962	20.00

MATHERS, JERRY Better known as "The Beaver."

Number	Title (A Side/B Side)	Yr	NM
45s			
ATLANTIC			
❑ 2156	Don'tcha Cry/Wind-Up Toy	1962	20.00
❑ 2156 [PS]	Don'tcha Cry/Wind-Up Toy	1962	40.00

MATHIS, BOBBY, AND THE SEVILLES

Number	Title (A Side/B Side)	Yr	NM
45s			
SIOUX			
❑ 51860	Girl in the Drugstore/ Going to the City	1960	150.00

MATHIS, JOHNNY

Number	Title (A Side/B Side)	Yr	NM
12-Inch Singles			
COLUMBIA			
❑ CAS 1400 [DJ]	Daydreamin' (same on both sides)	1988	10.00
❑ CAS 1805 [DJ]	In the Still of the Night (same on both sides)	1989	10.00
—With Take 6			
❑ AS 1867 [DJ]	Simple (Vocal Version 5:55)/ (Instrumental)	1984	10.00
❑ 38-05034	Simple/(Instrumental)	1984	6.00
❑ 38-07837	Begin the Beguine/Simple	198?	6.00
—"Mixed Masters" reissue			
❑ CAS 8322 [DJ]	Let Your Heart Remember/ (Dub Mix)	199?	10.00
❑ 23-11002	Begin the Beguine (Thompson Disco Remix 8:28)/ Gone, Gone, Gone (Luongo Disco Remix 6:30)	1979	15.00
45s			
COLUMBIA			
❑ (no #) [DJ]	Columbia Records Presents Johnny Mathis — Take 2	1957	30.00
—Promo-only gatefold sleeve containing white-label promos of 40784 and 40851			
❑ SS-7 [S]	The Best of Everything/The Theme from "A Summer Place"	1960	15.00
—B-side by Percy Faith; "Stereo Seven" single, small hole, plays at 33 1/3 rpm			
❑ AS 93 [DJ]	The Heart of a Woman (same on both sides)	1974	10.00
—Promo release for the Helena Rubenstein cosmetics firm			
❑ AS 93 [PS]	Helena Rubenstein Presents Johnny Mathis for Courant	1974	15.00
—Promo sleeve with above single			
❑ AE7 1148 [DJ]	Christmas Is/Sleigh Ride	1977	8.00
❑ AE7 1148 [PS]	Christmas Is/Sleigh Ride	1977	12.00
—Above single and sleeve were the 1977 Christmas Seals record			
❑ 18-02194	Nothing Between Us But Love/ Deep Purple	1981	3.00
❑ 38-03222	When the Lovin' Goes Out of the Lovin'/Warm	1982	3.00
❑ 38-04468	Simple/Lead Me to Your Love	1984	3.00
❑ 38-04856	Right From the Heart/Hold On	1985	3.00
❑ 38-05588	Just One Touch/I Need You (The Journey)	1985	3.00

Number	Title (A Side/B Side)	Yr	NM
❑ 38-06561	Where Can I Find Christmas?/It's Beginning to Look a Lot Like Christmas	1986	4.00
❑ 38-07797	I'm on the Outside Looking In/Just Like You	1988	3.00
❑ 38-08524	Daydreamin'/Love Brought Us Here Tonight	1988	3.00
❑ 10080	Sail On White Moon/The Heart of a Woman	1974	5.00
❑ 10112	I'm Stone in Love with You/Foolish	1975	5.00
❑ 10175	The Greatest Gift/You're As Right As Rain	1975	5.00
❑ 10250	Stardust/What I Did for Love	1975	5.00
❑ 3-10291	One Day in Your Life/Midnight Blue	1976	5.00
❑ 3-10350	Yellow Roses on Her Gown/Every Time You Touch Me (I Get High)	1976	5.00
❑ 3-10404	Do Me Wrong, But Do Me/Send In the Clowns	1976	5.00
❑ 3-10447	When a Child Is Born/Turn the Lights Down	1976	5.00
❑ 3-10496	Loving You, Losing You/World of Laughter	1977	5.00
❑ 3-10574	Arianne/99 Miles from L.A.	1977	5.00
❑ 3-10611	Hold Me, Thrill Me, Kiss Me/The Most Beautiful Girl	1977	5.00
❑ 3-10640	When a Child Is Born/Every Time You Touch Me (I Get High)	1977	5.00
❑ 3-10902	The Last Time I Felt Like This/As Time Goes By	1979	4.00
—A-side with Jane Olivor			
❑ 3-11001	Begin the Beguine/Gone, Gone, Gone	1979	4.00
❑ 1-11091	No One Else But the One You Love/To the Ends of the Earth	1979	4.00
—A-side with Stephanie Lawrence			
❑ 1-11158	Christmas in the City of the Angels/The Very First Christmas Day	1979	5.00
❑ 1-11313	Different Kinda Different/The Lights of Rio	1980	4.00
—A-side with Paulette			
❑ 11-11409	When a Child Is Born/The Lord's Prayer	1980	4.00
—With Gladys Knight and the Pips			
❑ 30355 [S]	Someone/Very Much in Love	1959	20.00
—"Stereo Seven" single, small hole, plays at 33 1/3 rpm			
❑ 30410 [S]	Small World/You Are Everything to Me	1959	20.00
—"Stereo Seven" single, small hole, plays at 33 1/3 rpm			
❑ 30483 [S]	Misty/The Story of Our Love	1959	20.00
—"Stereo Seven" single, small hole, plays at 33 1/3 rpm			
❑ 30583 [S]	The Best of Everything/Cherie	1959	20.00
—"Stereo Seven" single, small hole, plays at 33 1/3 rpm			
❑ 30598 [S]	Heavenly/Hello, Young Lovers	1959	15.00
—"Stereo Seven" single, small hole, plays at 33 1/3 rpm			
❑ 30599 [S]	Misty/Stranger in Paradise	1959	15.00
—"Stereo Seven" single, small hole, plays at 33 1/3 rpm			
❑ 30600 [S]	Tonight/Maria	1959	15.00
—"Stereo Seven" single, small hole, plays at 33 1/3 rpm			
❑ 30601 [S]	Secret Love/And This Is My Beloved	1959	15.00
—"Stereo Seven" single, small hole, plays at 33 1/3 rpm			
❑ 30684 [S]	Maria/Hey Love	1960	15.00
—"Stereo Seven" single, small hole, plays at 33 1/3 rpm			
❑ 30764 [S]	My Love for You/Oh That Feeling	1960	15.00
—"Stereo Seven" single, small hole, plays at 33 1/3 rpm			
❑ S7 30828 [S]	Everything's Coming Up Roses/I Wish I Were in Love Again	1960	12.00
❑ S7 30829 [S]	You Do Something To Me/Let's Misbehave	1960	12.00
❑ S7 30830 [S]	I Could Have Danced All Night/A Cock-Eyed Optimist	1960	12.00
❑ S7 30831 [S]	I Just Found Out About Love/Let's Do It	1960	12.00
❑ S7 30832 [S]	I Am in Love/Love Eyes	1960	12.00
—The above five are "Stereo Seven" 33 1/3 rpm jukebox singles from set "JS7-9" entitled "The Rhythms and Ballads of Broadway"			
❑ 30866 [S]	How to Handle a Woman/While You're Young	1960	15.00
—"Stereo Seven" single, small hole, plays at 33 1/3 rpm			
❑ 30980 [S]	You Set My Heart to Music/Jenny	1961	15.00
—"Stereo Seven" single, small hole, plays at 33 1/3 rpm			
❑ 31048 [S]	Laurie, My Love/Should I Wait	1961	15.00
—"Stereo Seven" single, small hole, plays at 33 1/3 rpm			
❑ 31238 [S]	Christmas Eve/My Kind of Christmas	1961	25.00
—"Stereo Seven" single, small hole, plays at 33 1/3 rpm			
❑ 31261 [S]	Sweet Thursday/One Look	1962	20.00
—"Stereo Seven" single, small hole, plays at 33 1/3 rpm			
❑ S7 31344 [S]	Live It Up/Just Friends	1962	12.00
❑ S7 31345 [S]	Why Not/On a Cold and Rainy Day	1962	12.00
❑ S7 31346 [S]	I Won't Dance/Johnny One Note	1962	12.00
❑ S7 31347 [S]	Crazy in the Heart/Too Much Too Soon	1962	12.00
❑ S7 31348 [S]	Hey Look Me Over/Love	1962	12.00
—The above five are "Stereo Seven" 33 1/3 rpm jukebox singles from set "JS7-47" entitled "Live It Up!"			
❑ 31420 [S]	Marianna/Unaccustomed As I Am	1962	20.00
—"Stereo Seven" single, small hole, plays at 33 1/3 rpm			
❑ 31509 [S]	That's the Way It Is/I'll Never Be Lonely Again	1962	20.00
—"Stereo Seven" single, small hole, plays at 33 1/3 rpm			
❑ 31582 [S]	Gina/I Love Her That's Why	1962	20.00
—"Stereo Seven" single, small hole, plays at 33 1/3 rpm			
❑ 31666 [S]	What Will Mary Say/Quiet Girl	1963	25.00
—"Stereo Seven" single, small hole, plays at 33 1/3 rpm			
❑ 31666 [S]	What Will My Mary Say/Quiet Girl	1963	25.00
—"Stereo Seven" single, small hole, plays at 33 1/3 rpm; revised A-side title			
❑ S7 31731 [S]	Rapture/Love Me As Though There Were No Tomorrow	1963	12.00
❑ S7 31732 [S]	Moments Like This/You've Come Home	1963	12.00
❑ S7 31733 [S]	Here I'll Stay/My Darling, My Darling	1963	12.00
❑ S7 31734 [S]	Stars Fell on Alabama/I Was Telling Her About You	1963	12.00
❑ S7 31735 [S]	Lost in Loveliness/Stella by Starlight	1963	12.00
—The above five are "Stereo Seven" 33 1/3 rpm jukebox singles from "JS7-76" entitled "Rapture"			
❑ 31799 [S]	Every Step of the Way/No Man Can Stand Alone	1963	15.00
—"Stereo Seven" single, small hole, plays at 33 1/3 rpm			
❑ 31836 [S]	Sooner or Later/In Wisconsin	1963	15.00
—"Stereo Seven" single, small hole, plays at 33 1/3 rpm			
❑ 31916 [S]	I'll Search My Heart/All the Sad Young Men	1963	15.00
—"Stereo Seven" single, small hole, plays at 33 1/3 rpm			
❑ 33001	It's Not for Me to Say/Chances Are	196?	6.00
—Red label			
❑ 33001	It's Not for Me to Say/Chances Are	198?	3.00
—Gray label			
❑ 3-33001	It's Not for Me to Say/Chances Are	196?	15.00
—"Hall of Fame Series"; "Columbia Single 33"; small hole			
❑ 33042	Maria/Misty	196?	6.00
—Red label			
❑ 33042	Maria/Misty	198?	3.00
—Gray label			
❑ 33048	Wonderful, Wonderful/The Twelfth of Never	196?	6.00
—Red label			
❑ 33048	Wonderful, Wonderful/The Twelfth of Never	198?	3.00
—Gray label			
❑ 33056	Small World/A Certain Smile	196?	6.00
—Red label			
❑ 33056	Small World/A Certain Smile	198?	3.00
—Gray label			
❑ 33142	Venus/Gina	196?	6.00
—Red label			
❑ 33142	Venus/Gina	198?	3.00
—Gray label			
❑ 33174	I'll Never Fall in Love Again/A Time for Us	197?	4.00
—Red label			
❑ 33174	I'll Never Fall in Love Again/A Time for Us	198?	3.00
—Gray label			
❑ 33226	What Will My Mary Say/Call Me	197?	4.00
—Red label			
❑ 33226	What Will My Mary Say/Call Me	198?	3.00
—Gray label			
❑ 33253	Show and Tell/Soul and Inspiration-Just Once in My Life	197?	4.00
—Red label			
❑ 33253	Show and Tell/Soul and Inspiration-Just Once in My Life	198?	3.00
—Gray label			
❑ 33264	I'm Coming Home/I'm Stone in Love with You	197?	4.00
—Red label			
❑ 33264	I'm Coming Home/I'm Stone in Love with You	198?	3.00
—Gray label			
❑ JZSP 39330 [DJ]	In Other Words (Complete Version)/In Other Words (Short Version)	1956	25.00
—Promo only, possibly his first single. Came with a "Columbia Records Introduces" sleeve, the presence of which doubles the value			
❑ 40784	Wonderful! Wonderful!/When Sunny Gets Blue	1956	12.00
❑ 40851	It's Not for Me to Say/Warm and Tender	1957	12.00
❑ 40993	Chances Are/The Twelfth of Never	1957	10.00
❑ 40993 [PS]	Chances Are/The Twelfth of Never	1957	20.00
❑ 41060	No Love (But Your Love)/Wild Is the Wind	1957	10.00
❑ 41060 [PS]	No Love (But Your Love)/Wild Is the Wind	1957	15.00
❑ 41082	Come to Me/When I Am With You	1957	10.00
❑ 41152	All the Time/Teacher, Teacher	1958	10.00
❑ 41193	A Certain Smile/Let It Rain	1958	10.00
❑ 41193 [PS]	A Certain Smile/Let It Rain	1958	15.00
❑ 41253	Call Me/Stairway to the Sea	1958	10.00
❑ 41253 [PS]	Call Me/Stairway to the Sea	1958	15.00
❑ 41304	Let's Love/You Are Beautiful	1958	10.00
❑ 41355	Someone/Very Much in Love	1959	10.00
❑ 41410	Small World/You Are Everything to Me	1959	10.00
❑ 41483	Misty/The Story of Our Love	1959	10.00
❑ 41483 [PS]	Misty/The Story of Our Love	1959	15.00
❑ 41491	The Best of Everything/Cherie	1959	10.00
❑ 41491 [PS]	The Best of Everything/Cherie	1959	15.00
❑ 41583	Starbright/All Is Well	1960	8.00
❑ 41583 [PS]	Starbright/All Is Well	1960	12.00
❑ 41684	Maria/Hey Love	1960	8.00
—Reissued in 1961 with the same catalog number			
❑ 41764	My Love for You/Oh That Feeling	1960	8.00
❑ 3-41764	My Love for You/Oh That Feeling	1960	15.00
—"Columbia Single 33"; small hole			
❑ 41866 [PS]	How to Handle a Woman/While You're Young	1960	12.00
❑ 41866	How to Handle a Woman/While You're Young	1960	8.00
❑ 3-41866	How to Handle a Woman/While You're Young	1960	15.00
—"Columbia Single 33"; small hole			
❑ 41980 [PS]	You Set My Heart to Music/Jenny	1961	12.00
❑ 41980	You Set My Heart to Music/Jenny	1961	8.00
❑ 3-41980	You Set My Heart to Music/Jenny	1961	15.00
—"Columbia Single 33"; small hole			
❑ 42005	Should I Wait/Oh How I Try	1961	—
—Unreleased?			
❑ 3-42005	Should I Wait/Oh How I Try	1961	—
—Unreleased?			
❑ 42048 [PS]	Laurie My Love/Should I Wait (Or Should I Run to Her)	1961	12.00
❑ 42048	Laurie My Love/Should I Wait (Or Should I Run to Her)	1961	8.00
❑ 3-42048	Laurie My Love/Should I Wait (Or Should I Run to Her)	1961	15.00
—"Columbia Single 33"; small hole			
❑ 42156 [PS]	Wasn't the Summer Short/There You Are	1961	12.00
❑ 42156	Wasn't the Summer Short/There You Are	1961	8.00
❑ 3-42156	Wasn't the Summer Short/There You Are	1961	15.00
—"Columbia Single 33"; small hole			
❑ 3-42238	My Kind of Christmas/Christmas Eve	1961	20.00
—"Columbia Single 33"; small hole			
❑ 4-42238	My Kind of Christmas/Christmas Eve	1961	12.00
❑ 4-42238 [PS]	My Kind of Christmas/Christmas Eve	1961	20.00
❑ 42261 [PS]	Sweet Thursday/One Look	1962	12.00
❑ 42261	Sweet Thursday/One Look	1962	8.00
❑ 3-42261	Sweet Thursday/One Look	1962	15.00
—"Columbia Single 33"; small hole			
❑ 42420 [PS]	Marianna/Unaccustomed As I Am	1962	12.00
❑ 42420	Marianna/Unaccustomed As I Am	1962	8.00
❑ 3-42420	Marianna/Unaccustomed As I Am	1962	15.00
—"Columbia Single 33"; small hole			
❑ 42509 [PS]	That's the Way It Is/I'll Never Be Lonely Again	1962	10.00
❑ 42509	That's the Way It Is/I'll Never Be Lonely Again	1962	8.00
❑ 3-42509	That's the Way It Is/I'll Never Be Lonely Again	1962	15.00
—"Columbia Single 33"; small hole			
❑ 42582 [DJ]	Gina (same on both sides)	1962	20.00
—Promo only on red vinyl			
❑ 42582 [PS]	Gina/I Love Her That's Why	1962	10.00
❑ 42582	Gina/I Love Her That's Why	1962	8.00
❑ 3-42582	Gina/I Love Her That's Why	1962	15.00
—"Columbia Single 33"; small hole			
❑ 42666 [DJ]	What Will My Mary Say (same on both sides)	1963	20.00
—Promo only on red vinyl			
❑ 42666 [PS]	What Will Mary Say/Quiet Girl	1963	12.00
❑ 42666	What Will My Mary Say/Quiet Girl	1963	8.00
—Revised A-side title			
❑ 42666	What Will Mary Say/Quiet Girl	1963	10.00
❑ 3-42666	What Will My Mary Say/Quiet Girl	1963	15.00
—"Columbia Single 33"; small hole; revised A-side title			
❑ 3-42666	What Will Mary Say/Quiet Girl	1963	20.00
—"Columbia Single 33"; small hole			
❑ 42799 [PS]	Every Step of the Way/No Man Can Stand Alone	1963	10.00
❑ 42799	Every Step of the Way/No Man Can Stand Alone	1963	8.00

Except when noted otherwise, VG = 25% of NM, and VG+ = 50% of NM. (Example: VG = $2.00, VG+ = $4.00 and NM = $8.00.)

Number	Title (A Side/B Side)	Yr	NM
3-42799	Every Step of the Way/No Man Can Stand Alone	1963	20.00

—"Columbia Single 33"; small hole

Number	Title (A Side/B Side)	Yr	NM
42836	Sooner or Later/In Wisconsin	1963	8.00
3-42836	Sooner or Later/In Wisconsin	1963	20.00

—"Columbia Single 33"; small hole

Number	Title (A Side/B Side)	Yr	NM
42916	I'll Search My Heart/All the Sad Young Men	1963	8.00
42916 [DJ]	I'll Search My Heart (same on both sides)	1963	20.00

—Promo only on red vinyl

Number	Title (A Side/B Side)	Yr	NM
44266	Misty Roses/Don't Talk to Me	1967	5.00
44357	Among the First to Know/Long Winter Nights	1967	5.00
44517	Venus/Don't Go Breakin' My Heart	1968	5.00
44637	You Make Me Think About You/Night Dreams	1968	5.00
44728	The End of the World/The 59th Street Bridge Song (Feelin' Groovy)	1968	5.00
44837	I'll Never Fall in Love Again/Whoever You Are, I Love You	1969	5.00
44915	Love Theme from Romeo and Juliet (A Time for Us)/The World I Threw Away	1969	5.00
JZSP 44991 [DJ]	The Christmas Song (Merry Christmas to You)/What Child Is This?	1958	20.00
45022	Midnight Cowboy/We	1969	5.00
45035	Give Me Your Love for Christmas/Calypso Noel	1969	6.00
45035 [PS]	Give Me Your Love for Christmas/Calypso Noel	1969	8.00
45100 [DJ]	Give Me Your Love for Christmas/Calypso Noel	1969	8.00
45100 [PS]	Give Me Your Love for Christmas/Calypso Noel	1969	10.00

—The above sleeve and record were the 1969 Christmas Seals promo

Number	Title (A Side/B Side)	Yr	NM
45104	For All We Know/Odds and Ends	1970	5.00
45183	The Last Time I Saw Her/Wherefore and Why	1970	5.00
45223	Darling Lili/Pieces of Dreams	1970	5.00
45263	Until It's Time for You to Go/Evil Ways	1970	5.00
JZSP 45265 [DJ]	An Open Fire/I Concentrate on You	1959	20.00
45281	Christmas Is/Sign of the Dove	1970	5.00
45323	I Was There/Ten Times Forever More	1971	5.00
45371	Evie/Think About Things	1971	5.00
45415	Long Ago and Far Away/For All We Know	1971	5.00
45470	How Can You Mend a Broken Heart/If We Only Have Love	1971	5.00
45513	Christmas Is/Sign of the Dove	1971	5.00
45559	If We Only Have Love/This Way, Mary	1972	5.00
45635	Make It Easy on Yourself/Sometimes	1972	5.00
45729	Soul and Inspiration-Just Once in My Life/I	1972	5.00
45777	Walking Tall (Theme)/Take Good Care of Her	1973	5.00
45835	Show and Tell/Happy (Theme from Lady Sings the Blues)	1973	5.00
45908	I'm Coming Home/Stop, Look, and Listen to Your Heart	1973	5.00
45975	Life Is a Song Worth Singing/I Just Wanted to Be Me	1973	5.00
46048	I'm Stone in Love with You/Sweet Child	1974	5.00
JZSP 55369 [DJ]	Maria/Tonight	1959	20.00
38-69092	In the Still of the Night/True Love Ways	1989	4.00

—A-side with Take 6

MERCURY

Number	Title (A Side/B Side)	Yr	NM
DJ-72 [DJ]	Chim Chim Cheree (same on both sides?)	1964	15.00
72184	Come Back/Your Teenage Dreams	1963	6.00
72184 [PS]	Come Back/Your Teenage Dreams	1963	10.00
72217	The Little Drummer Boy/Have Reindeer, Will Travel	1963	10.00
72217 [PS]	The Little Drummer Boy/Have Reindeer, Will Travel	1963	20.00
72229	Bye Bye Barbara/A Great Night for Cryin'	1964	6.00
72229 [PS]	Bye Bye Barbara/A Great Night for Cryin'	1964	10.00
72263	No More/The Fall of Love	1964	6.00
72287	Taste of Tears/White Roses from a Blue Valentine	1964	6.00
72339	Listen Lonely Girl/All I Wanted	1964	6.00
72339 [PS]	Listen Lonely Girl/All I Wanted	1964	10.00
72432	Dianacita/Take the Time	1965	6.00
72432 [PS]	Dianacita/Take the Time	1965	10.00
72464	Mirage/The Sweetheart Tree	1965	6.00
72464 [PS]	Mirage/The Sweetheart Tree	1965	10.00
72493	On a Clear Day You Can See Forever/Come Back to Me	1965	6.00
72539	Moment to Moment/Glass Mountain	1966	6.00
72568	The Shadow of Your Smile (Love Theme from "The Sandpiper")/The Sweetheart Tree	1966	6.00
72610	The Impossible Dream/So Nice	1966	6.00
72610 [PS]	The Impossible Dream/So Nice	1966	10.00
72653	Saturday Sunshine/Two Tickets and a Candy Heart	1967	6.00
72653 [PS]	Saturday Sunshine/Two Tickets and a Candy Heart	1967	10.00

7-Inch Extended Plays

COLUMBIA

Number	Title (A Side/B Side)	Yr	NM
B-2129	*It's Not for Me to Say/Warm and Tender/Wonderful, Wonderful/Babalu	1957	15.00
B-2129 [PS]	Songs from "Lizzie" and Other Favorites	1957	15.00
B-2143	Come to Me/Wild Is the Wind//No Love (But Your Love)/When I Am with You	1957	15.00
B-2143 [PS]	Johnny Mathis Sings	1957	15.00
B-2537	The Twelfth of Never/Chances Are//Wonderful, Wonderful/It's Not for Me to Say	1959	12.00
B-2537 [PS]	Johnny Mathis (Hall of Fame Series)	1959	12.00
B-2626	*Call Me/A Certain Smile/All the Time/When Sunny Gets Blue	195?	12.00
B-2626 [PS]	Johnny Mathis (Hall of Fame Series)	195?	12.00
B-2640	*Come to Me/Wild Is the Wind/Someone/You Are Beautiful	195?	12.00
B-2640 [PS]	Johnny Mathis (Hall of Fame Series)	195?	12.00
7-8634	Chances Are/The Twelfth of Never/Wonderful! Wonderful!//It's Not for Me to Say/Come to Me/Wild Is the Wind	1963	10.00

—Jukebox issue; small hole, plays at 33 1/3 rpm

Number	Title (A Side/B Side)	Yr	NM
7-8634 [PS]	Johnny's Greatest Hits	1963	10.00
B-8871	*Autumn in Rome/Love, Your Magic Spell Is Everywhere/Cabin in the Sky/In Other Words	1957	15.00
B-8871 [PS]	Johnny Mathis, Vol. 1	1957	15.00
B-8872	*Caravan/Star Eyes/It Might As Well Be Spring/Street of Dreams	1957	15.00
B-8872 [PS]	Johnny Mathis, Vol. 2	1957	15.00
B-8873	*Easy to Love/Prelude to a Kiss/Babalu/Angel Eyes	1957	15.00
B-8873 [PS]	Johnny Mathis, Vol. 3	1957	15.00
7-9637	I Say a Little Prayer/Love Is Blue/Never My Love//Venus/Moon River/Walk On By	1968	10.00

—Jukebox issue; small hole, plays at 33 1/3 rpm

Number	Title (A Side/B Side)	Yr	NM
7-9637 [PS]	Love Is Blue	1968	10.00
B-10281	Will I Find My Love Today/Looking at You//Let Me Love You/All Through the Night	1957	12.00
B-10281 [PS]	Looking at You	1957	12.00

—Same contents, different title

Number	Title (A Side/B Side)	Yr	NM
B-10281 [PS]	Will I Find My Love Today	1957	12.00
B-10282	*It Could Happen to You/That Old Black Magic/Too Close for Comfort/In the Wee Small Hours of the Morning	1957	12.00
B-10282 [PS]	Too Close for Comfort	1957	12.00
B-10283	*Year After Year/Early Autumn/You Stepped Out of a Dream/Day In, Day Out	1957	12.00
B-10283 [PS]	Day In, Day Out	1957	12.00
B-10781	Warm/A Handful of Stars//My One and Only Love/While We're Young	1958	12.00
B-10781 [PS]	Warm, Vol. 1	1958	12.00
B-10782	*By Myself/I've Grown Accustomed to Her Face/Baby, Baby, Baby/What'll I Do	1958	12.00
B-10782 [PS]	Warm, Vol. 2	1958	12.00
B-10783	*I'm Glad There Is You/The Lovely Things You Do/There Goes My Heart/Then I'll Be Tired of You	1958	12.00
B-10783 [PS]	Warm, Vol. 3	1958	12.00
B-11191	*Good Night, Dear Lord/I Heard a Forest Praying/Deep River/Swing Low, Sweet Chariot	1958	10.00
B-11191 [PS]	Good Night, Dear Lord	1958	10.00
B-11192	*Eli Eli/Kol Nidre/Where Can I Go?/One God	1958	10.00
B-11192 [PS]	Eli Eli	1958	10.00
B-11193	*Ave Maria (Bach-Gounod)/The Rosary/May the Good Lord Bless and Keep You/Ave Maria (Schubert)	1958	10.00
B-11193 [PS]	Ave Maria	1958	10.00
B-11651	To Be in Love/You'd Be So Nice to Come Home To//It's De-Lovely/I've Got the World on a String	1958	12.00
B-11651 [PS]	Swing Softly, Vol. 1	1958	12.00
B-11652	*Sweet Lorraine/Can't Get Out of This Mood/You Hit the Spot/Get Me to the Church on Time	1958	12.00
B-11652 [PS]	Swing Softly, Vol. 2	1958	12.00
B-11653	*Love Walked In/Easy to Say/This Heart of Mine/Like Someone in Love	1958	12.00
B-11653 [PS]	Swing Softly, Vol. 3	1958	12.00
B-11951	Winter Wonderland/Blue Christmas//White Christmas/Sleigh Ride	1958	12.00
B-11951 [PS]	Merry Christmas, Vol. 1	1958	12.00
B-11952	I'll Be Home for Christmas/Oh Holy Night//The Christmas Song/Silver Bells	1958	12.00
B-11952 [PS]	Merry Christmas, Vol. 2	1958	12.00
B-11953	The First Noel/It Came Upon a Midnight Clear//What Child Is This?/Silent Night, Holy Night	1958	12.00
B-11953 [PS]	Merry Christmas, Vol. 3	1958	12.00
B-12701	*Open Fire/Please Be Kind/Bye Bye Blackbird/Tenderly	1959	10.00
B-12701 [PS]	Open Fire, Two Guitars, Vol. 1	1959	10.00
B-12702	*Embraceable You/My Funny Valentine/I'll Be Seeing You/I'm Just a Boy in Love	1959	10.00
B-12702 [PS]	Open Fire, Two Guitars, Vol. 2	1959	10.00
B-12703	I Concentrate on You/You'll Never Know//When I Fall in Love/In the Still of the Night	1959	10.00
B-12703 [PS]	Open Fire, Two Guitars, Vol. 3	1959	10.00
B-13511	*Heavenly/Misty/Hello, Young Lovers/I'll Be Easy to Find	1959	10.00
B-13511 [PS]	Heavenly, Vol. 1	1959	10.00
B-13512	*Something I Dreamed Last Night/Moonlight Becomes You/They Say It's Wonderful/More Than You Know	1959	10.00
B-13512 [PS]	Heavenly, Vol. 2	1959	10.00
B-13513	A Lovely Way to Spend an Evening/That's All//A Ride on a Rainbow/Stranger in Paradise	1959	10.00
B-13513 [PS]	Heavenly, Vol. 3	1959	10.00
B-14221	Secret Love/Where Are You//Maria/Where Do You Think You're Going	1959	10.00
B-14221 [PS]	Faithfully, Vol. 1	1959	10.00
B-14222	*Faithfully/One Starry Night/Nobody Knows/You Better Go Now	1959	10.00
B-14222 [PS]	Faithfully, Vol. 2	1959	10.00
B-14223	And This Is My Beloved/Tonight//Follow Me/Blue Gardenia	1959	10.00
B-14223 [PS]	Faithfully, Vol. 3	1959	10.00
B-15261	Goodnight My Love/There's No You//Once/I'm So Lost	1960	10.00
B-15261 [PS]	Johnny's Mood, Vol. 1	1960	10.00
B-15262	*Corner to Corner/The Folks Who Live on the Hill/I'm in the Mood for Love/Stay Warm	1960	10.00
B-15262 [PS]	Johnny's Mood, Vol. 2	1960	10.00
B-15263	*I'm Gonna Laugh You Right Out of My Life/How High the Moon/April in Paris/In Return	1960	10.00
B-15263 [PS]	Johnny's Mood, Vol. 3	1960	10.00
7-30210	Come Saturday Morning/Yellow Days/(If You Can Let Me Make Love To You) Why Can't I Touch You//Until It's Time for You to Go/Everything Is Beautiful	1970	10.00

—Jukebox issue; small hole, plays at 33 1/3 rpm

Number	Title (A Side/B Side)	Yr	NM
7-30210 [PS]	Close to You	1970	10.00

MERCURY

Number	Title (A Side/B Side)	Yr	NM
SR-665-C	What Now My Love/What the World Needs Now Is Love/Man of La Mancha//I Will Wait for You/Elusive Butterfly/So Nice	1966	12.00

—Jukebox issue; small hole, plays at 33 1/3 rpm

Number	Title (A Side/B Side)	Yr	NM
SR-665-C [PS]	So Nice	1966	12.00

Albums

COLUMBIA

Number	Title (A Side/B Side)	Yr	NM
GP 2 [(2)]	Warm/Open Fire, Two Guitars	1969	15.00
C2L 17 [(2)M]	The Rhythms and Ballads of Broadway	1960	25.00

—Red and black label with six "eye" logos

M

Number	Title (A Side/B Side)	Yr	NM
❑ C2L 17 [(2)M]	The Rhythms and Ballads of Broadway	1962	20.00
—Red label with either "Guaranteed High Fidelity" or "360 Sound Mono"			
❑ C2L 34 [(2)M]	The Great Years	1964	15.00
❑ C2S 803 [(2)S]	The Rhythms and Ballads of Broadway	1960	30.00
—Red and black label with six "eye" logos			
❑ C2S 803 [(2)S]	The Rhythms and Ballads of Broadway	1962	25.00
—Red "360 Sound" label			
❑ C2S 834 [(2)S]	The Great Years	1964	20.00
—Red "360 Sound" label			
❑ CL 887 [M]	Johnny Mathis	1957	50.00
❑ CS 1005	Raindrops Keep Fallin' on My Head	1970	12.00
❑ CL 1028 [M]	Wonderful Wonderful	1957	30.00
—Red and black label with six "eye" logos			
❑ CL 1028 [M]	Wonderful Wonderful	1962	15.00
—Red label with either "Guaranteed High Fidelity" or "360 Sound Mono"			
❑ CL 1078 [M]	Warm	1957	30.00
—Red and black label with six "eye" logos			
❑ CL 1078 [M]	Warm	1962	15.00
—Red label with either "Guaranteed High Fidelity" or "360 Sound Mono"			
❑ CL 1119 [M]	Good Night, Dear Lord	1958	30.00
—Red and black label with six "eye" logos			
❑ CL 1119 [M]	Good Night, Dear Lord	1962	15.00
—Red label with either "Guaranteed High Fidelity" or "360 Sound Mono"			
❑ CL 1133 [M]	Johnny's Greatest Hits	1958	30.00
—Red and black label with six "eye" logos			
❑ CL 1133 [M]	Johnny's Greatest Hits	1962	15.00
—Red label with either "Guaranteed High Fidelity" or "360 Sound Mono"			
❑ CL 1165 [M]	Swing Softly	1958	30.00
—Red and black label with six "eye" logos			
❑ CL 1165 [M]	Swing Softly	1962	15.00
—Red label with either "Guaranteed High Fidelity" or "360 Sound Mono"			
❑ CL 1195 [M]	Merry Christmas	1958	40.00
—Original cover has Johnny standing, holding skis and poles			
❑ CL 1195 [M]	Merry Christmas	196?	30.00
—Second cover has Johnny sitting, with skis and poles in snow			
❑ CL 1270 [M]	Open Fire, Two Guitars	1959	30.00
—Red and black label with six "eye" logos			
❑ CL 1270 [M]	Open Fire, Two Guitars	1962	15.00
—Red label with either "Guaranteed High Fidelity" or "360 Sound Mono"			
❑ CL 1344 [M]	More Johnny's Greatest Hits	1959	25.00
—Red and black label with six "eye" logos			
❑ CL 1344 [M]	More Johnny's Greatest Hits	1962	15.00
—Red label with either "Guaranteed High Fidelity" or "360 Sound Mono"			
❑ CL 1351 [M]	Heavenly	1959	20.00
—Red and black label with six "eye" logos			
❑ CL 1351 [M]	Heavenly	1962	15.00
—Red label with either "Guaranteed High Fidelity" or "360 Sound Mono"			
❑ CL 1422 [M]	Faithfully	1959	20.00
—Red and black label with six "eye" logos			
❑ CL 1422 [M]	Faithfully	1962	15.00
—Red label with either "Guaranteed High Fidelity" or "360 Sound Mono"			
❑ CL 1526 [M]	Johnny's Mood	1960	20.00
—Red and black label with six "eye" logos			
❑ CL 1526 [M]	Johnny's Mood	1962	15.00
—Red label with either "Guaranteed High Fidelity" or "360 Sound Mono"			
❑ CL 1623 [M]	I'll Buy You a Star	1961	15.00
—Red and black label with six "eye" logos			
❑ CL 1623 [M]	I'll Buy You a Star	1962	12.00
—Red label with either "Guaranteed High Fidelity" or "360 Sound Mono"			
❑ CL 1644 [M]	Portrait of Johnny	1961	15.00
—Red and black label with six "eye" logos; add 1/3 if portrait is there			
❑ CL 1644 [M]	Portrait of Johnny	1962	12.00
—Red label with either "Guaranteed High Fidelity" or "360 Sound Mono"			
❑ CL 1711 [M]	Live It Up!	1962	12.00
—Red label with either "Guaranteed High Fidelity" or "360 Sound Mono"			
❑ CL 1711 [M]	Live It Up!	1962	15.00
—Red and black label with six "eye" logos			
❑ CL 1915 [M]	Rapture	1962	12.00
❑ CL 2016 [M]	Johnny's Newest Hits	1963	12.00
❑ CL 2044 [M]	Johnny	1963	12.00
❑ CL 2098 [M]	Romantically	1963	12.00
❑ CL 2143 [M]	I'll Search My Heart and Other Great Hits	1964	12.00
❑ CL 2223 [M]	The Ballads of Broadway	1964	12.00
❑ CL 2224 [M]	The Rhythms of Broadway	1964	12.00
❑ CL 2726 [M]	Up, Up and Away	1967	15.00
❑ CL 2837 [M]	Love Is Blue	1968	25.00
❑ CL 2905 [M]	Those Were the Days	1968	40.00
❑ CS 8012 [S]	Good Night, Dear Lord	1958	40.00
—Red and black label with six "eye" logos			
❑ CS 8012 [S]	Good Night, Dear Lord	1962	20.00
—Red "360 Sound" label			
❑ CS 8021 [S]	Merry Christmas	1959	25.00
—Original cover has Johnny standing, holding skis and poles; red and black label with six "eye" logos			
❑ CS 8021 [S]	Merry Christmas	196?	20.00
—Second cover has Johnny sitting, with skis and poles in snow			
❑ PC 8021 [S]	Merry Christmas	198?	6.00
—New prefix; original "standing" cover; bar code on back cover with "02" suffix			
❑ CS 8023 [S]	Swing Softly	1958	40.00
—Red and black label with six "eye" logos			
❑ CS 8039 [S]	Warm	1958	40.00
—Red and black label with six "eye" logos			
❑ CS 8039 [S]	Warm	1962	20.00
—Red "360 Sound" label			
❑ CS 8056 [S]	Open Fire, Two Guitars	1959	40.00
—Red and black label with six "eye" logos			
❑ CS 8056 [S]	Open Fire, Two Guitars	1962	20.00
—Red "360 Sound" label			
❑ CS 8150 [S]	More Johnny's Greatest Hits	1959	30.00
—Red and black label with six "eye" logos			
❑ CS 8150 [S]	More Johnny's Greatest Hits	1962	20.00
—Red "360 Sound" label			
❑ CS 8150 [S]	More Johnny's Greatest Hits	1971	10.00
—Orange label			
❑ PC 8150 [S]	More Johnny's Greatest Hits	198?	6.00
—Reissue with new prefix			
❑ CS 8152 [S]	Heavenly	1959	30.00
—Red and black label with six "eye" logos			
❑ CS 8152 [S]	Heavenly	1962	20.00
—Red "360 Sound" label			
❑ CS 8152 [S]	Heavenly	1971	10.00
—Orange label			
❑ PC 8152 [S]	Heavenly	198?	6.00
—Reissue with new prefix			
❑ CS 8219 [S]	Faithfully	1959	25.00
—Red and black label with six "eye" logos			
❑ CS 8219 [S]	Faithfully	1962	20.00
—Red "360 Sound" label			
❑ CS 8326 [S]	Johnny's Mood	1960	25.00
—Red and black label with six "eye" logos			
❑ CS 8326 [S]	Johnny's Mood	1962	20.00
—Red "360 Sound" label			
❑ CS 8423 [S]	I'll Buy You a Star	1961	20.00
—Red and black label with six "eye" logos			
❑ CS 8423 [S]	I'll Buy You a Star	1962	15.00
—Red "360 Sound" label			
❑ CS 8444 [S]	Portrait of Johnny	1961	20.00
—Red and black label with six "eye" logos; add 1/3 if portrait is there			
❑ CS 8444 [S]	Portrait of Johnny	1962	15.00
—Red "360 Sound" label			
❑ CS 8511 [S]	Live It Up!	1962	15.00
—Red "360 Sound" label			
❑ CS 8511 [S]	Live It Up!	1962	20.00
—Red and black label with six "eye" logos; add 1/3 if portrait is there			
❑ CS 8634 [R]	Johnny's Greatest Hits	1963	12.00
❑ CS 8715 [S]	Rapture	1962	15.00
—Red "360 Sound" label			
❑ CS 8816 [S]	Johnny's Newest Hits	1963	15.00
—Red "360 Sound" label			
❑ CS 8844 [S]	Johnny	1963	15.00
—Red "360 Sound" label			
❑ CS 8898 [S]	Romantically	1963	15.00
—Red "360 Sound" label			
❑ CS 8943 [S]	I'll Search My Heart and Other Great Hits	1964	15.00
—Red "360 Sound" label			
❑ CS 9023 [S]	The Ballads of Broadway	1964	15.00
—Red "360 Sound" label			
❑ CS 9024 [S]	The Ballads of Broadway	1964	15.00
—Red "360 Sound" label			
❑ CS 9046 [R]	Wonderful Wonderful	1964	12.00
❑ CS 9526 [S]	Up, Up and Away	1967	15.00
❑ CS 9637 [S]	Love Is Blue	1968	15.00
❑ CS 9705 [S]	Those Were the Days	1968	15.00
❑ CS 9871	People	1969	15.00
❑ CS 9872	The Impossible Dream	1969	15.00
—Red "360 Sound" label			
❑ CS 9872	The Impossible Dream	1971	10.00
—Orange label			
❑ PC 9872	The Impossible Dream	198?	6.00
—Reissue with new prefix			
❑ CS 9909	Love Theme from "Romeo and Juliet"	1969	15.00
—Red "360 Sound" label			
❑ CS 9909	Love Theme from "Romeo and Juliet"	1971	10.00
—Orange label			
❑ PC 9909	Love Theme from "Romeo and Juliet"	198?	6.00
—Reissue with new prefix			
❑ CS 9923	Give Me Your Love for Christmas	1969	12.00
❑ C 30210	Close to You	1970	12.00
❑ G 30350 [(2)]	Johnny Mathis Sings the Music of Bacharach & Kaempfert	1970	15.00
❑ C 30499	Love Story	1971	12.00
❑ PC 30499	Love Story	198?	8.00
—Budget-line reissue			
❑ C 30740	You've Got a Friend	1971	12.00
❑ CQ 30740 [Q]	You've Got a Friend	1972	20.00
❑ PC 30740	You've Got a Friend	198?	8.00
—Budget-line reissue			
❑ 2CQ 30979 [(2)Q]	Johnny Mathis In Person	1972	25.00
❑ KG 30979 [(2)]	Johnny Mathis In Person	1972	15.00
❑ CQ 31342 [Q]	The First Time Ever (I Saw Your Face)	1972	20.00
❑ KC 31342	The First Time Ever (I Saw Your Face)	1972	12.00
❑ PC 31342	The First Time Ever (I Saw Your Face)	198?	8.00
—Budget-line reissue			
❑ KG 31345 [(2)]	Johnny Mathis' All-Time Greatest Hits	1972	15.00
❑ CQ 31626 [Q]	Song Sung Blue	1972	20.00
❑ KC 31626	Song Sung Blue	1972	12.00
❑ CQ 32114 [Q]	Me and Mrs. Jones	1973	18.00
❑ KC 32114	Me and Mrs. Jones	1973	10.00
❑ KC 32258	Killing Me Softly with Her Song	1973	10.00
❑ CQ 32435 [Q]	I'm Coming Home	1973	18.00
❑ KC 32435	I'm Coming Home	1973	10.00
❑ PC 32435	I'm Coming Home	198?	8.00
—Budget-line reissue			
❑ C 32963	What'll I Do	1974	10.00
❑ KC 33251	The Heart of a Woman	1974	10.00
❑ PC 33420	When Will I See You Again	1975	10.00
❑ CG 33621 [(2)]	Heavenly/Faithfully	1975	12.00
❑ PC 33887	Feelings	1975	10.00
❑ PC 34117	I Only Have Eyes for You	1976	10.00
❑ PC 34441	Mathis Is...	1977	10.00
❑ PC 34667	Johnny Mathis' Greatest Hits	1977	10.00
❑ PC 34872	Hold Me, Thrill Me, Kiss Me	1977	10.00
❑ PC 35259	You Light Up My Life	1986	8.00
—Budget-line reissue			
❑ JC 35359	You Light Up My Life	1978	10.00
❑ C 35578	Romantically	1978	8.00
❑ JC 35649	The Best Days of My Life	1979	10.00
❑ PC 35649	The Best Days of My Life	1985	8.00
—Budget-line reissue			
❑ JC 36216	Mathis Magic	1979	10.00
❑ JC 36505	Different Kinda Different	1980	10.00
❑ JC 36871	The Best of Johnny Mathis 1975-1980	1980	10.00
❑ C2X 37440 [(2)]	The First 25 Years — The Silver Anniversary Album	1981	12.00
❑ FC 37748	Friends in Love	1982	10.00
❑ 3C 38306	Christmas with Johnny Mathis	1982	8.00
—Reissue of Columbia LE 10196 with same contents			
❑ FC 38699	Johnny Mathis Live	1983	10.00
❑ FC 38718	A Special Part of Me	1984	10.00
❑ PC 39468	For Christmas	1984	8.00
❑ FC 39601	Right from the Heart	1985	10.00
❑ FC 40372	The Hollywood Musicals	1986	10.00
—With Henry Mancini			
❑ FC 40447	Christmas Eve with Johnny Mathis	1986	10.00
❑ OC 44156	Once in a While	1988	10.00
❑ OC 44336	In the Still of the Night	1989	12.00

COLUMBIA LIMITED EDITION

Number	Title (A Side/B Side)	Yr	NM
❑ LE 10003	Portrait of Johnny	197?	10.00
❑ LE 10196	Christmas with Johnny Mathis	1976	10.00
—Reissue of Harmony KH 30684 with same contents			

COLUMBIA MUSICAL TREASURY

Number	Title (A Side/B Side)	Yr	NM
❑ 6P 6030 [(6)]	The Johnny Mathis Treasury	197?	30.00

COLUMBIA SPECIAL PRODUCTS

Number	Title (A Side/B Side)	Yr	NM
❑ C 10896	Merry Christmas	1972	12.00
—Reissue			
❑ P 11477	Romantically, Johnny Mathis	197?	12.00
❑ P3 11837 [(3)]	Romantically, Johnny Mathis	197?	25.00
❑ P6 14628 [(6)]	Misty Memories: The Complete Johnny Mathis Treasury	197?	30.00
—Maunfactured for Candelite Music			
❑ P 14658	Holidays at the Fireside	197?	20.00
—Bonus album with box set 14628			
❑ P 14908	The Heart of Johnny Mathis	197?	15.00
—Bonus album with box set 14628			
❑ P4 14971 [(4)]	Johnny	197?	25.00

HARMONY

Number	Title (A Side/B Side)	Yr	NM
❑ KH 30017	Johnny Mathis	1970	10.00
❑ KH 30684	Christmas with Johnny Mathis	1971	12.00
—Reissue of Mercury SR 60837 with two fewer tracks			
❑ KH 31935	Something for Everyone	1973	10.00

MERCURY

Number	Title (A Side/B Side)	Yr	NM
❑ MG 20837 [M]	Sounds of Christmas	1963	12.00
❑ MG-20890 [M]	Tender Is the Night	1964	12.00
❑ MG-20913 [M]	The Wonderful World of Make Believe	1964	12.00
❑ MG-20942 [M]	This Is Love	1964	12.00
❑ MG-20988 [M]	Johnny Mathis Ole	1965	12.00
❑ MG-20991 [M]	Love Is Everything	1965	12.00
❑ MG-21041 [M]	The Sweetheart Tree	1965	12.00
❑ MG-21073 [M]	The Shadow of Your Smile	1966	12.00
❑ MG-21093 [M]	So Nice	1966	12.00
❑ MG-21107 [M]	Johnny Mathis Sings	1967	15.00
❑ SR 60837 [S]	Sounds of Christmas	1963	15.00
❑ SR-60890 [S]	Tender Is the Night	1964	15.00

Number	Title (A Side/B Side)	Yr	NM
❑ SR-60913 [S]	The Wonderful World of Make Believe	1964	15.00
❑ SR-60942 [S]	This Is Love	1964	15.00
❑ SR-60988 [S]	Johnny Mathis Ole	1965	15.00
❑ SR-60991 [S]	Love Is Everything	1965	15.00
❑ SR-61041 [S]	The Sweetheart Tree	1965	15.00
❑ SR-61073 [S]	The Shadow of Your Smile	1966	15.00
❑ SR-61093 [S]	So Nice	1966	15.00
❑ SR-61107 [S]	Johnny Mathis Sings	1967	15.00

MOBILE FIDELITY

Number	Title (A Side/B Side)	Yr	NM
❑ 1-171	Heavenly	1985	25.00

—Audiophile vinyl

READER'S DIGEST

Number	Title (A Side/B Side)	Yr	NM
❑ RB4-097 [(6)]	His Greatest Hits and Finest Performances	198?	25.00

TIME-LIFE

Number	Title (A Side/B Side)	Yr	NM
❑ SLGD-08 [(2)]	Legendary Singers: Johnny Mathis	1985	15.00

MATHIS, JOHNNY/DENIECE WILLIAMS

Also see each artist's individual listings.

45s

COLUMBIA

Number	Title (A Side/B Side)	Yr	NM
❑ 38-04379	Love Won't Let Me Wait/ Lead Me to Your Love	1984	3.00
❑ 3-10693	Too Much, Too Little, Too Late/ Emotion	1978	5.00
❑ 3-10693	Too Much, Too Little, Too Late/ I Wrote a Symphony on My Guitar	1978	10.00

—B-side by Johnny Mathis solo

Number	Title (A Side/B Side)	Yr	NM
❑ 3-10772	You're All I Need to Get By/You're a Special Part of My Life	1978	5.00
❑ 3-10772 [PS]	You're All I Need to Get By	1978	10.00

—Sleeve is promo only

Number	Title (A Side/B Side)	Yr	NM
❑ 3-10826	That's What Friends Are For/ I Just Can't Get Over You	1978	5.00
❑ 33360	Too Much, Too Little, Too Late/ You're All I Need to Get By	198?	3.00

—Gray label

Number	Title (A Side/B Side)	Yr	NM
❑ 33360	Too Much, Too Little, Too Late/ You're All I Need to Get By	198?	4.00

—Red label

Albums

COLUMBIA

Number	Title (A Side/B Side)	Yr	NM
❑ JC 35435	That's What Friends Are For	1978	10.00
❑ PC 35435	That's What Friends Are For	198?	8.00

—Budget-line reissue

MATHIS BROTHERS, THE

See DEAN AND MARK; THE NEWBEATS.

MATTHEWS, FAT MAN

45s

BAYOU

Number	Title (A Side/B Side)	Yr	NM
❑ 016	I'm Thankful/Goin' Down	1952	150.00

IMPERIAL

Number	Title (A Side/B Side)	Yr	NM
❑ 5211	When Boy Meets Girl/Later Baby	1952	2000.

—VG 1000; VG+ 1500

Number	Title (A Side/B Side)	Yr	NM
❑ 5235	Down the Line/You Know It	1953	100.00

MATTHEWS, IAN

Also see MATTHEWS' SOUTHERN COMFORT.

45s

COLUMBIA

Number	Title (A Side/B Side)	Yr	NM
❑ 10374	Brown Eyed Girl/Steamboat	1976	5.00
❑ 10553	Tigers Will Survive/Times	1977	5.00

ELEKTRA

Number	Title (A Side/B Side)	Yr	NM
❑ 45851	These Days/Same Old Man	1973	5.00
❑ 45871	Seven Bridges Road/ You Fell Through My Mind	1973	5.00
❑ 45892	Dirty Work/A Wailing Goodbye	1974	5.00

MUSHROOM

Number	Title (A Side/B Side)	Yr	NM
❑ 7039	Shake It/Stealin' Home	1978	4.00
❑ 7040	Give Me an Inch/Let There Be Blues	1979	4.00
❑ 7041	Don't Hang Up Your Dancing Shoes/Slip Away	1979	4.00
❑ 7045	Anna/You Don't See Me	1980	4.00

VERTIGO

Number	Title (A Side/B Side)	Yr	NM
❑ 101	If You Saw Through My Eyes/ Hearts	1971	6.00
❑ 102	Reno, Nevada/Desert Inn	1971	6.00
❑ 103	Da Doo Ron Ron/House of Un-American Blues Activity Dream	1972	6.00
❑ 105	Tigers Will Survive/ Hope You Know	1972	6.00

Albums

COLUMBIA

Number	Title (A Side/B Side)	Yr	NM
❑ PC 34102	Go for Broke	1976	10.00
❑ PC 34671	Hit and Run	1977	10.00

ELEKTRA

Number	Title (A Side/B Side)	Yr	NM
❑ EKS-75051	Valley Hi	1973	12.00
❑ EKS-75078	Some Days You Eat the Bear	1974	12.00

MUSHROOM

Number	Title (A Side/B Side)	Yr	NM
❑ MRS-5012	Stealin' Home	1978	10.00
❑ MRS-5014	Siamese Friends	1979	10.00

RSO

Number	Title (A Side/B Side)	Yr	NM
❑ RS-1-3092	A Spot of Interference	1980	10.00

VERTIGO

Number	Title (A Side/B Side)	Yr	NM
❑ VEL-1002	If You Saw Thro' My Eyes	1971	12.00
❑ VEL-1010	Tigers Will Survive	1972	12.00

WINDHAM HILL

Number	Title (A Side/B Side)	Yr	NM
❑ WD-1070	Walking a Changing Line: The Songs of Jules Shear	1987	10.00

MATTHEWS' SOUTHERN COMFORT

45s

DECCA

Number	Title (A Side/B Side)	Yr	NM
❑ 32664	Colorado Springs Eternal/ The Watch	1970	5.00
❑ 32774	Woodstock/Ballad of Obray Ramsey	1971	6.00
❑ 32845	Mare, Take Me Home/Brand New Tennessee Waltz	1971	5.00
❑ 32874	Tell Me Why/To Love	1971	5.00

Albums

DECCA

Number	Title (A Side/B Side)	Yr	NM
❑ DL 75191	Matthews' Southern Comfort	1970	12.00
❑ DL 75242	Second Spring	1970	12.00
❑ DL 75264	Later That Same Year	1971	12.00

PICKWICK

Number	Title (A Side/B Side)	Yr	NM
❑ SPC-3698	Later That Same Year	197?	8.00

MATTY, JAY

45s

ERA

Number	Title (A Side/B Side)	Yr	NM
❑ 3008	Janie My Lover/Tall Tale	1959	15.00

LUTE

Number	Title (A Side/B Side)	Yr	NM
❑ 6021	Merry Twist Mas/ Teenage Monster	1961	20.00

MAUDS, THE

45s

DUNWICH

Number	Title (A Side/B Side)	Yr	NM
❑ 160	Hold On/C'mon and Move	1967	12.00

MERCURY

Number	Title (A Side/B Side)	Yr	NM
❑ 72694	Hold On/C'mon and Move	1967	8.00
❑ 72720	When Something Is Wrong (With My Baby)/You Make Me Feel So Bad	1967	8.00
❑ 72760	He Will Break Your Heart/ You Must Believe Me	1967	8.00
❑ 72832	Forever Gone/Soul Drippin'	1968	8.00
❑ 72877	Only Love Can Save You/ Sergeant Sunshine	1968	8.00
❑ 72919	Brother Chickie/ Satisfy My Hunger	1969	8.00

RCA VICTOR

Number	Title (A Side/B Side)	Yr	NM
❑ 74-0377	Forget It, I've Got It/A Man Without a Dream	1970	6.00

Albums

MERCURY

Number	Title (A Side/B Side)	Yr	NM
❑ MG-21135 [M]	The Mauds Hold On	1967	20.00
❑ SR-61135 [S]	The Mauds Hold On	1967	25.00

MAURA AND MARIA

45s

CAMEO

Number	Title (A Side/B Side)	Yr	NM
❑ 338	Rain, Rain/(Instrumental)	1965	10.00

Albums

WYNCOTE

Number	Title (A Side/B Side)	Yr	NM
❑ SW-9075 [S]	Songs Made Famous by Joan Baez	1965	12.00
❑ W-9075 [M]	Songs Made Famous by Joan Baez	1965	10.00

MAURIAT, PAUL

45s

MGM

Number	Title (A Side/B Side)	Yr	NM
❑ 14378	Love Theme from "The Godfather"/Butterfly	1972	4.00

PHILIPS

Number	Title (A Side/B Side)	Yr	NM
❑ 40348	I Know a Place/I Tried and I Tried	1966	6.00
❑ 40426	You Don't Have to Say You Love Me/Kiss Tomorrow Goodbye	1967	6.00
❑ 40440	Black Is Black/Reach Out I'll Be There	1967	6.00
❑ 40462	This Is My Song/Puppet on a String	1967	6.00
❑ 40495	Love Is Blue/Alone in the World	1967	6.00
❑ 40495	Love Is Blue/Sunny	1967	6.00
❑ 40530	Love in Every Room/ The English Nightingale	1968	6.00
❑ 40530 [PS]	Love in Every Room/ The English Nightingale	1968	10.00
❑ 40550	San Francisco (Be Sure to Wear Flowers in Your Hair)/ I Waited for You	1968	6.00
❑ 40574	Chitty Chitty Bang Bang/ Come Un Carcon	1968	6.00
❑ 40594	Hey Jude/Those Were the Days	1969	5.00
❑ 40595	Sweet Charity/Irresistible	1969	5.00
❑ 40642	Get Back/Goodbye	1969	5.00
❑ 40647	Je T'Aime…Moi Non Plus/I Want to Love	1969	5.00
❑ 40683	Gone Is Love/She Is a Little Bit Sweeter	1970	5.00
❑ 40700	Etude in the Form of Rhythm and Blues/El Condor Pasa	1971	5.00
❑ 40707	Valerie's Theme/To Be the One You Love	1971	5.00

VERVE

Number	Title (A Side/B Side)	Yr	NM
❑ 10682	Apres Toi (Come What May)/ Theme from "A Summer Place"	1972	4.00

Albums

FANTASY

Number	Title (A Side/B Side)	Yr	NM
❑ 8380	Paris by Night	1968	12.00
❑ 8389	Joyeux Noel	1968	12.00
❑ 8394	Latin Style	1969	12.00

MERCURY

Number	Title (A Side/B Side)	Yr	NM
❑ SRM-1-3746	Overseas	1978	10.00

MGM

Number	Title (A Side/B Side)	Yr	NM
❑ SE-4838	Love Theme from "The Godfather"	1972	10.00
❑ M3G-4999	Have You Never Been Mellow	1975	10.00

PHILIPS

Number	Title (A Side/B Side)	Yr	NM
❑ PHM 200197 [M]	Listen Too	1965	12.00
❑ PHM 200215 [M]	Of Vodka and Caviar	1966	12.00
❑ PHM 200226 [M]	More Mauriat	1967	15.00
❑ PHM 200248 [M]	Blooming Hits	1967	20.00
❑ PHM 200255 [M]	The Christmas Album	1967	20.00
❑ PHS 600197 [S]	Listen Too	1965	15.00
❑ PHS 600215 [S]	Of Vodka and Caviar	1966	15.00
❑ PHS 600226 [S]	More Mauriat	1967	15.00
❑ PHS 600248 [S]	Blooming Hits	1967	15.00

—Original copies have no "blurb" for "Love Is Blue" on front cover

Number	Title (A Side/B Side)	Yr	NM
❑ PHS 600248 [S]	Blooming Hits	1968	12.00

—With blurb for "Love Is Blue" on front cover

Number	Title (A Side/B Side)	Yr	NM
❑ PHS 600255 [S]	The Christmas Album	1967	15.00
❑ PHS 600270	Mauriat Magic	1968	15.00
❑ PHS 600280	Prevailing Airs	1968	15.00
❑ PHS 600292	Doing My Thing	1969	15.00
❑ PHS 600299	The Soul of Paul Mauriat	1969	15.00
❑ PHS 600320	L-O-V-E	1969	15.00
❑ PHS 600337	Midnight Cowboy/ Let the Sunshine In	1970	12.00
❑ PHS 600345	Gone Is Love	1970	12.00
❑ PHS 600352	El Condor Pasa	1970	12.00

VERVE

Number	Title (A Side/B Side)	Yr	NM
❑ V6-5087	Theme from "A Summer Place"	1973	10.00

MAXIMILLIAN

Organist/keyboard player on DEL SHANNON's biggest hit records of the early 1960s.

45s

BIG TOP

Number	Title (A Side/B Side)	Yr	NM
❑ 3068	The Wanderer/The Snake	1961	60.00
❑ 3095	The Twistin' Ghost/The Breeze and I-Peter Gunn Theme	1961	20.00

CUB

Number	Title (A Side/B Side)	Yr	NM
❑ 9046	Gee Baby, You're the Utmost/ Blowing My Brains Out (Over You)	1959	25.00

Albums

ABC

Number	Title (A Side/B Side)	Yr	NM
❑ S-696	Maximillian	1969	40.00

MAXWELL, HOLLY

45s

CONSTELLATION

Number	Title (A Side/B Side)	Yr	NM
❑ 152	One Thin Dime/It's Impossible	1965	200.00
❑ 162	Let Him Go for Himself/ Only When You're Lonely	1965	25.00

CURTOM

Number	Title (A Side/B Side)	Yr	NM
❑ 1942	No One Else/Suffer	1969	12.00

MAXWELL, ROBERT

45s

DECCA

Number	Title (A Side/B Side)	Yr	NM
❑ 25622	Shangri-La/That Old Black Magic	1964	8.00
❑ 25637	Peg o' My Heart/Little Dipper	1964	6.00
❑ 25671	A Summer Song/Summertime	1965	6.00
❑ 31668	One O'Clock Jump/Rosebud	1964	6.00

M

Number	Title (A Side/B Side)	Yr	NM
❑ 31734	April in Portugal/The Right to Love	1965	6.00
❑ 31839	Song of the Nairobi Trio/ Theme from "Morituri"	1965	6.00

MERCURY

Number	Title (A Side/B Side)	Yr	NM
❑ 5773	Chinatown, My Chinatown/ Shuffle Off to Buffalo	1952	15.00

—As "Bobby Maxwell"

Number	Title (A Side/B Side)	Yr	NM
❑ 5844	Limehouse Blues/ Plink, Plank, Plunk	1952	15.00
❑ 70033	Shangri-La/Mary Lou	1953	20.00

—As "Bobby Maxwell"

Number	Title (A Side/B Side)	Yr	NM
❑ 70159	Hindustan/Bobble, Bobble, Bobble	1953	15.00
❑ 70177	Rose Marie/Ebb Tide	1953	15.00

MGM

Number	Title (A Side/B Side)	Yr	NM
❑ 12215	The Nearness of You/ Midnight Breeze	1956	12.00
❑ 12254	Spaghetti Rag/Can't Keep Running	1956	12.00
❑ 12293	Hot Tamale/Freckles	1956	12.00
❑ 12351	Injury Music for Football Games/Cumana	1956	12.00
❑ 12410	Song of the Nairobi Trio/ Accidental Slip on an Oriental Rug	1957	12.00
❑ 12488	Mary Lou/Open Your Mouth and Sing	1957	12.00
❑ 12546	I've Told Every Little Star/ Come Follow Me Baby	1957	12.00

ROULETTE

Number	Title (A Side/B Side)	Yr	NM
❑ 4148	Little Dipper/Mexican Hop	1959	10.00
❑ 4180	Pink Parfait/Flower of Budapest	1959	10.00
❑ 4241	The Man with the Monocle/ Ver Boten Liebe	1960	10.00
❑ 4338	Bazaar in Barcelona/Little Dipper	1961	10.00

—Roulette titles as "Mickey Mozart"

Albums

COMMAND

Number	Title (A Side/B Side)	Yr	NM
❑ 33-913 [M]	Anytime	1967	15.00
❑ SD 913 [S]	Anytime	1967	12.00

DECCA

Number	Title (A Side/B Side)	Yr	NM
❑ DL 4421 [M]	Shangri-La	1964	12.00
❑ DL 4563 [M]	Peg o' My Heart	1964	12.00
❑ DL 4609 [M]	Songs for All Seasons	1965	12.00
❑ DL 4723 [M]	Let's Get Away from It All	1966	12.00
❑ DL 74421 [S]	Shangri-La	1964	15.00
❑ DL 74563 [S]	Peg o' My Heart	1964	15.00
❑ DL 74609 [S]	Songs for All Seasons	1965	15.00
❑ DL 74723 [S]	Let's Get Away from It All	1966	15.00

MGM

Number	Title (A Side/B Side)	Yr	NM
❑ E-4246 [M]	The Very Best of Robert Maxwell	1964	12.00
❑ SE-4246 [S]	The Very Best of Robert Maxwell	1964	15.00

MAY, BILLY

45s

CAPITOL

Number	Title (A Side/B Side)	Yr	NM
❑ KCF 329 [PS]	Big Band Bash	1952	10.00

—Empty box for 15859, 15860 and 15861

Number	Title (A Side/B Side)	Yr	NM
❑ CCF 349 [PS]	A Band Is Born!	1952	10.00

—Empty box for 15905, 15906 and 15907

Number	Title (A Side/B Side)	Yr	NM
❑ F1793	All of Me/Lean, Baby	1951	15.00
❑ F1794	Fat Man Boogie/My Silent Love	1951	15.00
❑ F1795	When My Sugar Walks Down the Street/I Guess I'll Have to Change My Plans	1951	15.00
❑ F1919	Charmaine/When I Take My Sugar to Tea	1952	15.00
❑ F1955	Unforgettable/Silver and Gold	1952	15.00
❑ F1995	Always/There Is No Greater Love	1952	15.00
❑ F2054	Honest and Truly/When the Swallows Come Back to Capistrano	1952	15.00
❑ F2113	Easy Street/Mayhem	1952	15.00
❑ F2157	Love Is Just Around the Corner/ Gin and Tonic	1952	15.00
❑ F2227	Orchids in the Moonlight/ Fat Man Mambo	1952	15.00
❑ F2284	High Noon/Do You Ever Think of Me	1952	15.00
❑ F2297	A Cute Piece of Property/ Driftwood	1952	15.00
❑ F2364	Cocktails for Two/ Little Brown Jug	1953	15.00
❑ F2474	Good Grief/From the Land of the Sky Blue Water	1953	15.00
❑ F2575	Gone with the Wind/Romance	1953	15.00
❑ F2653	Cool Water/Dixieland Band	1953	15.00
❑ F2721	The Breeze and I/Whistle Stop	1954	15.00
❑ F2759	Rose Marie/Bill and Sam	1954	15.00
❑ F2802	Young at Heart/Lemon Twist	1954	15.00
❑ F2840	Hernando's Hideaway/Anything Can Happen Mambo	1954	15.00
❑ F2849	Hi Fi/The Song Is You	1954	15.00
❑ F3066	How Important Can It Be?/ Let It Happen	1955	12.00
❑ F3104	Whatever Lola Wants/ Just Between Friends	1955	12.00
❑ F3123	Cha Cha Cha/Shaner Maidel	1955	12.00
❑ F3221	Oklahoma!/Por Favor	1955	12.00
❑ F3297	Street of Dreams/Suzette	1955	12.00
❑ F3372	Main Title — Theme from "The Man with the Golden Arm"/Our Melody	1956	12.00
❑ F3486	Nightmare/The Beat	1956	12.00
❑ F3598	Christopher Columbus/Floater	1956	12.00
❑ F3697	Theme from "The Strange One"/Laurel's Theme	1957	12.00
❑ F3846	Seventy-Six Trombones/ Young and Dangerous	1957	12.00
❑ 4752	Love Makes the World Go Round/The Sweetest Sounds	1962	10.00
❑ F15731	If I Had You/All of Me	1951	12.00
❑ 6F15859	You're Driving Me Crazy/ Tenderly	1952	10.00
❑ 6F15860	When Your Lover Has Gone/ Please Be Kind	1952	10.00
❑ 6F15861	Perfidia/Diane	1952	10.00

—Above three comprise box set KCF-329, "Big Band Bash"

Number	Title (A Side/B Side)	Yr	NM
❑ 6F15905	When My Sugar Walks Down the Street/I Guess I'll Have to Change My Plans	1952	10.00
❑ 6F15906	Charmaine/Lean, Baby	1952	10.00
❑ 6F15907	The Fat Man Boogie/ There Is No Greater Love	1952	10.00

—Above three comprise box set CCF-349, "A Band Is Born!"

MCA

Number	Title (A Side/B Side)	Yr	NM
❑ 40352	Front Page Rag/Reunion	1974	8.00

REPRISE

Number	Title (A Side/B Side)	Yr	NM
❑ 20054	Ballad of the Sergeants 3/ Sergeant Boswell's Rock	1962	10.00
❑ 20062	Sergeants 3 March/ Girls from the Antler Bar	1962	10.00

TIME

Number	Title (A Side/B Side)	Yr	NM
❑ 1050	Advise and Consent/ Bashful Billie	1962	10.00

7-Inch Extended Plays

CAPITOL

Number	Title (A Side/B Side)	Yr	NM
❑ EAP 1-562	(contents unknown)	195?	12.00
❑ EAP 1-562 [PS]	Sorta-May, Part 1	195?	12.00
❑ EAP 2-562	(contents unknown)	195?	12.00
❑ EAP 2-562 [PS]	Sorta-May, Part 2	195?	12.00
❑ EAP 3-562	You Go to My Head/In a Persian Market//Just One of Those Things	195?	12.00
❑ EAP 3-562 [PS]	Sorta-May, Part 3	195?	12.00
❑ EAP 1-1043	(contents unknown)	1958	10.00
❑ EAP 1-1043	Big Fat Brass, Part 1	1958	10.00

Albums

BAINBRIDGE

Number	Title (A Side/B Side)	Yr	NM
❑ ST 1001	I Believe in You	197?	12.00

CAPITOL

Number	Title (A Side/B Side)	Yr	NM
❑ H 237 [10]	Join the Band	1951	40.00
❑ L 329 [10]	Big Band Bash	1952	40.00
❑ T 329 [M]	Big Band Bash	195?	25.00

—Turquoise label original

Number	Title (A Side/B Side)	Yr	NM
❑ H 349 [10]	A Band Is Born!	1952	40.00
❑ T 349 [M]	A Band Is Born!	195?	25.00

—Turquoise label original

Number	Title (A Side/B Side)	Yr	NM
❑ H 374 [10]	Bacchanalia!	1953	40.00
❑ T 374 [M]	Bacchanalia!	195?	30.00

—Turquoise label original

Number	Title (A Side/B Side)	Yr	NM
❑ H 487 [10]	Billy May's Naughty Operetta!	1953	40.00
❑ T 487 [M]	Billy May's Naughty Operetta!	195?	25.00

—Turquoise label original

Number	Title (A Side/B Side)	Yr	NM
❑ M 562 [M]	Sorta-May	197?	10.00

—Reissue with new prefix

Number	Title (A Side/B Side)	Yr	NM
❑ T 562 [M]	Sorta-May	195?	25.00

—Turquoise label original

Number	Title (A Side/B Side)	Yr	NM
❑ T 677 [M]	Sorta-Dixie!	195?	25.00

—Turquoise label original

Number	Title (A Side/B Side)	Yr	NM
❑ T 771 [M]	Billy May Plays for Fancy Dancin'	1956	25.00

—Turquoise label original

Number	Title (A Side/B Side)	Yr	NM
❑ STAO 924 [S]	Jimmie Lunceford in Hi-Fi: Authentic Re-Creations of the Lunceford Style	1958	40.00

—Black colorband label, Capitol logo at left

Number	Title (A Side/B Side)	Yr	NM
❑ ST 1043 [S]	Big Fat Brass	1958	30.00

—Black colorband label, Capitol logo at left

Number	Title (A Side/B Side)	Yr	NM
❑ T 1043 [M]	Big Fat Brass	1958	20.00

—Black colorband label, Capitol logo at left

Number	Title (A Side/B Side)	Yr	NM
❑ ST 1329 [S]	Cha Cha!	1959	25.00

—Black colorband label, Capitol logo at left

Number	Title (A Side/B Side)	Yr	NM
❑ T 1329 [M]	Cha Cha!	1959	20.00

—Black colorband label, Capitol logo at left

Number	Title (A Side/B Side)	Yr	NM
❑ T 1367 [M]	Cha Cha Mambos	1959	20.00

—Black colorband label, logo at left

Number	Title (A Side/B Side)	Yr	NM
❑ T 1377 [M]	Pow!	1959	20.00

—Gold "The Star Line" label

Number	Title (A Side/B Side)	Yr	NM
❑ ST 1417 [S]	The Girls and Boys on Broadway	1960	20.00

—Black colorband label, Capitol logo at left

Number	Title (A Side/B Side)	Yr	NM
❑ T 1417 [M]	The Girls and Boys on Broadway	1960	15.00

—Black colorband label, Capitol logo at left

Number	Title (A Side/B Side)	Yr	NM
❑ ST 1581 [S]	The Great Jimmie Lunceford: Authentic Re-Creations of the Lunceford Style by Billy May	1961	20.00

—Gold "The Star Line" label

Number	Title (A Side/B Side)	Yr	NM
❑ T 1581 [M]	The Great Jimmie Lunceford: Authentic Re-Creations of the Lunceford Style by Billy May	1961	15.00

—Gold "The Star Line" label

Number	Title (A Side/B Side)	Yr	NM
❑ ST 1709 [S]	The Sweetest Swingin' Sounds of No Strings	196?	20.00
❑ T 1709 [M]	The Sweetest Swingin' Sounds of No Strings	196?	15.00
❑ ST 1888 [S]	Bill's Bag	1963	20.00
❑ T 1888 [M]	Bill's Bag	1963	15.00
❑ ST 2560 [S]	Billy May Today	1965	15.00
❑ T 2560 [M]	Billy May Today	1965	12.00
❑ M 11885 [M]	Sorta-Dixie!	197?	10.00

—Reissue of Capitol 677

CREATIVE WORLD

Number	Title (A Side/B Side)	Yr	NM
❑ ST-1051 [M]	Sorta-May	197?	12.00
❑ ST-1054	Sorta-Dixie!	197?	12.00

IMPERIAL

Number	Title (A Side/B Side)	Yr	NM
❑ LP-9042 [M]	Fuzzy Pink Nightgown	1957	50.00

—Movie soundtrack

PAUSA

Number	Title (A Side/B Side)	Yr	NM
❑ PR 9035	A Band Is Born!	198?	10.00

—Reissue of Capitol T 349

PICKWICK

Number	Title (A Side/B Side)	Yr	NM
❑ PC- 3010 [M]	Hey It's May	196?	15.00
❑ SPC- 3010 [R]	Hey It's May	196?	8.00

STEREO SOUNDS

Number	Title (A Side/B Side)	Yr	NM
❑ SA-12	Music for Uptight Guys	196?	15.00

TIME

Number	Title (A Side/B Side)	Yr	NM
❑ S-2064 [S]	Billy May and His Orchestra	1962	20.00
❑ 52064 [M]	Billy May and His Orchestra	1962	15.00

TIME-LIFE

Number	Title (A Side/B Side)	Yr	NM
❑ STL-340 [(3)]	The Swing Era: 1930-1936	197?	20.00

—Box set with hardcover book; re-creations of original big-band charts, with some contributions by the Glenn Gray Orchestra

Number	Title (A Side/B Side)	Yr	NM
❑ STL-341 [(3)]	The Swing Era: 1936-1937	197?	20.00

—Box set with hardcover book; re-creations of original big-band charts, with some contributions by the Glenn Gray Orchestra

Number	Title (A Side/B Side)	Yr	NM
❑ STL-342 [(3)]	The Swing Era: 1937-1938	197?	20.00

—Box set with hardcover book; re-creations of original big-band charts, with some contributions by the Glenn Gray Orchestra

Number	Title (A Side/B Side)	Yr	NM
❑ STL-343 [(3)]	The Swing Era: 1938-1939	197?	20.00

—Box set with hardcover book; re-creations of original big-band charts, with some contributions by the Glenn Gray Orchestra

Number	Title (A Side/B Side)	Yr	NM
❑ STL-344 [(3)]	The Swing Era: 1939-1940	197?	20.00

—Box set with hardcover book; re-creations of original big-band charts, with some contributions by the Glenn Gray Orchestra

Number	Title (A Side/B Side)	Yr	NM
❑ STL-345 [(3)]	The Swing Era: 1940-1941	197?	20.00

—Box set with hardcover book; re-creations of original big-band charts, with some contributions by the Glenn Gray Orchestra

Number	Title (A Side/B Side)	Yr	NM
❑ STL-346 [(3)]	The Swing Era: 1941-1942	197?	20.00

—Box set with hardcover book; re-creations of original big-band charts, with some contributions by the Glenn Gray Orchestra

Number	Title (A Side/B Side)	Yr	NM
❑ STL-347 [(3)]	The Swing Era: 1942-1944	197?	20.00

—Box set with hardcover book; re-creations of original big-band charts, with some contributions by the Glenn Gray Orchestra

Number	Title (A Side/B Side)	Yr	NM
❑ STL-348 [(3)]	The Swing Era: 1944-1945	197?	20.00

—Box set with hardcover book; re-creations of original big-band charts, with some contributions by the Glenn Gray Orchestra

Number	Title (A Side/B Side)	Yr	NM
❑ STL-349 [(3)]	The Swing Era: The Postwar Years	197?	20.00

—Box set with hardcover book; re-creations of original big-band charts, with some contributions by the Glenn Gray Orchestra

Number	Title (A Side/B Side)	Yr	NM
❑ STL-350 [(3)]	The Swing Era: Into the '50s	197?	20.00

—Box set with hardcover book; re-creations of original big-band charts, with some contributions by the Glenn Gray Orchestra

Number	Title (A Side/B Side)	Yr	NM
❑ STL-351 [(3)]	The Swing Era: Encore!	197?	20.00

—Box set with hardcover book; re-creations of original big-band charts, with some contributions by the Glenn Gray Orchestra

Number	Title (A Side/B Side)	Yr	NM
❑ STL-352 [(3)]	The Swing Era: Curtain Call	197?	20.00

—Box set with hardcover book; re-creations of original big-band charts, with some contributions by the Glenn Gray Orchestra

Number	Title (A Side/B Side)	Yr	NM
❑ STL-353 [(3)]	The Swing Era: One More Time	197?	20.00

—Box set with hardcover book; re-creations of original big-band charts, with some contributions by the Glenn Gray Orchestra

MAY BLITZ

Albums

PARAMOUNT

Number	Title (A Side/B Side)	Yr	NM
❑ PAS-5020	May Blitz	1970	30.00

MAYALL, JOHN

12-Inch Singles

ISLAND

Number	Title (A Side/B Side)	Yr	NM
❑ PR 2490 [DJ]	The Last Time (same on both sides)	1988	8.00
❑ PR 2595 [DJ]	Fascinatin' Lover/Interview (22:33)	1989	12.00

Number	Title (A Side/B Side)	Yr	NM
45s			
ABC			
❑ 12216	Sunshine/Turn Me Loose	1976	5.00
BLUE THUMB			
❑ 264	Step in the Sun/ Al Goldstein Blues	1975	5.00
IMMEDIATE			
❑ 502	Telephone Blues/I'm Your Witch Doctor	1967	8.00
LONDON			
❑ 20016	Key to Love/Parchman Farm	1966	10.00
❑ 20024	All Your Love/Hideaway	1966	10.00
❑ 20035	Oh, Pretty Woman/Suspicions	1967	8.00
❑ 20037	Jenny/Picture on the Wall	1967	8.00
❑ 20039	Broken Wings/Sonny Boy Blue	1967	8.00
❑ 20042	Living Alone/Walking on Sunset	1968	8.00
POLYDOR			
❑ 14004	Don't Waste My Time/ Don't Pick a Flower	1969	6.00
❑ 14010	Room to Move/Saw Mill Gulch Road	1969	6.00
❑ 14051	Nature's Disappearing/ My Pretty Girl	1970	6.00
❑ 14051 [PS]	Nature's Disappearing/ My Pretty Girl	1970	15.00
❑ 14117	Nobody Cares/Play the Harp	1972	6.00
❑ 14151	Moving On/Keep Our Country Green	1972	6.00
❑ 14243	The 1974 Gasoline Blues/ Brand New Band	1974	6.00
❑ 14253	Let Me Give/Passing Through	1974	6.00
Albums			
ABC			
❑ ABCD-926	Notice to Appear	1976	10.00
❑ D-958	A Banquet in Blues	1976	10.00
❑ D-992	Lots of People	1977	10.00
❑ D-1039	A Hard Core Package	1977	10.00
❑ D-1086	Last of the British Blues	1978	10.00
ACCORD			
❑ SN-7209	Roadshow Blues Band	1982	10.00
BLUE THUMB			
❑ BTS-6019	New Year, New Band, New Company	1975	10.00
DECAL			
❑ LIK-1	Some of My Best Friends Are Blues	1986	10.00
DJM			
❑ 23	The Bottom Line	1979	10.00
❑ 29	No More Interviews	1979	10.00
GNP CRESCENDO			
❑ 2184	Behind the Iron Curtain	1986	10.00
ISLAND			
❑ 91005	Chicago Line	1988	10.00
❑ 842795-1	A Sense of Place	1990	12.00
LONDON			
❑ PS 492 [S]	Blues Breakers with Eric Clapton	1966	40.00
❑ PS 502 [S]	A Hard Road	1967	20.00
❑ PS 529 [S]	Crusade	1967	20.00
❑ PS 534	The Blues Alone	1968	15.00
❑ PS 537	Bare Wires	1968	15.00
❑ PS 543	Raw Blues	1968	15.00
❑ PS 545	Blues from Laurel Canyon	1969	15.00
❑ PS 562	Looking Back	1969	15.00
❑ PS 570	The Diary of a Band	1970	12.00
❑ PS 589	Live in Europe	1971	12.00
❑ 2PS 600 [(2)]	Through the Years	1971	12.00
❑ 2PS 618 [(2)]	Down the Line	1973	10.00
❑ LL 3492 [M]	Blues Breakers with Eric Clapton	1966	30.00
❑ LL 3502 [M]	A Hard Road	1967	20.00
❑ LL 3529 [M]	Crusade	1967	20.00
❑ LC-50009	Blues Breakers with Eric Clapton	1977	10.00
—Reissue of London PS 492			
❑ 800086-1	Blues Breakers with Eric Clapton	1983	8.00
—Reissue of London 50009			
❑ 820320-1	Primal Solos	1985	8.00
❑ 820331-1	Looking Back	1985	8.00
—Reissue of London PS 562			
❑ 820342-1	Raw Blues	1985	8.00
—Reissue of London PS 543			
MCA			
❑ 716	Last of the British Blues	1980	8.00
—Reissue of ABC 1086			
❑ 795	Hard Core	1980	8.00
—Reissue of ABC 1039			
MOBILE FIDELITY			
❑ 1-183	Blues Breakers Featuring Eric Clapton	1985	50.00
—Audiophile vinyl			
❑ 1-246	The Blues Alone	1996	30.00
—Audiophile vinyl			
POLYDOR			
❑ 25-3002 [(2)]	Back to the Roots	1971	12.00

John Mayall, *Thru the Years*, London 2PS 600/1, 1971, 2 records, **$12.**

Number	Title (A Side/B Side)	Yr	NM
❑ PD2-3005 [(2)]	Ten Years Are Gone	1973	12.00
❑ PD2-3006 [(2)]	The Best of John Mayall	1973	12.00
❑ 24-4004	The Turning Point	1970	10.00
❑ 24-4010	Empty Rooms	1970	10.00
❑ 24-4022	U.S.A. Union	1970	10.00
❑ PD-5012	Memories	1971	10.00
❑ PD-5027	Jazz-Blues Fusion	1972	10.00
❑ PD-5036	Moving On	1972	10.00
❑ PD-6030	The Latest Edition	1974	12.00
❑ SKAO-93398	U.S.A. Union	1970	15.00
—Capitol Record Club edition			
❑ 823305-1	The Turning Point	1985	8.00
—Reissue of Polydor 24-4004			
❑ 837127-1	Archive to the Eighties	1988	8.00

MAYE, LEE Also recorded as "Arthur Lee Maye."

Number	Title (A Side/B Side)	Yr	NM
45s			
ABC			
❑ 11028	If You Leave Me/The Greatest Love I've Ever Known	1967	30.00
BUDDAH			
❑ 141	He'll Have to Go/Jus' Lookin'	1969	6.00
CASH			
❑ 1063	Will You Be Mine/Honey Honey	1958	150.00
❑ 1065	All I Want Is Someone to Love/ Pounding	1958	120.00
DIG			
❑ 124	This Is the Night for Love/ (B-side unknown)	1956	250.00
❑ 133	A Fool's Prayer/(B-side unknown)	1957	150.00
FLIP			
❑ 330	Hey Pretty Baby/'Cause You're Mine Alone	1958	80.00
—As "Arthur Lee Maye"			
IMPERIAL			
❑ 5790	Will You Be Mine/Honey Honey	1961	20.00
JAMIE			
❑ 1272	Who Made You What You Are/ Loving Fool	1964	10.00
❑ 1276	How's the World Treating You?/ Loving Fool	1964	40.00
—As "Lee Maye of the Milwaukee Braves"			
❑ 1284	Only a Dream/The Breaks of Life	1964	10.00
❑ 1287	Even a Nobody/Who Made You What You Are	1964	10.00
❑ 1295	(Don't Pretend) Just Lay It on the Line/Careless Hands	1965	8.00
—With Barbara Lynn			
LENOX			
❑ 5566	Half Way (Out of Love with You)/I Can't Please You	1963	20.00
MODERN			
❑ 944	Set My Heart Free/I Wanna Love	1954	600.00
—As "Arthur Lee Maye and the Crowns"			
RPM			
❑ 424	Truly/Oochie Pachie	1955	200.00
—As "Arthur Lee Maye and the Crowns"			
❑ 429	Loop De Loop/Love Me Always	1955	120.00
—As "Arthur Lee Maye"			
❑ 438	Do the Bop/Please Don't Leave Me	1955	150.00
—As "Arthur Lee Maye and the Crowns"			
SPECIALTY			
❑ 573	Gloria/Oo-Rooba-Lee	1956	60.00
—As "Arthur Lee Maye and the Crowns"			
TOWER			
❑ 243	When My Heart Hurts No More/ At the Party	1966	30.00

MAYER, NATHANIEL

Number	Title (A Side/B Side)	Yr	NM
45s			
FORTUNE			
❑ 449	Village of Love/I Want a Woman	1962	25.00
❑ 487	Hurting Love/Leave Me Alone	1962	30.00
—Fortune 449 and 487 were part of the United Artists numbering system			
❑ 542	My Last Dance with You/ My Little Darling	1962	20.00
❑ 545	Village of Love/I Want a Woman	1962	20.00
❑ 547	Hurting Love/Leave Me Alone	1962	20.00

Number	Title (A Side/B Side)	Yr	NM
❑ 550	Mr. Santa Claus/(B-side unknown)	1962	30.00
❑ 550	Work It Out/Well, I've Got News	1962	40.00
❑ 554	I Had a Dream/I'm Not Gonna Cry	1963	15.00
❑ 557	Going Back to the Village of Love/My Last Dance with You	1963	60.00
❑ 562	The Place I Know/ Don't Come Back	196?	15.00
❑ 563	Village of Love/I Want a Woman	196?	12.00
❑ 567	From Now On/I Want Love and Affection	196?	12.00

Albums

FORTUNE

Number	Title (A Side/B Side)	Yr	NM
❑ 8014 [M]	Goin' Back to the Village of Love	196?	60.00
—Yellow label			
❑ 8014 [M]	Goin' Back to the Village of Love	196?	150.00
—Purple label			
❑ 8014 [M]	Goin' Back to the Village of Love	1964	300.00
—Light blue label			
❑ 8014 [M]	Goin' Back to the Village of Love	197?	15.00
—Bluish purple label, with much more flexible vinyl than earlier pressings			

MAYFIELD, CURTIS

Also see THE IMPRESSIONS.

12-Inch Singles

CAPITOL

Number	Title (A Side/B Side)	Yr	NM
❑ V-15602	Superfly 1990 (6 versions)	1990	8.00
—With Ice-T			

CURTOM

Number	Title (A Side/B Side)	Yr	NM
❑ 12-PO-22 [DJ]	I Mo Git U Sucka/He's a Fly Guy	198?	10.00
❑ 12-PO-52 [DJ]	Got to Be Real/On and On	198?	10.00

RSO/CURTOM

Number	Title (A Side/B Side)	Yr	NM
❑ 1016 [DJ]	Tell Me, Tell Me (7:16)// Heartbeat/Over the Hump	1979	10.00

45s

ARISTA

Number	Title (A Side/B Side)	Yr	NM
❑ 9806	He's a Flyguy/(Instrumental)	1989	2.00
❑ 9806 [PS]	He's a Flyguy/(Instrumental)	1989	3.00
—With Fishbone			

BOARDWALK

Number	Title (A Side/B Side)	Yr	NM
❑ NB7-11-122	She Don't Let Nobody (But Me)/ You Get All My Love	1981	4.00
❑ NB7-11-132	Toot An'Toot An'Toot/ Come Free Your People	1981	4.00
❑ NB7-11-155	Hey Baby (Give It All to Me)/ Summer Hot	1982	4.00
❑ NB7-11-169	Dirty Laundry/Nobody But You	1982	4.00

COLUMBIA

Number	Title (A Side/B Side)	Yr	NM
❑ 10147	Stash That Butt, Sucker/Zanzibar	1975	5.00

CRC

Number	Title (A Side/B Side)	Yr	NM
❑ 001	Baby It's You/Breakin' in the Streets	1985	6.00

CURTOM

Number	Title (A Side/B Side)	Yr	NM
❑ 0105	So in Love/Hard Times	1975	5.00
❑ 0118	Only You Babe/Love to the People	1976	5.00
❑ 0122	Party Night/P.S. I Love You	1976	5.00
❑ 0125	Show Me Love/Just Want to Be with You	1977	5.00
❑ 0131	Do Do Wap Is Strong in Here/ Need Someone to Love	1977	5.00
❑ 0135	You Are, You Are/Get a Little Bit (Give, Get, Take and Have)	1978	5.00
❑ 0135 [PS]	You Are, You Are/Get a Little Bit (Give, Get, Take and Have)	1978	6.00
❑ 0141	Do It All Night/Party Party	1978	5.00
❑ 0142	In Love, In Love, In Love/Keeps Me Loving You	1978	5.00
❑ 1955	(Don't Worry) If There's a Hell Below We're All Going to Go/ The Makings of You	1970	6.00
❑ 1960	Beautiful Brother of Mine/ Give It Up	1971	6.00
❑ 1963	Mighty Mighty (Spade and Whitey)/(B-side unknown)	1971	6.00
❑ 1966	Get Down/We're a Winner	1971	6.00
❑ 1968	We Got to Have Peace/ We're a Winner	1972	6.00
❑ 1968 [PS]	We Got to Have Peace/ We're a Winner	1972	8.00
❑ 1972	Beautiful Brother of Mine/ Love to Keep You In My Mind	1972	6.00
❑ 1974	Move On Up/Underground	1972	6.00
❑ 1975	Freddie's Dead (Theme from "Superfly")/Underground	1972	6.00
❑ 1978	Superfly/Underground	1972	6.00
❑ 1978 [PS]	Superfly/Underground	1972	8.00
❑ 1987	Future Shock/The Other Side of Town	1973	6.00
❑ 1991	If I Were Only a Child Again/ Think	1973	6.00
❑ 1993	Can't Say Nothin'/Future Song	1973	6.00
❑ 1999	Kung Fu/Right On for the Darkness	1974	6.00
❑ 1999 [PS]	Kung Fu/Right On for the Darkness	1974	8.00
❑ 2005	Sweet Exorcist/Suffer	1974	6.00
❑ 2006	Mother's Son/Love Me	1974	6.00

RSO/CURTOM

Number	Title (A Side/B Side)	Yr	NM
❑ 919	This Year/(Instrumental)	1979	5.00
❑ 941	You're So Good to Me/Between You, Babe, and Me	1979	5.00
—With Linda Clifford			
❑ 1029	Love's Sweet Sensation/ (Instrumental)	1980	5.00
—With Linda Clifford			
❑ 1036	Love Me, Love Me Now/ It's Alright	1980	5.00
❑ 1046	Tripping Out/Never Stop Loving	1980	5.00

7-Inch Extended Plays

CURTOM

Number	Title (A Side/B Side)	Yr	NM
❑ CRS-8014-EP	Pusherman/Think (Instrumental)//Give Me Your Love/Eddie You Should Know Better/Junkie Chase (Instrumental)	1972	15.00
—Jukebox issue; small hole, plays at 33 1/3 rpm			
❑ CRS-8014-EP [PS]	Super Fly	1972	15.00

Albums

BOARDWALK

Number	Title (A Side/B Side)	Yr	NM
❑ NB1-33239	Love Is the Place	1981	10.00
❑ NB1-33256	Honesty	1982	10.00

CRC

Number	Title (A Side/B Side)	Yr	NM
❑ 2001	We Come in Peace with a Message of Love	1985	12.00

CURTOM

Number	Title (A Side/B Side)	Yr	NM
❑ CUR-2003	There's No Place Like America Today	198?	8.00
—Reissue of 5001			
❑ CUR-2005	Something to Believe In	198?	8.00
—Reissue of RSO 3077			
❑ CUR-2008	Take It to the Street	198?	10.00
❑ CUR-2901 [(2)]	Live in Europe	198?	12.00
❑ CUR-2902 [(2)]	Greatest Hits of All Time (Classic Collection)	198?	12.00
❑ CU 5001	There's No Place Like America Today	1975	12.00
❑ CU 5007	Give, Get, Take and Have	1976	12.00
❑ CU 5013	Never Say You Can't Survive	1977	12.00
❑ CUK 5022	Do It All Night	1978	12.00
❑ CRS-8005	Curtis	1970	15.00
❑ CRS-8008 [(2)]	Curtis/Live!	1971	20.00
❑ CRS-8009	Roots	1971	15.00
❑ CRS-8014	Superfly	1972	20.00
❑ CRS-8015	Back to the World	1973	15.00
❑ CRS-8018	Curtis in Chicago	1973	15.00
❑ CRS-8601	Sweet Exorcist	1974	12.00
❑ CRS-8604	Got to Find a Way	1974	12.00

RSO

Number	Title (A Side/B Side)	Yr	NM
❑ RS-1-3053	Heartbeat	1979	10.00
❑ RS-1-3077	Something to Believe In	1980	10.00

MAYFIELD, PERCY

45s

ATLANTIC

Number	Title (A Side/B Side)	Yr	NM
❑ 3207	I Don't Want to Be President/ Nothin' Stays the Same Forever	1974	5.00

BRUNSWICK

Number	Title (A Side/B Side)	Yr	NM
❑ 55390	Walking on a Tightrope/ P.M. Blues	1968	8.00

CHESS

Number	Title (A Side/B Side)	Yr	NM
❑ 1599	Double Dealing/Are You Out There	1955	60.00

IMPERIAL

Number	Title (A Side/B Side)	Yr	NM
❑ 5577	One Love/My Reward	1959	15.00
❑ 5620	My Heart Is a Prisoner/ My Memories	1959	15.00

KING

Number	Title (A Side/B Side)	Yr	NM
❑ 4480	Two Years of Torture/Half Awake	1951	60.00

RCA VICTOR

Number	Title (A Side/B Side)	Yr	NM
❑ 74-0307	To Live the Past/Lying Woman (Not Trustworthy)	1970	6.00
❑ 74-0348	A Highway Is Like a Woman/You Wear Your Hair Too Long	1970	6.00
❑ 74-0379	Daddy Wants You to Come Home/Weakness Is a Thing Called Man	1970	6.00
❑ 74-0462	The Flirt/California Blues	1971	6.00

SPECIALTY

Number	Title (A Side/B Side)	Yr	NM
❑ 375	Please Send Me Someone to Love/Strange Things Happening	1950	80.00
❑ 390	Lost Love/Life Is Suicide	1951	60.00
❑ 400	What a Fool I Was/ Nightless Lover	1951	60.00
❑ 408	Prayin' For Your Return/My Blues	1951	60.00
❑ 416	Cry Baby/Hopeless	1952	40.00
❑ 425	The Big Question/The Hurt Is On	1952	40.00
❑ 432	Louisiana/Two Hearts Are Greater Than One	1952	40.00
❑ 439	Lonesome Highway/My Heart	1952	40.00
❑ 460	Lost Mind/Lonely One	1953	40.00
—Black vinyl			
❑ 460	Lost Mind/Lonely One	1953	80.00
—Colored vinyl			
❑ 473	The Bachelor Blues/ How Deep Is the Well	1953	40.00
—Black vinyl			
❑ 473	The Bachelor Blues/ How Deep Is the Well	1953	80.00
—Colored vinyl			
❑ 485	I Need Love So Bad/Loose Lips	1954	40.00
❑ 499	You Don't Exist No More/ Sugar Mama, Peach Papa	1954	40.00
❑ 537	My Heart Is Cryin'/You Were Lyin' to Me	1954	40.00
❑ 544	Baby You're Rich/ The Voice Within	1955	30.00
❑ 607	Diggin' the Moonglow/ Please Believe Me	1956	30.00
❑ 690	When Did You Leave Heaven/ What Must I Do	1960	20.00
❑ 723	Lost Mind/River's Invitation	1973	6.00

TANGERINE

Number	Title (A Side/B Side)	Yr	NM
❑ 923	Never No More/I Reached for a Tear	1962	12.00
❑ 927	Never Say Now/Life Is Suicide	1963	10.00
❑ 931	River's Invitation/Baby Please	1963	10.00
❑ 934	The Hunt Is On/Cookin' in Style	1963	10.00
❑ 935	You Don't Exist No More/ Memory Pain	1964	10.00
❑ 941	Stranger in My Own Home Town/ Maybe It's Because of Love	1964	10.00
❑ 950	Fading Love/Stand By	1965	8.00
❑ 957	Give Me Time to Explain/ My Jug and I	1965	8.00
❑ 966	It's Time to Make a Change/ We Both Must Cry	1966	8.00
❑ 973	My Love/My Bottle Is My Companion	1966	8.00
❑ 977	As Long As You're Mine/ Ha Ha in the Daytime	1967	8.00
❑ 979	Don't Start Lyin' to Me/ Pretty Eyed Baby	1967	8.00

Albums

BRUNSWICK

Number	Title (A Side/B Side)	Yr	NM
❑ BL 754145	Walking on a Tightrope	1968	20.00

INTERMEDIA

Number	Title (A Side/B Side)	Yr	NM
❑ QS-5010	Please Send Me Someone to Love	198?	10.00

RCA VICTOR

Number	Title (A Side/B Side)	Yr	NM
❑ LSP-4269	Percy Mayfield Sings Percy Mayfield	1970	15.00
❑ LSP-4444	Weakness Is a Thing Called Man	1970	15.00
❑ LSP-4558	Blues And Then Some	1971	15.00

SPECIALTY

Number	Title (A Side/B Side)	Yr	NM
❑ SPS-2126	The Best of Percy Mayfield	1970	20.00
❑ SP-7001	Poet of the Blues	1990	15.00

TANGERINE

Number	Title (A Side/B Side)	Yr	NM
❑ TRC-1505 [M]	My Jug and I	1966	30.00
❑ TRCS-1505 [S]	My Jug and I	1966	50.00
❑ TRC-1510 [M]	Bought Blues	1967	30.00
❑ TRCS-1510 [S]	Bought Blues	1967	50.00

MAYO, DAVID

45s

TMI

Number	Title (A Side/B Side)	Yr	NM
❑ ZS7 9001	Beautiful/Plain Old Gone	1971	7.00
❑ ZS7 9007	One Woman Man/ (B-side unknown)	1971	7.00

MAYO, FRANKIE, AND THE FALCONS

45s

RCA VICTOR

Number	Title (A Side/B Side)	Yr	NM
❑ 47-7076	Stepping Stone/Jigsaw Puzzle	1957	25.00

MAYPOLE

Albums

COLOSSUS

Number	Title (A Side/B Side)	Yr	NM
❑ CS-1007	Maypole	1971	60.00

MAYS, WILLIE

45s

DUKE

Number	Title (A Side/B Side)	Yr	NM
❑ 350	My Sad Heart/If You Love Me	1962	10.00
❑ 418	My Sad Heart/If You Love Me	1967	8.00

Except when noted otherwise, VG = 25% of NM, and VG+ = 50% of NM. (Example: VG = $2.00, VG+ = $4.00 and NM = $8.00.)

Number	Title (A Side/B Side)	Yr	NM
EPIC			
❑ 9066	Say Hey (The Willie Mays Song)/ Out of the Bushes	1954	25.00
—With the Treniers			

MC5

45s

Number	Title (A Side/B Side)	Yr	NM
A-SQUARE			
❑ 333	Looking at You/Borderline	1967	80.00
—500 copies of this record were pressed			
❑ 333 [PS]	Looking at You/Borderline	1967	40.00
ALIVE/TOTAL ENERGY			
❑ NER 3012	Looking at You/Borderline	1998	6.00
—30th anniversary reissue			
❑ NER 3012 [PS]	Looking at You/Borderline	1998	6.00
AMG			
❑ 1000 [DJ]	I Can Only Give You Everything (same on both sides)	1966	50.00
❑ 1001	I Can Only Give You Everything/I Just Don't Know	1969	50.00
—Black label			
❑ 1001	I Can Only Give You Everything/One of the Guys	1969	50.00
—Yellow label			
ATLANTIC			
❑ 2678	Tonight/Looking at You	1969	15.00
❑ 2724	The American Ruse/ Shakin' Street	1970	15.00
ELEKTRA			
❑ MC5-1 [DJ]	Kick Out the Jams/ Motor City Is Burning	1968	70.00
—Distributed free at Fillmore East concert 12/12/68; A-side is an alternate take			
❑ 45648	Kick Out the Jams/ Motor City Is Burning	1969	20.00

Albums

Number	Title (A Side/B Side)	Yr	NM
ALIVE			
❑ 0005 [10]	Power Trip	1994	12.00
❑ 0008 [10]	Ice Pick Slim/Mad Like Eldridge Cleaver	1994	12.00
ATLANTIC			
❑ SD 8247	Back in the USA	1970	50.00
❑ SD 8285	High Time	1971	50.00
ELEKTRA			
❑ EKS-74042	Kick Out the Jams	1969	20.00
—All other editions			
❑ EKS-74042	Kick Out the Jams	1969	50.00
—Gatefold cover with John Sinclair liner notes in center spread; brownish label			
SUNDAZED			
❑ LP 5092	Kick Out the Jams	2001	20.00
—Reissue of original Elektra album, complete with uncensored liner notes			
❑ LP 5093	Back in the USA	2002	20.00
—Reissue on 180-gram vinyl			
❑ LP 5094	High Time	2002	20.00
—Reissue on 180-gram vinyl			
TOTAL ENERGY			
❑ 2001 [10]	The American Ruse	1994	12.00

MCCALL, C.W.

45s

Number	Title (A Side/B Side)	Yr	NM
AMERICAN GRAMAPHONE			
❑ 351	Old Home Filler-Up An' Keep On-a-Truckin' Café/Old 30	1974	15.00
MGM			
❑ 14738	Old Home Filler-Up An' Keep On-a-Truckin' Café/Old 30	1974	4.00
❑ 14764	Wolf Creek Pass/Sloan	1974	4.00
❑ 14801	Classified/I've Trucked All Over This Land	1975	4.00
❑ 14825	Black Bear Road/Four Wheel Drive	1975	4.00
❑ 14839	Convoy/Long Lonesome Road	1975	5.00
POLYDOR			
❑ 14310	There Won't Be No Country Music (There Won't Be No Rock 'n' Roll)/Green River	1976	4.00
❑ 14331	Crispy Critters/Jackson Hole	1976	4.00
❑ 14352	Four Wheel Cowboy/ Aurora Borealis	1976	4.00
❑ 14365	'Round the World with the Rubber Duck/Night Rider	1976	4.00
❑ 14377	Audubon/Ratchetjaw	1977	4.00
❑ 14420	Roses for Mama/Columbine	1977	4.00
❑ 14445	Sing Silent Night/Old Glory	1977	5.00
❑ 14458	Old Glory/Watch the Wildwood Flowers	1978	4.00
❑ 14527	Outlaws and Lone Star Beer/ Silver Cloud Breakdown	1978	4.00
❑ 14550	Milton/The Little Things in Life	1979	4.00

MC5, *Kick Out the Jams*, Elektra EKS-74042, 1969, gatefold cover with John Sinclair liner notes, **$50.**

Albums

Number	Title (A Side/B Side)	Yr	NM
MGM			
❑ M3G-4989	Wolf Creek Pass	1975	10.00
❑ M3G-5008	Black Bear Road	1975	10.00
POLYDOR			
❑ PD-1-6069	Wilderness	1976	10.00
❑ PD-1-6094	Rubber Duck	1977	10.00
❑ PD-1-6125	Roses for Mama	1978	10.00
❑ PD-1-6156	Greatest Hits	1978	10.00
❑ PD-1-6190	C.W. McCall & Co.	1979	10.00
❑ 825793-1	Greatest Hits	198?	8.00
—Reissue of 6156			

MCCALL, DARRELL

45s

Number	Title (A Side/B Side)	Yr	NM
ATLANTIC			
❑ 4019	There's Still a Lot of Love in San Antone/A Texas Honky Tonk	1974	5.00
❑ 4200	If You Don't Know Your Roses/ Where Is All That Love You Talked About	1974	5.00
AVCO			
❑ 609	Cold Beer Signs and Country Music/Face to the Wall	1975	6.00
❑ 615	Helpless/If You Don't Believe I Love You	1975	6.00
CAPITOL			
❑ 4543	My Kind of Lovin'/ Beyond Imagination	1961	12.00
❑ 4609	Call the Zoo/Lonesome	1961	12.00
COLUMBIA			
❑ 3-10296	Pins and Needles (In My Heart)/ Every Girl I See	1976	5.00
❑ 3-10410	I Come Home to Face the Music/ It's Been So Long, Darlin'	1976	5.00
❑ 3-10480	Lily Dale/Please Don't Leave Me	1976	5.00
—A-side with Willie Nelson			
❑ 3-10576	Dreams of a Dreamer/Sad Songs and Waltzes	1977	5.00
❑ 3-10653	Down the Roads of Daddy's Dreams/An Old Memory's Arms	1977	5.00
❑ 3-10723	The Weeds Outlived the Roses/ Love Didn't Drive My Good Woman Wild	1978	5.00
INDIGO			
❑ 304	Memphis in May/ (B-side unknown)	1984	6.00
PHILIPS			
❑ 40053	I Can Take His Baby Away/ A Man Can Change	1962	10.00
❑ 40079	A Stranger Was Here/ I'm a Little Bit Lonely	1962	10.00
❑ 40116	No Place to Hide/Hud	1963	10.00
❑ 40154	Keeping My Feet on the Ground/Got My Baby on My Mind	1963	10.00
RCA			
❑ PB-12033	Long Line of Empties/I Wonder Which One of Us Is to Blame	1980	4.00
WAYSIDE			
❑ 003	Hurry Up/Wedding Band	1969	6.00
❑ 005	Hide and Go Cheat/Tiny Ribbons	1969	6.00
❑ 008	The Arms of My Weakness/ Big Oak Tree	1970	6.00
❑ 011	Sally Bryson/(B-side unknown)	1970	6.00
❑ 1011	I'd Love to Live with You Again/ I Love You Baby	1968	7.00
❑ 1021	Wall of Pictures/I'd Die to See You Smile	1968	7.00

Albums

Number	Title (A Side/B Side)	Yr	NM
COLUMBIA			
❑ KC 34718	Lily Dale	1977	12.00
WAYSIDE			
❑ 1030	Meet Darrell McCall	1969	20.00

MCCALLS, THE

45s

HIT

Number	Title (A Side/B Side)	Yr	NM
❑ 236	Five O'Clock World/ As Tears Go By	1966	12.00
—B-side by the Chords (2)			
❑ 244	Daydream/19th Nervous Breakdown	1966	10.00
❑ 260	Hanky Panky/Hungry	1966	10.00
—B-side by the Gallicos			

MCCALLUM, DAVID

45s

CAPITOL

Number	Title (A Side/B Side)	Yr	NM
❑ 5571	My Carousel/Communications	1966	8.00
❑ 5571 [PS]	My Carousel/Communications	1966	12.00
❑ 5721	Three Bites of the Apple/ House on Breckinridge Lane	1966	8.00
❑ 5721 [PS]	Three Bites of the Apple/ House on Breckinridge Lane	1966	12.00
❑ 5802	A Man and a Woman/ House of Mirrors	1966	8.00

Albums

CAPITOL

Number	Title (A Side/B Side)	Yr	NM
❑ ST 2432 [S]	Music — A Part of Me	1966	15.00
❑ T 2432 [M]	Music — A Part of Me	1966	12.00
❑ ST 2498 [S]	Music: A Bit More of Me	1966	15.00
❑ T 2498 [M]	Music: A Bit More of Me	1966	12.00
❑ ST 2651 [S]	Music: It's Happening Now	1967	15.00
❑ T 2651 [M]	Music: It's Happening Now	1967	15.00
❑ ST 2748 [S]	McCallum	1967	15.00
❑ T 2748 [M]	McCallum	1967	15.00

M

MCCANN, LES

12-Inch Singles

A&M

Number	Title (A Side/B Side)	Yr	NM
❑ SP-17042 [DJ]	Just the Way You Are (6:31) (same on both sides)	1978	12.00

45s

A&M

Number	Title (A Side/B Side)	Yr	NM
❑ 2081	Just the Way You Are/How Can You (Live Without Love)	1978	4.00

ATLANTIC

Number	Title (A Side/B Side)	Yr	NM
❑ 2615	With These Hands/Burnin' Coal	1969	6.00
❑ 2713	What I Call Soul/Comment	1970	6.00
❑ 2918	What's Going On (Part 1)/ What's Going On (Part 2)	1972	5.00
❑ 3253	When It's Over/Someday We'll Meet Again	1975	5.00
❑ 3312	Us/Well, Cuss Me Daddy	1976	5.00

LIMELIGHT

Number	Title (A Side/B Side)	Yr	NM
❑ 3060	But Not Really/Jack V. Schwartz	1965	8.00
❑ 3066	Green Green Rocky Road/ Great City	1965	8.00
❑ 3077	All/Bucket O' Grease	1967	8.00
❑ 3078	Caper of the Golden Bulls/ Loves of July	1967	8.00
❑ 3081	The Shout (Part 1)/ The Shout (Part 2)	1967	8.00

PACIFIC JAZZ

Number	Title (A Side/B Side)	Yr	NM
❑ 306	C Jam Blues/The Shout	1960	12.00
❑ 309	Truth/Little Girl from Casper	1961	12.00
❑ 311	Fish This Week/Vacushna	1961	12.00
❑ 317	I Am in Love/Big Jim	1961	12.00
❑ 318	Gone Up and Get That Church (Part 1)/Gone Up and Get That Church (Part 2)	1961	12.00
❑ 329	Sweet Georgia Brown/ I Cried for You	1961	12.00
❑ 335	Next Spring/Wonder Why	1962	12.00
❑ 341	Twist Cha Cha/Little 3/4 for God & Co.	1962	12.00
❑ 350	Shampoo/Kathleen's Theme	1963	12.00
❑ 820	They Can't Take That Away from Me/Little Girl from Casper	1960	12.00

WORLD PACIFIC

Number	Title (A Side/B Side)	Yr	NM
❑ 387	The Gospel Truth/Send It On Down to Me	1963	10.00
❑ 389	Bye and Bye/Get That Soul	1963	10.00
❑ 404	Back at the Chicken Shack/ Sack o' Woe	1964	10.00
❑ 406	Bluesette/Spanish Castles	1964	10.00
❑ 411	Big City/Route 66	1964	10.00
❑ 418	It Had Better Be Tonight/ Que Rico	1964	10.00
❑ 422	Basuto Baby/McCanna	1965	10.00
❑ 88133	The Shout/Spanish Onions	1966	8.00

Albums

A&M

Number	Title (A Side/B Side)	Yr	NM
❑ SP-4718	The Man	1978	10.00
❑ SP-4780	Tall, Dark and Handsome	1979	10.00

ABC IMPULSE!

Number	Title (A Side/B Side)	Yr	NM
❑ AS-9329	The Music Lets Me Be	1977	10.00
❑ AS-9333	Live at the Roxy	1978	10.00

ATLANTIC

Number	Title (A Side/B Side)	Yr	NM
❑ SD 2-312 [(2)]	Live at Montreux	1974	15.00
❑ SD 1516	Much Les	1969	15.00
❑ SD 1547	Comment	1970	15.00
❑ 1603 [M]	Invitation to Openness	1972	25.00
—Mono is white label promo only with "d/j copy monaural" sticker on front cover			
❑ SD 1603 [S]	Invitation to Openness	1972	12.00
❑ SD 1619	Talk to the People	1972	12.00
❑ SD 1646	Layers	1973	12.00
❑ SD 1666	Another Beginning	1974	12.00
❑ SD 1679	Hustle to Survive	1975	12.00
❑ SD 1690	River High, River Low	1976	12.00

JAM

Number	Title (A Side/B Side)	Yr	NM
❑ 012	The Longer You Wait	1984	10.00
❑ 019	Les McCann's Music Box	1984	10.00

LIMELIGHT

Number	Title (A Side/B Side)	Yr	NM
❑ LM-82016 [M]	But Not Really	1965	15.00
❑ LM-82025 [M]	Poo Boo	1965	15.00
❑ LM-82031 [M]	Beaux J. Pooboo	1966	15.00
❑ LM-82036 [M]	Live at Shelly's Manne-Hole	1966	15.00
❑ LM-82041 [M]	Les McCann Plays the Hits	1966	15.00
❑ LM-82043 [M]	Bucket O' Grease	1967	20.00
❑ LM-82046 [M]	Live at the Bohemian Caverns, Washington, D.C.	1967	20.00
❑ LS-86016 [S]	But Not Really	1965	20.00
❑ LS-86025 [S]	Poo Boo	1965	20.00
❑ LS-86031 [S]	Beaux J. Pooboo	1966	20.00
❑ LS-86036 [S]	Live at Shelly's Manne-Hole	1966	20.00
❑ LS-86041 [S]	Les McCann Plays the Hits	1966	20.00
❑ LS-86043 [S]	Bucket O' Grease	1967	15.00
❑ LS-86046 [S]	Live at the Bohemian Caverns, Washington, D.C.	1967	15.00

PACIFIC JAZZ

Number	Title (A Side/B Side)	Yr	NM
❑ PJ-2 [M]	The Truth	1960	25.00
❑ ST-2 [S]	The Truth	1960	30.00
❑ PJ-7 [M]	The Shout	1960	25.00
❑ ST-7 [S]	The Shout	1960	30.00
❑ PJ-16 [M]	Les McCann in San Francisco	1961	25.00
❑ ST-16 [S]	Les McCann in San Francisco	1961	30.00
❑ PJ-25 [M]	Pretty Lady	1961	20.00
❑ ST-25 [S]	Pretty Lady	1961	25.00
❑ PJ-31 [M]	Les McCann Sings	1961	20.00
❑ ST-31 [S]	Les McCann Sings	1961	25.00
❑ PJ-45 [M]	Les McCann in New York	1962	20.00
❑ ST-45 [S]	Les McCann in New York	1962	25.00
❑ PJ-56 [M]	On Time	1962	20.00
—Black vinyl			
❑ PJ-56 [M]	On Time	1962	40.00
—Yellow vinyl			
❑ ST-56 [S]	On Time	1962	25.00
—Black vinyl			
❑ ST-56 [S]	On Time	1962	50.00
—Yellow vinyl			
❑ PJ-63 [M]	Shampoo	1962	15.00
❑ ST-63 [S]	Shampoo	1962	20.00
❑ PJ-69 [M]	The Gospel Truth	1963	15.00
❑ ST-69 [S]	The Gospel Truth	1963	20.00
❑ PJ-78 [M]	Soul Hits	1963	15.00
❑ ST-78 [S]	Soul Hits	1963	20.00
❑ PJ-81 [M]	Jazz Waltz	1964	15.00
❑ ST-81 [S]	Jazz Waltz	1964	20.00
❑ PJ-84 [M]	McCanna	1964	15.00
❑ ST-84 [S]	McCanna	1964	20.00
❑ PJ-91 [M]	McCann/Wilson	1965	15.00
—With Gerald Wilson			
❑ ST-91 [S]	McCann/Wilson	1965	20.00
—With Gerald Wilson			
❑ LN-10077	Les McCann in San Francisco	1980	8.00
—Budget-line reissue			
❑ LN-10078	Les McCann in New York	1980	8.00
—Budget-line reissue			
❑ LN-10079	Soul Hits	1980	8.00
—Budget-line reissue			
❑ LN-10083	The Shout	1980	8.00
—Budget-line reissue			
❑ PJ-10097 [M]	Spanish Onions	1966	15.00
❑ PJ-10107 [M]	A Bag of Gold	1966	15.00
❑ ST-20097 [S]	Spanish Onions	1966	20.00
❑ ST-20107 [S]	A Bag of Gold	1966	20.00

STONE

Number	Title (A Side/B Side)	Yr	NM
❑ 1906	Butterfly	1988	10.00

SUNSET

Number	Title (A Side/B Side)	Yr	NM
❑ SUS-5214	Django	1969	10.00
❑ SUS-5296	Unlimited	1970	10.00

WORLD PACIFIC

Number	Title (A Side/B Side)	Yr	NM
❑ ST-20166	More Or Les McCann	1969	15.00
❑ ST-20173	Les McCann Sings & Plays in the Big City	1970	15.00

MCCANN, LES, AND EDDIE HARRIS

45s

ATLANTIC

Number	Title (A Side/B Side)	Yr	NM
❑ 2694	Compared to What/Cold Duck	1969	6.00

Albums

ATLANTIC

Number	Title (A Side/B Side)	Yr	NM
❑ SD 1537	Swiss Movement	1969	15.00
❑ SD 1583	Second Movement	1971	15.00

MCCANNON, GEORGE, III

45s

AMOS

Number	Title (A Side/B Side)	Yr	NM
❑ 135	I Fall to Pieces/Birds of All Nations	1970	8.00
❑ 151	Tall Oak Tree/No Love at All	1970	8.00

BELL

Number	Title (A Side/B Side)	Yr	NM
❑ 702	I Miss Her/Without Your Sweet Lips on Mine	1968	12.00

MERCURY

Number	Title (A Side/B Side)	Yr	NM
❑ 72011	Sigma Alpha Lonely/Shy Boy	1962	12.00
❑ 72072	Thumblin'/Candle in the Wind	1963	12.00

PARKWAY

Number	Title (A Side/B Side)	Yr	NM
❑ 883	Lana/What Am I Gonna Do	1963	15.00

PHI-DAN

Number	Title (A Side/B Side)	Yr	NM
❑ 5007	Seven Million People/You Can't Grow Peaches on a Cherry Tree	1965	25.00

TOWER

Number	Title (A Side/B Side)	Yr	NM
❑ 198	Look for the Rainbow/She Only Makes Me Love You More	1966	12.00

MCCANTS, JUNIOR

45s

KING

Number	Title (A Side/B Side)	Yr	NM
❑ 6076	A Boy Needs a Girl/Help My Love	1967	100.00
❑ 6106	Try Me for Your New Love/ She Wrote It — I Read It	1967	4000.
—VG 2000; VG+ 3000			

MCCARTNEY, LINDA See PAUL McCARTNEY; SUZY AND THE RED STRIPES.

MCCARTNEY, PAUL Includes duets with Linda McCartney plus his work with Wings. Also see THE BEATLES; MICHAEL JACKSON AND PAUL McCARTNEY.

12-Inch Singles

ATLANTIC

Number	Title (A Side/B Side)	Yr	NM
❑ PR 388 [DJ]	Every Night/Lucille	1981	250.00

CAPITOL

Number	Title (A Side/B Side)	Yr	NM
❑ SPRO-8574 [DJ]	Maybe I'm Amazed (mono/stereo)	1976	80.00
—As "Wings"			
❑ SPRO-9556/7 [DJ]	Spies Like Us (4:40) (3:46)	1985	30.00
❑ SPRO-9763 [DJ]	Press (same on both sides)	1986	20.00
❑ SPRO-9797 [DJ]	Angry (same on both sides)	1986	30.00
❑ SPRO-9860/1 [DJ]	Stranglehold/Angry	1986	25.00
❑ SPRO-9928 [DJ]	Pretty Little Head (same on both sides)	1986	50.00
❑ V-15212	Spies Like Us (Party Mix)/ (Alternative Mix)// (DJ Version)/My Carnival	1985	15.00
—"MLP" on label instead of "MPL"			
❑ V-15212	Spies Like Us (Party Mix)/ (Alternative Mix)//(DJ Version)/ My Carnival	1985	20.00
—"MPL" correct on label			
❑ V-15235	Press (Video Mix 4:41)/It's Not True (5:51)//Hanglide (5:18)/ Press (Dub Mix 6:28)	1986	12.00
❑ V-15499	Ou Est Le Soleil? (7:10)/(Tub Dub Mix 4:27) (Instrumental 4:25)	1989	12.00

COLUMBIA

Number	Title (A Side/B Side)	Yr	NM
❑ AS 775 [DJ]	Coming Up/Coming Up (Live at Glasgow)	1980	50.00
—White label			
❑ AS 775 [DJ]	Coming Up/Coming Up (Live at Glasgow)	1980	60.00
—Red label			
❑ AS 1444 [DJ]	Ebony and Ivory//Ballroom Dancing/The Pound Is Sinking	1982	30.00
❑ AS 1940 [DJ]	No More Lonely Nights (Ballad) (same on both sides)	1984	20.00
❑ AS 1990 [DJ]	No More Lonely Nights (Special Dance Mix) (same on both sides)	1984	20.00
❑ 44-03019	Take It Away//I'll Give You a Ring/ Dress Me Up as a Robber	1982	12.00

Except when noted otherwise, VG = 25% of NM, and VG+ = 50% of NM. (Example: VG = $2.00, VG+ = $4.00 and NM = $8.00.)

Number	Title (A Side/B Side)	Yr	NM
❑ 44-05077	No More Lonely Nights (Playout Version)//Silly Love Songs/ No More Lonely Nights (Ballad)	1984	12.00
❑ 44-05077	No More Lonely Nights (Special Dance Mix)//Silly Love Songs/ No More Lonely Nights (Ballad)	1984	30.00
❑ 23-10940	Goodnight Tonight (7:25)/ Daytime Nighttime Suffering	1979	10.00
—Credited to "Wings"; generic white cover, no picture cover or sticker			
❑ 23-10940	Goodnight Tonight (7:25)/ Daytime Nighttime Suffering	1979	15.00
—Credited to "Wings"; with picture cover			
❑ 23-10940	Goodnight Tonight (7:25)/ Daytime Nighttime Suffering	1979	80.00
—Credited to "Wings"; generic white cover with large blue and white sticker			
❑ 23-10940 [DJ]	Goodnight Tonight (7:25)/ (4:18)	1979	25.00
—Credited to "Wings"; promo issue with two versions of the A-side			
❑ 8C8 39927 [PD]	No More Lonely Nights (Extended Version)//Silly Love Songs/No More Lonely Nights (Ballad)	1984	20.00
—Picture disc; despite having only the above three tracks, its number is in the CBS album (not singles) numbering system			

45s

APPLE

Number	Title (A Side/B Side)	Yr	NM
❑ 1829	Another Day/Oh Woman, Oh Why	1971	8.00
❑ 1829	Another Day/Oh Woman, Oh Why	1971	12.00
—With star on A-side label			
❑ 1837	Uncle Albert/Admiral Halsey// Too Many People	1971	8.00
—Paul and Linda McCartney; with no misspelling			
❑ 1837	Uncle Albert/Admiral Halsey// Too Many People	1971	15.00
—Paul and Linda McCartney; with "Pual" misspelling on producer credit			
❑ 1837	Uncle Albert/Admiral Halsey// Too Many People	1971	50.00
—Paul and Linda McCartney; with unsliced apple on B-side label			
❑ 1837	Uncle Albert/Admiral Halsey// Too Many People	1975	30.00
—Paul and Linda McCartney; with "All Rights Reserved" on label			
❑ 1847	Give Ireland Back to the Irish/ Give Ireland Back to the Irish (Version)	1972	10.00
—Wings			
❑ 1847 [PS]	Give Ireland Back to the Irish/ Give Ireland Back to the Irish (Version)	1972	30.00
—Wings; title sleeve with large center hole			
❑ 1851	Mary Had a Little Lamb/ Little Woman Love	1972	10.00
—Wings			
❑ 1851 [DJ]	Mary Had a Little Lamb/ Little Woman Love	1972	300.00
—White label promo, lists artist as Paul McCartney			
❑ 1851 [PS]	Mary Had a Little Lamb/ Little Woman Love	1972	25.00
—Wings; without "Little Woman Love" on sleeve			
❑ 1851 [PS]	Mary Had a Little Lamb/ Little Woman Love	1972	40.00
—Wings; with "Little Woman Love" on sleeve			
❑ 1857	Hi Hi Hi/C Moon	1972	10.00
—Wings; red label			
❑ 1861	My Love/The Mess	1973	8.00
—Paul McCartney and Wings; custom "Red Rose Speedway" label			
❑ 1861 [DJ]	My Love/The Mess	1973	200.00
—Paul McCartney and Wings; white label			
❑ 1863	Live and Let Die/I Lie Around	1973	8.00
—Wings			
❑ 1869	Helen Wheels/Country Dreamer	1973	8.00
—Paul McCartney and Wings			
❑ P-1869 [DJ]	Helen Wheels/Country Dreamer	1973	2000.
—Paul McCartney and Wings; a very rare promo, as most promos have the same song on both sides (see 6786 and 6787 below)			
❑ 1871	Jet/Let Me Roll It	1974	8.00
—Paul McCartney and Wings			
❑ 1871	Jet/Mamunia	1974	10.00
—Paul McCartney and Wings			
❑ 1871	Jet/Mamunia	1974	100.00
—Paul McCartney and Wings; A-side incorrectly listed as playing for 2:49			
❑ P-1871 [DJ]	Jet (Edited Mono)/Jet (Stereo)	1974	50.00
—Paul McCartney and Wings			
❑ 1873	Band on the Run/Nineteen Hundred and Eighty-Five	1974	8.00
—Paul McCartney and Wings			
❑ P-1873 [DJ]	Band on the Run (Edited Mono)/ Band on the Run (Full-length Stereo)	1974	40.00
—Paul McCartney and Wings			
❑ P-1873 [DJ]	Band on the Run (mono/stereo, both edits)	1974	100.00
—Paul McCartney and Wings			
❑ 1875	Junior's Farm/Sally G	1974	8.00
—Paul McCartney and Wings			
❑ 1875	Junior's Farm/Sally G	1975	80.00
—Paul McCartney and Wings; with "All Rights Reserved" on label			
❑ P-1875 [DJ]	Junior's Farm (Edited Mono)/ Junior's Farm (Full-length Stereo)	1974	50.00
—Paul McCartney and Wings			
❑ P-1875 [DJ]	Sally G (mono/stereo)	1974	80.00
—Paul McCartney and Wings			
❑ PRO-6193/4 [DJ]	Another Day/Oh Woman, Oh Why	1971	80.00
❑ PRO-6786 [DJ]	Helen Wheels (mono/stereo)	1973	50.00
—Paul McCartney and Wings			
❑ PRO-6787 [DJ]	Country Dreamer (mono/stereo)	1973	400.00
—Paul McCartney and Wings			

CAPITOL

Number	Title (A Side/B Side)	Yr	NM
❑ 1829	Another Day/Oh Woman, Oh Why	1976	15.00
—Black label			
❑ 1837	Uncle Albert/Admiral Halsey// Too Many People	1976	15.00
—Credited to "Paul and Linda McCartney"; black label			
❑ 1847	Give Ireland Back to the Irish/ Give Ireland Back to the Irish	1976	20.00
—Credited to "Wings"; black label			
❑ 1851	Mary Had a Little Lamb/ Little Woman Love	1976	12.00
—Credited to "Wings"; black label			
❑ 1857	Hi Hi Hi/C Moon	1976	15.00
—Credited to "Wings"; black label			
❑ 1861	My Love/The Mess	1976	20.00
—Credited to "Paul McCartney and Wings"; black label; "The Mess" plays normally			
❑ 1861	My Love/The Mess	1976	20.00
—Credited to "Paul McCartney and Wings"; black label; "The Mess" plays too fast			
❑ 1863	Live and Let Die/I Lie Around	1976	12.00
—Credited to "Wings"; black label			
❑ 1869	Helen Wheels/Country Dreamer	1976	15.00
—Credited to "Paul McCartney and Wings"; black label			
❑ 1871	Jet/Let Me Roll It	1976	15.00
—Credited to "Paul McCartney and Wings"; black label			
❑ 1873	Band on the Run/Nineteen Hundred and Eighty-Five	1976	15.00
—Credited to "Paul McCartney and Wings"; black label			
❑ 1875	Junior's Farm/Sally G	1976	15.00
—Credited to "Paul McCartney and Wings"; black label			
❑ 4091	Listen to What the Man Said/ Love in Song	1975	5.00
—Credited to "Wings"			
❑ 4091 [PS]	Listen to What the Man Said/ Love in Song	1975	12.00
❑ 4145	Letting Go/You Gave Me the Answer	1975	5.00
—Credited to "Wings"			
❑ 4175	Venus and Mars Rock Show/ Magneto and Titanium Man	1975	5.00
—Credited to "Wings"			
❑ 4256	Silly Love Songs/ Cook of the House	1976	4.00
—Credited to "Wings"; "Speed of Sound" label (more common version)			
❑ 4256	Silly Love Songs/ Cook of the House	1976	8.00
—Credited to "Wings"; black label			
❑ 4293	Let 'Em In/Beware My Love	1976	4.00
—Credited to "Wings"; "Speed of Sound" label			
❑ 4293	Let 'Em In/Beware My Love	1976	6.00
—Credited to "Wings"; black label (more common version)			
❑ 4385	Maybe I'm Amazed/Soily	1976	4.00
—Credited to "Wings"; custom label (more common version)			
❑ 4385	Maybe I'm Amazed/Soily	1976	20.00
—Credited to "Wings"; black label			
❑ 4504	Girls' School/Mull of Kintyre	1977	5.00
—Credited to "Wings"; black label (more common version)			
❑ 4504	Girls' School/Mull of Kintyre	1978	120.00
—Credited to "Wings"; purple label, label has reeded edge			
❑ 4504 [PS]	Girls' School/Mull of Kintyre	1977	12.00
❑ 4559	With a Little Luck/Backwards Traveller-Cuff Link	1978	4.00
—Credited to "Wings"			
❑ 4594	I've Had Enough/ Deliver Your Children	1978	4.00
—Credited to "Wings"			
❑ 4625	London Town/I'm Carrying	1978	4.00
—Credited to "Wings"			
❑ B-5537	Spies Like Us/My Carnival	1985	3.00
❑ B-5537 [PS]	Spies Like Us/My Carnival	1985	6.00
❑ B-5597	Press/It's Not True	1986	5.00
❑ B-5597 [PS]	Press/It's Not True	1986	5.00
❑ B-5636	Stranglehold/Angry	1986	5.00
❑ B-5636 [PS]	Stranglehold/Angry	1986	5.00
❑ B-5672	Only Love Remains/ Tough on a Tightrope	1987	5.00
❑ B-5672 [PS]	Only Love Remains/ Tough on a Tightrope	1987	5.00
❑ SPRO-8570/1 [DJ]	Maybe I'm Amazed (3:43) (stereo/mono)	1977	30.00
—As "Wings"			
❑ 7PRO-9552/3 [DJ]	Spies Like Us (4:40)/(3:46)	1985	20.00
❑ S7-17318	Off the Ground/ Cosmically Conscious	1993	6.00
—Black vinyl "error" issue			
❑ S7-17318	Off the Ground/ Cosmically Conscious	1993	6.00
—White vinyl standard issue			
❑ S7-17319	Biker Like an Icon/ Things We Said Today	1993	6.00
—Black vinyl "error" issue			
❑ S7-17319	Biker Like an Icon/ Things We Said Today	1993	6.00
—White vinyl standard issue			
❑ S7-17489	C'mon People/Down to the River	1993	8.00
—All copies on white vinyl			
❑ S7-17643	Wonderful Christmastime/ Rudolph, the Red-Nosed Reggae	1993	6.00
—Credited to "Paul McCartney & Wings"; red vinyl			
❑ B-44367	My Brave Face/ Flying to My Home	1989	5.00
—Version 3: Same as Version 2, time of A-side is "3:16"			
❑ B-44367	My Brave Face/ Flying to My Home	1989	8.00
—Version 2: Artist in custom print, title in block print, time of A-side is "3:17"			
❑ B-44367	My Brave Face/ Flying to My Home	1989	10.00
—Version 1: Both title and artist in block print, time of A-side is "3:17"			
❑ B-44367 [PS]	My Brave Face/ Flying to My Home	1989	5.00
❑ 50291	Freedom/From a Lover to a Friend	2001	4.00
❑ S7-56946	Hope of Deliverance/ Long Leather Coat	1993	6.00
❑ 58823	No Other Baby/Try Not to Cry	1999	4.00
❑ 58995	Maybe I'm Amazed/Band on the Run	2001	5.00
—Credited to "Wings"; gold vinyl; both sides feature spoken introductions by Paul			
❑ 77730	Your Loving Flame/Lonely Road	2002	4.00
❑ 7PRO-79074 [DJ]	Put It There (same on both sides)	1990	1000.
—Vinyl is promo only			
❑ 7PRO-79700 [DJ]	This One (same on both sides)	1989	400.00
—Vinyl is promo only			
❑ 7PRO-79889 [DJ]	Figure of Eight (same on both sides)	1989	100.00
—Test pressings with blank label; most known copies come in a Capitol sleeve; number taken from dead wax			

COLUMBIA

Number	Title (A Side/B Side)	Yr	NM
❑ AE7 1204 [DJ]	Coming Up (Live at Glasgow)/ (B-side blank)	1980	8.00
—Small hole, plays at 33 1/3 rpm; this was the bonus single included with most early pressings of the "McCartney II" LP (Columbia FC 36511) and was not distributed separately			
❑ 18-02171	Silly Love Songs/ Cook of the House	1981	25.00
—Credited to "Wings"; despite label information, this has an edited version of A-side			
❑ 18-03018	Take It Away/I'll Give You a Ring	1982	3.00
❑ 18-03018 [PS]	Take It Away/I'll Give You a Ring	1982	3.00
❑ 38-03235	Tug of War/Get It	1982	12.00
❑ 38-04127	Wonderful Christmastime/ Rudolph the Red-Nosed Reggae	1983	30.00
—Scarce reissue with B-side in stereo			
❑ 38-04296	So Bad/Pipes of Peace	1983	5.00
❑ 38-04296 [PS]	So Bad/Pipes of Peace	1983	5.00
❑ 38-04581	No More Lonely Nights/ (playout version)	1984	4.00
❑ 38-04581	No More Lonely Nights/ (Special Dance Version)	1984	40.00
❑ 38-04581 [PS]	No More Lonely Nights/ (playout version)	1984	5.00
—Title print in white, credit print in gray			
❑ 38-04581 [PS]	No More Lonely Nights/ (playout version)	1984	30.00
—Title print in gray, credit print in white			
❑ 3-10939	Goodnight Tonight/Daytime Nighttime Suffering	1979	6.00
—Credited to "Wings"			
❑ 3-11020	Getting Closer/Spin It On	1979	6.00
—Credited to "Wings"			
❑ 3-11020 [PS]	Getting Closer/Spin It On	1979	30.00
—Title sleeve with large center hole			
❑ 1-11070	Arrow Through Me/Old Siam, Sir	1979	6.00
—Credited to "Wings"			
❑ 1-11162	Wonderful Christmastime/ Rudolph the Red-Nosed Reggae	1979	10.00
❑ 1-11162 [PS]	Wonderful Christmastime/ Rudolph the Red-Nosed Reggae	1979	15.00
❑ 1-11263	Coming Up//Coming Up (Live at Glasgow)/Lunch Box-Odd Sox	1980	4.00
—The first song on side 2 is credited to "Paul McCartney & Wings"			

M

Number	Title (A Side/B Side)	Yr	NM
❑ 1-11263 [PS]	Coming Up//Coming Up (Live at Glasgow)/Lunch Box-Odd Sox	1980	5.00
❑ 1-11335	Waterfalls/Check My Machine	1980	6.00
❑ 1-11335 [PS]	Waterfalls/Check My Machine	1980	20.00
❑ 13-33405	Goodnight Tonight/ Getting Closer	1980	10.00

—Credited to "Wings"; red label "Hall of Fame" series

❑ 13-33407 My Love/Maybe I'm Amazed 1980 10.00

—Credited to "Paul McCartney and Wings"; red label "Hall of Fame" series; B-side is the studio version, making its first appearance on U.S. 45 here

❑ 13-33407 My Love/Maybe I'm Amazed 1985 30.00

—Credited to "Paul McCartney and Wings"; briefly available grayish label reissue

❑ 13-33408 Jet//Uncle Albert/Admiral Halsey 1980 10.00

—Credited to "Paul McCartney and Wings"; red label "Hall of Fame" series

❑ 13-33408 Jet//Uncle Albert/Admiral Halsey 1985 30.00

—Credited to "Paul McCartney and Wings"; briefly available grayish label reissue

❑ 13-33409 Band on the Run/Helen Wheels 1980 10.00

—Credited to "Paul McCartney and Wings"; red label "Hall of Fame" series

❑ 13-33409 Band on the Run/Helen Wheels 1985 30.00

—Credited to "Paul McCartney and Wings"; briefly available grayish label reissue

EMI

❑ 3977 Walking in the Park with Eloise/ Bridge on the River Suite 1974 60.00

❑ 3977 [PS] Walking in the Park with Eloise/ Bridge on the River Suite 1974 80.00

—As "The Country Hams"

Albums

APPLE

❑ SMAS-3363 McCartney 197? 20.00

—New prefix on label

❑ SMAS-3363 McCartney 1975 100.00

—With "All Rights Reserved" on label

❑ STAO-3363 McCartney 1970 20.00

—Only "McCartney" on label; back cover does NOT say "An Abkco managed company"

❑ STAO-3363 McCartney 1970 25.00

—"McCartney" and "Paul McCartney" on separate lines on label; New York address on back cover

❑ STAO-3363 McCartney 1970 25.00

—Only "McCartney" on label; back cover says "An Abkco managed company"

❑ STAO-3363 McCartney 1970 30.00

—"McCartney" and "Paul McCartney" on separate lines on label; California addess on back cover

❑ STAO-3363 McCartney 1970 80.00

—Apple label with small Capitol logo on B-side

❑ MAS-3375 [M] Ram 1971 4000.

—Credited to "Paul and Linda McCartney"; mono record in stereo cover for radio station use only

❑ SMAS-3375 Ram 1971 15.00

—Credited to "Paul and Linda McCartney"; unsliced apple on one label, sliced apple on other

❑ SMAS-3375 Ram 1971 30.00

—Credited to "Paul and Linda McCartney"; unsliced apple on both labels

❑ SMAS-3375 Ram 1971 50.00

—Credited to "Paul and Linda McCartney"; Apple label with small Capitol logo on B-side

❑ SMAS-3375 Ram 1975 100.00

—Credited to "Paul and Linda McCartney"; with "All Rights Reserved" on label

❑ SW-3386 Wild Life 1971 15.00

—Credited to "Wings"

❑ SMAL-3409 Red Rose Speedway 1973 20.00

—Credited to "Paul McCartney and Wings"; with bound-in booklet

❑ SO-3415 Band on the Run 1973 20.00

—Credited to "Paul McCartney and Wings"; with photo innersleeve and poster

❑ SPRO-6210 [DJ]Brung to Ewe By 1971 400.00

—Promo-only radio spots for "Ram"; counterfeits have uneven spacing between tracks

CAPITOL

❑ SMAS-3363 McCartney 1976 20.00

—Black label, "Manufactured by MPL Communications Inc" at top

❑ SMAS-3363 McCartney 1976 25.00

—Black label, "Manufactured by McCartney Music Inc" at top

❑ SMAS-3375 Ram 197? 20.00

—Credited to "Paul and Linda McCartney"; black label, "Manufactured by MPL Communications Inc" at top

❑ SMAS-3375 Ram 197? 40.00

—Credited to "Paul and Linda McCartney"; black label, "Manufactured by Capitol RecordsÕ" on label

❑ SMAS-3375 Ram 1976 30.00

—Credited to "Paul and Linda McCartney"; black label, "Manufactured by McCartney Music Inc" at top

❑ SW-3386 Wild Life 197? 20.00

—Credited to "Wings"; black label, "Manufactured by MPL Communications Inc" at top

❑ SW-3386 Wild Life 1976 30.00

—Credited to "Wings"; black label, "Manufactured by McCartney Music Inc" at top

❑ SMAL-3409 Red Rose Speedway 197? 25.00

—Credited to "Paul McCartney and Wings"; black label, "Manufactured by MPL Communications Inc" at top

❑ SMAL-3409 Red Rose Speedway 1976 30.00

—Credited to "Paul McCartney and Wings"; black label, "Manufactured by McCartney Music Inc" at top

❑ SO-3415 Band on the Run 197? 20.00

—Credited to "Paul McCartney and Wings"; black label, "Maunfactured by MPL Communications Inc." at top

❑ SO-3415 Band on the Run 197? 50.00

—Credited to "Paul McCartney and Wings"; black label, "Manufactured by Capitol Records..."

❑ SO-3415 Band on the Run 1975 20.00

—Credited to "Paul McCartney and Wings"; custom label with MPL logo

❑ SMAS-11419 Venus and Mars 1975 15.00

—Credited to "Wings"; with two posters and two stickers

❑ SW-11525 Wings at the Speed of Sound 1976 10.00

—Credited to "Wings"; custom label

❑ SW-11525 [DJ]Wings at the Speed of Sound 1976 300.00

—Credited to "Wings"; white label advance promo

❑ SWCO-11593 [(3)]Wings Over America 1976 25.00

—Credited to "Wings"; custom labels with poster

❑ ST-11642 Thrillington 1977 100.00

—Credited to "Percy 'Thrills' Thrillington"; instrumental versions of songs from Ram LP

❑ SW-11777 London Town 1978 15.00

—Credited to "Wings"; custom label with poster

❑ SEAX-11901 [PD]Band on the Run 1978 40.00

—Credited to "Paul McCartney and Wings"; picture disc

❑ SOO-11905 Wings Greatest 1978 15.00

—Credited to "Wings"; custom label with poster

❑ SOO-11905 [DJ]Wings Greatest 1978 400.00

—Credited to "Wings"; white label advance promo/test pressing

❑ PJAS-12475 Press to Play 1986 12.00

❑ CLW-48287 [(2)]All the Best! 1987 20.00

❑ C1-56500 Flaming Pie 1997 30.00

❑ C1-91653 Flowers in the Dirt 1989 20.00

❑ C1-94778 [(3)] Tripping the Live Fantastic 1990 60.00

❑ 99176 [(2)] Band on the Run 1999 40.00

—Limited-edition 180-gram reissue with original LP on one record and interviews and "The Making of.." on the second

❑ C1-595379 Tripping the Live Fantastic — Highlights! 1990 25.00

—Released on vinyl only through Columbia House; with Canada address on back cover, this was sold in the U.S. by Columbia House

❑ C1-595379 Tripping the Live Fantastic — Highlights! 1990 25.00

—Released on vinyl only through Columbia House; with U.S. address on back cover

COLUMBIA

❑ A2S 821 [(2)DJ]The McCartney Interview 1980 40.00

—Promo-only set; one LP is the entire interview, the other is banded for airplay; white labels with black print; counterfeits have blank white labels

❑ FC 36057 Back to the Egg 1979 10.00

—Credited to "Wings"; custom label

❑ FC 36057 [DJ] Back to the Egg 1979 40.00

—Credited to "Wings"; "Demonstration -- Not for Sale" on custom label

❑ PC 36057 Back to the Egg 1984 30.00

—Credited to "Wings"; "PC" cover with "FC" label

❑ PC 36057 Back to the Egg 1984 40.00

—Credited to "Wings"; "PC" cover with "PC" label

❑ JC 36478 McCartney 1979 15.00

❑ PC 36478 McCartney 1984 15.00

—Budget-line reissue

❑ JC 36479 Ram 1980 15.00

—Credited to "Paul and Linda McCartney"

❑ PC 36479 Ram 1984 15.00

—Credited to "Paul and Linda McCartney"; budget-line reissue

❑ JC 36480 Wild Life 1980 15.00

—Credited to "Wings"

❑ PC 36480 Wild Life 1982 15.00

—Credited to "Wings"; budget-line reissue

❑ JC 36481 Red Rose Speedway 1980 15.00

—Credited to "Paul McCartney and Wings"; flat or glossy cover

❑ PC 36481 Red Rose Speedway 198? 15.00

—Credited to "Paul McCartney and Wings"; not issued with booklet

❑ JC 36482 Band on the Run 198? 100.00

—Credited to "Paul McCartney and Wings"; white "MPL" logo on lower left front cover

❑ JC 36482 Band on the Run 1980 15.00

—Credited to "Paul McCartney and Wings"; custom label

❑ PC 36482 Band on the Run 198? 20.00

—Credited to "Paul McCartney and Wings"; "PC" cover with "JC" label

❑ PC 36482 Band on the Run 198? 30.00

—Credited to "Paul McCartney and Wings"; "PC" cover with "PC" label

❑ FC 36511 McCartney II 1980 10.00

—Add 80% if bonus single of "Coming Up (Live at Glasgow)" (AE7 1204) is with package

❑ FC 36511 [DJ] McCartney II 1980 30.00

—White label promo

❑ PC 36511 McCartney II 1984 25.00

—"PC" cover with "FC" label

❑ PC 36511 McCartney II 1984 100.00

—"PC" cover with "PC" label

❑ JC 36801 Venus and Mars 1980 15.00

—Credited to "Wings"; with one poster and two stickers

❑ PC 36801 Venus and Mars 1982 15.00

—Credited to "Wings"; budget-line reissue, not issued with inserts

❑ PC 36987 The McCartney Interview 1980 12.00

—Stock release of interview originally intended for promotional use only

❑ FC 37409 Wings at the Speed of Sound 1981 15.00

—Credited to "Wings"; custom label

❑ PC 37409 Wings at the Speed of Sound 1982 15.00

—Credited to "Wings"; regular Columbia label, budget-line reissue

❑ PC 37462 Tug of War 1984 30.00

—Custom label; "PC" cover with "TC" label

❑ PC 37462 Tug of War 1984 100.00

—Regular Columbia label; "PC" cover with "PC" label

❑ TC 37462 Tug of War 1982 10.00

❑ C3X 37990 [(3)]Wings Over America 1982 50.00

—Credited to "Wings"; custom labels, no poster

❑ QC 39149 Pipes of Peace 1983 12.00

❑ SC 39613 Give My Regards to Broad Street 1984 15.00

❑ HC 46382 Band on the Run 1981 50.00

—Credited to "Paul McCartney and Wings"; half-speed mastered edition

HEAR MUSIC

❑ HMLP-30383 Memory Almost Full 2007 15.00

MPL/PARLOPHONE

❑ 96413 Unplugged (The Official Bootleg) 1991 75.00

—No U.S. pressings; "American" copies were U.K. imports with liner notes in Spanish!

NATIONAL FEATURES CORP.

❑ 2955/6 Band on the Run Radio Interview Special 1973 1500.

—Promo-only interview disc

MCCARTNEY, PAUL, AND STEVIE WONDER

Also see each artist's individual listings.

12-Inch Singles

COLUMBIA

❑ 44-02878 Ebony and Ivory//Rainclouds/ Ebony and Ivory (Solo) 1982 12.00

—B-side by McCartney solo

45s

COLUMBIA

❑ 18-02860 Ebony and Ivory/Rainclouds 1982 4.00

—B-side by McCartney solo

❑ 18-02860 [PS] Ebony and Ivory/Rainclouds 1982 4.00

MCCLAY, YUL, AND THE MONDELLOS

See THE MONDELLOS.

MCCORD, SYLVESTER

45s

HIT

❑ 72 Tie Me Kangaroo Down, Sport/ Sukiyaki 1963 8.00

—B-side by the Music City Five

MCCORMICK, GAYLE

Also see SMITH.

45s

ABC DUNHILL

❑ 4281 Gonna Be Alright Now/Save Me 1971 5.00

❑ 4288 It's a Cryin' Shame/If Only You Believe 1971 5.00

❑ 4298 You Really Got a Hold on Me/ C'est La Vie 1972 5.00

DECCA

❑ 33030 Near You/Take Me Back 1972 5.00

MCA

❑ 40007 Sweet Feelings/Take Me Back 1973 4.00

SHADY BROOK

❑ 45017 Coming In Out of the Rain/ Simon Said 1977 10.00

Albums

ABC DUNHILL

❑ DS-50109 Gayle McCormick 1971 12.00

DECCA

❑ DL 75364 Flesh and Blood 1972 12.00

FANTASY

❑ 9467 One More Hour 1974 12.00

MCCORMICK, MAUREEN

Also see THE BRADY BUNCH; CHRIS KNIGHT AND MAUREEN McCORMICK.

45s

PARAMOUNT

❑ 0292 Love's in the Roses/Harmonize 1974 15.00

MCCOY, CHARLIE

45s

CADENCE

❑ 1390 Cherry Berry Wine/My Little Woman 1960 10.00

❑ 1415 I Just Want to Make Love to You/Rooster Blues 1962 10.00

MONUMENT

❑ 45-210 Summit Ridge Drive/Play It Again Charlie 1977 5.00

❑ 45-224 Amazing Grace/Squeezing 1977 5.00

❑ 45-239 Foggy River/Last Letter 1977 5.00

Except when noted otherwise, VG = 25% of NM, and VG+ = 50% of NM. (Example: VG = $2.00, VG+ = $4.00 and NM = $8.00.)

Number	Title (A Side/B Side)	Yr	NM
❑ 45-258	Fair and Tender Ladies/18th Century Rosewood Clock	1978	5.00
❑ 45-272	Drifting Lovers/West Virginia Mountain Melody	1978	5.00
❑ 45-282	Midnight Flyer/Cripple Creek	1979	5.00
❑ 45-289	Ramblin' Music Man/Red Haired Boy	1979	5.00
❑ 45-292	Carolina Morning/Appalachian Fever	1979	5.00
❑ 45-296	Cold, Cold Heart/Station Break	1980	5.00
❑ 842	My Babe/Will You Love Me Tomorrow	1964	12.00
❑ 870	I'm Ready/Harpoon Man	1965	8.00
❑ 893	Girl (Those Were the Good Old Days)/It's a Man Down There	1965	8.00
❑ 926	Let Him Go/Screamin', Shoutin', Beggin', Pleadin'	1966	8.00
❑ 975	Stubborn Kind of Fellow/My Baby's Back Again	1966	8.00
❑ 998	Cold Cold World/You've Got to Face Life	1967	8.00
❑ 1076	Gimme Some Lovin'/Boy from England	1968	6.00
❑ 1093	Harper Valley P.T.A./Juke	1968	6.00
❑ 1938	Blue Christmas/Christmas Cheer	1976	3.00
—"Golden Series" reissue			
❑ 03518	The State of Our Union/Just Doin' Nothin' with You (Is Really Somethin')	1983	4.00
—With Laney Hicks			
❑ 8529	I Started Loving You Again/The Real McCoy	1971	5.00
❑ 8546	I'm So Lonesome I Could Cry/Grade A	1972	5.00
❑ 8554	I Really Don't Want to Know/Minor, Minor	1972	5.00
❑ 8566	Orange Blossom Special/Hangin' On	1973	5.00
❑ 8576	Shenandoah/John Henry	1973	5.00
❑ 8589	Release Me/Fastest Harp in the South	1973	5.00
❑ 8600	Silver Threads and Golden Needles/I Just Can't Stand to See You Cry	1974	4.00
❑ 8611	Boogie Woogie (A/K/A T.D.'s Boogie Woogie)/Keep On Harpin'	1974	4.00
—With Barefoot Jerry			
❑ 8625	The Way We Were/I Can't Help It	1974	4.00
❑ 8633	Blue Christmas/Christmas Cheer	1974	5.00
❑ 8638	Everybody Stand Up and Holler for the Union/New River Gorge	1975	4.00
❑ 8650	Please Don't Tell Me How the Story Ends/Juke	1975	4.00
❑ 8660	Blues Stay Away from Me/Pots and Pans	1975	4.00
❑ 8672	Columbus Stockade Blues/(I Heard That) Lonesome Whistle	1975	4.00
❑ 8683	The Star-Spangled Banner/Silver Wings	1976	4.00
❑ 8703	Wabash Cannonball/Ode to Billie Joe	1976	4.00
❑ 21001	Until the Nights/I Love the Way You Love Me	1981	5.00
—With Laney Smallwood			

7-Inch Extended Plays

MONUMENT

Number	Title (A Side/B Side)	Yr	NM
❑ AEZ-00001 [DJ]	Jackson/Today I Started Loving You Again/Easy Lovin'//To Get to You/Rocky Top/I'm So Lonesome I Could Cry	1973	10.00
—Label calls this "Bonus Record"; contains excerpts of the above songs plus an interview with Frank Jones; small hole, plays at 33 1/3 rpm			
❑ AEZ-00001 [PS]	Free Bonus 7"	1973	10.00
—Sleeve with large flap at left; may have been included with purchase of certain Charlie McCoy LPs in 1973			

Albums

CMH

Number	Title (A Side/B Side)	Yr	NM
❑ 9030 [(2)]	Flat-Picking Spectacular	1984	12.00

MONUMENT

Number	Title (A Side/B Side)	Yr	NM
❑ 6623	The Real McCoy	1976	10.00
—Reissue of 31329			
❑ 6624	Charlie McCoy	1976	10.00
—Reissue of 31910			
❑ 6625	Good Time Charlie	1976	10.00
—Reissue of 32215			
❑ 6626	The Fastest Harp in the South	1976	10.00
—Reissue of 32749			
❑ 6627	The Nashville Hit Man	1976	10.00
—Reissue of 32922			
❑ 6628	Charlie My Boy!	1976	10.00
—Reissue of 33384			
❑ 6629	Harpin' the Blues	1976	10.00
—Reissue of 33802			
❑ 6630	Play It Again Charlie	1976	10.00
❑ 7612	Cookin'	1977	10.00
❑ 7622	Greatest Hits	1978	10.00
❑ 7632	Appalachian Fever	1979	10.00
❑ SLP-18097	The World of Charlie McCoy	1968	15.00
❑ Z 31329	The Real McCoy	1971	12.00
❑ KZ 31910	Charlie McCoy	1972	12.00
❑ KZ 32215	Good Time Charlie	1973	12.00
❑ KZ 32749	The Fastest Harp in the South	1974	12.00
❑ KZ 32922	The Nashville Hit Man	1974	12.00
❑ PZ 33384	Charlie My Boy!	1975	12.00
❑ PZ 33802	Harpin' the Blues	1975	12.00
❑ PW 38387	The Greatest Hits of Charlie McCoy	1982	8.00

MCCOY, VAN

12-Inch Singles

H&L

Number	Title (A Side/B Side)	Yr	NM
❑ 2002	Rhythms of the World (10:12)//Soul Cha Cha/That's the Joint	1976	20.00

45s

AVCO

Number	Title (A Side/B Side)	Yr	NM
❑ 4639	Love Is the Answer/Killing Me Softly	1974	5.00
❑ 4648	Boogie Down/Rainy Night in Georgia	1975	5.00
❑ 4653	The Hustle/Hey Girl, Come and Get It	1975	4.00
❑ 4660	Change with the Times/Goodnight Baby	1975	4.00

COLUMBIA

Number	Title (A Side/B Side)	Yr	NM
❑ 43415	Keep Loving Me/Butterfly	1965	12.00
❑ 43495	Starlight Starbright/This Is the Way We Fall in Love	1965	8.00
❑ 43694	I Will Wait for You/The House That Love Built	1966	8.00

EPIC

Number	Title (A Side/B Side)	Yr	NM
❑ 10470	I Started a Joke/Toney's Theme	1969	7.00

H&L

Number	Title (A Side/B Side)	Yr	NM
❑ 4653	The Hustle/Hey Girl, Come and Get It	197?	5.00
—Reissue of Avco 4653, but harder to find			
❑ 4667	Night Walk/Love Child	1976	4.00
❑ 4670	Party/The Disco Kid	1976	4.00
❑ 4677	The Shuffle/That's the Joint	1976	4.00
❑ 4682	Soul Cha Cha/Oriental Boogie	1977	4.00

LIBERTY

Number	Title (A Side/B Side)	Yr	NM
❑ 55457	Follow Your Heart/Lonely	1962	12.00

MCA

Number	Title (A Side/B Side)	Yr	NM
❑ 40885	My Favorite Fantasy/You're So Right for Me	1978	4.00
❑ 40938	Trying to Make the Best of It/Two Points	1978	4.00
❑ 40984	Lonely Dancer/Decisions	1979	4.00

ROCK'N

Number	Title (A Side/B Side)	Yr	NM
❑ 101	Mr. D.J./Never Trust a Friend	1961	50.00

Albums

AVCO

Number	Title (A Side/B Side)	Yr	NM
❑ AV-69002	Love Is the Answer	1974	10.00
❑ AV-69006	Disco Baby	1975	10.00
❑ AV-69009	The Disco Kid	1975	10.00

BUDDAH

Number	Title (A Side/B Side)	Yr	NM
❑ BDS-5103	Soul Improvisations	1971	15.00
❑ BDS-5648	From Disco to Love	1975	10.00
—Retitled reissue of 5103			

COLUMBIA

Number	Title (A Side/B Side)	Yr	NM
❑ CL 2497 [M]	Night Time Is the Lonely Time	1966	20.00
❑ CS 9297 [S]	Night Time Is the Lonely Time	1966	25.00

H&L

Number	Title (A Side/B Side)	Yr	NM
❑ HL-69002	Love Is the Answer	1976	8.00
—Reissue of Avco 69002			
❑ HL-69006	Disco Baby	1976	8.00
—Reissue of Avco 69006			
❑ HL-69009	The Disco Kid	1976	8.00
—Reissue of Avco 69009			
❑ HL-69012	The Real McCoy	1976	10.00
❑ HL-69014	Rhythms of the World	1976	10.00
❑ HL-69016	The Hustle and Best of Van McCoy	1976	10.00
❑ HL-69022	Van McCoy and His Magnificent Movie Machine	1977	10.00

MCA

Number	Title (A Side/B Side)	Yr	NM
❑ 3036	My Favorite Fantasy	1978	10.00
❑ 3054	A Woman Called Moses	1978	10.00
❑ 3071	Lovely Dancer	1979	10.00

MCCOYS, THE

Also see RICK DERRINGER.

45s

BANG

Number	Title (A Side/B Side)	Yr	NM
❑ 506	Hang On Sloopy/I Can't Explain It	1965	15.00
❑ 511	Fever/Sorrow	1965	10.00
❑ 516	Up and Down/If You Tell a Lie	1966	10.00
❑ 522	Come On Let's Go/Little People	1966	10.00
❑ 527	(You Make Me Feel) So Good/Runaway	1966	10.00
❑ 532	Don't Worry Mother, Your Son's Heart Is Pure/Ko-Ko	1966	10.00
❑ 538	I Got to Go Back (And Watch That Little Girl Dance)/Dynamite	1966	10.00
❑ 543	Beat the Clock/Like You Do to Me	1967	10.00
❑ 549	I Wonder If She Remembers Me/Say Those Magic Words	1967	10.00

MERCURY

Number	Title (A Side/B Side)	Yr	NM
❑ 72843	Jesse Brady/Resurrection	1968	8.00
❑ 72897	Daybreak/Epilogue	1969	8.00
❑ 72967	Don't Fight It/Rosa Rodriguez	1969	15.00

PHILCO-FORD

Number	Title (A Side/B Side)	Yr	NM
❑ HP-6	Fever/Hang On Sloopy	1967	20.00
—4-inch plastic "Hip Pocket Record" with color sleeve			

RCA VICTOR

Number	Title (A Side/B Side)	Yr	NM
❑ 47-7204	Daddy's Geisha Girl/Our Love Goes On and On	1958	20.00
❑ 47-7354	Full Grown Cat/Throwing Kisses	1958	25.00

Albums

BANG

Number	Title (A Side/B Side)	Yr	NM
❑ BLP-212 [M]	Hang On Sloopy	1965	30.00
❑ BLPS-212 [S]	Hang On Sloopy	1965	40.00
❑ BLP-213 [M]	You Make Me Feel So Good	1966	30.00
❑ BLPS-213 [S]	You Make Me Feel So Good	1966	40.00

MERCURY

Number	Title (A Side/B Side)	Yr	NM
❑ SR-61163	Infinite McCoys	1968	25.00
❑ SR-61207	Human Ball	1969	25.00

MCCRACKEN, HUGH

45s

CONGRESS

Number	Title (A Side/B Side)	Yr	NM
❑ 257	Buzz in My Head/You Blow My Mind	1965	25.00
❑ 261	Runnin', Runnin'/What I Gotta Do to Satisfy You	1966	25.00

MCCRACKLIN, JIMMY

45s

ART-TONE

Number	Title (A Side/B Side)	Yr	NM
❑ 825	Just Got to Know/The Drag	1961	12.00
❑ 826	Christmas Time (Part 1)/Christmas Time (Part 2)	1961	12.00
❑ 827	Shame, Shame, Shame/I'm the One	1962	12.00
❑ 831	That's No Big Thing/Susie and Pat	1962	12.00

CHECKER

Number	Title (A Side/B Side)	Yr	NM
❑ 885	The Walk/I'm to Blame	1958	25.00
❑ 893	Everybody Rock/Get Tough	1958	15.00

CHESS

Number	Title (A Side/B Side)	Yr	NM
❑ 1809	I Know/Later On	1961	10.00
❑ 1826	One Track Love/Trottin'	1962	10.00

HI

Number	Title (A Side/B Side)	Yr	NM
❑ 2023	Things I Meant to Say/Here Today and Gone Tomorrow	1960	12.00

HOLLYWOOD

Number	Title (A Side/B Side)	Yr	NM
❑ 1054	It's All Right/Fare You Well	1955	50.00

IMPERIAL

Number	Title (A Side/B Side)	Yr	NM
❑ 5892	Bitter Pill/Head Over Flip	1962	10.00
❑ 5906	I Don't Care/Just Got to Know	1963	10.00
❑ 5911	Advice/No No	1963	10.00
❑ 5926	The Bitter and the Sweet/Just Pretending	1963	10.00
❑ 5955	That's the Way (It Goes)/I'll See It Through	1963	10.00
❑ 5977	Every Night/The Slightest Idea	1963	10.00
❑ 5982	Sooner or Later/Looking for a Woman	1963	10.00
❑ 66010	I Did Wrong/Someone	1964	8.00
❑ 66035	Just Like It Is/Let's Do It All	1964	8.00
❑ 66067	Believe in Me/Set Six	1964	8.00
❑ 66094	Every Night, Every Day/Can't Raise Me	1965	8.00
❑ 66116	Arkansas (Part 1)/Arkansas (Part 2)	1965	8.00
❑ 66129	Think/Steppin' Up in Class	1965	8.00
❑ 66147	My Answer/Beulah	1966	8.00

M

Number	Title (A Side/B Side)	Yr	NM
❑ 66168	Come On Home (Back Where You Belong)/Something That Belongs to Me	1966	8.00
❑ 66180	Just Let Me Cry/These Boots Are Made for Walkin'	1966	8.00
❑ 66207	It's Got to Be Love/Sorry	1966	8.00
IRMA			
❑ 102	You're the One/I Wanna Make Love to You	1956	30.00
❑ 103	Take a Chance/Fare Well	1956	30.00
❑ 107	I'm the One/Savoy's Jump	1957	30.00
❑ 109	Beer Tavern Girl/Love for You	1957	30.00
KENT			
❑ 369	I've Got Eyes for You/I'm Gonna Tell Your Mother	1962	10.00
LIBERTY			
❑ 56198	Believe Me/I Never Thought	1970	5.00
MERCURY			
❑ 71412	The Wobble/With Your Love	1959	15.00
❑ 71516	Let's Do It (The Chicken Scratch)/Georgia Slop	1959	15.00
❑ 71613	Doomed Lover/By Myself	1960	12.00
❑ 71666	You Rascal You/No One to Love Me	1960	12.00
❑ 71747	What's That (Part 1)/The Bridge	1961	12.00
❑ 71766	No One to Love Me/(B-side unknown)	1961	12.00
MINIT			
❑ 32018	Let the Door Hit You/This Thing	1967	6.00
❑ 32022	Dog (Part 1)/Dog (Part 2)	1967	6.00
❑ 32033	Get Together/How You Like Your Love	1967	6.00
❑ 32044	Pretty Little Sweet Thing/A & I	1968	6.00
❑ 32052	Love, Love, Love/Married Life	1968	6.00
❑ 32064	Drown in My Own Tears/What's Going On	1969	6.00
❑ 32086	I Had to Get With It/You Ain't Nothin' But a Devil	1969	6.00
❑ 32092	Stick to My Mind/I Just Live by the Rules	1970	6.00
MODERN			
❑ 926	Blues Blasters' Boogie/The Panic's On	1954	40.00
❑ 934	Darlin' Share Your Love/Give My Heart a Break	1954	40.00
❑ 951	Please Forgive Me Baby/Couldn't Be a Dream	1954	40.00
❑ 967	Gonna Tell Your Mother/That Ain't Right	1955	40.00
PEACOCK			
❑ 1605	My Days Are Limited/She's Gone	1952	60.00
❑ 1615	She Felt Too Good/Share and Share Alike	1953	60.00
❑ 1634	I Cried/The End	1953	60.00
❑ 1639	The Cheater/My Story	1954	60.00
❑ 1683	I Need Your Loving/The Swinging Thing	1958	25.00
Albums			
CHESS			
❑ LP-1464 [M]	Jimmy McCracklin Sings	1961	120.00
CROWN			
❑ CLP-5244 [M]	Twist with Jimmy McCracklin	196?	15.00
—Black label, multi-color "Crown"			
❑ CLP-5244 [M]	Twist with Jimmy McCracklin	1962	25.00
—Gray label			
❑ CLP-5244 [M]	Twist with Jimmy McCracklin	1962	50.00
—Black label, silver "Crown"			
EVEJIM			
❑ EJR-4013	Same Lovin'	198?	12.00
IMPERIAL			
❑ LP-9219 [M]	I Just Gotta Know	1964	25.00
❑ LP-9285 [M]	Every Night, Every Day	1965	25.00
❑ LP-9297 [M]	Think	1965	25.00
❑ LP-9306 [M]	My Answer	1966	25.00
❑ LP-9316 [M]	The New Soul of Jimmy McCracklin	1966	25.00
❑ LP-12219 [S]	I Just Gotta Know	1964	30.00
❑ LP-12285 [S]	Every Night, Every Day	1965	30.00
❑ LP-12297 [S]	Think	1965	30.00
❑ LP-12306 [S]	My Answer	1966	30.00
❑ LP-12316 [S]	The New Soul of Jimmy McCracklin	1966	30.00
MINIT			
❑ LP-4009 [M]	The Best of Jimmy McCracklin	1967	30.00
❑ LP-24009 [S]	The Best of Jimmy McCracklin	1967	25.00
❑ LP-24011	Let's Get Together	1968	25.00
❑ LP-24017	Stinger Man	1969	25.00
STAX			
❑ STS-2047	Yesterday Is Gone	1972	20.00
❑ MPS-8506	High on the Blues	1980	10.00

M

MCCRAE, GEORGE

Number	Title (A Side/B Side)	Yr	NM
12-Inch Singles			
GOLD MOUNTAIN			
❑ 81205	Own the Night/Own the Night (Dub)	1984	8.00
T.K. DISCO			
❑ TKD-22	Love in Motion (5:00)/Givin' Back the Feeling (5:31)	1977	12.00
❑ TKD-62	Kiss Me (The Way I Like It) (3:42) (5:47)	1977	12.00
❑ TKD-91	Let's Dance (6:10)/Hey Sexy Dancer	1978	12.00
45s			
SOUL CITY			
❑ XW456	Taking It All Off/Please Help Me Find My Baby	1974	6.00
T.K.			
❑ 1004	Rock Your Baby (Part 1)/Rock Your Baby (Part 2)	1974	5.00
❑ 1006	I Get Lifted/I Can't Leave You Alone	1974	5.00
❑ 1011	Look At You/I Need Someone Like You	1975	5.00
❑ 1014	I Ain't Lyin'/You Don't Know	1975	5.00
❑ 1016	Honey I/Sing a Happy Song	1975	5.00
❑ 1021	I'm Gonna Stay with My Baby Tonight/Love in Motion	1977	5.00
❑ 1024	Kiss Me (The Way I Like It) Part 1/Kiss Me (The Way I Like It) Part 2	1977	5.00
❑ 1029	Let's Dance (People All Over the World)/Let George Do It	1978	5.00
❑ 1032	I Want You Around Me/Are You Looking for Love	1979	5.00
❑ 1034	Don't You Feel My Love/You Got Me Going Crazy	1979	5.00
UNITED ARTISTS			
❑ 50811	Taking It All Off/Please Help Me Find My Baby	1971	10.00
Albums			
GOLD MOUNTAIN			
❑ GM 80008	Own the Night	1984	10.00
T.K.			
❑ 501	Rock Your Baby	1974	10.00
❑ 602	George McCrae	1975	10.00
❑ 606	Diamond Touch	1977	10.00

MCCRAE, GEORGE AND GWEN

Also see each artist's individual listings.

Number	Title (A Side/B Side)	Yr	NM
45s			
CAT			
❑ 2002	Winners Together or Losers Apart/Homesick Lovesick	1976	5.00
❑ 2004	I'll Do the Rockin'/Mechanical Body	1976	5.00
Albums			
CAT			
❑ 2606	Together	1976	10.00

MCCRAE, GWEN

Number	Title (A Side/B Side)	Yr	NM
12-Inch Singles			
ATLANTIC			
❑ PR 387 [DJ]	Keep the Fire Burning (same on both sides)	1982	6.00
BLACK JACK			
❑ 0021	Do You Know What I Mean (Long Version) (Short Version) (Dub)	1984	8.00
45s			
ATLANTIC			
❑ 3853	Funky Sensation/Have a Good Time	1981	4.00
❑ 3881	Poison/(B-side unknown)	1981	4.00
❑ 89910	Keep the Fire Burning/Hang On	1982	4.00
❑ 89961	I Need to Be with You/(B-side unknown)	1982	4.00
CAT			
❑ 1987	He Keeps Something Groovy Goin' On/Your Love Is Worse Than a Cold Love	1973	5.00
❑ 1989	For Your Love/Your Love	1973	5.00
❑ 1992	It's Worth the Hurt/90% of Me Is You	1974	5.00
❑ 1994	Move Me Baby/He Don't Ever Lose His Groove	1974	5.00
❑ 1996	Rockin' Chair/It Keeps On Raining	1975	5.00
❑ 1999	Love Insurance/He Keeps Something Groovy Goin' On	1975	5.00
❑ 2000	Cradle of Love/Easy Rock	1976	5.00
❑ 2005	Damn Right It's Good/Love Without Sex	1976	5.00
❑ 2011	Starting All Over Again/At Bedtime	1977	5.00
❑ 2014	The Melody of Life/The Joy	197?	5.00
❑ 2015	Maybe I'll Find Somebody New/All This Love That I'm Givin'	197?	5.00
COLUMBIA			
❑ 45214	Lead Me On/Lay It On Me	1970	5.00
❑ 45320	Been So Long/Lay It On Me	1971	5.00
❑ 45448	Ain't Nothing You Can Do/Goin' Down the Road Feelin' Bad	1971	5.00
❑ 45578	You Were Always on My Mind/He's Not You	1972	5.00
❑ 45684	I'm Losing the Feeling/Leave the Driving to Us	1972	5.00
Albums			
ATLANTIC			
❑ 80014	On My Way	1982	10.00
CAT			
❑ 2603	Gwen McCrae	1974	10.00
❑ 2605	Rockin' Chair	1975	10.00
❑ 2608	Something So Right	1976	10.00

MCCREA, DARLENE

Number	Title (A Side/B Side)	Yr	NM
45s			
JUBILEE			
❑ 5524	I Feel a Little Bit Better/Soulful Feeling	1965	10.00
ROULETTE			
❑ 4173	You/You Made a Fool of Me	1959	12.00
TOWER			
❑ 104	Don't Worry Baby/Heart's Not In It	1964	10.00

MCCULLERS, MICKEY

Number	Title (A Side/B Side)	Yr	NM
45s			
TAMLA			
❑ 54064	Same Old Story/I'll Cry a Million Tears	1962	40.00
V.I.P.			
❑ 25009	Same Old Story/Who You Gonna Run To	1964	50.00

MCCULLOCH, DANNY

Number	Title (A Side/B Side)	Yr	NM
45s			
CAPITOL			
❑ 2363	Wings of a Man/Orange and Red Beans	1968	8.00
❑ 2488	Hold On/Hope	1969	8.00
Albums			
CAPITOL			
❑ ST-174	Wings of a Man	1969	20.00

MCCULLOUGH, CHARLES

Number	Title (A Side/B Side)	Yr	NM
45s			
DOOTO			
❑ 462	My Girl/Zorro	1961	12.00
❑ 465	You're Not Too Young/That's Alright	1962	12.00

MCCURN, GEORGE

Number	Title (A Side/B Side)	Yr	NM
45s			
A&M			
❑ 705	I'm Just a Country Boy/In My Little Corner of the World	1963	10.00
❑ 715	Please Send Me Someone to Love/How's the World Treating You	1963	25.00
❑ 726	When the Wind Blows (In Chicago)/Georgia Town	1963	10.00
❑ 731	Guess Who/I've Got to Move	1964	15.00
❑ 741	Well/Clap Your Hands	1964	15.00
❑ 748	Your Friend/While the Bloom Is On the Rose	1964	10.00
❑ 759	As Tears Go By/Georgia Town	1965	15.00
LIBERTY			
❑ 55418	Your Daughter's Hand/The Time Has Come	1962	20.00
REPRISE			
❑ 0479	You Say You Don't Want Me/Too Many Tears	1966	25.00
Albums			
A&M			
❑ LP-102 [M]	Country Boy Goes to Town!!!!!	1963	25.00

Except when noted otherwise, VG = 25% of NM, and VG+ = 50% of NM. (Example: VG = $2.00, VG+ = $4.00 and NM = $8.00.)

Number	Title (A Side/B Side)	Yr	NM

MCDANIELS, GENE

45s

ATLANTIC

Number	Title (A Side/B Side)	Yr	NM
❑ 2805	The Lord Is Back/ Tell Me Mr. President	1971	6.00

—As "Eugene McDaniels"

COLUMBIA

Number	Title (A Side/B Side)	Yr	NM
❑ 43800	Something Blue/ Cause I Love You So	1966	30.00
❑ 44010	Touch of Your Lips/Sweet Lover No More	1967	30.00

LIBERTY

Number	Title (A Side/B Side)	Yr	NM
❑ 55231	In Times Like These/Once Before	1959	15.00
❑ 55265	The Green Door/Facts of Life	1960	15.00
❑ 55308	A Hundred Pounds of Clay/ Take a Chance on Love	1961	16.00
❑ 55344	A Tear/She's Come Back	1961	15.00
❑ 55371	Tower of Strength/The Secret	1961	16.00
❑ 55405	Chip Chip/ Another Tear Falls	1962	15.00
❑ 55444	Funny/Chapel of Tears	1962	15.00
❑ 55480	Point of No Return/ Warmer Than a Whisper	1962	15.00
❑ 55510	Spanish Lace/ Somebody's Waiting	1962	15.00
❑ 55541	The Puzzle/Cry Baby Cry	1963	12.00
❑ 55597	It's a Lonely Town/ False Friends	1963	30.00
❑ 55637	Old Country/Anyone Else	1963	12.00
❑ 55723	Make Me a Present of You/In Times Like These	1964	12.00
❑ 55752	Emily/Forgotten Man	1964	100.00
❑ 55805	A Miracle/Walk with a Winner	1965	150.00
❑ 55834	Hang On/Will It Last Forever	1965	100.00

MGM

Number	Title (A Side/B Side)	Yr	NM
❑ 14613	Ol' Heartbreak Top Ten/River	1973	5.00

ODE

Number	Title (A Side/B Side)	Yr	NM
❑ 66107	Lady Fair/Natural Juices	1975	4.00

UNITED ARTISTS

Number	Title (A Side/B Side)	Yr	NM
❑ 0053	A Hundred Pounds of Clay/ Tower of Strength	1973	4.00

—"Silver Spotlight Series" reissue

Number	Title (A Side/B Side)	Yr	NM
❑ 0054	Chip Chip/Point of No Return	1973	4.00

—"Silver Spotlight Series" reissue

Albums

ATLANTIC

Number	Title (A Side/B Side)	Yr	NM
❑ SD 8259	Outlaw	1970	15.00
❑ SD 8281	Headless Heroes	1971	15.00

LIBERTY

Number	Title (A Side/B Side)	Yr	NM
❑ LRP-3146 [M]	In Times Like These	1960	30.00
❑ LRP-3175 [M]	Sometimes I'm Happy, Sometimes I'm Blue	1960	30.00
❑ LRP-3191 [M]	100 Lbs. of Clay!	1961	30.00
❑ LRP-3204 [M]	Gene McDaniels Sings Movie Memories	1962	30.00
❑ LRP-3215 [M]	Tower of Strength	1962	30.00
❑ LRP-3258 [M]	Hit After Hit	1962	30.00
❑ LRP-3275 [M]	Spanish Lace	1963	25.00
❑ LRP-3311 [M]	The Wonderful World of Gene McDaniels	1963	25.00
❑ LST-7146 [S]	In Times Like These	1960	40.00

—Black vinyl

Number	Title (A Side/B Side)	Yr	NM
❑ LST-7146 [S]	In Times Like These	1960	200.00

—Blue vinyl

Number	Title (A Side/B Side)	Yr	NM
❑ LST-7175 [S]	Sometimes I'm Happy, Sometimes I'm Blue	1960	40.00
❑ LST-7191 [S]	100 Lbs. of Clay!	1961	40.00
❑ LST-7204 [S]	Gene McDaniels Sings Movie Memories	1962	40.00
❑ LST-7215 [S]	Tower of Strength	1962	40.00
❑ LST-7258 [S]	Hit After Hit	1962	40.00
❑ LST-7275 [S]	Spanish Lace	1963	30.00
❑ LST-7311 [S]	The Wonderful World of Gene McDaniels	1963	30.00

ODE

Number	Title (A Side/B Side)	Yr	NM
❑ SP-77028	Natural Juices	1975	12.00

SUNSET

Number	Title (A Side/B Side)	Yr	NM
❑ SUM-1122 [M]	Facts of Life	1967	12.00
❑ SUS-5122 [S]	Facts of Life	1967	15.00

UNITED ARTISTS

Number	Title (A Side/B Side)	Yr	NM
❑ UA-LA447-E	The Very Best of Gene McDaniels	1975	10.00

MCDEVITT, CHAS., AND HIS SKIFFLE GROUP

45s

CHIC

Number	Title (A Side/B Side)	Yr	NM
❑ 1008	Freight Train/The Cotton Song	1957	15.00

EPIC

Number	Title (A Side/B Side)	Yr	NM
❑ 9244	Face in the Rain/Sporting Life	1957	15.00

KAPP

Number	Title (A Side/B Side)	Yr	NM
❑ 216	Sing, Sing, Sing/Johnny-O	1958	15.00
❑ 238	Stack-O-Lee/Real Love	1958	15.00

MCDONALD, COUNTRY JOE

See COUNTRY JOE AND THE FISH.

MCDONALD, KATHI

45s

CAPITOL

Number	Title (A Side/B Side)	Yr	NM
❑ 3835	Freak Lover/Bogart to Bowie	1974	10.00
❑ 3880	Heat Wave/Bogart to Bowie	1974	10.00

Albums

CAPITOL

Number	Title (A Side/B Side)	Yr	NM
❑ ST-11224	Insane Asylum	1974	30.00

MCDONALD, MICHAEL

Also see THE DOOBIE BROTHERS; THE REGENTS (5).

12-Inch Singles

MCA

Number	Title (A Side/B Side)	Yr	NM
❑ 23641	Sweet Freedom (Freedom Mix — Club Version 10:10) (12" Vocal Version 8:25) (Instrumental 9:25) (Son of Freedom Mix — Radio Edit 6:48)	1986	8.00

REPRISE

Number	Title (A Side/B Side)	Yr	NM
❑ PRO-A-4395 [DJ]	All We Got (It's Not Enough, It's Never Enough) (4 versions)	1990	12.00
❑ PRO-A-4398 [DJ]	Tear It Up (same on both sides)	1990	8.00
❑ PRO-A-6538 [DJ]	Hey Girl (Edit) (LP Version) (Radio Remix)	1993	15.00
❑ 21734	All We Got (It's Not Enough, It's Never Enough) (5 versions)/ Show Me	1990	8.00

WARNER BROS.

Number	Title (A Side/B Side)	Yr	NM
❑ PRO-A-2325 [DJ]	No Lookin' Back (same on both sides)	1985	10.00

45s

BELL

Number	Title (A Side/B Side)	Yr	NM
❑ 45182	Dear Me/I Think I Love You Again	1972	15.00

—As "Mike McDonald"

Number	Title (A Side/B Side)	Yr	NM
❑ 45219	Good Old Time Love Song/ When I'm Home	1972	15.00

—As "Mike McDonald"

Number	Title (A Side/B Side)	Yr	NM
❑ 45259 [DJ]	Drivin' Wheel/(B-side unknown)	1972	12.00

—As "Mike McDonald"; stock copy may not exist

Number	Title (A Side/B Side)	Yr	NM
❑ 45308 [DJ]	Where Do I Go from Here/ (B-side unknown)	1973	12.00

—As "Mike McDonald"; stock copy may not exist

MCA

Number	Title (A Side/B Side)	Yr	NM
❑ S45-17156 [DJ]	Sweet Freedom (Short Version 4:10)/(Radio Edit 6:48)	1986	8.00
❑ 52857	Sweet Freedom/The Freedom Eights	1986	3.00
❑ 52857 [PS]	Sweet Freedom/The Freedom Eights	1986	3.00

RCA VICTOR

Number	Title (A Side/B Side)	Yr	NM
❑ 74-0405	God Knows/If You Won't, I Will	1970	20.00

—As "Mike McDonald"

REPRISE

Number	Title (A Side/B Side)	Yr	NM
❑ 7-18469	I Stand for You/East of Eden	1993	4.00

WARNER BROS.

Number	Title (A Side/B Side)	Yr	NM
❑ GWB 0444	I Keep Forgettin' (Every Time You're Near)/I Gotta Try	198?	3.00

—"Back to Back Hits" reissue

Number	Title (A Side/B Side)	Yr	NM
❑ 7-28596	Our Love (Theme from "No Mercy")/Don't Let Me Down	1986	3.00
❑ 7-28596 [PS]	Our Love (Theme from "No Mercy")/Don't Let Me Down	1986	3.00
❑ 7-28847	Lost in the Parade/By Heart	1985	4.00
❑ 7-28847 [PS]	Lost in the Parade/By Heart	1985	4.00
❑ 7-28960	No Lookin' Back/Don't Let Me Down	1985	3.00
❑ 7-28960 [PS]	No Lookin' Back/Don't Let Me Down	1985	3.00
❑ 7-29743	Playin' by the Rules/Believe in It	1983	4.00
❑ 7-29862	I Gotta Try/Believe in It	1982	4.00
❑ 7-29862 [PS]	I Gotta Try/Believe in It	1982	4.00
❑ 7-29933	I Keep Forgettin' (Every Time You're Near)/Losin' End	1982	4.00

—Second pressing has subtitle on A-side

Number	Title (A Side/B Side)	Yr	NM
❑ 7-29933	I Keep Forgettin'/Losin' End	1982	6.00

—First pressing has no subtitle on A-side

Number	Title (A Side/B Side)	Yr	NM
❑ 7-29933 [PS]	I Keep Forgettin' (Every Time You're Near)/Losin' End	1982	4.00

—Second pressing has subtitle on A-side

Number	Title (A Side/B Side)	Yr	NM
❑ 7-29933 [PS]	I Keep Forgettin'/Losin' End	1982	6.00

—First pressing has no subtitle on A-side

Albums

ARISTA

Number	Title (A Side/B Side)	Yr	NM
❑ ABM-2006	That Was Then — The Early Recordings of Michael McDonald	1982	50.00

MOBILE FIDELITY

Number	Title (A Side/B Side)	Yr	NM
❑ 1-149	If That's What It Takes	1985	40.00

—Audiophile vinyl

REPRISE

Number	Title (A Side/B Side)	Yr	NM
❑ 25979	Take It to Heart	1990	15.00

WARNER BROS.

Number	Title (A Side/B Side)	Yr	NM
❑ 23703	If That's What It Takes	1982	10.00
❑ 25291	No Lookin' Back	1985	10.00

MCDONALD, SKEETS

45s

CAPITOL

Number	Title (A Side/B Side)	Yr	NM
❑ F1518	Scoot, Git and Begone/The Blues Is Bad News	1951	25.00
❑ F1570	Bless Your Little Old Heart/ Today I'm Moving Out	1951	25.00
❑ F1771	I'm Hurtin'/Ridin' with the Blues	1951	25.00
❑ F1890	Baby Brown Eyes/Fuss and Fight	1951	25.00
❑ F1967	Tell Me Why/Be My Life's Companion	1952	20.00
❑ F1993	Wheel of Fortune/Love That Hurt Me So	1952	20.00
❑ F2073	Curtain of Tears/Please Come Back	1952	20.00
❑ F2216	Don't Let the Stars Get In Your Eyes/Big Family Trouble	1952	20.00
❑ F2326	Let Me Know/I'm Sorry to Say I'm Sorry	1953	20.00
❑ F2434	I Can't Last Long/I've Got to Win Your Love Again	1953	20.00
❑ F2523	Baby I'm Courtin'/It's Your Life	1953	20.00
❑ F2573	Hi Diddle Dee/Worried Mind	1953	20.00

—With Helen O'Connell

Number	Title (A Side/B Side)	Yr	NM
❑ F2607	Looking at the Moon and Wishing/I Need Your Love	1953	20.00
❑ F2696	Look Who's Cryin' Now/Walkin' on Teardrops	1954	20.00
❑ F2774	I Love You Mama Mia/ Remember You're Mine	1954	20.00
❑ F2885	But I Do/Your Love Is Like a Faucet	1954	20.00
❑ F2976	Smoke Comes Out My Chimney/Each Time a New Love Dies	1954	20.00
❑ F3038	Number One in Your Heart/I Can't Stand It Any Longer	1955	20.00
❑ F3117	You're Too Late/A Losing Hand	1955	20.00
❑ F3215	Strollin'/You Turned Me Down	1955	20.00
❑ F3312	Baby I'm Lost Without You/I Got a New Field to Plow	1956	15.00
❑ F3378	Fallen Angel/It'll Take Me a Long, Long Time	1956	15.00
❑ F3461	You Oughta See Grandma Rock/Heart Breakin' Mama	1956	100.00
❑ F3525	You Gotta Be My Baby/ Somebody	1956	15.00
❑ F3600	Don't Push Me Too Far/You Better Not Go	1956	15.00
❑ F3679	Keep Her Off Your Mind/I Am Music	1957	15.00
❑ F3741	Welcome Home/Your Sweet Love Is Gone	1957	15.00
❑ F3778	Fingertips/Bless Your Little Ol' Heart	1957	15.00
❑ F3833	I'm Hurtin'/Love Wind	1957	15.00
❑ F4095	What I Know About Her/What Am I Doing Here	1958	15.00
❑ F4147	Baby Wait/What a Lonesome Life It's Been	1959	15.00

COLUMBIA

Number	Title (A Side/B Side)	Yr	NM
❑ 4-41556	Cheek to Cheek with the Blues/ Where You Go (I'll Follow)	1960	12.00
❑ 4-41667	Gotta Get Away from That Crowd/The Everglades	1960	12.00
❑ 4-41773	This Old Heart/Make Room for the Blues	1960	12.00
❑ 4-42001	You're Not Wicked, You're Just Weak/He'll Let You Live a Little	1961	12.00
❑ 4-42252	Same Old Town/I Write You Letters	1961	12.00
❑ 4-42421	You Warned Me/What a Fool I Was	1962	12.00
❑ 4-42655	Dear John/I've Gotta Show You	1962	12.00
❑ 4-42807	Call Me Mr. Brown/This Old Broken Heart	1963	10.00
❑ 4-42960	Chin Up, Chest Out/I'd Hate to See Him	1963	10.00
❑ 4-43065	Too Many Times Away from You/Think of Me	1964	10.00

M

Number	Title (A Side/B Side)	Yr	NM
❑ 4-43152	Down in Mexico/Teardrop Inn	1964	10.00
❑ 4-43275	Me and My Heart and My Shoes/Mrs. Right's Divorcing Mr. Wrong	1965	10.00
❑ 4-43425	Big Chief Buffalo Nickel (Desert Blues)/Day Sleeper	1965	10.00
❑ 4-43573	A Member of the Blues/Polly Brown	1966	10.00
❑ 4-43791	There Sits an Angel/She's Never Gone That Route	1966	10.00
❑ 4-43946	Mabel/Too Much of Me (Walked Away with You)	1966	10.00
UNI			
❑ 55041	It's Genuine/Old Indians Never Die	1967	10.00
7-Inch Extended Plays			
CAPITOL			
❑ EAP 1-451	*Don't Let the Stars Get In Your Eyes/Let Me Know/Bless Your Little Ol' Heart (You're Mine)/I'm Hurtin'	1954	15.00
❑ EAP 1-451 [PS]	Country & Hillbilly Songs	1954	15.00
Albums			
CAPITOL			
❑ T 1040 [M]	Goin' Steady with the Blues	1958	80.00
COLUMBIA			
❑ CL 2170 [M]	Call Me Skeets	1964	25.00
❑ CS 8970 [S]	Call Me Skeets	1964	30.00
FORTUNE			
❑ 3001	The Tattooed Lady and Other Songs	1969	50.00
SEARS			
❑ SPS-116 [R]	Skeets	196?	25.00

MCDOWELL, MISSISSIPPI FRED

Number	Title (A Side/B Side)	Yr	NM
Albums			
ARHOOLIE			
❑ F-1021 [M]	Delta Blues	1964	50.00
❑ F-1027 [M]	Delta Blues, Vol. 2	1966	50.00
❑ F-1046	Mississippi Fred McDowell and His Blues Boys	1970	30.00
❑ F-1068	Keep Your Lamp Trimmed and Burning	1973	20.00
CAPITOL			
❑ ST-403	I Do Not Play No Rock and Roll	1970	25.00
JUST SUNSHINE			
❑ JSS-4	Mississippi Fred McDowell 1904-1972	1973	15.00
MILESTONE			
❑ MLP-3003 [M]	Long Way from Home	1966	30.00
❑ MLS-93003 [S]	Long Way from Home	1966	40.00
SIRE			
❑ SES-97018	Mississippi Fred McDowell in London	1970	30.00

MCDOWELL, PAUL

Number	Title (A Side/B Side)	Yr	NM
45s			
BRAVE			
❑ 1030	Standing Room Only/Play Me a Song (I Can Cry To)	196?	15.00

MCDUFF, JACK

Number	Title (A Side/B Side)	Yr	NM
45s			
ATLANTIC			
❑ 2402	Can't Get Satisfied (Part 1)/Can't Get Satisfied (Part 2)	1967	7.00
❑ 2423	Do It Now/Mush Melon	1967	7.00
❑ 5069	A Change Is Gonna Come/Down in the Valley	1966	8.00
❑ 5075	Tobacco Road/This Bitter Earth	1966	8.00
BLUE NOTE			
❑ 1953	Theme from Electric Surfboard/Down Home Style	1969	6.00
❑ 1957	The Vibrator/Oblighetto	1970	6.00
❑ 1958	Hunk-O-Funk/Mystic John	1970	6.00
CADET			
❑ 5614	Let My People Go/Ain't It	1968	6.00
❑ 5632	Black Is?/Win, Lose or Draw	1969	6.00
❑ 5693	Ain't No Sunshine/The Prophet	1972	5.00
PRESTIGE			
❑ 169	Brother Jack/Organ Grinder's Swing	1960	12.00
❑ 184	Yeah Baby (Part 1)/Yeah Baby (Part 2)	196?	12.00
❑ 199	The Honeydripper (Part 1)/The Honeydripper (Part 2)	196?	12.00
❑ 211	Goodnight, It's Time to Go/Sanctified Waltz	1961	12.00
❑ 219	Mellow Gravy (Part 1)/Mellow Gravy (Part 2)	196?	10.00
❑ 232	He's a Real Gone Guy (Part 1)/He's a Real Gone Guy (Part 2)	196?	10.00
❑ 246	Screamin'/Somethin'	196?	10.00
❑ 255	Doin' the '68/Kirk's Work	196?	10.00
—With Roland Kirk			
❑ 265	Sanctified Samba/Whistle While You Work	196?	10.00
❑ 273	Rock Candy/Real Good'yn	196?	10.00
❑ 286	Passing Through/Somewhere in the Night	196?	10.00
❑ 299	Grease Monkey/Wink's Blues	1963	8.00
❑ 320	Oh, Look at Me Now/Prelude	1964	8.00
❑ 330	Once in a Lifetime/Rail Heat	196?	8.00
❑ 344	A Kettle of Fish/Carry Me Home	1964	8.00
❑ 351	The Girl from Ipanema/Lew's Place	196?	8.00
❑ 377	Silk 'n' Soul (Part 1)/Silk 'n' Soul (Part 2)	196?	8.00
❑ 388	Hot Barbecue/Three Day Thang	196?	8.00
❑ 399	Walk On By/Too Many Fish in the Sea	196?	8.00
❑ 423	For Those Who Choose/Talkin' 'Bout My Woman	196?	8.00
❑ 722	Grease Monkey/Rock Candy	197?	6.00
Albums			
ATLANTIC			
❑ 1463 [M]	A Change Is Gonna Come	1966	15.00
❑ SD 1463 [S]	A Change Is Gonna Come	1966	20.00
❑ 1472 [M]	Tobacco Road	1967	20.00
❑ SD 1472 [S]	Tobacco Road	1967	15.00
❑ SD 1498	Double Barreled Soul	1968	15.00
BLUE NOTE			
❑ BST-84322	Down Home Style	1969	15.00
❑ BST-84334	Moon Rappin'	1970	15.00
❑ BST-84348	To Seek a New Home	1970	15.00
❑ BST-84358	Who Knows	1971	15.00
CADET			
❑ LPS-812	Natural Thing	1968	15.00
❑ LPS-817	Getting Our Thing Together	1969	15.00
❑ LPS-831	Gin and Orange	1970	15.00
❑ CH-50024	Check This Out	1973	12.00
❑ CH-50051	Fourth Dimension	1974	12.00
❑ CH-60017	The Healin' System	1972	12.00
❑ CH-60031	Magnetic Feel	1975	12.00
CHESS			
❑ 19004	Sophisticated Funk	1976	12.00
FANTASY			
❑ OJC-222	The Honeydripper	198?	10.00
—Reissue of Prestige 7199			
❑ OJC-324	Tough 'Duff	1988	10.00
—Reissue of Prestige 7185			
❑ OJC-326	Brother Jack Meets the Boss	1988	10.00
—Reissue of Prestige 7228			
MUSE			
❑ MR-5361	The Re-Entry	1989	12.00
PRESTIGE			
❑ PRLP-7174 [M]	Brother Jack	1960	50.00
❑ PRLP-7185 [M]	Tough 'Duff	1960	50.00
❑ PRLP-7199 [M]	The Honeydripper	1961	50.00
❑ PRLP-7220 [M]	Goodnight, It's Time to Go	1961	40.00
❑ PRST-7220 [S]	Goodnight, It's Time to Go	1961	40.00
❑ PRLP-7228 [M]	Mellow Gravy — Brother Jack Meets the Boss	1962	40.00
❑ PRST-7228 [S]	Mellow Gravy — Brother Jack Meets the Boss	1962	40.00
❑ PRLP-7259 [M]	Screamin'	1963	40.00
❑ PRST-7259 [S]	Screamin'	1963	40.00
❑ PRLP-7265 [M]	Somethin' Slick!	1963	40.00
❑ PRST-7265 [S]	Somethin' Slick!	1963	40.00
❑ PRLP-7274 [M]	Live!	1963	40.00
❑ PRST-7274 [S]	Live!	1963	40.00
❑ PRLP-7286 [M]	Live! At the Jazz Workshop	1964	40.00
❑ PRST-7286 [S]	Live! At the Jazz Workshop	1964	40.00
❑ PRLP-7323 [M]	The Dynamic Jack McDuff	1964	40.00
❑ PRST-7323 [S]	The Dynamic Jack McDuff	1964	40.00
❑ PRLP-7333 [M]	Prelude	1964	25.00
❑ PRST-7333 [S]	Prelude	1964	30.00
❑ PRLP-7362 [M]	The Concert McDuff Recorded Live!	1965	25.00
❑ PRST-7362 [S]	The Concert McDuff Recorded Live!	1965	30.00
❑ PRLP-7404 [M]	Silk and Soul	1965	25.00
❑ PRST-7404 [S]	Silk and Soul	1965	30.00
❑ PRLP-7422 [M]	Hot Barbeque	1966	20.00
❑ PRST-7422 [S]	Hot Barbeque	1966	25.00
❑ PRLP-7476 [M]	Walk On By	1967	25.00
❑ PRST-7476 [S]	Walk On By	1967	20.00
❑ PRLP-7481 [M]	Brother Jack McDuff's Greatest Hits	1967	25.00
❑ PRST-7481 [S]	Brother Jack McDuff's Greatest Hits	1967	20.00
❑ PRLP-7492 [M]	Hallelujah Time!	1967	25.00
❑ PRST-7492 [S]	Hallelujah Time!	1967	20.00
❑ PRST-7529	The Midnight Sun	1968	20.00
❑ PRST-7567	Soul Circle	1968	20.00
❑ PRST-7596	Jack McDuff Plays for Beautiful People	1969	20.00
❑ PRST-7642	I Got a Woman	1969	20.00
❑ PRST-7666	Steppin' Out	1969	20.00
❑ PRST-7703	Live! The Best of Brother Jack McDuff	1969	20.00
❑ PRST-7771	Best of the Big Soul Band	1970	15.00
❑ PRST-7785	Brother Jack	1970	15.00
❑ PRST-7814	Tough Duff	1971	15.00
❑ PRST-7851	On With It	1973	12.00
❑ 24013 [(2)]	Rock Candy	1972	15.00

MCFADDEN, BOB

Number	Title (A Side/B Side)	Yr	NM
45s			
BRUNSWICK			
❑ 55120	Frankie and Igor at a Rock and Roll Party/Children Cross the Bridge	1959	25.00
❑ 55140	The Mummy/The Beat Generation	1959	25.00
—As "Bob McFadden and Dor"			
❑ 55140 [PS]	The Mummy/The Beat Generation	1959	40.00
—As "Bob McFadden and Dor"			
❑ 55156	Bingo/Shake, Rattle and Roll	1959	25.00
CORAL			
❑ 62209	Dracula Cha-Cha/Transylvania Polka	1959	30.00
Albums			
BRUNSWICK			
❑ BL 54056 [M]	Songs Our Mummy Taught Us	1959	200.00
❑ BL 754056 [S]	Songs Our Mummy Taught Us	1959	300.00

MCFARLAND, GARY

Number	Title (A Side/B Side)	Yr	NM
45s			
IMPULSE!			
❑ 250	Winter Samba/Summer's Gone Away	1966	8.00
PRESTIGE			
❑ 331	The Dreamer/River Gal	196?	10.00
SKYE			
❑ 453	By the Time I Get to Phoenix/Flea Market	1968	6.00
❑ 4511	80 Miles an Hour Through Beer-Can Country/(B-side unknown)	1969	6.00
❑ 4516	Slaves/(Instrumental)	1970	6.00
VERVE			
❑ 10272	How to Succeed in Business Without Really Trying/I Believe in You	1962	10.00
❑ 10342	And I Love Her/A Hard Day's Night	1964	10.00
❑ 10380	Fried Bananas/Wine and Bread	1966	10.00
Albums			
ABC IMPULSE!			
❑ AS-46 [S]	Points of Departure	1968	15.00
❑ AS-9104 [S]	Tijuana Jazz	1968	15.00
❑ AS-9112 [S]	Profiles	1968	15.00
❑ AS-9122 [S]	Simpatico	1968	15.00
BUDDAH			
❑ BDS 95001	Butterscotch Rum	1967	20.00
COBBLESTONE			
❑ CST 9019	Requiem for Gary McFarland	1972	20.00
IMPULSE!			
❑ A-46 [M]	Point of Departure	1963	30.00
❑ AS-46 [S]	Points of Departure	1963	40.00
❑ A-9104 [M]	Tijuana Jazz	1966	20.00
❑ AS-9104 [S]	Tijuana Jazz	1966	25.00
❑ A-9112 [M]	Profiles	1966	30.00
❑ AS-9112 [S]	Profiles	1966	40.00
❑ A-9122 [M]	Simpatico	1966	30.00
❑ AS-9122 [S]	Simpatico	1966	40.00
SKYE			
❑ SK-2	Does the Sun Really Shine on the Moon?	1968	20.00
❑ SK-8	America the Beautiful	1969	20.00
❑ SK-11	Slaves	1970	30.00
❑ SK-14	Today	1970	30.00
VERVE			
❑ V-8443 [M]	How to Succeed in Business Without Really Trying	1962	20.00
❑ V6-8443 [S]	How to Succeed in Business Without Really Trying	1962	25.00
❑ V-8518 [M]	The Gary McFarland Orchestra with Special Guest Soloist Bill Evans	1963	25.00
❑ V6-8518 [S]	The Gary McFarland Orchestra with Special Guest Soloist Bill Evans	1963	30.00
❑ V-8603 [M]	Soft Samba	1964	25.00
❑ V6-8603 [S]	Soft Samba	1964	30.00
❑ V-8632 [M]	The "In" Sound	1965	40.00

Except when noted otherwise, VG = 25% of NM, and VG+ = 50% of NM. (Example: VG = $2.00, VG+ = $4.00 and NM = $8.00.)

Number	Title (A Side/B Side)	Yr	NM
❑ V6-8632 [S]	The "In" Sound	1965	50.00
❑ V/V6-8674	Gary McFarland	1965	—
—Canceled			
❑ V-8682 [M]	Soft Samba Strings	1966	25.00
❑ V6-8682 [S]	Soft Samba Strings	1966	30.00
❑ V-8738 [M]	Scorpio and Other Signs	1967	50.00
❑ V6-8738 [S]	Scorpio and Other Signs	1967	40.00
❑ V6-8786	Sympathetic Vibrations	1969	25.00

MCGHEE, BROWNIE

45s

Number	Title (A Side/B Side)	Yr	NM
DOT			
❑ 1184	Cheatin' and Lyin'/Need Someone to Love	1954	250.00
HARLEM			
❑ 2323	Worrying Over You/Christina	1954	60.00
❑ 2329	My Confession (I Want to Thank You)/Bluebird, Bluebird	1954	60.00
JAX			
❑ 302	Smiling and Crying Blues/A Letter to Lightnin' Hopkins	1951	120.00
❑ 304	I Feel So Good/Key to the Highway	1952	120.00
❑ 307	Meet You in the Morning/Brownie's Blues	1952	120.00
❑ 310	Guitar Strangers Blues/Dissatisfied Woman	1952	120.00
❑ 312	I'm 10,000 Years Old/Cherry Red	1952	120.00
❑ 322	New Bad Blood Blues/Pawnshop Blues	1953	120.00
RED ROBIN			
❑ 111	Don't Dog Your Woman/Daisy	1953	250.00
SAVOY			
❑ 835	Diamond Ring/So Much Trouble	1952	30.00
❑ 872	Tell Me Baby/Bad Nerves	1952	30.00
❑ 899	Sweet Baby Blues/4 O'Clock in the Morning	1953	30.00
❑ 1177	I'd Love to Love You/Anna Mae	1955	20.00
❑ 1185	When It's Love Time/My Fault	1956	20.00
❑ 1564	Living with the Blues/Be My Friend	1959	15.00

Albums

Number	Title (A Side/B Side)	Yr	NM
BLUESVILLE			
❑ BVLP-1042 [M]	Brownie's Blues	1962	80.00
—Blue label, silver print			
❑ BVLP-1042 [M]	Brownie's Blues	1964	25.00
—Blue label, trident logo at right			
FANTASY			
❑ OBC-505	Brownie's Blues	198?	12.00
FOLKWAYS			
❑ FP-30 [10]	Brownie McGhee Blues	1951	120.00
❑ FA-2030 [10]	Brownie McGhee Blues	1951	100.00
❑ 2421/2 [(2)]	Traditional Blues Vol. 1 and 2	197?	15.00
❑ 3557	Brownie McGhee Sings the Blues	197?	12.00
SAVOY JAZZ			
❑ SJL-1204	Jumpin' the Blues	1989	12.00

MCGHEE, BROWNIE, AND SONNY TERRY

See SONNY TERRY AND BROWNIE McGHEE.

MCGHEE, STICK

45s

Number	Title (A Side/B Side)	Yr	NM
ATLANTIC			
❑ 873	Drinkin' Wine Spo-Dee-O-Dee/Blues Mixture (I'd Rather Drink Muddy Water)	1971	20.00
—Yellow label, "fan" logo at lower left; first issue of this number on 45			
❑ 955	Wee Wee Hours (Part 1)/Wee Wee Hours (Part 2)	1952	100.00
—Note: Stick McGhee records on Atlantic before 955 are unconfirmed on 45 rpm			
❑ 991	New Found Love/Meet You in the Morning	1953	80.00
HERALD			
❑ 553	Money Fever/Sleep-In Job	1960	15.00
KING			
❑ 4610	Little Things We Used to Do/Head Happy with Wine	1953	100.00
❑ 4628	Whiskey, Women and Loaded Dice/Blues in My Heart and Tears in My Eyes	1953	100.00
❑ 4672	Jungle Juice/Dealing from the Bottom	1953	100.00
❑ 4700	I'm Doin' All This Time/Wiggle Waggin' Woo	1954	100.00
❑ 4783	Double Crossin' Liquor/Six to Eight	1955	120.00
❑ 4800	Get Your Mind Out the Gutter/Sad, Bad, Glad	1955	100.00
LONDON			
❑ 978	You Gotta Have Something on the Ball/(B-side unknown)	1951	250.00
SAVOY			
❑ 1148	Things Have Changed/Help Me Baby	1955	30.00

MCGHEE, STICK, AND JOHN LEE HOOKER

Also see each artist's individual listings.

Albums

Number	Title (A Side/B Side)	Yr	NM
AUDIO LAB			
❑ AL-1520 [M]	Highway of Blues	1959	350.00

MCGILL, JERRY

45s

Number	Title (A Side/B Side)	Yr	NM
SUN			
❑ 326	Love Struck/I Wanna Make Sweet Love	1959	30.00

MCGONNIGLE, MEL

45s

Number	Title (A Side/B Side)	Yr	NM
ROCKET			
❑ 101	Rattle Shakin' Mama/I Want You	1958	700.00

MCGOVERN, MAUREEN

45s

Number	Title (A Side/B Side)	Yr	NM
CASABLANCA			
❑ 814604-7	The Morning After/Nice to Be Around	198?	3.00
—Reissue			
CBS			
❑ 39-07689	The Same Moon/Why Can't I Forget	1988	4.00
❑ 39-07689 [PS]	The Same Moon/Why Can't I Forget	1988	4.00
MAIDEN VOYAGE			
❑ 120	Halfway Home/You Love Me Too Late	1981	4.00
20TH CENTURY			
❑ TCR-2	The Morning After/Nice to Be Around	197?	4.00
—Reissue			
❑ 2010	The Morning After (Song from The Poseidon Adventure)/Midnight Storm	1973	4.00
❑ 2051	I Won't Last a Day Without You/Darlene	1973	4.00
❑ 2072	Nice to Be Around/If I Wrote You a Song	1974	4.00
❑ 2107	Give Me a Reason to Be Gone/Love Knots	1974	4.00
❑ 2158	We May Never Love Like This Again/Wherever Love Takes Me	1974	4.00
❑ 2213	Even Better Than I Know Myself/All I Want (All I Need)	1975	4.00
❑ 2234	Love Songs Are Getting Harder to Sing/Stop Me	1975	4.00
❑ 2234 [PS]	Love Songs Are Getting Harder to Sing/Stop Me	1975	8.00
—No titles on sleeve, but catalog number is on it plus the words "The new Maureen McGovern in more ways than one!"			
WARNER BROS.			
❑ 8750	Can You Read My Mind/You Love Me Too Late	1979	4.00
❑ 8835	Different Worlds/Carolina Moon	1979	4.00
❑ 49129	Can't Take My Eyes Off You/A Very Special Love	1979	4.00
❑ 49177	We Could Have It All/Don't Stop Now	1980	4.00
❑ 49525	Bottom Line/Don't Stop Now	1980	4.00

Albums

Number	Title (A Side/B Side)	Yr	NM
CBS			
❑ BFM 42314	Another Woman in Love	1987	10.00
❑ BFM 44500	State of the Heart	1988	10.00
20TH CENTURY			
❑ T-419	The Morning After	1973	12.00
❑ T-439	Nice to Be Around	1974	12.00
❑ T-474	Academy Award Performances	1975	12.00
WARNER BROS.			
❑ BSK 3329	Maureen McGovern	1979	10.00

MCGRATH, BAT, AND DON POTTER

45s

Number	Title (A Side/B Side)	Yr	NM
EPIC			
❑ 5-10562	Mr. Cadillac/Walking Bird	1969	8.00
❑ 5-10582	Me and Bobby McGee/Jefferson Queen	1970	10.00

Albums

Number	Title (A Side/B Side)	Yr	NM
EPIC			
❑ BN 26499	Introducing	1969	15.00

MCGRIFF, JIMMY

12-Inch Singles

Number	Title (A Side/B Side)	Yr	NM
T.K. DISCO			
❑ TKD-79	Sky Hawk/Tailgunner	1976	12.00

45s

Number	Title (A Side/B Side)	Yr	NM
BLUE NOTE			
❑ 1968	Black Pearl/Groove Alley	1971	5.00
CAPITOL			
❑ 2875	Sugar Sugar/Fat Cakes	1970	5.00
❑ 3019	The Bird/Plain Brown Bag	1971	5.00
GROOVE MERCHANT			
❑ 1003	Groove Grease/Mr. Lucky	1972	5.00
❑ 1006	Theme from Shaft/Let's Stay Together	1972	5.00
❑ 1014	Everyday I Have the Blues/It's You I Adore	1973	5.00
❑ 1025	If You're Ready (Come Go with Me)/(B-side unknown)	1974	5.00
❑ 1029	Main Squeeze/The Sermon	1975	5.00
❑ 1033	Stump Juice/The Worm Turns	1976	5.00
JELL			
❑ 503	Soul Song Of Christmas (Silent Nite)/Chip! Chip!	1965	8.00
MILESTONE			
❑ 313	I'm Walkin'/(B-side unknown)	1984	4.00
SOLID STATE			
❑ 2501	I Cover the Waterfront/Slow But Sure	1966	8.00
❑ 2502	Cherry/The Comeback	1966	8.00
❑ 2510	I Can't Give You Anything But Love, Baby/(I Can't Get No) Satisfaction	1967	8.00
❑ 2515	Tennessee Waltz/Swingin' Shepherd Blues	1967	8.00
❑ 2516	Days of Wine and Roses/You Are My Sunshine	1967	8.00
❑ 2520	I've Got a Woman/Kiko	1968	6.00
❑ 2522	Honey/Since You've Been Gone	1968	6.00
❑ 2524	The Worm/Keep Loose	1968	6.00
❑ 2528	Step One/South Wes	1969	6.00
❑ 2531	Charlotte/Trying to Come By	1969	6.00
❑ 2534	Back on the Street/Chris Cross	1970	6.00
SUE			
❑ 105	Hello Betty/Close Your Eyes	1964	8.00
❑ 110	All Day Long/When You're Smiling	1964	8.00
❑ 112	Topkapi/Theme from "The Man with the Golden Arm"	1964	8.00
❑ 120	Sho 'Nuff/Bilbo	1965	8.00
❑ 123	Discotheque U.S.A./People	1965	8.00
❑ 128	Turn Blue/Bump De Bump	1965	8.00
❑ 770	I've Got a Woman (Part 1)/I've Got a Woman (Part 2)	1962	10.00
❑ 777	All About My Girl/M.G. Blues	1963	8.00
❑ 786	The Last Minute (Part 1)/The Last Minute (Part 2)	1963	8.00
❑ 791	One of Mine/Broadway	1963	8.00
❑ 802	Lonely Avenue (Part 1)/Lonely Avenue (Part 2)	1963	8.00
❑ 804	Winter with McGriff Pt. 1/Winter with McGriff Pt. 2	1963	10.00
❑ 804	Christmas with McGriff Part 1/Part 2	1963	12.00
❑ 10001	Kiko/Jumpin' at the Woodside	1964	8.00
UNITED ARTISTS			
❑ 50826	Pretty Baby/I Need Love So Bad	1971	5.00
—With Junior Parker			

7-Inch Extended Plays

Number	Title (A Side/B Side)	Yr	NM
SOLID STATE			
❑ SSLP 9-18002	I Cover the Waterfront/Hallelujah//See See Rider/Boston Bust Out	196?	12.00
—Jukebox issue; small hole, plays at 33 1/3 rpm			
❑ SSLP 9-18002 [PS]	A Bag Full of Soul	196?	12.00

Albums

Number	Title (A Side/B Side)	Yr	NM
BLUE NOTE			
❑ BST-84350	Electric Funk	1970	15.00
❑ BST-84364	Something to Listen To	1971	15.00
❑ BST-84374	Black Pearl	1971	15.00
CAPITOL			
❑ ST-616	Soul Sugar	1970	15.00
COLLECTABLES			
❑ COL-5147	Blues for Mr. Jimmy	198?	10.00
GROOVE MERCHANT			
❑ 503	Groove Grease	1972	15.00

M

Number	Title (A Side/B Side)	Yr	NM
❑ 506	Let's Stay Together	1972	15.00
❑ 509	Fly Dude	1973	15.00
❑ 520	Come Together	1973	12.00
❑ 529	If You're Ready Come Go with Me	1974	12.00
❑ 534	Main Squeeze	1975	12.00
❑ 2203	Black and Blues	1971	15.00
❑ 2205	Good Things Don't Happen Every Day	1971	15.00
❑ 3300 [(2)]	Giants of the Organ In Concert	1974	15.00
❑ 3309	Stump Juice	1976	12.00
❑ 3311	Mean Machine	1976	12.00
❑ 4403 [(2)]	Flyin' Time	197?	15.00
JAM			
❑ 002	City Lights	1982	12.00
❑ 005	Movin' Upside the Blues	1983	12.00
LRC			
❑ 9316	Tailgunner	1977	15.00
❑ 9320	Outside Looking In	1978	15.00
MILESTONE			
❑ M-9116	Countdown	1984	10.00
❑ M-9126	Skywalk	1985	10.00
❑ M-9135	State of the Art	1986	10.00
❑ M-9148	The Starting Five	1987	10.00
❑ M-9163	Blue to the 'Bone	1988	10.00
QUINTESSENCE			
❑ 25061	Soul	1978	12.00
SOLID STATE			
❑ SM-17001 [M]	The Big Band of Jimmy McGriff	1966	15.00
❑ SM-17002 [M]	A Bag Full of Soul	1966	15.00
❑ SM-17006 [M]	Cherry	1967	20.00
❑ SS-18001 [S]	The Big Band of Jimmy McGriff	1966	20.00
❑ SS-18002 [S]	A Bag Full of Soul	1966	20.00
❑ SS-18006 [S]	Cherry	1967	20.00
❑ SS-18017	A Bag Full of Blues	1968	20.00
❑ SS-18030	I've Got a New Woman	1968	20.00
❑ SS-18036	Honey	1968	20.00
❑ SS-18045	The Worm	1968	20.00
❑ SS-18053	Step I	1969	20.00
❑ SS-18060	A Thing to Come By	1969	20.00
❑ SS-18063	The Way You Look Tonight	1970	20.00
SUE			
❑ LP-1012 [M]	I've Got a Woman	1962	30.00
❑ STLP-1012 [S]	I've Got a Woman	1962	40.00
❑ LP-1013 [M]	One of Mine	1963	30.00
❑ STLP-1013 [S]	One of Mine	1963	40.00
❑ LP-1017 [M]	Jimmy McGriff at the Apollo	1963	30.00
❑ STLP-1017 [S]	Jimmy McGriff at the Apollo	1963	40.00
❑ LP-1018 [M]	Christmas with McGriff	1963	30.00
❑ STLP-1018 [S]	Christmas with McGriff	1963	40.00
❑ LP-1020 [M]	Jimmy McGriff at the Organ	1963	30.00
❑ STLP-1020 [S]	Jimmy McGriff at the Organ	1963	40.00
❑ LP-1033 [M]	Topkapi	1964	30.00
❑ STLP-1033 [S]	Topkapi	1964	40.00
❑ LP-1039 [M]	Blues for Mister Jimmy	1965	30.00
❑ STLP-1039 [S]	Blues for Mister Jimmy	1965	40.00
❑ LP-1043 [M]	Toast to Greatest Hits	1966	20.00
❑ STLP-1043 [S]	Toast to Greatest Hits	1966	25.00
SUNSET			
❑ SUS-5264	The Great Jimmy McGriff	1969	10.00
VEEP			
❑ VP-13515 [M]	Live Where the Action Is	1966	20.00
❑ VP-13522 [M]	Greatest Organ Hits	1967	25.00
❑ VPS-16515 [S]	Live Where the Action Is	1966	25.00
❑ VPS-16522 [S]	Greatest Organ Hits	1967	20.00

MCGRIFF, JIMMY, AND JUNIOR PARKER

Also see each artist's individual listings.

Albums

Number	Title (A Side/B Side)	Yr	NM
CAPITOL			
❑ ST-569	Dudes Doin' Business	1971	15.00
UNITED ARTISTS			
❑ UAS-5597	Jimmy McGriff and Junior Parker	1972	15.00
❑ UAS-6814	100 Proof Black Magic	1971	15.00

MCGUINN, ROGER

Also see THE BYRDS.

45s

Number	Title (A Side/B Side)	Yr	NM
COLUMBIA			
❑ 10019	Gate of Horn/Same Old Sound	1974	6.00
❑ 10181	Somebody Loves You/Easy Does It	1975	6.00
❑ 10201	Lover of the Bayou/Easy Does It	1975	6.00
❑ 10385	Take Me Away/Friend	1976	6.00
❑ 10543	American Girl/I'm Not Lonely Anymore	1977	6.00
❑ 45931	Draggin'/Time Cube	1973	6.00

Albums

Number	Title (A Side/B Side)	Yr	NM
ARISTA			
❑ AL 8648	Back from Rio	1991	15.00
COLUMBIA			
❑ AS 353 [DJ]	The Roger McGuinn Airplay Anthology	1977	30.00
—Promo only; also includes Byrds tracks			
❑ KC 31946	Roger McGuinn	1973	12.00
❑ KC 32956	Peace On You	1974	12.00
❑ PC 33541	Roger McGuinn & Band	1975	12.00
❑ PC 34154	Cardiff Rose	1976	12.00
❑ PC 34656	Thunderbyrd	1977	12.00

MCGUINN, CLARK, & HILLMAN

45s

Number	Title (A Side/B Side)	Yr	NM
CAPITOL			
❑ 4693	Don't You Write Her Off/Sad Boy	1979	5.00
❑ 4739	Surrender to Me/Little Mama	1979	4.00
❑ 4763	Bye Bye Baby/Backstage Pass	1979	4.00
❑ 4821	Street Talk/One More Chance	1980	4.00
❑ 4855	Deeper/City	1980	4.00

Albums

Number	Title (A Side/B Side)	Yr	NM
CAPITOL			
❑ SW-11910	McGuinn, Clark & Hillman	1979	12.00
❑ ST-12043	City	1980	12.00

MCGUINNESS FLINT

Also see COULSON, DEAN, McGUINNESS, FLINT.

45s

Number	Title (A Side/B Side)	Yr	NM
CAPITOL			
❑ 3014	When I'm Dead and Gone/Lazy Afternoon	1971	6.00
❑ 3139	Rock On/Malt and Barley Blues	1971	6.00
❑ 3186	Friends of Mine/Happy Birthday, Ruthy Baby	1971	6.00

Albums

Number	Title (A Side/B Side)	Yr	NM
CAPITOL			
❑ SMAS-625	McGuinness Flint	1971	12.00
❑ ST-794	Happy Birthday, Ruthy Baby	1971	12.00

MCGUIRE, BARRY

Also see THE NEW CHRISTY MINSTRELS.

45s

Number	Title (A Side/B Side)	Yr	NM
DUNHILL			
❑ 4009	Eve of Destruction/What Exactly's the Matter with Me	1965	12.00
❑ 4014	Child of Our Times/Upon a Painted Ocean	1965	10.00
❑ 4014 [PS]	Child of Our Times/Upon a Painted Ocean	1965	15.00
❑ 4019	This Precious Time/Don't You Wonder Where It's At	1966	12.00
—A-side backing group: The Mamas and The Papas			
❑ 4028	Cloudy Summer Afternoon (Raindrops)/I'd Have to Be Outta My Mind	1966	10.00
❑ 4048	There's Nothing Else on My Mind/Why Not Stop and Dig It	1966	10.00
❑ 4098	Masters of War/Stop Now and Dig It While You Can	1967	8.00
❑ 4116	Lollipop Train/Inner-Manipulations	1968	8.00
❑ 4124	Grasshopper Song/Top o' the Hill	1968	10.00
❑ 4124 [PS]	Grasshopper Song/Top o' the Hill	1968	15.00
HORIZON			
❑ 4	One by One/Town and Country	1963	12.00
❑ 8	Oh, Miss Mary/So Long, Stay Well	1963	12.00
MIRA			
❑ 205	Greenback Dollar/Oh, Miss Mary	1965	10.00
MOSAIC			
❑ 1001	The Three/Theme from The Tree	1961	12.00
❑ 1004	I've Got a Secret/Cindy and Johnny	1962	12.00
MYRRH			
❑ 119	Love Is/David and Goliath	1973	5.00
ODE			
❑ 66010	Old Farm/South of the Border	1970	6.00
SPARROW			
❑ 1023	Cosmic Cowboy/What Good Would It Do	197?	6.00

7-Inch Extended Plays

Number	Title (A Side/B Side)	Yr	NM
DUNHILL			
❑ LP-DS-50005	This Precious Time/California Dreamin'/Hide Your Love Away//Let Me Be/Do You Believe in Magic/Don't You Wonder Where It's At	1966	12.00
—Jukebox issue, small hole, plays at 33 1/3 rpm			
❑ LP-DS-50005 [PS]	This Precious Time	1966	12.00

Albums

Number	Title (A Side/B Side)	Yr	NM
ABC DUNHILL			
❑ DS-50033	The World's Last Private Citizen	1968	25.00
DUNHILL			
❑ D-50003 [M]	Eve of Destruction	1965	30.00
❑ DS-50003 [S]	Eve of Destruction	1965	40.00
❑ D-50005 [M]	This Precious Time	1966	25.00
❑ DS-50005 [S]	This Precious Time	1966	30.00
HORIZON			
❑ ST-1636 [S]	The Barry McGuire Album	1963	40.00
❑ WP-1636 [M]	The Barry McGuire Album	1963	30.00
MIRA			
❑ LP-3000 [M]	The Barry McGuire Album	1965	20.00
—Reissue of Horizon LP			
❑ LPS-3000 [S]	The Barry McGuire Album	1965	25.00
—Reissue of Horizon LP			
MYRRH			
❑ MSA-6519	Seeds	1974	12.00
❑ MSA-6531	Lighten Up	1975	12.00
ODE			
❑ SP-77004	Barry McGuire with the Doctor	1970	15.00

MCGUIRE, BARRY, AND BARRY KANE

45s

Number	Title (A Side/B Side)	Yr	NM
HORIZON			
❑ 354	Another Man/Bull 'Gine Run	1962	12.00

Albums

Number	Title (A Side/B Side)	Yr	NM
HORIZON			
❑ SWP-1608 [S]	Barry and Barry: Here and Now!	1962	30.00
❑ WP-1608 [M]	Barry and Barry: Here and Now!	1962	25.00

MCKAY, SCOTTY

45s

Number	Title (A Side/B Side)	Yr	NM
ACE			
❑ 603	Let the Good Times Roll/Little Liza Jane	1960	50.00
❑ 608	Brown Eyed Handsome Man/Cry Me a River	1960	60.00
❑ 623	Ole King Cole/Pull Down the Sky	1961	50.00
❑ 636	I've Got My Eyes on You/Shattered Dreams	1961	40.00
❑ 652	Olive Learned to Pop-Eye/Shame	1962	40.00
❑ 8003	Half a Heartache/Little Miss Blue	1962	30.00
CLARIDGE			
❑ 309	Batman/All Around the World	1966	25.00
EVENT			
❑ 4295	Rollin' Dynamite/Evenin' Time	1959	50.00
HANNA-BARBERA			
❑ 495	I'm Gonna Love Ya/Waikiki Beach	1966	25.00
LAWN			
❑ 102	I've Been Thinkin'/It's a Fun Thing	1960	25.00
PARKWAY			
❑ 806	Rollin' Dynamite/Evenin' Time	1959	40.00
PHILIPS			
❑ 40109	Mess Around/Sittin' Down and Cryin'	1963	20.00
SAVANNAH SOUND			
❑ 501	Here Comes Batman/All Around the World	196?	40.00
SWAN			
❑ 4049	Little Lump of Sugar/Midnight Cryin' Time	1960	60.00
UNI			
❑ 55205	High on Life/If You Really Want Me To, I'll Go	1970	12.00

MCKENDREE SPRING

45s

Number	Title (A Side/B Side)	Yr	NM
DECCA			
❑ 32510	If the Sun Should Rise/What Will We Do with the Child	1969	6.00
❑ 32773	Because It's Time/Oh, Now My Friend	1971	6.00
❑ 32961	Down by the River/Flying Dutchmen	1972	6.00
❑ 33000	God Bless the Conspiracy/Flying Dutchmen	1972	6.00
MCA			
❑ 40024	Underground Railroad/Watch Those Pennies	1973	5.00
PYE			
❑ 71023	Easier Things Have Been Done/(B-side unknown)	1975	5.00

Except when noted otherwise, VG = 25% of NM, and VG+ = 50% of NM. (Example: VG = $2.00, VG+ = $4.00 and NM = $8.00.)

Number	Title (A Side/B Side)	Yr	NM
❑ 71060	Too Young to Feel This Old/I'm Gonna Lose That Game Again	1976	5.00

Albums

DECCA

Number	Title (A Side/B Side)	Yr	NM
❑ DL 75104	McKendree Spring	1969	15.00
❑ DL 75230	Second Thoughts	1970	15.00
❑ DL 75332	McKendree Spring 3	1972	15.00
❑ DL 75385	Tracks	1972	15.00

MCA

Number	Title (A Side/B Side)	Yr	NM
❑ 44	McKendree Spring 3	1973	10.00
—Reissue of Decca 75332			
❑ 50	Tracks	1973	10.00
—Reissue of Decca 75385			
❑ 277	McKendree Spring	1973	10.00
—Reissue of Decca 75104			
❑ 370	Spring Suite	1973	12.00

PYE

Number	Title (A Side/B Side)	Yr	NM
❑ 12108	Get Me to the Country	1975	12.00
❑ 12124	Too Young to Feel This Old	1976	12.00

MCKENZIE, SCOTT

Also see THE JOURNEYMEN (1); THE SMOOTHIES.

45s

CAPITOL

Number	Title (A Side/B Side)	Yr	NM
❑ 5348	All I Want Is You/Look in Your Eyes	1965	10.00
❑ 5500	There Stands the Glass/Wipe the Tears (From Your Face)	1965	10.00
❑ 5961	All I Want Is You/Look in Your Eyes	1967	6.00

EPIC

Number	Title (A Side/B Side)	Yr	NM
❑ 10124	No, No, No, No, No/I Want to Be Alone	1967	8.00
—B-side by McKenzie's Musicians			

ODE

Number	Title (A Side/B Side)	Yr	NM
❑ 103	San Francisco (Be Sure to Wear Flowers in Your Hair)/What's the Difference	1967	8.00
—Revised title and revised mix			
❑ 103	San Francisco "Wear Some Flowers in Your Hair"/What's the Difference	1967	15.00
—Original title; also has a different mix (echoey bass drum in bridge) than the later, more common version			
❑ 105	Like and Old Time Movie/What's the Difference, Chapter II	1967	6.00
❑ 107	Holy Man/What's the Difference, Chapter III	1968	6.00
❑ 66012	Going Home Again/Take a Moment	1970	5.00

Albums

ODE

Number	Title (A Side/B Side)	Yr	NM
❑ Z12 44001 [M]	The Voice of Scott McKenzie	1967	30.00
❑ Z12 44002 [S]	The Voice of Scott McKenzie	1967	20.00
❑ SP-77007	Stained Glass Morning	1970	15.00

MCKINLEYS, THE

45s

SWAN

Number	Title (A Side/B Side)	Yr	NM
❑ 4185	A Million Miles Away/Someone Cares for Me	1964	15.00

MCLAIN, DENNY

45s

CAPITOL

Number	Title (A Side/B Side)	Yr	NM
❑ 2282	Extra Innings/Lonely Is the Name	1968	12.00

Albums

CAPITOL

Number	Title (A Side/B Side)	Yr	NM
❑ ST-204	Denny McLain In Las Vegas	1969	25.00
❑ ST 2881	Denny McLain at the Organ	1968	25.00

MCLAIN, TOMMY

45s

CRAZY CAJUN

Number	Title (A Side/B Side)	Yr	NM
❑ 2015	Good Morning Lousiana/Mama Send a Dollar	197?	6.00
❑ 2018	Tender Years/Honky Tonk	197?	6.00
❑ 2027	Leaving This Town/Jukebox Songs	197?	6.00
❑ 2031	Send Me the Pillow/Following Him	197?	6.00
❑ 2033	Bartender, Play Me Some Freddie Fender/I Cried	197?	7.00
❑ 2037	Fannie Mae/Going Out with the Tide	198?	5.00
—With Freddy Fender			
❑ 2044	They'll Never Take That Away from Me/Lose the Blues	197?	6.00
❑ 2063	Going Honky Tonkin'/The Same Old Thing	198?	6.00

JIN

Number	Title (A Side/B Side)	Yr	NM
❑ 197	Sweet Dreams/I Need You So	1966	25.00
❑ 209	Think It Over/I Can't Take It No More	196?	10.00
❑ 216	You Wouldn't Know a Love/If You Would Be True	196?	10.00
❑ 221	Legend in My Time/I'm Glad for Your Sake	196?	10.00
❑ 228	Before I Grow Too Old/Domino '68	1968	10.00
❑ 229	Barefootin'/Together Again	1968	30.00
❑ 230	Tender Years/My Heart Remembers	1968	10.00
❑ 235	I Need You So/After Loving You	196?	10.00
❑ 236	Sticks and Stones/I'll Miss You	196?	10.00
❑ 317	When a Man Loves a Woman/I Can't Take It No More	197?	6.00
❑ 342	Tender Years/Think It Over	197?	6.00
❑ 368	Just Because I Thought I'd Never Fall in Love/(B-side unknown)	197?	5.00
—Promo-only version on Quiex II vinyl			

MSL

Number	Title (A Side/B Side)	Yr	NM
❑ 197	Sweet Dreams/I Need You So	1966	12.00
❑ 209	Think It Over/I Can't Take It No More	196?	10.00
❑ 213	Am I That Easy to Forget/I'm Gonna Cry	196?	10.00

STARFLITE

Number	Title (A Side/B Side)	Yr	NM
❑ 4901	(I Don't Love You) Since You Walked Out on Me/That's Good Enough for Me	1979	6.00

Albums

CRAZY CAJUN

Number	Title (A Side/B Side)	Yr	NM
❑ 1050	Good Mornin' Lousiana	1978	25.00

JIN

Number	Title (A Side/B Side)	Yr	NM
❑ 9009	Tommy McLain	1975	25.00

STARFLITE

Number	Title (A Side/B Side)	Yr	NM
❑ 36028	Backwoods Bayou Adventure	1979	15.00

MCLAUGHLIN, JOHN

Albums

CBS

Number	Title (A Side/B Side)	Yr	NM
❑ FM 45578	Mediterranean Concerto	1989	15.00

CELLULOID

Number	Title (A Side/B Side)	Yr	NM
❑ CEL-5010	Devotion	198?	10.00
—Reissue of Douglas 31568			

COLUMBIA

Number	Title (A Side/B Side)	Yr	NM
❑ PC 34162	Shakti with John McLaughlin	1976	12.00
—No bar code on cover			
❑ PC 34372	A Handful of Beauty	1977	12.00
—No bar code on cover			
❑ JC 34980	Natural Elements	1977	12.00
—No bar code on cover			
❑ JC 35326	Electric Guitarist	1978	12.00
—No bar code on cover			
❑ JC 35785	Electric Dreams	1979	10.00
❑ JC 36355	The Best of John McLaughlin	1980	12.00
❑ PC 36355	The Best of John McLaughlin	198?	8.00
—Reissue with new prefix			
❑ FC 37152	Friday Night in San Francisco	1981	10.00
—With Al DiMeola and Paco De Lucia			
❑ FC 38645	Passion, Grace & Fire	1983	10.00
—With Al DiMeola and Paco De Lucia			

DOUGLAS

Number	Title (A Side/B Side)	Yr	NM
❑ 4	Devotion	1970	20.00
❑ KZ 30766	My Goals Beyond	1971	15.00
—Original issue			
❑ KZ 31568	Devotion	1972	15.00
—Reissue of 4			

DOUGLAS CASABLANCA

Number	Title (A Side/B Side)	Yr	NM
❑ ADLP-6003	My Goals Beyond	1976	12.00
—Reissue of Douglas 30766; second issue of this album			

ELEKTRA/MUSICIAN

Number	Title (A Side/B Side)	Yr	NM
❑ E1-60031	My Goals Beyond	1982	12.00
—Third issue of this album			

POLYDOR

Number	Title (A Side/B Side)	Yr	NM
❑ PD-5510	Extrapolation	1972	20.00
❑ PD-1-6074	Extrapolation	1972	12.00
—Reissue of 5510			

PYE

Number	Title (A Side/B Side)	Yr	NM
❑ 12103	Where Fortune Smiles	1975	20.00
—Recorded in 1970; this was the first U.S. issue of this material			

RELATIVITY

Number	Title (A Side/B Side)	Yr	NM
❑ 88561-8061-1	Adventures in Radioland	1986	12.00

RYKO ANALOGUE

Number	Title (A Side/B Side)	Yr	NM
❑ RALP-0051	My Goals Beyond	1987	20.00
—Clear vinyl; fourth issue of this album			

WARNER BROS.

Number	Title (A Side/B Side)	Yr	NM
❑ BSK 3619	Belo Horizonte	1981	15.00
❑ 23723	Music Spoken Here	1982	10.00
❑ 25190	Mahavishnu	1985	10.00

MCLAWLER, SARAH

45s

KING

Number	Title (A Side/B Side)	Yr	NM
❑ 4549	Please Try to Love Me/Ready, Willing, and Able	1952	100.00
❑ 4561	Romance in the Dark/I'm Just Another One	1952	100.00

VEE JAY

Number	Title (A Side/B Side)	Yr	NM
❑ 199	Babe in the Woods/Flamingo	1956	30.00
❑ 239	Snowfall/Relax Miss Frisky	1957	30.00
—With Richard Otto			

Albums

VEE JAY

Number	Title (A Side/B Side)	Yr	NM
❑ LP-1030 [M]	At the Break of Day	1961	40.00
—With Richard Otto			

MCLEAN, DON

45s

ARISTA

Number	Title (A Side/B Side)	Yr	NM
❑ 0284	Prime Time/The Statue	1977	4.00
❑ 0379	It Doesn't Matter Anymore/If We Try	1978	4.00

CAPITOL

Number	Title (A Side/B Side)	Yr	NM
❑ B-44098	Perfect Love/Can't Blame the Train	1987	3.00
❑ B-44186	Love in the Heart/Every Day's a Miracle	1988	3.00
❑ B-44258	Eventually/It's Not Your Fault	1988	3.00

EMI

Number	Title (A Side/B Side)	Yr	NM
❑ 9100	American Pie/Vincent	1992	8.00
—Scarce reissue with entire 8:30 version of "American Pie" on one side			

EMI AMERICA

Number	Title (A Side/B Side)	Yr	NM
❑ 8375	He's Got You/To Have and To Hold	1987	3.00
❑ 43025	Superman's Ghost/(B-side unknown)	1987	3.00

MEDIARTS

Number	Title (A Side/B Side)	Yr	NM
❑ 108	And I Love You So/Castles in the Air	1970	10.00

MILLENNIUM

Number	Title (A Side/B Side)	Yr	NM
❑ YB-11799	Crying/Genesis (In the Beginning)	1980	4.00
❑ YB-11803	Lloras "Crying"/Genesis (In the Beginning)	1981	—
—Unreleased			
❑ YB-11804	Since I Don't Have You/Your Cheating Heart	1981	4.00
❑ YB-11809	It's Just the Sun/Words and Music	1981	4.00
❑ YB-11819	Castles in the Air/Crazy Eyes	1981	4.00
❑ YB-13106	Jerusalem/Left for Dead on the Road of Love	1982	4.00
❑ GB-13477	Crying/Since I Don't Have You	1983	3.00
—Gold Standard Series			

UNITED ARTISTS

Number	Title (A Side/B Side)	Yr	NM
❑ XW206	If We Try/The More You Pay	1973	4.00
❑ XW363	Fool's Paradise/Happy Trails	1973	4.00
❑ XW519	Vincent/Dreidel	1974	4.00
—Reissue			
❑ XW520	American Pie (Part 1)/American Pie (Part 2)	1974	4.00
—Reissue			
❑ XW541	Sitting on Top of the World/Mule Skinner Blues	1974	4.00
❑ XW579	Homeless Brothers/La La Love You	1974	4.00
❑ XW614	Wonderful Baby/Birthday Song	1975	4.00
❑ 50796	And I Love You So/Castles in the Air	1971	6.00
❑ 50856	American Pie/Empty Chairs	1971	—
—Unreleased?			
❑ 50856	American Pie — Part 1/American Pie — Part 2	1971	5.00
❑ 50856 [DJ]	American Pie (mono/stereo)	1971	8.00
—With a different edit than the Part 1/Part 2 stock copy			
❑ 50856 [PS]	American Pie	1971	10.00
—Comes with both promos and stock copies			
❑ 50887	Vincent/Castles in the Air	1972	5.00
❑ 50887 [PS]	Vincent/Castles in the Air	1972	10.00
❑ 51100	Dreidel/Bronco Bill's Lament	1973	4.00

Albums

ARISTA

Number	Title (A Side/B Side)	Yr	NM
❑ AL 4149	Prime Time	1978	10.00

CAPITOL

Number	Title (A Side/B Side)	Yr	NM
❑ C1-48080	Love Tracks	1988	10.00

CASABLANCA

Number	Title (A Side/B Side)	Yr	NM
❑ NBLP 7173	Chain Lightning	1979	—
—Canceled			

EMI AMERICA

Number	Title (A Side/B Side)	Yr	NM
❑ ST-17255	Don McLean's Greatest Hits, Then and Now	1987	10.00

M

Number	Title (A Side/B Side)	Yr	NM
LIBERTY			
❑ LN-10037	American Pie	1980	8.00
—Reissue of United Artists 5535			
❑ LN-10157	Tapestry	1982	8.00
—Reissue of United Artists 5522			
❑ LN-10211	Homeless Brother	198?	8.00
—Reissue of United Artists 315			
MEDIARTS			
❑ 41-4	Tapestry	1970	20.00
MILLENNIUM			
❑ BXL1-7756	Chain Lightning	1981	10.00
❑ BXL1-7762	Believers	1981	10.00
UNITED ARTISTS			
❑ UA-LA161-F	Playin' Favorites	1973	12.00
❑ UA-LA315-G	Homeless Brother	1974	12.00
❑ UA-LA652-H2 [(2)]	Solo	1976	15.00
❑ UAS-5522	Tapestry	1971	12.00
—Reissue of Mediarts LP			
❑ UAS-5535	American Pie	1971	12.00
❑ UAS-5651	Don McLean	1972	12.00

MCLEAN, PHIL

45s

Number	Title (A Side/B Side)	Yr	NM
VERSATILE			
❑ 107	Small Sad Sam/Chicken	1961	10.00
❑ 108	Big Mouth Bill/Come with Us	1962	10.00

MCLOLLIE, OSCAR

45s

Number	Title (A Side/B Side)	Yr	NM
CLASS			
❑ 206	Here I Am/Say	1957	15.00
❑ 228	Hey Girl — Hey Boy/Let Me Know Let Me Know	1958	15.00
—With Jeanette Baker			
❑ 238	Let's Get Together/Rock-a-Cha	1958	15.00
—With Jeanette Baker			
❑ 243	Convicted/My Heart Speaks	1959	15.00
❑ 265	The Honey Jump/Call It Love	1960	15.00
❑ 503	Rain/Casino	1956	20.00
MERCURY			
❑ 70964	Blue Velvet/The Penalty	1956	25.00
MODERN			
❑ 902	The Honey Jump (Part 1)/The Honey Jump (Part 2)	1952	60.00
❑ 915	Be Cool My Heart/All the Oil in Texas	1952	50.00
❑ 920	Falling in Love with You/Lolly Pop	1953	50.00
❑ 938	Hot Banana/Wiggle Toe	1954	40.00
❑ 943	God Gave Us Christmas/Dig That Crazy Santa Claus	1954	40.00
❑ 950	Pretty Girl/Hey Lolly Lolly	1955	40.00
❑ 955	Pagliacci (With a Broken Heart)/Eternal Love	1955	40.00
❑ 970	Roll, Hot Rod, Roll/Convicted	1955	40.00
❑ 976	God Gave Us Christmas/(B-side unknown)	1955	30.00
WING			
❑ 90083	God's Green Earth/Got Your Love in My Heart	1956	25.00

Albums

Number	Title (A Side/B Side)	Yr	NM
CROWN			
❑ CLP-5016 [M]	Oscar McLollie and His Honey Jumpers	1956	400.00
—Opinions differ as to whether this LP actually exists. Value is probably conservative.			

MCLUHAN

Albums

Number	Title (A Side/B Side)	Yr	NM
BRUNSWICK			
❑ BL 754177	Anomaly	1972	20.00

MCLUHAN, MARSHALL

Albums

Number	Title (A Side/B Side)	Yr	NM
COLUMBIA			
❑ CL 2701 [M]	The Medium Is the Message	1967	25.00
❑ CS 9501 [S]	The Medium Is the Message	1967	25.00

MCMAHON, ED

45s

Number	Title (A Side/B Side)	Yr	NM
CAMEO			
❑ 474	Beautiful Girl/The Loving Heart	1967	12.00

Albums

Number	Title (A Side/B Side)	Yr	NM
CAMEO			
❑ C-2009 [M]	And Me...I'm Ed McMahon	1967	25.00
❑ SC-2009 [S]	And Me...I'm Ed McMahon	1967	30.00
RCA CAMDEN			
❑ CAL-1083 [M]	What Do You Want to Be When You Grow Up?	1965	20.00
❑ CAS-1083 [S]	What Do You Want to Be When You Grow Up?	1965	25.00

MCMANUS, ROSS

45s

Number	Title (A Side/B Side)	Yr	NM
IMPERIAL			
❑ 66042	Patsy Girl/I'm the Greatest	1964	12.00

MCNABB, CECIL

45s

Number	Title (A Side/B Side)	Yr	NM
KING			
❑ 5116	Clock Tickin' Rhythm/Nothing Like This	1958	250.00

MCNAIR, BARBARA

45s

Number	Title (A Side/B Side)	Yr	NM
AUDIO FIDELITY			
❑ 153	Love Has a Way/(B-side unknown)	1969	10.00
❑ 162	After St. Francis/I Can Tell	1969	10.00
CORAL			
❑ 61923	Till There Was You/Bobby	1958	25.00
❑ 61972	He's Got the Whole World in His Hands/Flipped Over You	1958	30.00
❑ 61996	Indiscreet/Waltz Me Around	1958	25.00
❑ 62020	Too Late This Spring/See If I Care	1958	25.00
❑ 62071	Goin' Steady with the Moon/I Feel a Feeling	1959	25.00
❑ 62116	Lover's Prayer/Old Devil Moon	1959	25.00
KC			
❑ 109	Cross Over the Bridge/Gloryland	1962	50.00
❑ 112	A Little Bird Told Me/Nobody Rings My Bell	1963	40.00
MOTOWN			
❑ 1087	Touch of Time/You're Gonna Love My Baby	1965	300.00
❑ 1099	What a Day/Everything Is Good About You	1966	25.00
❑ 1106	Here I Am Baby/My World Is Empty Without You	1966	25.00
❑ 1112	Steal Away Tonight/For Once in My Life	1967	500.00
❑ 1123	Where Would I Be Without You/For Once in My Life	1968	25.00
❑ 1133	You Could Never Love Him/Fancy Passes	1968	25.00
SIGNATURE			
❑ 12024	He's a King/Murray, What's Your Hurry	1960	100.00
❑ 12033	All About Love/You Done Me Wrong	1960	20.00
❑ 12049	Kansas City/Love Talk	1960	20.00
WARNER BROS.			
❑ 5633	Wanted Me/It Was Never Like This	1965	150.00

Albums

Number	Title (A Side/B Side)	Yr	NM
AUDIO FIDELITY			
❑ AFSD-6222	More Today Than Yesterday	1969	20.00
❑ ST-92074	More Today Than Yesterday	1969	25.00
—Capitol Record Club edition			
MOTOWN			
❑ 644 [M]	Here I Am	1966	50.00
❑ S-644 [S]	Here I Am	1966	60.00
❑ S-680	The Real Barbara McNair	1969	30.00
SIGNATURE			
❑ SM 1042 [M]	Love Talk	1960	40.00
❑ SS 1042 [S]	Love Talk	1960	50.00
WARNER BROS.			
❑ W 1541 [M]	I Enjoy Being a Girl	1964	25.00
❑ WS 1541 [S]	I Enjoy Being a Girl	1964	30.00
❑ W 1570 [M]	The Livin' End	1964	25.00
❑ WS 1570 [S]	The Livin' End	1964	30.00

MCNAUGHTON, BYRON, AND HIS ALL NEWS ORCHESTRA

45s

Number	Title (A Side/B Side)	Yr	NM
JAMIE			
❑ 1427	Right from the Shark's Jaws (The Jaws Interview)/Jaws Jam	1975	10.00

MCNEELY, BIG JAY

45s

Number	Title (A Side/B Side)	Yr	NM
ALADDIN			
❑ 3242	Real Crazy Cool/Let's Split	1954	30.00
BAYOU			
❑ 014	Hometown Jamboree/Teenage Hop	1953	80.00
❑ 018	Catastrophe/Calamity	1953	80.00
FEDERAL			
❑ 12102	The Goof/Big Jay Shuffle	1952	40.00
❑ 12111	Just Crazy/Penthouse Serenade	1952	40.00
❑ 12141	Nervous Man, Nervous/Rock Candy	1953	40.00
❑ 12151	3-D/Texas Turkey	1953	40.00
❑ 12168	Mule Walk/Ice Water	1954	40.00
❑ 12179	Hot Cinders/Whipped Cream	1954	40.00
❑ 12186	Let's Work/Hard Tack	1954	40.00
❑ 12191	Beachcomber/Strip Tease Swing	1954	40.00
IMPERIAL			
❑ 5219	Deacon's Express/Jet Fury	1953	50.00
—Note: Earlier Big Jay McNeely releases on Imperial are unknown on 45 rpm			
SAVOY			
❑ 1143	Deacon Hop/The Hucklebuck	1955	30.00
—With Paul Williams			
SWINGIN'			
❑ 614	There Is Something on Your Mind/Back...Shack...Track	1959	25.00
❑ 618	I Got the Message/Psycho Serenade	1959	15.00
❑ 622	Minnie/My Darling Dear	1960	15.00
❑ 627	I Love You, Oh Darling/Oh, What a Fool	1960	15.00
❑ 629	After Midnight/Before Midnight	1961	15.00
❑ 637	Without a Love/The Squat	1962	15.00
VEE JAY			
❑ 142	Big Jay's Hop/Three Blind Mice	1955	40.00
❑ 212	Jay's Rock/The Convention	1956	60.00
—B-side by the Delegates			
WARNER BROS.			
❑ 5401	You Don't Have to Go/Big Jay's Count	1963	12.00

7-Inch Extended Plays

Number	Title (A Side/B Side)	Yr	NM
FEDERAL			
❑ EP-246	Big Jake Shuffle/3-D//Nervous Man Nervous/The Goof	1953	300.00
❑ EP-246 [PS]	Go! Go! Go! With Big Jay McNeely	1953	300.00
❑ EP-301	*Mule Milk/Hot Cinders/Ice Water/Whipped Cream	1954	200.00
❑ EP-301 [PS]	Big Jay McNeely, Vol. 2	1954	200.00
❑ EP-332	(contents unknown)	1954	200.00
❑ EP-332 [PS]	Wild Man of the Saxophone	1954	200.00
❑ EP-373	(contents unknown)	1955	100.00
❑ EP-373 [PS]	Just Crazy	1955	100.00

Albums

Number	Title (A Side/B Side)	Yr	NM
COLLECTABLES			
❑ COL-5133	Golden Classics	198?	10.00
FEDERAL			
❑ 295-96 [10]	Big Jay McNeely	1955	3000.
❑ 395-530 [M]	Big Jay McNeely in 3-D	1956	800.00
KING			
❑ 650 [M]	Big "J" in 3-D	1959	500.00
SAVOY			
❑ MG-15045 [10]	A Rhythm and Blues Concert	1955	2000.
—VG value 1000; VG+ value 1500			
WARNER BROS.			
❑ W 1533 [M]	Big Jay McNeely	1963	80.00
❑ WS 1533 [S]	Big Jay McNeely	1963	100.00

MCNICHOL, KRISTY AND JIMMY

Albums

Number	Title (A Side/B Side)	Yr	NM
RCA VICTOR			
❑ AFL1-2875	Kristy and Jimmy McNichol	1978	20.00

MCPHATTER, CLYDE

Also see THE DRIFTERS.

45s

Number	Title (A Side/B Side)	Yr	NM
AMY			
❑ 941	Everybody's Somebody's Fool/I Belong to You	1965	15.00
❑ 950	Little Bit of Sunshine/Everybody Loves a Good Time	1966	12.00
❑ 968	A Shot of Rhythm and Blues/I'm Not Going to Work Today	1966	12.00
❑ 975	Sweet and Innocent/Lavender Lace	1967	12.00
❑ 993	I Dreamt I Died/Lonely People Can't Afford to Cry	1967	300.00
ATLANTIC			
❑ 1070	Everybody's Laughing/Hot Ziggity	1955	30.00
❑ 1077	Love Has Joined Us Together/I Gotta Have You	1955	30.00
—With Ruth Brown			
❑ 1081	Seven Days/I'm Not Worthy	1956	30.00
❑ 1092	Treasure of Love/When You're Sincere	1956	40.00
❑ 1106	Thirty Days/I'm Lonely Tonight	1956	30.00

Except when noted otherwise, VG = 25% of NM, and VG+ = 50% of NM. (Example: VG = $2.00, VG+ = $4.00 and NM = $8.00.)

Number	Title (A Side/B Side)	Yr	NM
❑ 1117	Without Love (There Is Nothing)/I Make Believe	1956	30.00
❑ 1133	No Matter What/Just to Hold My Hand	1957	25.00
❑ 1149	Long Lonely Nights/ Heartaches	1957	25.00
❑ 1158	You'll Be There/Rock and Cry	1957	25.00
❑ 1170	That's Enough for Me/No Love Like Her Love	1958	25.00
❑ 1185	Come What May/Let Me Know	1958	25.00
❑ 1199	A Lover's Question/I Can't Stand Up Long	1958	25.00
❑ 2018	Lovey Dovey/My Island of Dreams	1959	20.00
❑ 2028	Since You've Been Gone/Try, Try Baby	1959	20.00
—B-side actually the "old" Drifters (uncredited)			
❑ 2038	You Went Back on Your Word/ There You Go	1959	20.00
—B-side actually the "old" Drifters (uncredited)			
❑ 2049	Just Give Me a Ring/Don't Dog Me	1960	20.00
—B-side actually the "old" Drifters (uncredited)			
❑ 2060	Deep Sea Ball/Let the Boogie-Woogie Roll	1960	20.00
—B-side actually the "old" Drifters (uncredited)			
❑ 2082	If I Didn't Love You Like I Do/ Go! Yes Go!	1960	20.00
—B-side actually the "old" Drifters (uncredited)			
DECCA			
❑ 32719	Book of Memories/I'll Belong to You	1970	8.00
❑ 32753	Why Can't We Get Together/ Mixed-Up Cup	1970	8.00
DERAM			
❑ 85032	Thank You Love/Only a Fool	1968	10.00
❑ 85039	Baby You've Got It/Baby I Could Be So Good at Loving You	1969	10.00
MERCURY			
❑ 71660	Ta Ta/I Ain't Givin' Up Nothin'	1960	15.00
❑ 71692	I Just Want to Love You/You're for Me	1960	15.00
❑ 71692 [PS]	I Just Want to Love You/You're for Me	1960	30.00
❑ 71740	One More Chance/Before I Fall in Love Again	1960	15.00
❑ 71740 [PS]	One More Chance/Before I Fall in Love Again	1960	30.00
❑ 71783	Tomorrow Is a-Comin'/I'll Love You Till the Cows Come Home	1961	15.00
❑ 71783 [PS]	Tomorrow Is a-Comin'/I'll Love You Till the Cows Come Home	1961	30.00
❑ 71809	A Whole Heap o'Love/You're Movin' Me	1961	15.00
❑ 71809 [PS]	A Whole Heap o'Love/You're Movin' Me	1961	30.00
❑ 71841	I Never Knew/Happiness	1961	15.00
❑ 71841 [PS]	I Never Knew/Happiness	1961	25.00
❑ 71868	Same Time, Same Place/Your Second Choice	1961	15.00
❑ 71868 [PS]	Same Time, Same Place/Your Second Choice	1961	30.00
❑ 71941	Lover Please/Let's Forget About the Past	1962	20.00
❑ 71941 [PS]	Lover Please/Let's Forget About the Past	1962	40.00
❑ 71987	Little Bitty Pretty One/Next to Me	1962	15.00
❑ 71987 [PS]	Little Bitty Pretty One/Next to Me	1962	40.00
❑ 72025	Maybe/I Do Believe	1962	15.00
❑ 72025 [PS]	Maybe/I Do Believe	1962	30.00
❑ 72051	The Best Man Cried/Stop	1962	15.00
❑ 72051 [PS]	The Best Man Cried/Stop	1962	30.00
❑ 72166	So Close to Being in Love/From One to One	1963	15.00
❑ 72166 [PS]	So Close to Being in Love/From One to One	1963	30.00
❑ 72220	Deep in the Heart of Harlem/ Happy Good Times	1963	15.00
❑ 72220 [PS]	Deep in the Heart of Harlem/ Happy Good Times	1963	30.00
❑ 72253	Second Window, Second Floor/In My Tenement	1964	15.00
❑ 72317	Lucille/Baby, Baby	1964	15.00
❑ 72407	Crying Won't Help You Now/ I Found My Love	1965	15.00
❑ 72407 [PS]	Crying Won't Help You Now/ I Found My Love	1965	30.00
MGM			
❑ 12780	I Told Myself a Lie/The Masquerade Is Over	1959	20.00
❑ 12816	Twice As Nice/Where Did I Make My Mistake	1959	20.00

Number	Title (A Side/B Side)	Yr	NM
❑ 12843 [M]	Let's Try Again/Bless You	1959	20.00
❑ 12877	Think Me a Kiss/When the Right Time Comes Along	1960	20.00
❑ 12949	One Right After Another/This Is Not Goodbye	1960	20.00
❑ 12988	The Glory of Love/Take a Step	1961	20.00
❑ SK-50134 [S]	Let's Try Again/Bless You	1959	40.00
7-Inch Extended Plays			
ATLANTIC			
❑ EP 584	*Without Love (There Is Nothing)/Thirty Days//I Make Believe/Treasure of Love	1958	250.00
❑ EP 584 [PS]	Clyde McPhatter	1958	250.00
❑ EP 605	*Honey Love/What'cha Gonna Do/Seven Days/Long Lonely Nights	1958	250.00
❑ EP 605 [PS]	Rock with Clyde McPhatter	1958	250.00
❑ EP 618	A Lover's Question/I Can't Stand Up Alone//Lovey Dovey/My Island of Dreams	1959	250.00
❑ EP 618 [PS]	Clyde McPhatter	1959	250.00
MERCURY			
❑ SR-619-C	Lover Please/Money Honey/ Don't Let Go//Little Bitty Pretty One/Sixty Minute Man/ I'm Movin' On	196?	30.00
—Jukebox issue; small hole, plays at 33 1/3 rpm			
❑ SR-619-C [PS]	Lover Please!	196?	30.00
Albums			
ALLEGIANCE			
❑ AV-5029	The Pretty One	198?	10.00
ATLANTIC			
❑ 8024 [M]	Love Ballads	1958	500.00
—Black label			
❑ 8024 [M]	Love Ballads	1960	200.00
—Brown and purple label			
❑ 8024 [M]	Love Ballads	1960	400.00
—White "bullseye" label			
❑ 8031 [M]	Clyde	1959	500.00
—Black label			
❑ 8031 [M]	Clyde	1960	200.00
—Brown and purple label			
❑ 8031 [M]	Clyde	1960	400.00
—White "bullseye" label			
❑ 8077 [M]	The Best of Clyde McPhatter	1963	200.00
DECCA			
❑ DL 75231	Welcome Home	1970	25.00
MERCURY			
❑ MG-20597 [M]	Ta Ta	1960	50.00
❑ MG-20655 [M]	Golden Blues Hits	1961	50.00
❑ MG-20711 [M]	Lover Please	1962	50.00
❑ MG-20750 [M]	Rhythm and Soul	1962	50.00
❑ MG-20783 [M]	Clyde McPhatter's Greatest Hits	1963	30.00
❑ MG-20902 [M]	Songs of the Big City	1964	30.00
❑ MG-20915 [M]	Live at the Apollo	1964	30.00
❑ SR-60262 [S]	Ta Ta	1960	70.00
❑ SR-60655 [S]	Golden Blues Hits	1961	70.00
❑ SR-60711 [S]	Lover Please	1962	70.00
❑ SR-60750 [S]	Rhythm and Soul	1962	70.00
❑ SR-60783 [S]	Clyde McPhatter's Greatest Hits	1963	40.00
❑ SR-60902 [S]	Songs of the Big City	1964	40.00
❑ SR-60915 [S]	Live at the Apollo	1964	40.00
MGM			
❑ E-3775 [M]	Let's Start Over Again	1959	150.00
❑ SE-3775 [S]	Let's Start Over Again	1959	200.00
❑ E-3866 [M]	Clyde McPhatter's Greatest Hits	1960	70.00
❑ SE-3866 [S]	Clyde McPhatter's Greatest Hits	1960	80.00
WING			
❑ MGW-12224 [M]	May I Sing for You?	1962	25.00
❑ SRW-16224 [S]	May I Sing for You?	1962	30.00

MCRAE, CARMEN

Number	Title (A Side/B Side)	Yr	NM
45s			
ATLANTIC			
❑ 2421	For Once in My Life/Got to Get You Into My Life	1967	6.00
❑ 2485	Elusive Butterfly/I'm Always Drunk in San Francisco	1968	6.00
❑ 2581	Gloomy Sunday/My Heart Reminds Me	1968	6.00
❑ 2691	I Love You More Than You'll Ever Know/Just a Dream Ago	1969	5.00
❑ 2736	I Want You/Just a Little Lovin'	1970	5.00
❑ 2776	Carry That Weight/Goodbye Joe	1971	5.00
❑ 2807	Silent Spring/I Love the Life I Lead	1971	5.00
BETHLEHEM			
❑ 11009	If I'm Lucky/Tip Toe Gently	1958	12.00

Number	Title (A Side/B Side)	Yr	NM
COLUMBIA			
❑ 42292	Take Five/Easy As You Go	1962	10.00
❑ 42376	How Does the Wine Taste/ Nightlife	1962	10.00
❑ 42642	Am I Going Out of Your Mind/ Baby, Baby	1962	10.00
DECCA			
❑ 29324	Ooh (What'cha Doin' to Me)/If I'm Lucky	1954	15.00
❑ 29398	Keep Me in Mind/They All Laughed	1954	15.00
❑ 29472	Whatever Lola Wants/Am I the One to Blame	1955	12.00
❑ 29555	Get Set/You Don't Have to Tell Me	1955	12.00
❑ 29620	I Go for You/A Fine Romance	1955	12.00
—With Sammy Davis, Jr.			
❑ 29675	Love Is Here to Stay/This Will Make You Laugh	1955	12.00
❑ 29749	The Next Time It Happens/ Come On, Come In	1955	12.00
❑ 29793	Come Down to Earth, Mr. Smith/I Guess I'll Dress for the Blues	1956	12.00
❑ 29890	Star Eyes/Tonight He's Out to Break Another Heart	1956	12.00
❑ 29949	You Don't Know Me/Never Loved Him Anyhow	1956	12.00
❑ 30004	Skyliner/If You Should Leave Me	1956	12.00
❑ 30075	I'm Putting All My Eggs in One Basket/Namely You	1956	12.00
❑ 30112	The Party's Over/I'm a Dreamer, Aren't We All	1956	12.00
❑ 30274	How Many Stars Have to Shine/ It's Like Gettin' a Donkey	1957	12.00
❑ 30468	Rich Man, Poor Man/Coax Me	1957	12.00
❑ 30540	Passing Fancy/As I Love You	1958	12.00
❑ 30618	Invitation/Lo and Behold	1958	12.00
❑ 30667	So Nice to Be Wrong/Moon Ray	1958	12.00
❑ 30727	I Love the Ground You Walk On/I'll Love You	1958	12.00
GROOVE MERCHANT			
❑ 1018	It Takes a Whole Lot of Human Feeling/Straighten Up and Fly Right	1973	5.00
❑ 1022	The Good Life/How Could I Settle for Less	1973	5.00
KAPP			
❑ 259	Which Way Is Love/ Play for Keeps	1959	10.00
❑ 290	Talk to Me/Show Me the Way	1959	10.00
❑ 302	The More I See You/ Don't Cry Joe	1959	10.00
❑ 327	Big Town/What Has She Got	1960	10.00
MAINSTREAM			
❑ 613	Haven't We Met?/Life Is Just a Bowl of Cherries	1965	8.00
❑ 630	Go and Buy Yourself a Dream/ (B-side unknown)	1965	8.00
❑ 650	Alfie/Modesty	1966	8.00
7-Inch Extended Plays			
ATLANTIC			
❑ EP-8165 [DJ]	Elusive Butterfly/I'm Always Drunk in San Francisco//Ask Any Woman/My Very Own Person	1968	15.00
—White label, large hole			
❑ EP-8165 [PS]	Portrait of Carmen	1968	15.00
DECCA			
❑ ED 2279	(contents unknown)	195?	12.00
❑ ED 2279 [PS]	By Special Request, Part 1	195?	12.00
❑ ED 2280	I Can't Get Started/Yardbird Suite//Just One of Those Things/This Will Make You Laugh	195?	12.00
❑ ED 2280 [PS]	By Special Request, Part 2	195?	12.00
❑ ED 2341	(contents unknown)	1956	12.00
❑ ED 2341 [PS]	Torchy! Part 1	1956	12.00
❑ ED 2342	But Beautiful/If You'd Stay the Way I Dream About You//I'm a Dreamer Aren't We All/ Good Morning Heartache	1956	12.00
❑ ED 2342 [PS]	Torchy! Part 2	1956	12.00
❑ ED 2343	(contents unknown)	1956	12.00
❑ ED 2343 [PS]	Torchy! Part 3	1956	12.00
Albums			
ACCORD			
❑ SN-7152	Love Songs	1981	10.00
ATLANTIC			
❑ SD 2-904 [(2)]	The Great American Songbook	1971	20.00
❑ SD 1568	Just a Little Lovin'	1971	12.00
❑ 8143 [M]	For Once in My Life	1967	20.00
❑ SD 8143 [S]	For Once in My Life	1967	15.00
❑ 8165 [M]	Portrait of Carmen	1968	30.00
❑ SD 8165 [S]	Portrait of Carmen	1968	15.00

M

Number	Title (A Side/B Side)	Yr	NM
❑ 8200 [M]	The Sound of Silence	1968	30.00
—Mono is white label promo only; "d/j copy monaural" sticker on front cover			
❑ SD 8200 [S]	The Sound of Silence	1968	15.00
BAINBRIDGE			
❑ 6221	The Sound of Silence	198?	10.00
BETHLEHEM			
❑ BCP-1023 [10]	Carmen McRae	1955	100.00
BLUE NOTE			
❑ BN-LA462-G	I Am Music	1975	12.00
❑ BN-LA635-G	Can't Hide Love	1976	12.00
❑ BN-LA709-H2 [(2)]	The Great Music Hall	1977	15.00
❑ LWB-709 [(2)]	The Great Music Hall	1981	12.00
—Reissue of BN-LA709-H2			
BUDDAH			
❑ B2D-6501 [(2)]	I'm Coming Home Again	1980	15.00
CATALYST			
❑ 7904	As Time Goes By	197?	12.00
COLUMBIA			
❑ CL 1730 [M]	Lover Man	1962	20.00
❑ CL 1943 [M]	Something Wonderful	1962	20.00
❑ CS 8530 [S]	Lover Man	1962	25.00
❑ CS 8743 [S]	Something Wonderful	1962	25.00
CONCORD JAZZ			
❑ CJ-128	Two for the Road	1980	10.00
❑ CJ-235	You're Looking at Me: A Collection of Nat King Cole Songs	1984	10.00
❑ CJ-342	Fine and Mellow	1988	10.00
DECCA			
❑ DL 8173 [M]	By Special Request	1955	50.00
—Black label, silver print			
❑ DL 8173 [M]	By Special Request	1960	20.00
—Black label with color bars			
❑ DL 8267 [M]	Torchy!	1956	50.00
—Black label, silver print			
❑ DL 8267 [M]	Torchy!	1960	20.00
—Black label with color bars			
❑ DL 8347 [M]	Blue Moon	1957	50.00
—Black label, silver print			
❑ DL 8347 [M]	Blue Moon	1960	20.00
—Black label with color bars			
❑ DL 8583 [M]	After Glow	1957	50.00
—Black label, silver print			
❑ DL 8583 [M]	After Glow	1960	20.00
—Black label with color bars			
❑ DL 8662 [M]	Mad About the Man	1958	50.00
—Black label, silver print			
❑ DL 8662 [M]	Mad About the Man	1960	20.00
—Black label with color bars			
❑ DL 8738 [M]	Carmen for Cool Ones	1958	50.00
—Black label, silver print			
❑ DL 8738 [M]	Carmen for Cool Ones	1960	20.00
—Black label with color bars			
❑ DL 8815 [M]	Birds of a Feather	1959	50.00
—Black label, silver print			
❑ DL 8815 [M]	Birds of a Feather	1960	20.00
—Black label with color bars			
FOCUS			
❑ FL-334 [M]	Bittersweet	1964	15.00
❑ FS-334 [S]	Bittersweet	1964	20.00
GROOVE MERCHANT			
❑ 522	A Whole Lot of Human Feeling	1973	12.00
❑ 531	Ms. Jazz	1974	12.00
❑ 4401 [(2)]	Velvet Soul	197?	15.00
HARMONY			
❑ HL 7452 [M]	Yesterdays	1968	20.00
❑ HS 11252 [S]	Yesterdays	1968	12.00
❑ KH 32177	Carmen McRae Sings Billie Holiday	1972	10.00
JAZZ MAN			
❑ 5004	Carmen McRae and the Kenny Clarke/Francy Boland Big Band	198?	10.00
KAPP			
❑ KL-1117 [M]	Book of Ballads	1958	25.00
❑ KL-1135 [M]	When You're Away	1959	25.00
❑ KL-1169 [M]	Something to Swing About	1960	25.00
❑ KL-1541 [M]	This Is Carmen McRae	1967	20.00
❑ KS-3000 [S]	Book of Ballads	1958	30.00
❑ KS-3018 [S]	When You're Away	1959	30.00
❑ KS-3053 [S]	Something to Swing About	1960	30.00
❑ KS-3541 [S]	This Is Carmen McRae	1967	15.00
MAINSTREAM			
❑ 309	Carmen McRae	1971	12.00
❑ 338	Carmen's Gold	1972	12.00
❑ 352	Carmen McRae In Person	1972	12.00
❑ 387	I Want You	1972	12.00
❑ 403	Live and Doin' It	1974	12.00
❑ 800 [(2)]	Alive!	1974	15.00
❑ S-6028 [S]	Second to None	1965	20.00
❑ S-6044 [S]	Haven't We Met?	1965	20.00
❑ S-6065 [S]	Woman Talk	1966	20.00
❑ S-6084 [S]	Alfie	1966	20.00
❑ S-6091 [S]	In Person/San Francisco	1967	15.00
❑ S-6110	Live & Wailin'	1968	15.00
❑ 56028 [M]	Second to None	1965	15.00
❑ 56044 [M]	Haven't We Met?	1965	15.00
❑ 56065 [M]	Woman Talk	1966	15.00
❑ 56084 [M]	Alfie	1966	15.00
❑ 56091 [M]	In Person/San Francisco	1967	20.00
MCA			
❑ 4111 [(2)]	The Greatest of Carmen McRae	197?	12.00
NOVUS			
❑ 3086-1-N	Carmen Sings Monk	1990	12.00
PAUSA			
❑ 9003	Can't Hide Love	198?	10.00
QUINTESSENCE			
❑ 25021	Ms. Jazz	1978	10.00
—Reissue of Groove Merchant 531			
STANYAN			
❑ 10115	Mad About the Man	197?	12.00
TEMPONIC			
❑ 29562	Carmen	1972	12.00
TIME			
❑ S-2104 [S]	Live at Sugar Hill	1960	25.00
❑ 52104 [M]	Live at Sugar Hill	1960	20.00
VOCALION			
❑ VL 3697 [M]	Carmen McRae	1963	15.00
❑ VL 73828	My Foolish Heart	1969	12.00

MCVIE, CHRISTINE Also see CHICKEN SHACK; FLEETWOOD MAC.

Number	Title (A Side/B Side)	Yr	NM
45s			
EPIC			
❑ 10536	I'd Rather Go Blind/Get Like You Used to Be	1969	12.00
—As "Christine Perfect"			
SIRE			
❑ 732	I'd Rather Go Blind/Close to Me	1976	8.00
WARNER BROS.			
❑ GWB 0488	Got a Hold on Me/Love Will Show Us How	1986	3.00
—"Back to Back Hits" series			
❑ 29160	I'm the One/The Challenge	1984	3.00
❑ 29313	Love Will Show Us How/The Challenge	1984	3.00
❑ 29313 [PS]	Love Will Show Us How/The Challenge	1984	3.00
❑ 29372	Got a Hold on Me/Who's Dreaming This Dream	1984	3.00
❑ 29372 [PS]	Got a Hold on Me/Who's Dreaming This Dream	1984	3.00
Albums			
SIRE			
❑ SR 6022	The Legendary Christine Perfect Album	1978	10.00
—Reissue with Warner Bros. distribution			
❑ SASD-7522	The Legendary Christine Perfect Album	1976	15.00
—Original with ABC distribution			
WARNER BROS.			
❑ 25059	Christine McVie	1984	8.00
❑ 25059 [DJ]	Christine McVie	1984	15.00
—Promo on Quiex II vinyl			

MCWILLIAMS, DAVID

Number	Title (A Side/B Side)	Yr	NM
45s			
COLUMBIA			
❑ 4-43793	Blue Eyes/God and My Country	1966	12.00
KAPP			
❑ 896	Days of Pearly Spencer/There's No Lock Upon My Door	1968	10.00
❑ 952	This Side of Heaven/Can I Get There by Candlelight?	1968	8.00
Albums			
KAPP			
❑ KS-3547	Days of Pearly Spencer	1968	25.00

ME & YOU

Number	Title (A Side/B Side)	Yr	NM
45s			
PARKWAY			
❑ 121	Let the World In/I've Got My Time Baby	1966	20.00

ME AND THEM

Number	Title (A Side/B Side)	Yr	NM
45s			
U.S. SONGS			
❑ 601	Everything I Do Is Wrong/Show You Mean It Too	1964	15.00

MEADER, VAUGHN

Number	Title (A Side/B Side)	Yr	NM
45s			
MGM			
❑ K13169	Elephant Song/No Hiding Place	1963	10.00
VERVE			
❑ 10309	St. Nick Visits the White House/'Twas the Night Before Christmas	1963	20.00
7-Inch Extended Plays			
CADENCE			
❑ CSBLL-1	The Experiment/After Dinner Conversations/Relatively Speaking/Motorcade//But Vote!/Economy Lunch/Press Conference	1962	10.00
—Jukebox issue; small hole, plays at 33 1/3 rpm			
❑ CSBLL-1 [PS]	The First Family	1962	10.00
Albums			
CADENCE			
❑ CLP 3060 [M]	The First Family	1962	10.00
❑ CLP 3065 [M]	The First Family, Vol. Two	1963	20.00
❑ CLP 25065 [S]	The First Family, Vol. Two	1963	30.00
KAMA SUTRA			
❑ KSBS-2038	The Second Coming	1971	15.00
LAURIE			
❑ LLP-2035 [M]	Take That!	1966	15.00
VERVE			
❑ V-15042 [M]	Have Some Nuts	1964	15.00
❑ V6-15042 [S]	Have Some Nuts	1964	20.00
❑ V-15050 [M]	If the Shoe Fits	1965	15.00

MEADOW Supposedly, Laura Branigan was in this group.

Number	Title (A Side/B Side)	Yr	NM
45s			
PARAMOUNT			
❑ 0187	Here I Am/Something Borrowed, Something Blue	1973	8.00
❑ 0208	Cane and Able/Something Borrowed, Something Blue	1973	8.00
Albums			
PARAMOUNT			
❑ PAS-6066	The Friend Ship	1973	20.00

MEADOWLARKS, THE See DON JULIAN AND THE MEADOWLARKS.

MEAT LOAF Also see STONEY AND MEATLOAF. MEAT LOAF also contributed vocals to TED NUGENT'S Free For All album. Also see THE POPCORN BLIZZARD; STONEY AND MEATLOAF.

Number	Title (A Side/B Side)	Yr	NM
12-Inch Singles			
ATLANTIC			
❑ PR 966 [DJ]	Getting Away with Murder (same on both sides)	1986	8.00
❑ PR 997 [DJ]	Rock and Roll Mercenaries (same on both sides)	1986	8.00
CLEVELAND INT'L.			
❑ AS 1277 [DJ]	I'm Gonna Love Her for Both of Us/Peel Out	1981	8.00
EPIC			
❑ AS 477 [DJ]	Paradise by the Dashboard Light (7:55)//same (6:58 with play-by-play)/same (6:58 without play-by-play)	1978	20.00
—With "Bat Out of Hell" picture cover			
RCA			
❑ JD-14050 [DJ]	(Give Me the Future with a) Modern Girl (LP Version) (7" Version)	1984	10.00
❑ JW-14141 [DJ]	Surf's Up (LP Version)//Surf's Up (Edit)/Bad Attitude	1984	15.00
45s			
ATLANTIC			
❑ 89303	Rock 'N' Roll Mercenaries/Execution Day	1987	3.00
—A-side with John Parr			
❑ 89303 [PS]	Rock 'N' Roll Mercenaries/Execution Day	1987	3.00
❑ 89340	Getting Away with Murder/Rock 'N' Roll Hero	1986	3.00
CLEVELAND INT'L.			
❑ 02490	I'm Gonna Love Her for Both of Us/Peel Out	1981	4.00
❑ 02607	Read 'Em and Weep/Peel Out	1981	4.00
❑ 04028	The Razor's Edge/You Never Can Be Too Sure About the Girl	1983	4.00

Except when noted otherwise, VG = 25% of NM, and VG+ = 50% of NM. (Example: VG = $2.00, VG+ = $4.00 and NM = $8.00.)

Number	Title (A Side/B Side)	Yr	NM
EPIC			
❑ 50467	You Took the Words Right Out of My Mouth/For Crying Out Loud	1977	8.00
❑ 50513	Two Out of Three Ain't Bad (3:50)/For Crying Out Loud	1978	5.00
❑ 50513	Two Out of Three Ain't Bad (5:12)/For Crying Out Loud	1978	6.00
❑ 50588	Paradise by the Dashboard Light/"Bat" Overture	1978	5.00
❑ 50634	You Took the Words Right Out of My Mouth/Paradise by the Dashboard Light	1978	5.00
MCA			
❑ 54626	I'd Do Anything for Love (But I Won't Do That) (Single Edit)/ I'd Do Anything for Love (But I Won't Do That) (Edit)	1993	4.00
❑ 54757	Rock and Roll Dreams Come Through/I'd Do Anything for Love (But I Won't Do That) (Live)	1993	4.00
❑ 54848	Objects in the Rear View Mirror May Appear Closer Than They Are/Two Out of Three Ain't Bad (Live)	1994	4.00
RCA			
❑ PB-14101	(Give Me the Future with a) Modern Girl/Sailor to a Siren	1985	3.00
❑ PB-14101 [PS]	(Give Me the Future with a) Modern Girl/Sailor to a Siren	1985	3.00
❑ PB-14149	Surf's Up/Jumpin' the Sun	1985	3.00
RSO			
❑ 407	More Than You Deserve/ Presence of the Lord	1974	12.00
Albums			
ATLANTIC			
❑ 81698	Blind Before I Stop	1986	8.00
CLEVELAND INT'L.			
❑ FE 36007	Dead Ringer	1981	8.00
❑ PE 36007	Dead Ringer	198?	6.00
—Budget-line reissue			
EPIC			
❑ E99 34974 [PD]	Bat Out of Hell	1978	20.00
❑ JE 34974	Bat Out of Hell	1979	8.00
—Dark blue label			
❑ PE 34974	Bat Out of Hell	1977	10.00
—Orange label; originals do not have bar code on back cover			
❑ PE 34974	Bat Out of Hell	1985	6.00
—Dark blue label; bar code on cover			
❑ FE 38444	Midnight at the Lost and Found	1983	8.00
❑ HE 44974	Bat Out of Hell	1981	40.00
—Half-speed mastered edition			
RCA VICTOR			
❑ AFL1-5451	Bad Attitude	1985	8.00
VIRGIN			
❑ 09463-63147-1 [(2)]	Bat Out of Hell III: The Monster Is Loose	2006	20.00

MEAT PUPPETS

Number	Title (A Side/B Side)	Yr	NM
12-Inch Singles			
SST			
❑ 100	I Am a Machine/Get On Down	1987	8.00
❑ 150	Paradise/I Can't Be Counted On	1987	8.00
45s			
LONDON			
❑ PRO 943 [DJ]	Sam/Bali Ha'i	1991	5.00
❑ PRO 943 [PS]	Sam/Bali Ha'i	1991	5.00
SST			
❑ E 39 [DJ]	Swimming Ground/ Up on the Sun	1985	6.00
❑ E 39 [PS]	Swimming Ground/ Up on the Sun	1985	6.00
—Stamped sleeve promoting upcoming LP			
7-Inch Extended Plays			
SST			
❑ 044	In a Car/Big House/Dolfin Field/ Out in the Gardiner/Foreign Lawns	1985	2.50
—Reissue of World Imitation EP			
❑ 044 [PS]	In a Car	1985	2.50
WORLD IMITATION			
❑ PRC-1	In a Car/Big House/Dolfin Field/ Out in the Gardiner/Foreign Lawns	1981	20.00
❑ PRC-1 [PS]	In a Car	1981	20.00
Albums			
LONDON			
❑ 1109 [10]	Raw Meat	1994	20.00
—Promo-only five-song 10-inch EP			
❑ 828484-1	Too High to Die	1994	20.00
—Includes bonus 10-inch EP (double value for DJ stamp on cover)			
MERCURY			
❑ 828665-1	No Joke!	1995	15.00
SST			
❑ 009	Meat Puppets	1982	15.00
❑ 019	Meat Puppets II	1984	15.00
❑ 039	Up on the Sun	1985	15.00
❑ 049 [10]	Out My Way	1986	10.00
—10-inch EP			
❑ 100	Mirage	1986	15.00
❑ 150	Huevos	1987	15.00
❑ 253	Monsters	1989	15.00
❑ 265 [(2)]	No Strings Attached	1990	18.00

MEDALLIONS, THE (1)

Number	Title (A Side/B Side)	Yr	NM
45s			
DOOTO			
❑ 419	For Better or For Worse/I Wonder, Wonder, Wonder	1957	30.00
—As "Vernon Green and the Medallions"			
❑ 425	A Lover's Prayer/Unseen	1957	30.00
—As "Vernon Green and the Medallions"			
❑ 446	Magic Mountain/59 Volvo	1959	25.00
—As "Vernon Green and the Medallions"			
❑ 454	Behind the Door/Rocket Ship	1959	25.00
—As "Vernon Green and the Medallions"			
DOOTONE			
❑ 347	The Letter/Buick 59	1955	60.00
—Black label			
❑ 347	The Letter/Buick 59	1955	200.00
—Red label			
❑ 357	The Telegram/Coupe de Ville Baby	1955	60.00
—Maroon label			
❑ 357	The Telegram/Coupe de Ville Baby	1955	150.00
—Blue label			
❑ 364	Edna/Speeding	1955	60.00
❑ 373	My Pretty Baby/I'll Never Love Again	1955	60.00
—As "Johnny Twovoice and the Medallions"			
❑ 379	Dear Darling/Don't Shoot Baby	1955	70.00
❑ 393	I Want a Love/Dance and Swing	1956	50.00
❑ 400	Shedding Tears for You/Push Button Automobile	1956	60.00
—As "Vernon Green and the Medallions"			
❑ 407	My Mary Lou/Did You Have Fun	1956	60.00
—As "Vernon Green and the Medallions"			
❑ 479	Can You Talk/You Don't Know	1964	15.00
MINIT			
❑ 32034	Look at Me, Look at Me/Am I Ever Gonna See My Baby	1968	20.00
—As "Vernon Green and the Medallions"			
PAN WORLD			
❑ 71	Dear Ann/Shimmy Shimmy Shake	1962	50.00
—As "Vernon Green and the Medallions"			
7-Inch Extended Plays			
DOOTONE			
❑ 202	(contents unknown)	1958	100.00
❑ 202 [PS]	Rhythm and Blues	1958	150.00

MEDALLIONS, THE (2)

Number	Title (A Side/B Side)	Yr	NM
45s			
ESSEX			
❑ 901	I Know/Laki-Lani	1955	400.00

MEDALLIONS, THE (3)

Number	Title (A Side/B Side)	Yr	NM
45s			
LENOX			
❑ 5556	You Are Irresistible/Why Do You Look at Me	1962	25.00

MEDALLIONS, THE (4)

Number	Title (A Side/B Side)	Yr	NM
45s			
SINGULAR			
❑ 1002	A Broken Heart/Lolo Baby	1957	50.00
SULTAN			
❑ 4004	Love That Girl/Caracahi	1959	80.00

MEDALLIONS, THE (U)

Could be group (1), (3) or (4), or a totally different group.

Number	Title (A Side/B Side)	Yr	NM
45s			
SARG			
❑ 191	I Love You True/My Baby's Gone	1961	40.00
❑ 194	Lovin' Time/Home Town	1961	40.00

MEDIUM

Number	Title (A Side/B Side)	Yr	NM
Albums			
GAMMA			
❑ GS-503	Medium	196?	100.00

MEDLEY, BILL

Also see THE RIGHTEOUS BROTHERS.

Number	Title (A Side/B Side)	Yr	NM
45s			
A&M			
❑ 1285	A Song for You/We've Only Just Begun	1971	5.00
❑ 1309	You've Lost That Lovin' Feeling/We've Only Just Begun	1971	5.00
❑ 1311	A Song for You/We've Only Just Begun	1971	4.00
❑ 1336	Help Me Make It Through the Night/Hung on You	1972	4.00
❑ 1350	Freedom for the Stallion/Damn Good Friend	1972	4.00
❑ 1371	A Simple Man/ Missing You Too Long	1972	4.00
❑ 1434	Put a Little Love Away/ It's Not Easy	1973	4.00
CURB			
❑ 10542	Most of All You/I'm Gonna Be Strong	1989	3.00
❑ 76890	Don't Let Go/Bridge Over Troubled Water	1990	3.00
ELEKTRA			
❑ 69281	Rude Awakening/ Leave Love Behind	1989	3.00
—B-side by Jonathan Elias			
LIBERTY			
❑ 1402	Don't Know Much/Woman	1981	4.00
❑ 1412	Stay the Night/Grandma and Grandpa	1981	4.00
MCA			
❑ 53443	Brown Eyed Woman/You've Lost That Lovin' Feelin'	1988	3.00
MGM			
❑ 13931	I Can't Make It Alone/One Day Girl	1968	8.00
❑ 13959	Brown Eyed Woman/Let the Good Times Roll	1968	8.00
❑ 14000	Peace Brother Peace/Winter Won't Come This Year	1968	8.00
❑ 14025	Something's So Wrong/This Is a Love Song	1969	8.00
❑ 14081	Reaching Back/Someone Is Standing Outside	1969	8.00
❑ 14099	Evie/Let Me Love Again	1969	8.00
❑ 14119	Hold On, I'm Comin'/ Makin' My Way	1970	6.00
❑ 14145	Nobody Knows/Something's So Wrong	1970	6.00
❑ 14179	Gone/What Have You Got to Lose	1970	6.00
❑ 14202	Wasn't It Easy/Gone	1970	6.00
PARAMOUNT			
❑ 0089	Swing Low, Sweet Chariot/ (B-side unknown)	1971	6.00
PLANET			
❑ YB-13317	Right Here and Now/ The Best of My Life	1982	4.00
❑ YB-13425	I'm No Angel/I Need You in My Life	1983	3.00
❑ YB-13474	For You/I Need You in My Life	1983	3.00
RCA			
❑ 5224-7-RX	(I've Had) The Time of My Life/ Love Is Strange	1987	3.00
—A-side: With Jennifer Warnes; B-side by Mickey and Sylvia			
❑ 5224-7-RX [PS]	(I've Had) The Time of My Life/ Love Is Strange	1987	4.00
—A-side: With Jennifer Warnes; B-side by Mickey and Sylvia			
❑ PB-13692	I've Got Dreams to Remember/ Till Your Memory's Gone	1983	3.00
❑ PB-13753	I Still Do/I've Got Dreams to Remember	1984	3.00
❑ PB-13851	Turn It Loose/I've Always Got the Heart to Sing the Blues	1984	3.00
❑ PB-13962	She Keeps Me in One Piece/ Old Friend	1984	—
—Unreleased			
❑ PB-14021	Is There Anything I Can Do/Old Friend	1985	3.00
❑ PB-14081	Women in Love/Stand Up	1985	3.00
REPRISE			
❑ 0413	I Surrender to Your Touch/ Leavin' Town	1965	15.00
SCOTTI BROTHERS			
❑ ZS4-07938	He Ain't Heavy, He's My Brother/The Bridge	1988	3.00
—B-side by Georgio Moroder			
❑ ZS4-07938 [PS]	He Ain't Heavy, He's My Brother/The Bridge	1988	3.00
UNITED ARTISTS			
❑ XW1256	Lay a Little Lovin' On Me/ Wasn't That You Last Night	1978	4.00

M

Number	Title (A Side/B Side)	Yr	NM
❑ XW1270	Statue of a Fool/Wasn't That You Last Night	1978	4.00
❑ 1349	Hello Rock & Roll/Still a Fool	1980	4.00

VERVE

Number	Title (A Side/B Side)	Yr	NM
❑ 10569	That Lucky Old Sun/My Darling Clementine	1967	10.00

Albums

A&M

Number	Title (A Side/B Side)	Yr	NM
❑ SP-3505	A Song for You	1971	12.00
❑ SP-3517	Smile	1972	12.00

LIBERTY

Number	Title (A Side/B Side)	Yr	NM
❑ LT-1097	Sweet Thunder	1981	8.00

—Reissue of United Artists 1097

MGM

Number	Title (A Side/B Side)	Yr	NM
❑ E-4583 [M]	Bill Medley 100%	1968	50.00

—Mono is yellow label promo only

Number	Title (A Side/B Side)	Yr	NM
❑ SE-4583 [S]	Bill Medley 100%	1968	20.00
❑ SE-4603	Soft and Soulful	1969	20.00
❑ SE-4640	Someone Is Standing Outside	1969	20.00
❑ SE-4702	Nobody Knows	1970	15.00
❑ SE-4741	Gone	1970	15.00

RCA VICTOR

Number	Title (A Side/B Side)	Yr	NM
❑ BXL1-4434	Right Here and Now	1982	10.00
❑ CPL1-5352	Still Hung Up on You	1984	10.00
❑ MHL1-8519 [EP]	I Still Do	1985	8.00

UNITED ARTISTS

Number	Title (A Side/B Side)	Yr	NM
❑ UA-LA929-H	Lay a Little Lovin' on Me	1978	10.00
❑ LT-1097	Sweet Thunder	1980	10.00

MEEHAN, DON

45s

DATE

Number	Title (A Side/B Side)	Yr	NM
❑ 2-1654	Sir, My Men Refuse to Go/That's the Reason Why	1969	10.00

MEEK, JOE

45s

LONDON

Number	Title (A Side/B Side)	Yr	NM
❑ 9634	Kennedy March/Theme of Freedom	1964	20.00

MEGATRONS, THE

45s

ACOUSTICON

Number	Title (A Side/B Side)	Yr	NM
❑ 101	Velvet Waters/The Merry Piper	1959	15.00

AUDICON

Number	Title (A Side/B Side)	Yr	NM
❑ 101	Velvet Waters/The Merry Piper	1959	12.00
❑ 104	Whispering Winds/Tootie Flutie	1960	10.00
❑ 107	Dance of the Silhouettes/Ranchero	1960	10.00
❑ 110	Julienne/By the Waters of the Minnetonka	1960	10.00

LAURIE

Number	Title (A Side/B Side)	Yr	NM
❑ 3291	Velvet Waters/The Merry Piper	1965	8.00
❑ 3310	A Love That Will Last Forever/The Detroit Sound	1965	8.00

MEISNER, RANDY

Also see EAGLES.

45s

ASYLUM

Number	Title (A Side/B Side)	Yr	NM
❑ 45502	I Really Want You Here Tonight/Heart Song	1978	5.00

EPIC

Number	Title (A Side/B Side)	Yr	NM
❑ 02059	Gotta Get Away/Trouble Ahead	1981	4.00
❑ 03032	Never Been in Love/Nothing Is Said ('Til the Artist Is Dead)	1982	4.00
❑ 03352	Strangers Still/Runnin'	1982	4.00
❑ 9-50939	Deep Inside My Heart/I Need You Bad	1980	4.00
❑ 50964	Hearts on Fire/Anyway Bye Bye	1981	4.00

Albums

ASYLUM

Number	Title (A Side/B Side)	Yr	NM
❑ 6E-140	Randy Meisner	1978	10.00

EPIC

Number	Title (A Side/B Side)	Yr	NM
❑ NJE 36748	One More Song	1980	10.00
❑ FE 38121	Randy Meisner	1982	10.00

MEL AND TIM

45s

BAMBOO

Number	Title (A Side/B Side)	Yr	NM
❑ 106	I've Got Puredee/(Instrumental)	1969	6.00
❑ 107	Backfield in Motion/Do It Right Baby	1969	6.00

—Multicolor label

Number	Title (A Side/B Side)	Yr	NM
❑ 107	Backfield in Motion/Do It Right Baby	1969	8.00

—White label, not a promo

Number	Title (A Side/B Side)	Yr	NM
❑ 109	Good Guys Only Win in the Movies/I Found That I Was Wrong	1970	6.00
❑ 112	Feeling Bad/I've Got Puredee	1970	6.00
❑ 114	Mail Call Time/Forget It, I've Got It	1970	6.00
❑ 116	We've Got a Groove to Move On/Never on Time	1970	6.00
❑ 118	I'm the One/Put An Extra Plus to Your Love	1971	6.00

STAX

Number	Title (A Side/B Side)	Yr	NM
❑ 0127	Starting All Over Again/It Hurts to Want It So Bad	1972	5.00
❑ 0154	I May Not Be What You Want/Too Much Wheelin' and Dealin'	1973	5.00
❑ 0160	Heaven Knows/Don't Mess with My Money, My Honey, Oh My Woman	1973	5.00
❑ 0202	Those Little Things That Count/The Same Folks	1974	5.00
❑ 0224	Forever and a Day/That's the Way I Want to Live My Life	1974	5.00

Albums

BAMBOO

Number	Title (A Side/B Side)	Yr	NM
❑ BMS-8001	Good Guys Only Win in the Movies	1970	25.00

STAX

Number	Title (A Side/B Side)	Yr	NM
❑ STS-3007	Starting All Over Again	1972	20.00
❑ STS-5501	Mel and Tim	1974	20.00

MEL-O-DOTS, THE

45s

APOLLO

Number	Title (A Side/B Side)	Yr	NM
❑ 1192	One More Time/Just How Long	1952	3000.

MELA, DENNY

45s

PARKWAY

Number	Title (A Side/B Side)	Yr	NM
❑ 802	Forget My Past/Blondie	1959	15.00

MELANIE

45s

AMHERST

Number	Title (A Side/B Side)	Yr	NM
❑ 300	Who's Been Sleeping in My Bed (Edited)/Who's Been Sleeping in My Bed	1985	4.00

ATLANTIC

Number	Title (A Side/B Side)	Yr	NM
❑ 3380	If I Needed You/Cyclone	1977	5.00

BLANCHE

Number	Title (A Side/B Side)	Yr	NM
❑ 1	Imaginary Heroes/Detroit or Buffalo	1982	4.00
❑ 110	When You're Dead and Gone/Detroit or Buffalo	1982	4.00

BUDDAH

Number	Title (A Side/B Side)	Yr	NM
❑ 113	Bo Bo's Party/I'm Back in Town	1969	6.00
❑ 135	Beautiful People/Any Guy	1969	6.00
❑ 161 [DJ]	Take Me Home (mono/stereo)	1970	6.00

—May be promo only

Number	Title (A Side/B Side)	Yr	NM
❑ 167	Lay Down (Candles in the Rain)/Candles in the Rain	1970	6.00
❑ 167 [PS]	Lay Down (Candles in the Rain)/Candles in the Rain	1970	8.00
❑ 186	Peace Will Come (According to Plan)/Close to It All	1970	5.00
❑ 186	Peace Will Come (According to Plan)/Stop (I Don't Want to Hear It Anymore)	1970	5.00
❑ 186 [PS]	Peace Will Come (According to Plan)/Stop (I Don't Want to Hear It Anymore)	1970	6.00
❑ 202	Ruby Tuesday/Merry Christmas	1970	5.00
❑ 202	Ruby Tuesday/Lovin Baby Girl	1971	6.00

—Scarcer than the original B-side

Number	Title (A Side/B Side)	Yr	NM
❑ 224	We Don't Know Where We're Going/The Good Book	1971	5.00
❑ 268	The Nickel Song/What Have They Done to My Song Ma	1971	5.00
❑ 268 [DJ]	The Nickel Song (stereo/mono)	1971	10.00

—Promo edition; custom light blue label with "Melanie" repeated seven times in white along the outer border

Number	Title (A Side/B Side)	Yr	NM
❑ 268 [PS]	The Nickel Song/What Have They Done to My Song Ma	1971	6.00
❑ 304	I'm Back in Town/Johnny Boy	1972	5.00

COLUMBIA

Number	Title (A Side/B Side)	Yr	NM
❑ 44349	My Beautiful People/God's Only Daughter	1967	10.00
❑ 44349 [PS]	My Beautiful People/God's Only Daughter	1967	20.00
❑ 44524	Garden in the City/Why Didn't My Mother Tell Me	1968	10.00
❑ 44524 [PS]	Garden in the City/Why Didn't My Mother Tell Me	1968	20.00

GORDIAN

Number	Title (A Side/B Side)	Yr	NM
❑ 1947	Rag Doll/(B-side unknown)	1985	4.00

MIDSONG INT'L.

Number	Title (A Side/B Side)	Yr	NM
❑ 40858	I'd Rather Leave While I'm in Love/Record People	1978	5.00
❑ 40903	Knock on Wood/Record People	1978	5.00

NEIGHBORHOOD

Number	Title (A Side/B Side)	Yr	NM
❑ 4201	Brand New Key/Some Say (I Got Devil)	1971	5.00

—Multicolor label

Number	Title (A Side/B Side)	Yr	NM
❑ 4201	Brand New Key/Some Say (I Got Devil)	1971	6.00

—White label (not a promo)

Number	Title (A Side/B Side)	Yr	NM
❑ 4202	Ring the Living Bell/Railroad	1972	4.00
❑ 4202 [PS]	Ring the Living Bell/Railroad	1972	5.00
❑ 4204	Steppin'/Someday I'll Be a Farmer	1972	4.00
❑ 4204 [PS]	Steppin'/Someday I'll Be a Farmer	1972	8.00
❑ 4207	Together Alone/Center of the Circle	1972	4.00
❑ 4207 [PS]	Together Alone/Center of the Circle	1972	5.00
❑ 4209	Stoneground Woman/Do You Believe	1972	4.00
❑ 4210	Bitter Bad/Do You Believe	1973	4.00
❑ 4212	Seeds/Some Say (I Got Devil)	1973	4.00
❑ 4213	Will You Love Me Tomorrow/Here I Am	1973	4.00
❑ 4213 [PS]	Will You Love Me Tomorrow/Here I Am	1973	5.00
❑ 4214	Love to Love Again/Fine and Feather	1974	4.00
❑ 4214 [PS]	Love to Love Again/Fine and Feather	1974	6.00
❑ 4215	Lover's Cross/Holding Out	1974	4.00
❑ 10000	You're Not a Bad Ghost, Just an Old Song/Eyes of Man	1975	4.00
❑ 10001	Sweet Misery/Record Machine	1975	4.00

PORTRAIT

Number	Title (A Side/B Side)	Yr	NM
❑ 51001	One More Try/Apathy	1981	4.00

STORK

Number	Title (A Side/B Side)	Yr	NM
❑ (no #)	Timothy Scott Bogart	1970	12.00

—One-sided promo of "Christopher Robin" to celebrate the birth of Neil Bogart's son

TOMATO

Number	Title (A Side/B Side)	Yr	NM
❑ 10007	Running After Love/Holding Out	1979	5.00

WORLD UNITED

Number	Title (A Side/B Side)	Yr	NM
❑ 1947	Oh Boy/Brand New Key	1978	5.00

7-Inch Extended Plays

BUDDAH

Number	Title (A Side/B Side)	Yr	NM
❑ SP 2 [DJ]	Merry Christmas/Christopher Robin//I'm Back In Town/I Really Loved Harold	1971	10.00
❑ SP 2 [PS]	I'm Back in Town	1971	10.00

Albums

ABC

Number	Title (A Side/B Side)	Yr	NM
❑ ABND-879	From the Beginning/Twelve Great Performances	1975	10.00

ACCORD

Number	Title (A Side/B Side)	Yr	NM
❑ SN-7109	What Have They Done to My Song Ma	1981	10.00
❑ SN-7191	Beautiful People	1982	10.00

AMHERST

Number	Title (A Side/B Side)	Yr	NM
❑ AMH-3302	Am I Real or What	1985	10.00

ATLANTIC

Number	Title (A Side/B Side)	Yr	NM
❑ SD 18190	Photograph	1976	10.00

BLANCHE

Number	Title (A Side/B Side)	Yr	NM
❑ BL 6177	Arabesque	1982	10.00

BUDDAH

Number	Title (A Side/B Side)	Yr	NM
❑ BDS-5024	Born to Be	1969	15.00
❑ BDS-5041	Melanie	1969	15.00
❑ BDS-5060	Candles in the Rain	1970	15.00
❑ BDS-5066	Leftover Wine	1970	15.00
❑ BDS-5074	My First Album	1971	12.00
❑ BDS-5095	Garden in the City	1971	12.00
❑ BDS-5132	Please Love Me	1973	12.00
❑ B2D-5664 [(2)]	The Best...Melanie	197?	15.00
❑ BDS-95000	The Good Book	1971	15.00
❑ BDS-95005 [(2)]	Four Sides of Melanie	1972	15.00

MIDSONG

Number	Title (A Side/B Side)	Yr	NM
❑ MCA-3033	Phonogenic: Not Just Another Pretty Face	1978	10.00

NEIGHBORHOOD

Number	Title (A Side/B Side)	Yr	NM
❑ 3000	As I See It Now	1974	12.00
❑ 3001	Sunsets and Other Beginnings	1975	12.00
❑ 47001	Gather Me	1971	12.00
❑ 47005	Stoneground Words	1972	12.00
❑ 48001	Madrugada	1974	12.00
❑ 49001 [(2)]	Melanie at Carnegie Hall	1973	15.00

Except when noted otherwise, VG = 25% of NM, and VG+ = 50% of NM. (Example: VG = $2.00, VG+ = $4.00 and NM = $8.00.)

PICKWICK

Number	Title (A Side/B Side)	Yr	NM
❑ SPC-3317	Try the Real Thing	197?	10.00

TOMATO

Number	Title (A Side/B Side)	Yr	NM
❑ TOM-2-9003 [(2)]	Ballroom Streets	1979	12.00

MELCHER, TERRY
Also see BRUCE AND TERRY.

45s
COLUMBIA

Number	Title (A Side/B Side)	Yr	NM
❑ 42427	I Waited Too Long/That's All I Want	1962	20.00
—As "Terry Day"			
❑ 42427 [PS]	I Waited Too Long/That's All I Want	1962	40.00
—As "Terry Day"			
❑ 42678	Be a Soldier/I Love You Betty	1963	20.00
—As "Terry Day"			
❑ 42678 [PS]	Be a Soldier/I Love You Betty	1963	40.00

RCA VICTOR

Number	Title (A Side/B Side)	Yr	NM
❑ PB-10587	Fire in a Rainstorm/So Right Tonight	1976	10.00

Albums
REPRISE

Number	Title (A Side/B Side)	Yr	NM
❑ MS 2185	Terry Melcher	1974	15.00

MELIS, JOSE

45s
COLUMBIA

Number	Title (A Side/B Side)	Yr	NM
❑ 4-39181	Moon Over Miami/Isle of Capri	1951	12.00
❑ 4-39182	On a Little Street in Singapore/Cherokee	1951	12.00
❑ 4-39183	The Love Nest/Moon Over Miami	1951	12.00
❑ 4-39184	Playera/Orientale	1951	12.00
—The above four comprise a box set			

MERCURY

Number	Title (A Side/B Side)	Yr	NM
❑ 1252x45	Five Foot Two, Eyes of Blue/(B-side unknown)	195?	12.00
❑ 5757x45	In a Little Spanish Town/Tamanaco	1952	15.00
❑ 70017x45	Vanos, Vanos/The Hour of Parting	1953	15.00
❑ 71821	Hello My Heart/Summertime in Venice	1961	8.00
❑ 72006	Meadowland/On Top of Old Smokey	1962	8.00

MGM

Number	Title (A Side/B Side)	Yr	NM
❑ K12464	Mandolina/Argentina Ballerina	1957	12.00

SEECO

Number	Title (A Side/B Side)	Yr	NM
❑ 6001	Sweet and Lovely/Bright Lights of Brussels	1958	10.00
❑ 6003	Chop Stick Rock/Rockin' the Keys	1958	10.00
❑ 6015	The Story Of Christmas/Sleigh Ride	1958	12.00
❑ 6019	Anniversary Song/Linger Awhile	1959	10.00

Albums
DIPLOMAT

Number	Title (A Side/B Side)	Yr	NM
❑ D-2260 [M]	Jose Melis and the Metropolitan Strings	196?	10.00
❑ DS-2260 [S]	Jose Melis and the Metropolitan Strings	196?	10.00

HARMONY

Number	Title (A Side/B Side)	Yr	NM
❑ HL 7150 [M]	Exciting TV Star Jose Melis	195?	12.00

MERCURY

Number	Title (A Side/B Side)	Yr	NM
❑ MG 20008 [M]	Classics the South American Way	195?	15.00
❑ MG 20127 [M]	Latin American Stylings	195?	15.00
❑ MG 20275 [M]	Tonight It's Music	195?	15.00
❑ MG 20610 [M]	Jose Melis on Broadway	1961	12.00
❑ MG 20648 [M]	Jose Melis in Movieland	1961	12.00
❑ MG 20684 [M]	Jose Melis at the Pops Concert	1962	12.00
❑ MG 20709 [M]	Jose Melis at the Opera	1962	12.00
❑ MG 20738 [M]	Everybody's Favorites	1962	12.00
❑ MG 25035 [10]	Jose Melis	195?	30.00
❑ MG 25119 [10]	Latin-American Piano	195?	30.00
❑ SR 60610 [S]	Jose Melis on Broadway	1961	15.00
❑ SR 60648 [S]	Jose Melis in Movieland	1961	15.00
❑ SR 60684 [S]	Jose Melis at the Pops Concert	1962	15.00
❑ SR 60709 [S]	Jose Melis at the Opera	1962	15.00
❑ SR 60738 [S]	Everybody's Favorites	1962	15.00

MGM

Number	Title (A Side/B Side)	Yr	NM
❑ E-262 [10]	The Jose Melis Trio	1955	30.00
❑ E-3527 [M]	Jose Melis of the Jack Paar Show	1957	15.00

MUSICOR

Number	Title (A Side/B Side)	Yr	NM
❑ MM-2071 [M]	Piano Classics the South American Way	1967	12.00
❑ MS-3071 [S]	Piano Classics the South American Way	1967	12.00

PALACE

Number	Title (A Side/B Side)	Yr	NM
❑ P-84 [M]	Dance Party with Jose Melis	195?	12.00

SEECO

Number	Title (A Side/B Side)	Yr	NM
❑ CELP-411 [M]	Tonight with Jose Melis	1958	15.00
❑ CELP-414 [M]	Jose Melis at Midnight	1959	15.00
❑ CELP 423 [M]	Christmas with Melis	1959	15.00
❑ CELP-436 [M]	The Many Moods of Jose Melis	1960	12.00
❑ CELP-445 [M]	Jose Melis Plays the Latin Way	1960	12.00
❑ CELP-462 [M]	Jose Melis Plays Jack Paar's Favorites	1960	12.00
❑ CELP-471 [M]	Our Love	1961	12.00
❑ CELP-4140 [S]	Jose Melis at Midnight	1959	20.00
❑ CELP-4360 [S]	The Many Moods of Jose Melis	1960	15.00
❑ CELP-4450 [S]	Jose Melis Plays the Latin Way	1960	15.00
❑ CELP-4620 [S]	Jose Melis Plays Jack Paar's Favorites	1960	15.00
❑ CELP-4710 [S]	Our Love	1961	15.00

MELLENCAMP, JOHN
Includes records as "Johnny Cougar," "John Cougar," and "John Cougar Mellencamp."

12-Inch Singles
ELEKTRA

Number	Title (A Side/B Side)	Yr	NM
❑ ED 5333 [DJ]	Rave On (same on both sides)	1988	10.00

MERCURY

Number	Title (A Side/B Side)	Yr	NM
❑ PRO 527-1 [DJ]	Paper in Fire (same on both sides)	1987	10.00

RIVA

Number	Title (A Side/B Side)	Yr	NM
❑ MK 116 [DJ]	I Need a Lover (Long) (Short)	1979	20.00
❑ MK 126 [DJ]	Small Paradise (same on both sides)	1979	20.00
❑ MK 152 [DJ]	This Time (Short Version 3:56) (Long Version 4:18)	1980	20.00
❑ MK 170 [DJ]	Ain't Even Done with the Night (Album Version) (Live Version)	1980	20.00
❑ MK 196 [DJ]	Hurts So Good (same on both sides)	1982	15.00
❑ MK 209 [DJ]	Jack and Diane (Long Version) (Short Version)	1982	20.00
❑ MK 219 [(2)DJ]	Hand to Hold On To/Thundering Hearts/I Need a Lover/Small Paradise/Ain't Even Done with the Night/A Little Night Dancin'	1982	30.00
❑ PRO 235-1 [DJ]	Crumblin' Down (same on both sides)	1983	15.00
❑ PRO 254-1 [DJ]	Play Guitar (Album Version) (Radio Version)/Pink Houses (Acoustic Version)	1984	15.00
❑ PRO 268-1 [DJ]	Authority Song (same on both sides)	1984	10.00
❑ PRO 283-1 [DJ]	Serious Business (same on both sides)	1984	15.00
❑ PRO 364-1 [DJ]	Lonely Ol' Night (same on both sides)	1985	10.00
❑ PRO 384-1 [DJ]	Small Town (Album Version)/(Acoustic Version)	1985	12.00
❑ PRO 412-1 [DJ]	Rain on the Scarecrow (same on both sides)	1986	12.00
❑ PRO 427-1 [DJ]	Rumbleseat (same on both sides)	1986	12.00
❑ 884455-1	R.O.C.K. in the U.S.A. (A Salute to 60's Rock)/Under the Boardwalk	1986	10.00

45s
COLUMBIA

Number	Title (A Side/B Side)	Yr	NM
❑ 38-79653	Peaceful World/In Our Lives	2001	3.00

ELEKTRA

Number	Title (A Side/B Side)	Yr	NM
❑ 69370	Rave On/Tutti Frutti	1988	3.00
—B-side by Little Richard			
❑ 69370 [PS]	Rave On/Tutti Frutti	1988	4.00

MCA

Number	Title (A Side/B Side)	Yr	NM
❑ 40634	American Dream/Oh, Pretty Woman	1976	10.00
—As "Johnny Cougar"			

MERCURY

Number	Title (A Side/B Side)	Yr	NM
❑ 574244-7	Key West Intermezzo (I Saw You First)/Just Another Day	1997	3.00
❑ 856258-7	Dance Naked/R.O.C.K. in the U.S.A.	1994	4.00
❑ 858738-7	Wild Night/Brothers	1994	4.00
—With Me'Shell NgedeOcelo			
❑ 862702-7	Human Wheels/Human Wheels (Edit)	1993	4.00
❑ 866414-7	Again Tonight/Get a Leg Up (Live)	1992	4.00
❑ 867890-7	Get a Leg Up (Family Version)/Whenever We Wanted	1991	4.00
❑ 870126-7	Check It Out/We Are the People	1988	3.00
—Mercury releases starting with "870" and "888" are by "John Cougar Mellencamp"			
❑ 870126-7 [PS]	Check It Out/We Are the People	1988	3.00
❑ 870327-7	Rooty Toot Toot/Check It Out	1988	3.00
❑ 870327-7 [PS]	Rooty Toot Toot/Check It Out	1988	3.00
❑ 874012-7	Pop Singer/J.M.'s Question	1989	3.00
❑ 874012-7 [PS]	Pop Singer/J.M.'s Question	1989	3.00
❑ 874644-7	Jackie Brown/Jackie Brown (Acoustic Version)	1989	3.00
❑ 874644-7 [PS]	Jackie Brown/Jackie Brown (Acoustic Version)	1989	3.00
❑ 874932-7	Let It All Hang Out/Country Gentleman	1989	4.00
❑ 874932-7 [PS]	Let It All Hang Out/Country Gentleman	1989	4.00
❑ 888763-7	Paper in Fire/Never Too Old	1987	3.00
❑ 888763-7 [PS]	Paper in Fire/Never Too Old	1987	3.00
❑ 888934-7	Cherry Bomb/Shama Lama Ding Dong	1987	3.00
❑ 888934-7 [PS]	Cherry Bomb/Shama Lama Ding Dong	1987	3.00

RIVA

Number	Title (A Side/B Side)	Yr	NM
❑ 202	I Need a Lover/Welcome to Chinatown	1979	4.00
—Riva 202-211 as "John Cougar"			
❑ 202 [DJ]	I Need a Lover (Short Version 3:40)/(Long Version 5:35)	1979	8.00
❑ 202 [PS]	I Need a Lover/Welcome to Chinatown	1979	10.00
❑ 203	Small Paradise/Sugar Marie	1980	4.00
❑ 204	A Little Night Dancin'/Pray for Me	1980	5.00
❑ 205	This Time/Don't Misunderstand Me	1980	4.00
❑ 207	Ain't Even Done with the Night/Make Me Feel	1981	4.00
❑ 209	Hurts So Good/Close Enough	1982	4.00
❑ 209 [PS]	Hurts So Good/Close Enough	1982	10.00
❑ 210	Jack and Diane/Can You Take It	1982	4.00
❑ 211	Hand to Hold On To/Small Paradise	1982	4.00
❑ 211 [PD]	Hand to Hold On To/Small Paradise	1982	20.00
—Promo-only 7-inch picture disc with small hole			
❑ 214	Crumblin' Down/Golden Gates	1983	4.00
—Riva 214 on as "John Cougar Mellencamp"			
❑ 214 [PS]	Crumblin' Down/Golden Gates	1983	5.00
❑ 215 [PS]	Pink Houses/Serious Business	1983	6.00
❑ 215 [DJ]	Pink Houses (Long Version 4:43)/(Short Version 3:59)	1983	20.00
❑ 215 [DJ]	Pink Houses (Long Version 4:43)/(Short Version 3:59)	1983	20.00
—Promo only on pink vinyl			
❑ 216	Authority Song/Pink Houses (Acoustic Version)	1984	4.00
❑ 216 [PS]	Authority Song/Pink Houses (Acoustic Version)	1984	5.00
❑ 880984-7	Lonely Ol' Night/The Kind of Fella I Am	1985	3.00
❑ 880984-7 [PS]	Lonely Ol' Night/The Kind of Fella I Am	1985	4.00
❑ 884202-7	Small Town/(Acoustic Version)	1985	3.00
❑ 884202-7 [PS]	Small Town/(Acoustic Version)	1985	4.00
❑ 884455-7	R.O.C.K. in the U.S.A. (A Salute to 60's Rock)/Under the Boardwalk	1986	3.00
❑ 884455-7 [PS]	R.O.C.K. in the U.S.A. (A Salute to 60's Rock)/Under the Boardwalk	1986	3.00
❑ 884635-7	Rain on the Scarecrow/Pretty Ballerina	1986	3.00
❑ 884635-7 [PS]	Rain on the Scarecrow/Pretty Ballerina	1986	3.00
❑ 884856-7	Rumbleseat/Cold Sweat	1986	3.00
❑ 884856-7 [PS]	Rumbleseat/Cold Sweat	1986	3.00

Albums
COLUMBIA

Number	Title (A Side/B Side)	Yr	NM
❑ C 69602	John Mellencamp	1998	15.00

HEAR MUSIC

Number	Title (A Side/B Side)	Yr	NM
❑ HRM 30895	Life, Death, Love and Freedom	2008	20.00

MCA

Number	Title (A Side/B Side)	Yr	NM
❑ 2225	Chestnut Street Incident	1977	25.00
—As "Johnny Cougar"			

MERCURY

Number	Title (A Side/B Side)	Yr	NM
❑ 832465-1	The Lonesome Jubilee	1987	8.00
❑ 838220-1	Big Daddy	1989	10.00

MOBILE FIDELITY

Number	Title (A Side/B Side)	Yr	NM
❑ 1-222	The Lonesome Jubilee	1995	40.00
—Audiophile vinyl			

RIVA

Number	Title (A Side/B Side)	Yr	NM
❑ RVL 7401	John Cougar	1979	10.00
—As "John Cougar"			
❑ RVL 7403	Nothin' Matters and What If It Did	1980	10.00
—As "John Cougar"			
❑ RVL 7501	American Fool	1982	8.00
—As "John Cougar"			
❑ RVL 7504	Uh-Huh	1983	8.00
—As "John Cougar Mellencamp"			
❑ 824865-1	Scarecrow	1985	8.00
—As "John Cougar Mellencamp"			

M

MELLO-HARPS, THE

45s

Number	Title (A Side/B Side)	Yr	NM
CASINO			
❑ 104	Gumma Gumma/No Good	1959	60.00
DO-RE-MI			
❑ 203	Love Is a Vow/Valerie	1956	8000.
—VG 4000; VG+ 6000			
TIN PAN ALLEY			
❑ 145/6	I Love Only You/Ain't Got the Money	1955	400.00
❑ 157/8	What Good Are My Dreams/ Gone	1956	600.00
❑ 159	I Couldn't Believe/My Bleeding Heart	1956	600.00

MELLO-KINGS, THE

45s

Number	Title (A Side/B Side)	Yr	NM
HERALD			
❑ 502	Tonite Tonite/Do Baby Do	1957	50.00
—Label corrected to "The Mello-Kings"; script print inside flag			
❑ 502	Tonite Tonite/Do Baby Do	1957	500.00
—First pressing credits "The Mellotones"			
❑ 502	Tonite Tonite/Do Baby Do	1961	25.00
—Reissue; block print inside flag			
❑ 507	Chapel on the Hill/Sassafras	1957	30.00
❑ 511	Baby Tell Me Why Why Why/ The Only Girl I'll Ever Know	1958	30.00
❑ 518	Valerie/She's Real Cool	1958	30.00
❑ 536	Chip Chip/Running to You	1959	30.00
—Both sides play as labeled			
❑ 536	Chip Chip/Running to You	1959	150.00
—Mispressing; plays "Rockin' at the Bandstand"/"Down in Cuba" by the Royal Holidays			
❑ 548	Our Love Is Beautiful/ Dear Mr. Jock	1960	25.00
❑ 554	Kid Stuff/I Promise	1960	25.00
❑ 561	Penny/Till There Were None	1961	25.00
❑ 567	Love at First Sight/ She's Real Cool	1961	25.00
LANA			
❑ 124	Tonite Tonite/Chip Chip	196?	10.00
LESCAY			
❑ 3009	Walk Softly/But You Lied	1962	30.00
LOST-NITE			
❑ 415	Tonite Tonite/Do Baby Do	197?	5.00
—Reissue			

7-Inch Extended Plays

Number	Title (A Side/B Side)	Yr	NM
HERALD			
❑ HEP-451	Tonite, Tonite/She's Real Cool/ /The Only Girl/Do Baby Do	1957	300.00
❑ HEP-451 [PS]	The Fabulous Mello-Kings	1957	400.00

Albums

Number	Title (A Side/B Side)	Yr	NM
COLLECTABLES			
❑ COL-5020	Greatest Hits	198?	10.00
HERALD			
❑ H-1013 [M]	Tonight-Tonight	196?	250.00
—Multi-color label			
❑ H-1013 [M]	Tonight-Tonight	1960	500.00
—Yellow label			
RELIC			
❑ LP-5035	Greatest Hits	198?	12.00

MELLO-MOODS, THE

45s

Number	Title (A Side/B Side)	Yr	NM
GAMBLE			
❑ 2512	Stop Taking My Love for Granted/ Inspirational Pleasure	1972	10.00
HAMILTON			
❑ 143	I'm Lost/I Woke Up This Morning	1953	100.00
LOST-NITE			
❑ 332	I Couldn't Sleep a Wink Last Night/And You Just Can't Go Through Life Alone	197?	5.00
—Reissue			
❑ 337	Where Are You (Now That I Need You)/How Could You	197?	5.00
—Reissue			
PRESTIGE			
❑ 799	Call on Me/I Tried and Tried and Tried	1953	700.00
❑ 856	I'm Lost/I Woke Up This Morning	1953	700.00
RED ROBIN			
❑ 104	I Couldn't Sleep a Wink Last Night/And You Just Can't Go Through Life Alone	1952	1000.
—Despite the lower number, this came out after Robin/Red Robin 105			
ROBIN			
❑ 105	Where Are You (Now That I Need You)/How Could You	1951	5000.
—Despite the higher number, this record pre-dates both of the Red Robin releases			

Selected 78s

Number	Title (A Side/B Side)	Yr	NM
ROBIN			
❑ 105	Where Are You (Now That I Need You)/How Could You	1951	1000.
—Despite the higher number, this came out before Red Robin 104			

MELLO-TONES, THE More than one group.

45s

Number	Title (A Side/B Side)	Yr	NM
COLUMBIA			
❑ 1-904	When the Rain Gates Unfold/ What Are They Doing in Heaven	1950	400.00
—Microgroove 33 1/3 rpm 7-inch record, small hole			
❑ 6-904	When the Rain Gates Unfold/ What Are They Doing in Heaven	1950	400.00
—Originally released on Columbia's short-lived special numbering system for 7-inch records			
❑ 39051	When the Rain Gates Unfold/ What Are They Doing in Heaven	1950	300.00
❑ 39215	Looking for a City/ Flysing Saucers	1951	300.00
DECCA			
❑ 48318	Winos on Parade/ Man Loves Woman	1954	400.00
❑ 48319	I'm Just Another One in Love with You/I'm Gonna Get	1954	400.00
FASCINATION			
❑ 1001	Rosie Lee/I'll Never Fall in Love Again	1957	150.00
GEE			
❑ 1037	Rosie Lee/I'll Never Fall in Love Again	1957	40.00
❑ 1040	Ca-Sandra/Rattle Shake Roll	1957	40.00
OKEH			
❑ 6828	Rough and Rocky Road/Cool by the River Banks	1951	300.00

MELLOW DROPS, THE

45s

Number	Title (A Side/B Side)	Yr	NM
IMPERIAL			
❑ 5324	When I Grow Too Old to Dream/ The Crazy Song	1955	200.00

MELLOWLARKS, THE

45s

Number	Title (A Side/B Side)	Yr	NM
ARGO			
❑ 5285	Sing a Silly Sing Song/ Farewell to You, My Nancy	1958	25.00

MELLOWS, THE

45s

Number	Title (A Side/B Side)	Yr	NM
CANDLELIGHT			
❑ 1011	Moon of Silver/You're Gone	1956	150.00
❑ 1012	Farewell Farewell/No More Loneliness	1956	150.00
CELESTE			
❑ 3002	Lucky Guy/My Darling	1956	120.00
❑ 3004	I'm Yours/Sweet Lorraine	1956	600.00
JAY DEE			
❑ 793	How Sentimental Can I Be/ Nothin' to Do	1954	200.00
❑ 797	Smoke from Your Cigarette/ Pretty Baby	1954	250.00
❑ 801	I Was a Fool to Let You Go/ I Still Care	1955	200.00
❑ 807	Yesterday's Memories/ Loveable Lilly	1955	150.00

MELO GENTS, THE

45s

Number	Title (A Side/B Side)	Yr	NM
WARNER BROS.			
❑ 5056	Baby Be Mine/Get Off My Back	1959	50.00

MELODEARS, THE

45s

Number	Title (A Side/B Side)	Yr	NM
GONE			
❑ 5033	Summer Romance/Charock	1958	15.00
❑ 5040	It's Love Because/ They Don't Say	1958	15.00

MELODY MAKERS, THE

45s

Number	Title (A Side/B Side)	Yr	NM
HOLLIS			
❑ 1001	Carolina Moon/Let's Make Love Worthwhile	1957	100.00
❑ 1002	The Nearnes of You/Gotta Go	1957	150.00

MELVIN, HAROLD, AND THE BLUE NOTES Also see THE BLUE NOTES (1).

12-Inch Singles

Number	Title (A Side/B Side)	Yr	NM
PHILLY WORLD			
❑ PR 751 [DJ]	Today's Your Lucky Day (6:20) (7:07)	1984	8.00
SOURCE			
❑ 13950	Prayin' (5:56)/Your Love Is Taking Me on a Journey (5:55)	1979	40.00

45s

Number	Title (A Side/B Side)	Yr	NM
ABC			
❑ 12240	Reaching for the World/ Stay Together	1976	5.00
❑ 12268	After You Love Me, Why Do You Leave Me/Big Singing Star	1977	5.00
—With Sharon Paige			
❑ 12327	Baby, You Got My Nose Open/ Try to Live a Day	1978	5.00
❑ 12368	Power of Love/Now Is the Time	1978	5.00
ARCTIC			
❑ 135	Go Away/What Can a Man Do	1967	75.00
LANDA			
❑ 703	Get Out (And Let Me Cry)/You May Not Love Me	1964	150.00
—As "The Blue Notes"			
MCA			
❑ 41291	Tonight's the Night/If You're Looking for Someone to Love	1980	4.00
—With Sharon Paige			
❑ 51190	Hang On In There/If You Love Me, Really Love Me	1982	4.00
PHILADELPHIA INT'L.			
❑ 3516	I Miss You (Part I)/I Miss You (Part II)	1972	5.00
❑ 3520	If You Don't Know Me By Now/ Let Me Into Your World	1972	5.00
❑ 3525	Yesterday I Had the Blues/ Ebony Woman	1973	5.00
❑ 3525 [PS]	Yesterday I Had the Blues/ Ebony Woman	1973	6.00
❑ 3533	The Love I Lost (Part 1)/The Love I Lost (Part 2)	1973	15.00
❑ 3543	Satisfaction Guaranteed (Or Take Your Love Back)/I'm Weak for You	1974	5.00
❑ 3552	Where Are All My Friends/Let It Be You	1974	15.00
❑ 3562	Bad Luck (Part 1)/Bad Luck (Part 2)	1975	5.00
❑ 3569	Hope That We Can Be Together Soon/Be for Real	1975	5.00
—With Sharon Paige			
❑ 3579	Wake Up Everybody (Part 1)/ Wake Up Everybody (Part 2)	1975	5.00
❑ 3588	Tell the World How I Feel About 'Cha Baby/You Know How to Make Me Feel So Good	1976	5.00
PHILLY WORLD			
❑ 99709	I Really Love You/I Can't Let Go	1984	4.00
❑ 99735	Today's Your Lucky Day (Long)/Today's Your Lucky Day (Short)	1984	4.00
❑ 99761	Don't Give Me Up/ (Instrumental)	1984	4.00
SOURCE			
❑ 41156	Prayin'/(Instrumental)	1979	30.00
❑ 41157	Tonight's the Night/Your Love Is Taking Me on a Journey	1979	4.00
—As "Sharon Paige with Harold Melvin and the Blue Notes"			
❑ 41231	I Should Be Your Lover (Part 1)/ I Should Be Your Lover (Part 2)	1980	4.00

7-Inch Extended Plays

Number	Title (A Side/B Side)	Yr	NM
PHILADELPHIA INT'L.			
❑ ZS7 31648	Be for Real//Ebony Woman/ Let It Be You	1971	20.00
—Stereo jukebox issue; small hole, plays at 33 1/3 rpm			
❑ ZS7 31648 [PS]	Harold Melvin and the Blue Notes	1971	20.00

Albums

Number	Title (A Side/B Side)	Yr	NM
ABC			
❑ AB-969	Reaching for the World	1977	10.00
❑ AB-1041	Now Is the Time	1978	10.00
MCA			
❑ 5261	All Things Happen in Time	1981	10.00
PHILADELPHIA INT'L.			
❑ KZ 31648	Harold Melvin and the Blue Notes	1972	12.00
❑ KZ 32407	Black & Blue	1973	12.00
❑ ZQ 32407 [Q]	Black & Blue	1973	20.00
❑ PZ 33148	To Be True	1975	12.00
❑ PZ 33808	Wake Up Everybody	1975	12.00
❑ PZQ 33808 [Q]	Wake Up Everybody	1975	20.00

Number	Title (A Side/B Side)	Yr	NM
❑ PZ 34232	Collector's Item — All Their Greatest Hits!	1976	12.00
PHILLY WORLD			
❑ 90187	Talk It Up (Tell Everybody)	1985	10.00
SOURCE			
❑ 3197	The Blue Album	1980	10.00
MELVINS, THE			
45s			
BONER			
❑ BR 21	Sweet Young Thing Ain't Sweet No More/I Dreamed I Dream	1989	25.00
—B-side by Steel Pole Bathtub; orange vinyl			
❑ BR 21 [PS]	Sweet Young Thing Ain't Sweet No More/I Dreamed I Dream	1989	25.00
LEOPARD GECKO			
❑ LG 004	Oven/Revulsion/We Reach	1989	20.00
—Originals on pink vinyl			
❑ LG 004 [PS]	Oven/Revulsion/We Reach	1989	20.00
—With insert of cut-out clothes			
MAKE 'EM BLEED AND SUFFER			
❑ (no #)	Symptom of the Universe/ Hate the Police (Live)	1988	25.00
—B-side by Mudhoney			
❑ (no #) [PS]	Symptom of the Universe/ Hate the Police (Live)	1988	25.00
—Actually a large envelope that contained this single, which was enclosed in a Japanese porno magazine			
RISE			
❑ RR 76 [PD]	Hooch/Sky Pup	1993	15.00
—Most of these picture discs were used as promos			
❑ RR 76 [PS]	Hooch/Sky Pup	1993	15.00
—Fold-around silk-screened sleeve by Frank Kozik			
SLAP A HAM			
❑ 13	Love Canal/Someday	199?	10.00
—5" single with clear vinyl			
❑ 13 [PS]	Love Canal/Someday	199?	10.00
—Plastic bag with stickers on both sides			
SYMPATHY FOR THE RECORD INDUSTRY			
❑ 81	With Yo Heart, Not Yo Hands/ 4-Letter Woman/Anal Satan	199?	4.00
—Yellow vinyl			
❑ 81 [PS]	With Yo Heart, Not Yo Hands/ 4-Letter Woman/Anal Satan	199?	4.00
7-Inch Extended Plays			
C/Z			
❑ 1705	Easy As It Was	1986	25.00
❑ 1705 [PS]	Easy As It Was	1986	25.00
MEMORIES, THE			
45s			
WAY-LIN			
❑ 101	Love Bells/I Promise	1959	400.00
MEMPHIS MINNIE			
45s			
CHECKER			
❑ 771	Broken Heart/Me and My Chauffeur	1953	3000.
—VG 1000; VG+ 2000			
J.O.B.			
❑ 1101	Kissing in the Dark/World of Trouble	1952	1000.
Albums			
MCA			
❑ 1370	Moanin' the Blues	198?	15.00
PORTRAIT			
❑ RJ 44072	I Ain't No Bad Gal	1988	15.00
MEMPHIS SLIM			
45s			
JOSIE			
❑ 973	Come Again/Little Lonely Girl	1967	10.00
KING			
❑ 6301	Messin' Around with the Blues/ Mistake in Life	1970	8.00
MERCURY			
❑ 8251x45	Train Time/Blue Evening	1951	50.00
❑ 8266x45	No Mail Blues/Gonna Need My Help Some Day	1952	50.00
❑ 8281x45	The Question/Never Let Me Love	1952	50.00
❑ 70063x45	The Train Is Coming/ Drivin' Me Mad	1953	40.00
MONEY			
❑ 212	My Country Gal/Treat Me Like I Treat You	1955	40.00
PEACOCK			
❑ 1602	Sitting and Thinking/Living Like a King	1952	50.00

Men At Work, "It's a Mistake," Columbia 03959, 1983, $3.

Number	Title (A Side/B Side)	Yr	NM
STRAND			
❑ 25041	Four Walls/Lonesome	1961	25.00
UNITED			
❑ 138	Back Alley/Living the Life I Love	1952	60.00
❑ 156	The Come Back/ Five O'Clock Blues	1953	60.00
—Black vinyl			
❑ 156	The Come Back/Five O'Clock Blues	1953	150.00
—Red vinyl			
❑ 166	Call Before You Go Home/ This Is My Lucky Day	1953	60.00
—Black vinyl			
❑ 166	Call Before You Go Home/ This Is My Lucky Day	1953	150.00
—Red vinyl			
❑ 176	Wish Me Well/Sassy Mae	1954	60.00
—Black vinyl			
❑ 176	Wish Me Well/Sassy Mae	1954	150.00
—Red vinyl			
❑ 182	I Love My Baby/Four Years of Torment	1954	50.00
❑ 186	Memphis Slim U.S.A./Blues All Around My Head	1954	50.00
❑ 189	She's Alright/Two of a Kind	1955	50.00
❑ 201	Go to Find My Baby/Blue and Lonesome	1956	40.00
VEE JAY			
❑ 271	Stroll On Little Girl/Guitar Cha Cha Cha	1958	20.00
❑ 294	This Time I'm Through/What's the Matter	1958	20.00
❑ 330	Steppin' Out/My Gal Keeps Me Crying	1959	20.00
❑ 343	The Come Back/Slim's Blues	1960	15.00
WARNER BROS.			
❑ 7500	Chicago Seven/Boogie Woogie 1-9-7-0	1971	8.00
Albums			
BATTLE			
❑ BM-6118 [M]	Alone with My Friends	1963	50.00

Number	Title (A Side/B Side)	Yr	NM
❑ BM-6122 [M]	Baby Please Come Home	1963	50.00
BLUESVILLE			
❑ BVLP-1018 [M]	Just Blues	1961	120.00
—Blue label, silver print			
❑ BVLP-1018 [M]	Just Blues	1964	30.00
—Blue label, trident logo at right			
❑ BVLP-1031 [M]	No Strain	1961	120.00
—Blue label, silver print			
❑ BVLP-1031 [M]	No Strain	1964	30.00
—Blue label, trident logo at right			
❑ BVLP-1053 [M]	All Kinds of Blues	1962	100.00
—Blue label, silver print			
❑ BVLP-1053 [M]	All Kinds of Blues	1964	30.00
—Blue label, trident logo at right			
❑ BVLP-1075 [M]	Steady Rollin' Blues	1963	100.00
—Blue label, silver print			
❑ BVLP-1075 [M]	Steady Rollin' Blues	1964	30.00
—Blue label, trident logo at right			
BUDDAH			
❑ BDS-7505	Mother Earth	1969	20.00
CANDID			
❑ CM-8023 [M]	Slim's Tribute to Big Bill Broonzy	1961	60.00
❑ CM-8024 [M]	Memphis Slim U.S.A.	1962	60.00
❑ CS-9023 [S]	Slim's Tribute to Big Bill Broonzy	1961	80.00
❑ CS-9024 [S]	Memphis Slim U.S.A.	1962	80.00
CHESS			
❑ LP-1455 [M]	Memphis Slim	1961	150.00
—Black label			
❑ LP-1510 [M]	The Real Folk Blues	1966	80.00
DISC			
❑ D-105 [M]	If the Rabbit Had a Gun	1964	40.00
FOLKWAYS			
❑ FG-3524 [M]	The Real Boogie Woogie	1959	100.00
❑ FG-3535 [M]	Memphis Slim...And the Real Honky Tonk	1960	100.00
❑ FG-3536 [M]	Chicago Blues	1961	100.00
JUBILEE			
❑ JGM-8003 [M]	Legend of the Blues	1967	25.00
❑ JGS-8003 [S]	Legend of the Blues	1967	25.00

M

KING

Number	Title (A Side/B Side)	Yr	NM
❑ 885 [M]	Memphis Slim Sings Folk Blues	1964	50.00

SCEPTER

Number	Title (A Side/B Side)	Yr	NM
❑ SM-535 [M]	Self Portrait	1966	20.00
❑ SMS-535 [S]	Self Portrait	1966	25.00

SPIN-O-RAMA

Number	Title (A Side/B Side)	Yr	NM
❑ 149 [M]	Lonesome Blues	196?	20.00

STRAND

Number	Title (A Side/B Side)	Yr	NM
❑ SL-1046 [M]	The World's Foremost Blues Singer	1962	40.00
❑ SLS-1046 [S]	The World's Foremost Blues Singer	1962	50.00

UNITED ARTISTS

Number	Title (A Side/B Side)	Yr	NM
❑ UAL-3137 [M]	Broken Soul Blues	1961	60.00
❑ UAS-6137 [S]	Broken Soul Blues	1961	80.00

VEE JAY

Number	Title (A Side/B Side)	Yr	NM
❑ LP-1012 [M]	Memphis Slim at the Gate of the Horn	1959	200.00
—Maroon label			
❑ LP-1012 [M]	Memphis Slim at the Gate of the Horn	1961	120.00
—Black rainbow label, oval logo			

MEN, THE

Albums

SNAT-5

Number	Title (A Side/B Side)	Yr	NM
❑ 2001	Hermeneutics	1981	25.00

MEN AT WORK

12-Inch Singles

COLUMBIA

Number	Title (A Side/B Side)	Yr	NM
❑ (no #) [DJ]	Who Can It Be Now? (same on both sides)	1982	15.00
❑ AS 1608 [DJ]	Be Good Johnny (same on both sides)	1983	8.00
❑ AS 1634 [DJ]	Overkill (same on both sides)	1983	12.00
❑ AS 1749 [DJ]	Dr. Heckle & Mr. Jive/Upstairs at My House (Live)/I Like To (Live)	1983	8.00
❑ CAS 2073 [DJ]	Everything I Need (same on both sides)	1985	8.00
❑ CAS 2152 [DJ]	Maria (same on both sides)	1985	8.00
❑ CAS 2189 [DJ]	Hard Luck Story (Single Version) (Album Version)	1985	10.00
❑ 44-03977	It's a Mistake//Who Can It Be Now/F 19	1983	10.00
❑ 44-05216	Everything I Need (Extended Version) (7" Version)	1985	8.00

45s

COLUMBIA

Number	Title (A Side/B Side)	Yr	NM
❑ AE7 1633 [DJ]	Overkill (same on both sides)	1983	5.00
❑ AE7 1633 [PS]	Overkill (same on both sides)	1983	5.00
—Special color sleeve, different from stock version			
❑ 18-02888	Who Can It Be Now?/Anyone for Tennis	1982	4.00
❑ 38-03303	Down Under/Crazy	1982	4.00
❑ CNR-03373	Down Under/(B-side blank)	1982	5.00
—One-sided budget release			
❑ 38-03552	Be Good Johnny/F 19	1983	—
—Scheduled but not released			
❑ 38-03795	Overkill/Till the Money Runs Out	1983	3.00
❑ 38-03795 [PS]	Overkill/Till the Money Runs Out	1983	3.00
❑ 38-03959	It's a Mistake/Shintano	1983	3.00
❑ 38-03959 [PS]	It's a Mistake/Shintano	1983	3.00
❑ 38-04111	Dr. Heckyll & Mr. Jive/I Like To (Live)	1983	3.00
❑ 38-04111 [PS]	Dr. Heckyll & Mr. Jive/I Like To (Live)	1983	3.00
❑ 38-04111 [PS]	Dr. Heckyll & Mr. Jive	1983	5.00
—"Demonstration -- Not for Sale" on rear			
❑ 38-04929	Everything I Need/Sail to You	1985	3.00
❑ 38-04929 [PS]	Everything I Need/Sail to You	1985	3.00
❑ 38-04929 [PS]	Everything I Need	1985	5.00
—"Demonstration – Not for Sale" on rear			
❑ 38-05454	Maria/Snakes and Ladders	1985	3.00
❑ 38-05454 [PS]	Maria/Snakes and Ladders	1985	3.00
❑ 38-05649	Hard Luck Story/Snakes and Ladders	1985	3.00

Albums

COLUMBIA

Number	Title (A Side/B Side)	Yr	NM
❑ A2S 1650 [(2)DJ]	Cargo (World Premiere Weekend)	1983	20.00
—Promo-only two-record package of interviews and music			
❑ ARC 37978	Business as Usual	1982	8.00
❑ FC 37978	Business as Usual	1982	6.00
—New prefix to reflect list-price increase			
❑ PC 38660	Cargo	198?	6.00
—Reissue with new prefix			
❑ QC 38660	Cargo	1983	6.00
❑ FC 40078	Two Hearts	1985	8.00
❑ HC 47978	Business as Usual	1983	25.00
—Half-speed mastered edition			
❑ HC 48660	Cargo	1983	25.00
—Half-speed mastered edition			

MEN WITHOUT HATS

12-Inch Singles

BACKSTREET

Number	Title (A Side/B Side)	Yr	NM
❑ 13969	The Safety Dance (extended)/Antarctica	1983	10.00

MCA

Number	Title (A Side/B Side)	Yr	NM
❑ L33-1164 [DJ]	I Got the Message (long)/I Got the Message (short)	1983	6.00
❑ L33-1217 [DJ]	Where Do the Boys Go/Where Do the Boys Go (Extended)	1984	6.00
❑ 23513	Where Do the Boys Go (2 versions)	1984	8.00

MERCURY

Number	Title (A Side/B Side)	Yr	NM
❑ 870153-1	Moonbeam (5 versions)	1988	10.00
❑ 888859-1	Pop Goes the World (4 versions)	1987	10.00

STIFF

Number	Title (A Side/B Side)	Yr	NM
❑ TEES-12-08	Nationale 7/Freeways	1981	12.00

45s

BACKSTREET

Number	Title (A Side/B Side)	Yr	NM
❑ 52232	The Safety Dance/Living in China	1983	3.00
❑ 52232 [PS]	The Safety Dance/Living in China	1983	5.00

MCA

Number	Title (A Side/B Side)	Yr	NM
❑ 52293	I Like/Things in My Life	1983	3.00
❑ 52293 [PS]	I Like/Things in My Life	1983	3.00
❑ 52332	I've Got the Message/Great Ones Remember	1983	3.00
❑ 52460	Where Do the Boys Go?/Unsatisfaction	1984	3.00

MERCURY

Number	Title (A Side/B Side)	Yr	NM
❑ 870153-7	Moonbeam/Jenny Wore Black	1988	3.00
❑ 870153-7 [PS]	Moonbeam/Jenny Wore Black	1988	3.00
❑ 870432-7	Walk on Water/Lose My Way	1988	3.00
❑ 888859-7	Pop Goes the World/End of the World	1987	3.00
❑ 888859-7 [PS]	Pop Goes the World/End of the World	1987	3.00

Albums

BACKSTREET

Number	Title (A Side/B Side)	Yr	NM
❑ 5436	Rhythm of Youth	1983	10.00
—Reissue			
❑ 39002	Rhythm of Youth	1983	12.00

MCA

Number	Title (A Side/B Side)	Yr	NM
❑ 5487	Folk of the 80's, Part 3	1984	10.00

MERCURY

Number	Title (A Side/B Side)	Yr	NM
❑ 842000-1	In the 21st Century	1989	10.00

STIFF

Number	Title (A Side/B Side)	Yr	NM
❑ TEES-12-01 [EP]	Folk of the 80's	1981	30.00
—Reissue of Trend 10-inch EP			

TREND

Number	Title (A Side/B Side)	Yr	NM
❑ HATS-001 [10]	Folk of the 80's	1981	30.00
—10-inch four-song EP; possibly released only in Canada			

MENDEL, ED

45s

HIT

Number	Title (A Side/B Side)	Yr	NM
❑ 32	I Remember You/Green Onions	1962	8.00
—B-side by the Dave Grundy Combo			

MENDES, SERGIO Includes Brasil '66, '77, '86, '88, etc.

12-Inch Singles

A&M

Number	Title (A Side/B Side)	Yr	NM
❑ 12103	Dance Attack (Club Mix)/Dance Attack (Dub)	1984	6.00
❑ 12195	Nonstop (Remix)/(Instrumental)	1986	6.00

ELEKTRA

Number	Title (A Side/B Side)	Yr	NM
❑ ED 5602 [DJ]	What Is This?/Fanfarra	1992	8.00

45s

A&M

Number	Title (A Side/B Side)	Yr	NM
❑ 807	Mas Que nada/The Joker	1966	6.00
❑ 814	Day Tripper/Slow Hot Wind	1966	6.00
❑ 825	Constant Rain (Chove Chuva)	1966	6.00
❑ 836	For Me/Gente	1967	6.00
❑ 853	Night and Day/Cinnamon and Clove	1967	5.00
❑ 872	Watch What Happens/The Frog	1967	5.00
❑ 872 [PS]	Watch What Happens/The Frog	1967	10.00
❑ 910	Look Around/With a Little Help from My Friends	1968	5.00
❑ 924	The Look of Love/Like a Lover	1968	5.00
❑ 924 [PS]	The Look of Love/Like a Lover	1968	8.00
❑ 961	The Fool on the Hill/So Many Stars	1968	5.00
❑ 961 [PS]	The Fool on the Hill/So Many Stars	1968	8.00
❑ 986	Scarborough Fair/Canto Triste	1968	5.00
❑ 986 [PS]	Scarborough Fair/Canto Triste	1968	8.00
❑ 1049	Pretty World/Fiesta	1969	5.00
❑ 1049 [PS]	Pretty World/Fiesta	1969	6.00
❑ 1073	(Sittin' On) The Dock of the Bay/Song of No Regrets	1969	5.00
❑ 1073 [PS]	(Sittin' On) The Dock of the Bay/Song of No Regrets	1969	6.00
❑ 1132	Wichita Lineman/Ye Me Le	1969	5.00
❑ 1164	Norwegian Wood/Masquerade	1970	4.00
❑ 1164 [PS]	Norwegian Wood/Masquerade	1970	8.00
❑ 1209	For What It's Worth/Vira Mundo	1970	4.00
❑ 1226	Chelsea Morning/Where Are You Coming From	1970	4.00
❑ 1245	Lost in Paradise/Righteous Life	1971	4.00
❑ 1257	Aza Branca/Sometimes in Winter	1971	4.00
❑ 1279	Zanzibar/So Many People	1971	4.00
❑ 1313	After Midnight/Morro Velho	1971	4.00
❑ 1346	After Sunrise/The Grab	1972	4.00
❑ 2429	Summer Love/Life in the Movies	1982	4.00
❑ 2540	Never Gonna Let You Go/Carnival	1983	3.00
❑ 2563	Rainbow's End/Carnival	1983	3.00
❑ 2623	Olympia/Carnival	1984	3.00
❑ 2623 [PS]	Olympia/Carnival	1984	4.00
❑ 2639	Alibis/Confetti	1984	3.00
❑ 2662	Let's Give a Little More This Time/Confetti	1984	3.00
❑ 2672	Real Life/Confetti	1984	3.00
❑ 2706	Let's Give a Little More This Time/Confetti	1985	3.00
❑ 2859	Non-Stop/Flower of Bahia (Flor de Bahia)	1986	3.00
❑ 2875	Take This Love/Your Smile	1986	3.00
❑ 2917	What Do We Mean to Each Other/Flower of Bahia (Flor de Bahia)	1987	3.00

ATLANTIC

Number	Title (A Side/B Side)	Yr	NM
❑ 2472	I Say a Little Prayer/Comin' Home Baby	1968	6.00
❑ 2502	My Favorite Things/Tempo Feliz	1968	6.00
❑ 5056	All My Loving/The Telephone Song	1967	6.00
❑ 5076	The Great Arrival/Monday, Monday	1969	6.00

BELL

Number	Title (A Side/B Side)	Yr	NM
❑ 45335	Love Music/Walk the Way You Walk	1973	4.00
❑ 45372	Where Is the Love/Hey, Look at the Sun	1973	4.00
❑ 45410	Put a Little Love Away/They Look at the Sun	1973	5.00

ELEKTRA

Number	Title (A Side/B Side)	Yr	NM
❑ 45235	If I Ever Lose This Heaven/You Been Away Too Long	1975	4.00
❑ 45249	The Trouble With Hello Is Goodbye/Davy	1975	4.00
❑ 45283	Someday We'll All Be Free/Emerio	1975	4.00
❑ 45310	Sunny Day/Tell Me in a Whisper	1976	4.00
❑ 45360	Home Cooking/Real Thing	1976	4.00
❑ 45405	Love Me Tomorrow/Peninsula	1977	4.00
❑ 45416	The Real Thing/Peninsula	1977	4.00
❑ 45453	Love City/Peninsula	1978	4.00
❑ 45494	Midnight Lovers/Misturada	1978	4.00
❑ 45512	Waters of March/Misturada	1978	4.00
❑ 46064	Summer Dream/Lonely Woman	1979	4.00
❑ 46567	I'll Tell You/Lonely Woman	1979	4.00
❑ 46618	Let It Go/Magic Lady	1980	4.00

7-Inch Extended Plays

A&M

Number	Title (A Side/B Side)	Yr	NM
❑ SP 437	With a Little Help from My Friends/Roda/The Frog//The Look of Love/Batucuda/Look Around	1968	12.00
—Jukebox issue; small hole, plays at 33 1/3 rpm			
❑ SP 437 [PS]	Look Around	1968	12.00

Albums

A&M

Number	Title (A Side/B Side)	Yr	NM
❑ LP-116 [M]	Sergio Mendes and Brasil '66	1966	12.00
❑ LP-122 [M]	Equinox	1967	15.00
❑ SP-3108	Fool on the Hill	198?	8.00
—Budget-line reissue			
❑ SP-3258	Greatest Hits	198?	8.00
—Budget-line reissue			
❑ SP-3522 [(2)]	The Sergio Mendes Foursider	1973	15.00
❑ SP-4116 [S]	Sergio Mendes and Brasil '66	1966	15.00
❑ SP-4122 [S]	Equinox	1967	15.00
❑ SP-4137	Look Around	1968	15.00
❑ SP-4160	Fool on the Hill	1968	15.00
❑ SP-4197	Crystal Illusions	1969	15.00
❑ SP-4236	Ye-Me-Le	1969	15.00

Except when noted otherwise, VG = 25% of NM, and VG+ = 50% of NM. (Example: VG = $2.00, VG+ = $4.00 and NM = $8.00.)

Number	Title (A Side/B Side)	Yr	NM
❑ SP-4252	Greatest Hits	1970	15.00
❑ SP-4284	Stillness	1970	15.00
❑ SP-4315	Pais Tropical	1971	12.00
❑ SP-4353	Primal Roots	1972	12.00
❑ SP-4937	Sergio Mendes	1983	10.00
❑ SP-4984	Confetti	1984	10.00
❑ SP-5135	Sergio Mendes and Brasil '86	1986	10.00
❑ SP-5250	Arara	1989	12.00
❑ SP-6012 [(2)]	The Sergio Mendes Foursider	198?	10.00

—Budget-line reissue

ATLANTIC

Number	Title (A Side/B Side)	Yr	NM
❑ 1434 [M]	The Swinger from Rio	1965	15.00
❑ SD 1434 [S]	The Swinger from Rio	1965	20.00
❑ 1466 [M]	Great Arrival	1966	15.00
❑ SD 1466 [S]	Great Arrival	1966	20.00
❑ 1480 [M]	The Beat of Brazil	1967	20.00
❑ SD 1480 [S]	The Beat of Brazil	1967	15.00
❑ 8112 [M]	Sergio Mendes In Person at the El Matador	1967	20.00
❑ SD 8112 [S]	Sergio Mendes In Person at the El Matador	1967	15.00
❑ 8177 [M]	Sergio Mendes' Favorite Things	1968	40.00

—White label promo only

Number	Title (A Side/B Side)	Yr	NM
❑ SD 8177 [S]	Sergio Mendes' Favorite Things	1968	20.00

BELL

Number	Title (A Side/B Side)	Yr	NM
❑ 1119	Love Music	1973	10.00
❑ 1305	Vintage 74	1974	10.00

CAPITOL

Number	Title (A Side/B Side)	Yr	NM
❑ ST 2294 [S]	In a Brazilan Bag	1965	60.00
❑ T 2294 [M]	In a Brazilan Bag	1965	50.00

ELEKTRA

Number	Title (A Side/B Side)	Yr	NM
❑ 6E-134	Sergio Mendes and Brasil '88	1978	10.00
❑ 6E-214	Magic Lady	1980	10.00
❑ 7E-1027	Sergio Mendes	1975	10.00
❑ EQ-1027 [Q]	Sergio Mendes	1975	15.00
❑ 7E-1055	Homecooking	1976	10.00
❑ 7E-1102	Sergio Mendes and the New Brasil '77	1977	10.00

MOBILE FIDELITY

Number	Title (A Side/B Side)	Yr	NM
❑ 1-118	Sergio Mendes and Brasil '66	1984	50.00

—Audiophile vinyl

PHILIPS

Number	Title (A Side/B Side)	Yr	NM
❑ PHM 200263 [M]	Quiet Nights	1968	20.00
❑ PHS 600263 [S]	Quiet Nights	1968	15.00

PICKWICK

Number	Title (A Side/B Side)	Yr	NM
❑ SPC-3149	So Nice	1972	10.00

TOWER

Number	Title (A Side/B Side)	Yr	NM
❑ ST 5052 [S]	In a Brazilan Bag	1966	50.00

—Reissue of Capitol 2294

Number	Title (A Side/B Side)	Yr	NM
❑ T 5052 [M]	In a Brazilan Bag	1966	40.00

—Reissue of Capitol 2294

MEPHISTOPHELES

45s

REPRISE

Number	Title (A Side/B Side)	Yr	NM
❑ 0832	Cricket Song/Take a Jet	1969	12.00

Albums

REPRISE

Number	Title (A Side/B Side)	Yr	NM
❑ RS 6355	In Frustration I Hear Singing	1969	40.00

MERCED BLUE NOTES, THE

45s

ACCENT

Number	Title (A Side/B Side)	Yr	NM
❑ 1069	Rufus/Your Tender Lips	1961	40.00

GALAXY

Number	Title (A Side/B Side)	Yr	NM
❑ 738	Rufus Jr./Thumping	1965	30.00
❑ 744	Mama Rufus/Bad Bad Whiskey	1965	30.00

SOUL

Number	Title (A Side/B Side)	Yr	NM
❑ 35007	Do the Pig/Thumping	1965	350.00

TRI-PHI

Number	Title (A Side/B Side)	Yr	NM
❑ 1011	Midnight Sessions (Part 1)/ Midnight Sessions (Part 2)	1962	50.00
❑ 1023	Whole Lotta Nothin'/Fragile	1963	40.00

MERCER, JOHNNY

45s

CAPITOL

Number	Title (A Side/B Side)	Yr	NM
❑ 54-582	Baby It's Cold Outside/I Never Heard You Say	1949	30.00

—With Margaret Whiting

Number	Title (A Side/B Side)	Yr	NM
❑ F853	Jamboree Jones/Dixieland Band	1950	20.00
❑ F982	She's Shimmyun on the Beach Again/At the Jazzland Ball	1950	20.00
❑ F1261	Jingle Bells/Santa Claus Is Comin' to Town	1950	15.00
❑ F1285	Winter Wonderland/Goofus	1950	15.00
❑ F1618	One for My Baby/St. Louis Blues	1951	15.00

—Reissue of material first issued on 78

Number	Title (A Side/B Side)	Yr	NM
❑ F1641	Sugar Blues/Goofus	1951	15.00

—Reissue of material first issued on 78

Number	Title (A Side/B Side)	Yr	NM
❑ F2248	The Glow-Worm/New Ashmolean	1952	15.00
❑ F15512	Candy/Ac-Cent-Tchu-Ate the Positive	1950	15.00
❑ F15513	G.I. Jive/I Lost My Sugar in Salt Lake City	1950	15.00
❑ F15514	On the Atchison, Topeka and the Santa Fe/Strip Polka	1950	15.00

—The above three comprise CCF-214; all are reissues of hits that charted from 1942-45

Number	Title (A Side/B Side)	Yr	NM
❑ 54-90041	Jingle Bells/Santa Claus Is Coming to Town	1949	30.00

Albums

CAPITOL

Number	Title (A Side/B Side)	Yr	NM
❑ H 210 [10]	Music of Jerome Kern	1950	80.00
❑ H 214 [10]	Johnny Mercer Sings	1950	80.00
❑ T 907 [M]	Ac-Cent-Tchu-Ate the Positive	1957	50.00

JUPITER

Number	Title (A Side/B Side)	Yr	NM
❑ JLP-1001 [M]	Johnny Mercer Sings Just for Fun	1956	50.00

PAUSA

Number	Title (A Side/B Side)	Yr	NM
❑ PR 9062	Jonny Mercer Sings Jonny Mercer	1986	10.00

—Name is indeed misspelled on the label as "Jonny"

MERCER, WILL

45s

CONSTELLATION

Number	Title (A Side/B Side)	Yr	NM
❑ 109	Penny Candy/ Willowy Billowy Land	1963	15.00

SUN

Number	Title (A Side/B Side)	Yr	NM
❑ 329	You're Just My Kind/ Ballad of St. Mark's	1959	25.00

MERCHANTS OF DREAM, THE

45s

A&M

Number	Title (A Side/B Side)	Yr	NM
❑ 989	Sing Me Life/Dorothy the Fairy Queen	1968	10.00

Albums

A&M

Number	Title (A Side/B Side)	Yr	NM
❑ SP-4149	Strange Night Voyage	1969	25.00

MERCURY, ERIC

45s

AVCO EMBASSY

Number	Title (A Side/B Side)	Yr	NM
❑ 4516	Hurdy Gurdy Man/Enter My Love	1969	20.00
❑ 4523	Everybody Has the Right to Know/You Bring Me to My Knees	1969	20.00

ENTERPRISE

Number	Title (A Side/B Side)	Yr	NM
❑ 9041	I Can Smell That Funky Music/ Listen with Your Eyes	1971	15.00
❑ 9047	The Truth Will Set You Free/ What's Usual Seems Natural	1972	15.00
❑ 9080	Love Is Taking Over/Take a Walk Down My Street	1973	12.00
❑ 9089	Sweet Sara/Don't Lose Faith in Me Lord	1973	12.00

SACK

Number	Title (A Side/B Side)	Yr	NM
❑ 001	Lonely Girl/(B-side unknown)	196?	2500.

—VG 1000 ; VG+ 1750

MERCURY, FREDDIE Also see QUEEN.

12-Inch Singles

COLUMBIA

Number	Title (A Side/B Side)	Yr	NM
❑ AS 1928 [DJ]	Love Kills (same on both sides)	1984	10.00
❑ 05314	Living on My Own (Extended Version) (7" Version)	1985	8.00

45s

ANTHEM

Number	Title (A Side/B Side)	Yr	NM
❑ 104	I Can Hear Music/Going Back	1973	100.00

—As "Larry Lurex"; A-side matrix number on label is "A-0009-REMIX"

Number	Title (A Side/B Side)	Yr	NM
❑ 104	I Can Hear Music/Going Back	1973	150.00

—As "Larry Lurex"; A-side matrix number on label is "A-0009"

CAPITOL

Number	Title (A Side/B Side)	Yr	NM
❑ B-5696	The Great Pretender/Exercises in Free Love	1987	3.00
❑ B-5696 [PS]	The Great Pretender/Exercises in Free Love	1987	4.00

COLUMBIA

Number	Title (A Side/B Side)	Yr	NM
❑ 04606	Love Kills/Rotwang's Party (Robot Dance)	1984	4.00
❑ 04606 [PS]	Love Kills/Rotwang's Party (Robot Dance)	1984	4.00
❑ 04869	I Was Born to Love You/.Stop All the Fighting	1985	4.00
❑ 04869 [PS]	I Was Born to Love You/.Stop All the Fighting	1985	4.00
❑ 05455	Living on My Own/She Blows Hot and Cold	1985	4.00

Albums

COLUMBIA

Number	Title (A Side/B Side)	Yr	NM
❑ FC 40071	Mr. Bad Guy	1985	12.00

MERCY

45s

SUNDI

Number	Title (A Side/B Side)	Yr	NM
❑ 6811	Love (Can Make You Happy)/ Fire Ball	1969	8.00

WARNER BROS.

Number	Title (A Side/B Side)	Yr	NM
❑ 7291	Love Can Make You Happy/ Happy As Can Be, La La La	1969	15.00

—Pressed in U.S. for export only; A-side is a re-recording of the hit on Sundi

Number	Title (A Side/B Side)	Yr	NM
❑ 7297	Forever/The Morning's Come	1969	6.00
❑ 7331	Hello Baby/ Heard You Went Away	1969	6.00

Albums

SUNDI

Number	Title (A Side/B Side)	Yr	NM
❑ SRLP-803	The Mercy & Love (Can Make You Happy)	1969	20.00

—Has the original version of the title song plus filler instrumentals

WARNER BROS.

Number	Title (A Side/B Side)	Yr	NM
❑ WS 1799	Love (Can Make You Happy)	1969	15.00

—"Love (Can Make You Happy)" was re-recorded for this LP

MEREDITH, BUDDY

45s

NASHVILLE

Number	Title (A Side/B Side)	Yr	NM
❑ 5015	Time/Please Stay a Little While	196?	20.00
❑ 5042	I May Fall Again/Haunted House	1962	20.00

RICE

Number	Title (A Side/B Side)	Yr	NM
❑ 5003	Almost Out of My Mind/ Trapper Man	1964	12.00
❑ 5011	New Girl in Town/ Lonely in Person	196?	10.00
❑ 5014	Sugarland U.S.A./ We Let Love Go to Sleep	196?	10.00
❑ 5017	Big Riverboat Gambler/Just Call My Name	196?	10.00
❑ 5019	For the Love of Mike/Little Black Bug	196?	10.00
❑ 5021	I Pledge Allegiance/I'm Comin' Back in Style	196?	10.00
❑ 5026	Flop Top Beer/We Let Love Go to Sleep	196?	10.00

STARDAY

Number	Title (A Side/B Side)	Yr	NM
❑ 603	Secret Sin/I Miss You All Over	1963	15.00
❑ 617	The Heart Is No Plaything/ Here I Am Again	1963	15.00

Albums

STARDAY

Number	Title (A Side/B Side)	Yr	NM
❑ SLP-225 [M]	Sing Me a Heart Song	1963	30.00

MERKIN

Albums

WINDI

Number	Title (A Side/B Side)	Yr	NM
❑ 1004/5	Music from Merkin	1972	400.00

MERLIN, JACK

45s

CAMEO

Number	Title (A Side/B Side)	Yr	NM
❑ 311	My Debbie/Drip Drop Sha-La-La Blues	1964	15.00

DOT

Number	Title (A Side/B Side)	Yr	NM
❑ 16332	Girl of My Dreams/I Beat the Blues	1962	50.00

HICKORY

Number	Title (A Side/B Side)	Yr	NM
❑ 1296	One Song/Mechanical Man	1965	50.00
❑ 1322	Are You/Love Life of Crime	1965	25.00

MERMAIDS, THE See THE MURMAIDS.

MERRI-MEN, THE Another group containing former members of BILL HALEY AND HIS COMETS.

45s

APT

Number	Title (A Side/B Side)	Yr	NM
❑ 25051	Big Daddy/St, Louis Blues	1960	25.00

MERRIAM, CHUCK

45s

CAMEO

Number	Title (A Side/B Side)	Yr	NM
❑ 301	Broken Glass/Chuck's Monster	1964	12.00

MERRY ELVES, THE

45s

ARGUS

Number	Title (A Side/B Side)	Yr	NM
❑ 250	Rock & Roll Around the Christmas Tree/I Love Christmas	1964	10.00

M

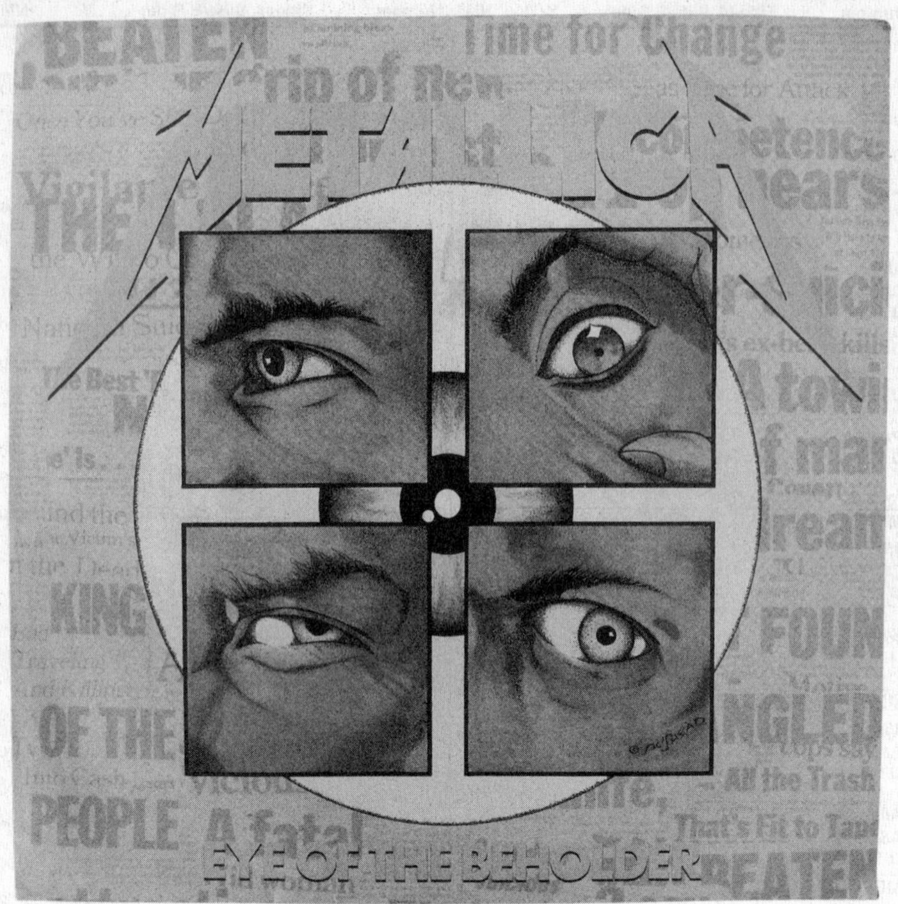

Metallica, "Eye of the Beholder," Elektra 69357, 1988, **$10**

MERRY-GO-ROUND, THE Also see EMMITT RHODES.

Number	Title (A Side/B Side)	Yr	NM
45s			
A&M			
❑ 834	Live/Time Will Show the Wiser	1967	10.00
❑ 857	Gonna Fight the World/We're in Love	1967	10.00
❑ 863	You're a Very Lovely Woman/ Where Have You Been All My Life	1967	10.00
❑ 886	Had to Run Around/She Laughed Loud	1967	10.00
❑ 920	Missing You/Listen, Listen	1968	10.00
❑ 957	Highway/'Til the Day After	1968	10.00
Albums			
A&M			
❑ LP-132 [M]	The Merry-Go-Round	1967	30.00
❑ SP-4132 [S]	The Merry-Go-Round	1967	20.00
RHINO			
❑ RNLP 126	The Best of the Merry-Go-Round	1985	10.00

MERRYWEATHER, NEIL

Number	Title (A Side/B Side)	Yr	NM
45s			
CAPITOL			
❑ 2537	Curiosity/Feeling of Freedom	1969	8.00
MERCURY			
❑ 73619	Hollywood Boulevard/High Altitude Hide and Seek	1974	5.00
Albums			
CAPITOL			
❑ SKAO-220	Merryweather	1969	15.00
❑ STBB-278 [(2)]	Word of Mouth	1969	20.00
KENT			
❑ KST-546	Neil Merryweather and the Boers	197?	15.00
MERCURY			
❑ SRM-1-1007	Space Rangers	1974	12.00
❑ SRM-1-1024	Kryptonite	1975	12.00

MERRYWEATHER AND CAREY

Number	Title (A Side/B Side)	Yr	NM
45s			
RCA VICTOR			
❑ 74-0429	Shop Around/If I Were You	1971	6.00
Albums			
RCA VICTOR			
❑ LSP-4442	Ivar Avenue Reunion	1970	15.00
❑ LSP-4485	Vacuum Cleaner	1971	15.00

MERSEY LADS, THE

Number	Title (A Side/B Side)	Yr	NM
45s			
MGM			
❑ 13481	Johnny No Love/What 'Cha Gonna Do Baby	1966	15.00

MERSEYBEATS, THE

Number	Title (A Side/B Side)	Yr	NM
45s			
FONTANA			
❑ 1513	It Would Take a Long Time/ Don't Let It Happen to Us	1965	15.00
❑ 1532	I Love You, Yes I Do/ See Me Back	1965	15.00
❑ 1882	Mr. Moonlight/I Think of You	1964	15.00
❑ 1905	Don't Turn Around/ Really Mystified	1964	15.00
❑ 1950	See Me Back/Last Night	1964	15.00
Albums			
ARC INTERNATIONAL			
❑ 834 [M]	England's Best Sellers	1964	40.00

MERSEYBOYS, THE

Number	Title (A Side/B Side)	Yr	NM
Albums			
VEE JAY			
❑ VJ-1101 [DJ]	The 15 Greatest Songs of the Beatles	1964	150.00
—White label, all-blue print; without typographical error on label: "Saluting Their Return To America"			
❑ VJ-1101 [DJ]	The 15 Greatest Songs of the Beatles	1964	150.00
—White label, blue and black print; with typographical error on label: "Saluting Their Return to Amercia"			
❑ VJ-1101 [M]	The 15 Greatest Songs of the Beatles	1964	100.00
—With typographical error on label "Saluting Their Return to Amercia"; this album is not known to exist in stereo			
❑ VJ-1101 [M]	The 15 Greatest Songs of the Beatles	1964	100.00
—Without typographical error on label "Saluting Their Return To America"; this album is not known to exist in stereo			

MERSEYS, THE

Number	Title (A Side/B Side)	Yr	NM
45s			
MERCURY			
❑ 72582	Sorrow/Some Other Day	1966	20.00

MESHEL, BILLY

Number	Title (A Side/B Side)	Yr	NM
45s			
OLD TOWN			
❑ 1181	My Little Angel/Tiger and the 71st Street Sharks	1965	12.00
PROBE			
❑ 459	I Say Hello When I'm Leaving/ (It Ain't Easy Being) Shirley Newman's Boyfriend	1969	10.00
❑ 462	Today Has Been Cancelled/ That's What Sends Him to the Bowery	1969	10.00
Albums			
PROBE			
❑ CPLP-4502	The Love Songs of A. Wilbur Meshel	1969	20.00

MESMERIZING EYE, THE

Number	Title (A Side/B Side)	Yr	NM
Albums			
SMASH			
❑ MGS-27090 [M]	Psychedelia — A Musical Light Show	1967	50.00
❑ SRS-67090 [S]	Psychedelia — A Musical Light Show	1967	60.00

MESSENGERS, THE (1) Milwaukee-based rock group.

Number	Title (A Side/B Side)	Yr	NM
45s			
RARE EARTH			
❑ 5032	That's the Way a Woman Is/I n the Jungle	1971	5.00
SOUL			
❑ 35037	Window Shopping/ California Soul	1967	30.00
U.S.A.			
❑ 866	Midnight Hour/Up 'Til Now	1967	12.00
—As "Michael and the Messengers"			
❑ 866	Midnight Hour/Hard Hard Year	1967	15.00
—As "The Messengers"			
❑ 874	Romeo and Juliet/Lies	1967	15.00
—As "Michael and the Messengers"			
Albums			
RARE EARTH			
❑ RS-509	The Messengers	1969	20.00

MESSENGERS, THE (2)

Number	Title (A Side/B Side)	Yr	NM
45s			
ERA			
❑ 3143	Let Me Be Your Man/You've Got Me Cryin'	1964	12.00

MESSENGERS, THE (3) British group.

Number	Title (A Side/B Side)	Yr	NM
45s			
MGM			
❑ 13293	I'm Stealin' Back/This Little Light of Mine	1964	12.00
❑ 13346	When Did You Leave Heaven/ More Pretty Girls Than One	1965	12.00

MESSENGERS, THE (4) Chicago group; after THE MESSENGERS (1) changed record labels, this group recorded as "Michael and the Messengers" on U.S.A.

Number	Title (A Side/B Side)	Yr	NM
45s			
U.S.A.			
❑ 889	Run and Hide/She Was the Girl	1967	8.00
—As "Michael and the Messengers"			
❑ 897	Gotta Take It Easy/ I Need Her Here	1968	8.00
—As "Michael and the Messengers"			

MESSINA, JIM Also see BUFFALO SPRINGFIELD; LOGGINS AND MESSINA; POCO.

Number	Title (A Side/B Side)	Yr	NM
45s			
AUDIO FIDELITY			
❑ 098	The Breeze and I/Straight Man	1964	30.00

Except when noted otherwise, VG = 25% of NM, and VG+ = 50% of NM. (Example: VG = $2.00, VG+ = $4.00 and NM = $8.00.)

Number	Title (A Side/B Side)	Yr	NM
COLUMBIA			
❑ 11094	New and Different Way/(Is This) Lovin' You Lady	1979	4.00
❑ 11182	Do You Want to Dance/Seeing You (For the First Time)	1980	4.00
FEATURE			
❑ 101	Panther Pounce/Tiger Tail	1964	30.00
ULTIMA			
❑ 705	Drag Bike Boogie/A-Rab	1964	30.00
VIV			
❑ 1000	Side Track/Sherrie	1965	25.00
WARNER BROS.			
❑ 29278	Big Tease/The Island	1984	4.00
❑ 29457	Forever My Love/One More Mile	1983	4.00
❑ 49784	Move Into Your Heart/Stay the Night	1981	4.00
—With Pauline Wilson			
❑ 49839	It's All Right Here/Move Into Your Heart	1981	4.00
Albums			
AUDIO FIDELITY			
❑ DFM-3037 [M]	The Dragsters	1964	80.00
❑ DFS-7037 [S]	The Dragsters	1964	100.00
COLUMBIA			
❑ JC 36141	Oasis	1979	10.00
THIMBLE			
❑ TLP-3	Jim Messina	197?	15.00
WARNER BROS.			
❑ BSK 3559	Messina	1981	10.00
❑ BSK 3559 [DJ]	Messina	1981	20.00
—Promo-only version on Quiex II vinyl			
❑ 23825	One More Mile	1983	10.00

METALLICA

Number	Title (A Side/B Side)	Yr	NM
45s			
ELEKTRA			
❑ 69329	One/The Prince	1988	7.00
❑ 69329 [PS]	One/The Prince	1988	12.00
❑ 69357	Eye of the Beholder/Breadfan	1988	10.00
❑ 69357 [PS]	Eye of the Beholder/Breadfan	1988	12.00
Albums			
ELEKTRA			
❑ 60396	Ride the Lightning	1984	20.00
❑ 60439	Master of Puppets	1986	20.00
❑ 60757 [EP]	Garage Days Re-Revisited	1987	50.00
❑ 60766	Kill 'Em All	1987	15.00
—Reissue of Megaforce 069 with two extra tracks			
❑ 60812 [(2)]	...And Justice for All	1988	25.00
❑ 61113 [(2)]	Metallica	1991	60.00
❑ 61923 [(2)]	Load	1996	20.00
❑ 62126 [(2)]	Re-Load	1997	30.00
❑ 62299 [(3)]	Garage Inc.	1998	25.00
❑ 62504 [(3)]	S&M	1999	20.00
❑ 62853 [(2)]	St. Anger	2003	30.00
MEGAFORCE			
❑ MRI 069	Kill 'Em All	1983	40.00
❑ MRI 069 [PD]	Kill 'Em All	1983	50.00
—Un-numbered version			
❑ MRI 069 [PD]	Kill 'Em All	1983	100.00
—Numbered limited edition version			
❑ MRI 769	Ride the Lightning	1984	40.00
RHINO			
❑ R1-76156 [(10)]	Vinyl Box Set	2004	200.00
—Limited edition of 5,000 numbered copies; includes their first four albums pressed on two records each, the "Garage Days Re-Revisited" EP and the picture disc "Creeping Death"			
WARNER BROS.			
❑ 343676	Kill 'Em All	2008	30.00
❑ 424572	Ride the Lightning	2008	16.00
❑ 470716 [(2)]	...And Justice for All	2008	20.00
❑ 470780 [(2)]	...And Justice for All	2008	50.00
❑ 470908	Master of Puppets	2008	30.00
❑ 508732 [(2)]	Death Magnetic	2008	20.00
❑ 511830 [(2)]	Metallica	2008	20.00
❑ 512119	Death Magnetic	2008	100.00
—Deluxe box			

METERS, THE

Also see AARON NEVILLE.

Number	Title (A Side/B Side)	Yr	NM
45s			
JOSIE			
❑ 1001	Sophisticated Cissy/Sehorn's Farm	1968	10.00
❑ 1005	Cissy Strut/Here Comes the Meter Man	1969	10.00
❑ 1008	Ease Back/Ann	1969	10.00
❑ 1013	Dry Spell/Look-Ka Py Py	1969	10.00
❑ 1015	Look-Ka Py Py/This Is My Last Affair	1970	10.00
❑ 1018	Chicken Strut/Hey! Last Minute	1970	10.00
❑ 1021	Hand Clapping Song/Joog	1970	10.00
❑ 1024	A Message from the Meters/Zony Mash	1970	10.00
❑ 1026	Stretch Your Rubber Band/Groovy Lady	1971	10.00
❑ 1029	(The World Is a Bit Under the Weather) Doodle-Oop/I Need More Time	1971	10.00
❑ 1031	Good Old Funky Music/Sassy Lady	1971	10.00
REPRISE			
❑ 1086	Do the Dirt/Smiling	1972	8.00
❑ 1106	Cabbage Alley/The Flower Song	1972	8.00
❑ 1135	Chug Chug Chug-A-Lug (Part 1)/Chug Chug Chug-A-Lug (Part 2)	1972	8.00
❑ 1307	Hey Pocky A-Way/Africa	1974	6.00
❑ 1314	People Say/Loving You Is On My Mind	1974	6.00
❑ 1338	Running Fast/They All Ask'd for You	1975	6.00
❑ 1357	Disco Is the Thing Today/Mister Moon	1976	6.00
❑ 1372	Trick Bag/Find Yourself	1976	6.00
WARNER BROS.			
❑ 8434	Be My Lady/No More Okey Doke	1977	5.00
Albums			
JOSIE			
❑ JOS-4010	The Meters	1969	80.00
❑ JOS-4011	Look-Ka Py Py	1970	80.00
❑ JOS-4012	Struttin'	1970	80.00
REPRISE			
❑ MS 2076	Cabbage Alley	1972	50.00
❑ MS 2200	Rejuvenation	1974	40.00
❑ MS 2228	Fire on the Bayou	1975	40.00
❑ MS 2252	Trick Bag	1976	40.00
ROUNDER			
❑ 2103	Look-Ka Py Py	1990	20.00
—Reissue of Josie 4011			
❑ 2104	Good Old Funky Music	1990	20.00
SUNDAZED			
❑ LP 5081	Kickback	2001	12.00
VIRGO			
❑ 12002	The Best of the Meters	1972	50.00
WARNER BROS.			
❑ BS 3042	New Directions	1977	30.00

METRONOMES, THE (1)

Number	Title (A Side/B Side)	Yr	NM
45s			
CADENCE			
❑ 1310	I Love My Girl/I'm Gonna Get Me a Girl Somehow	1957	100.00
❑ 1339	How Much I Love You/Dear Don	1957	120.00

METRONOMES, THE (2)

Number	Title (A Side/B Side)	Yr	NM
45s			
CHALLENGE			
❑ 9157	Hot Time/Tears, Tears, Tears	1962	15.00
MAUREEN			
❑ 1000	My Dearest Darling/The Chickie-Goo	1962	50.00

METRONOMES, THE (U)

Could be completely different groups.

Number	Title (A Side/B Side)	Yr	NM
Albums			
STRAND			
❑ SL-1057 [M]	The Fabulous Metronomes Sing the Standard Hits	1962	30.00
❑ SLS-1057 [S]	The Fabulous Metronomes Sing the Standard Hits	1962	40.00
WYNNE			
❑ 106 [M]	And Now... The Metronomes	1960	120.00

METROS, THE (1)

Number	Title (A Side/B Side)	Yr	NM
45s			
1-2-3			
❑ 1720	If You Can Feel/The Dampness from Your Kiss	1969	10.00
RCA VICTOR			
❑ 47-8994	Sweetest One/Time Changes Things	1966	30.00
❑ 47-9159	Since I Found My Baby/No Baby	1967	300.00
❑ 47-9331	Let's Groove/The Replacer	1967	60.00
Albums			
RCA VICTOR			
❑ LPM-3776 [M]	Sweetest One	1967	80.00
❑ LSP-3776 [S]	Sweetest One	1967	100.00

METROS, THE (2)

Number	Title (A Side/B Side)	Yr	NM
45s			
JUST			
❑ 1502	All of My Life/Lookin'	1959	400.00

METROS, THE (3)

Number	Title (A Side/B Side)	Yr	NM
45s			
MTM			
❑ B-72070	After the Passion's Gone/Don't Let Our Love Go (Baby)	1986	4.00
Albums			
MTM			
❑ ST-71054	The Metros	1986	12.00

METROTONES, THE

Number	Title (A Side/B Side)	Yr	NM
45s			
COLUMBIA			
❑ 40420	A-Ting-a-Ling/Tonight	1955	20.00
❑ 40486	Write Me Baby/Even Though	1955	20.00
RESERVE			
❑ 116	Please Come Back/Skitter Skatter	1957	250.00
7-Inch Extended Plays			
COLUMBIA			
❑ B-2026	(contents unknown)	1955	20.00
❑ B-2026 [PS]	Tops in Rock and Roll, Vol. 1	1955	20.00
❑ B-2027	Tweedlee Dee/Pledging My Love//Rock Love/Hearts of Stone	1955	20.00
❑ B-2027 [PS]	Tops in Rock and Roll, Vol. 2	1955	20.00
Albums			
COLUMBIA			
❑ CL 6341 [10]	Tops in Rock and Roll	1955	250.00

MFSB

Number	Title (A Side/B Side)	Yr	NM
45s			
PHILADELPHIA INT'L.			
❑ 3528	Family Affair/Layin' Low	1973	5.00
❑ 3540	TSOP (The Sound of Philadelphia)/Something for Nothing	1974	5.00
❑ 3547	Love Is the Message/My One and Only Love	1974	5.00
❑ 3567	Sexy/Human Machine	1975	5.00
❑ 3576	T.L.C. (Tender Lovin' Care)/Love Has No Time or Place	1975	5.00
❑ 3578	The Zip/My Mood	1975	5.00
❑ 3583	Smile Happy/When Your Love Is Gone	1976	5.00
❑ 3589	Philadelphia Freedom/South Philly	1976	5.00
❑ 3600	Summertime And I'm Feelin' Mellow/Hot Summer Nights	1976	5.00
❑ 3607	We Got the Time/(B-side unknown)	1976	5.00
❑ 3626	I'm On Your Side/Picnic in the Park	1977	5.00
❑ 3641	K-Jee/My Mood	1978	5.00
❑ 3650	Use Ta Be My Guy/Redwood Beach	1978	5.00
❑ 3663	Let's Party Down/To Be in Love	1978	5.00
❑ 3668	Dance with Me Tonight/Is It Something I Said	1979	5.00
TSOP			
❑ 02022	Mysteries of the World/Thank You Miss Scott	1981	4.00
❑ 4797	Manhattan Skyline/Metamorphosis	1980	4.00
Albums			
PHILADELPHIA INT'L.			
❑ KZ 32046	MFSB	1973	10.00
❑ KZ 32707	Love Is the Message	1974	10.00
❑ ZQ 32707 [Q]	Love Is the Message	1974	18.00
❑ PZ 33158	Universal Love	1975	10.00
❑ PZ 33845	Philadelphia Freedom	1975	10.00
❑ PZQ 33845 [Q]	Philadelphia Freedom	1975	18.00
❑ PZ 34238	Summertime	1976	10.00
❑ PZ 34658	The End of Phase One	1977	10.00
❑ JZ 35516	The Gamble-Huff Orchestra	1978	10.00
TSOP			
❑ JZ 36405	Mysteries of the World	1980	10.00

MIAMI SOUND MACHINE

Number	Title (A Side/B Side)	Yr	NM
12-Inch Singles			
AUDIOFON			
❑ AU-285	You've Broken My Heart/Live Again	1978	50.00
CBS INTERNATIONAL			
❑ DBS 10048	Dr. Beat (Long Version 6:26) (Instrumental 5:12)	1984	20.00

George Michael, "A Different Corner," Columbia 05888, 1986, **$3.**

Number	Title (A Side/B Side)	Yr	NM
ELECTRIC CAT			
❑ 1703	I Want You to Love Me/ Different Kind of Love	1978	120.00
EPIC			
❑ 49-05023	Dr. Beat (Long Version 6:26) (Instrumental 5:12)	1984	10.00
❑ 49-05127	I Need a Man (Album Version) (Instrumental)	1984	20.00
❑ 49-05253	Conga (Special Dance Mix 6:00) (Instrumental 4:52)	1985	10.00
❑ 49-05338	Bad Boy (Remix 6:11) (Dub Version 6:43)	1986	8.00
❑ 49-05966	Falling in Love (Uh-Oh) (6:07) (Dub Mix 5:18)	1986	8.00
❑ AED 6590 [DJ]	Jambala (The Main Mix 8:01) (Alt Mix) (Eutopia Mix 8:37) (Dub)	1994	12.00
❑ 49H-08147	Dr. Beat (Long Version 6:26)/I Need a Man (Album Version)	1988	15.00
—"Mixed Masters" reissue			
❑ 49-77707	Jambala (The Main Mix 8:01) (Eutopia Mix 8:37)/Love Is the Thing (Spike Boys Club Mix 9:03) (Spike Boys Dub Part 1 7:40)	1994	8.00
—"Love Is the Thing" by Donna Allen			

45s

Number	Title (A Side/B Side)	Yr	NM
AUDIOFON			
❑ AU-282	Live Again/(Instrumental)	1977	50.00
CBS INTERNATIONAL			
❑ DBS 10008	Regresa a Mi/Hombre Enamorado	1980	40.00
❑ DBS 10012	You're All I Have/Night Bring Me My Lover	1980	40.00
❑ DBS 10014	No Me Olvidaras (One Day)/ Asi Somos	1980	40.00
❑ DBS 10019	Baila Conmingo/Atiendeme	1981	25.00
❑ DBS 10029	Sola/Quedemos Como Amigos	1981	25.00
❑ DBS 10033 [DJ]	No Sera Facil (same on both sides)	1982	30.00
❑ DBS 10034	No Sera Facil/Dingui-li-Bangui	1982	25.00
❑ DBS 10038	No Mirare/Tu Sabes Quererme	1982	25.00
❑ DBS 10040	Yo Tambien Quiero Bailar/ Devuelveme el Amor	1982	25.00
❑ DBS 10044	Luchare/Dr. Beat	1984	20.00
❑ DBS 10049	Dr. Beat/Eyes of Innocence	1984	20.00
❑ DBS 10051	A Todo Maquine/Olivadate	1984	20.00
❑ DBS 10056	Comunicacion/Entregate	1985	20.00
❑ DBS 10070	Hablas De Mi/Conga	1985	20.00
❑ DBS 10080	Primitive Love/Words Get in the Way Spanish Version (No Me Vuelvo a Enamorar)	1986	20.00
❑ DBS 10120	Words Get in the Way/Spanish Version (No Me Vuelvo a Enamorar)	1986	20.00
ELECTRIC CAT			
❑ 1704	I Want You to Love Me/Different Kind of Love	1978	100.00
❑ 1717	You've Broken My Heart/Live Again	1978	100.00
EPIC			
❑ 34-04574	Dr. Beat/When Someone Comes Into Your Life	1984	10.00
❑ 34-04674	I Need a Man/Orange Express	1984	10.00
❑ 34-05457	Conga/Mucho Money	1985	3.00
❑ 34-05457 [PS]	Conga/Mucho Money	1985	4.00
❑ 34-05805	Bad Boy/Surrender Paradise	1986	3.00
❑ 34-05805 [PS]	Bad Boy/Surrender Paradise	1986	4.00
❑ 34-06120	Words Get In the Way/Movies	1986	3.00
—A picture sleeve is rumored to exist, but we've never seen one			
❑ 34-06352	Falling in Love (Uh-Oh)/ Primitive Love	1986	3.00
❑ 34-06352 [PS]	Falling in Love (Uh-Oh)/ Primitive Love	1986	4.00
❑ 15-69121	Conga/Bad Boy	1989	3.00
—Reissue			
❑ 15-69122	Words Get in the Way/Betcha Say That	1989	3.00
—Reissue; B-side as "Gloria Estefan and Miami Sound Machine"			

Albums

Number	Title (A Side/B Side)	Yr	NM
AUDIOFON			
❑ AUS 5426	Live Again — Renacer	1977	200.00
—The rest have a cover with a blue and yellow "tropical" background			
❑ AUS 5426	Live Again — Renacer	1977	300.00
—First 600 have a cover where the backdrop is clearly visible			
❑ AUS 5427	Miami Sound Machine	1978	200.00
—Spanish-language version			
CBS INTERNATIONAL			
❑ DML 10306	Imported	1980	50.00
—Reissue of 10455			
❑ DHL 10311	Miami Sound Machine	1980	100.00
—Different album than Electric Cat 226 and its later issues			
❑ DIL 10320	Otra Vez	1981	50.00
❑ DIL 10330	Rio	1982	50.00
❑ DSL 10335	7Up Presenta Los Hits de Miami Sound Machine	1983	150.00
—Only available in the Miami area from 7Up dealers			
❑ DIL 10349	A Toda Maquina	1984	40.00
—Spanish-language version of "Eyes of Innocence," their first all-English LP			
❑ DIL 10375	Primitive Love	1985	30.00
—Edition mostly distributed in Puerto Rico, with three Spanish-language tracks replacing three English tracks			
❑ DKL 10455	Imported	1979	100.00
—Reissue of MSM album			
ELECTRIC CAT			
❑ ECS 226	Miami Sound Machine	1978	200.00
—Mostly English-language version			
EPIC			
❑ BFE 39622	Eyes of Innocence	1984	15.00
—Original issue			
❑ PE 39622	Eyes of Innocence	1986	8.00
—Reissue with new prefix			
❑ BFE 40131	Primitive Love	1985	12.00
—The band's breakthrough LP to non-Hispanic audiences, and the last one not to have Gloria Estefan prominently credited; original issue			
❑ FE 40131	Primitive Love	1986	8.00
—Reissue with new prefix			
MSM			
❑ ERK 0714	Imported	1979	200.00
TOP HITS			
❑ TH-AM 2185	Live Again — Renacer	1982	80.00
—Reissue of Audiofon LP of the same name			
❑ TH-AM 2187	Miami Sound Machine	1982	100.00
—Reissue of Electric Cat LP of the same name			
❑ TH-AM 2228	Lo Mejor De Miami Sound Machine — A Portrait of the Originals	1983	50.00
—Compilation from first two Spanish-language LPs			

MICHAEL, GEORGE

12-Inch Singles

Number	Title (A Side/B Side)	Yr	NM
COLUMBIA			
❑ 44-06814	I Want Your Sex (Monogamy Mix 13:13: Rhythm 1 Lust, Rhythm 2 Brass in Love, Rhythm 3 A Last Request)/ Hard Day	1987	8.00
❑ 44-07466	Hard Day (Special Remix)/ Hard Day (Edit)/I Want Your Sex (Monogamy Mix)	1987	8.00
❑ 44-07478	Faith (Single Version) (Instrumental)/Hand to Mouth	1987	8.00
❑ 44-07547	Father Figure//Love's In Need of Love Today (Live)/Father Figure (Instrumental)	1987	10.00
❑ 44-07849	Monkey (3 versions)	1988	8.00
❑ 44-07898	Kissing a Fool (Vocal) (Instrumental)/A Last Request	1988	12.00
❑ 44-73584	Freedom (2 mixes)/Fantasy	1990	10.00
❑ 44-74352	Too Funky (Extended Version 5:37) (Digital Mix 6:25)/Too Jazzy (Happy Mix 5:53)/ Crazyman Dance Mix (5:52)	1992	10.00
DREAMWORKS			
❑ PRO-A-4894 [DJ]	Fastlove (Extended Version 9:27) (Full Version 5:24) (A/C Summer Mix)/ I'm Your Man '96	1996	15.00
❑ PRO-A-5001 [DJ]	Spinning the Wheel (Forthright Club Mix) (Dub Mix) (Forthright Edit Mix) (Jon Douglas Remix)	1996	15.00
❑ PRO-A-5021 [DJ]	Star People (Forthright Club Mix 9:16) (Club Dub Mix 7:15) (Forthright Dub Mix 7:27) (Galaxy Mix 8:08)	1997	12.00
❑ 58003	Star People (Galaxy Mix 8:08) (Forthright Club Mix 9:16) (MTV Unplugged Edit 4:31) (Forthright Dub Mix 7:27) (Club Dub Mix 7:15)/The Strangest Thing (Live) (6:01)	1997	10.00

Except when noted otherwise, VG = 25% of NM, and VG+ = 50% of NM. (Example: VG = $2.00, VG+ = $4.00 and NM = $8.00.)

Number | Title (A Side/B Side) | Yr | NM

EPIC
❑ EAS 41703 [DJ] Outside (4 versions) 1998 25.00

HOLLYWOOD
❑ ED 10327 [DJ] Killer/Papa Was a Rollin' Stone (12" Pop Mix) (12" House Mix) (12" Deep House Dub Mix) 1993 20.00
❑ ED 10329 [DJ] Killer/Papa Was a Rollin' Stone (NYC Club Mix) (Very Vocal Club Mix) (Killer Papa Dub) (Killer Techno) (X-Tended Mix) 1993 20.00
❑ HR 66289 Killer/Papa Was a Rollin' Stone (2 versions) 1993 10.00

45s

COLUMBIA
❑ 38-05888 A Different Corner/(Instrumental) 1986 3.00
❑ 38-05888 [PS] A Different Corner/(Instrumental) 1986 3.00
❑ 38-07164 I Want Your Sex (Rhythm 1 Lust)/(Rhythm 2 Brass in Love) 1987 3.00
❑ 38-07164 [PS] I Want Your Sex (Rhythm 1 Lust)/(Rhythm 2 Brass in Love) 1987 3.00
❑ 38-07623 Faith/Hand to Mouth 1987 3.00
❑ 38-07623 [PS] Faith/Hand to Mouth 1987 3.00
❑ 38-07682 Father Figure/(Instrumental) 1988 3.00
❑ 38-07682 [PS] Father Figure/(Instrumental) 1988 3.00
❑ 38-07773 One More Try/Look At Your Hands 1988 3.00
❑ 38-07773 [PS] One More Try/Look At Your Hands 1988 3.00
❑ 38-07941 Monkey/(Instrumental) 1988 3.00
❑ 38-07941 [PS] Monkey/(Instrumental) 1988 3.00
❑ 38-08050 Kissing a Fool/(Instrumental) 1988 3.00
❑ 38-08050 [PS] Kissing a Fool/Kissing a Fool (instrumental) 1988 3.00
❑ 38-68704 A Different Corner/(Instrumental) 1989 3.00
—Reissue
❑ 38-73512 Praying for Time/If You Were My Woman 1990 3.00
❑ 38-73559 Freedom/Fantasy 1990 3.00
❑ 38-73663 Waiting for That Day-You Can't Always Get What You Want/Mothers Pride 1991 3.00
❑ 38-73799 Soul Free/Cowboys and Angels 1991 —
—Canceled on 45
❑ 38-74086 Don't Let the Sun Go Down on Me/I Believe (When I Fall in Love It Will Be Forever) 1991 4.00
—A-side guest vocalist: Elton John
❑ 38-74114 Faith/Hand to Mouth 1991 3.00
—Reissue
❑ 38-74115 One More Try/Look At Your Hands 1991 3.00
—Reissue
❑ 38-74353 Too Funky/Crazyman Dance 1992 3.00

DREAMWORKS SKG
❑ 59000 Jesus to a Child/One More Try (Live Gospel Version) 1996 4.00
❑ 59001 Fastlove/I'm Your Man '96 1996 5.00

Albums

COLUMBIA
❑ OC 40867 Faith 1987 10.00
❑ C 46898 Listen Without Prejudice (Vol. 1) 1990 12.00

MICHAEL, GEORGE, AS GENE EARLHART

This George Michael was a disc jockey at WFIL in Philadelphia when this record was made.

45s

WFIL
❑ DM 84514 Between the Periods — The Fantastic Philadelphia Flyers (same on both sides) 1974 20.00

MICHAEL AND THE MESSENGERS

See THE MESSENGERS (1); THE MESSENGERS (4).

MICHAELS, DICK

45s

EXPLOSIVE
❑ 101/102 Coffee Date/Teen Age Blues 1961 60.00

MICHAELS, JERRI

45s

CAMEO
❑ 414 Give It All to Me/Like a Madness 1966 60.00

MICHAELS, LEE

45s

A&M
❑ 911 Sounding the Sleep/Love 1968 6.00
❑ 912 Tomorrow/Sounding the Sleep 1968 6.00
❑ 942 If I Lose You/My Friends 1968 6.00
❑ 1048 Goodbye, Goodbye/The War 1969 5.00
❑ 1095 Heighty Ho/Want My Baby 1969 5.00
❑ 1219 Ummmm My Lady/What Now America 1970 5.00
❑ 1262 Do You Know What I Mean/Keep the Circle Turning 1971 5.00
❑ 1262 [PS] Do You Know What I Mean/Keep the Circle Turning 1971 10.00
❑ 1303 Can I Get a Witness/You Are What You Do 1971 4.00
❑ 1303 [PS] Can I Get a Witness/You Are What You Do 1971 10.00
❑ 1326 Hold On to Freedom/Own Special Way 1972 4.00
❑ 1448 Rock Me Baby/Heighty Ho 1973 4.00

COLUMBIA
❑ 45874 Same Old Song/Rock and Roll Community 1973 5.00

Albums

A&M
❑ SP-3158 Lee Michaels 198? 8.00
—Budget-line reissue
❑ SP-3518 Live 1973 15.00
❑ SP-4140 Carnival of Life 1968 40.00
❑ SP-4152 Recital 1968 20.00
❑ SP-4199 Lee Michaels 1969 15.00
❑ SP-4249 Barrel 1970 15.00
❑ SP-4302 5th 1971 15.00
❑ SP-4336 Space and First Takes 1972 15.00

COLUMBIA
❑ CQ 32275 [Q] Nice Day for Something 1973 20.00
❑ KC 32275 Nice Day for Something 1973 12.00
❑ KC 32846 Tailface 1974 12.00

MICHAELS, MARILYN

45s

RCA VICTOR
❑ 47-7771 Tell Tommy I Miss Him/Everyone Was There But You 1960 20.00
❑ 47-7831 Past the Age of Innocence/Danny 1961 15.00

MICHAELS, TONY

45s

GOLDEN WORLD
❑ 41 I Love the Life I Live/Picture Me and You 1966 300.00

MICKEY AND KITTY

MICKEY BAKER (ex-MICKEY AND SYLVIA) and Kitty Noble.

45s

ATLANTIC
❑ 2024 Ooh-Sha-Lala/The Kid Brother 1959 15.00
❑ 2036 First Love/St. Louis Blues 1959 15.00
❑ 2046 My Reverie/Buttercup 1959 15.00

MICKEY AND SYLVIA

Also see MICKEY BAKER; SYLVIA (1).

45s

ALL PLATINUM
❑ 2307 Lovedrops/Because You Do It to Me 1969 6.00
❑ 2310 Anytime/Souling with Mickey and Sylvia 1969 6.00

CAT
❑ 102 Fine Love/Speedy Life 1954 40.00
—As "Little" Sylvia Vanderpool and Mickey Baker

GROOVE
❑ 0164 No Good Lover/Walkin' in the Rain 1956 30.00
❑ 0175 Love Is Strange/I'm Going Home 1956 30.00

KING
❑ 5737 Baby, Let's Dance/Oh Yea, Ah Ah 1963 12.00
❑ 6006 Love Is Strange/Darling 1965 10.00

RAINBOW
❑ 316 I'm So Glad/Se De Boom Run Dun 1955 30.00
❑ 318 Forever and a Day/Ride, Sally, Ride 1955 30.00

RCA
❑ 5224-7-RX Love Is Strange/(I've Had) The Time of My Life 1987 3.00
—B-side by Bill Medley and Jennifer Warnes

RCA VICTOR
❑ 37-7877 Love Is the Only Thing/Love Lesson 1961 50.00
—"Compact Single 33" (small hole, plays at LP speed)
❑ 47-7403 To the Valley/Oh Yeah! Uh-Huh 1958 20.00
❑ 47-7774 [M] Sweeter As the Days Go By/Mommy Out De Light 1960 15.00
❑ 47-7811 [M] What Would I Do/This Is My Story 1960 20.00
❑ 47-7877 Love Is the Only Thing/Love Lesson 1961 15.00
❑ 47-8517 Let's Shake Some More/Gypsy 1965 12.00
❑ 47-8582 Fallin' in Love/From the Beginning of Time 1965 12.00
❑ 61-7774 [S] Sweeter As the Days Go By/Mommy Out De Light 1960 40.00
—"Living Stereo" (large hole, plays at 45 rpm)
❑ 61-7811 [S] What Would I Do/This Is My Story 1960 40.00
—"Living Stereo" (large hole, plays at 45 rpm)
❑ APAO-0080 Love Is Strange/Dearest 1973 6.00

STANG
❑ 5004 Rocky Raccoon/Souling with Mickey and Sylvia 1969 8.00
❑ 5047 Baby You're So Fine/Anytime You Want To 1973 6.00

VIK
❑ 0252 Love Is Strange/I'm Going Home 1957 30.00
❑ 0267 There Oughta Be a Law/Dearest 1957 25.00
❑ 0280 Two Shadows on Your Window/Love Will Make You Fail in School 1957 25.00
❑ 0290 Love Is a Treasure/Let's Have a Picnic 1957 25.00
❑ 0297 There'll Be No Backin' Out/Where Is My Honey 1957 25.00
❑ 0324 Rock and Stroll Room/Bewildered 1958 20.00
❑ 0334 It's You I Love/True, True Love 1958 20.00

WILLOW
❑ 23000 Baby, You're So Fine/Lovedrops 1961 15.00
❑ 23002 Darling (I Miss You So)/I'm Guilty 1961 15.00
❑ 23004 Since I Fell for You/He Gave Me Everything 1962 15.00
❑ 23006 Love Is Strange/Walking in the Rain 1962 15.00

7-Inch Extended Plays

GROOVE
❑ EGA-18 Love Is Strange/I'm Going Home//Walkin' in the Rain/No Good Lover 1957 150.00
❑ EGA-18 [PS] Love Is Strange 1957 150.00

VIK
❑ 262 *There Oughta Be a Law/I'm So Glad/Dearest/Se De Boom Run Dun 1957 80.00
❑ 262 [PS] Love Is Strange 1957 80.00

Albums

RCA CAMDEN
❑ CAL-863 [M] Love Is Strange 1965 50.00
❑ CAS-863(e) [R] Love Is Strange 1965 30.00

RCA VICTOR
❑ APM1-0327 Do It Again 1973 12.00

VIK
❑ LX-1102 [M] New Sounds 1957 400.00

MIDDLE OF THE ROAD

45s

RCA VICTOR
❑ 74-0407 Chirpy Chirpy Cheep Cheep/Rainin' 'N Painin' 1970 5.00
❑ 74-0539 Tweedle Dee, Tweedle Dum/Give It Time 1971 4.00
❑ 74-0612 Soley Soley/To Remind Me 1971 4.00
❑ 74-0732 On This Land/Talk of All the U.S.A. 1972 4.00

Albums

RCA VICTOR
❑ LSP-4674 Acceleration 1972 12.00

MIDDLEBROOKS, HARRY

45s

CAPITOL
❑ 2079 Funny How Time Slips Away/You're the Reason I'm Living 1968 8.00

Albums

AVI
❑ AV-6033 Give It Time 197? 12.00

CAPITOL
❑ ST-2850 [S] Funny How Time Slips Away 1968 12.00
❑ T 2850 [M] Funny How Time Slips Away 1968 25.00

M

MIDDLETON, TONY
Also see THE WILLOWS.

45s

Number	Title (A Side/B Side)	Yr	NM
A&M			
❑ 1084	Angela/Keep On Dancing	1969	30.00
❑ 1124	Harlem Lady/Sound of Goodbye	1969	15.00
ABC-PARAMOUNT			
❑ 10695	You Spoiled My Reputation /If I Could Write a Song	1965	200.00
ALFA			
❑ 113	My Home Town/Please Take Me	1962	30.00
ALTO			
❑ 2001	Untouchable/I Need You	1960	12.00
BIG TOP			
❑ 3037	Unchained Melody/ Sweet Baby of Mine	1960	30.00
EL DORADO			
❑ 508	First Taste of Love/ Only My Heart	1957	30.00
GONE			
❑ 5015	Let's Fall in Love/Say Yeah	1957	60.00
MALA			
❑ 544	Out of This World/My Baby Likes to Boogaloo	1966	500.00
MGM			
❑ 13493	Don't Ever Leave Me/To the Ends of the Earth	1966	400.00
MR. G			
❑ 811	Let Me Down Easy (Part 1)/ Let Me Down Easy (Part 2)	1968	12.00
❑ 815	Good Morning World/ (B-side unknown)	1968	12.00
PALA			
❑ 45-006	Untouchable/I Need You	1960	20.00
PHILIPS			
❑ 40151	I Need You Tonight/ Send Me Away	1963	30.00
❑ 40184	Too Hot to Handle/I Just Couldn't Help Myself	1964	12.00
ROULETTE			
❑ 4345	Is It This or Is It That/I'm Gonna Try Love One More Time	1961	25.00
ROYAL FLUSH			
❑ 102	Lady Fingers/A Garden in the Ghetto	1976	6.00
SAXONY			
❑ 104	I'm On My Way/ (B-side unknown)	1958	50.00
SCEPTER			
❑ 12290	Border Song (Holy Moses)/ Silliest People	1970	10.00
TOY			
❑ 3803	Rock and Roll Lullaby/ Sittin' in the Sunshine	1972	8.00
TRIUMPH			
❑ 600	Count Your Blessings (See What Love Has Done)/ I Just Want Somebody	1959	25.00
❑ 605	The Universe/Blackjack	1959	25.00
UNITED ARTISTS			
❑ 410	Drifting/Memories Are Made of This	1962	40.00

MIDLER, BETTE

12-Inch Singles

Number	Title (A Side/B Side)	Yr	NM
ATLANTIC			
❑ DSKO 67 [DJ]	Strangers in the Night (same on both sides)	1976	20.00
❑ DSKO 187 [DJ]	Married Men (Long 7:58) (Short 5:32)	1979	10.00
❑ DSKO 201 [DJ]	Hang On In There Baby (5:36)/ My Knight in Black Leather (6:57)	1979	15.00
❑ DSKO 218 [DJ]	Big Noise from Winnetka (6:56) (same on both sides)	1979	15.00
❑ PR 548 [DJ]	Favorite Waste of Time (4:35)/ Only in Miami (2:43)	1983	10.00
❑ PR 578 [DJ]	Beast of Burden (same on both sides)	1983	12.00
❑ DMD 1655 [DJ]	Moonlight Dancing (Club Mix 7:07) (Enigmatic Dub with Acapella Intro 5:26) (Extacy Dub 6:26)	1990	8.00
❑ DMD 2259 [DJ]	To Deserve You (MK Club Mix) (MK Dub 1) (MK Dub 2) (Arif's Club Mix) (Bonzai's Club Mix)	1995	12.00
❑ PR 2547 [DJ]	Under the Boardwalk (Edit) (same on both sides)	1988	8.00
❑ DK 4800	Married Men (7:58)/Bang You're Dead (3:10)	1979	12.00
❑ 86027	Moonlight Dancing (Club Mix 7:07) (Enigmatic Dub with Acapella Intro 5:26) (Exstacy Dub 6:26)	1990	12.00
WARNER BROS.			
❑ PRO-A-9587 [DJ]	I'm Beautiful (Victor Calderone Main Vocal Mix 7:59) (Victor Calderone Dub 7:59) (Victor Calderone Drum Dub 4:30)	1999	12.00
❑ PRO-A-9591 [DJ]	I'm Beautiful (Danny Tenaglia Continental Club Mix 8:24) (Brinsley Evans Back to the Scene of the Crime Extended Mix 6:20) (Danny's D-Tour Dub 9:33) (Lil' D-Tour Groove 4:16)	1999	15.00
❑ 42360 [(2)]	In These Shoes (Sound Factory Vox Mix 9:07) (Other Side Mix 7:57) (Sound Factory Dub Mix 8:50) (Mark's Heels to Platforms Vocal Mix 8:35) (Radio Mix 4:10) (Extended Radio Mix 7:17) (Mark's Sole Dub 8:23)	2000	12.00
❑ 44586 [(2)]	I'm Beautiful (Danny Tenaglia Continental Club Mix 8:24) (Brinsley Evans Back to the Scene of the Crime Mix 4:20) (Victor Calderone Main Vocal Mix 7:59) (Album Version 3:55) (Danny's D-Tour Dub 9:33) (Lil' D-Tour Groove 4:16) (Victor Calderone Dub 7:59) (Victor Calderone Drum Dub 4:30)	1999	15.00
❑ PRO-A-100533-A [(2)DJ]	In These Shoes (Extended Radio Mix 7:23) (Sound Factory Vox Mix 9:08) (Other Side Mix 7:58) (Radio Mix 4:11) (Sound Factory Dub Mix 8:52)	2000	12.00
❑ PRO-A-100536 [DJ]	In These Shoes (Mark's Heels to Platforms Vocal Mix 8:35) (Mark's Sole Dub 8:23)	2000	10.00

45s

Number	Title (A Side/B Side)	Yr	NM
ATLANTIC			
❑ 2928	Do You Want to Dance/ Superstar	1972	5.00
❑ 2964	Boogie Woogie Bugle Boy/ Delta Dawn	1973	5.00
❑ 2980	Friends/Chapel of Love	1973	6.00
❑ 2980 [DJ]	Chapel of Love (stereo/mono)	1973	10.00
❑ 3004	In the Mood/Drinking Again	1974	6.00
❑ 3319	Stranger in the Night/ Samedi Et Vendredi	1976	6.00
❑ 3325	Old Cape Cod/Tragedy	1976	6.00
❑ 3379	You're Movin' Out Today/Let Me Just Follow Behind	1976	5.00
❑ 3431	Storybook Children (Daybreak)/Empty Bed Blues	1977	5.00
❑ 3475	Paradise/Red	1978	6.00
❑ 3582	Married Men/Bang, You're Dead	1979	5.00
❑ 3616	Hang On In There Baby/ Cradle Days	1979	6.00
❑ 3628	Big Noise from Winnetka/Rain	1979	6.00
❑ 3643	When a Man Loves a Woman/ Love Me with a Feeling	1980	4.00
❑ 3656	The Rose/Stay with Me	1980	4.00
❑ 3656 [PS]	The Rose/Stay with Me	1980	6.00
❑ 3771	My Mother's Eyes/Chapel of Love	1980	5.00
❑ 7-87572	Every Road Leads Back to You/ I Remember You-Dixie's Dream	1991	4.00
❑ 7-87820	From a Distance/One More Round	1990	4.00
❑ 7-87825	Night and Day/The Girl Is On to You	1990	4.00
❑ 7-88972	Wind Beneath My Wings/ Oh Industry	1989	3.00
❑ 7-88972 [PS]	Wind Beneath My Wings/ Oh Industry	1989	6.00
❑ 7-88976	Under the Boardwalk/ The Friendship Theme	1989	3.00
❑ 7-88976	Under the Boardwalk/ Otto Titsling	1989	5.00
❑ 7-88976 [PS]	Under the Boardwalk/ The Friendship Theme	1989	4.00
❑ 7-89712	Beast of Burden/ Come Back Jimmy Dean	1984	5.00
❑ 7-89761	Favorite Waste of Time/ My Eye on You	1983	5.00
❑ 7-89789	All I Need to Know/ My Eye on You	1983	5.00
❑ 7-89789 [DJ]	All I Need to Know (2:59)/(4:08)	1983	8.00
❑ 7-89789 [PS]	All I Need to Know/ My Eye on You	1983	6.00
ATLANTIC OLDIES SERIES			
❑ OS-13155	Boogie Woogie Bugle Boy/ Do You Want to Dance?	197?	4.00
—Gold label with "Oldies Series" at 3 o'clock			
❑ OS-13169	Friends/In the Mood	197?	4.00
—Gold label; "Oldies Series" at 3 o'clock			
❑ OS-13198	Old Cape Cod/Strangers in the Night	197?	4.00
❑ OS-13222	The Rose/When a Man Loves a Woman	198?	3.00
—Reissue			
❑ 7-84896	Wind Beneath My Wings/Under the Boardwalk	199?	3.00
—Reissue			

7-Inch Extended Plays

Number	Title (A Side/B Side)	Yr	NM
ATLANTIC			
❑ SD 7-7270	(contents unknown)	1973	15.00
—Jukebox issue; small hole, plays at 33 1/3 rpm			
❑ SD 7-7270 [PS]	Bette Midler	1973	15.00

Albums

Number	Title (A Side/B Side)	Yr	NM
ATLANTIC			
❑ PR 275 [DJ]	Live! At Last Specially Edited for Air Play	1977	15.00
—Promo-only 14-track sampler			
❑ 7238 [M]	The Divine Miss M	1972	30.00
—Mono is promo only; white label, "dj copy monaural" sticker on stereo cover			
❑ QD 7238 [Q]	The Divine Miss M	1973	20.00
❑ SD 7238 [S]	The Divine Miss M	1972	10.00
—"1841 Broadway" address on label			
❑ SD 7270	Bette Midler	1973	12.00
—"1841 Broadway" address on label; with poster			
❑ SD 2-9000 [(2)]	Live! At Last	1977	12.00
❑ SD 16004	Thighs and Whispers	1979	10.00
❑ SD 16010	The Rose	1979	10.00
❑ SD 16022	Divine Madness	1980	10.00
❑ SD 18155	Songs for the New Depression	1976	10.00
❑ SD 19151	Broken Blossom	1977	10.00
❑ 80070	No Frills	1983	10.00
❑ 81291	Mud Will Be Flung Tonight!	1985	10.00
❑ 81933	Beaches	1988	10.00
❑ 82129	Some People's Lives	1990	12.00
❑ SW-95507	Bette Midler	1973	20.00
—Longines Record Club edition			
❑ R 163898	Mud Will Be Flung Tonight!	1985	12.00
—RCA Music Service edition			

MIDNIGHT ANGELS, THE

45s

Number	Title (A Side/B Side)	Yr	NM
APEX			
❑ 77073	I'm Sufferin'/In the Moonlight	1967	30.00
❑ 77073 [PS]	I'm Sufferin'/In the Moonlight	1967	40.00

MIDNIGHT OIL

12-Inch Singles

Number	Title (A Side/B Side)	Yr	NM
COLUMBIA			
❑ AS 1746 [DJ]	The Power and the Passion/ Read About It/U.S. Forces	1982	8.00
❑ CAS 2020 [DJ]	Blue Sky Mine (Food On Table Mix) (same on both sides)	1990	8.00
❑ CAS 2107 [DJ]	Best of Both Worlds (same on both sides)	1984	12.00
❑ CAS 2911 [DJ]	Beds Are Burning (same on both sides)	1987	12.00
❑ 04238	The Power and the Passion/ Glitch Baby Glitch	1983	10.00
❑ 04976	The Power and the Passion/ Giltch Baby/Wedding Cake	1983	8.00

45s

Number	Title (A Side/B Side)	Yr	NM
COLUMBIA			
❑ 04349	The Power and the Passion/Tin Legs and Tin Mines	1984	3.00
❑ 04349 [PS]	The Power and the Passion/Tin Legs and Tin Mines	1984	3.00
❑ 04349 [PS]	The Power and the Passion	1984	5.00
—"Demonstration -- Not for Sale" on rear			
❑ 04470	Read About It/Outside World	1984	3.00
❑ 07433	Beds Are Burning/Bullroarer	1987	3.00
—With copyright notice "1987 CBS Records Pty. Ltd."			
❑ 07433	Beds Are Burning/Bullroarer	1987	4.00
—With copyright notice "1987 Midnight Oil"			
❑ 07964	The Dead Heart/Kosciusko	1988	3.00
❑ 07964 [PS]	The Dead Heart/Kosciusko	1988	3.00
❑ 08093	Dreamworld/Progress	1988	3.00
❑ 08093 [PS]	Dreamworld/Progress	1988	3.00
❑ 73250	Blue Sky Mine/ Wedding Cake Island	1990	—
—Cassette only			
❑ 73336	Forgotten Years/You May Not Be Released	1990	—
—Cassette only			

M

Except when noted otherwise, VG = 25% of NM, and VG+ = 50% of NM. (Example: VG = $2.00, VG+ = $4.00 and NM = $8.00.)

Number	Title (A Side/B Side)	Yr	NM
❑ 74933	Truganini/Drums of Heaven	1993	3.00
❑ 77090	Outbreak of Love/ Ships of Freedom	1993	3.00

Albums

COLUMBIA

Number	Title (A Side/B Side)	Yr	NM
❑ BFC 38996	10,9,8,7,6,5,4,3,2,1	1983	12.00
❑ BFC 39987	Red Sails in the Sunset	1984	12.00
❑ BFC 40967	Diesel and Dust	1987	12.00
❑ FC 40967	Diesel and Dust	1988	10.00
—Reissue; "02" added to rear-cover bar code			
❑ C 45398	Blue Sky Mining	1990	12.00
—All copies on blue vinyl			

MIDNIGHT STRING QUARTET

45s

VIVA

Number	Title (A Side/B Side)	Yr	NM
❑ 606	You Don't Have to Say You Love Me/The Lonely Bull	1966	6.00
❑ 616	Prophesy of Love/I Hear a Smyphony	1967	6.00
❑ 622	The Little Drummer Boy/Silent Night	1967	6.00
❑ 628	Midnight Memories/Classical Gas	1968	6.00

Albums

VIVA

Number	Title (A Side/B Side)	Yr	NM
❑ 2571 [(2)]	Best of the Midnight String Quartet	1971	12.00
❑ V-6001 [M]	Rhapsodies for Young Lovers	1966	12.00
❑ VS-6001 [S]	Rhapsodies for Young Lovers	1966	10.00
❑ V-6004 [M]	Spanish Rhapsodies for Young Lovers	1967	12.00
❑ V-6008 [M]	Rhapsodies for Young Lovers, Vol. Two	1967	12.00
❑ V-6010 [M]	Christmas Rhapsodies for Young Lovers	1967	15.00
❑ V-6013 [M]	Love Rhapsodies	1968	15.00
❑ V-36004 [S]	Spanish Rhapsodies for Young Lovers	1967	10.00
❑ V-36008 [S]	Rhapsodies for Young Lovers, Vol. Two	1967	10.00
❑ V-36010 [S]	Christmas Rhapsodies for Young Lovers	1967	10.00
❑ V-36013 [S]	Love Rhapsodies	1968	10.00
❑ V-36015	The Look of Love and Other Rhapsodies for Young Lovers	1968	10.00
❑ V-36019	Goodnight My Love and Other Rhapsodies for Young Lovers	1969	10.00
❑ V-36022	Rhapsodies for Young Lovers, Vol. Three	1969	10.00
❑ V-36024	Chamber Music for Young Lovers	1969	10.00

MIDNIGHTERS, THE

Also see HANK BALLARD AND THE MIDNIGHTERS; THE ROYALS (1).

45s

FEDERAL

Number	Title (A Side/B Side)	Yr	NM
❑ 12169	Work With Me Annie/Until I Die	1954	40.00
—All-green label; as "The Midnighters (Formerly Known As the Royals)"			
❑ 12169	Work With Me Annie/Until I Die	1954	100.00
—Silver top label; as " The Midnighters (Formerly Known As the Royals)"			
❑ 12177	Give It Up/That Woman	1954	80.00
—As "The Midnighters Formerly the Royals"			
❑ 12185	Sexy Ways/Don't Say Your Last Goodbye	1954	80.00
—As "The Midnighters Formerly the Royals"			
❑ 12195	Annie Had a Baby/ She's the One	1954	60.00
❑ 12200	Annie's Aunt Fanny/ Crazy Loving	1954	60.00
❑ 12202	Tell Them/Stingy Little Thing	1954	60.00
❑ 12205	She's the One/Moonrise	1955	60.00
❑ 12210	Ashamed of Myself/Ring-a-Ling-Ling	1955	60.00
❑ 12220	Why Are We Apart/Switchie, Witchie, Titchie	1955	60.00
❑ 12224	Henry's Got Flat Feet (Can't Dance No More)/Whatsoever You Do	1955	60.00
❑ 12227	It's Love Baby (24 Hours a Day)/Looka Here	1955	60.00
❑ 12230	Give It Up/That Woman	1955	60.00
❑ 12240	Rock and Roll Wedding/That House on the Hill	1955	60.00
❑ 12243	Don't Change Your Pretty Ways/ We'll Never Meet Again	1955	60.00
❑ 12251	Partners for Life/ Sweet Mama, Do Right	1956	60.00
❑ 12260	Rock Granny Roll/ Open Up the Back Door	1956	60.00
❑ 12270	Tore Up Over You/ Early One Morning	1956	50.00
❑ 12285	I'll Be Home Some Day/ Come On and Get It	1957	50.00
❑ 12288	Let Me Hold Your Hand/ Oh Bah Baby	1957	50.00
❑ 12293	E Basta Cosi/In the Doorway Crying	1957	50.00
❑ 12299	Oh, So Happy/Is Your Love for Real	1957	40.00
❑ 12305	Let 'Em Roll/What Made You Change Your Mind	1957	40.00
❑ 12317	Stay By My Side/ Daddy's Little Baby	1958	40.00
❑ 12339	Baby Please/Ow-Wow-Oo-Wee	1958	40.00

7-Inch Extended Plays

FEDERAL

Number	Title (A Side/B Side)	Yr	NM
❑ 333	Work with Me Annie/Moonrise// Sexy Ways/Get It	1955	150.00
—All-green label			
❑ 333	Work with Me Annie/Moonrise// Sexy Ways/Get It	1955	300.00
—Green label, silver top			
❑ 333 [PS]	The Midnighters Sing Their Greatest Hits	1955	200.00
—Pink cover			
❑ 333 [PS]	The Midnighters Sing Their Greatest Hits	1955	200.00
—Purple cover			

Albums

FEDERAL

Number	Title (A Side/B Side)	Yr	NM
❑ 295-90 [10]	Their Greatest Hits	1954	8000.
—VG value 4000; VG+ value 6000			
❑ 541 [M]	Their Greatest Hits	1955	1000.
—Yellow cover			
❑ 541 [M]	Their Greatest Hits	1955	1500.
—Red cover			
❑ 581 [M]	The Midnighters, Vol. 2	1955	1200.

KING

Number	Title (A Side/B Side)	Yr	NM
❑ 541 [M]	Their Greatest Jukebox Hits	1958	400.00
—Crownless black label, "King" is two inches wide on label			
❑ 541 [M]	Their Greatest Jukebox Hits	196?	200.00
—Reissue with Hank Ballard on cover			
❑ 541 [M]	Their Greatest Jukebox Hits	196?	300.00
—Crownless black label, "King" is three inches wide on label. Above two have a girl on the cover.			
❑ 581 [M]	The Midnighters, Vol. 2	1958	300.00
—Crownless black label, "King" is two inches wide on label			
❑ 581 [M]	The Midnighters, Vol. 2	196?	200.00
—Crownless black label, "King" is three inches wide on label			

MIDNIGHTERS, THE (2)

45s

20TH FOX

Number	Title (A Side/B Side)	Yr	NM
❑ 182	The Road Home/Taco	1960	12.00

MIGHTY AVENGERS, THE

45s

PRESS

Number	Title (A Side/B Side)	Yr	NM
❑ 9746	Blue Turns to Grey/I'm Lost Without You	1965	10.00

MIGHTY BABY

Albums

HEAD

Number	Title (A Side/B Side)	Yr	NM
❑ LPS-025	Mighty Baby	1969	100.00

MIGHTY CLOUDS OF JOY

12-Inch Singles

EPIC

Number	Title (A Side/B Side)	Yr	NM
❑ 50693	Joy in These Changing Times/ (Instrumental)	1979	12.00

45s

ABC

Number	Title (A Side/B Side)	Yr	NM
❑ 12164	Mighty High/Touch My Soul	1976	4.00
❑ 12196	You Are So Beautiful/ Everything Is All	1976	4.00
❑ 12241	There's Love in the World (Tell the Lonely People)/ (B-side unknown)	1976	4.00
❑ 12281	God Is Not Dead/ Music Is My Way of Life	1977	4.00
❑ 12322	Look on the Bright Side/ (B-side unknown)	1978	4.00

ABC DUNHILL

Number	Title (A Side/B Side)	Yr	NM
❑ 15012	Time/(B-side unknown)	1974	5.00
❑ 15025	Mighty Cloud of Joy/ Everything Is Going Up	1974	5.00

EPIC

Number	Title (A Side/B Side)	Yr	NM
❑ 50690	Joy in These Changing Times/ We're Gonna Have a Good Time	1979	4.00
❑ 50691	I've Been in the Storm Too Long/We're Blessed	1979	4.00
❑ 50788	I Get a Blessing Every Day/ Rainy Day Friend	1979	4.00
❑ 50875	What a Difference You've Made in My Life/We're Blessed	1980	4.00

MYRRH

Number	Title (A Side/B Side)	Yr	NM
❑ 241	Glow Love/(B-side unknown)	1982	4.00

PEACOCK

Number	Title (A Side/B Side)	Yr	NM
❑ 1823	Jesus Lead Us Safely/ Ain't Got Long Here	1961	12.00
❑ 1839	I'll Be Alright/My Religion	1961	12.00
❑ 1857	Time Has Changed/I Love Jesus	1962	10.00
❑ 1869	Family Circle/None But the Righteous	1962	10.00
❑ 1895	Glory Hallelujah/Lord Hold My Hand	1962	10.00
❑ 1896	Nearer to Thee/ You'll Never Know	1962	10.00
❑ 3025	I'll Go (Part 1)/I'll Go (Part 2)	1964	10.00
❑ 3050	A Friend in Jesus/Two Wings	1965	10.00
❑ 3064	He's Able/Swing Low	1965	10.00
❑ 3077	See How They Done My Lord/ Look for Me in Heaven	1966	10.00
❑ 3080	Nobody Can Turn Me Around/ Touch Me Lord	1966	10.00
❑ 3099	I'm Glad About It/Let Jesus Lead You	1966	10.00
❑ 3132	Somewhere Around God's Throne/The Holy Ghost	1967	8.00
❑ 3144	Pray for Me/Call Him Up	1968	8.00
❑ 3167	How Far Have I Strayed/Just to Behold His Face	1969	8.00
❑ 3175	In This World Alone/Why Do Men Treat the Lord	1970	8.00
❑ 3189	Heavy Load/I'll Be Alright Someday	1972	6.00

Albums

ABC

Number	Title (A Side/B Side)	Yr	NM
❑ D-899	Kickin'	1975	10.00
❑ D-986	The Truth Is the Power	1976	10.00
❑ D-1038	Live and Direct	1977	10.00

ABC DUNHILL

Number	Title (A Side/B Side)	Yr	NM
❑ DSX-50177	It's Time	1974	10.00

HOB

Number	Title (A Side/B Side)	Yr	NM
❑ 288	"Live" Zion Songs	196?	15.00

KING

Number	Title (A Side/B Side)	Yr	NM
❑ SG3-1107	Out Talking to Yourself	1970	15.00

MCA

Number	Title (A Side/B Side)	Yr	NM
❑ 1091 [(2)]	The Very Best of Mighty Clouds of Joy	198?	10.00
❑ 28008	Family Circle	198?	8.00
—Reissue of Peacock 114			
❑ 28012	The Bright Side	198?	8.00
—Reissue of Peacock 121			
❑ 28017	Mighty Clouds of Joy At the Music Hall	198?	8.00
—Reissue of Peacock 134			
❑ 28019	The Best of Mighty Clouds of Joy	198?	8.00
—Reissue of Peacock 136			
❑ 28025	The Untouchables	198?	8.00
—Reissue of Peacock 151			
❑ 28028	Songs of Rev. Julius Cheeks and the Nightingales	198?	8.00
—Reissue of Peacock 163			
❑ 28030	God Bless America	198?	8.00
—Reissue of Peacock 170			
❑ 28032	Live at the Apollo	198?	8.00
—Reissue of Peacock 173			
❑ 28040	The Best of Mighty Clouds of Joy — Vol. 2	198?	8.00

MYRRH

Number	Title (A Side/B Side)	Yr	NM
❑ MSB-6663	Cloudburst	1980	10.00
❑ MSB-6681	The Truth Is the Power	1981	10.00
❑ MSB-6694	Miracle Man	1982	10.00
❑ MSB-6712	Request Line	1983	10.00
❑ WR-8121	Mighty Clouds Alive	1984	10.00
❑ WR-8122	Sing and Shout	1984	10.00

PEACOCK

Number	Title (A Side/B Side)	Yr	NM
❑ 114	Family Circle	196?	20.00
❑ 121	The Bright Side	196?	20.00
❑ 134	Mighty Clouds of Joy At the Music Hall	196?	20.00
❑ 136	The Best of Mighty Clouds of Joy	196?	20.00
❑ 151	The Untouchables	196?	20.00
❑ 161	Out Talking to Yourself	196?	20.00
❑ 163	Songs of Rev. Julius Cheeks and the Nightingales	196?	20.00
❑ 170	God Bless America	1971	15.00
❑ 173	Live at the Apollo	1972	15.00

PRIORITY

Number	Title (A Side/B Side)	Yr	NM
❑ RV 37707	Changing Times	1982	10.00

Mike + The Mechanics, "Seeing is Believing," Atlantic 7-88921, 1988, $3.

Number	Title (A Side/B Side)	Yr	NM
MIGHTY JOE YOUNG			
45s			
POWERHAUS			
❑ MJ 004	(There'll Be Other Girls) Hoss/ Chump	1989	15.00
—1,000 copies were pressed			
❑ MJ 004 [PS]	(There'll Be Other Girls) Hoss/ Chump	1989	250.00
—Only 25 came with picture sleeves; value is conjecture			
MIGHTY LEMON DROPS, THE			
12-Inch Singles			
SIRE			
❑ PRO-A-2639 [DJ]	My Biggest Thrill (same on both sides)	1986	5.00
❑ PRO-A-2791 [DJ]	Out of Hand (Extended)/ Out of Hand (LP Version)	1987	5.00
❑ PRO-A-2963 [DJ]	Inside Out (12")/Inside Out (7")	1988	5.00
❑ PRO-A-3103 [DJ]	Fall Down (Remix)/Inside Out (Live)/Mighty Lemon Talk	1988	5.00
❑ PRO-A-3751 [DJ]	Into the Heart of Love (LP)/ Into the Heart of Love (Edit)	1989	5.00
45s			
SIRE			
❑ 27906	Inside Out/Head on the Block	1988	3.00
Albums			
REPRISE			
❑ 26017	Laughter	1989	10.00
SIRE			
❑ 25532	The Mighty Lemon Drops	1986	10.00
❑ 25595	Out of Hand	1987	10.00
❑ 25788	Happy Head	1988	10.00

Number	Title (A Side/B Side)	Yr	NM
MIGHTY MARVELOWS, THE See THE MARVELOWS.			
MIGHTY MIGHTY BOSSTONES			
12-Inch Singles			
MERCURY			
❑ 1156 [DJ]	Kinder Words/Chocolate Pudding/Pirate Ship	1994	10.00
45s			
BIG RIG			
❑ (no #)	The Impression That I Get/ At It Again	1997	5.00
—Green vinyl			
❑ (no #) [PS]	The Impression That I Get/ At It Again	1997	5.00
ISLAND			
❑ 314-562777-7	So Sad to Say/The Impression That I Get	2000	3.00
MERCURY			
❑ 858894-7	Detroit Rock City/ Detroit Rock City	1994	4.00
—B-side by Kiss; small center hole; green vinyl			
❑ 858894-7 [PS]	Detroit Rock City/ Detroit Rock City	1994	4.00
Albums			
BIG RIG			
❑ BR 101 [(2)]	Don't Know How to Party	1993	50.00
—Includes one 12-inch plaid picture disc and a 10-inch record called "Skacore"			
❑ BR 102 [(2)10]	Question the Answers	1994	50.00
—Two 10-inch records; includes one song not on the CD version			
BIG RIG/ISLAND			
❑ 314 542451-1 [(2)]	Pay Attention	2000	30.00
SIDE ONE DUMMY			
❑ SDLP- 1234	A Jackknife to a Swan	2002	25.00
TAANG!			
❑ 44	Devils Night Out	1991	30.00
❑ 49	More Noise & Other Disturbances	1991	25.00

Number	Title (A Side/B Side)	Yr	NM
MIGIL FIVE, THE			
45s			
CAMEO			
❑ 316	Mockin' Bird Hill/Long Ago (And Far Away)	1964	10.00
HICKORY			
❑ 1292	Your Cheatin' Heart/Boys and Girls	1965	10.00
❑ 1334	I'm in Love Again/One Hundred Years	1965	10.00
MERCURY			
❑ 72301	Near You/Don't Wanna Go On Shaking	1964	10.00
MIKE AND BILL			
45s			
ARISTA			
❑ 0130	Somebody's Gotta Go (Sho Ain't Me)/(Instrumental)	1975	15.00
❑ 0180	Things Won't Be This Bad Always/(Instrumental)	1976	10.00
MOVING UP			
❑ 124	Somebody's Gotta Go (Sho Ain't Me)/(Instrumental)	1975	25.00
YORK			
❑ 8501	Where Do I Stand/Wrong Choice	197?	100.00
MIKE AND LULU			
45s			
TOP RANK			
❑ 2036	Baby's Lullaby/Baby Talk	1959	12.00
MIKE AND THE CENSATIONS			
45s			
HIGHLAND			
❑ 1175	Victim of Circumstances Part 1/ Part 2	1967	20.00
❑ 1181	Don't Mess with Me/There Is Nothing I Can Do About It	1967	50.00
❑ 1186	Be Mine Forever/I Need Your Lovin'	1968	40.00
❑ 1189	Baby What You Gonna Do/ Don't Sell Your Soul	1968	60.00
❑ 1203	I Need Your Lovin'/Baby What You Gonna Do	1968	40.00
REVUE			
❑ 11041	Split Personality/You're Living a Lie	1969	30.00
❑ 11056	Shopping for Love/The Straw (That Broke the Camel's Back)	1969	30.00
❑ 11068	Gonna Try to Get You Back/A Man Ain't Nothin' But a Man	1970	70.00
MIKE AND THE JAYS			
45s			
DOYL			
❑ 1001	My Only Girl/Dingle Dangle Doll	1960	80.00
MIKE + THE MECHANICS			
12-Inch Singles			
ATLANTIC			
❑ PR 797 [DJ]	Silent Running (Long Version 6:11) (Short Version 4:10)	1985	10.00
❑ PR 900 [DJ]	Taken In (same on both sides)	1986	10.00
❑ PR 2522 [DJ]	Nobody's Perfect (Edit) (LP Version)	1989	8.00
ELEKTRA			
❑ ED 5394 [DJ]	Revolution (Edit) (same on both sides)	1989	15.00
45s			
ATLANTIC			
❑ 7-88921	Seeing Is Believing/Don't	1989	3.00
❑ 7-88921 [PS]	Seeing Is Believing/Don't	1989	3.00
❑ 7-88964	The Living Years/ Too Many Friends	1989	3.00
❑ 7-88964 [DJ]	The Living Years (Edit)/ (LP Version)	1989	5.00
❑ 7-88964 [PS]	The Living Years/ Too Many Friends	1989	8.00
❑ 7-88990	Nobody's Perfect/ Sunday Morning	1988	3.00
❑ 7-88990 [PS]	Nobody's Perfect/ Sunday Morning	1988	3.00
❑ 7-89404	Taken In/A Call to Arms	1986	3.00
❑ 7-89404 [PS]	Taken In/A Call to Arms	1986	4.00
❑ 7-89450	All I Need Is a Miracle/ You Are the One	1986	3.00
❑ 7-89450 [PS]	All I Need Is a Miracle/ You Are the One	1986	4.00
❑ 7-89488	Silent Running (On Dangerous Ground)/Par Avion	1985	3.00

Except when noted otherwise, VG = 25% of NM, and VG+ = 50% of NM. (Example: VG = $2.00, VG+ = $4.00 and NM = $8.00.)

Number	Title (A Side/B Side)	Yr	NM
❑ 7-89488 [PS]	Silent Running (On Dangerous Ground)/Par Avion	1985	4.00

ELEKTRA

Number	Title (A Side/B Side)	Yr	NM
❑ 7-69283	Revolution/Leave Love Behind	1989	3.00
—B-side by Jonathan Elias			
❑ 7-69283 [PS]	Revolution/Leave Love Behind	1989	5.00

Albums

ATLANTIC

Number	Title (A Side/B Side)	Yr	NM
❑ PR 820 [DJ]	Mike on Mike	1985	20.00
—Promo-only music and interviews			
❑ PR 2543 [DJ]	Mike on Mike II	1989	15.00
—Promo-only music and interviews			
❑ 81287	Mike + The Mechanics	1985	10.00
❑ 81923	Living Years	1989	10.00

MIKE AND THE MODIFIERS

45s

GORDY

Number	Title (A Side/B Side)	Yr	NM
❑ 7006	I Found Myself a Brand New Baby/It's Too Bad	1962	60.00

MIKE AND THE UTOPIANS

45s

CEE JAY

Number	Title (A Side/B Side)	Yr	NM
❑ 574	Erlene/I Found a Penny	1958	150.00
❑ 574	Erlene/I Wish	1958	300.00

MIKE, JOHN AND BILL

"Mike" is MICHAEL NESMITH, later of THE MONKEES.

45s

OMNIBUS

Number	Title (A Side/B Side)	Yr	NM
❑ 239	How Can You Kiss Me/Just a Little Love	1963	300.00

MILANO, BOBBY

45s

CAPITOL

Number	Title (A Side/B Side)	Yr	NM
❑ F-3012	A King or a Slave/If You Cared	1955	20.00

CHALLENGE

Number	Title (A Side/B Side)	Yr	NM
❑ 59005	Life Begins at 4 O'Clock/Double Talking Baby	1958	100.00

TIME

Number	Title (A Side/B Side)	Yr	NM
❑ 1019	Ruby/Do I Love You	1960	20.00

WARNER BROS.

Number	Title (A Side/B Side)	Yr	NM
❑ 5027	Water Under the Bridge/My Yiddishe Momma	1959	12.00

MILBURN, AMOS

45s

ALADDIN

Number	Title (A Side/B Side)	Yr	NM
❑ 3014	Chicken Shack Boogie/It Took a Long, Long Time	1950	200.00
—78 originally released in 1948			
❑ 3018	Bewildered/A and M Blues	1950	120.00
—78 originally released in 1948			
❑ 3068	Bad, Bad Whiskey/I'm Going to Tell My Mama	1950	500.00
—Note: Amos Milburn singles on Aladdin before 3068 are unconfirmed on 45 rpm except those listed			
❑ 3080	Let's Rock a While/Tears, Tears, Tears	1951	80.00
❑ 3090	Everybody Clap Hands/That Was Your Last Mistake	1951	80.00
❑ 3093	Ain't Nothin' Shaking/Just One More Drink	1951	80.00
❑ 3105	She's Gone Again/Boogie Woogie	1951	80.00
❑ 3124	Thinking and Drinking/Trouble in Mind	1952	80.00
❑ 3125	Flying Home/Put Something in My Hand	1952	80.00
❑ 3133	I Won't Be Your Fool Anymore/Roll Mr. Jelly	1952	80.00
❑ 3146	Button Your Lip/Everything I Do Is Wrong	1952	80.00
❑ 3150	Kiss Me Again/Greyhound	1952	80.00
❑ 3159	Rock, Rock, Rock/Boo Hoo	1953	60.00
❑ 3164	Let Me Go Home, Whiskey/Three Times a Fool	1953	60.00
❑ 3168	Long, Long Day/Please Mr. Johnson	1953	60.00
❑ 3197	One Scotch, One Bourbon, One Beer/What Can I Do	1953	100.00
❑ 3218	Good, Good Whiskey/Let's Have a Party	1954	80.00
❑ 3226	How Could You Hurt Me So/Rocky Mountain	1954	60.00
❑ 3240	Milk and Water/I'm Still a Fool for You	1954	60.00
❑ 3248	Glory of Love/Baby, Baby All the Time	1954	60.00
❑ 3253	Vicious, Vicious Vodka/I Done Done It	1954	60.00
❑ 3269	That's It/One, Two, Three Everybody	1954	60.00
❑ 3281	Why Don't You Do Right/I Love You Anyway	1955	40.00
❑ 3293	All Is Well/My Happiness Depends on You	1955	40.00
❑ 3306	House Party/I Guess I'll Go	1955	40.00
❑ 3320	French Fried Potatoes and Ketchup/I Need Someone	1956	40.00
❑ 3332	Chicken Shack Boogie/Juice, Juice, Juice	1956	40.00
❑ 3340	Girl of My Dreams/Everyday of the Week	1956	40.00
❑ 3363	Rum and Coca-Cola/Soft Pollow	1957	30.00
❑ 3370	Greyhound/Dear Angel	1957	30.00
❑ 3383	Thinking of You Baby/I f I Could Be with You	1957	30.00

IMPERIAL

Number	Title (A Side/B Side)	Yr	NM
❑ 5831	I'm Still a Fool for You/Rocky Mountain	1962	12.00

KING

Number	Title (A Side/B Side)	Yr	NM
❑ 5405	Christmas (Comes But Once a Year)/Please Come Home for Christmas	1960	12.00
—B-side by Charles Brown			
❑ 5464	I Wanna Go Back Home/My Little Baby	1961	12.00
—With Charles Brown			
❑ 5483	My Sweet Baby's Love/Heartaches That Make You Cry	1961	12.00
❑ 5529	Movin' Time/The Hammer	1961	12.00
❑ 6095	Whiz O Shoo Pepi/Same Old Thing	1967	10.00

MOTOWN

Number	Title (A Side/B Side)	Yr	NM
❑ 1038	I'll Make It Up to You Somehow/My Baby Gave Me Another Chance	1963	30.00
❑ 1046	My Daily Prayer/(B-side unknown)	1963	30.00

UNITED ARTISTS

Number	Title (A Side/B Side)	Yr	NM
❑ 0149	Chicken Shack Boogie/Revitalized	1973	4.00
—"Silver Spotlight Series" reissue			

Albums

ALADDIN

Number	Title (A Side/B Side)	Yr	NM
❑ LP-704 [10]	Rockin' the Boogie	1952	4000.
—Black vinyl			
❑ LP-704 [10]	Rockin' the Boogie	1952	8000.
—Red vinyl, blue cover			
❑ LP-810 [M]	Rockin' the Boogie	1957	—
—Canceled			

IMPERIAL

Number	Title (A Side/B Side)	Yr	NM
❑ LP-9176 [M]	Million Sellers	1962	500.00

MOSAIC

Number	Title (A Side/B Side)	Yr	NM
❑ MQ10-155 [(10)]	The Complete Aladdin Recordings of Amos Milburn	199?	180.00
—Limited editon of 3,500			

MOTOWN

Number	Title (A Side/B Side)	Yr	NM
❑ 608 [M]	The Return of Amos Milburn, "The" Blues Boss	1963	900.00

SCORE

Number	Title (A Side/B Side)	Yr	NM
❑ LP-4012 [M]	Let's Have a Party	1957	800.00
❑ LP-4035 [M]	Amos Milburn Sings the Blues	1958	—
—Canceled			

MILBURN, AMOS/WYNONIE HARRIS/ETC.

Albums

ALADDIN

Number	Title (A Side/B Side)	Yr	NM
❑ LP-703 [10]	Party After Hours	1952	4000.
—Black vinyl			
❑ LP-703 [10]	Party After Hours	1952	8000.
—Red vinyl, blue cover			

MILES, BUDDY

45s

ATLANTIC

Number	Title (A Side/B Side)	Yr	NM
❑ 3852 [DJ]	Can You Hold Me (same on both sides)	1981	4.00
—May be promo only			
❑ 4006 [DJ]	Sunshine of Your Love (same on both sides)	1982	4.00
—May be promo only			

CASABLANCA

Number	Title (A Side/B Side)	Yr	NM
❑ 839	Rockin' and Rollin' on the Streets of Hollywood/Livin' in the Right Space	1975	4.00
❑ 849	Nasty Disposition/Do It to Me	1975	4.00
❑ 859	Reuben "The Hurricane"/Where You Gonna Run To Lady	1976	4.00

COLUMBIA

Number	Title (A Side/B Side)	Yr	NM
❑ 10030	Pain/We Get Love	1974	15.00
❑ 10089	Pull Yourself Together/I'm Just a Kiss Away	1975	150.00
❑ 45826	Love Affair/Life Is What You Make It	1973	5.00
❑ 45876	Elvira/Hear No Evil	1973	5.00
❑ 45969	Crazy Love/Thinking of You	1973	5.00

MERCURY

Number	Title (A Side/B Side)	Yr	NM
❑ 72860	The Train (Part 1)/The Train (Part 2)	1968	8.00
❑ 72903	This Lady/'69 Freedom Special	1969	8.00
❑ 72945	Memphis Train/My Chant	1969	6.00
❑ 73008	Them Changes/Spot on the Wall	1970	6.00
❑ 73086	Down By the River/Hearts Delight	1970	6.00
❑ 73119	Dreams/Your Feeling Is Mine	1970	6.00
❑ 73159	We Got to Live Together (Part 1)/We Got to Live Together (Part 2)	1970	6.00
❑ 73170	Runaway Child/(B-side unknown)	1970	6.00
❑ 73205	Wholesale Love/That's the Way Life Is	1971	5.00
❑ 73238	Them Changes/The Way I Feel Tonight	1971	5.00
❑ 73261	Give Away None of My Love/Take It Off Him and Put It On Me	1972	5.00
❑ 73277	Life Is What You Make It (Part 1)/Life Is What You Make It (Part 2)	1972	5.00

Albums

ATLANTIC

Number	Title (A Side/B Side)	Yr	NM
❑ SD 2-4000 [(2)]	Sneak Attack	1982	12.00

CASABLANCA

Number	Title (A Side/B Side)	Yr	NM
❑ NBLP 7019	More Miles Per Gallon	1975	10.00
❑ NBLP 7024	Bicentennial Gathering of the Tribes	1976	10.00

COLUMBIA

Number	Title (A Side/B Side)	Yr	NM
❑ CQ 32048 [Q]	Chapter VII	1973	20.00
❑ KC 32048	Chapter VII	1973	12.00
❑ CQ 32694 [Q]	Booger Bear	1973	20.00
❑ KC 32694	Booger Bear	1973	12.00
❑ KC 33089	All the Faces	1974	12.00

MERCURY

Number	Title (A Side/B Side)	Yr	NM
❑ SRM-1-608	A Message to the People	1971	15.00
❑ SRM-2-7500 [(2)]	Buddy Miles Live	1971	15.00
❑ SR-61196	Expressway to Your Skull	1968	20.00
❑ SR-61222	Electric Church	1969	20.00
❑ SR-61280	Them Changes	1970	15.00
❑ SR-61313	We Got to Live Together	1970	15.00

MILES, GARRY

45s

LIBERTY

Number	Title (A Side/B Side)	Yr	NM
❑ 55261	Look for a Star/Afraid of Love	1960	15.00
❑ 55261 [PS]	Look for a Star/Afraid of Love	1960	30.00
❑ 55279	Wishing Well/Dream Girl	1960	12.00
❑ 55596	Candy/Do the Bug	1963	12.00
❑ 55685	What Kind of Girl Are You/What's New	1964	10.00
❑ 55714	Here Goes a Fool/Ecstasy	1964	10.00
❑ 55738	How Are Things in Paradise/Please Take the Time	1964	10.00

UNITED ARTISTS

Number	Title (A Side/B Side)	Yr	NM
❑ 0099	Look for a Star/Look for a Star	1973	5.00
—"Silver Spotlight Series" reissue; B-side by Garry Mills			

7-Inch Extended Plays

LIBERTY

Number	Title (A Side/B Side)	Yr	NM
❑ LSX-1005	Look for a Star/Wishing Well/I Miss You So/Afraid of Love	1960	50.00
❑ LSX-1005 [PS]	Look for a Star	1960	50.00

MILES, LENNY

45s

GROOVE

Number	Title (A Side/B Side)	Yr	NM
❑ 58-0001	Stay with Me/Hercules	1963	10.00
❑ 58-0010	I Wouldn't Be Here/Mind Your Own Biz	1963	10.00

SCEPTER

Number	Title (A Side/B Side)	Yr	NM
❑ 1212	Don't Believe Him Donna/Invisible	1960	12.00
❑ 1218	I Know Love/In Between Tears	1961	12.00

MILKWOOD (1)

Albums

A&M

Number	Title (A Side/B Side)	Yr	NM
❑ SP-4226	Under Milkwood	1969	300.00

MILKWOOD (2)

Albums

PARAMOUNT

Number	Title (A Side/B Side)	Yr	NM
❑ PAS-6046	How's the Weather?	1973	40.00

M

MILKWOOD TAPESTRY

Albums

METROMEDIA

Number	Title (A Side/B Side)	Yr	NM
MD-1007	Milkwood Tapestry	1969	75.00

MILLARD & DYCE

Albums

KAYMAR

Number	Title (A Side/B Side)	Yr	NM
KS-7-265	Open	1973	60.00

MILLENNIUM

45s

COLUMBIA

Number	Title (A Side/B Side)	Yr	NM
4-44546	I Just Want to Be Your Friend/ It's You	1968	10.00
4-44607	5 A.M./Prelude	1968	10.00

MILLER, BOBBY

45s

CONSTELLATION

Number	Title (A Side/B Side)	Yr	NM
103	The Big Question/I Don't Believe You	1963	20.00
111	The Big Question/ Uncle Willie Time	1963	20.00
116	Whoa (She's All Mine)/Take It in Stride	1964	20.00
127	This Is My Dance/Simon Says	1964	20.00
134	I'm For the Girls/Love Take the Case	1964	30.00

MILLER, CHUCK

45s

CAPITOL

Number	Title (A Side/B Side)	Yr	NM
F2613	Am I to Blame/Count Your Blessings	1953	20.00
F2700	The Pucker-Nut Free/After All	1954	20.00
F2766	Idaho Red/The Joker (In the Card Game of Life)	1954	20.00
—With Dave Cavanaugh			
F2841	Hopahula Boogie/I'll Know My Love	1954	20.00
F3187	No Baby Like You/Rouge River Valley	1955	15.00

MERCURY

Number	Title (A Side/B Side)	Yr	NM
70627	The House of Blue Lights/ Can't Help Wonderin'	1955	20.00
70697	Hawk Eye/Something to Live For	1955	15.00
70767	Boogie Along/Lookout Mountain	1955	15.00
70842	Bright Red Convertible/ Baltimore Jones	1956	15.00
70942	Vim Vam Vamoose/ Cool It Baby!	1956	15.00
71001	The Auctioneer/Baby Doll	1956	15.00
71056	Me Head in De Barrel/ Good Mornin' Darlin'	1957	12.00
71118	Rang Tang Ding Dong/ Bye Bye Love	1957	12.00
71173	Plaything/After Yesterday	1957	12.00
71308	Down the Road Apiece/ Mad About Her Blues	1958	12.00

Albums

MERCURY

Number	Title (A Side/B Side)	Yr	NM
MG-20195 [M]	After Hours	1956	80.00

MILLER, CLINT

45s

ABC-PARAMOUNT

Number	Title (A Side/B Side)	Yr	NM
9878	Bertha Lou/Doggone It Baby, I'm in Love	1957	50.00
9938	Polka Dotted Poliwampus/ Teenage Dance	1958	30.00
9938 [PS]	Polka Dotted Poliwampus/ Teenage Dance	1958	60.00
9979	A Lover's Prayer/ No, Never, My Love	1958	20.00

BIG TOP

Number	Title (A Side/B Side)	Yr	NM
3013	Lonely Traveler/You Must Have Read My Mind	1959	20.00

HEADLINE

Number	Title (A Side/B Side)	Yr	NM
1010	Silly Billy Boy/Do You Remember	1960	50.00
1011	London Town/Till the End of the World Rolls Around	1961	30.00
1013	I Still Write Your Name in the Sand/The Girl with a Ribbon in Her Hand	1961	30.00

LENOX

Number	Title (A Side/B Side)	Yr	NM
5557	Forget Me Nots/Drummer Boy of Shiloh	1962	12.00
5574	Bridge Across the River/Crabs Walk Sideways	1963	12.00

MILLER, DREW, AND THE BEL-AIRES

45s

MGM

Number	Title (A Side/B Side)	Yr	NM
11627	When Christmas Angels Sing/ Mystery Trail	1953	20.00

MILLER, HAL, AND THE RAYS

"The Rays" actually are the future FOUR SEASONS.

45s

AMY

Number	Title (A Side/B Side)	Yr	NM
909	I Still Care/On My Own Two Feet	1964	200.00
920	A Blessing in Disguise/ Cry Like the Rain	1965	80.00

TOPIX

Number	Title (A Side/B Side)	Yr	NM
6003	An Angel Cried/Faith, Hope, Dreams	1961	60.00

MILLER, JODY

45s

CAPITOL

Number	Title (A Side/B Side)	Yr	NM
2005	To Sir, With Love/Only When You're Lonely	1967	8.00
2066	I Knew You Well/I'm Into Lookin' for Someone to Love Me	1967	8.00
2187	It's My Time/Over the Edge	1968	8.00
2290	Long Black Limousine/Back in the Race	1968	8.00
2398	All the Crying in the World/ Bon Soir Cher	1969	6.00
2558	Times to Come/My Daddy's Thousand Dollars	1969	6.00
5090	He Walks Like a Man/Looking at the World Through a Tear	1963	10.00
5162	They Call My Guy a Tiger/ Wonderful Round of Indifference	1964	10.00
5192	In My Room/Fever	1964	10.00
5269	My Baby's Gone/ Warm Is the Love	1964	10.00
5298	This Is the Life/ Look for Small Pleasures	1964	10.00
5353	Be My Man/Never Let Him Go	1965	10.00
5402	Queen of the House/ The Greatest Actor	1965	8.00
5429	Silver Threads and Golden Needles/Melody for Robin	1965	8.00
5429 [PS]	Silver Threads and Golden Needles/Melody for Robin	1965	12.00
5483	Home of the Brave/ This Is the Life	1965	8.00
5483 [PS]	Home of the Brave/ This Is the Life	1965	12.00
5541	Magic Town/A Lonely Queen	1965	8.00
5594	We're Gonna Let the Good Times Roll/I Don't Care	1966	8.00
5671	I Remember Mama/Something in My Eye	1966	8.00
5743	Things/Quite a Long, Long Time	1966	8.00
5768	If You Were a Carpenter/ Let Me Walk with You	1966	8.00
5846	Crazy/How Do You Say Goodbye	1967	8.00
5911	Shutters and Boards/Kiss Me	1967	8.00

EPIC

Number	Title (A Side/B Side)	Yr	NM
5-10641	Look at Mine/Safe in These Lovin' Arms of Mine	1970	6.00
5-10692	If You Think I Love You Now (I've Just Started)/Looking Out My Back Door	1970	6.00
5-10734	He's So Fine/ You're Number Two	1971	6.00
5-10785	Baby I'm Yours/Good Lovin'	1971	6.00
5-10835	Be My Baby/Your Love's Been a Long Time Comin'	1972	5.00
5-10878	There's a Party Goin' On/ Love's the Answer	1972	5.00
5-10916	To Know Him Is to Love Him/ Make Me Your Kind of Woman	1972	5.00
5-10960	Good News/Soul Song	1973	5.00
5-11016	Darling, You Can Always Come Back Home/We'll Sing Our Song Together	1973	5.00
5-11056	The House of the Rising Sun/ In the Name of Love	1973	5.00
5-11076	Silent Night, Lonely Night/ (B-side unknown)	1973	6.00
5-11094	Reflections/One More Chance	1974	5.00
5-11134	Natural Woman/Jimmy's Roses	1974	5.00
50042	Country Girl/Safe in These Lovin' Arms of Mine	1974	4.00
50079	The Best in Me /I'm Alright 'Til I See	1975	4.00
50117	Don't Take It Away/ Long, Long Time	1975	4.00
50158	Will You Love Me Tomorrow/ Love, You Never Had It So Good	1975	4.00
50203	Ashes of Love/ She Calls Me Baby	1976	4.00
50304	When the New Wears Off Our Love/Silver and Gold	1976	4.00
50360	Spread a Little Love Around/ Montana Cowboy	1977	4.00
50432	Another Lonely Night/ All Night Long	1977	4.00
50512	Soft Lights and Slow Sexy Music/Home	1978	4.00
50568	(I Wanna) Love My Life Away/ I'm Gonna Write a Song	1978	4.00
50612	Kiss Away/Hold Me, Thrill Me, Kiss Me	1978	4.00
50673	I'm Gonna Make You Mine /I Don't Want Nobody (To Lead Me On)	1979	4.00
50734	Lay a Little Lovin' On Me /Crazy on You	1979	4.00

Albums

CAPITOL

Number	Title (A Side/B Side)	Yr	NM
ST 1913 [S]	Wednesday's Child Is Full of Woe	1963	40.00
T 1913 [M]	Wednesday's Child Is Full of Woe	1963	30.00
ST 2349 [S]	Queen of the House	1965	20.00
T 2349 [M]	Queen of the House	1965	15.00
ST 2412 [S]	Home of the Brave	1965	20.00
T 2412 [M]	Home of the Brave	1965	15.00
ST 2446 [S]	Jody Miller Sings the Great Hits of Buck Owens	1966	20.00
T 2446 [M]	Jody Miller Sings the Great Hits of Buck Owens	1966	15.00
ST 2996	The Nashville Sound of Jody Miller	1968	15.00
ST-11169	The Best of Jody Miller	1973	12.00

EPIC

Number	Title (A Side/B Side)	Yr	NM
E 30282	Look at Mine	1971	12.00
E 30659	He's So Fine	1971	12.00
KE 31706	There's a Party Goin' On	1972	12.00
KE 32386	Good News!	1973	12.00
KE 32569	House of the Rising Sun	1974	12.00
KE 33349	Country Girl	1975	12.00
KE 33934	Will You Love Me Tomorrow?	1976	12.00
PE 34446	Here's Jody	1977	12.00

MILLER, JODY, AND JOHNNY PAYCHECK

Also see each artist's individual listings.

45s

EPIC

Number	Title (A Side/B Side)	Yr	NM
5-10863	Let's All Go Down to the River/ In the Garden	1972	7.00

MILLER, LESLEY

45s

MGM

Number	Title (A Side/B Side)	Yr	NM
K13748	Teach Me to Love You/ Think of Rain	1967	15.00
K14074	You Ain't Goin' Nowhere/ Teach Me to Love You	1969	15.00

RCA VICTOR

Number	Title (A Side/B Side)	Yr	NM
47-8387	Just Another Fresh Boy/ Once a Fool	1964	15.00
47-8455	Heartache Is Over/Walk with Me	1964	15.00
47-8600	(You Got a Way of) Bringing Out My Tears/I Talk to Your Picture	1965	40.00
47-8753	He Doesn't Need Your Pity/I'm Going Back to My First Love	1965	30.00
47-8786	He Wore the Green Beret/ (You Got a Way of) Bringing Out My Tears	1966	30.00
47-8815	Mountain of Our Love/ Everybody Knows But Me	1966	30.00

MILLER, MICKEY

Albums

FOLKWAYS

Number	Title (A Side/B Side)	Yr	NM
FA-2393 [M]	American Folk Songs	1959	30.00

MILLER, MRS.

45s

AMARET

Number	Title (A Side/B Side)	Yr	NM
101	Up, Up and Away/Green Thumb	1969	8.00
114	I've Gotta Be Me/Renaissance of Smut	1970	8.00

CAPITOL

Number	Title (A Side/B Side)	Yr	NM
5640	Downtown/A Lover's Concerto	1966	10.00

Except when noted otherwise, VG = 25% of NM, and VG+ = 50% of NM. (Example: VG = $2.00, VG+ = $4.00 and NM = $8.00.)

Albums

AMAREST

Number	Title (A Side/B Side)	Yr	NM
❑ 5000	Mrs. Miller Does Her Thing	1969	20.00

CAPITOL

Number	Title (A Side/B Side)	Yr	NM
❑ ST 2494 [S]	Mrs. Miller's Greatest Hits	1966	30.00
❑ T 2494 [M]	Mrs. Miller's Greatest Hits	1966	25.00
❑ ST 2579 [S]	Will Success Spoil Mrs. Miller?	1966	30.00
❑ T 2579 [M]	Will Success Spoil Mrs. Miller?	1966	25.00
❑ ST 2734 [S]	The Country Soul of Mrs. Miller	1967	25.00
❑ T 2734 [M]	The Country Soul of Mrs. Miller	1967	25.00

MILLER, STEVE

As far as we know, no relation to the Steve Miller Band.

45s

HIT

Number	Title (A Side/B Side)	Yr	NM
❑ 313	Everlasting Love/In and Out of Love	1967	8.00
—B-side by Jenny and the Jewels			
❑ 330	This Guy's in Love with You/The Good, the Bad, and the Ugly	1968	8.00
—B-side by the New Society Group			

MILLER, STEVE, BAND

Also see THE GOLDBERG-MILLER BLUES BAND; BOZ SCAGGS.

12-Inch Singles

CAPITOL

Number	Title (A Side/B Side)	Yr	NM
❑ V-8613	Shangri-La (Extended)//Shangri-La (Dub)/Abracadabra	1984	10.00
❑ V-8632	Bongo Bongo (Born to Dance Mix)/Get On Home	1985	8.00
❑ V-8644	Italian X-Rays (Extended Version) (Edit)/Who Do You Love	1985	8.00
❑ SPRO 9008/10 [DJ]	True Fine Love/Dance, Dance, Dance	1977	15.00
❑ SPRO-9250/1 [DJ]	Shangri-La (Long Version) (Short Version)	1984	10.00
❑ SPRO 9252/3 [DJ]	Shangri-La (Extended) (7" Version) (Dub Version)	1984	8.00
❑ SPRO-9992 [DJ]	I Wanna Be Loved (same on both sides)	1986	15.00
—Promo only on blue vinyl			
❑ V-15270	I Want to Make the World Turn Around (3 versions)/Slinky	1986	6.00

45s

CAPITOL

Number	Title (A Side/B Side)	Yr	NM
❑ 2156	Roll With It/Sittin' in Circles	1968	12.00
❑ 2156 [PS]	Roll With It/Sittin' in Circles	1968	25.00
❑ 2287	Living in the U.S.A./Quicksilver Girl	1968	12.00
❑ 2447	Rock Love/(B-side unknown)	1969	10.00
❑ 2520	My Dark Hour/Song for Our Ancestors	1969	8.00
❑ 2638	Don't Let Nobody Turn You Around/Little Girl	1969	8.00
❑ 2878	Going to the Country/Never Kill Another Man	1970	6.00
❑ 2945	Going to Mexico/Steve Miller's Midnight Tango	1970	6.00
❑ 3228	Rock Love/Let Me Serve You	1971	6.00
❑ 3344	Fandango/Love's Riddle	1972	6.00
❑ 3732	The Joker/Something to Believe In	1973	5.00
❑ 3837	Your Cash Ain't Nothin' But Trash/Evil	1974	5.00
❑ 3884	Living in the U.S.A./Kow Kow Calqulator	1974	5.00
❑ 4260	Take the Money and Run/Sweet Maree	1976	4.00
❑ 4323	Rock'n Me/Shu Ba Du Da Ma Ma Ma Ma	1976	4.00
❑ 4323	Rockin' Me/Living in the U.S.A.	1976	5.00
❑ 4372	Fly Like an Eagle/Lovin' Cup	1976	4.00
❑ 4424	Jet Airliner/Babes in the Wood	1977	4.00
❑ 4466	Jungle Love/Wish Upon a Star	1977	4.00
❑ 4496	Swingtown/Winter Time	1977	4.00
❑ A-5068	Heart Like a Wheel/True Fine Love	1981	3.00
❑ A-5068 [PS]	Heart Like a Wheel/True Fine Love	1981	4.00
❑ A-5086	Circle of Love/(Instrumental)	1982	3.00
❑ B-5126	Abracadabra/Baby Wanna Dance	1982	3.00
❑ B-5126	Abracadabra/Give It Up	1982	4.00
❑ B-5126 [PS]	Abracadabra	1982	4.00
—Same sleeve has been found with record of either B-side			
❑ B-5162	Cool Magic/Young Girl's Heart	1982	3.00
❑ B-5162 [PS]	Cool Magic/Young Girl's Heart	1982	4.00
❑ B-5194	Give It Up/Heart Like a Wheel	1982	3.00
❑ B-5223	Buffalo's Serenade/Living in the U.S.A.	1983	3.00
❑ B-5407	Shangri-La/Circle of Love	1984	3.00
❑ B-5407 [PS]	Shangri-La/Circle of Love	1984	3.00
❑ B-5442	Bongo Bongo/Get On Home	1985	3.00
❑ B-5442 [PS]	Bongo Bongo/Get On Home	1985	3.00
❑ B-5476	Italian X-Rays/Who Do You Love	1985	3.00
❑ B-5646	I Want to Make the World Turn Around/Slinky	1986	3.00
❑ B-5646 [PS]	I Want to Make the World Turn Around/Slinky	1986	3.00
❑ B-5671	Nobody But You Baby/Maelstrom	1987	3.00
❑ B-5704	I Wanna Be Loved/I Wanna Be Loved	1987	3.00
❑ B-5704 [PS]	I Wanna Be Loved/I Wanna Be Loved	1987	3.00
❑ B-44222	Ya Ya/Filthy McNasty	1988	3.00
❑ B-44222 [PS]	Ya Ya/Filthy McNasty	1988	3.00

Albums

CAPITOL

Number	Title (A Side/B Side)	Yr	NM
❑ SKAO-184	Brave New World	1969	20.00
—Black label with colorband			
❑ SKAO-184	Brave New World	1970	15.00
—Green label			
❑ SKAO-8-0184	Brave New World	1969	25.00
—Capitol Record Club edition; black label with colorband			
❑ ST-331	Your Saving Grace	1969	15.00
❑ SKAO-436	Number 5	1970	15.00
❑ STBB-717 [(2)]	Children of the Future/Living in the U.S.A.	1971	15.00
—Repackage of 2920 and 2984 (with new title for the latter)			
❑ SW-748	Rock Love	1971	15.00
❑ SKAO 2920	Children of the Future	1968	25.00
—Black label with colorband			
❑ SKAO 2920	Children of the Future	1970	15.00
—Green label			
❑ ST 2984	Sailor	1968	25.00
—Black label with colorband			
❑ ST 2984	Sailor	1970	15.00
—Green label			
❑ SMAS-11022	Recall the Beginning…A Journey from Eden	1972	15.00
❑ SVBB-11114 [(2)]	Anthology	1972	15.00
❑ SMAS-11235	The Joker	1973	10.00
❑ ST-11497	Fly Like an Eagle	1976	10.00
❑ SO-11630	Book of Dreams	1977	10.00
❑ SOO-11872	Greatest Hits 1974-1978	1978	10.00
❑ SOO-11872 [DJ]	Greatest Hits 1974-1978	1978	30.00
—Promo only on blue vinyl			
❑ SEAX-11903 [PD]	Book of Dreams	1978	15.00
❑ ST-12121	Circle of Love	1981	10.00
❑ ST-12216	Abracadabra	1982	10.00
❑ ST-12263	Steve Miller Live	1983	10.00
❑ SJ-12339	Italian X-Rays	1985	10.00
❑ PJ-12445	Living in the 20th Century	1987	10.00
❑ SN-16078	Brave New World	1980	8.00
❑ SN-16079	Your Saving Grace	1980	8.00
❑ SN-16262	Children of the Future	1982	8.00
❑ SN-16263	Sailor	1982	8.00
❑ SN-16321	Greatest Hits 1974-1978	1984	8.00
❑ SN-16323	Book of Dreams	1984	8.00
❑ SN-16339	Fly Like an Eagle	1984	8.00
❑ SN-16357	Circle of Love	1985	8.00
❑ 21185	Fly Like an Eagle	1999	20.00
—Limited-edition reissue on 180-gram vinyl			
❑ C1-48303	Born 2 B Blue	1988	10.00
❑ SKAO-80436	Number 5	1970	20.00
—Capitol Record Club edition			
❑ R 223186 [(2)]	Anthology	197?	15.00
—RCA Music Service edition			

DCC COMPACT CLASSICS

Number	Title (A Side/B Side)	Yr	NM
❑ LPZ-2028	Greatest Hits 1974-1978	1996	50.00
—Audiophile vinyl			

MOBILE FIDELITY

Number	Title (A Side/B Side)	Yr	NM
❑ 1-021	Fly Like an Eagle	1979	50.00
—Audiophile vinyl			

MILLER, STEVE, BAND/QUICKSILVER MESSENGER SERVICE/THE BAND

Albums

CAPITOL

Number	Title (A Side/B Side)	Yr	NM
❑ STCR-288 [(3)]	Sailor/Quicksilver Messenger Service/Music from Big Pink	1969	30.00
—Special 3-LP box set combining these three LPs, also listed separately in each group's listing, in one package			

MILLER SISTERS, THE

45s

ACME

Number	Title (A Side/B Side)	Yr	NM
❑ 111	Let's Start Anew/The Flip Skip	1957	50.00
❑ 717	You Made Me a Promise/Crazy Billboard Song	1957	40.00
❑ 721	Let's Start Anew/The Flip Skip	1958	40.00

EMBER

Number	Title (A Side/B Side)	Yr	NM
❑ 1004	Guess Who/How Am I to Know	1956	30.00

FLIP

Number	Title (A Side/B Side)	Yr	NM
❑ 504	Someday You Will Pay/I Knew You Would	1955	200.00

GLODIS

Number	Title (A Side/B Side)	Yr	NM
❑ 1003	Pop Your Finger/You Got to Reap What You Sow	1961	15.00

GMC

Number	Title (A Side/B Side)	Yr	NM
❑ 10006	I'm Telling It Like It Is/Until You Come Home I'll Walk Alone	1967	10.00

HERALD

Number	Title (A Side/B Side)	Yr	NM
❑ 455	Hippity Ha/Until You're Mine	1955	50.00
❑ 527	Hippity Ha/Until You're Mine	1958	20.00

HULL

Number	Title (A Side/B Side)	Yr	NM
❑ 718	Please Don't Leave/Do You Wanna Go	1956	40.00
❑ 736	Just Wait and See/Black Pepper	1960	25.00
—B-side by Leo Price and Band			
❑ 750	Roll Back the Rug (And Twist)/Don't You Forget	1962	25.00
❑ 752	I Cried All Night/Hully Gully Reel	1962	20.00

MILLER

Number	Title (A Side/B Side)	Yr	NM
❑ 1140	Oh Lover/Remember That	1960	20.00
❑ 1141	Pony Dance/Give Me Some Old Fashioned Love	1960	20.00
❑ 1143	Please Mr. D.J./(B-side unknown)	1960	20.00

ONYX

Number	Title (A Side/B Side)	Yr	NM
❑ 507	Sugar Candy/My Own	1957	50.00

RAYNA

Number	Title (A Side/B Side)	Yr	NM
❑ 5001	I Miss You So/Dance Little Sister	1962	15.00
❑ 5004	Oh Why/Walk On	1962	15.00

RIVERSIDE

Number	Title (A Side/B Side)	Yr	NM
❑ 4535	Dance Close/Tell Him	1962	20.00

ROULETTE

Number	Title (A Side/B Side)	Yr	NM
❑ 4491	Baby Your Baby/Silly Girl	1963	12.00

STARDUST

Number	Title (A Side/B Side)	Yr	NM
❑ 3001	Feel Good/Concha	1964	10.00

SUN

Number	Title (A Side/B Side)	Yr	NM
❑ 230	There's No Right Way to Do Me Wrong/You Can Tell Me	1956	50.00
❑ 255	Finders Keepers/Ten Cats Down	1956	50.00
❑ 504	Someday You Will Pay/I Knew You Would	1955	150.00

YORKTOWN

Number	Title (A Side/B Side)	Yr	NM
❑ 75	Looking Over My Life/Si Senor	1965	10.00

MILLINDER, LUCKY

45s

KING

Number	Title (A Side/B Side)	Yr	NM
❑ 4449	Chew Tobacco Rag/Georgia Rose	1951	60.00
❑ 4453	I'm Waiting Just for You/Bongo Boogie	1951	60.00
❑ 4476	The Grape Vine/No One Else Could Be	1951	60.00
❑ 4496	The Right Kind of Love/It's Been a Long, Long Time	1951	60.00
❑ 4534	Ram-Bunk-Shush/Loaded with Love	1952	60.00
❑ 4545	When I Have You My Love/Please Be Careful	1952	100.00
❑ 4557	Lord Knows I Tried/Heavy Sugar	1952	100.00
❑ 4571	Backslider's Ball/Please Be Careful	1952	100.00
❑ 4792	It's a Sad, Sad Feeling/Ow	1955	80.00
—With the Admirals			
❑ 4803	Goody Good Love/I'm Here, Love	1955	30.00
❑ 5240	Heavy Sugar/Honeydripper	1959	12.00

RCA VICTOR

Number	Title (A Side/B Side)	Yr	NM
❑ 47-2961	Tomorrow/I Ain't Got Nothin' to Lose	1949	50.00
❑ 47-3005	Awful Natural/In the Middle of the Night	1949	50.00
❑ 47-3128	I'll Never Be Free/Journey's End	1949	50.00
❑ 50-0054	D Natural Blues/Little Girl, Don't Cry	1949	60.00
—Gray label, orange vinyl			
❑ 50-0088	Let It Be/Sweet Slumber	1950	50.00

WARWICK

Number	Title (A Side/B Side)	Yr	NM
❑ 582	Big Fat Mama/Slide My Trombone	1960	12.00

Albums

ALAMAC

Number	Title (A Side/B Side)	Yr	NM
❑ QSR-2425	Lucky Millinder and His Orchestra 1941-43	198?	10.00

HINDSIGHT

Number	Title (A Side/B Side)	Yr	NM
❑ HSR-233	The Uncollected Lucky Millinder and His Orchestra 1942	198?	10.00

M

MCA

Number	Title (A Side/B Side)	Yr	NM
❑ 1357	Let It Roll	198?	12.00

MILLS, GARRY

45s

IMPERIAL

Number	Title (A Side/B Side)	Yr	NM
❑ 5674	Look for a Star — Part 1/Look for a Star — Part 2	1960	15.00

LONDON

Number	Title (A Side/B Side)	Yr	NM
❑ 9504	I'll Step Down/Treasure Island	1962	15.00

TOP RANK

Number	Title (A Side/B Side)	Yr	NM
❑ 2071	Top Teen Baby/Don't Forget	1960	15.00

UNITED ARTISTS

Number	Title (A Side/B Side)	Yr	NM
❑ 0099	Look for a Star/Look for a Star	1973	5.00

—"Silver Spotlight Series" reissue; B-side by Gary Miles

MILLS, HAYLEY

45s

BUENA VISTA

Number	Title (A Side/B Side)	Yr	NM
❑ 385	Let's Get Together/Cobbler, Cobbler	1961	12.00
❑ 385 [PS]	Let's Get Together/Cobbler, Cobbler	1961	25.00
❑ 395	Johnny Jingo/Jeepers Creepers	1962	10.00
❑ 395 [PS]	Johnny Jingo/Jeepers Creepers	1962	25.00
❑ 401	Side by Side/Ching Ching and a Ring Ding Ding	1962	10.00
❑ 401 [PS]	Side by Side/Ching Ching and a Ring Ding Ding	1962	25.00
❑ 408	Castaway/Sweet River	1962	10.00
❑ 408 [PS]	Castaway/Sweet River	1962	25.00
❑ 409	Let's Climb/Enjoy It	1962	10.00
—With Maurice Chevalier			
❑ 409 [PS]	Let's Climb/Enjoy It	1962	25.00
❑ 420	Flitterin'/Beautiful Beulah	1963	10.00
—With Eddie Hodges			
❑ 420 [PS]	Flitterin'/Beautiful Beulah	1963	25.00

MAINSTREAM

Number	Title (A Side/B Side)	Yr	NM
❑ 656	Gypsy Girl/Younger Than Seventeen	1966	8.00

Albums

BUENA VISTA

Number	Title (A Side/B Side)	Yr	NM
❑ BV-3311 [M]	Let's Get Together	1962	20.00
❑ STER-3311 [S]	Let's Get Together	1962	30.00

MILLS, MRS.

45s

CAPITOL

Number	Title (A Side/B Side)	Yr	NM
❑ 4758	Bobbikins/Popcorn	1962	12.00

Albums

LIBERTY

Number	Title (A Side/B Side)	Yr	NM
❑ LRP-3359 [M]	My Mother — The Ragtime Piano Player	1964	12.00
❑ LST-7359 [S]	My Mother — The Ragtime Piano Player	1964	15.00

MIMMS, GARNET, AND THE ENCHANTERS

Includes Garnet Mimms credited alone. Also see THE ENCHANTERS (2).

45s

ARISTA

Number	Title (A Side/B Side)	Yr	NM
❑ 0239	What It Is (Part 1)/What It Is (Part 2)	1977	4.00
❑ 0289	Johnny Perter/Tail Snatcher	1977	4.00
❑ 0332	Right Here in the Palm of My Hand/Tail Snatcher	1978	4.00

GSF

Number	Title (A Side/B Side)	Yr	NM
❑ 6874	Another Place/Stop and Check Yourself	1972	6.00
❑ 6887	I'll Keep On Loving/Somebody, Someplace	1972	6.00

UNITED ARTISTS

Number	Title (A Side/B Side)	Yr	NM
❑ 0109	Cry Baby/For Your Precious Love	1973	4.00
—"Silver Spotlight Series" reissue			
❑ 629	Cry Baby/Don't Change Your Heart	1963	15.00
❑ 658	Baby Don't You Weep/For Your Precious Love	1963	20.00
❑ 658 [PS]	Baby Don't You Weep/For Your Precious Love	1963	30.00
❑ 694	Tell Me Baby/Anytime You Want Me	1964	15.00
❑ 715	One Girl/A Quiet Place	1964	20.00
❑ 773	One Woman Man/Look Away	1964	30.00
❑ 796	A Little Bit of Soap /I'll Make It Up to You	1964	20.00
❑ 848	So Close/It Was Easier to Hurt Her	1965	30.00
❑ 868	Welcome Home/The Adventures of Moll Flanders	1965	10.00
❑ 887	Everytime/That Goes to Show You	1965	15.00
❑ 951	Looking for You/More Than a Miracle	1965	200.00
❑ 995	Prove It to Me/I'll Take Good Care of You	1966	40.00
❑ 50058	My Baby/Keep On Smilin'	1966	—
—Unreleased			

VEEP

Number	Title (A Side/B Side)	Yr	NM
❑ 1232	Thinkin'/It's Been Such a Long Time Comin'	1966	20.00
❑ 1234	My Baby/Keep On Smilin'	1966	40.00
❑ 1252	All About Love/The Truth Hurts	1967	30.00

VERVE

Number	Title (A Side/B Side)	Yr	NM
❑ 10596	Stop and Think It Over/I Can Hear My Baby Crying	1968	30.00
❑ 10624	Can You Top This/We Can Find That Love	1968	30.00
❑ 10642	Take Me/Happy Landing	1969	15.00
❑ 10650	Sad Song/Get It While You Can	1970	30.00

Albums

ARISTA

Number	Title (A Side/B Side)	Yr	NM
❑ AL 4153	Garnet Mimms Has It All	1978	12.00

UNITED ARTISTS

Number	Title (A Side/B Side)	Yr	NM
❑ UAL 3305 [M]	Cry Baby and 11 Other Hits	1963	80.00
❑ UAL 3396 [M]	As Long As I Have You	1964	50.00
❑ UAL 3498 [M]	I'll Take Good Care of You	1966	50.00
❑ UAS 6305 [S]	Cry Baby and 11 Other Hits	1963	100.00
❑ UAS 6396 [S]	As Long As I Have You	1964	70.00
❑ UAS 6498 [S]	I'll Take Good Care of You	1966	70.00

MIND EXPANDERS, THE

Albums

DOT

Number	Title (A Side/B Side)	Yr	NM
❑ DLP-3773 [M]	What's Happening	1967	100.00
❑ DLP-25773 [S]	What's Happening	1967	80.00

MIND GARAGE, THE

45s

RCA VICTOR

Number	Title (A Side/B Side)	Yr	NM
❑ 47-9755	There Was a Time/What's Behind Those Eyes	1969	8.00
❑ 47-9812	Jailhouse Rock/Tobacco Road	1969	8.00

Albums

RCA VICTOR

Number	Title (A Side/B Side)	Yr	NM
❑ LSP-4218	The Mind Garage	1969	30.00
❑ LSP-4319	The Mind Garage Again!	1970	30.00

MINDBENDERS, THE

Also see WAYNE FONTANA AND THE MINDBENDERS.

45s

FONTANA

Number	Title (A Side/B Side)	Yr	NM
❑ 1541	A Groovy Kind of Love/Love Is Good	1966	12.00
❑ 1555	Ashes to Ashes/Don't Know About Love	1966	8.00
❑ 1571	I Want Her, She Wants Me/Morning After	1967	8.00
❑ 1595	It's Getting Harder All the Time/Off and Running	1967	8.00
❑ 1620	Yellow Brick Road/Blessed Are the Lonely	1968	8.00
❑ 1628	Uncle Joe the Ice Cream Man/The Man Who Loved Trees	1968	8.00

Albums

FONTANA

Number	Title (A Side/B Side)	Yr	NM
❑ MGF-27554 [M]	A Groovy Kind of Love	1966	25.00
—With "Ashes to Ashes"			
❑ MGF-27554 [M]	A Groovy Kind of Love	1966	30.00
—With "Don't Cry No More"			
❑ SRF-67554 [R]	A Groovy Kind of Love	1966	20.00
—With "Ashes to Ashes"			
❑ SRF-67554 [R]	A Groovy Kind of Love	1966	25.00
—With "Don't Cry No More"			

MINEO, SAL

45s

DECCA

Number	Title (A Side/B Side)	Yr	NM
❑ 31692	Why Don't You Love Me/A Girl Across the Way	1964	12.00

EPIC

Number	Title (A Side/B Side)	Yr	NM
❑ 9216	Start Movin' (In My Direction)/Love Affair	1957	25.00
❑ 9216 [PS]	Start Movin' (In My Direction)/Love Affair	1957	40.00
❑ 9227	Lasting Love/You Shouldn't Do That	1957	20.00
❑ 9227 [PS]	Lasting Love/You Shouldn't Do That	1957	30.00
❑ 9246	Party Time/The Words That I Whisper	1957	20.00
❑ 9246 [PS]	Party Time/The Words That I Whisper	1957	30.00
❑ 9260	Little Pigeon/Cuttin' In	1958	20.00
❑ 9260 [PS]	Little Pigeon/Cuttin' In	1958	—
—Rumored to exist, but without conclusive evidence, we will delete this from future editions			
❑ 9271	Seven Steps to Love/A Couple of Crazy Kids	1958	20.00
❑ 9287	Baby Face/Souvenirs of Summertime	1958	20.00
❑ 9327	Young As We Are/Make Believe Baby	1959	20.00
❑ 9327 [PS]	Young As We Are/Make Believe Baby	1959	30.00
❑ 9345	I'll Never Be Myself Again/The Words That I Whisper	1959	20.00

FONTANA

Number	Title (A Side/B Side)	Yr	NM
❑ 1504	Save the Last Dance for Me/Take Me Back	1965	12.00

7-Inch Extended Plays

EPIC

Number	Title (A Side/B Side)	Yr	NM
❑ EG-7187	(contents unknown)	1958	50.00
❑ EG-7187 [PS]	Sal Mineo	1958	50.00
❑ EG-7194	Baby Face/Too Young//The Words That I Whisper/Blue-Eyed Baby	1958	40.00
❑ EG-7194 [PS]	Sal	1958	40.00
❑ EG-7195	(contents unknown)	1958	40.00
❑ EG-7195 [PS]	Sal	1958	40.00
❑ EG-7204	Souvenirs of Summertime/Seven Steps to Love//A Couple of Crazy Kids/Secret Doorway	1959	50.00
❑ EG-7204 [PS]	Souvenirs of Summertime	1959	50.00
❑ ZTEP 27283/4	Too Young/Start Movin'//Baby Face/Little Pigeon	195?	60.00
—Special item for Scotch cellophane tape			
❑ ZTEP 27283/4 [PS]	Sal Sings	195?	80.00

Albums

EPIC

Number	Title (A Side/B Side)	Yr	NM
❑ LN 3405 [M]	Sal	1958	150.00

MINIATURE MEN, THE

45s

DOLTON

Number	Title (A Side/B Side)	Yr	NM
❑ 52	Miniature Blues/Soupy's Theme	1962	12.00
❑ 57	Baby Elephant Walk/Bool-Ya-Base	1962	12.00

MINISTRY

12-Inch Singles

ARISTA

Number	Title (A Side/B Side)	Yr	NM
❑ CP 726	Work for Love (3 mixes)	1983	15.00
❑ 9037	Work for Love/For Love	1983	15.00
❑ 9062	Revenge/Effigy/I Wanted to Tell Her	1983	15.00
❑ 9102	I Wanted to Tell Her (Tongue Tied Mix)/I Wanted to Tell Her	1983	15.00

SIRE

Number	Title (A Side/B Side)	Yr	NM
❑ PRO-A-3322 [DJ]	Stigmata/Tonight We Murder	1988	12.00
❑ 20401	Over the Shoulder/Isle of Man (Version 2)/Twitch (Version 2)	1986	8.00
❑ 21113	Stigmata/Tonight We Murder	1988	10.00
❑ 21384	Burning Inside/Thieves/Smothered Hope	1989	10.00
❑ 40211	Jesus Built My Hot Rod (2 mixes)/TV Song	1991	10.00

WAX TRAX!

Number	Title (A Side/B Side)	Yr	NM
❑ 003	Cold Life/Cold Life (Dub)/I'm Falling/Primental	1985	12.00
❑ 007	Every Day (Is Halloween)/All Day	198?	12.00
❑ 009	Nature of Love/Nature of Love (Cruelty Mix)	1985	8.00
❑ 020	Halloween (Remix)/Nature of Outtakes	1985	10.00
❑ 110072X	I'm Falling/Cold Life/Primental	1982	15.00

45s

ARISTA

Number	Title (A Side/B Side)	Yr	NM
❑ 9021	Revenge/She's Got a Cause	1983	6.00
❑ 9068	I Wanted to Tell Her/A Walk in the Park	1983	6.00

Albums

ARISTA

Number	Title (A Side/B Side)	Yr	NM
❑ AL 6608	With Sympathy	1983	14.00
❑ AL6 8016	With Sympathy	198?	10.00
—Reissue			

SIRE

Number	Title (A Side/B Side)	Yr	NM
❑ 25309	Twitch	1986	12.00
❑ 25799	The Land of Rape and Honey	1988	12.00
❑ 26004	The Mind Is a Terrible Thing to Taste	1989	12.00

WARNER BROS.

Number	Title (A Side/B Side)	Yr	NM
❑ 45838	Filth Pig	1996	20.00

Except when noted otherwise, VG = 25% of NM, and VG+ = 50% of NM. (Example: VG = $2.00, VG+ = $4.00 and NM = $8.00.)

Number	Title (A Side/B Side)	Yr	NM

WAX TRAX!

Number	Title (A Side/B Side)	Yr	NM
❑ 035	Twelve Inch Singles 1981-84	1985	15.00

MINNELLI, LIZA
Also see JUDY GARLAND AND LIZA MINNELLI.

12-Inch Singles

EPIC

Number	Title (A Side/B Side)	Yr	NM
❑ 68858	Losing My Mind (4 versions)	1989	10.00
❑ 73166	Love Pains (5 versions)	1989	10.00

45s

A&M

Number	Title (A Side/B Side)	Yr	NM
❑ 915	Married/You Better Sit Down Kids//Waiting for My Friends	1968	6.00
❑ 1018	Raggedy Ann and Raggedy Andy/Frank Mills	1969	6.00
❑ 1173	Come Saturday Morning/ Wherefore and Why	1970	6.00
❑ 1244	(I Wonder Where My) Easy Rider's Gone/The Man I Love	1971	6.00

CADENCE

Number	Title (A Side/B Side)	Yr	NM
❑ 1436	What Do You Think I Am/You Are For Living	1963	12.00

CAPITOL

Number	Title (A Side/B Side)	Yr	NM
❑ 4994	One Summer Love/ How Much Do I Love You	1963	10.00
❑ 5103	Day Dreaming/His Woman	1964	10.00
❑ 5473	Did I Hurt Your Feelings/Imprevu	1965	8.00
❑ 5761	I Who Have Nothing/ Middle of the Street	1966	8.00

COLUMBIA

Number	Title (A Side/B Side)	Yr	NM
❑ 10178	All That Jazz/My Own Best Friend	1975	4.00
❑ 45715	Ring Them Bells/It Was a Good Time	1972	5.00
❑ 45746	The Singer/Mr. Emery Won't Be Home	1972	5.00
❑ 45846	Don't Let Me Be Lonely Tonight/Mr. Emery Won't Be Home	1973	5.00
❑ 45995	Harbour/More Than I Like You	1974	5.00

EPIC

Number	Title (A Side/B Side)	Yr	NM
❑ 73011	Losing My Mind/ Tonight Is Forever	1989	5.00

UNITED ARTISTS

Number	Title (A Side/B Side)	Yr	NM
❑ XW1014	Theme from "New York, New York"/Hazy	1977	5.00

Albums

A&M

Number	Title (A Side/B Side)	Yr	NM
❑ SP-3524 [(2)]	Liza Minnelli Foursider	1973	15.00
❑ SP-4141 [M]	Liza Minnelli	1968	25.00

—Mono copies have stereo numbers, but the labels are mono white label promos

Number	Title (A Side/B Side)	Yr	NM
❑ SP-4141 [S]	Liza Minnelli	1968	15.00
❑ SP-4164	Come Saturday Morning	1969	15.00
❑ SP-4272	New Feelin'	1970	15.00
❑ SP-4345	Live at the Olympia	1971	15.00
❑ SP-6013 [(2)]	Liza Minnelli Foursider	198?	10.00

—Reissue of 3524

CAPITOL

Number	Title (A Side/B Side)	Yr	NM
❑ ST 2174 [S]	Liza! Liza!	1964	25.00
❑ T 2174 [M]	Liza! Liza!	1964	20.00
❑ SM-2271	It Amazes Me	1976	10.00

—Reissue with new prefix

Number	Title (A Side/B Side)	Yr	NM
❑ ST 2271 [S]	It Amazes Me	1965	25.00
❑ T 2271 [M]	It Amazes Me	1965	20.00
❑ ST 2448 [S]	There Is a Time	1966	25.00
❑ T 2448 [M]	There Is a Time	1966	20.00
❑ SM-11080	Maybe This Time	197?	10.00

—Reissue with new prefix

Number	Title (A Side/B Side)	Yr	NM
❑ ST-11080	Maybe This Time	1972	12.00
❑ SM-11803	There Is a Time	1978	10.00

—Reissue of ST 2448

COLUMBIA

Number	Title (A Side/B Side)	Yr	NM
❑ KC 31762	Liza with a "Z"	1972	15.00
❑ PC 31762	Liza with a "Z"	198?	8.00

—Budget-line reissue

Number	Title (A Side/B Side)	Yr	NM
❑ CQ 32149 [Q]	Liza Minnelli The Singer	1973	20.00
❑ KC 32149	Liza Minnelli The Singer	1973	15.00
❑ PC 32149	Liza Minnelli The Singer	198?	8.00

—Budget-line reissue

Number	Title (A Side/B Side)	Yr	NM
❑ PC 32854	Live at the Winter Garden	1974	15.00
❑ PC 34887	Tropical Nights	1977	12.00

EPIC

Number	Title (A Side/B Side)	Yr	NM
❑ OE 45098	Results	1989	15.00

TELARC

Number	Title (A Side/B Side)	Yr	NM
❑ 15502 [(2)]	Liza Minnelli at Carnegie Hall	1987	15.00

MINOR THREAT

45s

DISCHORD

Number	Title (A Side/B Side)	Yr	NM
❑ 15	Salad Days/Stumped/ Good Guys	1985	5.00
❑ 15 [PS]	Salad Days/Stumped/ Good Guys	1985	5.00

7-Inch Extended Plays

DISCHORD

Number	Title (A Side/B Side)	Yr	NM
❑ 3	Filler/I Don't Wanna Hear It/ Seeing Red/Straight Edge// Small Man, Big Mouth/ Screaming at a Wall/Bottled Violence/Minor Threat	1981	30.00

—Third and fourth pressings: Silver label

Number	Title (A Side/B Side)	Yr	NM
❑ 3	Filler/I Don't Wanna Hear It/ Seeing Red/Straight Edge// Small Man, Big Mouth/ Screaming at a Wall/Bottled Violence/Minor Threat	1981	35.00

—First pressing of 1000: Yellow label

Number	Title (A Side/B Side)	Yr	NM
❑ 3	Filler/I Don't Wanna Hear It/ Seeing Red/Straight Edge// Small Man, Big Mouth/ Screaming at a Wall/Bottled Violence/Minor Threat	1981	35.00

—Second pressing of 1000: Blue label

Number	Title (A Side/B Side)	Yr	NM
❑ 3 [PS]	Minor Threat	1981	30.00

—Fourth pressing of 2000: Blue cover

Number	Title (A Side/B Side)	Yr	NM
❑ 3 [PS]	Minor Threat	1981	35.00

—First pressing of 1000: Red cover

Number	Title (A Side/B Side)	Yr	NM
❑ 3 [PS]	Minor Threat	1981	35.00

—Second pressing of 1000: Yelow cover

Number	Title (A Side/B Side)	Yr	NM
❑ 3 [PS]	Minor Threat	1981	35.00

—Third pressing of 1000: Green cover

Number	Title (A Side/B Side)	Yr	NM
❑ 5	In My Eyes/Out of Step//Guilty of Being White/Steppin' Stone	1981	30.00

—Black vinyl, blue label

Number	Title (A Side/B Side)	Yr	NM
❑ 5	In My Eyes/Out of Step//Guilty of Being White/Steppin' Stone	1981	35.00

—Black vinyl, yellow label

Number	Title (A Side/B Side)	Yr	NM
❑ 5	In My Eyes/Out of Step//Guilty of Being White/Steppin' Stone	1981	35.00

—First pressing of 1000: Red vinyl

Number	Title (A Side/B Side)	Yr	NM
❑ 5 [PS]	In My Eyes/Out of Step//Guilty of Being White/Steppin' Stone	1981	30.00

—Heavy cover stock, as opposed to thinner paper stock

Number	Title (A Side/B Side)	Yr	NM
❑ 5 [PS]	In My Eyes/Out of Step//Guilty of Being White/Steppin' Stone	1981	35.00

—Printed, as opposed to photocopied, sleeve

Number	Title (A Side/B Side)	Yr	NM
❑ 5 [PS]	In My Eyes/Out of Step//Guilty of Being White/Steppin' Stone	1981	45.00

—First 125 issued with photocopied cover

Albums

DISCHORD

Number	Title (A Side/B Side)	Yr	NM
❑ 10	Out of Step	1983	20.00

—Second stock pressing, gray back cover with photos

Number	Title (A Side/B Side)	Yr	NM
❑ 10	Out of Step	1983	50.00

—First stock pressing, black back cover with lyrics

Number	Title (A Side/B Side)	Yr	NM
❑ 10 [DJ]	Out of Step	1983	500.00

—Test pressing of 50; black silkscreen cover with sheep logo; paste-on back cover; blank labels; plain innersleeve with rubber stamp

Number	Title (A Side/B Side)	Yr	NM
❑ 12 [EP]	The First Two 7" On a 12"	1984	15.00

MINORBOPS, THE

45s

LAMP

Number	Title (A Side/B Side)	Yr	NM
❑ 2012	Need You Tonight/ Want You for My Own	1957	250.00

MINT JULEPS, THE

45s

HERALD

Number	Title (A Side/B Side)	Yr	NM
❑ 481	Bells of Love/Vip-a-Dip	1956	25.00

—With block logo inside flag

Number	Title (A Side/B Side)	Yr	NM
❑ 481	Bells of Love/Vip-a-Dip	1956	100.00

—With script logo inside flag

LOST-NITE

Number	Title (A Side/B Side)	Yr	NM
❑ 424	Bells of Love/Vip-a-Dip	197?	5.00

—Reissue

MINT TATTOO

45s

DOT

Number	Title (A Side/B Side)	Yr	NM
❑ 17242	Mark of the Beast/ When Talking About You	1969	10.00

Albums

DOT

Number	Title (A Side/B Side)	Yr	NM
❑ DLP-25918	Mint Tattoo	1969	30.00

MINTS, THE
See KEN COPELAND.

MINUTE MEN, THE

45s

ARGO

Number	Title (A Side/B Side)	Yr	NM
❑ 5469	Please Keep the Beatles in England/My Love Is Gone	1964	15.00

MINUTEMEN
Also see FIREHOSE. Featuring Mike Watt.

45s

NEW ALLIANCE

Number	Title (A Side/B Side)	Yr	NM
❑ 004	Joy/Black Sheep//More Joy	1981	6.00
❑ 004 [PS]	Joy/Black Sheep//More Joy	1981	6.00

SST

Number	Title (A Side/B Side)	Yr	NM
❑ PSST E-58	Courage/What Is It?/Stories	1985	8.00
❑ PSST E-58 [PS]	Courage/What Is It?/Stories	1985	12.00

—Rubberstamped sleeve

Number	Title (A Side/B Side)	Yr	NM
❑ 214	Joy/Black Sheep//More Joy	199?	2.00

—Reissue of New Alliance 004

Number	Title (A Side/B Side)	Yr	NM
❑ 214 [PS]	Joy/Black Sheep//More Joy	199?	2.00

7-Inch Extended Plays

REFLEX

Number	Title (A Side/B Side)	Yr	NM
❑ L	Tour-Spiel	1984	12.50
❑ L [PS]	Tour-Spiel	1984	12.50

SST

Number	Title (A Side/B Side)	Yr	NM
❑ 002	Paranoid Time	1980	6.00
❑ 002 [PS]	Paranoid Time	1980	6.00

THERMIDOR

Number	Title (A Side/B Side)	Yr	NM
❑ 8	Bean-Spill	1981	8.00

—Came in generic Thermidor sleeve (add 25%)

Albums

NEW ALLIANCE

Number	Title (A Side/B Side)	Yr	NM
❑ 017	The Politics of Time	1984	12.00

SST

Number	Title (A Side/B Side)	Yr	NM
❑ 004	The Punch Line	1981	12.00
❑ 004	The Punch Line	1981	20.00

—Original copies have white labels

Number	Title (A Side/B Side)	Yr	NM
❑ 014	What Makes a Man Start Fires?	1983	10.00
❑ 014	What Makes a Man Start Fires?	1983	15.00

—Original version has yellow labels and no UPC code

Number	Title (A Side/B Side)	Yr	NM
❑ 016 [EP]	Buzz or Howl Under the Influence of Heat	1983	10.00
❑ 028 [(2)]	Double Nickels on the Dime	1984	12.00
❑ PSST E-28 [DJ]	Excerpts from Double Nickels on the Dime	1984	25.00

—One-sided promo LP with etched B-side and sticker on blank cover

Number	Title (A Side/B Side)	Yr	NM
❑ 034 [EP]	Project Mersh	1985	10.00
❑ 058	3-Way Tie (For Last)	1985	12.00
❑ 068 [(2)]	Ballot Result	1987	12.00
❑ 277	The Politics of Time	198?	10.00

—Reissue of New Alliance 017

MIRABAI

45s

ATLANTIC

Number	Title (A Side/B Side)	Yr	NM
❑ 3300	Cosmic Overload/To Be Young	1975	5.00

Albums

ATLANTIC

Number	Title (A Side/B Side)	Yr	NM
❑ SD 18144	Mirabai	1975	10.00

MIRACLES, THE
Includes records as "Smokey Robinson and the Miracles." Also see SMOKEY ROBINSON.

12-Inch Singles

COLUMBIA

Number	Title (A Side/B Side)	Yr	NM
❑ AS 283 [DJ]	Spy for Brotherhood (6:04) (same on both sides)	1976	20.00
❑ 23-10515	Spy for Brotherhood (6:04)/ Women (Make the World Go 'Round) (4:50)	1977	20.00

MOTOWN

Number	Title (A Side/B Side)	Yr	NM
❑ PR-129 [DJ]	The Tracks of My Tears/ I Second That Emotion// I Heard It Through the Grapevine (5:03)	1983	10.00

—As "Smokey Robinson and the Miracles"; B-side by Marvin Gaye; promo-only item issued in conjunction with the movie "The Big Chill"

45s

CHESS

Number	Title (A Side/B Side)	Yr	NM
❑ 1734	Bad Girl/I Love Your Baby	1959	60.00

—Blue label with vertical Chess logo (original)

Number	Title (A Side/B Side)	Yr	NM
❑ 1734	Bad Girl/I Love Your Baby	1963	25.00

—Black label

Number	Title (A Side/B Side)	Yr	NM
❑ 1734	Bad Girl/I Love Your Baby	1966	20.00

—Blue label with "Chess" at top

Number	Title (A Side/B Side)	Yr	NM
❑ 1768	I Need a Change/All I Want (Is You)	1960	40.00

COLUMBIA

Number	Title (A Side/B Side)	Yr	NM
❑ 3-10464	Spy for Brotherhood/The Bird Must Fly Away	1976	5.00
❑ 3-10517	Women (Make the World Go 'Round)/I Can Touch the Sky	1977	5.00
❑ 3-10706	Mean Machine/The Magic of Your Eyes (Laura's Eyes)	1978	5.00

END

Number	Title (A Side/B Side)	Yr	NM
❑ 1016	Got a Job/My Mama Done Told Me	1958	60.00
❑ 1029	Money/I Cry	1958	40.00

—Multicolor label with "A Division of Roulette Records Inc." on label

M

Number	Title (A Side/B Side)	Yr	NM
❑ 1029	Money/I Cry	1958	50.00
—Mostly gray-white label, no mention of Roulette Records			
❑ 1084	Money/I Cry	1961	25.00
MOTOWN			
❑ G 1/G 2	Bad Girl/I Love Your Baby	1959	2500.
—VG 1250; VG+ 1875			
❑ TLX-2207	Bad Girl/I Love Your Baby	1959	2500.
—VG 1250; VG+ 1875			
STANDARD GROOVE			
❑ 13090 [DJ]	I Care About Detroit	1968	150.00
—With no Tamla logo on label			
❑ 13090 [DJ]	I Care About Detroit	1968	200.00
—With Tamla globe logo on label			
TAMLA			
❑ EX-009 [DJ]	The Christmas Song/ Christmas Everyday	1963	200.00
❑ 54028	Way Over There/Depend On Me	1960	60.00
—With overdubbed strings on A-side			
❑ 54028	Way Over There/Depend On Me	1960	150.00
—No strings on A-side recording			
❑ 54028	The Feeling Is So Fine/You Can Depend On Me	1960	400.00
❑ 54028	The Feeling Is So Fine/You Can Depend On Me	1960	500.00
—With alternate take of B-side; matrix number followed by "A" in trail-off wax			
❑ 54034	Shop Around/Who's Lovin' You	196?	12.00
—Hit take; "L-1" in trail-off wax; globe label			
❑ 54034	Shop Around/Who's Lovin' You	1960	30.00
—Hit take; "L-1" in trail-off wax; horizontal lines label			
❑ 54034	Shop Around/Who's Lovin' You	1960	40.00
—Hit take; "ZTSC-67018" on label and in trail-off wax of Side 1 and "ZTSC-67019" on label and in trail-off wax of Side 2; horizontal lines label			
❑ 54034	Shop Around/Who's Lovin' You	1960	180.00
—Original take, withdrawn shortly after release; "H55518A" in trail-off wax			
❑ 54036	Ain't It Baby/The Only One I Love	1961	150.00
❑ 54044	Mighty Good Lovin'/ Broken Hearted	1961	50.00
❑ 54044 [PS]	Mighty Good Lovin'/ Broken Hearted	1961	150.00
❑ 54048	Everybody's Gotta Pay Some Dues/I Can't Believe	1961	50.00
❑ 54048	You Gotta Pay Some Dues/ I Can't Believe	1961	100.00
—Alternate A-side title			
❑ 54048 [PS]	Everybody's Gotta Pay Some Dues/I Can't Believe	1961	200.00
❑ 54053	What's So Good About Good-By/I've Been Good to You	1962	30.00
❑ 54053 [PS]	What's So Good About Good-By/I've Been Good to You	1962	120.00
❑ 54059	I'll Try Something New/You Never Miss a Good Thing	1962	20.00
❑ 54059 [PS]	I'll Try Something New/You Never Miss a Good Thing	1962	120.00
❑ 54069	Way Over There/If Your Mother Only Knew	1962	20.00
❑ 54073	You've Really Got a Hold on Me/Happy Landing	1962	20.00
❑ 54078	A Love She Can Count On/ I Can Take a Hint	1963	20.00
❑ 54083	Mickey's Monkey/Whatever Makes You Happy	1963	20.00
❑ 54089	I Gotta Dance to Keep from Crying/Such Is Love, Such Is Life	1963	15.00
❑ 54092	(You Can't Let the Boy Overpower) The Man in You/ Heartbreak Road	1964	15.00
❑ 54098	I Like It Like That/You're So Fine and Sweet	1964	15.00
❑ 54098 [PS]	I Like It Like That/You're So Fine and Sweet	1964	120.00
❑ 54102	That's What Love Is Made Of/ Would I Love You	1964	15.00
❑ 54109	Come On Do the Jerk/ Baby Don't You Go	1964	15.00
❑ 54113	Ooo Baby Baby/All That's Good	1965	15.00
❑ 54118	The Tracks of My Tears/ A Fork in the Road	1965	15.00
❑ 54123	My Girl Has Gone/Since You Won My Heart	1965	15.00
❑ 54127	Going to A-Go-Go/ Choosey Beggar	1965	15.00
❑ 54127 [PS]	Going to A-Go-Go/ Choosey Beggar	1965	100.00
❑ 54134	Whole Lot of Shakin' in My Heart (Since I Met You)/ Oh Be My Lover	1966	10.00
❑ 54140	Come 'Round Here — I'm the One You Need/Save Me	1966	10.00
❑ 54140 [PS]	Come 'Round Here — I'm the One You Need/Save Me	1966	100.00
❑ 54145	The Love I Saw in You Was Just a Mirage/Come Spy with Me	1967	8.00
—Starting here, through Tamla 54225, as "Smokey Robinson and the Miracles"			
❑ 54152	More Love/Swept for You Baby	1967	8.00
❑ 54159	I Second That Emotion/ You Must Be Love	1967	8.00
❑ 54162	If You Can Want/When the Words from Your Heart Get Caught Up in Your Throat	1968	8.00
—"Tamla" in box on label			
❑ 54162	If You Can Want/When the Words from Your Heart Get Caught Up in Your Throat	1968	15.00
—"Tamla" in globe on label			
❑ 54167	Yester Love/Much Better Off	1968	8.00
❑ 54172	Special Occasion/Give Her Up	1968	8.00
❑ 54178	Baby, Baby Don't Cry/Your Mother's Only Daughter	1968	8.00
❑ 54183	Here I Go Again/Doggone Right	1969	8.00
❑ 54184	Abraham, Martin, and John/ Much Better Off	1969	8.00
❑ 54189	Point It Out/Darling Dear	1969	8.00
❑ 54194	Who's Gonna Take the Blame/ I Gotta Thing For You	1970	8.00
❑ 54199	The Tears of a Clown/ Promise Me	1970	6.00
❑ 54205	I Don't Blame You at All/ That Girl	1971	6.00
❑ 54206	Crazy About the La La La/ Oh Baby Baby I Love You	1971	6.00
❑ 54211	Satisfaction/Flower Girl	1971	6.00
❑ 54220	We've Come Too Far to End It Now/When Sundown Comes	1972	6.00
❑ 54225	I Can't Stand to See You Cry/ With Your Love Came	1972	6.00
❑ 54237	Don't Let It End (Til You Let It Begin)/Wigs and Lashes	1973	5.00
—Starting here, name reverts to The Miracles			
❑ 54240	Give Me Just Another Day/ I Wanna Be with You	1973	5.00
❑ 54248	Do It Baby/I Wanna Be with You	1974	5.00
❑ 54256	Don't Cha Love It/Up Again	1974	5.00
❑ 54259	You Are Love/Gemini	1975	5.00
❑ 54262	Love Machine (Part 1)/ Love Machine (Part 2)	1975	5.00
❑ 54268	Night Life/Smog	1976	5.00
TOPPS/MOTOWN			
❑ 11	Shop Around	1967	75.00
—Cardboard record			

7-Inch Extended Plays

Number	Title (A Side/B Side)	Yr	NM
TAMLA			
❑ TM-60254	Mickey's Monkey/You've Really Got a Hold on Me/I Like It Like That//Shop Around/I've Been Good to You/What's So Good About Good-Bye	196?	50.00
—Jukebox issue; small hole, plays at 33 1/3 rpm			
❑ TM-60254 [PS]	Greatest Hits from the Beginning	196?	50.00
❑ TM-60267	The Tracks of My Tears/Going To a Go-Go/Ooo Baby Baby/ /My Girl Has Gone/Choosey Beggar/In Case You Need Love	1966	50.00
—Jukebox issue; small hole, plays at 33 1/3 rpm			
❑ TM-60267 [PS]	Going to a Go-Go	1966	50.00

Albums

Number	Title	Yr	NM
COLUMBIA			
❑ PC 34460	Love Crazy	1977	12.00
❑ PCQ 34460 [Q]	Love Crazy	1977	20.00
❑ JC 34910	The Miracles	1978	12.00
MOTOWN			
❑ M5-133V1	Do It Baby	1981	8.00
—Reissue of Tamla 334			
❑ M5-136V1	Away We a Go-Go	1981	8.00
—Reissue of Tamla 271			
❑ M5-156V1	The Tears of a Clown	1981	8.00
—Reissue of Tamla 276			
❑ M5-160V1	Hi, We're the Miracles	1981	8.00
—Reissue of Tamla 220			
❑ M5-210V1	Greatest Hits, Vol. 2	1981	8.00
—Reissue of Tamla 280			
❑ M5-217V1	Doin' Mickey's Monkey	1981	8.00
—Reissue of Tamla 245			
❑ M5-220V1	Recorded Live on Stage	1981	8.00
—Reissue of Tamla 241			
❑ M8-238M2 [(2)]	Greatest Hits from the Beginning	1982	12.00
—Reissue of Tamla 254			
❑ M 793R3 [(3)]	Smokey Robinson and the Miracles Anthology	1974	20.00
❑ 5253 ML	The Season for Miracles	1982	8.00
—Reissue of Tamla 307			
❑ 5254 ML	Christmas with the Miracles	1982	8.00
—Reissue of Tamla 236			
TAMLA			
❑ T 220 [M]	Hi We're the Miracles	1961	600.00
—White label			
❑ T 223 [M]	Cookin' with the Miracles	1962	800.00
—White label			
❑ T 230 [M]	I'll Try Something New	1962	600.00
—White label			
❑ T 236 [M]	Christmas with the Miracles	1963	300.00
—Originals have two globes on the top of the label			
❑ T 238 [M]	You've Really Got a Hold on Me	1963	200.00
—Retitled version of "The Fabulous Miracles"			
❑ T 238 [M]	The Fabulous Miracles	1963	300.00
❑ T 241 [M]	The Miracles On Stage	1963	200.00
❑ T 245 [M]	Doin' Mickey's Monkey	1963	200.00
❑ TS 245 [S]	Doin' Mickey's Monkey	1963	300.00
❑ T 254 [(2)M]	Greatest Hits from the Beginning	1965	50.00
❑ TS 254 [(2)P]	Greatest Hits from the Beginning	1965	40.00
❑ T 267 [M]	Going to a Go-Go	1966	30.00
❑ TS 267 [S]	Going to a Go-Go	1966	40.00
❑ T 271 [M]	Away We a Go-Go	1966	25.00
❑ TS 271 [S]	Away We a Go-Go	1966	30.00
❑ T 276 [M]	Make It Happen	1967	25.00
❑ TS 276 [S]	Make It Happen	1967	30.00
❑ TS 276 [S]	The Tears of a Clown	1970	15.00
—Retitled version of "Make It Happen"			
❑ TS 280	Greatest Hits, Vol. 2	1968	25.00
❑ TS 289	Live!	1969	20.00
❑ T 290 [M]	Special Occasion	1968	50.00
❑ TS 290 [S]	Special Occasion	1968	20.00
❑ TS 295	Time Out for Smokey Robinson & the Miracles	1969	20.00
❑ TS 297	Four in Blue	1969	20.00
❑ TS 301	What Love Has... Joined Together	1970	15.00
❑ TS 306	A Pocket Full of Miracles	1970	15.00
❑ TS 307	The Season for Miracles	1970	15.00
❑ TS 312	One Dozen Roses	1971	15.00
❑ TS 318	Flying High Together	1972	15.00
❑ TS 320 [(2)]	1957-1972	1972	20.00
❑ T 325F	Renaissance	1973	12.00
❑ T6-334	Do It Baby	1974	12.00
❑ T6-336	Don't Cha Love It	1975	12.00
❑ T6-339	City of Angels	1975	12.00
❑ T6-344	The Power of Music	1976	12.00
❑ T7-357	Greatest Hits	1977	12.00

MIRACLES, THE (2) No relation to the more famous group above.

45s

Number	Title (A Side/B Side)	Yr	NM
BATON			
❑ 210	A Lover's Chant/Come Home with Me	1955	150.00
CASH			
❑ 1008	You're An Angel/A Gal Named Jo	1955	200.00

MIRANDA, BOB Of THE HAPPENINGS.

45s

Number	Title (A Side/B Side)	Yr	NM
B.T. PUPPY			
❑ 544	Girl on a Swing/When I Lock My Door	1968	10.00
JUBILEE			
❑ 5709	Everybody Is a Star/Evergreen	1971	8.00

MIRETTES, THE Also see THE IKETTES.

45s

Number	Title (A Side/B Side)	Yr	NM
MINIT			
❑ 32045	Help Wanted/Play Fair	1968	10.00
MIRWOOD			
❑ 5514	He's Alright with Me/Your Kind Ain't No Good	1966	12.00
❑ 5531	He's Alright with Me/Now That I Found You Baby	1967	10.00
REVUE			
❑ 11004	In the Midnight Hour/ To Love Somebody	1968	10.00
❑ 11017	Take Me for a Little While/ Real Thing	1968	8.00
❑ 11029	First Love/I'm a Whole New Thing	1968	8.00
UNI			
❑ 55110	Stand By Your Man/If Everybody'd Help Somebody	1969	6.00
❑ 55126	Heart Full of Gladness/You Ain't Trying to Cross Over	1969	6.00
❑ 55147	Whirlpool/You Ain't Trying to Cross Over	1969	6.00
❑ 55161	Rap Run It On Down/ Sweet Soul Sister	1969	6.00
—A-side: Nate Turner and the Mirettes; B-side: Venetta Fields and the Mirettes			

Albums

Number	Title	Yr	NM
REVUE			
❑ RS-7205	In the Midnight Hour	1968	15.00
UNI			
❑ 73062	Whirlpool	1969	15.00

MISFITS, THE The famous punk band. Also see GLENN DANZIG; SAMHAIN.

45s

Number	Title (A Side/B Side)	Yr	NM
BLANK			
❑ A 101	Cough Cool/She	1977	200.00
—500 copies were pressed			

Except when noted otherwise, VG = 25% of NM, and VG+ = 50% of NM. (Example: VG = $2.00, VG+ = $4.00 and NM = $8.00.)

Number	Title (A Side/B Side)	Yr	NM
❑ A 101 [PS]	Cough Cool/She	1977	200.00
GEFFEN			
❑ PRO-S-1112 [DJ]	Dig Up Her Bones/Hate the Living, Love the Dead	1997	5.00
—All copies on blue vinyl			
❑ PRO-S-1112 [PS]	Dig Up Her Bones/Hate the Living, Love the Dead	1997	5.00
PLAN 9			
❑ PL 1001	Bullet/We Are 138/Attitude/ Hollywood Babylon	1978	100.00
—Black vinyl			
❑ PL 1001	Bullet/We Are 138/Attitude/ Hollywood Babylon	1978	125.00
—Red vinyl			
❑ PL 1001 [PS]	Bullet/We Are 138/Attitude/ Hollywood Babylon	1978	125.00
—First edition with gatefold and lyric sheet			
❑ PL 1001 [PS]	Bullet/We Are 138/Attitude/ Hollywood Babylon	1978	125.00
—Second edition with new back cover "Better Dead on Red"			
❑ PL 1009	Horror Business/Teenagers from Mars/Children in Heat	1979	60.00
—Yellow vinyl			
❑ PL 1009	Horror Business/Teenagers from Mars/Children in Heat	1979	6000.
—25 (!!) on black vinyl, no picture sleeve			
❑ PL 1009 [PS]	Horror Business/Teenagers from Mars/Children in Heat	1979	100.00
—With insert (deduct 40 percent if missing)			
❑ PL 1009 [PS]	Horror Business/Teenagers from Mars/Children in Heat	1979	300.00
—Withdrawn sleeve; these have a back cover with a group photo and were never used, but some have hit the collector's market			
❑ PL 1010	Night of the Living Dead/Where Eagles Dare/Ratt Fink	1979	60.00
❑ PL 1010 [PS]	Night of the Living Dead/Where Eagles Dare/Ratt Fink	1979	60.00
❑ PL 1013	London Dungeon/Horror Hotel/ Ghouls Night Out	1981	50.00
—3,000 with gray label			
❑ PL 1013	London Dungeon/Horror Hotel/ Ghouls Night Out	1981	50.00
—7,000 with orange label			
❑ PL 1013	London Dungeon/Horror Hotel/ Ghouls Night Out	1981	50.00
—Second pressing: 400 on black vinyl, smal center hole			
❑ PL 1013	London Dungeon/Horror Hotel/ Ghouls Night Out	1981	50.00
—Second pressing: 400 on white vinyl			
❑ PL 1013 [PS]	3 Hits from Hell: London Dungeon/Horror Hotel/ Ghouls Night Out	1981	50.00
❑ PL 1017	Halloween I/Halloween II	1981	50.00
❑ PL 1017 [PS]	Halloween I/Halloween II	1981	60.00
—Orange sleeve with lyric sheet			
❑ PL 1017 [PS]	Halloween I/Halloween II	1981	400.00
—Black and white test sleeve; approximately 10 were made			

7-Inch Extended Plays

Number	Title (A Side/B Side)	Yr	NM
PLAN 9			
❑ PL 1019	20 Eyes/Night Of The Living Dead/Astro Zombies/Horror Business//London Dungeon/ All Hell Breaks Loose/ We Are 138	1982	50.00
—Orange label			
❑ PL 1019	20 Eyes/Night Of The Living Dead/Astro Zombies/Horror Business//London Dungeon/ All Hell Breaks Loose/ We Are 138	1982	50.00
—Yellow label			
❑ PL 1019 [(3)]	Evilive	1982	800.00
—33 sets of 3 each with individual sleeves by the three band members, available through the Fiend Club (fan club)			
❑ PL 1019 [PS]	Evilive	1982	40.00
—Unnumbered sleeve			
❑ PL 1019 [PS]	Evilive	1982	75.00
—Numbered sleeve with insert			

Albums

Number	Title (A Side/B Side)	Yr	NM
CAROLINE			
❑ 7511	Static Age	1995	—
—Canceled; finally released on 7520			
❑ 7515	Collection II	1995	30.00
—Green vinyl (3,500 made); sealed copies have bar code roughly 1/4 to 1/2 inch from bottom of back cover			
❑ 7515	Collection II	1995	40.00
—Red vinyl (6,000 made); sealed copies have bar code roughly 1 inch from the bottom of back cover			
❑ 7515	Collection II	1995	100.00
—Clear vinyl (500 made); sealed copies have bar code at upper right or not at all			
❑ 7520	Static Age	1997	30.00
—Yellow vinyl (1,000 made)			
❑ 7520	Static Age	1997	40.00
—Red vinyl (2,000 made)			
❑ 7520	Static Age	1997	100.00
—Purple vinyl (500 made)			
GEFFEN			
❑ GEF 25126	American Psycho	1997	20.00
PLAN 9			
❑ PL9-02	Earth A.D.	1983	12.00
—At least 10,000 on black vinyl (distributed by Caroline)			
❑ PL9-02	Earth A.D.	1983	500.00
—500 on yellow vinyl			
❑ PL9-02	Earth A.D.	1983	600.00
—200 on clear vinyl with red and blue swirls			
❑ PL9-02	Earth A.D.	1983	800.00
—200 on dark purple vinyl			
❑ PL9-02	Earth A.D.	1983	1500.
—100 on green vinyl			
❑ PL9-03 [EP]	Die, Die My Darling	1984	12.00
—Common issue on black vinyl (distribuled by Caroline)			
❑ PL9-03 [EP]	Die, Die My Darling	1984	250.00
—500 on purple vinyl			
❑ PL9-03 [EP]	Die, Die My Darling	1984	250.00
—500 on white vinyl (distributed by Caroline)			
❑ PL9-06	Legacy of Brutality	1986	20.00
—Black vinyl (distributed by Caroline)			
❑ PL9-06	Legacy of Brutality	1986	300.00
—500 on white vinyl			
❑ PL9-06	Legacy of Brutality	1986	500.00
—500 on red vinyl			
❑ PL9-06	Legacy of Brutality	1986	5000.
—16 (!!) on pink vinyl; VG value 2000; VG+ value 3500			
❑ PL9-08 [EP]	Evilive	1987	20.00
—Black vinyl (distributed by Caroline)			
❑ PL9-08 [EP]	Evilive	1987	100.00
—2,000 on green vinyl (distributed by Caroline)			
❑ PL9-09	Misfits	1988	12.00
ROADRUNNER			
❑ RR 8658-1	Famous Monsters	1999	20.00
—Picture disc			
RUBY/SLASH			
❑ JRR 804	Walk Among Us	1982	50.00
—Purple cover with innersleeve and insert			
❑ JRR 804	Walk Among Us	1982	100.00
—Original red cover; has custom innersleeve and insert			
SLASH			
❑ 25756	Walk Among Us	1988	20.00
—Reissue of JRR 804; some copies came with a Halloween bag, which can double or even triple the value!			

MISFITS, THE (U)

More than one group. The punk band is outside the scope of this book and is not included.

45s

Number	Title (A Side/B Side)	Yr	NM
ARIES			
❑ 3	Midnight Star/I Don't Know	1961	200.00
HUSH			
❑ 105	Give Me Your Heart/ My Mother-in-Law	1960	400.00
IMPERIAL			
❑ 66054	This Little Piggy (I'm a Hog for You)/Lost Love	1964	25.00
JOEY			
❑ 117	Naughty Rooster/ Chicago Confidential	1961	12.00
SOUND STAGE 7			
❑ 2538	It's Up to You/Skiing Time	1965	25.00
TROY			
❑ 227	The Uncle Willie/Big Bad Wolf	196?	25.00

MISSING PERSONS

12-Inch Singles

Number	Title (A Side/B Side)	Yr	NM
CAPITOL			
❑ 8582	Give (dance mix)/ Clandestine People	1984	10.00
❑ SPRO 9081/2 [DJ]	Give (Long)/Give (Short)	1984	15.00
❑ SPRO 9123 [DJ]	Right Now (same on both sides)	1984	10.00
❑ SPRO 9187 [DJ]	Surrender Your Heart (same on both sides)	1984	6.00
❑ SPRO 9721 [DJ]	I Can't Think About Dancing (Extended)/I Can't Think About Dancing (LP)	1986	8.00
❑ SPRO 9837/8 [DJ]	Destination Unknown/ Walking in L.A.	1982	20.00
❑ SPRO 9853 [DJ]	Color in Your Life/ Go Against the Flow	1986	8.00
❑ SPRO 9885 [DJ]	Windows (same on both sides)	1982	10.00
❑ 15233	I Can't Think About Dancing (3 versions)/Face to Face	1988	6.00

45s

Number	Title (A Side/B Side)	Yr	NM
AMERICAN PIE			
❑ 9036	Words/Wildflower	198?	3.00
—Reissue; B-side by Skylark			
CAPITOL			
❑ 5127	Words/Hello, I Love You	1982	3.00
❑ 5127 [PS]	Words/Hello, I Love You	1982	3.00
❑ 5161	Destination Unknown/ No Way Out	1982	3.00
❑ 5161 [PS]	Destination Unknown/ No Way Out	1982	3.00
❑ 5200	Windows/Rock And Roll Suspension	1983	3.00
❑ 5200 [PS]	Windows/Rock And Roll Suspension	1983	3.00
❑ 5212	Walking in L.A./ Mental Hopscotch	1983	3.00
❑ 5326	Give/Clandestine People	1984	3.00
❑ 5326 [PS]	Give/Clandestine People	1984	3.00
❑ 5358	Right Now/Racing Against Time	1984	3.00
❑ 5381	Surrender Your Heart/ All Fall Down	1985	3.00
❑ 5381 [PS]	Surrender Your Heart/ All Fall Down	1985	3.00
❑ S7-18874	Destination Unknown/Windows	1995	3.00
—Reissue			

7-Inch Extended Plays

Number	Title (A Side/B Side)	Yr	NM
KOMOS			
❑ (# unknown)	I Like Boys	1980	25.00
❑ (# unknown) [PS]	I Like Boys	1980	25.00

Albums

Number	Title (A Side/B Side)	Yr	NM
CAPITOL			
❑ ST-12228	Spring Session M	1982	12.00
❑ ST-12315	Rhyme & Reason	1984	10.00
❑ ST-12465	Color in Your Life	1986	10.00
❑ MLP-15001 [EP]	Missing Persons	1982	12.00
❑ SN-16359	Rhyme & Reason	1985	8.00
—Budget-line reissue			
❑ SN-16460	Spring Session M	1987	8.00
—Budget-line reissue			

MISSOURI

Albums

Number	Title (A Side/B Side)	Yr	NM
PANAMA			
❑ 1022	Missouri	1977	30.00

MR. BIG (1)

45s

Number	Title (A Side/B Side)	Yr	NM
ARISTA			
❑ 0229	Romeo/Ain't Been a Man	1977	4.00
❑ 0248	Feel Like Calling Home/ (B-side unknown)	1977	5.00

Albums

Number	Title (A Side/B Side)	Yr	NM
ARISTA			
❑ AL 4083	Photographic Smile	1976	12.00

MR. BIG (2)

U.S.-based hard rock band featuring TALAS and DAVID LEE ROTH bassist Billy Sheehan.

45s

Number	Title (A Side/B Side)	Yr	NM
ATLANTIC			
❑ 7-87509	Just Take My Heart/ Road to Ruin	1992	4.00
❑ 7-87580	To Be with You/Green-Tinted Sixties Mind	1992	6.00
❑ 7-88860	Addicted to That Rush/ Blame It on My Youth	1989	5.00

Albums

Number	Title (A Side/B Side)	Yr	NM
ATLANTIC			
❑ 81990	Mr. Big	1989	10.00
❑ A1-82209	Lean Into It	1991	20.00
—U.S. version issued on vinyl only through Columbia House			

MR. BUNGLE

Features Mike Patton from FAITH NO MORE.

45s

Number	Title (A Side/B Side)	Yr	NM
WARNER BROS.			
❑ PRO-S-5452 [DJ]	Sudden Death/Ballrooms of Mars	1991	25.00
—"Soil Samples #6" on gray vinyl; B-side by the Flaming Lips			
❑ PRO-S-7829 [DJ]	Platypus/The Legendary Paper Project by the Secret Chiefs Trio	1995	12.00
—Bonus 45 with LP "Disco Volante"			

Albums

Number	Title (A Side/B Side)	Yr	NM
WARNER BROS.			
❑ 45963	Disco Volante	1995	20.00
—Originals have bonus 7-inch single (listed separately)			

MR. CLEAN

45s

Number	Title (A Side/B Side)	Yr	NM
ORIGINAL SOUND			
❑ 40	Mr. Clean/Jessie Lee	1964	150.00
—Written, produced and performed on by Frank Zappa			

Joni Mitchell, "Good Friends," Geffen 28840, 1985, **$5.**

Number	Title (A Side/B Side)	Yr	NM
MR. GASSER AND THE WEIRDOS			
Albums			
CAPITOL			
❑ ST 2010 [S]	Hot Rod Hootenanny	1963	120.00
❑ T 2010 [M]	Hot Rod Hootenanny	1963	100.00
❑ ST 2057 [S]	Rods n' Ratfinks	1963	120.00
—Add 25% if ratfink decal is enclosed			
❑ T 2057 [M]	Rods n' Ratfinks	1963	100.00
—Add 25% if ratfink decal is enclosed			
❑ ST 2114 [S]	Surfink!	1964	150.00
—Without bonus single			
❑ ST 2114 [S]	Surfink!	1964	200.00
—With bonus single in pocket on cover: "Santa Barbara"/"Midnight Run" by the Super Stocks			
❑ T 2114 [M]	Surfink!	1964	100.00
—Without bonus single			
❑ T 2114 [M]	Surfink!	1964	150.00
—With bonus single in pocket on cover: "Santa Barbara"/"Midnight Run" by the Super Stocks			
MR. LUCKY AND THE GAMBLERS			
45s			
DOT			
❑ 16930	Take a Look at Me/I Told You (Once Before)	1966	20.00
PANORAMA			
❑ 37	Take a Look at Me/I Told You (Once Before)	1966	20.00
❑ 52	Alice Designs/You Don't Need Me	1967	15.00
UNITED INT'L.			
❑ 1001	New Orleans/Searching	1965	20.00
❑ 4404	Koko Joe/I Told You (Once Before)	1966	20.00
MR. MIKE			
45s			
HICKORY			
❑ 1199	Cecilia/Stifelius	1962	12.00

Number	Title (A Side/B Side)	Yr	NM
MR. SHORT STUFF			
Albums			
SPIVEY			
❑ 1005	Mr. Short Stuff	196?	20.00
MR. SOUL			
45s			
GENUINE			
❑ 150	What Happened to Yesterday/ (B-side unknown)	196?	1800.
MR. SOUL BOWL			
45s			
ATLANTIC			
❑ 2823	Answer to the Want Ads/H-L-I-C	1971	6.00
MR. WIGGLES			
45s			
PARKWAY			
❑ 104	Fat Back Part 1/Part 2	1966	50.00
MITCHELL, BILLY			
45s			
ATLANTIC			
❑ 933	My Love, My Desire/ Pack Up All Your Bags	1951	300.00
❑ 950	If I Had Known/Verna Lee	1951	200.00
❑ 954	Let's Have a Ball Tonight/ Someday You'll Be Sorry	1952	200.00
❑ 974	Ghost Train/Bald Headed Woman	1952	200.00
—With Joe Morris			
CALLA			
❑ 165	Oh Happy Day/The Chokin' Kind	1969	8.00
❑ 167	Too Busy Thinking 'Bout My Baby/Crystal Blue Persuasion	1969	8.00
IMPERIAL			
❑ 5520	Satellite Be-Bop/Pickin' on the Wrong Chicken	1958	20.00

Number	Title (A Side/B Side)	Yr	NM
JUBILEE			
❑ 5400	Short Skirts/You Know I Do	1961	15.00
UNITED ARTISTS			
❑ 235	Call to Me (I'll Be Here)/Where	1960	15.00
WARWICK			
❑ 501	It Doesn't Matter to Me/ Stop a Little While	1959	15.00
MITCHELL, BOBBY			
45s			
IMPERIAL			
❑ 5236	I'm Cryin'/Rack 'Em Back	1953	200.00
❑ 5250	One Friday Morning/ Four-Eleven-Forty-Four	1953	200.00
❑ 5270	Baby's Gone/Sister Lucy	1954	120.00
❑ 5282	Angel Child/School Boy Blues	1954	120.00
❑ 5295	The Wedding Bells Are Ringing/Meant for Me	1954	120.00
❑ 5309	I'm a Young Man/ She Couldn't Be Found	1954	120.00
❑ 5326	I Wish I Knew/ Nothing Sweet As You	1955	80.00
❑ 5346	I Cried/I'm in Love	1955	60.00
❑ 5378	Try Rock and Roll/No, No, No	1956	50.00
❑ 5392	Goin' Round in Circles/ I Try So Hard	1956	50.00
❑ 5412	You Are My Angel/I've Got My Fingers Crossed	1956	50.00
❑ 5440	You Always Hurt the One You Love/I Would Like to Know	1957	40.00
❑ 5475	I'm Gonna Be a Wheel Someday/ You Better Go Home	1957	50.00
❑ 5511	I Love to Hold You/64 Hours	1958	40.00
❑ 5558	Hearts of Fire/You're Going to Be Sorry	1959	40.00
❑ 5882	My Southern Bell/ When First We Met	1962	12.00
❑ 5923	I Don't Want to Be a Wheel No More/I Got to Call That Number	1963	12.00
RON			
❑ 337	Sand Me Your Picture/ You're Doing Me Wrong	1961	12.00
❑ 342	Mama Don't Allow/There's Only One of You	1961	12.00
MITCHELL, JONI			
12-Inch Singles			
GEFFEN			
❑ PRO-A-2386 [DJ]	Good Friends (same on both sides)	1985	6.00
❑ PRO-A-2441 [DJ]	Shiny Toys (same on both sides)	1986	6.00
❑ PRO-A-3018 [DJ]	Snakes and Ladders (same on both sides)	1988	6.00
❑ PRO-A-3116 [DJ]	My Secret Place (Edit Version) (LP Version)	1988	6.00
45s			
ASYLUM			
❑ 11010	You Turn Me On, I'm a Radio/ Urge for Going	1972	5.00
❑ 11029	Raised on Robbery/ Court and Spark	1973	5.00
❑ 11034	Help Me/Just Like This Train	1974	5.00
❑ 11041	Free Man in Paris/People's Parties	1974	5.00
❑ 45221	Big Yellow Taxi/ Rainy Night House	1974	4.00
❑ 45244	Jericho/Carey	1975	4.00
❑ 45298	In France They Kiss on Main Street/Boho Dance	1976	4.00
❑ 45377	Coyote/Blue Motel Room	1976	4.00
❑ 45467	Dreamland/Jericho	1978	4.00
❑ 46506	The Dry Cleaner from Des Moines/God Must Be a Boogie Man	1979	4.00
❑ 47038	Why Do Fools Fall in Love/ Black Crow	1980	4.00
GEFFEN			
❑ 27887	My Secret Place/Lakota	1988	4.00
❑ 28675	Shiny Toys/Three Great Stimulants	1986	4.00
❑ 28840	Good Friends/Smokin' Empty (Try Another)	1985	4.00
❑ 28840 [PS]	Good Friends/Smokin' Empty (Try Another)	1985	5.00
❑ 29757	Underneath the Streetlight/ Be Cool	1983	4.00
❑ 29849	(You're So Square) Baby I Don't Care/Love	1982	4.00
❑ 29849 [PS]	(You're So Square) Baby I Don't Care/Love	1982	5.00

Except when noted otherwise, VG = 25% of NM, and VG+ = 50% of NM. (Example: VG = $2.00, VG+ = $4.00 and NM = $8.00.)

Number	Title (A Side/B Side)	Yr	NM
REPRISE			
❑ 0694	I Had a King/Night in the City	1968	8.00
❑ 0906	Big Yellow Taxi/Woodstock	1970	8.00
❑ 1029	Carey/This Flight Tonight	1971	8.00
❑ 1049	Case of You/California	1971	6.00
❑ 1154	Both Sides Now/Chelsea Morning	1972	5.00
—"Back to Back Hits" series			
❑ 1155	Big Yellow Taxi/Carey	1972	5.00
—"Back to Back Hits" series			
Albums			
ASYLUM			
❑ AB-202	Miles of Aisles	1974	10.00
❑ 5E-505	Mingus	1979	10.00
❑ BB-701 [(2)]	Don Juan's Reckless Daughter	1977	12.00
❑ BB-704 [(2)]	Shadows and Light	1980	12.00
❑ 7E-1001	Court and Spark	1974	10.00
❑ EQ-1001 [Q]	Court and Spark	1974	20.00
❑ 7E-1051	The Hissing of Summer Lawns	1975	10.00
❑ EQ-1051 [Q]	The Hissing of Summer Lawns	1975	20.00
❑ 7E-1087	Hejira	1976	10.00
❑ SD 5057	For the Roses	1972	10.00
DCC COMPACT CLASSICS			
❑ LPZ-2044	Court and Spark	1997	120.00
—Audiophile vinyl			
❑ LPZ-2069	Blue	2000	—
—Audiophile vinyl; canceled			
GEFFEN			
❑ PRO-A-1081 [DJ]	Wild Things Run Fast Sampler	1982	12.00
—Promo-only 4-song EP			
❑ GHS 2019	Wild Things Run Fast	1982	8.00
❑ GHS 24074	Dog Eat Dog	1985	8.00
❑ GHS 24172	Chalk Mark in a Rain Storm	1988	8.00
❑ GEF 24302	Night Ride Home	1991	15.00
NAUTILUS			
❑ NR-11	Court and Spark	1980	60.00
—Audiophile vinyl			
REPRISE			
❑ MS 2038	Blue	1970	15.00
❑ R 6293 [M]	Joni Mitchell	1968	40.00
—White label promo; evidently, no stock copies were issued in mono			
❑ RS 6293 [S]	Joni Mitchell	1968	20.00
—With "W7" and "r:" logos on two-tone orange label			
❑ RS 6293 [S]	Joni Mitchell	1970	12.00
—With only "r:" logo on all-orange (tan) label			
❑ RS 6341	Clouds	1969	20.00
—With "W7" and "r:" logos on two-tone orange label			
❑ RS 6341	Clouds	1970	12.00
—With only "r:" logo on all-orange (tan) label			
❑ RS 6376	Ladies of the Canyon	1970	12.00
—With only "r:" logo on all-orange (tan) label			
❑ RS 6376	Ladies of the Canyon	1970	20.00
—With "W7" and "r:" logos on two-tone orange label			
RHINO VINYL			
❑ 74842	Blue	2007	25.00
—Reissue on 180-gram vinyl; has replica Reprise label			

MITCHELL, LEE

Number	Title (A Side/B Side)	Yr	NM
45s			
PHILLIPS INT'L.			
❑ 3530	The Frog/A Little Bird Told Me	1958	15.00
SHARP			
❑ 0862	Rootie Tootie Baby/Who's That Big Man	1959	300.00

MITCHELL, MARLON

Number	Title (A Side/B Side)	Yr	NM
45s			
VENA			
❑ 100	Ice Cold Baby/Bermuda Shorts	1957	120.00

MITCHELL, PRISCILLA

Number	Title (A Side/B Side)	Yr	NM
45s			
MERCURY			
❑ 72499	It Comes and Goes/The Teen Years	1965	10.00
❑ 72565	Almost Everything a Lonely Girl Needs/Sweet Talk	1966	10.00
❑ 72635	Acres of Heartaches/Look at the Laughter	1966	10.00
❑ 72681	He's Not for Real/Take Me Home to Your Mama	1967	8.00
❑ 72757	Your Old Handy Man/Who's Cheating Who	1967	8.00
❑ 72807	Natch'illy Ain't No Good/You're Gonna Be Sorry	1968	8.00

MITCHELL, ROSE

Number	Title (A Side/B Side)	Yr	NM
45s			
IMPERIAL			
❑ 5243	Slipping In/I'm Searching	1953	60.00
❑ 5260	Live My Life/Baby Please Don't Go	1954	60.00

MITCHELL, STAN

Number	Title (A Side/B Side)	Yr	NM
45s			
GONE			
❑ 5106	Devil in Disguise/Lovin' Man	1961	30.00

MITCHELL, WILLIE

Number	Title (A Side/B Side)	Yr	NM
45s			
HI			
❑ 2044	The Crawl (Part 1)/The Crawl (Part 2)	1962	10.00
❑ 2053	Drippin'/Buddy Bear	1962	10.00
❑ 2058	Easy Now/Sunrise Serenade	1962	10.00
❑ 2066	Percolatin'/Empty Rooms	1963	10.00
❑ 2075	20-75/Secret Home	1964	8.00
❑ 2083	Percolatin'/Check Me	1964	8.00
❑ 2091	Buster Browne/Woodchopper's Ball	1965	8.00
❑ 2097	That Driving Beat/Everything Is Gonna Be Alright	1965	8.00
❑ 2103	Bad Eye/Sugar T	1966	6.00
❑ 2112	Mercy/Sticks and Stones	1966	6.00
❑ 2119	Misty/Barefootin'	1967	6.00
❑ 2125	Au Shucks/Slippin' and Slidin'	1967	6.00
❑ 2132	Lucky/Ooh Baby, You Turn Me On	1967	6.00
❑ 2140	Soul Serenade/Mercy, Mercy, Mercy	1968	6.00
❑ 2147	Prayer Meetin'/Run Daddy	1968	6.00
❑ 2151	Up-Hard/Beale Street Mood	1968	6.00
❑ 2151	Up-Hard/Red Light	1968	6.00
❑ 2151 [PS]	Up-Hard/Beale Street Mood	1968	10.00
❑ 2154	30-60-90/Take Five	1969	6.00
❑ 2158	Young People/Kitten Korner	1969	6.00
❑ 2167	My Babe/Teenie's Dream	1969	6.00
❑ 2175	Six to Go/Robin's Nest	1970	5.00
❑ 2181	Wade in the Water/Tails Out	1970	5.00
❑ 2190	Too Sweet/Restless	1971	5.00
❑ 2196	Breaking Point/Roadhouse	1971	5.00
❑ 2237	Last Tango in Paris/Six to Go	1973	4.00
HOME OF THE BLUES			
❑ 111	Thirty-Five Thirty/Yvonne	1960	12.00
❑ 119	One Mint Julep/I've Got a Right	1961	12.00
❑ 123	I Like It/Willie's House Party	1961	12.00
7-Inch Extended Plays			
HI			
❑ SBG-28	Hold It/You Can't Sit Down/The Dog//20-75/Mashed Potatoes/Last Date	1964	12.00
—Jukebox issue; small hole, plays at 33 1/3 rpm			
❑ SBG-28 [PS]	Hold It!! Here's Willie Mitchell	1964	12.00
❑ SBG-32	In the Mood/Woodchopper's Ball/Apple Jack//Ram-Bunk-Shush/Since I Met You Baby/When My Dreamboat Comes Home	1965	10.00
—Jukebox issue; small hole, plays at 33 1/3 rpm			
❑ SBG-32 [PS]	It's Dance Time	1965	10.00
❑ SBG-44	Everything Is Gonna Be Alright/Nick-O-Demus/The Champion Pt. 1//That Driving Beat/Fat Cat/Smiley	1966	10.00
—Jukebox issue; small hole, plays at 33 1/3 rpm			
❑ SBG-44 [PS]	The Driving Beat	1966	10.00
❑ SBG-47	Bad Eye/Shadow of Your Smile/Secret Agent Man//Taste of Honey/Hot Cha/What Now My Love	1966	10.00
—Jukebox issue; small hole, plays at 33 1/3 rpm			
❑ SBG-47 [PS]	It's What Happening	1966	10.00
❑ SBG-56	20-75/My Girl/Mustang Sally//Tequila/Honky Tonk/Pin Head	1968	10.00
—Jukebox issue; small hole, plays at 33 1/3 rpm			
❑ SBG-56 [PS]	Willie Mitchell Live	1968	10.00
❑ SBG-59	Soul Serenade/Ooh Baby, You Turn Me On/Soul Finger//Papa's Got a Brand New Bag/Sunny/Respect	1968	10.00
—Jukebox issue; small hole, plays at 33 1/3 rpm			
❑ SBG-59 [PS]	Soul Serenade	1968	10.00
❑ SBG-65	Grazing in the Grass/Sunrise Serenade/Up-Hard//Monkey Jump/Strawberry Solo/Hideaway	1968	10.00
—Jukebox issue; small hole, plays at 33 1/3 rpm			
❑ SBG-65 [PS]	Solid Soul	1968	10.00
❑ SBG-72	Take Five/Poppin'/Canadian Sunset//Louie, Louie/I Say a Little Prayer/Sunshine of Your Love	1969	10.00
—Jukebox issue; small hole, plays at 33 1/3 rpm			
❑ SBG-72 [PS]	On Top	1969	10.00
Albums			
BEARSVILLE			
❑ BRK 3520	... Listen ... Dance	1980	10.00
HI			
❑ 8002	Willie Mitchell Live	1977	10.00
❑ HL-32010 [M]	Sunrise Serenade	1963	40.00
❑ SHL-32010 [S]	Sunrise Serenade	1963	25.00
❑ HL-32021 [M]	Hold It	1964	25.00
❑ SHL-32021 [S]	Hold It	1964	30.00
❑ HL-32026 [M]	It's Dance Time	1965	25.00
❑ HL-32029 [M]	Driving Beat	1966	25.00
❑ SHL-32029 [S]	Driving Beat	1966	30.00
❑ HL-32034 [M]	The Hit Sound of Willie Mitchell	1967	30.00
❑ SHL-32034 [S]	The Hit Sound of Willie Mitchell	1967	25.00
❑ SHL-32036 [S]	It's Dance Time	1965	30.00
❑ HL-32039 [M]	Ooh Baby, You Turn Me On	1967	30.00
❑ SHL-32039 [S]	Ooh Baby, You Turn Me On	1967	25.00
❑ SHL-32042	Willie Mitchell Live	1968	25.00
❑ SHL-32045	Solid Soul	1968	25.00
❑ SHL-32048	On Top	1969	25.00
❑ SHL-32050	Soul Bag	1969	25.00
❑ SHL-32056	The Many Moods of Willie Mitchell	1970	25.00
❑ SHL-32058	Robin's Nest	1970	25.00
❑ SHL-32068/9 [(2)]	The Best of Willie Mitchell	1971	30.00

MITCHUM, ROBERT

Number	Title (A Side/B Side)	Yr	NM
45s			
CAPITOL			
❑ F3672	What Is This Generation Coming To/Mama Looka Boo Boo	1957	15.00
❑ 3741	The Ballad of Thunder Road/My Baby's Lovin' Arms	1973	6.00
❑ 3986	The Ballad of Thunder Road/My Honey's Lovin' Arms	1960	10.00
—Purple label, Capitol logo at left, no "F" prefix			
❑ 3986	The Ballad of Thunder Road/My Honey's Lovin' Arms	1962	8.00
—Orange and yellow swirl label, no "F" prefix			
❑ 3986	The Ballad of Thunder Road/My Honey's Lovin' Arms	1969	6.00
—Red and orange "target" label			
❑ 3986	The Ballad of Thunder Road/My Honey's Lovin' Arms	1973	4.00
—Orange label, "Capitol" at bottom			
❑ F3986	The Ballad of Thunder Road/My Honey's Lovin' Arms	1958	15.00
—Purple label with "F" prefix			
❑ F3986 [PS]	The Ballad of Thunder Road/My Honey's Lovin' Arms	1958	25.00
COLUMBIA			
❑ 03483	The Ballad of Thunder Road/That Little Ole Wine Drinker Me	1983	5.00
MONUMENT			
❑ 1006	Little Old Wine Drinker Me/Walker's Woods	1967	7.00
❑ 1025	You Deserve Each Other/That Man Right There	1967	7.00
Albums			
CAPITOL			
❑ T 853 [M]	Calypso — Is Like So...	1957	100.00
MONUMENT			
❑ MLP-8066 [M]	That Man, Robert Mitchum, Sings	1967	25.00
❑ SLP-18066 [S]	That Man, Robert Mitchum, Sings	1967	25.00

MIXTURES, THE (1)

Number	Title (A Side/B Side)	Yr	NM
45s			
LINDA			
❑ 104	Rainbow Stomp (Part 1)/Rainbow Stomp (Part 2)	1962	10.00
❑ 106	Jawbone/It's Gonna Work Out Fine	1962	10.00
❑ 108	Olive Oyl/Canadian Sunset	1963	10.00
❑ 109	Tiki/Poochum	1963	10.00
❑ 113	Chinese Checkers/Dig These Blues	1963	10.00
❑ 115	Sen-Say-Shun/The Last Minute	1964	10.00
Albums			
LINDA			
❑ 3301 [M]	Stompin' at the Rainbow	1962	100.00

MIXTURES, THE (2)

Number	Title (A Side/B Side)	Yr	NM
45s			
SIRE			
❑ 350	The Pushbike Song/Who Loves Ya	1971	6.00

MIZELL, HANK

Number	Title (A Side/B Side)	Yr	NM
45s			
AMAZON			
❑ 711	Jungle Rock/Then I'm In Your Arms	1963	50.00

M

Number	Title (A Side/B Side)	Yr	NM
EKO			
506	Jungle Rock/Then I'm In Your Arms	1958	600.00
—Issued as "Jim Bobo" on A-side and "Jim Bobo and Hank Mizell" on B-side			
KING			
5236	Jungle Rock/Then I'm In Your Arms	1959	300.00

MIZZY, VIC

Number	Title (A Side/B Side)	Yr	NM
45s			
RCA VICTOR			
47-8477	Main Theme: The Addams Family/Main Theme: Kentucky Jones	1964	20.00

MOB, THE These indeed are all the same group, led by Jim Holvay.

Number	Title (A Side/B Side)	Yr	NM
45s			
COLOSSUS			
130	I Dig Everything About You/Love Had a Hold on Me	1970	6.00
134	Give It to Me/I'd Like to See More of You	1971	6.00
134 [PS]	Give It to Me/I'd Like to See More of You	1971	8.00
145	Money/Once a Man, Twice a Child	1971	6.00
MERCURY			
72791	Disappear/I Wish You'd Leave Me Alone	1968	8.00
MGM			
14406	Feel Like Dancin'/You Give Me the Strength	1972	6.00
PRIVATE STOCK			
45,016	Rock and Roller/(B-side unknown)	1975	5.00
45,031	Hot Music/I Can't Stop This Love Song	1975	5.00
45,053	All the Dudes Are Dancing/(B-side unknown)	1975	5.00
45,084	Don't Let It Get You Down/(B-side unknown)	1976	5.00
45,159	Love Connection/(B-side unknown)	1977	5.00
Albums			
COLOSSUS			
CS-1006	The Mob	1971	20.00
MGM			
SE-4839	The Mob	1972	15.00
PRIVATE STOCK			
PS-2005	The Mob	1975	12.00

MOBY GRAPE Also see ALEXANDER "SKIP" SPENCE.

Number	Title (A Side/B Side)	Yr	NM
45s			
COLUMBIA			
44170	Changes/Fall on You	1967	8.00
44170 [PS]	Changes/Fall on You	1967	20.00
44171	Sitting by the Window/Indifference	1967	8.00
44171 [PS]	Sitting by the Window/Indifference	1967	20.00
44172	8:05/Mister Blues	1967	8.00
44172 [PS]	8:05/Mister Blues	1967	20.00
44173	Omaha/Someday	1967	8.00
44173 [PS]	Omaha/Someday	1967	20.00
44174	Hey Grandma/Come in the Morning	1967	8.00
44174 [PS]	Hey Grandma/Come in the Morning	1967	20.00
44567	Can't Be So Bad/Bitter Wind	1968	6.00
44789	If You Can't Learn From My Mistakes/Trucking Man	1969	6.00
44885	Ooh Mama Ooh/It's a Beautiful Day Today	1969	6.00
JZSP 118972 [DJ]	Omaha/8:05	1967	12.00
—Yellow label promo; "Rush Reservice"			
REPRISE			
1040	Gypsy Wedding/Apocalypse	1971	5.00
1055	Goin' Down to Texas/About Time	1971	5.00
1096	Gone Fishin'/Gypsy Wedding	1972	5.00
Albums			
COLUMBIA			
MGS 1	Grape Jam	1968	20.00
CXS 3 [(2)]	Wow/Grape Jam	1968	30.00
—Joint release of the two albums under one cover			
CXS 3 [(2)]	Wow/Grape Jam	1971	15.00
—Orange labels			
2698/9498	Moby Grape Poster	1967	8.00
—Poster has offending finger airbrushed out			
2698/9498	Moby Grape Poster	1967	15.00
—Poster has Don Stephenson "giving the finger" on his washboard			
CL 2698 [M]	Moby Grape	1967	20.00
—Cover has offending finger airbrushed out			
CL 2698 [M]	Moby Grape	1967	40.00
—Cover has Don Stephenson "giving the finger" on his washboard			
CS 9498	Moby Grape	1971	12.00
—Orange label; with poster			
CS 9498 [S]	Moby Grape	1967	20.00
—Cover has offending finger airbrushed out			
CS 9498 [S]	Moby Grape	1967	40.00
—Cover has Don Stephenson "giving the finger" on his washboard			
CS 9613	Wow	1968	20.00
CS 9613 [M]	Wow	1968	40.00
—"Special Mono Radio Station Copy" with white label			
CS 9696	Moby Grape '69	1969	20.00
CS 9912	Truly Fine Citizen	1969	20.00
C 31098	Great Grape	1972	15.00
ESCAPE			
ESA 1	Live Grape	1978	15.00
HARMONY			
KH 30392	Omaha	1971	15.00
REPRISE			
RS 6460	20 Granite Creek	1971	20.00
SUNDAZED			
LP-5225 [M]	Moby Grape	2007	25.00
—Reissue of Columbia 2698 with poster			
LP-5226	Wow	2007	20.00
—Reissue of Columbia 9613			
LP-5227	Grape Jam	2007	20.00
—Reissue of Columbia MGS 1			
LP-5228	Moby Grape '69	2007	15.00
—Reissue of Columbia 9696			

MOCEDADES

Number	Title (A Side/B Side)	Yr	NM
45s			
TARA			
100	Eres Tu (Touch the Wind)/Touch the Wind (Eres Tu)	1973	5.00
105	Dime Senor/I Ask the Lord	1974	4.00
105 [PS]	Dime Senor/I Ask the Lord	1974	6.00
Albums			
TARA			
53000	Eres Tu "Touch the Wind"	1974	12.00

MOCKINGBIRDS, THE With GRAHAM GOULDMAN and Kevin Godley, later of 10CC.

Number	Title (A Side/B Side)	Yr	NM
45s			
ABC-PARAMOUNT			
10653	That's How/I Never Should Have Kissed You	1965	15.00

MOD AND THE ROCKERS

Number	Title (A Side/B Side)	Yr	NM
Albums			
JUSTICE			
JLP-153	Mod and the Rockers Now!	1967	400.00

MODELS, THE

Number	Title (A Side/B Side)	Yr	NM
45s			
MGM			
13775	Bend Me, Shape Me/In a World of Pretty Faces	1967	20.00

MODERNAIRES, THE

Number	Title (A Side/B Side)	Yr	NM
45s			
CAPITOL			
2633	Theme from "The Mod Squad" (Alone Too Long)/I'll See Your Light	1969	8.00
COLUMBIA			
1-143 (?)	Johnny Get Your Girl/Busy Doing Nothing	1949	40.00
—Microgroove 33 1/3 rpm, 7-inch single, small hole			
1-245 (?)	Senora/Beautiful Blond from Bashful Bend	1949	40.00
—Microgroove 33 1/3 rpm 7-inch single, small hole			
1-468 (?)	Home Town Band/Olly Olly Oxen Free	1950	40.00
—Microgroove 33 1/3 rpm, 7-inch single, small hole			
1-472 (?)	The Big Movie Show in the Sky/The Yodel Blues	1950	40.00
—Microgroove 33 1/3 rpm 7-inch single, small hole			
1-612	Down the Lane/Rubber Knuckle Sam (Leader of the Washboard Band)	1950	40.00
—Microgroove 33 1/3 rpm 7-inch single, small hole			
1-704 (?)	Java Jive/Schenectady	1950	40.00
—Microgroove 33 1/3 rpm 7-inch single, small hole			
CORAL			
9-60408	Wishing You Were Here Tonight/Lovely Is the Evening	1951	20.00
9-60439	I'm Late/Alice in Wonderland	1951	20.00
9-60504	You'll Always Be the Sweetheart of My Dreams/Wings on My Wishes	1951	20.00
9-60525	You'll Always Be the Sweetheart of My Dreams/Whoo-ee Loo-ee-siana	1951	15.00
9-60609	October 32nd, 1992/Stompin' at the Savoy	1952	15.00
9-60658	I'll Always Be Following You/The Dipsy Doodle	1952	15.00
9-60726	Goody Goody/Bugle Call Rag	1952	15.00
9-60824	When My Love Comes Back to Me/Four or Five Times	1952	15.00
9-60881	Gotta Be This or That/Wild Flower	1952	15.00
9-60899	New Juke Box Saturday Night/Runnin' Wild	1953	15.00
9-60982	Say You're Mine Again/He Who Has Love	1953	15.00
9-61037	Put Some Money in the Juke Box/Rock-a-Bye Boogie	1953	15.00
9-61086	You'll Never Be Mine/The Other Side of You'll Never Be Mine	1953	15.00
9-61110	A Salute to Glenn Miller (Part 1)/(Part 2)	1953	12.00
9-61199	That's You, That's Me, That's Love/I Know Why	1954	12.00
9-61348	Mine, Mine, Mine/Birds and Puppies and Tropical Fish	1955	12.00
9-61378	Tops 'n Pops (Part 1)/(Part 2)	1955	12.00
9-61412	Wine, Women and Gold/Slue Foot	1955	12.00
—With Bob Crosby and His Bob Cats			
9-61449	Just Like We Used to Do/La Festa	1955	12.00
—With Bob Crosby and His Bob Cats			
9-61490	Wake Up the Place/Milkman's Matinee	1955	12.00
—With Les Brown and His Band of Renown			
9-61513	Alright, Okay, You Win/At My Front Door	1955	12.00
9-61547	Santa's Little Sleigh Bells/Sleepy Little Space Cadet	1955	15.00
9-61555	Go On with the Wedding/Ain't She Sweet	1956	12.00
9-61568	Let's Dance Medley (Part 1)/(Part 2)	1956	12.00
9-61599	April in Paris/Hi Diddlee I Di	1956	12.00
9-61674	Ninety-Eight Cents/Ask for Joe	1956	12.00
9-61764	I'm Ready to Love Again/Noah	1956	12.00
9-61779	Salute to Tommy Dorsey (Part 1)/(Part 2)	1957	10.00
9-61837	Cinderella Baby/Calypso Melody	1957	10.00
9-61873	A Foggy Day/Makin' Whoopee	1957	10.00
9-61949	Act Your Age/As Long As I Have You	1958	10.00
MERCURY			
71529	Like Young/Don't Dream	1959	10.00
UNITED ARTISTS			
422	Mr. Lucky/Bill Bailey (Won't You Please Come Home)	1962	8.00
Albums			
COLUMBIA			
CL 2490 [M]	The Modernaires Salute Herb Alpert and the Tijuana Brass	1966	12.00
CL 2584 [10]	Juke Box Saturday Night	1955	40.00
CL 6043 [10]	Tributes in Tempo	1950	40.00
CS 9290 [S]	The Modernaires Salute Herb Alpert and the Tijuana Brass	1966	15.00
HARMONY			
HL 7023 [M]	Juke Box Saturday Night	195?	20.00
LIBERTY			
LN-10215	The Modernaires Sing the Great Glenn Miller Instrumentals	198?	10.00
MERCURY			
MG-20546 [M]	Like Swung	1960	15.00
SR-60220 [S]	Like Swung	1960	20.00
UNITED ARTISTS			
WW 3510 [S]	The Modernaires Sing the Great Glenn Miller Instrumentals	196?	15.00
WW 7524 [M]	We Remember Tommy Dorsey, Too!	196?	15.00
WWS 8510 [S]	The Modernaires Sing the Great Glenn Miller Instrumentals	196?	20.00
WWS 8524 [S]	We Remember Tommy Dorsey, Too!	196?	20.00
WING			
MGW-12231 [M]	Like Swung	196?	12.00
SRW-16231 [S]	Like Swung	196?	15.00

MODUGNO, DOMENICO

Number	Title (A Side/B Side)	Yr	NM
45s			
DECCA			
30677	Nel Blu Dipinto Di Blu (Volare)/Mariti in Citta	1958	12.00

Except when noted otherwise, VG = 25% of NM, and VG+ = 50% of NM. (Example: VG = $2.00, VG+ = $4.00 and NM = $8.00.)

Number	Title (A Side/B Side)	Yr	NM
❑ 30747	Stay Here with Me/Io	1958	10.00
❑ 30777	Coma Prima/Strada 'Nfosa	1958	10.00
❑ 30845	Piove (Ciao, Ciao Bambino)/ Farfalle	1959	10.00
❑ 30950	The Bandit/Lunga Notte	1959	10.00
❑ 31071	Olympia/O Solo Mio	1960	8.00
❑ 31171	Ciao Ciao Bambino/Si, Si, Si	1960	8.00
❑ 31359	La Novia/Se Dio Vorra	1962	8.00
❑ 31401	Addio...Addio/Lupi E Percorelle	1962	8.00
❑ 31718	Tu Si' 'Na Casa Grande/ Tu Si O' Mare	1964	6.00

JUBILEE

Number	Title (A Side/B Side)	Yr	NM
❑ 5339	La Petit Reveil/Cavudduzzu	1958	10.00

MGM

Number	Title (A Side/B Side)	Yr	NM
❑ 13487	Dio, Come Ti Amo (English Version)/Dio, Come Ti Amo (Italian Version)	1966	6.00

RCA VICTOR

Number	Title (A Side/B Side)	Yr	NM
❑ 47-7321	Musetto/Io Mammeta E Tu	1958	10.00
❑ 47-9502	Meraviglioso (Part 1)/ Meraviglioso (Part 2)	1968	5.00
❑ 48-1022	Love Is Like the Wind/ How Did You	1972	4.00

7-Inch Extended Plays

DECCA

Number	Title (A Side/B Side)	Yr	NM
❑ ED 2633	*Nel Blu Dipinto Di Blu (Volare)/ Mariti in Citta/A Pizza C' 'A Pummarola/Ventu D'Estati	1958	15.00
❑ ED 2633 [PS]	Nel Blu Dipinto Di Blu (Volare) and Other Italian Favorites	1958	15.00

Albums

DECCA

Number	Title (A Side/B Side)	Yr	NM
❑ DL 4133 [M]	Viva Italia	1961	30.00
❑ DL 8808 [M]	Nel Blu Dipinto Di Blu (Volare) and Other Italian Favorites	1958	50.00
❑ DL 8853 [M]	Encore	1959	40.00

MODULATIONS, THE

45s

BUDDAH

Number	Title (A Side/B Side)	Yr	NM
❑ 398	I'm Hopelessly in Love/ What Good Am I	1974	60.00
❑ 418	I Can't Fight Your Love/Your Love Has Me Locked Up	1974	60.00
❑ 418	I Can't Fight Your Love/ I'm Hopelessly in Love	1974	20.00
❑ 497	Worth Your Weight in Gold/ I'll Always Love You	1975	20.00

MOZEL

Number	Title (A Side/B Side)	Yr	NM
❑ 101	Share Your Love/ Who's Going to Lose	197?	50.00

Albums

BUDDAH

Number	Title (A Side/B Side)	Yr	NM
❑ BDS-5638	It's Rough Out Here	1975	80.00

—Reproductions exist

MOE, ADRIAN, AND THE SCULPTORS

45s

COLUMBIA

Number	Title (A Side/B Side)	Yr	NM
❑ 4-43445	Love Train/Shotgun	1965	10.00
❑ 4-43445 [PS]	Love Train/Shotgun	1965	15.00

MOGEN DAVID AND THE GRAPES OF WRATH

45s

CHA CHA

Number	Title (A Side/B Side)	Yr	NM
❑ 757	Little Girl Gone/Go Away Girl	1967	4000.

—VG 2000; VG+ 3000

MOJO MEN, THE

45s

AUTUMN

Number	Title (A Side/B Side)	Yr	NM
❑ 11	Mama's Little Baby/Off the Hook	1965	15.00
❑ 19	Dance with Me/The Loneliest Boy in Town	1965	15.00
❑ 27	She's My Baby/Fire in My Heart	1966	15.00

GRT

Number	Title (A Side/B Side)	Yr	NM
❑ 5	Flower of Love/I Can't Let Go	1969	10.00
❑ 8	Candle to Burn/ Make You at Home	1969	10.00
❑ 16	Everyday Love/ There Goes My Mind	1969	10.00

REPRISE

Number	Title (A Side/B Side)	Yr	NM
❑ 0486	She's My Baby/ Do the Hanky Panky	1966	20.00
❑ 0539	Sit Down, I Think I Love You/Don't Leave Me Crying Like Before	1966	10.00
❑ 0580	Me About You/When You're in Love	1967	10.00
❑ 0617	Whatever Happened to Happy/ Make You at Home	1967	10.00
❑ 0661	Not Too Old to Start Crying/ New York City	1968	10.00
❑ 0689	Should I Cry/You to Me	1968	10.00
❑ 0707	Sit Down, I Think I Love You/ Me About You	1968	6.00

—"Back to Back Hits" series

Number	Title (A Side/B Side)	Yr	NM
❑ 0759	Don't Be Cruel/Let It Be Him	1968	10.00

TIDE

Number	Title (A Side/B Side)	Yr	NM
❑ 2000	Surfin' Fat Man/Paula	1964	40.00

Albums

GRT

Number	Title (A Side/B Side)	Yr	NM
❑ 10003	Mojo Magic	1969	25.00

MOJOS, THE

45s

PARROT

Number	Title (A Side/B Side)	Yr	NM
❑ 9707	Seven Daffodils/Nothin' at All	1964	10.00
❑ 45001	Everything's Alright/Give Your Loving to Me	1964	12.00
❑ 45002	Why Not Tonight/Don't Do It Anymore	1964	12.00

MOLES, GENE

45s

CHALLENGE

Number	Title (A Side/B Side)	Yr	NM
❑ 59249	Burning Rubber/Twin Pipes	1964	25.00

GARPAX

Number	Title (A Side/B Side)	Yr	NM
❑ 44176	Kaha Huna (Goddess of Surfing)/Maria (The Wind)	1963	25.00

MOLLERN, RONNIE

45s

KING

Number	Title (A Side/B Side)	Yr	NM
❑ 5365	Rockin' Up/Fat Mama	1960	150.00

MOLLY HATCHET

45s

EPIC

Number	Title (A Side/B Side)	Yr	NM
❑ 50669	The Creeper/Dreams I'll Never See	1979	4.00
❑ 50773	Gunsmoke/Jukin' City	1979	4.00
❑ 50809	It's All Over Now/Good Rockin'	1979	4.00
❑ 50822	Flirtin' with Disaster/Gunsmoke	1980	5.00
❑ 50943	Beatin' the Odds/ Few and Far Between	1980	4.00
❑ 50965	The Rambler/Get Her Back	1981	4.00

Albums

CAPITOL

Number	Title (A Side/B Side)	Yr	NM
❑ C1-92114	Lightning Strikes Twice	1989	12.00

EPIC

Number	Title (A Side/B Side)	Yr	NM
❑ AS99 694 [DJ]	Flirtin' with Disaster	1979	40.00
—Promo-only picture disc			
❑ AS99 844 [DJ]	Beatin' the Odds	1980	40.00
—Promo-only picture disc			
❑ AS99 1320 [DJ]	Take No Prisoners	1981	25.00
—Promo-only picture disc			
❑ JE 35347	Molly Hatchet	1978	12.00
—Orange label			
❑ JE 35347	Molly Hatchet	1979	10.00
—Dark blue label			
❑ PE 35347	Molly Hatchet	198?	8.00
—Budget-line reissue with new prefix			
❑ JE 36110	Flirtin' with Disaster	1979	10.00
❑ FE 36572	Beatin' the Odds	1980	10.00
❑ FE 37480	Take No Prisoners	1981	10.00
❑ PE 37480	Take No Prisoners	198?	8.00
—Budget-line reissue with new prefix			
❑ FE 38429	No Guts... No Glory	1983	10.00
❑ PE 38429	No Guts... No Glory	198?	8.00
—Budget-line reissue with new prefix			
❑ FE 39621	The Deed Is Done	1984	10.00
❑ E2 40137 [(2)]	Double Trouble Live	1985	15.00

MOLOCH

Albums

ENTERPRISE

Number	Title (A Side/B Side)	Yr	NM
❑ ENS-1002	Moloch	1969	30.00

MOM & DADS, THE

45s

GNP CRESCENDO

Number	Title (A Side/B Side)	Yr	NM
❑ 439	The Rangers Waltz/Quentin's E Flat Boogie	1971	5.00
❑ 451	In the Blue Canadian Rockies/ Blue Skirt Waltz	1972	5.00
❑ 455	Amazing Grace/ Rippling River Waltz	1972	5.00
❑ 460	Jingle Bell Rock/Auld Lang Syne	1972	5.00
❑ 461	Angry/Anniversary Waltz	1973	4.00
❑ 466	The Waltz You Saved for Me/ When the Saints Go Marching In	1973	4.00
❑ 472	Somewhere My Love/ My Happiness	1973	4.00
❑ 478	My Blue Heaven/ Your Cheatin' Heart	1974	4.00
❑ 485	Maiden's Prayer/ Wabash Cannonball	1974	4.00
❑ 496	Kentucky Waltz/ (B-side unknown)	1975	4.00
❑ 803	Silver Bells/Bill Bailey	1975	4.00

Albums

GNP CRESCENDO

Number	Title (A Side/B Side)	Yr	NM
❑ GNP-2061	The Rangers Waltz	1971	10.00
❑ GNP-2063	In the Blue Canadian Rockies	1972	10.00
❑ GNP-2065	Souvenirs	1972	10.00
❑ GNP-2068	Again!	1973	10.00
❑ GNP-2072	Reminiscing	1973	10.00
❑ GNP-2078	Dance with the Mom & Dads	1974	10.00
❑ GNP-2082	The Mom & Dads Play Your Favorite Hymns	1974	10.00
❑ GNP-2084	Love Is a Beautiful Song	1974	10.00
❑ GNP-2087	The Best of the Mom & Dads	1975	10.00
❑ GNP-2092	Dream	1975	10.00
❑ GNP-2096	Memories	1976	10.00
❑ GNP-2102	Summertime	1976	10.00
❑ GNP-2106	Down the River of Golden Dreams	1977	10.00
❑ GNP-2108	Whispering Hope	1977	10.00
❑ GNP-2110	One Dozen Roses	1977	10.00
❑ GNP-2117	Gratefully Yours	1978	10.00
❑ 2GNP-2123 [(2)]	Golden Country	1979	12.00
❑ GNP-2125	Love Letters in the Sand	1979	10.00
❑ 2GNP-2129 [(2)]	The Very Best of the Mom & Dads	1980	12.00
❑ GNP-2130	Blue Hawaii	1980	10.00
❑ GNP-2136	To Mom & Dad With Love from the Mom & Dads	1980	10.00
❑ GNP-2139	Waltz Across Texas	1981	10.00
❑ GNP-2150	Good Night Sweetheart	1985	8.00
❑ GNP-2173	20 Favorite Waltzes	1986	8.00
❑ GNP-2189	Red Sails in the Sunset	1987	8.00

MOM'S APPLE PIE

45s

BROWN BAG

Number	Title (A Side/B Side)	Yr	NM
❑ XW192	Love Plays a Song/ Can You Help Me	1973	10.00

Albums

BROWN BAG

Number	Title (A Side/B Side)	Yr	NM
❑ BB-LA073-F	Mom's Apple Pie #2	1973	15.00
❑ 14200	Mom's Apple Pie	1972	20.00
—With barbed wire wall covering the former opening. This is much rarer than the first version, though less sought-after			
❑ 14200	Mom's Apple Pie	1972	20.00
—With vulva showing in the apple pie			

MOMENTS, THE

Includes records as "Ray, Goodman and Brown." Records on Era and World Artists are by different groups and are outside the scope of this book. R&B trio. For legal reasons, their records on EMI America, EMI Manhattan, Panoramic and Polydor were issued under the name "Ray, Goodman and Brown."

45s

ALL PLATINUM

Number	Title (A Side/B Side)	Yr	NM
❑ 2350	Sho Nuff Boogie (Part 1)/ Sho Nuff Boogie (Part 2)	1974	5.00

—With Sylvia

EMI AMERICA

Number	Title (A Side/B Side)	Yr	NM
❑ 8365	Take It to the Limit/(Instrumental)	1986	3.00
❑ 8365 [PS]	Take It to the Limit/(Instrumental)	1986	3.00
❑ 8378	Celebrate Our Love/ (Instrumental)	1987	3.00
❑ 8378 [PS]	Celebrate Our Love/ (Instrumental)	1987	3.00
❑ 43022	Tonight (Baby)/Good Love	1987	3.00

EMI MANHATTAN

Number	Title (A Side/B Side)	Yr	NM
❑ 50155	Where Did You Get That Body, (Baby)?/Where Are You Now	1988	3.00
❑ 50155 [PS]	Where Did You Get That Body, (Baby)?/Where Are You Now	1988	3.00

HOG

Number	Title (A Side/B Side)	Yr	NM
❑ 1000	Baby I Want You/Pray for Me	196?	2000.

PANORAMIC

Number	Title (A Side/B Side)	Yr	NM
❑ 201	Who's Gonna Make the First Move/Look Like Lovers	1984	4.00

POLYDOR

Number	Title (A Side/B Side)	Yr	NM
❑ 2033	Special Lady/Deja Vu	1979	5.00
❑ 2077	Inside of You/Treat Her Right	1980	4.00
❑ 2116	My Prayer/The Way It Should Be	1980	4.00
❑ 2135	Happy Anniversary/You	1980	4.00
❑ 2159	Shoestrings/Me	1981	4.00
❑ 2191	How Can Love Be So Right (Yet So Wrong)/Each Time Is Like the First Time	1981	4.00
❑ 2203	Stay/Good Ole Days	1982	4.00
❑ 2208	Till the Right One Comes Along/Heaven in the Rain	1982	4.00
❑ 2222	Gambled on Your Love/ Pool of Love	1982	4.00
❑ 2227	After All/Love Minus One	1982	4.00

M

Number	Title (A Side/B Side)	Yr	NM
❑ 810056-7	Special Lady/My Prayer	1983	3.00
—Reissue			
STANG			
❑ (no #) [DJ]	Look at Me (I'm in Love) (French Version)/ Girls (French Version)	1975	12.00
—May be promo only			
❑ 5000	Not on the Outside/ Understanding	1968	8.00
❑ 5003	Sunday/Everybody Loves My Baby	1969	6.00
❑ 5005	I Do/Pocketful of Heartbreaks	1969	6.00
❑ 5008	I'm So Lost/Where	1969	6.00
❑ 5009	Lovely Way She Loves/I've Got to Keep On Loving, Love	1969	6.00
❑ 5012	Love on a Two-Way Street/ I Won't Do Anything	1970	8.00
❑ 5016	If I Didn't Care/You Make Me Feel Good	1970	6.00
❑ 5017	All I Have/The Hurt's On Me	1970	6.00
❑ 5020	I Can't Help It/To You with Love	1971	6.00
❑ 5024	That's How It Feels/ That's How It Feels (Long)	1971	6.00
❑ 5031	Lucky Me/I Lost One Bird in the Hand (Reaching Out for Two in the Bush)	1971	6.00
❑ 5033	To You with Love/ Key to My Happiness	1971	6.00
❑ 5036	Thanks a Lot/I Lost One Bird in the Hand (Reaching Out for Two in the Bush)	1972	6.00
❑ 5041	Just Because He Wants to Make Love (Doesn't Mean He Loves You)/So This Is Our Good-Bye	1972	6.00
❑ 5045	My Thing/Thanks a Lot	1972	6.00
❑ 5048	Girl I'm Gonna Miss You/ I Think So	1973	5.00
❑ 5050	Gotta Find a Way/Sweeter As the Days Go By	1973	5.00
❑ 5052	Sexy Mama/Where Can I Find Her	1973	6.00
❑ 5054	Sweet Sweet Lady/ Next Time I See You	1974	5.00
❑ 5056	What's Your Name/ Mama I Miss You	1974	5.00
❑ 5057	Girls (Part 1)/Girls (Part 2)	1974	5.00
—With the Whatnauts			
❑ 5060	Look at Me (I'm in Love)/ You've Come a Long Way	1975	5.00
❑ 5064	Got to Get to Know You/ I Feel So Bad	1975	5.00
❑ 5066	Nine Times/When the Morning Comes	1976	5.00
❑ 5068	With You/The Next Time I See You	1976	5.00
❑ 5071	We Don't Cry Out Loud/ Come In Girl	1977	5.00
❑ 5073	I Don't Wanna Go/Oh I Could Have Loved You	1977	5.00
❑ 5075	I Could Have Loved You/ Jack in the Box	1978	5.00
❑ 5076	Rain in My Backyard/Disco Man	1978	30.00
SUGAR HILL			
❑ 758	Baby Let's Rap Now (Part 1)/ Baby Let's Rap Now (Part 2)	1980	5.00
❑ 769	Record Breakin' Love Affair/ (B-side unknown)	1981	5.00
Albums			
CHESS			
❑ CH2-92517 [(2)]	Greatest Hits	198?	12.00
POLYDOR			
❑ PD-1-6240	Ray, Goodman & Brown	1979	10.00
❑ PD-1-6299	Ray, Goodman & Brown II	1980	10.00
❑ PD-1-6341	Stay	1981	10.00
STANG			
❑ ST-1000	Not On the Outside, But On the Inside Strong	1969	30.00
❑ ST-1002	The Moments On Top	1970	30.00
❑ ST-1003	A Moment with the Moments	1970	30.00
❑ ST-1004	Moments Greatest Hits	1971	20.00
❑ ST-1006	The Moments Live at the New York State Womans Prison	1971	25.00
❑ ST-1009	The Other Side of the Moments	1972	25.00
❑ ST-1015	Live at the Miss Black America Pageant	1972	20.00
❑ ST-1019	The Best of the Moments	1975	15.00
❑ ST-1022	My Thing	1973	15.00
❑ ST-1023	The Sexy Moments	1974	15.00
❑ ST-1026	Look at Me	1975	15.00
❑ ST-1030	Moments With You	1976	15.00
❑ 2ST-1033 [(2)]	Greatest Hits	1977	20.00
❑ ST-1034	Sharp	1978	15.00

MOMENTS, THE (2)

California studio group.

Number	Title (A Side/B Side)	Yr	NM
45s			
ERA			
❑ 3099	Walk Right In/(Instrumental)	1963	10.00
❑ 3104	Homework/Big Bound Wheel	1963	10.00
❑ 3114	Surfin' Train/Mamu Zey	1963	12.00
❑ 3128	In the Phonograph Booth/ Blues at Sandy Cove	1964	10.00

MOMENTS, THE (3)

Steve Marriott, later of SMALL FACES and HUMBLE PIE, was in this group.

Number	Title (A Side/B Side)	Yr	NM
45s			
WORLD ARTISTS			
❑ 1032	You Really Got Me/ Money, Money	1964	10.00

MONARCHS, THE (1)

Number	Title (A Side/B Side)	Yr	NM
45s			
MONUMENT			
❑ 03484	Look Homeward, Angel/ This Old Heart	1983	5.00
SOUND STAGE 7			
❑ 2502	This Old Heart/'Til I Hear It From You	1963	12.00
❑ 2516	Look Homeward, Angel/What Made You Change Your Mind	1964	12.00
❑ 2530	Climb Every Mountain/ Take Me Home	1964	12.00

MONARCHS, THE (2)

Number	Title (A Side/B Side)	Yr	NM
45s			
DOT			
❑ 15228	Gravy/Caravan Mambo	1954	40.00

MONARCHS, THE (3)

Number	Title (A Side/B Side)	Yr	NM
45s			
LOST-NITE			
❑ 120	Always Be Faithful/How Are You	196?	8.00
—Reissue			
MELBA			
❑ 101	Pretty Little Girl/In My Younger Days	1956	80.00
NEIL			
❑ 101	Pretty Little Girl/In My Younger Days	1956	150.00
❑ 103	Always Be Faithful/How Are You	1956	120.00

MONARCHS, THE (U)

Some of these could be by the above groups.

Number	Title (A Side/B Side)	Yr	NM
45s			
LIBAN			
❑ 1002	Love You That's Why/ Coming Home	1959	2000.
WING			
❑ 90040	Angels in the Sky/ Wanna Go Home	1955	80.00
YUCCA			
❑ 172	Forever Lost/Cuckoo	1964	50.00
ZONE			
❑ 1067	Friday Night/El Bandito	1963	15.00

MONDAY BLUES

Number	Title (A Side/B Side)	Yr	NM
45s			
VAULT			
❑ 963	Be My Baby/Do I Love You	1970	8.00
Albums			
VAULT			
❑ 133	The Phil Spector Song Book	1970	20.00

MONDAY MORNING QUARTERBACK, THE

Number	Title (A Side/B Side)	Yr	NM
45s			
WARNER BROS.			
❑ 7664	The Twelve Days of Christmas (The Game Plan to Beat Miami)//Santa Claus Medley: Santa Claus Is Comin' to Town/ Here Comes Santa Claus	1972	10.00
❑ 7664 [PS]	The Twelve Days of Christmas (The Game Plan to Beat Miami)//Santa Claus Medley: Santa Claus Is Comin' to Town/ Here Comes Santa Claus	1972	15.00
—Picture sleeve is a slick pasted onto a plain white sleeve			

MONDELLOS, THE

Number	Title (A Side/B Side)	Yr	NM
45s			
RHYTHM			
❑ 102	Come Back Home/100 Years from Today	1956	200.00
—As "Alice Jean and the Mondellos"			
❑ 105	Over the Rainbow/Never Leave Me Alone	1956	150.00
—As "Yul McClay and the Mondellos"			
❑ 106	That's What I Call Love/ Daylight Saving Time	1956	150.00
❑ 109	Hard to Please/Happiness Street	1957	150.00
❑ 114	My Heart/That's What I Call Love	1957	150.00
—As "Rudy Lambert and the Mondellos"			
❑ 128	That Old Feeling/ Sunday Kind of Love	1957	150.00
—As "Rudy Lambert and the Mondellos"			

MONEY, ZOOT

Number	Title (A Side/B Side)	Yr	NM
45s			
EPIC			
❑ 5-10077	Big Time Operator/ Zoot's Sermon	1966	10.00
Albums			
EPIC			
❑ LN 24241 [M]	All Happening Zoot Money's Big Roll Band at Klooks Kleek	1966	30.00

MONITORS, THE (1)

Number	Title (A Side/B Side)	Yr	NM
45s			
SOUL			
❑ 35049	Step by Step (Hand in Hand)/ Time Is Passing By	1968	15.00
V.I.P.			
❑ 25028	Say You/All for Someone	1965	30.00
❑ 25032	Greetings (This Is Uncle Sam)/ Number One in Your Heart	1965	40.00
❑ 25039	Since I Lost You Girl/Don't Put Off Till Tomorrow What You Can Do Today	1966	30.00
❑ 25046	Bring Back the Love/ The Further You Look, The Less You See	1967	20.00
❑ 25049	Step by Step (Hand in Hand)/ Time Is Passing By	1968	50.00
Albums			
SOUL			
❑ SS-714	Greetings, We're the Monitors	1969	60.00

MONITORS, THE (2)

Number	Title (A Side/B Side)	Yr	NM
45s			
ALADDIN			
❑ 3309	Tonight's the Night/ Candy Coated Kisses	1955	100.00

MONITORS, THE (U)

Some of these may be groups (1) or (2).

Number	Title (A Side/B Side)	Yr	NM
45s			
BUDDAH			
❑ 278	Fence Around Your Heart/ Have You Seen Her	1972	100.00
CIRCUS			
❑ 219	A Boyfriend's Prayer/Nita	1957	150.00
SPECIALTY			
❑ 595	Our Schooldays/ I've Got a Dream	1957	80.00
❑ 622	Closer to Heaven/ Rock 'N' Roll Forever	1957	200.00
❑ 636	Mamma Linda/Hop Scotch	1958	60.00

MONK, THELONIOUS

Number	Title (A Side/B Side)	Yr	NM
45s			
BLUE NOTE			
❑ 542	Thelonious/Suburban Eyes	195?	20.00
❑ 543	Round About Midnight/ Well You Needn't	195?	20.00
❑ 547	Evonce/Off Minor	195?	20.00
❑ 548	In Walked Bud/Epistrophy	195?	20.00
❑ 549	Evidence/Ruby My Dear	195?	20.00
❑ 1565	Monk's Mood/Who Knows	195?	15.00
❑ 1575	April in Paris/Nice Work	195?	15.00
❑ 1589	Straight No Chaser/Four in One	195?	15.00
❑ 1590	Criss Cross/Ebonel	195?	15.00
❑ 1602	Skippy/Let's Cool One	195?	15.00
❑ 1603	Carolina Moon/Hornin' In	195?	15.00
❑ 1664	'Round Midnight/In Walked Bud	195?	15.00
COLUMBIA			
❑ 42825	Bye-Ya/Hackensack	1963	10.00
❑ 44780	Just a Glance at Love/ Consecutive Seconds	1969	6.00
PRESTIGE			
❑ 162	Blue Monk/Bye-Ya	196?	10.00
❑ 795	Sweet and Lovely/Bye-Ya	195?	12.00
❑ 838	These Foolish Things/ Trinkle Tinkle	195?	12.00
❑ 850	Monk's Dream/ Little Rootie Tootie	195?	12.00
RIVERSIDE			
❑ 421	Coming on the Hudson /(B-side unknown)	195?	12.00

M

Except when noted otherwise, VG = 25% of NM, and VG+ = 50% of NM. (Example: VG = $2.00, VG+ = $4.00 and NM = $8.00.)

Number	Title (A Side/B Side)	Yr	NM
❑ 434	Blue Monk/(B-side unknown)	195?	12.00

Albums

ANALOGUE PRODUCTIONS

Number	Title (A Side/B Side)	Yr	NM
❑ AP-37 [(7)]	The Riverside Tenor Sessions	1999	250.00

BANDSTAND

Number	Title (A Side/B Side)	Yr	NM
❑ BDLP-1505	Blue Monk	1992	12.00
❑ BDLP-1516	April in Paris	1992	12.00

BLACK LION

Number	Title (A Side/B Side)	Yr	NM
❑ 152	Something in Blue	1972	20.00
❑ 197	The Man I Love	1973	20.00

BLUE NOTE

Number	Title (A Side/B Side)	Yr	NM
❑ BN-LA579-H2 [(2)]	The Complete Genius	1976	20.00
❑ LWB-579 [(2)]	The Complete Genius	1981	15.00
—Reissue of BN-LA579-H2			
❑ BLP-1510 [M]	Genius of Modern Music, Vol. 1	1956	400.00
—"Deep groove" version; Lexington Ave. address on label			
❑ BLP-1510 [M]	Genius of Modern Music, Vol. 1	1958	200.00
—"Deep groove" edition, W. 63rd St. address on label			
❑ BLP-1510 [M]	Genius of Modern Music, Vol. 1	1963	40.00
—"New York, USA" address on label			
❑ BLP-1511 [M]	Genius of Modern Music, Vol. 2	1956	400.00
—"Deep groove" version; Lexington Ave. address on label			
❑ BLP-1511 [M]	Genius of Modern Music, Vol. 2	1958	200.00
—"Deep groove" edition, W. 63rd St. address on label			
❑ BLP-1511 [M]	Genius of Modern Music, Vol. 2	1963	40.00
—"New York, USA" address on label			
❑ BLP-5002 [10]	Genius of Modern Music, Vol. 1	1952	800.00
❑ BLP-5009 [10]	Genius of Modern Music, Vol. 2	1952	800.00
❑ BLP-81510 [R]	Genius of Modern Music, Vol. 1	1968	20.00
—"A Division of Liberty Records" on label			
❑ BST-81510	Genius of Modern Music, Vol. 1	1985	12.00
—"The Finest in Jazz Since 1939" reissue			
❑ BLP-81511 [R]	Genius of Modern Music, Vol. 2	1968	20.00
—"A Division of Liberty Records" on label			
❑ BST-81511	Genius of Modern Music, Vol. 2	1985	12.00
—"The Finest in Jazz Since 1939" reissue			

COLUMBIA

Number	Title (A Side/B Side)	Yr	NM
❑ CL 1965 [M]	Monk's Dream	1963	30.00
—"Guaranteed High Fideilty" on label			
❑ CL 1965 [M]	Monk's Dream	1966	20.00
—"360 Sound Mono" on label			
❑ CL 2038 [M]	Criss-Cross	1963	30.00
—"Guaranteed High Fidelity" on label			
❑ CL 2038 [M]	Criss-Cross	1966	20.00
—"360 Sound Mono" on label			
❑ CL 2038 [M]	Criss-Cross	199?	12.00
—180-gram reissue			
❑ CL 2164 [M]	Monk Big Band and Quartet In Concert	1964	30.00
—"Guaranteed High Fidelity" on label			
❑ CL 2164 [M]	Monk Big Band and Quartet In Concert	1966	20.00
—"360 Sound Mono" on label			
❑ CL 2184 [M]	It's Monk's Time	1964	30.00
—"Guaranteed High Fidelity" on label			
❑ CL 2184 [M]	It's Monk's Time	1966	20.00
—"360 Sound Mono" on label			
❑ CL 2291 [M]	Monk	1965	30.00
—"Guaranteed High Fidelity" on label			
❑ CL 2291 [M]	Monk	1966	20.00
—"360 Sound Mono" on label			
❑ CL 2349 [M]	Solo Monk	1965	30.00
—"360 Sound Mono" on label			
❑ CL 2416 [M]	Misterioso	1966	25.00
—"360 Sound Mono" on label			
❑ CL 2416 [M]	Misterioso	199?	12.00
—180-gram reissue			
❑ CL 2651 [M]	Straight No Chaser	1967	50.00
—Red label with "Mono"			
❑ CS 8765 [S]	Monk's Dream	1963	70.00
—"360 Sound Stereo" in black on label			
❑ CS 8765 [S]	Monk's Dream	1966	25.00
—"360 Sound Stereo" in white on label			
❑ CS 8765 [S]	Monk's Dream	199?	12.00
—180-gram reissue			
❑ CS 8838 [S]	Criss-Cross	1963	60.00
—"360 Sound Stereo" in black on label			
❑ CS 8838 [S]	Criss-Cross	1966	25.00
—"360 Sound Stereo" in white on label			
❑ CS 8964 [S]	Monk Big Band and Quartet In Concert	1964	80.00
—"360 Sound Stereo" in black on label			
❑ CS 8964 [S]	Monk Big Band and Quartet In Concert	1966	25.00
—"360 Sound Stereo" in white on label			
❑ CS 8964 [S]	Monk Big Band and Quartet In Concert	199?	12.00
—180-gram reissue			
❑ CS 8984 [S]	It's Monk's Time	1964	70.00
—"360 Sound Stereo" in black on label			
❑ CS 8984 [S]	It's Monk's Time	1966	30.00
—"360 Sound Stereo" in white on label			
❑ CS 8984 [S]	It's Monk's Time	199?	12.00
—180-gram reissue			
❑ CS 9091 [S]	Monk	1965	50.00
—"360 Sound Stereo" in black on label			
❑ CS 9091 [S]	Monk	1966	25.00
—"360 Sound Stereo" in white on label			
❑ CS 9091 [S]	Monk	199?	12.00
—180-gram reissue			
❑ CS 9149	Solo Monk	1971	12.00
—Orange label			
❑ CS 9149 [S]	Solo Monk	1965	40.00
—Red "360 Sound" label			
❑ PC 9149	Solo Monk	198?	8.00
—Reissue with new prefix; most have bar codes			
❑ PC 9149	Solo Monk	199?	12.00
—180-gram reissue			
❑ CS 9216 [S]	Misterioso	1966	30.00
—"360 Sound Stereo" on red label			
❑ CS 9451	Straight No Chaser	1971	12.00
—Orange label			
❑ CS 9451 [S]	Straight No Chaser	1967	40.00
—Red "360 Sound" label			
❑ PC 9451	Straight No Chaser	198?	8.00
—Reissue with new prefix			
❑ PC 9451	Straight No Chaser	199?	12.00
—180-gram reissue			
❑ CS 9632	Underground	1971	12.00
—Orange label			
❑ CS 9632 [M]	Underground	1968	50.00
—White label promo only with stereo number; "Special Mono Radio Station Copy" sticker on stereo cover			
❑ CS 9632 [S]	Underground	1968	30.00
—Red "360 Sound" label			
❑ PC 9632	Underground	198?	8.00
—Reissue with new prefix			
❑ PC 9632	Underground	199?	12.00
—180-gram reissue			
❑ CS 9775	Greatest Hits	1969	20.00
—Red "360 Sound" label			
❑ CS 9775	Greatest Hits	1971	12.00
—Orange label			
❑ PC 9775	Greatest Hits	198?	8.00
—Reissue with new prefix			
❑ CS 9806	Monk's Blues	1969	80.00
—Red "360 Sound" label			
❑ CS 9806	Monk's Blues	1971	15.00
—Orange label			
❑ PC 9806	Monk's Blues	198?	8.00
—Reissue with new prefix; most have bar codes on back cover			
❑ PC 9806	Monk's Blues	199?	12.00
—180-gram reissue			
❑ KG 32892 [(2)]	Who's Afraid of the Big Band Monk	1974	25.00
❑ KG 32892 [(2)]	Who's Afraid of the Big Band Monk	199?	15.00
—180-gram reissue			
❑ JG 35720 [(2)]	Always Know	1979	20.00
❑ C2 38030 [(2)]	Live at the It Club	1983	25.00
—Original edition			
❑ C2 38030 [(2)]	Live at the It Club	199?	15.00
—180-gram reissue			
❑ C2 38269 [(2)]	Live at the Jazz Workshop	1983	25.00
❑ C2 38510 [(2)]	The Tokyo Concerts	1984	20.00
—Original edition			
❑ C2 38510 [(2)]	The Tokyo Concerts	199?	15.00
—180-gram reissue			

COLUMBIA JAZZ MASTERPIECES

Number	Title (A Side/B Side)	Yr	NM
❑ CJ 40785	Underground	1987	10.00
❑ CJ 40786	Monk's Dream	1987	10.00
❑ CJ 44297	The Composer	1988	12.00

COLUMBIA LIMITED EDITION

Number	Title (A Side/B Side)	Yr	NM
❑ LE 10122	Criss-Cross	197?	12.00

COLUMBIA MUSICAL TREASURY

Number	Title (A Side/B Side)	Yr	NM
❑ DS 338	Monk's Miracles	1967	30.00
—Columbia Record Club exclusive			

EVEREST ARCHIVE OF FOLK & JAZZ

Number	Title (A Side/B Side)	Yr	NM
❑ FS-336	Piano Solos	1978	12.00

FANTASY

Number	Title (A Side/B Side)	Yr	NM
❑ OJC-010	Thelonious Monk Trio	198?	12.00
❑ OJC-016	Monk	198?	12.00
❑ OJC-024	Thelonious Monk Plays Duke Ellington	198?	12.00
❑ OJC-026	Brilliant Corners	198?	12.00
❑ OJC-059	Thelonious Monk/Sonny Rollins	198?	12.00
❑ OJC-064	The Unique Thelonious Monk	198?	12.00
❑ OJC-084	Monk's Music	198?	12.00
❑ OJC-103	Thelonious in Action	198?	12.00
❑ OJC-135	Thelonious Monk at Town Hall	1984	12.00
❑ OJC-206	Misterioso	1985	12.00
❑ OJC-231	Alone in San Francisco	1987	12.00
❑ OJC-254	Thelonious Himself	1987	12.00
❑ OJC-301	Mulligan Meets Monk	1988	12.00
❑ OJC-305	Thelonious Monk at the Blackhawk	1988	12.00
❑ OJC-362	5 By Monk By 5	1989	12.00
❑ OJC-488	Monk in Italy	1991	12.00

GATEWAY

Number	Title (A Side/B Side)	Yr	NM
❑ GSLP-7023	Monk's Music	197?	15.00

GNP CRESCENDO

Number	Title (A Side/B Side)	Yr	NM
❑ 9008 [(2)]	Thelonious Monk	197?	15.00

JAZZ MAN

Number	Title (A Side/B Side)	Yr	NM
❑ 5017	Something in Blue	1980	12.00

MILESTONE

Number	Title (A Side/B Side)	Yr	NM
❑ M-9115	Evidence	1983	12.00
❑ M-9124	Blues Five Spot	1984	15.00
❑ M-47004 [(2)]	Pure Monk	1972	20.00
❑ M-47023 [(2)]	Brilliance	1975	25.00
❑ M-47033 [(2)]	Thelonious Monk In Person	1976	25.00
❑ M-47043 [(2)]	Thelonious Monk at the Five Spot	1978	20.00
❑ M-47052 [(2)]	The Riverside Trios	1980	20.00
❑ M-47060 [(2)]	April in Paris/Live	198?	20.00
❑ M-47064 [(2)]	Memorial Album	1982	20.00
❑ M-47067 [(2)]	'Round Midnight	198?	20.00

MOSAIC

Number	Title (A Side/B Side)	Yr	NM
❑ MR4-101 [(4)]	The Complete Blue Note Recordings of Thelonious Monk	198?	200.00
—Limited edition of 7,500			
❑ MR4-112 [(4)]	The Complete Black Lion and Vogue Recordings	199?	250.00
—Limited edition of 7,500			

PICCADILLY

Number	Title (A Side/B Side)	Yr	NM
❑ 3521	Monkisms	198?	12.00

PRESTIGE

Number	Title (A Side/B Side)	Yr	NM
❑ PRLP-142 [10]	Thelonious Monk Trio	1953	800.00
❑ PRLP-166 [10]	Thelonious Monk Quintet with Sonny Rollins and Julius Watkins	1953	800.00
❑ PRLP-180 [10]	Thelonious Monk Quintet	1954	800.00
❑ PRLP-189 [10]	Thelonious Monk Trio	1954	800.00
❑ PRLP-7027 [M]	Thelonious Monk	1956	300.00
—Reissue of 142 and 189 on one 12-inch record; yellow label with W. 50th St. address; label calls this "Thelonious Monk Trio"			
❑ PRLP-7053 [M]	Monk	1956	200.00
—Reissue of 150; yellow label with W. 50th St. address			
❑ PRLP-7075 [M]	Thelonious Monk/Sonny Rollins	1957	200.00
—Reissue of 166; yellow label with W. 50th St. address			
❑ PRLP-7159 [M]	Monk's Moods	1959	80.00
—Reissue of 7027; yellow label with Bergenfield, N.J. address			
❑ PRLP-7169 [M]	Work	1959	80.00
—Reissue of 7075			
❑ PRLP-7245 [M]	We See	1962	80.00
—Reissue of 7053			
❑ PRLP-7363 [M]	The Golden Monk	1965	30.00
—Reissue of 7245			
❑ PRST-7363 [R]	The Golden Monk	1965	20.00
❑ PRLP-7508 [M]	The High Priest	1967	50.00
—Reissue of 7159			
❑ PRST-7508 [R]	The High Priest	1967	20.00
❑ PRST-7656	The Genius of Thelonious Monk	1969	20.00
❑ PRST-7751	Reflections, Vol. 1	1970	20.00
❑ PRST-7848	Blue Monk, Vol. 2	197?	15.00
❑ PR-24006 [(2)]	Thelonious Monk	1971	20.00

RIVERSIDE

Number	Title (A Side/B Side)	Yr	NM
❑ R-022 [(22)]	The Complete Riverside Recordings	1987	500.00
❑ RLP 12-201 [M]	Thelonious Monk Plays Duke Ellington	1955	600.00
—White label with blue print			
❑ RLP 12-201 [M]	Thelonious Monk Plays Duke Ellington	1958	100.00
—Blue label with reel and microphone logo			
❑ RLP 12-209 [M]	The Unique Thelonious Monk	1956	500.00
—White label with blue print			
❑ RLP 12-209 [M]	The Unique Thelonious Monk	1958	100.00
—Blue label with reel and microphone logo			
❑ RLP 12-226 [M]	Brilliant Corners	1957	400.00
—White label with blue print			
❑ RLP 12-226 [M]	Brilliant Corners	1958	100.00
—Blue label with reel and microphone logo			
❑ RLP 12-235 [M]	Thelonious Himself	1957	400.00
—White label with blue print			
❑ RLP 12-235 [M]	Thelonious Himself	1958	100.00
—Blue label with reel and microphone logo			
❑ RLP 12-242 [M]	Monk's Music	1957	400.00
—White label with blue print			
❑ RLP 12-242 [M]	Monk's Music	1958	100.00
—Blue label with reel and microphone logo			
❑ RLP 12-247 [M]	Mulligan Meets Monk	1957	400.00
—White label with blue print			
❑ RLP 12-247 [M]	Mulligan Meets Monk	1958	100.00
—Blue label with reel and microphone logo			
❑ RLP 12-262 [M]	Thelonious in Action Recorded at the Five Spot Café, New York, With Johnny Griffn	1958	80.00
—Blue label with reel and microphone logo			
❑ RLP 12-279 [M]	Misterioso	1958	100.00
—Blue label with reel-and-microphone logo			
❑ RLP 12-300 [M]	The Thelonious Monk Orchestra at Town Hall	1959	60.00
—Blue label with reel and microphone logo			
❑ RLP 12-305 [M]	5 By Monk By 5	1959	60.00
—Blue label with reel and microphone logo			
❑ RLP 12-312 [M]	Thelonious Alone in San Francisco	1959	60.00
—Blue label with reel and microphone logo			
❑ RLP 12-323 [M]	Thelonious Monk Quartet Plus Two at the Blackhawk	1960	60.00
—Blue label with reel and microphone logo			
❑ RLP-421 [M]	Thelonious Monk's Greatest Hits	1962	25.00
❑ RLP-443 [M]	Thelonious Monk in Italy	1963	30.00

M

The Monkees, "That Was Then, This Is Now," Arista 9505, 1986, no mention of Micky Dolenz and Peter Tork on the sleeve, **$10.**

Number	Title (A Side/B Side)	Yr	NM
❑ RLP-460/1 [(2)M]	Two Hours with Thelonious Monk	1963	60.00
❑ RLP-483 [M]	The Thelonious Monk Story, Vol. 1	1965	30.00
❑ RLP-483/4 [(2)M]	The Thelonious Monk Story	1965	70.00
❑ RLP-484 [M]	The Thelonious Monk Story, Vol. 2	1965	30.00
❑ RLP-491 [M]	Monk in France	1965	30.00
❑ RLP 1101 [S]	Monk's Music	1959	60.00
—Black label with reel and microphone logo			
❑ RLP 1106 [S]	Mulligan Meets Monk	1959	60.00
—Black label with reel and microphone logo			
❑ RLP 1133 [S]	Misterioso	1958	70.00
—Black label with reel and microphone logo			
❑ RLP 1138 [S]	The Thelonious Monk Orchestra at Town Hall	1959	70.00
—Black label with reel and microphone logo			
❑ RLP 1150 [S]	5 By Monk By 5	1959	80.00
—Black label with reel and microphone logo			
❑ RLP 1158 [S]	Thelonious Alone in San Francisco	1959	70.00
—Black label with reel and microphone logo			
❑ RLP 1171 [S]	Thelonious Monk Quartet Plus Two at the Blackhawk	1960	70.00
—Black label with reel and microphone logo			
❑ RLP 1190 [S]	Thelonious in Action Recorded at the Five Spot Café, New York, With Johnny Griffn	1960	70.00
—Black label with reel and microphone logo			
❑ RM-3000 [M]	Mighty Monk	1967	40.00
❑ RS-3000 [S]	Mighty Monk	1967	30.00
❑ RM-3004 [M]	Monk's Music	1967	30.00
❑ RS-3004 [S]	Monk's Music	1967	20.00
❑ RS-3009 [R]	CT Meets Monk	1968	15.00
❑ RS-3015 [R]	Monk Plays Duke	1968	15.00
❑ RS-3020X [(2)R]	Two Hours with Thelonious Monk	1969	25.00
❑ RS-3037	Best of Thelonious Monk	1969	15.00
❑ RS-3047	Panorama!	1970	12.00
❑ 6039 [M]	Thelonious Monk Plays Duke Ellington	197?	12.00

Number	Title (A Side/B Side)	Yr	NM
❑ 6053 [M]	Thelonious Himself	197?	12.00
❑ 6068 [M]	The Unique Thelonious Monk	197?	12.00
❑ 6086	5 By Monk By 5	197?	12.00
❑ 6102	Thelonious in Action	197?	12.00
❑ 6107	Meet Thelonious Monk and Gerry Mulligan	197?	12.00
❑ 6119	Misterioso	197?	12.00
❑ 6163	Alone in San Francisco	198?	12.00
❑ 6183	Thelonious Monk at Town Hall	198?	12.00
❑ 6198	Thelonious Monk at the Blackhawk	198?	12.00
❑ 6207	Monk's Music	1983	12.00
❑ RS-9421 [S]	Thelonious Monk's Greatest Hits	1962	30.00
❑ RS-9443 [S]	Thelonious Monk in Italy	1963	40.00
❑ RS-9460/1 [(2)S]	Two Hours with Thelonious Monk	1963	80.00
❑ RS-9483 [S]	The Thelonious Monk Story, Vol. 1	1965	25.00
❑ RS-9483/4 [(2)S]	The Thelonious Monk Story	1965	60.00
❑ RS-9484 [S]	The Thelonious Monk Story, Vol. 2	1965	25.00
❑ RS-9491 [S]	Monk in France	1965	25.00
TRIP			
❑ 5022	Pure Monk	1974	12.00
XANADU			
❑ 202	Live at the Village Gate	1985	15.00

MONK, THELONIOUS, AND JOHN COLTRANE Also see each artist's individual listings.

Albums

Number	Title (A Side/B Side)	Yr	NM
FANTASY			
❑ OJC-039	Thelonious Monk with John Coltrane	198?	12.00
JAZZLAND			
❑ JLP-46 [M]	Thelonious Monk with John Coltrane	1961	100.00
❑ JLP-946 [S]	Thelonious Monk with John Coltrane	1961	80.00
MILESTONE			
❑ M-47011 [(2)]	Monk/Trane	1973	20.00
RIVERSIDE			
❑ RLP-490 [M]	Thelonious Monk with John Coltrane	1965	50.00
—Reissue of Jazzland 46			
❑ RS-9490 [S]	Thelonious Monk with John Coltrane	1965	40.00
—Reissue of Jazzland 946			

MONKEES, THE Also see DOLENZ, JONES & TORK; DOLENZ, JONES, BOYCE & HART; MICKEY DOLENZ; DAVY JONES; MICHAEL NESMITH.

12-Inch Singles

Number	Title (A Side/B Side)	Yr	NM
ARISTA			
❑ 9518	That Was Then, This Is Now/(Theme from) The Monkees	1986	8.00

45s

Number	Title (A Side/B Side)	Yr	NM
ARISTA			
❑ 0201	Daydream Believer/Monkee's Theme	1976	10.00
❑ 9505	That Was Then, This Is Now/(Theme from) The Monkees	1986	3.00
—With A-side artist listed as "Mickey Dolenz and Peter Tork (of the Monkees)"			
❑ 9505	That Was Then, This Is Now/(Theme from) The Monkees	1986	10.00
—First pressings list both sides' artist as "The Monkees"			
❑ 9505 [PS]	That Was Then, This Is Now/(Theme from) The Monkees	1986	3.00
—With "By Mickey Dolenz and Peter Tork (of the Monkees)" on sleeve			
❑ 9505 [PS]	That Was Then, This Is Now/(Theme from) The Monkees	1986	10.00
—Without "By Mickey Dolenz and Peter Tork (of the Monkees)" on sleeve			
❑ 9532	Daydream Believer/Randy Scouse Git	1986	4.00
❑ 9532 [PS]	Daydream Believer/Randy Scouse Git	1986	4.00
COLGEMS			
❑ 66-1001	Last Train to Clarksville/Take a Giant Step	1966	15.00
❑ 66-1001 [PS]	Last Train to Clarksville/Take a Giant Step	1966	20.00
—Version 3: Color photo, white strip at bottom of each side. Side 1 type reads "Ask For The Monkees LP Album"; Side 2 has "Write To Monkees." Note: At least one source claims that there are seven (7) different variations of the "Last Train to Clarksville" picture sleeve, but these are the ones we know about			
❑ 66-1001 [PS]	Last Train to Clarksville/Take a Giant Step	1966	25.00
—Version 2: Black & white photo, red strip at bottom with "Ask For The Monkees LP Album" in white			
❑ 66-1001 [PS]	Last Train to Clarksville/Take a Giant Step	1966	30.00
—Version 1: Black & white photo, no red strip at bottom			
❑ 66-1002	I'm a Believer/(I'm Not Your) Steppin' Stone	1966	15.00
❑ 66-1002 [PS]	I'm a Believer/(I'm Not Your) Steppin' Stone	1966	30.00
❑ 66-1003	A Little Bit Me, A Little Bit You/She Hangs Out	1967	—
—Unreleased			
❑ 66-1003 [PS]	A Little Bit Me, A Little Bit You/She Hangs Out	1967	1000.
—Though the record does not exist, this picture sleeve does. It uses the same photo that appears on the "Pleasant Valley Sunday" sleeve.			
❑ 66-1004	A Little Bit Me, A Little Bit You/The Girl I Knew Somewhere	1967	15.00
❑ 66-1007	Pleasant Valley Sunday/Words	1967	15.00
❑ 66-1007 [PS]	Pleasant Valley Sunday/Words	1967	30.00
❑ 66-1012	Daydream Believer/Goin' Down	1967	15.00
❑ 66-1012 [PS]	Daydream Believer/Goin' Down	1967	30.00
❑ 66-1019	Valleri/Tapioca Tundra	1968	10.00
❑ 66-1023	D.W. Washburn/It's Nice to Be with You	1968	10.00
❑ 66-1023 [PS]	D.W. Washburn/It's Nice to Be with You	1968	30.00
❑ 66-1031	Porpoise Song/As We Go Along	1968	10.00
❑ 66-1031 [PS]	Porpoise Song/As We Go Along	1968	20.00
❑ 66-5000	Tear Drop City/A Man Without a Dream	1969	10.00
❑ 66-5000 [PS]	Tear Drop City/A Man Without a Dream	1969	25.00
❑ 66-5004	Listen to the Band/Someday Man	1969	10.00
❑ 66-5004 [PS]	Someday Man/Listen to the Band	1969	20.00
—"Someday Man" listed first			
❑ 66-5004 [PS]	Listen to the Band/Someday Man	1969	25.00
—"Listen to the Band" listed first			
❑ 66-5005	Good Clean Fun/Mommy and Daddy	1969	15.00
❑ 66-5005 [PS]	Good Clean Fun/Mommy and Daddy	1969	25.00
❑ 66-5011	Oh My My/I Love You Better	1970	15.00
❑ 66-5011 [PS]	Oh My My/I Love You Better	1970	30.00
RHINO			
❑ 74408	Heart and Soul/M.G.B.G.T.	1987	3.00
—Black vinyl			
❑ 74408	Heart and Soul/M.G.B.G.T.	1987	10.00
—Pink vinyl			

Except when noted otherwise, VG = 25% of NM, and VG+ = 50% of NM. (Example: VG = $2.00, VG+ = $4.00 and NM = $8.00.)

Number	Title (A Side/B Side)	Yr	NM
74408 [PS]	Heart and Soul/M.G.B.G.T.	1987	4.00
74410	Every Step of the Way/ (I'll) Love You Forever	1987	3.00
74410 [PS]	Every Step of the Way/ (I'll) Love You Forever	1987	4.00
RNSI 74411	Every Step of the Way/ (I'll) Love You Forever	1987	10.00
—Picture disc in plastic sleeve with small hole			
7-Inch Extended Plays			
COLGEMS			
CGLP-101	Theme from The Monkees/ I Wanna Be Free/Take a Giant Step//Last Train to Clarksville/ Saturday's Child/Tomorrow's Gonna Be Another Day	1966	150.00
—Jukebox mini-LP, small hole, plays at 33 1/3 rpm			
CGLP-101 [PS]	The Monkees	1966	150.00
CGLP-102	I'm a Believer/Mary, Mary/ When Love Comes Knockin' (At Your Door)//(I'm Not Your) Steppin' Stone/The Kind of Girl I Could Love/She	1966	150.00
—Jukebox issue; small hole, plays at 33 1/3 rpm			
CGLP-102 [PS]	More of the Monkees	1966	150.00
Albums			
ARISTA			
AL 4089	The Monkees' Greatest Hits	1976	12.00
—Reissue of Bell LP			
AL8-8313	The Monkees' Greatest Hits	198?	8.00
—Reissue of Arista 4089			
AL9-8432	Then & Now...The Best of the Monkees	1986	12.00
AL-8524	The Monkees	1988	12.00
AL-8525	More of the Monkees	1988	12.00
BELL			
6081	Re-Focus	1972	30.00
COLGEMS			
COM-101 [M]	The Monkees	1966	20.00
—Second pressing: Side 1, Song 5 listed as "Papa Gene's Blues" (RE after number on upper right back cover)			
COM-101 [M]	The Monkees	1966	25.00
—First pressing: Side 1, Song 5 listed as "Papa Jean's Blues"			
COS-101 [S]	The Monkees	1966	20.00
—Second pressing: Side 1, Song 5 listed as "Papa Gene's Blues" (RE after number on upper right back cover)			
COS-101 [S]	The Monkees	1966	25.00
—First pressing: Side 1, Song 5 listed as "Papa Jean's Blues"			
COM-102 [M]	More of the Monkees	1966	20.00
COS-102 [S]	More of the Monkees	1966	20.00
COM-103 [M]	The Monkees' Headquarters	1967	20.00
—First pressing: Back cover, center bottom photo is of two of the LP's producers			
COM-103 [M]	The Monkees' Headquarters	1967	30.00
—Second pressing: Back cover, center bottom photo is of producers plus the Monkees with beards; "RE" on upper right back cover			
COS-103 [S]	The Monkees' Headquarters	1967	20.00
—First pressing: Back cover, center bottom photo is of two of the LP's producers			
COS-103 [S]	The Monkees' Headquarters	1967	30.00
—Second pressing: Back cover, center bottom photo is of producers plus the Monkees with beards; "RE" on upper right back cover			
COM-104 [M]	Pisces, Aquarius, Capricorn & Jones Ltd.	1967	40.00
COS-104 [S]	Pisces, Aquarius, Capricorn & Jones Ltd.	1967	20.00
COM-109 [M]	The Birds, the Bees & the Monkees	1968	100.00
COS-109 [S]	The Birds, the Bees & the Monkees	1968	20.00
COS-113	Instant Replay	1969	40.00
COS-115	The Monkees Greatest Hits	1969	40.00
COS-117	The Monkees Present	1969	50.00
COS-119	Changes	1970	80.00
PRS-329	The Monkees' Golden Hits	1971	100.00
—RCA Special Products edition			
SCOS-1001 [(2)]	A Barrel Full of Monkees	1971	75.00
COSO-5008	Head	1968	50.00
FSH			
71110	Live, 20th Anniversary Tour	1987	20.00
—Live album sold at tour stops			
LAURIE HOUSE			
LH-8009	The Monkees	1974	20.00
—TV mail-order offer			
PAIR			
ARPDL2-1109 [(2)]	Hit Factory	1986	20.00
RCA SPECIAL PRODUCTS			
DPL2-0188 [(2)]	The Monkees	1976	25.00
—TV mail-order offer			
RHINO			
RNLP-113	Monkee Flips	1984	12.00
RNLP-144	The Birds, the Bees and the Monkees	1985	12.00
RNLP-145	Head	1985	12.00
RNLP-146	Instant Replay	1985	12.00
RNLP-147	The Monkees Present	1985	12.00
RNLP-701 [PD]	Monkee Business	1982	15.00
RNLP-70139	Live 1967	1987	12.00
RNLP-70140	The Monkees	1986	12.00
RNLP-70141	Pisces, Aquarius, Capricorn & Jones Ltd.	1986	12.00
RNLP-70142	More of the Monkees	1986	12.00
RNLP-70143	The Monkees' Headquarters	1986	12.00
RNLP-70148	Changes	1986	12.00
RNLP-70150	Missing Links	1987	12.00
RNIN-70706	Pool It!	1987	10.00
SILHOUETTE			
SM-10012 [PD]	Tails of the Monkees	1983	15.00
SILVER EAGLE			
SE-1048 [(2)]	The Best of the Monkees	1986	15.00
—TV mail-order offer			
SUNDAZED			
LP 5045	The Monkees	1996	10.00
LP 5046	More of the Monkees	1996	10.00
LP 5047	The Monkees Headquarters	1996	10.00
LP 5048	Pisces, Aquarius, Capricorn & Jones Ltd.	1996	10.00
LP 5049	The Birds, the Bees, and the Monkees	1996	10.00
—All of the above are on colored vinyl with bonus tracks and posters			

MONORAYS, THE
More than one group?

Number	Title (A Side/B Side)	Yr	NM
45s			
ASTRA			
1018	Face in the Crowd/Step Right Up	196?	15.00
—Yellow vinyl			
RED ROCKET			
476	Guardian Angel/Five Minutes to Love You	1959	40.00
TAMMY			
1005	Guardian Angel/Five Minutes to Love You	1959	200.00
20TH CENTURY FOX			
594	You're No Good/Love	1965	200.00

MONOTONES, THE (1)
Male vocal group from New Jersey.

Number	Title (A Side/B Side)	Yr	NM
45s			
ARGO			
5290	Book of Love/You Never Loved Me	1958	30.00
5301	Tom Foolery/Zombi	1958	30.00
5321	The Legend of Sleepy Hollow/ Soft Shadows	1958	30.00
5339	Tell It to the Judge/ Fools Will Be Fools	1959	50.00
HULL			
735	Reading the Book of Love/Dream	1960	50.00
743	Daddy's Home, But Momma's Gone/Tattle Tale	1961	50.00
MASCOT			
124	Book of Love/You Never Loved Me	1957	800.00

MONOTONES, THE (2)
British group.

Number	Title (A Side/B Side)	Yr	NM
45s			
HICKORY			
1250	Is It Right/What Would You Do	1964	20.00
1306	When Will I Be Loved/ If You Can't Give Me All	1965	20.00

MONOTONES, THE (U)
Could be group (2); it's doubtful that it's group (1).

Number	Title (A Side/B Side)	Yr	NM
45s			
ABC-PARAMOUNT			
10796	Crystal Ball/A Thousand Faces	1966	20.00

MONRO, MATT

Number	Title (A Side/B Side)	Yr	NM
45s			
CAPITOL			
2058	Only the Night Wind Knows/ Fourth Blue Monday	1967	6.00
2103	Don't Answer Me/Pretty Polly	1968	5.00
2207	Yours Alone/The Music Played	1968	5.00
2318	Alguien Canto/De Repente Un Dea	1968	5.00
2390	Real Live Girl/When Joanna Loved Me	1969	5.00
2455	Love Song/Try to Remember	1969	5.00
2509	People/Southern Star	1969	5.00
2588	On Days Like These/Lily M'Lady	1969	5.00
2879	He Ain't Heavy, He's My Brother/We're Gonna Change the World	1970	4.00
3274	This Way Mary/Wish Now Was Then	1972	4.00
5623	Born Free/Other People	1966	6.00
5669	Honey on the Vine/Merci, Cherie	1966	6.00
5823	Wednesday's Child/ The Lady Smiles	1967	6.00
5947	These Years/What to Do	1967	6.00
LIBERTY			
55449	Softly, As I Leave You/ Is There Anything I Can Do	1962	10.00
55573	The Girl I Love/Leave Me Now	1963	8.00
55682	From Russia with Love/ Here and Now	1964	8.00
55725	Softly, As I Leave You/ I Love You Too	1964	8.00
55745	Walk Away/April Fool	1964	8.00
55763	For Mama/Going Places	1965	8.00
55786	Without You/Start Living	1965	8.00
55847	Yesterday/Just Yesterday	1965	8.00
55863	Beyond the Hill/Till Then My Love	1966	6.00
UNITED ARTISTS			
XW521	Softly, As I Leave You/ Walk Away	1974	4.00
—Reissue			
WARWICK			
624	Portrait of My Love/You're the Top of My Parade	1961	10.00
636	My Kind of Girl/This Time	1961	12.00
669	Why Not Now/Love Is the Same Anywhere	1961	10.00
Albums			
CAPITOL			
SKAO-152	Best of Matt Monro	1969	10.00
ST 2540 [S]	This Is the Life	1966	15.00
T 2540 [M]	This Is the Life	1966	12.00
ST 2608 [S]	Here's to My Lady	1966	15.00
T 2608 [M]	Here's to My Lady	1966	12.00
ST 2683 [S]	Invitation to Broadway	1967	15.00
T 2683 [M]	Invitation to Broadway	1967	12.00
ST 2730 [S]	Invitation to the Movies/Born Free	1967	12.00
T 2730 [M]	Invitation to the Movies/Born Free	1967	15.00
ST 2801 [S]	These Years	1968	12.00
T 2801 [M]	These Years	1968	15.00
LIBERTY			
LRP-3240 [M]	Matt Monro	1962	15.00
LRP-3256 [M]	From Hollywood With Love	1962	15.00
LRP-3402 [M]	Walk Away	1965	12.00
LRP-3423 [M]	All My Loving	1965	12.00
LRP-3437 [M]	Yesterday	1966	12.00
LRP-3459 [M]	Matt Monro's Best	1966	12.00
LST-7240 [S]	Matt Monro	1962	20.00
LST-7256 [S]	From Hollywood With Love	1962	20.00
LST-7402 [S]	Walk Away	1965	15.00
LST-7423 [S]	All My Loving	1965	15.00
LST-7437 [S]	Yesterday	1966	15.00
LST-7459 [S]	Matt Monro's Best	1966	15.00
LONDON			
LL 1611 [M]	Blue and Sentimental	1957	30.00
PICKWICK			
SPC-3147	This Is All I Ask	197?	10.00
WARWICK			
W 2045 [M]	My Kind of Girl	1961	30.00
WST 2045 [S]	My Kind of Girl	1961	50.00

MONROE, MARILYN

Number	Title (A Side/B Side)	Yr	NM
45s			
RCA VICTOR			
47-5745	River of No Return/ I'm Gonna File My Claim	1954	50.00
47-5745 [DJ]	River of No Return/ I'm Gonna File My Claim	1954	120.00
—Promo only with Marilyn Monroe's picture on label			
47-5745 [PS]	River of No Return/ I'm Gonna File My Claim	1954	120.00
47-6033	Heat Wave/After You Get What You Want	1955	30.00
47-6033 [PS]	Heat Wave/After You Get What You Want	1955	120.00
20TH FOX			
311	River of No Return/ One Silver Dollar	1962	20.00
311 [PS]	River of No Return/ One Silver Dollar	1962	80.00
UNITED ARTISTS			
161	I Wanna Be Loved By You/ I'm Through with Love	1959	20.00
Albums			
ASCOT			
AM-13008 [M]	Marilyn Monroe	1963	40.00
AS-16008 [S]	Marilyn Monroe	1963	50.00
MOVIETONE			
1016 [M]	The Unforgettable Marilyn Monroe	1967	25.00
72016 [R]	The Unforgettable Marilyn Monroe	1967	20.00

M

Number	Title (A Side/B Side)	Yr	NM
SANDY HOOK			
❑ SH-2013 [PD]	Rare Recordings 1948-1962	1980	25.00
STET			
❑ DS-15005	Never Before and Never Again	1980	15.00
20TH CENTURY			
❑ T-901	Remember Marilyn	1973	25.00
20TH FOX			
❑ F/SXG-5000	Marilyn Bonus Photo	1962	50.00
❑ FXG-5000 [M]	Marilyn	1962	150.00
❑ SXG-5000 [R]	Marilyn	1962	100.00

MONROES, THE

Albums

Number	Title (A Side/B Side)	Yr	NM
ALFA			
❑ AAE-15015 [EP]	The Monroes	1982	20.00

MONSTER MAGNET

45s

Number	Title (A Side/B Side)	Yr	NM
A&M			
❑ MM 1 [DJ]	Cage Around the Sun/ Superjudge	1993	7.50
—Sky blue vinyl			
❑ MM 1 [PS]	Cage Around the Sun/ Superjudge	1993	7.50
CIRCUIT			
❑ CIRCA 7001	Lizard Johnny/Freak Shop USA	1989	20.00
❑ CIRCA 7001	Lizard Johnny/Freak Shop USA	1989	60.00
—Red vinyl			
❑ CIRCA 7001 [PS]	Lizard Johnny/Freak Shop USA	1989	20.00
PRIMO SCREE			
❑ SCREE 2	Murder/Tractor	1990	15.00
❑ SCREE 2	Murder/Tractor	1990	40.00
—Green vinyl			
❑ SCREE 2 [DJ]	Murder/Tractor	1990	25.00
❑ SCREE 2 [PS]	Murder/Tractor	1990	15.00

MONTAGE

45s

Number	Title (A Side/B Side)	Yr	NM
LAURIE			
❑ 3438	I Shall Call Her Mary/ An Audience with Miss Priscilla Gray	1968	8.00
❑ 3453	Wake Up Jimmy/Tinsel and Ivy	1968	8.00

Albums

Number	Title (A Side/B Side)	Yr	NM
LAURIE			
❑ SLP-2049	Montage	1969	20.00

MONTANA SLIM

Also recorded extensively under his real name, "Wilf Carter." Other records are billed to both names.

45s

Number	Title (A Side/B Side)	Yr	NM
DECCA			
❑ 9-29384	My Mountain High Yodel Song/ Shoo Shoo Shoo Sh'La La	1954	25.00
❑ 9-29535	The Sunshine Bird/ Maple Leaf Rag	1955	20.00
❑ 9-29585	A Strawberry Roan/ Dynamite Trail	1955	20.00
❑ 9-29671	The Alpine Milkman/There's a Tree on Every Road	1955	20.00
❑ 9-29942	I'm Ragged But I'm Right/ Yodeling Song	1956	20.00
❑ 9-30079	My Little Lady/Silver Bell Yodel	1956	20.00
❑ 9-30340	Away Out on the Mountain/ Padlock on Your Heart	1957	20.00
❑ 9-30633	X's from Down in Texas/Let a Little Sunshine in Your Heart	1958	20.00
❑ 9-30907	My French Canadian Girl/ My Prairie Rose	1959	15.00
❑ 9-31034	Blind Boy's Prayer/There's a Bluebird on Your Windowsill	1959	15.00
RCA VICTOR			
❑ 45-5322	The Night Before Christmas/ Punkinhead	1951	30.00
❑ 47-4252	Wha' Hoppen/Tears Don't Always	1951	25.00
❑ 47-4303	The Night Before Christmas/ Punkinhead	1951	25.00
❑ 47-4446	My Oklahoma Rose/ I Wish There Were Three Days in the Year	1952	25.00
❑ 47-4523	Goodbye Maria/Driftwood on the River	1952	25.00
❑ 47-4846	Alabama Saturday Night/ Manhunt	1952	25.00
❑ 47-5045	Huggin' Squeezin' Kissin' Teasin'/Sweet Little Love	1952	25.00
❑ 47-5276	Sleep, Little One, Sleep/ Mockingbird Love	1953	25.00
❑ 47-8205	32 Wonderful Years/A Cashbox for a Heartache	1963	12.00
❑ 48-0054	Bluebird on Your Windowsill/All I Need Is Some More Lovin'	1949	40.00
—Originals on green vinyl			
❑ 48-0090	Streamlined Yodel Song/My Swiss Moonlight Lullaby	1949	40.00
—Originals on green vinyl			
❑ 48-0139	When the Ice Warms Next Again/Shackles and Chains	1950	40.00
—Originals on green vinyl			
❑ 48-0180	Unfaithful One/Give a Little, Take a Little	1950	40.00
—Originals on green vinyl			
❑ 48-0316	No, No, Don't Ring/A Little Shirt Mama Made for Me	1950	30.00
—Originals on green vinyl			
❑ 48-0352	Take It Easy Blues/Apple, Cherry, Mince, Chocolate	1950	30.00
—Originals on green vinyl			
❑ 48-0392	Jolly Old St. Nicholas/Rudolph the Red-Nosed Reindeer	1950	40.00
—Originals on green vinyl			
❑ 48-0397	The K.P. Blues/When That Love Bug Bites You	1950	30.00
—Originals on green vinyl			
❑ 48-0419	My Heart's Closed for Repairs/ Just a Woman's Smile	1951	30.00
❑ 48-0457	Let's Go Back to the Bible/ She'll Be There	1951	30.00
❑ 48-0477	My Wife Is On a Diet/ Sick, Sober and Sorry	1951	30.00
STARDAY			
❑ 686	Grandad's Yodeling Song/ The Little Shirt My Mother Made for Me	1964	12.00

Albums

Number	Title (A Side/B Side)	Yr	NM
DECCA			
❑ DL 4092 [M]	The Dynamite Trail	1960	50.00
❑ DL 8917 [M]	I'm Ragged But I'm Right	1959	60.00
❑ DL 74092 [S]	The Dynamite Trail	1960	60.00
RCA CAMDEN			
❑ CAL-527 [M]	Wilf Carter/Montana Slim	1958	40.00
❑ CAL-668 [M]	Reminiscin' with Montana Slim	1962	25.00
❑ CAL-846 [M]	32 Wonderful Years	1965	20.00
❑ CAS-846 [R]	32 Wonderful Years	1965	12.00
STARDAY			
❑ SLP-300 [M]	Wilf Carter As Montana Slim	1964	30.00
❑ SLP-389 [M]	Wilf Carter	1966	30.00

MONTCLAIRS, THE (1)

45s

Number	Title (A Side/B Side)	Yr	NM
PAULA			
❑ 345	Is This for Real/All I Really Care About Is You	1971	5.00
❑ 363	Dreaming Out of Season/ I Just Can't Get Away	1972	5.00
❑ 375	Beggin' Is Hard to Do/ Unwanted Love	1973	5.00
❑ 381	Make Up for Lost Time/ How Can One Man Live	1973	5.00
❑ 382	I Need You More Than Ever/ Prelude to a Heartbreak	1973	5.00
❑ 390	I'm Calling You/Hung Up on Your Love	1973	5.00
❑ 409	Baby, You Know I'm Gonna Miss You (Part 1)/Baby, You Know I'm Gonna Miss You (Part 2)	1974	5.00

MONTCLAIRS, THE (2)

45s

Number	Title (A Side/B Side)	Yr	NM
ABC-PARAMOUNT			
❑ 10463	I Believe (In Your Love)/No Baby	1963	15.00

MONTCLAIRS, THE (3)

45s

Number	Title (A Side/B Side)	Yr	NM
AUDICON			
❑ 111	Goodnight, Well, It's Time to Go/A Broken Promise	1961	30.00

MONTCLAIRS, THE (4)

45s

Number	Title (A Side/B Side)	Yr	NM
HI-Q			
❑ 5001	Golden Angel/Don Juan	1957	300.00
PREMIUM			
❑ 404	Give Me a Chance/ My Every Dream	1956	400.00
SONIC			
❑ 104	All I Want Is Love/I've Heard About You	1956	800.00

MONTCLAIRS, THE (U)

Some of these could be group (2) or (3).

45s

Number	Title (A Side/B Side)	Yr	NM
SUNBURST			
❑ 106	Wait for Me/Happy Feet Time	1965	12.00
❑ 115	Poopsie/Sore Feet	1965	12.00
UNITED INT'L.			
❑ 1007	Lisa/Tap Tap Daisy	1963	25.00
❑ 1013	Young Wings Can Fly/ Come On and Hold Me	1964	20.00
WICKWIRE			
❑ 13009	It's Gonna Work Out Fine/ If You Need Me	196?	12.00

MONTE, LOU

45s

Number	Title (A Side/B Side)	Yr	NM
AFE			
❑ 102	Darktown Strutters Ball/ The Sheik of Araby	1981	4.00
GWP			
❑ 530	I Really Don't Want to Know/ I Have an Angel in Heaven	1972	5.00
LAURIE			
❑ 3643	Paul Revere's Ride/Jerusalem, Jerusalem	1976	4.00
❑ 3652	Crabs Walk Sideways/Nicolena	1977	4.00
RCA VICTOR			
❑ 47-5382	Jealous of You/Angelina	1953	12.00
❑ 47-5496	Baby Cried/One Moment More	1953	12.00
❑ 47-5611	Darktown Strutters Ball/ I Know How You Feel	1954	15.00
❑ 47-5691	Somewhere There Is Someone/ Won't You Forgive Me	1954	12.00
❑ 47-5778	Veras Veranda/Chain Reaction	1954	12.00
❑ 47-5832	Italian Hucklebuck/Just Like Before	1954	12.00
❑ 47-5883	When I Hold You in My Arms/ In My Dreams	1954	12.00
❑ 47-5963	Cat's Whiskers/Roulette	1954	12.00
❑ 47-5993	How Important Can It Be/ Truly Yours	1955	10.00
❑ 47-6072	The Italian Wallflower/ Dreamboat	1955	10.00
❑ 47-6133	Bella Notte/With You Beside Me	1955	10.00
❑ 47-6246	King of the River/ Yaller Yaller Gold	1955	10.00
❑ 47-6287	Tombolee-Tombola/Rosina	1955	10.00
❑ 47-6320	Santo Natale/Italian Jingle Bells	1955	12.00
❑ 47-6403	Nina, the Queen of the Teeners/Pony Tail	1956	10.00
❑ 47-6522	If I Knew You Were Comin' I'd've Baked a Cake/Ask Your Heart	1956	10.00
❑ 47-6704	Elvis Presley for President/ If I Were a Millionaire	1956	30.00
❑ 47-6769	Roman Guitar/Some Cloud Above	1956	10.00
❑ 47-6848	Calypso Italiano/Someone Else Is Taking You Home	1957	10.00
❑ 47-6951	The Wife/Musica Bella	1957	10.00
❑ 47-7061	Ha! Ha! Ha!/Round and Round in My Heart	1957	10.00
❑ 47-7160	Lazy Mary/Angelique	1958	10.00
❑ 47-7265	Eh, Marie, Eh, Marie/ The Shiek of Araby	1958	8.00
❑ 47-7346	Marianne/Strada 'Nfosa	1958	8.00
❑ 47-7423	Where Do You Work, Marie/ Skinny Lena	1958	8.00
❑ 47-7467	The Italian Cowboy Song/Pizza Boy U.S.A.	1959	8.00
❑ 47-7523	The Angel in the Fountain/Sole Per Te (Only for You)	1959	8.00
❑ 47-7554	Pistol Packin' Mama/Have Another	1959	8.00
❑ 47-7641	Santa Nicola/All Because It's Christmas	1959	12.00
❑ 47-7689	Remember This Cumba/ Guardo Che Luna	1960	8.00
❑ 47-8716	Mama Get the Hammer (There's a Fly on Papa's Head)/Six O'Clock Supper	1965	6.00
❑ 47-8754	Paul Revere's Horse (Ba-Cha-Ca-Loop)/Oh Lonesome Me	1965	6.00
❑ 47-8831	Cheech the Cat/Makin' Whoopee	1966	6.00
❑ 47-9021	Oh How I Miss You Tonight/ Seventeen	1966	6.00
❑ 47-9216	When You Get What You Want/ There'll Be Some Changes Made	1967	6.00
❑ 47-9328	Digga Digga Baby/A Girl, A Girl	1967	6.00
❑ 47-9405	I Don't Play with Matches Anymore/All for the Kids	1967	6.00
REGALIA			
❑ 6600	Goombar Custer's Last Stand/ Tattooed Susie	1969	6.00
REPRISE			
❑ 0241	Down Little Doggie/La Luna Si Vuola Sposane	1963	6.00
❑ 0267	A Baby Cried/The Rooster and the Hen	1964	6.00
❑ 0284	Hello Dolly/Jungle Louie	1964	6.00

Except when noted otherwise, VG = 25% of NM, and VG+ = 50% of NM. (Example: VG = $2.00, VG+ = $4.00 and NM = $8.00.)

Number	Title (A Side/B Side)	Yr	NM
❑ 0302	You're So Bella, Isabella/ Too Fat Polka	1964	6.00
❑ 0326	I Want to Hold Your Hand/ My Parson's Across the Way	1964	8.00
❑ 0352	The Mixed-Up Bull from Palermo/ I Know How You Feel	1965	6.00
❑ 0384	Don't Wish Your Heartbreak on Me/No, No, Don't Cry, My Love	1965	6.00
❑ 0724	Pepino the Italian Mouse/What Did Washington Say (When He Crossed the Delaware)	1968	4.00
—"Back to Back Hits" series			
❑ 20015	A Good Man Is Hard to Find/ Sixteen Tons	1961	10.00
❑ 20037	Oh Mein Papa (Oh Mio Papa)/ Tici Ti Tici To Tici Ti	1961	10.00
❑ 20044	Twist Italiano/Oh Tessie	1962	10.00
❑ 20085	Please Mr. Columbus (Turn the Ship Around)/ Addio, Addio (Good-Bye)	1962	10.00
❑ 20106	Pepino the Italian Mouse/What Did Washington Say (When He Crossed the Delaware)	1962	8.00
❑ 20106 [PS]	Pepino the Italian Mouse/What Did Washington Say (When He Crossed the Delaware)	1962	12.00
❑ 20146	Pepino's Friend Pasqual (The Italian Pussy-Cat)/I Like You, You Like Me, Eh, Paisan?	1963	8.00
❑ 20146 [PS]	Pepino's Friend Pasqual (The Italian Pussy-Cat)/I Like You, You Like Me, Eh, Paisan?	1963	12.00
❑ 20171	Limbo Italiano/Bossa Nova Italiano	1963	8.00
❑ 20193	You're So Smart, You're So Smart Eh Papa/Paulucci	1963	8.00
❑ 20219	Hootenanny Italian Style/ Who Stole My Provolone	1963	8.00
ROULETTE			
❑ 4253	The Darktown Strutter's Ball/ Half a Love	1960	8.00
❑ 4266	Bim Bam Bu/Oh, Oh, Rosie	1960	8.00
❑ 4294	The Huckle-Buck/Always You	1960	8.00
❑ 4308	Christmas at Our House/ Dominick the Donkey	1960	12.00
❑ 4366	The Sheriff of Sicily/Katareena	1961	8.00
Albums			
RCA CAMDEN			
❑ CAL-455 [M]	Here's Lou Monte	195?	12.00
RCA VICTOR			
❑ LPM-1651 [M]	Lou Monte Sings for You	1957	25.00
❑ LPM-1877 [M]	Songs for Pizza Lovers	1958	25.00
❑ LPM-1976 [M]	Italian House Party	1959	20.00
❑ LSP-1976 [S]	Italian House Party	1959	25.00
❑ LPM-3672 [M]	The Best of Lou Monte	1966	15.00
❑ LSP-3672 [S]	The Best of Lou Monte	1966	12.00
❑ LPM-3705 [M]	Good Time Songs	1967	15.00
❑ LSP-3705 [S]	Good Time Songs	1967	12.00
REPRISE			
❑ R-6005 [M]	Great Italian-American Hits	1961	20.00
❑ R9-6005 [S]	Great Italian-American Hits	1961	25.00
❑ R-6014 [M]	Live in Person	1961	20.00
❑ R9-6014 [S]	Live in Person	1961	25.00
❑ R-6058 [M]	Pepino The Italian Mouse & Other Italian Fun Songs	1962	20.00
❑ R9-6058 [S]	Pepino The Italian Mouse & Other Italian Fun Songs	1962	25.00
❑ R-6099 [M]	More Italian Fun Songs	1963	20.00
❑ R9-6099 [S]	More Italian Fun Songs	1963	25.00
❑ R-6118 [M]	The Golden Hits of Lou Monte	1964	15.00
❑ RS-6118 [S]	The Golden Hits of Lou Monte	1964	20.00
ROULETTE			
❑ R-25126 [M]	Italiano U.S.A.	1960	20.00
❑ SR-25126 [S]	Italiano U.S.A.	1960	25.00
❑ R-25257 [M]	The Magic World of Italy	1963	15.00
❑ SR-25257 [S]	The Magic World of Italy	1963	20.00

MONTENEGRO, HUGO

Number	Title (A Side/B Side)	Yr	NM
45s			
GWP			
❑ 520	Lay Lady Lay/Blowin' in the Wind	1970	5.00
RCA VICTOR			
❑ 47-8369	Theme from The Long Ships/ Good Neighbor Sam	1964	6.00
❑ 47-8522	Candy's Theme/Polly	1965	6.00
❑ 47-8707	Theme from "Bunny Lake Is Missing"/Space Safari	1965	6.00
❑ 47-8747	Our Man Flint/Judith	1965	6.00
❑ 47-8847	Theme from "The Man from U.N.C.L.E."/Solo Busanova	1966	10.00
❑ 47-9050	Theme from The Professionals/ Jeannie	1966	6.00
❑ 47-9074	Hurry Sundown/Charlie's Trip	1967	6.00
❑ 47-9224	For a Few Dollars More/ The Gentle Rain	1967	6.00

Number	Title (A Side/B Side)	Yr	NM
❑ 47-9423	The Good, the Bad and The Ugly/March with Hope	1967	8.00
❑ 47-9554	Hang 'Em High/ Tomorrow;'s Love	1968	6.00
❑ 47-9638	Theme from "The Fox"/There's Got to Be a Better Way	1968	6.00
❑ 47-9712	Tony's Theme/Good Vibrations	1969	6.00
❑ 74-0160	Lady in Cement/Happy Together	1969	5.00
❑ 74-0302	Viva Max March/Don't Turn Back	1969	5.00
—With Al Hirt			
❑ 74-0515	Come Again/Lordy	1971	5.00
❑ 74-0607	Peace Train/Mammy Blue	1971	5.00
❑ 74-0690	Love Theme from "The Godfather"/Movin' On	1972	5.00
❑ 74-0875	Lost Horizon/Learn to Say Goodbye	1973	5.00
❑ 74-0954	Tara's Theme/Porcupine Pie	1973	5.00
❑ PB-10059	Living for the City/You Are the Sunshine of My Life	1974	4.00
❑ PB-10153	Love Said Goodbye/Shoo-Be-Doo-Be-Doo-Da-Day	1975	4.00
TIME			
❑ 1035	I Ain't Down Yet/If I Knew	1961	8.00
❑ 1040	The Young Savages/Majorca	1961	8.00
❑ 1043	Little Dutch Boy/Verdeales	1961	8.00
❑ 1048	Tarantella Twist/Nenella Bella	1962	8.00
❑ 1052	Palm Canyon Drive/Dark Eyes	1962	8.00
❑ 1058	Sherry/Get Off the Moon	1962	8.00
❑ 1062	Swanee River Boogie/ Hot Crawfish	1963	8.00
❑ 1064	How the West Was Won/ To Kill a Mockingbird	1963	10.00
—B-side by Dom Sebeskey			
❑ 1065	Have I Told You Lately/ Mom and Dad's Waltz	1963	8.00
❑ 1079	Be My Love/I Concentrate on You	1964	8.00
20TH FOX			
❑ 133	April Showers/La Primavera	1959	10.00
❑ 161	St. Louis Blues/Vaya Con Dios	1959	10.00
Albums			
BAINBRIDGE			
❑ 1002	American Musical Theatre, Vol. 1 (1924-1935)	198?	8.00
❑ 1003	American Musical Theatre, Vol. 2 (1935-1945)	198?	8.00
❑ 1004	American Musical Theatre, Vol. 3 (1946-1952)	198?	8.00
❑ 1005	American Musical Theatre, Vol. 4 (1953-1960)	198?	8.00
❑ 1009	Big Band Boogie	198?	8.00
❑ 1021	Camelot	198?	8.00
❑ 1028	Hugo Montenegro Plays the Movies	198?	8.00
GWP			
❑ 2003	The Dawn of Dylan	1971	15.00
MAINSTREAM			
❑ S-6101 [S]	Camelot	1967	12.00
❑ 56101 [M]	Camelot	1967	15.00
RCA CAMDEN			
❑ CAL-729 [M]	In a Sentimental Mood	196?	12.00
❑ CAS-729 [S]	In a Sentimental Mood	196?	12.00
❑ CAS-2309	Hawaiian Wedding Song	1969	10.00
RCA VICTOR			
❑ ARD1-0001 [Q]	Love Theme from "The Godfather"	1972	12.00
❑ APD1-0025 [Q]	Scenes and Themes	1973	20.00
❑ ARD1-0132 [Q]	Neil's Diamonds	1973	15.00
❑ APL1-0413	Hugo in Wonderland	1974	12.00
❑ ARD1-0413 [Q]	Hugo in Wonderland	1974	15.00
❑ ARD1-0784 [Q]	Others by Brothers	1974	15.00
❑ APD1-1024 [Q]	Rocket Man	1975	20.00
❑ APL1-1024	Rocket Man	1975	12.00
❑ ANL1-1094	Music from A Fistful of Dollars & For a Few Dollars More & The Good, The Bad and The Ugly	1975	10.00
❑ ANL1-2348	The Neil Diamond Songbook	1977	10.00
❑ LPM-2958 [M]	The Young Beat of Rome	1964	12.00
❑ LSP-2958 [S]	The Young Beat of Rome	1964	15.00
❑ LPM-3540 [M]	Come Spy with Me	1966	12.00
❑ LSP-3540 [S]	Come Spy with Me	1966	15.00
❑ LPM-3927 [M]	Music from A Fistful of Dollars & For a Few Dollars More & The Good, The Bad and The Ugly	1968	20.00
❑ LSP-3927 [S]	Music from A Fistful of Dollars & For a Few Dollars More & The Good, The Bad and The Ugly	1968	15.00
❑ LPM-4022 [M]	Hang 'Em High	1968	40.00
❑ LSP-4022 [S]	Hang 'Em High	1968	15.00
❑ LSP-4104	Good Vibrations	1969	15.00
❑ LSP-4170	Moog Power	1969	20.00
❑ LSP-4273	Colours of Love	1970	12.00
❑ AFL1-4361	The Best of Hugo Montenegro	1977	10.00
❑ LSP-4361	The Best of Hugo Montenegro	1970	12.00
❑ LSP-4537	People...One to One	1971	12.00
❑ LSP-4631	Mammy Blue	1971	12.00

Number	Title (A Side/B Side)	Yr	NM
❑ VPS-6036 [(2)]	This Is Hugo Montenegro	1971	15.00
TIME			
❑ S-2018 [S]	Cha Chas for Dancing	196?	20.00
❑ S-2020 [S]	Boogie Woogie and Bongos	196?	20.00
❑ S-2030 [S]	Arriba	196?	20.00
❑ S-2035 [S]	American Musical Theatre, Vol. 1 (1924-1935)	196?	15.00
❑ S-2036 [S]	American Musical Theatre, Vol. 2 (1935-1945)	196?	15.00
❑ S-2037 [S]	American Musical Theatre, Vol. 3 (1946-1952)	1961	15.00
❑ S-2038 [S]	American Musical Theatre, Vol. 4 (1953-1960)	1961	15.00
❑ S-2044 [S]	Great Songs from Motion Pictures Vol. 1 (1927-1937)	1961	15.00
❑ S-2045 [S]	Great Songs from Motion Pictures Vol. 2 (1938-1944)	1961	15.00
❑ S-2046 [S]	Great Songs from Motion Pictures Vol. 3 (1945-1960)	1961	15.00
❑ S-2051 [S]	Montenegro in Italy	196?	15.00
❑ TDM 3003 [(2)M]	Italy - Ciao	196?	15.00
❑ TDS 3003 [(2)S]	Italy - Ciao	196?	20.00
❑ 52018 [M]	Cha Chas for Dancing	196?	15.00
❑ 52020 [M]	Boogie Woogie and Bongos	196?	15.00
❑ 52030 [M]	Arriba	196?	15.00
❑ 52035 [M]	American Musical Theatre, Vol. 1 (1924-1935)	196?	12.00
❑ 52036 [M]	American Musical Theatre, Vol. 2 (1935-1945)	196?	12.00
❑ 52037 [M]	American Musical Theatre, Vol. 3 (1946-1952)	1961	12.00
❑ 52038 [M]	American Musical Theatre, Vol. 4 (1953-1960)	1961	12.00
❑ 52044 [M]	Great Songs from Motion Pictures Vol. 1 (1927-1937)	1961	12.00
❑ 52045 [M]	Great Songs from Motion Pictures Vol. 2 (1938-1944)	1961	12.00
❑ 52046 [M]	Great Songs from Motion Pictures Vol. 3 (1945-1960)	1961	12.00
❑ 52051 [M]	Montenegro in Italy	196?	12.00
20TH CENTURY FOX			
❑ S-4204	Lady in Cement	1968	20.00
20TH FOX			
❑ 3018 [M]	The 20th Century Strings, Vol. 1	1959	20.00
VIK			
❑ LX-1089 [M]	Loves of My Life	1957	25.00
❑ LX-1106 [M]	Ellington Fantasy	1957	25.00

MONTEREYS, THE

More than one group.

Number	Title (A Side/B Side)	Yr	NM
45s			
ARWIN			
❑ 130	Goodbye My Love/It Hurts Me So	1961	40.00
BLAST			
❑ 219	Face in the Crowd/Step Right Up	1965	400.00
DOMINION			
❑ 1019	First Kiss/Just One More Kiss	1964	40.00
EASTWEST			
❑ 121	I'll Love You Again/The American Teens	1958	25.00
GNP CRESCENDO			
❑ 314	For Sentimental Reasons/ I Still Love You	1964	25.00
IMPALA			
❑ 213	Without a Girl/So Deep	1959	120.00
MAJOR			
❑ 1009	A Crowded Room/You Said That You Loved Me	1959	70.00
PRINCE			
❑ 5060	Rita/Billy Bud	1960	15.00
ROSE			
❑ 109	You're the Girl for Me/Ape Shape	1958	100.00
SATURN			
❑ 1002	My Girl/With You	1956	40.00
TRANS AMERICAN			
❑ 1000/1	Darlin' Send Me a Letter/ Late Darlin'	1960	600.00

MONTEZ, CHRIS

Number	Title (A Side/B Side)	Yr	NM
45s			
A&M			
❑ 780	Call Me/Go Head On	1965	8.00
❑ 796	The More I See You/ You, I Love You	1966	10.00
❑ 810	There Will Never Be Another You/You Can Hurt the One You Love	1966	8.00
❑ 822	Keep Talkin'/Time After Time	1966	8.00
❑ 839	Because of You/Elena	1967	8.00
❑ 852	Just Friends/Twiggy	1967	6.00

M

Number	Title (A Side/B Side)	Yr	NM
❑ 855	Foollin' Around/Dindi (Jin-Jee)	1967	6.00
❑ 906	Once in a While/The Face I Love	1968	6.00
❑ 958	Love Is Here to Stay/ Nothing to Hide	1968	6.00
❑ 985	Where Are You Now/ Watch What Happens	1968	6.00

JAMIE

Number	Title (A Side/B Side)	Yr	NM
❑ 1410	Let's Dance/Somebody Loves You	1973	5.00

MONOGRAM

Number	Title (A Side/B Side)	Yr	NM
❑ 500	All You Had to Do (Was Tell Me)/Love Me	1962	12.00
❑ 505	Let's Dance/You're the One	1962	20.00
❑ 507	Some Kinda Fun/Tell Me	1962	12.00
❑ 508	Rockin' Blues/(Let's Do the) Limbo	1963	15.00
❑ 513	In An English Towne/ My Baby Loves to Dance	1963	12.00
❑ 516	No, No, No/Monkey Fever	1963	12.00
❑ 517	You're the One/All You Had to Do Was Tell Me	1964	12.00
—With Kathy Young			
❑ 520	It Takes Two/To Shoot the Curl	1964	12.00
—With Kathy Young			
❑ 522	(It's Not) Puppy Love/ He's Been Leading You On	1964	12.00

PARAMOUNT

Number	Title (A Side/B Side)	Yr	NM
❑ 0109	We Can Make the World a Whole Lot Brighter/ The End of the Line	1971	5.00

Albums

A&M

Number	Title (A Side/B Side)	Yr	NM
❑ LP-115 [M]	The More I See You/Call Me	1966	20.00
❑ LP-120 [M]	Time After Time	1966	15.00
❑ LP-128 [M]	Foolin' Around	1967	15.00
❑ LP-157 [M]	Watch What Happens	1967	15.00
❑ ST-4115 [S]	The More I See You/Call Me	1966	25.00
❑ SP-4120 [S]	Time After Time	1966	20.00
❑ SP-4128 [S]	Foolin' Around	1967	20.00
❑ SP-4157 [S]	Watch What Happens	1967	20.00

MONOGRAM

Number	Title (A Side/B Side)	Yr	NM
❑ M-100 [M]	Let's Dance and Have Some Kinda' Fun!!!	1963	400.00

MONTGOMERY, BOB

45s

BRUNSWICK

Number	Title (A Side/B Side)	Yr	NM
❑ 55157	Because I Love You/ Taste of the Blues	1959	40.00

MONTGOMERY, CHRISTOPHER

45s

DOLTON

Number	Title (A Side/B Side)	Yr	NM
❑ 84	My Paradise/Giants of Bombora	1963	30.00

MONTGOMERY, JACK

45s

AUSTONS

Number	Title (A Side/B Side)	Yr	NM
❑ 0001	Beauty Isn't Born/(Instrumental)	197?	150.00

BARRACUDA

Number	Title (A Side/B Side)	Yr	NM
❑ 101	Don't Turn Your Back on Me/ Never in a Million Years	196?	400.00

REVUE

Number	Title (A Side/B Side)	Yr	NM
❑ 11009	Baby, Baby, Take a Chance on Me/(Instrumental)	1968	150.00

SCEPTER

Number	Title (A Side/B Side)	Yr	NM
❑ 12152	Dearly Beloved/Do You Believe It	1966	300.00
—Correct title of A-side			
❑ 12152	My Dear Beloved/ Do You Believe It	1966	400.00
—Misprinted A-side title			

MONTGOMERY, MELBA

45s

CAPITOL

Number	Title (A Side/B Side)	Yr	NM
❑ 2513	As Far As My Forgetting's Got/ You Let Me Win	1969	8.00
❑ 2758	The Closer She Gets/ Where Do We Go from Here	1970	8.00
❑ 2825	Together Again/Eloy Crossing	1970	8.00
❑ 3091	He's My Man/We Don't Live Here Anymore	1971	8.00
❑ 3297	Hope I Never Love That Way Again/Say You'll Never Leave Me	1972	8.00
❑ 4290	He Called Me Baby/ Country Child	1976	4.00

COMPASS

Number	Title (A Side/B Side)	Yr	NM
❑ 45-7	Straight Talkin'/(B-side unknown)	1986	6.00

ELEKTRA

Number	Title (A Side/B Side)	Yr	NM
❑ 45211	If You Want the Rainbow/Love, I Need You	1974	5.00
❑ 45229	Don't Let the Good Times Fool You/It Sure Gets Lonely	1975	5.00
❑ 45247	Searchin' (For Someone Like You)/Hiding in the Darkness of My Mind	1975	5.00
❑ 45272	If I Ever Needed Someone/ He Loved You Right Out of My Mind	1975	5.00
❑ 45296	Love Was the Wind/I Never Dreamed That Love Could Be This Good	1975	5.00
❑ 45866	Wrap Your Love Around Me/ Let Me Show You How I Can	1973	6.00
❑ 45875	He'll Come Home/Country Written Up and Down Your Face	1973	6.00
❑ 45883	No Charge/I Love Him Because He's That Way	1974	6.00
❑ 45883	No Charge/Wrap Your Love Around Me	1974	6.00
❑ 45894	Your Pretty Roses Came Too Late/My Feel Good Sure Feels Fine	1974	6.00

KARI

Number	Title (A Side/B Side)	Yr	NM
❑ 111	The Star/Carolina in My Mind	1980	6.00

MUSICOR

Number	Title (A Side/B Side)	Yr	NM
❑ 1157	Don't Keep Me Lonely Too Long/I'm Looking for the Man	1966	10.00
❑ 1175	Crossing Over Jordan/The Dead Shall Live Again	1966	10.00
❑ 1182	He's Out There With Her Somewhere/My Tiny Music Box	1966	10.00
❑ 1209	He Stayed Away (Long As He Could)/Won't Take Long	1966	10.00
❑ 1241	What Can I Tell the Folks Back Home/The Right Time to Lose My Mind	1967	10.00
❑ 1278	The Day Your Memory Came to Town/Twilight Years	1967	10.00
❑ 1291	He Wrote Forgive Me/ You Put Me Here	1968	10.00
❑ 1311	Our Little Man/Tell Me Your Troubles	1968	10.00
❑ 1324	Hallelujah Road/ Life Beyond Death	1968	10.00
❑ 1344	What's to Become of What's Left of Me/Every Day's a Happy Day for Fools	1969	10.00

UNITED ARTISTS

Number	Title (A Side/B Side)	Yr	NM
❑ 576	Hall of Shame/What's Bad for You Is Good for Me	1963	12.00
❑ 652	The Greatest One of All/Lies Can't Hide What's On My Mind	1963	12.00
❑ 705	The Face/I Will Always Keep Loving You	1964	12.00
❑ 768	Big City Heartaches/ Why Does the Lady Cry	1964	12.00
❑ 803	I Can't Change Overnight/I Can't Get Used to Being Lonely	1965	12.00
❑ 850	White Lightning/I Saw It	1965	12.00
❑ 900	Yearning/I'll Wait Till Seven	1965	12.00
❑ 964	Big Joke/Constantly	1965	12.00
❑ XW1008	Never Ending Love Affair/You	1977	5.00
❑ XW1115	Angel of the Morning/ Pinkerton's Flowers	1977	5.00
❑ XW1175	Leavin' Me in Your Mind/We've Been Lyin' Here Too Long	1978	5.00

Albums

CAPITOL

Number	Title (A Side/B Side)	Yr	NM
❑ ST-328	The Big, Wonderful Country World of Melba Montgomery	1969	15.00
—This is the title on the cover; the label calls this "The Big, Beautiful Country World of Melba Montgomery"			
❑ ST-468	Don't Keep Me Lonely Too Long	1970	15.00

ELEKTRA

Number	Title (A Side/B Side)	Yr	NM
❑ CM-2	Don't Let the Good Times Fool You	1975	10.00
❑ CM-6	The Greatest Gift of All	1975	10.00
❑ EKS-75069	Melba Montgomery	1973	12.00
❑ EKS-75079	No Charge	1974	10.00

HILLTOP

Number	Title (A Side/B Side)	Yr	NM
❑ JS-6031	Miss Country Music	196?	12.00

MUSICOR

Number	Title (A Side/B Side)	Yr	NM
❑ MM-2074 [M]	Country Girl	1966	15.00
❑ MM-2097 [M]	The Hallelujah Road	1966	15.00
❑ MM-2113 [M]	Melba Toast	1967	20.00
❑ MM-2114 [M]	Don't Keep Me Lonely Too Long	1967	20.00
❑ MS-3074 [S]	Country Girl	1966	20.00
❑ MS-3097 [S]	The Hallelujah Road	1966	20.00
❑ MS-3113 [S]	Melba Toast	1967	20.00
❑ MS-3114 [S]	Don't Keep Me Lonely Too Long	1967	20.00

STARDAY

Number	Title (A Side/B Side)	Yr	NM
❑ SLP-352 [M]	Queen of Country Music	1965	25.00

UNITED ARTISTS

Number	Title (A Side/B Side)	Yr	NM
❑ UAL-3341 [M]	America's Number One Country and Western Girl Singer	1964	20.00
❑ UAL-3369 [M]	Down Home	1964	20.00
❑ UAL-3391 [M]	I Can't Get Used to Being Lonely	1965	20.00
❑ UAS-6341 [S]	America's Number One Country and Western Girl Singer	1964	25.00
❑ UAS-6369 [S]	Down Home	1964	25.00
❑ UAS-6391 [S]	I Can't Get Used to Being Lonely	1965	25.00

MONTGOMERY, TAMMY

Later known as TAMMI TERRELL.

45s

CHECKER

Number	Title (A Side/B Side)	Yr	NM
❑ 1072	If I Would Marry You/ This Time Tomorrow	1964	25.00
—Mostly blue label with red and black checkers			
❑ 1072	If I Would Marry You/ This Time Tomorrow	1964	40.00
—Maroon label			

SCEPTER

Number	Title (A Side/B Side)	Yr	NM
❑ 1224	If You See Bill/It's Mine	1961	60.00

TRY ME

Number	Title (A Side/B Side)	Yr	NM
❑ 28001	I Cried/If You Don't Think	1962	30.00
—As "Tana Montgomery"			

WAND

Number	Title (A Side/B Side)	Yr	NM
❑ 123	Voice of Experience/ I Wancha' to Be Sure	1962	30.00

MONTGOMERY, WES

45s

A&M

Number	Title (A Side/B Side)	Yr	NM
❑ 865	A Day in the Life (Part 1)/ A Day in the Life (Part 2)	1967	8.00
❑ 883	Windy/Watch What Happens	1967	8.00
❑ 916	Goin' On to Detroit/Wind Song	1968	8.00
❑ 940	Georgia on My Mind/ I Say a Little Prayer	1968	8.00
❑ 1008	Where Have All the Flowers Gone/Fly Me to the Moon	1968	8.00
❑ 1187	The Joker/Trust in Me	1970	6.00

PACIFIC JAZZ

Number	Title (A Side/B Side)	Yr	NM
❑ 301	Summertime/Fingerpickin'	1960	12.00

RIVERSIDE

Number	Title (A Side/B Side)	Yr	NM
❑ 431	Yesterdays/(B-side unknown)	1961	12.00
❑ 441	Airegan/Mr. Walker	196?	12.00
❑ 459	Movin' Along/Tune Up	196?	12.00
❑ 475	Full House/Cariba	196?	12.00

VERVE

Number	Title (A Side/B Side)	Yr	NM
❑ CS?-5 [(5)]	Celebrity Scene: Wes Montgomery	1966	60.00
—Box set of five singles (10440-10444). Price includes box, all 5 singles, jukebox title strips, bio. Records are sometimes found by themselves, so they are also listed separately.			
❑ 10373	Love Theme from "The Sandpiper"/Bumpin'	1965	8.00
❑ 10384	Goin' Out of My Head/Boss City	1966	8.00
❑ 10432	Tequila/Bumpin' On Sunset	1966	8.00
❑ 10440 [DJ]	Goin' Out of My Head/Tequila	1966	10.00
❑ 10441 [DJ]	Bumpin' (Part 1)/Bumpin' (Part 2)	1966	10.00
❑ 10442 [DJ]	Bumpin' on Sunset (Part 1)/ Bumpin' on Sunset (Part 2)	1966	10.00
❑ 10443 [DJ]	Phoenix Love Theme/Caravan	1966	10.00
❑ 10444 [DJ]	Love Theme from "The Sandpiper" (The Shadow of Your Smile)/A Quiet Thing	1966	10.00
—"CS2-5 Record Number 5"			
❑ 10489	California Dreaming/Mr. Walker	1967	8.00

Albums

A&M

Number	Title (A Side/B Side)	Yr	NM
❑ LP-2001 [M]	A Day in the Life	1967	20.00
❑ SP-3001 [S]	A Day in the Life	1967	12.00
❑ SP9-3001	A Day in the Life	1983	15.00
—"Audio Master Plus" reissue			
❑ SP-3006	Down Here on the Ground	1968	15.00
❑ SP9-3006	Down Here on the Ground	1983	15.00
—"Audio Master Plus" reissue			
❑ SP-3012	Road Song	1968	15.00
❑ SP9-3012	Road Song	1984	15.00
—"Audio Master Plus" reissue			
❑ SP-4247	Greatest Hits	1970	15.00

ACCORD

Number	Title (A Side/B Side)	Yr	NM
❑ SN-7170	The Classic Sound of Wes Montgomery	1981	10.00

BLUE NOTE

Number	Title (A Side/B Side)	Yr	NM
❑ BN-LA531-H2 [(2)]	Beginnings	1976	30.00
❑ LWB-531 [(2)]	Beginnings	1981	25.00
—Reissue of BN-LA531-H2			

DCC COMPACT CLASSICS

Number	Title (A Side/B Side)	Yr	NM
❑ LPZ-2014	Goin' Out of My Head	1996	40.00
—Audiophile vinyl			

Except when noted otherwise, VG = 25% of NM, and VG+ = 50% of NM. (Example: VG = $2.00, VG+ = $4.00 and NM = $8.00.)

Number	Title (A Side/B Side)	Yr	NM
FANTASY			
❑ OJC-034	A Dynamic New Sound	198?	12.00
❑ OJC-036	The Incredible Jazz Guitar of Wes Montgomery	198?	12.00
❑ OJC-089	Movin' Along	198?	12.00
❑ OJC-106	Full House	198?	12.00
❑ OJC-144	Portrait of Wes	198?	12.00
❑ OJC-233	So Much Guitar!	198?	12.00
❑ OJC-261	Boss Guitar	1987	12.00
❑ OJC-368	Fusion! Wes Montgomery with Strings	198?	12.00
❑ OJC-489	Guitar on the Go	1991	15.00
MGM			
❑ GAS-120	Wes Montgomery (Golden Archive Series)	1970	15.00
MILESTONE			
❑ 9110	Encores	1983	10.00
❑ 47003 [(2)]	While We're Young	1972	15.00
❑ 47013 [(2)]	Wes Montgomery and Friends	1973	15.00
❑ 47030 [(2)]	Pretty Blue	197?	12.00
❑ 47040 [(2)]	Movin'	197?	12.00
❑ 47051 [(2)]	Groove Brothers	1979	12.00
❑ 47057 [(2)]	Yesterdays	198?	12.00
❑ 47065 [(2)]	The Alternative Wes Montgomery	1982	12.00
MOBILE FIDELITY			
❑ MFSL-508	Bumpin'	198?	40.00
—"Original Master Recording" at top of cover			
PACIFIC JAZZ			
❑ PJ-5 [M]	Montgomeryland	1960	30.00
❑ ST-5 [S]	Montgomeryland	1960	40.00
❑ PJ-10104 [M]	Easy Groove	1966	15.00
❑ PJ-10130 [M]	Kismet	1967	20.00
❑ ST-20104 [S]	Easy Groove	1966	20.00
❑ ST-20130 [S]	Kismet	1967	15.00
❑ ST-20137	Portrait of Wes Montgomery	1968	15.00
PICCADILLY			
❑ 3584	Jazz Guitar	198?	10.00
RIVERSIDE			
❑ RLP 12-310 [M]	A Dynamic New Sound	1959	80.00
❑ RLP 12-320 [M]	The Incredible Jazz Guitar of Wes Montgomery	1960	60.00
❑ RLP-342 [M]	Movin' Along	1960	25.00
❑ RLP-382 [M]	So Much Guitar!	1961	25.00
❑ RLP-434 [M]	Full House	1962	30.00
❑ RLP-459 [M]	Boss Guitar	1963	80.00
❑ RLP-472 [M]	Fusion! Wes Montgomery with Strings	1964	20.00
❑ RLP-492 [M]	Portrait of Wes	1965	15.00
❑ RLP-494 [M]	Guitar on the Go	1965	15.00
❑ RLP 1156 [S]	New Concepts in Jazz Guitar	1959	30.00
❑ RLP 1169 [S]	The Incredible Jazz Guitar of Wes Montgomery	1960	30.00
❑ RM-3002 [M]	In the Wee Small Hours	1967	20.00
—Reissue of 472			
❑ RS-3002 [S]	In the Wee Small Hours	1967	15.00
—Reissue of 9472			
❑ RS-3012	This Is Wes Montgomery	1968	15.00
—Reissue of 9459			
❑ RS-3014	'Round Midnight	1968	15.00
—Reissue of 1156			
❑ RS-3036	March 6, 1925-June 15, 1968	1968	15.00
❑ RS-3039	The Best of Wes Montgomery	1968	12.00
❑ RS-3046	Panorama	1969	15.00
❑ 6046	The Incredible Jazz Guitar of Wes Montgomery	197?	10.00
❑ 6069	Full House	197?	10.00
❑ 6080	The Dynamic New Jazz Sound of Wes Montgomery	197?	10.00
❑ 6100	So Much Guitar!	197?	10.00
❑ 6111	Boss Guitar	197?	10.00
❑ 6168	Guitar on the Go	198?	10.00
❑ 6199	Movin' Along	198?	10.00
❑ 6202	Portrait of Wes	198?	10.00
❑ 6210	Fusion! Wes Montgomery with Strings	198?	10.00
❑ RS-9342 [S]	Movin' Along	1960	25.00
❑ RS-9382 [S]	So Much Guitar!	1961	25.00
❑ RS-9434 [S]	Full House	1962	30.00
❑ RS-9459 [S]	Boss Guitar	1963	25.00
❑ RS-9472 [S]	Fusion! Wes Montgomery with Strings	1964	25.00
❑ RS-9492 [S]	Portrait of Wes	1965	20.00
❑ RS-9494 [S]	Guitar on the Go	1965	20.00
VERVE			
❑ VE-2-2513 [(2)]	Small Group Recording	197?	15.00
❑ V-8610 [M]	Movin' Wes	1965	15.00
❑ V6-8610 [S]	Movin' Wes	1965	20.00
❑ V-8625 [M]	Bumpin'	1965	15.00
❑ V6-8625 [S]	Bumpin'	1965	20.00
❑ V-8642 [M]	Goin' Out of My Head	1966	15.00
❑ V6-8642 [S]	Goin' Out of My Head	1966	20.00
❑ V-8653 [M]	Tequila	1966	15.00
❑ V6-8653 [S]	Tequila	1966	20.00
❑ V-8672 [M]	California Dreaming	1967	20.00
❑ V6-8672 [S]	California Dreaming	1967	15.00
❑ V-8714 [M]	The Best of Wes Montgomery	1967	20.00
❑ V6-8714 [S]	The Best of Wes Montgomery	1967	15.00
❑ V6-8757	The Best of Wes Montgomery, Vol. 2	1968	15.00
❑ V6-8765	Willow Weep for Me	1969	15.00
❑ V6-8796	Eulogy	1970	15.00
❑ V6-8804	Just Walkin'	1971	12.00
❑ V6-8813 [(2)]	The History of Wes Montgomery	1972	15.00
❑ V3HB-8839 [(2)]	Return Engagement	1974	15.00

MONTGOMERYS, THE

Number	Title (A Side/B Side)	Yr	NM
45s			
AMY			
❑ 883	Promise of Love/Gotta Make a Hit Record	1963	250.00

MONTROSE

Number	Title (A Side/B Side)	Yr	NM
45s			
WARNER BROS.			
❑ 7776	Rock the Nation/One Thing on My Mind	1974	5.00
❑ 7814	Make It Last/Space Station No. 5	1974	5.00
❑ 8063	The Dreamer/Paper Money	1975	5.00
❑ 8080	Connection/We're Going Home	1975	5.00
❑ 8172	Clown Woman/Matriarch	1976	5.00
❑ 8281	Music Man/Tuft-Sedge	1976	5.00
❑ 8351	Let's Go/Merry-Go-Round	1977	5.00
Albums			
ENIGMA			
❑ ST-73264	Mean	1987	10.00
❑ D1-73323	Speed of Sound	1988	10.00
WARNER BROS.			
❑ BS 2740	Montrose	1974	12.00
❑ BS 2823	Paper Money	1974	10.00
❑ BS 2892	Warner Bros. Presents Montrose!	1975	10.00
❑ BS 2963	Jump On It	1976	10.00
❑ BSK 3106	Montrose	1978	8.00
—Reissue of 2740			

MONTY PYTHON

Number	Title (A Side/B Side)	Yr	NM
45s			
ARISTA			
❑ 0130	The Single/(B-side unknown)	1975	8.00
❑ 0578	They Won't Play This Song on the Radio/Sit on My Face-Farewell to John Denver	1980	8.00
WARNER BROS.			
❑ 49112	Always Look on the Bright Side of Life/Brian	1979	10.00
Albums			
ARISTA			
❑ SP-101 [DJ]	Monty Python's Contractual Obligation Sampler	1980	30.00
—One side is censored, the other is uncensored			
❑ AL 4039	Matching Tie & Handkerchief	1975	20.00
—Side 2 is "trick tracked," with two different routines depending on where you place the needle at the start			
❑ AL 4050	The Album of the Soundtrack of the Trailer of the Film of "Monty Python and the Holy Grail"	1975	20.00
❑ AL 4073	Monty Python Live! At City Center	1976	20.00
❑ AL 8296	The Monty Python Instant Record Collection	198?	8.00
—Reissue			
❑ AL 8343	Monty Python's Contractual Obligation Album	198?	8.00
—Reissue			
❑ AL 8353	Monty Python Live! At City Center	198?	8.00
—Reissue			
❑ AL 8355	The Album of the Soundtrack of the Trailer of the Film of "Monty Python and the Holy Grail"	198?	8.00
—Reissue			
❑ AL 8357	Matching Tie and Handkerchief	198?	8.00
—Reissue; we don't know whether Side 2 maintains the trick groove on this issue			
❑ AB 9536	Monty Python's Contractual Obligation Album	1980	20.00
❑ AB 9580	The Monty Python Instant Record Collection	1981	15.00
BBC			
❑ 22073	Monty Python's Flying Circus	1980	20.00
—Excerpts from TV shows; pressed by Columbia, possibly for exclusive use by the record club			
BUDDAH			
❑ BDS 5656 [(2)]	The Worst of Monty Python	1976	20.00
—Repackage of the two Charisma LPs			
CHARISMA			
❑ CAS 1049	Another Monty Python Record	1972	25.00
❑ CAS 1063	Monty Python's Previous Record	1972	25.00
MCA			
❑ 6121	Monty Python and the Meaning of Life	1983	12.00
PYE			
❑ 12116	Monty Python's Flying Circus	1975	20.00
VIRGIN			
❑ 90865 [(2)]	The Final Rip Off	1988	20.00
WARNER BROS.			
❑ BSK 3396	Life of Brian	1979	15.00

MOODS, THE (1)

Number	Title (A Side/B Side)	Yr	NM
45s			
BANG			
❑ 555	Gotta Figure Out/Genuine Jade	1968	8.00
WAND			
❑ 11224	Rainmaker/Lady Rain	1970	8.00

MOODS, THE (2)

Number	Title (A Side/B Side)	Yr	NM
45s			
KOOL			
❑ 1024	High School Days/The Broken Hip	1964	10.00
❑ 1028	Oop-Sy-Do/Stay with Me	1965	10.00
❑ 1032	Only the Young/(B-side unknown)	1965	10.00

MOODS, THE (3)

Number	Title (A Side/B Side)	Yr	NM
45s			
SARG			
❑ 162	Little Alice/Lady of the Sea	1959	80.00
❑ 176	Easy Going/Duck Walk	1959	40.00
❑ 179	Let Me Have Your Love/Broke Up	1959	50.00
❑ 184	Rockin' Santa Claus/Teenager's Past	1959	40.00
❑ 185	On the Move/Teenager's Past	1960	40.00

M

MOODY BLUES, THE

Also see GRAEME EDGE; JUSTIN HAYWARD; DENNY LAINE; RAY THOMAS.

Number	Title (A Side/B Side)	Yr	NM
12-Inch Singles			
POLYDOR			
❑ 431 [DJ]	The Other Side of Life (Edit) (LP Version)	1986	8.00
❑ 449 [DJ]	Running Out of Love (same on both sides)	1986	8.00
THRESHOLD			
❑ 174 [DJ]	Gemini Dream (same on both sides)	1981	8.00
❑ 224 [DJ]	Sitting at the Wheel (Edit) (LP Version)	1983	8.00
45s			
DERAM			
❑ 5N-67012	I'm Just a Singer (In a Rock and Roll Band)/For My Lady	197?	4.00
—Reissue of Threshold 67012			
❑ 85023	Nights in White Satin/Cities	1968	8.00
—Composer of "Nights in White Satin" listed as "Justin Hayward"			
❑ 85023	Nights in White Satin/Cities	1968	8.00
—Composers of "Nights in White Satin" listed as "Redwave-Hayward"			
❑ 85023	Nights in White Satin/Cities	1968	10.00
—Composer of "Nights in White Satin" listed as "Redwave"			
❑ 85028	Tuesday Afternoon (Forever Afternoon)/Another Morning	1968	8.00
❑ 85033	Ride My See-Saw/Voices in the Sky	1968	8.00
❑ 85044	Never Comes the Day/So Deep Within You	1969	8.00
LONDON			
❑ 270	Steppin' in a Slide Zone/I'll Be Level with You	1978	4.00
❑ 273	Driftwood/I'm Your Man	1978	5.00
❑ 1005	This Is My House (But Nobody Calls)/Boulevard de la Madelaine	1967	12.00
❑ 9726	Go Now!/Lose Your Money	1965	8.00
—Blue swirl label, "London" in black			
❑ 9726	Go Now!/Lose Your Money	1965	12.00
—Blue swirl label, "London" in white			
❑ 9726	Go Now!/Lose Your Money	1965	20.00
—White, purple and blue label			
❑ 9726V [DJ]	Go Now!/It's Easy Child	1965	20.00
—Orange and brown swirl label; may be promo only			
❑ 5N-9726	Go Now!/Lose Your Money	1975	6.00
—Blue swirl label; new prefix			
❑ 5N-9726	Go Now!/It's Easy Child	1978	6.00
—Reissue on "sunrise" label			
❑ 9764	From the Bottom of My Heart (I Love You)/And My Baby's Gone	1965	15.00
❑ 9799	Ev'ry Day/You Don't	1965	15.00
❑ 9810	Stop!/Bye Bye Bird	1966	15.00
❑ 20030	Fly Me High/I Really Haven't Got the Time	1967	12.00
POLYDOR			
❑ 870990-7	No More Lies/River of Endless Love	1988	3.00

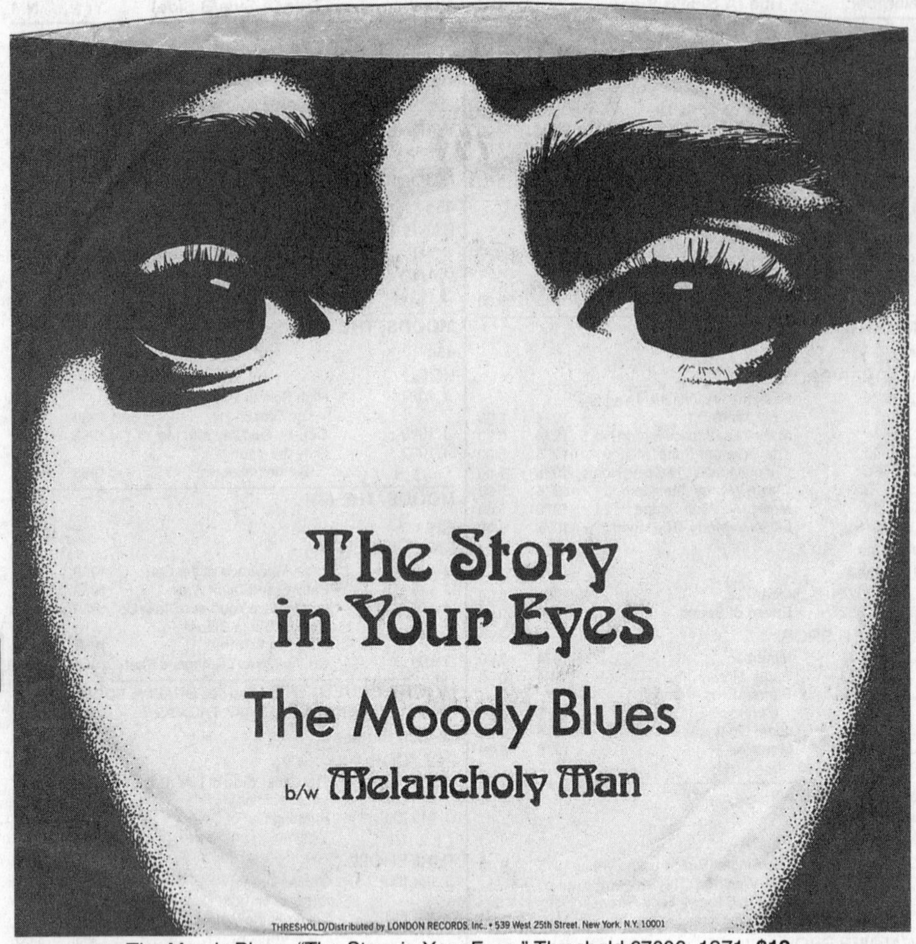

The Moody Blues, "The Story in Your Eyes," Threshold 67006, 1971, **$12.**

Number	Title (A Side/B Side)	Yr	NM
❑ 870990-7 [PS]	No More Lies/River of Endless Love	1988	3.00
❑ 871270-7	Al Fin Voy a Encontrarte (I Know You're Out There Somewhere — Spanish Version)/I Know You're Out There Somewhere	1989	5.00
❑ 883906-7	Your Wildest Dreams/ Talkin' Talkin'	1986	3.00
❑ 883906-7 [PS]	Your Wildest Dreams/ Talkin' Talkin'	1986	3.00
❑ 885201-7	The Other Side of Life/The Spirit	1986	5.00
—Blue vinyl			
❑ 885201-7 [PS]	The Other Side of Life/The Spirit	1986	5.00
—Special sleeve for blue vinyl version			
❑ 885212-7	The Other Side of Life/The Spirit	1986	3.00
❑ 885212-7 [PS]	The Other Side of Life/The Spirit	1986	3.00
❑ 887600-7	I Know You're Out There Somewhere/Miracle	1988	3.00
❑ 887600-7 [PS]	I Know You're Out There Somewhere/Miracle	1988	3.00
❑ 887815-7	Here Comes the Weekend/ River of Endless Love	1988	3.00
THRESHOLD			
❑ 601	Gemini Dream/Painted Smile	1981	4.00
❑ 602	The Voice/22,000 Days	1981	4.00
❑ 602 [PS]	The Voice/22,000 Days	1981	6.00
❑ 603	Talking Out of Turn/ Veteran Cosmic Rocker	1981	4.00
❑ 604	Sitting at the Wheel/ Going Nowhere	1983	4.00
❑ 604 [PS]	Sitting at the Wheel/ Going Nowhere	1983	6.00
❑ 605	Blue World/Sorry	1983	4.00
❑ 606	Running Water/Under My Feet	1983	4.00
❑ 67004	Question/Candle of Life	1970	6.00
❑ 67006	The Story in Your Eyes/ Melancholy Man	1971	6.00
❑ 67006 [PS]	The Story in Your Eyes/ Melancholy Man	1971	12.00
❑ 67009	Isn't Life Strange/ After You Came	1972	5.00
❑ 67012	I'm Just a Singer (In a Rock and Roll Band)/For My Lady	1973	5.00

Number	Title (A Side/B Side)	Yr	NM
Albums			
COMPLEAT			
❑ 672008 [(2)]	Early Blues	1985	15.00
—Reissue of London 1964-66 material			
DERAM			
❑ DE 16012 [M]	Days of Future Passed	1968	250.00
❑ DES 18012 [S]	Days of Future Passed	1968	20.00
—With large "DERAM" on top half of label			
❑ DES 18012 [S]	Days of Future Passed	1968	30.00
—With "LONDON" under "DERAM" on top half of label			
❑ DES 18017	In Search of the Lost Chord	1968	20.00
—Originals have gatefold covers			
❑ DES 18025	On the Threshold of a Dream	1969	20.00
—Originals have gatefold covers and lyric booklet			
❑ DES 18051 [R]	In the Beginning	1971	20.00
❑ 820006-1 [S]	Days of Future Passed	1985	8.00
❑ 820168-1	In Search of the Lost Chord	1985	8.00
❑ 820170-1	On the Threshold of a Dream	1985	8.00
LONDON			
❑ PS 428 [R]	Go Now — The Moody Blues #1	1965	40.00
❑ PS 690/1 [(2)]	Caught Live + 5	1977	12.00
❑ PS 708	Octave	1978	10.00
❑ PS 708 [DJ]	Octave	1978	30.00
—Promo only on blue vinyl			
❑ LL 3428 [M]	Go Now — The Moody Blues #1	1965	50.00
❑ 820161-1 [(2)]	Caught Live + 5	1985	8.00
❑ 820329-1	Octave	1986	8.00
MOBILE FIDELITY			
❑ 1-042	Days of Future Passed	1980	60.00
—Audiophile vinyl			
❑ 1-151	Seventh Sojourn	1984	70.00
—Audiophile vinyl			
❑ 1-215	On the Threshold of a Dream	1994	25.00
—Audiophile vinyl			
❑ 1-232	Every Good Boy Deserves Favour	1995	25.00
—Audiophile vinyl			
❑ 1-253	To Our Children's Children's Children	1996	60.00
—Audiophile vinyl			

Number	Title (A Side/B Side)	Yr	NM
NAUTILUS			
❑ NR-21	On the Threshold of a Dream	1981	50.00
—Audiophile vinyl; DBX-encoded version			
❑ NR-21	On the Threshold of a Dream	1981	60.00
—Audiophile vinyl			
POLYDOR			
❑ 829 179-1	The Other Side of Life	1986	10.00
❑ 835 756-1	Sur La Mer	1988	12.00
❑ 840 659-1	Greatest Hits (1967-1988)	1989	15.00
THRESHOLD			
❑ THS 1	To Our Children's Children's Children	1969	15.00
—White label with purple logo; gatefold cover			
❑ THS 1	To Our Children's Children's Children	197?	10.00
—Blue label; no gatefold			
❑ THS 3	A Question of Balance	197?	10.00
—Blue label; no gatefold			
❑ THS 3	A Question of Balance	1970	15.00
—White label with purple logo; gatefold cover			
❑ THS 5	Every Good Boy Deserves Favour	197?	10.00
—Blue label; no gatefold			
❑ THS 5	Every Good Boy Deserves Favour	197?	12.00
—Blue label; gatefold cover			
❑ THS 5	Every Good Boy Deserves Favour	1971	15.00
—White label with purple logo; gatefold cover			
❑ THS 7	Seventh Sojourn	197?	10.00
—Blue label; no gatefold			
❑ THS 7	Seventh Sojourn	197?	12.00
—Blue label; gatefold cover			
❑ THS 7	Seventh Sojourn	1972	15.00
—White label with purple logo; gatefold cover			
❑ THS 12/13 [(2)]	This Is the Moody Blues	1974	15.00
❑ THX-100 [DJ]	Special Interview Kit	1971	150.00
—Includes script			
❑ TR-1-2901	Long Distance Voyager	1981	10.00
❑ TR-1-2902	The Present	1982	10.00
❑ SMAS-93329	A Question of Balance	1971	20.00
—Capitol Record Club edition			
❑ 810119-1	The Present	1983	8.00
❑ 820007-1 [(2)]	This Is the Moody Blues	1985	8.00
❑ 820105-1	Long Distance Voyager	1985	8.00
❑ 820155-1	Voices in the Sky/The Best of the Moody Blues	1985	10.00
❑ 820159-1	Seventh Sojourn	1985	8.00
❑ 820160-1	Every Good Boy Deserves Favour	1985	8.00
❑ 820211-1	A Question of Balance	1985	8.00

MOOG MACHINE, THE

Number	Title (A Side/B Side)	Yr	NM
Albums			
COLUMBIA			
❑ CS 9921	Switched-On Rock	1969	20.00
❑ CS 9959	Christmas Becomes Electric	1969	20.00

MOON, KEITH
Also see THE WHO.

Number	Title (A Side/B Side)	Yr	NM
45s			
TRACK			
❑ 40316	Teenage Idol/Don't Worry Baby	1974	15.00
❑ 40387	Solid Gold/Move Over Ms. L.	1975	15.00
❑ 40435	In My Life/Crazy Like a Fox	1975	15.00
Albums			
TRACK/MCA			
❑ 2136	Two Sides of the Moon	1975	20.00

MOON, THE
With David Marks, ex-BEACH BOYS.

Number	Title (A Side/B Side)	Yr	NM
45s			
IMPERIAL			
❑ 66285	Mothers and Fathers/ Someday Girl	1968	30.00
❑ 66330	Faces/John Automaton	1968	25.00
❑ 66415	Not to Know/Pirate	1969	25.00
Albums			
IMPERIAL			
❑ LP-12381	Without Earth	1968	40.00
❑ LP-12444	The Moon	1969	40.00

MOON BEAMS, THE

Number	Title (A Side/B Side)	Yr	NM
45s			
GRATE			
❑ 100	A Lover's Plea/Don't Go Away	1959	150.00

MOONEY, ART

Number	Title (A Side/B Side)	Yr	NM
45s			
DECCA			
❑ 25551	Peg o' My Heart/The Banjo's Back in Town	196?	7.00
❑ 25569	Teasin'/Whispering	1962	7.00
KAPP			
❑ 598	Titena/Satin Doll	1964	7.00

Except when noted otherwise, VG = 25% of NM, and VG+ = 50% of NM. (Example: VG = $2.00, VG+ = $4.00 and NM = $8.00.)

Number	Title (A Side/B Side)	Yr	NM
MGM			
❑ 8014	I'm Looking Over a Four Leaf Clover/The Big Brass Band from Brazil	1949	30.00
—Originally issued on 78 in 1948 with the number 10119			
❑ K10765	Wham Bam Thank You Ma'am/ There'll Never Be Another You	1950	20.00
❑ K10822	Serenade in Blue/ I'm a Dreamer	1950	20.00
❑ K10839	I'll Never Be Free/To Think You've Chosen Me	1950	20.00
❑ K10906	Faithful/Just for Tonight	1951	15.00
❑ K10924	Sparrow in the Tree Top/ Beautiful Brown Eyes	1951	15.00
❑ K10969	Goodnight Cincinnati/Sarah Kelly from Plumbnelly	1951	15.00
❑ K10984	My Truly Fair/Love I'd Give My Life	1951	15.00
❑ K11015	The Song Is Ended/ Maybe It's Because	1951	15.00
❑ K11033	Stay Awhile/Oh How I Love You	1951	15.00
❑ K11072	Daddy/The Tinkle Song	1951	15.00
❑ K11115	Slow Poke/Keep On the Sunny Side	1951	15.00
❑ K11171	Blacksmith Blues/ You're Not Worth Tears	1952	15.00
❑ K11196	Move It Over/Honky Tonk Blues	1952	15.00
❑ K11258	I Painted It/I May Hate Myself in the Morning	1952	15.00
❑ K11306	Hesitation/You're the One I Care For	1952	15.00
❑ K11330	Over the Hill/Window Shopping	1952	15.00
❑ K11347	Lazy River/Honestly	1952	15.00
❑ K11386	Winter/Heartbreaker	1952	15.00
❑ K11434	I Just Can't Take It Baby/ I Played the Fool	1953	12.00
❑ K11456	Baby Don't Do It/All Night Long	1953	12.00
❑ K11486	Gee Whiz/Miss You	1953	12.00
❑ K11514	Kentucy/Seven-Twenty in the Books	1953	12.00
❑ K11542	O (Oh!)/Cloverleaf Special	1953	12.00
❑ K11570	Love Birds/Night Must Fall	1953	12.00
❑ K11610	Mogambo/Off Shore	1953	12.00
❑ K11651	The Creep/Plantation Waltz	1954	12.00
❑ K11669	Silhouette/Promises	1954	12.00
❑ K11690	Way, Paesano/Si Petite	1954	12.00
❑ K11725	Barefoot Days/Wanderlust Blues	1954	12.00
❑ K11772	Mothballs/Corn Belt Symphony	1954	12.00
❑ K11871	Bip Bam/Big Boy Blue	1954	12.00
❑ K11900	Honey-Babe/No Regrets	1955	12.00
❑ K12000	Alabama Jubilee/ Paddlin' Madeline Home	1955	12.00
❑ K12009	I'm Looking Over a Four Leaf Clover/Baby Face	1955	12.00
❑ K12039	Twenty Tiny Fingers/ A Happy Song	1955	12.00
❑ K12073	The Girl I Left Behind Me/Give Me a Band and My Baby	1955	12.00
❑ K12133	Memories of You/The Lord Is a Busy Man	1955	12.00
❑ K12165	Tutti-Frutti/You Can Take My Heart	1956	12.00
❑ K12190	The Phonograph Song/ Is There a Teen-Ager in the House	1956	12.00
❑ K12219	Tally Ho/You Are the One	1956	10.00
❑ K12277	Daydreams/Somebody Stole My Muchacha (Cha-Cha-Cha)	1956	10.00
❑ K12312	Theme from "Rebel Without a Cause"/Theme from "East of Eden"	1956	15.00
❑ K12312 [PS]	Theme from "Rebel Without a Cause"/Theme from "East of Eden"	1956	50.00
❑ K12320	Giant/Rock and Roll Tumbleweed	1956	10.00
❑ K12403	Sinner's Train/Wheeling, West Virginia	1957	10.00
❑ K12435	The Donkey Got Drunk/I Never Had a Worry in the World	1957	10.00
❑ K12461	A Face in the Crowd/ Mama Guitar	1957	10.00
❑ K12503	The Parade Is Passing Me By/ Honest Love	1957	10.00
❑ K12545	In Italy/Let the Rest of the World Go By	1957	10.00
❑ K12590	The River Kwai March and Colonel Bogey/Bullfight	1958	10.00
❑ K12649	Louella/Something's Always Happening on the River	1958	10.00
❑ K12703	Autumn Sunset/ Saw My Baby on TV	1958	10.00
❑ K12731	Night Train/The Fiddle, a Rifle, an Ax and a Bible	1958	10.00
❑ K12783	Underneath the Arches/ Wha-Chi-Bam-Ba	1959	10.00
❑ K12802	Smile/Sunset to Sunrise	1959	10.00

The Moody Blues, "I Know You're Out There Somewhere," Polydor 887600-7, 1988, **$3.**

Number	Title (A Side/B Side)	Yr	NM
❑ K12832	My Dreams Are Getting Better All the Time/Till the End of the World	1959	10.00
❑ K12869	Diddy Boppers/Goodtime Special, Part 2	1960	8.00
❑ K12908	Banjo Boy/Captain Buffalo	1960	8.00
❑ K12957	I Ain't Down Yet/'Till Tomorrow	1960	8.00
❑ K12989	Malibu/Yancey Special	1961	8.00
❑ K13246	I Ain't Down Yet/Dolce Far Niente	1964	8.00
—B-side by Leroy Holmes			
RIVERSIDE			
❑ 4543	St. Louis Blues Bossa Nova/ Sugar Loaf	1963	15.00
Albums			
CORONET			
❑ CX-138 [M]	Cha Cha Cha with Art Mooney	196?	10.00
❑ CXS-138 [S]	Cha Cha Cha with Art Mooney	196?	12.00
❑ CX-220 [M]	Dance and Dream	196?	12.00
❑ CXS-220 [S]	Dance and Dream	196?	12.00
DECCA			
❑ DL 4207 [M]	Songs Everybody Knows	1962	12.00
❑ DL 74207 [S]	Songs Everybody Knows	1962	15.00
DIPLOMAT			
❑ DS-2218 [S]	Cha Cha Cha with Art Mooney	196?	12.00
❑ DS-2246 [S]	Sing Along	196?	12.00
HURRAH			
❑ H-1002 [M]	Big Band Dance Time	1962	10.00
❑ HS-1002 [S]	Big Band Dance Time	1962	12.00
KAPP			
❑ KL-1405 [M]	Jump for Joy!	1964	12.00
❑ KL-1421 [M]	Sentimental Love Songs of World War II	1965	12.00
❑ KS-3405 [S]	Jump for Joy!	1964	15.00
❑ KS-3421 [S]	Sentimental Love Songs of World War II	1965	15.00
LION			
❑ L-70062 [M]	Those Happy Banjos	1958	15.00
MGM			
❑ E-121 [10]	Sunset to Sunrise	1952	30.00

Number	Title (A Side/B Side)	Yr	NM
❑ E-206 [10]	Banjo Bonanza	1953	30.00
❑ E-3431 [M]	Art Mooney Presents the Happy Minstrels	1956	25.00
❑ E-3616 [M]	Art Mooney in Hi-Fi Dixieland	1957	20.00
❑ E-3628 [M]	Sunrise to Sunrise	1958	40.00
—Quickly deleted and reissued as 3649 with a new title			
❑ E-3649 [M]	Art Mooney and His Orchestra in Hi-Fi Play for Dancing	1958	20.00
—Reissue of 3628 with new cover and title			
❑ E-3899 [M]	Spectacular Voices with Banjos	1961	12.00
❑ SE-3899 [S]	Spectacular Voices with Banjos	1961	15.00
PIROUETTE			
❑ FM-45 [M]	Cha Cha Cha with Art Mooney	196?	10.00
PROMENADE			
❑ 2218 [M]	Cha Cha Cha with Art Mooney	196?	10.00
❑ 2246 [M]	Sing Along	196?	10.00
RCA VICTOR			
❑ LPM-3739 [M]	The Best of Art Mooney	1967	20.00
❑ LSP-3739 [S]	The Best of Art Mooney	1967	12.00
SPIN-O-RAMA			
❑ S-45 [S]	Cha Cha Cha with Art Mooney	196?	12.00
❑ M-93 [M]	Dancetime	196?	10.00
❑ S-93 [S]	Dancetime	196?	12.00
❑ MK-3079 [M]	Cha Cha Cha with Art Mooney	196?	10.00
TIARA			
❑ TM-7545 [M]	Cha Cha Cha with Art Mooney	196?	10.00

MOONGLOWS, THE
Also see HARVEY.

Number	Title (A Side/B Side)	Yr	NM
45s			
BIG P			
❑ 101	Sincerely '72/You've Chosen Me	1972	10.00
CHAMPAGNE			
❑ 7500	I Just Can't Tell No Lie/I've Been Your Dog (Ever Since I've Been Your Man)	1952	1500.
CHANCE			
❑ 1147	Baby Please/Whistle My Love	1953	1000.
—Black vinyl			
❑ 1147	Baby Please/Whistle My Love	1953	3000.
—Red vinyl. VG 1500; VG+ 2250			

Number	Title (A Side/B Side)	Yr	NM
❑ 1150	Just a Lonely Christmas/Hey, Santa Claus	1953	3000.
—Red vinyl (this may not exist legitimately on black vinyl). VG 1500; VG+ 2250			
❑ 1152	Secret Love/Real Gone Mama	1954	1000.
—Yellow and black label			
❑ 1152	Secret Love/Real Gone Mama	1954	1500.
—Silver and blue label			
❑ 1156	I Was Wrong/Ooh Rockin' Daddy	1954	600.00
—Black and white label			
❑ 1156	I Was Wrong/Ooh Rockin' Daddy	1954	600.00
—Yellow and black label			
❑ 1161	My Gal/219 Train	1954	5000.
—VG 2500; VG+ 3750			
CHESS			
❑ 1581	Sincerely/Tempting	1954	60.00
—Blue label, silver top			
❑ 1589	Most of All/She's Gone	1955	60.00
—Blue label, silver top			
❑ 1598	Foolish Me/Slow Down	1955	60.00
—Blue label, silver top			
❑ 1605	Starlite/In Love	1955	60.00
—Blue label, silver top			
❑ 1611	In My Diary/Lover, Love Me	1955	60.00
—Blue label, silver top			
❑ 1619	We Go Together/Chickie Um Bah	1956	50.00
—Blue label, silver top			
❑ 1629	See Saw/When I'm With You	1956	50.00
—Blue label, silver top			
❑ 1646	Over and Over Again/I Knew from the Start	1957	50.00
—With normal version of A-side; blue label, silver top			
❑ 1646	Over and Over Again/I Knew from the Start	1957	60.00
—With slower version of A-side; "8189A" in in the run-off area			
❑ 1651	I'm Afraid the Masquerade Is Over/Don't Say Goodbye	1957	50.00
—Blue label, silver top			
❑ 1661	Please Send Me Someone to Love/Mr. Engineer (Bring Her Back to Me)	1957	50.00
—Blue label, silver top			
❑ 1669 [PS]	The Beating of My Heart/Confess It to Your Heart	1957	50.00
—In general, for the above singles, the blue label with vertical "Chess" versions are 60% of the above values; yellow early-1960s label versions and black mid-1960s versions are 40% of above; and blue late-1960s versions, with "Chess" on top, are about 20%			
❑ 1681	Too Late/Here I Am	1958	30.00
❑ 1689	In the Middle of the Night/Soda Pop	1958	30.00
❑ 1701	This Love/Sweeter Than Words	1958	30.00
❑ 1705	Ten Commandments of Love/Mean Old Blues	1958	30.00
—As "Harvey and the Moonglows"			
❑ 1717	Love Is a River/I'll Never Stop Wanting You	1959	25.00
❑ 1738	Mama Loocie/Unemployment	1959	25.00
—As "Harvey and the Moonglows"			
❑ 1770	Beatnick/Junior	1960	25.00
❑ 1811	Blue Velvet/Penny Arcade	1962	25.00
—As "Bobby Lester and the Moonglows"			
CRIMSON			
❑ 1003	My Imagination/Gee	1964	20.00
LANA			
❑ 130	Sincerely/Time After Time	196?	8.00
❑ 131	Most of All/What a Diffrence a Day Makes	196?	8.00
❑ 132	Blue Velvet/In My Diary	196?	8.00
❑ 133	See Saw/Love Is a River	196?	8.00
❑ 134	We Go Together/Shoo Doo Be Doo	196?	8.00
❑ 135	Ten Commandments of Love/Half a Heart	196?	8.00
LOST-NITE			
❑ 275	Just a Lonely Christmas/Baby Please	197?	6.00
—Reissue			
❑ 288	I Was Wrong/My Gal	197?	5.00
—Reissue			
❑ 294	Secret Love/Golden Teardrops	197?	5.00
—B-side by the Flamingos; reissue			
MELLO			
❑ 69	Just a Lonely Christmas/Hey, Santa Claus	19??	8.00
—Reissue			
RCA VICTOR			
❑ 74-0759	Sincerely/I Was Wrong	1972	5.00
❑ 74-0839	When I'm With You/You've Chosen Me	1972	5.00
VEE JAY			
❑ 423	Secret Love/Real Gone Mama	1962	25.00

7-Inch Extended Plays

Number	Title (A Side/B Side)	Yr	NM
CHESS			
❑ 5122	(contents unknown)	1959	250.00
❑ 5122 [PS]	Look! It's the Moonglows	1959	250.00
❑ 5123	True Love/Penny Arcade//I'll Stop Waiting/Sweeter Than Words	1959	250.00
❑ 5123 [PS]	Look! It's the Moonglows, Vol. 2	1959	250.00

Albums

Number	Title (A Side/B Side)	Yr	NM
CHESS			
❑ LP 1430 [M]	Look! It's the Moonglows	1959	500.00
❑ LP 1471 [M]	The Best of Bobby Lester & the Moonglows	1962	300.00
—Black label			
❑ LP 1471 [M]	The Best of Bobby Lester & the Moonglows	1966	50.00
—Blue, fading to white label			
❑ CH-9111	Their Greatest Sides	1986	12.00
❑ CH-9193	Look! It's the Moonglows	1987	12.00
—Reissue of 1430			
CONSTELLATION			
❑ C-2 [M]	Collectors Showcase — The Moonglows	1964	50.00
—Dark blue lettering			
❑ C-2 [M]	Collectors Showcase — The Moonglows	1964	100.00
—Light blue lettering			
LOST-NITE			
❑ LP-23 [10]	The Moonglows	1981	12.00
RCA VICTOR			
❑ LSP-4722	The Return of the Moonglows	1972	15.00

MOORE, BOB

45s

Number	Title (A Side/B Side)	Yr	NM
HICKORY			
❑ 1357	Only the Lonely/Skokiaan	1965	6.00
❑ 1372	Hell's Angels/I Can't Stop Loving You	1966	6.00
❑ 1407	Spanish Eyes/Elephant Rock	1966	6.00
❑ 1426	Acapulco/Parade of the Matadors	1966	6.00
❑ 1437	A White Sport Coat/Amigo No. 1	1967	6.00
❑ 1480	The Fastest Guitar Alive/The River	1967	6.00
❑ 1521	You Sit Around All Day/Amigo No. 1	1968	6.00
MONUMENT			
❑ 406	Theme from My Three Sons/Mais Oui	1959	15.00
❑ 437	Theme from My Three Sons/Mais Oui	1961	10.00
❑ 446	Mexico/Hot Spot	1961	8.00
❑ 457	Auf Wiederseh'n Marlene/Ooh La La	1962	8.00
❑ 457 [PS]	Auf Wiederseh'n Marlene/Ooh La La	1962	15.00
❑ 800	Flea Circus/Autumn Souvenirs	1962	8.00
❑ 814	Kentucky/Flowers of Florence	1963	8.00
❑ 834	Cologne/Hooten Trumpet	1964	8.00

Albums

Number	Title (A Side/B Side)	Yr	NM
HICKORY			
❑ LP-131 [M]	Viva Bob Moore	1965	15.00
❑ LPS-131 [S]	Viva Bob Moore	1965	20.00
MONUMENT			
❑ MLP-4005 [M]	Mexico and Other Great Hits!	1961	20.00
❑ SLP-4005 [S]	Mexico and Other Great Hits!	1961	25.00
❑ MLP-8008 [M]	Mexico	1967	12.00
❑ SLP-18008 [S]	Mexico	1967	15.00

MOORE, BOBBY, AND THE RHYTHM ACES

45s

Number	Title (A Side/B Side)	Yr	NM
CHECKER			
❑ 1129	Searching for My Love/Hey Mr. D.J.	1966	10.00
—Blue label			
❑ 1129	Searching for My Love/Hey Mr. D.J.	1966	15.00
—Maroon label, vertical "Checker"			
❑ 1156	Try My Love Again/Go Ahead and Burn Baby	1966	10.00
❑ 1180	Reaching Out/Chained to Your Heart	1967	10.00

Albums

Number	Title (A Side/B Side)	Yr	NM
CHECKER			
❑ LP-3000 [M]	Searching for My Love	1966	30.00
❑ LPS-3000 [R]	Searching for My Love	1966	20.00

MOORE, DOROTHY

12-Inch Singles

Number	Title (A Side/B Side)	Yr	NM
STREETKING			
❑ SKDS-1120	Just Another Broken Heart (Vocal 7:05) (Dub 4:41) (Edit 3:25)	1984	12.00
VOLT			
❑ 3106	Can't Get Over You (Once Again I'm Misty Blue) (4:24)/Don't Hold Your Breath	1988	12.00

45s

Number	Title (A Side/B Side)	Yr	NM
AVCO			
❑ 4590	See How They've Done My Love/(B-side unknown)	1972	12.00
❑ 4599	Same Old Feeling/(B-side unknown)	1972	12.00
CHIMNEYVILLE			
❑ 10204	Don't Let Go/Two of a Kind	1975	6.00
❑ 10207	We Can Love/Making Love	1975	6.00
—With King Floyd			
GSF			
❑ 6908	Cry Like a Baby/Just the One I've Been Looking For	1973	15.00
—B-side is sought by Northern Soul aficionados			
HANDSHAKE			
❑ WS9-02879	What's Forever For/Someone's Lover Before (But Never Someone's Girl)	1982	5.00
MALACO			
❑ 1029	Misty Blue/Here It Is	1976	6.00
❑ 1033	Funny How Time Slips Away/Ain't That a Mother's Luck	1976	6.00
❑ 1037	For Old Time Sake/Daddy's Eyes	1976	6.00
❑ 1040	We Should Really Be in Love/I'll Never Be Loved	1977	5.00
—With Eddie Floyd			
❑ 1042	I Believe You/Love Me	1977	6.00
❑ 1047	With Pen in Hand/Too Blind to See	1977	5.00
❑ 1048	Let the Music Play/1-2-3 (You and Me)	1978	5.00
❑ 1052	Special Occasion/Girl Overboard	1978	15.00
—B-side is sought by Northern Soul aficionados			
❑ 1054	(We Need More) Loving Time/Write a Little Prayer	1978	5.00
❑ 1059	Once or Twice/Love Me	1979	5.00
❑ 2062	Talk to Me-Every Beat of My Heart/Lonely	1980	5.00
❑ 2064	Angel of the Morning/Make It Soon	1980	5.00
❑ 2168	All Night Blue/Talk to Me	1990	5.00
❑ 2172	Be Strong Enough to Hold On/If You'll Give Me Your Heart	1991	4.00
❑ 2192	Read Me My Rights/Stay Close to Home	199?	4.00
PRELUDE			
❑ 8094	Just Came Apart at the Dreams/(Instrumental)	1984	10.00
STREETKING			
❑ SK-7120	Just Another Broken Heart/(Instrumental)	1984	5.00
VOLT			
❑ 301	Endless Summer Nights/Walk Through This Pain	1988	5.00
❑ 990	Can't Get Over You (Once Again I'm Misty Blue)/Don't Hold Your Breath	1988	5.00

Albums

Number	Title (A Side/B Side)	Yr	NM
MALACO			
❑ 6351	Misty Blue	1976	12.00
❑ 6353	Dorothy Moore	1977	15.00
❑ 6356	Once More with Feeling	1978	12.00
❑ 6359	Definitely Dorothy	1979	12.00
❑ 7363	Talk to Me	1980	15.00
❑ 7455	Feel the Love	1990	12.00
REJOICE/A&M			
❑ WR 8326	Givin' It Straight to You	1986	15.00
VOLT			
❑ 3401	Time Out for Me	1988	12.00
❑ 3405	Winner	1989	12.00

MOORE, DUDLEY

Albums

Number	Title (A Side/B Side)	Yr	NM
ATLANTIC			
❑ 1403 [M]	Beyond the Fringe and All That Jazz	1963	25.00
❑ SD 1403 [S]	Beyond the Fringe and All That Jazz	1963	30.00
LONDON			
❑ PS 558	Dudley Moore Trio	1969	25.00

MOORE, GATEMOUTH

45s

Number	Title (A Side/B Side)	Yr	NM
KING			
❑ 4492	Christmas Blues/Happy New Year, Darling	1951	50.00
—B-side by Lonnie Johnson			

Albums

Number	Title (A Side/B Side)	Yr	NM
AUDIO FIDEILITY			
❑ AFLP-1921 [M]	Revival!	196?	60.00
❑ AFSD-5921 [S]	Revival!	196?	80.00

Number	Title (A Side/B Side)	Yr	NM
BLUESWAY			
❑ BLS 6074	After 21 Years	1973	20.00
KING			
❑ 684 [M]	Gatemouth Moore Sings Blues	1960	5000.

MOORE, HARV

45s

Number	Title (A Side/B Side)	Yr	NM
AMERICAN ARTS			
❑ 20	Interview of the Fab Four /I Feel So Fine	1964	300.00

MOORE, JACKIE

12-Inch Singles

Number	Title (A Side/B Side)	Yr	NM
COLUMBIA			
❑ 10994	This Time Baby/Let's Go Somewhere and Make Love	1979	10.00
❑ 11136	How's Your Love Life Baby/ (Instrumental)	1979	10.00
❑ 11293	With Your Love/Helpless	1980	10.00
DIVA			
❑ 004	This Old Heart of Mine (4 versions)	198?	8.00
SUNNYVIEW			
❑ SUN 421	Love Is the Answer (4:23) (6:03)	1985	6.00

45s

Number	Title (A Side/B Side)	Yr	NM
ATLANTIC			
❑ 2681	Precious Precious/Will Power	1969	5.00
❑ 2798	Sometimes It's Got to Rain (In Your Love Life)/ Wonderful Marvelous	1971	5.00
❑ 2830	Time/Cover Me	1971	5.00
❑ 2861	Darling Baby/ Something in a Love	1972	5.00
❑ 2902	It Ain't Who You Know/They Tell Me of an Uncloudy Day	1972	5.00
❑ 2956	Sweet Charlie Babe/If	1973	5.00
❑ 2989	Both Ends Against the Middle/ Clean Up Your Own Yard	1973	5.00
CATAWBA			
❑ 1010	Holding Back/(B-side unknown)	1983	4.00
COLUMBIA			
❑ 04599	This Time Baby/Let's Go Somewhere and Make Love	1984	3.00
❑ 10779	Personally/Ain't No Trouble Like Love Trouble	1978	4.00
❑ 10993	This Time Baby/Let's Go Somewhere and Make Love	1979	4.00
❑ 11140	How's Your Love Life Baby/Do Ya Got What It Takes	1979	4.00
❑ 11288	Helpless/With Your Love	1980	4.00
❑ 11363	Love Won't Let Me Wait/With Your Love	1980	4.00
KAYVETTE			
❑ 5122	Make Me Feel Like a Woman/ Singin' Funky Music Turns Me On	1975	5.00
❑ 5124	Puttin' It Down to You/ Never Is Forever	1975	5.00
❑ 5125	It's Harder to Leave/ (B-side unknown)	1976	5.00
❑ 5127	Disco Body (Shake It to the East, Shake It to the West)/ Tired of Hiding	1976	5.00
❑ 5129	Make Me Yours/ Somebody Loves You	1977	5.00
❑ 5139	Heart Be Still/Singin' Funky Music Turns Me On	1981	4.00
❑ 5140	Who's Next/Singin' Funky Music Turns Me On	1981	4.00
SHOUT			
❑ 232	Dear John/Here I Am	1968	8.00
❑ 239	Why Don't You Call on Me/ (B-side unknown)	1968	8.00

Albums

Number	Title (A Side/B Side)	Yr	NM
ATLANTIC			
❑ SD 7285	Sweet Charlie Babe	1973	15.00
COLUMBIA			
❑ JC 35991	On My Way	1979	10.00
❑ JC 36455	With Your Love	1980	10.00
KAYVETTE			
❑ 801	Make Me Feel Like a Woman	1975	15.00

MOORE, LATTIE

45s

Number	Title (A Side/B Side)	Yr	NM
ARC			
❑ 8005	Juke Box Johnnie/ Pretty Woman Blues	1952	200.00
KING			
❑ 1194	Foolish Castles/I'm Gonna Tell You Something	1953	50.00
❑ 1250	I Gotta Go Home/A Brand New Case of Love	1953	50.00
❑ 1327	They're Not Worth the Paper They're Printed On/Under a Mexico Moon	1954	50.00
❑ 1350	Pull Down the Blinds/What Am I Supposed to Do	1954	50.00
❑ 4955	100,000 Women Can't Be Wrong/Lonesome Man Blues	1956	50.00
❑ 5370	Cajun Doll/Mine Again	1960	40.00
❑ 5413	Drunk Again/Driving Nails	1960	25.00
❑ 5526	Sundown and Sorrow/If the Good Lord's Willing	1961	20.00
❑ 5685	I Told You So/Heaven All Around Me	1962	15.00
❑ 5723	Out of Control/Just About Then	1963	15.00
❑ 5762	Honky Tonk Heaven/ Lonesome Man Blues	1963	15.00
SPEED			
❑ 101	Juke Joint Johnny/It's Good Enough for You	1952	400.00
STARDAY			
❑ 403	You Never Looked Sweeter/ Why Did You Lie to Me	1958	30.00
❑ 441	Too Hot to Handle/Just a-Waitin'	1959	30.00
WPL			
❑ 1001	Old Ex-Husbands/Beat Years of Your Life	1970	100.00

Albums

Number	Title (A Side/B Side)	Yr	NM
AUDIO LAB			
❑ AL-1555 [M]	The Best of Lattie Moore	1960	200.00
❑ AL-1573 [M]	Country Side	1962	150.00
DERBYTOWN			
❑ 102 [M]	Lattie Moore	196?	40.00

MOORE, MELBA

12-Inch Singles

Number	Title (A Side/B Side)	Yr	NM
CAPITOL			
❑ 8543	Mind Up Tonight (Extended) (Instrumental)	1982	6.00
❑ 8586	Love Me Right (Extended) (Instrumental)	1983	6.00
❑ 8627	Read My Lips/Got to Have Your Love	1985	8.00
❑ 8647	When You Love Me Like This/ Winner (Instrumental Edit)	1985	6.00
❑ SPRO-9335/6 [DJ]	Read My Lips (Special Mix) (Single Version)	1985	6.00
❑ SPRO-9381/2 [DJ]	Read My Lips (Remix) (Extended Version)	1985	6.00
❑ SPRO-9446/7 [DJ]	When You Love Me Like This (Club Mix) (Monster Groove Mix)	1985	8.00
❑ SPRO-9500 [DJ]	I Can't Believe (It's Over) (Extended Version) (Edit Version)	1985	8.00
❑ SPRO-9717 [DJ]	Love the One I'm With (5:44) (same on both sides)	1986	6.00
❑ SPRO-9776 [DJ]	Love the One I'm With (3 versions)	1986	6.00
❑ SPRO-9858/9980 [DJ]	Falling (Single Version) (LP Version)	1986	8.00
❑ V-15236	Love the One I'm With (5:44)/ Don't Go Away	1986	6.00
❑ V-15256	A Little Bit More (4:54) (4:15)/ When We Touch	1986	6.00
—With Freddie Jackson			
❑ V-15280	It's Been So Long (2 versions)/ Don't Go Away	1987	6.00
❑ V-15426	Love and Kisses (3 versions)/ I'm in Love	1988	6.00
❑ V-15561	Do You Really Want My Love (4 versions)	1990	6.00
EMI AMERICA			
❑ SPRO-9817 [DJ]	Love's Comin' At Ya (7" Version) (LP Version)	1981	8.00
EPIC			
❑ AS 660 [DJ]	Miss Thing (same on both sides)	1979	8.00
❑ 50665	Pick Me Up, I'll Dance/ (Instrumental)	1979	12.00
❑ 50771	Miss Thing/Need Love	1979	12.00
❑ 50807	Hot and Tasty/Night People	1979	12.00

45s

Number	Title (A Side/B Side)	Yr	NM
BUDDAH			
❑ 452	I Am His Lady/If I Lose You	1975	5.00
❑ 469	Natural Part of Everything/ Must Be Dues	1975	5.00
❑ 496	Starting to Fall/Must Be Dues	1975	5.00
—With Jo Ellen Cohn			
❑ 519	This Is It/Stay Awhile	1976	5.00
❑ 519 [PS]	This Is It/Stay Awhile	1976	8.00
❑ 535	Lean On Me/One Less Morning	1976	5.00
❑ 562	The Way You Make Me Feel/ So Many Mountains	1977	5.00
❑ 568	The Long and Winding Road/ Ain't No Love Lost	1977	5.00
❑ 572	My Sensitive, Passionate Man/ The Greatest Feeling	1977	5.00
❑ 572 [PS]	My Sensitive, Passionate Man/ The Greatest Feeling	1977	7.00
❑ 589	Standing Right Here/Living Free	1977	5.00
❑ 596	I Don't Know No One Else to Turn To/Just Another Link	1978	5.00
CAPITOL			
❑ B-5180	Mind Up Tonight/(Instrumental)	1982	3.00
❑ B-5208	Underlove/(Instrumental)	1983	3.00
❑ B-5288	Keepin' My Lover Satisfied/ (Instrumental)	1983	3.00
❑ B-5288 [PS]	Keepin' My Lover Satisfied/ (Instrumental)	1983	4.00
❑ B-5308	Livin' for Your Love/ Got to Have Your Love	1984	3.00
❑ B-5308 [PS]	Livin' for Your Love/Got to Have Your Love	1984	4.00
❑ B-5343	Love Me Right/Never Say Never	1984	3.00
❑ B-5343 [PS]	Love Me Right/Never Say Never	1984	4.00
❑ B-5415	(Can't Take Half) All of You/Let Me Be Yours	1984	3.00
—With Lillo Thomas			
❑ B-5415 [PS]	(Can't Take Half) All of You/ Let Me Be Yours	1984	4.00
❑ B-5437	Read My Lips/Got to Have Your Love	1985	3.00
❑ B-5437 [PS]	Read My Lips/Got to Have Your Love	1985	4.00
❑ B-5484	When You Love Me Like This/ Winner	1985	3.00
❑ B-5484 [PS]	When You Love Me Like This/ Winner	1985	4.00
❑ B-5520	I Can't Believe It (It's Over)/ King of No Heart	1985	3.00
❑ B-5577	Love the One I'm With (A Lot of Love)/Don't Go Away	1986	3.00
—With Kashif			
❑ B-5577 [PS]	Love the One I'm With (A Lot of Love)/Don't Go Away	1986	3.00
❑ B-5632	A Little Bit More/When We Touch	1986	3.00
—A-side with Freddie Jackson			
❑ B-5651	Falling/(B-side unknown)	1986	3.00
❑ B-5681	It's Been So Long/Don't Go Away	1987	3.00
❑ B-5681 [PS]	It's Been So Long/Don't Go Away	1987	3.00
❑ B-44012	I'm Not Gonna Let You Go/ Dreams	1987	3.00
❑ B-44012 [PS]	I'm Not Gonna Let You Go/ Dreams	1987	3.00
❑ B-44148	I Can't Complain/There I Go Falling in Love Again	1988	3.00
—A-side with Freddie Jackson			
❑ B-44148 [PS]	I Can't Complain/There I Go Falling in Love Again	1988	3.00
❑ B-44195	I'm in Love/Stay	1988	3.00
—With Kashif			
❑ B-44195 [PS]	I'm in Love/Stay	1988	3.00
❑ B-44265	Love and Kisses/I'm in Love	1988	3.00
EMI AMERICA			
❑ 8092	Take My Love/Just You, Just Me	1981	4.00
❑ 8104	Let's Stand Together/What a Woman Needs	1981	4.00
❑ 8114	Piece of the Rock/(Instrumental)	1982	4.00
❑ 8126	Love's Comin' At Ya/ (Instrumental)	1982	4.00
EPIC			
❑ 50600	You Stepped Into My Life/ There's No Other Like You	1978	4.00
❑ 50663	Pick Me Up, I'll Dance/Where Did You Ever Go	1979	4.00
❑ 50762	Miss Thing/Need Love	1979	4.00
❑ 50805	Hot and Tasty/Night People	1979	4.00
❑ 50909	Everything So Good About You/Next to You	1980	4.00
❑ 50954	Rest Inside My Love/ Something on My Mind	1980	4.00
MERCURY			
❑ 72942	I Messed Up a Good Thing/ I'll Do It All Over Again	1969	8.00
❑ 72989	We're Living to Give (Each Other)/(B-side unknown)	1969	8.00
❑ 73040	Time and Love/(B-side unknown)	1970	8.00
❑ 73072	I Got Love/I Love Making Love to You	1970	8.00

M

Number	Title (A Side/B Side)	Yr	NM
❑ 73134	Look What You're Doing to the Man/Patience Is Rewarded	1970	8.00
❑ 73183	If I Had a Million/Loving You Comes So Easy	1971	8.00
❑ 73217	He Ain't Heavy, He's My Brother/Take Up a Course in Happiness	1971	8.00
❑ 73289	Love Letters/I Ain't Got to Love Nobody Else	1972	8.00
MUSICOR			
❑ 1189	Does Love Believe in Me/Don't Cry, Sing Along with the Music	1966	10.00
Albums			
ACCORD			
❑ SN-7129	Sweet Melba	1981	10.00
BUDDAH			
❑ BDS-5629	Peach Melba	1975	10.00
❑ BDS-5657	This Is It	1976	10.00
❑ BDS-5677	Melba	1976	10.00
❑ BDS-5695	Portrait of Melba Moore	1977	10.00
❑ BDS-5720	Dancin' with Melba	1979	10.00
CAPITOL			
❑ ST-12243	The Other Side of the Rainbow	1982	10.00
❑ ST-12305	Never Say Never	1983	10.00
❑ ST-12382	Read My Lips	1985	10.00
❑ ST-12471	A Lot of Love	1986	10.00
❑ C1-92355	Soul Exposed	1990	12.00
EMI AMERICA			
❑ ST-17060	What a Woman Needs	1981	10.00
EPIC			
❑ JE 35507	Melba	1978	10.00
❑ JE 36128	Burn	1979	10.00
❑ JE 36412	Closer	1980	10.00
MERCURY			
❑ SRM-1-622	Live!	1972	12.00
❑ SR-61255	Living to Give	1970	15.00
❑ SR-61287	I Got Love	1970	15.00
❑ SR-61321	Look What You're Doing to the Man	1971	15.00

M

MOORE, MELVIN

Number	Title (A Side/B Side)	Yr	NM
45s			
KING			
❑ 4539	Possessed/Hold Me, Kiss Me, Squeeze Me	1952	100.00

MOORE, RUDY

Number	Title (A Side/B Side)	Yr	NM
45s			
FEDERAL			
❑ 12253	My Little Angel/I'm Mad with You	1956	50.00
❑ 12259	The Buggy Ride/Ring-a-Ling-Dong	1956	50.00
❑ 12276	Step It Up and Go/Let Me Come Home	1956	100.00
❑ 12280	Bobbie Dobbie/I'll Be Home to See You Tomorrow Night	1956	50.00

MOORE, SAM

Also see SAM AND DAVE.

Number	Title (A Side/B Side)	Yr	NM
45s			
ATLANTIC			
❑ 2762	Give You Plenty Lovin'/Tennessee Waltz	1970	6.00
❑ 2791	Keep On Sockin' It To Me/Stop	1971	6.00
❑ 2814	Shop Around/If I Should Lose Your Love	1971	6.00

MOORE, SAMMIE

Number	Title (A Side/B Side)	Yr	NM
45s			
HIT			
❑ 125	No Particular Place to Go/Once Upon a Time	1964	8.00
—B-side by Sam Baker and Nancy Cohen			

MOORE, SCOTTY

Original guitarist in ELVIS PRESLEY's backup band.

Number	Title (A Side/B Side)	Yr	NM
45s			
FERNWOOD			
❑ 107	Have Guitar Will Travel/Rest	1958	30.00
Albums			
EPIC			
❑ LN 24103 [M]	The Guitar That Changed the World	1964	50.00
❑ BN 26103 [S]	The Guitar That Changed the World	1964	75.00
GUINNESS			
❑ GNS-36038	What's Left	1977	15.00

MOORE, TIM

Number	Title (A Side/B Side)	Yr	NM
45s			
A SMALL RECORD COMPANY			
❑ 0601	Second Avenue/(B-side unknown)	1974	10.00
ABC DUNHILL			
❑ 4337	Fool Like You/Thinking About You	1973	5.00
ASYLUM			
❑ 45208	Second Avenue/Aviation Man	1974	4.00
❑ 45214	Charmer/I'll Be Your Time	1974	4.00
❑ 45214 [PS]	Charmer/I'll Be Your Time	1974	6.00
❑ 45265	If Somebody Needs It/Sweet Navel Lightning	1975	4.00
❑ 45276	Rock and Roll Love Letter/Sweet Navel Lightning	1975	4.00
❑ 45287	Lay Down the Line to Me/Sweet Navel Lightning	1975	4.00
❑ 45394	In the Middle/Strengthen My Love	1977	4.00
❑ 45427	Second Avenue/Strengthen My Love	1977	4.00
❑ 46047	Fallen Angel/Crisis in the Finyard	1979	4.00
Albums			
A SMALL RECORD COMPANY			
❑ SRS-10001	Tim Moore	1974	30.00
ABC DUNHILL			
❑ DSX-50132	Of Woodstock and Other Places	1973	12.00
ASYLUM			
❑ 6E-179	High Contrast	1979	10.00
❑ 7E-1019	Tim Moore	1974	10.00
❑ 7E-1042	Behind the Eyes	1975	10.00
❑ 7E-1088	White Shadows	1977	10.00
ELEKTRA			
❑ 60463	Flash Forward	1985	10.00

MORGAN, FREDDY

Number	Title (A Side/B Side)	Yr	NM
45s			
CHALLENGE			
❑ 59044	64 Rue Blondell/Side Saddle	1959	10.00

MORGAN, JANE

Number	Title (A Side/B Side)	Yr	NM
45s			
ABC			
❑ 10969	Somebody Someplace/This Is My World Without You	1967	6.00
❑ 11002	Him's a Dope/I Promise You	1967	6.00
❑ 11024	The Marvelous Toy/Smile	1967	6.00
❑ 11034	Masquerade/Smile	1968	5.00
❑ 11054	My Funny Valentine/A Child	1968	5.00
❑ 11092	Look What You've Done to Me/There's Nothing Else in My Mind	1968	5.00
COLPIX			
❑ 713	Does Goodnight Mean Goodbye/Bless 'Em All	1963	8.00
❑ 713 [PS]	Does Goodnight Mean Goodbye/Bless 'Em All	1963	12.00
❑ 727	Frum Russia with Love/The Song from Moulin Rouge (Where Is Your Heart)	1964	8.00
❑ 734	C'est Si Bon/Once Upon a Summertime	1964	8.00
❑ 754	Dominique/Funny World	1964	8.00
❑ 755	The Poor People of Paris/Funny World	1964	8.00
❑ 761	After the Fall/Oh, How I Lie	1965	8.00
EPIC			
❑ 9819	Maybe/Walking the Streets in the Rain	1965	8.00
❑ 9847	Side by Side/Till I Waltz Again with You	1965	8.00
❑ 9881	Little Hands/Everyone Come to My Party	1965	8.00
❑ 10012	I Will Wait for You/Love Me True	1966	6.00
❑ 10032	Kiss Away/1-2-3	1966	6.00
❑ 10058	Elusive Butterfly/Good Lovin'	1966	6.00
❑ 10113	Kiss Tomorrow Goodbye/Now and Forever	1966	6.00
❑ 10159	The Three Bells/I Want to Be with You	1967	6.00
KAPP			
❑ KJB-12	Love Makes the World Go 'Round/Fly Me to the Moon	196?	7.00
❑ KJB-14	Fascination/The Day the Rains Came	196?	6.00
—"Winners Circle Series" reissue			
❑ KJB-14 [PS]	Fascination/The Day the Rains Came	196?	10.00
❑ 104	Baseball, Baseball/Fairweather Friends	1954	15.00
❑ 111	I Try to Forget You/Why Don't They Leave Us Alone	1955	12.00
❑ 115	Flyin' High/Give Me Your World	1955	12.00
❑ 121	In Paree/Take Me Away	1955	12.00
❑ 140	Let's Go Steady/Take Care	1956	12.00
❑ 148	La Ronde/Midnight Blues	1956	12.00
❑ 161	Two Different Worlds/Nights in Verona	1956	10.00
—With Roger Williams			
❑ 172	Come Home, Come Home, Come Home/From the First Hello to Our Last Goodbye	1957	10.00
❑ 185	It's Not for Me to Say/Around the World	1957	10.00
❑ 191	Fascination/(Instrumental)	1957	10.00
❑ 191 [PS]	Fascination/(Instrumental)	1957	20.00
—With color picture of Jane Morgan only			
❑ 191 [PS]	Fascination/(Instrumental)	1957	30.00
—With photos of Gary Cooper, Audrey Hepbum and Jane Morgan on sleeve			
❑ 200	It's Been a Long, Long Time/I'm New at the Game of Romance	1957	10.00
❑ 214	Only One Love/I've Got Bells on My Heart	1958	10.00
❑ 221	Enchanted Island/Once More, My Love, Once More	1958	10.00
❑ 235	The Day the Rains Came/The Day the Rains Came (French Version)	1958	10.00
❑ 236	You'll Never Walk Alone/I May Never Pass This Way Again	1958	10.00
❑ 253	To Love and Be Loved/If Only I Could Live My Life Again	1958	10.00
❑ 264	To Each His Own/Love Is Like Champagne	1959	10.00
❑ 284	With Open Arms/I Can't Begin to Tell You	1959	10.00
❑ 284 [PS]	With Open Arms/I Can't Begin to Tell You	1959	15.00
❑ 304	I'm in Love/Was It Day, Was It Night	1959	10.00
❑ 305	Happy Anniversary/C'est La Vie, C'est L'Amour	1959	10.00
❑ 305 [PS]	Happy Anniversary/C'est La Vie, C'est L'Amour	1959	15.00
❑ 317	The Bells of St. Mary's/Ballad of Lady Jane	1960	10.00
❑ 332	I Am a Heart/Romantica	1960	10.00
❑ 351	Lord and Master/Where's the Boy (I Never Met)	1960	10.00
❑ 358	The Angry Sea/Somebody	1960	10.00
❑ 369	Jerusalem/Jerusalem (French Version)	1961	8.00
❑ 390	Love Makes the World Go 'Round/He Makes Me Feel I'm Lonely	1961	8.00
❑ 418	It Takes Love/Homesick for New England	1961	8.00
❑ 431	Moon River/Blue Hawaii	1961	8.00
❑ 450	What Now My Love/Forever My Love	1962	8.00
❑ 478	Ask Me to Dance/Waiting for Charlie to Come Home	1962	8.00
❑ AS-924X [DJ]	The Second Time Around (same on both sides)	1961	20.00
❑ AS-928X [DJ]	Black Coffee/Guess I'll Hang My Tears Out to Dry	1962	20.00
—"Special Disc Jockey Record" and "Album Sample"			
RCA VICTOR			
❑ 47-9727	Congratulations, I Guess/All of My Laughter	1969	5.00
❑ 47-9839	A Girl Named Johnny Cash/Charley	1970	5.00
❑ 47-9901	The First Day/I'm Only a Woman	1970	5.00
❑ 74-0153	Marry Me, Marry Me/Three Rest Stops	1969	5.00
❑ 74-0194	Traces/Where Do I Go	1969	5.00
❑ 74-0316	He Gives Me Love/He's Never Too Busy	1970	5.00
❑ 74-0395	Jamie Boy/Things of Life	1970	5.00
7-Inch Extended Plays			
EPIC			
❑ 5-26166 [PS]	In My Style	1965	10.00
❑ 5-26166 [S]	I'm Sorry/You Belong to Me/Downtown//Fascination/Why Don't You Believe Me/We'll Sing in the Sunshine	1965	10.00
—33 1/3 rpm, small hole, "For Jukebox Use Only"			
KAPP			
❑ SE-405	The Day the Rains Came/Everybody Loves a Lover//It's All in the Game/Wrap Your Troubles in Dreams	1959	25.00
—Stereo, large hole			
❑ SE-405 [PS]	(title unknown)	1959	25.00
❑ SE-406	You'll Never Walk Alone/Dancing in the Dark//Catch a Falling Star/Melodie d'Amour	1959	25.00
—Stereo, large hole			
❑ SE-406 [PS]	(title unknown)	1959	25.00
❑ SE-415	Fascination/My Heart Reminds Me//It's Not for Me to Say/Around the World	1959	25.00
—Stereo, large hole			

Except when noted otherwise, VG = 25% of NM, and VG+ = 50% of NM. (Example: VG = $2.00, VG+ = $4.00 and NM = $8.00.)

Number	Title (A Side/B Side)	Yr	NM
❑ SE-415 [PS]	Jane Morgan	1959	25.00
❑ KE-731	From the First Hello to the Last Goodbye/Come Home, Come Home, Come Home//I'll Be Seeing You/Thanks for the Memory	1957	15.00
❑ KE-731 [PS]	From the First Hello to the Last Goodbye	1957	15.00
❑ KE-747	Fascination/It's Not for Me to Say//My Heart Reminds Me/An Affair to Remember	1957	15.00
❑ KE-747 [PS]	Fascination	1957	15.00
❑ KE-752	All the Way/Till//Melodie d'Amour (Song of Love)/Tammy	1958	15.00
❑ KE-752 [PS]	All the Way	1958	15.00
❑ KE-756	Arrivederci Roma/Who's Sorry Now?//Catch a Falling Star/Be My Little Bumble Bee	1958	15.00
❑ KE-756 [PS]	Jane Morgan and the Troubadours	1958	15.00
❑ KE-758	The Day the Rains Came/Volare//It's All in the Game/Everybody Loves a Lover	1958	15.00
❑ KE-758 [PS]	Jane Morgan	1958	15.00
❑ KBS 958	Moon River/With Open Arms/Wrap Your Troubles in Dreams//The Day the Rains Came/Blue Hawaii/The Second Time Around	196?	15.00
—Jukebox edition; small hole, plays at 33 1/3 rpm			
❑ KBS 958 [PS]	More Golden Hits	196?	15.00
Albums			
ABC			
❑ S-638	A Jane Morgan Happening	1968	12.00
COLPIX			
❑ CP 469 [M]	The Last Time I Saw Paris	1964	20.00
❑ SCP 469 [S]	The Last Time I Saw Paris	1964	25.00
❑ CP 497 [M]	The Jane Morgan Album	1966	15.00
❑ SCP 497 [S]	The Jane Morgan Album	1966	20.00
EPIC			
❑ LN 24166 [M]	In My Style	1965	12.00
❑ LN 24190 [M]	Today's Hits...Tomorrow's Golden Favorites	1966	12.00
❑ LN 24211 [M]	Fresh Flavor	1966	12.00
❑ LN 24247 [M]	Kiss Tomorrow Goodbye	1967	15.00
❑ BN 26166 [S]	In My Style	1965	15.00
❑ BN 26190 [S]	Today's Hits...Tomorrow's Golden Favorites	1966	15.00
❑ BN 26211 [S]	Fresh Flavor	1966	15.00
❑ BN 26247 [S]	Kiss Tomorrow Goodbye	1967	12.00
HARMONY			
❑ HS 11398	Sounds of Silence	1970	10.00
KAPP			
❑ KJM-1 [DJ]	Radio Station Sampler	196?	25.00
—Promo only, gatefold cover			
❑ KL-1023 [M]	Jane Morgan	1956	30.00
❑ KL-1066 [M]	Fascination	1957	30.00
❑ KL-1080 [M]	All the Way	1958	30.00
❑ KL-1089 [M]	Something Old, New, Borrowed, Blue	1958	30.00
❑ KL-1089S [S]	Something Old, New, Borrowed, Blue	1958	40.00
❑ KL-1093 [M]	Jane Morgan	1958	30.00
❑ KL-1105 [M]	The Day the Rains Came	1958	30.00
❑ KL-1105S [S]	The Day the Rains Came	1958	40.00
❑ KL-1129 [M]	Jane in Spain	1959	25.00
❑ KL-1170 [M]	Jane Morgan Time	1959	20.00
❑ KL-1191 [M]	Ballads of Lady Jane	1960	15.00
❑ KL-1239 [M]	Second Time Around	1961	15.00
❑ KL-1246 [M]	The Great Golden Hits	1961	15.00
❑ KL-1247 [M]	Big Hits from Broadway	1961	15.00
❑ KL-1250 [M]	Love Makes the World Go 'Round	1961	15.00
❑ KL-1268 [M]	Jane Morgan at the Cocoanut Grove	1962	15.00
❑ KL-1275 [M]	More Golden Hits	1962	15.00
❑ KL-1296 [M]	What Now My Love	1962	15.00
❑ KL-1329 [M]	Jane Morgan's Greatest Hits	1963	12.00
❑ KS-3001 [S]	Broadway in Stereo	1959	30.00
❑ KS-3014 [S]	Jane in Spain	1959	30.00
❑ KS-3017 [S]	Fascination	1959	30.00
❑ KS-3054 [S]	Jane Morgan Time	1959	25.00
❑ KS-3066 [S]	Fascination	1962	20.00
❑ KS-3191 [S]	Ballads of Lady Jane	1960	20.00
❑ KS-3239 [S]	Second Time Around	1961	20.00
❑ KS-3246 [S]	The Great Golden Hits	1961	20.00
❑ KS-3247 [S]	Big Hits from Broadway	1961	20.00
❑ KS-3250 [S]	Love Makes the World Go 'Round	1961	20.00
❑ KS-3268 [S]	Jane Morgan at the Cocoanut Grove	1962	20.00
❑ KS-3275 [S]	More Golden Hits	1962	20.00
❑ KS-3296 [S]	What Now My Love	1962	20.00
❑ KS-3329 [S]	Jane Morgan's Greatest Hits	1963	15.00
❑ UXL-5006 [(2)M]	Great Songs from the Great Shows of the Century	195?	40.00
MCA			
❑ 537	Jane Morgan's Greatest Hits	197?	10.00
RCA VICTOR			
❑ LSP-4171	Traces of Love	1969	12.00
❑ LSP-4322	Jane Morgan in Nashville	1970	12.00

MORGAN, JAYE P.

Number	Title (A Side/B Side)	Yr	NM
45s			
ABC-PARAMOUNT			
❑ 10678	Put a Ring on My Finger/Life Is Just a Bowl of Cherries	1965	7.00
BEVERLY HILLS			
❑ 9337	Billy Sunshine/Love of a Gentle Man	1969	6.00
❑ 9344	What Are You Doing the Rest of Your Life/Applause	1970	6.00
❑ 9349	He's Too Good to Me/I've Got an Awful Lot of Losing You to Do	1970	6.00
❑ 9367	A Song fo You/Do You Really Have a Heart	1971	6.00
❑ 9386	That Man Is My Weakness/Love of a Gentle Man	1972	6.00
DECCA			
❑ 9-29501	Life Was Made for Living/Have You Ever Been Lonely	1955	12.00
❑ 9-29611	Just a Gigolo/Life Is Just a Bowl of Cherries	1955	12.00
❑ 9-29722	Nobody Met the Train/Baby Don't Do It	1955	12.00
DERBY			
❑ 828	Just a Gigolo/Wasted Tears	1953	20.00
❑ 837	Life Is Just a Bowl of Cherries/Operator 299	1953	20.00
❑ 843	Ring, Telephone, Ring/Don't Tell Him	1953	20.00
❑ 852	Life Was Meant for Living/Nobody Met the Train	1954	20.00
❑ 855	I Ain't Got the Man/Baby Don't Do It	1954	20.00
MGM			
❑ K12752	Are You Lonesome Tonight/Miss You	1959	10.00
❑ K12786	My Reputation/(It Took) One Kiss	1959	10.00
❑ K12815	Somebody Loses, Somebody Wins/Somebody Else Is Taking My Place	1959	10.00
❑ K12838	Left My Gal in the Mountains/That Funny Feeling	1959	10.00
❑ K12861	My Darling, My Darling/Thoughts of Love	1959	10.00
❑ K12879	Half As Much/I Don't Want to Walk Without You	1960	10.00
❑ K12904	I Understand/I Wish I Didn't Love You So	1960	10.00
❑ K12924	I Walk the Line/Wondering Where You Are	1960	10.00
❑ K12956	When You Get What You Want/World I Can't Live In	1960	10.00
❑ K12984	Catch Me a Kiss/Close Your Eyes	1961	8.00
❑ K13021	Let Me Know/No One to Cry To	1961	8.00
❑ K13049	Brotherhood of Man/Nobody's Sweetheart	1961	8.00
❑ K13076	He Thinks I Still Care/Heartache Named Johnny	1962	8.00
❑ K13114	Ma, He's Making Eyes at Me/Slowly	1962	8.00
❑ K13142	The Longest Walk/Will He Love Me	1963	8.00
RCA VICTOR			
❑ 47-5896	That's All I Want from You/Dawn	1954	15.00
❑ 47-6016	Danger! Heartbreak Ahead/Softly, Softly	1955	15.00
❑ 47-6137	Chee Chee O-Chee (Sang the Little Bird)/Two Lost Souls	1955	10.00
—With Perry Como			
❑ 47-6182	The Longest Walk/Swanee	1955	15.00
❑ 47-6282	If You Don't Want My Love/Pepper-Hot Baby	1955	15.00
❑ 47-6329	Not One Goodbye/My Bewildered Heart	1955	15.00
❑ 47-6441	Get Up! Get Up! (You Sleepyhead)/Sweet Lips	1956	12.00
❑ 47-6505	Lost in the Shuffle/Play for Keeps	1956	12.00
❑ 47-6565	Johnny Casanova/The West Point Dress Parade	1956	12.00
❑ 47-6653	Just Love Me/The Call of the Wild	1956	12.00
❑ 47-6708	Mutual Admiration Society/If'n	1956	15.00
—With Eddy Arnold			
❑ 47-6798	I Thought It Was Over/I Pledge Allegiance to Your Heart	1957	12.00
❑ 47-6842	One/Do You Love Me	1957	12.00
—With Eddy Arnold			
❑ 47-6938	Graduation Ring/You, You Romeo	1957	12.00
❑ 47-7064	There's a Dream in My Heart/Take a Chance	1957	12.00
❑ 47-7178	My Blind Date/Tell Me More	1958	10.00
❑ 47-7263	I Love You So Much It Hurts/I Know, I Know, I Know	1958	10.00
❑ 47-7326	Easy Does It/Star Dust	1958	10.00
❑ 47-7364	All I Have to Do Is Dream/Just You, Just Me	1958	10.00
Albums			
ALLEGRO ELITE			
❑ 4111 [M]	Jaye P. Morgan Sings	195?	12.00
BEVERLY HILLS			
❑ 24	What Are You Doing the Rest of Your Life	1970	30.00
MAYFAIR			
❑ 9739 [M]	Life Is Just a Bowl of Cherries	195?	15.00
MGM			
❑ E-3774 [M]	Slow and Easy	1959	25.00
❑ SE-3774 [S]	Slow and Easy	1959	30.00
❑ E-3830 [M]	Up North	1960	25.00
❑ SE-3830 [S]	Up North	1960	30.00
❑ E-3867 [M]	Down South	1960	25.00
❑ SE-3867 [S]	Down South	1960	30.00
❑ E-3940 [M]	That Country Sound	1961	25.00
❑ SE-3940 [S]	That Country Sound	1961	30.00
RCA VICTOR			
❑ LPM-1155 [M]	Jaye P. Morgan	1955	50.00
❑ LPM-1682 [M]	Just You, Just Me	1958	40.00
RONDO-LETTE			
❑ A-13 [M]	Jaye P. Morgan Sings	1958	25.00
ROYALE			
❑ 18147 [10]	Jaye P. Morgan and Orchestra	195?	20.00
TOPS			
❑ L-1739 [M]	Life Is Just a Bowl of Cherries	195?	15.00

M

MORGAN, LEE

Number	Title (A Side/B Side)	Yr	NM
45s			
BLUE NOTE			
❑ 1661	Gaza Strip/Reggie of Chester	195?	12.00
❑ 1692	A Night in Tunisia, Part 1/A Night in Tunisia, Part 2	1957	12.00
❑ 1911	The Sidewinder, Part 1/The Sidewinder, Part 2	1964	8.00
❑ 1918	The Rumproller, Part 1/The Rumproller, Part 2	1966	8.00
❑ 1930	Cornbread, Part 1/Cornbread, Part 2	1967	8.00
❑ 1947	Hey Chico/Sweet Honey Bee	1968	8.00
❑ 1951	Midnight Cowboy/Popi	1969	8.00
VEE JAY			
❑ 360	I'm a Fool to Want You/Terrible "T"	1960	12.00
❑ 401	Expoobedient/Just in Time	1961	12.00
Albums			
BLUE NOTE			
❑ BN-LA224-G	Memorial Album	1974	20.00
❑ BN-LA582-J2 [(2)]	Procrastinator	1977	30.00
❑ LT-987	Sonic Boom	1979	25.00
❑ LT-1031	Taru	1980	40.00
❑ LT-1058	Tom Cat	1980	40.00
❑ LT-1091	Infinity	1981	40.00
❑ BLP-1538 [M]	Lee Morgan Indeed!	1957	500.00
—"Deep groove" edition, W. 63rd St. address on label			
❑ BLP-1538 [M]	Lee Morgan Indeed!	1957	1500.
—"Deep groove" version; Lexington Ave. address on label			
❑ BLP-1538 [M]	Lee Morgan Indeed!	1963	50.00
—"New York, USA" address on label			
❑ BLP-1538 [M]	Lee Morgan Indeed!	200?	30.00
—200-gram edition; distributed by Classic Records			
❑ BLP-1541 [M]	Lee Morgan, Vol. 2	1957	400.00
—"Deep groove" edition, W. 63rd St. address on label			
❑ BLP-1541 [M]	Lee Morgan, Vol. 2	1957	1000.
—"Deep groove" version; Lexington Ave. address on label			
❑ BLP-1541 [M]	Lee Morgan, Vol. 2	1963	50.00
—"New York, USA" address on label			
❑ BLP-1557 [M]	Lee Morgan, Vol. 3	1957	300.00
—Regular edition, W. 63rd St. address on label			
❑ BLP-1557 [M]	Lee Morgan, Vol. 3	1957	900.00
—"Deep groove" version; W. 63rd St. address on label			
❑ BLP-1557 [M]	Lee Morgan, Vol. 3	1963	50.00
—"New York, USA" address on label			
❑ BLP-1575 [M]	City Lights	1958	200.00
—Regular edition, W. 63rd St. address on label			
❑ BLP-1575 [M]	City Lights	1958	600.00
—"Deep groove" version; W. 63rd St. address on label			
❑ BLP-1575 [M]	City Lights	1963	50.00
—"New York, USA" address on label			
❑ BST-1575 [S]	City Lights	1959	150.00
—Regular edition, W. 63rd St. address on label			
❑ BST-1575 [S]	City Lights	1959	300.00
—"Deep groove" version; W. 63rd St. address on label			

Number	Title (A Side/B Side)	Yr	NM
❑ BST-1575 [S]	City Lights	1963	25.00
—"New York, USA" address on label			
❑ BLP-1578 [M]	The Cooker	1958	200.00
—Regular edition, W. 63rd St. address on label			
❑ BLP-1578 [M]	The Cooker	1958	400.00
—"Deep groove" version; W. 63rd St. address on label			
❑ BLP-1578 [M]	The Cooker	1963	50.00
—"New York, USA" address on label			
❑ BST-1578 [S]	The Cooker	1959	200.00
—Regular edition, W. 63rd St. address on label			
❑ BST-1578 [S]	The Cooker	1959	300.00
—"Deep groove" version; W. 63rd St. address on label			
❑ BST-1578 [S]	The Cooker	1963	40.00
—"New York, USA" address on label			
❑ BLP-1590 [M]	Candy	1958	250.00
—Regular edition, W. 63rd St. address on label			
❑ BLP-1590 [M]	Candy	1958	500.00
—"Deep groove" version; W. 63rd St. address on label			
❑ BLP-1590 [M]	Candy	1963	50.00
—"New York, USA" address on label			
❑ BST-1590 [S]	Candy	1959	200.00
—Regular edition, W. 63rd St. address on label			
❑ BST-1590 [S]	Candy	1959	300.00
—"Deep groove" version; W. 63rd St. address on label			
❑ BST-1590 [S]	Candy	1963	40.00
—"New York, USA" address on label			
❑ BLP-4034 [M]	Lee-Way	1960	300.00
—Regular edition, W. 63rd St. address on label			
❑ BLP-4034 [M]	Lee-Way	1960	500.00
—"Deep groove" version; W. 63rd St. address on label			
❑ BLP-4034 [M]	Lee-Way	1963	50.00
—"New York, USA" address on label			
❑ BLP-4157 [M]	The Sidewinder	1964	100.00
—"New York, USA" on label			
❑ BLP-4169 [M]	Search for the New Land	1965	120.00
—"New York, USA" on label			
❑ BLP-4199 [M]	The Rumproller	1966	100.00
—"New York, USA" on label			
❑ BLP-4212 [M]	The Gigolo	1966	100.00
—"New York, USA" on label			
❑ BLP-4222 [M]	Cornbread	1967	80.00
—"New York, USA" on label			
❑ BLP-4243 [M]	Delightfulee Morgan	1967	120.00
❑ LN-10075	The Sidewinder	1981	15.00
—Budget-line reissue			
❑ B1-32089	Lee-Way	1995	20.00
❑ B1-33579	The Procrastinator	1995	20.00
❑ B1-46137	The Sidewinder	1997	20.00
❑ BST-81578 [S]	The Cooker	1968	25.00
—"A Division of Liberty Records" on label			
❑ BST-84034 [S]	Lee-Way	1960	150.00
—Regular edition, W. 63rd St. address on label			
❑ BST-84034 [S]	Lee-Way	1963	40.00
—"New York, USA" address on label			
❑ BST-84034 [S]	Lee-Way	1968	25.00
—"A Division of Liberty Records" on label			
❑ BST-84157	The Sidewinder	1985	12.00
—"The Finest in Jazz Since 1939" reissue			
❑ BST-84157 [S]	The Sidewinder	1964	80.00
—"New York, USA" address on label			
❑ BST-84157 [S]	The Sidewinder	1968	25.00
—"A Division of Liberty Records" on label			
❑ BST-84169 [S]	Search for the New Land	1965	80.00
—"New York, USA" address on label			
❑ BST-84169 [S]	Search for the New Land	1968	25.00
—"A Division of Liberty Records" on label			
❑ BST-84199 [S]	The Rumproller	1966	80.00
—"New York, USA" address on label			
❑ BST-84199 [S]	The Rumproller	1968	25.00
—"A Division of Liberty Records" on label			
❑ BST-84212	The Gigolo	1986	12.00
—"The Finest in Jazz Since 1939" reissue			
❑ BST-84212 [S]	The Gigolo	1966	80.00
—"New York, USA" address on label			
❑ BST-84212 [S]	The Gigolo	1968	25.00
—"A Division of Liberty Records" on label			
❑ BST-84222 [S]	Cornbread	1967	80.00
—"New York, USA" address on label			
❑ BST-84222 [S]	Cornbread	1968	25.00
—"A Division of Liberty Records" on label			
❑ BST-84243	Delightfulee Morgan	198?	12.00
—"The Finest in Jazz Since 1939" reissue			
❑ BST-84243 [S]	Delightfulee Morgan	1967	60.00
—"New York, USA" address on label			
❑ BST-84243 [S]	Delightfulee Morgan	1968	25.00
—"A Division of Liberty Records" on label			
❑ BST-84289	Caramba!	1969	80.00
—"A Division of Liberty Records" on label			
❑ BST-84312	Charisma	1969	50.00
—"A Division of Liberty Records" on label			
❑ BST-84335	The Sixth Sense	1969	60.00
—"A Division of Liberty Records" on label			
❑ BST-84426	The Rajah	1984	50.00
❑ BST-84901 [(2)]	Lee Morgan	1972	30.00
—"A Division of Unted Artists" on blue and white labels			
❑ BST-89906 [(2)]	Lee Morgan at the Lighthouse	1970	50.00
❑ B1-91138	The Best of Lee Morgan	1988	15.00
FANTASY			
❑ OJC-310	Take Twelve	198?	12.00
GNP CRESCENDO			
❑ GNP-2079 [(2)]	Lee Morgan	1973	20.00

Number	Title (A Side/B Side)	Yr	NM
JAZZLAND			
❑ JLP-80 [M]	Take Twelve	1962	50.00
❑ JLP-980 [S]	Take Twelve	1962	60.00
MOSAIC			
❑ MQ6-162 [(6)]	The Complete Blue Note Lee Morgan Fifties Sessions	1995	300.00
PRESTIGE			
❑ MPP-2510	Take Twelve	198?	12.00
SAVOY			
❑ MG-12091 [M]	Introducing Lee Morgan	1956	400.00
SUNSET			
❑ SUS-5269	All the Way	1969	15.00
TRADITION			
❑ 2079	The Genius of Lee Morgan	1969	20.00
TRIP			
❑ 5003 [(2)]	Two Sides of Lee Morgan	1974	25.00
❑ 5020	Speedball	1974	15.00
❑ 5029	One of a Kind	1974	15.00
❑ 5037	A Date with Lee	1974	15.00
❑ 5041 [(2)]	Live Sessions	1975	25.00
VEE JAY			
❑ VJ-2508 [M]	Lee Morgan Quintet	1965	60.00
❑ VJS-2508 [S]	Lee Morgan Quintet	1965	80.00
❑ LP-3007 [M]	Here's Lee Morgan	1960	60.00
❑ SR-3007 [S]	Here's Lee Morgan	1960	80.00
❑ VJS-3007	Here's Lee Morgan	1986	15.00
—Reissue on reactivated label			
❑ LP-3015 [M]	Expoobident	1960	80.00
❑ SR-3015 [S]	Expoobident	1960	120.00
❑ E-4000	Lee Morgan 1938-1972	198?	20.00

MORGAN, LOUMELL

Number	Title (A Side/B Side)	Yr	NM
45s			
ATLANTIC			
❑ 953	Charmaine/Jock-O-Mo	1952	200.00

MORGAN TWINS, THE

Number	Title (A Side/B Side)	Yr	NM
45s			
RCA VICTOR			
❑ 47-7300	TV Hop/This Feeling's Bound to Be Love	1958	25.00
❑ 47-7373	Let's Get Goin'/While It Lasted	1958	25.00

MORGEN

Number	Title (A Side/B Side)	Yr	NM
45s			
PROBE			
❑ 474	Of Dreams/She's the Nighttime	1969	20.00
Albums			
PROBE			
❑ CPLP-4507	Morgen	1969	150.00

MORISSETTE, ALANIS

Number	Title (A Side/B Side)	Yr	NM
45s			
LAMOR			
❑ LMR-10-12	Fate Stay With Me/Find the Right Man	1987	400.00
❑ LMR-10-12 [PS]	Fate Stay With Me/Find the Right Man	1987	400.00
—As "Alanis"; Canadian release only, this was her first record			
MAVERICK			
❑ 7-17644	You Learn/You Oughta Know (Live)	1996	4.00
❑ 7-17698	Ironic/Forgiven (Live)	1996	5.00
Albums			
MAVERICK			
❑ 47094 [(2)]	Supposed Former Infatuation Junkie	1998	15.00

MORLEY, COZY

Number	Title (A Side/B Side)	Yr	NM
45s			
ABC-PARAMOUNT			
❑ 9811	I Love My Girl/Why Don't You Fall in Love	1957	25.00

MORLY GREY

Number	Title (A Side/B Side)	Yr	NM
Albums			
STARSHINE			
❑ 69000	The Only Truth	1969	200.00

MORNING DEW, THE

Number	Title (A Side/B Side)	Yr	NM
Albums			
ROULETTE			
❑ SR-42049	The Morning Dew	1970	300.00

MORNING GLORY

Number	Title (A Side/B Side)	Yr	NM
45s			
FONTANA			
❑ 1613	Need Someone/I See a Light	1968	10.00
Albums			
FONTANA			
❑ SRF-67573	Two Suns Worth	1968	30.00

MORNINGLORY

Number	Title (A Side/B Side)	Yr	NM
Albums			
TOYA			
❑ STLP-003	Growing	1972	40.00

MORRIS, JOE

Number	Title (A Side/B Side)	Yr	NM
45s			
ATLANTIC			
❑ 914	Any Time, Any Place, Any Where/Come Back Daddy Daddy	1950	500.00
—With Laura Tate; Atlantic's earliest number on 45; Morris' 78s on Atlantic before 914 were not issued on 45			
❑ 985	I'm Goin' to Leave You/That's What Makes My Baby Fat	1953	100.00
❑ 1160	Going, Going, Gone/Sinner Woman	1957	20.00
HERALD			
❑ 420	Travelin' Man/No, It Can't Be Done	1954	40.00
—Black vinyl			
❑ 420	Travelin' Man/No, It Can't Be Done	1954	80.00
—Red vinyl			
❑ 446	Be Careful/Way Down Yonder	1955	30.00

MORRISON, VAN

Number	Title (A Side/B Side)	Yr	NM
12-Inch Singles			
MERCURY			
❑ 447 [DJ]	Got to Go Back (same on both sides)	1986	6.00
WARNER BROS.			
❑ PRO-A-755 [DJ]	Wavelength (6:07) (3:57)	1978	15.00
❑ PRO-A-911 [DJ]	Summertime in England (Edit)/Haunts	1980	10.00
45s			
BANG			
❑ 545	Brown Eyed Girl/Goodbye, Baby	1967	12.00
❑ 552	Chick-a-Boom/Ro Ro Rosey	1967	10.00
❑ 585	Spanish Rose/Midnight Special	1971	8.00
MERCURY			
❑ 880669-7	Haunts of Ancient Peace/Tore Down A La Rimbaud	1985	4.00
❑ 884841-7	Ivory Tower/New Kind of Man	1986	4.00
❑ 884841-7 [PS]	Ivory Tower/New Kind of Man	1986	4.00
PHILCO-FORD			
❑ HP-16	Brown Eyed Girl/Midnight Special	1968	20.00
—4-inch plastic "Hip Pocket Record" with color sleeve			
POINTBLANK			
❑ 38655	Precious Time/Jackie Wilson Said (I'm in Heaven When You Smile) (Live)	1999	4.00
POINTBLANK/VIRGIN/EXILE			
❑ 38754	No Way Pedro/Let's Talk About Us	2000	4.00
—With Linda Gail Lewis			
WARNER BROS.			
❑ 7383	Come Running/Crazy Love	1970	6.00
❑ 7434	Domino/Sweet Janine	1970	6.00
❑ 7462	Blue Money/Sweet Thing	1971	6.00
❑ 7488	Call Me Up in Dreamland/Street Choir	1971	6.00
❑ 7518	Wild Night/When That Evening Sun Goes Down	1971	6.00
❑ 7543	Tupelo Honey/Starting a New Life	1971	6.00
❑ 7573	Straight to My Heart Like a Cannonball/Old Old Woodstock	1972	5.00
❑ 7616	Jackie Wilson Said (I'm in Heaven When You Smile)/You've Got the Power	1972	5.00
❑ 7638	Redwood Tree/Saint Dominic's Preview	1972	5.00
❑ 7665	Gypsy/Saint Dominic's Preview	1972	5.00
❑ 7706	Warm Love/I Will Be There	1973	5.00
❑ 7744	Green/Wild Children	1973	5.00
❑ 7786	Gloria/(B-side unknown)	1973	5.00
❑ 7797	Ain't Nothin' You Can Do/Wild Children	1974	5.00
❑ 8029	Bulbs/Cul-De-Sac	1974	5.00
❑ 8411	Joyous Sound/Mechanical Bliss	1977	5.00
❑ 8450	Moondance/Cold Wind in August	1977	5.00
❑ 8661	Wavelength/Checkin' It Out	1978	5.00
❑ 8743	Lifetimes/Natalia	1979	4.00
❑ 8805	Checkin' It Out/Kingdom Hall	1979	4.00

M

Number	Title (A Side/B Side)	Yr	NM
❑ 49086	Rolling Hills/Bright Side of the Road	1979	4.00
❑ 49162	Full Force Gale/You Make Me Feel So Free	1980	4.00
❑ 50031	Scandinavia/Cleaning Windows	1982	4.00

Albums

BANG

Number	Title (A Side/B Side)	Yr	NM
❑ BLB-218 [M]	Blowin' Your Mind	1968	50.00
—With the censored "Brown Eyed Girl" lyric, "Laughin' and a-runnin', hey hey, behind the stadium with you," part of which was spliced in from another part of the song. This has been confirmed to exist in mono.			
❑ BLBS-218 [S]	Blowin' Your Mind	1968	20.00
—With the censored "Brown Eyed Girl" lyric, "Laughin' and a-runnin', hey hey, behind the stadium with you," part of which was spliced in from another part of the song!			
❑ BLP-218 [M]	Blowin' Your Mind	1967	30.00
—With the true "Brown Eyed Girl" lyric, "Makin' love in the green grass behind the stadium with you."			
❑ BLPS-218 [S]	Blowin' Your Mind	1967	40.00
—With the true "Brown Eyed Girl" lyric, "Makin' love in the green grass behind the stadium with you."			
❑ BLPS-222	The Best of Van Morrison	1970	15.00
❑ BLPS-400	T.B. Sheets	1973	20.00

DIRECT DISK

Number	Title (A Side/B Side)	Yr	NM
❑ SD-16604	Moondance	1981	100.00
—Audiophile vinyl			

LOST HIGHWAY

Number	Title (A Side/B Side)	Yr	NM
❑ B0005968-01	Pay the Devil	2006	12.00

MERCURY

Number	Title (A Side/B Side)	Yr	NM
❑ 818336-1	Live at the Grand Opera House, Belfast	1985	10.00
❑ 822895-1	A Sense of Wonder	1985	8.00
❑ 830077-1	No Guru, No Method, No Teacher	1986	8.00
❑ 832585-1	Poetic Champions Compose	1987	8.00
❑ 834496-1	Irish Heartbeat	1988	8.00
—With the Chieftains			
❑ 839262-1	Avalon Sunset	1989	10.00
❑ 841970-1	The Best of Van Morrison	1990	15.00
❑ 847100-1	Enlightenment	1990	15.00

POLYDOR

Number	Title (A Side/B Side)	Yr	NM
❑ 1775313	Tupelo Honey	2008	20.00
❑ 8391661 [(2)]	It's Too Late to Stop Now	2008	30.00

WARNER BROS.

Number	Title (A Side/B Side)	Yr	NM
❑ WBMS-102 [DJ]	Live at the Roxy	1978	40.00
❑ WS 1768	Astral Weeks	1968	25.00
—With "W7" logo on green label			
❑ WS 1768	Astral Weeks	1970	12.00
—With "WB" logo on green label			
❑ WS 1768	Astral Weeks	1973	10.00
—"Burbank" palm-tree label			
❑ WS 1768	Astral Weeks	1979	8.00
—Later white or tan label			
❑ WS 1835	Moondance	1969	20.00
—With "W7" logo on green label			
❑ WS 1835	Moondance	1970	12.00
—With "WB" logo on green label			
❑ WS 1835	Moondance	1973	10.00
—"Burbank" palm-tree label			
❑ WS 1884	His Band and the Street Choir	1970	15.00
—With "WB" logo on green label			
❑ WS 1884	His Band and the Street Choir	1973	10.00
—"Burbank" palm-tree label			
❑ WS 1884	His Band and the Street Choir	1979	8.00
—Later white or tan label			
❑ WS 1950	Tupelo Honey	1971	15.00
—With "WB" logo on green label, plus poster			
❑ WS 1950	Tupelo Honey	1973	10.00
—"Burbank" palm-tree label			
❑ WS 1950	Tupelo Honey	1979	8.00
—Later white or tan label			
❑ WS 2633	Saint Dominic's Preview	1972	15.00
—With "WB" logo on green label			
❑ WS 2633	Saint Dominic's Preview	1973	10.00
—"Burbank" palm-tree label			
❑ WS 2633	Saint Dominic's Preview	1979	8.00
—Later white or tan label			
❑ BS 2712	Hard Nose the Highway	1973	12.00
—"Burbank" palm-tree label			
❑ BS 2712	Hard Nose the Highway	1979	8.00
—Later white or tan label			
❑ 2BS 2760 [(2)]	It's Too Late to Stop Now	1974	15.00
—"Burbank" palm-tree labels			
❑ 2BS 2760 [(2)]	It's Too Late to Stop Now	1979	8.00
—Later white or tan label			
❑ BS 2805	Veedon Fleece	1974	12.00
—"Burbank" palm-tree labels			
❑ BS 2805	Veedon Fleece	1979	8.00
—Later white or tan label			
❑ BS 2987	A Period of Transition	1977	12.00
—"Burbank" palm-tree labels			
❑ BS 2987	A Period of Transition	1979	8.00
—Later white or tan label			
❑ BSK 3103	Moondance	1977	10.00
—Reissue with new number; "Burbank" palm-tree label			
❑ BSK 3103	Moondance	1979	8.00
—Later white or tan label			
❑ BSK 3212	Wavelength	1978	12.00
❑ HS 3390	Into the Music	1979	12.00
❑ BSK 3462	Common One	1980	12.00
❑ BSK 3652	Beautiful Vision	1981	12.00
❑ 23802	Inarticulate Speech of the Heart	1983	12.00

MORRISSEY

Also see THE SMITHS.

12-Inch Singles

SIRE

Number	Title (A Side/B Side)	Yr	NM
❑ 20877	Suedehead/I Know Very Well.../Hairdresser on Fire	1988	12.00
❑ 20986	Everyday Is Like Sunday/Sister I'm a Poet/Disappointed/I Never Will Marry	1988	15.00
❑ 21163	The Last of the Famous International Playboys/Lucky Lisp/Michael Bones	1989	15.00
❑ 21232	Interesting Drug/Such a Little Thing.../Sweet and Tender...	1989	12.00
❑ 21424	Ouija Board, Ouija Board/Yes, I Am Blind/East West	1989	12.00
❑ 21529	November Spawned a Monster/he Knows I'd Love to See Him/Girl Least Likely To	1990	10.00
❑ 40043	Our Frank/Journalists Who Lie/Tony the Pony	1991	10.00
❑ 40580	Tomorrow/Let the Right One Slip In/There Speaks a True Friend	1992	10.00

45s

ATTACK

Number	Title (A Side/B Side)	Yr	NM
❑ ATMDJ-85761-7 [DJ]	You Have Killed Me/Good Looking Man About Town	2006	5.00
—Small hole			
❑ ATMDJ-85761-7 [PS]	You Have Killed Me/Good Looking Man About Town	2006	5.00
—Cardboard sleeve, opens at right			

SIRE

Number	Title (A Side/B Side)	Yr	NM
❑ 18789	Tomorrow	1993	—
—Cassette only			
❑ 27837	Everyday Is Like Sunday/Disappointed	1988	6.00
❑ 27907	Suedehead/I Know Very Well How I Got My Name	1988	6.00

7-Inch Extended Plays

ATTACK

Number	Title (A Side/B Side)	Yr	NM
❑ 06076-86000-7	Irish Blood, English Heart/It's Hard to Walk Tall When You're Small//Munich Air Disaster 1958/The Never-Played Symphonies	2004	5.00
—Small hole, plays at 45 rpm			
❑ 06076-86000-7 [PS]	Irisb Blood, English Heart	2004	5.00
—Cardboard sleeve			
❑ 06076-86007-7	First of the Gang to Die/My Life Is a Succession of People Saying Goodbye//Teenage Dad on His Estate/Mexico	2004	5.00
—Small hole, plays at 45 rpm			
❑ 06076-86007-7 [PS]	First of the Gang to Die	2004	5.00
—Cardboard sleeve			

Albums

ATTACK

Number	Title (A Side/B Side)	Yr	NM
❑ 86001	You Are the Quarry	2004	25.00

DECCA

Number	Title (A Side/B Side)	Yr	NM
❑ SKL 6003	Greatest Hits	2008	30.00

LOST HIGHWAY

Number	Title (A Side/B Side)	Yr	NM
❑ 1257801	Years of Refusal	2009	20.00

SIRE

Number	Title (A Side/B Side)	Yr	NM
❑ 25699	Viva Hate	1988	12.00
❑ R 153729	Viva Hate	1988	16.00
—BMG Direct Marketing edition			

MORTIMER

45s

PHILIPS

Number	Title (A Side/B Side)	Yr	NM
❑ 40524	Dedicated Music Man/To Understand Someone	1968	8.00
❑ 40524 [PS]	Dedicated Music Man/To Understand Someone	1968	12.00
❑ 40567	Ingenue's Theme/Slicker Beauty Hints	1968	8.00

Albums

PHILIPS

Number	Title (A Side/B Side)	Yr	NM
❑ PHS 600267	Mortimer	1969	25.00

MORTIMER, AZIE

45s

BIG TOP

Number	Title (A Side/B Side)	Yr	NM
❑ 3041	Lips/Wrapped Up in a Dream	1960	400.00

EPIC

Number	Title (A Side/B Side)	Yr	NM
❑ 5-9584	Cry Me a River/Little Boy (I Keep On Changing My Mind)	1963	20.00

OKEH

Number	Title (A Side/B Side)	Yr	NM
❑ 4-7336	You Can't Take It Away/A One Way Love (Is a Wrong Way Love)	1970	12.00
❑ 4-7337	I Don't Care/Prove It	1970	12.00

PALETTE

Number	Title (A Side/B Side)	Yr	NM
❑ 5097	Mama, What Should I Do/When You're Talking Love	1962	20.00
—As "A.Z. Mortimer"			

RCA VICTOR

Number	Title (A Side/B Side)	Yr	NM
❑ 47-8985	Little Miss Everything/Best Years	1966	15.00

REGATTA

Number	Title (A Side/B Side)	Yr	NM
❑ 2002	Brother Love/Treat Me Like You Love Me	1961	25.00

SWAN

Number	Title (A Side/B Side)	Yr	NM
❑ 4158	Put Yourself in My Place/Bring Back Your Love	1963	15.00

TROY

Number	Title (A Side/B Side)	Yr	NM
❑ 103	Little Soldier/Battle Hymn of the Republic	196?	25.00
❑ 104	Forever Kind of Love/Little Playboy	196?	25.00
❑ 105	Untouched by Human Love/Bring Back Your Love	196?	25.00
❑ 106	Little Old Lady/Cool It	196?	25.00

UNITED ARTISTS

Number	Title (A Side/B Side)	Yr	NM
❑ 826	The Other Half of Me/Next Time	1965	—
—Canceled			
❑ 838	(I Get the Feeling) You're Ashamed of Me/Deeper in My Heart	1965	—
—Canceled			
❑ 847	The Other Half of Me/(I Get the Feeling) You're Ashamed of Me	1965	40.00

MOSBY, JOHNNY AND JONIE

45s

CAPITOL

Number	Title (A Side/B Side)	Yr	NM
❑ 2087	Mr. and Mrs. John Smith/Hello There Stranger	1968	6.00
❑ 2179	Our Golden Wedding Day/Two Dollar Honeymoon Room	1968	6.00
❑ 2258	Come In the Back Door (Go 'Round, Go 'Round)/You Be the Mama, I'll Be the Papa	1968	6.00
❑ 2384	Just Hold My Hand/Walkin' Papers	1969	6.00
❑ 2505	Hold Me, Thrill Me, Kiss Me/Comparing Him with You	1969	6.00
❑ 2608	I'll Never Be Free/Pattern of Our Lives	1969	6.00
❑ 2730	Third World/You Go Back to Your World (I'll Go Back to Mine)	1970	6.00
❑ 2796	I'm Leavin' It Up to You/If It's Left Up to Me	1970	6.00
❑ 2865	My Happiness/Let Your Sun Shine on Me	1970	6.00
❑ 2865 [PS]	My Happiness/Let Your Sun Shine on Me	1970	10.00
❑ 2978	A Little of Me, A Little of You/Someone to Take My Place	1970	6.00
❑ 3039	Oh, Love of Mine/Closing Time Till Dawn	1971	6.00
❑ 3141	Let's Get This Show on the Road/Souvenirs of Love	1971	6.00
❑ 3219	Just One More Time/Meet Me Tonight	1971	6.00
❑ 3277	Music to My Ears/I'll Say It Again	1972	6.00
❑ 3332	My Ecstasy/Ain't You Ever	1972	6.00
❑ 3613	Let's Try Love Again/It's All Because of You	1973	6.00
❑ 5980	Make a Left and Then a Right/Take Back the World	1967	6.00

CHALLENGE

Number	Title (A Side/B Side)	Yr	NM
❑ 59088	He Wouldn't Take Me Home to Meet His Mother/Hard Luck and Misery	1960	15.00

COLUMBIA

Number	Title (A Side/B Side)	Yr	NM
❑ 42668	Don't Call Me from a Honky Tonk/Wrong Side of Town	1963	10.00
❑ 42841	Trouble in My Arms/Who's Been Cheatin' Who	1963	10.00
❑ 43005	Keep Those Cards and Letters Coming In/Take Me Home	1964	10.00

M

Motley Crue, "Girls, Girls, Girls," Elektra 7-69465, 1987, **$3.**

Number	Title (A Side/B Side)	Yr	NM
❑ 43100	How the Other Half Lives/ Stolen Paradise	1964	10.00
❑ 43218	Strawberry Wine/ Wrong Company	1965	8.00
❑ 43344	The High Cost of Loving/The Home She's Tearing Down	1965	8.00
❑ 43631	Heartbreak U.S.A./Identity	1966	8.00
TOPPA			
❑ 1034	Unreceived, Address Unknown/A Cup of Coffee	1961	15.00
❑ 1039	Making Believe/Ain't You Ever	1961	15.00
❑ 1047	Dear Okie/You Can't Hurt Me Anymore	1962	15.00
Albums			
CAPITOL			
❑ ST-170	Just Hold My Hand	1969	15.00
❑ ST-286	Hold Me	1969	15.00
❑ ST-414	I'll Never Be Free	1970	15.00
❑ ST-556	My Happiness	1970	15.00
❑ ST-737	Oh, Love of Mine	1971	15.00
❑ ST 2903	Make a Left and Then a Right	1968	15.00
COLUMBIA			
❑ CL 2297 [M]	Mr. & Mrs. Country Music	1965	15.00
❑ CS 9097 [S]	Mr. & Mrs. Country Music	1965	20.00
HARMONY			
❑ HS 11389	Mr. & Mrs. Country Music	1970	10.00
STARDAY			
❑ SLP-328 [M]	The New Sweethearts of Country Music	1965	30.00

MOSES, JOHNNY

Number	Title (A Side/B Side)	Yr	NM
45s			
IMPERIAL			
❑ 5329	You're Torturing Me/Do You Love Me? Do You?	1955	40.00

MOSES, LEE

Number	Title (A Side/B Side)	Yr	NM
45s			
FRONT PAGE			
❑ 2301	Time and Place/I Can't Take No Chances	1970	20.00
GATES			
❑ 1502	Bad Girl/Dark End of the Street	1967	80.00
MUSICOR			
❑ 1242	Bad Girl (Part 1)/(Part 2)	1967	30.00

MOSLEY, BOB

Number	Title (A Side/B Side)	Yr	NM
Albums			
REPRISE			
❑ MS 2068	Bob Mosley	1972	20.00

MOSS, ROY

Number	Title (A Side/B Side)	Yr	NM
45s			
FASCINATION			
❑ 1002	Wiggle Walkin' Baby/(B-side unknown)	1957	200.00
MERCURY			
❑ 70770	You're My Big Baby Now/You Nearly Lost Your Mind	1955	200.00
❑ 70858	Corinne, Corinna/You Don't Know My Mind	1956	200.00

MOST, MICKIE

Number	Title (A Side/B Side)	Yr	NM
45s			
LAWN			
❑ 236	Sea Cruise/It's a Little Bit Hot	1964	20.00

MOTELS, THE

Also see MARTHA DAVIS.

Number	Title (A Side/B Side)	Yr	NM
12-Inch Singles			
CAPITOL			
❑ SPRO 9048 [DJ]	Remember the Nights (same on both sides)	1983	7.00
❑ SPRO 9267 [DJ]	Total Control/Your Place or Mine	1979	10.00
❑ SPRO 9436 [DJ]	Shame/Shame (Extended Mix)	1985	6.00
❑ SPRO 9515 [DJ]	Shock (same on both sides)	1985	6.00
45s			
AMERICAN PIE			
❑ 9045	Only the Lonely/ Suddenly Last Summer	198?	3.00
—Reissue			
CAPITOL			
❑ 4796	Total Control/Love Don't Help	1979	5.00
❑ 4796 [PS]	Total Control/Love Don't Help	1979	5.00
❑ 4896	Danger/Cry Baby	1980	5.00
❑ 4937	Envy/Whose Problem	1980	5.00
❑ 5114	Only the Lonely/Change My Mind	1982	3.00
❑ 5114 [PS]	Only the Lonely/Change My Mind	1982	4.00
—A moderately tough sleeve to find			
❑ 5149	Take the L/Mission of Mercy	1982	3.00
❑ 5149 [PS]	Take the L/Mission of Mercy	1982	3.00
❑ 5182	Forever Mine/So L.A.	1982	3.00
❑ 5182 [PS]	Forever Mine/So L.A.	1982	3.00
❑ 5246	Remember the Nights/ Mission of Mercy	1983	3.00
❑ 5246 [PS]	Remember the Nights/ Mission of Mercy	1983	3.00
❑ 5271	Suddenly Last Summer/ Some Things Never Change	1983	3.00
❑ 5271 [PS]	Suddenly Last Summer/ Some Things Never Change	1983	3.00
❑ 5497	Shame/Save the Last Dance for Love	1985	3.00
❑ 5497 [PS]	Shame/Save the Last Dance for Love	1985	3.00
❑ 5529	Shock/In the Jungle (Concrete Jungle)	1985	3.00
❑ 5529 [PS]	Shock/In the Jungle (Concrete Jungle)	1985	3.00
Albums			
CAPITOL			
❑ ST-11996	The Motels	1979	10.00
❑ ST-12070	Careful	1980	10.00
❑ ST-12177	All Four One	1982	10.00
❑ ST-12177 [DJ]	All Four One	1982	20.00
—Promo-only high-grade vinyl pressing (different front cover)			
❑ ST-12288	Little Robbers	1983	10.00
❑ SJ-12378	Shock	1985	10.00
❑ SN-16343	The Motels	1985	8.00
—Budget-line reissue			
❑ SN-16347	Careful	1985	8.00
—Budget-line reissue			
❑ SN-16355	Little Robbers	1985	8.00
—Budget-line reissue			
❑ SN-16420	All Four One	198?	8.00
—Budget-line reissue			

MOTHER EARTH

Also see TRACY NELSON.

Number	Title (A Side/B Side)	Yr	NM
45s			
MERCURY			
❑ 72878	Down So Long/Goodbye Nelda Greeby	1968	8.00
❑ 72909	Mother Earth/I Did My Part	1969	8.00
❑ 72943	Painted Girls and Wine/ Your Time's Comin'	1969	8.00
REPRISE			
❑ 1019	Soul of Sadness/Temptation Took Control of Me and I Fell	1971	6.00
❑ 1041	I'll Be Long Gone/Bring Me Home	1971	6.00
UNITED ARTISTS			
❑ 50303	Revolution/Stranger in My Own Home	1968	10.00
Albums			
MERCURY			
❑ SR-61194	Living with the Animals	1968	25.00
❑ SR-61226	Make a Joyful Noise	1969	20.00
❑ SR-61230	Tracy Nelson Country	1969	20.00
❑ SR-61270	Satisfied	1970	20.00
REPRISE			
❑ MS 2054	Tracy Nelson/Mother Earth	1972	15.00
❑ RS 6431	Bring Me Home	1971	15.00

MOTHER LOVE BONE

PEARL JAM related.

Number	Title (A Side/B Side)	Yr	NM
12-Inch Singles			
MERCURY			
❑ PRO 900 [DJ]	Shangri La (same on both sides)	1990	20.00
Albums			
POLYDOR			
❑ 843191-1	Apple	1990	40.00
STARDOG			
❑ 839011-1 [EP]	Shine	1989	40.00
—Four songs on side one, the same four songs on side two			

MOTHERLODE

Number	Title (A Side/B Side)	Yr	NM
45s			
BUDDAH			
❑ 131	When I Die/Hard Life	1969	8.00

Except when noted otherwise, VG = 25% of NM, and VG+ = 50% of NM. (Example: VG = $2.00, VG+ = $4.00 and NM = $8.00.)

Number	Title (A Side/B Side)	Yr	NM
❑ 144	What Does It Take (To Win Your Love)/Memories of a Broken Promise	1969	6.00
❑ 185	I'm So Glad You're You, Not Me/Whippoorwill	1970	6.00

Albums

BUDDAH

Number	Title	Yr	NM
❑ BDS-5046	When I Die	1969	15.00
❑ BDS-5108	Tapped Out	1970	15.00

MOTHERS OF INVENTION, THE See FRANK ZAPPA.

❑ MOTIONS, THE (1)

45s

ABC-PARAMOUNT

Number	Title	Yr	NM
❑ 10529	Big Chief/Where Is Your Heart	1964	12.00

CONGRESS

Number	Title	Yr	NM
❑ 237	It's Gone/I've Got Money	1965	12.00

MERCURY

Number	Title	Yr	NM
❑ 72297	Beatle Drums/Long Hair	1964	25.00
❑ 72368	I Can Dance/Land Beyond the Moon	1964	20.00
❑ 72413	Bumble Bee '65/Motions	1965	20.00

MOTIONS, THE (2)

45s

LAURIE

Number	Title	Yr	NM
❑ 3112	Make Me a Love/Mr. Night	1961	120.00

MOTIONS, THE (3)

45s

PHILIPS

Number	Title	Yr	NM
❑ 40624	Freedom/What's Your Name	1969	8.00

Albums

PHILIPS

Number	Title	Yr	NM
❑ PHS 600317	Electric Baby	1969	20.00

MOTLEY CRUE

12-Inch Singles

ELEKTRA

Number	Title	Yr	NM
❑ ED 4960 [DJ]	Too Young to Fall in Love (same on both sides)	1984	20.00
❑ ED 5070 [DJ]	Smokin' in the Boys' Room (same on both sides)	1985	15.00
❑ ED 5094 [DJ]	Home Sweet Home (same on both sides)	1985	15.00
❑ ED 5230 [DJ]	Girls, Girls, Girls (same on both sides)	1987	15.00
❑ ED 5267 [DJ]	All I Need (same on both sides)	1987	12.00
❑ ED 5405 [DJ]	Dr. Feelgood (same on both sides)	1989	10.00
❑ ED 5419 [DJ]	Kickstart My Heart (same on both sides)	1989	10.00
❑ ED 5442 [DJ]	Without You (same on both sides)	1990	10.00

45s

ELEKTRA

Number	Title	Yr	NM
❑ 7-64985	Without You/Slice of Your Pie	1990	3.00
❑ 7-69248	Kickstart My Heart/She Goes Down	1989	4.00
❑ 7-69271	Dr. Feelgood/Sticky Sweet	1989	3.00
❑ 7-69271 [PS]	Dr. Feelgood/Sticky Sweet	1989	3.00
❑ 7-69429	All I Need/All in the Name	1987	4.00
❑ 7-69449	Wild Side/Five Years Dead	1987	3.00
❑ 7-69449 [PS]	Wild Side/Five Years Dead	1987	3.00
❑ 7-69465	Girls, Girls, Girls/Sumthin' for Nuthin'	1987	3.00
❑ 7-69465 [PS]	Girls, Girls, Girls/Sumthin' for Nuthin'	1987	3.00
❑ 7-69591	Home Sweet Home/Red Hot	1985	5.00
❑ 7-69625	Smokin' in the Boys' Room/Use It or Lose It	1985	4.00
❑ 7-69625 [PS]	Smokin' in the Boys' Room/Use It or Lose It	1985	4.00
❑ 7-69732	Too Young to Fall in Love/Take Me to the Top	1984	5.00
❑ 7-69732 [PS]	Too Young to Fall in Love/Take Me to the Top	1984	5.00
❑ 7-69756	Looks That Kill/Piece of Your Action	1984	5.00
❑ 7-69756 [PS]	Looks That Kill/Piece of Your Action	1984	5.00

ELEKTRA SPUN GOLD

Number	Title	Yr	NM
❑ 7-65974	Smokin' in the Boys' Room/Home Sweet Home	198?	3.00
—Reissue			
❑ 7-65980	Looks That Kill/Too Young to Fall in Love	198?	3.00
—Reissue			

LEATHUR

Number	Title	Yr	NM
❑ 001	Stick to Your Guns/Toast of the Town	1981	80.00
❑ 001 [PS]	Stick to Your Guns/Toast of the Town	1981	120.00

Albums

ELEKTRA

Number	Title	Yr	NM
❑ 60174	Too Fast for Love	1982	12.00
—Reissue of Leathur LP with slight revisions			
❑ 60289	Shout at the Devil	1982	10.00
❑ 60395 [EP]	Helter Skelter	1984	40.00
—Picture disc with four songs; includes poster and insert (deduct 50 percent if missing)			
❑ 60418	Theatre of Pain	1985	10.00
❑ 60725	Girls, Girls, Girls	1987	10.00
❑ 60829	Dr. Feelgood	1989	12.00

LEATHUR

Number	Title	Yr	NM
❑ LR-1281	Too Fast for Love	1981	150.00
—Second pressing with red lettering on cover. Both Leathur pressings contain "Stick to Your Guns," which was not on the Elektra reissue			
❑ LR-1281	Too Fast for Love	1981	200.00
—First pressing with white lettering on cover			

MOTLEY/HIP-O SELECT

Number	Title	Yr	NM
❑ B0004791-01	Too Fast for Love	2005	20.00
—Reissue of Leathur LP with bonus 7-inch single, Stick to Your Guns/Toast of the Town			

MOTORHEAD

Albums

EMI AMERICA

Number	Title	Yr	NM
❑ LN-10340	On Parole	1986	20.00
—First U.S. issue of early U.K. LP			

ENIGMA

Number	Title	Yr	NM
❑ D1-73536	The Birthday Party	1990	15.00
❑ D1-75405	No Sleep at All	1988	12.00

ISLAND

Number	Title	Yr	NM
❑ 90233 [(2)]	No Remorse	1984	20.00
—Regular cover			
❑ 90236 [(2)]	No Remorse	1984	35.00
—Leather cover			

MERCURY

Number	Title	Yr	NM
❑ SRM-1-4011	Ace of Spades	1980	15.00
❑ SRM-1-4042	Iron Fist	1982	15.00
❑ 811365-1	Another Perfect Day	1983	15.00

PROFILE

Number	Title	Yr	NM
❑ PAL-1223	Orgasmatron	1986	12.00
❑ PAL-1240	Rock 'N' Roll	1987	10.00
❑ PRO-3241	Overkill	1986	10.00
—First U.S. issue of early U.K. LP			
❑ PRO-3242	Bomber	1986	10.00
—First U.S. issue of early U.K. LP			
❑ PRO-3243	Ace of Spades	1986	10.00
—Reissue of Mercury 4011			
❑ PRO-3244	No Sleep 'Til Hammersmith	1986	10.00
—Reissue of Mercury 4023			

SANCTUARY

Number	Title	Yr	NM
❑ 5312076	No Sleep 'Til Hammersmith	2008	20.00

WTG

Number	Title	Yr	NM
❑ N 46858	1916	1991	20.00

MOTORS, THE DUCKS DELUXE and BRAM TCHAIKOVSKY related.

45s

VIRGIN

Number	Title	Yr	NM
❑ ZS8 9515	Dancing the Night Away/Whiskey and Wine	1977	4.00
❑ ZS8 9517	Cold Love/Phoney Heaven	1977	4.00
❑ ZS8 9519	Airport/Mamma Rock 'N' Roller	1978	4.00
❑ ZS8 9520	Forget About You/Breathless	1978	4.00
❑ ZS8 9521	Today/The Hustler	1978	4.00
❑ 67007	Love and Loneliness/Time for Makeup	1980	3.00
❑ 67007 [PS]	Love and Loneliness/Time for Makeup	1980	3.00

Albums

VIRGIN

Number	Title	Yr	NM
❑ VA 13139	Tenement Steps	1980	10.00
❑ PZ 34924	The Motors	1977	12.00
❑ JZ 35348	Approved by the Motors	1978	10.00

MOTT THE HOOPLE Also see IAN HUNTER. Includes two albums as MOTT, after IAN HUNTER left the band.

45s

ATLANTIC

Number	Title	Yr	NM
❑ 2749	Rock and Roll Queen/Backsliding Fearlessly	1970	8.00

COLUMBIA

Number	Title	Yr	NM
❑ 3-10091	All the Young Dudes/Rose	1975	5.00
❑ 4-45673	All the Young Dudes/One of the Boys	1972	6.00
—A-side is the British single version with "unlocked cars" lyric; matrix number in dead wax ends in "1" plus a letter			
❑ 4-45673	All the Young Dudes/One of the Boys	1972	8.00
—A-side is the LP version with "Marks and Sparks" lyric; matrix number in dead wax ends in the number "2" plus a letter			
❑ 4-45673 [PS]	All the Young Dudes/One of the Boys	1972	20.00
❑ 45754	One of the Boys/Sucker	1973	5.00
❑ 45784	Sweet Jane/Jerkin' Crocus	1973	5.00
❑ 45882	Honaloochie Boogie/Rose	1973	5.00
❑ 45920	All the Way from Memphis/I Wish I Was Your Mother	1973	5.00
❑ 46035	The Golden Age of Rock 'N' Roll/Rest in Peace	1974	5.00
❑ 46076	Roll Away the Stone/Looking Glass	1974	5.00
❑ 74712	All the Young Dudes/Hanoloochie Boogie	1992	3.00
—Reissue			

Albums

ATLANTIC

Number	Title	Yr	NM
❑ SD 7297	Rock and Roll Queen	1974	20.00
❑ SD 8258	Mott the Hoople	1970	20.00
—With "1841 Broadway" address and no mention of Warner Communications on label			
❑ SD 8258	Mott the Hoople	198?	8.00
—With Warner Communications "W" logo on label			
❑ SD 8272	Mad Shadows	1970	20.00
❑ SD 8284	Wildlife	1971	20.00
❑ SD 8304	Brain Capers	1972	20.00

COLUMBIA

Number	Title	Yr	NM
❑ KC 31750	All the Young Dudes	1972	15.00
❑ PC 31750	All the Young Dudes	198?	8.00
—Budget-line reissue			
❑ KC 32425	Mott	1973	15.00
❑ PC 32425	Mott	198?	8.00
—Budget-line reissue			
❑ PC 32871	The Hoople	1974	15.00
❑ PCQ 32871 [Q]	The Hoople	1974	25.00
❑ PC 33282	Mott the Hoople Live	1974	15.00
—No bar code on cover			
❑ PC 33282	Mott the Hoople Live	198?	8.00
—Reissue with bar code on cover			
❑ PC 33705	Drive On	1975	15.00
❑ PC 34236	Shouting and Pointing	1976	15.00
❑ PC 34368	Mott the Hoople's Greatest Hits	1976	12.00
—No bar code on cover			
❑ PC 34368	Mott the Hoople's Greatest Hits	198?	8.00
—Reissue with bar code on cover			

MOTTOLA, TONY

45s

COMMAND

Number	Title	Yr	NM
❑ 4024	Nina/Tra Vegila E Sonno	1962	8.00
❑ 4058	Michelle/Boulevard of Broken Dreams	1964	8.00
❑ 4076	Brasilia/Sabor A Mi	1965	8.00

PROJECT 3

Number	Title	Yr	NM
❑ 1303	The Gang That Sang Heart of My Heart/Georgia on My Mind	1967	6.00
❑ 1318	Call Me/The World of Your Embrace	1967	6.00
❑ 1323	Spanish Harlem/I Love, I Live, I Love	1968	6.00
❑ 1329	Somethin' Stupid/Lush and Lovely	1968	6.00
❑ 1337	Love in Every Room/This Guy's in Love with You	1968	6.00
❑ 1352	I've Gotta Be Me/Guitar Underground	1969	5.00
❑ 1355	I'll Never Fall in Love Again/Those Were the Days	1969	5.00
❑ 1378	Something/Chewy Chewy Gum Gum	1970	5.00
❑ 1381	Tequila/Bluesette	1970	5.00
❑ 1402	It's Too Late/(B-side unknown)	1971	4.00
❑ 1413	Love/I Don't Know How to Love Him	1971	4.00
❑ 1430	Classical Gas/Galloping Guitars	197?	4.00
❑ 1431	Sugar Blues/Chicken A La Spring	197?	4.00
❑ 1437	Jelly Bean/One	197?	4.00
❑ 1438	Nadia's Theme/I Love My Wife	1976	4.00

Albums

ABC

Number	Title	Yr	NM
❑ S-738	16 Great Performances	1972	10.00
❑ X-770	Mister Guitar	1973	10.00

COMMAND

Number	Title	Yr	NM
❑ 33-807 [M]	Mr. Big	1961	12.00
❑ SD 807 [S]	Mr. Big	1961	15.00
❑ 33-816 [M]	Roman Guitar	1962	12.00
❑ SD 816 [S]	Roman Guitar	1962	15.00
❑ 33-823 [M]	Country and Western Folk Songs	1962	12.00
❑ SD 823 [S]	Country and Western Folk Songs	1962	15.00
❑ 33-828 [M]	String Band Strum-Along	1962	12.00
❑ SD 828 [S]	String Band Strum-Along	1962	15.00
❑ 33-836 [M]	Roman Guitar, Vol. Two	1962	12.00
❑ SD 836 [S]	Roman Guitar, Vol. Two	1962	15.00
❑ 33-841 [M]	Spanish Guitar	1963	12.00
❑ SD 841 [S]	Spanish Guitar	1963	15.00
❑ 33-847 [M]	Romantic Guitar	1963	12.00
❑ SD 847 [S]	Romantic Guitar	1963	15.00
❑ 33-864 [M]	Sentimental Guitar	1964	12.00
❑ SD 864 [S]	Sentimental Guitar	1964	15.00

Number	Title (A Side/B Side)	Yr	NM
❑ 33-877 [M]	Guitar — Paris	1964	12.00
❑ SD 877 [S]	Guitar — Paris	1964	15.00
❑ 33-885 [M]	Command Performance	1965	12.00
❑ SD 885 [S]	Command Performance	1965	15.00
❑ 33-889 [M]	Love Songs — Mexico/S.A.	1965	12.00
❑ SD 889 [S]	Love Songs — Mexico/S.A.	1965	15.00
❑ 33-900 [M]	Amor — Mexico/S.A.	1966	12.00
❑ SD 900 [S]	Amor — Mexico/S.A.	1966	15.00
❑ 33-908 [M]	Guitar — U.S.A.	1967	15.00
❑ SD 908 [S]	Guitar — U.S.A.	1967	12.00
❑ QD-40001 [Q]	Guitar — Paris	1972	20.00
PICKWICK			
❑ SPC-3610	Spanish Guitar	1978	8.00
PROJECT 3			
❑ PR-5003	Heart and Soul	1967	12.00
❑ PR-5010	A Latin Love-In	1967	12.00
❑ PR4C-5010 [Q]	A Latin Love-In	1973	18.00
❑ PR-5020	Lush, Latin & Lovely	1968	12.00
❑ PR4C-5020 [Q]	Lush, Latin & Lovely	1973	18.00
❑ PR-5025	Warm, Wild & Wonderful	1968	12.00
❑ PR4C-5025 [Q]	Warm, Wild & Wonderful	1973	18.00
❑ PR-5032	Roma Oggi/Rome Today	1969	12.00
❑ PR4C-5032 [Q]	Roma Oggi/Rome Today	1973	18.00
❑ PR-5035	Tony Mottola Joins the Guitar Underground	1969	12.00
❑ PR-5041	The Tony Touch	1970	12.00
❑ PR4C-5041 [Q]	The Tony Touch	1973	18.00
❑ PR-5044	Tony Mottola's Guitar Factory	1970	12.00
❑ PR-5050	Close to You	1971	12.00
❑ PR-5058	Warm Feelings	1971	12.00
❑ PR-5062	Superstar Guitar	1972	12.00
❑ PR4C-5062 [Q]	Superstar Guitar	1973	15.00
❑ PR-5069	Tony and Strings	1973	12.00
❑ PR4C-5069 [Q]	Tony and Strings	1973	18.00
❑ PR-5074	Two Guitars	1974	10.00
❑ PR4C-5078 [Q]	Tony Mottola with the Quad Guitars	1974	15.00
❑ PR-5082	Tony Mottola with the Brass Menagerie	1974	12.00
❑ PR-5094	I Only Have Eyes for You	197?	10.00
❑ PR-5101	Goin' Out of My Head	197?	10.00
❑ PR-6007/8 [(2)]	Favorite Things: The Best of Tony Mottola	1975	15.00
❑ PR-6025/6 [(2)]	Feelings	198?	12.00
❑ PR-6031/2 [(2)]	The Best of Tony Mottola	198?	12.00

MOULD, BOB Also see HUSKER DU; SUGAR.

Number	Title (A Side/B Side)	Yr	NM
12-Inch Singles			
VIRGIN			
❑ 2685 [DJ]	See a Little Light (same on both sides)	1989	6.00
❑ 2929 [DJ]	Wishing Well/If You're True + 4 live tracks	1989	25.00
45s			
VIRGIN			
❑ 99190	See a Little Light/All Those People Know	1989	4.00
❑ 99190 [PS]	See a Little Light/All Those People Know	1989	6.00
Albums			
VIRGIN			
❑ PR 3512 [EP]	Rust Bucket Coliseum	1990	15.00
—Promo-only five-track release			
❑ 91240	Workbook	1989	12.00
❑ 91395	Black Sheets of Rain	1990	12.00

MOULTRY, MARY

Number	Title (A Side/B Side)	Yr	NM
45s			
KING			
❑ 6038	Last Year's Senior Prom/They're Trying to Tear Us Apart	1966	30.00

MOUNT RUSHMORE

Number	Title (A Side/B Side)	Yr	NM
45s			
DOT			
❑ 17158	Stone Free/She's So Good to Me	1968	8.00
Albums			
DOT			
❑ DLP-25898	High on Mount Rushmore	1968	20.00
❑ DLP-25934	Mount Rushmore '69	1969	20.00

MOUNTAIN Also see FELIX PAPPALARDI; LESLIE WEST; WEST, BRUCE AND LAING.

Number	Title (A Side/B Side)	Yr	NM
45s			
COLUMBIA			
❑ 38-74711	Mississippi Queen/The Animal Trainer and the Toad	1992	4.00
—Reissue			
WINDFALL			
❑ 532	Mississippi Queen/The Laird	1970	8.00
❑ 533	For Yasgur's Farm/To My Friend	1970	8.00
❑ 534	The Animal Trainer and the Toad/Tired Angels	1971	12.00
❑ 535	Silver Paper/Travelin' in the Dark	1971	10.00
❑ 536	Roll Over Beethoven/Crossroader	1971	10.00
❑ 537	Waiting to Take You Away/(B-side unknown)	1972	10.00
Albums			
COLUMBIA			
❑ CQ 32079 [Q]	The Best of Mountain	1973	20.00
❑ KC 32079	The Best of Mountain	1973	12.00
❑ PC 32079	The Best of Mountain	198?	8.00
—Budget-line reissue			
❑ CG 32818 [(2)]	Twin Peaks	1974	15.00
❑ PG 32818 [(2)]	Twin Peaks	198?	10.00
—Budget-line reissue			
❑ CQ 33008 [Q]	Avalanche	1974	20.00
❑ KC 33008	Avalanche	1974	12.00
❑ PC 33008	Avalanche	197?	8.00
—Budget-line reissue			
SCOTTI BROTHERS			
❑ FZ 40006	Go for Your Life	1985	10.00
WINDFALL			
❑ 4501	Mountain Climbing!	1970	15.00
❑ 5500	Nantucket Sleighride	1971	15.00
—Deduct 20% if inserts are missing			
❑ 5501	Flowers of Evil	1971	15.00
❑ 5502	Mountain Live (The Road Goes Ever On)	1972	15.00

MOUNTAIN BUS

Number	Title (A Side/B Side)	Yr	NM
Albums			
GOOD			
❑ 101	Sundance	1971	200.00

MOURNING REIGN, THE

Number	Title (A Side/B Side)	Yr	NM
45s			
CONTOUR			
❑ 601	Evil Hearted You/Get Out of My Life, Woman	1967	25.00
LINK			
❑ 1	Satisfaction Guaranteed/Our Fate	1966	30.00
❑ 1 [PS]	Satisfaction Guaranteed/Our Fate	1966	600.00
❑ 2	Evil Hearted You/Get Out of My Life, Woman	1966	30.00
7-Inch Extended Plays			
SUNDAZED			
❑ SEP 115	*Satisfaction Guaranteed/Our Fate/Light Switch/Cut Back	199?	2.00
❑ SEP 115 [PS]	The Mourning Reign	199?	2.00
Albums			
BEAT ROCKET			
❑ BR 102	The Mourning Reign	1999	12.00

MOUSE AND THE TRAPS

Number	Title (A Side/B Side)	Yr	NM
45s			
CAPITOL			
❑ 2460	Streets of a Dusty Town/Mouse	1969	10.00
FRATERNITY			
❑ 956	A Public Execution/All for You	1966	20.00
❑ 966	Mad of Sugar/I Am the One	1966	15.00
❑ 971	Would You Believe/Like I Know You Do	1966	15.00
❑ 973	Promises, Promises/Do the Best You Can	1966	15.00
❑ 989	Ya Ya/Cryin' Inside	1967	15.00
❑ 1000	Beg, Borrow, and Steal/L.O.V.E. Love	1967	15.00
❑ 1005	Sometimes You Just Can't Win/Cryin' Inside	1968	15.00
❑ 1005 [PS]	Sometimes You Just Can't Win/Cryin' Inside	1968	80.00
❑ 1011	I Satisfy/Good Times	1968	15.00
❑ 1015	Look at the Sun/Requiem for Sarah	1968	15.00
SMUDGE			
❑ 0703	Bottom Line/Gypsy Girl	1981	12.00

MOUTH AND MACNEIL

Number	Title (A Side/B Side)	Yr	NM
45s			
PHILIPS			
❑ 40715	How Do You Do?/Land of Milk and Honey	1972	4.00
—Dark blue label			
❑ 40715	How Do You Do?/Land of Milk and Honey	1972	5.00
—Light blue label			
❑ 40717	Why Did You, Why?/Hey, You Love	1972	4.00
❑ 40721	Sing Along/Hello	1973	4.00
❑ 40721 [PS]	Sing Along/Hello	1973	12.00
❑ 40724	You-Kou-La-La-Lou-Pi/Let Your Life Lead by Love	1973	4.00
TARA			
❑ 110	I See a Star/My Friends	1974	4.00
Albums			
PHILIPS			
❑ PHS 700000	How Do You Do?	1972	12.00
❑ PHS 700003	Mouth & MacNeil II	1973	12.00

MOVE, THE Also see ELECTRIC LIGHT ORCHESTRA; ROY WOOD.

Number	Title (A Side/B Side)	Yr	NM
45s			
A&M			
❑ 884	Flowers in the Rain/(Here We Go Round the) Lemon Tree	1967	12.00
❑ 914	Walk Upon the Water/Fire Brigade	1968	15.00
❑ 966	Yellow Rainbow/Something	1968	12.00
❑ 1020	Blackberry Way/Something	1969	12.00
❑ 1119	This Time Tomorrow/Curly	1969	12.00
❑ 1197	Brontosaurus/Lightning Never Strikes Twice	1970	12.00
❑ 1239	When Alice Comes Back to the Farm/What?	1971	12.00
❑ 1546	Zing Went the Strings of My Heart/Wild Tiger Woman	1974	10.00
CAPITOL			
❑ 3126	Tonight/Don't Mess Me Up	1971	20.00
DERAM			
❑ 7504	The Disturbance/Night of Fear	1967	15.00
❑ 7506	I Can Hear the Grass Grow/Wave the Flag and Stop the Train	1967	15.00
MGM			
❑ 14332 [DJ]	Chinatown/Down by the Bay	1971	20.00
—Evidently not released as stock copy			
UNITED ARTISTS			
❑ XW202	Tonight/My Marge	1973	6.00
❑ 50876	Chinatown/Down on the Bay	1972	8.00
❑ 50928	Do Ya/California Man	1972	8.00
Albums			
A&M			
❑ SP-3181	Shazam	1982	10.00
—Budget-line reissue of 4259			
❑ SP-3625 [(2)]	The Best of the Move	1974	15.00
❑ SP-4259	Shazam	1969	20.00
CAPITOL			
❑ ST-658	Looking On	1971	20.00
❑ ST-811	Message from the Country	1971	20.00
UNITED ARTISTS			
❑ UAS-5666	Split Ends	1972	15.00

MOVING SIDEWALKS, THE With Billy Gibbons, later of ZZ TOP.

Number	Title (A Side/B Side)	Yr	NM
45s			
TANTARA			
❑ 3101	99th Floor/What Are You Going to Do	1967	40.00
❑ 3103	I Want to Hold Your Hand/Joe Blues	1968	40.00
❑ 3113	Flashback/(B-side unknown)	1969	30.00
WAND			
❑ 1156	99th Floor/What Are You Going to Do	1967	25.00
❑ 1167	Need Me/Every Night a New Surprise	1968	25.00
Albums			
TANTARA			
❑ 6919	Flash	1968	300.00

MOZART, MICKEY See ROBERT MAXWELL.

MUDCRUTCH Early Tom Petty and the Heartbreakers.

Number	Title (A Side/B Side)	Yr	NM
45s			
PEPPER			
❑ 9449	Up in Mississippi/Cause Is Understood	1971	400.00
SHELTER			
❑ 40357	Depot Street/Wild Eyes	1975	30.00

MUDHONEY Also see GREEN RIVER.

Number	Title (A Side/B Side)	Yr	NM
45s			
AMPHETAMINE REPTILE			
❑ Scale 36	She's Just Fifteen/Jagged Time Lapse	1991	7.50
—B-side by Halo of Flies; black vinyl			
❑ Scale 36	She's Just Fifteen/Jagged Time Lapse	1991	27.50
—B-side by Halo of Flies; burgundy vinyl			
❑ Scale 36 [PS]	She's Just Fifteen/Jagged Time Lapse	1991	7.50
❑ Scale 76	Goat Cheese/Porn Weasel	1995	5.00
—B-side by Strapping Fieldhands			
❑ Scale 76 [PS]	Porn #3: Goat Cheese/Porn Weasel	1995	5.00

Number	Title (A Side/B Side)	Yr	NM
EMPTY			
❑ MT-166	You Stupid Asshole/ Knife Manual	1991	6.00
—B-side by Gas Huffer; blue vinyl			
❑ MT-166	You Stupid Asshole/ Knife Manual	1991	6.00
—B-side by Gas Huffer; green vinyl			
❑ MT-166 [PS]	You Stupid Asshole/ Knife Manual	1991	6.00
FOX			
❑ 10012	Pump It Up/Stomp	1994	5.00
—B-side by George Clinton/Parliament Funkadelic			
❑ 10012 [PS]	Pump It Up/Stomp	1994	5.00
—B-side by George Clinton/Parliament Funkadelic			
MAKE 'EM BLEED AND SUFFER			
❑ (no #)	Hate the Police (Live)/ Symptom of the Universe	1988	25.00
—B-side by the Melvins			
❑ (no #) [PS]	Hate the Police (Live)/ Symptom of the Universe	1988	25.00
—Actually a large envelope that contained this single, which was enclosed in a Japanese porno magazine			
REPRISE			
❑ PRO-S-5740 [DJ]	Suck You Dry/Deception Pass	1992	15.00
❑ PRO-S-6025 [DJ]	Blinding Sun/King Sandbox	1993	15.00
SUB POP			
❑ 18	Touch Me I'm Sick/ Sweet Young Thing	1988	7.50
—Regular Sub Pop label, black vinyl			
❑ 18	Touch Me I'm Sick/ Sweet Young Thing	1988	90.00
—First 800 were pressed on brown vinyl			
❑ 18	Touch Me I'm Sick/ Sweet Young Thing	1988	100.00
—Standard black vinyl pressing, toilet label			
❑ 18	Touch Me I'm Sick/ Sweet Young Thing	1988	200.00
—Any of accidental purple, red, yellow or blueish vinyl pressings			
❑ 18 [PS]	Touch Me I'm Sick/Sweet Young Thing	1988	7.50
—Only accompanied regular Sub Pop label pressings			
❑ 26	Halloween/Touch Me I'm Sick	1988	15.00
—B-side by Sonic Youth; last 2,500 on black vinyl			
❑ 26	Halloween/Touch Me I'm Sick	1988	50.00
—B-side by Sonic Youth; first 500 on clear vinyl			
❑ 26 [PS]	Halloween/Touch Me I'm Sick	1988	20.00
—#2 in Sub Pop Singles Club series			
❑ 33	You Got It/Burn It Clean	1989	10.00
❑ 33	You Got It/Burn It Clean	1989	15.00
—White vinyl			
❑ 33 [PS]	You Got It/Burn It Clean	1989	5.00
—Regular picture sleeve			
❑ 33 [PS]	You Got It/Burn It Clean	1989	25.00
—Foldout poster sleeve			
❑ 44a	This Gift/Baby Help Me Forget	1989	5.00
❑ 44a	This Gift/Baby Help Me Forget	1989	30.00
—Purple vinyl			
❑ 44a [PS]	This Gift/Baby Help Me Forget	1989	5.00
❑ 63	You're Gone//Thorn/ You Make Me Die	1990	5.00
❑ 63	You're Gone//Thorn/ You Make Me Die	1990	20.00
—First 3,000 on pink vinyl			
❑ 63 [PS]	You're Gone//Thorn/ You Make Me Die	1990	5.00
❑ 95	Let It Slide//Ounce of Deception/Checkout Time	1991	3.00
❑ 95	Let It Slide//Ounce of Deception/Checkout Time	1991	25.00
—Clear chartreuse vinyl			
❑ 95 [PS]	Let It Slide//Ounce of Deception/Checkout Time	1991	5.00
❑ 248	Tonight I'm Gonna Go Downtown/Blinding Sun	1994	7.50
—B-side by Jimmie Dale Gilmore			
❑ 248 [PS]	Tonight I'm Gonna Go Downtown/Blinding Sun	1994	7.50
—B-side by Jimmie Dale Gilmore			
❑ 484	Butterfly Stroke/Editions of You	1999	5.00
—Brown vinyl			
❑ 484 [PS]	Butterfly Stroke/Editions of You	1999	5.00
—Fold-open poster sleeve; Sub Pop Singles Club, Nov 1999			
SUPER ELECTRO			
❑ SE 708	Into Your Shtik/You Give Me the Creeps	1995	4.00
❑ SE 708 [PS]	Into Your Shtik/You Give Me the Creeps	1995	5.00
❑ SE 716	Night of the Hunted/ Brand New Face	1998	4.00
❑ SE 716 [PS]	Night of the Hunted/ Brand New Face	1998	5.00
WARNER BROS.			
❑ PRO-S-5652 [DJ]	Who Is Who/Heat	1992	15.00
—Part of "Soil X Samples" series; orange vinyl; B-side by the Jesus and Mary Chain			
Albums			
REPRISE			
❑ 45477	Five Dollar Bob's Mock Cooter Stew	1993	15.00
❑ 45840	My Brother the Cow	1994	15.00
SUB POP			
❑ 21 [EP]	Superfuzz Bigmuff	1988	20.00
—Without poster			
❑ 21 [EP]	Superfuzz Bigmuff	1988	30.00
—With poster			
❑ 44	Mudhoney	1989	20.00
—Without gatefold and poster			
❑ 44	Mudhoney	1989	30.00
—First 3,000 have gatefold sleeve and poster			
❑ 105 PD [PD]	Every Good Boy Deserves Fudge	1991	30.00
—Picture disc — limited edition of 2,500			
❑ SP 500 [(3)]	March to Fuzz	2000	25.00
❑ SP-555	Since We've Become Translucent	2002	15.00
❑ 70765	Mudhoney	2008	14.00
SUPER ELECTRO			
❑ SE 10	Tomorrow Hit Today	1998	12.00

MUDLARKS, THE

Number	Title (A Side/B Side)	Yr	NM
45s			
ROULETTE			
❑ 4143	Love Game/My Grandfather's Clock	1959	12.00

MUDSLINGER, ROGER

Number	Title (A Side/B Side)	Yr	NM
45s			
RED BIRD			
❑ 10-013	The Election Year 1964 (Part 1)/ The Election Year 1964 (Part 2)	1964	20.00

MUEHLEISEN, MAURY

Lead guitarist for JIM CROCE on most, if not all, of his hits.

Number	Title (A Side/B Side)	Yr	NM
45s			
CAPITOL			
❑ 3076	I Have No Time/Just a Passing Thing	1971	6.00

MUGWUMPS, THE

Also see DENNY DOHERTY; CASS ELLIOT; ZALMAN YANOVSKY.

Number	Title (A Side/B Side)	Yr	NM
45s			
SIDEWALK			
❑ 900	Bald Headed Woman/ Jug Band Music	1966	25.00
❑ 909	Season of the Witch/My Gal	1967	20.00
WARNER BROS.			
❑ 5471	I'll Remember Tonight/ I Don't Wanna Know	1964	15.00
❑ 7018	Searchin'/Here It Is, Another Day	1967	10.00
Albums			
WARNER BROS.			
❑ W 1697 [M]	The Mugwumps	1967	25.00
❑ WS 1697 [S]	The Mugwumps	1967	30.00

MULBERRY FRUIT BAND, THE

Number	Title (A Side/B Side)	Yr	NM
45s			
BUDDAH			
❑ 1	Yes, We Have No Bananas/ The Audition	1967	12.00

MULDAUR, GEOFF

Number	Title (A Side/B Side)	Yr	NM
Albums			
FOLKLORE			
❑ FRLP-14004 [M]	Sleepy Man Blues	1964	30.00
❑ FRST-14004 [S]	Sleepy Man Blues	1964	40.00
PRESTIGE			
❑ PRST-7727	Sleepy Man Blues	1969	20.00
—Reissue of Folklore LP			

MULDAUR, GEOFF & MARIA

Number	Title (A Side/B Side)	Yr	NM
45s			
REPRISE			
❑ 0807	Open Up Your Soul/Sittin' Alone in the Moonlight	1969	8.00
Albums			
CARTHAGE			
❑ CGLP-4428	Pottery Pie	198?	10.00
REPRISE			
❑ MS 2073	Sweet Potatoes	1972	12.00

MULDAUR, MARIA

Number	Title (A Side/B Side)	Yr	NM
45s			
REPRISE			
❑ 1183	Midnight at the Oasis/ Any Old Time	1973	5.00
❑ 1319	I'm a Woman/Cool River	1974	4.00
❑ 1331	Oh Papa/Gringo de Mexico	1975	4.00
❑ 1352	Sad Eyes/Wild Bird	1976	4.00
❑ 1362	Sweet Harmony/ Jon the Generator	1976	4.00
WARNER BROS.			
❑ 8580	Make Love to the Music/I'll Keep My Light in My Window	1978	4.00
❑ 49058	Dancin' in the Street/Birds Fly South (When Winter Comes)	1979	4.00
❑ 49131	Fall in Love Again/Love Is Everything	1979	4.00
Albums			
MYRRH			
❑ MSB-6685	There Is a Love	1984	10.00
REPRISE			
❑ MS 2148	Maria Muldaur	1973	12.00
❑ MS 2194	Waitress in a Donut Shop	1974	12.00
❑ MS4-2194 [Q]	Waitress in a Donut Shop	1974	20.00
❑ MS 2235	Sweet Harmony	1976	12.00
TAKOMA			
❑ 7084	Gospel Nights	1980	10.00
TUDOR			
❑ 109902	Sweet & Sour	1983	10.00
WARNER BROS.			
❑ BSK 3162	Southern Winds	1978	10.00
❑ BSK 3305	Open Your Eyes	1979	10.00

MULL, MARTIN

Number	Title (A Side/B Side)	Yr	NM
45s			
ABC			
❑ 12251	Boogie Man/Bombed Away	1977	5.00
❑ 12304	Humming Song/Get Up, Get Down	1977	5.00
CAPRICORN			
❑ 0019	Dueling Tubas/2001 Polkas	1973	8.00
❑ 0024	In the Eyes of My Dog (Part 1)/ In the Eyes of My Dog (Part 2)	1973	8.00
❑ 0037	Santafly/Santa Doesn't Cop Out On Dope	1973	12.00
❑ 0241	Do the Dog/Thousands of Girls	1975	8.00
❑ 0282	Santafly/Santa Doesn't Cop Out On Dope	1977	10.00
ELEKTRA			
❑ 46056	The Fruit Song/Pig in a Blanket	1979	5.00
❑ 46057	Bernie Don't Disco/Bun and Run Part 1 and 3	1979	5.00
Albums			
ABC			
❑ AB-997	I'm Everyone I've Ever Loved	1977	10.00
❑ AA-1064	Sex and Violins	1978	10.00
CAPRICORN			
❑ CP 0106	Martin Mull	1972	12.00
❑ CP 0117	Martin Mull and His Fabulous Furniture	1973	12.00
❑ CP 0126	Normal	1974	12.00
❑ CP 0155	Days of Wine and Neurosis	1975	12.00
❑ CP 0195	No Hits Four Errors	1977	10.00
ELEKTRA			
❑ 6E-200	Near Perfect	1979	10.00
MCA			
❑ 795	I'm Everyone I've Ever Loved	1980	8.00
—Reissue of ABC 997			

MULTIPLICATION ROCK (SOUNDTRACK)

Number	Title (A Side/B Side)	Yr	NM
45s			
CAPITOL			
❑ 3693	Naughty Number Nine/I Got Six	1973	15.00
Albums			
CAPITOL			
❑ SJA-11174	Multiplication Rock	1973	40.00

MUMMIES, THE

Number	Title (A Side/B Side)	Yr	NM
45s			
HIT			
❑ 193	Tell Her No/For Me	1965	12.00
—B-side by Wayne Harris			

MUNGO JERRY

Number	Title (A Side/B Side)	Yr	NM
45s			
BELL			
❑ 45123	Lady Rose/Little Louis	1971	4.00
❑ 45383	Alright, Alright, Alright/ Little Miss Hipshake	1973	4.00
❑ 45427	Wild Love/Glad I'm a Rocker	1973	4.00
❑ 45451	Long Legged Woman Dressed in Black/Gonna Bop Till I Drop	1974	4.00
JANUS			
❑ 125	In the Summertime/Mighty Man	1970	6.00
❑ 128	Johnny B. Badde/My Friend	1970	5.00
❑ 148	Baby Jump/The Man Beside the Piano	1971	5.00

PYE

Number	Title (A Side/B Side)	Yr	NM
65003	You Don't Have to Be in the Army/O'Reilly	1972	4.00
65009	Going Back Home/Open Up	1972	4.00
71032	In the Summertime/(B-side unknown)	1975	4.00

Albums

JANUS

Number	Title (A Side/B Side)	Yr	NM
JLS-3027	Memoirs of a Stockbroker	1972	15.00
JXS-7000	Mungo Jerry	1970	15.00

MUNSTERS, THE

45s

DECCA

Number	Title (A Side/B Side)	Yr	NM
31670	Munster Creep/Make It Go Away	1964	20.00

Albums

DECCA

Number	Title (A Side/B Side)	Yr	NM
DL 4588 [M]	The Munsters	1964	100.00
DL 74588 [S]	The Munsters	1964	150.00

MURE, BILLY

45s

DANCO

Number	Title (A Side/B Side)	Yr	NM
506	Mon Coeur Brise (My Broken Heart)/Rose of Cherry Bay	1965	8.00

EVEREST

Number	Title (A Side/B Side)	Yr	NM
19335	Jambalaya (On the Bayou)/Kaw-Liga	1960	10.00

FORD

Number	Title (A Side/B Side)	Yr	NM
2552	See the Fait from the Air/See Lanny Ross	1963	10.00

MGM

Number	Title (A Side/B Side)	Yr	NM
K13161	Maria Elena/In the Cool of the Day	1963	8.00
K13190	Fascination/Mona Lisa	1963	8.00
K13252	Ma, What Time Is It/Sticky Fingers	1964	8.00

—With Benny Mure

Number	Title (A Side/B Side)	Yr	NM
K13565	Five Foot Two, Eyes of Blue/Yes Sir, That's My Baby	1966	8.00

PARIS

Number	Title (A Side/B Side)	Yr	NM
545	Theme for the Lonely/Ambush	1960	10.00

RCA VICTOR

Number	Title (A Side/B Side)	Yr	NM
47-7394	Haggis Baggis/Tara Lara	1958	15.00

RIVERSIDE

Number	Title (A Side/B Side)	Yr	NM
4547	Diamonds/String of Guitars	1963	10.00

SPLASH

Number	Title (A Side/B Side)	Yr	NM
800	A String of Trumpets/Tea and Trumpets	1959	12.00

—As "Billy Mure and the Trumpeteers"

Number	Title (A Side/B Side)	Yr	NM
800	A String of Trumpets/Tea and Trumpets	1959	12.00

—As "The Trumpeteers"

SRG

Number	Title (A Side/B Side)	Yr	NM
102	Theme for the Lonely/Little Reuben	1960	15.00

STRAND

Number	Title (A Side/B Side)	Yr	NM
25037	Hawaiian Drums/Pink Hawaii	1961	8.00

7-Inch Extended Plays

RCA VICTOR

Number	Title (A Side/B Side)	Yr	NM
EPA-4271	(contents unknown)	1958	12.00
EPA-4271 [PS]	The Big Guitar	1958	12.00

Albums

EVEREST

Number	Title (A Side/B Side)	Yr	NM
SDBR-1067 [S]	A String of Trumpets	1960	30.00
SDBR-1072 [S]	Songs of Hank Williams	1960	30.00
SDBR-1120 [S]	Strictly Cha-Cha-Cha	1961	30.00
LPBR-5067 [M]	A String of Trumpets	1960	20.00
LPBR-5072 [M]	Songs of Hank Williams	1960	20.00
LPBR-5120 [M]	Strictly Cha-Cha-Cha	1961	20.00

KAPP

Number	Title (A Side/B Side)	Yr	NM
KL-1253 [M]	Tough Strings	1961	20.00
KS-3253 [S]	Tough Strings	1961	30.00

MGM

Number	Title (A Side/B Side)	Yr	NM
E-3780 [M]	Supersonic Guitars	1959	30.00
SE-3780 [S]	Supersonic Guitars	1959	50.00
E-3807 [M]	Supersonic Guitars, Vol. 2	1959	30.00
SE-3807 [S]	Supersonic Guitars, Vol. 2	1959	50.00
E-4131 [M]	Teen Bossa Nova	1963	20.00
SE-4131 [S]	Teen Bossa Nova	1963	30.00
E-4189 [M]	Maria Elena and Other Great Songs	1964	20.00
SE-4189 [S]	Maria Elena and Other Great Songs	1964	30.00
E-4406 [M]	Happy Guitars	1966	20.00
SE-4406 [S]	Happy Guitars	1966	25.00

PREMIER

Number	Title (A Side/B Side)	Yr	NM
PM-9014 [M]	Blue Hawaii	196?	10.00

—Side 1 by Billy Mure; Side 2 by Harry Kaapuni and His Royal Hawaiians

RCA VICTOR

Number	Title (A Side/B Side)	Yr	NM
LPM-1536 [M]	Supersonic Guitars in Hi-Fi	1957	40.00
LPM-1694 [M]	Fireworks	1958	30.00
LSP-1694 [S]	Fireworks	1958	40.00
LPM-1869 [M]	Supersonic in Flight	1959	30.00
LSP-1869 [S]	Supersonic in Flight	1959	50.00

SPIN-O-RAMA

Number	Title (A Side/B Side)	Yr	NM
S 147 [M]	Blue Hawaii	196?	10.00

—Side 1 by Billy Mure; Side 2 by Harry Kaapuni and His Royal Hawaiians

Number	Title (A Side/B Side)	Yr	NM
S 157 [M]	Hawaiian Moods	196?	10.00

—One side by Billy Mure; one side by Luke Leilani

STRAND

Number	Title (A Side/B Side)	Yr	NM
SL-1010 [M]	Hawaiian Percussion	1961	25.00
SLS-1010 [S]	Hawaiian Percussion	1961	40.00
SL-1021 [M]	'Round the World in Percussion	1961	25.00
SLS-1021 [S]	'Round the World in Percussion	1961	40.00
SL-1070 [M]	Pink Hawaii	1962	20.00
SLS-1070 [S]	Pink Hawaii	1962	30.00

SUNSET

Number	Title (A Side/B Side)	Yr	NM
SUS-5173	Songs of Hank Williams	196?	12.00

—Reissue of Everest SDBR-1072 with fewer tracks

UNITED ARTISTS

Number	Title (A Side/B Side)	Yr	NM
UAL-3031 [M]	Bandstand Record Hop	1959	40.00
UAS-6031 [S]	Bandstand Record Hop	1959	60.00

MURMAIDS, THE

45s

CHATTAHOOCHIE

Number	Title (A Side/B Side)	Yr	NM
628	Popsicles and Icicles/Bunny Stomp	1963	15.00
628	Popsicles and Icicles/Comedy and Tragedy	1963	15.00
628	Popsicles and Icicles/Huntington Flats	1963	15.00
628	Popsicles and Icicles/Blue Dress	1963	20.00
636	Heartbreak Ahead/He's Good to Me	1964	10.00
641	Wild and Wonderful/Bull Talk	1964	10.00
668	Stuffed Animals/Little White Lies	1965	10.00
711	Little Boys/Go Away	1966	10.00

LIBERTY

Number	Title (A Side/B Side)	Yr	NM
56069	Paper Sun/Song Through Perception	1968	—

—Unreleased

Number	Title (A Side/B Side)	Yr	NM
56078	Paper Sun/Song Through Perception	1968	10.00

Albums

CHATTAHOOCHEE

Number	Title (A Side/B Side)	Yr	NM
CHLP-628 [M]	The Mermaids Resurface!	1981	30.00

MURPHEY, MICHAEL

Also includes records as "Michael Martin Murphey."

45s

A&M

Number	Title (A Side/B Side)	Yr	NM
1368	Geronimo's Cadillac/Boy from the Country	1972	5.00
1368 [PS]	Geronimo's Cadillac/Boy from the Country	1972	6.00
1447	Cosmic Cowboy/Temperature Train	1973	5.00
1459	Calico Silver/Blessing in Disguise	1973	5.00
1712	Geronimo's Cadillac/Blessing in Disguise	1975	4.00

EMI AMERICA

Number	Title (A Side/B Side)	Yr	NM
8243	What She Wants/Still Taking Chances	1984	3.00
8243 [PS]	What She Wants/Still Taking Chances	1984	3.00
8265	Carolina in the Pines/Cherokee Fiddle	1985	3.00

EPIC

Number	Title (A Side/B Side)	Yr	NM
02075	Take It As It Comes/Hard Country	1981	4.00

—A-side with Katy Moffatt

Number	Title (A Side/B Side)	Yr	NM
11130	Holy Roller/Rye By-The-Sea	1974	4.00
11130 [PS]	Holy Roller/Rye By-The-Sea	1974	6.00
50014	You Can Only Say So Much/Fort Worth, I Love You	1974	4.00
50084	Wildfire/Night Thunder	1975	5.00
50131	Carolina in the Pines/Without My Lady There	1975	4.00
50184	Mansion on the Hill/Renegade	1976	4.00
50214	Rhythm of the Road/Swans Against the Sun	1976	4.00
50319	Cherokee Fiddler/Running Wide Open	1976	4.00
50369	Changing Woman/A North Wind and a New Moon	1977	4.00
50540	Nothing Is Your Own/Song Day	1978	4.00
50572	Paradise Tonight/Song Dog	1978	4.00
50686	Lightning/Chain Gang	1979	4.00
50739	South Coast/Backsliders Wine	1979	4.00

LIBERTY

Number	Title (A Side/B Side)	Yr	NM
1455	Lost River/The Two-Step Is Easy	1982	3.00
1466	What's Forever For/Crystal	1982	3.00
1486	Still Taking Chances/Lost River	1982	3.00
1494	Crystal/Love Affairs	1983	3.00
1505	The Heart Never Lies/Don't Count the Rainy Days	1983	3.00
1505 [PS]	The Heart Never Lies/Don't Count the Rainy Days	1983	4.00
1514	Will It Be Love by Morning/Goodbye Money Mountain	1983	3.00
1514 [PS]	Will It Be Love by Morning/Goodbye Money Mountain	1983	4.00
1517	Disenchanted/Sacred Heart	1984	3.00

—Starting here, as "Michael Martin Murphey"

Number	Title (A Side/B Side)	Yr	NM
1523	Radio Land/The Heart Never Lies	1984	3.00

WARNER BROS.

Number	Title (A Side/B Side)	Yr	NM
PRO-S-2869 [DJ]	Colorado Christmas/The Cowboy's Christmas Ball	1987	6.00

—B-side by Nitty Gritty Dirt Band

Number	Title (A Side/B Side)	Yr	NM
7-18321	Big Iron/Cowboy Logic	1993	4.00
18928	I Don't Do Floors/I'm Gonna Miss You Girl	1992	3.00
19290	What Am I Doin' Here/Where Do Cowboys Go When They Die-Reincarnation	1991	3.00
19412	Let the Cowboy Dance/Red River Valley	1991	3.00
19724	Cowboy Logic/Spanish Is the Lovin' Tongue	1990	3.00
22666	Route 66/Juke Box	1990	3.00
22765	Family Tree/Wood Smoke in the Wind	1989	3.00
22970	Never Givin' Up on Love/Desperation Road	1989	3.00
22970 [PS]	Never Givin' Up on Love/Desperation Road	1989	4.00
27668	From the Word Go/Vanishing Breed	1989	3.00
27810	Pilgrims on the Way (Matthew's Song)/Still Got the Fire	1988	3.00
27947	Talkin' to the Wrong Man/What Am I Doin' Hangin' 'Round	1988	3.00
27947 [PS]	Talkin' to the Wrong Man/What Am I Doin' Hangin' 'Round	1988	3.00
28168	I'm Gonna Miss You, Girl/Running Blood	1987	3.00
28370	A Long Line of Love/Worlds Apart	1987	3.00
28471	A Face in the Crowd/You're History	1987	3.00

—With Holly Dunn

Number	Title (A Side/B Side)	Yr	NM
28598	Fiddlin' Man/Ghost Town (Messages from the Ghost Ranch)	1986	3.00
28694	Rollin' Nowhere/Face-2-Face with the Night	1986	3.00
28797	Tonight We Ride/Santa Fe Cantina	1986	3.00

Albums

A&M

Number	Title (A Side/B Side)	Yr	NM
SP-3134	Geronimo's Cadillac	198?	8.00

—Budget-line reissue

Number	Title (A Side/B Side)	Yr	NM
SP-3137	Cosmic Cowboy Souvenir	198?	8.00

—Budget-line reissue

Number	Title (A Side/B Side)	Yr	NM
SP-4358	Geronimo's Cadillac	1972	12.00
SP-4388	Cosmic Cowboy Souvenir	1973	12.00

EMI AMERICA

Number	Title (A Side/B Side)	Yr	NM
LN-10310	The Heart Never Lies	1986	8.00

—Budget-line reissue

Number	Title (A Side/B Side)	Yr	NM
ST-17143	The Best of Michael Martin Murphey	1984	10.00

EPIC

Number	Title (A Side/B Side)	Yr	NM
KE 32835	Michael Murphey	1974	12.00
KE 33290	Blue Sky — Night Thunder	1975	10.00
PE 33290	Blue Sky — Night Thunder	197?	8.00

—Reissue with new prefix & dark blue label

Number	Title (A Side/B Side)	Yr	NM
PE 33851	Swans Against the Sun	1975	10.00
PEQ 33851 [Q]	Swans Against the Sun	1975	16.00
PE 34220	Flowing Free Forever	1976	10.00
JE 35013	Lonewolf	1978	10.00
JE 35742	Peaks, Valleys, Honky-Tonks & Alleys	1979	10.00

LIBERTY

Number	Title (A Side/B Side)	Yr	NM
LT-51120	Michael Martin Murphey	1982	10.00
LT-51150	The Heart Never Lies	1983	10.00

WARNER BROS.

Number	Title (A Side/B Side)	Yr	NM
25369	Tonight We Ride	1986	10.00
25500	Americana	1987	10.00
25644	River of Time	1988	10.00
25894	Land of Enchantment	1989	12.00

MURPHY, BILL

45s

HIT

Number	Title (A Side/B Side)	Yr	NM
28	Devil Woman/Little Diane	1962	8.00

—B-side by Ed Van Zandt

MURPHY, KEITH, AND THE DAZE

45s

KING

Number	Title (A Side/B Side)	Yr	NM
❑ 6171	Dirty Ol' Sam/Slightly Reminiscent of Her	1968	100.00

MURRAY, JACK

45s

LAURIE

Number	Title (A Side/B Side)	Yr	NM
❑ 3199	Surfin' with Me/What Do You Think of Me Baby	1963	15.00

MURRAY, RAY, AND THE DYNAMICS

45s

ARBO

Number	Title (A Side/B Side)	Yr	NM
❑ 222	With All My Love/Baby, What You Want Me to Do	1960	100.00

MURRAY THE "K" Also see VARIOUS ARTISTS COLLECTIONS.

45s

Number	Title (A Side/B Side)	Yr	NM
BRS			
❑ 1/2	Murray the "K" and The Beatles As It Happened	1964	40.00
❑ 1/2 [PS]	Murray the "K" and The Beatles As It Happened	1964	120.00
IBC			
❑ F4KM-0082/3	Murray the "K" and The Beatles As It Happened	1976	10.00
❑ F4KM-0082/3 [PS]	Murray the "K" and The Beatles As It Happened	1976	10.00
RED BIRD			
❑ 10-045	It's What's Happening, Baby/Sins of a Family	1966	15.00

MUSIC ASYLUM, THE

45s

ASCOT

Number	Title (A Side/B Side)	Yr	NM
❑ 2238	Yesterday's Children/I Need Someone (The Painter)	1967	10.00

Albums

UNITED ARTISTS

Number	Title (A Side/B Side)	Yr	NM
❑ UAS-6778	Commit Thyself	1970	20.00

MUSIC CITY FIVE, THE

45s

HIT

Number	Title (A Side/B Side)	Yr	NM
❑ 62	Pipeline/Don't Say Nothin' Bad About My Baby	1963	8.00
—B-side by Clara Wilson			
❑ 72	Sukiyaki/Tie Me Kangaroo Down, Sport	1963	8.00
—B-side by Sylvester McCord			
❑ 76	Wipe Out/Judy's Turn to Cry	1963	8.00
—B-side by Katy Richards			
❑ 87	Washington Square/Donna the Prima Donna	1963	8.00
—As "The Music City Five & Ten"; B-side by Ed Hardin			
❑ 91	Maria Elena/The Matador	1963	8.00
—B-side by Harvey Frolic			

MUSIC CITY ORCHESTRA, THE

45s

HIT

Number	Title (A Side/B Side)	Yr	NM
❑ 20	The Stripper/Speedy Gonzales	1962	8.00
—B-side by Tom Walls			
❑ 49	Walk Right In/From a Jack to a King	1963	8.00
—B-side by Jackie Ott			
❑ 70	Sukiyaki/Hello Stranger	1963	8.00
—As "The Music City Chorus and Orchestra featuring Samayami"; B-side by Alpha Zoe			
❑ 195	Berlin Melody/Ferry Cross the Mersey	1965	8.00
—B-side by Johnny LaFlore			
❑ 210	Supercalifragilisticexpialidocious/Chim Chim Cheree	1965	8.00
—As "The Music City Orchestra and Chorus"			

MUSIC CITY SINGERS, THE

45s

HIT

Number	Title (A Side/B Side)	Yr	NM
❑ 112	Don't Let the Rain Come Down/Suspicion	1964	8.00
—B-side by Ed Hardin			
❑ 119	Love Me with All Your Heart/Cotton Candy	1964	8.00
—B-side by the Nashville Five			
❑ 129	Today/Beans in My Ears	1964	8.00

MUSIC CITY SOUNDS, THE

45s

MGM

Number	Title (A Side/B Side)	Yr	NM
❑ 14132	My Happiness/Gotta Travel On	1970	8.00
❑ 14168	Tennessee Waltz/Release Me	1970	8.00

Albums

MGM

Number	Title (A Side/B Side)	Yr	NM
❑ SE-4672	The Music City Sounds Featuring Lloyd Green and Pete Wade	1970	15.00

MUSIC COMPANY, THE

Albums

Number	Title (A Side/B Side)	Yr	NM
CRESTVIEW			
❑ CRS-3057	Hard and Heavy	196?	25.00
MIRWOOD			
❑ M-7002 [M]	Rubber Soul Jazz	1966	20.00
❑ MS-7002 [S]	Rubber Soul Jazz	1966	25.00

MUSIC EXPLOSION, THE

45s

Number	Title (A Side/B Side)	Yr	NM
ATTACK			
❑ 1404	The Little Black Egg/Stay By My Side	1966	25.00
LAURIE			
❑ 3380	Little Bit O'Soul/I See the Light	1967	12.00
❑ 3400	Can't Stop Now/Sunshine Games	1967	8.00
❑ 3414	We Gotta Go Home Hearts and Flowers	1967	8.00
❑ 3429	What You Want/Road Runner	1968	8.00
❑ 3440	Where Are We Going/Flash	1968	8.00
❑ 3454	Yes Sir/Dazzling	1968	8.00
❑ 3466	Jack in the Box/Rewind	1968	8.00
❑ 3479	What's Your Name/Call Me Anything	1969	8.00
❑ 3500	The Little Black Egg/Stay By My Side	1969	8.00

Albums

LAURIE

Number	Title (A Side/B Side)	Yr	NM
❑ LLP-2040 [M]	Little Bit O'Soul	1967	20.00
❑ SLLP-2040 [S]	Little Bit O'Soul	1967	25.00

MUSIC MACHINE, THE Also see T.S. BONNIWELL.

45s

Number	Title (A Side/B Side)	Yr	NM
BELL			
❑ 764	Mother Nature—Father Earth/Advise and Consent	1969	8.00
ORIGINAL SOUND			
❑ (no #) [PS]	The Music Machine	1967	10.00
—Custom sleeve, large center hole, not assigned to any one record, with pictures of band members on front and ads for "Oldies But Goodies" LPs on back			
❑ 61	Talk Talk/Come On In	1966	12.00
❑ 67	The People in Me/Masculine Institution	1967	10.00
❑ 71	Double Yellow Line/Absolutely Positive	1967	10.00
❑ 75	I've Loved You/The Eagle Never Hunts the Fly	1967	10.00
❑ 82	Hey Joe/Wrong	1968	10.00
SUNDAZED			
❑ 131	Point of No Return/King Mixer	199?	2.00
❑ 131 [PS]	Point of No Return/King Mixer	199?	2.00
WARNER BROS.			
❑ 7093	Bottom of the Soul/Astrologically Incompatible	1968	8.00
❑ 7093 [PS]	Bottom of the Soul/Astrologically Incompatible	1968	15.00
❑ 7199	To the Light/You'll Love Me Again	1968	8.00

Albums

Number	Title (A Side/B Side)	Yr	NM
ORIGINAL SOUND			
❑ 5015 [M]	(Turn On) The Music Machine	1966	40.00
❑ 8875 [S]	(Turn On) The Music Machine	1966	50.00
SUNDAZED			
❑ LP 5038	Ignition	2000	12.00
WARNER BROS.			
❑ W 1732 [M]	Bonniwell's Music Machine	1967	25.00
❑ WS 1732 [S]	Bonniwell's Music Machine	1967	40.00

MY BLOODY VALENTINE

12-Inch Singles

Number	Title (A Side/B Side)	Yr	NM
RELATIVITY			
❑ 88561-1016-1	Soft as Snow/Feed Me With Your Kiss/You're Still in a Dream/Slow/Instrumental	1989	20.00
SIRE			
❑ PRO-A-4512 [DJ]	Soon/Glider/Don't Ask Why/Off Your Face	1990	8.00

Albums

CREATION/RELATIVITY

Number	Title (A Side/B Side)	Yr	NM
❑ 1006	Isn't Anything	1989	30.00

MYDDLE CLASS, THE

45s

Number	Title (A Side/B Side)	Yr	NM
BUDDAH			
❑ 150	I Happen to Love You/Don't Let Me Sleep Too Long	1969	10.00
TOMORROW			
❑ 912	Don't Look Back/Wind Chimes Laughter	1966	20.00
❑ 7501	Gates of Eden/Free As the Wind	1966	20.00
❑ 7503	I Happen to Love You/Don't Let Me Sleep Too Long	1966	25.00

MYLES, BILLY

45s

Number	Title (A Side/B Side)	Yr	NM
DOT			
❑ 15809	King of Clowns/So In Need of You	1958	20.00
EMBER			
❑ 1026	The Joker (That's What They Call Me)/Honey Bee	1957	30.00
❑ 1040	Price of Your Love/I'm Too Sentimental	1958	25.00
❑ 1046	I'm Gonna Walk/Price of Your Love	1958	25.00
KING			
❑ 5395	Dance Little Girlie/Two Empty Arms	1960	15.00
LOST-NITE			
❑ 425	The Joker (That's What They Call Me)/Honey Bee	197?	5.00
—Reissue			

MYRICK, GARY, AND THE FIGURES

12-Inch Singles

Number	Title (A Side/B Side)	Yr	NM
EPIC			
❑ AS 1694 [DJ]	Guitar, Talk, Love & Drums (Extended Special Version)/(Short Special Version)	1983	10.00
—Etched cartoon on B-side			
GEFFEN			
❑ PRO-A-2349 [DJ]	When Angels Kiss/I Stand for Love	1985	8.00
❑ PRO-A-2403 [DJ]	Hearts Pound (Like a Rhythm Machine) (same on both sides)	1985	8.00

45s

Number	Title (A Side/B Side)	Yr	NM
EPIC			
❑ AE7 1303 [DJ]	Living in a Movie/My Girl (It's Simple)	1981	5.00
❑ AE7 1303 [PS]	Living in a Movie/My Girl (It's Simple)	1981	5.00
—"Film can" sleeve with bio insert			
❑ 04009	Message Is You/Glamorous	1983	3.00
❑ 50937	She Talks in Stereo/Model	1980	3.00
GEFFEN			
❑ 28905	When Angels Kiss/I Was a Painted Picture	1985	3.00

7-Inch Extended Plays

EPIC

Number	Title (A Side/B Side)	Yr	NM
❑ AE7 1207 [DJ]	She Talks in Stereo/Ever Since the World Began//Deep in the Heartland/The Party	1980	8.00

Albums

Number	Title (A Side/B Side)	Yr	NM
EPIC			
❑ AS 912 [DJ]	Talks in Stereo	1981	40.00
—Side one has studio tracks, side two has live versions of songs on side one			
❑ AS 1389 [DJ]	Live Sampler	1982	16.00
—Four live tracks, including one unreleased song			
❑ JE 36524	Gary Myrick and the Figures	1981	10.00
—Reissue with amended prefix			
❑ NJE 36524	Gary Myrick and the Figures	1980	12.00
❑ ARE 37429	Living in a Movie	1981	10.00
❑ B5E 38637 [EP]	Language	1983	10.00
GEFFEN			
❑ GHS 24076	Stand for Love	1985	10.00

MYSTERIOUS FLYING ORCHESTRA, THE

Albums

RCA VICTOR

Number	Title (A Side/B Side)	Yr	NM
❑ APL1-2137	The Mysterious Flying Orchestra	1977	20.00

MYSTERY TOUR, THE

45s

Number	Title (A Side/B Side)	Yr	NM
MGM			
❑ 14097	The Ballad of Paul/The Ballad of Paul (Follow the Bouncing Ball)	1969	25.00

MYSTIC ASTROLOGICAL CRYSTAL BAND, THE

45s

Number	Title (A Side/B Side)	Yr	NM
CAROLE			
❑ 1004	Flowers Never Cry/(B-side unknown)	1967	25.00

Albums

Number	Title (A Side/B Side)	Yr	NM
CAROLE			
❑ 8001 [M]	Mystic Astrological Crystal Band	1967	25.00
❑ S-8001 [S]	Mystic Astrological Crystal Band	1967	30.00
❑ S-8003	Clip Out, Put On Book	1968	30.00

MYSTIC MOODS ORCHESTRA, THE

45s

Number	Title (A Side/B Side)	Yr	NM
PHILIPS			
❑ 40366	Fire Island/A Dream	1966	6.00
❑ 40419	Theme from "The Sand Pebbles"/Wednesday's Child	1966	6.00
❑ 40581	Medley: Sounds of Silence-Canticle-Scarborough Fair/Homeward Bound	1969	5.00
❑ 40623	Early Morning Rain/Lalena	1969	5.00
❑ 40623 [PS]	Early Morning Rain/Lalena	1969	10.00
❑ 40659	Love Token/Green, Green Grass of Home	1970	5.00
❑ 40696	Love Grows (Where My Rosemary Goes)/Early in the Morning	1971	4.00
SOUNDBIRD			
❑ 5002	Honeytrippin'/Midnight Snack	197?	4.00
WARNER BROS.			
❑ 7686	Awakening/Cosmic Sea	1973	4.00
❑ 7743	Astral Trip/Drifting Thought	1973	4.00
❑ 7817	Your Place or Mine/Any Way You Want It	1974	4.00

Albums

Number	Title (A Side/B Side)	Yr	NM
BAINBRIDGE			
❑ 6201	More Than Music	1982	6.00
❑ 6202	Moods for a Stormy Night	1982	6.00
—Reissue of Sound Bird 7504			
❑ 6203	Mexico!	1982	6.00
❑ 6204	Nightide	1982	6.00
—Reissue of Sound Bird 7502			
❑ 6205	One Stormy Night	1982	6.00
—Reissue of Sound Bird 7501			
❑ 6206	Emotions	1982	6.00
—Reissue of Sound Bird 7505			
❑ 6207	Love Token	1982	6.00
❑ 6208	Stormy Weekend	1982	6.00
—Reissue of Sound Bird 7506			
❑ 6209	Highway One	1982	6.00
❑ 6210	English Muffins	1982	6.00
❑ 6211	Country Lovin' Folk	1982	6.00
—Reissue of Sound Bird 8512			
❑ 6212	Extensions	1982	6.00
❑ 6215	Erogenous	1982	6.00
—Reissue of Sound Bird 7509			
❑ 6216	Another Stormy Night	1983	8.00
❑ 6219	Summer Moods	1985	8.00
MOBILE FIDELITY			
❑ 1-001	Emotions	1979	25.00
—Audiophile vinyl			
❑ 1-002	Cosmic Forces	1979	25.00
—Audiophile vinyl			
❑ 1-003	Stormy Weekend	1979	25.00
—Audiophile vinyl			
PHILIPS			
❑ PHM 200205 [M]	One Stormy Night	1966	12.00
❑ PHM 200213 [M]	Nightide	1966	12.00
❑ PHM 200231 [M]	More Than Music	1967	15.00
❑ PHM 200250 [M]	Mexican Trip	1967	15.00
❑ PHM 200260 [M]	The Mystic Moods of Love	1968	15.00
❑ PHS 600205 [S]	One Stormy Night	1966	15.00
❑ PHS 600213 [S]	Nightide	1966	15.00
❑ PHS 600231 [S]	More Than Music	1967	12.00
❑ PHS 600250 [S]	Mexican Trip	1967	12.00
❑ PHS 600260 [S]	The Mystic Moods of Love	1968	12.00
❑ PHS 600277	Emotions	1968	12.00
❑ PHS 600301	Extensions	1969	12.00
❑ PHS 600321	Love Token	1969	12.00
❑ PHS 600342	Stormy Weekend	1970	12.00
❑ PHS 600349	English Muffins	1970	12.00
❑ PHS 600351	Country Lovin' Folk	1971	12.00
SOUND BIRD			
❑ 7501	One Stormy Night	1975	8.00
—Reissue of Warner Bros. 2594			
❑ 7502	Nightide	1975	8.00
—Reissue of Warner Bros. 2593			
❑ 7503	Man and...	1975	8.00
❑ 7504	Moods for a Stormy Night	1975	8.00
❑ 7505	Emotions	1975	8.00
❑ 7506	Stormy Weekend	1975	8.00
—Reissue of Warner Bros. 2596			
❑ 7507	Touch	1975	8.00
❑ SQ 7507 [Q]	Touch	1975	12.00
❑ 7508	Love the One You're With	1975	8.00
—Reissue of Warner Bros. 2577			
❑ SQ 7508 [Q]	Love the One You're With	1975	12.00
—Reissue of Warner Bros. BS4 2577			
❑ 7509	Erogenous	1975	8.00
—Reissue of Warner Bros. 2786			
❑ SQ 7509 [Q]	Erogenous	1975	12.00
—Reissue of Warner Bros. BS4 2786			
❑ 7510	Being with You	1976	10.00
❑ SQ 7510 [Q]	Being with You	1976	16.00
❑ 8503	Misty	1978	8.00
❑ 8505	Midnight	1978	8.00
❑ 8508	Alone Together	1978	8.00
❑ 8510	Being with You	1978	8.00
—Reissue of Sound Bird 7510			
❑ 8511	Cosmic Forces	1978	8.00
❑ 8512	Country Lovin' Folk	1978	8.00
❑ 8514	Simple	1978	8.00
WARNER BROS.			
❑ BS 2577	Love the One You're With	1972	12.00
❑ BS4 2577 [Q]	Love the One You're With	1974	16.00
❑ BS 2593	Nightide	1972	10.00
—Reissue of Philips 600-213			
❑ BS 2594	One Stormy Night	1972	10.00
—Reissue of Philips 600-205			
❑ BS 2595	Love Token	1972	10.00
—Reissue of Philips 600-321			
❑ BS 2596	Stormy Weekend	1972	10.00
—Reissue of Philips 600-342			
❑ BS 2597	Emotions	1972	10.00
—Reissue of Philips 600-277			
❑ BS 2598	The Mystic Moods of Love	1972	10.00
—Reissue of Philips 600-260			
❑ BS 2648	Highway One	1973	12.00
❑ BS4 2648 [Q]	Highway One	1974	16.00
❑ BS 2690	Awakening	1973	12.00
❑ BS4 2690 [Q]	Awakening	1974	16.00
❑ BS 2745	Clear Light	1974	12.00
❑ BS4 2745 [Q]	Clear Light	1974	16.00
❑ BS 2786	Erogenous	1974	10.00
❑ BS4 2786 [Q]	Erogenous	1974	16.00

MYSTIC NUMBER NATIONAL BANK, THE

Albums

Number	Title (A Side/B Side)	Yr	NM
PROBE			
❑ CPLP-4501	The Mystic Number National Bank	1969	20.00

MYSTIC SIVA

Albums

Number	Title (A Side/B Side)	Yr	NM
VO			
❑ 19713	Mystic Siva	1971	1000.

MYSTICS, THE

45s

Number	Title (A Side/B Side)	Yr	NM
AMBIENT SOUND			
❑ 02871	Now That Summer Is Here/Prayer to An Angel	1982	5.00
BLACK CAT			
❑ 101	Snoopy/Ooh Poo Pah Doo	1966	40.00
CONSTELLATION			
❑ 138	She's Got Everything/Just a Loser	1964	12.00
DOT			
❑ 16862	Now and For Always/Didn't We Have a Good Time	1966	10.00
KING			
❑ 5678	Mashed Potatoes With Me/The Hoppy Hop	1962	15.00
❑ 5735	The Jumpin' Bean/Just For Your Love	1963	15.00
LAURIE			
❑ 3028 [M]	Hushabye/Adam and Eve	1959	30.00
❑ S-3028 [S]	Hushabye/Adam and Eve	1959	120.00
❑ 3038	Don't Take the Stars/So Tenderly	1959	25.00
❑ 3047	All Through the Night/To Think of You Again	1960	25.00
❑ 3058	White Cliffs of Dover/Blue Star	1960	25.00
❑ 3086	Star Crossed Lovers/Goodbye Mr. Blue	1961	25.00
❑ 3104	Sunday Kind of Love/Darling I Know How	1961	30.00
NOLTA			
❑ 353	The Fox/Dan	1963	15.00

Albums

Number	Title (A Side/B Side)	Yr	NM
AMBIENT SOUND			
❑ FZ 37716	Crazy for You	1982	10.00
COLLECTABLES			
❑ COL-5043	16 Golden Classics	198?	10.00

N

N.W.A.

12-Inch Singles

Number	Title (A Side/B Side)	Yr	NM
PRIORITY			
❑ SPRO 81104 [DJ]	Express Yourself (Radio Edit) (Instrumental) (Explicit LP)/Straight Outta Comption (Radio Edit) (Instrumental) (Explicit LP)	1998	20.00
—A-side featuring Silkk The Shocker; B-side featuring King Tee, MC Eiht and Dre			
RUTHLESS			
❑ MRC 1034	Panic Zone/Dope Man (2 versions)/B-Ball (2 versions)	1987	40.00
❑ 7263	Gangsta Gangsta (LP Version) (Radio Edit)//Something Like That/Quiet on Tha Set/Something 2 Dance 2	1989	25.00
❑ 7291	100 Miles and Runnin' (unknown versions)	1990	12.00

45s

Number	Title (A Side/B Side)	Yr	NM
RUTHLESS			
❑ 7206	Express Yourself/Straight Outta Compton	1989	10.00
❑ 7206 [PS]	Express Yourself/Straight Outta Compton	1989	10.00

Albums

Number	Title (A Side/B Side)	Yr	NM
PRIORITY			
❑ SPRO 30080 [DJ]	Greatest Hits/In-Store Play	1996	20.00
—Promo-only "clean" versions for retailer use			
RUTHLESS			
❑ MRC 1057	N.W.A. and the Posse	1987	25.00
❑ 7224 [EP]	100 Miles and Runnin'	1990	15.00
❑ 50561 [(2)]	Greatest Hits	1996	15.00
❑ 57102	Straight Outta Compton	1989	20.00
❑ 57119	N.W.A. and the Posse	1990	15.00
—Reissue of MRC 1057			
❑ 57126	Efil4zaggin (Niggaz4life)	1991	20.00

NABAY

45s

Number	Title (A Side/B Side)	Yr	NM
IMPACT			
❑ 1032	Believe It or Not/(Instrumental)	1967	3000.

NADER, RICHARD

See VARIOUS ARTISTS COLLECTIONS.

NAGLE, RON

Albums

Number	Title (A Side/B Side)	Yr	NM
WARNER BROS.			
❑ WS 1902	Bad Rice	1970	20.00

NAKED RAYGUN

12-Inch Singles

Number	Title (A Side/B Side)	Yr	NM
CAROLINE			
❑ 1455	Treason//Mr. Gridlock/I Don't Know	199?	30.00
—Numbered limited edition of 2,500 on pink vinyl			

45s

Number	Title (A Side/B Side)	Yr	NM
SANDPOUNDER			
❑ SR 001	Vanilla Blue/Slim	1987	3.00
—Blue and white vinyl			
❑ SR 001 [PS]	Vanilla Blue/Slim	1987	3.00

7-Inch Extended Plays

Number	Title (A Side/B Side)	Yr	NM
RUTHLESS			
❑ (# unknown)	Flammable Solid	1983	50.00
❑ (# unknown) [PS]	Flammable Solid	1983	50.00
—With stickered cover and parchment lyric sheet			

Albums

Number	Title (A Side/B Side)	Yr	NM
CAROLINE			
❑ 1348	Jettison	1988	20.00
❑ 1371	Understand?	1989	20.00
❑ 1642	Raygun...Naked Raygun	1990	20.00
HAUNTED TOWN			
❑ HTR 11	Free Shit	2001	10.00
HOMESTEAD			
❑ HMS 008	Throb Throb	1984	20.00
—Second edition has lyric innersleeve			
❑ HMS 008	Throb Throb	1984	30.00
—First edition has lyric sheet			
❑ HMS 045	All Rise	1985	30.00

Except when noted otherwise, VG = 25% of NM, and VG+ = 50% of NM. (Example: VG = $2.00, VG+ = $4.00 and NM = $8.00.)

Number	Title (A Side/B Side)	Yr	NM
RUTHLESS			
❑ 03 [EP]	Basement Screams	1983	80.00

NAPOLEON XIV

Number	Title (A Side/B Side)	Yr	NM
45s			
WARNER BROS.			
❑ 5831	They're Coming to Take Me Away, Ha-Haaa!/Yawa Em Ekat ot Gnimoc Er'yeht, !Aaah-Ah	1966	12.00
❑ 5853	I'm in Love with My Little Red Tricycle/Doin' the Napoleon	1966	10.00
❑ 7726	They're Coming to Take Me Away, Ha-Haaa!/!Aaah-Ah, Yawa Em Ekat ot Gnimoc Er'yeht	1973	8.00
Albums			
RHINO			
❑ RNLP 816	They're Coming to Take Me Away, Ha-Haaa!	1985	12.00
WARNER BROS.			
❑ W 1661 [M]	They're Coming to Take Me Away, Ha-Haaa!	1966	60.00
❑ WS 1661 [S]	They're Coming to Take Me Away, Ha-Haaa!	1966	100.00

NARZ, JACK

Number	Title (A Side/B Side)	Yr	NM
Albums			
DOT			
❑ DLP-3244 [M]	Sing the Folk Hits with Jack Narz	1960	25.00
❑ DLP-25244 [S]	Sing the Folk Hits with Jack Narz	1960	30.00

NASH, GRAHAM Also see CROSBY, STILLS AND NASH; CROSBY, STILLS, NASH & YOUNG; THE HOLLIES.

Number	Title (A Side/B Side)	Yr	NM
45s			
ATLANTIC			
❑ 2804	Chicago/Simple Man	1971	6.00
❑ 2827	Military Madness/Sleep Song	1971	5.00
❑ 2840	Used to Be a King/Wounded Bird	1971	5.00
❑ 2990	Prison Song/Hey You (Looking at the Moon)	1973	5.00
❑ 89373	Chippin' Away/Newday	1986	3.00
❑ 89396	Sad Eyes/Newday	1986	3.00
❑ 89434	Innocent Eyes/I Got a Rock	1986	3.00
❑ 89434 [PS]	Innocent Eyes/I Got a Rock	1986	4.00
CAPITOL			
❑ 4812	In the 80's/T.V. Guide	1979	4.00
❑ 4849	Helicopter Song/ Out on the Island	1980	4.00
❑ 4879	Earth and Sky/Magical Child	1980	4.00
Albums			
ATLANTIC			
❑ SD 7204	Songs for Beginners	1971	12.00
❑ SD 7288	Wild Tales	1974	10.00
❑ 81633	Innocent Eyes	1986	8.00
CAPITOL			
❑ SWAK-12014	Earth & Sky	1980	10.00

NASH, GRAHAM, AND DAVID CROSBY
Also see each artist's individual listings.

Number	Title (A Side/B Side)	Yr	NM
45s			
ABC			
❑ 12140	Carry Me/Mama Lion	1975	4.00
❑ 12165	Bittersweet/Take the Money and Run	1976	4.00
❑ 12185	Love Workout/Bittersweet	1976	4.00
❑ 12199	Out of the Darkness/ Broken Bird	1976	4.00
❑ 12217	Foolish Man/Spotlight	1976	4.00
ATLANTIC			
❑ 2873	Immigration Man/Whole Cloth	1972	5.00
❑ 2892	Southbound Train/ The Wall Song	1972	5.00
Albums			
ABC			
❑ ABCD-902	Wind on the Water	1975	10.00
❑ ABCD-956	Whistling Down the Wire	1976	10.00
❑ AA-1042	Crosby/Nash — Live	1977	10.00
❑ AA-1102	The Best of Crosby/Nash	1978	10.00
ATLANTIC			
❑ SD 7220	Graham Nash/David Crosby	1972	12.00
MCA			
❑ 37007	Wind on the Water	198?	8.00
—Reissue of ABC 902			
❑ 37008	The Best of Crosby/Nash	198?	8.00
—Reissue of ABC 1102			

NASH, JOHNNY Also see PAUL ANKA/GEORGE HAMILTON IV/JOHNNY NASH.

Number	Title (A Side/B Side)	Yr	NM
45s			
ABC-PARAMOUNT			
❑ 9743	Out of Town/A Teenager Sings the Blues	1956	20.00
❑ 9844	The Ladder of Love/ I'll Walk Alone	1957	20.00
❑ 9874	A Very Special Love/Won't You Let Me Share My Love with You	1957	20.00
❑ 9894	My Pledge to You/It's So Easy to Say	1958	20.00
❑ 9927	Please Don't Go/I Lost My Love Last Night	1958	20.00
❑ 9942	Truly Love/You're Looking at Me	1958	20.00
❑ 9960	Almost in Your Arms/ Midnight Moonlight	1958	20.00
❑ 9989	Roots of Heaven/Walk with Faith in Your Heart	1958	20.00
❑ 9996	As Time Goes By/ The Voice of Love	1959	20.00
❑ 9996 [PS]	As Time Goes By/ The Voice of Love	1959	40.00
❑ 10026	And the Angels Sing/ Baby, Baby, Baby	1959	20.00
❑ 10046	Take a Giant Step/But Not for Me	1959	20.00
❑ 10060	The Wish/Too Proud	1959	20.00
❑ 10076	A Place in the Sun/Goodbye	1960	15.00
❑ 10095	Never My Love/(You've Got the) Love I Love	1960	15.00
❑ 10112	Let the Rest of the World Go By/ Music of Love	1960	15.00
❑ 10137	(Looks Like) The End of the World/We Kissed	1960	15.00
❑ 10160	Kisses/Somebody	1960	15.00
❑ 10181	World of Tears/Some of Your Lovin'	1961	100.00
❑ 10205	I Need Someone to Stand By/ A House on the Hill	1961	12.00
❑ 10212	A Thousand Miles Away/I Need Someone to Stand By Me	1961	12.00
❑ 10230	I'm Counting on You/ I Lost My Baby	1961	12.00
❑ 10251	Too Much Love/Love's Young Dream	1961	40.00
ARGO			
❑ 5471	Talk to Me/Love Ain't Nothin'	1964	75.00
❑ 5479	Then You Can Tell Me Goodbye/Always	1964	8.00
❑ 5492	Spring Is Here/Strange Feeling	1965	40.00
❑ 5501	Teardrops in the Rain/ I Know What I Want	1965	8.00
ATLANTIC			
❑ 2344	Big City/Somewhere	1966	20.00
CADET			
❑ 5528	Teardrops in the Rain/ Get Myself Together	1966	15.00
EPIC			
❑ 10873	Stir It Up/Cream Puff	1972	7.00
❑ 10902	I Can See Clearly Now/ How Good It Is	1972	6.00
❑ 10949	Stir It Up/Ooh Baby You've Been Good to Me	1973	6.00
❑ 11003	My Merry-Go-Round/We're Trying to Get Back to You	1973	5.00
❑ 11034	Ooh What a Feeling/ Yellow House	1973	5.00
❑ 11070	Loving You/Gonna Open Up My Heart Again	1973	5.00
❑ 50021	You Can't Go Halfway/ The Very First Time	1974	5.00
❑ 50051	Beautiful Baby/Celebrate Life	1974	5.00
❑ 50091	Good Vibrations/ The Very First Time	1975	5.00
❑ 50138	Tears on My Pillow (I Can't Take It)/Beautiful Baby	1975	5.00
❑ 50219	(What a) Wonderful World/Rock It Baby (We've Got a Date)	1976	5.00
❑ 50386	Back in Time/That Woman	1977	4.00
❑ 50737	Closer/Mr. Sea	1979	4.00
❑ 50821	You're the One/Don't Forget	1980	4.00
GROOVE			
❑ 58-0018	Helpless/I've Got a Lot to Offer, Darling	1963	10.00
❑ 58-0018 [PS]	Helpless/I've Got a Lot to Offer, Darling	1963	30.00
❑ 58-0021	Deep in the Heart of Harlem/ What Kind of Love Is This	1963	40.00
❑ 58-0021 [PS]	Deep in the Heart of Harlem/ What Kind of Love Is This	1963	50.00
❑ 58-0026	It's No Good for Me/ Town of Lonely Hearts	1963	10.00
❑ 58-0030	I'm Leaving/Oh Mary Don't You Weep	1964	10.00
JAD			
❑ 207	Hold Me Tight/Cupid	1968	8.00
—Mostly light green label with purple trim			
❑ 209	You Got Soul/Don't Cry	1968	8.00
❑ 214	Lovey Dovey/You Got Soul	1969	6.00
❑ 215	Sweet Charity/People in Love	1969	6.00
❑ 218	Love and Peace/People in Love	1969	6.00
❑ 220	Cupid/Hold Me Tight	1969	6.00
❑ 223	What a Groovy Feeling/ You Got Soul (Part 1)	1970	6.00
JANUS			
❑ 136	Falling In and Out of Love/You've Got to Change Your Ways	1970	6.00
JODA			
❑ 102	Let's Move and Groove (Together)/Understanding	1965	10.00
❑ 105	One More Time/Got to Find Her	1965	10.00
❑ 106	Somewhere/Big City	1966	10.00
MGM			
❑ 13637	Amen/Perfumed Flower	1966	8.00
❑ 13683	Good Goodness/ You Never Know	1967	8.00
❑ 13805	Stormy/(I'm So) Glad You're My Baby	1967	8.00
WARNER BROS.			
❑ 5270	Don't Take Your Love Away/ Moment of Weakness	1962	12.00
❑ 5301	Ol' Man River/My Dear Little Sweetheart	1962	12.00
❑ 5336	Cigarettes, Whiskey and Wild, Wild Women/I'm Movin' On	1963	12.00
Albums			
ABC-PARAMOUNT			
❑ 244 [M]	Johnny Nash	1958	30.00
❑ S-244 [S]	Johnny Nash	1959	40.00
❑ 276 [M]	Quiet Hour	1959	30.00
❑ S-276 [S]	Quiet Hour	1959	40.00
❑ 299 [M]	I Got Rhythm	1959	30.00
❑ S-299 [S]	I Got Rhythm	1959	40.00
❑ 344 [M]	Let's Get Lost	1960	30.00
❑ S-344 [S]	Let's Get Lost	1960	40.00
❑ 383 [M]	Studio Time	1961	30.00
❑ S-383 [S]	Studio Time	1961	40.00
ARGO			
❑ LP-4038 [M]	Composer's Choice	1964	20.00
❑ LPS-4038 [S]	Composer's Choice	1964	25.00
EPIC			
❑ KE 31607	I Can See Clearly Now	1972	15.00
—Yellow label			
❑ KE 31607	I Can See Clearly Now	1973	12.00
—Orange label			
❑ KE 32158	My Merry-Go-Round	1973	15.00
❑ PE 32828	Celebrate Life	1974	15.00
JAD			
❑ JS-1001	Prince of Peace	1969	25.00
❑ JS-1006	Folk Soul	1970	25.00
❑ JS-1207	Hold Me Tight	1968	30.00

NASHVILLE ALL STARS, THE

Number	Title (A Side/B Side)	Yr	NM
45s			
ROYAL AMERICAN			
❑ 63	Kansas City/Big Boss Man	1972	6.00
❑ 75	Workin' Man Blues/Hideaway	1973	6.00

NASHVILLE FIVE, THE

Number	Title (A Side/B Side)	Yr	NM
45s			
HIT			
❑ 119	Cotton Candy/Love Me with All Your Heart	1964	8.00
—B-side by the Music City Singers			
❑ 135	Walk Don't Run '64/Because	1964	10.00
—B-side by the Roamers			
❑ 231	A Taste of Honey/ England Swings	1965	8.00
—B-side by Bobby Brooks			
❑ 243	Batman Theme/Husbands and Wives	1966	8.00

NASHVILLE GUITARS, THE

Number	Title (A Side/B Side)	Yr	NM
Albums			
MONUMENT			
❑ MLP-8058 [M]	The Nashville Guitars	1966	15.00
❑ SLP-18058 [S]	The Nashville Guitars	1966	20.00
❑ MLP-18093	The Nashville Guitars at Home	1968	15.00

NASHVILLE TEENS, THE

Number	Title (A Side/B Side)	Yr	NM
45s			
LONDON			
❑ 9689	Tobacco Road/I Like It Like That	1964	15.00
❑ 9712	T.N.T./Google Eyes	1964	12.00
❑ 9736	Devil-in-Law/Find My Way Back Home	1965	12.00

N

Number	Title (A Side/B Side)	Yr	NM
MGM			
❑ 13357	Little Bird/Whatcha Gonna Do	1965	10.00
❑ 13406	I Know How It Feels to Be Loved/Soon Forgotten	1965	10.00
❑ 13483	The Hard Way/Upside Down	1966	10.00
❑ 13678	That's My Woman/Words	1967	10.00
UNITED ARTISTS			
❑ 50880	Tennessee Woman/Ella James	1972	20.00
Albums			
LONDON			
❑ PS 407 [R]	Tobacco Road	1964	80.00
❑ LL 3407 [M]	Tobacco Road	1964	100.00

NATIONAL GALLERY, THE

Number	Title (A Side/B Side)	Yr	NM
Albums			
PHILIPS			
❑ PHS 600266	The National Gallery (Performing Musical Interpretations of the Paintings of Paul Klee)	1968	20.00

NATIONAL LAMPOON Also see MELISSA MANCHESTER.

Number	Title (A Side/B Side)	Yr	NM
45s			
BANANA			
❑ 218	Deteriorata/Thise Fabulous Sixties	1972	8.00
❑ 233	Pizza Man/Lemmings Lament	1974	8.00
❑ 240	The Watergate Tapes/The Silent Majority	1973	8.00
LABEL 21			
❑ 202	What Were You Expecting — Rock 'n Roll?/(B-side unknown)	197?	6.00
❑ 202 [PS]	What Were You Expecting — Rock 'n Roll?/(B-side unknown)	197?	10.00
Albums			
BANANA			
❑ BTS 38	Radio Dinner	1972	15.00
❑ BTS 6006	Lemmings	1973	15.00
❑ BTS 6008	Missing White House Tapes	1974	15.00
EPIC			
❑ PE 33410	Gold Turkey	1974	12.00
—Orange label			
❑ PE 33410	Gold Turkey	1979	8.00
—Dark blue label			
❑ PE 33956	Goodbye Pop	1975	12.00
—Orange label			
❑ PE 33956	Goodbye Pop	1979	8.00
—Dark blue label			
LABEL 21			
❑ IMP-2001	That's Not Funny, That's Sick!	1978	10.00
❑ PIC-2001 [PD]	That's Not Funny, That's Sick!	1978	20.00
❑ IMP-2002	The White Album	1979	10.00
MCA			
❑ 27023	Lemmings	198?	8.00
❑ 27024	Radio Dinner	198?	8.00
PASSPORT			
❑ PB 6018	Sex, Drugs, Rock and Roll and the End of the World	1982	10.00
VISA			
❑ 2001	That's Not Funny, That's Sick!	198?	8.00
❑ 2002	The White Album	198?	8.00
❑ 7008	Greatest Hits of the National Lampoon	1978	12.00

NATIVE BOYS, THE

Number	Title (A Side/B Side)	Yr	NM
45s			
COMBO			
❑ 113	Strange Love/Cherrlyn	1956	60.00
❑ 115	Tears/When I Met You	1956	70.00
❑ 119	Laughing Love/Valley of Lovers	1956	70.00
❑ 120	Oh Let Me Dream/I've Got a Feeling	1956	60.00
LOST-NITE			
❑ 366	Strange Love/Cherrlyn	197?	5.00
—Reissue			
❑ 369	Tears/When I Met You	197?	5.00
—Reissue			
❑ 372	Laughing Love/Valley of Lovers	197?	5.00
—Reissue			
❑ 375	Oh Let Me Dream/I've Got a Feeling	197?	5.00
—Reissue			
MODERN			
❑ 939	Native Girl/It Won't Take Long	1954	400.00

NATURAL FOUR, THE

Number	Title (A Side/B Side)	Yr	NM
45s			
ABC			
❑ 11205	Why Should We Stop Now/You Did This for Me	1969	8.00
❑ 11236	Same Thing in Mind/The Situation Needs No Explanation	1969	12.00
❑ 11253	Hurt/I Thought You Were Mine	1969	25.00
❑ 11257	Message from a Black Man/Stepping On Up	1970	500.00
CURTOM			
❑ 0101	Heaven Right Here on Earth/While We're Away	1975	5.00
❑ 0104	Love's So Wonderful/What's Happening Here	1975	5.00
❑ 0114	It's the Music/It's the Music (Disco Version)	1976	5.00
❑ 0119	Free/Nothing Beats a Failure (But a Try)	1976	5.00
❑ 1981	Things Will Be Better Tomorrow/Eddie, You Should Know Better	1973	5.00
❑ 1984	Try Love Again/Eddie, You Should Know Better	1973	5.00
❑ 1990	Can This Be Real/Try Love Again	1973	5.00
❑ 1995	Love That Really Counts/Love's Society	1974	5.00
❑ 2000	You Bring Out the Best in Me/You Can't Keep Running Away	1974	5.00
Albums			
CURTOM			
❑ CU 5004	Heaven Right Here on Earth	1975	20.00
❑ CRT-8600	The Natural Four	1974	20.00

NATURALS, THE (1)

Number	Title (A Side/B Side)	Yr	NM
45s			
CALLA			
❑ 181	I Can't Share You/Young Generation	1972	6.00
MOTOWN			
❑ 1208	Good Things/Where Was I When Love Came By	1972	6.00
SHOUT			
❑ 307	Color Him Father/Crystal Blue Persuasion	197?	6.00
❑ 310	Cold Day in Hell/(B-side unknown)	197?	6.00

NATURALS, THE (2)

Number	Title (A Side/B Side)	Yr	NM
45s			
BEACON			
❑ 462	You Give Me So Much/What a Shape I'm In	1958	40.00

NATURALS, THE (3)

Number	Title (A Side/B Side)	Yr	NM
45s			
CHATTAHOOCHIE			
❑ 633	Just in Case You Change Your Mind/Why Don't They Understand	1963	12.00

NATURALS, THE (4)

Number	Title (A Side/B Side)	Yr	NM
45s			
ERA			
❑ 1089	The Mummy/Don't Send Me Away	1959	15.00

NATURALS, THE (5) Also see THE FOUR NATURALS.

Number	Title (A Side/B Side)	Yr	NM
45s			
HUNT			
❑ 325	Blue Moon/How Strange	1959	15.00
RED TOP			
❑ 113	Blue Moon/How Strange	1959	30.00

NATURALS, THE (6) British group.

Number	Title (A Side/B Side)	Yr	NM
45s			
LIBERTY			
❑ 55741	I Should Have Known Better/Didn't I	1964	12.00
❑ 55758	It Was You/Look at Me Now	1964	12.00

NATURALS, THE (7)

Number	Title (A Side/B Side)	Yr	NM
45s			
MGM			
❑ K11970	Marty/The Jitterbug Waltz	1955	15.00
❑ K11970 [PS]	Marty/The Jitterbug Waltz	1955	80.00
—With photos of Ernest Borgnine and Betsy Blair, plus a synopsis of the play			
❑ K12576	Patti Ann/Missing	1957	12.00
❑ K12576 [PS]	Patti Ann/Missing	1957	20.00

NATURALS, THE (8)

Number	Title (A Side/B Side)	Yr	NM
45s			
SMASH			
❑ 1925	Different Girls/Hey Fellas	1964	12.00

NATURALS, THE (U) We're not sure if this is a ninth different group.

Number	Title (A Side/B Side)	Yr	NM
45s			
CUB			
❑ 9026	The Flower Song/Three Young Men	1959	15.00
—B-side by Lee Davis			
20TH CENTURY FOX			
❑ 545	Caravan/Whole Lotta Rockin'	1964	12.00

NATURE BOY & FRIENDS

Number	Title (A Side/B Side)	Yr	NM
45s			
BERTRAM INT'L.			
❑ 255	Surfer John/John John	1964	40.00

NAVARRO, TOMMY

Number	Title (A Side/B Side)	Yr	NM
45s			
DE JAC			
❑ 1253	I Cried My Life Away/Club of Broken Hearts	196?	500.00

NAVARRO, TOMMY, AND THE SUNDIALERS

Number	Title (A Side/B Side)	Yr	NM
45s			
URANIA			
❑ 1401	I'll Be Satisfied/Summertime	1961	100.00
Albums			
URANIA			
❑ UR-900 [M]	Twist Around the Town	1961	100.00
❑ US-5900 [S]	Twist Around the Town	1961	150.00

NAYLOR, JERRY

Number	Title (A Side/B Side)	Yr	NM
45s			
COLUMBIA			
❑ 4-44809	The Chokin' Kind/Helga	1969	8.00
❑ 4-44874	Gotta Travel On/Posters on the Wall	1969	8.00
❑ 4-45106	But for Love/Angeline	1970	7.00
❑ 4-45170	Broken-Hearted Man/Mind Excursion	1970	7.00
❑ 4-45212	If I Promise/Marie	1970	7.00
❑ 4-45292	Come On Love/Las Virgenes Road	1970	7.00
HITSVILLE			
❑ 6041	The Bad Part of Me/I Hate to Drink Alone	1976	5.00
❑ 6046	The Last Time You Love Me/Born to Fool Around	1976	5.00
MC			
❑ 5004	If You Don't Want to Love Her/Love Away Her Memory Tonight	1978	5.00
❑ 5010	Rave On/Lady, Would You Like to Dance	1978	5.00
MELODYLAND			
❑ 6003	Is This All There Is to a Honky Tonk?/You're the One	1974	5.00
❑ 6012	He'll Have to Go/Once Again	1975	5.00
❑ 6020	What's a Nice Girl Like You Doing in a Honky Tonk/Prayin' for My Mind	1975	5.00
MGM			
❑ 14312	With This Ring/Goodtime Charlie	1971	6.00
❑ 14393	That'll Be the Day/Hands	1972	6.00
❑ 14439	Continental Highway/In This World	1972	6.00
❑ 14497	Bitter Memories/Love You Most of All	1973	6.00
❑ 14546	If You Don't Know Me by Now/Bitter Memories	1973	6.00
❑ 14637	Honky Tonk Women/You Are a Song	1973	6.00
OAK			
❑ 1014	Cheating Eyes/America, I'm Coming Home to You	1980	6.00
SKYLA			
❑ 1118	You're Thirteen/Stop Your Crying	1961	20.00
❑ 1123	Judee Malone/I'm Tired	1962	20.00
SMASH			
❑ 1971	I'll Take You Home/I Found You	1965	15.00
TOWER			
❑ 139	It's Only Make Believe/Leave Him and Come to My Loving Arms	1965	15.00
❑ 162	City Lights/Life	1965	15.00
❑ 214	My Special Angel/Would You Believe	1966	12.00
❑ 264	Almost Persuaded/I'll Get My Life the Way I Want It	1966	12.00
❑ 280	Drinkin' and Thinkin'/Johnny Brown	1966	12.00

Except when noted otherwise, VG = 25% of NM, and VG+ = 50% of NM. (Example: VG = $2.00, VG+ = $4.00 and NM = $8.00.)

Number	Title (A Side/B Side)	Yr	NM
❑ 327	Sweet Violets/Temptation Leads Me	1967	12.00
❑ 365	High on Happiness/Today and Tomorrow	1967	12.00
WARNER BROS.			
❑ 8767	But for Love/Part Time Lover, Full Time Fool	1979	5.00
❑ 8881	She Wears It Well/Part Time Lover, Full Time Fool	1979	5.00
WEST			
❑ 723	For Old Time Sake/ I Want to Be Loved	1986	6.00
❑ 726	Lean on Me/I Wanna Be Loved	1987	6.00

NAZARETH

45s

Number	Title (A Side/B Side)	Yr	NM
A&M			
❑ 1453	Broken Down Angel/Hard Living	1973	5.00
❑ 1469	Bad Bad Boy/Razamanaz	1973	5.00
❑ 1511	Go Down Fighting/ This Flight Tonight	1974	5.00
❑ 1548	Sunshine/This Flight Tonight	1974	5.00
❑ 1671	Love Hurts/Hair of the Dog	1975	4.00
❑ 1671 [PS]	Love Hurts/Hair of the Dog	1975	6.00
❑ 1854	Loretta/Lift the Lid	1976	4.00
❑ 1895	I Want To (Do Everything for You)/I Don't Want to Go On Without You	1976	4.00
❑ 1936	Somebody to Roll/ This Flight Tonight	1976	4.00
❑ 2009	Kentucky Fried Blues/ Shot Me Down	1978	4.00
❑ 2029	Gone Dead Train/ Kentucky Fried Blues	1978	4.00
❑ 2116	Expect No Mercy/ May the Sunshine	1979	4.00
❑ 2130	Whatever You Want Babe/ Expect No Mercy	1979	4.00
❑ 2158	Star/Expect No Mercy	1979	4.00
❑ 2219	Holiday/Ship of Dreams	1980	4.00
❑ 2237	Hearts Grown Cold/ Ship of Dreams	1980	4.00
❑ 2324	Dressed to Kill/Pop the Silo	1981	4.00
❑ 2378	Juicy Lucy/Morning Dew	1981	4.00
❑ 2389	Hair of the Dog/Holiday	1982	4.00
❑ 2421	Love Leads to Madness/ Take the Rap	1982	4.00
❑ 2444	Dream On/Take the Rap	1982	4.00
WARNER BROS.			
❑ 7599	Morning Dew (Take Me for a Walk)/Dear John	1972	8.00

Albums

Number	Title (A Side/B Side)	Yr	NM
A&M			
❑ SP-3109	Close Enough for Rock 'N' Roll	1981	8.00
—Budget-line reissue			
❑ SP-3168	Exercises	1982	8.00
—Reissue of Warner Bros. 2639			
❑ SP-3169	Nazareth	1982	8.00
—Reissue of Warner Bros. 2615			
❑ SP-3225	Hair of the Dog	1984	8.00
—Budget-line reissue			
❑ SP-3226	Hot Tracks	1984	8.00
—Budget-line reissue			
❑ SP-3609	Loud 'N' Proud	1974	10.00
❑ SP-3641	Rampant	1974	10.00
❑ SP-4396	Razamanaz	1973	15.00
—First edition with brown label			
❑ SP-4396	Razamanaz	1974	10.00
❑ SP-4511	Hair of the Dog	1975	10.00
❑ SP-4562	Close Enough for Rock 'N' Roll	1976	10.00
❑ SP-4610	Play 'N' the Game	1976	10.00
❑ SP-4643	Hot Tracks	1977	10.00
❑ SP-4666	Expect No Mercy	1977	10.00
❑ SP-4741	No Mean City	1979	10.00
❑ SP-4799	Malice in Wonderland	1980	10.00
❑ SP-4844	The Fool Circle	1981	10.00
❑ SP-4901	2XS	1982	10.00
❑ SP-6703 [(2)]	'Snaz	1981	12.00
MCA			
❑ 5458	Sound Elixir	1983	10.00
WARNER BROS.			
❑ BS 2615	Nazareth	1972	20.00
❑ BS 2639	Exercises	1972	20.00

NAZZ (1) Also see TODD RUNDGREN.

45s

Number	Title (A Side/B Side)	Yr	NM
SGC			
❑ 001	Hello It's Me/Open My Eyes	1969	8.00
—Third printing: Mostly green label with some yellow. Red vinyl copies on any label are bootlegs.			
❑ 001	Hello It's Me/Open My Eyes	1969	12.00
—Second pressing: Darker yellow label with horizontal lines			
❑ 001	Hello It's Me/Open My Eyes	1969	20.00
—First pressing: Light yellow label, no horizontal lines on label			
❑ 001 [PS]	Hello It's Me/Open My Eyes	1969	20.00
—Legitimate sleeves are paper, not cardboard			
❑ 006	Not Wrong Long/Under the Ice	1969	12.00
❑ 006 [PS]	Not Wrong Long/Under the Ice	1969	20.00
❑ 009	Magic Me/Some People	1970	12.00
❑ 009	Magic Me/Kicks	1970	25.00

Albums

Number	Title (A Side/B Side)	Yr	NM
RHINO			
❑ RNLP 109	Nazz	1984	15.00
❑ RNLP 110	Nazz Nazz	1984	15.00
❑ RNLP 111	Nazz III	1984	15.00
❑ RNLP 116	The Best of Nazz	1984	15.00
❑ R1 70116	The Best of Nazz	1987	12.00
SGC			
❑ SD 5001	Nazz	1968	40.00
❑ 5002 [M]	Nazz Nazz	1969	80.00
—Promo-only mono pressing on red vinyl			
❑ SD 5002 [S]	Nazz Nazz	1969	40.00
—Red vinyl			
❑ SD 5002 [S]	Nazz Nazz	1969	80.00
—Black vinyl			
❑ SD 5004	Nazz III	1970	40.00

NAZZ (2) Early ALICE COOPER.

45s

Number	Title (A Side/B Side)	Yr	NM
VERY			
❑ 001	Lay Down and Die, Goodbye/ Wonder Who's Loving Her Now	1967	2000.
—Warning! Reproductions of this record were made in the 1990s with white promo labels and picture sleeves. They are NOT the real thing. VG 1000; VG+ 1500			

NEAL, JERRY

45s

Number	Title (A Side/B Side)	Yr	NM
DOT			
❑ 15810	I Hates Rabbits/Scratchin'	1958	80.00
—With Eddie Cochran on guitar on B-side			

NED AND GARY

45s

Number	Title (A Side/B Side)	Yr	NM
LIBERTY			
❑ 55160	Lovin'/I Bust My Seams	1958	60.00

NED AND NELDA FRANK ZAPPA and Ray Collins.

45s

Number	Title (A Side/B Side)	Yr	NM
VIGAH			
❑ 002	Hey Nelda/Surf Along	1963	150.00

NEELY, SAM

45s

Number	Title (A Side/B Side)	Yr	NM
A&M			
❑ 1523	Come a Little Bit Closer/ Sadie Take a Lover	1974	4.00
❑ 1612	You Can Have Her/ It's a Fine Morning	1974	4.00
❑ 1651	I Fought the Law/Guitar Man	1974	4.00
❑ 1694	Sanctuary/Cajun Man	1975	4.00
CAPITOL			
❑ 3235	Long Road to Texas/Change a Sad to a Happy Song	1971	6.00
❑ 3358	Blue Time/Cry Me a Song	1972	6.00
❑ 3381	Loving You Just Crossed My Mind/Everyday Is the Same As Today	1972	5.00
❑ 3510	Rosalie/Try to Reason Why	1973	5.00
❑ 3586	Blue Time/Kiss the Morning Sunshine	1973	5.00
ELEKTRA			
❑ 45419	Sail Away/My Lover and My Friend	1977	4.00
❑ 45484	Your Love Is In Good Hands/ Things That Lovers Do	1978	4.00
MCA			
❑ 52194	The Party's Over (Everybody's Gone)/What Do I Tell My Heart	1983	3.00
❑ 52226	When You Leave That Way You Can Never Go Back/ Music Made Me Do It	1983	3.00
❑ 52269	Let's Fall in Love Again Tonight/ You're No Ordinary Memory	1983	3.00
❑ 52323	Old Photographs/ Somebody's Leaving	1983	3.00

Albums

Number	Title (A Side/B Side)	Yr	NM
A&M			
❑ SP-3626	Sam Neely	1974	12.00
CAPITOL			
❑ ST-873	Long Road to Texas	1972	15.00
❑ ST-11097	Loving You Just Crossed My Mind	1972	12.00
—Reissued version of ST-873			
❑ SMAS-11143	Sam Neely — 2	1973	12.00

NEGATIVLAND

Albums

Number	Title (A Side/B Side)	Yr	NM
SEELAND			
❑ 001	Negativland	1981	15.00
—Every copy has a different cover			
❑ 002	Points	1982	12.00
—Black vinyl			
❑ 002	Points	1982	15.00
—Blue vinyl			
❑ 003	A Big 10-8 Place	1985	12.00
SST			
❑ 133	Escape from Noise	1987	18.00
—With booklet			
❑ 252	Helter Stupid	1989	12.00
❑ 272 [EP]	U2	1990	100.00
—Withdrawn thanks to pressure from the record company of U2 (the band)			
❑ 292 [EP]	Guns	1992	8.00

NEIGHB'RHOOD CHILDREN

45s

Number	Title (A Side/B Side)	Yr	NM
ACTA			
❑ 813	Maintain/Just No Way	1967	20.00
—As "Neighborhood"			
❑ 823	Happy Child/Please Leave Me Alone	1968	15.00
❑ 828	Behold the Lilies/I Want Action	1968	20.00
DOT			
❑ 17238	On Our Way/Woman Thing	1969	15.00
NAM			
❑ 2014	Dancing in the Street/ (B-side unknown)	196?	15.00

Albums

Number	Title (A Side/B Side)	Yr	NM
ACTA			
❑ 8005 [M]	The Neighb'rhood Children	1968	80.00
❑ 38005 [S]	The Neighb'rhood Children	1968	100.00
SUNDAZED			
❑ LP 5023 [(2)]	Long Years in Space	199?	15.00

NEIGHBORHOOD, THE

45s

Number	Title (A Side/B Side)	Yr	NM
BIG TREE			
❑ 102	Big Yellow Taxi/You Could Be Born Again	1970	4.00
—Later pressings have red and yellow labels			
❑ 102	Big Yellow Taxi/You Could Be Born Again	1970	5.00
—Originals have white labels			
❑ 106	Laugh/Now's the Time for Love	1970	5.00

Albums

Number	Title (A Side/B Side)	Yr	NM
BIG TREE			
❑ 2001	Debut	1970	15.00

NEIGHBORHOOD KIDS, THE

45s

Number	Title (A Side/B Side)	Yr	NM
BRUNSWICK			
❑ 55466	The Christmas Party of the Eighth Reindeer/Christmas Is for Everyone	1971	8.00

NEIL, FRED Also see VINCE MARTIN AND FRED NEIL.

45s

Number	Title (A Side/B Side)	Yr	NM
BRUNSWICK			
❑ 55117	Listen Kitten/Take Me Back Again	1959	30.00
—As "Freddie Neil"			
CAPITOL			
❑ 2047	The Dolphins/I've Got a Secret	1967	30.00
❑ 2091	Felicity/Please Send Me Someone to Love	1968	30.00
❑ 2256	Everybody's Talkin'/ That's the Bag I'm In	1968	30.00
❑ 2604	Everybody's Talkin'/Badi-Da	1969	25.00
EPIC			
❑ 5-9334	Love's Funny/Secret, Secret	1959	20.00
❑ 5-9403	Slippin' Around/You Don't Have to Be a Baby to Cry	1960	20.00
❑ 5-9435	Four Chaplains/The Rainbow and the Rose	1961	20.00
LOOK			
❑ 1002	You Ain't Treatin' Me Right/ (B-side unknown)	1958	60.00
—As "Freddie Neil"			

Albums

Number	Title (A Side/B Side)	Yr	NM
CAPITOL			
❑ ST-294	Everybody's Talkin'	1969	25.00
❑ ST 2665 [S]	Fred Neil	1966	40.00
—With color photo on back			
❑ ST 2665 [S]	Fred Neil	1967	30.00
—With black & white photo on back			
❑ T 2665 [M]	Fred Neil	1966	30.00

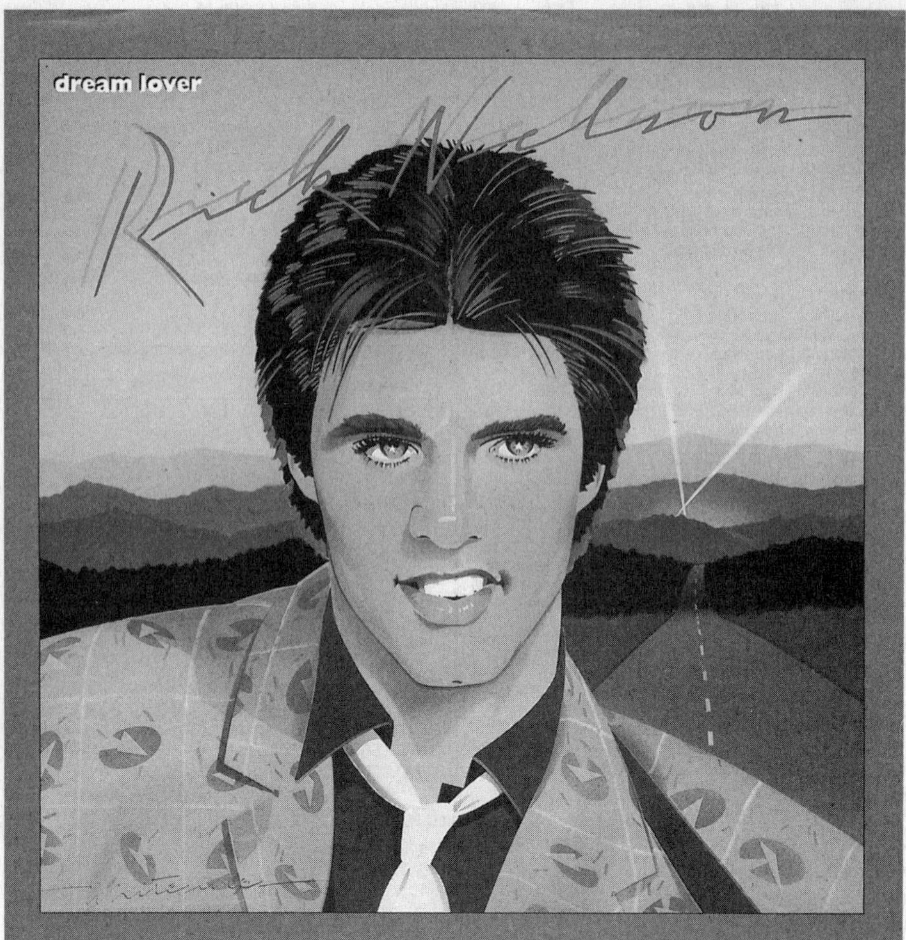

Rick Nelson, "Dream Lover," Epic 34-06066, 1986, $4,

Number	Title (A Side/B Side)	Yr	NM
❑ ST 2862 [S]	Fred Neil Sessions	1968	30.00
❑ T 2862 [M]	Fred Neil Sessions	1968	40.00

ELEKTRA

Number	Title (A Side/B Side)	Yr	NM
❑ EKL-293 [M]	Bleecker and MacDougal	1965	30.00
❑ EKS-7293 [S]	Bleecker and MacDougal	1965	40.00
❑ EKS-74073	Little Bit of Rain	1970	20.00

—Reissue of 7293

SUNDAZED

Number	Title (A Side/B Side)	Yr	NM
❑ LP 5107	Bleecker and MacDougal	2002	12.00

NEIL AND JACK
NEIL DIAMOND and Jack Parker.

45s

DUEL

Number	Title (A Side/B Side)	Yr	NM
❑ 508	What Will I Do/You Are My Love at Last	1962	400.00
❑ 517	I'm Afraid/Till You've Tried Love	1962	400.00

NEKTAR

45s

PASSPORT

Number	Title (A Side/B Side)	Yr	NM
❑ 7902	Remember the Future/Confusion	1974	6.00
❑ 7904	Astral Man/Nelly the Elephant	1975	5.00

Albums

PASSPORT

Number	Title (A Side/B Side)	Yr	NM
❑ PPS-98002	Remember the Future	1974	12.00
❑ PPSD-98005	Down to Earth	1975	12.00
❑ PPSD-98011	Recycled	1976	10.00
❑ PPSD-98017	A Tab in the Ocean	1976	10.00

POLYDOR

Number	Title (A Side/B Side)	Yr	NM
❑ PD-1-6115	Magic Is a Child	1977	10.00

VISA

Number	Title (A Side/B Side)	Yr	NM
❑ IMP 9001 [(2)]	Thru the Ears	1979	12.00

NELSON, KATHY

45s

LIBERTY

Number	Title (A Side/B Side)	Yr	NM
❑ 55115	Santa Dear/Gimmie a Little Kiss, Will Ya Huh?	1957	20.00

NELSON, RICKY
Includes records as "Rick Nelson."

45s

CAPITOL

Number	Title (A Side/B Side)	Yr	NM
❑ 4962	Almost Saturday Night/The Loser Babe Is You	1981	5.00
❑ 4974	Call It What You Want/It Hasn't Happened Yet	1981	5.00
❑ 4988	Believe What You Say/The Loser Babe Is You	1981	5.00
❑ B-5178	No Fair Falling in Love/Give 'Em My Number	1982	5.00
❑ 89574	The Christmas Song (Chestnuts Roasting on an Open Fire)/Jingle Bells	2000	8.00

—Red vinyl

COLLECTABLES

Number	Title (A Side/B Side)	Yr	NM
❑ 4471	I'm Walking/A Teenager's Romance	1992	3.00
❑ 6022	Hello Mary Lou/Poor Little Fool	1992	3.00
❑ 6102	Sweeter Than You/It's Late	1993	3.00
❑ 6125	Be Bop Baby/Lonesome Town	1993	3.00
❑ 6126	Travelin' Man/It's Up to You	1993	3.00

—A-side is probably the "cold ending" version that has become the common version on reissues since the start of the compact disc era

Number	Title (A Side/B Side)	Yr	NM
❑ 6127	Stood Up/Teenage Idol	1993	3.00
❑ 6210	Believe What You Say/Never Be Anyone Else But You	1994	3.00
❑ 6211	Waitin' in School/Just a Little Too Much	1994	3.00
❑ 6212	Young Emotions/Everlovin'	1994	3.00
❑ 90000	For You/Who Put the Bomp	199?	3.00

—B-side by Barry Mann

Number	Title (A Side/B Side)	Yr	NM
❑ 90052	Garden Party/So Long Mama	199?	3.00
❑ 90106	Fools Rush In (Where Angels Fear to Tread)/For You	199?	3.00

DECCA

Number	Title (A Side/B Side)	Yr	NM
❑ 31475	You Don't Love Me Anymore (And I Can Tell)/I Got a Woman	1963	15.00
❑ 31475 [PS]	You Don't Love Me Anymore (And I Can Tell)/I Got a Woman	1963	30.00
❑ 31495	String Along/Gypsy Woman	1963	15.00
❑ 31495 [PS]	String Along/Gypsy Woman	1963	30.00
❑ 31533	Fools Rush In/Down Home	1963	15.00
❑ 31533 [PS]	Fools Rush In/Down Home	1963	30.00
❑ 31574	For You/That's All She Wrote	1963	15.00
❑ 31574 [PS]	For You/That's All She Wrote	1963	30.00
❑ 31612	The Very Thought of You/I Wonder (If Your Love Will Ever Belong to Me)	1964	12.00
❑ 31612 [PS]	The Very Thought of You/I Wonder (If Your Love Will Ever Belong to Me)	1964	30.00
❑ 31656	There's Nothing I Can Say/Lonely Corner	1964	12.00
❑ 31656 [PS]	There's Nothing I Can Say/Lonely Corner	1964	30.00
❑ 31703	A Happy Guy/Don't Breathe a Word	1964	12.00
❑ 31703 [PS]	A Happy Guy/Don't Breathe a Word	1964	30.00
❑ 31756	Mean Old World/When the Chips Are Down	1965	12.00
❑ 31756 [PS]	Mean Old World/When the Chips Are Down	1965	30.00
❑ 31800	Yesterday's Love/Come Out Dancin'	1965	12.00
❑ 31800 [PS]	Yesterday's Love/Come Out Dancin'	1965	30.00
❑ 31845	Love and Kisses/Say You Love Me	1965	12.00
❑ 31845 [PS]	Love and Kisses/Say You Love Me	1965	40.00
❑ 31900	Your Kind of Lovin'/Fire Breathin' Dragon	1966	12.00
❑ 31900 [PS]	Your Kind of Lovin'/Fire Breathin' Dragon	1966	150.00
❑ 31956	Louisiana Man/You Just Can't Quit	1966	12.00
❑ 31956 [PS]	Louisiana Man/You Just Can't Quit	1966	60.00
❑ 32026	Alone/Things You Gave Me	1966	12.00
❑ 32026 [PS]	Alone/Things You Gave Me	1966	80.00
❑ 32055	They Don't Give Medals (To Yesterday's Heroes)/Take a Broken Heart	1966	12.00
❑ 32120	Take a City Bride/I'm Called Lonely	1967	10.00
❑ 32120 [PS]	Take a City Bride/I'm Called Lonely	1967	60.00
❑ 32176	Moonshine/Suzanne on a Sunday Morning	1967	10.00
❑ 32222	Dream Weaver/Baby Close Your Eyes	1967	10.00
❑ 32284	Don't Blame It on Your Wife/Promenade in Green	1968	10.00
❑ 32298	Barefoot Boy/Don't Make Promises	1968	10.00
❑ 32550	She Belongs to Me/Promises	1969	8.00
❑ 32635	Easy to Be Free/Come On In	1970	8.00
❑ 32635 [PS]	Easy to Be Free/Come On In	1970	15.00
❑ 32676	I Shall Be Released/If You Gotta Go, Go Now	1970	8.00
❑ 32711	Look at Mary/We Got Such a Long Way to Go	1970	8.00
❑ 32739	How Long/Down Along the Bayou Country	1970	8.00
❑ 32779	Life/California	1971	8.00
❑ 32860	Thank You Lord/Sing Me a Song	1971	8.00
❑ 32906	Love Minus Zero-No Limit/Gypsy Pilot	1971	8.00
❑ 32980	Garden Party/So Long Mama	1972	10.00
❑ 34193 [S]	Gypsy Woman/For Your Sweet Love	1963	100.00
❑ 34193/7 [PS]	Envelope, bonus photo and intact jukebox title strips for these 5 singles	1963	100.00
❑ 34194 [S]	Pick Up the Pieces/Every Time I See You Smilin'	1963	100.00
❑ 34195 [S]	One Boy Too Late/Everytime I Think About You	1963	100.00
❑ 34196 [S]	Let's Talk the Whole Thing Over/I Got a Woman	1963	100.00
❑ 34197 [S]	I Will Follow You/What Comes Next	1963	100.00

—34193-34197 are 33 1/3 rpm, small hole jukebox singles. The set came with a package, priced separately.

EPIC

Number	Title (A Side/B Side)	Yr	NM
❑ 34-06066	Dream Lover/Rave On	1986	4.00
❑ 34-06066 [PS]	Dream Lover/Rave On	1986	4.00
❑ 50458	It's Another Day/You Can't Dance	1977	5.00
❑ 50501	Gimme A Little Sign/Something You Can't Buy	1978	5.00
❑ 50674	Dream Lover/That Ain't the Way Love's Supposed to Be	1979	5.00

Except when noted otherwise, VG = 25% of NM, and VG+ = 50% of NM. (Example: VG = $2.00, VG+ = $4.00 and NM = $8.00.)

Number	Title (A Side/B Side)	Yr	NM
IMPERIAL			
❑ 5463	Be-Bop Baby/Have I Told You Lately That I Love You	1957	25.00
—Black label			
❑ 5463	Be-Bop Baby/Have I Told You Lately That I Love You	1957	50.00
—Red label			
❑ 5463 [PS]	Be-Bop Baby/Have I Told You Lately That I Love You	1957	80.00
❑ 5483	Stood Up/Waitin' in School	1957	25.00
—Black label			
❑ 5483	Stood Up/Waitin' in School	1957	40.00
—Red label			
❑ 5483 [PS]	Stood Up/Waitin' in School	1957	70.00
❑ 5503	Believe What You Say/My Bucket's Got a Hole in It	1958	30.00
—Black label			
❑ 5503	Believe What You Say/My Bucket's Got a Hole in It	1958	50.00
—Red label			
❑ 5503 [PS]	Believe What You Say/My Bucket's Got a Hole in It	1958	70.00
❑ 5528	Poor Little Fool/Don't Leave Me This Way	1958	30.00
❑ 5545	Lonesome Town/I Got a Feeling	1958	30.00
❑ 5545	Lonesome Town/I Got a Feeling	1958	600.00
—Red vinyl			
❑ 5545 [PS]	Lonesome Town/I Got a Feeling	1958	70.00
❑ 5565	Never Be Anyone Else But You/It's Late	1959	25.00
—Black label			
❑ 5565	Never Be Anyone Else But You/It's Late	1959	40.00
—Red label			
❑ 5565 [PS]	Never Be Anyone Else But You/It's Late	1959	80.00
❑ 5595	Just a Little Too Much/Sweeter Than You	1959	25.00
❑ 5595 [PS]	Just a Little Too Much/Sweeter Than You	1959	70.00
❑ 5614	I Wanna Be Loved/Mighty Good	1959	25.00
❑ 5614 [PS]	I Wanna Be Loved/Mighty Good	1959	70.00
❑ 5663	Young Emotions/Right By My Side	1960	25.00
❑ 5663 [PS]	Young Emotions/Right By My Side	1960	70.00
❑ 5685	I'm Not Afraid/Yes Sir, That's My Baby	1960	25.00
❑ 5685 [PS]	I'm Not Afraid/Yes Sir, That's My Baby	1960	70.00
❑ 5707	You Are the Only One/Milk Cow Blues	1960	25.00
❑ 5707 [PS]	You Are the Only One/Milk Cow Blues	1960	70.00
❑ 5741	Travelin' Man/Hello Mary Lou	1961	25.00
—Black vinyl			
❑ 5741	Travelin' Man/Hello Mary Lou	1961	800.00
—Red vinyl			
❑ 5741 [PS]	Travelin' Man/Hello Mary Lou	1961	70.00
❑ 5770	A Wonder Like You/Everlovin'	1961	20.00
—Starting here, Imperial singles by "Rick Nelson"			
❑ 5770 [PS]	A Wonder Like You/Everlovin'	1961	40.00
❑ 5805	Young World/Summertime	1962	20.00
❑ 5805 [PS]	Young World/Summertime	1962	40.00
❑ 5864	Teen Age Idol/I've Got My Eyes on You	1962	20.00
❑ 5864 [PS]	Teen Age Idol/I've Got My Eyes on You	1962	40.00
❑ 5901	It's Up to You/I Need You	1962	20.00
❑ 5901 [PS]	It's Up to You/I Need You	1962	40.00
❑ 5910	That's All/I'm in Love Again	1963	25.00
❑ 5935	Old Enough to Love/If You Can't Rock Me	1963	20.00
❑ 5935	Old Enough to Love/If You Can't Rock Me	1963	500.00
—Red vinyl			
❑ 5935 [PS]	Old Enough to Love/If You Can't Rock Me	1963	40.00
❑ 5958	A Long Vacation/Mad Mad World	1963	20.00
❑ 5958	A Long Vacation/Mad Mad World	1963	300.00
—Red vinyl			
❑ 5985	Time After Time/There's Not a Minute	1963	20.00
❑ 58896	Young World/A Wonder Like You	2000	5.00
—EMI-Capitol jukebox issue with Imperial logo at top			
❑ 66004	Today's Teardrops/Thank You Darlin'	1963	15.00
❑ 66004 [PS]	Today's Teardrops/Thank You Darlin'	1963	40.00
❑ 66017	Congratulations/One Minute to One	1964	15.00
❑ 66039	Everybody But Me/Lucky Star	1964	15.00
MCA			
❑ 40001	Palace Guard/A Flower Opens Gently By	1973	6.00
❑ 40130	Evil Woman Child/Lifestream	1973	6.00
❑ 40187	Windfall/Legacy	1974	6.00
❑ 40214	One Night Stand/Lifestream	1974	6.00
❑ 40392	Louisiana Belle/Try (Try to Fall in Love)	1975	6.00
❑ 40458	Rock and Roll Lady/Fadeaway	1975	6.00
❑ 52781	You Know What I Mean/Don't Leave Me This Way	1986	5.00
❑ 52781 [PS]	You Know What I Mean/Don't Leave Me This Way	1986	5.00
UNITED ARTISTS			
❑ 0071	Be-Bop Baby/Stood Up	1973	5.00
❑ 0072	Lonesome Town/It's Up to You	1973	5.00
❑ 0073	Poor Little Fool/My Bucket's Got a Hole in It	1973	5.00
❑ 0074	Travelin' Man/Believe What You Say	1973	5.00
❑ 0075	Teen Age Idol/Young Emotions	1973	5.00
❑ 0076	Never Be Anyone Else But You/That's All	1973	5.00
❑ 0077	Young World/It's Late	1973	5.00
❑ 0078	Just a Little Too Much/Waitin' in School	1973	5.00
❑ 0079	Hello Mary Lou/Sweeter Than You	1973	5.00
❑ 0080	A Wonder Like You/Everlovin'	1973	5.00
—0071 through 0080 are "Silver Spotlight Series" reissues			
UNIVERSAL PICTURES			
❑ CPM 7-112/3 [DJ]	Love and Kisses Radio Spots	1965	300.00
—Red vinyl; three segments on one side, three on the other; double the value if a six-page transcription is with the record			
VERVE			
❑ 10047	I'm Walkin'/A Teenager's Romance	1957	40.00
—Black and white label			
❑ 10047	I'm Walkin'/A Teenager's Romance	1957	50.00
—Orange and yellow label			
❑ 10070	You're My One and Only Love/Honey Rock	1957	40.00
—B-side by Barney Kessel			

7-Inch Extended Plays

Number	Title (A Side/B Side)	Yr	NM
DECCA			
❑ ED 2760	I Will Follow You/Pick Up the Pieces//One Boy Too Late/Let's Talk the Whole Thing Over	1963	150.00
❑ ED 2760 [PS]	One Boy Too Late	1963	150.00
❑ 7-34319 [PS]	Best Always	1965	30.00
—With title strips			
❑ 7-34319 [S]	I'm Not Ready for You Yet/Lonely Corner/Mean Old World//I Know a Place/It's Beginning to Hurt/When the Chips Are Down	1965	30.00
—33 1/3 rpm, small hole jukebox edition			
IMPERIAL			
❑ IMP 153	Be-Bop Baby/Have I Told You Lately That I Love You//Honeycomb/Boppin' the Blues	1957	50.00
❑ IMP 153 [PS]	Ricky (Honeycomb)	1957	50.00
❑ IMP 154	Teenage Doll/If You Can't Rock Me//Whole Lotta Shakin' Goin' On/Baby I'm Sorry	1957	50.00
❑ IMP 154 [PS]	Ricky, Vol. 2	1957	50.00
❑ IMP 155	Your True Love/True Love//Am I Blue/I'm Confessin'	1957	50.00
❑ IMP 155 [PS]	Ricky (True Love)	1957	50.00
❑ IMP 156	Shirley Lee/There's Good Rockin' Tonight//Someday/I'm Feelin' Sorry	1958	50.00
❑ IMP 156 [PS]	Ricky Nelson (Someday)	1958	50.00
❑ IMP 157	Down the Line/Don't Leave Me This Way//I'm in Love Again/My Babe	1958	50.00
❑ IMP 157 [PS]	Ricky Nelson (Down the Line)	1958	50.00
❑ IMP 158	Unchained Melody/I'll Walk Alone//There Goes My Baby/Poor Little Fool	1958	50.00
❑ IMP 158 [PS]	Ricky Nelson (Unchained Melody)	1958	50.00
❑ IMP 159	Be True to Me/One of These Mornings//Lonesome Town/It's Late	1959	50.00
❑ IMP 159 [PS]	Ricky Sings Again (Be True to Me)	1959	50.00
❑ IMP 160	Restless Kid/It's All in the Game//Believe What You Say/You Tear Me Up	1959	50.00
❑ IMP 160 [PS]	Ricky Sings Again (Restless Kid)	1959	50.00
❑ IMP 161	Old Enough to Love/Tryin' to Get to You//Never Be Anyone Else But You/I Can't Help It	1959	50.00
❑ IMP 161 [PS]	Ricky Sings Again (Old Enough to Love)	1959	50.00
❑ IMP 162	You'll Never Know What You're Missin'/I've Been Thinkin'//So Long/You're So Fine	1959	50.00
❑ IMP 162 [PS]	Songs by Ricky (You'll Never Know What You're Missin')	1959	50.00
❑ IMP 163	One Minute To One/Blood from a Stone//Half Breed/Just a Little Too Much	1959	50.00
❑ IMP 163 [PS]	Songs by Ricky (One Minute to One)	1959	50.00
❑ IMP 164	Don't Leave Me/That's All//Sweeter Than You/A Long Vacation	1959	50.00
—Original track order			
❑ IMP 164	Don't Leave Me/That's All//A Long Vacation/Sweeter Than You	1959	60.00
—Revised track order; "RE" before master number at 3 o'clock on label			
❑ IMP 164 [PS]	Songs by Ricky (Don't Leave Me)	1959	50.00
❑ IMP 165	Glory Train/I Bowed My Head in Shame//March with the Band of the Lord/If You Believe It	1959	100.00
❑ IMP 165 [PS]	Ricky Sings Spirituals	1959	100.00
❑ LP 4-2232	Travelin' Man/Never Be Anyone Else But You/It's Late//Young Emotions/Hello Mary Lou/Yes Sir, That's My Baby	1964	80.00
—33 1/3 rpm, small hole, jukebox edition			
❑ LP 4-2232 [PS]	Million Sellers	1964	80.00
VERVE			
❑ 5048	I'm Walkin'/A Teenager's Romance//You're My One and Only Love/Honey Rock	1957	150.00
❑ 5048 [PS]	Ricky	1957	200.00

Albums

Number	Title	Yr	NM
CAPITOL			
❑ SOO-12109	Playing to Win	1981	10.00
DECCA			
❑ DL 4419 [M]	For Your Sweet Love	1963	30.00
❑ DL 4479 [M]	Rick Nelson Sings "For You"	1963	35.00
❑ DL 4559 [M]	The Very Thought of You	1964	30.00
❑ DL 4608 [M]	Spotlight on Rick	1964	30.00
❑ DL 4660 [M]	Best Always	1965	30.00
❑ DL 4678 [M]	Love and Kisses	1965	30.00
❑ DL 4779 [M]	Bright Lights and Country Music	1966	25.00
❑ DL 4827 [M]	Country Fever	1967	25.00
❑ DL 4944 [M]	Another Side of Rick	1967	25.00
❑ DL 5014 [M]	Perspective	1968	50.00
—Mono copies are promo only			
❑ DL 74419 [S]	For Your Sweet Love	1963	40.00
❑ DL 74479 [S]	Rick Nelson Sings "For You"	1963	45.00
❑ DL 74559 [S]	The Very Thought of You	1964	40.00
❑ DL 74608 [S]	Spotlight on Rick	1964	40.00
❑ DL 74660 [S]	Best Always	1965	40.00
❑ DL 74678 [S]	Love and Kisses	1965	40.00
❑ DL 74779 [S]	Bright Lights and Country Music	1966	30.00
❑ DL 74827 [S]	Country Fever	1967	30.00
❑ DL 74944 [S]	Another Side of Rick	1967	30.00
❑ DL 75014 [S]	Perspective	1968	30.00
❑ DL 75162	Rick Nelson In Concert	1970	25.00
❑ DL 75236	Rick Sings Nelson	1970	25.00
—Deduct 20 percent if poster is missing			
❑ DL 75297	Rudy the Fifth	1971	25.00
❑ DL 75391	Garden Party	1972	25.00
EMI AMERICA			
❑ SQ-17192	The Very Best of Rick Nelson	1986	10.00
—Reissue of United Artists UA-LA330			
EPIC			
❑ JE 34420	Intakes	1977	12.00
❑ FE 40388	The Memphis Sessions	1986	10.00
EPIC/NU-DISK			
❑ 3E 36868 [10]	Four You	1981	12.00
IMPERIAL			
❑ LP 9048 [M]	Ricky	1957	100.00
—Black label with stars			
❑ LP 9048 [M]	Ricky	1964	25.00
—Black label with pink and white at left			
❑ LP 9048 [M]	Ricky	1966	20.00
—Black label with green and white at left			
❑ LP 9050 [M]	Ricky Nelson	1958	100.00
—Black label with stars			
❑ LP 9050 [M]	Ricky Nelson	1964	25.00
—Black label with pink and white at left			
❑ LP 9050 [M]	Ricky Nelson	1966	20.00
—Black label with green and white at left			
❑ LP 9061 [M]	Ricky Sings Again	1959	100.00
—Black label with stars			
❑ LP 9061 [M]	Ricky Sings Again	1964	25.00
—Black label with pink and white at left			
❑ LP 9061 [M]	Ricky Sings Again	1966	20.00
—Black label with green and white at left			
❑ LP 9082 [M]	Songs by Ricky	1959	75.00
—Black label with stars			
❑ LP 9082 [M]	Songs by Ricky	1964	25.00
—Black label with pink and white at left			
❑ LP 9082 [M]	Songs by Ricky	1966	20.00
—Black label with green and white at left			

N

Number	Title (A Side/B Side)	Yr	NM
❑ LP 9122 [M]	More Songs by Ricky	1960	75.00
—Black label with stars			
❑ LP 9122 [M]	More Songs by Ricky	1964	25.00
—Black label with pink and white at left			
❑ LP 9122 [M]	More Songs by Ricky	1966	20.00
—Black label with green and white at left			
❑ LP 9152 [M]	Rick Is 21	1961	40.00
—Black label with stars			
❑ LP 9152 [M]	Rick Is 21	1964	25.00
—Black label with pink and white at left			
❑ LP 9152 [M]	Rick Is 21	1966	20.00
—Black label with green and white at left			
❑ LP 9167 [M]	Album Seven by Rick	1962	40.00
—Black label with stars			
❑ LP 9167 [M]	Album Seven by Rick	1964	25.00
—Black label with pink and white at left			
❑ LP 9167 [M]	Album Seven by Rick	1966	20.00
—Black label with green and white at left			
❑ LP 9218 [M]	Best Sellers by Rick Nelson	1963	40.00
—Black label with stars			
❑ LP 9218 [M]	Best Sellers by Rick Nelson	1964	25.00
—Black label with pink and white at left			
❑ LP 9218 [M]	Best Sellers by Rick Nelson	1966	20.00
—Black label with green and white at left			
❑ LP 9223 [M]	It's Up to You	1963	40.00
—Black label with stars			
❑ LP 9223 [M]	It's Up to You	1964	25.00
—Black label with pink and white at left			
❑ LP 9223 [M]	It's Up to You	1966	20.00
—Black label with green and white at left			
❑ LP 9232 [M]	Million Sellers	1963	40.00
—Black label with stars			
❑ LP 9232 [M]	Million Sellers	1964	25.00
—Black label with pink and white at left			
❑ LP 9232 [M]	Million Sellers	1966	20.00
—Black label with green and white at left			
❑ LP 9244 [M]	A Long Vacation	1963	40.00
—Black label with stars			
❑ LP 9244 [M]	A Long Vacation	1964	25.00
—Black label with pink and white at left			
❑ LP 9244 [M]	A Long Vacation	1966	20.00
—Black label with green and white at left			
❑ LP 9251 [M]	Rick Nelson Sings for You	1964	25.00
—Black label with pink and white at left			
❑ LP 9251 [M]	Rick Nelson Sings for You	1964	40.00
—Black label with stars			
❑ LP 9251 [M]	Rick Nelson Sings for You	1966	20.00
—Black label with green and white at left			
❑ LP 12030 [S]	Songs by Ricky	1959	200.00
—Black label with silver print			
❑ LP 12030 [S]	Songs by Ricky	1964	40.00
—Black label with pink and white at left			
❑ LP 12030 [S]	Songs by Ricky	1966	25.00
—Black label with green and white at left			
❑ LP 12059 [DJ]	More Songs by Ricky	1960	1000.
—Promo copy on blue vinyl. Add 20 percent for enclosed poster.			
❑ LP 12059 [S]	More Songs by Ricky	1960	100.00
—Black label with silver print			
❑ LP 12059 [S]	More Songs by Ricky	1964	40.00
—Black label with pink and white at left			
❑ LP 12059 [S]	More Songs by Ricky	1966	25.00
—Black label with green and white at left			
❑ LP 12071 [S]	Rick Is 21	1961	100.00
—Black label with silver print			
❑ LP 12071 [S]	Rick Is 21	1964	40.00
—Black label with pink and white at left			
❑ LP 12071 [S]	Rick Is 21	1966	25.00
—Black label with green and white at left			
❑ LP 12082 [S]	Album Seven by Rick	1962	100.00
—Black label with silver print			
❑ LP 12082 [S]	Album Seven by Rick	1964	40.00
—Black label with pink and white at left			
❑ LP 12082 [S]	Album Seven by Rick	1966	25.00
—Black label with green and white at left			
❑ LP 12090 [S]	Ricky Sings Again	1962	150.00
—Black label with silver print			
❑ LP 12090 [S]	Ricky Sings Again	1964	40.00
—Black label with pink and white at left			
❑ LP 12090 [S]	Ricky Sings Again	1966	25.00
—Black label with green and white at left			
❑ LP 12218 [R]	Best Sellers	1964	20.00
—Black label with pink and white at left			
❑ LP 12218 [R]	Best Sellers	1966	15.00
—Black label with green and white at left			
❑ LP 12232 [R]	Million Sellers	1964	20.00
—Black label with pink and white at left			
❑ LP 12232 [R]	Million Sellers	1966	15.00
—Black label with green and white at left			
❑ LP 12244 [R]	A Long Vacation	1964	20.00
—Black label with pink and white at left			
❑ LP 12244 [R]	A Long Vacation	1966	15.00
—Black label with green and white at left			
❑ LP 12251 [R]	Rick Nelson Sings for You	1964	20.00
—Black label with pink and white at left			
❑ LP 12251 [R]	Rick Nelson Sings for You	1964	25.00
—Black label with silver print			
❑ LP 12251 [R]	Rick Nelson Sings for You	1966	15.00
—Black label with green and white at left			
❑ LP 12392 [R]	Ricky	1968	15.00
—Rechanneled reissue of 9048			
❑ LP 12393 [R]	Ricky Nelson	1968	15.00
—Rechanneled reissue of 9050			

N

LIBERTY

Number	Title (A Side/B Side)	Yr	NM
❑ LM-1004	Ricky	1981	8.00
—Reissue of United Artists 1004			
❑ LXB-9960 [(2)]	Legendary Masters	198?	12.00
—Reissue of United Artists 9960			
❑ LN-10134	Ricky Sings Again	1982	10.00
—Reissue of Imperial 12090			
❑ LN-10205	Souvenirs	1983	8.00
❑ LN-10253	Teen Age Idol	1984	8.00
❑ LN-10304	I Need You	1986	8.00
—Reissue of Sunset 5205			
❑ LN-10305	Ricky Nelson	1986	8.00
—Another reissue			
❑ LM-51004	Ricky	1983	8.00
—Reissue of Liberty 1004			

MCA

Number	Title (A Side/B Side)	Yr	NM
❑ 3	Rick Nelson In Concert	1973	12.00
—Reissue of Decca 75162			
❑ 20	Rick Sings Nelson	1973	12.00
—Reissue of Decca 75236			
❑ 37	Rudy the Fifth	1973	12.00
—Reissue of Decca 75297			
❑ 62	Garden Party	1973	12.00
—Reissue of Decca 75391			
❑ 383	Windfall	1974	15.00
❑ 1517	The Decca Years	1982	8.00
❑ 2-4004 [(2)]	Rick Nelson Country	1973	15.00
❑ 6163	All My Best	1986	10.00
❑ 25983	Rick Nelson In Concert The Troubadour, 1969	1987	10.00
—Reissue of MCA 3 with revised title			

RHINO

Number	Title (A Side/B Side)	Yr	NM
❑ RNLP 215	Greatest Hits	1985	12.00
❑ RNDF 259 [PD]	Greatest Hits	1985	15.00
❑ R1-70215	Greatest Hits	1987	10.00
❑ R1-71114	Live 1983-1985	1989	12.00

SUNSET

Number	Title (A Side/B Side)	Yr	NM
❑ SUM-1118 [M]	Ricky Nelson	1966	15.00
❑ SUS-5118 [P]	Ricky Nelson	1966	20.00
❑ SUS-5205	I Need You	1968	15.00

TIME-LIFE

Number	Title (A Side/B Side)	Yr	NM
❑ SRNR 31 [(2)]	Rick Nelson: 1957-1972	1989	15.00

UNITED ARTISTS

Number	Title (A Side/B Side)	Yr	NM
❑ UA-LA330-E	The Very Best of Rick Nelson	1974	12.00
❑ LM-1004	Ricky	1980	10.00
—Reissue of Imperial 9048			
❑ UAS-9960 [(2)]	Legendary Masters	1971	25.00

VERVE

Number	Title (A Side/B Side)	Yr	NM
❑ V 2083 [M]	Teen Time	1957	500.00
—Has three Ricky Nelson songs plus tracks by four others; usually treated as Rick's LP because of his prominence on the cover			

NELSON, SANDY

Also see THE GAMBLERS.

45s

IMPERIAL

Number	Title (A Side/B Side)	Yr	NM
❑ 5630	Drum Party/Big Noise from Winnetka	1959	12.00
❑ 5648	Party Time/The Wiggle	1960	12.00
❑ 5672	Bouncy/Lost Dreams	1960	12.00
❑ 5708	Cool Operator/Jive Talk	1960	12.00
❑ 5745	Big Noise from the Jungle/ Get With It	1961	12.00
❑ 5775	Let There Be Drums/ Quite a Beat	1961	15.00
❑ 5809	Drums Are My Beat/ The Birth of the Beat	1962	12.00
❑ 5829	Drummin' Up a Storm/ Drum Stomp	1962	12.00
❑ 5860	All Night Long/Rompin' and Stompin'	1962	12.00
❑ 5870	And Then There Were Drums/ Live It Up	1962	12.00
❑ 5884	Teenage House Party/Day Train	1962	12.00
❑ 5904	Be-Bop Baby/Let the Four Winds Blow	1962	12.00
❑ 5932	Ooh Poo Pah Doo/Feel So Good	1963	12.00
❑ 5940	You Name It/Alexis	1963	12.00
❑ 5965	Here We Go Again/Just Bill	1963	12.00
❑ 5988	Caravan/Sandy	1963	12.00
❑ 66019	Drum Shack/Kitty's Theme	1964	10.00
❑ 66034	Castle Rock/You Don't Say	1964	10.00
❑ 66060	Teen Beat '65/Kitty's Theme	1964	12.00
❑ 66093	Chop Chop/Reach for a Star	1965	10.00
❑ 66107	Land of 1000 Dances/ Let There Be Drums	1965	10.00
❑ 66127	Drums A-Go-Go/Caesar	1965	10.00
❑ 66146	A Lover's Concerto/ Treat Her Right	1965	10.00
❑ 66193	Rock It To 'Em J.B./The Charge	1966	10.00
❑ 66209	Let's Go Trippin'/Pipeline	1966	12.00
❑ 66246	The Drums Go On/ Lawdy Miss Clawdy	1967	10.00
❑ 66253	Peter Gunn/You Got Me Hummin'	1967	10.00
❑ 66284	Alligator Boogaloo/ Midnight Magic	1968	10.00
❑ 66350	Rebirth of the Beat/ Lion in Winter	1969	10.00
❑ 66375	Manhattan Spiritual/ The Stripper	1969	10.00
❑ 66402	Let There Be Drums and Brass/ Leap Frog	1969	10.00

ORIGINAL SOUND

Number	Title (A Side/B Side)	Yr	NM
❑ 5	Teen Beat/Big Jump	1959	25.00

UNITED ARTISTS

Number	Title (A Side/B Side)	Yr	NM
❑ 0082	Teen Beat/Let There Be Drums	1973	5.00
—"Silver Spotlight Series" reissue			
❑ XW383	You Are the Sunshine of My Life/Dance with the Devil	1974	10.00
❑ 50830	Sapporo '72	1971	—
—Unreleased			

VEEBLETRONICS

Number	Title (A Side/B Side)	Yr	NM
❑ 1	Drum Tunnel/Boogie #5	198?	5.00
❑ 2	Hunk of Drums/Witch Hunt	198?	5.00
❑ 3	A Drum Is a Woman/Boogie #5	198?	5.00

Albums

IMPERIAL

Number	Title (A Side/B Side)	Yr	NM
❑ LP 9105 [M]	Sandy Nelson Plays Teen Beat	1960	30.00
❑ LP 9136 [M]	He's a Drummer Boy	1961	30.00
❑ LP 9159 [M]	Let There Be Drums	1962	30.00
❑ LP 9168 [M]	Drums Are My Beat!	1962	20.00
—Black label with stars			
❑ LP 9168 [M]	Drums Are My Beat!	1964	15.00
—Pink, white and black label			
❑ LP 9189 [M]	Drummin' Up a Storm	1962	20.00
❑ LP 9202 [M]	Golden Hits	1962	20.00
❑ LP 9203 [M]	Country Style	1962	20.00
❑ LP 9203 [M]	On the Wild Side	1966	15.00
—Same LP as above, but new title on cover			
❑ LP 9204 [M]	Compelling Percussion	1962	20.00
❑ LP 9215 [M]	Teenage House Party	1963	20.00
❑ LP 9224 [M]	The Best of the Beats	1963	15.00
❑ LP 9237 [M]	Beat That Drum	1963	15.00
❑ LP 9249 [M]	Sandy Nelson Plays	1963	15.00
❑ LP 9258 [M]	Be True to Your School	1964	15.00
❑ LP 9272 [M]	Live! In Las Vegas	1964	20.00
❑ LP 9278 [M]	Teen Beat '65	1965	15.00
❑ LP 9283 [M]	Drum Discotheque	1965	15.00
❑ LP 9287 [M]	Drums A Go-Go	1965	15.00
❑ LP 9298 [M]	Boss Beat	1965	15.00
❑ LP 9305 [M]	"In" Beat	1966	15.00
❑ LP 9314 [M]	Super Drums	1966	15.00
❑ LP 9329 [M]	Beat That #!!@* Drum	1966	12.00
❑ LP 9340 [M]	Cheetah Beat	1967	12.00
❑ LP 9345 [M]	The Beat Goes On	1967	12.00
❑ LP 9362 [M]	Soul Drums	1967	15.00
❑ LP 12044 [S]	Sandy Nelson Plays Teen Beat	1960	40.00
❑ LP 12080 [R]	Let There Be Drums	1962	25.00
❑ LP 12083 [S]	Drums Are My Beat!	1962	25.00
❑ LP 12089 [R]	He's a Drummer Boy	1962	25.00
❑ LP 12189 [S]	Drummin' Up a Storm	1962	25.00
❑ LP 12202 [P]	Golden Hits	1962	25.00
❑ LP 12203 [S]	Country Style	1962	25.00
❑ LP 12203 [S]	On the Wild Side	1966	20.00
—Same LP as above, but new title on cover			
❑ LP 12204 [S]	Compelling Percussion	1962	25.00
❑ LP 12215 [S]	Teenage House Party	1963	25.00
❑ LP 12224 [S]	The Best of the Beats	1963	15.00
—Black, pink and white label			
❑ LP 12224 [S]	The Best of the Beats	1963	20.00
—Black label			
❑ LP 12237 [S]	Beat That Drum	1963	20.00
❑ LP 12249 [S]	Sandy Nelson Plays	1963	20.00
❑ LP 12258 [S]	Be True to Your School	1964	20.00
❑ LP 12272 [R]	Live! In Las Vegas	1964	15.00
❑ LP 12278 [S]	Teen Beat '65	1965	20.00
❑ LP 12283 [S]	Drum Discotheque	1965	20.00
❑ LP 12287 [S]	Drums A Go-Go	1965	20.00
❑ LP 12298 [S]	Boss Beat	1965	20.00
❑ LP 12305 [S]	"In" Beat	1966	20.00
❑ LP 12314 [S]	Super Drums	1966	20.00
❑ LP 12329 [S]	Beat That #!!@* Drum	1966	15.00
❑ LP 12340 [S]	Cheetah Beat	1967	15.00
❑ LP 12345 [S]	The Beat Goes On	1967	15.00
❑ LP 12362 [S]	Soul Drums	1967	12.00
❑ LP 12367	Boogaloo Beat	1968	12.00
❑ LP 12400	Rock and Roll Revival	1968	12.00
❑ LP 12424	Rebirth of the Beat	1969	12.00
❑ LP 12439	Manhattan Spiritual	1969	12.00
❑ LP 12451	Groovy	1970	12.00

LIBERTY

Number	Title (A Side/B Side)	Yr	NM
❑ LN-10172	The Very Best of Sandy Nelson	1982	8.00
❑ LN-10209	Collectors' Gems, Vol. 2	1983	8.00

PICKWICK

Number	Title (A Side/B Side)	Yr	NM
❑ SPC-3605	And Then There Were Drums	1978	10.00

SUNSET

Number	Title (A Side/B Side)	Yr	NM
❑ SUM-1114 [M]	Walking Beat	1966	10.00
❑ SUM-1166 [M]	Teen Drums	1967	10.00
❑ SUS-5114 [S]	Walking Beat	1966	12.00
❑ SUS-5166 [S]	Teen Drums	1967	12.00
❑ SUS-5224	And There Were Drums (Drums and More Drums)	1968	10.00

Except when noted otherwise, VG = 25% of NM, and VG+ = 50% of NM. (Example: VG = $2.00, VG+ = $4.00 and NM = $8.00.)

Number	Title (A Side/B Side)	Yr	NM
❑ SUS-5261	Heavy Drums	1969	10.00
❑ SUS-5291	Sandy Nelson Plays Fats Domino Hits	1970	10.00

UNITED ARTISTS

Number	Title (A Side/B Side)	Yr	NM
❑ UA-LA440-E	The Very Best of Sandy Nelson	1975	12.00

NELSON, TERI, GROUP

45s

KAMA SUTRA

Number	Title (A Side/B Side)	Yr	NM
❑ 245	Sweet Talkin' Willie/Back Side	1968	10.00

NELSON, TRACY Also see MOTHER EARTH; TRACY AND WILLIE NELSON.

45s

ATLANTIC

Number	Title (A Side/B Side)	Yr	NM
❑ 3235	It Takes a Lot to Laugh, It Takes a Train to Cry/Lean On Me	1975	5.00

CAPITOL

Number	Title (A Side/B Side)	Yr	NM
❑ 4442	Sad Situation/Let's Get Down to the Truth	1977	4.00

—With Larry Ballard

MCA

Number	Title (A Side/B Side)	Yr	NM
❑ 40479	Sweet Soul Music/ Nothing I Can't Handle	1975	4.00

MERCURY

Number	Title (A Side/B Side)	Yr	NM
❑ 72995	Sad Situation/Stay As Sweet As You Are	1970	8.00

Albums

ADELPHI

Number	Title (A Side/B Side)	Yr	NM
❑ 4119	Doin' It My Way	1981	10.00

ATLANTIC

Number	Title (A Side/B Side)	Yr	NM
❑ SD 7310	Tracy Nelson	1974	12.00

COLUMBIA

Number	Title (A Side/B Side)	Yr	NM
❑ KC 31759	Poor Man's Paradise	1973	12.00

FLYING FISH

Number	Title (A Side/B Side)	Yr	NM
❑ FF-052	Homemade Songs	1978	10.00
❑ FF-209	Come See About Me	1980	10.00

MCA

Number	Title (A Side/B Side)	Yr	NM
❑ 494	Sweet Soul Music	1975	12.00
❑ 2203	Time Is On My Side	1976	12.00

PRESTIGE

Number	Title (A Side/B Side)	Yr	NM
❑ PRLP 7393 [M]	Deep Are the Roots	1965	25.00
❑ PRST 7393 [S]	Deep Are the Roots	1965	30.00
❑ PRST 7726	Deep Are the Roots	1969	15.00

NELSON, TRACY AND WILLIE Also see each artist's individual listings.

45s

ATLANTIC

Number	Title (A Side/B Side)	Yr	NM
❑ 4028	After the Fire Is Gone/ Whiskey River	1976	5.00

NELSON, WILLIE Includes many duets not listed separately below. Also see HANK COCHRAN; DANNY DAVIS; MERLE HAGGARD; WAYLON JENNINGS; TRACY NELSON; WAYLON AND WILLIE.

45s

AMERICAN GOLD

Number	Title (A Side/B Side)	Yr	NM
❑ 7601	Night Life/Rainy Day Blues	1976	5.00

ATLANTIC

Number	Title (A Side/B Side)	Yr	NM
❑ 2968	Shotgun Willie/Sad Songs and Waltzes	1973	5.00
❑ 2979	Devil in a Sleepin' Bag/ Stay All Night	1973	5.00
❑ 3008	Heaven and Hell/I Still Can't Believe You're Gone	1974	5.00
❑ 3020	Phases and Stages/ Bloody Mary Morning	1974	5.00
❑ 3228	Sister's Coming Home/ Pick Up the Tempo	1974	5.00
❑ 3334	Heaven and Hell/I Still Can't Believe You're Gone	1976	5.00

BELLAIRE

Number	Title (A Side/B Side)	Yr	NM
❑ 107	Night Life/Rainy Day Blues	1963	30.00
❑ 107	Night Life/Rainy Day Blues	1963	60.00

—Colored vinyl

Number	Title (A Side/B Side)	Yr	NM
❑ 5000	Night Life '76/Man with the Blues	1976	5.00

BETTY

Number	Title (A Side/B Side)	Yr	NM
❑ 5702	What a Way to Love/ Misery Mansion	1964	20.00
❑ 5703	Man with the Blues/The Storm Has Just Begun	1964	20.00

CHALLENGE

Number	Title (A Side/B Side)	Yr	NM
❑ 59280	I'm Talking About Love/I'm in Love with a Dancing Girl Working at Metropole	1965	15.00

COLUMBIA

Number	Title (A Side/B Side)	Yr	NM
❑ AE7 1182 [DJ]	White Christmas/Blue Christmas	1979	25.00

—Green vinyl

Number	Title (A Side/B Side)	Yr	NM
❑ AE7 1183 [DJ]	Pretty Paper/Rudolph the Red-Nosed Reindeer	1979	25.00

—Red vinyl

Number	Title (A Side/B Side)	Yr	NM
❑ AE7 1775 [DJ]	Pretty Paper/White Christmas	1982	6.00
❑ 02000	Mona Lisa/Twinkle, Twinkle Little Star	1981	4.00
❑ 02166	On the Road Again/ September Song	1981	3.00

—Reissue

Number	Title (A Side/B Side)	Yr	NM
❑ 02187	I'm Gonna Sit Right Down and Write Myself a Letter/ Over the Rainbow	1981	4.00
❑ 02558	Heartaches of a Fool/ Uncloudy Day	1981	4.00
❑ 02741	Always on My Mind/ The Party's Over	1982	4.00
❑ 03073	Let It Be Me/Permanently Lonely	1982	4.00
❑ 03123	Angel Flying Too Close to the Ground/Mona Lisa	1982	3.00

—Reissue

Number	Title (A Side/B Side)	Yr	NM
❑ 03124	Heartache of a Fool/ Midnight Rider	1982	3.00

—Reissue

Number	Title (A Side/B Side)	Yr	NM
❑ 03385	Last Thing I Needed First Thing This Morning/Old Fords and a Natural Stone	1982	4.00
❑ 03476	Pretty Paper/White Christmas	1982	5.00
❑ 03674	Beer Barrel Polka/Little Old Fashioned Karma	1983	4.00
❑ 03965	Why Do I Have to Choose/ Would You Lay with Me (In a Field of Stone)	1983	4.00
❑ 04217	To All the Girls I've Loved Before/ I Don't Want to Wake You	1984	3.00

—Julio Iglesias & Willie Nelson; B-side by Julio Iglesias solo

Number	Title (A Side/B Side)	Yr	NM
❑ 04217 [PS]	To All the Girls I've Loved Before/ I Don't Want to Wake You	1984	4.00

—Julio Iglesias & Willie Nelson; second sleeve has artists' names in all capital letters

Number	Title (A Side/B Side)	Yr	NM
❑ 04217 [PS]	To All the Girls I've Loved Before/ I Don't Want to Wake You	1984	5.00

—Julio Iglesias & Willie Nelson; first sleeve has artists' names in both capital and small letters

Number	Title (A Side/B Side)	Yr	NM
❑ 04263	Without a Song/I Can't Begin to Tell You	1983	3.00
❑ 04495	As Time Goes By/ You'll Never Know	1984	25.00

—Willie Nelson and Julio Iglesias; withdrawn immediately upon release

Number	Title (A Side/B Side)	Yr	NM
❑ 04495 [PS]	As Time Goes By/ You'll Never Know	1984	25.00

—Willie Nelson and Julio Iglesias; withdrawn immediately upon release

Number	Title (A Side/B Side)	Yr	NM
❑ 04568	City of New Orleans/ Why Are You Pickin' On Me	1984	3.00
❑ 04568 [PS]	City of New Orleans/ Why Are You Pickin' On Me	1984	4.00
❑ 04715	Seven Spanish Angels/ Who Cares	1984	3.00

—A-side: Ray Charles and Willie Nelson; B-side: Ray Charles and Janie Frickie

Number	Title (A Side/B Side)	Yr	NM
❑ 04847	Forgiving You Was Easy/ You Wouldn't Cross the Street (To Say Goodbye)	1985	3.00
❑ 04881	Highwayman/The Human Condition	1985	3.00

—A-side: Willie Nelson/Waylon Jennings/Johnny Cash/Kris Kristofferson; B-side: Nelson, Cash

Number	Title (A Side/B Side)	Yr	NM
❑ 04881 [PS]	Highwayman/The Human Condition	1985	4.00

—A-side: Willie Nelson/Waylon Jennings/Johnny Cash/Kris Kristofferson; B-side: Nelson, Cash

Number	Title (A Side/B Side)	Yr	NM
❑ 05566	Are There Any More Real Cowboys/I'm a Memory	1985	3.00

—A-side with Neil Young

Number	Title (A Side/B Side)	Yr	NM
❑ 05594	Desperadoes Waiting for a Train/The Twentieth Century Is Almost Over	1985	3.00

—A-side: Willie Nelson/Waylon Jennings/Johnny Cash/Kris Kristofferson; B-side: Nelson, Cash

Number	Title (A Side/B Side)	Yr	NM
❑ 05597	Me and Paul/I Let My Mind Wander	1985	3.00
❑ 05677	Slow Movin' Outlaw/ They All Went to Mexico	1985	3.00

—A-side with Lacy J. Dalton; B-side with Carlos Santana

Number	Title (A Side/B Side)	Yr	NM
❑ 05749	I Told a Lie to My Heart/Slow Movin' Outlaw	1986	3.00

—A-side with Hank Williams, Jr.; B-side: with Lacy J. Dalton

Number	Title (A Side/B Side)	Yr	NM
❑ 05834	Living in the Promiseland/ Bach Minuet in G	1986	3.00
❑ 06246	I'm Not Trying to Forget You/ I've Got the Craziest Feeling	1986	3.00
❑ 06530	Partners After All/Home Away from Home	1986	3.00
❑ 07007	Heart of Gold/So Much Like My Dad	1987	3.00
❑ 07202	Island in the Sun/There Is No Easy Way (But There Is a Way)	1987	3.00
❑ 07636	Nobody There But Me/Wake Me When It's Over	1987	3.00
❑ 08044	Spanish Eyes/Ole Buttermilk Sky	1988	3.00

—With Julio Iglesias

Number	Title (A Side/B Side)	Yr	NM
❑ 08395	Living in the Promiseland/ Forgiving You Was Easy	1988	3.00

—Reissue

Number	Title (A Side/B Side)	Yr	NM
❑ 08406	Highwayman/Desperadoes Waiting for a Train	1988	3.00

—Waylon Jennings/Willie Nelson/Johnny Cash/Kris Kristofferson; reissue

Number	Title (A Side/B Side)	Yr	NM
❑ 08541	Twilight Time/Ac-Cent-Tchu-Ate the Positive	1989	3.00
❑ 10176	Blue Eyes Cryin' in the Rain/ Bandera	1975	5.00
❑ 10275	Remember Me/Time of the Preacher	1975	5.00
❑ 10327	I'd Have to Be Crazy/ Amazing Grace	1976	5.00
❑ 10383	If You've Got the Money, I've Got the Time/The Sound in Your Mind	1976	5.00
❑ 10453	Uncloudy Day/ Precious Memories	1976	5.00
❑ 10588	I Love You a Thousand Ways/ Mom and Dad's Waltz	1977	5.00
❑ 10644	Something to Brag About/ Anybody's Darlin' (Anybody But Mine)	1977	5.00

—With Mary Kay Place

Number	Title (A Side/B Side)	Yr	NM
❑ 10704	Georgia on My Mind/On the Sunny Side of the Street	1978	5.00
❑ 10784	Blue Skies/Moonlight in Vermont	1978	5.00
❑ 10834	All of Me/Unchained Melody	1978	5.00
❑ 10877	Whiskey River/Under the Double Eagle	1978	5.00
❑ 10929	September Song/Don't Get Around Much Anymore	1979	4.00
❑ 11126	Help Me Make It Through the Night/The Pilgrim: Chapter 33	1979	4.00
❑ 11186	My Heroes Have Always Been Cowboys/Rising Star (Love Theme)	1980	4.00
❑ 11257	Midnight Rider/Do You Think You're a Cowboy	1980	4.00
❑ 11351	On the Road Again/ Jumpin' Cotton-Eyed Joe	1980	4.00

—B-side by Johnny Gimble

Number	Title (A Side/B Side)	Yr	NM
❑ 11418	Angel Flying Too Close to the Ground/I Guess I've Come to Live Here in Your Eyes	1981	4.00
❑ 68923	Nothing I Can Do About It Now/ If I Were a Painting	1989	3.00
❑ 73015	There You Are/Spirit	1989	3.00
❑ 73233	Silver Stallion/America Remains	1990	3.00

—Waylon Jennings/Willie Nelson/Johnny Cash/Kris Kristofferson

Number	Title (A Side/B Side)	Yr	NM
❑ 73249	The Highway/Spirit	1990	3.00
❑ 73374	Is the Better Part Over/Mr. Record Man	1990	3.00
❑ 73381	Born and Raised in Black and White/Texas	1990	3.00

—The Highwaymen (Waylon Jennings/Willie Nelson/Johnny Cash/ Kris Kristofferson)

Number	Title (A Side/B Side)	Yr	NM
❑ 73518	It Ain't Necessarily So/ I Never Cared for You	1990	3.00
❑ 73572	American Remains/Texas	1990	3.00

—The Highwaymen (Waylon Jennings/Willie Nelson/Johnny Cash/ Kris Kristofferson)

Number	Title (A Side/B Side)	Yr	NM
❑ 73655	The Piper Came Today/ (I Don't Have a Reason) To Go to California Anymore	1991	3.00
❑ 73749	Ten with a Two/You Decide	1991	3.00
❑ 77184	Still Is Still Moving to Me/ Valentine	1993	3.00

D

Number	Title (A Side/B Side)	Yr	NM
❑ 1084	Man with the Blues/ The Storm Has Just Begun	1959	30.00
❑ 1131	What a Way to Love/ Misery Mansion	1960	30.00

ISLAND

Number	Title (A Side/B Side)	Yr	NM
❑ 572414-7	The Maker/I Never Cared for You	1998	3.00

LIBERTY

Number	Title (A Side/B Side)	Yr	NM
❑ S7-18486	It Is What It Is/The Devil's Right Hand	1995	3.00

—By The Highwaymen

Number	Title (A Side/B Side)	Yr	NM
❑ S7-18584	One After 909/Yesterday	1995	3.00

—B-side by Billy Dean

Number	Title (A Side/B Side)	Yr	NM
❑ 55386	Mr. Record Man/The Part Where I Cry	1961	20.00
❑ 55403	Willingly/Chain of Love	1962	15.00

—A-side with Shirley Collie

Number	Title (A Side/B Side)	Yr	NM
❑ 55439	Touch Me/Where My House Lives	1962	15.00
❑ 55468	You Dream About Me/ Is This My Destiny	1962	15.00

—A-side with Shirley Collie

Number	Title (A Side/B Side)	Yr	NM
❑ 55494	Wake Me When It's Over/There's Gonna Be Love in My House	1962	15.00
❑ 55532	Half a Man/The Last Letter	1963	12.00

N

Number	Title (A Side/B Side)	Yr	NM
❑ 55591	Take My Word/Feed It a Memory	1963	12.00
❑ 55638	How Long Is Forever/You Took My Happy Away	1963	12.00
❑ 55661	Am I Blue/There'll Be No Teardrops Tonight	1964	10.00
❑ 55697	River Boy/Opportunity to Cry	1964	10.00
❑ 56143	Right or Wrong/I Hope So	1969	6.00
LONE STAR			
❑ 703	The End of Understanding/Will You Remember Mine	1978	5.00
MERCURY			
❑ 088 172243-7	Mendocino County Line/Maria (Shut Up and Kiss Me)	2002	3.00
—A-side with Lee Ann Womack			
MONUMENT			
❑ 855	I Never Cared for You/You Left Me	1964	15.00
❑ 03408	Everything Is Beautiful (In Its Own Way)/Put It Off Until Tomorrow	1982	4.00
—A-side: Willie Nelson and Dolly Parton; B-side: Dolly Parton and Kris Kristofferson			
❑ 03781	You're Gonna Love Yourself (In the Morning)/What Do You Think About Lovin'	1983	4.00
—A-side: Willie Nelson and Brenda Lee; B-side: Dolly Parton and Brenda Lee			
PARADISE			
❑ 629	Wabash Cannonball/Tennessee Waltz	1984	4.00
—A-side with Hank Wilson (a.k.a. Leon Russell); B-side by Wilson solo			
RCA			
❑ PB-10969	I'm a Memory/It Should Be Easier Now	1977	5.00
—With Darrell McCall			
❑ PB-11061	You Ought to Hear Me Cry/One in a Row	1977	5.00
❑ PB-11235	If You Can Touch Her at All/Rainy Day Blues	1978	5.00
❑ PB-11465	Sweet Memories/Little Things	1979	5.00
❑ PB-11673	Crazy Arms/Hurricane Shirley	1979	5.00
—B-side by Bobby Bare			
❑ GB-11995	Sweet Memories/If You Can Touch Her At All	1980	3.00
—Gold Standard Series			
❑ PB-12254	Good Times/Where Do You Stand	1981	4.00
❑ PB-12254 [PS]	Good Times/Where Do You Stand	1981	5.00
❑ PB-12328	Mountain Dew/Laying My Burdens Down	1981	4.00
RCA VICTOR			
❑ 47-8484	Pretty Paper/What a Merry Christmas This Could Be	1964	15.00
❑ 47-8519	She's Not for You/Permanently Lonely	1965	12.00
❑ 47-8594	Healing Hands of Time/One Day at a Time	1965	12.00
❑ 47-8682	I Just Can't Let You Say Goodbye/And So Will You, My Love	1965	12.00
❑ 47-8801	Columbus Stockade Blues/He Sits at My Table	1966	12.00
❑ 47-8852	I'm Still Not Over You/I Love You Because	1966	12.00
❑ 47-8933	One in a Row/San Antonio Rose	1966	12.00
❑ 47-9029	Pretty Paper/What a Merry Christmas This Could Be	1966	12.00
❑ 47-9100	The Party's Over/Make Way for a Better Man	1967	10.00
❑ 47-9202	Blackjack County Chain/Some Other World	1967	10.00
❑ 47-9324	San Antonio/To Make a Long Story Short	1967	10.00
❑ 47-9427	Little Things/I'll Stay Around	1968	10.00
❑ 47-9536	Good Times/Don't You Ever Get Tired	1968	10.00
❑ 47-9605	Johnny One Time/She's Still Gone	1968	10.00
❑ 47-9684	Bring Me Sunshine/Don't Say Love or Nothing	1968	10.00
❑ 47-9778	Pretty Paper/What a Merry Christmas This Could Be	1969	—
—Unreleased			
❑ 47-9798	Who Do I Know in Dallas/Once More with Feeling	1969	8.00
❑ 47-9903	Laying My Burdens Down/Truth Number One	1970	8.00
❑ 47-9931	Pretty Paper/What a Merry Christmas This Could Be	1970	8.00
❑ 47-9951	I'm a Memory/I'm So Lonesome I Could Cry	1971	6.00
❑ 47-9984	Kneel at the Feet of Jesus/What Can You Do to Me Now	1971	6.00
❑ 74-0162	Jimmy's Road/Natural to Be Gone	1969	8.00
❑ 74-0542	Yesterday's Wine/Me and Paul	1971	6.00
❑ 74-0635	A Moment Isn't Very Long/Words Don't Fit the Picture	1972	6.00
❑ 74-0816	Mountain Dew/Phases, Stages, Circles, Cycles, and Scenes	1972	6.00
❑ PB-10429	I'm a Memory/Fire and Rain	1975	5.00
❑ PB-10461	Pretty Paper/What a Merry Christmas This Could Be	1975	8.00
❑ PB-10591	Summer of Roses/I Gotta Get Drunk	1976	5.00
SARG			
❑ 260	A Storm Has Just Begun/When I Sang My Last Hillbilly Song	196?	50.00
—Some sources say this came out in 1955, but that doesn't coincide with this label's history			
SONGBIRD			
❑ 41313	Family Bible/In God's Eyes	1980	4.00
UNITED ARTISTS			
❑ 641	Night Life/Rainy Day Blues	1963	15.00
❑ XW771	The Last Letter/There Goes a Man	1976	5.00
❑ XW1165	Hello Walls/The Last Letter	1978	5.00
❑ XW1254	There'll Be Teardrops Tonight/Blue Must Be the Color of the Blues	1978	5.00
WILLIE NELSON			
❑ 628	No Place for Me/The Lumberjack	1957	300.00

Albums

Number	Title	Yr	NM
ALLEGIANCE			
❑ AV-5005	Willie or Won't He	1983	10.00
❑ AV-5010	Wild & Willie	1983	10.00
ATLANTIC			
❑ SD 7262	Shotgun Willie	1973	20.00
❑ SD 7291	Phases and Stages	1974	20.00
COLUMBIA			
❑ KC 33482	Red Headed Stranger	1975	15.00
—No bar code on back cover			
❑ PC 33482	Red Headed Stranger	1979	8.00
—With bar code on back cover; budget-line reissue			
❑ PC 34092	The Sound in Your Mind	1976	12.00
—No bar code on back cover			
❑ PC 34092	The Sound in Your Mind	1979	8.00
—With bar code on back cover; budget-line reissue			
❑ KC 34112	The Troublemaker	1976	12.00
—No bar code on back cover			
❑ PC 34112	The Troublemaker	1979	8.00
—With bar code on back cover; budget-line reissue			
❑ JC 34695	To Lefty From Willie	1977	12.00
❑ PC 34695	To Lefty From Willie	1979	8.00
—Budget-line reissue			
❑ JC 35305	Stardust	1978	10.00
❑ JC 35305	Stardust	2000	25.00
—Classic Records reissue on audiophile vinyl			
❑ KC2 35642 [(2)]	Willie and Family Live	1978	15.00
❑ JC 36188	Willie Nelson Sings Kristofferson	1979	10.00
❑ PC 36188	Willie Nelson Sings Kristofferson	1980	8.00
—Budget-line reissue			
❑ JC 36189	Pretty Paper	1979	10.00
❑ JS 36327	The Electric Horseman	1979	10.00
—Side 2 by Dave Grusin			
❑ S2 36752 [(2)]	Honeysuckle Rose	1980	12.00
—Over half of the LP is by Willie			
❑ FC 36883	Somewhere Over the Rainbow	1981	10.00
❑ KC2 37542 [(2)]	Willie Nelson's Greatest Hits (& Some That Will Be)	1981	12.00
❑ FC 37951	Always on My Mind	1982	10.00
❑ PC 37951	Always on My Mind	1984	8.00
—Budget-line reissue			
❑ PC 38248	Tougher Than Leather	1984	8.00
—Budget-line reissue			
❑ QC 38248	Tougher Than Leather	1983	10.00
❑ CX 38250 [(10)]	Willie Nelson	1983	120.00
❑ FC 39110	Without a Song	1983	10.00
❑ PC 39110	Without a Song	1984	8.00
—Budget-line reissue			
❑ FC 39145	City of New Orleans	1984	10.00
❑ PC 39145	City of New Orleans	1985	8.00
—Budget-line reissue			
❑ FC 39363	Angel Eyes	1984	10.00
❑ PC 39363	Angel Eyes	1985	8.00
—Budget-line reissue			
❑ FC 39894	Partners	1986	10.00
❑ PC 39894	Partners	1987	8.00
—Budget-line reissue			
❑ 9C9 39943 [PD]	Always on My Mind	1985	20.00
❑ FC 39990	Half Nelson	1985	10.00
—Duets with 10 different artists			
❑ PC 39990	Half Nelson	1986	8.00
—Budget-line reissue			
❑ FC 40008	Me and Paul	1985	10.00
❑ PC 40008	Me and Paul	1986	8.00
—Budget-line reissue			
❑ FC 40056	Highwayman	1985	10.00
—Waylon Jennings/Willie Nelson/Johnny Cash/Kris Kristofferson			
❑ FC 40327	The Promiseland	1986	10.00
❑ FC 40487	Island in the Sea	1987	10.00
❑ HC 43482	Red Headed Stranger	1982	40.00
—Half-speed mastered edition			
❑ FC 44431	What a Wonderful World	1988	10.00
❑ FC 45046	A Horse Called Music	1989	10.00
❑ C 45240	Highwayman 2	1990	15.00
—Waylon Jennings/Willie Nelson/Johnny Cash/Kris Kristofferson			
❑ HC 45305	Stardust	1981	70.00
—Half-speed mastered edition			
❑ HC 47951	Always on My Mind	1982	50.00
—Half-speed mastered edition			
❑ HC 48248	Tougher Than Leather	1983	50.00
—Half-speed mastered edition			
DELTA			
❑ DLP-1157	Diamonds in the Rough	1982	10.00
HEARTLAND			
❑ HL 1038/9 [(2)]	The Best of Willie Nelson	1987	15.00
LIBERTY			
❑ LRP-3239 [M]	...And Then I Wrote	1962	40.00
❑ LRP-3308 [M]	Here's Willie Nelson	1963	40.00
❑ LST-7239 [S]	...And Then I Wrote	1962	50.00
❑ LST-7308 [S]	Here's Willie Nelson	1963	50.00
❑ LN-10013	Country Willie	1980	8.00
—Budget-line reissue			
❑ LN-10118	The Best of Willie Nelson	1982	8.00
—Budget-line reissue			
LOST HIGHWAY			
❑ B0004706-01	Countryman	2005	12.00
❑ B0006079-01	You Don't Know Me: The Songs of Cindy Walker	2006	12.00
❑ B0006939-01	Songbird	2006	15.00
PAIR			
❑ PDL2-1007 [(2)]	Country Winners	1986	12.00
❑ PDL2-1032 [(2)]	Once More with Feeling	1986	12.00
❑ PDL2-1114 [(2)]	Good Hearted Woman	1986	12.00
PICKWICK			
❑ ACL1-0326	Country Winners	1976	8.00
❑ ACL1-0705	Spotlight on Willie Nelson	1976	8.00
❑ SPC-3584	Hello Walls	1978	10.00
❑ ACL1-7018	Columbus Stockade Blues	1976	8.00
PLANTATION			
❑ PLP-24	The Longhorn Jamboree Presents: Willie Nelson & His Friends	1976	10.00
—Also includes tracks by David Allan Coe, Jerry Lee Lewis and Carl Perkins			
RCA CAMDEN			
❑ ACL1-0326	Country Winners	1973	12.00
❑ ACL1-0705	Spotlight on Willie Nelson	1974	12.00
❑ CAS-2444	Columbus Stockade Blues	1970	15.00
❑ ACL1-7018	Columbus Stockade Blues	1975	10.00
RCA VICTOR			
❑ ANL1-1102	Yesterday's Wine	1975	10.00
❑ APL1-1234	What Can You Do to Me Now	1975	12.00
❑ APL1-1487	Willie Nelson Live	1976	12.00
❑ APL1-2210	Before His Time	1977	10.00
❑ AHL1-3243	Sweet Memories	1979	10.00
❑ LPM-3418 [M]	Country Willie — His Own Songs	1965	20.00
❑ LSP-3418 [S]	Country Willie — His Own Songs	1965	25.00
❑ LPM-3528 [M]	Country Favorites, Willie Nelson Style	1966	20.00
❑ LSP-3528 [S]	Country Favorites, Willie Nelson Style	1966	25.00
❑ AHL1-3549	Danny Davis & Willie Nelson with the Nashville Brass	1980	10.00
❑ LPM-3659 [M]	Country Music Concert	1966	20.00
❑ LSP-3659 [S]	Country Music Concert	1966	25.00
❑ AYL1-3671	Before His Time	1980	8.00
—"Best Buy Series" reissue			
❑ LPM-3748 [M]	Make Way for Willie Nelson	1967	20.00
❑ LSP-3748 [S]	Make Way for Willie Nelson	1967	25.00
❑ AYL1-3800	Yesterday's Wine	1980	8.00
—"Best Buy Series" reissue			
❑ LPM-3858 [M]	The Party's Over and Other Great Willie Nelson Songs	1967	25.00
❑ LSP-3858 [S]	The Party's Over and Other Great Willie Nelson Songs	1967	20.00
❑ LPM-3937 [M]	Texas in My Soul	1968	100.00
❑ LSP-3937 [S]	Texas in My Soul	1968	20.00
❑ AYL1-3958	What Can You Do to Me Now	1981	8.00
—"Best Buy Series" reissue			
❑ AHL1-4045	The Minstrel Man	1981	10.00
❑ LSP-4057	Good Times	1968	20.00
❑ LSP-4111	My Own Peculiar Way	1969	20.00
❑ AYL1-4165	Willie Nelson Live	1981	8.00
—"Best Buy Series" reissue			
❑ LSP-4294	Both Sides Now	1970	20.00
❑ AYL1-4300	Sweet Memories	1982	8.00
❑ —"Best Buy Series" reissue			
❑ LSP-4404	Laying My Burdens Down	1970	20.00
❑ AHL1-4420	The Best of Willie Nelson	1982	10.00
❑ LSP-4489	Willie Nelson & Family	1971	20.00
❑ LSP-4568	Yesterday's Wine	1971	20.00
❑ LSP-4653	The Picture	1972	20.00
❑ LSP-4760	The Willie Way	1972	20.00

Except when noted otherwise, VG = 25% of NM, and VG+ = 50% of NM. (Example: VG = $2.00, VG+ = $4.00 and NM = $8.00.)

Number	Title (A Side/B Side)	Yr	NM
❑ AHL1-4819	My Own Way	1983	10.00
❑ AYL1-5143	The Best of Willie Nelson	1984	8.00
—"Best Buy Series" reissue			
❑ CPL1-5174	Don't You Ever Get Tired of Hurting Me	1984	10.00
❑ AYL1-5438	My Own Way	1985	8.00
—"Best Buy Series" reissue			
❑ AHL1-5470	Collector's Series	1985	10.00
❑ CPL1-7158	Willie	1986	10.00
SONGBIRD			
❑ 3258	Family Bible	1980	10.00
SUNSET			
❑ SUM-1138 [M]	Hello Walls	1966	15.00
❑ SUS-5138 [S]	Hello Walls	1966	20.00
TAKOMA			
❑ TAK-7104	The Legend Begins	1983	10.00
TIME-LIFE			
❑ P 16946 [(3)]	Country and Western Classics	1983	20.00
UNITED ARTISTS			
❑ UA-LA086-E	The Best of Willie Nelson	1973	15.00
—Reissue of Liberty tracks			
❑ UA-LA410-G	Country Willie	1975	15.00
❑ UA-LA574-H2 [(2)]	Texas Country	1975	18.00
❑ UA-LA930-G	There'll Be No Teardrops Tonight	1978	15.00

NELSON, WILLIE, AND DAVID ALLAN COE

Albums

Number	Title (A Side/B Side)	Yr	NM
PLANTATION			
❑ PLP 41	Willie and David	1980	10.00

—One side is solo songs by Willie Nelson, the other side solo songs by David Allan Coe

NELSON, WILLIE, AND KRIS KRISTOFFERSON

Also see each artist's individual listings.

45s

Number	Title (A Side/B Side)	Yr	NM
COLUMBIA			
❑ 38-04652	How Do You Feel About Foolin' Around/Eye of the Storm	1984	3.00

Albums

Number	Title (A Side/B Side)	Yr	NM
COLUMBIA			
❑ FC 39531	Music from Songwriter	1984	10.00

NELSON, WILLIE, AND ROGER MILLER

Also see each artist's individual listings.

45s

Number	Title (A Side/B Side)	Yr	NM
COLUMBIA			
❑ 02681	Old Friends/When a House Is Not a Home	1982	4.00
—With Ray Price			

Albums

Number	Title (A Side/B Side)	Yr	NM
COLUMBIA			
❑ FC 38013	Old Friends	1982	10.00
❑ PC 38013	Old Friends	198?	8.00
—Budget-line reissue			

NELSON, WILLIE, AND WEBB PIERCE

Also see each artist's individual listings.

45s

Number	Title (A Side/B Side)	Yr	NM
COLUMBIA			
❑ 03231	In the Jailhouse Now/Back Street Affair	1982	4.00

Albums

Number	Title (A Side/B Side)	Yr	NM
COLUMBIA			
❑ FC 38095	In the Jailhouse Now	1982	10.00
❑ PC 38095	In the Jailhouse Now	198?	8.00
—Budget-line reissue			

NELSON, WILLIE, AND RAY PRICE

Also see each artist's individual listings.

45s

Number	Title (A Side/B Side)	Yr	NM
COLUMBIA			
❑ 11329	Faded Love/This Cold World with You	1980	4.00
❑ 11405	Don't You Ever Get Tired (Of Loving Me)/Funny How Time Slips Away	1980	4.00

Albums

Number	Title (A Side/B Side)	Yr	NM
COLUMBIA			
❑ JC 36476	San Antonio Rose	1980	10.00
❑ PC 36476	San Antonio Rose	198?	8.00
—Budget-line reissue			

NELSON, WILLIE, AND LEON RUSSELL

Also see each artist's individual listings.

45s

Number	Title (A Side/B Side)	Yr	NM
COLUMBIA			
❑ 11023	Heartbreak Hotel/Sioux City Sue	1979	4.00
❑ 11119	Trouble in Mind/One for My Baby (And One More for the Road)	1979	4.00

Albums

Number	Title (A Side/B Side)	Yr	NM
COLUMBIA			
❑ KC2 36064 [(2)]	One for the Road	1979	15.00

NELSON, WILLIE, AND HANK SNOW

Albums

Number	Title (A Side/B Side)	Yr	NM
COLUMBIA			
❑ FC 39977	Brand on My Heart	1984	10.00
❑ PC 39977	Brand on My Heart	1985	8.00
—Budget-line reissue			

NELSON, WILLIE, AND FARON YOUNG

Albums

Number	Title (A Side/B Side)	Yr	NM
COLUMBIA			
❑ FC 39484	Funny How Time Slips Away	1984	10.00
❑ PC 39484	Funny How Time Slips Away	1985	8.00
—Budget-line reissue			

NELSON, WILLY

Cousin of RICKY NELSON, this isn't the famous country singer. It's confusing enough that he recorded for Liberty, for which the "other" Willie recorded in the early 1960s, but some pressings of this record were spelled "Willie"!

45s

Number	Title (A Side/B Side)	Yr	NM
LIBERTY			
❑ 55155	Susie/No Dough	1958	25.00
—As "Willy Nelson"			
❑ 55155	Susie/No Dough	1958	30.00
—As "Willie Nelson"			

NEON PHILHARMONIC, THE

45s

Number	Title (A Side/B Side)	Yr	NM
MCA			
❑ 40518	So Glad You're a Woman/Making Out the Best You Can	1976	5.00
TRX			
❑ 5039	Annie Poor/Love Will Find a Way	1972	5.00
WARNER BROS.			
❑ 7261	Morning Girl/Brilliant Colors	1969	8.00
❑ 7311	No One Is Going to Hurt You/You Lied	1969	6.00
❑ 7355	Clouds/Snow	1969	6.00
❑ 7380	Heighdy-Ho Princess/Don't Know My Way Around My Soul	1970	6.00
❑ 7419	Flowers for Your Pillow/To Be Continued	1970	6.00
❑ 7457	Something to Believe In/A Little Love	1971	6.00
❑ 7497	Gotta Feeling in My Bones/Keep the Faith in Me	1971	6.00

Albums

Number	Title (A Side/B Side)	Yr	NM
WARNER BROS.			
❑ WS 1769	The Moth Confesses	1968	25.00
❑ WS 1804	The Neon Philharmonic	1969	15.00

NEONS, THE (1)

45s

Number	Title (A Side/B Side)	Yr	NM
CHALLENGE			
❑ 9147	Magic Moment/Fat Girls	1962	100.00
❑ 59147	Magic Moment/Fat Girls	1962	50.00

NEONS, THE (2)

45s

Number	Title (A Side/B Side)	Yr	NM
GONE			
❑ 5090	Angel Face/Golden Dreams	1960	40.00
TETRA			
❑ 4444	Angel Face/Kiss Me Quickly	1956	80.00
❑ 4449	Road of Romance/My Chickadee	1957	80.00
VINTAGE			
❑ 1016	Honey Bun/Golden Dreams	1974	5.00

NEONS, THE (3)

45s

Number	Title (A Side/B Side)	Yr	NM
WALDON			
❑ 1001	My Lover/Tucson	1961	700.00

NEP-TUNES, THE

Albums

Number	Title (A Side/B Side)	Yr	NM
FAMILY			
❑ FLP-152 [M]	Surfer's Holiday	1963	200.00
❑ SFLP-152 [S]	Surfer's Holiday	1963	300.00

NEPTUNES, THE

Several different groups.

45s

Number	Title (A Side/B Side)	Yr	NM
CHECKER			
❑ 967	She'll Understand/So Little Time	1960	12.00
GEM			
❑ 100	Turn Around/Girl That's an Awful Thing to Say	196?	25.00
GLORY			
❑ 269	Fraidy Cat/As Long As	1959	20.00
INSTANT			
❑ 3255	Make a Memory/House of Heartaches	1963	50.00
PAYSON			
❑ 101/2	If You Care/She Went That-a-Way	1958	20.00
RCA VICTOR			
❑ 47-7931	Curiosity Killed the Cat/This Is Love	1961	12.00
VICTORIA			
❑ 102	I'm Coming Home/I Don't Cry Anymore	1964	300.00
WARNER BROS.			
❑ 5453	Shame Girl/I've Got Plans	1964	12.00

NERO, FRANCES

45s

Number	Title (A Side/B Side)	Yr	NM
SOUL			
❑ 35020	Keep On Lovin' Me/Fight Off Fire with Fire	1966	200.00

NERO, PETER

45s

Number	Title (A Side/B Side)	Yr	NM
ARIOLA AMERICA			
❑ 7635	There'll Be Time/Always Lovely Times	1976	4.00
❑ 7650	Tara's Theme/Always Lovely Times	1976	4.00
ARISTA			
❑ 0112	Emmanuelle/Soul Ballet	1975	4.00
❑ 0125	Theme from "The Young and the Restless"/Superstition	1975	4.00
COLUMBIA			
❑ 44846	Soulful Strut/For Once in My Life	1969	5.00
❑ 44934	Be-In/Theme from Picasso Summer	1969	5.00
❑ 45077	Come Saturday Morning/Maybe Tomorrow	1970	4.00
❑ 45167	Company/Raindrops Keep Fallin' on My Head	1970	4.00
❑ 45198	The Great Hits of Summer Medley/Something	1970	4.00
❑ 45279	Theme from "Love Story"/El Condor Pasa	1970	4.00
❑ 45399	Theme from "Summer of '42"/Theme from "Jesus Christ Superstar"	1971	4.00
❑ 45544	Brian's Song/Just for Her	1972	4.00
❑ 45651	Love Theme from "The Godfather"/A Love That Never Ends	1972	4.00
❑ 45731	Ben (Theme from "Ben")/His World	1972	4.00
❑ 45756	Lady Sings the Blues/Love Is Waiting	1973	4.00
❑ 45756 [PS]	Lady Sings the Blues/Love Is Waiting	1973	5.00
❑ 45825	Theme from "Baxter"/Love Is Waiting	1973	4.00
❑ 45959	The Morning After/Daydream	1973	4.00
RCA VICTOR			
❑ 47-7932	Maria/On the Street Where You Live	1961	8.00
❑ 47-7956	Theme from "Summer and Smoke"/Maria	1961	8.00
❑ 47-7956 [PS]	Theme from "Summer and Smoke"/Maria	1961	12.00
❑ 47-8161	Space Flight/It's a Darn Good Thing	1963	8.00
❑ 47-8322	Sunday in New York/More in Love	1964	6.00
❑ 47-8503	Theme from "36 Hours"/If You've Got a Heart	1965	6.00
❑ 47-8620	Ship of Fools/Why Did I Choose You	1965	6.00
❑ 47-8715	Thunderball/Theme from "The Spy Who Came In from the Cold"	1965	6.00
❑ 47-8892	Born Free/Who's Afraid	1966	6.00
❑ 47-9125	Theme from The Quiller Memorandum/Amy's Theme	1967	6.00
❑ 47-9247	Guantanamera/Xochimilco	1967	6.00
❑ 47-9429	Theme from The Fox/Who Will Answer	1968	6.00
❑ 47-9556	Elvira/A Heart Without Love	1968	6.00

Albums

Number	Title (A Side/B Side)	Yr	NM
ARISTA			
❑ AL 4034	Disco, Dance and Love Themes	1976	10.00
BAINBRIDGE			
❑ BT-6268	The Sounds of Love	1987	10.00
COLUMBIA			
❑ CS 1009	I'll Never Fall in Love Again	1970	10.00
❑ CS 9800	I've Gotta Be Me	1969	12.00

N

Number	Title (A Side/B Side)	Yr	NM
C 30586	Love Story	1971	10.00
CQ 31105 [Q]	Summer of '42	1971	15.00
KC 31105	Summer of '42	1971	10.00
KC 31335	The First Time Ever (I Saw Your Face)	1972	10.00
C2 31982 [(2)]	The World of Peter Nero	1972	12.00
KC 32689	Say, Has Anybody Seen My Sweet Gypsy Rose	1973	10.00
PC 33136	Greatest Hits	1974	10.00
CONCORD JAZZ			
CJ-48	Now	1978	10.00
CRYSTAL CLEAR			
6001	The Wiz	198?	20.00
—Direct-to-disc recording			
MODE			
LP-117 [M]	Bernie Nerow Trio	1957	120.00
—As "Bernie Nerow"			
PREMIER			
PM-2011 [M]	Just for You	1963	20.00
PS-2011 [R]	Just for You	1963	12.00
RCA CAMDEN			
CAL-2139 [M]	Peter Nero Plays Born Free and Others	1967	15.00
CAS-2139 [S]	Peter Nero Plays Born Free and Others	1967	12.00
CAL-2228 [M]	If Ever I Would Leave You	1968	15.00
CAS-2228 [S]	If Ever I Would Leave You	1968	12.00
RCA VICTOR			
PRM-241 [M]	Tender Is the Night	1967	15.00
PRS-241 [S]	Tender Is the Night	1967	20.00
—Special-products release			
ADL1-0284 [(2)]	Music Festival of Hits	1973	12.00
LPM-2334 [M]	Piano Forte	1961	15.00
LSP-2334 [S]	Piano Forte	1961	20.00
LPM-2383 [M]	New Piano in Town	1961	15.00
LSP-2383 [S]	New Piano in Town	1961	20.00
LPM-2484 [M]	Young and Warm and Wonderful	1962	15.00
LSP-2484 [S]	Young and Warm and Wonderful	1962	20.00
LPM-2536 [M]	For the Nero-Minded	1962	15.00
LSP-2536 [S]	For the Nero-Minded	1962	20.00
LPM-2618 [M]	The Colorful Peter Nero	1963	15.00
LSP-2618 [S]	The Colorful Peter Nero	1963	20.00
LPM-2638 [M]	Hail the Conquering Nero	1963	15.00
LSP-2638 [S]	Hail the Conquering Nero	1963	20.00
LPM-2710 [M]	Peter Nero in Person	1963	15.00
LSP-2710 [S]	Peter Nero in Person	1963	20.00
LPM-2827 [M]	Sunday in New York	1964	15.00
LSP-2827 [S]	Sunday in New York	1964	20.00
LPM-2853 [M]	Reflections	1964	15.00
LSP-2853 [S]	Reflections	1964	20.00
LPM-2935 [M]	Songs You Won't Forget	1964	15.00
LSP-2935 [S]	Songs You Won't Forget	1964	20.00
LPM-2978 [M]	The Best of Peter Nero	1965	15.00
LSP-2978 [S]	The Best of Peter Nero	1965	20.00
LPM-3313 [M]	Career Girls	1965	15.00
LSP-3313 [S]	Career Girls	1965	20.00
LPM-3496 [M]	The Screen Scene	1966	12.00
LSP-3496 [S]	The Screen Scene	1966	15.00
LPM-3550 [M]	Peter Nero — Up Close	1966	12.00
LSP-3550 [S]	Peter Nero — Up Close	1966	15.00
LPM-3610 [M]	Peter Nero On Tour	1966	12.00
LSP-3610 [S]	Peter Nero On Tour	1966	15.00
LPM-3720 [M]	Plays a Salute to Herb Alpert and the Tijuana Brass	1967	15.00
LSP-3720 [S]	Plays a Salute to Herb Alpert and the Tijuana Brass	1967	12.00
LPM-3814 [M]	Xochimilico	1967	15.00
LSP-3814 [S]	Xochimilico	1967	12.00
LPM-3871 [M]	Nero-ing In on the Hits	1968	15.00
LSP-3871 [S]	Nero-ing In on the Hits	1968	12.00
LPM-3936 [M]	Peter Nero Plays Love Is Blue and Ten Other Great Songs	1968	15.00
LSP-3936 [S]	Peter Nero Plays Love Is Blue and Ten Other Great Songs	1968	12.00
LSP-4072	Impressions (Great Songs of Burt Bacharach and Hal David)	1968	12.00
LSP-4205	Love Trip	1969	12.00

NEROW, BERNIE See PETER NERO.

Albums

Number	Title (A Side/B Side)	Yr	NM
			—

NERVES, THE

7-Inch Extended Plays

Number	Title (A Side/B Side)	Yr	NM
NERVES			
4501	Hanging on the Telephone	1976	20.00
4501 [PS]	Hanging on the Telephone	1976	20.00

NERVOUS EATERS

45s

Number	Title (A Side/B Side)	Yr	NM
ELEKTRA			
47025	No Sleep Tonite/Last Chance	1980	20.00
47025 [DJ]	No Sleep Tonite (mono/stereo)	1980	15.00
47072	Loretta/Get Stuffed	1980	20.00
47072 [DJ]	Loretta (mono/stereo)	1980	15.00
RAT			
528-G	Just Head/Get Stuffed	1979	40.00
5282	Loretta/Rock with Me	1979	10.00
5282 [PS]	Loretta/Rock with Me	1979	10.00
5282 [PS]	Loretta/Rock with Me	1979	40.00
—First pressing has cardboard sleeve			

Albums

Number	Title (A Side/B Side)	Yr	NM
ACE OF HEARTS			
1007	Hot Steel and Acid	1986	10.00
ELEKTRA			
6E-282	Nervous Eaters	1980	15.00

NERVOUS NORVUS

45s

Number	Title (A Side/B Side)	Yr	NM
BIG BEN			
101	Pure Gold/Let's Worship God Each Sunday	1960	25.00
DOT			
15470	Transfusion/Dig	1956	30.00
—Second pressings have black labels			
15470	Transfusion/Dig	1956	50.00
—Originals have maroon labels			
15485	Ape Call/Wild Dog of Kentucky	1956	20.00
—Second pressings have black labels			
15485	Ape Call/Wild Dog of Kentucky	1956	30.00
—Originals have maroon labels			
15500	The Fang/The Bullfrog	1956	20.00
—Second pressings have black labels			
15500	The Fang/The Bullfrog	1956	30.00
—Originals have maroon labels			
16765	Transfusion/Ape Call	1965	12.00
EMBEE			
117	I Like Girls/Stone Age Woo	1959	20.00

NESMITH, MICHAEL Also see MIKE, JOHN AND BILL; THE MONKEES.

45s

Number	Title (A Side/B Side)	Yr	NM
COLPIX			
787	The New Recruit/A Journey	1965	150.00
—As "Michael Blessing"			
792	Until It's Time for You to Go/What's the Trouble, Officer	1965	150.00
—As "Michael Blessing"			
EDAN			
1001	Just a Little Love/Curson Terrace	1965	120.00
HIGHNESS			
HN-13	Wanderin'/Well Well Well	1963	400.00
—As "Mike Nesmith"			
PACIFIC ARTS			
084	Life, the Unsuspecting Captive/Rio	1977	8.00
101	Roll with the Flow/I've Just Begun to Care	1978	6.00
PAC45-104	Rio/Casablanca Moonlight	1978	6.00
PAC45-104 [PS]	Rio/Casablanca Moonlight	1978	12.00
106	Magic (This Night Is Magic)/Dance	1979	6.00
108	Cruisin'/Horserace	1979	6.00
6373	Life, the Unsuspecting Captive/Rio	1976	10.00
6398	Navajo Trail/Love's First Kiss	1976	10.00
RCA VICTOR			
47-9853	Rose City Chimes/Little Red Rider	1970	10.00
74-0368	Joanne/One Rose	1970	12.00
74-0399	Silver Moon/Lady of the Valley	1970	10.00
74-0453	Nevada Fighter/Here I Am	1971	8.00
74-0453 [PS]	Nevada Fighter/Here I Am	1971	20.00
74-0491	Tumbling Tumbleweeds/Texas Morning	1971	8.00
74-0540	Only Bound/Propinquity	1971	8.00
74-0629	Lazy Lady/Mama Rocker	1971	8.00
74-0804	Roll with the Flow/Keep On	1972	8.00
447-0868	Joanne/Silver Moon	197?	5.00
—"Gold Standard Series"; red label			

Albums

Number	Title (A Side/B Side)	Yr	NM
PACIFIC ARTS			
(no #) [DJ]	The Michael Nesmith Radio Special	1979	40.00
11-101A	The Prison	197?	50.00
—Boxed set with booklet			
7-101	The Prison	197?	20.00
—Standard cover			
7-106	Compilation	1976	20.00
7-107	From a Radio Engine to the Photon Wing	1977	12.00
7-116	And the Hits Just Keep On Comin'	1978	15.00
—Reissue of RCA 4695			
7-117	Pretty Much Your Standard Ranch Stash	1978	15.00
—Reissue of RCA APL1-0164			
7-118	Live at the Palais	1978	15.00
7-130	Infinite Rider on the Big Dogma	1979	15.00
ILPA-9486	From a Radio Engine to the Photon Wing	1977	15.00
—Original issue			
RCA VICTOR			
APL1-0164	Pretty Much Your Standard Ranch Stash	1973	25.00
LSP-4371	Magnetic South	1970	30.00
LSP-4415	Loose Salute	1970	30.00
LSP-4497	Nevada Fighter	1971	25.00
LSP-4563	Tantamount to Treason	1971	25.00
LSP-4695	And the Hits Just Keep On Comin'	1972	25.00
RHINO			
R1-70168	The Newer Stuff	1989	12.00

NETHERWORLD

Albums

Number	Title (A Side/B Side)	Yr	NM
R.E.M.			
4441	Netherworld	196?	60.00

NEUMAN, ALFRED E., AND THE FURSHLUGGINER FIVE

45s

Number	Title (A Side/B Side)	Yr	NM
ABC-PARAMOUNT			
10013	What — Me Worry?/Potrzebie	1959	40.00
10013 [PS]	What — Me Worry?/Potrzebie	1959	60.00

NEVILLE, AARON Also see THE METERS; LINDA RONSTADT.

45s

Number	Title (A Side/B Side)	Yr	NM
A&M			
31458 0312 7	The Grand Tour/Don't Take Away My Heaven	1993	4.00
31458 0442 7	Please Come Home for Christmas/Louisiana Christmas Day	1993	5.00
31458 1112 7	For the Good Times/Crying in the Chapel	1995	4.00
75021 1563 7	Everybody Plays the Fool/House on a Hill	1991	4.00
BELL			
746	You Can Give, But You Can't Take/Where Is My Baby	1968	8.00
781	Speak to Me/You Don't Love Me Anymore	1969	8.00
834	All These Things/She's On My Mind	1969	8.00
MERCURY			
73310	Baby I'm-a Want You/Mojo Hannah	1972	6.00
73387	Hercules/Going Home	1973	150.00
MINIT			
612	Over You/Every Day	1960	15.00
—As "Arron Neville"			
618	Show Me the Way/Get Out of My Life	1960	12.00
624	Don't Cry/Reality	1961	12.00
631	Let's Live/I Found Another Love	1961	12.00
639	How Many Times/I'm Waitin' at the Station	1962	12.00
650	Humdinger/Sweet Little Mama	1962	12.00
657	Wrong Number/How Could I Help But Love You	1963	12.00
PAR-LO			
101	Tell It Like It Is/Why Worry	1966	20.00
—Black and white label			
101	Tell It Like It Is/Why Worry	1966	25.00
—Turquoise label, silver print			
101	Tell It Like It Is/Why Worry	1966	25.00
—Yellow label, red and black print			
103	She Took You for a Ride/Space Man	1967	8.00
POLYDOR			
14426	Greatest Love/Performance	1977	4.00
SAFARI			
201	Forever More/Ape Man	1967	10.00
WHO DAT?			
VPAG-4476/7	Who Dat? (The History of the Saints)/(Extended Version)	1987	8.00

Albums

Number	Title (A Side/B Side)	Yr	NM
MINIT			
LP 24007 [R]	Like It 'Tis	1967	30.00
LP 40007 [M]	Like It 'Tis	1967	40.00
PAR-LO			
1 [M]	Tell It Like It Is	1967	80.00
1 [S]	Tell It Like It Is	1967	200.00

NEVILLE, AARON, AND TRISHA YEARWOOD

45s

Number	Title (A Side/B Side)	Yr	NM
MCA			
54836	I Fall to Pieces/(Instrumental)	1994	4.00

Except when noted otherwise, VG = 25% of NM, and VG+ = 50% of NM. (Example: VG = $2.00, VG+ = $4.00 and NM = $8.00.)

NEVILLE BROTHERS, THE

Albums

CAPITOL

Number	Title (A Side/B Side)	Yr	NM
❑ ST-11865	The Neville Brothers	1978	30.00

NEW BIRTH, THE Also see LOVE, PEACE AND HAPPINESS; THE NITE-LITERS.

45s

Number	Title (A Side/B Side)	Yr	NM
ARIOLA AMERICA			
❑ 7760	I Love You/Fastest Gun	1979	4.00
BUDDAH			
❑ 464	Granddaddy (Part 1)/ Granddaddy (Part 2)	1975	4.00
❑ 470	Dream Merchant/Why Did It	1975	4.00
RCA VICTOR			
❑ 74-0400	What'll I Do/One Way Bus	1970	6.00
❑ 74-0520	It's Impossible/Honeybee	1971	5.00
❑ 74-0657	Unh Song/Two Kinds of People	1972	5.00
❑ 74-0774	Come Back in My Life (Part 1)/ Come Back in My Life (Part 2)	1972	5.00
❑ 74-0912	I Can Understand It/ Oh Baby, I Love the Way	1973	5.00
❑ APBO-0003	Until It's Time for You to Go/ You Are What I'm All About	1973	5.00
❑ APBO-0185	It's Been a Long Time/ Keep On Doin' It	1973	5.00
❑ APBO-0265	Wildflower/Got to Get a Knutt	1974	5.00
❑ PB-10017	I Wash My Hands of the Whole Damn Deal Part 1/Part 2	1974	5.00
❑ PB-10110	Comin' From All Sides/Patiently	1974	5.00
❑ PB-10242	Do It Again/Pretty Music	1975	5.00
WARNER BROS.			
❑ 8217	The Long and Winding Road/ Hurry Hurry	1976	4.00
❑ 8256	Fallin' in Love — Part I/ Fallin' in Love — Part II	1976	4.00
❑ 8292	We Are All God's Children — Part I/We Are All God's Children — Part II	1976	4.00
❑ 8422	Deeper/Deeper (Part 2)	1977	4.00
❑ 8499	The Mighty Army/Hurry Hurry	1977	4.00
❑ 8536	How Will I Live/Squeezing Too Much Living	1978	4.00

Albums

Number	Title (A Side/B Side)	Yr	NM
ARIOLA AMERICA			
❑ SW-50062	Platinum City	1979	10.00
BUDDAH			
❑ BDS-5636	Blind Baby	1975	10.00
COLLECTABLES			
❑ COL-5100	Golden Classics	1988	10.00
RCA VICTOR			
❑ APD1-0285 [Q]	It's Been a Long Time	1974	20.00
❑ APL1-0285	It's Been a Long Time	1974	10.00
❑ APL1-0494	Comin' From All Ends	1974	10.00
❑ APL1-1021	The Best of the New Birth	1975	10.00
❑ ANL1-2145	Birth Day	1977	10.00
—Reissue of 4797			
❑ AFL1-4411	I'm Back	1982	10.00
❑ LSP-4450	The New Birth	1970	15.00
❑ LSP-4526	Ain't No Big Thing, But It's Growing	1971	15.00
❑ LSP-4697	Coming Together	1972	15.00
❑ LSP-4797	Birth Day	1973	12.00
WARNER BROS.			
❑ BS 2953	Love Potion	1976	10.00
❑ BSK 3071	Behold the Mighty Army	1977	10.00

NEW BRICK WINDOW, THE

45s

VENDETTA

Number	Title (A Side/B Side)	Yr	NM
❑ 126	Little Girl/Baby Come Running	1968	50.00

NEW CHRISTY MINSTRELS, THE Also see BARRY McGUIRE; KENNY ROGERS.

45s

Number	Title (A Side/B Side)	Yr	NM
COLUMBIA			
❑ 42592	This Land Is Your Land/ Don't Cry, Suzanne	1962	10.00
❑ 42592 [PS]	This Land Is Your Land/ Don't Cry, Suzanne	1962	15.00
❑ 42673	Denver/Liza Lee	1963	10.00
❑ 42805	Green, Green/The Banjo	1963	10.00
❑ 42887	Saturday Night/ The Wheeler-Dealers	1963	10.00
❑ 43000	Today/Miss Katy Cruel	1964	8.00
❑ 43092	Silly Ol' Summertime/ The Far Side of the Hill	1964	8.00
❑ 43137	Same Ol' Huckleberry Finn/ The Ol' Riverboat	1964	8.00
❑ 43178	Down the Road I Go/ Gotta Get a-Goin'	1964	8.00
❑ 43215	Chim Chim Cheree/They Gotta Quit Kickin' My Dog Around	1965	8.00
❑ 43281	The River/Se Paingi, Se Ridi	1965	8.00
❑ 43347	Jim 'n' I, Him 'n' I, Flying in the Gemini/A Little Bit of Happiness	1965	8.00
❑ 43470	Born to Be Free/Everybody Loves Saturday Night	1965	8.00
❑ 43533	Dance My Troubles Away (Zorba's Dance)/ There But for Fortune	1966	6.00
❑ 43644	If I Could Start My Life Again/The Music of the World a-Turnin'	1966	6.00
❑ 43822	A Corner in the Sun/ Beautiful, Beautiful World	1966	6.00
❑ 43940	We Need a Little Christmas/ Oh Holy Night	1966	10.00
❑ 43961	It Should Have Been You/ Sleep Comes Easy	1967	6.00
❑ 44176	I'll Coat Your Mind with Honey/ Night and Day	1967	6.00
❑ 44355	The Clown/No Matter What People	1967	6.00
❑ 44528	Ballad for Americans/ Gallant Men	1968	5.00
❑ 44577	Alice's Restaurant/ Summertime Love	1968	5.00
❑ 4-44631	Chitty Chitty Bang Bang/ Me Old Bam-Boo	1968	6.00
❑ JZSP 116417/8 [DJ]	We Need a Little Christmas/ Sleigh Ride	1966	12.00
—White label			
❑ JZSP 116417/8 [DJ]	We Need a Little Christmas/ Sleigh Ride	1966	12.00
—Yellow label			
GREGAR			
❑ 71-0102	You Need Someone to Love/ South American Getaway	1970	4.00
❑ 71-0106	Brother/I Still Do	1970	4.00
❑ 71-0109	You Are Always On My Mind/ Where Are You Then	1971	4.00
❑ 71-0114	The Age of Not Believing/ Love It Along	1972	4.00

Albums

Number	Title (A Side/B Side)	Yr	NM
COLUMBIA			
❑ CL 1872 [M]	The New Christy Minstrels	1962	20.00
❑ CL 1941 [M]	The New Christy Minstrels In Person	1963	20.00
❑ CL 2017 [M]	Tall Tales! Legends & Nonsense	1963	20.00
❑ CL 2055 [M]	Ramblin' Feturing Green, Green	1963	20.00
❑ CL 2096 [M]	Merry Christmas	1963	20.00
❑ CL 2159 [M]	Today	1964	20.00
❑ CL 2187 [M]	Land of Giants	1964	20.00
❑ CL 2280 [M]	The Quiet Sides of the New Christy Minstrels	1965	20.00
❑ CL 2303 [M]	Cowboys and Indians	1965	20.00
❑ CL 2369 [M]	Chim Chim Cher-ee	1965	20.00
❑ CL 2384 [M]	The Wandering Minstrels	1965	20.00
❑ CL 2479 [M]	Greatest Hits	1966	20.00
❑ CL 2531 [M]	In Italy...In Italian	1966	20.00
❑ CL 2542 [M]	New Kick	1967	20.00
❑ CL 2556 [M]	Christmas with the Christies	1966	20.00
❑ CS 8672 [S]	The New Christy Minstrels	1962	25.00
❑ CS 8741 [S]	The New Christy Minstrels In Person	1963	25.00
❑ CS 8817 [S]	Tall Tales! Legends & Nonsense	1963	25.00
❑ CS 8855 [S]	Ramblin' Feturing Green, Green	1963	25.00
❑ CS 8896 [S]	Merry Christmas	1963	25.00
❑ CS 8959 [S]	Today	1964	25.00
❑ CS 8987 [S]	Land of Giants	1964	25.00
❑ CS 9080 [S]	The Quiet Sides of the New Christy Minstrels	1965	25.00
❑ CS 9103 [S]	Cowboys and Indians	1965	25.00
❑ CS 9169 [S]	Chim Chim Cher-ee	1965	25.00
❑ CS 9184 [S]	The Wandering Minstrels	1965	25.00
❑ CS 9279 [S]	Greatest Hits	1966	25.00
❑ CS 9331 [S]	In Italy...In Italian	1966	25.00
❑ CS 9342 [S]	New Kick	1967	25.00
❑ CS 9356 [S]	Christmas with the Christies	1966	25.00
❑ CS 9616 [M]	On Tour Through Motortown	1968	50.00
—White label promo only; "Special Mono Radio Station Copy" sticker on front			
❑ CS 9616 [S]	On Tour Through Motortown	1968	20.00

The New Colony Six, *Revelations*, Mercury SR-61165, 1968, **$30.**

New Order, "Blue Monday 1988," Qwest 7-27979, 1988, **$10.**

Number	Title (A Side/B Side)	Yr	NM
❑ CS 9709	Chitty Chitty Bang Bang	1969	20.00

GREGAR

Number	Title (A Side/B Side)	Yr	NM
❑ 102	You Need Someone to Love	1970	15.00

NEW COLONY SIX, THE

45s

CENTAUR

Number	Title (A Side/B Side)	Yr	NM
❑ 1201	I Confess/Dawn Is Breaking	1966	15.00
❑ 1202	I Like Awake/At the River's Edge	1966	15.00

MCA

Number	Title (A Side/B Side)	Yr	NM
❑ 40215	Never Be Lonely/ Long Time to Be Alone	1974	25.00
❑ 40288	I Really Don't Want to Go/Run	1974	30.00

MERCURY

Number	Title (A Side/B Side)	Yr	NM
❑ 72737	Treat Her Groovy/Rap-a-Tap	1967	10.00
—Orange and red swirl label			
❑ 72737	Treat Her Groovy/Rap-a-Tap	1967	12.00
—Red label with "Mercury" logo in all capital letters			
❑ 72737 [PS]	Treat Her Groovy/Rap-a-Tap	1967	15.00
❑ 72775	I Will Always Think About You/ Hold Me with Your Eyes	1968	10.00
—Orange and red swirl label			
❑ 72775	I Will Always Think About You/ Hold Me with Your Eyes	1968	12.00
—Red label with "Mercury" logo in all capital letters			
❑ 72817	Can't You See Me Cry/ Summertime's Another Name for Love	1968	8.00
❑ 72817 [PS]	Can't You See Me Cry/ Summertime's Another Name for Love	1968	15.00
❑ 72858	Things I'd Like to Say/Come and Give Your Love to Me	1968	10.00
—Red label with "Mercury" logo in an oval			
❑ 72858	Things I'd Like to Say/Come and Give Your Love to Me	1968	12.00
—Orange and red swirl label			
❑ 72920	I Could Never Lie to You/ Just Feel Worse	1969	8.00
❑ 72961	I Want You to Know/Free	1969	8.00
❑ 73004	Barbara, I Love You/Prairie Grey	1970	8.00
❑ 73063	People and Me/Ride the Wicked Wind	1970	15.00
❑ 73093	Close Your Eyes Little Girl/Love, That's the Best I Can Do	1970	20.00
—Promo copies go for less			

SENTAR

Number	Title (A Side/B Side)	Yr	NM
❑ 1203	Cadillac/Sunshine	1966	15.00
❑ 1204	(Ballad of the) Wingbat Marmaduke/Power of Love	1966	15.00
❑ 1205	Love You So Much/ Let Me Love You	1967	15.00
❑ 1206	You're Gonna Be Mine/Woman	1967	15.00
❑ 1207	I'm Just Waiting Anticipating for Her to Show Up/Hello Lonely	1967	15.00

SENTAUR

Number	Title (A Side/B Side)	Yr	NM
❑ 1202	I Like Awake/At the River's Edge	1966	20.00
—Reissue of Centaur 1202, but harder to find			

SUNLIGHT

Number	Title (A Side/B Side)	Yr	NM
❑ 1001	Roll On/If You Could See	1971	6.00
❑ 1004	Long Time to Be Alone/ Never Be Lonely	1971	6.00
❑ 1005	Someone, Sometime/ Come On Down	1972	8.00

TWILIGHT

Number	Title (A Side/B Side)	Yr	NM
❑ 1004	Long Time to Be Alone/ Never Be Lonely	1973	—
—The existence of this record as a US pressing has not been confirmed			

Albums

MERCURY

Number	Title (A Side/B Side)	Yr	NM
❑ SR-61165	Revelations	1968	30.00
❑ SR-61228	Attacking a Straw Man	1969	30.00

SENTAR

Number	Title (A Side/B Side)	Yr	NM
❑ LP-101 [M]	Breakthrough	1966	500.00
❑ SST-3001 [S]	Colonization	1967	60.00
❑ ST-3001 [M]	Colonization	1967	50.00

SUNDAZED

Number	Title (A Side/B Side)	Yr	NM
❑ LP 5007	At the River's Edge	1995	10.00

NEW DAWN, THE

45s

GARLAND

Number	Title (A Side/B Side)	Yr	NM
❑ 2020	Why Did You Go/Tears	1970	25.00

IMPERIAL

Number	Title (A Side/B Side)	Yr	NM
❑ 66397	Melody Fair/Sometimes in the Morning	1969	8.00

MAINSTREAM

Number	Title (A Side/B Side)	Yr	NM
❑ 652	If I Can't Have Your Love/Loser	1966	25.00
❑ 664	Slave of Desire/Funny Feeling	1966	25.00

RCA VICTOR

Number	Title (A Side/B Side)	Yr	NM
❑ 47-9569	Listen to the Music/Someday	1968	8.00

Albums

HOOT

Number	Title (A Side/B Side)	Yr	NM
❑ GR 704569	There's a New Dawn	1970	1000.

NEW ESTABLISHMENT, THE

May be more than one group.

45s

COLGEMS

Number	Title (A Side/B Side)	Yr	NM
❑ 66-5006	(One of These Days) Sunday's Gonna Come on Tuesday/ Baby, the Rain Must Fall	1969	8.00
❑ 66-5009	I'll Build a Bridge/Seattle	1969	8.00

MERCURY

Number	Title (A Side/B Side)	Yr	NM
❑ 72705	And We Were Strangers/ A Time for Everything	1967	10.00

UNITED WORLD

Number	Title (A Side/B Side)	Yr	NM
❑ 1001	Slums of the City/Riding High	197?	200.00

Albums

COLGEMS

Number	Title (A Side/B Side)	Yr	NM
❑ COS-118	The New Establishment	1970	—
—Scheduled but never released			

NEW FACES, THE

45s

DOT

Number	Title (A Side/B Side)	Yr	NM
❑ 16747	Blue Mist/So Small	1965	20.00
❑ 16777	Never Gonna Love Again/ You'll Be Too Late	1965	20.00

PARROT

Number	Title (A Side/B Side)	Yr	NM
❑ 40026	We Can Get There by Candlelight/The Yellow Road	1968	15.00
❑ 40030	If You Love Me/The Road and the Miles to Dundee	1968	15.00

NEW GROUP, THE

45s

ROULETTE

Number	Title (A Side/B Side)	Yr	NM
❑ R-4557	A World to Win/ Lulu's Back in Town	1964	10.00

NEW HOPE

See THE KIT KATS.

NEW KINGSTON TRIO, THE

See THE KINGSTON TRIO.

NEW MARKETTS, THE

See THE MARKETTS.

NEW MIX, THE

Albums

UNITED ARTISTS

Number	Title (A Side/B Side)	Yr	NM
❑ UAS-6678	The New Mix	1968	20.00

NEW ORDER

Also see JOY DIVISION.

12-Inch Singles

A&M

Number	Title (A Side/B Side)	Yr	NM
❑ SP-12174	Shellshock (9:41)/ Thieves Like Us (6:39)	1986	10.00
❑ SP-12174 [DJ]	Shellshock (Extended Version 9:41) (Dub Version 7:35)	1986	10.00

FACTORY

Number	Title (A Side/B Side)	Yr	NM
❑ FACTUS 10	Blue Monday/The Beach	1983	20.00

FFRR

Number	Title (A Side/B Side)	Yr	NM
❑ PR 400064 [DJ]	Here to Stay (Radio Edit) (Felix da Housecat — Thee Extended Glitz Mix) (Scumfrog Dub)	2002	15.00

LONDON

Number	Title (A Side/B Side)	Yr	NM
❑ PRO 3105 [(2)DJ]	Here to Stay (Radio Edit) (Extended Instrumental) (Felix da Housecat — Thee Extended Glitz Mix) (Scumfrog Dub)	2002	20.00

MINIMAL

Number	Title (A Side/B Side)	Yr	NM
❑ QAL-249	Confusion (Alternative Mix 5:30) (Essential Mix 5:10) (Trip 1- Ambient Confusion 3:40) (Accapella 1:17) (Con-om-fus-ars-ion 7:05) (Ooh-Wee Dub 6:50)	1990	10.00

Except when noted otherwise, VG = 25% of NM, and VG+ = 50% of NM. (Example: VG = $2.00, VG+ = $4.00 and NM = $8.00.)

QWEST

Number	Title (A Side/B Side)	Yr	NM
❑ PRO-A-2342 [DJ]	The Perfect Kiss (Live Video Version 5:18) (Single Edit 4:23)	1985	15.00
❑ PRO-A-2600 [DJ]	Bizarre Love Triangle (Edit 3:40) (Album Version 4:19)	1986	15.00
❑ PRO-A-2636 [DJ]	Bizarre Love Triangle (7" Edit 3:23) (Extended Edit 4:58)	1986	15.00
❑ PRO-A-2644 [DJ]	Way of Life (same on both sides)	1986	12.00
❑ PRO-A-2784 [DJ]	True Faith (LP Version) (Edit)	1987	12.00
❑ PRO-A-3037 [DJ]	Blue Monday 1988 (Club Mix 7:27)/Touched by the Hand of God (Remix 7:02) (Dub Version 5:30)	1988	15.00
❑ PRO-A-6276 [(2)DJ]	World (The Price of Love) (Perfecto Mix 7:33) (The Brothers Dubstrumental 5:39) (Pharmacy Dub 7:06) (Album Version 4:44) (The Brothers in Rhythm Mix 8:03) (The Sexy Disco Dub Mix 5:56) (World in Action Mix 5:51) (Radio Edit 3:39)	1993	25.00
❑ PRO-A-6318 [DJ]	Ruined in a Day (Reunited in a Day Mix 6:14) (Instrumental 6:14) (Album Version 4:25) (Bogle Mix 4:28) (Dance Hall Groove 5:25) (Rhythm Twins Dub 4:28)	1993	25.00
—			
❑ PRO-A-6729 [DJ]	Spooky (Stadium Mix 6:30) (Stadium Instrumental 6:32) (Night Tripper Mix 7:02) (Magimix 6:55) (Moulimix 5:49) (Boo! Dub Mix 4:56)	1993	15.00
—			
❑ PRO-A-7622 [DJ]	Bizarre Love Triangle (Shep's Extended Dance 6:41) (Shep's Dub Version 7:03) (Shep's 12" Alternate Mix 4:59) (Shep's Single Mix 3:43) (Original Album Version 4:19)	1995	15.00
❑ PRO-A-7622-A [DJ]	Bizarre Love Triangle (Shep's Extended Dance 6:41) (Shep's Dub Version 7:03) (Shep's 12" Alternate Mix 4:59) (Shep's Single Mix 3:43) (Original Album Version 4:19)	1995	25.00

—Label is white with no print except for "PRO-A-7622-A"; "Promotion Only. Not For Sale."; "Side 1" (or "Side 2"); and "33 1/3 RPM"; sleeve contains insert listing the versions

Number	Title (A Side/B Side)	Yr	NM
❑ 20330	The Perfect Kiss (8:46)/ The Kiss of Death (7:02)/ Perfect Pit (1:24)	1985	10.00
❑ 20332	Blue Monday/The Beach	1985	8.00
—Reissue of Factory FACTUS 10			
❑ 20390	Sub-Culture (Remix 7:26)/ Subvulture (7:57)/ Sub-Culture (4:57)	1985	10.00
❑ 20546	Bizarre Love Triangle (2 versions)/I Don't Care/ State of the Nation	1986	10.00
—Original with picture cover			
❑ 20546	Bizarre Love Triangle (2 versions)/I Don't Care/ State of the Nation	1995	6.00
—Reissue in generic sleeve			
❑ 20733	True Faith (Morning Sun Extended Remix 8:59) (Alternate Faith Dub 10:41)/ 1963 (5:32)	1987	12.00
❑ 20869	Blue Monday 1988 (Remix 7:09) (Dub 7:16)/Touched by the Hand of God (Remix 7:02) (Dub 5:30)	1988	12.00
❑ 21062	Round & Round (12" Version 6:50) (Club Mix 7:09) (12" Remix 6:53)/Best and Marsh (4:32)	1989	10.00
❑ 21107	Fine Time (7" Version 3:08) (LP Version 4:42)/Fine Line (4:43)/Fine Time (Silk Mix 6:15) (Messed Around Mix 4;35)/Don't Do It (4:30)	1988	10.00
❑ 21582	World in Motion (Carabinieri Mix 5:52) (No Alla Violenza Mix 5:35) (Subbuteo Mix 5:08) (Subbuteo Dub 5:08)	1990	8.00
❑ 40760	Regret (Fire Island Mix 7:15) (Junior Dub Mix 7:44) (New Order Mix 5:10) (Album Version 4:07)	1993	10.00
❑ 40966	World (The Price of Love) (The Perfecto Mix 7:33) (Sexy Disco Dub Mix 5:56) (World in Action Mix 5:51) (Brothers in Rhythm Mix 8:03)/Ruined in a Day (Reunited in a Day Mix 6:14) (Bogle Mix 4:28)	1993	10.00
❑ 41313	Spooky (Stadium Mix 6:30) (Night Tripper Mix 7:02) (Neworder in Heaven Mix 6:10) (Magimix 6:55) (Moulimix 5:49) (Boo! Dub Mix 4:56)	1993	8.00
❑ PRO-A-100604-A [DJ]	True Faith (Pink Noise Club Mix 8:50) (Pink Noise I've Taken Too Much Dub 6:50)	2001	25.00
❑ PRO-A-100645-A [(2)DJ]	True Faith (Morel's Extra Dub 8:24) (Philip Steir Dub 8:12) (Morel's Pink Noise Club Mix 8:50) (Philip Steir Club Mix 8:12) (Morel's Shifty Dub 7:22)	2001	25.00
❑ PRO-A-100663 [(2)DJ]	True Faith (Morel's Extra Dub 8:24) (Philip Steir Dub 8:12) (Morel's Pink Noise Club Mix 8:50) (Philip Steir Re-Order Mix 8:12) (Morel's Calling Shifty Dub 7:22)	2001	25.00

REPRISE

Number	Title (A Side/B Side)	Yr	NM
❑ 42397 [(2)]	Crystal (Digweed & Muir Bedrock Remix 12:52) (Lee Coombs Remix 8:44) (Digweed & Muir Bedrock Dub 10:34) (John Creamer & Stephane K Intro Mix 3:22) (John Creamer & Stephane K Main Mix 11:25)	2001	10.00
❑ PRO-A-100804 [(2)]	Someone Like You (Futureshock Vox Remix 8:04) (Funk D'Void Remix With Guitar & Vocals 9:56) (Gabriel & Dresden 911 Vocal Mix) (James Holden Heavy Dub 6:43) (Futureshock Stripdown Mix 7:49) (Gabriel & Dresden Voco-Tech Dub 11:10)	2001	30.00

STREETWISE

Number	Title (A Side/B Side)	Yr	NM
❑ SWRL 2213	Confusion (8:13) (Beats 5:19) (Instrumental 7:33) (Rough Mix 8:04)	1983	12.00
❑ SWRL 2213 [DJ]	Confusion (Rough Mix 8:04) (same on both sides)	1983	25.00

—Test pressing made for the New Music Seminar with label, titles and artist rubber-stamped or written on labels

45s

FACTORY

Number	Title (A Side/B Side)	Yr	NM
❑ FAC 53	Procession/Everything's Gone Green	1982	5.00
—All copies pressed in England; U.S. records are indistinguishable from records meant for U.K. distribution			
❑ FAC 53 [PS]	Procession/Everything's Gone Green	1982	25.00

—American edition; yellow print with gray background (all other colors are UK-only editions) and a "Rough Trade" sticker on cover

QWEST

Number	Title (A Side/B Side)	Yr	NM
❑ PRO-S-3450 [DJ]	Fine Time (7" Edit) (same on both sides)	1988	25.00
—May only exist as a test pressing			
❑ PRO-S-3464 [DJ]	Round and Round (Edit)/ Fine Time (7" Edit)	1989	12.00
❑ 7-18586	Regret/(New Order Mix)	1993	4.00
❑ 7-21887	True Faith/Blue Monday 1988	198?	3.00
—Reissue			
❑ 7-27524	Round & Round/Best and Marsh	1989	4.00
❑ 7-27524 [PS]	Round & Round/Best and Marsh	1989	4.00
❑ 7-27524DJ [DJ]	Round & Round (7" Version)/ (7" Edit)	1989	5.00
❑ 7-27979	Blue Monday 1988/Touched by the Hand of God	1988	8.00
❑ 7-27979 [PS]	Blue Monday 1988/Touched by the Hand of God	1988	10.00
❑ 7-28271	True Faith/1963	1987	4.00
❑ 7-28271 [PS]	True Faith/1963	1987	4.00
❑ 7-28271DJ [DJ]	True Faith (Album Edit)/(Remix)	1987	5.00
❑ 7-28421	Bizarre Love Triangle/ Every Little Bit Counts	1987	15.00
❑ 7-28421 [DJ]	Bizarre Love Triangle (same on both sides)	1987	8.00
❑ 7-28968	The Perfect Kiss/(Instrumental)	1985	6.00
❑ 7-28968 [PS]	The Perfect Kiss/(Instrumental)	1985	10.00

Albums

FACTORY

Number	Title (A Side/B Side)	Yr	NM
❑ FACTUS 8 [EP]	1981-1982	1983	20.00
❑ FACTUS 12	Power, Corruption and Lies	1983	20.00
❑ FACTUS 50	Movement	198?	12.00
—With bar code on cover			
❑ FACTUS 50	Movement	1981	20.00
—Originals have no bar code			
❑ FACTUS 50	Movement	1981	50.00

—Purple vinyl (looks more black, but will appear purple when held to a light)

QWEST

Number	Title (A Side/B Side)	Yr	NM
❑ PRO-A-5970 [DJ]	In Order	1993	40.00
—Promo only six-song, 44-minute compilation; orange vinyl			
❑ 25289	Low Life	1985	10.00
❑ 25308	Power, Corruption and Lies	1985	10.00
—Reissue of Factory FACTUS 12			
❑ 25511	Brotherhood	1986	10.00
❑ 25621 [(2)]	Substance	1987	15.00
❑ 25845	Technique	1989	12.00
❑ R 100938	Technique	1989	12.00

—BMG Direct Marketing edition

NEW ORDER, THE

45s

WARNER BROS.

Number	Title (A Side/B Side)	Yr	NM
❑ 5816	You've Got Me High/Meet Your Match	1966	30.00
❑ 5836	Why Can't I?/Pucci Girl	1966	20.00
❑ 5870	Sailing Ship/Had I Loved Her Less	1966	12.00

NEW ORLEANS BAND, THE

45s

HIT

Number	Title (A Side/B Side)	Yr	NM
❑ 275	Winchester Cathedral/Born Free	1966	8.00

—B-side by Floyd Tiller

NEW PHASE, THE

45s

GAYTIME EAST

Number	Title (A Side/B Side)	Yr	NM
❑ GT-1003	Love Is the Name of the Game (Part 1)/(Part 2)	196?	120.00

NEW RENAISSANCE SOCIETY, THE

Albums

HANNA-BARBERA

Number	Title (A Side/B Side)	Yr	NM
❑ HLP-9504 [M]	Baroque n' Stones	1966	20.00
❑ HST-9504 [S]	Baroque n' Stones	1966	25.00

NEW RIDERS OF THE PURPLE SAGE

JERRY GARCIA was briefly in this group.

45s

A&M

Number	Title (A Side/B Side)	Yr	NM
❑ 2327	Fly Right/Night for Making Love	1981	4.00
❑ 2352	Full Moon at Midnite/ No Other Love	1981	4.00

COLUMBIA

Number	Title (A Side/B Side)	Yr	NM
❑ 10067	You Angel You/Parson Brown	1974	5.00
❑ 45469	Louisiana Lady/The Last Lonely Eagle	1971	6.00
❑ 45526	Garden of Eden/I Don't Know You	1972	5.00
❑ 45607	I Don't Need No Doctor/ Runnin' Back to You	1972	5.00
❑ 45682	Rainbow/Dim Lights, Thick Smoke	1972	5.00
❑ 45763	Groupie/She's No Angel	1973	5.00
❑ 45976	Panama Red/Cement, Clay, and Glass	1973	6.00

MCA

Number	Title (A Side/B Side)	Yr	NM
❑ 40564	Don't Put Her Down/Fifteen Days Under the Hood	1976	4.00
❑ 40591	Dead Flowers/She's Looking Better Every Beer	1976	4.00
❑ 40686	Red Hot Women and Ice Cold Beer/Love Has Strange Ways	1977	4.00
❑ 40715	(Just) Another Night in Reno/ Home Grown	1977	4.00

Albums

A&M

Number	Title (A Side/B Side)	Yr	NM
❑ SP-4818	Feelin' All Right	1981	10.00

COLUMBIA

Number	Title (A Side/B Side)	Yr	NM
❑ KC 30888	New Riders of the Purple Sage	1971	15.00
❑ PC 30888	New Riders of the Purple Sage	1979	8.00
—Budget-line reissue			
❑ KC 31284	Powerglide	1972	15.00
❑ PC 31284	Powerglide	1979	8.00
—Budget-line reissue			
❑ KC 31930	Gypsy Cowboy	1972	15.00
❑ PC 31930	Gypsy Cowboy	1979	8.00

—Budget-line reissue

N

Number | Title (A Side/B Side) | Yr | NM

❑ CQ 32450 [Q] The Adventures of Panama Red 1974 20.00
❑ KC 32450 The Adventures of Panama Red 1973 15.00
❑ PC 32450 The Adventures of Panama Red 1979 8.00
—Budget-line reissue
❑ PC 32870 Home, Home on the R oad 1974 15.00
—Originals have no bar code
❑ PC 33145 Brujo 1974 15.00
—Originals have no bar code
❑ PC 33688 Oh, What a Mighty Time 1975 15.00
—Originals have no bar code
❑ PC 34367 The Best of New Riders of the Purple Sage 1976 12.00
—Originals have no bar code
❑ PC 34367 The Best of New Riders of the Purple Sage 1979 8.00
—Budget-line reissue with bar code

MCA
❑ 632 Marin County Line 1980 8.00
—Reissue of 2307
❑ 2196 New Riders 1976 12.00
❑ 2248 Who Are These Guys 1977 12.00
❑ 2307 Marin County Line 1977 12.00

RELIX
❑ RRLP-2024 Before Time Began 1986 8.00
❑ RRLP-2025 Vintage NRPS 1987 8.00

NEW SEEKERS, THE

45s

COCA-COLA
❑ (no #) [DJ] Buy the World a Coke// Bring a Little Sunshine/ It's the Real Thing 1971 12.00
—All three songs are Coca-Coca jingles. The A-side became "I'd Like to Teach the World to Sing"

COLUMBIA
❑ 10559 You Never Can Tell/ Give Me Love Your Way 1977 5.00

ELEKTRA
❑ 45699 Look What They've Done to My Song, Ma/It's a Beautiful Day 1970 6.00
❑ 45710 Beautiful People/When There's No Love Left 1970 5.00
❑ 45719 The Nickel Song/Cincinnati 1971 5.00
❑ 45734 Never Ending Song of Love/ All Right My Love 1971 —
—Unreleased
❑ 45747 Tonight/Sweet Louise 1971 5.00
❑ 45762 I'd Like to Teach the World to Sing/Boom Town 1971 6.00
❑ 45780 Beg, Steal or Borrow/ Mystic Queen 1972 5.00
❑ 45787 Circles/I Can Say You're Beautiful 1972 5.00
❑ 45805 Dance, Dance, Dance/I Can Say You're Beautiful 1972 5.00

MGM
❑ 14586 The Greatest Song I've Ever Heard/Woman Grows 1973 5.00
❑ 14683 Reach Out I'll Be There/ You Won't Find Another Fool Like Me 1973 5.00
❑ 14691 Song for You and Me/You Won't Find Another Fool Like Me 1974 5.00

MGM VERVE
❑ 10698 Come Softly to Me/ Unwithered Rose 1972 5.00
❑ 10698 [PS] Come Softly to Me/ Unwithered Rose 1972 5.00
❑ 10709 Pinball Wizard-See Me, Feel Me/Come Softly to Me 1973 5.00
❑ 10709 Pinball Wizard-See Me, Feel Me/Time Limit 1973 6.00

Albums

ELEKTRA
❑ EQ-5051 [Q] The Best of the New Seekers 1973 20.00
❑ EKS-74088 Beautiful People 1971 12.00
❑ EKS-74108 New Colours 1971 12.00
❑ EKS-74115 We'd Like to Teach the World to Sing 1971 12.00
❑ EKS-75034 Circles 1972 12.00
❑ EKS-75051 The Best of the New Seekers 1973 12.00

MGM VERVE
❑ V 5090 Come Softly to Me 1972 10.00
❑ V 5095 The History of the New Seekers 1973 10.00
❑ V 5098 Pinball Wizards 1973 10.00

NEW SOCIETY, THE

45s

RCA VICTOR
❑ 47-8807 Buttermilk/Do Not Ask for Love 1966 10.00
❑ 47-8958 We Have So Little Time/ Dawn of Sorrow 1966 10.00
❑ 47-9149 I've Been Thinking About You Baby/Love Thee Till I Die 1967 10.00

Number | Title (A Side/B Side) | Yr | NM

Albums

RCA VICTOR
❑ LPM-3676 [M] The Barock Sound of the New Society 1966 25.00
❑ LSP-3676 [S] The Barock Sound of the New Society 1966 30.00

NEW SOCIETY GROUP, THE

45s

HIT
❑ 280 Mercy, Mercy, Mercy/Green, Green Grass of Home 1967 8.00
—B-side by Ed Hardin
❑ 319 Love Is Blue/I Can Take or Leave Your Loving 1968 8.00
—B-side by the Chords (2)
❑ 330 The Good, the Bad, and the Ugly/ This Guy's in Love with You 1968 8.00
—B-side by Steve Miller
❑ 355 Soulful Strut/You Showed Me 1969 8.00
—B-side by the Fantastics

NEW SURVIVORS, THE

45s

SCEPTER
❑ 12227 The Pickle Protest/But I Know 1968 15.00

NEW THINGS, THE

45s

ACCENT
❑ 1228 Dumbo/I Want You Back 1967 40.00

NEW TWEEDY BROTHERS, THE

45s

DOT
❑ 16910 Good Time Car/Terms of You Love Me 1966 40.00

Albums

RIDON
❑ 234 The New Tweedy Brothers 1968 400.00
—With plain white cover
❑ 234 The New Tweedy Brothers 1968 2000.
—With oversized hexagonal cover designed to look like a sugar cube

NEW VAUDEVILLE BAND, THE

45s

FONTANA
❑ 1562 Winchester Cathedral/ Wait for Me Baby 1966 8.00
❑ 1573 Peek-A-Boo/Amy 1967 6.00
❑ 1589 Finchley Central/Sadie Moonshine 1967 6.00
❑ 1589 [PS] Finchley Central/Sadie Moonshine 1967 10.00
❑ 1598 Green Street Green/ Fourteen Lovely Women 1967 6.00
❑ 1612 Bonnie and Clyde/ Anniversary Song 1968 6.00

7-Inch Extended Plays

FONTANA
❑ SRF-752-C Winchester Cathedral/Tap Your Feet/A Nightingale Sang in Berkeley Square// Whispering/That's All for Now Sugar Baby/Lili Marlene 1966 15.00
❑ SRF-752-C [PS] Winchester Cathedral 1966 15.00

Albums

FONTANA
❑ MGF-27560 [M] Winchester Cathedral 1966 15.00
—With "Oh, Donna Clara"; record has mono number and actually plays in mono; the number "27560" is in the trail-off
❑ MGF-27560 [M] Winchester Cathedral 1966 15.00
—With "Whatever Happened to Phyllis Puke" and "Diana Goodbye"
❑ MGF-27560 [P] Winchester Cathedral 1966 12.00
—With "Oh, Donna Clara"; record has mono number, but plays stereo; the number "2/67560" is in trail-off area
❑ MGF-27688 [M] The New Vaudeville Band on Tour 1967 12.00
❑ SRF-67560 [P] Winchester Cathedral 1966 12.00
—With "Oh, Donna Clara"
❑ SRF-67560 [P] Winchester Cathedral 1966 15.00
—With "Whatever Happened to Phyllis Puke" and "Diana Goodbye"
❑ SRF-67688 [P] The New Vaudeville Band on Tour 1967 12.00

NEW WANDERERS, THE

45s

READY
❑ 1001 Let Me Render My Service to You/(B-side unknown) 196? 3000.
❑ 1006 This Man in Love/ (B-side unknown) 196? 500.00

Number | Title (A Side/B Side) | Yr | NM

NEW WAVE, THE

45s

CANTERBURY
❑ 503 Where Do We Go from Here/ Not from You 1967 10.00
❑ 512 Little Dreams/Autre Fois 1967 10.00

Albums

CANTERBURY
❑ CLPS-1501 The New Wave 1967 25.00

NEW WORLD

45s

RAK
❑ ZS7 4505 Tom Tom Turnaround/ Lay Me Down 1972 7.00
❑ ZS7 4509 First Steps/Sister Jane 1972 7.00
❑ ZS7 4514 Living Next Door to Alice/ Something to Say 1973 8.00

NEW YORK CITY

45s

CHELSEA
❑ BCBO-0025 Make Me Twice the Man/Uncle James 1973 5.00
❑ 78-0113 I'm Doin' Fine Now/Ain't It So 1973 5.00
❑ BCBO-0150 Quick, Fast, In a Hurry/Set the Record Straight 1973 5.00
❑ 3000 Happiness Is/Darling Take Me Back 1974 5.00
❑ 3008 Love Is What You Make It/Do You Remember Yesterday 1974 5.00
❑ 3010 Got to Get You Back In My Life/ Reach Out 1975 5.00
❑ 3031 Can't Survive Without My Sweets/Take My Hand 1975 5.00

Albums

CHELSEA
❑ BCL1-0198 I'm Doin' Fine Now 1973 15.00
❑ CHL 500 Soulful Road 1974 15.00
❑ CHL 514 The Best of New York City 1977 12.00

NEW YORK DOLLS

Also see DAVID JOHANSEN; SYLVAIN SYLVAIN.

45s

MERCURY
❑ DJ-378 [DJ] Trash (mono/stereo) 1973 15.00
❑ DJ-378 [PS] Trash (mono/stereo) 1973 75.00
—Promo-only numbered sleeve
❑ DJ-387 [DJ] Personality Crisis (mono/stereo) 1973 15.00
❑ 73414 Trash/Personality Crisis 1973 60.00
❑ 73414 [PS] Trash/Personality Crisis 1973 15.00
❑ 73478 Stranded in the Jungle/ Who Are the Mystery Girls 1974 15.00
❑ 73615 Puss 'N' Boots/Showmen 1974 20.00

Albums

MERCURY
❑ SRM-1-675 New York Dolls 1973 40.00
❑ SRM-1-1001 In Too Much Too Soon 1974 40.00
❑ 826094-1 Night of the Living Dolls 1985 12.00
❑ 1786413 New York Dolls 2008 20.00

NEW YORK ROCK ENSEMBLE, THE

Includes records as "The New York Rock and Roll Ensemble."

45s

ATCO
❑ AT-305X [DJ] Beautiful/Beautiful Too 1968 20.00
—"Composed and Recorded For The Bell System Film 'Operator' (Nell Cox Films)" on bottom of both sides' labels; possibly a Bell System promo item
❑ 6467 Biji/Biji Rock 1967 10.00
❑ 6501 Kiss Her Once/Suddenly 1967 10.00
❑ 6584 The Thing to Do/Pick Up in the Morning 1968 10.00
❑ 6671 Wait Until Tomorrow/ The Brandenburg 1969 10.00

COLUMBIA
❑ 45242 Running Down the Highway/ Law and Order 1970 5.00
❑ 45288 The King Is Dead/Beside You 1970 5.00
❑ 45367 Fields of Joy/Ride, Ride My Lady 1971 5.00
❑ 45574 Roll Over/A Whiter Shade of Pale 1972 5.00

Albums

ATCO
❑ SD 33-240 The New York Rock 'n' Roll Ensemble 1968 15.00
❑ SD 33-294 Faithful Friends 1969 15.00
❑ SD 33-312 Reflections 1970 15.00

COLUMBIA
❑ C 30033 Roll Over 1970 15.00
❑ KC 31317 Freedomburger 1972 15.00

Except when noted otherwise, VG = 25% of NM, and VG+ = 50% of NM. (Example: VG = $2.00, VG+ = $4.00 and NM = $8.00.)

Number	Title (A Side/B Side)	Yr	NM

NEW YORK SOUNDS, THE

45s

RED BIRD

Number	Title (A Side/B Side)	Yr	NM
❑ 10-060	Drag Street/Good Lovin'	1966	20.00

NEW YORKERS, THE (1) With FRED PARRIS of THE FIVE SATINS.

45s

WALL

Number	Title (A Side/B Side)	Yr	NM
❑ 547	Miss Fine/Dream a Little Dream	1961	30.00
❑ 548	Tears in My Eyes/A Little Bit	1961	30.00

NEW YORKERS, THE (2) Early version of THE HUDSON BROTHERS.

45s

DECCA

Number	Title (A Side/B Side)	Yr	NM
❑ 32569	I Guess the Lord Must Be in New York City/Do Wah Diddy	1969	10.00

JERDEN

Number	Title (A Side/B Side)	Yr	NM
❑ 906	Adrienne/Ice Cream World	1968	12.00
❑ 908	Land of Ur/Michael Glover	1969	12.00

SCEPTER

Number	Title (A Side/B Side)	Yr	NM
❑ 12190	You're Not My Girl/ When I'm Gone	1967	15.00
❑ 12199	Mr. Kirby/Seeds of Spring	1967	15.00
❑ 12207	Again/Show Me the Way to Love	1968	12.00

WARNER BROS.

Number	Title (A Side/B Side)	Yr	NM
❑ 7318	Lonely/There'll Come a Time	1969	10.00

NEW YORKERS, THE (3)

45s

TAC-FUL

Number	Title (A Side/B Side)	Yr	NM
❑ 101	You Should Have Told Me/ Don't Want to Be Your Fool	1964	50.00

NEW YORKERS FIVE, THE

45s

DANICE

Number	Title (A Side/B Side)	Yr	NM
❑ 801	Gloria My Darling/Cha Cha Baby	1955	400.00

NEWBAG, JOHNNY

45s

ATLANTIC

Number	Title (A Side/B Side)	Yr	NM
❑ 2355	The Poorer the Man (The Higher His Love)/Got to Get You Back	1966	100.00

PORT

Number	Title (A Side/B Side)	Yr	NM
❑ 3008	Sweet Thing/Little Samson	1965	100.00

NEWBEATS, THE Also see DEAN AND MARC.

45s

BUDDAH

Number	Title (A Side/B Side)	Yr	NM
❑ 390	The Way You Do the Things You Do/Does Your Body Need Lovin'	1973	8.00

HICKORY

Number	Title (A Side/B Side)	Yr	NM
❑ 326	Bread and Butter/ Tough Little Buggy	1974	6.00
❑ 1269	Bread and Butter/ Tough Little Buggy	1964	15.00
❑ 1282	Everything's All Right/ Pink Dally Rue	1964	12.00
❑ 1290	Break Away (From That Boy)/ Hey-O Daddy-O	1965	10.00
❑ 1305	(The Bees Are For the Birds) The Birds Are For the Bees/ Better Watch Your Step	1965	10.00
❑ 1320	Little Child/I Can't Hear You No More	1965	10.00
❑ 1332	Run, Baby, Run (Back Into My Arms)/Mean Wooly Willie	1965	12.00
❑ 1366	Shake Hands (And Come Out Crying)/Too Sweet to Be Forgotten	1966	10.00
❑ 1387	Short on Love/Crying My Heart Out	1966	8.00
❑ 1408	Bird Dog/Evil Eva	1966	8.00
❑ 1422	My Yesterday Love/ Patent on Love	1966	8.00
❑ 1436	So Fine/Top Secret	1967	8.00
❑ 1467	Hide the Moon/It's Really Goodbye	1967	8.00
❑ 1485	Don't Turn Me Loose/ You and Me and Happiness	1967	8.00
❑ 1496	Bad Dreams/Swinger	1968	8.00
❑ 1510	I've Been a Long Time Loving You/Michelle de Ann	1968	8.00
❑ 1522	Ain't That Lovin' You/The Girls and the Boys	1968	8.00
❑ 1539	Great Balls of Fire/ Thou Shalt Not Steal	1969	8.00
❑ 1552	Groovin' (Out on Life)/ Bread and Butter	1969	10.00
❑ 1562	Laura (What's He Got That I Ain't Got)/Break Away (From That Boy)	1970	6.00
❑ 1569	I'm a Teardrop/She Won't Hang Her Love (Out on the Line)	1970	6.00
❑ 1600	Am I Not My Brother's Keeper/ Run, Baby, Run (Back Into My Arms)	1971	10.00
❑ 1624	Oh, Pretty Woman/ Remember Love	1972	10.00
❑ 1637	Love Gets Sweeter/Eveything's All Right	1972	10.00

PLAYBOY

Number	Title (A Side/B Side)	Yr	NM
❑ 6013	I Believe I'm in Love with You/ I Know (You Don't Want Me No More)	1974	6.00

7-Inch Extended Plays

HICKORY

Number	Title (A Side/B Side)	Yr	NM
❑ HSP 120005	A Patent on Love/So Fine/Thou Shalt Not Steal//There Outa Be a Law/I'm Blue (The Gong Gong Song)/Ain't That Lovin' You Baby	1965	25.00

—Jukebox issue; small hole, plays at 33 1/3 rpm

Number	Title (A Side/B Side)	Yr	NM
❑ HSP 120005 [PS]	Bread & Butter	1965	40.00

—Sleeve calls this "Special Promotion Six-Pac" and calls the first song on side 2 "There Oughta Be a Law"

Albums

HICKORY

Number	Title (A Side/B Side)	Yr	NM
❑ LPM 120 [M]	Bread and Butter	1964	50.00
❑ LPS 120 [S]	Bread and Butter	1964	150.00
❑ LPM 122 [M]	Big Beat Sounds by the Newbeats	1965	50.00
❑ LPS 122 [S]	Big Beat Sounds by the Newbeats	1965	100.00
❑ LPM 128 [M]	Run Baby Run	1965	50.00
❑ LPS 128 [S]	Run Baby Run	1965	100.00
❑ DT 90701 [R]	Bread and Butter	1965	150.00
—Capitol Record Club edition			
❑ ST 90701 [S]	Bread and Butter	1965	200.00
—Capitol Record Club edition			
❑ T 90701 [M]	Bread and Butter	1965	150.00
—Capitol Record Club edition			

NEWBURY, MICKEY

45s

ABC HICKORY

Number	Title (A Side/B Side)	Yr	NM
❑ 54006	Hand Me Another of Those/ Leavin' Kentucky	1977	5.00
❑ 54015	Makes Me Wonder If I Ever Said Goodbye/Shenandoah	1977	5.00
❑ 54025	Gone to Alabama/Westphalia Texas Blues	1978	5.00
❑ 54034	It Don't Matter Anymore/ Wish I Was	1978	5.00
❑ 54042	Looking for the Sunshine/ A Weed Is a Weed	1979	5.00

AIRBORNE

Number	Title (A Side/B Side)	Yr	NM
❑ 10005	An American Trilogy/San Francisco Mabel Joy	1988	5.00

ELEKTRA

Number	Title (A Side/B Side)	Yr	NM
❑ 45206	You Only Live Once (In a While)/ Baby's Not Home	1974	5.00
❑ 45238	Lovers/Good Night	1975	5.00
❑ 45256	Sail Away/If You Ever Get to Houston	1975	5.00
❑ 45329	An American Trilogy/Sunshine	1976	5.00
❑ 45750	An American Trilogy/San Francisco Mable Joy	1971	10.00
❑ 45771	Mobile Blue/Frisco Depot	1972	6.00
❑ 45789	How I Love Them Old Songs/ Remember the Good	1972	6.00
❑ 45840	Heaven Help the Child/ Good Morning Dear	1973	5.00
❑ 45853	Sunshine/Song for Susan	1973	5.00
❑ 45889	If I Could Be/Love Look	1974	5.00

HICKORY

Number	Title (A Side/B Side)	Yr	NM
❑ 1312	Lonely Place/Well I Did (Last Night)	1965	10.00
❑ 1344	There Is a Time to Die/ Travelin' Man	1965	10.00
❑ 1370	Anyway You Want Me/ (It May Not Take) Too Much	1966	10.00
❑ 1419	After the Rains/Baby Just Said Goodbye	1966	10.00
❑ 1463	Dreamin' in the Rain/Leavin' Makes the Rain Come Down	1967	10.00
❑ 1673	America the Beautiful/Freedom	1980	5.00

MCA

Number	Title (A Side/B Side)	Yr	NM
❑ 41032	Blue Sky Shinin'/Darlin' Take Care of Yourself	1979	5.00

MERCURY

Number	Title (A Side/B Side)	Yr	NM
❑ 57061	Country Boy Saturday Night/ Let's Say Goodbye One More Time	1981	5.00
❑ 72975	Ten Tottle Tommy/San Francisco Mable Joy	1969	7.00
❑ 73036	Sunshine/Sad Satin Rhyme	1970	7.00

RCA VICTOR

Number	Title (A Side/B Side)	Yr	NM
❑ 47-9570	Weeping Annaleah/Are My Thoughts with You	1968	8.00
❑ 47-9632	Got Down on Saturday/ Sweet Memories	1968	8.00
❑ 47-9690	Organized Noise/The Queen	1968	8.00

Albums

ABC HICKORY

Number	Title (A Side/B Side)	Yr	NM
❑ HA-44002	Rusty Tracks	1977	10.00
❑ HA-44011	Eye on the Sparrow	1978	10.00
❑ HB-44017	The Sailor	1979	10.00

ELEKTRA

Number	Title (A Side/B Side)	Yr	NM
❑ EK-PROMO 20 [DJ]	Recorded Live at Montezuma Hall, San Diego State University, March 6, 1973	1973	40.00
❑ 7E-1007	I Came to Hear the Music	1974	10.00
❑ 7E-1030	Lovers	1975	10.00
❑ EQ-4107 [Q]	'Frisco Mabel Joy	1974	20.00
❑ EKS-74107	'Frisco Mabel Joy	1971	10.00
❑ EKS-75055	Heaven Help the Child	1973	10.00

MCA

Number	Title (A Side/B Side)	Yr	NM
❑ 802	Rusty Tracks	198?	8.00
—Reissue			
❑ 803	Eye on the Sparrow	198?	8.00
—Reissue			
❑ 804	The Sailor	198?	8.00
—Reissue			
❑ 945	Sweet Memories	1985	10.00

MERCURY

Number	Title (A Side/B Side)	Yr	NM
❑ SR 61236	Looks Like Rain	1969	15.00

RCA VICTOR

Number	Title (A Side/B Side)	Yr	NM
❑ LSP-4043	Harlequin Melodies	1968	15.00

NEWCOMERS, THE

45s

MERCURY

Number	Title (A Side/B Side)	Yr	NM
❑ 74011	Do Yourself a Favor/That's When You Know Your Woman Wants to Be Free	1978	30.00

STAX

Number	Title (A Side/B Side)	Yr	NM
❑ 0099	Pin the Tail on the Donkey/ Mannish Boy	1971	8.00

TRUTH

Number	Title (A Side/B Side)	Yr	NM
❑ 3204	Keep an Eye on Your Close Friends/(Instrumental)	1974	15.00
❑ 3213	(Too Much in Common to Be Lovers) Too Much Going to Say Good-Bye/The Whole World's a Picture Show	1974	30.00

VOLT

Number	Title (A Side/B Side)	Yr	NM
❑ 4022	Open Up Your Heart/ Girl, This Boy Loves You	1969	30.00
❑ 4049	You Put the Sunshine Back in My World/Still a Boy in My Heart	1971	30.00

NEWHART, BOB

Albums

HARMONY

Number	Title (A Side/B Side)	Yr	NM
❑ HS 11344	The Very Funny Bob Newhart	196?	12.00

MURRAY HILL

Number	Title (A Side/B Side)	Yr	NM
❑ OP 2529 [(2)]	The Best of the Button-Down Mind	197?	20.00

WARNER BROS.

Number	Title (A Side/B Side)	Yr	NM
❑ W 1379 [M]	The Button-Down Mind of Bob Newhart	1960	30.00
❑ WS 1379 [S]	The Button-Down Mind of Bob Newhart	1960	25.00
❑ W 1393 [M]	The Button-Down Mind Strikes Back!	1960	30.00
❑ WS 1393 [S]	The Button-Down Mind Strikes Back!	1960	25.00
❑ 2N 1399 [(2)M]	The Bob Newhart Deluxe Edition	1961	50.00
❑ 2NS 1399 [(2)S]	The Bob Newhart Deluxe Edition	1961	40.00
❑ W 1417 [M]	Behind the Button-Down Mind of Bob Newhart	1961	25.00
❑ WS 1417 [S]	Behind the Button-Down Mind of Bob Newhart	1961	20.00
❑ W 1467 [M]	The Button-Down Mind on TV	1962	25.00
❑ WS 1467 [S]	The Button-Down Mind on TV	1962	20.00
❑ W 1517 [M]	Bob Newhart Faces Bob Newhart (Faces Bob Newhart)	1964	25.00
❑ W 1588 [M]	The Windmills Are Weakening	1965	30.00
❑ W 1672 [M]	The Best of Bob Newhart	1966	30.00
❑ WS 1672 [S]	The Best of Bob Newhart	1966	25.00
—Gold label			

N

Number	Title (A Side/B Side)	Yr	NM
❑ WS 1672 [S]	The Best of Bob Newhart	1968	20.00
—Green "W7" label			
❑ WS 1672 [S]	The Best of Bob Newhart	1970	15.00
—Green "WB" label			
❑ WS 1672 [S]	The Best of Bob Newhart	1973	12.00
—"Burbank" palm-trees label			
❑ WS 1672 [S]	The Best of Bob Newhart	1979	8.00
—White or tan label			
❑ W 1717 [M]	This Is It	1967	30.00

NEWLYWEDS, THE

45s

HOMOGENIZED SOUL

Number	Title (A Side/B Side)	Yr	NM
❑ 601	Love Walked Out/The Quarrel	1961	3000.
—VG 1500; VG+ 2250			

NEWMAN, BOB

45s

KING

Number	Title (A Side/B Side)	Yr	NM
❑ 45-959	Lonesome Truck Driver's Blues/Turtle Dovin'	1951	60.00
❑ 45-973	It Hurts Me/Rover, Rover	1951	50.00
❑ 45-1008	Hangover Boogie/I'm Gonna Give You a Dose of Your Own Medicine	1951	50.00
❑ 45-1044	Haulin' Freight/Baby, Take Me Home with You	1952	50.00
❑ 45-1057	Around the Corner/ Lonesome Sailor's Dream	1952	50.00
❑ 45-1082	Chic-a-Choo Freight/ Sand Boogie	1952	50.00
❑ 45-1108	Tonight's the Night/Greetings	1952	50.00
❑ 45-1131	Phfft! You Were Gone/ Doodle Bug	1952	50.00
❑ 45-1155	Sweet Orchard Vine/ Strange Love	1953	50.00
❑ 45-1186	It's Momma, She's the One/ Sweet Music	1953	50.00
❑ 45-5216	Lonesome Truck Driver's Blues/Haulin' Freight	1959	25.00
❑ 45-5789	Lonesome Truck Driver's Blues/Haulin' Freight	1963	15.00

Albums

AUDIO LAB

Number	Title (A Side/B Side)	Yr	NM
❑ AL-1536 [M]	The Kentucky Colonel	1959	200.00

NEWMAN, PHYLLIS

45s

SIRE

Number	Title (A Side/B Side)	Yr	NM
❑ 4104	Frank Mills/World of Music	1969	10.00

Albums

SIRE

Number	Title (A Side/B Side)	Yr	NM
❑ SES-97002	Those Were the Days	1969	20.00

NEWMAN, RANDY

12-Inch Singles

WARNER BROS.

Number	Title (A Side/B Side)	Yr	NM
❑ PRO-A-860 [DJ]	Political Science/Spys	1979	8.00

45s

DOT

Number	Title (A Side/B Side)	Yr	NM
❑ 16411	Golden Gridiron Boy/ Country Boy	1962	50.00
—May be promo only			

REPRISE

Number	Title (A Side/B Side)	Yr	NM
❑ 0692	I Think It's Going to Rain Today/ The Beehive State	1968	15.00
❑ 0771	Last Night I Had a Dream/ I Think He's Hiding	1968	25.00
—May be promo only			
❑ 0917	Have You Seen My Baby/ Hold On	1970	15.00
❑ 0945	Gone Dead Train/Harry Flowers	1970	15.00
❑ 1102	Sail Away/Political Science	1972	6.00
❑ 1123	You Can Leave Your Hat On/ Memo to My Son	1972	6.00
❑ 1324	Guilty/Naked Man	1975	5.00
❑ 1387	Louisiana 1927/Marie	1977	5.00
❑ 22798	I'd Love to See You Smile/End Title (I'd Love to See You Smile)	1989	3.00
❑ 27709	It's Money That Matters/ Roll with the Punches	1988	3.00
❑ 27709 [PS]	It's Money That Matters/ Roll with the Punches	1988	3.00
❑ 27856	Falling in Love/Bad News from Home	1989	3.00

WARNER BROS.

Number	Title (A Side/B Side)	Yr	NM
❑ 8492	Short People/Old Man on the Farm	1977	5.00
❑ 8550	Baltimore/You Can't Fool the Fat Man	1978	4.00
❑ 8630	Rider in the Rain/Sigmund Freud's Impersonation of Albert Einstein in America	1978	4.00
❑ 29241	The Natural/The Natural (Final Game)	1984	4.00
❑ 29687	I Love L.A./Song for the Dead	1983	4.00
❑ 29803	The Blues/The Same Girl	1983	4.00
—A-side: With Paul Simon			
❑ 29803 [PS]	The Blues/The Same Girl	1983	4.00
❑ 49088	It's Money That I Love/Ghosts	1979	4.00
❑ 49149	Half a Man/The Story of a Rock and Roll Band	1979	4.00
❑ 49223	Spies/Political Science (Let's Drop the Big One)	1980	4.00

7-Inch Extended Plays

REPRISE

Number	Title (A Side/B Side)	Yr	NM
❑ PRO 374 [DJ]	Radio Spots for: 12 Songs	1970	20.00
—White label; three 60-second ads on each side; not issued with cover			

Albums

REPRISE

Number	Title (A Side/B Side)	Yr	NM
❑ MS 2064	Sail Away	1972	10.00
—With song titles listed on back			
❑ MS 2064	Sail Away	1972	15.00
—With no song titles listed on back			
❑ MS 2193	Good Old Boys	1974	10.00
❑ MS4 2193 [Q]	Good Old Boys	1974	15.00
❑ RS 6286	Randy Newman	1968	15.00
—Cover with close-up of Randy's face; "W7" and "r:" logos on two-tone orange label			
❑ RS 6286	Randy Newman	1968	20.00
—Cover with Randy standing in the clouds			
❑ RS 6286	Randy Newman	1970	12.00
—With only "r:" logo on all-orange (tan) label			
❑ RS 6373	12 Songs	1970	10.00
—With only "r:" logo on all-orange (tan) label			
❑ RS 6373	12 Songs	1970	15.00
—With "W7" and "r:" logos on two-tone orange label			
❑ RS 6459	Randy Newman/Live	1971	10.00
❑ 25773	Land of Dreams	1988	10.00

WARNER BROS.

Number	Title (A Side/B Side)	Yr	NM
❑ BSK 3079	Little Criminals	1977	10.00
❑ HS 3346	Born Again	1979	10.00
❑ 23755	Trouble in Paradise	1983	10.00

NEWMAN, TED

45s

RCA VICTOR

Number	Title (A Side/B Side)	Yr	NM
❑ 47-7197	It's Hot in Here/Why Did You Break My Heart	1958	15.00
❑ 47-7251	Hey Little Freshman/Brigette	1958	15.00

REV

Number	Title (A Side/B Side)	Yr	NM
❑ 3505	Plaything/Unlucky Me	1957	20.00
❑ 3511	I Double Dare You/ None of Your Tears	1957	15.00

NEWPORTS, THE (1)

45s

CRYSTAL BALL

Number	Title (A Side/B Side)	Yr	NM
❑ 129	Jingle Bells/My Juanita	1979	8.00

GUYDEN

Number	Title (A Side/B Side)	Yr	NM
❑ 2067	If I Could Tonight/A Fellow Needs a Girl	1962	30.00
❑ 2116	Tears/Disillusioned Love	1964	30.00

NEWPORTS, THE (2)

45s

KENT

Number	Title (A Side/B Side)	Yr	NM
❑ 380	The Wonder of Love/ Dixie Women	1962	300.00

NEWPORTS, THE (3)

45s

LAURIE

Number	Title (A Side/B Side)	Yr	NM
❑ 3327	The Trouble Is You/I Want You	1966	25.00

NEWPORTS, THE (U)

May be group (3), may be completely different.

45s

PARROT

Number	Title (A Side/B Side)	Yr	NM
❑ 45008	Party Night/Listen to Your Big Brother	1966	15.00

NEWTON, BOBBY

45s

ATLANTIC

Number	Title (A Side/B Side)	Yr	NM
❑ 2932	There's an Island/ A Little Bit of Soap	1973	20.00
❑ 2992	When the World's at Peace/ If You Can't Be My Woman	1973	30.00

FOXIE

Number	Title (A Side/B Side)	Yr	NM
❑ 7003	Dance Craze/These Empty Arms	1960	40.00

INTREPID

Number	Title (A Side/B Side)	Yr	NM
❑ 75014	Your Love Gets Sweeter Everyday/How Can I Thank You Enough	1969	25.00
—With Tina Blount			

LORRAINE

Number	Title (A Side/B Side)	Yr	NM
❑ 1401	Don't Fight the Feeling/ Alone and Lonely Nights	1966	25.00

MERCURY

Number	Title (A Side/B Side)	Yr	NM
❑ 72894	Do the Whip/(Instrumental)	1969	30.00

NEWTON, JUICE

45s

CAPITOL

Number	Title (A Side/B Side)	Yr	NM
❑ 4499	Come to Me/Save a Heart	1977	6.00
❑ 4552	It's a Heartache/Wouldn't Mind the Rain	1978	6.00
❑ 4611	Hey Baby/It's Not Impossible	1978	6.00
❑ 4679	Let's Keep It That Way/Tell My Baby Goodbye	1979	5.00
❑ 4714	Lay Back in the Arms of Someone/It's Not Impossible	1979	5.00
❑ 4768	Any Way That You Want Me/ A Dream Never Dies	1979	5.00
❑ 4793	Until Tonight/Lay Back in the Arms of Someone	1979	5.00
❑ 4818	Sunshine/Go Easy on Me	1980	4.00
❑ 4856	You Fill My Life/Tear It Up	1980	4.00
❑ 4976	Angel of the Morning/ Headin' for a Heartache	1981	3.00
❑ 4976 [PS]	Angel of the Morning/ Headin' for a Heartache	1981	4.00
❑ 4997	Queen of Hearts/River of Love	1981	3.00
❑ 4997 [PS]	Queen of Hearts/River of Love	1981	4.00
❑ A-5046	The Sweetest Thing (I've Ever Known)/Ride 'Em Cowboy	1981	3.00
❑ A-5046 [PS]	The Sweetest Thing (I've Ever Known)/Ride 'Em Cowboy	1981	4.00
❑ B-5120	Love's Been a Little Bit Hard on Me/Ever True	1982	3.00
❑ B-5120 [PS]	Love's Been a Little Bit Hard on Me/Ever True	1982	4.00
❑ B-5148	Break It to Me Gently/ Adios Mi Corazon	1982	3.00
❑ B-5148 [PS]	Break It to Me Gently/ Adios Mi Corazon	1982	4.00
❑ B-5192	Heart of the Night/Love Sail Away	1982	3.00
❑ B-5192 [PS]	Heart of the Night/Love Sail Away	1982	4.00
❑ B-5265	Tell Her No/Stranger at My Door	1983	3.00
❑ B-5265 [PS]	Tell Her No/Stranger at My Door	1983	4.00
❑ B-5289	Dirty Looks/20 Years Ago	1983	3.00
❑ B-5289 [PS]	Dirty Looks/20 Years Ago	1983	4.00
❑ B-5379	Ride 'Em Cowboy/ Love Sail Away	1984	3.00

RCA

Number	Title (A Side/B Side)	Yr	NM
❑ 5068-7-R	What Can I Do with My Heart/ Let Your Woman Take Care of You	1986	3.00
❑ 5170-7-R	First Time Caller/Til You Cry	1987	3.00
❑ 5283-7-R	Tell Me True/If I Didn't Love You	1987	3.00
❑ 8815-7-R	When Love Comes Around the Bend/(B-side unknown)	1989	3.00
❑ PB-10828	If I Ever/Bye, Bye Baby	1976	8.00
❑ PB-13823	A Little Love/Waiting for the Sun	1984	3.00
❑ PB-13823 [PS]	A Little Love/Waiting for the Sun	1984	4.00
❑ PB-13863	Can't Wait All Night/ Restless Heart	1984	3.00
❑ PB-13863 [PS]	Can't Wait All Night/ Restless Heart	1984	4.00
❑ PB-13907	Restless Heart/ Eye of a Hurricane	1984	3.00
❑ PB-14139	You Make Me Want to Make You Mine/Waiting for the Sun	1985	3.00
❑ PB-14139 [PS]	You Make Me Want to Make You Mine/Waiting for the Sun	1985	4.00
❑ PB-14199	Hurt/Eye of a Hurricane	1985	3.00
❑ PB-14295	Old Flame/One Touch	1986	3.00
❑ GB-14355	Hurt/You Make Me Want to Make You Mine	1986	3.00
❑ PB-14377	Both to Each Other (Friends and Lovers)/ A World Without Love	1986	3.00
—With Eddie Rabbitt			
❑ PB-14377 [PS]	Both to Each Other (Friends and Lovers)/ A World Without Love	1986	5.00
❑ PB-14417	Cheap Love/Old Flame	1986	3.00

RCA VICTOR

Number	Title (A Side/B Side)	Yr	NM
❑ PB-10354	Catwillow River/It's High Time	1975	8.00
—With Silver Spur			
❑ PB-10412	The Sweetest Thing (I've Ever Known)/ The Shelter of Your Love	1975	8.00
—With Silver Spur			
❑ PB-10538	Love Is a Word/The Sweetest Thing (I've Ever Known)	1976	8.00
—With Silver Spur			

Albums

CAPITOL

Number	Title (A Side/B Side)	Yr	NM
❑ ST-11682	Come to Me	1977	15.00
❑ ST-11811	Well-Kept Secret	1978	15.00

Except when noted otherwise, VG = 25% of NM, and VG+ = 50% of NM. (Example: VG = $2.00, VG+ = $4.00 and NM = $8.00.)

Number	Title (A Side/B Side)	Yr	NM
ST-12000	Take Heart	1980	15.00
ST-12136	Juice	1981	10.00
ST-12210	Quiet Lies	1982	10.00
ST-12294	Dirty Looks	1983	10.00
SJ-12353	Greatest Hits	1984	10.00
SN-16242	Come to Me	1982	8.00
—Budget-line reissue			
SN-16243	Well-Kept Secret	1982	8.00
—Budget-line reissue			
SN-16244	Take Heart	1982	8.00
—Budget-line reissue			
SN-16313	Juice	1984	8.00
—Budget-line reissue			
SN-16314	Quiet Lies	1984	8.00
—Budget-line reissue			
SN-16356	Dirty Looks	1985	8.00
—Budget-line reissue			
SN-16471	Greatest Hits	1987	8.00
—Budget-line reissue			
RCA			
5646-1-R	Old Flame	1986	10.00
—Reissue of 5493 with slightly different lineup			
6371-1-R	Emotion	1987	10.00
8376-1-R	Ain't Gonna Cry	1989	10.00
RCA VICTOR			
APL1-1004	Juice Newton and Silver Spur	1975	20.00
APL1-1722	After Dust Settled	1977	15.00
AYL1-4037	Juice Newton and Silver Spur	1982	8.00
—"Best Buy Series" reissue			
AYL1-4038	After Dust Settled	1982	8.00
—"Best Buy Series" reissue			
AFL1-4995	Can't Wait All Night	1984	10.00
AFL1-5493	Old Flame	1985	12.00

NEWTON, WAYNE Also see THE NEWTON BROTHERS.

45s

Number	Title (A Side/B Side)	Yr	NM
ARIES II			
101	You Stepped Into My Life/She Believes in Me	1979	4.00
107	I Apologize/It's Nice to Be with You	1979	4.00
108	Years/Rhythm Rhapsody	1980	4.00
CAPITOL			
2016	Love of the Common People/It's Still Loving You	1967	6.00
2917	Up Here in a Tree/Fallin'	1970	5.00
2980	For the Good Times/Little Dreamer	1970	5.00
3044	Apartment 21/Me and Bobby McGee	1971	5.00
3118	Remember the Good Times/Good Morning Dear	1971	5.00
3189	I Ain't That Easy to Love/Leavin' Ya Going My Way	1971	5.00
3241	Just a Memory/Higher Ground	1971	5.00
4920	Heart! (I Hear You Beating)/So Long Lucy	1963	10.00
4920	Heart/So Long Lucy	1963	12.00
—Original pressing has no subtitle on A-side			
4989	Danke Schoen/Better Now Than Later	1963	12.00
5058	Shirl Girl/Someone's Ahead of You	1963	10.00
5124	Dream Baby (How Long Must I Dream)/I'm Looking Over a Four-Leaf Clover	1964	10.00
5171	Bill Bailey/When the Saints Go Marching In	1964	10.00
5203	Only You/Too Late to Meet	1964	10.00
5338	Comin' On Too Strong/Lookin' Through a Tear	1965	25.00
—Bruce Johnston and Terry Melcher help out on this record			
5366	Red Roses for a Blue Lady/One More Memory	1965	8.00
5419	I'll Be With You in Apple Blossom Time/Laura Lee	1965	8.00
5470	Summer Wind/I'll Be Standing By	1965	8.00
5514	Keep the Lovin' Feelin'/Remember When	1965	8.00
5553	A Little Bit of Heaven/Some Sunday Morning	1965	8.00
5578	You Just Don't Know/After the Laughter	1966	8.00
5578 [PS]	You Just Don't Know/After the Laughter	1966	15.00
5643	Somebody to Love/Stagecoach to Cheyenne	1966	8.00
5643 [PS]	Somebody to Love/Stagecoach to Cheyenne	1966	15.00
5692	Excuse Me/How Loud a Sound	1966	8.00
5754	The Games That Lovers Play/Half a World Away	1966	8.00
5793	Happy Is Gone/How D'Ya Talk to a Girl	1966	8.00
5842	If I Only Had a Song to Sing/Sunny Day Girl	1967	6.00
5954	Dream Street Rose/Summer Colors	1967	6.00
5993	Through the Eyes of Love/Just a Memory	1967	6.00
CHALLENGE			
59228	I Want to Mean Everything to You/I Still Love You	1964	10.00
59238	The Little White Cloud That Cried/Born When You Kissed Me	1964	10.00
59238	The Little White Cloud That Cried/Calorie Date	1964	10.00
CHELSEA			
BCBO-0091	May the Road Rise to Meet You/Pour Me a Little More Wine	1973	4.00
78-0100	Daddy Don't You Walk So Fast/Echo Valley 2-6809	1972	5.00
—Mostly pink label			
78-0100	Daddy Don't You Walk So Fast/Echo Valley 2-6809	1972	6.00
—White label (not a promo)			
78-0105	Can't You Hear the Song?/You Don't Have to Ask	1972	4.00
78-0109	Anthem/Fool	1972	4.00
78-0116	Just Yesterday/While We're Still Young	1973	4.00
78-0124	Help Me Help You/We Didn't Know the Time of Day	1973	4.00
AMBO-0126	Daddy Don't You Walk So Fast/Fool	1973	4.00
—Gold Standard Series reissue			
3003	Lay Lady Lay/Walking in the Sand	1974	4.00
3018	All Alone Am I/You Don't Have to Ask	1975	4.00
3028	Run to Me/Lady Lonely	1975	4.00
3041	The Hungry Years/In Dreams	1976	4.00
3058	It Could Have Been a Wonderful Christmas/Jingle Bell Hustle	1976	5.00
CURB			
10520	Cowboy's Christmas/(B-side unknown)	1988	3.00
10559	While the Feeling's Good/Our Wedding Band	1989	3.00
—A-side with Tammy Wynette			
GEORGE			
7777	The Little White Cloud That Cried/(B-side unknown)	1962	20.00
MGM			
13891	All the Time/Like Everything Else	1968	5.00
13936	Remembering/Angelica	1968	5.00
13955	Dreams of the Everyday Housewife/The Tip of My Fingers	1968	5.00
13993	Silence Says/Town and Country	1968	5.00
14014	I Just Can't Help Believin'/Husbands and Wives	1968	5.00
14019	Christmas Prayer/Santa Claus Is Comin' to Town	1968	5.00
14046	Everything's in Love Today/The Silence Says	1969	5.00
14083	New York City/For the First Time	1969	5.00
14098	It's Such a Lonely Time of the Year/The Country	1969	5.00
14430	With Pen in Hand/Town and Country	1972	4.00
20TH CENTURY			
2393	Hold Me Like You Never Had Me/Housewife	1978	4.00
WARNER BROS.			
8415	I Want You with Me/Midnight Sun	1977	4.00

7-Inch Extended Plays

Number	Title (A Side/B Side)	Yr	NM
ARIES II			
102	White Christmas/It's the Season//I'll Be Home for Christmas/Blue Snow at Christmas	1979	4.00

Albums

Number	Title (A Side/B Side)	Yr	NM
ARIES II			
WY 201	Wayne Newton Christmas	1979	10.00
CAPITOL			
SKAO-137	The Best of Wayne Newton, Vol. 2	1968	15.00
STBB-487 [(2)]	Merry Christmas to You	1970	15.00
ST-617	How I Got This Way	1971	15.00
ST 1973 [S]	Danke Schoen	1963	20.00
T 1973 [M]	Danke Schoen	1963	15.00
ST 2029 [S]	Wayne Newton In Person	1964	20.00
T 2029 [M]	Wayne Newton In Person	1964	15.00
ST 2130 [S]	Wayne Newton Sings Hit Songs	1964	20.00
T 2130 [M]	Wayne Newton Sings Hit Songs	1964	15.00
SM-2335	Red Roses for a Blue Lady	197?	10.00
—Reissue			
ST 2335 [S]	Red Roses for a Blue Lady	1965	20.00
T 2335 [M]	Red Roses for a Blue Lady	1965	15.00
ST 2389 [S]	Summer Wind	1965	20.00
T 2389 [M]	Summer Wind	1965	15.00
ST 2445 [S]	Wayne Newton — Now!	1966	20.00
T 2445 [M]	Wayne Newton — Now!	1966	15.00
SM-2563	The Old Rugged Cross	197?	10.00
—Reissue			
ST 2563 [S]	The Old Rugged Cross	1966	20.00
T 2563 [M]	The Old Rugged Cross	1966	15.00
ST 2588 [S]	Songs for a Merry Christmas	1966	15.00
T 2588 [M]	Songs for a Merry Christmas	1966	12.00
ST 2635 [S]	It's Only the Good Times	1967	20.00
T 2635 [M]	It's Only the Good Times	1967	15.00
ST 2714 [S]	Song of the Year... Wayne Newton Style	1967	15.00
T 2714 [M]	Song of the Year... Wayne Newton Style	1967	20.00
ST 2797 [S]	The Best of Wayne Newton	1967	15.00
T 2797 [M]	The Best of Wayne Newton	1967	20.00
ST 2832 [S]	God Is Alive	1968	15.00
T 2832 [M]	God Is Alive	1968	20.00
ST 2847 [S]	Wayne Newton — The Greatest	1968	15.00
T 2847 [M]	Wayne Newton — The Greatest	1968	20.00
SM-11972	Danke Schoen	1979	10.00
—Reissue			
SN-16083	The Best of Wayne Newton	1980	8.00
—Budget-line reissue			
CAPITOL PICKWICK SERIES			
PC-3455 [M]	Somewhere My Love	196?	10.00
SPC-3455 [S]	Somewhere My Love	196?	10.00
PC-3459 [M]	Everybody Loves Somebody	196?	10.00
SPC-3459 [S]	Everybody Loves Somebody	196?	10.00
PC-3461 [M]	Michelle	196?	10.00
SPC-3461 [S]	Michelle	196?	10.00
PC-3464 [M]	Wow! Wayne Newton Live	196?	10.00
SPC-3464 [S]	Wow! Wayne Newton Live	196?	10.00
CHELSEA			
BCL1-0367	Pour Me a Little More Wine	1973	12.00
CHL-504	The Best of Wayne Newton Live	1974	10.00
CHL-507	Midnight Idol	1975	10.00
CHL-512	Tomorrow	1976	10.00
CHL-513	Daddy Don't You Walk So Fast	1976	10.00
—Reissue of 1001			
CHE 1001	Daddy Don't You Walk So Fast	1972	12.00
CHE 1003	Can't You Hear the Song?	1972	12.00
CHE 1006	While We're Still Young	1973	12.00
CURB			
10607	Coming Home	1989	12.00
MGM			
E-4523 [M]	Walking on New Grass	1968	20.00
SE-4523 [S]	Walking on New Grass	1968	12.00
E-4549 [M]	One More Time	1968	20.00
SE-4549 [S]	One More Time	1968	12.00
SE-4593	Christmas Isn't Christmas Without You	1968	12.00
SE-4594	Dreams of the Everyday Housewife/Town and Country	1969	12.00
20TH CENTURY			
T-576	Change of Heart	1979	10.00
WORD			
WST-8586	Only Believe	1972	12.00

NEWTON BROTHERS, THE With WAYNE NEWTON.

45s

Number	Title (A Side/B Side)	Yr	NM
CAPITOL			
F-4236	The Real Thing/I Spy	1959	80.00

NEWTON-JOHN, OLIVIA

12-Inch Singles

Number	Title (A Side/B Side)	Yr	NM
MCA			
L33-1150 [DJ]	Twist of Fate (2 versions)	1983	20.00
13987	Livin' in Desperate Times/Twist of Fate	1984	20.00
23593	Soul Kiss (Extended Dance Mix) (Dub Mix) (Instrumental Mix)	1985	8.00
23606	Toughen Up (Dance Remix) (Instrumental)	1986	8.00
23890	The Rumour (4 versions)	1988	8.00

45s

Number	Title (A Side/B Side)	Yr	NM
ATLANTIC			
89420	The Best of Me/Sage	1986	3.00
—With David Foster			
89420 [PS]	The Best of Me/Sage	1986	3.00
MCA			
40043	Take Me Home, Country Roads/Sail Into Tomorrow	1973	30.00
—This has (finally) been proven to exist			
40043 [DJ]	Take Me Home, Country Roads (mono/stereo)	1973	20.00
40101	Let Me Be There/Maybe Then I'll Think of You	1973	5.00
40209	If You Love Me (Let Me Know)/Brotherly Love	1974	5.00
40280	I Honestly Love You/Home Ain't Home Anymore	1974	5.00
40349	Have You Never Been Mellow/Water Under the Bridge	1974	5.00

N

Number	Title (A Side/B Side)	Yr	NM
❑ 40418	Please Mr. Please/ And In the Morning	1975	5.00
❑ 40418 [PS]	Please Mr. Please/ And In the Morning	1975	10.00
❑ 40459	Something Better to Do/ He's My Rock	1975	5.00
❑ 40459 [PS]	Something Better to Do/ He's My Rock	1975	6.00
❑ 40495	Let It Shine/He Ain't Heavy, He's My Brother	1975	5.00
❑ 40525	Come On Over/Small Talk and Pride	1976	4.00
❑ 40600	Don't Stop Believin'/ Greensleeves	1976	4.00
❑ 40600 [PS]	Don't Stop Believin'/ Greensleeves	1976	5.00
❑ 40642	Every Face Tells a Story/ Love You Hold the Key	1976	4.00
❑ 40670	Sam/I'll Bet You a Kangaroo	1976	4.00
❑ 40737	Making a Good Thing Better/ I Think I'll Say Goodbye	1977	4.00
❑ 40811	I Honestly Love You/Don't Cry for Me Argentina	1977	5.00
❑ 40811 [PS]	I Honestly Love You/Don't Cry for Me Argentina	1977	10.00
❑ 40975	A Little More Love/ Borrowed Time	1978	4.00
❑ 40975 [PS]	A Little More Love/ Borrowed Time	1978	5.00
❑ 41009	Deeper Than the Night/Please Don't Keep Me Waiting	1979	4.00
❑ 41074	Totally Hot/Dancing Round and Round	1979	4.00
❑ 41074 [PS]	Totally Hot/Dancing Round and Round	1979	5.00
❑ 41247	Magic/Fool Country	1980	4.00
—Standard blue rainbow label			
❑ 41247	Magic/Fool Country	1980	5.00
—Custom pink "Xanadu" label			
❑ 41247 [PS]	Magic/Fool Country	1980	5.00
❑ 41285	Xanadu/Whenever You're Away from Me	1980	4.00
—A-side with Electric Light Orchestra; B-side with Gene Kelly. Persistent rumors claim existence of a U.S. picture sleeve for this record, but we've never seen one.			
❑ 41286	Suddenly/You Made Me Love You	1980	5.00
—A-side with Cliff Richard			
❑ 51007	Suddenly/You Made Me Love You	1980	4.00
—A-side with Cliff Richard			
❑ 51007 [PS]	Suddenly/You Made Me Love You	1980	5.00
❑ 51182	Physical/The Promise (The Dolphin Song)	1981	3.00
❑ 51182 [PS]	Physical/The Promise (The Dolphin Song)	1981	4.00
❑ 52000	Make a Move on Me/Falling	1982	3.00
❑ 52000 [PS]	Make a Move on Me/Falling	1982	5.00
❑ 52069	Landslide/Recovery	1982	3.00
❑ 52069 [PS]	Landslide/Recovery	1982	4.00
❑ 52100	Heart Attack/Strangers Touch	1982	3.00
❑ 52100 [PS]	Heart Attack/Strangers Touch	1982	3.00
❑ 52155	Tied Up/Silvery Rain	1983	3.00
❑ 52155 [PS]	Tied Up/Silvery Rain	1983	3.00
❑ 52284	Twist of Fate/Take a Chance	1983	3.00
❑ 52284 [PS]	Twist of Fate/Take a Chance	1983	3.00
❑ 52341	Livin' in Desperate Times/ Landslide	1984	3.00
❑ 52341 [PS]	Livin' in Desperate Times/ Landslide	1984	3.00
❑ 52686	Soul Kiss/Electric	1985	3.00
❑ 52686 [PS]	Soul Kiss/Electric	1985	3.00
❑ 52757	Toughen Up/Driving Music	1986	3.00
❑ 52757 [PS]	Toughen Up/Driving Music	1986	3.00
❑ 53294	The Rumour/Winter Angel	1988	3.00
❑ 53294 [PS]	The Rumour/Winter Angel	1988	3.00
❑ 53438	Can't We Talk It Over in Bed/ Get Out	1988	3.00
❑ 53438 [PS]	Can't We Talk It Over in Bed/ Get Out	1988	4.00
❑ 72053	I Honestly Love You/I Honestly Love You (Remix)	1998	3.00
—New recordings			
MCA NASHVILLE			
❑ 72074	Back with a Heart/Under My Skin	1998	3.00
RSO			
❑ 903	Hopelessly Devoted to You/Love Is a Many-Splendored Thing	1978	4.00
UNI			
❑ 55281	If Not for You/The Biggest Clown	1971	10.00
❑ 55304	Banks of the Ohio/It's So Hard to Say Goodbye	1971	8.00
❑ 55317	What Is Life/I'm a Small and Lonely Light	1972	8.00
❑ 55348	Just a Little Too Much/ My Old Man's Gotta Gun	1972	12.00

Albums

Number	Title (A Side/B Side)	Yr	NM
GEFFEN			
❑ GHS 24257	Warm and Tender	1989	12.00
MCA			
❑ 389	Let Me Be There	1973	15.00
❑ 411	If You Love Me Let Me Know	1974	10.00
—With corrected song title: "I Honestly Love You"			
❑ 411	If You Love Me Let Me Know	1974	15.00
—Originals have incorrect song title: "I Love You, I Honestly Love You"			
❑ 2133	Have You Never Been Mellow	1975	10.00
❑ 2148	Clearly Love	1975	10.00
❑ 2186	Come On Over	1976	10.00
❑ 2223	Don't Stop Believin'	1976	10.00
❑ 2280	Making a Good Thing Better	1977	10.00
❑ 3012	Let Me Be There	1977	8.00
—Reissue			
❑ 3013	If You Love Me Let Me Know	1977	8.00
—Reissue			
❑ 3014	Have You Never Been Mellow	1977	8.00
—Reissue			
❑ 3015	Clearly Love	1977	8.00
—Reissue			
❑ 3016	Come On Over	1977	8.00
—Reissue			
❑ 3017	Don't Stop Believin'	1977	8.00
—Reissue			
❑ 3018	Making a Good Thing Better	1977	8.00
—Reissue			
❑ 3028	Olivia Newton-John's Greatest Hits	1977	10.00
❑ 3067	Totally Hot	1978	10.00
❑ 5229	Physical	1981	8.00
❑ 5347	Olivia's Greatest Hits, Vol. 2	1982	8.00
❑ 6151	Soul Kiss	1985	8.00
❑ 6245	The Rumour	1988	8.00
❑ 16011	Physical	1982	25.00
—Audiophile edition			
❑ 37061	Clearly Love	1980	8.00
—Reissue			
❑ 37062	Come On Over	1980	8.00
—Reissue			
❑ 37063	Don't Stop Believin'	1980	8.00
—Reissue			
❑ 37123	Totally Hot	1981	8.00
—Reissue			
MOBILE FIDELITY			
❑ 1-040	Totally Hot	1980	20.00
—Audiophile vinyl			
UNI			
❑ 73117	If Not for You	1971	80.00

NEXT MORNING, THE

Albums

Number	Title (A Side/B Side)	Yr	NM
CALLA			
❑ SC-2002	The Next Morning	1972	100.00

NIC NACS, THE

45s

Number	Title (A Side/B Side)	Yr	NM
RPM			
❑ 342	Gonna Have a Merry Christmas/ Found Me a Sugar Daddy	1951	200.00

NICE, THE

Keith Emerson, later of EMERSON, LAKE AND PALMER, was in this group.

45s

Number	Title (A Side/B Side)	Yr	NM
IMMEDIATE			
❑ 5004	Azrial (Angel of Death)/Thoughts of Emerlist Davjack	1968	12.00
❑ 5008	America/Diamnd Hard Apples of the Moon	1968	12.00
MERCURY			
❑ 73114	Country Pie/(B-side unknown)	1970	8.00
❑ 73272	Country Pie-Brandenburg Concerto No. 6 (Part 1)/ Finale-5th Bridge	1972	6.00

Albums

Number	Title (A Side/B Side)	Yr	NM
COLUMBIA SPECIAL PRODUCTS			
❑ P 11633	Thoughts of Emerlist Davjack	1973	12.00
❑ P 11634	Ars Longa Vita Brevis	1973	12.00
❑ P 11635	The Nice	1973	12.00
IMMEDIATE			
❑ Z12 52004	Thoughts of Emerlist Davjack	1968	20.00
❑ Z12-52020	Ars Longa Vita Brevis	1969	20.00
❑ Z12-52022	The Nice	1969	15.00
MERCURY			
❑ SRM-2-6500 [(2)]	Keith Emerson with The Nice	1972	15.00
❑ SR 61295	Five Bridges	1970	12.00
❑ SR 61324	Elegy	1971	12.00
SIRE			
❑ SASH-3710 [(2)]	The Vintage Years	1975	15.00

NICHOLAS, PAUL

45s

Number	Title (A Side/B Side)	Yr	NM
COLUMBIA			
❑ 46050	D.J. Saturday Night/Lovely Lady	1974	5.00
RSO			
❑ 851	Reggae Like It Used to Be/ Heat of the Night	1976	4.00
❑ 878	Heaven on the 7th Floor/ Do You Want My Love	1977	4.00
❑ 887	On the Strip/Beauty Queen	1978	4.00

Albums

Number	Title (A Side/B Side)	Yr	NM
RSO			
❑ RS-1-3028	Paul Nicholas	1977	12.00

NICHOLLS, ALLAN

45s

Number	Title (A Side/B Side)	Yr	NM
AVCO EMBASSY			
❑ 4520	Goin' Down/Sounds & Noises	1969	8.00
RARE EARTH			
❑ 5020	Coming Apart/Let the Music Play	1970	8.00

NICHOLS, MIKE, AND ELAINE MAY

Albums

Number	Title (A Side/B Side)	Yr	NM
MERCURY			
❑ SRM-2-628 [(2)]	Retrospect	1972	20.00
❑ OCM 2200 [M]	An Evening with Mike Nichols and Elaine May	1961	30.00
❑ OCS 6200 [S]	An Evening with Mike Nichols and Elaine May	1961	40.00
❑ MG 20376 [M]	Improvisations to Music	1959	30.00
❑ MG 20680 [M]	Nichols and May Examine Doctors	1962	25.00
❑ MG 20997 [M]	The Best of Nichols and May	1965	20.00
❑ SR 60040 [S]	Improvisations to Music	1959	40.00
❑ SR 60680 [S]	Nichols and May Examine Doctors	1962	30.00
❑ SR 60997 [S]	The Best of Nichols and May	1965	25.00

NICHOLS, NICHELLE

Albums

Number	Title (A Side/B Side)	Yr	NM
EPIC			
❑ LN 24351 [M]	Down to Earth	1968	80.00
—White label promo only; in stereo cover with "Mono" sticker			
❑ BN 26351 [S]	Down to Earth	1968	40.00

NICK AND THE JAGUARS

45s

Number	Title (A Side/B Side)	Yr	NM
TAMLA			
❑ 5501F	Ich-I-Bon #1/Cool and Crazy	1960	300.00

NICK AND THE NACKS

45s

Number	Title (A Side/B Side)	Yr	NM
BARRY			
❑ 108	The Night/That Old Black Magic	1964	400.00

NICK AND THE STINGRAYS

45s

Number	Title (A Side/B Side)	Yr	NM
MILL-MONT			
❑ 1628	You Are So Beautiful/ Broken Hearted Baby	196?	200.00

NICKEL BAG, THE

Albums

Number	Title (A Side/B Side)	Yr	NM
KAMA SUTRA			
❑ KLP-8066 [M]	Doing Their Love Thing	1968	60.00
—Both stock and promo copies exist			
❑ KLPS-8066 [S]	Doing Their Love Thing	1968	25.00

NICKIE AND THE NITELITES

With Nick Massi, later of THE FOUR SEASONS.

45s

Number	Title (A Side/B Side)	Yr	NM
BRUNSWICK			
❑ 55155	I'm Lonely/Tell Me You Care	1959	100.00

NICKS, STEVIE

Also see FLEETWOOD MAC; TOM PETTY AND THE HEARTBREAKERS.

12-Inch Singles

Number	Title (A Side/B Side)	Yr	NM
MODERN			
❑ PR 315 [DJ]	Edge of Seventeen (Live Full Length)/Edge of Seventeen (Live Edit)	1982	40.00
❑ PR 507 [DJ]	Stand Back (full length version)/ Stand Back (edit)	1983	20.00
❑ PR 807 [DJ]	Talk to Me (same on both sides)	1985	12.00
❑ PR 868 [DJ]	I Can't Wait (Rock Mix)/ Imperial Hotel	1986	20.00
❑ PR 925 [DJ]	I Can't Wait (4 versions)	1986	15.00
❑ 96825	I Can't Wait (4 versions)/ The Nightmare	1986	8.00

Except when noted otherwise, VG = 25% of NM, and VG+ = 50% of NM. (Example: VG = $2.00, VG+ = $4.00 and NM = $8.00.)

Number	Title (A Side/B Side)	Yr	NM
45s			
ATLANTIC OLDIES SERIES			
❑ OS 13236	Stop Draggin' My Heart Around/Leather and Lace	1983	3.00
❑ OS 13258	Edge of Seventeen/Stand Back	1985	3.00
❑ 84964	Talk to Me/I Can't Wait	1987	3.00
❑ 84998	If Anyone Falls/Nightbird	1986	3.00
MODERN			
❑ 3836	Stop Draggin' My Heart Around/Kind of Woman	1981	—
—Canceled; reassigned to 7336 (Atco series)			
❑ 7336	Stop Draggin' My Heart Around/Kind of Woman	1981	4.00
—With Tom Petty and the Heartbreakers			
❑ 7336 [PS]	Stop Draggin' My Heart Around/Kind of Woman	1981	6.00
❑ 7341	Leather and Lace/Bella Donna	1981	4.00
—With Don Henley; with no reference to Waylon Jennings and Jessi Colter on label			
❑ 7341	Leather and Lace/Bella Donna	1981	5.00
—With Don Henley; first pressing states "Written for Waylon Jennings and Jessi Colter"			
❑ 7341 [PS]	Leather and Lace/Bella Donna	1981	10.00
❑ 7401	Edge of Seventeen (Just Like the White Winged Dove)/Edge of Seventeen (Live)	1982	4.00
❑ 7401 [PS]	Edge of Seventeen (Just Like the White Winged Dove)/Edge of Seventeen (Live)	1982	6.00
❑ 7405	After the Glitter Fades/Think About It	1982	6.00
❑ 7405 [PS]	After the Glitter Fades/Think About It	1982	8.00
❑ 99150	Whole Lotta Trouble/Ghosts	1989	3.00
❑ 99150 [PS]	Whole Lotta Trouble/Ghosts	1989	—
—Rumored to exist, but without confirmation, this will be deleted from futire editions			
❑ 99179	Two Kinds of Love/Real Tears	1989	3.00
❑ 99179 [PS]	Two Kinds of Love/Real Tears	1989	5.00
❑ 99216	Rooms on Fire/Alice	1989	3.00
❑ 99216 [PS]	Rooms on Fire/Alice	1989	3.00
❑ 99532	Has Anyone Ever Written Anything for You/Imperial Hotel	1986	3.00
❑ 99532 [PS]	Has Anyone Ever Written Anything for You/Imperial Hotel	1986	8.00
❑ 99565	I Can't Wait/The Nightmare	1986	3.00
❑ 99565 [DJ]	I Can't Wait (Remix)/I Can't Wait (Soft Intro)	1986	8.00
❑ 99565 [PS]	I Can't Wait/The Nightmare	1986	3.00
❑ 99565 [PS]	I Can't Wait (Remix)/I Can't Wait (Soft Intro)	1986	12.00
❑ 99582	Talk to Me/One More Big Time Rock and Roll Star	1985	3.00
❑ 99582 [PS]	Talk to Me/One More Big Time Rock and Roll Star	1985	3.00
❑ 99799	Nightbird/Gate and Garden	1984	3.00
❑ 99799 [PS]	Nightbird/Gate and Garden	1984	50.00
❑ 99832	If Anyone Falls/Wild Heart	1983	4.00
❑ 99832 [PS]	If Anyone Falls/Wild Heart	1983	5.00
❑ 99863	Stand Back/Garbo	1983	3.00
❑ 99863 [PS]	Stand Back/Garbo	1983	4.00
WARNER SUNSET			
❑ 17132	If You Ever Did Believe/Crystal	1998	4.00
Albums			
ATLANTIC			
❑ 1P-8160	TimeSpace — The Best of Stevie Nicks	1991	20.00
—Columbia House edition; only US vinyl version			
MOBILE FIDELITY			
❑ 1-121	Bella Donna	1984	50.00
—Audiophile vinyl			
MODERN			
❑ MR 38-139	Bella Donna	1981	10.00
❑ PR-2881 [DJ]	Reflections from the Other Side of the Mirror	1989	20.00
—Promo-only interview album with script			
❑ 90084	The Wild Heart	1983	10.00
❑ 90479	Rock a Little	1985	10.00
❑ 91245	The Other Side of the Mirror	1989	10.00

NICKY AND THE NOBLES

Number	Title (A Side/B Side)	Yr	NM
45s			
END			
❑ 1021	Schoolhouse Rock/A Way to Tell Her	1958	50.00
❑ 1098	School Bells/School Day Crush	1961	25.00
GONE			
❑ 5039	School Bells/School Day Crush	1958	25.00
—Multicolor label			
❑ 5039	School Bells/School Day Crush	1958	60.00
—Black label			
❑ 5039	School Bells/School Days	1958	100.00
—With B-side title variation			

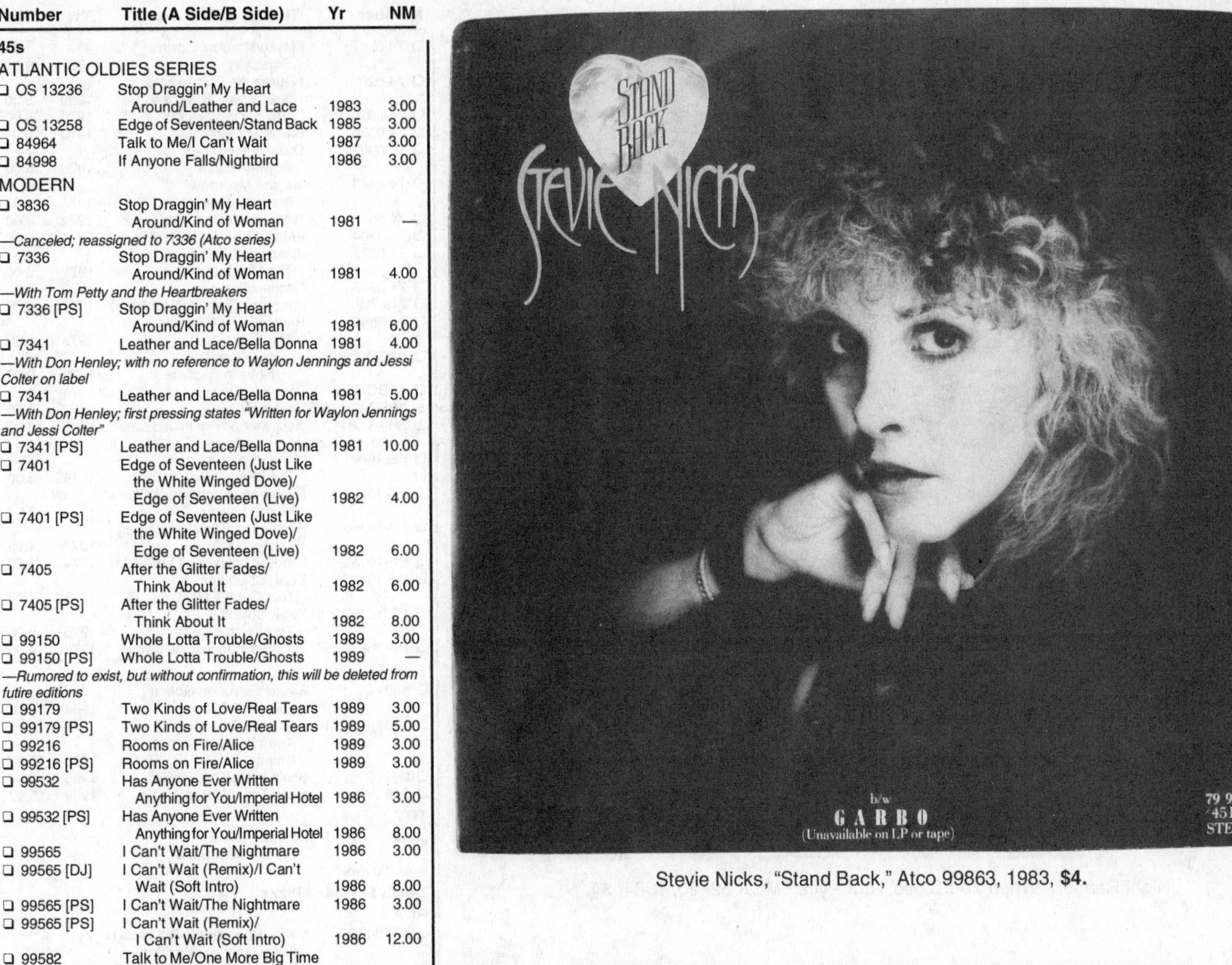

Stevie Nicks, "Stand Back," Atco 99863, 1983, $4.

NICO

Also see THE VELVET UNDERGROUND.

Number	Title (A Side/B Side)	Yr	NM
Albums			
ELEKTRA			
❑ EKS-74029	The Marble Index	1968	30.00
ISLAND			
❑ ILPS-9311	The End	1975	20.00
PVC			
❑ 8938	Camera Obscura	1985	15.00
REPRISE			
❑ RS 6424	Desert Shore	1970	25.00
VERVE			
❑ V-5032 [M]	Chelsea Girl	1967	30.00
❑ V6-5032 [S]	Chelsea Girl	1967	40.00

NICOL, JIMMY

His 15 minutes of fame came from his brief stint filling in for an ailing Ringo Starr on a 1964 Beatles tour.

Number	Title (A Side/B Side)	Yr	NM
45s			
ARGO			
❑ 5464	Night Train/Humpty Dumpty	1964	—
—Unreleased			
MAR MAR			
❑ 313	Night Train/Humpty Dumpty	1965	150.00
PARROT			
❑ 9752	Sweet Clementine/Roaring Blue	1965	25.00

NIEWOOD, GERRY

Number	Title (A Side/B Side)	Yr	NM
Albums			
A&M			
❑ SP-3409	Slow, Hot Wind	1977	10.00
HORIZON			
❑ SP-719	Gerry Niewood and Timepiece	1976	12.00

NIGHT RANGER

DAMN YANKEES related. Guitarist Brad Gillis was briefly in OZZY OSBOURNE's band.

Number	Title (A Side/B Side)	Yr	NM
45s			
BOARDWALK			
❑ NB7-11-171	Don't Tell Me You Love Me/Night Ranger	1983	5.00
❑ NB7-11-175	Sing Me Away/Play Rough	1983	5.00
❑ NB7-11-181	Young Girl in Love/Call My Name	1983	5.00
MCA			
❑ 52305	(You Can Still) Rock in America/Let Him Run	1983	4.00
❑ 52350	Sister Christian/Chippin' Away	1984	4.00
❑ 52420	When You Close Your Eyes/Why Does Love Have to Change	1984	3.00
❑ 52420 [PS]	When You Close Your Eyes/Why Does Love Have to Change	1984	4.00
❑ 53495	Don't Start Thinkin' (I'm Alone Tonight)/Kiss Me Where It Hurts	1989	3.00
MCA CAMEL			
❑ 52591	Sentimental Street/Night Machine	1985	3.00
❑ 52591 [PS]	Sentimental Street/Night Machine	1985	3.00
❑ 52661	Four in the Morning (I Can't Take Any More)/The Boy Needs to Rock	1985	3.00
❑ 52661 [PS]	Four in the Morning (I Can't Take Any More)/The Boy Needs to Rock	1985	3.00
❑ 52729	Goodbye/Seven Wishes	1985	3.00
❑ 52729 [PS]	Goodbye/Seven Wishes	1985	12.00
❑ 53013	The Secret of My Success/Carry On	1987	3.00
❑ 53013 [PS]	The Secret of My Success/Carry On	1987	3.00
❑ 53131	Hearts Away/Better Let it Go	1987	3.00
❑ 53364	I Did It for Love/Woman in Love	1988	3.00
❑ 53364 [PS]	I Did It for Love/Woman in Love	1988	3.00

N

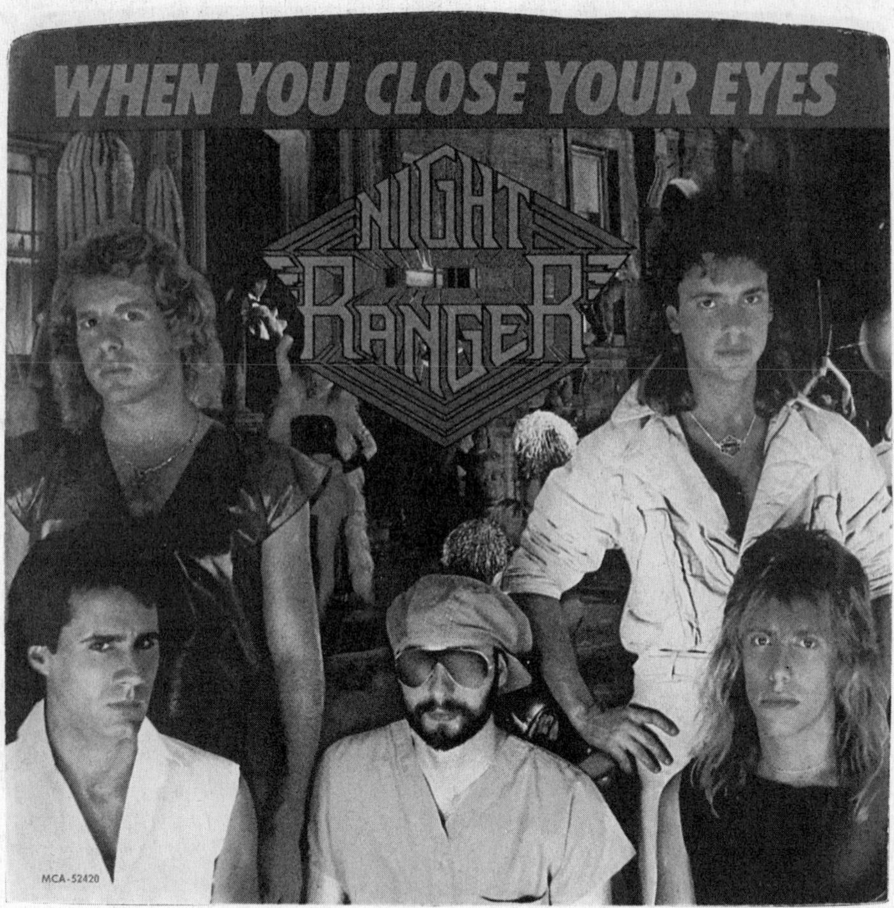

Night Ranger, "When You Close Your Eyes," MCA 52420, 1984, **$4.**

Number	Title (A Side/B Side)	Yr	NM
Albums			
BOARDWALK			
❑ NB1-33259	Dawn Patrol	1982	12.00
MCA			
❑ 5456	Midnight Madness	1984	8.00
❑ 5460	Dawn Patrol	1984	8.00
—Reissue of Boardwalk LP			
MCA CAMEL			
❑ 5593	7 Wishes	1985	8.00
❑ 5839	Big Life	1987	8.00

NIGHT WATCH, THE

Number	Title (A Side/B Side)	Yr	NM
45s			
ABC			
❑ 10862	Closed Time/Lips to Your Heart	1966	25.00

NIGHTCRAWLERS, THE

Number	Title (A Side/B Side)	Yr	NM
45s			
KAPP			
❑ KE-110	The Little Black Egg/You're Running Wild	1966	10.00
❑ 709	The Little Black Egg/You're Running Wild	1965	15.00
❑ 746	A Basket of Flowers/Washboard	1966	15.00
❑ 826	My Butterfly/Today I'm Happy	1967	30.00
LEE			
❑ 101	Cry/Marie	1964	60.00
❑ 1012	The Little Black Egg/You're Running Wild	1965	50.00
MARLIN			
❑ 1904	A Basket of Flowers/Washboard	1966	20.00
Albums			
KAPP			
❑ KL-1520 [M]	The Little Black Egg	1967	60.00
❑ KS-3520 [S]	The Little Black Egg	1967	40.00

NIGHTHAWK, ROBERT

Number	Title (A Side/B Side)	Yr	NM
45s			
STATES			
❑ 131	The Moon Is Rising/Maggie Campbell	1954	300.00

NILSSON Also see THE FOTO-FI FOUR; THE RIC-A-SHAYS.

Number	Title (A Side/B Side)	Yr	NM
45s			
CRUSADER			
❑ 103	Baa Baa Black Sheep/Baa Baa Black Sheep (Part 2)	1964	30.00
—As "Bo Pete"			
MUSICOR			
❑ 6308	Please Mr. Music Man/Foolish Clock	1977	4.00
POLYDOR			
❑ 881177-7	Silver Horse/Loneliness	1984	4.00
RCA			
❑ PB-10759	Just One Look-Baby I'm Yours/That Is All	1976	4.00
—With Lynda Lawrence			
❑ PB-11059	Perfect Day/Who Done It	1977	4.00
❑ PB-11059 [PS]	Perfect Day/Who Done It	1977	5.00
❑ PB-11144	All I Think About Is You/I Never Thought I'd Get This Lonely	1977	4.00
❑ PB-11193	Ain't It Kinda Wonderful/I'm Bringing a Red, Red Rose	1978	4.00
❑ PB-11318	Spaceman/Me and My Arrow	1978	4.00
RCA VICTOR			
❑ 47-9206	Without Her/Freckles	1967	8.00
❑ 47-9298	You Can't Do That/Ten Little Indians	1967	10.00
❑ 47-9383	River Deep Mountain High/She Sang Hymns Out of Tune	1967	8.00
❑ 47-9442	One/Sister Marie	1968	8.00
❑ 47-9544	Everybody's Talkin'/Don't Leave Me	1968	12.00
❑ 47-9675	Rainmaker/I Will Take You There	1968	8.00
❑ 74-0161	Everybody's Talkin'/Rainmaker	1969	10.00
❑ 74-0207	Maybe/Marchin' Down Broadway	1969	8.00
❑ 74-0261	I Guess the Lord Must Be in New York City/Maybe	1969	8.00
❑ 74-0310	I'll Be Home/Waiting	1970	6.00
❑ 74-0336	Caroline/Yellow Man	1970	6.00
❑ 74-0362	Down to the Valley/Buy My Album	1970	6.00
❑ 74-0443	Me and My Arrow/Are You Sleeping	1971	6.00
❑ 74-0524	Without Her/Good Old Desk	1971	6.00
❑ 74-0604	Without You/Gotta Get Up	1971	5.00
❑ 74-0673	Jump Into the Fire/The Moonbeam Song	1972	5.00
❑ 74-0718	Coconut/Down	1972	5.00
❑ 74-0788	Spaceman/Turn On Your Radio	1972	5.00
❑ 74-0855	Remember (Christmas)/The Lottery Song	1972	5.00
❑ APBO-0039	As Time Goes By/Lullabye in Ragtime	1973	6.00
❑ APBO-0246	Daybreak/Down	1974	4.00
❑ APBO-0246 [PS]	Daybreak/Down	1974	6.00
❑ SP-45-304 [DJ]	Jump Into the Fire (mono/stereo)	1972	10.00
—Promo-only number			
❑ PB-10001	Many Rivers to Cross/Don't Forget Me	1974	8.00
❑ PB-10078	Subterranean Homesick Blues/Mucho Mungo	1974	8.00
❑ PB-10130	Remember (Christmas)/The Lottery Song	1974	4.00
❑ PB-10139	Loop De Loop/Don't Forget Me	1974	4.00
❑ PB-10183	Kojak Columbo/Turn Out the Light	1975	4.00
❑ PB-10183 [PS]	Kojak Columbo/Turn Out the Light	1975	5.00
❑ PB-10634	Sail Away/Moonshine Bandit	1976	4.00
TOWER			
❑ 103	Sixteen Tons/I'm Gonna Lose My Mind	1964	15.00
❑ 136	You Can't Take Your Love Away from Me/Born in Grenada	1965	15.00
❑ 244	She's Yours/Growing Up	1966	15.00
❑ 518	Good Time/Growin' Up	1969	15.00
TRY			
❑ 501	Do You Wanna/Groovy Little Suzie	1964	40.00
—As "Bo Pete"			
7-Inch Extended Plays			
RCA			
❑ DTF0-2005	Makin' Whoopee/Nevertheless (I'm in Love with You)/You Made Me Love You (I Didn't Want to Do It)/I Wonder Who's Kissing Her Now/For Me and My Gal/It Had to Be You	1973	20.00
—Stereo jukebox issue; small hole, plays at 33 1/3 rpm			
❑ DTF0-2005 [PS]	A Little Touch of Schmilsson in the Night	1973	20.00
Albums			
MUSICOR			
❑ MUS-2505 [S]	Early Tymes	1977	15.00
PICKWICK			
❑ SPC-3321	Rock 'N' Roll	1977	10.00
RAPPLE			
❑ ABL1-0220	Son of Dracula	1974	12.00
RCA VICTOR			
❑ (no #) [M]	The True One	1967	200.00
—Boxed set with mono copy of RCA Victor 3874, two photos, button, poster, sticker, bios			
❑ APL1-0097	A Little Touch of Schmilsson in the Night	1973	12.00
❑ APL1-0203	Nilsson Sings Newman	1974	10.00
—Reissue of LSP-4289			
❑ APD1-0319 [Q]	Nilsson Schmilsson	1974	20.00
❑ SPS-33-567 [DJ]	Scatalogue	197?	100.00
❑ APD1-0570 [Q]	Pussy Cats	1974	30.00
❑ CPL1-0570	Pussy Cats	1974	20.00
❑ APD1-0817 [Q]	Duit On Mon Dei	1975	20.00
❑ APL1-0817	Duit On Mon Dei	1975	12.00
❑ LSPX-1003	The Point!	1971	12.00
❑ APD1-1031 [Q]	Sandman	1976	20.00
❑ APL1-1031	Sandman	1976	12.00
❑ APL1-1119	That's the Way It Is	1976	12.00
❑ AFL1-2276	Knnillssonn	1977	12.00
❑ AFL1-2798	Greatest Hits	1978	12.00
❑ ANL1-3464	Nilsson Schmilsson	1979	8.00
❑ AYL1-3761	A Little Touch of Schmilsson in the Night	1980	8.00
—"Best Buy Series" reissue			
❑ AYL1-3811	The Point!	1980	8.00
—"Best Buy Series" reissue			
❑ AYL1-3812	Son of Schmilsson	1980	8.00
—"Best Buy Series" reissue			
❑ LPM-3874 [M]	Pandemonium Shadow Show	1967	40.00

Number	Title (A Side/B Side)	Yr	NM
❑ LSP-3874 [S]	Pandemonium Shadow Show	1967	20.00
—"Stereo" on black label			
❑ LSP-3874 [S]	Pandemonium Shadow Show	1969	15.00
—Orange label			
❑ LPM-3956 [M]	Aerial Ballet	1968	50.00
❑ LSP-3956 [S]	Aerial Ballet	1968	20.00
—"Stereo" on black label			
❑ LSP-3956 [S]	Aerial Ballet	1969	15.00
—Orange label, non-flexible vinyl			
❑ LSP-4197	Harry	1969	15.00
—Orange label, non-flexible vinyl			
❑ LSP-4289	Nilsson Sings Newman	1970	12.00
—Orange label, non-flexible vinyl			
❑ LSP-4417	The Point!	1971	10.00
—Reissue of LSPX-1003			
❑ LSP-4515	Nilsson Schmilsson	1971	12.00
❑ LSP-4543	Aerial Pandemonium Ballet	1971	12.00
—Collection of tracks from 3874 and 3956, remixed with, in some cases, new vocals			
❑ LSP-4717	Son of Schmilsson	1972	12.00
—With custom black "Victor" label			
TOWER			
❑ ST 5095 [S]	Spotlight on Nilsson	1967	20.00
❑ T 5095 [M]	Spotlight on Nilsson	1967	20.00
❑ DT 5165 [R]	Spotlight on Nilsson	1969	15.00

NIMBLE, JACK B. AND THE QUICKS

45s

Number	Title (A Side/B Side)	Yr	NM
DEL RIO			
❑ 2303/4	Like Keyed/Babes in Toyland	1962	25.00
❑ 2305	Nut Rocker/Never on Sunday	1962	30.00
DOT			
❑ 16319	Nut Rocker/Never on Sunday	1962	15.00

NIMOY, LEONARD

45s

Number	Title (A Side/B Side)	Yr	NM
DOT			
❑ 17028	The Ballad of Bilbo Baggins/ Cotton Candy	1967	15.00
❑ 17038	Theme from "Star Trek"/ Visit to a Sad Planet	1967	20.00
❑ 17125	I'd Love Making Love to You/ Please Don't Try to Change My Mind	1968	15.00
❑ 17175	Consilium/Here We Go 'Round Again	1968	15.00
❑ 17330	The Sun Will Rise/ Time to Get It Together	1969	15.00

Albums

Number	Title (A Side/B Side)	Yr	NM
CAEDMON			
❑ TC-1466	The Martian Chronicles	1976	30.00
❑ TC-1479	The Illustrated Man	1976	30.00
❑ TC-1520	War of the Worlds	1977	30.00
❑ TC-1526	Green Hills of Earth	1977	30.00
DOT			
❑ DLP 3794 [M]	Mr. Spock's Music from Outer Space	1967	50.00
❑ DLP 3835 [M]	Two Sides of Leonard Nimoy	1968	50.00
❑ DLP 3883 [M]	The Way I Feel	1968	80.00
—Stereo cover with "Monaural" sticker; label is black stock copy			
❑ DLP 25794 [S]	Mr. Spock's Music from Outer Space	1967	80.00
❑ DLP 25835 [S]	Two Sides of Leonard Nimoy	1968	80.00
❑ DLP 25883 [S]	The Way I Feel	1968	60.00
❑ DLP 25910	The Touch of Leonard Nimoy	1969	60.00
❑ DLP 25966	The New World of Leonard Nimoy	1969	60.00
JRT			
❑ (# unknown)	The Mysterious Golem	1982	40.00
PARAMOUNT			
❑ PAS-1030 [(2)]	Outer Space/Inner Mind	1970	50.00
PICKWICK			
❑ SPC-3199	Space Odyssey	197?	50.00
SEARS			
❑ SPS-491	Leonard Nimoy	196?	80.00

NINCHUKS, THE

45s

Number	Title (A Side/B Side)	Yr	NM
BRYAN			
❑ BP-1 [DJ]	Bruce Lee's "Return of the Dragon" (mono/stereo)	1974	10.00
—Stock copies may not exist			

NINE INCH NAILS Industrial rock vehicle for Trent Reznor.

12-Inch Singles

Number	Title (A Side/B Side)	Yr	NM
NOTHING/INTERSCOPE			
❑ INT8P-6164/5/6 [(3)DJ]	The Perfect Drug Versions (Meat Beat Manifesto 7:34) (Nine Inch Nails 8:18) (Plug 6:54) (Aphrodite 6:10) (The Orb 6:13) (Spacetime Continuum 5:50)	1997	80.00
—Also called "Halo Eleven"; vinyl is promo only			
❑ INT8P-6641 [DJ]	The Day the World Went Away (4:03) (Quiet 6:20) (Porter Ricks)/Starfuckers, Inc. (5:24)	1999	20.00
❑ 97026	The Day the World Went Away (4:03) (Quiet 6:20) (Porter Ricks)	1999	10.00
—Also called "Halo Thirteen"			
NOTHING/TVT			
❑ 2611	Down In It (Skin 3:45) (Shred 6:55) (Singe 7:03)	1989	8.00
—Also called "Halo One"			
❑ 2614	Head Like a Hole (Slate 4:13) (Clay 4:30) (Copper 6:26) (Soil 6:38)/Terrible Lie (Sympathetic Mix 4:26) (Empathetic Mix 6:11)/You Know Who You Are (5:40)	1990	10.00
—Also called "Halo Three"			
❑ 2617	Sin (Short 4:19) (Long 5:50) (Dub 4:56)/Get Down Make Love (4:17)	1990	8.00
—Also called "Halo Four"			
NOTHING/TVT/INTERSCOPE			
❑ DMD 1941 [DJ]	Happiness in Slavery (Fixed Version 6:09) (Sherwood Slave Remix 2:17) (PK Slavery Remix 5:41) (Broken Version 5:21)	1993	30.00
—			
❑ DMD 1947 [DJ]	Wish (Fixed Remix 9:08) (Broken Version 3:47) (same on both sides)	1993	30.00
❑ DMD 2117 [(2)DJ]	Closer to God (5:25)/Closer (Precursor 7:16) (Deviation 6:15) (Internal 4:15) (Further Away 5:44) (Original 6:25)/ Heresy (Blind 5:38)/ Memorabilia (7:21)/March of the F**kheads (4:44)	1994	50.00
—Also called "Halo Nine"; vinyl is promo only			

Nilsson, "Daybreak," RCA APBO-0246, 1974, $6.

Number	Title (A Side/B Side)	Yr	NM
❑ PR 5539 [DJ]	March of the Pigs/Reptilian//All the Pigs, All Lined Up/A Violet Fluid/Underneath the Skin	1994	30.00
—Also called "Halo Seven"			

Albums

Number	Title (A Side/B Side)	Yr	NM
NOTHING			
❑ 1169701 [(2)S]	The Downward Spiral	2008	30.00
NOTHING/INTERSCOPE			
❑ B0004553-01 [(2)]	With Teeth	2005	25.00
❑ 490473 [(3)]	The Fragile	1999	100.00
—Also called "Halo Fourteen"			
❑ 490744 [(2)]	Things Falling Apart	2000	22.00
—Also called "Halo Sixteen"			
NOTHING/TVT			
❑ 2610	Pretty Hate Machine	1990	20.00
—Also called "Halo Two"			
NOTHING/TVT/INTERSCOPE			
❑ DMD 1903 [EP]	Broken	1992	30.00
—Also called "Halo Five"; promo-only vinyl release; six songs on one side of a 12-inch record and two bonus tracks, "Physical (You're So)" and "Suck," on a bonus 7-inch record			
❑ PR 5509 [(2)DJ]	The Downward Spiral	1994	60.00
—Also called "Halo Eight"; vinyl is promo only			
❑ 96093 [EP]	Fixed	1992	30.00
—Also called "Halo Six"			
RYKODISC			
❑ RLP 10386-1	Pretty Hate Machine	2006	20.00
—Reissue of TVT album of the same title			

999

12-Inch Singles

Number	Title (A Side/B Side)	Yr	NM
POLYDOR			
❑ PRO 155 [DJ]	Mercy Mercy/That's the Way It Goes/Obsessed/Taboo	1981	10.00

45s

Number	Title (A Side/B Side)	Yr	NM
POLYDOR			
❑ 2076	Boiler/Hollywood	1980	15.00

N

Nirvana, *MTV Unplugged in New York*, DGC 24727, 1994, **$20.**

Number	Title (A Side/B Side)	Yr	NM
❑ 2172	Obsessed/Fortune Teller	1981	15.00
Albums			
POLYDOR			
❑ PD1-6256	Biggest Prize in Sport	1980	14.00
❑ PD1-6307	Biggest Tour in Sport	1980	14.00
❑ PD1-6322	Concrete	1981	12.00
PVC			
❑ 7999	High Energy Plan	1979	12.00

1910 FRUITGUM COMPANY Also see KASENETZ-KATZ SINGING ORCHESTRAL CIRCUS.

Number	Title (A Side/B Side)	Yr	NM
45s			
ATTACK			
❑ 10293	Lawdy, Lawdy/The Clock	1970	12.00
BUDDAH			
❑ 24	Simon Says/Reflections from the Looking Glass	1968	10.00
❑ 39	May I Take a Giant Step (Into Your Heart)/(Poor Old) Mr. Jensen	1968	8.00
❑ 54	1,2,3, Red Light/Sticky, Sticky	1968	10.00
❑ 71	Goody Goody Gumdrops/Candy Kisses	1968	8.00
❑ 91	Indian Giver/Pow Wow	1969	10.00
❑ 114	Special Delivery/No Good Annie	1969	8.00
❑ 130	The Train/Eternal Light	1969	8.00
❑ 146	When We Get Married/Baby Sweet	1969	8.00
SUPER K			
❑ 115	Go Away/The Track	1970	12.00
Albums			
BUDDAH			
❑ BDM-5010 [M]	Simon Says	1968	50.00
—Appears to be promo only; "Mono" sticker on stereo cover			
❑ BDS-5010 [S]	Simon Says	1968	25.00
❑ BDS-5022	1,2,3 Red Light	1968	25.00
❑ BDS-5027	Goody, Goody Gumdrops	1969	25.00
❑ BDS-5036	Indian Giver	1969	25.00
❑ BDS-5043	Hard Ride	1969	25.00
❑ BDS-5057	Juiciest Fruitgum	1970	25.00

94 EAST

Number	Title (A Side/B Side)	Yr	NM
45s			
HOT PINK			
❑ 3223	Just Another Sucker/(B-side unknown)	1986	6.00
POLYDOR			
❑ 14414	Be My Fortune Teller/I Just Wanna Be	1977	—
—Unreleased?			
Albums			
HOT PINK			
❑ HLP 3223	Minneapolis Genius — 94 East	1977	40.00
—Deduct 25% for cut-outs			

NINO AND THE EBB TIDES

Number	Title (A Side/B Side)	Yr	NM
45s			
ACME			
❑ 720	Franny Franny/Darling I'll Love Only You	1958	300.00
MADISON			
❑ 162	Those Oldies But Goodies (Remind Me of You)/Don't Run Away	1961	40.00
❑ 166	Juke Box Saturday Night/(Someday) I'll Fall in Love	1961	30.00
MALA			
❑ 480	Automatic Reaction/Linda Lou Garrett Like 24 Karat	1964	20.00
MARCO			
❑ 105	Little Miss Blue/Someday	1961	50.00
MR. PEACOCK			
❑ 102	Wished I Was Home/Happy Guy	1961	25.00
❑ 117	Lovin' Time/Stamps, Baby, Stamps	1962	25.00
MR. PEEKE			
❑ 123	Tonight I'll Be Lonely/Nursery Rhymes	1963	25.00
RECORTE			
❑ 405	Puppy Love/You Make Me Rock 'N' Roll	1958	50.00
❑ 408	The Real Meaning of Christmas/Two Purple Shadows in the Snow	1958	300.00
❑ 409	I'm Confessin'/Tell the World I Do	1959	50.00
❑ 413	Don't Look Around/I Love Girls	1959	100.00

NIRVANA The 1990s grunge group. Dave Grohl now leads FOO FIGHTERS and is also in THEM CROOKED VULTURES.

Number	Title (A Side/B Side)	Yr	NM
12-Inch Singles			
DGC			
❑ PRO-A-4314 [DJ]	Smells Like Teen Spirit/Even In His Youth/Aneurysm	1991	20.00
—Promo only on yellow vinyl			
❑ 4416 [DJ]	Come As You Are (same on both sides)	1991	15.00
❑ 4558 [DJ]	Heart-Shaped Box/Gallons of Rubbin' Alcohol	1993	12.00
45s			
COMMUNION			
❑ 23	Here She Comes Now/Venus in Furs	1991	12.50
—B-side by The Melvins; blue vinyl			
❑ 23	Here She Comes Now/Venus in Furs	1991	12.50
—B-side by The Melvins; green vinyl			
❑ 23 [PS]	Here She Comes Now/Venus in Furs	1991	12.50
—B-side by The Melvins			
DGC			
❑ 19050	Smells Like Teen Spirit/Even In His Youth	1991	8.00
❑ 19120	Come As You Are/Drain You	1992	8.00
❑ 19134	Lithium/Been a Son	1992	—
—Cassette only			
SUB POP			
❑ 23	Love Buzz/Big Cheese	1988	500.00
—#1 in Sub Pop Singles Club series			
❑ 23 [PS]	Love Buzz/Big Cheese	1988	500.00
—Hand-numbered edition of 1,000			
❑ 73	Sliver/Dive	1990	10.00
—Black vinyl, no California address on label			
❑ 73	Sliver/Dive	1990	50.00
—Clear pink/lavender vinyl			
❑ 73 [PS]	Sliver/Dive	1990	3.00
—Later picture sleeves were seam sealed			
❑ 73 [PS]	Sliver/Dive	1990	10.00
—Original picture sleeves were fold-over, not seam sealed			
❑ 73	Sliver/Dive	1990	6.00
—Still later issues on black vinyl with California address on label			
❑ 73	Sliver/Dive	1990	8.00
—Later issues on pale yellow vinyl with California address on label			
❑ 73	Sliver/Dive	1990	40.00
—First 3,000 on blue vinyl			
❑ 97	Molly's Lips (Live)/Candy	1991	10.00
—B-side by Fluid; black vinyl			
❑ 97	Molly's Lips (Live)/Candy	1991	35.00
—B-side by Fluid; green vinyl			
❑ 97 [PS]	Molly's Lips (Live)/Candy	1991	10.00
—B-side by Fluid; #27 in Sub Pop Singles Club series			
Albums			
DGC			
❑ 24425	Nevermind	1991	30.00
—All copies on black vinyl			
❑ 24504	Incesticide	1992	30.00
—All copies on blue swirl vinyl			
❑ 24607	In Utero	1993	30.00
—All copies on clear vinyl			
❑ 24727	MTV Unplugged in New York	1994	20.00
—Black vinyl, issued simultaneously with white vinyl version; color of vinyl cannot be determined without opening the shrink wrap			
❑ 24727	MTV Unplugged in New York	1994	20.00
—White vinyl version			
❑ 25105 [(2)]	From the Muddy Banks of the Wishkah	1996	20.00
MOBILE FIDELITY			
❑ 1-258	Nevermind	1996	200.00
—Audiophile vinyl			
SUB POP			
❑ SP 34	Bleach	1989	20.00
—Red vinyl			
❑ SP 34	Bleach	1989	60.00
—Pink vinyl			
❑ SP 34	Bleach	1989	60.00
—Purple vinyl			
❑ SP 34	Bleach	1989	150.00
—Red and white swirl vinyl			
❑ SP 34	Bleach	1989	200.00
—First 1,000 were pressed on white vinyl			
❑ SP 34	Bleach	1989	200.00
—Second 1,000 were pressed on black vinyl and include a poster			
❑ 70034	Bleach	2000	18.00
—Reissue			

Except when noted otherwise, VG = 25% of NM, and VG+ = 50% of NM. (Example: VG = $2.00, VG+ = $4.00 and NM = $8.00.)

NIRVANA (1)

45s

BELL

Number	Title (A Side/B Side)	Yr	NM
❑ 715	We Can Help You/Pentecost Hotel	1968	10.00
❑ 730	You Are Just the One/Girl in the Park	1968	10.00
❑ 739	Trapeze/The Touchables	1968	10.00

Albums

BELL

Number	Title (A Side/B Side)	Yr	NM
❑ 6015	The Story of Simon Simopath	1968	50.00
❑ 6024	All of Us	1969	50.00

NIRVANA (2)

Albums

METROMEDIA

Number	Title (A Side/B Side)	Yr	NM
❑ MD-1018	Nirvana	1970	25.00

NITE RIDERS, THE

Possibly two different groups.

45s

MGM

Number	Title (A Side/B Side)	Yr	NM
❑ 12487	Sippin' Coffee/Tank Town	1957	30.00

TEEN

Number	Title (A Side/B Side)	Yr	NM
❑ 116	Starlight and You/I Know You're In There	1955	40.00
❑ 118	Got Me a Six-Button Benny/Don't Hang Up the Phone	1955	40.00
❑ 120	When a Man Cries/Waiting in the Schoolroom	1955	40.00

NITE ROCKERS, THE

45s

RCA VICTOR

Number	Title (A Side/B Side)	Yr	NM
❑ 47-7323	Nite Rock/Oh! Baby	1958	30.00

NITE-LITERS, THE

Also see LOVE, PEACE AND HAPPINESS; THE NEW BIRTH.

45s

RCA VICTOR

Number	Title (A Side/B Side)	Yr	NM
❑ 74-0374	Con-Funk-Shun/Down and Dirty	1970	6.00
❑ 74-0461	K-Jee/Tanga Boo Gonk	1971	5.00
❑ 74-0591	Afro-Strut/(We've Got to) Pull Together	1971	5.00
❑ 74-0714	Cherish Every Precious Moment/I've Got Dreams to Remember	1972	5.00
❑ 74-0812	Funky-Doo/Do the Granny	1972	5.00
❑ APBO-0244	Pe-Foul/Serenade for a Jive Turkey	1974	5.00

Albums

RCA VICTOR

Number	Title (A Side/B Side)	Yr	NM
❑ LSP-4493	Morning, Noon & The Nite-Liters	1971	15.00
❑ LSP-4580	Instrumental Directions	1972	15.00

NITTY GRITTY DIRT BAND

Includes The Dirt Band. Also see JOHN DENVER.

45s

DECCA

Number	Title (A Side/B Side)	Yr	NM
❑ 55206	Maybe Baby/Crying, Waiting, Hoping	1996	3.00

—B-side by Marty Stuart and Steve Earle

LIBERTY

Number	Title (A Side/B Side)	Yr	NM
❑ 1389	High School Yearbook/Too Good to Be True	1980	4.00
—As "The Dirt Band"			
❑ 1398	Nazamas Nuestra Magic (Make a Little Magic)/Jas' Moon	1981	4.00
—As "The Dirt Band"			
❑ 1429	Fire in the Sky/EZ Slow	1981	4.00
—As "The Dirt Band"			
❑ 1449	Badlands/Jealousy	1982	4.00
—As "The Dirt Band"			
❑ 1467	Too Close for Comfort/Circular Man	1982	4.00
—As "The Dirt Band"			
❑ 1499	Let's Go/Shot Full of Love	1983	4.00
❑ 1507	Mary Anne/Dance Little Jean	1983	4.00
❑ 1513	Colorado Christmas/Mr. Bojangles	1983	6.00
❑ 55948	Buy for Me the Rain/Candy Man	1967	10.00
❑ 55982	The Teddy Bear's Picnic/Truly Right	1967	8.00
❑ 55982 [PS]	The Teddy Bear's Picnic/Truly Right	1967	15.00
❑ 56054	These Days/Collegiana	1968	8.00
❑ 56134	Some of Shelley's Blues/Yukon Railroad	1969	6.00
❑ 56159	Rave On/The Cure	1970	6.00
❑ 56197	Mr. Bojangles/Mr. Bojangles (Prelude: Uncle Charlie and His Dog Teddy)	1970	6.00
❑ 56197	Mr. Bojangles (Prelude: Uncle Charlie and His Dog Teddy)/Spanish Fandango	1970	8.00
❑ S7-57766	I Fought the Law/Mr. Bojangles	1992	4.00

MCA

Number	Title (A Side/B Side)	Yr	NM
❑ 53795	One Step Over the Line/Riding Along	1990	3.00
—A-side: With Roseanne Cash; B-side: With Emmylou Harris			
❑ 53964	The Rest of the Dream/Snowballs	1990	3.00
❑ 55182	You Believed in Me/Atlanta Reel '96	1996	3.00
—A-side by Karla Bonoff and the Nitty Gritty Dirt Band; B-side by Michael Omartian			
❑ 79013	From Small Things (Big Things One Day Come)/Blues Berry Hill	1990	3.00
❑ 79075	You Make Life Good Again/Snowballs	1990	3.00

UNITED ARTISTS

Number	Title (A Side/B Side)	Yr	NM
❑ 0061	Mr. Bojangles/Buy for Me the Rain	1973	4.00
—"Silver Spotlight Series" reissue			
❑ XW177	Will the Circle Be Unbroken/Honky Tonkin'	1973	5.00
❑ XW177 [PS]	Will the Circle Be Unbroken/Honky Tonkin'	1973	8.00
❑ XW247	Grand Ole Opry Song/Orange Blossom Special	1973	5.00
❑ XW263	Cosmic Cowboy (Part 1)/Cosmic Cowboy (Part 2)	1973	5.00
❑ XW321	Tennessee Stud/Way Down Town	1973	5.00
—With Doc Watson			
❑ XW544	The Battle of New Orleans/Mountain Whipporwill	1974	5.00
❑ XW544 [PS]	The Battle of New Orleans/Mountain Whipporwill	1974	6.00
❑ XW655	(All I Have to Do Is) Dream/Raleigh-Durham Reel	1975	5.00
❑ XW741	Mother of Love/The Moon Just Turned Blue	1975	5.00
❑ XW830	Cosmic Cowboy/Stars and Stripes Forever	1976	4.00
—As "The Dirt Band"			
❑ XW889	Jamaica Lady/Bayou Jubilee-Sally Was a Goodun	1976	4.00
—As "The Dirt Band"			
❑ XW936	Buy for Me the Rain/Mother Earth (Provides for Me)	1976	4.00
—As "The Dirt Band"			
❑ XW1164	Orange Blossom Special/Will the Circle Be Unbroken	1978	4.00
❑ XW1228	Wild Nights/In for the Night	1978	4.00
—As "The Dirt Band"			
❑ XW1268	For a Little While/On the Loose	1978	4.00
—As "The Dirt Band"			
❑ 1312	In Her Eyes/Jas' Moon	1979	4.00
—As "The Dirt Band"			
❑ 1330	An American Dream/Take Me Back	1979	5.00
—As "The Dirt Band"			
❑ 1356	Make a Little Magic/Jas' Moon	1980	4.00
—As "The Dirt Band"			
❑ 1378	Badlands/Too Good to Be True	1980	4.00
—As "The Dirt Band"			
❑ 50769	House at Pooh Corner/Travelin' Mood	1971	6.00
❑ 50769 [PS]	House at Pooh Corner/Travelin' Mood	1971	8.00
❑ 50817	The Cure/Some of Shelly's Blues	1971	6.00
❑ 50849	Precious Jewel/I Saw the Light	1971	6.00
—With Roy Acuff			
❑ 50861	I Saw the Light/Sixteen Tracks	1971	6.00
❑ 50890	Jambalaya (On the Bayou)/Hoping to Say	1972	6.00
❑ 50890 [PS]	Jambalaya (On the Bayou)/Hoping to Say	1972	8.00
❑ 50921	Baltimore/Fish Song	1972	6.00
❑ 50965	Honky Tonkin'/Jamaica	1972	6.00

UNIVERSAL

Number	Title (A Side/B Side)	Yr	NM
❑ UVL-66009	Turn of the Century/Blueberry Hill	1989	3.00
❑ UVL-66023	When It's Gone/I'm Sittin' on Top of the World	1989	4.00

WARNER BROS

Number	Title (A Side/B Side)	Yr	NM
❑ PRO-S-2869 [DJ]	Colorado Christmas/The Cowboy's Christmas Ball	1987	6.00

—B-side by Michael Martin Murphey

WARNER BROS.

Number	Title (A Side/B Side)	Yr	NM
❑ 27679	Down That Road Tonight/A Lot Like Me	1989	3.00
❑ 27750	I've Been Lookin'/Must Be Love	1988	3.00
❑ 27940	Workin' Man/Brass Sky	1988	3.00
❑ 28173	Oh What a Love/America, My Sweetheart	1987	3.00
❑ 28173 [PS]	Oh What a Love/America, My Sweetheart	1987	4.00
❑ 28311	Fishin' in the Dark/Keepin' the Road Hot	1987	3.00
❑ 28443	Baby's Got a Hold on Me/Oleanna	1987	3.00
❑ 28547	Cadillac Ranch/Fire in the Sky	1986	3.00
❑ 28690	Stand a Little Rain/Miner's Night Out	1986	3.00
❑ 28780	Partners, Brothers and Friends/Redneck Riviera	1986	3.00
❑ 28897	Home Again in My Heart/Telluride	1985	4.00
❑ 29027	Modern Day Romance/Queen of the Road	1985	4.00
❑ 29099	High Horse/Must Be Love	1985	4.00
❑ 29203	I Love Only You/Face on the Cutting Room Floor	1984	4.00
❑ 29282	Long Hard Road (The Sharecropper's Dream)/Video Tape	1984	4.00

Albums

LIBERTY

Number	Title (A Side/B Side)	Yr	NM
❑ LWB-184 [(2)]	Stars and Stripes Forever	1981	10.00
❑ LKCL-670 [(3)]	Dirt, Silver and Gold	1981	12.00
❑ LO-974	An American Dream	1981	8.00
❑ LT-1042	Make a Little Magic	1981	8.00
❑ LRP-3501 [M]	The Nitty Gritty Dirt Band	1967	25.00
❑ LRP-3516 [M]	Ricochet	1967	25.00
❑ LMAS-5553	All the Good Times	1981	8.00
❑ LST-7501 [S]	The Nitty Gritty Dirt Band	1967	30.00
❑ LST-7516 [S]	Ricochet	1967	30.00
❑ LST-7540	Rare Junk	1968	25.00
❑ LST-7611	Alive	1969	25.00
❑ LST-7642	Uncle Charlie and His Dog Teddy	1970	25.00
—Standard issue of LP			
❑ LST-7642 [DJ]	Uncle Charlie and His Dog Teddy	1970	120.00
—Leatherette promo pack with LP, two other discs, photos, booklet			
❑ LTAO-7642	Uncle Charlie and His Dog Teddy	1981	8.00
❑ LT-51146	Let's Go	1982	10.00
❑ LWCL-51158 [(3)]	Will the Circle Be Unbroken	1986	15.00

MCA

Number	Title (A Side/B Side)	Yr	NM
❑ 6407	The Rest of the Dream	1990	12.00

UNITED ARTISTS

Number	Title (A Side/B Side)	Yr	NM
❑ UA-LA184-J2 [(2)]	Stars and Stripes Forever	1974	15.00
❑ UA-LA469-G	Dream	1975	12.00
❑ UA-LA670-L3 [(3)]	Dirt, Silver and Gold	1976	20.00
❑ UA-LA830-H	The Chicken Chronicles	1978	10.00
❑ UA-LA854-H	The Dirt Band	1978	10.00
❑ UA-LA974-H	An American Dream	1979	10.00
❑ LT-1042	Make a Little Magic	1980	10.00
❑ LW-1106	Jealousy	1981	10.00
❑ UAS-5553	All the Good Times	1972	15.00
❑ UAS-9801 [(3)]	Will the Circle Be Unbroken	1972	30.00

UNIVERSAL

Number	Title (A Side/B Side)	Yr	NM
❑ UVL2-12500 [(2)]	Will the Circle Be Unbroken, Vol. Two	1989	20.00

WARNER BROS.

Number	Title (A Side/B Side)	Yr	NM
❑ 25113	Plain Dirt Fashion	1984	8.00
❑ 25304	Partners, Brothers and Friends	1985	8.00
❑ 25382	Twenty Years of Dirt: The Best of the Nitty Gritty Dirt Band	1986	8.00
❑ 25573	Hold On	1987	8.00
❑ 25722	Workin' Band	1988	8.00
❑ 25830	More Great Dirt: The Best of the Nitty Gritty Dirt Band, Vol. 2	1989	10.00

NITZINGER

BLOODROCK related.

45s

CAPITOL

Number	Title (A Side/B Side)	Yr	NM
❑ 3359	Earth Eater/One Foot in History	1973	5.00

20TH CENTURY

Number	Title (A Side/B Side)	Yr	NM
❑ 2311	Yellow Dog/Are You With Me	1976	4.00

Albums

CAPITOL

Number	Title (A Side/B Side)	Yr	NM
❑ SMAS-11091	Nitzinger	1972	18.00
❑ SMAS-11122	One Foot in History	1973	18.00

20TH CENTURY

Number	Title (A Side/B Side)	Yr	NM
❑ T-518	Live Better Electrically	1976	12.00

NITZSCHE, JACK

45s

FANTASY

Number	Title (A Side/B Side)	Yr	NM
❑ 760	One Flew Over the Cuckoo's Next/The Last Dance	1976	6.00
❑ 760 [PS]	One Flew Over the Cuckoo's Next/The Last Dance	1976	10.00

—Jack Nicholson is pictured on the sleeve

MCA

Number	Title (A Side/B Side)	Yr	NM
❑ 40897	Coke Machine/Hard Workin' Man	1978	4.00

REPRISE

Number	Title (A Side/B Side)	Yr	NM
❑ 0262	The Last Race/Man with the Golden Arm	1964	20.00

Number	Title (A Side/B Side)	Yr	NM
❑ 0285	Theme from The Long Ships/ Zapata	1964	20.00
❑ 0337	The Green Grass of Texas/ Night Walker	1965	20.00
❑ 0364	Senorita from Detroit/ Puerto Vallarta	1965	20.00
❑ 20202	The Lonely Surfer/Song for a Summer Night	1963	30.00
❑ 20202 [PS]	The Lonely Surfer/Song for a Summer Night	1963	100.00
❑ 20225	Rumble/Theme for a Broken Heart	1963	20.00
Albums			
REPRISE			
❑ MS 2092	St. Giles Cripplegate	1972	20.00
❑ R 6101 [M]	The Lonely Surfer	1963	75.00
❑ R9-6101 [S]	The Lonely Surfer	1963	150.00
—Pink, gold and green label			
❑ RS 6101 [S]	The Lonely Surfer	197?	20.00
—With only "r:" logo on all-orange (tan) label			
❑ R 6115 [M]	Dance to the Hits of the Beatles	1964	50.00
❑ RS 6115 [S]	Dance to the Hits of the Beatles	1964	60.00
❑ R 6200 [M]	Chopin '66	1966	25.00
❑ RS 6200 [S]	Chopin '66	1966	30.00

NIX, DON

Number	Title (A Side/B Side)	Yr	NM
45s			
CREAM			
❑ 7604	A Demain (Until Tomorrow)/ A Demain (Until Tomorrow) (Edited Version)	1976	4.00
❑ 7608	Rollin' in My Dreams/ (B-side unknown)	1976	4.00
ELEKTRA			
❑ 45746	Olena/Riding the Blinds	1971	5.00
❑ 45776	Going Down/She Don't Want a Lover, She Just Needs a Friend	1972	5.00
ENTERPRISE			
❑ 9067	Black Cat Moan/The Train Don't Stop Here No More	1973	5.00
❑ 9083	She's a Friend of Mine/When I Lay My Burden Down	1973	5.00
Albums			
CREAM			
❑ 1001	Gone Too Long	1979	10.00
ELEKTRA			
❑ EKS-74101	Living by the Days	1971	12.00
ENTERPRISE			
❑ ENS-1032	Hobos, Heroes and Street Corner Clowns	1974	12.00

NIX, WILLIE

Number	Title (A Side/B Side)	Yr	NM
45s			
CHANCE			
❑ 1163	Nervous Wreck/No More Love	1954	3000.
SABRE			
❑ 104	All By Myself/Just Can't Stay	1953	2000.

NIXON, MOJO, AND SKID ROPER

Number	Title (A Side/B Side)	Yr	NM
12-Inch Singles			
ENIGMA			
❑ 054 [DJ]	I'm Gonna Dig Up Howlin' Wolf (same on both sides)	1987	6.00
Albums			
ENIGMA			
❑ ST-73272	Bo-Day-Shus!!!	1987	12.00
RESTLESS			
❑ 72056	Mojo Nixon and Skid Roper	1985	12.00
❑ 72127	Frenzy	1986	12.00
❑ 72185 [EP]	Get Out of My Way	1986	10.00
—Clear vinyl			

NO NAMES, THE

Number	Title (A Side/B Side)	Yr	NM
45s			
GUYDEN			
❑ 2114	Love/Jam	1964	50.00

NOBELLS, THE

Number	Title (A Side/B Side)	Yr	NM
45s			
MAR			
❑ 101	Searchin' for My Love/ Crying Over You	1962	100.00

NOBLE, NICK

Number	Title (A Side/B Side)	Yr	NM
45s			
CAPITOL			
❑ 3677	It's All Up to You/Let Me Be a Man	1973	5.00
CHESS			
❑ 1876	Sleep Walk/Flying Over Rainbows	1963	10.00
❑ 1879	Stay with Me/Flying Over Rainbows	1963	8.00
❑ 1909	Don't Forget/Not Like I Used to Be	1964	8.00
CHURCHILL			
❑ 7701	May God Be With You/ (B-side unknown)	1978	6.00
❑ 7713	Stay with Me/My Country Kind of Girl	1978	6.00
❑ 7755	Big Man's Cafe/My Country Kind of Girl	1980	6.00
COLUMBIA			
❑ 4-44887	I'm Gonna Make You Love Me/ I'm So Busy Being Broken Hearted	1969	6.00
CORAL			
❑ 9-62075	How Much Can a Heart Take/ My Darling's Earrings	1959	10.00
❑ 9-62124	I Need Someone/Thank Heaven for Little Girls	1959	10.00
❑ 9-62144	Somethin' Cha Cha/ I Surrender Dear	1959	10.00
❑ 62169	Violino/Lemons and Cloves	1960	10.00
❑ 62213	The Tip of My Fingers/ Sweet Love	1960	12.00
❑ 62233	Excuse Me (I Think I've Got a Heartache)/Island Farewell	1960	10.00
❑ 62246	Someplace to Cry/Over Someone's Shoulder	1961	10.00
❑ 62262	(I'm Gonna) Cry Some Tears/ They Call Me the Fool	1961	10.00
❑ 62280	For Just a Little While Tonight/ The Beat of My Soul	1961	10.00
❑ 62495	The Tip of My Fingers/ Someplace to Cry	1966	8.00
DATE			
❑ 2-1582	Until It's Time for You to Go/ You're the Right One for Me	1967	7.00
❑ 2-1616	My Marie/It Hurts to Say Goodbye	1968	7.00
❑ 2-1629	Lovely As I Leave You/ Take Me Back	1968	7.00
EPIC			
❑ 50327	Forgetting Someone/If We Could Live Our Life Away	1977	4.00
FRATERNITY			
❑ 817	Fountains Cry/There's a Church in Your Heart	1958	10.00
❑ 825	One Track Mind/Lonely Star	1958	10.00
LIBERTY			
❑ 55442	The Twelfth Dark Hour/My Heart Came Running Back to You	1962	8.00
❑ 55488	Hello Out There/We Could	1962	8.00
❑ 55534	A Legend in My Time/ Closer to Heaven	1963	8.00
❑ 55576	Gee Little Girl/A Rose and a Star	1963	8.00
MERCURY			
❑ 70397	Right or Wrong/Maybe Today	1954	15.00
❑ 70496	Tara's Theme/Please Don't Break My Heart	1954	15.00
❑ 70821	To You, My Love/You Are My Only Love	1956	12.00
❑ 70897	Keeping Cool (With Lemonade)/ You're Sensational	1956	12.00
❑ 70959	Autumn Concerto/Mom, Oh Mom	1956	12.00
❑ 71031	No One Sweeter Than You/ I'm a Visitor	1957	12.00
❑ 71117	A Fallen Star/They're Playing Our Song	1957	12.00
❑ 71124	A Fallen Star/Let Me Hold You in My Arms	1957	10.00
❑ 71169	Moonlight Swim/Lucy Lou	1957	10.00
❑ 71233	Halo of Love/Sweet Treat	1957	10.00
TMS			
❑ 601	The Girl on the Other Side/ Why Don't You Believe Me	1979	6.00
❑ 612	I Wanna Go Back/I Keep On Breathin' You	1979	6.00
20TH CENTURY FOX			
❑ 6612	The Girl with the Long Red Hair/ Simple, Simple	1965	8.00
WING			
❑ 90003	The Bible Tells Me So/ Army of the Lord	1955	12.00
❑ 90028	The Best Is Yet to Come/ If It Happened to You	1955	12.00
❑ 90042	Lovely Lies/Bella Bella Perzicella	1955	12.00
❑ 90045	To You My Love/You Are My Only Love	1955	15.00
Albums			
COLUMBIA			
❑ CS 9810	I'm Gonna Make You Love Me	1969	15.00
LIBERTY			
❑ LRP-3302 [M]	Relax	1963	20.00
❑ LST-7302 [M]	Relax	1963	25.00
MERCURY			
❑ MG-20182 [M]	You Don't Know What Love Is	1956	25.00
WING			
❑ MGW-12184 [M]	Music for Lovers	196?	15.00

NOBLES, CLIFF

Number	Title (A Side/B Side)	Yr	NM
45s			
ATLANTIC			
❑ 2352	My Love Is Getting Stronger/ Too Fond of You	1966	300.00
❑ 2380	Your Love Is All I Need/ Everybody Is Weak for Somebody	1967	75.00
JAMIE			
❑ 1406	The Horse/If You Don't	1972	15.00
MOON SHOT			
❑ 6710	Pony the Horse/Little Claudie	1969	25.00
PHIL-L.A. OF SOUL			
❑ 310	The More I Do for You Baby/ This Love Will Last	1968	8.00
❑ 313	The Horse/Love Is All Right	1968	10.00
❑ 318	Horse Fever/Judge Baby, I'm Back	1968	8.00
❑ 324	Switch It On/Burning Desire	1969	8.00
❑ 329	The Camel/Goin' Away	1969	8.00
ROULETTE			
❑ 7142	This Feeling of Loneliness/We Got Our Thing Together	1973	15.00
Albums			
MOON SHOT			
❑ 601	Pony the Horse	1969	40.00
PHIL-L.A. OF SOUL			
❑ 4001	The Horse	1968	60.00

NOBLES, THE (1)

Number	Title (A Side/B Side)	Yr	NM
45s			
ABC-PARAMOUNT			
❑ 9984	Till the End of Time/ Standing Loose	1958	25.00
❑ 10012	Just for Me/To Me	1959	25.00

NOBLES, THE (2)

Number	Title (A Side/B Side)	Yr	NM
45s			
KLIK			
❑ 305	Poor Rock and Roll/Ting-a-Ling	1958	200.00
LOST-NITE			
❑ 153	Poor Rock and Roll/Ting-a-Ling	196?	6.00
—Reissue			
TIMES SQUARE			
❑ 1	Poor Rock and Roll/Ting-a-Ling	1963	25.00
—Green vinyl			
❑ 1	Poor Rock and Roll/Ting-a-Ling	1963	30.00
—Blue vinyl			
❑ 12	Crime Doesn't Pay/Darkness	1963	20.00
—All copies on blue vinyl			
❑ 33	Why Be a Fool/The Search	1964	20.00

NOBLES, THE (3)

Number	Title (A Side/B Side)	Yr	NM
45s			
SELBON			
❑ 1005	Black Widow/Jaguar	1963	40.00

NOBLES, THE (4)

Number	Title (A Side/B Side)	Yr	NM
45s			
STACY			
❑ 926	Serenade/You Ain't Right	1962	40.00

NOBLES, THE (5)

Number	Title (A Side/B Side)	Yr	NM
45s			
U.S.A.			
❑ 788	Marlene/That Special One	1965	25.00

NOBLES, THE (U)

Number	Title (A Side/B Side)	Yr	NM
45s			
TEE GEE			
❑ 101	Oops Oh Lawdy/Stop Crying	1958	50.00

NOCTURNES, THE

Number	Title (A Side/B Side)	Yr	NM
45s			
CARLSON INT'L			
❑ 4105	My Christmas Star/ (B-side unknown)	1964	60.00
MGM			
❑ K10768	Oh! Marie/Lucky, Lucky, Lucky Me	1950	20.00
❑ K10835	Malaguena/After My Laughter Came Tears	1950	20.00

N

Except when noted otherwise, VG = 25% of NM, and VG+ = 50% of NM. (Example: VG = $2.00, VG+ = $4.00 and NM = $8.00.)

Number	Title (A Side/B Side)	Yr	NM
❑ K11158	Misirlou/I'll Never Let You Cry	1952	15.00
❑ K11525	As You Desire Me/ Giuseppe's Serenade	1953	15.00
❑ K11644	Poppa Piccolino/For the First Time in a Long Time	1953	12.00
❑ K11700	I Saw a Stranger/Sing It Paisan	1954	12.00
❑ K11783	Who Dat (Buck Dance)/ The Knicka-Knacka Song (My Old Gal)	1954	12.00
❑ K11863	Somebody Ought to Write a Song/Remember Mama	1954	12.00
❑ K11906	Hey Punchinello/These Are the Things We'll Share	1955	12.00
❑ K12057	Ballads, Boogie and Blues/Por Favor (Please)	1955	12.00
❑ K12084	Toodle-Oo Igaloo/Birmin'ham	1955	12.00
❑ K30594	Malaguena/Lilli Marlene	195?	15.00
Albums			
MGM			
❑ E-154 [10]	Melodies from Far Away Places	195?	60.00

NODAENS, THE With Dave Nowlen, formerly of THE SURVIVORS.

Number	Title (A Side/B Side)	Yr	NM
45s			
GOLD			
❑ 1001	Beach Girl/Gypsy	196?	80.00

NOEL, SID

Number	Title (A Side/B Side)	Yr	NM
45s			
ALADDIN			
❑ 3331	The Flying Saucer (Part 1)/ The Flying Saucer (Part 2)	1956	40.00

—Cover version of the Buchanan and Goodman break-in record

NOGUEZ, JACKY

Number	Title (A Side/B Side)	Yr	NM
45s			
JAMIE			
❑ 1127	Ciao, Ciao Bambina (Chiow, Chiow, Bambeena)/ De Serait Dommage	1959	12.00
❑ 1137	Marina/Adonis	1959	12.00
❑ 1148	Amapola/Mahzel	1959	12.00
❑ 1148 [PS]	Amapola/Mahzel	1959	15.00
Albums			
JAMIE			
❑ JLP-3007 [M]	Chow Chow Bambina	1959	20.00
❑ JLPS-3007 [S]	Chow Chow Bambina	1959	30.00
❑ JLP-3012 [M]	Jacky Noguez	1960	20.00
❑ JLPS-3012 [S]	Jacky Noguez	1960	30.00
❑ JLP-3013 [M]	Dance Along with Jacky Noguez	1960	20.00
❑ JLPS-3013 [S]	Dance Along with Jacky Noguez	1960	30.00

NOLAN See NOLAN PORTER.

NOLAN, FRANKIE

Number	Title (A Side/B Side)	Yr	NM
45s			
ABC-PARAMOUNT			
❑ 10231	I Still Care/(I Wish It Were) Summer All Year Round	1961	40.00

—Frankie Valli also appears on this record

NOLAND, TERRY

Number	Title (A Side/B Side)	Yr	NM
45s			
APT			
❑ 25065	There Goes a Girl/ Long Gone Baby	1962	15.00
BRUNSWICK			
❑ 55010	Hypnotized/Ten Little Women	1957	30.00
❑ 55036	Patty Baby/Don't Do Me This Way	1957	30.00
❑ 55054	Puppy Love/Oh Baby, Look at Me	1958	30.00
❑ 55069	Crazy Dream/Everyone But One	1958	30.00
❑ 55092	There Was a Fungus Among Us/Sugar Drop	1958	40.00
❑ 55122	Guess I'm Gonna Fall/ Teenage Teardrops	1959	30.00
CORAL			
❑ 62274	There Was a Fungus Among Us/Sugar Drop	1961	20.00
Albums			
BRUNSWICK			
❑ BL 54041 [M]	Terry Noland	1958	600.00

—Buddy Holly plays guitar

NON-CONFORMISTS, THE

Number	Title (A Side/B Side)	Yr	NM
45s			
SCEPTER			
❑ 12184	Two-Legged Big Eyed Yellow Haired Crying Canary/ Bird Walk	1967	30.00

NOONE, PETER Also see HERMAN'S HERMITS.

Number	Title (A Side/B Side)	Yr	NM
45s			
BELL			
❑ 45131	Oh You Pretty Thing/ Because You're There	1971	50.00
—Allegedly features David Bowie on A-side piano			
❑ 45266	Should I/(B-side unknown)	1972	8.00
CASABLANCA			
❑ 0017	Meet Me at the Corner Down at Joe's Cafe/(Blame It) On the Pony Express	1974	5.00
❑ 0106	Meet Me at the Corner Down at Joe's Cafe/(Blame It) On the Pony Express	1974	4.00
❑ 802	Meet Me at the Corner Down at Joe's Cafe/(Blame It) On the Pony Express	1974	4.00
❑ 823	Something Old, Something New/(B-side unknown)	1975	4.00
JOHNSTON			
❑ 02838	(I Don't Wanna Love You But) You Got Me Anyway/ I'm One of the Glory Boys	1982	4.00
PHILIPS			
❑ 40730	All SIng Together/ Getting Over You	1974	5.00
Albums			
JOHNSTON			
❑ ARZ 37369	One of the Glory Boys	1982	10.00

NORMAN, GENE, AND THE ROCKIN' ROCKETS

Number	Title (A Side/B Side)	Yr	NM
45s			
SNAG			
❑ 101	Snaggle Tooth Ann/ Long Gone Night Train	1958	1000.

NORMAN, JIMMY

Number	Title (A Side/B Side)	Yr	NM
45s			
BUDDAH			
❑ 439	Funk Don't Mean a Scent/In the Palm of Another's Hand	1974	15.00
❑ 504	I Wanna Make Love to You/ Fallin' in Love	1975	12.00
DOT			
❑ 16016	Green Stamps/Just to Get to You	1959	30.00
JOSIE			
❑ 994	Gangster of Love/Gangster of Love Pt. 2	1968	25.00
LITTLE STAR			
❑ 113	I Don't Love You No More (I Don't Care About You)/Tell Her for Me	1962	20.00
❑ 121	You Crack Me Up/I Know I'm in Love	1962	40.00
❑ 126	Love Is Wonderful/What's the Word, Do the Bird	1963	30.00
MUN-RAB			
❑ 102	You Win Again/Thank Him	1959	40.00
POLO			
❑ 211	Dotted Line/You Crack Me Up	1964	60.00
RAY STAR			
❑ 781	I'll Never Be Free/ Lovesick Feeling	1961	40.00
❑ 783	One of These Days/ Someone to Care For	1962	40.00
SAMAR			
❑ 112	You're Only Hurting Yourself/ That Little Old Groovemaker	1966	200.00
—Jimi Hendrix played guitar on these two sides			
❑ 116	Can You Blame Me/ This I Beg of You	1966	25.00

NORMAN, LARRY A founding father of Christian rock. Also see PEOPLE.

Number	Title (A Side/B Side)	Yr	NM
45s			
CAPITOL			
❑ 2766	Sweet Sweet Song of Salvation/ Walking Backwards Down the Stairs	1970	20.00
MGM			
❑ 14351	Righteous Rocker, Holy Rocker/ Peace, Pollution, Revolution	1972	15.00
❑ 14676	Christmas Time/ The Same Old Story	1973	15.00
❑ 14703	Nightmare/Baroquen Spirits	1974	15.00
SOLID ROCK			
❑ 202	Christmas Time/The Christmas Song	1976	8.00
VERVE			
❑ 10718	I've Got to Learn to Live Without You/Readers Digest	1973	20.00
❑ 10720	I've Got to Learn to Live Without You/The Outlaw	1973	20.00
Albums			
AB			
❑ 777	Streams of White Light Into Darkened Corners	1977	25.00
CAPITOL			
❑ ST-446	Upon This Rock	1970	30.00
IMPACT			
❑ 3121	Upon This Rock	197?	20.00
MGM			
❑ SE-4942	So Long Ago the Garden	1974	40.00
ONE WAY			
❑ 900	Bootleg	1972	30.00
—Regular cover			
❑ 4847	Bootleg	1972	40.00
—Gatefold cover			
❑ 7397	Street Level	1971	30.00
PHYDEAUX			
❑ ARF-777-6	Almost So Long Ago the Garden	1984	12.00
❑ BONE-777-6	Almost So Long Ago the Garden	1981	15.00
SOLID ROCK			
❑ 2001	In Another Land	1976	15.00
❑ 2007	Something New Under the Son	1981	15.00
STREET LEVEL			
❑ ROCK-888-5	Only Visiting This Planet	1978	12.00
—Regular cover			
❑ ROCK-888-5	Only Visiting This Planet	1978	15.00
—Gatefold cover			
VERVE			
❑ V6-5092	Only Visiting This Planet	1973	30.00
—Tri-fold cover			
❑ V6-5092	Only Visiting This Planet	1973	40.00
—Gatefold cover			

NORMANAIRES, THE

Number	Title (A Side/B Side)	Yr	NM
45s			
MGM			
❑ 11622	My Greatest Sin/Wrap It Up	1953	80.00

NORRIS, CHARLES

Number	Title (A Side/B Side)	Yr	NM
45s			
ATLANTIC			
❑ 994	Messin' Up/Let Me Know	1953	60.00

NORTH, FREDDIE

Number	Title (A Side/B Side)	Yr	NM
45s			
ABET			
❑ 9418	Don't Make Me Look So Bad/ Hold Back	1967	12.00
❑ 9430	I Have a Dream/(Instrumental)	1968	10.00
❑ 9436	Oh Lord, What Are You Doing to Me/Long Hard Road	1968	10.00
❑ 9439	Love to Hate/Thank That Woman	1969	10.00
❑ 9440	Follow the Lamb/From the Blind Side	1969	10.00
CAPITOL			
❑ 4832	Just to Please You/ Ninety-Pound Woman	1962	15.00
❑ 4873	Just to Please You/ Ninety-Pound Woman	1962	15.00
MANKIND			
❑ 12004	She's All I Got/Ain't Nothin' in the News (But the Blues)	1971	8.00
❑ 12009	You and Me Together Forever/ Did I Come Back Too Soon (Or Stay Away Too Long)	1972	8.00
❑ 12011	Sweeter Than Sweetness/ I Did the Woman Wrong	1972	8.00
❑ 12014	Roll Over (Play Like Love Ain't Dead)/Are You Thinking of Him	1972	8.00
❑ 12016	Song #29 (I'm Your Man)/ Laid Back and Easy	1972	8.00
❑ 12018	You're Killing Me Slowly But Surely/It's So Groovy Doing What You Want to Do	1973	8.00
❑ 12019	Lovin' on Back Streets/ Love to Hate	1973	8.00
❑ 12020	Taking Her Love Ain't Gonna Be Easy/Raining on a Sunny Day	1973	8.00
❑ 12022	Cuss the Wind/Love to Hate	1975	10.00
❑ 12025	I Loved Another Woman/ Rainy Night in Georgia	197?	8.00
PHILLIPS INT'L.			
❑ 3574	Don't Make Me Cry/Sometime She'll Come Along	1962	25.00
RIC			
❑ 119	The Hurt/It's No Good for Me	1964	200.00

N

Number	Title (A Side/B Side)	Yr	NM
UNIVERSITY			
❑ 605	How to Cry/OK, So What?	1960	30.00
Albums			
MANKIND			
❑ 204	Friend	1971	25.00
❑ 205	Cuss the Wind	1973	40.00

NORTH, JAY

Number	Title (A Side/B Side)	Yr	NM
45s			
KEM			
❑ 2756	The Cat And The Christmas Tree/Christmas For Tommy	1960	15.00
Albums			
KEM			
❑ 27	Look Who's Singing!	1960	100.00

NORTHCOTT, TOM

Number	Title (A Side/B Side)	Yr	NM
45s			
UNI			
❑ 55267	I Think It's Going to Rain Today/ It's True	1971	7.00
❑ 55288	Suzanne/Spaceship Races	1971	7.00
WARNER BROS.			
❑ 7051	Sunny Goodge Street/ Who Planted Thorns in Miss Alice's Garden	1967	10.00
❑ 7160	1941/Other Times	1968	8.00
❑ 7212	Girl from the north Country/ Landscape Grown Cold	1968	12.00
❑ 7283	Make Me an Island/High Hope	1969	12.00
❑ 7330	The Rainmaker/Cities Make the Country Colder	1969	12.00

NORTHERN LIGHT

Number	Title (A Side/B Side)	Yr	NM
45s			
COLUMBIA			
❑ 3-10136	Minnesota/Theme from Minnesota	1975	5.00
GLACIER			
❑ 4501	Minnesota/Theme from Minnesota	1974	8.00
❑ 4504	Runnin'/The Runner	197?	6.00

NORTHERN LIGHTS, THE

With Bjorn Ulvaeus, later of ABBA.

Number	Title (A Side/B Side)	Yr	NM
45s			
UNITED ARTISTS			
❑ 991	Time to Move Along/No Time	1966	20.00

NORWOOD, DOROTHY

Number	Title (A Side/B Side)	Yr	NM
45s			
GRC			
❑ 1011	There's Got to Be Rain in Your Life (To Appreciate the Sunshine)/Get Aboard the Soul Train	1973	8.00
❑ 2009	Mama Loves Her Children All the Time (Part 1)/(Part 2)	1974	8.00
❑ 2057	Let Your Feet Down Easy/ What a Beautiful World	1975	7.00
JEWEL			
❑ 262	He's a Friend/There Is Someone Who Cares for You	1978	6.00
SAVOY			
❑ 4204	Johnny and Jesus/Failure Is Not in God, It's in Me	1963	15.00
❑ 4223	I'm Thine, Oh Lord/ The Old Lady's House	1964	15.00
❑ 4261	A Boy and His Kite/ (B-side unknown)	1966	12.00
❑ 4282	The Singing Slave/ (B-side unknown)	1967	12.00
❑ 4301	In That Little Town/Prescription	1969	10.00
❑ 4325	Jesus Is a Soul Man/Our Prayer	1969	10.00
❑ 4338	Precious Lord/(B-side unknown)	1970	10.00
Albums			
I AM			
❑ 4002-1-M	A Wonderful Day	1990	15.00
JEWEL			
❑ 0134	He's a Friend	1978	15.00
SAVOY			
❑ SL-7042 [(2)]	The Mountain Climbers	1979	20.00
❑ MG 14083 [M]	Johnny and Jesus	196?	25.00
❑ MG 14093 [M]	The Old Lady's House	196?	25.00
❑ MG 14107 [M]	The Bell Didn't Toll	196?	25.00
❑ MG 14127 [M]	He Will Never Let Go My Hand	196?	25.00
❑ MG 14140 [M]	Denied Mother	196?	25.00
❑ MG 14157 [M]	Soldier from Vietnam	196?	25.00
❑ MG 14169 [M]	The Dorothy Norwood Singers	196?	25.00
❑ MG 14175 [M]	The Singing Slave	196?	25.00
❑ MG 14190 [M]	Bereaved Child	196?	25.00
❑ MG 14212	The Stories Behind the Songs	196?	25.00
❑ MG 14217	Just in Time	196?	25.00
❑ MG 14244	Brother Came Too Late	196?	25.00
❑ MG 14259	Jesus Picked Up the Pieces	196?	25.00
❑ MG 14266	Despondent Wife	196?	25.00
❑ MG 14282	Three Little Pigs	197?	25.00
—With Lois Snead			
❑ MG 14295	Just the Two of Us	1972	25.00
—With Lois Snead			
❑ MG 14309	Come By Here	1973	25.00
❑ SL-14515	Faithful Daughter	198?	15.00
❑ SL-14557	God Can	198?	15.00
❑ SL-14598	Answer Me Dear Jesus	198?	15.00
❑ SL-14630	Look What They've Done to My Child	198?	15.00
❑ SL-14651	Somebody Here	198?	15.00
—With the Allen Darling Ensemble			
❑ SL-14716	Up Where We Belong	1983	15.00
WORD			
❑ WR-8420	Mother's Son	1988	10.00

NOSY PARKER

Number	Title (A Side/B Side)	Yr	NM
Albums			
(NO LABEL)			
❑ (no #)	Nosy Parker	1975	250.00

NOTE-TORIALS, THE

Number	Title (A Side/B Side)	Yr	NM
45s			
IMPALA			
❑ 201	Valerie/Loved and Lost	1958	1000.
SUNBEAM			
❑ 119	Valerie/Loved and Lost	1958	200.00

NOTES, THE

Number	Title (A Side/B Side)	Yr	NM
45s			
CAPITOL			
❑ F3332	Don't Leave Me Now/ Cha Jezebel	1956	300.00
MGM			
❑ 12338	Trust in Me/Round and Round	1956	200.00
SARG			
❑ 177	Little Girl/G.I. Blues	1959	50.00

NOVA LOCAL, THE

Number	Title (A Side/B Side)	Yr	NM
45s			
DECCA			
❑ 32138	Games/If You Only Had the Time	1967	20.00
❑ 32194	Other Girls/John Knight's Body (I Wanna Get Out)	1967	20.00
Albums			
DECCA			
❑ DL 74977	Nova 1	1968	70.00

NOVAS, THE

Number	Title (A Side/B Side)	Yr	NM
45s			
PARROT			
❑ 45005	The Crusher/Take 7	1964	80.00
TWIN TOWN			
❑ 713	Novas Coaster/On the Road Again	1965	40.00

NOVELLS, THE

Number	Title (A Side/B Side)	Yr	NM
Albums			
MOTHER'S			
❑ MLPS-73	A Happening	1968	50.00

NRBQ

Number	Title (A Side/B Side)	Yr	NM
45s			
BEARSVILLE			
❑ 29588	Rain at the Drive-In/Shackaroo	1983	5.00
BUTTON			
❑ 037	Froggy Went a-Courtin'/ Bless Your Beautiful Hide	1975	50.00
COLUMBIA			
❑ 44865	Stomp/I Didn't Know Myself	1969	6.00
❑ 44937	C'mon Everybody/Rocket No. 9	1969	6.00
❑ 45019	Sure to Fall (In Love With You)/ Down in My Heart	1969	6.00
KAMA SUTRA			
❑ 544	Howard Johnson's Got His Hojo Workin'/Do You Feel It	1972	6.00
❑ 549	Only You/Magnet	1972	6.00
❑ 575	C'mon If You're Comin'/ RC Cola and a Moon Pie	1973	6.00
❑ 586	Get That Gasoline Blues/Mona	1974	6.00
MERCURY			
❑ 73991	Green Lights/I Love Her, She Loves Me	1978	5.00
RED ROOSTER			
❑ 1001	Ridin' in My Car/Do the Bump	1977	10.00
❑ 1002	I Got a Rocket in My Pocket/ Tapdancin' Bats	1977	6.00
❑ 1002 [PS]	I Got a Rocket in My Pocket/ Tapdancin' Bats	1977	10.00
❑ 1006	Christmas Wish/ Jolly Old St. Nicholas	1978	10.00
❑ 1006 [PS]	Christmas Wish/ Jolly Old St. Nicholas	1978	10.00
ROUNDER			
❑ 1010	Captain Lou!/Boardin' House Pie	1982	4.00
❑ 1010 [PS]	Captain Lou!/Boardin' House Pie	1982	4.00
❑ 4521	Hot Biscuits and Sweet Marie/ She Don't Look Good	1979	5.00
❑ 4522	Get That Gasoline Blues/ Wacky Tobacky	1979	5.00
❑ 4525	Christmas Wish/Jolly Old St. Nicholas	1979	5.00
❑ 4525 [PS]	Christmas Wish/Jolly Old St. Nicholas	1979	6.00
❑ 4531	Me and the Boys/People	1980	5.00
❑ 4531 [PS]	Me and the Boys/People	1980	10.00
❑ 4539	Never Take the Place of You/ Captain Lou Albano for Tiddlywinks	1980	5.00
❑ 4556	Things to Do/I Can't Stop Loving You Now	1985	4.00
—With Skeeter Davis			
SCEPTER			
❑ 12322	Sho' Need Love/Don't Talk About My Music1	1971	50.00
—As "The Dickens"			
SELECT-O-HIT			
❑ 022	Sourpuss/Rumors	1974	50.00
VIRGIN			
❑ 99130	If I Don't Have You/ Boozoo, That's Who	1989	4.00
❑ 99161 [DJ]	Wild Weekend/This Love Is True	1989	4.00
7-Inch Extended Plays			
RED ROOSTER			
❑ EP-1	Christmas Wish/Here Comes Santa Claus//God Rest Ye Merry Gentlemen/Message from the North Pole	1979	15.00
—Called "Merry Christmas from NRBQ"; not issued with cover			
Albums			
ANNUIT COEPTIS			
❑ 1001/2 [(2)]	Scraps/Workshop	1976	20.00
—Reissue of Kama Sutra LPs			
BEARSVILLE			
❑ 23817	Grooves in Orbit	1983	10.00
COLUMBIA			
❑ CS 9858	NRBQ	1969	25.00
—"360 Sound Stereo" label			
❑ CS 9858	NRBQ	1970	12.00
—Orange label			
❑ PC 9858	NRBQ	198?	8.00
—Budget-line reissue			
KAMA SUTRA			
❑ KSBS-2045	Scraps	1972	30.00
❑ KSBS-2065	Workshop	1973	40.00
MERCURY			
❑ SRM-1-3712	NRBQ at Yankee Stadium	1978	15.00
❑ 824462-1	NRBQ at Yankee Stadium	1984	10.00
—Reissue			
RED ROOSTER			
❑ 101	All Hopped Up	1977	15.00
ROUNDER			
❑ EP-2501 [EP]	Christmas Wish	1985	12.00
❑ 3029	All Hopped Up	1979	12.00
❑ 3030	Kick Me Hard	1979	12.00
❑ 3048	Tiddlywinks	1980	12.00
❑ 3055	Scraps	1982	10.00
❑ 3066	Tapdancin' Bats	1983	10.00
❑ 3090	RC Cola & a Moon Pie	1987	10.00
❑ 3098	Lou and the Q	1986	10.00
—With pro wrestler Captain Lou Albano			
❑ 3108	God Bless Us All	1988	10.00
❑ 3109	Live! Diggin' Uncle Q	1988	10.00
SUNDAZED			
❑ LP-5162	Atsa My Band	2003	15.00
❑ LP-5184	Scraps	2007	15.00
—Reissue of Kama Sutra 2045			
❑ LP-5185	Workshop	2007	15.00
—Reissue of Kama Sutra 2065			
VIRGIN			
❑ 91291	Wild Weekend	1989	10.00

NU-TONES, THE

Number	Title (A Side/B Side)	Yr	NM
45s			
COMBO			
❑ 127	At Midnight/Beans 'N' Greens	1957	150.00
HOLLYWOOD STAR			
❑ 798	You're No Barking Dog/Believe	1955	600.00
❑ 798	Annie Kicked the Bucket/Believe	1955	8000.

Except when noted otherwise, VG = 25% of NM, and VG+ = 50% of NM. (Example: VG = $2.00, VG+ = $4.00 and NM = $8.00.)

NU TORNADOS, THE

45s

CARLTON

Number	Title (A Side/B Side)	Yr	NM
❑ 492	Philadelphia, U.S.A./ Magic Record	1959	25.00
❑ 497	The "Ole Mummers" Strut/ Let's Have a Party	1959	20.00

FELSTED

Number	Title (A Side/B Side)	Yr	NM
❑ 8577	Cry Baby Cry/Keep a Flower Growing in Your Heart	1959	20.00

NUGENT, TED

Also see THE AMBOY DUKES; ST. PARADISE. One-time vocalist Charlie Huhn is now in FOGHAT.

45s

ATLANTIC

Number	Title (A Side/B Side)	Yr	NM
❑ 89436	Little Miss Dangerous/ Angry Young Man	1986	3.00
❑ 89442	High Heels in Motion/ Angry Young Man	1986	3.00
❑ 89442 [PS]	High Heels in Motion/ Angry Young Man	1986	4.00
❑ 89661	Lean Mean R&R Machine/ (Where Do You) Draw the Line	1984	3.00
❑ 89705	Tied Up in Love/Lean Mean R&R Machine	1984	5.00
—Promo copies, with "Tied Up in Love" on both sides, go for less			
❑ 89705 [PS]	Tied Up in Love/Lean Mean R&R Machine	1984	5.00
❑ 89978	No, No, No/Habitual Offender	1982	3.00
❑ 89998	Bound and Gagged/ Habitual Offender	1982	3.00
❑ 89998 [PS]	Bound and Gagged/ Habitual Offender	1982	5.00

EPIC

Number	Title (A Side/B Side)	Yr	NM
❑ 01046	Land of a Thousand Dances/ The TNT Overture	1981	4.00
❑ 50172	Motor City Madness/Where Have You Been All My Life	1975	5.00
❑ 50197	Hey Baby/Stormtroopin'	1976	5.00
❑ 50301	Dog Eat Dog/Light My Way	1976	5.00
❑ 50363	Free-for-All/Street Rags	1977	4.00
❑ 50425	Cat Scratch Fever/Wang Dang Sweet Poontang	1977	5.00
❑ 50493	Death by Misadventure/ Home Bound	1977	4.00
❑ 50533	Yank Me, Crank Me/ Cat Scratch Fever	1978	4.00
❑ 50648	Need You Bad/I Got the Feelin'	1979	4.00
❑ 50713	I Want to Tell You/ Bite Down Hard	1979	4.00
❑ 50907	Wango Tango/Scream Dream	1980	4.00

Albums

ATLANTIC

Number	Title (A Side/B Side)	Yr	NM
❑ SD 19365	Nugent	1982	10.00
❑ 80125	Penetrator	1984	10.00
❑ 81632	Little Miss Dangerous	1986	10.00
❑ 81812	If You Can't Lick 'Em...Lick 'Em	1988	10.00

EPIC

Number	Title (A Side/B Side)	Yr	NM
❑ AS99-607 [PD]	State of Shock	1979	30.00
—Promo-only picture disc			
❑ PE 33692	Ted Nugent	1975	12.00
—Orange label			
❑ PE 33692	Ted Nugent	1979	8.00
—Reissue with dark blue label and bar code			
❑ PE 34121	Free-for-All	1976	12.00
—Orange label			
❑ PE 34121	Free-for-All	1979	8.00
—Reissue with dark blue label and bar code			
❑ PEQ 34121 [Q]	Free-for-All	1976	20.00
❑ JE 34700	Cat Scratch Fever	1977	12.00
—Orange label			
❑ PE 34700	Cat Scratch Fever	198?	8.00
—Reissue with dark blue label and bar code			
❑ KE2 35069 [(2)]	Double Live Gonzo!	1978	15.00
—Orange labels			
❑ FE 35551	Weekend Warriors	1978	12.00
—Orange label			
❑ PE 35551	Weekend Warriors	198?	8.00
—Reissue with dark blue label and bar code			
❑ FE 36000	State of Shock	1979	10.00
❑ PE 36000	State of Shock	198?	8.00
—Budget-line reissue			
❑ FE 36404	Scream Dream	1980	10.00
❑ FE 37084	Intensities in 10 Cities	1981	10.00
❑ PE 37084	Intensities in 10 Cities	198?	8.00
—Budget-line reissue			
❑ FE 37667	Great Gonzos! The Best of Ted Nugent	1981	10.00
❑ PE 37667	Great Gonzos! The Best of Ted Nugent	198?	8.00
—Budget-line reissue			

NUGGETS, THE (1)

45s

CAPITOL

Number	Title (A Side/B Side)	Yr	NM
❑ F-2989	So Help Me I Love You/ Quirl Up in My Arms	1954	20.00
❑ F-3052	Anxious Heart/Shtiggy Boom	1955	15.00

NUGGETS, THE (2)

45s

RCA VICTOR

Number	Title (A Side/B Side)	Yr	NM
❑ 47-7930	Before We Say Goodnight/ Angel on the Dance Floor	1961	30.00
❑ 47-8031	Just a Friend/Cat Snapper	1962	15.00

NUMAN, GARY

12-Inch Singles

I.R.S.

Number	Title (A Side/B Side)	Yr	NM
❑ 13824	My World Storm (2 versions)/ Are Friends Electric (2 versions)	1991	10.00

45s

ATCO

Number	Title (A Side/B Side)	Yr	NM
❑ 7206	Are Friends Electric?/ You Are In My Vision	1979	4.00
❑ 7211	Cars/Metal	1980	4.00
❑ 7308	I Die; You Die/Sleep by Windows	1980	4.00
❑ 7316	Remind Me to Smile	1981	4.00

ATLANTIC

Number	Title (A Side/B Side)	Yr	NM
❑ 13224	Cars/I Die; You Die	198?	3.00
—"Oldies Series" reissue			

Albums

ATCO

Number	Title (A Side/B Side)	Yr	NM
❑ SD 32-103	Telekon	1980	10.00
❑ SD 32-106	Tubeway Army: The First Album	1980	10.00
—First American issue of U.K. debut			
❑ SD 38-117	Replicas	1979	10.00
—With Tubeway Army			
❑ SD 38-120	The Pleasure Principle	1979	12.00
❑ SD 38-143	Dance	1981	10.00
❑ 90014	I, Assassin	1982	12.00

I.R.S.

Number	Title (A Side/B Side)	Yr	NM
❑ 82003	New Anger	1988	10.00

NUMA

Number	Title (A Side/B Side)	Yr	NM
❑ 1005	Strange Charm	1985	10.00

NUMBERS, THE

45s

BONNEVILLE

Number	Title (A Side/B Side)	Yr	NM
❑ 101	Big Red/My Pillow	1962	200.00

DORE

Number	Title (A Side/B Side)	Yr	NM
❑ 641	Big Red/My Pillow	1962	50.00

NUNS, THE

45s

415 RECORDS

Number	Title (A Side/B Side)	Yr	NM
❑ S-0001	Savage/Decadent Jew/ Suicide Child	1978	20.00
❑ S-0001 [PS]	Savage/Decadent Jew/ Suicide Child	1978	20.00

ROSCO

Number	Title (A Side/B Side)	Yr	NM
❑ (no #) [PS]	The Beat/Media Control	1979	15.00
❑ (no #)	The Beat/Media Control	1979	15.00
❑ 4166	World War III/Cock in My Pocket	1980	15.00
❑ 4166 [PS]	World War III/Cock in My Pocket	1980	15.00
—Insert and rubberstamped sleeve			

Albums

BOMP!

Number	Title (A Side/B Side)	Yr	NM
❑ 4010	The Nuns	1980	18.00

POSH BOY

Number	Title (A Side/B Side)	Yr	NM
❑ 105	The Nuns	1980	18.00
—Same album as the Bomp! release			

NUTMEGS, THE

45s

BABY GRAND

Number	Title (A Side/B Side)	Yr	NM
❑ 800	Story Untold '72/Tell Me	1972	8.00

HERALD

Number	Title (A Side/B Side)	Yr	NM
❑ 452	Story Untold/Make Me Lose My Mind	1955	70.00
❑ 459	Ship of Love/Rock Me	1955	40.00
❑ 466	Whispering Sorrows/Betty Lou	1955	50.00
❑ 475	Key to the Kingdom (Of Your Heart)/ Gift O' Gabbin' Woman	1956	50.00
❑ 492	Love So True/Comin' Home	1956	40.00
❑ 538	My Sweet Dream/My Story	1959	40.00
❑ 574	Rip Van Winkle/Crazy 'Bout You	1962	25.00

LANA

Number	Title (A Side/B Side)	Yr	NM
❑ 128	Story Untold/Beautiful Dreamer	196?	10.00
❑ 129	Tingaling/Ship of Love	196?	10.00

LOST-NITE

Number	Title (A Side/B Side)	Yr	NM
❑ 412	Story Untold/Make Me Lose My Mind	197?	5.00
—Reissue			
❑ 430	Ship of Love/Rock Me	197?	5.00
—Reissue			
❑ 445	Love So True/Comin' Home	197?	5.00
—Reissue			

NIGHTRAIN

Number	Title (A Side/B Side)	Yr	NM
❑ 905	Shifting Sands/Take Me and Make Me	1973	8.00

TEL

Number	Title (A Side/B Side)	Yr	NM
❑ 1014	A Dream of Love/Someone, Somewhere (Help Me)	1960	100.00

TIMES SQUARE

Number	Title (A Side/B Side)	Yr	NM
❑ 6	Let Me Tell You/Hello	1963	25.00
—Blue vinyl			
❑ 14	The Way Love Should Be/ Wide Hoop Skirts	1963	20.00
❑ 19	Down to Earth/Coo Coo Cuddle Coo	1963	20.00
—B-side by the Admirations			
❑ 22	Why Must We Go to School/Ink Dries Quicker Than Tears	1963	20.00
—B-side by the Vol.s			
❑ 27	Down in Mexico/ My Sweet Dreams	1964	20.00
❑ 103	You're Crying/Wa-Do-Wa	1964	20.00

7-Inch Extended Plays

HERALD

Number	Title (A Side/B Side)	Yr	NM
❑ 452	*Story Untold/Betty Lou/Comin' Home/Whispering Sorrows	1960	100.00
❑ 452 [PS]	Story Untold	1960	120.00

Albums

COLLECTABLES

Number	Title (A Side/B Side)	Yr	NM
❑ COL-5018	Greatest Hits	198?	10.00

QUICKSILVER

Number	Title (A Side/B Side)	Yr	NM
❑ QS-1001	Shoo-Wop-a-Doo-Wop	198?	10.00

RELIC

Number	Title (A Side/B Side)	Yr	NM
❑ LP-5002	The Nutmegs Featuring Leroy Griffin	198?	10.00
❑ LP-5011	Greatest Hits (1955-1959)	198?	10.00

NUTTY SQUIRRELS, THE

45s

COLUMBIA

Number	Title (A Side/B Side)	Yr	NM
❑ 41818	Please Don't Take Our Tree for Christmas/Nutty Noel	1960	20.00
❑ 41818 [PS]	Please Don't Take Our Tree for Christmas/Nutty Noel	1960	40.00

HANOVER

Number	Title (A Side/B Side)	Yr	NM
❑ 4540	Uh! Oh! (Part 1)/Uh! Oh! (Part 2)	1959	25.00
❑ 4540 [PS]	Uh! Oh! (Part 1)/Uh! Oh! (Part 2)	1959	50.00
❑ 4551	Eager Beaver/Zowee	1960	20.00

RCA VICTOR

Number	Title (A Side/B Side)	Yr	NM
❑ 47-8287	Hello Again/Bluesette	1963	15.00

7-Inch Extended Plays

HANOVER

Number	Title (A Side/B Side)	Yr	NM
❑ 301	Uh-Huh/Ding Dong// Salt Peanuts/Zowee	1960	40.00
❑ 301 [PS]	(title unknown)	1960	60.00
—Paper sleeve (not cardboard)			

Albums

COLUMBIA

Number	Title (A Side/B Side)	Yr	NM
❑ CL 1589 [M]	Bird Watching	1961	30.00
❑ CS 8389 [S]	Bird Watching	1961	40.00

HANOVER

Number	Title (A Side/B Side)	Yr	NM
❑ HML-8014 [M]	The Nutty Squirrels	1960	50.00

MGM

Number	Title (A Side/B Side)	Yr	NM
❑ E-4272 [M]	A Hard Day's Night	1964	25.00
❑ SE-4272 [S]	A Hard Day's Night	1964	30.00

NYRO, LAURA

45s

COLUMBIA

Number	Title (A Side/B Side)	Yr	NM
❑ 44531	Sweet Blindness/Eli's Comin'	1968	8.00
❑ 44786	Once It Was Alright (Farmer Joe)/Lu	1969	6.00
❑ 45041	Time and Love/A Man Who Sends Me Home	1969	6.00
❑ 45089	Save the Country/ New York Tendaberry	1970	6.00
❑ 45230	Up On the Roof/ Captain Saint Lucifer	1970	6.00
❑ 45298	When I Was a Freeport and You Were the Main Drag/ Been On a Train	1971	6.00
❑ JZSP139152/3 [DJ]	Sweet Blindness/ Stoned Soul Picnic	1968	15.00

Number	Title (A Side/B Side)	Yr	NM
VERVE FOLKWAYS			
❑ 5024	Wedding Bell Blues/ Stoney End	1966	10.00
❑ 5038	Billie's Blues/Goodbye Joe	1967	10.00
❑ 5051	And When I Die/Flim Flam Man	1967	10.00
VERVE FORECAST			
❑ 5095	Stoney End/Flim Flam Man	1968	8.00
❑ 5104	And When I Die/I Never Meant to Hurt You	1969	8.00
❑ 5112	Goodbye Joe/I Never Meant to Hurt You	1969	8.00

Albums

Number	Title (A Side/B Side)	Yr	NM
COLUMBIA			
❑ CL 2826 [M]	Eli and the Thirteenth Confession	1968	40.00
❑ CS 9626	Eli and the Thirteenth Confession	1970	10.00
—Orange label			
❑ CS 9626 [S]	Eli and the Thirteenth Confession	1968	15.00
—"360 Sound Stereo" label			
❑ PC 9626	Eli and the Thirteenth Confession	198?	8.00
—Budget-line reissue			
❑ CS 9737	New York Tendaberry	1969	15.00
—"360 Sound Stereo" label			
❑ CS 9737	New York Tendaberry	1970	10.00
—Orange label			
❑ PC 9737	New York Tendaberry	198?	8.00
—Budget-line reissue			
❑ KC 30259	Christmas and the Beads of Sweat	1970	10.00
—Orange label			
❑ KC 30259	Christmas and the Beads of Sweat	1970	15.00
—"360 Sound Stereo" label			
❑ PC 30259	Christmas and the Beads of Sweat	198?	8.00
—Budget-line reissue			
❑ KC 30987	Gonna Take a Miracle	1971	15.00
❑ PC 30987	Gonna Take a Miracle	197?	8.00
—Budget-line reissue			
❑ KC 31410	The First Songs	1973	15.00
—Reissue of Verve Forecast 3020			
❑ PC 31410	The First Songs	197?	8.00
—Budget-line reissue			
❑ PC 33912	Smile	1976	12.00
—No bar code on cover			
❑ PC2 34331 [(2)DJ]	Season of Lights…Laura Nyro in Concert	1977	50.00
—Promo only in plain cardboard jacket; this LP was edited to one LP for release			
❑ JC 34786	Season of Lights…Laura Nyro in Concert	1977	12.00
—Edited version of above			
❑ JC 35449	Nested	1978	12.00
❑ PC 35449	Nested	198?	8.00
—Budget-line reissue			
❑ FC 39215	Mother's Spiritual	1984	10.00
VERVE FOLKWAYS			
❑ FT-3020 [M]	Laura Nyro — More Than a New Discovery	1967	30.00
❑ FTS-3020 [S]	Laura Nyro — More Than a New Discovery	1967	30.00
VERVE FORECAST			
❑ FTS-3020 [S]	Laura Nyro (The First Songs)	1967	20.00
—"The First Songs" is found on the label and back cover, but not on the front cover or the spine; this has the same material as the Verve Folkways LP but in a different order			
❑ FTS-3029	Laura Nyro	1968	—
—Canceled			
❑ ST 93036	Laura Nyro — More Than a New Discovery	1968	25.00
—Capitol Record Club edition			

O

O'BRIAN, HUGH

7-Inch Extended Plays

Number	Title (A Side/B Side)	Yr	NM
ABC-PARAMOUNT			
❑ A-203	(contents unknown)	1957	20.00
❑ A-203 [PS]	Hugh O'Brian (TV's Wyatt Earp) Sings, Vol. I	1957	20.00
❑ B-203	(contents unknown)	1957	20.00
❑ B-203 [PS]	Hugh O'Brian (TV's Wyatt Earp) Sings, Vol. II	1957	20.00
❑ C-203	Don't Move/Timothy//I'm Walkin' Away/Down in the Meadow	1957	20.00
❑ C-203 [PS]	Hugh O'Brian (TV's Wyatt Earp) Sings, Vol. III	1957	20.00

Albums

Number	Title (A Side/B Side)	Yr	NM
ABC-PARAMOUNT			
❑ ABC-203 [M]	TV's Wyatt Earp Sings	1957	60.00

O'BRIEN, RHYS

45s

Number	Title (A Side/B Side)	Yr	NM
MGM			
❑ 13862	The Word Called Love/ Christmas Morning	1967	8.00

O'BRIEN, TIMMY

45s

Number	Title (A Side/B Side)	Yr	NM
RASON			
❑ 1001	Just In Time For Christmas/ I Been A Good Boy	1959	12.00

O'CONNOR, CARROLL

Albums

Number	Title (A Side/B Side)	Yr	NM
A&M			
❑ SP-4340	Remembering You	1972	25.00
AUDIO FIDELITY			
❑ AFSD-6727	Carroll O'Connor Sings for Old P.F.A.R.T.S.	1976	25.00

O'CONNOR, CARROLL, AND JEAN STAPLETON

45s

Number	Title (A Side/B Side)	Yr	NM
ATLANTIC			
❑ 2847	Those Were the Days/ Those Were the Days	1971	5.00
❑ 2847 [PS]	Those Were the Days/ Those Were the Days	1971	8.00

O'DELL, KENNY

45s

Number	Title (A Side/B Side)	Yr	NM
CAPRICORN			
❑ 0020	Rock and Roll Man/ Ain't Gonna Study No More	1973	5.00
❑ 0038	You Bet Your Sweet. Sweet Love/Let's Go Find Some Country Music	1973	5.00
❑ 0203	I Take It On Home/ I'll Find Another Way	1974	4.00
❑ 0219	Soulful Woman/Let's Get On the Road	1975	4.00
❑ 0233	My Honky Tonk Ways/ Behind Closed Doors	1975	4.00
❑ 0247	Together This Christmas/ I Can't Think When You're Doing That to Me	1975	4.00
❑ 0301	Let's Shake Hands and Come Out Lovin'/We Might Be All Night	1978	4.00
❑ 0309	As Long As I Can Wake Up in Your Arms/Soulful Woman	1978	4.00
❑ 0317	Medicine Woman/Who Do I Know in Denver	1979	4.00
EPIC			
❑ 10693	If I Was a Rambler/High on Life	1971	5.00
❑ 10730	I Was a Loser (But Now I've Got You)/Jubal	1971	5.00
❑ 10791	I Was a Loser (But Now I've Got You)/Jubal	1971	5.00
KAPP			
❑ 2169	Two for the Road/Why Don't We Go Somewhere and Love	1972	5.00
❑ 2178	Lizzie and the Rainman/ Homecoming Queen	1972	5.00
MAR-KAY			
❑ 3696	Old Time Lovin'/ Take Another Look	1966	10.00
VEGAS			
❑ 718	Beautiful People/Flower Girl	1967	8.00
❑ 722	Springfield Plane/ I'm Gonna Take It	1968	6.00
❑ 724	Happy with You/Couldn't Love You	1968	6.00
WHITE WHALE			
❑ 319	No Obligation/(B-side unknown)	1969	6.00
❑ 331	Groovy Relationship/ (B-side unknown)	1969	6.00

Albums

Number	Title (A Side/B Side)	Yr	NM
CAPRICORN			
❑ CP 0140	Kenny O'Dell	1974	12.00
❑ CPN 0211	Let's Shake Hands and Come Out Lovin'	1978	12.00
VEGAS			
❑ 401	Beautiful People	1968	25.00

O'HENRY, LENNY

45s

Number	Title (A Side/B Side)	Yr	NM
ABC-PARAMOUNT			
❑ 10222	Billy the Continental Kid/ Cheated Heart	1961	15.00
❑ 10272	Goin' to a Party/Touch of You	1961	15.00
ATCO			
❑ 6291	Across the Street/Saturday Angel	1964	12.00
❑ 6312	Sweet Young Love/ Savin' All My Love	1964	12.00
❑ 6525	Across the Street/Saturday Angel	1967	8.00
SMASH			
❑ 1800	Burning Memories/Mr. Moonlight	1963	12.00

O'JAYS, THE

12-Inch Singles

Number	Title (A Side/B Side)	Yr	NM
EMI			
❑ SPRO-04305/24 [DJ]	Have You Had Your Love Today (2 versions)/ Lovin' You	1989	10.00
❑ 4853/4 [DJ]	Merry Christmas Baby/ The Christmas Song	1991	10.00
❑ V-56127	Have You Had Your Love Today (4 versions)	1989	6.00
❑ V-56207	Don't Let Me Down (6 versions)	1990	8.00
PHILADELPHIA INT'L.			
❑ 4Z8-3708	Sing a Happy Song (5:00)/ Get On Out and Party (5:02)	1979	15.00
❑ 4Z8-3713	I Love Music (6:33)/Livin' for the Weekend (6:29)	1979	25.00
—First issue of these two dance hits on a 12-inch single			
❑ 4Z9-05000	Extraordinary Girl (5:18)/ (Instrumental)	1984	10.00
❑ 4Z9-05040	Let Me Show You (How Much I Really Love You) (unknown versions)	1984	10.00
❑ V-56049	Don't Take Your Love Away (3 versions)/I Just Want Somebody to Love Me	1987	8.00
❑ SPRO-79129/30 [DJ]	Lovin' You (5:15)/Don't Let the Dream Get Away (4:16)	1987	10.00
VOLCANO			
❑ 34272	What's Stopping You (4 versions)	1997	6.00
❑ 37226	Pay the Bills (Main Mix) (Instrumental)/ (same on both sides)	1997	10.00

45s

Number	Title (A Side/B Side)	Yr	NM
APOLLO			
❑ 759	Miracles/Can't Take It	1961	30.00
ASTROSCOPE			
❑ 106	Wisdom of a Child/Peace	1974	8.00
❑ 110	Peace/Don't You Know a True Love (When You See Her)	1974	8.00
BELL			
❑ 691	I'll Be Sweeter Tomorrow (Than I Was Today)/I Dig Your Act	1967	10.00
❑ 704	Look Over Your Shoulder/ I'm So Glad I Found You	1968	10.00
❑ 737	The Choice/Going, Going, Gone	1968	10.00
❑ 749	I Miss You/Now That I Found You	1968	10.00
❑ 770	Don't You Know a True Love/ That's All Right	1969	8.00
❑ 45378	Look Over Your Shoulder/ Four for the Price of One	1973	5.00
EMI			
❑ S7-17491	Somebody Else Will/Decisions	1993	4.00
❑ S7-18914	Have Yourself a Merry Little Christmas/I Can Hardly Wait 'Til Christmas	1995	4.00
❑ B-50180	Have You Had Your Love Today/ Pot Can't Call the Kettle Black	1989	3.00
❑ B-50212	Out of My Mind (Radio Mix)/ (Soul 2 Mix)	1989	3.00
❑ B-50230	Serious Hold on Me/ (Instrumental)	1989	4.00
IMPERIAL			
❑ 5942	How Does It Feel/ Crack Up Laughing	1963	15.00
❑ 5976	Lonely Drifter/That's Enough	1963	10.00
❑ 66007	Stand Tall/The Storm Is Over	1963	10.00
❑ 66025	I'll Never Stop Loving You/ My Dearest Beloved	1964	10.00
❑ 66037	You're on Top/Lovely Dee	1964	10.00
❑ 66076	Girl Machine/Oh How You Hurt Me	1964	10.00
❑ 66102	Lipstick Traces/Think It Over, Baby	1965	10.00
❑ 66121	Whip It On Me Baby/ I've Cried My Last Tear	1965	10.00
❑ 66131	You're the One (You're the Only One)/Let It All Come Out	1965	10.00
❑ 66145	I'll Never Let You Go/ It Won't Hurt	1965	10.00
❑ 66162	I'll Never Forget You/ Pretty Words	1966	300.00
❑ 66177	No Time for You/ It's a Blowin' Wind	1966	10.00
❑ 66197	Friday Night/Stand In for Love	1966	10.00

Except when noted otherwise, VG = 25% of NM, and VG+ = 50% of NM. (Example: VG = $2.00, VG+ = $4.00 and NM = $8.00.)

Number	Title (A Side/B Side)	Yr	NM
❑ 66200	Lonely Drifter/That's Enough	1966	10.00
LITTLE STAR			
❑ 124	How Does It Feel/ Crack Up Laughing	1963	25.00
❑ 125	Dream Girl/Joey St. Vincent	1963	25.00
❑ 1401	Now He's Home/ Just to Be with You	1962	25.00
MINIT			
❑ 32015	Hold On/Working on Your Case	1967	10.00
NEPTUNE			
❑ 12	One Night Affair/ There's Someone (Waiting Back Home)	1969	8.00
❑ 18	Branded Bad/You're the Best Thing Since Candy	1969	8.00
❑ 20	Christmas Ain't Christmas New Year's Ain't New Year's Without the One You Love/ There's Someone Waiting	1969	10.00
❑ 22	Deeper (In Love with You)/ I've Got the Groove	1970	8.00
❑ 31	Looky Looky (Look at Me Girl)/ Let Me in Your World	1970	8.00
❑ 33	Christmas Ain't Christmas New Year's Ain't New Year's Without the One You Love/ Just Can't Get Enough	1970	8.00
PHILADELPHIA INT'L.			
❑ ZS8-02096	Forever Mine/Girl, Don't Let It Get You Down	1981	3.00
—Reissue			
❑ ZS5-02834	I Just Want to Satisfy/ Don't Walk Away Mad	1982	4.00
❑ ZS4-02982	My Favorite Person/One by One	1982	4.00
❑ ZS5-03009	Your Body's Here with Me (But Your Mind's on the Other Side of Town)/Out in the Real World	1982	4.00
❑ 3101	Hurry Up and Come Back/Identify	1979	5.00
❑ 3517	Back Stabbers/Sunshine	1972	5.00
❑ 3522	992 Arguments/Listen to the Clock on the Wall	1972	5.00
❑ 3524	Love Train/Who Am I	1973	5.00
❑ 3531	Time to Get Down/Shiftless, Shady, Jealous Kind of People	1973	5.00
❑ 3535	Put Your Hands Together/ You Got Your Hooks in Me	1973	5.00
❑ 3537	Christmas Ain't Christmas New Year's Ain't New Year's Without the One You Love/ Just Can't Get Enough	1973	6.00
❑ 3544	For the Love of Money/ People Keep Tellin' Me	1974	5.00
❑ 3558	Sunshine (Part 1)/ Sunshine (Part 2)	1974	5.00
❑ 3565	Give the People What They Want/What Am I Waiting For	1975	5.00
❑ 3573	Let Me Make Love to You/ Survival	1975	5.00
❑ 3577	I Love Music (Part 1)/ I Love Music (Part 2)	1975	5.00
❑ 3581	Christmas Ain't Christmas New Year's Ain't New Year's Without the One You Love/ Just Can't Get Enough	1975	5.00
❑ 3587	Livin' for the Weekend/ Stairway to Heaven	1976	5.00
❑ 3596	Family Reunion/Unity	1976	5.00
❑ 3601	Message in Our Music/ She's Only a Woman	1976	5.00
❑ 3610	Darlin' Darlin' Baby (Sweet, Tender, Love)/A Prayer	1976	5.00
❑ 3631	Work On Me/Let's Spend Some Time Together	1977	5.00
❑ 3642	Use Ta Be My Girl/ This Time Baby	1978	5.00
❑ 3652	Brandy/Take Me to the Stars	1978	5.00
❑ 3666	Cry Together/Strokety Stroke	1978	5.00
❑ 3707	Sing a Happy Song/ One in a Million (Girl)	1979	5.00
❑ 3726	I Want You Here with Me/ Get On Out and Party	1979	5.00
❑ 3727	Forever Mine/Get On Out and Party	1979	5.00
❑ ZS4-03892	I Can't Stand the Pain/ A Letter to My Friends	1983	4.00
❑ ZS4-04069	Put Our Heads Together/ Nice and Easy	1983	4.00
❑ ZS4-04437	Extraordinary Girl/I Really Need You Now	1984	4.00
❑ ZS4-04535	Let Me Show You (How Much I Really Love You)/Love You Direct	1984	4.00
❑ B-50013	Just Another Lonely Night/ What Good Are These Arms of Mine	1985	3.00
❑ B-50021	What a Woman/I Love America	1985	3.00
❑ B-50067	Don't Take Your Love Away/ I Just Want Somebody to Love Me	1987	3.00
❑ B-50084	Lovin' You/Don't Let the Dream Get Away	1987	3.00
❑ B-50104	Let Me Touch You/ Undercover Lover	1987	3.00
❑ B-50122	I Just Want Someone to Love Me/Lovin' You	1988	3.00
SARU			
❑ 1220	Shattered Man/La De Da (Means I'm Out to Get You)	1971	6.00
TSOP			
❑ 3771	Christmas Ain't Christmas New Year's Ain't New Year's Without the One You Love/ Just Can't Get Enough	1980	5.00
❑ 4790	Girl, Don't Let It Get You Down/ You're the Girl of My Dreams	1980	4.00
❑ 4791	Once Is Not Enough/ To Prove I Love You	1980	4.00
❑ 70050	You Won't Fall/You'll Never Know (All There Is to Know 'Bout Love)	1981	4.00
Albums			
BELL			
❑ 6014	Back on Top	1968	20.00
❑ 6082	The O'Jays	1973	12.00
EMI			
❑ E1-90921	Serious	1989	10.00
❑ E1-93390	Emotionally Yours	1991	15.00
❑ E1-96420	Home for Christmas	1991	15.00
IMPERIAL			
❑ LP 9290 [M]	Comin' Through	1965	40.00
❑ LP 12290 [S]	Comin' Through	1965	50.00
KORY			
❑ 1006	The O'Jays	1977	10.00
LIBERTY			
❑ LN-10119	Greatest Hits	1980	8.00
—Budget-line reissue of Imperial material			
MINIT			
❑ LP-24008 [S]	Soul Sounds	1967	50.00
❑ LP-40008 [M]	Soul Sounds	1967	40.00
NEPTUNE			
❑ 202	The O'Jays in Philadelphia	1969	30.00
PHILADELPHIA INT'L.			
❑ ASZ 140 [DJ]	Everything You Always Wanted to Hear by the O'Jays But Were Afraid to Ask For	1975	15.00
❑ KZ 31712	Back Stabbers	1972	12.00
❑ KZ 32120	The O'Jays in Philadelphia	1973	12.00
—Reissue of Neptune LP			
❑ KZ 32408	Ship Ahoy	1973	10.00
❑ PZ 32408	Ship Ahoy	198?	8.00
—Budget-line reissue			
❑ PZQ 32408 [Q]	Ship Ahoy	1974	15.00
❑ KZ 32953	The O'Jays Live in London	1974	10.00
❑ PZQ 32953 [Q]	The O'Jays Live in London	1974	15.00
❑ PZ 33150	Survival	1975	10.00
❑ PZ 33807	Family Reunion	1975	10.00
—No bar code on back cover			
❑ PZ 33807	Family Reunion	198?	8.00
—Budget-line reissue with bar code			
❑ PZQ 33807 [Q]	Family Reunion	1975	15.00
❑ PZ 34245	Message in the Music	1976	10.00
❑ PZ 34684	Travelin' at the Speed of Thought	1977	10.00
❑ PZG 35024 [(2)]	The O'Jays: Collector's Items	1978	12.00
❑ Z2 35024 [(2)]	The O'Jays: Collector's Items	198?	10.00
—Reissue			
❑ JZ 35355	So Full of Love	1978	10.00
❑ PZ 35355	So Full of Love	198?	8.00
—Budget-line reissue			
❑ FZ 36027	Identify Yourself	1979	10.00
❑ FZ 37999	My Favorite Person	1982	10.00
❑ FZ 38518	When Will I See You Again	1983	10.00
❑ PZ 38518	When Will I See You Again	1985	8.00
—Budget-line reissue			
❑ FZ 39251	Greatest Hits	1984	10.00
❑ 53015	Love Fever	1985	10.00
❑ 53036	Let Me Touch You	1987	10.00
SUNSET			
❑ SUS-5222	Full of Soul	1968	15.00
—Reissue of Imperial LP			
TSOP			
❑ FZ 36416	The Year 2000	1980	10.00
UNITED ARTISTS			
❑ UAS-5655	The O'Jays Greatest Hits	1972	12.00
VOLCANO			
❑ 31149	Love You to Tears	1997	15.00

O'KAYSIONS, THE

Number	Title (A Side/B Side)	Yr	NM
45s			
ABC			
❑ 11094	Girl Watcher/Deal Me In	1968	8.00
❑ 11153	Love Machine/Dedicated to the One I Love	1968	6.00
❑ 11207	Twenty-Four Hours from Tulsa/ Colors	1969	6.00
COTILLION			
❑ 44089	Happiness/Watch Out Girl	1970	5.00
❑ 44134	Life and Things/Travelin' Life	1971	5.00
NORTH STATE			
❑ 1001	Girl Watcher/Deal Me In	1968	100.00
❑ 1001 [PS]	Girl Watcher/Deal Me In	1968	300.00
Albums			
ABC			
❑ S-664	Girl Watcher	1968	40.00

O'KEEFE, DANNY

Number	Title (A Side/B Side)	Yr	NM
45s			
ATLANTIC			
❑ 2978	Angel, Spread Your Wings/ Mad Ruth the Babe	1973	5.00
❑ 3267	The Delta Queen/Quits	1975	5.00
JERDEN			
❑ 806	Don't Wake Me in the Morning/ That Old Sweet Song	1966	10.00
PICCADILLY			
❑ 228	Don't Wake Me in the Morning/ That Old Sweet Song	1967	8.00
❑ 237	Today One Day Later/Baby	1967	8.00
SIGNPOST			
❑ 70006	Good Time Charlie's Got the Blues/The Valentine Pieces	1972	6.00
❑ 70012	The Road/I'm Sober Now	1972	5.00
WARNER BROS.			
❑ 8435	You Look Just Like a Girl Again/ On Discovering a Missing Person	1977	5.00
❑ 8489	The Runaway/Just Jones	1977	5.00
Albums			
ATLANTIC			
❑ SD 7264	Breezy Stories	1973	12.00
❑ SD 18125	So Long, Harry Truman	1975	12.00
COTILLION			
❑ SD 9036	Danny O'Keefe	1971	15.00
FIRST AMERICAN			
❑ 7700	The Seattle Tapes	1977	12.00
❑ 7721	The Seattle Tapes, Vol. 2	1979	12.00
PANORAMA			
❑ 105	Introducing Danny O'Keefe	1966	40.00
SIGNPOST			
❑ SD 8404	O'Keefe	1972	12.00
WARNER BROS.			
❑ PRO 760 [DJ]	The O'Keefe File	1977	15.00
❑ BS 3050	American Roulette	1977	10.00
❑ BSK 3314	Global Blues	1978	10.00

O'KEEFE, JOHNNY

Number	Title (A Side/B Side)	Yr	NM
45s			
BRUNSWICK			
❑ 55067	Real Wild Child/ Shake Baby Shake	1958	200.00
LIBERTY			
❑ 55223	She's My Baby/Own True Self	1959	40.00
❑ 55228	She's My Baby/It's Too Late	1959	30.00
❑ 55228 [PS]	She's My Baby/It's Too Late	1959	50.00
❑ 55262	Come On and Take My Hand/ Don't You Know Little Baby	1960	40.00
MR. PEACOCK			
❑ 111	I'm Counting on You/ The Steady Game	1962	40.00
SIMS			
❑ 337	So Why/Cryin' Is the One Thing I Do Very Well	1968	8.00

O'KEEFE, PAUL

Number	Title (A Side/B Side)	Yr	NM
45s			
EVEREST			
❑ 19322	(Santa Claus) What Would You Like for Christmas?/ A Baby in a Basket	1959	12.00
❑ 19322 [PS]	(Santa Claus) What Would You Like for Christmas?/ A Baby in a Basket	1959	15.00

O

O'NEIL, TOM

45s

COLONIAL

Number	Title (A Side/B Side)	Yr	NM
❑ 7012	Who's Sorry Now/Georgia on My Mind	196?	15.00
❑ 7015	I Get the Blues When It Rains/ A Song for Anita	196?	15.00

PETAL

Number	Title (A Side/B Side)	Yr	NM
❑ 1001	St. Louis Blues/A Song for Anita	196?	20.00
❑ 1010	I Get the Blues When It Rains/ I Ain't Got Nobody	196?	20.00

O'SULLIVAN, GILBERT

45s

EPIC

Number	Title (A Side/B Side)	Yr	NM
❑ 50415	You Got Me Going/Call On Me	1977	4.00
❑ 50967	What's in a Kiss/ Down, Down, Down	1981	4.00

MAM

Number	Title (A Side/B Side)	Yr	NM
❑ 3602	Nothing Rhymed/ Everybody Knows	1971	6.00
❑ 3607	Underneath the Blanket Go/ (B-side unknown)	1971	6.00
❑ 3613	We Will/I Didn't Know What to Do	1971	6.00
❑ 3617	No Matter How I Try/ If I Don't Get You Back	1972	5.00
❑ 3619	Alone Again (Naturally)/Save It	1972	6.00
❑ 3626	Clair/Ooh Wakka Doo Wakka Day	1972	5.00
❑ 3626 [PS]	Clair/Ooh Wakka Doo Wakka Day	1972	6.00
❑ 3628	Out of the Question/ Everybody Knows	1973	5.00
❑ 3629	Get Down/A Very Extraordinary Sort of Girl	1973	5.00
❑ 3633	Ooh Baby/Good Company	1973	4.00
❑ 3636	Happiness Is Me and You/ Breakfast, Dinner and Tea	1974	4.00
❑ 3641	A Woman's Place/Too Bad	1974	4.00
❑ 3642	You Are You/To Cut a Long Story Short	1974	4.00
❑ 3643	Marriage Machine/Tell Me Why	1975	4.00
❑ 3644	I Don't Love You But I Think I Like You/That's a Fact	1975	4.00
❑ 3645	Christmas Song/Just As You Are	1975	5.00

Albums

EPIC

Number	Title (A Side/B Side)	Yr	NM
❑ JE 37013	Off Centre	1981	10.00

MAM

Number	Title (A Side/B Side)	Yr	NM
❑ 4	Gilbert O'Sullivan — Himself	1972	15.00
❑ 5	Back to Front	1972	15.00
❑ 7	I'm a Writer, Not a Fighter	1973	15.00
❑ 10	Stranger in My Own Backyard	1974	15.00

OBOLER, ARCH

Albums

CAPITOL

Number	Title (A Side/B Side)	Yr	NM
❑ ST 1763 [S]	Drop Dead! An Exercise in Horror	1962	30.00
❑ T 1763 [M]	Drop Dead! An Exercise in Horror	1962	25.00

OBSESSIONS, THE

45s

ACCENT

Number	Title (A Side/B Side)	Yr	NM
❑ 1182	Love Always/A Fool	1964	200.00

OCEAN

45s

KAMA SUTRA

Number	Title (A Side/B Side)	Yr	NM
❑ 519	Put Your Hand in the Hand/ Tear Down the Fences	1971	5.00
❑ 525	Deep Enough for Me/ No Other Woman	1971	4.00
❑ 529	We Got a Dream/Will the Circle Be Unbroken	1971	4.00
❑ 556	One More Chance/Will the Circle Be Unbroken	1972	4.00

Albums

KAMA SUTRA

Number	Title (A Side/B Side)	Yr	NM
❑ KSBS-2033	Put Your Hand in the Hand	1971	12.00
❑ KSBS-2064	Give Tomorrow's Children One More Chance	1972	12.00

OCHS, PHIL

45s

A&M

Number	Title (A Side/B Side)	Yr	NM
❑ 881	Flower Lady/Cross My Heart	1967	10.00
❑ 891	Outside of a Small Circle of Friends/Miranda	1967	10.00
❑ 932	The War Is Over/The Harder They Fall	1968	8.00
❑ 1070	My Life/The World Began in Eden and Ended in Los Angeles	1969	8.00
❑ 1180	My Kingdom for a Car/ One Way Ticket Home	1970	8.00
❑ 1376	Kansas City Bomber/ Gas Station Woman	1972	8.00
❑ 1509	Here's to the State of Richard Nixon/Power and Glory	1974	8.00

Albums

A&M

Number	Title (A Side/B Side)	Yr	NM
❑ LP-133 [M]	Pleasures of the Harbor	1967	25.00
❑ LP-148 [M]	Tape from California	1968	50.00
—Mono is white label promo only; "Monaural" sticker at upper right corner of stereo cover			
❑ SP-3125	Phil Ochs Greatest Hits	198?	8.00
—Budget-line reissue			
❑ SP-4133 [S]	Pleasures of the Harbor	1967	20.00
❑ SP-4148 [S]	Tape from California	1968	20.00
❑ SP-4181	Rehearsals for Retirement	1969	20.00
❑ SP-4253	Phil Ochs Greatest Hits	1970	20.00
❑ SP-4599 [(2)]	Chords of Fame	1974	25.00
—Original edition			
❑ SP-6511 [(2)]	Chords of Fame	1976	15.00
—Reissue of 4599			

CARTHAGE

Number	Title (A Side/B Side)	Yr	NM
❑ CGLP-4422	I Ain't Marching Anymore	198?	10.00
❑ CGLP-4427	All the News That's Fit to Sing	198?	10.00

ELEKTRA

Number	Title (A Side/B Side)	Yr	NM
❑ EKL-269 [M]	All the News That's Fit to Sing	1964	30.00
—Gold label with "guitar player" logo			
❑ EKL-269 [M]	All the News That's Fit to Sing	1966	20.00
—Gold label with stylized "E" logo			
❑ EKL-287 [M]	I Ain't Marching Anymore	1965	30.00
—Gold label with "guitar player" logo			
❑ EKL-287 [M]	I Ain't Marching Anymore	1966	20.00
—Gold label with stylized "E" logo			
❑ EKL-310 [M]	Phil Ochs in Concert	1966	20.00
❑ EKS-7269 [S]	All the News That's Fit to Sing	1964	40.00
—Gold label with "guitar player" logo			
❑ EKS-7269 [S]	All the News That's Fit to Sing	1966	25.00
—Gold label with stylized "E" logo			
❑ EKS-7287 [S]	I Ain't Marching Anymore	1965	40.00
—Gold label with "guitar player" logo			
❑ EKS-7287 [S]	I Ain't Marching Anymore	1966	25.00
—Gold label with stylized "E" logo			
❑ EKS-7287 [S]	I Ain't Marching Anymore	1975	12.00
—Butterfly label with small Warner Communications logo			
❑ EKS-7310 [S]	Phil Ochs in Concert	1966	25.00

FOLKWAYS

Number	Title (A Side/B Side)	Yr	NM
❑ FB-5320	Phil Ochs Sings Songs for Broadside (#10)	1976	12.00
❑ FB-5321	Phil Ochs Interviews	197?	12.00
❑ FD-5362	Broadside Tapes 1 (#14)	1979	12.00

PICKWICK

Number	Title (A Side/B Side)	Yr	NM
❑ SPC-3707	Rehearsals for Retirement	197?	10.00

RHINO

Number	Title (A Side/B Side)	Yr	NM
❑ RNLP-70080	A Toast to Those Who Are Gone	1986	10.00

SMITHSONIAN/FOLKWAYS

Number	Title (A Side/B Side)	Yr	NM
❑ SF-40008	Broadside Tapes 1 (#14)	1989	12.00

OCTAVES, THE

45s

VAL

Number	Title (A Side/B Side)	Yr	NM
❑ 1001	You're Too Young/ Mambo Carolyn	1958	75.00

OCTOBER COUNTRY

45s

EPIC

Number	Title (A Side/B Side)	Yr	NM
❑ 5-10252	October Country/ Baby What I Mean	1967	10.00
❑ 5-10320	My Girlfriend Is a Witch/ I Just Don't Know	1968	10.00

Albums

EPIC

Number	Title (A Side/B Side)	Yr	NM
❑ BN 26381	October Country	1968	20.00

ODA

Albums

LOUD

Number	Title (A Side/B Side)	Yr	NM
❑ A 0011	Oda	1973	200.00

ODDIS, RAY

45s

V.I.P.

Number	Title (A Side/B Side)	Yr	NM
❑ 25012	Happy Ghoul Tide/ Ray the Newspaper Boy	1964	20.00

ODDS AND ENDS

45s

RED BIRD

Number	Title (A Side/B Side)	Yr	NM
❑ 10-083	Before You Go (Hey Little Girl)/ Never Learn	1967	12.00

ODETTA

45s

ABC DUNHILL

Number	Title (A Side/B Side)	Yr	NM
❑ 4213	Ballad of Easy Rider/Visa Versa	1969	6.00

POLYDOR

Number	Title (A Side/B Side)	Yr	NM
❑ 14045	Take Me to the Pilot/Hit or Miss	1970	5.00

RCA VICTOR

Number	Title (A Side/B Side)	Yr	NM
❑ 47-8262	Got My Mind on Freedom/ It's a Mighty World	1963	10.00

RIVERSIDE

Number	Title (A Side/B Side)	Yr	NM
❑ 4524	Make Me a Pallet on Your Floor/ Oh, My Babe	1962	10.00

VANGUARD

Number	Title (A Side/B Side)	Yr	NM
❑ 35007	Motherless Children/ The Ox-Driver Song	1959	12.00

VERVE FOLKWAYS

Number	Title (A Side/B Side)	Yr	NM
❑ 5030	Until It's Time for You to Go/ Clown Town	1966	8.00

VERVE FORECAST

Number	Title (A Side/B Side)	Yr	NM
❑ 5087	Peace and Harmony/Until It's Time for You to Go	1968	6.00

Albums

ALCAZAR

Number	Title (A Side/B Side)	Yr	NM
❑ ALC-104	Christmas Spirituals	198?	10.00

EVEREST ARCHIVE OF FOLK & JAZZ

Number	Title (A Side/B Side)	Yr	NM
❑ 273	Odetta	1973	12.00

FANTASY

Number	Title (A Side/B Side)	Yr	NM
❑ 3-15 [10]	Odetta and Larry	1955	50.00
❑ OBC-509	Odetta and the Blues	198?	10.00
—Reissue of Riverside LP			
❑ F-3252 [M]	Odetta and Larry	1957	50.00
—Dark red vinyl			
❑ F-3252 [M]	Odetta and Larry	1958	30.00
❑ F-8345	Odetta and Larry	1963	10.00
—Reissue of 3252			

RCA VICTOR

Number	Title (A Side/B Side)	Yr	NM
❑ LPM-2573 [M]	Sometimes I Feel Like Crying	1962	20.00
❑ LSP-2573 [S]	Sometimes I Feel Like Crying	1962	25.00
❑ LPM-2643 [M]	Odetta Sings Folk Songs	1963	20.00
❑ LSP-2643 [S]	Odetta Sings Folk Songs	1963	25.00
❑ LPM-2792 [M]	It's a Mighty World	1964	15.00
❑ LSP-2792 [S]	It's a Mighty World	1964	20.00
❑ LPM-2923 [M]	Odetta Sings of Many Things	1964	15.00
❑ LSP-2923 [S]	Odetta Sings of Many Things	1964	20.00
❑ LPM-3324 [M]	Odetta Sings Dylan	1965	15.00
❑ LSP-3324 [S]	Odetta Sings Dylan	1965	20.00
❑ LPM-3457 [M]	Odetta in Japan	1965	15.00
❑ LSP-3457 [S]	Odetta in Japan	1965	20.00

RIVERSIDE

Number	Title (A Side/B Side)	Yr	NM
❑ RLP-417 [M]	Odetta and the Blues	1962	25.00
❑ RS-9417 [S]	Odetta and the Blues	1962	30.00

ROSE QUARTZ

Number	Title (A Side/B Side)	Yr	NM
❑ RQ-101	Movin' It On	1987	10.00

TRADITION

Number	Title (A Side/B Side)	Yr	NM
❑ TRP-1010 [M]	Odetta Sings Ballads and Blues	1957	30.00
❑ TRP-1025 [M]	Odetta at the Gate of Horn	1958	30.00
❑ TRP-1052 [M]	The Best of Odetta	1967	20.00
❑ TRS-2052 [R]	The Best of Odetta	1967	15.00

VANGUARD

Number	Title (A Side/B Side)	Yr	NM
❑ VSD-43/44 [(2)]	Essential Odetta	1973	15.00
❑ VSD-2046 [S]	My Eyes Have Seen	1960	25.00
❑ VSD-2057 [S]	Ballads for Americans	1960	25.00
❑ VSD-2072 [S]	Odetta at Carnegie Hall	1961	25.00
❑ VSD-2079 [S]	Christmas Spirituals	1961	25.00
❑ VSD-2109 [S]	Odetta at Town Hall	1962	25.00
❑ VSD-2153 [S]	One Grain of Sand	1963	25.00
❑ VRS-3003 [M]	Odetta at Carnegie Hall	1967	15.00
❑ VRS-9059 [M]	My Eyes Have Seen	1960	20.00
❑ VRS-9066 [M]	Ballads for Americans	1960	20.00
❑ VRS-9076 [M]	Odetta at Carnegie Hall	1961	20.00
❑ VRS-9079 [M]	Christmas Spirituals	1961	20.00
❑ VRS-9103 [M]	Odetta at Town Hall	1962	20.00
❑ VRS-9137 [M]	One Grain of Sand	1963	20.00
❑ VSD-73003 [S]	Odetta at Carnegie Hall	1967	20.00

OFF KEYS, THE

45s

ROWE

Number	Title (A Side/B Side)	Yr	NM
❑ 003	Our Wedding Day/Singing Bells	1962	100.00

TECHNICHORD

Number	Title (A Side/B Side)	Yr	NM
❑ 1001	Our Wedding Day/Singing Bells	1962	25.00
—Flat maroon label			
❑ 1001	Our Wedding Day/Singing Bells	1962	50.00
—Glossy red label			

OGNIR AND THE NIGHT PEOPLE

45s

SAMRON

Number	Title (A Side/B Side)	Yr	NM
❑ 102	I Found a New Love/All My Heart	1965	40.00

O

Except when noted otherwise, VG = 25% of NM, and VG+ = 50% of NM. (Example: VG = $2.00, VG+ = $4.00 and NM = $8.00.)

Number	Title (A Side/B Side)	Yr	NM
WARNER BROS.			
❑ 5687	I Found a New Love/All My Heart	1965	25.00

OHIO EXPRESS, THE Also see THE RARE BREED.

45s

Number	Title (A Side/B Side)	Yr	NM
BUDDAH			
❑ 38	Yummy Yummy Yummy/Zig Zag	1968	10.00
❑ 56	Down at Lulu's/She's Not Coming Home	1968	8.00
❑ 70	Chewy Chewy/Firebird	1968	10.00
❑ 92	Sweeter Than Sugar/ Bitter Than Lemon	1969	8.00
❑ 102	Mercy/Roll It Up	1969	8.00
❑ 117	Pinch Me (Baby, Convince Me)/ Peanuts	1969	8.00
❑ 129	Sausalito (Is the Place to Go)/ Make Love Not War	1969	8.00
—With Graham Gouldman, later of 10CC, on lead vocal			
❑ 147	Cowboy Convention/ The Race (That Took Place)	1970	8.00
❑ 160	Love Equals Love/Peanuts	1970	8.00
❑ 386	Wham Bam/Slow and Steady	1973	15.00
—As "Ohio Ltd."			
CAMEO			
❑ 483	Beg, Borrow and Steal/Maybe	1967	12.00
❑ 2001	Try It/Soul Struttin'	1967	12.00
SUPER K			
❑ 114	Hot Dog/Ooh La La	1970	10.00

Albums

Number	Title (A Side/B Side)	Yr	NM
BUDDAH			
❑ BDM 1018 [M]	The Ohio Express	1968	40.00
—Stereo cover with "mono" sticker attached; white label promo			
❑ BDS 5018 [S]	The Ohio Express	1968	20.00
❑ BDS 5026	Chewy, Chewy	1969	20.00
❑ BDS 5037	Mercy	1969	20.00
❑ BDS 5058	The Very Best of the Ohio Express	1970	20.00
CAMEO			
❑ C 20000 [M]	Beg, Borrow and Steal	1967	30.00
❑ CS 20000 [S]	Beg, Borrow and Steal	1967	40.00

OHIO PLAYERS, THE Also see THE OHIO UNTOUCHABLES.

12-Inch Singles

Number	Title (A Side/B Side)	Yr	NM
AIR CITY			
❑ A-402	Sight for Sore Eyes/ (Instrumental)	1984	6.00
ARISTA			
❑ SP-46 [DJ]	Everybody Up (9:32) (3:57)	1979	12.00
BOARDWALK			
❑ AS 941 [DJ]	Try a Little Tenderness/ DDDDDDDance	1981	15.00
—B-side by Rox			
MERCURY			
❑ MK-43 [DJ]	Magic Trick/Good Luck Charm	1976	15.00
TRACK			
❑ 58813	Sweat (3 versions)/ Rock the House	1988	6.00

45s

Number	Title (A Side/B Side)	Yr	NM
AIR CITY			
❑ 402	Sight for Sore Eyes/ (Instrumental)	1984	4.00
❑ 402 [PS]	Sight for Sore Eyes/ (Instrumental)	1984	4.00
❑ 1007	Follow Me/(B-side unknown)	1984	5.00
ARISTA			
❑ 0408	Everybody Up/Take De Funk Off, Fly	1979	4.00
❑ 0440	Don't Say Goodbye/Say It	1979	4.00
BOARDWALK			
❑ NB7-11-133	Star of the Party/I Better Take a Coffee Break	1981	25.00
❑ WS8-02063	Skinny/Call Me	1981	4.00
❑ 5708	Try a Little Tenderness/ Try to Be a Man	1981	4.00
CAPITOL			
❑ 2385	Bad Bargain/Here Today and Gone Tomorrow	1969	10.00
❑ 2523	Find Someone to Love/ Over the Rainbow	1969	10.00
COMPASS			
❑ 7015	Tresspassin'/You Don't Mean It	1967	50.00
❑ 7018	It's a Crying Shame/I've Got to Hold On	1968	25.00
MERCURY			
❑ 73480	Jive Turkey (Part 1)/ Streakin' Cheek to Cheek	1974	5.00
❑ 73609	Skin Tight/Heaven Must Be Like This	1974	5.00
❑ 73643	Fire/Together	1974	5.00
❑ 73675	I Want to Be Free/Smoke	1975	5.00
❑ 73713	Sweet Sticky Thing/Alone	1975	5.00
❑ 73734	Love Rollercoaster/It's All Over	1975	5.00
❑ 73753	Happy Holidays (Part 1)/ Happy Holidays (Part 2)	1975	6.00
❑ 73775	Fopp/Let's Love	1976	5.00
❑ 73814	Who'd She Coo?/Bi-Centennial	1976	5.00
❑ 73860	Far East Mississippi/Only a Child Can Love	1976	5.00
❑ 73881	Feel the Beat (Everybody Disco)/Contradiction	1976	5.00
❑ 73913	Body Vibes/Don't Fight My Love	1977	5.00
❑ 73932	O-H-I-O/Can You Still Love Me	1977	5.00
❑ 73956	Merry Go Round/Angel	1977	5.00
❑ 73974	Good Luck Charm (Part 1)/ Good Luck Charm (Part 2)	1977	5.00
❑ 73983	Magic Trick/Mr. Mean	1978	5.00
❑ 74014	Funk-O-Nots/Sleepwalkin'	1978	5.00
❑ 74031	Time Slips Away/Nott Enuff	1978	5.00
TANGERINE			
❑ 978	Neighbors/A Thing Called Love	1967	25.00
TRACK			
❑ 58812	Let's Play (From Now On)/ Show Off	1988	3.00
❑ 58815	Sweat/Rock the House	1988	3.00
WESTBOUND			
❑ 188	Pain (Part 1)/Pain (Part 2)	1971	6.00
❑ 204	Pleasure/I Wanna Hear from You	1972	6.00
❑ 208	Walt's First Trip/Varce Is Love	1972	6.00
❑ 214	Funky Worm/Paint Me	1973	6.00
❑ 216	Ecstasy/Not So Sad and Lonely	1973	6.00
❑ 228	Sleep Talk/Food Stamps Y'All	1974	6.00
❑ 5018	Rattlesnake/Gone Forever	1976	6.00

Albums

Number	Title (A Side/B Side)	Yr	NM
ACCORD			
❑ SN-7102	Young and Ready	1981	8.00
ARISTA			
❑ AB 4226	Everybody Up	1979	8.00
BOARDWALK			
❑ FW 37090	Tenderness	1981	8.00
CAPITOL			
❑ ST-192	Observations in Time	1969	50.00
❑ ST-11291	The Ohio Players	1974	12.00
—Reissue of 192			
MERCURY			
❑ SRM-1-705	Skin Tight	1974	10.00
—Chicago skyline label			
❑ SRM-1-705	Skin Tight	1974	12.00
—Red label			
❑ SRM-1-1013	Fire	1974	10.00
❑ SRM-1-1038	Honey	1975	10.00
❑ SRM-1-1088	Contradiction	1976	10.00
❑ SRM-1-1122	Ohio Players Gold	1976	10.00
❑ SRM-1-3701	Angel	1977	10.00
❑ SRM-1-3707	Mr. Mean	1977	10.00
❑ SRM-1-3730	Jass-Ay-Lay-Dee	1978	10.00
❑ 824461-1	Ohio Players Gold	198?	8.00
—Reissue of 1122			
TRACK			
❑ TRK 58810	Back	1988	10.00
TRIP			
❑ 8029	First Impression	1972	12.00
UNITED ARTISTS			
❑ UA-LA502-E	The Very Best of The Ohio Players	1975	12.00
WESTBOUND			
❑ 211	Rattlesnake	1975	12.00
❑ 219	Pain	1976	12.00
—Reissue of 2015			
❑ 220	Pleasure	1976	12.00
—Reissue of 2017			
❑ 222	Ecstasy	1976	12.00
—Reissue of 2021			
❑ 304	The Best of the Early Years	1977	15.00
❑ 1003	Climax	1974	15.00
❑ 1005	Ohio Players Greatest Hits	1975	15.00
❑ 2015	Pain	1972	20.00
❑ 2017	Pleasure	1973	20.00
❑ 2021	Ecstasy	1973	20.00

OHIO UNTOUCHABLES, THE Early version of THE OHIO PLAYERS.

45s

Number	Title (A Side/B Side)	Yr	NM
LUPINE			
❑ 109	She's My Heart's Desire/ What to Do	1962	50.00
❑ 110	Love Is Amazing/ Forgive Me Darling	1962	50.00
❑ 116/7	I'm Tired/Uptown	1962	40.00
❑ 1009	She's My Heart's Desire/ What to Do	1964	20.00
❑ 1010	Love Is Amazing/ Forgive Me Darling	1964	20.00
❑ 1011	I'm Tired/Uptown	1964	15.00

OINGO BOINGO

12-Inch Singles

Number	Title (A Side/B Side)	Yr	NM
A&M			
❑ SP-17203 [DJ]	Private Life/Whole Day Off/ Nothing to Fear/Grey Matter	1982	12.00
❑ SP-17240 [DJ]	Wake Up (It's 1984) (4:39) (3:00)	1983	12.00
❑ SP-17242 [DJ]	Nothing Bad Ever Happens/ Who Do You Want to Be	1983	15.00
I.R.S.			
❑ SP-70951	Only a Lad (4:18)/ Ain't This the Life	1980	25.00
❑ SP-70953 [DJ]	Only a Lad (same on both sides)	1980	30.00
MCA			
❑ L33-17022 [DJ]	Weird Science (3:45) (same on both sides)	1985	10.00
❑ L33-17048 [DJ]	Weird Science (6:00) (6:38)	1985	10.00
❑ L33-17078 [DJ]	Just Another Day (5:10) (3:58)	1985	10.00
❑ L33-17193 [DJ]	Pain (same on both sides)	1986	10.00
❑ L33-17288 [DJ]	Not My Slave (same on both sides)	1987	8.00
❑ L33-17660 [DJ]	Cinderella Undercover/ Winning Side	1988	8.00
❑ L33-18005 [DJ]	Flesh and Blood (3 versions)	1989	12.00
❑ 23574	Weird Science (3 versions)	1985	8.00
❑ 23638	Stay (Stay Late Mix)/ Dead Man's Party (Party 'Til You're Dead Mix)	1986	12.00
❑ 23696	Pain (4 versions)	1986	8.00
❑ 23752	Not My Slave (7:40) (5:52)	1987	10.00
❑ 24022	Out of Control (6 versions)	1990	10.00

45s

Number	Title (A Side/B Side)	Yr	NM
A&M			
❑ 2439	Private Life/Islands	1982	5.00
❑ 2504 [DJ]	Whole Day Off (stereo/mono)	1982	10.00
—Apparently, no stock copy exists			
❑ 2610	Wake Up (It's 1984)/ No Spill Blood	1983	5.00
MCA			
❑ 42013 [(5)]	BOI-NGO	1987	50.00
—Boxed set of five 45s, comprising the album of the same name			
❑ 52633	Weird Science/Weird Mama	1985	4.00
—B-side by Ira & the Geeks			
❑ 52633 [PS]	Weird Science/Weird Mama	1985	4.00
❑ 52726	Just Another Day/ Dead Man's Party	1985	4.00
❑ 52726 [PS]	Just Another Day/ Dead Man's Party	1985	4.00
❑ 52789	Stay/Heard Somebody Cry	1986	4.00
❑ 52789 [PS]	Stay/Heard Somebody Cry	1986	4.00
❑ 53050	Not My Slave/Where Do All My Friends Go	1987	4.00
❑ 53050 [PS]	Not My Slave/Where Do All My Friends Go	1987	4.00
❑ 53105	We Close Our Eyes/Where Do All My Friends Go	1987	4.00
❑ 53105 [PS]	We Close Our Eyes/Where Do All My Friends Go	1987	4.00
PELICAN			
❑ 1001	You Got Your Baby Back/ Ballad of the Caveman	1976	100.00
—As "The Mystic Knights of the Oingo Boingo"			
❑ 1001 [PS]	You Got Your Baby Back/ Ballad of the Caveman	1976	100.00
—As "The Mystic Knights of the Oingo Boingo"			

Albums

Number	Title (A Side/B Side)	Yr	NM
A&M			
❑ SP-3250	Only a Lad	1984	8.00
—Reissue of 4863			
❑ SP-3251	Nothing to Fear	1984	8.00
—Reissue of 4930			
❑ SP-3252	Good for Your Soul	1984	8.00
—Reissue of 4959			
❑ SP-4863	Only a Lad	1981	10.00
❑ SP-4903	Nothing to Fear	1982	10.00
❑ SP-4959	Good for Your Soul	1983	10.00
❑ SP-5217	Skeletons in the Closet	1988	10.00
I.R.S.			
❑ SP-70400	Oingo Boingo	1980	12.00
—Limited edition 12" version			
❑ SP-70400 [10]	Oingo Boingo	1980	12.00
—Four-song 10-inch EP			
MCA			
❑ 5665	Dead Man's Party	1985	10.00
❑ 5811	BOI-NGO	1987	10.00
❑ 6365	Dark at the End of the Tunnel	1990	10.00
❑ 8030 [(2)]	Boingo Alive	1988	12.00
❑ L33-18137 [DJ]	Dark at the End of the Tunnel	1990	40.00
—Promo-only picture disc			

O

OKLAHOMA WRANGLERS, THE

Number	Title (A Side/B Side)	Yr	NM
45s			
RCA VICTOR			
❑ 47-4376	Unhappy New Year/Savannah River Rag	1951	15.00

OLA AND THE JANGLERS

Number	Title (A Side/B Side)	Yr	NM
45s			
GNP CRESCENDO			
❑ 423	Let's Dance/Strolling Along	1969	8.00
❑ 427	What a Way to Die/That's Why I Cry	1969	8.00
❑ 432	California Sun/Baby, Baby, Baby	1970	8.00
LONDON			
❑ 20034	Eeny Meeny Miney Moe /I Can Wait	1967	10.00
Albums			
GNP CRESCENDO			
❑ GNPS-2050	Let's Dance/What a Way to Die	1969	20.00

OLD & IN THE WAY

JERRY GARCIA heads a bluegrass band!

Number	Title (A Side/B Side)	Yr	NM
Albums			
ROUND			
❑ RX-103	Old & In the Way	1975	25.00
SUGAR HILL			
❑ SH-3746	Old & In the Way	1987	10.00
	—Reissue of Round LP		

OLDFIELD, MIKE

Number	Title (A Side/B Side)	Yr	NM
10-Inch Singles			
VIRGIN			
❑ PR 361 [DJ]	Guilty//North Star/Platinum Finale	1979	100.00
12-Inch Singles			
KINETIC			
❑ PRO-A-9752 [DJ]	Far Above the Clouds (Jam & Spoon Mix) (Timewriters Big Bag of Secrets Mix) (Jam & Spoon Deep Inside Club) (Far Below the Bass)	1999	30.00
❑ 44669	Far Above the Clouds (Jam & Spoon Mix) (Timewriters Big Bag of Secrets Mix) (Jam & Spoon Deep Inside Club) (Far Below the Bass)	1999	12.00
REPRISE			
❑ PRO-A-7992 [(2)DJ]	Let There Be Light (BT's Pure Luminescence Remix)/(The Ultraviolet Mix Edit)//(Hardfloor Remix) (Hardfloor Dub)/(BT's Entropic Dub)	1995	25.00
❑ 40749	Sentinel Restructure (Trance Mix) (Tubular Beats)/The Bell (Edit)//Sentinel Restructure (Satoshi Tomii Interpretation) (Global Lust Mix)	1992	20.00
❑ 43561	Let There Be Light (BT's Pure Luminescense Remix) (BT's Entropic Dub)	1995	15.00
VIRGIN			
❑ PR 2113 [DJ]	Magic Touch (same on both sides)	1988	20.00
❑ PR 2181 [DJ]	Wind Chimes Part 2/North Point	1988	50.00
VIRGIN/EPIC			
❑ AS 1424 [DJ]	Five Miles Out/Family Man	1982	30.00
45s			
VIRGIN			
❑ PR 199 [DJ]	Tubular Bells (same on both sides?)	1974	25.00
❑ PR 223 [DJ]	Hergest Ridge (two different edits?)	1974	20.00
❑ 9505	Theme: From Ommadawn/ On Horseback	1975	6.00
❑ 9510	Portsmouth/Argiers	1975	6.00
❑ 55100	Tubular Bells (Now the Original Theme from the Movie "The Exorcist")/Tubular Bells	1973	8.00
❑ 99402	Magic Touch/Wind Chimes Part 1	1987	4.00
❑ 99402 [PS]	Magic Touch/Wind Chimes Part 1	1987	4.00
VIRGIN/EPIC			
❑ 14-02877	Family Man/Mount Teidi	1982	6.00
7-Inch Extended Plays			
VIRGIN			
❑ PR 196 [DJ]	Tubular Bells Excerpts	1974	25.00
	—Six different edits; promo only		
Albums			
VIRGIN			
❑ QD 13-105 [Q]	Tubular Bells	1974	25.00
❑ VR 13-105	Tubular Bells	1973	15.00
	—First stereo issue of this album		
❑ VR 13-109	Hergest Ridge	1974	12.00
	—First issue of this album		
❑ VR 13-109 [DJ]	Hergest Ridge	1974	20.00
	—Promo only; banded for airplay		
❑ VR 13-115	The Orchestral Tubular Bells	1975	12.00
❑ VR 13135	Tubular Bells	1979	10.00
	—Third stereo issue of this album		
❑ VR 13143 [(2)]	Airborn	1980	15.00
	—U.S.-only compilation, which may make it much more valuable overseas		
❑ PZ 33913	Ommadawn	1975	12.00
	—Original U.S. issue of this album		
❑ PZ 33913 [DJ]	Ommadawn	1975	20.00
	—Promo only; banded for airplay		
❑ PZQ 33913 [Q]	Ommadawn	1975	20.00
❑ PZ 34116	Tubular Bells	1976	12.00
	—Second stereo issue of this album (note the "PZ" prefix)		
❑ 90589	Tubular Bells	1987	8.00
	—Fifth stereo issue of this album		
❑ 90590	Hergest Ridge	1987	8.00
	—Reissue of Virgin International 2013		
❑ 90591	The Killing Fields	1987	10.00
❑ 90645	Islands	1988	10.00
❑ 90894	The Orchestral Tubular Bells	1989	10.00
	—Reissue of 13-115		
❑ 91270	Earth Moving	1990	12.00
VIRGIN INTERNATIONAL			
❑ VI-2013	Hergest Ridge	1979	10.00
	—Reissue of 13-109; not to be confused with UK pressings that have only a "V" prefix		
❑ VI-2043	Ommadawn	1979	10.00
	—Reissue of 33913; not to be confused with UK pressings that have only a "V" prefix		
VIRGIN/EPIC			
❑ PE 34116	Tubular Bells	1982	8.00
	—Fourth stereo issue of this album (note the "PE" prefix)		
❑ FE 37358	QE2	1981	10.00
❑ ARE 37983	Five Miles Out	1982	10.00
❑ HE 44116	Tubular Bells	1982	30.00
	—Half-speed mastered edition		

OLDHAM, ANDREW

Number	Title (A Side/B Side)	Yr	NM
45s			
PARROT			
❑ 9684	Theme from The Dick Van Dyke Show/I'd Like to See Me on the "B" Side	1964	30.00
❑ 9745	I Get Around/Save It For Me	1965	30.00
Albums			
LONDON			
❑ PS 457 [S]	The Rolling Stones Songbook	1965	150.00
❑ LL 3457 [M]	The Rolling Stones Songbook	1965	100.00
PARROT			
❑ PA 61003 [M]	East Meets West	1965	80.00
❑ PAS 71003 [S]	East Meets West	1965	100.00

OLENN, JOHNNY

Number	Title (A Side/B Side)	Yr	NM
45s			
ANTLER			
❑ 1101	My Sweetie Pie/For the First Time	1959	40.00
❑ 1105	Born Reckless/You, Loveable You	1959	40.00
❑ 4009	My Sweetie Pie/Smile	1957	40.00
❑ 4018	The Magic Touch/Football Freddy	1957	40.00
ENTREE			
❑ AM-2000/3	Gotta' Keep Movin' (Keep Movin' On)/You've Got the Magic Touch	195?	30.00
LIBERTY			
❑ 55053	Candy Kisses/My Idea of Love	1957	25.00
PERSONALITY			
❑ 1002	Teenie/Devil Darling	1959	50.00
TNT			
❑ 1016	Candy Kisses/Sally Let Your Bangs Hang Down	1955	50.00
❑ 1018	I Ain't Gonna Cry No More/Blues Stay Away from Me	1955	50.00
Albums			
LIBERTY			
❑ LRP-3029 [M]	Just Rollin' with Johnny Olenn	1956	300.00

OLIVA, TONY

Number	Title (A Side/B Side)	Yr	NM
Albums			
KUBANY			
❑ SD-600	My Favorite Music	1966	30.00

OLIVER, WARD

Number	Title (A Side/B Side)	Yr	NM
45s			
HIT			
❑ 36	Next Door to an Angel/He's a Rebel	1962	10.00
	—B-side by the Gleams		

OLIVER AND THE TWISTERS

Number	Title (A Side/B Side)	Yr	NM
45s			
COLPIX			
❑ 615	Mother Goose Twist/Locomotion Twist	1961	12.00
❑ 615 [PS]	Mother Goose Twist/Locomotion Twist	1961	25.00
Albums			
COLPIX			
❑ CP-423 [M]	Look Who's Twistin' Everybody	1961	40.00

OLIVERS, THE

Number	Title (A Side/B Side)	Yr	NM
45s			
PHALANX			
❑ 1022	Bleecker Street/I Saw What You Did	1967	60.00
RCA VICTOR			
❑ 47-9113	Bleecker Street/I Saw What You Did	1967	20.00

OLIVES, THE

Number	Title (A Side/B Side)	Yr	NM
45s			
HIT			
❑ 306	How Can I Be Sure/Come Back When You Grow Up	1967	8.00
	—B-side by Jimmy Lewis and the Elfs		

OLLIE AND THE NIGHTINGALES

Number	Title (A Side/B Side)	Yr	NM
45s			
STAX			
❑ 0014	You're Leaving Me/Showered with Love	1968	6.00
❑ 0027	The Mellow Way You Treat Your Man/Don't Do What I Did	1969	6.00
❑ 0045	I've Got a Feeling/You'll Never Do Wrong	1969	6.00
❑ 0065	I'll Be Your Anything/Bracing Myself for the Fall	1970	6.00
❑ 245	I Got a Sure Thing/Girl You Have My Heart Singing	1968	8.00
Albums			
STAX			
❑ STS-2021	Ollie and the Nightingales	1969	50.00

OLSEN, DOROTHY

Number	Title (A Side/B Side)	Yr	NM
45s			
RCA VICTOR			
❑ 47-7654	The Christmas Spirit/Little Donkey	1959	15.00

OLSSON, NIGEL

Drummer in ELTON JOHN's band.

Number	Title (A Side/B Side)	Yr	NM
12-Inch Singles			
BANG			
❑ 2Z8-4801	Little Bit of Soap (5:28)/Cassey Blue-Au Revoir (6:24)	1979	15.00
45s			
BANG			
❑ 740	Dancin' Shoes/Living in a Fantasy	1978	5.00
❑ 4800	Little Bit of Soap/Thinking of You	1979	4.00
❑ 4803	Part of the Chosen Few/All It Takes	1979	4.00
COLUMBIA			
❑ 10733	Rainy Day/Right or Wrong	1978	5.00
ROCKET			
❑ 40337	Only One Woman/In Good Time	1974	5.00
❑ 40455	Something Lacking in Me/Songs I Sing	1975	5.00
❑ 40491	A Girl Like You/Girl, We've Got to Keep On	1975	5.00
UNI			
❑ 55291	Some Sweet Day/Weirdhouse	1971	6.00
	—As "Nigel Olsson's Drum Orchestra"		
❑ 55308	And I Know in My Heart/Sunshine Looks Like Rain	1971	6.00
Albums			
BANG			
❑ JZ 35792	Nigel	1979	10.00
❑ JZ 36491	Changing Tides	1980	10.00
ROCKET			
❑ L33-1962 [DJ]	Drummers Can Sing Too!	1975	20.00
	—Promo-only interview album		
❑ PIG-2158	Nigel Olsson	1975	12.00

Number	Title (A Side/B Side)	Yr	NM
UNI			
❑ 73113	Nigel Olsson's Drum Orchestra	1971	15.00

OLYMPIC RUNNERS PETE WINGFIELD was in this group.

Number	Title (A Side/B Side)	Yr	NM
45s			
LONDON			
❑ 202	Do It Over/Put the Music Where Your Mouth Is	1974	5.00
❑ 216	Grab It/Let Your Fingers Do the Talking	1974	5.00
❑ 217	Sproutin' Out/Be My Main Squeeze	1975	5.00
❑ 219	Drag It Over Here/Mac B. Coolie	1975	5.00
❑ 227	Dump the Bump/Exit City	1976	5.00
❑ 233	Party Time Is Here to Stay/ 'Til the Sun Comes Up	1976	5.00
❑ 247	Say What You Wanna But It Sure Is Funny/It's Only Love	1976	5.00
❑ 261	Keep It Up/The Kool Gent	1977	5.00
POLYDOR			
❑ 2008	The Bitch/Onya	1979	4.00
❑ 2030	God Bless You/The Bitch	1979	4.00
Albums			
LONDON			
❑ PS 653	Put the Music Where Your Mouth Is	1974	15.00
❑ PS 658	Out in Front	1975	15.00
❑ PS 668	Don't Let Up	1975	15.00
❑ PS 678	Hot to Trot	1977	15.00
POLYDOR			
❑ PD-1-6196	Dancealot	1979	12.00

OLYMPICS, THE Also see THE CHALLENGERS (3); WALTER WARD AND THE CHALLENGERS.

Number	Title (A Side/B Side)	Yr	NM
45s			
ARVEE			
❑ 562	(Baby) Hully Gully/Private Eye	1959	25.00
❑ 595	Big Boy Pete/The Slop	1960	25.00
❑ 5006	Shimmy Like Kate/Workin' Hard	1960	20.00
❑ 5020	Dance by the Light of the Moon/ Dodge City	1960	20.00
❑ 5023	Little Pedro/The Bullfight	1961	20.00
❑ 5031	Stay Where You Are/Dooley	1961	40.00
❑ 5044	Mash Them 'Taters/The Stomp	1961	20.00
❑ 5051	Everybody Likes to Cha Cha Cha/The Twist	1962	15.00
❑ 5056	Baby It's Hot/The Scotch	1962	15.00
❑ 5073	What'd I Say (Part 1)/ What'd I Say (Part 2)	1963	15.00
❑ 6501	Big Boy Pete '65/ Stay Where You Are	1965	12.00
DEMON			
❑ 1508	Western Movies/Well!	1958	30.00
❑ 1512	Dance with the Teacher/ Everybody Needs Love	1958	25.00
❑ 1514	Your Love/The Chicken	1959	25.00
DUO DISC			
❑ 104	The Boogler (Part 1)/ The Boogler (Part 2)	1964	12.00
❑ 105	Return of Big Boy Pete/ Return of the Watusi	1964	12.00
JUBILEE			
❑ 5674	The Cartoon Song/Things That Make Me Laugh	1969	8.00
LOMA			
❑ 2010	I'm Comin' Home/ Rainin' in My Heart	1965	10.00
❑ 2013	Good Lovin'/Olympic Shuffle	1965	10.00
❑ 2017	Baby I'm Yours/No More Will I Cry	1965	10.00
LOST-NITE			
❑ 311	Big Boy Pete/Mine Exclusively	197?	5.00
MGM			
❑ 14505	Worm in Your Wheatgerm/ The Apartment	1973	5.00
MIRWOOD			
❑ 5504	We Go Together (Pretty Baby)/ Secret Agents	1966	8.00
❑ 5513	Mine Exclusively/Secret Agents	1966	8.00
❑ 5523	Baby Do the Philly Dog/ Western Movies	1966	8.00
❑ 5525	The Bounce/The Duck	1966	8.00
❑ 5529	The Same Old Thing/ I'll Do a Little Bit More	1967	8.00
❑ 5533	Big Boy Pete/(Baby) Hully Gully	1967	8.00
PARKWAY			
❑ 6003	Lookin' for a Love/Good Things	1968	8.00
TITAN			
❑ 1718	The Chicken/Cool Short	1961	25.00

Yoko Ono, *Feeling The Space*, Apple SW-3412, 1973, **$20.**

Number	Title (A Side/B Side)	Yr	NM
TRI DISC			
❑ 105	Return of Big Boy Pete/ Return of the Watusi	1962	15.00
❑ 106	The Bounce/Fireworks	1963	15.00
❑ 107	Dancin' Holiday/Do the Slauson Shuffle	1963	15.00
❑ 110	Bounce Again/A New Dancin' Partner	1963	15.00
❑ 112	The Broken Hip/So Goodbye	1963	15.00
WARNER BROS.			
❑ 7369	Girl, You're My Kind of People/ Please, Please, Please	1970	6.00
7-Inch Extended Plays			
ARVEE			
❑ 423	(contents unknown)	1960	200.00
❑ 423 [PS]	Doin' the Hully Gully	1960	200.00
Albums			
ARVEE			
❑ A-423 [M]	Doin' the Hully Gully	1960	160.00
❑ A-424 [M]	Dance by the Light of the Moon	1961	120.00
❑ A-429 [M]	Party Time	1961	120.00
EVEREST			
❑ 4109	The Olympics	1981	10.00
MIRWOOD			
❑ MS-7003 [S]	Something Old, Something New	1966	50.00
❑ MW-7003 [M]	Something Old, Something New	1966	40.00
POST			
❑ 8000	The Olympics Sing	196?	25.00
RHINO			
❑ RNDF-207	The Official Record Album of the Olympics	1983	12.00
TRI-DISC			
❑ 1001 [M]	Do the Bounce	1963	80.00

OMEGAS, THE (1)

Number	Title (A Side/B Side)	Yr	NM
45s			
DECCA			
❑ 31008	When You Touch Me/Froze	1959	20.00
❑ 31094	So How Come (No One Loves Me)/Study Hall	1960	20.00
❑ 31138	Falling in Love/No One Will Ever Know	1960	20.00
GROOVE			
❑ 4	I Wanna Go Home/Midnight Run	1961	15.00

OMEGAS, THE (2)

Number	Title (A Side/B Side)	Yr	NM
45s			
UNITED ARTISTS			
❑ 50247	I Can't Believe/Mr. Yates	1968	30.00

OMNIBUS

Number	Title (A Side/B Side)	Yr	NM
45s			
UNITED ARTISTS			
❑ 50631	It's All in Your Heart/ The Man Song	1970	8.00
Albums			
UNITED ARTISTS			
❑ UAS-6743	Omnibus	1970	40.00

100 PROOF AGED IN SOUL

Number	Title (A Side/B Side)	Yr	NM
45s			
HOT WAX			
❑ 6904	Too Many Cooks (Spoil the Soup)/Not Enough Love to Satisfy	1969	6.00
—Later pressings as "100 Proof Aged in Soul"			
❑ 6904	Too Many Cooks (Spoil the Soup)/Not Enough Love to Satisfy	1969	12.00
—First pressings as "Aged in Soul"			
❑ 7004	Somebody's Been Sleeping/ I've Come to Save You	1970	6.00
❑ 7009	One Man's Leftovers (Is Another Man's Feast)/ If I Could See the Light in the Window	1970	6.00
❑ 7104	Driveway/Love Is Sweeter	1971	6.00

Roy Orbison, "Crying," Monument 447, 1961, $40.

Number	Title (A Side/B Side)	Yr	NM
❑ 7108	90 Day Freeze (On Her Love)/ Not Enough Love to Satisfy	1971	6.00
❑ 7202	Everything Good Is Bad/I'd Rather Fight Than Switch	1972	6.00
❑ 7206	Don't Scratch/If I Could See the Light in the Window	1972	6.00
❑ 7211	Nothing Sweeter Than Love/ Since You've Been Gone	1972	6.00

Albums

HOT WAX

Number	Title (A Side/B Side)	Yr	NM
❑ 704	Somebody's Been Sleeping in My Bed	1970	15.00
❑ 712	100 Proof Aged in Soul	1971	15.00

ONO, YOKO

Also see JOHN LENNON.

12-Inch Singles

GEFFEN

Number	Title (A Side/B Side)	Yr	NM
❑ PRO-A-934 [DJ]	Walking on Thin Ice (3:23) (5:58)	1981	15.00
❑ PRO-A-975 [DJ]	No, No, No/Dogtown/I Don't Know Why/She Gets Down on Her Knees	1981	20.00

POLYDOR

Number	Title (A Side/B Side)	Yr	NM
❑ PRO 192 [DJ]	My Man/Let the Tears Dry	1982	10.00
❑ 810575-1	Never Say Goodbye (Remix)/ Loneliness (Remix)	1983	15.00
❑ 883455-1	Hell in Paradise (Club Version) (Dub Version) (Single Version)	1985	8.00
❑ 883872-1 [DJ]	Walking on Thin Ice (Remix 7:17)/Cape Clear (2 versions)	1986	15.00

45s

APPLE

Number	Title (A Side/B Side)	Yr	NM
❑ GM/OYB-1 [DJ]	Greenfield Morning/ Open Your Box	1971	800.00
—Exactly six copies made for the personal use of Yoko Ono.			
❑ 1839	Mrs. Lennon/Midsummer New York	1971	7.00
—As "Yoko Ono/Plastic Ono Band"			
❑ 1853	Now or Never/Move On Fast	1972	7.00
❑ 1853 [PS]	Now or Never/Move On Fast	1972	8.00
❑ 1859	Death of Samantha/Yang Yang	1973	7.00
❑ 1867	Woman Power/Men, Men, Men	1973	7.00

CAPITOL

Number	Title (A Side/B Side)	Yr	NM
❑ S7-18550	Never Say Goodbye/ We're All Water	1995	4.00

GEFFEN

Number	Title (A Side/B Side)	Yr	NM
❑ PRO-S-935 [DJ]	Walking on Thin Ice (3:23) (5:58)	1981	12.00
❑ 49683	Walking on Thin Ice/It Happened	1981	5.00
❑ 49683 [PS]	Walking on Thin Ice/It Happened	1981	5.00
—Includes picture sleeve and lyric insert			
❑ 49802	No, No, No/Will You Touch Me	1981	5.00
❑ 49802 [PS]	No, No, No/Will You Touch Me	1981	5.00
❑ 49849	Goodbye Sadness/ I Don't Know Why	1981	5.00

POLYDOR

Number	Title (A Side/B Side)	Yr	NM
❑ 2224	My Man/Let the Tears Dry	1982	4.00
❑ 2224 [PS]	My Man/Let the Tears Dry	1982	4.00
❑ 883455-7	Hell in Paradise/(Instrumental)	1985	4.00
❑ 883455-7 [PS]	Hell in Paradise/(Instrumental)	1985	4.00

Albums

APPLE

Number	Title (A Side/B Side)	Yr	NM
❑ SW-3373	Yoko Ono Plastic Ono Band	1970	20.00
❑ SVBB-3380 [(2)]	Fly	1971	25.00
❑ SVBB-3399 [(2)]	Approximately Infinite Universe	1973	25.00
❑ SW-3412	Feeling the Space	1973	20.00

CAPITOL

Number	Title (A Side/B Side)	Yr	NM
❑ SPRO-11219 [DJ]	Rising Mixes	1996	12.00
—Promo-only vinyl EP of six remixes from the CD "Rising"			

GEFFEN

Number	Title (A Side/B Side)	Yr	NM
❑ GHS 2004	Season of Glass	1981	12.00

POLYDOR

Number	Title (A Side/B Side)	Yr	NM
❑ PD-1-6364	It's Alright (I See Rainbows)	1982	10.00
❑ 823289-1	It's Alright (I See Rainbows)	1984	8.00
—Reissue			
❑ 827530-1	Starpeace	1985	12.00

OPALS, THE (1)

45s

APOLLO

Number	Title (A Side/B Side)	Yr	NM
❑ 462	My Heart's Desire/ Oh But She Did	1954	200.00
—Original with flat (non-glossy) label			
❑ 462	My Heart's Desire/ Oh But She Did	1958	40.00
—Reissue with glossy label			

OPALS, THE (2)

45s

BELTONE

Number	Title (A Side/B Side)	Yr	NM
❑ 2025	Love/Two-Sided Love	1962	25.00

OPALS, THE (3)

45s

OKEH

Number	Title (A Side/B Side)	Yr	NM
❑ 7188	Does It Matter/Tender Lover	1964	25.00
❑ 7202	You Can't Hurt Me No More/ Rhythm	1964	25.00
❑ 7224	I'm So Afraid/Restless Lover	1965	25.00

OPALS, THE (U)

May be group (3); could be a different group.

45s

LAURIE

Number	Title (A Side/B Side)	Yr	NM
❑ 3288	No, No, Never Again/ Just Like a Little Bitty Baby	1965	12.00

ORANG UTAN

Albums

BELL

Number	Title (A Side/B Side)	Yr	NM
❑ 6054	Orang Utan	1971	40.00

ORANGE COLORED SKY

45s

UNI

Number	Title (A Side/B Side)	Yr	NM
❑ 55088	Orange Colored Sky/ The Shadow of Summer	1968	12.00
❑ 55115	Happiness Is/Another Sky	1969	12.00
❑ 55156	The Sun and I/Sweet Potato	1969	12.00

Albums

UNI

Number	Title (A Side/B Side)	Yr	NM
❑ 73031	Orange Colored Sky	1968	50.00

ORANGE WEDGE

Albums

(NO LABEL)

Number	Title (A Side/B Side)	Yr	NM
❑ (no #)	No One Left But Me	1975	300.00
❑ (no #)	Wedge	1975	300.00

ORBISON, ROY

12-Inch Singles

VIRGIN

Number	Title (A Side/B Side)	Yr	NM
❑ PR 2593 [DJ]	You Got It (same on both sides)	1989	12.00
❑ PR 2667 [DJ]	She's a Mystery to Me (same on both sides)	1989	15.00

45s

ASYLUM

Number	Title (A Side/B Side)	Yr	NM
❑ 46048	Tears/Easy Way Out	1979	5.00
❑ 46541	Poor Baby/Lay It Down	1979	5.00

ERIC

Number	Title (A Side/B Side)	Yr	NM
❑ 7101	Pretty Paper/Oh Pretty Woman	197?	4.00

JE-WEL

Number	Title (A Side/B Side)	Yr	NM
❑ 101	Ooby Dooby/Tryin' to Get to You	1956	4000.
—As "The Teen Kings"; with "Vocal: Roy Oribson" credit (spelled incorrectly). VG 1500 ; VG+ 2750			
❑ 101	Ooby Dooby/Tryin' to Get to You	1956	4000.
—As "The Teen Kings"; with "Vocal: Roy Orbison" credit (spelled correctly). VG 1500; VG+ 2750			

MERCURY

Number	Title (A Side/B Side)	Yr	NM
❑ 73610	Sweet Mama Blue/Heartache	1974	8.00
❑ 73652	Hung Up onYou/Spanish Nights	1975	6.00
❑ 73705	It's Lonely/Still	1975	6.00

MGM

Number	Title (A Side/B Side)	Yr	NM
❑ CS9-5	Celebrity Scene: Roy Orbison	1967	100.00
—Box set of five singles (13756-13760). Price includes box, all 5 singles, jukebox title strips, bio. Records are sometimes found by themselves, so they are also listed separately.			
❑ 13386	Ride Away/Wonderin'	1965	10.00
❑ 13386 [PS]	Ride Away/Wonderin'	1965	20.00
❑ 13410	Crawling Back/If You Can't Say Something Nice	1965	10.00
❑ 13410 [PS]	Crawling Back/If You Can't Say Something Nice	1965	20.00
❑ 13446	Breakin' Up Is Breakin' My Heart/ Wait	1966	10.00
❑ 13446 [PS]	Breakin' Up Is Breakin' My Heart/ Wait	1966	20.00
❑ 13498	Twinkle Toes/Where Is Tomorrow	1966	10.00
❑ 13498 [PS]	Twinkle Toes/Where Is Tomorrow	1966	20.00
❑ 13549	Too Soon to Know/You'll Never Be Sixteen Again	1966	10.00
❑ 13549 [PS]	Too Soon to Know/You'll Never Be Sixteen Again	1966	100.00
❑ 13634	Communication Breakdown/ Going Back to Gloria	1966	10.00

Except when noted otherwise, VG = 25% of NM, and VG+ = 50% of NM. (Example: VG = $2.00, VG+ = $4.00 and NM = $8.00.)

Number	Title (A Side/B Side)	Yr	NM
❑ 13685	So Good/Memories	1967	10.00
❑ 13756	Ride Away/Crawlin' Back	1967	15.00
—Part of Celebrity Scene CS9-5			
❑ 13757	Breakin' Up Is Breakin' My Heart/Too Soon to Know	1967	15.00
—Part of Celebrity Scene CS9-5			
❑ 13758	Twinkle Toes/Where Is Tomorrow?	1967	15.00
—Part of Celebrity Scene CS9-5			
❑ 13759	Sweet Dreams/Going Back to Gloria	1967	15.00
—Part of Celebrity Scene CS9-5			
❑ 13760	You'll Never Be Sixteen Again/There Won't Be Many Coming Home	1967	15.00
—Part of Celebrity Scene CS9-5			
❑ 13764	Cry Softly Lonely One/Pistolero	1967	10.00
❑ 13764 [PS]	Cry Softly Lonely One/Pistolero	1967	20.00
❑ 13817	She/Here Comes the Rain Baby	1967	10.00
❑ 13889	Shy Away/Born to Be Loved by You	1968	10.00
❑ 13950	Flowers/Walk On	1968	10.00
❑ 13991	Heartache/Sugar Man	1968	10.00
❑ 14039	Southbound Jericho Parkway/My Friend	1969	10.00
❑ 14079	Penny Arcade/Tennessee Own My Soul	1969	10.00
❑ 14105	How Do You Start Over/She Cheats on Me	1970	10.00
❑ 14121	So Young/If I Had a Woman Like You	1970	10.00
❑ 14293	Close Again/Last Night	1971	10.00
❑ 14358	Changes/God Loves You	1972	10.00
❑ 14413	Remember the Good/Harlem Woman	1972	10.00
❑ 14413	Remember the Good/If Only for a While	1972	10.00
❑ 14441	I Can Read Between the Lines/Memphis, Tennessee	1972	10.00
❑ 14552	Rain Rain (Coming Down)/Sooner or Later	1973	10.00
❑ 14626	I Wanna Live/You Lay So Easy on My Mind	1973	10.00

MONUMENT

Number	Title (A Side/B Side)	Yr	NM
❑ 45-200	(I'm a) Southern Man/Born to Love Me	1976	5.00
❑ 45-215	Drifting Away/Under Suspicion	1977	5.00
❑ 409	Paper Boy/With the Bug	1959	80.00
—White label with vertical lines			
❑ 412	Uptown/Pretty One	1959	30.00
❑ 421	Only the Lonely (Know the Way I Feel)/Here Comes That Song Again	1960	25.00
❑ 425	Blue Angel/Today's Teardrops	1960	20.00
❑ 433	I'm Hurtin'/I Can't Stop Loving You	1960	20.00
❑ 433 [PS]	I'm Hurtin'/I Can't Stop Loving You	1960	120.00
❑ 438	Running Scared/Love Hurts	1961	20.00
❑ 438 [PS]	Running Scared/Love Hurts	1961	40.00
❑ 447	Crying/Candy Man	1961	20.00
❑ 447 [PS]	Crying/Candy Man	1961	40.00
❑ 456	Dream Baby (How Long Must I Dream)/The Actress	1962	20.00
❑ 456 [PS]	Dream Baby (How Long Must I Dream)/The Actress	1962	40.00
❑ 461	The Crowd/Mama	1962	20.00
❑ 461 [PS]	The Crowd/Mama	1962	40.00
❑ 467	Leah/Workin' for the Man	1962	20.00
❑ 467 [PS]	Leah/Workin' for the Man	1962	40.00
❑ 503	Paper Boy/With the Bug	196?	12.00
—Reissue of 409			
❑ 505	Uptown/Pretty One	196?	12.00
—Reissue of 412			
❑ 508	Only the Lonely (Know the Way I Feel)/Here Comes That Song Again	196?	12.00
—Reissue of 421			
❑ 509	Blue Angel/Today's Teardrops	196?	12.00
—Reissue of 425			
❑ 510	I'm Hurtin'/I Can't Stop Loving You	196?	12.00
—Reissue of 433			
❑ 514	Running Scared/Love Hurts	196?	12.00
—Reissue of 438			
❑ 517	Crying/Candy Man	196?	12.00
—Reissue of 447			
❑ 519	Dream Baby (How Long Must I Dream)/The Actress	196?	12.00
—Reissue of 456			
❑ 520	The Crowd/Mama	196?	12.00
—Reissue of 461			
❑ 521	Leah/Working for the Man	196?	12.00
—Reissue of 467; note that the B-side title is slightly different here than on 467			
❑ 526	In Dreams/Shahdaroba	196?	12.00
—Reissue of 806			
❑ 527	Falling/Distant Drums	196?	12.00
—Reissue of 815			
❑ 530	Mean Woman Blues/Blue Bayou	196?	12.00
—Reissue of 824			
❑ 531	Pretty Paper/Beautiful Dreamer	196?	12.00
—Reissue of 830			
❑ 533	It's Over/Indian Wedding	196?	12.00
—Reissue of 837			
❑ 806	In Dreams/Shahdaroba	1963	20.00
❑ 806 [PS]	In Dreams/Shahdaroba	1963	40.00
❑ 815	Falling/Distant Drums	1963	20.00
❑ 815 [PS]	Falling/Distant Drums	1963	50.00
❑ 824	Mean Woman Blues/Blue Bayou	1963	20.00
❑ 830	Pretty Paper/Beautiful Dreamer	1963	20.00
❑ 837	It's Over/Indian Wedding	1964	20.00
❑ 837 [PS]	It's Over/Indian Wedding	1964	40.00
❑ 851	Oh Pretty Woman/Yo Te Amo Maria	1964	20.00
—Revised title			
❑ 851	Pretty Woman/Yo Te Amo Maria	1964	30.00
—Original title			
❑ 873	Goodnight/Only with You	1965	15.00
❑ 891	(Say) You're My Girl/Sleepy Hollow	1965	15.00
❑ 906	Let the Good Times Roll/Distant Drums	1965	15.00
❑ 939	Lana/Our Summer Song	1966	15.00
❑ 1900	Running Scared/Love Hurts	197?	4.00
—"Golden Series" reissue			
❑ 1901	Crying/Candy Man	197?	4.00
—"Golden Series" reissue			
❑ 1902	Leah/Workin' for the Man	197?	4.00
—"Golden Series" reissue			
❑ 1903	Mean Woman Blues/Blue Bayou	197?	4.00
—"Golden Series" reissue			
❑ 1904	Falling/Distant Drums	197?	4.00
—"Golden Series" reissue			
❑ 1906	Only the Lonely (Know the Way I Feel)/Uptown	197?	4.00
—"Golden Series" reissue			
❑ 1907	Dream Baby (How Long Must I Dream)/I'm Hurtin'	197?	4.00
—"Golden Series" reissue			
❑ 1908	In Dreams/The Crowd	197?	4.00
—"Golden Series" reissue			
❑ 1910	Oh Pretty Woman/It's Over	197?	4.00
—"Golden Series" reissue			
❑ 1915	Blue Angel/Paper Boy	197?	4.00
—"Golden Series" reissue			
❑ 1936	Pretty Paper/Beautiful Dreamer	1976	4.00
—"Golden Series" reissue			
❑ 8690	Belinda/All These Chains	1976	5.00

NORTON

Number	Title (A Side/B Side)	Yr	NM
❑ 45-846	Domino/Everybody's Tryin' to Kiss My Baby	2001	4.00
—B-side by Gene Ross; includes custom company sleeve; Sun Records outtakes			

RCA VICTOR

Number	Title (A Side/B Side)	Yr	NM
❑ 47-7381	Sweet and Innocent/Seems to Me	1958	40.00
❑ 47-7447	Almost Eighteen/Julie	1959	40.00

SUN

Number	Title (A Side/B Side)	Yr	NM
❑ 242	Ooby Dooby/Go! Go! Go!	1956	100.00
❑ 251	Rockhouse/You're My Baby	1956	60.00
❑ 265	Devil Doll/Sweet and Easy to Love	1957	80.00
❑ 284	Chicken Hearted/I Like Love	1958	50.00
❑ 353	Devil Doll/Sweet and Easy to Love	1960	250.00

VIRGIN

Number	Title (A Side/B Side)	Yr	NM
❑ 99159	Oh Pretty Woman/Claudette	1989	3.00
❑ 99159 [PS]	Oh Pretty Woman/Claudette	1989	3.00
❑ 99202	California Blue/In Dreams	1989	3.00
❑ 99202 [PS]	California Blue/In Dreams	1989	3.00
❑ 99227	She's a Mystery to Me/Dream Baby	1989	3.00
❑ 99227 [PS]	She's a Mystery to Me/Dream Baby	1989	3.00
❑ 99245	You Got It/Crying	1989	4.00
—B-side with k.d. lang			
❑ 99245	You Got It/The Only One	1989	3.00
❑ 99245 [PS]	You Got It	1989	3.00
—The same sleeve may have come with both issues of the 45			
❑ 99388	Crying/Falling	1988	3.00
—A-side with k.d. lang			
❑ 99388 [PS]	Crying/Falling	1988	3.00
❑ 99434	In Dreams/Leah	1987	3.00
❑ 99434 [PS]	In Dreams/Leah	1987	4.00

WARNER BROS.

Number	Title (A Side/B Side)	Yr	NM
❑ 49262	That Lovin' You Feeling Again/Lola	1980	5.00
—A-side with Emmylou Harris; B-side by Craig Hundley			

7-Inch Extended Plays

MONUMENT

Number	Title (A Side/B Side)	Yr	NM
❑ MSP-2	Crying/Our Summer Song/Let's Make a Memory//Lana/Loneliness/Night Life	1962	100.00
—Probably a jukebox single; small hole, plays at 33 1/3 rpm; picture sleeve is unconfirmed			
❑ MSP-003	In Dreams/Lonely Wine/Shadharoba//Dream/Blue Bayou/Gigolette (They Call You)	1963	50.00
—Stereo jukebox issue; small hole, plays at 33 1/3 rpm			
❑ MSP-003 [PS]	Roy Orbison	1963	50.00
❑ SSP-512	Oh, Pretty Woman/Dance/Let the Good Times Roll//(I Get So) Sentimental/Wedding Day/I'd Be a Legend in My Time	1965	40.00
—Jukebox issue; small hole, plays at 33 1/3 rpm			
❑ SSP-512 [PS]	Orbisongs, Vol. One	1965	40.00

Albums

ACCORD

Number	Title	Yr	NM
❑ SN-7150	Ooby Dooby	1981	8.00

ASYLUM

Number	Title	Yr	NM
❑ 6E-198	Laminar Flow	1979	12.00

BUCKBOARD

Number	Title	Yr	NM
❑ BBS-1015	Roy Orbison's Golden Hits	197?	10.00

CANDELITE

Number	Title	Yr	NM
❑ P2 12946 [(2)]	The Living Legend of Roy Orbison	1976	15.00

DCC COMPACT CLASSICS

Number	Title	Yr	NM
❑ LPZ-2042 [(2)]	The All-Time Greatest Hits of Roy Orbison	1997	120.00
—Audiophile vinyl			

DESIGN

Number	Title	Yr	NM
❑ DLP-164 [M]	Orbiting with Roy Orbison	196?	15.00
❑ DLPS-164 [R]	Orbiting with Roy Orbison	196?	10.00

HALLMARK

Number	Title	Yr	NM
❑ SHM-824	The Exciting Roy Orbison	197?	8.00

HITS UNLIMITED

Number	Title	Yr	NM
❑ 233-0	My Spell on You	1982	8.00

MERCURY

Number	Title	Yr	NM
❑ SRM-1-1045	I'm Still in Love with You	1975	12.00

MGM

Number	Title	Yr	NM
❑ E-4308 [M]	There Is Only One Roy Orbison	1965	25.00
❑ SE-4308 [S]	There Is Only One Roy Orbison	1965	35.00
❑ E-4322 [M]	The Orbison Way	1965	25.00
❑ SE-4322 [S]	The Orbison Way	1965	35.00
❑ E-4379 [M]	The Classic Roy Orbison	1966	25.00
❑ SE-4379 [S]	The Classic Roy Orbison	1966	35.00
❑ E-4424 [M]	Roy Orbison Sings Don Gibson	1967	25.00
❑ SE-4424 [S]	Roy Orbison Sings Don Gibson	1967	35.00
❑ E-4514 [M]	Cry Softly, Lonely One	1967	25.00
❑ SE-4514 [S]	Cry Softly, Lonely One	1967	35.00
❑ SE-4636	The Many Moods of Roy Orbison	1969	25.00
❑ SE-4659	The Great Songs of Roy Orbison	1970	25.00
❑ SE-4683	Hank Williams the Roy Orbison Way	1970	25.00
❑ SE-4835	Roy Orbison Sings	1972	15.00
❑ SE-4867	Memphis	1972	15.00
❑ SE-4934	Milestones	1973	15.00
❑ ST 90454 [S]	There Is Only One Roy Orbison	1965	40.00
—Capitol Record Club edition			
❑ T 90454 [M]	There Is Only One Roy Orbison	1965	40.00
—Capitol Record Club edition			
❑ ST-90631 [S]	The Orbison Way	1965	35.00
—Capitol Record Club edition			
❑ T-90631 [M]	The Orbison Way	1965	35.00
—Capitol Record Club edition			
❑ ST-90928 [S]	The Classic Roy Orbison	1966	35.00
—Capitol Record Club edition			
❑ T-90928 [M]	The Classic Roy Orbison	1966	35.00
—Capitol Record Club edition			
❑ ST-91173 [S]	Roy Orbison Sings Don Gibson	1967	35.00
—Capitol Record Club edition			
❑ T-91173 [M]	Roy Orbison Sings Don Gibson	1967	35.00
—Capitol Record Club edition			

MONUMENT

Number	Title	Yr	NM
❑ M-4002 [M]	Lonely and Blue	1961	150.00
❑ M-4007 [M]	Crying	1962	120.00
❑ M-4009 [M]	Roy Orbison's Greatest Hits	1962	50.00
❑ MC-6619	Roy Orbison's Greatest Hits	1977	12.00
❑ MC-6620	In Dreams	1977	12.00
❑ MC-6621	More of Roy Orbison's Greatest Hits	1977	12.00
❑ MC-6622	The Very Best of Roy Orbison	1977	12.00
❑ MG-7600	Regeneration	1976	15.00
❑ MLP-8000 [M]	Roy Orbison's Greatest Hits	1963	30.00
❑ MLP-8003 [M]	In Dreams	1963	50.00
—White and rainbow label			
❑ MLP-8003 [M]	In Dreams	1964	30.00
—Green and gold label			
❑ MLP-8023 [M]	Early Orbison	1964	30.00
❑ MLP-8024 [M]	More of Roy Orbison's Greatest Hits	1964	30.00

Except when noted otherwise, VG = 25% of NM, and VG+ = 50% of NM. (Example: VG = $2.00, VG+ = $4.00 and NM = $8.00.)

Orchestral Manoeuvres in the Dark, "(Forever) Live and Die," A&M 2872, 1986, $3.

Number	Title (A Side/B Side)	Yr	NM
❑ MLP-8035 [M]	Orbisongs	1965	25.00
❑ MLP-8045 [M]	The Very Best of Roy Orbison	1966	25.00
❑ MP-8600 [(2)]	The All-Time Greatest Hits of Roy Orbison	1977	16.00
❑ SM-14002 [S]	Lonely and Blue	1961	600.00
❑ SM-14007 [S]	Crying	1962	600.00
❑ SM-14009 [S]	Roy Orbison's Greatest Hits	1962	80.00
❑ SLP-18000 [S]	Roy Orbison's Greatest Hits	1963	40.00
❑ SLP-18003 [S]	In Dreams	1963	100.00
—White and rainbow label			
❑ SLP-18003 [S]	In Dreams	1964	50.00
—Green and gold label			
❑ SLP-18023 [S]	Early Orbison	1964	50.00
❑ SLP-18024 [S]	More of Roy Orbison's Greatest Hits	1964	40.00
❑ SLP-18035 [S]	Orbisongs	1965	35.00
❑ SLP-18045 [P]	The Very Best of Roy Orbison	1966	35.00
—"It's Over" is rechanneled			
❑ KZG 31484 [(2)]	The All-Time Greatest Hits of Roy Orbison	1972	25.00
❑ KWG 38384 [(2)]	The All-Time Greatest Hits of Roy Orbison	1982	10.00
RHINO			
❑ R1 70711	The Classic Roy Orbison	1989	12.00
❑ R1 70916	The Sun Years	1989	15.00
❑ R1 71493 [(2)]	For the Lonely: A Roy Orbison Anthology	1988	12.00
S&P			
❑ 507 [(2)]	The All-Time Greatest Hits of Roy Orbison	2004	40.00
—Reissue on 180-gram vinyl			
SUN			
❑ 113	The Original Sound	1969	12.00
❑ LP-1260 [M]	Roy Orbison at the Rock House	1961	600.00
TIME-LIFE			
❑ SRNR 34 [(2)]	Roy Orbison 1960-1965	1990	20.00
—Box set in "The Rock 'n' Roll Era" series			
TRIP			
❑ TLX-8505	The Best of Roy Orbison	197?	8.00

Number	Title (A Side/B Side)	Yr	NM
VIRGIN			
❑ 90604 [(2)]	In Dreams: The Greatest Hits	1987	12.00
—Re-recordings of his original hits			
❑ 91058	Mystery Girl	1989	10.00
❑ 91295	A Black and White Night	1990	15.00

ORBITS, THE

More than one group.

45s

Number	Title (A Side/B Side)	Yr	NM
ARGO			
❑ 5286	Who Are You/Mr. Bad Luck	1958	40.00
DOOTO			
❑ 601	Tell Me Baby/Two Crazy Scientists	196?	20.00
FLAIR-X			
❑ 5000	Message of Love/I Really Do	1956	30.00
NU-KAT			
❑ 116/7	Knock Her Down/My Love	1959	30.00
SPACE			
❑ 1116	Queen Bee/Darlin'	1960	400.00

ORCHESTRAL MANOEUVRES IN THE DARK

12-Inch Singles

Number	Title (A Side/B Side)	Yr	NM
A&M			
❑ SP-12108	Locomotion/Her Body in My Soul/The Avenue	1984	10.00
❑ SP-12120	Tesla Girls (3 versions)	1984	10.00
❑ SP-12143	So in Love (Special American Remix)/Concrete Hands (Extended)	1985	10.00
❑ SP-12161	Secret (remix)/Firegun/ The Naive Daughters of Golden West	1985	10.00
❑ SP-12176	If You Leave (Extended)/ La Femme Accident (Remix)	1986	12.00
❑ SP-12202	(Forever) Live and Die (2 versions)/This Town	1986	10.00
❑ SP-12215	We Love You (Extended Version) (7" Version) (Dub Version)	1986	10.00
❑ SP-12258	Dreaming (Club Mix) (Radio Edit) (Dub)/Satellite	1988	8.00
❑ SP-12272	Secret (3 versions)/ Telegraph (Live)	1988	8.00
❑ SP-12285	Brides of Frankenstein (Remix) (Dub)	1988	8.00
❑ SP-17332 [DJ]	So in Love (same on both sides?)	1985	8.00
❑ SP-17367 [DJ]	If You Leave/Pretty in Pink	1986	15.00
—B-side by Psychedelic Furs; promo from movie "Pretty in Pink"			
❑ SP-17428 [DJ]	(Forever) Live and Die (same on both sides)	1986	10.00
❑ SP-17441 [DJ]	We Love You (7")/(Remix)	1986	8.00
VIRGIN			
❑ DMD 1665 [DJ]	Pandora's Box (4 versions)/ Sugar Tax	1991	10.00
❑ DMD 1802 [DJ]	Sailing on the Seven Seas (5 versions)	1991	10.00
❑ SPRO 12777 [DJ]	Stand Above Me (3 versions)	1993	10.00
VIRGIN/EPIC			
❑ AE 1247 [DJ]	Enola Gay/Messages	1980	15.00
❑ AE 1403 [DJ]	Georgia/Souvenir/She's Leaving/Joan of Arc	1981	15.00
❑ AE 1658 [DJ]	Telegraph (LP Version) (Edit)/ Radio Waves	1983	15.00

45s

Number	Title (A Side/B Side)	Yr	NM
A&M			
❑ 1209	Secret/Telegraph (Live)	1988	3.00
❑ 1209 [PS]	Secret/Telegraph (Live)	1988	3.00
❑ 2671	Locomotion/Her Body in My Soul	1984	4.00
❑ 2671 [PS]	Locomotion/Her Body in My Soul	1984	4.00
❑ 2746	So in Love/Concrete Hands	1985	3.00
❑ 2746 [PS]	So in Love/Concrete Hands	1985	3.00
❑ 2794	Secret/Firegun	1985	3.00
❑ 2794 [PS]	Secret/Firegun	1985	3.00
❑ 2811	If You Leave/La Femme Accident (6:15)	1986	3.00
❑ 2811	If You Leave/La Femme Accident (2:42)	1986	5.00
❑ 2811 [PS]	If You Leave/La Femme Accident	1986	5.00
❑ 2872	(Forever) Live and Die/This Town	1986	3.00
—Black label			
❑ 2872	(Forever) Live and Die/This Town	1986	5.00
—White label stock copy			
❑ 2872 [PS]	(Forever) Live and Die/This Town	1986	3.00
—The same sleeve was used with both stock pressings			
❑ 2897	We Love You/(Dub)	1986	5.00
❑ 2897 [PS]	We Love You/(Dub)	1986	15.00
❑ 3002	Dreaming/Satellite	1988	3.00
❑ 3002 [PS]	Dreaming/Satellite	1988	3.00
❑ 8669	If You Leave/Secret	198?	3.00
—Reissue			
VIRGIN			
❑ S7-17597	Dream of Me (Based on "Love's Theme")/Strange Sensations	1993	4.00
VIRGIN/EPIC			
❑ 14-02766	Souvenir/New Stone Age	1982	5.00
❑ 34-03891	Telegraph/This Is Helena	1983	6.00

Albums

Number	Title (A Side/B Side)	Yr	NM
A&M			
❑ SP6-5027	Junk Culture	1984	8.00
❑ SP-5077	Crush	1985	8.00
❑ SP-5144	The Pacific Age	1986	10.00
❑ SP-5186	The Best of O.M.D.	1988	10.00
❑ R 114546	The Pacific Age	1986	12.00
—RCA Music Service edition			
❑ R 184156	The Best of O.M.D.	1988	12.00
—BMG Direct Marketing edition			
VIRGIN			
❑ 90611	Orchestral Manoeuvres in the Dark	1987	10.00
—Reissue			
❑ 90612	Organisation	1987	10.00
—First U.S. issue of early LP			
❑ 91006	Dazzle Ships	1988	10.00
—Reissue			
VIRGIN/EPIC			
❑ FE 37411	Orchestral Manoeuvres in the Dark	1981	15.00
❑ ARE 37721	Architecture and Morality	1981	15.00
VIRGN/EPIC			
❑ BFE 38543	Dazzle Ships	1983	12.00

ORCHIDS, THE (1)

45s

Number	Title (A Side/B Side)	Yr	NM
COLUMBIA			
❑ 42913	That Boy Is Messin' Up My Mind/Harlem Tango	1963	20.00
❑ 43066	Tell Me a Story/From Bad to Worse	1964	20.00
❑ 43175	Christmas Is the Time to Be With Your Baby/It Doesn't Matter	1964	20.00

Except when noted otherwise, VG = 25% of NM, and VG+ = 50% of NM. (Example: VG = $2.00, VG+ = $4.00 and NM = $8.00.)

Number	Title (A Side/B Side)	Yr	NM
ORCHIDS, THE (2)			
45s			
HARLOW			
❑ 101	I Don't Think You Missed Me/ We're in Love	1962	20.00
ORCHIDS, THE (3)			
45s			
KING			
❑ 4661	Oh Why/All Night Baby	1953	400.00
❑ 4663	I've Been a Fool from the Start/ Beginning to Miss You	1953	400.00
LOST-NITE			
❑ 150	I Can't Refuse/You Said You Loved Me	196?	6.00
—Reissue			
❑ 159	Newly Wed/You're Everything to Me	196?	6.00
—Reissue			
PARROT			
❑ 815	Newly Wed/You're Everything to Me	1955	400.00
❑ 819	I Can't Refuse/You Said You Loved Me	1955	250.00
ORCHIDS, THE (U) Some of these could be group (1) or (2).			
45s			
ROULETTE			
❑ 4412	Pony Walk/Good Time Stomp	1962	20.00
❑ 4633	Good Good Time/Love Is What You Make It	1965	12.00
UNITED ARTISTS			
❑ 375	You'll Never Know/Say Yes	1961	20.00
WALL			
❑ 549	Soft Shadows/Good Gully	1961	20.00
Albums			
ROULETTE			
❑ R-25169 [M]	Twistin' at the Roundtable	1962	20.00
❑ SR-25169 [S]	Twistin' at the Roundtable	1962	25.00
ORGAN GRINDERS, THE			
45s			
SMASH			
❑ 2242	Babylon/Precious Time	1969	10.00
Albums			
MERCURY			
❑ SR-61282	Out of the Egg	1970	30.00
ORIENT EXPRESS, THE			
Albums			
MAINSTREAN			
❑ S-6117	The Orient Express	1969	80.00
ORIENTS, THE			
45s			
LAURIE			
❑ 3232	Queen of the Angels/Shouldn't I	1964	40.00
ORIGINAL CADILLACS, THE See THE CADILLACS.			
ORIGINAL CASUALS, THE			
45s			
BACK BEAT			
❑ 503	So Tough/I Love My Darling	1958	25.00
❑ 503	So Tough/I Love My Darling	1958	40.00
—Original pressings by "The Casuals"			
❑ 510	Ju-Judy/Don't Pass Me By	1958	25.00
❑ 514	Three Kisses Past Midnight/ It's Been a Long Time	1958	25.00
ORIGINAL LAST POETS, THE See THE LAST POETS.			
ORIGINAL SURFARIS, THE See THE SURFARIS (2).			
ORIGINAL TWISTERS, THE			
Albums			
WING			
❑ MGW-12217 [M]	Come On and Twist	1962	20.00
❑ SRW-16217 [S]	Come On and Twist	1962	25.00
ORIGINALS, THE (1)			
12-Inch Singles			
FANTASY			
❑ D-118	Blue Moon (8:27)/While the Cat's Away (7:34)	1979	12.00
❑ D-130	J-E-A-L-O-U-S (Means I Love You)/Jezebel (You've Got Me Under Your Spell)	1979	12.00
PHASE II			
❑ AS 917 [DJ]	Waitin' on a Letter/Mr. Postman (8:40) (Instrumental 8:56)	1981	10.00
❑ 4W8-5655	Waitin' on a Letter/Mr. Postman (8:40)//The Magic Is You (5:00)	1981	8.00
SOUL			
❑ M 00001D1	Down to Love Town (5:55)/Let's Be Young Tonight (5:07)	1976	20.00
—B-side by Jermaine Jackson on Motown			
45s			
FANTASY			
❑ 820	Take This Love/Ladies (We Need You)	1978	5.00
❑ 847	Blue Moon/Ladies (We Need You)	1979	5.00
❑ 856	J-E-A-L-O-U-S (Means I Love You)/Jezebel (You've Got Me Under Your Spell)	1979	5.00
MOTOWN			
❑ PR-1 [DJ]	Young Train (same on both sides?)	1973	200.00
❑ 1355	Good Lovin' Is Just a Dime Away/Nothing Can Take the Place (Of Your Love)	1975	6.00
❑ 1370	50 Years/Financial Affair	1975	6.00
❑ 1379	Everybody's Got to Do Something/(Instrumental)	1975	6.00
PHASE II			
❑ WS8-02061	Baby I'm for Real/ Share Your Love with Me	1981	4.00
❑ WS8-02147	The Magic Is You/Let Me Dance	1981	4.00
❑ ZS5-02724	Baby I'm for Real/ The Magic Is You	1982	4.00
—As "Hank Dixon and the Originals"			
❑ 5653	Waitin' on a Letter/Mr. Postman// (B-side unknown)	1981	5.00
SOUL			
❑ 35029	Goodnight Irene/Need Your Loving (Want It Back)	1967	12.00
❑ 35056	We've Got a Way Out Love/ You're the One	1969	12.00
❑ 35061	Green Grow the Lilacs/ You're the One	1969	12.00
❑ 35066	Baby I'm for Real/ The Moment of Truth	1969	8.00
❑ 35069	The Bells/I'll Wait for You	1970	8.00
❑ 35074	We Can Make It Baby/ I Like Your Style	1970	8.00
❑ 35074	We Can Make It/I Like Your Style	1970	12.00
❑ 35079	God Bless Whoever Sent You/ Desperate Young Man	1970	8.00
❑ 35085	Keep Me/A Man Without Love	1971	6.00
❑ 35093	I'm Someone Who Cares/ Once I Have You	1972	6.00
❑ 35102	Be My Love/Endlessly Love	1973	6.00
❑ 35109	First Lady (Sweet Mother's Love)/There's a Chance When You Love, You Love	1973	6.00
❑ 35112	Supernatural Voodoo Woman (Part 1)/Supernatural Voodoo Woman (Part 2)	1974	6.00
❑ 35113	Game Called Love/Ooh You Put a Spell on Me	1974	6.00
❑ 35115	You're My Only World/ So Near (And Yet So Far)	1974	6.00
❑ 35117	Touch/Ooh You Put a Spell on Me	1975	6.00
❑ 35119	Down to Love Town/ Just to Be Closer to You	1976	6.00
❑ 35121 [DJ]	Call On Your Six Million Dollar Man (mono/stereo)	1977	6.00
Albums			
FANTASY			
❑ F-9546	Another Time, Another Place	1978	10.00
❑ F-9577	Come Away with Me	1979	10.00
MOTOWN			
❑ M5-110V	Motown Superstar Series, Vol. 10	1982	10.00
❑ M7-826	California Sunset	1975	15.00
PHASE II			
❑ JW 37075	Yesterday and Today	1981	12.00
SOUL			
❑ SS-716	Baby I'm for Real	1969	40.00
❑ SS-724	Portrait of the Originals	1970	25.00
❑ SS-729	Naturally Together	1971	25.00
❑ SS-734	Definitions	1971	20.00
❑ SS-740	The Game Called...	1973	15.00
❑ SS-743	California Sunset	1974	—
—Unreleased			
❑ S7-746	Communique	1976	15.00
❑ S7-749	Down to Love Town	1977	15.00
ORIGINALS, THE (2)			
45s			
DIAMOND			
❑ 102	At Times Like These/Gimme a Little Kiss, Will Ya, Huh?	1961	40.00
❑ 116	Summer Schoo/You and I	1962	40.00
ORIGINALS, THE (3) CHUCK RIO was in this group.			
45s			
JACKPOT			
❑ 48007	The Whip/The Blue Kat	1959	30.00
❑ 48012	Anna/Sleepless Nights	1959	30.00
ORIGINALS, THE (4) TONY ALLEN was in this group.			
45s			
ORIGINAL SOUND			
❑ 10	Wishing Star/Let Me Hear You Say Yeah	1960	30.00
❑ 13	Little Lonely Girl/I Still Love You	1960	20.00
—As "Tony Allan and the Originals"			
ORIOLES, THE Also see SONNY TIL.			
45s			
ABNER			
❑ 1016	Sugar Girl/Didn't I Say	1958	60.00
CHARLIE PARKER			
❑ 211	Secret Love/The Wobble	1962	20.00
❑ 212	In the Chapel in the Moonlight/ Hey! Little Woman	1962	20.00
❑ 213	Back to the Chapel Again/ (It's Gonna Be a) Lonely Christmas	1962	20.00
❑ 214	What Are You Doing New Year's Eve/Don't Mess Around with My Love	1962	20.00
❑ 215	It's Too Soon to Know/ I Miss You So	1963	15.00
❑ 216	Write and Tell Me Why/Don't Tell Her What Happens to Me	1963	15.00
❑ 219	I Miss You So/Hey! Little Woman	1963	15.00
HARLEM SOUND			
❑ 1001	Lonely Christmas/What Are You Doing New Year's Eve	19??	5.00
JUBILEE			
❑ 5000	It's Too Soon to Know/ Barbara Lee	1951	4000.
❑ 5005	Tell Me So/Deacon Jones	1951	2000.
❑ 5016	So Much/Forgive and Forget	1951	2000.
❑ 5017	What Are You Doing New Year's Eve/Lonely Christmas	1951	800.00
❑ 5017 [PS]	What Are You Doing New Year's Eve/Lonely Christmas	1954	1000.
❑ 5025	At Night/Every Dog-Gone Time	1951	1000.
❑ 5040	I Cross My Fingers/Can't Seem to Laugh Anymore	1951	2000.
❑ 5045	Oh Holy Night/The Lord's Prayer	1951	600.00
—Original on blue label			
❑ 5045	Oh Holy Night/The Lord's Prayer	196?	25.00
—Reissue on black label			
❑ 5045 [PS]	Oh Holy Night/The Lord's Prayer	1954	600.00
❑ 5051	I Miss You So/You Are My First Love	1951	800.00
❑ 5051	I Miss You So/You Are My First Love	1951	2000.
—Red vinyl. VG 1000; VG+ 1500			
❑ 5055	Pal of Mine/Happy Go Lucky Local Blues	1951	800.00
❑ 5061	I'm Just a Fool in Love/ Hold Me, Squeeze Me	1951	800.00
❑ 5065	Baby, Please Don't Go/Don't Tell Her What's Happened to Me	1951	600.00
—Black vinyl			
❑ 5065	Baby, Please Don't Go/Don't Tell Her What's Happened to Me	1951	2000.
—Red vinyl. VG 1,000; VG+ 1,500			
❑ 5071	When You're Not Around/ How Blind Can You Be	1952	600.00
❑ 5074	Trust in Me/Shrimp Boats	1952	500.00
❑ 5076	Proud of You/You Never Cared for Me	1952	500.00
❑ 5082	It's All Over Because We're Through/Waiting	1952	500.00
❑ 5084	Barfly/Getting Tired, Tired, Tired	1952	400.00
❑ 5092	Don't Cry Baby/See See Rider	1952	400.00
❑ 5092	Don't Cry Baby/See See Rider	1952	1500.
—Red vinyl			
❑ 5102	You Belong to Me/I Don't Want to Take a Chance	1952	500.00
❑ 5107	I Miss You So/Till Then	1952	400.00
❑ 5107	I Miss You So/Till Then	1952	1500.
—Red vinyl			
❑ 5107	I Miss You So/Till Then	1963	25.00
—Reissue, credited to "Sonny Til and the Orioles"			
❑ 5108	Teardrops on My Pillow/Hold Me, Thrill Me, Kiss Me	1953	400.00
❑ 5108	Teardrops on My Pillow/Hold Me, Thrill Me, Kiss Me	1953	1500.
—Red vinyl			
❑ 5115	Bad Little Girl/Dem Days	1953	400.00
❑ 5120	I Cover the Waterfront/ One More Time	1953	400.00

O

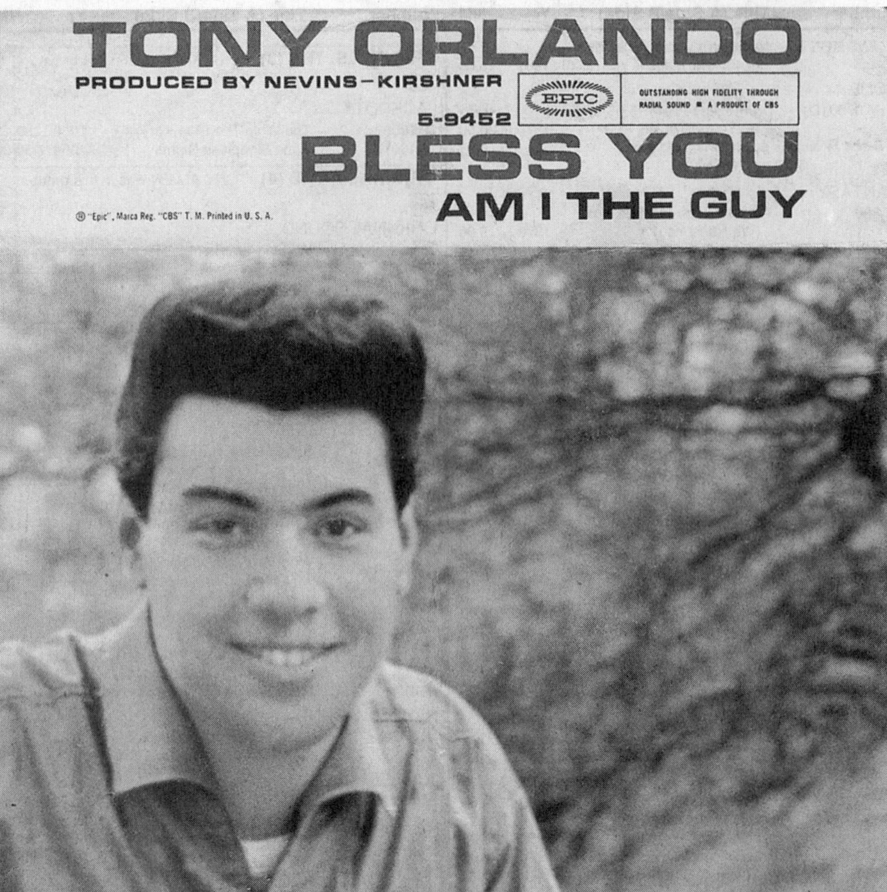

Tony Orlando, "Bless You," Epic 5-9452, 1961, **$25.**

Number	Title (A Side/B Side)	Yr	NM
❑ 5120	I Cover the Waterfront/ One More Time	1953	1200.
—Red vinyl			
❑ 5122	Crying in the Chapel/Don't You Think I Ought to Know	1953	80.00
❑ 5127	In the Mission of St. Augustine/ Write and Tell Me Why	1953	50.00
❑ 5134	There's No One But You/ Robe of Calvary	1954	50.00
❑ 5137	Secret Love/Don't Go to Strangers	1954	50.00
❑ 5143	Maybe You'll Be There/ Drowining Every Hope I Ever Had	1954	80.00
❑ 5154	In the Chapel in the Moonlight/ Thank the Lord, Thank the Lord	1954	50.00
❑ 5161	If You Believe/Longing	1954	50.00
❑ 5172	Runaround/Count Your Blessings Instead of Sheep	1954	50.00
❑ 5177	I Love You Mostly/Fair Exchange	1955	40.00
❑ 5189	I Need You Baby/The Good Lord Will Smile	1955	40.00
❑ 5221	Please Sing My Blues Tonight/ Moody Over You	1955	40.00
❑ 5231	Angel/Don't Go to Strangers	1956	60.00
❑ 5363	Tell Me So/At Night	1959	15.00
—As "Sonny Til and the Orioles"			
❑ 5384	Come On Home/The First of Summer	1960	15.00
—As "Sonny Til and the Orioles"			
❑ 6001	Crying in the Chapel/ Forgive and Forget	1959	15.00
—As "Sonny Til and the Orioles"			
LANA			
❑ 109	What Are You Doing New Year's Eve/Crying in the Chapel	196?	8.00
—Oldies reissue			
VEE JAY			
❑ 196	I Just Got Lucky/ Happy 'Til the Letter	1956	30.00
❑ 228	For All We Know/ Never Leave Me Baby	1956	30.00
❑ 244	Sugar Girl/Didn't I Say	1957	40.00

Number	Title (A Side/B Side)	Yr	NM
VIRGO			
❑ 6017	What Are You Doing New Year's Eve/Crying in the Chapel	1972	4.00
7-Inch Extended Plays			
JUBILEE			
❑ 5000	Too Soon to Know/Forgive and Forget//Tell Me So/At Night	1954	1000.
❑ 5000 [PS]	The Orioles Sing	1954	1000.
Albums			
BIG A			
❑ LP-2001	The Orioles' Greatest All-Time Hits	1969	30.00
CHARLIE PARKER			
❑ PLP-816 [M]	Modern Sounds of the Orioles	1962	80.00
❑ PLP-816S [S]	Modern Sounds of the Orioles	1962	100.00
COLLECTABLES			
❑ COL-5014	Sonny Til and the Orioles' Greatest Hits	198?	12.00
MURRAY HILL			
❑ M 61234 [(5)]	For Collectors Only	1983	40.00

ORION Also see JIMMY ELLIS.

Number	Title (A Side/B Side)	Yr	NM
45s			
KRISTAL			
❑ 2292/2308	I'm Saving Up My Pennies/ I'm Starting Over	1985	4.00
❑ 2338	100 Pounds of Clay/Because He Lived	1986	4.00
RADIOACTIVE			
❑ 18772-1 [DJ]	Unchained Melody (same on both sides)	1987	5.00
STARGEM			
❑ 2465 [DJ]	Only a Woman Like You (same on both sides)	1990	5.00
❑ 2469	I Want You, I Need You, I Love You/Plastic Saddle	1990	5.00
❑ 2502	Love It Back Together/ If That Isn't Love	1990	5.00
—Red vinyl			
❑ 2502 [PS]	Love It Back Together/ If That Isn't Love	1990	5.00
SUN			
❑ 1142	Honey/Ebony Eyes	1979	4.00
❑ 1147	Before the Next Teardrop Falls/ Washing Machine	1979	4.00
❑ 1148	Remember Bethlehem/ Silent Night	1979	4.00
❑ 1148 [DJ]	Remember Bethlehem (same on both sides)	1979	10.00
—Yellow vinyl promo			
❑ 1151	Be-Bop-a-Lula/The Breakup	1980	4.00
—A-side with Jerry Lee Lewis; B-side with Charlie Rich			
❑ 1152	It Ain't No Mystery/ Stranger in My Place	1980	4.00
❑ 1152 [DJ]	It Ain't No Mystery (same on both sides)	1980	10.00
—Yellow vinyl promo			
❑ 1153	Texas Tea/Faded Love	1980	4.00
❑ 1153 [DJ]	Texas Tea (same on both sides)	1980	10.00
—Yellow vinyl promo			
❑ 1156	Am I That Easy to Forget/ Crazy Arms	1980	4.00
❑ 1156 [DJ]	Am I That Easy to Forget (same on both sides)	1980	10.00
—Yellow vinyl promo			
❑ 1159	Rockabilly Rebel/Memphis Sun	1980	4.00
❑ 1159 [DJ]	Rockabilly Rebel (same on both sides)	1980	10.00
—Yellow vinyl promo			
❑ 1162	Crazy Little Thing Called Love/ Matchbox	1981	4.00
❑ 1165	Born/If I Can't Have You	1981	4.00
❑ 1165 [DJ]	Born (same on both sides)	1981	10.00
—Yellow vinyl promo			
❑ 1170	Some You Win, Some You Lose/Ain't No Good	1981	4.00
❑ 1170 [DJ]	Some You Win, Some You Lose (same on both sides)	1981	10.00
—Yellow vinyl promo			
❑ 1172	Baby Please Say Yes/Feelings	1982	4.00
❑ 1175	Honky Tonk Heaven/ Morning, Noon and Night	1982	4.00
❑ 1175 [DJ]	Honky Tonk Heaven (same on both sides)	1982	10.00
—Yellow vinyl promo			
7-Inch Extended Plays			
SUN			
❑ 1152 [DJ]	Stranger in My Place Greetings: Wedding Anniversary/Good Music/Great Station//Favorite Station/Best Music/Birthday	1981	40.00
—Came with insert but no cover			
Albums			
SUN			
❑ 1012	Orion Reborn	1978	10.00
—Blue cover			
❑ 1012	Orion Reborn	1978	30.00
—White cover, also known as the "coffin cover"			
❑ 1017	Sunrise	1979	10.00
❑ 1019	Orion Country	1980	10.00
❑ 1021	Rockabilly	1981	10.00
❑ 1025	Glory	1982	10.00
❑ 1028	Fresh	1983	10.00

ORION, P.J., AND THE MAGNATES

Number	Title (A Side/B Side)	Yr	NM
Albums			
MAGNATE			
❑ 122459	P.J. Orion and the Magnates	196?	150.00

ORION THE HUNTER With Barry Goudreau, formerly of BOSTON.

Number	Title (A Side/B Side)	Yr	NM
45s			
PORTRAIT			
❑ 37-04483	So You Ran/Fast Talk	1984	5.00
❑ 37-04571	Joanne/I Call It Love	1984	5.00
Albums			
PORTRAIT			
❑ BFR 39239	Orion the Hunter	1984	15.00

ORLANDO, TONY Also see BERTELL DACHE; DAWN (1).

Number	Title (A Side/B Side)	Yr	NM
12-Inch Singles			
CASABLANCA			
❑ NBD 20158	They're Playing Our Song (8:06)/(B-side blank)	1979	10.00
45s			
ATCO			
❑ 6376	Think Before You Act/She Loves Me (For What I Am)	1965	10.00
CAMEO			
❑ 471	Sweet Sweet/Manuelito (Little Manuel)	1967	10.00

Except when noted otherwise, VG = 25% of NM, and VG+ = 50% of NM. (Example: VG = $2.00, VG+ = $4.00 and NM = $8.00.)

Number	Title (A Side/B Side)	Yr	NM
CASABLANCA			
❑ 967	They're Playing Our Song (Medley)/Moonlight	1979	4.00
❑ 991	Sweets for My Sweet/ High Steppin'	1979	4.00
❑ 2229	San Pedros Children/ High Steppin'	1979	4.00
❑ 2249	Pullin' Together/ She Always Knew	1980	4.00
EPIC			
❑ 9441	Halfway to Paradise/ Lonely Tomorrows	1961	15.00
❑ 9441 [PS]	Halfway to Paradise/ Lonely Tomorrows	1961	25.00
❑ 9452	Bless You/Am I the Guy	1961	15.00
❑ 9452 [PS]	Bless You/Am I the Guy	1961	25.00
❑ 9476	Hapy Times (Are Here to Stay)/ Lonely Am I	1961	12.00
❑ 9476 [PS]	Hapy Times (Are Here to Stay)/ Lonely Am I	1961	25.00
❑ 9491	My Baby's a Starnger/ Talkin' About You	1962	12.00
❑ 9491 [PS]	My Baby's a Starnger/ Talkin' About You	1962	25.00
❑ 9502	I'd Never Find Another You/ Love on Your Lips	1962	12.00
❑ 9519	At the Edge of Tears/Chills	1962	12.00
❑ 9519 [PS]	At the Edge of Tears/Chills	1962	25.00
❑ 9562	Beautiful Dreamer/ The Loneliest	1962	10.00
❑ 9570	Joanie/Shirley	1963	10.00
❑ 9622	I'll Be There/What Am I Gonna Do	1963	10.00
❑ 9668	She Doesn't Know It/Tell Me What I Can Do	1964	10.00
❑ 9715	To Wait for Love/Accept It	1964	10.00
Albums			
CASABLANCA			
❑ NBLP 7153	I Got Rhythm	1979	10.00
❑ NBLP 7209	Living for the Music	1980	10.00
EPIC			
❑ BN 611 [S]	Bless You and 11 Other Great Hits	1961	40.00
❑ LN 3808 [M]	Bless You and 11 Other Great Hits	1961	30.00
❑ BG 33785 [(2)]	Before Dawn	1975	15.00

ORLANDO, TONY (2) This is not by the same singer as the rest.

Number	Title (A Side/B Side)	Yr	NM
45s			
MILO			
❑ 101	Ding Dong/You and Only You	1959	100.00

ORLANDO, TONY, AND DAWN See DAWN (1).

ORLEANS

Number	Title (A Side/B Side)	Yr	NM
12-Inch Singles			
INFINITY			
❑ L33-1004 [DJ]	Love Takes Time (same on both sides)	1979	10.00
45s			
ABC			
❑ 11408	Please Be There/Mountains	1973	5.00
❑ 11420	If/Stoned	1974	5.00
ASYLUM			
❑ 45243	Let There Be Music/ Give One Heart	1975	4.00
❑ 45261	Dance with Me/Ending of a Song	1975	5.00
❑ 45336	Still the One/Siam Sam	1976	5.00
—Clouds label			
❑ 45336	Still the One/Siam Sam	1976	6.00
—Dark blue label with white stylized "a" at top			
❑ 45375	Reach/Sweet Destiny	1976	4.00
❑ 45391	The Bum/Spring Fever	1977	4.00
❑ 45447	Business As Usual/ Time Passes On	1977	4.00
ATLANTIC AMERICA			
❑ 99981	One of a Kind/Beatin' Around the Bush	1982	4.00
INFINITY			
❑ 50006	Love Takes Time/Isn't It Easy	1979	4.00
❑ 50017	Don't Throw Our Love Away/ The Flame and the Moth	1979	4.00
❑ 50036	Forever/Keep On Rollin'	1979	4.00
MCA			
❑ 41228	Change Your Mind/When Are You Coming Home	1980	4.00
❑ 41283	No Ordinary Lady/Dukie's Tune	1980	4.00
❑ 52862	Lady Liberty/On Hold	1986	3.00
❑ 52909	Grown-Up Children/On Hold	1986	3.00
❑ 52963	You're Mine/Language of Love	1986	3.00
Albums			
ABC			
❑ ABCX-795	Orleans	1973	15.00
❑ AA-1058-2 [(2)]	Before the Dance	1977	12.00
❑ AC-30011	The ABC Collection	1976	10.00
ASYLUM			
❑ 7E-1029	Let There Be Music	1975	10.00
❑ 7E-1070	Waking and Dreaming	1976	10.00
INFINITY			
❑ INF-9006	Forever	1979	10.00
MCA			
❑ 5110	Orleans	1980	10.00
❑ 5767	Grown Up Children	1986	8.00
RADIO			
❑ 90012	One of a Kind	1982	10.00

ORLONS, THE

Number	Title (A Side/B Side)	Yr	NM
45s			
ABC			
❑ 10894	Everything/Keep Your Hands Off My Baby	1967	10.00
❑ 10948	Kissin' Time/Once Upon a Time	1967	10.00
CALLA			
❑ 113	Spinnin' Top/Anyone Who Had a Heart	1966	10.00
CAMEO			
❑ 105 [DJ]	Big Girls Don't Cry/Pop Pop Pop-Pie	1962	40.00
—Yellow label, black print, promo only			
❑ 198	I'll Be True/Heart Darling Angel	1961	50.00
❑ 211	Mr. 21/Please Let It Be Me	1961	50.00
❑ 218	The Wah-Watusi/Holiday Hill	1962	20.00
❑ 231	Don't Hang Up/The Conservative	1962	20.00
❑ 231 [PS]	Don't Hang Up/The Conservative	1962	40.00
❑ 243	South Street/Them Terrible Boots	1963	20.00
❑ 243 [PS]	South Street/Them Terrible Boots	1963	40.00
❑ 257	Not Me/My Best Friend	1963	20.00
❑ 257 [PS]	Not Me/My Best Friend	1963	30.00
❑ 273	Cross Fire!/It's No Big Thing	1963	20.00
❑ 273 [PS]	Cross Fire!/It's No Big Thing	1963	30.00
❑ 287	Bon-Doo-Wah/Don't Throw Your Love Away	1963	15.00
❑ 287 [PS]	Bon-Doo-Wah/Don't Throw Your Love Away	1963	30.00
❑ 295	Shimmy Shimmy/ Everything Nice	1964	15.00
❑ 295 [PS]	Shimmy Shimmy/ Everything Nice	1964	25.00
❑ 319	Rules of Love/Heartbreak Hotel	1964	15.00
❑ 319 [PS]	Rules of Love/Heartbreak Hotel	1964	25.00
❑ 332	Knock! Knock! (Who's There)/ Goin' Places	1964	15.00
❑ 332 [PS]	Knock! Knock! (Who's There)/ Goin' Places	1964	25.00
❑ 346	I Ain't Coming Back/Envy (In My Eyes)	1965	12.00
❑ 352	Come On Down Baby/ I Ain't Coming Back	1965	12.00
❑ 372	Don't You Want My Lovin'/ I Can't Take It	1965	12.00
❑ 384	No Love But Your Love/ Envy (In My Eyes)	1965	40.00
Albums			
CAMEO			
❑ C 1020 [M]	The Wah-Watusi	1962	60.00
❑ C 1033 [M]	All the Hits by the Orlons	1962	60.00
❑ C 1041 [M]	South Street	1963	60.00
❑ C 1054 [M]	Not Me	1963	50.00
❑ C 1061 [M]	The Orlons' Biggest Hits	1964	50.00
❑ C 1073 [M]	Down Memory Lane with the Orlons	1964	50.00

ORLONS, THE / THE DOVELLS Also see each artist's individual listings.

Number	Title (A Side/B Side)	Yr	NM
Albums			
CAMEO			
❑ C 1067 [M]	Golden Hits of the Orlons and the Dovells	1964	50.00

ORPHAN EGG

Number	Title (A Side/B Side)	Yr	NM
Albums			
CAROLE			
❑ CARS-8004	Orphan Egg	1968	40.00

ORPHANS, THE

Number	Title (A Side/B Side)	Yr	NM
45s			
EPIC			
❑ 10288	There's No Flowers in My Garden/One Spoken Word	1968	10.00
❑ 10348	This Is the Time/Deserted	1968	10.00

ORPHEUS

Number	Title (A Side/B Side)	Yr	NM
45s			
BELL			
❑ 45128	Big Green Pearl/Sweet Life	1971	5.00
MGM			
❑ 13882	Can't Find the Time/Lesley's Girl	1967	10.00
—Originals have black labels			
❑ 13882	Can't Find the Time/Lesley's Girl	1969	6.00
—Reissues (same number) have blue and gold labels			
❑ 13947	I've Never Seen Love Like This/ Congress Alley	1968	6.00
❑ 14022	Brown Arms in Houston/ I Can Make the Sun Rise	1969	6.00
❑ 14022 [PS]	Brown Arms in Houston/ I Can Make the Sun Rise	1969	10.00
❑ 14139	Joyful/By the Size of My Shoes	1970	6.00
RED BIRD			
❑ 10-041	My Life/Music Minus Orpheus	1965	15.00
Albums			
MGM			
❑ E-4524 [M]	Orpheus	1968	20.00
❑ SE-4524 [S]	Orpheus	1968	15.00
❑ E-4569 [M]	Ascending	1968	30.00
—Known copies are yellow label promos with "DJ Monaural" sticker on stereo cover			
❑ SE-4569 [S]	Ascending	1968	20.00
❑ SE-4599	Joyful	1969	20.00

ORR, J.D.

Number	Title (A Side/B Side)	Yr	NM
45s			
SUMMIT			
❑ 105	Hula-Hoop Boogie/ Lonesome Hearted Blues	1958	400.00

ORSI, PHIL, AND THE LITTLE KINGS

Number	Title (A Side/B Side)	Yr	NM
45s			
LUCKY			
❑ 1009	Come On Everybody/ Oh My Darling	1963	75.00
❑ 1015	Don't You Just Know It/ (B-side unknown)	1964	25.00
U.S.A.			
❑ 837	Stay/Whoever He May Be	1965	25.00
❑ 841	Sorry (I Ran All the Way Home)/ Whoever He May Be	1965	25.00

OSBORNE, ARTHUR

Number	Title (A Side/B Side)	Yr	NM
45s			
BRUNSWICK			
❑ 55068	Hey Ruby/Don't Give Me Heartaches	1958	60.00

OSBORNE, KELL, AND THE CHICKS

Number	Title (A Side/B Side)	Yr	NM
45s			
CLASS			
❑ 302	Little Chick-A-Dee/Do You Mind	1962	15.00
HIGHLAND			
❑ 1182	Law Against a Heartbreaker/ Trouble Trouble Baby	196?	2500.
—VG 1000; VG+ 1750			
LOMA			
❑ 2023	That's What's Happening/You Can't Outsmart a Woman	1965	200.00
TITANIC			
❑ 5008	Quicksand/Lonely Boy Song	1963	600.00
TREY			
❑ 3006	The Bells of St. Mary's/ That's Alright, Baby	1960	25.00

OSBORNE BROTHERS, THE

Number	Title (A Side/B Side)	Yr	NM
45s			
CMH			
❑ 1522	Shackles and Chains/ Midnight Flyer	1979	4.00
—With Mac Wiseman			
❑ 1524	I Can Hear Kentucky Calling Me/Shawnee	1980	4.00
DECCA			
❑ 31546	Take This Hammer/ Don't Even Look at Me	1963	8.00
❑ 31595	Bluegrass Express/Cuckoo Bird	1964	8.00
❑ 31655	Charlie Cotton/This Heart of Mine	1964	8.00
❑ 31751	Hey, Hey, Bartender/ Me and My Old Banjo	1965	8.00
❑ 31823	Lonesome Day/I'll Be Alright Tomorrow	1965	8.00
❑ 31886	Up This Hill and Down/Memories	1965	8.00
❑ 31977	Hard Times/A World of Unwanted	1966	8.00
❑ 32052	The Kind of Woman I Got/ One Tear	1966	8.00

Ozzy Osbourne, "Flying High Again," Jet 02582, 1981, $5.

Number	Title (A Side/B Side)	Yr	NM
❑ 32137	Roll Muddy River/Making Plans	1967	8.00
❑ 32242	Rocky Top/My Favorite Memory	1967	8.00
❑ 32325	Cut the Cornbread, Mama/ If I Could Count on You	1968	8.00
❑ 32382	Son of a Sawmill Man/That Was Yesterday	1968	8.00
❑ 32451	Working Man/World of Forgotten	1969	8.00
❑ 32516	Tennessee Hound Dog/Thanks for All the Yesterdays	1969	8.00
❑ 32598	Ruby, Are You Mad/Sempre	1969	8.00
❑ 32680	Listen to the Rain/Midnight Angel	1970	8.00
❑ 32746	My Old Kentucky Home (Turpentine and Dandelion Wine)/No Good Son of a Gun	1970	8.00
❑ 32794	Georgia Pineywoods/ Searching for Yesterday	1971	8.00
❑ 32864	Muddy Bottom/Beneath Still Waters	1971	8.00
❑ 32908	Take Me Home, Country Roads/ Tears Are No Stranger	1971	8.00
❑ 32942	Windy City/Shelly's Winter Love	1972	8.00
❑ 32979	Miss You Mississippi/Today I Started Loving You Again	1972	8.00
❑ 33028	Midnight Flyer/Tears Will Kiss the Morning Dew	1972	8.00
❑ 55274	Rocky Top (Radio Mix)/ Rocky Top (Original Version)	1996	4.00
MCA			
❑ 40028	Lizzie Lou/Tears	1973	4.00
❑ 40113	Blue Heartache/You're Heavy on My Mind	1973	4.00
❑ 40169	Sled Ridin'/Fastest Grass Alive	1973	4.00
❑ 40226	Bluegrass Melodies/The Seventh of December	1974	4.00
❑ 40346	El Rancho/A Heartache Looking for a Home	1974	4.00
❑ 40509	Don't Let Smokey Mountain Smoke Get In Your Eyes/ Born a Ramblin' Man	1976	4.00

Number	Title (A Side/B Side)	Yr	NM
MGM			
❑ 12308	My Aching Heart/ Ruby Are You Mad	1956	15.00
—With Red Allen			
❑ 12383	Whu Dun It/Teardrops in My Eyes	1956	15.00
—With Red Allen			
❑ 12420	Ho Honey Ho/Down in the Willow Garden	1957	12.00
—With Red Allen			
❑ 12527	Della Mae/Wild Mountain Honey	1957	12.00
—With Red Allen			
❑ 12583	Once More/She's No Angel	1957	12.00
—With Red Allen			
❑ 12633	My Destiny/If You Don't Somebody Else Will	1958	12.00
—With Red Allen			
❑ 12689	Love Pains/It Hurts to Know	1958	12.00
—With Red Allen			
❑ 12762	I Love You Only/Give This Message to Your Heart	1959	12.00
❑ 12805	Lost Highway/You'll Never Know	1959	12.00
❑ 12839	Sweethearts Again/There's a Woman Behind Every Man	1959	12.00
❑ 12930	Blame Me/Lonely, Lonely Me	1960	10.00
❑ 12970	At the First Fall of Snow/Fair and Tender Ladies	1960	10.00
❑ 13045	Black Sheep Returned to the Fold/Each Season Changes You	1961	10.00
❑ 13073	Five Days of Heaven/It Ain't Gonna Rain No Mo'	1962	10.00
❑ 13098	Banjo Boys/Poor Old Cora	1962	10.00
❑ 13126	Mule Skinner Blues/Lovey Told Me Goodbye	1963	10.00
RCA			
❑ PB-13097	Rocky Top/Old Flames Can't Hold a Candle to You	1982	4.00
Albums			
CMH			
❑ 4501	Greatest Bluegrass Hits, Vol. 1	198?	12.00
❑ 6206	#1	197?	12.00

Number	Title (A Side/B Side)	Yr	NM
❑ 6231	Bluegrass Concerto	197?	12.00
❑ 6244	Kentucky Calling Me	1980	12.00
❑ 6256	Bobby and His Mandolin	1981	12.00
❑ 9008 [(2)]	From Rocky Top to Muddy Bottom	1977	15.00
❑ 9011 [(2)]	Bluegrass Collection	1978	15.00
❑ 9016 [(2)]	The Essential Bluegrass Album	1979	15.00
—With MacWiseman			
DECCA			
❑ DL 4602 [M]	Voices in the Bluegrass	1965	15.00
❑ DL 4767 [M]	Up This Hill and Down	1966	15.00
❑ DL 4903 [M]	Modern Sounds of Bluegrass Music	1967	15.00
❑ DL 4993 [M]	Yesterday, Today and The Osborne Brothers	1968	25.00
❑ DL 74602 [S]	Voices in the Bluegrass	1965	20.00
❑ DL 74767 [S]	Up This Hill and Down	1966	20.00
❑ DL 74903 [S]	Modern Sounds of Bluegrass Music	1967	20.00
❑ DL 74993 [S]	Yesterday, Today and The Osborne Brothers	1968	20.00
❑ DL 75079	Favorite Hymns by the Osborne Brothers	1969	20.00
❑ DL 75128	Up to Date and Down to Earth	1969	20.00
❑ DL 75204	Ru-Beeeee	1970	20.00
❑ DL 75271	The Osborne Brothers	1971	15.00
❑ DL 75321	Country Roads	1971	15.00
❑ DL 75356	Bobby & Sonny	1972	15.00
MCA			
❑ 105	Voices in the Bluegrass	1973	12.00
—Reissue of Decca 74602			
❑ 119	Yesterday, Today and The Osborne Brothers	1973	12.00
—Reissue of Decca 74993			
❑ 125	Favorite Hymns by the Osborne Brothers	1973	12.00
—Reissue of Decca 75079			
❑ 135	Ru-Beeeee	1973	12.00
—Reissue of Decca 75204			
❑ 4086 [(2)]	The Best of the Osborne Brothers	1974	15.00
MGM			
❑ GAS 140	The Osborne Brothers (Golden Archives Series)	1970	20.00
❑ E-3734 [M]	Country Pickin' and Hillside Singin'	1959	50.00
❑ E-4018 [M]	Bluegrass Music	1962	25.00
❑ SE-4018 [S]	Bluegrass Music	1962	30.00
❑ E-4090 [M]	Bluegrass Instrumentals	1962	25.00
❑ SE-4090 [S]	Bluegrass Instrumentals	1962	30.00
❑ E-4149 [M]	Cuttin' Grass	1963	25.00
❑ SE-4149 [S]	Cuttin' Grass	1963	30.00
RCA VICTOR			
❑ AHL1-4324	Bluegrass Spectacular	1982	10.00
❑ AYL1-5436	Bluegrass Spectacular	1985	8.00
—"Best Buy Series" reissue			
ROUNDER			
❑ SS-03	The Osborne Brothers with Red Allen	1981	12.00
❑ SS-04	The Osborne Brothers	198?	12.00
SUGAR HILL			
❑ SH-3740	Some Things I Want to Sing About	1984	10.00
❑ SH-3754	Once More, Vol. 1	1986	10.00
❑ SH-3758	Once More, Vol. 2	1987	10.00
❑ SH-3764	Singing, Shouting Praises	1988	10.00

OSBOURNE, OZZY Also see BLACK SABBATH; QUIET RIOT; URIAH HEEP; RAINBOW; BADLANDS; NIGHT RANGER.

12-Inch Singles

Number	Title (A Side/B Side)	Yr	NM
CBS ASSOCIATED			
❑ AS 1305 [DJ]	Miracle Man (same on both sides)	1988	20.00
❑ ZAS 2261 [DJ]	Shot in the Dark (4:25) (same on both sides)	1986	15.00

45s

Number	Title (A Side/B Side)	Yr	NM
CBS ASSOCIATED			
❑ ZS4-04318	Bark at the Moon/Spiders	1984	5.00
❑ ZS4-04383	So Tired/"B" Side	1984	5.00
❑ ZS4-05810	Shot in the Dark/You Said It All	1986	4.00
❑ ZS4-05810 [PS]	Shot in the Dark/You Said It All	1986	6.00
❑ ZS4-07168	Crazy Train (Live)/ Crazy Train (Original)	1987	5.00
❑ ZS8-08463	Shot in the Dark/Crazy Train	1988	4.00
—Reissue			
❑ ZS4-08516	Miracle Man/Man You Said It All	1988	5.00
❑ ZS4-68534	Crazy Babies/Demon Alcohol	1989	5.00
EPIC			
❑ 34-74986	Changes/No More Tears	1993	4.00
❑ 34-79651	Gets Me Through (same on both sides)	2001	5.00
EPIC ASSOCIATED			
❑ 35-73973	No More Tears/S.I.N.	1991	4.00
❑ 35-74093	Mama, I'm Coming Home/ Don't Blame Me	1991	5.00

Except when noted otherwise, VG = 25% of NM, and VG+ = 50% of NM. (Example: VG = $2.00, VG+ = $4.00 and NM = $8.00.)

Number	Title (A Side/B Side)	Yr	NM
JET			
❑ ZS6-02079	Crazy Train/Steal Away (The Night)	1981	6.00
❑ ZS5-02582	Flying High Again/I Don't Know	1981	5.00
❑ ZS5-02707	Tonight/Little Dolls	1982	5.00
❑ ZS4-03392	Paranoid/Iron Man	1982	5.00
❑ ZS4-03534	Never Say Die/Paranoid	1983	5.00
Albums			
CBS ASSOCIATED			
❑ AS 1828 [DJ]	Interview with Ozzy	1984	30.00
❑ FZ 38987	Bark at the Moon	1983	10.00
❑ PZ 38987	Bark at the Moon	1985	8.00
—Budget-line reissue with new prefix			
❑ FZ 40026	The Ultimate Sin	1986	10.00
❑ 9Z9 40543 [EP]	The Ultimate Live Ozzy	1986	40.00
—Picture disc with live material			
❑ ZX2 40714	Ozzy Osbourne/Randy Rhoads Tribute	1987	12.00
❑ FZ 44245	No Rest for the Wicked	1988	10.00
❑ Z 46795	No More Tears	1991	20.00
JET			
❑ AS99 1372 [PD]	Diary of a Madman	1981	30.00
—Promo-only picture disc			
❑ JZ 36812	Blizzard of Ozz	1981	10.00
❑ FZ 37492	Diary of a Madman	1981	10.00
❑ 8Z8 37640 [EP]	Mr. Crowley	1982	30.00
—Three-song picture disc with live material			
❑ ZX2 38350 [(2)]	Speak of the Devil	1982	15.00

OSCAR See CARROLL SPINNEY.

OSHINS, MILT

Number	Title (A Side/B Side)	Yr	NM
45s			
PELVIS			
❑ 169	All About Elvis/All About Elvis (Part 2)	1956	75.00

OSIBISA

Number	Title (A Side/B Side)	Yr	NM
45s			
DECCA			
❑ 32920	Woyaya/Music for Gong Gong	1972	5.00
❑ 32957	Move On/Survival	1972	5.00
❑ 32994	Ana-Bo/Wango Wango	1972	5.00
ISLAND			
❑ 053	Sunshine Day/Bum to Bum	1976	4.00
❑ 064	Dance the Body Music/ Right Now	1976	4.00
❑ 080	The Coffee Song/The Warrior	1977	4.00
WARNER BROS.			
❑ 7770	Adwoa/Fire	1974	5.00
❑ 8031	Rokoto/Who's Got the Paper	1974	5.00
Albums			
ANTILLES			
❑ 7051	Welcome Home	1978	10.00
❑ 7058	Ojah Awake	1978	10.00
BUDDAH			
❑ BDS-5136	Super Fly T.N.T.	1973	30.00
DECCA			
❑ DL 75285	Osibisa	1971	15.00
❑ DL 75327	Woyaya	1972	15.00
❑ DL 75368	Heads	1972	15.00
ISLAND			
❑ ILPS 9355	Welcome Home	1976	10.00
❑ ILPS 9411	Ojah Awake	1977	10.00
MCA			
❑ 32	Osibisa	1973	10.00
—Reissue of Decca 75285			
❑ 43	Woyaya	1973	10.00
—Reissue of Decca 75327			
WARNER BROS.			
❑ BS 2732	Happy Children	1973	10.00
❑ BS 2802	Osibirock	1974	10.00

OSMOND, DONNY

Also see DONNY AND MARIE OSMOND; THE OSMONDS.

Number	Title (A Side/B Side)	Yr	NM
12-Inch Singles			
CAPITOL			
❑ V-15505	Hold On (5 versions)	1989	6.00
❑ V-15642	My Love Is a Fire (3 versions)	1990	6.00
❑ V-15666	Sure Lookin' (5 versions)	1990	10.00
❑ SPRO-79419 [DJ]	My Love Is a Fire (3 versions)	1990	8.00
45s			
CAPITOL			
❑ B-44369	Soldier of Love/My Secret Touch	1989	3.00
❑ B-44369 [PS]	Soldier of Love/My Secret Touch	1989	5.00
❑ B-44379	Sacred Emotion/Groove	1989	3.00
❑ 7PRO-79585	Soldier of Love (same on both sides)	1989	8.00
—Promo-only pressing			

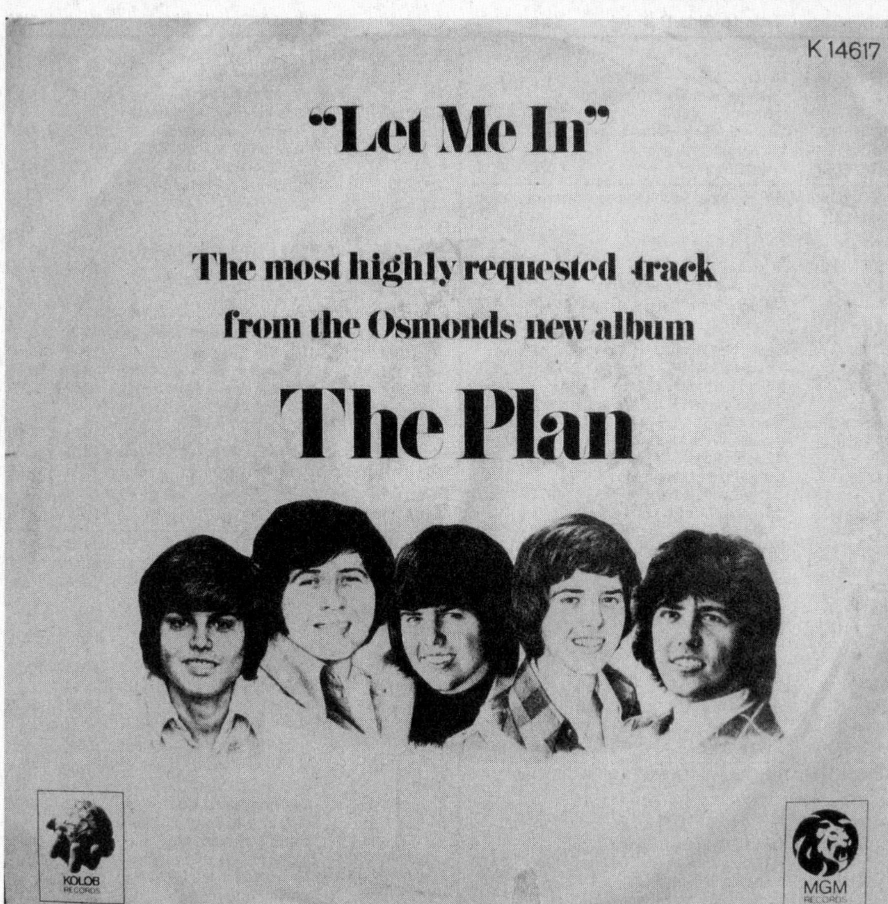

The Osmonds, "Let Me In," MGM 14617, 1973, **8$.**

Number	Title (A Side/B Side)	Yr	NM
❑ 7PRO-79608	Sacred Emotion (same on both sides)	1989	5.00
—7-inch vinyl originally was promo only			
❑ 7PRO-79608 [PS]	Sacred Emotion (same on both sides)	1989	5.00
—Picture sleeve appears to have been released only with promo copies			
❑ 7PRO-79683	Hold On (same on both sides)	1989	6.00
—7-inch vinyl is promo only			
❑ 7PRO-79912/3	I'll Be Good to You (1/2 Guitar Solo)/(Extended Guitar Mix)	1990	6.00
—7-inch vinyl is promo only			
MGM			
❑ 14227	Sweet and Innocent/Flirtin'	1971	6.00
❑ 14227 [PS]	Sweet and Innocent/Flirtin'	1971	8.00
❑ 14285	Go Away Little Girl/The Wild Rover (Time to Ride)	1971	5.00
—Altered B-side title			
❑ 14285	Go Away Little Girl/Time to Ride	1971	6.00
❑ 14322	Hey Girl/I Knew You When	1971	6.00
❑ 14367	Puppy Love/Let My People Go	1972	6.00
❑ 14407	Too Young/Love Me	1972	6.00
❑ 14424	Lonely Boy/Why	1972	6.00
❑ 14503	The Twelfth of Never/Life Is Just What You Make It	1973	5.00
❑ 14503 [PS]	The Twelfth of Never/Life Is Just What You Make It	1973	8.00
❑ 14583	A Million to One/Young Love	1973	5.00
❑ 14677	Are You Lonesome Tonight/ When I Fall in Love	1973	5.00
❑ 14781	I Have a Dream/I'm Dyin'	1975	4.00
POLYDOR			
❑ 14320	C'mon Marianne/ Ol' Man Auctioneer	1976	4.00
❑ 14417	You Got Me Dangling on a String/ I'm Sorry	1977	4.00
Albums			
CAPITOL			
❑ C1-92354	Donny Osmond	1989	12.00
❑ C1-94051	Eyes Don't Lie	1990	15.00
MGM			
❑ SE-4782	The Donny Osmond Album	1971	12.00
❑ SE-4797	To You with Love, Donny	1971	10.00
❑ SE-4820	Portrait of Donny	1972	10.00
❑ SE-4854	Too Young	1972	10.00
❑ SE-4872	My Best to You	1972	10.00
❑ SE-4886	Alone Together	1973	25.00
—With tear-off 10x10 photo intact; deduct 60 percent if missing			
❑ M3G-4930	A Time for Us	1973	10.00
❑ M3G-4978	Donny	1974	10.00
POLYDOR			
❑ PD-1-6067	Disco Train	1976	8.00
❑ PD-1-6109	Donald Clark Osmond	1977	8.00

OSMOND, DONNY AND MARIE

Also see DONNY OSMOND; MARIE OSMOND; THE OSMONDS.

Number	Title (A Side/B Side)	Yr	NM
45s			
MGM			
❑ 14735	I'm Leaving It (All) Up to You/ The Umbrella Song	1974	5.00
❑ 14765	Morning Side of the Mountain/ One of These Days	1974	4.00
❑ 14807	Make the World Go Away/ Living on My Suspicion	1975	4.00
❑ 14840	Deep Purple/Take Me Back Again	1975	4.00
POLYDOR			
❑ 14363	Ain't Nothin' Like the Real Thing/ Sing	1976	4.00
❑ 14439	(You're My) Soul and Inspiration/ Now We're Together	1977	4.00
❑ 14456	Baby, I'm Sold on You/ Sure Would Be Nice	1978	4.00
❑ 14474	May Tomorrow Be a Perfect Day/ I Want to Give You My Everything	1978	4.00
❑ 14510	On the Shelf/Certified Honey	1978	4.00
Albums			
MGM			
❑ M3G-4968	I'm Leaving It All Up to You	1974	10.00
❑ M3G-4996	Make the World Go Away	1975	10.00

Number	Title (A Side/B Side)	Yr	NM
POLYDOR			
❑ PD-1-6068	Donny & Marie — Featuring Songs from Their Television Show	1976	8.00
❑ PD-1-6083	Donny & Marie — New Season	1976	8.00
❑ PD-1-6127	Winning Combination	1978	8.00
❑ PD-1-6169	Goin' Coconuts	1978	8.00

OSMOND, JIMMY

Youngest of the first generation of singing Osmonds.

45s

Number	Title (A Side/B Side)	Yr	NM
MERCURY			
❑ 74005	Life Is Just What You Make It/Theme from "The Great Brain"	1978	4.00
MGM			
❑ 14199	Santa, No Chimney/I Hope You Have a Merry Christmas	1970	6.00
❑ 14328	If Santa Were My Daddy/Silent Night	1971	6.00
—As "Little Jimmy Osmond"			
❑ 14328 [PS]	If Santa Were My Daddy/Silent Night	1971	8.00
❑ 14376	Long Haired Lover from Liverpool/Mother of Mine	1972	5.00
❑ 14468	Tweedlee Dee/Mama'd Know What to Do	1972	5.00
❑ 14687	I'm Gonna Knock on Your Door/Give Me a Good Old Mammy Song	1973	5.00
❑ 14770	Yes Virginia, There Is a Santa Claus/If Santa Were My Daddy	1974	6.00
❑ 14771	Don't You Remember/Little Arrows	1974	5.00

Albums

Number	Title (A Side/B Side)	Yr	NM
MGM			
❑ SE-4855	Killer Joe	1972	10.00
❑ M3G-4916	Little Arrows	1975	12.00

O

OSMOND, MARIE

Also see DONNY AND MARIE OSMOND.

45s

Number	Title (A Side/B Side)	Yr	NM
CAPITOL			
❑ B-5445	Until I Fall in Love Again/I Don't Want to Go Too Far	1985	3.00
❑ B-5478	Meet Me in Montana/What Do Lonely People Do	1985	3.00
—With Dan Seals			
❑ B-5478 [PS]	Meet Me in Montana/What Do Lonely People Do	1985	4.00
❑ B-5521	There's No Stopping Your Heart/Blue Sky Shinin'	1985	3.00
❑ B-5521 [PS]	There's No Stopping Your Heart/Blue Sky Shinin'	1985	5.00
❑ B-5563	Read My Lips/That Old Devil Moon	1986	3.00
❑ B-5613	You're Still New to Me/New Love	1986	3.00
—With Paul Davis			
❑ B-5613 [PS]	You're Still New to Me/New Love	1986	4.00
❑ B-5663	I Only Wanted You/We're Gonna Need a Love Song	1986	3.00
❑ B-5703	Everybody's Crazy 'Bout My Baby/Making Music	1987	3.00
❑ B-44044	Cry Just a Little/More Than Dancing	1987	3.00
❑ B-44176	Without a Trace/Baby's Blue Eyes	1988	3.00
❑ B-44215	Sweet Life/My Home Town Boy	1988	3.00
—A-side: With Paul Davis			
❑ B-44269	I'm in Love and He's in Dallas/My Home Town Boy	1989	3.00
❑ B-44412	Steppin' Stone/What Would You Do About Me If You Were Me	1989	3.00
❑ B-44468	Slowly But Surely/What Would You Do About You	1989	4.00
❑ NR-44505	Let Me Be the First/What's a Little Lovin' Between Friends	1990	5.00
❑ 7PRO-79808	Slowly But Surely (same on both sides)	1989	5.00
—Vinyl originally was promo only			
CURB			
❑ 76840	Like a Hurricane/I'll Be Faithful to You	1990	4.00
❑ 76851	Paper Roses/Think with Your Heart	1990	4.00
ELEKTRA			
❑ 69882	I'm Learning/Look Who's Getting Over Who	1982	4.00
❑ 69995	Back to Believing Again/Look Who's Getting Over Who	1982	4.00
MGM			
❑ 14609	Paper Roses/Least of All You	1973	5.00
❑ 14609 [PS]	Paper Roses/Least of All You	1973	8.00
❑ 14694	My Little Corner of the World/It's Just the Other Way Around	1974	4.00
❑ 14786	Who's Sorry Now/This I Promise You	1975	4.00
POLYDOR			
❑ 14333	"A" My Name Is Alice/Weeping Willow	1976	4.00
❑ 14385	This Is the Way That I Feel/Play the Music Loud	1977	4.00
❑ 14385 [PS]	This Is the Way That I Feel/Play the Music Loud	1977	5.00
❑ 14405	Cry, Baby, Cry/Please Tell Him I Said Hello	1977	4.00
RCA			
❑ PB-13680	Who's Counting/'Til the Best Comes Along	1983	4.00

Albums

Number	Title (A Side/B Side)	Yr	NM
CAPITOL			
❑ ST-12414	There's No Stopping Your Heart	1985	8.00
❑ ST-12516	I Only Wanted You	1986	8.00
❑ C1-48968	All in Love	1988	8.00
❑ C1-91781	Steppin' Stone	1989	10.00
MGM			
❑ SE-4910	Paper Roses	1973	12.00
❑ M3G-4944	In My Little Corner of the World	1974	12.00
❑ M3G-4979	Who's Sorry Now	1975	12.00
POLYDOR			
❑ PD-1-6099	This Is the Way That I Feel	1977	8.00

OSMONDS, THE

Includes records as "The Osmond Brothers." (Most of these were pre-1970, before Donny was a member of the group.) Also see DONNY OSMOND.

45s

Number	Title (A Side/B Side)	Yr	NM
BARNABY			
❑ 2002	Mary Elizabeth/Speak Like a Child	1968	10.00
❑ 2004	I've Got Loving on My Mind/Mollie- "A"	1968	10.00
❑ 2005	Taking a Chance on Love/Groove With What You Got	1969	10.00
ELEKTRA			
❑ 47438	I Think About Your Lovin'/Working Man's Blues	1982	4.00
❑ 69883	Never Ending Song of Love/You'll Be Seeing Me	1982	4.00
❑ 69969	It's Like Falling in Love/Your Leaving Was the Last Thing on My Mind	1982	4.00
EMI AMERICA			
❑ 8298	Baby When Your Heart Breaks Down/Love Burning Down	1985	3.00
❑ 8313	Baby Wants/Lovin' Proof	1986	3.00
❑ 8325	You Look Like the One I Love/It's Only a Heartache	1986	3.00
❑ 8360	Looking for Suzanne/Back in Your Arms	1986	3.00
❑ 43033	Slow Ride/Heartbreak Radio	1987	3.00
MERCURY			
❑ 74056	Love on the Line/You're Mine	1979	4.00
❑ 74079	Emily/Rainin'	1979	4.00
MGM			
❑ 13162	Be My Little Baby Bumble Bee/I Wouldn't Trade the Silver in My Mother's Hair	1963	15.00
❑ 13174	Theme from "The Travels of Jamie McPheeters"/Aura Lee	1963	15.00
❑ 13174 [PS]	Theme from "The Travels of Jamie McPheeters"/Aura Lee	1963	30.00
❑ 13281	Mr. Sandman/My Mom	1964	20.00
❑ 13281 [PS]	Mr. Sandman/My Mom	1964	50.00
❑ 14159	Movin' Along/Open Up Your Heart	1970	8.00
❑ 14193	One Bad Apple/He Ain't Heavy, He's My Brother	1970	6.00
❑ 14193 [PS]	One Bad Apple/He Ain't Heavy, He's My Brother	1970	50.00
—Sleeve calls the group "The Osmond Brothers," rather than "The Osmonds" as the 45 does, which may explain its rarity			
❑ 14259	Double Lovin'/Chilly Winds	1971	6.00
❑ 14295	Yo-Yo/Keep on My Side	1971	6.00
❑ 14324	Down by the Lazy River/He's the Light of the World	1971	6.00
❑ 14405	Hold Her Tight/Love Is	1972	5.00
❑ 14450	Crazy Horses/That's My Girl	1972	5.00
❑ 14562	Goin' Home/Are You Up There	1973	5.00
❑ 14617	Let Me In/One Way Ticket to Anywhere	1973	5.00
❑ 14617 [PS]	Let Me In/One Way Ticket to Anywhere	1973	8.00
❑ 14746	Love Me for a Reason/Fever	1974	5.00
❑ 14791	The Proud One/The Last Day Is Coming	1975	5.00
❑ 14831	Thank You/I'm Still Gonna Need You	1975	5.00
❑ 14831 [PS]	Thank You/I'm Still Gonna Need You	1975	6.00
POLYDOR			
❑ 14348	Check It Out/I Can't Live a Dream	1976	4.00
UNI			
❑ 55015	I Can't Stop/Flower Music	1967	10.00
❑ 55276	I Can't Stop/Flower Music	1971	6.00
WARNER BROS.			
❑ 28982	Any Time/Desperately	1985	3.00
❑ 29312	If Every Man Had a Woman Like You/Come Back to Me	1984	4.00
❑ 29387	Where Does An Angel Go When She Cries/One More for Lovers	1984	4.00
❑ 29594	She's Ready for Someone to Love Her/You Make the Long Road Shorter with Your Love	1983	4.00

Albums

Number	Title (A Side/B Side)	Yr	NM
ELEKTRA			
❑ 60180	The Osmond Brothers	1982	10.00
MERCURY			
❑ SRM-1-3766	Steppin' Out	1979	10.00
METRO			
❑ M 543 [M]	We Sing You a Merry Christmas	1965	15.00
—Reissue of 4187 with one track missing and remaining contents rearranged			
❑ MS 543 [S]	We Sing You a Merry Christmas	1965	20.00
MGM			
❑ PM-7 [M]	The Travels of Jaimie McPheeters	1963	50.00
—Side 1: Dialogue from TV show; Side 2: Osmond Brothers tracks. AC Spark Plugs promo.			
❑ PM-9 [M]	We Sing You a Merry Christmas	1963	40.00
—Special-products issue for AC Spark Plug dealers			
❑ E-4146 [M]	Songs We Sang on the Andy Williams Show	1963	25.00
❑ SE-4146 [S]	Songs We Sang on the Andy Williams Show	1963	30.00
—As "The Osmond Brothers"			
❑ E-4187 [M]	We Sing You a Merry Christmas	1963	25.00
—As "The Osmond Brothers"			
❑ SE-4187 [S]	We Sing You a Merry Christmas	1963	30.00
❑ E-4235 [M]	The Osmond Brothers Sing the All-Time Hymn Favorites	1964	20.00
❑ SE-4235 [S]	The Osmond Brothers Sing the All-Time Hymn Favorites	1964	25.00
❑ E-4291 [M]	The New Sound of the Osmond Brothers	1965	20.00
❑ SE-4291 [S]	The New Sound of the Osmond Brothers	1965	25.00
❑ SE-4724	Osmonds	1971	12.00
❑ SE-4770	Homemade	1971	30.00
—With tear-off poster intact; deduct 60 percent if poster is not attached			
❑ SE-4796	Phase-III	1972	12.00
❑ SE-4826 [(2)]	The Osmonds "Live"	1972	15.00
❑ SE-4851	Crazy Horses	1972	12.00
❑ SE-4902	The Plan	1973	10.00
❑ M3G-4939	Love Me for a Reason	1974	10.00
❑ M3G-4993	The Proud One	1975	10.00
❑ MG-2-5012 [(2)]	Around the World — Live in Concert	1975	12.00
❑ ST 90403 [S]	The New Sound of the Osmond Brothers	1965	40.00
—Capitol Record Club edition			
❑ T 90403 [M]	The New Sound of the Osmond Brothers	1965	40.00
—Capitol Record Club edition			
POLYDOR			
❑ PD-1-6077	Brainstorm	1976	10.00
❑ PD-2-8001 [(2)]	The Osmond Christmas Album	1976	15.00
—Includes group, solo and duet recordings			
❑ PD-2-9005	The Osmonds Greatest Hits	1977	12.00
WARNER BROS.			
❑ 25070	One Way Rider	1984	8.00

OSWALD, LEE HARVEY

Albums

Number	Title (A Side/B Side)	Yr	NM
EYEWITNESS			
❑ 1002	Lee Harvey Oswald Speaks	1967	80.00
INCA			
❑ 1001	Oswald: Self Portrait in Red	1965	100.00
KEY			
❑ 880	The President's Assassin Speaks	1964	100.00

OTHER HALF, THE (1)

45s

Number	Title (A Side/B Side)	Yr	NM
ACTA			
❑ 801	Flight of the Dragon Lady/Wonderful Day	1967	20.00
❑ 806	I Need You/No Doubt About It	1967	20.00
❑ 819	What Can I Do for You/Bad Day	1968	15.00
❑ 825	Morning Fire/Ozlee Eaves Drop	1968	15.00
GNP CRESCENDO			
❑ 378	I've Come So Far/Mr. Pharmacist	1966	20.00

Albums

Number	Title (A Side/B Side)	Yr	NM
ACTA			
❑ 38004	The Other Half	1968	100.00

Except when noted otherwise, VG = 25% of NM, and VG+ = 50% of NM. (Example: VG = $2.00, VG+ = $4.00 and NM = $8.00.)

OTHER HALF, THE (2)

Albums

7/2

Number	Title (A Side/B Side)	Yr	NM
❑ (no #)	The Other Half	1966	1500.

—Album has been counterfeited, but those records are translucent when held to a light, originals are not

OTHER ONES, THE

45s

ABC-PARAMOUNT

Number	Title (A Side/B Side)	Yr	NM
❑ 10793	Stop/Dreaming Out Loud	1966	12.00

OTHER TIKIS, THE See THE TIKIS.

OTHERS, THE (1) British group.

45s

FONTANA

Number	Title (A Side/B Side)	Yr	NM
❑ 1944	Oh Yeah!/I'm Taking Her Home	1964	30.00

OTHERS, THE (2)

45s

MERCURY

Number	Title (A Side/B Side)	Yr	NM
❑ 72602	Revenge/I'm in Need	1966	30.00

OTHERS, THE (U)

45s

RCA VICTOR

Number	Title (A Side/B Side)	Yr	NM
❑ 47-8669	I Can't Stand This Love, Goodbye/Until I Heard It From You	1965	30.00
❑ 47-8776	Lonely Street/(I Remember) The First Time I Saw You	1965	15.00

OTIS, JOHNNY

45s

ATLANTIC

Number	Title (A Side/B Side)	Yr	NM
❑ 2409	Keep the Faith — Part I/Keep the Faith — Part II	1967	12.00

CAPITOL

Number	Title (A Side/B Side)	Yr	NM
❑ F3799	Can't You Hear Me Callin'/My Ding-a-Ling	1957	50.00
❑ F3799/3802	The Johnny Otis Show	1957	400.00

—Four-record set with four-pocket cover. Price is for entire set. Records alone are valued separately below.

Number	Title (A Side/B Side)	Yr	NM
❑ F3800	Ma, He's Makin' Eyes at Me/In the Dark	1957	50.00
❑ F3801	Stay with Me/Tell Me So	1957	50.00
❑ F3802	It's Too Soon to Know/Star of Love	1957	50.00
❑ F3852	Bye Bye Baby/Good Golly	1957	25.00
❑ F3889	Well, Well, Well/You Just Kissed Me Goodbye	1958	25.00
❑ F3966	Willie and the Hand Jive/Ring-a-Ling	1958	30.00
❑ F4060	Willie Did the Cha Cha/Crazy Country Hop	1958	25.00
❑ F4156	My Dear/You	1959	20.00
❑ F4168 [M]	Castin' My Spell/Telephone Baby	1959	20.00
❑ F4168 [S]	Castin' My Spell/Telephone Baby	1959	50.00
❑ F4226	Three Girls Named Molly (Doin' the Hully Gully)/I'll Do the Same for You	1959	20.00
❑ F4260	Let the Sun Shine in My Life/Baby, Just You	1959	20.00
❑ 4326	Mumblin' Mosie/Hey Baby, Don't You Know	1960	15.00

DIG

Number	Title (A Side/B Side)	Yr	NM
❑ 119	Hey! Hey! Hey! Hey!/Let the Sunshine in My Heart	1956	30.00
❑ 122	The Midnite Creeper (Part 1)/The Midnite Creeper (Part 2)	1956	30.00
❑ 132	My Eyes Are Full of Tears/Turtle Dove	1957	30.00
❑ 134	Wa Wa (Part 1)/Wa Wa (Part 2)	1957	30.00
❑ 139	Stop, Look and Love Me/The Night Is Young	1957	30.00

ELDO

Number	Title (A Side/B Side)	Yr	NM
❑ 106	The New Bo Diddley/The Jelly Roll	1960	15.00
❑ 152	Keep the Faith (Part 1)/Keep the Faith (Part 2)	1968	8.00
❑ 153	Long Distance/Banana Peels	1968	8.00

EPIC

Number	Title (A Side/B Side)	Yr	NM
❑ 5-10606	You Can Depend on Me/The Watts Breakaway	1970	6.00
❑ 5-10757	Willie and the Hand Jive/Goin' Back to L.A.	1971	6.00

—B-side with Delmar Evans

HAWK SOUND

Number	Title (A Side/B Side)	Yr	NM
❑ 1003	Jaws/Good to the Last Drop	1975	5.00

KENT

Number	Title (A Side/B Side)	Yr	NM
❑ 506	Country Girl/Bye Bye Baby	1969	8.00
❑ 4521	Shuggie's Blues/Cool Ade	1969	8.00

KING

Number	Title (A Side/B Side)	Yr	NM
❑ 5581	Hand Jive One More Time/Baby I Got News for You	1961	15.00
❑ 5606	She's All Right/It Must Be Love	1962	15.00
❑ 5634	Queen of the Twist/I Know My Love Is True	1962	15.00
❑ 5690	The Hey Hey Hey Song/Early in the Morning Blues	1962	15.00
❑ 5707	Somebody Call the Station/Yes	1963	12.00
❑ 5790	Bye, Bye Baby/The Hash	1963	12.00

MERCURY

Number	Title (A Side/B Side)	Yr	NM
❑ 8263	Oopy Doo/Stardust	1952	50.00
❑ 8273	One-Nighter Blues/Goomp Blues	1952	50.00
❑ 8289	Call Operator 210/Baby Baby Blues	1952	50.00
❑ 8295	Gypsy Blues/The Candle's Burning Low	1952	50.00
❑ 70038	Why Don't You Believe Me/Wishing Well	1953	50.00
❑ 70050	Love Bug Boogie/Brown Skin Butterball	1953	50.00

OKEH

Number	Title (A Side/B Side)	Yr	NM
❑ 7332	Watts Breakaway/You Can Depend On Me	1969	6.00

PEACOCK

Number	Title (A Side/B Side)	Yr	NM
❑ 1625	Young Girl/Rock Me Baby	1953	80.00
❑ 1636	Shake It/I Won't Be Your Fool No More	1954	50.00
❑ 1648	Sittin' Here Drinkin'/You Got Me Crying	1955	50.00
❑ 1675	Butter Ball/Dandy's Boogie	1957	50.00

SAVOY

Number	Title (A Side/B Side)	Yr	NM
❑ 731	Double Crossing Blues/Back Alley Blues	1950	100.00

—B-side by the Beale Street Gang

Number	Title (A Side/B Side)	Yr	NM
❑ 731	Double Crossing Blues/Ain't Nothin' Shakin'	1950	120.00
❑ 750	Cupid Boogie/Just Can't Get Free	1950	60.00
❑ 764	Wedding Blues/Far Away Blues (Xmas Blues)	1950	60.00
❑ 766	Rockin' Blues/My Heart Tells Me	1950	60.00
❑ 777	Gee Baby/Mambo Boogie	1951	50.00
❑ 780	Doggin' Blues/Living and Loving You	1951	50.00
❑ 787	I Dream/Hangover Blues	1951	50.00
❑ 788	All Nite Long/New Love	1951	50.00
❑ 812	Warning Blues/I'll Ask My Heart	1951	50.00
❑ 815	Harlem Nocturne/Midnight in the Barrelhouse	1951	50.00
❑ 824	Get Together Blues/Chittlin' Switch	1951	50.00
❑ 855	It Ain't the Beauty/Gonna Take a Train	1952	50.00

7-Inch Extended Plays

CAPITOL

Number	Title (A Side/B Side)	Yr	NM
❑ EAP 1-940	Hum Ding a Ling/It's Too Soon to Know//Stay with Me/Ma (He's Makin' Eyes at Me)	1958	150.00
❑ EAP 1-940 [PS]	The Johnny Otis Show	1958	150.00

Albums

ALLIGATOR

Number	Title (A Side/B Side)	Yr	NM
❑ AL-4726	The New Johnny Otis Show	1982	10.00

CAPITOL

Number	Title (A Side/B Side)	Yr	NM
❑ T 940 [M]	The Johnny Otis Show	1958	250.00
❑ C1-92858 [(2)]	The Capitol Years	1989	15.00

DIG

Number	Title (A Side/B Side)	Yr	NM
❑ 104 [M]	Rock and Roll Hit Parade, Vol. 1	1957	900.00

—Gold cover with thick cardboard and thick vinyl records. Counterfeits have noticeably thinner vinyl.

Number	Title (A Side/B Side)	Yr	NM
❑ 104 [M]	Rock and Roll Hit Parade, Vol. 1	1958	600.00

—Yellow cover with thick cardboard and thick vinyl records. Counterfeits have noticeably thinner vinyl.

EPIC

Number	Title (A Side/B Side)	Yr	NM
❑ BN 26524	Cuttin' Up	1970	25.00
❑ EG 30473 [(2)]	The Johnny Otis Show Live at Monterey	1971	30.00

KENT

Number	Title (A Side/B Side)	Yr	NM
❑ KST-534	Cold Shot	1968	25.00

SAVOY

Number	Title (A Side/B Side)	Yr	NM
❑ SJL-2230 [(2)]	The Original Johnny Otis Show	1978	15.00
❑ SJL-2252 [(2)]	The Original Johnny Otis Show, Vol. 2	1980	15.00

OTIS, SHUGGIE

45s

EPIC

Number	Title (A Side/B Side)	Yr	NM
❑ 10603	Hurricane/Jennie Lee	1970	6.00
❑ 10798	Strawberry Letter 23/Ice Cold Daydream	1971	8.00
❑ 10978	Purple (Part 1)/Purple (Part 2)	1973	6.00
❑ 50054	Inspiration Information/Aht Uh Mi Hed	1975	6.00

LUAKA BOP

Number	Title (A Side/B Side)	Yr	NM
❑ 77666	Aht Uh Mi Hed/Strawberry Letter 23	2001	4.00

Albums

EPIC

Number	Title (A Side/B Side)	Yr	NM
❑ BN 26511	Here Comes Shuggie Otis	1970	15.00
❑ KE 30752	Freedom Flight	1971	15.00
❑ PE 33059	Inspiration Information	1975	15.00

OTIS AND CARLA

45s

ATCO

Number	Title (A Side/B Side)	Yr	NM
❑ 6665	When Something Is Wrong with My Baby/Ooh Carla, Ooh Otis	1968	10.00

STAX

Number	Title (A Side/B Side)	Yr	NM
❑ 216	Tramp/Tell It Like It Is	1967	10.00
❑ 228	Knock on Wood/Let Me Be Good to You	1967	10.00
❑ 244	Lovey Dovey/New Year's Resolution	1968	10.00

Albums

STAX

Number	Title (A Side/B Side)	Yr	NM
❑ ST-716 [M]	King and Queen	1967	35.00
❑ STS-716 [S]	King and Queen	1967	50.00

SUNDAZED

Number	Title (A Side/B Side)	Yr	NM
❑ LP 5069 [S]	King and Queen	2001	12.00

—Reissue on 180-gram vinyl

OTT, JACKIE

45s

HIT

Number	Title (A Side/B Side)	Yr	NM
❑ 49	From a Jack to a King/Walk Right In	1963	8.00

—B-side by the Music City Orchestra

Number	Title (A Side/B Side)	Yr	NM
❑ 58	Out of My Mind/Young Lovers	1963	8.00

—B-side by Bob and Bobbie

O

OUR GANG

45s

BR'ER BIRD

Number	Title (A Side/B Side)	Yr	NM
❑ 001	Summertime Summertime/Theme from Leon's Garage	1966	200.00

OUTCASTS, THE (1) Garage-rock band from San Antonio, Texas.

45s

ASKEL

Number	Title (A Side/B Side)	Yr	NM
❑ 102	I'm in Pittsburgh (And It's Raining)/Price of Victory	1966	80.00
❑ 104	I'll Set You Free/Everyday	1966	30.00
❑ 107	Route 66/Everyday	1966	30.00

GALLANT

Number	Title (A Side/B Side)	Yr	NM
❑ 101	1523 Blair/Smokestack Lightning	1967	50.00

OUTCAST

Number	Title (A Side/B Side)	Yr	NM
❑ 6865	Nothing Ever Comes Easy/Oriental Express	1965	60.00

OUTCASTS, THE (2) Garage-rock band from Long Island.

45s

CAMEO

Number	Title (A Side/B Side)	Yr	NM
❑ 477	Today's the Day/I Didn't Have to Love Her Anymore	1967	25.00

DECCA

Number	Title (A Side/B Side)	Yr	NM
❑ 32036	Set Me Free/You'd Be Surprised	1966	15.00

Albums

CICADELIC

Number	Title (A Side/B Side)	Yr	NM
❑ CIC-987	Meet the Outcasts	1985	15.00
❑ CIC-988	Live! Standing Room Only	1985	15.00

OUTCASTS, THE (U) Definitely not (1); probably not (2); likely more than one additional group.

45s

DOT

Number	Title (A Side/B Side)	Yr	NM
❑ 16828	I Gotta Find Cupid/Mexican Maiden	1966	12.00
❑ 16897	I'll Keep Coming Back/Hava Nagila	1966	12.00

KARATE

Number	Title (A Side/B Side)	Yr	NM
❑ 531	I Found Out About You/I Can't Get Through to You	196?	30.00

SHORE BIRD

Number	Title (A Side/B Side)	Yr	NM
❑ 1005	I Wanted You/Little Bitty Man	196?	20.00

SOLA

Number	Title (A Side/B Side)	Yr	NM
❑ 12	People/You're Teaching Me	196?	30.00

STUDIO CITY

Number	Title (A Side/B Side)	Yr	NM
❑ 1040	You Do Me Wrong/Love Eternal	1962	30.00

OUTLAW BLUES BAND, THE

Albums

BLUESWAY

Number	Title (A Side/B Side)	Yr	NM
❑ BLS-6020	Breakin' In	1969	25.00
❑ BLS-6021	The Outlaw Blues Band	1968	25.00

OUTLAWS "Southern rock" band; few, if any, of their releases used the word "The" before their name. Also see LYNYRD SKYNYRD.

12-Inch Singles

ARISTA

Number	Title (A Side/B Side)	Yr	NM
❑ SP-39 [DJ]	You Are the Show/ If Dreams Came True	1979	15.00

PASHA

Number	Title (A Side/B Side)	Yr	NM
❑ AS 2513 [DJ]	Soldiers of Fortune (2 versions?)	1986	20.00
❑ AS 2570 [DJ]	One Last Ride (2 versions?)	1987	15.00

45s

ARISTA

Number	Title (A Side/B Side)	Yr	NM
❑ 0150	There Goes Another Love Song/Keep Prayin'	1975	4.00
❑ 0188	Breaker-Breaker/South Carolina	1976	4.00
❑ 0213	Green Grass and High Tides/ Prisoner	1976	5.00
❑ 0258	Hurry Sundown/So Afraid	1977	4.00
❑ 0282	Hearin' My Heart Talkin'/Holiday	1977	4.00
❑ 0338	Green Grass and High Tides/ Holiday	1978	4.00
❑ 0378	Take It Anyway You Want It/Cry Some More	1978	4.00
❑ 0397	You Are the Show/ If Dreams Came True	1979	4.00
❑ 0582	(Ghost) Riders in the Sky/ Devil's Road	1981	4.00
❑ 0597	Wishing Well/I Can't Stop Loving You	1981	4.00
❑ 0678	Running/(B-side unknown)	1982	4.00

PASHA

Number	Title (A Side/B Side)	Yr	NM
❑ ZS4-06550	One Last Ride/Saved by the Bell	1987	3.00

Albums

ARISTA

Number	Title (A Side/B Side)	Yr	NM
❑ SP-132 [EP]	Radio Remixes	1982	12.00
—Promo-only four-song sampler			
❑ AL 4042	Outlaws	1975	10.00
❑ AL 4070	Lady in Waiting	1976	10.00
❑ AQ 4070 [Q]	Lady in Waiting	1976	15.00
❑ AL 4135	Hurry Sundown	1977	10.00
❑ AB 4205	Playin' to Win	1978	10.00
❑ A2L 8114 [(2)]	Bring It Back Alive	198?	10.00
—Second reissue			
❑ A2L 8300 [(2)]	Bring It Back Alive	1978	12.00
❑ AL 8301	Outlaws	198?	8.00
—Reissue			
❑ AL 8319	Greatest Hits of the Outlaws/ High Tides Forever	198?	8.00
—Reissue			
❑ AL 8369	Hurry Sundown	198?	8.00
—Reissue			
❑ A2L 8608 [(2)]	Bring It Back Alive	198?	10.00
—Reissue			
❑ AL 9507	In the Eye of the Storm	1979	10.00
❑ AL 9542	Ghost Riders	1980	10.00
❑ AL 9584	Los Hombres Malo	1982	10.00
❑ AL 9614	Greatest Hits of the Outlaws/ High Tides Forever	1982	10.00

DIRECT DISC

Number	Title (A Side/B Side)	Yr	NM
❑ SD 16617	Outlaws	198?	50.00
—Audiophile vinyl			

PAIR

Number	Title (A Side/B Side)	Yr	NM
❑ PDL2-1050 [(2)]	The Outlaws	1986	12.00

PASHA

Number	Title (A Side/B Side)	Yr	NM
❑ BFZ 40512	Soldiers of Fortune	1986	8.00

OUTLAWS, THE (2)

45s

CRUSADE

Number	Title (A Side/B Side)	Yr	NM
❑ 92765	Chains/(B-side unknown)	1965	30.00

OUTLAWS, THE (3)

45s

DOT

Number	Title (A Side/B Side)	Yr	NM
❑ 16512	Hold-Up/Somethin' Else	1963	40.00

OUTLAWS, THE (U) Could be group (2); could be a completely different group.

45s

SMASH

Number	Title (A Side/B Side)	Yr	NM
❑ 2025	Don't Cry/Only for You	1966	12.00

OUTSIDERS, THE Lead singer Sonny Geraci later sang with CLIMAX.

45s

BELL

Number	Title (A Side/B Side)	Yr	NM
❑ 904	Changes/Lost in My World	1970	6.00

CAPITOL

Number	Title (A Side/B Side)	Yr	NM
❑ 2055	Little Bit of Lovin'/I Will Love You	1967	8.00
❑ 2216	Oh How It Hurts/We Ain't Gonna Make It	1968	8.00
❑ 5573	Time Won't Let Me/ Was It Really Real	1966	12.00
❑ 5646	Girl in Love/What Makes You So Bad	1966	10.00
❑ 5646 [PS]	Girl in Love/What Makes You So Bad	1966	20.00
❑ 5701	Respectable/Lost in My World	1966	10.00
❑ 5759	Help Me Girl/You Gotta Look	1966	10.00
❑ 5759 [PS]	Help Me Girl/You Gotta Look	1966	20.00
❑ 5843	I'll Give You Time/I'm Not Trying to Hurt You	1967	8.00
❑ 5843 [PS]	I'll Give You Time/I'm Not Trying to Hurt You	1967	20.00
❑ 5892	I Just Can't See You Anymore/ Gotta Leave Us Alone	1967	8.00
❑ 5955	I'll See You in the Summertime/ And Now You Want My Sympathy	1967	8.00
❑ 5955 [PS]	I'll See You in the Summertime/ And Now You Want My Sympathy	1967	20.00

ELLEN

Number	Title (A Side/B Side)	Yr	NM
❑ 503	Rickity-Boom-Bal-Aye/The Bird Rattle	196?	15.00

KAPP

Number	Title (A Side/B Side)	Yr	NM
❑ 2104	Tinker, Tailor/Oh You're Not So Pretty	1970	6.00

Albums

CAPITOL

Number	Title (A Side/B Side)	Yr	NM
❑ ST 2501 [S]	Time Won't Let Me	1966	30.00
❑ T 2501 [M]	Time Won't Let Me	1966	25.00
❑ ST 2558 [S]	The Outsiders Album #2	1966	30.00
❑ T 2568 [M]	The Outsiders Album #2	1966	25.00
❑ ST 2636 [S]	In	1967	25.00
❑ T 2636 [M]	In	1967	30.00
❑ ST 2745 [S]	Happening "Live!"	1967	25.00
❑ T 2745 [M]	Happening "Live!"	1967	30.00

RHINO

Number	Title (A Side/B Side)	Yr	NM
❑ RNLP-70132	The Best of the Outsiders (1965-1968)	1986	10.00

OUTSIDERS, THE (U) Probably not the same group as above.

45s

KARATE

Number	Title (A Side/B Side)	Yr	NM
❑ 505	The Guy with the Long Liverpool Hair/Outsider	1964	20.00

OVATIONS, THE (1) R&B vocal group. In essence this is two versions of the same group; the later records featured former members of OLLIE AND THE NIGHTINGALES.

45s

GOLDWAX

Number	Title (A Side/B Side)	Yr	NM
❑ 110	Pretty Little Angel/ Won't You Call	1964	15.00
❑ 113	It's Wonderful to Be in Love/ Dance Party	1965	15.00
❑ 117	I'm Living Good/Recipe for Love	1965	15.00
❑ 300	Don't Cry/I Need a Lot of Loving	1966	15.00
❑ 306	I Believe I'll Go Back Home/ Qualifications	1966	15.00
❑ 314	Me and My Imagination/ They Say	1967	15.00
❑ 322	I've Gotta Go/Kiss My Troubles and Blues Away	1967	15.00
❑ 341	Happiness/Rockin' Chair	1969	15.00
❑ 342	You Had Your Choice/ I'm Living Good	1969	15.00

MGM

Number	Title (A Side/B Side)	Yr	NM
❑ 14623	"Having a Party" Medley/ Just Too Good to Be True	1973	8.00
❑ 14705	I'm in Love/Don't Say You Love Me	1974	8.00
—As "Louis Williams and the Ovations"			

SOUNDS OF MEMPHIS

Number	Title (A Side/B Side)	Yr	NM
❑ 708	Touching Me/Don't Break Your Promise	1972	8.00
❑ 712	Hooked on a Feeling/Take It From One Who Knows	1972	8.00
❑ 717	One in a Million/So Nice to Be Loved by You	1973	8.00

Albums

MGM

Number	Title (A Side/B Side)	Yr	NM
❑ SE-4945	Having a Party	1973	15.00

SOUNDS OF MEMPHIS

Number	Title (A Side/B Side)	Yr	NM
❑ 7001	Hooked on a Feeling	1972	20.00

OVATIONS, THE (2)

45s

ANDIE

Number	Title (A Side/B Side)	Yr	NM
❑ 5017	My Lullaby/Whole Wide World	1960	40.00

BARRY

Number	Title (A Side/B Side)	Yr	NM
❑ 101	My Lullaby/The Day We Fell in Love	1961	40.00

EPIC

Number	Title (A Side/B Side)	Yr	NM
❑ 9470	Oh, What a Day/Real True Love	1961	40.00

OVATIONS, THE (3)

45s

CAPITOL

Number	Title (A Side/B Side)	Yr	NM
❑ 5082	I Just Don't Wanna Cry/Loneliness Never Entered My Mind	1963	30.00

OVATIONS, THE (U) Each of these could be by one of the above groups.

45s

HAWK

Number	Title (A Side/B Side)	Yr	NM
❑ 153	I Still Love You/Runaround	1963	200.00

JOSIE

Number	Title (A Side/B Side)	Yr	NM
❑ 916	Who Needs Love/Remembering	1964	25.00

OVERKILL

Albums

MEGAFORCE

Number	Title (A Side/B Side)	Yr	NM
❑ MRI 1469	Feel the Fire	1985	12.00

MEGAFORCE/ATLANTIC

Number	Title (A Side/B Side)	Yr	NM
❑ 81735	Taking Over	1987	10.00
❑ 81792 [EP]	Fuck You!	1987	10.00
❑ 81865	Under the Influence	1988	10.00
❑ 82045	The Years of Decay	1989	12.00

OVERMAN, RUNE

45s

PARKWAY

Number	Title (A Side/B Side)	Yr	NM
❑ 859	Madison Piano/Big Bass Boogie	1962	15.00

STACY

Number	Title (A Side/B Side)	Yr	NM
❑ 970	Beatnik Walk/Smorgasbord	1964	10.00

OWEN, MACK

45s

SUN

Number	Title (A Side/B Side)	Yr	NM
❑ 336	Walkin' and Talkin'/ Somebody Like You	1960	20.00

OWEN-B

Albums

MUS-I-COL

Number	Title (A Side/B Side)	Yr	NM
❑ 101209	Owen-B	1970	60.00

OWENS, BONNIE

45s

CAPITOL

Number	Title (A Side/B Side)	Yr	NM
❑ 2029	Don't Tell Me/ Somewhere Between	1967	8.00
❑ 2210	How Can Our Cheatin' Be Wrong/Yes I Love You Only	1968	8.00
❑ 2340	Lead Me On/I'll Always Be Glad to Take You Back	1968	8.00
❑ 2586	It Don't Take Much to Make Me Cry/My Hi-Fi to Cry By	1969	8.00
❑ 2716	Philadelphia Lawyer/ That Little Boy of Mine	1970	8.00
❑ 5459	Number One Heel/ The Longer You Wait	1965	10.00
❑ 5529	Excuse Me for Living/Souvenirs	1965	10.00
❑ 5618	Merry-Go-Round/ Livin' on Your Love	1966	10.00
❑ 5688	You Don't Even Try/ What's It Gonna Cost Me	1966	10.00
❑ 5755	Consider the Children/ I Know He Loves Me	1966	10.00
❑ 5847	Someone Else You've Known/ The Best Part of Me	1967	10.00
❑ 5977	I'd Be More of a Woman/ Everything That's Fastened Down Is Coming Loose	1967	10.00

MAR-VEL

Number	Title (A Side/B Side)	Yr	NM
❑ 102	A Dear John Letter/ Wonderful World	1953	50.00
—With Fuzzy Owens			

 Except when noted otherwise, VG = 25% of NM, and VG+ = 50% of NM. (Example: VG = $2.00, VG+ = $4.00 and NM = $8.00.)

Number	Title (A Side/B Side)	Yr	NM
TALLY			
❑ 149	Why Don't Daddy Live Here Anymore/Waggin' Tongues	1963	25.00
❑ 156	Don't Take Advantage of Me/Stop the World	1964	25.00
❑ 184	Lie a Little/I'll Try Again Tomorrow	1964	25.00
"X"			
❑ 0028	I Traded My Heart for His Gold/Take Me	1954	40.00
❑ 0065	No Tomorrow/Just a Love for Someone to Steal	1954	40.00

Albums

Number	Title	Yr	NM
CAPITOL			
❑ ST-195	Lead Me On	1969	25.00
❑ ST-341	Hi-Fi to Cry By	1969	25.00
❑ ST-557	Mother's Favorite Hymns	1970	25.00
❑ ST 2403 [S]	Don't Take Advantage of Me	1965	25.00
❑ T 2403 [M]	Don't Take Advantage of Me	1965	20.00
❑ ST 2600 [S]	All of Me Belongs to You	1967	25.00
❑ T 2600 [M]	All of Me Belongs to You	1967	25.00
❑ ST 2861	Somewhere Between	1968	25.00

OWENS, BUCK

45s

Number	Title (A Side/B Side)	Yr	NM
CAPITOL			
❑ 2001	It Takes People Like You (To Make People Like Me)/You Left Her Lonely Too Long	1967	8.00
❑ 2001 [PS]	It Takes People Like You (To Make People Like Me)/You Left Her Lonely Too Long	1967	12.00
❑ 2080	How Long Will My Baby Be Gone/Everybody Needs Somebody	1968	8.00
❑ 2080 [PS]	How Long Will My Baby Be Gone/Everybody Needs Somebody	1968	12.00
❑ 2142	Sweet Rosie Jones/Happy Times Are Here Again	1968	8.00
❑ 2142 [PS]	Sweet Rosie Jones/Happy Times Are Here Again	1968	12.00
❑ 2237	Let the World Keep On a-Turnin'/I'll Love You Forever and Ever	1968	8.00
—With Buddy Alan			
❑ 2237 [PS]	Let the World Keep On a-Turnin'/I'll Love You Forever and Ever	1968	12.00
—As "Buck Owens and Buddy Alan and the Buckaroos"			
❑ 2300	I've Got You on My Mind Again/That's All Right with Me (If It's All Right with You)	1968	8.00
❑ 2300 [PS]	I've Got You on My Mind Again/That's All Right with Me (If It's All Right with You)	1968	12.00
❑ 2328	Christmas Shopping/One of Everything You Got	1968	8.00
❑ 2330	Turkish Holiday/Things I Saw Happening at the Fountain	1968	8.00
❑ 2377	Who's Gonna Mow Your Grass/There's Gotta Be Some Chances Made	1969	8.00
❑ 2377 [PS]	Who's Gonna Mow Your Grass/There's Gotta Be Some Chances Made	1969	12.00
❑ 2485	Johnny B. Goode/Maybe If I Close My Eyes (It'll Go Away)	1969	8.00
❑ 2485 [PS]	Johnny B. Goode/Maybe If I Close My Eyes (It'll Go Away)	1969	12.00
❑ 2570	Tall Dark Stranger/Sing That Kind of Song	1969	8.00
❑ 2570 [PS]	Tall Dark Stranger/Sing That Kind of Song	1969	12.00
❑ 2646	Big in Vegas/White Satin Bed	1969	8.00
❑ 2646 [PS]	Big in Vegas/White Satin Bed	1969	12.00
❑ 2783	The Kansas City Song/I'd Love to Be Your Man	1970	8.00
❑ 2783 [PS]	The Kansas City Song/I'd Love to Be Your Man	1970	10.00
❑ 2947	I Wouldn't Live in New York City (If They Gave Me the Whole Dang Town)/No Milk and Honey in Baltimore	1970	8.00
❑ 2947 [PS]	I Wouldn't Live in New York City (If They Gave Me the Whole Dang Town)/No Milk and Honey in Baltimore	1970	10.00
❑ 2962	Buckaroo/Okie from Muskogee	1970	12.00
—As "Buck Owens' Bakersfield Brass"			
❑ 3011	Act Naturally/My Heart Skips a Beat	1971	12.00
—As "Buck Owens' Bakersfield Brass"			
❑ 3023	Bridge Over Troubled Water/(I'm Goin') Home	1971	6.00
❑ 3023 [PS]	Bridge Over Troubled Water/(I'm Goin') Home	1971	10.00
❑ 3066	Cajun Brass/Waitin' in Your Welfare Line	1971	10.00
—As "Buck Owens' Bakersfield Brass"			
❑ 3096	Ruby (Are You Mad)/Heartbreak Mountain	1971	6.00
❑ 3164	Rollin' in My Sweet Baby's Arms/Corn Likker	1971	6.00
❑ 3164 [PS]	Rollin' in My Sweet Baby's Arms/Corn Likker	1971	10.00
❑ 3215	Too Old to Cut the Mustard/'Wham Bam	1971	6.00
—As "Buck and Buddy" (Buck Owens and BUDDY ALAN)			
❑ 3215 [PS]	Too Old to Cut the Mustard/Wham Bam	1971	10.00
❑ 3262	I'll Still Be Waiting for You/Full Time Daddy	1972	6.00
❑ 3314	Made in Japan/Black Texas Dirt	1972	6.00
❑ 3429	You Ain't Gonna Have Ol' Buck to Kick Around No More/I Love You So Much It Hurts	1972	6.00
❑ 3504	In the Palm of Your Hand/Get Out of Town Before Sundown	1972	6.00
❑ 3563	Ain't It Amazing, Gracie/The Good Old Days	1973	6.00
❑ 3688	Arms Full of Empty/Songwriter's Lament	1973	6.00
❑ 3769	Big Game Hunter/That Loving Feeling	1973	6.00
❑ F3824	Come Back/I Know What It Means	1957	20.00
❑ 3841	On the Cover of the Music City News/Stony Mountain, West Virginia	1974	6.00
❑ 3907	(It's a) Monsters' Holiday/Great Expectations	1974	6.00
❑ F3957	Sweet Thing/I Only Know That I Love You So	1957	20.00
❑ 3976	Great Expectations/Let the Fun Begin	1974	6.00
❑ 4043	41st Street Lonely Hearts Club/Weekend Daddy	1975	6.00
❑ F4090	I'll Take a Chance on Loving You/Walk the Floor	1958	20.00
❑ 4138	The Battle of New Orleans/Run Him to the Roundhouse Nellie	1975	6.00
❑ F4172	Second Fiddle/Everlasting Love	1959	20.00
❑ 4181	Meanwhile Back at the Ranch/Country Singer's Prayer	1976	6.00
❑ F4245	Under Your Spell Again/Tired of Livin'	1959	20.00
❑ 4337	Above and Beyond/Till These Dreams Come True	1960	15.00
❑ 4412	Excuse Me (I Think I've Got a Heartache)/I've Got a Right to Know	1960	15.00
❑ 4496	Foolin' Around/High As the Mountains	1961	15.00
❑ 4602	Under the Influence of Love/Bad Bad Dream	1961	15.00
❑ 4679	Nobody's Fool But Yours/Mirror Mirror on the Wall	1962	15.00
❑ 4765	Save the Last Dance for Me/King of Fools	1962	15.00
❑ 4826	Kickin' Our Hearts Around/I Can't Stop (My Lovin' You)	1962	15.00
❑ 4872	You're for Me/House Down the Block	1962	15.00
❑ 4937	Act Naturally/Over and Over Again	1963	15.00
❑ 5025	Love's Gonna Live Here/Getting Used to Losing You	1963	12.00
❑ 5136	My Heart Skips a Beat/Together Again	1964	12.00
❑ 5240	I Don't Care (Just As Long As You Love Me)/Don't Let Her Know	1964	12.00
❑ 5336	I've Got a Tiger by the Tail/Cryin' Time	1965	10.00
❑ 5336 [PS]	I've Got a Tiger by the Tail/Cryin' Time	1965	15.00
❑ 5410	Before You Go/No One But You	1965	10.00
❑ 5410 [PS]	Before You Go/No One But You	1965	15.00
❑ 5465	Only You (Can Break My Heart)/Gonna Have Love	1965	10.00
❑ 5465 [PS]	Only You (Can Break My Heart)/Gonna Have Love	1965	15.00
❑ 5517	Buckaroo/If You Want a Love	1965	10.00
❑ 5537	Santa Looked a Lot Like Daddy/All I Want for Christmas Dear Is You	1965	10.00
❑ 5537	Santa Looked a Lot Like Daddy/All I Want for Christmas Dear Is You	1973	4.00
—Orange label, "Capitol" at bottom			
❑ 5537 [PS]	Santa Looked a Lot Like Daddy/All I Want for Christmas Dear Is You	1965	15.00
❑ 5566	Waitin' in Your Welfare Line/In the Palm of Your Hand	1965	10.00
❑ 5647	Think of Me/Heart of Glass	1966	10.00
❑ 5647 [PS]	Think of Me/Heart of Glass	1966	15.00
❑ 5705	Open Up Your Heart/No More Me and You	1966	10.00
❑ 5705 [PS]	Open Up Your Heart/No More Me and You	1966	15.00
❑ 5811	Where Does the Good Times Go/The Way That I Love You	1967	8.00
❑ 5811 [PS]	Where Does the Good Times Go/The Way That I Love You	1967	12.00
❑ 5865	Sam's Place/Don't Ever Tell Me Goodbye	1967	8.00
❑ 5865 [PS]	Sam's Place/Don't Ever Tell Me Goodbye	1967	12.00
❑ 5942	Your Tender Loving Care/What a Liar I Am	1967	8.00
❑ 5942 [PS]	Your Tender Loving Care/What a Liar I Am	1967	12.00
❑ B-44248	Hot Dog/Second Fiddle	1988	4.00
❑ B-44248 [PS]	Hot Dog/Second Fiddle	1988	5.00
❑ B-44295	A-11/Sweethearts in Heaven	1989	4.00
❑ B-44356	Put a Quarter in the Jukebox/Don't Let Her Know	1989	4.00
❑ B-44409	Act Naturally/The Key's in the Mailbox	1989	15.00
—A-side with Ringo Starr			
❑ 7PRO-79805 [DJ]	Gonna Have Love (same on both sides)	1989	10.00
—Vinyl is promo only			
DIXIE			
❑ 505	Hot Dog/Rhythm and Booze	1956	400.00
—As "Corky Jones"			
PEP			
❑ 105	It Don't Show on Me/Down on the Corner of Love	1956	50.00
❑ 106	The House Down the Block/Right After the Dance	1956	50.00
❑ 107	Hot Dog/Rhythm and Booze	1956	250.00
—As "Corky Jones"			
❑ 109	There Goes My Love/Sweethearts in Heaven	1957	50.00
REPRISE			
❑ 27964	Streets of Bakersfield/One More Name	1988	3.00
—With Dwight Yoakam			
❑ 27964 [PS]	Streets of Bakersfield/One More Name	1988	4.00
STARDAY			
❑ 571	There Goes My Love/It Don't Show on Me	1961	15.00
❑ 588	Down on the Corner of Love/Right After the Dance	1962	15.00
❑ 7010	Sweethearts in Heaven/Down on the Corner of Love	196?	5.00
❑ 8004	Sweethearts in Heaven/Down on the Corner of Love	197?	4.00
WARNER BROS.			
❑ 8223	Hollywood Waltz/Rain on Your Parade	1976	5.00
❑ 8255	California Okie/Child Support	1976	5.00
❑ 8316	World Famous Paradise Inn/He Don't Deserve You Anymore	1977	5.00
❑ 8316	World Famous Holiday Inn/He Don't Deserve You Anymore	1977	10.00
❑ 8395	It's Been a Long, Long Time/Rain on Your Parade	1977	5.00
❑ 8433	Our Old Mansion/How Come My God Don't Bark	1977	5.00
❑ 8486	Let the Good Times Roll/Texas Tornado	1977	5.00
❑ 8614	Nights Are Forever Without You/When I Need You	1978	4.00
❑ 8701	Do You Wanna Make Love/Seasons of My Heart	1978	4.00
❑ 8830	Play Together Again Again/He Don't Deserve You Anymore	1979	4.00
—A-side with Emmylou Harris			
❑ 49046	Hangin' In and Hangin' On/Sweet Molly Brown's	1979	4.00
❑ 49118	Let Jesse Rob the Train/Victim of Life's Circumstances	1979	4.00
❑ 49200	Love Is a Warm Cowboy/I Don't Want to Live in San Francisco	1980	4.00
❑ 49278	Moonlight and Magnolia/Nickels and Dimes	1980	4.00
❑ 49651	Without You/Love Don't Make the Bars	1981	4.00

7-Inch Extended Plays

Number	Title	Yr	NM
CAPITOL			
❑ SXA-1777	You're for Me/Down on the Corner of Love/Fool Me Again//Country Polka/Under the Influence of Love/Nobody's Fool But Yours	196?	20.00
—Jukebox issue; small hole, plays at 33 1/3 rpm			

O

Number	Title (A Side/B Side)	Yr	NM
SXA-1777 [PS]	You're for Me	196?	20.00
SXA-2186	I Don't Care/Don't Let Her Know/Playboy//You're Welcome Anytime/Bud's Bounce/Understand Your Man	196?	20.00
—Jukebox issue; small hole, plays at 33 1/3 rpm			
SXA-2186 [PS]	I Don't Care	196?	20.00
SXA-2283	I've Got a Tiger by the Tail/Trouble and Me/Wham Bam//Fallin' for You/We're Gonna Let the Good Times Roll/Memphis	1965	20.00
—Jukebox issue; small hole, plays at 33 1/3 rpm			
SXA-2283 [PS]	I've Got a Tiger by the Tail	1965	20.00
SU-2353	No Fool Like an Old Fool/Steel Guitar Rag/I Betcha Didn't Know//There's Gonna Come a Day/Raz-Ma-Taz Polka/Charlie Brown	196?	20.00
—Jukebox issue; small hole, plays at 33 1/3 rpm			
SU-2353 [PS]	Before You Go/No One But You	196?	20.00
R-5446	Memphis/Let the Bad Times Roll On//Fallin' for You/If You Fall Out of Love	1965	15.00
R-5446 [PS]	4-By Buck Owens	1965	25.00
Albums			
CAPITOL			
ST-131	I've Got You on My Mind Again	1969	20.00
SKAO-145	The Best of Buck Owens, Vol. 3	1969	20.00
ST-194	Anywhere U.S.A.	1969	20.00
ST-212	Tall Dark Stranger	1969	20.00
ST 8-0232	Buck Owens in London	1969	25.00
—Capitol Record Club edition			
ST-232	Buck Owens in London	1969	20.00
SWBB-257 [(2)]	Close-Up	1969	20.00
—Reissue of "Together Again" and "No One But You"			
ST-439	Your Mother's Prayer	1970	20.00
ST-476	The Kansas City Song	1970	20.00
STBB-486 [(2)]	A Merry "Hee Haw" Christmas	1970	25.00
STCL-574 [(3)]	Buck Owens	1970	40.00
ST-628	I Wouldn't Live in New York City	1970	20.00
ST-685	Bridge Over Troubled Water	1971	15.00
ST-830	The Best of Buck Owens, Vol. 4	1971	15.00
ST 1482 [S]	Buck Owens Sings Harlan Howard	1961	50.00
T 1482 [M]	Buck Owens Sings Harlan Howard	1961	40.00
DT 1489 [R]	Under Your Spell Again	1968	25.00
—"Duophonic" reissue of mono original with new title			
T 1489 [M]	Buck Owens	1961	40.00
—Black colorband label, Capitol logo at left			
T 1489 [M]	Buck Owens	1962	30.00
—Black colorband label, Capitol logo at top			
ST 1777 [S]	You're for Me	1962	50.00
T 1777 [M]	You're for Me	1962	40.00
ST 1879 [S]	On the Bandstand	1963	50.00
T 1879 [M]	On the Bandstand	1963	40.00
ST 1989 [S]	Buck Owens Sings Tommy Collins	1963	50.00
T 1989 [M]	Buck Owens Sings Tommy Collins	1963	40.00
ST 2105 [S]	The Best of Buck Owens	1964	30.00
T 2105 [M]	The Best of Buck Owens	1964	25.00
ST 2135 [S]	Together Again/My Heart Skips a Beat	1964	30.00
T 2135 [M]	Together Again/My Heart Skips a Beat	1964	25.00
ST 2186 [S]	I Don't Care	1964	30.00
T 2186 [M]	I Don't Care	1964	25.00
ST 2283 [S]	I've Got a Tiger by the Tail	1965	30.00
T 2283 [M]	I've Got a Tiger by the Tail	1965	25.00
ST 2353 [S]	Before You Go/No One But You	1965	30.00
T 2353 [M]	Before You Go/No One But You	1965	25.00
ST 2367 [S]	The Instrumental Hits of Buck Owens & the Buckaroos	1965	30.00
T 2367 [M]	The Instrumental Hits of Buck Owens & the Buckaroos	1965	25.00
ST 2396 [S]	Christmas with Buck Owens and His Buckaroos	1965	30.00
T 2396 [M]	Christmas with Buck Owens and His Buckaroos	1965	20.00
ST 2443 [S]	Roll Out the Red Carpet for Buck Owens & The Buckaroos	1966	25.00
T 2443 [M]	Roll Out the Red Carpet for Buck Owens & The Buckaroos	1966	20.00
ST 2497 [S]	Dust on Mother's Bible	1966	25.00
T 2497 [M]	Dust on Mother's Bible	1966	20.00
ST 2556 [S]	Carnegie Hall Concert	1966	25.00
T 2556 [M]	Carnegie Hall Concert	1966	20.00
ST 2650 [S]	Open Up Your Heart	1967	25.00
T 2650 [M]	Open Up Your Heart	1967	20.00
ST 2715 [S]	Buck Owens and His Buckaroos in Japan	1967	25.00
T 2715 [M]	Buck Owens and His Buckaroos in Japan	1967	20.00
ST 2760 [S]	Your Tender Loving Care	1967	25.00
T 2760 [M]	Your Tender Loving Care	1967	25.00
ST 2841 [S]	It Takes People Like You to Make People Like Me	1968	25.00
T 2841 [M]	It Takes People Like You to Make People Like Me	1968	40.00
ST 2897	The Best of Buck Owens, Vol. 2	1968	25.00
ST 2902	A Night on the Town	1968	25.00
ST 2962	Sweet Rosie Jones	1968	25.00
ST 2977	Christmas Shopping	1968	25.00
SPRO 2980/1 [DJ]	Minute Masters	1966	50.00
—Promo-only excerpts of 24 songs			
ST 2994	Buck Owens, The Guitar Player	1968	25.00
ST-11105	Live at the White House	1972	15.00
ST-11136	In the Palm of Your Hand	1973	15.00
SMAS-11180	Ain't It Amazing, Gracie	1973	15.00
ST-11222	Arms Full of Empty	1972	15.00
ST-11273	The Best of Buck Owens Vol. 5	1973	15.00
ST-11332	Monster's Holiday	1974	15.00
ST-11390	Weekend Daddy	1974	15.00
ST-11471	The Best of Buck Owens, Vol. 6	1976	15.00
C1-91132	Hot Dog!	1988	12.00
C1-92893	Act Naturally	1989	15.00
COUNTRY MUSIC FOUNDATION			
CMF-012	Live at Carnegie Hall	198?	12.00
LABREA			
1017 [M]	Buck Owens	1961	100.00
8017 [S]	Buck Owens	1961	150.00
STARDAY			
SLP-172	The Fabulous Country Music Sound of Buck Owens	1962	50.00
SLP-324	Coutnry Hit Maker #1	1964	25.00
TIME-LIFE			
STW-114	Country Music	1981	10.00
WARNER BROS.			
BS 2952	Buck 'Em	1976	12.00
BS 3087	Our Old Mansion	1977	12.00

OWENS, BUCK, AND ROSE MADDOX

Number	Title (A Side/B Side)	Yr	NM
45s			
CAPITOL			
4550	Mental Cruelty/Loose Talk	1961	15.00
4992	We're the Talk of the Town/Sweethearts in Heaven	1963	15.00

OWENS, BUCK, AND SUSAN RAYE

Also see each artist's individual listings.

Number	Title (A Side/B Side)	Yr	NM
45s			
CAPITOL			
2731	We're Gonna Get Together/Everybody Needs Somebody	1970	8.00
2731 [PS]	We're Gonna Get Together/Everybody Needs Somebody	1970	10.00
2791	Togetherness/Fallin' for You	1970	8.00
2791 [PS]	Togetherness/Fallin' for You	1970	10.00
2871	The Great White Horse/Your Tender Loving Care	1970	8.00
2871 [PS]	The Great White Horse/Your Tender Loving Care	1970	10.00
3225	Santa's Gonna Come in a Stagecoach/One of Everything You Got	1971	8.00
3368	Looking Back to See/Cryin' Time	1972	6.00
3368 [PS]	Looking Back to See/Cryin' Time	1972	10.00
3601	The Good Old Days (Are Here Again)/When You Get to Heaven (I'll Be There)	1973	6.00
4100	Love Is Strange/Sweethearts in Heaven	1975	6.00
Albums			
CAPITOL			
ST-448	We're Gonna Get Together	1970	20.00
ST-558	Great White Horse	1970	15.00
ST-837	Merry Christmas from Buck Owens and Susan Raye	1971	15.00
ST-11084	The Best of Buck Owens and Susan Raye	1972	15.00
ST-11204	The Good Old Days (Are Here Again)	1973	15.00

OWENS BROTHERS, THE

Number	Title (A Side/B Side)	Yr	NM
45s			
ABC-PARAMOUNT			
9775	Night Train/Don't Cry	1956	40.00
—Also released on Sheraton by the Four Chaps.			

OXFORD CIRCLE, THE

Number	Title (A Side/B Side)	Yr	NM
45s			
WORLD UNITED			
002	Mind Destruction/Foolsih Woman	196?	50.00

OXFORD CIRCUS, THE

Number	Title (A Side/B Side)	Yr	NM
45s			
ZIG ZAG			
101	Tracy/4th Street Carnival	1967	40.00

OZ KNOZZ

Number	Title (A Side/B Side)	Yr	NM
Albums			
OZONE			
O2-1000	Ruff Mix	1975	500.00

OZARK MOUNTAIN DAREDEVILS

Number	Title (A Side/B Side)	Yr	NM
12-Inch Singles			
COLUMBIA			
AS 766 [DJ]	Take You Tonight (same on both sides)	1980	15.00
45s			
A&M			
1477	Country Girl/Within Without	1973	5.00
1515	If You Wanna Get to Heaven/Spaceship Orion	1974	5.00
1623	Look Away/It Probably Always Will	1974	4.00
1654	Jackie Blue/Better Days	1974	4.00
1654 [PS]	Jackie Blue/Better Days	1974	6.00
1709	Colorado Song/Thin Ice	1975	4.00
1772	If I Only Knew/Dreams	1975	4.00
1808	Keep On Churnin'/Time Warp	1976	4.00
1809	You Make It Right/Dreams	1976	4.00
1842	Chicken Train Stomp/Journey to the Center of Your Heart	1976	4.00
1880	Noah (Let It Rain)/Red Plum	1976	4.00
1888	You Know Like I Know/Arroyo	1976	4.00
1888 [PS]	You Know Like I Know/Arroyo	1976	6.00
1989	Crazy Lovin'/Stinghead	1977	4.00
2016	Following (The Way That I Feel)/Snowbound	1978	4.00
COLUMBIA			
1-11247	Take You Tonight/Runnin' Out	1980	4.00
1-11357	Oh Darlin'/Sailin' Around the World	1980	4.00
Albums			
A&M			
SP-3110	The Ozark Mountain Daredevils	198?	8.00
—Budget-line reissue			
SP-3192	It'll Shine When It Shines	198?	8.00
—Budget-line reissue			
SP-3202	The Best of Ozark Mountain Daredevils	1982	10.00
SP-3654	It'll Shine When It Shines	1974	12.00
SP-4411	The Ozark Mountain Daredevils	1973	12.00
SP-4549	The Car Over the Lake Album	1975	12.00
SP-4601	Men from Earth	1976	12.00
SP-4662	Don't Look Down	1977	12.00
SP-6006 [(2)]	It's Alive	1978	15.00
COLUMBIA			
JC 36375	Ozark Mountain Daredevils	1980	10.00
SOUNDS GREAT			
SG-5004	The Lost Cabin Sessions	1985	10.00

OZONE, MAKOTO

Number	Title (A Side/B Side)	Yr	NM
Albums			
COLUMBIA			
BFC 39624	Makoto Ozone	1985	10.00
FC 40240	After	1986	10.00
FC 40676	Now You Know	1987	10.00

P

P.F.M.

Number	Title (A Side/B Side)	Yr	NM
45s			
MANTICORE			
2002	Celebration/(B-side unknown)	1973	6.00
7003	Mr. Nine Til Five/Celebration	1974	5.00
Albums			
ASYLUM			
7E-1071	Chocolate Kings	1976	10.00
7E-1101	Jet Lag	1977	10.00
MANTICORE			
MA6-502	P.F.M. 'Cook'	1974	12.00
MC 66668	Photos of Ghosts	1973	12.00
MC 66673	The World Became the World	1974	12.00

P.J.

Number	Title (A Side/B Side)	Yr	NM
45s			
TAMLA			
54215	T.L.C./It Takes a Man to Teach a Woman How to Love	1972	25.00
V.I.P.			
25062	It Takes a Man to Teach a Woman How to Love/The Best Years of My Life	1970	40.00

Except when noted otherwise, VG = 25% of NM, and VG+ = 50% of NM. (Example: VG = $2.00, VG+ = $4.00 and NM = $8.00.)

Number	Title (A Side/B Side)	Yr	NM
PACERS, THE More than one group.			
45s			
CALICO			
❑ 101/2	I Found a Dream/I Wanna Dance with You	1958	30.00
CORAL			
❑ 62398	Sassy Sue/You Got Me Bugged	1964	10.00
GUYDEN			
❑ 2064	How Sweet/No Wonder	1962	1500.
RAZORBACK			
❑ 103	Fright Street/Sooie	1958	25.00
❑ 108	Confound It/Skeeter Dape	1960	25.00
❑ 112	Don't Get Around Much/ Sad Sad	1962	25.00
❑ 115	West Memphis/Dollar, Two Ninety-Eight	1963	25.00
❑ 118	Tennessee Stud/ Beautiful Debbie	1964	20.00
❑ 123	The Pit/Pace Setter	1965	20.00
❑ 125	Batman/Gotham City	1966	20.00
❑ 137	Short Squashed Texan/ Sock It To 'Em Soobey	1967	20.00
Albums			
RAZORBACK			
❑ 121 [M]	You Asked For It	1965	100.00
PACIFIC DRIFT			
45s			
DERAM			
❑ 85063	Tomorrow Morning Brings/ Yes You Do	1970	8.00
Albums			
DERAM			
❑ DES 18040	Feelin' Free	1970	20.00
PACIFIC GAS & ELECTRIC			
45s			
COLUMBIA			
❑ 45009	Redneck/Bluebuster	1969	6.00
❑ 45158	Are You Ready?/Staggolee	1970	6.00
—Available with at least three different label variations, all equal in value			
❑ 45221	Elvira/Father Come On Home	1970	5.00
❑ 45304	The Time Has Come Death Row No. 172	1971	5.00
❑ 45444	One More River to Cross/ Rocky Roller's Lament	1971	5.00
❑ 45519	Thank God for You Baby/ See the Monkey Run	1971	5.00
❑ 45621	Heat Wave/We Did What We Could	1972	5.00
KENT			
❑ 4538	The Hunter/Long Handled Shovel	1971	12.00
POWER			
❑ 1701	Wade in the Water/Live Love	1969	10.00
Albums			
ABC DUNHILL			
❑ DSX-50157	Pacific Gas and Electric Starring Charlie Allen	1974	12.00
BRIGHT ORANGE			
❑ 701	Get It On	1968	40.00
COLUMBIA			
❑ CS 1017	Are You Ready	1970	12.00
—Orange label			
❑ CS 1017	Are You Ready	1970	15.00
—"360 Sound" label			
❑ CS 9900	Pacific Gas and Electric	1969	15.00
—"360 Sound" label			
❑ CS 9900	Pacific Gas and Electric	1970	12.00
—Orange label			
❑ C 30362	PG&E	1971	12.00
❑ C 32019	The Best of Pacific Gas & Electric	1972	12.00
POWER			
❑ 701	Get It On	1969	25.00
PACKARDS, THE			
45s			
PARADISE			
❑ 105	Dream of Love/Ding Dong	1956	400.00
PLA-BAC			
❑ 106	Ladise/My Doctor of Love	1956	2000.
PADDY, KLAUS AND GIBSON			
45s			
CHESS			
❑ 1956	No Good Without You Baby/ Rejected	1966	8.00

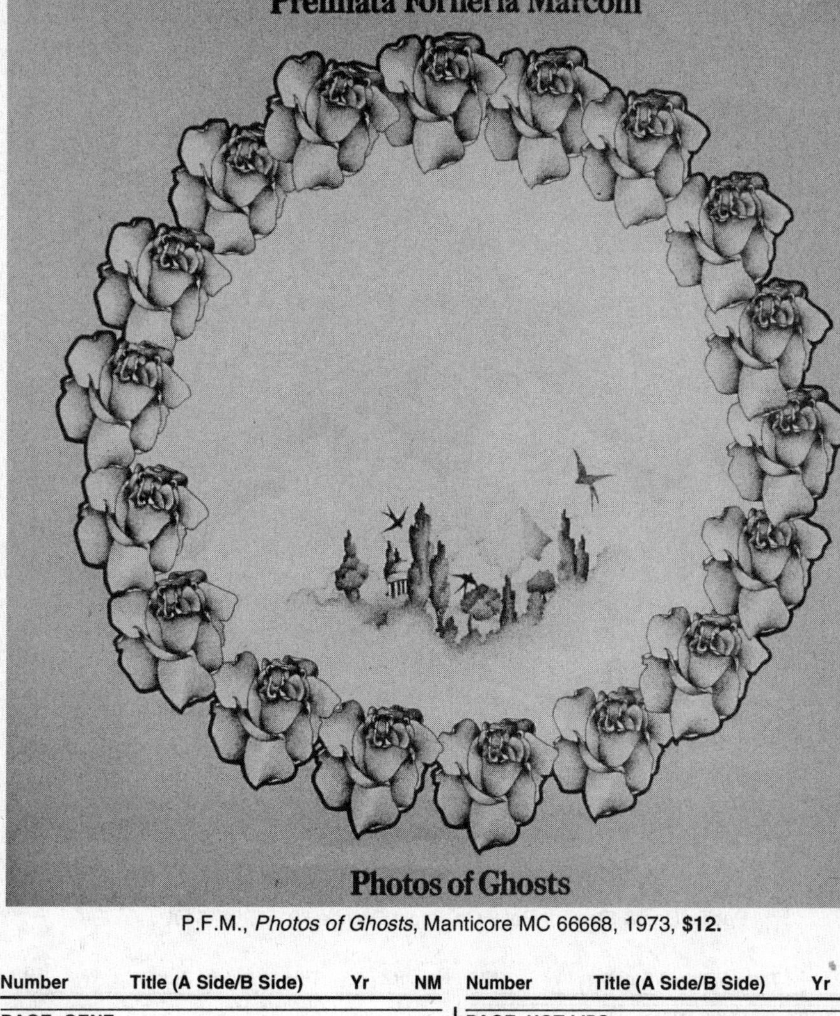

P.F.M., *Photos of Ghosts*, Manticore MC 66668, 1973, **$12.**

Number	Title (A Side/B Side)	Yr	NM
PAGE, GENE			
12-Inch Singles			
ARISTA			
❑ SP-13 [DJ]	Close Encounters of the Third Kind (6:00) (3:38)	1978	10.00
ATLANTIC			
❑ DSKO 69 [DJ]	Wild Cherry (6:00) (same on both sides)	1976	12.00
45s			
ARISTA			
❑ 0302	Close Encounters of the Third Kind/When You Wish Upon a Star	1978	5.00
❑ 0322	Theme from "Star Trek"/Sho Like to Ride on a Star	1978	5.00
❑ 0337	Moonglow-Love Theme/ Beyond the Hole in Space	1978	5.00
❑ 0492	Love Starts After Dark/ I Wanna Dance	1980	4.00
❑ 0516	Put a Little Love in Your Lovin'/ With You in the Night	1980	4.00
ATLANTIC			
❑ 3247	All My Dreams Are Coming True/Cream Corner	1975	5.00
❑ 3322	Wild Cherry/Fantasy Woman	1976	5.00
❑ 3338	Into My Thing/Organ Grinder	1976	5.00
Albums			
ARISTA			
❑ AL 4174	Close Encounters	1978	10.00
❑ AL 4262	Love Starts After Dark	1980	10.00
ATLANTIC			
❑ SD 18111	Hot City	1974	12.00
❑ SD 18161	Lovelock!	1975	12.00

Number	Title (A Side/B Side)	Yr	NM
PAGE, HOT LIPS			
45s			
KING			
❑ 1404	Cadillac Song/ Ain't Nothing Wrong	1954	100.00
❑ 4584	Last Call for Alcohol/Old Parie	1952	300.00
❑ 4594	I Bongo You/Ruby	1953	200.00
❑ 4616	Jungle King/What Shall I Do	1953	150.00
RCA VICTOR			
❑ 50-0120	Let Me In/That's the One for Me	1951	100.00
❑ 50-0129	Strike While the Iron's Hot/ I Wanna Ride Like the Cowboys Do	1951	100.00
Albums			
CONTINENTAL			
❑ 16007 [M]	Hot and Cozy	1962	30.00
ONYX			
❑ 207	After Hours	197?	12.00
XANADU			
❑ 107	Trumpet at Minton's	197?	12.00
PAGE, JIMMY Also see LED ZEPPELIN; JIMMY PAGE AND ROBERT PLANT; THE YARDBIRDS; THE FIRM; HONEYDRIPPERS.			
45s			
GEFFEN			
❑ 27821	Wasting My Time/Fires of Winter	1988	5.00
Albums			
GEFFEN			
❑ GHS 24188	Outrider	1988	10.00
SPRINGBOARD			
❑ SPB-4038	Special Early Works	1972	25.00

P

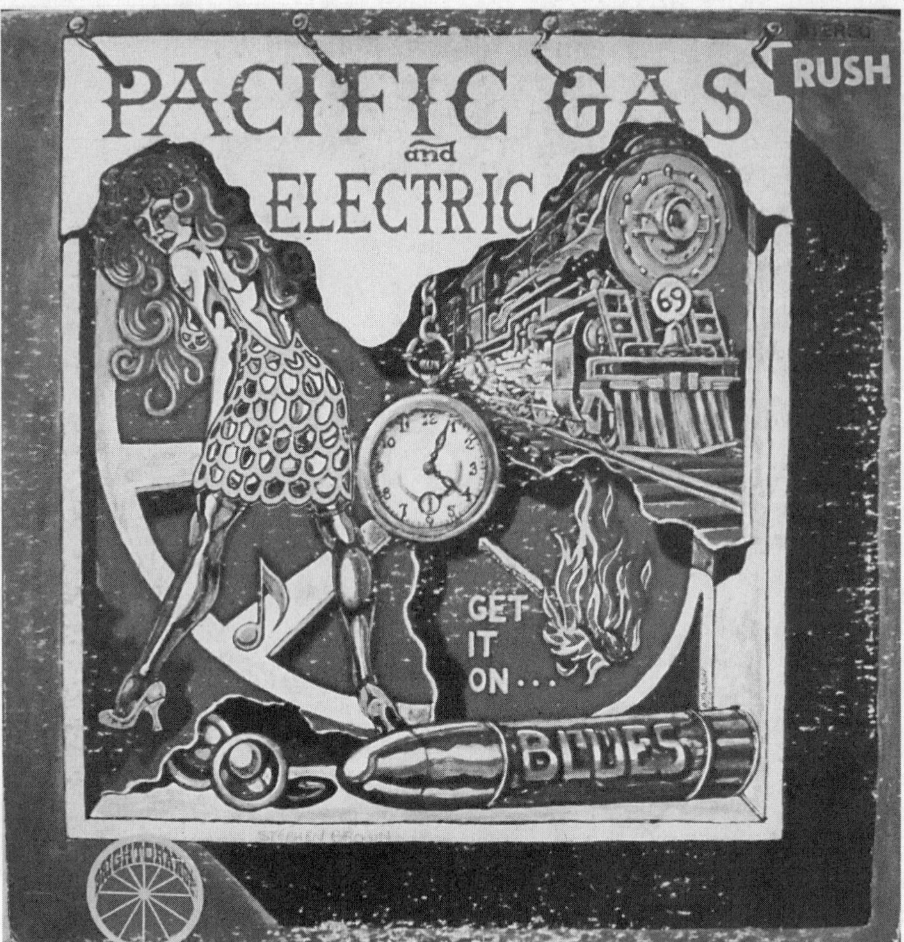

Pacific Gas & Electric, *Get It On*, Bright Orange 701, 1968, **$40.**

Number	Title (A Side/B Side)	Yr	NM
PAGE, LARRY, ORCHESTRA			
45s			
CALLA			
❑ 126	Jo Jo/Waltzing to Jazz	1966	12.00
❑ 144	Girl on a Swing/The Last Waltz	1967	10.00
LONDON			
❑ 259	I'm Hooked on You/Erotic Soul	1977	4.00
PAGE ONE			
❑ 21010	Hey Jude/Those Were the Days	1969	8.00
❑ 21018	Promises, Promises/ Wichita Lineman	1969	8.00
Albums			
RHINO			
❑ RNLP-058	Kinky Music	1984	10.00
❑ RNDF-257 [PD]	Kinky Music	1984	12.00
PAGE BOYS, THE Probably more than one group.			
45s			
ABC-PARAMOUNT			
❑ 10323	Lonely Sea/Road of Life	1962	10.00
BIG B			
❑ 1017	Santa's Snowdeer/ White Wonderland	19??	8.00
DECCA			
❑ 31505	If Tears Could Speak/ Ole Buttermilk Skies	1963	12.00
HAMILTON			
❑ 50025	Barracuda/Peter Gunn	1960	12.00
PREP			
❑ 117	Waiting/This I Give to You	1957	25.00
PAGENTS, THE			
45s			
BAMBOO			
❑ 525	Pa-Cha/Sad and Lonely	1963	50.00
ERA			
❑ 3119	Enchanted/The Big Daddy	1963	30.00
❑ 3124	Glenda/Shake	1964	30.00
❑ 3134	Pa-Cha/Sad and Lonely	1964	25.00
IKE			
❑ 631	Enchanted Surf/The Big Daddy	1963	100.00
PAIGE, HAL			
45s			
ATLANTIC			
❑ 996	Drive It Home/Break of Day Blues	1953	150.00
❑ 1032	Big Foot May/Please Say You Do	1954	150.00
CHECKER			
❑ 873	Don't Have to Cry No More/ Pour the Corn	1957	20.00
FURY			
❑ 1002	Don't Have to Cry No More/ Pour the Corn	1957	80.00
❑ 1024	After Hours Blues/Going Back to My Home Town	1959	20.00
J&S			
❑ 1601	Thunderbird/Sugar Bare	1957	30.00
PAIR, THE			
45s			
LIBERTY			
❑ 55820	Get Up Off It Baby/Donna Lee	1965	—
—Canceled			
❑ 55910	Run for Your Life/Girl, I Think I Love You	1966	8.00
Albums			
LIBERTY			
❑ LRP-3410 [M]	The Pair Live! At the Ice House	1965	20.00
❑ LRP-3440 [M]	The Pair Extraordinaire	1966	15.00
❑ LRP-3461 [M]	"In"-Citement	1966	15.00
❑ LRP-3504 [M]	It's a Wonderful World	1967	15.00
❑ LST-7410 [S]	The Pair Live! At the Ice House	1965	25.00
❑ LST-7440 [S]	The Pair Extraordinaire	1966	20.00
❑ LST-7461 [S]	"In"-Citement	1966	20.00
❑ LST-7504 [S]	It's a Wonderful World	1967	20.00
PAISLEYS, THE			
Albums			
AUDIO CITY			
❑ 70	Cosmic Mind at Play	1970	200.00
PALACE GUARD, THE			
45s			
ORANGE EMPIRE			
❑ 331	All Night Long/Playgirl	1965	15.00
❑ 332	A Girl You Can Depend On/ If You Need Me	1965	15.00
❑ 400	Falling Sugar/Oh Blue	1965	15.00
PARKWAY			
❑ 111	Saturday's Child/Party Lights	1966	12.00
❑ 124	Calliope/Creed	1966	12.00
VERVE			
❑ 10410	Falling Sugar/Oh Blue	1966	10.00
PALANCE, JACK			
Albums			
WARNER BROS.			
❑ WS 1865	Palance	1970	30.00
PALISADES, THE More than one group.			
45s			
CALICO			
❑ 113	Close Your Eyes/I Can't Quit	1960	20.00
CHAIRMAN			
❑ 4401	Heaven Is Being with You/ Make the Night a Little Longer	1963	25.00
—With Carole King			
DEBRA			
❑ 1003	Chapel Bells/She Can't Stop Dancing	1963	150.00
—Also released credited to "The Magics"			
DORE			
❑ 609	Hometown Girl/Oh My Love	1961	15.00
LEADER			
❑ 806	Dear Joan/The Shrine	1960	20.00
MEDIEVAL			
❑ 205	This Is the Night/Relic Rock	1962	20.00
PALM BEACH BAND BOYS, THE			
45s			
RCA VICTOR			
❑ 47-9003	Bend It/Gypsy Caravan	1966	6.00
❑ 47-9026	I'm Gonna Sit Right Down and Write Myself a Letter/I Don't Want to Set the World on Fire	1966	6.00
❑ 47-9207	More and More/Fernanda's Theme	1967	6.00
❑ 47-9141	The Object of My Affection/ Strangers in the Night	1967	6.00
Albums			
RCA VICTOR			
❑ LPM-3734 [M]	Winchester Cathedral	1966	12.00
❑ LSP-3734 [S]	Winchester Cathedral	1966	10.00
❑ LPM-3808 [M]	The Palm Beach Band Boys Strike Again	1967	15.00
❑ LSP-3808 [S]	The Palm Beach Band Boys Strike Again	1967	10.00
PALMER, BRUCE			
Albums			
VERVE FORECAST			
❑ FTS-3086	The Cycle Is Complete	1970	20.00
PALMER, ROBERT Also see VINEGAR JOE.			
12-Inch Singles			
EMI			
❑ SPRO 4739/45 [DJ]	Mercy Mercy Me (The Ecology)-I Want You (4 versions)	1991	8.00
❑ V-56140	Tell Me I'm Not Dreaming (5 versions)	1989	6.00
EMI MANHATTAN			
❑ SPRO 04074 [DJ]	Simply Irresistible (same on both sides)	1988	6.00
❑ SPRO 04192 [DJ]	More Than Ever (LP Version)/ More Than Ever (Live)	1988	6.00
❑ 56113	Early in the Morning (3 versions)/ Disturbing Behavior	1988	6.00
ISLAND			
❑ PR 635 [DJ]	You Are in My System (6:06) (2:57)	1983	6.00
❑ PR 678 [DJ]	Pride (3 versions)	1983	8.00
❑ PR 791 [DJ]	Discipline of Love (6:44) (3:20)	1985	6.00

Except when noted otherwise, VG = 25% of NM, and VG+ = 50% of NM. (Example: VG = $2.00, VG+ = $4.00 and NM = $8.00.)

Number	Title (A Side/B Side)	Yr	NM
❑ PR 827 [DJ]	Addicted to Love (6:01) (same on both sides)	1986	8.00
❑ PR 830 [DJ]	Addicted to Love (Edit 4:04) (same on both sides)	1986	15.00
❑ PR 879 [DJ]	Hyperactive (same on both sides)	1986	6.00
❑ PR 891 [DJ]	I Didn't Mean to Turn You On (same on both sides)	1986	6.00
❑ PRO-A-906 [DJ]	Johnny and Mary	1980	8.00
—B-side is blank			
❑ PRO-A-922 [DJ]	Looking for Clues (same on both sides)	1980	8.00
❑ PR 969 [DJ]	I Didn't Mean to Turn You On (3 versions)/Addicted to Love	1986	10.00
❑ 2236 [DJ]	Sweet Lies (same on both sides)	1988	6.00
❑ 96804	I Didn't Mean to Turn You On (3 versions)/Addicted to Love	1986	8.00
❑ 96840	Discipline of Love//Woke Up Laughing/Dance for Me	1985	6.00
❑ 96984	Pride (Remix)/Pride (Dub)	1983	8.00

45s

EMI

Number	Title (A Side/B Side)	Yr	NM
❑ 7PRO-04311 [DJ]	Tell Me I'm Not Dreaming/Tell Me I'm Not Dreaming (12" Edit)	1989	5.00
—Vinyl is promo only			
❑ S7-18129	Know By Now/In the Stars	1994	3.00
❑ 50183	She Makes My Day/ Casting a Spell	1989	3.00
❑ 50183 [PS]	She Makes My Day/ Casting a Spell	1989	3.00

EMI MANHATTAN

Number	Title (A Side/B Side)	Yr	NM
❑ 50133	Simply Irresistible/Nova	1988	3.00
❑ 50133 [PS]	Simply Irresistible/Nova	1988	3.00
❑ 50157	Early in the Morning/ Disturbing Behavior	1988	3.00
❑ 50157 [PS]	Early in the Morning/ Disturbing Behavior	1988	3.00

ISLAND

Number	Title (A Side/B Side)	Yr	NM
❑ 006	Sneakin' Sally Through the Alley/ Epidemic	1974	5.00
❑ 015	Get Ta Steppin'/ Get Right On Down	1975	5.00
❑ 042	Which One of Us Is the Fool/ Get Outside	1975	5.00
❑ 049	Pressure Drop/Give Me an Inch Girl	1976	5.00
❑ 075	Man Smart, Woman Smarter/ Keep in Touch	1976	5.00
❑ 081	One Last Look/Some People Can Do What They Want	1977	5.00
❑ 100	Every Kinda People/ How Much Fun	1978	4.00
❑ 105	You Overwhelm Me/Come Over	1978	4.00
❑ 8697	Where Can It Go/You're Gonna Get What's Coming	1978	4.00
❑ 49016	Bad Case of Loving You (Doctor, Doctor)/ Love Can Run Faster	1979	4.00
❑ 49094	In Walks Love Again/Jealous	1979	4.00
❑ 49137	Can We Still Be Friends/ Remember to Remember	1979	4.00
❑ 49554	Style Kills/Johnny and Mary	1980	4.00
❑ 49620	Looking for Clues/Woke Up Laughing	1980	4.00
❑ 50042	Some Guys Have All the Luck/ Too Good to Be True	1982	4.00
❑ 99139	Bad Case of Loving You/ Sweet Lies	1989	3.00
❑ 99139 [PS]	Bad Case of Loving You/ Sweet Lies	1989	4.00
❑ 99377	Sweet Lies/Want You More	1988	3.00
❑ 99377 [PS]	Sweet Lies/Want You More	1988	3.00
❑ 99537	I Didn't Mean to Turn You On/ Get It Through Your Heart	1986	3.00
❑ 99537 [PS]	I Didn't Mean to Turn You On/ Get It Through Your Heart	1986	3.00
❑ 99545	Hyperactive/Woke Up Laughing	1986	3.00
❑ 99570	Addicted to Love/Let's Fall in Love Tonight	1986	3.00
❑ 99570 [PS]	Addicted to Love/Let's Fall in Love Tonight	1986	4.00
—First version: Close-up photo of Robert Palmer			
❑ 99570 [PS]	Addicted to Love/Let's Fall in Love Tonight	1986	4.00
—Second version: Photo of "models" band from video			
❑ 99597	Discipline of Love (Why Did You Do It)/Dance for Me	1985	3.00
❑ 99597 [PS]	Discipline of Love (Why Did You Do It)/Dance for Me	1985	3.00
❑ 99835	Pride/(B-side unknown)	1983	3.00
❑ 99835 [PS]	Pride/(B-side unknown)	1983	4.00
❑ 99866	You Are In My System/Deadline	1983	3.00
❑ 99866 [PS]	You Are In My System/Deadline	1983	3.00

MCA

Number	Title (A Side/B Side)	Yr	NM
❑ 52643	All Around the World/ It's Not Difficult	1985	3.00

Albums

EMI MANHATTAN

Number	Title (A Side/B Side)	Yr	NM
❑ E1-48057	Heavy Nova	1988	10.00

ISLAND

Number	Title (A Side/B Side)	Yr	NM
❑ PRO-819 [DJ]	Secrets	1979	30.00
—Promo-only picture disc			
❑ ILPS 9294	Sneakin' Sally Through the Alley	1975	12.00
❑ ILPS 9372	Pressure Drop	1976	12.00
❑ ILPS 9420	Some People Can Do What They Like	1977	12.00
❑ ILPS 9476	Double Fun	1978	12.00
—Original copies of the above four albums were NOT distributed by Warner Bros.			
❑ ILPS 9544	Secrets	1979	10.00
❑ ILPS 9595	Clues	1980	10.00
❑ ILPS 9665	Maybe It's Live	1982	10.00
❑ 90065	Pride	1983	10.00
❑ 90086	Sneakin' Sally Through the Alley	1984	8.00
❑ 90087	Pressure Drop	1984	8.00
❑ 90089	Secrets	1984	8.00
❑ 90471	Riptide	1985	10.00
❑ 90493	Clues	1986	8.00
❑ 90494	Double Fun	1986	8.00
❑ 91318	Addictions Vol. I	1989	12.00
—Original pressing available only for a short time			
❑ 842301-1	Addictions Vol. I	1990	10.00

WARNER BROS.

Number	Title (A Side/B Side)	Yr	NM
❑ WBMS-111 [DJ]	Live in Boston	1979	20.00
—Part of "The Warner Bros. Music Show"			

PALS, THE

45s

GUYDEN

Number	Title (A Side/B Side)	Yr	NM
❑ 2019	My Baby Likes to Rock/ Summer Is Here	1959	20.00

TURF

Number	Title (A Side/B Side)	Yr	NM
❑ 1000	My Baby Likes to Rock/ Summer Is Here	1958	40.00

PANDIT, KORLA

45s

FANTASY

Number	Title (A Side/B Side)	Yr	NM
❑ 545	Turkish Dance/Brazilian Brion	195?	15.00

VITA

Number	Title (A Side/B Side)	Yr	NM
❑ V-1	White Christmas/ Merry Christmas	195?	15.00
❑ V-2	Ave Maria/Bist Du Bi Mir	195?	15.00
❑ V-3	Adeste Fideles//Jesu Bambino/ Silent Night	195?	15.00
❑ V-4	Joy to the World/Hark! The Herald Angels Sing	195?	15.00
❑ 220	Remembering/They Say	195?	20.00

Albums

FANTASY

Number	Title (A Side/B Side)	Yr	NM
❑ 3272 [M]	Music of the Exotic East	1958	25.00
—Black vinyl			
❑ 3272 [M]	Music of the Exotic East	1958	40.00
—Red vinyl			
❑ 3284 [M]	Latin Holiday	1959	25.00
—Black vinyl			
❑ 3284 [M]	Latin Holiday	1959	40.00
—Red vinyl			
❑ 3286 [M]	Korla Pandit at the Pipe Organ	1959	25.00
—Black vinyl			
❑ 3286 [M]	Korla Pandit at the Pipe Organ	1959	40.00
—Red vinyl			
❑ 3288 [M]	Tropical Magic	1959	25.00
—Black vinyl			
❑ 3288 [M]	Tropical Magic	1959	40.00
—Red vinyl			
❑ 3293 [M]	Speak to Me of Love	1959	25.00
—Black vinyl			
❑ 3293 [M]	Speak to Me of Love	1959	40.00
—Red vinyl			
❑ 3304 [M]	Korla Pandit in Concert	1960	25.00
—Black vinyl			
❑ 3304 [M]	Korla Pandit in Concert	1960	40.00
—Red vinyl			
❑ 3320 [M]	Music of Mystery and Romance	1961	25.00
—Black vinyl			
❑ 3320 [M]	Music of Mystery and Romance	1961	40.00
—Red vinyl			
❑ 3327 [M]	Love Letters	1961	25.00
—Black vinyl			
❑ 3327 [M]	Love Letters	1961	40.00
—Red vinyl			
❑ 3329 [M]	Hypnotique	1961	25.00
—Black vinyl			
❑ 3329 [M]	Hypnotique	1961	40.00
—Red vinyl			
❑ 3334 [M]	Music of Hollywood	1962	25.00
—Black vinyl			
❑ 3334 [M]	Music of Hollywood	1962	40.00
—Red vinyl			
❑ 3342 [M]	Music for Meditation	1962	25.00
—Black vinyl			
❑ 3342 [M]	Music for Meditation	1962	40.00
—Red vinyl			
❑ 3347 [M]	Korla Pandit in Paris	1962	25.00
❑ 3350 [M]	Christmas with Korla Pandit	1962	25.00
—Black vinyl			
❑ 3350 [M]	Christmas with Korla Pandit	1962	40.00
—Red vinyl			
❑ 8013 [S]	Music of the Exotic East	1960	30.00
—Black vinyl			
❑ 8013 [S]	Music of the Exotic East	1960	50.00
—Blue vinyl			
❑ 8018 [S]	Korla Pandit at the Pipe Organ	1960	30.00
—Black vinyl			
❑ 8018 [S]	Korla Pandit at the Pipe Organ	1960	50.00
—Blue vinyl			
❑ 8027 [S]	Latin Holiday	1960	30.00
—Black vinyl			
❑ 8027 [S]	Latin Holiday	1960	50.00
—Blue vinyl			
❑ 8034 [S]	Tropical Magic	1960	30.00
—Black vinyl			
❑ 8034 [S]	Tropical Magic	1960	50.00
—Blue vinyl			
❑ 8039 [S]	Speak to Me of Love	1960	30.00
—Black vinyl			
❑ 8039 [S]	Speak to Me of Love	1960	50.00
—Blue vinyl			
❑ 8049 [S]	Korla Pandit in Concert	1960	30.00
—Black vinyl			
❑ 8049 [S]	Korla Pandit in Concert	1960	50.00
—Blue vinyl			
❑ 8061 [S]	Music of Mystery and Romance	1961	30.00
—Black vinyl			
❑ 8061 [S]	Music of Mystery and Romance	1961	50.00
—Blue vinyl			
❑ 8070 [S]	Love Letters	1961	30.00
—Black vinyl			
❑ 8070 [S]	Love Letters	1961	50.00
—Blue vinyl			
❑ 8075 [S]	Hypnotique	1961	30.00
—Black vinyl			
❑ 8075 [S]	Hypnotique	1961	50.00
—Blue vinyl			
❑ 8086 [S]	Music of Hollywood	1962	30.00
—Black vinyl			
❑ 8086 [S]	Music of Hollywood	1962	50.00
—Blue vinyl			
❑ 8342 [S]	Music for Meditation	1962	30.00
—Black vinyl			
❑ 8342 [S]	Music for Meditation	1962	50.00
—Blue vinyl			
❑ 8347 [S]	Korla Pandit in Paris	1962	30.00
❑ 8350 [S]	Christmas with Korla Pandit	1962	30.00
—Black vinyl			
❑ 8350 [S]	Christmas with Korla Pandit	1962	50.00
—Blue vinyl			

NATIONAL CUSTOM

Number	Title (A Side/B Side)	Yr	NM
❑ NCR 12-574	Fantastique!	196?	30.00

SYMPATHY FOR THE RECORD INDUSTRY

Number	Title (A Side/B Side)	Yr	NM
❑ SFTRI 387	Exotica 2000	1996	12.00

VITA

Number	Title (A Side/B Side)	Yr	NM
❑ VLP-14 [10]	Rememb'ring with Korla Pandit	195?	80.00

PANICS, THE

45s

ABC-PARAMOUNT

Number	Title (A Side/B Side)	Yr	NM
❑ 10072	Heartaches/You're Driving Me Crazy	1959	15.00

CHANCELLOR

Number	Title (A Side/B Side)	Yr	NM
❑ 1109	Panicsville/Bony Moronie	1962	15.00
❑ 1127	Skinnie Minnie Olive Oil/ Voodoo Walk	1962	15.00

PHILIPS

Number	Title (A Side/B Side)	Yr	NM
❑ 40230	The Kangaroo/It Ain't What You Got	1964	12.00

SHOESTRING

Number	Title (A Side/B Side)	Yr	NM
❑ 107	No More/I Pretend	196?	10.00

SWAN

Number	Title (A Side/B Side)	Yr	NM
❑ 4247	Beans/Show Her You Care	1966	12.00

Albums

CHANCELLOR

Number	Title (A Side/B Side)	Yr	NM
❑ CHL-5026 [M]	Panicsville	1962	30.00
❑ CHLS-5026 [S]	Panicsville	1962	40.00

PHILIPS

Number	Title (A Side/B Side)	Yr	NM
❑ PHM 200159 [M]	Discotheque Dance Party	1964	15.00
❑ PHS 600159 [S]	Discotheque Dance Party	1964	20.00

PANTERA

Offshoots include DOWN, SUPERJOINT RITUAL, DAMAGEPLAN, REBEL MEETS REBEL and HELLYEAH!.

Albums

EASTWEST

Number	Title (A Side/B Side)	Yr	NM
❑ 61908	The Great Southern Trendkill	1996	30.00
❑ 62068 [(2)]	Official Live: 101 Proof	1997	100.00

Number | Title (A Side/B Side) | Yr | NM

❑ 92302 Far Beyond Driven 1994 200.00

ELEKTRA

❑ 62451 Reinventing the Steel 2000 35.00

METAL MAGIC

❑ MMR 1283 Metal Magic 1983 150.00
❑ MMR 1984 Projects in the Jungle 1984 100.00
❑ MMR 1985 I Am the Night 1985 100.00
❑ MMR 1988 Power Metal 1988 120.00

PAPA DOO RUN RUN With BRUCE JOHNSTON.

45s

BLUE PACIFIC

❑ 1-001 Lady Love/Slow Down 197? 4.00
❑ 1-001 [PS] Lady Love/Slow Down 197? 4.00

EQUINOX

❑ PB-10404 Disney Girls/Be True to Your School 1975 10.00

Albums

TELARC

❑ 70501 California Project 1985 10.00

PAPER DOLLS, THE

45s

MGM

❑ 13766 'Cause I Love You/You're the Boy I Want to Marry 1967 12.00

UNI

❑ 55104 Someday/Any Old Time You're Lonely and Sad 1969 10.00

WARNER BROS.

❑ 7191 All the Time in the World/Something Here in My Heart (Keeps a-Tellin' Me No) 1968 10.00

PAPER GARDEN, THE

Albums

MUSICOR

❑ MS-(# unknown)The Paper Garden 1968 40.00

PAPER LACE

45s

BANG

❑ 700 Martha/You Can't Touch Me 1972 5.00
❑ 704 Ragamuffin Man/Elsie 1973 5.00
❑ 711 Ragamuffin Man/Elsie 1974
—Canceled

MERCURY

❑ 73479 Billy, Don't Be a Hero/Celia 1974 6.00
❑ 73492 The Night Chicago Died/Can You Get It When You Want It 1974 4.00
—Chicago skyline label
❑ 73492 The Night Chicago Died/Can You Get It When You Want It 1974 6.00
—Red label
❑ 73620 The Black-Eyed Boys/Jean 1974 4.00
❑ 73694 So What If I Am/Himalayan Lullaby 1975 4.00

Albums

MERCURY

❑ SRM-1-1008 Paper Lace 1974 12.00

PAPPALARDI, FELIX Also see MOUNTAIN.

45s

COLUMBIA

❑ 43773 Love Someday/You Lie to Me 1966 25.00

Albums

A&M

❑ SP-4586 Creation 1976 10.00
❑ SP-4729 Don't Worry Me 1979 10.00

PARADE, THE

45s

A&M

❑ 841 Sunshine Girl/This Old Melody 1967 10.00
❑ 867 She's Got the Magic/Welcome, You're in Love 1967 6.00
❑ 887 Frog Prince/Hallelujah Rocket 1967 6.00
❑ 904 I Can See Love/Radio Song 1968 6.00
❑ 950 A.C.-D.C./She Sleeps Alone 1968 6.00
❑ 970 Laughing Lady/Hallelujah Rocket 1968 6.00

PARADONS, THE

45s

MILESTONE

❑ 2003 Diamonds and Pearls/I Want Love 1960 20.00
—Green label
❑ 2003 Diamonds and Pearls/I Want Love 1960 30.00
—Red label
❑ 2003 Diamonds and Pearls/I Want Love 1960 50.00
—Maroon label
❑ 2005 Bells Ring/Please Tell Me 1960 30.00
❑ 2015 I Had a Dream/Never, Never 1962 40.00

TUFFEST

❑ 102 Never Again/This Is Love 1961 150.00

WARNER BROS.

❑ 5186 Take All of Me/So Fine, So Fine, So Fine 1960 20.00

PARAGONS, THE

45s

BUDDAH

❑ 478 Oh Lovin' You/Con Me 1975 6.00

LOST-NITE

❑ 121 The Vows of Love/Stick with Me Baby 196? 8.00
❑ 125 Let's Start All Over Again/Stick With Me Baby 196? 8.00
—Reissue
❑ 128 Hey Little School Girl/Florence 196? 8.00
—Reissue
❑ 130 Two Hearts Are Better Than One/Give Me Love 196? 8.00
—Reissue
❑ 133 Twilight/Stick with Me Baby 196? 8.00
❑ 160 So You Will Know/Don't Cry Baby 196? 8.00
—Reissue

MUSIC CLEF

❑ 3001/2 Time After Time/Baby, Take My Hand 1963 20.00

MUSICRAFT

❑ 1102 Wedding Bells/Blue Velvet 1960 25.00

TAP

❑ 500 If/Hey Baby 1961 50.00
❑ 503 In the Midst of the Night/Begin the Beguine 1961 40.00
❑ 504 These Are the Things I Love/If You Love Me 1961 40.00

TIMES SQUARE

❑ 9 So You Will Know/Don't Cry Baby 1963 20.00

WINLEY

❑ 215 Hey Little School Girl/Florence 1957 50.00
❑ 220 Let's Start All Over Again/Stick With Me Baby 1957 50.00
❑ 223 Two Hearts Are Better Than One/Give Me Love 1958 40.00
❑ 227 The Vows of Love/Twilight 1958 40.00
❑ 227 The Wows of Love/Twilight 1958 1000.
—With misspelled A-side title
❑ 228 Don't Cry Baby/So You Will Know 1958 40.00
❑ 236 Darling, I Love You/Doll Baby 1959 40.00
❑ 240 So You Will Know/Doll Baby 1959 30.00
❑ 250 Kneel and Pray/Just a Moment 1961 30.00

Albums

COLLECTABLES

❑ COL-5035 The Best of the Paragons 198? 10.00

LOST-NITE

❑ LLP-4 [10] The Best of the Paragons 1981 10.00
—Red vinyl; in die-cut cover with sticker

PARAGONS, THE & THE HARPTONES

Albums

MUSICTONE

❑ M-8001 [M] The Paragons vs. the Harptones 1964 40.00

PARAGONS, THE & THE JESTERS

Albums

JOSIE

❑ 4008 [M] The Paragons Meet the Jesters 1962 200.00

JUBILEE

❑ JLP-1098 [M] The Paragons Meet the Jesters 1959 300.00
—Blue label, black vinyl
❑ JLP-1098 [M] The Paragons Meet the Jesters 1959 1500.
—Multi-color splash vinyl; VG value 750; VG+ value 1125
❑ JLP-1098 [M] The Paragons Meet the Jesters 196? 60.00
—Black label with multi-color logo
❑ JLP-1098 [M] The Paragons Meet the Jesters 196? 150.00
—Flat black label

WINLEY

❑ LP-6003 [M] War! The Jesters vs. the Paragons 195? 500.00

PARAGONS, THE (2) Not the same group as the others.

45s

CENTURY CUSTOM

❑ 19317 Surf Drums/Sunday Morning 196? 60.00
—B-side by the Samohi Serenaders

PARAKEETS, THE (1)

45s

BIG TOP

❑ 3130 I Love You Like I Do/I Want You Right Now 1962 20.00

JUBILEE

❑ 5407 Come Back/Shangri-La 1961 25.00

PARAKEETS, THE (2)

45s

GEM

❑ 218 Give Me Time/I'm Losing My Mind Over You 1954 400.00

PARAMOR, NORRIE

45s

CAPITOL

❑ F3629 Every Street's a Boulevard/Magic Banjo 1957 10.00
❑ F3714 Taurus Tango/Gemini Waltz 1957 10.00
❑ F4266 Waltzing Matilda/Barcelona 1959 10.00

ESSEX

❑ 337 Callahan's Monkey/Melodia 1953 15.00
❑ 356 Wedding Day/Luxembourg Polka 1954 12.00

Albums

CAPITOL

❑ ST 2071 [S] In London…In Love Again 1964 15.00
❑ T 2071 [M] In London…In Love Again 1964 12.00
❑ ST 2357 [S] Warm and Willing 1965 15.00
❑ T 2357 [M] Warm and Willing 1965 12.00
❑ ST 2526 [S] In Tokyo — In Love 1966 15.00
❑ T 2526 [M] In Tokyo — In Love 1966 12.00
❑ ST 10025 [S] In London…In Love 196? 15.00
❑ T 10025 [M] In London…In Love 196? 12.00
❑ T 10052 [M] London After Dark 196? 12.00
❑ T 10130 [M] Norrie Paramor's Moods 196? 12.00
❑ ST 10212 [S] Autumn 196? 15.00
❑ T 10212 [M] Autumn 196? 12.00
❑ ST 10238 [S] Amor Amor 196? 15.00
❑ T 10238 [M] Amor Amor 196? 12.00

POLYDOR

❑ 24-6006 Love at First Sight 1970 10.00

PARAMOUNTS, THE (1)

45s

CARLTON

❑ 524 Girl Friend/Trying 1960 40.00

PARAMOUNTS, THE (2)

45s

CENTAUR

❑ 103 When I Dream/Where's Carolyn Tonight 1963 60.00

PARAMOUNTS, THE (3) ROBERT KNIGHT was in this group.

45s

DOT

❑ 16175 Why Do You Have to Go/Congratulations 1961 25.00
❑ 16201 When You Dance/Year 17 1961 25.00

PARAMOUNTS, THE (4) British group; an early incarnation of PROCOL HARUM.

45s

LIVERPOOL SOUND

❑ 903 Poison Ivy/I Feel Good All Over 1964 75.00

PARAMOUNTS, THE (U) Could be any of the above groups except (4), or they could be entirely different.

45s

COMBO

❑ 156 Take My Heart/Thunderbird Baby 1960 120.00

FLEETWOOD

❑ 1014 I Know You'll Be My Love/Christopher Columbus 1960 100.00

LAURIE

❑ 3201 Just to Be with You/One More for the Road 1963 30.00

LOST-NITE

❑ 374 Take My Heart/Thunderbird Baby 197? 5.00
—Reissue

MAGNUM

❑ 722 Time Will Bring a Change/Under Your Spell 1964 30.00

Number	Title (A Side/B Side)	Yr	NM
MERCURY			
❑ 72429	Girl with the Big Black Boots/I Won't Share Your Love	1965	12.00

PARAMOURS, THE BIL MEDLEY and BOBBY HATFIELD, later THE RIGHTEOUS BROTHERS.

45s

Number	Title (A Side/B Side)	Yr	NM
MOONGLOW			
❑ 214	That's All I Want Tonight/There She Goes	1962	20.00
❑ 214	That's All I Want Tonight/There She Goes	1962	40.00
—Red vinyl			
SMASH			
❑ 1701	That's the Way We Love/Prison Break	1961	20.00
❑ 1718	Cutie Cutie/Miss Social Climber	1961	20.00

PARFAYS, THE

45s

Number	Title (A Side/B Side)	Yr	NM
FONTANA			
❑ 1526	You've Got a Good Thing Goin'/Boy/In the Beginning	1965	30.00

PARIS With Bob Welch, ex-FLEETWOOD MAC.

45s

Number	Title (A Side/B Side)	Yr	NM
CAPITOL			
❑ 4356	Blue Robin/Big Towne, 2061	1976	5.00
Albums			
CAPITOL			
❑ ST-11464	Paris	1975	12.00
❑ ST-11560	Big Towne, 2061	1976	12.00

PARIS, BOBBY

45s

Number	Title (A Side/B Side)	Yr	NM
CAMEO			
❑ 396	Night Owl/Tears on My Pillow	1966	200.00
CAPITOL			
❑ 3592	Baby, Spread Your Love on Me/You're a Friend	1973	10.00
❑ 3664	You're a Friend/Baby Spread Your Love on Me	1973	20.00
❑ 3727	Love Looks So Good on You/Day Dreamer	1973	10.00
❑ 5929	I Walked Away/Kansas City	1967	500.00
—Counterfeits exist with B-sides by other artists			
CHATTAHOOCHEE			
❑ 631	Little Miss Dreamer/Who Needs You	1963	12.00
❑ 672	Love Passed Me By/The Fight	1965	15.00
JAIRICK			
❑ 204	Are You the One/Torch Is Out	1963	15.00
JOLAR			
❑ 1001	Is It You/Wishing Well	1962	15.00
MAGENTA			
❑ 03	Dark Continent (Part 1)/(Part 2)	1961	25.00
TETRAGRAMMATON			
❑ 1504	Per-So-Nal-Ly/Tragedy	1968	80.00
—Authentic copies are on styrene; counterfeits are on vinyl			
❑ 1509	Let Me Show You the Way/Bye, Bye, Blackbird	1968	20.00
❑ 1517	Let the Sunshine In (The Flesh Failures)/You	1969	10.00
Albums			
TETRAGRAMMATON			
❑ T-105 [S]	Let Me Show You the Way	1968	40.00
❑ M-2105 [M]	Let Me Show You the Way	1968	100.00

PARIS, FREDDIE No relation to FRED PARRIS.

45s

Number	Title (A Side/B Side)	Yr	NM
RCA VICTOR			
❑ 47-9232	Take Me As I Am/It's Okay to Cry Now	1967	10.00
❑ 47-9358	Little Things Can Make a Woman Cry/Face It, Boy, It's Over	1967	10.00
❑ 47-9571	There She Goes/Young Hearts, Young Hands	1968	20.00
Albums			
RCA VICTOR			
❑ LSP-4064	Lovin' Mood	1968	20.00

PARIS BROTHERS, THE

45s

Number	Title (A Side/B Side)	Yr	NM
BRUNSWICK			
❑ 55132	This Is It/Our Love Is Here to Stay	1959	30.00
CORAL			
❑ 62220	Funny Feeling/(B-side unknown)	1959	20.00

PARIS PILOT

Albums

Number	Title (A Side/B Side)	Yr	NM
HIP			
❑ 7004	Paris Pilot	1970	25.00

PARIS SISTERS, THE

45s

Number	Title (A Side/B Side)	Yr	NM
CAPITOL			
❑ 2081	Golden Days/Greener Days	1968	8.00
CAVALIER			
❑ 828	Christmas in My Home Town/Man with the Mistletoe Moustache	197?	6.00
DECCA			
❑ 29372	Ooh La La/Whose Arms Are You Missing	1954	25.00
❑ 29488	Baby, Honey, Baby/Huckleberry Pie	1955	25.00
❑ 29527	His and Hers/Truly Do	1955	25.00
—With Gary Crosby			
❑ 29574	The Know How/I Wanna	1955	25.00
❑ 29744	Lover Boy/Oh Yes You Do	1955	25.00
❑ 29891	I Love You Dear/Mistaken	1956	25.00
❑ 29970	Daughter! Daughter!/So Much — So Very Much	1956	25.00
❑ 30554	Don't Tell Anybody/Mind Reader	1958	20.00
GNP CRESCENDO			
❑ 410	Stand Naked Clown/Ugliest Girl in Town	1968	8.00
GREGMARK			
❑ 2	Be My Boy/I'll Be Crying Tomorrow	1961	20.00
❑ 6	I Love How You Love Me/All Through the Night	1961	25.00
❑ 10	He Knows I Love Him Too Much/Lonely Girl's Prayer	1962	20.00
❑ 12	Let Me Be the One/What Am I to Do	1962	20.00
❑ 13	Yes I Love You/Once Upon a While Ago	1962	20.00
—All the Gregmark records were Phil Spector productions			
IMPERIAL			
❑ 5465	Old Enough to Cry/Tell Me More	1957	20.00
❑ 5487	Some Day/My Original Love	1958	20.00
MERCURY			
❑ 72320	Once Upon a Time/When I Fall in Love	1964	10.00
❑ 72320 [PS]	Once Upon a Time/When I Fall in Love	1964	20.00
❑ 72468	Always Waitin'/Why Do I Take It from You	1965	10.00
❑ 72468 [PS]	Always Waitin'/Why Do I Take It from You	1965	20.00
MGM			
❑ 13236	Dream Lover/Lonely Girl	1964	15.00
❑ 13236 [PS]	Dream Lover/Lonely Girl	1964	25.00
REPRISE			
❑ 0440	Sincerely/Too Good to Be True	1965	10.00
❑ 0472	I'm Me/You	1966	10.00
❑ 0511	It's My Party/My Good Friend	1966	10.00
❑ 0548	Some of Your Lovin'/Long After Tonight Is All Over	1967	10.00
Albums			
REPRISE			
❑ R-6259 [M]	Everything Under the Sun	1967	40.00
❑ RS-6359 [S]	Everything Under the Sun	1967	60.00
SIDEWALK			
❑ DT 5906 [R]	Golden Hits of the Paris Sisters	1967	30.00
❑ T 5906 [M]	Golden Hits of the Paris Sisters	1967	50.00
UNIFILMS			
❑ 505 [M]	The Paris Sisters Sing Songs from Glass House	1966	40.00
❑ S-505 [S]	The Paris Sisters Sing Songs from Glass House	1966	50.00

PARISH HALL

Albums

Number	Title (A Side/B Side)	Yr	NM
FANTASY			
❑ 8398	Parish Hall	1969	20.00

PARKER, BILLIE JEAN

Albums

Number	Title (A Side/B Side)	Yr	NM
RCA VICTOR			
❑ LPM-3967 [M]	The Truth About Bonnie and Clyde	1968	40.00
❑ LSP-3967 [S]	The Truth About Bonnie and Clyde	1968	15.00

PARKER, BILLY (1)

45s

Number	Title (A Side/B Side)	Yr	NM
SOUNDWAVES			
❑ 4686	Too Many Irons in the Fire/Honky Tonk Girl	1982	5.00
—A-side with Cal Smith			

PARKER, BOBBY

45s

Number	Title (A Side/B Side)	Yr	NM
V-TONE			
❑ 223	Watch Your Step/Steal Your Heart Away	1961	15.00
—"223-AAX" in hit side trail-off area			
❑ 223	Watch Your Step/Steal Your Heart Away	1961	20.00
—"45-V Tone 223-A" in hit side trail-off area			
VEE JAY			
❑ 279	You Got What It Takes/Blues Get Off My Shoulder	1958	30.00

PARKER, CHARLIE

45s

Number	Title (A Side/B Side)	Yr	NM
CLEF			
❑ 89129	Cosmic Rays/Kim	1955	25.00
❑ 89138	I Remember You/Chi Chi	1955	25.00
❑ 89144	I Hear Music/Laird Baird	1955	25.00
MERCURY			
❑ 11070	You Came Along from Out of Nowhere/East of the Sun	195?	100.00
—Red vinyl; part of Album C-509, which means there must be others like it, but this is the only one we've confirmed			
7-Inch Extended Plays			
CLEF			
❑ EP 255	Summertime/I Didn't Know What Time It Was//Bloom Dido/Melancholy Baby	195?	50.00
❑ EP 255 [PS]	(title unknown)	195?	50.00
Albums			
ALAMAC			
❑ QSR 2430	Charlie Parker's All Stars 1950	198?	12.00
AMERICAN RECORDING SOCIETY			
❑ G-441 [M]	Now's the Time	1957	50.00
BARONET			
❑ B-105 [M]	A Handful of Modern Jazz	1962	20.00
❑ BS-105 [R]	A Handful of Modern Jazz	1962	12.00
❑ B-107 [M]	The Early Bird	1962	20.00
❑ BS-107 [R]	The Early Bird	1962	12.00
BIRDLAND			
❑ 425 [10]	A Night at Carnegie Hall	1956	300.00
BLUE NOTE			
❑ BT-85108	Charlie Parker at Storyville	198?	12.00
BLUE RIBBON			
❑ 8011 [M]	The Early Bird	1962	20.00
❑ S-8011 [R]	The Early Bird	1962	12.00
CHARLIE PARKER			
❑ PLP-401 [M]	Bird Is Free	1961	40.00
❑ PLP-404 [M]	The Happy Bird	1961	40.00
❑ PLP-406 [M]	Charlie Parker	1961	40.00
❑ PLP-407 [M]	Bird Symbols	1961	40.00
❑ PLP-408 [M]	Once There Was Bird	1961	40.00
❑ CP-2-502 [(2)M]	Live at Rockland Palace, September 26, 1952	1961	50.00
❑ CP-513 [M]	Charlie Parker Plus Strings	196?	40.00
❑ PLP-701 [(3)]	Historical Masterpieces	196?	60.00
CLEF			
❑ MGC-101 [10]	Charlie Parker with Strings	1958	—
—Canceled			
❑ MGC-157 [10]	Charlie Parker	1954	400.00
❑ MGC-501 [10]	Charlie Parker with Strings	1954	400.00
—Reissue of Mercury 501			
❑ MGC-509 [10]	Charlie Parker with Strings, No. 2	1954	400.00
—Reissue of Mercury 509			
❑ MGC-512 [10]	Bird and Diz	1954	400.00
—Reissue of Mercury 512			
❑ MGC-513 [10]	South of the Border	1954	400.00
—Reissue of Mercury 513			
❑ MGC-609 [M]	Charlie Parker Big Band	1954	400.00
❑ MGC-646 [M]	The Magnificent Charlie Parker	1955	400.00
❑ MGC-675 [M]	Charlie Parker with Strings	1955	400.00
❑ MGC-725 [M]	Night and Day	1956	120.00
COLUMBIA			
❑ C2 34808 [(2)]	One Night in Birdland	198?	12.00
—Reissue with new prefix			
❑ JG 34808 [(2)]	One Night in Birdland	1977	15.00
❑ JC 34831	Summit Meeting	1977	12.00
❑ JC 34832	Bird with Strings Live	1977	12.00
CONCERT HALL JAZZ			
❑ 1004 [10]	The Fabulous Bird	1955	60.00
❑ 1017 [10]	The Art of Charlie Parker, Vol. 2	1955	60.00

Number	Title (A Side/B Side)	Yr	NM
CONTINENTAL			
❑ 16004 [M]	Bird Lives	1962	40.00
DEBUT			
❑ DEB-611 [M]	Bird on 52nd Street	196?	50.00
DIAL			
❑ LP-201 [10]	Charlie Parker Quintet	1949	800.00
❑ LP-202 [10]	Charlie Parker Quintet	1949	800.00
❑ LP-203 [10]	Charlie Parker	1949	800.00
❑ LP-207 [10]	Charlie Parker Sextet	1949	800.00
❑ LP-901 [M]	The Bird Blows the Blues	1949	4000.
—Limited edition of 300 copies on opaque red vinyl; designed as a mail-order offer; issued with a generic gray cover; also has a pale yellow Dial label similiar to the label's 78 rpm design			
❑ LP-901 [M]	The Bird Blows the Blues	1950	600.00
—Commercial version of mail-order album			
❑ LP-904 [M]	Alternate Masters	1951	600.00
❑ LP-905 [M]	Alternate Masters	1951	600.00
ELEKTRA/MUSICIAN			
❑ 60019	One Night in Washington	1982	10.00
ESP-DISK'			
❑ ESP-BIRD-2	Broadcast Performances 1948-1949, Vol. 2	1973	20.00
EVEREST ARCHIVE OF FOLK & JAZZ			
❑ 214	Charlie Parker	1969	12.00
❑ 232	Charlie Parker, Vol. 2	1970	10.00
❑ 254	Charlie Parker, Vol. 3	197?	10.00
❑ 295	Charlie Parker, Vol. 4	197?	10.00
❑ 315	Charlie Parker, Vol. 5	197?	10.00
FANTASY			
❑ OJC-041	Bird at St. Nick's	1983	10.00
❑ OJC-044	Jazz at Massey Hall	198?	10.00
❑ OJC-114	Bird on 52nd St.	198?	10.00
❑ 6011 [M]	Bird on 52nd St.	1964	30.00
❑ 6012 [M]	Bird at St. Nick's	1964	30.00
❑ 86011 [R]	Bird on 52nd St.	1964	15.00
❑ 86012 [R]	Bird at St. Nick's	1964	15.00
HALL OF FAME			
❑ 617	Giants of Jazz	197?	10.00
❑ 620	Takin' Off	197?	10.00
JAZZ WORKSHOP			
❑ JWS-500 [M]	Bird at St. Nick's	1958	120.00
❑ JWS-501 [M]	Bird on 52nd Street	1958	120.00
JAZZTONE			
❑ J-(# unk) [M]	The Art of Charlie Parker, Vol. 2	1955	50.00
❑ J-1204 [M]	Giants of Modern Jazz	1955	50.00
❑ J-1214 [M]	The Fabulous Bird	1955	50.00
❑ J-1240 [M]	The Saxes of Stan Getz and Charlie Parker	1957	50.00
LES JAZZ COOL			
❑ 101 [M]	Les Jazz Cool, Vol. 1	1960	50.00
❑ 102 [M]	Les Jazz Cool, Vol. 2	1960	50.00
❑ 103 [M]	Les Jazz Cool, Vol. 3	1960	50.00
MERCURY			
❑ MGC-101 [10]	Charlie Parker with Strings	1950	500.00
—Reissue of 35010			
❑ MGC-109 [10]	Charlie Parker with Strings, Vol. 2	1950	500.00
❑ MGC-501 [10]	Charlie Parker with Strings	1951	500.00
—Reissue of 101 with new number			
❑ MGC-509 [10]	Charlie Parker with Strings, Vol. 2	1952	500.00
—Reissue of 109 with new number			
❑ MGC-512 [10]	Bird and Diz	1952	500.00
❑ MGC-513 [10]	South of the Border	1952	500.00
❑ MG-35010 [10]	Charlie Parker with Strings	1950	600.00
MGM			
❑ M3G-4949	Archetypes	1974	12.00
MOSAIC			
❑ MR10-129 [(10)]	The Complete Dean Benedetti Recordings of Charlie Parker	199?	100.00
ONYX			
❑ 221	First Recordings with Jay McShann	197?	12.00
PHOENIX			
❑ 10	New Bird	197?	10.00
❑ 12	New Bird, Vol. 2	197?	10.00
❑ 17	Yardbird in Lotusland	197?	10.00
PICKWICK			
❑ PC-3054 [M]	Yardbird	196?	12.00
❑ SPC-3054 [R]	Yardbird	196?	10.00
PRESTIGE			
❑ 24009 [(2)]	Charlie Parker	197?	15.00
❑ 24024 [(2)]	Parker/Powell/Mingus/Roach	197?	15.00
ROOST			
❑ LP-2210 [M]	All Star Sextet	1958	120.00
❑ LP-2257 [M]	The World of Charlie Parker	1963	40.00
SAVOY			
❑ MG-9000 [10]	Charlie Parker	1950	500.00
❑ MG-9001 [10]	Charlie Parker, Vol. 2	1951	500.00
❑ MG-9010 [10]	Charlie Parker, Vol. 3	1952	500.00
❑ MG-9011 [10]	Charlie Parker, Vol. 4	1952	500.00
❑ MG-12000 [M]	Charlie Parker Memorial	1955	100.00
❑ MG-12001 [M]	The Immortal Charlie Parker	1955	100.00
❑ MG-12009 [M]	Charlie Parker Memorial, Vol. 2	1955	100.00
❑ MG-12014 [M]	The Genius of Charlie Parker	1955	100.00
❑ MG-12079 [M]	The Charlie Parker Story	1956	100.00
❑ MG-12138 [M]	Bird's Night — The Music of Charlie Parker	1958	50.00
❑ MG-12152 [M]	An Evening at Home with the Bird	196?	40.00
❑ MG-12179 [M]	The "Bird" Returns	196?	30.00
❑ MG-12186 [M]	Newly Discovered Sides by the Immortal Charlie Parker	1966	30.00
SAVOY JAZZ			
❑ SJL-1107	Encores	197?	12.00
❑ SJL-1108	Bird at the Roost	197?	12.00
❑ SJL-1129	Encores, Vol. 2	198?	10.00
❑ SJL-1132	One Night in Chicago	198?	10.00
❑ SJL-1173	Bird at the Roost, Vol. 3	1987	10.00
❑ SJL-1208	Original Bird: The Best on Savoy	198?	10.00
❑ SJL-2201 [(2)]	Bird: The Savoy Recordings	1976	15.00
❑ SJL-2259 [(2)]	Bird at the Roost: The Complete Royal Roost Performances, Vol. 1	198?	15.00
❑ SJL-2260 [(2)]	Bird at the Roost: The Complete Royal Roost Performances, Vol. 2	1986	15.00
❑ SJL-5500 [(5)]	The Complete Savoy Studio Sessions	197?	30.00
SPOTLITE			
❑ 101	Charlie Parker on Dial, Vol. 1	197?	10.00
❑ 102	Charlie Parker on Dial, Vol. 2	197?	10.00
❑ 103	Charlie Parker on Dial, Vol. 3	197?	10.00
❑ 104	Charlie Parker on Dial, Vol. 4	197?	10.00
❑ 105	Charlie Parker on Dial, Vol. 5	197?	10.00
❑ 106	Charlie Parker on Dial, Vol. 6	197?	10.00
STASH			
❑ ST-260	Birth of the Bebop	1986	10.00
❑ ST-280	The Bird You Never Heard	1988	10.00
TRIP			
❑ 5035 [(2)]	The Master	197?	12.00
❑ 5039 [(2)]	Birdology	197?	15.00
UPFRONT			
❑ UPF-172	Live Sessions	197?	10.00
VERVE			
❑ VSP-23 [M]	Bird Wings	1966	20.00
❑ VSPS-23 [R]	Bird Wings	1966	12.00
❑ UMV-2029	Now's the Time	198?	10.00
❑ UMV-2030	Swedish Schnapps	198?	10.00
❑ VE-2-2501 [(2)]	The Verve Years 1948-50	197?	15.00
❑ VE-2-2508 [(2)]	Charlie Parker Sides	197?	15.00
❑ VE-2-2512 [(2)]	The Verve Years 1950-51	197?	15.00
❑ VE-2-2523 [(2)]	The Verve Years 1952-54	197?	15.00
❑ UMV-2562	Charlie Parker with Strings	198?	10.00
❑ UMV-2617	Jazz Perennial	198?	10.00
❑ 50-5263 [M]	April in Paris (The Genius of Charlie Parker #2)	197?	15.00
—Book-of-the-Month Club edition of 8004			
❑ MGV-8000 [M]	The Charlie Parker Story, Vol. 1	1957	80.00
❑ V-8000 [M]	The Charlie Parker Story, Vol. 1	1961	25.00
❑ V6-8000 [R]	The Charlie Parker Story, Vol. 1	196?	12.00
❑ MGV-8001 [M]	The Charlie Parker Story, Vol. 2	1957	80.00
❑ V-8001 [M]	The Charlie Parker Story, Vol. 2	1961	25.00
❑ V6-8001 [R]	The Charlie Parker Story, Vol. 2	196?	12.00
❑ MGV-8002 [M]	The Charlie Parker Story, Vol. 3	1957	80.00
❑ V-8002 [M]	The Charlie Parker Story, Vol. 3	1961	25.00
❑ V6-8002 [R]	The Charlie Parker Story, Vol. 3	196?	12.00
❑ MGV-8003 [M]	Night and Day (The Genius of Charlie Parker #1)	1957	80.00
❑ V-8003 [M]	Night and Day (The Genius of Charlie Parker #1)	1961	25.00
❑ V6-8003 [R]	Night and Day (The Genius of Charlie Parker #1)	196?	12.00
❑ MGV-8004 [M]	April in Paris (The Genius of Charlie Parker #2)	1957	80.00
❑ V-8004 [M]	April in Paris (The Genius of Charlie Parker #2)	1961	25.00
❑ V6-8004 [R]	April in Paris (The Genius of Charlie Parker #2)	196?	12.00
❑ MGV-8005 [M]	Now's the Time (The Genius of Charlie Parker #3)	1957	80.00
❑ V-8005 [M]	Now's the Time (The Genius of Charlie Parker #3)	1961	25.00
❑ V6-8005 [R]	Now's the Time (The Genius of Charlie Parker #3)	196?	12.00
❑ MGV-8006 [M]	Bird and Diz (The Genius of Charlie Parker #4)	1957	80.00
❑ V-8006 [M]	Bird and Diz (The Genius of Charlie Parker #4)	1961	25.00
❑ V6-8006 [R]	Bird and Diz (The Genius of Charlie Parker #4)	196?	12.00
❑ MGV-8007 [M]	Charlie Parker Plays Cole Porter (The Genius of Charlie Parker #5)	1957	80.00
❑ V-8007 [M]	Charlie Parker Plays Cole Porter (The Genius of Charlie Parker #5)	1961	25.00
❑ V6-8007 [R]	Charlie Parker Plays Cole Porter (The Genius of Charlie Parker #5)	196?	12.00
❑ MGV-8008 [M]	Fiesta (The Genius of Charlie Parker #6)	1957	80.00
❑ V-8008 [M]	Fiesta (The Genius of Charlie Parker #6)	1961	25.00
❑ V6-8008 [R]	Fiesta (The Genius of Charlie Parker #6)	196?	12.00
❑ MGV-8009 [M]	Jazz Perennial (The Genius of Charlie Parker #7)	1957	80.00
❑ V-8009 [M]	Jazz Perennial (The Genius of Charlie Parker #7)	1961	25.00
❑ V6-8009 [R]	Jazz Perennial (The Genius of Charlie Parker #7)	196?	12.00
❑ MGV-8010 [M]	Swedish Schnapps (The Genius of Charlie Parker #8)	1957	80.00
❑ V-8010 [M]	Swedish Schnapps (The Genius of Charlie Parker #8)	1961	25.00
❑ V6-8010 [R]	Swedish Schnapps (The Genius of Charlie Parker #8)	196?	12.00
❑ MGV-8100-3 [(3)M]	The Charlie Parker Story	1957	150.00
—Combines 8000, 8001 and 8002 in a box set			
❑ V-8100-3 [(3)M]	The Charlie Parker Story	1961	60.00
—Combines 8000, 8001 and 8002 in a box set			
❑ V-8409 [M]	The Essential Charlie Parker	1961	25.00
❑ V6-8409 [R]	The Essential Charlie Parker	196?	12.00
❑ V6-8787 [R]	Bird Set	1969	15.00
❑ V3HB-8840 [(2)]	Return Engagement	197?	15.00
❑ 817442-1	Bird on Verve, Vol. 1: Charlie Parker with Strings	1985	10.00
❑ 817443-1	Bird on Verve, Vol. 2: Bird and Diz	1985	10.00
❑ 817444-1	Bird on Verve, Vol. 3: More Charlie Parker with Strings	1985	10.00
❑ 817445-1	Bird on Verve, Vol. 4: Afro-Cuban Jazz	1985	10.00
❑ 817446-1	Bird on Verve, Vol. 5: Charlie Parker	1985	10.00
❑ 817447-1	Bird on Verve, Vol. 6: South of the Border	1985	10.00
❑ 817448-1	Bird on Verve, Vol. 7: Big Band	1985	10.00
❑ 817449-1	Bird on Verve, Vol. 8: Charlie Parker in Hi-Fi	1985	10.00
❑ 823250-1	The Cole Porter Songbook	1986	10.00
❑ 833564-1	Charlie Parker Sides	198?	10.00
❑ 837176-1	Bird: The Original Recordings of Charlie Parker	1987	10.00
VOGUE			
❑ LAE-12002 [M]	Memorial Album	1955	150.00
WARNER BROS.			
❑ 6BS 3159 [(6)]	The Complete Dial Recordings	1977	80.00
—Limited edition of 4,000 box sets			
❑ 2WB 3198 [(2)]	The Very Best of Bird	1977	20.00
ZIM			
❑ 1001	Lullaby in Rhythm	197?	12.00
❑ 1003	At the Pershing Ballroom, Chicago, 1950	197?	12.00
❑ 1006	Apartment Jam	197?	12.00

PARKER, CHARLIE/STAN GETZ/WARDELL GRAY

Albums

Number	Title (A Side/B Side)	Yr	NM
DESIGN			
❑ DLP-183 [M]	Charlie Parker/Stan Getz/ Wardell Gray	196?	15.00

PARKER, CHARLIE/DIZZY GILLESPIE

Albums

Number	Title (A Side/B Side)	Yr	NM
EMUS			
❑ ES-12027 [R]	Charlie Parker / Dizzy Gillespie	197?	12.00

PARKER, CHARLIE; DIZZY GILLESPIE; RED NORVO

Albums

Number	Title (A Side/B Side)	Yr	NM
DIAL			
❑ LP-903 [M]	Fabulous Jam Session	1951	600.00

PARKER, CHARLIE/DIZZY GILLESPIE/BUD POWELL/MAX ROACH

Albums

Number	Title (A Side/B Side)	Yr	NM
SAVOY			
❑ MG-9034 [10]	Bird, Diz, Bud, Max	1953	600.00

PARKER, CHARLIE/COLEMAN HAWKINS/ GEORGIE AULD

Albums

Number	Title (A Side/B Side)	Yr	NM
JAM			
❑ 5006	Unearthed Masters, Vol. 1	198?	10.00

PARKER, FESS

45s

Number	Title (A Side/B Side)	Yr	NM
BUENA VISTA			
❑ F-426	Ballad of Davy Crockett/Farewell	1963	12.00
❑ F-426 [PS]	Ballad of Davy Crockett/Farewell	1963	15.00

P

Except when noted otherwise, VG = 25% of NM, and VG+ = 50% of NM. (Example: VG = $2.00, VG+ = $4.00 and NM = $8.00.)

Number	Title (A Side/B Side)	Yr	NM
CASCADE			
❑ 5910	Eyes of an Angel/Strong Man	1959	15.00
❑ 5913	Lonely/Jayhawkers	1959	15.00
COLUMBIA			
❑ J4-242	Ballad of Davy Crockett/I Gave My Love (Riddle Song)	1955	20.00
—Yellow label "Children's Series" release			
❑ J4-242 [PS]	Ballad of Davy Crockett/I Gave My Love (Riddle Song)	1955	40.00
—Yellow label "Children's Series" release			
❑ 4-40449	Ballad of Davy Crockett/I Gave My Love (Riddle Song)	1955	15.00
❑ 4-40450	Farewell/I'm Lonely My Darlin'	1955	15.00
❑ 4-40568	Yaller Yaller Gold/King of the River	1955	25.00
DISNEYLAND			
❑ F-039	Wringle Wrangle/(Instrumental)	1957	30.00
—B-side by Camarata			
❑ F-043	Wringle Wrangle/The Ballad of John Coulter	1957	12.00
❑ F-043 [PS]	Wringle Wrangle/The Ballad of John Coulter	1957	25.00
❑ F-045	Pioneer's Prayer/The Ballad of John Coulter	1957	12.00
❑ F-045 [PS]	Pioneer's Prayer/The Ballad of John Coulter	1957	25.00
❑ F-049	A Hole in the Sky/Wedding Bell Calypso	1957	12.00
❑ F-049 [PS]	A Hole in the Sky/Wedding Bell Calypso	1957	25.00
❑ F-053	Gonna Find Me a Bluebird/Catch Me Fish	1957	25.00
GUSTO			
❑ 900	Ballad of Davy Crockett/Lonely	1963	10.00
RCA VICTOR			
❑ 47-8429	Daniel Boone/The Ballad of Davy Crockett	1964	12.00
❑ 47-8429 [PS]	Daniel Boone/The Ballad of Davy Crockett	1964	20.00
❑ 74-0249	Comin' After Jimmy/Sittin' Here Drinkin'	1969	10.00
Albums			
COLUMBIA			
❑ CL 666 [M]	Walt Disney's Davy Crockett, King of the Wild Frontier	1955	100.00
DISNEYLAND			
❑ WDL-1007 [M]	Yarns and Songs of the West	1959	30.00
—Reissue of 3006			
❑ DQ-1269 [M]	Pecos Bill and Other Stories in Song	1965	30.00
❑ DQ-1315 [M]	Three Adventures of Davy Crockett	1968	25.00
—Another reissue, this time of 1926			
❑ DQ-1336	Cowboy and Indian Songs	1969	30.00
❑ ST-1926 [M]	Three Adventures of Davy Crockett	1963	30.00
—Reissue of 3602			
❑ WDL-3006 [M]	Yarns and Songs	1957	40.00
❑ WDL-3041 [M]	Westward Ho the Wagons	1959	30.00
—Reissue of 4008			
❑ WDA-3602 [M]	Three Adventures of Davy Crockett	1958	50.00
—Reissue of Columbia 666			
❑ WDL-4006 [M]	Westward Ho the Wagons	1956	80.00
RCA VICTOR			
❑ LPM-2973 [M]	Fess Parker Sings About Daniel Boone, Davy Crockett and Abe Lincoln	1964	25.00
❑ LSP-2973 [S]	Fess Parker Sings About Daniel Boone, Davy Crockett and Abe Lincoln	1964	30.00

PARKER, FESS, AND BUDDY EBSEN

45s

Number	Title (A Side/B Side)	Yr	NM
COLUMBIA			
❑ B-2031	Davy Crockett, Indian Fighter	1955	40.00
—Cover for 40476 and 40477			
❑ B-2032	Davy Crockett Goes to Congress	1955	40.00
—Cover for 40478 and 40479			
❑ B-2033	Davy Crockett at the Alamo	1955	40.00
—Cover for 40480 and 40481			
❑ 4-40476	Davy Crockett, Indian Fighter (Part 1)/Davy Crockett, Indian Fighter (Part 4)	1955	20.00
❑ 4-40477	Davy Crockett, Indian Fighter (Part 2)/Davy Crockett, Indian Fighter (Part 3)	1955	20.00
❑ 4-40478	Davy Crockett Goes to Congress (Part 1)/Davy Crockett Goes to Congress (Part 4)	1955	20.00
❑ 4-40479	Davy Crockett Goes to Congress (Part 2)/Davy Crockett Goes to Congress (Part 3)	1955	20.00
❑ 4-40480	Davy Crockett at the Alamo (Part 1)/Davy Crockett at the Alamo (Part 4)	1955	20.00
❑ 4-40481	Davy Crockett at the Alamo (Part 2)/Davy Crockett at the Alamo (Part 3)	1955	20.00
❑ 4-40510	Be Sure You're Right (Then Go Ahead)/Old Betsy (Davy Crockett's Rifle)	1955	20.00

PARKER, GRAHAM

Includes records with THE RUMOUR. Includes records with THE RUMOUR.

12-Inch Singles

Number	Title (A Side/B Side)	Yr	NM
ARISTA			
❑ SP-130 [DJ]	You Hit the Spot/You Hit the Spot (Extended)	1982	6.00
❑ SP-118 [DJ]	Temporary Beauty/No More Excuses (Instrumental)	1982	7.00
❑ SP-65 [DJ]	Mercury Poisoning/I Want You Back (Alive)	1979	12.00
❑ SP-41 [DJ]	Mercury Poisoning (one-sided)	1979	12.00
—Gray vinyl with custom labels			
❑ SP-54 [DJ]	Local Girls/I Want You Back (Alive)	1979	6.00
❑ SP-65 [DJ]	Mercury Poisoning/I Want You Back (Alive)	1979	12.00
❑ SP-118 [DJ]	Temporary Beauty/No More Excuses (Instrumental)	1982	7.00
❑ SP-130 [DJ]	You Hit the Spot/You Hit the Spot (Extended)	1982	6.00
❑ 9098 [DJ]	You Can't Take Love for Granted (2 versions)	1983	6.00
❑ 9098 [DJ]	You Can't Take Love for Granted (2 versions)	1983	6.00
ELEKTRA			
❑ ED 5040 [DJ]	Wake Up (Next to You) (Long Version)/Wake Up (Next to You) (Short Version)	1984	5.00
❑ ED5040 [DJ]	Wake Up (Next to You) (Long Version)/Wake Up (Next to You) (Short Version)	1984	5.00
❑ ED 5078 [DJ]	The Weekend's Too Short (same on both sides)	1985	5.00
❑ ED5078 [DJ]	The Weekend's Too Short (same on both sides)	1985	5.00
MERCURY			
❑ MK-28 [DJ]	Hold Back the Night/(Let Me Get) Sweet on You//White Honey/Soul Shoes	1977	30.00
—Promo-only 12-inch version of "The Pink Parker"			
❑ MK-28 [DJ]	Hold Back the Night/(Let Me Get) Sweet on You//White Honey/Soul Shoes	1977	30.00
—Promo-only 12-inch version of "The Pink Parker"			
RCA			
❑ 8336-1 [DJ]	Start a Fire (LP version)/Start a Fire (Edit)	1988	6.00
❑ 8685-1 [DJ]	Don't Let It Break You Down (same on both sides)	1988	6.00
❑ 8336 [DJ]	Start a Fire/Start a Fire (Edit)	1988	6.00
❑ 8336 [DJ]	Start a Fire/Start a Fire (Edit)	1988	6.00
❑ 8336-1 [DJ]	Start a Fire (LP version)/Start a Fire (Edit)	1988	6.00
❑ 8685-1 [DJ]	Don't Let It Break You Down (same on both sides)	1988	6.00
❑ 9178-RD	Everything Goes (extended)/That Thing Is Rockin'	1990	10.00

45s

Number	Title (A Side/B Side)	Yr	NM
ARISTA			
❑ 0420	Local Girls/I Want You Back	1979	4.00
❑ 0420 [PS]	Local Girls/I Want You Back	1979	4.00
❑ 0439	Mercury Poisoning/I Want You Back (Alive)	1979	4.00
❑ 0523	Stupefaction/Women in Charge	1980	4.00
❑ 0523 [PS]	Stupefaction/Women in Charge	1980	4.00
❑ 0549	Endless Nights/No Holding Back	1980	4.00
—A-side: Guest vocals by Bruce Springsteen			
❑ 0652	Temporary Beauty/No More Excuses	1981	4.00
❑ 0687	You Hit the Spot/Habit Worth Forming	1982	3.00
❑ 9065	Life Gets Better/Beyond a Joke	1983	3.00
ELEKTRA			
❑ 69654	Wake Up (Next to You)/Bricks and Mortar	1985	4.00
❑ 69654 [PS]	Wake Up (Next to You)/Bricks and Mortar	1985	5.00
MERCURY			
❑ DJ-531 [DJ]	Stick to Me (same on both sides)	1977	12.00
❑ DJ-491 [DJ]	Hold Back the Night (same on both sides)	1977	12.00
❑ DJ-491 [DJ]	Hold Back the Night (same on both sides)	1977	12.00
❑ DJ-531 [DJ]	Stick to Me (same on both sides)	1977	12.00
❑ 73834	Soul Shoes/You've Got to Be Kidding	1976	8.00
❑ 73876	Heat Treatment/Back Door Love	1976	8.00
❑ 73970	Stick to Me/The Heat in Harlem	1977	8.00
❑ 74000	Hold Back the Night/(Let Me Get) Sweet on You//White Honey/Soul Shoes	1977	5.00
—Pink vinyl			
❑ 74000	Hold Back the Night/(Let Me Get) Sweet on You//White Honey/Soul Shoes	1977	7.00
—Also on black vinyl; scarcer than pink version			
❑ 74000 [PS]	"The Pink Parker": Hold Back the Night/(Let Me Get) Sweet on You//White Honey/Soul Shoes, The	1977	5.00
RCA			
❑ 8639-7-R	(Get Started) Start a Fire/Ordinary Girl	1988	3.00
❑ 8639-7-R [PS]	(Get Started) Start a Fire/Ordinary Girl	1988	3.00

Albums

Number	Title (A Side/B Side)	Yr	NM
ARISTA			
❑ SP-63 [DJ]	Live Sparks	1979	20.00
❑ SP-63 [DJ]	Live Sparks	1979	20.00
❑ AL 4223	Squeezing Out Sparks	1979	12.00
❑ AL8-8023	The Real Macaw	1983	10.00
❑ AL6-8352	The Real Macaw	1985	8.00
—Budget-line reissue			
❑ AL6-8356	The Up Escalator	1985	8.00
—Budget-line reissue			
❑ AL6-8363	Squeezing Out Sparks	1985	8.00
—Budget-line reissue			
❑ AL6-8374	Another Grey Area	1985	8.00
—Budget-line reissue			
❑ AL6-8391	Look Back in Anger	1985	10.00
❑ AL 9517	The Up Escalator	1980	10.00
❑ AL 9589	Another Grey Area	1982	10.00
ELEKTRA			
❑ 60388	Steady Nerves	1985	10.00
MERCURY			
❑ SRM-2-100 [(2)]	The Parkerilla	1978	18.00
—Originals have gatefold sleeves			
❑ SRM-1-1095	Howlin' Wind	1976	15.00
❑ SRM-1-1117	Heat Treatment	1976	15.00
❑ SRM-1-3706	Stick to Me	1977	15.00
❑ 824808-1	Stick to Me	1985	12.00
—Reissue with new number			
❑ 826097-1	Pourin' It All Out: The Mercury Years	1985	12.00
RCA			
❑ 8316-1-R	The Mona Lisa's Sister	1988	10.00
❑ 9876-1-R	Human Soul	1989	10.00
ROCK THE HOUSE			
❑ RTH-2817-1	12 Haunted Episodes	1995	15.00

PARKER, JUNIOR

Also includes records as "Little Junior Parker." Also see JIMMY McGRIFF AND JUNIOR PARKER.

45s

Number	Title (A Side/B Side)	Yr	NM
BLUE ROCK			
❑ 4064	I Got Money/Lover to Friend	1968	8.00
❑ 4067	Reconsider Baby/Lovin' Man on Your Hands	1968	8.00
❑ 4080	Ain't Gon' Be No Cuttin' Loose/I'm So Satisfied	1969	8.00
❑ 4088	Easy Lovin'/You Can't Keep a Good Woman Down	1969	8.00
CAPITOL			
❑ 2857	The Outside Man/Darling, Depend on Me	1970	6.00
❑ 2951	Lady Madonna/Tomorrow Never Knows	1970	10.00
❑ 2997	Drownin' on Dry Land/River's Invitation	1970	6.00
DUKE			
❑ 120	Dirty Friend Blues/Can't Understand	1954	60.00
❑ 127	Please Baby Please/Sittin', Drinkin' and Thinkin'	1954	60.00
❑ 137	Backtracking/I Wanna Ramble	1954	70.00
❑ 147	Driving Me/There Better Not Be No Feel	1956	50.00
❑ 157	Mother-in-Law Blues/That's My Baby	1956	50.00
❑ 164	Next Time You See Me/My Dolly Bee	1957	30.00
❑ 168	That's Alright/Pretty Baby	1957	30.00
❑ 177	Peaches/Pretty Little Doll	1957	30.00
❑ 184	Wondering/Sitting and Thinking	1958	25.00
❑ 193	Barefoot Rock/What Did I Do	1958	25.00
❑ 301	Sweet Home Chicago/Sometimes	1959	20.00
❑ 306	Five Long Years/I'm Holding On	1959	20.00
❑ 309	Stranded/Blue Letter	1959	20.00
❑ 315	Dangerous Woman/Belinda Marie	1960	15.00

Number	Title (A Side/B Side)	Yr	NM
❑ 317	The Next Time/You're On My Mind	1960	15.00
❑ 326	I'll Learn to Love Again/ That's Just Alright	1960	15.00
❑ 330	Stand By Me/I'll Forget About You	1960	15.00
❑ 335	Driving Wheel/Seven Days	1961	25.00
❑ 341	In the Dark/How Long Can This Go On	1961	12.00
❑ 345	Annie Get Your Yo-Yo/Mary Jo	1961	12.00
❑ 351	I Feel Alright Again/Sweeter As the Days Go By	1962	12.00
❑ 357	Foxy Devil/Someone Somewhere	1962	12.00
❑ 362	It's a Pity/Last Night	1963	12.00
❑ 364	If You Don't Love Me/ I Can't Forget About You	1963	12.00
❑ 367	The Tables Have Turned/ Yonders Wall	1963	12.00
❑ 371	Strange Things Happening/I'm Gonna Stop	1964	12.00
❑ 376	Things I Used to Do/That's Why I'm Always Crying	1964	12.00
❑ 384	I'm in Love/Jivin' Woman	1964	12.00
❑ 389	Crying for My Baby/Guess You Don't Know (The Golden Rule)	1965	12.00
❑ 394	These Kind of Blues (Part 1)/ These Kind of Blues (Part 2)	1966	12.00
❑ 398	Walking the Floor Over You/ Goodbye Little Girl	1966	12.00
❑ 406	Get Away Blues/Why Do You Make Me Cry	1966	12.00
❑ 413	Man or Mouse/Wait for Another Day	1966	12.00
GROOVE MERCHANT			
❑ 1002	Way Back Home/ (B-side unknown)	1971	12.00
❑ 1004	I Like Your Style/I Need Love So Bad	1972	10.00
❑ 1010	Love Ain't Nothin' But a Business Goin' On/Losing Battle	1972	10.00
MERCURY			
❑ 72620	Baby Please/Just Like a Fish	1966	10.00
❑ 72651	You Can Make It If You Care/ Ooh Wee Baby, That's the Way You Make Me Feel	1967	10.00
❑ 72672	Country Girl/Sometimes I Wonder	1967	10.00
❑ 72699	I Can't Put My Finger On It/ If I Had Your Love	1967	10.00
❑ 72733	Hurtin' Inside/What a Fool I Was	1967	10.00
❑ 72793	It Must Be Love/Your Love's All Over	1968	8.00
MINIT			
❑ 32080	Worried Life Blues/Let the Good Times Roll	1969	6.00
SUN			
❑ 187	Feelin' Good/Fussin' and Fightin' Blues	1953	400.00
—As "Little Junior's Blue Flames"			
❑ 192	Mystery Train/Love My Baby	1954	300.00
—As "Little Junior's Blue Flames"			
UNITED ARTISTS			
❑ 50855	Funny How Time Slips Away/ No One Knows	1971	10.00
Albums			
ABC			
❑ AC-30010	The ABC Collection	1976	15.00
ABC DUKE			
❑ DLP-76	Driving Wheel	1974	15.00
❑ DLP-83	The Best of Junior Parker	1974	15.00
BLUE ROCK			
❑ SRB-64004	Honey-Drippin' Blues	1969	15.00
BLUESWAY			
❑ BLS-6066	Sometime Tomorrow	1973	15.00
CAPITOL			
❑ ST-564	Outside Man	1970	15.00
DUKE			
❑ DLP-76 [M]	Driving Wheel	196?	100.00
—With Wagon Wheel on front cover			
❑ DLP-76 [M]	Driving Wheel	1962	150.00
—With Cadillac on front cover			
❑ DLP-83 [M]	The Best of Junior Parker	1967	50.00
❑ DLPS-83 [P]	The Best of Junior Parker	1967	40.00
GROOVE MERCHANT			
❑ 513	Love Ain't Nothin'	1974	15.00
MCA			
❑ 27046	The Best of Junior Parker	1980	10.00
MERCURY			
❑ MG-21101 [M]	Like It Is	1967	30.00
❑ SR-61101 [S]	Like It Is	1967	25.00
MINIT			
❑ 24024	Blues Man	1969	25.00
UNITED ARTISTS			
❑ UAS-6823	I Tell Stories Sad and True	1971	15.00

PARKER, JUNIOR, AND BOBBY BLAND

Also see each artist's individual listings.

Number	Title (A Side/B Side)	Yr	NM
Albums			
ABC DUKE			
❑ DLP-72	Blues Consolidated	1974	15.00
DUKE			
❑ DLP-72 [M]	Blues Consolidated	1961	150.00

PARKER, ROBERT

Number	Title (A Side/B Side)	Yr	NM
45s			
IMPERIAL			
❑ 5842	Mash Potatoes All Night Long/ Twistin' Out of Space	1962	12.00
❑ 5889	You're Lookin' Good/ Little Things Mean a Lot	1962	12.00
❑ 5916	Please Forgive Me/You Got It	1963	12.00
ISLAND			
❑ 044	Give Me the Country Side of Life/It's Hard But It's Fair	1975	4.00
❑ 074	A Little Bit Something/Better Luck in the Summer	1976	4.00
NOLA			
❑ 721	Barefootin'/Let's Go Baby (Where the Action Is)	1966	20.00
❑ 724	Ring Around the Roses/ She's Coming Home	1966	12.00
❑ 726	Happy Feet/The Scratch	1966	12.00
❑ 729	Tip Toe/Soul Kind of Loving	1966	12.00
❑ 730	A Letter To Santa/C.C. Rider	1966	12.00
❑ 733	Yak Yak Yak/Secret Agents	1967	12.00
❑ 735	Everybody's Hip-Hugging/ Foxy Mama	1967	12.00
❑ 738	I Caught You in a Lie/Holdin' Out	1967	12.00
❑ 739	Barefootin' Boogaloo/Soul Sister	196?	15.00
RON			
❑ 327	All Nite Long (Part 1)/ All Nite Long (Part 2)	1959	15.00
❑ 331	Walkin'/Across the Track	1960	15.00
SILVER FOX			
❑ 12	You Shakin' Things Up/ You See Me	1969	6.00
Albums			
NOLA			
❑ LP-1001 [M]	Barefootin'	1966	40.00

PARKS, GINO

Number	Title (A Side/B Side)	Yr	NM
45s			
CRAZY HORSE			
❑ 1303	Nerves of Steel/Help Me Somebody	1968	100.00
FORTUNE			
❑ 528	Last Night I Cried/Just Go	1957	80.00
GOLDEN WORLD			
❑ 32	My Sophisticated Lady/ Talkin' About My Baby	1966	20.00
MIRACLE			
❑ 3	Don't Say Bye Bye/ Blibber Blabber	1960	800.00
TAMLA			
❑ 54042	That's No Lie/Same Thing	1961	100.00
❑ 54066	For This I Thank You/Fire	1962	80.00

PARKS, MICHAEL

Number	Title (A Side/B Side)	Yr	NM
45s			
MGM			
❑ 14092	Tie Me to Your Apron Strings Again/Won't You Ride in My Little Red Wagon	1969	5.00
❑ 14104	Long Lonesome Highway/ Mountain High	1970	6.00
❑ 14154	Sally/Save a Little, Spend a Little	1970	5.00
❑ 14363	Won't You Ride in My Little Red Wagon/Big "T" Water	1972	5.00
VERVE			
❑ 10653	Drownin' on Dry Land/ River's Invitation	1971	5.00
Albums			
FIRST AMERICAN			
❑ 7781	You Don't Know Me	1983	10.00
MGM			
❑ SE-4646	Closing the Gap	1969	15.00
❑ SE-4662	Long Lonesome Highway	1970	15.00
❑ SE-4717	Blue	1970	15.00
❑ SE-4784	The Best of Michael Parks	1971	15.00
VERVE			
❑ V6-5079	Lost and Found	1971	15.00

PARKS, RAY

Number	Title (A Side/B Side)	Yr	NM
45s			
CAPITOL			
❑ F3580	You're Gonna Have to Bawl, That's All/Just a-Hangin' Around	1956	70.00

PARKS, VAN DYKE

Number	Title (A Side/B Side)	Yr	NM
45s			
MGM			
❑ 13441	Do What You Wanta/ Number Nine	1966	12.00
❑ 13570	Come to the Sunshine/ Farther Along	1966	12.00
WARNER BROS.			
❑ 7026	Donovan's Colors Part 1/Part 2	1967	12.00
—As "George Washington Brown"			
❑ 7409	On the Rolling Sea When Jesus Speaks to Me/The Eagle and Me	1970	10.00
❑ 7609	Occapella/Ode to Tobago	1972	6.00
❑ 7632	Riverboat/John Jones	1972	6.00
Albums			
SUNDAZED			
❑ LP- 5140	Song Cycle	2002	15.00
—Reissue on 180-gram vinyl			
❑ LP-5141	Discover America	2002	15.00
—Reissue on 180-gram vinyl			
WARNER BROS.			
❑ WS 1727	Song Cycle	1968	15.00
—Green label with "W7" box logo			
❑ WS 1727	Song Cycle	1968	25.00
—Gold label			
❑ WS 1727	Song Cycle	1970	12.00
—Green label with "WB" shield logo			
❑ BS 2589	Discover America	1972	12.00
❑ BS 2878	Clang of the Yankee Reaper	1975	12.00
❑ 23829	Jump!	1984	12.00
❑ 25968	Tokyo Rose	1989	12.00

PARLET

Number	Title (A Side/B Side)	Yr	NM
12-Inch Singles			
CASABLANCA			
❑ NBD 20161	Ridin' High (9:40)/(B-side blank)	1979	20.00
45s			
CASABLANCA			
❑ 919	Pleasure Principle/(Pt. 2)	1978	5.00
❑ 932	Cookie Jar/Are You Dreaming	1978	5.00
❑ 975	Ridin' High/(Pt. 2)	1979	5.00
❑ 995	Don't Ever Stop/Huff-N-Puff	1979	5.00
❑ 2260	Wolf Tickets/(Pt. II)	1980	5.00
❑ 2293	Help from My Friends/ Watch Me Do My Thang	1980	5.00
Albums			
CASABLANCA			
❑ NBLP 7094	Pleasure Principle	1978	20.00
❑ NBLP 7146	Invasion of the Booty Snatchers	1979	20.00

PARLETTES, THE

Number	Title (A Side/B Side)	Yr	NM
45s			
JUBILEE			
❑ 5467	Tonight I Met An Angel/ Because We're Very Young	1964	12.00

PARLIAMENT

Also see GEORGE CLINTON; FUNKADELIC; THE PARLIAMENTS.

Number	Title (A Side/B Side)	Yr	NM
12-Inch Singles			
CASABLANCA			
❑ NBD 20113	Flash Light (10:31)/ (B-side blank)	1977	40.00
❑ NBD 20208	Theme from The Black Hole/ Big Bang Theory// (B-side blank)	1979	20.00
❑ 876585-1	Flash Light (10:31)/P-Funk (Wants to Get Funked Up) (7:34)	198?	10.00
—"Timepieces" reissue			
45s			
CASABLANCA			
❑ 0003	The Goose (Part 1)/ The Goose (Part 2)	1974	6.00
❑ 0013	Up for the Down Stroke/ Presence of a Brain	1974	6.00
❑ 0104	Up for the Down Stroke/ Presence of a Brain	1974	5.00
❑ 803	Up for the Down Stroke/ Presence of a Brain	1974	5.00
❑ 811	Testify/I Can Move You	1974	5.00
❑ 831	Chocolate City/ Chocolate City (Part 2)	1975	5.00
❑ 843	Ride On/Big Footin'	1975	5.00

Except when noted otherwise, VG = 25% of NM, and VG+ = 50% of NM. (Example: VG = $2.00, VG+ = $4.00 and NM = $8.00.)

Number	Title (A Side/B Side)	Yr	NM
❑ 852	P. Funk (Wants to Get Funked Up)/Night of the Tempasaurus Peoples	1976	5.00
❑ 856	Tear the Roof Off the Sucker (Give Up the Funk)/P-Funk	1976	4.00
—Tan label			
❑ 856	Tear the Roof Off the Sucker (Give Up the Funk)/P-Funk	1976	5.00
—Blue label			
❑ 864	Star Child (Mothership Connection)/ Supergroovealistic	1976	5.00
❑ 871	Do That Stuff/Handcuffs	1976	5.00
❑ 875	Dr. Funkenstein/ Children of Production	1977	5.00
❑ 892	Fantasy Is Reality/The Landing (Of the Mothership)	1977	5.00
❑ 900	Bop Gun (Endangered Species)/ I've Been Watchin' You	1977	5.00
❑ 909	Flash Light/Swing Down, Sweet Chariot	1978	5.00
❑ 921	Funkentelechy/Funkentelechy (Part 2)	1978	5.00
❑ 950	Aqua Boogie (A Psychoal-phadiscobetabioaquad oloop)/(You're a Fish and I'm a) Water Sign	1978	5.00
❑ 950 [PS]	Aqua Boogie (A Psychoal-phadiscobetabioaquado-loop)/(You're a Fish and I'm a) Water Sign	1978	10.00
❑ 976	Rumpofsteelskin/ Liquid Sunshine	1979	5.00
❑ 2222	Party People/Party People (Part 2)	1979	5.00
❑ 2235	Theme from The Black Hole/ (You're a Fish and I'm a) Water Sign	1980	5.00
❑ 2250	The Big Bang Theory/The Big Bang Theory (Part 2)	1980	5.00
❑ 2317	Agony of DeFeet/The Freeze	1980	5.00
❑ 2330	Crush It/Body Language	1981	5.00
INVICTUS			
❑ 9077	I Call My Baby Pussy Cat/ Little Ole Country Boy	1970	10.00
❑ 9091	Red Hot Mama/Little Ole Country Boy	1971	10.00
❑ 9095	Breakdown/Little Ole Country Boy	1971	10.00
❑ 9123	Come In Out of the Rain/ Little Ole Country Boy	1972	8.00

Albums

Number	Title	Yr	NM
CASABLANCA			
❑ NBLP 7002	Up for the Down Stroke	1974	75.00
❑ NBLP 7014	Chocolate City	1975	75.00
❑ NBLP 7022	Mothership Connection	1976	65.00
❑ NBLP 7034	The Clones of Dr. Funkenstein	1976	65.00
❑ NBLP 7053 [(2)]	Parliament Live/ P. Funk Earth Tour	1977	75.00
❑ NBLP 7084	Funkentelechy vs. the Placebo Syndrome	1977	65.00
❑ NBLP 7125	Motor-Booty Affair	1978	65.00
❑ NBPIX 7125 [PD]	Motor-Booty Affair	1978	75.00
❑ NBLP 7195	Gloryhallastoopid (Or Pin the Tale on the Funky)	1979	65.00
❑ NBLP 7249	Trombipulation	1980	65.00
❑ NBLP 9003	Up for the Down Stroke	1974	60.00
—Original pressing, distributed by Warner Bros.			
❑ 822637-1	Greatest Hits	1984	20.00
❑ 824501-1	Funkentelechy vs. the Placebo Syndrome	1985	20.00
❑ 824502-1	Mothership Connection	1985	20.00
INVICTUS			
❑ ST-7302	Osmium	1970	150.00

PARLIAMENTS, THE All of the below are probably the same group, a Detriot-based R&B group led by GEORGE CLINTON that evolved into PARLIAMENT and FUNKADELIC.

45s

Number	Title (A Side/B Side)	Yr	NM
APT			
❑ 25036	Poor Willie/Party Boys	1959	40.00
ATCO			
❑ 6675	A New Day Begins/I'll Wait	1969	20.00
FLIPP			
❑ 100/1	Lonely Island/You Make Me Wanna Cry	1960	30.00
—Yellow label			
❑ 100/1	Lonely Island/You Make Me Wanna Cry	1960	40.00
—Red label			
GOLDEN WORLD			
❑ 46	Heart Trouble/That Was My Girl	1966	150.00

Parliament, "Aqua Boogie," Casablanca 950, 1978, **$10.**

Number	Title (A Side/B Side)	Yr	NM
LEN			
❑ 101	Don't Need You Anymore/ Honey, Take Me Home with You	1958	80.00
REVILOT			
❑ 207	(I Wanna) Testify/I Can Feel the Ice Melting	1967	15.00
❑ 211	All Your Goodies Are Gone (The Loser's Seat)/ Don't Be Sore at Me	1967	15.00
❑ 214	Little Man/The Goose (That Laid the Golden Egg)	1968	15.00
❑ 217	Look at What I Almost Missed/ What You Been Growing	1968	15.00
❑ 223	Good Old Music/Time	1968	15.00
❑ 228	A New Day Begins/I'll Wait	1968	200.00
SYMBOL			
❑ 917	You're Cute/I'll Get You Yet	1962	25.00
U.S.A.			
❑ 719	My Only Love/To Be Alone	1961	20.00

PARRIS, FRED Not to be confused with FREDDIE PARIS. Also see THE CHAMPLAINS; THE CHEROKEES (5); THE FIVE SATINS; THE NEW YORKERS (1).

45s

Number	Title (A Side/B Side)	Yr	NM
ATCO			
❑ 6439	Land of the Broken Hearts/ Bring It Home to Daddy	1966	10.00
BIRTH			
❑ 101	Dark at the Top of My Heart/ Benediction	196?	8.00
CHECKER			
❑ 1108	No Use in Crying/Walk a Little Faster	1965	10.00
GREEN SEA			
❑ 106	Blushing Bride/Giving My Love to You	1966	10.00
❑ 107	I'll Be Hangin' On/ I Can Really Satisfy	1966	10.00
KLIK			
❑ 7905	The Voice/She's Gone (With the Wind)	1958	200.00
—With the Scarlets and Passionettes			
MAMA SADIE			
❑ 1001	In the Still of the Nite "67"/Heck No	1967	10.00

PARROTS, THE (1)

45s

Number	Title (A Side/B Side)	Yr	NM
CHECKER			
❑ 772	Don't Leave Me/ Weep, Weep, Weep	1953	500.00

PARROTS, THE (2)

45s

Number	Title (A Side/B Side)	Yr	NM
MALA			
❑ 558	They All Got Carried Away/Hey, Put the Clock Back on the Wall	1967	12.00

PARSONS, ALAN, PROJECT

12-Inch Singles

Number	Title (A Side/B Side)	Yr	NM
ARISTA			
❑ ADP-9438 [DJ]	Stereotomy (4:13) (7:15)	1985	10.00
❑ ADP-9548 [DJ]	Standing on Higher Ground (Album Version 5:02) (Edited Version 4:20)	1987	12.00

45s

Number	Title (A Side/B Side)	Yr	NM
ARISTA			
❑ 0260	I Wouldn't Want to Be Like You/ Nucleus	1977	4.00
❑ 0288	I Robot/Don't Let It Show	1977	4.00
❑ 0310	Day After Day/Breakdown	1978	4.00
❑ 0352	What Goes Up/In the Lap of the Gods	1978	4.00
❑ 0454	Damned If I Do/If I Could Change Your Mind	1979	4.00
❑ 0491	You Won't Be There/ Secret Garden	1980	4.00
❑ 0502	You Lie Down with Dogs/Lucifer	1980	4.00
❑ 0573	Games People Play/ Ace of Swords	1980	4.00

Alan Parsons Project, *Eve*, Arista AL 8318, 1979, **$8.**

Number	Title (A Side/B Side)	Yr	NM
❑ 0598	Time/The Gold Bug	1981	4.00
❑ 0635	Snake Eyes/I Don't Wanna Go Home	1981	4.00
❑ 0696	Eye in the Sky/Gemini	1982	4.00
❑ 1029	Psychobabble/ Children of the Moon	1982	4.00
❑ 1048	Old and Wise/You're Gonna Get Your Fingers Burned	1983	4.00
❑ 9108	You Don't Believe/Lucifer	1983	4.00
❑ 9160	Don't Answer Me/ Don't Let It Show	1984	3.00
❑ 9160 [PS]	Don't Answer Me/ Don't Let It Show	1984	3.00
❑ 9208	Prime Time/Gold Bug	1984	3.00
❑ 9282	Let's Talk About Me/Hawkeye	1984	3.00
❑ 9282 [PS]	Let's Talk About Me/Hawkeye	1984	3.00
❑ 9349	Days Are Numbers (The Traveller)/ Somebody Out There	1985	3.00
❑ 9443	Stereotomy/Urbania	1985	3.00
❑ 9576	Standing on Higher Ground/ Inside Looking Out	1987	3.00
❑ 9576 [PS]	Standing on Higher Ground/ Inside Looking Out	1987	3.00
20TH CENTURY			
❑ 2297	(The System of) Doctor Tarr and Professor Fether/ Dream Within a Dream	1976	5.00
❑ 2308	The Raven/Prelude to Fall of the House of Usher	1976	5.00
❑ 2333	To One in Paradise/ The Cask of Amontillado	1977	6.00

Albums

Number	Title (A Side/B Side)	Yr	NM
ARISTA			
❑ SP-140 [(8)DJ]	Complete Audio Guide to the Alan Parsons Project	1982	80.00
—Contains first six APP LPs plus a two-record set of other Parsons work			
❑ SP-68 [(6)DJ]	Audio Guide to the Alan Parsons Project	1979	50.00
—Contains first four APP LPs plus a two-record set of other Parsons work			
❑ SP-68 [(6)DJ]	Audio Guide to the Alan Parsons Project	1979	50.00
—Contains first four APP LPs plus a two-record set of other Parsons work			
❑ SP-140 [(8)DJ]	Complete Audio Guide to the Alan Parsons Project	1982	80.00
—Contains first six APP LPs plus a two-record set of other Parsons work			
❑ AB 4180	Pyramid	1978	10.00
❑ AL 7002	I Robot	1977	10.00
❑ AL 8040	I Robot	1983	8.00
—Reissue			
❑ AL 8193	The Best of the Alan Parsons Project	1983	8.00
❑ AL 8204	Ammonia Avenue	1984	10.00
❑ AL 8263	Vulture Culture	1985	8.00
❑ ALPD 8263 [DJ]	Vulture Culture	1985	25.00
—Promo-only picture disc			
❑ ALPD8263 [DJ]	Vulture Culture	1985	25.00
—Promo-only picture disc			
❑ AL 8289	Ammonia Avenue	1985	8.00
—Reissue			
❑ AL 8290	Eye in the Sky	1985	8.00
—Reissue			
❑ AL 8315	The Turn of a Friendly Card	1985	8.00
—Reissue			
❑ AL 8318	Eve	1985	8.00
—Reissue			
❑ AL 8320	Pyramid	1985	8.00
—Reissue			
❑ AL 8384	Stereotomy	1986	8.00
—With regular LP jacket			
❑ AL 8384	Stereotomy	1986	15.00
—First editions came in an oversize vinyl jacket			
❑ AL 8448	Gaudi	1987	8.00
❑ AL 8486	The Best of the Alan Parsons Project, Vol. 2	1987	8.00
❑ AL 8487	The Instrumental Works of the Alan Parsons Project	1988	10.00
❑ AB 9504	Eve	1979	10.00
❑ AL 9518	The Turn of a Friendly Card	1980	10.00
❑ AL 9599	Eye in the Sky	1982	10.00
CASABLANCA			
❑ 822784-1	Tales of Mystery and Imagination - Edgar Allan Poe	1984	10.00
—Reissue of 20th Century LP			
MOBILE FIDELITY			
❑ 1-084	I Robot	1982	60.00
—Audiophile vinyl			
❑ MFQR 1-084	I Robot	1982	100.00
—Audiophile vinyl; Ultra High Quality pressing in box			
❑ 1-204	Tales of Mystery and Imagination - Edgar Allan Poe	1994	60.00
—Audiophile vinyl			
20TH CENTURY			
❑ T-508	Tales of Mystery and Imagination - Edgar Allan Poe	1976	15.00

PARSONS, BILL Also see BOBBY BARE.

45s

Number	Title (A Side/B Side)	Yr	NM
FRATERNITY			
❑ 835	The All American Boy/ Rubber Dolly	1959	40.00
—This record is actually by Bobby Bare miscredited			
❑ 838	Educated Rock and Roll/ Carefree Wanderer	1959	30.00
STARDAY			
❑ 526	Hod Rod Volkswagen/ Guitar Blues	1960	30.00
❑ 544	The Price We Pay for Livin'/ A-Waitin'	1960	20.00

PARSONS, GRAM Also see THE BYRDS; THE FLYING BURRITO BROTHERS; THE INTERNATIONAL SUBMARINE BAND.

45s

Number	Title (A Side/B Side)	Yr	NM
REPRISE			
❑ 1139	That's All It Took/She	1972	6.00
❑ 1192	Love Hurts/In My Hour of Darkness	1974	6.00
SIERRA			
❑ 104	Medley (Bony Moronie/40 Days/Almost Grown)// Conversations/Hot Burrito #1	1982	5.00
—Second song on side 2 by Gene Parsons			
❑ 104 [PS]	Gram Parsons and the Fallen Angels	1982	7.00
❑ 105	Love Hurts/The New Soft Shoe	1982	5.00
WARNER BROS.			
❑ 50013	Return of the Grievous Angel/ Hearts on Fire	1982	5.00

Albums

Number	Title (A Side/B Side)	Yr	NM
REPRISE			
❑ MS 2123	G.P.	1973	15.00
❑ MS 2171	Grievous Angel	1974	15.00
SIERRA			
❑ SP-1963	Early Years, Vol. 1 (1963-65)	198?	8.00
—Reissue of 8702			
❑ GP-1973	Gram Parsons and the Fallen Angels Live '73	1982	10.00
❑ 8702	Early Years, Vol. 1 (1963-65)	1979	10.00
SUNDAZED			
❑ LP 5076	Another Side of This Life	2000	12.00

PARTON, DOLLY Also see KENNY ROGERS AND DOLLY PARTON; PORTER WAGONER AND DOLLY PARTON.

12-Inch Singles

Number	Title (A Side/B Side)	Yr	NM
RCA			
❑ JD-11425 [DJ]	Baby I'm Burning/ I Wanna Fall in Love	1978	10.00
—Promo version on black vinyl			
❑ PD-11425	Baby I'm Burnin'/ I Wanna Fall in Love	1978	15.00
—Pink vinyl			
❑ PW-13545 [DJ]	Potential New Boyfriend (Long Version)/(Instrumental) (Short Version)	1983	10.00
❑ PW-13712 [DJ]	Save the Last Dance for Me (Long Version)/(Instrumetnal) (Short Version)	1983	8.00

45s

Number	Title (A Side/B Side)	Yr	NM
COLUMBIA			
❑ 07665	The River Unbroken/ More Than I Can Say	1988	3.00
❑ 07665 [PS]	The River Unbroken/ More Than I Can Say	1988	3.00
❑ 07727	I Know You by Heart/Could I Have Your Autograph	1988	3.00
—With Smokey Robinson			
❑ 07727 [PS]	I Know You by Heart/Could I Have Your Autograph	1988	3.00
❑ 07995	Make Love Mine/Two Lovers	1988	3.00
❑ 68760	Why'd You Come In Here Lookin' Like That/Wait Til I Get You Home	1989	3.00

Except when noted otherwise, VG = 25% of NM, and VG+ = 50% of NM. (Example: VG = $2.00, VG+ = $4.00 and NM = $8.00.)

Number	Title (A Side/B Side)	Yr	NM
❑ 69040	Yellow Roses/Wait Til I Get You Home	1989	3.00
❑ 73200	He's Alive/What Is It We Love	1990	3.00
❑ 73226	Time for Me to Fly/The Moon, the Stars, and Me	1990	3.00
❑ 73341	White Limozeen/The Moon, the Stars, and Me	1990	3.00
❑ 73498	Slow Healin' Heart/Take Me Back to the Country	1990	3.00
❑ 73711	Rockin' Years/What a Heartache	1991	3.00
—A-side with Ricky Van Shelton			
❑ 73826	Silver and Gold/Runaway Feelin'	1991	3.00
❑ 74011	Eagle When She Flies/Wildest Dreams	1991	3.00
❑ 74183	The Best Woman Wins/Country Road	1992	3.00
—A-side with Lorrie Morgan			
❑ 74876	Romeo/The High and the Mighty	1993	3.00
—A-side: "Dolly Parton and Friends"			
❑ 74954	More Where That Came From/I'll Make Your Bed	1993	3.00
❑ 77083	Full Circle/What Will Baby Be	1993	3.00
❑ 77294	Silver Threads and Golden Needles/Let Her Fly	1993	3.00
—Dolly Parton/Tammy Wynette/Loretta Lynn			
❑ 77723	To Daddy/PMS Blues	1994	3.00
❑ 78079	I Will Always Love You/Speakin' of the Devil	1995	3.00
—A-side: "With Special Guest Vince Gill"			

DECCA

Number	Title (A Side/B Side)	Yr	NM
❑ 72061	Honky Tonk Songs/Paradise Road	1998	3.00
❑ 72080	The Salt in My Tears/Hungry Again	1998	3.00

GOLDBAND

Number	Title (A Side/B Side)	Yr	NM
❑ 1086	Puppy Love/Girl Left Alone	1959	600.00
—Originals have a red label			
❑ 1086	Puppy Love/Girl Left Alone	198?	6.00
—Reissue; has a white label with a photo of Dolly			

MERCURY

Number	Title (A Side/B Side)	Yr	NM
❑ 71982	It's Sure Gonna Hurt/The Love You Gave	1962	300.00

MONUMENT

Number	Title (A Side/B Side)	Yr	NM
❑ 869	I Wasted My Tears/What Do You Think About Lovin'	1965	15.00
❑ 897	Old Enough to Know Better (Too Young to Resist)/Happy, Happy Birthday Baby	1965	15.00
❑ 913	Busy Signal/I Took Him for Granted	1965	15.00
❑ 922	Control Yourself/Don't Drop Out	1966	15.00
❑ 948	Little Things/I'll Put It Off Until Tomorrow	1966	15.00
❑ 982	Dumb Blonde/The Giving and the Taking	1967	10.00
❑ 1007	Something Fishy/I've Lived My Life	1967	10.00
❑ 1032	Why, Why, Why/I Couldn't Wait Forever	1967	10.00
❑ 1047	I'm Not Worth the Tears/Ping Pong	1968	8.00
❑ 03408	Everything Is Beautiful (In Its Own Way)/Put It Off Until Tomorrow	1982	4.00
—A-side with Willie Nelson; B-side with Kris Kristofferson			
❑ 03781	What Do You Think About Lovin'/You're Gonna Love Yourself (In the Morning)	1983	4.00
—A-side: Dolly Parton and Brenda Lee; B-side: Willie Nelson and Brenda Lee			

RCA

Number	Title (A Side/B Side)	Yr	NM
❑ 5001-7-R	Do I Ever Cross Your Mind/We Had It All	1986	3.00
❑ PB-10935	Light of a Clear Blue Morning/There	1977	4.00
❑ PB-11123	Here You Come Again/Me and Little Andy	1977	4.00
❑ PB-11240	Two Doors Down/It's All Wrong, But It's All Right	1978	4.00
❑ JB-11296 [DJ]	Heartbreaker (same on both sides)	1978	10.00
—Promo only on red vinyl			
❑ PB-11296	Heartbreaker/Sure Thing	1978	4.00
❑ JB-11420 [DJ]	Baby I'm Burning (same on both sides)	1978	10.00
—Promo only on red vinyl			
❑ PB-11420	Baby I'm Burning/I Really Got the Feeling	1978	4.00
❑ GB-11505	Here You Come Again/Two Doors Down	1979	3.00
—Gold Standard Series			
❑ PB-11577	You're the Only One/Down	1979	4.00
❑ JB-11705 [DJ]	Great Balls of Fire (same on both sides)	1979	10.00
—Promo only on red vinyl			
❑ PB-11705	Sweet Summer Lovin'/Great Balls of Fire	1979	4.00
❑ JH-11926 [DJ]	Starting Over Again (same on both sides)	1980	12.00
—Promo only on green vinyl			
❑ PB-11926	Starting Over Again/Sweet Agony	1980	4.00
❑ GB-11993	Baby I'm Burnin'/Heartbreaker	1980	3.00
—Gold Standard Series			
❑ PB-12040	Old Flames Can't Hold a Candle to You/I Knew You When	1980	4.00
❑ JH-12133 [DJ]	9 to 5 (same on both sides)	1980	15.00
—Promo only on blue vinyl			
❑ PB-12133	9 to 5/Sing for the Common Man	1980	4.00
❑ PB-12133 [PS]	9 to 5/Sing for the Common Man	1980	5.00
❑ PB-12200	But You Know I Love You/Poor Folks' Town	1981	4.00
❑ PB-12282	The House of the Rising Sun/Working Girl	1981	4.00
❑ GB-12316	9 to 5/Old Flames Can't Hold a Candle to You	1981	3.00
—Gold Standard Series			
❑ JK-13057 [DJ]	Single Women (same on both sides)	1982	12.00
—Promo only on red vinyl			
❑ PB-13057	Single Women/Barbara on Your Mind	1982	4.00
❑ PB-13234	Heartbreak Express/Act Like a Fool	1982	4.00
❑ PB-13260	I Will Always Love You/Do I Ever Cross Your Mind	1982	4.00
—A-side is the same song, but a different recording than that on APBO-0234			
❑ PB-13260 [PS]	I Will Always Love You/Do I Ever Cross Your Mind	1982	5.00
❑ JK-13361 [DJ]	Hard Candy Christmas (same on both sides)	1982	12.00
—Promo only on red vinyl			
❑ PB-13361	Hard Candy Christmas/Me and Little Andy	1982	4.00
❑ JK-13514 [DJ]	Potential New Boyfriend (Short) (same on both sides)	1983	12.00
—Promo only on yellow vinyl			
❑ JK-13514 [DJ]	Potential New Boyfriend (same on both sides)	1983	12.00
—Promo only on blue vinyl			
❑ PB-13514	Potential New Boyfriend/One of Those Days	1983	3.00
❑ PB-13619	Tennessee Homesick Blues/Butterflies	1984	3.00
❑ JK-13703 [DJ]	Save the Last Dance for Me (same on both sides)	1983	10.00
—Promo only on green vinyl			
❑ PB-13703	Save the Last Dance for Me/Elusive Butterfly	1983	3.00
❑ PB-13756	The Great Pretender/Downtown	1984	3.00
❑ PB-13756 [PS]	The Great Pretender/Downtown	1984	3.00
❑ PB-13856	Sweet Lovin' Friends/Too Much Water	1984	
—Unreleased			
❑ PB-13883	Sweet Lovin' Friends/God Won't Get You	1984	3.00
—With Sylvester Stallone			
❑ JK-13944 [DJ]	Medley: Winter Wonderland/Sleigh Ride (same on both sides)	1984	4.00
❑ PB-13944	Medley: Winter Wonderland-Sleigh Ride/The Christmas Song	1984	3.00
—B-side by Kenny Rogers			
❑ PB-13987	Don't Call It Love/We Got Too Much	1985	3.00
❑ GB-14070	Tennessee Homesick Blues/Hard Candy Christmas	1985	3.00
—Gold Standard Series			
❑ PB-14218	Think About Love/Come Back to Me	1985	3.00
❑ PB-14297	Tie Our Love (In a Double Knot)/I Hope You're Never Happy	1986	3.00
❑ GB-14346	Don't Call It Love/Real Love	1986	3.00
—Gold Standard Series			

RCA VICTOR

Number	Title (A Side/B Side)	Yr	NM
❑ 47-9548	Just Because I'm a Woman/I Wish I Felt This Way at Home	1968	8.00
❑ 47-9657	In the Good Old Days (When Times Were Bad)/Try Being Lonely	1968	8.00
❑ 47-9784	Daddy Come and Get Me/Chas	1969	6.00
❑ 47-9863	Mule Skinner Blues/More Than Their Share	1970	6.00
❑ 47-9928	Joshua/I'm Doing This for Your Sake	1970	6.00
❑ 47-9971	Comin' For to Carry Me Home/Golden Streets of Glory	1971	10.00
❑ 47-9999	My Blue Tears/The Mystery of the Mystery	1971	6.00
❑ 74-0132	Daddy/He's a Go-Getter	1969	6.00
❑ 74-0192	In the Ghetto/Bridge	1969	6.00
❑ 74-0243	My Blue Ridge Mountain Boy/'Til Death Do Us Part	1969	6.00
❑ 74-0538	Coat of Many Colors/Here I Am	1971	6.00
❑ 74-0538 [PS]	Coat of Many Colors/Here I Am	1971	10.00
❑ 74-0662	Touch Your Woman/Mission Chapel Memories	1972	5.00
❑ 74-0757	Washday Blues/Just As Good As Gone	1972	10.00
❑ 74-0797	Lord, Hold My Hand/When I Sing for Him	1972	5.00
❑ 74-0868	My Tennessee Mountain Home/Better Part of Life	1973	5.00
❑ 74-0950	Traveling Man/I Remember	1973	5.00
❑ APBO-0145	Jolene/Love, You're So Beautiful Tonight	1973	5.00
❑ APBO-0234	I Will Always Love You/Lonely Comin' Down	1974	5.00
❑ PB-10031	Love Is Like a Butterfly/Sacred Memories	1974	4.00
❑ PB-10164	The Bargain Store/I'll Never Forget	1975	4.00
❑ GB-10165	Jolene/My Tennessee Mountain Home	1975	3.00
—Gold Standard Series			
❑ PB-10310	The Seeker/Love with Feeling	1975	8.00
❑ PB-10396	We Used To/My Heart Started Breaking	1975	4.00
❑ GB-10504	Love Is Like a Butterfly/Sacred Memories	1975	3.00
—Gold Standard Series			
❑ GB-10505	I Will Always Love You/Lovely Comin' Down	1975	3.00
—Gold Standard Series			
❑ PB-10564	Hey, Lucky Lady/Most of All, Why	1976	4.00
❑ GB-10676	The Bargain Store/The Seeker	1976	3.00
—Gold Standard Series			
❑ PB-10730	All I Can Do/Falling Out of Love with Me	1976	4.00

RISING TIDE

Number	Title (A Side/B Side)	Yr	NM
❑ 56041	Just When I Needed You Most/For the Good Times	1996	3.00

Albums

COLUMBIA

Number	Title	Yr	NM
❑ FC 40968	Rainbow	1987	10.00
❑ FC 44384	White Limozeen	1989	12.00
❑ C 46882	Eagle When She Flies	1991	20.00
—Available on vinyl only through Columbia House			

MONUMENT

Number	Title	Yr	NM
❑ 7623	In the Beginning	197?	12.00
❑ MLP-8085 [M]	Hello, I'm Dolly	1967	30.00
❑ SLP-18085 [S]	Hello, I'm Dolly	1967	40.00
❑ SLP-18136	As Long As I Love	1970	20.00
❑ KZG 31913 [(2)]	The World of Dolly	1972	20.00
❑ KZG 33876 [(2)]	Hello, I'm Dolly	1975	20.00

PAIR

Number	Title	Yr	NM
❑ PDL2-1009 [(2)]	Just the Way I Am	1986	12.00
❑ PDL2-1116 [(2)]	Portrait	1986	12.00

RCA

Number	Title	Yr	NM
❑ 5706-1-R	The Best of Dolly Parton, Vol. 3	1987	10.00
❑ 6497-1-R	The Best There Is	1987	10.00

RCA CAMDEN

Number	Title	Yr	NM
❑ ACL1-0307	Mine	1973	10.00
❑ CAS-2583	Just the Way I Am	1972	10.00

RCA VICTOR

Number	Title	Yr	NM
❑ APL1-0033	My Tennessee Mountain Home	1973	12.00
❑ APD1-0286 [Q]	Bubbling Over	1974	20.00
❑ APL1-0286	Bubbling Over	1973	12.00
❑ APL1-0473	Jolene	1974	12.00
❑ APL1-0712	Love Is Like a Butterfly	1974	12.00
❑ APL1-0950	The Bargain Store	1975	12.00
❑ APL1-1117	The Best of Dolly Parton	1975	12.00
❑ APL1-1221	Dolly	1975	12.00
❑ APL1-1665	All I Can Do	1976	12.00
❑ APL1-2188	New Harvest...First Gathering	1977	12.00
❑ DJL1-2314 [DJ]	Personal Music Dialogue with Dolly Parton	1976	25.00
❑ AFL1-2544	Here You Come Again	1977	12.00
❑ AFL1-2797	Heartbreaker	1978	12.00
❑ AHL1-3361	Great Balls of Fire	1979	12.00
❑ AHL1-3546	Dolly Dolly Dolly	1980	12.00
❑ AYL1-3665	Heartbreaker	1980	8.00
—"Best Buy Series" reissue			
❑ AYL1-3764	My Tennessee Mountain Home	1980	8.00
—"Best Buy Series" reissue			
❑ AHL1-3852	9 to 5 and Odd Jobs	1980	12.00
❑ AYL1-3898	Jolene	1981	8.00
—"Best Buy Series" reissue			
❑ LPM-3949 [M]	Just Because I'm a Woman	1968	100.00
❑ LSP-3949 [S]	Just Because I'm a Woman	1968	20.00
—Orange label			
❑ LSP-3949 [S]	Just Because I'm a Woman	1968	30.00
—"Stereo" on black label			
❑ AYL1-3980	New Harvest	1981	8.00
—"Best Buy Series" reissue			
❑ LSP-4099	In the Good Old Days	1969	20.00
❑ LSP-4188	My Blue Ridge Mountain Boy	1969	20.00
❑ LSP-4288	The Fairest of Them All	1970	20.00
❑ AHL1-4289	Heartbreak Express	1982	12.00

Number	Title (A Side/B Side)	Yr	NM
❑ LSP-4387	A Real Live Dolly	1970	25.00
—Four songs feature Porter Wagoner			
❑ LSP-4398	Golden Streets of Glory	1971	20.00
❑ AHL1-4422	Greatest Hits	1982	12.00
❑ LSP-4449	The Best of Dolly Parton	1970	20.00
❑ LSP-4507	Joshua	1971	20.00
❑ LSP-4603	Coat of Many Colors	1971	20.00
❑ LSP-4686	Touch Your Woman	1972	20.00
❑ AHL1-4691	Burlap & Satin	1983	10.00
❑ LSP-4752	My Favorite Song Writer: Porter Wagoner	1972	20.00
❑ LSP-4762	Dolly Parton Sings	1972	15.00
❑ AYL1-4829	Here You Come Again	1984	8.00
—"Best Buy Series" reissue			
❑ AYL1-4830	9 to 5 and Odd Jobs	1984	8.00
—"Best Buy Series" reissue			
❑ AHL1-4940	The Great Pretender	1984	10.00
❑ AYL1-5146	The Best of Dolly Parton	1984	8.00
—"Best Buy Series" reissue			
❑ AHL1-5414	Real Love	1985	10.00
❑ AYL1-5437	Burlap & Satin	1985	8.00
—"Best Buy Series" reissue			
❑ AHL1-5471	Collector's Series	1985	10.00
❑ AHL1-9508	Think About Love	1986	10.00

TIME-LIFE

Number	Title (A Side/B Side)	Yr	NM
❑ STW-107	Country Music	1981	10.00

PARTON, DOLLY/GEORGE JONES

Albums

STARDAY

Number	Title (A Side/B Side)	Yr	NM
❑ LP 429 [P]	Dolly Parton and George Jones	1968	40.00

—One side of Dolly in stereo, one side of "Possum" in rechanneled stereo

PARTON, DOLLY/FAYE TUCKER

Albums

SOMERSET

Number	Title (A Side/B Side)	Yr	NM
❑ S-9700 [M]	Hits Made Famous by Country Queens	1963	25.00
❑ SF-19700 [S]	Hits Made Famous by Country Queens	1963	30.00
—Dolly Parton sings songs made famous by Kitty Wells			
❑ SF-29400	Dolly Parton Sings Country Oldies	1968	15.00

TIME

Number	Title (A Side/B Side)	Yr	NM
❑ 2108	Country & Western Soul	1963	40.00

PARTRIDGE FAMILY, THE

Also see DANNY BONADUCE; DAVID CASSIDY.

45s

BELL

Number	Title (A Side/B Side)	Yr	NM
❑ 910	I Think I Love You/Somebody Wants to Love You	1970	5.00
❑ 910	I Think I Love You/Somebody Wants to Love You	1970	25.00
—Artist erroneously listed on both sides as "The PATRIDGE Family"			
❑ 910 [PS]	I Think I Love You/Somebody Wants to Love You	1970	6.00
❑ 963	Doesn't Somebody Want to Be Wanted/You Are Always on My Mind	1971	5.00
❑ 963 [PS]	Doesn't Somebody Want to Be Wanted/You Are Always on My Mind	1971	6.00
❑ 996	I'll Meet You Halfway/Morning Rider on the Road	1971	5.00
❑ 45130	I Woke Up in Love This Morning/Twenty-Four Hours a Day	1971	5.00
❑ 45160	It's One of Those Nights (Yes Love)/One Night Stand	1971	5.00
❑ 45200	Am I Losing You/If You Ever Go	1972	4.00
❑ 45235	Breaking Up Is Hard to Do/I'm Here, You're Here	1972	4.00
❑ 45301	Looking Through the Eyes of Love/Storybook Love	1972	4.00
❑ 45336	Friend and a Lover/Something's Wrong	1973	4.00
❑ 45414	Lookin' for a Good Time/Money Money	1973	40.00
—Extremely rare as a stock copy			
❑ 45414 [PS]	Lookin' for a Good Time/Money Money	1973	40.00

Albums

BELL

Number	Title (A Side/B Side)	Yr	NM
❑ 1107	The Partridge Family At Home with Their Greatest Hits	1972	20.00
❑ 1111	The Partridge Family Notebook	1972	25.00
❑ 1122	Crossword Puzzle	1973	30.00
❑ 1137	Bulletin Board	1973	50.00
❑ 1319 [(2)]	The World of the Partridge Family	1974	40.00
❑ 6050	The Partridge Family Album Bonus Photo	1970	10.00
❑ 6050	The Partridge Family Album	1970	20.00
❑ 6059	Up to Date Book Cover	1971	10.00
❑ 6059	Up to Date	1971	20.00
❑ 6064	The Partridge Family Sound Magazine	1971	20.00
❑ 6066	A Partridge Family Christmas Card	1971	15.00
—Without Christmas card			
❑ 6066	A Partridge Family Christmas Card	1971	25.00
—With attached Christmas card			
❑ 6066	A Partridge Family Christmas Card	1971	40.00
—With Christmas card printed on the cover (later pressing)			
❑ 6072	The Partridge Family Shopping Bag Bonus Shopping Bag	1972	10.00
❑ 6072	The Partridge Family Shopping Bag	1972	20.00

LAURIE HOUSE

Number	Title (A Side/B Side)	Yr	NM
❑ H-8014 [(2)]	The Partridge Family	197?	50.00

PARTY BROTHERS, THE

45s

CANUSA

Number	Title (A Side/B Side)	Yr	NM
❑ 505	A&T's Party/Let Me Be the One	1967	40.00

REVUE

Number	Title (A Side/B Side)	Yr	NM
❑ 11046	Do the Ground Hog/Nassau Daddy	1969	40.00

PASSIONS, THE (1)

45s

ABC-PARAMOUNT

Number	Title (A Side/B Side)	Yr	NM
❑ 10436	The Bully/The Empty Seat	1963	25.00

AUDICON

Number	Title (A Side/B Side)	Yr	NM
❑ 102	Just to Be with You/Oh Melancholy Me	1959	40.00
❑ 105	I Only Want You/This Is My Love	1960	20.00
—Red, black and white label			
❑ 105	I Only Want You/This Is My Love	1960	30.00
—Red label			
❑ 106	Gloria/Jungle Drums	1960	30.00
❑ 108	Beautiful Dreamer/One Look Is All It Took	1960	30.00
❑ 112	Made for Lovers/You Don't Have Me Anymore	1961	40.00

DIAMOND

Number	Title (A Side/B Side)	Yr	NM
❑ 146	Sixteen Candles/The Third Floor	1963	40.00

JUBILEE

Number	Title (A Side/B Side)	Yr	NM
❑ 5406	Lonely Road/One Look Is All It Took	1961	20.00

OCTAVIA

Number	Title (A Side/B Side)	Yr	NM
❑ 8005	Aphrodite/I've Gotta Know	1962	800.00

PASSIONS, THE (2)

45s

BACK BEAT

Number	Title (A Side/B Side)	Yr	NM
❑ 573	Baby I Do/Man About Town	1966	10.00

TOWER

Number	Title (A Side/B Side)	Yr	NM
❑ 424	Without a Warning/Just Like a Rolling Seal	1968	8.00
❑ 443	I Can See My Way Through/Just Another Reason	1968	8.00
❑ 443	I Can See My Way Through/Without a Warning	1968	8.00
❑ 474	Just Like a Rolling Stone/Just Another	1969	8.00
❑ 485	Hijacked/Hijacked	1969	8.00

PASSIONS, THE (3)

45s

CAPITOL

Number	Title (A Side/B Side)	Yr	NM
❑ F3963	Jackie Brown/My Aching Heart	1958	30.00

ERA

Number	Title (A Side/B Side)	Yr	NM
❑ 1063	Jackie Brown/My Aching Heart	1957	40.00

PASSIONS, THE (U)

Could be group (1) or (3), or a completely different group.

45s

DORE

Number	Title (A Side/B Side)	Yr	NM
❑ 505	Nervous About Sally/Tango of Love	1958	30.00

GSF

Number	Title (A Side/B Side)	Yr	NM
❑ 6880	One Night Affair/A Toast (May There Be No Last Time)	1972	30.00

TOPAZ

Number	Title (A Side/B Side)	Yr	NM
❑ 1317	It Ain't Fair/I'm So Afraid	196?	10.00

PASSPORT

12-Inch Singles

ATLANTIC

Number	Title (A Side/B Side)	Yr	NM
❑ DMD 843 [DJ]	Running in Real Time (Extended Mix 7:24) (Dub Mix 6:33) (7 Inch Edit 3:19)	1986	8.00

45s

ATCO

Number	Title (A Side/B Side)	Yr	NM
❑ 7054	Ju-Ju Man/(B-side unknown)	1976	4.00

ATLANTIC

Number	Title (A Side/B Side)	Yr	NM
❑ 3487	Loco-Motive/Mandrake	1978	5.00
❑ 3659	Departure/(B-side unknown)	1979	5.00
❑ 3857	Rambling/Riding on a Cloud	1981	5.00
❑ 89558	Running in Real Time/(B-side unknown)	1986	5.00
❑ 89697	Man in the Mirror/(B-side unknown)	1983	5.00
❑ 89925	New Moon/(B-side unknown)	1982	5.00

Albums

ATCO

Number	Title (A Side/B Side)	Yr	NM
❑ SD 36-107	Cross-Collateral	1975	12.00
❑ SD 36-132	Infinity Machine	1976	12.00
❑ SD 36-149	Iguacu	1977	10.00
❑ SD 7042	Looking Thru	1974	12.00

ATLANTIC

Number	Title (A Side/B Side)	Yr	NM
❑ SD 18162	Doldinger Jubilee '75	1976	12.00
❑ SD 19177	Sky Blue	1978	10.00
❑ SD 19233	Garden of Eden	1979	10.00
❑ SD 19265	Oceanliner	1980	10.00
❑ SD 19304	Blue Tattoo	1981	10.00
❑ 80034	Earthborn	1982	10.00
❑ 80144	Man in the Mirror	1983	10.00
❑ 81251	Running in Real Time	1985	10.00
❑ 81727	Heavy Nights	1986	10.00
❑ 81937	Talk Back	1989	10.00

REPRISE

Number	Title (A Side/B Side)	Yr	NM
❑ MS 2143	Doldinger	1973	15.00

PASTEL SIX, THE

45s

CHATTAHOOCHIE

Number	Title (A Side/B Side)	Yr	NM
❑ 696	I Can't Dance/Red River Quetzal	1966	10.00

DOWNEY

Number	Title (A Side/B Side)	Yr	NM
❑ 101	Twitchin'/Open House at the Cinder	1962	30.00
❑ 101	Twitchin'/Wino Stomp	1962	30.00
❑ 102	Braum's Nightmare/Open House at the Cinder	1962	25.00

ZEN

Number	Title (A Side/B Side)	Yr	NM
❑ 102	The Cinnamon Cinder (It's a Very Nice Dance)/Bandido	1962	25.00
❑ 105	Sing Along Song/The Strange Ghost	1963	25.00
❑ 108	The Milkshake/Parchman Farm	1963	25.00
❑ 111	Miss Sue/Baby Please Don't Go	1963	25.00

Albums

ZEN

Number	Title (A Side/B Side)	Yr	NM
❑ 1001 [M]	The Cinnamon Cinder	1963	100.00

PASTELS, THE

45s

ARGO

Number	Title (A Side/B Side)	Yr	NM
❑ 5287	Been So Long/My One and Only Dream	1958	25.00
❑ 5297	You Don't Love Me Anymore/Let's Go to the Rock 'N' Roll Ball	1958	30.00
❑ 5314	So Far Away/Don't Knock	1958	25.00

ARK

Number	Title (A Side/B Side)	Yr	NM
❑ 298	Jungle Run/K-Nif	196?	50.00

JUBILEE

Number	Title (A Side/B Side)	Yr	NM
❑ 5495	First Star/Tokyo Melody	1965	12.00

MASCOT

Number	Title (A Side/B Side)	Yr	NM
❑ 123	Been So Long/My One and Only Dream	1957	300.00

UNITED

Number	Title (A Side/B Side)	Yr	NM
❑ 196	Put Your Arms Around Me/Boom De De Boom	1957	80.00

PATCHETT, TOM, AND JAY TARSES

45s

DECCA

Number	Title (A Side/B Side)	Yr	NM
❑ 32892	Howard Hardsell/Run to Daylight	1971	5.00

—B-side by H.B. Barnum

Albums

DECCA

Number	Title (A Side/B Side)	Yr	NM
❑ DL 75300	Instant Replay (Two Sides of Football)	1971	15.00

PATIENCE AND PRUDENCE

45s

CHATATHOOCHIE

Number	Title (A Side/B Side)	Yr	NM
❑ 665	Tonight You Belong to Me (New Version)/How Can I Tell Him	1965	10.00

LIBERTY

Number	Title (A Side/B Side)	Yr	NM
❑ 55022	Tonight You Belong to Me/A Smile and a Ribbon	1956	30.00
❑ 55040	Gonna Get Along Without Ya Now/The Money Tree	1956	25.00

—Blue-green label, silver print

Except when noted otherwise, VG = 25% of NM, and VG+ = 50% of NM. (Example: VG = $2.00, VG+ = $4.00 and NM = $8.00.)

Number	Title (A Side/B Side)	Yr	NM
❑ 55040	Gonna Get Along Without Ya Now/The Money Tree	1956	40.00
—Maroon label, gold print			
❑ 55058	Dreamer's Bay/We Can't Sing Rhythm and Blues	1957	25.00
❑ 55084	You Tattletale/Very Nice in Bali Bali	1957	25.00
❑ 55084 [PS]	You Tattletale/Very Nice in Bali Bali	1957	50.00
❑ 55107	Witchcraft/Over Here	1957	25.00
❑ 55125	Heavenly Angel/Little Wheel	1958	25.00
❑ 55154	All I Do Is Dream of You/ Your Careless Love	1958	25.00
❑ 55169	Golly Oh Gee/Tom Thumb's Tune	1958	25.00
❑ 55207	Should I/Whisper Whisper	1959	15.00
—With Mike Clifford			
UNITED ARTISTS			
❑ 0012	Tonight You Belong to Me/ Gonna Get Along Without You Now	1973	5.00
—"Silver Spotlight Series" reissue			

PATRICK, MILT

45s

Number	Title (A Side/B Side)	Yr	NM
CAPITOL			
❑ 4634	Up to My Ears in Tears/ When I Met You	1961	10.00
DEMON			
❑ 1518	A Fountain of Love/You Are My Inspiration	1959	12.00
EVEREST			
❑ 2014	I Don't Think I Wanna Do It/ No Fool Like an Old Fool	1963	8.00
TERRI-ANN			
❑ 101	Merry Twistmas/Just A Doggone Dream	1962	10.00

PATRON SAINTS, THE

Albums

Number	Title (A Side/B Side)	Yr	NM
(NO LABEL)			
❑ JT-1001	Fohhob Bohob	1969	3000.
—100 copies were pressed; VG value 1000; VG+ value 2000			
PATRON SAINT			
❑ JT-1001	Fohhob Bohob	1997	25.00
—Authorized reissue with bonus 7-inch single; numbered edition of 500			

PATTERSON, MIKE, AND THE FUGITIVES

45s

Number	Title (A Side/B Side)	Yr	NM
IMPERIAL			
❑ 66083	Cookin' Beans/Jerky	1965	12.00
❑ 66118	Don't You Just Know It/ Righteous Theme	1965	12.00

PATTO Also see SPOOKY TOOTH.

45s

Number	Title (A Side/B Side)	Yr	NM
ISLAND			
❑ 1208	Mummy/Singing the Blues on Reds	1972	6.00

Albums

Number	Title (A Side/B Side)	Yr	NM
ISLAND			
❑ SW-9322	Roll 'Em, Smoke 'Em, Put Another Line Out	1972	30.00
VERTIGO			
❑ VEL-1001	Patto	1971	35.00
❑ VEL-1008	Hold Your Fire	1972	35.00

PATTON, JIMMY

45s

Number	Title (A Side/B Side)	Yr	NM
SAGE AND SAND			
❑ 261	Call Me/Forty-Nine Women	1958	120.00
❑ 282	Ocean Full of Tears/ Twinklin' Teardrops	1959	40.00
SIMS			
❑ 103	Careful/Guilty	1955	50.00
—With Ann Jones			
❑ 104	Teenage Haert/Jalopy	1955	50.00
❑ 105	Ocean of Tears/I Don't Want It	1955	50.00
❑ 117	Okie's in the Pokie/Lonely Nights	1960	200.00
❑ 227	Blue Darling/Preacher and a Girl in the Night	1965	12.00
❑ 256	Can't Shake the Blues/ (B-side unknown)	1965	12.00

Albums

Number	Title (A Side/B Side)	Yr	NM
MOON			
❑ 101 [M]	Make Room for the Blues	1966	40.00
SIMS			
❑ 127 [M]	Blue Darlin'	1965	40.00
SOURDOUGH			
❑ 127 [M]	Blue Darlin'	1965	50.00
STEREOPHONIC			
❑ LP-1002 [S]	Take 30 Minutes with Jimmy Patton	196?	120.00

PATTY AND THE EMBLEMS

45s

Number	Title (A Side/B Side)	Yr	NM
CONGRESS			
❑ 263	Easy Come, Easy Go/ It's the Little Things	1966	20.00
HERALD			
❑ 590	Mixed-Up, Shook-Up, Girl/ Ordinary Guy	1964	20.00
❑ 593	The Sound of Music Makes Me Want to Dance/You Took Advantage of a Good Thing	1964	15.00
❑ 595	And We Danced/You Can't Get Away from Me	1964	15.00
KAPP			
❑ 791	Let Him Go Little Heart/Try It, You Won't Forget It	1966	20.00
❑ 850	Please Don't Ever Leave Me/ All My Tomorrows Are Gone	1967	20.00
❑ 870	I'll Cry Later/One Man Woman	1967	20.00
❑ 897	I'm Gonna Love You a Long, Long Time/My Heart's So Full of You	1968	15.00
LOST-NITE			
❑ 420	Mixed-Up, Shook-Up, Girl/ Ordinary Guy	197?	5.00
—Reissue			

PATTY FLABBIE'S COUGHED ENGINE

45s

Number	Title (A Side/B Side)	Yr	NM
DIAMOND			
❑ 252	Billy Got a Goat/Tin Can Eater	1968	15.00

PAUL See RAY HILDEBRAND.

PAUL, BILLY

12-Inch Singles

Number	Title (A Side/B Side)	Yr	NM
PHILADELPHIA INT'L.			
❑ 3678	Bring the Family Back (5:53)/ It's Critical (6:33)	1979	12.00
❑ 3706	False Faces (6:52)/ (B-side unknown)	1979	12.00

45s

Number	Title (A Side/B Side)	Yr	NM
GAMBLE			
❑ 232	Somewhere/Bluesette	1968	12.00
JUBILEE			
❑ 5081	That's Why I Dream/Why Am I	1952	30.00
❑ 5086	You Didn't Know/The Stars Are Mine	1952	30.00
NEPTUNE			
❑ 30	Mrs. Robinson/Let's Fall in Love All Over	1970	10.00
PHILADELPHIA INT'L.			
❑ 3120	Jesus Boy (You Only Look Like a Man)/Love Buddies	1980	5.00
❑ 3509	Love Buddies/Magic Carpet Ride	1971	6.00
❑ 3515	This Is Your Life/I Wish It Were Yesterday	1972	6.00
❑ 3521	Me and Mrs. Jones/Your Song	1972	5.00
❑ 3526	Am I Black Enough for You/ I'm Gonna Make It This Time	1973	5.00
❑ 3538	Thanks for Saving My Life/ I Was Married	1974	5.00
❑ 3551	Be Truthful to Me/I Wish It Was Yesterday	1974	5.00
❑ 3563	Billy's Back Home/I've Got So Much to Live For	1975	5.00
❑ 3572	When It's Your Turn to Go/ July, July, July, July	1975	5.00
❑ 3584	Let's Make a Baby/ My Head's On Straight	1976	5.00
❑ 3593	People Power/I Want Cha Baby	1976	5.00
❑ 3613	How Good Is Your Game/I Think I'll Stay Home Today	1977	5.00
❑ 3621	Let 'Em In/We All Got a Mission	1977	5.00
❑ 3630	I Trust You/Love Won't Come Easy	1977	5.00
❑ 3635	Only the Strong Survive/ Where I Belong	1977	5.00
❑ 3639	Everybody's Breakin' Up/ Sooner or Later	1978	5.00
❑ 3645	One Man's Junk/Don't Give Up on Love	1978	5.00
❑ 3676	Bring the Family Back/It's Critical	1979	5.00
❑ 3699	False Faces/I Gotta Put This Life Down	1979	5.00
❑ 3736	You're My Sweetness/ (B-side unknown)	1979	5.00
❑ ZS9 3737	Jesus Boy (You Only Look Like a Man)/(B-side unknown)	1979	6.00
TOTAL EXPERIENCE			
❑ 2419	Lately/(Instrumental)	1985	5.00
❑ 2434	Sexual Therapy/Hot Date	1986	5.00

7-Inch Extended Plays

Number	Title (A Side/B Side)	Yr	NM
PHILADELPHIA INT'L.			
❑ ZS7 31793	I'm Just a Prisoner//Am I Black Enough for You/I'm Gonna Make It This Time	1972	12.00
—Jukebox issue; small hole, plays at 33 1/3 rpm			
❑ ZS7 31793 [PS]	360 Degrees of Billy Paul	1972	12.00

Albums

Number	Title (A Side/B Side)	Yr	NM
GAMBLE			
❑ SG-5002	Feeling Good at the Cadillac Club	1968	30.00
ICHIBAN			
❑ ICH-1025	Wide Open	198?	10.00
NEPTUNE			
❑ 201	Ebony Woman	1970	20.00
PHILADELPHIA INT'L.			
❑ Z 30580	Going East	1971	12.00
❑ KZ 31793	360 Degrees of Billy Paul	1972	12.00
❑ ZQ 31793 [Q]	360 Degrees of Billy Paul	1972	20.00
❑ KZ 32118	Ebony Woman	1973	12.00
—Reissue of Neptune LP			
❑ KZ 32119	Feeling Good at the Cadillac Club	1973	12.00
—Reissue of Gamble LP			
❑ KZ 32409	War of the Gods	1973	10.00
❑ ZQ 32409 [Q]	War of the Gods	1973	20.00
❑ KZ 32952	Live in Europe	1974	10.00
❑ ZQ 32952 [Q]	Live in Europe	1974	20.00
❑ PZ 33157	Got My Head On Straight	1975	10.00
❑ PZ 33843	When Love Is New	1975	10.00
❑ PZ 34389	Let 'Em In	1976	10.00
❑ PZ 34923	Only the Strong Survive	1977	10.00
❑ JZ 35756	First Class	1979	10.00
❑ Z2 36314 [(2)]	The Best of Billy Paul	1980	15.00
TOTAL EXPERIENCE			
❑ TEL8-5711	Lately	1985	10.00

PAUL, BUNNY

45s

Number	Title (A Side/B Side)	Yr	NM
BRUNSWICK			
❑ 55003	Poor Joe/Buzz Me	1957	15.00
❑ 55022	Breedle-Lump-Bump/ The One You Love	1957	15.00
CAPITOL			
❑ F3074	Please Have Mercy/These Are the Things We'll Share	1955	15.00
❑ F3109	Two Castanets/Leave My Heart Alone	1955	15.00
❑ F3178	Song of the Dreamer/For the Very First Time	1955	15.00
❑ F3224	Take a Chance/Tell the Man	1955	15.00
❑ F3288	Open the Door/Who Am I Foolin'	1955	15.00
DOT			
❑ 15107	Magic Guitar/Never Let Me Go	1953	25.00
ESSEX			
❑ 344	New Love/You'll Never Leave My Side	1954	100.00
❑ 352	Such a Night/I'm Gonna Have Some Fun	1954	60.00
❑ 359	Lovey Dovey/Answer the Call	1954	60.00
❑ 364	Honey Love/I'll Never Tell	1954	100.00
❑ 371	You Are Always in My Heart/ You Came a Long Way from St. Louis	1954	60.00
❑ 385	Brown Jug/Pam-Poo-Dey	1955	60.00
GORDY			
❑ 7017	We're Only Young Once/ I'm Hooked	1963	20.00
POINT			
❑ 5	Sweet Talk/History	1956	40.00
ROULETTE			
❑ 4186	Such a Night/A Million Miles from Nowhere	1959	15.00

PAUL, LES See note under LES PAUL AND MARY FORD.

45s

Number	Title (A Side/B Side)	Yr	NM
DECCA			
❑ 27903	Blue Skies/Dark Eyes	1951	15.00
❑ 29013	Steel Guitar Rag/Guitar Boogie	1954	15.00
LONDON			
❑ 120	Los Angeles/The System	1969	6.00

Albums

Number	Title (A Side/B Side)	Yr	NM
CAPITOL			
❑ N-16286	Early Les Paul	1982	8.00
DECCA			
❑ DL-5018 [10]	Hawaiian Paradise	1949	100.00
❑ DL-5376 [10]	Galloping Guitars	1952	100.00
❑ DL 8589 [M]	More of Les	1957	40.00

P

GLENDALE

Number	Title (A Side/B Side)	Yr	NM
6014	The Les Paul Trio	198?	10.00

LONDON

Number	Title (A Side/B Side)	Yr	NM
50016	Multi-Trackin'	1979	12.00

LONDON PHASE 4

Number	Title (A Side/B Side)	Yr	NM
SP-44101	Les Paul Now!	1968	15.00

VOCALION

Number	Title (A Side/B Side)	Yr	NM
VL 3849 [M]	The Guitar Artistry of Les Paul	196?	12.00
VL 73849 [R]	The Guitar Artistry of Les Paul	196?	10.00

PAUL, LES, AND MARY FORD

Included in the Capitol listings are LES PAUL solo works. Some of these appear on B-sides of duet hits.

45s

CAPITOL

Number	Title (A Side/B Side)	Yr	NM
PRO 233/4 [DJ]	Magic Melody/Magic Melody — Part II	1955	30.00
—Promo-only release; B-side's running time listed as "One Second"!			
CCF-286 [PS]	The New Sound! Vol. II	1951	15.00
—Box for 3-record set (F15748, F15749, F15750)			
F1014	Nola/Jealous	1950	20.00
F1088	Dry My Tears/Cryin'	1950	20.00
F1192	Goofus/Sugar Sweet	1950	20.00
F1316	Tennessee Waltz/Little Rock Getaway	1950	20.00
F1373	Mockin' Bird Hill/Chicken Reel	1951	20.00
F1451	How High the Moon/Walkin' Whistlin' Blues	1951	25.00
F1592	Josephine/I Wish I Had Never Seen Sunshine	1951	15.00
F1600	Brazil/Lover	1951	12.00
—As "Les Paul"			
F1621	Nola/Jealous	1951	12.00
—Reissue			
F1675	How High the Moon/Josephine	195?	12.00
—Reissue			
F1676	Tennessee Waltz/Mockin' Bird Hill	195?	12.00
—Reissue			
F1690	Meet Mister Callaghan/My Baby's Comin' Home	195?	12.00
—Reissue			
F1748	The World Is Waiting for the Sunrise/Whispering	1951	15.00
F1825	Just One More Chance/Jazz Me Blues	1951	15.00
F1881	Jingle Bells/Silent Night	1951	15.00
F1920	Tiger Rag/It's a Lonesome Old Town	1951	15.00
F2080	I'm Confessin' (That I Love You)/Carioca	1952	15.00
F2123	Smoke Rings/In the Good Old Summertime	1952	15.00
F2193	Meet Mister Callaghan/Take Me in Your Arms and Hold Me	1952	15.00
F2265	My Baby's Coming Home/Lady of Spain	1952	15.00
F2316	Bye Bye Blues/Mammy's Boogie	1953	15.00
F2400	I'm Sitting on Top of the World/Sleep	1953	15.00
F2486	Vaya Con Dios (May God Be With You)/Johnny (Is the Boy for Me)	1953	15.00
F2614	Don'cha Hear Them Bells/The Kangaroo	1953	15.00
F2617	Jungle Bells (Dingo-Dango-Day)/White Christmas	1953	15.00
F2735	I Really Don't Want to Know/South	1954	12.00
F2839	I'm a Fool to Care/Auctioneer	1954	12.00
F2928	Whither Thou Goest/Mandolino	1954	12.00
F3015	Someday Sweetheart/Song in Blue	1955	12.00
F3108	No Letter Today/Genuine Love	1955	12.00
F3165	Hummingbird/Goodbye My Love	1955	12.00
F3248	Amukiriki (The Lord Willing)/Magic Melody	1955	12.00
F3301	Texas Lady/Alabamy Bound	1955	12.00
F3302	Rudolph the Red-Nosed Reindeer/Santa Claus Is Comin' to Town	1955	12.00
F3329	Moritat (Theme from Threepenny Opera)/Nuevo Laredo	1956	10.00
F3389	Say the Words I Love to Hear/Send Me Some Money	1956	10.00
F3444	Cimarron/San Antonio Rose	1956	10.00
F3570	Blow the Smoke Away/Running Wild	1956	10.00
F3612	Cinco Robles (Five Oaks)/Ro-Ro-Robinson	1957	10.00
F3725	Tuxedos and Flowers/Hummin' and Waltzin'	1957	10.00
F3776	I Don't Want You No More/Strollin' Blues	1957	10.00
F3825	A Pair of Fools/Fire	1957	10.00
F3858	Goodnight My Someone/The Night of the Fourth	1957	10.00
F3934	More and More Each Day/A Small Island	1958	10.00
F15748	In the Good Old Summertime/La Rosita	1951	15.00
—"Part 1" and "Part 6" of CCF-286			
F15749	Three Little Words/Moon Over Manakoora	1951	15.00
—"Part 2" and "Part 5" of CCF-286			
F15750	I'm Forever Blowing Bubbles/The Lonesome Road	1951	15.00
—"Part 3" and "Part 4" of CCF-286			

COLUMBIA

Number	Title (A Side/B Side)	Yr	NM
S7 31385 [S]	'Deed I Do/Makin' Whoopee!	1962	12.00
S7 31386 [S]	A Cottage for Sale/Chasing Shadows	1962	12.00
S7 31387 [S]	It's Been a Long, Long Time/After You've Gone	1962	12.00
S7 31388 [S]	Am I Blue/You Brought a New Kind of Love to Me	1962	12.00
S7 31389 [S]	(titles unknown)	1962	12.00
—The above five are "Stereo Seven" 33 1/3 rpm jukebox singles from "JS7-52"			
41222	Put a Ring on My Finger/Fantasy	1958	10.00
41222 [PS]	Put a Ring on My Finger/Fantasy	1958	15.00
41278	Jealous Heart/Big Eyed Gal	1958	10.00
41350	All I Need Is You/At the Save-a-Penny Super Store	1959	10.00
41592	The Poor People of Paris/All Night Long	1960	8.00
41660	Wonderful Rain/Take a Warning	1960	8.00
41994	Jura (I Swear I Love You)/It's Been a Long, Long Time	1961	8.00
41994 [PS]	Jura (I Swear I Love You)/It's Been a Long, Long Time	1961	12.00
42179	It's Too Late/Mountain Railroad	1961	8.00
42241	Goodnight Irene/Lonely Guitar	1961	8.00
42241 [PS]	Goodnight Irene/Lonely Guitar	1961	12.00
42419	Your Cheatin' Heart/Another Town, Another Time	1962	8.00
42419 [PS]	Your Cheatin' Heart/Another Town, Another Time	1962	12.00
42602	Playing Make Believe/I Just Don't Understand	1962	8.00
42602 [PS]	Playing Make Believe/I Just Don't Understand	1962	12.00
42754	Gentle Is Your Love/Move Along Baby (Don't Waste My Time)	1963	8.00
42754 [PS]	Gentle Is Your Love/Move Along Baby (Don't Waste My Time)	1963	12.00

7-Inch Extended Plays

CAPITOL

Number	Title (A Side/B Side)	Yr	NM
1-286	In the Good Old Summertime/Three Little Words//La Rosita/Just One More Chance	195?	20.00
2-286	The Lonesome Road/Jazz Me Blues//I'm Forever Blowing Bubbles/Moon of Manakoora	195?	20.00
EBF-286 [PS]	Les Paul's New Sound, Vol. 2	195?	30.00
—Gatefold sleeve for 1-286 and 2-286 (we don't know if the EP records also were issued individually with separate "Part 1" and "Part 2" sleeves)			
1-356	(contents unknown)	195?	20.00
2-356	(contents unknown)	195?	20.00
EBF-356 [PS]	Bye Bye Blues	195?	30.00
—Gatefold sleeve for 1-356 and 2-356 (we don't know if the EP records also were issued individually with separate "Part 1" and "Part 2"sleeves)			
EAP 1-416	How High the Moon/Josephine//Mockin' Bird Hill/Whispering	195?	20.00
EAP 1-416 [PS]	The Hit Makers, Part 1	195?	20.00
EAP 2-416	*Meet Mister Callaghan/Tiger Rag/Tennessee Waltz/The World Is Waiting for the Sunrise	195?	20.00
EAP 2-416 [PS]	The Hit Makers, Part 2	195?	20.00
EAP 1-495	Vaya Con Dios (May God Be With You)/Sleep//Lady of Spain/My Baby's Comin' Home	195?	20.00
EAP 1-495 [PS]	Vaya Con Dios	195?	20.00
EAP 1-540	I'm Sitting on Top of the World/South//Smoke Rings/Jazz Me Blues	195?	20.00
EAP 1-540 [PS]	Sitting on Top of the World	195?	20.00
EAP 1-543	Jingle Bells/White Christmas//Santa Claus Is Comin' to Town/Silent Night	195?	20.00
EAP 1-543 [PS]	Christmas Cheer	195?	20.00
EAP 1-554	I'm a Fool to Care/I Really Don't Want to Know//Auctioneer/It's a Lonesome Old Town	1956	15.00
EAP 1-554 [PS]	I'm a Fool to Care	1956	15.00
EAP 1-559	Whither Thou Goest/Nola//Take Me in Your Arms and Hold Me/Mandolino	1955	20.00
EAP 1-559 [PS]	Whither Thou Goest	1955	20.00
EAP 1-577	Falling in Love with Love/On the Sunny Side of the Street//Just One of Those Things/Twelfth Street Rag	1955	15.00
EAP 1-577 [PS]	Les and Mary, Part 1	1955	15.00
EAP 2-577	Lies/Turista//Swing Low Sweet Chariot/Nuevo Laredo	1955	15.00
EAP 2-577 [PS]	Les and Mary, Part 2	1955	15.00
EAP 3-577	The Best Things in Life Are Free/Theme from "Laughing Eyes"//Some of These Days/Tico Tico	1955	15.00
EAP 3-577 [PS]	Les and Mary, Part 3	1955	15.00
EAP 4-577	Baby Won't You Please Come Home/Dangerous Curves//I'm Movin' On/Farewell for Just Awhile	1955	15.00
EAP 4-577 [PS]	Les and Mary, Part 4	195?	15.00
EBF 1-577 [PS]	Les and Mary, Parts 1 and 2	1955	20.00
EBF 2-577 [PS]	Les and Mary, Parts 3 and 4	1955	20.00
—Gatefold cover for some editions of 3-577 and 4-577			
EAP 1-695	(contents unknown)	195?	15.00
EAP 1-695 [PS]	Songs for Today	195?	15.00
EAP 1-802	(contents unknown)	1956	15.00
EAP 1-802 [PS]	Time to Dream, Vol. 1	1956	15.00
EAP 2-802	(contents unknown)	1956	15.00
EAP 2-802 [PS]	Time to Dream, Vol. 2	1956	15.00
EAP 3-802	(contents unknown)	1956	15.00
EAP 3-802 [PS]	Time to Dream, Vol. 3	1956	15.00
EAP 1-9121	Mister Sandman/That's What I Like//I Need You Now/The Things I Didn't Do	1955	15.00
EAP 1-9121 [PS]	Les Paul and Mary Ford	1955	15.00

Albums

CAPITOL

Number	Title (A Side/B Side)	Yr	NM
H 226 [10]	The New Sound, Vol. 1	1950	80.00
T 226 [M]	The New Sound, Vol. 1	1955	50.00
H 286 [10]	The New Sound, Vol. 2	1951	80.00
SM-286	The New Sound, Vol. 2	197?	10.00
T 286 [M]	The New Sound, Vol. 2	1955	50.00
H 356 [10]	Bye Bye Blues	1952	80.00
T 356 [M]	Bye Bye Blues	1955	50.00
H 416 [10]	The Hit Makers	1953	80.00
T 416 [M]	The Hit Makers	1955	50.00
H 577 [10]	Les and Mary	1955	80.00
W 577 [M]	Les and Mary	1955	50.00
T 802 [M]	Time to Dream	1956	50.00
DT 1476 [R]	The Hits of Les and Mary	1960	20.00
T 1476 [M]	The Hits of Les and Mary	1960	25.00
SM-11308	The World Is Still Waiting for the Sunrise	197?	10.00
—Reissue with new prefix			
ST-11308	The World Is Still Waiting for the Sunrise	1974	12.00

CAPITOL SPECIAL MARKETS

Number	Title (A Side/B Side)	Yr	NM
SLCR-8130 [(3)]	The All-Time Greatest Hits of Les Paul and Mary Ford	1980	20.00
—Produced for Murray Hill Records (979462)			

COLUMBIA

Number	Title (A Side/B Side)	Yr	NM
CL 1276 [M]	Lovers' Luau	1959	20.00
CL 1688 [M]	Warm and Wonderful	1962	20.00
CL 1821 [M]	Bouquet of Roses	1962	20.00
CL 1928 [M]	Swingin' South	1963	15.00
CS 8086 [S]	Lovers' Luau	1959	30.00
CS 8488 [S]	Warm and Wonderful	1962	25.00
CS 8621 [S]	Bouquet of Roses	1962	25.00
CS 8728 [S]	Swingin' South	1963	20.00

HARMONY

Number	Title (A Side/B Side)	Yr	NM
HL 7333 [M]	The Fabulous Les Paul and Mary Ford	1965	12.00
HS 11133 [S]	The Fabulous Les Paul and Mary Ford	1965	12.00

PICKWICK

Number	Title (A Side/B Side)	Yr	NM
SPC-3122	Brazil	197?	10.00

PAUL, LOUIS

45s

COTILLION

Number	Title (A Side/B Side)	Yr	NM
44064	Annie Mae/Railroad Man	1970	10.00

ENTERPRISE

Number	Title (A Side/B Side)	Yr	NM
9056	Gotta Get Away/With a Little Bit of Love	1972	6.00
9060	It's Christmas Time/Santa Claus Is on His Way Again	1972	6.00
9077	Merry-Go-Round/Mister Crystal	1973	6.00
9094	I Like Rock and Roll/My Dream	1974	6.00

Albums

ENTERPRISE

Number	Title (A Side/B Side)	Yr	NM
ENS-1034	Reflections of the Way It Really Is	1971	15.00

PAUL AND PAULA

Also see RAY HILDEBRAND; JILL JACKSON.

45s

LE CAM

Number	Title (A Side/B Side)	Yr	NM
99	The Beginning of Love/All I Want Is You	1963	20.00
305	From the Top of the World/All I Want Is You	197?	4.00
—As "Jill and Ray"			

Except when noted otherwise, VG = 25% of NM, and VG+ = 50% of NM. (Example: VG = $2.00, VG+ = $4.00 and NM = $8.00.)

Number	Title (A Side/B Side)	Yr	NM
❑ 315	Hey Paula ('77 Disco)/(Instrumental)	1977	4.00
❑ 321	Hey Paula/Paula (My Love)	1978	4.00
—Reissued in 1982 with the same catalog number			
❑ 354	Hey Paula/Elmer's Tune	198?	4.00
❑ 979	Hey Paula/Bobbie Is the One	1962	50.00
—As "Jill and Ray"			
PHILIPS			
❑ 40084	Hey Paula/Bobby Is the One	1962	15.00
❑ 40096	Young Lovers/Ba-Hey-Be	1963	12.00
❑ 40096 [PS]	Young Lovers/Ba-Hey-Be	1963	20.00
❑ 40114	First Quarrel/School Is Thru	1963	12.00
❑ 40114 [PS]	First Quarrel/School Is Thru	1963	20.00
❑ 40130	Something Old, Something New/Flipped Over You	1963	12.00
❑ 40142	First Day Back at School/A Perfect Pair	1963	12.00
❑ 40158	Holiday for Teens/Holiday Hootenanny	1963	12.00
❑ 40168	We'll Never Break Up for Good/Crazy Little Things	1964	10.00
❑ 40209	The Young Years/Darlin'	1964	10.00
❑ 40234	No Other Baby/Too Dark to See	1964	10.00
❑ 40268	True Love/Any Way You Want Me	1965	8.00
❑ 40296	Dear Paula/All the Love	1965	8.00
❑ 40352	All I Want Is You/The Beginning of Love	1966	10.00
UNI			
❑ 55052	All These Things/Wedding	1968	8.00
UNITED ARTISTS			
❑ 50712	Moments Like These/Mrs. Bean	1970	6.00
Albums			
PHILIPS			
❑ PHM 200078 [M]	Paul and Paula Sing for Young Lovers	1963	30.00
❑ PHM 200089 [M]	We Go Together	1963	30.00
❑ PHM 200101 [M]	Holiday for Teens	1963	30.00
❑ PHS 600078 [S]	Paul and Paula Sing for Young Lovers	1963	40.00
❑ PHS 600089 [S]	We Go Together	1963	40.00
❑ PHS 600101 [S]	Holiday for Teens	1963	40.00

PAULA, MARLENA

Number	Title (A Side/B Side)	Yr	NM
45s			
REGENT			
❑ 7506	I Wanna Spend Christmas with Elvis/Once More It's Christmas	1956	50.00

PAULSON, BUTCH

Number	Title (A Side/B Side)	Yr	NM
45s			
VIRGELLE			
❑ 708	Man from Mars/My Own Brother	195?	100.00
❑ 718	Candy Lou/Today Was Blue Tomorrow	195?	50.00

PAULSON, PAT

Number	Title (A Side/B Side)	Yr	NM
Albums			
RUBICON/MERCURY			
❑ SR 61179	Pat Paulson for President	1968	20.00
❑ SR 61251	Live at the Ice House	1970	15.00

PAUPERS, THE

Number	Title (A Side/B Side)	Yr	NM
45s			
VERVE FOLKWAYS			
❑ 5033	Copper Penny/If I Call You by Some Other Name	1966	10.00
❑ 5043	Let Me Be/Simple Deed	1967	10.00
VERVE FORECAST			
❑ 5056	One Rainy Day/Tudor Impressions	1967	10.00
❑ 5062	Magic People/Black Thank You Package	1967	10.00
❑ 5074	Think I Care/White Song	1967	10.00
❑ 5094	Another Man's Hair on My Razor/Cairo Hotel	1968	10.00
Albums			
VERVE FORECAST			
❑ FT-3026 [M]	Magic People	1967	20.00
❑ FTS-3026 [S]	Magic People	1967	20.00
❑ FTS-3051	Ellis Island	1968	15.00

PAVLOV'S DOG

Number	Title (A Side/B Side)	Yr	NM
45s			
ABC			
❑ 12086	Episode/Julia	1975	10.00
Albums			
ABC			
❑ D-866	Pampered Menial	1975	25.00
COLUMBIA			
❑ PC 33552	Pampered Menial	1976	12.00
—Reissue of ABC album			
❑ PC 33964	At the Sound of the Bell	1976	12.00

PAVONE, RITA

Number	Title (A Side/B Side)	Yr	NM
45s			
POLYDOR			
❑ 15011	'Til Tomorrow/Try It and See	1970	6.00
RCA VICTOR			
❑ 47-8212	Cuore/Ballo del Mattone	1963	8.00
❑ 47-8365	Remember Me/Just One More	1964	8.00
❑ 47-8365 [PS]	Remember Me/Just One More	1964	10.00
❑ 47-8420	Wait for Me/It's Not Easy	1964	8.00
❑ 47-8420 [PS]	Wait for Me/It's Not Easy	1964	10.00
❑ 47-8538	I Don't Wanna Be Hurt/Eyes of Mine	1965	8.00
❑ 47-8612	Oh My Mama/Right Now	1965	8.00
❑ 47-9485	Okay, Okay/Wenn Ich Ein Junge War	1968	10.00
Albums			
RCA VICTOR			
❑ LPM-2900 [M]	Rita Pavone	1964	15.00
❑ LSP-2900 [S]	Rita Pavone	1964	20.00
❑ LPM-2996 [M]	Small Wonder	1965	15.00
❑ LSP-2996 [S]	Small Wonder	1965	20.00

PAXTON, GARY
Also see THE HOLLYWOOD ARGYLES; THE PLEDGES; SKIP AND FLIP.

Number	Title (A Side/B Side)	Yr	NM
45s			
CAPITOL			
❑ 5467	My Heart Won't Let My Lips Say Goodbye/It's My Way (Of Lovin' You)	1965	15.00
❑ 5707	Goin' Through the Motions/You Got to Do the Best You Can	1966	15.00
❑ 5975	Mother-in-Law/Miles and Cities	1967	15.00
FELSTED			
❑ 8691	Sweet Senorita from Santa Fe/Kansas City	1964	20.00
GARPAX			
❑ 44172	It Had to Be You/We're Going Back Together	1963	20.00
❑ 44177	The Scavenger/How to Be a Fool (In Six Easy Lessons)	1963	20.00
❑ 44180	Two Duel Bump Camel Named Robert E. Lee/Your Past Is Back Again	1964	20.00
LIBERTY			
❑ 55407	Teen Age Crush/It's So Funny I Could Cry	1962	20.00
❑ 55485	Stop Twistin' Baby/Alley Oop Was a Two Dab Man	1962	20.00
❑ 55584	Spooky Movies (Part 1)/Spooky Movies (Part 2)	1963	20.00
LONDON			
❑ 5208	Super Torque/Cute Little Coly	1964	20.00
LUTE			
❑ 5801	You're Ruinin' My Gladness/The Way I See It	1960	20.00
MGM			
❑ 14306	Carin' for Karen/Out on a Limb	1971	6.00
❑ 14362	Rocky Top/Parchman Farm	1972	6.00
NEW PAX			
❑ 6	Different World/(B-side unknown)	1976	8.00
❑ 5349	Lord I Need You Right Now/(B-side unknown)	197?	8.00
PAX			
❑ 2406	The Big A/The Big M	197?	6.00
—Red vinyl			
PRIVATE STOCK			
❑ 45,007	The Clone Affair/(B-side unknown)	1975	5.00
RCA VICTOR			
❑ 74-0916	Shadow of Your Memory/This Little Light of Mine	1973	5.00
❑ APBO-0081	It's Hard to Be a Rock and Roll Star When You're Old and Fat/White Tornado Alias Gary S. Paxton	1973	5.00
❑ PB-10449	Too Far Gone (To Care What You Do to Me)/Freedom Lives in a Country Song	1975	5.00
W.I.N.			
❑ 28	The Race Driver's Song/Someday Darling I'll Give You	197?	15.00
❑ 28 [PS]	The Race Driver's Song/Someday Darling I'll Give You	197?	25.00
—Sponsored by NAPA			
Albums			
NEW PAX			
❑ NP-33005	The Astonishing, Outrageous, Amazing, Incredible, Unbelievably Different World of Gary S. Paxton	1976	12.00
❑ NP-33033	More from the Astonishing, Outrageous, Amazing, Incredible, Unbelievable World of Gary S. Paxton	1977	12.00
❑ NP-33048	The Gospel According to Gary S.	1979	12.00
❑ NP-33080	(Some of) The Best of Gary S. Paxton (So Far)	1980	12.00
PAX			
❑ R-2406	Terminally Weird but Godly Right/Anchored in the Rock of Ages	1978	12.00
❑ R-2411	Gary Sanford Paxton	1979	12.00

PAXTON, TOM

Number	Title (A Side/B Side)	Yr	NM
45s			
ELEKTRA			
❑ 45667	Crazy John/Things I Notice Now	1969	6.00
❑ 45674	Jimmy Newman/Forest Lawn	1970	6.00
❑ 45703	Whose Garden Was This/Annie's Going to Sing Her Song	1970	6.00
REPRISE			
❑ 1110	Peace Will Come (According to Plan)/Jesus Christ S.R.O.	1972	5.00
VANGUARD			
❑ 35206	The Death of Stephen Biko/Anita O.J.	1977	5.00
Albums			
ELEKTRA			
❑ EKL-277 [M]	Ramblin' Boy	1964	20.00
❑ EKL-298 [M]	Ain't That News	1965	20.00
❑ EKL-317 [M]	Outward Bound	1966	20.00
❑ 7E-2003 [(2)]	The Compleat Tom Paxton	1971	20.00
❑ EKS-7277 [S]	Ramblin' Boy	1964	25.00
❑ EKS-7298 [S]	Ain't That News	1965	25.00
❑ EKS-7317 [S]	Outward Bound	1966	25.00
❑ EKS-74019	Morning Again	1968	20.00
❑ EKS-74043	The Things I Notice Now	1969	15.00
❑ EKS-74066	Tom Paxton 6	1970	15.00
FLYING FISH			
❑ FF-280	Even a Gray Day	1983	10.00
❑ FF-356	One Million Lawyers... And Other Disasters	1986	10.00
❑ FF-408	The Marvellous Toy and Other Gallimaufry	1987	10.00
❑ FF-414	And Loving You	1987	10.00
❑ FF-486	Politics	199?	12.00
❑ FF-519	The Very Best of Tom Paxton	199?	12.00
GASLIGHT			
❑ GV-116 [M]	I'm the Man Who Built the Bridges	1962	80.00
HOGEYE			
❑ 004	Bulletin...We Interrupt This Record	198?	10.00
MOUNTAIN RAILROAD			
❑ 52792	Up and Up	1980	12.00
❑ 52796	The Paxton Report	198?	12.00
PRIVATE STOCK			
❑ PS-2002	Something in My Life	1975	12.00
REPRISE			
❑ MS 2096	Peace Will Come	1972	15.00
❑ MS 2144	New Songs for Old Friends	1973	15.00
❑ RS 6443	How Come the Sun	1971	15.00
VANGUARD			
❑ VSD-79395	New Songs from the Briarpatch	1977	12.00
❑ VSD-79411	Heroes	1978	12.00

PAYCHECK, JOHNNY

Number	Title (A Side/B Side)	Yr	NM
45s			
AMI			
❑ 1322	I Never Got Over You/Ole Pay Ain't Checked Out Yet	1984	5.00
❑ 1323	You're Every Step I Take/I Can't Stop Drinking	1985	5.00
❑ 1327	Everything Is Changing/Palimony	1985	5.00
BIG A			
❑ A-100	Nothing Lasts Forever/No One Ever Lost More	1967	12.00
CERTRON			
❑ 10003	Forever Ended Yesterday/It's For Sure I Can't Go On	1970	8.00
DAMASCUS			
❑ 2001	Scars/(B-side unknown)	1989	6.00

Number	Title (A Side/B Side)	Yr	NM
DECCA			
9-30763	On This Mountaintop/It's Been a Long, Long Time for Me	1958	30.00
—A-side as "Donny Young and Roger Miller"; B-side as "Donny Young"			
9-30881	The Old Man and the River/Pictures Can't Talk Back	1959	25.00
—As "Donny Young"			
31077	Shakin' the Blues/Miracle of Love	1960	40.00
—As "Donny Young"			
31283	Go Ring the Bells/I Guess I Had It Coming	1961	25.00
—As "Donny Young"			
DESPERADO			
1001	Out of Beer/Oklahoma Lady	1988	6.00
EPIC			
19-02144	Yesterday's News (Just Hit Home Today)/Someone Told My Story	1981	4.00
14-02684	The Highlight of '81/Sharon Rae	1982	4.00
14-02817	No Way Out/We've All Gone Crazy	1982	4.00
14-03052	D.O.A. (Drunk On Arrival)/Gonna Get Right (And Do Something Wrong)	1982	4.00
5-10783	She's All I Got/You Touched My Life	1971	7.00
5-10836	Someone to Give My Love To/Love Sure Is Beautiful	1972	7.00
5-10876	Love Is a Good Thing/High on the Thought of You	1972	7.00
5-10912	Somebody Loves Me/Without You	1972	7.00
5-10947	Something About You I Love/Your Love Is the Key to It All	1973	6.00
5-10999	Mr. Lovemaker/Once You've Had the Best	1973	6.00
5-11046	Song and Dance Man/Love Is a Strange and Wonderful Thing	1973	6.00
5-11090	My Part of Forever/If Love Gets Any Better	1974	6.00
5-11142	Keep On Lovin' Me/The Ballad of Thunder Road	1974	6.00
8-50040	For a Minute There/She's All I Live For	1974	6.00
8-50073	Loving You Beats All I've Ever Seen/Touch of the Master's Hand	1975	6.00
8-50111	I Didn't Love Her Anymore/Loving Her Is All I Thought It Would Be	1975	6.00
8-50146	All-American Man/The Fool Strikes Again	1975	6.00
8-50193	The Feminine Touch/Rhythm Guitar	1976	6.00
8-50215	Gone at Last/Live with Me	1976	6.00
8-50249	11 Months and 29 Days/Live with Me (Till I Can Learn to Live Again)	1976	6.00
8-50291	I Can See Me Lovin' You Again/I Sleep with Her Memory Every Night	1976	6.00
8-50334	Slide Off of Your Satin Sheets/That's What the Outlaws in Texas Want to Hear	1977	6.00
8-50391	I'm the Only Hell (Mama Ever Raised)/She's Still Lookin' Good	1977	6.00
8-50469	Take This Job and Shove It/Colorado Kool-Aid	1977	8.00
8-50539	Georgia in a Jug/Me and the I.R.S.	1978	6.00
8-50621	Friend, Lover, Wife/Leave It to Me	1978	6.00
8-50655	The Outlaw's Prayer/Armed and Crazy	1979	6.00
9-50777	(Stay Away From) The Cocaine Train/Billy Bardo	1979	5.00
9-50818	Drinkin' and Drivin'/Just Makin' Love Don't Make It Love	1979	5.00
9-50863	Fifteen Beers/Who Was That Man Who Beat Me So	1980	5.00
9-50923	In Memory of a Memory/New York Town	1980	5.00
HILLTOP			
3002	Don't Start Countin' on Me/I'd Rather Be Your Fool	1964	20.00
3006	For Those Who Think Young/The Girl They Talk About	1965	15.00
3007	A-11/Where (In the World)	1965	15.00
3009	Heartbreak Tennessee/Help Me Hank, I'm Fallin'	1966	15.00
3015	I'm Barely Hangin' On to Me/The Real Mr. Heartache	1966	15.00
LITTLE DARLIN'			
008	The Lovin' Machine/Pride Covered Ears	1966	10.00
0011	The Ballad of the Green Berets/A Dying Hero	1966	10.00
0014	Right Back Where We Parted/The Way Things Were Going	1966	10.00
—With Micki Evans			
0016	Motel Time Again/If You Should Come Back Today	1966	10.00
0020	Jukebox Charlie/Something in Your World	1967	10.00
0032	The Cave/Then Love Dies	1967	10.00
0035	Don't Monkey with Another Monkey's Monkey/You'll Recover in Time	1967	10.00
0042	(It Won't Be Long) And I'll Be Hating You/Fools Hall of Fame	1968	10.00
0043	The Old Year Is Gone/According to the Bible	1968	10.00
0046	My Heart Keeps Running to You/Yesterday, Today and Tomorrow	1968	10.00
0052	If I'm Gonna Sink/The Loser	1968	10.00
0055	Jingle Bells/The Old Year Is Gone	1968	10.00
0057	My World of Memories/(B-side unknown)	1969	10.00
0060	Wherever You Are/I Can't Promise You Won't Get Lonely	1969	10.00
0072	Wildfire/Basin Street Mama	1969	10.00
7804	It Won't Be Long/If I'm Gonna Sink (Might As Well Go to the Bottom)	1978	6.00
7808	Down on the Corner at a Bar Named Kelly's/Something He'll Have to Learn	1978	6.00
7810	I'll Place My Order Early/The Old Year Is Gone	1978	6.00
7918	California Dreams/The Loser	1979	6.00
7923	Gentle on My Mind/Everything You Touch Turns to Hurt	1979	6.00
MERCURY			
71900	On Second Thought/One Day a Week	1962	20.00
—As "Donny Young"			
71981	Not Much I Don't/I'd Come Back to Me	1962	20.00
—As "Donny Young"			
884720-7	Old Violin/Comin' Home to Baby	1986	4.00
888088-7	Don't Bury Me 'Til I'm Ready/Ex-Wives and Lovers	1986	4.00
888341-7	Come to Me/Ragtime Redneck	1987	4.00
888651-7	I Grow Old Too Fast (And Smart Too Slow)/Caught Between a Rock and a Soft Place	1987	4.00
888925-7	Modern Times/She Don't Love Me All the Time	1987	4.00
TODD			
1098	Don't You Get Lonesome Without Me/I'm Glad to Have Her Back Again	1964	20.00
—As "Donny Young"			

Albums

Number	Title	Yr	NM
ACCORD			
SN-7173	Extra Special	1981	10.00
ALLEGIANCE			
AV-435	I Don't Need to Know That Right Now	198?	8.00
CERTRON			
7002	Johnny Paycheck Again	1970	15.00
EPIC			
E 31141	She's All I Got	1971	12.00
KE 31449	Someone to Give My Love To	1972	12.00
KE 31702	Somebody Loves Me	1972	12.00
KE 32387	Something About You I Love	1973	12.00
KE 32570	Song and Dance Man	1973	12.00
KE 33091	Greatest Hits	1974	10.00
PE 33091	Greatest Hits	198?	8.00
—Budget-line reissue			
KE 33354	Loving You Beats All I've Ever Seen	1975	10.00
KE 33943	11 Months and 29 Days	1975	10.00
PE 34693	Slide Off of Your Satin Sheets	1976	10.00
KE 35045	Take This Job and Shove It	1977	10.00
PE 35045	Take This Job and Shove It	198?	8.00
—Budget-line reissue			
KE 35444	Armed and Crazy	1978	10.00
KE 35623	Greatest Hits, Vol. 2	1978	10.00
PE 35623	Greatest Hits, Vol. 2	198?	8.00
—Budget-line reissue			
JE 36200	Everybody's Got a Family — Meet Mine	1979	10.00
JE 36496	New York Town	1980	10.00
FE 36761	Mr. Hag Told My Story	1981	10.00
PE 36761	Mr. Hag Told My Story	1981	8.00
—Budget-line reissue			
FE 37345	Encore	1981	10.00
PE 37345	Encore	198?	8.00
—Budget-line reissue			
FE 37933	Lovers and Losers	1982	10.00
FE 38322	Johnny Paycheck's Biggest Hits	1983	10.00
PE 39943	John Austin Paycheck	1984	8.00
INTERMEDIA			
QS-5018	Back On the Job	198?	8.00
LITTLE DARLIN'			
LD-4001 [M]	Johnny Paycheck at Carnegie Hall	1966	20.00
LD-4003 [M]	The Lovin' Machine	1966	20.00
LD-4004 [M]	Gospeltime in My Fashion	1967	20.00
LD-4006 [M]	Johnny Paycheck Sings Jukebox Charlie	1967	25.00
SLD-8001 [S]	Johnny Paycheck at Carnegie Hall	1966	25.00
SLD-8003 [S]	The Lovin' Machine	1966	25.00
SLD-8004 [S]	Gospeltime in My Fashion	1967	25.00
SLD-8006 [S]	Johnny Paycheck Sings Jukebox Charlie	1967	25.00
SLD-8010	Country Soul	1968	25.00
SLD-8012	Johnny Paycheck's Greatest Hits	1968	25.00
SLD-8023	Wherever You Are	1969	25.00
MERCURY			
830404-1	Modern Times	1987	10.00
POWER PAK			
PO-284	Johnny Paycheck At His Best	197?	8.00

PAYCHECK, JOHNNY, AND MERLE HAGGARD

Also see each artist's individual listings.

45s

Number	Title (A Side/B Side)	Yr	NM
EPIC			
19-51012	I Can't Hold Myself in Line/Carolyn	1981	4.00

PAYNE, FREDA

12-Inch Singles

Number	Title (A Side/B Side)	Yr	NM
CAPITOL			
8509	I'll Do Anything for You (7:40)/(Instrumental)	1978	12.00
SPRO-8922/3 [DJ]	Happy Days Are Here Again-Happy Music/I'll Do Anything for You	1978	15.00
SPRO-9219 [DJ]	Red Hot (7:01) (same on both sides)	1979	10.00
SUTRA			
SUD 009	In Motion (5:35)/(Instrumental)	1982	15.00

45s

Number	Title (A Side/B Side)	Yr	NM
ABC			
12079	Shadows on the Wall/I Get Carried Away	1975	5.00
12139	Lost in Love/You	1975	5.00
ABC DUNHILL			
15018	It's Yours to Have/Run for Life	1974	5.00
ABC-PARAMOUNT			
10366	Desafinado/He Who Laughs Last	1962	20.00
10437	Pretty Baby/Grin and Bear It	1963	20.00
CAPITOL			
4383	I Can't Live on a Memory/I Get High (On Your Memory)	1976	5.00
4431	Baby, You've Got What It Takes/Bring Back the Joy	1977	5.00
4494	Love Magnet/Loving You Means So Much to Me	1977	5.00
4537	Feed Me Your Love/Stares and Whispers	1978	5.00
4631	Happy Days Are Here Again-Happy Music (Dance the Night Away)/Falling in Love	1978	5.00
4695	I'll Do Anything for You (Part 1)/I'll Do Anything for You (Part 2)	1979	5.00
4775	Red Hot/Longest Night	1979	5.00
4805	Can't Wait/Longest Night	1979	5.00
IMPULSE!			
221	It's Time/Sweet September	1963	20.00
INVICTUS			
1255	Two Wrongs Don't Make a Right/We've Gotta Find a Way Back to Love	1973	6.00
1257	For No Reason/Mother Misery's Favorite Child	1973	6.00
9073	The Unhooked Generation/Easiest Way to Fall	1969	6.00
9075	Band of Gold/Easiest Way to Fall	1970	6.00
9080	Deeper and Deeper/The Unhooked Genration	1970	6.00
9085	Cherish What Is Dear to You (While It Is Near to You)/They Don't Owe Me a Thing	1971	6.00

Except when noted otherwise, VG = 25% of NM, and VG+ = 50% of NM. (Example: VG = $2.00, VG+ = $4.00 and NM = $8.00.)

Number	Title (A Side/B Side)	Yr	NM
❑ 9085 [PS]	Cherish What Is Dear to You (While It Is Near to You)/ They Don't Owe Me a Thing	1971	10.00
❑ 9092	Bring the Boys Home/ I Shall Not Be Moved	1971	6.00
❑ 9100	You Brought the Joy/ Suddenly It's Yesterday	1971	6.00
❑ 9109	I'm Not Getting Any Better/ The Road We Didn't Take	1972	6.00
❑ 9128	She's in My Life/Through the Memory of My Mind	1972	6.00
MGM			
❑ 13509	You've Lost That Lovin' Feelin'/ Sad Sad September	1966	20.00
SUTRA			
❑ 117	In Motion/(Instrumental)	1982	5.00
Albums			
ABC			
❑ D-901	Out of Payne Comes Love	1976	12.00
ABC DUNHILL			
❑ DSX-50176	Payne and Pleasure	1974	15.00
ABC IMPULSE!			
❑ AS-53 [S]	After the Lights Go Down Low…And Much More	1968	15.00
CAPITOL			
❑ ST-11700	Stares and Whispers	1977	12.00
❑ ST-11864	Supernatural	1978	12.00
❑ ST-12003	Hot	1979	12.00
IMPULSE!			
❑ A-53 [M]	After the Lights Go Down Low…And Much More	1964	30.00
❑ AS-53 [S]	After the Lights Go Down Low…And Much More	1964	40.00
INVICTUS			
❑ ST-7301	Band of Gold	1970	15.00
❑ SMAS-7307	Contact	1971	15.00
❑ ST-9804	The Best of Freda Payne	1972	15.00
❑ Z 32493	Reaching Out	1973	15.00
MGM			
❑ GAS-128	Freda Payne (Golden Archive Series)	1970	15.00
❑ E-4370 [M]	How Do You Say I Don't Love You Anymore	1966	20.00
❑ SE-4370 [S]	How Do You Say I Don't Love You Anymore	1966	25.00

PEACE, JOE

Number	Title (A Side/B Side)	Yr	NM
Albums			
RITE			
❑ 29917	Finding Peace	1972	200.00

PEACHEROOS, THE

Number	Title (A Side/B Side)	Yr	NM
45s			
EXCELLO			
❑ 2044	Be-Bop Baby/Everyday My Love Is True	1954	400.00

PEACHES AND HERB

Herb Fame with at least three different female singers who were "Peaches."

Number	Title (A Side/B Side)	Yr	NM
12-Inch Singles			
POLYDOR			
❑ PRO 055 [DJ]	Shake Your Groove Thing (6:36) (same on both sides)	1978	50.00
❑ PRO 116 [DJ]	Roller-Skatin' Mate (6:48) (same on both sides)	1979	10.00
❑ PRO 165 [DJ]	Freeway (6:03) (same on both sides)	1981	12.00
45s			
COLUMBIA			
❑ 03872	Remember/Come to Me	1983	4.00
❑ 04081	In My World/Keep On Smiling	1983	4.00
❑ 45386	The Sound of Silence/ The Two of Us	1971	5.00
❑ 45554	God Save This World/I Can't Forget the One I Love	1972	5.00
DATE			
❑ 1523	Let's Fall in Love/We're In This Thing Together	1966	10.00
❑ 1549	Close Your Eyes/ I Will Watch Over You	1967	10.00
❑ 1549 [PS]	Close Your Eyes/ I Will Watch Over You	1967	15.00
❑ 1555	Cupid-Venus/Darling, How Long	1967	15.00
❑ 1563	For Your Love/I Need Your Love So Desperately	1967	10.00
❑ 1563 [PS]	For Your Love/I Need Your Love So Desperately	1967	15.00
❑ 1574	Love Is Strange/It's True I Love You	1967	10.00
❑ 1574 [PS]	Love Is Strange/It's True I Love You	1967	15.00
❑ 1586	Two Little Kids/We've Got to Love One Another	1967	8.00
❑ 1592	The Ten Commandments of Love/What a Lovely Way (To Say Goodnight)	1968	8.00
❑ 1603	United/Thank You	1968	8.00
❑ 1603 [PS]	United/Thank You	1968	15.00
❑ 1623	Let's Make a Promise/ Me and You	1968	8.00
❑ 1623 [PS]	Let's Make a Promise/ Me and You	1968	15.00
❑ 1633	We've Got to Love One Another/So True	1968	10.00
❑ 1637	When He Touches Me (Nothing Else Matters)/Thank You	1969	8.00
❑ 1649	Let Me Be the One/I Need Your Love So Desperately	1969	8.00
❑ 1655	Cupid/Darling, How Long	1969	8.00
❑ 1669	It's Just a Game, Love/ Satisfy My Hunger	1970	8.00
❑ 1676	Soothe Me with Your Love/ We're So Much in Love	1970	8.00
MCA			
❑ 40701	We're Still Together/ Love Is Here Beside Us	1977	5.00
❑ 40782	It Will Never Be the Same Again/I'm Counting on You	1977	5.00
MERCURY			
❑ 73350	Keep It Coming/ I'm a-Hurtin' Inside	1973	5.00
❑ 73388	Can't It Wait/Thank Heaven for You	1973	5.00
POLYDOR			
❑ 2031	Roller-Skatin' Mate (Part 1)/ Roller-Skatin' Mate (Part 2)	1979	4.00
❑ 2053	I Pledge My Love/(I Want Us) Back Together	1980	4.00
❑ 2115	Funtime (Part 1)/Funtime (Part 2)	1980	4.00
❑ 2140	One Child of Love/Hearsay	1980	4.00
❑ 2157	Surrender/Love Stealers	1981	4.00
❑ 2178	Freeway/Pickin' Up the Pieces	1981	4.00
❑ 2187	Bluer Than Blue/Go with the Flow	1981	4.00
❑ 14514	Shake Your Groove Thing/All Your Love (Get It Here)	1978	4.00
❑ 14547	Reunited/Easy as Pie	1979	4.00
❑ 14577	We've Got Love/ Four's a Traffic Jam	1979	4.00
Albums			
COLUMBIA			
❑ FC 38746	Remember	1983	10.00
DATE			
❑ TEM 3004 [M]	Let's Fall in Love	1967	20.00
❑ TEM 3005 [M]	For Your Love	1967	25.00
❑ TEM 3007 [M]	Golden Duets	1968	30.00
❑ TES 4004 [S]	Let's Fall in Love	1967	25.00
❑ TES 4005 [S]	For Your Love	1967	20.00
❑ TES 4007 [S]	Golden Duets	1968	20.00
❑ TES 4012	Peaches and Herb's Greatest Hits	1968	20.00
EPIC			
❑ E 36089	Love Is Strange	1979	10.00
—Reissue of Date material			
❑ JE 36099	Peaches and Herb's Greatest Hits	1979	10.00
—Reissue of Date 4012			
MCA			
❑ 2261	Peaches and Herb	1977	12.00
POLYDOR			
❑ PD-1-6172	2 Hot!	1978	10.00
❑ PD-1-6239	Twice the Fire	1979	10.00
❑ PD-1-6298	Worth the Wait	1980	10.00
❑ PD-1-6332	Sayin' Something!	1981	10.00

PEANUT BUTTER CONSPIRACY, THE

Number	Title (A Side/B Side)	Yr	NM
45s			
CHALLENGE			
❑ 500	Back in L.A./Have a Little Faith	1969	8.00
❑ 500 [PS]	Back in L.A./Have a Little Faith	1969	40.00
COLUMBIA			
❑ 43985	It's a Happening Thing/ Twice Is Life	1967	10.00
❑ 43985 [PS]	It's a Happening Thing/ Twice Is Life	1967	50.00
❑ 44063	Then Came Love/ Dark on You Now	1967	8.00
❑ 44356	Turn On a Friend (To the Good Life)/Captain Sandwich	1967	8.00
❑ 44667	I'm a Fool/It's So Hard	1968	8.00
VAULT			
❑ 933	Time Is After You/Floating Dream	1966	15.00
Albums			
CHALLENGE			
❑ 2000	For Children of All Ages	1969	30.00
COLUMBIA			
❑ CL 2654 [M]	The Peanut Butter Conspiracy Is Spreading	1967	30.00
❑ CL 2790 [M]	The Great Conspiracy	1968	40.00
❑ CS 9454 [S]	The Peanut Butter Conspiracy Is Spreading	1967	30.00
❑ CS 9590 [S]	The Great Conspiracy	1968	30.00

PEARL JAM

Also see GREEN RIVER; MOTHER LOVE BONE; SOUNDGARDEN.

Number	Title (A Side/B Side)	Yr	NM
10-Inch Singles			
EPIC			
❑ 3ES 58120	Reach Down/I Believe in Miracles	2003	20.00
—2003 fan club release; in "Come Back! It's Christmas ..." cardboard picture cover			
45s			
EPIC			
❑ ES7 3857 [DJ]	Happy When I'm Crying/L ive for Today	1997	10.00
—B-side by R.E.M.			
❑ ES7 3857 [PS]	Happy When I'm Crying/ Live for Today	1997	10.00
—1997 fan club single			
❑ ZS7 4906 [DJ]	Sonic Reducer/Ramblings Continued	1992	20.00
❑ ZS7 4906 [PS]	Sonic Reducer/Ramblings Continued	1992	20.00
—Picture sleeve front states "Who Killed Rudolph?"; 1992 fan-club single			
❑ ZS7 5610 [DJ]	Angel/Ramblings	1993	20.00
❑ ZS7 5610 [PS]	Angel/Ramblings	1993	20.00
—1993 fan-club single			
❑ ZSS 7628 [PS]	History Never Repeats/Sonic Reducer//Swallow My Pride/ My Way	1995	15.00
—1995 fan club double single (there was no 1994 fan club release)			
❑ ZSS 7628-1 [DJ]	History Never Repeats/ Sonic Reducer	1995	15.00
❑ ZSS 7628-2 [DJ]	Swallow My Pride/My Way	1995	15.00
—The above two were in the same sleeve (below)			
❑ ES7 9358 [DJ]	Olympic Platinum/Smile	1996	15.00
❑ ES7 9358 [PS]	Olympic Platinum/Smile	1996	15.00
—1996 fan club single			
❑ ES7 16450 [DJ]	Crown of Thorns/Can't Help Falling in Love with You	2000	15.00
❑ ES7 16450 [PS]	Crown of Thorns/Can't Help Falling in Love with You	2000	15.00
—2000 fan club single			
❑ ES7 41700 [DJ]	Soldier of Love/Last Kiss	1998	15.00
❑ ES7 41700 [PS]	Soldier of Love/Last Kiss	1998	15.00
—1998 fan club single			
❑ ES7 49997 [DJ]	Strangest Tribe/Drifting	1999	10.00
❑ ES7 49997 [PS]	Strangest Tribe/Drifting	1999	10.00
—1999 fan club single			
❑ ES7 56680-1 [DJ]	Last Soldier/Indifference	2001	10.00
—One record of 2-record set			
❑ ES7 56680-2 [DJ]	Gimme Some Truth/I Just Want to Have Something to Do	2001	10.00
—One record of 2-record set			
❑ ES7 56680-2 [PS]	I Just Want to Have Something to Do	2001	10.00
—2001 fan club single			
❑ ES7 58540 [DJ]	Don't Believe in Christmas/ Sleepless Nights	2002	10.00
❑ ES7 58540 [PS]	Don't Believe in Christmas/ Sleepless Nights	2002	10.00
—2002 fan club single			
❑ ES7 59252 [DJ]	Bu$hleaguer/Down	2002	5.00
❑ ES7 59252 [PS]	Bu$hleaguer/Down	2002	5.00
❑ 74745	Jeremy/Alive	1995	4.00
—Gray-label reissue with Collectables logo			
❑ 74745	Jeremy/Alive	1997	3.00
—Dark-blue label reissue			
❑ 77771	Spin the Black Circle/ Tremor Christ	1994	3.00
❑ 77771 [PS]	Spin the Black Circle/ Tremor Christ	1994	5.00
❑ 77772	Not for You/Out of My Mind	1995	4.00
❑ 77772 [PS]	Not for You/Out of My Mind	1995	5.00
❑ 77873	Immortality/Rearviewmirror	1995	4.00
—B-side by The Frogs			
❑ 77873 [PS]	Immortality/Rearviewmirror	1995	5.00
❑ 78199	I Got ID/Long Road	1995	4.00
❑ 78199 [PS]	I Got ID/Long Road	1995	5.00
—"Merkinball" cardboard sleeve			
❑ 78389	Who You Are/Habit	1996	4.00
❑ 78389 [PS]	Who You Are/Habit	1996	5.00
❑ 78491	Off He Goes/Dead Man	1996	4.00
❑ 78491 [PS]	Off He Goes/Dead Man	1996	5.00
❑ 78797	Given to Fly//Pilate/Leatherman	1997	4.00
❑ 78797 [PS]	Given to Fly//Pilate/Leatherman	1997	5.00
❑ 78896 [PS]	Wishlist//U/Brain of J	1998	2.00
❑ 78896	Wishlist//U/Brain of J	1998	5.00
❑ 34 79809	I Am Mine/Undone	2002	5.00

P

Number	Title (A Side/B Side)	Yr	NM
❑ 34 79809 [PS]	I Am Mine/Undone	2002	2.00
EPIC ASSOCIATED			
❑ ZS7 4354 [DJ]	Let Me Sleep (Christmas Time)/Ramblings	1991	50.00
—Small hole, plays at 33 1-3 RPM			
❑ ZS7 4354 [PS]	Let Me Sleep (Christmas Time)/Ramblings	1991	50.00
—1991 fan-club single and by far the rarest			
❑ 74745	Jeremy/Alive	1992	20.00
—White label; deleted upon release, then briefly available again in 1995			
R.E.M. FAN CLUB			
❑ REM 97 [DJ]	Happy When I'm Crying/Live for Today	1997	15.00
—B-side by R.E.M.			
❑ REM 97 [PS]	Happy When I'm Crying/Live for Today	1997	15.00
—1997 R.E.M. fan club single			
Albums			
EPIC			
❑ E 53136	Vs.	1993	20.00
❑ E2 63365 [(2)]	Binaural	2000	50.00
❑ E 66900	Vitalogy	1994	20.00
❑ E 67500	No Code	1996	25.00
—Includes one of four sets of six 12x12 trading cards			
❑ E 68164	Yield	1998	50.00
❑ E2 69752 [(2)]	Live on Two Legs	1998	50.00
❑ E3 85738 [(3)]	Lost Dogs	2004	25.00
—CD version was issued in 2003			
❑ E2 86825 [(2)]	Riot Act	2002	50.00
❑ E4 93535 [(4)]	Rearviewmirror: Greatest Hits	2004	50.00
EPIC ASSOCIATED			
❑ Z 47857	Ten	1991	10.00
—Album not released on U.S. vinyl until 1994			
J			
❑ 82876-71467-1 [(2)]	Pearl Jam	2006	20.00
—With 36-page lyric booklet; number is nowhere on the packaging or labels, but is only in the trail-off wax of the records			

PEARLS, THE (1)

Number	Title (A Side/B Side)	Yr	NM
45s			
AMBER			
❑ 2003	I Cried/It Must Be Love	1961	500.00
—Originals have matrix muber stamped into trail-off wax			

PEARLS, THE (2)

Number	Title (A Side/B Side)	Yr	NM
45s			
ATCO			
❑ 6057	Shadows of Love/Yum Yummy	1956	30.00
❑ 6066	Bells of Love/Come On Home	1956	40.00
LOST-NITE			
❑ 393	Let's You and I Go Steady/Zippidy Zippidy Zoom	197?	5.00
—Reissue			
ON THE SQUARE			
❑ 320	Band of Angels/Ugly Face	1959	20.00
ONYX			
❑ 503	Let's You and I Go Steady/Zippidy Zippidy Zoom	1956	60.00
❑ 506	My Oh My/Tree in the Meadow	1956	150.00
❑ 510	Your Cheatin' Heart/I Sure Need You	1957	60.00
❑ 511	Ice Cream Baby/Yuz-a-Ma-Tuz	1957	60.00
❑ 516	The Wheel of Love/It's Love, Love, Love	1957	120.00

PEARLS, THE (3)

Number	Title (A Side/B Side)	Yr	NM
45s			
BELL			
❑ 45342	You Came, You Saw, You Conquered/(B-side unknown)	1973	5.00
PRIVATE STOCK			
❑ 45-060	Pearly/I'll See You in My Dreams	1975	5.00

PEARLS, THE (4)

Number	Title (A Side/B Side)	Yr	NM
45s			
WARNER BROS.			
❑ 5300	Happy Over You/If I Had a Choice	1962	20.00

PEARLS BEFORE SWINE

Number	Title (A Side/B Side)	Yr	NM
45s			
ESP-DISK'			
❑ 4554	Morning Song/Drop Out	1967	30.00
❑ 4575	Images of April/There Was a Man	1968	40.00
❑ 4576	I Saw the World/(B-side unknown)	1968	40.00
REPRISE			
❑ 0873	If You Don't Want To/These Things Too	1969	12.00
❑ 0916	God Save the Child/Rocket Man	1970	12.00
❑ 0949	The Jeweler/Rocket Man	1970	12.00
Albums			
ADELPHI			
❑ 4111 [(2)]	The Best of Pearls Before Swine	198?	15.00
ESP-DISK			
❑ 1054	One Nation Under Ground Bonus Poster	1967	25.00
❑ 1054 [M]	One Nation Under Ground	1967	50.00
❑ 1054 [S]	One Nation Under Ground	1967	50.00
—Black and white cover			
❑ 1054 [S]	One Nation Under Ground	1967	50.00
—Sepia-tone cover with no border			
❑ 1054 [S]	One Nation Under Ground	1967	50.00
—Sepia-tone cover with white border			
❑ 1054 [S]	One Nation Under Ground	1968	30.00
—Full-color cover			
❑ 1075	Balaklava	1968	40.00
REPRISE			
❑ RS 6364	These Things Too	1969	30.00
❑ RS 6405	The Use of Ashes	1970	30.00
❑ RS 6442	City of Gold	1971	40.00
❑ RS 6467	Beautiful Lies You Could Live In	1971	40.00

PEARSON, DUKE

Number	Title (A Side/B Side)	Yr	NM
45s			
BLUE NOTE			
❑ 1754	Black Coffee/Gate City	1960	10.00
❑ 1755	Taboo/Like Somebody in Love	1960	10.00
❑ 1931	Ready Rudy/Sweet Honey Bee	1966	8.00
Albums			
ATLANTIC			
❑ 3002 [M]	Honeybuns	196?	15.00
❑ SD 3002 [S]	Honeybuns	196?	15.00
❑ SD 3005	Prairie Dog	196?	15.00
BLUE NOTE			
❑ BN-LA317-G	It Could Only Happen with You	1974	15.00
❑ BLP-4022 [M]	Profile — Duke Pearson	1959	80.00
—Regular version with W. 63rd St. address on label			
❑ BLP-4022 [M]	Profile — Duke Pearson	1959	120.00
—"Deep groove" version (deep indentation under label on both sides)			
❑ BLP-4022 [M]	Profile — Duke Pearson	1963	25.00
—With New York, USA address on label			
❑ BLP-4035 [M]	Tender Feelin's	1960	80.00
—Regular version with W. 63rd St. address on label			
❑ BLP-4035 [M]	Tender Feelin's	1960	120.00
—"Deep groove" version (deep indentation under label on both sides)			
❑ BLP-4035 [M]	Tender Feelin's	1963	25.00
—With New York, USA address on label			
❑ BLP-4191 [M]	Wahoo!	1965	30.00
❑ BLP-4252 [M]	Sweet Honey Bee	1966	30.00
❑ B1-28269	The Right Touch	1994	12.00
—Reissue of 84267			
❑ B1-35220	I Don't Care Who Knows It	1996	12.00
❑ BST-84022 [S]	Profile — Duke Pearson	1959	60.00
—With W. 63rd St. address on label			
❑ BST-84022 [S]	Profile — Duke Pearson	1963	20.00
—With New York, USA address on label			
❑ BST-84022 [S]	Profile — Duke Pearson	1967	12.00
—With "A Division of Liberty Records" on label			
❑ BST-84035 [S]	Tender Feelin's	1960	60.00
—With W. 63rd St. address on label			
❑ BST-84035 [S]	Tender Feelin's	1963	20.00
—With New York, USA address on label			
❑ BST-84035 [S]	Tender Feelin's	1967	12.00
—With "A Division of Liberty Records" on label			
❑ B1-84191	Wahoo!	1986	12.00
—"The Finest in Jazz Since 1939" reissue			
❑ BST-84191 [S]	Wahoo!	1965	30.00
—With New York, USA address on label			
❑ BST-84191 [S]	Wahoo!	1967	12.00
—With "A Division of Liberty Records" on label			
❑ BST-84252 [S]	Sweet Honey Bee	1966	30.00
—With New York, USA address on label			
❑ BST-84252 [S]	Sweet Honey Bee	1967	12.00
—With "A Division of Liberty Records" on label			
❑ BST-84267	The Right Touch	1968	25.00
❑ BST-84276	Introducing Duke Pearson's Big Band	1968	25.00
❑ BST-84293	The Phantom	1969	25.00
❑ BST-84308	Now Hear This	1969	25.00
❑ BST-84323	Merry Ole Soul	1970	20.00
❑ BST-84344	How Insensitive	1970	20.00
❑ B1-89792	Sweet Honey Bee	1993	12.00
—Reissue of 84252			
JAZZTIME			
❑ 33-02 [M]	Hush!	1962	40.00
PRESTIGE			
❑ PRST-7729	Dedication	1970	15.00

PEBBLES AND BAMM BAMM

Number	Title (A Side/B Side)	Yr	NM
45s			
HANNA-BARBERA			
❑ 449	Open Up Your Heart/The Lord Is Counting on You	1965	25.00
❑ 449 [PS]	Open Up Your Heart/The Lord Is Counting on You	1965	50.00
❑ 484	The World Is Full of Toys/Daddy	1966	25.00
7-Inch Extended Plays			
HANNA-BARBERA			
❑ CS 7044	Little Drummer Boy/We Three Kings//Silent Night/It Came Upon a Midnight Clear	1965	50.00
❑ CS 7044 [PS]	We Wish You a Merry Christmas	1965	100.00
Albums			
HANNA-BARBERA			
❑ HLP-2033 [M]	Pebbles and Bamm-Bamm Sing Songs of Christmas	1965	120.00
❑ HLP-2040 [M]	On the Good Ship Lollipop	1966	100.00

PEDICIN, MIKE

Number	Title (A Side/B Side)	Yr	NM
45s			
ABC-PARAMOUNT			
❑ 10303	Gotta Twist/When the Cats Come Twistin' In	1962	12.00
APOLLO			
❑ 534	Hey Pop, Give Me the Keys/St. James Infirmary	1959	40.00
CAMEO			
❑ 125	Shake a Hand/The Dickie Doo	1957	25.00
FEDERAL			
❑ 12417	Burnt Toast/You Gotta Go, You Gotta Go	1961	15.00
MALVERN			
❑ 101	The Dickie Doo/(B-side unknown)	1957	30.00
RCA VICTOR			
❑ 47-6043	I'm Hip/I Wanna Hug You, Kiss You, Squeeze You	1955	25.00
❑ 47-6051	Mambo Rock/D-E-V-I-L	1955	25.00
❑ 47-6150	Fe-Fi-Fo-Fum/The Hot Barcarolle	1955	25.00
❑ 47-6235	You Gotta Go/The Banjo Rock	1955	25.00
❑ 47-6285	Jackpot/When the Cats Come Marching In	1955	25.00
❑ 47-6369	The Large, Large House/Hotter Than a Pistol	1955	25.00
❑ 47-6546	The Beat/Save Us, Preacher Davis	1956	25.00
❑ 47-6676	Teenage Fairy Tales/Close All the Doors	1956	25.00
❑ 47-6847	The Hucklebuck/Calypso Rock	1957	25.00
20TH CENTURY			
❑ 75006	My Heart Is Breaking/I'll Always Love You Some	195?	30.00
❑ 75009	Kiss, Kiss, Kiss/L ove Every Moment	195?	30.00
❑ 75012	Never Mind/M-m-Boy	195?	30.00
❑ 75019	I've Got a Feeling It's Love/Is That What You Call Love	195?	30.00
❑ 75021	Disc Jockey's Boogie/Tiger Rag	195?	30.00
❑ 75023	It's My Heart to Give/Kiss Me Before You Say Goodbye	195?	30.00
❑ 75027	Shake a Hand!/Disc Jockey's Boogie	195?	40.00
❑ 75027	Shake a Hand!/When We Met	195?	40.00
❑ 75029	Not Somebody Else Just Me/Sweet Georgia Brown	195?	30.00
Albums			
APOLLO			
❑ LP-484 [M]	Musical Medicine	1957	150.00

PEDRICK, BOBBY, JR. See ROBERT JOHN.

PEEBLES, ANN

Number	Title (A Side/B Side)	Yr	NM
12-Inch Singles			
HI			
❑ 78519	I Didn't Take Your Man/(B-side unknown)	1978	12.00
45s			
HI			
❑ 2157	Walk Away/I Can't Let You Go	1969	6.00
❑ 2165	Give Me Some Credit/Solid Foundation	1969	6.00
❑ 2173	Generation Gap Between Us/I'll Get Along	1970	6.00
❑ 2178	Part Time Love/I Still Love You	1970	6.00
❑ 2186	I Pity the Fool/Heartaches, Heartaches	1971	6.00
❑ 2198	Slipped, Tripped and Fell in Love/99 Lbs.	1971	6.00
❑ 2205	Breaking Up Somebody's Home/Troubles, Heartaches and Sadness	1972	6.00
❑ 2219	Somebody's On Your Case/I've Been There Before	1972	6.00
❑ 2232	I'm Gonna Tear Your Playhouse Down/One Way Street	1973	6.00
❑ 2248	I Can't Stand the Rain/I've Been There Before	1973	6.00

Except when noted otherwise, VG = 25% of NM, and VG+ = 50% of NM. (Example: VG = $2.00, VG+ = $4.00 and NM = $8.00.)

Number	Title (A Side/B Side)	Yr	NM
❑ 2265	(You Keep Me) Hangin' On/Heartaches, Heartaches	1974	6.00
❑ 2271	Do I Need You/Love Vibration	1974	6.00
❑ 2278	Until You Came Into My Life/Put Yourself in My Place	1974	6.00
❑ 2284	Beware/You Got to Feed the Fire	1975	6.00
❑ 2294	Come to Mama/I'm Leaving You	1975	6.00
❑ 2302	Dr. Love Power/I Still Love You	1976	6.00
❑ 2309	I Don't Lend My Man/I Need Somebody	1976	6.00
❑ 2320	Fill This World with Love/It Was Jealousy	1976	6.00
❑ 77502	If This Is Heaven/Sailing	1977	5.00
❑ 78509	Old Man with Young Ideas/A Good Day for Lovin'	1978	5.00
❑ 78518	I Didn't Take Your Man/Being Here with You	1978	5.00
❑ 79528	If You've Got the Time (I've Got the Love)/Let Your Lovelight Shine	1979	5.00
❑ 80533	I'd Rather Leave While I'm in Love/Heartaches	1980	5.00
❑ 81534	Mon Belle-Amour/(B-side unknown)	1981	5.00

Albums

HI

Number	Title	Yr	NM
❑ HLP-6002	If This Is Heaven	1977	12.00
❑ HLP-6007	The Handwriting Is On the Wall	1978	12.00
❑ HLP-8005	Part Time Love	197?	12.00
—Reissue of 32059			
❑ HLP-8009	Straight from the Heart	197?	12.00
—Reissue of 32065			
❑ SHL-32059	Part Time Love	1971	20.00
❑ SHL-32065	Straight from the Heart	1972	20.00
❑ XSHL-32079	I Can't Stand the Rain	1974	20.00
❑ SHL-32091	Tellin' It	1975	20.00

PEEL, DAVID

45s

APPLE

Number	Title	Yr	NM
❑ PRO-6498/9 [DJ]	F Is Not a Dirty Word/The Ballad of New York City	1972	120.00
❑ PRO-6545/6 [DJ]	Hippie from New York City/The Ballad of New York City	1972	120.00

ORANGE

Number	Title	Yr	NM
❑ 1001	Bring Back the Beatles/Imagine	1977	10.00

Albums

APPLE

Number	Title	Yr	NM
❑ SW-3391	The Pope Smokes Dope	1972	40.00

ELEKTRA

Number	Title	Yr	NM
❑ EKS-74032	Have a Marijuana	1968	25.00
❑ EKS-74069	The American Revolution	1970	20.00

PEELS, THE

45s

KARATE

Number	Title	Yr	NM
❑ 522	Juanita Banana/Fun	1966	12.00
❑ 527	Scrooey Mooey/Time Marches On	1966	8.00
❑ 533	Juanita Banana II/Rosita Tomato	1966	10.00

Albums

KARATE

Number	Title	Yr	NM
❑ 5402 [M]	Juanita Banana	1966	80.00

PEEPS, THE

45s

PHILIPS

Number	Title	Yr	NM
❑ 40315	Now Is the Time/Got Plenty of Love	1965	10.00

PEIL, DANNY

45s

RAYNARD

Number	Title	Yr	NM
❑ 602	Jingle Jump/Flip Side	1964	15.00
—As "Danny Peil and the Apollos" with the B-side credited to "The Apollos"			
❑ 602	Jingle Jump/Flip Side	1964	15.00
—As "Danny Peil and the Tigers"			

PEJOE, MORRIS

45s

CHECKER

Number	Title	Yr	NM
❑ 766	Tired of Crying Over You/Gonna Buy Me a Telephone	1953	500.00
—Black vinyl			
❑ 766	Tired of Crying Over You/Gonna Buy Me a Telephone	1953	3000.
—Red vinyl. VG 1500; VG+ 2250			
❑ 781	Can't Get Along/It'll Plumb Get It	1953	400.00
—Black vinyl			
❑ 781	Can't Get Along/It'll Plumb Get It	1953	1000.
—Red vinyl			

VEE JAY

Number	Title	Yr	NM
❑ 148	You're Gonna Need Me/Hurt My Feelings	1955	60.00

PELICANS, THE

45s

IMPERIAL

Number	Title	Yr	NM
❑ 5307	Chimes/Ain't Gonna Do It	1954	1000.

LOST-NITE

Number	Title	Yr	NM
❑ 155	White Cliffs of Dover/Aurelia	196?	8.00
—Reissue			

PARROT

Number	Title	Yr	NM
❑ 793	White Cliffs of Dover/Aurelia	1954	3000.
—Black vinyl			
❑ 793	White Cliffs of Dover/Aurelia	1954	6000.
—Red vinyl. VG 3000; VG+ 4500			

PENDARVIS, TRACY

45s

SUN

Number	Title	Yr	NM
❑ 335	A Thousand Guitars/Is It Too Late	1960	20.00
❑ 345	Is It Me/South Bound Line	1960	25.00
❑ 359	Eternally/Belle of the Swanee	1961	20.00

PENDERGRASS, TEDDY

45s

ASYLUM

Number	Title	Yr	NM
❑ 69401	Joy/Let Me Be Closer	1988	3.00
❑ 69422	2 A.M./(Instrumental)	1988	4.00
❑ 69538	Lert Me Be Closer/Love Emergency	1986	4.00
❑ 69568	Love 4/2//One of Us Feels in Love	1986	4.00
❑ 69595	Never Felt Like Dancin'/Love Emergency	1985	4.00
❑ 69628	Somewhere I Belong/Hot Love	1985	4.00
❑ 69628 [PS]	Somewhere I Belong/Hot Love	1985	4.00
❑ 69669	In My Time/Stay with Me	1985	4.00
❑ 69696	You're My Choice Tonight (Choose Me)/So Sad the Song	1984	4.00
❑ 69720	Hold Me/Love	1984	4.00
—With Whitney Houston			
❑ 69720 [PS]	Hold Me/Love	1984	4.00

ELEKTRA

Number	Title	Yr	NM
❑ 69312	The Last Time/(B-side unknown)	1989	3.00
❑ 69358	Love Is the Power/I'm Ready	1988	3.00
❑ 69358 [PS]	Love Is the Power/I'm Ready	1988	3.00
❑ 69422	2 A.M./(Instrumental)	1988	3.00

PHILADELPHIA INT'L.

Number	Title	Yr	NM
❑ 02095	Can't You Try/Love T.K.O.	1981	4.00
❑ 02462	I Can't Live Without Your Love/You Must Live On	1981	4.00
❑ 02619	You're My Latest, Greatest Inspiration/Keep On Lovin' Me	1981	4.00
❑ 02856	Nine Times Out of Ten/This Gift of Life	1982	4.00
❑ 3107	Can't We Try/Plenty Good Lovin'	1980	5.00
❑ 3116	Love T.K.O./I Just Called to Say	1980	5.00
❑ 03116	Love T.K.O./I Just Called to Say	1982	3.00
—Reissue			
❑ 03284	I Can't Win for Losing/Don't Lead Me Out Along the Road	1982	4.00
❑ 03325	I Can't Win for Losing	1982	6.00
—One-sided budget release			
❑ 3622	I Don't Love You Anymore/Somebody Told Me	1977	5.00
❑ 3633	The Whole Town's Laughing at Me/The More I Get, The More I Want	1977	5.00
❑ 3648	Close the Door/Get Up, Get Down, Get Funky, Get Loose	1978	5.00
❑ 3657	Only You/It Don't Hurt Now	1978	5.00
❑ 3669	Life Is a Song Worth Singing/Cold, Cold World	1978	5.00
❑ 3696	Turn Off the Lights/If You Know Like I Know	1979	5.00
❑ 3717	Come Go with Me/Do Me	1979	5.00
❑ 3733	Shout and Scream/Close the Door	1979	5.00
❑ 3742	It's You I Love/Where Did All the Lovin' Go	1980	5.00
❑ 04302	Life Is for the Living/I Want My Baby Back	1984	4.00
❑ 70062	Is It Still Good to You/Girl You Know	1981	4.00

Albums

ASYLUM

Number	Title	Yr	NM
❑ 60317	Love Language	1984	8.00
❑ 60447	Workin' It Back	1985	8.00

ELEKTRA

Number	Title	Yr	NM
❑ 60775	Joy	1988	8.00

PHILADELPHIA INT'L.

Number	Title	Yr	NM
❑ PZ 34390	Teddy Pendergrass	1977	10.00
—No bar code on back cover			
❑ PZ 34390	Teddy Pendergrass	198?	8.00
—With bar code on back cover			
❑ PZ 35095	Life Is a Song Worth Singing	1978	10.00
—No bar code on back cover			
❑ PZ 35095	Life Is a Song Worth Singing	198?	8.00
—With bar code on back cover			
❑ FZ 36003	Teddy	1979	10.00
❑ PZ 36003	Teddy	198?	8.00
—Budget-line reissue with new prefix			
❑ KZ2 36294 [(2)]	Teddy Live! Coast to Coast	1979	12.00
❑ FZ 36745	TP	1980	10.00
❑ PZ 36745	TP	198?	8.00
—Budget-line reissue with new prefix			
❑ FZ 37491	It's Time for Love	1981	10.00
❑ PZ 37491	It's Time for Love	198?	8.00
—Budget-line reissue with new prefix			
❑ FZ 38118	This One's for You	1982	10.00
❑ PZ 38118	This One's for You	198?	8.00
—Budget-line reissue with new prefix			
❑ FZ 38646	Heaven Only Knows	1983	10.00
❑ PZ 38646	Heaven Only Knows	1985	8.00
—Budget-line reissue with new prefix			
❑ FZ 39252	Greatest Hits	1984	10.00
❑ HZ 47491	It's Time for Love	198?	40.00
—Half-speed mastered edition			

PENDLETONS, THE

45s

DOT

Number	Title	Yr	NM
❑ 16511	Board Party/Barefoot Adventure	1963	100.00

RENDEZVOUS

Number	Title	Yr	NM
❑ 194	The Waddle/Itchy Bon Mash	1962	40.00

PENDULUM, THE

45s

KAMA SUTRA

Number	Title	Yr	NM
❑ 253	Silly Sally Sunday/I Do You	1968	8.00
❑ 257	Dead Dog/Now I'll Cry	1968	8.00
❑ 268	High on a Hill/She Can Blow Your Mind	1969	10.00

PENETRATIONS, THE

45s

ICON

Number	Title	Yr	NM
❑ 1002	Bring 'Em Back Alive/Fackin' Out	196?	30.00
—Black vinyl; note slightly different A-side title			
❑ 1002	Bring 'Em In/Fackin' Out	196?	60.00
—Blue vinyl			

PENGUINS, THE

45s

ATLANTIC

Number	Title	Yr	NM
❑ 1132	Pledge of Love/I Knew I'd Fall in Love	1957	30.00

DOOTO

Number	Title	Yr	NM
❑ 348	Earth Angel/Hey Senorita	1959	20.00
—Reissue on altered label name and yellow label			
❑ 428	That's How Much I Need You/Be My Lovin' Baby	1957	40.00
❑ 432	Sweet Love/Let Me Make Up Your Mind	1958	30.00
❑ 435	Do Not Pretend/If You're Mine	1958	30.00

DOOTONE

Number	Title	Yr	NM
❑ 345	No There Ain't No News Today/When I Am Gone	1954	300.00
—B-side by Dootsie Williams Orchestra			
❑ 348	Earth Angel/Hey Senorita	1954	150.00
—First pressings on glossy red labels			
❑ 348	Earth Angel/Hey Senorita	1955	30.00
—Black label			
❑ 348	Earth Angel/Hey Senorita	1955	40.00
—Blue label			
❑ 348	Earth Angel/Hey Senorita	1955	50.00
—Maroon label			
❑ 353	Love Will Make Your Mind Go Wild/Ookey Ook	1954	70.00
—First pressings on glossy red label			
❑ 353	Love Will Make Your Mind Go Wild/Ookey Ook	1955	30.00
—Black label			
❑ 353	Love Will Make Your Mind Go Wild/Ookey Ook	1955	40.00
—Blue label			
❑ 353	Love Will Make Your Mind Go Wild/Ookey Ook	1955	50.00
—Maroon label			
❑ 362	Baby, Let's Make Some Love/Kiss a Fool Goodbye	1955	50.00

ELDO

Number	Title	Yr	NM
❑ 119	Universal Twist/To Keep Our Love	1962	20.00

GLENVILLE

Number	Title	Yr	NM
❑ 101	Earth Angel/Hey Senorita	197?	6.00
—Reissue			

The Pentangle, *Basket of Light*, Reprise RS 6372, 1969, **$20.**

Number	Title (A Side/B Side)	Yr	NM
MERCURY			
❑ 70610	Don't Do It/Be Mine or Be a Fool	1955	50.00
—Black vinyl			
❑ 70610	Don't Do It/Be Mine or Be a Fool	1955	200.00
—Red vinyl			
❑ 70654	Walkin' Down Broadway/ It Only Happens with You	1955	50.00
❑ 70703	Promises, Promises, Promises/ The Devil That I See	1955	50.00
❑ 70762	A Christmas Prayer/Jingle Jangle	1955	80.00
❑ 70799	My Troubles Are Not At an End/ She's Gone, Gone	1956	25.00
—Black label			
❑ 70799	My Troubles Are Not At an End/ She's Gone, Gone	1956	50.00
—Maroon label			
❑ 70943	Earth Angel/Ice	1956	40.00
—Not the same recording as the hit on Dootone			
❑ 71033	Cool Baby Cool/Will You Be Mine	1957	40.00
ORIGINAL SOUND			
❑ 27	Memories of El Monte/Be Mine	1963	50.00
—Black and silver label; A-side written by Frank Zappa			
❑ 27	Memories of El Monte/Be Mine	1963	100.00
—Black and red label			
❑ 54	Heavenly Angel/Big Bobo's Party Train	1965	25.00
POWER			
❑ 7023	Earth Angel/Hey Senorita	195?	8.00
—Reissue from "S.P.C. Newark, N.J."			
❑ 7023 [PS]	Earth Angel/Hey Senorita	195?	12.00
SUN STATE			
❑ 001	Believe Me/The Pony Rock	1962	25.00
WING			
❑ 90076	Dealer of Dreams/Peace of Mind	1956	30.00
7-Inch Extended Plays			
DOOTO			
❑ 241	Butterball/Heart of a Fool// Money Talks/Lover or Fool	1959	120.00
❑ 241 [PS]	The Cool, Cool Penguins Vol. 1	1959	120.00
❑ 243	(contents unknown)	1959	120.00
❑ 243 [PS]	The Cool, Cool Penguins, Vol. 2	1959	120.00
❑ 244	(contents unknown)	1959	120.00
❑ 244 [PS]	The Cool, Cool Penguins, Vol. 3	1959	120.00
DOOTONE			
❑ 101	Earth Angel/I Ain't Gonna Cry No More//Love Will Make Your Mind Go Wild/Baby Let's Make Some Love	1955	250.00
❑ 101 [PS]	The Penguins	1955	250.00
—Issued in "Dootone" jacket rather than custom jacket			
Albums			
COLLECTABLES			
❑ COL-5045	Golden Classics	198?	10.00
DOOTO			
❑ DTL-204 [M]	The Best Vocal Groups... Rhythm and Blues	1959	200.00
—Reissue of Dootone 204; blue and yellow label			
❑ DTL-204 [M]	The Best Vocal Groups...Rhythm and Blues	196?	100.00
—Black label with gold/orange/blue ring. This is NOT a counterfeit.			
❑ DTL-242 [M]	The Cool, Cool Penguins	1959	700.00
—Blue and yellow label			
❑ DTL-242 [M]	The Cool, Cool Penguins	1959	700.00
—Red and yellow label			
❑ DTL-242 [M]	The Cool, Cool Penguins	196?	200.00
—Black label with gold/orange/blue ring. This is NOT a counterfeit.			
DOOTONE			
❑ DTL-204 [M]	The Best Vocal Groups... Rhythm and Blues	195?	500.00
—As above; glossy maroon label			
❑ DTL-204 [M]	The Best Vocal Groups... Rhythm and Blues	1957	1500.
—Also includes tracks by the Medallions, Don Julian and the Meadowlarks, and the Dootones. Flat maroon label.			

PENN, LITTLE "LAMBSIE"

Number	Title (A Side/B Side)	Yr	NM
45s			
ATCO			
❑ 6082	I Wanna Spend Christmas With Elvis/Painted Lips and Pigtails	1956	50.00

PENN, WILLIAM, AND THE QUAKERS

Number	Title (A Side/B Side)	Yr	NM
45s			
DUANE			
❑ 104	Coming Up My Way/Care Free	196?	40.00
HUSH			
❑ 230	Little Girl/Somebody's Dum Dum	196?	50.00
MELRON			
❑ 5013	California Sun/No More Love	1966	50.00
❑ 5024	Santa Needs Ear Muffs on His Nose/Philly	1966	60.00
❑ 5024	Santa Needs Ear Muffs on His Nose/Sweet Caroline	1966	60.00
THUNDERBIRD			
❑ 502	Blow My Mind/Swami	1966	40.00
—As the "William Penn Fyve"			
TWILIGHT			
❑ 410	Ghost of the Monks/ Goodbye My Love	1967	30.00
UPTOWN			
❑ 745	Chrome Dome Wheeler Dealer/ Scrapped	1967	40.00

PENNANTS, THE

Number	Title (A Side/B Side)	Yr	NM
45s			
WORLD			
❑ 102	Don't Go/Workin' Man	1961	100.00

PENNER, DICK

Number	Title (A Side/B Side)	Yr	NM
45s			
SUN			
❑ 282	Cindy Lou/Your Honey Love	1958	50.00

PENNINGTON, RAY

Number	Title (A Side/B Side)	Yr	NM
45s			
CAPITOL			
❑ 2006	Who's Gonna Walk the Dog (And Put Out the Cat)/You Turned the Lights On	1967	8.00
❑ 2118	Hush, Hush, Sweet Charlotte/ Someday You'll Fall Back to Me	1968	8.00
❑ 5751	Who's Been Mowing the Lawn (While I Was Gone)/I Don't Feel at Home	1966	8.00
❑ 5855	Ramblin' Man/Let Go	1967	8.00
DIMENSION			
❑ 1039	For Christmas/Don't Let Me Lie Again	1982	5.00
❑ 1043	While I Was Slippin' In (She Was Steppin' Out)/ I Can Forget About You	1983	5.00
EMH			
❑ 0022	The Memories That Last/ Nothing to Go On	1983	5.00
❑ 0027	For Christmas/Dark Haired Woman	1983	5.00
❑ 0029	Drowning My Troubles (Till They've Learned How to Swim)/Till the Fear Slips Away	1984	5.00
❑ 0033	Nothing's Changed, Nothing's New/The Devil's Den	1984	5.00
KING			
❑ 5783	The First Step Down Is the Longest/Your Diary	1963	12.00
LEE			
❑ 502	Boogie Woogie Country Girl/ (B-side unknown)	1958	250.00
❑ 504	My Steady Baby/ (B-side unknown)	1958	150.00
MONUMENT			
❑ 1109	Raining in My Heart/My Mind Is No Match for Your Memory	1968	7.00
❑ 1134	After I'm Number One/ Cold, Gray Light of Dawn	1969	7.00
❑ 1145	What Eva Doesn't Have/Denver	1969	7.00
❑ 1170	This Song Don't Care Who Sings It/I Wouldn't Treat a Doggone Dog (The Way You're Treatin' Me)	1969	7.00
❑ 1194	You Don't Know Me/ Country Blues	1970	7.00
❑ 1208	The Other Woman/I Know Love	1970	7.00
❑ 1231	Bubbles in My Beer/Don't Build No Fences for Me	1970	7.00
❑ 8527	The Best Worst Thing/My Daddy Was a Travelin' Man	1971	6.00
❑ 8537	My Church/This Song Don't Care Who Sings It	1971	6.00
❑ 8540	Woman Go On Home/ Dark Haired Woman	1972	6.00
❑ 8553	Let Them Talk/Happy Times	1972	6.00

Except when noted otherwise, VG = 25% of NM, and VG+ = 50% of NM. (Example: VG = $2.00, VG+ = $4.00 and NM = $8.00.)

Number	Title (A Side/B Side)	Yr	NM
MRC			
❑ 1022	She Wanted a Little Bit More/ (B-side unknown)	1978	5.00
RUBY			
❑ 290	Fancy Free/You'll Want Me Back But I Won't Care	1957	60.00
STEP ONE			
❑ 340	Deep Water/Faded Love	198?	5.00
❑ 343	Cincinnati Blues/Before You Turn Me Down	198?	5.00
❑ 403	Blue of a Kind/Fat Boy Rag	1989	5.00
ZODIAC			
❑ 1003	I Can't Get Up Myself/ (B-side unknown)	1976	6.00
❑ 1010	Steppin' Aside Just Ain't My Style/The Good Old Days Are Right Now	1976	6.00
Albums			
DIMENSION			
❑ DLP-5007	Memories	1983	12.00
MONUMENT			
❑ SLP-18145	Ray Pennington Sings for the Other Woman	1970	15.00

PENNSYLVANIA PLAYERS, THE See DICKIE GOODMAN.

PENNY AND JEAN

Number	Title (A Side/B Side)	Yr	NM
45s			
RCA VICTOR			
❑ 47-7844	I Forgot More Than You'll Ever Know/How Come I'm Crying Now?	1961	12.00
Albums			
RCA VICTOR			
❑ LPM-2244 [M]	Two for the Road	1961	20.00
❑ LSP-2244 [S]	Two for the Road	1961	25.00

PENNY AND THE OVERTONES

Number	Title (A Side/B Side)	Yr	NM
45s			
RIM			
❑ 2021	What Made You Forget/ (B-side unknown)	1958	100.00

PENTAGON

Number	Title (A Side/B Side)	Yr	NM
Albums			
EAST WIND			
❑ 10002	Pentagon	1979	20.00

PENTAGONS, THE

Number	Title (A Side/B Side)	Yr	NM
45s			
DONNA			
❑ 1337	To Be Loved (Forever)/ Down at the Beach	1961	30.00
❑ 1344	I Like the Way You Look (At Me)/ For a Love That Is Mine	1961	30.00
FLEET INT'L.			
❑ 100	Down at the Beach/To Be Loved (Forever)	1960	200.00
—Original record has "Down at the Beach" labeled as "100-1" and "To Be Loved (Forever)" as "100-2"			
JAMIE			
❑ 1201	I Wonder/She's Mine	1961	15.00
❑ 1210	Until Then/I'm in Love	1962	15.00
LOST-NITE			
❑ 210	To Be Loved (Forever)/ Down at the Beach	196?	5.00
—Reissue			

PENTANGLE, THE

Number	Title (A Side/B Side)	Yr	NM
45s			
REPRISE			
❑ PRO 391 [DJ]	Light Flight/Sally Go 'Round the Roses	1969	10.00
❑ 0784	Let No Man Steal Your Throne/ Way Behind the Sun	1968	8.00
❑ 0843	I Saw an Angel/Once I Had a Sweetheart	1969	8.00

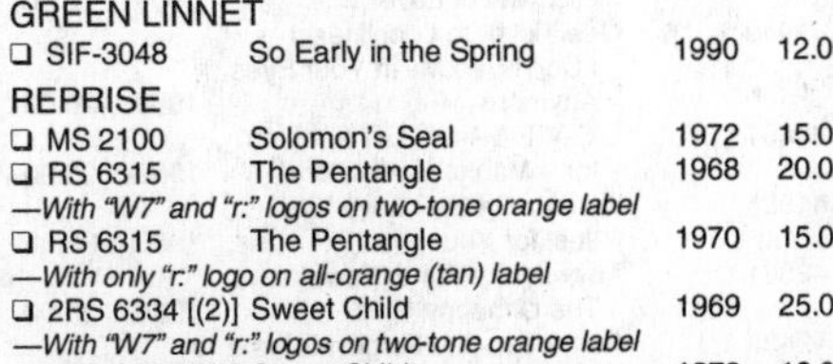

Number	Title (A Side/B Side)	Yr	NM
Albums			
GREEN LINNET			
❑ SIF-3048	So Early in the Spring	1990	12.00
REPRISE			
❑ MS 2100	Solomon's Seal	1972	15.00
❑ RS 6315	The Pentangle	1968	20.00
—With "W7" and "r:" logos on two-tone orange label			
❑ RS 6315	The Pentangle	1970	15.00
—With only "r:" logo on all-orange (tan) label			
❑ 2RS 6334 [(2)]	Sweet Child	1969	25.00
—With "W7" and "r:" logos on two-tone orange label			
❑ 2RS 6334 [(2)]	Sweet Child	1970	18.00
—With only "r:" logo on all-orange (tan) label			

Pere Ubu, *Dub Housing*, Chrysalis CHR 1207, 1979, **$25.**

Number	Title (A Side/B Side)	Yr	NM
❑ RS 6372	Basket of Light	1969	20.00
—With "W7" and "r:" logos on two-tone orange label			
❑ RS 6372	Basket of Light	1970	15.00
—With only "r:" logo on all-orange (tan) label			
❑ RS 6430	Cruel Sister	1971	15.00
❑ RS 6463	Reflection	1971	15.00
SHANACHIE			
❑ 79066	A Maid That's Deep in Love	198?	10.00
VARRICK			
❑ VR-017	Open the Door	1985	10.00
❑ VR-026	In the Round	1986	10.00

PEOPLE Also see LARRY NORMAN.

Number	Title (A Side/B Side)	Yr	NM
45s			
CAPITOL			
❑ 2078	I Love You/Somebody Tell Me My Name	1968	12.00
❑ 2251	Apple Cider/Ashes of Me	1968	10.00
❑ 2499	Turnin' Me In/Ulla	1969	10.00
❑ 5920	Organ Grinder/Riding High	1967	10.00
PARAMOUNT			
❑ 0005	Love Will Take Us Higher and Higher/Livin' It Up	1969	6.00
❑ 0011	Sunshine Lady/Crosstown Bus	1969	6.00
❑ 0019	For What It's Worth/Maple Street	1970	6.00
❑ 0028	One Chain Don't Make No Prison/Keep It Alive	1970	6.00
POLYDOR			
❑ 14087	Chant for Peace/ I Don't Carry No Guns	1971	6.00
ZEBRA			
❑ 102	Come Back Beatles (same on both sides)	1978	10.00
Albums			
CAPITOL			
❑ ST-151	Both Sides of People	1969	20.00
❑ ST 2924	I Love You	1968	20.00
PARAMOUNT			
❑ PAS-5013	There Are People	1970	20.00

PEOPLE'S CHOICE

Number	Title (A Side/B Side)	Yr	NM
45s			
CASABLANCA			
❑ 2322	My Feet Won't Move, But My Shoes Did the Boogie/ You Ought to Be Dancin'	1980	4.00
PALMER			
❑ 5020	Easy to Be True/Savin' My Love for You	1967	250.00
PHIL-L.A. OF SOUL			
❑ 349	I Likes to Do It/Big Ladies Man	1971	6.00
❑ 352	Wootie-T-Woo/'Cause That's the Way I Know	1971	6.00
❑ 356	Magic/Oh How I Love It	1972	6.00
❑ 358	Let Me Do My Thing/ On a Cloudy Day	1972	6.00
PHILADELPHIA INT'L.			
❑ 3649	Turn Me Loose/Soft and Tender	1978	4.00
❑ 3658	Rough-Ride/Stay with Me	1978	4.00
PHILIPS			
❑ 40653	Keep On Holding On/ Just Look What You've Done	1969	12.00
TSOP			
❑ 4751	Love Shot/The Big Hurt	1973	5.00
❑ 4759	Party Is a Groovy Thing/ Asking for Trouble	1974	5.00
❑ 4769	Do It Any Way You Wanna/ The Big Hurt	1975	5.00
❑ 4773	Nursery Rhymes (Part 1)/ Nursery Rhymes (Part 2)	1975	5.00
❑ 4781	Here We Go Again/Mickey D's	1976	5.00
❑ 4782	Movin' In All Directions/ Mellow Hood	1976	5.00
❑ 4784	Cold Blooded & Down-Right Funky/Jam, Jam, Jam (All Night Long)	1976	5.00

Pere Ubu, *The Art of Walking*, Rough Trade ROUGH US 4, 1980, **$40.**

Number	Title (A Side/B Side)	Yr	NM
❑ 4786	If You Gonna Do It (Put Your Mind To It) (Part I)/If You Gonna Do It (Put Your Mind To It) (Part II)	1977	5.00
Albums			
PHILADELPHIA INT'L.			
❑ JZ 35363	Turn Me Loose	1978	10.00
TSOP			
❑ KZ 33154	Boogie Down U.S.A.	1975	10.00
❑ PZ 34124	We Got the Rhythm	1976	10.00

PEPE AND THE ASTROS

Number	Title (A Side/B Side)	Yr	NM
45s			
SWAMI			
❑ 553/4	Judy My Love/Now, Ain't That a Shame	1961	50.00

PEPP, GEORGE

Number	Title (A Side/B Side)	Yr	NM
45s			
COLEMAN			
❑ 80	The Feeling Is Real/(B-side unknown)	196?	1200.

PEPPERMINT RAINBOW, THE

Number	Title (A Side/B Side)	Yr	NM
45s			
DECCA			
❑ 32316	Pink Lemonade/Walking in Different Circles	1968	8.00
❑ 32410	Will You Be Staying After Sunday/And I'll Be There	1968	10.00
❑ 32498	Don't Wake Me Up in the Morning, Michael/Rosemary	1969	8.00
❑ 32498 [PS]	Don't Wake Me Up in the Morning, Michael/Rosemary	1969	12.00
❑ 32562	You're the Sound of Love/Jamais	1969	8.00
❑ 32601	Good Morning Means Goodbye/Don't Love Me Unless It's Forever	1969	8.00
Albums			
DECCA			
❑ DL 75129	Will You Be Staying After Sunday	1969	20.00

PEPPERMINT TROLLEY COMPANY, THE

Number	Title (A Side/B Side)	Yr	NM
45s			
ACTA			
❑ 807	She's the Kind of Girl/Little Miss Sunshine	1967	8.00
❑ 809	It's a Lazy Summer Day/Blue Eyes	1967	8.00
❑ 815	Baby You Come Rollin' Across My Mind/9 O'Clock Business Man	1968	10.00
❑ 829	Trust/I Remember Long Along	1968	8.00
❑ 834	The Last Thing on My Mind/Memphis City Letter	1969	15.00
❑ 835	Spinnin' 'n' Whirlin' Around/New York City	1969	8.00
VALIANT			
❑ 752	Lollipop Train/Bored to Tears	1966	20.00
Albums			
ACTA			
❑ A-8007 [M]	The Peppermint Trolley Company	1968	50.00
—In stereo cover with "Monaural" sticker			
❑ A-38007 [S]	The Peppermint Trolley Company	1968	25.00

PEPS, THE See THE FABULOUS PEPS.

PERE UBU Pioneering Cleveland industrialists, featuring Dave Thomas.

Number	Title (A Side/B Side)	Yr	NM
12-Inch Singles			
FONTANA			
❑ PRO 747 [DJ]	Breathe/Bang the Drum/Over My Head/Universal Vibration	1989	10.00
RESTLESS			
❑ 72340	We Have the Technology/Postman Drove a Caddy/The B Side	1988	6.00
45s			
HEARTHAN			
❑ HR-101	30 Seconds Over Tokyo/Heart of Darkness	1975	35.00
—Second issue: Brown on white label			
❑ HR-101	30 Seconds Over Tokyo/Heart of Darkness	1975	50.00
—First issue: Black label			
❑ HR-101 [PS]	30 Seconds Over Tokyo/Heart of Darkness	1975	100.00
—First 1,000 issued with picture sleeve			
❑ HR-102	Final Solution/Cloud 149	1976	25.00
❑ HR-102 [PS]	Final Solution/Cloud 149	1976	150.00
—First 600 issued with picture sleeve			
❑ HR-103	Street Waves/My Dark Ages	1976	25.00
❑ HR-103 [PS]	Street Waves/My Dark Ages	1976	50.00
—Most issued with picture sleeve			
❑ HR-104	The Modern Dance/Heaven	1977	25.00
❑ HR-104 [PS]	The Modern Dance/Heaven	1977	50.00
—First 1,000 issued with picture sleeve			
ROUGH TRADE			
❑ RT US 004	Not Happy/Lonesome Cowboy Dave	1981	10.00
❑ RT US 004 [PS]	Not Happy/Lonesome Cowboy Dave	1981	15.00
Albums			
BLANK			
❑ 001	The Modern Dance	1978	40.00
CHRYSALIS			
❑ CHR 1207	Dub Housing	1979	25.00
ENIGMA			
❑ D1-73343	The Tenement Year	1988	15.00
FONTANA			
❑ 838237-1	Cloudland	1989	12.00
ROUGH TRADE			
❑ ROUGH US 4	The Art of Walking	1980	20.00
—Revised version: Vocal added on "Arabia"; "Miles" is shortened			
❑ ROUGH US 4	The Art of Walking	1980	40.00
—First 1,800 were incorrectly mastered			
❑ ROUGH US 7	The Modern Dance	1981	20.00
—Reissue of Blank 001			
❑ ROUGH US 10	390 Degrees of Simulated Stereo	1981	20.00
❑ ROUGH US 21	Song of the Bailing Man	1982	20.00

PERENNIALS, THE

Number	Title (A Side/B Side)	Yr	NM
45s			
BALL			
❑ 1016	My Big Mistake/I'm Yours 'Til the End	1963	400.00

PERFECT, CHRISTINE See CHRISTINE McVIE.

PERFIDIANS, THE

Number	Title (A Side/B Side)	Yr	NM
45s			
HUSKY			
❑ 1	La Paz/Whiplash	1962	40.00
—Black vinyl			
❑ 1	La Paz/Whiplash	1962	80.00
—Red vinyl			

PERHACS, LINDA

Number	Title (A Side/B Side)	Yr	NM
Albums			
KAPP			
❑ KS-3636	Parallelograms	1970	200.00

PERKINS, CARL

Number	Title (A Side/B Side)	Yr	NM
45s			
COLUMBIA			
❑ 41131	Pink Pedal Pushers/Jive After Five	1958	30.00
❑ 41131 [PS]	Pink Pedal Pushers/Jive After Five	1958	120.00
❑ 41207	Levi Jacket/Pop, Let Me Have the Car	1958	25.00
❑ 41296	Y-O-U/This Life I Live	1958	25.00
❑ 41379	Pointed Toe Shoes/Highway of Love	1959	25.00
❑ 41449	One Ticket to Loneliness/I Don't See Me in Your Eyes Anymore	1959	25.00
❑ 41651	L-O-V-E-V-I-L-L-E/Too Much for a Man to Understand	1960	25.00
❑ 41825	Honey, 'Cause I Love You/Just for You	1960	25.00
❑ 42061	Anyway the Wind Blows/The Unhappy Girls	1961	25.00
❑ 42403	Hollywood City/Forget Me Next Time Around	1962	—
—Unreleased?			

Except when noted otherwise, VG = 25% of NM, and VG+ = 50% of NM. (Example: VG = $2.00, VG+ = $4.00 and NM = $8.00.)

Number	Title (A Side/B Side)	Yr	NM
❑ 42405	Hollywood City/The Fool I Used to Be	1962	25.00
❑ 42405 [PS]	Hollywood City/The Fool I Used to Be	1962	120.00
❑ 42514	Sister Twister/Hambone	1962	25.00
❑ 42514 [PS]	Sister Twister/Hambone	1962	400.00
❑ 42753	I Just Got Back from There/Forget Me Next Time Around	1963	25.00
❑ 44723	Restless/1143	1968	8.00
❑ 44883	For Your Love/Four Letter Word	1969	8.00
❑ 44993	C.C. Rider/Soul Beat	1969	8.00
❑ 45107	All Mama's Children/Step Aside	1970	8.00
—With NRBQ			
❑ 45132	State of Confusion/My Son, My Son	1970	6.00
❑ 45253	What Every Little Boy Ought to Know/Just As Long	1970	5.00
❑ 45347	Me Without You/Red Headed Woman	1971	5.00
❑ 45466	Cotton Top/About All I Can Give You Is My Love	1971	5.00
❑ 45582	High on Love/Take Me Back to Memphis	1972	5.00
❑ 45694	Someday/The Trip	1972	5.00
DECCA			
❑ 31548	Help Me Find My Baby/For a Little While	1963	15.00
❑ 31591	After Sundown/I Wouldn't Have Told You	1964	15.00
❑ 31709	The Monkeyshine/Let My Baby Be	1964	15.00
❑ 31786	One of These Days/Mama of My Song	1965	15.00
DOLLIE			
❑ 505	Country Boy's Dream/If I Could Come Back	1966	12.00
❑ 508	Shine, Shine, Shine/Almost Love	1967	12.00
❑ 512	Without You/You Can Take the Boy Out of the Country	1967	12.00
❑ 514	My Old Home Town/Back to Tennessee	1967	12.00
❑ 516	It's You/Lake County Cotton Country	1968	12.00
FLIP			
❑ 501	Movie Magg/Turn Around	1955	1000.
JET			
❑ 5054	Blue Suede Shoes/Rock Around the World	1979	4.00
MERCURY			
❑ 55009	The E.P. Express/Big Bad Blues	1977	4.00
❑ 73425	(Let's Get) Dixiefried/One More Loser Goin' Home	1973	6.00
❑ 73489	Ruby, Don't Take Your Love to Town/Sing My Song	1974	5.00
❑ 73653	You'll Always Be a Lady to Me/Low Class	1974	5.00
❑ 73690	The E.P. Express/Big Bad Blues	1975	5.00
❑ 73993	Help Me Dream/You Tore My Heaven All to Hell	1973	6.00
MMI			
❑ 1016	Don't Get Off Gettin' It On/Georgia Court Room	1977	4.00
❑ 1019	Standing in the Need of Love/Georgia Court Room	1977	4.00
MUSIC MILL			
❑ 1007	Born to Boogie/Take Me Back	1976	4.00
SMASH			
❑ 884760-7	Birth of Rock and Roll/Rock and Roll (Fais-Do-Do)	1986	4.00
—B-side with Jerry Lee Lewis, Roy Orbison and Johnny Cash			
❑ 884760-7 [PS]	Birth of Rock and Roll/Rock and Roll (Fais-Do-Do)	1986	4.00
—B-side with Jerry Lee Lewis, Roy Orbison and Johnny Cash			
❑ 884934-7	Sixteen Candles/Rock & Roll (Fais-Do-Do)	1986	4.00
—B-side with Jerry Lee Lewis, Roy Orbison and Johnny Cash; A-side by Jerry Lee Lewis			
❑ 888142-7	Class of '55/We Remember the King	1987	4.00
—B-side with Jerry Lee Lewis, Roy Orbison and Johnny Cash			
SUEDE			
❑ 101	I Don't Want to Fall in Love Again/We Did It in '54	1978	4.00
❑ 102	Rock-a-Billy Fever/Till You Get Through with Me	1978	4.00
❑ 6777	Little Teardrops/Green Grass of Home	1977	4.00
SUN			
❑ 224	Gone, Gone, Gone/Let the Jukebox Keep On Playing	1955	100.00
❑ 234	Blue Suede Shoes/Honey Don't	1956	60.00
❑ 235	Sure to Fall/Tennessee	1956	—
—Unreleased			
❑ 243	Boppin' the Blues/All Mama's Children	1956	40.00
❑ 249	Dixie Fried/I'm Sorry, I'm Not Sorry	1956	30.00
❑ 261	Matchbox/Your True Love	1957	30.00
❑ 274	That's Right/Forever Yours	1957	30.00
❑ 287	Glad All Over/Lend Me Your Comb	1958	30.00
UNIVERSAL			
❑ UVL-66002	Charlene/Love Makes Dreams Come True	1989	4.00
❑ UVL-66019	Hambone/Love Makes Dreams Come True	1989	4.00
7-Inch Extended Plays			
COLUMBIA			
❑ B-12341	Whole Lotta Shakin' Goin' On/That's All Right//Tutti Frutti/I Got a Woman	1958	200.00
❑ B-12341 [PS]	Whole Lotta Shakin'	1958	200.00
SUN			
❑ EPA-115	Blue Suede Shoes/Movie Magg//Sure to Fall/Gone, Gone, Gone	1958	400.00
❑ EPA-115 [PS]	Carl Perkins	1958	400.00
Albums			
ACCORD			
❑ SN-7169	Presenting Carl Perkins	1982	10.00
ALBUM GLOBE			
❑ 8118	Country Soul	1980	10.00
❑ 9037	Goin' Back to Memphis	1980	10.00
ALLEGIANCE			
❑ AV-5001	The Heart and Soul of Carl Perkins	198?	10.00
BULLDOG			
❑ BDL-2034	Twenty Golden Pieces	198?	10.00
COLUMBIA			
❑ CL 1234 [DJ]	Whole Lotta Shakin'	1958	800.00
—White label promo			
❑ CL 1234 [M]	Whole Lotta Shakin'	1958	400.00
❑ CS 9833	Carl Perkins' Greatest Hits	1969	25.00
—Red "360 Sound Stereo" label			
❑ CS 9931	Carl Perkins On Top	1969	25.00
—Red "360 Sound Stereo" label			
❑ CS 9981	Boppin' the Blues	1970	12.00
—Orange label			
❑ CS 9981	Boppin' the Blues	1970	25.00
—Red "360 Sound Stereo" label			
❑ PC 9981	Boppin' the Blues	198?	8.00
—Budget-line reissue			
❑ FC 37961	The Survivors	1982	10.00
—With Johnny Cash and Jerry Lee Lewis			
❑ PC 37961	The Survivors	198?	8.00
—Budget-line reissue			
COLUMBIA LIMITED EDITION			
❑ LE 10117	Carl Perkins' Greatest Hits	1974	12.00
—"Limited Edition" brown label			
DESIGN			
❑ DLP-611 [M]	Tennessee	1963	30.00
❑ SDLP-611 [R]	Tennessee	1963	20.00
DOLLIE			
❑ 4001	Country Boy's Dream	1967	30.00
❑ ST-91428	Country Boy's Dream	1967	40.00
—Capitol Record Club edition			
HARMONY			
❑ HS 11385	Carl Perkins	1970	15.00
❑ KH 31179	Brown Eyed Handsome Man	1971	12.00
❑ KH 31792	Greatest Hits	1972	12.00
HILLTOP			
❑ 6103	Matchbox	197?	12.00
JET			
❑ JT-LA856-H	Ol' Blue Suede's Back	1978	15.00
❑ JZ 35604	Ol' Blue Suede's Back	1978	10.00
KOALA			
❑ AW 14164	Country Soul	198?	10.00
MCA DOT			
❑ 39035	Carl Perkins	1985	10.00
MERCURY			
❑ SRM-1-691	My Kind of Country	1973	12.00
RHINO			
❑ RNLP-70221	Original Sun Greatest Hits (1955-1957)	1986	12.00
ROUNDER			
❑ SS-27	Honky Tonk Gal: Rare and Unissued Sun Masters	1989	12.00
SMASH			
❑ 830002-1	Class of '55	1986	12.00
—With Jerry Lee Lewis, Roy Orbison and Johnny Cash			
SUEDE			
❑ 002	Live at Austin City Limits	1981	10.00
SUN			
❑ LP-111	Original Golden Hits	1969	12.00
❑ LP-112	Blue Suede Shoes	1969	12.00
❑ SLP-1225 [M]	The Dance Album of Carl Perkins	1957	1200.
❑ SLP-1225 [M]	Teen Beat — The Best of Carl Perkins	1961	500.00
—Reissue with new title			
SUNNYVALE			
❑ 9330803	The Sun Story, Vol. 3	1977	12.00
TRIP			
❑ TLP-8503 [(2)]	The Best of Carl Perkins	1974	12.00
UNIVERSAL			
❑ UVL-76001	Born to Rock	1989	15.00

PERKINS, LAURA LEE

Number	Title (A Side/B Side)	Yr	NM
45s			
IMPERIAL			
❑ 5493	Kiss Me Baby/I Just Don't Like This Kind of Lovin'	1958	40.00
❑ 5507	Don't Wait Up/Oh La Baby	1958	40.00

PERKINS, ROY

Number	Title (A Side/B Side)	Yr	NM
45s			
MELADEE			
❑ 111	Bye Bye Baby/You're on My Mind	1958	100.00
❑ 112	You're Gone/Here Am I	1958	600.00
MERCURY			
❑ 71278	Drop Top/That's What the Mailman Had to Say	1958	40.00

PERKINS, TONY

Number	Title (A Side/B Side)	Yr	NM
45s			
EPIC			
❑ 9165	If You'll Be Mine/A Little Love Can Go a Long Way	1956	20.00
—As "Anthony Perkins"			
❑ 9181	Friendly Persuasion/If You Were the Only Girl	1956	20.00
—As "Anthony Perkins"			
❑ 9201	A Fool in Love/Melody for Lovers	1957	20.00
—As "Anthony Perkins"			
RCA VICTOR			
❑ 47-7020	Moon-Light Swim/First Romance	1957	12.00
❑ 47-7078	When School Starts Again/Rocket to the Moon	1957	12.00
❑ 47-7155	Indian Giver/Just Being of Age	1958	12.00
❑ 47-7155 [PS]	Indian Giver/Just Being of Age	1958	25.00
❑ 47-7244	The Prettiest Girl in School/No, No, No	1958	12.00
❑ 47-7295	Moonlight Swim/She Used to Be My Girl	1958	12.00
❑ 47-7415	Treasure Island/Gonna Get Some Lovin'	1958	12.00
Albums			
EPIC			
❑ LN 3394 [M]	Tony Perkins	1957	50.00
RCA VICTOR			
❑ LPM-1679 [M]	From My Heart	1958	40.00
❑ LSP-1679 [S]	From My Heart	1958	60.00
❑ LPM-1853 [M]	On a Rainy Afternoon	1958	40.00
❑ LSP-1853 [S]	On a Rainy Afternoon	1958	60.00

PERPETUAL MOTION

Number	Title (A Side/B Side)	Yr	NM
45s			
DIAL			
❑ 4078	Neckin' Don't Make It/Get Ready	1968	12.00

PERRIN, SUE

Number	Title (A Side/B Side)	Yr	NM
45s			
GOLDEN WORLD			
❑ 2	Candy Store Man/Recipe of Love	1963	30.00
J&W			
❑ 1001	Can't Let Go/Clickety Clack Heart	196?	150.00

PERRINE, PEP

Number	Title (A Side/B Side)	Yr	NM
Albums			
HIDEOUT			
❑ 1003 [M]	Pep Perrine Live and In Person	196?	120.00

PERSIANS, THE (1)

Number	Title (A Side/B Side)	Yr	NM
45s			
ABC			
❑ 11087	Too Much Pride/That's If You Want Me To	1968	8.00
❑ 11145	I Only Have Eyes for You/The Sun's Gotta Shine in Your Heart	1968	8.00
CAPITOL			
❑ 3230	Your Love/Keep On Moving	1971	6.00
❑ 3333	I Want to Go Home/Baby Come Back Home	1972	6.00
❑ 3414	Give Me a Little Tune/I Won't Cry for You Anymore	1972	6.00

Number	Title (A Side/B Side)	Yr	NM
GWP			
509	I Don't Know How (To Fall Out of Love)/Here It Comes	1969	7.00
GWP'S GRAPEVINE			
201	Detour/(B-side unknown)	1970	7.00

PERSIANS, THE (2)

Number	Title (A Side/B Side)	Yr	NM
45s			
GOLD EAGLE			
1813	Love Me Tonight/Gee What a Girl	1962	25.00
GOLDISC			
1	Teardrops Are Falling/Vault of Memories	1963	60.00
17	Let's Monkey Again/When You Said Let's Get Married	1963	30.00
MUSIC WORLD			
102	Let's Monkey Again/When You Said Let's Get Married	1963	12.00
PAGEANT			
601	Get a Hold of Yourself/The Steady Kind	1963	15.00
RSVP			
114	Tears of Love/Dance Now	1962	30.00
RTO			
100	Sunday Kind of Love/When We Get Married	1963	15.00

PERSONALITIES, THE

Number	Title (A Side/B Side)	Yr	NM
45s			
SAFARI			
1002	Woe Woe Baby/Yours to Command	1957	50.00
—No giraffe on label			
1002	Woe Woe Baby/Yours to Command	1957	200.00
—With giraffe on label			

PERSUADERS, THE More than one group?

Number	Title (A Side/B Side)	Yr	NM
45s			
ATCO			
6822	Thin Line Between Love and Hate/Thigh Spy	1971	10.00
6919	Bad, Bold and Beautiful Girl/Please Stay	1973	7.00
6943	Some Guys Have All the Luck/Love Attack	1973	8.00
6956	Best Thing That Ever Happened to Me/The Way She Is	1974	7.00
6964	All Strung Out on You/Once in a Lifetime Thing	1974	7.00
7012	I've Been Through This Before/Stay with Me	1975	7.00
BUM BUM			
701	Miserlou/World of Wonder	196?	30.00
CALLA			
3006	I Need Love/Sure Shot	1977	6.00
3007	Trying to Love Two Women/Quickest Way Out	1977	6.00
CARLTON			
568	Arabella/Viva El Matador	1962	15.00
WIN OR LOSE			
220	Love Gonna Pack Up (And Walk Out)/You Musta Put Something In Your Love	1971	8.00
222	If This Is What You Call Love (I Don't Want No Part of It)/Thanks for Loving Me	1972	8.00
225	Peace in the Valley of Love/What Is the Definition of Love	1972	8.00
WINLEY			
235	Tears/What Could It Be	1959	150.00
Albums			
ATCO			
SD 7021	The Persuaders	1973	20.00
SD 7046	Best Thing That Ever Happened to Me	1974	20.00
CALLA			
PZ 34802	It's All About Love	1977	15.00
COLLECTABLES			
COL-5139	Thin Line Between Love and Hate (Golden Classics)	198?	10.00
WIN OR LOSE			
SD 33-387	Thin Line Between Love and Hate	1972	25.00

PERSUADERS, THE (2)

Number	Title (A Side/B Side)	Yr	NM
45s			
SATURN			
404	Surfing Strip/Hanging Ten	1963	30.00
405	Caught in the Soup/Gremmie Bread	1963	30.00
Albums			
SATURN			
SAT-5000 [M]	Surfer's Nightmare	1963	300.00
SATS-5000 [S]	Surfer's Nightmare	1963	400.00

PERSUASIONS, THE

Number	Title (A Side/B Side)	Yr	NM
45s			
A&M			
1531	I Really Got It Bad for You/We're All Goin' Home	1974	6.00
1631	With This Ring/Somewhere to Lay My Head	1974	6.00
1658	I Just Want to Sing with My Friends/Somewhere to Lay My Head	1975	6.00
1698	One Thing on My Mind/Darlin'	1975	6.00
CAPITOL			
3162	Let It Be/It's You That I Need	1971	8.00
3242	Don't Know Why I Love You/Tempts Jam	1971	8.00
3317	People Get Ready/Buffalo Soldier	1972	8.00
3425	The Ten Commandments of Love/Good Times	1972	8.00
3492	Three Angels (Part 1)/Three Angels (Part 2)	1972	8.00
ELEKTRA			
45396	Papa-Oom-Mow-Mow/Women and Drinkin'	1977	5.00
MCA			
40080	Good Old Accapella/You Must Believe in Me	1973	6.00
40118	Chapel of Love/Love You Most of All	1973	6.00
REPRISE			
0977	Since I Fell for You/Without a Song	1970	8.00
TOWER			
146	Try Me/I'll Go Crazy	1965	10.00
197	Big Brother/Deep Down Love	1966	10.00
Albums			
A&M			
SP-3635	More Than Before	1974	12.00
SP-3656	I Just Want to Sing with My Friends	1974	12.00
CAPITOL			
SM-791	We Came to Play	197?	10.00
—Reissue with new prefix			
ST-791	We Came to Play	1971	25.00
ST-872	Street Corner Symphony	1972	25.00
ST-11101	Spread the Word	1972	25.00
CATAMOUNT			
905	Stardust	197?	40.00
ELEKTRA			
7E-1099	Chirpin'	1977	12.00
FLYING FISH			
FF-093	Comin' At Ya	1979	12.00
MCA			
326	We Still Ain't Got No Band	1973	15.00
REPRISE			
RS 6394	Acapella	1970	30.00
ROUNDER			
3053	Good News	1981	10.00
3083	No Frills	1984	10.00

PETER AND GORDON Also see GORDON WALLER.

Number	Title (A Side/B Side)	Yr	NM
45s			
CAPITOL			
2071	Greener Days/Never Ever	1968	10.00
2214	You've Had Better Times/Sipping My Wine	1968	10.00
2544	I Can Remember (Not Too Long Ago)/Hard Time, Rainy Day	1969	10.00
PRO4587	You've Had Better Times/Sipping My Wine	1968	15.00
5175	A World Without Love/If I Were You	1964	12.00
5211	Nobody I Know/You Don't Have to Tell Me	1964	12.00
5211 [PS]	Nobody I Know/You Don't Have to Tell Me	1964	16.00
5272	I Don't Want to See You Again/I Would Buy You Presents	1964	12.00
5272 [PS]	I Don't Want to See You Again/I Would Buy You Presents	1964	16.00
5335	I Go to Pieces/Love Me, Baby	1965	12.00
5335 [PS]	I Go to Pieces/Love Me, Baby	1965	16.00
5406	True Love Ways/If You Wish	1965	12.00
5406 [PS]	True Love Ways/If You Wish	1965	16.00
5461	To Know You Is to Love You/I Told You So	1965	10.00
5461 [PS]	To Know You Is to Love You/I Told You So	1965	15.00
5532	Don't Pity Me/Crying in the Rain	1965	10.00
5579	Woman/Wrong from the Start	1966	10.00
—A-side composer listed as "A. Smith"			
5579	Woman/Wrong from the Start	1966	12.00
—A-side composer listed as "Bernard Webb"			
5650	There's No Living Without Your Loving/A Stranger with a Black Dove	1966	10.00
5650 [PS]	There's No Living Without Your Loving/A Stranger with a Black Dove	1966	15.00
5684	To Show I Love You/Start Trying Someone Else	1966	10.00
5684 [PS]	To Show I Love You/Start Trying Someone Else	1966	15.00
5740	Lady Godiva/Morning's Calling	1966	10.00
5740	Lady Godiva/The House I Live In	1966	15.00
5808	Knight in Rusty Armour/Flower Lady	1966	10.00
5808 [PS]	Knight in Rusty Armour/Flower Lady	1966	15.00
5864	Sunday for Tea/Hurtin' Is Lovin'	1967	10.00
5864 [PS]	Sunday for Tea/Hurtin' Is Lovin'	1967	15.00
5919	The Jokers/Red Cream and Velvet	1967	10.00
CAPITOL CREATIVE PRODUCTS			
51 [DJ]	Wrong from the Start/You've Lost That Lovin' Feelin'	1966	12.00
—B-side by the Lettermen			
CAPITOL STARLINE			
6076	A World Without Love/Nobody I Know	1965	8.00
—Green swirl label original			
6103	I Go to Pieces/Love Me Baby	1966	8.00
—Green swirl label original			
6104	There's No Living Without Your Loving/Stranger with a Black Dove	1966	8.00
—Green swirl label original			
6155	I Don't Want to See You Again/Woman	197?	6.00
—Red and white "bullseye" label original			
6156	Lady Godiva/You've Had Better Times	197?	6.00
—Red and white "bullseye" label original			
Albums			
CAPITOL			
ST 2115 [S]	A World Without Love	1964	25.00
T 2115 [M]	A World Without Love	1964	20.00
ST 2220 [S]	I Don't Want to See You Again	1964	25.00
T 2220 [M]	I Don't Want to See You Again	1964	20.00
ST 2324 [S]	I Go to Pieces	1965	25.00
T 2324 [M]	I Go to Pieces	1965	20.00
ST 2368 [S]	True Love Ways	1965	25.00
T 2368 [M]	True Love Ways	1965	20.00
ST 2430 [S]	Peter and Gordon Sing the Hits of Nashville	1966	25.00
T 2430 [M]	Peter and Gordon Sing the Hits of Nashville	1966	20.00
ST 2477 [P]	Woman	1966	25.00
—"Woman" is rechanneled			
T 2477 [M]	Woman	1966	20.00
ST 2549 [P]	The Best of Peter and Gordon	1966	18.00
—Black label with colorband; "Woman" is rechanneled			
ST 2549 [P]	The Best of Peter and Gordon	1967	15.00
—"Starline" label			
T 2549 [M]	The Best of Peter and Gordon	1966	15.00
—Black label with colorband			
T 2549 [M]	The Best of Peter and Gordon	1967	12.00
—"Starline" label			
ST 2664 [S]	Lady Godiva	1967	20.00
T 2664 [M]	Lady Godiva	1967	15.00
ST 2729 [S]	Knight in Rusty Armour	1967	20.00
T 2729 [M]	Knight in Rusty Armour	1967	15.00
ST 2747 [S]	In London for Tea	1967	20.00
T 2747 [M]	In London for Tea	1967	15.00
ST 2882 [S]	Hot, Cold and Custard	1968	25.00
SN-16084 [S]	The Best of Peter and Gordon	1979	8.00

PETER, PAUL AND MARY Also see PAUL STOOKEY; MARY TRAVERS; PETER YARROW.

Number	Title (A Side/B Side)	Yr	NM
45s			
(NO LABEL)			
(no #) [DJ]	Eugene McCarthy for President	1968	25.00
(no #) [DJ]	El Salvador/Light One Candle	1983	15.00
WARNER BROS.			
(no #)	A-Soalin' (mono/stereo)	196?	12.00
—Green custom label			
(no #) [PS]	A-Soalin' (mono/stereo)	196?	20.00
—Illustrated book with lyrics			

Except when noted otherwise, VG = 25% of NM, and VG+ = 50% of NM. (Example: VG = $2.00, VG+ = $4.00 and NM = $8.00.)

Number	Title (A Side/B Side)	Yr	NM
❑ PRO 149 [DJ]	Morning Train/Gone the Rainbow	1963	15.00
—Stereo 33 1/3 rpm, 7-inch single with small hole; "Promotion" at 10 o'clock on label			
❑ S 155 [DJ]	Quit Your Low Down Ways/Freight Train	1963	15.00
—Stereo 33 1/3 rpm, 7-inch single with small hole; "Promotion" at bottom of label			
❑ 5274	Lemon Tree/Early in the Morning	1962	10.00
❑ 5296	If I Had a Hammer/Gone the Rainbow	1962	10.00
❑ 5325	Big Boat/Tiny Sparrow	1962	10.00
❑ 5325 [PS]	Big Boat/Tiny Sparrow	1962	20.00
❑ 5334	Settle Down (Goin' Down That Highway)/500 Miles	1963	10.00
❑ 5348	Puff (The Magic Dragon)/Pretty Mary	1963	10.00
—Later pressings add subtitle			
❑ 5348	Puff/Pretty Mary	1963	12.00
—First pressings have no subtitle on A-side			
❑ 5368	Blowin' in the Wind/Flora	1963	10.00
❑ 5385	Don't Think Twice, It's All Right/Autumn to May	1963	10.00
❑ 5399	Stewball/The Cruel War	1963	10.00
❑ 5402	A-Soalin'/High-A-Bye	1963	12.00
❑ 5402 [PS]	A-Soalin'/High-A-Bye	1963	20.00
❑ 5418	Tell It on the Mountain/Old Coat	1964	10.00
❑ 5442	Oh, Rock My Soul (Part 1)/Oh, Rock My Soul (Part 2)	1964	10.00
❑ 5496	For Lovin' Me/Monday Morning	1965	8.00
❑ 5625	When the Ship Comes In/The Times They Are a-Changin'	1965	8.00
❑ 5659	Early Morning Rain/The Rising of the Moon	1965	8.00
❑ 5809	The Cruel War/Mon Vrai Destin	1966	8.00
❑ 5842	Hurry Sundown/Sometime Lover	1966	—
—Unreleased?			
❑ 5849	The Other Side of This Life/Sometime Lover	1966	8.00
❑ 5883	For Baby (For Bobbie)/Hurry Sundown	1967	8.00
❑ 7067	I Dig Rock and Roll Music/The Great Mandella (The Wheel of Life)	1967	10.00
❑ 7092	Too Much of Nothing/The House Song	1967	8.00
❑ 7232	Yesterday's Tomorrow/Love City (Postcards to Duluth)	1968	8.00
❑ 7279	Day Is Done/Make Believe Town	1969	8.00
❑ 7340	Leaving on a Jet Plane/The House Song	1969	10.00
❑ 7359	Christmas Dinner/The Marvelous Toy	1969	10.00
❑ 8684	Like the First Time/Best of Friends	1978	4.00
❑ 8728	Forever Young/Best of Friends	1978	4.00
7-Inch Extended Plays			
WARNER BROS.			
❑ S 1473	(Moving)	196?	12.00
❑ S 1473	Settle Down/Gone the Rainbow/Pretty Mary//This Land Is Your Land/Man Come Into Egypt/Morning Train	196?	12.00
—Jukebox issue; small hole, plays at 33 1/3 rpm			
❑ S 1507	Very Last Day/Tell It on the Mountain/Freight Train//Rocky Road/Quit Your Low Down Ways/Stewball	196?	12.00
—Jukebox issue; small hole, plays at 33 1/3 rpm, "Promotion" on label			
❑ S 1507-1	Tell It on the Mountain/Blowin' in the Wind/Very Last Day//Freight Train/All My Trials/Quit Your Low Down Ways	196?	12.00
—Jukebox issue; small hole, plays at 33 1/3 rpm, "Promotion" on label			
❑ S 1507-1 [PS]	In the Wind	196?	12.00
❑ S 1751	Moments of Soft Persuasion/Too Much of Nothing/Reason to Believe//She Dreams/Hymn/I Shall Be Released	1968	10.00
—Jukebox issue; small hole, plays at 33 1/3 rpm			
❑ S 1751 [PS]	Late Again	1968	10.00
Albums			
GOLD CASTLE			
❑ D1-71301	No Easy Walk to Freedom	1988	10.00
—Reissue of 171001			
❑ D1-71316	A Holiday Celebration	1988	10.00
❑ R 164086	A Holiday Celebration	1988	12.00
—Same as above, except BMG Direct Marketing edition			
❑ 171001	No Easy Walk to Freedom	1987	12.00
PETER, PAUL AND MARY			
❑ 830331	Such Is Love	1983	20.00
WARNER BROS.			
❑ W 1449 [M]	Peter, Paul and Mary	1962	20.00
❑ WS 1449 [S]	Peter, Paul and Mary	1962	25.00
—Gold label			
❑ WS 1449 [S]	Peter, Paul and Mary	1968	12.00
—Green "W7" label			
❑ WS 1449 [S]	Peter, Paul and Mary	1970	10.00
—Any later Warner Bros. label (green "WB", palm trees, white label)			
❑ W 1473 [M]	(Moving)	1963	20.00
❑ WS 1473 [S]	(Moving)	1963	25.00
—Gold label			
❑ WS 1473 [S]	(Moving)	1968	10.00
—Any later Warner Bros. label (green "W7", green "WB", palm trees, white label)			
❑ W 1507 [M]	In the Wind	1963	20.00
❑ WS 1507 [S]	In the Wind	1963	25.00
—Gold label			
❑ WS 1507 [S]	In the Wind	1968	10.00
—Any later Warner Bros. label			
❑ 2W 1555 [(2)M]	Peter, Paul and Mary In Concert	1964	25.00
❑ 2WS 1555 [(2)S]	Peter, Paul and Mary In Concert	1964	30.00
—Gold labels			
❑ 2WS 1555 [(2)S]	Peter, Paul and Mary In Concert	1968	12.00
—Any later Warner Bros. label			
❑ W 1589 [M]	A Song Will Rise	1965	20.00
❑ WS 1589 [S]	A Song Will Rise	1965	25.00
—Gold label			
❑ WS 1589 [S]	A Song Will Rise	1968	10.00
—Any later Warner Bros. label			
❑ W 1615 [M]	See What Tomorrow Brings	1965	20.00
❑ WS 1615 [S]	See What Tomorrow Brings	1965	25.00
—Gold label			
❑ WS 1615 [S]	See What Tomorrow Brings	1968	10.00
—Any later Warner Bros. label			
❑ W 1648 [M]	Peter, Paul and Mary Album	1966	20.00
❑ WS 1648 [S]	Peter, Paul and Mary Album	1966	25.00
—Gold label			
❑ WS 1648 [S]	Peter, Paul and Mary Album	1968	10.00
—Any later Warner Bros. label			
❑ W 1700 [M]	Album 1700	1967	25.00
❑ WS 1700 [S]	Album 1700	1967	25.00
—Gold label			
❑ WS 1700 [S]	Album 1700	1968	12.00
—Green "W7" label			
❑ WS 1700 [S]	Album 1700	1970	10.00
—Any later Warner Bros. label			
❑ WS 1751	Late Again	1968	15.00
—Green "W7" label			
❑ WS 1751	Late Again	1970	10.00
—Any later Warner Bros. label			
❑ WS 1785	Peter, Paul and Mommy	1969	15.00
—Green "W7" label			
❑ WS 1785	Peter, Paul and Mommy	1970	10.00
—Any later Warner Bros. label			
❑ BS 2552	(Ten) Years Together — The Best of Peter, Paul and Mary	1970	15.00
—Green "WB" label			
❑ BS 2552	(Ten) Years Together — The Best of Peter, Paul and Mary	1973	12.00
—"Burbank" palm-trees label			
❑ BSK 3105	(Ten) Years Together — The Best of Peter, Paul and Mary	1977	10.00
—"Burbank" palm-trees label			
❑ BSK 3105	(Ten) Years Together — The Best of Peter, Paul and Mary	1979	8.00
—White or tan label			
❑ BSK 3231	Reunion	1978	10.00

PETERSEN, PAUL

Also see JAMES DARREN/SHELLEY FABARES/PAUL PETERSEN.

Number	Title (A Side/B Side)	Yr	NM
45s			
COLPIX			
❑ 620	She Can't Find Her Keys/Very Likely	1962	15.00
❑ 620 [PS]	She Can't Find Her Keys/Very Likely	1962	30.00
—Sleeve spells his last name "Peterson" in error			
❑ 631	What Did They Do Before Rock and Roll/Very Unlikely	1962	20.00
—With Shelly Fabares			
❑ 631 [PS]	What Did They Do Before Rock and Roll/Very Unlikely	1962	400.00
❑ 632	Keep Your Love Locked (Deep in Your Heart)/Be Everything to Anyone You Love	1962	12.00
❑ 632 [PS]	Keep Your Love Locked (Deep in Your Heart)/Be Everything to Anyone You Love	1962	30.00
❑ 649	Lollipops and Roses/Please Mr. Sun	1962	12.00
❑ 663	My Dad/Little Boy Sad	1962	15.00
❑ 663 [PS]	My Dad/Little Boy Sad	1962	30.00
❑ 676	Amy/Goody Goody	1963	12.00
❑ 676	Amy/I Only Have Eyes for You	1963	12.00
❑ 697	Girls in the Summertime/Mama, Your Little Boy Fell	1963	12.00
❑ 707	The Cheer Leader/Polka Dots and Moonbeams	1963	12.00
❑ 720	She Rides with Me/Poorest Boy in Town	1964	80.00
—A-side produced by Brian Wilson			
❑ 730	Where Is She/Hey There Beautiful	1964	12.00
❑ 763	Happy/Little Dreamer	1965	12.00
❑ 785	The Ring/You Don't Need Money	1965	12.00
MOTOWN			
❑ 1108	Chained/Don't Let It Happen	1967	20.00
❑ 1129	A Little Bit for Sandy/Your Love's Got Me Runnin'	1968	20.00
Albums			
COLPIX			
❑ CP-429 [M]	Lollipops and Roses	1962	50.00
❑ SCP-429 [S]	Lollipops and Roses	1962	60.00
❑ CP-442 [M]	My Dad	1963	50.00
❑ SCP-442 [S]	My Dad	1963	60.00

PETERSON, EARL

Number	Title (A Side/B Side)	Yr	NM
45s			
COLUMBIA			
❑ 21364	Boogie Blues/Believe Me	1955	50.00
❑ 21406	Be Careful of the Heart You're Going to Break/I'm Not Buying Baby	1955	50.00
❑ 21467	I Ain't Gonna Fall in Love/I'll Live My Life Alone	1955	50.00
❑ 21540	You Gotta Be My Baby/World of Make Believe	1956	40.00
SUN			
❑ 197	Boogie Blues/In the Dark	1954	500.00

PETERSON, OSCAR

Number	Title (A Side/B Side)	Yr	NM
45s			
CLEF			
❑ 89076	I Was Doing All Right/Oh, Lady Be Good	1953	15.00
❑ 89077	Begin the Beguine/Let's Do It	1953	15.00
❑ 89078	Cheek to Cheek/I've Got My Love to Keep Me Warm	1953	15.00
❑ 89079	Sophisticated Lady/Cottontail	1953	15.00
❑ 89093	Autumn in New York/I Hear Music	1954	15.00
❑ 89106	One for My Baby/Polka Dots and Moonbeams	1954	15.00
❑ 89113	It's Easy to Remember/Pooper	1954	15.00
❑ 89124	Unforgettable/Angel Eyes	1954	15.00
❑ 89130	Nuages/Dark Eyes	1955	12.00
❑ 89139	Pettiford's Tune/(B-side unknown)	1955	12.00
❑ 89148	Soft Winds/Sweet Lorraine	1955	12.00
LIMELIGHT			
❑ 3056	March Past/Place St. Henri	1965	8.00
❑ 3062	Lover's Promenade/The Smudge	1965	8.00
❑ 3072	Straighten Up and Fly Right/When My Sugar Walks Down the Street	1966	8.00
MERCURY			
❑ 8917	Debut/Tenderly	1950	25.00
❑ 8921	Lover Come Back to Me/They Didn't Believe Me	1950	20.00
❑ 8922	Where or When/Oscar's Blues	1950	20.00
❑ 8923	All the Things You Are/Three O'Clock in the Morning	1950	20.00
❑ 8926	Little White Lies/Lover	1951	20.00
❑ 8930	Exactly Like You/Robin's Nest	1951	20.00
❑ 8933	Get Happy/Jumping with Symphony Sid	1951	20.00
❑ 8940	Squatty Roo/Salute to Garne	1951	20.00
❑ 8943	How High the Moon/Nameless	1951	20.00
❑ 8952	What's New/I Get a Kick Out of You	1951	20.00
❑ 8959	Love for Sale/Until the Real Thing Comes Along	1952	20.00
❑ 8976	Rough Ridin'/But Not for Me	1952	20.00
❑ 8999	Just One of Those Things/Willow Weep for Me	1952	20.00
❑ 72342	Incoherent Blues/Mumbles	1964	8.00
❑ 89006	You Go to My Head/You Turn the Tables on Me	1952	15.00
❑ 89007	I Can't Get Started/Small Hotel	1952	15.00
❑ 89008	East of the Moon (West of the Sun)/These Foolish Things	1952	15.00
❑ 89009	Blue Moon/They Can't Take That Away from Me	1952	15.00
❑ 89038	The Man I Love/It Ain't Necessarily So	1953	15.00
❑ 89039	Blue Skies/Isn't This a Lovely Day	1953	15.00
❑ 89040	In the Still of the Night/What Is This Thing Called Love	1953	15.00
❑ 89041	Prelude to a Kiss/John Hardy's Wife	1953	15.00
❑ 89062	I Can't Give You Anything But Love, Baby/Spring Is Here	1953	15.00
PRESTIGE			
❑ 711	Sandy's Blues (Part 1)/Sandy's Blues (Part 2)	1969	6.00
❑ 727	Girl Talk/On a Clear Day	1969	6.00
VERVE			
❑ 10056	Soft Sands/Echoes	1957	12.00
❑ 10073	Why, Oh Why/I've Never Left Your Arms	1957	12.00

P

Number	Title (A Side/B Side)	Yr	NM
❑ 10084	Song to the Stars/Chanel	1957	12.00
❑ 10145	Bye Bye Blackbird/Golden Striker	1958	12.00
❑ 10192	On the Street Where You Live/I Could Have Danced All Night	1959	12.00
❑ 10207	Gentleman Jimmy/'Til Tomorrow	1960	10.00
❑ 10268	Billy Boy/Yours Is My Heart Alone	1962	10.00
❑ 10292	This Could Be the Start of Something Big/Gravy Waltz	1963	10.00
❑ 10302	Hallelujah Time/ Hymn to Freedom	1963	10.00
❑ 10320	Someday My Prince Will Come/ Come Sunday	1964	8.00
❑ 10354	People/Quiet Nights of Quiet Stars	1965	8.00

Albums

AMERICAN RECORDING SOCIETY

Number	Title (A Side/B Side)	Yr	NM
❑ G-415 [M]	An Oscar for Peterson	1957	40.00
❑ G-438 [M]	Oscar Peterson Trio at Newport	1957	40.00

BASF

Number	Title (A Side/B Side)	Yr	NM
❑ MC 20668	A Rare Mood	1976	15.00
❑ 20713	Motions and Emotions	1972	12.00
❑ 20734	Tristeza on Piano	1972	12.00
❑ 20868	Walking the Line	1973	12.00
❑ 20869	Another Day	1975	15.00
❑ MC 20879	Tracks	1974	15.00
❑ 20905	In Tune	1973	12.00
❑ 20908	Reunion Blues	1973	15.00
❑ MC 21281	Great Connection	1974	15.00
❑ 25101 [(2)]	Exclusively for My Friends	1972	15.00
❑ 25156 [(2)]	In a Mellow Mood	1973	15.00

BOOK-OF-THE-MONTH

Number	Title (A Side/B Side)	Yr	NM
❑ 61-7546 [(4)]	Easy Does It	1984	25.00

CLEF

Number	Title (A Side/B Side)	Yr	NM
❑ MGC-106 [10]	Oscar Peterson Piano Solos	1951	100.00
—Reissue of Mercury 25024			
❑ MGC-107 [10]	Oscar Peterson at Carnegie Hall	1951	100.00
❑ MGC-110 [10]	Oscar Peterson Collates	1952	100.00
❑ MGC-116 [10]	The Oscar Peterson Quartet	1952	100.00
❑ MGC-119 [10]	Oscar Peterson Plays Pretty	1952	100.00
❑ MGC-127 [10]	Oscar Peterson Collates No. 2	1953	80.00
❑ MGC-145 [10]	Oscar Peterson Sings	1954	80.00
❑ MGC-155 [10]	Oscar Peterson Plays Pretty No. 2	1954	80.00
❑ MGC-168 [10]	The Oscar Peterson Quartet No. 2	1954	80.00
❑ MGC-603 [M]	Oscar Peterson Plays Cole Porter	1953	60.00
❑ MGC-604 [M]	Oscar Peterson Plays Irving Berlin	1953	60.00
❑ MGC-605 [M]	Oscar Peterson Plays George Gershwin	1953	60.00
❑ MGC-606 [M]	Oscar Peterson Plays Duke Ellington	1953	60.00
❑ MGC-623 [M]	Oscar Peterson Plays Jerome Kern	1954	50.00
❑ MGC-624 [M]	Oscar Peterson Plays Richard Rodgers	1954	50.00
❑ MGC-625 [M]	Oscar Peterson Plays Vincent Youmans	1954	50.00
❑ MGC-648 [M]	Oscar Peterson Plays Harry Warren	1955	50.00
❑ MGC-649 [M]	Oscar Peterson Plays Harold Arlen	1955	50.00
❑ MGC-650 [M]	Oscar Peterson Plays Jimmy McHugh	1955	50.00
❑ MGC-688 [M]	The Oscar Peterson Quartet	1956	50.00
—Reissue of 116			
❑ MGC-694 [M]	Recital by Oscar Peterson	1956	50.00
❑ MGC-695 [M]	Nostalgic Memories by Oscar Peterson	1956	50.00
❑ MGC-696 [M]	Tenderly — Music by Oscar Peterson	1956	50.00
❑ MGC-697 [M]	Keyboard Music by Oscar Peterson	1956	50.00
❑ MGC-698 [M]	An Evening with the Oscar Peterson Duo/Quartet	1956	50.00
❑ MGC-708 [M]	Oscar Peterson Plays Count Basie	1956	50.00
❑ MGC-751 [M]	The Oscar Peterson Trio at the Stratford Shakesperean Festival, Vol. 1	1955	—
—Canceled			
❑ MGC-752 [M]	The Oscar Peterson Trio at the Stratford Shakesperean Festival, Vol. 2	1955	—
—Canceled			

DCC COMPACT CLASSICS

Number	Title (A Side/B Side)	Yr	NM
❑ LPZ-2021	West Side Story	1996	100.00
—Audiophile vinyl			

EMARCY

Number	Title (A Side/B Side)	Yr	NM
❑ 405 [(2)]	Oscar Peterson Trio Transition	1976	15.00

FANTASY

Number	Title (A Side/B Side)	Yr	NM
❑ OJC-378	Oscar Peterson Jam — Montreux '77	1989	10.00
❑ OJC-383	Oscar Peterson and the Bassists — Montreux '77	1989	10.00
❑ OJC-498	Skol	1991	10.00
❑ OJC-603	Trumpet Summit Meets the Oscar Peterson Big Four	1991	10.00
❑ OJC-627	The Good Life	1991	10.00

LIMELIGHT

Number	Title (A Side/B Side)	Yr	NM
❑ LM-82010 [M]	Canadiana Suite	1965	15.00
❑ LM-82023 [M]	Eloquence	1965	15.00
❑ LM-82029 [M]	With Respect to Nat	1966	15.00
❑ LM-82039 [M]	Blues Etude	1966	15.00
❑ LM-82044 [M]	Soul Espanol	1967	20.00
❑ LS-86010 [S]	Canadiana Suite	1965	20.00
❑ LS-86023 [S]	Eloquence	1965	20.00
❑ LS-86029 [S]	With Respect to Nat	1966	20.00
❑ LS-86039 [S]	Blues Etude	1966	15.00
❑ LS-86044 [S]	Soul Espanol	1967	15.00

MERCURY

Number	Title (A Side/B Side)	Yr	NM
❑ MGC-106 [10]	Oscar Peterson Piano Solos	1951	120.00
❑ MGC-107 [10]	Oscar Peterson at Carnegie Hall	1951	120.00
❑ MGC-110 [10]	Oscar Peterson Collates	1952	120.00
❑ MGC-116 [10]	The Oscar Peterson Quartet	1952	120.00
❑ MGC-119 [10]	Oscar Peterson Plays Pretty	1952	120.00
❑ MGC-603 [M]	Oscar Peterson Plays Cole Porter	1953	100.00
❑ MGC-604 [M]	Oscar Peterson Plays Irving Berlin	1953	100.00
❑ MGC-605 [M]	Oscar Peterson Plays George Gershwin	1953	100.00
❑ MGC-606 [M]	Oscar Peterson Plays Duke Ellington	1953	100.00
❑ MG-20975 [M]	Oscar Peterson Trio + One	1964	25.00
❑ MG-25024 [10]	Oscar Peterson Piano Solos	1950	150.00
❑ SR-60975 [S]	Oscar Peterson Trio + One	1964	30.00

MGM

Number	Title (A Side/B Side)	Yr	NM
❑ GAS-133	Oscar Peterson (Golden Archive Series)	1970	12.00

MOBILE FIDELITY

Number	Title (A Side/B Side)	Yr	NM
❑ 1-243	Very Tall	1995	50.00
—Audiophile vinyl			

PABLO

Number	Title (A Side/B Side)	Yr	NM
❑ 2310701	The Trio	1975	12.00
❑ 2310739	Oscar Peterson and Roy Eldridge	1976	12.00
❑ 2310740	Oscar Peterson and Dizzy Gillespie	1976	12.00
❑ 2310741	Oscar Peterson and Harry Edison	1976	12.00
❑ 2310742	Oscar Peterson and Clark Terry	1976	12.00
❑ 2310743	Oscar Peterson and Jon Faddis	1976	12.00
❑ 2310747	Montreux '75	1976	12.00
❑ 2310779	Porgy and Bess	1976	12.00
❑ 2310796	Giants	1977	12.00
❑ 2310817	Jousts	1979	12.00
❑ 2310895	History of An Artist, Vol. 2	1983	12.00
❑ 2310918	If You Could See Me Now	1987	10.00
❑ 2310927	Oscar Peterson + Harry Edison + Eddie "Cleanhead" Vinson	1988	10.00
❑ 2310940	Live	1990	10.00
❑ 2625702 [(2)]	History of An Artist	1975	15.00
❑ 2625705 [(2)]	A Salle Pleyel	1975	15.00
❑ 2625711 [(2)]	Oscar Peterson in Russia	1976	12.00
❑ 2640101 [(2)]	Freedom Songbook	1983	15.00

PABLO LIVE

Number	Title (A Side/B Side)	Yr	NM
❑ 2308208	Oscar Peterson Jam — Montreux '77	1977	12.00
❑ 2308213	Oscar Peterson and the Bassists — Montreux '77	1978	12.00
❑ 2308224	Digital at Montreux	1980	12.00
❑ 2308231	Nigerian Marketplace	1982	12.00
❑ 2308232	Skol	1982	12.00
❑ 2308241	The Good Life	1983	12.00
❑ 2620111 [(2)]	The London Concert	1979	15.00
❑ 2620112 [(2)]	The Paris Concert	1979	15.00
❑ 2620115 [(2)]	Live at the Northsea Jazz Festival, 1980	1981	15.00

PABLO TODAY

Number	Title (A Side/B Side)	Yr	NM
❑ 2312108	Night Child	1979	12.00
❑ 2312129	A Royal Wedding Suite	198?	12.00
❑ 2312135	The Personal Touch	1982	12.00
❑ 2313103	Silent Partner	1980	12.00

PAUSA

Number	Title (A Side/B Side)	Yr	NM
❑ PR 7044	Mellow Mood	1979	10.00
❑ PR 7059	Action	1980	10.00
❑ PR 7064	Girl Talk	1980	10.00
❑ PR 7069	My Favorite Instrument	1980	10.00
❑ PR 7073	In Tune	1980	10.00
—Reissue of BASF 20905			
❑ PR 7080	The Way I Really Play	1981	10.00
❑ PR 7099	Reunion Blues	1981	10.00
—Reissue of BASF 20908			
❑ PR 7102	Motions and Emotions	1982	10.00
—Reissue of BASF 20713			
❑ PR 7113	Great Connection	1983	10.00
—Reissue of BASF 21281			
❑ PR 7124	Tristeza on Piano	1983	10.00
—Reissue of BASF 20734			
❑ PR 7135	Another Day	1983	10.00
—Reissue of BASF 20869			

PRESTIGE

Number	Title (A Side/B Side)	Yr	NM
❑ PRST-7595	Soul-O!	1968	15.00
❑ PRST-7620	The Great Oscar Peterson on Prestige!	1969	15.00
❑ PRST-7649	Oscar Peterson Plays for Lovers	1969	15.00
❑ PRST-7690	Easy Walker	1969	15.00

RCA VICTOR

Number	Title (A Side/B Side)	Yr	NM
❑ LPT-3006 [10]	This Is Oscar Peterson	1952	120.00

TRIP

Number	Title (A Side/B Side)	Yr	NM
❑ 5560	Eloquence	197?	10.00

VERVE

Number	Title (A Side/B Side)	Yr	NM
❑ VSP-11 [M]	Stage Right	1966	12.00
❑ VSPS-11 [S]	Stage Right	1966	15.00
❑ MGV-2002 [M]	In a Romantic Mood — Oscar Peterson with Strings	1956	40.00
❑ V-2002 [M]	In a Romantic Mood — Oscar Peterson with Strings	1961	20.00
❑ MGV-2004 [M]	Pastel Moods by Oscar Peterson	1956	40.00
❑ V-2004 [M]	Pastel Moods by Oscar Peterson	1961	20.00
❑ MGV-2012 [M]	Romance — The Vocal Styling of Oscar Peterson	1956	40.00
—Reissue of Clef 145			
❑ V-2012 [M]	Romance — The Vocal Styling of Oscar Peterson	1961	20.00
❑ MGV-2044 [M]	Recital by Oscar Peterson	1957	40.00
—Reissue of Clef 694			
❑ V-2044 [M]	Recital by Oscar Peterson	1961	20.00
❑ MGV-2045 [M]	Nostalgic Memories by Oscar Peterson	1957	40.00
—Reissue of Clef 695			
❑ V-2045 [M]	Nostalgic Memories by Oscar Peterson	1961	20.00
❑ MGV-2046 [M]	Tenderly — Music by Oscar Peterson	1957	40.00
—Reissue of Clef 696			
❑ V-2046 [M]	Tenderly — Music by Oscar Peterson	1961	20.00
❑ MGV-2047 [M]	Keyboard Music by Oscar Peterson	1957	40.00
—Reissue of Clef 697			
❑ V-2047 [M]	Keyboard Music by Oscar Peterson	1961	20.00
❑ MGV-2048 [M]	An Evening with Oscar Peterson	1957	40.00
—Reissue of Clef 698			
❑ V-2048 [M]	An Evening with Oscar Peterson	1961	20.00
❑ MGV-2052 [M]	Oscar Peterson Plays the Cole Porter Songbook	1957	40.00
—Reissue of Clef 603			
❑ V-2052 [M]	Oscar Peterson Plays the Cole Porter Songbook	1961	20.00
❑ V6-2052 [S]	Oscar Peterson Plays the Cole Porter Songbook	1961	15.00
—Reissue of 6083			
❑ MGV-2053 [M]	Oscar Peterson Plays the Irving Berlin Songbook	1957	40.00
—Reissue of Clef 604			
❑ V-2053 [M]	Oscar Peterson Plays the Irving Berlin Songbook	1961	20.00
❑ V6-2053 [S]	Oscar Peterson Plays the Irving Berlin Songbook	1961	15.00
—Reissue of 6084			
❑ MGV-2054 [M]	Oscar Peterson Plays the George Gershwin Songbook	1957	40.00
—Reissue of Clef 605			
❑ V-2054 [M]	Oscar Peterson Plays the George Gershwin Songbook	1961	20.00
❑ V6-2054 [S]	Oscar Peterson Plays the George Gershwin Songbook	1961	15.00
—Reissue of 6085			
❑ MGV-2055 [M]	Oscar Peterson Plays the Duke Ellington Songbook	1957	40.00
—Reissue of Clef 606			
❑ V-2055 [M]	Oscar Peterson Plays the Duke Ellington Songbook	1961	20.00
❑ V6-2055 [S]	Oscar Peterson Plays the Duke Ellington Songbook	1961	15.00
—Reissue of 6086			
❑ MGV-2056 [M]	Oscar Peterson Plays the Jerome Kern Songbook	1957	40.00
—Reissue of Clef 623			
❑ V-2056 [M]	Oscar Peterson Plays the Jerome Kern Songbook	1961	20.00
❑ V6-2056 [S]	Oscar Peterson Plays the Jerome Kern Songbook	1961	15.00
—Reissue of 6087			
❑ MGV-2057 [M]	Oscar Peterson Plays the Richard Rodgers Songbook	1957	40.00
—Reissue of Clef 624			
❑ V-2057 [M]	Oscar Peterson Plays the Richard Rodgers Songbook	1961	20.00
❑ V6-2057 [S]	Oscar Peterson Plays the Richard Rodgers Songbook	1961	15.00
—Reissue of 6088			
❑ MGV-2058 [M]	Oscar Peterson Plays the Vincent Youmans Songbook	1957	—
—Reissue planned but canceled			

Number	Title (A Side/B Side)	Yr	NM
❑ MGV-2059 [M]	Oscar Peterson Plays the Harry Warren Songbook	1957	40.00
—Reissue of Clef 648			
❑ V-2059 [M]	Oscar Peterson Plays the Harry Warren Songbook	1961	20.00
❑ V6-2059 [S]	Oscar Peterson Plays the Harry Warren Songbook	1961	15.00
—Reissue of 6090			
❑ MGV-2060 [M]	Oscar Peterson Plays the Harold Arlen Songbook	1957	40.00
—Reissue of Clef 649			
❑ V-2060 [M]	Oscar Peterson Plays the Harold Arlen Songbook	1961	20.00
❑ V6-2060 [S]	Oscar Peterson Plays the Harold Arlen Songbook	1961	15.00
—Reissue of 6091			
❑ MGV-2061 [M]	Oscar Peterson Plays the Jimmy McHugh Songbook	1957	40.00
—Reissue of Clef 650			
❑ V-2061 [M]	Oscar Peterson Plays the Jimmy McHugh Songbook	1961	20.00
❑ V6-2061 [S]	Oscar Peterson Plays the Jimmy McHugh Songbook	1961	15.00
—Reissue of 6092			
❑ MGV-2079 [M]	Soft Sands	1957	40.00
❑ V-2079 [M]	Soft Sands	1961	20.00
❑ MGV-2119 [M]	Oscar Peterson Plays "My Fair Lady"	1958	40.00
❑ V-2119 [M]	Oscar Peterson Plays "My Fair Lady"	1961	20.00
❑ V6-2119 [S]	Oscar Peterson Plays "My Fair Lady"	1961	15.00
—Reissue of 6060			
❑ MGV-2156 [M]	The Oscar Peterson Trio with David Rose	1958	—
—Canceled			
❑ UMV-2502	Oscar Peterson at the Stratford Shakespearean Festival	198?	10.00
❑ UMV-2626	Oscar Peterson at the Concertgebouw	198?	10.00
❑ BOMC 70-5601 [S]	Night Train	197?	25.00
—Book-of-the-Month Club edition			
❑ 30-5606 [M]	The Oscar Peterson Quartet #1	197?	12.00
—Book-of-the-Month Club edition			
❑ MGVS-6036 [S]	A Night on the Town	1960	—
—Canceled			
❑ MGVS-6060 [S]	Oscar Peterson Plays "My Fair Lady"	1960	30.00
❑ MGVS-6069 [S]	The Oscar Peterson Trio with the Modern Jazz Quartet at the Opera House	1960	30.00
❑ MGVS-6071 [S]	Songs for a Swingin' Affair — A Jazz Portrait of Sinatra	1960	40.00
❑ MGVS-6083 [S]	Oscar Peterson Plays the Cole Porter Songbook	1960	30.00
❑ MGVS-6084 [S]	Oscar Peterson Plays the Irving Berlin Songbook	1960	30.00
❑ MGVS-6085 [S]	Oscar Peterson Plays the George Gershwin Songbook	1960	30.00
❑ MGVS-6086 [S]	Oscar Peterson Plays the Duke Ellington Songbook	1960	30.00
❑ MGVS-6087 [S]	Oscar Peterson Plays the Jerome Kern Songbook	1960	30.00
❑ MGVS-6088 [S]	Oscar Peterson Plays the Richard Rodgers Songbook	1960	30.00
❑ MGVS-6089 [S]	Oscar Peterson Plays the Vincent Youmans Songbook	1960	—
—Canceled			
❑ MGVS-6090 [S]	Oscar Peterson Plays the Harry Warren Songbook	1960	30.00
❑ MGVS-6091 [S]	Oscar Peterson Plays the Harold Arlen Songbook	1960	30.00
❑ MGVS-6092 [S]	Oscar Peterson Plays the Jimmy McHugh Songbook	1960	30.00
❑ MGVS-6098 [S]	Porgy and Bess	1960	—
—Canceled			
❑ MGVS-6116 [S]	The Jazz Soul of Oscar Peterson	1960	—
—Canceled			
❑ MGVS-6119 [S]	Swinging Brass with the Oscar Peterson Trio	1960	30.00
❑ MGVS-6134 [S]	The Music from "Fiorello!"	1960	—
—Canceled			
❑ MGV-8024 [M]	The Oscar Peterson Trio at the Stratford Shakespearean Festival	1957	40.00
❑ V-8024 [M]	The Oscar Peterson Trio at the Stratford Shakespearean Festival	1961	20.00
❑ MGV-8072 [M]	The Oscar Peterson Quartet No. 1	1957	40.00
❑ V-8072 [M]	The Oscar Peterson Quartet No. 1	1961	20.00
❑ MGV-8078 [M]	Recital by Oscar Peterson	1957	—
—Canceled			
❑ MGV-8079 [M]	Nostalgic Memories by Oscar Peterson	1957	—
—Canceled			

Number	Title (A Side/B Side)	Yr	NM
❑ MGV-8080 [M]	Tenderly — Music by Oscar Peterson	1957	—
—Canceled			
❑ MGV-8081 [M]	Keyboard Music by Oscar Peterson	1957	—
—Canceled			
❑ MGV-8082 [M]	An Evening with Oscar Peterson	1957	—
—Canceled			
❑ MGV-8092 [M]	Oscar Peterson Plays Count Basie	1957	40.00
—Reissue of Clef 708			
❑ V-8092 [M]	Oscar Peterson Plays Count Basie	1961	20.00
❑ MGV-8239 [M]	The Oscar Peterson Trio with Sonny Stitt, Roy Eldredge and Jo Jones at Newport	1958	40.00
❑ V-8239 [M]	The Oscar Peterson Trio with Sonny Stitt, Roy Eldredge and Jo Jones at Newport	1961	20.00
❑ MGV-8268 [M]	The Oscar Peterson Trio at the Concertgebouw	1958	40.00
❑ V-8268 [M]	The Oscar Peterson Trio at the Concertgebouw	1961	20.00
❑ MGV-8269 [M]	The Oscar Peterson Trio with the Modern Jazz Quartet at the Opera House	1958	40.00
❑ V-8269 [M]	The Oscar Peterson Trio with the Modern Jazz Quartet at the Opera House	1961	20.00
❑ V6-8269 [S]	The Oscar Peterson Trio with the Modern Jazz Quartet at the Opera House	1961	15.00
—Reissue of 6069			
❑ MGV-8287 [M]	A Night on the Town	1958	40.00
❑ V-8287 [M]	A Night on the Town	1961	20.00
❑ MGV-8334 [M]	Songs for a Swingin' Affair — A Jazz Portrait of Sinatra	1959	50.00
❑ V-8334 [M]	Songs for a Swingin' Affair — A Jazz Portrait of Sinatra	1961	20.00
❑ V6-8334 [S]	Songs for a Swingin' Affair — A Jazz Portrait of Sinatra	1961	15.00
—Reissue of 6071			
❑ MGV-8340 [M]	Porgy and Bess	1959	40.00
❑ V-8340 [M]	Porgy and Bess	1961	20.00
❑ V6-8340 [S]	Porgy and Bess	1961	15.00
❑ MGV-8351 [M]	The Jazz Soul of Oscar Peterson	1959	40.00
❑ V-8351 [M]	The Jazz Soul of Oscar Peterson	1961	20.00
❑ MGV-8364 [M]	Swinging Brass with the Oscar Peterson Trio	1959	40.00
❑ V-8364 [M]	Swinging Brass with the Oscar Peterson Trio	1961	20.00
❑ V6-8364 [S]	Swinging Brass with the Oscar Peterson Trio	1961	15.00
—Reissue of 6119			
❑ MGV-8366 [M]	The Music from "Fiorello!"	1960	40.00
❑ V-8366 [M]	The Music from "Fiorello!"	1961	20.00
❑ MGV-8368 [M]	The Oscar Peterson Trio at J.A.T.P.	1960	40.00
❑ V-8368 [M]	The Oscar Peterson Trio at J.A.T.P.	1961	20.00
❑ MGV-8399 [M]	Carnival	1960	—
—Canceled			
❑ V-8420 [M]	The Trio — Live from Chicago	1961	25.00
❑ V6-8420 [S]	The Trio — Live from Chicago	1961	30.00
❑ V-8429 [M]	Very Tall	1962	25.00
❑ V6-8429 [S]	Very Tall	1962	30.00
❑ V-8454 [M]	West Side Story	1962	25.00
❑ V6-8454 [S]	West Side Story	1962	30.00
❑ V-8476 [M]	Bursting Out with the All Star Big Band!	1962	25.00
❑ V6-8476 [S]	Bursting Out with the All Star Big Band!	1962	30.00
❑ V-8480 [M]	The Sound of the Trio	1962	25.00
❑ V6-8480 [S]	The Sound of the Trio	1962	30.00
❑ V-8482 [M]	The Modern Jazz Quartet and the Oscar Petereson Trio at the Opera House	1962	20.00
—Reissue of 8269			
❑ V6-8482 [S]	The Modern Jazz Quartet and the Oscar Petereson Trio at the Opera House	1962	20.00
—Reissue of 8269			
❑ V-8516 [M]	Affinity	1963	25.00
❑ V6-8516 [S]	Affinity	1963	30.00
❑ V-8538 [M]	Night Train	1963	25.00
❑ V6-8538 [S]	Night Train	1963	30.00
❑ V-8562 [M]	The Oscar Peterson Trio with Nelson Riddle	1963	25.00
❑ V6-8562 [S]	The Oscar Peterson Trio with Nelson Riddle	1963	30.00
❑ V-8581 [M]	Oscar Peterson Plays "My Fair Lady"	1964	15.00
❑ V6-8581 [S]	Oscar Peterson Plays "My Fair Lady"	1964	20.00
❑ V-8591 [M]	The Oscar Peterson Trio Plays	1964	15.00
❑ V6-8591 [S]	The Oscar Peterson Trio Plays	1964	20.00
❑ V-8606 [M]	We Get Requests	1965	15.00
❑ V6-8606 [S]	We Get Requests	1965	20.00
❑ V-8660 [M]	Put On a Happy Face	1966	15.00

Number	Title (A Side/B Side)	Yr	NM
❑ V6-8660 [S]	Put On a Happy Face	1966	20.00
❑ V-8681 [M]	Something Warm	1966	15.00
❑ V6-8681 [S]	Something Warm	1966	20.00
❑ V-8700 [M]	Thoroughly Modern '20s	1967	15.00
❑ V6-8700 [S]	Thoroughly Modern '20s	1967	15.00
❑ V-8740 [M]	Night Train, Vol. 2	1967	20.00
❑ V6-8740 [S]	Night Train, Vol. 2	1967	15.00
❑ V6-8775	Oscars — Oscar Peterson Plays the Academy Awards	1969	15.00
❑ V6-8810 [(2)]	The Oscar Peterson Collection	1972	15.00
❑ V3G-8828	The Newport Years	1974	12.00
❑ V3HB-8842 [(2)]	Return Engagement	1975	15.00
❑ 810047-1	We Get Requests	1986	10.00
❑ 821289-1	Motions and Emotions	1984	10.00
—Reissue			
❑ 821663-1	Travelin' On	1985	10.00
❑ 821849-1	Tracks	1985	10.00
❑ 821987-1	Oscar Peterson Plays the Cole Porter Songbook	1986	10.00
—Reissue of 2053			
❑ 823249-1	Oscar Peterson Plays the George Gershwin Songbook	1985	10.00
—Reissue of 2054			
❑ 825099-1	The Oscar Peterson Trio Set	1985	10.00
❑ 825769-1	Songs for a Swingin' Affair — A Jazz Portrait of Sinatra	1985	10.00
—Reissue of 8334			
❑ 825865-1	Oscar Peterson Plays the Jerome Kern Songbook	1985	10.00
—Reissue of 2056			
❑ 833552 [(2)]	Return Engagement	198?	12.00
—Reissue of 8842 (though the labels may still use the old number)			
WING			
❑ SRW 16351	Canadiana Suite	1969	12.00

PETERSON, OSCAR, AND HERB ELLIS

Albums

Number	Title (A Side/B Side)	Yr	NM
BASF			
❑ 20723	Hello Herbie	1969	15.00
PAUSA			
❑ PR 7085	Hello Herbie	1981	10.00
—Reissue			

PETERSON, OSCAR, AND STEPHANE GRAPPELLI

Albums

Number	Title (A Side/B Side)	Yr	NM
JAZZ MAN			
❑ 5054	Time After Time	1983	12.00
PABLO			
❑ 2310907	Violins No End	198?	12.00
—With Stuff Smith			
PRESTIGE			
❑ 24041 [(2)]	Oscar Peterson Featuring Stephane Grappelli	1974	15.00

PETERSON, OSCAR, AND MILT JACKSON

Albums

Number	Title (A Side/B Side)	Yr	NM
PABLO			
❑ 2310881	Two of the Few	1983	12.00

PETERSON, OSCAR/GERRY MULLIGAN

Albums

Number	Title (A Side/B Side)	Yr	NM
VERVE			
❑ V-8559 [M]	The Oscar Peterson Trio and the Gerry Mulligan Four at Newport	1963	25.00
❑ V6-8559 [S]	The Oscar Peterson Trio and the Gerry Mulligan Four at Newport	1963	30.00

PETERSON, RAY

45s

Number	Title (A Side/B Side)	Yr	NM
CLOUD 9			
❑ 134	Nobody But Me/(B-side unknown)	1975	5.00
DECCA			
❑ 32861	Stamp Out Loneliness/There's a Better Way	1971	5.00
DUNES			
❑ 2002	Corrina, Corinna/Be My Girl	1960	25.00
—Produced by Phil Spector			
❑ 2002 [PS]	Corrina, Corinna/Be My Girl	1960	60.00
❑ 2004	Sweet Little Kathy/You Didn't Care	1961	15.00
❑ 2006	Missing You/You Thrill Me	1961	15.00
❑ 2009	I Could Have Loved You So Well/Why Don't You Write Me	1961	20.00
—Produced by Phil Spector			
❑ 2013	You Know Me Much Too Well/You Didn't Care	1962	15.00
❑ 2018	If Only Tomorrow/You Didn't Care	1962	15.00
❑ 2019	Is It Wrong/Slowly	1963	15.00
❑ 2022	A Love to Remember/I'm Not Jimmy	1963	15.00
❑ 2024	Where Are You/Deep Are the Roots	1963	15.00

P

Number	Title (A Side/B Side)	Yr	NM
❑ 2025	Give Us Your Blessing/Without Love (There Is Nothing)	1963	15.00
❑ 2027	I Forgot What It Was Like/ Be My Girl	1963	15.00
❑ 2030	Promises/Sweet Little Kathy	1963	15.00
MGM			
❑ 13269	If You Were Here/Oh No	1964	10.00
❑ 13269 [PS]	If You Were Here/Oh No	1964	15.00
❑ 13299	Across the Street (Is a Million Miles Away)/When I Stop Dreaming	1964	10.00
❑ 13330	Unchained Melody/That's All	1965	8.00
❑ 13336	A House Without Windows/ Wish I Could Say No to You	1965	8.00
❑ 13388	I'm Only Human/ One Lonesome Rose	1965	8.00
❑ 13436	Love Hurts/Everybody	1966	8.00
❑ 13508	Amanda/I'm Gonna Change Everything	1966	8.00
❑ 13564	Just One Smile/The Whole World's Goin' Crazy	1966	8.00
RCA			
❑ GB-11758	Tell Laura I Love Her/The Wonder of You	1979	3.00
—Gold Standard Series			
RCA VICTOR			
❑ 37-7845	My Blue Angel/I'm Tired	1961	50.00
—"Compact Single 33" (small hole, plays at LP speed)			
❑ 47-7087	Fever/We're Old Enough to Cry	1957	25.00
❑ 47-7165	Let's Try Romance/ Shirley Purley	1958	20.00
❑ 47-7255	Suddenly/Tall Light	1958	20.00
❑ 47-7303	Patricia/The Blue-Eyed Baby	1958	20.00
❑ 47-7336	Dream Way/I'll Always Want You Near	1958	20.00
❑ 47-7404	Richer Than I/Love Is a Woman	1958	20.00
❑ 47-7513	The Wonder of You/I'm Gone	1959	25.00
❑ 47-7578	My Blue Angel/Come and Get It	1959	20.00
❑ 47-7635	Goodnight My Love (Pleasant Dreams)/Till Then	1959	20.00
❑ 47-7635 [PS]	Goodnight My Love (Pleasant Dreams)/Till Then	1959	30.00
❑ 47-7703	Answer Me, My Love/What Do You Want to Make Those Eyes At Me For	1960	20.00
❑ 47-7745	Tell Laura I Love Her/ Wedding Days	1960	25.00
❑ 47-7779	Teenage Heartache /I'll Always Want You Near	1960	20.00
❑ 47-7845	My Blue Angel/I'm Tired	1961	20.00
❑ 47-8333	The Wonder of You/Goodnight My Love	1964	10.00
❑ 61-7578 [S]	My Blue Angel/Come and Get It	1959	80.00
—"Living Stereo" (large hole, plays at 45 rpm)			
❑ 61-7745 [S]	Tell Laura I Love Her/ Wedding Days	1960	100.00
—"Living Stereo" (large hole, plays at 45 rpm)			
REPRISE			
❑ 0811	Love Rules the World/Together	1969	8.00
UNI			
❑ 55249	Love the Understanding Way/ Oklahoma City Rimes	1970	8.00
❑ 55268	Tell Laura I Love Her/ To Wait for Love	1971	6.00
❑ 55275	Fever/Changes	1971	6.00

7-Inch Extended Plays

Number	Title (A Side/B Side)	Yr	NM
RCA VICTOR			
❑ EPA-4367	Tell Laura I Love Her/Suddenly// Fever/The Wonder of You	1960	120.00
❑ EPA-4367 [PS]	Tell Laura I Love Her	1960	120.00

Albums

Number	Title (A Side/B Side)	Yr	NM
DECCA			
❑ DL 75307	Ray Peterson Country	1971	20.00
MGM			
❑ E-4250 [M]	The Very Best of Ray Peterson	1964	25.00
❑ SE-4250 [S]	The Very Best of Ray Peterson	1964	30.00
❑ E-4277 [M]	The Other Side of Ray Peterson	1965	25.00
❑ SE-4277 [S]	The Other Side of Ray Peterson	1965	30.00
RCA CAMDEN			
❑ CAL-2119 [M]	Goodnight My Love	1966	12.00
❑ CAS-2119 [S]	Goodnight My Love	1966	12.00
RCA VICTOR			
❑ LPM-2297 [M]	Tell Laura I Love Her	1960	100.00
❑ LSP-2297 [S]	Tell Laura I Love Her	1960	150.00
UNI			
❑ 73078	Missing You/Featuring His Greatest Hits!	1969	20.00

PETRIFIED FOREST, THE

45s

Number	Title (A Side/B Side)	Yr	NM
FONTANA			
❑ 1596	So Mystifying/She's the Only Thing That's Kept Me Going	1967	15.00

PETS, THE

45s

Number	Title (A Side/B Side)	Yr	NM
ARWIN			
❑ 109	Cha-Hua-Hua/Cha-Kow-Ski	1958	15.00
❑ 112	Wow-Ee!!!/Beyond the Sea	1958	15.00
❑ 116	Guitarro/Whatever Will Be, Will Be	1958	15.00

PETTICOATS, THE (1)

45s

Number	Title (A Side/B Side)	Yr	NM
CHALLENGE			
❑ 9211	Surfin' Sally/Why Does Billy Play in Your Yard	1963	25.00

PETTICOATS, THE (2)

45s

Number	Title (A Side/B Side)	Yr	NM
DOT			
❑ 16052	By the Light of the Silvery Moon/ Troubadour	1960	20.00
❑ 16155	For Sentimental Reasons/ Cincinnati	1960	20.00

PETTICOATS, THE (3)

45s

Number	Title (A Side/B Side)	Yr	NM
PREP			
❑ 125	I Ain't Gonna Do It No More/ Manhattan Mountains	1957	20.00
UNIQUE			
❑ 344	The Motorboat Song/ The First One	1956	20.00
❑ 363	High Heels/I'll Go Along with You	1956	20.00
❑ 387	In My Loving Heart/ Michigan Bankroll	1957	20.00

PETTY, NORMAN, TRIO

Also see THE PICKS.

45s

Number	Title (A Side/B Side)	Yr	NM
ABC-PARAMOUNT			
❑ 9787	Almost Paradise/It's Been a Long, Long Time	1957	12.00
COLUMBIA			
❑ 40929	The First Kiss/(Instrumental)	1957	12.00
❑ 41039	Moondreams/Toy Boy	1957	100.00
—With Buddy Holly on guitar			
FELSTED			
❑ 8647	Mood Indigo/On the Alamo	1962	10.00
JARO			
❑ 77027	Ditty Dum/Bring Your Heart	1960	12.00
"X"			
❑ 0040	Mood Indigo/Petty's Little Polka	1954	12.00
❑ 0071	On the Alamo/Echo Polka	1954	12.00
❑ 0104	I Wonder Why/Three Little Kisses	1955	12.00
❑ 0130	Oh! You Pretty Woman/ Hey! Good Lookin'	1955	12.00
❑ 0167	Solitude/When It's Darkness on the Delta	1955	12.00

7-Inch Extended Plays

Number	Title (A Side/B Side)	Yr	NM
COLUMBIA			
❑ B-10921	(contents unknown)	1958	100.00
❑ B-10921 [PS]	Moondreams	1958	100.00
"X"			
❑ EXA-82	(contents unknown)	1955	20.00
❑ EXA-82 [PS]	The Norman Petty Trio In Full Fidelity	1955	20.00

Albums

Number	Title (A Side/B Side)	Yr	NM
COLUMBIA			
❑ CL 1092 [M]	Moondreams	1958	150.00
TOP RANK			
❑ R-639 [M]	Petty for Your Thoughts	1960	30.00
❑ RS-639 [S]	Petty for Your Thoughts	1960	40.00
VIK			
❑ LX-1073 [M]	Corsage	1957	70.00

PETTY, TOM, AND THE HEARTBREAKERS

Includes Tom Petty solo. Also see STEVIE NICKS; TRAVELING WILBURYS. Includes Tom Petty solo. Also see STEVIE NICKS; TRAVELING WILBURYS.

12-Inch Singles

Number	Title (A Side/B Side)	Yr	NM
MCA			
❑ L33-17033 [DJ]	Rebels (LP Version 5:20) (Special Live Version 6:19)	1985	12.00

45s

Number	Title (A Side/B Side)	Yr	NM
BACKSTREET			
❑ 41138	Don't Do Me Like That/ Casa Dega	1979	4.00
❑ 41138 [PS]	Don't Do Me Like That/ Casa Dega	1979	5.00
❑ 41169	Refugee/It's Rainin' Again	1980	4.00
❑ 41169 [PS]	Refugee/It's Rainin' Again	1980	5.00
❑ 41227	Here Comes My Girl/ Louisiana Rain	1980	4.00
❑ 41227 [PS]	Here Comes My Girl/ Louisiana Rain	1980	5.00
❑ 51100	The Waiting/Nightwatchman	1981	4.00
❑ 51100 [PS]	The Waiting/Nightwatchman	1981	4.00
❑ 51136	A Woman in Love (It's Not Me)/ Gator on the Lawn	1981	4.00
❑ 51136 [PS]	A Woman in Love (It's Not Me)/ Gator on the Lawn	1981	4.00
❑ 52144	You Got Lucky/Between Two Worlds	1982	4.00
❑ 52144 [PS]	You Got Lucky/Between Two Worlds	1982	4.00
❑ 52181	Change of Heart/ Heartbreakers Beach Party	1983	3.00
❑ 52181	Change of Heart/ Heartbreakers Beach Party	1983	8.00
—Red vinyl in clear plastic sleeve with sticker			
❑ 52181 [PS]	Change of Heart/ Heartbreakers Beach Party	1983	4.00
—Only issued with black-vinyl versions			
MCA			
❑ 52496	Don't Come Around Here No More/Trailer	1985	4.00
—Second pressings feature a 5-plus-minute version of the A-side			
❑ 52496	Don't Come Around Here No More/Trailer	1985	4.00
—Original copies have a 4:19 version of the A-side			
❑ 52496 [PS]	Don't Come Around Here No More/Trailer	1985	4.00
❑ 52605	Make It Better (Forget About Me)/Crackin' Up	1985	3.00
❑ 52605 [PS]	Make It Better (Forget About Me)/Crackin' Up	1985	3.00
❑ 52658	Rebels/Southern Accents	1985	3.00
❑ 52658 [PS]	Rebels/Southern Accents	1985	3.00
❑ 52772	Needles and Pins/Spike	1985	3.00
—A-side: With Stevie Nicks			
❑ 52772 [PS]	Needles and Pins/Spike	1985	3.00
❑ 53065	Jammin' Me/Make That Connection	1987	3.00
❑ 53065 [PS]	Jammin' Me/Make That Connection	1987	3.00
❑ 53153	All Mixed Up/Let Me Up (I've Had Enough)	1987	3.00
❑ 53153 [PS]	All Mixed Up/Let Me Up (I've Had Enough)	1987	3.00
❑ 53369	I Won't Back Down/ The Apartment Song	1989	4.00
❑ 53369	I Won't Back Down/ The Apartment Song	1989	25.00
—Special vinyl promo cover			
❑ 53682	Runnin' Down a Dream/ Alright for Now	1989	4.00
❑ 53748	Free Fallin'/Down the Line	1989	5.00
❑ 53781	A Face in the Crowd/A Mind with a Heart of Its Own	1990	4.00
❑ 54124	Learning to Fly/Too Good to Be True	1991	4.00
❑ 54131	Into the Great Wide Open/ Makin' Some Noise	1991	4.00
❑ 54387	King's Highway/All or Nothin'	1992	4.00
❑ 54732	Mary Jane's Last Dance/ The Waiting	1993	4.00
❑ 79030	Yer So Bad/Love Is a Long Road	1990	4.00
SHELTER			
❑ 62006	Breakdown/The Wild One, Forever	1976	—
—Unreleased?			
❑ 62006 [DJ]	Breakdown (Mono)/ Breakdown (Stereo)	1976	10.00
❑ 62006 [DJ]	Breakdown (Mono)/ Breakdown (Stereo)	1976	10.00
❑ 62007	American Girl/Luna	1977	6.00
❑ 62008	Breakdown/Fooled Again (I Can't Take It)	1977	6.00
❑ 62010	I Need to Know/No Second Thoughts	1978	5.00
❑ 62011	Listen to Her Heart/I Don't Know What to Say to You	1978	5.00
❑ 62011 [PS]	Listen to Her Heart/I Don't Know What to Say to You	1978	5.00
WARNER BROS.			
❑ 17593	Walls (Circus)/Walls (No. 3)	1996	3.00
❑ 17925	It's Good to Be King/Cabin Down Below	1995	3.00
❑ 18026	A Higher Place/Only a Broken Heart	1995	3.00
❑ 18030	You Don't Know How It Feels/ Girl on LSD	1994	3.00

Albums

Number	Title (A Side/B Side)	Yr	NM
AMERICAN			
❑ 44285-1 [(2)]	Highway Companion	2007	25.00
—180-gram issue; CD released in 2006			
BACKSTREET			
❑ BSR-5105	Damn the Torpedoes	1979	10.00

Except when noted otherwise, VG = 25% of NM, and VG+ = 50% of NM. (Example: VG = $2.00, VG+ = $4.00 and NM = $8.00.)

Number	Title (A Side/B Side)	Yr	NM
❑ BSR-5160	Hard Promises	1981	10.00
❑ BSR-5360	Long After Dark	1982	10.00
MCA			
❑ 1486	Damn the Torpedoes	1987	8.00
❑ 5486	Southern Accents	1985	10.00
❑ 5836	Let Me Up (I've Had Enough)	1987	10.00
❑ 6253	Full Moon Fever	1989	10.00
❑ 2-8021 [(2)]	Pack Up the Plantation — Live!	1985	12.00
❑ 10317	Into the Great Wide Open	1991	20.00
❑ 37116	You're Gonna Get It!	1982	8.00
❑ 37143	Tom Petty and the Heartbreakers	1982	8.00
❑ 37239	Hard Promises	1984	8.00
SHELTER			
❑ DA-52029 [DJ]	You're Gonna Get It!	1978	25.00
—Promo only on red vinyl			
❑ TP-12677 [DJ]	Official Live 'Leg	1977	40.00
—Promo-only live album with letter to radio (has been counterfeited)			
❑ TP-12677 [DJ]	Official Live 'Leg	1977	40.00
—Promo-only live album with letter to radio (has been counterfeited)			
❑ SRL-52006	Tom Petty and the Heartbreakers	1976	15.00
—Original copies were distributed by ABC			
❑ SRL-52006	Tom Petty and the Heartbreakers	1979	12.00
—Later copies were distributed by MCA			
❑ DA-52029	You're Gonna Get It!	1978	15.00
—Original copies were distributed by ABC			
❑ DA-52029	You're Gonna Get It!	1979	12.00
—Later copies were distributed by MCA			
❑ DA-52029 [DJ]	You're Gonna Get It!	1978	25.00
—Promo only on red vinyl			
WARNER BROS.			
❑ 45759 [(2)]	Wildflowers	1994	30.00
❑ 46285	Songs and Music from the Motion Picture "She's the One"	1996	10.00
❑ 47294 [(2)]	Echo	1999	20.00
❑ 47955	The Last DJ	2002	20.00
PHAETONS, THE			
45s			
HI-Q			
❑ 5012	Fling/Homemade	1959	20.00
SAHARA			
❑ 102	I'm So Lonely/Road of Blues	1963	20.00
❑ 103	The Beatle Walk/Frantic	1964	50.00
—B-side by the Premiers			
VIN			
❑ 1015	I Love My Baby/As You Know	1959	60.00
WARNER BROS.			
❑ 7082	She Came Like the Rain/Three Weeks, Four Days and Fifteen Hours	1967	10.00
❑ 7205	Leave It to Me/You'd Better Come Home	1968	10.00
PHAFNER			
45s			
DRAGON			
❑ 1001	Overdrive/Plea from the Soul	1971	200.00
Albums			
DRAGON			
❑ LP-101	Overdrive	1971	3000.
—VG value 1000; VG+ value 2000			
PHANTOM, THE (1)			
45s			
CAPITOL			
❑ F3427	Whispering/Five Foot Two, Eyes of Blue	1956	20.00
PHANTOM, THE (2)			
45s			
DOT			
❑ 16056	Love Me/Whisper Your Love	1960	150.00
❑ 16056 [PS]	Love Me/Whisper Your Love	1960	300.00
PHANTOM'S DIVINE COMEDY			
45s			
HIDEOUT			
❑ 1080	Calm Before the Storm/Black Magic, White Magic	1974	20.00
Albums			
CAPITOL			
❑ ST-11313	The Phantom's Divine Comedy, Part One	1974	75.00
PHELPS, JAMES			
45s			
ARGO			
❑ 5499	Love Is a Five-Letter Word/I'll Do the Best I Can	1965	8.00
❑ 5509	La De Da, I'm a Fool in Love/Wasting Time	1965	8.00
CADET			
❑ 5534	Oh, What a Feeling/Action	1966	8.00
FONTANA			
❑ 1581	Don't Be a Cry Baby/Walking the Floor Over You	1967	6.00
❑ 1600	Fabulous One/The Wrong Number	1967	6.00
PARAMOUNT			
❑ 0136	My Lover's Prayer/Check Yourself	1971	5.00
PHIL AND DEL			
45s			
LINDA			
❑ 105	My Girl/Don't Play with Love	1962	12.00
RAMPART			
❑ 656	It Hurts Me/These Feelings	196?	10.00
PHIL AND HARV			
45s			
RAMPART			
❑ 611	Darling (Please Bring Your Love)/Friendship	196?	12.00
❑ 612	Sweeter Than Candy/The Facts of Love	196?	12.00
PHILADELPHIA EXPERIMENT, THE			
Albums			
ATLANTIC			
❑ 93042 [(2)]	The Philadelphia Experiment	2001	15.00
PHILADELPHIA STRUMMERS, THE			
45s			
PARKWAY			
❑ 816	I Ain't Down Yet/Every Moment You Live	1961	10.00
PHILBIN, REGIS			
Albums			
MERCURY			
❑ SR-61169	It's Time for Regis!	1968	25.00
PHILIP AND STEPHAN P.F. SLOAN and STEVE BARRI, again.			
45s			
INTERPHON			
❑ 7711	Meet Me Tonight Little Girl/When You're Near, You're So Far Away	1964	15.00
PHILIPS, TERRY			
45s			
CORAL			
❑ 62247	Fear/Find a Horseshoe	1961	15.00
UNITED ARTISTS			
❑ 351	My Foolish Ways/Hands of a Fool	1961	80.00
PHILLIPS, CHARLIE			
45s			
ARA			
❑ 1001	Rambling Guitar Man/Kiss Her Once for Me	196?	12.00
COLUMBIA			
❑ 42035	No More Sugartime/Welcome to the Wedding	1961	12.00
❑ 42289	I Guess I'll Never Learn/Now That It's Over	1962	10.00
❑ 42526	Cancel the Call/You're Moving Away	1962	10.00
❑ 42691	No One to Love/'Til Sunday	1963	10.00
❑ 42851	Later Tonight/This Is the House	1963	10.00
❑ 43014	Street of Loneliness/Please Help Me Believe	1964	10.00
CORAL			
❑ 61908	Sugartime/One Faded Rose	1958	25.00
❑ 61970	Be My Bride/Too Many Tears	1958	25.00
K-ARK			
❑ 874	Your Going Is Coming/Just Let the Flowers Grow	197?	8.00
LONGHORN			
❑ 574	Rainbow in the Valley/The Big Ball Is in Cowtown	1966	10.00
—As "Charlie 'Sugartime' Phillips"			
REPRISE			
❑ 0581	Be Careful, Go Easy, Go Slow/Souvenirs of Sorrow	1967	8.00
PHILLIPS, ESTHER Includes records as "Little Esther" and "Little Esther Phillips."			
12-Inch Singles			
MERCURY			
❑ 90 [DJ]	Oo-Oop-Oo-Oop (Long Version)/Oo-Oop-Oo-Oop (Edit)	1979	12.00
❑ 101 [DJ]	Our Day Will Come (same on both sides)	1979	12.00
WINNING			
❑ 1002	Turn Me Out (4:39) (5:51)	1983	10.00
45s			
ATLANTIC			
❑ 2223	Hello Walls/Double Crossing Blues	1964	15.00
—With Jimmy Ricks			
❑ 2229	No Headstone on My Grave/Mo Jo Hannah	1964	15.00
❑ 2251	It's Too Soon to Know/You're the Reason I'm Living	1964	15.00
❑ 2265	Half a Heart/Some Things You Never Get Used To	1964	15.00
❑ 2281	And I Love Him/Shangri-La	1965	12.00
❑ 2294	Moonglow & Theme from Picnic/Makin' Whoopee	1965	12.00
❑ 2304	Let Me Know When It's Over/I Saw Me	1965	12.00
❑ 2324	Just Say Goodbye/I Could Have Told You	1966	12.00
❑ 2335	When a Woman Loves a Man/Ups and Downs	1966	12.00
❑ 2360	Somebody Else Is Taking My Place/When Love Comes to the Human Race	1966	12.00
❑ 2370	Fever/Try Me	1966	12.00
❑ 2411	Release Me/Don't Feel Rained	1967	10.00
❑ 2417	I'm Sorry/Cheater Man	1967	10.00
❑ 2745	Brand New Day/Set Me Free	1970	6.00
❑ 2775	Crazy Love/All God Has Is Us	1970	6.00
❑ 2783	Catch Me I'm Falling/Woman Will Do Wrong	1971	6.00
❑ 2800	Cry Me a River Blues/I'm Getting 'Long Alright	1971	6.00
DECCA			
❑ 28804	If You Want Me/Talkin' All Out of My Head	1953	40.00
❑ 48305	Please Don't Send Me/Stop Crying	1953	40.00
❑ 48314	Sit Back Down/He's a No Good Man	1954	60.00
FEDERAL			
❑ 12023	I'm a Bad, Bad Girl/Don't Make a Fool Out of Me	1951	80.00
❑ 12036	Heart to Heart/Looking for a Man to Satisfy My Soul	1951	500.00
—With the Dominoes			
❑ 12042	Cryin' and Singin' the Blues/Tell Him That I Need Him	1951	80.00
❑ 12055	Ring-a-Ding-Doo/The Crying Blues	1952	70.00
❑ 12063	Summertime/The Storm	1952	70.00
❑ 12065	Better Beware/I'll Be There	1952	70.00
❑ 12078	Aged and Mellow/Bring My Lovin' Back to Me	1952	70.00
❑ 12090	Somebody New/Ramblin' Blues	1952	70.00
❑ 12100	Saturday Night Daddy/Mainliner	1952	300.00
—With Bobby Nunn			
❑ 12108	Last Laugh Blues/Flesh, Blood and Bones	1952	70.00
—With Little Willie Littlefield			
❑ 12115	Hollerin' and Screamin'/Turn the Lamp Down Low	1953	70.00
—With Little Willie Littlefield			
❑ 12122	You Took My Love Too Fast/Street Lights	1953	300.00
—With Bobby Nunn			
❑ 12126	Hound Dog/Sweet Lips	1953	70.00
❑ 12142	Cherry Wine/Love Oh Love	1953	70.00
KUDU			
❑ 904	Home Is Where the Hatred Is/Til My Back Ain't Got No Bone	1972	5.00
❑ 906	Baby I'm for Real/That's All Right with Me	1972	5.00
❑ 910	I've Never Found a Man (To Love Me Like You Do)/Cherry Red	1972	5.00
❑ 915	Use Me/Let Me in Your Life	1973	5.00
❑ 917	Justified/Too Many Roads	1973	5.00
❑ 921	Such a Night/Can't Trust Your Neighbor	1974	5.00
❑ 922	Disposable Society/(B-side unknown)	1974	5.00
❑ 925	What a Difference a Day Makes/Turn Around, Look at Me	1975	5.00
❑ 929	For All We Know/Fever	1976	5.00

P

Number	Title (A Side/B Side)	Yr	NM
❑ 936	Boy I Really Tied One On/ Magic's in the Air	1976	5.00
❑ 938	Higher and Higher/ All the Way Down	1976	5.00
LENOX			
❑ 5555	Release Me/Don't Feel Rained On	1962	30.00
❑ 5560	Am I That Easy to Forget/ I Really Don't Want to Know	1963	20.00
❑ 5565	You Never Miss Your Water (Till the Well Runs Dry)/ If You Want It (I've Got It)	1963	20.00
—As "Little Esther Phillips and Big Al Downing"			
❑ 5570	Why Should We Try Anymore/ While It Lasted	1963	20.00
❑ 5575	Don't Let Me Go/Why Was I Born	1963	20.00
❑ 5577	A Lover's Hymn/God Bless the Child Who's Got His Own	1963	20.00
MERCURY			
❑ 73967	Love Addict/I've Never Been a Woman Before	1977	4.00
❑ 74030	There You Go Again (There She Goes Again)/Stormy Weather	1978	4.00
❑ 74060	Oo-Oop-Oo-Oop/ I'll Close My Eyes	1979	4.00
❑ 74077	Our Day Will Come/Mr. Melody	1979	4.00
ROULETTE			
❑ 7031	Too Late to Worry, Too Blue to Cry/I'm in the Mood for Love	1969	7.00
❑ 7049	Tonight I'll Be Staying Here with You/Sweet Dreams	1969	7.00
❑ 7059	Nobody But You/Too Much of a Man	1969	7.00
SAVOY			
❑ 1193	You Can Bet Your Life/ 'Tain't Whatcha Say It's Whatcha Do	1956	25.00
❑ 1516	Longing in My Heart/ If It's News to Me	1957	20.00
❑ 1563	It's So Good/Do You Ever Think of Me	1959	15.00
WARWICK			
❑ 610	Gee Baby/Wild Child	1961	15.00
WINNING			
❑ 1001	Turn Me Out/(B-side unknown)	1983	5.00

Albums

Number	Title	Yr	NM
ATLANTIC			
❑ SD 1565	Burnin'	1970	25.00
❑ SD 1680	Confessin' the Blues	1975	15.00
❑ 8102 [M]	And I Love Him	1965	50.00
—Cover has a pink Cupid on it			
❑ 8102 [M]	And I Love Him	1966	30.00
—Cover has a black photo on it			
❑ SD 8102 [S]	And I Love Him	1965	80.00
—Cover has a pink Cupid on it			
❑ SD 8102 [S]	And I Love Him	1966	40.00
—Cover has a black photo on it			
❑ 8122 [M]	Esther	1966	30.00
❑ SD 8122 [S]	Esther	1966	40.00
❑ 8130 [M]	The Country Side of Esther Phillips	1966	30.00
—Reissue of Lenox 227			
❑ SD 8130 [S]	The Country Side of Esther Phillips	1966	40.00
—Reissue of Lenox S-227			
❑ 90670	Confessin' the Blues	1987	10.00
—Reissue of 1680			
CBS ASSOCIATED			
❑ PZ 40710	What a Diff'rence a Day Makes	1987	8.00
—Reissue of Kudu 23			
❑ PZ 40935	From a Whisper to a Scream	1988	8.00
—Reissue of Kudu 05			
KING			
❑ 622 [M]	Memory Lane	1959	4000.
KUDU			
❑ 05	From a Whisper to a Scream	1972	12.00
❑ 09	Alone Again, Naturally	1972	12.00
❑ 14	Black-Eyed Blues	1973	12.00
❑ 18	Performance	1974	12.00
❑ 23	What a Diff'rence a Day Makes	1975	12.00
❑ 28	For All We Know	1976	12.00
❑ 31	Capricorn Princess	1976	12.00
LENOX			
❑ 227 [M]	Release Me	1962	100.00
❑ S-227 [S]	Release Me	1962	200.00
MERCURY			
❑ SRM-1-1187	You've Come a Long Way, Baby	1977	10.00
❑ SRM-1-3733	All About Esther Phillips	1978	10.00
❑ SRM-1-3769	Here's Esther—Are You Ready?	1979	10.00
❑ SRM-1-4005	A Good Black Is Hard to Crack	1981	10.00
MUSE			
❑ MR-5302	A Way to Say Goodbye	1986	12.00
SAVOY JAZZ			
❑ SJL-2258	The Complete Savoy Recordings	1984	10.00

PHILLIPS, GENE

Albums

Number	Title	Yr	NM
CROWN			
❑ CLP-5375 [M]	Gene Phillips and the Rockers	1963	30.00

PHILLIPS, JOHN

Also see THE JOURNEYMEN; THE MAMAS AND THE PAPAS; THE SMOOTHIES.

45s

Number	Title (A Side/B Side)	Yr	NM
ABC DUNHILL			
❑ 4236	Mississippi/April Anne	1970	6.00
ATCO			
❑ 6960	Green-Eyed Lady/Lion	1974	6.00
COLUMBIA			
❑ 45737	Revolution on Vacation/ Cup of Tea	1972	5.00

Albums

Number	Title	Yr	NM
ABC DUNHILL			
❑ DS-50077	John Phillips (John the Wolfking of L.A.)	1970	15.00

PHILLIPS, MICHELLE

Also see THE MAMAS AND THE PAPAS.

45s

Number	Title (A Side/B Side)	Yr	NM
A&M			
❑ 1740	There She Goes/Aloha Louie	1975	5.00
❑ 1824	No Love Today/Aloha Louie	1976	4.00
❑ 1824 [PS]	No Love Today/Aloha Louie	1976	6.00
❑ 1996	The Aching Kind/Lady of Fantasy	1977	5.00
❑ 2021	There She Goes/ Victim of Romance	1978	5.00

Albums

Number	Title	Yr	NM
A&M			
❑ SP-4651	Victim of Romance	1977	15.00

PHILLIPS, PHIL

45s

Number	Title (A Side/B Side)	Yr	NM
KHOURY'S			
❑ 711	Sea of Love/Juella	1959	1500.
MERCURY			
❑ 10021 [S]	Take This Heart/Verdie Mae	1959	50.00
❑ 71465	Sea of Love/Juella	1959	25.00
❑ 71531 [M]	Take This Heart/Verdie Mae	1959	20.00
❑ 71550	Providing/Don't Leave Me	1960	20.00
❑ 71611	What Will I Tell My Heart/ Your True Love Once More	1960	20.00
❑ 71649	Stormy Weather/Don't Cry Baby	1960	20.00
❑ 71657	Come BackMy Darling/Nobody Knows-Nobody Cares	1960	20.00
❑ 71817	Sweet Affection/Betray	1961	25.00

PHILLIPS, RICHARD

45s

Number	Title (A Side/B Side)	Yr	NM
HIT			
❑ 225	Kansas City Star/Yesterday	1965	12.00
—B-side by the Jalopy Five			

PHILLIPS, SHAWN

45s

Number	Title (A Side/B Side)	Yr	NM
A&M			
❑ 1238	A Christmas Song/Lovely Lady	1970	10.00
❑ 1238 [PS]	A Christmas Song/Lovely Lady	1970	10.00
❑ 1402	We/"L" Ballade	1972	5.00
❑ 1405	Lost Horizon/Landscape	1973	5.00
❑ 1435	Anella/Hey Miss Lonely	1973	5.00
❑ 1482	Dream Queen/Bright White	1973	5.00
❑ 1507	All the Kings and Castles/ Salty Tears	1974	5.00
❑ 1750	Do You Wonder/ Summer Vignette	1975	5.00
ASCOT			
❑ 2152	The New Frankie and Johnny Song/Cloudy Summer Afternoon	1964	12.00

Albums

Number	Title	Yr	NM
A&M			
❑ SP-3128	Second Contribution	198?	8.00
—Budget-line reissue			
❑ SP-3135	Faces	198?	8.00
—Budget-line reissue			
❑ SP-3662	Furthermore	1974	12.00
❑ SP-4241	Contribution	1970	15.00
❑ SP-4282	Second Contribution	1971	15.00
❑ SP-4324	Collaboration	1972	15.00
❑ SP-4363	Faces	1972	12.00
❑ SP-4402	Bright White	1973	12.00
❑ SP-4539	Do You Wonder	1975	12.00
❑ SP-4582	Rumpelstiltskin's Resolve	1976	12.00
❑ SP-4650	Spaced	1977	12.00
CHAMELEON			
❑ D1-74764	Beyond Here Be Dragons	1988	10.00
RCA VICTOR			
❑ AFL1-3028	Transcendence	1978	10.00
❑ AYL1-3873	Transcendence	1981	8.00
—"Best Buy Series" reissue			

PHILOSOPHERS, THE

Albums

Number	Title	Yr	NM
PHILO			
❑ 1001	After Sundown	1969	150.00

PHLUPH

45s

Number	Title (A Side/B Side)	Yr	NM
VERVE			
❑ 10564	Another Day/Doctor Mind	1967	15.00
❑ 10575	Patterns/In Her Way	1967	20.00

Albums

Number	Title	Yr	NM
VERVE			
❑ V6-5054	Phluph	1968	30.00

PHONETICS, THE

45s

Number	Title (A Side/B Side)	Yr	NM
TRUDEL			
❑ 1005	Pretty Girl/Don't Let Love Get You Down	196?	400.00
❑ 1007	Just a Boy's Dream/Don't Let Love Get You Down	196?	1500.
❑ 1010	Ghosts/It's Jerkin' and Twinin' Time	196?	40.00
❑ 1012	What Good (Am I Without You)/ Don't Let Love Get You Down	196?	500.00

PIANO RED

Also see DR. FEELGOOD AND THE INTERNS.

45s

Number	Title (A Side/B Side)	Yr	NM
CHECKER			
❑ 911	Get Up Mare/So Worried	1958	30.00
GROOVE			
❑ 0023	Decatur Street Blues/ Big Rock Joe from Kokomo	1954	30.00
❑ 0101	Pay It No Mind/Jump, Man, Jump	1955	30.00
❑ 0118	Six O'Clock Bounce/Goodbye	1955	30.00
❑ 0126	Red's Blues/Gordy's Rock	1955	30.00
❑ 0136	Jumpin' with Daddy/ She Knocks Me Out	1956	30.00
❑ 0145	I'm Nobody's Fool/ That's My Desire	1956	30.00
❑ 0169	Woo-Ee/You Were Mine for Awhile	1956	30.00
JAX			
❑ 1000	This Old World/I Feel Good	1959	15.00
❑ 1006	Guitar Walk/I've Been Walkin'	1959	15.00
KING			
❑ 6330	I Want a Bowlegged Woman/ Underground Atlanta	1970	5.00
RCA VICTOR			
❑ 47-4265	Diggin' the Boogie/Let's Have a Good Time Tonight	1951	60.00
❑ 47-4380	Hey Good Lookin'/It Makes No Difference Now	1951	60.00
❑ 47-4524	Bouncin' with Red/Count the Days I'm Gone	1952	60.00
❑ 47-4766	She Walks Right In/Sales Tax Boogie	1952	60.00
❑ 47-4957	Yoo Doopee Doo/Daybreak	1952	60.00
❑ 47-5101	I'm Gonna Rock Some More/ Everybody's Boogie	1952	50.00
❑ 47-5224	She's Dynamite/I'm Gonna Tell Everybody	1953	40.00
❑ 47-5337	Decatur Street Boogie/Your Mouth's Got a Hole In It	1953	40.00
❑ 47-5544	Right and Ready, Taxi, Taxi 6963	1953	40.00
❑ 47-6856	Wild Fire/Rock Baby	1957	20.00
❑ 47-6953	Peachtree Parade/Please Don't Talk About Me	1957	20.00
❑ 47-7065	South/Coo Cha	1957	20.00
❑ 47-7217	Comin' On/One Glimpse of Heaven	1958	20.00
❑ 50-0099	Rockin' with Red/Red's Boogie	1950	150.00
—Gray label, orange vinyl			
❑ 50-0106	The Wrong Yo-Yo/My Gal Jo	1951	60.00
❑ 50-0118	Jumpin' the Boogie/Just Right Bounce	1951	60.00
❑ 50-0130	Layin' the Boogie/Baby What's Wrong	1951	60.00

7-Inch Extended Plays

Number	Title	Yr	NM
GROOVE			
❑ EGA-3	(contents unknown)	1956	100.00
❑ EGA-3 [PS]	Jump, Man, Jump	1956	100.00
❑ EGA-26	(contents unknown)	1956	60.00
❑ EGA-26 [PS]	Piano Red In Concert, Vol. 1	1956	60.00
❑ EGA-27	(contents unknown)	1956	60.00
❑ EGA-27 [PS]	Piano Red In Concert, Vol. 2	1956	60.00

Except when noted otherwise, VG = 25% of NM, and VG+ = 50% of NM. (Example: VG = $2.00, VG+ = $4.00 and NM = $8.00.)

Number	Title (A Side/B Side)	Yr	NM
❑ EGA-28	(contents unknown)	1956	60.00
❑ EGA-28 [PS]	Piano Red In Concert, Vol. 3	1956	60.00

RCA VICTOR

Number	Title (A Side/B Side)	Yr	NM
❑ EPA-587	Rockin' with Red/I'm Gonna Rock Some More//Red's Boogie/Diggin' the Boogie	1954	100.00
❑ EPA-587 [PS]	Rockin' with Red	1954	100.00
❑ EPA-5091	(contents unknown)	1959	50.00
—Black label			
❑ EPA-5091	(contents unknown)	1959	100.00
—Maroon label			
❑ EPA-5091 [PS]	Rockin' with Red	1959	50.00

Albums

ARHOOLIE

Number	Title (A Side/B Side)	Yr	NM
❑ 1064	William Perryman (Alone with Piano)	197?	12.00

EUPHONIC

Number	Title (A Side/B Side)	Yr	NM
❑ 1212	Percussive Piano	198?	10.00

GROOVE

Number	Title (A Side/B Side)	Yr	NM
❑ LG-1001 [M]	Jump Man, Jump	1956	—
—The existence of this LP has not been confirmed			
❑ LG-1002 [M]	Piano Red in Concert	1956	600.00

KING

Number	Title (A Side/B Side)	Yr	NM
❑ KS-1117	Happiness Is Piano Red	1970	20.00

RCA CAMDEN

Number	Title (A Side/B Side)	Yr	NM
❑ ACL1-0547	Rockin' with Red	1974	12.00

SOUTHLAND

Number	Title (A Side/B Side)	Yr	NM
❑ 8	Willie Perryman-Piano Red-Dr. Feelgood	1983	15.00

PICKETT, BOBBY "BORIS"

45s

ANTHEM

Number	Title (A Side/B Side)	Yr	NM
❑ 205	Monster Concert/Am I	1973	6.00

CAPITOL

Number	Title (A Side/B Side)	Yr	NM
❑ 5063	Simon the Sensible Surfer/ Simon Says So What	1963	25.00

GARPAX

Number	Title (A Side/B Side)	Yr	NM
❑ P-1	Monster Mash/Monster's Mash Party	1962	30.00
—Orange label, first release of 44167?			
❑ 724	I'm Down to My Last Heartbreak/I Can't Stop	1962	25.00
❑ 44167	Monster Mash/Monster's Mash Party	1962	25.00
❑ 44167 [PS]	Monster Mash/Monster's Mash Party	1962	60.00
❑ 44171	Monster's Holiday/ Monster's Motion	1962	25.00
❑ 44171 [PS]	Monster's Holiday/ Monster's Motion	1962	40.00
❑ 44175	Graduation Day/The Humpty Dumpty	1963	25.00
❑ 44175 [PS]	Graduation Day/The Humpty Dumpty	1963	40.00
❑ 44185	Blood Bank Blues/ Me and My Mummy	1965	25.00

METROMEDIA

Number	Title (A Side/B Side)	Yr	NM
❑ BMBO-0089	Me and My Mummy/It's Not the Same Without You	1973	10.00
—B-side by Pickett and Payne			

PARROT

Number	Title (A Side/B Side)	Yr	NM
❑ 348	Monster Mash/Monster's Mash Party	1970	10.00
—Reissued in 1973 with the same number and label design			
❑ 366	Monster's Holiday/Monster Minuet	1971	10.00

PIZZERIA

Number	Title (A Side/B Side)	Yr	NM
❑ 1	Star Drek/Mangy Old Sidewinder	1977	10.00
—With Peter Ferrara; originals are autographed on the label by both			

POLYDOR

Number	Title (A Side/B Side)	Yr	NM
❑ 14361	King Kong (Your Song)/ Disco Kong	1976	5.00
—With Peter Ferrara			

RCA VICTOR

Number	Title (A Side/B Side)	Yr	NM
❑ 47-8312	Smoke! Smoke! Smoke! (That Cigarette)/Gotta Leave This Town	1964	15.00
❑ 47-8459	The Werewolf Watusi/ Monster Swim	1964	15.00

WHITE WHALE

Number	Title (A Side/B Side)	Yr	NM
❑ 363	Monster Man Jam/Am I	1970	25.00
—B-side by Bobby and Joan Pickett			
❑ 365	Monster Concert/ (B-side unknown)	1970	25.00

Albums

GARPAX

Number	Title (A Side/B Side)	Yr	NM
❑ GPX 57001 [M]	The Original Monster Mash	1962	150.00
❑ SGP 67001 [S]	The Original Monster Mash	1962	250.00

PARROT

Number	Title (A Side/B Side)	Yr	NM
❑ XPAS 71063 [R]	The Original Monster Mash	1973	25.00
—Reissue of Garpax LP with four tracks deleted and one added			

PICKETT, WILSON

Also see THE FALCONS.

12-Inch Singles

MOTOWN

Number	Title (A Side/B Side)	Yr	NM
❑ 217	Land of a Thousand Dances (4 versions)/Just Let Her Know	1987	8.00

45s

ATLANTIC

Number	Title (A Side/B Side)	Yr	NM
❑ 2233	I'm Gonna Cry/For Better or Worse	1964	15.00
❑ 2271	Come Home Baby/ Take a Little Love	1965	15.00
❑ 2289	In the Midnight Hour/I'm Not Tired	1965	15.00
❑ 2306	Don't Fight It/It's All Over	1965	15.00
❑ 2320	634-5789 (Soulsville, U.S.A.)/ That's a Man's Way	1966	15.00
❑ 2334	Ninety-Nine and a Half (Won't Do)/Danger Zone	1966	15.00
❑ 2348	Land of 1000 Dances/ You're So Fine	1966	15.00
❑ 2365	Mustang Sally/Three Time Loser	1966	15.00
❑ 2381	Eveybody Needs Somebody to Love/Nothing You Can Do	1967	12.00
❑ 2394	I Found a Love — Part I/I Found a Love — Part II	1967	12.00
❑ 2412	Soul Dance Number Three/ You Can't Stand Alone	1967	12.00
❑ 2430	Funky Broadway/I'm Sorry About That	1967	12.00
❑ 2448	Stag-O-Lee/I'm In Love	1967	12.00
❑ 2484	Jealous Love/I've Come a Long Way	1968	10.00
❑ 2504	She's Lookin' Good/ We've Got to Have Love	1968	10.00
❑ 2528	I'm a Midnight Mover/Deborah	1968	10.00
❑ 2558	I Found a True Love/ For Better or Worse	1968	10.00
❑ 2575	A Man and a Half/People Make the World (What It Is)	1968	10.00
❑ 2591	Hey Jude/Search Your Heart	1968	10.00
❑ 2611	Mini-Skirt Minnie/ Back in Your Arms	1969	8.00
❑ 2631	Born to Be Wild/Toe Hold	1969	8.00
❑ 2648	Hey Joe/Night Owl	1969	8.00
❑ 2682	You Keep Me Hangin' On/Now You See Me, Now You Don't	1969	8.00
❑ 2722	Sugar, Sugar/Cole, Cooke, and Redding	1970	8.00
❑ 2753	She Said Yes/It's Still Good	1970	6.00
❑ 2765	Engine Number Nine/ International Playboy	1970	6.00
❑ 2781	Don't Let the Green Grass Fool You/Ain't No Doubt About It	1971	6.00
❑ 2797	Don't Knock My Love (Part 1)/ Don't Knock My Love (Part 2)	1971	6.00
❑ 2824	Call My Name, I'll Be There/ Woman Let Me Down Home	1971	6.00
❑ 2852	Fire and Water/Pledging My Love	1971	6.00
❑ 2878	Funk Factory/One Step Away	1972	6.00
❑ 2909	Mama Told Me Not to Come/ Covering the Same Old Ground	1972	6.00
❑ 2961	Come Right Here/ International Playboy	1973	6.00

BIG TREE

Number	Title (A Side/B Side)	Yr	NM
❑ 16121	Who Turned You On/ Dance You Down	1978	5.00
❑ 16129	Groovin'/Time to Let the Sun Shine In	1978	5.00

CORREC-TONE

Number	Title (A Side/B Side)	Yr	NM
❑ 501	Let Me Be Your Boy/ My Heart Belongs to You	1962	60.00

CUB

Number	Title (A Side/B Side)	Yr	NM
❑ 9113	Let Me Be Your Boy/ My Heart Belongs to You	1962	30.00

DOUBLE L

Number	Title (A Side/B Side)	Yr	NM
❑ 713	If You Need Me/Baby Call on Me	1963	20.00
❑ 717	It's Too Late/I'm Gonna Love You	1963	20.00
❑ 724	I'm Down to My Last Heartbreak/I Can't Stop	1963	15.00

EMI AMERICA

Number	Title (A Side/B Side)	Yr	NM
❑ 8027	I Want You/Love of My Life	1979	5.00
❑ 8034	Live with Me/Granny	1980	5.00
❑ 8070	Ain't Gonna Give You No More/ Don't Underestimate the Power of Love	1981	5.00
❑ 8082	Back on the Right Track/It's You	1981	5.00

ERVA

Number	Title (A Side/B Side)	Yr	NM
❑ 318	Love Dagger/Time to Let the Sun Shine on Me	1977	5.00

MOTOWN

Number	Title (A Side/B Side)	Yr	NM
❑ 1898	Don't Turn Away/Can't Stop Now	1987	4.00
❑ 1916	In the Midnight Hour/ Just Let Her Know	1987	4.00
❑ 1938	Love Never Let Me Down/ Just Let Her Know	1988	4.00
❑ 53407	Love Never Let Me Down/ Just Let Her Know	1988	4.00

PHILCO-FORD

Number	Title (A Side/B Side)	Yr	NM
❑ HP-11	Land of a 1000 Dances/ Midnight Hour	1967	15.00
—4-inch plastic "Hip Pocket Record" with color sleeve			

RCA VICTOR

Number	Title (A Side/B Side)	Yr	NM
❑ 74-0908	Mr. Magic Man/I Sho' Love You	1973	6.00
❑ APBO-0049	Take a Closer Look at the Woman You're With/ Two Woman and a Wife	1973	6.00
❑ APBO-0174	Soft Soul Boogie Woogie/ Take That Pollution Out of Your Throat	1973	6.00
❑ APBO-0309	Take Your Pleasure Where You FInd It/What Good Is a Lie	1974	6.00
❑ PB-10067	I Was Too Nice/Isn't That So	1974	6.00

VERVE

Number	Title (A Side/B Side)	Yr	NM
❑ 10378	Let Me Be Your Boy/My Heart Belongs to You	1966	20.00

WICKED

Number	Title (A Side/B Side)	Yr	NM
❑ 8101	The Best Part of a Man/How Will I Ever Know	1975	6.00
❑ 8102	Love Will Keep Us Together/ It's Gonna Be Good	1976	6.00

7-Inch Extended Plays

ATLANTIC

Number	Title (A Side/B Side)	Yr	NM
❑ SD 8129	Something You Got/Barefootin'/ Land of 1000 Dances//In the Midnight Hour/Ninety-Nine and a Half (Won't Do)/I'm Drifting	1966	15.00
—Jukebox issue; small hole, plays at 33 1/3 rpm			
❑ SD 8129 [PS]	The Exciting Wilson Pickett	1966	15.00
❑ SD 7-8250	Groovy Little Woman/ Funky Way/It's Still Good// This Old Town/You Keep Me Hangin' On	1970	12.00
—Jukebox issue; small hole, plays at 33 1/3 rpm			
❑ SD 7-8250 [PS]	Right On	1970	12.00

Albums

ATLANTIC

Number	Title (A Side/B Side)	Yr	NM
❑ SD 2-501 [(2)]	Wilson Pickett's Greatest Hits	1973	20.00
❑ 8114 [M]	In the Midnight Hour	1965	40.00
❑ SD 8114 [R]	In the Midnight Hour	1965	30.00
❑ 8129 [M]	The Exciting Wilson Pickett	1966	40.00
❑ SD 8129 [R]	The Exciting Wilson Pickett	1966	30.00
❑ 8136 [M]	The Wicked Pickett	1967	40.00
❑ SD 8136 [R]	The Wicked Pickett	1967	30.00
❑ 8145 [M]	The Sound of Wilson Pickett	1967	40.00
❑ SD 8145 [P]	The Sound of Wilson Pickett	1967	40.00
❑ 8151 [M]	The Best of Wilson Pickett	1967	40.00
❑ SD 8151 [R]	The Best of Wilson Pickett	1967	20.00
❑ SD 8175	I'm in Love	1968	25.00
❑ SD 8183	The Midnight Mover	1968	25.00
❑ SD 8215	Hey Jude	1969	20.00
❑ SD 8250	Right On	1970	20.00
❑ SD 8270	Wilson Pickett in Philadelphia	1970	20.00
❑ 8290 [M]	The Best of Wilson Pickett, Vol. II	1971	25.00
—Mono copies are promo only			
❑ SD 8290 [S]	The Best of Wilson Pickett, Vol. II	1971	15.00
❑ SD 8300	Don't Knock My Love	1971	15.00
❑ 81283	The Best of Wilson Pickett	1985	10.00

BIG TREE

Number	Title (A Side/B Side)	Yr	NM
❑ SD 76011	Funky Situation	1978	12.00

DOUBLE-L

Number	Title (A Side/B Side)	Yr	NM
❑ DL-2300 [M]	It's Too Late	1963	50.00
❑ SDL-8300 [S]	It's Too Late	1963	70.00

EMI AMERICA

Number	Title (A Side/B Side)	Yr	NM
❑ SW-17019	I Want You	1979	12.00
❑ SW-17043	Right Track	1981	12.00

MOTOWN

Number	Title (A Side/B Side)	Yr	NM
❑ 6244 ML	American Soul Man	1987	10.00

RCA VICTOR

Number	Title (A Side/B Side)	Yr	NM
❑ APL1-0312	Miz Lena's Boy	1973	15.00
❑ APL1-0495	Pickett in the Pocket	1974	15.00
❑ APL1-0856	Join Me and Let's Be Free	1975	15.00
❑ ANL1-2149	Join Me and Let's Be Free	1977	10.00
—Reissue			
❑ LSP-4858	Mr. Magic Man	1973	15.00

TRIP

Number	Title (A Side/B Side)	Yr	NM
❑ 8010	Wickedness	1972	10.00

UPFRONT

Number	Title (A Side/B Side)	Yr	NM
❑ UPF-127 [S]	It's Too Late	197?	10.00

WAND

Number	Title (A Side/B Side)	Yr	NM
❑ WD-672 [M]	Great Wilson Pickett Hits	1966	30.00
❑ WDS-672 [R]	Great Wilson Pickett Hits	1966	20.00

P

Number	Title (A Side/B Side)	Yr	NM
WICKED			
❑ 9001	Chocolate Mountain	1976	25.00

PICKS, THE
Also see NORMAN PETTY TRIO.

45s

Number	Title (A Side/B Side)	Yr	NM
COLUMBIA			
❑ 41096	Moondreams/Look to the Future	1958	50.00

PICKWICKS, THE

45s

Number	Title (A Side/B Side)	Yr	NM
PARROT			
❑ 9679	Apple Blossom Time/I Don't Want to Tell You Again	1964	15.00
WARNER BROS.			
❑ 5492	Little by Little/I Took My Baby Home	1965	15.00

PIERCE, WEBB

45s

Number	Title (A Side/B Side)	Yr	NM
DECCA			
❑ 9-28091	That Heart Belongs to Me/So Used to Loving You	1952	25.00
❑ 9-28369	Back Street Affair/I'll Always Take Care of You	1952	25.00
❑ 9-28431	Bow Thy Head/The Country Church	1952	30.00
❑ 9-28534	I'll Go On Alone/That's Me Without You	1953	25.00
❑ 9-28594	The Last Waltz/I Haven't Got the Heart	1953	25.00
❑ 9-28725	It's Been So Long/Don't Throw Your Life Away	1953	25.00
❑ 9-28834	There Stands the Glass/I'm Walking the Dog	1953	25.00
❑ 9-28991	Slowly/You Just Can't Be True	1954	25.00
❑ 9-29107	Even Tho/Sparkling Brown Eyes	1954	25.00
❑ 9-29155	Mother Calling My Name in Prayer/Bugle Call from Heaven	1954	30.00
❑ 9-29252	More and More/You're Not Mine Anymore	1954	25.00
❑ 9-29391	In the Jailhouse Now/I'm Gonna Fall Out of Love with You	1955	20.00
❑ 9-29480	I Don't Care/Your Good for Nothing Heart	1955	20.00
❑ 9-29662	Love, Love, Love/If You Were Me	1955	20.00
❑ 9-29805	Yes, I Know Why/'Cause I Love You	1956	20.00
❑ 9-29974	Any Old Time/We'll Find a Way	1956	20.00
❑ 9-30045	Teenage Boogie/I'm Really Glad You Hurt Me	1956	40.00
❑ 9-30155	I'm Tired/It's My Way	1956	20.00
❑ 9-30255	Honky Tonk Song/Someday	1957	20.00
❑ 9-30321	Bye Bye, Love/Missing You	1957	15.00
❑ 9-30419	Holiday for Love/Don't Do It Darlin'	1957	15.00
❑ 9-30550	New Panhandle Rag/How Long?	1958	15.00
❑ 9-30623	Cryin' Over You/You'll Come Back	1958	15.00
❑ 9-30711	Tupelo County Jail/Falling Back to You	1958	15.00
❑ 9-30789	I'm Letting You Go/Sittin' Alone	1958	15.00
❑ 9-30858	A Thousand Miles Ago/What Goes On in Your Heart	1959	15.00
❑ 9-30923	I Ain't Never/Shanghaied	1959	15.00
❑ 9-31021	No Love Have I/Whirlpool of Love	1959	15.00
❑ 31058	Is It Wrong (For Loving You)/(Doin' the) Lovers Leap	1960	12.00
❑ 31118	Drifting Texas Sand/All I Need Is You	1960	12.00
❑ 31165	Fallen Angel/Truck Driver's Blues	1960	12.00
❑ 31197	Let Forgiveness In/There's More Pretty Girls Than One	1961	12.00
❑ 31249	Sweet Lips/Last Night	1961	12.00
❑ 31298	Walking the Streets/How Do You Talk to a Baby	1961	12.00
❑ 31347	Alla My Love/You Are My Life	1962	12.00
❑ 31380	Take Time/Crazy Wild Desire	1962	12.00
❑ 31421	Cow Town/Sooner or Later	1962	12.00
❑ 31451	Sawmill/If I Could Come Back	1963	10.00
❑ 31488	Sands of Gold/Nobody's Darlin' But Mine	1963	10.00
❑ 31544	Those Wonderful Years/If the Back Door Could Talk	1963	10.00
❑ 31582	Waiting a Lifetime/Love Come to Me	1964	10.00
❑ 31617	Memory No. 1/French Riviera	1964	10.00
❑ 31704	That's Where My Money Goes/Broken Engagement	1964	10.00
❑ 31737	Loving You Then Losing You/Let Me Live a Little	1965	10.00
❑ 31816	Who Do I Think I Am/Hobo and the Rose	1965	10.00
❑ 31867	Christmas at Home/Sweet Memories	1965	12.00
❑ 31924	You Ain't No Better Than Me/The Champ	1966	10.00
❑ 31982	Love's Something (I Can't Understand)/A Loner	1966	10.00
❑ 32033	Where'd Ya Stay Last Night/She's Twenty-One	1966	10.00
❑ 32098	Goodbye City, Goodbye Girl/That Same Old Street	1967	8.00
❑ 32167	Fool Fool Fool/Bottles and Babies	1967	8.00
❑ 32246	Luzianna/Somebody Please Kiss My Sweet Thing	1967	8.00
❑ 32339	Stranger in a Strange, Strange City/In Another World	1968	8.00
❑ 32388	Saturday Night/I Tried Everything to Please	1968	8.00
❑ 32438	If I Had Last Night to Live Over/No Tears Tonight	1969	8.00
❑ 32508	This Thing/Does My Memory Ever Cross Your Mind	1969	8.00
❑ 32577	Love Ain't Never Gonna Be No Better/The Other Side of You	1969	8.00
❑ 32641	Merry-Go-Round World/Fools Night Out	1970	8.00
❑ 32694	The Man You Want Me to Be/Too Long	1970	8.00
❑ 32762	Showing His Dollar/The Way We Were Back Then	1970	8.00
❑ 32787	Tell Him That You Love Him/Heartaches Are for Lovers, Not for Friends	1971	8.00
❑ 32855	Someone Stepped In (And Stole Me Blind)/I Miss the Little Things	1971	8.00
❑ 32924	Hey Good Lookin'/Wonderful, Wonderful	1972	8.00
❑ 32973	I'm Gonna Be a Swinger/Someday	1972	8.00
❑ 33015	There Stands the Glass/Valentino of the Hobos	1972	8.00
❑ 33044	Let the Children Pick the Flowers/You're Letting Me Go	1973	8.00
❑ 7-34014 [S]	Hideaway Heart/(B-side unknown)	1962	15.00
—33 1/3 rpm jukebox single, small hole			
❑ 7-34015 [S]	Cow Town/(B-side unknown)	1962	15.00
—33 1/3 rpm jukebox single, small hole			
❑ 7-34016 [S]	First to Have a Second Chance/(B-side unknown)	1962	15.00
—33 1/3 rpm jukebox single, small hole			
❑ 7-34017 [S]	Tennessee Waltz/(B-side unknown)	1962	15.00
—33 1/3 rpm jukebox single, small hole			
❑ 7-34018 [S]	I'm Walking Behind You/(B-side unknown)	1962	15.00
—33 1/3 rpm jukebox single, small hole			
❑ 7-34076 [S]	Waterloo/Cry, Cry Darling	1962	15.00
—33 1/3 rpm jukebox single, small hole			
❑ 7-34135 [S]	I've Got a New Heartache/(B-side unknown)	1963	15.00
—33 1/3 rpm jukebox single, small hole			
❑ 7-34136 [S]	What Good Will It Do/One More Time	1963	15.00
—33 1/3 rpm jukebox single, small hole			
❑ 7-34137 [S]	Are You Sincere?/(B-side unknown)	1963	15.00
—33 1/3 rpm jukebox single, small hole			
❑ 7-34138 [S]	I Can't Stop Loving You/(B-side unknown)	1963	15.00
—33 1/3 rpm jukebox single, small hole			
❑ 7-34139 [S]	If I Lost Your Love/(B-side unknown)	1963	15.00
—33 1/3 rpm jukebox single, small hole			
❑ 7-38099 [S]	In the Jailhouse Now/Poison Love	1959	20.00
—Small hole, plays at 33 1/3 rpm			
❑ 7-38223 [S]	Drinkin' My Blues Away/Let Me Be the First to Know	196?	20.00
—33 1/3 rpm jukebox single, small hole			
❑ 7-38224 [S]	I Think of You/You Make Love to Everyone	196?	20.00
—33 1/3 rpm jukebox single, small hole			
❑ 9-46322	If Crying Would Make You Care/Drifting Texas Sand	1951	30.00
❑ 9-46332	California Blues/You Scared the Love Right Out of Me	1951	30.00
❑ 9-46364	Wondering/New Silver Bells	1951	25.00
❑ 9-46385	I'm Gonna See My Baby/You Know I'm Still in Love	1952	25.00
4 STAR			
❑ 1601	Heebie Jeebie Blues/High Geared Daddy	1952	30.00
❑ 1610	Hawaiian Echoes/I Saw Your Face in the Moon	1952	30.00
❑ 1616	Georgia Rag/Lucky Lee	1952	30.00
❑ 1629	Jilted Love/I'm Happy You Hurt Me	1953	30.00
KING			
❑ 5366	New Panhandle Rag/It's All Between the Lines	1960	12.00
❑ 5429	Jilted Love/Georgia Rag	1960	12.00
MCA			
❑ 40128	Lo-Lenna/When You're Living in Hell	1973	6.00
❑ 40181	I'd Be Number One/You Better Treat Her Right	1974	6.00
❑ 40255	Honey (Open That Door)/Take the Time It Takes	1974	6.00
❑ 40310	I Know, I Know, I Know/I'm Ashamed to Be Here	1974	6.00
PLANTATION			
❑ 131	The Good Lord Giveth (And Uncle Sam Taketh Away)/Send My Love to Me	1975	6.00
❑ 136	I've Got Leaving on My Mind/Shame, Shame, Shame	1976	6.00
❑ 141	That's Me Without You/Appleton	1976	6.00
❑ 145	Christmas Time's a Coming/The Family Christmas Tree	1976	6.00
❑ 149	Got You on My Mind/Love Brought Us Together	1977	5.00
—With Carol Channing			
❑ 154	Rhinestone Cowboy Club/Sparkling Brown Eyes	1977	6.00

7-Inch Extended Plays

Number	Title (A Side/B Side)	Yr	NM
DECCA			
❑ ED 2144	The Wondering Boy, Part 1	195?	20.00
❑ ED 2144	Wondering/There Stands the Glass//That's Me Without You/Don't Throw Your Life Away	195?	20.00
❑ ED 2145	Back Street Affair/It's Been So Long//Slowly/That Heart Belongs to Me	195?	20.00
❑ ED 2145	The Wondering Boy, Part 2	195?	20.00
❑ ED 2241	(contents unknown)	195?	20.00
❑ ED 2241 [PS]	Webb Pierce, Vol. 1	195?	20.00
❑ ED 2242	(contents unknown)	195?	20.00
❑ ED 2242 [PS]	Webb Pierce, Vol. 2	195?	20.00
❑ ED 2243	(contents unknown)	195?	20.00
❑ ED 2243 [PS]	Webb Pierce, Vol. 3	195?	20.00
❑ ED 2355	(contents unknown)	1956	20.00
❑ ED 2355 [PS]	The Country Church	1956	20.00
❑ ED 2364	(contents unknown)	1956	20.00
❑ ED 2364 [PS]	The Wondering Boy, Vol. 3	1956	20.00
❑ ED 2581	*New Love Affair/I Care No More/Just Imagination/I Love	1958	20.00
❑ ED 2581 [PS]	Just Imagination	1958	20.00
❑ ED 2653 [M]	*After the Boy Gets the Girl/I Owe It to Myself/My Shoes Keep Walking Back to You/Life to Go	1959	20.00
❑ ED 2653 [PS]	Webb	1959	20.00
❑ ED 7-2653 [PS]	Webb	1959	30.00
❑ ED 7-2653 [S]	*After the Boy Gets the Girl/I Owe It to Myself/My Shoes Keep Walking Back to You/Life to Go	1959	30.00
❑ ED 2668 [M]	*I Ain't Never/Shanghaied/A Thousand Miles Ago/What Goes On in Your Heart	1959	20.00
❑ ED 2668 [PS]	I Ain't Never	1959	20.00
❑ ED 7-2668 [PS]	I Ain't Never	1959	30.00
❑ ED 7-2668 [S]	*I Ain't Never/Shanghaied/A Thousand Miles Ago/What Goes On in Your Heart	1959	30.00
❑ ED 2685	*Walking the Streets/All I Need Is You/Drifting Texas Sand/Drinking My Blues Away	1960	25.00
❑ ED 2685 [PS]	Walking the Streets	1960	25.00
❑ ED 2694	*Is It Wrong/Lover's Leap/No Love Have I/Whirlpool of Love	1961	25.00
❑ ED 2694 [PS]	Is It Wrong	1961	25.00
❑ ED 2709	*Hideaway Heart/Tender Years/Pictures on the Wall/First to Have a Second Chance	1962	25.00
❑ ED 2709 [PS]	Hideaway Heart	1962	25.00
❑ ED 2715	Alla My Love/You Are My Life//Sweet Lips/How Do You Talk to a Baby	1962	25.00
❑ ED 2715 [PS]	Alla My Love	1962	25.00
❑ ED 2719	(contents unknown)	1962	25.00
❑ ED 2719 [PS]	Webb Pierce	1962	25.00
❑ ED 2734	*Crazy Wild Desire/Take Time/I'm Falling in Love with You/There's More Pretty Girls Than One	1962	25.00
❑ ED 2734 [PS]	Crazy Wild Desire	1962	25.00
❑ ED 2748	(contents unknown)	1963	30.00
❑ ED 2748 [PS]	Fallen Angel	1963	30.00
❑ ED 2761	*Cow Town/If I Could Come Back/Sooner or Later/Sawmill	1964	30.00
❑ ED 2761 [PS]	Cow Town	1964	30.00
❑ ED 2785	(contents unknown)	1965	40.00
❑ ED 2785 [PS]	Nobody's Darling But Mine	1965	40.00
❑ ED 2786	Softly and Tenderly/If Jesus Came to Your House//What Would You Give in Exchange for Your Soul/Bow Thy Head	1965	40.00
❑ ED 2786 [PS]	Softly and Tenderly	1965	40.00
❑ ED 2799	(contents unknown)	1966	40.00

Except when noted otherwise, VG = 25% of NM, and VG+ = 50% of NM. (Example: VG = $2.00, VG+ = $4.00 and NM = $8.00.)

Number	Title (A Side/B Side)	Yr	NM
❑ ED 2799 [PS]	Loving You Then Losing You	1966	40.00
❑ 7-34042	Heartaches by the Number/You Are My Life/Waterloo// Someday You'll Call My Name/ Alla My Love/I Close My Eyes	196?	20.00
—Stereo jukebox issue; small hole, plays at 33 1/3 rpm			
❑ 7-34042 [PS]	Cross Country	196?	20.00
❑ 7-34110	Walk On By/Are You Sincere/ I've Got a New Heartache// Little Bitty Tear/If I Could Come Back/One More Time	196?	15.00
—Jukebox issue; small hole, plays at 33 1/3 rpm			
❑ 7-34110 [PS]	I've Got a New Heartache	196?	15.00
Albums			
DECCA			
❑ DXB 181 [(2)M]	The Webb Pierce Story	1964	30.00
—Deduct 25% if booklet is missing			
❑ DL 4015 [M]	Webb with a Beat	1960	30.00
❑ DL 4079 [M]	Walking the Streets	1960	30.00
❑ DL 4110 [M]	Golden Favorites	1961	30.00
❑ DL 4144 [M]	Fallen Angel	1961	30.00
❑ DL 4218 [M]	Hideaway Heart	1962	30.00
❑ DL 4294 [M]	Cross Country	1962	30.00
❑ DL 4358 [M]	I've Got a New Heartache	1963	25.00
❑ DL 4384 [M]	Bow Thy Head	1963	25.00
❑ DL 4486 [M]	Sands of Gold	1964	25.00
❑ DL 4604 [M]	Memory #1	1965	25.00
❑ DL 4659 [M]	Country Music Time	1965	25.00
❑ DL 4739 [M]	Sweet Memories	1966	25.00
❑ DL 4782 [M]	Webb's Choice	1966	25.00
❑ DL 4844 [M]	Where'd Ya Stay Last Night	1967	30.00
❑ DL 4964 [M]	Fool, Fool, Fool	1968	50.00
❑ DL 5536 [10]	That Wondering Boy	1954	120.00
❑ DXSB 7181 [(2)S]	The Webb Pierce Story	1964	40.00
—Deduct 25% if booklet is missing			
❑ DL 8129 [M]	Webb Pierce	1955	60.00
—Black label, silver print			
❑ DL 8129 [M]	Webb Pierce	196?	30.00
—Black label with color bar			
❑ DL 8295 [M]	That Wondering Boy	1956	60.00
—Black label, silver print			
❑ DL 8295 [M]	That Wondering Boy	196?	30.00
—Black label with color bar			
❑ DL 8728 [M]	Just Imagination	1957	50.00
—Black label, silver print			
❑ DL 8728 [M]	Just Imagination	196?	30.00
—Black label with color bar			
❑ DL 8889 [M]	Bound for the Kingdom	1959	40.00
—Black label, silver print			
❑ DL 8889 [M]	Bound for the Kingdom	196?	25.00
—Black label with color bar			
❑ DL 8899 [M]	Webb!	1959	40.00
—Black label, silver print			
❑ DL 8899 [M]	Webb!	196?	25.00
—Black label with color bar			
❑ DL 74015 [S]	Webb with a Beat	1960	40.00
❑ DL 74079 [S]	Walking the Streets	1960	40.00
❑ DL 74110 [S]	Golden Favorites	1961	40.00
❑ DL 74144 [S]	Fallen Angel	1961	40.00
❑ DL 74218 [S]	Hideaway Heart	1962	40.00
❑ DL 74294 [S]	Cross Country	1962	40.00
❑ DL 74358 [S]	I've Got a New Heartache	1963	30.00
❑ DL 74384 [S]	Bow Thy Head	1963	30.00
❑ DL 74486 [S]	Sands of Gold	1964	30.00
❑ DL 74604 [S]	Memory #1	1965	30.00
❑ DL 74659 [S]	Country Music Time	1965	30.00
❑ DL 74739 [S]	Sweet Memories	1966	30.00
❑ DL 74782 [S]	Webb's Choice	1966	30.00
❑ DL 74844 [S]	Where'd Ya Stay Last Night	1967	25.00
❑ DL 74964 [S]	Fool, Fool, Fool	1968	25.00
❑ DL 74999	Webb Pierce's Greatest Hits	1968	25.00
❑ DL 75071	Saturday Night	1969	25.00
❑ DL 75132	Webb Pierce Sings This Thing	1969	25.00
❑ DL 75168	Love Ain't Never Gonna Be No Better	1970	25.00
❑ DL 75210	Merry-Go-Round World	1970	20.00
❑ DL 75280	The Webb Pierce Road Show	1971	20.00
❑ DL 75393	I'm Gonna Be a Swinger	1972	20.00
❑ DL 78889 [S]	Bound for the Kingdom	1959	50.00
—Black label, silver print			
❑ DL 78889 [S]	Bound for the Kingdom	196?	30.00
—Black label with color bar			
❑ DL 78899 [M]	Webb!	196?	30.00
—Black label with color bar			
❑ DL 78899 [S]	Webb!	1959	50.00
—Black label, silver print			
KING			
❑ 648 [M]	The One and Only Webb Pierce	1959	70.00
MCA			
❑ 130	Greatest Hits	1973	12.00
❑ 513	I'm Gonna Be a Swinger	197?	12.00
—Reissue of Decca 75393			
❑ 4087 [(2)]	The Best of Webb Pierce	1974	15.00
VOCALION			
❑ VL 73830	Country Songs	1968	12.00
❑ VL 73911	Country Favorites	1970	15.00

Pink Floyd, *A Momentary Lapse of Reason*, Columbia OC 40599, 1987, **$10.**

Number	Title (A Side/B Side)	Yr	NM
PIERCE, WEBB AND DEBBIE			
45s			
MCA			
❑ 40048	Foreign Girl/What the People Say	1973	6.00
PLANTATION			
❑ 189	On My Way Out/I'm Coming Home Again	1980	5.00
❑ 191	Reality of Life/My Memory Remembers	1980	5.00
❑ 196	Happy Birthday Jesus/ (B-side unknown)	1980	6.00
PIERCE, WEBB, AND NANCY DEE			
45s			
DECCA			
❑ 32884	Above Suspicion/ I Owe It to My Heart	1971	8.00
PILOT (1)			
45s			
ARISTA			
❑ AS 0259	One Good Reason Why/ Get Up and Go	1977	4.00
EMI			
❑ 3992	Magic/Just Let Me Be	1974	5.00
❑ 4135	Don't Speak Loudly/Just a Smile	1975	4.00
❑ 4202	January/Do Me Good	1975	4.00
❑ 4305	Canada/Mover	1976	4.00
Albums			
EMI			
❑ ST-11368	Pilot	1975	10.00
❑ ST-11488	January	1976	10.00
PILOT (2)			
45s			
RCA VICTOR			
❑ 74-0770	Rider/Miss Sandy	1972	6.00
Albums			
RCA VICTOR			
❑ LSP-4730	Pilot	1972	12.00
❑ LSP-4825	Point of View	1973	20.00
PILTDOWN MEN, THE			
45s			
CAPITOL			
❑ 4414	Brontosaurus Stomp/ McDonald's Cave	1960	20.00
❑ 4460	Piltdown Rides Again/ Bubbles in the Tar	1960	15.00
❑ 4501	Goodnight Mrs. Flintstone/ The Great Impostor	1961	15.00
❑ 4581	Fossil Rock/Gargantua	1961	15.00
❑ 4703	Big Lizard/A Pretty Girl Is Like a Melody	1962	15.00
❑ 4875	Tequila Bossa Nova/Night Surfin'	1962	15.00
PIN-UPS, THE			
45s			
STORK			
❑ STK-1	Lookin' for Boys/Kenny	1964	15.00
PINERA, MIKE			
45s			
CAPRICORN			
❑ 0288	Alone with You/Lady Divine	1978	6.00
SPECTOR			
❑ 00002	Can't You Believe/ I Am the Bubble	1979	6.00
❑ 00003	Goodnight My Love/ Looking for the Light	1979	12.00
Albums			
CAPRICORN			
❑ CPN 0202	Isla	1978	12.00
SPECTOR			
❑ 00001	Forever, Mike Pinera	1979	12.00

P

PING PONGS, THE

45s

CUB

Number	Title (A Side/B Side)	Yr	NM
❑ 9062	Big Ben/In the Chapel in the Moonlight	1960	20.00

UNITED ARTISTS

Number	Title (A Side/B Side)	Yr	NM
❑ 236	Zyzzle/Summer Reverie	1960	20.00

PINK CLOUD, THE

45s

TOWER

Number	Title (A Side/B Side)	Yr	NM
❑ 376	Midnight Sun (Vocal)/ Midnight Sun (Instrumental)	1967	20.00

PINK FLOYD Also see SYD BARRETT; ROGER WATERS; RICHARD WRIGHT.

12-Inch Singles

COLUMBIA

Number	Title (A Side/B Side)	Yr	NM
❑ AS 777 [DJ]	Run Like Hell/Don't Leave Me Now	1980	20.00
❑ AS 1334 [DJ]	Money/Another Brick in the Wall, Part 2	1981	25.00
—Pink vinyl			
❑ AS 1541 [DJ]	When the Tigers Broke Free/ Bring the Boys Back Home	1982	12.00
❑ AS 1635 [DJ]	Your Possible Pasts/ The Final Cut	1982	12.00
❑ CAS 2775 [DJ]	Learning to Fly (Edit)/ Learning to Fly (LP)	1987	12.00
❑ CAS 2878 [DJ]	On the Turning Away (7" Edit)/ On the Turning Away (Live)	1987	12.00

45s

CAPITOL

Number	Title (A Side/B Side)	Yr	NM
❑ 58884	Money (Single Edit)/ Time (Single Edit)	2000	6.00
❑ 58885	Wish You Were Here/ Have a Cigar	2000	6.00

COLUMBIA

Number	Title (A Side/B Side)	Yr	NM
❑ AE7 1653 [DJ]	Not Now John (Obscured Version) (same on both sides)	1983	10.00
❑ AE7 1653 [PS]	Not Now John (Obscured Version) (same on both sides)	1983	10.00
❑ 02165	Run Like Hell/Comfortably Numb	1981	3.00
—Reissue			
❑ 03118	Another Brick in the Wall, Part 2/One of My Turns	1982	3.00
—Reissue			
❑ 03142	When the Tigers Broke Free/ Bring the Boys Back Home	1982	4.00
❑ 03142 [PS]	When the Tigers Broke Free/ Bring the Boys Back Home	1982	8.00
—Fold-open cardboard sleeve			
❑ X18-03176	When the Tigers Broke Free/ Bring the Boys Back Home	1982	10.00
❑ X18-03176 [PS]	When the Tigers Broke Free/ Bring the Boys Back Home	1982	10.00
—Fold-open cardboard sleeve			
❑ 03905	Not Now John (Obscured Version)/The Heroes Return	1983	4.00
❑ 03905 [PS]	Not Now John (Obscured Version)/The Heroes Return	1983	8.00
❑ 07363	Learning to Fly/Terminal Frost	1987	4.00
❑ 07363 [PS]	Learning to Fly/Terminal Frost	1987	4.00
❑ 07660	On the Turning Away/ Run Like Hell	1987	4.00
❑ 07660 [PS]	On the Turning Away/ Run Like Hell	1987	8.00
❑ 10248	Have a Cigar/Welcome to the Machine	1975	12.00
❑ 11187	Another Brick in the Wall (Part 2)/One of My Turns	1980	4.00
—Regular Columbia orange label			
❑ 11187	Another Brick in the Wall (Part 2)/One of My Turns	1980	5.00
—Custom "wall" label			
❑ 11187 [PS]	Another Brick in the Wall (Part 2)/One of My Turns	1980	8.00
❑ 11265	Run Like Hell/Don't Leave Me Now	1980	4.00
❑ 11311	Comfortably Numb/Hey You	1980	4.00
❑ CS7 51388 [DJ]	Another Brick in the Wall (Part II) (Live) (same on both sides)	2005	10.00
—White vinyl; given at Best Buy to buyers of The Wall DVD			
❑ 77493	Take It Back/Astronomy Domine (Live)	1994	4.00

HARVEST

Number	Title (A Side/B Side)	Yr	NM
❑ 3240	Fearless/One of These Days	1971	20.00
❑ 3391	Stay/Free Four	1972	20.00
❑ 3609	Money/Any Colour You Like	1973	15.00
❑ P-3609 [DJ]	Money (Edited Mono)/Money (Edited Stereo)	1973	20.00
❑ 3832	Time/Us and Them	1974	20.00
❑ SPRO-6669 [DJ]	Money (Censored Edited Mono)/ Money (Censored Edited Stereo)	1973	15.00
—This promo was sent to radio stations with a frantic note telling them to disregard the first promo			

TOWER

Number	Title (A Side/B Side)	Yr	NM
❑ 333	Arnold Layne/Candy and a Currant Bun	1967	200.00
❑ 333 [PS]	Arnold Layne/Candy and a Currant Bun	1967	700.00
—Only issued with promotional copies			
❑ 356	See Emily Play/Scarecrow	1967	200.00
❑ 356 [PS]	See Emily Play/Scarecrow	1967	700.00
—Title sleeve; only issued with some promotional copies			
❑ 356 [PS]	See Emily Play/Scarecrow	1967	800.00
—Photo sleeve; only issued with some promotional copies			
❑ 378	The Gnome/Flaming	1967	150.00
❑ 426	It Would Be So Nice/Julia Dream	1968	250.00
❑ 440	Let There Be More Light/ Remember a Day	1968	300.00

Albums

CAPITOL

Number	Title (A Side/B Side)	Yr	NM
❑ SPRO-8116/7 [DJ]	Pink Floyd Tour '75	1975	80.00
❑ SEAX-11902 [PD]	The Dark Side of the Moon	1978	50.00
❑ ST-12276	Works	1983	10.00
❑ SN-16230	More	1982	10.00
—Budget-line reissue			
❑ SN-16234	Relics	1982	10.00
—Budget-line reissue			
❑ SN-16330	Obscured by Clouds	1985	10.00
—Budget-line reissue			
❑ SN-16337	Atom Heart Mother	1985	10.00
—Budget-line reissue			

COLUMBIA

Number	Title (A Side/B Side)	Yr	NM
❑ AP-1 [DJ]	Animals	1977	150.00
—White cover, with the song "Pigs" edited for airplay			
❑ AS 736 [DJ]	Off the Wall	1979	150.00
—Sampler from 2-LP set			
❑ AS 1636 [DJ]	The Final Cut	1983	25.00
—White label, record banded for airplay			
❑ HC 33453	Wish You Were Here	1981	60.00
—Half-speed mastered edition (original)			
❑ PC 33453	Wish You Were Here	1975	12.00
—Standard copy (no blue wraparound) without bar code			
❑ PC 33453	Wish You Were Here	1975	25.00
—Original copies had a blue wraparound with title/artist sticker. Most buyers threw this out upon opening the LP!			
❑ PC 33453 [DJ]	Wish You Were Here	1975	250.00
—White cover, "Special DJ Copy"; banded for airplay			
❑ PC 33453 [DJ]	Wish You Were Here	1975	300.00
—Blue cover with photo and title on jacket; unbanded record			
❑ PCQ 33453 [Q]	Wish You Were Here	1975	200.00
❑ JC 34474	Animals	1977	10.00
❑ JC 34474 [DJ]	Animals	1977	100.00
—"Demonstration Not for Sale" on label; also has insert			
❑ PC2 36183 [(2)]	The Wall	1979	15.00
❑ PC 37680	A Collection of Great Dance Songs	198?	8.00
—Budget-line reissue			
❑ TC 37680	A Collection of Great Dance Songs	1981	10.00
❑ QC 38243	The Final Cut	1983	10.00
❑ OC 40599	A Momentary Lapse of Reason	1987	10.00
❑ HC 43453	Wish You Were Here	1982	40.00
—Half-speed mastered edition (reissue)			
❑ PC2 44484 [(2)]	Delicate Sound of Thunder	1988	20.00
❑ HC2 46183 [(2)]	The Wall	1983	250.00
—Half-speed mastered edition			
❑ HC 47680	A Collection of Great Dance Songs	1982	50.00
—Half-speed mastered edition			
❑ C 64200	The Division Bell	1994	100.00
—U.S. pressings on blue vinyl			

EMI

Number	Title (A Side/B Side)	Yr	NM
❑ 32700 [(4)]	Pulse	1995	100.00
—Pressed in U.K. for U.S. release; box set with 12x12 hardback book; identical to British pressings except for American bar code (67065) on shrink wrap			

HARVEST

Number	Title (A Side/B Side)	Yr	NM
❑ SKAO-382	Atom Heart Mother	197?	15.00
—With title on front cover			
❑ SKAO-382	Atom Heart Mother	1970	25.00
—Without title on front cover			
❑ SKBB-388 [(2)]	Ummagumma	1969	40.00
—With the soundtrack LP from "Gigi" leaning against wall on front cover			
❑ SKBB-388 [(2)]	Ummagumma	1970	20.00
—With white LP cover leaning against wall on front cover			
❑ SW-759	Relics	1971	15.00
❑ SMAS-832	Meddle	1971	15.00
❑ ST-11078	Obscured by Clouds	1972	15.00
❑ SMAS-11163	The Dark Side of the Moon	1973	12.00
—With no inserts			
❑ SMAS-11163	The Dark Side of the Moon	1973	25.00
—With poster and two stickers			
❑ ST-11198	More	1973	12.00
—Reissue of Tower 5169			
❑ SABB-11257 [(2)]	A Nice Pair	1973	15.00

MOBILE FIDELITY

Number	Title (A Side/B Side)	Yr	NM
❑ 1-017	The Dark Side of the Moon	1980	50.00
—Audiophile vinyl			
❑ MFQR-017	The Dark Side of the Moon	1982	300.00
—Audiophile vinyl; "Ultra High Quality Recording" in box			
❑ 1-190	Meddle	1987	75.00
—Audiophile vinyl			
❑ 1-202	Atom Heart Mother	1994	75.00
—Audiophile vinyl			

TOWER

Number	Title (A Side/B Side)	Yr	NM
❑ ST 5093 [S]	Pink Floyd (The Piper at the Gates of Dawn)	1967	80.00
—Orange label			
❑ ST 5093 [S]	Pink Floyd (The Piper at the Gates of Dawn)	1968	40.00
—Multi-color striped label			
❑ T 5093 [M]	Pink Floyd (The Piper at the Gates of Dawn)	1967	250.00
❑ ST 5131	A Saucerful of Secrets	1968	40.00
—Multi-color striped label			
❑ ST 5131	A Saucerful of Secrets	1968	80.00
—Orange label			
❑ ST 5169	More	1968	50.00

PINKERTON'S ASSORTED COLOURS

45s

LONDON

Number	Title (A Side/B Side)	Yr	NM
❑ 9820	Mirror, Mirror/She Don't Care	1966	20.00

PARROT

Number	Title (A Side/B Side)	Yr	NM
❑ 40001	Don't Stop Loving Me Baby/ Will You	1966	20.00

PINKNEY, BILL Also see THE DRIFTERS.

45s

FONTANA

Number	Title (A Side/B Side)	Yr	NM
❑ 1956	Don't Call Me/I Do the Jerk	1964	12.00

GAME

Number	Title (A Side/B Side)	Yr	NM
❑ 394	Ol' Man River/Millionaire	196?	50.00

PHILLIPS INT'L.

Number	Title (A Side/B Side)	Yr	NM
❑ 3524	After the Hop/Sally's Got a Sister	1958	20.00
—As "Bill Pinky"			

VEEP

Number	Title (A Side/B Side)	Yr	NM
❑ 1264	I Found Some Lovin'/ The Masquerade Is Over	1967	10.00

PIPES, THE (1)

45s

CARLTON

Number	Title (A Side/B Side)	Yr	NM
❑ 575	Teamwork/Soon I Will Be Done	1962	20.00

PIPES, THE (2)

45s

DOOTO

Number	Title (A Side/B Side)	Yr	NM
❑ 388	Be Fair/Let Me Give You Money	1958	25.00
❑ 401	You Are An Angel/I Love the Life I Live	1958	25.00

DOOTONE

Number	Title (A Side/B Side)	Yr	NM
❑ 388	Be Fair/Let Me Give You Money	1956	300.00
❑ 401	You Are An Angel/I Love the Life I Live	1956	300.00

PIPKINS, THE

45s

CAPITOL

Number	Title (A Side/B Side)	Yr	NM
❑ 2819	Gimme Dat Ding/To Love You	1970	6.00
❑ 2874	Sugar and Spice-Are You Cookin' Goose/Yakety Yak	1970	5.00

Albums

CAPITOL

Number	Title (A Side/B Side)	Yr	NM
❑ ST-483	Gimme Dat Ding	1970	25.00

PIPS, THE See GLADYS KNIGHT AND THE PIPS.

PIPSQUEEKS, THE

45s

WARNER BROS.

Number	Title (A Side/B Side)	Yr	NM
❑ 5878	Santa's Little Helpers/ Santa's Magic Flute	1966	10.00

PIRANHAS, THE

Albums

CUSTOM FIDELITY

Number	Title (A Side/B Side)	Yr	NM
❑ 1452	Somethin' Fishy	1969	150.00

Except when noted otherwise, VG = 25% of NM, and VG+ = 50% of NM. (Example: VG = $2.00, VG+ = $4.00 and NM = $8.00.)

PIRATES, THE
Early version of THE TEMPTATIONS.

45s

MEL-O-DY

Number	Title (A Side/B Side)	Yr	NM
105	Mind Over Matter (I'm Gonna Make You Mine)/I'll Love You Till I Die	1962	100.00

PISTILLI, GENE
Also see CASHMAN, PISTILLI & WEST; MANHATTAN TRANSFER.

45s

ATCO

Number	Title (A Side/B Side)	Yr	NM
6850	Benn Down So Long It Looks Like Up to Me/Lettin' Down an Old Friend	1971	5.00

CAPITOL

Number	Title (A Side/B Side)	Yr	NM
2627	Mr. Bojangles/Ruby Tuesday	1969	5.00

PITNEY, GENE

45s

BLAZE

Number	Title (A Side/B Side)	Yr	NM
351	Going Back to My Love/Cradle of My Arms	1958	30.00
—As "Billy Bryan"			

EPIC

Number	Title (A Side/B Side)	Yr	NM
50332	Dedication AKA This Song I Want to Dedicate to You/Sandman	1977	5.00
50461	It's Over, It's Over/Walkin' in the Sun	1977	5.00

FESTIVAL

Number	Title (A Side/B Side)	Yr	NM
25002	Please Come Back/I'll Find You	1960	30.00

MUSICOR

Number	Title (A Side/B Side)	Yr	NM
1002	(I Wanna) Love My Life Away/I Laughed So Hard I Cried	1960	15.00
1002 [PS]	(I Wanna) Love My Life Away/I Laughed So Hard I Cried	1960	40.00
1006	Louisiana Mama/Take Me Tonight	1961	15.00
1006 [PS]	Louisiana Mama/Take Me Tonight	1961	30.00
1009	Town Without Pity/Air Mail Special Delivery	1961	15.00
1011	Every Breath I Take/Mr. Moon, Mr. Cupid and I	1961	20.00
—Produced by Phil Spector; mostly brown label			
1011	Every Breath I Take/Mr. Moon, Mr. Cupid and I	1961	30.00
—Produced by Phil Spector; mostly gunmetal gray label with color inserts			
1011 [PS]	Every Breath I Take/Mr. Moon, Mr. Cupid and I	1961	25.00
1020	(The Man Who Shot) Liberty Valance/Take It Like a Man	1962	15.00
—Mostly brown label			
1022	Only Love Can Break a Heart/If I Didn't Have a Dime	1962	15.00
—Mostly brown label			
1026	Half Heaven-Half Heartache/Tower Tall	1962	15.00
—Mostly black label			
1026	Half Heaven-Half Heartache/Tower Tall	1962	25.00
—Mostly brown label			
1028	Mecca/Teardrop by Teardrop	1963	15.00
1028 [PS]	Mecca/Teardrop by Teardrop	1963	20.00
1032	True Love Never Runs Smooth/Donna Means Heartbreak	1963	15.00
1034	Twenty-Four Hours from Tulsa/Lonely Night Dream	1963	15.00
1034 [PS]	Twenty-Four Hours from Tulsa/Lonely Night Dream	1963	20.00
1036	That Girl Belongs to Yesterday/Who Needs It	1964	20.00
—A-side written by Mick Jagger and Keith Richards and produced by Andrew Oldham			
1036 [PS]	That Girl Belongs to Yesterday/Who Needs It	1964	25.00
1038	Yesterday's Hero/Cornflower Blue	1964	15.00
1039	I'm Gonna Find Myself a Girl/Lips Are Redder	1964	—
—Unreleased?			
1040	It Hurts to Be in Love/Hawaii	1964	15.00
1040 [PS]	It Hurts to Be in Love/Hawaii	1964	20.00
1045	I'm Gonna Be Strong/E Se Domani	1964	15.00
1045	I'm Gonna Be Strong/Aladdin's Lamp	1964	20.00
1045 [PS]	I'm Gonna Be Strong/E Se Domani	1964	20.00
1065	Amici Miri/I Tuoi Anni Piu Belli	1965	—
—Unreleased?			
1070	I Must Be Seeing Things/Marianne	1965	12.00
1070 [PS]	I Must Be Seeing Things/Marianne	1965	15.00
1093	Last Chance to Turn Around/Save Your Love	1965	12.00
1103	Looking Through the Eyes of Love/There's No Living Without Your Loving	1965	12.00
1130	Princess in Rags/Amore Mio	1965	12.00
1150	Me Voy Para El Compo/Hojas Muertas	1966	—
—Unreleased?			
1155	Lei Mi Aspetta/Nessuno Mi Puo' Guidcare	1966	15.00
1171	Backstage/Blue Color	1966	10.00
1171 [PS]	Backstage/Blue Color	1966	15.00
1200	(In the) Cold Light of Day/The Boss' Daughter	1966	10.00
1200 [PS]	(In the) Cold Light of Day/The Boss' Daughter	1966	15.00
1219	Just One Smile/Innamorato	1966	10.00
1233	For Me, This Is Happy/I'm Gonna Listen to Me	1967	10.00
1235	Don't Mean to Be a Preacher/Animal Crackers (In Cellophane Boxes)	1967	10.00
1245	Tremblin'/Where Did the Magic Go	1967	10.00
1252	Somethin' Gotten Hold of My Heart/Building Up My Dream World	1967	10.00
1299	The More I Saw of Her/Won't Take Long	1968	8.00
1306	She's a Heartbreaker/Conquistador	1968	10.00
1308	Somewhere in the Country/Lonely Drifter	1968	8.00
1331	Billy, You're My Friend/Lonely Drifter	1968	8.00
1331	Billy, You're My Friend/She Believes in Me	1968	8.00
1331 [PS]	Billy, You're My Friend/Lonely Drifter	1968	12.00
1348	Baby, You're My Kind of Woman/Hate	1969	8.00
1358	Maria Elena/The French Horn	1969	8.00
1361	Playing Games of Love/California	1969	8.00
1384	She Lets Her Hair Down (Early in the Morning)/I Remember	1969	8.00
1394	All the Young Women/I Remember	1970	6.00
1405	A Street Called Hope/Think of Us	1970	6.00
1419	Shady Lady/Billy, You're My Friend	1970	6.00
1439	Higher and Higher/Beautiful Sounds	1971	6.00
1442	A Thousand Arms (Five Hundred Hearts)/Gene, Are You There?	1971	6.00
1453	I Just Can't Help Myself/Beautiful Sounds	1972	6.00
1461	Summertime Dreaming/A Thousand Arms (Five Hundred Hearts)	1972	6.00
1474	Shady Lady/Run, Run Roadrunner	1973	6.00

Albums

MUSIC DISC

Number	Title	Yr	NM
MDS 1003	The Man Who Shot Liberty Valance	1969	12.00
MDS 1005	Town Without Pity	1969	12.00
MDS 1006	America's Greatest Country Songs	1969	12.00
MDS 1008	Twenty Four Hours from Tulsa	1969	12.00
MDS 1014	Baby, I Need Your Lovin'	1969	12.00

MUSICOR

Number	Title	Yr	NM
MM-2001 [M]	The Many Sides of Gene Pitney	1962	50.00
—Brown label			
MM-2001 [M]	The Many Sides of Gene Pitney	1963	25.00
—Black label			
MM-2003 [M]	Only Love Can Break a Heart	1962	40.00
—Brown label			
MM-2003 [M]	Only Love Can Break a Heart	1963	25.00
—Black label			
MM-2004 [M]	Gene Pitney Sings Just for You	1963	30.00
MM-2005 [M]	World-Wide Winners	1963	30.00
MM-2006 [M]	Blue Gene	1963	30.00
MM-2007 [M]	Gene Pitney Meets the Fair Young Ladies of Folkland	1964	30.00
MM-2008 [M]	Gene Pitney's Big Sixteen	1964	30.00
MM-2015 [M]	Gene Italiano	1964	25.00
MM-2019 [M]	It Hurts to Be in Love	1964	25.00
MM-2043 [M]	Gene Pitney's More Big Sixteen	1965	25.00
MM-2056 [M]	I Must Be Seeing Things	1965	25.00
MM-2069 [M]	Looking Through the Eyes of Love	1965	25.00
MM-2072 [M]	Gene Pitney En Espanol	1965	25.00
MM-2085 [M]	Big Sixteen, Vol. 3	1966	20.00
MM-2095 [M]	Backstage I'm Lonely	1966	20.00
MM-2100 [M]	Messumo Mi Puo Giudicare	1966	20.00
MM-2101 [M]	The Gene Pitney Show	1966	20.00
MM-2102 [M]	Greatest Hits of All Times	1966	20.00
MM-2104 [M]	The Country Side of Gene Pitney	1967	20.00
MM-2108 [M]	Young and Warm and Wonderful	1967	20.00
MM-2117 [M]	Just One Smile	1967	20.00
MM-2134 [M]	Golden Greats	1967	25.00
MS-3001 [R]	The Many Sides of Gene Pitney	1962	30.00
—Brown label			
MS-3001 [R]	The Many Sides of Gene Pitney	1963	20.00
—Black label			
MS-3003 [S]	Only Love Can Break a Heart	1962	50.00
—Brown label			
MS-3003 [S]	Only Love Can Break a Heart	1963	30.00
—Black label			
MS-3004 [S]	Gene Pitney Sings Just for You	1963	40.00
MS-3005 [P]	World-Wide Winners	1963	40.00
MS-3006 [S]	Blue Gene	1963	40.00
MS-3007 [S]	Gene Pitney Meets the Fair Young Ladies of Folkland	1964	40.00
MS-3008 [P]	Gene Pitney's Big Sixteen	1964	40.00
MS-3015 [S]	Gene Italiano	1964	30.00
MS-3019 [P]	It Hurts to Be in Love	1964	30.00
MS-3043 [P]	Gene Pitney's More Big Sixteen	1965	30.00
MS-3056 [S]	I Must Be Seeing Things	1965	30.00
MS-3069 [S]	Looking Through the Eyes of Love	1965	30.00
MS-3072 [S]	Gene Pitney En Espanol	1965	30.00
MS-3085 [S]	Big Sixteen, Vol. 3	1966	25.00
MS-3095 [S]	Backstage I'm Lonely	1966	25.00
MS-3100 [S]	Messumo Mi Puo Giudicare	1966	25.00
MS-3101 [S]	The Gene Pitney Show	1966	25.00
MS-3102 [P]	Greatest Hits of All Times	1966	25.00
MS-3104 [S]	The Country Side of Gene Pitney	1967	25.00
MS-3108 [S]	Young and Warm and Wonderful	1967	25.00
MS-3117 [S]	Just One Smile	1967	25.00
MS-3134 [S]	Golden Greats	1967	20.00
M2-3148 [(2)M]	The Gene Pitney Story	1968	40.00
—Mono is promo only			
M2S-3148 [(2)S]	The Gene Pitney Story	1968	25.00
—Add 40% if bonus photo is enclosed			
MS-3161	Gene Pitney Sings Burt Bacharach	1968	20.00
MS-3164	She's a Heartbreaker	1968	20.00
MS-3174	The Greatest Hits of Gene Pitney	1969	20.00
MS-3183	Gene Pitney Sings the Platters' Golden Platters	1970	15.00
MS-3193	Gene Pitney Super Star	1971	15.00
MS-3206	Ten Years After	1971	15.00
MS-3233	Golden Hour	1972	15.00
MUX-4600 [(2)]	The Best of Gene Pitney (Double Gold Series)	1977	15.00

RHINO

Number	Title	Yr	NM
RNDA-1102 [(2)]	Anthology (1961-1968)	1984	12.00

SPRINGBOARD

Number	Title	Yr	NM
SPB-4057	Gene Pitney	1975	10.00

PITNEY, GENE, AND GEORGE JONES
Also see each artist's individual listings.

45s

MUSICOR

Number	Title (A Side/B Side)	Yr	NM
1066	I've Got Five Dollars and It's Saturday Night/Wreck on the Highway	1965	12.00
1071	I've Got a New Heartache/My Shoes Keep Walking Back to You	1965	—
—Unreleased?			
1097	I'm a Fool to Care/Louisiana Man	1965	12.00
1097 [PS]	I'm a Fool to Care/Louisiana Man	1965	15.00
1115	Your Old Standby/Big Job	1965	12.00
1115 [PS]	Your Old Standby/Big Job	1965	15.00
1165	Y'All Come/That's All It Took	1966	10.00

Albums

MUSICOR

Number	Title	Yr	NM
MM-2044 [M]	For the First Time! Two Great Singers Together: George Jones and Gene Pitney	1965	25.00
MM-2065 [M]	It's Country Time Again	1965	25.00
MS-3044 [S]	For the First Time! Two Great Singers Together: George Jones and Gene Pitney	1965	30.00
MS-3065 [S]	It's Country Time Again	1965	30.00

PITNEY, GENE, AND MELBA MONTGOMERY
Also see each artist's individual listings.

45s

MUSICOR

Number	Title (A Side/B Side)	Yr	NM
1135	Baby, Ain't That Fine/Everybody Knows But You and Me	1965	12.00
1173	King and Queen/Being Together	1966	10.00

Albums

MUSICOR

Number	Title	Yr	NM
MM-2077 [M]	Being Together	1966	25.00
MS-3077 [S]	Being Together	1966	30.00

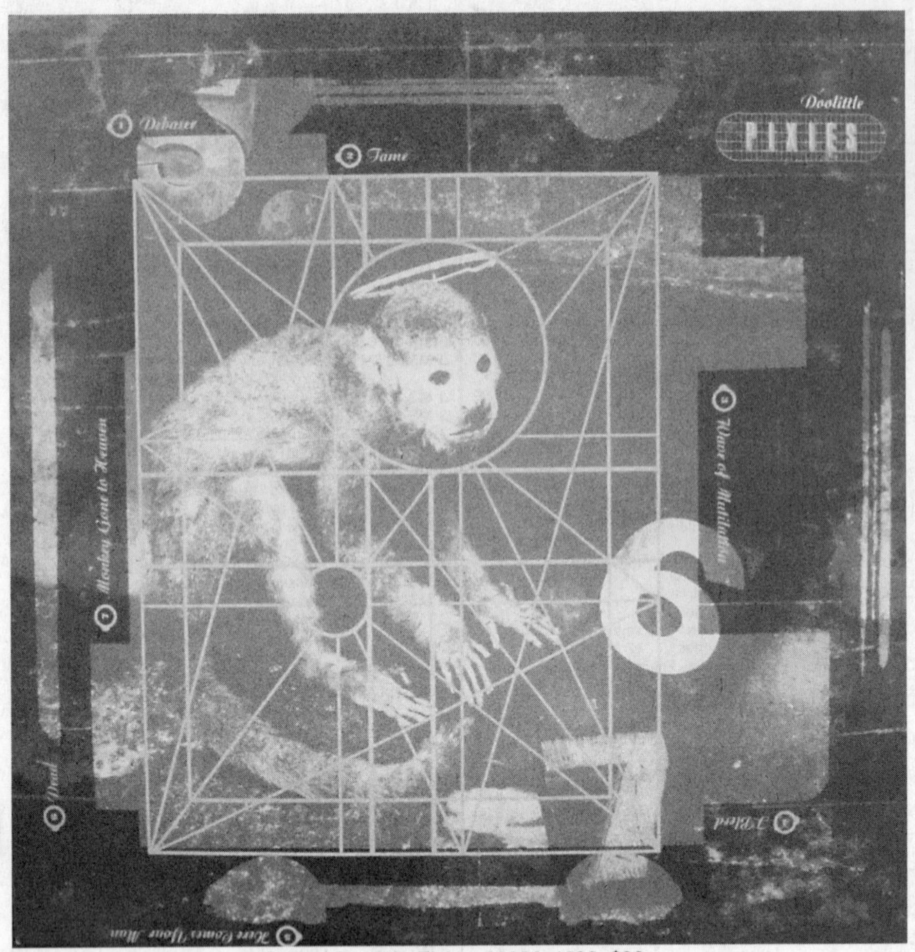

Pixies, *Doolittle*, Elektra 60856, 1989, **$20.**

Number	Title (A Side/B Side)	Yr	NM
PITTMAN, BARBARA			
45s			
PHILLIPS INT'L.			
❑ 3518	Two Young Fools in Love/I'm Getting Better All the Time	1957	40.00
❑ 3527	Cold, Cold Heart/ Everlasting Love	1958	40.00
❑ 3553	Handsome Man/The Eleventh Commandment	1960	20.00
SUN			
❑ 253	I Need a Man/No Matter Who's to Blame	1956	150.00
PITTS, GLORIA JEAN			
45s			
IMPERIAL			
❑ 5406	I Don't Stand No Quittin'/ Things You Should Know	1956	50.00
PIXIES Features Frank Black, now a prolific solo artist.			
12-Inch Singles			
ELEKTRA			
❑ ED 5386 [DJ]	Here Comes Your Man (same on both sides)	1989	6.00
❑ ED 5476 [DJ]	Velouria/Make Believe/I've Been Waiting for You/The Thing	1990	10.00
45s			
ELEKTRA			
❑ 69287	Here Comes Your Man/ Into the White	1989	8.00
Albums			
ELEKTRA			
❑ PR-8127 [DJ]	Live	1989	50.00
—Promo-only seven-song live collection of mostly songs from their pre-Elektra days			
❑ 60856 [DJ]	Doolittle	1989	12.00
—Promo-only on audiophile vinyl			
❑ 60856	Doolittle	1989	20.00
❑ 60963	Bossanova	1990	15.00

Number	Title (A Side/B Side)	Yr	NM
4AD			
❑ 70010	Bossanova	2008	15.00
❑ 71014	Trompe La Monde	2008	15.00
ROUGH TRADE			
❑ ROUGH US 38	Surfer Rosa	1988	20.00
PIXIES THREE, THE			
45s			
MERCURY			
❑ 72130	Birthday Party/Our Love	1963	15.00
❑ 72130 [PS]	Birthday Party/Our Love	1963	25.00
❑ 72208	Cold, Cold Winter/442 Glenwood Avenue	1963	15.00
❑ 72208 [PS]	Cold, Cold Winter/442 Glenwood Avenue	1963	25.00
❑ 72250	Gee/After the Party	1964	15.00
❑ 72250 [PS]	Gee/After the Party	1964	30.00
❑ 72288	It's Summertime U.S.A./ The Hootch	1964	15.00
❑ 72288 [PS]	It's Summertime U.S.A./ The Hootch	1964	25.00
❑ 72331	Love Walked In/Orphan Boy	1964	15.00
❑ 72357	Love Me, Love Me/Your Way	1964	15.00
Albums			
MERCURY			
❑ MG-20912 [M]	Party with the Pixies Three	1964	150.00
❑ SR-60912 [S]	Party with the Pixies Three	1964	200.00
PLAIDS, THE			
45s			
DARL			
❑ 1001	Keeper of My Heart/I Sing for You	1956	20.00
❑ 1003	Halfway to Heaven/ Al-Lee-O, Al-Lee-Ay	1956	20.00
ERA			
❑ 3002	Around the Corner/He Stole Flo	1959	20.00
LIBERTY			
❑ 55167	Hungry for Your Love/Chit-Chat	1958	400.00

Number	Title (A Side/B Side)	Yr	NM
NASCO			
❑ 6011	Till the End of the Dance/My Pretty Baby	1958	20.00
PLANET P Features Tony Carey of RAINBOW and solo fame.			
45s			
GEFFEN			
❑ 29705	Why Me?/Only You and Me	1983	3.00
❑ 29705 [PS]	Why Me?/Only You and Me	1983	3.00
MCA			
❑ 52515	What I See/Beyond the Barrier	1984	3.00
—As "Planet P Project"			
❑ 52515 [DJ]	What I See (same on both sides)	1984	8.00
—Pink vinyl; as "Planet P Project"			
Albums			
GEFFEN			
❑ GHS 4000	Planet P	1983	12.00
MCA			
❑ L33-1227 [EP]	Pink World	1984	12.00
—Promo-only pink vinyl EP			
❑ 8019 [(2)]	Pink World	1984	20.00
—As "Planet P Project"			
PLANET PATROL			
12-Inch Singles			
TOMMY BOY			
❑ TB 319	Play at Your Own Risk (Lil' John Remix Main 6.25) (Lil' John Remix Instrumental 6.20) (Lil' John Remix Radio Edit 4.03) (Original Version 7.50)	1998	8.00
❑ TB 825	Play at Your Own Risk (Vocal 7:59) (Instrumental 8:20)	1982	25.00
❑ TB 835	Chea p Thrills (Vocal) (Instrumental)	1983	15.00
❑ TB 837	I Didn't Know I Loved You (Till I Saw You Rock & Roll) (Vocal) (Instrumental)/ Play at Your Own Risk	1983	20.00
❑ TB 843	It Wouldn't Have Made Any Difference/Don't Tell Me	1983	15.00
❑ TB 846	Danger Zone (Vocal) (Instrumental) (A Cappella)	1984	20.00
Albums			
TOMMY BOY			
❑ TBLP-1002	Planet Patrol	1983	15.00
—Black vinyl			
❑ TBLP-1002	Planet Patrol	1983	40.00
—Originals on purple vinyl			
PLANETS, THE (1)			
45s			
ALJON			
❑ 1244	Be Sure/Once Upon a Lifetime	1962	300.00
PLANETS, THE (2)			
45s			
ERA			
❑ 1038	Never Again/Stand There Mountain	1957	50.00
❑ 1049	Be Sure/Wild Leaves	1957	50.00
NU-CLEAR			
❑ 7422	I Need You So/Sharin' Lockers	1959	60.00
PLANETS, THE (3)			
45s			
ROULETTE			
❑ 4551	You Are My Sunshine/Mr. Moon	1964	15.00
PLANT, ROBERT Also see LED ZEPPELIN; JIMMY PAGE AND ROBERT PLANT; HONEYDRIPPERS.			
45s			
ES PARANZA			
❑ 99333	Ship of Fools/Billy's Revenge	1988	3.00
❑ 99333 [PS]	Ship of Fools/Billy's Revenge	1988	3.00
❑ 99348	Tall Cool One/White, Clean and Neat	1988	3.00
❑ 99348 [PS]	Tall Cool One/White, Clean and Neat	1988	10.00
❑ 99373	Heaven Knows/Walking Towards Paradise	1988	3.00
❑ 99373 [PS]	Heaven Knows/Walking Towards Paradise	1988	3.00
❑ 99622	Too Loud/Kallalou Kallalou	1985	3.00
❑ 99622 [PS]	Too Loud/Kallalou Kallalou	1985	4.00
❑ 99644	Little by Little/Trouble Your Money	1985	3.00
❑ 99644 [PS]	Little by Little/Trouble Your Money	1985	4.00
❑ 99820	In the Mood/Horizontal Departure	1983	3.00
❑ 99820 [PS]	In the Mood/Horizontal Departure	1983	5.00
❑ 99844	Big Log/Far Post	1983	3.00
❑ 99844 [PS]	Big Log/Far Post	1983	5.00

Except when noted otherwise, VG = 25% of NM, and VG+ = 50% of NM. (Example: VG = $2.00, VG+ = $4.00 and NM = $8.00.)

Number	Title (A Side/B Side)	Yr	NM
SWAN SONG			
❑ 99952	Pledge Pin/Fat Lip	1982	4.00
❑ 99952 [PS]	Pledge Pin/Fat Lip	1982	30.00
❑ 99979	Burning Down One Side/ Moonlight in Samosa	1982	4.00
❑ 99979 [PS]	Burning Down One Side/ Moonlight in Samosa	1982	6.00
Albums			
ES PARANZA			
❑ PR 2244 [(2)DJ]	Non-Stop Go	1988	25.00
—Promo-only interview album			
❑ 90101	The Principle of Moments	1983	8.00
❑ 90265	Shaken 'n' Stirred	1985	8.00
❑ 90485 [EP]	Little by Little Collector's Edition	1985	8.00
❑ 90863	Now and Zen	1988	8.00
❑ 91336	Manic Nirvana	1990	15.00
SWAN SONG			
❑ SS 8512	Pictures at Eleven	1982	10.00

PLANT & SEE

Number	Title (A Side/B Side)	Yr	NM
45s			
WHITE WHALE			
❑ 309	Henrietta/Put Out the Fire	1969	12.00
Albums			
WHITE WHALE			
❑ WWS-7120	Plant & See	1969	25.00

PLANT LIFE

Number	Title (A Side/B Side)	Yr	NM
45s			
DATE			
❑ 1572	Flower Girl/Say It Over Again	1967	10.00

PLANTS, THE

Number	Title (A Side/B Side)	Yr	NM
45s			
J&S			
❑ 248/9	I Searched the Seven Seas/I Took a Trip Way Over the Sea	1956	400.00
❑ 1602	Dear, I Swear/It's You	1957	40.00
—No address under label name			
❑ 1602	Dear, I Swear/It's You	1957	400.00
—Address under label name			

PLASMATICS

Number	Title (A Side/B Side)	Yr	NM
45s			
VICE SQUAD			
❑ VS 101/102	Butcher Baby/Fast Food Service/Concrete Shoes	1978	20.00
—All copies on red vinyl			
❑ VS 101/102 [PS]	Butcher Baby/Fast Food Service/ Concrete Shoes	1978	20.00
❑ VS 103/104	Dream Lover/Corruption/Want You Baby	1978	20.00
—All copies on purple vinyl			
❑ VS 103/104 [PS]	Dream Lover/Corruption/Want You Baby	1978	20.00
Albums			
CAPITOL			
❑ ST-12237	Coup d'Etat	1982	15.00
PVC			
❑ 6908	Metal Priestess	1983	15.00
—Reissue of Stiff WOW-666			
❑ 8929	Beyond the Valley of 1984	1983	15.00
—Reissue of Stiff USE-11			
STIFF			
❑ USE-9	New Hope for the Wretched	1980	25.00
❑ USE-11	Beyond the Valley of 1984	1981	25.00
❑ WOW-666 [EP]	Metal Priestess	1981	25.00
VICE SQUAD			
❑ VS 105/106 [EP]	Meet the Plasmatics	1979	50.00

PLASTER CASTERS, THE

Number	Title (A Side/B Side)	Yr	NM
Albums			
BLUESTIME			
❑ BTS-9001	The Plaster Casters Blues Band	1969	50.00

PLASTIC COW, THE

Number	Title (A Side/B Side)	Yr	NM
45s			
DOT			
❑ 17284	The Plastic Cow/Medicine Man	1969	10.00
❑ 17300	Lady Jane/One Many, One Vault	1969	10.00
Albums			
DOT			
❑ DLP 25961	The Plastic Cow Goes Moooooog	1969	20.00

PLASTIC ONO BAND See JOHN LENNON; YOKO ONO.

❑ PLATO

Number	Title (A Side/B Side)	Yr	NM
45s			
PARKWAY			
❑ 914	Copy Cat/Claude's Theme	1964	10.00

Planet P, *Planet P*, Geffen GHS 4000, 1983, **$12.**

PLATTERS, THE

More than one group has used this name over the years, but all are related. Also see TONY WILLIAMS.

Number	Title (A Side/B Side)	Yr	NM
45s			
ANTLER			
❑ 3000/1	I Do It All the Time/Shake What Your Mama Gave You	1982	6.00
AVALANCHE			
❑ XW224	Sunday with You/If the World Loved	1973	8.00
—As "The Buck Ram Platters"			
ENTREE			
❑ 107	Won't You Be My Friend/Run While It's Dark	1965	8.00
—As "The Platters 1965"			
FEDERAL			
❑ 12153	Give Thanks/Hey Now	1953	400.00
—As "Tony Williams and the Platters"			
❑ 12164	I'll Cry When You're Gone/ I Need You All the Time	1954	1000.
❑ 12181	Roses of Picardy/ Beer Barrel Polka	1954	300.00
❑ 12188	Tell the World/Love All Night	1954	200.00
❑ 12198	Voo-Vee-Ah-Bee/ Shake It Up Mambo	1954	200.00
❑ 12204	Maggie Doesn't Work Here Anymore/Take Me Back, Take Me Back	1955	200.00
❑ 12244	Only You (And You Alone)/ You Made Me Cry	1955	300.00
❑ 12250	Tell the World/I Need You All the Time	1956	120.00
❑ 12271	Give Thanks/I Need You All the Time	1956	80.00
MERCURY			
❑ 10001 [S]	Smoke Gets In Your Eyes/ No Matter What You Are	1959	50.00
❑ 10007 [S]	Remember When/ Love of a Lifetime	1959	40.00
❑ 70633	Only You (And You Alone)/ Bark, Battle and Ball	1955	40.00
—Black label			
❑ 70633	Only You (And You Alone)/ Bark, Battle and Ball	1955	50.00
—Earliest pressings have pink labels			
❑ 70753	The Great Pretender/I'm Just a Dancing Partner	1955	20.00
—Black label			
❑ 70753	The Great Pretender/I'm Just a Dancing Partner	1955	40.00
—Maroon label			
❑ 70819	(You've Got) The Magic Touch/ Winner Take All	1956	20.00
—Black label			
❑ 70819	(You've Got) The Magic Touch/ Winner Take All	1956	40.00
—Maroon label			
❑ 70893	My Prayer/Heaven on Earth	1956	20.00
—Black label			
❑ 70893	My Prayer/Heaven on Earth	1956	40.00
—Maroon label			
❑ 70948	You'll Never Never Know/ It Isn't Right	1956	20.00
—Black label			
❑ 70948	You'll Never Never Know/ It Isn't Right	1956	30.00
—Maroon label			
❑ 71011	One in a Million/On My Word of Honor	1956	30.00
❑ 71032	I'm Sorry/He's Mine	1957	20.00
—Black label			
❑ 71032	I'm Sorry/He's Mine	1957	30.00
—Maroon label			
❑ 71093	My Dream/I Wanna	1957	20.00
—Black label			
❑ 71093	My Dream/I Wanna	1957	30.00
—Maroon label			
❑ 71184	Only Because/The Mystery of You	1957	25.00
❑ 71246	Helpless/Indifferent	1957	25.00
❑ 71289	Twilight Time/Out of My Mind	1958	25.00
❑ 71320	You're Making a Mistake/ My Old Flame	1958	25.00

Number	Title (A Side/B Side)	Yr	NM
❑ 71353	I Wish/It's Raining Outside	1958	25.00
—Black label			
❑ 71353	I Wish/It's Raining Outside	1958	30.00
—Blue label			
❑ 71383	Smoke Gets In Your Eyes/ No Matter What You Are	1958	25.00
—Black label			
❑ 71383	Smoke Gets In Your Eyes/ No Matter What You Are	1958	30.00
—Blue label			
❑ 71427	Enchanted/The Sound and the Fury	1959	20.00
❑ 71467 [M]	Remember When/ Love of a Lifetime	1959	20.00
❑ 71502	Where/Wish It Were Me	1959	20.00
❑ 71538	My Secret/What Does It Matter	1959	20.00
❑ 71563	Harbor Lights/Sleepy Lagoon	1960	20.00
❑ 71563 [PS]	Harbor Lights/Sleepy Lagoon	1960	40.00
❑ 71624	Ebb Tide/(I'll Be With You) In Apple Blossom Time	1960	20.00
❑ 71656	Red Sails in the Sunset/Sad River	1960	20.00
❑ 71656 [PS]	Red Sails in the Sunset/Sad River	1960	30.00
❑ 71697	To Each His Own/Down the River of Golden Dreams	1960	20.00
❑ 71697 [PS]	To Each His Own/Down the River of Golden Dreams	1960	30.00
❑ 71749	If I Didn't Care/True Lover	1961	15.00
❑ 71749 [PS]	If I Didn't Care/True Lover	1961	30.00
❑ 71791	Trees/Immortal Love	1961	15.00
❑ 71791 [PS]	Trees/Immortal Love	1961	30.00
❑ 71847	I'll Never Smile Again/ You Don't Say	1961	15.00
❑ 71847 [PS]	I'll Never Smile Again/ You Don't Say	1961	30.00
❑ 71904	Song for the Lonely/ You'll Never Know	1961	15.00
❑ 71904 [PS]	Song for the Lonely/ You'll Never Know	1961	30.00
❑ 71921	It's Magic/Reaching for a Star	1962	15.00
❑ 71921 [PS]	It's Magic/Reaching for a Star	1962	30.00
❑ 71986	More Than You Know/ Every Little Moment	1962	12.00
❑ 72060	Memories/Heartbreak	1962	12.00
❑ 72107	Once in a While/I'll See You in My Dreams	1963	10.00
❑ 72129	Strangers/Here Comes Heaven Again	1963	10.00
❑ 72194	Viva Ju Joy/Quando Caliente El Sol	1963	10.00
❑ 72242	Java Jive/Michael Row the Boat Ashore	1964	10.00
❑ 72305	Sincerely/P.S. I Love You	1964	10.00
❑ 72359	Love Me Tender/Little Things Mean a Lot	1964	10.00
❑ 76160	Platterama Medley/Red Sails in the Sunset	1982	6.00
MUSICOR			
❑ 1166	I Love You 1000 Times/Don't Hear, Speak, See No Evil	1966	8.00
❑ 1195	Alone in the Light (Without You)/ Devri	1966	8.00
❑ 1211	I'll Be Home/(You've Got) The Magic Touch	1966	8.00
❑ 1229	With This Ring/If I Had a Love	1967	10.00
❑ 1251	Washed Ashore (On a Lonely Island in the Sea)/One in a Million	1967	8.00
❑ 1251	Washed Ashore (On a Lonely Island in the Sea)/What Name Shall I Give You, My Love	1967	8.00
❑ 1262	On Top of My Mind/ Shing-a-Ling-a-Loo	1967	8.00
❑ 1275	Sweet, Sweet Lovin'/Sonata	1967	8.00
❑ 1288	Love Must Go On/How Beautiful Our Love Is	1968	8.00
❑ 1302	So Many Tears/Think Before You Walk Away	1968	8.00
❑ 1322	Hard to Get a Thing Called Love/ Why	1968	8.00
❑ 1341	Fear of Loving You/Sonata	1968	8.00
❑ 1443	Be My Love/Sweet Sweet Lovin'	1971	8.00
OWL			
❑ 320	Sixteen Tons/Are You Sincere	1973	8.00
POWER			
❑ 7012	Only You/Voo Vee Ah Bee	195?	8.00
—Reissue from "S.P.C. Newark, N.J."			
RAM			
❑ 1002	Only You/Here Comes the Boogie Man	1977	8.00
❑ 1004/5	My Ship Is Coming In/Guilty	1977	8.00
❑ 4852	Personality/Who's Sorry Now	1978	8.00
7-Inch Extended Plays			
FEDERAL			
❑ EP-378	*Only You (And You Alone)/ I Need You All the Time// Tell the World/Give Thanks	1956	400.00
❑ EP-378 [PS]	The Platters Sing for Only You	1956	400.00
KING			
❑ 378	(contents unknown)	1956	150.00
❑ 378 [PS]	The Platters	1956	150.00
—Reissue of Federal EP			
❑ 651	(contents unknown)	1956	160.00
—"Federal" 651 is a counterfeit; all originals are on King			
❑ 651 [PS]	The Platters	1956	160.00
MERCURY			
❑ SR 621	Summertime/People Will Say We're in Love/More Than You Know//Stormy Weather/Every Little Movement/Poor Butterfly	196?	30.00
—Jukebox issue; small hole, plays at 33 1/3 rpm			
❑ SR 621 [PS]	Encore of Broadway Golden Hits	196?	30.00
❑ EP 1-3336	My Prayer/Have Mercy//On My Word of Honor/I'm Sorry	1957	40.00
❑ EP 1-3336 [PS]	The Platters	1957	40.00
❑ EP 1-3343	Heart of Stone/I'd Climb the Highest Mountain//September in the Rain/You've Changed	1957	40.00
❑ EP 1-3343 [PS]	The Platters (Part 1)	1957	40.00
❑ EP 1-3344	I'll Get By/I'll Give You My Word//In the Still of the Night/ Wagon Wheels	1957	40.00
❑ EP 1-3344 [PS]	The Platters (Part 2)	1957	40.00
❑ EP 1-3345	Take Me in Your Arms/You Can Depend on Me//Temptation/ I Don't Know Why	1957	40.00
❑ EP 1-3345 [PS]	The Platters (Part 3)	1957	40.00
❑ EP 1-3353	No Power on Earth/You Are Too Beautiful//Darktown Strutter's Ball/Sweet Sixteen	1958	40.00
❑ EP 1-3353 [PS]	The Flying Platters (Part 1)	1958	40.00
❑ EP 1-3354	Only Because/Love, You Funny Thing//I'm Gonna Sit Right Down and Write Myself a Letter/In the Middle of Nowhere	1958	40.00
❑ EP 1-3354 [PS]	The Flying Platters (Part 2)	1958	40.00
❑ EP 1-3355	Mean to Me/Oh Promise Me// Time and Tide/Don't Forget	1958	40.00
❑ EP 1-3355 [PS]	The Flying Platters	1958	40.00
❑ EP 1-3393	Twilight Time/For the First Time//Don't Blame Me/But Not Like You	1958	40.00
❑ EP 1-3393 [PS]	Twilight Time	1958	40.00
❑ EP1-4029	Twilight Time/My Prayer// Smoke Gets in Your Eyes/ Remember When	196?	30.00
❑ EP1-4029 [PS]	Encore of Golden Hits - Vol. 1	196?	30.00
Albums			
CANDELITE MUSIC			
❑ CMI 1000 [(5)]	The 50 Golden Hits of the Platters	197?	40.00
COLUMBIA SPECIAL PRODUCTS			
❑ P 11834 [S]	Christmas with the Platters	1973	15.00
—Reissue of Mercury SR-60841 with fewer tracks			
FEDERAL			
❑ 549 [M]	The Platters	1957	1600.
—Records on Federal 651 are bootlegs from the 1970s			
KING			
❑ 651 [M]	The Platters	1959	800.00
—Records on Federal 651 are bootlegs from the 1970s			
❑ KLP-651 [M]	The Platters	1987	10.00
—Reissue with "Highland Records" on label			
❑ 5002	19 Hits of the Platters	197?	12.00
MERCURY			
❑ SRM-1-4050	Platterama	1982	10.00
❑ MG-20146 [M]	The Platters	1956	100.00
❑ MG-20216 [M]	The Platters, Vol. Two	1956	100.00
❑ MG-20298 [M]	The Flying Platters	1957	100.00
❑ MG-20366 [M]	The Flying Platters Around the World	1958	30.00
❑ MG-20410 [M]	Remember When?	1959	30.00
❑ MG-20472 [M]	Encore of Golden Hits	1960	30.00
❑ MG-20481 [M]	Reflections	1960	25.00
❑ MG-20589 [M]	Life Is Just a Bowl of Cherries	1960	25.00
❑ MG-20591 [M]	More Encore of Golden Hits	1960	25.00
❑ MG-20613 [M]	Encore of Broadway Golden Hits	1961	20.00
❑ MG-20669 [M]	Song for the Lonely	1962	20.00
❑ MG-20759 [M]	Moonlight Memories	1963	20.00
❑ MG-20782 [M]	The Platters Present All-Time Movie Hits	1963	20.00
❑ MG-20808 [M]	The Platters Sing Latino	1963	20.00
❑ MG-20841 [M]	Christmas with the Platters	1963	30.00
❑ MG-20893 [M]	Encore of Golden Hits of the Groups	1964	20.00
❑ MG-20933 [M]	10th Anniversary Album	1964	20.00
❑ MG-20983 [M]	The New Soul of the Platters	1965	15.00
❑ SR-60043 [S]	The Flying Platters Around the World	1959	50.00
❑ SR-60087 [S]	Remember When?	1959	50.00
❑ SR-60160 [S]	Reflections	1960	30.00
❑ SR-60243 [P]	Encore of Golden Hits	1960	40.00
—Original: Black label, silver print; 12 songs on LP			
❑ SR-60243 [P]	Encore of Golden Hits	1965	25.00
—Second edition: Red label, "MERCURY" in white across top; may or may not have "Gold Record Award" insignia on back cover; 12 songs on LP			
❑ SR-60243 [P]	Encore of Golden Hits	1975	12.00
—Chicago skyline label; album has 10 songs			
❑ SR-60245 [S]	Life Is Just a Bowl of Cherries	1960	30.00
❑ SR-60252 [S]	More Encore of Golden Hits	1960	30.00
❑ SR-60613 [S]	Encore of Broadway Golden Hits	1961	25.00
❑ SR-60669 [S]	Song for the Lonely	1962	25.00
❑ SR-60759 [S]	Moonlight Memories	1963	25.00
❑ SR-60782 [S]	The Platters Present All-Time Movie Hits	1963	25.00
❑ SR-60808 [S]	The Platters Sing Latino	1963	25.00
❑ SR-60841 [S]	Christmas with the Platters	1963	40.00
—Same as above, but in stereo			
❑ SR-60893 [S]	Encore of Golden Hits of the Groups	1964	25.00
❑ SR-60933 [S]	10th Anniversary Album	1964	25.00
❑ SR-60983 [S]	The New Soul of the Platters	1965	20.00
❑ 828246-1	More Encore of Golden Hits	198?	8.00
—Reissue			
❑ 828254-1	Encore of Golden Hits	198?	8.00
—Reissue			
MUSIC DISC			
❑ MDS-1002	Only You	1969	12.00
MUSICOR			
❑ MM-2091 [M]	I Love You 1,000 Times	1966	15.00
❑ MM-2111 [M]	The Platters Have the Magic Touch	1966	15.00
❑ MM-2125 [M]	Going Back to Detroit	1967	15.00
❑ MM-2141 [M]	New Golden Hits of the Platters	1967	20.00
❑ MS-3091 [S]	I Love You 1,000 Times	1966	20.00
❑ MS-3111 [S]	The Platters Have the Magic Touch	1966	20.00
❑ MS-3125 [S]	Going Back to Detroit	1967	15.00
❑ MS-3141 [S]	New Golden Hits of the Platters	1967	15.00
❑ MS-3156	Sweet, Sweet Lovin'	1968	15.00
❑ MS-3171	I Get the Sweetest Feeling	1968	15.00
❑ MS-3185	Singing the Great Hits Our Way	1969	15.00
❑ MS-3231	Golden Hour	1973	12.00
❑ MS-3254	The Golden Hits of the Platters	1973	12.00
PICKWICK			
❑ PTP-2083 [(2)]	Only You	1973	12.00
❑ SPC-3236	Super Hits	197?	10.00
RHINO			
❑ RNFP-71495 [(2)]	Anthology (1955-1967)	1986	12.00
SPRINGBOARD			
❑ SPB-4059	The Platters	197?	10.00
WING			
❑ MGW-12112 [M]	Encores!	1959	30.00
—With liner notes on back cover			
❑ MGW-12112 [M]	Encores!	196?	15.00
—With photos of other Wing LPs on back cover			
❑ MGW-12226 [M]	Flying Platters	1963	12.00
❑ MGW-12272 [M]	Reflections	1964	12.00
❑ MGW-12346 [M]	10th Anniversary Album	196?	12.00
❑ SRW-16112 [R]	Encores!	196?	12.00
❑ SRW-16226 [S]	Flying Platters	1963	12.00
❑ SRW-16272 [S]	Reflections	1964	12.00
❑ SRW-16346 [S]	10th Anniversary Album	196?	12.00

PLAYBOYS, THE (1)

The only of the many Playboys groups to have a national hit (other than Gary Lewis' or John Fred's bands).

Number	Title (A Side/B Side)	Yr	NM
45s			
CAMEO			
❑ 142	Over the Weekend/Double Talk	1958	20.00
MARTINIQUE			
❑ 101	Over the Weekend/Double Talk	1958	50.00
❑ 400	Please Forgive Me/Sing Along	1959	40.00

PLAYBOYS, THE (2)

Number	Title (A Side/B Side)	Yr	NM
45s			
ABC-PARAMOUNT			
❑ 10070	You're All I See/Memories	1959	20.00

PLAYBOYS, THE (3)

Number	Title (A Side/B Side)	Yr	NM
45s			
ACE			
❑ 670	Gotta Feelin'/How Could You Forget	1963	12.00

PLAYBOYS, THE (4)

Number	Title (A Side/B Side)	Yr	NM
45s			
CAT			
❑ 108	Tell Me/Rock, Moan and Cry	1954	50.00
❑ 115	Good Golly Miss Molly/ Honey Run	1955	50.00

Number	Title (A Side/B Side)	Yr	NM
PLAYBOYS, THE (5)			
45s			
CATALINA			
❑ 1069	Shortnin' Bread/Cheater Stomp	1964	30.00
PLAYBOYS, THE (6)			
45s			
TETRA			
❑ 4447	One Question/So Good	1956	150.00
PLAYBOYS, THE (U) Many of these could be by the above groups; many probably are not.			
45s			
CHANCELLOR			
❑ 1074	Boston Hop/What'd I Say	1961	15.00
—B-side by the Cousins			
❑ 1106	Duck Walk/If I Had My Way	1962	15.00
COTTON			
❑ 1008	Careful with My Heart/Girl of My Dreams	1962	25.00
DOLTON			
❑ 8	Party Ice/Icy Fingers	1959	20.00
HEARTBEAT			
❑ 60	Harlem Nocturne/Blue Moon	1963	20.00
IMPERIAL			
❑ 5586	Sweet Talk/Crazy Daisy	1959	20.00
LEGATO			
❑ 101	Mope De Mope/The Night Before Christmas	1963	30.00
MERCURY			
❑ 71228	Why Do I Love You, Why Do I Care/Don't Do Me Wrong	1957	25.00
RIK			
❑ 572	Jungle Fever/Shotgun	1959	25.00
SOUVENIR			
❑ 1001	Believe It or Not/Hawaiian War Chant	1959	15.00
TITAN			
❑ 1732	The Scramble/Cat Walk	1963	20.00
ZIPP			
❑ 101	Sweet Talk/Crazy Daisy	1959	40.00

Number	Title (A Side/B Side)	Yr	NM
PLAYMATES, THE			
45s			
ABC-PARAMOUNT			
❑ 10422	"A" My Name Is Alice/Just a Little Bit	1963	10.00
❑ 10468	She Never Looked Better/But Not Through Tears	1963	10.00
❑ 10492	I Cross My Fingers/I'll Never Get Over You	1963	10.00
❑ 10522	Guy Behind the Wheel/One Guy Left on the Corner	1964	10.00
BELL			
❑ 45149	Foundation of Love/Davenu	1971	6.00
COLPIX			
❑ 760	Fiddler on the Roof/Piece of the Sky	1964	8.00
❑ 769	One by One the Roses Died/Spanish Perfume	1965	8.00
CONGRESS			
❑ 245	Ballad of Stanley the Lifeguard/Should I Ask Someone Else to Tell Her	1965	8.00
RAINBOW			
❑ 360	Nickelodeon Rag/I Have Only Myself to Blame	1956	30.00
ROULETTE			
❑ 4003	Barefoot Girl/Pretty Woman	1957	15.00
❑ 4022	Darling It's Wonderful/Island Girl	1957	15.00
❑ 4022	Darling It's Wonderful/Magic Shoes	1957	15.00
❑ 4037	Jo-Ann/You Can't Stop Me from Dreaming	1957	25.00
❑ 4056	Let's Be Lovers/Give Me Another Chance	1958	15.00
❑ 4072	Don't Go Home/Can't You Get It Through Your Head	1958	15.00
❑ 4100	The Day I Died/While the Record Goes Around	1958	15.00
❑ 4115	Beep Beep/Your Love	1958	25.00
❑ 4136	Star Love/The Thing-A-Ma-Jig	1959	12.00
❑ 4160	What Is Love/I Am	1959	12.00
❑ 4200	First Love/A-Ciu-E	1959	12.00
❑ 4211	On the Beach/The Song Everybody's Singing	1959	12.00
❑ 4227	Second Chance/These Things I Offer You	1960	12.00

The Plimsouls, *Everywhere at Once*, Geffen GHS 4002, 1983, **$12.**

Number	Title (A Side/B Side)	Yr	NM
❑ 4252	Parade of Pretty Girls/Our Wedding Day	1960	12.00
❑ 4276	Wait for Me/Eyes of Angel	1960	12.00
❑ 4322	Little Mis Stuck-Up/Real Life	1961	12.00
❑ 4370	Tell Me What She Said/Cowboys Never Cry	1961	12.00
❑ 4393	Wimoweh/One Little Kiss	1961	12.00
❑ 4417	A Rose and a Star/Bachelor Flat	1962	10.00
❑ 4432	Keep Your Hands in Your Pocket/The Cop on the Beat	1962	10.00
❑ 4464	What a Funny Way to Show It/Petticoats Fly	1962	10.00
Albums			
FORUM			
❑ F-9012 [M]	At Play with the Playmates	196?	12.00
❑ SF-9012 [S]	At Play with the Playmates	196?	15.00
❑ F-9021 [M]	Broadway Show Stoppers	196?	12.00
❑ SF-9021 [S]	Broadway Show Stoppers	196?	15.00
❑ F-16001 [M]	The Playmates Visit West of the Indies	1960	15.00
❑ SF-16001 [S]	The Playmates Visit West of the Indies	1960	20.00
ROULETTE			
❑ R-25001 [M]	Calypso	1957	25.00
❑ R-25043 [M]	At Play with the Playmates	1958	25.00
❑ SR-25043 [S]	At Play with the Playmates	1958	30.00
❑ R-25059 [M]	Rock and Roll Record Hop	1959	20.00
❑ SR-25059 [S]	Rock and Roll Record Hop	1959	25.00
❑ R-25068 [M]	Cuttin' Capers	1960	20.00
❑ SR-25068 [S]	Cuttin' Capers	1960	25.00
❑ R-25084 [M]	Broadway Show Stoppers	1961	20.00
❑ SR-25084 [S]	Broadway Show Stoppers	1961	25.00
PLEASE, BOBBY			
45s			
ERA			
❑ 1044	Heartache Street/Your Driver's License Please	1957	15.00
IMPERIAL			
❑ 5508	I'm Girl Crazy/My Tummy Flip	1958	15.00

Number	Title (A Side/B Side)	Yr	NM
JAMIE			
❑ 1118	The Monster/The Switch	1959	15.00
PLEASURE FAIR, THE With Robb Royer, later of BREAD.			
45s			
UNI			
❑ 55016	Morning Glory Days/Fade In, Fade Out	1967	8.00
❑ 55078	Today/I'm Gonna Hafta Let You Go	1968	8.00
Albums			
UNI			
❑ 3008 [M]	The Pleasure Fair	1967	20.00
❑ 73008 [S]	The Pleasure Fair	1967	20.00
PLEASURE SEEKERS SUZI QUATRO was in this group.			
45s			
CAPITOL			
❑ 2050	(Theme from) Valley of the Dolls/If You Climb on the Tiger's Back	1967	20.00
HIDEOUT			
❑ 1006	Never Thought You'd Leave Me/What a Way to Die	1967	100.00
MERCURY			
❑ 72800	Good Kind of Hurt/Light of Love	1968	25.00
PLEBS, THE			
45s			
MGM			
❑ 13320	Bad Blood/Babe I'm Gonna Leave You	1965	12.00
PLEDGES, THE Actually Clyde Battin and GARY PAXTON, who recorded as SKIP AND FLIP.			
45s			
REV			
❑ 3517	Betty Jean/Her Bermuda Shorts	1958	25.00

Except when noted otherwise, VG = 25% of NM, and VG+ = 50% of NM. (Example: VG = $2.00, VG+ = $4.00 and NM = $8.00.)

Poco, *Crazy Eyes*, Epic KE 32354, 1979, **$12.**

PLIMSOULS, THE

Number	Title (A Side/B Side)	Yr	NM
12-Inch Singles			
GEFFEN			
❑ PRO-A-2068 [DJ]	A Million Miles Away/The Oldest Story/Magic Touch	1983	12.00
SHAKY CITY			
❑ 12134	A Million Miles Away/I'll Get Lucky	1982	20.00
45s			
GEFFEN			
❑ 29496	Oldest Story in the World/Hobo	1983	10.00
❑ 29600	A Million Miles Away/ Play the Breaks	1983	4.00
❑ 29600 [PS]	A Million Miles Away/ Play the Breaks	1983	12.00
PLANET			
❑ 47923	Now/When You Find Out	1981	30.00
❑ 47930	Zero Hour//Hush Hush/ Dizzy Miss Lizzie	1981	60.00
SHAKY CITY			
❑ 134	A Million Miles Away/I'll Get Lucky	1982	4.00
❑ 134 [PS]	A Million Miles Away/I'll Get Lucky	1982	4.00
Albums			
BEAT			
❑ BE-1001 [EP]	Zero Hour	1980	25.00
GEFFEN			
❑ GHS 4002	Everywhere at Once	1983	12.00
PLANET			
❑ 13	The Plimsouls	1981	20.00

PLUGZ

Number	Title (A Side/B Side)	Yr	NM
45s			
FATIMA			
❑ 79	La Bamba/Achin'	1981	15.00
❑ 79 [PS]	La Bamba/Achin'	1981	15.00
SLASH			
❑ 102	Move/Let Go/Mindless Contentment	1978	20.00
❑ 102 [PS]	Move/Let Go/Mindless Contentment	1978	20.00
—Gray folder with necktie and "Singi" button artwork			
❑ 102 [PS]	Move/Let Go/Mindless Contentment	1978	100.00
—Black on yellow sleeve with band photo and lyrics			
Albums			
FATIMA			
❑ 80	Better Luck	1981	25.00
PLUG/REAL LIFE			
❑ 001	Electrify Me	1979	60.00

PLUM NELLY

Number	Title (A Side/B Side)	Yr	NM
Albums			
CAPITOL			
❑ ST-692	Deceptive Lines	1971	20.00

PLUMB, EVE

"Jan Brady" of THE BRADY BUNCH.

Number	Title (A Side/B Side)	Yr	NM
45s			
RCA VICTOR			
❑ 74-0409	How Will It Be/ Fortune Cookie Song	1970	15.00
❑ 74-0409 [PS]	How Will It Be/ Fortune Cookie Song	1970	20.00

PLUMMER, DAVE, AND THE PLUNGERS

Number	Title (A Side/B Side)	Yr	NM
45s			
MAYBROOK			
❑ 320	Surfin' Monster/King of the Road	196?	40.00

POCO

Also see JIM MESSINA.

Number	Title (A Side/B Side)	Yr	NM
12-Inch Singles			
MCA			
❑ 2314 [DJ]	Under the Gun (same on both sides)	1980	8.00
RCA			
❑ 9039-1-RAB [DJ]	Call It Love (Edit)/ Call It Love (LP)	1989	6.00
45s			
ABC			
❑ 12126	Keep On Tryin'/Georgia, Bind My Ties	1975	5.00
❑ 12159	Makin' Love/Flyin' Solo	1976	5.00
❑ 12204	Rose of Cimarron/ Tulsa Turnaround	1976	5.00
❑ 12295	Indian Summer/Me and You	1977	5.00
❑ 12439	Crazy Love/Barbados	1978	5.00
ATLANTIC			
❑ 89629	Save a Corner of Your Heart/ The Storm	1984	5.00
❑ 89650	This Old Flame/The Storm	1984	3.00
❑ 89674	Days Gone By/Daylight	1984	3.00
❑ 89851	Break of Hearts/Love's So Cruel	1983	5.00
❑ 89919	Shoot for the Moon/ The Midnight Rodeo	1982	3.00
❑ 89970	Ghostown/High Sierra	1982	3.00
❑ 89970 [PS]	Ghostown/High Sierra	1982	4.00
EPIC			
❑ 10501	Pickin' Up the Pieces/First Love	1969	10.00
❑ 10543	My Kind of Love/Hard Luck	1969	10.00
❑ 10636	You Better Think Twice/ Anyway, Bye Bye	1970	8.00
❑ 10714	C'Mon/I Guess You Made It	1971	8.00
❑ 10804	Just for Me and You/Ol' Forgiver	1971	8.00
❑ 10816	You Are the One/Railroad Days	1971	8.00
❑ 10890	Good Feeling to Know/ Early Times	1972	6.00
❑ 10958	I Can See Everything/ Go and Say Goodbye	1973	6.00
❑ 11055	Here We Go Again/Fools Gold	1973	6.00
❑ 11092	Magnolia/Blue Water	1974	6.00
❑ 11141	Rocky Mountain Breakdown/ Faith in the Families	1974	6.00
❑ 50076	Bitter Blue/High and Dry	1975	6.00
MCA			
❑ 41023	Heart of the Night/Last Goodbye	1979	4.00
❑ 41103	Legend/Indian Summer	1979	4.00
❑ 41269	Under the Gun/Reputation	1980	4.00
❑ 41269 [PS]	Under the Gun/Reputation	1980	6.00
❑ 41326	Midnight Rain/Fool's Paradise	1980	4.00
❑ 51034	Everlasting Kind/Friends in the Distance	1980	4.00
❑ 51172	Down on the River Again/ Widowmaker	1981	4.00
❑ 52001	Seas of Heartbreaks/Feudin'	1982	4.00
RCA			
❑ 9038-7-R	Call It Love/Lovin' You Every Minute	1989	3.00
❑ 9038-7-R [PS]	Call It Love/Lovin' You Every Minute	1989	3.00
❑ 9131-7-R	Nothin' to Hide/If It Wasn't for You	1989	3.00
❑ 9131-7-R [PS]	Nothin' to Hide/If It Wasn't for You	1989	3.00
Albums			
ABC			
❑ D-890	Head Over Heels	1975	10.00
❑ D-946	Rose of Cimarron	1976	10.00
❑ D-989	Indian Summer	1977	10.00
❑ AA-1099	Legend	1978	12.00
ATLANTIC			
❑ 80008	Ghost Town	1982	10.00
❑ 80148	Inamorata	1984	10.00
EPIC			
❑ BN 26460	Pickin' Up the Pieces	1969	15.00
—Yellow label			
❑ BN 26460	Pickin' Up the Pieces	1973	10.00
—Orange label			
❑ BN 26522	Poco	1970	15.00
—Yellow label			
❑ BN 26522	Poco	1973	10.00
—Orange label			
❑ EQ 30209 [Q]	Deliverin'	1972	20.00
❑ KE 30209	Deliverin'	1971	15.00
—Yellow label			
❑ KE 30209	Deliverin'	1973	10.00
—Orange label			
❑ E 30753	From the Inside	1973	10.00
—Reissue with new prefix			
❑ KE 30753	From the Inside	1971	15.00
—Yellow label			
❑ KE 30753	From the Inside	1973	10.00
—Orange label			
❑ KE 31601	A Good Feelin' to Know	1972	15.00
—Yellow label			
❑ KE 31601	A Good Feelin' to Know	1973	10.00
—Orange label			
❑ PE 31601	A Good Feelin' to Know	198?	8.00
—Budget-line reissue			
❑ EQ 32354 [Q]	Crazy Eyes	1973	20.00
❑ KE 32354	Crazy Eyes	1973	12.00
—Orange label			
❑ PE 32354	Crazy Eyes	1979	8.00
—Blue label			
❑ EQ 32895 [Q]	Seven	1974	20.00

Except when noted otherwise, VG = 25% of NM, and VG+ = 50% of NM. (Example: VG = $2.00, VG+ = $4.00 and NM = $8.00.)

Number	Title (A Side/B Side)	Yr	NM
❑ KE 32895	Seven	1974	12.00
—Orange label			
❑ PCQ 33192 [Q]	Cantamos	1974	20.00
❑ PE 33192	Cantamos	1974	12.00
—Orange label			
❑ PE 33336	Live	1976	12.00
—Orange label			
❑ PEG 33537 [(2)]	The Very Best of Poco	1975	15.00
—Orange labels			
❑ JE 36210	The Songs of Paul Cotton	1980	10.00
❑ JE 36211	The Songs of Richie Furay	1980	10.00
MCA			
❑ AA-1099	Legend	1979	10.00
—Reissue of ABC 1099			
❑ 5132	Under the Gun	1980	10.00
❑ 5227	Blue and Gray	1981	10.00
❑ 5288	Cowboys & Englishmen	1982	10.00
❑ 5363	Backtracks	1983	10.00
❑ 37009	Head Over Heels	1980	8.00
—Budget-line reissue			
❑ 37010	Rose of Cimarron	1980	8.00
—Budget-line reissue			
❑ 37011	Indian Summer	1980	8.00
—Budget-line reissue			
❑ 37117	Legend	1981	8.00
—Budget-line reissue			
❑ 37160	Under the Gun	198?	8.00
—Budget-line reissue			
MOBILE FIDELITY			
❑ 1-020	Legend	1979	40.00
—Audiophile vinyl			
RCA			
❑ 9694-1-R	Legacy	1989	10.00

POETS, THE (1)

45s

Number	Title (A Side/B Side)	Yr	NM
SYMBOL			
❑ 214	She Blew a Good Thing/Out to Lunch	1966	15.00
❑ 216	So Young (And So Innocent)/A Sure Thing	1966	12.00
❑ 219	I'm Particular/I've Only Two Hearts	1966	12.00
VEEP			
❑ 1286	The Hustler/Soul Brothers Holiday	1968	20.00

POETS, THE (2) British group.

45s

Number	Title (A Side/B Side)	Yr	NM
DYNO VOX			
❑ 201	Now We're Thru/There Are Some	1965	25.00

POETS, THE (3)

45s

Number	Title (A Side/B Side)	Yr	NM
FLASH			
❑ 129	Vowels of Love/Dead	1958	60.00
—Maroon label			
❑ 129	Vowels of Love/Dead	1958	200.00
—Black label			

POETS, THE (4)

45s

Number	Title (A Side/B Side)	Yr	NM
IMPERIAL			
❑ 5664	Honey Chile/I'm in Love	1960	15.00

POETS, THE (U) These could be group (1) or (2).

45s

Number	Title (A Side/B Side)	Yr	NM
CHAIRMAN			
❑ 4408	Coffee House/Number One (More Time)	1963	12.00
J-2			
❑ 1302	Wrapped Around Your Finger/(B-side unknown)	196?	1000.
RED BIRD			
❑ 10-046	Merry Christmas Baby/I'm Stuck on You	1965	12.00
TRY ME			
❑ 28006	Devil's Den (Part 1)/(Part 2)	196?	20.00

POGUES, THE

12-Inch Singles

Number	Title (A Side/B Side)	Yr	NM
ISLAND			
❑ 2607 [DJ]	Yeah Yeah Yeah Yeah Yeah (2 versions)/The Limerick Raka	1988	7.00
❑ 96578	Yeah, Yeah, Yeah, Yeah, Yeah (2 versions)/The Limerick Rake	1988	7.00

Albums

Number	Title (A Side/B Side)	Yr	NM
ENIGMA			
❑ ST-73225	Red Roses for Me	1986	25.00
ISLAND			
❑ 90872	If I Should Fall from Grace With God	1988	12.00
STIFF/MCA			
❑ 5744	Rum, Sodomy and the Lash	1985	20.00
❑ 36015 [EP]	Poguetry in Motion	1986	20.00

POI DOG PONDERING

12-Inch Singles

Number	Title (A Side/B Side)	Yr	NM
COLUMBIA			
❑ CAS 1777 [DJ]	Living with the Dreaming Body/Fact of Life	1989	6.00
❑ CAS 1995 [DJ]	U Li La Lu/Bury Me Deep	1990	8.00
—One-sided 12-inch with etched B-side			

45s

Number	Title (A Side/B Side)	Yr	NM
COLUMBIA			
❑ CS7 2000 [DJ]	Big Beautiful Spoon/Sugarbush Cushman	1990	8.00

Albums

Number	Title (A Side/B Side)	Yr	NM
COLUMBIA			
❑ CAS 1856 [DJ]	Interchords	1989	20.00
—Promo-only interview and music			
❑ CAS 2219 [EP]	Untitled (Fruitless)	1990	15.00
—Promo-only six-song sampler			
❑ C 45403	Wishing Like a Mountain and Thinking Like the Sea	1990	12.00
TEXAS HOTEL			
❑ 11 [EP]	Poi Dog Pondering	1988	8.00
❑ 16 [EP]	Circle Around the Sun	198?	8.00

POINDEXTER, DON, AND THE STARLITE WRANGLERS

45s

Number	Title (A Side/B Side)	Yr	NM
SUN			
❑ 202	Now She Cares No More for Me/My Kind of Love	1954	2000.

POINTER SISTERS, THE

12-Inch Singles

Number	Title (A Side/B Side)	Yr	NM
COLUMBIA			
❑ 07883	Power of Persuasion (3 versions)	1988	6.00
MCA			
❑ 23769	Be There (4 versions)	1987	6.00
MOTOWN			
❑ 4661	Friend's Advice (Don't Take It) (3 versions)	1990	6.00
❑ L33-17922 [DJ]	Friend's Advice (Don't Take It) (5 versions)	1990	8.00
PLANET			
❑ 11403 [DJ]	Happiness (same on both sides)	1979	8.00
❑ 11406 [DJ]	Come and Get Your Love/Dirty Work/Echoes of Love/Hypnotized	1979	12.00
❑ 11407 [DJ]	Fire/Happiness	1979	12.00
—Red vinyl			
❑ JD-13328 [DJ]	I'm So Excited	1982	10.00
—One-sided promo			
❑ YD-13429	I'm So Excited/If You Wanna Get Back My Love	1983	10.00
❑ YD-13721	Automatic (4:48) (6:06)	1984	8.00
❑ YD-13781	Jump (For My Love) (6:24)/(Instrumental)/Heartbeat	1984	8.00
❑ JR-13858 [DJ]	I'm So Excited (same on both sides)	1984	10.00
❑ YD-13952	Neutron Dance (4:59)/Telegraph Your Love	1984	8.00
❑ YD-14042	Baby Come and Get It (7:14)/Operator	1985	8.00
RCA			
❑ 5774-1-RDAC [DJ]	Goldmine (2 versions)/Sexual Power	1986	6.00
❑ 6491-1-RDAC [DJ]	Mercury Rising (3 versions)	1986	6.00
❑ 6865-1-RD	He Turned Me Out (4 versions)	1988	6.00
❑ PD-14127	Dare Me (Long) (Instrumental)/I'll Be There	1985	6.00
❑ PD-14196	Twist My Arm (Dance Mix)/(Instrumental)/Easy Persuasion	1985	8.00
❑ PD-14225	Freedom (4:18) (6:21)	1985	6.00

45s

Number	Title (A Side/B Side)	Yr	NM
ATLANTIC			
❑ 2845	Don't Try to Take the Fifth/Tulsa County	1971	20.00
❑ 2893	Destination No More Heartaches/Send Him Back	1972	40.00
BLUE THUMB			
❑ 229	Yes We Can Can/Jada	1973	6.00
❑ 243	Wang Dang Doodle/Cloudburst	1973	6.00
❑ 248	Steam Heat/Shaky Flat Blues	1974	6.00
❑ 254	Fairytale/Love In Them Thar Hills	1974	5.00
—Second pressing has a multicolor label with ABC logo			
❑ 254	Fairytale/Love In Them Thar Hills	1974	10.00
—First pressing has a gray to white label and no reference to ABC			
❑ 262	Live Your Life Before You Die/Shaky Flat Blues	1975	5.00
❑ 265	How Long (Betcha' Got a Chick on the Side)/Easy Days	1975	5.00
❑ 268	Going Down Slowly/Sleeping Alone	1975	5.00
❑ 271	You Gotta Believe/Shaky Flat Blues	1976	5.00
❑ 275	Having a Party/Lonely Gal	1977	5.00
❑ 277	I Need a Man/I'll Get By Without You	1978	5.00
COLUMBIA			
❑ 08015	Power of Persuasion/(Instrumental)	1988	3.00
❑ 08015 [PS]	Power of Persuasion/(Instrumental)	1988	3.00
MCA			
❑ 53120	Be There/(Instrumental)	1987	3.00
❑ 53120 [PS]	Be There/(Instrumental)	1987	3.00
MOTOWN			
❑ 902	Friends' Advice (Don't Take It)/Friends' Advice (Don't Take It) (Dub)	1990	4.00
PLANET			
❑ YB-13254	American Music/I Want to Do It with You	1982	4.00
❑ YB-13327	I'm So Excited/Nothing But a Heartache (Live)	1982	4.00
❑ YB-13430	If You Wanna Get Back Your Lady/I'm So Excited	1983	4.00
❑ GB-13485	American Music/I'm So Excited	1983	3.00
—Gold Standard Series			
❑ YB-13639	I Need You/If You Wanna Get Back Your Lady	1983	4.00
❑ YB-13730	Automatic/Nightline	1984	4.00
❑ YB-13780	Jump (For My Love)/Heart Beat	1984	4.00
❑ GB-13795	I Need You/If You Wanna Get Back Your Lady	1984	3.00
—Gold Standard Series			
❑ YB-13857	I'm So Excited/Dance Electric	1984	4.00
❑ YB-13951	Neutron Dance/Telegraph Your Love	1984	4.00
❑ YB-14041	Baby Come and Get It/Operator	1985	4.00
❑ YB-14041 [PS]	Baby Come and Get It/Operator	1985	4.00
❑ GB-14072	Jump (For My Love)/Automatic	1985	3.00
—Gold Standard Series			
❑ GB-14076	Fire/He's So Shy	1985	3.00
—Gold Standard Series			
❑ GB-14077	Slow Hand/Should I Do It	1985	3.00
—Gold Standard Series			
❑ 45901	Fire/Love Is Like a Rolling Stone	1978	4.00
❑ 45901 [PS]	Fire/Love Is Like a Rolling Stone	1978	6.00
❑ 45902	Happiness/Too Late	1979	4.00
❑ 45906	Blind Faith/The Shape I'm In	1979	4.00
❑ 47916	He's So Shy/Movin' On	1980	4.00
❑ 47918	Es Tan Timido/Cosas Especiales	1980	6.00
❑ 47920	Could I Be Dreaming/Evil	1980	4.00
❑ 47925	Where Did the Time Go/Special Things	1981	4.00
❑ 47929	Slow Hand/Holdin' Out for Love	1981	4.00
❑ 47937	What a Surprise/Fall in Love Again	1981	4.00
❑ 47945	Sweet Lover Man/Got to Find Love	1981	4.00
❑ 47960	Should I Do It/We're Gonna Make It	1982	4.00
RCA			
❑ 5062-7-R	Goldmine/Sexual Power	1986	3.00
❑ 5062-7-R [PS]	Goldmine/Sexual Power	1986	3.00
❑ 5112-7-R	All I Know Is the Way I Feel/Translation	1987	3.00
❑ 5230-7-R	Mercury Rising/Say the Word	1987	3.00
❑ 6865-7-R	He Turned Me Out/Translation	1988	3.00
❑ 6865-7-R [PS]	He Turned Me Out/Translation	1988	3.00
❑ 8378-7-R	I'm in Love/Uh-Oh	1988	3.00
❑ PB-14126	Dare Me/I'll Be There	1985	3.00
❑ PB-14126 [PS]	Dare Me/I'll Be There	1985	3.00
❑ PB-14197	Twist My Arm/Easy Persuasion	1986	3.00
❑ PB-14197 [PS]	Twist My Arm/Easy Persuasion	1986	3.00
❑ PB-14224	Freedom/Telegraph Your Love	1985	3.00
❑ PB-14224 [PS]	Freedom/Telegraph Your Love	1985	3.00
❑ GB-14354	Neutron Dance/Baby Come and Get It	1986	3.00
—Gold Standard Series			
SBK			
❑ S7-17637	Don't Walk Away/Tell It to My Heart	1993	4.00

Albums

Number	Title (A Side/B Side)	Yr	NM
ABC BLUE THUMB			
❑ BT-6021	Steppin	1975	12.00
❑ BT-6023	Having a Party	1977	12.00
❑ BTSY-6026 [(2)]	The Best of the Pointer Sisters	1976	15.00
BLUE THUMB			
❑ BTS-48	The Pointer Sisters	1973	12.00
❑ BTS-6009	That's a Plenty	1974	12.00

P

Number	Title (A Side/B Side)	Yr	NM
❑ BTS-8002 [(2)]	Live at the Opera House	1974	15.00

MCA

Number	Title (A Side/B Side)	Yr	NM
❑ 3275	Retrospect	1981	10.00
—Reissue of Blue Thumb material			

MOTOWN

Number	Title (A Side/B Side)	Yr	NM
❑ 6287 ML	Right Rhythm	1990	12.00

PLANET

Number	Title (A Side/B Side)	Yr	NM
❑ P-1	Energy	1978	10.00
❑ P-9	Special Things	1980	10.00
❑ P-18	Black and White	1981	10.00
❑ BXL1-4355	So Excited!	1982	10.00
❑ BEL1-4705A	Break Out	1984	8.00
—Reissue has "I'm So Excited" plus a remix of "Jump (For My Love)"			
❑ BXL1-4705	Break Out	1983	10.00
—Original does not have "I'm So Excited"			
❑ P-9003	Priority	1979	10.00
❑ 60203	Pointer Sisters' Greatest Hits	1982	10.00

RCA

Number	Title (A Side/B Side)	Yr	NM
❑ 5609-1-R	Hot Together	1986	10.00
❑ 6562-1-R	Serious Slammin'	1988	10.00

RCA VICTOR

Number	Title (A Side/B Side)	Yr	NM
❑ AYL1-5088	Special Things	1985	8.00
—Budget-line reissue			
❑ AYL1-5089	Priority	1985	8.00
—Budget-line reissue			
❑ AYL1-5091	Energy	1985	8.00
—Budget-line reissue			
❑ AYL1-5092	Black and White	1985	8.00
—Budget-line reissue			
❑ AJL1-5487	Contact	1985	10.00

POISON

First name in "hair metal."

45s

CAPITOL

Number	Title (A Side/B Side)	Yr	NM
❑ B-5686	Talk Dirty to Me/Want Some, Need Some	1987	3.00
—Originals have Capitol logo at top with colorband			
❑ B-5686 [PS]	Talk Dirty to Me/Want Some, Need Some	1987	4.00
❑ S7-56969	Stand/Until You Suffer Some (Fire and Ice)	1993	4.00
—Black vinyl			
❑ S7-56969	Stand/Until You Suffer Some (Fire and Ice)	1993	6.00
—Blue vinyl			
❑ 88643	Shut Up, Make Love/ Every Rose Has Its Thorn	2000	3.00

ENIGMA

Number	Title (A Side/B Side)	Yr	NM
❑ B-44004	I Want Action/Play Dirty	1987	3.00
❑ B-44004 [PS]	I Want Action/Play Dirty	1987	4.00
—Fold-out poster sleeve			
❑ B-44038	I Won't Forget You/ Blame It on You	1987	3.00
❑ B-44038 [PS]	I Won't Forget You/ Blame It on You	1987	3.00
❑ B-44145	Nothin' But a Good Time/ Look But You Can't Touch	1988	3.00
❑ B-44145 [PS]	Nothin' But a Good Time/ Look But You Can't Touch	1988	3.00
❑ B-44191	Fallen Angel/Bad to Be Good	1988	3.00
❑ B-44191 [PS]	Fallen Angel/Bad to Be Good	1988	3.00
❑ B-44203	Every Rose Has Its Thorn/ Livin' for the Minute	1988	3.00
❑ B-44203 [PS]	Every Rose Has Its Thorn/ Livin' for the Minute	1988	3.00
❑ B-44293	Your Mama Don't Dance/Look What the Cat Dragged In	1989	3.00
❑ B-44293 [PS]	Your Mama Don't Dance/Look What the Cat Dragged In	1989	3.00
❑ NR-44584	Swamp Juice (Soul-O)-Unskinny Bop/Valley of Lost Souls	1990	4.00

Albums

CAPITOL

Number	Title (A Side/B Side)	Yr	NM
❑ C1-598046 [(2)]	Swallow This Live	1991	40.00
—Vinyl version available only from Columbia House			

CAPITOL/ENIGMA

Number	Title (A Side/B Side)	Yr	NM
❑ ST-12523	Look What the Cat Dragged In	1986	8.00
❑ C1-48493	Open Up and Say...Ahh!	1988	8.00
—With cropped front cover photo (woman's tongue is cut off; large black bars at top and bottom of cover)			
❑ C1-48493	Open Up and Say...Ahh!	1988	12.00
—With uncropped front cover photo (woman's tongue is fully visible)			
❑ SPRO 79319/22 [(2)]	Open Up and Say...Ahh! World Premiere Weekend	1988	25.00
—Special radio-only version to promote the LP's release			
❑ C1-91813	Flesh & Blood	1990	12.00
—With blood airbrushed out of front cover photo			
❑ C1-91813	Flesh & Blood	1990	12.00
—With blood dripping from letters "Flesh & Blood"			
❑ R 144402	Look What the Cat Dragged In	1986	10.00
—BMG Direct Marketing club edition			
❑ ST-512523	Look What the Cat Dragged In	1986	10.00
—Columbia House club edition			
❑ C1-591813	Flesh & Blood	1990	12.00
—Columbia House club edition			

POISON IDEA

45s

AMERICAN LEATHER

Number	Title (A Side/B Side)	Yr	NM
❑ 002 [PD]	Just to Get Away/ Kick Out the Jams	198?	15.00
❑ 003	Discontent/Jailhouse Stomp	1990	5.00
❑ 003 [PS]	Discontent/Jailhouse Stomp	1990	5.00

SUB POP

Number	Title (A Side/B Side)	Yr	NM
❑ 86	We Got the Beat/ Taken by Surprise	1990	7.50
—Last 1,500 on black vinyl			
❑ 86	We Got the Beat/ Taken by Surprise	1990	22.50
—First 3,000 on mint green vinyl			
❑ 86 [PS]	We Got the Beat/ Taken by Surprise	1990	7.50
—#25 in Sub Pop Singles Club series			

TIM/KERR

Number	Title (A Side/B Side)	Yr	NM
❑ 9370 [PD]	Santa Claus Is Back In Town/ I'm Mad At The Fat Man	1993	8.00
—B-side by Ray and Clover; picture disc			

7-Inch Extended Plays

AMERICAN LEATHER

Number	Title (A Side/B Side)	Yr	NM
❑ 001	Darby Crash Rides Again	1988	15.00
—Blue vinyl			
❑ 001 [PS]	Darby Crash Rides Again	1988	15.00
—Black and white sleeve			

FATAL ERECTION

Number	Title (A Side/B Side)	Yr	NM
❑ TR-001	Pick Your King	1983	12.50
—Third pressing on blue vinyl			
❑ TR-001	Pick Your King	1983	20.00
—Second pressing on black vinyl			
❑ TR-001	Pick Your King	1983	37.50
—First pressing on clear vinyl			
❑ TR-001 [PS]	Pick Your King	1983	12.50
—Third sleeve: Cream or white, no inserts			
❑ TR-001 [PS]	Pick Your King	1983	20.00
—Second sleeve: Blue, no inserts			
❑ TR-001 [PS]	Pick Your King	1983	37.50
—First sleeve: white with two inserts			

SHITFOOL

Number	Title (A Side/B Side)	Yr	NM
❑ (# unknown)	Filth Kick	1988	12.00
❑ (# unknown) [PS]	Filth Kick	1988	12.00
—2,000 pressed			

POITIER, SIDNEY

Albums

WARNER BROS.

Number	Title (A Side/B Side)	Yr	NM
❑ W 1561 [M]	Poitier Meets Plato	1965	25.00
❑ WS 1561 [S]	Poitier Meets Plato	1965	30.00

POLICE, THE

Also see STEWART COPELAND; KLARK KENT; STING; ANDY SUMMERS.

12-Inch Singles

A&M

Number	Title (A Side/B Side)	Yr	NM
❑ SP-12207	Don't Stand So Close to Me '86 (2 versions)/Don't Stand So Close to Me (Original & Live)	1986	8.00
❑ SP-17122 [DJ]	Message in a Bottle//Message in a Bottle (Live)/Landlord	1979	20.00
❑ SP-17137 [DJ]	Voices Inside My Head/When the World Is Running Down...	1980	8.00
❑ SP-17173 [DJ]	One World (Not Three)/Too Much Information	1981	10.00
❑ SP-17182 [DJ]	Spirits in the Material World/ Secret Journey	1981	12.00
❑ SP-17230 [DJ]	Every Breath You Take (same on both sides)	1983	10.00
❑ SP-17432 [DJ]	Don't Stand So Close to Me '86 (same on both sides)	1986	7.00
❑ SP-17449 [DJ]	Walking on the Moon (same on both sides)	1986	8.00

45s

A&M

Number	Title (A Side/B Side)	Yr	NM
❑ (no #) [(5)DJ]	The Police File	1985	50.00
—Boxed set of five "A&M Memories" singles released to radio. Price is mostly for the box.			
❑ 2096	Roxanne/Dead End Job	1978	6.00
❑ 2147	Can't Stand Losing You/ No Time This Time	1979	5.00
❑ 2147 [PS]	Can't Stand Losing You/ No Time This Time	1979	10.00
❑ AM-2147 [PD]	Roxanne/Can't Stand Losing You	1979	10.00
—Badge-shaped picture disc			
❑ 2190	Message in a Bottle/Landlord	1979	5.00
❑ 2190 [PS]	Message in a Bottle/Landlord	1979	10.00
—Fold-out poster sleeve			
❑ 2190 [PS]	Message in a Bottle/Landlord	1979	12.00
—Regular sleeve			
❑ 2218	Bring On the Night/ Visions of the Night	1980	5.00
❑ 2275	De Do Do Do, De Da Da Da/ Friends	1980	3.00
—Yellowish custom label with blueish triangle (most common version)			
❑ 2275	De Do Do Do, De Da Da Da/ Friends	1980	4.00
—Red custom label with silver triangle			
❑ 2275	De Do Do Do, De Da Da Da/ Friends	1980	4.00
—Standard A&M late-1970s label			
❑ 2275 [PS]	De Do Do Do, De Da Da Da/ Friends	1980	6.00
—Actually a title sleeve with large center hole			
❑ 2301	Don't Stand So Close to Me/ A Sermon	1981	3.00
❑ 2301 [PS]	Don't Stand So Close to Me/ A Sermon	1981	3.00
❑ 2371	Every Little Thing She Does Is Magic/Shambelle	1981	3.00
❑ 2371 [PS]	Every Little Thing She Does Is Magic/Shambelle	1981	3.00
❑ 2390	Spirits in the Material World/ Flexible Strategies	1982	3.00
❑ 2390 [PS]	Spirits in the Material World/ Flexible Strategies	1982	3.00
❑ 2408	Secret Journey/Darkness	1982	3.00
❑ 2408 [PS]	Secret Journey/Darkness	1982	3.00
❑ 2542	Every Breath You Take/ Murder by Numbers	1983	3.00
❑ 2542 [PS]	Every Breath You Take/ Murder by Numbers	1983	3.00
❑ 2569	King of Pain/Someone to Talk To	1983	3.00
❑ 2569 [PS]	King of Pain/Someone to Talk To	1983	3.00
❑ 2571	Synchronicity II/Once Upon a Daydream	1983	3.00
❑ 2571 [PS]	Synchronicity II/Once Upon a Daydream	1983	3.00
❑ 2614	Wrapped Around Your Finger/ Tea in the Sahara (Live)	1984	3.00
❑ 2614 [PS]	Wrapped Around Your Finger/ Tea in the Sahara (Live)	1984	3.00
❑ 2879	Don't Stand So Close to Me '86/ Don't Stand So Close to Me (Live)	1986	3.00
❑ 2879 [PS]	Don't Stand So Close to Me '86/ Don't Stand So Close to Me (Live)	1986	3.00
❑ 2908	Walking on the Moon/ Message in a Bottle	1986	5.00
❑ 2908 [PS]	Walking on the Moon/Message in a Bottle	1986	5.00
❑ PR-4400 [PD]	Message in a Bottle/Message in a Bottle (Live)	1980	10.00
—Star-shaped badge picture disc in folder; promo only			
❑ PR-4401 [PD]	Don't Stand So Close to Me/De Do Do Do, De Da Da Da	1981	10.00
—Star-shaped badge picture disc in folder; promo only			
❑ 8622	Roxanne/Can't Stand Losing You	198?	3.00
—Reissue			
❑ 8631	De Do Do Do, De Da Da Da/ Don't Stand So Close to Me	198?	3.00
—Reissue			
❑ 8633	Every Little Thing She Does Is Magic/Spirits in the Material World	198?	3.00
—Reissue			
❑ 8640	Every Breath You Take/ Wrapped Around Your Finger	198?	3.00
—Reissue			
❑ 8649	King of Pain/Synchronicity II	198?	3.00
—Reissue			
❑ 75021 8738 7	Canary in a Coal Mine/ Message in a Bottle	1996	3.00
—Oldies reissue; first appearance of A-side on U.S. 45			
❑ 25000	De Do Do Do, De Da Da Da (Japanese)/De Do Do Do, De Da Da Da (Spanish)	1981	5.00
—Small center hole			
❑ 25000 [PS]	De Do Do Do, De Da Da Da (Japanese)/De Do Do Do, De Da Da Da (Spanish)	1981	5.00

Albums

A&M

Number	Title (A Side/B Side)	Yr	NM
❑ SP-3311	Outlandos d'Amour	198?	8.00
—Reissue			
❑ SP-3312	Reggatta de Blanc	198?	8.00
—Reissue			
❑ SP-3713 [(2)10]	Reggatta de Blanc	1979	30.00
—Two 10" records with poster			
❑ SP-3720	Zenyatta Mondatta	1980	10.00
❑ SP-3730	Ghost in the Machine	1981	10.00
❑ SP-3730 [DJ]	Ghost in the Machine	1981	1000.
—Special prototype picture disc that lights up when placed on a turntable			
❑ SP-3735	Synchronicity	1983	10.00
—With blue, yellow and red color bands; 93 versions of this cover exist, none more valuable than any other			

Except when noted otherwise, VG = 25% of NM, and VG+ = 50% of NM. (Example: VG = $2.00, VG+ = $4.00 and NM = $8.00.)

Number	Title (A Side/B Side)	Yr	NM
❑ SP-3735	Synchronicity	1983	40.00
—With gold, silver and bronze color bands on cover; used on audiophile pressings			
❑ SP-3902	Every Breath You Take — The Singles	1986	10.00
❑ SP-4753	Outlandos d'Amour	1979	12.00
❑ SP-4792	Reggatta de Blanc	1979	12.00
❑ SP-6018 [(2)10]	Reggatta de Blanc	1980	30.00
—Reissue of SP-3713			
❑ R 123571	Ghost in the Machine	1981	12.00
—RCA Music Service edition			
❑ R 124159	Outlandos d'Amour	1979	12.00
—RCA Music Service edition			
❑ R 130108	Zenyatta Mondatta	1980	12.00
—RCA Music Service edition			
❑ R 134070	Synchronicity	1983	12.00
—RCA Music Service edition			
❑ R 153349	Reggatta de Blanc	1979	12.00
—RCA Music Service edition			
❑ R 173924	Every Breath You Take — The Singles	1986	12.00
—BMG Direct Marketing edition			
❑ 1775311	Zenyatta Mondatta	2008	20.00
❑ 3937351	Synchronicity	2008	20.00
—Black & white cover			
NAUTILUS			
❑ NR-19	Zenyatta Mondatta	1981	40.00
—Audiophile vinyl			
❑ NR-40	Ghost in the Machine	1982	40.00
—Audiophile vinyl			

POLLARD, RAY

45s

Number	Title (A Side/B Side)	Yr	NM
DECCA			
❑ 32111	Lie, Lips, Lie/This Is My Song	1967	40.00
❑ 32189	This Is No Laughing Matter/ Wanderlust	1967	120.00
OMNIPOTENT			
❑ 1001	Soulmate?/(B-side unknown)	1973	800.00
SHRINE			
❑ 0103	No One Likes Me/This Time (I'm Gonna Be True)	1965	800.00
UNITED ARTISTS			
❑ 856	Darling Take Me Back/ My Girl and I	1965	80.00
❑ 916	The Drifter/Let Him Go (And Let Me Love You)	1965	80.00
❑ 50012	All the Things You Are/ It's a Sad Thing	1966	100.00

POLLUTION

45s

Number	Title (A Side/B Side)	Yr	NM
CAPITOL			
❑ 2458	Getting Together/Angela Jerome	1969	10.00
PROPHECY			
❑ 55001	Do You Really Have a Heart/ (B-side unknown)	1971	8.00
❑ 55003	The River/(B-side unknown)	1972	8.00

Albums

Number	Title (A Side/B Side)	Yr	NM
CAPITOL			
❑ ST-205	Heir: Pollution	1969	20.00
PROPHECY			
❑ SD 6051	Pollution	1971	20.00
❑ SD 6067	Pollution II	1972	20.00

POLNAREFF, MICHEL

45s

Number	Title (A Side/B Side)	Yr	NM
ATLANTIC			
❑ 3314	Since I Saw You/If You Only Believe	1976	5.00
❑ 3330	Lipstick (Part 1)/ Lipstick (Part 2)	1976	5.00
4 CORNERS OF THE WORLD			
❑ 141	Time Will Tell/Under What Star Was I Born	1967	15.00
KAPP			
❑ 786	Love Me, Please Love Me/ No, No, No, No, No	1966	8.00

Albums

Number	Title (A Side/B Side)	Yr	NM
ATLANTIC			
❑ SD 18153	Michel Polnareff	1976	10.00
4 CORNERS OF THE WORLD			
❑ FCL-4240 [M]	French Rock-Blues	1967	12.00
❑ FCS-4240 [S]	French Rock-Blues	1967	15.00

PONCHER, JERRY

45s

Number	Title (A Side/B Side)	Yr	NM
HIT			
❑ 124	What'd I Say/Every Little Bit Hurts	1964	8.00
—B-side by Peggy Gaines			

PONI-TAILS, THE

45s

Number	Title (A Side/B Side)	Yr	NM
ABC-PARAMOUNT			
❑ 9846	Wild Eyes and Tender Lips/ It's Just My Luck to Be Fifteen	1957	20.00
❑ 9934	Born Too Late/Come On Joey Dance With Me	1958	25.00
❑ 9934 [DJ]	Born Too Late/Come On Joey Dance With Me	1958	50.00
—White label promo with artist's name spelled "Pony-Tails"			
❑ 9969	Close Friends/Seven Minutes in Heaven	1958	20.00
❑ 9995	Early to Bed/Father Time	1959	20.00
❑ 10027	Moody/Ooh-Pah Polka	1959	20.00
❑ 10047	I'll Be Seeing You/I'll Keep Tryin'	1959	20.00
❑ 10077	Before We Say Goodnight/ Come Be My Love	1960	20.00
❑ 10114	Who, When and Why/ Oh My, You	1960	20.00
MARC			
❑ 1001	Can I Be Sure/Still in Your Teens	1957	25.00
POINT			
❑ 8	Your Wild Heart/Que La Bozena	1957	25.00

PONTY, JEAN-LUC

12-Inch Singles

Number	Title (A Side/B Side)	Yr	NM
ATLANTIC			
❑ PR 420 [DJ]	As (3:15) (5:45)	1982	6.00
❑ PR 524 [DJ]	Far from Beaten Paths (3:50) (5:58)	1983	6.00
❑ PR 801 [DJ]	Open Mind (Edit) (Extended)	1984	6.00
❑ PR 809 [DJ]	Infinite Pursuit (same on both sides)	1985	6.00

45s

Number	Title (A Side/B Side)	Yr	NM
ATLANTIC			
❑ 3368	New Country/Renaissance	1976	5.00
❑ 3523	Cosmic Messenger/ The Art of Happiness	1978	5.00
❑ 3639	Beach Girl/Sunset Drive	1979	8.00
❑ 3778	Demagomania/ (B-side unknown)	1980	4.00
❑ 4009	As/Rhythms of Hope	1982	4.00
❑ 89787	Far from Beaten Paths/ (B-side unknown)	1983	4.00

Albums

Number	Title (A Side/B Side)	Yr	NM
ATLANTIC			
❑ SD 16020	Civilized Evil	1980	10.00
❑ SD 18138	Upon the Wings of Music	1975	10.00
❑ SD 18163	Aurora	1976	10.00
❑ SD 18195	Imaginary Voyage	1976	10.00
❑ SD 19110	Enigmatic Ocean	1977	10.00
❑ SD 19136	Imaginary Voyage	1978	8.00
—Reissue of 18195			
❑ SD 19158	Aurora	1978	8.00
—Reissue of 18163			
❑ SD 19189	Cosmic Messenger	1978	10.00
❑ SD 19229	Jean-Luc Ponty: Live	1979	10.00
❑ SD 19253	A Taste for Passion	1979	10.00
❑ SD 19333	Mystical Adventures	1982	10.00
❑ A1-80098	Individual Choice	1983	8.00
❑ 80185	Open Mind	1984	8.00
❑ 81276	Fables	1985	8.00
BASF			
❑ 20645	Sunday Walk	1972	20.00
❑ 21288	Open Strings	1973	20.00
BLUE NOTE			
❑ BN-LA632-H2 [(2)]	Cantaloupe Island	1976	20.00
❑ LWB-632 [(2)]	Cantaloupe Island	1981	12.00
—Reissue of BN-LA632-H2			
❑ LT-1102	Live at Donte's	1981	10.00
COLUMBIA			
❑ FC 40983	The Gift of Time	1987	8.00
❑ FC 45252	Storytelling	1989	15.00
DIRECT DISC			
❑ SD-16603	Cosmic Messenger	1980	30.00
—Audiophile vinyl			
INNER CITY			
❑ IC-1003	Live at Montreux: Sonata Erotica	1976	15.00
❑ IC-1005	Jean-Luc Ponty and Stephane Grappelli	197?	10.00
PAUSA			
❑ PR-7014	Jean-Luc Ponty Meets Giorgio Gaslini	1979	10.00
❑ PR-7033	Sunday Walk	1980	10.00
—Reissue of BASF 20645			
❑ PR-7065	Open Strings	1980	10.00
—Reissue of BASF 21288			
❑ PA 9001	The Jean-Luc Ponty Experience	1982	20.00
PRESTIGE			
❑ PRST-7676	Critic's Choice	1969	20.00
WORLD PACIFIC			
❑ ST-20134	More Than Meets the Ear	1969	20.00
❑ ST-20156	Electric Connection	1969	25.00
WORLD PACIFIC JAZZ			
❑ ST-20168	The Jean-Luc Ponty Experience	1969	25.00
❑ ST-20172	King Kong — Jean-Luc Ponty Plays the Music of Frank Zappa	1970	40.00

POOBAH

45s

Number	Title (A Side/B Side)	Yr	NM
A.E.I.			
❑ 004/005	Through These Eyes/Watch Me!	1976	50.00
OPEN HEARTH			
❑ 582-26	Your Way, My Way/Let's Rock	197?	50.00

Albums

Number	Title (A Side/B Side)	Yr	NM
A.E.I.			
❑ A-LP-1	U.S. Rock	1976	250.00
PEPPERMINT			
❑ PP-1180	Steamroller	1979	150.00
RITE			
❑ (no #)	Let Me In	1972	600.00

POOH AND THE HEFFALUMPS

45s

Number	Title (A Side/B Side)	Yr	NM
LAURIE			
❑ 3281	Lady Godiva/Rooty Toot	1965	12.00

POOLE, BRIAN

Also see BRIAN POOLE AND THE TREMELOES.

45s

Number	Title (A Side/B Side)	Yr	NM
DATE			
❑ 1539	Everything I Touch Turns to Tears/I Need Her Tonight	1966	10.00

POOLE, BRIAN, AND THE TREMELOES

Also see BRIAN POOLE; THE TREMELOES.

45s

Number	Title (A Side/B Side)	Yr	NM
AUDIO FIDELITY			
❑ 112	I Go Crazy/Love Me Baby	1965	10.00
❑ 121	Good Lovin'/Could It Be You	1966	10.00
LONDON			
❑ 9600	Keep On Dancing/Blue	1963	15.00
❑ 9625	Do You Love Me/Why Can't You Love Me	1964	15.00
MONUMENT			
❑ 840	Candy Man/I Can Dream	1964	12.00
❑ 846	Someone, Someone/(Meet Me) Where We Used to Meet	1964	12.00
❑ 882	After a While/Don't Cry	1965	12.00

Albums

Number	Title (A Side/B Side)	Yr	NM
AUDIO FIDELITY			
❑ AFLP 2151 [M]	Brian Poole Is Here	1966	40.00
❑ AFSD 2151 [R]	Brian Poole Is Here	1966	30.00
❑ AFLP 2177 [M]	The Tremeloes Are Here	1967	40.00
—Reissue of above album with new title			
❑ AFSD 2177 [R]	The Tremeloes Are Here	1967	30.00
—Reissue of above album with new title			

POP WILL EAT ITSELF

12-Inch Singles

Number	Title (A Side/B Side)	Yr	NM
NOTHING			
❑ 2141	RSVP (4 versions)	1994	12.00
RCA			
❑ 2732	Dance of the Mad (2 versions)/ Preaching to the Perverted/ Touched by the Hand of God	1990	10.00
❑ 2763	X, Y & Zee (3 versions)	1991	12.00
❑ 2845	Another Man's Rhubarb (3 versions)	1990	10.00
❑ 9001	Can U Dig It? (4 versions)	1989	12.00
❑ 9009 [DJ]	Can U Dig It?/Can You Dig It? (7" English Mix)	1989	10.00

Albums

Number	Title (A Side/B Side)	Yr	NM
NOTHING			
❑ 95887	Amalgamation	1994	10.00
RCA			
❑ 9742-1-R	This Is the Day...This Is the Hour...This Is This!	1989	15.00
ROUGH TRADE			
❑ ROUGH 22	Now for a Feast	198?	15.00
❑ ROUGH 33	Box Frenzy!	1988	15.00

POPCORN AND THE MOHAWKS

45s

Number	Title (A Side/B Side)	Yr	NM
MOTOWN			
❑ 1002	Custer's Last Man/Shimmy Gully	1960	60.00

P

POPCORN BLIZZARD, THE (1)

Number	Title (A Side/B Side)	Yr	NM
45s			
DE-LITE			
❑ 516	Good Thing Going/My Suzanne	1969	20.00
❑ 522	Good Good Day/ I Just Saw a Face	1969	20.00
Albums			
DE-LITE			
❑ DE-2004	Explode!	1969	40.00

POPCORN BLIZZARD, THE (2)

Number	Title (A Side/B Side)	Yr	NM
45s			
MAGENDA			
❑ 7411	Once Upon a Time/Hello!	1967	100.00
—The first recorded performance by MEAT LOAF			

POPE, RAYMOND, AND THE LOVETONES

Number	Title (A Side/B Side)	Yr	NM
45s			
SQUALOR			
❑ 1313	I Love Nadine/Star	1962	150.00

POPE JOHN XXIII

Number	Title (A Side/B Side)	Yr	NM
Albums			
MERCURY			
❑ 200 [M]	Pope John XXIII	1963	15.00
—Tribute album released after his death			

POPPIES, THE

Dorothy Moore of "Misty Blue" fame was in this group.

Number	Title (A Side/B Side)	Yr	NM
45s			
EPIC			
❑ 9893	I Wonder Why/Lullaby of Love	1966	10.00
❑ 10019	He's Ready/He's Got Real Love	1966	10.00
❑ 10019 [PS]	He's Ready/He's Got Real Love	1966	20.00
❑ 10059	Do It with Soul/He Means So Much to Me	1966	12.00
❑ 10086	There's a Pain in My Heart/My Love and I	1966	25.00
TUFF			
❑ 372	Johnny Don't Cry/(Instrumental)	1964	15.00
Albums			
EPIC			
❑ LN 24200 [M]	Lullaby of Love	1966	40.00
❑ BN 26200 [S]	Lullaby of Love	1966	50.00

POPPY FAMILY, THE

Also see TERRY JACKS.

Number	Title (A Side/B Side)	Yr	NM
45s			
LONDON			
❑ 128	Another Year, Another Day/ You Don't Know What Love Is	1970	10.00
—Deleted quickly; a more common Margaret Whiting single was also issued as London 128			
❑ 129	Which Way You Goin' Billy/ Endless Sleep	1970	6.00
❑ 139	That's When I Went Wrong/ Shadows on My Wall	1970	5.00
❑ 148	I Was Wondering/ Where Evil Grows	1971	5.00
❑ 164	No Good to Cry/I'll See You There	1971	5.00
❑ 172	Good Friends/Tryin'	1972	5.00
Albums			
LONDON			
❑ PS 574	Which Way You Goin' Billy?	1970	15.00
❑ PS 599	Seeds	1971	15.00

POPSICLES, THE (1)

Number	Title (A Side/B Side)	Yr	NM
45s			
GNP CRESCENDO			
❑ 336	I Don't Want to Be Your Baby Anymore/Baby I Miss You	1965	10.00

POPSICLES, THE (2)

Number	Title (A Side/B Side)	Yr	NM
45s			
KNIGHT			
❑ 2002	Thumb Print/This Is the End	1958	40.00

POPULAIRES, THE

Number	Title (A Side/B Side)	Yr	NM
45s			
MARVELLO			
❑ 5001	Island of Paradise/I Lost My Heart	1957	200.00

PORCELAIN BEARMEAT

Number	Title (A Side/B Side)	Yr	NM
Albums			
DILL PICKLE			
❑ 3468	Free Love, Free Sex, Free Music	1971	20.00

PORTER, DAVID

Number	Title (A Side/B Side)	Yr	NM
45s			
ENTERPRISE			
❑ 9014	Can't See You When I Want To/ One Part, Two Parts	1970	6.00
❑ 9049	Ain't That Loving You (For More Reasons Than One)/ Baby I'm-a Want You	1972	5.00
—With Isaac Hayes			
❑ 9050	I'm Afraid the Masquerade Is Over/Sloopy	1972	5.00
❑ 9055	Wanna Be Your Somebody/ When the Chips Are Down	1972	5.00
❑ 9071	As Long As You're the One Somebody in the World/ When You Have to Sneak	1973	5.00
❑ 9090	Falling Out, Falling In/ I Got You and I'm Glad	1973	5.00
STAX			
❑ 163	Can't See You When I Want To/ Win You Over	1965	20.00
Albums			
ENTERPRISE			
❑ ENS-1009	Gritty, Groovy, & Gettin' It	1970	20.00
❑ ENS-1012	David Porter…Into a Real Thing	1971	20.00
❑ ENS-1019	Victim of the Joke?	1972	20.00
❑ ENS-1026	Sweat and Love	1973	20.00

PORTER, JIM

Number	Title (A Side/B Side)	Yr	NM
45s			
HIT			
❑ 05	Dr. Feelgood/Shout	1962	8.00
—B-side by Bill Austin			

PORTER, NOLAN

Number	Title (A Side/B Side)	Yr	NM
45s			
ABC			
❑ 11343	If I Could Only Be Sure/ Work It Out in the Morning	1972	100.00
❑ 11367	Singer Man/Oh Baby	1973	60.00
❑ 11367 [DJ]	Singer Man (mono/stereo)	1973	6.00
LIZARD			
❑ 1008	I Like What You Give/ Somebody's Cryin'	1971	15.00
—As "Nolan"			
❑ 1010	Keep On Keeping On/ Don't Make Me Color My Black Face Blue	1971	40.00
—As "N.F. Porter"			
❑ 21003	Crazy Love/What Would You Do (If I Did That to You)	1971	12.00
—As "Nolan"			
Albums			
ABC			
❑ ABCX-766	Nolan	1973	120.00
LIZARD			
❑ A-20102	No Apologies	1971	30.00
—As "Nolan"			

PORTER, ROYCE

Number	Title (A Side/B Side)	Yr	NM
45s			
D			
❑ 1026	Lookin'/I Still Belong to You	1958	100.00
LOOK			
❑ 1001	Yes I Do/(B-side unknown)	1957	250.00
MERCURY			
❑ 71314	Good Time/Beach of Love	1958	100.00

PORTRAITS, THE (1)

Number	Title (A Side/B Side)	Yr	NM
45s			
CAPITOL			
❑ F-4181	Close to You/Easy Cash	1959	30.00

PORTRAITS, THE (2)

Number	Title (A Side/B Side)	Yr	NM
45s			
SIDEWALK			
❑ 928	A Million to One/Let's Tell the World	1967	15.00
❑ 935	Over the Rainbow/ Runaround Girl	1968	20.00

PORTRAITS, THE (3)

Number	Title (A Side/B Side)	Yr	NM
45s			
TRI-DISC			
❑ 109	We're Gonna Party/ Three Blind Mice	1963	15.00

PORTRAITS, THE (U)

Could be group (1) or (3).

Number	Title (A Side/B Side)	Yr	NM
45s			
RCA VICTOR			
❑ 47-7900	Yo-Yo Girl/My Big Brother's Friend	1961	15.00

POSEY, SANDY

Number	Title (A Side/B Side)	Yr	NM
45s			
AUDIOGRAPH			
❑ 449	Can't Get Used to Sleeping Without You/(B-side unknown)	1983	4.00
COLUMBIA			
❑ 45360	Losing Out on You/You Say Beautiful Things to Me	1971	5.00
❑ 45458	Bring Him Safely Home To Me/ A Man in Need of Love	1971	5.00
❑ 45596	Why Don't We Go Somewhere and Love/Together	1972	5.00
❑ 45703	Happy Happy Birthday Baby/ Thank the Lord for New York City	1972	5.00
❑ 45828	Don't/Thank the Lord for New York City	1973	5.00
MGM			
❑ 13501	Born a Woman/ Caution to the Wind	1967	8.00
❑ 13612	Single Girl/Blue Is My Best Color	1966	8.00
❑ 13612 [PS]	Single Girl/Blue Is My Best Color	1966	12.00
❑ 13702	What a Woman in Love Won't Do/Shattered	1967	8.00
❑ 13744	I Take It Back/The Boy I Love	1967	8.00
❑ 13744 [PS]	I Take It Back/The Boy I Love	1967	12.00
❑ 13824	Are You Never Coming Home/ I Can Show You How to Live	1967	8.00
❑ 13892	Silly Girl, Silly Boy/ Something I'll Remember	1968	6.00
❑ 13967	Ways of the World/Wonderful World of Summer	1968	6.00
❑ 14006	All Hung Up in Your Green Eyes/ Your Conception of Love	1968	6.00
MONUMENT			
❑ 8698	Trying to Live Without You Kind of Days/Why Do We Carry On	1976	5.00
WARNER BROS.			
❑ 8289	It's Midnight (Do You Know Where Your Baby Is)/ Long Distance Kissing	1976	4.00
❑ 8540	Born to Be with You/ It's Not Too Late	1978	4.00
❑ 8610	Love, Love, Love-Chapel of Love/I Believe in Love	1978	4.00
❑ 8731	Love Is Sometimes Easy/ I Believe in Love	1979	4.00
❑ 8852	Try Home/Love Is Sometimes Easy	1979	4.00
❑ 49104	Black Is the Night/ Best Things in My Life	1979	4.00
Albums			
COLUMBIA			
❑ KC 31594	Why Don't We Go Somewhere and Love	1972	12.00
MGM			
❑ GAS-125	Sandy Posey (Golden Archive Series)	1970	15.00
❑ E-4418 [M]	Born a Woman	1966	15.00
❑ SE-4418 [S]	Born a Woman	1966	20.00
❑ E-4455 [M]	Single Girl	1967	20.00
❑ SE-4455 [S]	Single Girl	1967	20.00
❑ E-4480 [M]	I Take It Back	1967	20.00
❑ SE-4480 [S]	I Take It Back	1967	20.00
❑ E-4509 [M]	The Best of Sandy Posey	1967	25.00
❑ SE-4509 [S]	The Best of Sandy Posey	1967	20.00
❑ E-4525 [M]	Looking at You	1968	25.00
❑ SE-4525 [S]	Looking at You	1968	15.00
❑ ST-91110	Single Girl	1967	25.00
—Capitol Record Club issue			

POSEY, SANDY/ SKEETER DAVIS

Also see each artist's individual listings.

Number	Title (A Side/B Side)	Yr	NM
Albums			
GUSTO			
❑ 0005	The Best of Sandy Posey/ Skeeter Davis	198?	8.00

POSITIVELY 13 O'CLOCK

Number	Title (A Side/B Side)	Yr	NM
45s			
HANNA-BARBERA			
❑ 500	Psychotic Reaction/13 O'Clock Theme for Psychotics	1966	40.00

POSSESSIONS, THE

Number	Title (A Side/B Side)	Yr	NM
45s			
BRITTON			
❑ 1003	No More Love/You and Your Lies	1964	40.00
❑ 1003	No More Love/You and Your Lies	1964	70.00
—Blue vinyl			
PARKWAY			
❑ 930	No More Love/You and Your Lies	1964	20.00

Except when noted otherwise, VG = 25% of NM, and VG+ = 50% of NM. (Example: VG = $2.00, VG+ = $4.00 and NM = $8.00.)

Number	Title (A Side/B Side)	Yr	NM

POSSUM Possibly two different groups.

45s

HIGHLAND			
❑ 10	The Cockroach That Ate Cincinnati/Chula Vista	1966	15.00

Albums

CAPITOL			
❑ ST-648	Possum	1970	12.00

POSSUM HUNTERS, THE

Albums

TAKOMA			
❑ C-1010	Death on Lee Highway	1970	20.00

POST, MIKE

45s

BELL			
❑ 45155	Nicholas and Alexandra's Theme/Kotch	1971	5.00
ELEKTRA			
❑ 47186	The Theme from Hill Street Blues/Aaron's Tune	1981	4.00
❑ 47186 [PS]	The Theme from Hill Street Blues/Aaron's Tune	1981	4.00
❑ 47400	Theme from Magnum, P.I./Gumbus Bed	1982	4.00
❑ 47400 [PS]	Theme from Magnum, P.I./Gumbus Bed	1982	4.00
❑ 47477	School's Out/Aaron's Tune	1982	4.00
EPIC			
❑ 50325	Theme from "Baa Baa Black Sheep"/Southbound	1976	4.00
MGM			
❑ 14772	The Rockford Files/Dixie Lullabye	1974	5.00
❑ 14829	Manhattan Spiritual/Lay Back Lafayette	1975	4.00
MUSIC FACTORY			
❑ 419	Harper Valley P.T.A./Walking to San Francisco	1968	8.00
POLYDOR			
❑ 887145-7	Theme from "L.A. Law"/Jenny's Ayre	1987	4.00
❑ 887145-7 [PS]	Theme from "L.A. Law"/Jenny's Ayre	1987	4.00
RCA			
❑ PB-13859	The A Team//6/24	1984	5.00
REPRISE			
❑ 0406	For My Home/Long Time Alone	1965	10.00
❑ 0468	Hard Times/Louisiana Man	1966	10.00
WARNER BROS.			
❑ 7357	Bubble Gum Breakthrough/Not a Blade of Grass	1969	8.00

Albums

ELEKTRA			
❑ 60028 [EP]	Television Theme Songs	1982	8.00
MGM			
❑ M3G-5005	Railhead Overture	1975	10.00
POLYDOR			
❑ 833985-1	Theme from L.A. Law and Otherwise	1987	8.00
RCA VICTOR			
❑ AFL1-5415	Mike Post	1985	10.00

POSTA, ADRIENNE

45s

LONDON			
❑ 9782	When a Girl Really Loves You/Winds That Bloe	1966	10.00

POTLIQUOR

45s

CAPITOL			
❑ 4795	Misery/Oh So Long	1979	4.00
❑ 4819	Boy Oh Boy/Red Stick	1980	4.00
JANUS			
❑ 139	Down the River Boogie/Riverboat	1970	5.00
❑ 179	Cheer/Chattanooga	1972	5.00
❑ 186	Beyond the River Jordan/(B-side unknown)	1972	5.00
❑ 195	Waitin' for Me at the River/(B-side unknown)	1972	5.00

Albums

CAPITOL			
❑ ST-11998	Potliquor	1979	12.00
JANUS			
❑ JLS-3002	Potliquor	1970	20.00
❑ JLS-3033	Levee Blues	1972	20.00
❑ JLS-3036	Louisiana Rock and Roll	1973	20.00

POWDER PUFFS, THE

45s

IMPERIAL			
❑ 66014	(You Can't Take) My Boyfriend's Woody/Woody Wagon	1964	25.00

POWELL, ADAM CLAYTON

Albums

JUBILEE			
❑ JGM 2062 [M]	Keep the Faith, Baby!	1967	15.00

POWELL, AUSTIN

45s

ATLANTIC			
❑ 968	Wrong Again/What More Can I Ask	1952	200.00
DECCA			
❑ 48206	All This Can't Be True/Some Other Spring	1951	80.00

POWELL, CHRIS, AND THE FIVE BLUE FLAMES

45s

COLUMBIA			
❑ 39272	Country Girl Blues/Man with a Horn	1951	150.00
❑ 39407	My Love Has Gone/In the Cool of the Evening	1951	500.00
GRAND			
❑ 108	Sweet Sue Mambo/Uh Uh Baby	1953	50.00
❑ 112	Secret Love Mambo/I Love Paris Mambo	1954	50.00
❑ 116	Dinah/Song of the Vagabond	1954	50.00
❑ 120	Mr. Sandman/Mambo Gunch	1954	50.00
❑ 124	Anniversary Waltz/Sweet Georgia Brown	1955	40.00
❑ 127	Mandolin Mambo/The Whiffenpoof Song	1955	40.00
GROOVE			
❑ 0105	Break It Up/Love Ya Like Crazy	1955	20.00
❑ 0111	Unchained Melody/Something's Gotta Give	1955	20.00
❑ 0128	Goodbye Little Girl/Chinatown	1955	20.00
❑ 0144	Moritat/The Poor People of Paris	1956	20.00
OKEH			
❑ 6818	The Masquerade Is Over/Talkin'	1951	300.00
❑ 6850	October Twilight/That's Right	1952	100.00
❑ 6875	Ida Red/Darn That Dream	1952	100.00
❑ 6900	Blue Boy/I Come from Jamaica	1952	100.00

POWELL, JEROME

45s

PARKWAY			
❑ 927	Home to Stay/Live and Let Live	1964	12.00

POWELL, JIMMY (1) British singer.

45s

DECCA			
❑ 32685	Stranger on a Train/Sugar Man	1970	6.00
LONDON			
❑ 9545	I Love You/Dance Her By Me (One More Time)	1962	10.00

POWELL, JIMMY (2) American instrumentalist.

45s

JUBILEE			
❑ 5533	The Shadow of Your Smile/On a Clear Day You Can See Forever	1966	8.00

Albums

JUBILEE			
❑ JGM 8001 [M]	In a Sentimental Mood	1966	15.00

POWELL, SANDY

45s

HERALD			
❑ 557	Bon Bon/Pistol-Packin' Mama	1961	100.00
IMPALA			
❑ 211	Bon Bon/Pistol-Packin' Mama	1961	300.00
SINGULAR			
❑ 714	My Jimmie/Next Thing to Paradise	1958	25.00

POWELL, WILLIAM

45s

POWERHOUSE			
❑ 101	Heartache Souvenirs/(B-side unknown)	196?	1500.

POWER, DUFFY

45s

EPIC			
❑ 10650	Hellhound/Hummingbird	1970	6.00
VEEP			
❑ 1204	Where Am I/I Don't Care	1964	20.00

Albums

GSF			
❑ 1005	Duffy Power	1973	10.00

POWERS, JETT See P.J. PROBY.

POWERS, JOEY

45s

AMY			
❑ 892	Midnight Mary/Where Do You Want the World Delivered	1963	12.00
❑ 898	Billy Old Buddy/In the Morning Gloria	1964	10.00
❑ 903	Love Is a Season/You Comb Her Hair	1964	10.00
❑ 914	Tears Keep Falling/Where Did the Summer Go	1964	10.00
❑ 986	Gimmie Gimmie/Baila Maria	1967	8.00
MGM			
❑ 13421	I Love You/Leave Me Alone	1965	8.00
RCA VICTOR			
❑ 47-8039	Two Tickets and a Candy Heart/Jenny, Won't You Walk Up?	1962	10.00
❑ 47-8119	Don't Envy Me/Me, Myself and I	1962	10.00
❑ 47-9790	Hard to Be Without You/You're in a Bad Way	1969	5.00
—As "Joey Powers' Flower"			
❑ 74-0326	Land of the Midnight Sun/So Sing the Children on the Avenue	1970	5.00
—As "Joey Powers' Flower"			

Albums

AMY			
❑ 8001 [M]	Midnight Mary	1964	30.00

POWERS, JOHNNY

45s

FORTUNE			
❑ 199	Honey Let's Go (To a Rock and Roll Show)/Your Love	1955	200.00
FOX			
❑ 916	Rock Rock/Long Blonde Hair, Red Rose Lips	1957	500.00
HI-Q			
❑ 5044	Rock the Universe/Honey Let's Go (To a Rock and Roll Show)	1958	100.00
SUN			
❑ 327	With Your Love, With Your Kiss/Be Mine, All Mine	1959	50.00
TRIODEX			
❑ 103	A Teenage Prayer/A Young Boy's Heart	1960	25.00

POWERS, TINA

45s

PARKWAY			
❑ 847	Making Up Is Fun to Do/Back to School	1962	20.00

POWERS OF BLUE, THE

45s

MTA			
❑ 113	Good Lovin'/(I Can't Get No) Satisfaction	1966	10.00
❑ 118	Cool Jerk/You Blow My Mind	1967	8.00

Albums

MTA			
❑ 1002 [M]	Flipout	1967	30.00
❑ 5002 [S]	Flipout	1967	30.00

POZO-SECO SINGERS, THE DON WILLIAMS was in this group.

45s

CERTRON			
❑ 10006	Apartment #9/Comin' Apart	1970	5.00
❑ 10020	Strawberry Fields & Something/There's Never Been a Time	1970	5.00
❑ 10033	Bringing It Down to Me/He's a Friend of Mine	1971	5.00
COLUMBIA			
❑ 43437	Time/Down the Road I Go	1965	8.00
❑ 43646	I'll Be Gone/It Ain't Worth the Lonely Road Back	1966	8.00

P

Number	Title (A Side/B Side)	Yr	NM
❑ 43784	I Can Make It With You/Come a Little Bit Closer	1966	8.00
❑ 43927	Look What You've Done/Almost Persuaded	1966	8.00
❑ 44041	I Believed It All/Excuse Me Dear Martha	1967	8.00
❑ 44168	It's All Right/Morning Dew	1967	8.00
❑ 44263	Louisiana Man/Tomorrow Proper	1967	8.00
❑ 44598	Gotta Come Up with Something/The Renegade	1968	6.00
❑ 44690	Good Morning Today/Remember Suzie	1968	6.00
❑ 44841	Leavin'/Creole Woman	1969	6.00
❑ 44979	Woman in Love/God Save the Children	1969	6.00
—As "Susan Taylor and Pozo Seco"			
❑ 44980	Morning Mama Memories/The Proper Mrs. Brown	1969	10.00
—As "Don Williams and Pozo Seco"; his first "solo" credit			
❑ 45065	High on Life/Till You Hear Your Mama Call	1970	6.00
EDMARK			
❑ 10017	Time/Down the Road I Go	1965	20.00

Albums

Number	Title (A Side/B Side)	Yr	NM
CERTRON			
❑ CS-7007	Spend Some Time with Me	1970	15.00
COLUMBIA			
❑ CL 2515 [M]	Time/I'll Be Gone	1966	15.00
❑ CL 2600 [M]	I Can Make It with You	1967	20.00
❑ CS 9315 [S]	Time/I'll Be Gone	1966	20.00
❑ CS 9400 [S]	I Can Make It with You	1967	15.00
❑ CS 9656	Shades of Time	1968	15.00
POWER PAK			
❑ 285	The Pozo-Seco Singers with Don Williams	198?	10.00

PRADO, PEREZ

45s

Number	Title (A Side/B Side)	Yr	NM
RCA VICTOR			
❑ 47-3782	El Mambo/Mambo #5	1950	20.00
❑ 47-3873	Chattanoogie Shoe Shine Boy/More Mambo Jambo	1950	15.00
❑ 47-3917	Mambo #8/Babarabatiri	1950	15.00
❑ 47-3918	Pachito E-Che/Mambo #5	1950	15.00
❑ 47-3988	Cuban Mambo/Mambo del Papelero	1950	15.00
❑ 47-4196	Syncopated Clock Mambo/Broadway Mambo	1951	15.00
❑ 47-4319	C'est Si Bon Mambo/In a Little Spanish Town Mambo	1951	15.00
❑ 47-5281	A La Billy May/Beautiful	1953	12.00
❑ 47-5367	Anna/Silvana Mangano	1953	12.00
❑ 47-5738	Such a Night/Ballin' the Jack	1954	12.00
❑ 47-5820	St. Louis Blues Mambo/Tomcat Mambo	1954	12.00
❑ 47-5839	Skokiaan/The High and the Mighty	1954	12.00
❑ 47-5892	Marilyn Monroe Mambo/Steam Heat Mambo	1954	25.00
❑ 47-5965	Cherry Pink and Apple Blossom White/Rhythm Sticks	1954	12.00
❑ 47-6085	Mood Indigo/Back Bay Shuffle (Mambo)	1955	10.00
❑ 47-6122	Whatever Lola Wants/Dilo (Mambo)	1955	10.00
❑ 47-6214	Crazy, Crazy/Monitor Mambo	1955	10.00
❑ 47-6277	Pretty Doll/La Macarena	1955	10.00
❑ 47-6375	Red River Valley Mambo/Black Horse Mambo	1955	10.00
❑ 47-6477	The Story of Love/Tomorrow I Will Live	1956	10.00
❑ 47-6538	Cuban Rock/Hawaiian War Chant	1956	12.00
❑ 47-6684	Petticoats of Portugal/Bandido	1956	10.00
❑ 47-6752	Bongo Bash/Donna	1956	10.00
❑ 47-6776	Hawaiian Cha Cha Cha/Mambo Japanese	1956	10.00
❑ 47-6882	Rum and Coca-Cola/Cose, Cose, Cose	1957	10.00
❑ 47-6960	Calypso Man/Cucara Cha Cha Cha	1957	10.00
❑ 47-6990	Beautiful Margaret/Leyende Mexicana (Legend of Mexico)	1957	10.00
❑ 47-7120	A Lo Loco/Kilindini Dance	1957	10.00
❑ 47-7245	Patricia/Why Wait	1958	10.00
❑ 47-7337	Guaglione/Paris	1958	8.00
❑ 47-7456	The Millionaire/Catalania	1959	8.00
❑ 47-7540	Tic Toc Polly Woc/My Roberta	1959	8.00
❑ 47-7630	Clap Hands/Divina	1959	8.00
❑ 47-7768	Oh, Oh, Rosie/Rockambo Baby	1960	8.00
❑ 47-7826	Julie Is Her Name/Be True to Me	1960	8.00
❑ 47-7873	Teresita La Chunga/Ritmo De Chunga	1961	8.00
❑ 47-7963	Arrivederci Roma/Moliendo Café	1961	8.00
❑ 47-8006	Patricia Twist/Ti-Pi-Tin Twist	1962	8.00
❑ 47-8077	La Raggaza (The Girl)/Via Veneto	1962	8.00
❑ 47-8204	Katanga/Teresita	1963	8.00
❑ 47-8259	Natalia Dengue/El Dengue	1963	8.00
❑ 47-8356	Caravan/Papa Mi	1964	8.00
❑ 61-8520 [S]	You're Driving Me Crazy! (What Did I Do?)/Taking a Chance on Love	1960	25.00
—"Living Stereo" (large hole, plays at 45 rpm)			
❑ 47-5393	Suby/Jazz Me Blues	1953	12.00
UNITED ARTISTS			
❑ 765	The Girl with the Green Eyes/Woman of Straw	1964	8.00

7-Inch Extended Plays

Number	Title (A Side/B Side)	Yr	NM
RCA VICTOR			
❑ LPC-114	Cherry Pink and Apple Blossom White/Mambo No. 5//In a Little Spanish Town/Patricia	1961	12.00
—"Compact 33 Double"; small hole, plays at 33 1/3 rpm			
❑ LPC-114 [PS]	Big Hits by Prado	1961	12.00
❑ EPA-404	Cuban Mambo/In a Little Spanish Town ('Twas on a Night Like This)//Mambo Jambo/Perdido	195?	15.00
❑ EPA-404 [PS]	Perez Prado and His Orchestra	195?	15.00
❑ EPA-732	Mambo Jambo/Mambo No. 5//Perdido/Mambo No. 8	1956	12.00
❑ EPA-732 [PS]	(title unknown)	1956	12.00
❑ EPA-4322	Patricia/Mood Indigo//Pretty Doll/Whistling Rock	1958	12.00
❑ EPA-4322 [PS]	Patricia	1958	12.00
❑ EPA-5022	Cherry Pink and Apple Blossom White/St. Louis Blues Mambo//Mambo Jambo/Mambo No. 5	1958	12.00
❑ EPA-5022 [PS]	Perez Prado (Gold Standard Series)	1958	12.00

Albums

Number	Title (A Side/B Side)	Yr	NM
RCA CAMDEN			
❑ CAL-409 [M]	Mambo Happy!	1957	20.00
❑ CAL-547 [M]	Latino!	1960	20.00
RCA VICTOR			
❑ LPM-21 [10]	Perez Prado Plays Mucho Mambo for Dancing	1951	60.00
❑ LPM-1075 [M]	Mambo Mania	1955	40.00
❑ LPM-1101 [M]	Voodoo Suite (and Six All-Time Greats)	1955	40.00
❑ LPM-1196 [M]	Mambo by the King	1956	40.00
❑ LPM-1257 [M]	Havana 3 A.M.	1956	40.00
❑ LPM-1459 [M]	Latin Satin	1957	40.00
❑ LPM-1556 [M]	"Prez"	1958	30.00
❑ LSP-1556 [S]	"Prez"	1959	40.00
❑ LPM-1883 [M]	Dilo (Ugh!)	1958	30.00
❑ LSP-1883 [S]	Dilo (Ugh!)	1959	40.00
❑ ANL1-1941	Pure Gold	1975	10.00
❑ LPM-2028 [M]	Pops and Prado	1959	30.00
❑ LSP-2028 [S]	Pops and Prado	1959	40.00
❑ LPM-2104 [M]	Big Hits by Prado	1959	30.00
❑ LSP-2104 [S]	Big Hits by Prado	1959	40.00
❑ LPM-2133 [M]	A Touch of Tabasco	1960	20.00
❑ LSP-2133 [S]	A Touch of Tabasco	1960	30.00
❑ LPM-2308 [M]	Rockambo	1961	20.00
❑ LSP-2308 [S]	Rockambo	1961	30.00
❑ LPM-2379 [M]	The New Dance La Chunga	1961	20.00
❑ LSP-2379 [S]	The New Dance La Chunga	1961	30.00
❑ LPM-2524 [M]	The Twist Goes Latin	1962	20.00
❑ LSP-2524 [S]	The Twist Goes Latin	1962	30.00
❑ LPM-2571 [M]	Exotic Suite	1962	20.00
❑ LSP-2571 [S]	Exotic Suite	1962	30.00
❑ LPM-2610 [M]	Our Man in Latin America	1963	20.00
❑ LSP-2610 [S]	Our Man in Latin America	1963	30.00
❑ LPM-3108 [10]	Mambo by the King	1953	60.00
❑ LPM-3330 [M]	Dance Latino	1965	15.00
❑ LSP-3330 [S]	Dance Latino	1965	20.00
❑ LPM-3732 [M]	The Best of Perez Prado	1967	20.00
❑ LSP-3732 [S]	The Best of Perez Prado	1967	15.00
❑ VPS-6066 [(2)]	This Is Perez Prado	1972	15.00
UNITED ARTISTS			
❑ LS-61032	Estas Si Viven (The Living End)	196?	15.00

PRATT, ANDY

45s

Number	Title (A Side/B Side)	Yr	NM
COLUMBIA			
❑ 45804	Avenging Annie/So Fine (It's Frightening)	1973	5.00
NEMPEROR			
❑ 007	If You Could See Yourself (Through My Eyes)/(B-side unknown)	1976	4.00
❑ 008	Some Things Go On Forever/That's When Miracles Occur	1976	4.00
❑ 013	All I Want Is You/(B-side unknown)	1977	4.00

Albums

Number	Title (A Side/B Side)	Yr	NM
COLUMBIA			
❑ KC 31722	Andy Pratt	1973	10.00
NEMPEROR			
❑ SD 438	Resolution	1976	10.00
❑ SD 443	Shiver in the Night	1977	10.00
POLYDOR			
❑ 24-4015	Records Are Like Life	1970	12.00

PRATT & MCCLAIN

45s

Number	Title (A Side/B Side)	Yr	NM
ABC DUNHILL			
❑ 4387	Spirit of Love/When My Ship Comes In	1974	5.00
❑ 15004	Turn, Turn, Turn/Here I Am	1974	5.00
❑ 15024	We've Lost the Magic/When My Ship Comes In	1974	5.00
REPRISE			
❑ 1351	Happy Days/Cruisin' with the Fonz	1976	5.00
❑ 1361	Devil with a Blue Dress/Tonight We're Gonna Fall in Love	1976	4.00
❑ 1367	One Way or the Other/Tonight We're Gonna Fall in Love	1976	—
—Canceled?			
❑ 1373	Whachersign/Who Needs It	1976	4.00

Albums

Number	Title (A Side/B Side)	Yr	NM
ABC DUNHILL			
❑ DSX-50164	Pratt-McClain	1974	12.00
REPRISE			
❑ MS 2250	Pratt & McClain Featuring "Happy Days"	1976	10.00

PREACHERS, THE

45s

Number	Title (A Side/B Side)	Yr	NM
CHALLENGE			
❑ 501	Vitamin L.O.V.E./Till the Dawn	1969	12.00
MOONGLOW			
❑ 240	Who Do You Love/Chicken Poppa	1965	25.00
❑ 5006	Pain and Sorrow/Stay Out of My World	1965	20.00

PRECISIONS, THE (1)

45s

Number	Title (A Side/B Side)	Yr	NM
ATCO			
❑ 6643	Don't Double (With Trouble)/Into My Life	1969	12.00
❑ 6669	New York City/You're the Best (That Ever Did It)	1969	12.00
D-TOWN			
❑ 1033	My Lover Come Back/I Wanna Tell My Baby	1965	200.00
❑ 1055	Mexican Love Song/You're Sweet	1965	25.00
DREW			
❑ 1001	Such Misery/A Lover's Plea	1967	25.00
❑ 1002	Why Girl/What I Want	1967	15.00
❑ 1002	Why Girl/Sugar Ain't Sweet	1967	2500.
—VG 1000; VG+ 1750			
❑ 1003	If This Is Love (I'd Rather Be Lonely)/You'll Soon Be Gone	1967	25.00
❑ 1004	Instant Heartbreak (Just Add Tears)/Dream Girl	1968	15.00
❑ 1005	Never Let Her Go/A Place	1968	15.00

PRECISIONS, THE (2)

45s

Number	Title (A Side/B Side)	Yr	NM
HIGHLAND			
❑ 300	Eight Reasons Why I Love You/(B-side unknown)	1962	400.00

PRECISIONS, THE (U)

May be group (2); could be someone else.

45s

Number	Title (A Side/B Side)	Yr	NM
RAYNA			
❑ 1001	White Christmas/Silent Night	19??	100.00

PRELUDE

45s

Number	Title (A Side/B Side)	Yr	NM
ISLAND			
❑ IXPI 1 [DJ]	Christmas Message (same on both sides)	1974	10.00
❑ 002	After the Goldrush/Johnson Boy	1974	6.00
❑ 018	Fly/Lady from a Small Town	1975	5.00
PYE			
❑ 71045	For a Dancer/Best of a Bad Time	1975	5.00

Albums

Number	Title (A Side/B Side)	Yr	NM
ISLAND			
❑ ILPS 9282	After the Gold Rush	1974	12.00
PYE			
❑ 12120	Owlcreek Incident	1975	12.00
❑ 12139	Back Into the Light	1976	12.00

PRELUDES, THE (1)

45s

Number	Title (A Side/B Side)	Yr	NM
ARLISS			
❑ 1004	Lorraine/Oh Please, Genie	1961	80.00
OCTAVIA			
❑ 8008	A Place for You (In My Heart)/That Would Be So Good	1962	40.00

PRELUDES, THE (2)

45s

Number	Title (A Side/B Side)	Yr	NM
CUB			
❑ 9005	Kingdom of Love/Vanishing Angel	1958	150.00

PRELUDES, THE (3)

45s

Number	Title (A Side/B Side)	Yr	NM
EMPIRE			
❑ 103	Don't Fall in Love Too Soon/I Want Your Arms Around Me (All the Time)	1956	100.00

PRELUDES FIVE, THE

45s

Number	Title (A Side/B Side)	Yr	NM
PIK			
❑ 231	Starlight/Don't You Know Love?	1961	25.00

PREMEERS, THE

45s

Number	Title (A Side/B Side)	Yr	NM
HERALD			
❑ 577	Diary of Our Love/Gee Oh Gee	1963	30.00

PREMIATA FORNERIA MARCONI See P.F.M.

PREMIERS, THE (1)

45s

Number	Title (A Side/B Side)	Yr	NM
FARO			
❑ 615	Farmer John/Duffy's Blues	1964	30.00
❑ 621	Get Your Baby/Little Ways	1965	12.00
❑ 624	Come On and Dance/Get On the Plane	1966	12.00
❑ 627	Ring Around My Rosie (Part 1)/Ring Around My Rosie (Part 2)	1967	12.00
WARNER BROS.			
❑ 5443	Farmer John/Duffy's Blues	1964	15.00
❑ 5464	Annie Oakley/Blues for Arlene	1964	12.00

Albums

Number	Title (A Side/B Side)	Yr	NM
WARNER BROS.			
❑ W 1565 [M]	Farmer John	1964	40.00
❑ WS 1565 [S]	Farmer John	1964	50.00

PREMIERS, THE (2)

45s

Number	Title (A Side/B Side)	Yr	NM
ALERT			
❑ 706	Jolene/Oh, Theresa	1959	100.00
FURY			
❑ 1029	I Pray/Pigtails, Eyes Are Blue	1960	40.00
RUST			
❑ 5032	Falling Star/She Gives Me Fever	1961	100.00

PREMIERS, THE (3)

45s

Number	Title (A Side/B Side)	Yr	NM
CINDY			
❑ 3008	China Doll/Life Is Grand	1958	80.00
DIG			
❑ 106	New Moon/Baby	1956	150.00
❑ 113	My Darling/Have a Heart	1956	250.00
FORTUNE			
❑ 527	When You Are in Love/The Trap of Love	1956	80.00
GONE			
❑ 5009	Is It a Dream/Valerie	1957	200.00
—With "Let Me Share Your Dream" by The Deltas (Gone 5010) on Side 1 by mistake			
❑ 5009	Is It a Dream/Valerie	1957	500.00
—With correct track on side 1			
RCA VICTOR			
❑ 47-6958	Run Along Baby/Hey Miss Fancy	1957	80.00

PREMIERS, THE (4)

45s

Number	Title (A Side/B Side)	Yr	NM
KING			
❑ 6061	She's Always There/I'm Better Off Now	1966	20.00
STAX			
❑ 177	Make It Me/You Make a Strong Girl Weak	1965	30.00

PREMIERS, THE (5)

45s

Number	Title (A Side/B Side)	Yr	NM
MINK			
❑ 21	Tonight/I Think I Love You	1959	100.00
PARKWAY			
❑ 807	Tonight/I Think I Love You	1959	20.00

PREMIERS, THE (6)

45s

Number	Title (A Side/B Side)	Yr	NM
NU-PHI			
❑ 367/8	Cruisin'/(B-side unknown)	1959	30.00
❑ 701	Firewater/Younger Than You	1960	30.00

PREMIERS, THE (U)

Could be one of the above groups; could be a completely different group.

45s

Number	Title (A Side/B Side)	Yr	NM
BOND			
❑ 5803/4	Hop and Skip/Uh-Huh	1958	20.00

PRESENT, THE

45s

Number	Title (A Side/B Side)	Yr	NM
PHILIPS			
❑ 40466	I Know/Many's the Slip Twixt the Cup and the Lip	1966	30.00

PRESIDENTS, THE (1)

45s

Number	Title (A Side/B Side)	Yr	NM
SUSSEX			
❑ 200	For You/Gotta Keep Movin'	1970	7.00
❑ 207	5-10-15-20 (25-30 Years of Love)/I'm Still Dancing	1970	8.00
❑ 212	Triangle of Love (Hey Diddle Diddle)/Sweet Magic	1971	7.00
❑ 217	The Sweetest Thing This Side of Heaven/It's All Over Now	1971	7.00

Albums

Number	Title (A Side/B Side)	Yr	NM
SUSSEX			
❑ SXBX-7005	5-10-15-20 (25-30 Years of Love)	1970	25.00

PRESIDENTS, THE (2)

Not the same as group (1). The Sussex group's success forced this group to change its name, as reflected in the label credit on their final DeLuxe 45.

45s

Number	Title (A Side/B Side)	Yr	NM
DELUXE			
❑ 113	Gold Walk/I Want My Baby	1969	8.00
❑ 120	Snoopy/Stinky	1969	8.00
❑ 127	Which Way/Peter Rabbit	1970	8.00
❑ 134	Lover's Psalm/Our Meeting	1971	6.00
—As "The President's Band"			

PRESIDENTS, THE (3)

45s

Number	Title (A Side/B Side)	Yr	NM
MERCURY			
❑ 72016	Pots 'n' Pans/The Toasts	1962	20.00

PRESIDENTS, THE (U)

The Hollywood record could be group (1) or (2); the Warner Bros. record could be group (3).

45s

Number	Title (A Side/B Side)	Yr	NM
HOLLYWOOD			
❑ 1137	Shoeshine (Part 1)/Shoeshine (Part 2)	1968	10.00
PLUM			
❑ 31	Mighty Fly Do/Love Pain	197?	10.00
WARNER BROS.			
❑ 5240	Hot Toddy March/I Do Love You (Do I Love You)	1961	15.00

PRESLEY, ELVIS

12-Inch Singles

Number	Title (A Side/B Side)	Yr	NM
RCA			
❑ EP-0517 [DJ]	Little Sister/Rip It Up	1983	100.00
❑ 07863-60570-1	A Little Less Conversation (12" Extended Remix)/(Radio Remix Edit)/(Original Version)	2002	12.00
—Credited to "Elvis vs JXL"; includes record and custom cover			

45s

Number	Title (A Side/B Side)	Yr	NM
BMG			
❑ DPC-13558	That's All Right (same on both sides)	2003	1000.
—Gray label; used as a promotion for buyers of an Elvis Presley Illuminated CD/Record Player Radio			
❑ 56193	Rubberneckin' (Paul Oakenfold Remix Radio Edit)/(Original)	2003	5.00
COLLECTABLES			
❑ COL-0103 [(23)]	Elvis #1 Hit Singles Collection	2001	100.00
—Contains reproductions, on red vinyl, of 18 RCA singles and all five Sun singles, using facsimiles of original labels and reproductions of original picture sleeves, and all-new sleeves for those songs not issued originally with picture sleeves; with poster and all in wooden box			
❑ COL-0134 [(23)]	Elvis Hit Singles Collection Vol. 2	2002	100.00
—Contains reproductions, on red vinyl, of 23 RCA singles not in the first box, using facsimiles of original labels and reproductions of original picture sleeves, and all-new sleeves for those songs not issued originally with picture sleeves; with poster and all in wooden box			
❑ COL-4500	Good Rockin' Tonight/I Don't Care If the Sun Don't Shine	1986	3.00
—Black vinyl			
❑ COL-4500	Good Rockin' Tonight/I Don't Care If the Sun Don't Shine	1992	4.00
—Gold vinyl			
❑ COL-4501	You're a Heartbreaker/Milkcow Blues Boogie	1986	3.00
—Black vinyl			
❑ COL-4501	You're a Heartbreaker/Milkcow Blues Boogie	1992	4.00
—Gold vinyl			
❑ COL-4502	Baby Let's Play House/I'm Left, You're Right, She's Gone	1986	3.00
—Black vinyl			
❑ COL-4502	Baby Let's Play House/I'm Left, You're Right, She's Gone	1992	4.00
—Gold vinyl			
❑ COL-4503	I Got a Woman/I'm Counting on You	1986	3.00
—Black vinyl			
❑ COL-4503	I Got a Woman/I'm Counting on You	1992	4.00
—Gold vinyl			
❑ COL-4504	I'll Never Let You Go (Little Darlin')/I'm Gonna Sit Right Down and Cry (Over You)	1986	3.00
—Black vinyl			
❑ COL-4504	I'll Never Let You Go (Little Darlin')/I'm Gonna Sit Right Down and Cry (Over You)	1992	4.00
—Gold vinyl			
❑ COL-4505	Tryin' to Get to You/I Love You Because	1986	3.00
—Black vinyl			
❑ COL-4505	Tryin' to Get to You/I Love You Because	1992	4.00
—Gold vinyl			
❑ COL-4506	Money Honey/One-Sided Love Affair	1986	3.00
—Black vinyl			
❑ COL-4506	Money Honey/One-Sided Love Affair	1992	4.00
—Gold vinyl			
❑ COL-4507	Too Much/Playing for Keeps	1986	3.00
—Black vinyl			
❑ COL-4507	Too Much/Playing for Keeps	1992	4.00
—Gold vinyl			
❑ COL-4508	A Big Hunk o'Love/My Wish Came True	1986	3.00
—Black vinyl			
❑ COL-4508	A Big Hunk o'Love/My Wish Came True	1992	4.00
—Gold vinyl			
❑ COL-4509	Stuck on You/Fame and Fortune	1986	3.00
—Black vinyl			
❑ COL-4509	Stuck on You/Fame and Fortune	1992	4.00
—Gold vinyl			
❑ COL-4510	I Feel So Bad/Wild in the Country	1986	3.00
—Black vinyl			
❑ COL-4510	I Feel So Bad/Wild in the Country	1992	4.00
—Gold vinyl			
❑ COL-4511	She's Not You/Jailhouse Rock	1986	3.00
—Black vinyl			
❑ COL-4511	She's Not You/Jailhouse Rock	1992	4.00
—Gold vinyl			
❑ COL-4512	One Broken Heart for Sale/Devil in Disguise	1986	3.00
—Black vinyl			
❑ COL-4512	One Broken Heart for Sale/Devil in Disguise	1992	4.00
—Gold vinyl			
❑ COL-4513	Bossa Nova Baby/Such a Night	1986	3.00
—Black vinyl			
❑ COL-4513	Bossa Nova Baby/Such a Night	1992	4.00
—Gold vinyl			
❑ COL-4514	Love Me/Flaming Star	1986	3.00
—Black vinyl			
❑ COL-4514	Love Me/Flaming Star	1992	4.00
—Gold vinyl			
❑ COL-4515	Follow That Dream/When My Blue Moon Turns to Gold Again	1986	3.00
—Black vinyl			
❑ COL-4515	Follow That Dream/When My Blue Moon Turns to Gold Again	1992	4.00
—Gold vinyl			
❑ COL-4516	Frankie and Johnny/Love Letters	1986	3.00
—Black vinyl			
❑ COL-4516	Frankie and Johnny/Love Letters	1992	4.00
—Gold vinyl			
❑ COL-4517	U.S. Male/Until It's Time for You to Go	1986	3.00
—Black vinyl			

P

Number	Title (A Side/B Side)	Yr	NM
COL-4517	U.S. Male/Until It's Time for You to Go	1992	4.00
—Gold vinyl			
COL-4518	Old Shep/You'll Never Walk Alone	1986	3.00
—Black vinyl			
COL-4518	Old Shep/You'll Never Walk Alone	1992	4.00
—Gold vinyl			
COL-4519	Poor Boy/An American Trilogy	1986	3.00
—Black vinyl			
COL-4519	Poor Boy/An American Trilogy	1992	4.00
—Gold vinyl			
COL-4520	How Great Thou Art/His Hand in Mine	1986	3.00
—Black vinyl			
COL-4520	How Great Thou Art/His Hand in Mine	1992	4.00
—Gold vinyl			
COL-4521	Big Boss Man/Paralyzed	1986	3.00
—Black vinyl			
COL-4521	Big Boss Man/Paralyzed	1992	4.00
—Gold vinyl			
COL-4522	Fools Fall in Love/Blue Suede Shoes	1986	3.00
—Black vinyl			
COL-4522	Fools Fall in Love/Blue Suede Shoes	1992	4.00
—Gold vinyl			
COL-4564	The Elvis Medley/Always on My Mind	1986	3.00
COL-4738	Ask Me/The Girl of My Best Friend	1997	3.00
COL-4743	Girls! Girls! Girls!/Ain't That Loving You Baby	1997	3.00
COL-4744	It's Only Love/Beyond the Reef	1997	3.00
04764	Witchcraft/Spinout	1997	3.00
80000	(Now and Then There's) A Fool Such As I/I Need Your Love Tonight	1997	4.00
—Gray marbled vinyl			
80001	Separate Ways/Always on My Mind	1997	4.00
—Gray marbled vinyl			
80002	An American Trilogy/Until It's Time for You to Go	1997	4.00
—Gray marbled vinyl			
80003	Crying in the Chapel/I Believe in the Man in the Sky	1997	4.00
—Gray marbled vinyl			
80004	Don't/I Beg of You	1997	4.00
—Gray marbled vinyl			
80005	Don't Cry Daddy/Rubberneckin'	1997	4.00
—Gray marbled vinyl			
80006	Good Luck Charm/Anything That's Part of You	1997	4.00
—Gray marbled vinyl			
80007	Guitar Man/Hi-Heel Sneakers	1997	4.00
—Gray marbled vinyl			
80008	Hard Headed Woman/Don't Ask Me Why	1997	4.00
—Gray marbled vinyl			
80009	Heartbreak Hotel/I Was the One	1997	4.00
—Gray marbled vinyl			
80010	Mystery Train/I Forgot to Remember to Forget	1997	4.00
—Gray marbled vinyl			
80011	One Night/I Got Stung	1997	4.00
—Gray marbled vinyl			
80012	I Really Don't Want to Know/There Goes My Everything	1997	4.00
—Gray marbled vinyl			
80013	I Want You, I Need You, I Love You/My Baby Left Me	1997	4.00
—Gray marbled vinyl			
80014	If I Can Dream/Edge of Reality	1997	4.00
—Gray marbled vinyl			
80015	Kentucky Rain/My Little Friend	1997	4.00
—Gray marbled vinyl			
80016	Kiss Me Quick/Suspicion	1997	4.00
—Gray marbled vinyl			
80017	Kissin' Cousins/It Hurts Me	1997	4.00
—Gray marbled vinyl			
80018	Marie's the Name His Latest Flame/Little Sister	1997	4.00
—Gray marbled vinyl			
80019	(Let Me Be You) Teddy Bear/Loving You	1997	4.00
—Gray marbled vinyl			
80020	The Wonder of You/Mama Liked the Roses	1997	4.00
—Gray marbled vinyl			
80021	Memories/Charro	1997	4.00
—Gray marbled vinyl			
80022	My Boy/Thinking About You	1997	4.00
—Gray marbled vinyl			
80023	Way Down/My Way	1997	4.00
—Gray marbled vinyl			
80024	Patch It Up/You Don't Have to Say You Love Me	1997	4.00
—Gray marbled vinyl			

Number	Title (A Side/B Side)	Yr	NM
80025	Surrender/Lonely Man	1997	4.00
—Gray marbled vinyl			
80026	That's All Right/Blue Moon of Kentucky	1997	4.00
—Gray marbled vinyl			
80027	Wear My Ring Around Your Neck/Doncha' Think It's Time	1997	4.00
—Gray marbled vinyl			
80028	Puppet on a String/Wooden Heart	1997	4.00
—Gray marbled vinyl			
RCA			
447-0600	I Forgot to Remember to Forget/Mystery Train	1977	4.00
—Note: All RCA releases with a "447" prefix are from the Gold Standard Series and are black label, dog near top			
447-0601	That's All Right/Blue Moon of Kentucky	1977	4.00
447-0602	Good Rockin' Tonight/I Don't Care If the Sun Don't Shine	1977	4.00
447-0603	Milkcow Blues Boogie/You're a Heartbreaker	1977	4.00
447-0604	Baby Let's Play House/I'm Left, You're Right, She's Gone	1977	4.00
447-0605	Heartbreak Hotel/I Was the One	1977	4.00
447-0607	I Want You, I Need You, I Love You/My Baby Left Me	1977	4.00
447-0608	Hound Dog/Don't Be Cruel	1977	4.00
447-0609	Blue Suede Shoes/Tutti Frutti	1977	4.00
447-0613	Blue Moon/Just Because	1977	4.00
447-0614	Money Honey/One-Sided Love Affair	1977	4.00
447-0615	Lawdy Miss Clawdy/Shake, Rattle, and Roll	1977	4.00
447-0616	Love Me Tender/Anyway You Want Me (That's How I Will Be)	1977	4.00
447-0617	Too Much/Playing for Keeps	1977	4.00
447-0618	All Shook Up/That's When Your Heartaches Begin	1977	4.00
447-0619	Jailhouse Rock/Treat Me Nice	1977	4.00
447-0620	(Let Me Be Your) Teddy Bear/Loving You	1977	4.00
447-0621	Don't/I Beg of You	1977	4.00
447-0622	Wear My Ring Around Your Neck/Don'tcha Think It's Time	1977	4.00
447-0623	Hard Headed Woman/Don't Ask Me Why	1977	4.00
447-0624	One Night/I Got Stung	1977	4.00
447-0625	(Now and Then There's) A Fool Such As I/I Need Your Love Tonight	1977	4.00
447-0626	A Big Hunk o' Love/My Wish Came True	1977	4.00
447-0627	Stuck on You/Fame and Fortune	1977	4.00
447-0628	It's Now or Never/A Mess of Blues	1977	4.00
447-0629	Are You Lonesome To-Night?/I Gotta Know	1977	4.00
447-0630	Surrender/Lonely Man	1977	4.00
447-0631	I Feel So Bad/Wild in the Country	1977	4.00
447-0634	(Marie's the Name) His Latest Flame/Little Sister	1977	4.00
447-0635	Can't Help Falling in Love/Rock-a-Hula Baby	1977	4.00
447-0636	Good Luck Charm/Anything That's Part of You	1977	4.00
447-0637	She's Not You/Just Tell Her Jim Said Hello	1977	4.00
447-0638	Return to Sender/Where Do You Come From	1977	4.00
447-0639	Kiss Me Quick/Suspicion	1977	4.00
447-0640	One Broken Heart for Sale/They Remind Me Too Much of You	1977	4.00
447-0641	(You're the) Devil in Disguise/Please Don't Drag That String Around	1977	4.00
447-0642	Bossa Nova Baby/Witchcraft	1977	4.00
447-0643	Crying in the Chapel/I Believe in the Man in the Sky	1977	4.00
447-0644	Kissin' Cousins/It Hurts Me	1977	4.00
447-0645	Such a Night/Never Ending	1977	4.00
447-0646	Viva Las Vegas/What'd I Say	1977	4.00
447-0647	Blue Christmas/Santa Claus Is Back in Town	1977	4.00
447-0647 [PS]	Blue Christmas/Santa Claus Is Back in Town	1977	10.00
—Does not mention "Gold Standard Series" on sleeve			
447-0648	Do the Clam/You'll Be Gone	1977	4.00
447-0649	Ain't That Loving You Baby/Ask Me	1977	4.00
447-0650	Puppet on a String/Wooden Heart	1977	4.00
447-0651	Joshua Fit the Battle/Known Only to Him	1977	4.00
447-0653	(Such An) Easy Question/It Feels So Right	1977	4.00
447-0654	I'm Yours/(It's a) Long, Lonely Highway	1977	4.00
447-0655	Tell Me Why/Blue River	1977	4.00

Number	Title (A Side/B Side)	Yr	NM
447-0656	Frankie and Johnny/Please Don't Stop Loving Me	1977	4.00
447-0657	Love Letters/Come What May	1977	4.00
447-0658	Spinout/All That I Am	1977	4.00
447-0659	Indescribably Blue/Fools Fall in Love	1977	4.00
447-0661	There's Always Me/Judy	1977	4.00
447-0662	Big Boss Man/You Don't Know Me	1977	4.00
447-0663	Guitar Man/High Heel Sneakers	1977	4.00
447-0664	U.S. Male/Stay Away	1977	5.00
447-0665	You'll Never Walk Alone/We Call on Him	1977	4.00
447-0666	Let Yourself Go/Your Time Hasn't Come Yet, Baby	1977	4.00
447-0667	A Little Less Conversation/Almost in Love	1977	4.00
447-0668	If I Can Dream/Edge of Reality	1977	4.00
447-0669	Memories/Charro	1977	4.00
447-0670	How Great Thou Art/His Hand in Mine	1977	4.00
447-0671	In the Ghetto/Any Day Now	1977	4.00
447-0672	Clean Up Your Own Back Yard/The Fair Is Moving On	1977	4.00
447-0673	Suspicious Minds/You'll Think of Me	1977	4.00
447-0674	Don't Cry Daddy/Rubberneckin'	1977	4.00
447-0675	Kentucky Rain/My Little Friend	1977	4.00
447-0676	The Wonder of You/Mama Liked the Roses	1977	4.00
447-0677	I've Lost You/The Next Step Is Love	1977	4.00
447-0678	You Don't Have to Say You Love Me/Patch It Up	1977	4.00
447-0679	I Really Don't Want to Know/There Goes My Everything	1977	4.00
447-0680	Where Did They Go, Lord/Rags to Riches	1977	4.00
447-0681	If Every Day Was Like Christmas/How Would You Like to Be	1977	4.00
447-0682	Life/Only Believe	1977	4.00
447-0683	I'm Leavin'/Heart of Rome	1977	4.00
447-0684	It's Only Love/The Sound of Your Cry	1977	4.00
447-0685	An American Trilogy/Until It's Time for You to Go	1977	4.00
DME1-1803	King of the Whole Wide World/King Creole	1997	8.00
—Gold vinyl (about 7,000 pressed)			
DME1-1803 [DJ]	King of the Whole Wide World/King Creole	1997	400.00
—Test pressings of above on green, blue, white and clear vinyl. Value is for any of them.			
DME1-1803 [PS]	King of the Whole Wide World/King Creole	1997	8.00
—Same picture sleeve with either edition			
DME1-1803R	King of the Whole Wide World/King Creole	1997	15.00
—Red vinyl, marked as a promotional copy (about 3,000 pressed)			
8760-7-R	Heartbreak Hotel/Heartbreak Hotel	1988	5.00
—B-side by "David Keith & Charlie Schlatter with Zulu Time"			
8760-7-R [PS]	Heartbreak Hotel/Heartbreak Hotel	1988	6.00
—Stock version with pink Cadillac pictured			
8760-7-RA1 [DJ]	Heartbreak Hotel/Heartbreak Hotel	1988	25.00
—B-side by "David Keith & Charlie Schlatter with Zulu Time"; white label promo, "Not for Sale" on label			
8760-7-RA1 [PS]	Heartbreak Hotel/Heartbreak Hotel	1988	80.00
—Promo-only sleeve with "The Infamous Butch Waugh as Elvis Presley"			
GB-10485	Take Good Care of Her/I've Got a Thing About You, Baby	1977	4.00
—Gold Standard Series; black label			
GB-10486	Separate Ways/Always on My Mind	1977	4.00
—Gold Standard Series; black label			
GB-10487	T-R-O-U-B-L-E/Mr. Songman	1977	4.00
—Gold Standard Series; black label			
GB-10488	Promised Land/It's Midnight	1977	4.00
—Gold Standard Series; black label			
GB-10489	My Boy/Thinking About You	1977	4.00
—Gold Standard Series; black label			
PB-10601	Hurt/For the Heart	1976	100.00
—Second pressings (very rare) on the 1976-88 "dog near top" black label			
JB-10857 [DJ]	Moody Blue/She Thinks I Still Care	1976	15.00
—Light yellow label promo, "Not for Sale" on label			
JB-10857 [DJ]	Moody Blue/She Thinks I Still Care	1976	1000.
—Colored vinyl pressings exist in five different colors — red, white, gold, blue, green. Value is for any of them.			
PB-10857	Moody Blue/She Thinks I Still Care	1976	5.00
PB-10857 [PS]	Moody Blue/She Thinks I Still Care	1976	10.00

Except when noted otherwise, VG = 25% of NM, and VG+ = 50% of NM. (Example: VG = $2.00, VG+ = $4.00 and NM = $8.00.)

Number	Title (A Side/B Side)	Yr	NM
❑ JH-10951 [DJ]	Let Me Be There (mono/stereo)	1977	200.00
—Promo only			
❑ JB-10998 [DJ]	Way Down/Pledging My Love	1977	20.00
—Light yellow label promo, "Not for Sale" on label			
❑ JB-10998 [DJ]	Way Down/Pledging My Love	1977	120.00
—White label promo, "Elvis Presley" is twice as large as the song titles			
❑ PB-10998	Way Down/Pledging My Love	1977	5.00
❑ PB-10998 [PS]	Way Down/Pledging My Love	1977	10.00
❑ PB-11099	Hound Dog/Don't Be Cruel	1977	4.00
❑ PB-11099 [PS]	Hound Dog/Don't Be Cruel	1977	4.00
—From boxes "15 Golden Records, 30 Golden Hits" and "20 Golden Hits in Full Color Sleeves"			
❑ PB-11100	In the Ghetto/Any Day Now	1977	4.00
❑ PB-11100 [PS]	In the Ghetto/Any Day Now	1977	4.00
—From boxes "15 Golden Records, 30 Golden Hits" and "20 Golden Hits in Full Color Sleeves"			
❑ PB-11101	Jailhouse Rock/Treat Me Nice	1977	4.00
❑ PB-11101 [PS]	Jailhouse Rock/Treat Me Nice	1977	4.00
—From box "15 Golden Records, 30 Golden Hits"			
❑ PB-11102	Can't Help Falling in Love/ Rock-a-Hula Baby	1977	4.00
❑ PB-11102 [PS]	Can't Help Falling in Love/ Rock-a-Hula Baby	1977	4.00
—From boxes "15 Golden Records, 30 Golden Hits" and "20 Golden Hits in Full Color Sleeves"			
❑ PB-11103	Suspicious Minds/ You'll Think of Me	1977	4.00
❑ PB-11103 [PS]	Suspicious Minds/ You'll Think of Me	1977	4.00
—From box "15 Golden Records, 30 Golden Hits"			
❑ PB-11104	Are You Lonesome To-Night?/ I Gotta Know	1977	4.00
❑ PB-11104 [PS]	Are You Lonesome To-Night?/ I Gotta Know	1977	4.00
—From boxes "15 Golden Records, 30 Golden Hits" and "20 Golden Hits in Full Color Sleeves"			
❑ PB-11105	Heartbreak Hotel/I Was the One	1977	4.00
❑ PB-11105 [PS]	Heartbreak Hotel/I Was the One	1977	4.00
—From boxes "15 Golden Records, 30 Golden Hits" and "20 Golden Hits in Full Color Sleeves"			
❑ PB-11106	All Shook Up/That's When Your Heartaches Begin	1977	4.00
❑ PB-11106 [PS]	All Shook Up/That's When Your Heartaches Begin	1977	4.00
—From boxes "15 Golden Records, 30 Golden Hits" and "20 Golden Hits in Full Color Sleeves"			
❑ PB-11107	Blue Suede Shoes/Tutti Frutti	1977	4.00
❑ PB-11107 [PS]	Blue Suede Shoes/Tutti Frutti	1977	4.00
—From boxes "15 Golden Records, 30 Golden Hits" and "20 Golden Hits in Full Color Sleeves"			
❑ PB-11108	Love Me Tender/Any Way You Want Me (That's How I Will Be)	1977	4.00
❑ PB-11108 [PS]	Love Me Tender/Any Way You Want Me (That's How I Will Be)	1977	4.00
—From boxes "15 Golden Records, 30 Golden Hits" and "20 Golden Hits in Full Color Sleeves"			
❑ PB-11109	(Let Me Be Your) Teddy Bear/ Loving You	1977	4.00
❑ PB-11109 [PS]	(Let Me Be Your) Teddy Bear/ Loving You	1977	4.00
—From boxes "15 Golden Records, 30 Golden Hits" and "20 Golden Hits in Full Color Sleeves"			
❑ PB-11110	It's Now or Never/A Mess of Blues	1977	4.00
❑ PB-11110 [PS]	It's Now or Never/A Mess of Blues	1977	4.00
—From box "15 Golden Records, 30 Golden Hits"			
❑ PB-11111	Return to Sender/Where Do You Come From	1977	4.00
❑ PB-11111 [PS]	Return to Sender/Where Do You Come From	1977	4.00
—From boxes "15 Golden Records, 30 Golden Hits" and "20 Golden Hits in Full Color Sleeves"			
❑ PB-11112	One Night/I Got Stung	1977	4.00
❑ PB-11112 [PS]	One Night/I Got Stung	1977	4.00
—From box "15 Golden Records, 30 Golden Hits"			
❑ PB-11113	Crying in the Chapel/I Believe in the Man in the Sky	1977	4.00
❑ PB-11113 [PS]	Crying in the Chapel/I Believe in the Man in the Sky	1977	4.00
—From box "15 Golden Records, 30 Golden Hits"			
❑ JH-11165 [DJ]	My Way/America	1977	20.00
—Light yellow label promo, "Not for Sale" on label			
❑ PB-11165	My Way/America	1977	5.00
❑ PB-11165	My Way/America the Beautiful	1977	20.00
❑ PB-11165 [PS]	My Way/America	1977	10.00
❑ PB-11165 [PS]	My Way/America the Beautiful	1977	25.00
❑ JH-11212 [DJ]	Unchained Melody/ Softly, As I Leave You	1978	20.00
—Light yellow label promo, "Not for Sale" on label			
❑ PB-11212	Unchained Melody/ Softly, As I Leave You	1978	5.00
—No credit to Sherrill Nielsen on the "Unchained Melody" side			
❑ PB-11212	Unchained Melody/ Softly, As I Leave You	1978	10.00
—Erroneously states "Vocal Accompaniment by Sherrill Nielsen" on "Unchained Melody" side			
❑ PB-11212 [PS]	Unchained Melody/ Softly, As I Leave You	1978	10.00
❑ PP-11301	15 Golden Records, 30 Golden Hits	1977	60.00
—Includes 15 records (11099-11113) and outer box			

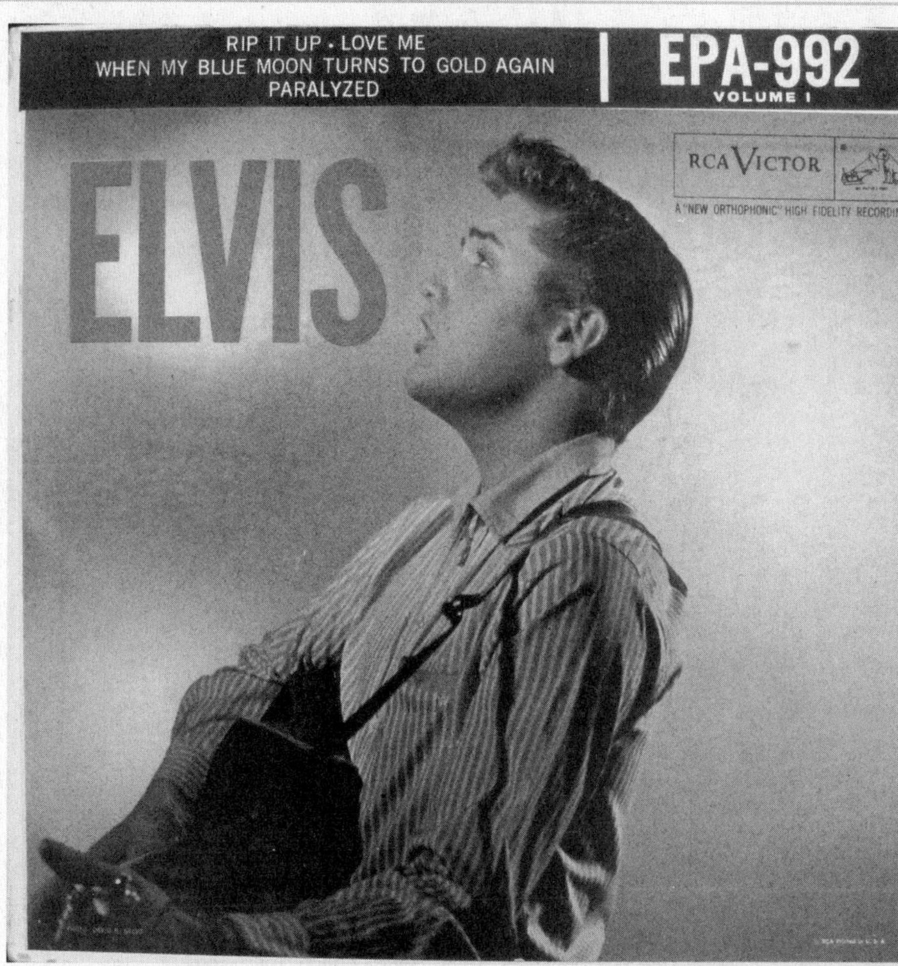

Elvis Presley, *Elvis (Volume 1)*, RCA Victor EPA-992, 1956, **$50.**

Number	Title (A Side/B Side)	Yr	NM
❑ JH-11320 [DJ]	(Let Me Be Your) Teddy Bear/ Puppet on a String	1978	15.00
—Light yellow label promo, "Not for Sale" on label			
❑ PB-11320	(Let Me Be Your) Teddy Bear/ Puppet on a String	1978	5.00
❑ PB-11320 [PS]	(Let Me Be Your) Teddy Bear/ Puppet on a String	1978	10.00
❑ GB-11326	Moody Blue/For the Heart	1978	4.00
—Gold Standard Series			
❑ PP-11340	20 Golden Hits in Full Color Sleeves	1977	80.00
—Includes 10 records (11099, 11100, 11102, 11104-11109, 11111) and outer box			
❑ GB-11504	Way Down/My Way	1979	4.00
—Gold Standard Series			
❑ JB-11533 [DJ]	Are You Sincere/Solitaire	1979	10.00
—Yellow label, dog near top, "Not for Sale" on label			
❑ PB-11533	Are You Sincere/Solitaire	1979	5.00
❑ PB-11533 [PS]	Are You Sincere/Solitaire	1979	10.00
❑ JB-11679 [DJ]	There's a Honky Tonk Angel (Who Will Take Me Back In)/ I Got a Feelin' in My Body	1979	12.00
—Light yellow label promo, "Not for Sale" on label			
❑ PB-11679	There's a Honky Tonk Angel (Who Will Take Me Back In)/ I Got a Feelin' in My Body	1979	5.00
—Has production credits removed; only producers are listed			
❑ PB-11679	There's a Honky Tonk Angel (Who Will Take Me Back In)/ I Got a Feelin' in My Body	1979	15.00
—Has full production credits (background vocals, strings) listed in error on both sides			
❑ PB-11679 [PS]	There's a Honky Tonk Angel (Who Will Take Me Back In)/ I Got a Feelin' in My Body	1979	10.00
❑ GB-11988	Unchained Melody/ Are You Sincere	1980	4.00
—Gold Standard Series			
❑ JH-12158 [DJ]	Guitar Man (mono/stereo)	1981	15.00
—Promo only on black vinyl			
❑ JH-12158 [DJ]	Guitar Man (mono/stereo)	1981	300.00
—Promo only on red vinyl			
❑ PB-12158	Guitar Man/Faded Love	1981	5.00
❑ PB-12158 [PS]	Guitar Man/Faded Love	1981	10.00

Number	Title (A Side/B Side)	Yr	NM
❑ JB-12205 [DJ]	Lovin' Arms/You Asked Me To	1981	15.00
—Yellow label promo, "Not for Sale" on label, black vinyl			
❑ JB-12205 [DJ]	Lovin' Arms/You Asked Me To	1981	300.00
—Yellow label promo, "Not for Sale" on label, green vinyl			
❑ PB-12205	Lovin' Arms/You Asked Me To	1981	6.00
—Not issued with picture sleeve (bootlegs exist)			
❑ JB-13058 [DJ]	There Goes My Everything/ You'll Never Walk Alone	1982	15.00
—Light yellow label promo, "Not for Sale" on label			
❑ PB-13058	There Goes My Everything/ You'll Never Walk Alone	1982	5.00
❑ PB-13058 [PS]	There Goes My Everything/ You'll Never Walk Alone	1982	10.00
❑ GB-13275	Suspicious Minds/ You'll Think of Me	1982	4.00
—Gold Standard Series			
❑ JH-13302	The Impossible Dream (The Quest)/An American Trilogy	1982	100.00
❑ JH-13302 [PS]	The Impossible Dream (The Quest)/An American Trilogy	1982	100.00
—Promo only, distributed to visitors to Elvis' birthplace in Tupelo, Mississippi, in 1982.			
❑ JB-13351 [DJ]	The Elvis Medley (Long Version)/ The Elvis Medley (Short Version)	1982	15.00
—Promo only on black vinyl			
❑ JB-13351 [DJ]	The Elvis Medley (Long Version)/ The Elvis Medley (Short Version)	1982	300.00
—Promo only on gold vinyl			
❑ PB-13351	The Elvis Medley/ Always on My Mind	1982	5.00
❑ PB-13351 [PS]	The Elvis Medley/ Always on My Mind	1982	10.00
❑ JB-13500 [DJ]	I Was the One/Wear My Ring Around Your Neck	1983	15.00
—Promo only on black vinyl, "Not for Sale" on label			
❑ JB-13500 [DJ]	I Was the One/Wear My Ring Around Your Neck	1983	300.00
—Promo only on gold vinyl			
❑ PB-13500	I Was the One/Wear My Ring Around Your Neck	1983	5.00
❑ PB-13500 [PS]	I Was the One/Wear My Ring Around Your Neck	1983	10.00

Elvis Presley, "Too Much," RCA Victor 47-6800, 1957, **$90.**

Number	Title (A Side/B Side)	Yr	NM
❑ JB-13547 [DJ]	Little Sister/Paralyzed	1983	15.00
—Promo only, black vinyl, "Not for Sale" on label			
❑ JB-13547 [DJ]	Little Sister/Paralyzed	1983	300.00
—Promo only on blue vinyl			
❑ PB-13547	Little Sister/Paralyzed	1983	5.00
❑ PB-13547 [PS]	Little Sister/Paralyzed	1983	10.00
❑ JB-13875 [DJ]	Baby Let's Play House/ Hound Dog	1984	200.00
—Gold vinyl, custom label			
❑ PB-13875	Baby Let's Play House/ Hound Dog	1984	40.00
—Gold vinyl, custom label			
❑ PB-13875 [PS]	Baby Let's Play House/ Hound Dog	1984	40.00
❑ PB-13885	Blue Suede Shoes/Tutti Frutti	1984	4.00
—From box "Elvis' Greatest Hits, Golden Singles, Vol. 1"; gold vinyl			
❑ PB-13885 [PS]	Blue Suede Shoes/Tutti Frutti	1984	4.00
❑ PB-13886	Don't Be Cruel/Hound Dog	1984	4.00
—From box "Elvis' Greatest Hits, Golden Singles, Vol. 1"; gold vinyl			
❑ PB-13886 [PS]	Don't Be Cruel/Hound Dog	1984	4.00
❑ PB-13887	I Want You, I Need You, I Love You/Love Me	1984	4.00
—From box "Elvis' Greatest Hits, Golden Singles, Vol. 1"; gold vinyl			
❑ PB-13887 [PS]	I Want You, I Need You, I Love You/Love Me	1984	4.00
❑ PB-13888	All Shook Up/(Let Me Be Your) Teddy Bear	1984	4.00
—From box "Elvis' Greatest Hits, Golden Singles, Vol. 1"; gold vinyl			
❑ PB-13888 [PS]	All Shook Up/(Let Me Be Your) Teddy Bear	1984	4.00
❑ PB-13889	It's Now or Never/Surrender	1984	4.00
—From box "Elvis' Greatest Hits, Golden Singles, Vol. 1"; gold vinyl			
❑ PB-13889 [PS]	It's Now or Never/Surrender	1984	4.00
❑ PB-13890	In the Ghetto/If I Can Dream	1984	4.00
—From box "Elvis' Greatest Hits, Golden Singles, Vol. 1"; gold vinyl			
❑ PB-13890 [PS]	In the Ghetto/If I Can Dream	1984	4.00
❑ PB-13891	That's All Right/Blue Moon of Kentucky	1984	4.00
—From box "Elvis' Greatest Hits, Golden Singles, Vol. 2"; gold vinyl			
❑ PB-13891 [PS]	That's All Right/Blue Moon of Kentucky	1984	4.00
❑ PB-13892	Heartbreak Hotel/Jailhouse Rock	1984	4.00
—From box "Elvis' Greatest Hits, Golden Singles, Vol. 2"; gold vinyl			
❑ PB-13892 [PS]	Heartbreak Hotel/Jailhouse Rock	1984	4.00

Number	Title (A Side/B Side)	Yr	NM
❑ PB-13893	Love Me Tender/Loving You	1984	4.00
—From box "Elvis' Greatest Hits, Golden Singles, Vol. 2"; gold vinyl			
❑ PB-13893 [PS]	Love Me Tender/Loving You	1984	4.00
❑ PB-13894	(Marie's the Name) His Latest Flame/Little Sister	1984	4.00
—From box "Elvis' Greatest Hits, Golden Singles, Vol. 2"; gold vinyl			
❑ PB-13894 [PS]	(Marie's the Name) His Latest Flame/Little Sister	1984	4.00
❑ PB-13895	Are You Lonesome Tonight/ Can't Help Falling in Love	1984	4.00
—From box "Elvis' Greatest Hits, Golden Singles, Vol. 2"; gold vinyl			
❑ PB-13895 [PS]	Are You Lonesome Tonight/ Can't Help Falling in Love	1984	4.00
❑ PB-13896	Suspicious Minds/Burning Love	1984	4.00
—From box "Elvis' Greatest Hits, Golden Singles, Vol. 2"; gold vinyl			
❑ PB-13896 [PS]	Suspicious Minds/Burning Love	1984	4.00
❑ PB-13897	Elvis' Greatest Hits, Golden Singles, Vol. 1	1984	15.00
—Box set of six 45s with sleeves (13885-13890) with box			
❑ PB-13898	Elvis' Greatest Hits, Golden Singles, Vol. 2	1984	15.00
—Box set of six 45s with sleeves (13891-13896) with box			
❑ JK-13929 [DJ]	Blue Suede Shoes (same on both sides)	1984	25.00
—Blue vinyl promo, "Not for Sale" on label			
❑ PB-13929	Blue Suede Shoes/ Promised Land	1984	12.00
—Blue vinyl; correct label — "Blue Suede Shoes" side says "Mono" and "Promised Land" side says "Stereo"			
❑ PB-13929	Blue Suede Shoes/ Promised Land	1984	15.00
—Blue vinyl; incorrect label — "Blue Suede Shoes" side says "Stereo" and "Promised Land" side says "Mono"			
❑ PB-13929 [PS]	Blue Suede Shoes/ Promised Land	1984	10.00
❑ JK-14090 [DJ]	Always on My Mind (same on both sides)	1985	20.00
—Purple vinyl; "Not for Sale" on label			
❑ PB-14090	Always on My Mind/My Boy	1985	10.00
—Purple vinyl			
❑ PB-14090 [PS]	Always on My Mind/My Boy	1985	10.00
❑ PB-14237	Merry Christmas Baby/Santa Claus Is Back in Town	1985	5.00
—Normal black RCA label			

Number	Title (A Side/B Side)	Yr	NM
❑ PB-14237	Merry Christmas Baby/Santa Claus Is Back in Town	1985	15.00
—"Elvis 50th Anniversary" label			
❑ PB-14237	Merry Christmas Baby/Santa Claus Is Back in Town	1985	15.00
—Green vinyl			
❑ PB-14237 [PS]	Merry Christmas Baby/Santa Claus Is Back in Town	1985	12.00
❑ 60575	A Little Less Conversation (JXL Radio Edit Remix)/ (Original Version)	2002	8.00
—Credited to "Elvis Presley: Elvis vs JXL"			
❑ 62402	Don't Be Cruel/Ain't That Lovin' You Baby (Fast Version)	1992	5.00
❑ 62402 [PS]	Don't Be Cruel/Ain't That Lovin' You Baby (Fast Version)	1992	5.00
—Generic white sleeve with "Elvis — The King of Rock 'n' Roll" sticker			
❑ 62403	Blue Christmas/Love Me Tender	1992	5.00
❑ 62403 [PS]	Blue Christmas/Love Me Tender	1992	5.00
—Generic white sleeve with "Elvis — The King of Rock 'n' Roll" sticker			
❑ 62411	Silver Bells (Unreleased Version)/Silver Bells	1993	5.00
❑ 62449	Heartbreak Hotel/Hound Dog	1992	5.00
❑ 64476	Heartbreak Hotel/I Was the One//Heartbreak Hotel (Alternate Take 5)/I Was the One (Alternate Take 2)	1996	3.00
❑ 64476 [PS]	Heartbreak Hotel/I Was the One//Heartbreak Hotel (Alternate Take 5)/I Was the One (Alternate Take 2)	1996	3.00
RCA VICTOR			
❑ 37-7850	Surrender/Lonely Man	1961	600.00
—"Compact Single 33" (small hole, plays at LP speed)			
❑ 37-7850 [PS]	Surrender/Lonely Man	1961	1000.
—Special picture sleeve for above record			
❑ 37-7880	I Feel So Bad/Wild in the Country	1961	1000.
—"Compact Single 33" (small hole, plays at LP speed)			
❑ 37-7880 [PS]	I Feel So Bad/Wild in the Country	1961	1200.
—Special picture sleeve for above record			
❑ 37-7908	(Marie's the Name) His Latest Flame/Little Sister	1961	1500.
—"Compact Single 33" (small hole, plays at LP speed)			
❑ 47-6357	I Forgot to Remember to Forget/ Mystery Train	1955	60.00
—No horizontal line on label			
❑ 47-6357	I Forgot to Remember to Forget/ Mystery Train	1955	60.00
—With horizontal line on label			
❑ 47-6357 [PS]	This Is His Life: Elvis Presley	1955	1500.
—Promo-only sleeve issued with above single; no stock picture sleeve was issued. This was formerly listed under "I Want You, I Need You, I Love You," as the sleeve does not have a number. Consensus opinion now places it with "Mystery Train."			
❑ 47-6380	That's All Right/ Blue Moon of Kentucky	1955	60.00
—No horizontal line on label			
❑ 47-6380	That's All Right/ Blue Moon of Kentucky	1955	60.00
—With horizontal line on label			
❑ 47-6381	Good Rockin' Tonight/I Don't Care If the Sun Don't Shine	1955	60.00
—No horizontal line on label			
❑ 47-6381	Good Rockin' Tonight/I Don't Care If the Sun Don't Shine	1955	60.00
—With horizontal line on label			
❑ 47-6382	Milkcow Blues Boogie/You're a Heartbreaker	1955	60.00
—No horizontal line on label			
❑ 47-6382	Milkcow Blues Boogie/ You're a Heartbreaker	1955	60.00
—With horizontal line on label			
❑ 47-6383	Baby Let's Play House/I'm Left, You're Right, She's Gone	1955	60.00
—No horizontal line on label			
❑ 47-6383	Baby Let's Play House/I'm Left, You're Right, She's Gone	1955	60.00
—With horizontal line on label			
❑ 47-6420	Heartbreak Hotel/I Was the One	1956	40.00
—No horizontal line on label			
❑ 47-6420	Heartbreak Hotel/I Was the One	1956	40.00
—With horizontal line on label			
❑ 47-6540	I Want You, I Need You, I Love You/My Baby Left Me	1956	40.00
—No horizontal line on label			
❑ 47-6540	I Want You, I Need You, I Love You/My Baby Left Me	1956	40.00
—With horizontal line on label			
❑ 47-6604	Don't Be Cruel/Hound Dog	1956	30.00
—No horizontal line on label			
❑ 47-6604	Don't Be Cruel/Hound Dog	1956	30.00
—With horizontal line on label			
❑ 47-6604 [PS]	Don't Be Cruel/Hound Dog	1956	120.00
—"Hound Dog!" listed on top of "Don't Be Cruel"			
❑ 47-6604 [PS]	Don't Be Cruel/Hound Dog	1956	200.00
—"Don't Be Cruel" listed on top of "Hound Dog!"			
❑ 47-6636	Blue Suede Shoes/Tutti Frutti	1956	80.00
—No horizontal line on label			
❑ 47-6636	Blue Suede Shoes/Tutti Frutti	1956	80.00
—With horizontal line on label			

Except when noted otherwise, VG = 25% of NM, and VG+ = 50% of NM. (Example: VG = $2.00, VG+ = $4.00 and NM = $8.00.)

Number	Title (A Side/B Side)	Yr	NM
❑ 47-6637	I Got a Woman/ I'm Countin' On You	1956	80.00
—No horizontal line on label			
❑ 47-6637	I Got a Woman/ I'm Countin' On You	1956	80.00
—With horizontal line on label			
❑ 47-6638	I'm Gonna Sit Right Down and Cry (Over You)/I'll Never Let You Go (Little Darlin')	1956	70.00
—No horizontal line on label			
❑ 47-6638	I'm Gonna Sit Right Down and Cry (Over You)/I'll Never Let You Go (Little Darlin')	1956	70.00
—With horizontal line on label			
❑ 47-6639	Tryin' to Get to You/ I Love You Because	1956	70.00
—No horizontal line on label			
❑ 47-6639	Tryin' to Get to You/ I Love You Because	1956	70.00
—With horizontal line on label			
❑ 47-6640	Blue Moon/Just Because	1956	60.00
—No horizontal line on label			
❑ 47-6640	Blue Moon/Just Because	1956	60.00
—With horizontal line on label			
❑ 47-6641	Money Honey/One-Sided Love Affair	1956	50.00
—No horizontal line on label			
❑ 47-6641	Money Honey/One-Sided Love Affair	1956	50.00
—With horizontal line on label			
❑ 47-6642	Lawdy Miss Clawdy/ Shake, Rattle, and Roll	1956	40.00
—No horizontal line on label			
❑ 47-6642	Lawdy Miss Clawdy/ Shake, Rattle, and Roll	1956	40.00
—With horizontal line on label, dog on label as usual			
❑ 47-6642	Lawdy Miss Clawdy/ Shake, Rattle, and Roll	1956	200.00
—With horizontal line on label, but with no dog			
❑ 47-6643	Love Me Tender/Anyway You Want Me (That's How I Will Be)	1956	30.00
—No horizontal line on label			
❑ 47-6643	Love Me Tender/Anyway You Want Me (That's How I Will Be)	1956	30.00
—With horizontal line on label			
❑ 47-6643	Love Me Tender/Anyway You Want Me (That's How I Will Be)	1956	40.00
—No reference to the movie "Love Me Tender" on label			
❑ 47-6643 [PS]	Love Me Tender/Anyway You Want Me (That's How I Will Be)	1956	30.00
—Black and light pink sleeve			
❑ 47-6643 [PS]	Love Me Tender/Anyway You Want Me (That's How I Will Be)	1956	40.00
—Black and dark pink sleeve			
❑ 47-6643 [PS]	Love Me Tender/Anyway You Want Me (That's How I Will Be)	1956	75.00
—Black and green sleeve			
❑ 47-6643 [PS]	Love Me Tender/Anyway You Want Me (That's How I Will Be)	1956	180.00
—Black and white sleeve			
❑ 47-6800	Too Much/Playing for Keeps	1957	30.00
—No horizontal line on label			
❑ 47-6800	Too Much/Playing for Keeps	1957	30.00
—With horizontal line on label, dog on label as normal			
❑ 47-6800	Too Much/Playing for Keeps	1957	200.00
—With horizontal line on label, but with no dog			
❑ 47-6800 [PS]	Too Much/Playing for Keeps	1957	90.00
❑ 47-6870	All Shook Up/That's When Your Heartaches Begin	1957	30.00
—No horizontal line on label			
❑ 47-6870	All Shook Up/That's When Your Heartaches Begin	1957	30.00
—With horizontal line on label			
❑ 47-6870 [PS]	All Shook Up/That's When Your Heartaches Begin	1957	90.00
❑ 47-7000	(Let Me Be Your) Teddy Bear/ Loving You	1957	30.00
—Parentheses around "Let Me Be Your", no horizontal line on label			
❑ 47-7000	(Let Me Be Your) Teddy Bear/ Loving You	1957	30.00
—Parentheses around "Let Me Be Your", with horizontal line on label			
❑ 47-7000	(Let Me Be Your) Teddy Bear/ Loving You	1957	40.00
—Label says "Let Me Be Your TEDDY BEAR" (no parentheses)			
❑ 47-7000 [PS]	(Let Me Be Your) Teddy Bear/ Loving You	1957	120.00
❑ 47-7035	Jailhouse Rock/Treat Me Nice	1957	30.00
—No horizontal line on label			
❑ 47-7035	Jailhouse Rock/Treat Me Nice	1957	30.00
—With horizontal line on label			
❑ 47-7035 [PS]	Jailhouse Rock/Treat Me Nice	1957	100.00
❑ 47-7150	Don't/I Beg of You	1958	25.00
—No horizontal line on label			
❑ 47-7150	Don't/I Beg of You	1958	25.00
—With horizontal line on label			
❑ 47-7150 [PS]	Don't/I Beg of You	1958	90.00
❑ 47-7240	Wear My Ring Around Your Neck/Don'tcha Think It's Time	1958	25.00
❑ 47-7240 [PS]	Wear My Ring Around Your Neck/Don'tcha Think It's Time	1958	90.00
❑ 47-7280	Hard Headed Woman/ Don't Ask Me Why	1958	25.00
❑ 47-7280 [PS]	Hard Headed Woman/ Don't Ask Me Why	1958	70.00
❑ 47-7410	One Night/I Got Stung	1958	25.00
❑ 47-7410 [PS]	One Night/I Got Stung	1958	70.00
❑ 47-7506	(Now and Then There's) A Fool Such As I/ I Need Your Love Tonight	1959	25.00
❑ 47-7506 [PS]	(Now and Then There's) A Fool Such As I/ I Need Your Love Tonight	1959	60.00
—Sleeve lists Elvis' EPs and Gold Standard singles			
❑ 47-7506 [PS]	(Now and Then There's) A Fool Such As I/ I Need Your Love Tonight	1959	1000.
—Sleeve promotes the "Elvis Sails" EP			
❑ 47-7600	A Big Hunk o'Love/ My Wish Came True	1959	25.00
❑ 47-7600 [PS]	A Big Hunk o'Love/ My Wish Came True	1959	70.00
❑ 47-7740	Stuck on You/Fame and Fortune	1960	20.00
❑ 47-7740 [PS]	Stuck on You/Fame and Fortune	1960	60.00
❑ 47-7777	It's Now or Never/ A Mess of Blues	1960	20.00
—All other pressings with overdubbed piano			
❑ 47-7777	It's Now or Never/ A Mess of Blues	1960	1000.
—An early mispress is missing the piano part on the A-side. Has the number "L2WW-0100-3S" or "L2WW-0100-4S" in trail-off wax.			
❑ 47-7777 [PS]	It's Now or Never/A Mess of Blues	1960	60.00
❑ 47-7810	Are You Lonesome To-Night?/ I Gotta Know	1960	20.00
❑ 47-7810 [PS]	Are You Lonesome To-Night?/ I Gotta Know	1960	60.00
❑ 47-7850	Surrender/Lonely Man	1961	20.00
❑ 47-7850 [PS]	Surrender/Lonely Man	1961	60.00
❑ 47-7880	I Feel So Bad/Wild in the Country	1961	20.00
❑ 47-7880 [PS]	I Feel So Bad/Wild in the Country	1961	50.00
❑ 47-7908	(Marie's the Name) His Latest Flame/Little Sister	1961	20.00
—All copies of this record actually read "Marie's the Name HIS LATEST FLAME" (no parentheses)			
❑ 47-7908 [PS]	(Marie's the Name) His Latest Flame/Little Sister	1961	50.00
❑ 47-7968	Can't Help Falling in Love/ Rock-a-Hula Baby	1961	20.00
❑ 47-7968 [PS]	Can't Help Falling in Love/ Rock-a-Hula Baby	1961	40.00
❑ 47-7992	Good Luck Charm/Anything That's Part of You	1962	20.00
❑ 47-7992 [PS]	Good Luck Charm/Anything That's Part of You	1962	40.00
—Titles in blue and pink letters			
❑ 47-7992 [PS]	Good Luck Charm/Anything That's Part of You	1962	40.00
—Titles in rust and lavender letters			
❑ 47-8041	She's Not You/Just Tell Her Jim Said Hello	1962	20.00
❑ 47-8041 [PS]	She's Not You/Just Tell Her Jim Said Hello	1962	40.00
❑ 47-8100	Return to Sender/Where Do You Come From	1962	20.00
❑ 47-8100 [PS]	Return to Sender/Where Do You Come From	1962	40.00
❑ 47-8134	One Broken Heart for Sale/ They Remind Me Too Much of You	1963	12.00
❑ 47-8134 [PS]	One Broken Heart for Sale/ They Remind Me Too Much of You	1963	30.00
❑ 47-8188	(You're the) Devil in Disguise/ Please Don't Drag That String Around	1963	12.00
—Second pressing with correct B-side title			
❑ 47-8188	(You're the) Devil in Disguise/ Please Don't Drag That String Along	1963	200.00
—First pressing with incorrect B-side title			
❑ 47-8188 [PS]	(You're the) Devil in Disguise/ Please Don't Drag That String Around	1963	30.00
—All sleeves have correct B-side title			
❑ 47-8243	Bossa Nova Baby/Witchcraft	1963	12.00
❑ 47-8243 [PS]	Bossa Nova Baby/Witchcraft	1963	30.00
—"Ask For" on sleeve			
❑ 47-8243 [PS]	Bossa Nova Baby/Witchcraft	1963	30.00
—"Coming Soon" on sleeve			
❑ 47-8243 [PS]	Bossa Nova Baby/Witchcraft	1963	30.00
—No reference to another album on sleeve			
❑ 47-8307	Kissin' Cousins/It Hurts Me	1964	12.00
❑ 47-8307 [PS]	Kissin' Cousins/It Hurts Me	1964	25.00
❑ 47-8360	Viva Las Vegas/What'd I Say	1964	12.00
❑ 47-8360 [PS]	Viva Las Vegas/What'd I Say	1964	25.00
—"Coming Soon" on sleeve			
❑ 47-8360 [PS]	Viva Las Vegas/What'd I Say	1964	50.00
—"Ask For" on sleeve			
❑ 47-8400	Such a Night/Never Ending	1964	12.00
❑ 47-8400 [PS]	Such a Night/Never Ending	1964	25.00
❑ 47-8440	Ain't That Loving You Baby/ Ask Me	1964	10.00
❑ 47-8440 [PS]	Ain't That Loving You Baby/ Ask Me	1964	25.00
—"Ask For" on sleeve			
❑ 47-8440 [PS]	Ain't That Loving You Baby/ Ask Me	1964	25.00
—"Coming Soon" on sleeve			
❑ 47-8500	Do the Clam/You'll Be Gone	1965	10.00
❑ 47-8500 [PS]	Do the Clam/You'll Be Gone	1965	25.00
❑ 47-8585	(Such An) Easy Question/ It Feels So Right	1965	10.00
❑ 47-8585 [PS]	(Such An) Easy Question/ It Feels So Right	1965	25.00
—"Ask For" on sleeve			
❑ 47-8585 [PS]	(Such An) Easy Question/ It Feels So Right	1965	25.00
—"Coming Soon" on sleeve			
❑ 47-8657	I'm Yours/(It's a) Long, Lonely Highway	1965	10.00
❑ 47-8657 [PS]	I'm Yours/(It's a) Long, Lonely Highway	1965	25.00
❑ 47-8740	Tell Me Why/Blue River	1965	10.00
❑ 47-8740 [PS]	Tell Me Why/Blue River	1965	25.00
❑ 47-8780	Frankie and Johnny/Please Don't Stop Loving Me	1966	10.00
❑ 47-8780 [PS]	Frankie and Johnny/Please Don't Stop Loving Me	1966	25.00
❑ 47-8870	Love Letters/Come What May	1966	10.00
❑ 47-8870 [PS]	Love Letters/Come What May	1966	25.00
—"Ask For" on sleeve			
❑ 47-8870 [PS]	Love Letters/Come What May	1966	25.00
—"Coming Soon" on sleeve			
❑ 47-8941	Spinout/All That I Am	1966	10.00
❑ 47-8941 [PS]	Spinout/All That I Am	1966	25.00
—"Ask For" on sleeve			
❑ 47-8941 [PS]	Spinout/All That I Am	1966	25.00
—"Watch For" on sleeve			
❑ 47-8950	If Every Day Was Like Christmas/ How Would You Like to Be	1966	20.00
❑ 47-8950 [PS]	If Every Day Was Like Christmas/ How Would You Like to Be	1966	40.00
❑ 47-9056	Indescribably Blue/ Fools Fall in Love	1966	10.00
❑ 47-9056 [PS]	Indescribably Blue/ Fools Fall in Love	1966	25.00
❑ 47-9115	Long Legged Girl (With the Short Dress On)/That's Someone You Never Forget	1967	10.00
❑ 47-9115 [PS]	Long Legged Girl (With the Short Dress On)/That's Someone You Never Forget	1967	25.00
—"Ask For" on sleeve			
❑ 47-9115 [PS]	Long Legged Girl (With the Short Dress On)/That's Someone You Never Forget	1967	25.00
—"Coming Soon" on sleeve			
❑ 47-9287	There's Always Me/Judy	1967	10.00
❑ 47-9287 [PS]	There's Always Me/Judy	1967	25.00
❑ 47-9341	Big Boss Man/ You Don't Know Me	1967	10.00
❑ 47-9341 [PS]	Big Boss Man/ You Don't Know Me	1967	25.00
❑ 47-9425	Guitar Man/High Heel Sneakers	1968	10.00
❑ 47-9425 [PS]	Guitar Man/High Heel Sneakers	1968	25.00
—"Ask For" on sleeve			
❑ 47-9425 [PS]	Guitar Man/High Heel Sneakers	1968	25.00
—"Coming Soon" on sleeve			
❑ 47-9465	U.S. Male/Stay Away	1968	10.00
❑ 47-9465 [PS]	U.S. Male/Stay Away	1968	25.00
❑ 47-9547	Let Yourself Go/Your Time Hasn't Come Yet, Baby	1968	10.00
❑ 47-9547 [PS]	Let Yourself Go/Your Time Hasn't Come Yet, Baby	1968	25.00
—"Ask For" on sleeve			
❑ 47-9547 [PS]	Let Yourself Go/Your Time Hasn't Come Yet, Baby	1968	25.00
—"Coming Soon" on sleeve			
❑ 47-9600	You'll Never Walk Alone/ We Call on Him	1968	12.00
❑ 47-9600 [PS]	You'll Never Walk Alone/ We Call on Him	1968	100.00
❑ 47-9610	A Little Less Conversation/ Almost in Love	1968	10.00
❑ 47-9610 [PS]	A Little Less Conversation/ Almost in Love	1968	25.00
❑ 47-9670	If I Can Dream/Edge of Reality	1968	8.00
—First Elvis single on orange label			
❑ 47-9670 [PS]	If I Can Dream/Edge of Reality	1968	20.00
—Does not mention his NBC-TV special on sleeve			
❑ 47-9670 [PS]	If I Can Dream/Edge of Reality	1968	20.00
—Mentions his NBC-TV special on sleeve			
❑ 47-9731	Memories/Charro	1969	8.00
❑ 47-9731 [PS]	Memories/Charro	1969	20.00
❑ 47-9741	In the Ghetto/Any Day Now	1969	8.00
❑ 47-9741 [PS]	In the Ghetto/Any Day Now	1969	20.00
—"Ask For" on sleeve			
❑ 47-9741 [PS]	In the Ghetto/Any Day Now	1969	20.00
—"Coming Soon" on sleeve			

P

Number	Title (A Side/B Side)	Yr	NM
❑ 47-9747	Clean Up Your Own Back Yard/The Fair Is Moving On	1969	8.00
❑ 47-9747 [PS]	Clean Up Your Own Back Yard/The Fair Is Moving On	1969	20.00
❑ 47-9764	Suspicious Minds/You'll Think of Me	1969	8.00
❑ 47-9764 [PS]	Suspicious Minds/You'll Think of Me	1969	20.00
❑ 47-9768	Don't Cry Daddy/Rubberneckin'	1969	8.00
❑ 47-9768 [PS]	Don't Cry Daddy/Rubberneckin'	1969	15.00
❑ 47-9791	Kentucky Rain/My Little Friend	1969	8.00
❑ 47-9791 [PS]	Kentucky Rain/My Little Friend	1969	15.00
❑ 47-9835	The Wonder of You/Mama Liked the Roses	1970	8.00
❑ 47-9835 [PS]	The Wonder of You/Mama Liked the Roses	1970	15.00
❑ 47-9873	I've Lost You/The Next Step Is Love	1970	6.00
❑ 47-9873 [PS]	I've Lost You/The Next Step Is Love	1970	15.00
❑ 47-9916	You Don't Have to Say You Love Me/Patch It Up	1970	6.00
❑ 47-9916 [PS]	You Don't Have to Say You Love Me/Patch It Up	1970	15.00
❑ 47-9960	I Really Don't Want to Know/There Goes My Everything	1971	6.00
❑ 47-9960 [PS]	I Really Don't Want to Know/There Goes My Everything	1971	15.00
—"Ask For" on sleeve			
❑ 47-9960 [PS]	I Really Don't Want to Know/There Goes My Everything	1971	15.00
—"Coming Soon" on sleeve			
❑ 47-9980	Where Did They Go, Lord/Rags to Riches	1971	6.00
❑ 47-9980 [PS]	Where Did They Go, Lord/Rags to Riches	1971	20.00
❑ 47-9985	Life/Only Believe	1971	6.00
❑ 47-9985 [PS]	Life/Only Believe	1971	30.00
❑ 47-9998	I'm Leavin'/Heart of Rome	1971	6.00
❑ 47-9998 [PS]	I'm Leavin'/Heart of Rome	1971	20.00
❑ 48-1017	It's Only Love/The Sound of Your Cry	1971	6.00
❑ 48-1017 [PS]	It's Only Love/The Sound of Your Cry	1971	15.00
❑ 61-7740 [S]	Stuck on You/Fame and Fortune	1960	400.00
—"Living Stereo" (large hole, plays at 45 rpm)			
❑ 61-7777 [S]	It's Now or Never/A Mess of Blues	1960	400.00
—"Living Stereo" (large hole, plays at 45 rpm)			
❑ 61-7810 [S]	Are You Lonesome To-Night?/I Gotta Know	1960	600.00
—"Living Stereo" (large hole, plays at 45 rpm)			
❑ 61-7850 [S]	Surrender/Lonely Man	1961	800.00
—"Living Stereo" (large hole, plays at 45 rpm)			
❑ 74-0130	How Great Thou Art/His Hand in Mine	1969	25.00
❑ 74-0130 [PS]	How Great Thou Art/His Hand in Mine	1969	150.00
❑ 74-0572	Merry Christmas Baby/O Come All Ye Faithful	1971	15.00
❑ 74-0572 [PS]	Merry Christmas Baby/O Come All Ye Faithful	1971	40.00
❑ 74-0619	Until It's Time for You to Go/We Can Make the Morning	1971	6.00
❑ 74-0619 [PS]	Until It's Time for You to Go/We Can Make the Morning	1971	15.00
❑ 74-0651	He Touched Me/The Bosom of Abraham	1972	8.00
—"He Touched Me" plays correctly. A-side has "APKS-1277" stamped in trail-off wax.			
❑ 74-0651	He Touched Me/The Bosom of Abraham	1972	150.00
—"He Touched Me" actually plays at about 35 rpm in error. A-side has "AWKS-1277" stamped in trail-off wax.			
❑ 74-0651 [PS]	He Touched Me/The Bosom of Abraham	1972	120.00
❑ 74-0672	An American Trilogy/The First Time Ever I Saw Your Face	1972	20.00
❑ 74-0672 [PS]	An American Trilogy/The First Time Ever I Saw Your Face	1972	40.00
❑ 74-0769	Burning Love/It's a Matter of Time	1972	6.00
—Originals have orange labels			
❑ 74-0769	Burning Love/It's a Matter of Time	1974	150.00
—Very rare reissues have gray labels			
❑ 74-0769 [PS]	Burning Love/It's a Matter of Time	1972	15.00
❑ 74-0815	Separate Ways/Always on My Mind	1972	6.00
❑ 74-0815 [PS]	Separate Ways/Always on My Mind	1972	15.00
❑ 74-0910	Steamroller Blues/Fool	1973	6.00
❑ 74-0910 [PS]	Steamroller Blues/Fool	1973	15.00
❑ 37-7908 [PS]	(Marie's the Name) His Latest Flame/Little Sister	1961	2000.
—Special picture sleeve for above record. VG 1000 ; VG+ 1500			
❑ 37-7908 [PS]	(Marie's the Name) His Latest Flame/Little Sister	1961	2250.
—Special picture sleeve for above record; says "Stereo-Orthophonic" on sleeve in error. VG 2250; VG+ 1687.50			

Number	Title (A Side/B Side)	Yr	NM
❑ 37-7968	Can't Help Falling in Love/Rock-a-Hula Baby	1961	2000.
—"Compact Single 33" (small hole, plays at LP speed). VG 1000; VG+ 1500			
❑ 37-7968 [PS]	Can't Help Falling in Love/Rock-a-Hula Baby	1961	4000.
—Special picture sleeve for above record. VG 2000; VG+ 3000			
❑ 37-7992	Good Luck Charm/Anything That's Part of You	1962	2500.
—"Compact Single 33" (small hole, plays at LP speed). VG 1250; VG+ 1875			
❑ 37-7992 [PS]	Good Luck Charm/Anything That's Part of You	1962	5000.
—Special picture sleeve for above record. VG 2500; VG+ 3750			
❑ 47-6420	Heartbreak Hotel/I Was the One	2001	4.00
—Black label, dog on top; red vinyl; "DRE1 3034" in trail-off wax, from box "Elvis #1 Hit Singles Collection"			
❑ 47-6420 [PS]	Heartbreak Hotel/I Was the One	2001	4.00
—"The RCA logo is TMK(s) Æ Registered Marca(s) Registrada(s) RCA Corporation" on rear at lower left; this is the only official sleeve for this number			
❑ 47-6540	I Want You, I Need You, I Love You/My Baby Left Me	2001	4.00
—Black label, dog on top; red vinyl; "DRE-13056" in trail-off wax; from box "Elvis #1 Hit Singles Collection"			
❑ 47-6540 [PS]	I Want You, I Need You, I Love You/My Baby Left Me	2001	4.00
—"The RCA logo is TMK(s) Æ Registered Marca(s) Registrada(s) RCA Corporation" on rear at lower left; this is the only official sleeve for this number			
❑ 47-6604	Don't Be Cruel/Hound Dog	2001	4.00
—Black label, dog on top; red vinyl; "DRE-13035" in trail-off wax; from box "Elvis #1 Hit Singles Collection"			
❑ 47-6604 [PS]	Don't Be Cruel/Hound Dog	2001	4.00
—"Hound Dog!" listed above "Don't Be Cruel"; "This is a replica of the original packaging" on rear at lower left edge			
❑ 47-6636	Blue Suede Shoes/Tutti Frutti	2002	4.00
—Black label, dog on top; red vinyl; "DRE 13222" in trail-off wax; from box "Elvis Hit Singles Collection, Vol. 2"			
❑ 47-6636 [PS]	Blue Suede Shoes/Tutti Frutti	2002	4.00
—"This is a replica of the original packaging" on rear along lower right edge, though no prior sleeve was legitimately made; this is the only official picture sleeve for this number			
❑ 47-6643	Love Me Tender/Any Way You Want Me (That's How I Will Be)	2001	4.00
—Black label, dog on top; red vinyl; "DRE1-3036" in trail-off wax; from box "Elvis #1 Hit Singles Collection"			
❑ 47-6643 [PS]	Love Me Tender/Any Way You Want Me (That's How I Will Be)	2001	4.00
—Black and light pink version; "This is a replica of the original packaging" on rear along bottom			
❑ 47-6800	Too Much/Playing for Keeps	2001	4.00
—Black label, dog on top; red vinyl; "DRE1-3037" in trail-off wax; from box "Elvis #1 Hit Singles Collection"			
❑ 47-6800 [PS]	Too Much/Playing for Keeps	2001	4.00
—"This is a replica of the original packaging" on rear along bottom			
❑ 47-6840	All Shook Up/That's When Your Heartaches Begin	2001	4.00
—Black label, dog on top; red vinyl; "DRE1 3038" in trail-off wax; from box "Elvis #1 Hit Singles Collection"			
❑ 47-6870 [PS]	All Shook Up/That's When Your Heartaches Begin	2001	4.00
—"This is a replica of the original packaging" on rear at bottom			
❑ 47-7000	(Let Me Be Your) Teddy Bear/Loving You	2001	4.00
—Parentheses around "Let Me Be Your"; black label, dog on top; red vinyl; "DRE1 3039" in trail-off wax; from box "Elvis #1 Hit Singles Collection"			
❑ 47-7000 [PS]	(Let Me Be Your) Teddy Bear/Loving You	2001	4.00
—"This is a replica of the original packaging" on rear along right edge			
❑ 47-7035	Jailhouse Rock/Treat Me Nice	1957	10000.
—Gold label; gold vinyl. VG 5000; VG+ 7500			
❑ 47-7035	Jailhouse Rock/Treat Me Nice	2001	4.00
—Black label, dog on top; red vinyl; "DRE1 3040" in trail-off wax; from box "Elvis #1 Hit Singles Collection"			
❑ 47-7035 [PS]	Jailhouse Rock/Treat Me Nice	2001	4.00
—"This is a replica of the original packaging" on rear along lower right edge			
❑ 47-7150	Don't/I Beg of You	2001	4.00
—Black label, dog on top; red vinyl; "DRC-13041" in trail-off wax; from box "Elvis #1 Hit Singles Collection"			
❑ 47-7150 [PS]	Don't/I Beg of You	2001	4.00
—"This is a replica of the original packaging" on rear at lower right			
❑ 47-7240	Wear My Ring Around Your Neck/Don'tcha Think It's Time	2002	4.00
—Black label, dog on top; red vinyl; "DRE 13238" in trail-off wax; from box "Elvis Hit Singles Collection, Vol. 2"			
❑ 47-7240 [PS]	Wear My Ring Around Your Neck/Don'tcha Think It's Time	2002	4.00
—"This is a replica of the original packaging" on rear along lower right edge			
❑ 47-7280	Hard Headed Woman/Don't Ask Me Why	2001	4.00
—Black label, dog on top; red vinyl; "DRE-13042" in trail-off wax; from box "Elvis #1 Hit Singles Collection"			
❑ 47-7280 [PS]	Hard Headed Woman/Don't Ask Me Why	2001	4.00
—"This is a replica of the original packaging" on rear along right edge			

Number	Title (A Side/B Side)	Yr	NM
❑ 47-7410	One Night/I Got Stung	2002	4.00
—Black label, dog on top; red vinyl; "DRE 13237" in trail-off wax; from box "Elvis Hit Singles Collection, Vol. 2"			
❑ 47-7410 [PS]	One Night/I Got Stung	2002	4.00
—"This is a replica of the original packaging" on rear at lower right			
❑ 47-7506	(Now and Then There's) A Fool Such As I/I Need Your Love Tonight	2002	4.00
—Black label, dog at top; red vinyl; "DRE 13220" in trail-off wax; from box "Elvis Hit Singles Collection, Vol. 2"			
❑ 47-7506 [PS]	(Now and Then There's) A Fool Such As I/I Need Your Love Tonight	2002	4.00
—Lists Elvis' EPs and Gold Standard singles on back; "This is a replica of the original packaging" on rear along lower right edge			
❑ 47-7600	A Big Hunk o'Love/My Wish Came True	2001	4.00
—Black label, dog on top; red vinyl; "DRC-13043" in trail-off wax; from box "Elvis #1 Hit Singles Collection"			
❑ 47-7600 [PS]	A Big Hunk o'Love/My Wish Came True	2001	4.00
—"This is a replica of the original packaging" on rear at lower left			
❑ 47-7740	Stuck on You/Fame and Fortune	2001	4.00
—Black label, dog on top; red vinyl; "DRE1-3044" in trail-off wax; from box "Elvis #1 Hit Singles Collection"			
❑ 47-7740 [PS]	Stuck on You/Fame and Fortune	2001	4.00
—"This is a replica of the original packaging" on rear along bottom left edge			
❑ 47-7777	It's Now or Never/A Mess of Blues	2001	4.00
—Black label, dog on top; red vinyl; "DRE1 3045" in trail-off wax; from box "Elvis #1 Hit Singles Collection"			
❑ 47-7777 [PS]	It's Now or Never/A Mess of Blues	2001	4.00
—"This is a replica of the original packaging" on rear along bottom left edge			
❑ 47-7810	Are You Lonesome To-Night?/I Gotta Know	2001	4.00
—Black label, dog on top; red vinyl; "DRE1 3046" in trail-off wax; from box "Elvis #1 Hit Singles Collection"			
❑ 47-7810 [PS]	Are You Lonesome To-Night?/I Gotta Know	2001	4.00
—"This is a replica of the original packaging" on rear along left edge			
❑ 47-7850	Surrender/Lonely Man	2001	4.00
—Black label, dog on top; red vinyl; "DRE1 3047" in trail-off wax; from box "Elvis #1 Hit Singles Collection"			
❑ 47-7850 [PS]	Surrender/Lonely Man	2001	4.00
—"This is a replica of the original packaging" on rear along lower right edge			
❑ 47-7880	I Feel So Bad/Wild in the Country	2002	4.00
—Black label, dog on top; red vinyl; "DRE 13225" in trail-off wax; from box "Elvis Hit Singles Collection, Vol. 2"			
❑ 47-7880 [PS]	I Feel So Bad/Wild in the Country	2002	4.00
—"This is a replica of the original packaging" on rear along lower right edge			
❑ 47-7908	(Marie's the Name) His Latest Flame/Little Sister	2002	4.00
—Black label, dog on top; red vinyl; "DRE 13226" in trail-off wax; from box "Elvis Hit Singles Collection, Vol. 2"			
❑ 47-7908 [PS]	(Marie's the Name) His Latest Flame/Little Sister	2002	4.00
—"This is a replica of the original packaging" on rear along lower right edge			
❑ 47-7968	Can't Help Falling in Love/Rock-a-Hula Baby	2002	4.00
—Black label, dog near top, no "Victor" on label; red vinyl; "DRE 13241" in trail-off wax; from box "Elvis Hit Singles Collection, Vol. 2"			
❑ 47-7968 [PS]	Can't Help Falling in Love/Rock-a-Hula Baby	2002	4.00
—"This is a replica of the original packaging" on back along lower left edge			
❑ 47-7992	Good Luck Charm/Anything That's Part of You	2001	4.00
—Black label, dog on top; red vinyl; "DRE1 3045" in trail-off wax; from box "Elvis #1 Hit Singles Collection"			
❑ 47-7992 [PS]	Good Luck Charm/Anything That's Part of You	2001	4.00
—Titles in rust and lavender letters; "This is a replica of the original packaging" on rear at lower left edge			
❑ 47-8041	She's Not You/Just Tell Her Jim Said Hello	2002	4.00
—Black label, dog near top, no "Victor" on label; red vinyl; "DRE 13240" in trail-off wax; from box "Elvis Hit Singles Collection, Vol. 2"			
❑ 47-8041 [PS]	She's Not You/Just Tell Her Jim Said Hello	2002	4.00
—"This is a replica of the original packaging" on rear along lower right edge			
❑ 47-8100	Return to Sender/Where Do You Come From	2002	4.00
—Black label, dog near top, no "Victor" on label; red vinyl; "DRE 13223" in trail-off wax; from box "Elvis Hit Singles Collection, Vol. 2"			
❑ 47-8100 [PS]	Return to Sender/Where Do You Come From	2002	4.00
—"This is a replica of the original packaging" on rear at lower left			
❑ 47-8134	One Broken Heart for Sale/They Remind Me Too Much of You	2002	4.00
—Black label, dog on top; red vinyl; "DRE 13219" in trail-off wax; from box "Elvis Hit Singles Collection, Vol. 2"			
❑ 47-8134 [PS]	One Broken Heart for Sale/They Remind Me Too Much of You	2002	4.00
—"This is a replica of the original packaging" on rear along right edge			

P

Except when noted otherwise, VG = 25% of NM, and VG+ = 50% of NM. (Example: VG = $2.00, VG+ = $4.00 and NM = $8.00.)

Number	Title (A Side/B Side)	Yr	NM
❑ 47-8188	(You're the) Devil in Disguise/ Please Don't Drag That String Around	2002	4.00
—Black label, dog on top; red vinyl; "DRE 13235" in trail-off wax; from box "Elvis Hit Singles Collection, Vol. 2"			
❑ 47-8188 [PS]	(You're the) Devil in Disguise/ Please Don't Drag That String Around	2002	4.00
—"This is a replica of the original packaging" on rear along lower right edge			
❑ 47-8243	Bossa Nova Baby/Witchcraft	2002	4.00
—Black label, dog on top; red vinyl; "DRE 13221" in trail-off wax; from box "Elvis Hit Singles Collection, Vol. 2"			
❑ 47-8243 [PS]	Bossa Nova Baby/Witchcraft	2002	4.00
—"Coming Soon! Special! 'Fun in Acapulco' LP Album" on sleeve; "This is a replica of the original packaging" on rear at bottom			
❑ 47-8360	Viva Las Vegas/What'd I Say	2002	4.00
—Black label, dog on top; red vinyl; "DRE 13232" in trail-off wax; from box "Elvis Hit Singles Collection, Vol. 2"			
❑ 47-8360 [DJ]	Viva Las Vegas/What'd I Say	1964	50.00
—White label promo, "Not for Sale" on label			
❑ 47-8360 [PS]	Viva Las Vegas/What'd I Say	2002	4.00
—"Coming Soon! Special 'Viva Las Vegas' EP - 4 New Songs" on sleeve; "This is a replica of the original packaging" on rear along lower right edge			
❑ 47-8400 [DJ]	Such a Night/Never Ending	1964	5000.
—White label promo, "Not for Sale" on label. VG 2500; VG+ 3750			
❑ 47-8440	Ain't That Loving You Baby/ Ask Me	2002	4.00
—Black label, dog on top; red vinyl; "DRE 13231" in trail-off wax; from box "Elvis Hit Singles Collection, Vol. 2"			
❑ 47-8440 [DJ]	Ain't That Loving You Baby/ Ask Me	1964	60.00
—White label promo			
❑ 47-8440 [PS]	Ain't That Loving You Baby/ Ask Me	2002	4.00
—"Ask For 'Roustabout' LP Album" on sleeve, "This is a replica of the original packaging" on rear at bottom right			
❑ 47-8500 [DJ]	Do the Clam/You'll Be Gone	1965	50.00
—White label promo, "Not for Sale" on label			
❑ 47-8585 [DJ]	(Such An) Easy Question/ It Feels So Right	1965	50.00
—White label promo, "Not for Sale" on label			
❑ 47-8657	I'm Yours/(It's a) Long, Lonely Highway	2002	4.00
—Black label, dog on left; red vinyl; "DRE 13233" in trail-off wax; from box "Elvis Hit Singles Collection, Vol. 2"			
❑ 47-8657 [DJ]	I'm Yours/(It's a) Long, Lonely Highway	1965	40.00
—White label promo, "Not for Sale" on label			
❑ 47-8657 [PS]	I'm Yours/(It's a) Long, Lonely Highway	2002	4.00
—"This is a replica of the original packaging" on rear at bottom			
❑ 47-8740 [DJ]	Tell Me Why/Blue River	1965	50.00
—White label promo, "Not for Sale" on label			
❑ 47-8780 [DJ]	Frankie and Johnny/ Please Don't Stop Loving Me	1966	50.00
—White label promo, "Not for Sale" on label			
❑ 47-8870 [DJ]	Love Letters/Come What May	1966	50.00
—White label promo, "Not for Sale" on label			
❑ 47-8941 [DJ]	Spinout/All That I Am	1966	50.00
—White label promo, "Not for Sale" on label			
❑ 47-8950 [DJ]	If Every Day Was Like Christmas/ How Would You Like to Be	1966	50.00
—White label promo, "Not for Sale" on label			
❑ 47-9056 [DJ]	Indescribably Blue/ Fools Fall in Love	1966	40.00
—White label promo, "Not for Sale" on label			
❑ 47-9115 [DJ]	Long Legged Girl (With the Short Dress On)/That's Someone You Never Forget	1967	40.00
—White label promo, "Not for Sale" on label			
❑ 47-9287 [DJ]	There's Always Me/Judy	1967	40.00
—White label promo, "Not for Sale" on label			
❑ 47-9341 [DJ]	Big Boss Man/You Don't Know Me	1967	40.00
—White label promo, "Not for Sale" on label			
❑ 47-9425 [DJ]	Guitar Man/High Heel Sneakers	1968	30.00
—White label promo, "Not for Sale" on label			
❑ 47-9465 [DJ]	U.S. Male/Stay Away	1968	40.00
—Yellow label promo, "Not for Sale" on label			
❑ 47-9547 [DJ]	Let Yourself Go/Your Time Hasn't Come Yet, Baby	1968	60.00
—Yellow label promo, "Not for Sale" on label			
❑ 47-9600 [DJ]	You'll Never Walk Alone/ We Call on Him	1968	30.00
—Yellow label promo, "Not for Sale" on label			
❑ 47-9610 [DJ]	A Little Less Conversation/ Almost in Love	1968	40.00
—Yellow label promo, "Not for Sale" on label			
❑ 47-9670	If I Can Dream/Edge of Reality	2002	4.00
—Orange label; red vinyl; "DRE 13229" in trail-off wax; from box "Elvis Hit Singles Collection, Vol. 2"			
❑ 47-9670 [DJ]	If I Can Dream/Edge of Reality	1968	30.00
—Yellow label promo, "Not for Sale" on label			
❑ 47-9670 [PS]	If I Can Dream/Edge of Reality	2002	4.00
—With no mention of his NBC-TV special on sleeve; "This is a replica of the original packaging" on rear at lower left			
❑ 47-9731 [DJ]	Memories/Charro	1969	30.00
—Yellow label promo, "Not for Sale" on label			
❑ 47-9741	In the Ghetto/Any Day Now	2002	4.00
—Orange label; red vinyl; "DRE 13239" in trail-off wax; from box "Elvis Hit Singles Collection, Vol. 2"			
❑ 47-9741 [DJ]	In the Ghetto/Any Day Now	1969	30.00
—Yellow label promo, "Not for Sale" on label			
❑ 47-9741 [PS]	In the Ghetto/Any Day Now	2002	4.00
—"Ask For From Elvis in Memphis LP Album" on sleeve; "This is a replica of the original packaging" on rear at lower right			
❑ 47-9747 [DJ]	Clean Up Your Own Back Yard/ The Fair Is Moving On	1969	30.00
—Yellow label promo, "Not for Sale" on label			
❑ 47-9764	Suspicious Minds/ You'll Think of Me	2001	4.00
—Orange label; red vinyl; "DRE1-3050" in trail-off wax; from box "Elvis #1 Hit Singles Collection"			
❑ 47-9764 [DJ]	Suspicious Minds/ You'll Think of Me	1969	30.00
—Yellow label promo, "Not for Sale" on label			
❑ 47-9764 [PS]	Suspicious Minds/ You'll Think of Me	2001	4.00
—"This is a replica of the original packaging" on rear along lower right edge			
❑ 47-9768	Don't Cry Daddy/Rubberneckin'	2002	4.00
—Orange label; red vinyl; "DRE 13224" in trail-off wax; from box "Elvis Hit Singles Collection, Vol. 2"			
❑ 47-9768 [DJ]	Don't Cry Daddy/Rubberneckin'	1969	30.00
—Yellow label promo, "Not for Sale" on label			
❑ 47-9768 [PS]	Don't Cry Daddy/Rubberneckin'	2002	4.00
—"This is a replica of the original packaging" on rear at lower right edge			
❑ 47-9791	Kentucky Rain/My Little Friend	2002	4.00
—Orange label; red vinyl; "DRE 13228" in trail-off wax; from box "Elvis Hit Singles Collection, Vol. 2"			
❑ 47-9791 [DJ]	Kentucky Rain/My Little Friend	1969	30.00
—Yellow label promo, "Not for Sale" on label			
❑ 47-9791 [PS]	Kentucky Rain/My Little Friend	2002	4.00
—"This is a replica of the original packaging" on rear along right edge			
❑ 47-9835	The Wonder of You/ Mama Liked the Roses	2002	4.00
—Orange label; red vinyl; "DRE 13230" in trail-off wax; from box "Elvis Hit Singles Collection, Vol. 2"			
❑ 47-9835 [DJ]	The Wonder of You/ Mama Liked the Roses	1970	30.00
—Yellow label promo, "Not for Sale" on label			
❑ 47-9835 [PS]	The Wonder of You/ Mama Liked the Roses	2002	4.00
—"This is a replica of the original packaging" on rear along lower right edge			
❑ 47-9873 [DJ]	I've Lost You/The Next Step Is Love	1970	25.00
—Yellow label promo, "Not for Sale" on label			
❑ 47-9916	You Don't Have to Say You Love Me/Patch It Up	2002	4.00
—Orange label; red vinyl; "DRE 13227" in trail-off wax; from box "Elvis Hit Singles Collection, Vol. 2"			
❑ 47-9916 [DJ]	You Don't Have to Say You Love Me/Patch It Up	1970	25.00
—Yellow label promo, "Not for Sale" on label			
❑ 47-9919 [PS]	You Don't Have to Say You Love Me/Patch It Up	2002	4.00
—"This is a replica of the original packaging" on rear at bottom			
❑ 47-9960 [DJ]	I Really Don't Want to Know/ There Goes My Everything	1971	25.00
—Yellow label promo, "Not for Sale" on label			
❑ 47-9980 [DJ]	Where Did They Go, Lord/Rags to Riches	1971	30.00
—Yellow label promo, "Not for Sale" on label			
❑ 47-9985 [DJ]	Life/Only Believe	1971	30.00
—Yellow label promo, "Not for Sale" on label			
❑ 47-9998 [DJ]	I'm Leavin'/Heart of Rome	1971	25.00
—Yellow label promo, "Not for Sale" on label			
❑ 48-1017 [DJ]	It's Only Love/The Sound of Your Cry	1971	30.00
—Yellow label promo, "Not for Sale" on label			
❑ 68-7850 [S]	Surrender/Lonely Man	1961	2000.
—"Compact Stereo 33" in "Living Stereo". VG 1000; VG+ 1500			
❑ 74-0130 [DJ]	How Great Thou Art/ His Hand in Mine	1969	120.00
—Yellow label promo, "Not for Sale" on label			
❑ 74-0572 [DJ]	Merry Christmas Baby/ O Come All Ye Faithful	1971	30.00
—Yellow label promo, "Not for Sale" on label			
❑ 74-0619 [DJ]	Until It's Time for You to Go/ We Can Make the Morning	1971	30.00
—Yellow label promo, "Not for Sale" on label			
❑ 74-0651 [DJ]	He Touched Me/The Bosom of Abraham	1972	120.00
—Yellow label promo, "Not for Sale" on label			
❑ 74-0672 [DJ]	An American Trilogy/The First Time Ever I Saw Your Face	1972	25.00
—Yellow label promo, "Not for Sale" on label			
❑ 74-0769	Burning Love/It's a Matter of Time	2002	4.00
—Orange label; red vinyl; "DRE 13234" in trail-off wax; from box "Elvis Hit Singles Collection, Vol. 2"			
❑ 74-0769 [DJ]	Burning Love/It's a Matter of Time	1972	25.00
—Yellow label promo, "Not for Sale" on label			
❑ 74-0769 [PS]	Burning Love/It's a Matter of Time	2002	4.00
—"This is a replica of the original packaging" on rear along lower right edge			
❑ 74-0815 [DJ]	Separate Ways/ Always on My Mind	1972	25.00
—Yellow label promo, "Not for Sale" on label			
❑ 74-0910 [DJ]	Steamroller Blues/Fool	1973	15.00
—Light yellow label promo, "Not for Sale" on label			
❑ 447-0600	I Forgot to Remember to Forget/Mystery Train	1959	15.00
—Note: All RCA Victor releases with a "447" prefix are from the Gold Standard Series. Black label, dog on top			
❑ 447-0600	I Forgot to Remember to Forget/Mystery Train	1965	10.00
—Black label, dog on left			
❑ 447-0600	I Forgot to Remember to Forget/Mystery Train	1969	25.00
—Orange label			
❑ 447-0600	I Forgot to Remember to Forget/Mystery Train	1970	8.00
—Red label			
❑ 447-0601	That's All Right/Blue Moon of Kentucky	1959	15.00
—Black label, dog on top			
❑ 447-0601	That's All Right/Blue Moon of Kentucky	1965	10.00
—Black label, dog on left			
❑ 447-0601	That's All Right/Blue Moon of Kentucky	1969	8.00
—Red label; B-side artist credit is misspelled "Elvis Presely"			
❑ 447-0601 [DJ]	That's All Right/Blue Moon of Kentucky	1964	100.00
❑ 447-0601 [PS]	That's All Right/Blue Moon of Kentucky	1964	200.00
❑ 447-0602	Good Rockin' Tonight/I Don't Care If the Sun Don't Shine	1959	15.00
—Black label, dog on top			
❑ 447-0602	Good Rockin' Tonight/I Don't Care If the Sun Don't Shine	1959	6000.
—One-of-a-kind red vinyl pressing. VG 2000; VG+ 4000			
❑ 447-0602	Good Rockin' Tonight/I Don't Care If the Sun Don't Shine	1965	10.00
—Black label, dog on left			
❑ 447-0602	Good Rockin' Tonight/I Don't Care If the Sun Don't Shine	1970	8.00
—Red label			
❑ 447-0602 [DJ]	Good Rockin' Tonight/I Don't Care If the Sun Don't Shine	1964	100.00
❑ 447-0602 [PS]	Good Rockin' Tonight/I Don't Care If the Sun Don't Shine	1964	200.00
❑ 447-0603	Milkcow Blues Boogie/ You're a Heartbreaker	1959	15.00
—Black label, dog on top			
❑ 447-0603	Milkcow Blues Boogie/ You're a Heartbreaker	1965	10.00
—Black label, dog on left			
❑ 447-0603	Milkcow Blues Boogie/ You're a Heartbreaker	1969	25.00
—Orange label			
❑ 447-0603	Milkcow Blues Boogie/ You're a Heartbreaker	1970	8.00
—Red label			
❑ 447-0604	Baby Let's Play House/I'm Left, You're Right, She's Gone	1959	15.00
—Black label, dog on top			
❑ 447-0604	Baby Let's Play House/I'm Left, You're Right, She's Gone	1965	10.00
—Black label, dog on left			
❑ 447-0604	Baby Let's Play House/I'm Left, You're Right, She's Gone	1970	8.00
—Red label			
❑ 447-0605	Heartbreak Hotel/I Was the One	1959	15.00
—Black label, dog on top			
❑ 447-0605	Heartbreak Hotel/I Was the One	1965	10.00
—Black label, dog on left			
❑ 447-0605	Heartbreak Hotel/I Was the One	1969	25.00
—Orange label			
❑ 447-0605	Heartbreak Hotel/I Was the One	1970	8.00
—Red label			
❑ 447-0605 [DJ]	Heartbreak Hotel/I Was the One	1964	100.00
❑ 447-0605 [PS]	Heartbreak Hotel/I Was the One	1964	200.00
❑ 447-0607	I Want You, I Need You, I Love You/My Baby Left Me	1959	15.00
—Black label, dog on top			
❑ 447-0607	I Want You, I Need You, I Love You/My Baby Left Me	1965	10.00
—Black label, dog on left			
❑ 447-0607	I Want You, I Need You, I Love You/My Baby Left Me	1969	25.00
—Orange label			
❑ 447-0607	I Want You, I Need You, I Love You/My Baby Left Me	1970	8.00
—Red label			
❑ 447-0608	Hound Dog/Don't Be Cruel	1959	15.00
—Black label, dog on top			
❑ 447-0608	Hound Dog/Don't Be Cruel	1965	10.00
—Black label, dog on left			
❑ 447-0608	Hound Dog/Don't Be Cruel	1969	25.00
—Orange label			
❑ 447-0608	Hound Dog/Don't Be Cruel	1970	8.00
—Red label			
❑ 447-0608 [DJ]	Hound Dog/Don't Be Cruel	1964	100.00
❑ 447-0608 [PS]	Hound Dog/Don't Be Cruel	1964	200.00
❑ 447-0609	Blue Suede Shoes/Tutti Frutti	1959	15.00
—Black label, dog on top			
❑ 447-0609	Blue Suede Shoes/Tutti Frutti	1965	10.00
—Black label, dog on left			

P

Number	Title (A Side/B Side)	Yr	NM
❑ 447-0609	Blue Suede Shoes/Tutti Frutti	1969	25.00
—Orange label			
❑ 447-0609	Blue Suede Shoes/Tutti Frutti	1970	8.00
—Red label			
❑ 447-0610	I Got a Woman/I'm Countin' On You	1959	15.00
—Black label, dog on top			
❑ 447-0611	I'm Gonna Sit Right Down and Cry (Over You)/I'll Never Let You Go (Little Darlin')	1959	15.00
—Black label, dog on top			
❑ 447-0612	Tryin' to Get to You/I Love You Because	1959	15.00
—Black label, dog on top			
❑ 447-0613	Blue Moon/Just Because	1959	15.00
—Black label, dog on top			
❑ 447-0613	Blue Moon/Just Because	1965	10.00
—Black label, dog on left			
❑ 447-0613	Blue Moon/Just Because	1969	25.00
—Orange label			
❑ 447-0613	Blue Moon/Just Because	1970	8.00
—Red label			
❑ 447-0614	Money Honey/One-Sided Love Affair	1959	15.00
—Black label, dog on top			
❑ 447-0614	Money Honey/One-Sided Love Affair	1965	10.00
—Black label, dog on left			
❑ 447-0614	Money Honey/One-Sided Love Affair	1969	25.00
—Orange label			
❑ 447-0614	Money Honey/One-Sided Love Affair	1970	8.00
—Red label			
❑ 447-0615	Lawdy Miss Clawdy/Shake, Rattle, and Roll	1959	15.00
—Black label, dog on top			
❑ 447-0615	Lawdy Miss Clawdy/Shake, Rattle, and Roll	1965	10.00
—Black label, dog on left			
❑ 447-0615	Lawdy Miss Clawdy/Shake, Rattle, and Roll	1969	25.00
—Orange label			
❑ 447-0615	Lawdy Miss Clawdy/Shake, Rattle, and Roll	1970	8.00
—Red label			
❑ 447-0616	Love Me Tender/Anyway You Want Me (That's How I Will Be)	1959	15.00
—Black label, dog on top			
❑ 447-0616	Love Me Tender/Anyway You Want Me (That's How I Will Be)	1965	10.00
—Black label, dog on left			
❑ 447-0616	Love Me Tender/Anyway You Want Me (That's How I Will Be)	1969	25.00
—Orange label			
❑ 447-0616	Love Me Tender/Anyway You Want Me (That's How I Will Be)	1970	8.00
—Red label			
❑ 447-0617	Too Much/Playing for Keeps	1959	15.00
—Black label, dog on top			
❑ 447-0617	Too Much/Playing for Keeps	1965	10.00
—Black label, dog on left			
❑ 447-0617	Too Much/Playing for Keeps	1969	25.00
—Orange label			
❑ 447-0617	Too Much/Playing for Keeps	1970	8.00
—Red label			
❑ 447-0618	All Shook Up/That's When Your Heartaches Begin	1959	15.00
—Black label, dog on top			
❑ 447-0618	All Shook Up/That's When Your Heartaches Begin	1965	10.00
—Black label, dog on left			
❑ 447-0618	All Shook Up/That's When Your Heartaches Begin	1969	25.00
—Orange label			
❑ 447-0618	All Shook Up/That's When Your Heartaches Begin	1970	8.00
—Red label			
❑ 447-0618 [DJ]	All Shook Up/That's When Your Heartaches Begin	1964	100.00
❑ 447-0618 [PS]	All Shook Up/That's When Your Heartaches Begin	1964	200.00
❑ 447-0619	Jailhouse Rock/Treat Me Nice	1959	15.00
—Black label, dog on top			
❑ 447-0619	Jailhouse Rock/Treat Me Nice	1965	10.00
—Black label, dog on left			
❑ 447-0619	Jailhouse Rock/Treat Me Nice	1969	25.00
—Orange label			
❑ 447-0619	Jailhouse Rock/Treat Me Nice	1970	8.00
—Red label			
❑ 447-0620	(Let Me Be Your) Teddy Bear/Loving You	1959	15.00
—Black label, dog on top			
❑ 447-0620	(Let Me Be Your) Teddy Bear/Loving You	1965	10.00
—Black label, dog on left			
❑ 447-0620	(Let Me Be Your) Teddy Bear/Loving You	1969	25.00
—Orange label			
❑ 447-0620	(Let Me Be Your) Teddy Bear/Loving You	1970	8.00
—Red label			
❑ 447-0621	Don't/I Beg of You	1961	12.00
—Black label, dog on top			
❑ 447-0621	Don't/I Beg of You	1965	10.00
—Black label, dog on left			
❑ 447-0621	Don't/I Beg of You	1969	25.00
—Orange label			
❑ 447-0621	Don't/I Beg of You	1970	8.00
—Red label			
❑ 447-0622	Wear My Ring Around Your Neck/Don'tcha Think It's Time	1961	12.00
—Black label, dog on top			
❑ 447-0622	Wear My Ring Around Your Neck/Don'tcha Think It's Time	1965	10.00
—Black label, dog on left			
❑ 447-0622	Wear My Ring Around Your Neck/Don'tcha Think It's Time	1969	25.00
—Orange label			
❑ 447-0622	Wear My Ring Around Your Neck/Don'tcha Think It's Time	1970	8.00
—Red label			
❑ 447-0623	Hard Headed Woman/Don't Ask Me Why	1961	15.00
—Black label, dog on top			
❑ 447-0623	Hard Headed Woman/Don't Ask Me Why	1965	10.00
—Black label, dog on left			
❑ 447-0623	Hard Headed Woman/Don't Ask Me Why	1969	25.00
—Orange label			
❑ 447-0623	Hard Headed Woman/Don't Ask Me Why	1970	8.00
—Red label			
❑ 447-0624	One Night/I Got Stung	1961	12.00
—Black label, dog on top			
❑ 447-0624	One Night/I Got Stung	1965	10.00
—Black label, dog on left			
❑ 447-0624	One Night/I Got Stung	1969	25.00
—Orange label			
❑ 447-0624	One Night/I Got Stung	1970	8.00
—Red label			
❑ 447-0625	(Now and Then There's) A Fool Such As I/I Need Your Love Tonight	1961	15.00
—Black label, dog on top			
❑ 447-0625	(Now and Then There's) A Fool Such As I/I Need Your Love Tonight	1965	10.00
—Black label, dog on left			
❑ 447-0625	(Now and Then There's) A Fool Such As I/I Need Your Love Tonight	1969	25.00
—Orange label			
❑ 447-0625	(Now and Then There's) A Fool Such As I/I Need Your Love Tonight	1970	8.00
—Red label			
❑ 447-0626	A Big Hunk o'Love/My Wish Came True	1962	15.00
—Black label, dog on top			
❑ 447-0626	A Big Hunk o'Love/My Wish Came True	1965	10.00
—Black label, dog on left			
❑ 447-0626	A Big Hunk o'Love/My Wish Came True	1969	25.00
—Orange label			
❑ 447-0626	A Big Hunk o'Love/My Wish Came True	1970	8.00
—Red label			
❑ 447-0627	Stuck on You/Fame and Fortune	1962	12.00
—Black label, dog on top			
❑ 447-0627	Stuck on You/Fame and Fortune	1965	10.00
—Black label, dog on left			
❑ 447-0627	Stuck on You/Fame and Fortune	1969	25.00
—Orange label			
❑ 447-0627	Stuck on You/Fame and Fortune	1970	8.00
—Red label			
❑ 447-0628	It's Now or Never/A Mess of Blues	1962	12.00
—Black label, dog on top			
❑ 447-0628	It's Now or Never/A Mess of Blues	1965	10.00
—Black label, dog on left			
❑ 447-0628	It's Now or Never/A Mess of Blues	1969	25.00
—Orange label			
❑ 447-0628	It's Now or Never/A Mess of Blues	1970	8.00
—Red label			
❑ 447-0629	Are You Lonesome To-Night?/I Gotta Know	1962	15.00
—Black label, dog on top			
❑ 447-0629	Are You Lonesome To-Night?/I Gotta Know	1965	10.00
—Black label, dog on left			
❑ 447-0629	Are You Lonesome To-Night?/I Gotta Know	1969	25.00
—Orange label			
❑ 447-0629	Are You Lonesome To-Night?/I Gotta Know	1970	8.00
—Red label			
❑ 447-0630	Surrender/Lonely Man	1962	25.00
—Black label, dog on top			
❑ 447-0630	Surrender/Lonely Man	1965	10.00
—Black label, dog on left			
❑ 447-0630	Surrender/Lonely Man	1969	25.00
—Orange label			
❑ 447-0630	Surrender/Lonely Man	1970	8.00
—Red label			
❑ 447-0631	I Feel So Bad/Wild in the Country	1962	12.00
—Black label, dog on top			
❑ 447-0631	I Feel So Bad/Wild in the Country	1965	10.00
—Black label, dog on left			
❑ 447-0631	I Feel So Bad/Wild in the Country	1970	8.00
—Red label			
❑ 447-0634	(Marie's the Name) His Latest Flame/Little Sister	1962	12.00
—Black label, dog on top			
❑ 447-0634	(Marie's the Name) His Latest Flame/Little Sister	1965	10.00
—Black label, dog on left			
❑ 447-0634	(Marie's the Name) His Latest Flame/Little Sister	1969	25.00
—Orange label			
❑ 447-0634	(Marie's the Name) His Latest Flame/Little Sister	1970	8.00
—Red label			
❑ 447-0635	Can't Help Falling in Love/Rock-a-Hula Baby	1962	12.00
—Black label, dog on top			
❑ 447-0635	Can't Help Falling in Love/Rock-a-Hula Baby	1965	10.00
—Black label, dog on left			
❑ 447-0635	Can't Help Falling in Love/Rock-a-Hula Baby	1969	25.00
—Orange label			
❑ 447-0635	Can't Help Falling in Love/Rock-a-Hula Baby	1970	8.00
—Red label			
❑ 447-0636	Good Luck Charm/Anything That's Part of You	1962	12.00
—Black label, dog on top			
❑ 447-0636	Good Luck Charm/Anything That's Part of You	1965	10.00
—Black label, dog on left			
❑ 447-0636	Good Luck Charm/Anything That's Part of You	1969	25.00
—Orange label			
❑ 447-0636	Good Luck Charm/Anything That's Part of You	1970	8.00
—Red label			
❑ 447-0637	She's Not You/Just Tell Her Jim Said Hello	1963	12.00
—Black label, dog on top			
❑ 447-0637	She's Not You/Just Tell Her Jim Said Hello	1965	10.00
—Black label, dog on left			
❑ 447-0637	She's Not You/Just Tell Her Jim Said Hello	1969	25.00
—Orange label			
❑ 447-0637	She's Not You/Just Tell Her Jim Said Hello	1970	8.00
—Red label			
❑ 447-0638	Return to Sender/Where Do You Come From	1963	12.00
—Black label, dog on top			
❑ 447-0638	Return to Sender/Where Do You Come From	1965	10.00
—Black label, dog on left			
❑ 447-0638	Return to Sender/Where Do You Come From	1969	25.00
—Orange label			
❑ 447-0638	Return to Sender/Where Do You Come From	1970	8.00
—Red label			
❑ 447-0639	Kiss Me Quick/Suspicion	1964	10.00
—Black label, dog on top			
❑ 447-0639	Kiss Me Quick/Suspicion	1969	25.00
—Orange label			
❑ 447-0639	Kiss Me Quick/Suspicion	1970	8.00
—Red label			
❑ 447-0639 [DJ]	Kiss Me Quick/Suspicion	1964	50.00
—White label promo, "Not for Sale" on label			
❑ 447-0639 [PS]	Kiss Me Quick/Suspicion	1964	40.00
❑ 447-0640	One Broken Heart for Sale/They Remind Me Too Much of You	1964	25.00
—Black label, dog on top			
❑ 447-0640	One Broken Heart for Sale/They Remind Me Too Much of You	1965	10.00
—Black label, dog on left			
❑ 447-0640	One Broken Heart for Sale/They Remind Me Too Much of You	1969	25.00
—Orange label			
❑ 447-0640	One Broken Heart for Sale/They Remind Me Too Much of You	1970	8.00
—Red label			
❑ 447-0641	(You're the) Devil in Disguise/Please Don't Drag That String Around	1964	25.00
—Black label, dog on top			
❑ 447-0641	(You're the) Devil in Disguise/Please Don't Drag That String Around	1965	10.00
—Black label, dog on left			

Except when noted otherwise, VG = 25% of NM, and VG+ = 50% of NM. (Example: VG = $2.00, VG+ = $4.00 and NM = $8.00.)

Number	Title (A Side/B Side)	Yr	NM
❑ 447-0641	(You're the) Devil in Disguise/ Please Don't Drag That String Around	1970	8.00
—Red label			
❑ 447-0642	Bossa Nova Baby/Witchcraft	1964	25.00
—Black label, dog on top			
❑ 447-0642	Bossa Nova Baby/Witchcraft	1965	10.00
—Black label, dog on left			
❑ 447-0642	Bossa Nova Baby/Witchcraft	1969	25.00
—Orange label			
❑ 447-0642	Bossa Nova Baby/Witchcraft	1970	8.00
—Red label			
❑ 447-0643	Crying in the Chapel/I Believe in the Man in the Sky	1965	10.00
—Black label, dog on left			
❑ 447-0643	Crying in the Chapel/I Believe in the Man in the Sky	1970	8.00
—Red label			
❑ 447-0643	Crying in the Chapel/I Believe in the Man in the Sky	2002	4.00
—Black label, dog on left; red vinyl; "DRE 13236" in trail-off wax; from box "Elvis Hit Singles Collection, Vol. 2"			
❑ 447-0643 [DJ]	Crying in the Chapel/I Believe in the Man in the Sky	1965	30.00
—White label promo, "Not for Sale" on label			
❑ 447-0643 [PS]	Crying in the Chapel/I Believe in the Man in the Sky	1965	30.00
❑ 447-0643 [PS]	Crying in the Chapel/I Believe in the Man in the Sky	2002	4.00
—"This is a replica of the original packaging" on back at lower left			
❑ 447-0644	Kissin' Cousins/It Hurts Me	1965	10.00
—Black label, dog on left			
❑ 447-0644	Kissin' Cousins/It Hurts Me	1969	25.00
—Orange label			
❑ 447-0644	Kissin' Cousins/It Hurts Me	1970	8.00
—Red label			
❑ 447-0645	Such a Night/Never Ending	1965	10.00
—Black label, dog on left			
❑ 447-0645	Such a Night/Never Ending	1965	40.00
—Black label, dog on top			
❑ 447-0645	Such a Night/Never Ending	1969	25.00
—Orange label			
❑ 447-0645	Such a Night/Never Ending	1970	8.00
—Red label			
❑ 447-0646	Viva Las Vegas/What'd I Say	1965	10.00
—Black label, dog on left			
❑ 447-0646	Viva Las Vegas/What'd I Say	1965	25.00
—Black label, dog on top			
❑ 447-0646	Viva Las Vegas/What'd I Say	1969	25.00
—Orange label			
❑ 447-0646	Viva Las Vegas/What'd I Say	1970	8.00
—Red label			
❑ 447-0647	Blue Christmas/Santa Claus Is Back in Town	1965	12.00
—Black label, dog on side			
❑ 447-0647	Blue Christmas/Santa Claus Is Back in Town	1969	25.00
—Orange label			
❑ 447-0647	Blue Christmas/Santa Claus Is Back in Town	1970	8.00
—Red label			
❑ 447-0647 [DJ]	Blue Christmas/Santa Claus Is Back in Town	1965	40.00
—White label promo, "Not for Sale" on label			
❑ 447-0647 [PS]	Blue Christmas/Santa Claus Is Back in Town	1965	30.00
—Has "Gold Standard Series" on sleeve			
❑ 447-0648	Do the Clam/You'll Be Gone	1965	10.00
—Black label, dog on left			
❑ 447-0648	Do the Clam/You'll Be Gone	1970	10.00
—Red label			
❑ 447-0649	Ain't That Loving You Baby/ Ask Me	1965	10.00
—Black label, dog on left			
❑ 447-0649	Ain't That Loving You Baby/ Ask Me	1970	8.00
—Red label			
❑ 447-0650	Puppet on a String/ Wooden Heart	1965	10.00
—Black label, dog on left			
❑ 447-0650	Puppet on a String/ Wooden Heart	1970	8.00
—Red label			
❑ 447-0650 [DJ]	Puppet on a String/ Wooden Heart	1965	30.00
—White label promo, "Not for Sale" on label			
❑ 447-0650 [PS]	Puppet on a String/ Wooden Heart	1965	30.00
❑ 447-0651	Joshua Fit the Battle/ Known Only to Him	1966	15.00
—Black label, dog on left			
❑ 447-0651	Joshua Fit the Battle/ Known Only to Him	1970	8.00
—Red label			
❑ 447-0651 [DJ]	Joshua Fit the Battle/ Known Only to Him	1966	120.00
—White label promo, "Not for Sale" on label			
❑ 447-0651 [PS]	Joshua Fit the Battle/ Known Only to Him	1966	200.00

Number	Title (A Side/B Side)	Yr	NM
❑ 447-0652	Milky White Way/Swing Down Sweet Chariot	1966	15.00
—Black label, dog on left			
❑ 447-0652	Milky White Way/Swing Down Sweet Chariot	1970	8.00
—Red label			
❑ 447-0652 [DJ]	Milky White Way/Swing Down Sweet Chariot	1966	120.00
—White label promo, "Not for Sale" on label			
❑ 447-0652 [PS]	Milky White Way/Swing Down Sweet Chariot	1966	200.00
❑ 447-0653	(Such An) Easy Question/ It Feels So Right	1966	10.00
—Black label, dog on left			
❑ 447-0653	(Such An) Easy Question/ It Feels So Right	1970	8.00
—Red label			
❑ 447-0654	I'm Yours/(It's a) Long, Lonely Highway	1966	10.00
—Black label, dog on left			
❑ 447-0654	I'm Yours/(It's a) Long, Lonely Highway	1970	8.00
—Red label			
❑ 447-0655	Tell Me Why/Blue River	1968	10.00
—Black label, dog on left			
❑ 447-0655	Tell Me Why/Blue River	1970	8.00
—Red label			
❑ 447-0656	Frankie and Johnny/Please Don't Stop Loving Me	1968	10.00
—Black label, dog on left			
❑ 447-0656	Frankie and Johnny/Please Don't Stop Loving Me	1969	25.00
—Orange label			
❑ 447-0656	Frankie and Johnny/Please Don't Stop Loving Me	1970	8.00
—Red label			
❑ 447-0657	Love Letters/Come What May	1968	10.00
—Black label, dog on left			
❑ 447-0657	Love Letters/Come What May	1970	8.00
—Red label			
❑ 447-0658	Spinout/All That I Am	1968	10.00
—Black label, dog on left			
❑ 447-0658	Spinout/All That I Am	1970	8.00
—Red label			
❑ 447-0659	Indescribably Blue/ Fools Fall in Love	1969	25.00
—Orange label			
❑ 447-0659	Indescribably Blue/ Fools Fall in Love	1970	8.00
—Red label			
❑ 447-0660	Long Legged Girl (With the Short Dress On)/That's Someone You Never Forget	1970	40.00
❑ 447-0661	There's Always Me/Judy	1970	15.00
❑ 447-0662	Big Boss Man/You Don't Know Me	1970	10.00
❑ 447-0663	Guitar Man/High Heel Sneakers	1970	8.00
❑ 447-0664	U.S. Male/Stay Away	1970	8.00
❑ 447-0665	You'll Never Walk Alone/ We Call on Him	1970	10.00
❑ 447-0666	Let Yourself Go/Your Time Hasn't Come Yet, Baby	1970	8.00
❑ 447-0667	A Little Less Conversation/ Almost in Love	1970	8.00
❑ 447-0668	If I Can Dream/Edge of Reality	1970	8.00
❑ 447-0669	Memories/Charro	1970	8.00
❑ 447-0670	How Great Thou Art/ His Hand in Mine	1970	10.00
❑ 447-0671	In the Ghetto/Any Day Now	1970	8.00
❑ 447-0672	Clean Up Your Own Back Yard/ The Fair Is Moving On	1970	8.00
❑ 447-0673	Suspicious Minds/ You'll Think of Me	1970	8.00
❑ 447-0674	Don't Cry Daddy/ Rubberneckin'	1970	8.00
❑ 447-0675	Kentucky Rain/My Little Friend	1971	8.00
❑ 447-0676	The Wonder of You/Mama Liked the Roses	1971	8.00
❑ 447-0677	I've Lost You/The Next Step Is Love	1971	8.00
❑ 447-0678	You Don't Have to Say You Love Me/Patch It Up	1972	8.00
❑ 447-0679	I Really Don't Want to Know/ There Goes My Everything	1972	8.00
❑ 447-0680	Where Did They Go, Lord/ Rags to Riches	1972	8.00
❑ 447-0681	If Every Day Was Like Christmas/ How Would You Like to Be	1972	8.00
❑ 447-0682	Life/Only Believe	1972	8.00
❑ 447-0683	I'm Leavin'/Heart of Rome	1972	8.00
❑ 447-0684	It's Only Love/The Sound of Your Cry	1972	8.00
❑ 447-0685	An American Trilogy/Until It's Time for You to Go	1973	8.00
❑ 447-0720	Blue Christmas/Wooden Heart	1964	15.00
❑ 447-0720	Blue Christmas/Wooden Heart	2001	4.00
—Black label, dog on top; red vinyl; "DRE1 3049" in trail-off wax; from box "Elvis #1 Hit Singles Collection"			
❑ 447-0720 [DJ]	Blue Christmas/Wooden Heart	1964	40.00
—White label promo, "Not for Sale" on label			

Number	Title (A Side/B Side)	Yr	NM
❑ 447-0720 [PS]	Blue Christmas/Wooden Heart	1964	60.00
❑ 447-0720 [PS]	Blue Christmas/Wooden Heart	2001	4.00
—"This is a replica of the original packaging" on rear along left edge			
❑ CR-15 [DJ]	Old Shep	1956	1000.
—One-sided promo			
❑ SP-45-76 [DJ]	Don't/Wear My Ring Around Your Neck	1960	800.00
❑ SP-45-76 [PS]	Don't/Wear My Ring Around Your Neck	1960	2000.
—VG 1000; VG+ 1500			
❑ APBO-0088	Raised on Rock/ For Ol' Times Sake	1973	6.00
❑ APBO-0088 [PS]	Raised on Rock/ For Ol' Times Sake	1973	15.00
❑ DJAO-0088 [DJ]	Raised on Rock/ For Ol' Times Sake	1973	20.00
—Light yellow label promo, "Not for Sale" on label; both sides are mono			
❑ 4-834-115 [DJ]	I'll Be Back	1966	8000.
—One-sided promo with designation "For Special Academy Consideration Only". VG 4000; VG+ 6000			
❑ SP-45-118 [DJ]	King of the Whole Wide World/ Home Is Where the Heart Is	1962	200.00
❑ SP-45-118 [PS]	King of the Whole Wide World/ Home Is Where the Heart Is	1962	300.00
❑ SP-45-139 [DJ]	Roustabout/One Track Heart	1964	300.00
❑ SP-45-162 [DJ]	How Great Thou Art/So High	1967	150.00
❑ SP-45-162 [PS]	How Great Thou Art/So High	1967	200.00
❑ APBO-0196	Take Good Care of Her/I've Got a Thing About You, Baby	1973	6.00
❑ APBO-0196 [PS]	Take Good Care of Her/I've Got a Thing About You, Baby	1973	15.00
❑ DJBO-0196 [DJ]	Take Good Care of Her/I've Got a Thing About You, Baby	1973	25.00
—Light yellow label promo, "Not for Sale" on label			
❑ APBO-0280	If You Talk in Your Sleep/Help Me	1974	6.00
—On label, the title "If You Talk" is on one line and "In Your Sleep" is on another line			
❑ APBO-0280	If You Talk in Your Sleep/Help Me	1974	12.00
—On label, the title "If You Talk in Your Sleep" is all on one line			
❑ APBO-0280 [PS]	If You Talk in Your Sleep/Help Me	1974	15.00
❑ DJAO-0280 [DJ]	If You Talk in Your Sleep/Help Me	1974	25.00
—Light yellow label promo, "Not for Sale" on label; both sides are mono			
❑ HO7W-0808 [DJ]	Blue Christmas (same on both sides)	1957	1500.
❑ RCA-2458EX	My Boy/Loving Arms	1975	500.00
—Gray label; pressed in the U.S. for export			
❑ RCA-2458EX [PS]	My Boy/Loving Arms	1975	200.00
—Not a sleeve, but a paper insert with no number on it; white with green and black print			
❑ JA-10074 [DJ]	Promised Land/It's Midnight	1974	25.00
—Light yellow label promo, "Not for Sale" on label; both sides are mono			
❑ PB-10074	Promised Land/It's Midnight	1974	5.00
—Gray label (available at the same time as orange label)			
❑ PB-10074	Promised Land/It's Midnight	1974	5.00
—Orange label (available at the same time as gray label)			
❑ PB-10074	Promised Land/It's Midnight	1975	25.00
—Tan label (reissue)			
❑ PB-10074 [PS]	Promised Land/It's Midnight	1975	10.00
❑ GB-10156	Burning Love/Steamroller Blues	1975	8.00
—Gold Standard Series; red label			
❑ GB-10156	Burning Love/Steamroller Blues	1977	4.00
—Gold Standard Series; black label			
❑ GB-10157	Raised on Rock/If You Talk in Your Sleep	1975	8.00
—Gold Standard Series; red label			
❑ GB-10157	Raised on Rock/If You Talk in Your Sleep	1977	4.00
—Gold Standard Series; black label			
❑ JH-10191 [DJ]	My Boy (mono/stereo)	1975	30.00
—Light yellow label promo, "Not for Sale" on label			
❑ PB-10191	My Boy/Thinking About You	1975	5.00
—Orange label			
❑ PB-10191	My Boy/Thinking About You	1975	5.00
—Tan label			
❑ PB-10191 [PS]	My Boy/Thinking About You	1975	10.00
❑ JH-10278 [DJ]	T-R-O-U-B-L-E (mono/stereo)	1975	30.00
—Light yellow label promo, "Not for Sale" on label			
❑ PB-10278	T-R-O-U-B-L-E/Mr. Songman	1975	5.00
—Orange label			
❑ PB-10278	T-R-O-U-B-L-E/Mr. Songman	1975	10.00
—Tan label			
❑ PB-10278	T-R-O-U-B-L-E/Mr. Songman	1975	100.00
—Gray label			
❑ PB-10278 [PS]	T-R-O-U-B-L-E/Mr. Songman	1975	10.00
❑ JA-10401 [DJ]	Bringing It Back/Pieces of My Life	1975	25.00
—Yellow label promo; both sides are mono			
❑ PB-10401	Bringing It Back/Pieces of My Life	1975	5.00
—Tan label			
❑ PB-10401	Bringing It Back/Pieces of My Life	1975	200.00
—Orange label			
❑ PB-10401 [PS]	Bringing It Back/Pieces of My Life	1975	10.00
❑ GB-10485	Take Good Care of Her/I've Got a Thing About You, Baby	1975	8.00
—Gold Standard Series; red label			

P

Number	Title (A Side/B Side)	Yr	NM
❑ GB-10486	Separate Ways/Always on My Mind	1975	8.00
—Gold Standard Series; red label			
❑ GB-10487	T-R-O-U-B-L-E/Mr. Songman	1975	8.00
—Gold Standard Series; red label			
❑ GB-10488	Promised Land/It's Midnight	1975	8.00
—Gold Standard Series; red label			
❑ GB-10489	My Boy/Thinking About You	1975	8.00
—Gold Standard Series; red label			
❑ JB-10601 [DJ]	Hurt/For the Heart	1976	25.00
—Yellow label promo, "Not for Sale" on label			
❑ PB-10601	Hurt/For the Heart	1976	5.00
—Originals on tan labels			
❑ PB-10601 [PS]	Hurt/For the Heart	1976	10.00

SUN

Number	Title (A Side/B Side)	Yr	NM
❑ 209	That's All Right/Blue Moon of Kentucky	1954	6000.
—A mint copy of this has sold for over $17,000, but so far that is an aberration. VG 2000 ; VG+ 4000			
❑ 209	That's All Right/Blue Moon of Kentucky	2001	4.00
—Red vinyl; "DRE1-3051" in trail-off wax; from box "Elvis #1 Hit Singles Collection"			
❑ 209 [PS]	That's All Right/Blue Moon of Kentucky	2001	4.00
—"Sun Æ Records is a registered trademark" on rear along lower left edge; this is the only official sleeve for this number			
❑ 210	Good Rockin' Tonight/I Don't Care If the Sun Don't Shine	1954	3500.
—VG 1500; VG+ 2500			
❑ 210	Good Rockin' Tonight/I Don't Care If the Sun Don't Shine	2001	4.00
—Red vinyl; "DRE1 3052" in trail-off wax; from box "Elvis #1 Hit Singles Collection"			
❑ 210 [PS]	Good Rockin' Tonight/I Don't Care If the Sun Don't Shine	2001	4.00
—"Sun Æ Records is a registered trademark" on rear along lower left edge; this is the only official sleeve for this number			
❑ 215	Milkcow Blues Boogie/You're a Heartbreaker	1955	5000.
—VG 2000 ; VG+ 3500			
❑ 215	Milkcow Blues Boogie/You're a Heartbreaker	2001	4.00
—Red vinyl, "DRE-13053" in trail-off wax, from box "Elvis #1 Hit Singles Collection"			
❑ 215 [PS]	Milkcow Blues Boogie/You're a Heartbreaker	2001	4.00
—"Sun Æ Records is a registered trademark" on rear along lower left edge; this is the only official sleeve for this number			
❑ 217	Baby Let's Play House/I'm Left, You're Right, She's Gone	1955	3000.
—VG 1,000; VG+ 2,000			
❑ 217	Baby Let's Play House/I'm Left, You're Right, She's Gone	2001	4.00
—Red vinyl; "DRE1 3054" in trail-off wax; from box "Elvis #1 Hit Singles Collection"			
❑ 217 [PS]	Baby Let's Play House/I'm Left, You're Right, She's Gone	2001	4.00
—"Sun Æ Records is a registered trademark" on rear along lower left edge; this is the only official picture sleeve for this number			
❑ 223	I Forgot to Remember to Forget/Mystery Train	1955	2500.
❑ 223	I Forgot to Remember to Forget/Mystery Train	2001	4.00
—Red vinyl; "DRE-1-3055" in trail-off wax; from box "Elvis #1 Hit Singles Collection"			
❑ 223 [PS]	I Forgot to Remember to Forget/Mystery Train	2001	4.00
—"Sun Æ Records is a registered trademark" on rear along bottom; this is the only official sleeve for this number			

7-Inch Extended Plays

RCA

Number	Title (A Side/B Side)	Yr	NM
❑ DTF0-2006 [PS]	Aloha from Hawaii Via Satellite	1973	100.00
❑ DTF0-2006 [S]	Something/You Gave Me a Mountain/I Can't Stop Loving You//My Way/What Now My Love/I'm So Lonesome I Could Cry	1973	80.00
—Jukebox issue; small hole, plays at 33 1/3 rpm			

RCA VICTOR

Number	Title (A Side/B Side)	Yr	NM
❑ DJ-7 [DJ]	Love Me Tender/Anyway You Want Me (That's How I Will Be)//Welcome to the Club/I Won't Be Rockin' Tonight	1956	200.00
—B-side tracks by Jean Chapel; white label; each side is labeled with the corresponding nuimber for the regular 45 rpm issue			
❑ SPD-22 [(2)]	Elvis Presley	1956	400.00
—Value is for both discs together			
❑ SPD-22 [PS]	Elvis Presley	1956	400.00
—Bonus given to buyers of a Victrola			
❑ SPD-23 [(3)]	Elvis Presley	1956	3000.
—Value is for all three discs together. VG 1000; VG+ 2000			
❑ SPD-23 [PS]	Elvis Presley	1956	3000.
—Bonus given to buyers of a more expensive Victrola. VG 1000; VG+ 2000			
❑ SPA-7-37 [DJ]	Perfect for Parties	1956	60.00
—With horizontal line on label			
❑ SPA-7-37 [DJ]	Perfect for Parties	1956	60.00
—Without horizontal line on label			
❑ SPA-7-37 [PS]	Perfect for Parties	1956	60.00
❑ DJ-56 [DJ]	Too Much/Playing for Keeps//Chantez-Chantez/Honkytonk Heart	1956	200.00
—B-side tracks by Dinah Shore; white label; each side is labeled with the corresponding number for the regular 45 rpm issue			
❑ LPC-128	Flaming Star/Summer Kisses, Winter Tears//Are You Lonesone To-Night?/It's Now or Never	1961	40.00
—"Compact 33 Double" with small hole			
❑ LPC-128 [PS]	Elvis By Request	1961	40.00
❑ EPA-747	Blue Suede Shoes/Tutti Frutti//I Got a Woman/Just Because	1956	50.00
—With horizontal line on label			
❑ EPA-747	Blue Suede Shoes/Tutti Frutti//I Got a Woman/Just Because	1956	50.00
—Without horizontal line on label			
❑ EPA-747	Blue Suede Shoes/Tutti Frutti//I Got a Woman/Just Because	1956	200.00
—With horizontal line on label, but with no dog			
❑ EPA-747	Blue Suede Shoes/Tutti Frutti//I Got a Woman/Just Because	1956	200.00
—With incorrect label on Side 1 that lists, as song 3, "I'm Gonna Sit Right Down and Cry (Over You)," which does not appear on this record. Known copies of this version do not have horizontal line on label.			
❑ EPA-747	Blue Suede Shoes/Tutti Frutti//I Got a Woman/Just Because	1965	30.00
—Black label, dog on left			
❑ EPA-747	Blue Suede Shoes/Tutti Frutti//I Got a Woman/Just Because	1969	80.00
—Orange label			
❑ EPA-747 [PS]	Elvis Presley	1956	50.00
—Five different back covers exist, all with titles on front cover; any are of equal value			
❑ EPA-747 [PS]	Elvis Presley	1956	600.00
—Temporary envelope sleeve with black print, "Blue Suede Shoes by Elvis Presley" in big letters			
❑ EPA-747 [PS]	Elvis Presley	1956	1000.
—Temporary envelope sleeve with dark blue print, "Blue Suede Shoes by Elvis Presley" in big letters			
❑ EPA-747 [PS]	Elvis Presley	1965	30.00
—No titles at top of front cover			
❑ EPA-821	Heartbreak Hotel/I Was the One//Money Honey/I Forgot to Remember to Forget	1956	50.00
—With horizontal line on label			
❑ EPA-821	Heartbreak Hotel/I Was the One//Money Honey/I Forgot to Remember to Forget	1956	50.00
—Without horizontal line on label			
❑ EPA-821	Heartbreak Hotel/I Was the One//Money Honey/I Forgot to Remember to Forget	1956	200.00
—With horizontal line on label, but with no dog			
❑ EPA-821	Heartbreak Hotel/I Was the One//Money Honey/I Forgot to Remember to Forget	1965	30.00
—Black label, dog on left			
❑ EPA-821	Heartbreak Hotel/I Was the One//Money Honey/I Forgot to Remember to Forget	1969	80.00
—Orange label			
❑ EPA-821 [PS]	Heartbreak Hotel	1956	50.00
❑ EPA-830	Shake, Rattle and Roll/I Love You Because//Blue Moon/Lawdy, Miss Clawdy	1956	50.00
—With horizontal line on label			
❑ EPA-830	Shake, Rattle and Roll/I Love You Because//Blue Moon/Lawdy, Miss Clawdy	1956	50.00
—Without horizontal line on label			
❑ EPA-830	Shake, Rattle and Roll/I Love You Because//Blue Moon/Lawdy, Miss Clawdy	1956	200.00
—With horizontal line on label, but with no dog			
❑ EPA-830	Shake, Rattle and Roll/I Love You Because//Blue Moon/Lawdy, Miss Clawdy	1965	30.00
—Black label, dog on left			
❑ EPA-830	Shake, Rattle and Roll/I Love You Because//Blue Moon/Lawdy, Miss Clawdy	1969	80.00
—Orange label			
❑ EPA-830 [PS]	Elvis Presley	1956	50.00
❑ EPA-940	Don't Be Cruel/I Want You, I Need You, I Love You//Hound Dog/My Baby Left Me	1956	50.00
—With horizontal line on label			
❑ EPA-940	Don't Be Cruel/I Want You, I Need You, I Love You//Hound Dog/My Baby Left Me	1956	50.00
—Without horizontal line on label			
❑ EPA-940	Don't Be Cruel/I Want You, I Need You, I Love You//Hound Dog/My Baby Left Me	1956	200.00
—With horizontal line on label, but with no dog			
❑ EPA-940 [PS]	The Real Elvis	1956	50.00
❑ EPA-965	Anyway You Want Me (That's How I Will Be)/I'm Left, You're Right, She's Gone//I Don't Care If the Sun Don't Shine/Mystery Train	1956	40.00
—With horizontal line on label			
❑ EPA-965	Anyway You Want Me (That's How I Will Be)/I'm Left, You're Right, She's Gone//I Don't Care If the Sun Don't Shine/Mystery Train	1956	40.00
—Without horizontal line on label			
❑ EPA-965	Anyway You Want Me (That's How I Will Be)/I'm Left, You're Right, She's Gone//I Don't Care If the Sun Don't Shine/Mystery Train	1956	200.00
—With horizontal line on label, but with no dog			
❑ EPA-965	Anyway You Want Me (That's How I Will Be)/I'm Left, You're Right, She's Gone//I Don't Care If the Sun Don't Shine/Mystery Train	1965	30.00
—Black label, dog on left			
❑ EPA-965	Anyway You Want Me (That's How I Will Be)/I'm Left, You're Right, She's Gone//I Don't Care If the Sun Don't Shine/Mystery Train	1969	80.00
—Orange label			
❑ EPA-965 [PS]	Anyway You Want Me	1956	50.00
—With song titles and catalog number on front			
❑ EPA-965 [PS]	Anyway You Want Me	196?	40.00
—Without song titles and catalog number on front			
❑ EPA-992	Rip It Up/Love Me//When My Blue Moon Turns to Gold Again/Paralyzed	1956	40.00
—With horizontal line on label			
❑ EPA-992	Rip It Up/Love Me//When My Blue Moon Turns to Gold Again/Paralyzed	1956	40.00
—Without horizontal line on label			
❑ EPA-992	Rip It Up/Love Me//When My Blue Moon Turns to Gold Again/Paralyzed	1956	200.00
—With horizontal line on label; but with no dog			
❑ EPA-992	Rip It Up/Love Me//When My Blue Moon Turns to Gold Again/Paralyzed	1965	30.00
—Black label, dog on left			
❑ EPA-992	Rip It Up/Love Me//When My Blue Moon Turns to Gold Again/Paralyzed	1969	80.00
—Orange label			
❑ EPA-992 [PS]	Elvis (Vol. 1)	1956	50.00
❑ EPA-993	So Glad You're Mine/Old Shep//Ready Teddy/Anyplace Is Paradise	1956	40.00
—With horizontal line on label			
❑ EPA-993	So Glad You're Mine/Old Shep//Ready Teddy/Anyplace Is Paradise	1956	40.00
—Without horizontal line on label			
❑ EPA-993	So Glad You're Mine/Old Shep//Ready Teddy/Anyplace Is Paradise	1956	200.00
—With horizontal line on label, but with no dog			
❑ EPA-993	So Glad You're Mine/Old Shep//Ready Teddy/Anyplace Is Paradise	1965	30.00
—Black label, dog on left			
❑ EPA-993	So Glad You're Mine/Old Shep//Ready Teddy/Anyplace Is Paradise	1969	80.00
—Orange label			
❑ EPA-993 [PS]	Elvis (Vol. 2)	1956	50.00
—Titles at top of front cover			
❑ EPA-993 [PS]	Elvis (Vol. 2)	1965	30.00
—No titles at top of front cover			
❑ EPA-994	Long Tall Sally/First in Line//How Do You Think I Feel/How's the World Treating You	1956	50.00
—With horizontal line on label			
❑ EPA-994	Long Tall Sally/First in Line//How Do You Think I Feel/How's the World Treating You	1956	50.00
—Without horizontal line on label			
❑ EPA-994	Long Tall Sally/First in Line//How Do You Think I Feel/How's the World Treating You	1956	200.00
—With horizontal line on label, but with no dog			
❑ EPA-994	Long Tall Sally/First in Line//How Do You Think I Feel/How's the World Treating You	1965	30.00
—Black label, dog on left			
❑ EPA-994	Long Tall Sally/First in Line//How Do You Think I Feel/How's the World Treating You	1969	80.00
—Orange label			

Except when noted otherwise, VG = 25% of NM, and VG+ = 50% of NM. (Example: VG = $2.00, VG+ = $4.00 and NM = $8.00.)

Number	Title (A Side/B Side)	Yr	NM
❑ EPA-994 [PS]	Strictly Elvis (Elvis, Vol. 3)	1956	50.00
—With titles listed on front cover			
❑ EPA-994 [PS]	Strictly Elvis (Elvis, Vol. 3)	1965	30.00
—No titles listed on front cover			
❑ EPB-1254 [(2)]	Elvis Presley	1956	200.00
—With horizontal line on label; eight songs on two discs; value is for both discs together			
❑ EPB-1254 [(2)]	Elvis Presley	1956	200.00
—Without horizontal line on label; eight songs on two discs; value is for both discs together			
❑ EPB-1254 [(2)]	Elvis Presley	1956	1500.
—Two records have three songs on each side (12 total), as opposed to the two of the standard release			
❑ EPB-1254 [PS]	Elvis Presley	1956	150.00
—With no hype of other non-Elvis releases on back			
❑ EPB-1254 [PS]	Elvis Presley	1956	200.00
—Three different back covers exist hyping other non-Elvis RCA Victor releases; any are of equal value			
❑ EPB-1254 [PS]	Elvis Presley... the most talked-about new personality in the last ten years of recorded music	1956	1500.
❑ EPA-1-1515	Loving You/Party//(Let Me Be Your) Teddy Bear/True Love	1957	40.00
—With horizontal line on label			
❑ EPA-1-1515	Loving You/Party//(Let Me Be Your) Teddy Bear/True Love	1957	40.00
—Without horizontal line on label			
❑ EPA-1-1515	Loving You/Party//(Let Me Be Your) Teddy Bear/True Love	1965	30.00
—Black label, dog on left			
❑ EPA-1-1515	Loving You/Party//(Let Me Be Your) Teddy Bear/True Love	1969	80.00
—Orange label			
❑ EPA-1-1515 [PS]	Loving You, Vol. I	1957	40.00
❑ EPA-2-1515	Lonesome Cowboy/Hot Dog//Mean Woman Blues/Got a Lot of Livin' to Do	1957	40.00
—With horizontal line on label			
❑ EPA-2-1515	Lonesome Cowboy/Hot Dog//Mean Woman Blues/Got a Lot of Livin' to Do	1957	40.00
—Without horizontal line on label			
❑ EPA-2-1515	Lonesome Cowboy/Hot Dog//Mean Woman Blues/Got a Lot of Livin' to Do	1965	30.00
—Black label, dog on left			
❑ EPA-2-1515	Lonesome Cowboy/Hot Dog//Mean Woman Blues/Got a Lot of Livin' to Do	1969	80.00
—Orange label			
❑ EPA-2-1515 [PS]	Loving You, Vol. II	1957	40.00
—With song titles on top of front cover			
❑ EPA-2-1515 [PS]	Loving You, Vol. II	1965	30.00
—No song titles on top of front cover			
❑ EPA-4006	Love Me Tender/Let Me//Poor Boy/We're Gonna Move	1956	50.00
—With horizontal line on label			
❑ EPA-4006	Love Me Tender/Let Me//Poor Boy/We're Gonna Move	1956	50.00
—Without horizontal line on label			
❑ EPA-4006	Love Me Tender/Let Me//Poor Boy/We're Gonna Move	1956	200.00
—With horizontal line on label, but with no dog			
❑ EPA-4006	Love Me Tender/Let Me//Poor Boy/We're Gonna Move	1965	30.00
—Black label, dog on left			
❑ EPA-4006	Love Me Tender/Let Me//Poor Boy/We're Gonna Move	1969	80.00
—Orange label			
❑ EPA-4006 [PS]	Love Me Tender	1956	50.00
—With song titles on top of front cover			
❑ EPA-4006 [PS]	Love Me Tender	1965	30.00
—No song titles on top of front cover			
❑ EPA-4041	I Need You So/Have I Told You Lately//Blueberry Hill/Is It So Strange	1957	50.00
—With horizontal line on label			
❑ EPA-4041	I Need You So/Have I Told You Lately//Blueberry Hill/Is It So Strange	1957	50.00
—Without horizontal line on label			
❑ EPA-4041	I Need You So/Have I Told You Lately//Blueberry Hill/Is It So Strange	1957	200.00
—With horizontal line on label, but with no dog			
❑ EPA-4041	I Need You So/Have I Told You Lately//Blueberry Hill/Is It So Strange	1965	30.00
—Black label, dog on left			
❑ EPA-4041	I Need You So/Have I Told You Lately//Blueberry Hill/Is It So Strange	1969	80.00
—Orange label			
❑ EPA-4041 [PS]	Just for You (Elvis Presley)	1957	50.00
❑ EPA-4054	(There'll Be) Peace in the Valley (For Me)/It Is No Secret (What God Can Do)//I Believe/Take My Hand, Precious Lord	1957	40.00
—With horizontal line on label			
❑ EPA-4054	(There'll Be) Peace in the Valley (For Me)/It Is No Secret (What God Can Do)//I Believe/Take My Hand, Precious Lord	1957	40.00
—Without horizontal line on label			
❑ EPA-4054 [PS]	Peace in the Valley	1957	40.00
❑ EPA-4108	Santa Bring My Baby Back (To Me)/Blue Christmas//Santa Claus Is Back in Town/I'll Be Home for Christmas	1957	40.00
—Black label, dog on top			
❑ EPA-4108	Santa Bring My Baby Back (To Me)/Blue Christmas//Santa Claus Is Back in Town/I'll Be Home for Christmas	1965	30.00
—Black label, dog on left			
❑ EPA-4108	Santa Bring My Baby Back (To Me)/Blue Christmas//Santa Claus Is Back in Town/I'll Be Home for Christmas	1969	80.00
—Orange label			
❑ EPA-4108 [PS]	Elvis Sings Christmas Songs	1957	40.00
❑ EPA-4114	Jailhouse Rock/Young and Beautiful//I Want to Be Free/Don't Leave Me Now//(You're So Square) Baby I Don't Care	1957	40.00
—Black label, dog on top			
❑ EPA-4114	Jailhouse Rock/Young and Beautiful//I Want to Be Free/Don't Leave Me Now//(You're So Square) Baby I Don't Care	1965	30.00
—Black label, dog on left			
❑ EPA-4114	Jailhouse Rock/Young and Beautiful//I Want to Be Free/Don't Leave Me Now//(You're So Square) Baby I Don't Care	1969	80.00
—Orange label			
❑ EPA-4114 [PS]	Jailhouse Rock	1957	40.00
❑ EPA-4319	King Creole/New Orleans//As Long As I Have You/Lover Doll	1958	40.00
❑ EPA-4319 [PS]	King Creole	1958	40.00
—Without copyright notice on front cover			
❑ EPA-4319 [PS]	King Creole	1958	50.00
—With copyright notice on front cover			
❑ EPA-4321	Trouble/Young Dreams//Crawfish/Dixieland Rock	1958	40.00
—Black label, dog on top			
❑ EPA-4321	Trouble/Young Dreams//Crawfish/Dixieland Rock	1965	30.00
—Black label, dog on left			
❑ EPA-4321	Trouble/Young Dreams//Crawfish/Dixieland Rock	1969	80.00
—Orange label			
❑ EPA-4321 [PS]	King Creole, Vol. 2	1958	40.00
❑ EPA-4325	Press Interview with Elvis Presley/Elvis Presley's Newsreel Interview/Pat Hernon Interviews Elvis...	1958	80.00
❑ EPA-4325 [PS]	Elvis Sails	1958	80.00
—With 1959 calendar and a hole to make it suitable for hanging			
❑ EPA-4340	White Christmas/Here Comes Santa Claus//Oh Little Town of Bethlehem/Silent Night	1958	70.00
—Black label, dog on top			
❑ EPA-4340	White Christmas/Here Comes Santa Claus//Oh Little Town of Bethlehem/Silent Night	1965	40.00
—Black label, dog on left			
❑ EPA-4340	White Christmas/Here Comes Santa Claus//Oh Little Town of Bethlehem/Silent Night	1969	80.00
—Orange label			
❑ EPA-4340 [PS]	Christmas with Elvis	1958	80.00
—With copyright notice and "Printed in U.S.A." at lower right			
❑ EPA-4340 [PS]	Christmas with Elvis	1965	40.00
—Without copyright notice and "Printed in U.S.A." at lower right			
❑ EPA-4368	Follow That Dream/Angel//What a Wonderful Life/I'm Not the Marrying Kind	1962	30.00
—Black label, dog on top, no playing times on label			
❑ EPA-4368	Follow That Dream/Angel//What a Wonderful Life/I'm Not the Marrying Kind	1962	40.00
—Black label, dog on top, with playing times on label			
❑ EPA-4368	Follow That Dream/Angel//What a Wonderful Life/I'm Not the Marrying Kind	1965	25.00
—Black label, dog on left			
❑ EPA-4368	Follow That Dream/Angel//What a Wonderful Life/I'm Not the Marrying Kind	1969	80.00
—Orange label			
❑ EPA-4368 [PS]	Follow That Dream	1962	40.00
—Incorrect playing times on back cover; "Follow That Dream" is listed as 1:35 but is actually 1:38, and two others are wrong also			
❑ EPA-4368 [PS]	Follow That Dream	1962	150.00
—Paper sleeve with "Coin Operator — DJ Prevue" at top; print is in red			
❑ EPA-4368 [PS]	Follow That Dream	1965	25.00
—Correct playing times on back cover			
❑ EPA-4371	King of the Whole Wide World/This Is Living/Riding the Rainbow//Home Is Where the Heart Is/I Got Lucky/A Whistling Tune	1962	40.00
—Black label, dog on top			
❑ EPA-4371	King of the Whole Wide World/This Is Living/Riding the Rainbow//Home Is Where the Heart Is/I Got Lucky/A Whistling Tune	1965	30.00
—Black label, dog on left			
❑ EPA-4371	King of the Whole Wide World/This Is Living/Riding the Rainbow//Home Is Where the Heart Is/I Got Lucky/A Whistling Tune	1969	80.00
—Orange label			
❑ EPA-4371 [PS]	Kid Galahad	1962	40.00
❑ EPA-4382	If You Think I Don't Need You/I Need Somebody to Lean On//C'mon Everybody/Today, Tomorrow and Forever	1964	40.00
—Black label, dog on top			
❑ EPA-4382	If You Think I Don't Need You/I Need Somebody to Lean On//C'mon Everybody/Today, Tomorrow and Forever	1965	30.00
—Black label, dog on left			
❑ EPA-4382	If You Think I Don't Need You/I Need Somebody to Lean On//C'mon Everybody/Today, Tomorrow and Forever	1969	80.00
—Orange label			
❑ EPA-4382 [PS]	Viva Las Vegas	1964	40.00
❑ EPA-4383	I Feel That I've Known You Forever/Slowly But Surely//Night Rider/Dirty Feeling	1965	30.00
—Black label, dog on left			
❑ EPA-4383	I Feel That I've Known You Forever/Slowly But Surely//Night Rider/Dirty Feeling	1969	80.00
—Orange label			
❑ EPA-4383 [PS]	Tickle Me	1965	30.00
—"Ask For" on front cover			
❑ EPA-4383 [PS]	Tickle Me	1965	30.00
—"Coming Soon" on front cover			
❑ EPA-4383 [PS]	Tickle Me	1969	35.00
—No blurb for new album on front cover			
❑ EPA-4387	Easy Come, Easy Go/The Love Machine/Yoga Is As Yoga Does//You Gotta Shop/Sing You Children/I'll Take Love	1967	30.00
—All copies appear to be black label, dog on left			
❑ EPA-4387 [PS]	Easy Come, Easy Go	1967	30.00
❑ EPA-5088	Hard Headed Woman/Good Rockin' Tonight//Don't/I Beg of You	1959	60.00
—Black label, dog on top			
❑ EPA-5088	Hard Headed Woman/Good Rockin' Tonight//Don't/I Beg of You	1959	400.00
—Maroon label			
❑ EPA-5088	Hard Headed Woman/Good Rockin' Tonight//Don't/I Beg of You	1965	30.00
—Black label, dog on left			
❑ EPA-5088	Hard Headed Woman/Good Rockin' Tonight//Don't/I Beg of You	1969	80.00
—Orange label			
❑ EPA-5088 [PS]	A Touch of Gold	1959	60.00
❑ EPA-5101	Wear My Ring Around Your Neck/Treat Me Nice//One Night/That's All Right	1959	60.00
—Black label, dog on top			
❑ EPA-5101	Wear My Ring Around Your Neck/Treat Me Nice//One Night/That's All Right	1959	400.00
—Maroon label			
❑ EPA-5101	Wear My Ring Around Your Neck/Treat Me Nice//One Night/That's All Right	1965	30.00
—Black label, dog on left			
❑ EPA-5101	Wear My Ring Around Your Neck/Treat Me Nice//One Night/That's All Right	1969	80.00
—Orange label			
❑ EPA-5101 [PS]	A Touch of Gold, Vol. II	1959	60.00
❑ EPA-5120	Don't Be Cruel/I Want You, I Need You, I Love You//Hound Dog/My Baby Left Me	1959	60.00
—Black label, dog on top			

P

Number	Title (A Side/B Side)	Yr	NM
❑ EPA-5120	Don't Be Cruel/I Want You, I Need You, I Love You//Hound Dog/My Baby Left Me	1959	600.00
—Maroon label			
❑ EPA-5120	Don't Be Cruel/I Want You, I Need You, I Love You//Hound Dog/My Baby Left Me	1965	25.00
—Black label, dog on left			
❑ EPA-5120	Don't Be Cruel/I Want You, I Need You, I Love You//Hound Dog/My Baby Left Me	1969	80.00
—Orange label			
❑ EPA-5120 [PS]	The Real Elvis	1959	60.00
❑ EPA-5121	(There'll Be) Peace in the Valley (For Me)/It Is No Secret (What God Can Do)//I Believe/Take My Hand, Precious Lord	1959	30.00
—Black label, dog on top			
❑ EPA-5121	(There'll Be) Peace in the Valley (For Me)/It Is No Secret (What God Can Do)//I Believe/Take My Hand, Precious Lord	1959	400.00
—Maroon label			
❑ EPA-5121	(There'll Be) Peace in the Valley (For Me)/It Is No Secret (What God Can Do)//I Believe/Take My Hand, Precious Lord	1965	25.00
—Black label, dog on left			
❑ EPA-5121	(There'll Be) Peace in the Valley (For Me)/It Is No Secret (What God Can Do)//I Believe/Take My Hand, Precious Lord	1969	80.00
—Orange label			
❑ EPA-5121 [PS]	Peace in the Valley	1959	40.00
—Three slightly different cover variations with no difference in value			
❑ EPA-5122	King Creole/New Orleans//As Long As I Have You/Lover Doll	1959	30.00
—Black label, dog on top			
❑ EPA-5122	King Creole/New Orleans//As Long As I Have You/Lover Doll	1959	2000.
—Maroon label. VG 1000; VG+ 1500			
❑ EPA-5122	King Creole/New Orleans//As Long As I Have You/Lover Doll	1965	25.00
—Black label, dog on left			
❑ EPA-5122	King Creole/New Orleans//As Long As I Have You/Lover Doll	1969	80.00
—Orange label			
❑ EPA-5122 [PS]	King Creole	1959	40.00
—With "Gold Standard Series" on front cover			
❑ EPA-5122 [PS]	King Creole	1965	30.00
—Without "Gold Standard Series" on front cover			
❑ EPA-5141	All Shook Up/Don't Ask Me Why//Too Much/Blue Moon of Kentucky	1959	30.00
—Black label, dog on left			
❑ EPA-5141	All Shook Up/Don't Ask Me Why//Too Much/Blue Moon of Kentucky	1959	70.00
—Black label, dog on top			
❑ EPA-5141	All Shook Up/Don't Ask Me Why//Too Much/Blue Moon of Kentucky	1959	80.00
—Orange label			
❑ EPA-5141	All Shook Up/Don't Ask Me Why//Too Much/Blue Moon of Kentucky	1959	400.00
—Maroon label			
❑ EPA-5141 [PS]	A Touch of Gold, Vol. 3	1959	70.00
❑ EPA-5157	Press Interview with Elvis Presley//Elvis Presley's Newsreel Interview/Pat Hernon Interviews Elvis...	1965	30.00
—Black label, dog on top			
❑ EPA-5157	Press Interview with Elvis Presley//Elvis Presley's Newsreel Interview/Pat Hernon Interviews Elvis...	1969	80.00
—Orange label			
❑ EPA-5157 [PS]	Elvis Sails	1965	30.00
❑ G8-MW-8705 [DJ]	TV Guide Presents Elvis Presley	1956	1200.
—Blue label, locked grooves (needle has to be lifted to play each of the four excerpts)			
❑ 599-9141	Blue Moon of Kentucky/Love Me Tender//Mystery Train/Milkcow Boogie Blues	1957	400.00
—This is "Side 6" and "Side 15" of various artists box set SPD-26, "Great Country/Western Hits"; notice the error in title on the second side			

Albums

BMG/SUN

Number	Title	Yr	NM
❑ 82876-61205-1	Elvis at Sun	2004	15.00

BOXCAR

Number	Title	Yr	NM
❑ (no #)	Having Fun with Elvis on Stage	1974	150.00
—All-talking record sold at Elvis concerts in 1974			

COLLECTABLES

Number	Title	Yr	NM
❑ COL-0165 [(6)]	Elvis Top Album Collection, Vol. 1	2003	100.00
—Contains reproductions, on red vinyl, of five RCA albums (LPM-1254, LPM-1382, LSP-2370, LSP-2426 and APL2-2587) using facsimiles of original labels, covers, inner sleeves and inserts; with poster and all in wooden box			
❑ COL-0166 [(6)]	Elvis Top Album Collection, Vol. 2	2003	100.00
—Contains reproductions, on red vinyl, of five RCA albums (LPM-1515, LOC-1035, LSP-2256, LSP-2999 and CPL2-2642) using facsimiles of original labels, covers, inner sleeves and inserts; with poster and all in wooden box			

DCC COMPACT CLASSICS

Number	Title	Yr	NM
❑ LPZ-2037 [S]	Elvis Is Back!	1997	120.00
—Audiophile vinyl			
❑ LPZ-2040 [(2)]	24 Karat Hits!	1997	120.00
—Audiophile vinyl			

FOTOPLAY

Number	Title	Yr	NM
❑ FSP-1001 [PD]	To Elvis: Love Still Burning	1978	15.00
—In black cardboard cover with white printing			
❑ FSP-1001 [PD]	To Elvis: Love Still Burning	1978	25.00
—Tribute-song picture disc of Elvis; in plastic bag with 11x11 insert			
❑ FSP-1001 [PD]	To Elvis: Love Still Burning	1978	30.00
—In white cardboard cover with black printing			

GOLDEN EDITIONS

Number	Title	Yr	NM
❑ KING-1	The First Year (Elvis, Scotty and Bill)	1979	15.00
❑ GEL-101	The First Year (Elvis, Scotty and Bill)	1979	20.00

GREAT NORTHWEST

Number	Title	Yr	NM
❑ GV-2004	The King Speaks (February 1961, Memphis, Tennessee)	1977	10.00
—Label says this is on "Green Valley" while sleeve says "Great Northwest"			
❑ GNW-4005	The Elvis Tapes	1977	12.00
❑ GNW-4006	The King Speaks (February 1961, Memphis, Tennessee)	1977	8.00
—Both label and sleeve say this is on "Great Northwest"			

GREEN VALLEY

Number	Title	Yr	NM
❑ GV-2001	Elvis Exclusive Live Press Conference (Memphis, Tennessee, February 1961)	1977	40.00
—Issued with two slightly different covers			
❑ GV-2001/3 [(2)]	Elvis (Speaks to You)	1978	30.00
—Elvis interviews plus tracks by the Jordanaires			

GUSTO

Number	Title	Yr	NM
❑ SD-995	Interviews with Elvis (Canada 1957)	1978	40.00
—Reissue of Great Northwest album			

HALW

Number	Title	Yr	NM
❑ HALW-0001	The First Years	1978	20.00
—Without limited edition number			
❑ HALW-0001	The First Years	1978	30.00
—With stamped, limited edition number			

K-TEL

Number	Title	Yr	NM
❑ NU 9900	Love Songs	1981	20.00

LOUISIANA HAYRIDE

Number	Title	Yr	NM
❑ LH-3061	Beginning Years	1984	20.00
—With booklet and facsimile contract			

MARVENCO

Number	Title	Yr	NM
❑ 101	Beginning (1954-1955)	1988	15.00
—Pink vinyl with booklet and facsimile contract			

MOBILE FIDELITY

Number	Title	Yr	NM
❑ 1-059	From Elvis in Memphis	1982	50.00
—Audiophile vinyl			

MUSIC WORKS

Number	Title	Yr	NM
❑ PB-3601	The First Live Recordings	1984	15.00
❑ PB-3602	The Hillbilly Cat	1984	15.00

OAK

Number	Title	Yr	NM
❑ 1003	Vintage 1955 Elvis	1990	60.00

PAIR

Number	Title	Yr	NM
❑ PDL2-1010 [(2)]	Double Dynamite	1982	20.00
❑ PDL2-1037 [(2)]	Remembering	1983	30.00
❑ PDL2-1185 [(2)]	Elvis Aron Presley Forever	1988	20.00

PICKWICK

Number	Title	Yr	NM
❑ (no #) [(7)]	The Pickwick Pack (unofficial title)	1978	60.00
—Seven Pickwick albums in special package and cardboard wrapper; one of the LPs is Elvis' Christmas Album			
❑ (no #) [(7)]	The Pickwick Pack (unofficial title)	1979	60.00
—Seven Pickwick albums in special package and cardboard wrapper; one of the LPs is Frankie and Johnny			
❑ CAS-2304	Elvis Sings Flaming Star	1976	10.00
❑ CAS-2408	Let's Be Friends	1975	10.00
❑ CAS-2428 [M]	Elvis' Christmas Album	1975	12.00
—Same contents as RCA Camden LP; no Christmas trim on border; despite the "CAS" catalog number, this album is mono			
❑ CAS-2428 [M]	Elvis' Christmas Album	1976	10.00
—Same as above, but with Christmas trim on cover border; despite the "CAS" catalog number, this album is mono			
❑ CAS-2440	Almost in Love	1975	10.00
❑ CAL-2472	You'll Never Walk Alone	1975	10.00
❑ CAL-2518	C'mon Everybody	1975	10.00
❑ CAS-2533	I Got Lucky	1975	10.00
❑ CAS-2567	Elvis Sings Hits from His Movies, Vol. 1	1975	10.00
❑ CAS-2595	Burning Love And Hits from His Movies, Vol. 2	1975	12.00
—First cover contains a notice about the upcoming "Aloha from Hawaii" show			
❑ CAS-2595	Burning Love And Hits from His Movies, Vol. 2	1976	8.00
—Reissue deletes the "Aloha from Hawaii" notice			
❑ CAS-2611	Separate Ways	1975	10.00
❑ DL2-5001 [(2)]	Double Dynamite	1975	25.00
❑ ACL-7007	Frankie and Johnny	1976	10.00
❑ ACL-7064	Mahalo from Elvis	1978	20.00

PREMORE

Number	Title	Yr	NM
❑ PL-589	Early Elvis (1954-1956 Live at the Louisiana Hayride)	1989	30.00

RCA

Number	Title	Yr	NM
❑ 2023-1-R	The Million Dollar Quartet	1990	12.00
—With Jerry Lee Lewis, Carl Perkins, and perhaps Johnny Cash			
❑ 2227-1-R	The Great Performances	1990	40.00
❑ 3114-1-R [(3)]	Collectors Gold	1991	200.00
❑ 5600-1-R	Return of the Rocker	1986	20.00
❑ 6221-1-R [(2)]	The Memphis Record	1987	30.00
❑ 6313-1-R	Elvis Talks!	1987	30.00
❑ 6382-1-R	The Number One Hits	1987	30.00
❑ 6383-1-R [(2)]	The Top Ten Hits	1987	30.00
❑ 6414-1-R [(2)]	The Complete Sun Sessions	1987	30.00
❑ 6738-1-R	Essential Elvis: The First Movies	1988	25.00
❑ 6985-1-R	The Alternate Aloha	1988	20.00
❑ 8468-1-R	Elvis in Nashville (1956-1971)	1988	40.00
❑ 9586-1-R	Elvis Gospel 1957-1971 (Known Only to Him)	1989	40.00
❑ 9589-1-R	Essential Elvis, Vol. 2 (Stereo '57)	1989	25.00
❑ 82876-51108-1 [(2)]	2nd to None	2003	20.00
❑ 07863-67642-1	Elvis' Golden Records	1997	30.00
—Reissue for the Tower Records chain with 6 bonus tracks			
❑ 07863-67643-1	Elvis' Gold Records Vol. 2 — 50,000,000 Elvis Fans Can't Be Wrong	1997	30.00
—Reissue for the Tower Records chain with 10 bonus tracks			
❑ 07863-68079-1 [(2)]	30 #1 Hits	2002	20.00

RCA CAMDEN

Number	Title	Yr	NM
❑ CAS-2304	Elvis Sings Flaming Star	1969	30.00
❑ CAS-2408	Let's Be Friends	1970	30.00
❑ CAL-2428 [M]	Elvis' Christmas Album	1970	30.00
—Blue label, non-flexible vinyl			
❑ CAL-2428 [M]	Elvis' Christmas Album	1971	12.00
—Blue label, flexible vinyl			
❑ CAS-2440	Almost in Love	1970	40.00
—Last song on Side 2 is "Stay Away, Joe"			
❑ CAS-2440	Almost in Love	1973	25.00
—Last song on Side 2 is "Stay Away"			
❑ CAL-2472	You'll Never Walk Alone	1974	30.00
❑ CALX-2472	You'll Never Walk Alone	1971	15.00
❑ CAL-2518	C'mon Everybody	1971	20.00
❑ CAL-2533	I Got Lucky	1971	25.00
❑ CAS-2567	Elvis Sings Hits from His Movies, Vol. 1	1972	20.00
❑ CAS-2595	Burning Love And Hits from His Movies, Vol. 2	1972	10.00
—No star on cover, no bonus photo			
❑ CAS-2595	Burning Love And Hits from His Movies, Vol. 2	1972	25.00
—With star on front cover advertising a bonus photo, the presence of which doubles the value of this LP			
❑ CAS-2611	Separate Ways	1973	30.00

RCA SPECIAL PRODUCTS

Number	Title	Yr	NM
❑ DPL2-0056(e) [(2)]	Elvis	1973	25.00
—Blue labels			
❑ DPL2-0056(e) [(2)]	Elvis	1973	50.00
—Mustard labels			
❑ DPL2-0056(e) [(2)]	Elvis Commemorative Album	1978	80.00
—Reissue of "Elvis" (same number) with new title and gold vinyl			
❑ DPL2-0168 [(2)]	Elvis in Hollywood	1976	60.00
—Blue labels; with 20-page booklet			
❑ DML5-0263 [(5)]	The Elvis Story	1977	60.00
—Available through Candelite Music via mail order			
❑ DML1-0264	His Songs of Inspiration	1977	15.00
❑ DPL5-0347 [(5)]	Memories of Elvis (A Lasting Tribute to the King of Rock 'N' Roll)	1978	80.00
❑ DML1-0348	The Greatest Show on Earth	1978	15.00
❑ DML6-0412 [(6)]	The Legendary Recordings of Elvis Presley	1979	100.00
❑ DML1-0413	The Greatest Moments in Music	1980	15.00
❑ DML1-0437	Rock 'N Roll Forever	1981	15.00
❑ DVL1-0461	The Legendary Magic of Elvis Presley	1980	15.00
❑ DML3-0632 [(3)]	The Elvis Presley Collection	1984	80.00
—Available through Candelite Music via mail order			
❑ DPL1-0647	Elvis Country	1984	30.00
❑ DVM1-0704	Elvis (One Night with You)	1984	60.00
—With poster (deduct 25% if missing)			

Except when noted otherwise, VG = 25% of NM, and VG+ = 50% of NM. (Example: VG = $2.00, VG+ = $4.00 and NM = $8.00.)

Number | Title (A Side/B Side) | Yr | NM

❑ SVL3-0710 [(3)] 50 Years — 50 Hits 1985 30.00
❑ DVL2-0728 [(2)] His Songs of Faith and Inspiration 1986 50.00
❑ SVL2-0824 [(2)] Good Rockin' Tonight 1988 20.00
❑ CAL-2428 [M] Elvis' Christmas Album 1986 30.00
—Reissue for The Special Music Company

RCA VICTOR

❑ (no #) International Hotel, Las Vegas Nevada, Presents Elvis, 1969 1969 2500.
—Gift box to guests at Elvis' July 31-Aug, 1, 1969 shows. Includes LPM-4088 and LSP-4155; press release; 1969 catalog; three photos; and thank-you note from Elvis and the Colonel. Most of the value is for the box; VG value 1250; VG+ value 1875
❑ (no #) International Hotel, Las Vegas Nevada, Presents Elvis, 1970 1970 2500.
—Gift box to guests at Elvis' Jan. 28, 1970 show. Includes LSP-6020 and 47-9791; press release; 1970 catalog; photo; booklet; and dinner menu. Most of the value is for the box; VG value 1250; VG+ value 1875
❑ PRS-279 Singer Presents Elvis Singing Flaming Star and Others 1968 100.00
—Sold only at Singer sewing machine dealers; reissued on RCA Camden 2304
❑ APL1-0283 Elvis 1973 50.00
❑ CPL1-0341 A Legendary Performer, Vol. 1 1974 25.00
—Includes booklet (deduct 40% if missing); with die-cut hole in front cover
❑ CPL1-0341 A Legendary Performer, Vol. 1 1986 15.00
—No die-cut hole in cover and no booklet
❑ APL1-0388 Raised on Rock/ For Ol' Times Sake 1973 30.00
—Orange label
❑ APL1-0388 Raised on Rock/ For Ol' Times Sake 1975 30.00
—Tan label
❑ APL1-0388 Raised on Rock/ For Ol' Times Sake 1977 12.00
—Black label, dog near top
❑ SP-33-461 [DJ] Special Palm Sunday Programming 1967 700.00
—White label promo. Add 25% for cue sheet.
❑ AFL1-0475 Good Times 1977 12.00
—Black label, dog near top; includes copies with sticker wrapped around spine with new number
❑ CPL1-0475 Good Times 1974 50.00
—Orange label
❑ CPL1-0475 Good Times 1976 12.00
—Black label, dog near top
❑ SPS-33-571 [DJ] Elvis As Recorded at Madison Square Garden 1972 300.00
—"Radio Station Banded Special Version"; came in plain white cover with stickers
❑ AFL1-0606 Elvis Recorded Live on Stage in Memphis 1977 12.00
—Black label, dog near top; includes copies with sticker wrapped around spine with new number
❑ APD1-0606 [Q] Elvis Recorded Live on Stage in Memphis 1974 200.00
—"RCA QuadraDisc" labels
❑ CPL1-0606 Elvis Recorded Live on Stage in Memphis 1974 25.00
—Orange label
❑ CPL1-0606 Elvis Recorded Live on Stage in Memphis 1975 25.00
—Tan label
❑ DJL1-0606 [DJ] Elvis Recorded Live on Stage in Memphis 1974 300.00
—Special banded version for radio airplay
❑ AFM1-0818 Having Fun with Elvis on Stage 1977 25.00
—Black label, dog near top
❑ CPM1-0818 Having Fun with Elvis on Stage 1974 30.00
—Commercial issue of Boxcar LP; orange label
❑ CPM1-0818 Having Fun with Elvis on Stage 1975 20.00
—Tan label
❑ DJM1-0835 [DJ] Elvis Presley Interview Record: An Audio Self-Portrait 1984 80.00
—Promotional item for "50th Anniversary" series; later issued as RCA 6313-1-R
❑ AFL1-0873 Promised Land 1977 15.00
—Black label, dog near top
❑ APD1-0873 [Q] Promised Land 1975 200.00
—"RCA QuadraDisc" label
❑ APD1-0873 [Q] Promised Land 1977 120.00
—Black label, dog near top; quadraphonic reissue
❑ APL1-0873 Promised Land 1975 20.00
—Tan label
❑ APL1-0873 Promised Land 1975 60.00
—Orange label
❑ ANL1-0971(e) Pure Gold 1975 15.00
—Orange label
❑ ANL1-0971(e) Pure Gold 1976 12.00
—Yellow label
❑ LOC-1035 [M] Elvis' Christmas Album Sticker 1957 150.00
—Gold sticker with "To_______" and "From_______" blanks
❑ LOC-1035 [M] Elvis' Christmas Album 1957 500.00
—Gatefold cover; title printed in gold on LP spine; includes bound-in booklet but not sticker
❑ LOC-1035 [M] Elvis' Christmas Album 1957 500.00
—Gatefold cover; title printed in silver on LP spine; includes bound-in booklet but not sticker
❑ LOC-1035 [M] Elvis' Christmas Album 1957 15000.
—Red vinyl; unique; VG value 7500; VG+ value 11250

Number | Title (A Side/B Side) | Yr | NM

❑ LOC-1035 [M] Elvis' Christmas Album 2003 20.00
—Red vinyl; not to be mistaken for the unique 1957 version, as this has "DRL 13265" number in trail-off wax and BMG Special Products logo and "This is a replica of the original packaging" on back cover; from box "Elvis Top Album Collection Vol. 2"
❑ AFL1-1039 Elvis Today 1977 12.00
—Black label, dog near top; includes copies with sticker wrapped around spine with new number
❑ APD1-1039 [Q] Elvis Today 1975 200.00
—"RCA QuadraDisc" labels
❑ APD1-1039 [Q] Elvis Today 1977 150.00
—Black label, dog near top; quadraphonic reissue
❑ APL1-1039 Elvis Today 1975 30.00
—Tan label
❑ APL1-1039 Elvis Today 1975 60.00
—Orange label
❑ AFL1-1254(e) [R] Elvis Presley 1977 12.00
—Black label, dog near top; includes copies with sticker wrapped around spine with new number
❑ LPM-1254 [M] Elvis Presley 1956 250.00
—Version 3: "Long Play" on label; "Elvis" in pale pink, "Presley" in neon green on cover; black logo box in upper right front cover
❑ LPM-1254 [M] Elvis Presley 1956 400.00
—Version 2: "Long Play" on label; "Elvis" in pale pink, "Presley" in neon green on cover; neon green logo box in upper right front cover
❑ LPM-1254 [M] Elvis Presley 1956 500.00
—Version 1: "Long Play" on label; "Elvis" in pale pink, "Presley" in pale green on cover; pale green logo box in upper right front cover
❑ LPM-1254 [M] Elvis Presley 1958 200.00
—Version 4: "Long Play" on label; "Elvis" in neon pink, almost red, "Presley" in neon green on cover; black logo box in upper right front cover
❑ LPM-1254 [M] Elvis Presley 1963 120.00
—"Mono" on label; cover photo is slightly left of center, otherwise same as Version 4 above
❑ LPM-1254 [M] Elvis Presley 1964 60.00
—"Monaural" on label
❑ LPM-1254 [M] Elvis Presley 2003 20.00
—Red vinyl; "DRL 13272" in trail-off wax; "BMG Special Products" logo on back cover; from box "Elvis Top Album Collection Vol. 1"
❑ LSP-1254(e) [R] Elvis Presley 1962 200.00
—"Stereo Electronically Reprocessed" and silver "RCA Victor" on label
❑ LSP-1254(e) [R] Elvis Presley 1965 40.00
—"Stereo Electronically Reprocessed" and white "RCA Victor" on label
❑ LSP-1254(e) [R] Elvis Presley 1968 30.00
—Orange label, non-flexible vinyl
❑ LSP-1254(e) [R] Elvis Presley 1975 15.00
—Tan label
❑ LSP-1254(e) [R] Elvis Presley 1976 12.00
—Black label, dog near top
❑ ANL1-1319 [S] His Hand in Mine 1976 15.00
—Reissue with more tightly cropped photo of Elvis on front cover
❑ CPL1-1349 A Legendary Performer, Vol. 2 1976 30.00
—Includes booklet (deduct 40% if missing); with die-cut hole in front cover
❑ CPL1-1349 A Legendary Performer, Vol. 2 1976 60.00
—Without false starts and outtakes of "Such a Night" and "Cane and a High Starched Collar," which are supposed to be there. End of matrix number may be "31."
❑ CPL1-1349 A Legendary Performer, Vol. 2 1986 15.00
—No die-cut hole in cover and no booklet
❑ AFL1-1382(e) [R] Elvis 1977 12.00
—Black label, dog near top; includes copies with sticker wrapped around spine with new number
❑ LPM-1382 [M] Elvis 1956 300.00
—Back cover has ads for other albums. At least 11 different variations of this are known, all of equal value.
❑ LPM-1382 [M] Elvis 1956 300.00
—Back cover has no ads for other albums. "Long Play" on label.
❑ LPM-1382 [M] Elvis 1956 400.00
—With tracks listed on labels as "Band 1" through "Band 6"
❑ LPM-1382 [M] Elvis 1956 800.00
—With alternate take of "Old Shep" on side 2. Matrix number on the "Old Shep" side ends in "15S," "17S" or "19S," but should be played for positive ID. On alternate take, Elvis sings "he grew old AND his eyes were growing dim" (no AND on standard press)
❑ LPM-1382 [M] Elvis 1963 80.00
—"Mono" on label
❑ LPM-1382 [M] Elvis 1965 60.00
—"Monaural" on label
❑ LPM-1382 [M] Elvis 2003 20.00
—Red vinyl; "DRC 13271" in trail-off wax; "BMG Special Products" logo on back cover; from box "Elvis Top Album Collection Vol. 1"
❑ LSP-1382(e) [R] Elvis 1962 200.00
—"Stereo Electronically Reprocessed" and silver "RCA Victor" on label
❑ LSP-1382(e) [R] Elvis 1964 50.00
—"Stereo Electronically Reprocessed" and white "RCA Victor" on label
❑ LSP-1382(e) [R] Elvis 1968 30.00
—Orange label, non-flexible vinyl
❑ LSP-1382(e) [R] Elvis 1971 20.00
—Orange label, flexible vinyl
❑ LSP-1382(e) [R] Elvis 1975 15.00
—Tan label
❑ LSP-1382(e) [R] Elvis 1976 12.00
—Black label, dog near top
❑ AFL1-1506 From Elvis Presley Boulevard, Memphis, Tennessee 1977 10.00
—Black label, dog near top; new number is on cover and label

Number | Title (A Side/B Side) | Yr | NM

❑ AFL1-1506 From Elvis Presley Boulevard, Memphis, Tennessee 1977 12.00
—Black label, dog near top; with sticker wrapped around spine with new number (old number still on label)
❑ APL1-1506 From Elvis Presley Boulevard, Memphis, Tennessee 1976 30.00
—Tan label
❑ AFL1-1515(e) [R] Loving You 1977 12.00
—Black label, dog near top; includes copies with sticker wrapped around spine with new number
❑ LPM-1515 [M] Loving You 1957 300.00
—"Long Play" on label
❑ LPM-1515 [M] Loving You 1963 100.00
—"Mono" on label
❑ LPM-1515 [M] Loving You 1964 50.00
—"Monaural" on label
❑ LPM-1515 [M] Loving You 2003 20.00
—Red vinyl; "DRL 13268" in trail-off wax; "BMG Special Products" logo on back cover; from box "Elvis Top Album Collection Vol. 2"
❑ LSP-1515(e) [R] Loving You 1962 150.00
—"Stereo Electronically Reprocessed" and silver "RCA Victor" on label
❑ LSP-1515(e) [R] Loving You 1964 50.00
—"Stereo Electronically Reprocessed" and white "RCA Victor" on label
❑ LSP-1515(e) [R] Loving You 1968 40.00
—Orange label, non-flexible vinyl
❑ LSP-1515(e) [R] Loving You 1971 20.00
—Orange label, flexible vinyl
❑ LSP-1515(e) [R] Loving You 1975 20.00
—Tan label
❑ LSP-1515(e) [R] Loving You 1976 12.00
—Black label, dog near top
❑ AFM1-1675 The Sun Sessions 1977 15.00
—Black label, dog near top; includes copies with sticker wrapped around spine with new number
❑ APM1-1675 The Sun Sessions 1976 12.00
—Black label, dog near top
❑ APM1-1675 The Sun Sessions 1976 20.00
—Tan label
❑ AFL1-1707(e) [R] Elvis' Golden Records 1977 12.00
—Black label, dog near top; includes copies with sticker wrapped around spine with new number
❑ AQL1-1707(e) [R] Elvis' Golden Records 1979 10.00
—Another reissue with new prefix
❑ LPM-1707 [M] Elvis' Golden Records 1958 150.00
—Title on cover in light blue letters; no song titles listed on front cover; "RE" on back cover
❑ LPM-1707 [M] Elvis' Golden Records 1958 250.00
—Title on cover in light blue letters; no song titles listed on front cover
❑ LPM-1707 [M] Elvis' Golden Records 1963 60.00
—"Mono" on label; title on cover in white letters; song titles added to front cover
❑ LPM-1707 [M] Elvis' Golden Records 1964 40.00
—"Monaural" on label; "RE2" on back cover
❑ LSP-1707(e) [R] Elvis' Golden Records 1962 200.00
—"Stereo Electronically Reprocessed" and silver "RCA Victor" on label
❑ LSP-1707(e) [R] Elvis' Golden Records 1964 50.00
—"Stereo Electronically Reprocessed" and white "RCA Victor" on label
❑ LSP-1707(e) [R] Elvis' Golden Records 1968 30.00
—Orange label, non-flexible vinyl
❑ LSP-1707(e) [R] Elvis' Golden Records 1971 20.00
—Orange label, flexible vinyl
❑ LSP-1707(e) [R] Elvis' Golden Records 1975 20.00
—Tan label
❑ LSP-1707(e) [R] Elvis' Golden Records 1976 12.00
—Black label, dog near top
❑ AFL1-1884(e) [R] King Creole 1977 12.00
—Black label, dog near top; includes copies with sticker wrapped around spine with new number
❑ LPM-1884 [M] King Creole 1958 200.00
—"Long Play" on label; contrary to some other sources, this was NOT issued with a bonus photo
❑ LPM-1884 [M] King Creole 1963 80.00
—"Mono" on label
❑ LPM-1884 [M] King Creole 1964 60.00
—"Monaural" on label
❑ LSP-1884(e) [R] King Creole 1962 150.00
—"Stereo Electronically Reprocessed" and silver "RCA Victor" on label
❑ LSP-1884(e) [R] King Creole 1964 60.00
—"Stereo Electronically Reprocessed" and white "RCA Victor" on label
❑ LSP-1884(e) [R] King Creole 1968 40.00
—Orange label, non-flexible vinyl
❑ LSP-1884(e) [R] King Creole 1971 20.00
—Orange label, flexible vinyl
❑ LSP-1884(e) [R] King Creole 1975 20.00
—Tan label
❑ LSP-1884(e) [R] King Creole 1976 12.00
—Black label, dog near top
❑ ANL1-1936 Elvis Sings the Wonderful World of Christmas 1975 15.00
—New number; same contents as LSP-4579. Orange label.
❑ ANL1-1936 Elvis Sings the Wonderful World of Christmas 1976 12.00
—Tan label
❑ ANL1-1936 Elvis Sings the Wonderful World of Christmas 1977 10.00
—Black label, dog near top
❑ LPM-1951 [M] Elvis' Christmas Album 1958 150.00
—Same contents as LOC-1035, but with non-gatefold blue cover; "Long Play" at bottom of label

P

Number Title (A Side/B Side) Yr NM

❑ LPM-1951 [M] Elvis' Christmas Album 1963 70.00
—"Mono" at bottom of label: "RE" on lower left front cover (photos on back were altered)
❑ LPM-1951 [M] Elvis' Christmas Album 1964 40.00
—"Monaural" at bottom of label; "RE" on lower left front cover
❑ LSP-1951(e) [R]Elvis' Christmas Album 1964 50.00
—Black label, dog on top; "Stereo Electronically Reprocessed" at bottom of label
❑ LSP-1951(e) [R] Elvis' Christmas Album 1968 60.00
—Orange label, non-flexible vinyl
❑ AFL1-1990(e) [R] For LP Fans Only 1977 12.00
—Black label, dog near top; includes copies with sticker wrapped around spine with new number
❑ LPM-1990 [M] For LP Fans Only 1959 250.00
—"Long Play" on label
❑ LPM-1990 [M] For LP Fans Only 1963 80.00
—"Mono" on label
❑ LPM-1990 [M] For LP Fans Only 1964 50.00
—"Monaural" on label
❑ LSP-1990(e) [R]For LP Fans Only 1965 50.00
—"Stereo Electronically Reprocessed" on label; normal cover with different front and back cover photos
❑ LSP-1990(e) [R]For LP Fans Only 1965 300.00
—"Stereo Electronically Reprocessed" on label; error cover with same photo on both front and back
❑ LSP-1990(e) [R]For LP Fans Only 1968 30.00
—Orange label, non-flexible vinyl
❑ LSP-1990(e) [R]For LP Fans Only 1975 20.00
—Tan label
❑ LSP-1990(e) [R]For LP Fans Only 1976 12.00
—Black label, dog near top
❑ AFL1-2011(e) [R] A Date with Elvis 1977 12.00
—Black label, dog near top; includes copies with sticker wrapped around spine with new number
❑ LPM-2011 [M] A Date with Elvis 1959 400.00
—"Long Play" on label; gatefold cover, no sticker on cover
❑ LPM-2011 [M] A Date with Elvis 1959 500.00
—"Long Play" on label; gatefold cover, with sticker on cover
❑ LPM-2011 [M] A Date with Elvis 1963 100.00
—"Mono" on label; no gatefold cover
❑ LPM-2011 [M] A Date with Elvis 1965 50.00
—"Monaural" on label
❑ LSP-2011(e) [R] A Date with Elvis 1965 50.00
—Black label, "Stereo Electronically Reprocessed" on label
❑ LSP-2011(e) [R] A Date with Elvis 1968 30.00
—Orange label, non-flexible vinyl
❑ LSP-2011(e) [R] A Date with Elvis 1971 20.00
—Orange label, flexible vinyl
❑ LSP-2011(e) [R] A Date with Elvis 1975 20.00
—Tan label
❑ LSP-2011(e) [R] A Date with Elvis 1977 12.00
—Black label, dog near top
❑ AFL1-2075(e) [R] Elvis' Gold Records Vol. 2 — 50,000,000 Elvis Fans Can't Be Wrong 1977 12.00
—Black label, dog near top; includes copies with sticker wrapped around spine with new number
❑ LPM-2075 [M] Elvis' Gold Records Vol. 2 — 50,000,000 Elvis Fans Can't Be Wrong 1960 200.00
—"Long Play" on label; "Magic Millions" on upper right front cover with RCA Victor logo
❑ LPM-2075 [M] Elvis' Gold Records Vol. 2 — 50,000,000 Elvis Fans Can't Be Wrong 1963 80.00
—"Mono" on label; "RE" on lower right front cover
❑ LPM-2075 [M] Elvis' Gold Records Vol. 2 — 50,000,000 Elvis Fans Can't Be Wrong 1964 50.00
—"Monaural" on label; label has words "50,000,000 Elvis Presley Fans Can't Be Wrong"
❑ LPM-2075 [M] Elvis' Gold Records Vol. 2 — 50,000,000 Elvis Fans Can't Be Wrong 1964 50.00
—"Monaural" on label; label only has "Elvis' Gold Records - Vol. 2"
❑ LSP-2075(e) [R]Elvis' Gold Records Vol. 2 — 50,000,000 Elvis Fans Can't Be Wrong 1962 150.00
—"Stereo Electronically Reprocessed" on label; label has words "50,000,000 Elvis Presley Fans Can't Be Wrong"
❑ LSP-2075(e) [R]Elvis' Gold Records Vol. 2 — 50,000,000 Elvis Fans Can't Be Wrong 1964 50.00
—"Stereo Electronically Reprocessed" and white "RCA Victor" on label
❑ LSP-2075(e) [R]Elvis' Gold Records Vol. 2 — 50,000,000 Elvis Fans Can't Be Wrong 1968 30.00
—Orange label, non-flexible vinyl
❑ LSP-2075(e) [R]Elvis' Gold Records Vol. 2 — 50,000,000 Elvis Fans Can't Be Wrong 1971 20.00
—Orange label, flexible vinyl
❑ LSP-2075(e) [R]Elvis' Gold Records Vol. 2 — 50,000,000 Elvis Fans Can't Be Wrong 1975 20.00
—Tan label
❑ LSP-2075(e) [R]Elvis' Gold Records Vol. 2 — 50,000,000 Elvis Fans Can't Be Wrong 1976 12.00
—Black label, dog near top
❑ AFL1-2231 [S] Elvis Is Back! 1977 12.00
—Black label, dog near top; includes copies with sticker wrapped around spine with new number
❑ LPM-2231 [M] Elvis Is Back! 1960 150.00
—With sticker attached to front cover. Side 2, Song 4 is listed as "The Girl Next Door Went a-Walking."
❑ LPM-2231 [M] Elvis Is Back! 1960 150.00
—With sticker attached to front cover. Side 2, Song 4 is listed as "The Girl Next Door."
❑ LPM-2231 [M] Elvis Is Back! 1960 200.00
—With no sticker attached to front cover. Side 2, Song 4 is listed as "The Girl Next Door Went a-Walking."
❑ LPM-2231 [M] Elvis Is Back! 1960 200.00
—With no sticker attached to front cover. Side 2, Song 4 is listed as "The Girl Next Door."
❑ LPM-2231 [M] Elvis Is Back! 1963 60.00
—"Mono" on label; song titles printed on front cover
❑ LPM-2231 [M] Elvis Is Back! 1964 60.00
—"Monaural" on label
❑ LSP-2231 [S] Elvis Is Back! 1960 300.00
—"Living Stereo" on label; with no sticker attached to front cover. Side 2, Song 4 is listed as "The Girl Next Door Went a-Walking."
❑ LSP-2231 [S] Elvis Is Back! 1960 300.00
—"Living Stereo" on label; with no sticker attached to front cover. Side 2, Song 4 is listed as "The Girl Next Door."
❑ LSP-2231 [S] Elvis Is Back! 1960 300.00
—"Living Stereo" on label; with sticker attached to front cover. Side 2, Song 4 is listed as "The Girl Next Door Went a-Walking."
❑ LSP-2231 [S] Elvis Is Back! 1960 300.00
—"Living Stereo" on label; with sticker attached to front cover. Side 2, Song 4 is listed as "The Girl Next Door."
❑ LSP-2231 [S] Elvis Is Back! 1964 60.00
—"Stereo" on label; song titles printed on front cover
❑ LSP-2231 [S] Elvis Is Back! 1968 40.00
—Orange label, non-flexible vinyl
❑ LSP-2231 [S] Elvis Is Back! 1975 20.00
—Tan label
❑ LSP-2231 [S] Elvis Is Back! 1976 15.00
—Black label, dog on top
❑ AFL1-2256 [S] G.I. Blues 1977 12.00
—Black label, dog near top; includes copies with sticker wrapped around spine with new number
❑ LPM-2256 [M] G.I. Blues 1960 120.00
—"Long Play" on label; with no sticker on front cover
❑ LPM-2256 [M] G.I. Blues 1960 500.00
—"Long Play" on label; with sticker on front cover advertising the presence of "Wooden Heart"
❑ LPM-2256 [M] G.I. Blues 1963 100.00
—"Mono" on label
❑ LPM-2256 [M] G.I. Blues 1964 50.00
—"Monaural" on label
❑ LSP-2256 [S] G.I. Blues 1960 100.00
—"Living Stereo" on label; with no sticker on front cover
❑ LSP-2256 [S] G.I. Blues 1960 600.00
—"Living Stereo" on label; with sticker on front cover advertising the presence of "Wooden Heart"
❑ LSP-2256 [S] G.I. Blues 1964 50.00
—"Stereo" on black label
❑ LSP-2256 [S] G.I. Blues 1968 40.00
—Orange label, non-flexible vinyl
❑ LSP-2256 [S] G.I. Blues 1971 20.00
—Orange label, flexible vinyl
❑ LSP-2256 [S] G.I. Blues 1975 25.00
—Tan label
❑ LSP-2256 [S] G.I. Blues 1976 12.00
—Black label, dog near top
❑ LSP-2256 [S] G.I. Blues 2003 20.00
—Red vinyl; "DRL 13273" in trail-off wax; "BMG Special Products" logo on back cover; from box "Elvis Top Album Collection Vol. 2"
❑ AFL1-2274 Welcome to My World 1977 12.00
—Black label, dog near top; includes copies with sticker wrapped around spine with new number
❑ APL1-2274 Welcome to My World 1977 20.00
—Black label, dog near top
❑ AQL1-2274 Welcome to My World 1979 10.00
—Black label, dog near top; includes copies with sticker wrapped around spine with new number
❑ LPM-2328 [M] His Hand in Mine 1960 120.00
—"Long Play" on label
❑ LPM-2328 [M] His Hand in Mine 1963 60.00
—"Mono" on label
❑ LPM-2328 [M] His Hand in Mine 1964 50.00
—"Monaural" on label
❑ LSP-2328 [S] His Hand in Mine 1960 200.00
—"Living Stereo" on label
❑ LSP-2328 [S] His Hand in Mine 1964 100.00
—"Stereo" and white "RCA Victor" on black label
❑ LSP-2328 [S] His Hand in Mine 1964 600.00
—"Stereo" and silver "RCA Victor" on black label
❑ LSP-2328 [S] His Hand in Mine 1968 50.00
—Orange label, non-flexible vinyl
❑ LSP-2328 [S] His Hand in Mine 197? 20.00
—Orange label, flexible vinyl
❑ LSP-2328 [S] His Hand in Mine 1975 20.00
—Tan label
❑ AHL1-2347 Greatest Hits, Vol. One 1981 25.00
—With embossed cover
❑ AHL1-2347 Greatest Hits, Vol. One 1983 15.00
—Without embossed cover
❑ AFL1-2370 [S] Something for Everybody 1977 12.00
—Black label, dog near top; includes copies with sticker wrapped around spine with new number
❑ LPM-2370 [M] Something for Everybody 1961 120.00
—"Long Play" on label; back cover advertises RCA Compact 33 singles and doubles
❑ LPM-2370 [M] Something for Everybody 1963 80.00
—"Mono" on label; back cover advertises "Viva Las Vegas" EP
❑ LPM-2370 [M] Something for Everybody 1964 50.00
—"Monaural" on label; back cover advertises "Viva Las Vegas" EP
❑ LSP-2370 [S] Something for Everybody 1961 200.00
—"Living Stereo" on label; back cover advertises RCA Compact 33 singles and doubles
❑ LSP-2370 [S] Something for Everybody 1963 100.00
—"Stereo" and silver "RCA Victor" on black label; back cover advertises Elvis' Christmas Album and His Hand in Mine LPs and "Viva Las Vegas" EP
❑ LSP-2370 [S] Something for Everybody 1964 50.00
—"Stereo" and white "RCA Victor" on black label; back cover advertises "Viva Las Vegas" EP
❑ LSP-2370 [S] Something for Everybody 1968 40.00
—Orange label, non-flexible vinyl; final back cover change advertises Elvis (NBC-TV Special), Elvis' Christmas Album and His Hand in Mine LPs
❑ LSP-2370 [S] Something for Everybody 1971 20.00
—Orange label, flexible vinyl
❑ LSP-2370 [S] Something for Everybody 1975 20.00
—Tan label
❑ LSP-2370 [S] Something for Everybody 1976 12.00
—Black label, dog near top
❑ LSP-2370 [S] Something for Everybody 2003 20.00
—Red vinyl; "DRL 13270" in trail-off wax; "BMG Special Products" logo on back cover; from box "Elvis Top Album Collection Vol. 1"
❑ AFL1-2426 [S] Blue Hawaii 1977 12.00
—Black label, dog near top; with sticker wrapped around spine with new number
❑ LPM-2426 [M] Blue Hawaii 1961 100.00
—"Long Play" on label; with sticker on cover advertising the presence of "Can't Help Falling in Love" and "Rock-a-Hula Baby"
❑ LPM-2426 [M] Blue Hawaii 1962 60.00
—"Long Play" on label; no sticker on front cover
❑ LPM-2426 [M] Blue Hawaii 1963 50.00
—"Mono" on label
❑ LPM-2426 [M] Blue Hawaii 1964 40.00
—"Monaural" on label
❑ LSP-2426 [S] Blue Hawaii 1961 150.00
—"Living Stereo" on label and upper right front cover; with sticker on cover advertising the presence of "Can't Help Falling in Love" and "Rock-a-Hula Baby"
❑ LSP-2426 [S] Blue Hawaii 1962 80.00
—"Living Stereo" on label and upper right front cover; no sticker on front cover
❑ LSP-2426 [S] Blue Hawaii 1964 50.00
—"Stereo" on label; "Victor Stereo" on upper right front cover
❑ LSP-2426 [S] Blue Hawaii 1968 40.00
—Orange label, non-flexible vinyl
❑ LSP-2426 [S] Blue Hawaii 197? 1000.
—One-of-a-kind blue vinyl pressing with black label, dog near top
❑ LSP-2426 [S] Blue Hawaii 1971 20.00
—Orange label, flexible vinyl
❑ LSP-2426 [S] Blue Hawaii 1975 20.00
—Tan label
❑ LSP-2426 [S] Blue Hawaii 1977 12.00
—Black label, dog near top
❑ LSP-2426 [S] Blue Hawaii 2003 20.00
—Red vinyl; "DRL 13358" in trail-off wax; "BMG Special Products" logo on back cover; from box "Elvis Top Album Collection Vol. 1"
❑ AFK1-2428 Moody Blue 1977 3000.
—Alternate cover slick (never put on an actual cover), with the words "Moody Blue" inside the large word "Elvis." See any late-1970s Elvis inner sleeve for a black and white photo of the scrapped cover; VG value 1500; VG+ value 2250
❑ AFL1-2428 Moody Blue 1977 10.00
—Blue vinyl
❑ AFL1-2428 Moody Blue 1977 200.00
—Black vinyl
❑ AFL1-2428 [DJ] Moody Blue 1977 2000.
—Experimental colored vinyl pressings (with no cover), any color or combination except blue or black
❑ AQL1-2428 Moody Blue 1979 25.00
—Reissue with new prefix
❑ AFL1-2523 [S] Pot Luck with Elvis 1977 12.00
—Black label, dog near top; includes copies with sticker wrapped around spine with new number
❑ LPM-2523 [M] Pot Luck with Elvis 1962 100.00
—"Long Play" on label
❑ LPM-2523 [M] Pot Luck with Elvis 1964 120.00
—"Monaural" on label
❑ LSP-2523 [S] Pot Luck with Elvis 1962 150.00
—"Living Stereo" on label
❑ LSP-2523 [S] Pot Luck with Elvis 1964 60.00
—"Stereo" on black label
❑ LSP-2523 [S] Pot Luck with Elvis 1968 40.00
—Orange label, non-flexible vinyl
❑ LSP-2523 [S] Pot Luck with Elvis 1975 20.00
—Tan label

Number	Title (A Side/B Side)	Yr	NM
❑ LSP-2523 [S]	Pot Luck with Elvis	1976	12.00
—Black label, dog near top			
❑ APL1-2558 [S]	Harum Scarum	1977	12.00
—Black label, dog near top			
❑ APL1-2560 [S]	Spinout	1977	12.00
—Black label, dog near top			
❑ APL1-2564 [S]	Double Trouble	1977	12.00
—Black label, dog near top; includes copies with sticker wrapped around spine with new number			
❑ APL1-2565	Clambake	1977	12.00
❑ APL1-2568 [S]	It Happened at the World's Fair	1977	12.00
❑ AFL2-2587 [(2)]	Elvis in Concert	197?	1000.
—Both records on translucent blue vinyl; possibly an in-house demo at the RCA Indianapolis pressing plant			
❑ APL2-2587 [(2)]	Elvis in Concert	1977	25.00
❑ APL2-2587 [(2)]	Elvis in Concert	2003	20.00
—Red vinyl; "DRL 13360" in trail-off wax; "This is a replica of the original packaging" on back cover and all inserts; "DRL-23360" on back cover; from box "Elvis Top Album Collection Vol. 1"			
❑ CPL2-2587 [(2)]	Elvis in Concert	1982	40.00
❑ AFL1-2621 [S]	Girls! Girls! Girls!	1977	12.00
—Black label, dog near top; includes copies with sticker wrapped around spine with new number			
❑ LPM-2621 [M]	Girls! Girls! Girls!	1962	80.00
—"Long Play" on label			
❑ LPM-2621 [M]	Girls! Girls! Girls!	1963	60.00
—"Mono" on label			
❑ LPM-2621 [M]	Girls! Girls! Girls!	1964	40.00
—"Monaural" on label			
❑ LPM/LSP-2621	Girls! Girls! Girls! Bonus 1963 Calendar	1962	150.00
—With listing of other Elvis records on back			
❑ LSP-2621 [S]	Girls! Girls! Girls!	1962	150.00
—"Living Stereo" on label			
❑ LSP-2621 [S]	Girls! Girls! Girls!	1964	60.00
—"Stereo" on black label			
❑ LSP-2621 [S]	Girls! Girls! Girls!	1968	40.00
—Orange label, non-flexible vinyl			
❑ LSP-2621 [S]	Girls! Girls! Girls!	1971	20.00
—Orange label, flexible vinyl			
❑ LSP-2621 [S]	Girls! Girls! Girls!	1975	25.00
—Tan label			
❑ LSP-2621 [S]	Girls! Girls! Girls!	1976	12.00
—Black label, dog near top			
❑ CPD2-2642 [(2)Q]	Aloha from Hawaii Via Satellite	1975	30.00
—Orange labels			
❑ CPD2-2642 [(2)Q]	Aloha from Hawaii Via Satellite	1977	80.00
—Black labels, dog near top			
❑ CPL2-2642 [(2)Q]	Aloha from Hawaii Via Satellite	1984	12.00
—New prefix; single-pocket instead of gatefold jacket			
❑ CPL2-2642 [(2)S]	Aloha from Hawaii Via Satellite	2003	20.00
—Red vinyl, "DRL 13359" in trail-off wax, "DRL-23359" on back cover, "BMG Special Products" logo on back cover, from box "Elvis Top Album Collection Vol. 2"			
❑ LPM-2697 [M]	It Happened at the World's Fair	1963	120.00
❑ LPM/LSP-2697	It Happened at the World's Fair Photo	1963	250.00
❑ LSP-2697 [S]	It Happened at the World's Fair	1963	200.00
—"Living Stereo" and silver "RCA Victor" on black label			
❑ LSP-2697 [S]	It Happened at the World's Fair	1964	80.00
—"Stereo" and white "RCA Victor" on black label			
❑ AFL1-2756 [S]	Fun in Acapulco	1977	12.00
—Black label, dog near top; includes copies with sticker wrapped around spine with new number			
❑ LPM-2756 [M]	Fun in Acapulco	1963	80.00
—"Mono" on label			
❑ LPM-2756 [M]	Fun in Acapulco	1964	50.00
—"Monaural" on label			
❑ LSP-2756 [S]	Fun in Acapulco	1963	100.00
—"Stereo" and silver "RCA Victor" on black label			
❑ LSP-2756 [S]	Fun in Acapulco	1964	60.00
—"Stereo" and white "RCA Victor" on black label			
❑ LSP-2756 [S]	Fun in Acapulco	1968	40.00
—Orange label, non-flexible vinyl			
❑ LSP-2756 [S]	Fun in Acapulco	1975	25.00
—Tan label			
❑ LSP-2756 [S]	Fun in Acapulco	1976	12.00
—Black label, dog near top			
❑ AFL1-2765 [S]	Elvis' Golden Records, Vol. 3	1977	12.00
—Black label, dog near top; includes copies with sticker wrapped around spine with new number			
❑ LPM-2765 [M]	Elvis' Golden Records, Vol. 3	1963	100.00
—"Mono" on label			
❑ LPM-2765 [M]	Elvis' Golden Records, Vol. 3	1964	60.00
—"Monaural" on label			
❑ LSP-2765 [S]	Elvis' Golden Records, Vol. 3	1963	150.00
—"Stereo" and silver "RCA Victor" on black label			
❑ LSP-2765 [S]	Elvis' Golden Records, Vol. 3	1964	50.00
—"Stereo" and white "RCA Victor" on black label			
❑ LSP-2765 [S]	Elvis' Golden Records, Vol. 3	1968	40.00
—Orange label, non-flexible vinyl			
❑ LSP-2765 [S]	Elvis' Golden Records, Vol. 3	1975	20.00
—Tan label			
❑ LSP-2765 [S]	Elvis' Golden Records, Vol. 3	1976	12.00
—Black label, dog near top			
❑ AFL1-2772	He Walks Beside Me	1978	25.00
—Includes 20-page photo booklet			

Elvis Presley, "She's Not You," RCA Victor 47-8041, 1962, **$40.**

Number	Title (A Side/B Side)	Yr	NM
❑ AFL1-2894 [S]	Kissin' Cousins	1977	12.00
—Black label, dog near top; includes copies with sticker wrapped around spine with new number			
❑ LPM-2894 [M]	Kissin' Cousins	1964	80.00
—"Mono" on label; front cover has a small black and white photo of six cast members in lower right			
❑ LPM-2894 [M]	Kissin' Cousins	1964	100.00
—"Monaural" on label; front cover has a small black and white photo of six cast members in lower right			
❑ LPM-2894 [M]	Kissin' Cousins	1964	200.00
—"Monaural" on label; front cover does NOT have black and white photo in lower right			
❑ LPM-2894 [M]	Kissin' Cousins	1964	200.00
—"Mono" on label; front cover does NOT have black and white photo in lower right			
❑ LSP-2894 [S]	Kissin' Cousins	1964	60.00
—"Stereo" and white "RCA Victor" on black label; all front covers have the cast photo in lower right			
❑ LSP-2894 [S]	Kissin' Cousins	1964	120.00
—"Stereo" and silver "RCA Victor" on black label; front cover has a small black and white photo of six cast members in lower right			
❑ LSP-2894 [S]	Kissin' Cousins	1964	200.00
—"Stereo" and silver "RCA Victor" on black label; front cover does NOT have black and white photo in lower right			
❑ LSP-2894 [S]	Kissin' Cousins	1968	40.00
—Orange label, non-flexible vinyl			
❑ LSP-2894 [S]	Kissin' Cousins	1971	20.00
—Orange label, flexible vinyl			
❑ LSP-2894 [S]	Kissin' Cousins	1975	25.00
—Tan label			
❑ LSP-2894 [S]	Kissin' Cousins	1976	12.00
—Black label, dog near top			
❑ LSP-2894 [S]	Kissin' Cousins	1976	1500.
—Black label, dog near top; blue vinyl			
❑ CPL1-2901	Elvis Sings for Children and Grownups Too!	1978	10.00
—With greeting card graphic printed on back cover, and no slits on back cover			
❑ CPL1-2901	Elvis Sings for Children and Grownups Too!	1978	20.00
—With two slits for removable greeting card on back cover (card should be with package)			
❑ AFL1-2999 [S]	Roustabout	1977	12.00
—Black label, dog near top; includes copies with sticker wrapped around spine with new number			

Number	Title (A Side/B Side)	Yr	NM
❑ LPM-2999 [M]	Roustabout	1964	100.00
—"Mono" on label			
❑ LPM-2999 [M]	Roustabout	1965	60.00
—"Monaural" on label			
❑ LSP-2999 [S]	Roustabout	1964	60.00
—"Stereo" and white "RCA Victor" on black label			
❑ LSP-2999 [S]	Roustabout	1964	600.00
—"Stereo" and silver "RCA Victor" on black label			
❑ LSP-2999 [S]	Roustabout	1968	40.00
—Orange label, non-flexible vinyl			
❑ LSP-2999 [S]	Roustabout	1971	20.00
—Orange label, flexible vinyl			
❑ LSP-2999 [S]	Roustabout	1975	20.00
—Tan label			
❑ LSP-2999 [S]	Roustabout	1976	12.00
—Black label, dog near top			
❑ LSP-2999 [S]	Roustabout	2003	20.00
—Red vinyl, "DRL 13269" in trail-off wax; "BMG Special Products" logo on back cover; from box "Elvis Top Album Collection Vol. 2"			
❑ CPL1-3078 [PD]	A Legendary Performer, Vol. 3	1978	25.00
—Picture disc applied to blue vinyl LP; with booklet (deduct 40% if missing)			
❑ CPL1-3082	A Legendary Performer, Vol. 3	1978	25.00
—Includes booklet (deduct 40% if missing); with die-cut hole in front cover			
❑ CPL1-3082	A Legendary Performer, Vol. 3	1986	8.00
—No die-cut hole in cover and no booklet			
❑ AQL1-3279	Our Memories of Elvis	1979	20.00
❑ AFL1-3338 [S]	Girl Happy	1977	12.00
—Black label, dog near top; includes copies with sticker wrapped around spine with new number			
❑ LPM-3338 [M]	Girl Happy	1965	60.00
❑ LSP-3338 [S]	Girl Happy	1965	60.00
—"Stereo" on black label			
❑ LSP-3338 [S]	Girl Happy	1968	40.00
—Orange label, non-flexible vinyl			
❑ LSP-3338 [S]	Girl Happy	1971	20.00
—Orange label, flexible vinyl			
❑ LSP-3338 [S]	Girl Happy	1975	25.00
—Tan label			
❑ LSP-3338 [S]	Girl Happy	1976	12.00
—Black label, dog near top			
❑ AQL1-3448	Our Memories of Elvis, Vol. 2	1979	20.00

Number | Title (A Side/B Side) | Yr | NM

❑ AFL1-3450 [P] Elvis for Everyone 1977 12.00
—Black label, dog near top; includes copies with sticker wrapped around spine with new number
❑ LPM-3450 [M] Elvis for Everyone 1965 60.00
❑ LSP-3450 [P] Elvis for Everyone 1965 60.00
—Black label, "Stereo" on label
❑ LSP-3450 [P] Elvis for Everyone 1968 40.00
—Orange label, non-flexible vinyl
❑ LSP-3450 [P] Elvis for Everyone 1971 20.00
—Orange label, flexible vinyl
❑ LSP-3450 [P] Elvis for Everyone 1975 20.00
—Tan label
❑ LSP-3450 [P] Elvis for Everyone 1976 12.00
—Black label, dog near top
❑ DJL1-3455 [DJ] Pure Elvis 1979 600.00
—Promo-only item for Our Memories of Elvis, Vol. 2; contains original version of five songs on one side, "unsweetened" versions of same songs on the other
❑ LPM-3468 [M] Harum Scarum 1965 60.00
❑ LPM/LSP-3468 Harum Scarum Bonus Photo 1965 60.00
❑ LSP-3468 [S] Harum Scarum 1965 60.00
—"Stereo" on black label
❑ LPM-3553 [M] Frankie and Johnny 1966 60.00
❑ LPM/LSP-3553 Frankie and Johnny Bonus Print 1966 60.00
❑ LSP-3553 [S] Frankie and Johnny 1966 60.00
—"Stereo" on black label
❑ AFL1-3643 [S] Paradise, Hawaiian Style 1977 12.00
—Black label, dog near top; includes copies with sticker wrapped around spine with new number
❑ LPM-3643 [M] Paradise, Hawaiian Style 1966 60.00
❑ LSP-3643 [S] Paradise, Hawaiian Style 1966 60.00
—"Stereo" on black label
❑ LSP-3643 [S] Paradise, Hawaiian Style 1968 40.00
—Orange label, non-flexible vinyl
❑ LSP-3643 [S] Paradise, Hawaiian Style 1971 20.00
—Orange label, flexible vinyl
❑ LSP-3643 [S] Paradise, Hawaiian Style 1975 15.00
—Tan label
❑ LSP-3643 [S] Paradise, Hawaiian Style 1976 12.00
—Black label, dog near top
❑ AYL1-3683 [S] Blue Hawaii 1980 10.00
—"Best Buy Series" reissue
❑ AYL1-3684 [S] Spinout 1980 8.00
—"Best Buy Series" reissue
❑ CPL8-3699 [(8)] Elvis Aron Presley 1980 100.00
—Box set; regular issue with booklet
❑ CPL8-3699 [(8)] Elvis Aron Presley 1980 250.00
—Box set; "Reviewer Series" edition (will be identified as such on the cover)
❑ LPM-3702 [M] Spinout 1966 60.00
❑ LPM/LSP-3702 Spinout Bonus Photo 1966 60.00
❑ LSP-3702 [S] Spinout 1966 60.00
—"Stereo" on black label
❑ DJL1-3729 [DJ] Elvis Aron Presley (Excerpts) 1980 120.00
—Promo-only excerpts of songs from box set
❑ AYL1-3732 Pure Gold 1980 8.00
—"Best Buy Series" reissue
❑ AYL1-3733 [R] King Creole 1980 8.00
—"Best Buy Series" reissue; includes copies with sticker wrapped around spine with new number
❑ AYL1-3734 [S] Harum Scarum 1980 8.00
—"Best Buy Series" reissue
❑ AYL1-3735 [S] G.I. Blues 1980 8.00
—"Best Buy Series" reissue
❑ AFL1-3758 [S] How Great Thou Art 1977 12.00
—Black label, dog near top; includes copies with sticker wrapped around spine with new number
❑ AQL1-3758 [S] How Great Thou Art 1979 10.00
—Reissue with new prefix
❑ LPM-3758 [M] How Great Thou Art 1967 60.00
—"Mono Dynagroove" on label
❑ LSP-3758 [S] How Great Thou Art 1967 60.00
—"Stereo Dynagroove" on black label
❑ LSP-3758 [S] How Great Thou Art 1968 40.00
—Orange label, non-flexible vinyl
❑ LSP-3758 [S] How Great Thou Art 1971 25.00
—Orange label, flexible vinyl
❑ LSP-3758 [S] How Great Thou Art 1975 20.00
—Tan label
❑ LSP-3758 [S] How Great Thou Art 1976 12.00
—Black label, dog near top
❑ DJL1-3781 [DJ] Elvis Aron Presley (Selections) 1980 120.00
—Promo-only complete versions of songs from box set
❑ LPM-3787 [M] Double Trouble 1967 60.00
—With bonus photo announcement on cover
❑ LPM-3787 [M] Double Trouble 1967 80.00
—With no bonus photo announcement on cover
❑ LPM/LSP-3787 Double Trouble Bonus Photo 1967 50.00
❑ LSP-3787 [S] Double Trouble 1967 60.00
—With bonus photo announcement on cover
❑ LSP-3787 [S] Double Trouble 1967 70.00
—With no bonus photo announcement on cover; black label "Stereo"
❑ LSP-3787 [S] Double Trouble 1968 40.00
—Orange label, non-flexible vinyl
❑ LSP-3787 [S] Double Trouble 1975 20.00
—Tan label
❑ LSP-3787 [S] Double Trouble 1977 12.00
—Black label, dog near top
❑ AYL1-3892 Elvis in Person at the International Hotel, Las Vegas, Nevada 1981 8.00
—"Best Buy Series" reissue

❑ AYM1-3893 The Sun Sessions 1981 8.00
—"Best Buy Series" reissue; includes copies with sticker wrapped around spine with new number
❑ LPM-3893 [M] Clambake 1967 250.00
❑ LPM/LSP-3893 Clambake Bonus Photo 1967 50.00
❑ LSP-3893 [S] Clambake 1967 60.00
❑ AYM1-3894 Elvis (NBC-TV Special) 1981 8.00
—"Best Buy Series" reissue
❑ AAL1-3917 Guitar Man 1981 30.00
❑ AFL1-3921 [P] Elvis' Gold Records, Vol. 4 1976 15.00
—Tan label with new prefix
❑ AFL1-3921 [P] Elvis' Gold Records, Vol. 4 1977 12.00
—Black label, dog near top; includes copies with sticker wrapped around spine with new number
❑ LPM-3921 [M] Elvis' Gold Records, Vol. 4 1968 2000.
—"Monaural" on label
❑ LSP-3921 [P] Elvis' Gold Records, Vol. 4 1968 40.00
—Orange label, non-flexible vinyl
❑ LSP-3921 [P] Elvis' Gold Records, Vol. 4 1968 50.00
—"Stereo" and white "RCA Victor" on black label
❑ LSP-3921 [P] Elvis' Gold Records, Vol. 4 197? 20.00
—Orange label, flexible vinyl
❑ LSP-3921 [P] Elvis' Gold Records, Vol. 4 1975 25.00
—Tan label
❑ LSP-3921 [P] Elvis' Gold Records, Vol. 4 1976 12.00
—Black label, dog near top
❑ AYL1-3935 [S] His Hand in Mine 1981 8.00
—"Best Buy Series" reissue; includes copies with sticker wrapped around spine with new number
❑ AYL1-3956 Elvis Country ("I'm 10,000 Years Old") 1981 8.00
—"Best Buy Series" reissue
❑ AFL1-3989 [S] Speedway 1977 12.00
—Black label, dog near top; includes copies with sticker wrapped around spine with new number
❑ LPM-3989 [M] Speedway 1968 2000.
❑ LPM/LSP-3989 Speedway Bonus Photo 1968 50.00
❑ LSP-3989 [S] Speedway 1968 40.00
—Orange label, non-flexible vinyl
❑ LSP-3989 [S] Speedway 1968 60.00
—"Stereo" on black label
❑ LSP-3989 [S] Speedway 1971 20.00
—Orange label, flexible vinyl
❑ LSP-3989 [S] Speedway 1975 20.00
—Tan label
❑ LSP-3989 [S] Speedway 1976 12.00
—Black label, dog near top
❑ CPL2-4031 [(2)] This Is Elvis 1980 15.00
❑ AFM1-4088 Elvis (NBC-TV Special) 1977 12.00
—Black label, dog near top; includes copies with sticker wrapped around spine with new number
❑ LPM-4088 Elvis (NBC-TV Special) 1968 40.00
—Orange label, non-flexible vinyl
❑ LPM-4088 Elvis (NBC-TV Special) 1971 30.00
—Orange label, flexible vinyl
❑ LPM-4088 Elvis (NBC-TV Special) 1975 20.00
—Tan label
❑ LPM-4088 Elvis (NBC-TV Special) 1976 15.00
—Black label, dog near top
❑ AYL1-4114 That's the Way It Is 1981 8.00
—"Best Buy Series" reissue; includes copies with sticker wrapped around spine with new number
❑ AYL1-4115 [S] Kissin' Cousins 1981 8.00
—"Best Buy Series" reissue; includes copies with sticker wrapped around spine with new number
❑ AYL1-4116 [S] Something for Everybody 1981 8.00
—"Best Buy Series" reissue; includes copies with sticker wrapped around spine with new number
❑ AFL1-4155 From Elvis in Memphis 1977 12.00
—Black label, dog near top; includes copies with sticker wrapped around spine with new number
❑ LSP-4155 From Elvis in Memphis 1969 40.00
—Orange label, non-flexible vinyl
❑ LSP-4155 From Elvis in Memphis Bonus Photo 1969 40.00
❑ LSP-4155 From Elvis in Memphis 1971 30.00
—Orange label, flexible vinyl
❑ LSP-4155 From Elvis in Memphis 1975 25.00
—Tan label
❑ LSP-4155 From Elvis in Memphis 1976 15.00
—Black label, dog near top
❑ AYL1-4232 [P] Elvis for Everyone 1982 8.00
—"Best Buy Series" reissue
❑ AFL1-4362 On Stage February, 1970 1977 12.00
—Black label, dog near top; includes copies with sticker wrapped around spine with new number
❑ AQL1-4362 On Stage February, 1970 1983 8.00
—Reissue with some cover changes
❑ LSP-4362 On Stage February, 1970 1970 40.00
—Orange label, non-flexible vinyl
❑ LSP-4362 On Stage February, 1970 1971 25.00
—Orange label, flexible vinyl
❑ LSP-4362 On Stage February, 1970 1975 25.00
—Tan label
❑ LSP-4362 On Stage February, 1970 1976 30.00
—Black label, dog near top
❑ CPL1-4395 Memories of Christmas 1982 15.00
—With greeting card (deduct 1/3 if missing)

❑ AFL1-4428 Elvis in Person at the International Hotel, Las Vegas, Nevada 1977 12.00
—Black label, dog near top; includes copies with sticker wrapped around spine with new number
❑ LSP-4428 Elvis in Person at the International Hotel, Las Vegas, Nevada 1970 50.00
—Orange label, non-flexible vinyl
❑ LSP-4428 Elvis in Person at the International Hotel, Las Vegas, Nevada 1971 40.00
—Orange label, flexible vinyl
❑ LSP-4428 Elvis in Person at the International Hotel, Las Vegas, Nevada 1975 25.00
—Tan label
❑ LSP-4428 Elvis in Person at the International Hotel, Las Vegas, Nevada 1976 15.00
—Black label, dog near top
❑ AFL1-4429 Back in Memphis 1977 12.00
—Black label, dog near top; with sticker wrapped around spine with new number
❑ LSP-4429 Back in Memphis 1970 40.00
—Orange label, non-flexible vinyl
❑ LSP-4429 Back in Memphis 1971 30.00
—Orange label, flexible vinyl
❑ LSP-4429 Back in Memphis 1975 25.00
—Tan label
❑ LSP-4429 Back in Memphis 1977 15.00
—Black label, dog near top
❑ AFL1-4445 That's the Way It Is 1977 12.00
—Black label, dog near top; includes copies with sticker wrapped around spine with new number
❑ LSP-4445 That's the Way It Is 1970 80.00
—Orange label, non-flexible vinyl
❑ LSP-4445 That's the Way It Is 1971 25.00
—Orange label, flexible vinyl
❑ LSP-4445 That's the Way It Is 1975 20.00
—Tan label
❑ LSP-4445 That's the Way It Is 1976 15.00
—Black label, dog near top
❑ AFL1-4460 Elvis Country ("I'm 10,000 Years Old") 1977 12.00
—Black label, dog near top; includes copies with sticker wrapped around spine with new number
❑ LSP-4460 Elvis Country ("I'm 10,000 Years Old") 197? 2000.
—Green vinyl; black label, dog near top
❑ LSP-4460 Elvis Country ("I'm 10,000 Years Old") Bonus Photo 1971 15.00
—Available in either orange-label pressing
❑ LSP-4460 Elvis Country ("I'm 10,000 Years Old") 1971 25.00
—Orange label, flexible vinyl
❑ LSP-4460 Elvis Country ("I'm 10,000 Years Old") 1971 40.00
—Orange label, non-flexible vinyl
❑ LSP-4460 Elvis Country ("I'm 10,000 Years Old") 1975 25.00
—Tan label
❑ LSP-4460 Elvis Country ("I'm 10,000 Years Old") 1976 15.00
—Black label, dog near top
❑ AFL1-4530 Love Letters from Elvis 1977 12.00
—Black label, dog near top; includes copies with sticker wrapped around spine with new number
❑ AHL1-4530 The Elvis Medley 1982 12.00
❑ LSP-4530 Love Letters from Elvis 1971 30.00
—Orange label; "Love Letters" on one line of cover; "from" on a second line, "Elvis" on a third line
❑ LSP-4530 Love Letters from Elvis 1971 40.00
—Orange label; "Love Letters from" on one line of cover, "Elvis" on a second line
❑ LSP-4530 Love Letters from Elvis 1975 25.00
—Tan label; "Love Letters" on one line of cover; "from" on a second line, "Elvis" on a third line
❑ LSP-4530 Love Letters from Elvis 1975 30.00
—Tan label; "Love Letters from" on one line of cover, "Elvis" on a second line
❑ LSP-4530 Love Letters from Elvis 1976 20.00
—Black label, dog near top
❑ LSP-4579 Elvis Sings the Wonderful World of Christmas Postcard 1971 20.00
❑ LSP-4579 Elvis Sings the Wonderful World of Christmas 1971 30.00
—Orange label. Bonus postcard is priced separately
❑ AFL1-4671 Elvis Now 1977 12.00
—Black label, dog near top; includes copies with sticker wrapped around spine with new number
❑ LSP-4671 Elvis Now 1972 30.00
—Orange label
❑ LSP-4671 Elvis Now 1975 25.00
—Tan label
❑ LSP-4671 Elvis Now 1976 15.00
—Black label, dog near top

Except when noted otherwise, VG = 25% of NM, and VG+ = 50% of NM. (Example: VG = $2.00, VG+ = $4.00 and NM = $8.00.)

Number	Title (A Side/B Side)	Yr	NM
❑ LSP-4671 [DJ]	Elvis Now	1972	100.00
—Orange label; with white timing sticker on front cover			
❑ AHL1-4678	I Was the One	1983	10.00
❑ AFL1-4690	He Touched Me	1977	12.00
—Black label, dog near top; includes copies with sticker wrapped around spine with new number			
❑ LSP-4690	He Touched Me	1972	40.00
—Orange label			
❑ LSP-4690	He Touched Me	1975	20.00
—Tan label			
❑ LSP-4690	He Touched Me	1976	15.00
—Black label, dog near top			
❑ LSP-4690 [DJ]	He Touched Me	1972	100.00
—Orange label; with white timing sticker on front cover			
❑ AFL1-4776	Elvis As Recorded at Madison Square Garden	1977	12.00
—Black label, dog near top; includes copies with sticker wrapped around spine with new number			
❑ AQL1-4776	Elvis As Recorded at Madison Square Garden	1980	8.00
—Another reissue with new prefix			
❑ LSP-4776	Elvis As Recorded at Madison Square Garden	1972	30.00
—Orange label			
❑ LSP-4776	Elvis As Recorded at Madison Square Garden	1975	20.00
—Tan label			
❑ LSP-4776	Elvis As Recorded at Madison Square Garden	1976	15.00
—Black label, dog near top			
❑ LSP-4776 [DJ]	Elvis As Recorded at Madison Square Garden	1972	100.00
—Orange label; with white timing sticker on front cover			
❑ CPL1-4848	A Legendary Performer, Vol. 4	1983	30.00
—Includes booklet (deduct 40% if missing); with die-cut hole in front cover			
❑ CPL1-4848	A Legendary Performer, Vol. 4	1986	20.00
—No die-cut hole in cover			
❑ AFL1-4941	Elvis' Gold Records, Vol. 5	1984	10.00
❑ CPM6-5172 [(6)]	A Golden Celebration	1984	100.00
❑ AFM1-5182	Rocker	1984	20.00
❑ AFM1-5196 [M]	Elvis' Golden Records	1984	20.00
—50th Anniversary reissue in mono with banner			
❑ AFM1-5197 [M]	Elvis' Gold Records Vol. 2 — 50,000,000 Elvis Fans Can't Be Wrong	1984	20.00
—50th Anniversary reissue in mono with banner			
❑ AFM1-5198 [M]	Elvis Presley	1984	20.00
—50th Anniversary reissue in mono with banner			
❑ AFM1-5199 [M]	Elvis	1984	20.00
—50th Anniversary reissue in mono with banner			
❑ AFL1-5353	A Valentine Gift for You	1985	10.00
—Black vinyl			
❑ AFL1-5353	A Valentine Gift for You	1985	20.00
—Red vinyl			
❑ AFL1-5418	Reconsider Baby	1985	20.00
—All copies on blue vinyl			
❑ AFL1-5430	Always on My Mind	1985	20.00
—All copies on purple vinyl			
❑ AFM1-5486 [M]	Elvis' Christmas Album	1985	15.00
—Same as LOC-1035; black vinyl with booklet			
❑ AFM1-5486 [M]	Elvis' Christmas Album	1985	20.00
—Same as LOC-1035; green vinyl with booklet			
❑ UNRM-5697/8 [DJ]	Special Christmas Programming	1967	1200.
—White label promo. Add 25% for script.			
❑ LSP-6020	From Memphis to Vegas/ From Vegas to Memphis Bonus Photos	1969	50.00
—Four different photos came with LP, but no more than two per set. Value is for any two different of the four photos.			
❑ LSP-6020 [(2)]	From Memphis to Vegas/ From Vegas to Memphis	1969	100.00
—Orange labels, non-flexible vinyl; with composers of "Words" correctly listed as Barry, Robin and Maurice Gibb			
❑ LSP-6020 [(2)]	From Memphis to Vegas/ From Vegas to Memphis	1969	150.00
—Orange labels, non-flexible vinyl; with composers of "Words" incorrectly listed as Tommy Boyce and Bobby Hart			
❑ LSP-6020 [(2)]	From Memphis to Vegas/ From Vegas to Memphis	1971	40.00
—Orange labels, flexible vinyl			
❑ LSP-6020 [(2)]	From Memphis to Vegas/ From Vegas to Memphis Bonus Photos	1975	30.00
—Tan labels			
❑ LSP-6020 [(2)]	From Memphis to Vegas/ From Vegas to Memphis Bonus Photos	1976	20.00
—Black label, dog near top			
❑ VPSX-6089 [(2)DJ]	Aloha from Hawaii Via Satellite	1973	2000.
—Orange or dark orange label; with white timing sticker on front cover			
❑ VPSX-6089 [(2)Q]	Aloha from Hawaii Via Satellite	1973	40.00
—Lighter orange labels, "RCA" on side			
❑ VPSX-6089 [(2)Q]	Aloha from Hawaii Via Satellite	1973	100.00
—Dark orange labels, "QuadraDisc" on top, "RCA" on bottom			
❑ VPSX-6089 [(2)Q]	Aloha from Hawaii Via Satellite	1973	5000.
—Stokely-Van Camp employee version with Saturn-shaped sticker on front cover with "Chicken of the Sea" and mermaid (beware: this has been counterfeited); VG value 2500; VG+ value 3750			
❑ LPM-6401	Worldwide 50 Gold Award Hits, Vol. 1 Photo Book	1970	40.00
—Two different books have been found in this LP box; price is for either			
❑ LPM-6401 [(4)]	Worldwide 50 Gold Award Hits, Vol. 1	1970	80.00
—Orange labels, non-flexible vinyl; with blurb for photo book on cover			
❑ LPM-6401 [(4)]	Worldwide 50 Gold Award Hits, Vol. 1	1970	80.00
—Orange labels, flexible vinyl; with blurb for photo book on cover			
❑ LPM-6401 [(4)]	Worldwide 50 Gold Award Hits, Vol. 1	1975	40.00
—Tan labels			
❑ LPM-6401 [(4)]	Worldwide 50 Gold Award Hits, Vol. 1	1977	30.00
—Black labels, dog near top			
❑ LPM-6402	The Other Sides: Worldwide 50 Gold Award Hits, Vol. 2 Poster	1971	25.00
❑ LPM-6402	The Other Sides: Worldwide 50 Gold Award Hits, Vol. 2 Swatch and Envelope	1971	25.00
❑ LPM-6402 [(4)]	The Other Sides: Worldwide 50 Gold Award Hits, Vol. 2	1971	70.00
—Orange labels, flexible vinyl; with blurb for inserts on cover			
❑ LPM-6402 [(4)]	The Other Sides: Worldwide 50 Gold Award Hits, Vol. 2	1975	30.00
—Tan labels			
❑ LPM-6402 [(4)]	The Other Sides: Worldwide 50 Gold Award Hits, Vol. 2	1977	20.00
—Black labels, dog near top			
❑ KKL1-7065	A Canadian Tribute	1978	20.00
—Gold vinyl, embossed cover			
❑ R 213690 [(2)]	Worldwide Gold Award Hits, Parts 1 & 2	1974	40.00
—RCA Record Club version; tan labels			
❑ R 213690 [(2)]	Worldwide Gold Award Hits, Parts 1 & 2	1974	120.00
—RCA Record Club version; one label is orange, the other is tan (orange label on both records is unknown)			
❑ R 213690 [(2)]	Worldwide Gold Award Hits, Parts 1 & 2	1977	25.00
—RCA Record Club version; black labels, dog near top			
❑ R 213736 [(2)S]	Aloha from Hawaii Via Satellite	1973	70.00
—RCA Record Club edition in stereo instead of quadraphonic; orange labels			
❑ R 213736 [(2)S]	Aloha from Hawaii Via Satellite	1975	60.00
—RCA Record Club edition in stereo instead of quadraphonic; tan labels			
❑ R 213736 [(2)S]	Aloha from Hawaii Via Satellite	1977	30.00
—RCA Record Club edition in stereo instead of quadraphonic; black labels, dog near top			
❑ R 214657 [(2)]	Worldwide Gold Award Hits, Parts 3 & 4	1978	20.00
—RCA Record Club version; black labels, dog near top			
❑ R 233299(e) [(2)]	Country Classics	1980	40.00
—RCA Music Service exclusive			
❑ R 234340 [(2)]	From Elvis with Love	1978	40.00
—RCA Music Service exclusive			
❑ R 244047 [(2)]	The Legendary Concert Performances	1978	40.00
—RCA Music Service exclusive			
❑ R 244069 [(2)]	Country Memories	1978	40.00
—RCA Music Service exclusive			

READER'S DIGEST

Number	Title (A Side/B Side)	Yr	NM
❑ 010/A [(7)]	His Greatest Hits	1983	60.00
—Yellow box			
❑ 010/A [(7)]	His Greatest Hits	1990	40.00
—White box			
❑ RD-10/A [(8)]	His Greatest Hits	1979	400.00
—White box			
❑ RBA-072/D	Great Hits of 1956-57	1987	20.00
❑ RD4A-181/D	Elvis Sings Inspirational Favorites	1983	20.00
❑ RB4-191/A [(7)]	The Legend Lives On	1986	60.00
❑ RDA-242/D	Elvis Sings Country Favorites	1984	60.00

SHOW-LAND

Number	Title (A Side/B Side)	Yr	NM
❑ LP-2001	The First of Elvis	1979	100.00

SILHOUETTE

Number	Title (A Side/B Side)	Yr	NM
❑ 10001/2 [(2)]	Personally Elvis	1979	30.00
—Interview records; no music			

SUN

Number	Title (A Side/B Side)	Yr	NM
❑ 1001	The Sun Years — Interviews and Memories	1977	8.00
—With "Nashville, U.S.A." on label; white cover with brown print			
❑ 1001	The Sun Years — Interviews and Memories	1977	15.00
—With "Nashville, U.S.A." on label; dark yellow cover with brown print			
❑ 1001	The Sun Years — Interviews and Memories	1977	25.00
—With "Memphis, Tennessee" on label			

TIME-LIFE

Number	Title (A Side/B Side)	Yr	NM
❑ STL-106 [(2)]	Elvis Presley: 1954-1961	1986	30.00
❑ STW-106	Country Music	1981	20.00
❑ STL-126 [(2)]	Elvis the King: 1954-1965	1989	80.00

PRESTON, BILLY

12-Inch Singles

MEGATONE

Number	Title (A Side/B Side)	Yr	NM
❑ 124	And Dance (5:41)/Kick It (5:46)	1984	6.00

MOTOWN

Number	Title (A Side/B Side)	Yr	NM
❑ PR-64 [DJ]	Give It Up Hot/Sock-It, Rocket	1979	12.00
❑ 4570	Since I Held You Close (3 versions)/It Don't Get Better Than This	1986	6.00

45s

A&M

Number	Title (A Side/B Side)	Yr	NM
❑ 1320	Outa-Space/I Wrote a Simple Song	1972	5.00
❑ 1340	Should Have Known Better/ The Bus	1972	5.00
❑ 1380	Slaughter/God Loves You	1972	5.00
❑ 1380 [PS]	Slaughter/God Loves You	1972	6.00
❑ 1411	Will It Go Round in Circles/ Blackbird	1973	4.00
❑ 1463	Space Race/We're Gonna Make It	1973	4.00
❑ 1463 [PS]	Space Race/We're Gonna Make It	1973	6.00
❑ 1492	You're So Unique/How Long Has the Train Been Gone	1973	4.00
❑ 1536	Creature Feature/My Soul Is a Witness	1974	4.00
❑ 1544	Nothing from Nothing/ My Soul Is a Witness	1974	4.00
❑ 1544 [PS]	Nothing from Nothing/ My Soul Is a Witness	1974	6.00
❑ 1644	Struttin'/You Are So Beautiful	1974	4.00
❑ 1735	Fancy Lady/Song of Joy	1975	4.00
❑ 1735 [PS]	Fancy Lady/Song of Joy	1975	6.00
❑ 1768	Do It While You Can/Song of Joy	1975	4.00
❑ 1892	Do What You Want/ I've Got the Spirit	1976	4.00
❑ 1925	Girl/Ecstasy	1977	4.00
❑ 1954	Wide Stride/When You Are Mine	1977	4.00
❑ 1980	A Whole New Thing/Wide Stride	1977	4.00
❑ 2012	I Really Miss You/Attitudes	1978	4.00
❑ 2071	Get Back/Space Race	1978	4.00

APPLE

Number	Title (A Side/B Side)	Yr	NM
❑ 1808	That's the Way God Planned It/ What About You	1969	8.00
❑ 1808	That's the Way God Planned It/ What About You	1972	8.00
—With "Mono" on both sides of record and reference to LP			
❑ 1808 [PS]	That's the Way God Planned It/ What About You	1969	10.00
❑ P-1808/PRO 6555 [DJ]	That's the Way God Planned It (Parts 1 & 2) (mono/stereo)	1969	60.00
❑ 1814	Everything's All Right/I Want to Thank You	1969	8.00
❑ 1817	All That I've Got (I'm Gonna Give It to You)/As I Get Older	1970	8.00
❑ 1817 [PS]	All That I've Got (I'm Gonna Give It to You)/As I Get Older	1970	15.00
❑ 1826	My Sweet Lord/Little Girl	1970	8.00
❑ 1826	My Sweet Lord/Little Girl	1970	12.00
—With star on A-side label			

APPLE/AMERICOM

Number	Title (A Side/B Side)	Yr	NM
❑ 1808P/M-433	That's the Way God Planned It (Edit)/What About You	1969	400.00
—Four-inch flexi-disc sold from vending machines			

CAPITOL

Number	Title (A Side/B Side)	Yr	NM
❑ 2309	Hey Brother (Part 1)/ Hey Brother (Part 2)	1968	8.00
❑ 5611	The Girl's Got "It"/The Night	1966	8.00
❑ 5660	In the Midnight Hour/Advice	1966	8.00
❑ 5730	Sunny/Let the Music Play	1966	8.00
❑ 5797	Phony Friends/Can't She Tell	1966	8.00

CONTRACT

Number	Title (A Side/B Side)	Yr	NM
❑ 5102	Volcano/Young Heartaches	1961	300.00

DERBY

Number	Title (A Side/B Side)	Yr	NM
❑ 1002	Greazee (Part 1)/(Part 2)	1963	25.00

MGM

Number	Title (A Side/B Side)	Yr	NM
❑ 14001	The Split/It's Just a Love Game	1968	8.00

MOTOWN

Number	Title (A Side/B Side)	Yr	NM
❑ 1470	It Will Come In Time/All I Wanted Was You	1979	4.00
❑ 1505	Sock-It Rocket/Hope	1981	4.00
❑ 1511	A Change Is Gonna Come/You	1981	4.00
❑ 1625	I'm Never Gonna Say Goodbye/Love You So	1982	4.00

MYRRH

Number	Title (A Side/B Side)	Yr	NM
❑ 216	One with the Lord/Universal Love	1979	8.00

VEE JAY

Number	Title (A Side/B Side)	Yr	NM
646	Don't Let the Sun Catch You Cryin'/(B-side unknown)	1965	—
—Canceled?			
653	Don't Let the Sun Catch You Cryin'/Billy's Bag	1965	10.00
692	Log Cabin/Drown in My Own Tears	1965	10.00

Albums

A&M

Number	Title (A Side/B Side)	Yr	NM
SP-3205	The Best of Billy Preston	1982	10.00
SP-3507	I Wrote a Simple Song	1971	12.00
SP-3516	Music Is My Life	1972	12.00
SP-3526	Everybody Likes Some Kind of Music	1973	12.00
SP-3637	Live European Tour	1974	12.00
SP-3645	The Kids & Me	1974	12.00
SP-4532	It's My Pleasure	1975	12.00
SP-4587	Billy Preston	1976	12.00
SP-4657	It's a Whole New Thing	1977	12.00

APPLE

Number	Title (A Side/B Side)	Yr	NM
ST-3359	That's the Way God Planned It	1969	50.00
—Cover has close-up of Billy Preston			
ST-3359	That's the Way God Planned It	1972	20.00
—Cover has multiple images of Billy Preston			
ST-3370	Encouraging Words	1970	20.00

BUDDAH

Number	Title (A Side/B Side)	Yr	NM
BDS-7502	Billy Preston	1969	15.00

CAPITOL

Number	Title (A Side/B Side)	Yr	NM
ST 2532 [S]	Wildest Organ in Town!	1966	40.00
T 2532 [M]	Wildest Organ in Town!	1966	30.00
DT 2607 [R]	Club Meetin'	1967	—
T 2607 [M]	Club Meetin'	1967	—
—The above versions of Club Meetin' may not exist			

DERBY

Number	Title (A Side/B Side)	Yr	NM
LPM-701 [M]	16 Year Old Soul	1963	250.00

EXODUS

Number	Title (A Side/B Side)	Yr	NM
304 [M]	Early Hits of 1965	1965	25.00

GNP CRESCENDO

Number	Title (A Side/B Side)	Yr	NM
GNPS-2071 [(2)]	Soul'd Out	1973	15.00

MCA

Number	Title (A Side/B Side)	Yr	NM
28037	Gospel Soul	198?	8.00
—Reissue of Peacock LP			

MOTOWN

Number	Title (A Side/B Side)	Yr	NM
M7-925	Late at Night	1980	10.00
M8-941	The Way I Am	1981	10.00
M7-958	Billy Preston & Syreeta	1981	10.00
6020 ML	Pressin' On	1982	10.00

MYRRH

Number	Title (A Side/B Side)	Yr	NM
MSB-6605	Behold	1978	12.00
MSB-6607	Universal Love	1979	12.00

PEACOCK

Number	Title (A Side/B Side)	Yr	NM
179	Gospel Soul	197?	12.00

PICKWICK

Number	Title (A Side/B Side)	Yr	NM
SPC-3315	Organ Transplant	197?	10.00

VEE JAY

Number	Title (A Side/B Side)	Yr	NM
LP-1123 [M]	The Most Exciting Organ Ever	1965	30.00
LPS-1123 [S]	The Most Exciting Organ Ever	1965	50.00
LP-1142 [M]	Greatest Hits	1966	30.00
LPS-1142 [S]	Greatest Hits	1966	50.00

PRESTON, BILLY, AND SYREETA

Also see each artist's individual listings.

45s

MOTOWN

Number	Title (A Side/B Side)	Yr	NM
1460	With You I'm Born Again/Go For It	1979	5.00
1477	With You I'm Born Again/All I Wanted Was You	1979	4.00
1520	Searchin'/Hey You	1981	4.00
1522	Just for You (Put the Boogie in Your Body)/Hey You	1981	4.00

TAMLA

Number	Title (A Side/B Side)	Yr	NM
54312	Dance For Me Children/One More Time for Love	1980	4.00
54319	Please Stay/Signed, Sealed, Delivered (I'm Yours)	1980	4.00

PRESTON, JACKIE

45s

HIT

Number	Title (A Side/B Side)	Yr	NM
144	Tottle-Dee Doodle, Dee Doo/We'll Sing in the Sunshine	1964	8.00
—B-side by Betty Coleson			

PRESTON, JOHN

45s

HIT

Number	Title (A Side/B Side)	Yr	NM
69	Blue on Blue/Those Lazy-Hazy-Crazy Days of Summer	1963	8.00
—B-side by Frank Clark			
92	Walking Proud/500 Miles Away from Home	1963	8.00
—B-side by Mitch Wood			
155	Ringo/The Spirit of This Land	1964	8.00
—B-side by Charlie Rogers			
177	Speaking of Broken Hearts/You're Nobody Till Somebody Loves You	1965	8.00
—B-side by Marty Wood			
194	You Were Gone/Can't You Hear My Heartbeat	1965	8.00
—B-side by Jackie Harris			
207	Long Lonely Nights/Once You've Been in Love	1965	8.00

PRESTON, JOHNNY

45s

ABC

Number	Title (A Side/B Side)	Yr	NM
11085	I'm Only Human/There's No One Like You	1968	10.00
11187	Kick the Can/I've Just Been Wasting My Time	1969	10.00

HALLWAY

Number	Title (A Side/B Side)	Yr	NM
1201	All Around the World/Just Plain Hurt	1964	15.00
1204	Willie and the Hand Jive/I've Got My Eyes on You	1964	15.00
1927	Running Bear '65/Dedicated to the One I Love	1965	15.00

IMPERIAL

Number	Title (A Side/B Side)	Yr	NM
5924	This Little Bitty Tear/The Day the World Stood Still	1963	10.00
5947	I've Got My Eyes on You/I Couldn't Take It Again	1963	10.00

MERCURY

Number	Title (A Side/B Side)	Yr	NM
10027 [S]	Cradle of Love/City of Tears	1960	50.00
10036 [S]	Feel So Fine/I'm Starting to Go Steady	1960	60.00
71474	Running Bear/My Heart Knows	1959	25.00
71598 [M]	Cradle of Love/City of Tears	1960	20.00
71598 [PS]	Cradle of Love/City of Tears	1960	30.00
71651 [M]	Feel So Fine/I'm Starting to Go Steady	1960	20.00
71651 [PS]	Feel So Fine/I'm Starting to Go Steady	1960	30.00
71691	Charming Billy/Up in the Air	1960	20.00
71728	New Baby for Christmas/(I Want a) Rock and Roll Guitar	1960	20.00
71761	Leave My Kitten Alone/Token of Love	1961	20.00
71761 [PS]	Leave My Kitten Alone/Token of Love	1961	30.00
71803	I Feel Good/Willy Walk	1961	20.00
71803 [PS]	I Feel Good/Willy Walk	1961	40.00
71865	Let Them Talk/She Once Belonged to Me	1961	20.00
71908	Free Me/Kissin' Tree	1961	20.00
71908 [PS]	Free Me/Kissin' Tree	1961	30.00
71951	Let's Leave It That Way/Broken Hearts Anonymous	1962	15.00
72049	Let the Big Boss Man (Pull You Through)/The Day After Forever	1962	15.00

TCF HALL

Number	Title (A Side/B Side)	Yr	NM
101	Running Bear '65/Dedicated to the One I Love	1965	10.00
110	Sounds Like Trouble/You Can Make It If You Try	1965	15.00
120	I'm Askin' Forgiveness/Good Good Lovin'	1965	10.00

Albums

MERCURY

Number	Title (A Side/B Side)	Yr	NM
MG-20592 [M]	Running Bear	1960	100.00
MG-20609 [M]	Come Rock with Me	1960	100.00
SR-60250 [S]	Running Bear	1960	150.00
—Black label			
SR-60250 [S]	Running Bear	1981	12.00
—Reissue on Chicago skyline label			
SR-60609 [S]	Come Rock with Me	1960	150.00

WING

Number	Title (A Side/B Side)	Yr	NM
MGW-12246 [M]	Running Bear	1963	20.00
SRW-16246 [S]	Running Bear	1963	25.00

PRESTON, MIKE

45s

LONDON

Number	Title (A Side/B Side)	Yr	NM
1834	A House, a Car and a Wedding Ring/My Lucky Love	1958	12.00
1865	Girl Without a Heart/In Surabaya	1959	10.00
1903	'Till Tomorrow/An Ordinary Couple	1960	10.00
1981	Girl Without a Heart/Marry Me	1960	10.00
9601	Careless Love/Little Grain of Sand	1963	10.00

PRESTON, TERRY

See FERLIN HUSKY.

PRETENDERS

12-Inch Singles

POLYDOR

Number	Title (A Side/B Side)	Yr	NM
632 [DJ]	Windows of the World/1969	1988	8.00

SIRE

Number	Title (A Side/B Side)	Yr	NM
PRO-A-1085 [DJ]	Back on the Chain Gang/My City Was Gone	1982	8.00
PRO-A-2106 [DJ]	Middle of the Road/2000 Miles	1983	6.00
PRO-A-2128 [DJ]	Show Me/Time the Avenger	1984	7.00
PRO-A-2154 [DJ]	Thin Line Between Love and Hate/Thumbelina	1984	7.00
PRO-A-2627 [DJ]	Room Full of Mirrors (same on both sides)	1986	6.00
PRO-A-2677 [DJ]	Tradition of Love (long)/Tradition of Love (edit)	1986	6.00
PRO-A-2732 [DJ]	Hymn to Her (Edit)/Hym to Her (LP Version)	1986	7.00

45s

AMERICAN PIE

Number	Title (A Side/B Side)	Yr	NM
9014	Stop Your Sobbing/Talk of the Town	198?	3.00
—Reissue label; first appearance of B-side on U.S. stock 45			

MCA

Number	Title (A Side/B Side)	Yr	NM
54615	I'm Not in Love/I'm Not in Love (instrumental)	1993	3.00

POLYDOR

Number	Title (A Side/B Side)	Yr	NM
887816-7	Window of the World/1969	1988	3.00
887816-7 [PS]	Window of the World/1969	1988	3.00

SIRE

Number	Title (A Side/B Side)	Yr	NM
GSRE 0448	Back on the Chain Gang/My City Was Gone	198?	3.00
—"Back to Back Hits" reissue			
GSRE 0474	Brass in Pocket/Middle of the Road	198?	3.00
—"Back to Back Hits" reissue			
GSRE 0496	Show Me/Thin Line Between Love and Hate	198?	3.00
—"Back to Back Hits" reissue			
PRO-S-942 [DJ]	Message of Love/Talk of the Town	1981	10.00
18160	I'll Stand By You/Rebel Rock Me	1994	3.00
18163	Night in My Veins/Angel of the Morning	1994	3.00
19820	Never Do That	1990	—
—Cassette only			
28354	Hymn to Her (She Will Always Carry On)/Tradition of Love	1987	3.00
28354 [PS]	Hymn to Her (She Will Always Carry On)/Tradition of Love	1987	3.00
28496	My Baby/Room Full of Mirrors	1987	3.00
28496 [PS]	My Baby/Room Full of Mirrors	1987	3.00
28630	Don't Get Me Wrong/Dance!	1986	3.00
28630 [PS]	Don't Get Me Wrong/Dance!	1986	3.00
29249	Thin Line Between Love and Hate/Time the Avenger	1984	3.00
29249 [PS]	Thin Line Between Love and Hate/Time the Avenger	1984	3.00
29317	Show Me/Fast or Slow (The Law Is The Law)	1984	3.00
29317 [PS]	Show Me/Fast or Slow (The Law Is The Law)	1984	3.00
29444	Middle of the Road/2000 Miles	1983	3.00
29444 [PS]	Middle of the Road/2000 Miles	1983	3.00
29840	Back on the Chain Gang/My City Was Gone	1982	3.00
29840 [PS]	Back on the Chain Gang/My City Was Gone	1982	3.00
49181	Brass in Pocket (I'm Special)/Space Invader	1980	4.00
49506	Stop Your Sobbing/Phone Call	1980	4.00
49506 [PS]	Stop Your Sobbing/Phone Call	1980	8.00
49533	Kid/Tattooed Love Boys	1980	4.00
49819	Louie Louie/In the Sticks	1981	4.00
49819 [PS]	Louie Louie/In the Sticks	1981	4.00
49861	I Go to Sleep/Waste Not Want Not	1981	4.00

WARNER BROS.

Number	Title (A Side/B Side)	Yr	NM
28259	If There Was a Man/Into Vienna	1987	3.00
—B-side by John Barry			

Number	Title (A Side/B Side)	Yr	NM
❑ 28259 [PS]	If There Was a Man/Into Vienna	1987	3.00

—B-side by John Barry

WEA/REAL

Number	Title (A Side/B Side)	Yr	NM
❑ ARE 20	2000 Miles/Fast Or Slow (The Law's The Law)	1983	5.00
❑ ARE 20 [PS]	2000 Miles/Fast Or Slow (The Law's The Law)	1983	5.00

—Above record and sleeve are U.K. imports

Albums

NAUTILUS

Number	Title (A Side/B Side)	Yr	NM
❑ NR-38	Pretenders	1982	50.00

—Audiophile vinyl

SIRE

Number	Title (A Side/B Side)	Yr	NM
❑ MINI 3563 [EP]	Extended Play	1981	10.00
❑ SRK 3572	Pretenders II	1981	10.00
❑ SRK 6083	Pretenders	1980	10.00
❑ 23980	Learning to Crawl	1983	10.00
❑ 23980 [DJ]	Learning to Crawl	1983	12.00

—Promo-only Quiex II pressing; otherwise, same as above

Number	Title (A Side/B Side)	Yr	NM
❑ 25488	Get Close	1986	10.00
❑ 25664	The Singles	1987	10.00
❑ 26219	Packed!	1990	12.00
❑ R 133248	The Singles	1987	12.00

—BMG Direct Marketing edition; otherwise, same as 25664

Number	Title (A Side/B Side)	Yr	NM
❑ R 144453	Get Close	1986	12.00

—RCA Music Service edition

WARNER BROS.

Number	Title (A Side/B Side)	Yr	NM
❑ WBMS-114 [DJ]	Pretenders Live	1980	20.00

—Part of "The Warner Bros. Music Show" series; comes in red die-cut cover

Number	Title (A Side/B Side)	Yr	NM
❑ WBMS-121 [DJ]	Pretenders Live (Star Fleet)	1982	20.00

—Part of "The Warner Bros. Music Show" series; comes in black cover with white sticker

Number	Title (A Side/B Side)	Yr	NM
❑ WBMS-142 [DJ]	Get Close Interview	1987	20.00

—Part of "The Warner Bros. Music Show" series

PRETENDERS, THE (2) Also see JIMMY JONES.

45s

APT

Number	Title (A Side/B Side)	Yr	NM
❑ 25026	Blue and Lonely/Daddy Needs Baby	1959	500.00

CENTRAL

Number	Title (A Side/B Side)	Yr	NM
❑ 2605	Blue and Lonely/Daddy Needs Baby	1958	1500.

PRETENDERS, THE (3)

45s

BETHLEHEM

Number	Title (A Side/B Side)	Yr	NM
❑ 3050	The Day You Are Mine/Ding Dong Bells	1962	200.00

PRETENDERS, THE (4)

45s

CHATTAHOOCHIE

Number	Title (A Side/B Side)	Yr	NM
❑ 685	Pepita's Theme/Tijuana Taxi	1965	20.00

PRETENDERS, THE (U) The Rama and Whirlin' Disc records could be by group (2). None of these, or any of the above, are by the group fronted by Chrissie Hynde; they are outside the scope of this book.

45s

LOST-NITE

Number	Title (A Side/B Side)	Yr	NM
❑ 353	Close Your Eyes/Part-Time Sweetheart	197?	5.00

—Reissue

POWER-MARTIN

Number	Title (A Side/B Side)	Yr	NM
❑ 1001	Smile/I'm So Happy	1961	100.00

RAMA

Number	Title (A Side/B Side)	Yr	NM
❑ 198	Possessive Love/I've Got to Have You Baby	1956	120.00

WHIRLIN' DISC

Number	Title (A Side/B Side)	Yr	NM
❑ 106	Close Your Eyes/Part-Time Sweetheart	1957	250.00

PRETTY BOY See DON COVAY.

PRETTY THINGS, THE

45s

FONTANA

Number	Title (A Side/B Side)	Yr	NM
❑ 1508	I Can Never Say/Honey, I Need	1965	25.00
❑ 1518	Cry to Me/Judgment Day	1965	15.00
❑ 1518	Cry to Me/I Can Never Say	1965	35.00
❑ 1540	Midnight to Six Man/Can't Stand Pain	1966	25.00
❑ 1550	Come See Me/Judgment Day	1966	25.00
❑ 1550	Come See Me/Progress	1966	35.00
❑ 1916	Big Boss Man/Rosalyn	1964	25.00
❑ 1941	Don't Bring Me Down/We'll Be Together	1964	25.00

LAURIE

Number	Title (A Side/B Side)	Yr	NM
❑ 3458	Talkin' About the Good Times/Walking Through My Dreams	1968	50.00

NORTON

Number	Title (A Side/B Side)	Yr	NM
❑ 45-084	All Light Up/Vivian Prince	1999	2.00
❑ 45-084 [PS]	All Light Up/Vivian Prince	1999	2.00
❑ PT 109	All Light Up/Pretty Beat	1999	4.00

—Red vinyl, small hole, called "The Pretty Things U.S. Tour 45"

RARE EARTH

Number	Title (A Side/B Side)	Yr	NM
❑ 5005	Private Sorrow/Balloon Burning	1969	25.00

SWAN SONG

Number	Title (A Side/B Side)	Yr	NM
❑ 70104	Come Home Momma/Joey	1975	5.00
❑ 70107	It Isn't Rock & Roll/Remember That Boy	1975	5.00

7-Inch Extended Plays

NORTON

Number	Title (A Side/B Side)	Yr	NM
❑ EP-501	Rosalyn/Judgement Day//Roadrunner/Don't Bring Me Down	1999	2.00
❑ EP-501 [PS]	Rosalyn	1999	2.00
❑ EP-502	Big City/I Can Never Say//Get Yourself Home/Honey I Need	1999	2.00
❑ EP-502 [PS]	Big City	1999	2.00
❑ EP-503	You Don't Believe Me/Buzz the Jerk//You'll Never Do It Baby/Come See Me	1999	2.00
❑ EP-503 [PS]	Buzz the Jerk	1999	2.00
❑ EP-504	Midnight to Six Man/Can't Stand the Pain//LSD/Me Needing You	1999	2.00
❑ EP-504 [PS]	Midnight to Six Man	1999	2.00
❑ EP-505	A House in the Country/Progress//Tripping/Photographer	1999	2.00
❑ EP-505 [PS]	A House in the Country	1999	2.00

Albums

BIG BEAT

Number	Title (A Side/B Side)	Yr	NM
❑ WIK-24	Live at Heartbreak Hotel	1985	10.00

FONTANA

Number	Title (A Side/B Side)	Yr	NM
❑ MGF-27544 [M]	The Pretty Things	1965	80.00
❑ SRF-67544 [P]	The Pretty Things	1965	80.00

NORTON

Number	Title (A Side/B Side)	Yr	NM
❑ 282	The Pretty Things	2000	12.00
❑ 283	Get the Picture?	2000	12.00
❑ 284	Midnight to Six	2000	12.00
❑ TED-1001 [10]	Defecting Grey	2000	8.00

RARE EARTH

Number	Title (A Side/B Side)	Yr	NM
❑ RS 506	S.F. Sorrow	1969	30.00

—Later copies are standard in shape

Number	Title (A Side/B Side)	Yr	NM
❑ RS 506	S.F. Sorrow	1969	50.00

—Original covers are rounded at top

Number	Title (A Side/B Side)	Yr	NM
❑ RS 515	Parachute	1970	20.00
❑ R 549R2 [(2)]	Real Pretty	1976	15.00

—The two prior Rare Earth albums in one package

SIRE

Number	Title (A Side/B Side)	Yr	NM
❑ SASH-3713 [(2)]	The Vintage Years	1976	15.00

SWAN SONG

Number	Title (A Side/B Side)	Yr	NM
❑ SS 8411	Silk Torpedo	1975	10.00
❑ SS 8414	Savage Eye	1976	10.00

WARNER BROS.

Number	Title (A Side/B Side)	Yr	NM
❑ BS 2680	Freeway Madness	1973	10.00
❑ BSK 3466	Cross Talk	1980	10.00

PREVIN, ANDRE

45s

COLUMBIA

Number	Title (A Side/B Side)	Yr	NM
❑ 30833 [S]	(titles unknown)	1960	10.00
❑ 30834 [S]	(titles unknown)	1960	10.00
❑ 30835 [S]	(titles unknown)	1960	10.00
❑ 30836 [S]	(titles unknown)	1960	10.00
❑ 30837 [S]	(titles unknown)	1960	10.00
❑ 31074 [S]	(titles unknown)	1961	10.00
❑ 31075 [S]	(titles unknown)	1961	10.00
❑ 31076 [S]	(titles unknown)	1961	10.00
❑ 31077 [S]	(titles unknown)	1961	10.00
❑ 31078 [S]	(titles unknown)	1961	10.00
❑ 31540 [S]	(titles unknown)	1962	10.00
❑ 31541 [S]	(titles unknown)	1962	10.00
❑ 31542 [S]	(titles unknown)	1962	10.00
❑ 31543 [S]	(titles unknown)	1962	10.00
❑ 31544 [S]	(titles unknown)	1962	10.00

—Anyone who can fill in these gaps — the above 15 all are Columbia "Stereo 7" singles — please let us know.

Number	Title (A Side/B Side)	Yr	NM
❑ 41683	Love Me or Leave Me/Like Love	1960	8.00
❑ 42596	Song from "Two for the Seesaw"/Song from "Long Day's Journey Into Night"	1962	8.00
❑ 43136	Goodbye, Charlie/Kiss Me, Stupid	1964	8.00
❑ JZSP 55071/0 [DJ]	God Rest Ye Merry, Gentlemen/Let No Walls Divide	1961	12.00

—B-side by Doris Day

DECCA

Number	Title (A Side/B Side)	Yr	NM
❑ 25529	Moonlight Becomes You/Let's Fall in Love	1961	8.00

MGM

Number	Title (A Side/B Side)	Yr	NM
❑ 12792	Like Young/Young Man's Lament	1959	10.00

—With David Rose

Number	Title (A Side/B Side)	Yr	NM
❑ 12840	Young and Tender/Too Young to Be True	1959	10.00

RCA VICTOR

Number	Title (A Side/B Side)	Yr	NM
❑ 47-2764	But Not for Me/Hallelujah	1949	15.00
❑ 47-2765	My Shining Hour/This Can't Be Love	1949	15.00
❑ 47-2766	Mad About the Boy/Just One of Those Things	1949	15.00

—The above three comprise box set WP-214, "Andre Previn Plays the Piano"

Number	Title (A Side/B Side)	Yr	NM
❑ 47-2767	I Didn't Know What Time It Was/Should I	1949	15.00
❑ 47-3080	Dardanella/The Gypsy in My Soul	1949	15.00
❑ 47-3123	Anything Goes/Bewitched, Bothered and Bewildered	1949	15.00
❑ 47-3124	You're the Top/I'm Old Fashioned	1949	15.00
❑ 47-3125	Who Cares/Who	1949	15.00

—The above three comprise a box set

Number	Title (A Side/B Side)	Yr	NM
❑ 47-3263	I Didn't Know What Time It Was/Should I	1949	15.00
❑ 47-3836	Three Little Words/Thinking of You	1950	15.00
❑ 47-3837	Who's Sorry Now/All Alone	1950	15.00
❑ 47-4161	Skylark/You Took Advantage of Me	1951	15.00
❑ 47-4163	Dearly Beloved/Love Is Just Around the Corner	1951	15.00
❑ 47-4351	Lullaby of Broadway/I Only Have Eyes for You	1951	12.00
❑ 47-4352	This Head of Mine/September in the Rain	1951	12.00
❑ 47-4353	This Heart of Mine/I Know Why and So Do You	1951	12.00
❑ 47-4354	I'll String Along/Jeepers Creepers	1951	12.00

—The above four comprise a box set

Number	Title (A Side/B Side)	Yr	NM
❑ 47-4780	The Story of a Piano (Part 1)/Romance, Op. 28, No. 2	1952	12.00
❑ 47-4781	The Story of a Piano (Part 2)/Valse Brilliance in A Minor	1952	12.00
❑ 47-4782	The Story of a Piano (Part 3)/Traumere Op. 15	1952	12.00
❑ 47-4783	The Story of a Piano (Part 4)/Adagio Cantabile	1952	12.00

—The above four comprise a box set

Number	Title (A Side/B Side)	Yr	NM
❑ 47-9122	Theme from Hotel/The Bad Guys	1967	6.00
❑ WP 214 [PS]	Andre Previn Plays the Piano	1949	15.00

—Empty box for 47-2764, 47-2765 and 47-2766

UNITED ARTISTS

Number	Title (A Side/B Side)	Yr	NM
❑ 50080	Bad Guys/Waltz of the Fortune Cookie	1966	6.00

Albums

ANGEL

Number	Title (A Side/B Side)	Yr	NM
❑ DS-37780	A Different Kind of Blues	1981	10.00
❑ S-1-37799	It's a Breeze	1981	10.00

COLUMBIA

Number	Title (A Side/B Side)	Yr	NM
❑ CL 1437 [M]	Like Love	1960	15.00

—Red and black label with six "eye" logos

Number	Title (A Side/B Side)	Yr	NM
❑ CL 1437 [M]	Like Love	1963	12.00

—Red label with "Guaranteed High Fidelity" or "360 Sound Mono" at bottom

Number	Title (A Side/B Side)	Yr	NM
❑ CL 1495 [M]	Rhapsody in Blue	1960	15.00

—Red and black label with six "eye" logos

Number	Title (A Side/B Side)	Yr	NM
❑ CL 1495 [M]	Rhapsody in Blue	1963	12.00

—Red label with "Guaranteed High Fidelity" or "360 Sound Mono" at bottom

Number	Title (A Side/B Side)	Yr	NM
❑ CL 1530 [M]	Give My Regards to Broadway	1960	20.00

—Red and black label with six "eye" logos

Number	Title (A Side/B Side)	Yr	NM
❑ CL 1530 [M]	Give My Regards to Broadway	1963	12.00

—Red label with "Guaranteed High Fidelity" or "360 Sound Mono" at bottom

Number	Title (A Side/B Side)	Yr	NM
❑ CL 1569 [M]	Camelot	1961	20.00

—Red and black label with six "eye" logos

Number	Title (A Side/B Side)	Yr	NM
❑ CL 1569 [M]	Camelot	1963	12.00

—Red label with "Guaranteed High Fidelity" or "360 Sound Mono" at bottom

Number	Title (A Side/B Side)	Yr	NM
❑ CL 1595 [M]	Thinking of You	1961	20.00

—Red and black label with six "eye" logos

Number	Title (A Side/B Side)	Yr	NM
❑ CL 1595 [M]	Thinking of You	1963	12.00

—Red label with "Guaranteed High Fidelity" or "360 Sound Mono" at bottom

Number	Title (A Side/B Side)	Yr	NM
❑ CL 1649 [M]	A Touch of Elegance	1961	20.00

—Red and black label with six "eye" logos

Number	Title (A Side/B Side)	Yr	NM
❑ CL 1741 [M]	Mack the Knife and Other Kurt Weill Music	1962	20.00

—Red and black label with six "eye" logos

Number	Title (A Side/B Side)	Yr	NM
❑ CL 1741 [M]	Mack the Knife and Other Kurt Weill Music	1963	12.00

—Red label with "Guaranteed High Fidelity" or "360 Sound Mono" at bottom

P

Number	Title (A Side/B Side)	Yr	NM
❑ CL 1786 [M]	Faraway Part of Town	1962	20.00
—Red and black label with six "eye" logos			
❑ CL 1786 [M]	Faraway Part of Town	1963	12.00
—Red label with "Guaranteed High Fidelity" or "360 Sound Mono" at bottom			
❑ CL 1888 [M]	The Light Fantastic	1962	20.00
—Red and black label with six "eye" logos			
❑ CL 1888 [M]	The Light Fantastic	1963	12.00
—Red label with "Guaranteed High Fidelity" or "360 Sound Mono" at bottom			
❑ CL 1933 [M]	Sittin' on a Rainbow: The Music of Harold Arlen	1963	15.00
—"Guaranteed High Fidelity" on label			
❑ CL 2034 [M]	Andre Previn in Hollywood	1963	15.00
—Red label with "Guaranteed High Fidelity" at bottom			
❑ CL 2034 [M]	Andre Previn in Hollywood	1966	12.00
—Red label with "360 Sound Mono" at bottom			
❑ CL 2114 [M]	The Soft and Swinging Music of Jimmy McHugh	1964	15.00
—Red label with "Guaranteed High Fidelity" at bottom			
❑ CL 2114 [M]	The Soft and Swinging Music of Jimmy McHugh	1966	12.00
—Red label with "360 Sound Mono" at bottom			
❑ CL 2195 [M]	My Fair Lady	1964	15.00
—Red label with "Guaranteed High Fidelity" at bottom			
❑ CL 2195 [M]	My Fair Lady	1966	12.00
—Red label with "360 Sound Mono" at bottom			
❑ CL 2294 [M]	Popular Previn	1965	15.00
—Red label with "Guaranteed High Fidelity" at bottom			
❑ CL 2294 [M]	Popular Previn	1966	12.00
—Red label with "360 Sound Mono" at bottom			
❑ CS 8233 [S]	Like Love	1960	20.00
—Red and black label with six "eye" logos			
❑ CS 8233 [S]	Like Love	1963	15.00
—Red label with "360 Sound Stereo" at bottom			
❑ CS 8286 [S]	Rhapsody in Blue	1960	20.00
—Red and black label with six "eye" logos			
❑ CS 8286 [S]	Rhapsody in Blue	1963	15.00
—Red label with "360 Sound Stereo" at bottom			
❑ CS 8330 [S]	Give My Regards to Broadway	1960	15.00
—Red label with "360 Sound Stereo" at bottom			
❑ CS 8330 [S]	Give My Regards to Broadway	1960	25.00
—Red and black label with six "eye" logos			
❑ CS 8369 [S]	Camelot	1961	25.00
—Red and black label with six "eye" logos			
❑ CS 8369 [S]	Camelot	1963	15.00
—Red label with "360 Sound Stereo" at bottom			
❑ CS 8395 [S]	Thinking of You	1961	25.00
—Red and black label with six "eye" logos			
❑ CS 8395 [S]	Thinking of You	1963	15.00
—Red label with "360 Sound Stereo" at bottom			
❑ CS 8449 [S]	A Touch of Elegance	1961	25.00
—Red and black label with six "eye" logos			
❑ CS 8541 [S]	Mack the Knife and Other Kurt Weill Music	1962	15.00
—Red label with "360 Sound Stereo" at bottom			
❑ CS 8541 [S]	Mack the Knife and Other Kurt Weill Music	1962	25.00
—Red and black label with six "eye" logos			
❑ CS 8586 [S]	Faraway Part of Town	1962	25.00
—Red and black label with six "eye" logos			
❑ CS 8586 [S]	Faraway Part of Town	1963	15.00
—Red label with "360 Sound Stereo" at bottom			
❑ CS 8688 [S]	The Light Fantastic	1962	25.00
—Red and black label with six "eye" logos			
❑ CS 8688 [S]	The Light Fantastic	1963	15.00
—Red label with "360 Sound Stereo" at bottom			
❑ CS 8733 [S]	Sittin' on a Rainbow: The Music of Harold Arlen	1963	20.00
—Red label, "360 Sound Stereo" in black at bottom			
❑ CS 8834 [S]	Andre Previn in Hollywood	1963	20.00
—Red label with "360 Sound Stereo" in black at bottom			
❑ CS 8834 [S]	Andre Previn in Hollywood	1966	15.00
—Red label with "360 Sound Stereo" in white at bottom			
❑ CS 8914 [S]	The Soft and Swinging Music of Jimmy McHugh	1964	20.00
—Red label with "360 Sound Stereo" in black at bottom			
❑ CS 8914 [S]	The Soft and Swinging Music of Jimmy McHugh	1966	15.00
—Red label with "360 Sound Stereo" in white at bottom			
❑ CS 8995 [S]	My Fair Lady	1964	20.00
—Red label with "360 Sound Stereo" in black at bottom			
❑ CS 8995 [S]	My Fair Lady	1966	15.00
—Red label with "360 Sound Stereo" in white at bottom			
❑ CS 9094 [S]	Popular Previn	1965	20.00
—Red label with "360 Sound Stereo" in black at bottom			
❑ CS 9094 [S]	Popular Previn	1966	15.00
—Red label with "360 Sound Stereo" in white at bottom			
CONTEMPORARY			
❑ C-3543 [M]	Pal Joey	1957	50.00
❑ C-3548 [M]	Gigi	1958	50.00
❑ M-3558 [M]	Andre Previn Plays Vernon Duke	1959	50.00
❑ M-3567 [M]	Andre Previn Plays Jerome Kern	1959	50.00
❑ M-3570 [M]	Jazz Trio, King Size	1959	50.00
❑ M-3572 [M]	West Side Story	1960	40.00
❑ M-3575 [M]	Like Previn	1960	40.00
❑ M-3586 [M]	Andre Previn Plays Harold Arlen	1960	40.00
❑ S-7543 [S]	Pal Joey	1959	40.00
❑ S-7548 [S]	Gigi	1959	40.00
❑ S-7558 [S]	Andre Previn Plays Vernon Duke	1959	40.00
❑ S-7567 [S]	Andre Previn Plays Jerome Kern	1959	40.00
❑ S-7570 [S]	Jazz Trio, King Size	1959	40.00
❑ S-7572 [S]	West Side Story	1960	30.00
❑ S-7575 [S]	Like Previn	1960	30.00
❑ S-7586 [S]	Andre Previn Plays Harold Arlen	1960	30.00
CORONET			
❑ 170	Featuring Andre Previn	196?	12.00
❑ 181	The Magic Sounds of Andre Previn	196?	12.00
DECCA			
❑ DL 4115 [M]	Andre Previn Plays Pretty	1961	12.00
❑ DL 4350 [M]	But Beautiful	1963	12.00
❑ DL 8131 [M]	Let's Get Away from It All	1955	40.00
❑ DL 8341 [M]	Hollywood at Midnight	1957	40.00
❑ DL 74115 [S]	Andre Previn Plays Pretty	1961	15.00
❑ DL 74350 [S]	But Beautiful	1963	15.00
EVEREST ARCHIVE OF FOLK & JAZZ			
❑ 247	Early Years	1970	10.00
FANTASY			
❑ OJC-157	Double Play!	198?	10.00
—Reissue of Contemporary 7011			
❑ OJC-170	Like Previn	198?	10.00
—Reissue of Contemporary 7575			
❑ OJC-422	West Side Story	1990	10.00
❑ OJC-637	Pal Joey	1991	12.00
GUEST STAR			
❑ 1436	Piano Greats	196?	12.00
HARMONY			
❑ HL 7348 [M]	Misty	1965	12.00
❑ HL 7407 [M]	Starlight Piano	196?	12.00
❑ HL 7429 [M]	Camelot	1967	12.00
❑ HS 11148 [S]	Misty	1965	12.00
❑ HS 11207 [S]	Starlight Piano	196?	12.00
❑ HS 11229 [S]	Camelot	1967	12.00
JAZZ ODYSSEY			
❑ 32160260	Mack the Knife and Other Kurt Weill Music	196?	12.00
—Reissue of Columbia 8541			
MGM			
❑ E-3716 [M]	Secret Songs for Young Lovers	1959	20.00
❑ SE-3716 [S]	Secret Songs for Young Lovers	1959	25.00
❑ E-3811 [M]	Like Blue	1960	20.00
❑ SE-3811 [S]	Like Blue	1960	25.00
❑ E-4186 [M]	Andre Previn — Composer, Conductor, Arranger, Pianist	1964	15.00
❑ SE-4186 [S]	Andre Previn — Composer, Conductor, Arranger, Pianist	1964	20.00
MOBILE FIDELITY			
❑ 1-095	West Side Story	1982	25.00
—Audiophile vinyl			
MONARCH			
❑ 203 [10]	All Star Jazz	1952	80.00
❑ 204 [10]	Andre Previn Plays Duke	1952	80.00
PRI			
❑ 3026 [S]	The World's Most Honored Pianist	1962	25.00
—Issued on yellow vinyl			
RCA CAMDEN			
❑ CAL-792 [M]	Love Walked In	1964	12.00
❑ CAS-792 [R]	Love Walked In	1964	10.00
RCA VICTOR			
❑ LPM-36 [10]	Andre Previn By Request	1951	80.00
❑ LPM-1011 [M]	Gershwin	1955	40.00
❑ LPM-1356 [M]	Three Little Words	1957	40.00
❑ ANL1-2805	Pure Gold	1978	10.00
❑ LPT-3002 [10]	Andre Previn Plays Harry Warren	1952	80.00
❑ LPM-3491 [M]	Andre Previn Plays Music of the Young Hollywood Composers	1966	12.00
❑ LSP-3491 [S]	Andre Previn Plays Music of the Young Hollywood Composers	1966	15.00
❑ LPM-3551 [M]	Andre Previn with Voices	1966	12.00
❑ LSP-3551 [S]	Andre Previn with Voices	1966	15.00
❑ LPM-3806 [M]	All Alone	1967	15.00
❑ LSP-3806 [S]	All Alone	1967	12.00
SPRINGBOARD			
❑ SPB-4053	After Dark	197?	10.00
STEREO RECORDS			
❑ S-7004 [S]	Pal Joey	1958	50.00
❑ S-7020 [S]	Gigi	1958	50.00
STRAND			
❑ SL 1074 [M]	Andre Previn Plays	1962	12.00
❑ SLS 1074 [S]	Andre Previn Plays	1962	15.00
VERVE			
❑ V-8565 [M]	The Essential Andre Previn	1963	12.00
❑ V6-8565 [S]	The Essential Andre Previn	1963	15.00

PREVIN, ANDRE; HERB ELLIS; SHELLY MANNE; RAY BROWN

Albums

Number	Title (A Side/B Side)	Yr	NM
COLUMBIA			
❑ CL 2018 [M]	Four to Go	1963	20.00
❑ CS 8818 [S]	Four to Go	1963	25.00

PREVIN, ANDRE, AND RUSS FREEMAN

Albums

Number	Title (A Side/B Side)	Yr	NM
CONTEMPORARY			
❑ C-3537 [M]	Double Play!	1957	50.00
❑ S-7011 [S]	Double Play!	1959	40.00
STEREO RECORDS			
❑ S-7011 [S]	Double Play!	1958	50.00

PRICE, ALAN

Also see THE ANIMALS.

45s

Number	Title (A Side/B Side)	Yr	NM
COTILLION			
❑ 44044	Falling in Love Again/Sly Sadie	1969	6.00
—Might be promo only			
EPIC			
❑ 04319	I Don't Feel No Pain No More (Time and Tide)/Rowf and Snitter Run to Sea	1984	4.00
—Might be promo only			
JET			
❑ XW1119	I Wanna Dance/Just for You	1978	4.00
❑ 5056	This Is Your Lucky Day/Mama Don't Go Home	1979	4.00
PARROT			
❑ 3001	I Put a Spell on You/Iechyd-Da	1966	10.00
❑ 3007	Hi-Lili, Hi-Lo/Take Me Home	1966	10.00
❑ 3009	Tickle Me/Simon Smith and His Amazing Dancing Bears	1966	10.00
❑ 3013	Who Cares/The House That Jack Built	1967	8.00
❑ 3014	Shame/Don't Do That Again	1967	8.00
❑ 3019	Not Born to Follow/To Ramona	1968	8.00
WARNER BROS.			
❑ 7717	Poor People/O Lucky Man	1973	5.00

Albums

Number	Title (A Side/B Side)	Yr	NM
ACCORD			
❑ SJA-7904	It's Priceless	1982	10.00
JET			
❑ JT-LA809-H	Alan Price	1977	10.00
—The "H" suffix is on the label, but the front and back cover, inner sleeve and spine have a "G" prefix; it's not known if any labels have a "G" prefix			
❑ JZ 35710	Lucky Day	1979	10.00
❑ NJZ 36510	Rising Sun	1980	10.00
PARROT			
❑ PAS 71018 [P]	The Price Is Right	1968	30.00
TOWNHOUSE			
❑ SN-7126	House of the Rising Sun	1981	10.00
WARNER BROS.			
❑ BS 2710	O Lucky Man	1973	12.00
❑ BS 2783	Between Today and Yesterday	1974	12.00

PRICE, LLOYD

45s

Number	Title (A Side/B Side)	Yr	NM
ABC			
❑ 1237	Stagger Lee/Personality	1969	6.00
—"Golden Treasure Chest" reissue; contains the "samitized" version of "Stagger Lee" with Mr. Lee and Billy arguing over a woman			
❑ 11016	Personality/Just Because	1967	8.00
ABC-PARAMOUNT			
❑ 9792	Just Because/Why	1957	20.00
❑ 9972 [M]	Stagger Lee/You Need Love	1958	20.00
—Most, if not all, copies contain the "raunchy" version of "Stagger Lee" with Mr. Lee and Billy playing cards			
❑ S-9972 [S]	Stagger Lee/You Need Love	1958	40.00
❑ 9997 [M]	Where Were You (On Our Wedding Day)?/Is It Really Love	1959	20.00
❑ S-9997 [S]	Where Were You (On Our Wedding Day)?/Is It Really Love	1959	40.00
❑ 10018 [M]	(You've Got) Personality/ Have You Ever Had the Blues	1959	20.00
—Note longer title			
❑ 10018 [M]	Personality/Have You Ever Had the Blues	1959	20.00
❑ S-10018 [S]	Personality/Have You Ever Had the Blues	1959	50.00
❑ 10032 [M]	I'm Gonna Get Married/ Three Little Pigs	1959	20.00
❑ S-10032 [S]	I'm Gonna Get Married/ Three Little Pigs	1959	50.00
❑ 10062	Come Into My Heart/ Won't Cha Come Home	1959	15.00

P

Number	Title (A Side/B Side)	Yr	NM
❑ S-10062 [S]	Come Into My Heart/ Won't Cha Come Home	1959	50.00
❑ 10075	Lady Luck/Never Let Me Go	1960	15.00
❑ 10102	No If's — No And's/For Love	1960	15.00
❑ 10123	Question/If I Look a Little Blue	1960	15.00
❑ 10139	Just Call Me (And I'll Understand)/Who Could've Told You	1960	15.00
❑ 10162	(You Better) Know What You're Doin'/That's Why Tears Come and Go	1960	15.00
❑ 10177	Boo Hoo/I Made You Cry	1961	15.00
❑ 10197	One Hundred Percent/ Say I'm the One	1961	15.00
❑ 10206	String of Pearls/Chantilly Lace	1961	15.00
❑ 10221	Mary and Man-O/I Ain't Givin' Up Nothin'	1961	15.00
❑ 10229	Talk to Me/I Cover the Waterfront	1961	15.00
❑ 10288	Be a Leader/'Nother Fairy Tale	1962	15.00
❑ 10299	Twistin' the Blues/Pop Eye's Irresistable You	1962	15.00
❑ 10342	Counterfeit Friends/Your Picture	1962	15.00
❑ 10372	Under Your Spell Again/Happy Birthday Mama	1962	15.00
❑ 10412	Who's Sorry Now/Hello Bill	1963	15.00
DOUBLE-L			
❑ 714	Pistol Packin' Mama/ Tennessee Waltz	1963	10.00
❑ 722	Misty/Cry On	1963	10.00
❑ 728	Merry Christmas Mama/Auld Lang Syne	1963	12.00
❑ 729	Billie Baby/Try a Little Bit of Tenderness	1964	10.00
❑ 729 [PS]	Billie Baby/Try a Little Bit of Tenderness	1964	25.00
❑ 730	I'll Be a Fool for You/ You're Nobody Till Somebody Loves You	1964	10.00
❑ 736	Go On Little Girl/ You're Reading Me	1965	10.00
❑ 739	Every Night/Peeping and Hiding	1966	10.00
❑ 740	Send Me Some Loving/ Somewhere Along the Way	1966	10.00
GSF			
❑ 6882	Sing a Song/(B-side unknown)	1972	6.00
❑ 6894	Love Music/Just for Baby	1973	6.00
❑ 6904	Trying to Slip (Away)/ They Get Down	1973	6.00
HURD			
❑ 82	Misty '66/Saturday Night	1966	8.00
JAD			
❑ 208	Luv, Luv, Luv/Take All	1968	8.00
❑ 212	Don't Stop Now/The Truth	1968	8.00
KRC			
❑ 301	Lonely Chair/The Chicken and the Bop	1957	50.00
❑ 303	Hello Little Girl/Georgianna	1957	25.00
❑ 305	How Many Times/To Love and Be Loved	1957	25.00
❑ 587	Just Because/Why	1957	80.00
❑ 5000	No Limit to Love/Such a Mess	195?	25.00
❑ 5002	Gonna Let You Come Back Home/Down by the River	195?	25.00
LPG			
❑ 111	What Did You Do with My Love/ Love Music	1976	6.00
LUDIX			
❑ 4747	Feelin' Good/Cupid's Bandwagon	197?	6.00
MONUMENT			
❑ 856	Don't Cry/I Love You, I Just Love You	1964	10.00
❑ 865	Amen/I'd Fight the World	1964	10.00
❑ 877	Oh, Lady Luck/Woman	1965	10.00
❑ 887	If I Had My Life to Live Over/ Two for Love	1965	10.00
PARAMOUNT			
❑ 0168	In the Eyes of God/The Legend of Nigger Charley	1972	6.00
REPRISE			
❑ 0499	I Won't Cry Anymore/The Man Who Took the Valise Off the Floor at Grand Central Station at Noon	1966	8.00
SCEPTER			
❑ 12310	Hooked on a Feeling/If You Really Love Him	1971	6.00
❑ 12327	Mr. and Mrs. Untrue/ Natural SInner	1971	6.00
SPECIALTY			
❑ 428	Lawdy Miss Clawdy/ Mailman Blues	1952	250.00

Number	Title (A Side/B Side)	Yr	NM
❑ 428	Lawdy Miss Clawdy/ Mailman Blues	1952	1500.
—Red vinyl			
❑ 440	Oooh-Oooh-Oooh/ Restless Heart	1952	100.00
❑ 452	Ain't It a Shame?/Tell Me Pretty Baby	1953	100.00
❑ 452	Ain't It a Shame?/ Tell Me Pretty Baby	1953	200.00
—Red vinyl			
❑ 457	What's the Matter Now/So Long	1953	100.00
❑ 457	What's the Matter Now/So Long	1953	200.00
—Red vinyl			
❑ 463	Where You At?/Baby Don't Turn Your Back on Me	1953	100.00
❑ 463	Where You At?/Baby Don't Turn Your Back on Me	1953	200.00
—Red vinyl			
❑ 471	I Wish Your Picture Was You/ Frog Legs	1953	100.00
❑ 483	Let Me Come Home, Baby/ Too Late for Tears	1954	80.00
❑ 483	Let Me Come Home, Baby/ Too Late for Tears	1954	200.00
—Red vinyl			
❑ 494	Walkin' the Track/Jimmie Lee	1954	80.00
❑ 535	Oo-Ee Baby/Chee-Koo Baby	1954	40.00
❑ 540	Trying to Find Someone to Love/Lord, Lord, Amen!	1955	40.00
❑ 571	Woe Ho Ho/I Yi Yi Gomen-a-Sai (I'm Sorry)	1956	40.00
❑ 578	Country Boy Rock/ Rock 'N' Dance	1956	50.00
❑ 582	Forgive Me, Clawdy/I'm Glad	1956	30.00
❑ 602	Baby Please Come Home/ Breaking My Heart (All Over Again)	1957	30.00
❑ 661	Lawdy Miss Clawdy/ Mailman Blues	1959	20.00
TURNTABLE			
❑ 501	I Understand/The Grass Will Sing (For You)	1969	8.00
❑ 502	I Heard It Through the Grapevine/It's Your Thing	1969	8.00
❑ 506	Bad Conditions/The Truth	1969	8.00
❑ 509	Lawdy Miss Clawdy/Little Volcano	1969	8.00
7-Inch Extended Plays			
ABC-PARAMOUNT			
❑ A-277 [PS]	Lawdy Miss Clawdy/Just Because//You Need Love/Why	1959	100.00
❑ A-277 [PS]	The Exciting Lloyd Price	1959	100.00
❑ A-315	Ain't Nobody's Business/Just to Hold Your Hand//Talk to Me/ I Cover the Waterfront	1960	100.00
❑ A-315 [PS]	Mr. Personality Sings the Blues	1960	100.00
❑ A-324	Lady Luck/Personality//Stagger Lee/I'm Gonna Get Married	1960	100.00
❑ A-324 [PS]	Mr. Personality's Big Hits	1960	100.00
Albums			
ABC			
❑ S-297	Mr. Personality	1967	15.00
—Reissue on revised label			
❑ S-324 [R]	Mr. Personality's Big 15	1968	15.00
—Reissue on revised label			
❑ X-763	16 Greatest Hits	1972	15.00
❑ AC-30006	The ABC Collection	1976	15.00
❑ DW-94842	16 Greatest Hits	1972	20.00
—Capitol Record Club edition			
ABC-PARAMOUNT			
❑ ABC-277 [M]	The Exciting Lloyd Price	1959	40.00
❑ ABCS-277 [S]	The Exciting Lloyd Price	1959	80.00
❑ ABC-297 [M]	Mr. Personality	1959	40.00
❑ ABCS-297 [S]	Mr. Personality	1959	80.00
❑ ABC-315 [M]	Mr. Personality Sings the Blues	1960	40.00
❑ ABCS-315 [S]	Mr. Personality Sings the Blues	1960	80.00
❑ ABC-324 [M]	Mr. Personality's 15 Hits	1960	40.00
—Label calls this "Mr. Personality's Big Hits"			
❑ ABC-346 [M]	The Fantastic Lloyd Price	1960	40.00
❑ ABCS-346 [R]	The Fantastic Lloyd Price	196?	25.00
❑ ABC-366 [M]	Lloyd Price Sings the Million Sellers	1961	40.00
❑ ABCS-366 [S]	Lloyd Price Sings the Million Sellers	1961	50.00
❑ ABC-382 [M]	Cookin' with Lloyd Price	1961	40.00
❑ ABCS-382 [S]	Cookin' with Lloyd Price	1961	50.00
DOUBLE-L			
❑ DL-2301 [M]	The Lloyd Price Orchestra	1963	25.00
❑ DL-2303 [M]	Misty	1963	25.00
❑ SDL-8301 [S]	The Lloyd Price Orchestra	1963	40.00
❑ SDL-8303 [S]	Misty	1963	40.00
GRAND PRIX			
❑ 422 [M]	Mr. Rhythm and Blues	196?	12.00
❑ S-422 [R]	Mr. Rhythm and Blues	196?	10.00
GUEST STAR			
❑ G-1910 [M]	Come to Me	196?	12.00

Number	Title (A Side/B Side)	Yr	NM
❑ GS-1910 [R]	Come to Me	196?	10.00
JAD			
❑ 1002	Lloyd Price Now	1969	25.00
LPG			
❑ 001	Music…Music	1976	10.00
MCA			
❑ 1503	Greatest Hits	1982	8.00
MONUMENT			
❑ MLP-8032 [M]	Lloyd Swings for Sammy	1965	25.00
❑ SLP-18032 [S]	Lloyd Swings for Sammy	1965	40.00
PICKWICK			
❑ SPC-3518	Big Hits	197?	8.00
SCEPTER CITATION			
❑ CTN-18006	The Best of Lloyd Price	1972	10.00
SPECIALTY			
❑ SP-2105	Lloyd Price	198?	12.00
—1980s reissue			
❑ SP-2105 [M]	Lloyd Price	1959	180.00
TRIP			
❑ TOP 16-5	16 Greatest Hits	1976	10.00
TURNTABLE			
❑ TTS-5001	Lloyd Price Now	197?	15.00
UPFRONT			
❑ UPF-126	Misty	197?	12.00

PRIDE

Albums

Number	Title (A Side/B Side)	Yr	NM
WARNER BROS.			
❑ WS 1848	Pride	1970	25.00

PRIDE, CHARLEY

Includes releases as "Country Charley Pride."

45s

Number	Title (A Side/B Side)	Yr	NM
RCA			
❑ 2723-7-R	The Easy Part's Over/ The Right to Do Wrong	1990	3.00
—"Gold Standard Series" reissue			
❑ PB-10757	A Whole Lotta Things to Sing About/The Hardest Part of Livin's Lovin' Me	1976	4.00
❑ PB-10875	She's Just An Old Love Turned Memory/Country Music	1977	4.00
❑ PB-10975	I'll Be Leaving Alone/ We Need Lovin'	1977	4.00
❑ PB-11086	More to Me/Heaven Watches Over Fools Like Me	1977	4.00
❑ PB-11201	Someone Loves You Honey/ Days of Our Lives	1978	4.00
❑ PB-11287	When I Stop Leaving (I'll Be Gone)/I Can See the Lovin' in Your Eyes	1978	4.00
❑ GB-11331	My Eyes Can Only See As Far As You/A Whole Lotta Things to Sing About	1978	3.00
—"Gold Standard Series" reissue			
❑ PB-11391	Burgers and Fries/Nothing's Prettier Than Rose Is	1978	4.00
❑ PB-11477	Where Do I Put Her Memory/ The Best in the World	1979	4.00
❑ GB-11498	Someone Loves You Honey/ When I Stop Leaving (I'll Be Gone)	1979	3.00
—"Gold Standard Series" reissue			
❑ PB-11655	You're My Jamaica/Let Me Have a Chance to Love You	1979	4.00
❑ PB-11736	Dallas Cowboys/When I Stop Leaving	1979	6.00
—Regular black-label edition			
❑ PB-11736	Dallas Cowboys/When I Stop Leaving	1979	12.00
—Special blue and silver label edition			
❑ PB-11751	Missin' You/Heartbreak Mountain	1979	4.00
❑ PB-11912	Honky Tonk Blues/I'm So Lonesome I Could Cry	1980	3.00
❑ GB-11992	Burgers and Fries/Where Do I Put Her Memory	1980	3.00
—"Gold Standard Series" reissue			
❑ PB-12002	You Win Again/There's a Little Bit of Hank in Me	1980	3.00
❑ PB-12100	You Almost Slipped My Mind/ Ghost Written Love Letters	1980	3.00
❑ PB-12178	Roll On Mississippi/ Fall Back on Me	1981	3.00
❑ PB-12294	Never Been So Loved (In All My Life)/I Call Her My Girl	1981	3.00
❑ GB-12371	Honky Tonk Blues/ You Win Again	1981	3.00
—"Gold Standard Series" reissue			
❑ PB-13014	Mountain of Love/Love Is a Shadow	1981	3.00
❑ PB-13096	I Don't Think She's in Love Anymore/Oh What a Beautiful Love Song	1982	3.00

P

Number	Title (A Side/B Side)	Yr	NM
❑ PB-13293	You're So Good When You're Bad/I Haven't Loved This Way in Years	1982	3.00
❑ PB-13359	Let It Snow, Let It Snow, Let It Snow/Peace on Earth	1982	5.00

—B-side by Razzy Bailey

Number	Title (A Side/B Side)	Yr	NM
❑ PB-13397	Why Baby Why/It's So Good to Be Together	1982	3.00
❑ PB-13451	More and More/Radio Heroes	1983	3.00
❑ PB-13542	Night Games/I Could Let Her Get Close to Me	1983	3.00
❑ PB-13648	Ev'ry Heart Should Have One/Lovin' It Up (Livin' It Down)	1983	3.00
❑ PB-13667	Let It Snow, Let It Snow, Let It Snow/O Holy Night	1983	4.00
❑ PB-13732	The Late Show/Love on a Blue Rainy Day	1984	4.00
❑ JK-13754	Stagger Lee (same on both sides)	1984	10.00

—Promo on red vinyl

Number	Title (A Side/B Side)	Yr	NM
❑ PB-13821	The Power of Love/Ellie	1984	3.00
❑ PB-13936	Missin' Mississippi/Falling in Love Again	1984	3.00
❑ PB-14045	Down on the Farm/Now and Then	1985	3.00
❑ PB-14134	Let a Little Love Come In/Night Games	1985	3.00
❑ PB-14265	The Best There Is/The Tumbleweed and the Rose	1986	3.00
❑ PB-14296	Love on a Blue Rainy Day/I Used It All on You	1986	3.00

RCA VICTOR

Number	Title (A Side/B Side)	Yr	NM
❑ 47-8738	Atlantic Coastal Line/Snakes Crawl at Night	1966	15.00
❑ 47-8862	Miller's Cave/Before I Met You	1966	15.00
❑ 47-9000	Just Between You and Me/Detroit City	1966	12.00
❑ 47-9162	I Know One/The Best Banjo Picker	1967	12.00
❑ 47-9281	Does My Ring Hurt Your Finger/The Spell of the Freight Train	1967	12.00

—Above three labeled as "Country Charley Pride"

Number	Title (A Side/B Side)	Yr	NM
❑ 47-9403	The Day the World Stood Still/Gone, On the Other Hand	1967	8.00
❑ 47-9514	The Easy Part's Over/Right to Do Wrong	1968	8.00
❑ 47-9622	Let the Chips Fall/She Made Me Go	1968	8.00
❑ 47-9716	Kaw-Liga/Little Folks	1969	8.00
❑ 47-9777	Wings of a Dove/They Stood in Silent Prayer	1969	12.00
❑ 47-9806	Is Anybody Goin' to San Antone/Things Are Looking Up	1970	6.00
❑ 47-9855	Wonder Could I Live There Anymore/Piroque Joe	1970	6.00
❑ 47-9902	I Can't Believe That You've Stopped Loving Me/Time	1970	6.00
❑ 47-9933	Christmas in My Home Town/Santa and the Kids	1970	8.00
❑ 47-9952	I'd Rather Love You/You Don't Belong	1971	6.00
❑ 47-9974	Let Me Live/Did You Think to Pray	1971	8.00
❑ 47-9996	I'm Just Me/A Place for the Lonesome	1971	6.00
❑ 74-0167	All I Have to Offer You (Is Me)/Brand New Bed of Roses	1969	8.00
❑ 74-0265	(I'm So) Afraid of Losing You Again/Good Chance of Tear-Fall Tonight	1969	8.00
❑ 74-0550	Kiss an Angel Good Mornin'/No One Could Ever Take Me from You	1971	6.00
❑ 74-0624	All His Children/You'll Still Be the One	1972	5.00
❑ 74-0707	It's Gonna Take a Little Bit Longer/You're Wanting Me to Stop Loving You	1972	5.00
❑ 74-0707 [PS]	It's Gonna Take a Little Bit Longer/You're Wanting Me to Stop Loving You	1972	8.00
❑ 74-0802	She's Too Good to Be True/She's That Kind	1972	5.00
❑ 74-0884	A Shoulder to Cry On/I'm Learning to Love Her	1973	5.00
❑ 74-0942	Don't Fight the Feelings of Love/Tennessee Girl	1973	5.00
❑ 447-0920	I'm Just Me/Jeanie Norman	1972	6.00

—Gold Standard Series on red label; B-side makes its first 45 rpm appearance here

Number	Title (A Side/B Side)	Yr	NM
❑ 447-0921	You'll Still Be the One/Crystal Chandelier	1972	6.00

—Gold Standard Series on red label; B-side makes its first 45 rpm appearance here

Number	Title (A Side/B Side)	Yr	NM
❑ 447-0935	Christmas in My Home Town/Santa and the Kids	1972	4.00

—Gold Standard Series

Number	Title (A Side/B Side)	Yr	NM
❑ APBO-0073	Amazing Love/Blue Ridge Mountains Turnin' Green	1973	5.00
❑ AMBO-0128	A Shoulder to Cry On/Don't Fight the Feelings of Love	1973	4.00

—"Gold Standard Series" reissue

Number	Title (A Side/B Side)	Yr	NM
❑ APBO-0257	We Could/Love Put a Song in My Heart	1974	5.00
❑ PB-10030	Mississippi Cotton Picking Delta Town/Mary Go Round	1974	4.00
❑ PB-10126	Then Who Am I/Completely Helpless	1974	4.00
❑ PB-10236	I Ain't All Bad/Hard Times Will Be the Best Times	1975	4.00
❑ PB-10344	Hope You're Feelin' Me (Like I'm Feelin' You)/Searching for the Morning Sun	1975	4.00
❑ PB-10455	The Happiness of Having You/Right Back Missing You Again	1975	4.00
❑ GB-10507	Then Who Am I/Completely Helpless	1975	3.00

—"Gold Standard Series" reissue

Number	Title (A Side/B Side)	Yr	NM
❑ GB-10508	Mississippi Cotton Picking Delta Town/Mary Go Round	1975	3.00

—"Gold Standard Series" reissue

Number	Title (A Side/B Side)	Yr	NM
❑ GB-10509	Amazing Love/Blue Ridge Mountains Turning Green	1975	3.00

—"Gold Standard Series" reissue

Number	Title (A Side/B Side)	Yr	NM
❑ PB-10592	My Eyes Can Only See As Far As You/Oklahoma Morning	1976	4.00
❑ PB-10643	In Jesus' Name I Pray/I Don't Deserve a Mansion	1976	6.00
❑ GB-10674	I Ain't All Bad/Hope You're Feelin' Me (Like I'm Feelin' You)	1976	4.00

—"Gold Standard Series" reissue

16TH AVENUE

Number	Title (A Side/B Side)	Yr	NM
❑ 70400	Have I Got Some Blues for You/Ever Knowin'	1987	4.00
❑ 70402	If You Still Want a Fool Around/You Took Me There	1987	4.00
❑ 70408	Shouldn't It Be Easier Than This/Look in Your Mirror	1987	4.00
❑ 70414	I'm Gonna Love Her on the Radio/Shouldn't It Be Easier Than This	1988	4.00
❑ 70420	Where Was I/A Whole Lotta Lovin' (Goes a Long, Long Way)	1988	4.00
❑ 70425	White Houses/Shouldn't It Be Easier Than This	1989	4.00
❑ 70429	The More I Do/Heaven Help Us All	1989	4.00
❑ 70435	Amy's Eyes/I Made Love to You in My Mind	1989	4.00
❑ 70440	Moody Woman/Shouldn't It Be Easier Than This	1990	5.00
❑ 70446	Whole Lotta Love on the Line/Plenty Good Lovin'	1990	5.00

Albums

PAIR

Number	Title	Yr	NM
❑ PDL2-1023 [(2)]	Country in My Soul	1986	12.00

RCA CAMDEN

Number	Title	Yr	NM
❑ CAS-2584	The Incomparable Charley Pride	1972	15.00

RCA VICTOR

Number	Title	Yr	NM
❑ APD1-0217 [Q]	Sweet Country	1973	25.00
❑ APL1-0217	Sweet Country	1973	15.00
❑ APL1-0315	Charley Pride Presents the Pridesmen	1973	15.00
❑ APD1-0397 [Q]	Amazing Love	1974	25.00
❑ APL1-0397	Amazing Love	1974	15.00
❑ APL1-0534	Country Feelin'	1974	15.00
❑ APD1-0757 [Q]	Pride of America	1974	25.00
❑ APL1-0757	Pride of America	1974	15.00
❑ ANL1-0996	Charley Pride — In Person	1975	10.00

—Reissue of LSP-4094

Number	Title	Yr	NM
❑ APD1-1038 [Q]	Charley	1975	25.00
❑ APL1-1038	Charley	1975	15.00
❑ ANL1-1214	I'm Just Me	1975	10.00

—Reissue of LSP-4560

Number	Title	Yr	NM
❑ APD1-1241 [Q]	The Happiness of Having You	1975	25.00
❑ APL1-1241	The Happiness of Having You	1975	15.00
❑ APD1-1359 [Q]	Sunday Morning with Charley Pride	1976	25.00
❑ APL1-1359	Sunday Morning with Charley Pride	1976	15.00
❑ ANL1-1934	Christmas in My Home Town	1976	8.00

—Reissue of LSP-4406

Number	Title	Yr	NM
❑ APL1-2023	The Best of Charley Pride, Vol. III	1976	12.00
❑ APL1-2261	She's Just an Old Love Turned Memory	1977	12.00
❑ AHL1-2478	Someone Loves You Honey	1978	12.00
❑ AHL1-2963	Burgers and Fries	1978	12.00
❑ AHL1-3441	You're My Jamaica	1979	12.00
❑ AHL1-3548	There's a Little Bit of Hank in Me	1980	12.00
❑ LPM-3645 [M]	Country Charley Pride	1966	25.00
❑ LSP-3645 [S]	Country Charley Pride	1966	30.00
❑ AYL1-3676	Someone Loves You Honey	1980	8.00

—"Best Buy Series" reissue

Number	Title	Yr	NM
❑ AYL1-3740	Sunday Morning with Charley Pride	1980	8.00

—"Best Buy Series" reissue

Number	Title	Yr	NM
❑ LPM-3775 [M]	The Pride of Country Music	1967	25.00
❑ LSP-3775 [S]	The Pride of Country Music	1967	20.00
❑ AYL1-3874	I'm Just Me	1981	8.00

—"Best Buy Series" reissue

Number	Title	Yr	NM
❑ LPM-3895 [M]	The Country Way	1967	25.00
❑ LSP-3895 [S]	The Country Way	1967	20.00
❑ AHL1-3905	Roll On Mississippi	1981	10.00
❑ AYL1-3943	The Happiness of Having You	1981	8.00

—"Best Buy Series" reissue

Number	Title	Yr	NM
❑ LPM-3952 [M]	Make Mine Country	1968	60.00
❑ LSP-3952 [S]	Make Mine Country	1968	20.00
❑ LSP-4041	Songs of Pride — Charley, That Is	1968	20.00
❑ AYL1-4074	Amazing Love	1981	8.00

—"Best Buy Series" reissue

Number	Title	Yr	NM
❑ LSP-4094	Charley Pride — In Person	1969	20.00
❑ AHL1-4151	Greatest Hits	1981	10.00
❑ LSP-4153	The Sensational Charley Pride	1969	20.00
❑ AYL1-4166	She's Just an Old Love Turned Memory	1981	8.00

—"Best Buy Series" reissue

Number	Title	Yr	NM
❑ AHL1-4223	The Best of Charley Pride	198?	10.00

—Reissue of LSP-4223

Number	Title	Yr	NM
❑ LSP-4223	The Best of Charley Pride	1969	20.00
❑ AYL1-4252	Burgers and Fries	1982	8.00

—"Best Buy Series" reissue

Number	Title	Yr	NM
❑ AHL1-4287	Charley Pride Sings Everybody's Choice	1982	10.00
❑ LSP-4290	Just Plain Charley	1970	20.00
❑ LSP-4367	Charley Pride's 10th Album	1970	20.00
❑ LSP-4406	Christmas in My Home Town	1970	20.00
❑ LSP-4468	From Me to You	1971	20.00
❑ LSP-4513	Did You Think to Pray	1971	20.00
❑ AHL1-4524	Charley Pride Live	1983	10.00
❑ LSP-4560	I'm Just Me	1971	20.00
❑ LSP-4617	Charley Pride Sings Heart Songs	1971	20.00
❑ AHL1-4662	Country Classics	1983	10.00
❑ AHL1-4682	The Best of Charley Pride, Vol. 2	198?	10.00

—Reissue of LSP-4682

Number	Title	Yr	NM
❑ LSP-4682	The Best of Charley Pride, Vol. 2	1972	20.00
❑ LSP-4742	A Sunshiny Day with Charley Pride	1972	20.00
❑ AHL1-4822	Night Games	1983	10.00
❑ AYL1-4831	There's a Little Bit of Hank in Me	1983	8.00

—"Best Buy Series" reissue

Number	Title	Yr	NM
❑ LSP-4837	Songs of Love by Charley Pride	1973	15.00
❑ AHL1-5031	The Power of Love	1984	10.00
❑ AYL1-5147	Greatest Hits	1984	8.00

—"Best Buy Series" reissue

Number	Title	Yr	NM
❑ AYL1-5148	The Best of Charley Pride	1984	8.00

—"Best Buy Series" reissue

Number	Title	Yr	NM
❑ AHL1-5426	Greatest Hits, Vol. 2	1985	10.00
❑ AHL1-5851	Back to the Country	1986	10.00
❑ CPL1-7049	Collector's Series	1985	10.00
❑ AHL1-7174	The Best There Is	1986	10.00

READER'S DIGEST

Number	Title	Yr	NM
❑ RDA-217 [(6)]	Charley Pride's Country	1979	40.00

16TH AVENUE

Number	Title	Yr	NM
❑ ST-70550	After All This Time	1987	12.00
❑ D1-70551	I'm Gonna Love Her on the Radio	1988	12.00
❑ D1-70554	Moody Woman	1989	12.00

TEE VEE/RCA SPECIAL PRODUCTS

Number	Title	Yr	NM
❑ DVL2-0208 [(2)]	Favorites	1976	15.00

—Label calls this "Charley's Favorites"

TIME-LIFE

Number	Title	Yr	NM
❑ STW-101	Country Music	1981	10.00

PRIESMAN, MAGEL

45s

SUN

Number	Title (A Side/B Side)	Yr	NM
❑ 294	Memories of You/I Feel So Blue	1958	25.00

PRIMETTES, THE

Early version of THE SUPREMES.

45s

LUPINE

Number	Title (A Side/B Side)	Yr	NM
❑ 120	Tears of Sorrow/Pretty	1962	300.00

PRIMITIVES, THE (1)

45s

PARKWAY

Number	Title (A Side/B Side)	Yr	NM
❑ 940	Help Me/Let Them Fall	1965	20.00

PRIMITIVES, THE (2)

LOU REED was in this group.

45s

PICKWICK

Number	Title (A Side/B Side)	Yr	NM
❑ 1001	The Ostrich/Sneaky Pete	1964	300.00

PRIMUS

Albums

CAROLINE

Number	Title	Yr	NM
❑ CAROL1619	Frizzle Fry	1990	80.00

—Red vinyl

Number	Title	Yr	NM
❑ CAROL1620	Suck on This	1990	60.00

—Clear vinyl

Except when noted otherwise, VG = 25% of NM, and VG+ = 50% of NM. (Example: VG = $2.00, VG+ = $4.00 and NM = $8.00.)

Number	Title (A Side/B Side)	Yr	NM
INTERSCOPE			
❑ INT2-90126 [(2)]	Brown Album	1997	50.00
❑ 92553 [(2)]	Tales from the Punchbowl	1995	80.00
❑ 069-490414-01 [(2)]	Antipop	1999	30.00
MOBILE FIDELITY			
❑ LMF45-001 [EP]	Animals Should Not Try to Act Like Humans	2004	30.00
—"Original Master Recording" at top of cover; plays at 45 rpm			
PRAWN SONG/INTERSCOPE			
❑ 7-72738-1 [(2)]	Pork Soda	1993	60.00

PRINCE

12-Inch Singles

Number	Title (A Side/B Side)	Yr	NM
(NO LABEL)			
❑ JUN 7 [DJ]	Gett Off (Approx: Damn Near 10 Min.)/(B-side blank)	1991	200.00
—1500 copies were pressed; catalog number is Prince's birthday (June 7)			
❑ L-39777 [DJ]	Sexy MF (5:25) (same on both sides)	1992	40.00
—Gold vinyl record; with generic "Jacket Made in Canada" cover and none of the other goodies			
❑ L-39777 [DJ]	Sexy MF (5:25) (same on both sides)	1992	100.00
—Gold vinyl record; with custom cover, "Sexy MF" sticker, card, envelope and fan (deduct for missing items)			
ARISTA			
❑ ARDP-3750 [(2)DJ]	The Greatest Romance Ever Sold (Radio Edit Featuring Eve 4:32) (Jason Nevins Romance Beats 6:03)/(Neptunes Extended Remix Featuring Q-Tip 5:08) (Jason Nevins Remix Edit 3:36)//(Adam & Eve Remix Featuring Eve 4:30) (Album Version 5:29)/(Jason Nevins Extended Remix 6:41) (Neptunes Remix Edit Featuring Q-Tip 3:42)	1999	20.00
❑ ARDP-3764 [DJ]	The Greatest Romance Ever Sold (Album Version 5:30) (Radio Edit 4:30)/(Adam & Eve Remix Featuring Eve 4:28) (Radio Edit Featuring Eve 4:32)	1999	12.00
❑ ARDP-3783 [DJ]	The Greatest Romance Ever Sold—Jason Nevins Mixes (4 versions)	1999	15.00
❑ 13750 [(2)]	The Greatest Romance Ever Sold (Radio Edit Featuring Eve 4:32) (Jason Nevins Romance Beats 6:03)/(Neptunes Extended Remix Featuring Q-Tip 5:08) (Jason Nevins Remix Edit 3:36)//(Adam & Eve Remix Featuring Eve 4:30) (Album Version 5:29)/(Jason Nevins Extended Remix 6:41) (Neptunes Remix Edit Featuring Q-Tip 3:42)	1999	10.00
NPG			
❑ SPRO-11672 [DJ]	Somebody's Somebody (Ultrafantasy Edit 3:45)/(Radio Edit 4:30) (Live Studio Mix 3:45)	1996	15.00
❑ SPRO-11698 [DJ]	Face Down (X-tended Rap Money Mix 4:56) (Instrumental Money Mix 3:58)//I Can't Make You Love Me (Album Version 6:38)/Face Down (A Cappella 2:21)	1997	20.00
❑ 19991 [DJ]	1999 (The New Master 7:09) (Rosario 1:19) (The Inevitable Mix 5:44) (Keep Steppin' 4:33)/(Rosie and Doug E. in a Deep House 6:23) (The New Master Single Edit 4:30) (Acapella 5:11)	1998	20.00
—Promo only on purple vinyl			
NPG/BELLMARK			
❑ 72514	The Most Beautiful Girl in the World/Beautiful	1994	8.00
❑ SPRO 72516 [DJ]	The Most Beautiful Girl in the World (Staxowax 5:00) (Mustang Mix 6:22) (Brian's Mix 4:30)/(Beautiful 5:55) (Original Mix 4:39)	1994	15.00
PAISLEY PARK			
❑ PRO-A-2300 [DJ]	America (3:40) (same on both sides)	1985	15.00

Prince, "Uptown," Warner Bros. 49559, 1980, **$15.**

Number	Title (A Side/B Side)	Yr	NM
❑ PRO-A-2313 [DJ]	Raspberry Beret (3:31) (same on both sides)	1985	15.00
❑ PRO-A-2331 [DJ]	Pop Life (3:43) (same on both sides)	1985	15.00
❑ PRO-A-2448 [DJ]	Kiss (Edit 3:46) (same on both sides)	1986	12.00
❑ PRO-A-2458 [DJ]	Kiss (Extended Version 7:16) (same on both sides)	1986	15.00
❑ PRO-A-2476 [DJ]	Mountains (LP Version 3:58) (Extended Version 10:03)	1986	15.00
❑ PRO-A-2687 [DJ]	Sign "O" the Times (Edit 3:44) (LP Version 4:57)	1987	10.00
❑ PRO-A-2758 [DJ]	If I Was Your Girlfriend (4:54) (same on both sides)	1987	12.00
❑ PRO-A-2770 [DJ]	I Could Never Take the Place of Your Man (Fade 3:39) (LP Version 6:31)	1987	15.00
❑ PRO-A-2771 [DJ]	U Got the Look (Long Look 6:45) (same on both sides)	1987	15.00
❑ PRO-A-2927 [DJ]	Hot Thing (Edit 3:40) (Extended Remix 8:32)	1987	20.00
❑ PRO-A-3283 [DJ]	I Wish U Heaven (LP Version 2:43) (same on both sides)	1988	12.00
❑ PRO-A-4345 [DJ]	Thieves in the Temple (Album Version 3:20) (same on both sides)	1990	10.00
❑ PRO-A-4515 [DJ]	New Power Generation (Album Version 3:15) (same on both sides)	1990	10.00
❑ PRO-A-4578 [DJ]	New Power Generation (Funky Weapon Remix 5:01) (same on both sides)	1990	15.00
❑ PRO-A-4977 [DJ]	Gett Off (Urge Mix) (Urge Dub) (Flutestramental)/(Thrust Mix) (Thrust Dub) (Rosie's Dub)	1991	15.00
❑ PRO-A-5137 [DJ]	Cream (Remixes)	1991	30.00
—Price is for Specialty test pressing; it's not known if any actual promo 12-inch singles with this number were pressed			
❑ PRO-A-5141 [DJ]	Insatiable (Edit 4:01) (Album Version 6:37)	1991	15.00
❑ PRO-A-5148 [DJ]	Diamonds and Pearls (Edit 4:20) (Album Version 4:45)	1991	15.00
❑ PRO-A-5298 [DJ]	Money Don't Matter 2 Night (Edit 4:11) (Album Version 4:48)	1992	15.00
❑ PRO-A-5301 [DJ]	Willing and Able (Edit 4:15) (Album Version 4:59)	1992	40.00
❑ PRO-A-5570 [DJ]	Sexy MF (5:25) (same on both sides)	1992	12.00
❑ PRO-A-5770 [DJ]	My Name Is Prince (Edit 4:05) (6:36)	1992	15.00
❑ PRO-A-5890 [DJ]	Damn U (Album Version 4:01) (same on both sides)	1992	12.00
❑ PRO-A-5985 [DJ]	The Morning Papers (Album Version 3:57) (same on both sides)	1993	12.00

Number	Title (A Side/B Side)	Yr	NM
❑ PRO-A-5993 [DJ]	Pink Cashmere (Vocal Version 3:56)/(Guitar Version 3:58) (Album Version 6:12)	1993	25.00
—With picture cover (deduct 40% if missing)			
❑ PRO-A-5994 [DJ]	Nothing Compares 2 U (Edit 4:17) (Album Version 4:58)	1993	12.00
❑ 20355	Raspberry Beret (New Mix 7:25)/She's Always in My Hair (New Mix 6:48)	1985	15.00
❑ 20357	Pop Life (Fresh Dance Mix 6:16)/Hello (Fresh Dance Mix 6:38)	1985	10.00
❑ 20389	America (21:46)/Girl (7:36)	1985	10.00
❑ 20442	Kiss (Extended Version 7:16)/Love or $ (Extended Version)	1986	12.00
❑ 20465	Mountains (Extended Version 10:03)/Alexa de Paris (Extended Version 4:54)	1986	12.00
❑ 20516	Anotherloverholenyohead (Extended Version 7:52)/Girls and Boys (LP Version 5:30)	1986	10.00
❑ 20648	Sign "O" the Times (LP Version 4:57)/La, La, La, He, He, Hee (Highly Explosive 10:32)	1987	10.00
❑ 20697	If I Was Your Girlfriend (4:54)/Shockadelica (Extended Version 6:12)	1987	10.00
❑ 20727	U Got the Look (Long Look 6:45) (Single Cut 3:58)/Housequake (Album Cut 4:38) (7 Minutes MoQuake 7:15)	1987	15.00
❑ 20728	I Could Never Take the Place of Your Man (LP Version 6:31)/Hot Thing (Edit 3:40)//(Extended Remix 8:32) (Dub Version 6:53)	1987	10.00
❑ 20930	Alphabet St. (Album Version 5:40)/Alphabet St. "This is not music, this is a trip" (7:48)	1988	10.00
❑ 21005	Glam Slam (Remix 8:52)/Escape (Free yo mind from this rat race) (6:26)	1988	10.00
❑ 21074	I Wish U Heaven (Part 1, 2 and 3)/Scarlet Pussy (6:09)	1988	10.00
❑ 21598	Thieves in the Temple (Remix 8:03) (Thieves in the House Mix 6:50) (Temple House Dub 5:06)	1990	8.00
❑ 21783	New Power Generation (Funky Weapon Remix 5:01)/T.C.'s Rap (Featuring T.C. Ellis 3:11)/Brother with a Purpose (Featuring Tony Mosley 4:18)//Get Off (4:41)/The Lubricated Lady (2:39)/Loveleft, Loveright (5:00)	1990	8.00
❑ 40138	Gett Off (Extended Remix 8:31) (Houstyle 8:20)/Violet the Organ Grinder (4:59)/Gett Off (Flutestramental 7:26)/Gangster Glam (6:04)/Clockin' the Jizz (Instrumental 4:51)	1991	10.00
❑ 40197	Cream (Album Version 4:12) (N.P.G. Mix 5:47)/Things Have Gotta Change (Tony M. Rap 3:57)/2 the Wire (Creamy Instrumental 3:13)/Get Some Solo (1:31)//Do Your Dance (KC's Remix 5:58)/Housebangers (4:23)/Q in Doubt (Instrumental 4:00)/Ethereal Mix (4:43)	1991	10.00
❑ 40574	7 (Album Version 5:09) (After 6 Edit 4:20) (After 6 Long Version 5:15)//(Acoustic Version 3:54) (Album Edit 4:23)/2 Whom It May Concern (4:01)	1992	10.00
❑ 40700	My Name Is Prince (12" Club Mix 8:11) (House Mix 7:18)//(Original Mix Edit 8:06) (Hard Core 12" Mix 7:55)/Sexy M.F. (12" Remix 7:34)	1992	10.00
❑ 40700 [DJ]	My Name Is Prince (12" Club Mix 8:11) (House Mix 7:18)//(Original Mix Edit 8:06) (Hard Core 12" Mix 7:55)/Sexy M.F. (12" Remix 7:34)	1992	25.00
—White label promo in generic cover			

WARNER BROS.

Number	Title (A Side/B Side)	Yr	NM
❑ PRO-A-741 [DJ]	Just As Long As We're Together/Soft and Wet	1978	100.00
—The only Prince 12-inch single with the "Burbank" label			
❑ PRO-A-781 [DJ]	Soft and Wet (same on both sides)	1978	80.00
❑ PRO-A-832 [DJ]	I Wanna Be Your Lover (same on both sides)	1979	80.00
❑ PRO-A-848 [DJ]	Why You Wanna Treat Me So Bad?/Bambi	1979	80.00
❑ PRO-A-870 [DJ]	Still Waiting/Why You Wanna Treat Me So Bad?//Sexy Dancer	1980	60.00
❑ PRO-A-904 [DJ]	Uptown (Edit 4:09) (Long Version 5:29)	1980	60.00
❑ PRO-A-915 [DJ]	Head/Sister/Partyup//(B-side blank)	1980	80.00
❑ PRO-A-916 [DJ]	When You Were Mine/Gotta Broken Heart Again//Uptown	1980	60.00
❑ PRO-A-929 [DJ]	Dirty Mind (same on both sides)	1980	60.00
❑ PRO-A-937 [DJ]	Gotta Stop (Messin' About)/Partyup (Edit)//Head/When U Were Mine/Uptown	1981	80.00
❑ PRO-A-938 [DJ]	Gotta Stop (Messin' About) (same on both sides)	1981	60.00
❑ PRO-A-980 [DJ]	Controversy (3:39) (Long Version 7:18)	1981	50.00
❑ PRO-A-1002 [DJ]	Let's Work (Dance Remix, Long Version 8:02)/(7" Single Version 2:56)	1982	60.00
❑ PRO-A-1035 [DJ]	Do Me, Baby (Edit 3:57)/Private Joy (4:25)	1982	60.00
❑ PRO-A-1070 [DJ]	1999 (Album Version) (S ingle Version 3:35)	1982	60.00
❑ PRO-A-1082 [DJ]	Let's Pretend We're Married/D.M.S.R.//Automatic	1982	50.00
❑ PRO-A-2001 [DJ]	Little Red Corvette (LP Version 4:58) (Dance Remix 8:00)	1983	40.00
❑ PRO-A-2042 [DJ]	1999 (Single Version 3:35)//Free/Automatic	1983	50.00
❑ PRO-A-2080 [DJ]	Delirious (LP Version 3:56) (Single Edit 2:36)	1983	30.00
❑ PRO-A-2139 [DJ]	When Doves Cry (Long Version 5:52)(Short Version 3:49)	1984	25.00
❑ PRO-A-2173 [DJ]	Let's Go Crazy (Edit 3:46) (Album Version 4:40)	1984	30.00
❑ PRO-A-2182 [DJ]	Let's Go Crazy (Special Dance Mix 7:35) (Album Version 4:40)	1984	40.00
❑ PRO-A-2192 [DJ]	Purple Rain (Edit 4:02) (LP Version 8:45)	1984	40.00
—Purple vinyl			
❑ PRO-A-2233 [DJ]	I Would Die 4 U (2:57) (same on both sides)	1984	20.00
❑ PRO-A-2263 [DJ]	Take Me With U (same on both sides)	1985	30.00
❑ PRO-A-3579 [DJ]	Batdance (Edit 4:06) (LP Version 6:13)	1989	10.00
❑ PRO-A-3702 [DJ]	Batdance (The Batmix 7:15) (Radio Edit 4:09)/(Vicki Vale Mix 5:55) (Radio Edit 4:13)	1989	12.00
❑ PRO-A-3704 [DJ]	Scandalous (LP Version 6:15) (Edit 4:12)	1989	15.00
❑ PRO-A-3705 [DJ]	Partyman (LP Version 3:11) (same on both sides)	1989	10.00
❑ PRO-A-7000 [DJ]	Letitgo (Edit 4:17) (Album Version 5:33)	1994	15.00
❑ PRO-A-7481 [DJ]	Purple Medley (Edit 3:34)/(11:03)	1995	20.00
❑ PRO-A-7594 [DJ]	I Hate U (Edit 4:27) (5:58)	1995	15.00
❑ PRO-A-7941 [DJ]	Gold (Album Version 7:23) (Radio Edit with Guitar Solo 4:22)//Rock 'N' Roll Is Alive! (and it lives in Minneapolis)/Gold (Alternate Radio Mix with Guitar Solo 4:36)	1995	20.00
—Promo only on gold vinyl			
❑ 20120	1999/Little Red Corvette	1983	25.00
❑ 20170	Let's Pretend We're Married (7:20)/Irresistible Bitch (4:11)	1983	20.00
❑ 20228	When Doves Cry (5:54)/17 Days (3:54)	1984	10.00
❑ 20246	Let's Go Crazy (Special Dance Mix 7:35)/Erotic City (7:24)	1984	10.00
❑ 20267	Purple Rain (8:45)/God (3:59)	1984	—
—Black vinyl; can someone confirm the existence of this record as a stock copy?			
❑ 20267	Purple Rain (8:45)/God (3:59)	1984	25.00
—Purple vinyl			
❑ 20291	I Would Die 4 U (Extended Version 10:00)/Another Lonely Christmas (6:47)	1984	15.00
—Oversized picture label with die-cut custom sleeve			
❑ 21257	Batdance (The Batmix 7:15)//(Vicki Vale Mix 5:55)/200 Balloons (5:05)	1989	10.00
❑ 21370	Partyman (The Purple Party Mix 6:02) (Partyman Music Mix 4:31)//(The Video Mix 6:20)/Feel U Up (Short Stroke 3:42)	1989	10.00
❑ 21422	The Scandalous Sex Suite (The Crime 6:24/The Passion 6:14/The Rapture 6:39)//Sex (7:02)/When 2 R in Love (4:02)	1989	10.00
❑ 41745	Letitgo (Caviar Radio Edit 4:49) (Cavi' Street Edit 5:02) (Instrumental 5:02) (On the Cool-Out Tip Radio Edit 4:34)/(Sherm Stick Edit 5:42) (- Sherm Stick Edit 5:42) (Original Radio Edit 4:15) (Original Album Version 5:33)	1994	8.00
❑ 41745-A [DJ]	Letitgo (Caviar Radio Edit 4:49) (Cavi' Street Edit 5:02) (Instrumental 5:02) (On the Cool-Out Tip Radio Edit 4:34)/(Sherm Stick Edit 5:42) (- Sherm Stick Edit 5:42) (Original Radio Edit 4:15) (Original Album Version 5:33)	1994	12.00
—White promo label, "Advance Only." on label, generic white jacket			
❑ 41833	Space (Universal Love Radio Remix 3:58) (Universal Love Remix 6:10) (Funky Stuff Remix 5:41)/(Acoustic Remix 4:41) (Funky Stuff Dub 4:48)	1994	8.00
❑ 41833-A [DJ]	Space (Universal Love Radio Remix 3:58) (Universal Love Remix 6:10) (Funky Stuff Remix 5:41)/(Acoustic Remix 4:41) (Funky Stuff Dub 4:48)	1994	12.00
—White label promo, "Advance Only." on label			
❑ 43503	Purple Medley (11:03) (Edit 3:14)/Kirk J's B Sides Remix (7:01)	1995	10.00
❑ 43592	I Hate U (Extended Remix 6:17) (7" Edit 4:27)/(Quiet Night Mix by Eric Leeds 3:55) (Album Version 6:07)	1995	8.00
❑ DWBS 50028	Let's Work (Dance Remix, Long Version 8:02)/Gotta Stop (Messin' About) (2:55)	1982	60.00

45s

PAISLEY PARK

Number	Title (A Side/B Side)	Yr	NM
❑ GWB 0528	Purple Rain/Raspberry Beret	1986	3.00
—"Back to Back Hits" reissue			
❑ GWB 0529	Pop Life/America	1986	3.00
—"Back to Back Hits" reissue			
❑ PRO-S-2939 [DJ]	Hot Thing (same on both sides)	1987	12.00
❑ PRO-S-3211 [DJ]	Glam Slam (Shep Pettibone Remix 4:22)/(Edit 3:28)	1988	15.00
❑ PRO-S-3371 [DJ]	I Wish U Heaven (Radio Edit of Remix 4:25)/(Single Edit of Remix 5:45)	1988	15.00
❑ 15990	Insatiable/Diamonds and Pearls	1993	3.00
—"Back to Back Hits" reissue			
❑ 15991	Cream/Gett Off	1993	3.00
—"Back to Back Hits" reissue			
❑ 18371	Pink Cashmere/Soft and Wet	1993	3.00
❑ 18372	Peach/Nothing Compares 2 U (Live)	1993	3.00
❑ 18583	The Morning Papers/Live 4 Love	1993	3.00
❑ 18700	Damn U/2 Whom It May Concern	1993	3.00
❑ 18707	My Name Is Prince/Sexy Mutha	1992	3.00
❑ 18817	Sexy M.F./Strollin'	1992	3.00
❑ 18824	7/(Acoustic Version)	1992	3.00
❑ 19020	Money Don't Matter 2 Night/Call the Law	1992	3.00
❑ 19083	Diamonds and Pearls/X-Cerpts	1991	3.00
❑ 19090	Insatiable/I Love U in Me	1991	3.00
❑ 19175	Cream/Horny Pony	1991	3.00
❑ 19225	Gett Off/Horny Pony	1991	3.00
❑ 19525	New Power Generation/New Power Generation (Part II)	1990	3.00
❑ 19751	Thieves in the Temple/Thieves in the Temple Part II	1990	3.00
❑ 27745	I Wish U Heaven/Scarlet Pussy	1988	3.00
❑ 27745 [DJ]	I Wish U Heaven (same on both sides)	1988	8.00
❑ 27745 [PS]	I Wish U Heaven/Scarlet Pussy	1988	5.00
❑ 27806	Glam Slam/Escape	1988	3.00
❑ 27806 [DJ]	Glam Slam (same on both sides)	1988	8.00
❑ 27806 [PS]	Glam Slam/Escape	1988	3.00
—Heavy plastic sleeve with title sticker			
❑ 27900	Alphabet St./Alphabet St. (Cont.)	1988	3.00
❑ 27900 [DJ]	Alphabet St./Alphabet St. (Cont.)	1988	8.00
❑ 27900 [PS]	Alphabet St./Alphabet St. (Cont.)	1988	3.00
—Heavy PVC sleeve with title sticker			
❑ 28288	I Could Never Take the Place of Your Man/Hot Thing	1987	3.00
❑ 28288 [DJ]	I Could Never Take the Place of Your Man (same on both sides)	1987	8.00
❑ 28288 [PS]	I Could Never Take the Place of Your Man/Hot Thing	1987	3.00
❑ 28289	U Got the Look/Housequake	1987	3.00
❑ 28289 [DJ]	U Got the Look (same on both sides)	1987	8.00
❑ 28289 [PS]	U Got the Look/Housequake	1987	3.00
❑ 28334	If I Was Your Girlfriend/Shockadelica	1987	3.00
❑ 28334 [DJ]	If I Was Your Girlfriend (same on both sides)	1987	8.00

Number	Title (A Side/B Side)	Yr	NM
❑ 28334 [PS]	If I Was Your Girlfriend/Shockadelica	1987	3.00
❑ 28399	Sign "O" the Times/La, La, La, Hee, Hee, Hee	1987	3.00
❑ 28399 [DJ]	Sign "O" the Times (same on both sides)	1987	8.00
❑ 28399 [PS]	Sign "O" the Times/La, La, La, Hee, Hee, Hee	1987	3.00
❑ 28620	Anotherloverholenyohead/Girls and Boys	1986	3.00
❑ 28620 [DJ]	Anotherloverholenyohead (same on both sides)	1986	8.00
❑ 28620 [DJ]	Girls and Boys (same on both sides)	1986	12.00
❑ 28620 [PS]	Anotherloverholenyohead/Girls and Boys	1986	3.00
❑ 28711	Mountains/Alexa de Paris	1986	3.00
❑ 28711 [DJ]	Mountains (same on both sides)	1986	8.00
❑ 28711 [PS]	Mountains/Alexa de Paris	1986	3.00
❑ 28751	Kiss/Love or $	1986	3.00
❑ 28751 [DJ]	Kiss (same on both sides)	1986	8.00
❑ 28751 [PS]	Kiss/Love or $	1986	3.00
❑ 28972	Raspberry Beret/She's Always In My Hair	1985	3.00
❑ 28972 [DJ]	Raspberry Beret (same on both sides)	1985	8.00
—Unlike stock copies, the promo does not have custom labels; the "Paisley Park" logo is at 9 o'clock, a color "WB" shield is at 3 o'clock			
❑ 28972 [PS]	Raspberry Beret/She's Always In My Hair	1985	3.00
❑ 28998	Pop Life/Hello	1985	3.00
❑ 28998 [DJ]	Pop Life (same on both sides)	1985	8.00
❑ 28998 [PS]	Pop Life/Hello	1985	3.00
❑ 28999	America/Girl	1985	4.00
❑ 28999 [DJ]	America (same on both sides)	1985	8.00
❑ 28999 [PS]	America/Girl	1985	4.00
❑ 29052	Paisley Park/She's Always In My Hair	1985	—
—Unreleased in U.S.; this pairing, with similar numbers, exists in many European countries			
❑ 29052 [PS]	Paisley Park/She's Always In My Hair	1985	500.00
—Evidently, some U.S. picture sleeves exist (not to be confused with European sleeves for this record)			
WARNER BROS.			
❑ GWB 0392	I Wanna Be Your Lover/Why You Wanna Treat Me So Bad?	1982	4.00
—"Back to Back Hits" reissue			
❑ GWB 0468	1999/Little Red Corvette	1984	3.00
—"Back to Back Hits" reissue			
❑ GWB 0476	Delirious/Let's Pretend We're Married	1984	3.00
—"Back to Back Hits" reissue			
❑ GWB 0516	When Doves Cry/Let's Go Crazy	1985	3.00
—"Back to Back Hits" reissue			
❑ GWB 0517	I Would Die 4 U/Take Me With U	1985	3.00
—"Back to Back Hits" reissue			
❑ 8619	Soft and Wet/So Blue	1978	30.00
—Two slightly different variations exist; one has the time of each side under the catalog number, the other has the time of each side after the titles			
❑ 8619 [DJ]	Soft and Wet (stereo/mono)	1978	15.00
❑ 8713	Just As Long As We're Together/In Love	1978	30.00
❑ 8713 [DJ]	Just As Long As We're Together (stereo/mono)	1978	15.00
❑ 17715	Gold/Rock 'N' Roll Is Alive! (and it lives in Minneapolis)	1995	3.00
❑ 17811	I Hate U (Edit)/(Quite Night Mix by Eric Leeds)	1995	3.00
❑ 17903	Purple Medley/Kirk J's B Sides Remix	1995	3.00
❑ 18012	Space (Universal Love Radio Remix)/(Album Version)	1994	3.00
❑ 18074	Letitgo/Solo	1994	3.00
❑ 20129 [PD]	Little Red Corvette/1999	1983	40.00
—7-inch picture disc with custom sticker; numbered as if a 12-inch single			
❑ 21858	I Could Never Take the Place of Your Man/Alphabet St.	1989	3.00
—"Back to Back Hits" series			
❑ 21859	Batdance/Partyman	1989	3.00
—"Back to Back Hits" series			
❑ 21938	Sign "O" the Times/U Got the Look	1988	3.00
—"Back to Back Hits" series			
❑ 21980	Anotherloverholenyohead/Mountains	1987	3.00
—"Back to Back Hits" series			
❑ 21981	Uptown/Controversy	1987	3.00
—"Back to Back Hits" series			
❑ 21982	Kiss/Soft and Wet	1987	3.00
—"Back to Back Hits" series			
❑ 22757	The Arms of Orion/I Love U in Me	1989	3.00
❑ 22757 [PS]	The Arms of Orion/I Love U in Me	1989	3.00
—With Sheena Easton			
❑ 22814	Partyman/Feel U Up	1989	3.00
❑ 22814 [DJ]	Partyman (same on both sides)	1989	12.00
❑ 22814 [PS]	Partyman/Feel U Up	1989	3.00
❑ 22824	Scandalous/When 2 R In Love	1989	3.00
❑ 22824 [DJ]	Scandalous (same on both sides)	1989	20.00
—The last Prince promo 45 -- though "Partyman" has a lower number, it was released earlier, as opposed to the usual backwards numbering of Warner Bros. from 1982 on			
❑ 22824 [PS]	Scandalous/When 2 R In Love	1989	3.00
❑ 22924	Batdance/200 Balloons	1989	3.00
❑ 22924 [DJ]	Batdance (same on both sides)	1989	10.00
❑ 22924 [PS]	Batdance/200 Balloons	1989	3.00
❑ 29079	Take Me With U/Baby I'm a Star	1985	4.00
❑ 29079 [DJ]	Take Me With U (same on both sides)	1985	8.00
❑ 29079 [PS]	Take Me With U/Baby I'm a Star	1985	4.00
❑ 29121	I Would Die 4 U/Another Lonely Christmas	1984	4.00
❑ 29121 [DJ]	I Would Die 4 U (same on both sides)	1984	8.00
❑ 29121 [PS]	I Would Die 4 U/Another Lonely Christmas	1984	4.00
❑ 29174	Purple Rain/God	1984	—
—Black vinyl; can someone confirm the existence of this record as a stock copy?			
❑ 29174	Purple Rain/God	1984	4.00
—Purple vinyl			
❑ 29174 [DJ]	Purple Rain (same on both sides)	1984	8.00
—Purple vinyl			
❑ 29174 [PS]	Purple Rain/God	1984	8.00
—Plastic semi-transparent sleeve			
❑ 29216	Let's Go Crazy/Erotic City	1984	4.00
❑ 29216 [DJ]	Let's Go Crazy (same on both sides)	1984	8.00
❑ 29216 [PS]	Let's Go Crazy/Erotic City	1984	8.00
❑ 29286	When Doves Cry/17 Days	1984	3.00
—Black vinyl			
❑ 29286	When Doves Cry/17 Days	1984	20.00
—Purple vinyl			
❑ 29286 [DJ]	When Doves Cry (3:49)/(5:52)	1984	8.00
—Black vinyl			
❑ 29286 [DJ]	When Doves Cry (3:49)/(5:52)	1984	10.00
—Purple vinyl promo			
❑ 29286 [PS]	When Doves Cry/17 Days	1984	3.00
❑ 29503	Delirious/Horny Toad	1983	5.00
—Label lists correct A-side time of 2:36			
❑ 29503	Delirious/Horny Toad	1983	6.00
—Label erroneously lists A-side time at 3:56			
❑ 29503 [DJ]	Delirious (stereo/mono)	1983	10.00
—Label on both sides lists incorrect A-side time of 3:56			
❑ 29503 [PS]	Delirious/Horny Toad	1983	50.00
—Fold-out poster sleeve			
❑ 29548	Let's Pretend We're Married/Irresistible Bitch	1983	5.00
❑ 29548 [DJ]	Let's Pretend We're Married (stereo/mono)	1983	8.00
❑ 29548 [PS]	Let's Pretend We're Married/Irresistible Bitch	1983	10.00
❑ 29746	Little Red Corvette/All the Critics Love U in New York	1983	5.00
❑ 29746 [DJ]	Little Red Corvette (Edit 3:08)/(Dance Remix 4:32)	1983	12.00
❑ 29896	1999/How Come U Don't Call Me Anymore?	1982	5.00
❑ 29896 [DJ]	1999 (stereo/mono)	1982	8.00
❑ 29896 [PS]	1999/How Come U Don't Call Me Anymore?	1982	10.00
❑ 29942	Do Me, Baby/Private Joy	1982	15.00
❑ 29942 [DJ]	Do Me, Baby (stereo/mono)	1982	7.50
❑ 49050	I Wanna Be Your Lover/My Love Is Forever	1979	10.00
❑ 49050 [DJ]	I Wanna Be Your Lover (stereo/mono)	1979	15.00
❑ 49050 [DJ]	My Love Is Forever (stereo/mono)	1979	20.00
❑ 49050 [PS]	My Love Is Forever	1979	80.00
—Promo-only sleeve; withdrawn when "I Wanna Be Your Lover" was pushed as the A-side			
❑ 49178	Why You Wanna Treat Me So Bad?/Baby	1980	30.00
❑ 49178 [DJ]	Why You Wanna Treat Me So Bad? (stereo/mono)	1980	15.00
❑ 49178 [PS]	Why You Wanna Treat Me So Bad?/Baby	1980	60.00
❑ 49226	Still Waiting/Bambi	1980	15.00
❑ 49226 [DJ]	Still Waiting (stereo/mono)	1980	8.00
❑ 49559	Uptown/Crazy You	1980	15.00
❑ 49559 [DJ]	Uptown (stereo/mono)	1980	7.50
❑ 49559 [PS]	Uptown/Crazy You	1980	15.00
❑ 49638	Dirty Mind/When We're Dancing Close and Slow	1980	15.00
❑ 49638 [DJ]	Dirty Mind (stereo/mono)	1980	7.50
❑ 49808	Controversy/When You Were Mine	1981	15.00
❑ 49808 [DJ]	Controversy (stereo/mono)	1981	8.00
❑ 50002	Let's Work/Ronnie Talk to Russia	1982	15.00
❑ 50002 [DJ]	Let's Work (stereo/mono)	1982	8.00
Albums			
ARISTA			
❑ 14624 [(2)]	Rave Un2 the Joy Fantastic	1999	12.00
NPG/BELLMARK			
❑ 71003 [EP]	The Beautiful Experience	1994	20.00
NPG/REDLINE			
❑ 70004 [(2)]	The Rainbow Children	2001	150.00
PAISLEY PARK			
❑ 25286	Around the World in a Day	1985	10.00
—Original copies have a fold-over flap (deduct 25% or more if missing)			
❑ 25395	Parade	1986	8.00
❑ 25577 [(2)]	Sign "O" The Times	1987	15.00
❑ W1-25577 [(2)]	Sign "O" The Times	1987	18.00
—Columbia House edition			
❑ 25677-DJ [(2)]	The Black Album	1987	3000.
—Entire album on two 12-inch records that play at 45 RPM			
❑ 25677	The Black Album	1987	1500.
—Withdrawn prior to release, though a few copies escaped. Numerous counterfeits exist on other labels and colored vinyl.			
❑ 25720	Lovesexy	1988	12.00
❑ 25720-DJ [DJ]	Lovesexy	1988	20.00
—Gold stamped and stickered cover (no UPC) with promo labels; tracks are banded			
❑ 27493 [(2)]	Graffiti Bridge	1990	15.00
—Also includes The Time, Tevin Campbell			
❑ R 124370	Around the World in a Day	1985	12.00
—RCA Music Service edition			
❑ R 140234	Parade	1986	12.00
—RCA Music Service edition			
❑ R 154087	Lovesexy	1988	14.00
—BMG Direct Marketing edition			
❑ R 234107 [(2)]	Graffiti Bridge	1990	18.00
—Also includes The Time, Tevin Campbell; BMG Direct Marketing edition			
❑ R 261991 [(2)]	Sign "O" The Times	1987	18.00
—BMG Direct Marketing edition			
WARNER BROS.			
❑ BSK 3150	For You	1978	12.00
—White WB label			
❑ BSK 3150	For You	1978	20.00
—First edition on Burbank "palm trees" label			
❑ BSK 3366	Prince	1979	12.00
❑ BSK 3478	Dirty Mind	1980	12.00
❑ BSK 3601	Controversy	1981	12.00
❑ PRO-A-7270 [(2)DJ]	Come	1994	30.00
—Promo-only vinyl			
❑ PRO-A-7330 [DJ]	The Black Album	1994	30.00
—Promo-only vinyl			
❑ PRO-A-7835 [(2)DJ]	The Gold Experience	1995	80.00
—Promo-only gold vinyl with numbered gold foil jacket			
❑ 23720 [(2)]	1999	1982	15.00
❑ 25110	Purple Rain	1984	10.00
—With poster			
❑ 25110	Purple Rain	1984	50.00
—Purple vinyl; comes with poster			
❑ 25936	Batman (Soundtrack)	1989	10.00
❑ 45793 [DJ]	The Black Album	1994	100.00
—Peach vinyl; 1,000 copies			
❑ 45793 [DJ]	The Black Album	1994	200.00
—White vinyl; 300 copies, numbered in gold on the label (from 051 to 350)			
❑ 45793 [DJ]	The Black Album	1994	500.00
—Gray marbled vinyl; 50 copies			
❑ R 160175	Purple Rain	1984	12.00
—RCA Music Service edition; includes poster			
❑ R 160344	Batman (Soundtrack)	1989	12.00
—BMG Direct Marketing edition			
❑ R 252483 [(2)]	1999	1982	18.00
—RCA Music Service edition			

PRINCE, BOB

Number	Title (A Side/B Side)	Yr	NM
Albums			
RCA VICTOR			
❑ LPM-2435 [M]	Opus Jazz	1961	20.00
❑ LSP-2435 [S]	Opus Jazz	1961	25.00
WARNER BROS.			
❑ W 1240 [M]	N.Y. Export: Op. Jazz from Ballets U.S.A.; Ballet Music from Leonard Bernstein's West Side Story	1958	20.00
❑ WS 1240 [S]	N.Y. Export: Op. Jazz from Ballets U.S.A.; Ballet Music from Leonard Bernstein's West Side Story	1958	25.00
❑ W 1276 [M]	Charleston 1970	1959	20.00
❑ WS 1276 [S]	Charleston 1970	1959	25.00

PRINCE, BOBBY

Number	Title (A Side/B Side)	Yr	NM
45s			
CHANCE			
❑ 1128	Tell Me Why, Why, Why/I Want to Hold You	1953	500.00
❑ 1158	Better Think It Over/If You Only Knew	1954	400.00
EXCELLO			
❑ 2039	Too Many Keys/Please Give Me Your Love	1954	80.00

Procol Harum, "A Whiter Shade of Pale," A&M 1389, **$5.**

Number	Title (A Side/B Side)	Yr	NM
PRINCE BUSTER			
45s			
AMY			
❑ 906	Everybody Ska/ 30 Pieces of Silver	1964	15.00
ATLANTIC			
❑ 2231	Don't Make Me Cry/ That Lucky Old Sun	1964	15.00
PHILIPS			
❑ 40427	Ten Commandments/ Don't Make Me Cry	1967	12.00
RCA VICTOR			
❑ 47-9114	Ten Commandments from Woman to Man/Ain't That Saying a Lot	1967	12.00
Albums			
RCA VICTOR			
❑ LPM-3792 [M]	Ten Commandments	1967	25.00
❑ LSP-3792 [S]	Ten Commandments	1967	30.00
PRINE, JOHN			
45s			
ASYLUM			
❑ 45509	Fish and Whistle/Sabu Visits the Twin Cities Alone	1978	4.00
❑ 45550	There She Goes/That's the Way That the World Goes 'Round	1978	4.00
❑ 46562	Ubangi Stomp/Automobile	1979	4.00
ATLANTIC			
❑ 2815	Sam Stone/Blue Umbrella	1971	5.00
❑ 2857	Quiet Man/Illegal Smile	1972	5.00
❑ 2925	Clocks and Spoons/Everybody	1972	5.00
❑ 3013	Grandpa Was a Carpenter/ Onomatopoeia	1974	4.00
❑ 3218	Quiet Man/Illegal Smile	1974	4.00
❑ 3276	Middle Man/Saddle in the Rain	1975	4.00
❑ 3297	Common Sense/Come Back to Us Barbara Lewis, Harre Krishna, Beauregard	1975	4.00
OH BOY			
❑ 001	I Saw Mommy Kissing Santa Claus/Silver Bells	198?	10.00
—Red vinyl			
❑ 001 [PS]	I Saw Mommy Kissing Santa Claus/Silver Bells	198?	12.00
Albums			
ASYLUM			
❑ 6E-139	Bruised Orange	1978	12.00
❑ 6E-222	Pink Cadillac	1979	12.00
❑ 6E-286	Storm Windows	1980	12.00
ATLANTIC			
❑ SD 7240	Diamonds in the Rough	1972	12.00
❑ SD 7274	Sweet Revenge	1973	12.00
❑ SD 8296	John Prine	1971	12.00
❑ SD 18127	Common Sense	1975	12.00
❑ SD 18202	Prime Prine — The Best of John Prine	1976	12.00
❑ SD 19156	John Prine	1978	10.00
—Reissue of 8296			
OH BOY			
❑ 002	Aimless Love	198?	10.00
❑ 003	German Afternoons	198?	10.00
❑ 005 [(2)]	John Prine Live	1986	15.00
❑ OBR-034 [(2)]	Fair & Square	2007	25.00
—Contains four bonus tracks not on the CD version			
PRISCO, TOMMY			
45s			
EPIC			
❑ 5-9219	Maybe Someday/Teardrops in My Heart	1957	20.00
❑ 5-9239	I Don't Want to Love You/ Hasty Words	1957	20.00
❑ 5-9267	Chewin' Gum/O Bella Mia	1958	20.00
❑ 5-9302	Till There Was You/ For Me and My Girl	1959	20.00
❑ 5-9315	Stingaree/Only Once	1959	30.00
PRISONAIRES, THE			
45s			
SUN			
❑ 186	Just Walking in the Rain/ Baby Please	1953	500.00
❑ 186	Just Walking in the Rain/ Baby Please	1953	5000.
—Red vinyl. VG 2500; VG+ 3750			
❑ 189	Softly and Tenderly/ My God Is Real	1953	700.00
❑ 191	A Prisoner's Prayer/I Know	1953	500.00
❑ 207	There Is Love in You/ What'll You Do Next	1954	12000.
—VG 5000; VG+ 8500			
PRIZES, THE			
45s			
PARKWAY			
❑ 917	Summer's Here at Last/ I Found Someone New	1964	10.00
PROBY, P.J.			
45s			
BETA			
❑ 1008	Loud Perfume/(B-side unknown)	1958	200.00
—As "Jett Powers"			
DESIGN			
❑ 811	Go Girl Go/Teen-Age Quarrel	1957	300.00
—As "Jett Powers"			
IMPERIAL			
❑ 66079	Rocking Pneumonia/ Just Call, I'll Be There	1964	15.00
❑ 66084	Somewhere/Just Like Him	1965	—
—Unreleased			
LIBERTY			
❑ 55367	There Stands the One/ Try to Forget Her	1961	15.00
❑ 55505	The Other Side of Town/ Watch Me Walk Away	1962	15.00
❑ 55588	So Do I/I Can't Take It Like You Can	1963	15.00
❑ 55757	Somewhere/Just Like Him	1964	12.00
❑ 55777	Rocking Pneumonia/I Apologize	1965	12.00
❑ 55791	Stagger Lee/Mission Bell	1965	12.00
❑ 55806	That Means a Lot/Let the Water Run Down	1965	25.00
—The A-side is a Lennon-McCartney song; the Beatles' own version was not released until 1996			
❑ 55850	Good Things Are Coming My Way/Maria	1965	12.00
❑ 55875	My Prayer/Wicked Woman	1966	12.00
❑ 55915	I Can't Make It Alone/ If I Ruled the World	1966	12.00
❑ 55915 [PS]	I Can't Make It Alone/ If I Ruled the World	1966	15.00
❑ 55936	Niki-Hoeky/Good Things Are Coming My Way	1966	10.00
❑ 55974	Work with Me Annie/You Can't Come Home Again (If You Leave Me Now)	1967	10.00
❑ 55974 [PS]	Work with Me Annie/You Can't Come Home Again (If You Leave Me Now)	1967	15.00
❑ 55989	Butterfly High/Just Holding On	1967	10.00
❑ 56031	It's Your Day Today/I Apologize	1968	8.00
❑ 56051	What's Wrong with My World/ Turn Her Away	1968	8.00
LONDON			
❑ 9648	Hold Me/The Tip of My Fingers	1964	15.00
❑ 9688	Hold Me/The Tip of My Fingers	1964	15.00
❑ 9705	Sweet and Tender Romance/ Together	1964	15.00
SURFSIDE			
❑ 714	You Got Me Crying/I Need Love	1965	20.00
UNITED ARTISTS			
❑ 0070	Niki-Hoeky/Let the Water Run Down	1973	4.00
—"Silver Spotlight Series" reissue			
Albums			
LIBERTY			
❑ LRP-3406 [M]	Somewhere/Go Go P.J. Proby	1965	20.00
❑ LRP-3421 [M]	P.J. Proby	1965	20.00
❑ LRP-3497 [M]	Enigma	1967	20.00
❑ LRP-3515 [M]	Phenomenon	1967	20.00
❑ LST-7406 [S]	Somewhere/Go Go P.J. Proby	1965	25.00
❑ LST-7421 [S]	P.J. Proby	1965	25.00
❑ LST-7497 [S]	Enigma	1967	25.00
❑ LST-7515 [S]	Phenomenon	1967	25.00
❑ LST-7561	What's Wrong with My World?	1968	25.00

Except when noted otherwise, VG = 25% of NM, and VG+ = 50% of NM. (Example: VG = $2.00, VG+ = $4.00 and NM = $8.00.)

PROCESSION

Number	Title (A Side/B Side)	Yr	NM
45s			
SMASH			
❑ 2225	Adelaide, Adelaide/One Day in Every Week	1969	8.00
❑ 2239	Every American Citizen/You-Me	1969	8.00
Albums			
SMASH			
❑ SRS-67122	Procession	1969	20.00

PROCOL HARUM

Also see THE PARAMOUNTS (4); ROBIN TROWER.

Number	Title (A Side/B Side)	Yr	NM
45s			
A&M			
❑ 885	Homburg/Good Captain Clack	1967	12.00
❑ 927	In the Wee Small Hours of Sixpence/Quite Rightly So	1968	12.00
❑ 1069	A Salty Dog/Long Gone Geek	1969	8.00
❑ 1111	The Devil Came from Kansas/Boredom	1969	8.00
❑ 1218	Whiskey Train/About to Die	1970	6.00
❑ 1264	Power Failure/Broken Barricades	1971	6.00
❑ 1287	Song for a Dreamer/Simple Sister	1971	6.00
❑ 1347	Conquistador/A Salty Dog	1972	5.00
❑ 1347 [PS]	Conquistador/A Salty Dog	1972	8.00
❑ 1389	A Whiter Shade of Pale/Lime Street Blues	1972	5.00
❑ 1389 [PS]	A Whiter Shade of Pale/Lime Street Blues	1972	5.00
CHRYSALIS			
❑ 2011 [DJ]	Bringing Home the Bacon (mono/stereo)	1973	8.00
—May be promo only			
❑ 2013	Grand Hotel/Fires	1973	5.00
❑ 2013 [PS]	Grand Hotel/Fires	1973	10.00
❑ 2032	Nothing But the Truth/Drunk Again	1973	5.00
❑ 2109	Pandora's Box/Piper's Tune	1975	5.00
DERAM			
❑ 7507	A Whiter Shade of Pale/Lime Street Blues	1967	15.00
WARNER BROS.			
❑ CRS 2115	Wizard Man/Something Magic	1977	6.00
—Warner Bros. label with Chrysalis number; possible factory mispress?			
Albums			
A&M			
❑ SP-3123	A Salty Dog	1979	8.00
—Reissue of 4179			
❑ SP-3259	The Best of Procol Harum	198?	8.00
—Reissue of 4401			
❑ SP-4151	Shine On Brightly	1968	25.00
❑ SP-4179	A Salty Dog	1969	15.00
❑ SP-4261	Home	1970	12.00
❑ SP-4294	Broken Barricades	1971	12.00
❑ SP-4335	Procol Harum Live in Concert with the Edmonton Symphony Orchestra	1972	12.00
❑ SP-4373	A Whiter Shade of Pale	1972	12.00
—Reissue of Deram 18008 with one more track			
❑ SP-4401	The Best of Procol Harum	1973	12.00
❑ SP-8503 [DJ]	Procol Harum Lives	197?	25.00
—Interview LP alone			
❑ SP-8503 [DJ]	Procol Harum Lives	197?	300.00
—Promo-only box set with press kit, photos, keychain and interview LP			
CHRYSALIS			
❑ CHR 1037	Grand Hotel	1973	12.00
—Green label with "3300 Warner Blvd." address			
❑ CHR 1037	Grand Hotel	1977	10.00
—Blue label with New York address			
❑ CHR 1058	Exotic Birds and Fruit	1974	12.00
—Green label with "3300 Warner Blvd." address			
❑ CHR 1058	Exotic Birds and Fruit	1977	10.00
—Blue label with New York address			
❑ CHR 1080	Procol's Ninth	1975	12.00
—Green label with "3300 Warner Blvd." address			
❑ CHR 1080	Procol's Ninth	1977	10.00
—Blue label with New York address			
❑ CHR 1130	Something Magic	1977	10.00
❑ PV 41037	Grand Hotel	1985	8.00
❑ PV 41058	Exotic Birds and Fruit	1985	8.00
❑ PV 41080	Procol's Ninth	1985	8.00
DERAM			
❑ DE 16008 [M]	Procol Harum	1967	80.00
❑ DE/S 16008/18008	Procol Harum Poster	1967	25.00
❑ DES 18008 [R]	Procol Harum	1967	40.00

PROCTOR, BILLY

Number	Title (A Side/B Side)	Yr	NM
45s			
EPIC			
❑ 50160	(I'm Gonna) Chop Down That Oak Tree/Keeping Up with the Joneses	1975	5.00
SOUL			
❑ 35099	What Is Black/I Can Take It All	1972	20.00

PROFESSOR MORRISON'S LOLLIPOP

Number	Title (A Side/B Side)	Yr	NM
45s			
WHITE WHALE			
❑ 275	Gypsy Lady/You Got the Love	1968	10.00
❑ 288	Angela/Duba Duba Doo	1968	10.00
❑ 293	Oo Poo Pah Susie/You Can Take It	1969	10.00

PROFFITT, RANDY, AND THE BEACHCOMBERS

Number	Title (A Side/B Side)	Yr	NM
45s			
BETT-COE			
❑ 103	Check That Baby Out One Time/Young Love in Spring	196?	50.00

PROFILES, THE (1)

Number	Title (A Side/B Side)	Yr	NM
45s			
BAMBOO			
❑ 104	Got to Be Love (Something Stupid)/You Don't Care About Me	1969	8.00
❑ 108	Be Careful/I Still Love You	1969	8.00
❑ 115	A Little Misunderstanding/Got to Be Love	1970	8.00
DUO			
❑ 7449	If I Didn't Love You/(B-side unknown)	1968	10.00

PROFILES, THE (2)

Number	Title (A Side/B Side)	Yr	NM
45s			
GAIT			
❑ 1444	Never/Right By Her Side	1962	200.00

PROGRESSIVES, THE

Number	Title (A Side/B Side)	Yr	NM
45s			
DOT			
❑ 16514	Hot Cinders/Man of Mystery	1963	20.00

PROPHETS, THE

Number	Title (A Side/B Side)	Yr	NM
45s			
DELPHI			
❑ 007	Talk Don't Bother Me/Don't Look Back	1967	150.00
❑ 009	Don't You Think It's Time/I Don't Love You No More	1967	120.00
JUBILEE			
❑ 5565	Talk Don't Bother Me/Don't Look Back	1967	25.00
❑ 5596	Don't You Think It's Time/I Don't Love You No More	1967	30.00
SHRINE			
❑ 116	If I Had One Gold Piece/Huh Baby	1966	3000.
—VG 1500; VG+ 2250			
SMASH			
❑ 2161	I Got the Fever/Soul Control	1967	10.00
STEPHANYE			
❑ 335	My Kind of Girl/I Can't Make It	196?	30.00

PROVINE, DOROTHY

Number	Title (A Side/B Side)	Yr	NM
45s			
WARNER BROS.			
❑ 5202	Bye Bye Blackbird/Crazy Words-Crazy Tune	1961	12.00
❑ 5249	The Whisper Song/Don't Bring Lulu	1961	12.00
Albums			
WARNER BROS.			
❑ W 1394 [M]	The Roaring 20's	1961	20.00
❑ WS 1394 [S]	The Roaring 20's	1961	25.00
❑ W 1419 [M]	The Vamp of the Roaring 20's	1961	20.00
❑ WS 1419 [S]	The Vamp of the Roaring 20's	1961	25.00

PROVISOR, DENNY

Number	Title (A Side/B Side)	Yr	NM
45s			
20TH CENTURY-FOX			
❑ 506	Mickey Mouse/Walk On with Him	1964	12.00
VALIANT			
❑ 717	Little Girl Lost/Dead Letter	1965	12.00
❑ 728	She's Not Mine Anymore/It Really Tears Me Up	1965	12.00

PROW, JIMMY LEE

Number	Title (A Side/B Side)	Yr	NM
45s			
KING			
❑ 4929	Shopping List/You Tell Her, I Stutter	1956	30.00

PRUETT, JEANNE

Number	Title (A Side/B Side)	Yr	NM
45s			
AUDIOGRAPH			
❑ 441	Star-Studded Nights/Wild Side of Life	1984	4.00
❑ 454	Love Me/Safely in the Arms of Jesus	1983	5.00
—A-side with Marty Robbins			
❑ 467	Lady of the Eighties/Ain't No Way to Make a Bad Love Grow	1983	4.00
❑ 477	We Came So Close/(B-side unknown)	1983	4.00
DECCA			
❑ 32383	One Woman Man/One Day Ahead of My Tears	1968	8.00
❑ 32435	Make Me Feel Like a Woman Again/Don't Hold Your Breath	1969	8.00
❑ 32614	It Ain't Fair That It Ain't Right/At the Sight of You	1970	6.00
❑ 32703	King Size Bed/One Day Ahead of My Tears	1970	6.00
❑ 32857	Hold On to My Unchanging Love/He's Calling Me Baby Again	1971	6.00
❑ 32929	Love Me/I'm Out Looking for You	1972	6.00
❑ 32977	Call On Me/Stay on His Mind	1972	6.00
❑ 33013	I Forgot More Than You'll Ever Know (About Him)/Don't Hold Your Breath	1972	6.00
IBC			
❑ 0002	Please Sing Satin Sheets for Me/Love All the Leavin' Out of You	1979	5.00
❑ 0005	Back to Back/Wild Side of Life	1979	5.00
❑ 0008	Temporarily Yours/Ain't We Sad Today	1980	5.00
❑ 00010	It's Too Late/I Can't Feel at Home	1980	5.00
MCA			
❑ 40015	Satin Sheets/Sweet Sweetheart	1973	6.00
❑ 40116	I'm Your Woman/Your Memory's Comin' On	1973	4.00
❑ 40207	You Don't Need to Move a Mountain/Hopefully	1974	4.00
❑ 40284	Welcome to the Sunshine (Sweet Baby Jane)/What My Thoughts Do All the Time	1974	4.00
❑ 40340	Just Like Your Daddy/One More Time	1974	4.00
❑ 40395	Honey on His Hands/One of These Days	1975	4.00
❑ 40440	A Poor Man's Woman/Momma Let Me Find Shelter (In Your Sweet Woman's Arms)	1975	4.00
❑ 40490	My Baby's Gone/But Not Today	1975	4.00
❑ 40527	Driftin' Too Far Away/Sweet Sorrow	1976	4.00
❑ 40569	It Doesn't Hurt to Ask/If I'm Not Girl Enough to Hold You	1976	4.00
❑ 40605	I've Taken/Sweet and Warm and Right	1976	4.00
❑ 40678	I'm Living a Lie/My First Pay Day	1977	4.00
❑ 40723	She's Still All Over You/Fancy Place to Cry	1977	4.00
MERCURY			
❑ 55017	I'm a Woman/Midnight Exchange	1978	4.00
❑ 55034	I Guess I'm Not That Good at Being Bad/Where Do You Draw the Line	1978	4.00
MSR			
❑ 1956	Rented Room/(B-side unknown)	1987	4.00
PAID			
❑ 118	Sad Ole Shade of Gray/When I Stop Dreaming	1981	4.00
❑ 136	I Ought to Feel Guilty/Who'll Turn Out the Lights (In Your World)	1981	4.00
RCA VICTOR			
❑ 47-8157	Another Heart to Break/Just a Little After Heartaches	1963	15.00
❑ 47-8232	Little Black Book/The Things I Don't Know	1963	15.00
❑ 47-8297	As a Matter of Fact/Sing Me a Song I Can Cry By	1963	15.00
Albums			
ALLEGIANCE			
❑ AV-5028	Stand By Your Man	1984	10.00
DECCA			
❑ DL 75360	Love Me	1972	15.00

Number	Title (A Side/B Side)	Yr	NM
DOT/MCA			
❑ 39031	Jeanne Pruett	1985	10.00
MCA			
❑ 338	Satin Sheets	1973	12.00
❑ 388	Jeanne Pruett	1974	12.00
❑ 479	Honey on His Hands	1975	12.00
❑ 503	Love Me	1975	12.00
—Reissue of Decca LP			

PRYOR, RICHARD

Albums

Number	Title (A Side/B Side)	Yr	NM
AUDIOFIDELITY			
❑ 349 [PD]	Richard Pryor Live	198?	15.00
DOVE			
❑ RS 6325	Richard Pryor	1968	20.00
LAFF			
❑ (# unknown)	Supernigger	198?	8.00
❑ A 146	Craps: After Hours	1971	12.00
❑ A 170	Pryor Goes Foxx Hunting	197?	12.00
❑ A 184	Down 'N' Dirty	197?	12.00
❑ A 188	Richard Pryor Meets Richard and Willie and the S.L.A.	1976	12.00
❑ A 196	Are You Serious???	1977	12.00
❑ A 198	Who Me? I'm Not Him	1977	12.00
❑ A 200	Black Ben	1978	10.00
❑ A 202	Wizard of Comedy	1978	10.00
❑ A 206	Outrageous	1979	10.00
❑ A 209	Insane	1980	10.00
❑ A 212	Holy Smoke	1980	10.00
❑ A 216	Rev. Du Rite	1981	10.00
❑ A 221	The Very Best of Richard Pryor	1982	10.00
❑ 226	Blackjack	198?	8.00
—Reissue of 146			
❑ 227	Show Biz	198?	8.00
—Reissue of 200			
❑ 279	Richard Pryor Live	198?	8.00
PARTEE			
❑ PBS-2404	That Nigger's Crazy	1974	15.00
REPRISE			
❑ MS 2227	Is It Something I Said?	1975	12.00
❑ MS 2241	That Nigger's Crazy	197?	12.00
—Reissue of Partee LP			
❑ MSK 2285	Is It Something I Said?	1977	10.00
—Reissue of 2227			
❑ MSK 2287	That Nigger's Crazy	1977	10.00
—Reissue of Reprise 2241			
❑ RS 6325	Richard Pryor	197?	12.00
—Reissue of Dove LP			
TIGER LILY			
❑ TL 14023	L.A. Jail	1977	12.00
WARNER BROS.			
❑ BS 2960	Bicentennial Nigger	1976	12.00
❑ BSK 3057	Richard Pryor's Greatest Hits	1977	10.00
❑ BSK 3114	Bicentennial Nigger	1977	10.00
—Reissue of 2960			
❑ 2BSK 3364 [(2)]	Wanted	1978	12.00
❑ BSK 3660	Richard Pryor Live on the Sunset Strip	1982	10.00
❑ 23981	Richard Pryor: Here and Now	1983	10.00

PRYOR, SNOOKY

45s

Number	Title (A Side/B Side)	Yr	NM
J.O.B.			
❑ 1014	Cryin' Shame/Eight, Nine, Ten	1953	400.00
❑ 1126	Uncle Sam, Don't Take My Man/Boogie Twist	1963	200.00
PARROT			
❑ 807	Crosstown Blues/I Want You for Myself	1954	1500.
—Black vinyl			
❑ 807	Crosstown Blues/I Want You for Myself	1954	2500.
—Red vinyl			
VEE JAY			
❑ 215	Judgment Day/Someone to Love Me	1956	120.00

PRYSOCK, ARTHUR

45s

Number	Title (A Side/B Side)	Yr	NM
BETHLEHEM			
❑ 3100	The Girls I Never Kissed/Funny World	1972	6.00
DECCA			
❑ 25684	When Day Is Done/What Will I Tell My Heart	1965	8.00
❑ 27722	Blue Velvet/Morning Side Of the Mountain	1951	15.00
❑ 27769	Sin/The Love of a Gypsy	1951	15.00
❑ 27871	A Man Ain't Supposed to Cry/I Didn't Sleep a Wink Last Night	1951	15.00
❑ 27967	Wheel of Fortune/'Til the Stars Fall in the Ocean	1952	15.00
❑ 27978	I Hear a Rhapsody/Am I to Blame	1952	15.00
❑ 28270	School of Love/Sentimental Fool	1952	15.00
❑ 28700	I'd Give Anything/This Is the Time	1953	15.00
❑ 28867	My Mood/Temptation	1953	15.00
❑ 28950	Nobody Cares/Jean	1953	15.00
❑ 29118	Baby Don't You Cry/My Last Goodbye	1954	15.00
❑ 31710	Wheel of Fortune/I Cover the Waterfront	1964	8.00
❑ 31775	Baby, Don't You Cry/I Didn't Sleep a Wink Last Night	1965	8.00
GUSTO			
❑ 9023	Today I Started Loving You Again/It Ain't No Big Thing	1979	6.00
KING			
❑ 6243	Soul Soliloquy/(I Wanna Go) Where the Soul Trees Grow	1969	6.00
❑ 6271	The 23rd Psalm/I Believe	1969	6.00
❑ 6276	Save Your Love for Me/If I Were Young Again	1969	6.00
❑ 6279	Go Ahead and Fly/How Do I Tell Her	1969	6.00
❑ 6307	Have a Good Time/Frisco Line	1970	6.00
❑ 6315	Lord, Is That Me/My Home Is Not a Home Without You	1970	6.00
❑ 6353	Cry/Unforgettable	1971	6.00
❑ 6354	It Ain't No Big Thing/Big Blue Diamonds	1971	6.00
❑ 6364	Precious Memories/Just a Closer Walk with Thee	1971	6.00
MCA			
❑ 40943	Here's to Good Friends/All I Can Do Is Cry	1978	8.00
—The song that became the "Tonight, let it be Lowenbrau" commercial			
MERCURY			
❑ 70352	Take Care of Yourself/I'll Never Let You Cry	1954	15.00
❑ 70414	This I Know/If You Don't, Somebody Will	1954	15.00
❑ 70502	Show Me How to Mambo/I'm in Heaven Tonight	1954	15.00
❑ 70599	I Have Lied/Morning, Noon and Night	1955	15.00
OLD TOWN			
❑ 100	In the Rain/Thank Heaven for You	1973	5.00
❑ 103	Color My World/Good Morning News	1974	5.00
❑ 106	Hurt So Bad/Love Makes It Right	1974	5.00
❑ 108	I Wantcha Baby/One Broken Heart	1975	5.00
❑ 1000	When Love Is New/All I Need Is You	1976	5.00
❑ 1001	I Wantcha Baby/One Broken Heart	1977	5.00
❑ 1002	You Can Do It/You Can Do It (Part 2)	1977	5.00
❑ 1003	Since I Fell for You/Between Hello and Goodbye	1978	5.00
❑ 1055	I Love You So/The Greatest Gift	1958	12.00
❑ 1060	I Just Want to Make Love to You/Keep a Light in the Window	1958	12.00
❑ 1073	I Worry About You/My Faith	1959	12.00
❑ 1079	The Very Thought of You/If Ever I Should Fall in Love	1960	10.00
❑ 1087	This Is My Love/Do You Believe	1960	10.00
❑ 1092	Good Rockin' Tonight/My Everything	1960	10.00
❑ 1101	This Time/I Wonder Where Our Love Has Gone	1961	10.00
❑ 1106	One More Time/Speak to Me	1961	10.00
❑ 1115	April in Paris/When I Fall in Love	1962	10.00
❑ 1125	Where Can I Go/Pianissimo	1962	10.00
❑ 1132	Our Love Will Last/Come and See This Old Fool	1963	10.00
❑ 1138	My Special Prayer/You Can't Come In	1963	10.00
❑ 1144	There Will Never Be Another You/Crawdad	1963	10.00
❑ 1146	Stella by Starlight/My Wish	1963	10.00
❑ 1155	Ebb Tide/Are You Ready for a Laugh	1964	8.00
❑ 1163	Close Your Eyes/My Everlasting Love	1964	8.00
❑ 1170	Fly Me to the Moon/Without the One You Love	1964	8.00
❑ 1174	Full Moon and Empty Arms/You Always Hurt the One You Love	1964	8.00
❑ 1177	Teardrops in the Rain/I'm Crossing Over	1965	8.00
❑ 1183	It's Too Late, Baby Too Late/Who Can I Turn To	1965	8.00
❑ 1185	Open Up Your Heart/Only a Fool Breaks His Own Heart	1965	8.00
❑ 1188	Again/I Got the Blues So Bad	1965	8.00
❑ 1191	My Funny Valentine/House by the Side of the Road	1966	8.00
❑ 1196	Because/Let It Be Me	1966	8.00
VERVE			
❑ 10470	You Don't Have to Say You Love Me/10,000 Kisses, 10,000 Hugs	1966	6.00
❑ 10515	Love Me/She's a Woman	1967	6.00
❑ 10544	Before You Break My Heart/Goodbye, So Long	1967	6.00
❑ 10574	A Working Man's Prayer/No More in Life	1967	6.00
❑ 10592	Madam/No Sun Today	1968	6.00
❑ 10620	I Must Be Doing Something Right/Young Runaways	1968	6.00
❑ 10633	My Special Prayer/Pretty Girl	1969	6.00

Albums

Number	Title (A Side/B Side)	Yr	NM
DECCA			
❑ DL 4581 [M]	Strictly Sentimental	1965	15.00
❑ DL 4628 [M]	Showcase	1965	15.00
❑ DL 74581 [S]	Strictly Sentimental	1965	20.00
❑ DL 74628 [S]	Showcase	1965	20.00
KING			
❑ KS-1064	The Country Side of Arthur Prysock	1969	12.00
❑ KS-1066	Where the Soul Trees Go	1970	12.00
❑ KS-1067	The Lord Is My Shepherd	1970	12.00
❑ KS-1088	Fly My Love	1970	12.00
❑ KS-1134	Unforgettable	1971	12.00
MCA			
❑ 3061	Here's To Good Friends	1978	10.00
MGM			
❑ GAS-134	Arthur Prysock (Golden Archive Series)	1970	12.00
❑ SE-4694	Arthur Prysock	1970	12.00
MILESTONE			
❑ M-9139	A Rockin' Good Way	1986	10.00
❑ M-9146	This Guy's in Love with You	1987	10.00
❑ M-9157	Today's Love Songs, Tomorrow's Blues	1988	10.00
OLD TOWN			
❑ 12-001	Arthur Prysock '74	1973	12.00
❑ 12-002	Love Makes It Right	1974	12.00
❑ 12-004	All My Life	1976	12.00
❑ LP-102 [M]	I Worry About You	1962	50.00
❑ LP-2004 [M]	Arthur Prysock Sings Only for You	1962	50.00
❑ LP-2005 [M]	Coast to Coast	1963	40.00
❑ LP-2006 [M]	A Portrait of Arthur Prysock	1963	40.00
❑ LP-2007 [M]	Everlasting Songs for Everlasting Lovers	1964	40.00
❑ LP-2008 [M]	Intimately Yours	1964	40.00
❑ LP-2009 [M]	A Double Header with Arthur Prysock	1965	40.00
❑ LP-2010 [M]	In a Mood	1965	40.00
❑ OT 12005	Arthur Prysock Does It Again	1977	12.00
❑ ST-90604 [S]	A Portrait of Arthur Prysock	1965	40.00
—Capitol Record Club edition			
❑ T-90604 [M]	A Portrait of Arthur Prysock	1965	40.00
—Capitol Record Club edition			
POLYDOR			
❑ PD-2-8901 [(2)]	Silk and Satin	1977	15.00
VERVE			
❑ V6-650 [(2)]	24 Karat Hits	1969	15.00
❑ V-5009 [M]	Art and Soul	1966	12.00
❑ V6-5009 [S]	Art and Soul	1966	15.00
❑ V-5011 [M]	The Best of Arthur Prysock	1967	12.00
❑ V6-5011 [S]	The Best of Arthur Prysock	1967	15.00
❑ V-5012 [M]	A Portrait of Arthur Prysock	1967	15.00
❑ V6-5012 [S]	A Portrait of Arthur Prysock	1967	15.00
❑ V-5014 [M]	Mister Prysock	1967	15.00
❑ V6-5014 [S]	Mister Prysock	1967	15.00
❑ V-5029 [M]	Love Me	1968	15.00
❑ V6-5029 [S]	Love Me	1968	12.00
❑ V-5038 [M]	The Best of Arthur Prysock, Number 2	1968	20.00
—All mono copies appear to be yellow label promos			
❑ V6-5038 [S]	The Best of Arthur Prysock, Number 2	1968	12.00
❑ V-5048 [M]	To Love or Not to Love	1968	30.00
—May be promo only			
❑ V6-5048 [S]	To Love or Not to Love	1968	12.00
❑ V6-5059	I Must Be Doing Something Right	1968	12.00
❑ V6-5070	This Is My Beloved	1969	12.00

PRYSOCK, ARTHUR/COUNT BASIE Also see each artist's individual listings.

Albums

Number	Title (A Side/B Side)	Yr	NM
VERVE			
❑ V-8646 [M]	Arthur Prysock/Count Basie	1966	15.00
❑ V6-8646 [S]	Arthur Prysock/Count Basie	1966	20.00
❑ 827011-1	Arthur Prysock/Count Basie	1985	8.00
—Reissue			

Number	Title (A Side/B Side)	Yr	NM

PRYSOCK, RED

45s

CHESS

Number	Title (A Side/B Side)	Yr	NM
❑ 2042	I Heard It Through the Grapevine/ Groovy Sax	1968	8.00

KING

Number	Title (A Side/B Side)	Yr	NM
❑ 5595	Hand Clapping One More Time/ Smokestack	1962	10.00
❑ 5644	Quick as a Flash/Old Folks	1962	10.00
❑ 5669	Harem Girl/Ride Away	1962	10.00
❑ 5704	Here We Go Again/ Can't Sit Down	1963	10.00

MERCURY

Number	Title (A Side/B Side)	Yr	NM
❑ 70367	Jump Red Jump/Body and Soul	1954	20.00
❑ 70419	Happy Feet/Blow Your Horn	1954	20.00
❑ 70460	Hey There/Fats' Place	1954	20.00
❑ 70540	Rock 'n' Roll/Little Jamie	1955	20.00
❑ 70602	The Zonked/Horn Blows	1955	20.00
❑ 70674	Hand Clappin'/Shoe String	1955	20.00
❑ 70698	Jumbo/Hand Clappin'	1955	20.00
❑ 70733	Finger Tips/Short Circuit	1955	20.00
❑ 70787	Zip/Red Speaks	1956	15.00
❑ 70918	Rock and Roll Party/ Rock and Roll Mambo	1956	15.00
❑ 70985	Teen-Age Rock/Paquino Walk	1956	15.00
❑ 71054	Head Snappin'/Pog Wog	1957	15.00
❑ 71175	Rooster Walk/Two Point Eight	1957	15.00
❑ 71214	What's the Word, Thunderbird/ Satellite	1957	15.00
❑ 71358	Billie's Blues/Willow Weep for Me	1958	12.00
❑ 71411	Margie/Chop Suey	1959	12.00
❑ 71476	Riffin' with Red/And the Angels Sing	1959	12.00
❑ 71573	Deep Purple/Offshore	1960	12.00
❑ 71735	More Handclappin'/ Twistin' 'n' Bendin'	1960	12.00
❑ 71786	Charleston Twist/Bony Maronie	1961	12.00

RED ROBIN

Number	Title (A Side/B Side)	Yr	NM
❑ 107	Wiggles/Crying My Heart Out	1952	120.00
❑ 117	Hard Rock/Jump for George	1953	100.00
❑ 139	Jackpot/The Hammer	1956	80.00

Albums

MERCURY

Number	Title (A Side/B Side)	Yr	NM
❑ MG-20088 [M]	Rock 'n Roll	1955	200.00
❑ MG-20211 [M]	Fruit Boots	1957	120.00
❑ MG-20307 [M]	The Beat	1957	80.00
❑ MG-20512 [M]	Swing Softly Red	1958	50.00
❑ SR-60188 [S]	Swing Softly Red	1959	80.00

WING

Number	Title (A Side/B Side)	Yr	NM
❑ MGW-12007 [M]	Fruit Boots	1959	40.00
—Originals have liner notes on back cover			
❑ MGW-12007 [M]	Fruit Boots	196?	20.00
—Reissues have other LPs listed on back cover			
❑ SRW-16007 [R]	Fruit Boots	196?	12.00

PSYCHEDELIC FURS

12-Inch Singles

A&M

Number	Title (A Side/B Side)	Yr	NM
❑ 17367 [DJ]	Pretty in Pink/If You Leave	1986	10.00
—B-side by Orchestral Manoeuvres in the Dark; promo from movie "Pretty in Pink"			
❑ 17367 [DJ]	Pretty in Pink/If You Leave	1986	10.00
—B-side by Orchestral Manoeuvres in the Dark; promo from movie "Pretty in Pink"			

COLUMBIA

Number	Title (A Side/B Side)	Yr	NM
❑ AS 879 [DJ]	We Love You/Sister Europe	1980	8.00
❑ AS879 [DJ]	We Love You/Sister Europe	1980	8.00
❑ AS 1538 [DJ]	Love My Way/Forever Now/ President Gas/Angels	1980	20.00
❑ AS1538 [DJ]	Love My Way/Forever Now/ President Gas/Angels	1980	20.00
❑ AS 1839 [DJ]	The Ghost in You (Edit)/The Ghost in You (LP Version)	1984	8.00
❑ AS1839 [DJ]	The Ghost in You (Edit)/The Ghost in You (LP Version)	1984	8.00
❑ CAS 1877	Should God Forget/Badman	1989	8.00
❑ AS 1908 [DJ]	Here Comes Cowboy (Remix Edit)/Here Comes Cowboy (LP Version)	1984	8.00
❑ AS1908 [DJ]	Here Comes Cowboy (Remix Edit)/Here Comes Cowboy (LP Version)	1984	8.00
❑ CAS 2538 [DJ]	Heartbreak Beat (LP version)/ Heartbreak Beat (7" version)	1986	6.00
❑ CAS2538 [DJ]	Heartbreak Beat (LP version)/ Heartbreak Beat (7" version)	1986	6.00
❑ CAS2829 [DJ]	Angels Don't Cry (LP version)/ Angels Don't Cry (7" Remix)	1987	6.00
❑ CAS 02829 [DJ]	Angels Don't Cry (LP version)/ Angels Don't Cry (7" Remix)	1987	6.00
❑ 03197	Love My Way/Goodbye/ Aeroplane	1982	6.00
❑ 04984	The Ghost in You/Heartbeat (New York Mix)	1984	6.00
❑ 05696	Heartbreak Beat (Extended)/ Heartbreak Beat (Dub)/ New Dream	1987	6.00
❑ 06862	Shock (3 versions)	1987	6.00
❑ 07862	All That Money Wants (Special Version)	1988	6.00

45s

A&M

Number	Title (A Side/B Side)	Yr	NM
❑ 2826	Pretty in Pink (Long)/ Pretty in Pink (Short)	1986	3.00
❑ 2826 [PS]	Pretty in Pink (Long)/ Pretty in Pink (Short)	1986	25.00

COLUMBIA

Number	Title (A Side/B Side)	Yr	NM
❑ 03340	Love My Way/I Don't Want to Be Your Shadow	1982	4.00
❑ 03930	Run and Run/President Gas	1983	3.00
❑ 04416	The Ghost in You/ Heartbeat (Remix)	1984	3.00
❑ 04416 [PS]	The Ghost in You/ Heartbeat (Remix)	1984	3.00
❑ 04577	Here Come Cowboys/ Another Edge	1984	3.00
❑ 04627	Heaven/Alice's House	1984	3.00
❑ 06420	Heartbreak Beat/New Dream	1986	3.00
❑ 06420 [PS]	Heartbreak Beat/New Dream	1986	3.00
❑ 07224	Shock/President Gas (Live)	1987	3.00
❑ 07440	Angels Don't Cry/Mack the Knife	1987	3.00
❑ 07974	All That Money Wants/Birdland	1988	3.00
❑ 07974 [PS]	All That Money Wants/Birdland	1988	3.00
❑ 08499	Heaven/India	1988	3.00
❑ 74055	Until She Comes/Sometimes	1991	—
—Cassette only			

Albums

COLUMBIA

Number	Title (A Side/B Side)	Yr	NM
❑ AS 1296 [DJ]	Interchords	1981	15.00
❑ AS1296 [DJ]	Interchords	1981	25.00
❑ CAS1310 [DJ]	Interchords with Richard Butler	1988	20.00
❑ CAS 01310 [DJ]	Interchords with Richard Butler	1988	15.00
❑ CAS 2719 [DJ]	Richard Butler Interview	1987	15.00
❑ CAS2719 [DJ]	Richard Butler Interview	1987	15.00
❑ NFC 36791	Psychedelic Furs	1980	12.00
❑ PC 36791	The Psychedelic Furs	198?	8.00
—Budget-line reissue			
❑ NFC 37339	Talk Talk Talk	1981	10.00
❑ PC 37339	Talk Talk Talk	1983	8.00
—Budget-line reissue			
❑ ARC 38261	Forever Now	1982	10.00
❑ PC 38261	Forever Now	198?	8.00
—Budget-line reissue			
❑ BFC 39278	Mirror Moves	1984	10.00
❑ PC 39278	Mirror Moves	198?	8.00
—Budget-line reissue			
❑ FC 40466	Midnight to Midnight	1987	10.00
❑ FC 44377	All of This and Nothing	1988	10.00
❑ FC 45412	Book of Days	1989	10.00

PSYCHOTIC PINEAPPLE, THE

45s

PYNOTIC

Number	Title (A Side/B Side)	Yr	NM
❑ (no #)	I Want Her So Bad/Say That You Will	1978	20.00
❑ (no #) [PS]	I Want Her So Bad/Say That You Will	1978	20.00

RICHMOND

Number	Title (A Side/B Side)	Yr	NM
❑ 1	I Wanna Wanna Wanna Wanna Wanna Wanna Wanna Get Rid of You/Ahead of My Time	1979	7.50
❑ 1 [PS]	I Wanna Wanna Wanna Wanna Wanna Wanna Wanna Get Rid of You/Ahead of My Time	1979	7.50

Albums

RICHMOND

Number	Title (A Side/B Side)	Yr	NM
❑ 6026	Where's the Party	1980	25.00

PUBLIC IMAGE LTD.

Includes Johnny Rotten - now as Lydon - from the SEX PISTOLS. Includes Johnny Rotten - now as Lydon - from the SEX PISTOLS.

12-Inch Singles

ELEKTRA

Number	Title (A Side/B Side)	Yr	NM
❑ ED 5129 [DJ]	Rise (3 versions)	1986	8.00
❑ ED5129 [DJ]	Rise (3 versions)	1986	8.00

VIRGIN

Number	Title (A Side/B Side)	Yr	NM
❑ 1120 [DJ]	Seattle (12" Mix)/Body (12" Mix)	1987	8.00
❑ 1120 [DJ]	Seattle (12" Mix)/Body (12" Mix)	1987	8.00
❑ 1406 [DJ]	Happy (3 versions)	1989	6.00
❑ 1406 [DJ]	Happy (3 versions)	1989	6.00
❑ 2247 [DJ]	Body (Remix)/Body (7" version)	1988	8.00
❑ 2247 [DJ]	Body (Remix)/Body (7" version)	1988	8.00
❑ 2709 [DJ]	Disappointed (3 versions)	1989	10.00
❑ 2709 [DJ]	Disappointed (3 versions)	1989	10.00
❑ 96519	Warriors (2 versions)/Happy (2 versions)	1989	8.00
❑ 96729	Seattle (12" Mix)/Body (12" Mix)	1987	6.00

Albums

ELEKTRA

Number	Title (A Side/B Side)	Yr	NM
❑ 60365	This Is What You Want... This Is What You'll Get	1984	10.00
❑ 60438	Public Image Ltd. Album	1986	10.00
❑ 60491	Live in Tokyo	1985	10.00

ISLAND

Number	Title (A Side/B Side)	Yr	NM
❑ 2WX 3288 [(2)]	Second Edition	1980	18.00

VIRGIN

Number	Title (A Side/B Side)	Yr	NM
❑ 90642	Happy	1987	10.00
❑ 91062	9	1989	10.00

WARNER BROS.

Number	Title (A Side/B Side)	Yr	NM
❑ 2WX 3288 [(2)]	Second Edition	198?	12.00
—Reissue			
❑ BSK 3536	Flowers of Romance	1981	12.00

PUCKETT, GARY, AND THE UNION GAP

Includes Gary Puckett solo and records credited to "The Union Gap Featuring Gary Puckett."

45s

COLUMBIA

Number	Title (A Side/B Side)	Yr	NM
❑ 44297	Woman, Woman/ Don't Make Promises	1967	8.00
❑ 44297 [PS]	Woman, Woman/ Don't Make Promises	1967	12.00
—As "The Union Gap"			
❑ 44450	Young Girl/I'm Losing You	1968	8.00
—As "The Union Gap Featuring Gary Puckett"			
❑ 44450 [PS]	Young Girl/I'm Losing You	1968	12.00
—As "The Union Gap featuring Gary Puckett"			
❑ 44547	Lady Willpower/ Daylight Strangers	1968	8.00
❑ 44547 [PS]	Lady Willpower/ Daylight Strangers	1968	12.00
—As "The Union Gap"			
❑ 44644	Over You/If the Day Would Come	1968	6.00
❑ 44644 [PS]	Over You/If the Day Would Come	1968	12.00
❑ 44788	Don't Give In to Him/Could I	1969	6.00
❑ 44967	This Girl Is a Woman Now/ His Other Woman	1969	6.00
❑ 45097	Let's Give Adam and Eve Another Chance/The Beggar	1970	6.00
❑ 45097 [PS]	Let's Give Adam and Eve Another Chance/The Beggar	1970	8.00
❑ 45249	I Just Don't Know What to Do With Myself/All That Matters	1970	5.00
❑ 45303	Keep the Customer Satisfied/ No One Really Knows	1971	5.00
❑ 45358	Life Has Its Little Ups and Downs/Shimmering Eyes	1971	5.00
❑ 45438	Hello Morning/Gentle Woman	1971	5.00
❑ 45509	Hello Morning/I Can't Hold On	1971	5.00
❑ 45678	Bless the Child/Leavin' in the Morning	1972	5.00

Albums

COLUMBIA

Number	Title (A Side/B Side)	Yr	NM
❑ CS 1042	Gary Puckett and the Union Gap's Greatest Hits	1970	20.00
❑ CL 2812 [M]	Woman, Woman	1968	40.00
—As "The Union Gap Featuring Gary Puckett"			
❑ CL 2864 [M]	Young Girl	1968	50.00
—Red label stock copy with "Mono" on label; this has been confirmed to exist			
❑ CL 2915 [M]	Incredible	1968	60.00
—Red label stock copy with "Mono" on label; this has been confirmed to exist			
❑ CS 9612 [S]	Woman, Woman	1968	20.00
—As "The Union Gap Featuring Gary Puckett"			
❑ CS 9664 [M]	Young Girl	1968	40.00
—White label promo with stereo number and "Mono" on label; "Special Mono Radio Station Copy" sticker and timing strip on front cover			
❑ CS 9664 [S]	Young Girl	1968	20.00
❑ CS 9715 [S]	Incredible	1968	20.00
❑ CS 9935	The New Gary Puckett and the Union Gap Album	1969	20.00
❑ C 30862	The Gary Puckett Album	1971	15.00

HARMONY

Number	Title (A Side/B Side)	Yr	NM
❑ KH 31184	Lady Willpower	1972	10.00

PUFNSTUF

45s

DECCA

Number	Title (A Side/B Side)	Yr	NM
❑ 32702	Pufnstuf/Nonsense	1970	15.00

PUGSLEY MUNION

Albums

J&S

Number	Title (A Side/B Side)	Yr	NM
❑ SLP-001	Just Like You	1969	100.00

P

Except when noted otherwise, VG = 25% of NM, and VG+ = 50% of NM. (Example: VG = $2.00, VG+ = $4.00 and NM = $8.00.)

PULLEN, DWIGHT See WHITEY PULLEN.

PULLEN, WHITEY

45s

CARLTON

Number	Title (A Side/B Side)	Yr	NM
❑ 455	Sunglasses After Dark/ Teenage Bug	1958	300.00
—As "Dwight Pullen"			

DELTA

Number	Title (A Side/B Side)	Yr	NM
❑ 1503	Broke Waiting for a Break/ I'm Beggin' Your Pardon	196?	50.00

ROLLIN' ROCK

Number	Title (A Side/B Side)	Yr	NM
❑ 005	Let's All Go Wild/ Moonshine Liquor	1978	5.00
❑ 010	Drinkin' Wine/Everybody's Rockin'	1978	5.00
❑ 017	Tuscaloosa Lucy/Tight Slacks	1979	5.00

SAGE

Number	Title (A Side/B Side)	Yr	NM
❑ 274	Walk My Way Back Home/ Don't Make Me Cry	1958	250.00
❑ 279	By You, By the Bayou/ It's Over With	1959	200.00
—As "Dwight Pullen"			
❑ 283	I Live a Lifetime Last Night/ You'll Get Yours Some Day	1959	200.00
—As "Dwight Pullen"			
❑ 294	Let's All Go Wild Tonight/Gently	1959	150.00
❑ 303	I'm Beggin' Your Pardon/Let Your Left Hand Know	1960	100.00
❑ 313	Tuscaloosa Lucy/Waltz of the Steel Guitar	1960	120.00
❑ 372	Crazy in Love/I Won the Day I Lost You	1962	40.00

PUMPKIN

45s

BRUNSWICK

Number	Title (A Side/B Side)	Yr	NM
❑ 55004	Half Past Seventeen/ Boom Boom	1957	40.00

PURCELL, BOOTS, COMBO

45s

HIT

Number	Title (A Side/B Side)	Yr	NM
❑ 26	Rinky Dink/Vacation	1962	8.00
—B-side by Connie Landers			
❑ 39	Desafinado/Release Me	1962	8.00
—B-side by Lucille Johns			

PURE LOVE AND PLEASURE

45s

ABC DUNHILL

Number	Title (A Side/B Side)	Yr	NM
❑ 4232	All in My Mind/What Cha Gonna Do	1970	8.00

Albums

ABC DUNHILL

Number	Title (A Side/B Side)	Yr	NM
❑ DS-50076	A Record of Pure Love and Pleasure	1970	15.00

PURE PRAIRIE LEAGUE

45s

CASABLANCA

Number	Title (A Side/B Side)	Yr	NM
❑ 2266	Let Me Love You Tonight/ Janny Lou	1980	4.00
❑ 2294	I'm Almost Ready/ You're My True Love	1980	4.00
❑ 2319	I Can't Stop the Feelin'/ A Lifetime of Nightime	1980	4.00
❑ 2332	Still Right Here in My Heart/ Don't Keep Me Hangin'	1981	4.00
❑ 2337	You're Mine Tonight.Do You Love Me Truly, Julie	1981	4.00

RCA

Number	Title (A Side/B Side)	Yr	NM
❑ PB-10829	Dance/Help Yourself	1976	4.00
❑ PB-10880	All the Way/Fade Away	1977	4.00
❑ PB-11148	The Sun Shone Lightly/ Lucille Crawfield	1977	4.00
❑ PB-11260	Working in the Coal Mine/ Bad Cream	1978	4.00
❑ PB-11282	Love Will Grow/Slim Pickin's	1978	4.00
❑ PB-11678	Can't Hold Back/ Restless Woman	1979	4.00

RCA VICTOR

Number	Title (A Side/B Side)	Yr	NM
❑ 48-1028	Tears/You're Between Me	1972	6.00
❑ 74-0742	Woman/She Darked the Sun	1972	6.00
❑ 74-0794	Early Morning Riser/ Angel #9	1972	6.00
❑ PB-10184	Amie/Memories	1975	5.00
❑ PB-10302	Two-Lane Highway/ Sister's Keeper	1975	4.00
❑ PB-10382	Just Can't Believe It/ Kentucky Moonshine	1975	4.00
❑ GB-10490	Amie/Memories	1975	3.00
—Gold Standard Series			
❑ PB-10580	Long Cold Winter/The Sun Shone Brightly	1976	4.00
❑ PB-10679	That'll Be the Day/I Can Only Dream of You	1976	4.00

Albums

CASABLANCA

Number	Title (A Side/B Side)	Yr	NM
❑ NBLP-7212	Firin' Up	1980	10.00
❑ NBLP-7255	Something in the Night	1981	10.00

PAIR

Number	Title (A Side/B Side)	Yr	NM
❑ PDL2-1034 [(2)]	Home on the Range	1986	12.00

RCA VICTOR

Number	Title (A Side/B Side)	Yr	NM
❑ APD1-0933 [Q]	Two Lane Highway	1975	20.00
❑ APL1-0933	Two Lane Highway	1975	12.00
❑ APD1-1247 [Q]	If the Shoe Fits	1976	20.00
❑ APL1-1247	If the Shoe Fits	1976	12.00
❑ APL1-1924	Dance	1976	12.00
❑ CPL2-2404 [(2)]	Live!! Takin' the Stage	1977	15.00
❑ AFL1-2590	Just Fly	1978	12.00
❑ AFL1-3335	Can't Hold Back	1979	12.00
❑ AYL1-3669	Two Lane Highway	1980	8.00
—"Best Buy Series" reissue			
❑ AYL1-3717	If the Shoe Fits	1981	8.00
—"Best Buy Series" reissue			
❑ AYL1-3718	Just Fly	1981	8.00
—"Best Buy Series" reissue			
❑ AYL1-3719	Pure Prairie League	1981	8.00
—"Best Buy Series" reissue			
❑ AYL1-3723	Dance	1981	8.00
—"Best Buy Series" reissue			
❑ AFL1-4650	Pure Prairie League	1977	10.00
—Reissue of LSP-4650			
❑ LSP-4650	Pure Prairie League	1972	12.00
❑ AYL1-4656	Bustin' Out	1984	8.00
—"Best Buy Series" reissue			
❑ AFL1-4769	Bustin' Out	1977	10.00
—Reissue of LSP-4769			
❑ LSP-4769	Bustin' Out	1972	12.00

PURIFY, JAMES AND BOBBY

45s

BELL

Number	Title (A Side/B Side)	Yr	NM
❑ 648	I'm Your Puppet/So Many Reasons	1966	15.00
❑ 660	Wish You Didn't Have to Go/ You Can't Keep a Good Man Down	1967	8.00
❑ 669	Shake a Tail Feather/ Goodness Gracious	1967	12.00
❑ 680	I Take What I Want/Sixteen Tons	1967	8.00
❑ 685	Let Love Come Between Us/ I Don't Want to Have to Wait	1967	8.00
❑ 700	Do Unto Me/Everybody Needs Somebody	1967	8.00
❑ 721	I Can Remember/I Was Born to Lose Out	1968	8.00
❑ 735	Help Yourself (To All of My Lovin')/Last Piece of Love	1968	8.00
❑ 751	Untie Me/We're Finally Gonna Make It	1968	8.00
❑ 774	I Don't Know What It Is You Got/ Section C	1969	8.00

CASABLANCA

Number	Title (A Side/B Side)	Yr	NM
❑ 812	Do Your Thing/Why Love	1974	5.00
❑ 827	Man Can't Be a Man Without a Woman/You and Me Together Forever	1975	5.00
❑ 830	All the Love I Got/ (B-side unknown)	1975	5.00

MERCURY

Number	Title (A Side/B Side)	Yr	NM
❑ 73767	I'm Your Puppet/ Lay Me Down Easy	1976	5.00
❑ 73806	Morning Glory/Turning Back the Pages	1976	5.00
❑ 73884	I Ain't Got to Love Nobody Else/ What's Better Than Love	1977	5.00
❑ 73893	Get Closer/What's Better Than Love	1977	5.00

PHILCO-FORD

Number	Title (A Side/B Side)	Yr	NM
❑ HP-28	I'm Your Puppet/ Goodnight Gracious	1968	15.00
—4-inch plastic "Hip Pocket Record" with color sleeve			

SPHERE SOUND

Number	Title (A Side/B Side)	Yr	NM
❑ 77004	I'm Your Puppet/Everybody Needs Somebody	196?	8.00

Albums

BELL

Number	Title (A Side/B Side)	Yr	NM
❑ 6003 [M]	James and Bobby Purify	1966	25.00
❑ S-6003 [S]	James and Bobby Purify	1966	30.00
❑ 6010 [M]	The Pure Sound of the Purifys	1967	25.00
❑ S-6010 [S]	The Pure Sound of the Purifys	1967	30.00

MERCURY

Number	Title (A Side/B Side)	Yr	NM
❑ SRM-1-1134	The Purify Brothers	1977	12.00

PURIM, FLORA

45s

MILESTONE

Number	Title (A Side/B Side)	Yr	NM
❑ 301	Casa Forte/Search for Peace	1975	5.00
❑ 303	Open Your Eyes, You Can Fly/ Andei (I Walked)	1976	5.00

WARNER BROS.

Number	Title (A Side/B Side)	Yr	NM
❑ 8392	Angels/Fairy Tale Song	1977	5.00
❑ 8650	Everyday, Everynight/ Walking Away	1978	5.00

Albums

FANTASY

Number	Title (A Side/B Side)	Yr	NM
❑ OJC-315	Butterfly Dreams	1988	8.00
—Reissue of Milestone 9052			
❑ OJC-619	Stories to Tell	1991	12.00
—Reissue of Milestone 9058			

MILESTONE

Number	Title (A Side/B Side)	Yr	NM
❑ FPM-4005 [Q]	Stories to Tell	1975	25.00
❑ M-9052	Butterfly Dreams	1973	15.00
❑ M-9058	Stories to Tell	1974	15.00
❑ M-9065	Open Your Eyes You Can Fly	1976	15.00
❑ M-9070	500 Miles High	1976	12.00
❑ M-9075	Nothing Will Be As It Was... Tomorrow	1977	20.00
❑ M-9077	Encounter	1977	15.00
❑ M-9081	That's What She Said	1978	12.00
❑ M-9095	Love Reborn	1980	12.00

VIRGIN

Number	Title (A Side/B Side)	Yr	NM
❑ 90995	The Midnight Sun	1988	12.00

WARNER BROS.

Number	Title (A Side/B Side)	Yr	NM
❑ BS 2985	Nothing Will Be As It Was... Tomorrow	1977	12.00
❑ BSK 3168	Everyday, Everynight	1978	12.00
❑ BSK 3344	Carry On	1979	15.00

PURIM, FLORA, AND AIRTO

Albums

CROSSOVER

Number	Title (A Side/B Side)	Yr	NM
❑ CR-5001	The Magicians	1988	10.00
❑ CR-5003	The Sun Is Out	1989	15.00

GEORGE WEIN COLLECTION

Number	Title (A Side/B Side)	Yr	NM
❑ GW-3007	Humble People	1986	10.00

PURPLE GANG, THE

Albums

SIRE

Number	Title (A Side/B Side)	Yr	NM
❑ SES 97006	The Purple Gang Strikes	1969	20.00

PURPLE IMAGE

Albums

MAP CITY

Number	Title (A Side/B Side)	Yr	NM
❑ 3015	Purple Image	1971	50.00

PURSELL, BILL

45s

COLUMBIA

Number	Title (A Side/B Side)	Yr	NM
❑ 42619	Our Winter Love/A Wound Can't Erase	1962	8.00
❑ 42780	Loved/Stranger	1963	6.00
❑ 42832	Pride/Farewell to Adra	1963	6.00
❑ 42876	Dark Alley/Autumn Magic	1963	6.00
❑ 42970	The Theme from Captain Newman/Remember Me (I'm the One Who Loves You)	1964	6.00
❑ 43090	Crying/I'll Never Be Free	1964	6.00
❑ 43255	Madrilena/Remembered Love	1965	6.00
❑ 43380	You've Lost That Lovin' Feelin'/ Quiet Nights of Quiet Stars	1965	6.00
❑ 43593	Love Theme from Superman/ Soul Shall It Be	1966	10.00

DOT

Number	Title (A Side/B Side)	Yr	NM
❑ 17217	Geary Street/Winter Waves	1969	5.00

Albums

COLUMBIA

Number	Title (A Side/B Side)	Yr	NM
❑ CL 1992 [M]	Our Winter Love	1963	15.00
❑ CL 2077 [M]	Chasing a Dream	1964	15.00
❑ CL 2421 [M]	Remembered Love	1965	15.00
❑ CS 8792 [S]	Our Winter Love	1963	20.00
❑ CS 8877 [S]	Chasing a Dream	1964	20.00
❑ CS 9221 [S]	Remembered Love	1965	20.00

PUZZLE

45s

ABC

Number	Title (A Side/B Side)	Yr	NM
❑ 11181	Hey Medusa/Make the Children Happy	1969	8.00

Albums

ABC

Number	Title (A Side/B Side)	Yr	NM
❑ ABCS-671	Puzzle	1969	20.00

PYLE, ARTIMUS

Albums

MCA

Number	Title (A Side/B Side)	Yr	NM
❑ 5313	A.P.B.	1982	25.00
❑ 39003	Nightcaller	1983	25.00

Number	Title (A Side/B Side)	Yr	NM

PYRAMIDS, THE (1) Surf instrumental group.

45s

BEST

Number	Title (A Side/B Side)	Yr	NM
❑ 1	Pyramid's Stomp/Paul	1963	30.00
❑ 102	Penetration/Here Comes Marsha	1963	40.00
❑ 13001	Pyramid's Stomp/Paul	1963	20.00
❑ 13002	Penetration/Here Comes Marsha	1964	15.00
—With "Dist. by London" or similar wording on label			
❑ 13002	Penetration/Here Comes Marsha	1964	20.00
—No mention of London Records on label			
❑ 13002 [PS]	Penetration/Here Comes Marsha	1964	40.00
—Black sleeve			
❑ 13002 [PS]	Penetration/Here Comes Marsha	1964	40.00
—Red sleeve			

CEDWICKE

Number	Title (A Side/B Side)	Yr	NM
❑ 13005	Midnight Run/Custom Caravan	1964	40.00
❑ 13006	Contact/Pressure	1964	40.00

Albums

BEST

Number	Title (A Side/B Side)	Yr	NM
❑ LPM-1001 [M]	The Original Penetration! And Other Favorites	1964	250.00
—Original issue with "Walkin' the Dog"			
❑ BR 16501 [M]	The Original Penetration! And Other Favorites	1964	200.00
—Reissue with "Road Runnah"			
❑ BS 36501 [R]	The Original Penetration! And Other Favorites	1964	120.00

SUNDAZED

Number	Title (A Side/B Side)	Yr	NM
❑ LP-5012	Penetration! The Best of the Pyramids	1995	10.00

PYRAMIDS, THE (2) Black vocal group.

45s

CUB

Number	Title (A Side/B Side)	Yr	NM
❑ 9112	I'm the Playboy/Cryin'	1962	20.00

SONBERT

Number	Title (A Side/B Side)	Yr	NM
❑ 82861	I'm the Playboy/Cryin'	1962	40.00

VEE JAY

Number	Title (A Side/B Side)	Yr	NM
❑ 489	What Is Love/Shakin' Fit	1963	25.00

PYRAMIDS, THE (U) Neither group (1) nor (2), but probably not all the same.

45s

DAVIS

Number	Title (A Side/B Side)	Yr	NM
❑ 453	At Any Cost/Okay, Baby!	1956	50.00
❑ 457	Why Did You Go/Before It's Too Late	1957	50.00

FEDERAL

Number	Title (A Side/B Side)	Yr	NM
❑ 12233	Deep in My Heart for You/ And I Need You	1955	400.00

HOLLYWOOD

Number	Title (A Side/B Side)	Yr	NM
❑ 1047	Someday/Bow Wow	1955	500.00

RCA VICTOR

Number	Title (A Side/B Side)	Yr	NM
❑ 47-7556	Long Long Time/Oh No You Won't (Oh Yes You Will)	1959	15.00

SHELL

Number	Title (A Side/B Side)	Yr	NM
❑ 304	Ankle Bracelet/ Hot Dog Dooly Wah	1961	25.00
—As "The Original Pyramids"			
❑ 711	Ankle Bracelet/ Hot Dog Dooly Wah	1958	50.00

PYTHON LEE JACKSON With ROD STEWART on vocals.

45s

GNP CRESCENDO

Number	Title (A Side/B Side)	Yr	NM
❑ 449	In a Broken Dream/Doin' Fine	1972	6.00
❑ 449	In a Broken Dream/ Turn the Music Down	1972	6.00
❑ 462	Cloud Nine/Rod's Blues	1973	6.00

Albums

GNP CRESCENDO

Number	Title (A Side/B Side)	Yr	NM
❑ GNPS-2066	In a Broken Dream	1972	15.00

Q

QUADRANGLE, THE

45s

PHILIPS

Number	Title (A Side/B Side)	Yr	NM
❑ 40408	She's Too Familiar Now/ No More Time	1966	30.00

Quarterflash, "Right Kind of Love," Geffen 29994, 1982, **$4.**

QUADRELLS, THE

45s

WHIRLIN' DISC

Number	Title (A Side/B Side)	Yr	NM
❑ 103	What Can the Matter Be/ Come to Me	1957	70.00

QUADS, THE

45s

VAULT

Number	Title (A Side/B Side)	Yr	NM
❑ 907	Surfin' Hearse/Little Queenie	1963	40.00

QUAILS, THE (1) See BILL ROBINSON AND THE QUAILS.

QUAILS, THE (2)

45s

HARVEY

Number	Title (A Side/B Side)	Yr	NM
❑ 116	My Love/Never Felt Like This Before	1961	50.00
❑ 120	I Thought/Over the Hump	1963	50.00

QUAITE, CHRISTINE

45s

WORLD ARTISTS

Number	Title (A Side/B Side)	Yr	NM
❑ 1022	Tell Me Mamma/In the Middle of the Floor	1964	12.00
❑ 1028	Mr. Stuck Up/Will You Be the Same Tomorrow	1964	12.00

QUAKER CITY BOYS, THE

45s

SWAN

Number	Title (A Side/B Side)	Yr	NM
❑ 4023	Teasin'/Won't Ya Come Out Mary Ann	1958	12.00
❑ 4026	Everywhere You Go/ Love Me Tonight	1959	10.00
❑ 4045	Goodbye 50's, Hello 60's/ You Call Everybody Darlin'	1959	10.00

QUARTER NOTES, THE (1)

45s

BISON

Number	Title (A Side/B Side)	Yr	NM
❑ 757	Frantic Flip/Canadian Sunset	1960	30.00

IMPERIAL

Number	Title (A Side/B Side)	Yr	NM
❑ 5647	Frantic Flip/Canadian Sunset	1960	15.00

WIZZ

Number	Title (A Side/B Side)	Yr	NM
❑ 715	Record Hop Blues/ Suki-Yaki-Rocki	1959	25.00

QUARTER NOTES, THE (2)

45s

BOOM

Number	Title (A Side/B Side)	Yr	NM
❑ 60018	Hey Little Girl/I've Been Loved	1966	15.00

QUARTER NOTES, THE (3)

45s

DELUXE

Number	Title (A Side/B Side)	Yr	NM
❑ 6116	Loneliness/Come De Nite	1957	25.00
❑ 6129	My Fantasy/Ten Minutes to Midnight	1957	25.00

QUARTER NOTES, THE (U) Some of these could be group (1) or (3).

45s

DOT

Number	Title (A Side/B Side)	Yr	NM
❑ 15685	Please Come Home/ Like You Bug Me	1958	25.00

GUYDEN

Number	Title (A Side/B Side)	Yr	NM
❑ 2083	Pretty Pretty Eyes/I Don't Wanna Go Home	1963	20.00

RCA VICTOR

Number	Title (A Side/B Side)	Yr	NM
❑ 47-7327	The Interview/Punkanilla	1958	15.00

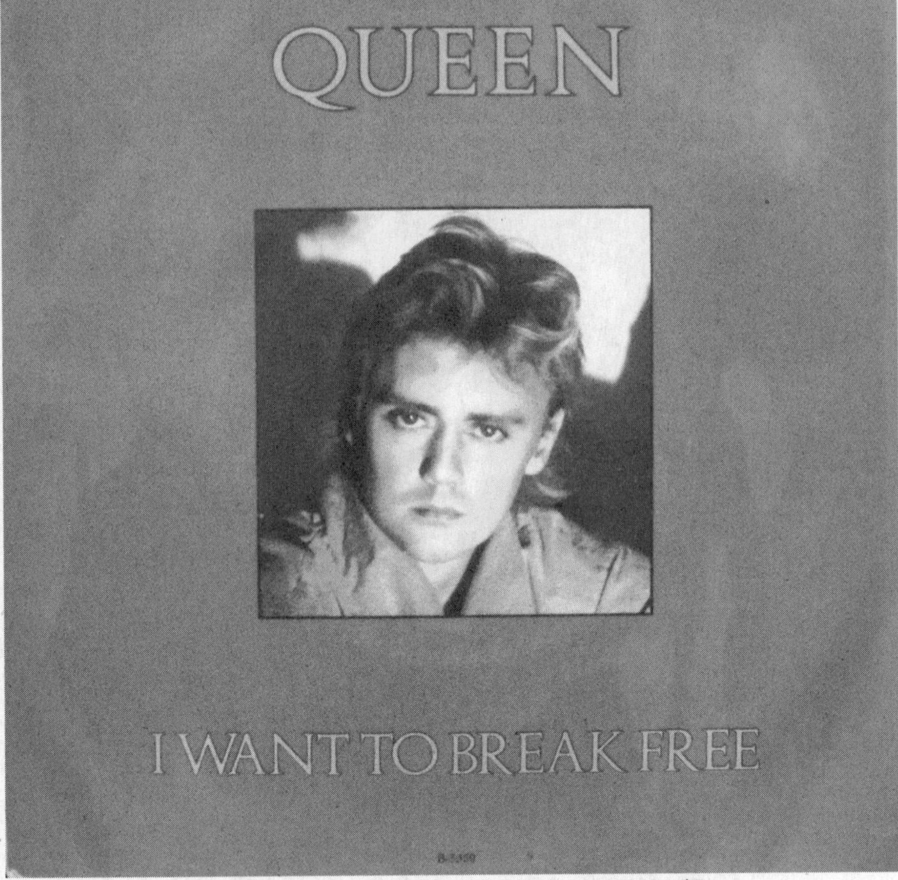

Queen, "I Want to Break Free," Capitol B-5350, 1984, **$5.**

QUARTERFLASH

12-Inch Singles

GEFFEN

Number	Title (A Side/B Side)	Yr	NM
❑ PRO-A-1009 [DJ]	Find Another Fool (Edit) (LP Version)	1982	10.00
❑ PRO-A-2034 [DJ]	Take Me to Heart (same on both sides?)	1983	8.00
❑ PRO-A-2077 [DJ]	Take Another Picture/ It Don't Move Me	1983	10.00
❑ PRO-A-2400 [DJ]	Walking on Ice (3;45) (same on both sides)	1985	8.00

45s

GEFFEN

Number	Title (A Side/B Side)	Yr	NM
❑ GGEF 0426	Harden My Heart/Find Another Fool	1983	3.00
—"Back to Back Hits" reissue series			
❑ PRO-S-1012 [DJ]	Find Another Fool (Remix Edit)/ (LP Version)	1982	8.00
❑ 28894	Walking on Ice/Come to Me	1985	3.00
❑ 28894 [PS]	Walking on Ice/Come to Me	1985	3.00
❑ 28908	Talk to Me/Grace Under Fire	1985	3.00
❑ 28908 [PS]	Talk to Me/Grace Under Fire	1985	3.00
❑ 29523	Take Another Picture/ One More Round to Go	1983	4.00
❑ 29523 [PS]	Take Another Picture/ One More Round to Go	1983	4.00
❑ 29603	Take Me to Heart/ Nowhere Left to Hide	1983	4.00
❑ 29603 [PS]	Take Me to Heart/ Nowhere Left to Hide	1983	4.00
❑ 29882	Critical Times/Try to Make It True	1982	4.00
❑ 29994	Right Kind of Love/ You're Holdin' Me Back	1982	4.00
❑ 29994 [PS]	Right Kind of Love/ You're Holdin' Me Back	1982	4.00
❑ 49824	Harden My Heart/ Don't Be Lonely	1981	4.00
❑ 50006	Find Another Fool/Cruisin' with the Deuce	1982	4.00
❑ 50006 [PS]	Find Another Fool/Cruisin' with the Deuce	1982	4.00

WARNER BROS.

Number	Title (A Side/B Side)	Yr	NM
❑ 29932	Night Shift/Love Should Be So Kind	1982	4.00

Albums

GEFFEN

Number	Title (A Side/B Side)	Yr	NM
❑ GHS 2003	Quarterflash	1981	8.00
❑ GHS 4011	Take Another Picture	1983	8.00
❑ GHS 24078	Back Into Blue	1985	8.00

QUATEMAN, BILL

45s

COLUMBIA

Number	Title (A Side/B Side)	Yr	NM
❑ 4-45792	Only Love/Keep Dreaming	1973	5.00
❑ 4-45792 [PS]	Only Love/Keep Dreaming	1973	8.00
❑ 4-45858	Get It Right On Out There/ Your Love Can Make It Real	1973	5.00

RCA

Number	Title (A Side/B Side)	Yr	NM
❑ PB-10912	Night After Night/Your Money or Your Life	1977	4.00
❑ PB-11180	Wait Until Tomorrow/Josephine	1977	4.00
❑ PB-11254	Shot in the Dark/All Over Now	1978	4.00
❑ PB-11588	Just Like You/It's Alright	1979	4.00

Albums

COLUMBIA

Number	Title (A Side/B Side)	Yr	NM
❑ KC 31761	Bill Quateman	1973	12.00

RCA VICTOR

Number	Title (A Side/B Side)	Yr	NM
❑ APL1-2027	Night After Night	1977	10.00
❑ APL1-2434	Shot in the Dark	1977	10.00

QUATERMASS

Albums

HARVEST

Number	Title (A Side/B Side)	Yr	NM
❑ SKAO-314	Quatermass	1970	30.00

QUATRO, SUZI

Also see THE PLEASURE SEEKERS.

12-Inch Singles

DREAMLAND

Number	Title (A Side/B Side)	Yr	NM
❑ DPR 1204 [DJ]	Rock Hard (same on both sides)	1980	10.00

45s

ARISTA

Number	Title (A Side/B Side)	Yr	NM
❑ 0106	Your Mama Won't Like Me/ Peter Peter	1975	6.00

BELL

Number	Title (A Side/B Side)	Yr	NM
❑ 45401	48 Crash/Little Bitch Blue	1973	6.00
❑ 45416	Can the Can/Ain't Ya Somethin' Honey	1973	7.00
❑ 45477	All Shook Up/Glycerine Queen	1974	6.00
❑ 45609	Devil Gate Drive/In the Morning	1974	6.00
❑ 45615	Keep a-Knockin'/Cat Size	1974	6.00

BIG TREE

Number	Title (A Side/B Side)	Yr	NM
❑ 16053	Can the Can/Don't Mess Around	1975	6.00

DREAMLAND

Number	Title (A Side/B Side)	Yr	NM
❑ 104	Rock Hard/State of Mind	1980	4.00
❑ 104 [PS]	Rock Hard/State of Mind	1980	4.00
❑ 107	Lipstick/Woman Cry	1980	4.00

RAK

Number	Title (A Side/B Side)	Yr	NM
❑ 4512	Brain Confusion (For All the Lonely People)/Rolling Stone	1972	12.00

RSO

Number	Title (A Side/B Side)	Yr	NM
❑ 917	Stumblin' In/A Stranger to Paradise	1979	4.00
—With Chris Norman (lead singer of Smokie)			
❑ 929	If You Can't Give Me Love/ Non-Citizen	1979	4.00
❑ 1001	I've Never Been in Love/ Space Cadets	1979	4.00
❑ 1014	She's in Love with You/ Starlight Lady	1979	4.00

Albums

ARISTA

Number	Title (A Side/B Side)	Yr	NM
❑ AL 4035	Your Mama Won't Like Me	1975	12.00

BELL

Number	Title (A Side/B Side)	Yr	NM
❑ 1302	Suzi Quatro	1974	15.00
❑ 1313	Quatro	1974	15.00

DREAMLAND

Number	Title (A Side/B Side)	Yr	NM
❑ DL-1-5006	Rock Hard	1980	10.00

RSO

Number	Title (A Side/B Side)	Yr	NM
❑ RS-1-3044	If You Knew Suzi...	1979	10.00
❑ RS-1-3064	Suzi...And Other Four Letter Words	1980	10.00

QUATTLEBAUM, DOUG

45s

GOTHAM

Number	Title (A Side/B Side)	Yr	NM
❑ 519	Don't Be Funny Baby/Lizzie Lou	1953	100.00

Albums

BLUESVILLE

Number	Title (A Side/B Side)	Yr	NM
❑ BVLP-1065 [M]	Softee Man Blues	1963	60.00
—Blue label, silver print			
❑ BVLP-1065 [M]	Softee Man Blues	1964	20.00
—Blue label, trident logo at right			

QUAZAR

45s

ARISTA

Number	Title (A Side/B Side)	Yr	NM
❑ 0349	Funk 'n' Roll (Dancin' in the Funkshine)/Savin' My Love for a Rainy Day	1978	6.00
❑ 0349 [PS]	Funk 'n' Roll (Dancin' in the Funkshine)/Savin' My Love for a Rainy Day	1978	6.00
❑ 0386	Funk with a Big Foot/ Starlight Circus	1979	5.00

Albums

ARISTA

Number	Title (A Side/B Side)	Yr	NM
❑ AB 4187	Quazar	1978	12.00

QUEEN

Also see BRIAN MAY AND FRIENDS; FREDDIE MERCURY; ROGER TAYLOR.

12-Inch Singles

CAPITOL

Number	Title (A Side/B Side)	Yr	NM
❑ V-8575	Radio Ga Ga (Vocal) (Instrumental)/I Go Crazy	1984	12.00
❑ V-8590	I Want to Break Free/Machines (Or Back to Humans)	1984	12.00
—We don't know if this 12-inch single has four different covers the way the 45 has four different picture sleeves			
❑ V-8622	Thank God It's Christmas/Keep Passing the Open Windows (Extended)/Man on the Prowl (Extended)	1984	20.00
❑ SPRO-9064 [DJ]	Radio Ga Ga (same on both sides)	1984	15.00

Except when noted otherwise, VG = 25% of NM, and VG+ = 50% of NM. (Example: VG = $2.00, VG+ = $4.00 and NM = $8.00.)

Number	Title (A Side/B Side)	Yr	NM
❑ SPRO-9160 [DJ]	It's a Hard Life (same on both sides?)	1984	20.00
❑ SPRO-9271/6 [DJ]	Hammer to Fall (Headbanger Mix) (Single Edit)	1984	20.00
❑ SPRO-9537 [DJ]	One Vision (same on both sides)	1985	15.00
❑ SPRO-9649 [DJ]	Princes of the Universe (same on both sides)	1986	20.00
❑ SPRO-9714/5 [DJ]	A Kind of Magic (4:30) (6:30)	1986	15.00
❑ V-15210	One Vision (Extended Version)/Blurred Vision	1985	15.00
❑ V-15232	A Kind of Magic (Extended Version)/Gimme the Prize (Kurgan's Theme)	1986	15.00
❑ V-15260	Pain Is So Close to Pleasure (2 versions)/Don't Lose Your Head	1986	15.00
DREAMWORKS			
❑ PRO-A-5105 [DJ]	Another One Bites the Dust (4 versions)	1998	12.00
❑ PRO-A-5113 [DJ]	Another One Bites the Dust (3 versions)	1998	15.00
❑ PRO-A-5118 [DJ]	Another One Bites the Dust (7 versions)	1998	15.00
ELEKTRA			
❑ 12-77DJ [DJ]	We Are the Champions/We Will Rock You//We Will Rock You/We Are the Champions	1977	80.00
❑ AS 11401 [DJ]	Bicycle Race/Fat Bottomed Girls (both stereo)//same (both mono)	1978	25.00
❑ AS 11461 [DJ]	Another One Bites the Dust (same on both sides)	1980	15.00
❑ AS 11481 [DJ]	Flash's Theme AKA Flash (stereo/mono)	1980	15.00
❑ AS 11567 [DJ]	Body Language (stereo/mono)	1982	12.00
❑ 67954	Back Chat/Staying Power	1982	20.00
HOLLYWOOD			
❑ ED 5529 [DJ]	We Will Rock You (7 versions)/We Are the Champions	1991	15.00
❑ ED 10607 [DJ]	You Don't Fool Me (3 versions)	1996	20.00
❑ HR-66003	You Don't Fool Me (4 versions)	1996	8.00

45s

Number	Title (A Side/B Side)	Yr	NM
CAPITOL			
❑ B-5317	Radio Ga Ga/I Go Crazy	1984	4.00
❑ B-5317 [PS]	Radio Ga Ga/I Go Crazy	1984	5.00
❑ B-5350	I Want to Break Free/Machines (Or Back to Humans)	1984	4.00
❑ B-5350 [PS]	I Want to Break Free/Machines (Or Back to Humans)	1984	5.00
—With Brian May in center			
❑ B-5350 [PS]	I Want to Break Free/Machines (Or Back to Humans)	1984	5.00
—With Freddie Mercury in center			
❑ B-5350 [PS]	I Want to Break Free/Machines (Or Back to Humans)	1984	5.00
—With John Deacon in center			
❑ B-5350 [PS]	I Want to Break Free/Machines (Or Back to Humans)	1984	5.00
—With Roger Taylor in center			
❑ B-5372	It's a Hard Life/Is This the World We Created?	1984	5.00
❑ B-5372 [PS]	It's a Hard Life/Is This the World We Created?	1984	6.00
❑ B-5424	Hammer to Fall/Tear It Up	1984	5.00
❑ B-5424 [PS]	Hammer to Fall/Tear It Up	1984	5.00
❑ B-5530	One Vision/Blurred Vision	1985	4.00
❑ B-5530 [PS]	One Vision/Blurred Vision	1985	5.00
❑ B-5568	Princes of the Universe/A Dozen Red Roses for My Darling	1985	4.00
❑ B-5568 [PS]	Princes of the Universe/A Dozen Red Roses for My Darling	1985	5.00
❑ B-5590	A Kind of Magic/Gimme the Prize (Kurgan's Theme)	1986	4.00
❑ B-5590 [PS]	A Kind of Magic/Gimme the Prize (Kurgan's Theme)	1986	5.00
—Later sleeves have either the correct B-side, or no B-side at all, listed			
❑ B-5590 [PS]	A Kind of Magic/A Dozen Red Roses for My Darling	1986	6.00
—First edition of sleeve has wrong B-side listed; this was the British pairing for this single, but we don't think this pairing was issued in the U.S.			
❑ B-5633	Pain Is So Close to Pleasure/Don't Lose Your Head	1986	4.00
❑ B-5633 [PS]	Pain Is So Close to Pleasure/Don't Lose Your Head	1986	5.00
❑ 7PRO-9114 [DJ]	I Want to Break Free (same on both sides)	1984	12.00
—White label, no song title or name of group on label			
❑ 7PRO-9546/7 [DJ]	One Vision (4:00)/(3:46)	1985	12.00

Queen, "Pain is so Close to Pleasure," Capitol B-5633, 1986, **$5.**

Number	Title (A Side/B Side)	Yr	NM
❑ B-44372	I Want It All/Hang On In There	1989	5.00
❑ B-44372 [PS]	I Want It All/Hang On In There	1989	5.00
❑ 7PRO-79685	Breakthru (same on both sides)	1989	12.00
—Vinyl is promo only			
❑ 7PRO-79779	Scandal (same on both sides)	1989	12.00
—Vinyl is promo only			
ELEKTRA			
❑ 45080	Killer Queen/Liar	1977	4.00
—"Spun Gold" reissue			
❑ 45083	Bohemian Rhapsody/You're My Best Friend	1977	4.00
—"Spun Gold" reissue			
❑ 45090	We Are the Champions/We Will Rock You	1979	4.00
—"Spun Gold" reissue			
❑ 45103	Crazy Little Thing Called Love/Bicycle Race	1981	4.00
—"Spun Gold" reissue			
❑ 45106	Another One Bites the Dust/Keep Yourself Alive	1981	4.00
—"Spun Gold" reissue			
❑ 45226	Killer Queen/Flick of the Wrist	1975	8.00
—Butterfly label			
❑ 45226	Killer Queen/Flick of the Wrist	1975	10.00
—Caterpillar label			
❑ 45268	Keep Yourself Alive//Lily of the Valley/God Save the Queen	1975	8.00
❑ 45297	Bohemian Rhapsody/I'm in Love with My Car	1975	8.00
—Butterfly label			
❑ 45297	Bohemian Rhapsody/I'm in Love with My Car	1976	10.00
—Red label, much scarcer than butterfly label			
❑ 45318	You're My Best Friend/'39	1976	6.00
—Butterfly label			
❑ 45318	You're My Best Friend/'39	1976	10.00
—Red label, much scarcer than butterfly label			
❑ 45362	Somebody to Love/White Man	1976	6.00
—Butterfly label			
❑ 45362	Somebody to Love/White Man	1976	10.00
—Red label, much scarcer than butterfly label			
❑ 45385	Tie Your Mother Down/Drowse	1977	6.00
❑ 45412	Long Away/You and I	1977	8.00
❑ 45441	We Are the Champions/We Will Rock You	1977	6.00
❑ 45441 [PS]	We Are the Champions/We Will Rock You	1977	10.00
❑ 45478	It's Late/Sheer Heart Attack	1978	6.00
❑ 45478 [PS]	It's Late/Sheer Heart Attack	1978	10.00
❑ 45541	Bicycle Race/Fat Bottomed Girls	1978	6.00
❑ 45541 [PS]	Bicycle Race/Fat Bottomed Girls	1978	12.00
❑ 45863	Keep Yourself Alive/Son and Daughter	1973	25.00
❑ 45884	Liar/Doing All Right	1974	20.00
❑ 45891	Seven Seas of Rhye/See What a Fool I've Been	1974	20.00
❑ 46008	Don't Stop Me Now/More of That Jazz	1979	6.00
❑ 46039	Jealousy/Fun It	1979	6.00
❑ 46532	We Will Rock You (Live)/Let Me Entertain You	1979	8.00
❑ 46579	Crazy Little Thing Called Love/Spread Your Wings	1979	4.00
❑ 46652	Play the Game/A Human Body	1980	4.00
❑ 46652 [PS]	Play the Game/A Human Body	1980	5.00
❑ 47031	Another One Bites the Dust/Don't Try Suicide	1980	4.00
❑ 47086	Need Your Loving Tonight/Rock It (prime jive)	1980	4.00
❑ 47092	Flash's Theme AKA Flash/Football Fight	1980	4.00
❑ 47092 [PS]	Flash's Theme AKA Flash/Football Fight	1980	5.00
❑ 47235	Under Pressure/Soul Brother	1981	4.00
—A-side with David Bowie			
❑ 47235 [PS]	Under Pressure/Soul Brother	1981	6.00
❑ 47452	Body Language/Life Is Real (Song for Lennon)	1982	4.00
—Most copies of this did not come with picture sleeves			
❑ 47452 [PS]	Body Language/Life Is Real (Song for Lennon)	1982	10.00
—All-white sleeve			
❑ 47452 [PS]	Body Language/Life Is Real (Song for Lennon)	1982	15.00
—Nude bodies sleeve			
❑ 69941	Back Chat/Staying Power	1982	4.00

Q

Number | Title (A Side/B Side) | Yr | NM

❑ 69941 [PS] Back Chat/Staying Power 1982 5.00
❑ 69981 Calling All Girls/Put Out the Fire 1982 4.00
❑ 69981 [PS] Calling All Girls/Put Out the Fire 1982 6.00

HOLLYWOOD
❑ 64725 We Are the Champions/These Are the Days of Our Lives 1992 4.00
❑ 64794 Bohemian Rhapsody/ The Show Must Go On 1992 4.00

Albums

CAPITOL
❑ ST-12322 The Works 1984 10.00
❑ SMAS-12476 A Kind of Magic 1986 10.00
❑ C1-92357 The Miracle 1989 15.00

DCC COMPACT CLASSICS
❑ LPZ-2072 A Night at the Opera 2000 50.00
—Audiophile vinyl

ELEKTRA
❑ 6E-101 A Day at the Races 1977 10.00
—Butterfly, red, or red/black labels
❑ 6E-112 News of the World 1977 10.00
❑ 6E-112 [DJ] News of the World 1977 150.00
—White label promo with oversize cover and press kit
❑ 6E-166 Jazz 1978 8.00
—Without poster of the nude bicycle race. Some copies had a sticker on the shrink wrap with an address at which the poster was available free.
❑ 6E-166 Jazz 1978 12.00
—With poster of the nude bicycle race
❑ 5E-513 The Game 1980 10.00
—With dull gray cover; all copies have custom white labels
❑ 5E-513 The Game 1980 15.00
—With shiny, mirrorlike cover; all copies have custom white labels
❑ 5E-564 Queen's Greatest Hits 1981 12.00
❑ BB-702 [(2)] Live Killers 1979 12.00
❑ 7E-1026 Sheer Heart Attack 1974 10.00
—Butterfly, red, or red/black labels
❑ 7E-1026 [DJ] Sheer Heart Attack 1974 50.00
—White label promo
❑ 7E-1053 A Night at the Opera 1975 10.00
—Butterfly, red, or red/black labels
❑ EQ-5064 [Q] Queen 1973 40.00
❑ 60128 Hot Space 1982 10.00
❑ EKS-75064 Queen 1973 10.00
—With "Queen" printed on the cover; butterfly, red, or red/black labels
❑ EKS-75064 Queen 1973 30.00
—With "Queen" gold-embossed on the cover
❑ EKS-75064 [DJ] Queen 1973 50.00
—White label promo
❑ EKS-75082 Queen II 1974 10.00
—Butterfly, red, or red/black labels
❑ EKS-75082 [DJ] Queen II 1974 50.00
—White label promo

HOLLYWOOD
❑ ED-62005 [PD] Queen at the BBC 1995 100.00
—Promo-only picture disc (no U.S. stock vinyl)
❑ 62017 Made in Heaven 1996 20.00
—White vinyl; imported from Europe; the only distinguishing mark to make this a U.S. version is the Hollywood bar code, which was stuck to the shrink wrap
❑ D 261801 Queen II 2008 20.00
❑ D 261901 Sheer Heart Attack 2008 20.00
❑ D 262001 A Night at the Opera 2008 20.00
❑ D 262101 A Day at the Races 2008 20.00
❑ D 436301 Queen 2009 20.00
❑ D 436401 News of the World 2009 20.00
❑ D 436501 Flash Gordon 2009 20.00
❑ D 436601 A Kind of Magic 2009 20.00
❑ D 436701 Innuendo 2009 20.00

MOBILE FIDELITY
❑ 1-067 A Night at the Opera 1980 100.00
—Audiophile vinyl
❑ 1-211 The Game 1995 90.00
—Audiophile vinyl
❑ 1-256 A Day at the Races 1996 95.00
—Audiophile vinyl

QUEEN, THE

45s

MERCURY
❑ 71389 Honky Tonky/Somewhere Along the Line 1958 20.00

QUEEN & PAUL RODGERS

Albums

HOLLYWOOD
❑ D 261601 [(2)] The Cosmos Rocks 2008 30.00

QUEEN'S NECTORINE MACHINE, THE

45s

ABC
❑ 11172 I Got Trouble/Gypsy Lady 1969 15.00

Albums

ABC
❑ S-666 The Mystical Powers of Roving Tarot Gamble 1969 40.00

QUEENSRYCHE

12-Inch Singles

EMI
❑ SPRO 04195 [DJ] Eyes of a Stranger (same on both sides) 1989 10.00
❑ SPRO 04341 [DJ] I Don't Believe in Love (5:36) (4:23) 1989 12.00

EMI AMERICA
❑ SPRO-9040 [DJ] Queen of the Reich/ The Lady Wore Black 1983 15.00
❑ SPRO-9326/7 [DJ] Warning (Studio) (Live) 1984 15.00
❑ SPRO-9692 [DJ] Walk in the Shadows (same on both sides) 1986 10.00
❑ SPRO-9781 [DJ] Gonna Get Close to You (same on both sides) 1986 10.00
❑ SPRO-9862 [DJ] The Whisper/I Dream in Infrared 1986 10.00

EMI MANHATTAN
❑ SPRO 04048 [DJ] Breaking the Silence (same on both sides) 1988 10.00
❑ SPRO 04141 [DJ] Revolution Calling (same on both sides) 1988 10.00

45s

EMI
❑ 7PRO-04281 Eyes of a Stranger (same on both sides) 1989 10.00
—Promo only number
❑ 7PRO-04345 I Don't Believe in Love (same on both sides) 1989 10.00
—Vinyl is promo only
❑ S7-18305 Bridge/I Am I 1995 4.00
❑ S7-18553 Disconnected/Bridge 1995 4.00
❑ B-50201 Eyes of a Stranger/The Mission 1989 8.00
❑ S7-57752 Anybody Listening?/ Silent Lucidity 1992 8.00

Albums

EMI
❑ E1-30711 Promised Land 1994 20.00
❑ E1-92806 Empire 1990 15.00

EMI AMERICA
❑ ST-17134 The Warning 1984 10.00
❑ ST-17134 [DJ] The Warning 1984 40.00
—Promo-only "High Quality Vinyl" pressing
❑ ST-17197 Rage for Order 1986 10.00
—Black circle on front cover
❑ ST-17197 Rage for Order 1986 15.00
—Blue circle on front cover
❑ MLP-19006 [EP] Queensryche 1983 12.00
❑ SPRO-MLP-19006 [DJ] Queensryche 1983 40.00
—White label version in film can

EMI MANHATTAN
❑ SPRO-04136/7 [PD] Operation: Mindcrime 1988 80.00
—Promo-only picture disc
❑ SPRO-04194 [DJ] Speak the Word 1988 20.00
—Promo-only interview album
❑ E1-48640 Operation: Mindcrime 1988 12.00

RHINO
❑ R1-73306 [(2)] Operation: Mindcrime II 2006 20.00

206 RECORDS
❑ R-101 [EP] Queensryche 1983 75.00

QUESTELL, CONNIE

45s

DECCA
❑ 31783 Don't Let It Break Your Heart/ Straighten Up 1965 100.00
❑ 31855 Give Up Girl/World of Trouble 1965 200.00
❑ 31986 Girl Can't Take It/Tell Me What to Do 1966 100.00

? (QUESTION MARK) AND THE MYSTERIANS

45s

ABKCO
❑ 4020 96 Tears/Can't Get Enough of You, Baby 1973 12.00
—Reissue; contains full-length version of A-side (most Cameo singles are edited)
❑ 4033 I Need Somebody/Girl (You Captivate Me) 1973 12.00
—Reissue

CAMEO
❑ 428 96 Tears/Midnight Hour 1966 15.00
—Contains an early fade of the A-side and the LP version of the B-side; trail-off wax markings are "C 428 A R" and "C 428 B R"; composer of both songs listed as "The Mysterians"
❑ 428 96 Tears/Midnight Hour 1966 20.00
—Contains an early fade of the A-side and the LP version of the B-side; trail-off wax markings are "C 428 A R" and "C 428 B R"; composer of both songs listed as "Rudy Martinez"
❑ 428 96 Tears/Midnight Hour 1966 30.00
—Contains the LP version of the A-side and an alternate version (different vocal and words) of the B-side; trail-off wax markings are "C 428 A-1A" and "C 428 B-1B"
❑ 428 96 Tears/Midnight Hour 1966 15.00
—Label credit is "? and the Mysterians"; contains an early fade of the A-side (even though the time is listed as "2:53") and the LP version of the B-side; trail-off wax markings are "C 428 A" and "62831" on Side 1 and "C 428 B" and "62831-X" on Side 2; composer of both songs listed as "The Mysterians"
❑ 441 I Need Somebody/"8" Teen 1966 15.00
❑ 467 Can't Get Enough of You, Baby/ Smokes 1967 15.00
❑ 479 Girl (You Captivate Me)/Got To 1967 15.00
❑ 496 Do Something to Me/ Love Me, Baby 1967 15.00

CAPITOL
❑ 2162 Make You Mine/I Love You, Baby (Like Nobody's Business) 1968 50.00

CHICORY
❑ 410 Talk Is Cheap/She Goes to Church on Sunday 1968 50.00

COLLECTABLES
❑ 4050 96 Tears/Midnight Hour 1997 4.00
—Yellow-orange vinyl; new recordings by the original group

LUV
❑ 159 Funky Lady/Hot N' Groovin' 1975 20.00

NORTON
❑ 45-083 Are You for Real?/I'll Be Back 1999 2.00
—1966 demo recordings
❑ 45-083 [PS] Are You for Real?/I'll Be Back 1999 2.00
❑ 45-096 Sally Go Round the Roses/ It's Not Easy 2000 2.00
❑ 45-096 [PS] Sally Go Round the Roses/ It's Not Easy 2000 2.00

PA-GO-GO
❑ 102 96 Tears/Midnight Hour 1965 300.00

SUPER K
❑ 102 Hang In/Sha La La 1969 15.00

TANGERINE
❑ 989 Ain't It a Shame/Turn Around Baby (Don't Ever Look Back) 1970 40.00

Albums

CAMEO
❑ C-2004 [M] 96 Tears 1966 100.00
❑ CS-2004 [P] 96 Tears 1966 80.00
—"96 Tears," "I Need Somebody," "Up Side" and "8-Teen" are rechanneled
❑ C-2006 [M] Action 1967 150.00
❑ CS-2006 [P] Action 1967 100.00
—"Don't Hold It Against Me," "Like a Rose" and "Girl (You Captivate Me)" are rechanneled

COLLECTABLES
❑ COL 2004 Featuring 96 Tears 1997 12.00
—Re-recorded tracks; orange vinyl

NORTON
❑ 262 [(2)] Do You Feel It Baby? 1998 15.00
—Live album recorded in 1997

QUICK, THE

Featuring ERIC CARMEN.

45s

EPIC
❑ 10516 Ain't Nothing Gonna Stop Me/ Southern Comfort 1969 25.00

QUICKLY, TOMMY

45s

LIBERTY
❑ 55732 It's As Simple As That/You Might As Well Forget Him 1964 10.00
❑ 55753 Wild Side of Life/Forget the Other Guy 1964 10.00

QUICKSILVER MESSENGER SERVICE

Includes records as "Quicksilver." Also see DINO VALENTI.

45s

CAPITOL
❑ 2194 Pride of Man/Dino's Song 1968 15.00
❑ 2320 Stand By Me/Bears 1968 15.00
❑ 2320 [PS] Stand By Me/Bears 1968 750.00
❑ 2557 Who Do You Love/ Which Do You Love 1969 15.00
❑ 2670 Words Can't Say/Holy Holy 1969 15.00

Q

Number	Title (A Side/B Side)	Yr	NM
❑ 2800	Shady Grove/Three or Four Feet from Home	1970	15.00
❑ 2920	Fresh Air/Freeway Flyer	1970	10.00
❑ 3046	Good Old Rock and Roll/ What About Me	1971	8.00
❑ 3233	Hope/I Found Love	1971	8.00
❑ 3349	Doin' Time in the U.S.A./ Changes	1972	8.00
❑ 3417	Fresh Air/Freeway Flyer	1972	8.00
❑ 4206	Gypsy Lights/Witches' Moon	1976	6.00

Albums

CAPITOL

Number	Title (A Side/B Side)	Yr	NM
❑ ST-120	Happy Trails	1969	30.00
—Black label with colorband			
❑ ST-120	Happy Trails	1973	12.00
—Orange label			
❑ SKAO-391	Shady Grove	1969	25.00
—Lime green label			
❑ SKAO-391	Shady Grove	1973	12.00
—Orange label			
❑ SM-391	Shady Grove	1976	10.00
—Reissue on yellow label and new prefix			
❑ SMAS-498	Just for Love	1970	25.00
—Lime green label			
❑ SMAS-498	Just for Love	1973	12.00
—Orange label			
❑ SMAS-630	What About Me	1970	25.00
—Lime green label			
❑ SMAS-630	What About Me	1973	12.00
—Orange label			
❑ SW-819	Quicksilver	1971	25.00
—Red label with stylized "C" at top			
❑ SW-819	Quicksilver	1973	12.00
—Orange label			
❑ ST 2904	Quicksilver Messenger Service	1968	40.00
—Black label with colorband; glossy black cover with red and silver foil-like printing			
❑ ST-2904	Quicksilver Messenger Service	1969	20.00
—Lime green or red label			
❑ ST-2904	Quicksilver Messenger Service	1973	12.00
—Orange label			
❑ SMAS-11002	Comin' Thru	1972	15.00
❑ SVBB-11165 [(2)]	Anthology	1973	20.00
❑ ST-11462	Solid Silver	1975	15.00
❑ SM-11820	Solid Silver	1978	10.00
—Reissue of 11462			
❑ ST-12496	Peace By Piece	1986	10.00
❑ SN-16089	Quicksilver Messenger Service	1980	8.00
—Budget-line reissue			
❑ SN-16090	Happy Trails	1980	8.00
—Budget-line reissue			
❑ SN-16091	Quicksilver	1980	8.00
—Budget-line reissue			
❑ SN-16092	What About Me	1980	8.00
—Budget-line reissue			
❑ SN-16093	Just for Love	1980	8.00
—Budget-line reissue			
❑ SN-16094	Shady Grove	1980	8.00
—Budget-line reissue			

QUIET RIOT

OZZY OSBOURNE guitarist Randy Rhoads was on this band's first two albums, issued only in Japan.

12-Inch Singles

PASHA

Number	Title (A Side/B Side)	Yr	NM
❑ ZAS 01306 [DJ]	Stay with Me Tonight (same on both sides)	1988	7.00
❑ AS 1880 [DJ]	Mama Weer All Crazee Now (same on both sides)	1984	10.00
❑ AS 1922 [DJ]	Party All Nite (same on both sides)	1984	10.00
❑ ZAS 2382 [DJ]	The Wild and the Young (same on both sides)	1986	8.00
❑ ZAS 2534 [DJ]	Twilight Hotel (same on both sides)	1986	8.00
❑ 4Z9-05038	Mama Weer All Crazee Now// Metal Health/Let's Get Crazy (Live)	1984	10.00

45s

PASHA

Number	Title (A Side/B Side)	Yr	NM
❑ ZS4-04005	Cum On Feel the Noize/ Run for Cover	1983	4.00
❑ ZS4-04267	Bang Your Head (Metal Health)/ (Live)	1983	4.00
❑ ZS4-04267 [PS]	Bang Your Head (Metal Health)/ (Live)	1983	4.00
❑ ZS4-04505	Mama Weer All Crazee Now/ Bad Boy	1984	4.00
❑ ZS4-04505 [PS]	Mama Weer All Crazee Now/ Bad Boy	1984	4.00
❑ ZS4-06174	The Wild and the Young/ Rise or Fall	1986	4.00
❑ ZS4-06174 [PS]	The Wild and the Young/ Rise or Fall	1986	4.00
❑ ZS4-08096	Stay With Me Tonight/ Callin' the Shots	1988	5.00

Albums

PASHA

Number	Title (A Side/B Side)	Yr	NM
❑ BFZ 38443	Metal Health	1983	8.00
—Original edition with full prefix			
❑ FZ 38443	Metal Health	1983	8.00
—Later edition with shorter prefix			
❑ PZ 38443	Metal Health	198?	6.00
—Later edition yet with new prefix and longer bar code on back			
❑ 8Z8 39203	Metal Health	1983	18.00
—Picture disc in plastic sleeve with sticker			
❑ QZ 39516	Condition Critical	1984	8.00
❑ OZ 40321	QR III	1986	8.00
❑ OZ 40981	Quiet Riot	1988	8.00

QUILL

Albums

COTILLION

Number	Title (A Side/B Side)	Yr	NM
❑ SD 9017	Quill	1970	25.00

QUIN-TONES, THE

45s

HUNT

Number	Title (A Side/B Side)	Yr	NM
❑ 321	Down the Aisle of Love/ Please Dear	1958	50.00
❑ 322	There'll Be No Sorrow/ What Am I to Do	1958	60.00

RED TOP

Number	Title (A Side/B Side)	Yr	NM
❑ 108	Down the Aisle of Love/ Please Dear	1958	40.00
❑ 108	Down the Aisle of Love/ Please Dear	1958	120.00
—Red label			
❑ 116	Heavenly Father/ I Watch the Stars	1959	100.00

QUINN, CAROLE

45s

MGM

Number	Title (A Side/B Side)	Yr	NM
❑ K-13265	Good Boy Gone Bad/What's So Sweet About Sweet Sixteen	1964	10.00
❑ K-13326	Do Those Little Things/ I'll Do It for You	1965	10.00

QUINNS, THE

45s

LOST-NITE

Number	Title (A Side/B Side)	Yr	NM
❑ 127	Oh Starlight/Hong Kong	196?	8.00
—Reissue			

QUINTEROS, EDDIE

45s

BRENT

Number	Title (A Side/B Side)	Yr	NM
❑ 7009	Come Dance with Me/Vivian	1960	30.00
❑ 7012	Please Don't Go/ Lookin' for My Baby	1960	35.00
❑ 7014	Slow Down Sandy/Lindy Lou	1960	50.00

QUINTESSENCE

Albums

ISLAND

Number	Title (A Side/B Side)	Yr	NM
❑ SMAS-9301	Quintessence	1971	30.00
❑ SW-9305	Dive Deep	1971	30.00

QUINTET, THE

Albums

UNITED ARTISTS

Number	Title (A Side/B Side)	Yr	NM
❑ UAS-5514	Future Tense	1971	15.00
❑ UAS-5599	The Quintet	1972	15.00

QUINTONES, THE (1)

45s

CHESS

Number	Title (A Side/B Side)	Yr	NM
❑ 1685	I Try So Hard/Ding Dong	1957	40.00

QUINTONES, THE (2)

45s

GEE

Number	Title (A Side/B Side)	Yr	NM
❑ 1009	I'm Willing/Strange As It Seems	1956	1000.

QUINTONES, THE (3)

45s

PHILLIPS INT'L.

Number	Title (A Side/B Side)	Yr	NM
❑ 3586	Times Sho' Gettin' Ruff/Softie	1963	20.00

QUINTONES, THE (U)

45s

PARK

Number	Title (A Side/B Side)	Yr	NM
❑ 111/2	South Sea Island/ More Than a Notion	1957	400.00

QUIVER

Also see SUTHERLAND BROTHERS AND QUIVER.

Albums

WARNER BROS.

Number	Title (A Side/B Side)	Yr	NM
❑ WS 1939	Quiver	1971	15.00
❑ BS 2630	Gone in the Morning	1972	15.00

QUOTATIONS, THE

Several different groups.

45s

ADMIRAL

Number	Title (A Side/B Side)	Yr	NM
❑ 753	In the Night/Oh No, I Still Love Her	1964	20.00

DEVENUS

Number	Title (A Side/B Side)	Yr	NM
❑ 107	It Can Happen to You/You Don't Have to Worry	1968	12.00

DOWNSTAIRS

Number	Title (A Side/B Side)	Yr	NM
❑ 1003	Night/Why Do You Do Me Like You Do	1970	8.00

IMPERIAL

Number	Title (A Side/B Side)	Yr	NM
❑ 66338	Havin' a Good Time/Can I Have Someone	1968	10.00
❑ 66368	Havin' a Good Time (With My Baby)/Can I Have Someone (For Once)	1969	10.00

LIBERTY

Number	Title (A Side/B Side)	Yr	NM
❑ 55527	Listen, My Children, And You Shall Hear/Speak Softly and Carry a Big Horn	1962	25.00

VERVE

Number	Title (A Side/B Side)	Yr	NM
❑ 10245	Imagination/Ala-Men-Say	1961	30.00
❑ 10252	This Love of Mine/We'll Reach Heaven Together	1962	30.00
❑ 10261	See You in September/ Sumemrtime Goodbye	1962	50.00

R

R.E.M.

12-Inch Singles

I.R.S.

Number	Title (A Side/B Side)	Yr	NM
❑ L33-17034 [DJ]	Driver 8/Driver 8 (Live)	1985	25.00
❑ L33-17060 [DJ]	Life and How to Live It/ Bandwagon/Crazy	1985	25.00
❑ L33-17159 [DJ]	Fall on Me (same on both sides)	1986	25.00
❑ L33-17199 [DJ]	I Believe/Toys in the Attic	1986	18.00
❑ L33-17200 [DJ]	Superman (same on both sides)	1986	15.00
❑ L33-17384 [DJ]	The One I Love (same on both sides)	1987	20.00
❑ L33-17430 [DJ]	It's the End of the World As We Know It (And I Feel Fine)/ Disturbance Heroin House (Live)	1987	20.00
❑ L33-17510 [DJ]	Finest Worksong (same on both sides)	1988	15.00
❑ 23792	The One I Love/The One I Love (Live)/Maps and Legends	1987	12.00
❑ 23850	Finest Worksong (Dub)/ Finest Worksong (Other)/ Time After Time (Live)	1988	15.00
❑ 70416 [DJ]	Ages of You (same on both sides)	1987	8.00
❑ 70982 [DJ]	(Don't Go Back to) Rockville (Edit)/Catapult (Live)	1984	25.00

WARNER BROS.

Number	Title (A Side/B Side)	Yr	NM
❑ PRO-A-3306 [DJ]	Orange (same on both sides)	1988	20.00
—Orange vinyl, custom labels			
❑ PRO-A-5263 [DJ]	Radio Song (Tower of Luv Bug Mix)/Radio Song (Monster Remix)	1991	25.00
❑ 40229	Radio Song (Tower of Luv Bug Mix)/Love Is All Around/ Belong (Live)	1991	8.00
❑ 41857	Bang and Blame/Losing My Religion (Live)/Country Feedback (Live)/Begin the Begin (Live)	1994	8.00
❑ 42363	Imitation of Life/The Lifting/ Beat a Drum/2JN	2001	10.00
—Orange vinyl; in clear PVC sleeve with sticker (which, stupidly, holds the flap of the cover down, thus making it nearly impossible to open the way it's supposed to open without damaging the sticker)			

45s

EPIC

Number	Title (A Side/B Side)	Yr	NM
❑ ES7 3857 [DJ]	Live for Today/Happy When I'm Crying	1997	25.00
—B-side by Pearl Jam			
❑ ES7 3857 [PS]	Live for Today/Happy When I'm Crying	1997	10.00
—1997 Pearl Jam fan club single			

R.E.M., "Superman," I.R.S. 52971, 1986, **$5.**

Number	Title (A Side/B Side)	Yr	NM
EVATONE			
❑ 105900-15	Dark Globe (one-sided)	1989	6.00
—5-inch black flexi-disc included in issue of Sassy magazine (double value if record is still attached to magazine)			
FAN CLUB			
❑ REM 92 [DJ]	Where's Captain Kirk?/Toyland	1992	25.00
❑ REM 92 [PS]	Where's Captain Kirk?/Toyland	1992	25.00
—Any of three variations of a gray sleeve			
❑ REM 92 [PS]	Where's Captain Kirk?/Toyland	1992	25.00
—White sleeve			
❑ REM 94 [DJ]	Sex Bomb/Christmas in Tunisia	1994	25.00
❑ REM 94 [PS]	Sex Bomb/Christmas in Tunisia	1994	25.00
—Picture sleeve also included a magnet, stamps and sticker			
❑ REM 95 [DJ]	Wicked Game/Java	1995	15.00
❑ REM 95 [PS]	Wicked Game/Java	1995	15.00
❑ REM 96 [DJ]	Only in America/I Will Survive	1996	15.00
❑ REM 96 [PS]	Only in America/I Will Survive	1996	15.00
❑ REM 97 [DJ]	Live for Today/Happy When I'm Crying	1997	15.00
—B-side by Pearl Jam			
❑ REM 97 [PS]	Live for Today/Happy When I'm Crying	1997	15.00
❑ REM 1993 [DJ]	Silver Bells/Christmas Time Is Here	1993	25.00
❑ REM 1993 [PS]	Silver Bells/Christmas Time Is Here	1993	25.00
❑ 2000 [DJ]	Christmas Time (Is Here Again)//Hastings and Main/Take Seven	2000	10.00
—Blue vinyl, small hole			
❑ 2000 [PS]	Christmas Time (Is Here Again)//Hastings and Main/Take Seven	2000	10.00
—Die-cut sleeve			
❑ U-23518M [DJ]	Parade of the Wooden Soldiers/See No Evil	1988	60.00
—Green vinyl			
❑ U-23518M [PS]	Parade of the Wooden Soldiers/See No Evil	1988	60.00
❑ 122589 [DJ]	Good King Wenceslas/Academy Fight Song	1989	50.00
❑ 122589 [PS]	Good King Wenceslas/Academy Fight Song	1989	50.00
—Fold-out poster sleeve			
❑ 122590 [DJ]	Ghost Reindeer in the Sky/Summertime	1990	40.00
❑ 122590 [PS]	Ghost Reindeer in the Sky/Summertime	1990	40.00
❑ 122591 [DJ]	Baby Baby/Christmas Griping	1991	40.00
❑ 122591 [PS]	Baby Baby/Christmas Griping	1991	40.00
HIB-TONE			
❑ HT-0001	Radio Free Europe/Sitting Still	1981	50.00
—Second pressing, with Hib-Tone address			
❑ HT-0001	Radio Free Europe/Sitting Still	1981	75.00
—First pressing, with no address for Hib-Tone Records on label			
❑ HT-0001 [PS]	Radio Free Europe/Sitting Still	1981	75.00
I.R.S.			
❑ 9916	Radio Free Europe/There She Goes Again	1983	10.00
❑ 9916 [PS]	Radio Free Europe/There She Goes Again	1983	30.00
❑ 9927	So. Central Rain (I'm Sorry)/King of the Road	1984	6.00
❑ 9927 [PS]	So. Central Rain (I'm Sorry)/King of the Road	1984	15.00
❑ 9931	(Don't Go Back to) Rockville/Catapult (Live)	1984	10.00
❑ 9931 [PS]	(Don't Go Back to) Rockville/Catapult (Live)	1984	15.00
❑ 52642	Can't Get There from Here/Bandwagon	1985	6.00
❑ 52642 [PS]	Can't Get There from Here/Bandwagon	1985	6.00
❑ 52678	Driver 8/Crazy	1985	6.00
❑ 52678 [PS]	Driver 8/Crazy	1985	6.00
❑ 52883	Fall on Me/Rotary Ten	1986	5.00
❑ 52883 [PS]	Fall on Me/Rotary Ten	1986	5.00
❑ 52971	Superman/White Tornado	1986	5.00
❑ 52971 [PS]	Superman/White Tornado	1986	5.00
❑ 53171	The One I Love/Maps and Legends	1987	3.00
❑ 53171 [PS]	The One I Love/Maps and Legends	1987	3.00
❑ 53220	It's the End of the World As We Know It (And I Feel Fine)/Last Date	1987	3.00
❑ 53220 [PS]	It's the End of the World As We Know It (And I Feel Fine)/Last Date	1987	4.00
THE BOB			
❑ 5	Tighten Up (one-sided)	198?	18.00
❑ 20	Femme Fatale (one-sided)	1986	15.00
—Flexi-disc included with The Bob magazine; black			
❑ 20	Femme Fatale (one-sided)	1986	15.00
—Flexi-disc included with The Bob magazine; red			
❑ 20 [PS]	Femme Fatale (one-sided)	1986	40.00
—Picture sleeve sent to The Bob subscribers only			
WARNER BROS.			
❑ W-2960	Orange Crush/Ghost Riders	1989	—
—Import, issued in U.S. with some copies of Warner Bros. 22780			
❑ W-2960 [PS]	Orange Crush/Ghost Riders	1989	—
—Import, issued in U.S. with some copies of Warner Bros. 22780			
❑ 16504	Bad Day/Favorite Writer	2003	4.00
❑ 16888	The Great Beyond/Man on the Moon (Live)	2000	4.00
❑ 17129	Daysleeper/Emphysema	1998	3.00
❑ 17446	Electrolite/The Wake-Up Bomb-Live	1997	3.00
❑ 17490	Bittersweet Me/Undertow	1996	3.00
❑ 17529	E-Bow the Letter/Tricycle	1996	3.00
❑ 17737	Tongue/Tongue (Live)	1995	3.00
❑ 17900	Strange Currencies/(Instrumental)	1995	3.00
❑ 17994	Bang and Blame/(Instrumental)	1995	3.00
❑ 18050	What's the Frequency, Kenneth?/(Instrumental)	1994	3.00
❑ 18523	The Sidewinder Sleeps Tonite/The Lion Sleeps Tonight	1993	3.00
❑ 18638	Everybody Hurts/Mandolin Strum	1993	3.00
❑ 18642	Man on the Moon/New Orleans Instrumental #2	1992	3.00
❑ 18729	Drive/Winged Mammal Theme	1992	3.00
❑ 19242	Shiny Happy People/Forty Second Song	1991	3.00
❑ 19246	Radio Song/Love Is All Around	1991	3.00
❑ 19392	Losing My Religion/Rotary Eleven	1991	3.00
❑ 21864	Stand/Pop Song 89	1989	3.00
—"Back to Back Hits" series			
❑ 22780	Singleactiongreen	1989	25.00
—Box set of 4 7-inch 45s, each with picture sleeve, plus poster. All have WB 27688, 27640 and 22791; all also are supposed to have W2960, but some contain 927 652 in error. No difference in value.			
❑ 22791	Get Up/Funtime	1989	3.00
❑ 22791 [PS]	Get Up/Funtime	1989	3.00
❑ 27640	Pop Song 89/Pop Song 89 (Acoustic Version)	1989	3.00
❑ 27640 [PS]	Pop Song 89/Pop Song 89 (Acoustic Version)	1989	—
—Only issued as part of Warner Bros. 22780; not available otherwise			
❑ 27688	Stand/Memphis Train Blues	1988	3.00
❑ 27688 [PS]	Stand/Memphis Train Blues	1988	3.00
❑ 927652	Orange Crush/Memphis Train Blues	1989	—
—Import with large hole, issued in U.S. with some copies of Warner Bros. 22780			
❑ 927652 [PS]	Orange Crush/Memphis Train Blues	1989	—
—Import, issued in U.S. with some copies of Warner Bros. 22780			

Albums

Number	Title	Yr	NM
A&M			
❑ B 1301501	Murmur	2009	20.00
❑ B 1302901	Reckoning	2009	20.00
I.R.S.			
❑ 5592	Fables of the Reconstruction	1985	12.00
❑ 5783	Lifes Rich Pageant	1986	12.00
❑ 6262	Eponymous	1988	10.00
❑ 42059	Document	1987	10.00
❑ SP-70014	Murmur	1983	12.00
—Reissue?			
❑ SP-70044	Reckoning	1984	12.00
❑ SP-70054	Dead Letter Office	1987	12.00
❑ SP-70502 [EP]	Chronic Town	1982	6.00
—Later pressings have a standard I.R.S. label			
❑ SP-70502 [EP]	Chronic Town	1982	12.00
—Original pressings have a custom gargoyle label			
❑ SP-70604	Murmur	1983	15.00
—Original number?			
❑ R 100701	Eponymous	1988	12.00
—BMG Direct Marketing edition			
❑ R 163503	Document	1987	12.00
—BMG Direct Marketing edition			
❑ R 173669	Lifes Rich Pageant	1986	14.00
—RCA Music Service edition			
MOBILE FIDELITY			
❑ 1-231	Murmur	1995	50.00
—Audiophile vinyl			
❑ 1-261	Reckoning	1996	80.00
—Audiophile vinyl			

Except when noted otherwise, VG = 25% of NM, and VG+ = 50% of NM. (Example: VG = $2.00, VG+ = $4.00 and NM = $8.00.)

Number	Title (A Side/B Side)	Yr	NM
WARNER BROS.			
❑ PRO-A-3377 [(2)DJ]	Should We Talk About the Weather?	1988	40.00
—Promo-only interviews and music			
❑ 25795	Green	1988	12.00
❑ W1-25795	Green	1988	15.00
—Columbia House edition			
❑ 26496	Out of Time	1991	16.00
❑ 45055	Automatic for the People	1992	10.00
❑ 45740	Monster	1994	10.00
❑ 46320 [(2)]	New Adventures in Hi-Fi	1996	15.00
❑ 47112 [(2)]	Up	1998	15.00
❑ 47946	Reveal	2001	20.00
❑ R1-78422 [(2)]	Around the Sun	2004	20.00
❑ R 100715	Green	1988	12.00
—BMG Direct Marketing edition			
❑ R 124762	Out of Time	1991	18.00
—BMG Direct Marketing edition; one of the last BMG vinyl releases			
❑ 303740 [(3)]	R.E.M. Live	2008	40.00
❑ 418620	Accelerate	2008	25.00

R.P.S.

Albums

Number	Title (A Side/B Side)	Yr	NM
MARS			
❑ (# unknown)	R.P.S.	197?	80.00

RABBLE, THE

Albums

Number	Title (A Side/B Side)	Yr	NM
ROULETTE			
❑ SR-42010	The Rabble	1968	150.00

RABIN, MIKE, AND THE DEMONS

Also see FREDDIE AND THE DREAMERS.

45s

Number	Title (A Side/B Side)	Yr	NM
TOWER			
❑ 109	Head Over Heels/I'm Leaving You	1964	15.00

RACHEL AND THE REVOLVERS

45s

Number	Title (A Side/B Side)	Yr	NM
DOT			
❑ 16392	The Revo-Lution/Number One	1962	500.00
—Produced by Brian Wilson			

RACKET SQUAD, THE

45s

Number	Title (A Side/B Side)	Yr	NM
JUBILEE			
❑ 5591	Hung Up/Higher Than High	1967	30.00
❑ 5601	Little Red Wagon/(Just Like) Romeo and Juliet	1967	20.00
❑ 5613	The Loser/No Fair at All	1968	20.00
❑ 5623	Let's Dance to the Beat of My Heart/Higher Than High	1968	20.00
❑ 5628	That's How Much I Love My Baby/Movin' In	1968	20.00
❑ 5638	Suburban Life/The Loser	1968	20.00
❑ 5657	I'll Never Forget Your Love/(B-side unknown)	1969	20.00
❑ 5682	In Your Arms/(B-side unknown)	1969	30.00
❑ 5694	Roller Coaster Ride/Coal Town	1970	30.00

Albums

Number	Title (A Side/B Side)	Yr	NM
JUBILEE			
❑ JGS-8015	The Racket Squad	1968	40.00
❑ JGS-8026	Corners of Your Mind	1969	40.00

RADHA KRISHNA TEMPLE

45s

Number	Title (A Side/B Side)	Yr	NM
APPLE			
❑ 1810	Hare Krishna Mantra/Prayer to the Spiritual Masters	1969	8.00
❑ 1810 [PS]	Hare Krishna Mantra/Prayer to the Spiritual Masters	1969	400.00
—Only one copy is known to exist. The price is highly speculative.			
❑ 1821	Govinda/Govinda Jai Jai	1970	8.00
❑ 1821	Govinda/Govinda Jai Jai	1970	10.00
—With Capitol logo on B-side label bottom			
❑ 1821 [PS]	Govinda/Govinda Jai Jai	1970	10.00
❑ PRO-5013/4 [DJ]	Govinda/Govinda Jai Jai	1970	25.00
—With an edit of the A-side			
❑ SPRO-5067/8 [DJ]	Govinda (Edit)/Govinda	1970	40.00

Albums

Number	Title (A Side/B Side)	Yr	NM
APPLE			
❑ SKAO-3376	The Radha Krishna Temple	1971	20.00

RADIANTS, THE

45s

Number	Title (A Side/B Side)	Yr	NM
ABC			
❑ 12394	I Need a Vacation/Just Like You	1978	5.00
CHESS			
❑ 1832	Father Knows Best/One Day I'll SHow You	1962	15.00
❑ 1849	Please Don't Leave Me/Heartbreak Society	1963	15.00
❑ 1872	I'm in Love/Shy Guy	1963	15.00
❑ 1887	Noble the Bargain Man/I Got to Dance to Keep My Baby	1964	15.00
❑ 1904	Voice Your Choice/If I Only Had You	1964	12.00
❑ 1925	It Ain't No Big Thing/I Got a Girl	1965	12.00
❑ 1939	Whole Lot of Love/Tomorrow	1965	12.00
❑ 1954	I Want to Thank You, Baby/Baby You've Got It	1966	12.00
—As "Maurice and the Radiants"			
❑ 1986	(Don't It Make You) Feel Kind of Bad/Anything You Do Is Alright	1967	12.00
❑ 2021	Don't Take Your Love/The Clown Is Clever	1967	12.00
❑ 2037	Hold On/I'm Glad I'm the Loser	1968	12.00
❑ 2057	Tears of a Clown/I'm Just a Man	1968	12.00
❑ 2066	Choo Choo/Ida Mae Foster	1969	10.00
❑ 2078	Book of Love/Another Mule Is Kicking In Your Stall	1969	10.00
❑ 2083	I'm So Glad I'm the Loser/Shadow of a Doubt	1970	10.00
TWINIGHT			
❑ 153	My Sunshine Girl/Don't Wanna Face the Truth	1971	8.00

RADICE, MARK

45s

Number	Title (A Side/B Side)	Yr	NM
DECCA			
❑ 32349	Natural Morning/You Took the Words Right Out of My Mouth	1968	12.00
❑ 32411	Three Cheers/Ten Thousand Year Old Blues	1968	40.00
—Supposedly includes Steve Tallerico (a.k.a. Steve Tyler), later of Aerosmith			
❑ 732525	Richest Man in the World/Girl by the Meter	1969	20.00
PARAMOUNT			
❑ 0170	Hey, My Love/Your Love Is Like Fire	1972	10.00
RCA VICTOR			
❑ 47-9420	Save Your Money/Wooden Girl	1967	15.00
❑ 47-9420 [PS]	Save Your Money/Wooden Girl	1967	30.00
UNITED ARTISTS			
❑ UA-XW840-Y	If You Can't Beat 'Em, Join' Em/The Whole Wide World Ain't Nothin' But a Party	1976	8.00
❑ UA-XW897-Y	The Answer Is You/Monkey See, Monkey Do	1976	8.00

Albums

Number	Title (A Side/B Side)	Yr	NM
PARAMOUNT			
❑ PAS-6033	Mark Radice	1972	40.00
ROADSHOW			
❑ RS-LA788-G	Intense	1977	15.00
UNITED ARTISTS			
❑ UA-LA629-G	Ain't Nothin' But a Party	1976	15.00

RADIO BIRDMAN

45s

Number	Title (A Side/B Side)	Yr	NM
SIRE			
❑ 1014	Murder City Nights/What Gives	1978	6.00

Albums

Number	Title (A Side/B Side)	Yr	NM
SIRE			
❑ SRK 6050	Radio Appears	1978	40.00

RAE, CHARLOTTE

Albums

Number	Title (A Side/B Side)	Yr	NM
VANGUARD			
❑ VRS-9004 [M]	Songs I Taught My Mother	1956	40.00

RAELETTS, THE

Backing vocalists for RAY CHARLES.

45s

Number	Title (A Side/B Side)	Yr	NM
TANGERINE			
❑ 972	One Hurt Deserves Another/One Room Paradise	1967	8.00
❑ 976	Into Something Fine/Lover's Blues	1967	8.00
❑ 984	I'm Gett'n Long Alright/All I Need Is His Love	1968	8.00
❑ 986	I Want to Thank You/It's Almost Here	1968	8.00
❑ 1006	I Want To (Do Everything for You)/Keep It to Yourself	1970	8.00
❑ 1014	Bad Water/That Goes to Show You	1970	8.00
❑ 1017	Here I Go Again/Leave My Man Alone	1971	8.00
❑ 1024	Come Get It, I Got It/Try a Little Kindness	197?	8.00
❑ 1029	You Must Be Doing Alright/You Have a Way with Me	197?	8.00
❑ 1031	Many Rivers to Cross/If You Wanna Keep Him	197?	8.00

Albums

Number	Title (A Side/B Side)	Yr	NM
TANGERINE			
❑ TRCS-1515	Yesterday, Today, Tomorrow	1972	15.00

RAFFERTY, GERRY

Also see THE HUMBLEBUMS; STEALERS WHEEL

45s

Number	Title (A Side/B Side)	Yr	NM
BLUE THUMB			
❑ 231	Can I Have My Money Back/Sign on the Dotted Line	1973	8.00
LIBERTY			
❑ 1482	Good Intentions/Standing at the Gates	1982	4.00
SIGNPOST			
❑ 70001	Make You, Break You/Mary Skeffington	1972	10.00
UNITED ARTISTS			
❑ XW1098	Mattie's Rag/City to City	1977	5.00
❑ XW1192	Baker Street/Big Change in the Weather	1978	4.00
—Regular press with the edited, slightly sped-up version of "Baker Street" on A-side			
❑ XW1192	Baker Street/Big Change in the Weather	1978	8.00
—Mispress with the full-length album version of "Baker Street" on A-side There is no "E" in the trail-off wax.			
❑ XW1233	Right Down the Line/Waiting for the Day	1978	4.00
❑ XW1233 [PS]	Right Down the Line/Waiting for the Day	1978	5.00
❑ XW1266	Home and Dry/Mattie's Rag	1978	4.00
❑ XW1298	Days Gone Down (Still Got That Light in Your Eyes)/Why Won't You Talk to Me	1979	4.00
❑ 1316	Get It Right Next Time/It's Gonna Be a Long Night	1979	4.00
❑ 1366	The Royal Mile/In Transit	1980	4.00

Albums

Number	Title (A Side/B Side)	Yr	NM
ABC/BLUE THUMB			
❑ 6031	Can I Have My Money Back?	1978	12.00
BLUE THUMB			
❑ BTS-58	Can I Have My Money Back?	1973	20.00
LIBERTY			
❑ LO-840	City to City	1981	8.00
—Reissue of United Artists 840			
❑ LOO-958	Night and Day	1981	8.00
—Reissue of United Artists 958			
❑ LOO-1039	Snakes and Ladders	1981	8.00
—Reissue of United Artists 1039			
❑ LT-51132	Sleepwalking	1982	10.00
MOBILE FIDELITY			
❑ 1-058	City to City	1980	40.00
—Audiophile vinyl			
POLYDOR			
❑ 835449-1	North and South	1988	10.00
UNITED ARTISTS			
❑ UA-LA840-H	City to City	1978	10.00
❑ UA-LA958-I	Night Owl	1979	10.00
❑ LOO-1039	Snakes and Ladders	1980	10.00
VISA			
❑ 7006	Gerry Rafferty	1978	10.00
—Reissue of Blue Thumb material			

RAG DOLLS, THE

45s

Number	Title (A Side/B Side)	Yr	NM
MALA			
❑ 493	Dusty/Hey Hoagy	1964	10.00
❑ 499	Baby's Gone/We Almost Made It	1965	10.00
❑ 506	Little Girl Tears/Put a Ring on My Finger	1965	10.00
PARKWAY			
❑ 921	Society Girl/Ragen (Society Girl Bossa Nova)	1964	12.00

RAGING STORMS, THE

45s

Number	Title (A Side/B Side)	Yr	NM
FLAME			
❑ 1019	High Octane/Madison Blues	1959	40.00
TRANS ATLAS			
❑ 677	The Dribble (Twist)/Hound Dog	1962	10.00
❑ 691	So Hard to Take/Down at the Corner	1962	10.00
WARWICK			
❑ 677	The Dribble (Twist)/Hound Dog	1962	10.00

RAGLAND, LOU

45s

Number	Title (A Side/B Side)	Yr	NM
AMY			
❑ 988	Travel Alone/Big Wheel	1967	200.00

R

Number	Title (A Side/B Side)	Yr	NM
RAIDERS, THE (1) See PAUL REVERE AND THE RAIDERS.			
RAIDERS, THE (2)			
45s			
ANDEX			
❑ 4015	Yoo Hoo/Hocus Pocus	1958	120.00
ATCO			
❑ 6125	Raiders from Outer Space/ The Castle of Love	1958	80.00
BRUNSWICK			
❑ 55090	Walking Through the Jungle/ My Steady Girl	1958	40.00
RAIDERS, THE (3)			
45s			
LIBERTY			
❑ 55393	Dardanella/What Time Is It	1961	30.00
Albums			
LIBERTY			
❑ LRP-3225 [M]	Twistin' the Country Classics	1962	25.00
❑ LST-7225 [S]	Twistin' the Country Classics	1962	30.00
RAIDERS, THE (4)			
45s			
SPRING-DALE			
❑ 102	Raiders' Rhythm/Tall Texas Women	1964	50.00
RAIDERS, THE (5)			
45s			
VAN			
❑ 00262	Stick Shift/Skipping Around	1962	50.00
❑ 00663	On a Straight Away/ It's Motivation	1963	20.00
❑ 00763	Supercharger/Cruisin' Low	1963	20.00
❑ 01064	Raisin' Cain/Repetition	1964	20.00
VEE JAY			
❑ 504	Stick Shift/Skipping Around	1963	20.00
RAIN At least two different groups.			
45s			
A.P.I.			
❑ 336	Outta My Life/E.S.P.	1967	50.00
❑ 337	Substitute/Hear You Cry	1967	50.00
BELL			
❑ 45206	Caught in the Middle of It/Stop Me from Believing in You	1972	5.00
LONDON			
❑ 107	Outta My Life/E.S.P.	1967	40.00
❑ 111	Substitute/Hear You Cry	1967	40.00
MGM			
❑ 13622	Take It Away/City Lovin'	1966	25.00
PARAMOUNT			
❑ 0087	Show Me the Road Home/ Funky Junky Blues	1971	20.00
Albums			
PROJECT 3			
❑ PR 5072 SD	New Rock Group	1972	25.00
WHAZOO			
❑ USR-3049	Live Christmas Night	1969	150.00
—Issued with no cover			
RAINBO Sissy Spacek is on this record.			
45s			
ROULETTE			
❑ 7030	John You Went Too Far This Time/C'mon Teach Me to Live	1969	20.00
RAINBOW Also see DEEP PURPLE; ELF; DIO; RONNIE DIO; FANDANGO; YNGWIE MALMSTEEN; MSG.			
45s			
MERCURY			
❑ 76146	Stone Cold/Rock Fever	1982	4.00
❑ 76146 [PS]	Stone Cold/Rock Fever	1982	5.00
❑ 815660-7	Street of Dreams/Anybody There	1983	4.00
❑ 815660-7 [PS]	Street of Dreams/Anybody There	1983	4.00
POLYDOR			
❑ 2014	Since You Been Gone/Bad Girls	1979	4.00
❑ 2163	I Surrender/Vielleicht Das Nachster Leit	1981	4.00
❑ 14290	Snake Charmer/Man on the Silver Mountain	1975	6.00
—As "Blackmore's Rainbow"			
❑ 14481	Long Live Rock 'n Roll/ Sensitive to Light	1978	4.00
Albums			
MERCURY			
❑ SRM-1-4041	Straight Between the Eyes	1982	10.00
❑ 815305-1	Bent Out of Shape	1983	10.00

Number	Title (A Side/B Side)	Yr	NM
❑ 827987-1 [(2)]	Finyl Vinyl	1986	14.00
OYSTER			
❑ OY-1-1601	Rainbow Rising	1976	12.00
❑ OY-2-1801 [(2)]	On Stage	1977	15.00
❑ OY-6049	Ritchie Blackmore's Rainbow	1975	15.00
POLYDOR			
❑ PX-1-502 [EP]	Jealous Lover	1981	8.00
❑ PD-1-6143	Long Live Rock 'n' Roll	1978	10.00
❑ PD-1-6221	Down to Earth	1979	10.00
❑ PD-1-6316	Difficult to Cure	1981	10.00
❑ 823655-1	Rainbow Rising	1985	8.00
—Reissue			
❑ 823656-1 [(2)]	On Stage	1985	12.00
—Reissue			
❑ 823705-1	Down to Earth	1985	8.00
—Reissue			
❑ 825089-1	Ritchie Blackmore's Rainbow	1985	9.00
—Reissue			
❑ 825090-1	Long Live Rock 'n' Roll	1985	8.00
—Reissue			
❑ 825383-1	Difficult to Cure	1985	8.00
—Reissue			
❑ 881516-1 [EP]	Jealous Lover	1985	6.00
—Reissue			
RAINBOW (2)			
Albums			
GNP CRESCENDO			
❑ GNPS-2049	After the Storm	1969	25.00
RAINBOW PRESS, THE			
45s			
MR. G			
❑ 817	There's a War On/Better Way	1968	15.00
❑ 821	Great White Whale/ The Last Platoon	1969	15.00
Albums			
MR. G			
❑ 9003	There's a War On	1968	30.00
❑ 9004	Sunday Funnies	1969	30.00
RAINBOW PROMISE, THE			
Albums			
NEW WINE			
❑ LPS-251-01	The Rainbow Promise	1970	300.00
RAINBOWS, THE (1)			
45s			
ARGYLE			
❑ 1012	Shirley/Stay	1962	25.00
FIRE			
❑ 1012	Mary Lee/Evening	1960	20.00
LOST-NITE			
❑ 340	Mary Lee/Evening	197?	5.00
—Reissue			
PILGRIM			
❑ 703	Mary Lee/Evening	1956	50.00
❑ 711	Shirley/Stay	1956	200.00
RAMA			
❑ 209	Minnie/They Say	1956	600.00
RED ROBIN			
❑ 134	Mary Lee/Evening	1955	600.00
—Note: Red Robin 141 is a bootleg			
RAINBOWS, THE (2)			
45s			
DAVE			
❑ 908	I Know/Only a Picture	1963	30.00
❑ 909	It Wouldn't Be Right/ Family Monkey	1963	30.00
RAINBOWS, THE (3)			
45s			
DOT			
❑ 16612	My Ringo/He's Hooked on J's	1964	15.00
❑ 16920	Color of Love/Down the Block	1966	10.00
RAINBOWS, THE (4)			
45s			
EPIC			
❑ 9900	Balla Balla/Ju Ju Hand	1966	10.00
JAMIE			
❑ 1339	Balla Balla/Ju Ju Hand	1967	8.00
RAINBOWS, THE (U) Some of these could be by groups (2), (3) or (4).			
45s			
GRAMO			
❑ 5508	Till Tomorrow/Mama, Take Your Daughter Back	196?	20.00

Number	Title (A Side/B Side)	Yr	NM
MERCURY			
❑ 72068	Gonna Go Down/Dreamwalk	1962	15.00
MGM			
❑ 13058	Old Man's Twist/Straight Ahead	1962	20.00
RONNIE			
❑ 202	The Christmas Song/Love Me	19??	10.00
—B-side by the Mellow Moods			
RAINCOATS, THE			
Albums			
ROUGH TRADE			
❑ ROUGH US 13	Odyshape	1981	25.00
SOUNDS LIKE			
❑ 12 [EP]	The Raincoats	1994	8.00
RAINDROPS, THE (1) JEFF BARRY and ELLIE GREENWICH.			
45s			
JUBILEE			
❑ 5444	What a Guy/It's So Wonderful	1963	20.00
❑ 5455	The Kind of Boy You Can't Forget/Even Though You Can't Dance	1963	25.00
❑ 5466	That Boy John/Hanky Panky	1963	25.00
❑ 5469	Book of Love/I Won't Cry	1964	20.00
❑ 5475	Let;s,Go Together/ You Got What I Like	1964	20.00
❑ 5487	One More Tear/Another Boy Like Mine	1964	20.00
❑ 5497	Don't Let Go/My Mama Don't Like Him	1965	20.00
❑ 5531	Hanky Panky/Hanky Panky	1965	50.00
—Very rare promo release			
Albums			
JUBILEE			
❑ JGM-5023 [M]	The Raindrops	1963	150.00
❑ JGS-5023 [S]	The Raindrops	1963	300.00
RAINDROPS, THE (2)			
45s			
CAPITOL			
❑ F-4136	Rockababy Rock/Rain	1959	30.00
RAINDROPS, THE (3)			
45s			
CORSAIR			
❑ 104	Maybe/Love Is Like a Mountain	1960	80.00
DORE			
❑ 561	Maybe/Love Is Like a Mountain	1960	25.00
RAINDROPS, THE (4)			
45s			
IMPERIAL			
❑ 5785	I Remember in the Still of the Night/Sweet Song	1961	30.00
RAINDROPS, THE (5)			
45s			
SPIN-IT			
❑ 104	(I Found) Heaven in Love/ I Prayed for Gold	1956	200.00
❑ 106	Little One/Rockin' on the Farm	1956	200.00
RAINDROPS, THE (U) Not sure which group this is.			
45s			
HAMILTON			
❑ 50021	Oh Why/Without Love, Love, Love	1960	20.00
RAINES, RITA			
45s			
CADENCE			
❑ 1331	I Told a Stranger/Sleepy Sunday Afternoon	1957	10.00
DEED			
❑ 1003	If I Were You/Boy Meets Girl	1955	12.00
❑ 1006	Don't Touch Me/Until Death Do Us Part	1955	12.00
❑ 1006	Don't Touch Me/Wedding Song	1955	12.00
❑ 1010	Such a Day (So Ein Tag)/ Ol' Devil Moon	1956	10.00
❑ 1015	I'm Crying/Little Mary	1956	10.00
❑ 1018	Young Adventurer/A Woman Needs to Be Told	1956	10.00
❑ 1020	There's a Time/I Volunteer	1956	10.00
JAMIE			
❑ 1036	Someone Else/Silence Is Golden	1957	15.00
❑ 1041	I Told a Stranger/Sleepy Sunday Afternoon	1957	15.00

Except when noted otherwise, VG = 25% of NM, and VG+ = 50% of NM. (Example: VG = $2.00, VG+ = $4.00 and NM = $8.00.)

Number	Title (A Side/B Side)	Yr	NM

RAINWATER, MARVIN

45s

(NO LABEL)

Number	Title (A Side/B Side)	Yr	NM
❑ MR 1 [DJ]	Hearts Hall of Fame//Gotta Go Get My Baby/Albino Stallion	195?	100.00

—Called "Especially for Friends by Marvin Rainwater"; white label

BRAVE

Number	Title (A Side/B Side)	Yr	NM
❑ 1001	Part Time Lover/ That Aching Heart	1963	10.00
—With Bill Guess			
❑ 1003	Love's Prison/ These Thoughts of You	196?	10.00
—With Bill Guess			
❑ 1004	Bad Girl/I Saw Your New Love Today	196?	10.00
—With Bill Guess			
❑ 1017	The Old Gang's Gone/Run for Your Life Boy	196?	8.00
❑ 1028	Oklahoma Hills/Wedding Rings	196?	8.00

CORAL

Number	Title (A Side/B Side)	Yr	NM
❑ 9-61342	I Gotta Go Get My Baby/Daddy's Glad You Came Home	1955	20.00

HILLTOP

Number	Title (A Side/B Side)	Yr	NM
❑ G-12	Tainted Gold/I Gotta Get to My Baby	196?	7.00

MGM

Number	Title (A Side/B Side)	Yr	NM
❑ 12071	Sticks and Stones/Albino Stallion	1955	20.00
❑ 12090	Tennessee Houn' Dog Yodel/ Tea Bag Romeo	1955	20.00
❑ 12152	Where Do We Go from Here/ Dem Low Down Blues	1955	20.00
❑ 12240	Hot and Cold/Mr. Blues	1956	40.00
❑ 12313	Why Did You Have to Go and Leave Me/What Am I Supposed to Do	1956	20.00
❑ 12370	Get Off the Stool/(Sometimes) I Feel Like Leaving Town	1956	30.00
❑ 12412	Gonna Find Me a Bluebird/So You Think You've Got Troubles	1957	20.00
❑ 12511	My Brand of Blues/ My Love Is Real	1957	20.00
❑ 12586	Lucky Star/Look for Me	1957	20.00
❑ 12609	Whole Lotta Woman/ Baby Don't Go	1958	20.00
❑ 12653	Moanin' the Blues/Gamblin' Man	1958	25.00
❑ 12665	I Dig You Baby/Moanin' the Blues	1958	20.00
❑ 12701	Nothin' Needs Nothin' (Like I Need You)/(There's Always) A Need for Love	1958	20.00
❑ 12739	Lonely Island/Born to Be Lonesome	1958	20.00
❑ 12773	Love Me Baby (Like There's No Tomorrow)/That's When I'll Stop Loving You	1959	20.00
❑ 12803	Half-Breed/A Song of Love	1959	20.00
❑ 12829	Young Girls/Valley of the Moon	1959	20.00
❑ 12865	Pale Faced Indian/ Wayward Angel	1960	15.00
❑ 12891	Hard Luck Blues/She's Gone	1960	15.00
❑ 12938	You're Not Happy ('Til I'm Cryin')/ Yesterday's Kisses	1960	15.00

NU TRAYL

Number	Title (A Side/B Side)	Yr	NM
❑ 902	Haircut/Looking Good	1976	6.00

RALPH HIMSELF

Number	Title (A Side/B Side)	Yr	NM
❑ 17094	Little Ralph the Robot (Poem)/ Little Ralph the Robot (Song)	197?	5.00

UNITED ARTISTS

Number	Title (A Side/B Side)	Yr	NM
❑ 837	It Wasn't Enough/ My Old Home Town	1965	10.00
❑ 917	Black Sheet/Indian Burial Ground	1965	10.00
❑ 50023	Sorrow Brings a Good Man Down/The Troubles My Little Boy Had	1966	10.00

WARNER BROS.

Number	Title (A Side/B Side)	Yr	NM
❑ 7373	Let Me Live Again/ I Love My Country	1970	7.00

WARWICK

Number	Title (A Side/B Side)	Yr	NM
❑ 666	Boo Hoo/I Can't Forget	1961	40.00
❑ 674	Tough Top Cat/(There's a) Honky Tonk in Your Heart	1962	25.00

7-Inch Extended Plays

MGM

Number	Title (A Side/B Side)	Yr	NM
❑ X1464	Gonna Find Me a Bluebird/ Where Do We Go from Here// Dem Lowdown Blues/Cause I'm a Dreamer	1957	25.00
❑ X1464 [PS]	Songs by Marvin Rainwater, Vol. 1	1957	25.00
❑ X1465	Tennessee Houn' Dog Yodel/ What Am I Supposed to Do// Why Did You Have to Go and Leave Me/Mr. Blues	1957	25.00
❑ X1465 [PS]	Songs by Marvin Rainwater Vol. 2	1957	25.00
❑ X1466	(contents unknown)	1957	25.00
❑ X1466 [PS]	Songs by Marvin Rainwater, Vol. 3	1957	25.00

Albums

CROWN

Number	Title (A Side/B Side)	Yr	NM
❑ CST-307 [R]	Marvin Rainwater	196?	12.00
❑ CLP-5307 [M]	Marvin Rainwater	196?	12.00

GUEST STAR

Number	Title (A Side/B Side)	Yr	NM
❑ GS-1435 [M]	Country and Western Star	196?	12.00

MGM

Number	Title (A Side/B Side)	Yr	NM
❑ E-3534 [M]	Songs by Marvin Rainwater	1957	150.00
❑ E-3721 [M]	Marvin Rainwater Sings with a Beat	1958	120.00
❑ E-4046 [M]	Gonna Find Me a Bluebird	1962	80.00
❑ SE-4046 [R]	Gonna Find Me a Bluebird	1962	50.00

SPIN-O-RAMA

Number	Title (A Side/B Side)	Yr	NM
❑ SPM-109 [M]	Golden Country Hits	196?	12.00

RAINY DAYS, THE

45s

JUBILEE

Number	Title (A Side/B Side)	Yr	NM
❑ 5517	He Was a Friend of Mine/ Don't Want No Fool	1965	12.00

PANIK

Number	Title (A Side/B Side)	Yr	NM
❑ 7542	Turn on Your Lovelight/ Go On and Cry	1966	25.00
❑ 7566	I Can Only Give You Anything/ (B-side unknown)	1966	25.00

RAINY DAZE, THE

45s

CHICORY

Number	Title (A Side/B Side)	Yr	NM
❑ 404	That Acapulco Gold/In My Mind Lives a Forest	1967	15.00

UNI

Number	Title (A Side/B Side)	Yr	NM
❑ 55002	That Acapulco Gold/In My Mind Lives a Forest	1967	10.00
❑ 55011	Discount City/Good Morning, Mr. Smith	1967	10.00
❑ 55026	Stop Sign/Blood of Oblivion	1967	10.00
❑ 55026	Fe Fi Fo Fum/Fe Fi Fo Fum	1967	25.00

—Original title of song (first pressing)

WHITE WHALE

Number	Title (A Side/B Side)	Yr	NM
❑ 279	My Door Is Always Open/ Make Me Laugh	1968	10.00

Albums

UNI

Number	Title (A Side/B Side)	Yr	NM
❑ 3002 [M]	That Acapulco Gold	1967	20.00
❑ 73002 [S]	That Acapulco Gold	1967	25.00

RAITT, BONNIE

12-Inch Singles

WARNER BROS.

Number	Title (A Side/B Side)	Yr	NM
❑ PRO-A-1030 [DJ]	Me and the Boys (same on both sides)	1982	12.00
❑ PRO-A-2536 [DJ]	No Way to Treat a Lady (same on both sides)	1986	6.00
❑ PRO-A-2613 [DJ]	Who But a Fool (same on both sides)	1986	6.00
❑ PRO-A-2655 [DJ]	Crimes of Passion (same on both sides)	1986	6.00

45s

A&M

Number	Title (A Side/B Side)	Yr	NM
❑ 1249	Baby Mine/Mickey Mouse March	1988	4.00
—A-side with Was (Not Was); B-side by Aaron Neville			
❑ 1249 [PS]	Baby Mine/Mickey Mouse March	1988	4.00

ARISTA

Number	Title (A Side/B Side)	Yr	NM
❑ 12795	You Got It/Feeling of Falling	1995	3.00

CAPITOL

Number	Title (A Side/B Side)	Yr	NM
❑ S7-17818	Love Sneakin' Up on You/ Hell to Pay	1994	3.00
❑ S7-18039	You/Feeling of Falling	1994	4.00
—Red vinyl			
❑ S7-18299	Storm Warning/Longing in Their Hearts	1995	3.00
❑ B-44364	Nick of Time/The Road's My Middle Name	1989	4.00
❑ B-44365	Thing Called Love/The Road's My Middle Name	1989	4.00
❑ B-44365 [PS]	Thing Called Love/The Road's My Middle Name	1989	4.00
❑ NR-44729	I Can't Make You Love Me/ Come to Me	1991	4.00
—White label, but not a promo			
❑ S7-56799	All at Once/Come to Me	1992	4.00
❑ S7-57698	Not the Only One/All at Once	1992	4.00
❑ S7-57741	I Can't Make You Love Me/ Something to Talk About	1992	4.00
❑ S7-57879	Good Man, Good Woman/ Nick of Time	1992	4.00
—A-side: Duet with Delbert McClinton			
❑ 58844	The Fundamental Things/ Cold, Cold, Cold	2000	3.00
❑ 77731	I Can't Help You Now/ Gnawin' On It	2002	4.00
❑ 7PRO-79940 [DJ]	Have a Heart (same on both sides)	1990	8.00
—Vinyl is promo only			

FULL MOON

Number	Title (A Side/B Side)	Yr	NM
❑ 49612	Once in a Lifetime/ You're Only Lonely	1980	4.00
—B-side by J.D. Souther			

FULL MOON/ASYLUM

Number	Title (A Side/B Side)	Yr	NM
❑ 47033	Don't It Make You Wanna Dance/ Orange Blossom Special	1980	5.00
—B-side by Gilley's Urban Cowboy Band			
❑ 47033 [PS]	Don't It Make You Wanna Dance/Orange Blossom Special	1980	6.00

REPRISE

Number	Title (A Side/B Side)	Yr	NM
❑ 1370	When You Touch Me This Way/ Since I've Been With You Babe	1976	5.00
—By Geoff Muldaur and Bonnie Raitt			

WARNER BROS.

Number	Title (A Side/B Side)	Yr	NM
❑ 7554	Bluebird/Women Be Wise	1972	8.00
❑ 7645	Too Long at the Fair/ Under the Falling Sky	1972	8.00
❑ 7645 [DJ]	Too Long at the Fair/ Under the Falling Sky	1972	15.00
—Cardboard picture sleeve and booklet			
❑ 7758	Everybody's Cryin' Mercy/ You've Been in Love Too Long	1973	6.00
❑ 8044	I Got Plenty/You Got to Be Ready for Love	1974	6.00
❑ 8166	Good Enough/My First Night Alone Without You	1975	6.00
❑ 8189	Run Like a Thief/ Walk Out the Front Door	1976	5.00
❑ 8382	Runaway/Louise	1977	5.00
❑ 8430	Two Lives/Three Time Loser	1977	5.00
❑ 8485	Gamblin' Man/About to Make Me Leave Home	1977	5.00
❑ 28450	Crimes of Passion/ Stand Up to the Night	1987	4.00
❑ 28615	No Way to Treat a Lady/ Stand Up to the Night	1986	4.00
❑ 29992	River of Tears/Me and the Boys	1982	4.00
❑ 49116	You're Gonna Get What's Comin'/The Glow	1979	4.00
❑ 49116 [PS]	You're Gonna Get What's Comin'/The Glow	1979	8.00
❑ 49185	Wild for You Baby/ (I Could Have Been Your) Best Old Friend	1980	4.00
❑ 50022	Can't Get Enough/Keep This Heart in Mind	1982	4.00

Albums

CAPITOL

Number	Title (A Side/B Side)	Yr	NM
❑ C1-91268	Nick of Time	1989	12.00
❑ C1-96111	Luck of the Draw	1991	15.00

DCC COMPACT CLASSICS

Number	Title (A Side/B Side)	Yr	NM
❑ LPZ-2025	Nick of Time	1996	80.00
—Audiophile vinyl			
❑ LPZ-2031	Luck of the Draw	1997	80.00
—Audiophile vinyl			

WARNER BROS.

Number	Title (A Side/B Side)	Yr	NM
❑ WS 1953	Bonnie Raitt	1971	15.00
—Green "WB" label			
❑ WS 1953	Bonnie Raitt	1973	12.00
—"Burbank" palm trees label			
❑ WS 1953	Bonnie Raitt	1979	8.00
—White or tan label			
❑ BS 2643	Give It Up	1972	15.00
—Green "WB" label			
❑ BS 2643	Give It Up	1973	12.00
—"Burbank" palm trees label			
❑ BS 2643	Give It Up	1979	8.00
—White or tan label			
❑ BS 2729	Takin' My Time	1973	12.00
—"Burbank" palm trees label			
❑ BS 2729	Takin' My Time	1979	8.00
—White or tan label			
❑ BS 2818	Streetlights	1974	12.00
—"Burbank" palm trees label			
❑ BS 2818	Streetlights	1979	8.00
—White or tan label			
❑ BS 2864	Home Plate	1975	12.00
—"Burbank" palm trees label			
❑ BS 2864	Home Plate	1979	8.00
—White or tan label			
❑ BS 2990	Sweet Forgiveness	1977	12.00
—"Burbank" palm trees label			

R

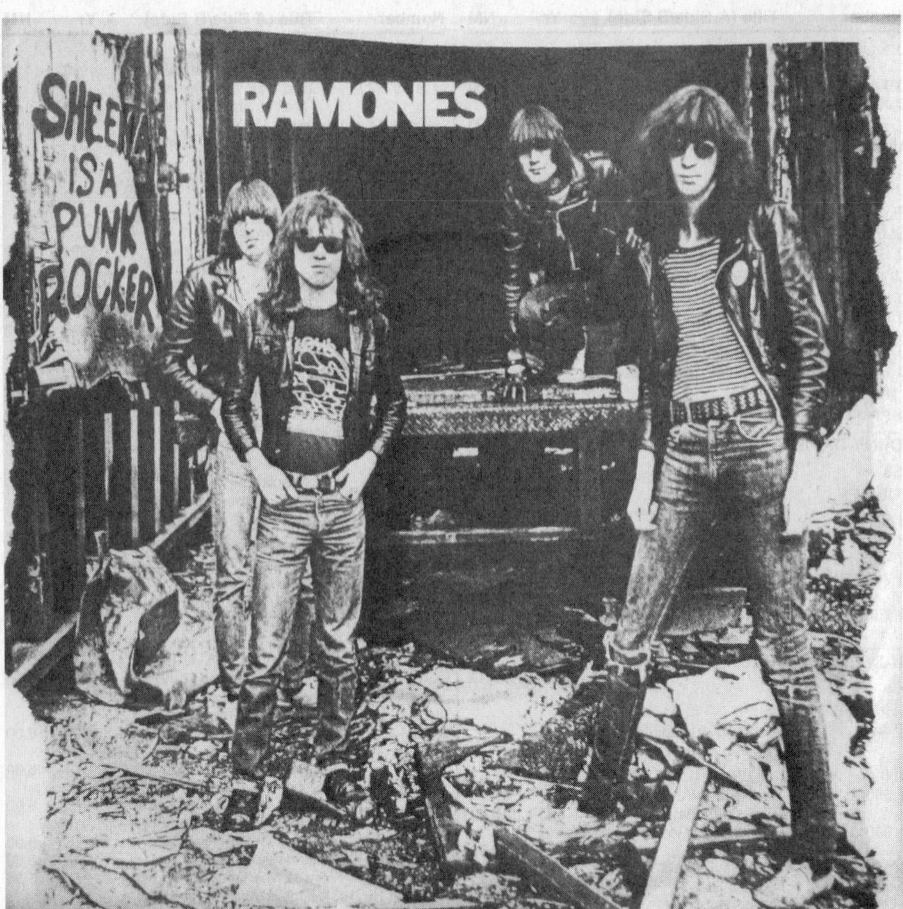

Ramones, "Sheena is a Punk Rocker," Sire 1006, 1977, **$10.**

Number	Title (A Side/B Side)	Yr	NM
❑ BS 2990	Sweet Forgiveness	1979	8.00
—White or tan label			
❑ HS 3369	The Glow	1979	12.00
❑ BSK 3630	Green Light	1982	12.00
❑ 25486	Nine Lives	1986	10.00

RAJAHS, THE

45s

KLIK

Number	Title (A Side/B Side)	Yr	NM
❑ 7805	I Fell in Love/Shifting Sands	1957	300.00

RALLY PACKS, THE STEVE BARRI and P.F. SLOAN with JAN AND DEAN.

45s

IMPERIAL

Number	Title (A Side/B Side)	Yr	NM
❑ 66036	Move Out Little Mustang/ Bucket Seats	1964	60.00

RAM

45s

POLYDOR

Number	Title (A Side/B Side)	Yr	NM
❑ 14099	The Want in You/ Mother's Day Song	1971	8.00

Albums

POLYDOR

Number	Title (A Side/B Side)	Yr	NM
❑ 24-5013	Where (In Conclusion)	1972	25.00

RAM JAM

45s

EPIC

Number	Title (A Side/B Side)	Yr	NM
❑ 50357	Black Betty/I Should Have Known	1977	5.00
❑ 50451	Keep Your Hands on the Wheel/Right on the Money	1977	4.00
❑ 50587	Pretty Poison/ Runaway Runaway	1978	6.00

Albums

EPIC

Number	Title (A Side/B Side)	Yr	NM
❑ PE 34885	Ram Jam	1977	12.00
❑ JE 35287	Portrait of the Artist as a Young Ram	1978	14.00

RAMAL, BILL

45s

MGM

Number	Title (A Side/B Side)	Yr	NM
❑ 13123	Hard Times/Sax Fifth Ave.	1963	10.00

20TH CENTURY FOX

Number	Title (A Side/B Side)	Yr	NM
❑ 432	Exodus/Theme from "Dr. No"	1963	10.00

RAMATAM

45s

ATLANTIC

Number	Title (A Side/B Side)	Yr	NM
❑ 2916	Changing Days/Wild Like Wind	1972	5.00

Albums

ATLANTIC

Number	Title (A Side/B Side)	Yr	NM
❑ SD 7236	Ramatam	1972	15.00
❑ SD 7261	In April Came the Dawning of the Red Suns	1973	15.00

RAMBEAU, EDDIE

45s

BELL

Number	Title (A Side/B Side)	Yr	NM
❑ 847	Who Will Buy-Where Is Love/ Solitary Man	1969	6.00
❑ 873	Don't Leave Me/Solitary Man	1970	6.00

DYNO VOICE

Number	Title (A Side/B Side)	Yr	NM
❑ 204	Concrete and Clay/ Don't Believe Him	1965	10.00
❑ 207	I Just Need Your Love/ My Name Is Mud	1965	8.00
❑ 211	The Train/Yesterday's Newspapers	1966	8.00
❑ 217	I Just Need Your Love/I'm the Sky	1966	8.00
❑ 221	I Miss You/Thinkin' About You Baby	1966	8.00
❑ 225	The Clock/If I Were You	1966	8.00

SWAN

Number	Title (A Side/B Side)	Yr	NM
❑ 4077	Skin Divin'/Toni	1961	10.00
❑ 4105	My Four Leaf Clover/Anyone Want More Flowers	1962	10.00
❑ 4112	Summertime Guy/Last Night Was My Last Night with You	1962	10.00
❑ 4145	Lover's Medley/The Car Hop and the Hard Top	1963	10.00

20TH CENTURY FOX

Number	Title (A Side/B Side)	Yr	NM
❑ 491	Come Closer/She's Smilin' at Me	1964	10.00

Albums

DYNO VOICE

Number	Title (A Side/B Side)	Yr	NM
❑ 9001 [M]	Concrete and Clay	1965	20.00
❑ DS-9001 [S]	Concrete and Clay	1965	25.00

RAMBLERS, THE (1)

45s

ADDIT

Number	Title (A Side/B Side)	Yr	NM
❑ 1257	Rambling/Devil Train	1960	30.00

RAMBLERS, THE (2)

45s

ALMONT

Number	Title (A Side/B Side)	Yr	NM
❑ 311	Father Sebastian/ Barbara (I Loved You)	1964	25.00
❑ 313	School Girl/Birdland Baby	1964	20.00
❑ 315	Surfin' Santa/Silly Little Boy	1964	25.00

RAMBLERS, THE (3)

45s

FEDERAL

Number	Title (A Side/B Side)	Yr	NM
❑ 12286	Don't You Know?/The Heaven and Earth	1957	150.00

RAMBLERS, THE (4)

45s

JAX

Number	Title (A Side/B Side)	Yr	NM
❑ 319	Search My Heart/50-50 Love	1953	500.00
—Red vinyl			

RAMBLERS, THE (5)

45s

MGM

Number	Title (A Side/B Side)	Yr	NM
❑ 11850	Vadunt-Un-Va-Da Song (Oui Oui Baby)/Please Bring Yourself Back Home	1954	300.00
❑ 55006	Bad Girl/Rickey-Do, Rickey-Do	1955	150.00

RAMBLERS, THE (6)

45s

TRUMPET

Number	Title (A Side/B Side)	Yr	NM
❑ 102	So Sad/Come On Back	1963	1000.

RAMBLERS, THE (U) Some of these could be by some of the above groups.

45s

IMPACT

Number	Title (A Side/B Side)	Yr	NM
❑ 10	Yaba Daba Ah Doo/ Funny Papers	1961	25.00

RCA VICTOR

Number	Title (A Side/B Side)	Yr	NM
❑ 47-5240	Mama He Treats Your Daughter Mean/And the Bull Walked Around Olay	1953	400.00

SIDEWINDER

Number	Title (A Side/B Side)	Yr	NM
❑ 101	Ticonderoga/Mozart Stomp	1964	40.00

RAMISTELLA, JOHNNY See JOHNNY RIVERS.

RAMONE, DEE DEE

12-Inch Singles

ROCK HOTEL

Number	Title (A Side/B Side)	Yr	NM
❑ 7159	Funky Man	1987	10.00

Albums

SIRE

Number	Title (A Side/B Side)	Yr	NM
❑ 25884	Standing in the Spotlight	1988	15.00

RAMONES, THE Marky Ramone was in DUST; also see DEE DEE RAMONE.

12-Inch Singles

BEGGARS BANQUET

Number	Title (A Side/B Side)	Yr	NM
❑ BEG 201T	Merry Christmas (I Don't Want to Fight Tonight) Extended/ I Wanna Live	1987	20.00
—U.K. import			

SIRE

Number	Title (A Side/B Side)	Yr	NM
❑ PRO-A-2219 [DJ]	Howling at the Moon/ Chasing the Night	1984	12.00
❑ PRO-A-2816 [DJ]	I Wanna Live (same on both sides)	1987	8.00
❑ PRO-A-3193 [DJ]	I Wanna Be Sedated/Sedated (Ramones On 45 Mega-Mix)/ Indian Giver	1988	20.00

Except when noted otherwise, VG = 25% of NM, and VG+ = 50% of NM. (Example: VG = $2.00, VG+ = $4.00 and NM = $8.00.)

Number	Title (A Side/B Side)	Yr	NM
45s			
BEGGARS BANQUET			
❑ BEG-201	Merry Christmas (I Don't Want to Fight Tonight)/I Wanna Live	1987	6.00
❑ BEG-201 [PS]	Merry Christmas (I Don't Want to Fight Tonight)/I Wanna Live	1987	6.00
—Above record and sleeve are U.K. imports			
NORTON			
❑ 45-065	I Wanna Be Your Boyfriend/ Judy Is a Punk	1997	5.00
—1975 demo versions			
❑ 45-065 [PS]	I Wanna Be Your Boyfriend/ Judy Is a Punk	1997	6.00
RSO			
❑ 1055	I Wanna Be Sedated/The Return of Jackie and Judy	1980	8.00
SIRE			
❑ 725	Blitzkrieg Bop/Havana Affair	1976	40.00
—Promo copies worth slightly less			
❑ 734 [PS]	I Wanna Be Your Boyfriend// California Sun/I Don't Wanna Walk Around with You	1976	14.00
❑ 734	I Wanna Be Your Boyfriend// California Sun/I Don't Wanna Walk Around with You	1976	9.00
❑ 738 [PS]	Swallow My Pride/Pinhead	1977	12.00
❑ 738	Swallow My Pride/Pinhead	1977	10.00
❑ 746 [PS]	Sheena Is a Punk Rocker/ I Don't Care	1977	12.00
❑ 746	Sheena Is a Punk Rocker/ I Don't Care	1977	10.00
❑ 1006	Sheena Is a Punk Rocker/ I Don't Care	1977	8.00
❑ 1006 [PS]	Sheena Is a Punk Rocker/ I Don't Care	1977	10.00
❑ 1008	Rockaway Beach/Locket Love	1977	8.00
❑ 1008 [PS]	Rockaway Beach/Locket Love	1977	14.00
❑ 1017 [PS]	Do You Wanna Dance?/ Baby Sitter	1978	30.00
❑ 1017	Do You Wanna Dance?/ Baby Sitter	1978	10.00
❑ 1025	Don't Come Close/ I Don't Want You	1978	8.00
❑ 1045	Needles and Pins/ I Wanted Everything	1979	8.00
❑ 1051 [PS]	Rock 'N' Roll High School/ Do You Wanna Dance	1979	8.00
❑ 1051	Rock 'N' Roll High School/ Do You Wanna Dance	1979	5.00
❑ 22911 [PS]	Pet Sematary/Sheena Is a Punk Rocker	1989	5.00
❑ 22911	Pet Sematary/Sheena Is a Punk Rocker	1989	6.00
❑ 27663 [PS]	I Wanna Be Sedated/I Wanna Be Sedated (Ramones On 45 Mega-Mix)	1988	6.00
❑ 27663	I Wanna Be Sedated/I Wanna Be Sedated (Ramones On 45 Mega-Mix)	1988	6.00
❑ 28599	Something to Believe In/ Animal Boy	1986	8.00
❑ 29107	Howling at the Moon (Sha La La)/Wart Hog	1985	8.00
❑ 29606	The Time Has Come Today/ Psycho Therapy	1983	7.00
❑ 49182	Baby I Love You/ High Risk Insurance	1980	6.00
❑ 49261	Do You Remember Rock & Roll Radio/Let's Go	1980	8.00
❑ 49812	We Want the Airwaves/All's Quiet on the Western Front	1981	8.00
Albums			
RADIOACTIVE			
❑ 10615	Mondo Bizarro	1992	15.00
❑ 11273	Adios Amigos!	1995	15.00
SIRE			
❑ PRO-A-605 [DJ]	Rock 'n' Roll High School Radio Sampler	1979	25.00
❑ PRO-A-756 [DJ]	Road to Ruin Radio Sampler	1978	35.00
❑ PRO-A-996 [DJ]	Pleasant Dreams Radio Sampler	1980	30.00
❑ SRK 3571	Pleasant Dreams	1981	15.00
❑ SR 6020	Ramones	1978	18.00
—Reissue, distributed by Warner Bros.; originals have no bar code			
❑ SR 6031	Ramones Leave Home	1978	18.00
—Third issue, distributed by Warner Bros., tracks as on second issue; originals have no bar code			
❑ SRK 6042	Rocket to Russia	1978	15.00
❑ SRK 6063	Road to Ruin	1979	15.00
❑ SRK 6077	End of the Century	1980	15.00
❑ SASD-7520	Ramones	1976	25.00
—First issue, distributed by ABC			
❑ SA-7528	Ramones Leave Home	1977	25.00
—Second issue, distributed by ABC, with "Sheena Is a Punk Rocker" replacing "Carbona Not Glue"			
❑ SA-7528	Ramones Leave Home	1977	50.00
—First issue, distributed by ABC, with "Carbona Not Glue"			
❑ 23800	Subterranean Jungle	1983	15.00
❑ 25187	Too Tough to Die	1984	15.00
❑ 25433	Animal Boy	1986	15.00
❑ 25641	Halfway to Sanity	1987	15.00
❑ 25709 [(2)]	RamonesMania	1988	20.00
❑ 25905	Brain Drain	1989	15.00

RAMRODS

Number	Title (A Side/B Side)	Yr	NM
45s			
AMY			
❑ 813	(Ghost) Riders in the Sky/Zig Zag	1961	25.00
❑ 817	Loch Lomond Rock/Take Me Back to My Boots and Saddle	1961	20.00
❑ 846	War Cry/Boing!	1962	20.00
QUEEN			
❑ 240145	Slee-Zee/Slouchee	1962	20.00
R&H			
❑ 1001	Moonlight Surf/Night Ride	1963	50.00

RAMS, THE

Number	Title (A Side/B Side)	Yr	NM
45s			
FLAIR			
❑ 1066	Sweet Thing/Rock Bottom	1955	150.00

RAN-DELLS, THE

Number	Title (A Side/B Side)	Yr	NM
45s			
CHAIRMAN			
❑ 4403	Martian Hop/Forgive Me, Darling (I Have Lied)	1963	20.00
❑ 4403 [PS]	Martian Hop/Forgive Me, Darling (I Have Lied)	1963	50.00
❑ 4407	Sound of the Sun/Come On and Love Me	1964	15.00
R.S.V.P.			
❑ 1104	Beyond the Stars/Wintertime	1964	15.00

RANCHEROS, THE

Number	Title (A Side/B Side)	Yr	NM
45s			
DOT			
❑ 16572	Linda's Tune/Little Linda	1964	25.00
LONNIE			
❑ 5005	Linda's Tune/Little Linda	1963	50.00

RANDAZZO, TEDDY

Also see THE THREE CHUCKLES.

Number	Title (A Side/B Side)	Yr	NM
45s			
ABC-PARAMOUNT			
❑ 9998	Papito/You Are Always in My Heart	1959	12.00
❑ 10014	Laughing on the Outside/ Awkward Age	1959	12.00
❑ 10043	Lies/I'm On a Merry-Go Round	1959	12.00
❑ 10068	How I Need You/You Don't Care Anymore	1959	12.00
❑ 10088	The Way of a Clown/Cherie	1960	12.00
❑ 10103	Triste Pagliaccio (The Way of a Clown)/Cherie	1960	15.00
❑ 10127	But You Broke My Heart/Misery	1960	12.00
❑ 10131	Journey of Love/Misery	1960	12.00
❑ 10193	Happy Ending/But You Broke My Heart	1961	10.00
❑ 10228	Broken Bell/Let the Sunshine In	1961	10.00
❑ 10247	Don't Go Away/ One More Chance	1961	10.00
❑ 10287	Mother Goose Twist/ It's a Pity to Say Goodbye	1961	10.00
❑ 10312	Teenage Senorita/ Blue Hawaii Moon	1962	10.00
❑ 10350	Dance to the Locomotion/ Cotton Fields	1962	10.00
❑ 10377	Echoes/It Wasn't a Dream	1962	10.00
COLPIX			
❑ 662	Big Wide World/Be Sure My Love	1962	12.00
❑ 684	Dear Heart/Just Hold My Hand	1963	10.00
DCP			
❑ 1003	Pretty Blue Eyes/Doo Dah	1964	8.00
❑ 1108	Less Than Tomorrow/ Lost Without You	1964	8.00
❑ 1134	You Don't Need a Heart/ As Long As I Live	1965	8.00
❑ 1153	You're Not That Girl Anymore/ Soul	1966	8.00
MGM			
❑ 13448	Lara's Theme/The Old and the New	1966	8.00
❑ 13449	Theme from "A Patch of Blue"/ The Old and the New	1966	8.00
❑ 13511	Watch What Happens/ Per Un Pugno Di Dollari	1966	8.00
❑ 13648	I'm Losing You/Trick or Treat	1966	8.00
❑ 13682	A Fistful of Dollars/Take Me Back	1967	8.00
VERVE FOLKWAYS			
❑ 5050	A World Without Love/Just One More Time	1967	8.00
VIK			
❑ 0277	Next Stop Paradise/How Could You Know?	1957	12.00
❑ 0289	Kiddio/I Was the Last One to Know	1957	12.00
❑ 0310	I'll Never Smile Again/ Red Ruby Lips	1957	12.00
❑ 0319	Dutch Treat/To Belong	1958	12.00
❑ 0330	Little Serenade/Be My Kitten, Little Chicken	1958	15.00
Albums			
ABC-PARAMOUNT			
❑ 352 [M]	Journey to Love	1961	30.00
❑ S-352 [S]	Journey to Love	1961	40.00
❑ 421 [M]	Teddy Randazzo Twists	1962	30.00
❑ S-421 [S]	Teddy Randazzo Twists	1962	40.00
COLPIX			
❑ CP-445 [M]	Big Wide World	1963	30.00
❑ SCP-445 [S]	Big Wide World	1963	40.00
VIK			
❑ LX-1121 [M]	I'm Confessin'	1958	200.00

RANDELL, BUDDY

Number	Title (A Side/B Side)	Yr	NM
45s			
UNI			
❑ 55209	Be My Baby/Randi Randi	1970	6.00

RANDELL, LYNNE

Number	Title (A Side/B Side)	Yr	NM
45s			
ABC			
❑ 11112	Open Letter/Right to Cry	1968	20.00
EPIC			
❑ 10147	Stranger in My Arms/Ciao Baby	1967	30.00
❑ 10197	I Need You Boy/That's a Hoe-Down	1967	30.00

RANDLE, BOBBY

Number	Title (A Side/B Side)	Yr	NM
45s			
SHAD			
❑ 5007	Karen/Walking in the Shadows	1959	30.00

RANDOLPH, BARBARA

Number	Title (A Side/B Side)	Yr	NM
SOUL			
❑ 35038	I Got a Feeling/You Got Me Hurtin' All Over	1967	20.00
❑ 35050	Can I Get a Witness/You Got Me Hurtin' All Over	1968	20.00

R

RANDOLPH, BOOTS

Number	Title (A Side/B Side)	Yr	NM
45s			
MONUMENT			
❑ 45-209	Honky Tonk/Memphis	1977	4.00
❑ 45-227	Jive Talkin'/Blueberry Hill	1977	4.00
❑ 45-263	You Light Up My Life/ Movin' On Up	1978	4.00
❑ 45-294	I Write the Songs/ Motherland-Oluwa	1980	4.00
❑ 443	Fancy Dan/Hey, Daddy Daddy	1961	10.00
❑ 460	Bluebird of Happiness/Keep a Light in Your Window Tonight	1962	10.00
❑ 804	Yakety Sax/I Really Don't Want to Know	1963	10.00
❑ 821	Lonely Street/Windy and Warm	1963	8.00
❑ 835	Hey, Mr. Sax Man/Baby, Go to Sleep	1964	8.00
❑ 852	Mickey's Tune/I'll Take You Home Again, Kathleen	1964	8.00
❑ 884	King of the Road/Theme from a Dream	1965	8.00
❑ 928	These Boots Are Made for Walking/Honey in Your Heart	1966	8.00
❑ 950	Yodeling Sax/Miss You	1966	8.00
❑ 976	The Shadow of Your Smile/ I'll Just Walk Away	1966	8.00
❑ 1009	Temptation/You've Lost That Lovin' Feelin'	1967	6.00
❑ 1038	Love Letters/Big Daddy	1967	6.00
❑ 1056	Wonderland by Night/Fred	1968	6.00
❑ 1081	Gentle on My Mind/Jackson	1968	6.00
❑ 1125	Games People Play/By the Time I Get to Phoenix	1969	6.00
❑ 1165	Hey Jude/Down Yonder	1969	6.00
❑ 1176	Sleigh Ride/White Christmas	1969	8.00
❑ 1199	Spanish Harlem/Anna	1970	5.00
❑ 1219	Sunday Morning Coming Down/Those Were the Days	1970	5.00
❑ 1226	Proud Mary/Without Love (There Is Nothing)	1970	5.00
❑ 1233	Take a Letter Maria/ See See Rider	1970	5.00
❑ 1937	Sleigh Ride/White Christmas	1976	4.00
—Golden Series			
❑ 8500	My Sweet Lord/(B-side unknown)	1971	5.00
❑ 8534	Lookin'/Alligator Annie	1972	4.00

Number	Title (A Side/B Side)	Yr	NM
8541	Lonesome Ladies/Mountain Minuet	1972	4.00
8552	Love Theme from "The Godfather"/Rocky Top	1972	4.00
8588	Marie/Sentimental Journey	1973	4.00
8616	Behind Closed Doors/Old Joe Clarke	1974	4.00
8632	Sleigh Ride/White Christmas	1974	5.00
8634	Sanford & Son Theme/Ebb Tide	1974	5.00

RCA VICTOR

Number	Title (A Side/B Side)	Yr	NM
47-7278	Difficult/I'm Getting Your Message Baby	1958	15.00
—As "Randy Randolph"			
47-7395	Yakety Sax/Percolator	1958	20.00
—As "Randy Randolph"			
47-7515	Blue Guitar/Greenback Dollar	1959	12.00
—As "Randy Randolph"			
47-7611	Temptation/Sweet Talk	1959	12.00
47-7721	Red Light/La Golondrina	1960	12.00
47-7835	Bog Daddy/Bongo Band	1961	12.00

7-Inch Extended Plays

MONUMENT

Number	Title (A Side/B Side)	Yr	NM
SMN-361 [DJ]	Sleigh Ride/Rudolph The Red-Nosed Reindeer//White Christmas/I'll Be Home For Christmas	1969	20.00

Albums

MONUMENT

Number	Title (A Side/B Side)	Yr	NM
DS 632	King of Yakety	197?	15.00
—Manufactured by CBS Direct Marketing Services			
6600	Boots Randolph's Yakety Sax	197?	10.00
—Reissue of 18002			
6601	Hip Boots	197?	10.00
—Reissue of 18015			
6602	Boots Randolph Plays More Yakety Sax	197?	10.00
—Reissue of 18037			
6603	The Fantastic Boots Randolph	197?	10.00
—Reissue of 18042			
6604	Boots with Strings	197?	10.00
—Reissue of 18066			
MC 6605	Sax-Sational	1976	10.00
—Reissue of 18079			
6606	Boots Randolph with the Knightsbridge Strings & Voices	197?	10.00
—Reissue of 18082			
6607	Sunday Sax	197?	10.00
—Reissue of 18092			
6608	The Sound of Boots	197?	10.00
—Reissue of 18099			
6609	...With Love/The Seductive Sax of Boots Randolph	197?	10.00
—Reissue of 18111			
6610	Boots and Stockings	197?	10.00
—Reissue of 18127			
6611	Yakety Revisited	197?	10.00
—Reissue of 18128			
6612	Hit Boots 1970	197?	10.00
—Reissue of 18144			
6613	Boots with Brass	197?	10.00
—Reissue of 18147			
6614	Homer Louis Randolph, III	197?	10.00
—Reissue of 30678			
6615	Boots Randolph Plays the Great Hits of Today	197?	10.00
—Reissue of 31908			
6616	Sentimental Journey	197?	10.00
—Reissue of 32292			
6617	Country Boots	197?	10.00
—Reissue of 32912			
6618	Cool Boots	197?	10.00
—Reissue of 33803			
7602	Greatest Hits	1977	10.00
7611	Sax Appeal	1977	10.00
7627	Put a Little Sax	1978	10.00
MLP-8002 [M]	Boots Randolph's Yakety Sax	1963	20.00
MLP-8015 [M]	Hip Boots	1964	15.00
MLP-8029 [M]	12 Monstrous Sax Hits	1965	15.00
MLP-8037 [M]	Boots Randolph Plays More Yakety Sax	1965	15.00
MLP-8042 [M]	The Fantastic Boots Randolph	1966	15.00
MLP-8066 [M]	Boots with Strings	1966	15.00
MLP-8079 [M]	Sax-Sational	1967	20.00
MLP-8082 [M]	Boots Randolph with the Knightsbridge Strings & Voices	1967	20.00
8604 [(2)]	Party Boots	197?	12.00
—Reissue of 34082			
SLP-18002 [S]	Boots Randolph's Yakety Sax	1963	25.00
SLP-18015 [S]	Hip Boots	1964	20.00
SLP-18029 [S]	12 Monstrous Sax Hits	1965	20.00
SLP-18037 [S]	Boots Randolph Plays More Yakety Sax	1965	20.00
SLP-18042 [S]	The Fantastic Boots Randolph	1966	20.00
SLP-18066 [S]	Boots with Strings	1966	20.00
SLP-18079 [S]	Sax-Sational	1967	15.00
SLP-18082 [S]	Boots Randolph with the Knightsbridge Strings & Voices	1967	15.00
SLP-18092	Sunday Sax	1968	20.00
SLP-18099	The Sound of Boots	1968	20.00
SLP-18111	...With Love/The Seductive Sax of Boots Randolph	1969	15.00
SLP 18127	Boots and Stockings	1969	15.00
SLP-18128	Yakety Revisited	1969	15.00
SLP-18144	Hit Boots 1970	1970	15.00
SLP-18147	Boots with Brass	1970	15.00
Z 30678	Homer Louis Randolph, III	1971	12.00
ZG 30963 [(2)]	The World of Boots Randolph	1971	15.00
KZ 31908	Boots Randolph Plays the Great Hits of Today	1972	12.00
KZ 32292	Sentimental Journey	1973	12.00
KZ 32912	Country Boots	1974	12.00
KZ 33298	Boots Randolph's Yakety Sax	1974	12.00
KZ 33803	Cool Boots	1975	12.00
BZ 33852 [(2)]	Boots with Strings	1975	15.00
Z2 34082 [(2)]	Party Boots	1976	15.00
PW 38388	Greatest Hits	1983	10.00
JW 38396	Dedication	1983	10.00

RCA CAMDEN

Number	Title (A Side/B Side)	Yr	NM
CAL-825 [M]	Yakin' Sax Man	1964	15.00
CAS-825 [S]	Yakin' Sax Man	1964	15.00
CAL-865 [M]	Sweet Talk	1965	15.00
CAS-865 [R]	Sweet Talk	1965	12.00
ACL-9003 [(2)]	Yakety Sax	1972	12.00

RCA VICTOR

Number	Title (A Side/B Side)	Yr	NM
LPM-2165 [M]	Yakety Sax	1960	40.00
LSP-2165 [S]	Yakety Sax	1960	50.00

RANDOLPH, WILLIAM

45s

HIT

Number	Title (A Side/B Side)	Yr	NM
173	Song of Love/The Wedding	1965	8.00
—B-side by Betty Coleson			
188	Swinging Spiritual/No Arms Can Ever Hold You	1965	8.00
—B-side by Danny Woods			
196	Madrid/Red Roses for a Blue Lady	1965	8.00
201	I'm in a Very Romantic Mood/I Know a Place	1965	8.00
—B-side by Betty Coleson			
205	Theme from "Peyton Place"/Tower Suite	1965	8.00
214	Come Back to Me/I'll Never Find Another You	1965	8.00
—B-side by the Broadway Singers			

RANDY AND THE RADIANTS

45s

SUN

Number	Title (A Side/B Side)	Yr	NM
395	The Mountain's High/Peek-a-Boo	1965	25.00
398	My Way of Thinking/Truth from My Eyes	1966	25.00

RANDY AND THE RAINBOWS

45s

AMBIENT SOUND

Number	Title (A Side/B Side)	Yr	NM
02872	Debbie/Try the Impossible	1982	5.00

B.T. PUPPY

Number	Title (A Side/B Side)	Yr	NM
535	I'll Be Seeing You/Oh to Get Away	1967	10.00

MIKE

Number	Title (A Side/B Side)	Yr	NM
4001	Lovely Lies/I'll Forget Her Tomorrow	1966	12.00
4004	Quarter to Three/He's a Fugitive	1966	12.00
4008	Bonnie's Part of Town/Can It Be	1966	12.00

RUST

Number	Title (A Side/B Side)	Yr	NM
5059	Denise/Come Back	1963	20.00
—Mostly white label			
5059	Denise/Come Back	1963	30.00
—Blue label			
5059	Denise/Come Back	197?	10.00
—Later pressing on gold label			
5073	She's My Angel/Why Do Kids Grow Up	1964	15.00
5080	Happy Teenager/Dry Your Eyes	1964	15.00
5091	Little Star/Sharin'	1964	15.00
5101	Joy Ride/Little Hot Rod Suzie	1965	15.00

Albums

AMBIENT SOUND

Number	Title (A Side/B Side)	Yr	NM
ASR-601	Remember	1985	12.00
FZ 37715	C'mon, Let's Go	1982	12.00

RANDY AND THE ROCKETS

45s

AZALEA

Number	Title (A Side/B Side)	Yr	NM
138	Over the Waves/New Chapel Hill	196?	20.00

JIN

Number	Title (A Side/B Side)	Yr	NM
161	Let's Do the Cajun Twist/Rockets' Twist	196?	15.00
165	No More Trouble/Bye Bye Baby	196?	15.00

VIKING

Number	Title (A Side/B Side)	Yr	NM
1000	If You Really Care/Genevieve	1959	20.00
1003	Is It True/Crazy Notion	1959	20.00
1004	That's Life/Sweet Love	1959	20.00

RANGERS, THE

45s

CHALLENGE

Number	Title (A Side/B Side)	Yr	NM
59229	Snow Skiing/Mogul Monster	1964	20.00
59239	Justine/Reputation	1964	20.00

FTP

Number	Title (A Side/B Side)	Yr	NM
404	Four on the Floor/Riders in the Sky	1961	30.00

RANGLIN, ERNEST

45s

STUDIO

Number	Title (A Side/B Side)	Yr	NM
1	Surfing (Part 1)/Surfing (Part 2)	196?	50.00

RANK, KEN

45s

FENTON

Number	Title (A Side/B Side)	Yr	NM
2194	Twin City Saucer/Ken's Thing	1968	30.00

RANKIN, KENNY

45s

ABC-PARAMOUNT

Number	Title (A Side/B Side)	Yr	NM
10268	Funny That's Love/Go Home Little Girl	1961	12.00
—As "Ken Rankin"			

ATLANTIC

Number	Title (A Side/B Side)	Yr	NM
3663	Regrets/(B-side unknown)	1980	4.00

COLUMBIA

Number	Title (A Side/B Side)	Yr	NM
42881	Soft Guitar/Baby Goodbye	1963	10.00
43036	Where Did My Little Girl Go/U.S. Mail	1964	10.00
4-43201	Knowing I Won't Go Back There/There'll Be No Other Love	1964	10.00
43885	Haven't We Met/In the Name of Love	1966	10.00

DECCA

Number	Title (A Side/B Side)	Yr	NM
30485	Saturday After the Game/I'll Be Waiting	1957	20.00
30691	My Popular Baby/You Be the Judge	1958	15.00
30852	Cindy Loo/Catch Love	1959	15.00
30954	I Cry By Night/Have Pity Miss Kitty	1959	15.00
31054	What Do You Want to Make Those Eyes at Me For/Tonight I'm Speaking Love	1960	12.00
31124	Casey Jones/It Started in Naples	1960	12.00
31162	Sure As You're Born/Teasin' Heart	1960	12.00

LITTLE DAVID

Number	Title (A Side/B Side)	Yr	NM
725	String Man/Comin' Down	1972	5.00
726	Peaceful/Sometimes	1973	5.00
727	Why Do Fools Fall in Love/(B-side unknown)	1973	5.00
728	Penny Lane/Killed a Cat	1974	5.00
729	Catfish/Silver Morning	1975	5.00
732	Sunday Kind of Love/Inside	1975	5.00
733	Creepin'/Lost Up in Loving You	1976	5.00
735	On and On/Through the Eyes of the Eagle	1977	5.00
737	When Sunny Gets Blue/I Love You	1977	5.00
8072	Penny Lane/Killed a Cat	1975	5.00
8093	Catfish/Silver Morning	1975	5.00

MERCURY

Number	Title (A Side/B Side)	Yr	NM
72768	Peaceful/The Dolphin	1968	8.00
72768 [PS]	Peaceful/The Dolphin	1968	12.00
72956	Minuet/Peaceful	1969	8.00

Albums

ATLANTIC

Number	Title (A Side/B Side)	Yr	NM
SD 19271	After the Roses	1980	10.00

LITTLE DAVID

Number	Title (A Side/B Side)	Yr	NM
LD 1003	Like a Seed	1972	10.00
LD 1009	Inside	1975	10.00
LD 1013	The Kenny Rankin Album	1977	10.00
SD 3000	Silver Morning	1974	10.00
90131	Silver Morning	1984	8.00
—Reissue of 3000			

MERCURY

Number	Title (A Side/B Side)	Yr	NM
MG-21141 [M]	Mind Dusters	1967	15.00
SR-61141 [S]	Mind Dusters	1967	12.00
SR-61240	Family	1969	12.00

RARE BIRD

45s

Number	Title (A Side/B Side)	Yr	NM
ABC			
❑ 11284	Hammerhead/What You Want to Know	1970	6.00
POLYDOR			
❑ 15079	Birdman (Part 1)/Birdman (Part 2)	1973	5.00
❑ 15081	The Darkest Hour/Hey Man	1973	5.00
❑ 15087	Somebody's Watching (Part 1)/ Somebody's Watching (Part 2)	1974	5.00
❑ 15093	Body and Soul/ (B-side unassigned)	1974	—
—Canceled			
PROBE			
❑ 477	Sympathy/Beautiful Scarlet	1970	8.00

Albums

Number	Title (A Side/B Side)	Yr	NM
ABC			
❑ X-715	As Your Mind Flies	1972	15.00
POLYDOR			
❑ PD 5530	Epic Forest	1973	15.00
❑ PD 6502	Somebody's Watching	1974	15.00
❑ PD 6506	Born Again	1974	15.00
PROBE			
❑ 4514	Rare Bird	1970	25.00

RARE BREED, THE

Later known as THE OHIO EXPRESS.

45s

Number	Title (A Side/B Side)	Yr	NM
ATTACK			
❑ 1401	Beg, Borrow and Steal/ Jeri's Theme	1966	30.00
❑ 1403	Come and Take a Ride in My Boat/Take Me to This World of Yours	1966	20.00

RARE EARTH

45s

Number	Title (A Side/B Side)	Yr	NM
PRODIGAL			
❑ 0637	Crazy Love/Is Your Teacher Cool	1977	5.00
❑ 0640	Warm Ride/Would You Like to Come Along	1978	5.00
❑ 0643	I Can Feel My Love Risin'/ S.O.S. (Stop Her On Sight)	1978	5.00
RARE EARTH			
❑ 960/961 [DJ]	What'd I Say (stereo/mono)	1972	25.00
—Blue vinyl, promo only, white label			
❑ 5010	Generation (Light of the Sky)/ Magic Key	1969	12.00
❑ 5012	Get Ready/Magic Key	1970	6.00
❑ 5017	(I Know) I'm Losing You/ When Joanie Smiles	1970	6.00
❑ 5021	Born to Wander/Here Comes the Night	1970	6.00
❑ 5031	I Just Want to Celebrate/ The Seed	1971	6.00
❑ 5031 [PS]	I Just Want to Celebrate/ The Seed	1971	10.00
❑ 5038	Hey Big Brother/ Under God's Light	1971	6.00
❑ 5043	What'd I Say/Nice to Be with You	1972	6.00
❑ 5048	Good Time Sally/ Love Shines Down	1972	6.00
❑ 5052	We're Gonna Have a Good Time/Would You Like to Come Along	1973	6.00
❑ 5053	Ma/(Instrumental)	1973	6.00
❑ 5054	Hum Along and Dance/ Come with Me	1973	6.00
❑ 5056	Big John Is My Name/Ma	1974	6.00
❑ 5057	Chained/Fresh from the Can	1974	6.00
❑ 5058	It Makes You Happy (But It Ain't Gonna Last Too Long)/ Boogie with Me Children	1975	6.00
❑ 5059	Let Me Be Your Sunshine/ Keep Me Out of the Storm	1976	6.00
❑ 5060	Midnight Lady/Walking Shtick	1976	6.00
RCA			
❑ PB-13076	Howzabout Some Love/ Let Me Take You Out	1982	—
—Unreleased			
VERVE			
❑ 10622	Stop-Where Did Our Love Go/ Mother's Oats	1968	12.00

Albums

Number	Title (A Side/B Side)	Yr	NM
MOTOWN			
❑ M5-116V1	Motown Superstar Series, Vol. 16	1981	10.00
❑ M5-202V1	Ecology	1981	8.00
❑ 5229 ML	Get Ready	1982	8.00
PRODIGAL			
❑ P6-10019	Rare Earth	1977	10.00
❑ P7-10025	Band Together	1978	10.00
❑ P7-10027	Grand Slam	1979	10.00

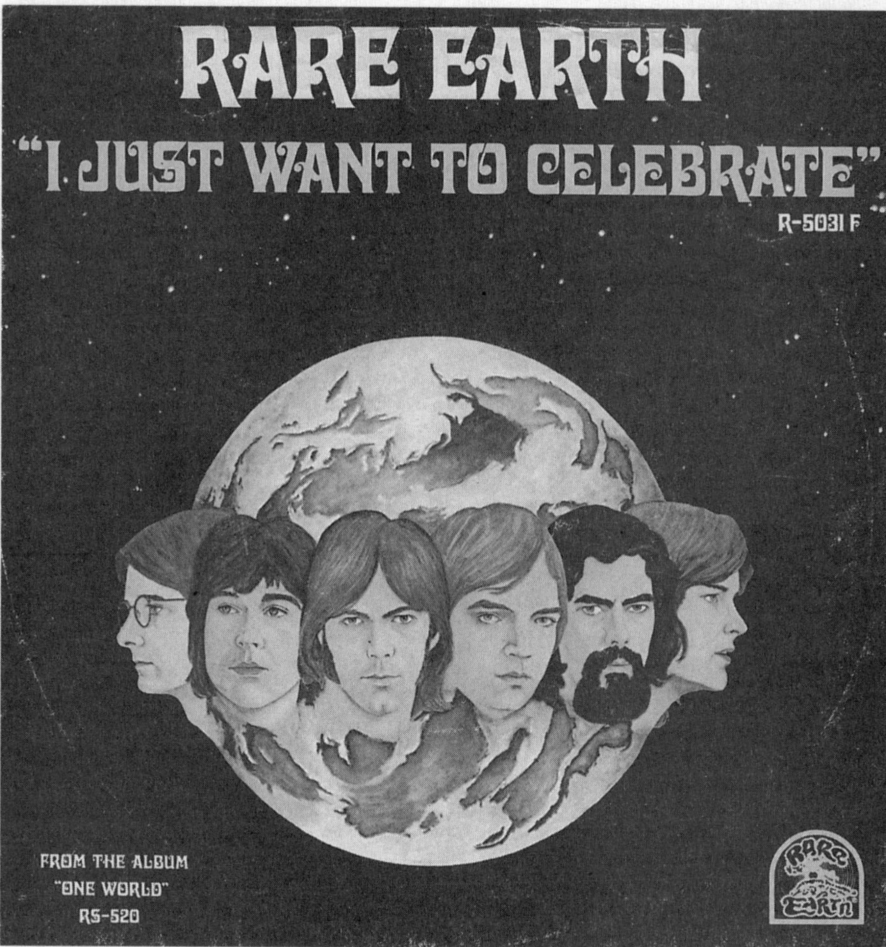

Rare Earth, "I Just Want to Celebrate," Rare Earth 5031, 1971, **$10.**

Number	Title (A Side/B Side)	Yr	NM
RARE EARTH			
❑ RS 507	Get Ready	1969	30.00
—Original cover has a rounded top			
❑ RS 507	Get Ready	1970	12.00
—Regular square cover			
❑ RS 510	Generation	1970	500.00
—At least one copy of this album has been confirmed to exist			
❑ RS 514	Ecology	1970	15.00
❑ RS 520	One World	1971	15.00
❑ R 534 [(2)]	Rare Earth in Concert	1971	15.00
❑ R 543	Willie Remembers	1972	12.00
❑ R6-546	Ma	1973	12.00
❑ R6-548	Back to Earth	1975	12.00
❑ R7-550	Midnight Lady	1976	12.00
VERVE			
❑ V6-5066	Dreams/Answers	1968	50.00

RASCALS, THE

Includes "The Young Rascals." Also see FELIX CAVALIERE; GENE CORNISH; FELIX AND THE ESCORTS.

45s

Number	Title (A Side/B Side)	Yr	NM
ATLANTIC			
❑ 2312	I Ain't Gonna Eat Out My Heart Anymore/Slow Down	1965	15.00
—From here through Atlantic 2463, as "The Young Rascals"			
❑ 2321	Good Lovin'/Mustang Sally	1966	15.00
❑ 2338	You Better Run/Love Is a Beautiful Thing	1966	10.00
❑ 2338 [PS]	You Better Run/Love Is a Beautiful Thing	1966	20.00
❑ 2353	Come On Up/What Is the Reason	1966	10.00
❑ 2377	I've Been Lonely Too Long/ If You Knew	1967	10.00
❑ 2377 [PS]	I've Been Lonely Too Long/ If You Knew	1967	20.00
❑ 2401	Groovin'/Sueno	1967	8.00
❑ 2401 [PS]	Groovin'/Sueno	1967	20.00
❑ 2424	A Girl Like You/It's Love	1967	8.00
❑ 2424 [PS]	A Girl Like You/It's Love	1967	20.00
❑ 2428	Groovin' (Spanish)/ Groovin' (Italian)	1967	20.00
❑ 2438	How Can I Be Sure/ I'm So Happy Now	1967	8.00
❑ 2463	It's Wonderful/Of Course	1967	8.00
❑ 2493	A Beautiful Morning/Rainy Day	1968	6.00
—First record as "The Rascals"			
❑ 2493 [PS]	A Beautiful Morning/Rainy Day	1968	20.00
❑ 2537	People Got to Be Free/My World	1968	6.00
❑ 2537 [PS]	People Got to Be Free/My World	1968	12.00
❑ 2584	A Ray of Hope/Any Dance'll Do	1968	6.00
❑ 2584 [PS]	A Ray of Hope/Any Dance'll Do	1968	12.00
❑ 2599	Heaven/Baby I'm Blue	1969	6.00
❑ 2634	See/Away Away	1969	6.00
❑ 2634 [PS]	See/Away Away	1969	12.00
❑ 2664	Carry Me Back/Real Thing	1969	6.00
❑ 2664 [PS]	Carry Me Back/Real Thing	1969	12.00
❑ 2695	Hold On/I Believe	1969	6.00
❑ 2695 [PS]	Hold On/I Believe	1969	12.00
❑ 2743	Glory Glory/You Don't Know	1970	6.00
❑ 2743 [PS]	Glory Glory/You Don't Know	1970	12.00
❑ 2773	Right On/Almost Home	1970	6.00
COLUMBIA			
❑ 45400	Love Me/Happy Song	1971	6.00
❑ 45491	Lucky Day/Love Letter	1971	6.00
❑ 45568	Brother Tree/Saga of New York	1972	6.00
❑ 45600	Echoes/Hummin' Song	1972	6.00
❑ 45649	Jungle Walk/Saga of New York	1972	10.00
PHILCO-FORD			
❑ HP-18	A Girl Like You/I've Been Lonely Too Long	1967	15.00
—4-inch plastic "Hip Pocket Record" with color sleeve			

7-Inch Extended Plays

Number	Title (A Side/B Side)	Yr	NM
ATLANTIC			
❑ SD 7-8169	Please Love Me/It's Wonderful/ I'm Gonna Love You//Easy Rollin'/Rainy Day	1968	20.00
—Jukebox issue; small hole, plays at 33 1/3 rpm			
❑ SD 7-8169 [PS]	Once Upon a Dream	1968	20.00

Albums

Number	Title (A Side/B Side)	Yr	NM
ATLANTIC			
❑ ST-137 [DJ]	Freedom Suite Sampler	1969	50.00
❑ SD 2-901 [(2)]	Freedom Suite	1969	20.00

R

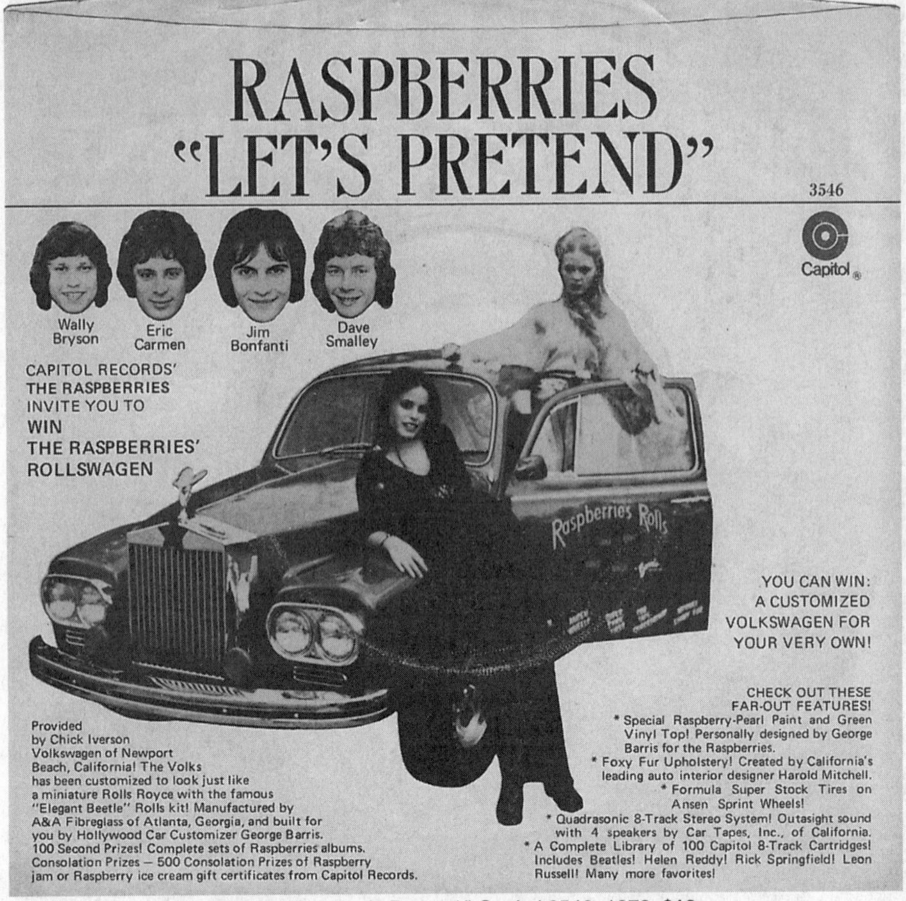

Raspberries, "Let's Pretend," Capitol 3546, 1973, **$12.**

Number	Title (A Side/B Side)	Yr	NM
❑ 8123 [M]	The Young Rascals	1966	30.00
❑ SD 8123 [S]	The Young Rascals	1966	40.00
—Green and blue label			
❑ SD 8123 [S]	The Young Rascals	1966	50.00
—Purple and green label			
❑ SD 8123 [S]	The Young Rascals	1969	12.00
—Red and green label			
❑ 8134 [M]	Collections	1967	25.00
❑ SD 8134 [S]	Collections	1967	30.00
—Green and blue label			
❑ SD 8134 [S]	Collections	1969	12.00
—Red and green label			
❑ 8148 [M]	Groovin'	1967	25.00
❑ SD 8148 [S]	Groovin'	1967	30.00
—Green and blue label			
❑ SD 8148 [S]	Groovin'	1969	12.00
—Red and green label			
❑ 8169 [M]	Once Upon a Dream	1968	40.00
❑ SD 8169 [S]	Once Upon a Dream	1968	25.00
—Green and blue label			
❑ SD 8169 [S]	Once Upon a Dream	1969	12.00
—Red and green label			
❑ 8190 [M]	Time Peace/The Rascals' Greatest Hits	1968	50.00
—Mono is promo only			
❑ SD 8190 [S]	Time Peace/The Rascals' Greatest Hits	1968	15.00
—Purple and gold label			
❑ SD 8190 [S]	Time Peace/The Rascals' Greatest Hits	1968	25.00
—Green and blue label			
❑ SD 8190 [S]	Time Peace/The Rascals' Greatest Hits	1969	12.00
—Red and green label			
❑ 8246 [M]	See	1969	50.00
—Mono is promo only; cover has "dj copy monaural" sticker on front			
❑ SD 8246 [S]	See	1969	15.00
❑ 8276 [M]	Search and Nearness	1970	50.00
—Mono is promo only; cover has "dj copy monaural" sticker on front			
❑ SD 8276 [S]	Search and Nearness	1970	15.00
COLUMBIA			
❑ G 30462 [(2)]	Peaceful World	1971	15.00
❑ KC 31103	The Island of Real	1972	12.00
PAIR			
❑ PDL2-1106 [(2)]	Rock and Roll Treasures	1986	15.00
RHINO			
❑ RNLP 70237	The Young Rascals	1988	10.00
❑ RNLP 70238	Collections	1988	10.00
❑ RNLP 70239	Groovin'	1988	10.00
❑ R1-70240	Once Upon a Dream	1988	10.00
❑ R1-70241	Freedom Suite	1988	10.00
❑ R1-70242	Searching for Ecstasy: The Rest of the Rascals 1969-1972	1988	10.00
SUNDAZED			
❑ LP 5116	The Young Rascals	2002	12.00
❑ LP 5117	Collections	2002	12.00
❑ LP 5118	Groovin'	2002	12.00
❑ LP 5119	Once Upon a Dream	2002	12.00
WARNER SPECIAL PRODUCTS			
❑ SP-2502 [(2)]	24 Greatest Hits	1971	20.00
WES FARRELL			
❑ PFT-1002 [DJ]	Songs from the Rascals	197?	25.00
—Promo-only publisher's demo			

RASPBERRIES Also see ERIC CARMEN; THE CHOIR.

45s

Number	Title (A Side/B Side)	Yr	NM
CAPITOL			
❑ 3280	Don't Want to Say Goodbye/Rock and Roll Mama	1972	8.00
❑ 3280 [PS]	Don't Want to Say Goodbye/Rock and Roll Mama	1972	25.00
❑ 3348	Go All the Way/With You in My Life	1972	6.00
❑ 3473	I Wanna Be with You/Goin' Nowhere Tonight	1972	6.00
❑ 3546	Let's Pretend/Every Way I Can	1973	6.00
❑ 3546 [PS]	Let's Pretend/Every Way I Can	1973	12.00
❑ 3610	Tonight/Had to Get Over a Heartbreak	1973	6.00
❑ 3765	I'm a Rocker/Money Down	1973	6.00
❑ 3826	Don't Want to Say Goodbye/Ecstasy	1974	6.00
❑ 3885	Drivin' Around/Might As Well	1974	6.00
❑ 3946	Overnight Sensation (Hit Record)/Hands on You	1974	6.00
❑ 4001	The Party's Over/Cruisin' Music	1974	6.00
❑ PRO-6426 [DJ]	Don't Want to Say Goodbye (3:48 Mono)/(5:00 Stereo)	1972	20.00

Albums

Number	Title (A Side/B Side)	Yr	NM
CAPITOL			
❑ SK-11036	Raspberries	1972	30.00
—Originals have red labels and a "scratch 'n' sniff" cover, the smell of which fades over time			
❑ ST-11036	Raspberries	1973	20.00
—Orange label, "Capitol" at bottom			
❑ ST-11123	Fresh	1972	20.00
❑ SMAS-11220	Side 3	1973	20.00
—With cover cut in the shape of a basket of raspberries			
❑ ST-11329	Starting Over	1974	20.00
❑ ST-11524	Raspberries' Best Featuring Eric Carmen	1976	15.00
❑ SN-16095	Raspberries' Best Featuring Eric Carmen	1979	10.00

RATCHELL

45s

Number	Title (A Side/B Side)	Yr	NM
DECCA			
❑ 32893	Lazy Lady/Problems	1971	6.00
❑ 32958	Julie My Woman/Out of Hand	1972	5.00
❑ 32981	Peace of Mind/My My	1972	5.00

Albums

Number	Title (A Side/B Side)	Yr	NM
DECCA			
❑ DL 75330	Ratchell	1972	15.00
❑ DL 75365	Ratchell 2	1972	15.00

RATIONALS, THE

45s

Number	Title (A Side/B Side)	Yr	NM
A-SQUARE			
❑ 101	Look What You're Doin'/Gave My Love	1966	25.00
❑ 103	Feelin' Lost/Little Girls Cry	1966	20.00
❑ 103	Feelin' Lost/Respect	1966	25.00
❑ 104	Leavin' Here/Respect	1966	30.00
—This is the original issue of this single			
❑ 104/3	Leavin' Here/Feelin' Lost	1966	25.00
❑ 107	I Need You/Out in the Streets	1968	20.00
❑ 402	I Need You/Get the Picture	1967	25.00
—B-side by SRC (Scott Richard Case)			
CAMEO			
❑ 437	Respect/Feelin' Lost	1966	12.00
❑ 455	Hold On Baby/Sing	1967	15.00
❑ 481	Leavin' Here/Not Like It Is	1967	15.00
CAPITOL			
❑ 2124	I Need You/Out in the Streets	1968	15.00
CREWE			
❑ 340	Handbags and Gladrags/Guitar Army	1969	15.00
DANBY'S			
❑ (no #)	Turn On/Irrational	1966	50.00
—Made for Danby's clothiers			
GENESIS			
❑ 1	Guitar Army/Sunset	1969	15.00

Albums

Number	Title (A Side/B Side)	Yr	NM
CREWE			
❑ CR-1334	The Rationals	1969	40.00

RATS, THE

45s

Number	Title (A Side/B Side)	Yr	NM
LAURIE			
❑ 3276	Spoonful/I've Got My Eyes on You Baby	1964	12.00
RUST			
❑ TR-2	Spoonful/I've Got My Eyes on You Baby	1965	15.00

RATTLES, THE Also see THE SEARCHERS.

45s

Number	Title (A Side/B Side)	Yr	NM
LONDON			
❑ 1037	Devil's on the Loose/I Know You Don't Know	1972	5.00
❑ 1047	Devil's Sun/Why Do I Care	1973	5.00
MERCURY			
❑ 72403	Shame, Shame, Shame/Someone Who Is Just Like You	1965	12.00
❑ 72554	Sha La La La Lee/Dance	1966	12.00
PROBE			
❑ 480	The Witch/Geraldine	1970	8.00

Albums

Number	Title (A Side/B Side)	Yr	NM
MERCURY			
❑ MG 21127 [M]	The Rattles' Greatest Hits	1967	80.00
❑ SR 61127 [R]	The Rattles' Greatest Hits	1967	50.00

Except when noted otherwise, VG = 25% of NM, and VG+ = 50% of NM. (Example: VG = $2.00, VG+ = $4.00 and NM = $8.00.)

RAVEN, PAUL
See GARY GLITTER.

RAVENAIRS, THE

45s

ALGONQUIN

Number	Title (A Side/B Side)	Yr	NM
718	A Night to Remember/Together Forever	1958	100.00

—Originally released as "The Rivieras"

RAVENS, THE
Also see JIMMY RICKS.

45s

ARGO

Number	Title (A Side/B Side)	Yr	NM
5255	Kneel and Pray/I Can't Believe	1956	40.00
5261	A Simple Prayer/Water Boy	1956	80.00
5276	That'll Be the Day/Dear One	1957	30.00
5284	Here Is My Heart/Lazy Mule	1957	30.00

CHECKER

Number	Title (A Side/B Side)	Yr	NM
871	That'll Be the Day/Dear One	1957	20.00

COLUMBIA

Number	Title (A Side/B Side)	Yr	NM
1-903	Don't Look Now/Time Takes Care of Everything	1950	1500.
—Microgroove 33 1/3 single			
6-903	Don't Look Now/Time Takes Care of Everything	1950	700.00
1-925	My Baby's Gone/I'm So Crazy for Love	1950	1500.
—Microgroove 33 1/3 single			
6-925	My Baby's Gone/I'm So Crazy for Love	1950	600.00
4-39112	You Don't Have to Drop a Heart/Midnight Blues	1950	2000.
4-39194	You're Always in My Dreams/Gotta Find My Baby	1951	2000.
4-39408	You Foolish Thing/Honey I Don't Want You	1951	2000.

JUBILEE

Number	Title (A Side/B Side)	Yr	NM
45-5184	Bye Bye Baby Blues/Happy Go Lucky Baby	1955	30.00
45-5203	Green Eyes/The Bells of San Rafael	1955	30.00
—As "Jimmy Ricks and the Ravens"			
45-5217	On Chapel Hill/We'll Raise a Ruckus Tonight	1955	30.00
45-5237	I'll Always Be in Love with You/(Take Me Back To My) Boots and Saddles	1956	30.00
—As "Jimmy Ricks and the Ravens"			

MERCURY

Number	Title (A Side/B Side)	Yr	NM
5764x45	There's No Use Pretending/Wagon Wheels	1951	300.00
5800x45	Begin the Beguine/Looking for My Baby	1952	250.00
5853x45	Why Did You Leave Me/Chloe	1952	250.00
8259x45	There's No Use Pretending/Wagon Wheels	1951	400.00
8291x45	Rock Me All Night Long/One Sweet Letter	1952	150.00
70060x45	I'll Be Back/Don't Mention My Name	1953	200.00
70119x45	Come a Little Bit Closer/She's Got to Go	1953	150.00
70213x45	Who'll Be the Fool/Rough Ridin'	1953	150.00
70240x45	Without a Song/Walkin' My Blues Away	1953	150.00
70307x45	September Song/Escortin' Or Courtin'	1954	150.00
70330x45	Going Home/Lonesome Road	1954	150.00
70413x45	I've Got You Under My Skin/Love Is No Dream	1954	100.00
—Black label			
70413x45	I've Got You Under My Skin/Love Is No Dream	1954	250.00
—Pink label			
70505x45	White Christmas/Silent Night	1954	100.00
—Black label			
70505x45	White Christmas/Silent Night	1954	200.00
—Pink label			
70554x45	Ol' Man River/Write Me a Letter	1955	100.00
—Black label			
70554x45	Ol' Man River/Write Me a Letter	1955	200.00
—Pink label			

NATIONAL

Number	Title (A Side/B Side)	Yr	NM
9111-X45	Count Every Star/I'm Gonna Paper All My Walls with Your Love	1950	3000.

—The only known Ravens single on a National 45. VG 1500; VG+ 2250

OKEH

Number	Title (A Side/B Side)	Yr	NM
6825	The Whiffenpoof Song/I Get All My Lovin' on a Saturday Night	1951	500.00
6843	That Old Gang of Mine/Everything But You	1951	500.00
6888	Mam'selle/Calypso Song	1952	400.00

SAVOY

Number	Title (A Side/B Side)	Yr	NM
1540	White Christmas/Silent Night	1958	20.00

TOP RANK

Number	Title (A Side/B Side)	Yr	NM
2003	Into the Shadows/The Rising Sun	1959	25.00
2016	Solitude/Hole in the Middle of the Moon	1959	25.00

7-Inch Extended Plays

KING

Number	Title (A Side/B Side)	Yr	NM
310	*Honey/Bye Bye Baby Blues/Out of a Dream/My Sugar Is So Refined	1954	500.00
310 [PS]	The Ravens Featuring Jimmy Ricks	1954	500.00

RENDITION

Number	Title (A Side/B Side)	Yr	NM
104	(contents unknown)	195?	1500.
104 [PS]	Ol' Man River	195?	2000.

Albums

HARLEM HIT PARADE

Number	Title (A Side/B Side)	Yr	NM
1007	The Ravens	1975	10.00

REGENT

Number	Title (A Side/B Side)	Yr	NM
MG-6062 [M]	Write Me a Letter	195?	150.00
—Red label			
MG-6062 [M]	Write Me a Letter	1957	300.00
—Green label			

SAVOY JAZZ

Number	Title (A Side/B Side)	Yr	NM
SJL-2227 [(2)]	The Greatest Group of Them All	1978	12.00

RAW

Albums

CORAL

Number	Title (A Side/B Side)	Yr	NM
CRL 757515	Raw Holly	1971	30.00

RAW SPITT

45s

UNITED ARTISTS

Number	Title (A Side/B Side)	Yr	NM
50813	That Ain't My Wife/Song to Sing	1971	12.00

Albums

UNITED ARTISTS

Number	Title (A Side/B Side)	Yr	NM
UAS-6795	Maybe You Ain't Black	1971	25.00

RAY, ALDER

45s

LIBERTY

Number	Title (A Side/B Side)	Yr	NM
55715	'Cause I Love Him/A Little Love (Will Go a Long Way)	1964	15.00

MINIT

Number	Title (A Side/B Side)	Yr	NM
32005	I Need You Baby/My Heart Is in Danger	1966	10.00

REVUE

Number	Title (A Side/B Side)	Yr	NM
11014	Love Will Let You Down/Run, Baby, Run	1968	8.00

RAY, DANNY

45s

VIN

Number	Title (A Side/B Side)	Yr	NM
1025	Love Me/Gone	1960	100.00

RAY, DAVE

Albums

ELEKTRA

Number	Title (A Side/B Side)	Yr	NM
EKL-284 [M]	Snaker's Here	1965	20.00
EKL-319 [M]	Fine Soft Land	1966	20.00
EKS-7284 [S]	Snaker's Here	1965	25.00
EKS-7319 [S]	Fine Soft Land	1966	25.00

RAY, DIANE

45s

MERCURY

Number	Title (A Side/B Side)	Yr	NM
72117	Please Don't Talk to the Lifeguard/That's All I Want from You	1963	15.00
72117 [PS]	Please Don't Talk to the Lifeguard/That's All I Want from You	1963	100.00
72195	My Summer Love/Where Is the Boy	1963	15.00
72195 [PS]	My Summer Love/Where Is the Boy	1963	60.00
72223	Snow Man/Just So Bobby Can See	1963	15.00
72223 [PS]	Snow Man/Just So Bobby Can See	1963	60.00
72248	No Arms Can Ever Hold You/Tied Up with Mary	1964	15.00
72276	Happy Happy Birthday Baby/That Boy's Gonna Be Mine	1964	15.00

Albums

MERCURY

Number	Title (A Side/B Side)	Yr	NM
MG-20903 [M]	The Exciting Years	1964	80.00
SR-60903 [S]	The Exciting Years	1964	100.00

RAY, JAMES

45s

CAPRICE

Number	Title (A Side/B Side)	Yr	NM
110	If You Gotta Make a Fool of Somebody/It's Been a Drag	1961	30.00
114	Itty Bitty Pieces/You Remember the Face	1962	25.00
117	Things Are Gonna Be Different/A Miracle	1962	25.00

CONGRESS

Number	Title (A Side/B Side)	Yr	NM
109	Marie/The Old Man and the Mule	1963	20.00
201	Do the Monkey/Put Me in Your Diary	1963	20.00
203	The Masquerade Is Over/One by One	1963	20.00
218	We Got a Thing Goin' On/On That Day	1964	20.00

DYNAMIC SOUND

Number	Title (A Side/B Side)	Yr	NM
503	I've Got My Mind Set on You/Always	1963	40.00

—The A-side was remade by George Harrison in 1987 as "Got My Mind Set on You"

7-Inch Extended Plays

CAPRICE

Number	Title (A Side/B Side)	Yr	NM
1002	The Old Man & the Mule/Lazy Bones//Come Rain or Come Shine/St. James Infirmary	1962	50.00
1002 [PS]	James Ray	1962	50.00

Albums

CAPRICE

Number	Title (A Side/B Side)	Yr	NM
LP-1002 [M]	James Ray	1962	80.00
SLP-1002 [S]	James Ray	1962	120.00

RAY AND ELLEN

45s

CAMEO

Number	Title (A Side/B Side)	Yr	NM
383	All Right/Two Little People	1965	15.00

RAY AND THE DARCHAES

45s

ALJON

Number	Title (A Side/B Side)	Yr	NM
1249	Carol/Little Girl So Fine	1962	120.00

BUZZY

Number	Title (A Side/B Side)	Yr	NM
202	Darling Forever/There Will Always Be	1962	100.00

RAY, GOODMAN AND BROWN
See THE MOMENTS.

RAY-O-VACS, THE

45s

ATCO

Number	Title (A Side/B Side)	Yr	NM
6085	Party Time/Crying All Alone	1957	25.00

DECCA

Number	Title (A Side/B Side)	Yr	NM
48162	Besame Mucho/You Gotta Love My Baby Too	1950	25.00
48181	A Kiss in the Dark/Got Two Arms	1950	25.00
48197	Goodnight My Love/Take Me Back to My Boots and Saddle	1951	25.00
48211	You Can Depend on Me/If You Ever Should Leave Me	1951	25.00
48221	My Baby's Gone/Let's	1951	25.00
48234	What's Mine Is Mine/I Still Love You Baby	1951	25.00
48260	Charmaine/Hands Across the Table	1951	25.00
48274	When the Swallows Come Back to Capistrano/She's a Real Lovin' Baby	1952	25.00

JOSIE

Number	Title (A Side/B Side)	Yr	NM
763	Darling/Ridin' High	1954	30.00
781	I Still Love You/Daddy	1955	30.00

JUBILEE

Number	Title (A Side/B Side)	Yr	NM
5098	What Can I Say/Start Lovin' Me	1952	30.00
5124	Outside of Paradise/You Know	1953	30.00

KAISER

Number	Title (A Side/B Side)	Yr	NM
384	Crying All Alone/Party Time	1956	30.00
389	Wine-O/Hong Kong	1956	30.00

SHARP

Number	Title (A Side/B Side)	Yr	NM
103	I'll Always Be in Love with You/Little Boy	1960	20.00

RAY-VONS, THE

45s

LAURIE

Number	Title (A Side/B Side)	Yr	NM
3248	Judy/Regina	1964	80.00

R

Number	Title (A Side/B Side)	Yr	NM
RAYE, SUSAN Also see BUCK OWENS AND SUSAN RAYE.			
45s			
CAPITOL			
❑ 2620	I Ain't Gonna Be Treated That-a-Way/Maybe If I Close My Eyes (It'll Go Away)	1969	6.00
❑ 2701	Put a Little Love in Your Heart/ I've Carried This Torch Much Too Long	1969	6.00
❑ 2833	One Night Stand/She Don't Deserve You Anymore	1970	6.00
❑ 2950	Willy Jones/I'll Love You Forever (If You're Sure You'll Want Me Then)	1970	6.00
❑ 3035	L.A. International Airport/ Merry-Go-Round of Love	1971	6.00
❑ 3129	Pitty, Pitty, Patter/I'll Be Gone	1971	6.00
❑ 3209	(I've Got a) Happy Heart/How Long Will My Baby Be Gone	1971	6.00
❑ 3289	A Song to Sing/Adios, Farewell, Goodbye, Good Luck, So Long	1972	5.00
❑ 3327	My Heart Has a Mind of Its Own/ You'll Never Miss the Water	1972	5.00
❑ 3438	Wheel of Fortune/My Heart Skips a Beat	1972	5.00
❑ 3499	Love Sure Feels Good in My Heart/I've Got You on My Mind Again	1972	5.00
❑ 3569	Cheating Game/I'll Love You Forever and Ever	1973	5.00
❑ 3699	Plastic Trains, Paper Planes/ I Won't Be Needing You	1973	5.00
❑ 3782	When You Get Back from Nashville/Nobody's Fool But Yours	1973	5.00
❑ 3850	Stop the World (And Let Me Off)/Love's Ups and Downs	1974	4.00
❑ 3927	You Can Sure See It from Here/ I Wish I Was a Butterfly	1974	4.00
❑ 3980	Whatcha Gonna Do with a Dog Like That/That Loving Feeling	1974	4.00
❑ 4063	Ghost Story/Beginner's Luck	1975	4.00
❑ 4140	He Gives Me Something (To Forgive Him For)/You're the Piece That's Always Gone	1975	4.00
❑ 4197	Honey Toast and Sunshine/Only a Good Love Lasts Forever	1975	4.00
UNITED ARTISTS			
❑ XW870	Ozark Mountain Lullaby/ Johnny Sunshine	1976	4.00
❑ XW934	Mr. Heartache/Turn Away	1977	4.00
❑ XW976	Saturday Night to Sunday Quiet/My Hiding Place	1977	4.00
❑ XW1026	It Didn't Have to Be a Diamond/ My Hiding Place	1977	4.00
WESTEXAS AMERICA			
❑ 1	Put Another Notch in Your Belt/ I Just Can't Take the Leaving Anymore	1984	4.00
Albums			
CAPITOL			
❑ ST-543	One Night Stand	1970	15.00
❑ ST-736	Willy Jones	1971	15.00
❑ ST-807	Pitty, Pitty, Patter	1971	15.00
❑ ST-875	(I've Got a) Happy Heart	1972	15.00
❑ ST-11055	My Heart Has a Mind of Its Own	1972	12.00
❑ ST-11106	Wheel of Fortune	1972	12.00
❑ ST-11135	Love Sure Feels Good in My Heart	1973	12.00
❑ ST-11179	Cheating Game	1973	12.00
❑ ST-11223	Plastic Trains, Paper Planes	1973	12.00
❑ ST-11255	Hymns by Susan Raye	1974	12.00
❑ ST-11282	The Best of Susan Raye	1974	12.00
❑ ST-11333	Singing	1974	12.00
❑ ST-11393	Whatch Gonna Do with a Dog Like That	1975	12.00
UNITED ARTISTS			
❑ UA-LA764-G	Susan Raye	1977	12.00
RAYS, THE			
45s			
AMY			
❑ 900	Love Another Girl/Sad Saturday	1964	8.00
CAMEO			
❑ 117	Silhouettes/Daddy Cool	1957	25.00
❑ 128	Rendezvous/Triangle	1958	30.00
❑ 133	Rags to Riches/The Man Above	1958	30.00
CHESS			
❑ 1613	Tippity Top/Moo-Goo-Gai-Pan	1956	25.00
❑ 1678	How Long Must I Wait/ Second Fiddle	1957	25.00
UNART			
❑ 2001	Souvenirs of Summertime/ Elevator Operator	1958	40.00
XYZ			
❑ 100	My Steady Girl/No One Loves You Like I Do	1957	60.00
❑ 102	Silhouettes/Daddy Cool	1957	60.00
—Blue label			
❑ 102	Silhouettes/Daddy Cool	1957	200.00
—Gray label			
❑ 106	Souvenirs of Summertime/ Elevator Operator	1958	50.00
❑ 600	Why Do You Look the Other Way/Zimbo Lula	1959	50.00
❑ 605	It's a Cryin' Shame/ Mediterranean Moon	1959	40.00
❑ 607	Magic Moon/Louie Hoo Hoo	1960	25.00
—Red label			
❑ 607	Magic Moon/Louie Hoo Hoo	1960	40.00
—Blue label			
❑ 608	Old Devil Moon/Silver Starlight	1960	25.00
7-Inch Extended Plays			
CHESS			
❑ 5120	(contents unknown)	1958	400.00
❑ 5120 [PS]	The Rays	1958	400.00
RAYS, THE (2)			
45s			
PERRI			
❑ 1004	Are You Happy Now/ Bright Brown Eyes	1962	30.00
—Frankie Valli performed on this record			
RE'VELLS, THE			
45s			
ROMAN PRESS			
❑ 201	Let It Please Be You/ Love Walked In	1962	100.00
RE-VELS, THE			
45s			
ATLAS			
❑ 1035	My Lost Love/Love Me, Baby	1954	400.00
—As "The Re-Vels Quartette"			
CHESS			
❑ 1708	False Alarm/When You Come Back to Me	1958	150.00
SOUND			
❑ 129	You Lied to Me/Later, Later Baby	1956	150.00
❑ 135	Dream, My Darlin', Dream/ Cha Cha Toni	1956	150.00
TEEN			
❑ 122	So in Love/It Happened to Me	1955	600.00
REACTORS, THE			
45s			
CAMEO			
❑ 446	Do That Thing/1-A	1966	20.00
REAL ORIGINAL BEATLES, THE Yeah, right.			
45s			
DOT			
❑ 16655	The Beatle Story (Part 1)/ The Beatle Story (Part 2)	1964	20.00
REBECCA AND THE SUNNY BROOK FARMERS			
Albums			
MUSICOR			
❑ MS-3176	Rebecca and the Sunny Brook Farmers	1969	40.00
REBELS, THE (1) See ROCKIN' REBELS.			
REBELS, THE (2)			
45s			
KING'S X			
❑ 3362	In the Park/In My Heart	1959	1000.
REBELS, THE (3)			
45s			
PEACOCK			
❑ 1909	The Donkey Step/Just Give Me Your Heart	1962	20.00
REBENACK, MAC See DR. JOHN.			
REBIRTH			
Albums			
AVANT GARDE			
❑ AVS-135	Rebirth	1971	50.00
REBOUNDS, THE This is not the group that became the Stampeders, according to a former member of the band.			
45s			
TOWER			
❑ 288	Since I Fell for You/I'm Not Your Steppin' Stone	1966	15.00
REBS, THE			
Albums			
FREDLO			
❑ 6830	1968 A.D. Break Through	1968	400.00
RECALLS, THE			
45s			
ARROW			
❑ 2002	No Reason/Nobody's Guy	196?	80.00
RECORDS, THE			
12-Inch Singles			
VIRGIN			
❑ PR 337 [DJ]	Starry Eyes/Paint Her Face/ Another Star	1989	15.00
❑ PR 365 [DJ]	Rumour Sets the Woods Alight/ Hearts in Her Eyes	1980	8.00
45s			
VIRGIN			
❑ 67000	Starry Eyes/Paint Her Face	1979	4.00
❑ 67000 [PS]	Starry Eyes/Paint Her Face	1979	4.00
❑ 67002	Teenarama/Held Up High	1979	4.00
❑ 67002 [PS]	Teenarama/Held Up High	1979	4.00
❑ 67008	Hearts in Her Eyes/So Sorry	1980	4.00
❑ 67008 [PS]	Hearts in Her Eyes/So Sorry	1980	5.00
7-Inch Extended Plays			
VIRGIN			
❑ PR 338	Abracadabra/See My Friends/ 1984/Have You Seen Your Mother, Baby	1979	3.00
❑ PR 338 [PS]	Abracadabra/See My Friends/ 1984/Have You Seen Your Mother, Baby	1979	3.00
—Came with their Virgin LP			
Albums			
VIRGIN			
❑ VA 13130	The Records	1979	15.00
—With bonus 4-song EP "Abracadabra" (deduct 33% if missing)			
❑ VA 13140	Crashes	1980	12.00
VIRGIN INTERNATIONAL			
❑ VI 2206	Music on Both Sides	1982	10.00
RED CRAYOLA, THE			
Albums			
INTERNATIONAL ARTISTS			
❑ 2	Parable of the Arable Land	1979	15.00
—Reissue with "Masterfonics" in trail-off wax			
❑ 2 [M]	Parable of the Arable Land	1968	100.00
❑ 2 [S]	Parable of the Arable Land	1968	60.00
❑ 7	God Bless the Red Crayola	1968	60.00
❑ 7	God Bless the Red Crayola	1979	15.00
—Reissue with "Masterfonics" in trail-off wax			
RED HOT CHILI PEPPERS Drummer Chad Smith is also in CHICKENFOOT.			
12-Inch Singles			
EMI			
❑ SPRO 04385 [DJ]	Stone Cold Bush/Fire/ Nobody Weird Like Me + 1	1989	15.00
❑ SPRO 04387 [DJ]	Higher Ground (2 versions)	1989	10.00
❑ SPRO 04504 [DJ]	Taste the Pain/Castles (Live)/ Special Secret Sauce (Live)/ F.U. (Live)	1989	20.00
❑ SPRO 04542 [DJ]	Show Me Your Soul (same on both sides)	1990	10.00
❑ SPRO 04896 [DJ]	Higher Ground (3 mixes)/ If You Want Me to Stay (2 versions)	1992	15.00
EMI AMERICA			
❑ SPRO 04002 [DJ]	Behind the Sun/Special Secret Song	1987	8.00
❑ 7839	Get Up and Jump/Baby Appeal	1984	12.00
❑ 7862	Hollywood (Extended)/ Hollywood (Dub)/Never Mind	1985	10.00
❑ SPRO 9466 [DJ]	Jungle Man/Nevermind/ Stranded	1986	8.00

R

Except when noted otherwise, VG = 25% of NM, and VG+ = 50% of NM. (Example: VG = $2.00, VG+ = $4.00 and NM = $8.00.)

Number	Title (A Side/B Side)	Yr	NM
EMI MANHATTAN			
❑ SPRO 79147 [DJ]	Fight Like a Brave (same on both sides)	1988	7.00
WARNER BROS.			
❑ PRO-A-5182 [DJ]	Give It Away (3 versions)	1991	12.00
45s			
EMI			
❑ S7-18210	Deck the Halls/Knock Me Down	1994	5.00
—Red vinyl			
❑ S7-56949	Behind the Sun/Fire	1993	4.00
❑ S7-57992	Higher Ground/If You Want Me to Stay	1992	4.00
EMI AMERICA			
❑ B-8280	Hollywood (Africa)/Nevermind	198?	10.00
WARNER BROS.			
❑ 15993	Under the Bridge/Give It Away	1992	3.00
—Reissue; first release of B-side on U.S. 45			
❑ 7-16875	Otherside/How Strong	2000	3.00
❑ 16913	Scar Tissue/Gong Li	1999	3.00
❑ 18401	Soul to Squeeze/Nobody Weird Like Me	1993	3.00
❑ 18978	Under the Bridge/The Righteous and the Wicked	1992	4.00
❑ 18988	Breaking the Girl	1992	—
—Cassette only			
❑ 19147	Give It Away	1992	—
—Cassette only			
WTG			
❑ 68678	Taste the Rain/All for Love	1989	4.00
—B-side by Nancy Wilson (of Heart)			
Albums			
EMI			
❑ E1-29665	Out in L.A.	1994	14.00
❑ E1-92152	Mother's Milk	1989	18.00
EMI AMERICA			
❑ ST-17128	Red Hot Chili Peppers	1984	15.00
❑ ST-17168	Freaky Styley	1985	15.00
❑ E1-48036	The Uplift Mofo Party Plan	1987	15.00
EMI MANHATTAN			
❑ E1-90869 [EP]	The Abbey Road E.P.	1988	8.00
WARNER BROS.			
❑ PRO-A-5170 [(2)DJ]	Blood Sugar Sex Magik	1991	40.00
—"Radio-ready" version of LP, this is the only U.S. vinyl release of this album			
❑ 43391-1 [(4)]	Stadium Arcadium	2006	40.00
—150-gram version; records are contained in two gatefold sleeves inside a slipcase			
❑ 47386 [(2)]	Californication	1999	60.00
❑ 48140 [(2)]	By the Way	2002	25.00
❑ 49996-1 [(4)]	Stadium Arcadium	2006	80.00
—180-gram version; box set contains records in individual sleeves plus two 12x12 booklets			

REDBONE Also see PAT AND LOLLY VEGAS.

Number	Title (A Side/B Side)	Yr	NM
45s			
EPIC			
❑ 10597	Crazy Cajun Cade Walk Band/Night Come Down	1970	6.00
❑ 10670	Maggie/New Blue Sermonette	1970	6.00
❑ 10712	Who Can Say/Light as a Feather	1971	6.00
❑ 10749	The Witch Queen of New Orleans/Chant: 13th Hour	1971	6.00
❑ 10839	When You Got Trouble/(B-side unknown)	1972	5.00
❑ 10866	One Monkey (Don't Stop No Show)/Message from a Drum	1972	5.00
❑ 10910	Already Here/Fais-Do	1972	5.00
❑ 10946	Poison Ivy/Condition Your Condition	1973	5.00
❑ 10979	We Were All Wounded at Wounded Knee/Speakeasy	1973	5.00
❑ 11035	Come and Get Your Love/Day to Day Life	1973	5.00
❑ 11035	Come and Get Your Love/Your Miserable Face	1973	5.00
❑ 11131	Wovoka/Clouds in My Sunshine	1974	4.00
❑ 50015	Suzie Girl/Interstate Highway 101	1974	4.00
❑ 50043	One More Time/Blood, Sweat and Tears	1974	4.00
❑ 50074	Only You and Rock and Roll/Interstate Highway 101	1975	4.00
❑ 50107	Physical Attraction/I've Got to Find the Right Woman	1975	4.00
RCA			
❑ PB-11096	Give Our Love Another Try/Funny Silk	1977	4.00
❑ PB-11182	Checkin' It Out/Funky Silk	1977	4.00

Red Hot Chili Peppers, *Mother's Milk*, EMI E1-92152, 1989, **$12.**

Number	Title (A Side/B Side)	Yr	NM
Albums			
EPIC			
❑ EGP 501 [(2)]	Redbone	1970	20.00
❑ E 30109	Potlatch	1970	15.00
❑ EQ 30815 [Q]	Message from a Drum	1973	20.00
❑ KE 30815	Message from a Drum	1972	15.00
❑ KE 31598	Already Here	1972	15.00
❑ KE 32462	Wovoka	1974	15.00
❑ EQ 33053 [Q]	Bearded Dreams Through Turquoise Eyes	1974	20.00
❑ KE 33053	Bearded Dreams Through Turquoise Eyes	1974	15.00
❑ KEG 33456 [(2)]	Come & Get Your Redbone	1975	20.00
RCA VICTOR			
❑ AFL1-2352	Cycles	1977	12.00

REDCOATS, THE Also see STEVE ALAIMO.

Number	Title (A Side/B Side)	Yr	NM
45s			
KITE			
❑ 2003	Perkin/Hi Ho	1957	50.00
❑ 2003	Perkins/Hi Ho	1957	50.00
—Note slight variation in A-side title			

REDD, BARBARA

Number	Title (A Side/B Side)	Yr	NM
45s			
S.P.Q.R.			
❑ 3311	I'll Be All Alone/Dancing Teardrops	1963	600.00

REDD, GENE

Number	Title (A Side/B Side)	Yr	NM
45s			
FEDERAL			
❑ 12119	I Dreamed the Blues/In the Redd	1953	30.00
KING			
❑ 5250	Red River Valley Rock/Kentucky Home Rock	1959	12.00
❑ 5262	Teen Beat/Old Virginny Rock	1959	12.00
❑ 5399	New Annie Laurie/New Sidewalks of New York	1960	12.00

REDD KROSS

Number	Title (A Side/B Side)	Yr	NM
Albums			
ATLANTIC			
❑ 82148	Third Eye	1990	10.00
BIG TIME			
❑ 6034-1	Neurotica	1987	12.00
FRONTIER			
❑ FLP 1018	Born Innocent	1986	12.00
—Reissue			
❑ 4609-1-L	Born Innocent	1991	10.00
—Reissue			
GASATANKA			
❑ E 1170	Teen Babies from Monsanto	1984	12.00
POSH BOY			
❑ 1010 [EP]	Red Cross	1980	15.00
❑ 1010 [EP]	Annette's Got the Hits	1987	10.00
—Reissue			
SMOKE			
❑ SMK7-103	Born Innocent	1982	15.00
SYMPATHY FOR THE RECORD INDUSTRY			
❑ 260 [10]	2,500 Redd Kross Fans Can't Be Wrong	1993	10.00

REDDING, OTIS Also see OTIS AND CARLA; THE SHOOTERS.

Number	Title (A Side/B Side)	Yr	NM
45s			
ATCO			
❑ 6592	Hard to Handle/Amen	1968	10.00
❑ 6612	I've Got Dreams to Remember/Nobody's Fault But Mine	1968	10.00
❑ 6631	White Christmas/Merry Christmas, Baby	1968	10.00
❑ 6636	Papa's Got a Brand New Bag/Direct Me	1968	10.00
❑ 6654	A Lover's Question/You Made a Man Out of Me	1969	10.00
❑ 6677	Love Man/I Can't Turn You Loose	1969	10.00
❑ 6700	Free Me/Higher and Higher	1969	10.00

R

Number	Title (A Side/B Side)	Yr	NM
❑ 6723	Look at the Girl/ That's a Good Idea	1969	10.00
❑ 6742	Demonstration/ Johnny's Heartbreak	1970	8.00
❑ 6766	Giving Away None of My Love/ Snatch a Little Piece	1970	8.00
❑ 6802	Try a Little Tenderness/I've Been Loving You Too Long (To Stop Now)	1971	6.00
❑ 6907	My Girl/Good to Me	1972	5.00
❑ 7069	White Christmas/ Merry Christmas, Baby	1976	5.00
❑ 7321	White Christmas/ Merry Christmas, Baby	1980	4.00
❑ 99955	White Christmas/ Merry Christmas, Baby	1982	4.00
BETHLEHEM			
❑ 3083	Shout Bamalama/Fat Girl	1964	20.00
CONFEDERATE			
❑ 135	Shout Bamalama/Fat Girl	1962	50.00
FINER ARTS			
❑ 2016	She's Alright/Tough Enuff	1961	50.00
—Originally released on Trans World by "The Shooters"			
KING			
❑ 6149	Shout Bamalama/Fat Girl	1968	10.00
ORBIT			
❑ 135	Shout Bamalama/Fat Girl	1961	300.00
PHILCO-FORD			
❑ HP-13	Shake/Fa-Fa-Fa-Fa-Fa	1967	20.00
—4-inch plastic "Hip Pocket Record" with color sleeve			
STONE			
❑ 209	You Left the Water Running/ The Otis Jam	1976	12.00
—B-side by the Memphis Studio Band			
VOLT			
❑ 103	These Arms of Mine/ Hey, Hey Baby	1962	20.00
❑ 109	That's What My Heart Needs/ Mary's Little Lamb	1963	20.00
❑ 112	Pain in My Heart/Something Is Worrying Me	1963	20.00
❑ 116	Come to Me/Don't Leave Me This Way	1964	15.00
❑ 117	Security/I Want to Thank You	1964	15.00
❑ 121	Chained and Bound/ Your One and Only Man	1964	15.00
❑ 124	Mr. Pitiful/That's How Strong My Love Is	1965	15.00
❑ 126	I've Been Loving You Too Long (To Stop Now)/I'm Depending on You	1965	15.00
❑ 128	Respect/Ole Man Trouble	1965	15.00
❑ 130	I Can't Turn You Loose/ Just One More Day	1965	15.00
❑ 132	Satisfaction/Any Ole Way	1966	15.00
❑ 136	My Lover's Prayer/ Don't Mess with Cupid	1966	15.00
❑ 138	Fa-Fa-Fa-Fa-Fa (Sad Song)/ Good to Me	1966	15.00
❑ 141	Try a Little Tenderness/ I'm Sick Y'All	1966	15.00
❑ 146	I Love You More Than Words Can Say/Let Me Come On Home	1967	12.00
❑ 149	Shake/You Don't Miss Your Water	1967	12.00
❑ 152	Glory of Love/I'm Coming Home	1967	12.00
❑ 157	(Sittin' On) The Dock of the Bay/ Sweet Lorene	1968	10.00
—Multicolor (mostly brown) label			
❑ 157	(Sittin' On) The Dock of the Bay/ Sweet Lorene	1968	12.00
—Black and red label			
❑ 163	The Happy Song (Dum-Dum)/ Open That Door	1968	10.00

7-Inch Extended Plays

Number	Title (A Side/B Side)	Yr	NM
ATCO			
❑ SD 37-265	I Can't Turn You Loose/Pain in My Heart//Mr. Pitiful/Any Ole Way/Respect	1968	25.00
—Stereo jukebox issue; small hole, plays at 33 1/3 rpm			
❑ SD 37-265 [PS]	Otis Redding In Person at the Whiskey A-Go-Go	1968	25.00
ATLANTIC			
❑ SD 70419	(Sittin' on) The Dock of the Bay/ Let Me Come On Home/Open the Door//The Glory of Love/ Tramp/Ole Man Trouble	1968	25.00
—Stereo jukebox issue; small hole, plays at 33 1/3 rpm			
❑ SD 70419 [PS]	The Dock of the Bay	1968	25.00
—Cover says "Volt" but the label of the record is Atlantic			

Albums

Number	Title (A Side/B Side)	Yr	NM
ATCO			
❑ 33-161 [M]	Pain in My Heart	1964	250.00
❑ SD 33-161 [R]	Pain in My Heart	1968	250.00
❑ 33-252 [M]	The Immortal Otis Redding	1968	50.00
—Mono is white label promo only			
❑ SD 33-252 [S]	The Immortal Otis Redding	1968	15.00
❑ SD 33-261	History of Otis Redding	1968	15.00
—Reissue of Volt 418			
❑ SD 33-265	Otis Redding In Person at the Whiskey A-Go-Go	1968	15.00
❑ SD 33-284	Otis Blue/Otis Redding Sings Soul	1969	15.00
—Reissue of Volt 412			
❑ SD 33-285	The Soul Album	1969	15.00
—Reissue of Volt 413			
❑ SD 33-286	Otis Redding Live in Europe	1969	15.00
—Reissue of Volt 416			
❑ SD 33-287	Complete & Unbelievable…The Otis Redding Dictionary of Soul	1969	15.00
—Reissue of Volt 415			
❑ SD 33-288	The Dock of the Bay	1969	15.00
—Reissue of Volt 419			
❑ SD 33-289	Love Man	1969	15.00
❑ SD 33-333	Tell the Truth	1970	15.00
❑ SD 2-801 [(2)]	The Best of Otis Redding	1972	20.00
ATLANTIC			
❑ SD 19346	Recorded Live	198?	10.00
❑ 81282	The Best of Otis Redding	1985	10.00
❑ 81762 [(4)]	The Otis Redding Story	1987	30.00
4 MEN WITH BEARDS			
❑ 4M 105	The Great Otis Redding Sings Soul Ballads	2002	15.00
—Reissue on 180-gram vinyl			
PAIR			
❑ PDL2-1062 [(2)]	The Legend of Otis Redding	1984	15.00
SUNDAZED			
❑ LP 5063 [M]	Complete & Unbelievable … The Otis Redding Dictionary of Soul	2001	12.00
—Reissue on 180-gram vinyl			
❑ LP 5064 [M]	Otis Blue/Otis Redding Sings Soul	2001	12.00
—Reissue on 180-gram vinyl			
❑ LP 5132 [M]	The Soul Album	2003	12.00
—Reissue on 180-gram vinyl			
❑ LP 5133 [S]	Otis Redding In Person at the Whiskey A-Go-Go	2003	12.00
—Reissue on 180-gram vinyl			
❑ LP 5134 [S]	Otis Redding Live in Europe	2003	12.00
—Reissue on 180-gram vinyl			
❑ LP 5172 [S]	The Dock of the Bay	2003	12.00
—Reissue on 180-gram vinyl			
VOLT			
❑ 411 [M]	The Great Otis Redding Sings Soul Ballads	1965	90.00
❑ S-411 [R]	The Great Otis Redding Sings Soul Ballads	1968	110.00
❑ 412 [M]	Otis Blue/Otis Redding Sings Soul	1965	40.00
❑ S-412 [S]	Otis Blue/Otis Redding Sings Soul	1965	50.00
❑ 413 [M]	The Soul Album	1966	40.00
❑ S-413 [S]	The Soul Album	1966	50.00
❑ 415 [M]	Complete & Unbelievable…The Otis Redding Dictionary of Soul	1966	40.00
❑ S-415 [S]	Complete & Unbelievable…The Otis Redding Dictionary of Soul	1966	50.00
❑ 416 [M]	Otis Redding Live in Europe	1967	30.00
❑ S-416 [S]	Otis Redding Live in Europe	1967	40.00
❑ 418 [M]	History of Otis Redding	1967	40.00
❑ S-418 [S]	History of Otis Redding	1967	30.00
❑ S-419	The Dock of the Bay	1968	30.00

REDELL, TEDDY

45s

Number	Title (A Side/B Side)	Yr	NM
ATCO			
❑ 6162	Judy/Can't You See	1960	20.00
HI			
❑ 2024	Pipeliner/I Want to Hold You	1960	20.00
VADEN			
❑ 110	Knockin' on the Backside/ Before It Began	1960	120.00
❑ 115	Goldust/Corrine, Corrina	1960	120.00
❑ 116	Judy/Can't You See	1960	120.00
❑ 117	Pipeliner/I Want to Hold You	1960	120.00
❑ 301	Pipeliner/I Want to Hold You	1961	80.00
❑ 305	I'll Sail My Ship Alone/ Don't Grow Old Alone	1961	80.00

REDEYE

45s

Number	Title (A Side/B Side)	Yr	NM
PENTAGRAM			
❑ 202	Mississippi State Line/199 Thoughts Too Late	1970	6.00
❑ 204	Games/Collections of Yesterday and Now	1970	6.00
❑ 206	Red Eye Blues/Making of a Hero	1971	6.00
❑ 209	Homebound Feelin'/ I'm Going Blind	1971	6.00
❑ 213	Mountain Annie/Just a Little More	1971	6.00

Albums

Number	Title (A Side/B Side)	Yr	NM
PENTAGRAM			
❑ PE-10003	Redeye	1970	15.00
❑ PR-10006	One Man's Poison	1971	15.00

REDJACKS, THE

45s

Number	Title (A Side/B Side)	Yr	NM
APT			
❑ 25006	Big Brown Eyes/ To Make You Mine	1958	20.00
OKLAHOMA			
❑ 5005	Big Brown Eyes/ To Make You Mine	1958	50.00

REDNOW, EIVETS

See STEVIE WONDER.

❑ REDWOODS, THE

JEFF BARRY was involved with this group.

45s

Number	Title (A Side/B Side)	Yr	NM
EPIC			
❑ 9447	Shake, Shake Sherry/ The Memory Lingers On	1961	30.00
—As "The Redwoods"			
❑ 9447	Shake, Shake Sherry/ The Memory Lingers On	1961	40.00
—As "The Flairs"			
❑ 9473	Never Take It Away/ Unemployment Insurance	1961	30.00
❑ 9505	Please, Mr. Scientist/Where You Need to Be	1962	40.00

REED, A.C.

45s

Number	Title (A Side/B Side)	Yr	NM
AGE			
❑ 29101	This Little Voice/ Apache War Dance	1961	30.00
—B-side by Earl Hooker			
❑ 29103	Come On Home/ I Wanna Be Free	1961	30.00
❑ 29112	Mean Cop/That Ain't Right	1962	30.00
❑ 29123	I Stay Mad/Whole Lotta Lovin'	1964	30.00
COOL			
❑ 5001	My Baby's Been Cheating (I Know)/My Baby Is Fine	1966	200.00
ICE CUBE			
❑ 5926	I Am Fed Up with This Music (X-Rated)/Got the Blues	1982	6.00
❑ 5927	I Am Fed Up with This Music (DJ Version)/Got the Blues	1982	10.00
❑ 5928	Fast Food Annie/This Little Voice	1982	8.00
NIKE			
❑ 2002	Boogaloo - Tramp/Talkin' 'Bout My Friends	1966	40.00
U.S.A.			
❑ 813	I'd Rather Fight Than Switch/ I've Got Money to Burn	1963	25.00

Albums

Number	Title (A Side/B Side)	Yr	NM
ALLIGATOR			
❑ AL-4757	I'm in the Wrong Business!	1988	12.00
ICE CUBE			
❑ 1057	Take These Blues and Shove 'Em!	1982	15.00
ROOSTER BLUES			
❑ R 7606	Take These Blues and Shove 'Em!	1982	10.00

REED, DEAN

45s

Number	Title (A Side/B Side)	Yr	NM
CAPITOL			
❑ F4121	The Search/Annabelle	1959	15.00
❑ F4198	A Pair of Scissors/ I Kissed a Queen	1959	15.00
❑ F4273	Our Summer Romance/ I Ain't Got You	1959	15.00
❑ 4384	Don't Let Her Go/No Wonder	1960	15.00
❑ 4438	Pistolero/Hummingbird	1960	15.00
IMPERIAL			
❑ 5733	I Forgot More Than You'll Ever Know/Once Again	1961	12.00

REED, JAMES

45s

Number	Title (A Side/B Side)	Yr	NM
BIG TOWN			
❑ 117	Things Ain't What They Used to Be/You Better Hold Me	1954	150.00
FLAIR			
❑ 1034	My Mama Told Me/ This Is the End	1954	200.00
❑ 1042	Dr. Brown/You Better Hold Me	1954	200.00
MONEY			
❑ 201	Oh People/My Love Is Real	1954	200.00

Except when noted otherwise, VG = 25% of NM, and VG+ = 50% of NM. (Example: VG = $2.00, VG+ = $4.00 and NM = $8.00.)

Number	Title (A Side/B Side)	Yr	NM
RHYTHM			
❑ 1775	Tin Pan Alley/Biggest Place in Town	1954	500.00
REED, JERRY			
45s			
CAPITOL			
❑ F3294	If the Good Lord's Willing and the Creeks Don't Rise/Here I Am	1955	20.00
❑ F3381	I'm a Lover, Not a Fighter/Honey Chile	1956	20.00
❑ F3429	When I Found You/Mister Whiz	1956	20.00
❑ F3504	Just a Romeo/This Great Big Empty Room	1956	20.00
❑ F3592	Too Busy Cryin' the Blues/You're Braggin', Boy	1956	20.00
❑ F3657	It's High Time/Forever	1957	15.00
❑ F3731	Rockin' in Bagdad/Oh Lonely Heart	1957	15.00
❑ F3823	In My Own Back Yard/Ba-Bee	1957	15.00
❑ F3882	Too Young to Be Blue/Bessie Baby	1958	15.00
❑ F3992	How Can I Go On This Way/Your Money Makes You Purty	1958	15.00
❑ B-5531	Big Time Fool/What Comes Around	1985	3.00
❑ B-5556	Country's Alive and Doing Well/Let It Go	1986	3.00
❑ B-5612	This Missin' You's a Whole Lotta Fun/There Was You	1986	3.00
❑ B-5660	You Can't Get the Hell Out of Texas/Old Fashioned Heart	1986	3.00
COLUMBIA			
❑ 42047	Love and War (Ain't Much Difference in the Two)/Love Is the Cause of It All	1961	10.00
❑ 42183	Hit and Run/Sure Is Blue Out Tonight	1961	10.00
❑ 42311	Pity the Fool/I've Got Everybody Fooled But Me	1962	10.00
❑ 42417	I'm Movin' On/Goodnight Irene	1962	10.00
❑ 42533	Twist-a-Roo/Hully Gully Guitar	1962	10.00
❑ 42533 [PS]	Twist-a-Roo/Hully Gully Guitar	1962	30.00
❑ 42639	Too Old to Cut the Mustard/Overlooked and Underloved	1962	10.00
❑ 42704	I Want to Be Loved/I'll See You in My Dreams	1963	10.00
❑ 42808	The Shock/Let's Get Ready for the Summer	1963	10.00
❑ 42863	The Mountain Man/Love Don't Grow on Trees	1963	10.00
❑ 43052	June Night/Spilled Milk	1964	10.00
NRC			
❑ 014	Have Blues Will Travel/This Can't Be Happening to Me	1958	15.00
❑ 032	Just Right/Stone Eternal	1959	12.00
❑ 5008	Little Lovin' Liza/Soldier's Joy	1959	12.00
RCA			
❑ PB-10784	Remembering/Babe	1976	4.00
❑ PB-10893	Semolita/Phantom of the Opry	1977	4.00
❑ PB-11008	With His Pants in His Hand/We Called It Everything Else	1977	4.00
❑ PB-11056	East Bound and Down/(I'm Just A) Redneck in a Rock and Roll Bar	1977	4.00
❑ PB-11164	You Know What/Louisiana Lady	1977	4.00
—With Seidina			
❑ PB-11232	Sweet Love Feelings/You're Gonna Need Someone	1978	4.00
❑ PB-11281	(I Love You) What Can I Say/High Rollin'	1978	4.00
❑ PB-11281	(I Love You) What Can I Say/I Feel for You	1978	4.00
❑ PB-11370	Stars and Stripes Forever/Reedology	1978	4.00
❑ PB-11407	Gimme Back My Blues/Honkin'	1978	4.00
❑ PB-11472	Second-Hand Satin Lady (And a Bargain Basement Boy)/Jiffy Jam	1979	4.00
❑ PB-11638	(Who Was the Man Who Put) The Line in Gasoline/Piece of Cake	1979	4.00
❑ PB-11698	Hot Stuff/Nervous Breakdown	1979	4.00
❑ PB-11764	Sugar Foot Rag/I Wanna Go Back Home to Georgia	1979	4.00
❑ PB-11944	Age/Workin' at the Car Wash Blues	1980	4.00
❑ GB-11986	East Bound and Down/(I'm Just A) Redneck in a Rock and Roll Bar	1980	3.00
—Gold Standard Series			
❑ PB-12034	The Friendly Family Inn/Bandit	1980	4.00
❑ PB-12083	Texas Bound and Flyin'/Concrete Sailor	1980	4.00
❑ PB-12157	Caffein, Nicotine, Benzedrine (And Wish Me Luck)/If Love's Not Around the House	1981	4.00
❑ PB-12210	The Testimony of Soddy Hoe/Dreaming Fairy Tales	1981	4.00
❑ PB-12253	Good Friends Make Good Lovers/The Devil Went Down to Georgia	1981	4.00
❑ JK-12318 [DJ]	Patches (same on both sides)	1981	10.00
—Promo only on blue vinyl			
❑ PB-12318	Patches/Stray Dogs and Stray Women	1981	4.00
❑ PB-13081	The Man with the Golden Thumb/East Bound and Down	1982	4.00
❑ PB-13268	She Got the Goldmine (I Got the Shaft)/44	1982	5.00
❑ PB-13355	The Bird/The Hobo	1982	5.00
—As "Jerry Reed and Friends"			
❑ JK-13422 [DJ]	Down on the Corner (same on both sides)	1983	10.00
—Promo only on green vinyl			
❑ PB-13422	Down on the Corner/Good Times	1983	4.00
❑ JB-13527 [DJ]	Good Ole Boys/She's Ready for Someone to Love Her	1983	12.00
—Promo only on blue vinyl			
❑ JK-13527 [DJ]	Good Ole Boys (same on both sides)	1983	10.00
—Promo only on green vinyl			
❑ PB-13527	Good Ole Boys/She's Ready for Someone to Love Her	1983	4.00
❑ PB-13663	I'm a Slave/Nobody Ever Loved Me	1983	4.00
❑ JK-13666 [DJ]	Christmas Time's a-Coming (same on both sides)	1983	5.00
❑ PB-13666	Christmas Time's a-Coming/The Best I Ever Had	1983	5.00
❑ GB-14069	She Got the Goldmine (I Got the Shaft)/The Bird	1985	3.00
—Gold Standard Series			
RCA VICTOR			
❑ 47-8565	If I Don't Live Up to It/I Feel a Sin Coming On	1965	8.00
❑ 47-8667	Ain't That Just Like a Fool/Love's Battleground	1965	8.00
❑ 47-8730	Fighting for the U.S.A./Navy Blues	1965	8.00
❑ 47-8957	Woman Shy/I Feel for You	1966	8.00
❑ 47-9152	Guitar Man/It Don't Work That Way	1967	10.00
❑ 47-9334	Tupelo Mississippi Flash/Wabash Cannonball	1967	8.00
❑ 47-9493	Remembering/Fine on My Mind	1968	8.00
❑ 47-9623	Alabama Wild Man/Twelve Bar Midnight	1968	8.00
❑ 47-9701	Oh, What a Woman/Losing Your Love	1968	8.00
❑ 47-9794	Turn It Around in Your Mind/Long Gone	1969	—
—Unreleased			
❑ 47-9804	Talk About the Good Times/Alabama Jubilee	1969	6.00
❑ 47-9870	Georgia Sunshine/Swinging '69	1970	6.00
❑ 47-9890	Tennessee Stud/Cannonball Rag	1970	6.00
—With Chet Atkins			
❑ 47-9904	Amos Moses/The Preacher and the Bear	1970	6.00
❑ 47-9976	When You're Hot, You're Hot/You've Been Crying Again	1971	6.00
❑ 48-1011	Ko Ko Joe/I Feel for You	1971	6.00
❑ 74-0124	Blues Land/There's Better Things in Life	1969	6.00
❑ 74-0211	Are You From Dixie/A Worried Man	1969	6.00
❑ 74-0242	A Thing Called Love/Hallelujah I Love Her So	1969	—
—Unreleased			
❑ 74-0613	Another Puff/Love Man	1971	5.00
❑ 74-0667	Smell the Flowers/f It Comes to That	1972	5.00
❑ 74-0738	Alabama Wildman/Take It Easy	1972	5.00
❑ 74-0775	Nashtownville/Jerry's Breakdown	1972	5.00
—With Chet Atkins			
❑ 74-0857	You Took All the Ramblin' Out of Me/I'm Not Playing Games	1972	5.00
❑ 74-0960	Lord, Mr. Ford/2-Timin'	1973	5.00
❑ 74-0738 [PS]	Alabama Wildman/Take It Easy	1972	10.00
❑ APBO-0194	The Uptown Poker Club/Honkin'	1973	5.00
❑ APBO-0224	The Crude Oil Blues/Pickie, Pickie, Pickie	1974	5.00
❑ APBO-0273	A Good Woman's Love/Everybody Needs Someone	1974	5.00
❑ PB-10013	You've Got It/Lightning Rod	1974	5.00
❑ PB-10063	Boogie Woogie Rock and Roll/In Between	1974	5.00
❑ PB-10132	Let's Sing Our Song/Grab Bag	1974	5.00
❑ PB-10247	Mind Your Love/Struttin'	1975	5.00
❑ PB-10325	The Telephone/City of New Orleans	1975	5.00
❑ PB-10389	You Got a Lock on Me/Reedology	1975	5.00
❑ GB-10510	Lord, Mr. Ford/Two-Timin'	1975	3.00
—Gold Standard Series			
❑ PB-10717	Gator/Good for Him	1976	5.00
Albums			
CAPITOL			
❑ ST-12492	Lookin' at You	1986	8.00
HARMONY			
❑ H 30547	I'm Movin' On	1971	10.00
RCA CAMDEN			
❑ ACL1-0331	Tupelo Mississippi Flash	1973	10.00
❑ CAS-2585	Oh What a Woman!	1972	10.00
RCA VICTOR			
❑ APD1-0238 [Q]	Lord, Mr. Ford	1973	25.00
❑ APL1-0238	Lord, Mr. Ford	1973	12.00
❑ APL1-0356	The Uptown Poker Club	1973	12.00
❑ APL1-0544	A Good Woman's Love	1974	12.00
❑ APL1-0787	Mind Your Love	1974	12.00
❑ APL1-1226	Red Hot Picker	1975	12.00
❑ ANL1-1345	When You're Hot, You're Hot	1975	10.00
—Reissue of 4506			
❑ APL1-1861	Both Barrels	1976	12.00
❑ ANL1-2167	Me and Chet	1976	10.00
—Reissue of 4707			
❑ AHL1-2346	Jerry Reed Rides Again	1977	12.00
❑ AHL1-2516	East Bound and Down	1977	12.00
❑ AHL1-2764	Sweet Love Feelings	1978	12.00
❑ AHL1-3359	Half Singin' & Half Pickin'	1979	12.00
❑ AHL1-3453	Jerry Reed Live!	1979	12.00
❑ AHL1-3604	Jerry Reed Sings Jim Croce	1980	12.00
❑ AYL1-3677	East Bound and Down	1980	8.00
—"Best Buy Series" reissue			
❑ LPM-3756 [M]	The Unbelievable Guitar and Voice of Jerry Reed	1967	25.00
❑ LSP-3756 [S]	The Unbelievable Guitar and Voice of Jerry Reed	1967	20.00
❑ AHL1-3771	Texas Bound and Flyin'	1980	12.00
❑ LPM-3978 [M]	Nashville Underground	1968	50.00
❑ LSP-3978 [S]	Nashville Underground	1968	20.00
❑ AHL1-4021	Dixie Dreams	1981	12.00
❑ LSP-4069	Alabama Wild Man	1968	20.00
❑ LSP-4147	Better Things in Life	1969	20.00
❑ AYL1-4167	Jerry Reed Live!	1982	8.00
—"Best Buy Series" reissue			
❑ LSP-4204	Jerry Reed Explores Guitar Country	1969	20.00
❑ LSP-4293	Cookin'	1970	20.00
❑ AHL1-4315	The Man with the Golden Thumb	1982	10.00
❑ LSP-4391	Georgia Sunshine	1970	20.00
❑ AYL1-4394	Texas Bound and Flyin'	1982	8.00
—"Best Buy Series" reissue			
❑ LSP-4506	When You're Hot, You're Hot	1971	15.00
❑ AHL1-4529	The Bird	1982	10.00
❑ LSP-4596	Ko-Ko Joe	1971	15.00
❑ LSP-4660	Smell the Flowers	1972	15.00
❑ AHL1-4692	Ready	1983	10.00
❑ LSP-4707	Me and Chet	1972	15.00
—With Chet Atkins			
❑ LSP-4729	The Best of Jerry Reed	1972	15.00
❑ LSP-4750	Jerry Reed	1972	15.00
❑ LSP-4838	Hot A' Mighty!	1973	15.00
❑ AYL1-5151	The Bird	1984	8.00
—"Best Buy Series" reissue			
❑ AHL1-5176	Greatest Hits	1984	10.00
❑ AHL1-5472	Collector's Series	1985	10.00
REED, JIMMY			
45s			
ABC			
❑ 10887	Got Nowhere to Go/Two Ways to Skin (A Cat)	1966	8.00
BLUESWAY			
❑ 61003	I Wanna Know/Two Heads Are Better Than One	1967	8.00
❑ 61006	Don't Press Your Luck Woman/Feel Like I Want to Ramble	1967	8.00
❑ 61013	Buy Me a Hound Dog/Crazy About Oklahoma	1968	8.00
❑ 61020	Peepin' and Hidin'/My Baby Told Me	1968	8.00
❑ 61025	Don't Light My Fire/The Judge Should Know	1969	8.00
CANYON			
❑ 38	Hard Walkin' Hannah (Part 1)/Hard Walkin' Hannah (Part 2)	196?	8.00
CHANCE			
❑ 1142	High and Lonesome/Roll and Rhumba	1953	2100.
—VG 700; VG+ 1400			
EXODUS			
❑ 2005	Knockin' At Your Door/Dedication to Sonny	1966	10.00

Lou Reed, *Transformer*, RCA Victor LSP-4807, 1972, orange label, **$20.**

Number	Title (A Side/B Side)	Yr	NM
❑ 2008	Cousin Peaches/ Crazy 'Bout Oklahoma	1966	10.00
RRG			
❑ 44001	Christmas Present Blues/ Crying Blind	19??	8.00
VEE JAY			
❑ 100	High and Lonesome/ Roll and Rumba	1953	600.00
❑ 100	High and Lonesome/ Roll and Rumba	1953	1200.
—Red vinyl			
❑ 105	I Found My Baby/Jimmy's Boogie	1953	200.00
❑ 105	I Found My Baby/Jimmy's Boogie	1953	400.00
—Red vinyl			
❑ 119	You Don't Have to Go/ Boogie in the Dark	1954	80.00
❑ 119	You Don't Have to Go/ Boogie in the Dark	1954	300.00
—Red vinyl			
❑ 132	Pretty Thing/I'm Gonna Ruin You	1955	100.00
❑ 153	I Don't Go for That/She Don't Want Me No More	1955	50.00
❑ 168	Ain't That Lovin' You Baby/Baby, Don't Say That No More	1956	40.00
❑ 186	Can't Stand to See You Go/ Rockin' with Reed	1956	40.00
❑ 203	I Love You Baby/My First Plea	1956	30.00
❑ 226	You've Got Me Dizzy/Honey, Don't Let Me Go	1956	30.00
❑ 237	Honey, Where You Going/ Little Rain	1957	30.00
❑ 248	The Sun Is Shining/Baby, What's On Your Mind	1957	30.00
❑ 253	Honest I Do/Signals of Love	1957	30.00
❑ 270	You're Something Else/ A String to My Heart	1958	30.00
❑ 275	You Got Me Crying/ Go On to School	1958	30.00
❑ 287	I Know It's a Sin/Down in Virginia	1958	30.00
❑ 298	I'm Gonna Get My Baby/ Odds and Ends	1958	30.00
❑ 304	I Told You Baby/Ends and Odds (Instrumental)	1958	30.00

Number	Title (A Side/B Side)	Yr	NM
❑ 314	Take Out Some Insurance/ You Know I Love You	1959	30.00
❑ 326	I Wanna Be Loved/ Going to New York	1959	30.00
❑ 333	Baby What You Want Me to Do/ Caress Me, Baby	1959	30.00
❑ 347	Found Love/Where Can You Be	1960	25.00
❑ 357	Hush Hush/Going to the River, Part 2	1960	25.00
❑ 373	Laughing at the Blues/ Close Together	1961	25.00
❑ 380	Big Boss Man/I'm a Love You	1961	25.00
❑ 398	Bright Lights, Big City/ I'm Mr. Luck	1961	25.00
❑ 425	Aw, Shucks, Hush Your Mouth/ Baby, What's Wrong	1962	20.00
❑ 449	Tell Me You Love Me/ Good Lover	1962	20.00
❑ 459	I'll Change My Style/Too Much	1962	20.00
❑ 473	Let's Get Together/Oh, John	1962	20.00
❑ 509	There'll Be a Day/Shame, Shame, Shame	1963	15.00
❑ 552	Mary Mary/I'm Gonna Help You	1963	15.00
❑ 570	Outskirts of Town/St. Louis Blues	1963	15.00
❑ 584	See See Rider/Wee Wee Baby Blues	1964	15.00
❑ 593	Help Yourself/Heading for a Fall	1964	15.00
❑ 616	Oh John/Down in Mississippi	1964	15.00
❑ 622	I'm Going Upside Your Head/ The Devil's Shoestring	1964	15.00
❑ 642	I Wanna Be Loved/A New Leaf	1965	15.00
❑ 702	I'm the Man Down There/ Left Handed Woman	1965	15.00
❑ 709	Don't Think I'm Through/ When Girls Do It	1966	15.00
Albums			
ANTILLES			
❑ 7007	Cold Chills	197?	15.00
BLUESVILLE			
❑ BLS-6054	I Ain't From Chicago	1973	15.00
❑ BLS-6067	The Ultimate Jimmy Reed	1973	15.00
❑ BLS-6073 [(2)]	Jimmy Reed at Carnegie Hall	1973	20.00

Number	Title (A Side/B Side)	Yr	NM
BLUESWAY			
❑ BL-6004 [M]	The New Jimmy Reed Album	1967	20.00
❑ BLS-6004 [S]	The New Jimmy Reed Album	1967	20.00
❑ BL-6009 [M]	Soulin'	1967	20.00
❑ BLS-6009 [S]	Soulin'	1967	20.00
❑ BLS-6015	Big Boss Man	1968	20.00
❑ BLS-6024	Down in Virginia	1969	20.00
BUDDAH			
❑ BDS-4003	The Very Best of Jimmy Reed	1969	15.00
—Reissue of Vee Jay 1039			
CHAMELEON			
❑ D1-74762	Bright Lights, Big City	1988	10.00
EVEREST ARCHIVE OF FOLK & JAZZ			
❑ 234	Jimmy Reed	197?	12.00
GNP CRESCENDO			
❑ GNPS-10006 [(2)]	The Best of Jimmy Reed	1974	15.00
SUNSET			
❑ SUS-5218	Somethin' Else	1968	12.00
TRADITION			
❑ 2069	Wailin' the Blues	1969	12.00
TRIP			
❑ 8012 [(2)]	History of Jimmy Reed	1971	15.00
VEE JAY			
❑ LP-1004 [M]	I'm Jimmy Reed	1958	220.00
—Maroon label			
❑ LP-1004 [M]	I'm Jimmy Reed	1961	80.00
—Black label with colorband			
❑ VJLP-1004	I'm Jimmy Reed	198?	10.00
—Reissue with glossy labels			
❑ LP-1008 [M]	Rockin' with Reed	1959	200.00
—Maroon label			
❑ LP-1008 [M]	Rockin' with Reed	1961	80.00
—Black label with colorband			
❑ VJLP-1008	Rockin' with Reed	198?	10.00
—Reissue with glossy labels			
❑ LP-1022 [M]	Found Love	1959	200.00
—Maroon label			
❑ LP-1022 [M]	Found Love	1961	80.00
—Black label with colorband			
❑ LP-1025 [M]	Now Appearing	1960	80.00
❑ VJLP-1025	Now Appearing	198?	10.00
—Reissue with glossy labels			
❑ 2LP-1035 [(2)M]	Jimmy Reed at Carnegie Hall	1961	50.00
❑ 2SR-1035 [(2)S]	Jimmy Reed at Carnegie Hall	1961	70.00
❑ VJLP2-1035 [(2)]	Jimmy Reed at Carnegie Hall	198?	12.00
—Reissue with glossy labels			
❑ LP-1039 [M]	The Best of Jimmy Reed	1962	40.00
❑ SR-1039 [S]	The Best of Jimmy Reed	1962	60.00
❑ VJLP-1039	The Best of Jimmy Reed	198?	10.00
—Reissue with glossy labels			
❑ LP-1050 [M]	Just Jimmy Reed	1962	40.00
❑ SR-1050 [S]	Just Jimmy Reed	1962	60.00
❑ LP-1067 [M]	T'Ain't No Big Thing… But He Is Jimmy Reed	1963	40.00
❑ SR-1067 [S]	T'Ain't No Big Thing… But He Is Jimmy Reed	1963	60.00
❑ LP-1072 [M]	The Best of the Blues	1963	40.00
❑ LP-1073 [M]	The 12 String Guitar Blues	1963	40.00
❑ SR-1073 [S]	The 12 String Guitar Blues	1963	150.00
❑ LP-1080 [M]	More of the Best of Jimmy Reed	1964	40.00
❑ SR-1080 [S]	More of the Best of Jimmy Reed	1964	150.00
❑ LP-1095 [M]	Jimmy Reed at Soul City	1964	40.00
❑ VJLP-1095	Jimmy Reed at Soul City	198?	10.00
—Reissue with glossy labels			
❑ VJS-7303	Blues Is My Business	198?	10.00
❑ LP-8501 [M]	The Legend, The Man	1965	40.00
❑ VJLP-8501	The Legend, The Man	198?	10.00
—Reissue with glossy labels			
❑ VJS-8501 [S]	The Legend, The Man	1965	150.00

REED, LOU Also see THE PRMITIVES; THE VELVET UNDERGROUND.

12-Inch Singles

Number	Title (A Side/B Side)	Yr	NM
A&M			
❑ 17352 [DJ]	September Song/September Song (7" Version)	1986	6.00
ARISTA			
❑ SP-14 [DJ]	Street Hassle (stereo)/Street Hassle (mono)	1978	10.00
❑ SP-36 [DJ]	Walk on the Wild Side/Coney Island Baby/Satellite of Love	1978	10.00
❑ SP-56 [DJ]	Disco Mystic/I Wanna Boogie with You	1979	10.00
❑ SP-84 [DJ]	How Do You Speak to An Angel/Keep Away/The Power of Positive Drinking/ Standing on Ceremony	1980	15.00
❑ 9375 [DJ]	Hot Hips (same on both sides)	1985	10.00
ATLANTIC			
❑ 819 [DJ]	My Love Is Chemical (same on both sides)	1985	7.00

Except when noted otherwise, VG = 25% of NM, and VG+ = 50% of NM. (Example: VG = $2.00, VG+ = $4.00 and NM = $8.00.)

Number	Title (A Side/B Side)	Yr	NM
RCA			
❑ 5711-1	Original Wrapper (2 versions)/ Video Violence (2 versions)	198?	8.00
❑ JR-13849 [DJ]	I Love You, Suzanne (same on both sides)	1984	7.00
❑ PD-13928	My Red Joystick (remix) (instrumental)/ I Love You Suzanne	1984	10.00
❑ JR-14343 [DJ]	No Money Down (same on both sides)	1986	12.00
—Green vinyl			
❑ PD-14388	No Money Down (Extended)/ No Money Down (Dub)/ Don't Hurt a Woman	1986	8.00
❑ JR-14420 [DJ]	Video Violence (same on both sides)	1986	8.00
❑ PD-14427	The Original Wrapper (3 mixes)/ Video Violence	1986	8.00
SIRE			
❑ PRO-A-3359 [DJ]	Dirty Blvd. (Radio Edit)/Dirty Blvd. (LP Version)	1988	8.00
45s			
A&M			
❑ 2781	September Song/Oh Heavenly Salvation	1985	4.00
—B-side by Mark Bingham/Johnny Adams/Aaron Neville			
❑ 2883	Soul Man/Sweet Sarah	1986	3.00
—With Sam Moore			
ARISTA			
❑ 0215	I Believe in Love/ Senselessly Cruel	1976	4.00
❑ 0431	City Lights/I Want to Boogie with You	1979	4.00
❑ 0535	Growing Up in Public/The Power of Positive Drinking	1980	4.00
ATLANTIC			
❑ 89468	My Love Is Chemical/ People Have Got to Move	1985	3.00
—B-side by Jenny Burton			
❑ 89468 [PS]	My Love Is Chemical/ People Have Got to Move	1985	5.00
RCA			
❑ JB-13558	Martial Law/Don't Talk to Me About Work	1983	3.00
❑ PB-13841	I Love You Suzanne/ My Friend George	1984	3.00
❑ PB-14368	No Money Down/ Don't Hurt a Woman	1986	3.00
RCA VICTOR			
❑ 74-0727	I Can't Stand It/Going Down	1972	6.00
❑ 74-0784	Walk and Talk It/Wild Child	1972	6.00
❑ 74-0887	Walk on the Wild Side/ Perfect Day	1973	6.00
❑ 74-0964	Satellite of Love/Walk and Talk It	1973	6.00
❑ APBO-0054	Vicious/Good Night Ladies	1973	5.00
❑ APBO-0172	Lady Day/How Do You Think It Feels	1973	5.00
❑ APBO-0238	Sweet Jane/Lady Day	1974	30.00
—Part of U.S. numbering system, but pressed for export.			
❑ PB-10053	Sally Can't Dance/Vicious	1974	4.00
❑ PB-10081	Sally Can't Dance/Ennui	1974	4.00
❑ GB-10162	Walk on the Wild Side/Vicious	1975	3.00
—Gold Standard Series reissue			
❑ PB-10573	Charley's Girl/Nowhere At All	1976	4.00
❑ PB-10648	Crazy Feeling/Nowhere At All	1976	4.00
SIRE			
❑ 22876	Romeo Had Juliette/ Busload of Faith	1989	3.00
❑ 22876 [PS]	Romeo Had Juliette/ Busload of Faith	1989	5.00
7-Inch Extended Plays			
NORTON			
❑ EP-097	Your Love/Merry Go Round// So Blue/Leave Her for Me	2000	4.00
—Early recordings; Side 1 credited to "Lewis Reed"; Side 2 credited to "The Jades"			
❑ EP-097 [PS]	All Tomorrow's Dance Parties	2000	4.00
Albums			
ARISTA			
❑ AL 4100	Rock and Roll Heart	1976	15.00
—Originals on light blue labels			
❑ AL 4169	Street Hassle	1978	15.00
❑ AL 4229	The Bells	1979	12.00
❑ ALB6-8390	City Lights — Classic Performances by Lou Reed	1985	10.00
❑ AL11 8434 [(2)]	Rock and Roll Diary 1967-1980	198?	16.00
—Reissue			
❑ AL 8502 [(2)]	Live! Take No Prisoners	1978	25.00
❑ A2L 8603 [(2)]	Rock and Roll Diary 1967-1980	1980	18.00
❑ AL 9522	Growing Up in Public	1980	12.00
❑ R 252506 [(2)]	Rock and Roll Diary 1967-1980	1980	18.00
—RCA Music Service edition			

Number	Title (A Side/B Side)	Yr	NM
DIRECT DISK			
❑ (no #) [DJ]	The Blue Mask	1982	150.00
—Only exists on test pressings; no stock copies made			
RCA VICTOR			
❑ APL1-0207	Berlin	1973	12.00
❑ AFL1-0472	Rock & Roll Animal	1977	8.00
—Reissue			
❑ APL1-0472	Rock & Roll Animal	1974	12.00
❑ AFL1-0611	Sally Can't Dance	1977	8.00
—Reissue			
❑ CPL1-0611	Sally Can't Dance	1974	20.00
❑ APL1-0915	Coney Island Baby	1976	16.00
❑ AFL1-0959	Lou Reed Live	1977	8.00
—Reissue			
❑ APL1-0959	Lou Reed Live	1975	15.00
❑ CPD2-1101 [(2)Q]	Metal Machine Music	1975	150.00
❑ CPL2-1101 [(2)]	Metal Machine Music	1975	50.00
—Orange or brown label			
❑ AFL1-2001	Walk on the Wild Side	1978	8.00
—Reissue			
❑ APL1-2001	Walk on the Wild Side	1977	12.00
❑ ANL1-2480	Coney Island Baby	1977	8.00
—Reissue			
❑ AYL1-3664	Rock & Roll Animal	1980	8.00
—Best Buy Series reissue			
❑ AYL1-3752	Lou Reed Live	1980	8.00
—Best Buy Series reissue			
❑ AYL1-3753	Walk on the Wild Side	1980	8.00
—Best Buy Series reissue			
❑ AYL1-3806	Transformer	1980	8.00
—Best Buy Series reissue			
❑ AYL1-3807	Coney Island Baby	1980	8.00
—Best Buy Series reissue			
❑ AFL1-4221	The Blue Mask	1982	10.00
❑ DJL1-4266 [DJ]	Special Radio Series, Vol. XVII	1980	25.00
—Promo-only with insert			
❑ DJL1-4267	The Blue Mask Interview Album	1982	25.00
❑ DJL1-4345 [DJ]	The Blue Mask Sampler	1982	12.00
—Three-song EP released to radio			
❑ AYL1-4388	Berlin	1983	8.00
—Best Buy Series reissue			
❑ AYL1-4555	Sally Can't Dance	1983	8.00
—Best Buy Series reissue			
❑ AFL1-4568	Legendary Hearts	1983	10.00
❑ LSP-4701	Lou Reed	1972	20.00
❑ AYL1-4780	The Blue Mask	1984	8.00
—Best Buy Series reissue			
❑ AFL1-4807	Transformer	1977	8.00
—Reissue			
❑ LSP-4807	Transformer	1972	20.00
❑ AFL1-4998	New Sensations	1984	8.00
❑ AFL1-7190	Mistrial	1986	12.00
SIRE			
❑ 25829	New York	1989	10.00
❑ R 101058	New York	1989	12.00
—BMG Music Service edition			
REED, LOU, AND JOHN CALE			
Albums			
SIRE			
❑ 26140	Songs for Drella	1990	10.00
REED, TAWNEY			
45s			
CONGRESS			
❑ 270	My Heart Cried/ Can't Take It Away	1966	12.00
RED BIRD			
❑ 10-044	Needle in a Haystack/ I Got a Feeling	1965	40.00
REED, URSULA			
45s			
OLD TOWN			
❑ 1001	Your're Laffin' "Cause I'm Cryin'/Ursula's Blues	1954	400.00
REED, VIVIAN			
12-Inch Singles			
UNITED ARTISTS			
❑ SP-181 [DJ]	It's Alright (This Feeling I'm Feeling) (5:26)/Sweet Harmony (4:20)	1978	15.00
❑ SP-189 [DJ]	Start Dancin' (6:50) (same on both sides)	1979	15.00
❑ UA P-5004	Ready and Waiting (7:08) (same on both sides)	1979	15.00
45s			
ATCO			
❑ 6938	Save Your Love for Me/I Didn't Mean to Love You	1973	600.00
EPIC			
❑ 5-10290	Baby, Baby/I	1968	15.00
❑ 5-10319	Yours Until Tomorrow/ I Wanna Be Free	1968	15.00

Number	Title (A Side/B Side)	Yr	NM
❑ 5-10382	Mama Open the Door/Medley: Soul and Inspiration-You've Lost That Lovin' Feelin'	1968	15.00
❑ 5-10422	Somewhere/Shape of Things to Come	1968	15.00
❑ 5-10453	Walk on My Side/ Look the Other Way	1969	25.00
❑ 5-10533	Then I'll Be Over You/ Unbelievable	1969	20.00
❑ 5-10683	Lean on Me/Missing You	1970	15.00
❑ 5-10752	I Feel the Earth Move/Don't Close the Door on Me	1971	30.00
H&L			
❑ 4666	Bubbling Brown Sugar/ (B-side unknown)	1976	8.00
❑ 4672	God Bless the Child/ Sweet Georgia Brown	1976	8.00
UNITED ARTISTS			
❑ X-1239-Y	It's Alright (This Feeling I'm Feeling)/When You Touch Me	1978	15.00
❑ X-1260-Y	Start Dancin'/Sweet Harmony	1979	12.00
❑ X-1296-Y	Ready and Waiting/ (B-side unknown)	1979	15.00
Albums			
EPIC			
❑ BN 26412	Vivian Reed	1968	40.00
H&L			
❑ 69017	Brown Sugar	1976	20.00
UNITED ARTISTS			
❑ UA-LA911-H	Another Side	1978	15.00
❑ UA-LA970-H	Ready and Waiting	1979	15.00
REEDER, BILL			
45s			
FERNWOOD			
❑ 121	You're My Baby/Where Were You Last Night	1960	80.00
HI			
❑ 2037	Till I Waltz Again with You/ There Was a Time	1961	80.00
❑ 2041	Secret Love/Judy	1961	20.00
VOLL			
❑ 100	Till I Waltz Again with You/ There Was a Time	1961	200.00
REEKERS, THE			
45s			
RY-JAC			
❑ 13	Grindin'/Don't Call Me Flyface	1964	50.00
REESE, JAXON May also be known as "Jackson Reese."			
45s			
PARKWAY			
❑ 129	Hurry Sundown/How Do You Speak to an Angel	1967	40.00
❑ 142	Pretty Girl/Cry Me a River	1967	40.00
REEVES, DEL			
45s			
CAPITOL			
❑ F3819	Love, Love, Love/You're Not the Changing Kind	1957	30.00
—With Chester Smith			
❑ F3979	The Trot/Cool Drool	1958	30.00
❑ F4045	Two Teen Hearts/ Baby I Love You	1958	30.00
CHART			
❑ 5082	Stand In/Bad, Bad Tuesday	1970	8.00
COLUMBIA			
❑ 4-43044	Talking to the Night Lights/ Not Since Adam	1964	10.00
DECCA			
❑ 31307	Be Quiet Mind/As Far As I Can See	1961	12.00
❑ 31417	He Stands Real Tall/ Empty House	1962	12.00
KOALA			
❑ 324	Good Ole Girls/Doin' Soft Time	1980	5.00
❑ 329	White Christmas/White Christmas (Second Version)	1980	5.00
❑ 333	Swinging Doors/Who Left the Door to Heaven Open	1981	5.00
❑ 336	Slow Hand/Take Off Time	1981	5.00
❑ 339	Ain't Nobody Gonna Get My Body But You/Let's Think About Livin'	1981	5.00
❑ 347	That's What I Like About the South/(B-side unknown)	1982	5.00
❑ 584	Take Me to Your Heart/What the Love of a Lady Can Do	1980	5.00
❑ 594	What Am I Gonna Do?/Night Out	1980	5.00

R

Jim Reeves, "Am I Losing You," RCA Victor 47-7800, 1960, **$20.**

Number	Title (A Side/B Side)	Yr	NM
PEACH			
❑ 739	You Must Be an Angel/I Watched You Walk Away	1960	25.00
❑ 746	Time After Time/I Don't Wonder	1961	20.00
❑ 748	You Must Be an Angel/I Watched You Walk Away	1961	20.00
PLAYBACK			
❑ 1103	The Second Time Around/(B-side unknown)	1986	5.00
❑ 1301	Dear Dr. Ruth/Anywhere U.S.A.	1988	6.00
❑ 1302	Louisiana Legs/(B-side unknown)	1988	6.00
❑ 1303	I Used My Doodle-De-Doos/I Wish I Had Loved	1988	6.00
REPRISE			
❑ 20158	The Only Girl I Can't Forget/The Love She Offered Me	1963	10.00
❑ 20228	I Closed My Eyes and Saw the Light/Once a Fool	1963	10.00
UNITED ARTISTS			
❑ 0141	Girl on the Billboard/Bar Room Talk	1973	4.00
—*"Silver Spotlight Series" reissue*			
❑ XW249	Mm-Mm Good/Bridge That Wouldn't Burn	1973	5.00
❑ XW308	Lay a Little Lovin' on Me/Lay Me to Sleep	1973	5.00
❑ XW378	What a Way to Go/Sometimes Woman	1974	5.00
❑ XW427	Prayer from a Mobile Home/Three Years Late	1974	5.00
❑ XW532	She Likes Country Bands/A Rose Is Hard to Beat	1974	5.00
❑ XW564	Pour It All on Me/Belles of Broadway	1974	5.00
❑ XW593	But I Do/One More Round of Gin	1975	5.00
❑ XW639	Puttin' In Overtime at Home/Homemade Love	1975	5.00
❑ XW702	You Comb Her Hair Every Morning/Hell and Half of Georgia	1975	5.00

Number	Title (A Side/B Side)	Yr	NM
❑ XW760	I Ain't Got Nobody/I Would Like to See You Again	1976	5.00
❑ 824	Girl on the Billboard/Eyes Don't Come Crying to Me	1965	8.00
❑ XW829	Nobody Touches My Baby/She's the Best Thing I Ever Almost Had	1976	5.00
❑ XW885	My Better Half/Dig a Little Deeper in the Well	1976	5.00
❑ 890	The Belles of Southern Bell/Nothing to Write Home About	1965	8.00
❑ 940	Women Do Funny Things to Me/My Half of Our Part	1965	8.00
❑ XW989	Ladies Night/Cryin' in Arkansas Tonight	1977	5.00
❑ XW1047	Am I in Heaven/Rita Ballow	1977	5.00
❑ XW1191	When My Angel Turns Into a Devil/How Can Anything That Feels So Good (Hurt So Bad)	1978	5.00
❑ XW1230	Dig Down Deep/Darlin' I Love You	1978	5.00
❑ 50001	One Bum Town/Dead and Gone	1966	8.00
❑ 50035	Gettin' Any Feed for Your Chickens/Plain as the Tears on My Face	1966	8.00
❑ 50081	This Must Be the Bottom/Laughter Keeps Running Down My Cheeks	1966	8.00
❑ 50115	Christmas Is Lonely/Sajo	1966	10.00
❑ 50128	Blame It On My Do Wrong/I Don't Have Sense Enough	1967	8.00
❑ 50157	The Private/Things Her Memory Makes	1967	8.00
❑ 50157 [PS]	The Private/Things Her Memory Makes	1967	20.00
❑ 50210	A Dime at a Time/So Much Got Lost	1967	8.00
❑ 50270	Wild Blood/Lest We Forget	1968	7.00
❑ 50332	Looking at the World Through a Windshield/If I Lived Here (I'd Be Home Now)	1968	7.00
❑ 50487	Good Time Charlie's/These Feet	1968	7.00
❑ 50531	Be Glad/Moccasin Branch	1969	7.00

Number	Title (A Side/B Side)	Yr	NM
❑ 50564	There Wouldn't Be a Lonely Heart in Town/Little Bit of Somethin' Else	1969	7.00
❑ 50622	A Lover's Question/Spare Me	1970	7.00
❑ 50667	Son of a Coal Man/The Chair That Rocked Us All	1970	7.00
❑ 50714	Right Back Loving You Again/Gardenia Brown	1970	7.00
❑ 50743	Bar Room Talk/I'm Not Through Loving You	1971	6.00
❑ 50763	Working Like the Devil (For the Lord)/Sidewalks of Chicago	1971	6.00
❑ 50802	The Philadelphia Fillies/Belles of Broadway	1971	6.00
❑ 50840	A Dozen Pairs of Boots/A Rose Is Hard to Beat	1971	6.00
❑ 50877	The Best Is Yet to Come/Truth Can Hurt a Woman	1972	6.00
❑ 50906	No Rings — No Strings/Hey, Anybody Here Seen Cupid	1972	6.00
❑ 50964	Before Goodbye/Buck Jones Guitar	1972	6.00
❑ 51106	Trucker's Paradise/Gathering of My Memories	1973	6.00

Albums

Number	Title	Yr	NM
KOALA			
❑ KO 14188	Del Reeves	1980	12.00
PLAYBACK			
❑ 12002	Here's Del Reeves	1988	15.00
STARDAY			
❑ 998	Greatest Hits	197?	10.00
SUNSET			
❑ SUS-5230	Wonderful World of Country Music	1968	12.00
❑ SUS-5279	Country Concert Live!	1969	12.00
❑ SUS-5321	Out in the Country	1970	12.00
UNITED ARTISTS			
❑ UA-LA044-F	Trucker's Paradise	1973	15.00
❑ UA-LA204-G	Live at the Palomino Club	1974	15.00
❑ UA-LA235	The Very Best of Del Reeves	1974	15.00
❑ UA-LA364-G	Del Reeves with Strings and Things	1975	15.00
❑ UA-LA687-G	10th Anniversary	1977	12.00
❑ UAL-3441 [M]	Del Reeves Sings Girl on the Billboard	1965	25.00
❑ UAL-3458 [M]	Doodle-Oo-Doo-Doo	1965	20.00
❑ UAL-3468 [M]	Del Reeves Sings Jim Reeves	1966	20.00
❑ UAL-3488 [M]	Special Delivery	1966	20.00
❑ UAL-3528 [M]	Santa's Boy	1966	20.00
❑ UAL-3530 [M]	Gettin' Any Feed for Your Chickens?	1966	20.00
❑ UAL-3571 [M]	Struttin' My Stuff	1967	25.00
❑ UAL-3595 [M]	Six of One, Half a Dozen of the Other	1967	25.00
❑ UAL-3612 [M]	The Little Church in the Dell	1967	30.00
❑ UAS-6441 [S]	Del Reeves Sings Girl on the Billboard	1965	30.00
❑ UAS-6458 [S]	Doodle-Oo-Doo-Doo	1965	25.00
❑ UAS-6468 [S]	Del Reeves Sings Jim Reeves	1966	25.00
❑ UAS-6488 [S]	Special Delivery	1966	25.00
❑ UAS-6528 [S]	Santa's Boy	1966	25.00
❑ UAS-6530 [S]	Gettin' Any Feed for Your Chickens?	1966	25.00
❑ UAS-6571 [S]	Struttin' My Stuff	1967	20.00
❑ UAS-6595 [S]	Six of One, Half a Dozen of the Other	1967	20.00
❑ UAS-6612 [S]	The Little Church in the Dell	1967	25.00
❑ UAS-6635	The Best of Del Reeves	1968	20.00
❑ UAS-6643	Running Wild	1968	20.00
❑ UAS-6674	Looking at the World Through a Windshield	1968	20.00
❑ UAS-6705	Down at Good Time Charlie's	1969	20.00
❑ UAS-6733	Big Daddy Del	1970	20.00
❑ UAS-6758	The Best of Del Reeves, Vol. 2	1970	20.00
❑ UAS-6789	Friends and Neighbors	1971	20.00
❑ UAS-6820	The Del Reeves Album	1971	20.00
❑ UAS-6830	Before Goodbye	1972	20.00

REEVES, DEL, AND BOBBY GOLDSBORO

Also see each artist's individual listings.

45s

Number	Title (A Side/B Side)	Yr	NM
UNITED ARTISTS			
❑ 50591	She Thinks I Still Care/Take a Little Good Will Home	1969	7.00

Albums

Number	Title	Yr	NM
UNITED ARTISTS			
❑ UAL 3615 [M]	Our Way of Life	1967	20.00
❑ UAS 6615 [S]	Our Way of Life	1967	20.00

REEVES, JIM

45s

Number	Title (A Side/B Side)	Yr	NM
ABBOTT			
❑ 115	Wagon Load of Love/What Were You Doing Last Nite	1953	25.00

Except when noted otherwise, VG = 25% of NM, and VG+ = 50% of NM. (Example: VG = $2.00, VG+ = $4.00 and NM = $8.00.)

Number	Title (A Side/B Side)	Yr	NM
❑ 115	Wagon Load of Love/What Were You Doing Last Nite	1953	60.00
—Red vinyl			
❑ 116	Mexican Joe/I Could Cry	1953	25.00
❑ 116	Mexican Joe/I Could Cry	1953	60.00
—Red vinyl			
❑ 137	Let Me Love You Just a Little/Butterfly Love	1953	25.00
❑ 137	Let Me Love You Just a Little/Butterfly Love	1953	60.00
—Red vinyl			
❑ 143	El Rancho Del Rio/It's Hard to Love Just One	1953	25.00
❑ 143	El Rancho Del Rio/It's Hard to Love Just One	1953	60.00
—Red vinyl			
❑ 148	Bimbo/Gypsy Heart	1953	60.00
—Red vinyl			
❑ 148	Bimbo/Gypsy Heart	1953	25.00
—Black vinyl			
❑ 160	Echo Bonita/Then I'll Stop Loving You	1954	20.00
❑ 164	Ramblin' Heart/Beatin' on the Ding Dong	1954	20.00
❑ 168	Padre of Old San Antone/Mother Went A-Walkin'	1954	20.00
❑ 170	Penny Candy/I'll Follow You	1954	20.00
❑ 174	Where Does a Broken Heart Go/The Wilder Your Heart Beats, The Sweeter You Love	1954	20.00
❑ 178	Drinking Tequila/Red Eyed and Rowdy	1955	20.00
❑ 180	Give Me One More Kiss/Tahiti	1955	20.00
❑ 184	Are You the One/How Many	1955	20.00
—With Alvadean Coker			
❑ 186	Let Me Remember/Hillbilly Waltz	1956	20.00

RCA

Number	Title (A Side/B Side)	Yr	NM
❑ PB-10956	It's Nothin' to Me/I Won't Forget You	1977	4.00
❑ PB-11060	Little Ole Dime/A Letter to My Heart	1977	4.00
❑ PB-11187	You're the Only Good Thing (That's Happened to Me)/When You Are Gone	1978	4.00
❑ PB-11564	Don't Let Me Cross Over/I've Enjoyed As Much of This As I Can Stand	1979	4.00
❑ PB-11737	Oh, How I Miss You Tonight/The Talking Walls	1979	4.00
❑ PB-11946	Take Me in Your Arms and Hold Me/Missing Angel	1980	4.00
—A-side with Deborah Allen (overdubbed)			
❑ PB-12118	There's Always Me/Somewhere Along the Line	1980	4.00
❑ PB-13410	The Jim Reeves Medley/He'll Have to Go	1982	4.00
❑ PB-13693	The Image of Me/Won't Come In While He's There	1983	4.00

RCA VICTOR

Number	Title (A Side/B Side)	Yr	NM
❑ 47-6200	Yonder Comes a Sucker/I'm Hurtin' Inside	1955	20.00
❑ 47-6274	I've Lived a Lot in My Time/Jimbo Jenkins	1955	20.00
❑ 47-6401	If You Were Mine/That's a Sad Affair	1956	20.00
❑ 47-6517	My Lips Are Sealed/Pickin' a Chicken	1956	20.00
❑ 47-6620	According to My Heart/The Mother of a Honky Tonk Girl	1956	20.00
—With Carol Johnson			
❑ 47-6625	Bimbo/Penny Candy	1956	20.00
❑ 47-6626	Mexican Joe/How Many	1956	20.00
❑ 47-6627	Then I'll Stop Loving You/Drinking Tequila	1956	20.00
❑ 47-6749	Am I Losing You/Waitin' for a Train	1956	20.00
❑ 47-6874	Four Walls/I Know and You Know	1957	15.00
❑ 47-6973	Young Hearts/Two Shadows on Your Window	1957	15.00
❑ 47-7070	Anna Marie/Everywhere You Go	1957	15.00
❑ 47-7171	I Love You More/Overnight	1958	15.00
❑ 47-7266	Blue Boy/Theme of Love (I Love to Say I Love You)	1958	15.00
❑ 47-7380	Billy Bayou/I'd Like to Be	1958	15.00
❑ 47-7479	Home/If Heartache Is the Fashion	1959	15.00
❑ 47-7557	Partners/I'm Beginning to Forget You	1959	15.00
❑ 47-7643	He'll Have to Go/In a Mansion Stands My Love	1959	12.00
❑ 47-7756	I'm Gettin' Better/I Know One	1960	12.00
❑ 47-7756 [PS]	I'm Gettin' Better/I Know One	1960	20.00
❑ 47-7800	Am I Losing You/I Missed Me	1960	12.00
❑ 47-7800 [PS]	Am I Losing You/I Missed Me	1960	20.00
❑ 47-7855	The Blizzard/Danny Boy	1961	12.00
❑ 47-7905	What Would You Do?/Stand At Your Window	1961	12.00
❑ 47-7950	Losing Your Love/(How Can I Write on Paper) What I Feel in My Heart	1961	12.00
❑ 47-8019	Adios Amigo/A Letter to My Heart	1962	10.00
❑ 47-8080	I'm Gonna Change Everything/Pride Goes Before a Fall	1962	10.00
❑ 47-8127	Is This Me?/Missing Angel	1963	10.00
❑ 47-8127 [PS]	Is This Me?/Missing Angel	1963	25.00
❑ 47-8193	Guilty/Little Ole You	1963	10.00
❑ 47-8193 [PS]	Guilty/Little Ole You	1963	15.00
❑ 47-8252	An Old Christmas Card/Senor Santa Claus	1963	15.00
❑ 47-8252 [PS]	An Old Christmas Card/Senor Santa Claus	1963	40.00
❑ 47-8289	Welcome to My World/Good Morning Self	1963	10.00
❑ 47-8324	Love Is No Excuse/Look Who's Talking	1964	10.00
—With Dottie West			
❑ 47-8383	I Guess I'm Crazy/Not Until the Next Time	1964	10.00
❑ 47-8461	I Won't Forget You/Highway to Nowhere	1964	10.00
❑ 47-8508	This Is It/There's That Smile Again	1965	8.00
❑ 47-8625	Is It Really Over?/Rosa Rio	1965	8.00
❑ 47-8625 [PS]	Is It Really Over?/Rosa Rio	1965	12.00
❑ 47-8719	Snowflake/Take My Hand, Precious Lord	1965	8.00
❑ 47-8789	Distant Drums/Old Tige	1966	8.00
❑ 47-8902	Blue Side of Lonesome/It Hurts So Much (To See You Go)	1966	8.00
❑ 47-9057	I Won't Come In While He's There/Maureen	1966	8.00
❑ 47-9238	The Storm/Trying to Forget	1967	8.00
❑ 47-9343	I Heard a Heart Break Last Night/Golden Memories and Silver Tears	1967	8.00
❑ 47-9455	That's When I See the Blues (In Your Pretty Brown Eyes)/I've Lived a Lot in My Time	1968	8.00
❑ 47-9614	When You Are Gone/How Can I Write on Paper	1968	8.00
❑ 47-9880	Angels Don't Lie/You Kept Me Awake Last Night	1970	6.00
❑ 47-9969	Gypsy Feet/He Will	1971	6.00
❑ 74-0135	When Two Worlds Collide/Could I Be Falling in Love	1969	6.00
❑ 74-0286	Why Do I Love You (Melody of Love)/Nobody's Fool	1969	6.00
❑ 74-0626	The Writing on the Wall/You're Free to Go	1971	6.00
❑ 74-0744	Missing You/The Tie That Binds	1972	5.00
❑ 74-0859	Blue Christmas/Snowflake	1972	5.00
❑ 74-0963	Am I That Easy to Forget/Rosa Rio	1973	4.00
❑ 447-0884	An Old Christmas Card/Senor Santa Claus	1972	4.00
—Gold Standard Series			
❑ 447-0885	Snowflake/Take My Hand, Precious Lord	1972	4.00
—Gold Standard Series			
❑ APBO-0255	I'd Fight the World/What's In It for Me	1974	4.00
❑ EP-10133	He Will/We Thank Thee	1974	4.00
❑ PB-10299	You Belong to Me/Maureen	1975	4.00
❑ PB-10418	You'll Never Know/There's That Smile Again	1975	4.00
❑ GB-10511	Missing You/I'd Fight the World	1975	4.00
—Gold Standard Series			

7-Inch Extended Plays

RCA VICTOR

Number	Title (A Side/B Side)	Yr	NM
❑ EPA-757	Roly Poly/Have I Told You Lately That I Love You//Tweedle O'Twill/Each Time You Leave	1956	20.00
❑ EPA-757 [PS]	(title unknown)	1956	20.00
❑ VLP-3482	Welcome to My World/I Guess I'm Crazy/Is This Me?//My Lips Are Sealed/Mexican Joe/According to My Heart	196?	15.00
—Jukebox issue; small hole, plays at 33 1/3 rpm			
❑ VLP-3482 [PS]	The Best of Jim Reeves, Vol. II	196?	15.00
❑ VLP-3793	Blue Side of Lonesome/Trying to Forget/I Know One//I Won't Come In While He's There/Teardrops on the Rocks/Deep Dark Water	1967	15.00
—Stereo jukebox issue; small hole, plays at 33 1/3 rpm			
❑ VLP-3793 [PS]	Blue Side of Lonesome	1967	15.00
❑ EPA-4357	He'll Have to Go/Wishful Thinking//Please Come Home/After Awhile	1960	20.00
❑ EPA-4357 [PS]	He'll Have to Go	1960	20.00
❑ EPA-5124	Four Walls/Blue Boy//Bimbo/Mexican Joe	1958	15.00
❑ EPA-5124 [PS]	Jim Reeves' Hits (Gold Standard Series)	1958	15.00
❑ EPA-5145	Am I Losing You/Home//Billy Bayou/Partners	1958	15.00
❑ EPA-5145 [PS]	Am I Losing You (Gold Standard Series)	1958	15.00

Albums

ABBOTT

Number	Title	Yr	NM
❑ LP-5001 [M]	Jim Reeves Sings	1956	2000.
—VG value 1000; VG+ value 1500			

COUNTRY MUSIC FOUNDATION

Number	Title	Yr	NM
❑ CMF-008	Live at the Opry	198?	10.00

PAIR

Number	Title	Yr	NM
❑ PDL2-1002 [(2)]	The Country Side of Jim Reeves	1986	12.00

RCA CAMDEN

Number	Title	Yr	NM
❑ ACL1-0123	Kimberley Jim	1973	15.00
❑ CAL-583 [M]	According to My Heart	1960	20.00
❑ CAS-583 [R]	According to My Heart	1960	20.00
❑ CAL-686 [M]	The Country Side of Jim Reeves	1962	20.00
❑ CAS-686 [S]	The Country Side of Jim Reeves	1962	20.00
❑ CAL-784 [M]	Good 'N' Country	1963	20.00
❑ CAS-784 [S]	Good 'N' Country	1963	20.00
❑ CAL-842 [M]	Have I Told You Lately That I Love You?	1964	20.00
❑ CAS-842 [S]	Have I Told You Lately That I Love You?	1964	20.00
❑ CAS-2532	Young and Country	1971	15.00
❑ CAX-9001 [(2)]	Jim Reeves	1972	20.00

RCA VICTOR

Number	Title	Yr	NM
❑ APL1-0039	Am I That Easy to Forget	1973	20.00
❑ APL1-0330	Great Moments with Jim Reeves	1973	20.00
❑ APL1-0537	I'd Fight the World	1974	20.00
❑ APL1-0793	The Best of Jim Reeves Sacred Songs	1974	20.00
❑ APL1-1037	Songs of Love	1975	20.00
❑ APL1-1224	I Love You Because	1976	20.00
❑ LPM-1256 [M]	Singing Down the Lane	1956	200.00
❑ LPM-1410 [M]	Bimbo	1957	200.00
—Reissue of Abbott LP			
❑ LPM-1576 [M]	Jim Reeves	1957	80.00
❑ LPM-1685 [M]	Girls I Have Known	1958	60.00
❑ CPL1-1891	A Legendary Performer	1976	20.00
❑ ANL1-1927	Twelve Songs of Christmas	1976	8.00
—Reissue of LSP-2758			
❑ LPM-1950 [M]	God Be With You	1958	40.00
❑ LSP-1950 [S]	God Be With You	1958	50.00
❑ LPM-2001 [M]	Songs to Warm the Heart	1959	40.00
❑ LSP-2001 [S]	Songs to Warm the Heart	1959	50.00
❑ LPM-2216 [M]	The Intimate Jim Reeves	1960	30.00
❑ LSP-2216 [S]	The Intimate Jim Reeves	1960	40.00
❑ LPM-2223 [M]	Featuring He'll Have to Go and Other Favorites	1960	30.00
—Black and white cover (original)			
❑ LPM-2223 [M]	Featuring He'll Have to Go and Other Favorites	1962	20.00
—Color cover (reissue)			
❑ LSP-2223 [S]	Featuring He'll Have to Go and Other Favorites	1960	40.00
—Black and white cover (original)			
❑ LSP-2223 [S]	Featuring He'll Have to Go and Other Favorites	1962	25.00
—Color cover (reissue)			
❑ LPM-2284 [M]	Tall Tales and Short Tempers	1961	25.00
❑ LSP-2284 [S]	Tall Tales and Short Tempers	1961	30.00
❑ APL1-2309	It's Nothin' to Me	1977	15.00
❑ LPM-2339 [M]	Talkin' to Your Heart	1961	25.00
❑ LSP-2339 [S]	Talkin' to Your Heart	1961	30.00
❑ LPM-2487 [M]	A Touch of Velvet	1962	25.00
❑ LSP-2487 [S]	A Touch of Velvet	1962	30.00
❑ LPM-2552 [M]	We Thank Thee	1962	25.00
❑ LSP-2552 [S]	We Thank Thee	1962	30.00
❑ LPM-2605 [M]	Gentleman Jim	1963	25.00
❑ LSP-2605 [S]	Gentleman Jim	1963	30.00
❑ LPM-2704 [M]	The International Jim Reeves	1963	25.00
❑ LSP-2704 [S]	The International Jim Reeves	1963	30.00
❑ AHL1-2720	Jim Reeves	1978	15.00
❑ LPM-2758 [M]	Twelve Songs of Christmas	1963	25.00
❑ LSP-2758 [S]	Twelve Songs of Christmas	1963	30.00
❑ LPM-2780 [M]	Kimberley Jim	1964	25.00
❑ LSP-2780 [S]	Kimberley Jim	1964	30.00
❑ LPM-2854 [M]	Moonlight and Roses	1964	25.00
❑ LSP-2854 [S]	Moonlight and Roses	1964	30.00
❑ LPM-2890 [M]	The Best of Jim Reeves	1964	20.00
❑ LSP-2890 [S]	The Best of Jim Reeves	1964	25.00
❑ LPM-2968 [M]	The Jim Reeves Way	1965	20.00
❑ LSP-2968 [S]	The Jim Reeves Way	1965	25.00
❑ ANL1-3014	Pure Gold, Vol. 1	1978	12.00
❑ AHL1-3271	The Best of Jim Reeves, Vol. IV	1979	15.00
❑ LPM-3427 [M]	Up Through the Years	1965	20.00
❑ LSP-3427 [S]	Up Through the Years	1965	25.00
❑ AHL1-3454	Don't Let Me Cross Over	1979	15.00
❑ LPM-3482 [M]	The Best of Jim Reeves, Vol. II	1966	20.00
❑ LSP-3482(e) [P]	The Best of Jim Reeves, Vol. II	1966	25.00
—This album is at least partially, and possibly entirely, in rechanneled stereo			
❑ LPM-3542 [M]	Distant Drums	1966	20.00
❑ LSP-3542 [P]	Distant Drums	1966	25.00
—"Overnight" and "The Gods Were Angry with Me" are rechanneled			

R

Number	Title (A Side/B Side)	Yr	NM
❑ AYL1-3678	The Best of Jim Reeves	1980	12.00
—"Best Buy Series" reissue			
❑ LPM-3709 [M]	Yours Sincerely, Jim Reeves	1966	20.00
❑ LSP-3709(e) [P]	Yours Sincerely, Jim Reeves	1966	25.00
—This album is at least partially, and possibly entirely, in rechanneled stereo			
❑ AYL1-3765	The Best of Jim Reeves Sacred Songs	1980	10.00
—"Best Buy Series" reissue			
❑ LPM-3793 [M]	Blue Side of Lonesome	1967	25.00
❑ LSP-3793 [S]	Blue Side of Lonesome	1967	20.00
❑ AHL1-3827	There's Always Me	1980	12.00
❑ LPM-3903 [M]	My Cathedral	1967	30.00
❑ LSP-3903 [S]	My Cathedral	1967	25.00
❑ AYL1-3936	Pure Gold, Vol. 1	1980	10.00
—"Best Buy Series" reissue			
❑ LPM-3987 [M]	A Touch of Sadness	1968	60.00
❑ LSP-3987 [S]	A Touch of Sadness	1968	20.00
❑ LSP-4062	Jim Reeves On Stage	1968	20.00
❑ AYL1-4075	The Best of Jim Reeves, Vol. IV	1981	10.00
—"Best Buy Series" reissue			
❑ LSP-4112	Jim Reeves and Some Friends	1969	20.00
❑ AYL1-4168	The Best of Jim Reeves, Vol. II	1981	10.00
—"Best Buy Series" reissue			
❑ LSP-4187	The Best of Jim Reeves Vol. III	1969	20.00
❑ LSP-4475	Jim Reeves Writes You a Record	1971	20.00
❑ LSP-4528	Something Special	1971	20.00
❑ AHL1-4531	The Jim Reeves Medley	1983	10.00
❑ LSP-4646	My Friend	1972	20.00
❑ LSP-4749	Missing You	1972	20.00
❑ AYL1-4833	Don't Let Me Cross Over	1983	10.00
—"Best Buy Series" reissue			
❑ AYL1-4835	I Love You Because	1983	10.00
—"Best Buy Series" reissue			
❑ AYL1-4836	Songs of Love	1983	10.00
—"Best Buy Series" reissue			
❑ AYL1-4838	The Best of Jim Reeves Vol. III	1983	10.00
—"Best Buy Series" reissue			
❑ AYL1-4839	There's Always Me	1983	10.00
—"Best Buy Series" reissue			
❑ AYL1-4840	We Thank Thee	1983	10.00
—"Best Buy Series" reissue			
❑ AHL1-4865	A Special Collection	1983	12.00
❑ CPL2-5044 [(2)]	Just for You	1984	15.00
❑ AHL1-5424	Collector's Series	1985	12.00
TIME-LIFE			
❑ STW-113	Country Music	1981	10.00

REEVES, JIM, AND PATSY CLINE Also see each artist's individual listings. Their duets were created electronically; they never actually recorded together.

Number	Title (A Side/B Side)	Yr	NM
45s			
MCA			
❑ 52052	So Wrong/I Fall to Pieces	1982	4.00
RCA			
❑ PB-12346	Have You Ever Been Lonely (Have You Ever Been Blue)/Welcome to My World	1981	4.00
Albums			
MCA			
❑ 5319	Remembering Jim Reeves and Patsy Cline	1982	15.00
RCA VICTOR			
❑ AHL1-4127	Greatest Hits	1981	15.00
❑ AYL1-5152	Greatest Hits	1984	10.00
—"Best Buy Series" reissue			

REEVES, MARTHA Also see MARTHA AND THE VANDELLAS.

Number	Title (A Side/B Side)	Yr	NM
45s			
ARISTA			
❑ 0124	Love Blind/This Time I'll Be Sweeter	1975	5.00
—Also see "Martha and the Vandellas"			
❑ 0160	Now That We Found Love/Higher and Higher	1975	4.00
❑ 0211	The Rest of My Life/Thank You	1976	4.00
❑ 0228	You've Lost That Lovin' Feelin'/Now That We Found Love	1977	4.00
FANTASY			
❑ 825	Love Don't Come No Stronger/You're Like Sunshine	1978	4.00
❑ 868	Dancin' in the Streets (Skatin' in the Streets)/When You Came	1979	4.00
❑ 887	Really Like Your Rap/That's What I Want	1979	4.00
MCA			
❑ 40194	Power of Love/Stand By Me	1974	5.00
❑ 40274	Stand By Me/Wild Night	1974	5.00
❑ 40329	My Man/Facsimile	1974	5.00
Albums			
ARISTA			
❑ AL 4105	The Rest of My Life	1976	12.00
FANTASY			
❑ F-9549	We'll Meet Again	1978	12.00
❑ F-9591	Gotta Keep Moving	1980	12.00
MCA			
❑ 414	Martha Reeves	1974	12.00

REFLECTIONS, THE (1) Detroit-based rock group.

Number	Title (A Side/B Side)	Yr	NM
45s			
ABC			
❑ 10794	Like Adam and Eve/Vito's House	1966	100.00
❑ 10822	You're Gonna Find Out (You Love Me)/Long Cigarette	1966	30.00
GOLDEN WORLD			
❑ 9	(Just Like) Romeo and Juliet/Can't You Tell By the Look in His Eyes	1964	20.00
❑ 12	Like Columbus Did/Lonely Girl	1964	15.00
❑ 15	Oowee Now/Talkin' Bout My Girl	1964	15.00
❑ 16	Henpecked Guy/Don't Do That to Me	1964	15.00
❑ 19	You're My Baby/Shabby Little Hut	1964	15.00
❑ 20	Poor Man's Son/Comin' At You	1965	15.00
❑ 22	Wheelin' and Dealin'/Deborah Ann	1965	15.00
❑ 24	June Bride/Out of the Picture	1965	15.00
❑ 29	Girl in the Candy Store/Your Kind of Love	1965	15.00
LANA			
❑ 140	(Just Like) Romeo and Juliet/Can't You Tell by the Look in My Eyes	196?	6.00
—Oldies reissue			
Albums			
GOLDEN WORLD			
❑ 300 [M]	(Just Like) Romeo and Juliet	1964	150.00

REFLECTIONS, THE (2) R&B group from New York.

Number	Title (A Side/B Side)	Yr	NM
45s			
CAPITOL			
❑ 4078	Three Steps from True Love/How Could We Let the Love Get Away	1975	6.00
❑ 4137	Love on Delivery/One Into One	1975	5.00
❑ 4222	Are You Ready (Here I Am)/Day After Day (Night After Night)	1976	5.00
❑ 4358	Gift Wrap My Love/She's My Summer Breeze	1976	25.00
RCA			
❑ PB-11408	Boogie City/I'm Gonna Let You Go This Time	1978	5.00

REFLECTIONS, THE (3)

Number	Title (A Side/B Side)	Yr	NM
45s			
CROSSROADS			
❑ 401	I Really Must Know/Maybe Tomorrow	1961	60.00
❑ 402	Rocket to the Moon/Because of You	1962	80.00

REFLECTIONS, THE (U) These could be either group (1) or (3).

Number	Title (A Side/B Side)	Yr	NM
45s			
KAY-KO			
❑ 1003	Helpless/You Said Goodbye	1963	200.00
TIGRE			
❑ 602	In the Still of the Night/Tic Toc	1962	40.00

REGALS, THE (1)

Number	Title (A Side/B Side)	Yr	NM
45s			
ALADDIN			
❑ 3266	Run Pretty Baby/May the Good Lord Bless and Keep You	1954	120.00
ATLANTIC			
❑ 1062	I'm So Lonely/Got the Water Boiling	1955	60.00
MGM			
❑ 11869	There'll Always Be a Christmas/When You're Home with the Ones You Love	1954	40.00

REGALS, THE (2)

Number	Title (A Side/B Side)	Yr	NM
45s			
LAST CHANCE			
❑ 109	See You in the Morning/Yes My Love	1961	10.00
LAVENDER			
❑ 1452	See You in the Morning/Yes My Love	1960	30.00
UNITED ARTISTS			
❑ 380	Icy Fingers/Tiger Tears	1961	30.00

REGAN, DENISE

Number	Title (A Side/B Side)	Yr	NM
45s			
DEE GEE			
❑ 3005	A Date with Santa Claus/Hole in the Stocking	1965	10.00
❑ 3005 [PS]	A Date with Santa Claus/Hole in the Stocking	1965	20.00

REGAN, EDDIE

Number	Title (A Side/B Side)	Yr	NM
45s			
ABC			
❑ 10795	Playin' Hide and Seek/Talk About Heartaches	1966	30.00

REGAN, RUSS

Number	Title (A Side/B Side)	Yr	NM
45s			
ABC-PARAMOUNT			
❑ 9949	Junior, Junior, Junior/I Never Knew	1958	20.00
CAPITOL			
❑ F4169	Joan of Love/That's When I Ran	1959	12.00
❑ F4280	Adults Only/Just the Two of Us	1959	12.00
CORVETTE			
❑ 1002	Junior, Junior, Junior/I Never Knew	1958	50.00

REGAN, TOMMY

Number	Title (A Side/B Side)	Yr	NM
45s			
COLPIX			
❑ 725	I'll Never Stop Loving You/This Time I'm Losing You	1964	100.00
TELL STAR			
❑ 5001	Santa Twist/(B-side unknown)	1962	12.00
WORLD ARTISTS			
❑ 1049	I Adore You/9 to 5	1965	15.00

REGENTS, THE (1)

Number	Title (A Side/B Side)	Yr	NM
45s			
COUSINS			
❑ 1002	Barbara-Ann/I'm So Lonely	1961	1200.
GEE			
❑ 1065	Barbara-Ann/I'm So Lonely	1961	30.00
❑ 1071	Runaround/Laura My Darling	1961	25.00
❑ 1073	Don't Be a Fool/Liar	1961	25.00
❑ 1075	Lonesome Boy/Oh Baby	1961	25.00
Albums			
GEE			
❑ GLP-706 [M]	Barbara Ann	1961	150.00
❑ SGLP-706	Barbara Ann	197?	25.00
—Reissue by Publishers Central Bureau (clearly marked as such on cover)			
❑ SGLP-706 [S]	Barbara Ann	1961	250.00

REGENTS, THE (2)

Number	Title (A Side/B Side)	Yr	NM
45s			
ARGO			
❑ 5268	Isle of Trinidad/Bamboo Tree	1957	25.00

REGENTS, THE (3)

Number	Title (A Side/B Side)	Yr	NM
45s			
BLUE CAT			
❑ 110	Playmates/Me and You	1965	10.00
DOT			
❑ 16970	The Russian Spy and I/Bald Headed Woman	1966	10.00
PENTHOUSE			
❑ 502	Words/Worryin' Kind	1966	10.00

REGENTS, THE (4)

Number	Title (A Side/B Side)	Yr	NM
45s			
KAYO			
❑ 101	(That's What I Call) A Real Good Time/No Hard Feelings	1960	25.00
PEORIA			
❑ 8	Summertime Blues/(B-side unknown)	196?	15.00

REGENTS, THE (5) MICHAEL McDONALD, later of THE DOOBIE BROTHERS, was in this group.

Number	Title (A Side/B Side)	Yr	NM
45s			
REPRISE			
❑ 0430	She's Got Her Own Way of Lovin'/When I Die, Don't You Cry	1965	30.00

REGENTS, THE (U)

Number	Title (A Side/B Side)	Yr	NM
Albums			
CAPITOL			
❑ KAO 2153 [M]	Live at the AM-PM Discotheque	1964	50.00

R

Except when noted otherwise, VG = 25% of NM, and VG+ = 50% of NM. (Example: VG = $2.00, VG+ = $4.00 and NM = $8.00.)

Number	Title (A Side/B Side)	Yr	NM
❑ SKAO 2153 [S]	Live at the AM-PM Discotheque	1964	60.00

REID, CLARENCE

45s

Number	Title (A Side/B Side)	Yr	NM
ALSTON			
❑ 3717	Baptize Me in Your Love/Whatever It Takes	1975	5.00
❑ 3720	Come On With It/Mr. Smith's Wife	1976	5.00
❑ 3723	Shake Your Butt/Caution! Love Ahead	1976	5.00
❑ 3733	Just Another Guy in the Band/I'm Excited	1977	5.00
❑ 3748	You Get Me Up/It's Hell Trying to Get to Heaven	1979	5.00
❑ 4572	Fools Are Not Born (They Are Made)/Part-Time Lover	1969	8.00
❑ 4574	Nobody But You Babe/Send Me Back My Money	1969	8.00
❑ 4578	I'm a Man of My Word/I'm Gonna Tear You a New Heart	1969	8.00
❑ 4582	I've Been Trying/Don't Look Too Hard	1970	6.00
❑ 4584	Chicken Hawk/That's How It Is	1970	6.00
❑ 4588	Masterpiece/Down the Road of Love	1970	6.00
❑ 4592	Direct Me/You Knock Me Out	1971	6.00
❑ 4597	You Got to Fight/Three Is a Crowd	1971	6.00
❑ 4598	I Get My Kicks/Gotta Take It Home to Mother	1971	6.00
❑ 4602	Love Every Woman You Can/Ten Tons of Dynamite	1971	6.00
❑ 4603	Good Old Days/Ten Tons of Dynamite	1972	6.00
❑ 4608	I'm Gonna Do Something Good to You/Real Woman	1972	6.00
❑ 4613	Ruby/Two People in Love	1972	6.00
❑ 4616	Till I Get My Share/With Friends Like These	1973	6.00
❑ 4621	Funky Party/Winter Man	1974	6.00
ATCO			
❑ 7025	See Through/I Bet You Believe Me Now	1975	8.00
DIAL			
❑ 3018	I Got My Shake/There'll Come a Day	1964	15.00
❑ 4019	I Refuse to Give Up/Somebody Will	1965	12.00
❑ 4040	Gimmie a Try/Part of Your Love	1966	12.00
PHIL-L.A. OF SOUL			
❑ 301	Cadillac Annie/Tired Blood	1967	10.00
WAND			
❑ 1106	Somebody Will/I Refuse to Give Up	1966	25.00
❑ 1121	I'm Your Yes Man/Your Love Is All the Help I Need	1966	200.00

Albums

Number	Title (A Side/B Side)	Yr	NM
ATCO			
❑ SD 33-307	Dancin' with Nobody But You Babe	1969	30.00

REID, MATTHEW

45s

Number	Title (A Side/B Side)	Yr	NM
ABC-PARAMOUNT			
❑ 10259	Jane/Why Start	1961	25.00
❑ 10305	Tarzan Twist (Bwana Ungava)/Through My Tears	1962	25.00
DECCA			
❑ 31662	One More Minute/Hurt Me	1964	12.00
PHILIPS			
❑ 40634	Outward Bound/Hey There Sweet Sue	1969	10.00
SCEPTER			
❑ 1238	Faded Roses/Tomorrow	1962	25.00
TOPIX			
❑ 6006	Cry Myself to Sleep/Lollipops Went Out of Style	1961	40.00

REID, TERRY

45s

Number	Title (A Side/B Side)	Yr	NM
ABC			
❑ 12209	Ooh Baby (Make Me Feel So Young)/Brace Awakening	1976	5.00
EPIC			
❑ 10498	May Fly/Superlungs My Supergirl	1969	8.00

Albums

Number	Title (A Side/B Side)	Yr	NM
ABC			
❑ X-935	Seed of Memory	1976	12.00
ATLANTIC			
❑ SD 7259	River	1973	12.00
CAPITOL			
❑ SW-11857	Rogue Waves	1978	12.00
EPIC			
❑ BN 26427	Bang, Bang You're Terry Reid	1968	15.00
❑ BN 26477	Terry Reid	1969	15.00

REINER, CARL, AND MEL BROOKS

Albums

Number	Title (A Side/B Side)	Yr	NM
CAPITOL			
❑ SW 1529 [S]	2000 Years	1961	20.00
❑ W 1529 [M]	2000 Years	1961	15.00
❑ SW 1618 [S]	2000 and One Years	1961	20.00
❑ W 1618 [M]	2000 and One Years	1961	15.00
❑ SW 1815 [S]	At the Cannes Film Festival	1962	20.00
❑ W 1815 [M]	At the Cannes Film Festival	1962	15.00
❑ ST 2981	The Best of the 2000 Year Old Man	1968	15.00
WARNER BROS.			
❑ BS 2741	2000 and Thirteen	1973	15.00
❑ 3XX 2744 [(3)]	The Incomplete Works of Reiner and Brooks	1973	25.00
WORLD PACIFIC			
❑ WP-1401 [M]	2000 Years	1960	30.00

RELATIVES, THE

45s

Number	Title (A Side/B Side)	Yr	NM
ALMONT			
❑ 306	Never Will I Love You Again/I'm Just Looking for Love	1964	40.00
MUSICOR			
❑ 1063	Eternally/Hadn't Been for Baby	1965	10.00

RELF, KEITH Lead singer of THE YARDBIRDS. Also see ARMAGEDDON (2); RENAISSANCE.

45s

Number	Title (A Side/B Side)	Yr	NM
EPIC			
❑ 10044	Mr. Zero/Knowing	1966	50.00
❑ 10044 [DJ]	Mr. Zero/Knowing	1966	150.00
—Promo on red vinyl... Reportedly, two promos were released for this single; the second, a different mix, was accompanied by a note telling the radio people not to play the first one, but to use the second one instead. This has not been confirmed.			
❑ 10110	Shapes in My Mind/Blue Sands	1966	50.00
❑ 10110 [DJ]	Shapes in My Mind (same on both sides)	1966	150.00
—Promo on red vinyl			
❑ 10110 [PS]	Shapes in My Mind/Blue Sands	1966	100.00
MCCM			
❑ 002	Together Now/All the Falling Angels	1989	5.00
—Purple marbled vinyl			
❑ 002 [PS]	Together Now/All the Falling Angels	1989	6.00

RELLA, CINDY

45s

Number	Title (A Side/B Side)	Yr	NM
CARLTON			
❑ 583	He Don't Love Me Anymore/I Want Him to Come Back Home	1962	12.00
❑ 601	Phil Will/To Tommy with Love	1964	12.00
DRUM BOY			
❑ 112	Bring Me A Beatle for Christmas/Cla-wence	1964	12.00

REMAINS, THE

45s

Number	Title (A Side/B Side)	Yr	NM
EPIC			
❑ 9777	You Say You're Sorry/I'm Talking About You	1965	80.00
❑ 9783	My Babe/Why Do I Cry	1965	80.00
❑ 9872	But I Ain't Got You/I Can't Get Away from You	1965	80.00
❑ 10001	Diddy Wah Diddy/Once Before	1966	80.00
❑ 10001 [DJ]	Diddy Wah Diddy/Once Before	1966	150.00
—Promo on red vinyl			
❑ 10001 [PS]	To Be Seen and Heard: Diddy Wah Diddy	1966	100.00
—Promo-only sleeve			
❑ 10060	Don't Look Back/Me Right Now	1966	80.00
SPOONFED			
❑ SR-4505	Why Do I Cry/Mercy, Mercy	1978	10.00
❑ SR-4505 [PS]	Why Do I Cry/Mercy, Mercy	1978	15.00
SUNDAZED			
❑ S 181	Diddy Wah Diddy/Once Before	2006	3.00
—Replica "Epic" white promo label; red vinyl			
❑ S 181 [PS]	Diddy Wah Diddy/Once Before	2006	3.00
—Cardboard sleeve			

Albums

Number	Title (A Side/B Side)	Yr	NM
EPIC			
❑ LN 24214 [M]	The Remains	1966	200.00
❑ BN 26214 [S]	The Remains	1966	300.00
SPOONFED			
❑ SFD-3205	The Remains	1978	15.00
—Red vinyl			
SUNDAZED			
❑ SEP 10-162 [10]	The Remains	2000	8.00
❑ LP 5015	A Session with the Remains	199?	10.00
❑ LP 5055	The Remains	1999	12.00

REMARKABLES, THE

45s

Number	Title (A Side/B Side)	Yr	NM
CHASE			
❑ 1600	Write Me/Whirl-A-Round	1964	250.00

REMINISCENTS, THE

45s

Number	Title (A Side/B Side)	Yr	NM
DAY			
❑ 1000	Zoom Zoom Zoom/Oh Let Me Dream	1963	50.00
—Blue vinyl			
MARCEL			
❑ 1000	Cards of Love/Flames	1962	120.00

REMUS, EUGENE

45s

Number	Title (A Side/B Side)	Yr	NM
MOTOWN			
❑ 1001	You Never Miss a Good Thing/Gotta Have Your Lovin'	1960	500.00
❑ 1001	You Never Miss a Good Thing/Hold Me Tight	1960	600.00

RENAISSANCE Actually two diffferent groups, though treated by collectors as one. The first, on Elektra, featured KEITH RELF and other ex-YARDBIRDS. The later group was that group's spiritual heir, but had all new members.

45s

Number	Title (A Side/B Side)	Yr	NM
CAPITOL			
❑ 3487	Prologue/Spare Some Love	1972	8.00
❑ 3715	Carpet of the Sun/Bound for Infinity	1973	8.00
I.R.S.			
❑ 9904	Remember/Bon Jour Swan Song	1982	5.00
❑ 9914	Richard IX/(B-side unknown)	1982	5.00
SIRE			
❑ 714	Mother Russia/I Think of You	1974	6.00
❑ 728	Carpet of the Sun/Kiev	1976	6.00
❑ 740	Midas Man/Captive Heart	1977	6.00
❑ 1022	Northern Lights/Opening Out	1978	5.00
❑ 1041	Northern Lights/Opening Out	1979	5.00
❑ 49041	Forever Changing/Jekyll and Hyde	1979	5.00

Albums

Number	Title (A Side/B Side)	Yr	NM
CAPITOL/SOVEREIGN			
❑ SMAS-11116	Prologue	1972	15.00
❑ ST-11216	Ashes Are Burning	1973	15.00
❑ SWBC-11871 [(2)]	In the Beginning	1978	15.00
—Combines 11116 and 11216 in one package			
ELEKTRA			
❑ EKS-74068	Renaissance	1969	30.00
I.R.S.			
❑ SP-70019	Camera Camera	1981	10.00
❑ SP-70033	Time Line	1983	10.00
MOBILE FIDELITY			
❑ 1-099	Scheherazade and Other Stories	1982	50.00
—Audiophile vinyl			
SIRE			
❑ SASD-3902 [(2)]	Live at Carnegie Hall	1976	15.00
❑ SR 6015	Turn of the Cards	1977	10.00
—Reissue of 7502			
❑ SR 6017	Scheherazade and Other Stories	1977	10.00
—Reissue of 7510			
❑ SR 6024	Novella	1977	10.00
—Reissue of 7526			
❑ 2XS 6029 [(2)]	Live at Carnegie Hall	1977	12.00
—Reissue of 3902			
❑ SRK 6049	A Song for All Seasons	1978	12.00
❑ SRK 6068	Azure d'Or	1979	12.00
❑ SAS-7502	Turn of the Cards	1974	12.00
❑ SASD-7510	Scheherazade and Other Stories	1975	12.00
❑ SASD-7526	Novella	1977	12.00

RENAY, DIANE

45s

Number	Title (A Side/B Side)	Yr	NM
ATCO			
❑ 6240	Falling Star/Little White Lies	1962	12.00
❑ 6262	Dime a Dozen/Tender	1963	12.00
FONTANA			
❑ 1679	Hold Me, Thrill Me, Kiss Me/Yesterday	1969	10.00

R

Number	Title (A Side/B Side)	Yr	NM
MGM			
❑ 13296	Billy Blue Eyes/Watch Out Sally	1964	10.00
❑ 13335	I Had a Dream/Troublemaker	1965	20.00
NEW VOICE			
❑ 800	Words/The Company You Keep	1965	10.00
❑ 803	Cross My Heart, Hope to Die/ Happy Birthday, Broken Heart	1965	10.00
20TH CENTURY FOX			
❑ 456	Navy Blue/Unbelievable Boy	1964	15.00
❑ 477	Kiss Me Sailor/Soft Spoken Guy	1964	10.00
❑ 514	Growin' Up Too Fast/ Waitin' for Joey	1964	10.00
❑ 533	It's In Your Tears/ Present from Eddie	1964	10.00
UNITED ARTISTS			
❑ 50048	Dynamite/Please Gypsy	1966	15.00
Albums			
20TH CENTURY FOX			
❑ TF-3133 [M]	Navy Blue	1964	80.00
❑ TFS-4133 [S]	Navy Blue	1964	150.00

RENDEZVOUS

Number	Title (A Side/B Side)	Yr	NM
45s			
REPRISE			
❑ 20089	Congratulations Baby/Faithfully	1962	30.00
RUST			
❑ 5041	It Breaks My Heart/Take a Break	1961	40.00

RENDEZVOUS STOMPERS, THE

Number	Title (A Side/B Side)	Yr	NM
45s			
DORE			
❑ 626	Gremmies Unite/Rock Me Gently	1962	40.00

RENE, GOOGIE

Number	Title (A Side/B Side)	Yr	NM
45s			
CLASS			
❑ 201	Wham Bam/Sad Fool	1957	40.00
—B-side by the Rollettes			
❑ 205	Midnight/Big Time	1957	20.00
❑ 208	Side-Track/Break It Up	1957	20.00
❑ 212	Beautiful Weekend/ Rock-a-Boogie	1957	20.00
❑ 214	At the Break of Dawn/ Twilight Walk	1957	20.00
❑ 221	Wiggle Tail (Part 1)/(Part 2)	1958	15.00
❑ 227	Swingin' Summer Love/Shine On Harvest Moon	1958	15.00
❑ 233	Sunrise/Moonglow	1958	15.00
❑ 239	Big Foot/Rebecca	1958	15.00
❑ 248	Rock-a-Bye Baby/Skumbo	1959	15.00
❑ 258	Romesville/Caesar's Pad	1959	15.00
❑ 258	Romesville/Farewell to Rome	1959	15.00
❑ 262	Caesar's Pad/Serenade in the Night	1959	15.00
❑ 264	Ez-Zee/Forever	1960	15.00
❑ 270	Cool It at the Coliseum/ Cafe Roman Candle	1960	15.00
❑ 305	Flapjacks (Part I)/(Part II)	1962	15.00
❑ 307	Jazzberry Jam/Country Walk	1963	15.00
❑ 309	Tamba Shake/Bossa Baby	1963	15.00
❑ 310	Soul Zone/Walk Right In	1963	20.00
❑ 312	The Chiller/Young Folk	1964	20.00
❑ 702	Soul Zone '65/Wild Bird	1965	20.00
❑ 706	Cool Swimming Pool/ (B-side unknown)	1965	20.00
❑ 1515	There I Was/Vikki's Lament	1965	200.00
❑ 1517	Smokey Joe's La La/ Needing You	1966	25.00
❑ 1518	Chica-Boo/Mercy Mercy	1966	25.00
❑ 1519	Downtown/Beautiful Weekend	1966	15.00
RENDEZVOUS			
❑ 134	The Slide (Part 1)/(Part 2)	1960	20.00
❑ 134 [PS]	The Slide (Part 1)/(Part 2)	1960	30.00
❑ 144	April Is Her Name/ Little Cupid Blues	1961	15.00
❑ 157	Caesar's Pad/Ez-Zee	1961	15.00
Albums			
CLASS			
❑ LP-200 [M]	Flapjacks	1963	20.00
❑ LP-5001 [M]	Beautiful Weekend	1957	30.00
❑ LP-5003 [M]	Googie Rene Presents Romesville	1959	25.00
RENDEZVOUS			
❑ M-1311 [M]	Beautiful Weekend	196?	15.00
❑ M-1313 [M]	Romseville	196?	15.00

RENE AND RENE

Number	Title (A Side/B Side)	Yr	NM
45s			
ABC			
❑ 10699	Chantilly Lace/I'm Not the Only One (No Soy El Unico)	1965	8.00
ARV INTERNATIONAL			
❑ A-5011	Lo Mucho Que Te Quiero/Mornin'	1968	12.00
—Blue label			
❑ A-5011	Lo Mucho Que Te Quiero/Mornin'	1968	15.00
—Silver label			
❑ A-5022	Kiss Me One More Time/ Should You Ever Leave Me	196?	10.00
CERTRON			
❑ 10011	My Amigo Jose/Good Old Days	1970	5.00
COLUMBIA			
❑ 43045	Angelito/Write Me Soon	1964	8.00
❑ 43045 [PS]	Angelito/Write Me Soon	1964	12.00
❑ 4-43140	Yo Te Lo Dije (I Could Have Told You)/Pretty Flowers Fade Away	1964	8.00
❑ 43163	Please Don't Bother/ Undecided	1964	8.00
EAST BEND			
❑ 209	Really Hurtin' This Guy/ El Mexicano	196?	10.00
❑ 213	Put Me in Jail (Gastigueme Ya)/ El Bandito	196?	10.00
EPIC			
❑ 10443	Muchachita/Our Day Will Come	1969	5.00
JOX			
❑ 017	Angelito/Write Me Soon	1964	12.00
❑ 025	Pretty Flowers/Fade Away	1965	10.00
❑ 032	Chantilly Lace/I'm Not the Only One	1965	10.00
❑ 041	Little Peanuts/Little Vagabond	1965	10.00
❑ 050	Loving You Could Hurt Me So/ Little Diamonds	1966	10.00
WHITE WHALE			
❑ 281	Lo Mucho Que Te Quiero/ Lloraras	1968	6.00
❑ 287	Lo Mucho Que Te Quiero/Mornin'	1968	5.00
❑ 298	Las Cosas/You Will Cry	1969	5.00
❑ 303	Enchilada Jose/Lloraras	1969	5.00
❑ 327	Love Is for the Two of Us/ Sally Tosis	1969	5.00
Albums			
WHITE WHALE			
❑ WWS-7119	Lo Mucho Que Te Quiero	1968	15.00

RENEGADES, THE (1)

Number	Title (A Side/B Side)	Yr	NM
45s			
AMERICAN INT'L.			
❑ 537	Charge/Geronimo	1959	50.00

RENEGADES, THE (2)

Number	Title (A Side/B Side)	Yr	NM
45s			
CONGRESS			
❑ 241	Cadillac/Matelot (Sailor Boy)	1965	30.00

RENEGADES, THE (3)

Number	Title (A Side/B Side)	Yr	NM
45s			
DORSET			
❑ 5007	Stolen Angel/Keep Laughin'	1961	50.00

RENEGADES, THE (U)

If these are any of the above, they are most likely group (2).

Number	Title (A Side/B Side)	Yr	NM
45s			
GARLAND			
❑ 2036	I'm a Loner/Travelin' Through This Countryside	196?	10.00
KARATE			
❑ 519	Take a Heart/If It Gets Lonesome	1966	15.00

RENO, AL

Number	Title (A Side/B Side)	Yr	NM
45s			
KAPP			
❑ 432	Cheryl/Congratulations	1961	40.00

REO SPEEDWAGON

Number	Title (A Side/B Side)	Yr	NM
12-Inch Singles			
EPIC			
❑ AS 314 [DJ]	Ridin' the Storm Out (mono/stereo)	1977	12.00
❑ AS 1489 [DJ]	Keep the Fire Burnin' (same on both sides)	1982	10.00
❑ AS 1947 [DJ]	I Do'Wanna Know (same on both sides)	1984	10.00
❑ EAS 2091 [DJ]	Gotta Feel More (Special Album Radio Mix Long Version 5:29) (LP Version 4:26) (Special Album Radio Mix Short Version 4:17)	1985	10.00
❑ EAS 2709 [DJ]	Variety Tonight (Long Version) (Short Version)	1987	7.00
❑ EAS 2747 [DJ]	In My Dreams (same on both sides)	1987	7.00
45s			
EPIC			
❑ 19-01054	Take It on the Run/ Someone Tonight	1981	4.00
❑ 19-02127	Don't Let Him Go/ I Wish You Were There	1981	4.00
❑ 19-02127 [PS]	Don't Let Him Go/ I Wish You Were There	1981	5.00
❑ 15-02153	Keep On Loving You/ Time for Me to Fly	1981	3.00
—Reissue			
❑ 14-02457	In Your Letter/Shakin' It Loose	1981	4.00
❑ 14-02967	Keep the Fire Burnin'/ I'll Follow You	1982	4.00
❑ 14-03175	Sweet Time/Stillness of the Night	1982	4.00
❑ 14-03175 [PS]	Sweet Time/Stillness of the Night	1982	5.00
❑ ENR-03264	Sweet Time/(B-side blank)	1982	5.00
—One-sided budget release			
❑ 34-03400	The Key/Let's Be-Bop	1982	4.00
❑ 15-03846	Keep the Fire Burnin'/ Take It on the Run	1983	3.00
—Reissue			
❑ 15-03847	In Your Letter/Don't Let Him Go	1983	3.00
—Reissue			
❑ 34-04659	I Do'Wanna Know/ Rock 'N Roll Star	1984	3.00
❑ 34-04659 [PS]	I Do'Wanna Know/ Rock 'N Roll Star	1984	4.00
❑ 34-04713	Can't Fight This Feeling/ Break His Spell	1984	3.00
❑ 34-04713 [PS]	Can't Fight This Feeling /Break His Spell	1984	6.00
❑ 34-04848	One Lonely Night/ Wheels Are Turnin'	1985	3.00
❑ 34-04848 [PS]	One Lonely Night/ Wheels Are Turnin'	1985	4.00
❑ 34-05412	Live Every Moment/ Gotta Feel More	1985	3.00
❑ 34-06656	That Ain't Love/ Accidents Can Happen	1987	3.00
❑ 34-06656 [PS]	That Ain't Love/ Accidents Can Happen	1987	3.00
❑ 34-07055	Variety Tonight/ Tired of Gettin' Nowhere	1987	3.00
❑ 34-07055 [DJ]	Variety Tonight (Long Version)/ (Short Version)	1987	4.00
❑ 34-07055 [PS]	Variety Tonight/ Tired of Gettin' Nowhere	1987	3.00
❑ 34-07255	In My Dreams/Over the Edge	1987	3.00
❑ 34-07255 [PS]	In My Dreams/Over the Edge	1987	3.00
❑ 34-07901	Here with Me/Wherever You're Goin' (It's Alright)	1988	3.00
❑ 34-07901 [DJ]	Here with Me (4:29)/(4:53)	1988	4.00
❑ 34-07901 [PS]	Here with Me/Wherever You're Goin' (It's Alright)	1988	3.00
❑ 34-08030	I Don't Want to Lose You/ On the Road Again	1988	3.00
❑ 5-10827	Sophisticated Lady/ Prison Women	1972	15.00
❑ 5-10827 [DJ]	Sophisticated Lady (stereo/mono)	1972	6.00
❑ 5-10847	157 Riverside Avenue/Five Men Were Killed Today	1972	15.00
❑ 5-10847 [DJ]	157 Riverside Avenue (stereo/mono)	1972	8.00
❑ 5-10892	Lay Me Down/Gypsy Woman's Passion	1972	15.00
❑ 5-10892 [DJ]	Lay Me Down (stereo/mono)	1972	8.00
❑ 5-10975	Little Queenie/Golden Country	1973	15.00
❑ 5-10975 [DJ]	Little Queenie (stereo/mono)	1973	8.00
❑ 5-11078	Ridin' the Storm Out/ Whiskey Night	1974	15.00
❑ 5-11078 [DJ]	Ridin' the Storm Out (stereo/mono)	1974	8.00
❑ 5-11132	Open Up/Start a New Life	1974	12.00
❑ 5-11132 [DJ]	Open Up (stereo/mono)	1974	6.00
❑ 8-50059	Throw the Chains Away/ Sky Blues	1975	8.00
❑ 8-50120	Out of Control/Running Blind	1975	8.00
❑ 8-50180	Reelin'/Headed for a Fall	1975	8.00
❑ 8-50254	Keep Pushin'/Tonight	1976	8.00
❑ 8-50288	Keep Pushin'/Flying Turkey Trot	1976	8.00
❑ 8-50367	Ridin' the Storm Out/Being Kind	1977	8.00
❑ 8-50459	Keep Pushin'/Flying Turkey Trot	1977	7.00
❑ 8-50545	Roll with the Changes/The Unidentified Flying Tuna Trot	1978	6.00
❑ 8-50582	Time for Me to Fly/Runnin' Blind	1978	6.00
❑ 9-50764	Easy Money/I Need You Tonight	1979	6.00
❑ 9-50790	Only the Strong Survive/ Drop It (An Old Disguise)	1979	6.00
❑ 9-50858	Time for Me to Fly/Lightning	1980	5.00
❑ 19-50953	Keep On Loving You/ Follow My Heart	1980	4.00
❑ 19-51006	Take It on the Run/ Someone Tonight	1981	—
—Unreleased; reassigned to 19-01054			
❑ 34-73499	Live It Up/All Heaven Broke Loose	1990	4.00
❑ 34-73540	Love Is a Rock/Go for Broke	1990	4.00

Except when noted otherwise, VG = 25% of NM, and VG+ = 50% of NM. (Example: VG = $2.00, VG+ = $4.00 and NM = $8.00.)

Number	Title (A Side/B Side)	Yr	NM
Albums			
EPIC			
❑ E 31089	REO Speedwagon	1972	15.00
—Yellow label original			
❑ KE 31089	REO Speedwagon	1973	12.00
—Orange label			
❑ PE 31089	REO Speedwagon	1979	8.00
—Dark blue label			
❑ KE 31745	R.E.O./T.W.O.	1972	15.00
—Yellow label original			
❑ KE 31745	R.E.O./T.W.O.	1973	12.00
—Orange label			
❑ PE 31745	R.E.O./T.W.O.	1979	8.00
—Dark blue label			
❑ KE 32378	Ridin' the Storm Out	1973	12.00
—Orange label			
❑ PE 32378	Ridin' the Storm Out	1979	8.00
—Dark blue label			
❑ PE 32948	Lost in a Dream	1974	12.00
—Orange label			
❑ PE 32948	Lost in a Dream	1979	8.00
—Dark blue label			
❑ PEQ 32948 [Q]	Lost in a Dream	1974	20.00
❑ PE 33338	This Time We Mean It	1975	12.00
—Orange label			
❑ PE 33338	This Time We Mean It	1979	8.00
—Dark blue label			
❑ PEQ 33338 [Q]	This Time We Mean It	1975	20.00
❑ PE 34143	R.E.O.	1976	12.00
—Orange label			
❑ PE 34143	R.E.O.	1979	8.00
—Dark blue label			
❑ PEG 34494 [(2)]	REO Speedwagon Live/You Get What You Play For	1977	15.00
—Orange labels			
❑ PEG 34494 [(2)]	REO Speedwagon Live/You Get What You Play For	1979	12.00
—Dark blue labels			
❑ JE 35082	You Can Tune a Piano, But You Can't Tuna Fish	1978	10.00
—Orange label; with bar code on back cover			
❑ JE 35082	You Can Tune a Piano, But You Can't Tuna Fish	1978	12.00
—Orange label; no bar code on back cover			
❑ JE 35082	You Can Tune a Piano, But You Can't Tuna Fish	1979	8.00
—Dark blue label			
❑ PE 35082	You Can Tune a Piano, But You Can't Tuna Fish	198?	8.00
❑ FE 35988	Nine Lives	1979	10.00
❑ PE 35988	Nine Lives	198?	8.00
—Budget-line reissue			
❑ KE2 36444 [(2)]	A Decade of Rock and Roll 1970 to 1980	1980	12.00
❑ FE 36844	Hi Infidelity	1980	8.00
❑ FE 38100	Good Trouble	1982	10.00
❑ PE 38100	Good Trouble	198?	8.00
—Budget-line reissue			
❑ QE 39593	Wheels Are Turnin'	1984	8.00
❑ FE 40444	Life As We Know It	1987	8.00
❑ OE 44202	The Hits	1988	10.00
❑ HE 45082	You Can Tune a Piano, But You Can't Tuna Fish	198?	40.00
—Half-speed mastered edition			
❑ E 45246	The Earth, a Small Man, His Dog and a Chicken	1990	12.00
❑ HE 46844	Hi Infidelity	1982	30.00
—Half-speed mastered edition			
❑ HE 48100	Good Trouble	1982	30.00
—Half-speed mastered edition			

REPARATA AND THE DELRONS

Number	Title (A Side/B Side)	Yr	NM
45s			
BIG TREE			
❑ 114	Just You/There's So Little Time	1971	5.00
KAPP			
❑ 989	(That's What Sends Men to) The Bowery/I've Got an Awful Lot of Losing to Do	1969	6.00
❑ 2010	San Juan/We're Gonna Hold the Night	1969	6.00
❑ 2050	Waking in the Rain/ Got Fear of Losing You	1969	6.00
LAURIE			
❑ 3252	Your Big Mistake/Leave Us Alone	1964	30.00
—As "The Delrons"			
❑ 3589	Octopus' Garden/ Your Life Is Gone	1972	5.00
—As "Reparata"			
MALA			
❑ 573	I Believe/It's Waiting There for You	1967	6.00
❑ 589	Captain of Your Ship/Toom Toom Is a Little Boy	1968	12.00
❑ 12000	Saturday Night Didn't Happen/ Panic	1968	6.00
❑ 12016	You Can't Change a Young Boy's Mind/Weather Forecast	1968	6.00
❑ 12026	Heaven Only Knows/ Summer Laughter	1968	6.00
NAMI			
❑ N-2024	Whenever a Teenager Cries/ Whenever a Teenager Cries	1974	6.00
—Remake			
POLYDOR			
❑ 14271	Shoes/Song for All	1975	4.00
—As "Reparata"			
❑ 14298	Jezebee Lancer the Belly Dancer/We Need You	1975	—
—Unreleased			
RCA VICTOR			
❑ 47-8721	I Can Tell/Take a Look Around You	1965	10.00
❑ 47-8820	I'm Nobody's Baby Now/ The Loneliest Girl in Town	1966	15.00
❑ 47-8921	Mama's Little Girl/He Don't Want You	1966	10.00
❑ 47-9123	Boys and Girls/That Kind of Trouble That I Love	1967	10.00
❑ 47-9185	I Can Hear the Rain/ Always Waitin'	1967	10.00
WORLD ARTISTS			
❑ 1036	Whenever a Teenager Cries/ He's My Guy	1964	12.00
❑ 1051	Tommy/Mama Don't Allow	1965	12.00
❑ 1057	He's the Greatest/ A Summer Thought	1965	12.00
❑ 1062	The Boy I Love/I Found My Place	1965	12.00
Albums			
AVCO EMBASSY			
❑ AVE-33008	Rock and Roll Revolution	1970	25.00
WORLD ARTISTS			
❑ WAM-2006 [M]	Whenever a Teenager Cries	1965	50.00
❑ WAS-3006 [S]	Whenever a Teenager Cries	1965	60.00

The Replacements, *Tim*, Sire 25330, 1985, **$12.**

REPLACEMENTS, THE Featuring PAUL WESTERBERG.

Number	Title (A Side/B Side)	Yr	NM
12-Inch Singles			
SIRE			
❑ PRO-A-2412 [DJ]	Kiss Me on the Bus (same on both sides)	1985	15.00
❑ PRO-A-2727 [DJ]	The Ledge (same on both sides)	1987	8.00
❑ PRO-A-2761 [DJ]	Alex Chilton (same on both sides)	1987	15.00
❑ PRO-A-2863 [DJ]	Can't Hardly Wait (Remix) (LP Version)	1987	12.00
❑ PRO-A-3419 [DJ]	I'll Be You (same on both sides)	1989	12.00
TWIN/TONE			
❑ TTR 8440	I Will Dare/20th Century Boy/ Hey Good Lookin' (Live)	1984	20.00
45s			
SIRE			
❑ 7-22992	I'll Be You/Date to Church	1989	4.00
❑ 7-22992 [PS]	I'll Be You/Date to Church	1989	7.00
❑ 7-28151	Can't Hardly Wait/Cool Water	1987	5.00
❑ 7-28151 [PS]	Can't Hardly Wait/Cool Water	1987	9.00
TWIN/TONE			
❑ TTR 8120	I'm in Trouble/If Only You Were Lonely	1981	40.00
❑ TTR 8120 [PS]	I'm in Trouble/If Only You Were Lonely	1981	40.00
Albums			
RHINO			
❑ 25330	Tim	2008	18.00
❑ 25557	Pleased to Meet Me	2008	18.00

Number | Title (A Side/B Side) | Yr | NM

SIRE
❑ PRO-A-3633 [DJ] Live Inconcerated 1989 50.00
—Five live tracks and one studio track, each of which is repeated on the other side
❑ PRO-A-4632 [DJ] Don't Sell Or Buy...It's Crap 1991 25.00
—Promo-only 5-track sampler
❑ 25330 Tim 1985 12.00
❑ 25557 Pleased to Meet Me 1987 12.00
❑ 25831 Don't Tell a Soul 1989 12.00
❑ R 101024 Don't Tell a Soul 1989 15.00
—BMG Music Service edition

TWIN/TONE
❑ TTR 8123 Sorry, Ma, Forgot to Take Out the Trash 1981 25.00
❑ TTR 8228 [EP] The Replacements Stink 1982 25.00
❑ TTR 8332 Hootenanny 1983 20.00
❑ TTR 8441 Let It Be 1984 20.00

WARNER BROS.
❑ WBMS-148 [DJ] An Interview with Paul Westerberg 1987 40.00
—Part of "The Warner Bros. Music Show" promotional series

REPRISE REPERTORY THEATRE, THE Artists who were signed to Reprise Records at the time, including ROSEMARY CLOONEY, BING CROSBY, SAMMY DAVIS, JR., DEAN MARTIN, FRANK SINATRA and JO STAFFORD, perform new versions of famous musicals under this collective name.

Albums

REPRISE
❑ F-2015 [M] Finian's Rainbow 196? 20.00
—Standard cover
❑ F-2015 [M] Finian's Rainbow 1964 30.00
—Gatefold cover
❑ FS-2015 [S] Finian's Rainbow 196? 25.00
—Standard cover
❑ FS-2015 [S] Finian's Rainbow 1964 40.00
—Gatefold cover
❑ F-2016 [M] Guys and Dolls 196? 20.00
—Standard cover
❑ F-2016 [M] Guys and Dolls 1964 30.00
—Gatefold cover
❑ FS-2016 [S] Guys and Dolls 196? 25.00
—Standard cover
❑ FS-2016 [S] Guys and Dolls 1964 40.00
—Gatefold cover
❑ F-2017 [M] Kiss Me, Kate 196? 20.00
—Standard cover
❑ F-2017 [M] Kiss Me, Kate 1964 30.00
—Gatefold cover
❑ FS-2017 [S] Kiss Me, Kate 196? 25.00
—Standard cover
❑ FS-2017 [S] Kiss Me, Kate 1964 40.00
—Gatefold cover
❑ F-2018 [M] South Pacific 196? 20.00
—Standard cover
❑ F-2018 [M] South Pacific 1964 30.00
—Gatefold cover
❑ FS-2018 [S] South Pacific 196? 25.00
—Standard cover
❑ FS-2018 [S] South Pacific 1964 40.00
—Gatefold cover
❑ F-2019 [(4)M] The Reprise Repertory Theatre 1964 200.00
—Box set of all four of the above LPs in gatefold covers
❑ FS-2019 [(4)S] The Reprise Repertory Theatre 1964 300.00
—Box set of all four of the above LPs in gatefold covers

RESIDENTS, THE

12-Inch Singles

RALPH
❑ RZ 8006-D Diskomo/Goosebump 1980 10.00
❑ RZ 8006-D Diskomo/Goosebump 1980 20.00
—Green vinyl
❑ RR 8721 Hit the Road Jack (Dance Mix)/Jambalaya-Firefly-The Big Bubble-Cry for the Fire 1987 8.00

45s

CRYPTIC
❑ RZ-SP-1SP 1 Earth Vs. the Flying Saucers 1986 20.00
—Green vinyl, one-sided, bonus with collector's edition of book "The Cryptic Guide to the Residents"

EVA-TONE
❑ 10371900-1 Diskomo (Live) 1988 5.00
—Flexi-disc included with April 1988 issue of Reflex

RALPH
❑ RR 0577 Beyond the Valley of A Day in the Life/Flying 1977 150.00
❑ RR 0577 [PS] Beyond the Valley of A Day in the Life/Flying 1977 150.00
—Also known as "The Residents Meet the Beatles and The Beatles Meet the Residents"
❑ RR 0776 Satisfaction/Loser Is Congruent to Weed 1976 150.00
❑ RR 0776 [PS] Satisfaction/Loser Is Congruent to Weed 1976 150.00
❑ RR 1272 Fire/Aircraft Damage 1972 200.00
—Part of "Santa Dog" two-7" single set
❑ RR 1272 Lightning/Explosion 1972 200.00
—Part of "Santa Dog" two-7" single set
❑ RR 1272 [PS] Santa Dog: Fire/Aircraft Damage; Lightning/Explosion 1972 600.00
—Signed, intentionally misnumbered sleeve for above two records
❑ RR 7803 Satisfaction/Loser Is Congruent to Weed 1978 4.00
❑ RR 7803 [PS] Satisfaction/Loser Is Congruent to Weed 1978 4.00
❑ RR 7812 Santa Dog '78/Fire 1978 20.00
❑ RR 7812 [PS] Santa Dog '78/Fire 1978 20.00
❑ RZ 8422 It's a Man's Man's Man's World/Safety Is a Cootie Wootie 1984 5.00
—Black vinyl
❑ RZ 8422 It's a Man's Man's Man's World/Safety Is a Cootie Wootie 1984 15.00
—White vinyl; blue "iris" label and plastic sleeve with red lines; corrected labels
❑ RZ 8422 It's a Man's Man's Man's World/Safety Is a Cootie Wootie 1984 20.00
—White vinyl; blue "iris" label and plastic sleeve with red lines; labels reversed
❑ RZ 8422 [PS] It's a Man's Man's Man's World/Safety Is a Cootie Wootie 1984 5.00
—Sleeve with black vinyl edition
❑ RZ 8621 Kaw-Liga/Stars and Stripes Forever 1986 15.00
—Picture disc
❑ RZ 8622 Kaw-Liga/Stars and Stripes Forever 1986 3.00
❑ RZ 8622 Kaw-Liga/Stars and Stripes Forever 1986 10.00
—White vinyl
❑ RZ 8622 [PS] Kaw-Liga/Stars and Stripes Forever 1986 3.00
❑ RR 8721 [PD] Hit the Road Jack/For Elsie (Excerpt) 1987 15.00
—Picture disc
❑ RR 8722 Hit the Road Jack/For Elsie (Excerpt) 1987 3.00
❑ RR 8722 [PS] Hit the Road Jack/For Elsie (Excerpt) 1987 3.00

7-Inch Extended Plays

RALPH
❑ WEIRD 1 Babyfingers 1981 20.00
—Pink vinyl on labels left over from fan club issue
❑ WEIRD 1 [PS] Babyfingers 1981 20.00
❑ RR 0377 *Monstrous Intro/Death in Barstow/Melon Collie Lassie/Flight of the Bumble Roach/Walter Westinghouse 1979 100.00
—Also known as "Babyfingers"; first edition not issued with picture sleeve
❑ RR 0377 *Monstrous Intro/Death in Barstow/Melon Collie Lassie/Flight of the Bumble Roach/Walter Westinghouse 1979 200.00
—Label hand-decorated with felt-tip pens
❑ RR 0377 [PS] Babyfingers 1979 200.00
—Actually a modified "Santa Dog '78" sleeve; this was sent with the felt-tip decorated copies to 10 people who had been waiting two years for a limited-edition copy of "The Third Reich 'n' Roll" LP
❑ RR 1177 *Laughing Song/Blue Rosebuds/Constantinople/The Booker Tease/Sinister Exaggerator/Bach Is Dead/Elvis and His Boss 1978 8.00
—Red label
❑ RR 1177 [PS] Duck Stab 1978 5.00
—Matte cover
❑ RR 1177 [PS] Duck Stab 1978 45.00
—Shiny cover

W.E.I.R.D.
❑ WEIRD 1 Babyfingers 1981 20.00
—Fan club reissue
❑ WEIRD 1 [PS] Babyfingers 1981 20.00

Albums

CRYPTIC
❑ S-18335 SP-2 For Elsie 1987 100.00
—Green vinyl one-sided LP

ENIGMA
❑ 73547 The King & Eye 1989 15.00

EPISODE
❑ ED 21 The Census Taker (Soundtrack) 1985 20.00
❑ ED 21 The Census Taker (Soundtrack) 1985 80.00
—Red vinyl

RALPH
❑ Mole Show 001 The Mole Show (The Roxy) 1983 30.00
❑ C-002A The Mole Show (The Roxy) 1983 40.00
—Picture disc
❑ OP-011 [DJ] Freak Show 1991 80.00
—Promo-only black vinyl pressing; 400 made
❑ OP-011 [PD] Freak Show 1991 40.00
—Picture disc
❑ RR 0274 Meet the Residents 1974 200.00
—First version: "Meet the Beatles" LP parody cover and "First Edition" on back cover
❑ RR 0278 Duck Stab 1978 10.00
—Second version: Yellow titles box on back
❑ RR 0278 Duck Stab 1978 12.00
—First version: Green titles box on back
❑ RR 0677 Meet the Residents 1977 12.00
—Fourth version: same cover as second version, modified and orange back cover
❑ RR 0677 Meet the Residents 1977 15.00
—Third version: same cover as second version, black "a" Ralph logo
❑ RR 0677 Meet the Residents 1977 20.00
—Second version: "She Loves You" picture sleeve parody cover, split "a" Ralph logo
❑ RR 1075 The Third Reich 'N' Roll 1976 10.00
—Fourth version: Gray carrot, black "a" Ralph logo
❑ RR 1075 The Third Reich 'N' Roll 1976 12.00
—Third version: Orange carrot, black "a" Ralph logo
❑ RR 1075 The Third Reich 'N' Roll 1976 15.00
—Second version: Gray carrot, split "a" Ralph logo
❑ RR 1075 The Third Reich 'N' Roll 1976 50.00
—Censored cover with swastikas obscured, pressed in U.S. for export to Germany
❑ RR 1075 The Third Reich 'N' Roll 1976 50.00
—First version of 1,000: Liner notes inside, orange carrot
❑ RR 1075 The Third Reich 'N' Roll 1976 1500.
—Numbered box set on marbled vinyl, silkscreened cover and lithographs inside
❑ RR 1174 Not Available 1978 10.00
—Green label, address is "109 Minna"
❑ RR 1174 Not Available 1978 12.00
—Green label, address is "444 Grove"
❑ RR 1174 Not Available 1978 15.00
—Orange label, remastered, "Re-3" in trail-off vinyl
❑ RR 1174 Not Available 1978 25.00
—Purple label, mis-mastered, "Re-1" in trail-off vinyl
❑ RR 1276 Fingerprince 1977 10.00
—Third version: Color cover
❑ RR 1276 Fingerprince 1977 20.00
—Second version: Lighter brown cover
❑ RR 1276 Fingerprince 1977 80.00
—First version: Dark brown cover, "First Pressing" written on back cover
❑ RZ 7707 [PD] Meet the Residents 1986 30.00
—Picture disc, with original cover on one side, replacement cover on other
❑ DJ 7901 [DJ] Please Do Not Steal It! 1979 40.00
—Promo-only sampler
❑ ESK 7906 Eskimo 1979 10.00
—Third version: Black vinyl, standard cover
❑ ESK 7906 Eskimo 1979 15.00
—Second version: Black vinyl, gatefold
❑ ESK 7906 Eskimo 1979 25.00
—First version: White vinyl, gatefold cover
❑ RZ 7906 [PD] Eskimo 1979 30.00
—Picture disc
❑ RZ 8052 The Residents Commercial Album 1980 12.00
—Third version: Green vinyl
❑ RZ 8052 The Residents Commercial Album 1980 15.00
—Second version: Corrected song order, green logo
❑ RZ 8052 The Residents Commercial Album 1980 20.00
—First version: Purple Ralph logo, songs listed in wrong order
❑ RZ 8152 Mark of the Mole 1981 10.00
❑ RZ 8152 Mark of the Mole 1981 50.00
—Signed brown vinyl edition with lyrics
❑ RZ 8202 The Tunes of Two Cities 1982 10.00
—Second edition: "109 Minna Street" address
❑ RZ 8202 The Tunes of Two Cities 1982 12.00
—First edition: "444 Grove Street" address
❑ RZ 8252 Intermission 1982 12.00
❑ RZ 8252 Intermission 1982 14.00
—Red vinyl
❑ RZ 8302 Residue 1983 12.00
❑ RR 8315 Title in Limbo 1983 12.00
—With Renaldo and The Loaf
❑ RZ 8402 George & James 1984 10.00
—Second edition: Approved mix with "Re-5" in trail-off
❑ RZ 8402 George & James 1984 30.00
—First edition: Rejected mix with "Re-1" in trail-off
❑ RZ 8402 George & James 1984 50.00
—"Re-5" in trail-off, clear vinyl
❑ RZ 8452 Whatever Happened to Vileness Fats? 1984 12.00
❑ RZ 8452 Whatever Happened to Vileness Fats? 1984 80.00
—Red vinyl
❑ RZ 8552 The Big Bubble 1985 12.00
❑ RZ 8552 The Big Bubble 1985 80.00
—Pink vinyl
❑ RZ 8602 The Eyeball Show (The 13th Anniversary Show) Live in Japan 1986 10.00
❑ RZ 8602 The Eyeball Show (The 13th Anniversary Show) Live in Japan 1986 80.00
—White vinyl
❑ RZ 8652 Stars & Hank Forever 1986 10.00

R

Number	Title (A Side/B Side)	Yr	NM
RZ 8652	Stars & Hank Forever	1986	40.00
—Blue vinyl			
RR 82761	Fingerprince	1988	10.00
—New number, black vinyl			
RR 82761	Fingerprince	1988	12.00
—New number, purple vinyl			
RR 87521	Duck Stab	1988	10.00
—New number, black vinyl			
RR 87521	Duck Stab	1988	12.00
—New number, red vinyl			
RR 88521	Meet the Residents	1988	12.00
—Original "Meet the Beatles" parody cover restored, black vinyl			
RR 88521	Meet the Residents	1988	15.00
—Original "Meet the Beatles" parody cover restored, white vinyl			

RYKO ANALOGUE

Number	Title (A Side/B Side)	Yr	NM
RALP-0044-2 [(2)]	God in Three Persons	1988	20.00
—Clear vinyl			
RALP-0045-2	God in Three Persons Instrumental	1988	15.00
—Clear vinyl			

UWEB

Number	Title (A Side/B Side)	Yr	NM
0011	Stranger Than Supper	1990	25.00
—Fan club issue			

RESTIVO, JOHNNY

45s

CAMEO

Number	Title (A Side/B Side)	Yr	NM
416	I'm Just a Boy (Looking for a Girl)/Suzanne	1966	20.00

EPIC

Number	Title (A Side/B Side)	Yr	NM
9537	My Reputation/You Can't Turn Back the Clock	1962	15.00

RCA VICTOR

Number	Title (A Side/B Side)	Yr	NM
47-7559 [M]	The Shape I'm In/Ya Ya	1959	20.00
47-7559 [PS]	The Shape I'm In/Ya Ya	1959	50.00
47-7601	Dear Someone/I Like Girls	1959	15.00
47-7601 [PS]	Dear Someone/I Like Girls	1959	30.00
47-7636	Our Wedding Day/Come Closer	1959	20.00
47-7697	High School Play/But I Love You	1960	15.00
47-7758	That's Good That's Bad/I Can't Take It	1960	15.00
47-7818	Two Crazy Kids/Give Me a Little Whistle (And I'll Be There)	1960	15.00
61-7559 [S]	The Shape I'm In/Ya Ya	1959	50.00
—"Living Stereo" issue with large hole			

20TH FOX

Number	Title (A Side/B Side)	Yr	NM
260	Sweet Lovin'/Looka Here Now	1961	15.00
279	Doctor Love/The Magic Age Is Seventeen	1961	15.00
279 [PS]	Doctor Love/The Magic Age Is Seventeen	1961	30.00

Albums

RCA VICTOR

Number	Title (A Side/B Side)	Yr	NM
LPM-2149 [M]	Oh, Johnny!	1959	60.00
LSP-2149 [S]	Oh, Johnny!	1959	100.00

RETURN TO FOREVER

Also see CHICK COREA.

45s

COLUMBIA

Number	Title (A Side/B Side)	Yr	NM
10497	Musicmagic/When Love Is New	1977	4.00

POLYDOR

Number	Title (A Side/B Side)	Yr	NM
15067	Spain/Captain Marvel	1973	6.00
—As "Chick Corea and Return to Forever"			
15094	Earth Juice/Beyond the Seventh Galaxy	1974	5.00
—As "Chick Corea and Return to Forever"			
15099	An Excerpt from the First Movement of Heavy Metal/Jungle Waterfall	1975	5.00
—As "Chick Corea and Return to Forever"			

Albums

COLUMBIA

Number	Title (A Side/B Side)	Yr	NM
PC 34076	Romantic Warrior	1976	12.00
—No bar code on cover			
PC 34076	Romantic Warrior	198?	8.00
—Reissue with bar code			
PC 34682	Musicmagic	1977	12.00
—No bar code on cover			
PC 34682	Musicmagic	1985	8.00
—Reissue with bar code			
PCQ 34682 [Q]	Musicmagic	1977	20.00
JC 35281	Return to Forever Live	1979	10.00
JC 36359	The Best of Return to Forever	1980	12.00
PC 36359	The Best of Return to Forever	198?	10.00
—Budget-line reissue with new prefix			

ECM

Number	Title (A Side/B Side)	Yr	NM
1022 ST	Return to Forever	197?	15.00
—Original issue; made in Germany?			
ECM-1-1022	Return to Forever	197?	12.00
—Distributed by Polydor			

POLYDOR

Number	Title (A Side/B Side)	Yr	NM
PD-5525	Light as a Feather	1973	12.00
PD-5536	Hymn of the Seventh Galaxy	1973	12.00
PD-6509	Where Have I Known You Before	1974	12.00
PD-6512	No Mystery	1975	12.00
825336-1	Hymn of the Seventh Galaxy	198?	8.00
—Reissue			

REUNION

45s

A&M

Number	Title (A Side/B Side)	Yr	NM
1308	City Song/No Good Alone	1971	4.00

BELL

Number	Title (A Side/B Side)	Yr	NM
45222	Smile (Theme from Modern Times)/Turn Back the Hands of Time (Gotta Have You Back)	1972	4.00
45287	Living Together, Growing Together/Just Say Goodbye	1974	4.00

RCA VICTOR

Number	Title (A Side/B Side)	Yr	NM
PB-10056	Life Is a Rock (But the Radio Rolled Me)/Are You Ready to Believe	1974	5.00
PB-10150	Disco-Tekin/Goodstuff	1975	4.00
PB-10252	They Don't Make 'Em Like That Anymore/Goodstuff	1975	4.00
GB-10491	Life Is a Rock (But the Radio Rolled Me)/Are You Ready to Believe	1975	3.00
—Gold Standard Series			

REV-LONS, THE

45s

GARPAX

Number	Title (A Side/B Side)	Yr	NM
44168	Boy Trouble/Give Me One More Chance	1962	15.00

REPRISE

Number	Title (A Side/B Side)	Yr	NM
0251	After Last Night/It's Gonna Happen Someday	1964	12.00
20200	I Can't Forget About You/Love Can't Be a One-Way Deal	1963	12.00

REVALONS, THE

45s

PET

Number	Title (A Side/B Side)	Yr	NM
802	Dreams Are for Fools/This Is the Moment	1958	120.00

REVELLS, THE

Albums

REPRISE

Number	Title (A Side/B Side)	Yr	NM
R-6160 [M]	The Go Sound of the Slots	1965	150.00
RS-6160 [S]	The Go Sound of the Slots	1965	200.00

REVELS, THE (1)

45s

NORGOLDE

Number	Title (A Side/B Side)	Yr	NM
103	Midnight Stroll/Talking to My Heart	1959	25.00
—Same A-side as above, but with revised title			
103	Dead Man's Stroll/Talking to My Heart	1959	120.00
104	Tweedlee Dee/Foo Man Choo	1959	20.00

REVELS, THE (2)

45s

CT

Number	Title (A Side/B Side)	Yr	NM
1	Church Key/Vesuvius	1960	100.00

DOWNEY

Number	Title (A Side/B Side)	Yr	NM
123	Intoxica/Comanche	1964	25.00

IMPACT

Number	Title (A Side/B Side)	Yr	NM
1	Church Key/Vesuvius	1960	25.00
—Black vinyl			
1	Church Key/Vesuvius	1960	50.00
—Red vinyl			
3	Intoxica/Tequila	1961	25.00
7	Comanche/Rampage	1961	25.00
—Black vinyl			
7	Comanche/Rampage	1961	50.00
—Yellow vinyl			
13	Party Time/Soft Top	1961	25.00
22	Conga Twist/Revellion	1962	25.00
—Black vinyl			
22	The Monkey Bird/Revellion	1962	25.00
—Black vinyl			
22	Conga Twist/Revellion	1962	50.00
—Yellow vinyl; Both A-sides of Impact 22 are the same song			
22	The Monkey Bird/Revellion	1962	50.00
—Yellow vinyl			

LYNN

Number	Title (A Side/B Side)	Yr	NM
1302	Six Pak/Good Grief	1960	60.00

SWINGIN'

Number	Title (A Side/B Side)	Yr	NM
620	Six Pak/Good Grief	1960	40.00

WESTCO

Number	Title (A Side/B Side)	Yr	NM
3/4	Party Time/Soft Top	1963	50.00
—Red and yellow vinyl			

Albums

IMPACT

Number	Title (A Side/B Side)	Yr	NM
LPM-1 [M]	Revels on a Rampage	1964	500.00

SUNDAZED

Number	Title (A Side/B Side)	Yr	NM
LP 5010	Intoxica! The Best of the Revels	1994	10.00

REVELS, THE (3)

45s

DIAMOND

Number	Title (A Side/B Side)	Yr	NM
143	Lots of Luck/Gonna Have Some Fun	1963	15.00

REVELS, THE (4)

45s

JAMIE

Number	Title (A Side/B Side)	Yr	NM
1318	True Love/Everybody Can Do the New Dog But Me	1966	10.00

REVELS, THE (U)

It's doubtful that any of these are group (2), and they probably aren't group (1), either. Group (3) and (4) are not out of the question, though.

45s

ANDIE

Number	Title (A Side/B Side)	Yr	NM
5077	Please/Two Little Monkeys (In a Banana Tree)	1960	20.00

KAPP

Number	Title (A Side/B Side)	Yr	NM
621	Downtown/Dollar Sign	1964	30.00

PALETTE

Number	Title (A Side/B Side)	Yr	NM
5074	O How I Love You/I Met My Lost Love	1961	20.00

REVENGERS, THE

45s

MGM

Number	Title (A Side/B Side)	Yr	NM
13465	Batman Theme/Back Side Blues	1966	12.00

Albums

METRO

Number	Title (A Side/B Side)	Yr	NM
M-565 [M]	Batman and Other Supermen	1966	30.00
MS-565 [S]	Batman and Other Supermen	1966	40.00

REVERE, PAUL, AND THE RAIDERS

Includes records as "Raiders" in the early 1970s. Also see MARK LINDSAY; JIM VALLEY; FREDDY WELLER.

45s

COLUMBIA

Number	Title (A Side/B Side)	Yr	NM
CSP-262	SS 396/Corvair Baby	1965	25.00
CSM-466	SS 396/Camaro	1967	25.00
—B-side by The Cyrkle			
CSM-466 [PS]	SS 396/Camaro	1967	50.00
—B-side by The Cyrkle			
10126	Gonna Have a Good Time/Your Love (Is the Only Love)	1975	10.00
42814	Louie Louie/Night Train	1963	40.00
43008	Louie Go Home/Have Love Will Travel	1964	15.00
43114	Over You/Swim	1964	15.00
43273	Ooh Poo Pah Doo/Sometimes	1965	15.00
43375	Steppin' Out/Blue Fox	1965	10.00
43375 [DJ]	Steppin' Out (same on both sides)	1965	50.00
—Red vinyl promo			
43461	Just Like Me/B.F.R.D.F. Blues	1965	10.00
43461 [DJ]	Just Like Me (same on both sides)	1965	50.00
—Red vinyl promo			
43556	Kicks/Shake It Up	1966	10.00
43556 [DJ]	Kicks (same on both sides)	1966	50.00
—Red vinyl promo			
43678	Hungry/There She Goes	1966	10.00
43678 [DJ]	Hungry (same on both sides)	1966	50.00
—Red vinyl promo			
43678 [PS]	Hungry/There She Goes	1966	20.00
43810	The Great Airplane Strike/In My Community	1966	10.00
43810 [DJ]	The Great Airplane Strike (same on both sides)	1966	50.00
—Red vinyl promo			
43810 [PS]	The Great Airplane Strike/In My Community	1966	15.00
43907	Good Thing/Undecided Man	1966	10.00
43907 [PS]	Good Thing/Undecided Man	1966	20.00
44018	Ups and Downs/Leslie	1967	10.00
44018 [PS]	Ups and Downs/Leslie	1967	15.00
44094	Him or Me — What's It Gonna Be?/Legend of Paul Revere	1967	10.00
44094 [PS]	Him or Me — What's It Gonna Be?/Legend of Paul Revere	1967	15.00
44227	I Had a Dream/Upon Your Leaving	1967	8.00
44227 [PS]	I Had a Dream/Upon Your Leaving	1967	10.00
44335	Peace of Mind/Do Unto Others	1967	8.00
44335 [PS]	Peace of Mind/Do Unto Others	1967	10.00

Number	Title (A Side/B Side)	Yr	NM
❑ 44376	Rain, Sleet or Snow/Brotherly Love	1967	—
—Canceled			
❑ 44444	Too Much Talk/Happening '68	1968	8.00
❑ 44444 [PS]	Too Much Talk/Happening '68	1968	10.00
❑ 44553	Don't Take It Too Hard/Observation from Flight 285 (In 3/4 Time)	1968	6.00
❑ 44553 [PS]	Don't Take It Too Hard/Observation from Flight 285 (In 3/4 Time)	1968	10.00
❑ 44655	Cinderella Sunshine/It's Happening	1968	8.00
❑ 44744	Mr. Sun, Mr. Moon/Without You	1969	6.00
❑ 44744 [PS]	Mr. Sun, Mr. Moon/Without You	1969	10.00
❑ 44854	Let Me/I Don't Know	1969	6.00
❑ 44970	We Gotta All Get Together/Frankfort Side Street	1969	6.00
❑ 45082	Just Seventeen/Sorceress with Blue Eyes	1970	6.00
—As "Raiders"			
❑ 45150	Gone Movin' On/Interlude (To Be Forgotten)	1970	6.00
—As "Raiders"			
❑ 45332	Indian Reservation (The Lament of the Cherokee Reservation Indian)/Terry's Tune	1971	6.00
—As "Raiders"; orange label with "Columbia" background print			
❑ 45332	Indian Reservation (The Lament of the Cherokee Reservation Indian)/Terry's Tune	1971	8.00
—As "Raiders"; red label, black print			
❑ 45453	Birds of a Feather/The Turkey	1971	6.00
—As "Raiders"			
❑ 45535	Country Wine/It's So Hard Getting Up Today	1972	5.00
—As "The Raiders"; gray label			
❑ 45535	Country Wine/It's So Hard Getting Up Today	1972	6.00
—As "The Raiders"; orange label with "COLUMBIA" background			
❑ 45601	Powder Blue Mercedes Queen/Golden Girls Sometimes	1972	8.00
—As "Raiders"			
❑ 45688	Song Seller/A Simple Song	1972	8.00
—As "Raiders"			
❑ 45759	Love Music/Goodbye, No. 9	1973	8.00
—As "Raiders"			
❑ 45898	All Over You/Seaboard Line Boogie	1973	8.00
—As "Raiders"			

DRIVE

Number	Title (A Side/B Side)	Yr	NM
❑ 6248	Ain't Nothing Wrong/You're Really Saying Something	1976	5.00

GARDENA

Number	Title (A Side/B Side)	Yr	NM
❑ 106	Beatnick Sticks/Orbit (The Spy)	1960	30.00
❑ 115	Paul Revere's Ride/Unfinished Fifth	1960	40.00
❑ 116	Like, Long Hair/Sharon	1961	30.00
❑ 118	Like, Charleston/Midnite Ride	1961	25.00
❑ 124	All Night Long/Groovey	1962	40.00
❑ 127	Like, Bluegrass/Leatherneck	1962	40.00
❑ 131	Shake It Up (Part 1)/Shake It Up (Part 2)	1962	40.00
❑ 137	Tall Cool One/Road Runner	1963	50.00

HITBOUND

Number	Title (A Side/B Side)	Yr	NM
❑ X-2	Jingle Bell Rock/Jingle Bells	1983	12.00
—B-side by Mike Love and Dean Torrence			
❑ X-2 [PS]	Jingle Bell Rock/Jingle Bells	1983	20.00
—B-side by Mike Love and Dean Torrence			

JERDEN

Number	Title (A Side/B Side)	Yr	NM
❑ 807	So Fine/Blues Stay Away	1966	25.00

SANDE

Number	Title (A Side/B Side)	Yr	NM
❑ 101	Louie Louie/Night Train	1963	250.00

20TH CENTURY

Number	Title (A Side/B Side)	Yr	NM
❑ 2283	The British Are Coming/Surrender at Appomattox	1976	6.00
—B-side by Susie Allanson			

7-Inch Extended Plays

COLUMBIA

Number	Title (A Side/B Side)	Yr	NM
❑ 7-9665	Happening '68/Communication Part 1/Communication Part 2//Happens Every Day/Love Makes the World Go Round (Don't You Let It Stop Now)/Free	1968	25.00
—Jukebox issue, small hole, plays at 33 1/3 rpm			
❑ 7-9665 [PS]	Happening '68	1968	25.00

JERDEN

Number	Title (A Side/B Side)	Yr	NM
❑ LP JRLS-7004	Shake Rattle & Roll/Work with Me Annie/So Fine//Mojo Workout/Blues Stay Away/Irresistible You	1966	50.00
—Jukebox issue; small hole, plays at 33 1/3 rpm			
❑ LP JRLS-7004 [PS]	In the Beginning	1966	50.00

Albums

COLUMBIA

Number	Title (A Side/B Side)	Yr	NM
❑ GP 12 [(2)]	Two All Time Great Selling LPs	1969	25.00
—Combines 9395 and 9521 in one package; red labels			
❑ GP 12	Two All Time Great Selling LPs	1971	20.00
—Combines 9395 and 9521 in one package; orange labels			
❑ CL 2307 [M]	Here They Come!	1965	20.00
—"360 Sound Mono" on label			
❑ CL 2307 [M]	Here They Come!	1965	30.00
—"Guaranteed High Fidelity" on label			
❑ CL 2451 [M]	Just Like Us!	1966	25.00
❑ CL 2508 [M]	Midnight Ride	1966	25.00
❑ CL 2595 [M]	The Spirit of '67	1966	25.00
❑ KCL 2662 [M]	Greatest Hits	1967	30.00
—Add 20% if booklet is included; at least some copies actually are stereo with the "XSS" prefix on the label's master numbers rather than "XLP," though we don't know if all of them are			
❑ CL 2721 [M]	Revolution!	1967	30.00
❑ CL 2755 [M]	A Christmas Present...And Past	1967	60.00
❑ CL 2805 [M]	Goin' to Memphis	1968	80.00
❑ CS 9107 [S]	Here They Come!	1965	25.00
—"360 Sound Stereo" in white on label			
❑ CS 9107 [S]	Here They Come!	1965	40.00
—"360 Sound Stereo" in black on label			
❑ CS 9251 [S]	Just Like Us!	1966	30.00
❑ CS 9308 [S]	Midnight Ride	1966	30.00
❑ CS 9395 [S]	The Spirit of '67	1966	30.00
❑ KCS 9462 [P]	Greatest Hits	1967	25.00
—Add 20% if booklet is included			
❑ CS 9521 [S]	Revolution!	1967	25.00
❑ CS 9555 [S]	A Christmas Present...And Past	1967	25.00
❑ CS 9605 [S]	Goin' to Memphis	1968	20.00
❑ CS 9665	Something Happening	1968	20.00
❑ CS 9753	Hard 'N' Heavy (With Marshmallow)	1969	20.00
—Black and white cover			
❑ CS 9753	Hard 'N' Heavy (With Marshmallow)	1969	30.00
—Color cover			
❑ CS 9905	Alias Pink Puzz	1969	20.00
❑ CS 9964	Collage	1970	20.00
❑ C 30386	Greatest Hits, Vol. 2	1971	20.00
❑ C 30768	Indian Reservation	1971	15.00
❑ KC 31106	Country Wine	1972	15.00
❑ KG 31464 [(2)]	All-Time Greatest Hits	1972	20.00
❑ PC 35593	Greatest Hits	1978	10.00

COLUMBIA LIMITED EDITION

Number	Title (A Side/B Side)	Yr	NM
❑ LE 10170 [S]	Midnight Ride	197?	15.00
—Reissue of 9308			

COLUMBIA SPECIAL PRODUCTS

Number	Title (A Side/B Side)	Yr	NM
❑ P 13512	Goin' to Memphis	197?	15.00

ERA

Number	Title (A Side/B Side)	Yr	NM
❑ NU 5880	The Great Raider Reunion	1983	12.00
—Re-recordings			

GARDENA

Number	Title (A Side/B Side)	Yr	NM
❑ LP-G-1000 [M]	Like, Long Hair	1961	600.00

HARMONY

Number	Title (A Side/B Side)	Yr	NM
❑ H 30089	Paul Revere and the Raiders Featuring Mark Lindsay	1970	12.00
❑ KH 30975	Good Thing	1971	12.00
❑ KH 31183	Movin' On	1972	12.00

JERDEN

Number	Title (A Side/B Side)	Yr	NM
❑ JRL-7004 [M]	Paul Revere and the Raiders In the Beginning	1966	60.00
❑ JRS-7004 [R]	Paul Revere and the Raiders In the Beginning	1966	30.00
❑ DT-90709 [R]	Paul Revere and the Raiders In the Beginning	1966	50.00
—Capitol Record Club edition			
❑ T-90709 [M]	Paul Revere and the Raiders In the Beginning	1966	70.00
—Capitol Record Club edition			

PICKWICK

Number	Title (A Side/B Side)	Yr	NM
❑ SPC-3176 [R]	Paul Revere and the Raiders	1969	10.00

SANDE

Number	Title (A Side/B Side)	Yr	NM
❑ S-1001 [M]	Paul Revere and the Raiders	1963	1200.
—Original version with "Sande" and no mention of "Etiquette" in trail-off area			
❑ S-1001 [M]	Paul Revere and the Raiders	1979	25.00
—Legitimate reissue with "Sande" and "Etiquette" in trail-off area			

SEARS

Number	Title (A Side/B Side)	Yr	NM
❑ SPS-493	Paul Revere and the Raiders	1969	25.00

REVEREND HORTON HEAT

45s

SUB POP

Number	Title (A Side/B Side)	Yr	NM
❑ 96	Psychobilly Freakout/Baby You Know Who	1990	6.00
—2,500 on black vinyl			
❑ 96 [PS]	Psychobilly Freakout/Baby You Know Who	1990	6.00
—#26 in Sub Pop Singles Club series; yes, this and 10-inch LP have the same number!			
❑ 96	Psychobilly Freakout/Baby You Know Who	1990	8.00
—First 4,000 on blue vinyl			

Albums

SUB POP

Number	Title (A Side/B Side)	Yr	NM
❑ 96 [10]	Smoke 'Em If You Got 'Em	1991	12.00
❑ 202	The Full Custom Gospel Sounds of Reverend Horton Heat	1993	12.00
❑ 250	Liquor in the Front	1994	12.00

REVERES, THE (1)

45s

GLORY

Number	Title (A Side/B Side)	Yr	NM
❑ 272	Leonore/Honeystroller	1958	20.00
—B-side by the Honeystrollers			

REVERES, THE (2)

45s

JUBILEE

Number	Title (A Side/B Side)	Yr	NM
❑ 5463	Beyond the Sea/The Show Must Go On	1963	25.00

REVERES, THE (3)

BRUCE JOHNSTON appears on this record.

45s

VALIANT

Number	Title (A Side/B Side)	Yr	NM
❑ 6041	Big "T"/Me and My Spider	1964	50.00

REVLONS, THE

More than one group.

45s

CAPITOL

Number	Title (A Side/B Side)	Yr	NM
❑ 4739	Dry Your Eyes/She'll Come to Me	1962	30.00

PARKWAY

Number	Title (A Side/B Side)	Yr	NM
❑ 107	Ya Ya/It Could Happen to You	1966	12.00

RAE COX

Number	Title (A Side/B Side)	Yr	NM
❑ 105	This Restless Heart/I Promise Love	1961	30.00

TIMES SQUARE

Number	Title (A Side/B Side)	Yr	NM
❑ 15	Ride Awy/Betty	1963	25.00
—B-side by the Centuries			

TOY

Number	Title (A Side/B Side)	Yr	NM
❑ 101	What a Love This Is/Did I Make a Mistake	1962	20.00

REVOLTING COCKS

12-Inch Singles

SIRE

Number	Title (A Side/B Side)	Yr	NM
❑ 41088	Do Ya Think I'm Sexy/Sergio Guitar/Wrong Sexy Mix	1993	6.00
❑ 41383	Crackin' Up (2 mixes)/Gila Copter (Version 2)	1994	8.00

WAX TRAX!

Number	Title (A Side/B Side)	Yr	NM
❑ 011	No Devotion/Attack Ships/On Fire	1985	10.00
❑ 022	You Often Forget (Benign Mix)/You Often Forget (Malignant Mix)	1986	10.00
❑ 042	Stainless Steel Providers/At the Top/TV Mind	1988	8.00
❑ 9086	(Let's Get) Physical/(Let's Talk) Physical	1989	8.00
❑ 9149	Beers Steers and Queers (2 mixes)/Stainless Steel Provider/Public Image (Live)	1990	8.00

Albums

WAX TRAX!

Number	Title (A Side/B Side)	Yr	NM
❑ 017	Big Sexy Land	1986	12.00
❑ 037	You Goddamned Son of a Bitch	1988	12.00
❑ 7063	Beers Steers and Queers	1990	12.00

REX

Hard rock band with two records; later solo albums are as REX SMITH.

45s

COLUMBIA

Number	Title (A Side/B Side)	Yr	NM
❑ AE7 1116 [DJ]	Trouble/Call Her Easy	1976	6.00
—Small hole, white label			
❑ AE7 1116 [PS]	Trouble/Call Her Easy	1976	9.00

Albums

COLUMBIA

Number	Title (A Side/B Side)	Yr	NM
❑ PC 34399	Rex	1976	15.00
❑ PC 34865	Where Do We Go from Here	1977	15.00

REYNOLDS, DEBBIE

45s

ABC-PARAMOUNT

Number	Title (A Side/B Side)	Yr	NM
❑ 10709	The Sweetheart Tree/From Where I Sit	1965	8.00

BEVERLY HILLS

Number	Title (A Side/B Side)	Yr	NM
❑ 9375	The Age of Not Believing/(B-side unknown)	1972	6.00

Except when noted otherwise, VG = 25% of NM, and VG+ = 50% of NM. (Example: VG = $2.00, VG+ = $4.00 and NM = $8.00.)

Number	Title (A Side/B Side)	Yr	NM
CORAL			
❑ 9-61851	Tammy/French Heels	1957	15.00
❑ 9-61897	A Very Special Love/ I Saw a Country Boy	1957	12.00
❑ 9-61986	This Happy Feeling/ Hillside in Scotland	1958	12.00
❑ 9-62030	Hungry Eyes/Faces There Are Fairer	1958	12.00
DOT			
❑ 15884	Aba Daba Honeymoon/ Love Is a Thing	1958	12.00
❑ 15937	Love Is a Simple Thing/ I Can't Love You Anymore	1959	10.00
❑ 15985	Am I That Easy to Forget/ Ask Me to Go Steady	1959	10.00
❑ 15985 [PS]	Am I That Easy to Forget/ Ask Me to Go Steady	1959	15.00
❑ 16071	City Lights/Just for a Touch of Your Love	1960	10.00
❑ 16071 [PS]	City Lights/Just for a Touch of Your Love	1960	15.00
❑ 16119	Please/I'll Pretend	1960	10.00
❑ 16156	It Looks Like Rain in Cherry Blossom Lane/Satisfied, Part 2	1960	10.00
❑ 16199	Lonely People/Just a Little Girl	1961	10.00
❑ 16225	Right or Wrong/Are You for Real	1961	10.00
❑ 16337	People Will Say We're in Love/ (Answer to) You Better Move On	1961	10.00
❑ 16446	Tammy/Am I That Easy to Forget	1963	8.00
❑ 16465	Home in the Meadow/ My Six Loves	1963	8.00
❑ 16473	Is Goodbye That Easy to Say/The Apple, the Wind and the Storm	1963	8.00
JANUS			
❑ 111	With a Little Love/Conversations	1970	6.00
MGM			
❑ K11939	Carolina in the Morning/Never Mind the Noise in the Market	1955	15.00
❑ K12086	Canoodlin' Rag/The Tender Trap	1955	15.00
❑ K12560	All Grown Up/Wall Flower	1957	15.00
❑ K12761	The Mating Game/Right Away	1959	10.00
❑ K12819	Love Is a Gamble/ It Started with a Kiss	1959	10.00
❑ K13140	Home in the Meadow/ Raise a Ruckus Tonight	1963	8.00
❑ K13492	Dominique/Brother John	1966	8.00
❑ K30282	Aba Daba Honeymoon/ Row, Row, Row	1951	20.00
—Credited to "Debbie Reynolds and Carleton Carpenter"			
❑ K30493	Ooops!/Oogie Oogie Wa Wa	1951	20.00
PARAMOUNT			
❑ 0220	Mother Earth and Father Time/ Charlotte's Web	1973	10.00
7-Inch Extended Plays			
MGM			
❑ X1141	Never Mind the Noise in the Market/Carolina in the Morning//What Good Is a Gal? (Without a Guy)/Am I in Love?	1955	
❑ X1141 [PS]	(title unknown)	1955	—
Albums			
DOT			
❑ DLP-3191 [M]	Debbie	1959	30.00
❑ DLP-3295 [M]	Am I That Easy to Forget?	1960	30.00
❑ DLP-3298 [M]	Fine and Dandy	1960	20.00
❑ DLP-3492 [M]	Tammy	1963	20.00
❑ DLP-25191 [S]	Debbie	1959	40.00
❑ DLP-25295 [S]	Am I That Easy to Forget?	1960	40.00
—Black vinyl			
❑ DLP-25295 [S]	Am I That Easy to Forget?	1960	80.00
—Blue vinyl			
❑ DLP-25298 [S]	Fine and Dandy	1960	25.00
❑ DLP-25492 [S]	Tammy	1963	25.00
K-TEL			
❑ NU 9190	Do It Debbie's Way	1983	10.00
—Exercise record			
METRO			
❑ M-535 [M]	Raise a Ruckus	196?	20.00
❑ MS-535 [S]	Raise a Ruckus	196?	20.00
MGM			
❑ E-3806 [M]	From Debbie with Love	1959	40.00

REYNOLDS, JODY

Number	Title (A Side/B Side)	Yr	NM
45s			
BRENT			
❑ 7042	Raggedy Ann/The Girl from King Marie	1963	10.00
DEMON			
❑ 1507	Endless Sleep/Tight Capris	1958	30.00
❑ 1509	Fire of Love/Daisy Mae	1958	25.00
❑ 1511	Closin' In/Elope with Me	1958	25.00
❑ 1515	Golden Idol/Beulah Lee	1959	25.00
❑ 1519	The Storm/Please Remember	1959	25.00
❑ 1523	Whipping Post/I Wanna Be with You Tonight	1960	25.00
❑ 1524	Stone Cold/(The Girl with) The Raven Hair	1960	25.00
INDIGO			
❑ 127	Tarantula/Thunder	1961	50.00
PULSAR			
❑ 2419	Endless Sleep/My Baby's Eyes	1969	6.00
SMASH			
❑ 1810	Don't Jmp/Stormy	1963	12.00
TITAN			
❑ 1734	Devil Girl/A Tear for Hesse	1963	15.00
❑ 1736	Requiem for Love/Stranger in the Mirror	1963	15.00
—With Bobbie Gentry			
Albums			
TRU-GEMS			
❑ 1002	Endless Sleep	1978	12.00

RHINOCEROS

Number	Title (A Side/B Side)	Yr	NM
45s			
ELEKTRA			
❑ 45640	You're My Girl/ I Will Serenade You	1968	6.00
❑ 45647	Apricot Brandy/When You Say You're Sorry	1969	8.00
❑ 45659	I Need Love/Velvuekus	1969	6.00
❑ 45677	Back Door/In a Little Room	1970	6.00
❑ 45691	Let's Party/Old Age	1970	6.00
❑ 45694	Better Times/It's a Groovy World	1970	6.00
Albums			
ELEKTRA			
❑ EKS-74030	Rhinoceros	1968	25.00
❑ EKS-74056	Satin Chickens	1969	20.00
❑ EKS-74075	Better Times Are Coming	1970	20.00

RHODES, EMITT

Also see THE MERRY-GO-ROUND.

Number	Title (A Side/B Side)	Yr	NM
45s			
A&M			
❑ 1254	Till the Day After/You're a Very Lovely Woman	1971	6.00
—As "Emitt Rhodes with the Merry-Go-Round"			
ABC DUNHILL			
❑ 4267	Fresh as a Daisy/You Take the Dark Out of the Night	1970	6.00
❑ 4274	Live Till You Die/ Promises I've Made	1971	5.00
❑ 4280	A Lullaby/With My Face on the Floor	1971	5.00
❑ 4295	Really Wanted You/ Love Will Stone You	1971	5.00
❑ 4303	Take You Far Away/ Golden Child of God	1972	5.00
❑ 4315	Tame the Lion/ Golden Child of God	1972	5.00
❑ 4315	Tame the Lion/ Golden Child of God	1972	15.00
—With insert			
Albums			
A&M			
❑ SP-4254	The American Dream	1970	25.00
—Original album contains "You're a Very Lovely Woman" and has Rhodes in front of a paint-covered backdrop on cover			
❑ SP-4254	The American Dream	1971	15.00
—Reissue contains "Saturday Night" and a framed photo of Rhodes on cover			
ABC DUNHILL			
❑ DS-50089	Emitt Rhodes	1970	12.00
❑ DS-50111	Mirror	1971	12.00
❑ DS-50122	Farewell to Paradise	1972	12.00

RHODES, SLIM

Number	Title (A Side/B Side)	Yr	NM
45s			
RHODES			
❑ 101	Brothers Frank and Jesse James/(B-side unknown)	195?	50.00
SUN			
❑ 216	Don't Believe/Uncertain Blues	1955	100.00
❑ 225	Are You Ashamed of Me/ The House of Sin	1955	300.00
❑ 238	Bad Girl/Gonna Romp and Stomp	1956	100.00
❑ 256	Do What I Do/Take and Give	1956	50.00

RHODES, TODD

Number	Title (A Side/B Side)	Yr	NM
45s			
KING			
❑ 4469	Gin, Gin, Gin/I Shouldn't Cry But I Do	1951	100.00
❑ 4486	Good Man/Evening Breeze	1951	60.00
❑ 4509	Your Daddy's Doggin' Around/ Red Boy Is Back	1952	60.00
❑ 4528	Rocket 69/Possessed	1952	50.00
❑ 4556	Snuff Dipper/Trying	1952	50.00
—B-side by La Vern Baker			
❑ 4566	Pig Latin Blues/Blue Autumn	1952	50.00
❑ 4583	Hog Maw and Cabbage Slaw/ Must I Cry Again	1952	50.00
—B-side by La Vern Baker			
❑ 4601	Thunderbolt Boogie/Lost Child	1953	50.00
—B-side by La Vern Baker			
❑ 4648	Your Mouth Got a Hole In It/ Feathers	1953	40.00
❑ 4666	Let Down Blues/Beet Patch	1953	40.00
❑ 4736	Silver Sunset/Specks	1954	30.00
❑ 4755	Chicken Strut/Echoes	1954	30.00
Albums			
KING			
❑ 295-88 [10]	Todd Rhodes Playing His Greatest Hits	1954	1500.
❑ 658 [M]	Dance Music	1960	800.00

RHYTHM, JOHNNY

Number	Title (A Side/B Side)	Yr	NM
45s			
MGM			
❑ 13043	This Is It/Wouldn't It Be Nice	1961	40.00

RHYTHM ACES, THE (1)

Number	Title (A Side/B Side)	Yr	NM
45s			
ACE			
❑ 518	Rock and Roll March/ Look What You've Done	1956	40.00
—B-side by Bob Douglas			
VEE JAY			
❑ 124	I Wonder Why/Get Lost	1954	200.00
—Black vinyl			
❑ 124	I Wonder Why/Get Lost	1954	2000.
—Red vinyl			
❑ 138	Whisper to Me/ Olly, Olly, Oxsen Free	1955	200.00
—Black vinyl			
❑ 138	Whisper to Me/ Olly, Olly, Oxsen Free	1955	2000.
—Red vinyl			
❑ 160	That's My Sugar/Flippety Flop	1955	120.00

RHYTHM ACES, THE (2)

Number	Title (A Side/B Side)	Yr	NM
45s			
MARK-X			
❑ 8004	Boppin' Sloppin' Baby/Crazy Jealousy	1960	30.00

RHYTHM ACES, THE (3)

Number	Title (A Side/B Side)	Yr	NM
45s			
ROULETTE			
❑ 4268	Mohawk Rock/It'll Do	1960	15.00
❑ 4426	Raunchy Twist/ Mockin' Bird Twist	1962	15.00
SIOUX			
❑ 82260	Allan's Rock/Go Get It	1960	30.00
❑ 102261	Yahma/What'd I Say Twist	1961	30.00
UNIVERSAL ARTISTS			
❑ 3160	Mohawk Rock/It'll Do	1960	40.00

RHYTHM CADETS, THE

Number	Title (A Side/B Side)	Yr	NM
45s			
VESTA			
❑ 501/2	Dearest Doryce/Rocking Jimmy	1957	800.00

RHYTHM DEVILS, THE

Number	Title (A Side/B Side)	Yr	NM
Albums			
PASSPORT			
❑ PB-9844	The Rhythm Devils Play River Music	1980	20.00

RHYTHM HERITAGE

Number	Title (A Side/B Side)	Yr	NM
45s			
ABC			
❑ 12063	Theme from "Young Frankenstein"/I Wouldn't Treat a Dog (The Way You Treated Me)	1975	5.00
❑ 12135	Theme from S.W.A.T./I Wouldn't Treat a Dog (The Way You Treated Me)	1975	4.00
—Version 2: With long version of A-side; "RE-1" on label next to matrix number			
❑ 12135	Theme from S.W.A.T./I Wouldn't Treat a Dog (The Way You Treated Me)	1975	5.00
—Version 1: With short version of A-side			
❑ 12177	Baretta's Theme (Keep Your Eye on the Sparrow)/My Cherie Amour	1976	4.00

R

Except when noted otherwise, VG = 25% of NM, and VG+ = 50% of NM. (Example: VG = $2.00, VG+ = $4.00 and NM = $8.00.)

Number	Title (A Side/B Side)	Yr	NM
❑ 12205	Disco-Fied/(It's Time to) Boogie Down	1976	4.00
❑ 12243	Gonna Fly Now (Theme from "Rocky")/Last Night on Earth	1976	4.00
❑ 12273	Theme from "Starsky and Hutch"/Disco Queen	1977	4.00
❑ 12334 [DJ]	Holdin' Out for You Love (mono/stereo)	1978	4.00
—May be promo only			
❑ 12378	Language of Love/Sail Away with Me	1978	4.00

Albums

ABC

Number	Title	Yr	NM
❑ D-934	Disco-Fied	1976	10.00
❑ D-987	Last Night on Earth	1977	10.00
❑ AA-1037	The Sky's the Limit	1978	10.00

RHYTHM MASTERS, THE (1)

45s

ACE

Number	Title	Yr	NM
❑ 610	The Devil and His Old Suitcase/Holding My Savior's Hand	1961	20.00

Albums

ACE

Number	Title	Yr	NM
❑ LP-1010 [M]	Hymns and Spirituals	1961	100.00

RHYTHM MASTERS, THE (2)

45s

FLIP

Number	Title	Yr	NM
❑ 314	Baby We Two/Patricia	1956	300.00

RHYTHM ROCKERS (1)

45s

CHALLENGE

Number	Title	Yr	NM
❑ 9196	Rendezvous Stomp/The Slide	1963	25.00

Albums

CHALLENGE

Number	Title	Yr	NM
❑ CHL-617 [M]	Soul Surfin'	1963	90.00

RHYTHM ROCKERS (2)

45s

SATIN

Number	Title	Yr	NM
❑ 921	Oh Boy/We Belong Together	1960	60.00
❑ 921 [PS]	Oh Boy/We Belong Together	1960	100.00

RHYTHM ROCKERS (3)

45s

SUN

Number	Title	Yr	NM
❑ 248	Fiddle Bop/Juke Box, Help Me Find My Baby	1956	100.00

RHYTHM ROCKERS (U) These could be by group (1) or (2).

45s

FENTON

Number	Title	Yr	NM
❑ 944	Surf Around/Three Strikes	1962	50.00

WIPE OUT

Number	Title	Yr	NM
❑ 1001	Foot Cruising/Get It On	1962	40.00

RHYTHMETTES, THE

45s

BRUNSWICK

Number	Title	Yr	NM
❑ 55012	Mind Reader/Mister Love	1957	15.00
❑ 55050	That's a-Plenty/Till My Baby Comes Home	1958	12.00
❑ 55083	Elaine/Bow Legged Woman	1958	12.00
❑ 55097	I'll Be With You in Apple Blossom Time/Page from the Future	1958	12.00

CORAL

Number	Title	Yr	NM
❑ 62186	High School Lovers/Snow Queen	1960	10.00

RCA VICTOR

Number	Title	Yr	NM
❑ 47-6089	Only You/Him	1955	20.00
❑ 47-6244	Show Me the Way/The Bridge of Love	1955	15.00
❑ 47-6349	Take My Hand, Show Me the Way/I've Got to Know	1955	15.00
❑ 47-6539	Homin' Pigeon/Boom-Boom	1956	15.00
❑ 47-6742	Winter Snow/Take a Look in the Mirror	1956	15.00

RHYZE

12-Inch Singles

SAM

Number	Title	Yr	NM
❑ S-12332	Just How Sweet Is Your Love/I Found Love in You	1980	25.00
❑ S-12334	Free/Singing and Dancing	1980	30.00

20TH CENTURY

Number	Title	Yr	NM
❑ TCD-134	Rhyze to the Top (6:15)/Party of Parties	1981	15.00
❑ TCD-137	Tonight's Gonna Be My Night (5:48)/Tazmania	1982	15.00

45s

SAM

Number	Title	Yr	NM
❑ 80-5014	Just How Sweet Is Your Love/I Found Love in You	1980	6.00
❑ 80-5016	Free/Singing and Dancing	1980	8.00

20TH CENTURY

Number	Title	Yr	NM
❑ 2509	Rhyze to the Top/Party of Parties	1981	10.00
❑ 2603	Tonight's Gonna Be My Night/What Can I Do About This Feelin'	1982	10.00

Albums

20TH CENTURY

Number	Title	Yr	NM
❑ T-639	Rhyze to the Top	1981	30.00

RIA AND THE REASONS

45s

AMY

Number	Title	Yr	NM
❑ 888	Memories Linger On/Sorry I Lied	1963	25.00
❑ 888	Memories Linger On/Sorry I Lied	1963	80.00
—Blue vinyl			

RSVP

Number	Title	Yr	NM
❑ 1110	He's Not There/She Fell in Love	1965	20.00
—As "Ria and the Revellons"			

RIALTOS, THE

45s

CB

Number	Title	Yr	NM
❑ 5009	Let Me In/It Hurts	1962	300.00

RIBBONS, THE

45s

MARSH

Number	Title	Yr	NM
❑ 202	Ain't Gonna Kiss Ya/My Baby Said	1963	15.00
❑ 203	After Last Night/This Is Our Melody	1963	12.00

PARKWAY

Number	Title	Yr	NM
❑ 912	Meoldie D'Amour/They Played a Sad Song	1964	12.00

RIC-A-SHAYS, THE Harry NILSSON was in this group.

45s

LOLA

Number	Title	Yr	NM
❑ 002	Groovy/Turn On	1964	25.00

RICARDOS, THE

45s

STAR-X

Number	Title	Yr	NM
❑ 512	Mary's Little Lamb/I Mean Really	1958	160.00

RICE, JIMMY

45s

RED BIRD

Number	Title	Yr	NM
❑ 10-022	The Grass Is Always Greener/Spanish Perfume	1965	20.00
❑ 10-027	Nobody But You/Or Not at All	1965	20.00

RICE, TONY

45s

ACTION

Number	Title	Yr	NM
❑ 100	My Darling Y-O-U/I Thank You Baby	1961	30.00

PRINCETON

Number	Title	Yr	NM
❑ 101	Summer's Love/Please Don't	1960	60.00

RAE COX

Number	Title	Yr	NM
❑ 106	Little School Girl/Blue Bird of Happiness	1961	20.00

RICH, BUDDY

45s

ARGO

Number	Title	Yr	NM
❑ 5384	Makin' Whoopee/Lulu's Back in Town	1961	8.00

CLEF

Number	Title	Yr	NM
❑ 89066	Sleepyhead/Bugle Call Rag	1953	12.00
❑ 89094	Let's Fall in Love/Me and My Jaguar	1954	12.00

GROOVE MERCHANT

Number	Title	Yr	NM
❑ 1031	The Bull/Nik Nik	197?	4.00

MCA

Number	Title	Yr	NM
❑ 51116	Fantasy/Listen Here Goes Funky	1981	4.00

PACIFIC JAZZ

Number	Title	Yr	NM
❑ 88136	Uptight/Sister Sadie	1966	5.00
❑ 88139	Norwegian Wood/Monitor Theme	1967	5.00
❑ 88140	The Beat Goes On/Mexicali Rose	1967	5.00
❑ 88145	Mercy, Mercy, Mercy/Big Mama Cass	1968	6.00

RCA VICTOR

Number	Title	Yr	NM
❑ PB-10712	Speak No Evil/Sophisticated Lady (She's a Different Lady)	1976	4.00

Albums

ARGO

Number	Title	Yr	NM
❑ LP-676 [M]	Playtime	1961	30.00
❑ LPS-676 [S]	Playtime	1961	40.00

EMARCY

Number	Title	Yr	NM
❑ EMS-2-402 [(2)]	Both Sides	1976	15.00
❑ 66006	Driver	1967	20.00

EVEREST ARCHIVE OF FOLK & JAZZ

Number	Title	Yr	NM
❑ 260	Buddy Rich	197?	15.00

GREAT AMERICAN

Number	Title	Yr	NM
❑ 1030	Class of '78	1978	20.00
—Direct-to-disc version of Gryphon 781			

GROOVE MERCHANT

Number	Title	Yr	NM
❑ 528	The Roar of '74	1974	12.00
❑ 3301	Very Live at Buddy's Place	1974	12.00
❑ 3303	The Last Blues Album, Vol. 1	1975	12.00
❑ 3307	The Big Band Machine	1976	12.00
❑ 4407 [(2)]	Tuff Dude!	197?	15.00

GRYPHON

Number	Title	Yr	NM
❑ 781	Class of '78	1978	12.00

LIBERTY

Number	Title	Yr	NM
❑ 11006	Keep the Customer Satisfied	1970	15.00

MCA

Number	Title	Yr	NM
❑ 5186	The Buddy Rich Band	1981	10.00

MERCURY

Number	Title	Yr	NM
❑ MG-20451 [M]	Richcraft	1959	60.00
❑ MG-20461 [M]	The Voice Is Rich	1959	50.00
❑ SR-60136 [S]	Richcraft	1959	70.00
❑ SR-60144 [S]	The Voice Is Rich	1959	60.00

NORGRAN

Number	Title	Yr	NM
❑ MGN-26 [10]	Buddy Rich Swingin'	1954	120.00
❑ MGN-1031 [M]	Sing and Swing with Buddy Rich	1955	80.00
❑ MGN-1052 [M]	The Swingin' Buddy Rich	1955	60.00
—Reissue of 26			
❑ MGN-1078 [M]	The Wailing Buddy Rich	1956	60.00
❑ MGN-1088 [M]	This One's for Basie	1956	60.00

PACIFIC JAZZ

Number	Title	Yr	NM
❑ LN-10089	Swingin' New Big Band	1981	8.00
—Budget-line reissue			
❑ LN-10090	Big Swing Face	1981	8.00
—Budget-line reissue			
❑ PJ-10113 [M]	Swingin' New Big Band	1966	25.00
❑ PJ-10117 [M]	Big Swing Face	1967	25.00
❑ ST-20113 [S]	Swingin' New Big Band	1966	20.00
❑ ST-20117 [S]	Big Swing Face	1967	20.00
❑ ST-20126	A New One	1968	20.00

PAUSA

Number	Title	Yr	NM
❑ 9004	Buddy & Soul	1983	10.00

QUINTESSENCE

Number	Title	Yr	NM
❑ 25051	Mr. Drums	1978	12.00

RCA VICTOR

Number	Title	Yr	NM
❑ ANL1-1090	A Different Drummer	1975	10.00
—Reissue of 4593			
❑ APL1-1503	Speak No Evil	1976	12.00
❑ CPL2-2273 [(2)]	Buddy Rich Plays & Plays & Plays	1977	15.00
❑ LSP-4593	A Different Drummer	1971	12.00
❑ AFL1-4666	Rich in London	1977	10.00
—Reissue with new prefix			
❑ LSP-4666	Rich in London	1972	12.00
❑ AFL1-4802	Stick It	1977	10.00
—Reissue with new prefix			
❑ LSP-4802	Stick It	1972	12.00

UNITED ARTISTS

Number	Title	Yr	NM
❑ UXS-86 [(2)]	Buddy Rich Superpak	1972	15.00

VERVE

Number	Title	Yr	NM
❑ VSP-40 [M]	Buddy Rich at J.A.T.P.	1966	15.00
❑ VSPS-40 [R]	Buddy Rich at J.A.T.P.	1966	12.00
❑ MGV-2009 [M]	Buddy Rich Sings Johnny Mercer	1956	60.00
❑ V-2009 [M]	Buddy Rich Sings Johnny Mercer	1961	20.00
❑ MGV-2075 [M]	Buddy Rich Just Sings	1957	60.00
❑ V-2075 [M]	Buddy Rich Just Sings	1961	20.00
❑ MGV-8142 [M]	The Swingin' Buddy Rich	1957	50.00
—Reissue of Norgran 1052			
❑ V-8142 [M]	The Swingin' Buddy Rich	1961	20.00
❑ MGV-8168 [M]	The Wailing Buddy Rich	1957	50.00
—Reissue of Norgran 1078			
❑ V-8168 [M]	The Wailing Buddy Rich	1961	20.00
❑ MGV-8176 [M]	This One's for Basie	1957	50.00
—Reissue of Norgran 1086			
❑ V-8176 [M]	This One's for Basie	1961	20.00
❑ MGV-8285 [M]	Buddy Rich in Miami	1958	60.00
❑ V-8285 [M]	Buddy Rich in Miami	1961	20.00
❑ V-8425 [M]	Blues Caravan	1962	25.00
❑ V6-8425 [S]	Blues Caravan	1962	30.00
❑ V-8471 [M]	Burnin' Beat	1962	25.00
❑ V6-8471 [S]	Burnin' Beat	1962	30.00
❑ V-8484 [M]	Drum Battle: Gene Krupa vs. Buddy Rich	1962	25.00

R

Except when noted otherwise, VG = 25% of NM, and VG+ = 50% of NM. (Example: VG = $2.00, VG+ = $4.00 and NM = $8.00.)

Number	Title (A Side/B Side)	Yr	NM
❑ V6-8484 [S]	Drum Battle: Gene Krupa vs. Buddy Rich	1962	30.00
❑ V-8712 [M]	Big Band Shout	1967	20.00
❑ V6-8712 [S]	Big Band Shout	1967	15.00
❑ V6-8778	Super Rich	1969	15.00
❑ V6-8824 [(2)]	Monster	1973	15.00

WHO'S WHO IN JAZZ

Number	Title (A Side/B Side)	Yr	NM
❑ 21006	Lionel Hampton Presents Buddy Rich	1978	12.00

WORLD PACIFIC

Number	Title (A Side/B Side)	Yr	NM
❑ WPS-20113	The Buddy Rich Big Band	1968	15.00
❑ WPS-20133	Mercy, Mercy	1968	15.00
❑ WPS-20158	Buddy & Soul	1969	15.00
❑ WPS-20169	The Best of Buddy Rich	1970	15.00

RICH, BUDDY, AND SWEETS EDISON

Albums

NORGRAN

Number	Title (A Side/B Side)	Yr	NM
❑ MGN-1038 [M]	Buddy Rich and Sweets Edison	1955	80.00

VERVE

Number	Title (A Side/B Side)	Yr	NM
❑ MGV-8129 [M]	Buddy and Sweets	1957	50.00

—Reissue of Norgran 1038

Number	Title (A Side/B Side)	Yr	NM
❑ V-8129 [M]	Buddy and Sweets	1961	20.00

RICH, BUDDY, AND MAX ROACH

Albums

MERCURY

Number	Title (A Side/B Side)	Yr	NM
❑ MG-20448 [M]	Rich Versus Roach	1959	60.00
❑ SR-60133 [S]	Rich Versus Roach	1959	70.00

RICH, CHARLIE

45s

ELEKTRA

Number	Title (A Side/B Side)	Yr	NM
❑ 45553	I'll Wake You Up When I Get Home/Salty Dog Blues	1978	4.00
❑ 47047	A Man Just Doesn't Know What a Woman Goes Through/Marie	1980	4.00
❑ 47104	Are We Dreamin' the Same Dream/Angelina	1981	4.00

EPIC

Number	Title (A Side/B Side)	Yr	NM
❑ 02058	You Made It Beautiful/How Good It Used to Be	1981	4.00
❑ 03165	Try a Little Tenderness/As Time Goes By	1982	4.00
❑ 10287	Set Me Free/I'll Just Go Away	1968	6.00
❑ 10358	Raggedy Ann/Nothing in the World	1968	6.00
❑ 10492	Life's Little Ups and Downs/It Takes Time	1969	6.00
❑ 10585	July 12, 1939/I'm Flying to Nashville Tonight	1970	6.00
❑ 10662	Nice 'N' Easy/I Can't Even Drink It Away	1970	6.00
❑ 10745	A Woman Left Lonely/Have a Heart	1971	5.00
❑ 10809	A Part of Your Life/A Sunday Kind of Woman	1971	5.00
❑ 10867	I Take It On Home/Peace on You	1972	5.00
❑ 10950	Behind Closed Doors/A Sunday Kind of Woman	1973	4.00

—Repressings have orange labels

Number	Title (A Side/B Side)	Yr	NM
❑ 10950	Behind Closed Doors/A Sunday Kind of Woman	1973	5.00

—Originals have yellow labels

Number	Title (A Side/B Side)	Yr	NM
❑ 11040	The Most Beautiful Girl/I Feel Like Going Home	1973	4.00
❑ 11091	A Very Special Love Song/I Can't Even Drink It Away	1974	4.00
❑ 20006	I Love My Friend/Why Oh Why	1974	4.00
❑ 50064	My Elusive Dreams/Whatever Happened	1975	4.00
❑ 50103	Every Time You Touch Me (I Get High)/Pass On By	1975	4.00
❑ 50142	All Over Me/You & I	1975	4.00
❑ 50182	Since I Fell for You/She	1975	4.00
❑ 50222	America the Beautiful (1976)/Down By the Riverside	1976	4.00
❑ 50268	Road Song/The Grass Is Always Greener	1976	4.00
❑ 50328	Easy Look/My Lady	1976	4.00
❑ 50392	Rollin' with the Flow/To Sing a Love Song	1977	4.00
❑ 50562	Beautiful Woman/Everybody Wrote That Song for Me	1978	4.00
❑ 50616	On My Knees/Mellow Melody	1978	4.00
❑ 50701	Spanish Eyes/I Do My Swingin' at Home	1979	4.00
❑ 50869	Even a Fool Would Let Go/Pretty People	1980	4.00

GROOVE

Number	Title (A Side/B Side)	Yr	NM
❑ 58-0020	The Grass Is Always Greener/She Loved Everybody But Me	1963	15.00
❑ 58-0020 [PS]	The Grass Is Always Greener/She Loved Everybody But Me	1963	30.00
❑ 58-0025	Big Boss Man/Let Me Go My Merry Way	1963	15.00
❑ 58-0032	Lady Love/Why, Oh Why	1964	15.00
❑ 58-0035	The Ways of a Woman in Love/My Mountain Dew	1964	15.00
❑ 58-0041	Nice 'N' Easy/Turn Around and Face Me	1964	15.00

HI

Number	Title (A Side/B Side)	Yr	NM
❑ 2116	Love Is After Me/Pass On By	1966	10.00
❑ 2123	My Heart Would Know/Nobody's Lonesome for Me	1967	10.00
❑ 2134	Hurry Up Freight Train/Only Me	1967	10.00

MERCURY

Number	Title (A Side/B Side)	Yr	NM
❑ 73466	I Washed My Hands in Muddy Water/No Home	1974	5.00
❑ 73498	A Field of Yellow Daisies/Party Girl	1974	5.00
❑ 73646	Something Just Came Over Me/Best Years	1974	5.00

PHILLIPS INT'L.

Number	Title (A Side/B Side)	Yr	NM
❑ 3532	Whirlwind/Philadelphia Baby	1959	25.00
❑ 3542	Rebound/Big Man	1959	25.00
❑ 3552	Lonely Weekends/Everything I Do Is Wrong	1960	25.00
❑ 3560	School Days/Gonna Be Waiting	1960	25.00
❑ 3562	On My Knees/Stay	1960	25.00
❑ 3566	Who Will the Next Fool Be/Caught in the Middle	1961	25.00
❑ 3572	Just a Little Sweet/It's Too Late	1962	20.00
❑ 3576	Easy Money/Midnight Blues	1962	20.00
❑ 3582	Sittin' and Thinkin'/Finally Found Out	1962	20.00
❑ 3584	There's Another Place I Can't Go/I Need Your Love	1963	20.00

RCA

Number	Title (A Side/B Side)	Yr	NM
❑ PB-10859	My Mountain Dew/Nice 'N Easy	1976	4.00
❑ PB-10966	Nice 'N Easy/It's All Over Now	1977	4.00

RCA VICTOR

Number	Title (A Side/B Side)	Yr	NM
❑ 47-8468	It's All Over Now/Too Many Teardrops	1964	15.00
❑ 47-8536	There Won't Be Anymore/Gentleman Jim	1965	20.00
❑ 47-8817	Nice 'N' Easy/Ol' Man River	1966	12.00
❑ 74-0983	Tomorrow Night/The Ways of a Woman in Love	1973	4.00
❑ APBO-0195	There Won't Be Anymore/It's All Over Now	1973	5.00
❑ APBO-0260	I Don't See Me in Your Eyes Anymore/No Room to Dance	1974	4.00
❑ PB-10062	She Called Me Baby/$10 and a Clean White Shirt	1974	4.00
❑ GB-10159	There Won't Be Anymore/Tomorrow Night	1975	3.00

—Gold Standard Series

Number	Title (A Side/B Side)	Yr	NM
❑ PB-10256	It's All Over Now/Big Jack	1975	4.00
❑ PB-10458	Not Everybody Knows/I've Got You Under My Skin	1975	4.00
❑ GB-10512	She Called Me Baby/$10 and a Clean White Shirt	1975	3.00

—Gold Standard Series

SMASH

Number	Title (A Side/B Side)	Yr	NM
❑ 1993	Mohair Sam/I Washed My Hands in Muddy Water	1965	20.00
❑ 2012	Dance of Love/I Can't Go On	1965	15.00
❑ 2022	Hawg Jaw/Something Just Came Over Me	1966	15.00
❑ 2038	No Home/Tears a-Go-Go	1966	15.00
❑ 2060	That's the Way/When My Baby Comes Home	1966	15.00

SUN

Number	Title (A Side/B Side)	Yr	NM
❑ 1110	Who Will the Next Fool Be/Stay	1970	5.00
❑ 1151	The Breakup/Be-Bop-a-Lula	1980	4.00

—B-side by Jerry Lee Lewis; both sides are duets with Orion

UNITED ARTISTS

Number	Title (A Side/B Side)	Yr	NM
❑ XW1193	Puttin' In Overtime at Home/Ghost of Another Man	1978	4.00
❑ XW1223	I Still Believe in Love/Wishful Thinking	1978	4.00
❑ XW1269	The Fool Strikes Again/I Loved You All the Way	1978	4.00
❑ XW1280	I Lost My Head/She Knows Just How to Touch Me	1979	4.00
❑ XW1307	Life Goes On/Standing Tall	1979	4.00
❑ 1325	You're Gonna Love Yourself in the Morning/Top of the Stairs	1979	4.00
❑ 1340	I'd Build a Bridge/All You Ever Have to Do Is Touch Me	1980	4.00

7-Inch Extended Plays

EPIC

Number	Title (A Side/B Side)	Yr	NM
❑ AE7 1065 [DJ]	Big Boss Man/Nice 'n' Easy//Life Has Its Little Ups and Downs/I Take It on Home	1972	6.00

—Small hole, plays at 33 1/3 rpm; came as a bonus with some copies of KE 31933, "The Best of Charlie Rich"

Number	Title (A Side/B Side)	Yr	NM
❑ AE7 1065 [PS]	The Best of Charlie Rich Bonus Record	1972	6.00

—Special sleeve for above disc; came as a bonus with some copies of KE 31933, "The Best of Charlie Rich"

Albums

BUCKBOARD

Number	Title (A Side/B Side)	Yr	NM
❑ 1019	The Entertainer	197?	10.00

COLUMBIA SPECIAL PRODUCTS

Number	Title (A Side/B Side)	Yr	NM
❑ P2 13663 [(2)]	Super Hits	197?	15.00

ELEKTRA

Number	Title (A Side/B Side)	Yr	NM
❑ 6E-301	Once a Drifter	1981	10.00

EPIC

Number	Title (A Side/B Side)	Yr	NM
❑ AS 50 [DJ]	Charlie Rich	1973	30.00

—Promo-only compilation

Number	Title (A Side/B Side)	Yr	NM
❑ AS 139 [DJ]	Everything You Always Wanted to Hear by Charlie Rich But Were Afraid to Ask For	1976	25.00

—Promo-only sampler

Number	Title (A Side/B Side)	Yr	NM
❑ BN 26376	Set Me Free	1968	20.00
❑ BN 26516	The Fabulous Charlie Rich	1970	20.00
❑ E 30214	Boss Man	1970	20.00
❑ CQ 31933 [Q]	The Best of Charlie Rich	1972	20.00
❑ KE 31933	The Best of Charlie Rich	1972	15.00

—Yellow label; add 80 percent if bonus record AE7 1065 and its special sleeve are still there

Number	Title (A Side/B Side)	Yr	NM
❑ KE 31933	The Best of Charlie Rich	1973	12.00

—Orange label

Number	Title (A Side/B Side)	Yr	NM
❑ CQ 32247 [Q]	Behind Closed Doors	1973	20.00
❑ KE 32247	Behind Closed Doors	1973	12.00
❑ PE 32247	Behind Closed Doors	197?	8.00

—Reissue

Number	Title (A Side/B Side)	Yr	NM
❑ PE 32531	Very Special Love Songs	1974	12.00
❑ PEQ 32531 [Q]	Very Special Love Songs	1974	20.00
❑ PE 33250	The Silver Fox	1974	12.00
❑ PEQ 33250 [Q]	The Silver Fox	1974	20.00
❑ PE 33455	Every Time You Touch Me (I Get High)	1975	12.00
❑ PEQ 33455 [Q]	Every Time You Touch Me (I Get High)	1975	20.00
❑ PE 33545	Silver Linings	1976	10.00
❑ PE 34240	Greatest Hits	1976	10.00

—Without bar code on cover

Number	Title (A Side/B Side)	Yr	NM
❑ PE 34240	Greatest Hits	1979	8.00

—With bar code on cover

Number	Title (A Side/B Side)	Yr	NM
❑ PE 34444	Take Me	1977	10.00
❑ PE 34444	Take Me	1977	10.00
❑ PE 34891	Rollin' with the Flow	1977	10.00
❑ JE 35394	Classic Rich, Vol. 1	1978	10.00
❑ JE 35624	Classic Rich, Vol. 2	1978	10.00

GROOVE

Number	Title (A Side/B Side)	Yr	NM
❑ GM-1000 [M]	Charlie Rich	1964	150.00
❑ GS-1000 [S]	Charlie Rich	1964	300.00

HARMONY

Number	Title (A Side/B Side)	Yr	NM
❑ KH 32166	I Do My Swingin' at Home	1973	12.00

HI

Number	Title (A Side/B Side)	Yr	NM
❑ 8006	I'm So Lonesome I Could Cry	198?	8.00

—Reissue of Hi 32084

Number	Title (A Side/B Side)	Yr	NM
❑ HL 12037 [M]	Charlie Rich Sings Country and Western	1967	30.00
❑ SHL 32037 [S]	Charlie Rich Sings Country and Western	1967	20.00
❑ SHL 32084	Charlie Rich Sings the Songs of Hank Williams & Others	1974	12.00

—Reissue of 32037

HILLTOP

Number	Title (A Side/B Side)	Yr	NM
❑ 6139	Lonely Weekends	197?	10.00
❑ 6149	Songs for Beautiful Girls	1974	10.00
❑ 6160	Entertainer of the Year	197?	10.00

MERCURY

Number	Title (A Side/B Side)	Yr	NM
❑ SRM-2-7505 [(2)]	Fully Realized	1974	15.00

PHILLIPS INTERNATIONAL

Number	Title (A Side/B Side)	Yr	NM
❑ PLP-1970 [M]	Lonely Weekends	1960	600.00

PICKWICK

Number	Title (A Side/B Side)	Yr	NM
❑ ACL-7001	Too Many Teardrops	1975	10.00

POWER PAK

Number	Title (A Side/B Side)	Yr	NM
❑ PO-241	There Won't Be Anymore	197?	10.00
❑ PO-245	Arkansas Traveler	197?	10.00
❑ PO-252	The Silver Fox	197?	10.00

QUICKSILVER

Number	Title (A Side/B Side)	Yr	NM
❑ QS-1005	Midnight Blue	198?	12.00

RCA CAMDEN

Number	Title (A Side/B Side)	Yr	NM
❑ CAS-2417	The Versatile and Talented Charlie Rich	1970	10.00

RCA VICTOR

Number	Title (A Side/B Side)	Yr	NM
❑ APL1-0258	Tomorrow Night	1973	12.00
❑ APL1-0433	There Won't Be Anymore	1974	12.00
❑ APL1-0686	She Called Me Baby	1974	12.00
❑ APL1-0857	Greatest Hits	1975	12.00
❑ APL1-1242	Now Everybody Knows	1975	12.00
❑ ANL1-1542	Tomorrow Night	1976	10.00

—Reissue

R

Number	Title (A Side/B Side)	Yr	NM
❑ APL1-2260	Big Boss Man/My Mountain Dew	1977	12.00
❑ ANL1-2424	She Called Me Baby	1977	10.00
—Reissue of APL1-0686			
❑ LPM-3352 [M]	That's Rich	1965	40.00
❑ LSP-3352 [S]	That's Rich	1965	50.00
❑ LPM-3537 [M]	Big Boss Man	1966	40.00
❑ LSP-3557 [S]	Big Boss Man	1966	50.00
❑ AHL1-5496	Collector's Series	1985	8.00
SMASH			
❑ MGS-27070 [M]	The Many New Sides of Charlie Rich	1965	30.00
❑ MGS-27078 [M]	The Best Years	1966	30.00
❑ SRS-67070 [S]	The Many New Sides of Charlie Rich	1965	40.00
❑ SRS-67070 [S]	The Best Years	1966	40.00
SUN			
❑ LP 110	Lonely Weekend	1970	12.00
❑ LP 123	A Time for Tears	1971	12.00
❑ LP 132	The Early Years	1974	12.00
❑ LP 133	The Memphis Sound of Charlie Rich	1974	12.00
❑ LP 134	Golden Treasures	1974	12.00
❑ LP 135	Sun's Best of Charlie Rich	1974	12.00
❑ 1003	20 Golden Hits	1979	10.00
—Gold vinyl			
❑ 1007	The Original Charlie Rich	1979	10.00
SUNNYVALE			
❑ 9330	The Sun Story Vol. 2	1977	10.00
TIME-LIFE			
❑ STW-115	Country Music	1981	10.00
TRIP			
❑ TLP-8502 [(2)]	The Best of Charlie Rich	1974	12.00
UNITED ARTISTS			
❑ UA-LA876-H	I Still Believe in Love	1978	12.00
❑ UA-LA925-H	The Fool Strikes Again	1978	10.00
WING			
❑ SRW-16375	A Lonely Weekend	1969	12.00

RICH, DAVE

45s

Number	Title (A Side/B Side)	Yr	NM
BRAGG			
❑ 210	Big Hands/Sin Pays	196?	15.00
DECCA			
❑ 31513	The Great Speckled Bird/I Want to Know You Lord	1963	12.00
❑ 31573	It's Not for Me to Understand/When They Ring Those Golden Bells	1963	12.00
MONUMENT			
❑ 918	The Runt/Hang On Till the Goin' On Comes On	1966	10.00
RCA VICTOR			
❑ 47-6327	I Forgot/I Think I'm Gonna Die	1955	30.00
❑ 47-6435	I'm Glad/Darling, I'm Lonesome	1956	30.00
❑ 47-6595	Your Pretty Blue Eyes/Ain't It Fine	1956	40.00
❑ 47-6687	I'm Sorry, Goodbye/I Love 'Em All	1956	30.00
❑ 47-6753	Lonely Street/Didn't Work Out, Did It	1956	30.00
❑ 47-6824	Tuggin' on My Heart Strings/Our Last Night Together	1957	30.00
❑ 47-6926	The Key to My Heart/Red Sweater	1957	30.00
❑ 47-7045	Chicken House/I've Learned	1957	30.00
❑ 47-7141	School Blues/I've Thought It Over	1958	30.00
❑ 47-7247	City Lights/Burn On Love Fire	1958	30.00
❑ 47-7334	Rosie Let's Get Cozy/Sunshine in My Heart	1958	30.00
❑ 47-7656	Where Else Would I Want to Be/Brand New Feeling	1959	25.00
REPUBLIC			
❑ 390	Because You're Gone/Cheatin', Stealin', Steel Guitar Man	1977	5.00
STOP			
❑ 122	When I've Learned/I Don't Need Nobody Else	196?	8.00
❑ 132	I Never Gave Up/On the Battlefield	196?	8.00
❑ 171	I Believe/Peace On Earth Begins Today	196?	8.00
TRUE			
❑ 116	The Sea of Galilee/King Jesus	1978	6.00
❑ 118	Love Is Running Out of My Eyes/When I Need Love	197?	6.00
❑ 201	I Come Apart/Don't You Ever Go Back	197?	6.00

Albums

Number	Title (A Side/B Side)	Yr	NM
STOP			
❑ 10007	Soul Brother	196?	30.00

RICH KIDS, THE

45s

Number	Title (A Side/B Side)	Yr	NM
STEED			
❑ 702	Plastic Flowers/Got to Find a Woman	1967	10.00
❑ 706	You Made Me a Man/I Tried to Tell You	1968	10.00

RICHARD, CLIFF Also see THE SHADOWS.

45s

Number	Title (A Side/B Side)	Yr	NM
ABC-PARAMOUNT			
❑ 10042	Living Doll/Apron Strings	1959	25.00
❑ 10066	Travellin' Light/Dynamite	1959	20.00
❑ 10093	Voice in the Wilderness/Don't Be Mad at Me	1960	20.00
❑ 10109	Fall in Love with You/Choppin' 'N' Changin'	1960	20.00
❑ 10136	Please Don't Tease/Where Is My Heart	1960	20.00
❑ 10175	Catch Me, I'm Falling/"D" in Love	1961	20.00
❑ 10195	Theme for a Dream/Mumblin' Mosie	1961	40.00
BIG TOP			
❑ 3101	The Young Ones/We Say Yeah	1962	20.00
CAPITOL			
❑ F4096	Move It/High Class Baby	1958	40.00
❑ F4154	Livin' Lovin' Doll/Steady with You	1959	40.00
DOT			
❑ 16399	Wonderful to Be Young/Got a Funny Feeling	1962	20.00
EMI			
❑ S7-19767	Mistletoe and Wine/Have Yourself a Merry Little Christmas	1997	4.00
EMI AMERICA			
❑ 8025	We Don't Talk Anymore/Count Me Out	1979	4.00
❑ 8035	Carrie/Language of Love	1980	4.00
❑ 8057	Dreaming/Dynamite	1980	4.00
—Gray label			
❑ 8057	Dreaming/Dynamite	1980	5.00
—Green label			
❑ 8068	A Little in Love/Everyman	1980	4.00
❑ 8076	Give a Little Bit More/Keep Lookin'	1981	4.00
❑ 8076 [PS]	Give a Little Bit More/Keep Lookin'	1981	5.00
❑ 8095	Wired for Sound/Hold On	1981	4.00
❑ 8103	Daddy's Home/Summer Rain	1982	4.00
❑ 8135	The Only Way Out/Be in My Heart	1982	4.00
❑ 8149	Little Town/Be in My Heart	1982	4.00
❑ 8180	Never Say Die (Give a Little Bit More)/Front Page	1983	4.00
❑ 8193	Donna/Ocean Deep	1984	4.00
EPIC			
❑ 9597	Lucky Lips/Next Time	1963	20.00
❑ 9597 [PS]	Lucky Lips/Next Time	1963	25.00
❑ 9633	It's All in the Game/I'm Looking Out the Window	1963	20.00
❑ 9633 [PS]	It's All in the Game/I'm Looking Out the Window	1963	—
—Rumored to exist, but without conclusive evidence, we will delete this from future editions			
❑ 9670	I'm the Lonely One/I Only Have Eyes for You	1964	20.00
❑ 9670 [PS]	I'm the Lonely One/I Only Have Eyes for You	1964	25.00
❑ 9691	Bachelor Boy/True, True Lovin'	1964	20.00
❑ 9737	I Don't Wanna Love You/Look in My Eyes Maria	1964	15.00
❑ 9757	Again/The Minute You're Gone	1965	15.00
❑ 9810	I Could Easily Fall (In Love with You)/On My Word	1965	15.00
❑ 9839	The Twelfth of Never/Paradise Lost	1965	15.00
❑ 9866	Wind Me Up (and Let Me Go)/Eye of a Needle	1965	15.00
❑ 10018	Blue Turns to Grey/I'll Walk Alone	1966	15.00
❑ 10070	Visions/Quando, Quando, Quando	1966	15.00
❑ 10101	Time Drags By/The La La La Song	1966	15.00
❑ 10178	It's All Over/Heartbeat	1967	15.00
MONUMENT			
❑ 1211	Goodbye Sam, Hello Samantha/You Never Can Tell	1970	6.00
❑ 1229	I Ain't Got Time Anymore/Morning Comes Too Soon	1970	6.00
POLYDOR			
❑ 885336-7	All I Ask of You/Phantom of the Opera Overture, Act 2	1987	3.00
—With Sarah Brightman			
❑ 885336-7 [PS]	All I Ask of You/Phantom of the Opera Overture, Act 2	1987	3.00
ROCKET			
❑ YB-11463	Green Light/Needing a Friend	1979	4.00
❑ 40531	Miss You Nights/Love Enough	1976	4.00
❑ 40574	Devil Woman/Love On (Shine On)	1976	5.00
❑ 40652	Junior Cowboy/I Can't Ask for Anymore Than You	1976	4.00
❑ 40724	Don't Turn the Light Out/Nothing Left for Me to Say	1977	4.00
❑ 40771	You've Got Me Wondering/Try a Smile	1977	4.00
SIRE			
❑ 703	Living in Harmony/Jesus	1973	5.00
❑ 707	Power to All Our Friends/Come Back Billie Joe	1973	5.00
STRIPED HORSE			
❑ 7008	My Pretty One/Love Ya	1988	3.00
❑ 7008 [PS]	My Pretty One/Love Ya	1988	3.00
❑ 7011	Some People/Love Ya	1988	3.00
❑ 7011 [PS]	Some People/Love Ya	1988	3.00
UNI			
❑ 55061	All My Love/Our Story Book	1968	10.00
❑ 55069	Congratulations/High 'N' Dry	1968	10.00
❑ 55145	The Day I Met Marie/Sweet Little Jesus Boy	1969	12.00
WARNER BROS.			
❑ 7344	Throw Down a Line/Reflections	1969	8.00
—A-side by Cliff and Hank (Marvin)			

Albums

Number	Title (A Side/B Side)	Yr	NM
ABC-PARAMOUNT			
❑ 321 [M]	Cliff Sings	1960	80.00
❑ S-321 [S]	Cliff Sings	1960	100.00
❑ 391 [M]	Listen to Cliff	1961	80.00
❑ S-391 [S]	Listen to Cliff	1961	100.00
EMI AMERICA			
❑ SN-16220	Green Light	1981	8.00
❑ SN-16221	I'm Nearly Famous	1981	8.00
❑ SN-16253	Every Face Tells a Story	1981	8.00
❑ SW-17018	We Don't Talk Anymore	1979	10.00
❑ SW-17039	I'm No Hero	1980	10.00
❑ SW-17059	Wired for Sound	1981	10.00
❑ ST-17081	Now You See Me, Now You Don't	1982	10.00
❑ ST-17105	Give a Little Bit More	1983	10.00
EPIC			
❑ LN 24063 [M]	Summer Holiday	1963	40.00
❑ LN 24089 [M]	It's All in the Game	1964	30.00
❑ LN 24115 [M]	Cliff Richard in Spain	1965	30.00
❑ BN 26063 [S]	Summer Holiday	1963	50.00
❑ BN 26089 [S]	It's All in the Game	1964	40.00
❑ BN 26115 [S]	Cliff Richard in Spain	1965	40.00
ROCKET			
❑ PIG-2210	I'm Nearly Famous	1976	12.00
❑ PIG-2268	Every Face Tells a Story	1977	12.00
❑ BXL1-2958	Green Light	1978	12.00
WORD			
❑ WR-8306	Walking in the Light	1985	12.00

RICHARD AND THE YOUNG LIONS

45s

Number	Title (A Side/B Side)	Yr	NM
PHILIPS			
❑ 40381 [PS]	Open Up Your Door/Once Upon Your Smile	1966	20.00
❑ 40381	Open Up Your Door/Once Upon Your Smile	1966	20.00
❑ 40414	Nasty/Lost and Found	1966	25.00
❑ 40438	To Have and to Hold/You Can Make It	1967	40.00

RICHARDS, BETTY

45s

Number	Title (A Side/B Side)	Yr	NM
HIT			
❑ 241	These Boots Are Made for Walking/Working My Way Back to You	1966	8.00
—B-side by the Chellows			
❑ 254	How Does That Grab You Darlin'/Leaning on the Lamp Post	1966	8.00
—B-side by the Chords (2)			

RICHARDS, KATY

45s

Number	Title (A Side/B Side)	Yr	NM
HIT			
❑ 34	All Alone Am I/He Thinks I Still Care	1962	8.00
—B-side by Connie Landers			
❑ 66	Losing You/Still	1963	10.00
—B-side by Bobby Russell			
❑ 76	Judy's Turn to Cry/Wipe Out	1963	8.00
—B-side by the Music City Five			

R

Except when noted otherwise, VG = 25% of NM, and VG+ = 50% of NM. (Example: VG = $2.00, VG+ = $4.00 and NM = $8.00.)

RICHARDS, KEITH

12-Inch Singles

VIRGIN

Number	Title (A Side/B Side)	Yr	NM
❑ PR 2395 [DJ]	Take It So Hard (same on both sides)	1988	30.00
❑ PR 2558 [DJ]	You Don't Move Me (same on both sides?)	1988	40.00
❑ PR 2632 [DJ]	Struggle (Edit) (LP Version)/Make No Mistake	1988	40.00

45s

ROLLING STONES

Number	Title (A Side/B Side)	Yr	NM
❑ 19311	Run Rudolph Run/The Harder They Come	1978	30.00
❑ 19311 [DJ]	Run Rudolph Run (same on both sides)	1978	15.00

VIRGIN

Number	Title (A Side/B Side)	Yr	NM
❑ S7-56955	Eileen/Wicked As It Seems	1993	4.00
❑ 99240	Make No Mistake/It Means a Lot	1988	4.00
❑ 99240 [PS]	Make No Mistake/It Means a Lot	1988	7.00
❑ 99297	Take It So Hard/I Could Have Stood You Up	1988	4.00
❑ 99297 [PS]	Take It So Hard/I Could Have Stood You Up	1988	7.00

Albums

VIRGIN

Number	Title (A Side/B Side)	Yr	NM
❑ 90973	Talk Is Cheap	1988	12.00

RICHARDS, SYLVIA

45s

HIT

Number	Title (A Side/B Side)	Yr	NM
❑ 53	Blame It on the Bossa Nova/Let's Limbo Some More	1963	8.00

—B-side by Leroy Jones

RICHARDSON, JAPE See THE BIG BOPPER.

RICHARDSON, RUDI

45s

SUN

Number	Title (A Side/B Side)	Yr	NM
❑ 271	Fools Hall of Fame/Why Should I Cry	1957	30.00

RICHARDSON, WARREN S., JR.

Albums

COTILLION

Number	Title (A Side/B Side)	Yr	NM
❑ SD 9013	Warren S. Richardson, Jr.	1970	30.00

RICHEY, GEORGE

45s

ASCOT

Number	Title (A Side/B Side)	Yr	NM
❑ 2149	Silent Telephone/Lonely Part of Town	1964	10.00

RICHIE, LITTLE JOE See LITTLE JOE.

RICHIE AND THE ROYALS

45s

GOLDEN CREST

Number	Title (A Side/B Side)	Yr	NM
❑ 573	Be My Girl/We're Strollin'	1962	50.00

RELLO

Number	Title (A Side/B Side)	Yr	NM
❑ 1	And When I'm Near You/Goody Goody	1961	80.00
❑ 3	Be My Girl/We're Strollin'	1962	200.00

RICHIE AND THE SAXONS

45s

TIP

Number	Title (A Side/B Side)	Yr	NM
❑ 1020	Bottom of the Barrel/Easy Now	196?	50.00

RICHMAN, JONATHAN, AND THE MODERN LOVERS

45s

BESERKLEY

Number	Title (A Side/B Side)	Yr	NM
❑ 5701	Roadrunner/Friday on My Mind	1975	10.00
—B-side by Earth Quake			
❑ 5701 [PS]	Roadrunner/Friday on My Mind	1975	10.00
❑ 5743	New England/Here Come the Martians	1976	10.00
❑ 5743 [PS]	New England/Here Come the Martians	1976	10.00

Albums

BESERKLEY

Number	Title (A Side/B Side)	Yr	NM
❑ BZ-0048	Jonathan Richman and the Modern Lovers	1976	30.00
—Distributed by GRT			
❑ JBZ 0048	Jonathan Richman and the Modern Lovers	1976	25.00
—Distributed by Playboy/CBS			
❑ BZ-0050	The Modern Lovers	1976	30.00
—Distributed by GRT			
❑ JBZ 0050	The Modern Lovers	1978	25.00
—Distributed by Playboy/CBS			

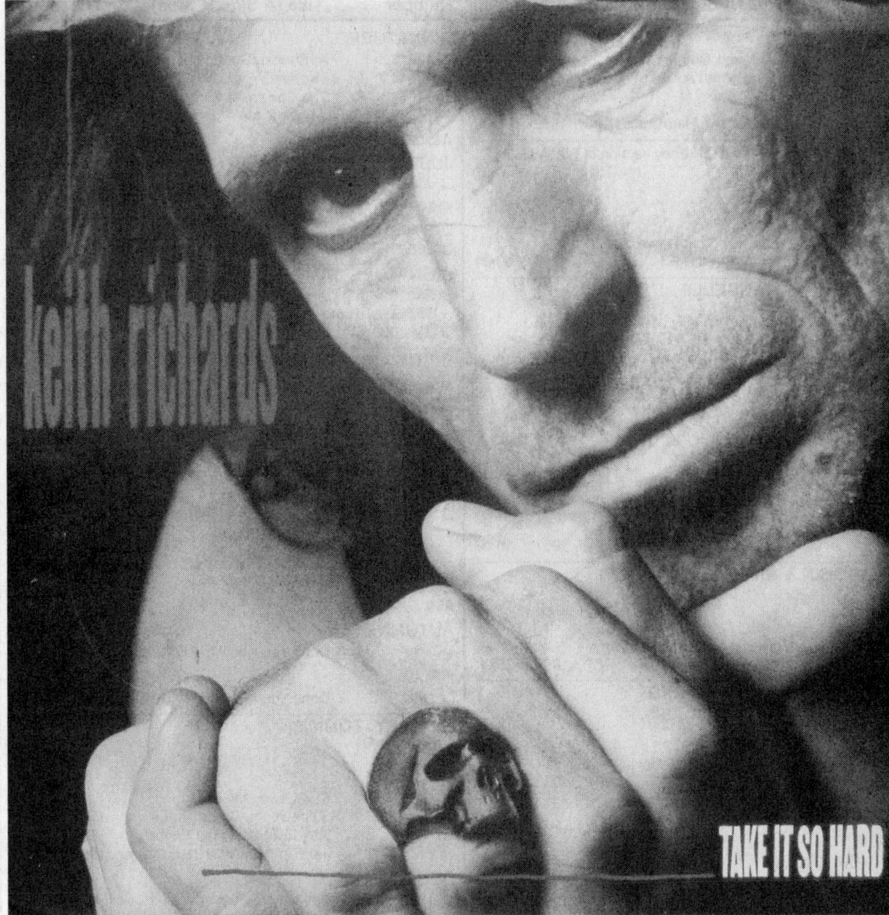

Keith Richards, "Take it So Hard," Virgin 99297, 1988, $5.

Number	Title (A Side/B Side)	Yr	NM
❑ BZ-0053	Rock 'N' Roll with the Modern Lovers	1977	18.00
—Distributed by Janus/GRT			
❑ JBZ 0055	Modern Lovers "Live"	1978	14.00
—Distributed by Playboy/CBS			
❑ JBZ 0060	Back in Your Life	1979	10.00
—Distributed by Playboy/CBS			
❑ 10060	Back in Your Life	1980	12.00
—Reissue -- change in distributing label to Elektra			
❑ PZ 34800	Rock 'N' Roll with the Modern Lovers	1977	14.00
—Distributed by Playboy/CBS			

BOMP!

Number	Title (A Side/B Side)	Yr	NM
❑ 4021	The Original Modern Lovers	1981	20.00
—Same album as Mohawk releasse			

HOME OF THE HITS

Number	Title (A Side/B Side)	Yr	NM
❑ HH-1910	The Modern Lovers	1975	50.00

MOHAWK

Number	Title (A Side/B Side)	Yr	NM
❑ SCALP 0002	The Original Modern Lovers	1981	25.00

RHINO

Number	Title (A Side/B Side)	Yr	NM
❑ RNLP 70091	The Modern Lovers	1986	12.00
—Reissue			
❑ RNLP 70092	Jonathan Richman and the Modern Lovers	1986	12.00
—Reissue			
❑ RNLP 70093	Rock 'N' Roll with the Modern Lovers	1986	12.00
—Reissue			
❑ RNLP 70094	Modern Lovers "Live"	1986	12.00
—Reissue			
❑ RNLP 70095	Back in Your Life	1986	12.00
—Reissue			

ROUNDER

Number	Title (A Side/B Side)	Yr	NM
❑ 9014	Modern Lovers '88	1988	12.00
❑ 9021	Jonathan Richman	1989	12.00
❑ 9024	Jonathan Goes Country	1990	12.00

SIRE

Number	Title (A Side/B Side)	Yr	NM
❑ 23939	Jonathan Sings!	1983	12.00

VAPOR

Number	Title (A Side/B Side)	Yr	NM
❑ 47086	I'm So Confused	1998	15.00
❑ 48216	Her Mystery Not of High Heels and Eye Shadow	2001	15.00

RICHY, PAUL

45s

SUN

Number	Title (A Side/B Side)	Yr	NM
❑ 338	The Legend of the Big Steeple/Broken Hearted Willie	1960	20.00

RICK AND DONNA

45s

A&M

Number	Title (A Side/B Side)	Yr	NM
❑ 710	I'm a Losing Guy/Wedding Bells Will Ring	1963	12.00

TOWER

Number	Title (A Side/B Side)	Yr	NM
❑ 112	A.B.C./What Good Is Love	1965	10.00

RICK AND THE KEENS

45s

AUSTIN

Number	Title (A Side/B Side)	Yr	NM
❑ 303	Peanuts/I'll Be Home	1961	50.00

JAMIE

Number	Title (A Side/B Side)	Yr	NM
❑ 1219	Your Turn ot Cry/Tender Years	1962	20.00

LE CAM

Number	Title (A Side/B Side)	Yr	NM
❑ 133	Darla/Someone New	1964	30.00
❑ 721	Peanuts/I'll Be Home	1961	50.00

SMASH

Number	Title (A Side/B Side)	Yr	NM
❑ 1705	Peanuts/I'll Be Home	1961	20.00
❑ 1722	Maybe/Popcorn	1961	20.00

TOLLIE

Number	Title (A Side/B Side)	Yr	NM
❑ 9016	Darla/Someone New	1964	20.00

RICK AND THE MASTERS

45s

CAMEO

Number	Title (A Side/B Side)	Yr	NM
❑ 226	Flame of Love/Here Come Nancy	1962	50.00
❑ 247	Let It Please Be You/I Don't Want Your Love	1963	50.00

Number	Title (A Side/B Side)	Yr	NM
HARAL			
❑ 776	Bewitched, Bothered and Bewildered/A Kissin' Friend	1962	60.00
TABA			
❑ 101	Flame of Love/Here Come Nancy	1962	150.00

RICK AND THE RAIDERS Early version of THE McCOYS. Also see RICK DERRINGER.

Number	Title (A Side/B Side)	Yr	NM
45s			
SONIC			
❑ 76234	You Know That I Love You/What Can I Do?	1963	50.00

RICK AND THE RANDELLS

Number	Title (A Side/B Side)	Yr	NM
45s			
ABC-PARAMOUNT			
❑ 10055	Let It Be You/Honey Doll	1959	40.00

RICK AND THE RAVENS With RAY MANZAREK, later of THE DOORS.

Number	Title (A Side/B Side)	Yr	NM
45s			
AURA			
❑ 4506	Henrietta/Just for Me	1965	60.00
❑ 4511	Soul Train/Geraldine	1965	50.00
POSAE			
❑ 101	Big Bucket "T"/Rampage	196?	80.00

RICK, ROBIN & HIM

Number	Title (A Side/B Side)	Yr	NM
45s			
V.I.P.			
❑ 25035	Three Choruses of Despair/Cause You Know Me	1965	25.00

RICKIE AND THE HALLMARKS

Number	Title (A Side/B Side)	Yr	NM
45s			
AMY			
❑ 877	Wherever You Are/Joanie Don't You Cry	1963	40.00

RICKLES, DON

Number	Title (A Side/B Side)	Yr	NM
Albums			
WARNER BROS.			
❑ WS 1745	Hello Dummy!	1968	15.00
❑ WS 1779	Don Rickles Speaks!	1969	15.00

R

RICKS, JIMMY Also see THE RAVENS.

Number	Title (A Side/B Side)	Yr	NM
45s			
ARNOLD			
❑ 1011	Canadian Sunset/Change of Heart	1961	15.00
ATCO			
❑ 6220	Daddy Rolling Stone/Homesick	1962	20.00
ATLANTIC			
❑ 2246	Trouble in Mind/Romance in the Dark	1964	15.00
BATON			
❑ 236	I'm a Fool to Want You/Bad Man of Missouri	1957	40.00
DECCA			
❑ 30443	What Have I Done/Lazy Mule	1957	25.00
FELSTED			
❑ 8560	Secret Love/If It Didn't Hurt So Much	1959	25.00
❑ 8582	Leaning On Your Love/Here Come the Tears Again	1959	25.00
FURY			
❑ 1070	I Wonder/Let Me Down Easy	1962	20.00
JOSIE			
❑ 796	She's Fine, She's Mine/The Unbeliever	1956	40.00
JUBILEE			
❑ 5559	Lonely Man/If You Ever Loved Someone	1967	12.00
❑ 5561	Wigglin' and Gigglin'/Long, Long Arm of Love	1967	12.00
❑ 5579	Don't Go to Strangers/Lonely Man	1967	12.00
❑ 5608	It's All in the Game/Baby Don't Leave Me	1967	12.00
❑ 5619	Snap Your Fingers/Wigglin' and Gigglin'	1968	12.00
MAINSTREAM			
❑ 625	Girl of My Dreams/Glow Worm	1965	15.00
MERCURY			
❑ 8296	Love Is the Thing/Too Soon	1952	80.00
PARIS			
❑ 504	Do You Promise/The Sugar Man Song	1957	30.00
SIGNATURE			
❑ 12013	At Sunrise/Goodnight My Love	1959	25.00
❑ 12040	I Needed Your Love/Timber	1960	20.00
❑ 12051	The Christmas Song/Love Is the Thing	1960	20.00
Albums			
JUBILEE			
❑ JGS-8021	Tell Her You Love Her	1969	50.00
MAINSTREAM			
❑ S-6050 [S]	Vibrations	1965	60.00
❑ 56050 [M]	Vibrations	1965	50.00
SIGNATURE			
❑ SM-1032 [M]	Jimmy Ricks	1961	200.00
—White label promo			
❑ SM-1032 [M]	Jimmy Ricks	1961	300.00

RICKY AND THE VACELS

Number	Title (A Side/B Side)	Yr	NM
45s			
EXPRESS			
❑ 711	Lorraine/Bubble Gum	1962	30.00
FARGO			
❑ 1050	His Girl/Don't Want Your Love No More	1963	30.00
❑ 1050	His Girl/Don't Want Your Love No More	1963	80.00
—Blue vinyl			

RICO AND THE RAVENS

Number	Title (A Side/B Side)	Yr	NM
45s			
AUTUMN			
❑ 6	Don't You Know/In My Heart	1965	15.00
RALLY			
❑ 1601	Don't You Know/In My Heart	1965	40.00

RIDGLEY, TOMMY

Number	Title (A Side/B Side)	Yr	NM
45s			
ATLANTIC			
❑ 1009	Ooh Lawdy My Baby/I'm Gonna Cross That River	1953	60.00
❑ 1039	Jam Up/Wish I Had Never	1954	40.00
❑ 2136	Jam Up Twist/Wish I Had Never	1962	15.00
DECCA			
❑ 48226	Anything But Love/Once in a Lifetime	1951	80.00
HERALD			
❑ 501	When I Meet My Girl/Whatcha Gonna Do	1957	20.00
❑ 508	Baby Do Liddle/Just a Memory	1957	20.00
❑ 513	Come back Baby/Woncha Gone	1958	20.00
❑ 526	Mairzy Doats and Dozy Doats/I've Heard That Story Before	1958	20.00
❑ 537	I'll Be True/Girl Across the Street	1959	20.00
❑ 540	Tina/How I Feel	1959	20.00
IMPERIAL			
❑ 5198	I Live My Life/Lavinia	1952	150.00
❑ 5203	Looped/Junie Mae	1952	150.00
❑ 5214	Monkey Man/Nobody Cares	1953	150.00
❑ 5223	Good Times/A Day Is Coming	1953	150.00
RIC			
❑ 968	Is It True/Let's Try and Talk It Over	1959	15.00
❑ 973	Do You Remember/Please Hurry Home	1960	15.00
❑ 978	Double Eye Whammy/Should I Ever Love Again	1961	15.00
❑ 982	Three Times/The Only Girl for Me	1961	15.00
❑ 984	The Girl from Kooka Monga/In the Same Old Way	1961	15.00
❑ 990	My Ordinary Girl/She's Got What It Takes	1962	12.00
❑ 993	Heavenly/I Love You Yes I Do	1963	12.00
❑ 994	Honest I Do/I've Heard That Story Before	1963	12.00
RONN			
❑ 36	It's the Same Old Way/I'm Not the Same Person	1969	10.00
WHITE CLIFFS			
❑ 260	Hey Little Chick/Did You Tell Him	1967	10.00

RIFFS, THE

Number	Title (A Side/B Side)	Yr	NM
45s			
JAMIE			
❑ 1296	Tell Her/I Been Thinkin'	1965	12.00
OLD TOWN			
❑ 1179	Tell Tale Friends/Why Are the Nights So Cold	1965	50.00
SUNNY			
❑ 22	Little Girl/Why Are the Nights So Cold	1964	200.00

RIG

Number	Title (A Side/B Side)	Yr	NM
45s			
CAPITOL			
❑ 2855	Quiet Lady/Sister Liza Bookman	1970	12.00
❑ 2952	Last Time Around/Have a Cigar	1970	12.00
Albums			
CAPITOL			
❑ ST-473	Rig	1970	20.00

RIGHTEOUS BROTHERS, THE Also see BOBBY HATFIELD; BILL MEDLEY; THE PARAMOURS; PHIL SPECTOR.

Number	Title (A Side/B Side)	Yr	NM
45s			
HAVEN			
❑ 800	Hold On to What You Got/Let Me Make the Music	1976	4.00
❑ 7002	Rock and Roll Heaven/I Just Wanna Be Me	1974	5.00
❑ 7004	Give It to the People/Love Is Not a Dirty Word	1974	4.00
❑ 7006	Dream On/Dr. Rock and Roll	1974	4.00
❑ 7011	High Blood Pressure/Never Say I Love You	1975	4.00
❑ 7014	Young Blood/Substitute	1975	4.00
MOONGLOW			
❑ 215	Little Latin Lupe Lu/I'm So Lonely	1963	20.00
❑ 215 [DJ]	Little Latin Lupe Lu/I'm So Lonely	1963	50.00
—Red vinyl promo			
❑ 221	Gotta Tell You How I Feel/If You're Lying, You'll Be Crying	1963	20.00
❑ 223	My Babe/Fee-Fi-Fidily-I-Oh	1963	20.00
❑ 224	Ko Ko Joe/B-Flat Blues	1963	20.00
❑ 231	Try to Find Another Man/I Still Love You	1964	20.00
❑ 234	Bring Your Love to Me/If You're Lying, You'll Be Crying	1964	20.00
❑ 235	This Little Girl of Mine/If You're Lying, You'll Be Crying	1964	15.00
❑ 238	Bring Your Love to Me/Fannie Mae	1965	15.00
❑ 239	You Can Have Her/Love or Magic	1965	15.00
❑ 242	Justine/In That Great Gettin' Up Morning	1965	15.00
❑ 243	For Your Love/Gotta Tell You How I Feel	1965	15.00
❑ 244	Georgia on My Mind/My Tears Will Go Away	1966	15.00
❑ 245	I Need a Girl/Bring Your Love to Me	1966	15.00
PHILLES			
❑ 124	You've Lost That Lovin' Feelin'/There's a Woman	1964	15.00
❑ 127	Just Once in My Life/The Blues	1965	15.00
❑ 127 [PS]	Just Once in My Life/The Blues	1965	30.00
❑ 129	Unchained Melody/Hung on You	1965	15.00
—With "Producer: Phil Spector" on the "Unchained Melody" side			
❑ 129	Unchained Melody/Hung on You	1965	30.00
—With no producer credit on the "Unchained Melody" side			
❑ 130	Ebb Tide/(I Love You) For Sentimental Reasons	1965	15.00
❑ 130 [PS]	Ebb Tide/(I Love You) For Sentimental Reasons	1965	30.00
❑ 132	The White Cliffs of Dover/She's Mine, All Mine	1966	20.00
❑ 132 [PS]	The White Cliffs of Dover/She's Mine, All Mine	1966	40.00
VERVE			
❑ CS8-5	Celebrity Scene: The Righteous Brothers	1967	60.00
—Box set of five singles (10520-10524). Price includes box, all 5 singles, jukebox title strips, bio. Records are sometimes found by themselves, so they are also listed separately.			
❑ 10383	(You're My) Soul and Inspiration/B Side Blues	1966	15.00
❑ 10383 [PS]	(You're My) Soul and Inspiration/B Side Blues	1966	30.00
❑ 10403	Rat Race/Green Onions	1966	15.00
❑ 10406	He/He Will Break Your Heart	1966	10.00
❑ 10406 [PS]	He/He Will Break Your Heart	1966	20.00
❑ 10430	Go Ahead and Cry/Things Didn't Go Your Way	1966	10.00
❑ 10449	On This Side of Goodbye/A Man Without a Dream	1966	10.00
❑ 10479	Along Came Jones/Jimmy's Blues	1967	8.00
❑ 10507	Melancholy Music Man/Don't Give Up on Me	1967	8.00
❑ 10520	(You're My) Soul and Inspiration/Go Ahead and Cry	1967	10.00
❑ 10521	Hold On, I'm Coming/He Will Break Your Heart	1967	10.00
❑ 10522	Melancholy Music Man/I Believe	1967	10.00
❑ 10523	I (Who Have Nothing)/Island in the Sun	1967	10.00
❑ 10524	My Girl/Something You Got	1967	10.00

Except when noted otherwise, VG = 25% of NM, and VG+ = 50% of NM. (Example: VG = $2.00, VG+ = $4.00 and NM = $8.00.)

Number	Title (A Side/B Side)	Yr	NM
❑ 10551	Stranded in the Middle of No Place/Been So Nice	1967	8.00
❑ 10551 [PS]	Stranded in the Middle of No Place/Been So Nice	1967	15.00
❑ 10577	Here I Am/So Many Lonely Nights Ahead	1968	8.00
❑ 10637	Let the Good Times Roll/You've Lost That Lovin' Feelin'	1968	8.00
❑ 10648	And the Party Goes On/Woman, Man Needs Ya	1968	8.00
❑ 10649	Good N' Nuff/Po' Folks	1968	8.00
❑ 871882-7	Unchained Melody/Hung on You	1989	4.00
7-Inch Extended Plays			
MOONGLOW			
❑ SD 71004	Little Latin Lupe Lu/Georgia on My Mind/Bye Bye Love//Fannie Mae/My Prayer/This Little Girl of Mine	1965	30.00
—Jukebox issue; small hole, plays at 33 1/3 rpm			
❑ SD 71004 [PS]	The Best of the Righteous Brothers	1965	30.00
Albums			
HAVEN			
❑ ST-9201	Give It to the People	1974	15.00
❑ ST-9203	Sons of Mrs. Righteous	1975	15.00
MGM			
❑ GAS-102	The Righteous Brothers (Golden Archive Series)	1970	15.00
❑ SE-4885	The History of the Righteous Brothers	1973	15.00
MOONGLOW			
❑ MLP-1001 [M]	Right Now!	1963	40.00
❑ MSP-1001 [S]	Right Now!	1963	60.00
❑ MLP-1002 [M]	Some Blue-Eyed Soul	1964	40.00
❑ MSP-1002 [S]	Some Blue-Eyed Soul	1964	60.00
❑ MLP-1003 [M]	This Is New!	1965	40.00
❑ MSP-1003 [S]	This Is New!	1965	60.00
❑ MLP-1004 [M]	The Best of the Righteous Brothers	1966	25.00
❑ MSP-1004 [S]	The Best of the Righteous Brothers	1966	30.00
PHILLES			
❑ PHLP-4007 [M]	You've Lost That Lovin' Feelin'	1964	25.00
❑ PHLPS-4007 [S]	You've Lost That Lovin' Feelin'	1964	40.00
❑ PHLP-4008 [M]	Just Once in My Life	1965	25.00
❑ PHLPS-4008 [S]	Just Once in My Life	1965	40.00
❑ PHLP-4009 [M]	Back to Back	1965	25.00
❑ PHLPS-4009 [S]	Back to Back	1965	40.00
❑ ST-90677 [S]	Back to Back	1965	40.00
—Capitol Record Club edition			
❑ T-90677 [M]	Back to Back	1965	30.00
—Capitol Record Club edition			
❑ ST-90692 [S]	You've Lost That Lovin' Feelin'	1965	50.00
—Capitol Record Club edition			
❑ T-90692 [M]	You've Lost That Lovin' Feelin'	1965	50.00
—Capitol Record Club edition			
RHINO			
❑ R1-71488 [(2)]	Anthology	1989	15.00
VERVE			
❑ V-5001 [M]	Soul and Inspiration	1966	20.00
❑ V6-5001 [S]	Soul and Inspiration	1966	25.00
❑ V-5004 [M]	Go Ahead and Cry	1966	20.00
❑ V6-5004 [S]	Go Ahead and Cry	1966	25.00
❑ V-5010 [M]	Sayin' Somethin'	1967	20.00
❑ V6-5010 [S]	Sayin' Somethin'	1967	25.00
❑ V-5020 [M]	Greatest Hits	1967	25.00
❑ V6-5020 [S]	Greatest Hits	1967	20.00
❑ V-5031 [M]	Souled Out	1967	30.00
❑ V6-5031 [S]	Souled Out	1967	20.00
❑ V6-5051	Standards	1968	20.00
❑ V6-5058	One for the Road	1968	20.00
—Without The Blossoms credited on the back cover			
❑ V6-5058	One for the Road	1968	30.00
—With The Blossoms credited on the back cover			
❑ V6-5071	Greatest Hits, Vol. 2	1969	20.00
❑ V6-5076	Re-Birth	1970	20.00
❑ ST-90669 [S]	Soul and Inspiration	1966	30.00
—Capitol Record Club edition			
❑ ST-90921 [S]	Go Ahead and Cry	1966	30.00
—Capitol Record Club edition			
❑ ST-91057 [S]	Sayin' Somethin'	1967	25.00
—Capitol Record Club edition			
❑ T-91057 [M]	Sayin' Somethin'	1967	30.00
—Capitol Record Club edition			
❑ 823662-1	Greatest Hits	198?	10.00

RILEY, BILLY LEE

Number	Title (A Side/B Side)	Yr	NM
45s			
ATLANTIC			
❑ 2525	Sittin' and a Waitin'/Happy Man	1968	8.00
BRUNSWICK			
❑ 55085	Rockin' on the Moon/Is That All to the Ball	1958	200.00
ENTRANCE			
❑ 7508	I Got a Thing About You Baby/You Don't Love Me	1972	5.00
GNP CRESCENDO			
❑ 371	Gonna Find a Cave/That's the Bag I'm In	1966	10.00
❑ 377	The Way I Feel/St. James Infirmary	1966	10.00
HIP			
❑ 8006	Family Portrait/Going Back to Memphis	1968	8.00
❑ 8011	Show Me Your Soul/Midnight Hour	1968	8.00
HOME OF THE BLUES			
❑ 233	Flip, Flop, and Fly/Teenage Letter	1961	30.00
MERCURY			
❑ 72314	Bo Diddley/Memphis	1964	15.00
❑ 72385	Mojo Workout/Charlene	1965	12.00
MOJO			
❑ 1933	Southern Soul/Midnight Hour	1967	10.00
SUN			
❑ 245	Trouble Bound/Rock with Me, Baby	1956	120.00
❑ 260	Flying Saucers Rock and Roll/I Want You Baby	1957	100.00
❑ 277	Red Hot/Pearly Lee	1957	60.00
❑ 289	Baby Please Don't Go/Wouldn't You Know	1958	50.00
❑ 313	Down by the Riverside/No Name Girl	1959	25.00
❑ 322	One More Time/Got the Water Boilin'	1959	50.00
❑ 1100	Kay/Looking for Her Heart	1969	6.00
❑ 1105	Pilot Town L.A./Workin' on the River	1969	6.00
❑ 1116	Tallahassee/Old Home Place	1970	5.00
Albums			
GNP CRESCENDO			
❑ GNP-2020 [M]	Billy Lee Riley	1966	15.00
❑ GNPS-2020 [S]	Billy Lee Riley	1966	20.00
MERCURY			
❑ MG-20958 [M]	The Whiskey A-Go-Go Presents Billy Lee Riley	1964	20.00
❑ MG-20965 [M]	Big Harmonica Special	1964	20.00
❑ MG-20974 [M]	Beatlemania Harmonica	1965	20.00
❑ SR-60958 [S]	The Whiskey A-Go-Go Presents Billy Lee Riley	1964	25.00
❑ SR-60965 [S]	Big Harmonica Special	1964	25.00
❑ SR-60974 [S]	Beatlemania Harmonica	1965	25.00

RILEY, BOB

Number	Title (A Side/B Side)	Yr	NM
45s			
CORAL			
❑ 62125	I Think It's a Shame/Blue Guitar Waltz	1959	20.00
DOT			
❑ 15625	Baby Sittin'/Without Your Love	1957	25.00
MGM			
❑ 12612	Wanda Jean/The Midnight Line	1958	150.00

RINCON SURFSIDE BAND, THE

Another creation of P.F. SLOAN and STEVE BARRI.

Number	Title (A Side/B Side)	Yr	NM
Albums			
DUNHILL			
❑ D 50001 [M]	Surfing Songbook	1965	200.00
❑ DS 50001 [S]	Surfing Songbook	1965	300.00

RINGO, JIMMY

Number	Title (A Side/B Side)	Yr	NM
45s			
DOT			
❑ 15787	I Like This Kind of Music/No One Else	1958	30.00
❑ 15997	I Like This Kind of Music/No One Else	1959	20.00

RINKY-DINKS, THE

See BOBBY DARIN.

RIO, BOBBY

Number	Title (A Side/B Side)	Yr	NM
45s			
ABC-PARAMOUNT			
❑ 10656	Boy Meets Girl/Don't Break My Heart and Run Away	1965	15.00
LENOX			
❑ 5569	Don Diddley/I Got You	1963	15.00

RIO, CHUCK

Also see THE CHAMPS; THE ORIGINALS (3).

Number	Title (A Side/B Side)	Yr	NM
45s			
CHALLENGE			
❑ 59019	Bad Boy/Denise	1958	20.00
❑ 59073	Ramblin' Through Dixie/Akiko	1960	20.00
FLAIR			
❑ 103	You Don't Have to Be a Baby to Cry/Big Boy	1962	40.00
JACKPOT			
❑ 48016	Margarita/C'est La Vie	1960	30.00
KENT			
❑ 308	Bye Bye Baby/No Matter What You Do	1958	20.00
SATURN			
❑ 402	Kreschendo Stomp/Rock-A-Nova	1962	50.00
TEQUILA			
❑ 100	Caravan/El Bracero	1961	20.00
❑ 103	La Cha Cha Twist/If You Were the Only Girl in the World	1961	20.00

RIOS, AUGIE

Number	Title (A Side/B Side)	Yr	NM
45s			
METRO			
❑ 20010	Donde Esta Santa Claus?/Ol' Fatso	1958	40.00
❑ 20016	Run Rattler Run/Hop, Skip and Jump	1959	30.00
❑ 20027	Trip to the Island/Teacher Walked Out of the Room	1959	30.00
MGM			
❑ 12966	Feliz Navidades/Gypsy Boy	1960	20.00
❑ 13292	Donde Esta Santa Claus?/Ol' Fatso	1964	12.00
SHELLEY			
❑ 181	I've Got a Girl/There's a Girl Down the Way	1963	40.00
❑ 186	When You Dance/No One	1963	30.00
❑ 192	Teach Me Tonight/Linda Lou	1964	20.00

RIOS, MIGUEL

Number	Title (A Side/B Side)	Yr	NM
45s			
A&M			
❑ 1193	A Song of Joy (Himno A La Alegria)/El Rio	1970	5.00
❑ 1193 [PS]	A Song of Joy (Himno A La Alegria)/El Rio	1970	8.00
❑ 1203	Himno A La Alegria/El Rio	1970	6.00
Albums			
A&M			
❑ SPX-4267	A Song of Joy	1970	15.00

RIOS, WALDO DE LOS

Number	Title (A Side/B Side)	Yr	NM
45s			
UNITED ARTISTS			
❑ 50772	Mozart Symphony No. 40 in G Minor, K.550, 1st Movement/Ode to Joy	1971	5.00
❑ 50821	Serenata #13/Concerto Para Piano	1971	4.00
❑ 50871	Elvira Madigan Theme/A Night of Music	1972	4.00
VAULT			
❑ 952	Those Were the Days/Aranguez (Mon Amour)	1969	5.00
WARNER BROS.			
❑ 8034	Elixir de Amor/Nabucco	1974	4.00
Albums			
UNITED ARTISTS			
❑ UAS-5554	Mozartmania	1972	12.00
❑ UAS-6802	Sinfonias	1971	12.00
VAULT			
❑ VS-126	International Hits	1969	15.00
WARNER BROS.			
❑ BS 2801	Operas	1974	12.00

RIOT

Number	Title (A Side/B Side)	Yr	NM
Albums			
ARIOLA			
❑ ARL 5007	Rock City	1977	15.00
CAPITOL			
❑ ST 12081	Narita	1979	12.00
❑ SN 16271	Narita	1982	10.00
CBS			
❑ BFZ 44232	Thundersteel	1988	12.00
❑ Z 45132	The Privilege of Power	1990	14.00
ELEKTRA			
❑ 55546	Fire Down Under	1981	12.00
❑ 60134	Restless Breed	1982	10.00
❑ 67969	Riot Live	1982	22.00
FIRE-SIGN			
❑ 87001	Rock City	1977	30.00
GRAND SLAMM			
❑ SLAM 6	Born In America	1989	14.00

R

Number	Title (A Side/B Side)	Yr	NM
QUALITY			
❑ QUS 1008	Born In America	1983	12.00

RIOT SQUAD, THE

45s

Number	Title (A Side/B Side)	Yr	NM
HANNA-BARBERA			
❑ 485	I Take It That We're Through/ Working Man	1966	15.00
REPRISE			
❑ 0457	Cry, Cry, Cry/How Is It Done?	1966	15.00
ROULETTE			
❑ 4621	Gonna Make You Mine/I Wanna Talk About My Baby	1965	15.00
❑ 4621 [PS]	Gonna Make You Mine/I Wanna Talk About My Baby	1965	50.00
—Promotional copy			

RIP CHORDS, THE

45s

Number	Title (A Side/B Side)	Yr	NM
COLUMBIA			
❑ 42687	Here I Stand/Karen	1963	15.00
❑ 42687 [DJ]	Here I Stand (same on both sides)	1963	20.00
—Black vinyl promo			
❑ 42687 [DJ]	Here I Stand (same on both sides)	1963	50.00
—Green vinyl promo			
❑ 42687 [PS]	Here I Stand	1963	50.00
—Sleeve is promo only			
❑ 42812	Gone/She Thinks I Still Care	1963	15.00
❑ 42812 [DJ]	Gone (same on both sides)	1963	50.00
—Blue vinyl promo			
❑ 42812 [PS]	Gone (same on both sides)	1963	50.00
—Sleeve is promo only			
❑ 42921	Hey, Little Cobra/The Queen	1963	20.00
❑ 42921 [DJ]	Hey, Little Cobra (same on both sides)	1963	50.00
—Yellow vinyl promo			
❑ 43035	Three Window Coupe/ Hot Rod U.S.A.	1964	15.00
❑ 43035 [DJ]	Three Window Coupe (same on both sides)	1964	50.00
—Red vinyl promo			
❑ 43093	One Piece Topless Bathing Suit/Wah-Wahini	1964	15.00
❑ 43221	Don't Be Scared/Bunny Hill	1965	15.00
SUNDAZED			
❑ SEP 188	Sting Ray//Red Hot Roadster/ Shut Down	2006	3.00
—Yellow vinyl			
❑ SEP 188 [PS]	Sting Ray//Red Hot Roadster/ Shut Down	2006	3.00
—Cardboard sleeve			

Albums

Number	Title (A Side/B Side)	Yr	NM
COLUMBIA			
❑ CL 2151 [M]	Hey Little Cobra and Other Hot Rod Hits	1964	40.00
—"Guaranteed High Fidelity" on label			
❑ CL 2151 [M]	Hey Little Cobra and Other Hot Rod Hits	1966	25.00
—"360 Sound Mono" on label			
❑ CL 2216 [M]	Three Window Coupe	1964	50.00
❑ CS 8951 [S]	Hey Little Cobra and Other Hot Rod Hits	1964	50.00
❑ CS 9016 [S]	Three Window Coupe	1964	70.00

RIP-CHORDS, THE

45s

Number	Title (A Side/B Side)	Yr	NM
ABCO			
❑ 105	I Love You the Most/Let's Do the Razzle Dazzle	1956	600.00
—Black vinyl			
❑ 105	I Love You the Most/Let's Do the Razzle Dazzle	1956	1500.
—Red vinyl			

RIPERTON, MINNIE

Also see ROTARY CONNECTION.

45s

Number	Title (A Side/B Side)	Yr	NM
CAPITOL			
❑ 4706	Memory Lane/I'm a Woman	1979	4.00
❑ 4761	Lover and Friend/ Return to Forever	1979	4.00
❑ 4902	Here We Go/Return to Forever	1980	4.00
❑ 4955	Give Me Time/Island in the Sun	1980	4.00
CHESS			
❑ 1980	Lonely Girl/You Gave Me Soul	1966	10.00
—As "Andrea Davis"			
EPIC			
❑ 11139	Every Time He Comes Around/ Reasons	1974	5.00
❑ 50020	Edge of a Dream/Seeing You This Way	1974	5.00
❑ 50057	Lovin' You/Edge of a Dream	1974	5.00
❑ 50128	Don't Let Anyone Bring You Down/Inside My Love	1975	5.00
❑ 50155	When It Comes Down To It/ Minnie's Lament	1975	5.00
❑ 50166	Simple Things/Minnie's Lament	1975	5.00
❑ 50190	Adventures in Paradise/ When It Comes Down To It	1976	5.00
❑ 50337	Stick Together (Part One)/ Stick Together (Part Two)	1977	5.00
❑ 50351	Young, Willing and Able/ Stick Together	1977	5.00
❑ 50394	Wouldn't Matter Where You Are	1977	5.00
❑ 50427	How Could I Love You More/ Young, Willing and Able	1977	5.00
GRT			
❑ 42	Oh! By the Way/Le Fleur	1972	6.00

Albums

Number	Title (A Side/B Side)	Yr	NM
ACCORD			
❑ SN-7205	Wistful Memories	1981	10.00
CAPITOL			
❑ SO-11936	Minnie	1979	10.00
❑ SN-12004	Perfect Angel	1979	10.00
—Reissue of Epic 32561			
❑ SN-12005	Adventures in Paradise	1979	10.00
—Reissue of Epic 33454			
❑ SN-12006	Stay in Love	1979	10.00
—Reissue of Epic 34191			
❑ SOO-12097	Love Lives Forever	1980	10.00
❑ ST-12189	The Best of Minnie Riperton	1981	10.00
❑ SN-16145	Perfect Angel	1980	8.00
—Budget-line reissue			
❑ SN-16146	Adventures in Paradise	1980	8.00
—Budget-line reissue			
❑ SN-16147	Stay in Love	1980	8.00
—Budget-line reissue			
EPIC			
❑ EQ 32561 [Q]	Perfect Angel	1974	20.00
❑ KE 32561	Perfect Angel	1974	12.00
❑ PE 33454	Adventures in Paradise	1975	12.00
❑ PEQ 33454 [Q]	Adventures in Paradise	1975	20.00
❑ PE 34191	Stay in Love	1977	12.00
GRT			
❑ 30001	Come To My Garden	1970	15.00
JANUS			
❑ 7011	Come To My Garden	1974	12.00
—Reissue of GRT LP			

RIPPLES AND WAVES PLUS MICHAEL, THE

Contrary to popular opinion, there is no Michael Jackson or any other Jackson Five involvement with this record.

45s

Number	Title (A Side/B Side)	Yr	NM
STEELTOWN			
❑ 689	Let Me Carry Your School Books/I Never Had a Girl	1969	80.00

RIPPY, RODNEY ALLEN

45s

Number	Title (A Side/B Side)	Yr	NM
BELL			
❑ 45403	Take Life a Little Easier/ World of Love	1973	8.00

Albums

Number	Title (A Side/B Side)	Yr	NM
BELL			
❑ 1311	Take Life a Little Easier	1974	20.00

RISERS, THE

Albums

Number	Title (A Side/B Side)	Yr	NM
IMPERIAL			
❑ LP-9269 [M]	She's a Bad Motorcycle	1964	100.00
❑ LP-12269 [S]	She's a Bad Motorcycle	1964	150.00

RISING STORM, THE

Albums

Number	Title (A Side/B Side)	Yr	NM
ARF! ARF!			
❑ 007	Alive in Anover Again	1983	120.00
REMNANT			
❑ BBA-3571	Calm Before the Rising Storm	1968	1200.
—VG value 600; VG+ value 900			
STANTON PARK			
❑ 001	Calm Before the Rising Storm	1991	20.00
—Reissue of Remnant album			

RISING SUNS, THE

Among the members of this group were RY COODER and TAJ MAHAL.

45s

Number	Title (A Side/B Side)	Yr	NM
COLUMBIA			
❑ 43534	Candy Man/The Devil's Got My Woman	1966	40.00

RITA AND THE TIARAS

45s

Number	Title (A Side/B Side)	Yr	NM
DORE			
❑ 783	Gone with the Wind Is My Love/ Wild Times	1967	1200.

RITA MARIE

45s

Number	Title (A Side/B Side)	Yr	NM
SUN			
❑ 1106	Lottie's Lament/Trouble	1969	5.00

RITCHIE FAMILY, THE

12-Inch Singles

Number	Title (A Side/B Side)	Yr	NM
CASABLANCA			
❑ NBD 20192	Put Your Feet to the Beat (6:58)/Bad Reputation (6:01)	1979	15.00
RCA			
❑ PD-13093	I'll Do My Best (For You Baby)/ You've Got Me Dancin'	1982	6.00
❑ PD-13551	All Night All Right/Fantasy	1983	6.00

45s

Number	Title (A Side/B Side)	Yr	NM
CASABLANCA			
❑ 2206	Put Your Feet to the Beat/ It's a Man's World	1979	4.00
❑ 2259	Give Me a Break/Bad Reputation	1980	4.00
❑ 2292	All My Love/I'll Never Be Able to Set You Free	1980	4.00
MARLIN			
❑ 3306	The Best Disco in Town/The Best Disco in Town (Part 2)	1976	4.00
❑ 3309	Life Is Music/Lady Luck	1977	4.00
❑ 3316	Quiet Village/Voodoo	1977	4.00
❑ 3323	American Generation/ Music Man	1978	4.00
RCA			
❑ PB-13092	I'll Do My Best (For You Baby)/ You've Got Me Dancin'	1982	3.00
❑ PB-13281	Walk with Me/Tonight I Need to Have Your Love	1982	3.00
❑ PB-13550	All Night All Right/Fantasy	1983	3.00
20TH CENTURY			
❑ 2218	Brazil/Hot Trip	1975	4.00
❑ 2252	I Want to Dance with You (Dance with Me)/ Lady Champagne	1975	4.00

Albums

Number	Title (A Side/B Side)	Yr	NM
CASABLANCA			
❑ NBLP-7166	Bad Reputation	1979	10.00
❑ NBLP-7223	Give Me a Break	1980	10.00
MARLIN			
❑ 2201	Arabian Nights	1976	10.00
❑ 2203	Life Is Music	1977	10.00
❑ 2206	African Queens	1977	10.00
❑ 2215	American Generation	1978	10.00
RCA VICTOR			
❑ AFL1-4324	I'll Do My Best	1982	10.00
❑ AFL1-4601	All Night, All Night	1983	10.00
20TH CENTURY			
❑ T-498	Brazil	1975	10.00

RITES, THE

45s

Number	Title (A Side/B Side)	Yr	NM
DECCA			
❑ 32218	Things/Hour Glass	1967	25.00

RITES OF SPRING, THE

45s

Number	Title (A Side/B Side)	Yr	NM
PARKWAY			
❑ 109	Why/Comin' On to Me	1966	30.00

RITTER, TEX

45s

Number	Title (A Side/B Side)	Yr	NM
CAPITOL			
❑ F885	Deck of Cards/Rye Whiskey	1950	30.00
❑ F928	Boogie Woogie Cowboy/He's a Cowboy Auctioneer	1950	40.00
❑ F1058	Bad Brahma Bull/ Blood on the Saddle	1950	30.00
❑ F1071	I've Got $5 and It's Saturday Night/Boiled Crawfish	1950	30.00
❑ F1098	Thief on the Cross/Beautiful Life	1950	30.00
❑ F1141	The Pledge of Allegiance/ Fiery Bear	1950	30.00
❑ F1188	Coal Smoke, Valve Oil and Steam/Nobody's Fool	1950	30.00
❑ F1264	Merry Christmas Polka/ Christmas Carols by the Old Corral	1950	30.00
❑ F1267	Daddy's Last Letter/ Onward Christian Soldiers	1950	30.00
❑ F1334	Stay Away from My Heart/ Big Blue Diamonds	1950	30.00
❑ F1388	You're Always Brand New/ My Bucket's Been Fixed	1951	25.00
❑ F1453	If I Could Steal You/There's No One to Cry Over Me	1951	25.00

Except when noted otherwise, VG = 25% of NM, and VG+ = 50% of NM. (Example: VG = $2.00, VG+ = $4.00 and NM = $8.00.)

Number	Title (A Side/B Side)	Yr	NM
❑ F1581	Wearin' Out Your Walkin' Shoes/Coffee Pot	1951	25.00
❑ F1629	Jealous Heart/Green Grow the Lilacs	1951	25.00
—Reissue of 1940s material first issued on 78			
❑ F1631	Rye Whiskey/Blood on the Saddle	1951	25.00
—Reissue of 1940s material first issued on 78			
❑ F1665	Deck of Cards/Ol' Shorty	195?	25.00
—Reissue of 1940s material first issued on 78			
❑ F1698	High Noon (Do Not Forsake Me)/Let Me Go Devil	195?	15.00
—Reissue			
❑ F1783	Tennessee Blues/Rock All Babies	1951	25.00
❑ PRO.1886 [DJ]	The Pledge of Allegiance (same on both sides)	196?	20.00
—Promo only; light blue label, dark blue print			
❑ F1977	As Long As the River Flows On/When My Blue Moon Turns to Gold	1952	25.00
❑ F2034	The Letter Edged in Black/There Shall Be Showers	1952	25.00
❑ 2097	Bump Tiddle Dee Bum Bum/I Just Can't Get Away	1968	8.00
❑ F2120	High Noon (Do Not Forsake Me)/Go On! Get Out!	1952	30.00
❑ F2174	Boll Weevil Song/Have I Told You Lately That I Love You	1952	25.00
❑ 2232	Texas/Stranger on Boot Hill	1968	8.00
❑ F2368	My Woman Ain't Pretty/Buffalo Dream	1953	25.00
❑ 2388	A Funny Thing Happened (On the Way to Miami)/The Governor and the Kid	1969	8.00
❑ F2475	The Marshall's Daughter/The San Antone Story	1953	25.00
❑ 2541	Growin' Up/A Letter to My Sons	1969	8.00
❑ F2594	Let Me Go, Devil!/Long Black Rifle	1953	25.00
❑ 2677	Wand'rin' Star/Chuckwagon Son of a Gun	1969	8.00
❑ F2686	Red Deck of Cards/Lord Send Me an Angel	1953	25.00
❑ F2756	Brave Man/Turn Around Boy	1954	20.00
❑ 2815	Green Green Valley/God Bless America Again	1970	7.00
❑ F2836	Lovely Veil of White/The Best Time of All	1954	20.00
❑ F2916	Prairie Home (Theme from The Vanishing Prairie)/The Bandit	1954	20.00
❑ F2957	Is There a Santa Claus/Ole Tex Kringle	1954	20.00
❑ F3003	A Whale of a Tale/High on a Mountain Top	1954	25.00
❑ 3154	Fall Away/Looking Back	1971	7.00
❑ F3179	Wichita/September Song	1955	20.00
❑ F3230	Gunsmoke/Remember the Alamo	1955	25.00
❑ 3286	Bourbon Man/Little Peanut Shell (Gotta Make It Grow)	1972	7.00
❑ F3324	These Hands/The Last Frontier	1956	20.00
❑ 3357	Lorena/The Keeper of the Key	1972	7.00
❑ F3363	If Jesus Came to Your House/Touch of the Master's Hand	1956	20.00
❑ F3430	The Wayward Wind/The Searchers (Ride Away)	1956	20.00
❑ 3457	Comin' After Jinny/You Will Have to Pay for Your Yesterday	1972	7.00
❑ F3538	The Last Wagon/Paul Bunyan Love	1956	20.00
❑ 3570	One Night for Willie/Sweet Bird of Youth	1973	6.00
❑ F3589	Green Grow the Lilacs/He Is There	1956	20.00
❑ F3640	Children and Fools/I Leaned on a Man	1957	20.00
❑ 3705	Willie, the Wandering Gypsy, and Me/Wind of Oklahoma	1973	6.00
❑ F3754	Trooper Hook (Chapter 1)/Trooper Hook (Chapter 2)	1957	20.00
❑ 3814	The Americans (A Canadian's Opinion)/He Who Is Without Sin	1974	6.00
❑ F3903	Here Was a Man/It Came Upon the Midnight Clear	1959	15.00
❑ F4006	Jealous Heart/Burning Sand	1958	15.00
❑ F4043	The History Song/I Look for a Love	1958	15.00
❑ F4217	Conversation with a Gun/Rye Whiskey	1959	15.00
❑ 4239	God Bless America Again/Lucy Let Your Lovelight Shine	1976	5.00
❑ F4285	Deck of Cards/Conversation with a Gun	1959	15.00
❑ 4364	The Vanishing American/The Gun, The Gold, and the Girl	1960	15.00
❑ 4567	I Dreamed of a Hill-Billy Heaven/The Wind and the Tree	1961	12.00
❑ 4644	Lonely Soldier Boy/Strange Little Melody	1961	12.00
❑ 4753	The Pledge of Allegiance/Ol' Shorty	1962	12.00
❑ 4849	Coo Se Coo/The Cookson Hills	1962	12.00
❑ 5004	The Gods Were Angry with Me/Will	1963	10.00
❑ 5159	That Son of a Saginaw Fisherman/Gallows Pole	1964	10.00
❑ 5224	Fool's Paradise/Gimme Some	1964	10.00
❑ 5347	She Loved This House/I Dreamed of a Hill-Billy Heaven	1965	10.00
❑ 5474	Bummin' Around/Take Him Fishin'	1965	10.00
❑ 5574	The Men in My Little Girl's Life/Custody	1966	8.00
❑ 5697	Mommy, Daddy, Tell Us/Remember Us	1966	8.00
❑ 5839	Just Beyond the Moon/Greedy Old Dog	1967	8.00
❑ 5966	A Working Man's Prayer/William Barrett Travis: A Message from the Alamo	1967	8.00
❑ 54-40179	The Chisholm Trail/San Antonio Rose	1949	30.00
❑ 54-40180	Try Me One More Time/Boll Weevil Song	1949	30.00
❑ 54-40181	Blood on the Saddle/Rounded Up in Glory	1949	30.00
❑ 54-40182	Rye Whiskey/Bad Brahma Bull	1949	30.00
—The above four comprise a box set			
❑ F40248	Never Mind My Tears/Some Sweet Day	1949	40.00

7-Inch Extended Plays

CAPITOL

Number	Title (A Side/B Side)	Yr	NM
❑ EAP 1-431	High Noon (Do Not Forsake Me)/Green Grow the Lilacs//I'm Wastin' My Tears on You/Jealous Heart	195?	20.00
❑ EAP 1-431 [PS]	Tex Ritter Sings	195?	20.00

Albums

BUCKBOARD

Number	Title (A Side/B Side)	Yr	NM
❑ BBS 1030	Tex Ritter	198?	10.00

CAPITOL

Number	Title (A Side/B Side)	Yr	NM
❑ ST-213	Chuck Wagon Days	1969	20.00
❑ ST-467	Green Green Valley	1970	20.00
❑ T 971 [M]	Songs from the Western Screen	1958	80.00
—Turquoise or gray label			
❑ T 971 [M]	Songs from the Western Screen	1959	40.00
—Black colorband label, logo at left			
❑ T 971 [M]	Songs from the Western Screen	1962	25.00
—Black colorband label, logo at top			
❑ T 1100 [M]	Psalms	1959	50.00
—Black colorband label, logo at left			
❑ T 1100 [M]	Psalms	1962	25.00
—Black colorband label, logo at top			
❑ ST 1292 [S]	Blood on the Saddle	1960	40.00
—Black colorband label, logo at left			
❑ ST 1292 [S]	Blood on the Saddle	1962	25.00
—Black colorband label, logo at top			
❑ T 1292 [M]	Blood on the Saddle	1960	30.00
—Black colorband label, logo at left			
❑ T 1292 [M]	Blood on the Saddle	1962	20.00
—Black colorband label, logo at top			
❑ SW 1562 [S]	The Lincoln Hymns	1961	40.00
❑ W 1562 [M]	The Lincoln Hymns	1961	30.00
❑ SM-1623	Hillbilly Heaven	1976	10.00
—Reissue with new prefix			
❑ ST 1623 [S]	Hillbilly Heaven	1961	40.00
—Black colorband label, logo at left			
❑ ST 1623 [S]	Hillbilly Heaven	1962	25.00
—Black colorband label, logo at top			
❑ T 1623 [M]	Hillbilly Heaven	1961	30.00
—Black colorband label, logo at left			
❑ T 1623 [M]	Hillbilly Heaven	1962	20.00
—Black colorband label, logo at top			
❑ ST 1910 [S]	Border Affair	1963	25.00
❑ T 1910 [M]	Border Affair	1963	20.00
❑ ST 2402 [S]	The Friendly Voice of Tex Ritter	1965	25.00
❑ T 2402 [M]	The Friendly Voice of Tex Ritter	1965	20.00
❑ DT 2595 [R]	The Best of Tex Ritter	1966	15.00
❑ T 2595 [M]	The Best of Tex Ritter	1966	25.00
❑ ST 2743 [S]	Sweet Land of Liberty	1967	25.00
❑ T 2743 [M]	Sweet Land of Liberty	1967	30.00
❑ ST 2786 [S]	Just Beyond the Moon	1967	25.00
❑ T 2786 [M]	Just Beyond the Moon	1967	30.00
❑ ST 2890 [S]	Bum Tiddil Dee Bum Bum!	1968	25.00
❑ T 2890 [M]	Bum Tiddil Dee Bum Bum!	1968	50.00
❑ ST 2974	Tex Ritter's Wild West	1968	25.00
❑ H 4004 [10]	Cowboy Favorites	195?	180.00
❑ ST-11037	Supercountrylegendary	1972	15.00
❑ SKC-11241 [(3)]	An American Legend	1973	30.00
❑ ST-11351	Fall Away	1974	15.00
❑ ST-11503	Comin' After Jinny	1976	15.00

HILLTOP

Number	Title (A Side/B Side)	Yr	NM
❑ PTP-2020 [(2)]	My Kinda Songs	197?	15.00
❑ JS-6043	Tex Ritter Sings His Hits	196?	12.00
❑ JS-6075	Love You As Big As Texas	196?	12.00
❑ JS-6138	High Noon	196?	12.00
❑ JS-6155	Tex	197?	12.00

LABREA

Number	Title (A Side/B Side)	Yr	NM
❑ L-8036 [M]	Jamboree, Nashville Style	196?	20.00
❑ LS-8036 [S]	Jamboree, Nashville Style	196?	25.00

PREMIER

Number	Title (A Side/B Side)	Yr	NM
❑ 9023	Tex Ritter and the Rio Grande River Boys	196?	12.00

RITUALS, THE

Featuring Arnie Ginsburg, formerly of JAN AND ARNIE.

45s

ARWIN

Number	Title (A Side/B Side)	Yr	NM
❑ 120	Girl in Zanzibar/Guitarro	1963	30.00
❑ 127	This Is Paradise/Gone	1964	30.00
❑ 128	Surfers Rule/Gone	1964	40.00

RIVERA, LUCY

45s

END

Number	Title (A Side/B Side)	Yr	NM
❑ 1041	Make Me Queen/Ific	1959	20.00

RIVERS, JOHNNY

45s

ATLANTIC

Number	Title (A Side/B Side)	Yr	NM
❑ 3011	Sitting in Limbo/Artists and Poets	1974	5.00
❑ 3028	Six Days on the Road/Artists and Poets	1974	5.00
❑ 3230	John Lee Hooker '74/Get It Up for Love	1974	5.00

BIG TREE

Number	Title (A Side/B Side)	Yr	NM
❑ 16094	Swayin' to the Music (Slow Dancin')/Outside Help	1977	4.00
❑ 16106	Curious Mind (Um, Um, Um, Um, Um, Um)/Ashes and Sand	1977	4.00

CAPITOL

Number	Title (A Side/B Side)	Yr	NM
❑ 4850	Long Black Veil/This Could Be the One	1962	15.00
❑ 4913	If You Want It, I've Got It/My Heart Is In Your Hands	1963	15.00
❑ 5232	Long Black Veil/Don't Look Now	1964	15.00

CHANCELLOR

Number	Title (A Side/B Side)	Yr	NM
❑ 1070	I Get So Doggone Lonesome/Knock Three Times	1961	20.00
❑ 1108	To Be Loved/Too Good to Last	1962	20.00

CORAL

Number	Title (A Side/B Side)	Yr	NM
❑ 62425	That's My Baby/Your First and Last Love	1964	15.00

CUB

Number	Title (A Side/B Side)	Yr	NM
❑ 9047	Everyday/Darling Talk to Me	1959	25.00
❑ 9058	Answer Me My Love/The Customary Thing	1960	20.00

DEE DEE

Number	Title (A Side/B Side)	Yr	NM
❑ 239	The White Cliffs of Dover/Your First and Last Love	1959	20.00

EPIC

Number	Title (A Side/B Side)	Yr	NM
❑ 50121	Help Me Rhonda/New Lovers and Old Friends	1975	5.00
—A-side features Brian Wilson on backing vocals			
❑ 50150	Can I Change My Mind/John Lee Hooker	1975	4.00
❑ 50208	Welcome Home/Outside Help	1976	4.00
❑ 50248	Linda Lue/Outside Help	1976	4.00

ERA

Number	Title (A Side/B Side)	Yr	NM
❑ 3037	Call Me/Andersonville	1961	20.00

GONE

Number	Title (A Side/B Side)	Yr	NM
❑ 5026	Baby Come Back/Long Long Walk	1958	40.00

GUYDEN

Number	Title (A Side/B Side)	Yr	NM
❑ 2003	You're the One/A Hole in the Ground	1958	25.00
❑ 2110	You're the One/A Hole in the Ground	1964	15.00

IMPERIAL

Number	Title (A Side/B Side)	Yr	NM
❑ 66032	Memphis/It Wouldn't Happen with Me	1964	12.00
❑ 66056	Maybelline/Walk Myself On Home	1964	10.00
❑ 66056 [PS]	Maybelline/Walk Myself On Home	1964	15.00
❑ 66075	Mountain of Love/Moody River	1964	10.00
❑ 66087	Midnight Special/Cupid	1965	10.00
❑ 66112	Seventh Son/Unsquare Dance	1965	10.00
❑ 66112 [PS]	Seventh Son/Unsquare Dance	1965	15.00
❑ 66133	Where Have All the Flowers Gone/Love Me While You Can	1965	10.00

R

Number	Title (A Side/B Side)	Yr	NM
❑ 66144	Under Your Spell Again/ Long Time Man	1965	10.00
❑ 66144 [PS]	Under Your Spell Again/ Long Time Man	1965	15.00
❑ 66159	Secret Agent Man/You Dig	1966	12.00
❑ 66159 [PS]	Secret Agent Man/You Dig	1966	15.00
❑ 66175	(I Washed My Hands In) Muddy Water/Roogalator	1966	10.00
❑ 66205	Poor Side of Town/ A Man Can Cry	1966	12.00
❑ 66205 [PS]	Poor Side of Town/ A Man Can Cry	1966	15.00
❑ 66227	Baby I Need Your Lovin'/ Gettin' Ready for Tomorrow	1967	10.00
❑ 66227 [PS]	Baby I Need Your Lovin'/ Gettin' Ready for Tomorrow	1967	15.00
❑ 66244	The Tracks of My Tears/ Rewind Medley	1967	10.00
❑ 66244 [PS]	The Tracks of My Tears/ Rewind Medley	1967	15.00
❑ 66267	Summer Rain/Memory of the Coming Good	1967	10.00
❑ 66286	Look To Your Soul/ Something's Strange	1968	8.00
❑ 66286 [PS]	Look To Your Soul/ Something's Strange	1968	12.00
❑ 66314	Everybody's Talkin'/ The Way We Live	1968	—
—Unreleased			
❑ 66335	Right Relations/Better Life	1968	8.00
❑ 66335 [PS]	Right Relations/Better Life	1968	12.00
❑ 66360	These Are Not My People/ Going Back to Big Sur	1969	8.00
❑ 66386	Muddy River/Resurrection	1969	8.00
❑ 66386 [PS]	Muddy River/Resurrection	1969	12.00
❑ 66418	One Woman/Ode to John Lee	1969	8.00
❑ 66448	Into the Mystic/Jesus Is a Soul Man	1970	8.00
❑ 66453	Fire and Rain/Apple Tree	1970	8.00
MCA			
❑ 52502	Heartbreak Love/Why Can't We Communicate	1984	4.00
MGM			
❑ 13266	Answer Me, My Love/ Customary Thing	1964	15.00
RIVERAIRE			
❑ 1001	Don't Bug Me Baby/ Haunting Black Eyes	1959	30.00
ROULETTE			
❑ 4565	Baby Come Back/ Long Long Walk	1964	20.00
RSO			
❑ 1030	Romance (Give Me a Chance)/ Don't Need No Other Now	1980	4.00
❑ 1045	China/The Price	1980	4.00
SOUL CITY			
❑ 007	Ashes and Sand/Outside Help	1977	5.00
❑ 008	Swayin' to the Music (Slow Dancin')/Outside Help	1977	8.00
❑ 010	Little White Lie/Be My Baby	1980	5.00
❑ 014	RSVP/The Price	1982	5.00
SUEDE			
❑ 1401	Little Girl/Two by Two	1957	100.00
—As "Johnny Ramistella"			
UNITED ARTISTS			
❑ 0101	Memphis/Secret Agent Man	1973	4.00
❑ 0102	Mountain of Love/Maybellene	1973	4.00
❑ 0103	Seventh Son/Midnight Special	1973	4.00
❑ 0104	Poor Side of Town/ Baby I Need Your Lovin'	1973	4.00
❑ 0105	Summer Rain/The Tracks of My Tears	1973	4.00
—0101 through 0105 are "Silver Spotlight Series" reissues			
❑ XW198	Blue Suede Shoes/Stories to a Child	1973	5.00
❑ XW226	Searchin'-So Fine/ New York City Dues	1973	5.00
❑ XW310	I'll Feel a Whole Lot Better/ Over the Line	1973	5.00
❑ XW522	Rockin' Pneumonia-Boogie Woogie Flu/Blue Suede Shoes	1974	4.00
—Reissue			
❑ XW523	Where Have All the Flowers Gone/(I Washed My Hands in) Muddy Water	1974	4.00
—Reissue			
❑ 741	Oh What a Kiss/ Knock Three Times	1964	12.00
❑ 769	Dream Doll/To Be Loved	1964	12.00
❑ 50778	Sea Cruise/Our Lady of the Well	1971	6.00
❑ 50822	Think His Name/ Permanent Change	1971	6.00
❑ 50948	On the Borderline/ Come Home America	1972	5.00

R

Number	Title (A Side/B Side)	Yr	NM
❑ 50960	Rockin' Pneumonia-Boogie Woogie Flu/Come Home America	1972	6.00
—On some pressings, the intro of the A-side is not repeated (lasts about 20 seconds)			
❑ 50960	Rockin' Pneumonia-Boogie Woogie Flu/Come Home America	1972	6.00
—On most pressings, the intro of the A-side lasts about 35 seconds			
7-Inch Extended Plays			
IMPERIAL			
❑ LP-4-2293	Where Have All the Flowers Gone/Michael (Row the Boat Ashore)/Tall Oak Tree// Mr. Tambourine Man/Green, Green/Blowin' in the Wind	196?	25.00
—Stereo jukebox issue; small hole, plays at 33 1/3 rpm			
❑ LP-4-2293 [PS]	Johnny Rivers Rocks the Folk	196?	25.00
Albums			
ATLANTIC			
❑ SD 7301	The Road	1974	12.00
BIG TREE			
❑ BT 76004	Outside Help	1977	12.00
CAPITOL			
❑ ST 2161 [S]	The Sensational Johnny Rivers	1964	25.00
❑ T 2161 [M]	The Sensational Johnny Rivers	1964	20.00
COLUMBIA			
❑ FE 38429	Not a Through Street	1983	10.00
❑ PE 38429	Not a Through Street	1985	8.00
—Budget-line reissue			
EPIC			
❑ PE 33681	New Lovers and Old Friends	1975	12.00
IMPERIAL			
❑ LP-9264 [M]	Johnny Rivers at the Whiskey A-Go-Go	1964	20.00
—Black label with pink and white at left			
❑ LP-9264 [M]	Johnny Rivers at the Whiskey A-Go-Go	1966	12.00
—Black label with green and white at left			
❑ LP-9274 [M]	Here We A-Go-Go Again!	1964	20.00
—Black label with pink and white at left			
❑ LP-9274 [M]	Here We A-Go-Go Again!	1966	12.00
—Black label with green and white at left			
❑ LP-9280 [M]	Johnny Rivers In Action!	1965	20.00
—Black label with pink and white at left			
❑ LP-9280 [M]	Johnny Rivers In Action!	1966	12.00
—Black label with green and white at left			
❑ LP-9284 [M]	Meanwhile Back at the Whiskey a-Go-Go	1965	20.00
—Black label with pink and white at left			
❑ LP-9284 [M]	Meanwhile Back at the Whiskey a-Go-Go	1966	12.00
—Black label with green and white at left			
❑ LP-9293 [M]	Johnny Rivers Rocks the Folk	1965	20.00
—Black label with pink and white at left			
❑ LP-9293 [M]	Johnny Rivers Rocks the Folk	1966	12.00
—Black label with green and white at left			
❑ LP-9307 [M]	...And I Know You Wanna Dance	1966	12.00
—Black label with green and white at left			
❑ LP-9307 [M]	...And I Know You Wanna Dance	1966	20.00
—Black label with pink and white at left			
❑ LP-9324 [M]	Johnny Rivers' Golden Hits	1966	15.00
❑ LP-9334 [M]	Changes	1966	15.00
❑ LP-9341 [M]	Rewind	1967	20.00
❑ LP-9372 [M]	Realization	1968	40.00
❑ LP-12264 [S]	Johnny Rivers at the Whiskey A-Go-Go	1964	25.00
—Black label with pink and white at left			
❑ LP-12264 [S]	Johnny Rivers at the Whiskey A-Go-Go	1966	15.00
—Black label with green and white at left			
❑ LP-12274 [S]	Here We A-Go-Go Again!	1964	25.00
—Black label with pink and white at left			
❑ LP-12274 [S]	Here We A-Go-Go Again!	1966	15.00
—Black label with green and white at left			
❑ LP-12280 [S]	Johnny Rivers In Action!	1965	25.00
—Black label with pink and white at left			
❑ LP-12280 [S]	Johnny Rivers In Action!	1966	15.00
—Black label with green and white at left			
❑ LP-12284 [S]	Meanwhile Back at the Whiskey a-Go-Go	1965	25.00
—Black label with pink and white at left			
❑ LP-12284 [S]	Meanwhile Back at the Whiskey a-Go-Go	1966	15.00
—Black label with green and white at left			
❑ LP-12293 [S]	Johnny Rivers Rocks the Folk	1965	25.00
—Black label with pink and white at left			
❑ LP-12293 [S]	Johnny Rivers Rocks the Folk	1966	15.00
—Black label with green and white at left			
❑ LP-12307 [S]	...And I Know You Wanna Dance	1966	15.00
—Black label with green and white at left			
❑ LP-12307 [S]	...And I Know You Wanna Dance	1966	25.00
—Black label with pink and white at left			
❑ LP-12324 [S]	Johnny Rivers' Golden Hits	1966	20.00
❑ LP-12334 [S]	Changes	1966	20.00
❑ LP-12341 [S]	Rewind	1967	20.00
❑ LP-12372 [S]	Realization	1968	20.00

Number	Title (A Side/B Side)	Yr	NM
❑ LP-12427	A Touch of Gold	1969	20.00
❑ LP-16001	Slim Slo Slider	1970	20.00
LIBERTY			
❑ LN-10120	The Best of Johnny Rivers	1981	8.00
❑ LN-10121	Changes	1981	8.00
—Budget-line reissue			
❑ LN-10154	Blue Suede Shoes	1981	8.00
—Budget-line reissue			
❑ LO-12324	Johnny Rivers' Golden Hits	198?	8.00
—Budget-line reissue			
❑ LW-12427	A Touch of Gold	198?	8.00
—Budget-line reissue			
MCA			
❑ 917	Greatest Hits	1985	10.00
PICKWICK			
❑ PC-3022 [M]	Johnny Rivers	196?	15.00
❑ SPC-3022 [R]	Johnny Rivers	196?	10.00
—Later covers have "electronically enhanced for STEREO" at upper right			
❑ SPC-3022 [R]	Johnny Rivers	196?	12.00
—First pressing covers have no "electronically enhanced for STEREO" at upper right			
❑ SPC-3191	If You Want It, I Got It	196?	12.00
RSO			
❑ RS-1-3082	Borrowed Time	1980	10.00
SEARS			
❑ SPS-417	Mr. Teenage	196?	25.00
❑ SPS-487	Groovin'	1968	25.00
SOUL CITY			
❑ SC 1007-1	Greatest Hits	1998	20.00
—500 copies, each autographed by Johnny Rivers			
SUNSET			
❑ SUM-1157 [M]	Whiskey A-Go-Go Revisited	1967	12.00
❑ SUS-5157 [S]	Whiskey A-Go-Go Revisited	1967	10.00
❑ SUS-5251	The Early Years	1969	10.00
UNART			
❑ M-20007 [M]	The Great Johnny Rivers	1967	12.00
❑ S-21007 [S]	The Great Johnny Rivers	1967	12.00
UNITED ARTISTS			
❑ UA-LA075-F	Blue Suede Shoes	1973	12.00
❑ USX-93 [(2)]	Johnny Rivers Superpak	1971	20.00
❑ UA-LA253-G	The Very Best of Johnny Rivers	1974	12.00
❑ UA-LA387-E	The Very Best of Johnny Rivers	1975	12.00
❑ UA-LA486-G	Wild Night	1976	12.00
❑ UAL-3386 [M]	Go, Johnny, Go	1964	20.00
❑ UAS-5532	Home Grown	1971	15.00
❑ UAS-5650	L.A. Reggae	1972	15.00
❑ UAS-6386 [S]	Go, Johnny, Go	1964	25.00
❑ ST-90813 [S]	Go, Johnny, Go	1965	30.00
—Capitol Record Club edition			
❑ T-90813 [M]	Go, Johnny, Go	1965	25.00
—Capitol Record Club edition			
WARNER BROS.			
❑ R133498 [S]	Johnny Rivers' Golden Hits	197?	30.00
—RCA Music Service edition of Imperial LP-12324 on "Burbank" palm trees label; why this was pressed on Warner Bros. is anyone's guess, but it doesn't appear to be an error			

RIVERS, TONY, AND THE CASTAWAYS

Number	Title (A Side/B Side)	Yr	NM
45s			
CONSTELLATION			
❑ 128	I Love the Way You Walk/ I Love You	1964	15.00

RIVIERAS, THE (1) R&B vocal group from northern New Jersey.

Number	Title (A Side/B Side)	Yr	NM
45s			
COED			
❑ 503	Count Every Star/True Love Is Hard to Find	1958	50.00
❑ 508	Moonlight Serenade/ Neither Rain Nor Snow	1959	40.00
❑ 513	Our Love/Midnight Flyer	1959	30.00
❑ 513	Our Love/True Love Is Hard to Find	1959	30.00
❑ 522	Since I Made You Cry/ 11th Hour Melody	1959	30.00
❑ 529	Blessing of Love/ Moonlight Cocktails	1960	25.00
❑ 538	My Friend/Great Big Eyes	1960	25.00
❑ 542	Easy to Remember/ Stay in My Heart	1960	25.00
❑ 551	El Doraado/Refrigerator	1961	25.00
❑ 592	Moonlight Cocktails/Midnight Flyer	1964	15.00
LOST-NITE			
❑ 162	Blessing of Love/ Moonlight Cocktails	196?	6.00
—Reissue			
❑ 164	Count Every Star/True Love Is Hard to Find	196?	6.00
—Reissue			

Except when noted otherwise, VG = 25% of NM, and VG+ = 50% of NM. (Example: VG = $2.00, VG+ = $4.00 and NM = $8.00.)

Number	Title (A Side/B Side)	Yr	NM
❑ 167	Moonlight Serenade/Neither Rain Nor Snow	196?	6.00
—Reissue			
❑ 169	Our Love/True Love Is Hard to Find	196?	6.00
—Reissue			
❑ 170	Easy to Remember/ Stay in My Heart	196?	6.00
—Reissue			
❑ 172	Since I Made You Cry/ 11th Hour Melody	196?	6.00
—Reissue			
Albums			
POST			
❑ 2000	The Rivieras Sing	196?	40.00

RIVIERAS, THE (2) Surf-garage rock band from South Bend, Indiana.

Number	Title (A Side/B Side)	Yr	NM
45s			
LANA			
❑ 136	California Sun/H.B. Goose Step	196?	8.00
—Oldies reissue			
RIVIERA			
❑ 1401	California Sun/H.B. Goose Step	1964	20.00
❑ 1401	California Sun/Played On	1964	40.00
—Possibly as few as 1,000 were pressed with this B-side			
❑ 1402	Little Donna/Let's Have a Party	1964	15.00
❑ 1403	Rockin' Robin/Battle Line	1964	15.00
❑ 1405	Whole Lotta Shakin'/Rip It Up	1965	15.00
❑ 1405	Whole Lotta Shakin'/ Lakeview Lane	1965	20.00
❑ 1406	Let's Go to Hawaii/ Lakeview Lane	1965	15.00
❑ 1407	Somebody Asked Me/ Somebody New	1965	15.00
—Credited to the Rivieras, but actually by Bobby Whiteside			
❑ 1409	Bug Juice/Never Feel the Pain	1965	20.00
Albums			
RIVIERA			
❑ 701 [M]	Campus Party	1964	250.00
U.S.A.			
❑ 102 [M]	Let's Have a Party	1964	150.00

RIVIERAS, THE (3)

Number	Title (A Side/B Side)	Yr	NM
45s			
ALGONQUIN			
❑ 718	Together Forever/ A Night to Remember	1958	200.00
—Reissued as "The Ravenairs"			

RIVILEERS, THE

Number	Title (A Side/B Side)	Yr	NM
45s			
BATON			
❑ 200	A Thousand Stars/Hey Chiquita	1953	200.00
❑ 201	Forever/Darling Farewell	1954	120.00
❑ 205	Carolyn/Eternal Love	1954	120.00
❑ 207	(I Love You) For Sentimental Reasons/I Want to See My Baby	1955	60.00
❑ 209	Little Girl/Don't Ever Leave Me	1955	60.00
❑ 241	A Thousand Stars/Who Is the Girl	1957	40.00

RIVINGTONS, THE

Number	Title (A Side/B Side)	Yr	NM
45s			
A.R.E. AMERICAN			
❑ 100	All That Glitters/ You Move Me Baby	1964	15.00
AGC			
❑ 5	I Lost the Love/Mind Your Man	1968	8.00
BATON MASTER			
❑ 202	Teach Me Tonight/ Reach Our Goal	1967	8.00
COLUMBIA			
❑ 43581	A Rose Growing in the Ruins/ Tend to Business	1966	12.00
❑ 43772	Yadi Yadi Yum Yum/ Yadi Yadi Revisited	1966	12.00
J.D.			
❑ 122	Don't Hate Your Father (Part 1)/ Don't Hate Your Father (Part 2)	1976	5.00
LIBERTY			
❑ 1484 [DJ]	Papa-Oom-Mow-Mow (same on both sides)	1982	6.00
—Reissue; promo only			
❑ 55427	Papa-Oom-Mow-Mow/ Deep Water	1962	25.00
❑ 55513	Kickapoo Joy Juice/My Reward	1962	15.00
❑ 55528	Mama-Oom-Mow-Mow/Waiting	1962	15.00
❑ 55553	The Bird's the Word/ I'm Losing My Grip	1963	20.00
❑ 55585	The Shaky Bird (Part 1)/ The Shaky Bird (Part 2)	1963	15.00
❑ 55610	Little Sally Walker/Cherry	1963	30.00
❑ 55671	Fairy Tales/Wee Jee Walk	1964	15.00
QUAN			
❑ 1379	I Don't Want a New Baby/ You're Gonna Pay	1967	10.00
RCA VICTOR			
❑ 74-0301	Pop Your Corn (Part 1)/ Pop Your Corn (Part 2)	1969	8.00
REPRISE			
❑ 0293	I Tried/One Monkey Don't Stop No Show	1964	12.00
UNITED ARTISTS			
❑ 0096	Papa-Oom-Mow-Mow/T he Bird's the Word	1973	4.00
—"Silver Spotlight Series" reissue			
VEE JAY			
❑ 634	All That Glitters/ You Move Me Baby	1964	12.00
❑ 649	I Love You Always/ Years of Tears	1965	12.00
❑ 677	The Willy/Just Got to Be Mine	1965	12.00
WAND			
❑ 11253	Papa-Oom-Mow-Mow/ I Don't Want a New Baby	1973	5.00
Albums			
LIBERTY			
❑ LRP-3282 [M]	Doin' the Bird	1963	100.00
❑ LST-7282 [S]	Doin' the Bird	1963	200.00

ROACH, MAX

Number	Title (A Side/B Side)	Yr	NM
Albums			
ABC IMPULSE!			
❑ AS-8 [S]	Percussion Bitter Sweet	1968	20.00
❑ AS-16 [S]	It's Time	1968	40.00
ARGO			
❑ LP-623 [M]	Max	1958	50.00
❑ LPS-623 [S]	Max	1958	40.00
ATLANTIC			
❑ 1435 [M]	Max Roach Trio Featuring the Legendary Hasaan	1965	20.00
❑ SD 1435 [S]	Max Roach Trio Featuring the Legendary Hasaan	1965	25.00
❑ 1467 [M]	Drums Unlimited	1966	20.00
❑ SD 1467 [S]	Drums Unlimited	1966	25.00
❑ SD 1510 [S]	Members Don't Get Weary	1968	20.00
❑ SD 1587	Lift Every Voice and Sing	1972	12.00
BAINBRIDGE			
❑ 1042	Max Roach	198?	10.00
❑ 1044	Max Roach/George Duvivier/ Sonny Clark	198?	10.00
CANDID			
❑ CD-8002 [M]	We Insist — Freedom Now Suite	1960	60.00
❑ CS-9002 [S]	We Insist — Freedom Now Suite	1960	60.00
DEBUT			
❑ DLP-13 [10]	Max Roach Quartet Featuring Hank Mobley	1954	400.00
EMARCY			
❑ MG-36098 [M]	Max Roach + 4	1957	100.00
❑ MG-36108 [M]	Jazz in 3/4 Time	1957	80.00
❑ MG-36127 [M]	The Max Roach 4 Plays Charlie Parker	1958	80.00
❑ MG-36132 [M]	Max Roach + 4 on the Chicago Scene	1958	60.00
❑ MG-36140 [M]	Max Roach Plus Four At Newport	1958	60.00
❑ MG-36144 [M]	Max Roach with the Boston Percussion Ensemble	1958	60.00
❑ SR-80001 [S]	Max Roach + 4	1959	80.00
❑ SR-80002 [S]	Jazz in 3/4 Time	1959	60.00
❑ SR-80010 [S]	Max Roach Plus Four At Newport	1959	50.00
❑ SR-80015 [S]	Max Roach with the Boston Percussion Ensemble	1959	50.00
❑ SR-80019 [S]	The Max Roach 4 Plays Charlie Parker	1959	60.00
❑ 814190-1 [(2)]	Standard Time	198?	12.00
❑ 826456-1	Jazz in 3/4 Time	1986	10.00
FANTASY			
❑ OJC-202	Max Roach Quartet Featuring Hank Mobley	1985	10.00
❑ OJC-304	Deeds, Not Words	1988	10.00
❑ 6007 [M]	Speak Brother, Speak	1963	25.00
❑ 86007 [S]	Speak Brother, Speak	1963	30.00
HAT ART			
❑ 4026 [(4)]	The Long March	1986	30.00
IMPULSE!			
❑ A-8 [M]	Percussion Bitter Sweet	1961	30.00
❑ AS-8 [S]	Percussion Bitter Sweet	1961	40.00
❑ A-16 [M]	It's Time	1962	20.00
❑ AS-16 [S]	It's Time	1962	30.00
JAZZLAND			
❑ JLP-79 [M]	Conversation	1962	30.00
❑ JLP-979 [S]	Conversation	1962	25.00
MCA			
❑ 29053	It's Time	1980	10.00
MERCURY			
❑ MG-20491 [M]	Quiet As It's Kept	1959	40.00
❑ MG-20539 [M]	Moon Faced and Starry-Eyed	1960	40.00
❑ MG-20760 [M]	Parisian Sketches	1962	30.00
❑ MG-20911 [M]	The Many Sides of Max	1964	25.00
❑ SR-60170 [S]	Quiet As It's Kept	1959	50.00
❑ SR-60215 [S]	Moon Faced and Starry-Eyed	1960	50.00
❑ SR-60760 [S]	Parisian Sketches	1962	40.00
❑ SR-60911 [S]	The Many Sides of Max	1964	30.00
MILESTONE			
❑ 47061 [(2)]	Conversations	198?	15.00
RIVERSIDE			
❑ RLP 12-280 [M]	Deeds, Not Words	1958	50.00
❑ RLP-1122 [S]	Deeds, Not Words	1959	40.00
❑ RS-3018 [S]	Deeds, Not Words	1968	15.00
SOUL NOTE			
❑ SN-1003	Pictures in a Frame	198?	12.00
❑ SN-1053	In the Light	1982	12.00
❑ SN-1093	Survivors	1985	12.00
❑ SN-1103	Scott Free	1985	12.00
❑ SN-1109	Easy Winners	1985	12.00
TIME			
❑ S-2087 [S]	Max Roach	1962	40.00
❑ 52087 [M]	Max Roach	1962	40.00
❑ ST-70003 [S]	Award Winning Drummer	1959	60.00
❑ T-70003 [M]	Award Winning Drummer	1959	80.00
TRIP			
❑ TLP-5522	Max Roach + 4	197?	12.00
❑ TLP-5559	Jazz in 3/4 Time	197?	12.00

ROACH, MAX/ART BLAKEY

Number	Title (A Side/B Side)	Yr	NM
Albums			
BLUE NOTE			
❑ BLP-5010 [10]	Max Roach Quintet / Art Blakey and His Band	1952	1000.

ROACH, MAX, AND ANTHONY BRAXTON

Number	Title (A Side/B Side)	Yr	NM
Albums			
BLACK SAINT			
❑ BSR-0024	Birth and Rebirth	198?	12.00
HAT HUT			
❑ 06 [(2)]	One in Two — Two in One	1980	20.00

ROACH, MAX, AND CLIFFORD BROWN

ROACH, MAX; SONNY CLARK; GEORGE DUVIVIER

Number	Title (A Side/B Side)	Yr	NM
Albums			
TIME			
❑ S-2101 [S]	Max Roach, Sonny Clark, George Duvivier	1962	40.00
❑ 52101 [M]	Max Roach, Sonny Clark, George Duvivier	1962	30.00

ROACH, MAX, AND CONNIE CROTHERS

Number	Title (A Side/B Side)	Yr	NM
Albums			
NEW ARTISTS			
❑ NA-1001	Swish	198?	12.00

ROACH, MAX, AND STAN LEVEY

Number	Title (A Side/B Side)	Yr	NM
Albums			
LIBERTY			
❑ LRP-3064 [M]	Drummin' the Blues	1957	80.00

ROACH, MAX, AND ARCHIE SHEPP

Number	Title (A Side/B Side)	Yr	NM
Albums			
HAT HUT			
❑ 13 [(2)]	The Long March	1980	20.00

ROACH, MAX, AND CECIL TAYLOR

Number	Title (A Side/B Side)	Yr	NM
Albums			
SOUL NOTE			
❑ SN-1100/1 [(2)]	Historic Concerts	1985	15.00

ROAD, THE

Number	Title (A Side/B Side)	Yr	NM
45s			
BLUE ONION			
❑ 106	It's So Hard to Find/You Rub Me the Wrong Way	1969	30.00
KAMA SUTRA			
❑ 256	She's Not There/A Bummer	1968	8.00
❑ 266	The Grass Looks Greener on the Other Side/In Love	1969	8.00
❑ 267	Mr. Soul/I Can Only Give You Everything	1969	8.00
❑ 504	Mr. Soul/The Grass Looks Greener on the Other Side	1970	6.00
❑ 531	Alone/If You Ever Needed a Woman	1971	6.00

Number	Title (A Side/B Side)	Yr	NM
Albums			
KAMA SUTRA			
❑ KSBS-2012	The Road	1970	15.00
—Reissue of 8075			
❑ KSBS-2032 [(2)]	Cognition	1970	20.00
❑ KLPS-8075	The Road	1969	20.00

ROAD RUNNERS, THE
More than one group. Also see GARY PAXTON.

Number	Title (A Side/B Side)	Yr	NM
45s			
CHALLENGE			
❑ 9197	Dead Man/Pretty Girls	1963	20.00
FELSTED			
❑ 8692	Quasimoto/Road Runnah	1964	40.00
MIRAMAR			
❑ 116	Take Me/I'll Make It Up to You	1965	15.00
MOROCCO			
❑ 001	Goodbye/Tell Her You Love Her	1966	20.00
REPRISE			
❑ 0418	Take Me/I'll Make It Up to You	1965	15.00
Albums			
LONDON			
❑ PS 381 [S]	The New Mustang (And Other Hot Rod Hits)	1964	300.00
❑ LL 3381 [M]	The New Mustang (And Other Hot Rod Hits)	1964	200.00

ROAMERS, THE

Number	Title (A Side/B Side)	Yr	NM
45s			
HIT			
❑ 94	Be True to Your School/Wonderful Summer	1963	8.00
—B-side by Joanne Kay			
❑ 102	Hey Little Cobra/Daisy Petal Pickin'	1964	8.00
—B-side by Ricky Dickens			
❑ 115	Dead Man's Curve/Ronnie	1964	8.00
—B-side by the Chellows			
❑ 118	Bits and Pieces/(Just Like) Romeo and Juliet	1964	10.00
❑ 126	I Get Around/Yesterday's Gone	1964	8.00
❑ 132	The Little Old Lady from Pasadena/Can't You See That She's Mine	1964	10.00
—B-side by the Jalopy Five			
❑ 135	Because/Walk Don't Run '64	1964	10.00
—B-side by the Nashville Five			
❑ 140	G.T.O./In the Misty Moonlight	1964	8.00
—B-side by Marty Wood			
❑ 141	Save It for Me/Selfish One	1964	8.00
—B-side by Betty Wrigley			
❑ 147	When I Grow Up (To Be a Man)/Matchbox	1964	10.00
—B-side by the Jalopy Five			
❑ 151	Tobacco Road/I Know Johnny Loves Me	1964	10.00
—B-side by Amy and the Jarretts			
❑ 152	Ride the Wild Surf/You're the Only Girl for Me	1964	8.00
❑ 158	Everything's Alright/Dance, Dance, Dance	1964	12.00
—B-side by the Spartas			
❑ 160	We Build a 409/Big Man in Town	1964	12.00
—B-side by the Chellows			
❑ 172	Love Potion Number Nine/Never Forget Me	1965	12.00
❑ 217	I Want Candy/(I Can't Get No) Satisfaction	1965	12.00
—B-side by the Jalopy Five			
❑ 218	I Want Candy/I Like It Like That	1965	12.00
—B-side by the Jalopy Five			
❑ 221	Eve of Destruction/I Got You Babe	1965	12.00
—B-side by Wayne and Dee			
❑ 222	Hang On Sloopy/The "In" Crowd	1965	12.00
—B-side by Just Three			
❑ 224	You Were On My Mind/Baby Don't Go	1965	10.00
—B-side by Jimmy and Pat			
❑ 227	Treat Her Right/You're the One	1965	8.00
—As "Cal York and the Roamers"; B-side by the Crests (2)			
❑ 250	Be True to Your School/Wonderful Summer	1966	8.00
—B-side by Joanne Kay			

ROBB, DEE
Later of THE ROBBS.

Number	Title (A Side/B Side)	Yr	NM
45s			
ARGO			
❑ 5439	Bye Bye Baby/The Prom	1963	12.00
SCORE			
❑ 1006	He's Got the Whole World in His Hands/Say That Thing	1964	15.00

ROBBINS, EDDIE

Number	Title (A Side/B Side)	Yr	NM
45s			
DAVID			
❑ 1001	Janice/It Was Fun	196?	25.00
DOT			
❑ 15702	A Girl Like You/Dear Parents	1958	40.00
POWER			
❑ 214	A Girl Like You/Dear Parents	1958	120.00

ROBBINS, MARTY

Number	Title (A Side/B Side)	Yr	NM
45s			
COLUMBIA			
❑ 02444	Jumper Cable Man/Good Hearted Woman	1981	4.00
❑ 02575	Teardrops on My Heart/Honeycomb	1981	4.00
❑ 02854	Lover, Lover/Some Memories Just Won't Die	1982	4.00
❑ 03236	Tie Your Dream to Mine/That's All She Wrote	1982	4.00
❑ 03789	Change of Heart/Devil in a Cowboy Hat	1983	4.00
❑ 03927	Baby That's Love/What If I Said I Love You	1983	4.00
❑ 10305	El Paso City/When I'm Gone	1976	5.00
❑ 10396	Among My Souvenirs/She's Just a Drifter	1976	5.00
❑ 10472	Adios Amigo/Helen	1977	5.00
❑ 10536	I Don't Know Why (I Just Do)/Inspiration for a Song	1977	5.00
❑ 10629	Don't Let Me Touch You/Tomorrow, Tomorrow, Tomorrow	1977	5.00
❑ 10673	Return to Me/More Than Anything, I Miss You	1978	5.00
❑ 10821	Please Don't Play a Love Song/Jenny	1978	5.00
❑ 10905	Touch Me with Magic/Confused and Lonely	1979	5.00
❑ 11016	All Around Cowboy/The Dreamer	1979	5.00
❑ 11102	Buenos Dias Argentina/Ballad of a Small Man	1979	5.00
❑ 11240	She's Made of Faith/Misery in My Soul	1980	4.00
❑ 11291	One Man's Trash (Is Another Man's Treasure)/I Can't Wait Until Tomorrow	1980	4.00
❑ 11372	An Occasional Rose/Holding On to You	1980	4.00
❑ 11425	Completely Out of Love/Another Cup of Coffee	1981	4.00
❑ 20925	Tomorrow You'll Be Gone/Love Me or Leave Me Alone	1952	30.00
❑ 20965	Crying 'Cause I Love You/I Wish Somebody Loved Me	1952	30.00
❑ 21022	I'll Go On Alone/You're Breaking My Heart	1952	30.00
❑ 21032	My Isle of Golden Dreams/Sweet Hawaiian Dream	1952	—
—Unreleased			
❑ 21075	I Couldn't Keep from Crying/After You Leave	1953	30.00
❑ 21111	A Castle in the Sky/A Half-Way Chance with You	1953	30.00
❑ 21145	Sing Me Something Sentimental/At the End of Long, Lonely Days	1953	30.00
❑ 21172	Blesserd Jesus Should I Fall Don't Let Me Lay/Kneel and Let the Lord Take Your Load	1953	30.00
❑ 21176	Don't Make Me Ashamed/It's a Long, Long Ride	1953	30.00
❑ 21213	My Isle of Golden Dreams/Aloha Oe	1954	30.00
❑ 21246	Pretty Words/Your Heart's Turn to Break	1954	30.00
❑ 21291	Call Me Up (And I'll Come Calling on You)/I'm Too Big to Cry	1954	30.00
❑ 21324	Time Goes By/It's a Pity What Money Can Do	1954	30.00
❑ 21351	That's All Right/Gossip	1955	50.00
❑ 21352	God Understands/Have Thine Own Way, Lord	1955	25.00
❑ 21388	Daddy Loves You/Pray for Me, Mother of Mine	1955	25.00
❑ 21414	It Looks Like I'm Just in the Way/I'll Love You Till the Day I Die	1955	25.00
❑ 21446	Maybellene/This Broken Heart of Mine	1955	50.00
❑ 21461	Pretty Mama/Don't Let Me Hang Around	1955	50.00
❑ 21477	Tennessee Toddy/Mean Mama Blues	1955	50.00
❑ 21508	Singing the Blues/I Can't Quit (I've Gone Too Far)	1956	40.00
❑ 21525	I'll Know You're Gone/How Long Will It Be	1956	25.00
—With Lee Emerson			
❑ 21545	Singing the Blues/I Can't Quit (I've Gone Too Far)	1956	30.00
❑ S7 30511 [S]	El Paso/Running Gun	1959	30.00
—"Stereo Seven" (small hole, plays at 33 1/3 rpm)			
❑ S7 30589 [S]	Big Iron/Saddle Tramp	1960	30.00
—"Stereo Seven" single (small hole, plays at 33 1/3 rpm)			
❑ S7 30771 [S]	Five Brothers/Ride, Cowboy, Ride	1960	30.00
—"Stereo Seven" single (small hole, plays at 33 1/3 rpm)			
❑ S7 30809 [S]	Ballad of the Alamo/A Time and a Place for Everything	1960	30.00
—"Stereo Seven" single (small hole, plays at 33 1/3 rpm)			
❑ S7 31124 [S]	To Each His Own/I Can't Help It	1961	20.00
❑ S7 31125 [S]	Answer Me My Love/Clara	1961	20.00
❑ S7 31126 [S]	Half As Much/Unchained Melody	1961	20.00
❑ S7 31127 [S]	Are You Sincere?/Guess I'll Be Going	1961	20.00
❑ S7 31128 [S]	To Think You've Chosen Me/Too Young	1961	20.00
—The above five are "Stereo Seven" 33 1/3 rpm jukebox singles from set "JS7-32" entitled "Just a Little Sentimental"			
❑ S7 31190 [S]	Just a Little Sentimental/Hurt	1961	20.00
❑ S7 31191 [S]	To Each His Own/I Can't Help It	1961	20.00
❑ S7 31192 [S]	Answer Me My Love/Half As Much	1961	20.00
❑ S7 31193 [S]	Unchained Melody/Are You Sincere?	1961	20.00
❑ S7 31747 [S]	Devil Woman/Time Can't Make Me Forget	1963	20.00
—"Stereo Seven" single, small hole, plays at 33 1/3 rpm			
❑ S7 31748 [S]	In the Ashes of an Old Love Affair/The Hands You're Holding Now	1963	20.00
—"Stereo Seven" single, small hole, plays at 33 1/3 rpm			
❑ S7 31749 [S]	Worried/Little Rich Girl	1963	20.00
—"Stereo Seven" single, small hole, plays at 33 1/3 rpm			
❑ S7 31750 [S]	Progressive Love/Love Is a Hurting Thing	1963	20.00
—"Stereo Seven" single, small hole, plays at 33 1/3 rpm			
❑ S7 31751 [S]	Kinda Halfway Feel/The Wine Flowed Freely	1963	20.00
—The above five are "Stereo Seven" 33 1/3 rpm jukebox singles from set "JS7-78" entitled "Devil Woman"			
❑ 3-39020 [S]	Change That Dial/You Won't Have Her Long	1964	30.00
—Jukebox single, small hole, plays at 33 1/3 rpm; rather than the usual rainbow "target" label of Columbia "Stereo Seven" singles, this one has green labels			
❑ 40679	Long Tall Sally/Mr. Teardrop	1956	50.00
❑ 40706	Respectfully Miss Brooks/You Don't Owe Me a Thing	1956	50.00
❑ 40815	Knee Deep in the Blues/The Same Two Lips	1957	25.00
❑ 40864	A White Sport Coat (And a Pink Carnation)/Grown Up Tears	1957	25.00
❑ 40864 [PS]	A White Sport Coat (And a Pink Carnation)/Grown Up Tears	1957	40.00
❑ 40868	I Cried Like a Baby/Where D'Ja Go	1957	25.00
—With Lee Emerson			
❑ 40969	Please Don't Blame Me/Teen-Age Dream	1957	25.00
❑ 41013	The Story of My Life/Once-a-Week Date	1957	25.00
❑ 41013 [PS]	The Story of My Life/Once-a-Week Date	1957	40.00
❑ 41143	Just Married/Stairway of Love	1958	20.00
❑ 41208	She Was Only Seventeen (He Was One Year More)/Sittin' in a Tree House	1958	20.00
❑ 41208 [PS]	She Was Only Seventeen (He Was One Year More)/Sittin' in a Tree House	1958	40.00
❑ 41282	Ain't I the Lucky One/The Last Time I Saw My Heart	1958	20.00
❑ 41325	The Hanging Tree/The Blues, Country Style	1959	20.00
❑ 41325 [PS]	The Hanging Tree/The Blues, Country Style	1959	40.00
❑ 41408	Cap and Gown/Last Night About This Time	1959	20.00
❑ 41511 [M]	El Paso/Running Gun	1959	20.00
❑ 41511 [PS]	El Paso/Running Gun	1959	30.00
❑ 41589 [M]	Big Iron/Saddle Tramp	1960	15.00
❑ 41686	Is There Any Chance/I Told My Heart	1960	15.00
❑ 41766	Don't Worry/A Time and a Place for Everything	1960	—
—Unreleased			
❑ 41771 [M]	Five Brothers/Ride, Cowboy, Ride	1960	15.00
❑ 41809 [M]	Ballad of the Alamo/A Time and a Place for Everything	1960	15.00
❑ 41809 [PS]	Ballad of the Alamo/A Time and a Place for Everything	1960	30.00
❑ 41922	Don't Worry/Like All the Other Times	1961	15.00

Except when noted otherwise, VG = 25% of NM, and VG+ = 50% of NM. (Example: VG = $2.00, VG+ = $4.00 and NM = $8.00.)

Number	Title (A Side/B Side)	Yr	NM
❑ 41922 [PS]	Don't Worry/Like All the Other Times	1961	25.00
❑ 42008	Jimmy Martinez/Ghost Train	1961	15.00
❑ 42008 [PS]	Jimmy Martinez/Ghost Train	1961	25.00
❑ 42065	It's Your World/You Told Me So	1961	15.00
❑ 42065 [PS]	It's Your World/You Told Me So	1961	25.00
❑ 42246	I Told the Brook/Sometimes I'm Tempted	1961	15.00
❑ 42246 [PS]	I Told the Brook/Sometimes I'm Tempted	1961	25.00
❑ 42375	Love Can't Wait/Too Far Gone	1962	15.00
❑ 42375 [PS]	Love Can't Wait/Too Far Gone	1962	25.00
❑ 42486	Devil Woman/April Fool's Day	1962	15.00
❑ 42486 [PS]	Devil Woman/April Fool's Day	1962	25.00
—Sleeve has a photo of Marty with a brown background			
❑ 42486 [PS]	Devil Woman/April Fool's Day	1962	25.00
—Sleeve has a photo of Marty with a green background			
❑ 42614	Ruby Ann/Won't You Forgive	1962	15.00
❑ 42614 [PS]	Ruby Ann/Won't You Forgive	1962	25.00
❑ 42672	Hawaii's Calling Me/Ka-Lu-A	1963	12.00
❑ 42701	Cigarettes and Coffee Blues/Teenager's Dad	1963	12.00
❑ 42701 [PS]	Cigarettes and Coffee Blues/Teenager's Dad	1963	25.00
❑ 42781	No Sign of Loneliness Here/I'm Not Ready Yet	1963	12.00
❑ 42781 [PS]	No Sign of Loneliness Here/I'm Not Ready Yet	1963	25.00
❑ 42831	Not So Long Ago/I Hope You Learn a Lot	1963	12.00
❑ 42890	Begging to You/Over High Mountain	1963	12.00
❑ 42968	Girl from Spanish Town/Kingston Girl	1964	10.00
❑ 43049	The Cowboy in the Continental Suit/Man Walks Among Us	1964	10.00
❑ 43134	One of These Days/Up in the Air	1964	10.00
❑ 43196	I Eish-Tay-Mah-Su (I Love You)/A Whole Lot Easier	1964	10.00
❑ 43258	Ribbon of Darkness/Little Robin	1965	10.00
❑ 43377	Old Red/Matilda	1965	8.00
❑ 43428	While You're Dancing/Lonely Too Long	1965	8.00
❑ 43500	Count Me Out/Private Wilson White	1965	8.00
❑ 43651	Ain't I Right/My Own Native Land	1966	—
—Unreleased			
❑ 43680	The Shoe Goes On the Other Foot Tonight/It Kind of Reminds Me of You	1966	8.00
❑ 43845	No Tears Milady/Fly Butterfly Fly	1966	8.00
❑ 43870	Mr. Shorty/Tall Handsome Strangers	1966	8.00
❑ 44128	Tonight Carmen/Waiting in Reno	1967	6.00
❑ 44271	Gardenias in Her Hair/In the Valley of the Rio Grande	1967	6.00
❑ 44509	Love Is In the Air/I've Been Leaving Everyday	1968	6.00
❑ 44633	I Walk Alone/Lily of the Valley	1968	6.00
❑ 44641	It Finally Happened/Big Mouthin' Around	1968	6.00
—By "Marty Robbins Jr. and Sr."			
❑ 44739	It's a Sin/I Feel Another Heartache Coming On	1969	5.00
❑ 44895	I Can't Say Goodbye/Hello Daily News	1969	5.00
❑ 44968	Girl from Spanish Town/Kingston Girl	1969	8.00
❑ 45024	Camelia/Virginia	1969	5.00
❑ 45091	My Woman, My Woman, My Wife/Martha Ellen Jenkins	1970	5.00
❑ 45215	Jolie Girl/The City	1970	5.00
❑ 45273	Padre/At Times	1970	6.00
❑ 45346	Little Spot in Heaven/Wait a Little Longer Please, Jesus	1971	6.00
❑ 45377	The Chair/Seventeen Years	1971	5.00
❑ 45442	Early Morning Sunshine/Another Day Has Gone By	1971	5.00
❑ 45520	The Best Part of Living/Gone with the Wind	1971	5.00
❑ 45668	I've Got a Woman's Love/A Little Spot in Heaven	1972	5.00
❑ 45775	Laura (What's He Got That I Ain't Got)/It Kind of Reminds Me of You	1973	5.00
❑ JZSP 49158/48863 [DJ]	El Paso (2:58)/El Paso (4:37)	1959	40.00
DECCA			
❑ 33006	This Much a Man/Guess I'll Stand Here Looking Dumb	1972	7.00
MCA			
❑ 40012	Franklin, Tennessee/Walking Piece of Heaven	1973	5.00
❑ 40067	A Man and a Train/Las Vegas, Nevada	1973	5.00
❑ 40134	Love Me/Crawling on My Knees	1973	5.00
❑ 40172	I'm Wanting To/Twentieth Century Drifter	1973	5.00

Number	Title (A Side/B Side)	Yr	NM
❑ 40236	Don't You Think/I Couldn't Believe It Was True	1974	5.00
❑ 40296	Two-Gun Daddy/Queen of the Big Rodeo	1974	5.00
❑ 40342	Life/It Takes Faith	1974	5.00
❑ 40425	These Are My Souvenirs/Shotgun Rider	1975	5.00
❑ 52197	Two Gun Daddy/Life	1983	5.00
WARNER BROS.			
❑ 29847	Honkytonk Man/Shotgun Rag	1982	4.00
—B-side by Johnny Gimble and the Texas Swing Band			

7-Inch Extended Plays

Number	Title (A Side/B Side)	Yr	NM
COLUMBIA			
❑ H-1785	I'll Go On Alone/Crying 'Cause I Love You//I Couldn't Keep from Crying/A Half-Way Chance with You	1953	60.00
❑ H-1785 [PS]	Marty Robbins	1953	60.00
❑ B-2116	*Singing the Blues/I Can't Quit/Long Gone Lonesome Blues/Lorelei	1956	50.00
❑ B-2116 [PS]	Singing the Blues	1956	50.00
❑ B-2134	A White Sport Coat/Mean Mama Blues//Grown-Up Tears/Long Tall Sally	1957	40.00
❑ B-2134 [PS]	A White Sport Coat	1957	40.00
❑ B-2153	The Letter Edged in Black/The Little Rosewood Casket//The Dream of the Miner's Child/The Convict and the Rose	1957	30.00
❑ B-2153 [PS]	Marty Robbins	1957	30.00
❑ B-2808	I Couldn't Keep from Crying/Sing Me Something Sentimental//Tennessee Toddy/You Don't Owe Me a Thing	1957	50.00
❑ B-2808 [PS]	Marty Robbins (Hall of Fame Series)	1957	50.00
❑ B-2814	A White Sport Coat/Singing the Blues//The Story of My Life/I'm So Lonesome I Could Cry	1958	12.00
❑ B-2814 [PS]	Marty Robbins	1958	12.00
❑ 7-8718	*The Wine Flowed Freely/Kinda Halfway Feel/Worried/Love Is a Hurting Thing/Devil Woman/In the Ashes of an Old Love Affair	196?	15.00
—Jukebox issue; small hole, plays at 33 1/3 rpm			
❑ 7-8718 [PS]	Devil Woman	196?	15.00
—Jukebox issue; small hole, plays at 33 1/3 rpm			
❑ 7-9020	*Everybody's Darling Plus Mine/Southern Dixie Flyer/Only a Picture Stops Time/Making Excuses/Rainbow/I Lived a Lifetime in a Day	196?	15.00
—Jukebox issue; small hole, plays at 33 1/3 rpm			
❑ 7-9020 [PS]	R.F.D.	196?	15.00
❑ B-9761	Lovesick Blues/I'm So Lonesome I Could Cry//It's Too Late Now/Rose of Ol' Pawnee	1957	15.00
❑ B-9761 [PS]	The Song of Robbins Vol. I	1957	15.00
❑ B-9762	I Never Let You Cross My Mind/I Hang My Head and Cry//You Only Want Me When You're Lonely/Moanin' the Blues	1957	15.00
❑ B-9762 [PS]	The Song of Robbins Vol. II	1957	15.00
❑ B-9763	I'll Step Aside/All the World Is Lonely Now//Bouquet of Roses/Have I Told You Lately That I Love You?	1957	15.00
❑ B-9763 [PS]	The Song of Robbins, Vol. III	1957	15.00
❑ B-10871	*Song of the Islands/Now Is the Hour/Sweet Leilani/Aloha Oe	1957	15.00
❑ B-10871 [PS]	Song of the Islands	1957	15.00
❑ B-11891	Kaw-Liga/Waltz of the Wind//Then I Turned and Walked Slowly Away/A House with Everything But Love	1958	15.00
❑ B-11891 [PS]	Marty Robbins	1958	15.00
❑ B-13491	El Paso/A Hundred and Sixty Acres//They're Hanging Me Tonight/The Strawberry Roan	1959	12.00
❑ B-13491 [PS]	Gunfighter Ballads and Trail Songs, Vol. I	1959	12.00
❑ B-13492	Big Iron/In the Valley//Running Gun/Utah Carol	1959	12.00
❑ B-13492 [PS]	Gunfighter Ballads and Trail Songs, Vol. II	1959	12.00
❑ B-13493	Cool Water/The Master's Call//Billy the Kid/The Little Green Valley	1959	15.00
❑ B-13493 [PS]	Gunfighter Ballads and Trail Songs, Vol. III	1959	15.00
❑ B-14811	*San Angelo/Prairie Fire/Streets of Laredo	1960	12.00
❑ B-14811 [PS]	More Gunfighter Ballads and Trail Songs, Vol. I	1960	12.00
❑ B-14812	*Five Brothers/Little Joe the Wrangler/Song of the Bandit/I've Got No Use for the Woman	1960	12.00
❑ B-14812 [PS]	More Gunfighter Ballads and Trail Songs, Vol. II	1960	12.00
❑ B-14813	*She Was Young and She Was Pretty/My Love/Ride Cowboy Ride/This Peaceful Sod	1960	12.00
❑ B-14813 [PS]	More Gunfighter Ballads and Trail Songs, Vol. III	1960	12.00

Albums

Number	Title (A Side/B Side)	Yr	NM
ARTCO			
❑ 110	The Best of Marty Robbins	1973	40.00
CBS SPECIAL PRODUCTS			
❑ P 17730	The Great Love Songs	1984	10.00
COLUMBIA			
❑ GP 15 [(2)]	Marty's Country	1969	25.00
❑ CL 976 [M]	The Song of Robbins	1957	100.00
—Red and black label with six "eye" logos			
❑ CL 976 [M]	The Song of Robbins	1963	20.00
—Red label with "Guaranteed High Fidelity" or "360 Sound Mono"			
❑ CL 1087 [M]	Song of the Islands	1957	120.00
—Red and black label with six "eye" logos			
❑ CL 1087 [M]	Song of the Islands	1963	20.00
—Red label with "Guaranteed High Fidelity" or "360 Sound Mono"			
❑ CL 1189 [M]	Marty Robbins	1958	80.00
—Red and black label with six "eye" logos			
❑ CL 1189 [M]	Marty Robbins	1963	20.00
—Red label with "Guaranteed High Fidelity" or "360 Sound Mono"			
❑ CL 1325 [M]	Marty's Greatest Hits	1959	80.00
—Red and black label with six "eye" logos			
❑ CL 1325 [M]	Marty's Greatest Hits	1963	20.00
—Red label with "Guaranteed High Fidelity" or "360 Sound Mono"			
❑ CL 1349 [M]	Gunfighter Ballads and Trail Songs	1959	30.00
—Red and black label with six "eye" logos			
❑ CL 1349 [M]	Gunfighter Ballads and Trail Songs	1963	15.00
—Red label with "Guaranteed High Fidelity" or "360 Sound Mono"			
❑ CL 1481 [M]	More Gunfighter Ballads and Trail Songs	1960	30.00
—Red and black label with six "eye" logos			
❑ CL 1481 [M]	More Gunfighter Ballads and Trail Songs	1963	15.00
—Red label with "Guaranteed High Fidelity" or "360 Sound Mono"			
❑ CL 1635 [M]	More Greatest Hits	1961	25.00
—Red and black label with six "eye" logos			
❑ CL 1635 [M]	More Greatest Hits	1963	15.00
—Red label with "Guaranteed High Fidelity" or "360 Sound Mono"			
❑ CL 1666 [M]	Just a Little Sentimental	1961	25.00
—Red and black label with six "eye" logos			
❑ CL 1666 [M]	Just a Little Sentimental	1963	15.00
—Red label with "Guaranteed High Fidelity" or "360 Sound Mono"			
❑ CL 1801 [M]	Marty After Midnight	1962	20.00
—Red label with "Guaranteed High Fidelity"			
❑ CL 1801 [M]	Marty After Midnight	1962	50.00
—Red and black label with six "eye" logos			
❑ CL 1801 [M]	Marty After Midnight	1965	15.00
—Red label with "360 Sound Mono"			
❑ CL 1855 [M]	Portrait of Marty	1962	40.00
❑ CL 1855/CS 8655	Portrait of Marty Bonus Photo	1962	30.00
❑ CL 1918 [M]	Devil Woman	1962	25.00
—Red label with "Guaranteed High Fidelity"			
❑ CL 1918 [M]	Devil Woman	1965	15.00
—Red label with "360 Sound Mono"			
❑ CL 2040 [M]	Hawaii's Calling Me	1963	25.00
—Red label with "Guaranteed High Fidelity"			
❑ CL 2040 [M]	Hawaii's Calling Me	1965	15.00
—Red label with "360 Sound Mono"			
❑ CL 2072 [M]	Return of the Gunfighter	1963	20.00
—Red label with "Guaranteed High Fidelity"			
❑ CL 2072 [M]	Return of the Gunfighter	1965	15.00
—Red label with "360 Sound Mono"			
❑ CL 2176 [M]	Island Woman	1964	30.00
—Red label with "Guaranteed High Fidelity"			
❑ CL 2176 [M]	Island Woman	1965	20.00
—Red label with "360 Sound Mono"			
❑ CL 2220 [M]	R.F.D.	1964	20.00
—Red label with "Guaranteed High Fidelity"			
❑ CL 2220 [M]	R.F.D.	1965	15.00
—Red label with "360 Sound Mono"			
❑ CL 2304 [M]	Turn the Lights Down Low	1965	15.00
—Red label with "360 Sound Mono"			
❑ CL 2304 [M]	Turn the Lights Down Low	1965	25.00
—Red label with "Guaranteed High Fidelity"			
❑ CL 2448 [M]	What God Has Done	1966	15.00
❑ CL 2527 [M]	The Drifter	1966	15.00
❑ CL 2601 [10]	Rock 'N Roll 'N Robbins	1956	1000.
❑ CL 2645 [M]	My Kind of Country	1967	25.00
❑ CL 2725 [M]	Tonight Carmen	1967	30.00
❑ CL 2735 [M]	Christmas with Marty Robbins	1967	50.00
❑ CL 2817 [M]	By the Time I Get to Phoenix	1968	60.00
❑ CS 8158 [S]	Gunfighter Ballads and Trail Songs	1959	40.00
—Red and black label with six "eye" logos			
❑ CS 8158 [S]	Gunfighter Ballads and Trail Songs	1963	20.00
—Red label with "360 Sound Stereo"			

Number	Title (A Side/B Side)	Yr	NM
❑ CS 8158 [S]	Gunfighter Ballads and Trail Songs	1971	10.00
—Orange label			
❑ PC 8158	Gunfighter Ballads and Trail Songs	198?	8.00
—Reissue with new prefix			
❑ CS 8272 [S]	More Gunfighter Ballads and Trail Songs	1960	40.00
—Red and black label with six "eye" logos			
❑ CS 8272 [S]	More Gunfighter Ballads and Trail Songs	1963	20.00
—Red label with "360 Sound Stereo"			
❑ CS 8272 [S]	More Gunfighter Ballads and Trail Songs	1971	10.00
—Orange label			
❑ PC 8272	More Gunfighter Ballads and Trail Songs❑ More	198?	8.00
—Reissue with new prefix			
❑ CS 8435 [S]	More Greatest Hits	1961	30.00
—Red and black label with six "eye" logos			
❑ CS 8435 [S]	More Greatest Hits	1963	20.00
—Red label with "360 Sound Stereo"			
❑ CS 8435 [S]	More Greatest Hits	1971	10.00
—Orange label			
❑ PC 8435	More Greatest Hits	198?	8.00
—Reissue with new prefix			
❑ CS 8466 [S]	Just a Little Sentimental	1961	30.00
—Red and black label with six "eye" logos			
❑ CS 8466 [S]	Just a Little Sentimental	1963	20.00
—Red label with "360 Sound Stereo"			
❑ CS 8601 [S]	Marty After Midnight	1962	30.00
—Red label with "360 Sound Stereo" in black			
❑ CS 8601 [S]	Marty After Midnight	1962	80.00
—Red and black label with six "eye" logos			
❑ CS 8601 [S]	Marty After Midnight	1965	20.00
—Red label with "360 Sound Stereo" in white			
❑ CS 8639 [P]	Marty's Greatest Hits	1962	30.00
—Red label with "360 Sound Stereo" in black			
❑ CS 8639 [P]	Marty's Greatest Hits	1965	20.00
—Red label with "360 Sound Stereo" in white			
❑ CS 8639 [P]	Marty's Greatest Hits	1970	10.00
—Orange label			
❑ PC 8639	Marty's Greatest Hits	198?	8.00
—Reissue with new prefix			
❑ CS 8655 [S]	Portrait of Marty	1962	50.00
❑ CS 8718 [S]	Devil Woman	1962	30.00
—Red label with "360 Sound Stereo" in black			
❑ CS 8718 [S]	Devil Woman	1965	20.00
—Red label with "360 Sound Stereo" in white			
❑ CS 8718 [S]	Devil Woman	1970	10.00
—Orange label			
❑ CS 8840 [S]	Hawaii's Calling Me	1963	30.00
—Red label with "360 Sound Stereo" in black			
❑ CS 8840 [S]	Hawaii's Calling Me	1965	20.00
—Red label with "360 Sound Stereo" in white			
❑ CS 8872 [S]	Return of the Gunfighter	1963	25.00
—Red label with "360 Sound Stereo" in black			
❑ CS 8872 [S]	Return of the Gunfighter	1965	20.00
—Red label with "360 Sound Stereo" in white			
❑ CS 8872 [S]	Return of the Gunfighter	1970	10.00
—Orange label			
❑ CS 8976 [S]	Island Woman	1964	40.00
—Red label with "360 Sound Stereo" in black			
❑ CS 8976 [S]	Island Woman	1965	30.00
—Red label with "360 Sound Stereo" in white			
❑ CS 9020 [S]	R.F.D.	1964	25.00
—Red label with "360 Sound Stereo" in black			
❑ CS 9020 [S]	R.F.D.	1965	20.00
—Red label with "360 Sound Stereo" in white			
❑ CS 9104 [S]	Turn the Lights Down Low	1965	20.00
—Red label with "360 Sound Stereo" in white			
❑ CS 9104 [S]	Turn the Lights Down Low	1965	30.00
—Red label with "360 Sound Stereo" in black			
❑ CS 9248 [S]	What God Has Done	1966	20.00
—Red "360 Sound" label			
❑ CS 9248 [S]	What God Has Done	1970	10.00
—Orange label			
❑ CS 9327 [S]	The Drifter	1966	20.00
—Red "360 Sound" label			
❑ CS 9327 [S]	The Drifter	1970	10.00
—Orange label			
❑ CS 9421 [R]	The Song of Robbins	1967	15.00
—Red "360 Sound" label			
❑ CS 9421 [R]	The Song of Robbins	1970	10.00
—Orange label			
❑ CS 9425 [R]	Song of the Islands	1967	15.00
❑ CS 9445 [S]	My Kind of Country	1967	20.00
❑ CS 9525 [S]	Tonight Carmen	1967	20.00
—Red "360 Sound" label			
❑ CS 9525 [S]	Tonight Carmen	1970	10.00
—Orange label			
❑ 3C 9535	Christmas with Marty Robbins	198?	10.00
—Budget-line reissue			
❑ CS 9535 [S]	Christmas with Marty Robbins	1967	30.00
❑ CS 9617 [M]	By the Time I Get to Phoenix	1968	50.00
—"Special Mono Radio Station Copy" with stereo number and "Mono" on white label			
❑ CS 9617 [S]	By the Time I Get to Phoenix	1968	20.00
❑ CS 9725	I Walk Alone	1968	20.00
—Red "360 Sound" label			
❑ CS 9725	I Walk Alone	1970	10.00
—Orange label			

Number	Title (A Side/B Side)	Yr	NM
❑ CS 9811	It's a Sin	1969	20.00
—Red "360 Sound" label			
❑ CS 9811	It's a Sin	1970	10.00
—Orange label			
❑ CS 9978	My Woman, My Woman, My Wife	1970	15.00
—Orange label			
❑ CS 9978	My Woman, My Woman, My Wife	1970	20.00
—Red "360 Sound" label			
❑ PC 30316	El Paso	198?	8.00
—Reissue of Harmony 30316			
❑ C 30571	Marty Robbins' Greatest Hits Vol. III	1971	15.00
❑ PC 30571	Marty Robbins' Greatest Hits Vol. III	198?	8.00
—Budget-line reissue			
❑ C 30816	Today	1971	15.00
❑ G 30881 [(2)]	The World of Marty Robbins	1971	20.00
❑ KC 31341	Bound for Old Mexico (Great Hits from South of the Border)	1973	15.00
❑ CG 31361 [(2)]	All Time Greatest Hits	1972	18.00
❑ KG 31361 [(2)]	Marty Robbins' All-Time Greatest Hits	1972	20.00
❑ KC 31628	I've Got a Woman's Love	1972	15.00
❑ KC 32586	Have I Told You Lately That I Love You	1974	15.00
❑ KC 33476	No Sign of Loneliness Here	1976	12.00
❑ CG 33630 [(2)]	Gunfighter Ballads and Trail Songs/My Woman, My Woman, My Wife	1976	15.00
❑ PC 34303	El Paso City	1976	12.00
—No bar code on cover			
❑ PC 34303	El Paso City	198?	8.00
—With bar code on cover			
❑ PC 34448	Adios Amigo	1977	12.00
—No bar code on cover			
❑ PC 34448	Adios Amigo	198?	8.00
—With bar code on cover			
❑ KC 35040	Don't Let Me Touch You	1977	12.00
❑ JC 35446	The Performer	1979	12.00
❑ KC 35629	Greatest Hits Vol. IV	1978	12.00
❑ JC 36085	All Around Cowboy	1979	12.00
❑ PC 36085	All Around Cowboy	198?	8.00
—Budget-line reissue			
❑ JC 36507	With Love	1980	12.00
❑ JC 36860	Everything I've Always Wanted	1981	12.00
❑ FC 37353	Encore	1981	12.00
❑ PC 37353	Encore	198?	8.00
—Budget-line reissue			
❑ FC 37541	The Legend	1982	12.00
❑ PC 37541	The Legend	1985	8.00
—Budget-line reissue			
❑ FC 37995	Come Back to Me	1982	12.00
❑ PC 37995	Come Back to Me	198?	8.00
—Budget-line reissue			
❑ FC 38309	Biggest Hits	1982	12.00
❑ FC 38603	Some Memories Just Won't Die	1983	12.00
❑ C2 38870 [(2)]	A Lifetime of Song 1951-1982	1983	15.00
❑ KC2 39575 [(2)]	Long, Long Ago	1984	15.00

COLUMBIA LIMITED EDITION

Number	Title (A Side/B Side)	Yr	NM
❑ LE 10022	Portrait of Marty	197?	10.00
❑ LE 10030	It's a Sin	197?	10.00
❑ LE 10033	My Kind of Country	197?	10.00
❑ LE 10045	By the Time I Get to Phoenix	197?	10.00
❑ LE 10046	Today	197?	10.00
❑ LE 10144	R.F.D.	197?	10.00
❑ LE 10145	Turn the Lights Down Low	197?	10.00
❑ LE 10189	Tonight Carmen	197?	10.00
❑ LE 10575	From the Heart	197?	10.00
❑ LE 10576	Streets of Laredo	197?	10.00
❑ LE 10577	The Story of My Life	197?	10.00
❑ LE 10578	The Song of Robbins	197?	10.00
❑ LE 10579	Devil Woman	197?	10.00

COLUMBIA MUSICAL TREASURY

Number	Title (A Side/B Side)	Yr	NM
❑ P5S 5812 [(5)]	Marty	1972	40.00

COLUMBIA RECORD CLUB

Number	Title (A Side/B Side)	Yr	NM
❑ DS 445	Bend in the River	1968	40.00

COLUMBIA SPECIAL PRODUCTS

Number	Title (A Side/B Side)	Yr	NM
❑ C 10980 [S]	Christmas with Marty Robbins	1972	15.00
—Stereo reissue; "Distributed by Apex Rendezvous, Inc." on back cover			
❑ C 11122	Marty's Greatest Hits	1972	12.00
❑ C 11311	By the Time I Get to Phoenix	1972	15.00
❑ C 11513	By the Time I Get to Phoenix	1973	15.00
❑ P 12416	Marty Robbins' Own Favorites	1974	15.00
❑ P 13358	Christmas with Marty Robbins	1976	12.00
❑ P 14035	Legendary Music Man	1977	12.00
❑ P 14613	The Best of Marty Robbins	1978	10.00
❑ P 15594	The Number One Cowboy	1981	10.00
❑ P 15812	Marty Robbins' Best	1982	10.00
❑ P 16561	Reflections	1982	10.00
❑ 3P 16578 [(3)]	Classics	1983	20.00
❑ P 16914	Country Classics	1983	10.00
❑ P 17120	Sincerely	1983	10.00
❑ P 17136	Forever Yours	1983	10.00
❑ P 17137	That Country Feeling	1983	10.00
❑ P 17138	Banquet of Songs	1983	10.00
❑ P 17159	The Great Marty Robbins	1983	10.00
❑ P 17206	The Legendary Marty Robbins	1983	10.00
❑ P 17209	Country Cowboy	1983	10.00
❑ P 17367	Song of the Islands	1983	10.00

DECCA

Number	Title (A Side/B Side)	Yr	NM
❑ DL 75389	This Much a Man	1972	15.00

HARMONY

Number	Title (A Side/B Side)	Yr	NM
❑ HS 11338	Singing the Blues	1969	15.00
❑ HS 11409	The Story of My Life	1970	15.00
❑ KH 30316	El Paso	1971	12.00
❑ KH 31257	Marty Robbins Favorites	1972	12.00
❑ H 31258	Songs of the Islands	1972	20.00
❑ KH 32286	Streets of Laredo	1973	12.00

MCA

Number	Title (A Side/B Side)	Yr	NM
❑ 61	This Much a Man	1973	12.00
—Reissue of Decca LP			
❑ 342	Marty Robbins	1973	15.00
❑ 421	Good'n Country	1974	15.00
❑ 27060	20th Century Drifter	1983	15.00
—Reissue of older material			

READER'S DIGEST

Number	Title (A Side/B Side)	Yr	NM
❑ RDA-054/A [(5)]	His Greatest Hits and Finest Performances	1983	30.00

TIME-LIFE

Number	Title (A Side/B Side)	Yr	NM
❑ STW-109	Country Music	1981	12.00

ROBBINS, MEL

45s

ARGO

Number	Title (A Side/B Side)	Yr	NM
❑ 5340	Save It/To Know You	1959	100.00

ROBBS, THE

Also see DEE ROBB.

45s

ABC

Number	Title (A Side/B Side)	Yr	NM
❑ 11270	I'll Never Get Enough/It All Comes Back	1970	6.00

ABC DUNHILL

Number	Title (A Side/B Side)	Yr	NM
❑ 4208	Write to You/Movin'	1969	10.00
❑ 4233	Written in the Dust/Last of the Wine	1970	8.00

ATLANTIC

Number	Title (A Side/B Side)	Yr	NM
❑ 2511	Castles in the Air/I Don't Want to Discuss It	1968	10.00
❑ 2578	A Good Time Song/Changin' Winds	1968	10.00

MERCURY

Number	Title (A Side/B Side)	Yr	NM
❑ 72579	Race with the Wind/In a Funny Sort of Way	1966	10.00
❑ 72616	I Don't Feel Alone/Next Time You Call Me	1966	10.00
❑ 72641	Bittersweet/End of the Week	1966	10.00
❑ 72641 [PS]	Bittersweet/End of the Week	1966	15.00
❑ 72678	Rapid Transit/Cynthia Loves	1967	10.00
❑ 72730	Girls, Girls/Violets of Dawn	1967	10.00

Albums

MERCURY

Number	Title (A Side/B Side)	Yr	NM
❑ MG-21130 [M]	The Robbs	1967	40.00
❑ SR-61130 [S]	The Robbs	1967	30.00

ROBBY AND THE ROBBINS

45s

TODD

Number	Title (A Side/B Side)	Yr	NM
❑ 1089	Surfer's Life/She Cried	1963	40.00

ROBERT AND JOHNNY

45s

OLD TOWN

Number	Title (A Side/B Side)	Yr	NM
❑ 1021	I Believe You/Train to Paradise	1956	50.00
❑ 1029	You're Mine/Million Dollar Bills	1956	40.00
❑ 1038	Don't Do It/Baby Come Home	1957	40.00
❑ 1043	Broken Hearted Man/Indian Marriage	1957	40.00
❑ 1047	We Belong Together/In the Rain	1958	50.00
❑ 1052	I Believe in You/Marry Me	1958	40.00
❑ 1052	I Know/Marry Me	1958	40.00
❑ 1058	Eternity with You/I'm Truly, Truly Yours	1958	30.00
❑ 1065	Give Me the Key to Your Heart/Truly in Love	1959	30.00
❑ 1068	Dream Girl/Oh My Love	1959	30.00
❑ 1072	Wear This Ring/Bad Dan	1959	30.00
❑ 1078	Hear My Heartbeat/Try Me Pretty Baby	1960	25.00
❑ 1086	We Belong Together/In the Rain	1960	25.00
❑ 1100	You're Mine/Please Me Please	1961	20.00
❑ 1108	Togetherness/I Got You	1961	20.00
❑ 1117	Wear This Ring/Broken Hearted Man	1962	20.00

SUE

Number	Title (A Side/B Side)	Yr	NM
❑ 792	A Perfect Wife/Brown, Pretty Brown Eyes	1963	25.00

Except when noted otherwise, VG = 25% of NM, and VG+ = 50% of NM. (Example: VG = $2.00, VG+ = $4.00 and NM = $8.00.)

Number	Title (A Side/B Side)	Yr	NM
ROBERTINO			
45s			
4 CORNERS OF THE WORLD			
101	Santo Natale/Caro Gesu Bambino	1963	8.00
KAPP			
416	O Sole Mio/Romantica	1961	8.00
445	Ave Maria/Santa Lucia	1962	8.00
474	Papa/Parlami D'Amore	1962	8.00
Albums			
KAPP			
KL-1252 [M]	O Sole Mio	1962	15.00
KL-1293 [M]	The Young Italian Singing Sensation	1962	15.00
KL-1338 [M]	Italia Mia	1963	15.00
KL-1471 [M]	The Best of Robertino	1966	12.00
KS-3252 [S]	O Sole Mio	1962	20.00
KS-3293 [S]	The Young Italian Singing Sensation	1962	20.00
KS-3338 [S]	Italia Mia	1963	20.00
KS-3471 [S]	The Best of Robertino	1966	15.00
ROBERTS, ART			
45s			
IMPERIAL			
5504	Give Her the Ax, Max/Terrible Ivan	1958	25.00
ROBERTS, BOBBY			
45s			
HUT			
881	Cravin'/Hop Skip and Jump	1958	250.00
KING			
4837	I'm Gonna Comb You Outta My Hair/My Undecided Heart	1955	50.00
4868	Her and My Best Friend/I'm Pullin' Stakes and Leavin' You	1956	100.00
SKY			
56-101	Big Sandy/She's My Woman	1956	2000.
—VG 1000; VG+ 1500			
ROBERTS, BOBBY, AND THE RAVONS			
45s			
CAMEO			
339	How Can I Make Her Mine/I'm in Love Again	1965	30.00
GMA			
10	How Can I Make Her Mine/I'm in Love Again	1964	120.00
15	Jenny, Jenny/Red Hot	1965	100.00
ROBERTS, DEREK			
45s			
ROULETTE			
4656	There Won't Be Any Snow (Christmas In The Jungle)/A World Without Sunshine	1965	10.00
ROBERTS, JOEY, JR.			
45s			
CAMEO			
418	Once in a Lifetime/That Man's Got No Luck	1966	15.00
440	Raggedy Ann/La La La La La	1966	15.00
ROBERTS, LANCE			
45s			
SUN			
348	The Good Guy Always Wins/The Time Is Right	1960	20.00
ROBERTS, LOU			
45s			
GENIE			
101	Rattle Snake Shake/(B-side unknown)	1965	80.00
MGM			
13347	Gettin' Ready/You Fooled Me	1965	30.00
13387	Don't Count on Me/Ten to One	1965	25.00
ROBERTS, ROCKY, AND THE AIREDALES			
45s			
BRUNSWICK			
55357	Buzz Buzz Buzz/Too Much	1967	10.00
55368	Tell Me/Gotta Thing Going	1968	10.00
Albums			
BRUNSWICK			
BL 54133 [M]	Rocky Roberts and the Airedales	1968	50.00
—Mono is yellow label promo only			
BL 754133 [S]	Rocky Roberts and the Airedales	1968	20.00
ROBERTS, TINA			
45s			
SECURITY			
1366	One Way or the Other/(B-side unknown)	196?	1000.
ROBERTSON, DON			
45s			
CAPITOL			
F3391	The Happy Whistler/You're Free to Go	1956	15.00
F3527	You/Every Day That I Live	1956	12.00
F3625	Rockaway/Fantasy	1957	12.00
F4282	Mery Men/A Fine Day	1959	12.00
JIMMY MCHUGH			
401	Let's Have an Old Fashioned Christmas/Ol' Kris Kringle	198?	5.00
—With Lou Dinning; B-side by the Mitchell Boy Choir			
MONUMENT			
ZS8 8674	Must Be a Better Way to Say Goodbye/Marguerita	1975	5.00
ZS8 8694	She Comes Home to Me/When I Was With You	1976	5.00
RCA VICTOR			
47-7862	Bobby-O/Buttons and Bows	1961	10.00
47-7909	Feather in the Wind/Tennessee Waltz	1961	10.00
47-8059	You Don't Need Me Anymore/Stand In	1962	10.00
47-8177	It's Hard for a King to Step Down/Life Goes On	1963	10.00
47-8269	Dictionary Song/What a Day	1963	10.00
47-8584	Ninety-Nine Miles an Hour/Born to Be with You	1965	10.00
47-9289	Don't Keep Me Lonely Too Long/Jamaica Rum	1967	8.00
47-9659	Earl's Breakdown/You Still Turn Me On	1968	7.00
47-9721	Honey Eyed Girl/I'm Yours	1969	7.00
Albums			
RCA VICTOR			
LPM-3348 [M]	Heart on My Sleeve	1965	20.00
LSP-3348 [S]	Heart on My Sleeve	1965	25.00
ROBINS, THE (1) Vocal group from Los Angeles. Part of the group splintered off and became the core of THE COASTERS.			
45s			
ATCO			
6059	Smokey Joe's Cafe/Just Like a Fool	1956	50.00
CROWN			
106	I Made a Vow/Double Crossing Baby	1954	400.00
120	Key to My Heart/All I Do Is Rock	1954	300.00
KNIGHT			
2001	Quarter to Twelve/Pretty Little Dolly	1958	50.00
2008	It's Never Too Late/A Little Bird Told Me	1958	80.00
RCA VICTOR			
47-5175	(Now and Then There's) A Fool Such As I/My Heart's the Biggest Fool	1953	500.00
47-5271	Oh Why/All Night Baby	1953	400.00
47-5434	How Would You Know/Let's Go to the Dance	1953	400.00
47-5486	My Baby Done Told Me/I'll Do It	1953	300.00
47-5489	Ten Days in Jail/Empty Bottles	1953	200.00
47-5564	Get It Off Your Mind/Don't Stop Now	1953	200.00
SPARK			
103	Riot in Cell Block #9/Wrap It Up	1954	300.00
—Copies on yellow labels are bootlegs			
107	Loop De Loop Mambo/Framed	1954	100.00
—Red label			
107	Loop De Loop Mambo/Framed	1954	300.00
—Silver top label			
110	If Teardrops Were Kisses/Whadaya Want	1955	100.00
—Blue label			
110	If Teardrops Were Kisses/Whadaya Want	1955	300.00
—Red label			
113	One Kiss/I Love Paris	1955	300.00
116	I Must Be Dreamin'/The Hatchet Man	1955	50.00
—Yellow label			
116	I Must Be Dreamin'/The Hatchet Man	1955	200.00
—Red label			
122	Smokey Joe's Cafe/Just Like a Fool	1955	350.00
WHIPPET			
200	Cherry Lips/Out of the Picture	1956	80.00
201	Hurt Me/Merry-Go-Rock	1956	70.00
203	That Old Black Magic/Since I First Met You	1956	70.00
206	A Fool in Love/All of a Sudden My Heart Sings	1957	70.00
208	Every Night/Where's the Fire	1957	70.00
211	In My Dreams/Keep Your Mind on Me	1957	70.00
212	Snowball/You Wanted Fun	1958	70.00
Albums			
GNP CRESCENDO			
GNPS-9034	The Best of the Robins	1975	15.00
WHIPPET			
WLP-703 [M]	Rock 'n' Roll with the Robins	1958	800.00
ROBINS, THE (2)			
45s			
ARDENT			
106	Batman/Batarang	1966	30.00
ROBINS, THE (3)			
45s			
LAVENDER			
001	The White Cliffs of Dover/How Many More Times	1961	40.00
002	Magic of a Dream/Mary Lou Loves to Hootchy Kootchy Koo	1961	40.00
ROBINS, THE (4)			
45s			
NEW HIT			
3010	Johnny/Doing the Popeye	1963	15.00
SWEET TAFFY			
400	Johnny/Doing the Popeye	1963	30.00
ROBINS, THE (U) These could be by any of the above, or none of the above.			
45s			
ARVEE			
5001	Just Like That/Whole Lot of Imagination	1960	25.00
5013	Live Wire Suzie/Oh No	1960	25.00
DOT			
16519	Blue Grass Blues/Top 40 Blues	1963	12.00
GONE			
5101	Baby Love/We Loved	1961	30.00
MUSICOR			
1050	Cry Over You/Lucy Watusi	1964	15.00
ROBINSON, BILL, AND THE QUAILS			
45s			
DATE			
1620	Do I Love You/Lay My Head on Your Shoulder	1969	10.00
DELUXE			
6030	Lonely Star/Quit Pushin'	1954	200.00
6047	I Know She's Gone/Baby Don't Want Me No More	1954	300.00
6057	A Little Bit of Love/Somewhere Somebody Cares	1954	200.00
6059	Why Do I Wait/Heaven Is the Place	1954	200.00
6074	Love of My Life/Oh Sugar	1955	150.00
6085	The Things She Used to Do/Pretty Huggin' Baby	1955	70.00
—As "The Quails"			
ROBINSON, FLOYD			
45s			
DOT			
16290	The Art of Making Love/Don't Let Me Fall	1961	12.00
16352	I Need You/Show Boat	1961	12.00
GROOVE			
58-0040	My Little Martian/Surprise	1964	80.00
JAMIE			
1186	Mother Nature/Is There Something I Ought to Know?	1961	15.00
RCA VICTOR			
47-7529	Makin' Love/My Girl	1959	20.00
47-7637	Tonight You Belong to Me/Let It Be Me	1959	15.00
47-7685	Little Sir Echo/Alphabet Song	1960	15.00
47-7693	Tattletale/I Believe in Love	1960	25.00
47-7736	Boys and Girls/Sonja	1960	15.00
47-7789	A Girl Like You/Why Can't It Go On	1960	15.00
47-7827	Out of Gas/Magic Lamp	1960	30.00

R

Tom Robinson Band, "2-4-6-8 Motorway," Harvest 4533, 1978, $3.

Number	Title (A Side/B Side)	Yr	NM
UNITED ARTISTS			
❑ 534	Heartaches/I've Got a Sweetheart	1963	12.00
❑ 986	Sidewalk Surfer/Motorcycle Man	1966	15.00
7-Inch Extended Plays			
RCA VICTOR			
❑ EPA-4350	(contents unknown)	1959	50.00
❑ EPA-4350 [PS]	Makin' Love	1959	50.00
Albums			
RCA VICTOR			
❑ LPM-2162 [M]	Floyd Robinson	1960	80.00
❑ LSP-2162 [S]	Floyd Robinson	1960	120.00

ROBINSON, FREDDY

Number	Title (A Side/B Side)	Yr	NM
45s			
CHECKER			
❑ 1143	The Creeper/Go Go Girl	1966	10.00
LIBERTY			
❑ 56214	Carmalita/Stone Stallion	1970	6.00
LIMELIGHT			
❑ 3005	Not Like Now/Five Feet of Lovin'	1963	12.00
MERCURY			
❑ 71270	Be Mine/You and Me	1958	12.00
PACIFIC JAZZ			
❑ 88152	Before Six/The Coming Atlantis	1969	6.00
❑ 88155	Black Fox/The Oogue Boogum Song	1970	6.00
QUEEN			
❑ 24005	The Buzzard/The Hawk	196?	10.00
Albums			
ENTERPRISE			
❑ ENS-1025	Freddy Robinson at the Drive-In	1972	12.00
PACIFIC JAZZ			
❑ ST-20162	The Coming Atlantis	1970	15.00
❑ ST-20176	Hot Fun in the Summertime	1971	15.00

ROBINSON, JOHNNY

Number	Title (A Side/B Side)	Yr	NM
45s			
EPIC			
❑ 10578	God Is Love/Kansas City	1970	10.00
❑ 10607	Person to Person/Lady Doctor	1970	10.00
MERCURY			
❑ 72434	I Gotta Kick the Habit (Part 1)/ I Gotta Kick the Habit (Part 2)	1965	20.00
OKEH			
❑ 7307	Gone But Not Forgotten/ I Need Your Love So Bad	1968	100.00
❑ 7317	Poor Man/When a Man Cries	1968	20.00
❑ 7328	Green Green Grass of Home/ You've Been With Him	1969	20.00
Albums			
EPIC			
❑ BN 26528	Memphis High	1970	20.00

ROBINSON, MARK

Number	Title (A Side/B Side)	Yr	NM
45s			
JAMIE			
❑ 1103	Pretty Jane/Want Me	1958	25.00
TEE GEE			
❑ 104	Pretty Jane/Want Me	1958	40.00

ROBINSON, SMOKEY Also see THE MIRACLES; RON AND BILL.

Number	Title (A Side/B Side)	Yr	NM
12-Inch Singles			
MOTOWN			
❑ M00004D1	Vitamin U/Chalk It Up	1977	20.00
—B-side by Jerry Butler			
❑ 00027	Get Ready/(Instrumental)	1979	12.00
❑ PR-92 [DJ]	Tell Me Tomorrow/Right in the Middle (vocal) (instrumental)	1982	10.00
—B-side by Bettye Lavette			
❑ L33-17828 [DJ]	(It's the) Same Old Love (3 versions)	1990	6.00
❑ L33-18141 [DJ]	Everything You Touch (3 versions)/It's the Same Old Feeling	1990	6.00
❑ 50109	Everything You Touch (3 versions)/It's the Same Old Feeling	1990	7.00
TAMLA			
❑ 145 [DJ]	And I Don't Love You (7:10)/ And I Don't Love You (Dub)	1984	8.00
45s			
COLUMBIA			
❑ 07727	I Know You by Heart/Could I Have Your Autograph	1988	3.00
—With Dolly Parton			
MOTOWN			
❑ 914	(It's the) Same Old Love/ (Instrumental)	1990	4.00
❑ 1877	Just to See Her/I'm Gonna Love You Like There's No Tomorrow	1987	3.00
❑ 1877 [PS]	Just to See Her/I'm Gonna Love You Like There's No Tomorrow	1987	8.00
❑ 1897	One Heartbeat/Love Will Set You Free (Theme from Solarbabies)	1987	3.00
❑ 1897 [PS]	One Heartbeat/Love Will Set You Free (Theme from Solarbabies)	1987	6.00
❑ 1911	What's Too Much/I've Made Love to You a Thousand Times	1987	3.00
❑ 1911 [PS]	What's Too Much/I've Made Love to You a Thousand Times	1987	5.00
❑ 1925	Love Don't Give No Reason/ Hanging On by a Thread	1988	3.00
❑ 1925 [PS]	Love Don't Give No Reason/ Hanging On by a Thread	1988	5.00
SBK			
❑ 07379	Double Good Everything/ Guess What I Got for You	1991	4.00
TAMLA			
❑ 1601	Tell Me Tomorrow (Part 1)/ Tell Me Tomorrow (Part 2)	1982	4.00
❑ 1615	Old Fashioned Love/Destiny	1982	4.00
❑ 1630	Are You Still Here/ Yes It's You Lady	1982	4.00
❑ 1655	I've Made Love to You a Thousand Times/Into Each Rain Some Life Must Fall	1983	4.00
❑ 1678	Touch the Sky/All My Life's a Lie	1983	4.00
❑ 1684	Blame It on Love/Even Tho'	1983	4.00
—With Barbara Mitchell			
❑ 1700	Don't Play Another Love Song/ Wouldn't You Like to Know	1983	4.00
❑ 1735	And I Don't Love You/Dynamite	1984	4.00
❑ 1756	I Can't Find/Gimme What You Want	1984	4.00
❑ 1786	First Time on a Ferris Wheel/ Train of Thought	1985	4.00
❑ 1828	Hold On to Your Love/ Train of Thought	1985	4.00
❑ 1828 [PS]	Hold On to Your Love/ Train of Thought	1985	6.00
❑ 1839	Sleepless Nights/Close Encounters of the First Kind	1986	4.00
❑ 1839 [PS]	Sleepless Nights/Close Encounters of the First Kind	1986	5.00
❑ 1855	Girl I'm Standing There/ Because of You (It's the Best It's Ever Been)	1986	4.00
❑ 1868	Love Will Set You Free (Theme 'from Solarbabies) (Parts 1 & 2)	1986	4.00
❑ 54233	Sweet Harmony/Want to Know My Mind	1973	5.00
❑ 54239	Baby Come Close/A Silent Partner in a Three-Way Love Affair	1973	5.00
❑ 54246	It's Her Turn to Live/Just My Soul Responding	1974	5.00
❑ 54250	Virgin Man/Fulfill Your Need	1974	5.00
❑ 54251	I Am, I Am/The Family Song	1974	5.00
❑ 54258	Baby That's Backatcha/ Just Passing Through	1975	5.00
❑ 54261	The Agony and the Ecstasy/ Wedding Song	1975	5.00
❑ 54265	Quiet Storm/Asleep on My Love	1975	5.00
❑ 54267	Open/Coincidentally	1976	5.00
❑ 54272	An Old Fashioned Man/ (B-side unassigned)	1976	—
—Unreleased			
❑ 54276	An Old Fashioned Man/ Just Passing Through	1976	5.00
❑ 54279	There Will Come a Day (I'm Gonna Happen to You)/ Humming Song	1977	5.00
❑ 54284	Vitamin U/Holly	1977	5.00

Except when noted otherwise, VG = 25% of NM, and VG+ = 50% of NM. (Example: VG = $2.00, VG+ = $4.00 and NM = $8.00.)

Number	Title (A Side/B Side)	Yr	NM
❑ 54288	Theme from Big Time (Part 1)/ Theme from Big Time (Part 2)	1977	5.00
❑ 54293	Daylight and Darkness/Why You Wanna See My Bad Side	1978	5.00
❑ 54296	I'm Loving You Softly/Shoe Soul	1978	5.00
❑ 54301	Get Ready/Ever Had a Dream	1979	4.00
❑ 54306	Cruisin'/Ever Had a Dream	1979	4.00
❑ 54311	Let Me Be the Clock/ Travelin' Through	1980	4.00
❑ 54313	Heavy on Pride/I Love the Nearness of You	1980	4.00
❑ 54318	I Want to Be Your Love/ Wine, Women and Song	1980	4.00
❑ 54321	Being with You/What's In Your Life for Me	1981	4.00
❑ 54325	Aquicontigo/Being with You (Aquicontigo)	1981	4.00
❑ 54327	You Are Forever/I Hear the Children Singing	1981	4.00
❑ 54332	Who's Sad/Food for Thought	1981	4.00

Albums

MOTOWN

Number	Title (A Side/B Side)	Yr	NM
❑ M5-118V1	Motown Superstar Series, Vol. 18	1981	10.00
❑ M5-134V1	Smokey	1981	8.00
—Reissue of Tamla 328			
❑ M5-154V1	Deep in My Soul	1981	8.00
—Reissue of Tamla 350			
❑ M5-168V1	Pure Smokey	1981	8.00
—Reissue of Tamla 331			
❑ M5-197V1	A Quiet Storm	1981	8.00
—Reissue of Tamla 337			
❑ 5267ML	Where There;s Smoke	1982	8.00
—Reissue of Tamla 366			
❑ 5349ML	Being with You	1983	8.00
—Reissue of Tamla 375			
❑ MOT-6226	One Heartbeat	1987	10.00
❑ MOT-6268	Love, Smokey	1990	12.00

TAMLA

Number	Title (A Side/B Side)	Yr	NM
❑ T 328	Smokey	1973	12.00
❑ T6-331	Pure Smokey	1974	12.00
❑ T6-337	A Quiet Storm	1975	12.00
❑ T6-341	Smokey's Family Robinson	1976	12.00
❑ T6-350	Deep in My Soul	1977	12.00
❑ T7-359	Love Breeze	1978	12.00
❑ T9-363 [(2)]	Smokin'	1979	15.00
❑ T7-366	Where There's Smoke	1979	10.00
❑ T8-367	Warm Thoughts	1980	10.00
❑ T8-375	Being with You	1981	10.00
❑ 6001TL	Yes It's You Lady	1982	10.00
❑ 6030TL	Touch the Sky	1983	10.00
❑ 6064TL	Blame It on Love & All the Great Hits	1983	10.00
❑ 6098TL	Essar	1984	10.00
❑ 6156TL	Smoke Signals	1986	10.00

UNIVERSAL MOTOWN

Number	Title (A Side/B Side)	Yr	NM
❑ 5316009	A Quiet Storm	2009	20.00

ROBINSON, SMOKEY, AND THE MIRACLES

See THE MIRACLES.

❑ ROBINSON, SUGAR CHILE

45s

CAPITOL

Number	Title (A Side/B Side)	Yr	NM
❑ F1386	Broken Down Piano/ I'll Get My Spinach	1951	25.00
❑ F1526	Baby Blues/The Donkey Song	1951	25.00
❑ F1719	The Hunkie Man/The Green Grass Grows All Around	1951	25.00

ROBINSON, SUGAR RAY

Albums

CONTINENTAL

Number	Title (A Side/B Side)	Yr	NM
❑ CLP-16009	I'm Still Swinging	195?	20.00

ROBINSON, TOM, BAND

12-Inch Singles

GEFFEN

Number	Title (A Side/B Side)	Yr	NM
❑ PRO-A-2209 [DJ]	War Baby/Atmospherics/Listen to the Radio/Rikki Don't Lose That Number	1984	6.00

I.R.S.

Number	Title (A Side/B Side)	Yr	NM
❑ 70960	Now Martin's Gone (2 versions)/ Bonfire	1982	5.00

45s

GEFFEN

Number	Title (A Side/B Side)	Yr	NM
❑ 29130	War Baby/Hell Yes	1984	3.00

HARVEST

Number	Title (A Side/B Side)	Yr	NM
❑ 4533	2-4-6-8 Motorway/ I Shall Be Released	1978	3.00
❑ 4568	Glad to Be Gay/Right On Sister	1978	3.00
❑ 4726	Our People/Bully for You	1979	3.00

I.R.S.

Number	Title (A Side/B Side)	Yr	NM
❑ 9503	Can't Keep Away// Mary Lynn/Dungannon	1981	3.00
❑ 9503 [PS]	Can't Keep Away// Mary Lynn/Dungannon	1981	3.00

Albums

GEFFEN

Number	Title (A Side/B Side)	Yr	NM
❑ GHS 24053	Hope and Glory	1984	10.00

HARVEST

Number	Title (A Side/B Side)	Yr	NM
❑ STBB-11778 [(2)]	Power in the Darkness	1978	12.00
❑ ST-11930	TRB 2	1979	12.00

I.R.S.

Number	Title (A Side/B Side)	Yr	NM
❑ SP-70013	Tom Robinson's Sector 27	1980	12.00

ROBINSON, VICKI SUE

12-Inch Singles

PRELUDE

Number	Title (A Side/B Side)	Yr	NM
❑ 532	Hot Summer Night/(Version)	1981	12.00

PROFILE

Number	Title (A Side/B Side)	Yr	NM
❑ 7025	To Sir with Love/(Instrumental)	1983	8.00
❑ 7039	Everlasting Love/(Instrumental)	1983	8.00

RCA

Number	Title (A Side/B Side)	Yr	NM
❑ PD-11029	Hold Tight/Falling in Love	1977	15.00
❑ PD-11228	Trust in Me (7:03)/Don't Try to Win Me Back Again (6:06)	1978	12.00
❑ PD-11442	Nighttime Fantasy (8:15)/Feels So Good It Must Be Wrong	1979	12.00
❑ PC-11507	Turn the Beat Around/Hold Tight	1979	12.00
❑ PC-11520	Nighttime Fantasy (8:15)/Feels So Good It Must Be Wrong	1980	8.00
❑ PD-11721	What's Happening in My Life (5:42)/Movin' On	1979	12.00

45s

PRELUDE

Number	Title (A Side/B Side)	Yr	NM
❑ 8038	Hot Summer Nights/(Version)	1981	4.00

PROFILE

Number	Title (A Side/B Side)	Yr	NM
❑ 5025	To Sir with Love/(Instrumental)	1983	4.00
❑ 5039	Everlasting Love/(Instrumental)	1983	4.00

RCA

Number	Title (A Side/B Side)	Yr	NM
❑ PB-10775	Daylight/Never Gonna Let You Go	1976	4.00
❑ PB-10863	Should I Stay-I Won't Let You Go/When You're Loving Me	1976	4.00
❑ GB-10944	Turn the Beat Around/Daylight	1977	3.00
—Gold Standard Series			
❑ PB-11028	Falling in Love/Hold Tight	1977	4.00
❑ PB-11227	Trust in Me/Don't Try to Win Me Back Again	1978	4.00
❑ PB-11280	Freeway Song/Half and Half	1978	4.00
❑ PB-11384	Jealousy/We Found Each Other	1978	4.00
❑ PB-11441	Nighttime Fantasy/Feel So Good It Must Be Wrong	1978	4.00
❑ PB-11720	What's Happening in My Life/ Movin' On	1979	4.00

RCA VICTOR

Number	Title (A Side/B Side)	Yr	NM
❑ PB-10282	Baby, Now That I've Found You/Thanks a Million	1975	4.00
❑ PB-10435	Never Gonna Let You Go (Part 1)/Never Gonna Let You Go (Part 2)	1975	4.00
❑ PB-10562	Turn the Beat Around/ Lack of Respect	1976	5.00

Albums

RCA VICTOR

Number	Title (A Side/B Side)	Yr	NM
❑ APL1-1256	Never Gonna Let You Go	1976	12.00
❑ APL1-1829	Vicki Sue Robinson	1977	12.00
❑ AFL1-2294	Half and Half	1978	12.00
❑ AYL1-3949	Turn the Beat Around	1981	8.00

ROBINSON, WANDA

45s

PERCEPTION

Number	Title (A Side/B Side)	Yr	NM
❑ 505	John Harvey's Blues/Final Hour	1971	8.00

Albums

PERCEPTION

Number	Title (A Side/B Side)	Yr	NM
❑ 18	Black Ivory	1971	12.00

ROCCO, LENNY

45s

DELSEY

Number	Title (A Side/B Side)	Yr	NM
❑ 301	Sugar Girl/Rochelle	1961	300.00

ROCHELL AND THE CANDLES

45s

CHALLENGE

Number	Title (A Side/B Side)	Yr	NM
❑ 9158	Turn Her Down/Each Night	1962	40.00
❑ 9191	Annie's Not an Orphan Anymore/Let's Run Away and Get Married	1963	20.00

SWINGIN'

Number	Title (A Side/B Side)	Yr	NM
❑ 623	Once Upon a Time/ When My Baby Is Gone	1960	20.00
❑ 634	So Far Away/Hey, Pretty Baby	1961	20.00
❑ 640	Peg of My Heart/Squat with Me, Baby	1962	20.00
❑ 652	Big Boy Pete/A Long Time Ago	1963	20.00

ROCHES, THE

45s

WARNER BROS.

Number	Title (A Side/B Side)	Yr	NM
❑ 29815	The Hallelujah Chorus/ Second Family	1982	20.00

Albums

MCA

Number	Title (A Side/B Side)	Yr	NM
❑ 10020	We Three Kings	1990	20.00

RHINO

Number	Title (A Side/B Side)	Yr	NM
❑ RNEP-70616 [EP]	No Trespassing	1987	10.00

WARNER BROS.

Number	Title (A Side/B Side)	Yr	NM
❑ BSK 3298	The Roches	1979	10.00
❑ BSK 3475	Nurds	1980	10.00
❑ 23735	Keep On Doing	1982	10.00
❑ 25321	Another World	1985	10.00

ROCK BROTHERS, THE

45s

KING

Number	Title (A Side/B Side)	Yr	NM
❑ 4851	Dungaree Doll/Livin' It Up	1955	30.00
❑ 4882	Oh, Didn't I Ramble/ I Gotta Get Back	1956	25.00

ROCK GARDEN, THE

45s

B.T. PUPPY

Number	Title (A Side/B Side)	Yr	NM
❑ 536	Sweet Pajamas/Perhaps the Joy of Giving	1967	10.00

ROCK ISLAND

45s

PROJECT 3

Number	Title (A Side/B Side)	Yr	NM
❑ 1382	Babe I'm Gonna Leave You/ Hard and Never Easy	1970	10.00

Albums

PROJECT 3

Number	Title (A Side/B Side)	Yr	NM
❑ PR-4005 SD	Rock Island	1970	30.00

ROCK-A-FELLAS, THE

45s

ABC-PARAMOUNT

Number	Title (A Side/B Side)	Yr	NM
❑ 9923	Don't Torment Me/Red Lips	1958	20.00

DEVERE

Number	Title (A Side/B Side)	Yr	NM
❑ 313	Don't Torment Me/Red Lips	1958	50.00

ROCK-A-TEENS, THE

45s

DORAN

Number	Title (A Side/B Side)	Yr	NM
❑ 3515	Woo Hoo/Untrue	1959	150.00

ROULETTE

Number	Title (A Side/B Side)	Yr	NM
❑ 4192	Woo Hoo/Untrue	1959	30.00
❑ 4217	Twangy/Doggone It, Baby	1959	25.00

Albums

ROULETTE

Number	Title (A Side/B Side)	Yr	NM
❑ R-25109 [M]	Woo-Hoo	1960	150.00
❑ SR-25109 [S]	Woo-Hoo	1960	250.00

ROCKA, BILLY

45s

BRUNSWICK

Number	Title (A Side/B Side)	Yr	NM
❑ 55049	Listen Pretty Baby/I'm Gonna Sit Right Down and Cry	1958	60.00

ROCKATS

Albums

ISLAND

Number	Title (A Side/B Side)	Yr	NM
❑ ILPS 9626	Live at the Ritz	1981	25.00

ROCKAWAYS, THE

45s

RED BIRD

Number	Title (A Side/B Side)	Yr	NM
❑ 10-005	Top Down Time/Don't Cry	1964	25.00

ROCKERS, THE

45s

CARTER

Number	Title (A Side/B Side)	Yr	NM
❑ 3029	Tell Me Why/Count Every Star	1955	800.00

FEDERAL

Number	Title (A Side/B Side)	Yr	NM
❑ 12267	What Am I to Do/I'll Die in Love with You	1956	200.00
❑ 12273	Down in the Bottom/ Why Don't You Believe Me	1956	100.00

R

ROCKETEERS, THE (1)

Number	Title (A Side/B Side)	Yr	NM
45s			
GLAD HAMP			
❑ 2017	Drag Strip/Summertime	1963	40.00

ROCKETEERS, THE (2)

Number	Title (A Side/B Side)	Yr	NM
45s			
HERALD			
❑ 415	Foolish One/Gonna Feed My Baby Poison	1953	700.00
—Black vinyl			
❑ 415	Foolish One/Gonna Feed My Baby Poison	1953	2000.
—Red vinyl			

ROCKETEERS, THE (3)

Number	Title (A Side/B Side)	Yr	NM
45s			
MODERN			
❑ 999	Talk It Over Baby/Hey Rube	1956	50.00

ROCKETEERS, THE (4)

Number	Title (A Side/B Side)	Yr	NM
45s			
M.J.C.			
❑ 501	My Reckless Heart/They Turned the Party Out Down at Bessie's House	1958	2000.

ROCKETEERS, THE (U)

Number	Title (A Side/B Side)	Yr	NM
45s			
VAL-UE			
❑ 102	Rippin' and Rockin'/Downtown	1960	30.00

ROCKETONES, THE

Number	Title (A Side/B Side)	Yr	NM
45s			
MELBA			
❑ 113	Mexico/Dee I	1957	50.00
❑ 113	Mexico/I Do	1957	60.00

ROCKETS, THE (2)

Number	Title (A Side/B Side)	Yr	NM
45s			
ATLANTIC			
❑ 988	Open the Door/Big Leg Mama	1953	100.00

ROCKETS, THE (3)

Number	Title (A Side/B Side)	Yr	NM
45s			
COLUMBIA			
❑ 41512	Gibraltar Rock/Walkin' Home	1959	25.00

ROCKETS, THE (4)

Number	Title (A Side/B Side)	Yr	NM
45s			
MODERN			
❑ 992	You Are the First One/Be Lovey Dovey	1956	40.00
Albums			
WHITE WHALE			
❑ WWS-7116	The Rockets	1968	25.00

ROCKETS, THE (5)

Features three future members of CRAZY HORSE.

Number	Title (A Side/B Side)	Yr	NM
45s			
WHITE WHALE			
❑ 270	Hole in My Pocket/Let Me Go	1968	15.00

ROCKETTES, THE

Number	Title (A Side/B Side)	Yr	NM
45s			
PARROT			
❑ 789	I Can't Forget/Love Nobody	1954	3000.
—VG 1000; VG+ 2000			

ROCKIN' BERRIES, THE

Number	Title (A Side/B Side)	Yr	NM
45s			
REPRISE			
❑ 0329	He's in Town/Flashbook	1964	12.00
❑ 0355	What in the World's Come Over You/You Don't Know What to Do	1965	10.00
❑ 0377	Poor Man's Son/Follow Me	1965	10.00
❑ 0400	You're My Girl/Brother Bill (Last Clean Shirt)	1965	10.00
❑ 0442	Doesn't Time Fly/The Water Is Over My Head	1965	10.00

ROCKIN' CHAIRS, THE

Number	Title (A Side/B Side)	Yr	NM
45s			
RECORTE			
❑ 402	Rockin' Chair Boogie/A Kiss Is a Kiss	1958	100.00
❑ 404	Please Mary/Come On Baby	1958	50.00
❑ 412	Memories of Love/Girl of Mine	1959	50.00

ROCKIN' DUKES, THE

Number	Title (A Side/B Side)	Yr	NM
45s			
O.J.			
❑ 1007	Angel and a Rose/My Baby Left Me	1957	300.00

ROCKIN' KIDS, THE

Number	Title (A Side/B Side)	Yr	NM
45s			
DOT			
❑ 15749	Black Stockings/Yea Yea (I'm in the Mood)	1958	30.00

ROCKIN' R'S, THE

Number	Title (A Side/B Side)	Yr	NM
45s			
STEPHENY			
❑ 1842	Walkin' You to School/Bewitched (Bothered and Bewildered)	1960	25.00
TEMPUS			
❑ 1507	Nameless/Heat	1959	30.00
❑ 1515	Mustang/I'm Still in Love with You	1959	30.00
❑ 7541	Crazy Baby/The Beat	1959	40.00
VEE JAY			
❑ 334	Mustang/I'm Still in Love with You	1959	20.00
❑ 346	Hum Bug/The Mix	1960	20.00

ROCKIN' RAMRODS, THE

Number	Title (A Side/B Side)	Yr	NM
45s			
BON-BON			
❑ 1315	She Lies/The Girl Can't Help It	1964	150.00
CLARIDGE			
❑ 301	Don't Fool with Fu Manchu/Tears	1965	40.00
❑ 317	Play It/Got My Mojo Workin'	1966	30.00
PLYMOUTH			
❑ 2961	I Wanna Be Your Man/I'll Be On My Way	1964	50.00
❑ 2961 [PS]	I Wanna Be Your Man/I'll Be On My Way	1964	100.00
❑ 2963	Mister Wind/Bright Lit Blue Skies	1966	25.00
—As "The Ramrods"			
❑ 2965	Flowers in My Mind/Mary, Mary	1967	30.00
—As "The Ramrods"			
SOUTHERN SOUND			
❑ SS305	Wild About You/Cry in My Room	1965	50.00
❑ SS305	Wild About You/Cry in My Room	1965	50.00
—Promo only			

ROCKIN' REBELS, THE

Includes records by "The Hot-Toddys" and "The Rebels."

Number	Title (A Side/B Side)	Yr	NM
45s			
CORSICAN			
❑ 0056	Rockin' Crickets/Shakin' and Stompin'	1959	40.00
—As "The Hot-Toddys"			
ITZY			
❑ 8	Wild Weekend/Wild Weekend Cha Cha	1963	20.00
LOST-NITE			
❑ 239	Wild Weekend/Donkey Twine	196?	5.00
—Reissue			
MAR-LEE			
❑ 0094	Wild Weekend/Wild Weekend Cha Cha	1960	100.00
—As "The Rebels"			
❑ 0095	Buffalo Blues/Donkey Walk	1961	30.00
—As "The Buffalo Rebels"			
❑ 0096	Theme from Rebel/Any Way You Want Me	1961	30.00
—As "The Buffalo Rebels"			
SHAN-TODD			
❑ 0056	Rockin' Crickets/Shakin' and Stompin'	1959	80.00
—As "The Hot-Toddys"			
STORK			
❑ STK-3	Bongo Blue Beat/Burn Baby Burn	1964	25.00
SWAN			
❑ 4125	Wild Weekend/Wild Weekend Cha Cha	1962	30.00
—Second pressings credit "Rockin' Rebels" and do not have "Don't Drop Out" on the label			
❑ 4125	Wild Weekend/Wild Weekend Cha Cha	1962	40.00
—First pressings credit "The Rebels"			
❑ 4125	Wild Weekend/Wild Weekend Cha Cha	1963	20.00
—Later pressings credit "Rockin' Rebels" and have "Don't Drop Out" on the label			
❑ 4140	Rockin' Crickets/Hully Gully Rock	1963	25.00
—A-side is the same recording as on Corsican and Shan-Todd			
❑ 4150	Another Wild Weekend/Happy Popcorn	1963	25.00
❑ 4161	Monday Morning/Flibbity Jibbit	1963	25.00
❑ 4248	Wild Weekend/Donkey Twine	1966	20.00
Albums			
SWAN			
❑ SLP-509 [M]	Wild Weekend	1963	200.00

ROCKIN' SAINTS, THE

Number	Title (A Side/B Side)	Yr	NM
45s			
DECCA			
❑ 30990	Saints Rock/Alright Baby	1959	30.00
❑ 31144	Cheat on Me, Baby/Half and Half	1960	80.00

ROCKIN' SIDNEY

Number	Title (A Side/B Side)	Yr	NM
45s			
EPIC			
❑ 34-05430	My Toot Toot/Jalapeno Lena	1985	4.00
GOLDBAND			
❑ 1158	Actions Speak Louder Than Words/Lais Per La Patate	196?	12.00
❑ 1159	My Poor Heart/Something Working Baby	196?	12.00
❑ 1163	Deedle Didie Da/Life Without Love	196?	10.00
❑ 1170	Gonna Be Looking/Shed So Many Tears	196?	10.00
❑ 1177	Corpus Christi/(B-side unknown)	196?	12.00
❑ 1178	Trust/Put On It	196?	10.00
❑ 1183	Soul Christmas (Part 1)/Soul Christmas (Part 2)	1966	12.00
❑ 1186	The Grandpa/Feel Delicious	1967	10.00
JIN			
❑ 110	My Little Girl/Don't Say Goodbye	1959	50.00
❑ 141	Walking Out on You/Rocky	1960	30.00
❑ 156	No Good Woman/You Ain't Nothin' But Fine	1960	30.00
❑ 164	Send Me Some Lovin'/Past Bedtime	196?	30.00
❑ 168	No Good Man/If I Could, I Win	196?	30.00
❑ 170	Don't Let Me Cross Over/You Don't Have to Go	196?	30.00
❑ 174	Something's Wrong/It Really Is a Hurtin' Thing	196?	30.00
❑ 177	Ya Ya/Wasted Days and Wasted Nights	196?	30.00
MAISON DE SOUL			
❑ 1017	Good Time Woman/You Ain't Nothin' But Fine	198?	6.00
❑ 1020	Dance and Show Off/Relax and Go Slow	198?	6.00
❑ 1021	Boogie for Me/Sweet Li'l Woman	198?	6.00
❑ 1024	My Toot Toot/Zydeco Shoes	1984	8.00
❑ 1025	Party This Christmas/Christmas Without You	1984	6.00
Albums			
EPIC			
❑ B5E 40153 [EP]	My Toot Toot	1985	8.00
ZBC			
❑ LP-100	A Holiday Celebration with Rockin' Sidney	1983	15.00

ROCKIN' STOCKIN', THE

Number	Title (A Side/B Side)	Yr	NM
45s			
SUN			
❑ 350	Rockin' Lang Syne/Yuleville U.S.A.	1960	30.00
❑ 1960	Rockin' Lang Syne/Yuleville U.S.A.	197?	15.00
—Reissue with green and red print on a white label with original Sun logo			

ROCKIN' VICKERS

Number	Title (A Side/B Side)	Yr	NM
45s			
COLUMBIA			
❑ 43818	Dandy/I Don't Need Your Love	1966	15.00

ROCKING BROTHERS, THE

Number	Title (A Side/B Side)	Yr	NM
45s			
IMPERIAL			
❑ 5333	Rock It/Behind the Sun	1955	30.00
❑ 5341	Blow Torch/Evening Shadows	1955	30.00
SAVOY			
❑ 1144	Play Boy Hop/The Grinder	1955	50.00
WHIPPET			
❑ 207	Yeah! Yeah!/Little Mike	1957	20.00

ROCKPILE

Also see DAVE EDMUNDS; NICK LOWE.

Number	Title (A Side/B Side)	Yr	NM
45s			
COLUMBIA			
❑ AE7 1218 [DJ]	Teacher Teacher/You Ain't Nothin' But Fine	1980	7.00
—White label promo; small hole			
❑ 11388	Teacher Teacher/Fool Too Long	1980	4.00

Number | Title (A Side/B Side) | Yr | NM

❑ 11388 [PS] Teacher Teacher/Fool Too Long 1980 7.00
—Promo-only sleeve detailing the history of Rockpile
❑ 60503 Heart/Take a Message to Mary 1981 4.00
—B-side by Dave Edmunds and Nick Lowe

Albums

COLUMBIA
❑ JC 36886 Seconds of Pleasure 1980 15.00
—Includes bonus EP, "Nick Lowe and Dave Edmunds Sing the Everly Brothers."

ROCKY AND HIS FRIENDS

45s

TOWER
❑ 178 Riot City/You're Not Wrong 1965 12.00

ROCKY FELLERS, THE

45s

DONNA
❑ 1383 Don't Sit Down/The Beachcomber Song 1963 12.00

PARKWAY
❑ 836 Long Tall Sally/South Pacific Twist 1962 12.00

SCEPTER
❑ 1245 Santa Santa/Great Big World 1962 20.00
—A-side is a very early Neil Diamond composition
❑ 1245 [DJ] Santa Santa (same on both sides) 196? 8.00
—Promo reissue; white label with mid-1960s Scepter Records logo (black oval)
❑ 1245 [DJ] Santa Santa/Santa's Grove 1963 12.00
—Promo reissue with new B-side. All-white label (no black oval)
❑ 1246 Killer Joe/Lonely Teardrops 1963 15.00
❑ 1254 Like the Big Guys Do/Great Big World 1963 12.00
❑ 1254 [PS] Like the Big Guys Do/Great Big World 1963 20.00
❑ 1258 Ching-a-Ling Baby/Hey Little Donkey 1963 12.00
❑ 1263 Bye Bye Baby/She Makes Me Wanna Dance 1963 12.00
❑ 1271 My Prayer/Two Guys from Trinidad 1964 12.00

VALMOR
❑ 2004 Opus/Orange Peel 1962 15.00

WARNER BROS.
❑ 5440 (Everybody Wants to Be a) Tiger/Jeannie Memsoh 1964 10.00
❑ 5459 Better Let Her Go/Nina 1964 10.00
❑ 5497 Man with the Blue Guitar/Don't Throw My Toys Away 1965 10.00
❑ 5613 Rented Tuxedo/Two Steps Downstairs in the Basement 1965 10.00

Albums

SCEPTER
❑ SP-512 [M] Killer Joe 1964 30.00
❑ SPS-512 [S] Killer Joe 1964 40.00

ROD AND CAROLYN

45s

PARKWAY
❑ 918 Young Love/Talk to Me 1964 10.00
❑ 934 Love Is Where You Are/I've Got You on My Mind 1964 10.00

RODGERS, JIMMIE (1)

Legendary country & western singer known as "The Singing Brakeman."

45s

RCA VICTOR
❑ 27-0098 Blue Yodel (T for Texas)/Away Out on the Mountain 1950 20.00
❑ 27-0099 Never No Mo' Blues/Daddy and Home 1950 20.00
❑ 27-0100 Frankie and Johnny/The Brakeman's Blues 1950 20.00
—The above three comprise box set WPT 21
❑ 27-0101 Blue Yodel No. 4/Waiting for a Train 1950 20.00
❑ 27-0102 My Old Pal/Desert Blues 1950 20.00
❑ 27-0103 Blue Yodel No. 3/I'm Sorry We Met 1950 20.00
—The above three comprise box set WPT 22
❑ 27-0104 Sleep, Baby, Sleep/My Carolina Sunshine Girl 1950 20.00
❑ 27-0105 Blue Yodel No. 2/Tuck Away My Lonesome Blues 1950 20.00
❑ 27-0106 Blue Yodel No. 6/Dear Old Sunny South by the Sea 1950 20.00
—The above three comprise box set WPT 23
❑ 47-6092 In the Jailhouse Now No. 2/Peach Pickin' Time Down in Georgia 1955 20.00
❑ 47-6205 Mule Skinner Blues/Mother, the Queen of My Heart 1955 20.00
❑ 47-6408 Never No Mo' Blues/Daddy and Home 1955 20.00
❑ WPT 21 [PS] Yodelingly Yours, Jimmie Rodgers, Vol. 1 1950 20.00
—Box for 27-0098, 27-0099 and 27-0100
❑ WPT 22 [PS] Yodelingly Yours, Jimmie Rodgers, Vol. 2 1950 20.00
—Box for 27-0101, 27-0102 and 27-0103
❑ WPT 23 [PS] Yodelingly Yours, Jimmie Rodgers, Vol. 3 1950 20.00
—Box for 27-0104, 27-0105 and 27-0106
❑ AMAO-0130 Mule Skinner Blues/Waiting for a Train 1973 8.00
—Gold Standard Series reissue

7-Inch Extended Plays

RCA VICTOR
❑ EPAT 23 *My Carolina Sunshine Girl/Sleep, Baby, Sleep/Blue Yodel No. 2/Tuck Away My Lonesome Blues 1952 20.00
❑ EPAT 23 [PS] Yodelingly Yours, Jimmie Rodgers, Vol. 3 1952 20.00
❑ EPAT 409 Never No Mo' Blues/Daddy and Home//Waiting for a Train/Blue Yodel No. 4 (California Blues) 1953 20.00
❑ EPAT 409 [PS] Yodelingly Yours, Jimmie Rodgers, Vol. 4 1953 20.00
❑ EPAT 410 (contents unknown) 195? 20.00
❑ EPAT 410 [PS] Yodelingly Yours, Jimmie Rodgers, Vol. 5 195? 20.00
❑ EPAT 411 *You and My Old Guitar/Prairie Lullaby/Old Pal of My Heart/My Little Lady 195? 20.00
❑ EPAT 411 [PS] Yodelingly Yours, Jimmie Rodgers, Vol. 6 195? 20.00
❑ 547-0901 Never No Mo' Blues/Daddy and Home//Jimmie's Mean Mama Blues/Old Pal of My Heart 1955 20.00
—"Side 1" and "Side 4" of EPB-1232
❑ 547-0902 Blue Yodel No. 4/Waiting for a Train//Prairie Lullaby/Blue Yodel No. 6 1955 20.00
—"Side 2" and "Side 3" of EPB-1232
❑ EPB-1232 [PS] Never No Mo' Blues — Jimmie Rodgers Memorial Album 1955 20.00
—Gatefold cover for 547-0901 and 547-0902

Albums

RCA VICTOR
❑ DPL2-0075 [(2)] The Legendary Jimmie Rodgers, Vol. 1 1974 40.00
—Special-products issue for Country Music Magazine
❑ ANL1-1209 My Rough and Rowdy Ways 1976 10.00
❑ LPM-1232 [M] Never No Mo' Blues — A Memorial Album 1955 150.00
❑ LPM-1640 [M] Train Whistle Blues 1957 150.00
❑ LPM-2112 [M] My Rough and Rowdy Ways 1960 80.00
❑ LPM-2213 [M] Jimmie the Kid 1961 80.00
❑ CPL1-2504 A Legendary Performer 1977 10.00
❑ LPM-2531 [M] Country Music Hall of Fame 1962 80.00
❑ LPM-2634 [M] The Short But Brilliant Life of Jimmie Rodgers 1963 80.00
❑ LPM-2865 [M] My Time Ain't Long 1964 50.00
❑ LPT-3037 [10] Yodelingly Yours Jimmie Rodgers, Vol. 1 1953 400.00
❑ LPT-3038 [10] Yodelingly Yours Jimmie Rodgers, Vol. 2 1953 400.00
❑ LPT-3039 [10] Yodelingly Yours Jimmie Rodgers, Vol. 3 1953 400.00
❑ LPM-3073 [10] Travelin' Blues 1952 400.00
❑ AHL1-3315 The Best of the Legendary Jimmie Rodgers 197? 8.00
—Reissue with new prefix
❑ LPM-3315 [M] The Best of the Legendary Jimmie Rodgers 1965 40.00
❑ LSP-3315 [R] The Best of the Legendary Jimmie Rodgers 1965 20.00
❑ VPS-6091(e) [(2)] This Is Jimmie Rodgers 1971 20.00

ROUNDER
❑ 1056 First Sessions 1927-1928 1990 12.00
❑ 1057 The Early Years 1928-1929 1990 12.00

RODGERS, JIMMIE (2)

Pop-country vocalist, no relation to the above.

45s

A&M
❑ 842 I'll Say Goodbye/Shadows 1967 6.00
❑ 871 Child of Clay/Turnaround 1967 6.00
❑ 898 If I Were the Man/What a Strange Town 1967 6.00
❑ 902 I Believe It All/You Pass Me By 1968 6.00
❑ 930 How Do You Say Goodbye/I Wanna Be Free 1968 6.00
❑ 976 Today/The Lovers 1968 6.00
❑ 1055 The Windmills of Your Mind/L.A. Break Down (And Take Me Back In) 1969 6.00
❑ 1120 Father Paul/Me About You 1969 6.00
❑ 1152 Cycles/Tomorrow My Friends 1969 6.00
❑ 1213 Troubled Times/The Dum Dum Song 1970 5.00

DOT
❑ 16378 No One Will Ever Know/Because 1962 10.00
❑ 16378 [PS] No One Will Ever Know/Because 1962 15.00
❑ 16407 Rainbow at Midnight/Rhumba Boogie 1962 10.00
❑ 16428 I'll Never Stand in Your Way/Afraid 1963 10.00
❑ 16450 Lonely Tears/A Face in the Crowd 1963 10.00
❑ 16467 (I Don't Know Why) I Just Do/Load 'Em Up (And Keep a Steppin') 1963 10.00
❑ 16490 Poor Little Raggedy Ann/I'm Gonna Be the Winner 1963 10.00
❑ 16527 Two-Ten Six-Eighteen (Doesn't Anybody Know My Name)/The Banana Boat Song 1963 10.00
❑ 16561 Together/Mama Was a Cotton Picker 1963 10.00
❑ 16595 The World I Used to Know/I Forgot More Than You'll Ever Know 1964 10.00
❑ 16653 Water Boy/Someplace Green 1964 10.00
❑ 16673 Two Tickets/I Forgot More Than You'll Ever Know 1964 10.00
❑ 16694 (All My Friends Are Gonna Be) Strangers/Bon Soir Mademoiselle 1965 8.00
❑ 16720 Careless Love/When I'm Right You Don't Remember 1965 8.00
❑ 16749 Are You Going My Way (Little Beachcomber)/Little Schoolgirl 1965 8.00
❑ 16781 Bye Bye Love/Hollow Words 1965 8.00
❑ 16795 The Chipmunk Song (Christmas Don't Be Late)/In the Snow 1965 8.00
❑ 16826 A Falen Star/Brother, Where Are You 1966 8.00
❑ 16861 It's Over/Anita, You're Dreaming 1966 10.00
❑ 16916 Morning Means Tomorrow/New Ideas 1966 8.00
❑ 16973 Love Me, Please Love Me/Wonderful You 1966 8.00
❑ 17040 Time/Yours and Mine 1967 8.00

EPIC
❑ 10828 Froggy's Fable/Daylight Lights the Dawning 1972 5.00
❑ 10857 Kick the Can/Go On By 1972 5.00

MGM
❑ 11732 Mama, Don't Cry at My Wedding/You Don't Live Here No More 1954 25.00

ROULETTE
❑ 4015 Honeycomb/Their Hearts Were Full of Spring 1957 20.00
❑ 4031 Kisses Sweeter Than Wine/Better Loved You'll Never Be 1957 20.00
❑ 4045 Oh-Oh, I'm Falling in Love Again/The Long Hot Summer 1958 15.00
—White label with colored spokes
❑ 4045 Oh-Oh, I'm Falling in Love Again/The Long Hot Summer 1958 20.00
—Red label
❑ 4070 Secretly/Make Me a Miracle 1958 20.00
❑ 4070 [PS] Secretly/Make Me a Miracle 1958 40.00
❑ 4090 Are You Really Mine/The Wizard 1958 15.00
❑ 4090 [PS] Are You Really Mine/The Wizard 1958 40.00
❑ 4116 Bimbombey/You Understand Me 1958 15.00
❑ 4129 I'm Never Gonna Tell/Because You're Young 1959 15.00
❑ 4158 [M] Ring-a-Ling-a-Lario/Wonderful You 1959 15.00
❑ 4158 [PS] Ring-a-Ling-a-Lario/Wonderful You 1959 25.00
❑ SSR-4158 [S] Ring-a-Ling-a-Lario/Wonderful You 1959 30.00
❑ 4191 Tucumcari/That Night You Became Seventeen 1959 15.00
❑ 4205 It's Christmas Once Again/Wistful Willie 1959 20.00
❑ 4218 [M] T.L.C. Tender Love and Care/Waltzing Matilda 1960 12.00
❑ SSR-4218 [S] T.L.C. Tender Love and Care/Waltzing Matilda 1960 30.00
❑ 4234 Just a Closer Walk with Thee/Joshua Fit the Battle of Jericho 1960 12.00
❑ 4260 The Wreck of the John B/Four Little Girls in Boston 1960 12.00
❑ 4293 Woman from Liberia/Come Along Julie 1960 12.00
❑ 4293 [PS] Woman from Liberia/Come Along Julie 1960 20.00

R

Number	Title (A Side/B Side)	Yr	NM
4318	When Love Is Young/The Little Shepherd of Kingdom Come	1960	12.00
4349	Everytime My Heart Sings/ I'm On My Way	1961	12.00
4371	John Brown's Baby/ I'm Going Home	1961	12.00
4384	A Little Dog Cried/Englidh Country Garden	1961	12.00
4439	You Are Everything to Me/ Wanderin' Eyes	1962	12.00
SSR-8001 [S]	Bo Diddley/Soldier Won't You Marry Me	1959	30.00
SSR-8007 [S]	Froggy Went a-Courtin'/Lisa	1959	30.00
SSR-8010 [S]	St. James Infirmary/ Just a Wearyin' for You	1959	30.00
SCRIMSHAW			
1313	A Good Woman Likes to Drink with the Boys/Dancing on the Moon	1977	4.00
1314	Everytime I Sing a Love Song/ Just a Little Time	1978	4.00
1316	When Our Love Began (Cowboys and Indians)/ (B-side unknown)	1978	4.00
1318	Secretly/Shovelin' Coal	1978	4.00
1319/20	Easy to Love/Easy	1979	4.00
—With Michele			
7-Inch Extended Plays			
ROULETTE			
EPR-1-303	Woman from Liberia/ The Mating Call//Hey Little Baby/Water Boy	1957	50.00
EPR-1-303 [PS]	Jimmie Rodgers	1957	50.00
EPR-1-312	*Honeycomb/Oh-Oh, I'm Falling in Love Again/ The Preacher/Better Loved You'll Never Be	195?	50.00
EPR-1-312 [PS]	Jimmie Rodgers Sings	195?	50.00
EPR-1-313	Tammy/The Song from Moulin Rouge//Love Letters in the Sand/Hey There	195?	50.00
EPR-1-313 [PS]	The Number One Ballads, Part 1	195?	50.00
EPR-1-315	Bo Diddley/Riddle Song// The Fox and the Goose/ Black Is the Color	1960	50.00
EPR-1-315 [PS]	Jimmie Rodgers Sings Folk Songs, Part I	1960	50.00
EPR-1-316	Waltzing Matilda/The Crocodile// Lord Randal/Gotta Lotta Tunes in My Guitar	195?	50.00
EPR-1-316 [PS]	Jimmie Rodgers Sings Folk Songs, Part II	195?	50.00
EPR-1-317	Soldier, Won't You Marry Me?/ Lassie O'Mine//Liza/ Froggy Went a-Courtin'	1960	50.00
EPR-1-317 [PS]	Jimmie Rodgers Sings Folk Songs, Part III	1960	50.00
Albums			
A&M			
SP-130 [M]	Child of Clay	1967	25.00
SP-4130 [S]	Child of Clay	1967	15.00
SP-4187	Windmills of Your Mind	1969	15.00
SP-4242	Troubled Times	1970	15.00
ACCORD			
SN-7198	Honeycomb & Other Hits	198?	10.00
DOT			
DLP-3453 [M]	No One Will Ever Know	1962	15.00
DLP-3496 [M]	Jimmie Rodgers Folk Concert	1963	15.00
DLP-3502 [M]	My Favorite Hymns	1963	15.00
DLP-3525 [M]	Honeycomb & Kisses Sweeter Than Wine	1963	15.00
DLP-3556 [M]	The World I Used to Know	1964	15.00
—Retitled version of above			
DLP-3556 [M]	Town and Country	1964	20.00
DLP-3579 [M]	12 Great Hits	1964	15.00
DLP-3614 [M]	Deep Purple	1965	15.00
DLP 3657 [M]	Christmas with Jimmie	1965	12.00
DLP-3687 [M]	The Nashville Sound	1966	15.00
DLP-3710 [M]	Country Music 1966	1966	15.00
DLP-3717 [M]	It's Over	1966	15.00
DLP-3780 [M]	Love Me, Please Love Me	1967	15.00
DLP-3815 [M]	Golden Hits/15 Hits of Jimmie Rodgers	1967	20.00
DLP-25453 [S]	No One Will Ever Know	1962	20.00
DLP-25496 [S]	Jimmie Rodgers Folk Concert	1963	20.00
DLP-25502 [S]	My Favorite Hymns	1963	20.00
DLP-25525 [S]	Honeycomb & Kisses Sweeter Than Wine	1963	20.00
DLP-25556 [S]	The World I Used to Know	1964	20.00
—Retitled version of above			
DLP-25556 [S]	Town and Country	1964	25.00
DLP-25579 [S]	12 Great Hits	1964	20.00
DLP-25614 [S]	Deep Purple	1965	20.00
DLP 25657 [S]	Christmas with Jimmie	1965	15.00
DLP-25687 [S]	The Nashville Sound	1966	20.00
DLP-25710 [S]	Country Music 1966	1966	20.00

Number	Title (A Side/B Side)	Yr	NM
DLP-25717 [S]	It's Over	1966	20.00
DLP-25780 [S]	Love Me, Please Love Me	1967	20.00
DLP-25815 [S]	Golden Hits/15 Hits of Jimmie Rodgers	1967	15.00
FORUM			
F-9025 [M]	At Home with Jimmie Rodgers: An Evening of Folk Songs	196?	12.00
SF-9025 [S]	At Home with Jimmie Rodgers: An Evening of Folk Songs	196?	12.00
F-9049 [M]	Just for You	196?	12.00
SF-9049 [S]	Just for You	196?	12.00
F-9059 [M]	Jimmie Rodgers Sings Folk Songs	196?	12.00
SF-9059 [S]	Jimmie Rodgers Sings Folk Songs	196?	12.00
HAMILTON			
HL-114 [M]	6 Favorite Hymns and 6 Favorite Folk Ballads	1964	12.00
HL-148 [M]	12 Immortal Songs	196?	12.00
HS-12114 [S]	6 Favorite Hymns and 6 Favorite Folk Ballads	1964	12.00
HS-12148 [S]	12 Immortal Songs	196?	12.00
PARAMOUNT			
PAS-2-1042 [(2)]	Honeycomb	1974	15.00
PICKWICK			
PC-3040 [M]	Jimmie Rodgers	196?	12.00
SPC-3040 [S]	Jimmie Rodgers	196?	12.00
SPC-3106	Am I That Easy to Forget	196?	12.00
SPC-3599	Big Hits	197?	10.00
ROULETTE			
R-25020 [M]	Jimmie Rodgers	1957	50.00
—Black label			
R-25020 [M]	Jimmie Rodgers	1959	25.00
—White label with colored spokes			
R-25033 [M]	Number One Ballads	1958	50.00
—Black label			
R-25033 [M]	Number One Ballads	1959	25.00
—White label with colored spokes			
R-25042 [M]	Jimmie Rodgers Sings Folk Songs	1958	50.00
—Black label			
R-25042 [M]	Jimmie Rodgers Sings Folk Songs	1959	25.00
—White label with colored spokes			
R-25057 [M]	His Golden Year	1959	25.00
R-25071 [M]	TV Favorites	1959	30.00
SR-25071 [S]	TV Favorites	1959	50.00
R-25081 [M]	Twilight on the Trail	1959	30.00
SR-25081 [S]	Twilight on the Trail	1959	50.00
R 25095 [M]	It's Christmas Once Again	1959	30.00
SR 25095 [S]	It's Christmas Once Again	1959	50.00
R-25103 [M]	When the Spirit Moves You	1960	30.00
SR-25103 [S]	When the Spirit Moves You	1960	40.00
R-25128 [M]	At Home with Jimmie Rodgers: An Evening of Folk Songs	1960	30.00
SR-25128 [S]	At Home with Jimmie Rodgers: An Evening of Folk Songs	1960	40.00
R-25150 [M]	The Folk Song World of Jimmie Rodgers	1961	30.00
SR-25150 [S]	The Folk Song World of Jimmie Rodgers	1961	40.00
R-25160 [M]	The Best of Jimmie Rodgers' Folk Tunes	1961	30.00
SR-25160 [S]	The Best of Jimmie Rodgers' Folk Tunes	1961	40.00
—Black vinyl			
SR-25160 [S]	The Best of Jimmie Rodgers' Folk Tunes	1961	250.00
—Red vinyl			
R-25179 [M]	15 Million Sellers	1962	25.00
SR-25179 [P]	15 Million Sellers	1962	20.00
—Orange and yellow label			
SR-25179 [P]	15 Million Sellers	1962	30.00
—White label with colored spokes			
R-25199 [M]	Folk Songs	1963	20.00
SR-25199 [S]	Folk Songs	1963	25.00
SR-42006	Yours Truly	1968	15.00

RODRIGUEZ, JOHNNY

Number	Title (A Side/B Side)	Yr	NM
45s			
CAPITOL			
B-44071	I Didn't (Every Chance I Had)/I'm Not That Good at Goodbye	1987	4.00
B-44204	I Wanta Wake Up with You/ Someday I'm Gonna Finish Leaving You	1988	4.00
B-44245	You Might Want to Use Me Again/She Loves Austin	1988	4.00
B-44325	No Chance to Dance/ Back to Stay	1989	4.00
B-44403	Back to Stay/Someday I'm Gonna Finish Leaving You	1989	4.00
COLUMBIA			
02987	The Most Beautiful Girl/Too Far Gone	1982	4.00
—With Ray Conniff; B-side by Zella Lehr with Ray Conniff			
EPIC			
01033	I Want You Tonight/Your Love Isn't Mine Anymore	1981	3.00
02411	Trying Not to Love You/ Mexico Rain	1981	3.00
02638	It's Not the Same Old You/ Born with the Blues	1981	3.00
03275	He's Not Entitled to Your Love/ Starting All Over Again	1982	3.00
03598	Foolin'/Because of You	1983	3.00
03972	How Could I Love Her So Much/ Somethin' About a Jukebox	1983	3.00
04206	Back on Her Mind Again/ Eleven Roses	1983	3.00
04336	Too Late to Go Home/No Memories Hangin' 'Round	1984	3.00
04460	Let's Leave the Lights On Tonight/What a Movie You'd Make	1984	3.00
04562	First Time Burned/Hand Me Another of Those	1984	3.00
04628	Rose of My Heart/Down in the Boondocks	1984	3.00
04838	Here I Am Again/Full Circle	1985	3.00
05732	She Don't Cry Like She Used To/Back on Her Mind Again	1985	3.00
05863	Maxine/Full Circle	1986	3.00
50671	Down on the Rio Grande/ Mexico Holiday	1979	4.00
50735	Fools for Each Other/ Street Walker	1979	4.00
50791	I Hate the Way I Love It/ Almost Persuaded	1979	4.00
—With Charly McClain			
50808	What'll I Tell Virginia/Whatever Gets Me Through the Night	1979	4.00
50859	Love, Look At Us Now/ Where Did It Go	1980	4.00
50932	North of the Border/When She Gets Around to Me	1980	4.00
MERCURY			
55004	Eres Tu/You Put a Hold on Me	1977	4.00
55012	Savin' This Love Song for You/ Que Te Quiero	1977	4.00
55020	We Believe in Happy Endings/ The Immigrant	1978	4.00
55029	Love Me with All Your Heart (Cuando Caliente El Sol)	1978	4.00
55050	Alibis/Rest Your Love on Me	1978	4.00
73334	Pass Me By (If You're Only Passing Through)/ Jealous Heart	1972	5.00
73368	You Always Come Back (To Hurting Me)/I Wonder Where You Are Tonight	1973	5.00
73416	Ridin' My Thumb to Mexico/ Release Me	1973	5.00
73446	That's the Way Love Goes /I Really Don't Want to Know	1973	5.00
73471	Something/Born to Lose	1974	5.00
73493	Dance with Me (Just One More Time)/Faded Love	1974	4.00
—Chicago skyline label			
73493	Dance with Me (Just One More Time)/Faded Love	1974	5.00
—Red label			
73621	We're Over/Oh I Miss You	1974	4.00
73659	I Just Can't Get Her Out of My Mind/Have I Told You Lately	1975	4.00
73682	Just Get Up and Close the Door/ Am I That Easy to Forget	1975	4.00
73715	Love Put a Song in My Heart/ Steppin' Out on You	1975	4.00
73769	I Couldn't Be Me Without You/ Sometimes I Wish I Were You	1976	4.00
73815	I Wonder If I Ever Said Goodbye/Louisiana	1976	4.00
73855	Hillbilly Heart/Commonly Known As the Blues	1976	4.00
73878	Desperado/There'll Always Be Honky-Tonks in Texas	1976	4.00
73914	If Practice Makes Perfect/ Hard Times	1977	4.00
Albums			
CAPITOL			
C1-90040	Gracias	1988	10.00
EPIC			
JE 36014	Rodriguez	1979	10.00
JE 36274	Through My Eyes	1980	10.00
JE 36587	Gypsy	1980	10.00
FE 37103	After the Rain	1981	10.00
FE 38321	Biggest Hits	1982	10.00
FE 38806	For Every Rose	1983	10.00
FE 39172	Foolin' with Fire	1984	10.00
FE 39583	Full Circle	1985	10.00
MERCURY			
SRM-1-686	All I Ever Meant to Do Was Sing	1973	15.00

Except when noted otherwise, VG = 25% of NM, and VG+ = 50% of NM. (Example: VG = $2.00, VG+ = $4.00 and NM = $8.00.)

Number	Title (A Side/B Side)	Yr	NM
❑ SRM-1-699	My Third Album	1974	15.00
❑ SRM-1-1012	Songs About Ladies and Love	1974	15.00
❑ SRM-1-1032	Just Get Up and Close the Door	1975	15.00
❑ SRM-1-1057	Love Put a Song in My Heart	1975	15.00
❑ SRM-1-1078	The Greatest Hits of Johnny Rodriguez	1976	15.00
❑ SRM-1-1110	Reflecting	1976	12.00
❑ SRM-1-1144	Practice Makes Perfect	1977	12.00
❑ SRM-1-5003	Just for You	1977	12.00
❑ SRM-1-5011	Love Me with All You Heart	1978	12.00
❑ SRM-1-5015	Johnny Rodriguez Was Here	1979	12.00
❑ SRM-1-5022	Sketches	1980	12.00
❑ SR-61378	Introducing Johnny Rodriguez	1973	15.00
❑ 826271-1	The Greatest Hits of Johnny Rodriguez	1985	8.00

—Reissue

ROE, TOMMY

45s

ABC

Number	Title (A Side/B Side)	Yr	NM
❑ 10762	Sweet Pea/Much More Love	1966	10.00
—Reissue; this was the common version when this song was a hit; earliest copies have "ABC Records" standing alone (not in a circle)			
❑ 10852	Hooray for Hazel/Need Your Love	1966	10.00
❑ 10888	It's Now Winters Day/Kick Me Charlie	1966	8.00
❑ 10888 [PS]	It's Now Winters Day/Kick Me Charlie	1966	15.00
❑ 10908	Sing Along with Me/Night Time	1967	8.00
❑ 10933	Moon Talk/Sweet Sounds	1967	8.00
❑ 10945	Little Miss Sunshine/You I Need	1967	8.00
❑ 10989	Melancholy Mood/Paisley Dreams	1967	8.00
❑ 11039	Dottie I Like It/Soft Words	1968	8.00
❑ 11076	An Oldie But a Goodie/Sugar Cane	1968	8.00
❑ 11140	It's Gonna Hurt Me/Gotta Keep Rolling Along	1968	8.00
❑ 11164	Dizzy/The You I Need	1969	10.00
❑ 11211	Heather Honey/Money Is My Pay	1969	6.00
❑ 11229	Jack and Jill/Tip Toe Tina	1969	6.00
❑ 11247	Jam Up Jelly Tight/Moontalk	1969	8.00
❑ 11247 [PS]	Jam Up Jelly Tight/Moontalk	1969	12.00
❑ 11258	Stir It Up and Serve It/Fire Fly	1970	6.00
❑ 11266	Pearl/A Dollar's Worth of Pennies	1970	6.00
❑ 11273	We Can Make Music/Gotta Keep Rolling Along	1970	6.00
❑ 11273 [PS]	We Can Make Music/Gotta Keep Rolling Along	1970	6.00
❑ 11281	King of Fools/Brush a Little Sunshine	1970	6.00
❑ 11287	Little Miss Goodie Two Shoes/Traffic Jam	1971	6.00
❑ 11293	King of Fools/Pistol-Legged Mama	1971	6.00
❑ 11307	Stagger Lee/Back Streets and Alleys	1971	6.00

ABC-PARAMOUNT

Number	Title (A Side/B Side)	Yr	NM
❑ 10329	Sheila/Save Your Kisses	1962	15.00
❑ 10362	Susie Darlin'/Piddle De Pat	1962	12.00
❑ 10362 [PS]	Susie Darlin'/Piddle De Pat	1962	25.00
❑ 10379	Town Crier/Rainbow	1962	12.00
❑ 10379 [PS]	Town Crier/Rainbow	1962	30.00
❑ 10389	Don't Cry Donna/Gonna Take a Chance	1962	12.00
❑ 10423	The Folk Singer/Count on Me	1963	10.00
❑ 10454	Kiss and Run/What Makes the Blues	1963	10.00
❑ 10478	Everybody/Sorry I'm Late, Lisa	1963	15.00
❑ 10515	Come On/There Will Be Better Years	1964	10.00
❑ 10543	Carol/Be a Good Little Girl	1964	10.00
❑ 10555	Dance with Henry/Wild Water Skiing Weekend	1964	20.00
❑ 10579	Oh So Right/I Think I Love You	1964	12.00
❑ 10604	Party Girl/Oh How I Could Love You	1964	10.00
❑ 10623	Love Me, Love Me/Diane from Manchester Square	1965	12.00
❑ 10665	Fourteen Pair of Shoes/Combo Music	1965	10.00
❑ 10696	The Gunfighter/I'm a Rambler, I'm a Gambler	1965	20.00
❑ 10706	I Keep Remembering (Things I Forgot)/Wish You Didn't Have to Go	1965	10.00
❑ 10738	Doesn't Anybody Know My Name/Everytime a Bluebird Cries	1965	10.00
❑ 10762	Sweet Pea/Much More Love	1966	25.00

AWESOME

Number	Title (A Side/B Side)	Yr	NM
❑ 104	First Things First/(B-side unknown)	1984	6.00
❑ 108	Sittin' on a Mood/(B-side unknown)	1984	6.00

BGO

Number	Title (A Side/B Side)	Yr	NM
❑ 1003	She Do Run Run/(B-side unknown)	1982	10.00

JUDD

Number	Title (A Side/B Side)	Yr	NM
❑ 1018	Caveman/I Gotta Girl	1960	50.00
❑ 1022	Sheila/Pretty Girl	1960	150.00

MARK IV

Number	Title (A Side/B Side)	Yr	NM
❑ 001	Caveman/I Gotta Girl	1960	100.00

MCA CURB

Number	Title (A Side/B Side)	Yr	NM
❑ 52711	Some Such Foolishness/Barbara Lou	1985	4.00
❑ 52778	Radio Romance/Barbara Lou	1986	4.00

MERCURY

Number	Title (A Side/B Side)	Yr	NM
❑ 888206-7	Let's Be Fools Like That Again/Barbara Lou	1986	3.00
❑ 888497-7	Back When It Really Mattered/Radio Romance	1987	3.00

MGM SOUTH

Number	Title (A Side/B Side)	Yr	NM
❑ 7001	Mean Little Woman, Rosalie/Skyline	1972	5.00
❑ 7008	Sarah My Love/Chewing on Sugar Cane	1972	5.00
❑ 7013	Working Class Hero/Sun in My Eyes	1973	5.00
❑ 7025	Silver Eyes/Memphis Me	1973	6.00

MONUMENT

Number	Title (A Side/B Side)	Yr	NM
❑ 45-205	Early in the Morning/Bad News	1976	5.00
❑ 45-228	Your Love Will See Me Through/Working Class Hero	1977	5.00
❑ 8644	Glitter and Gleam/Bad News	1975	5.00
❑ 8662	Snowing Me Under/Rita and Her Band	1975	5.00
❑ 8684	Slow Dancing/Burn On Love Light	1976	5.00
❑ 8705	Everybody/Energy	1976	5.00

TRUMPET

Number	Title (A Side/B Side)	Yr	NM
❑ 1401	Caveman/I Gotta Girl	1960	200.00

WARNER BROS.

Number	Title (A Side/B Side)	Yr	NM
❑ 8660	Dreamin' Again/Love the Way You Love Me Up	1978	4.00
❑ 8720	Just Look at Me/Love the Way You Love Me Up	1978	5.00
❑ 8800	Massachusetts/Just Look at Me	1979	5.00
❑ 49085	You Better Move On/Just Look at Me	1979	4.00
❑ 49235	Charlie, I Love Your Wife/There Is No Sun on Sunset Boulevard	1980	4.00

Albums

ABC

Number	Title (A Side/B Side)	Yr	NM
❑ S-467 [R]	Something for Everybody	1968	50.00
—Issued in rechanneled stereo four years after its original release			
❑ 594 [M]	It's Now Winters Day	1967	20.00
❑ S-594 [S]	It's Now Winters Day	1967	25.00
❑ 610 [M]	Phantasy	1967	40.00
❑ S-610 [S]	Phantasy	1967	40.00
❑ S-683	Dizzy	1969	20.00
❑ S-700	12 in a Roe/A Collection of Tommy Roe's Greatest Hits	1969	20.00
❑ S-714	We Can Make Music	1970	15.00
❑ S-732	Beginnings	1971	15.00
❑ X-762	16 Greatest Hits	1972	15.00
❑ ST-90883 [S]	Sweet Pea	1966	40.00
—Capitol Record Club issue			
❑ T-90883 [M]	Sweet Pea	1966	40.00
—Capitol Record Club issue			

ABC-PARAMOUNT

Number	Title (A Side/B Side)	Yr	NM
❑ 432 [M]	Sheila	1962	40.00
❑ S-432 [S]	Sheila	1962	50.00
❑ 467 [M]	Something for Everybody	1964	30.00
❑ 575 [M]	Sweet Pea	1966	30.00
❑ S-575 [S]	Sweet Pea	1966	40.00

ACCORD

Number	Title (A Side/B Side)	Yr	NM
❑ SN-7155	Sheila	1981	10.00

MCA

Number	Title (A Side/B Side)	Yr	NM
❑ 1519	Collectibles — Greatest Hits	1982	8.00

MONUMENT

Number	Title (A Side/B Side)	Yr	NM
❑ 7604	Energy	1977	10.00
—Reissue of 34182			
❑ 7614	Full Bloom	1977	10.00
❑ PZ 34182	Energy	1976	12.00

PICKWICK

Number	Title (A Side/B Side)	Yr	NM
❑ SPC-3361	Dizzy	197?	10.00

ROECKER, SHERRILL

45s

SWAN

Number	Title (A Side/B Side)	Yr	NM
❑ 4173	Don't Say Nothin' (If You Can't Say Anything Nice)/It's All Over	1964	10.00

ROEMANS, THE

TOMMY ROE's backing group.

45s

ABC

Number	Title (A Side/B Side)	Yr	NM
❑ 10814	When the Sun Shines in the Mornin'/Love (That's All I Want)	1966	15.00
❑ 10871	All the Good Things/Pleasing You Pleases Me	1966	15.00

ABC-PARAMOUNT

Number	Title (A Side/B Side)	Yr	NM
❑ 10583	Give Me a Chance/Your Friend	1964	20.00
❑ 10671	Miserlou/Don't	1965	20.00
❑ 10723	Universal Soldier/Lost Little Girl	1965	20.00
❑ 10757	Listen to Me/You Make Me Feel Good	1965	20.00

ROGER AND THE TRAVELERS

45s

EMBER

Number	Title (A Side/B Side)	Yr	NM
❑ 1079	You're Daddy's Little Girl/Just Gonna Be That Way	1961	100.00

LOST-NITE

Number	Title (A Side/B Side)	Yr	NM
❑ 421	You're Daddy's Little Girl/Just Gonna Be That Way	197?	6.00

—Reissue

ROGERS, CHARLIE

45s

HIT

Number	Title (A Side/B Side)	Yr	NM
❑ 155	The Spirit of This Land/Ringo	1964	8.00

—B-side by John Preston

ROGERS, JIMMY

45s

CHESS

Number	Title (A Side/B Side)	Yr	NM
❑ 1506	I Used to Love a Woman/Back Door Friend	1952	200.00
—Earlier Jimmy Rogers 45s on Chess are not known to exist			
❑ 1519	The Last Time/Out on the Road	1952	200.00
❑ 1543	Left Me with a Broken Heart/Act Like You Love Me	1953	200.00
❑ 1574	Chicago Bound/Sloppy Drunk	1954	300.00
❑ 1616	You're the One/Blues All Day Long	1956	50.00
❑ 1643	Walking By Myself/If It Ain't Me	1956	50.00
❑ 1659	One Kiss/I Can't Believe	1957	50.00
❑ 1687	What Have I Done/Trace of You	1958	40.00
❑ 1721	Rock This House/My Last Meal	1959	30.00

R

ROGERS, JULIE

45s

MEGA

Number	Title (A Side/B Side)	Yr	NM
❑ 0075	Almost Close to You/Where Do You Go	1972	5.00

MERCURY

Number	Title (A Side/B Side)	Yr	NM
❑ 72332	The Wedding/Without Your Love	1964	8.00
—Red label			
❑ 72332	The Wedding/Without Your Love	1964	10.00
—Black label			
❑ 72380	Like a Child/The Love of a Boy	1965	8.00
❑ 72380 [PS]	Like a Child/The Love of a Boy	1965	12.00
❑ 72426	Hawaiian Wedding Song/Turn Around, Look at Me	1965	8.00
❑ 72535	Another Year, Another Love, Another Heartache/Don't Waste Your Young Years on Him	1966	8.00
❑ 72646	Climb Ev'ry Mountain/While the Angelus Was Ringing	1966	8.00

Albums

MERCURY

Number	Title (A Side/B Side)	Yr	NM
❑ MG-20981 [M]	Julie Rogers	1965	15.00
❑ SR-60981 [S]	Julie Rogers	1965	20.00

ROGERS, MORRIS, AND THE CONTINENTALS

45s

DELTA

Number	Title (A Side/B Side)	Yr	NM
❑ 601/2	The Leg/Wonders of Love	1963	200.00

ROGERS, TIMMIE

45s

CADET

Number	Title (A Side/B Side)	Yr	NM
❑ 5685	Super Soul Brothers/It Rolls Through Everything	1971	5.00

CAMEO

Number	Title (A Side/B Side)	Yr	NM
❑ 116	Back to School Again/I've Got a Dog Who Loves Me	1957	30.00
❑ 131	Take Me to Your Leader/Fla-Ga-La-Pa	1958	25.00

CAPITOL

Number	Title (A Side/B Side)	Yr	NM
❑ F2406	Saturday Night/If I Were You, Baby	1953	25.00
❑ F2509	Oh Yeah/Nothin' Wrong with Nothin'	1953	25.00

The Rolling Stones, "In Another Land," London 907, 1967, **$75.**

Number	Title (A Side/B Side)	Yr	NM
EPIC			
❑ 9813	If You Can't Smile and Say Yes (Please Don't Cry and Say No)/Chum Goy Turn Toy Fricasee (Soy Soy Soo)	1965	8.00
❑ 9899	Everybody Wants to Go to Heaven, But Nobody Wants to Die/Too Young to Go Steady	1966	8.00
MERCURY			
❑ 70451	If I Give My Heart to You/ Teedle-Dee Teedle-Dum	1954	40.00
PAR-TEE			
❑ 1303	Watergate/Snake Hips	1973	5.00
PARKWAY			
❑ 814	I Love Ya, I Love Ya, I Love Ya/ Tee-Hee	1960	15.00
PHILIPS			
❑ 40074	Oh Yeah/Fla-Ga-La-Pa	1962	10.00
SIGNATURE			
❑ 12037	First Proposal/Underwater Cha Cha Cha	1960	15.00

Albums

Number	Title	Yr	NM
PHILIPS			
❑ PHM 200088 [M]	If I Were President	1963	20.00
❑ PHS 600088 [S]	If I Were President	1963	25.00

ROGERS, WELDON

45s

Number	Title (A Side/B Side)	Yr	NM
IMPERIAL			
❑ 5451	So Long, Good Luck and Goodbye/Trying to Get to You	1957	200.00
—B-side is actually The Teen Kings' version rather than Rogers'; by mistake, the wrong recording left Norman Petty's studio for Imperial.			
JE-WEL			
❑ 103	Everybody Wants You/ This Song's Just for You	1956	1000.

ROKES, THE

45s

Number	Title (A Side/B Side)	Yr	NM
RCA VICTOR			
❑ 47-9199	Let's Live for Today/ Change of Papers	1967	12.00
❑ 47-9546	When the Wind Arises/The Works of Bartholomew	1968	12.00

Albums

Number	Title	Yr	NM
RCA VICTOR INTERNATIONAL			
❑ FPM-185 [M]	Che Mondo Strano	1967	80.00

ROLLERS, THE

45s

Number	Title (A Side/B Side)	Yr	NM
LIBERTY			
❑ 55303	Bonneville/Got My Eye on You	1961	20.00
❑ 55320	The Continental Walk/ I Want You So	1961	20.00
❑ 55357	The Bounce/Teenager's Waltz	1961	20.00

ROLLETTES, THE

45s

Number	Title (A Side/B Side)	Yr	NM
CLASS			
❑ 201	Sad Fool/Wham Bam	1957	40.00
—B-side by Googie Rene			
❑ 203	Kiss Me Benny/ More Than You Realize	1957	40.00
MELKER			
❑ 103	An Understanding/I'm Trying (To Make You Love Me)	1960	2000.

ROLLING STONES, THE

Also see BRIAN JONES; RONNIE WOOD; MICK TAYLOR; MICK JAGGER; KEITH RICHARDS.

12-Inch Singles

Number	Title (A Side/B Side)	Yr	NM
ROLLING STONES			
❑ PR 70 [DJ]	Hot Stuff/Crazy Mama	1976	80.00
—Black and blue "splash" vinyl (counterfeits have black spots in blue vinyl)			
❑ DSKO 119 [DJ]	Miss You (8:36) (same on both sides)	1978	50.00
❑ DSKO 174 [DJ]	Miss You (8:34)/Hot Stuff (5:21)	1979	40.00
❑ DMD 253 [DJ]	If I Was a Dancer (Dance Pt. II)/ Dance (Instrumental)	1981	30.00
❑ PR 367 [DJ]	Emotional Rescue (4:18) (5:38)	1980	40.00
❑ PR 397 [DJ]	Start Me Up (same on both sides)	1981	30.00
❑ PR 574 [DJ]	She Was Hot/Think I'm Going Mad	1983	40.00
❑ DMD 685 [DJ]	Undercover of the Night (6:22) (Album Version 4:31)	1983	15.00
—Yellow label promo			
❑ PR 692 [DJ]	Too Much Blood (12:33)/ (Dub 8:00) (Album 6:25)	1983	20.00
❑ CAS 1765 [DJ]	Mixed Emotions (Chris Kimsey's 12" Mix 6:12)/ (LP Version 4:00)	1989	40.00
❑ CAS 2275 [DJ]	Harlem Shuffle (same on both sides)	1986	15.00
❑ CAS 2340 [DJ]	One Hit (To the Body) (London Mix 7:00) (Edit) (LP Version)	1986	20.00
❑ CAS 4051 [DJ]	Sexdrive (Club Version 6:00)/ (Edited Club Version 4:32) (Single Edit 4:26)	1991	60.00
❑ DK 4609	Miss You (8:36)/ Far Away Eyes (4:24)	1978	10.00
—With "Atlantic/Atco Disco" sleeve			
❑ DK 4609	Miss You (8:36)/ Far Away Eyes (4:24)	1978	12.00
—With "The Rolling Stones Miss You" die-cut sleeve			
❑ DK 4616	Miss You (8:34)/Hot Stuff (5:21)	1979	30.00
❑ 44-05365	Harlem Shuffle (NY Mix 6:25)/ (London Mix 6:19)	1986	10.00
❑ 44-05388	One Hit (To the Body) (London Mix 7:00)//One Hit (To the Body) (Edit)/Fight	1986	8.00
❑ 44-73133	Rock and a Hard Place (Dance Mix 6:54) (Oh-Oh Hard Dub Mix 6:50)/(Michael Brauer Mix 6:57) (Bonus Beats 4:02)	1989	15.00
❑ 96902	Too Much Blood (12:33)/ (Dub 8:00) (Album 6:25)	1984	15.00
❑ 96978	Undercover of the Night (6:22)/ Feel On Baby (Instrumental 6:27)	1983	10.00
VIRGIN			
❑ SPRO-12746 [DJ]	Anybody Seen My Baby? (Armand van Helden Rolling Steelo Mix 4:08) (Soul Solution Vocal Dub 3:44) (Casanova New Vocal Mix 4:00)	1997	40.00
❑ SPRO-12788 [(2)DJ]	Saint of Me (Deep Dish Club Mix 7:35)/(Deep Dish Grunge Garage Dub 7:23) (Deep Dish Rolling Dub 7:16)// (Todd Terry Extended Remix 6:00) (Todd Terry Fade 3:35)/ (Todd Terry's Freeze Dub 7:45) (Todd Terry Dub #2 7:45)	1998	70.00
❑ Y-38446	Love Is Strong (Teddy Riley Extended Remix 5:02) (Teddy Riley Extended Rock Remix 4:47) (Teddy Riley Dub Remix 4:05)/(Joe the Butcher Club Mix 5:26) (Album Version 3:46) (Teddy Riley Instrumental 4:47)	1994	8.00
❑ Y-38468	You Got Me Rocking (Perfecto Mix 5:00) (Sexy Dub Mix 6:16)//(Trance Mix 4:58) (Album Version 3:34)/Jump on Top of Me	1995	8.00
❑ Y-38626	Saint of Me (Deep Dish Club Mix 7:35) (Deep Dish Grunge Dub 7:23)//(Todd Terry Extended Remix 6:00)/ Anyway You Look at It	1998	8.00

45s

Number	Title (A Side/B Side)	Yr	NM
ABKCO			
❑ 4701	I Don't Know Why/ Try a Little Harder	1975	5.00
—With A-side writing credits of "Wonder, Riser, Hunter, Hardaway"			
❑ 4701	I Don't Know Why/ Try a Little Harder	1975	10.00
—With A-side writing credits of "Jagger, Richards, Taylor"			
❑ 4701 [DJ]	I Don't Know Why (same on both sides)	1975	25.00
❑ 4702	Out of Time/Jiving Sister Fanny	1975	6.00
❑ 4702 [DJ]	Out of Time/Jiving Sister Fanny	1975	25.00
LONDON			
❑ 901	Paint It, Black/Stupid Girl	1966	15.00
❑ 901 [DJ]	Paint It, Black/Stupid Girl	1966	75.00
—Orange swirl label			
❑ 901 [PS]	Paint It, Black/Stupid Girl	1966	60.00
❑ 902	Mothers Little Helper/Lady Jane	1966	15.00
❑ 902 [DJ]	Mothers Little Helper/Lady Jane	1966	75.00
—Orange swirl label			
❑ 902 [PS]	Mothers Little Helper/Lady Jane	1966	60.00

Except when noted otherwise, VG = 25% of NM, and VG+ = 50% of NM. (Example: VG = $2.00, VG+ = $4.00 and NM = $8.00.)

Number	Title (A Side/B Side)	Yr	NM
❑ 903	Have You Seen Your Mother, Baby, Standing in the Shadow?/Who's Driving My Plane	1966	15.00
❑ 903 [DJ]	Have You Seen Your Mother, Baby, Standing in the Shadow?/Who's Driving My Plane	1966	75.00
—Orange swirl label			
❑ 903 [PS]	Have You Seen Your Mother, Baby, Standing in the Shadow?/Who's Driving My Plane	1966	60.00
❑ 904	Ruby Tuesday/Let's Spend the Night Together	1967	15.00
❑ 904 [DJ]	Ruby Tuesday/Let's Spend the Night Together	1967	75.00
—Orange swirl label			
❑ 904 [PS]	Let's Spend the Night Together/ Ruby Tuesday	1967	60.00
❑ 905	Dandelion/We Love You	1967	20.00
❑ 905 [DJ]	Dandelion/We Love You	1967	75.00
—With full-length version of "We Love You"; orange swirl label			
❑ 905 [DJ]	Dandelion/We Love You	1967	150.00
—With 3:10 edited version of "We Love You"; orange swirl label			
❑ 905 [PS]	We Love You/Dandelion	1967	600.00
❑ 906	She's a Rainbow/2000 Light Years from Home	1967	20.00
❑ 906 [DJ]	She's a Rainbow/2000 Light Years from Home	1967	75.00
—Orange swirl label			
❑ 906 [PS]	She's a Rainbow/2000 Light Years from Home	1967	50.00
❑ 907	In Another Land/The Lantern	1967	25.00
—A-side credited to Bill Wyman, though taken from "Their Satanic Majesties Request"			
❑ 907 [DJ]	In Another Land/The Lantern	1967	75.00
—A-side credited to Bill Wyman; orange swirl label			
❑ 907 [PS]	In Another Land/The Lantern	1967	75.00
❑ 908	Jumpin' Jack Flash/ Child of the Moon	1968	15.00
❑ 908 [DJ]	Jumpin' Jack Flash/ Child of the Moon	1968	75.00
—Orange swirl label			
❑ 908 [PS]	Jumpin' Jack Flash/ Child of the Moon	1968	40.00
❑ 909	Street Fighting Man/ No Expectations	1968	20.00
❑ 909 [DJ]	Street Fighting Man/ No Expectations	1968	75.00
—Orange swirl label			
❑ 909 [PS]	Street Fighting Man/ No Expectations	1968	10000.
—VG 4000; VG+ 8000			
❑ 910	Honky Tonk Women/You Can't Always Get What You Want	1969	15.00
❑ 910 [PS]	Honky Tonk Women/You Can't Always Get What You Want	1969	30.00
❑ 9641 [DJ]	I Wanna Be Your Man/Stoned	1964	1000.
—With similar label to stock copy, except in white, black and gray			
❑ 9641 [DJ]	I Wanna Be Your Man/Stoned	1964	1500.
—White label, black print, script "London" at top			
❑ 9641	I Wanna Be Your Man/Stoned	1964	9000.
—VG 3000; VG+ 6000			
❑ 9657	Not Fade Away/I Wanna Be Your Man	1964	8.00
—Blue swirl label			
❑ 9657	Not Fade Away/I Wanna Be Your Man	1964	40.00
—White, purple and blue label			
❑ 9657 [DJ]	Not Fade Away/I Wanna Be Your Man	1964	900.00
—With similar label to original stock copy, except in white, black and gray			
❑ 9657 [DJ]	Not Fade Away/I Wanna Be Your Man	1964	1000.
—White label, black print, script "London" at top			
❑ 9657 [PS]	Not Fade Away/I Wanna Be Your Man	1964	450.00
❑ 9682	Tell Me (You're Coming Back)/ I Just Want to Make Love to You	1964	10.00
—Blue swirl label			
❑ 9682	Tell Me (You're Coming Back)/ I Just Want to Make Love to You	1964	40.00
—White, purple and blue label			
❑ 9682 [DJ]	Tell Me (You're Coming Back)/ I Just Want to Make Love to You	1964	75.00
—Orange swirl label			
❑ 9682 [PS]	Tell Me (You're Coming Back)/ I Just Want to Make Love to You	1964	175.00
❑ 5N 9682	Tell Me (You're Coming Back)/ I Just Want to Make Love to You	1977	12.00
—Sunrise label; this version plays the LP version rather than the single edit, even though the label says "Time: 2:35"; number in trail-off wax is "5N-9682-A"			

The Rolling Stones, "She's a Rainbow," London 906, 1967, **$50.**

Number	Title (A Side/B Side)	Yr	NM
❑ 9687	It's All Over Now/Good Times Bad Times	1964	10.00
—Blue swirl label			
❑ 9687	It's All Over Now/ Good Times, Bad Times	1964	40.00
—White, purple and blue label			
❑ 9687 [DJ]	It's All Over Now/ Good Times, Bad Times	1964	75.00
—Orange swirl label			
❑ 9687 [PS]	It's All Over Now/ Good Times, Bad Times	1964	125.00
❑ 9708	Time Is On My Side/ Congratulations	1964	10.00
—Blue swirl label			
❑ 9708	Time Is On My Side/ Congratulations	1964	30.00
—White, purple and blue label			
❑ 9708 [DJ]	Time Is On My Side/ Congratulations	1964	75.00
—Orange swirl label			
❑ 9708 [PS]	Time Is On My Side/ Congratulations	1964	100.00
❑ 9725	Heart of Stone/What a Shame	1964	10.00
—Blue swirl label			
❑ 9725	Heart of Stone/What a Shame	1964	30.00
—White, purple and blue label			
❑ 9725 [DJ]	Heart of Stone/What a Shame	1964	75.00
—Orange swirl label			
❑ 9725 [PS]	Heart of Stone/What a Shame	1964	800.00
❑ 9741	The Last Time/Play with Fire	1965	10.00
—Blue swirl label, "London" in black letters			
❑ 9741	The Last Time/Play with Fire	1965	15.00
—Blue swirl label, "London" in white letters			
❑ 9741	The Last Time/Play with Fire	1965	25.00
—White, purple and blue label			
❑ 9741 [DJ]	The Last Time/Play with Fire	1965	75.00
—Orange swirl label			
❑ 9741 [PS]	The Last Time/Play with Fire	1965	150.00
❑ 9766	(I Can't Get No) Satisfaction/ The Under Assistant West Coast Promotion Man	1965	20.00

Number	Title (A Side/B Side)	Yr	NM
❑ 9766 [DJ]	(I Can't Get No) Satisfaction/ The Under Assistant West Coast Promotion Man	1965	75.00
—Orange swirl label			
❑ 9766 [PS]	(I Can't Get No) Satisfaction/ The Under Assistant West Coast Promotion Man	1965	500.00
❑ 5N-9766 [DJ]	(I Can't Get No) Satisfaction/ The Under Assistant West Coast Promotion Man	1975	60.00
—Promo reissue; orange swirl label			
❑ 9792	Get Off of My Cloud/I'm Free	1965	20.00
❑ 9792 [DJ]	Get Off of My Cloud/I'm Free	1965	75.00
—Orange swirl label			
❑ 9792 [PS]	Get Off of My Cloud/I'm Free	1965	60.00
❑ 9808	As Tears Go By/Gotta Get Away	1965	15.00
❑ 9808 [DJ]	As Tears Go By/Gotta Get Away	1965	75.00
—Orange swirl label			
❑ 9808 [PS]	As Tears Go By/Gotta Get Away	1965	60.00
❑ 9823	19th Nervous Breakdown/ Sad Day	1966	15.00
❑ 9823 [DJ]	19th Nervous Breakdown/ Sad Day	1966	75.00
—Orange swirl label			
❑ 9823 [PS]	19th Nervous Breakdown/ Sad Day	1966	60.00
ROLLING STONES			
❑ (no #)	Tongue Sleeve	1972	8.00
—Sleeve used on some copies of "Tumbling Dice" and "Hang Fire," and possibly some other Rolling Stones Records 45s			
❑ PR 228 [DJ]	Time Waits for No One (mono/stereo)	1974	75.00
❑ PR 228 [PS]	Time Waits for No One (mono/stereo)	1974	175.00
❑ PR 316 [DJ]	Before They Make Me Run (mono/stereo)	1978	25.00
❑ PR 316 [PS]	Before They Make Me Run (mono/stereo)	1978	50.00
❑ 38-05802	Harlem Shuffle/Had It with You	1986	3.00
❑ 38-05802 [DJ]	Harlem Shuffle (same on both sides)	1986	20.00
❑ 38-05802 [PS]	Harlem Shuffle/Had It with You	1986	3.00

Number	Title (A Side/B Side)	Yr	NM
❑ 38-05802 [PS]	Harlem Shuffle	1986	20.00
—"Demonstration Not for Sale" on sleeve, and no B-side listed			
❑ 38-05906	One Hit (To the Body)/Fight	1986	3.00
❑ 38-05906 [DJ]	One Hit (To the Body) (same on both sides)	1986	20.00
❑ 38-05906 [PS]	One Hit (To the Body)/Fight	1986	3.00
❑ 38-05906 [PS]	One Hit (To the Body)	1986	20.00
—"Demonstration Not for Sale" on sleeve, and no B-side listed			
❑ 19100	Brown Sugar/Bitch	1971	5.00
❑ 19100 [DJ]	Brown Sugar (mono/stereo)	1971	30.00
❑ 19101	Wild Horses/Sway	1971	5.00
❑ 19101 [DJ]	Wild Horses (mono/stereo, both full length)	1971	30.00
❑ 19101 [DJ]	Wild Horses (long version/ short version)	1971	50.00
❑ 19103	Tumbling Dice/ Sweet Black Angel	1972	5.00
❑ 19103 [DJ]	Tumbling Dice (mono/stereo)	1972	30.00
❑ 19104	Happy/All Down the Line	1972	5.00
❑ 19104 [DJ]	Happy/All Down the Line	1972	30.00
❑ 19105	Angie/Silver Train	1973	5.00
—With "Angie" listed as "Side One" and "Silver Train" listed as "Side Two", or with no reference at all to "Side One" and "Side Two"			
❑ 19105	Silver Train/Angie	1973	12.00
—With "Silver Train" listed as "Side One" and "Angie" listed as "Side Two"			
❑ 19105 [DJ]	Angie (mono/stereo)	1973	30.00
❑ 19109	Doo Doo Doo Doo Doo (Heartbreaker)/ Dancing with Mr. D.	1973	5.00
❑ 19109 [DJ]	Doo Doo Doo Doo Doo (Heartbreaker) (mono/stereo)	1973	30.00
❑ 19301	It's Only Rock 'N' Roll (But I Like It)/Through the Lonely Nights	1974	5.00
❑ 19301 [DJ]	It's Only Rock 'N' Roll (But I Like It) (Edit/Long Version)	1974	30.00
❑ 19302	Ain't Too Proud to Beg/ Dance Little Sister	1974	5.00
❑ 19302 [DJ]	Ain't Too Proud to Beg (mono/stereo)	1974	30.00
❑ 19304	Fool to Cry/Crazy Mama	1976	—
—Promotional 12-inch singles exist with this coupling, but do U.S. 45s? Please advise.			
❑ 19304	Fool to Cry/Hot Stuff	1976	4.00
❑ 19304 [DJ]	Fool to Cry (same on both sides)	1976	30.00
❑ 19304 [DJ]	Hot Stuff (same on both sides)	1976	30.00
❑ 19304 [DJ]	Fool to Cry (long/short versions)	1976	35.00
❑ 19304 [DJ]	Hot Stuff (long/short versions)	1976	35.00
❑ 19304 [DJ]	Fool to Cry/Hot Stuff	1976	200.00
❑ 19307	Miss You/Far Away Eyes	1978	4.00
❑ 19307 [DJ]	Miss You (same on both sides)	1978	30.00
❑ 19307 [DJ]	Far Away Eyes (same on both sides)	1978	250.00
❑ 19307 [PS]	Miss You/Far Away Eyes	1978	4.00
❑ 19309	Beast of Burden/When the Whip Comes Down	1978	4.00
❑ 19309 [DJ]	Beast of Burden (long/short versions)	1978	30.00
❑ 19309 [PS]	Beast of Burden/When the Whip Comes Down	1978	2000.
—Beware of counterfeits! Original copies have a 1/2-inch inner fold on the inside of the picture sleeve (counterfeits have a much smaller fold). Also, the originals are a light lavender, almost pink, color (counterfeits are a grape or purple color).. VG 1000 ; VG+ 1500			
❑ 19310	Shattered/Everything Is Turning to Gold	1978	4.00
❑ 19310 [DJ]	Shattered (same on both sides)	1978	20.00
❑ 19310 [PS]	Shattered/Everything Is Turning to Gold	1978	6.00
❑ 20001	Emotional Rescue/ Down in the Hole	1980	4.00
❑ 20001 [DJ]	Emotional Rescue (edit/LP versions)	1980	20.00
❑ 20001 [PS]	Emotional Rescue/ Down in the Hole	1980	4.00
❑ 21001	She's So Cold/Send It to Me	1980	4.00
❑ 21001 [DJ]	She's So Cold (edit/LP versions)	1980	20.00
❑ 21001 [PS]	She's So Cold/Send It to Me	1980	6.00
❑ 21003	Start Me Up/No Use in Crying	1981	4.00
❑ 21003 [DJ]	Start Me Up (same on both sides)	1981	20.00
❑ 21003 [PS]	Start Me Up/No Use in Crying	1981	4.00
❑ 21004	Waiting on a Friend/Little T & A	1981	4.00
❑ 21004 [DJ]	Waiting on a Friend (same on both sides)	1981	20.00
❑ 21004 [PS]	Waiting on a Friend/Little T & A	1981	4.00
❑ 21300	Hang Fire/Neighbours	1982	4.00
❑ 21300 [DJ]	Hang Fire (same on both sides)	1982	20.00
❑ 21301	Going to A-Go-Go/ Beast of Burden	1982	4.00
❑ 21301 [DJ]	Going to A-Go-Go/ Beast of Burden	1982	20.00
❑ 21301 [PS]	Going to A-Go-Go/ Beast of Burden	1982	4.00
❑ 38-69008	Mixed Emotions/ Fancy Man Blues	1989	3.00
❑ 38-69008 [DJ]	Mixed Emotions (same on both sides)	1989	45.00
❑ 38-73057	Rock and a Hard Place/ Cook Cook Blues	1989	3.00
❑ 38-73093	Almost Hear You Sigh/ Break the Spell	1989	3.00
❑ 38-73742	Highwire/2000 Light Years from Home	1991	5.00
❑ 38-73789	Sexdrive/Undercover of the Night	1991	8.00
❑ 99724	Too Tough/Miss You	1984	40.00
❑ 99724 [DJ]	Miss You (same on both sides)	1984	30.00
❑ 99788	She Was Hot/Think I'm Going Mad	1984	3.00
❑ 99788 [DJ]	She Was Hot (long/short versions)	1984	30.00
❑ 99788 [PS]	She Was Hot/Think I'm Going Mad	1984	3.00
❑ 99813	Undercover of the Night/ All the Way Down	1983	3.00
❑ 99813 [DJ]	Undercover of the Night (same on both sides)	1983	20.00
❑ 99813 [PS]	Undercover of the Night/ All the Way Down	1983	3.00
❑ 99978	Time Is On My Side (Live)/ Twenty Flight Rock	1982	5.00
❑ 99978 [DJ]	Time Is On My Side (Live) (same on both sides)	1982	20.00
❑ 99978 [PS]	Time Is On My Side (Live)/ Twenty Flight Rock	1982	5.00

VIRGIN

Number	Title (A Side/B Side)	Yr	NM
❑ NR-38446	Love Is Strong//The Storm/Love Is Strong (Teddy Riley Remix)	1994	5.00
❑ NR-38446 [PS]	Love Is Strong//The Storm/Love Is Strong (Teddy Riley Remix)	1994	5.00
❑ NR-38459	Out of Tears//Out of Tears (Bob Clearmountain Remix Edit)/ I'm Gonna Drive	1994	5.00
❑ NR-38459 [PS]	Out of Tears//Out of Tears (Bob Clearmountain Remix Edit)/ I'm Gonna Drive	1994	5.00
❑ NR-38626	Saint of Me/Anyway You Look At It	1998	2.00
❑ NR-38626 [PS]	Saint of Me/Anyway You Look At It	1998	2.00

7-Inch Extended Plays

LONDON

Number	Title (A Side/B Side)	Yr	NM
❑ SBG 23	Around and Around/2120 South Michigan Avenue/ Confessin' the Blues//Time Is On My Side/Grown Up Wrong/It's All Over Now	1964	200.00
—Jukebox issue; small hole, plays at 33 1/3 rpm			
❑ SBG 23 [PS]	12x5	1964	200.00
❑ SBG 34	Down the Road Apiece/Off the Hook/Oh Baby (We Got a Good Thing Goin')// Everybody Needs Somebody to Love/Heart of Stone/ Surprise, Surprise	1965	200.00
—Jukebox issue; small hole, plays at 33 1/3 rpm			
❑ SBG 34 [PS]	The Rolling Stones, Now!	1965	200.00
❑ SBG 37	The Spider and the Fly/One More Try/Hitch Hike//The Last Time/ Good Times/Mercy Mercy	1965	200.00
—Jukebox issue; small hole, plays at 33 1/3 rpm			
❑ SBG 37 [PS]	Out of Our Heads	1965	200.00
❑ SBG 43	Talkin' 'Bout You/Look What You've Done/Get Off of My Cloud//I'm Free/Gotta Get Away/As Tears Go By	1965	200.00
—Jukebox issue; small hole, plays at 33 1/3 rpm			
❑ SBG 43 [PS]	December's Children (and Everybody's)	1965	200.00
❑ SBG 54	She's a Rainbow/2,000 Light Years from Home//In Another Land/Citadel/2000 Man	1967	250.00
—Jukebox issue; small hole, plays at 33 1/3 rpm			
❑ SBG 54 [PS]	Their Satanic Majesties Request	1967	250.00

ROLLING STONES

Number	Title (A Side/B Side)	Yr	NM
❑ PR 287 [DJ]	If You Can't Rock Me/Get Off of My Cloud/Brown Sugar// Jumpin' Jack Flash/Hot Stuff	1977	30.00
—Large hole; promo-only sampler from "Love You Live"			
❑ PR 287 [PS]	Love You Live	1977	50.00
❑ COC 7-22900	Rip This Joint/Hip Shake/ Tumbling Dice//Rocks Off/ Sweet Virginia	1972	80.00
—Jukebox issue; small hole, plays at 33 1/3 rpm			
❑ COC 7-22900 [PS]	Exile on Main St.	1972	80.00
—Part of "Little LP" series (LLP #199)			
❑ CO7-59101	Star Star/Hide Your Love//Can You Hear the Music/100 Years Ago	1973	80.00
—Jukebox issue; small hole, plays at 33 1/3 rpm			
❑ CO7-59101 [PS]	Goats Head Soup	1973	80.00

Albums

ABKCO

Number	Title (A Side/B Side)	Yr	NM
❑ ANA 1 [P]	Metamorphosis	1975	12.00
❑ MPD-1 [DJ]	Songs of the Rolling Stones	1975	700.00
—"Band in field" cover			
❑ MPD-1 [DJ]	Songs of the Rolling Stones	1975	3000.
—"Rock and Roll Circus" cover; VG value 1000; VG+ value 2000			
❑ DVL2-0268 [(2)P]	The Rolling Stones' Greatest Hits	1977	20.00
—RCA Special Products mail-order offer			
❑ 1218-1 [(4)]	Singles Collection: The London Years	1989	50.00
❑ AB-4224	Necrophilia	1973	8000.
—Canceled; covers exist. Value is for complete tri-fold cover.			
❑ 18771-9001-1	Big Hits (High Tide and Green Grass)	2003	20.00
—180-gram vinyl reissue pressed in U.S. by RTI, though cover says "Made in E.U."; with loose outer bag; number on cover is "882 322-1"			
❑ 18771-9002-1	Their Satanic Majesties Request	2003	20.00
—180-gram vinyl reissue pressed in U.S. by RTI, though cover says "Made in E.U."; with loose outer bag; cover has number "882 329-1"			
❑ 18771-9004-1	Let It Bleed	2003	20.00
—180-gram vinyl reissue pressed in U.S. by RTI, though cover says "Made in E.U."; with loose outer bag; cover has number "882 332-1"			
❑ 18771-9005-1	Get Yer Ya-Ya's Out!	2003	20.00
—180-gram vinyl reissue pressed in U.S. by RTI, though cover says "Made in E.U."; with loose outer bag; cover has number "882 333-1"			
❑ 18771-9006-1	Metamorphosis	2003	20.00
—180-gram vinyl reissue pressed in U.S. by RTI, though cover says "Made in E.U."; with loose outer bag; cover has number "882 344-1"			
❑ 18771-9375-1	England's Newest Hit Makers — The Rolling Stones	2003	20.00
—180-gram vinyl reissue pressed in U.S. by RTI, though cover says "Made in E.U."; with loose outer bag; cover has number "882 316-1"			
❑ 18771-9430-1	Out of Our Heads UK	2003	20.00
—180-gram vinyl reissue pressed in U.S. by RTI, though cover says "Made in E.U."; with loose outer bag; cover has number "882 319-1"			
❑ 18771-9477-1	Aftermath UK	2003	20.00
—180-gram vinyl reissue pressed in U.S. by RTI, though cover says "Made in E.U."; with loose outer bag; cover has number "882 323-1"			
❑ 18771-9500-1	Between the Buttons UK	2003	20.00
—180-gram vinyl reissue pressed in U.S. by RTI, though cover says "Made in E.U."; with loose outer bag; cover has number "882 326-1"			
❑ 18771-9539-1	Beggars Banquet	2003	20.00
—180-gram vinyl reissue pressed in U.S. by RTI, though cover says "Made in E.U."; with loose outer bag; cover has number "882 330-1"			
❑ 18771-9667-1 [(2)]	Hot Rocks 1964-1971	2003	40.00
—180-gram vinyl reissue pressed in U.S. by RTI, though cover says "Made in E.U."; with loose outer bag; cover has number "882 334-1"			

LONDON

Number	Title (A Side/B Side)	Yr	NM
❑ NP 1 [M]	Big Hits (High Tide and Green Grass)	1966	40.00
—With five lines of type on the front cover, all in capital letters			
❑ NP 1 [M]	Big Hits (High Tide and Green Grass)	1966	8000.
—With two lines of type on the front cover, all in small letters			
❑ NPS 1 [R]	Big Hits (High Tide and Green Grass)	1966	10.00
❑ RSD-1 [DJ]	The Rolling Stones — The Promotional Album	1969	3000.
—Not to be confused with imports of this rare promo; VG value 1000; VG+ value 2000			
❑ NP 2 [M]	Their Satanic Majesties Request	1967	250.00
❑ NPS 2 [S]	Their Satanic Majesties Request	1967	40.00
—With 3-D cover			
❑ NPS 2 [S]	Their Satanic Majesties Request	197?	8.00
—Without 3-D cover			
❑ NPS 3 [P]	Through the Past, Darkly (Big Hits Vol. 2)	1969	10.00
—With hexagonal cover			
❑ NPS 3 [P]	Through the Past, Darkly (Big Hits Vol. 2)	197?	20.00
—Reissue with regular square cover			
❑ NPS 3 [PD]	Through the Past, Darkly (Big Hits Vol. 2)	1969	6000.
—Prototype picture discs that used the cover art from "Big Hits (High Tide and Green Grass)" either on one or both sides; VG value 3000; VG+ value 4500			
❑ NPS 4 [S]	Let It Bleed	1969	10.00
—Without poster			
❑ NPS 4 [S]	Let It Bleed	1969	15.00
—With poster			
❑ NPS-4	Let It Bleed	1970	10000.
—One-of-a-kind red/yellow/blue/green vinyl (all on the same record!); VG value 5000; VG+ value 7500			
❑ NPS 5 [S]	Get Yer Ya-Ya's Out!	1970	10.00
❑ PS 375 [R]	England's Newest Hit Makers — The Rolling Stones	1964	300.00
—Dark blue label; lower left-hand corner of cover advertises a bonus photo			
❑ PS 375 [R]	England's Newest Hit Makers — The Rolling Stones	1965	25.00
—Dark blue label with "London" unboxed at top			
❑ PS 375 [R]	England's Newest Hit Makers — The Rolling Stones	1966	10.00
—Dark blue label with "London" boxed at top			
❑ PS 402 [R]	12 x 5	1964	25.00
—Dark blue label with "London" unboxed at top			
❑ PS 402 [R]	12 x 5	1965	10.00
—Dark blue label with "London" boxed at top			

Except when noted otherwise, VG = 25% of NM, and VG+ = 50% of NM. (Example: VG = $2.00, VG+ = $4.00 and NM = $8.00.)

Number — Title (A Side/B Side) — Yr — NM

❑ PS 420 [R] The Rolling Stones, Now! 1965 25.00
—Dark blue label with "London" unboxed at top. Add 20% for complete liner notes (or sticker) on back cover (both columns of type about equal in length).
❑ PS 420 [R] The Rolling Stones, Now! 1966 10.00
—Dark blue label with "London" boxed at top. Add 20% for censored liner notes (or sticker) on back cover (second column an inch shorter than the first column; "offensive" notes were quietly restored in the 1970s).
❑ PS 429 [R] Out of Our Heads 1965 10.00
—Dark blue label with "London" boxed at top
❑ PS 429 [R] Out of Our Heads 1965 25.00
—Dark blue label with "London" unboxed at top
❑ PS 429 [R] Out of Our Heads 1965 100.00
—Dark blue label with "London/ffrr" in a box at top and "Made in England by the Decca Record Co. Ltd." at top edge
❑ PS 451 [P] December's Children (and Everybody's) 1965 25.00
—Dark blue label with "London" unboxed at top
❑ PS 451 [P] December's Children (and Everybody's) 1966 10.00
—Dark blue label with "London" boxed at top. "Look What You've Done" is in true stereo; all other tracks are rechanneled.
❑ PS 476 [S] Aftermath 1966 10.00
❑ PS 493 [P] Got Live If You Want It! 1966 10.00
—"Fortune Teller" is rechanneled (it's actually an early studio recording with overdubbed crowd noise)
❑ PS 499 [S] Between the Buttons 1967 10.00
❑ PS 509 Back Behind and In Front 1967 5000.
—Prototype cover slick for an unreleased LP; the same number was used for "Flowers"
❑ PS 509 [M] Flowers 197? 8.00
—Some later "stereo" copies of this LP are actually entirely in mono
❑ PS 509 [P] Flowers 1967 10.00
—"Have You Seen Your Mother, Baby, Standing in the Shadow?" and "Mother's Little Helper" are rechanneled; all others are true stereo
❑ PS 539 Beggars Banquet 1968 10000.
—Original "toilet graffiti" cover slick (not on a cover)
❑ PS 539 [S] Beggars Banquet 1968 10.00
—With "Rev. Wilkins: credited as composer of "Prodigal Son"
❑ PS 539 [S] Beggars Banquet 1968 25.00
—With all songs credited to "Jagger-Richard"
❑ 2PS 606/7 [(2)P] Hot Rocks 1964-1971 1971 20.00
—With regular versions of all tracks. All of Side 1 and "Mothers Little Helper" and "19th Nervous Breakdown" on Side 2 are rechanneled. All of Side 3 and 4 are stereo.
❑ 2PS 606/7 [(2)P] Hot Rocks 1964-1971 1971 1000.
—With alternate versions of "Brown Sugar" and "Wild Horses" unavailable elsewhere. The date "11-5-71" or "11-18-71" is in the Side 4 trail-off area.
❑ 2PS 626/7 [(2)P] More Hot Rocks (Big Hits and Fazed Cookies) 1972 20.00
—All of Sides 1 and 4 are rechanneled; Side 2 and 3, except "Have You Seen Your Mother, Baby, Standing in the Shadow?" are in true stereo
❑ LL 3375 England's Newest Hit Makers — The Rolling Stones Bonus Photo 1964 200.00
❑ LL 3375 [DJ] England's Newest Hit Makers — The Rolling Stones 1964 3000.
—White label promo
❑ LL 3375 [M] England's Newest Hit Makers — The Rolling Stones 1964 300.00
—Maroon label with "Full Frequency Range Recording" inside horizontal lines that go through the center hole; lower left-hand corner of cover advertises a bonus photo
❑ LL 3375 [M] England's Newest Hit Makers — The Rolling Stones 1965 60.00
—Maroon label with "London" unboxed at top
❑ LL 3375 [M] England's Newest Hit Makers — The Rolling Stones 1966 40.00
—Red or maroon label with "London" boxed at top
❑ LL 3402 [M] 12 x 5 1964 60.00
—Maroon label with "London" unboxed at top
❑ LL 3402 [M] 12 x 5 1964 200.00
—Maroon label with "London/ffrr" in a box at top
❑ LL 3402 [M] 12 x 5 1964 10000.
—Maroon label with "London" unboxed at top; possibly unique blue vinyl pressing; VG value 5000; VG+ value 7500
❑ LL 3402 [M] 12 x 5 1965 40.00
—Red or maroon label with "London" boxed at top
❑ LL 3420 [M] The Rolling Stones, Now! 1965 60.00
—Maroon label with "London" unboxed at top and no lines on label. Add 20% for complete liner notes (or sticker) on back cover (both columns of type about equal in length).
❑ LL 3420 [M] The Rolling Stones, Now! 1965 200.00
—Maroon label with "London/ffrr" in a box at top. Add 20% for complete liner notes (or sticker) on back cover (both columns of type about equal in length).
❑ LL 3420 [M] The Rolling Stones, Now! 1965 400.00
—Maroon label with "London" unboxed, but with "ffrr" ear above "London" and "Full Frequency Range Recording" inside horizontal lines that go through the center hole
❑ LL 3420 [M] The Rolling Stones, Now! 1965 400.00
—Maroon label with "London" unboxed, with horizontal lines that go through the center hole, but with NO "ffrr" ear at the top and NO "Full Frequency Range Recording" between the horizonal lines
❑ LL 3420 [M] The Rolling Stones, Now! 1966 40.00
—Red or maroon label with "London" boxed at top and censored liner notes (second column an inch shorter than the first column)
❑ LL 3429 [M] Out of Our Heads 1965 40.00
—Maroon label with "London" unboxed at top
❑ LL 3429 [M] Out of Our Heads 1965 200.00
—Maroon label with "London/ffrr" in a box at top
❑ LL 3429 [M] Out of Our Heads 1966 25.00
—Red or maroon label with "London" boxed at top
❑ LL 3451 [M] December's Children (and Everybody's) 1965 40.00
—Maroon label with "London" unboxed at top
❑ LL 3451 [M] December's Children (and Everybody's) 1966 25.00
—Maroon label with "London" boxed at top
❑ LL 3476 [M] Aftermath 1966 40.00
❑ LL 3493 [M] Got Live If You Want It! 1966 40.00
❑ LL 3499 [M] Between the Buttons 1967 40.00
❑ LL 3509 [M] Flowers 1967 50.00

LONDON/ABKCO

❑ 62671 [(2)P] Hot Rocks 1964-1971 1986 15.00
—"Digitally Remastered from Original Master Recording" on cover; red label; same stereo content as original
❑ 62671 [(2)P] More Hot Rocks (Big Hits and Fazed Cookies) 1986 15.00
—"Digitally Remastered from Original Master Recording" on cover; red label
❑ 73751 [M] England's Newest Hit Makers — The Rolling Stones 1986 8.00
—"Digitally Remastered from Original Master Recording" on cover; red label
❑ 74021 [M] 12 x 5 1986 8.00
—"Digitally Remastered from Original Master Recording" on cover; red label
❑ 74201 [P] The Rolling Stones, Now! 1986 8.00
—"Digitally Remastered from Original Master Recording" on cover; red label; four tracks are in true stereo
❑ 74291 [P] Out of Our Heads 1986 8.00
—"Digitally Remastered from Original Master Recording" on cover; red label
❑ 74511 [M] December's Children (and Everybody's) 1986 8.00
—"Digitally Remastered from Original Master Recording" on cover; red label
❑ 74761 [S] Aftermath 1986 8.00
—"Digitally Remastered from Original Master Recording" on cover; red label
❑ 74931 [S] Got Live If You Want It! 1986 8.00
—"Digitally Remastered from Original Master Recording" on cover; red label
❑ 74991 [S] Between the Buttons 1986 8.00
—"Digitally Remastered from Original Master Recording" on cover; red label
❑ 75091 [S] Flowers 1986 8.00
—"Digitally Remastered from Original Master Recording" on cover; red label
❑ 75391 [S] Beggars Banquet 1986 12.00
—"Digitally Remastered from Original Master Recording" on cover; red label; original banned "toilet cover" released for the first time on this reissue
❑ 80011 [M] Big Hits (High Tide and Green Grass) 1986 8.00
—"Digitally Remastered from Original Master Recording" on cover; red label
❑ 80021 [S] Their Satanic Majesties Request 1986 8.00
—"Digitally Remastered from Original Master Recording" on cover; red label
❑ 80031 [S] Through the Past, Darkly (Big Hits Vol. 2) 1986 8.00
—"Digitally Remastered from Original Master Recording" on cover; red label
❑ 80041 Let It Bleed 1986 8.00
—"Digitally Remastered from Original Master Recording" on cover; red label
❑ 80051 Get Yer Ya-Ya's Out! 1986 8.00
—"Digitally Remastered from Original Master Recording" on cover; red label

MOBILE FIDELITY

❑ RC-1 [(11)] The Rolling Stones 1984 500.00
—London LPs pressed on audiophile vinyl in box
❑ 1-060 Sticky Fingers 1980 75.00
—Audiophile vinyl
❑ 1-087 Some Girls 1982 75.00
—Audiophile vinyl

RADIO PULSEBEAT NEWS

❑ 4 It's Here Luv!! 1965 180.00
—Ed Rudy interview album; this has been counterfeited, but originals can be identified thus: Charlie Watts' jacket should be completely black with no white marks; the label is very clear; the vinyl is all black

ROLLING STONES

❑ PR 164 [DJ] Interview with Mick Jagger by Tom Donahue 1971 200.00
—Yellow label
❑ COC 2-2900 [(2)] Exile on Main St. 1972 15.00
—Original covers have Unipak design — cover has to be opened to remove the records. Add 33% for sheet of postcards.
❑ COC 2-2900 [(2)] Exile on Main St. 1973 12.00
—Reissue covers have two pockets, one for each record
❑ COC 2-9001 [(2)] Love You Live 1977 12.00
❑ COC 16015 Emotional Rescue 1980 10.00
—Without poster
❑ COC 16015 Emotional Rescue 1980 15.00
—Originally released with a large poster wrapped around the outside of the record jacket
❑ COC 16028 Sucking in the Seventies 1981 10.00
❑ COC 16052 Tattoo You 1981 10.00
❑ COC 39100 Jamming with Edward 1972 15.00
—Not an official Stones album, this includes Jagger, Watts and Wyman with Ry Cooder and Nicky Hopkins
❑ COC 39100 [DJ] Jamming with Edward 1972 175.00
—White label stereo promo
❑ COC 39100 [M] Jamming with Edward 1972 250.00
—White label mono promo
❑ COC 39105 Sticky Fingers 1977 8.00
—Reissue on Atlantic with photo of zipper only
❑ COC 39105 Sticky Fingers 1977 10.00
—Reissue on Atlantic with working zipper
❑ COC 39106 Goats Head Soup 1977 8.00
—Reissue on Atlantic
❑ COC 39107 Made in the Shade 1977 8.00
—Reissue on Atlantic
❑ COC 39108 Some Girls 1978 10.00
—With "cover under reconstruction." Nine different color schemes exist for the front cover.
❑ COC 39108 Some Girls 1978 15.00
—With all women's faces visible. Nine different color schemes exist for the front cover.
❑ COC 39113 Still Life (American Concert 1981) 1982 10.00
❑ COC 39114 [PD] Still Life (American Concert 1981) 1982 40.00
❑ OC 40250 Dirty Work 1986 8.00
—Originals came with red shrink wrap; add 50% if it is still with the package
❑ FC 40488 Sticky Fingers 1986 8.00
—Reissue on CBS with photo of zipper only
❑ CG2 40489 [(2)] Exile on Main St. 1986 10.00
—Reissue on CBS
❑ FC 40492 Goats Head Soup 1986 8.00
—Reissue on CBS
❑ FC 40493 It's Only Rock 'n' Roll 1986 8.00
—Reissue on CBS
❑ FC 40494 Made in the Shade 1986 8.00
—Reissue on CBS
❑ FC 40495 Black and Blue 1986 8.00
—Reissue on CBS
❑ CG2 40496 [(2)] Love You Live 1986 10.00
—Reissue on CBS
❑ FC 40499 Some Girls 1986 8.00
—Reissue on CBS
❑ FC 40500 Emotional Rescue 1986 8.00
—Reissue on CBS
❑ FC 40501 Sucking in the Seventies 1986 8.00
—Reissue on CBS
❑ FC 40502 Tattoo You 1986 8.00
—Reissue on CBS
❑ FC 40503 Still Life (American Concert 1981) 1986 8.00
—Reissue on CBS
❑ FC 40504 Undercover 1986 8.00
—Reissue on CBS has no stickers on cover
❑ FC 40505 Rewind (1971-1984) 1986 8.00
—Reissue on CBS
❑ OC 45333 Steel Wheels 1989 10.00
❑ C 47456 Flashpoint 1991 20.00
❑ COC 59100 Sticky Fingers 1971 12.00
—With working zipper
❑ COC 59100 [DJ] Sticky Fingers 1971 300.00
—White label stereo promo
❑ COC 59100 [M] Sticky Fingers 1971 500.00
—White label mono promo
❑ COC 59101 Goats Head Soup 1973 10.00
—Without bonus photo
❑ COC 59101 Goats Head Soup 1973 15.00
—With bonus photo
❑ COC 79101 It's Only Rock 'n' Roll 1974 10.00
❑ COC 79102 Made in the Shade 1975 10.00
❑ COC 79104 Black and Blue 1976 10.00
❑ 90120 Undercover 1983 8.00
—With stickers peeled off
❑ 90120 Undercover 1983 12.00
—With stickers intact
❑ 90176 Rewind (1971-1984) 1984 25.00

VIRGIN

❑ V 2750 (8 39782 1) [(2)] Voodoo Lounge 1994 25.00
—U.S. versions pressed in U.K., but have UPC code paste-over and blue sticker "Marketed by Caroline"
❑ V 2801 (8 41040 1) [(2)] Stripped 1995 15.00
—U.S. versions pressed in U.K., but have UPC code paste-over with "Marketed and Distributed by Caroline Records"
❑ V 3012 [(2)] A Bigger Bang 2005 15.00
—Alternate number is "00946 3300671 3"; pressed in the EU for U.S. distribution

R

Number | Title (A Side/B Side) | Yr | NM

❑ 8 44712 1 [(2)] Bridges to Babylon 1997 80.00
—U.S. versions pressed in U.K., but have "Virgin Records America Inc." on back cover
❑ 8 46740 1 [(2)] No Security 1998 15.00
—U.S. versions pressed in U.K., but have "Virgin Records America Inc." on back cover
❑ 47863 Sticky Fingers 1999 25.00
—Limited-edition reissue with 180-gram vinyl and original working zipper cover
❑ 47864 [(2)] Exile on Main St. 1999 50.00
—Limited-edition reissue with 180-gram vinyl and all original inserts
❑ 47867 Some Girls 1999 25.00
—Limited-edition reissue with 180-gram vinyl and original inserts (except it has the "cover under reconstruction" inner sleeve)

ROLLINS, SONNY

45s

BLUE NOTE
❑ 1669 Decision (Part 1)/ Decision (Part 2) 1957 12.00
❑ 1670 Plain Jane (Part 1)/ Plain Jane (Part 2) 1957 12.00
❑ 1687 You Stepped Out of a Dream/ Why Don't Ewe 1957 12.00
❑ 1698 Sonny Moon for Two (Part 1)/ Sonny Moonfor Two (Part 2) 1958 12.00

IMPULSE!
❑ 247 Alfie's Theme (Part 1)/ Alfie's Theme (Part 2) 1966 8.00

MILESTONE
❑ 305 Isn't She Lovely/Arroz Con Pollo 1977 5.00
❑ 307 Harlem Boys/My Ideal 197? 5.00

PRESTIGE
❑ 108 St. Thomas (Part 1)/ St. Thomas (Part 2) 196? 10.00
❑ 128 They Can't Take That Away from Me/Ee-Ah 196? 10.00
❑ 173 Mack the Knife/The Stopper 196? 10.00
❑ 284 Almost Like Being in Love/In a Sentimental Mood 196? 10.00
❑ 769 Mambo Bounce/ This Love of Mine 195? 15.00
❑ 780 With a Song in My Heart/ Shadrack 195? 15.00
❑ 874 In a Sentimental Mood/Stopper 195? 12.00
❑ 905 Almost Like Being in Love/ No Moe 195? 12.00

RCA VICTOR
❑ 47-8111 If Ever I Would Leave You/ Brown Skin Girl 1962 8.00

Albums

ABC IMPULSE!
❑ AS-91 [S] Sonny Rollins On Impulse! 1968 25.00
—Black label with red ring
❑ AS-9121 [S] East Broadway Run Down 1968 15.00
—Black label with red ring
❑ AS-9236 [(2)] Reevaluation: The Impulse Years 1973 20.00
❑ IA-9349 There Will Never Be Another You 1978 15.00

ANALOGUE PRODUCTIONS
❑ AP 008 Way Out West 199? 25.00
—180-gram audiophile vinyl

BLUE NOTE
❑ BN-LA401-H2 [(2)]Sonny Rollins 1975 30.00
❑ BN-LA475-H2 [(2)]More from the Vanguard 1975 15.00
❑ BLP-1542 [M] Sonny Rollins 1957 1000.
—"Deep groove" version; Lexington Ave. address on label
❑ BLP-1542 [M] Sonny Rollins 1958 500.00
—"Deep groove" version, W. 63rd St. address on label
❑ BLP-1542 [M] Sonny Rollins 1963 80.00
—With "New York, USA" address on label
❑ BLP-1558 [M] Sonny Rollins, Vol. 2 1957 400.00
—Regular version, W. 63rd St. address on label
❑ BLP-1558 [M] Sonny Rollins, Vol. 2 1957 1000.
—"Deep groove" version; W. 63rd St. address on label
❑ BLP-1558 [M] Sonny Rollins, Vol. 2 1963 80.00
—With "New York, USA" address on label
❑ BLP-1581 [M] A Night at the Village Vanguard 1958 250.00
—Regular version, W. 63rd St. address on label
❑ BLP-1581 [M] A Night at the Village Vanguard 1958 400.00
—"Deep groove" version; W. 63rd St. address on label
❑ BLP-1581 [M] A Night at the Village Vanguard 1963 50.00
—With "New York, USA" address on label
❑ BLP-4001 [M] Newk's Time 1958 150.00
—Regular version, W. 63rd St. address on label
❑ BLP-4001 [M] Newk's Time 1958 300.00
—"Deep groove" version; W. 63rd St. address on label
❑ BLP-4001 [M] Newk's Time 1963 60.00
—With "New York, USA" address on label
❑ BST-4001 [S] Newk's Time 1959 120.00
—Regular version, W. 63rd St. address on label
❑ BST-4001 [S] Newk's Time 1959 250.00
—"Deep groove" version; W. 63rd St. address on label
❑ BST-4001 [S] Newk's Time 1963 40.00
—With "New York, USA" address on label

Number | Title (A Side/B Side) | Yr | NM

❑ BST-81542 [M] Sonny Rollins 1985 12.00
—"The Finest in Jazz Since 1939" reissue
❑ BST-81542 [R] Sonny Rollins 1967 15.00
—With "A Division of Liberty Records" on label
❑ BST-81558 [M] Sonny Rollins, Vol. 2 1985 12.00
—"The Finest in Jazz Since 1939" reissue
❑ BST-81558 [R] Sonny Rollins, Vol. 2 1967 15.00
—With "A Division of Liberty Records" on label
❑ BST-81581 [M] A Night at the Village Vanguard, Vol. 1 1987 12.00
—"The Finest in Jazz Since 1939" reissue
❑ BST-81581 [R] A Night at the Village Vanguard 1967 15.00
—With "A Division of Liberty Records" on label
❑ BST-84001 [S] Newk's Time 1967 20.00
—With "A Division of Liberty Records" on label
❑ BST-84001 [S] Newk's Time 198? 12.00
—"The Finest in Jazz Since 1939" reissue
❑ B1-93203 The Best of Sonny Rollins 1989 15.00

BLUEBIRD
❑ 5634-1-RB [(2)] The Quartets Featuring Jim Hall 1986 20.00

CONTEMPORARY
❑ C-3530 [M] Way Out West 1957 250.00
❑ M-3564 [M] Sonny Rollins and the Contemporary Leaders 1959 250.00
❑ S-7530 [S] Way Out West 1959 150.00
❑ S-7564 [S] Sonny Rollins and the Contemporary Leaders 1959 200.00
❑ C-7651 Alternate Takes 1986 15.00

DCC COMPACT CLASSICS
❑ LPZ-2008 Saxophone Colossus 1995 100.00
—180-gram audiophile vinyl
❑ LPZ-2022 Tenor Madness 1996 150.00
—180-gram audiophile vinyl

EVEREST ARCHIVE OF FOLK & JAZZ
❑ FS-220 [R] Sonny Rollins with Guest Artist Thad Jones 1968 12.00

FANTASY
❑ OJC-007 Work Time 1982 12.00
❑ OJC-011 Sonny Rollins with the Modern Jazz Quartet 1982 12.00
❑ OJC=029 The Sound of Sonny 198? 12.00
❑ OJC-058 Moving Out 198? 12.00
❑ OJC-067 Freedom Suite 198? 12.00
❑ OJC-124 Tenor Madness 198? 12.00
❑ OJC-214 Sonny Rollins Plays for Bird 198? 12.00
❑ OJC-243 Sonny Rollins Plus 4 1987 12.00
❑ OJC-291 Saxophone Colossus 198? 12.00
❑ OJC-312 The Next Album 1988 12.00
❑ OJC-314 Horn Culture 198? 12.00
❑ OJC-337 Way Out West 198? 12.00
❑ OJC-340 Sonny Rollins and the Contemporary Leaders 198? 15.00
❑ OJC-348 Sonny Boy 198? 12.00
❑ OJC-468 The Cutting Edge: Montreux 1974 198? 12.00
❑ OJC-620 Nucleus 1991 15.00

GATEWAY
❑ GS-7204 The Sound of Sonny 1977 10.00

GRP IMPULSE!
❑ IMP-161 [M] East Broadway Run Down 199? 20.00
—180-gram audiophile reissue
❑ IMP-223 Sonny Rollins On Impulse! 1997 20.00
—180-gram reissue

IMPULSE!
❑ A-91 [M] Sonny Rollins On Impulse! 1966 60.00
❑ AS-91 [S] Sonny Rollins On Impulse! 1966 80.00
❑ A-9121 [M] East Broadway Run Down 1967 80.00
❑ AS-9121 [S] East Broadway Run Down 1967 50.00

JAZZLAND
❑ JLP-72 [M] Sonny's Time 1962 80.00
❑ JLP-86 [M] Shadow Waltz 1962 80.00
❑ JLP-972 [S] Sonny's Time 1962 70.00
❑ JLP-986 [S] Shadow Waltz 1962 70.00

MCA
❑ 4127 [(2)] Great Moments with Sonny Rollins 198? 12.00
❑ 29054 Sonny Rollins On Impulse! 1980 10.00
❑ 29055 There Will Never Be Another You 1980 10.00

MCA IMPULSE!
❑ MCA-5655 Sonny Rollins On Impulse! 1986 10.00

METROJAZZ
❑ E-1002 [M] Sonny Rollins and the Big Brass 1958 120.00
❑ SE-1002 [S] Sonny Rollins and the Big Brass 1958 80.00
❑ E-1011 [M] Sonny Rollins at Music Inn 1958 120.00
❑ SE-1011 [S] Sonny Rollins at Music Inn 1958 100.00

MILESTONE
❑ M-9042 The Next Album 197? 12.00
❑ M-9051 Horn Culture 1974 12.00
❑ M-9059 The Cutting Edge: Montreux 1974 1975 12.00
❑ M-9064 Nucleus 1975 12.00
❑ M-9074 The Way I Feel 1976 12.00
❑ M-9080 Easy Living 1977 12.00

Number | Title (A Side/B Side) | Yr | NM

❑ M-9090 Don't Ask 1979 12.00
❑ M-9098 Love at First Sight 1980 12.00
❑ M-9104 No Problem 1981 10.00
❑ M-9108 Reel Life 1982 10.00
❑ M-9122 Sunny Days, Starry Nights 1984 10.00
❑ M-9150 G-Man 1987 12.00
❑ M-9155 Dancing in the Dark 1988 12.00
❑ M-9179 Falling in Love with Jazz 1990 15.00
❑ M-47007 [(2)] Freedom Suite Plus 1973 20.00
❑ M-55005 [(2)] Don't Stop the Carnival 1978 20.00

PRESTIGE
❑ PRLP-137 [10] Sonny Rollins Quartet 1952 800.00
❑ PRLP-186 [10] Sonny Rollins Quartet 1954 700.00
❑ PRLP-190 [10] Sonny Rollins 1954 600.00
❑ PRLP-7020 [M] Work Time 1956 500.00
—Yellow label with W. 50th St. address
❑ PRLP-7029 [M] Sonny Rollins with the Modern Jazz Quartet 1956 250.00
—Brown and yellow cover; catalog number at upper left is "Prestige Hi-Fil LP 7029"; record has yellow label with W. 50th St. address
❑ PRLP-7029 [M] Sonny Rollins with the Modern Jazz Quartet 1956 300.00
—Orange cover; second edition has the correct catalog number, "Prestige LP 7029," in upper left inside an orange box
❑ PRLP-7029 [M] Sonny Rollins with the Modern Jazz Quartet 1956 400.00
—Orange cover; original edition has the wrong catalog number at upper left (PR 7020), but the record has the correct number
❑ PRLP-7038 [M] Sonny Rollins Plus 4 1956 300.00
—Yellow label with W. 50th St. address
❑ PRLP-7047 [M] Tenor Madness 1956 300.00
—Yellow label with W. 50th St. address
❑ PRLP-7047 [M] Tenor Madness 1958 200.00
—Yellow label with Bergenfield, N.J. address
❑ PRLP-7058 [M] Moving Out 1956 300.00
—Yellow label with W. 50th St. address
❑ PRLP-7058 [M] Moving Out 1958 80.00
—Yellow label with Bergenfield, N.J. address
❑ PRLP-7079 [M] Saxophone Colossus 1957 400.00
—Yellow label with W. 50th St. address
❑ PRLP-7095 [M] Rollins Plays for Bird 1957 200.00
—Yellow label with W. 50th St. address
❑ PRLP-7126 [M] Tour de Force 1957 200.00
—Yellow label with W. 50th St. address
❑ PRLP-7207 [M] Sonny Boy 1961 100.00
❑ PRLP-7246 [M] Work Time 1962 80.00
❑ PRST-7246 [R] Work Time 1962 40.00
❑ PRLP-7269 [M] Sonny and the Stars 1963 80.00
❑ PRST-7269 [R] Sonny and the Stars 1963 40.00
❑ PRLP-7326 [M] Saxophone Colossus 1964 60.00
❑ PRST-7326 [R] Saxophone Colossus 1964 30.00
❑ PRLP-7433 [M] Sonny Rollins Plays Jazz Classics 1967 100.00
❑ PRST-7433 [R] Sonny Rollins Plays Jazz Classics 1967 30.00
❑ PRST-7553 [R] Sonny Rollins Plays for Bird 1968 30.00
❑ PRST-7657 [R] Tenor Madness 1969 25.00
❑ PRST-7750 Worktime 1970 12.00
❑ PRST-7856 The First Recordings 1972 12.00
❑ PR-24004 [(2)] Sonny Rollins 1972 25.00
❑ P-24050 [(2)] Saxophone Colossus and More 1974 20.00
❑ P-24082 [(2)] Taking Care of Business 1978 20.00
❑ P-24096 [(2)] Vintage Sessions 1981 20.00

QUINTESSENCE
❑ QJ-25181 Green Dolphin Street 1978 12.00

RCA VICTOR
❑ AFL1-0859 The Bridge 1977 12.00
—Reissue with new prefix; black label, dog at 1 o'clock
❑ APL1-0859 The Bridge 1975 20.00
—Reissue of LSP-2527; orange or tan label
❑ LPM-2527 [M] The Bridge 1962 40.00
—Black label, dog on top, "Long 33 1/3 Play" at bottom
❑ LSP-2527 [S] The Bridge 1962 70.00
—Black label, dog on top, "Living Stereo" at bottom
❑ LSP-2527 [S] The Bridge 199? 30.00
—Classic Records reissue on audiophile vinyl
❑ LSP-2527-45 [(4)]The Bridge 1999 60.00
—Classic Records reissue; 4 single-sided LPs that play at 45 rpm
❑ LPM-2572 [M] What's New? 1962 30.00
❑ LSP-2572 [S] What's New? 1962 60.00
❑ LPM-2612 [M] Our Man In Jazz 1962 30.00
❑ LSP-2612 [S] Our Man In Jazz 1962 60.00
❑ LSP-2612 [S] Our Man In Jazz 199? 25.00
—Classic Records reissue on audiophile vinyl
❑ LPM-2712 [M] Sonny Meets Hawk! 1963 30.00
❑ LSP-2712 [S] Sonny Meets Hawk! 1963 60.00
❑ LSP-2712 [S] Sonny Meets Hawk! 199? 25.00
—Classic Records reissue on audiophile vinyl
❑ ANL1-2809 Pure Gold 1978 10.00
❑ LPM-2927 [M] Now's the Time 1964 25.00
❑ LSP-2927 [S] Now's the Time! 1964 30.00
❑ LSP-2927 [S] Now's the Time! 199? 25.00
—Classic Records reissue on audiophile vinyl
❑ LPM-3355 [M] The Standard Sonny Rollins 1965 25.00
❑ LSP-3355 [S] The Standard Sonny Rollins 1965 30.00

RIVERSIDE
❑ RLP 12-241 [M] The Sound of Sonny 1957 400.00
—White label, blue print

Number	Title (A Side/B Side)	Yr	NM
❑ RLP 12-241 [M]	The Sound of Sonny	1959	200.00
—Blue label, microphone logo at top			
❑ RLP-258 [M]	Freedom Suite	1958	200.00
❑ RLP-1124 [S]	The Sound of Sonny	1959	200.00
❑ RS-3010 [S]	Freedom Suite	1968	30.00
❑ SMJ-6044	Freedom Suite	1974	20.00

STEREO RECORDS

Number	Title (A Side/B Side)	Yr	NM
❑ S-7017 [S]	Way Out West	1958	200.00

VERVE

Number	Title (A Side/B Side)	Yr	NM
❑ VSP-32 [M]	Tenor Titan	1966	15.00
❑ VSPS-32 [S]	Tenor Titan	1966	12.00
❑ UMV-2555	Sonny Rollins/Brass, Sonny Rollins/Trio	198?	10.00
❑ V-8430 [M]	Sonny Rollins/Brass, Sonny Rollins/Trio	1962	40.00
❑ V6-8430 [S]	Sonny Rollins/Brass, Sonny Rollins/Trio	1962	30.00

ROLLINS, SONNY; CLIFFORD BROWN; MAX ROACH

Albums

PRESTIGE

Number	Title (A Side/B Side)	Yr	NM
❑ PRLP-7291 [M]	Three Giants	1964	40.00
❑ PRST-7291 [R]	Three Giants	1964	25.00
❑ PRST-7821	Three Giants	1971	12.00

ROLLINS, SONNY/JIMMY CLEVELAND

Albums

PERIOD

Number	Title (A Side/B Side)	Yr	NM
❑ SPL-1204 [M]	Sonny Rollins Plays/Jimmy Cleveland Plays	1956	100.00

ROLLINS BAND, THE As in Henry Rollins of BLACK FLAG.

45s

SUB POP

Number	Title (A Side/B Side)	Yr	NM
❑ 72	Earache My Eye/You Know Me	1990	15.00
—Black vinyl pressing of 2,000			
❑ 72	Earache My Eye/You Know Me	1990	25.00
—Pink and red vinyl pressing of 2,000			
❑ 72 [PS]	Earache My Eye/You Know Me	1990	15.00
—#21 in Sub Pop Singles Club series			

Albums

IMAGO

Number	Title (A Side/B Side)	Yr	NM
❑ 21034	Weight	1994	15.00

1/4 STICK

Number	Title (A Side/B Side)	Yr	NM
❑ 0002	Turned On	1990	15.00

ROMAN NUMERALS, THE

45s

COLUMBIA

Number	Title (A Side/B Side)	Yr	NM
❑ 44314	The Come-On/Matchstick in a Whirlpool	1967	20.00
❑ 44314 [PS]	The Come-On/Matchstick in a Whirlpool	1967	30.00

ROME, RICHARD

45s

PARKWAY

Number	Title (A Side/B Side)	Yr	NM
❑ 978	Happiness Is/Back in Sixty Seconds	1966	10.00

SWAN

Number	Title (A Side/B Side)	Yr	NM
❑ 4021	Bluebird of Happiness/Leaf in the Wind	1959	12.00

ROMEO VOID

12-Inch Singles

COLUMBIA

Number	Title (A Side/B Side)	Yr	NM
❑ 05103	A Girl in Trouble (Is a Temporary Thing)/Six Days and One	1984	6.00
❑ 05135	Say No/Out on My Own	1984	7.00

45s

COLUMBIA

Number	Title (A Side/B Side)	Yr	NM
❑ 03378	Never Say Never/Guards	1982	3.00
❑ 04534	A Girl in Trouble (Is a Temporary Thing)/Going to Be Neon	1984	3.00
❑ 04704	Say No/Six Days and One	1984	3.00
❑ 04704 [PS]	Say No/Six Days and One	1984	3.00
❑ 04704 [PS]	Say No	1984	5.00
—"Demonstration – Not for Sale" on back			

415 RECORDS

Number	Title (A Side/B Side)	Yr	NM
❑ 0012	White Sweater/Apache	1982	3.00
❑ 0012 [PS]	White Sweater/Apache	1982	3.00

Albums

COLUMBIA

Number	Title (A Side/B Side)	Yr	NM
❑ PC 38178 [EP]	Never Say Never	1982	12.00
—Reissue			
❑ ARC 38182	Benefactor	1982	10.00
❑ PC 38182	Benefactor	198?	8.00
—Reissue			
❑ BFC 39155	Instincts	1984	10.00
❑ PC 39155	Instincts	1985	8.00
—Reissue			

415 RECORDS

Number	Title (A Side/B Side)	Yr	NM
❑ A-0004	It's a Condition	1981	15.00
❑ A-0007 [EP]	Never Say Never	1981	25.00

ROMEOS, THE (1) Featuring Philly Soul producers KENNY GAMBLE and Leon Huff.

45s

MARK II

Number	Title (A Side/B Side)	Yr	NM
❑ 101	Precious Memories/Juicy Lucy	1967	15.00
❑ 103	A Tear and a Smile/Seaching	1967	15.00

Albums

MARK II

Number	Title (A Side/B Side)	Yr	NM
❑ 1001	Precious Memories	1967	25.00

ROMEOS, THE (2)

45s

AMY

Number	Title (A Side/B Side)	Yr	NM
❑ 840	The Tiger's Wide Awake (The Lion Sleeps Tonight)/Hitch-Hikin'	1962	15.00

ROMEOS, THE (3)

45s

APOLLO

Number	Title (A Side/B Side)	Yr	NM
❑ 461	Love Me/I Beg You Please	1954	600.00

ROMEOS, THE (4)

45s

ATCO

Number	Title (A Side/B Side)	Yr	NM
❑ 6107	Moments to Remember You By/Fine, Fine Baby	1958	60.00

FOX

Number	Title (A Side/B Side)	Yr	NM
❑ 749	Gone, Gone, Get Away/Let's Be Partners	1957	120.00
—Yellow label			
❑ 749	Gone, Gone, Get Away/Let's Be Partners	1957	300.00
—Cream label			
❑ 846	Moments to Remember You By/Fine, Fine Baby	1957	120.00
—Yellow label			
❑ 846	Moments to Remember You By/Fine, Fine Baby	1957	500.00
—Cream label			

ROMEOS, THE (5)

45s

COLUMBIA

Number	Title (A Side/B Side)	Yr	NM
❑ 43074	Baby Stay in Line/Two of the Chosen Few	1964	10.00

ROMEOS, THE (U) If these are any of the above groups, the most likely contenders are groups (1), (2) or (5).

45s

FELSTED

Number	Title (A Side/B Side)	Yr	NM
❑ 8528	Two Innocent Loves/Love-Mobile	1958	30.00
❑ 8672	Julie/I'm Gonna Rebuild This World	1963	20.00

LOMA

Number	Title (A Side/B Side)	Yr	NM
❑ 2028	Mucho Soul/Are You Ready for That	1966	12.00
❑ 2041	Calypso Chili/Mon Petite Chow	1966	12.00

ROMERO, CHAN

45s

CHALLENGE

Number	Title (A Side/B Side)	Yr	NM
❑ 59285	The Funniest Things/It's Not Fine	1965	15.00

DEL-FI

Number	Title (A Side/B Side)	Yr	NM
❑ 4119	The Hippy Hippy Shake/If I Had My Way	1959	100.00
❑ 4126	I Don't Care Now/My Little Rudy	1959	60.00

PHILIPS

Number	Title (A Side/B Side)	Yr	NM
❑ 40391	Humpy Bumpy/Man Can't Dog a Woman	1966	10.00

RON AND BILL Ron White and Bill "SMOKEY" ROBINSON.

45s

ARGO

Number	Title (A Side/B Side)	Yr	NM
❑ 5350	It/Don't Say Bye Bye	1959	50.00

TAMLA

Number	Title (A Side/B Side)	Yr	NM
❑ 54025	It/Don't Say Bye Bye	1960	120.00

RON-DELLS, THE

45s

ARLEN

Number	Title (A Side/B Side)	Yr	NM
❑ 723	I'll Be Gone/Slow Down	1963	15.00

RON-DELS, THE Delbert McClinton was in this group.

45s

BROWNFIELD

Number	Title (A Side/B Side)	Yr	NM
❑ 18	If You Really Want Me To, I'll Go/Walk About	1965	25.00

DOT

Number	Title (A Side/B Side)	Yr	NM
❑ 16593	Far Horizons/On the Run	1964	25.00
❑ 17323	Matilda/Tina	1970	10.00

SHALIMAR

Number	Title (A Side/B Side)	Yr	NM
❑ 104	Matilda/Tina	1963	15.00

SMASH

Number	Title (A Side/B Side)	Yr	NM
❑ 1986	If You Really Want Me To, I'll Go/Walk About	1965	10.00
❑ 2002	She's My Girl/Over	1965	8.00
❑ 2014	A Picture of You/Lose Your Money	1965	8.00

RONDELLS, THE More than one group.

45s

ABC-PARAMOUNT

Number	Title (A Side/B Side)	Yr	NM
❑ 10690	Don't Say That You Love Me/Parking in the Ko Ko Mo	1965	15.00

CARLTON

Number	Title (A Side/B Side)	Yr	NM
❑ 467	Good Good/Dreamy	1958	20.00

RONDELS, THE

45s

AMY

Number	Title (A Side/B Side)	Yr	NM
❑ 825	Back Beat #1/Shades of Green	1961	25.00
❑ 830	My Prayer/Satan's Theme	1961	25.00
❑ 839	Caldonia/110 Lbs. of Drums	1962	25.00
❑ 844	Red Peppers/Flute Salad	1962	25.00
❑ 857	Meet Us at the Peppermint Lounge/Cover Charge	1962	25.00

RONDO, DON

45s

ATLANTIC

Number	Title (A Side/B Side)	Yr	NM
❑ 2194	Malibu/So Did I	1963	8.00

CARLTON

Number	Title (A Side/B Side)	Yr	NM
❑ 531	Friends/Hoot an' a Holler	1960	8.00
❑ 536	Wanderlust/The King of Holiday Island	1960	8.00
❑ 551	You'll Never Walk Alone/They Were You	1961	8.00

DECCA

Number	Title (A Side/B Side)	Yr	NM
❑ 29738	Evening Star/Beyond the Mighty River	1955	12.00
❑ 30248	I Offer You My Heart Evening Star	1957	12.00
❑ 32561	Statue of a Fool/I'll Be True	1969	5.00

JUBILEE

Number	Title (A Side/B Side)	Yr	NM
❑ 5256	Two Different Worlds/He Made You Mine	1956	12.00
❑ 5270	Don't/The Love I Never Had	1957	12.00
❑ 5282	To Belong/On Forgotten Street	1957	12.00
❑ 5288	White Silver Sands/Stars Fell on Alabama	1957	12.00
❑ 5297	Forsaking All Others/There's Only You	1957	12.00
❑ 5305	Wanderin' Heart/In Chi-Chi-Chihuahua	1957	10.00
❑ 5313	Made for Each Other/What a Shame	1958	10.00
❑ 5319	There Goes My Heart Again/Blonde Bombshell	1958	10.00
❑ 5320	School Dance/I've Got Bells in My Heart	1958	10.00
❑ 5325	Dormi, Dormi, Dormi/Her Hair Was Yellow	1958	10.00
❑ 5334	City Lights/As Long As I Have You	1958	10.00
❑ 5341	I Could Be a Mountain/Great Adventure	1958	10.00
❑ 5354	Song from "Geisha Boy"/Gretna Green	1958	10.00
❑ 5364	My Foolish Heart/Leave Your Trouble on My Lips	1959	10.00
❑ 5372	You're On My Mind Again/Cuckoo Girl	1959	10.00
❑ 5381	Because of You/Alone in the World	1960	8.00
❑ 5421	Two Different Worlds/Blonde Bombshell	1962	8.00
❑ 5522	Love Me Back/Play the Other Side	1966	6.00

ROULETTE

Number	Title (A Side/B Side)	Yr	NM
❑ 4202	Batch of Love/Quiet Girl	1959	10.00
❑ 4216	Wall to Wall Tears/The Golden Rule	1959	10.00
❑ 4236	That's My Girl/Even the Heavens Cried	1960	10.00

Number	Title (A Side/B Side)	Yr	NM
TUBA			
❑ 1301	My Way/A Warmer World	1965	8.00
❑ 1302	No Tears, No Regrets (After the Ball)/A Woman Is a Many Thing	1965	8.00
UNITED ARTISTS			
❑ 50111	Till the World Knows You're Mine/Is There Room in Your Tomorrow	1967	6.00
❑ 50191	Let's Live for Today/Oh Why My Love	1967	6.00
Albums			
JUBILEE			
❑ JLP-1052 [M]	Rondo	195?	20.00
❑ JLP-1081 [M]	Have You Met Don Rondo	195?	20.00
VOCALION			
❑ VL 73897	Two Different Worlds	1970	12.00

RONETTES, THE

Also see RONNIE SPECTOR.

Number	Title (A Side/B Side)	Yr	NM
45s			
A&M			
❑ 1040	You Came, You Saw, You Conquered/Oh, I Love You	1969	16.00
BUDDAH			
❑ 384	Go Out and Get It/Lover, Lover	1973	20.00
	—As "Ronnie Spector and the Ronettes"		
❑ 408	I Wish I Never Saw the Sunshine/I Wonder What He's Doing	1974	20.00
COLPIX			
❑ 601	I Want a Boy/Sweet Sixteen	1961	100.00
	—As "Ronnie and the Relatives"		
❑ 646	I'm Gonna Quit While I'm Ahead/I'm On the Wagon	1962	60.00
DIMENSION			
❑ 1046	He Did It/Recipe for Love	1965	50.00
MAY			
❑ 111	My Darling Angel/I'm Gonna Quit While I'm Ahead	1961	150.00
	—As "Ronnie and the Relatives"		
❑ 114	Silhouettes/You Bet I Would	1962	50.00
❑ 138	Memory/Good Girls	1963	50.00
PAVILLION			
❑ 03333	I Saw Mommy Kissing Santa Claus/Rudolph the Red-Nosed Reindeer	1982	5.00
	—B-side by The Crystals		
PHILLES			
❑ 116	Be My Baby/Tedesco and Pittman	1963	30.00
❑ 118	Baby I Love You/Miss Joan and Mr. Sam	1963	30.00
❑ 120	(The Best Part of) Breakin' Up/Big Red	1964	30.00
❑ 121	Do I Love You?/Bebe and Susu	1964	30.00
❑ 123	Walkin' in the Rain/How Does It Feel	1964	40.00
❑ 123 [PS]	Walkin' in the Rain/How Does It Feel	1964	150.00
❑ 126	Born to Be Together/Blues for Baby	1965	25.00
❑ 126 [PS]	Born to Be Together/Blues for Baby	1965	150.00
❑ 128	Is This What I Get for Loving You?/Oh, I Love You	1965	25.00
❑ 128 [PS]	Is This What I Get for Loving You?/Oh, I Love You	1965	150.00
❑ 133	I Can Hear Music/When I Saw You	1966	30.00
Albums			
COLPIX			
❑ CP-486 [M]	The Ronettes Featuring Veronica	1965	100.00
	—Blue label		
❑ CP-486 [M]	The Ronettes Featuring Veronica	1965	200.00
	—Gold label		
❑ SCP-486 [S]	The Ronettes Featuring Veronica	1965	150.00
	—Blue label		
❑ SCP-486 [S]	The Ronettes Featuring Veronica	1965	300.00
	—Gold label		
PHILLES			
❑ PHLP-4006 [M]	Presenting the Fabulous Ronettes Featuring Veronica	1964	400.00
	—Yellow and red label		
❑ PHLP-4006 [M]	Presenting the Fabulous Ronettes Featuring Veronica	1964	800.00
	—Blue and black label		
❑ PHLP-ST-4006 [S]	Presenting the Fabulous Ronettes Featuring Veronica	1965	600.00
❑ ST-90721 [S]	Presenting the Fabulous Ronettes Featuring Veronica	1965	400.00
	—Capitol Record Club edition		
❑ T-90721 [M]	Presenting the Fabulous Ronettes Featuring Veronica	1965	250.00
	—Capitol Record Club edition		

RONNIE AND THE DEL-AIRES

See THE DEL-AIRES.

RONNIE AND THE HI-LITES

Number	Title (A Side/B Side)	Yr	NM
45s			
ABC-PARAMOUNT			
❑ 10685	High School Romance/Too Young	1965	20.00
JOY			
❑ 260	I Wish That We Were Married/Twistin' and Kissin'	1962	25.00
❑ 265	Be Kind/Send My Love (Special Delivery)	1962	20.00
RAVEN			
❑ 8000	Valerie/The Fact of the Matter	1963	20.00
WIN			
❑ 250	A Slow Dance/What the Next Day May Bring	1963	20.00
❑ 251	The Fact of the Matter/You Keep Me Guessin'	1963	20.00
❑ 252	High School Romance/Uptown-Downtown	1963	25.00

RONNIE AND THE POMONA CASUALS

Number	Title (A Side/B Side)	Yr	NM
45s			
DONNA			
❑ 1400	Swimming at the Rainbow/Casual Blues	1964	12.00
❑ 1402	I Wanna Do the Jerk/Sloopy	1965	12.00
Albums			
DONNA			
❑ 2113 [M]	Everybody Jerk	1965	30.00

RONNIE AND THE RED CAPS

The first released record by RONNIE DIO.

Number	Title (A Side/B Side)	Yr	NM
45s			
REB			
❑ 45-105	Conquest/Lover	1958	250.00

RONNIE AND THE RELATIVES

See THE RONETTES.

RONNIE AND THE ROCKIN' KINGS

Number	Title (A Side/B Side)	Yr	NM
45s			
RCA VICTOR			
❑ 47-7248	Rock and Roll Sal/You Know	1958	40.00

RONNY AND THE DAYTONAS

Number	Title (A Side/B Side)	Yr	NM
45s			
MALA			
❑ 481	G.T.O./Hot Rod Baby	1964	25.00
❑ 490	California Bound/Hey Little Girl	1964	20.00
❑ 492	Bucket "T"/Little Rail Job	1964	20.00
❑ 497	Little Scrambler/Teenage Years	1965	20.00
❑ 503	Beach Boy/No Wheels	1965	25.00
❑ 513	Sandy/(Instrumental)	1965	20.00
❑ 525	Goodbye Baby/Somebody to Love Me	1966	20.00
❑ 531	Antique '32 Studebaker Dictator Coupe/Then the Rains Came	1966	20.00
❑ 542	I'll Think of Summer/Little Scrambler	1966	15.00
RCA VICTOR			
❑ 47-8896	All American Girl/Dianne, Dianne	1966	12.00
❑ 47-8896 [PS]	All American Girl/Dianne, Dianne	1966	25.00
❑ 47-9022	Winter Weather/Young	1966	12.00
❑ 47-9107	Walk with the Sun/The Last Letter	1967	12.00
❑ 47-9253	Brave New World/Hold Onto Your Heart	1968	12.00
❑ 47-9435	The Girls and the Boys/Alfie	1968	12.00
SHOW BIZ			
❑ 21207 [DJ]	4-Cast She'll Love Me Again	1968	20.00
	—One-sided promo		
Albums			
BEAT ROCKET			
❑ BR 119	G.T.O.	199?	12.00
	—Reissue of Mala 4001 with four bonus tracks		
❑ BR 120	Sandy	199?	12.00
	—Reissue of Mala 4002 with three bonus tracks		
MALA			
❑ 4001 [M]	G.T.O.	1964	120.00
❑ 4002 [M]	Sandy	1966	80.00
❑ 4002S [S]	Sandy	1966	100.00
SUNDAZED			
❑ LP 5050	G.T.O. — Best of the Mala Recordings	1997	10.00

RONSON, MICK

Also see DAVID BOWIE; MOTT THE HOOPLE.

Number	Title (A Side/B Side)	Yr	NM
45s			
RCA VICTOR			
❑ APBO-0212	Love Me Tender/Only After Dark	1974	6.00
❑ APBO-0291	Slaughter on Tenth Avenue/Leave My Heart Alone	1974	6.00
❑ PB-10237	Easy Days/Billy Porter	1975	6.00
7-Inch Extended Plays			
RCA VICTOR			
❑ DJEO-0259 [DJ]	Slaughter on 10th Avenue/Growing Up and I'm Fine//All Cut Up on You/Andy Warhol	1974	12.00
	—Promo-only EP with B-side by Dana Gillespie		
Albums			
RCA VICTOR			
❑ APL1-0353	Slaughter on 10th Avenue	1974	12.00
❑ APL1-0681	Play Don't Worry	1975	12.00

RONSTADT, LINDA

Number	Title (A Side/B Side)	Yr	NM
12-Inch Singles			
ASYLUM			
❑ ED 4935 [DJ]	What's New (same on both sides)	1983	10.00
❑ AS 11431 [DJ]	Blue Bayou/Lago Azul	1977	30.00
	—Blue vinyl		
❑ 67973 [DJ]	Get Closer (same on both sides)	1982	20.00
CAPITOL			
❑ ST-1003 [DJ]	Living Like a Fool (same on both sides)	1977	30.00
	—Red vinyl; yellow label, "Capitol" in red at bottom		
❑ ST-1003 [DJ]	Living Like a Fool (same on both sides)	1977	40.00
	—Red vinyl; yellow "SM" label with Capitol tower		
45s			
ASYLUM			
❑ 11026	Love Has No Pride/I Can Almost See It	1973	5.00
❑ 11032	Silver Threads and Golden Needles/Don't Cry Now	1974	5.00
❑ 11039	Desperado/Colorado	1974	5.00
❑ 45271	Love Is a Rose/Silver Blue	1975	6.00
❑ 45282	Heat Wave/Love Is a Rose	1975	4.00
❑ 45295	Tracks of My Tears/The Sweetest Gift	1975	4.00
	—B-side with Emmylou Harris		
❑ 45340	That'll Be the Day/Try Me Again	1976	4.00
	—Clouds label		
❑ 45340	That'll Be the Day/Try Me Again	1976	5.00
	—All-blue label		
❑ 45361	Someone to Lay Down Beside Me/Crazy	1976	4.00
❑ 45402	Lose Again/Lo Siento Mi Vida	1977	8.00
❑ 45431	Blue Bayou/Old Paint	1977	4.00
❑ 45438	It's So Easy/Lo Siento Mi Vida	1977	4.00
❑ 45462	Poor Poor Pitiful Me/Simple Man, Simple Dream	1978	4.00
❑ 45464	Lago Azul/Lo Siento Mi Vida	1978	12.00
❑ 45479	Tumbling Dice/I Never Will Marry	1978	4.00
❑ 45519	Back in the U.S.A./White Rhythm and Blues	1978	4.00
❑ 45519 [PS]	Back in the U.S.A./White Rhythm and Blues	1978	6.00
❑ 45546	Ooh Baby Baby/Blowing Away	1978	4.00
❑ 46011	Just One Look/Love Me Tender	1979	4.00
❑ 46034	Alison/Mohammed's Radio	1979	4.00
❑ 46602	How Do I Make You/Rambler Gambler	1980	4.00
❑ 46602 [PS]	How Do I Make You/Rambler Gambler	1980	5.00
❑ 46624	Hurt So Bad/Justine	1980	4.00
❑ 46654	I Can't Let Go/Look Out for My Love	1980	4.00
❑ 69476	(I Love You) For Sentimental Reasons/Straighten Up and Fly Right	1987	4.00
❑ 69507	When You Wish Upon a Star/Little Girl Blue	1986	4.00
❑ 69507 [PS]	When You Wish Upon a Star/Little Girl Blue	1986	4.00
❑ 69653	When I Fall in Love/It Never Entered My Mind	1985	4.00
❑ 69671	Lush Life/Skylark	1985	4.00
❑ 69725	Someone to Watch Over Me/What'll I Do	1984	4.00
❑ 69752	I've Got a Crush on You/Lover Man	1984	4.00
❑ 69780	What's New/Crazy He Calls Me	1983	4.00
❑ 69838	Easy for You to Say/Mr. Radio	1983	4.00
❑ 69853	I Knew You When/Talk to Me of Mendocino	1982	4.00
❑ 69853 [PS]	I Knew You When/Talk to Me of Mendocino	1982	5.00

Except when noted otherwise, VG = 25% of NM, and VG+ = 50% of NM. (Example: VG = $2.00, VG+ = $4.00 and NM = $8.00.)

Number | Title (A Side/B Side) | Yr | NM

❑ 69948 Get Closer/Sometimes You Just Can't Win 1982 4.00
❑ 69948 [PS] Get Closer/Sometimes You Just Can't Win 1982 5.00

CAPITOL
❑ 2438 Dolphins/The Long Way Around 1969 12.00
❑ 2767 Lovesick Blues/Will You Love Me Tomorrow 1970 8.00
❑ 2846 Long Long Time/Nobody's 1970 8.00
❑ 3021 The Long Way Around/(She's a) Very Lovely Woman 1971 6.00
❑ 3210 I Fall to Pieces/Can It Be True 1971 6.00
❑ 3273 Rock Me on the Water/Crazy Arms 1972 6.00
❑ 3990 You're No Good/I Can't Help It (If I'm Still in Love with You) 1974 4.00
❑ 4050 When Will I Be Loved/It Doesn't Matter Anymore 1975 4.00

ELEKTRA
❑ 64427 The Waiting/Walk On 1995 3.00
❑ 64987 All My Life/Shattered 1990 3.00
—With Aaron Neville
❑ 69261 Don't Know Much/Cry Like a Rainstorm 1989 3.00
—With Aaron Neville

ELEKTRA SPUN GOLD
❑ 45073 Love Has No Pride/Silver Threads and Golden Needles 1975 4.00
—Reissue
❑ 45081 Heat Wave/Tracks of My Tears 1977 3.00
—Reissue
❑ 45089 Blue Bayou/It's So Easy 1979 3.00
—Reissue
❑ 45092 Poor, Poor, Pitiful Me/Tumbling Dice 1979 3.00
—Reissue
❑ 45102 Back in the U.S.A./Ooh, Baby, Baby 1980 3.00
—Reissue
❑ 45116 Hurt So Bad/How Do I Make You 1981 3.00
—Reissue
❑ 65934 Don't Know Much/When Something Is Wrong with My Baby 1993 8.00
—With Aaron Neville; B-side's only appearance on U.S. 45
❑ 65965 When You Wish Upon a Star/(I Love You) For Sentimental Reasons 1988 3.00
—Reissue
❑ 65988 What's New/I've Got a Crush on You 1985 3.00
—Reissue
❑ 65989 I Knew You When/Get Closer 1985 3.00
—Reissue

MCA
❑ 52973 Somewhere Out There/(Instrumental) 1986 3.00
—With James Ingram
❑ 52973 [PS] Somewhere Out There/(Instrumental) 1986 4.00

Albums

ASYLUM
❑ 6E-104 Simple Dreams 1977 10.00
❑ 6E-106 Greatest Hits 1977 10.00
❑ 6E-155 Living in the U.S.A. 1978 10.00
❑ DP-401 [PD] Living in the U.S.A. 1978 18.00
❑ 5E-510 Mad Love 1980 10.00
❑ 5E-516 Greatest Hits, Vol. 2 1980 10.00
❑ 5E-540 Keeping Out of Mischief 1981 —
—Canceled
❑ 7E-1045 Prisoner in Disguise 1975 10.00
❑ 7E-1072 Hasten Down the Wind 1976 10.00
—"Clouds" label
❑ 7E-1072 Hasten Down the Wind 1976 15.00
—Solid blue label with white stylized "a" at top
❑ 7E-1092 Greatest Hits 1976 12.00
❑ SD 5064 Don't Cry Now 1973 10.00
❑ 60185 Get Closer 1982 10.00
❑ 60260 What's New 1983 10.00
❑ 60387 Lush Life 1984 10.00
❑ 60474 For Sentimental Reasons 1987 10.00
❑ 60489 [(3)] 'Round Midnight: The Nelson Riddle Sessions 1987 25.00
❑ 60765 Canciones De Mi Padre 1988 12.00

CAPITOL
❑ ST-208 Hand Sown...Home Grown 1969 20.00
—Black label with colorband
❑ ST-208 Hand Sown...Home Grown 1970 15.00
—Green label
❑ ST-208 Hand Sown...Home Grown 1971 12.00
—Red label
❑ ST-407 Silk Purse 1970 15.00
—Green label
❑ ST-407 Silk Purse 1971 12.00
—Red label
❑ ST-8-0407 Silk Purse 1970 20.00
—Capitol Record Club edition
❑ SMAS-635 Linda Ronstadt 1972 12.00
❑ ST-11269 Different Drum 1974 12.00
—Also includes Stone Poneys tracks
❑ ST-11358 Heart Like a Wheel 1974 12.00
❑ SW-11358 Heart Like a Wheel 1975 10.00
❑ SKBB-11629 [(2)]A Retrospective 1977 15.00
—Also includes Stone Poneys tracks
❑ SN-16130 Hand Sown...Home Grown 1980 8.00
❑ SN-16131 Silk Purse 1980 8.00
❑ SN-16132 Linda Ronstadt 1980 8.00
❑ SN-16133 Beginnings 1980 8.00
❑ SN-16299 Different Drum 198? 8.00
—Budget-line reissue

DCC COMPACT CLASSICS
❑ LPZ-2048 Greatest Hits 1997 80.00
—Audiophile vinyl
❑ LPZ-2065 Greatest Hits, Vol. Two 1998 40.00
—Audiophile vinyl

ELEKTRA
❑ 60872 Cry Like a Rainstorm, Howl Like the Wind 1989 12.00

MOBILE FIDELITY
❑ 1-158 What's New 1984 50.00
—Audiophile vinyl

NAUTILUS
❑ NR-26 Simple Dreams 1982 50.00
—Audiophile vinyl

PAIR
❑ PDL2-1070 [(2)]Prime of Life 1986 12.00
❑ PDL2-1125 [(2)]Rockfile 1986 12.00

TPM/RHINO EXCLUSIVE
❑ 306 Prisoner in Disguise 2008 22.00

RONSTADT, LINDA, AND THE STONE PONEYS
See STONE PONEYS.

ROOFTOP SINGERS, THE

45s

ATCO
❑ 6526 My Life Is My Own/Kites 1967 6.00

PHILCO-FORD
❑ HP-37 Walk Right In/Tom Cat 1969 15.00
—4-inch plastic "Hip Pocket Record" with color sleeve

VANGUARD
❑ 35017 Walk Right In/Cool Water 1962 10.00
❑ 35017 [PS] Walk Right In/Cool Water 1962 25.00
❑ 35019 Tom Cat/Shoes 1963 8.00
❑ 35019 [PS] Tom Cat/Shoes 1963 12.00
❑ 35020 Mama Don't Allow/It Don't Mean a Thing 1963 8.00
❑ 35020 [PS] Mama Don't Allow/It Don't Mean a Thing 1963 12.00
❑ 35024 Sail Away Ladies/Twelve String 1964 8.00
❑ 35029 Rainy Day/Buddy Won't You Roll Down the Line 1964 8.00
❑ 35034 Ham and Eggs/Somebody Came Home 1965 8.00

Albums

VANGUARD
❑ VSD-2136 [S] Walk Right In 1963 20.00
❑ VRS-9123 [M] Walk Right In 1963 15.00
❑ VRS-9134 [M] Good Time 1964 15.00
❑ VRS-9190 [M] Rainy River 1965 15.00
❑ VSD-79134 [S] Good Time 1964 20.00
❑ VSD-79190 [S] Rainy River 1965 20.00

ROOMATES, THE
Also see CATHY JEAN AND THE ROOMATES.

45s

BAN
❑ 691 A Place Called Love/Knowing You 1985 5.00

CAMEO
❑ 233 Sunday Kind of Love/A Lovely Way to Spend An Evening 1962 30.00

CANADIAN AMERICAN
❑ 166 My Heart/Just for Tonight 1964 40.00

PHILIPS
❑ 40105 Gee/Answer Me, My Love 1963 25.00
❑ 40153 The Nearness of You/Don't Cheat on Me 1963 25.00

PROMO
❑ 2211 I Want a Little Girl/Making Believe 196? 20.00
—Sources conflict as to date (1960 or 1964)

VALMOR
❑ 008 Glory of Love/Never Know 1961 20.00
❑ 010 Band of Gold/O Baby Love 1961 20.00
❑ 013 My Foolish Heart/My Kisses for Your Thoughts 1962 20.00

ROONEY, TEDDY

45s

IMPERIAL
❑ 5644 Bite Your Tongue/After the Dance 1960 40.00

ROOSTERS, THE
More than one group.

45s

A&M
❑ 746 Shake a Tail Feather/Rooster Walk 1964 12.00

EPIC
❑ 9487 Let's Try Again/Pretty Girl 1962 15.00

FELSTED
❑ 8642 Chicken Hop/Fun House 1962 15.00

PHILIPS
❑ 40504 Love Machine/I'm Suspectin' 1968 10.00
❑ 40559 Good Good Lovin'/Home Down Right 1968 8.00

SHAR-DEE
❑ 704 Chicken Hop/Fun House 1959 20.00

ROSE, BIFF

45s

BUDDAH
❑ 218 The Captain/I Forgot to Tell You 1971 5.00

TETRAGRAMMATON
❑ 1506 What's Gnawing at Me/Molly 1969 6.00
❑ 1510 Buzz the Fuzz/Gentle People 1969 6.00
❑ 1543 Take Care of My Brother/Myrtle's Files 1970 6.00

Albums

BUDDAH
❑ BDS-5069 Ride On! 1970 12.00
❑ BDS-5075 The Thorn in Mrs. Rose's Side 1971 12.00
—Reissue of Tetragrammaton 103
❑ BDS-5076 Children of Light 1971 12.00
—Reissue of Tetragrammaton 116
❑ BDS-5078 Half Live at the Bitter End 1971 12.00

TETRAGRAMMATON
❑ T-103 The Thorn in Mrs. Rose's Side 1968 15.00
❑ T-116 Children of Light 1969 15.00

UNITED ARTISTS
❑ UAS-5594 Uncle Jesus Auntie Christ 1972 12.00

ROSE, DAVID

45s

CAPITOL
❑ 2094 Theme from The High Chaparral/Merci, Cherie 1968 7.00
❑ 2094 [PS] Theme from The High Chaparral/Merci, Cherie 1968 10.00
❑ 2662 Those Were the Days/Happy Heart 1969 7.00
❑ 5762 Theme from The Bible/King of Kings 1966 7.00
❑ 5837 Blowup/Theme from Hombre 1967 7.00

KAPP
❑ AS-920X [DJ] I'm in the Mood for Love/Exactly Like You 195? 12.00

MGM
❑ 8009 Bewitched (Bothered and Bewildered)/Moon of Manakoora 1950 25.00
—Original 45 rpm issue
❑ K12243 Forbidden Planet/Theme from "The Swan" 1956 12.00
❑ K12270 Cool Tango/Catered Affair (Theme) 1956 12.00
❑ K12305 A Kiss Is Forever/Dance of Fury 1956 12.00
❑ K12336 Friendly Persuasion (Thee I Love)/There's Never Been Anyone Else 1956 12.00
❑ K12376 Holiday for Trombones/Midnight on the Cliffs 1956 12.00
❑ K12430 Calypso Melody/Theme from "Wings of Eagles" 1957 12.00
❑ K12492 Ama Casa Portuguesa/Arianne 1957 12.00
❑ K12525 A Night in Trinidad/Captain's Paradise 1957 12.00
❑ K12554 Ca, C'est L'Amour/Autumn Holiday 1957 12.00
❑ K12585 Savanna/Little Bisquit 1957 12.00
❑ K12608 Swinging Shepherd Blues/Rock Fiddle 1958 12.00
❑ K12631 The Night They Invented Champagne/Waltz at Maxim's 1958 12.00
❑ K12652 Chapo/Punch and Judy 1958 12.00
❑ K12714 How High the Moon/Stroll Along 1958 12.00

Number	Title (A Side/B Side)	Yr	NM
❑ K12750	Circus Elephants/Our Waltz	1959	10.00
❑ K12792	Like Young/Young Man's Lament	1959	10.00
—With Andre Previn			
❑ K12965	Theme from "Bonanza"/Choria's Theme (From "Butterfield-8")	1960	10.00
❑ K12974	Spellbound/Cimarron	1960	10.00
❑ K12997	Silent Thunder/Theme from "Carnival"	1961	10.00
❑ K13006	Too Young to Go Steady/It's a Most Unusual Day	1961	10.00
❑ K13030	Concerto/The Truth	1961	10.00
❑ K13064	The Stripper/Ebb Tide	1962	10.00
❑ K13086	Theme from "The Wonderful World of the Brothers Grimm"/Black and Tan Fantasy	1962	10.00
❑ K13118	The Runaway/Sunset Strip	1963	8.00
❑ K13131	How the West Was Won/Whistle Bait	1963	8.00
❑ K13211	Bird Brain/The Grasshopper	1964	8.00
❑ K13245	March from the River Kwai/Our Waltz	1964	8.00
❑ K13250	Love Theme from "The Carpetbaggers"/Lefty Louie	1964	8.00
❑ K13289	Emily/A World of Our Own	1964	8.00
❑ K13314	Fiddler on the Roof/Theme from "Quick, Before It Melts"	1965	8.00
❑ K13377	Brazilian Summer/Mae	1965	8.00
❑ K13427	Never Too Late/Tennessee Waltz	1965	8.00
❑ K30017	Holiday for Strings/Deserted City	1950	20.00
❑ K30018	Sweet Sue — Just You/Laura	1950	20.00
❑ K30019	Estrellita/4:20 A.M.	1950	20.00
❑ K30020	Intermezzo/Manhattan Square Dance	1950	20.00
❑ K30120	Bewitched (Bothered and Bewildered)/Moon of Manakoora	1950	20.00
❑ K30123	Serenade/Penny Serenade	1950	20.00
❑ K30124	Sunrise Serenade/Penthouse Serenade	1950	20.00
❑ K30125	Gaucho Serenade/Serenade in Blue	1950	20.00
❑ K30126	Serenade to a Lemonade/Puppet Serenade	1950	20.00
❑ K30259	Rose of Bel Air/Dance of the Spanish Onion	195?	15.00
❑ K30279	Wonderful One/The Tina Lina	195?	15.00
❑ K30291	An American in Paris/Liza	195?	15.00
❑ K30300	Star Dust/Sentimental Journey	195?	15.00
❑ K30301	When the Wind Was Green/Time and Time Again	195?	15.00
❑ K30302	Deep Purple/Moon of Manakoora	195?	15.00
❑ K30303	How High the Moon/Bewitched (Bothered and Bewildered)	195?	15.00
❑ K30324	Fiddlin' for Fun/Zing Zing, Zoom Zoom	195?	15.00
❑ K30334	May the Good Lord Bless (And Keep You)/The Vision of Bernadette	195?	15.00
❑ K30353	Syncopated Clock/Mask Waltz	195?	15.00
❑ K30384	Tenderly/Flying Horse	195?	15.00
❑ K30407	Rhapsody in Blue/Embraceable You	195?	15.00
❑ K30408	Somebody Loves Me/Someone to Watch Over Me	195?	15.00
❑ K30409	An American in Paris/Liza	195?	15.00
❑ K30410	Summertime/Love Is Here to Stay	195?	15.00
❑ K30464	Love Makes the World Go Round/Portrait of a Flirt	195?	15.00
❑ K30521	Paris Oui Oui/Why Do You Pass Me	195?	15.00
❑ K30619	All the Things You Are/Vanessa	195?	15.00
❑ K30669	Flavia/Magic Music Box	195?	15.00
❑ K30724	Beautiful Music to Love By/Suddenly	195?	15.00
❑ K30773	Waltz of the Bubbles/Lonesome on Main Street	195?	15.00
❑ K30783	Return to Paradise/The Bad and the Beautiful	195?	15.00
❑ K30796	All I Desire/No Other Love	195?	15.00
❑ K30802	Nostalgia/September Song	1954	12.00
❑ K30824	Parade of the Clowns/Our Waltz	1954	12.00
❑ K30839	I Live for You/Migraine Melody	1955	12.00
❑ K30850	I've Got the World on a String/It's Only a Paper Moon	1955	12.00
❑ K30858	Satan and the Polar Bear/Sleepy Lagoon	1955	12.00
❑ K30865	Love Walked In/Fascinating Rhythm	1955	12.00
❑ K30875	Take My Love/Love Is Eternal	1955	12.00
❑ K30882	Violin/Summertime in Venus	1955	12.00
❑ K30883	Love Is a Many-Splendored Thing/You and You Alone (Gelsomina)	1955	12.00
❑ K30885	Time for Parting/Barcelona	1955	12.00
❑ K30886	That Old Black Magic/Happiness Is a Thing Called Joe	1955	12.00
❑ K30887	Pam Pam/Serenade	1955	12.00
❑ SK-50105 [S]	The Night They Invented Champagne/Gigi	1958	20.00
❑ SK-50114 [S]	Chief Rocky Boy/Sorry for Myself	1959	20.00
❑ SK-50124 [S]	Like Young/Young Man's Lament	1959	20.00
—With Andre Previn			
❑ SK-50132 [S]	Young and Tender/Too Young to Be True	1959	20.00
—With Andre Previn			

POLYDOR

Number	Title (A Side/B Side)	Yr	NM
❑ 871886-7	The Stripper/Love Is a Many-Splendored Thing	198?	4.00
—"Timepieces" reissue			

RCA VICTOR

Number	Title (A Side/B Side)	Yr	NM
❑ 47-2752	What Is This Thing Called Love/I've Got You Under My Skin	1949	25.00
❑ 47-2753	Begin the Beguine/Love for Sale	1949	25.00
❑ 47-2754	Night and Day/Easy to Love	1949	25.00
❑ 47-2755	I Get a Kick Out of You/In the Still of the Night	1949	25.00
❑ WP 158 [PS]	Cole Porter Review	1949	25.00
—Box for 47-2752, 2753, 2754 and 2755			

7-Inch Extended Plays

MGM

Number	Title (A Side/B Side)	Yr	NM
❑ X1001	(contents unknown)	1952	10.00
❑ X1001 [PS]	Portrait of a Flirt	1952	10.00
❑ X1016	(contents unknown)	1952	10.00
❑ X1016 [PS]	Motion Picture Themes	1952	10.00
❑ X1089	*Beautiful Music to Love By/Suddenly/Lonesome on Main Street/Wonderful One	195?	10.00
❑ X1089 [PS]	Beautiful Music to Love By, Vol. 1	195?	10.00
❑ X1090	(contents unknown)	195?	10.00
❑ X1090 [PS]	Beautiful Music to Love By, Vol. 2	195?	10.00
❑ X1178	Serenade in Blue/Sunrise Serenade//Puppet Serenade/The Gaucho Serenade	1955	10.00
❑ X1178 [PS]	Lover's Serenade, Vol. 2	1955	10.00
❑ X1179	(contents unknown)	1955	10.00
❑ X1179 [PS]	Lover's Serenade, Vol. 3	1955	10.00
❑ X1531	*Blue Autumn/'Tis Autumn/Shine On Harvest Moon/Autumn Serenade	195?	10.00
❑ X1531 [PS]	Autumn Leaves, Vol. 2	195?	10.00
❑ X1532	*Autumn Nocturne/Autumn in New York/October Mist/Autumn Holiday	195?	10.00
❑ X1532 [PS]	Autumn Leaves, Vol. 3	195?	10.00

Albums

CAPITOL

Number	Title	Yr	NM
❑ ST-124	Something Fresh	1969	15.00
❑ ST-290	The Little Drummer Boy	1969	12.00
—Reissue of 2853			
❑ ST 2627 [S]	The Bible	1966	15.00
❑ T 2627 [M]	The Bible	1966	12.00
❑ ST 2717 [S]	Holiday for Strings	1967	12.00
❑ T 2717 [M]	Holiday for Strings	1967	15.00
❑ ST 2853	Christmas Album	1968	15.00

DINO

Number	Title	Yr	NM
❑ DP-3001	Miracle	1972	12.00

KAPP

Number	Title	Yr	NM
❑ K-1100-S [S]	Great Waltzes of the Fabulous Century	1958	25.00
❑ KL-1100 [M]	Great Waltzes of the Fabulous Century	1958	20.00
❑ KL-1205 [M]	Songs of the Fabulous Thirties, Vol. 1	1960	15.00
❑ KL-1206 [M]	Songs of the Fabulous Thirties, Vol. 2	1960	15.00
❑ KS-3010 [S]	Waltzes in Stereo	1959	30.00
❑ KS-3205 [S]	Songs of the Fabulous Thirties, Vol. 1	1960	20.00
❑ KS-3206 [S]	Songs of the Fabulous Thirties, Vol. 2	1960	20.00
❑ KX-5004-S [(2)S]	Songs of the Fabulous Thirties	1958	30.00
❑ KXL-5004 [(2)M]	Songs of the Fabulous Thirties	1958	25.00

LION

Number	Title	Yr	NM
❑ L-70109 [M]	Magic Melodies	1959	20.00

METRO

Number	Title	Yr	NM
❑ M 502 [M]	Deep Purple	1965	12.00
❑ MS 502 [R]	Deep Purple	1965	12.00
❑ M 585 [M]	Among the Stars	1966	12.00
❑ MS 585 [S]	Among the Stars	1966	12.00

MGM

Number	Title	Yr	NM
❑ E-85 [10]	David Rose and His Orchestra Play Music of George Gershwin	1951	40.00
❑ GAS-129	David Rose and His Orchestra (Golden Archive Series)	1970	10.00
❑ E-196 [10]	The Magic Music Box	1953	40.00
❑ E-506 [10]	Holiday for Strings	1950	60.00
❑ E-515 [10]	Serenades	1950	60.00
❑ E-532 [10]	A Sentimental Journey with David Rose	1950	60.00
❑ E-3067 [M]	Beautiful Music to Love By	1953	30.00
—Yellow label			
❑ E-3101 [M]	Let's Fall in Love	1954	30.00
—Yellow label			
❑ E-3108 [M]	Fiddlin' for Fun	1954	30.00
—Yellow label			
❑ E-3123 [M]	Love Walked In — The Music of George Gershwin	1954	30.00
—Yellow label			
❑ E-3134 [M]	Nostalgia	1954	30.00
—Yellow label			
❑ E-3215 [M]	Holiday for Strings	1955	30.00
—Yellow label			
❑ E-3255 [M]	Sentimental Journey	1955	30.00
—Yellow label			
❑ E-3289 [M]	Lover's Serenade	1955	30.00
—Yellow label			
❑ E-3397 [M]	Music from Motion Pictures	1956	30.00
—Yellow label			
❑ E-3469 [M]	A Merry Christmas to You	1956	30.00
—Yellow label			
❑ E-3469 [M]	A Merry Christmas to You	1960	15.00
—Black label			
❑ E-3481 [M]	Hi Fiddles	1957	25.00
—Yellow label			
❑ E-3555 [M]	The Song Is You — Melodies of Jerome Kern	1957	25.00
—Yellow label			
❑ E-3592 [M]	Autumn Leaves	1957	25.00
—Yellow label			
❑ SE-3592 [S]	Autumn Leaves	1959	30.00
—Yellow label			
❑ E-3603 [M]	Reflections in the Water	1957	25.00
—Yellow label			
❑ E-3612 [M]	Music from Jamaica	1957	25.00
—Yellow label			
❑ E-3640 [M]	David Rose Plays Music from "Gigi"	1958	25.00
—Yellow label			
❑ SE-3640 [S]	David Rose Plays Music from "Gigi"	1958	30.00
—Yellow label			
❑ E-3716 [M]	Secret Songs for Young Lovers	1959	20.00
—With Andre Previn; yellow label			
❑ SE-3716 [S]	Secret Songs for Young Lovers	1959	30.00
—With Andre Previn; yellow label			
❑ E-3746 [M]	David Rose Plays the Music from "Whoop Up!"	1959	20.00
—Yellow label			
❑ SE-3746 [S]	David Rose Plays the Music from "Whoop Up!"	1959	30.00
—Yellow label			
❑ E-3748 [M]	David Rose Plays David Rose	1959	20.00
—Yellow label			
❑ SE-3748 [S]	David Rose Plays David Rose	1959	20.00
—Yellow label			
❑ E-3852 [M]	Concert with a Beat!	1960	15.00
❑ SE-3852 [S]	Concert with a Beat!	1960	20.00
❑ E-3894 [M]	Box-Office Blockbusters	1961	15.00
❑ SE-3894 [S]	Box-Office Blockbusters	1961	20.00
❑ E-3895 [M]	Spectacular Strings	1961	15.00
❑ SE-3895 [S]	Spectacular Strings	1961	20.00
❑ E-3950 [M]	Exodus	1961	15.00
❑ SE-3950 [S]	Exodus	1961	20.00
❑ E-3952 [M]	Butterfield-8	1961	15.00
❑ SE-3952 [S]	Butterfield-8	1961	20.00
❑ E-3953 [M]	Cimarron	1961	15.00
❑ SE-3953 [S]	Cimarron	1961	20.00
❑ E-3960 [M]	David Rose and His Concert Orchestra Play His Dramatic Music from the NBC-TV Series "Bonanza"	1961	30.00
❑ SE-3960 [S]	David Rose and His Concert Orchestra Play His Dramatic Music from the NBC-TV Series "Bonanza"	1961	40.00
❑ E-4004 [M]	21 Channel Sound	1962	15.00
❑ SE-4004 [S]	21 Channel Sound	1962	20.00
❑ E-4062 [M]	The Stripper and Other Fun Songs for the Family	1962	15.00
—Black label			
❑ SE-4062 [S]	The Stripper and Other Fun Songs for the Family	1962	20.00
—Black label			
❑ SE-4062 [S]	The Stripper and Other Fun Songs for the Family	1968	12.00
—Blue and gold label			

Except when noted otherwise, VG = 25% of NM, and VG+ = 50% of NM. (Example: VG = $2.00, VG+ = $4.00 and NM = $8.00.)

Number	Title (A Side/B Side)	Yr	NM
❑ E-4077 [M]	The Wonderful World of the Brothers Grimm	1962	15.00
❑ SE-4077 [S]	The Wonderful World of the Brothers Grimm	1962	20.00
❑ E-4099 [M]	More, More, More, Music of the Stripper	1963	15.00
❑ SE-4099 [S]	More, More, More, Music of the Stripper	1963	20.00
❑ E-4144 [M]	Love Theme from "Cleopatra" and Music from Other Great Motion Pictures	1963	15.00
❑ SE-4144 [S]	Love Theme from "Cleopatra" and Music from Other Great Motion Pictures	1963	20.00
❑ E-4155 [M]	The Very Best of David Rose	1963	12.00
❑ SE-4155 [S]	The Very Best of David Rose	1963	15.00
❑ E-4271 [M]	The Americanization of Emily and Other Great Movie Themes	1964	15.00
❑ SE-4271 [S]	The Americanization of Emily and Other Great Movie Themes	1964	20.00
❑ E-4285 [M]	Quick, Before It Melts and Other Selections	1965	15.00
❑ SE-4285 [S]	Quick, Before It Melts and Other Selections	1965	20.00
❑ E-4307 [M]	The Velvet Beat	1965	12.00
❑ SE-4307 [S]	The Velvet Beat	1965	15.00
❑ ST-90534 [S]	The Stripper and Other Fun Songs for the Family	1965	20.00
—Capitol Record Club edition			
❑ T-90534 [M]	The Stripper and Other Fun Songs for the Family	1965	20.00
—Capitol Record Club edition			
❑ ST-90754 [S]	The Velvet Beat	1965	20.00
—Capitol Record Club edition			

ROSE, TIM

45s

CAPITOL

Number	Title (A Side/B Side)	Yr	NM
❑ 3001	I've Gotta Get a Message to You/Janie Sue	1970	6.00

COLUMBIA

Number	Title (A Side/B Side)	Yr	NM
❑ 43563	I'm Bringing It Home/Mother, Father, Where Are You	1966	8.00
❑ 43648	Hey Joe/The Lonely Blue King	1966	8.00
❑ 43722	Where Was I/I Gotta Do Things My Way	1966	8.00
❑ 43958	I'm Gonna Be Strong/I Got a Loneliness	1967	8.00
❑ 44031	Morning Dew/You're Slipping Away from Me	1967	8.00
❑ 44387	Long Time Man/Come Away Melinda	1967	8.00
❑ 44603	Long-Haired Boy/Looking at a Baby	1968	6.00
❑ 44792	Angela/Whatcha Gonna Do	1969	6.00
❑ 44849	Babe Do You Turn Me On/Roanoke	1969	6.00

PLAYBOY

Number	Title (A Side/B Side)	Yr	NM
❑ 50005	It Takes a Little Longer/Ride Your Love Away	1972	5.00
❑ 50012	Goin' Down in Hollywood/(B-side unknown)	1972	5.00

Albums

CAPITOL

Number	Title (A Side/B Side)	Yr	NM
❑ ST-673	Love, A Kind of Hate Story	1970	12.00

COLUMBIA

Number	Title (A Side/B Side)	Yr	NM
❑ CS 9577	Tim Rose	1968	12.00
❑ CS 9772	Thru Rose Colored Glasses	1969	12.00

PLAYBOY

Number	Title (A Side/B Side)	Yr	NM
❑ P-101	Tim Rose	1972	12.00

ROSE GARDEN, THE

45s

ATCO

Number	Title (A Side/B Side)	Yr	NM
❑ 6510	Next Plane to London/Flower Town	1967	12.00
❑ 6564	Here's Today/If My World Falls Through	1968	10.00

7-Inch Extended Plays

ATCO

Number	Title (A Side/B Side)	Yr	NM
❑ EP-C-4522 [DJ]	Rider/Long Time//February Sunshine/I'm Only Second	1967	20.00
—White label, red print			
❑ EP-C-4522 [PS]	The Rose Garden	1967	30.00

Albums

ATCO

Number	Title (A Side/B Side)	Yr	NM
❑ 33-225 [M]	The Rose Garden	1968	60.00
❑ SD 33-225 [S]	The Rose Garden	1968	25.00

ROSEBUDS, THE (1)

45s

GEE

Number	Title (A Side/B Side)	Yr	NM
❑ 1033	Dearest Darling/Unconditional Surrender	1957	50.00

LANCER

Number	Title (A Side/B Side)	Yr	NM
❑ 102	Kiss Me Goodnight/Joey	1959	60.00

ROSEBUDS, THE (2)

45s

TOWER

Number	Title (A Side/B Side)	Yr	NM
❑ 104	Say You'll Be Mine/Mama Said	1964	12.00

ROSELLA, CARMELA

45s

NANCY

Number	Title (A Side/B Side)	Yr	NM
❑ 1004	Oh, It Was Elvis/Where?	1961	40.00

ROSELLI, JIMMY

45s

LENOX

Number	Title (A Side/B Side)	Yr	NM
❑ 5571	Mala Femmina/Her Eyes Shone Like Diamonds	1963	8.00
❑ 5576	Passione/Satte Vincino A Me	1963	8.00

M&R

Number	Title (A Side/B Side)	Yr	NM
❑ 2010	When Your Old Wedding Ring Was New/Little Pal	1982	8.00

RIC

Number	Title (A Side/B Side)	Yr	NM
❑ 138	Yellow and Green Make Blue/Anema E Core	1964	8.00
❑ 148	Don't Cry Little Girl, Don't Cry/Just Say I Love Her	1965	8.00

UNITED ARTISTS

Number	Title (A Side/B Side)	Yr	NM
❑ 866	Laugh It Off/Why Don't We Do This More Often	1965	6.00
❑ 928	Have You Ever Been Lonely/Rage to Live	1965	6.00
❑ 957	New York: My Port of Call/This Is My Kind of Love	1965	6.00
❑ 996	I'll Never Let You Cry/I'm Gonna Change Everything	1966	6.00
❑ 1659	Buon Natale (Means Merry Christmas To You)/Christmas	1966	6.00
—"Silver Spotlight Series"			
❑ 50059	Love Me Love/Lusingame	1966	6.00
❑ 50064	This Planet Earth/Who Can Say (Africa Addio)	1966	6.00
❑ 50179	There Must Be a Way/I'm Yours to Command	1967	6.00
❑ 50217	Walkin' My Baby Back Home/All the Time	1967	6.00
❑ 50234	I Don't Want to Walk Without You/Please Believe Me	1967	6.00
❑ 50273	Bella/O Surdato 'Enammurato	1968	6.00
❑ 50287	Get Out of My Heart/Oh What It Seemed to Be	1968	6.00
❑ 50480	My Heart Cries for You/Why Did You Leave Me	1969	5.00
❑ 50490	Buona Sera, Mrs. Campbell/I'll Take Care of You	1969	5.00
❑ 50496	Buona Sera, Mrs. Campbell (Italian)/Te Purtavo Na Rosa	1969	8.00
❑ 50546	E Rose Parlano/Senza Mamma E Inamurata	1969	5.00
❑ 50624	I'm Coming Home, Los Angeles/Angelina	1970	5.00

Albums

UNITED ARTISTS

Number	Title (A Side/B Side)	Yr	NM
❑ UXS-83 [(2)]	Jimmy Roselli Superpak	1972	15.00
❑ UAL-3429 [M]	Life & Love Italian Style	1965	12.00
❑ UAL-3430 [M]	Mala Femmina	1965	12.00
❑ UAL-3438 [M]	The Great Ones!	1965	12.00
❑ UAL-3451 [M]	Saloon Songs	1966	12.00
❑ UAL-3467 [M]	New York: My Port of Call	1966	12.00
❑ UAL 3539 [M]	The Christmas Album	1966	12.00
❑ UAL-3544 [M]	The Italian Album	1966	12.00
❑ UAL-3564 [M]	Sold Out	1967	12.00
❑ UAL-3585 [M]	Saloon Songs, Vol. 2	1967	12.00
❑ UAL-3611 [M]	There Must Be a Way	1967	15.00
❑ UAS-5641	Simmo 'e Napule	1972	15.00
❑ UAS-6429 [S]	Life & Love Italian Style	1965	15.00
❑ UAS-6430 [S]	Mala Femmina	1965	15.00
❑ UAS-6438 [S]	The Great Ones!	1965	15.00
❑ UAS-6451 [S]	Saloon Songs	1966	15.00
❑ UAS-6467 [S]	New York: My Port of Call	1966	15.00
❑ UAS 6539 [S]	The Christmas Album	1966	15.00
❑ UAS-6544 [S]	The Italian Album	1966	15.00
❑ UAS-6564 [S]	Sold Out	1967	15.00
❑ UAS-6585 [S]	Saloon Songs, Vol. 2	1967	15.00
❑ UAS-6611 [S]	There Must Be a Way	1967	15.00
❑ UAS-6635	Core Napulitano	1968	15.00
❑ UAS-6645	The Best of Jimmy Roselli	1968	15.00
❑ UAS-6665	3 A.M.	1968	12.00
❑ UAS-6698	Core Spezzato	1969	15.00
❑ UAS-6724	Let Me Sing	1969	12.00
❑ UAS-6747	It's Been Swell	1970	12.00
❑ UAS-6775	I'te Voglio Bene Assale	1970	12.00

ROSES, THE

45s

DOT

Number	Title (A Side/B Side)	Yr	NM
❑ 15816	Almost Paradise/I Kissed An Angel	1958	25.00

ROSIE AND THE ORIGINALS

45s

BRUNSWICK

Number	Title (A Side/B Side)	Yr	NM
❑ 55205	Lonely Blue Nights/We'll Have a Chance	1961	25.00
—By "Rosie, formerly with the Originals"			
❑ 55212	My Darling Forever/The Time Is Near	1961	25.00
—By "Rosie, formerly with the Originals"			

ERA BACK TO BACK HITS

Number	Title (A Side/B Side)	Yr	NM
❑ 038	Angel Baby/Bumble Boogie	197?	6.00
—B-side by B. Bumble and the Stingers			

HIGHLAND

Number	Title (A Side/B Side)	Yr	NM
❑ 1011	Angel Baby/Give Me Love	1960	25.00
❑ 1025	Why Did You Leave Me/Angel from Above	196?	20.00
❑ 1032	Lonely Blue Nights/We'll Have a Chance	196?	25.00
—Actually a reissue of Brunswick 55205, but harder to find			

Albums

BRUNSWICK

Number	Title (A Side/B Side)	Yr	NM
❑ BL 54102 [M]	Lonely Blue Nights with Rosie	1961	150.00
❑ BL 754102 [S]	Lonely Blue Nights with Rosie	1961	200.00

ROSS, DIANA

Also see THE SUPREMES.

12-Inch Singles

MCA

Number	Title (A Side/B Side)	Yr	NM
❑ L33-1801 [DJ]	Ease On Down the Road (6:02) (same on both sides)	1978	60.00
—With Michael Jackson			

MOTOWN

Number	Title (A Side/B Side)	Yr	NM
❑ M 00010D1	Your Love Is So Good for Me (6:32)/I Can't Go On Living Without Your Love (4:32)	1978	25.00
—B-side by Thelma Houston			
❑ M 00011D1	What You Gave Me (6:06)/Free Me from My Freedom-Tie Me to a Tree (Handcuff Me) (8:25)	1978	20.00
—B-side by Bonnie Pointer			
❑ PR-16 [DJ]	Love Hangover (7:49)/I Want You (Vocal 4:33) (Instrumental 4:36)	1976	200.00
—B-side by Marvin Gaye on Tamla label			
❑ M 00026D1	The Boss (Remix 7:23)/Lovin', Livin' and Givin' (5:11)	1979	15.00
❑ PR 42 [DJ]	What You Gave Me (6:06) (same on both sides)	1978	15.00
❑ PR 54 [DJ]	It's My House//No One Gets the Prize/The Boss	1979	20.00
—No label name on label			
❑ PR 72 [DJ]	Upside Down (4:05)/Big Time (6:27)	1980	50.00
—No label name on label; B-side by Rick James			
❑ PR-75 [DJ]	I'm Coming Out (5:23)//Rock and Roll Me (3:38)/Shake It Lady (3:09)	1980	50.00
—No label name on label; first song on B-side by Mira Waters; second song on B-side by Legend			
❑ P12-1008 [DJ]	You're Gonna Love It (6 versions)	1991	8.00
❑ 37463 1011 1	Waiting in the Wings (LP Version) (Remix Edit) (Extended)	1992	20.00
❑ P12-1014 [DJ]	You're Gonna Love It (E-Smoove's Groovy Radio Edit 4:51) (E-Smoove's Groovy Remix 6:20) (E-Smoove's Groovy Instrumental 6:20)/(Underground Mix 7:29) (The Reel House Mix 6:59) (Mo's Flutestrumental 7:10)	1991	8.00
❑ 37463 1212 1	The Boss (EP Version) (Radio Edit) (BYC Mix)/I'm Coming Out (EP Version (Radio Edit) (Monstrumental)	1994	20.00
❑ 37463 1322 1	Take Me Higher (6 versions)	1995	12.00
❑ 37463 1379 1	If You're Not Gonna Love Me Right (4 versions)	1996	12.00
❑ 37463 1392 1	Voice of the Heart/If You're Not Gonna Love Me Right	1996	10.00
❑ U8P-1519 [DJ]	Until We Meet Again (4 versions)	1999	12.00
❑ L33-1643 [DJ]	When You Tell Me That You Love Me (same on both sides)	1991	12.00
❑ 37463 3001 1	I Will Survive (12" Vocal Mix) (LP Version) (7" Vocal Mix) (12" Instrumental) (7" Acapella)	1997	15.00
❑ MOT-4632	Love Hangover '89 (12" Version) (Urban Remix) (Dance Mix)	1989	8.00
❑ MOT-4639	Workin' Overtime (3 versions)	1989	10.00

R

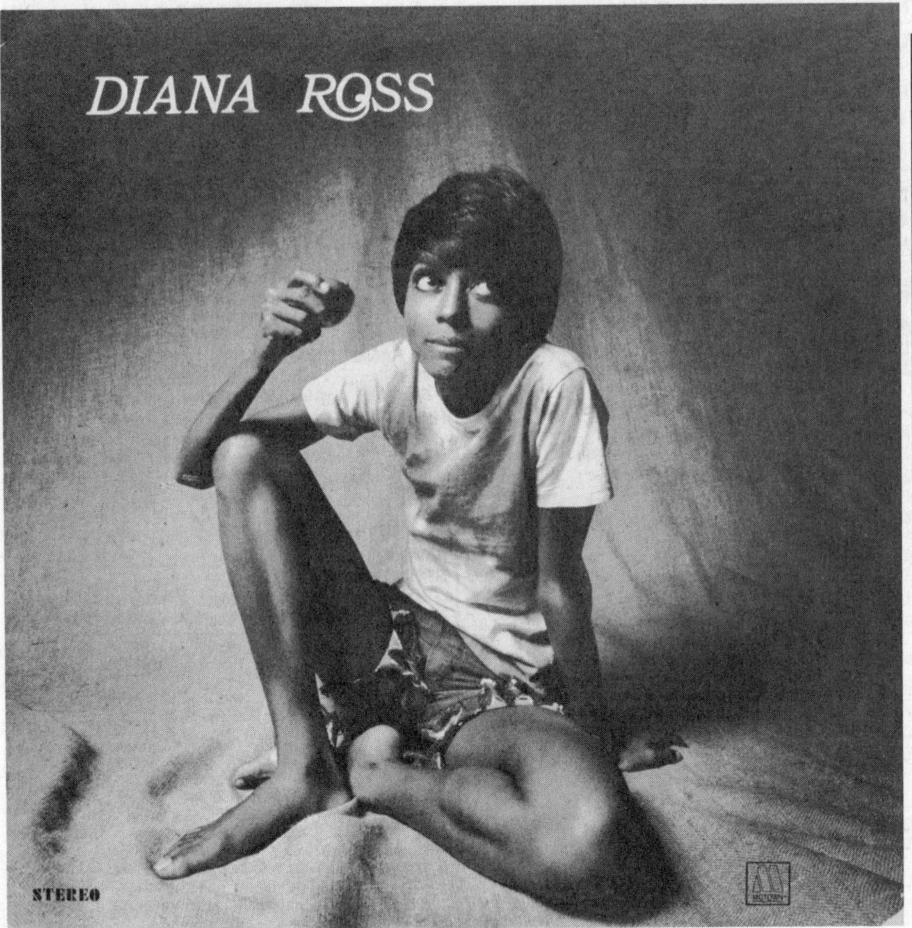

Diana Ross, *Diana Ross*, Motown MS 711, 1970, **$15.**

Number	Title (A Side/B Side)	Yr	NM
❑ MOT-4678	Bottom Line (3 versions)	1989	8.00
❑ 37463 4812 1	You're Gonna Love It (4 versions)	1991	6.00
❑ L33-17770 [DJ]	Love Hangover '89 (5 versions)	1989	8.00
❑ L33-17827 [DJ]	Workin' Overtime (6 versions)	1989	8.00
❑ L33-17909 [DJ]	Paradise (Club Mix 7:45) (Dub Mix 8:08) (7" Version 3:58)	1989	10.00
❑ L33-17963 [DJ]	This House (4:20) (5:34)	1989	8.00
❑ L33-18048 [DJ]	Bottom Line (7" Remix) (Extended Remix) (LP Version) (Instrumental)	1989	8.00
❑ 56266	Until We Meet Again (4 versions)	1999	8.00
RCA			
❑ 6416-1-RD	Dirty Looks (Remix Version 7:43) (Bonus Beats) (Instrumental Version 5:51)	1987	10.00
❑ PD-13022	Mirror, Mirror (6:06)/ Sweet Nothings	1981	15.00
❑ PD-13202	Work That Body (6:32)/ Two Can Make It	1982	12.00
❑ PD-13382	Muscles (6:38)/I Am Me	1982	10.00
❑ PD-13568	Pieces of Ice (7:19)/ (Instrumental)	1983	10.00
❑ PD-13625	Up Front (Special Club Remix 6:56)/Love or Loneliness	1983	15.00
❑ PD-13672	Let's Go Up/Girls	1983	10.00
❑ JD-13865 [DJ]	Swept Away (Long Version 7:37)/(Shorter Version 5:20)	1984	15.00
❑ PD-13865	Swept Away (Long Version 7:37)/(Instrumental 7:14)	1984	10.00
❑ JR-14033 [DJ]	Telephone (4:08) (same on both sides)	1985	12.00
❑ JD-14183 [DJ]	Eaten Alive (Extended Version 5:51)/(Instrumental 5:51)	1985	10.00
—White label, different prefix from stock copy			
❑ PD-14183	Eaten Alive (Extended Version 5:51)/(Instrumental 5:51)	1985	10.00
❑ JD-14245 [DJ]	Chain Reaction (3:47) (same on both sides)	1985	10.00
❑ JR-14267 [DJ]	Chain Reaction (6:52) (same on both sides)	1985	8.00
❑ PD-14267	Chain Reaction (6:52)/ More and More	1985	10.00

Number	Title (A Side/B Side)	Yr	NM
45s			
MCA			
❑ 40947	Ease On Down the Road/ Poppy Girls	1978	5.00
—With Michael Jackson; B-side by Quincy Jones			
❑ 40947 [PS]	Ease On Down the Road/ Poppy Girls	1978	5.00
—With Michael Jackson			
❑ 53448	If We Hold On Together/ (Instrumental)	1988	3.00
❑ 53448 [PS]	If We Hold On Together/ (Instrumental)	1988	3.00
MOTOWN			
❑ (no #) [PS]	Diana Ross TV Special 4/8/71	1971	8.00
—Special sleeve issued with some Motown (usually Diana Ross) 45s in March and April 1971			
❑ 1165	Reach Out and Touch (Somebody's Hand)/ Dark Side of the World	1970	5.00
❑ 1165 [PS]	Reach Out and Touch (Somebody's Hand)/ Dark Side of the World	1970	12.00
❑ 1169	Ain't No Mountain High Enough/ Can't It Wait Until Tomorrow	1970	5.00
❑ 1169 [PS]	Ain't No Mountain High Enough/ Can't It Wait Until Tomorrow	1970	12.00
❑ 1176	Remember Me/What About You	1971	5.00
❑ 1176 [PS]	Remember Me/What About You	1971	12.00
❑ 1184	Reach Out I'll Be There/ Close to You	1971	5.00
❑ 1188	Surrender/I'm a Winner	1971	5.00
❑ 1192	I'm Still Waiting/A Simple Thing Like Cry	1971	5.00
❑ 1211	Good Morning Heartache/ God Bless the Child	1972	5.00
❑ 1211 [PS]	Good Morning Heartache/ God Bless the Child	1972	10.00
❑ 1239	Touch Me in the Morning/I Won't Last a Day Without You	1973	5.00
❑ 1278	Last Time I Saw Him/ Save the Children	1973	5.00
❑ 1295	Sleepin'/You	1974	5.00

Number	Title (A Side/B Side)	Yr	NM
❑ 1335	Sorry Doesn't Always Make It Right/Together	1975	5.00
❑ 1335 [PS]	Sorry Doesn't Always Make It Right/Together	1975	12.00
❑ 1377	Theme from Mahogany (Do You Know Where You're Going To)/ No One's Gonna Be a Fool Forever	1975	5.00
❑ 1377	Do You Know Where You're Going To/No One's Gonna Be a Fool Forever	1975	12.00
—Possibly Canadian release only, with different A-side title			
❑ 1377 [PS]	Theme from Mahogany (Do You Know Where You're Going To)/No One's Gonna Be a Fool Forever	1975	20.00
❑ 1387	I Thought It Took a Little Time (But Today I Fell in Love)/ After You	1976	5.00
❑ 1387 [PS]	I Thought It Took a Little Time (But Today I Fell in Love)/ After You	1976	10.00
❑ 1392	Love Hangover/Kiss Me Now	1976	5.00
❑ 1398	One Love in My Lifetime/Smile	1976	5.00
❑ 1427	Gettin' Ready for Love/ Confide in Me	1977	5.00
❑ 1436	Your Love Is So Good for Me/ Baby It's Me	1978	5.00
❑ 1442	You Got It/Too Shy to Say	1978	5.00
❑ 1449 [DJ]	Top of the World (same on both sides)	1978	50.00
—Promo only; withdrawn before stock copies were pressed			
❑ 1450	Lovin' Livin' and Givin'/ Baby It's Me	1978	—
—Unreleased			
❑ 1456	What You Gave Me/Together	1979	4.00
❑ 1462	The Boss/I'm in the World	1979	4.00
❑ 1471	It's My House/Sparkle	1979	4.00
❑ 1491	I'm Coming Out/Give Up	1980	4.00
❑ 1494	Upside Down/Friend to Friend	1980	4.00
❑ 1496	It's My Turn/Together	1980	4.00
❑ 1496 [PS]	It's My Turn/Together	1980	12.00
❑ 1508	One More Chance/After You	1981	4.00
❑ 1513	To Love Again/Crying My Heart Out for You	1981	4.00
❑ 1519	Endless Love/(Instrumental)	1981	4.00
—With Lionel Richie			
❑ 1531	My Old Piano/Now That You're Gone	1981	4.00
❑ 1626	We Can Never Light That Old Flame Again/Old Funky Rolls	1982	4.00
❑ 1964	Workin' Overtime/(Instrumental)	1989	3.00
❑ 1964 [PS]	Workin' Overtime/(Instrumental)	1989	3.00
❑ 1998	This House/Paradise	1989	3.00
❑ 2003	Bottom Line/(Instrumental)	1989	3.00
❑ 2139	When You Tell Me That You Love Me/You and I	1991	4.00
❑ S45-17886 [DJ]	Workin' Overtime (4:18) (same on both sides)	1989	10.00
RCA			
❑ 5172-7-R	Dirty Looks/So Close	1987	3.00
❑ 5172-7-R [PS]	Dirty Looks/So Close	1987	3.00
❑ 5297-7-R	Tell Me Again/I Am Me	1987	3.00
❑ 5297-7-R [PS]	Tell Me Again/I Am Me	1987	3.00
❑ PB-12349	Why Do Fools Fall in Love/ Think I'm in Love	1981	4.00
❑ JB-13013 [DJ]	Endless Love (Long)/(Short)	1981	12.00
—Promo only			
❑ PB-13021	Mirror, Mirror/Sweet Nothings	1981	4.00
❑ PB-13201	Work That Body/You Can Make It	1982	4.00
❑ PB-13348	Muscles/I Am Me	1982	4.00
❑ PB-13348 [PS]	Muscles/I Am Me	1982	4.00
❑ PB-13424	So Close/Fool for Your Love	1983	4.00
❑ GB-13479	Why Do Fools Fall in Love/ Mirror, Mirror	1983	3.00
—Gold Standard Series			
❑ PB-13549	Pieces of Ice/Still in Love	1983	4.00
❑ PB-13549 [PS]	Pieces of Ice/Still in Love	1983	4.00
❑ PB-13624	Up Front/Love or Loneliness	1983	4.00
❑ PB-13671	Let's Go Up/Girls	1983	4.00
❑ GB-13798	Muscles/Pieces of Ice	1984	3.00
—Gold Standard Series			
❑ PB-13864	Swept Away/Fight for It	1984	3.00
❑ PB-13864 [PS]	Swept Away/Fight for It	1984	3.00
❑ PB-13966	Missing You/We Are the Children of the World	1984	3.00
❑ PB-13966 [PS]	Missing You/We Are the Children of the World	1984	3.00
❑ PB-14032	Telephone/Fool for Your Love	1985	3.00
❑ PB-14032 [PS]	Telephone/Fool for Your Love	1985	3.00
❑ PB-14181	Eaten Alive/(Instrumental)	1985	3.00
❑ PB-14181 [PS]	Eaten Alive/(Instrumental)	1985	3.00
❑ PB-14244	Chain Reaction/More and More	1985	4.00
❑ PB-14244	Chain Reaction (Special New Mix)/More and More	1986	3.00
❑ PB-14244 [PS]	Chain Reaction/More and More	1985	3.00
❑ GB-14342	Missing You/Swept Away	1986	3.00
—Gold Standard Series			

Except when noted otherwise, VG = 25% of NM, and VG+ = 50% of NM. (Example: VG = $2.00, VG+ = $4.00 and NM = $8.00.)

7-Inch Extended Plays

MOTOWN

Number	Title (A Side/B Side)	Yr	NM
❑ M 60724	My Place/Baby It's Love/The Long and Winding Road//How About You/I'm Still Waiting/Everything Is Everything	1970	12.00

—Jukebox issue; small hole, plays at 33 1/3 rpm

Number	Title (A Side/B Side)	Yr	NM
❑ M 60724 [PS]	Everything Is Everything	1970	12.00

—Part of "Little LP" series (LLP #133)

Albums

MOTOWN

Number	Title (A Side/B Side)	Yr	NM
❑ M5-135V1	Diana Ross	1981	8.00
—Reissue of 711			
❑ M5-155V1	Diana!	1981	8.00
—Reissue of 719			
❑ M5-163V1	Touch Me in the Morning	1981	8.00
—Reissue of 772			
❑ M5-169V1	Diana Ross Live at Caesars Palace	1981	8.00
—Reissue of 801			
❑ M5-198V1	The Boss	1981	8.00
—Reissue of 923			
❑ M5-214V1	Duets with Diana	1981	10.00
❑ MS-711	Diana Ross	1970	15.00
❑ MS-719	Diana!	1971	15.00
❑ MS-723	Surrender	1971	15.00
❑ MS-724	Everything Is Everything	1970	15.00
❑ M-758D [(2)]	Lady Sings the Blues	1972	15.00
—With booklet; all but four tracks are by Diana Ross			
❑ M-772L	Touch Me in the Morning	1973	15.00
❑ M6-801S1	Diana Ross Live at Caesars Palace	1974	12.00
❑ M7-812V1	Last Time I Saw Him	1974	12.00
❑ M6-861S1	Diana Ross	1976	12.00
❑ M6-869S1	Diana Ross' Greatest Hits	1976	12.00
❑ M7-877R2 [(2)]	An Evening with Diana Ross	1977	15.00
❑ M7-890R1	Baby It's Me	1977	12.00
❑ M7-907R1	Ross	1978	12.00
❑ M8-923M1	The Boss	1979	10.00
❑ M8-936	Diana	1980	10.00
❑ M8-951M1	To Love Again	1981	10.00
❑ M13-960C2 [(2)]	All the Great Hits	1981	12.00
❑ 5294 ML	Diana Ross	1983	8.00
—Reissue of 861			
❑ 6049 ML2 [(2)]	Diana Ross Anthology	1983	15.00
❑ MOT-6274	Workin' Overtime	1989	10.00
❑ 37463-6377-1	The Remixes	1994	12.00

NAUTILUS

Number	Title (A Side/B Side)	Yr	NM
❑ NR-37	Diana	1981	40.00

—Audiophile vinyl

RCA VICTOR

Number	Title (A Side/B Side)	Yr	NM
❑ AFL1-4153	Why Do Fools Fall in Love	1981	10.00
❑ AFL1-4384	Silk Electric	1982	10.00
❑ AFL1-4677	Ross	1983	8.00
❑ AFL1-5009	Swept Away	1984	8.00
❑ AYL1-5162	Why Do Fools Fall in Love	1985	6.00
—"Best Buy Series" reissue			
❑ AFL1-5422	Eaten Alive	1985	8.00
❑ 6388-1-R	Red Hot Rhythm and Blues	1987	8.00

ROSS, DIANA, AND MARVIN GAYE
Also see each artist's individual listings.

45s

MOTOWN

Number	Title (A Side/B Side)	Yr	NM
❑ 1269	My Mistake (Was to Love You)/Include Me in Your Life	1973	5.00
❑ 1280	You're a Special Part of Me/I'm Falling in Love with You	1973	5.00
❑ 1296	Don't Knock My Love/Just Say Just Say	1974	5.00

Albums

MOTOWN

Number	Title (A Side/B Side)	Yr	NM
❑ M5-124V1	Diana & Marvin	1981	8.00
—Reissue			
❑ M7-803	Diana & Marvin	1973	15.00

ROSS, DIANA; MARVIN GAYE; SMOKEY ROBINSON; AND STEVIE WONDER
Also see each artist's individual listings.

12-Inch Singles

MOTOWN

Number	Title (A Side/B Side)	Yr	NM
❑ M00015 D1	Pops, We Love You (6:32) (same on both sides)	1979	12.00

45s

MOTOWN

Number	Title (A Side/B Side)	Yr	NM
❑ 1455	Pops, We Love You/(Instrumental)	1979	4.00
—Later version is 3:30 and has no monologue			
❑ 1455	Pops, We Love You/(Instrumental)	1979	8.00
—Original version is 3:59 and has a monologue by Diana Ross			
❑ 1455 [DJ]	Pops, We Love You (same on both sides)	1979	10.00
—Original version is 3:59 and has a monologue by Diana Ross			
❑ M9-1455	Pops, We Love You/(Instrumental)	1979	15.00
—Heart-shaped red vinyl record in plastic sleeve			

ROSS, DIANA, AND THE SUPREMES
See THE SUPREMES.

ROSS, JACKIE

45s

BRUNSWICK

Number	Title (A Side/B Side)	Yr	NM
❑ 55325	Keep Your Chin Up/Love Is Easy to Lose	1967	8.00
❑ 55361	Mr. Sunshine/Walk on My Side	1968	8.00

CAPITOL

Number	Title (A Side/B Side)	Yr	NM
❑ 4308	I Can't Stand to See You Go/Ain't No Fun to Me	1976	4.00

CHESS

Number	Title (A Side/B Side)	Yr	NM
❑ 1903	Selfish One/Everything But Love	1964	8.00
❑ 1913	I've Got the Skill/Change Your Ways	1964	8.00
❑ 1915	Haste Makes Waste/Wasting Time	1964	8.00
❑ 1920	Jerk and Twine/New Lover	1965	8.00
❑ 1929	You Really Know How to Hurt a Girl/Dynamite Lovin'	1965	8.00
❑ 1938	Take Me for a Little While/Honey Dear	1965	8.00
❑ 1940	We Can Do It/Honey Dear	1965	8.00

GSF

Number	Title (A Side/B Side)	Yr	NM
❑ 6886	Woman Get Nothing from Love/Do I	1972	5.00
❑ 6895	A One Woman Man/Take the Weight Off Me	1973	5.00

MERCURY

Number	Title (A Side/B Side)	Yr	NM
❑ 73041	Angel of the Morning/Showcase	1970	6.00
❑ 73185	Glory Be/I Must Give You Time	1971	6.00

SAR

Number	Title (A Side/B Side)	Yr	NM
❑ 129	Hard Times/Hold Me	1962	15.00

—As "Jacki Ross"

SCEPTER

Number	Title (A Side/B Side)	Yr	NM
❑ 12345	The World's in a Hell of a Shape/What Would You Give	1972	5.00

Albums

CHESS

Number	Title (A Side/B Side)	Yr	NM
❑ LP-1489 [M]	In Full Bloom	1966	30.00
❑ LPS-1489 [S]	In Full Bloom	1966	40.00

ROSSINI, TONI

45s

SUN

Number	Title (A Side/B Side)	Yr	NM
❑ 349	I Gotta Know/Is It Too Late	1960	20.00
❑ 366	Well I Ask Ya/Darlena	1961	20.00
❑ 378	Meet Me After School/Just Around the Corner	1962	20.00
❑ 380	New Girl in Town/You Made It Sound So Easy	1962	20.00
❑ 387	Nobody/Moved to Kansas City	1964	20.00

ROTARY CONNECTION
Also see MINNIE RIPERTON.

45s

CADET CONCEPT

Number	Title (A Side/B Side)	Yr	NM
❑ DJ-1 [DJ]	Lady Jane/Amen	1968	15.00
❑ 7000	Like a Rollin' Stone/Turn Me On	1967	10.00
❑ 7002	Ruby Tuesday/Soul Man	1968	10.00
❑ 7007	Paper Castle/Teach Me How to Fly	1968	10.00
❑ 7008	Aladdin/Magical World	1968	10.00
❑ 7009	Silent Night Chant/Peace At Least	1968	12.00
❑ 7014	The Weight/Respect	1969	10.00
❑ 7018	Want You to Know/Memory Band	1969	10.00
❑ 7021	Love Me Now/May Our Amens Be True	1970	10.00
❑ 7027	Stormy Monday Blues/Teach Me How to Fly	1970	10.00
❑ 7028	Hey Love/If I Sing My Song	1971	10.00

—As "New Rotary Connection"

JANUS

Number	Title (A Side/B Side)	Yr	NM
❑ 249	Living Alone/Magical World	1975	5.00

—As "Minnie Riperton and Rotary Connection"

Albums

CADET

Number	Title (A Side/B Side)	Yr	NM
❑ CS-50006	Hey Love	1971	20.00

CADET CONCEPT

Number	Title (A Side/B Side)	Yr	NM
❑ LP-312 [M]	Rotary Connection	1968	60.00
—Mono appears to be promo only			
❑ LPS-312 [S]	Rotary Connection	1968	25.00
❑ LPS-317	Aladdin	1968	25.00
❑ LPS 318	Peace	1969	20.00
❑ LPS-322	Songs	1969	25.00
❑ LSP-328	Dinner Music	1970	25.00

ROTATIONS, THE (1)

45s

FRANTIC

Number	Title (A Side/B Side)	Yr	NM
❑ 200	Put a Nickel on D-9 (Pt. 1)/Put a Nickel on D-9 (Pt. 2)	1965	150.00
❑ 202	Changed Man/Heartaches	1967	100.00

MALA

Number	Title (A Side/B Side)	Yr	NM
❑ 576	Misty Roses/Trying to Make You My Own	1967	30.00

ROTATIONS, THE (2)

45s

ORIGINAL SOUND

Number	Title (A Side/B Side)	Yr	NM
❑ 41	The Crusher/Heavies	1964	100.00

—Produced by FRANK ZAPPA

ROTH, DAVID LEE
Also see VAN HALEN.

12-Inch Singles

WARNER BROS.

Number	Title (A Side/B Side)	Yr	NM
❑ PRO-A-2235 [DJ]	California Girls (same on both sides)	1985	12.00
❑ PRO-A-2277 [DJ]	Just a Gigolo/I Ain't Got Nobody (Medley) (same on both sides)	1985	15.00
❑ PRO-A-2513 [DJ]	Yankee Rose (same on both sides)	1986	8.00
❑ PRO-A-2547 [DJ]	Tobacco Road (same on both sides)	1986	12.00
❑ PRO-A-2564 [DJ]	Goin' Crazy! (same on both sides)	1986	10.00
❑ PRO-A-2619 [DJ]	That's Life/Bump and Grind	1986	10.00
❑ PRO-A-2919 [DJ]	Just Like Paradise (same on both sides)	1988	8.00
❑ PRO-A-3133 [DJ]	Stand Up (Extended Edit: The Long 1!) (Swank Remix: E.Z. to Swallow)	1988	8.00

45s

WARNER BROS.

Number	Title (A Side/B Side)	Yr	NM
❑ 27825	Damn Good/Skyscraper	1988	3.00
❑ 27825 [PS]	Damn Good/Skyscraper	1988	3.00
❑ 28108	Stand Up/Knucklebones	1988	3.00
❑ 28108 [PS]	Stand Up/Knucklebones	1988	3.00
❑ 28119	Just Like Paradise/Bottom Line	1988	3.00
❑ 28119 [PS]	Just Like Paradise/Bottom Line	1988	3.00
❑ 28511	That's Life/Bump and Grind	1986	3.00
❑ 28511 [PS]	That's Life/Bump and Grind	1986	3.00
❑ 28584	Goin' Crazy!/Loco Del Calor!	1986	3.00
❑ 28584 [PS]	Goin' Crazy!/Loco Del Calor!	1986	3.00
❑ 28656	Yankee Rose/Shyboy	1986	3.00
❑ 28656 [PS]	Yankee Rose/Shyboy	1986	3.00
❑ 29040	Just a Gigolo-I Ain't Got Nobody/Just a Gigolo-I Ain't Got Nobody	1985	3.00
❑ 29040 [PS]	Just a Gigolo-I Ain't Got Nobody/Just a Gigolo-I Ain't Got Nobody	1985	3.00
❑ 29102	California Girls/California Girls (Remix)	1985	3.00
❑ 29102 [PS]	California Girls/California Girls (Remix)	1985	3.00

Albums

WARNER BROS.

Number	Title (A Side/B Side)	Yr	NM
❑ 25222 [EP]	Crazy from the Heat	1985	6.00
❑ 25470	Eat 'Em and Smile	1986	8.00
❑ 25671	Skyscraper	1988	8.00
❑ 26477	A Little Ain't Enough	1991	15.00

ROULETTES, THE
More than one group.

45s

ANGLE

Number	Title (A Side/B Side)	Yr	NM
❑ 1001	Surfer's Charge/Archibald II (Duke of Nothing)	1963	50.00

CHAMP

Number	Title (A Side/B Side)	Yr	NM
❑ 102	I See a Star/Come On, Baby	1958	80.00

EBB

Number	Title (A Side/B Side)	Yr	NM
❑ 124	The Way You Carry On/You Don't Care Anymore	1957	30.00

LOST-NITE

Number	Title (A Side/B Side)	Yr	NM
❑ 233	I See a Star/Come On, Baby	196?	5.00

—Reissue

SCEPTER

Number	Title (A Side/B Side)	Yr	NM
❑ 1204	Hasten Jason/Wouldn't It Be Goin' Steady	1959	600.00

UNITED ARTISTS

Number	Title (A Side/B Side)	Yr	NM
❑ 718	Can You Go/Soon You'll Be Leaving Me	1964	20.00
❑ 990	Long Cigarette/Junk	1966	10.00

ROUND, JONATHAN

45s

WESTBOUND

Number	Title (A Side/B Side)	Yr	NM
❑ 186	Don't It Make You Want to Go Home/Train a-Comin'	1971	8.00
❑ 199	Sympathy for the Devil/Travelin' Mama Blues	1972	10.00

Albums

WESTBOUND

Number	Title (A Side/B Side)	Yr	NM
❑ 2009	Jonathan Round	1971	30.00
—Round cover			
❑ 2009	Jonathan Round	1972	15.00
—Square cover			

ROUND ROBIN

45s

CAPITOL

Number	Title (A Side/B Side)	Yr	NM
❑ 5962	Ton of Joy/Vulture	1967	12.00

DOMAIN

Number	Title (A Side/B Side)	Yr	NM
❑ 1019	Do the Slauson/Slauson Shuffle Time	1963	15.00
❑ 1400	Do the Slauson/Slauson Shuffle Time	1963	15.00
❑ 1402	Slauson Town/Malloy, The Engineer	1963	15.00
❑ 1405	The Roundest of Them All/8069 Vineland	1964	15.00
❑ 1406	I Know/Giddyap Kick	1964	15.00
❑ 1407	Don't Let Go/Up and Down	1964	15.00
❑ 1420	Land of 1000 Dances/Yea Yea	1965	12.00
❑ 1422	Sit and Dance/Little People	1965	12.00
❑ 1424	I'm the Wolfman/Sit and Dance	1965	12.00

ROUTERS, THE

45s

MERCURY

Number	Title (A Side/B Side)	Yr	NM
❑ 73418	Superbird/Sack of Woe	1973	6.00

WARNER BROS.

Number	Title (A Side/B Side)	Yr	NM
❑ 5283	Let's Go (pony)/Mashy	1962	15.00
❑ 5332	Half Time/Make It Snappy	1963	12.00
❑ 5349	Sting Ray/Snap Happy	1963	12.00
❑ 5379	A-Ooga/Big Band	1963	12.00
❑ 5403	Snap, Crackle and Pop/Amoeba	1963	12.00
❑ 5444	Crack Up/Let's Dance	1964	12.00
❑ 5467	Stamp and Shake/Ah-Ya	1964	12.00
❑ 7117	Let's Go (pony)/Mashy	1967	10.00

Albums

WARNER BROS.

Number	Title (A Side/B Side)	Yr	NM
❑ W 1490 [M]	Let's Go! with the Routers	1963	25.00
❑ WS 1490 [S]	Let's Go! with the Routers	1963	30.00
❑ W 1524 [M]	1963's Great Instrumental Hits	1964	30.00
❑ WS 1524 [S]	1963's Great Instrumental Hits	1964	40.00
❑ W 1559 [M]	Charge!	1964	25.00
❑ WS 1559 [S]	Charge!	1964	30.00
❑ W 1595 [M]	Go Go Go with the Chuck Berry Songbook	1965	20.00
❑ WS 1595 [S]	Go Go Go with the Chuck Berry Songbook	1965	25.00

ROUZAN SISTERS, THE

45s

FRISCO

Number	Title (A Side/B Side)	Yr	NM
❑ 113	Men of War/Dance Every Dance	1965	10.00

ROVA

Albums

BLACK SAINT

Number	Title (A Side/B Side)	Yr	NM
❑ BSR-0076	Rova Plays Lacy — Favorite Street	1984	12.00
❑ 120126	Beat Kennel	1987	12.00

HAT ART

Number	Title (A Side/B Side)	Yr	NM
❑ 2013 [(2)]	Saxophone Diplomacy	1986	15.00
❑ 2032 [(2)]	The Crowd	198?	15.00

METALANGUAGE

Number	Title (A Side/B Side)	Yr	NM
❑ (# unknown)	Daredevils	1979	20.00
❑ 101	Cinema Rovate	1978	20.00
❑ 106	The Removal of Secrecy	1979	20.00
❑ 118	As Was	1981	15.00

ROVER BOYS, THE

45s

ABC-PARAMOUNT

Number	Title (A Side/B Side)	Yr	NM
❑ 9659	Come to Me/Love Me Again	1955	15.00
❑ 9678	My Queen/Sixteen Teens	1956	15.00
❑ 9700	Graduation Day/I Hear Music	1956	15.00
❑ 9732	From a School Ring to a Wedding Ring/Young Love	1956	15.00
❑ 9760	The Piano Tuner/Whoop Doodly Baby	1956	15.00
❑ 9779	Little Did I Know/Again and Again	1957	15.00

CORAL

Number	Title (A Side/B Side)	Yr	NM
❑ 61271	Show Me/You've Got It	1954	20.00

DECCA

Number	Title (A Side/B Side)	Yr	NM
❑ 31485	Shalom/I Hear Havana	1963	8.00

RCA VICTOR

Number	Title (A Side/B Side)	Yr	NM
❑ 47-7432	Magic Lamp/Little Darlin'	1959	12.00
❑ 47-7482	Sweet Violets/Julia	1959	12.00

UNITED ARTISTS

Number	Title (A Side/B Side)	Yr	NM
❑ 288	Is It Me/Marry Young	1961	10.00
❑ 331	For Every Boy or Girl/If You Plant a Little Kiss	1961	10.00

VIK

Number	Title (A Side/B Side)	Yr	NM
❑ 0283	Soft Sands/My Baby's Steppin' Out	1957	20.00
❑ 0302	What Can I Do for a Heartache/I Got to You	1957	20.00
❑ 0313	Blue Willow/You're My Everything	1958	20.00
❑ 0317	Blind Date/Make Room for Me	1958	20.00
❑ 0338	S'Agapo/Ask Me Who Loves You	1958	20.00

ROVERS, THE (1)

45s

CAPITOL

Number	Title (A Side/B Side)	Yr	NM
❑ F3078	Why Oh-h/Ichi-Bon Tami Dachi	1955	50.00

MUSIC CITY

Number	Title (A Side/B Side)	Yr	NM
❑ 750	Why Oh-h/Ichi-Bon Tami Dachi	1954	80.00
—Black vinyl			
❑ 750	Why Oh-h/Ichi-Bon Tami Dachi	1954	250.00
—Red vinyl			
❑ 780	Salute to Johnny Ace/Jadda	1955	80.00
—Black vinyl			
❑ 780	Salute to Johnny Ace/Jadda	1955	250.00
—Red vinyl			

ROVERS, THE (2)

45s

CHATTAHOOCHIE

Number	Title (A Side/B Side)	Yr	NM
❑ 653	The Web/Can't Be the First	1964	10.00

ROVERS, THE (3)

45s

KAPP

Number	Title (A Side/B Side)	Yr	NM
❑ 278	Delia's Gone/I Know Where I'm Goin'	1959	12.00

ROVIN' KIND, THE

45s

DUNWICH

Number	Title (A Side/B Side)	Yr	NM
❑ 146	My Generation/Girl	1967	20.00
❑ 154	She/Didn't Want to Have to Do It	1967	20.00

ROULETTE

Number	Title (A Side/B Side)	Yr	NM
❑ 4687	Right on Time/Night People	1966	15.00

ROWLES, JOHN

Albums

KAPP

Number	Title (A Side/B Side)	Yr	NM
❑ KS-3597	Exciting	1969	15.00
❑ KS-3637	Cheryl Moana Marie	1971	15.00

MCA

Number	Title (A Side/B Side)	Yr	NM
❑ 549	John Rowles	197?	10.00

ROXY MUSIC

Also see BRYAN FERRY.

12-Inch Singles

WARNER BROS.

Number	Title (A Side/B Side)	Yr	NM
❑ PRO-A-1056 [DJ]	Take a Chance with Me (2 versions)/More Than This/Avalon	1982	12.00
❑ PRO-A-2033 [DJ]	More Than This/Avalon	1982	10.00

45s

ATCO

Number	Title (A Side/B Side)	Yr	NM
❑ 7018	The Thrill of It All/The Application Failed	1975	4.00
❑ 7042	Love Is the Drug/Both Ends Burning	1975	4.00
❑ 7100	Dance Away/Trash 2	1979	4.00
❑ 7204	Angel Eyes/My Little Girl	1979	4.00
❑ 7301	Over You/My Only Love	1980	4.00
❑ 7310	Oh Yeah (On the Radio)/Rain, Rain, Rain	1980	4.00
❑ 7315	In the Midnight Hour/(B-side unknown)	1980	4.00
❑ 7329	Jealous Guy/To Turn You On	1981	4.00
❑ 7329 [PS]	Jealous Guy/To Turn You On	1981	4.00

ATLANTIC OLDIES SERIES

Number	Title (A Side/B Side)	Yr	NM
❑ 13269	Love Is the Drug/Dance Away	198?	3.00
—Reissue			

REPRISE

Number	Title (A Side/B Side)	Yr	NM
❑ 1124	Virginia Plan/The Numberer	1972	10.00

WARNER BROS.

Number	Title (A Side/B Side)	Yr	NM
❑ GWB 0316	Do the Strand/Virginia Plain	197?	3.00
—"Back to Back Hits" series			
❑ 7719	Do the Strand/Editions of You	1973	10.00
❑ 29912	More Than This/Always Unknowing	1982	3.00
❑ 29978	Take a Chance with Me/India	1982	3.00
❑ 29978 [PS]	Take a Chance with Me/India	1982	4.00

Albums

ATCO

Number	Title (A Side/B Side)	Yr	NM
❑ SD 32-102	Flesh + Blood	1980	10.00
❑ SD 38-103	Greatest Hits	1977	10.00
❑ SD 36-106	Country Life	1975	25.00
—Original cover shows two semi-naked women on a grassy background			
❑ SD 36-106A	Country Life	1975	10.00
—Revised cover deletes women, leaves only the grassy background			
❑ SD 38-114	Manifesto	1979	10.00
❑ SD 38-114 [PD]	Manifesto	1979	30.00
—Picture disc			
❑ SD 36-127	Siren	1975	10.00
—Originals have yellow labels			
❑ SD 36-133	The First Roxy Music Album	1975	12.00
—Reissue of Reprise MS 2114; originals have yellow labels			
❑ SD 36-134	For Your Pleasure	1975	12.00
—Reissue of Warner Bros. BS 2696; originals have yellow labels			
❑ SD 36-139	Viva! Roxy Music (Live)	1976	10.00
—Originals have yellow labels			
❑ SD 7045	Stranded	1974	12.00
❑ 90122	The Atlantic Years (1973-80)	1983	10.00

REPRISE

Number	Title (A Side/B Side)	Yr	NM
❑ MS 2114	Roxy Music	1972	30.00
❑ 25857 [(2)]	Street Life: 20 Greatest Hits	1989	15.00
—By "Bryan Ferry & Roxy Music"			

WARNER BROS.

Number	Title (A Side/B Side)	Yr	NM
❑ BS 2696	For Your Pleasure	1973	25.00
❑ 23686	Avalon	1982	10.00
❑ 23808 [EP]	Musique — The High Road	1983	8.00

ROY C

45s

ALAGA

Number	Title (A Side/B Side)	Yr	NM
❑ 1000	In Divorce Court/I Don't Want to Worry	1970	10.00
❑ 1003	Falling in Love/I Found a Man in My Bed	1970	10.00
❑ 1005	A Merry Black Christmas/I Don't Want To Worry	1970	10.00
❑ 1006	Got to Get Enough (Of Your Sweet Love Stuff)/An Open Letter to the President	1971	10.00
❑ 1007	I Wasn't There/Those Days Are Gone	1971	10.00
❑ 1008	I'll Never Leave You Lonely/I'm Gonna Love (Somebody Else's Woman)	1972	10.00
❑ 1009	Since I Met You Baby/Lonely I Was	1972	10.00
—With Linda Caver			
❑ 1013	I Caught You in the Act/Back Into My Arms	1973	10.00
❑ 1014	Since God Made a Woman/We're On the Road to Hell	1973	10.00

BLACK HAWK

Number	Title (A Side/B Side)	Yr	NM
❑ 12101	Shotgun Wedding/I'm Gonna Make It	1965	12.00

MERCURY

Number	Title (A Side/B Side)	Yr	NM
❑ 73391	Don't Blame the Man/I'm Bustin' My Rocks	1973	6.00
❑ 73445	She Kept On Walkin'/Back Into My Arms	1973	6.00
❑ 73605	Loneliness Has Got a Hold on Me/If I Could Love You Forever	1974	5.00
❑ 73672	Love Me Till Tomorrow Comes/Virgin Girl	1975	5.00
❑ 73735	My Girl (Reggae)/The Second Time Around	1975	5.00
❑ 73780	Every Woman Has a Right/Don't Stop Short of Satisfaction	1976	5.00
❑ 73848	You Can't Judge a Man (By the Color of His Skin)/I Wanna Do It Again	1976	5.00
❑ 73981	From the Outside Looking In (He Used to Be My Friend)/After Loving You	1977	5.00

SHOUT

Number	Title (A Side/B Side)	Yr	NM
❑ 206	Gone Gone/Stop What You're Doing	1966	10.00

Except when noted otherwise, VG = 25% of NM, and VG+ = 50% of NM. (Example: VG = $2.00, VG+ = $4.00 and NM = $8.00.)

Number	Title (A Side/B Side)	Yr	NM
UPTOWN			
❑ 731	Shotgun Wedding/High School Dropout	1966	10.00
Albums			
MERCURY			
❑ SRM-1-678	Sex and Soul	1974	15.00
❑ SRM-1-1056	Nice	1976	15.00
❑ SRM-1-1192	More	1978	15.00

ROYAL, BILLY JOE

45s

Number	Title (A Side/B Side)	Yr	NM
ALL WOOD			
❑ 401	Wait for Me Baby/If It Wasn't for a Woman	1962	20.00
ATLANTIC			
❑ 2328	Never in a Hundred Years/We Haven't a Moment to Lose	1966	10.00
❑ 87770	If the Jukebox Took Teardrops/ How Could You	1991	4.00
❑ 87867	Ring Where a Ring Used to Be/ We Need to Walk	1990	4.00
❑ 87933	Searchin' for Some Kind of Clue/This Too Shall Pass	1990	4.00
❑ 88815	Till I Can't Take It Anymore/ He Don't Know	1990	4.00
ATLANTIC AMERICA			
❑ 99217	Love Has No Right/Cross My Heart and Hope to Try	1989	3.00
❑ 99217 [PS]	Love Has No Right/Cross My Heart and Hope to Try	1989	4.00
❑ 99242	Tell It Like It Is/Losing You	1989	3.00
❑ 99242 [PS]	Tell It Like It Is/Losing You	1989	4.00
❑ 99295	It Keeps Right On Hurtin'/ Let It Rain	1988	3.00
❑ 99295 [PS]	It Keeps Right On Hurtin'/ Let It Rain	1988	3.00
❑ 99364	Out of Sight and On My Mind/She Don't Cry Like She Used To	1988	3.00
❑ 99364 [PS]	Out of Sight and On My Mind/She Don't Cry Like She Used To	1988	3.00
❑ 99404	I'll Pin a Note on Your Pillow/ A Place for a Heartache	1987	3.00
❑ 99404 [PS]	I'll Pin a Note on Your Pillow/ A Place for a Heartache	1987	3.00
❑ 99485	Old Bridges Burn Slow/We've Both Got a Lot to Learn	1987	3.00
❑ 99485 [PS]	Old Bridges Burn Slow/We've Both Got a Lot to Learn	1987	3.00
❑ 99519	I Miss You Already/ Another Endless Night	1986	3.00
❑ 99555	Boardwalk Angel/Out of Sight and On My Mind	1986	3.00
❑ 99599	Burned Like a Rocket/ Lonely Loving You	1985	3.00
COLUMBIA			
❑ 43305	Down in the Boondocks/ Oh, What a Night	1965	10.00
❑ 43305 [DJ]	Down in the Boondocks (same on both sides)	1965	40.00
—Red vinyl promo			
❑ 43390	I Knew You When/Steal Away	1965	10.00
❑ 43390 [DJ]	I Knew You When (same on both sides)	1965	40.00
—Red vinyl promo			
❑ 43465	I've Got to Be Somebody/You Make Me Feel Like a Man	1965	8.00
❑ 43465 [DJ]	I've Got to Be Somebody (same on both sides)	1965	30.00
—Red vinyl promo			
❑ 43538	It's a Good Time/Don't Wait Up for Me Mama	1966	8.00
❑ 43622	Heart's Desire/Keep Inside Me	1966	8.00
❑ 43740	Campfire Girls/Should I Come Back	1966	8.00
❑ 43883	Yo-Yo/We Tried	1966	8.00
❑ 44003	Wisdom of a Fool/Everything Turned Blue	1967	8.00
❑ 44103	These Are Not My People/ The Greatest Love	1967	8.00
❑ 44277	Hush/Watching from the Bandstand	1967	8.00
❑ 44468	Don't You Be Ashamed (To Call My Name)/ Don't You Think It's Time	1968	8.00
❑ 44574	Storybook Children/Just Between You and Me	1968	8.00
❑ 44677	Movies in My Mind/Gabriel	1968	6.00
❑ 44743	Bed of Roses/The Greatest Love	1969	6.00
❑ 44814	Nobody Loves You But Me/ Baby I'm Thinking of You	1969	5.00
❑ 44902	Cherry Hill Park/Helping Hand	1969	8.00
❑ 45085	Mama's Song/Me Without You	1970	5.00
❑ 45220	Burning a Hole/Every Night	1970	5.00
❑ 45289	Tulsa/Pick Up the Pieces	1970	5.00
❑ 45406	Poor Little Pearl/Lady Lives to Love	1971	5.00
❑ 45495	Colorado Rain/We Go Back	1971	5.00
❑ 45557	Later/The Family	1972	6.00
❑ 45620	Child of Mine/Natchez Trace	1972	6.00
FAIRLANE			
❑ 21009	Never in a Hundred Years/We Haven't a Moment to Lose	1961	30.00
❑ 21013	Dark Glasses/Perhaps	1962	30.00
KAT FAMILY			
❑ 01044	(Who is Like You) Sweet America/No Love Like a First Love	1981	4.00
❑ 02074	You Really Got a Hold on Me/ No Love Like a First Love	1981	4.00
❑ 02297	Wasted Time/Outrun the Sun	1981	4.00
MERCURY			
❑ 76069	Mr. Kool/Let's Talk It Over	1980	4.00
MGM SOUTH			
❑ 7011	This Magic Moment/ Mountain Woman	1973	5.00
❑ 7018	Summertime Skies/ Look What I Found	1973	5.00
❑ 7022	If This Is the Last Time/ Perfect Harmony	1973	5.00
❑ 7032	Star Again/Sugar Blue	1974	5.00
PLAYER'S			
❑ 1	I'm Specialized/Really You	1965	20.00
PRIVATE STOCK			
❑ 45,192	Under the Boardwalk/ Precious Time	1978	5.00
❑ 45,212 [DJ]	Anchors Aweigh (mono/stereo)	1979	5.00
SCEPTER			
❑ 12419	All Night Rain/Time Don't Pass By Here	1976	4.00
TOLLIE			
❑ 9011	Mama Didn't Raise No Fools/ Get Behind Me, Devil	1964	15.00
Albums			
ATLANTIC AMERICA			
❑ 90508	Looking Ahead	1986	10.00
❑ 90658	The Royal Treatment	1987	10.00
❑ 91064	Tell It Like It Is	1989	10.00
COLUMBIA			
❑ CL 2403 [M]	Down in the Boondocks	1965	20.00
❑ CL 2781 [M]	Billy Joe Royal	1967	25.00
❑ CS 9203 [S]	Down in the Boondocks	1965	25.00
❑ CS 9581 [S]	Billy Joe Royal	1967	25.00
❑ CS 9974	Cherry Hill Park	1969	25.00
KAT FAMILY			
❑ JW 37342	Billy Joe Royal	1982	10.00
MERCURY			
❑ SRM-1-3837	Billy Joe Royal	1980	10.00

ROYAL DEBS, THE

45s

Number	Title (A Side/B Side)	Yr	NM
TIFCO			
❑ 826	I Do/Jerry	1962	25.00

ROYAL DRIFTERS, THE

45s

Number	Title (A Side/B Side)	Yr	NM
TEEN			
❑ 506	S'Why Hard/Little Linda	1959	100.00
❑ 508	To Each His Own/Da Kind	1959	150.00

ROYAL GUARDSMEN, THE

45s

Number	Title (A Side/B Side)	Yr	NM
LAURIE			
❑ 112	Snoopy's Christmas/ The Smallest Astronaut	197?	4.00
—B-side by Barry Winslow; reissue			
❑ 3359	Baby Let's Wait/Leaving Me	1966	75.00
❑ 3366	Snoopy vs. the Red Baron/ I Needed You	1966	12.00
—Regular red, black and white label			
❑ 3366	Snoopy vs. the Red Baron/ I Needed You	1966	15.00
—Light blue label			
❑ 3379	The Return of the Red Baron/ Sweetmeats Slide	1967	10.00
❑ 3391	Airplane Song (My Airplane)/Om	1967	8.00
❑ 3397	Wednesday/So Right (To Be in Love)	1967	8.00
❑ 3416	Snoopy's Christmas/It Kinda Looks Like Christmas	1967	10.00
❑ 3416 [PS]	Snoopy's Christmas/It Kinda Looks Like Christmas	1967	20.00
❑ 3428	I Say Love/I'm Not Gonna Stay	1968	8.00
❑ 3451	Snoopy for President/Down Behind the Lines	1968	8.00
❑ 3461	Baby Let's Wait/ Biplane "Evermore"	1968	8.00
❑ 3461	Baby Let's Wait/So Right (To Be in Love)	1968	8.00
❑ 3494	Magic Window/Mother, Where's Your Daughter	1969	20.00
❑ 3590	Snoopy for President/ Down Behind the Lines	1972	6.00
❑ 3646	Snoopy for President/ Sweetmeats Slide	1976	5.00
Albums			
HOLIDAY			
❑ HDY 1913	Merry Snoopy's Christmas	1980	10.00
—Reissue of Laurie 2042			
LAURIE			
❑ LLP-2038 [M]	Snoopy vs. the Red Baron	1967	20.00
❑ SLP-2038 [S]	Snoopy vs. the Red Baron	1967	25.00
❑ LLP-2039 [M]	The Return of the Red Baron	1967	20.00
❑ SLP-2039 [S]	The Return of the Red Baron	1967	25.00
❑ LLP 2042 [M]	Snoopy and His Friends	1967	15.00
—With "Merry Snoopy's Christmas" poster missing			
❑ LLP 2042 [M]	Snoopy and His Friends	1967	25.00
—With "Merry Snoopy's Christmas" poster still attached to back cover			
❑ SLP 2042 [S]	Snoopy and His Friends	1967	20.00
—With "Merry Snoopy's Christmas" poster missing			
❑ SLP 2042 [S]	Snoopy and His Friends	1967	30.00
—With "Merry Snoopy's Christmas" poster still attached to back cover			
❑ SLP-2046	Snoopy for President	1968	25.00

ROYAL HALOS, THE

45s

Number	Title (A Side/B Side)	Yr	NM
ALADDIN			
❑ 3460	My Love Is True/Nobody But Me and My Girl	1959	40.00

ROYAL HOLIDAYS, THE

45s

Number	Title (A Side/B Side)	Yr	NM
CARLTON			
❑ 472	Margaret/I'm Sorry	1958	25.00
HERALD			
❑ 536	Rockin' at the Bandstand/ Down in Cuba	1959	150.00
—Most, and perhaps all, copies were labeled "Chip Chip"/"Running to You" by the Mello-Kings			
PENTHOUSE			
❑ 9357	Margaret/I'm Sorry	1958	150.00

ROYAL PLAYBOYS, THE

Albums

Number	Title (A Side/B Side)	Yr	NM
WALDORF			
❑ 33-136 [10]	Rock and Roll/ New Orleans Blues	195?	500.00

ROYAL ROBINS, THE

45s

Number	Title (A Side/B Side)	Yr	NM
ABC-PARAMOUNT			
❑ 10504	Turn Me Loose/Country Fool	1963	30.00
❑ 10542	How High the Moon/ Something You've Got, Baby	1964	30.00

ROYAL TEENS, THE

Bob Gaudio, later of THE FOUR SEASONS, was in this group.

45s

Number	Title (A Side/B Side)	Yr	NM
ABC-PARAMOUNT			
❑ 9882	Short Shorts/Planet Rock	1958	30.00
❑ 9918	Big Name Button/Sham Rock	1958	25.00
❑ 9945	Harvey's Got a Girl Friend/ Hangin' Around	1958	25.00
❑ 9955	Open the Door/My Kind of Dream	1958	25.00
ALLNEW			
❑ 1415	Short Short Twist/Royal Twist	1962	20.00
ASTRA			
❑ 1012	Mad Gass/Sittin' with My Baby	196?	15.00
CAPITOL			
❑ F4261	Believe Me/Little Cricket	1959	30.00
❑ 4335	The Moon's Not Meant for Lovers/Was It a Dream	1960	30.00
❑ 4402	With You/It's the Talk of the Town	1960	30.00
JUBILEE			
❑ 5418	Short Short Twist/Royal Twist	1962	15.00
MIGHTY			
❑ 111	Leotards/Royal Blues	1959	25.00
❑ 112	Cave Man/Wounded Heart	1959	30.00
❑ 200	My Memories of You/Little Trixie	1961	40.00
MUSICOR			
❑ 1398	Smile a Little Smile for Me/ Hey Jude	1969	10.00
POWER			
❑ 113	Mad Gass/Sittin' with My Baby	1959	40.00
❑ 215	Short Shorts/Planet Rock	1957	150.00
SWAN			
❑ 4200	I'll Love You ('Til the End of Time)/(Instrumental)	1965	100.00
TCF HALL			
❑ 117	Bad Girl/Do the Montoona	1965	15.00

R

Number	Title (A Side/B Side)	Yr	NM
Albums			
COLLECTABLES			
❑ COL-5094	Short Shorts: Golden Classics	198?	10.00
MUSICOR			
❑ MS-3186	Newies But Oldies	1970	20.00
TRU-GEMS			
❑ 1001	Short Shorts & Others	1975	20.00

ROYAL TONES, THE

Number	Title (A Side/B Side)	Yr	NM
45s			
TITANIC			
❑ 5014	Black Lightnin'/Surfer's Junction	1964	60.00

ROYALETTES, THE

Number	Title (A Side/B Side)	Yr	NM
45s			
CHANCELLOR			
❑ 1133	No Big Thing/Yesterday's Lovers	1963	20.00
❑ 1140	Willie the Wolf/Blue Summer	1963	15.00
MGM			
❑ 13283	He's Gone/Don't You Cry	1964	12.00
❑ 13327	Poor Boy/Watch What Happens	1965	12.00
❑ 13366	It's Gonna Take a Miracle/Out of Sight, Out of Mind	1965	15.00
❑ 13405	I Want to Meet Him/Never Again	1965	12.00
❑ 13451	You Bring Me Down/ Only When You're Lonely	1966	12.00
❑ 13507	It's a Big Mistake/It's Better Not to Know	1966	12.00
❑ 13544	I Don't Want to Be the One/ An Affair to Remember	1966	12.00
❑ 13588	Love Without An End/When Summer's Gone	1966	12.00
❑ 13627	My Man/Take My Love	1966	12.00
ROULETTE			
❑ 4768	River of Ters/Something Wonderful	1967	10.00
WARNER BROS.			
❑ 5439	There He Goes/Come to Me	1964	15.00
Albums			
MGM			
❑ E-4332 [M]	It's Gonna Take a Miracle	1965	20.00
❑ SE-4332 [S]	It's Gonna Take a Miracle	1965	25.00
❑ E-4366 [M]	The Elegant Sound of the Royalettes	1966	20.00
❑ SE-4366 [S]	The Elegant Sound of the Royalettes	1966	25.00

ROYALS, THE (1) Later known as THE MIDNIGHTERS. Also see HANK BALLARD AND THE MIDNIGHTERS.

Number	Title (A Side/B Side)	Yr	NM
45s			
FEDERAL			
❑ 12064	Every Beat of My Heart/All Night Long	1952	1500.
❑ 12064AA	Every Beat of My Heart/ All Night Long	1952	3000.
—Blue vinyl. VG 1,000; VG+ 2,000			
❑ 12077	I Know I Love You So/ Starting From Tonight	1952	2500.
❑ 12088	Moonrise/Fifth Street Blues	1952	2000.
❑ 12088	Moonrise/Fifth Street Blues	1952	3000.
—Blue vinyl. VG 1000; VG+ 2000			
❑ 12098	A Love in My Heart/ I'll Never Let You Go	1952	1000.
❑ 12113	Are You Forgetting?/ What Did I Do	1952	600.00
❑ 12121	The Shrine of St. Cecelia/ I Feel So Blue	1953	800.00
❑ 12133	Get It/No It Ain't	1953	200.00
❑ 12150	Hello Miss Fine/I Feel That-A-Way	1953	200.00
❑ 12160	That's It/Someone Like You	1953	250.00
❑ 12169	Work With Me Annie/Until I Die	1954	250.00
—Original pressing; for reissues, see "Midnighters, The"			
❑ 12177 [DJ]	Give It Up/That Woman	1954	300.00
—Evidently, some promos exist crediting The Royals			
Albums			
FEDERAL			
❑ 567	The Best of the Royals	197?	15.00
—This is a bootleg album			

ROYALS, THE (2) Also see CHUCK WILLIS.

Number	Title (A Side/B Side)	Yr	NM
45s			
OKEH			
❑ 6832	If You Love Me/Dreams of You	1951	1000.

ROYALS, THE (3)

Number	Title (A Side/B Side)	Yr	NM
45s			
PENGUIN			
❑ 1008	Thunder Wagon/Teen Beat	1959	30.00

ROYALS, THE (4)

Number	Title (A Side/B Side)	Yr	NM
45s			
VAGABOND			
❑ 134	Surfin' Lagoon/Wild Safari	1962	50.00
❑ 444	Christmas Party/ White Christmas	1963	50.00
—Black vinyl			
❑ 444	Christmas Party/ White Christmas	1963	100.00
—Red vinyl			

ROYALS, THE (5) This Royals later became The Scooters.

Number	Title (A Side/B Side)	Yr	NM
45s			
VENUS			
❑ 103	Someday We'll Meet Again/ I Want You to Be My Mambo Baby	1954	400.00

ROYALTONES, THE

Number	Title (A Side/B Side)	Yr	NM
45s			
GOLDISC			
❑ 3004	Short Line/Big Wheel	1960	10.00
❑ 3011	Flamingo Express/Secret Love	1960	10.00
❑ 3011	Flamingo Express/Tacos	1960	10.00
❑ 3016	Butterscotch/Dixie Cup	1961	8.00
❑ 3017	Royal Whirl/Dixie Rock	1961	8.00
❑ 3026	Peppermint Twist/ Scotch and Soda	1962	8.00
❑ 3028	Do the Early Bird/ Scotch and Soda	1962	8.00
JUBILEE			
❑ 5338	Poor Boy/Wail!	1958	15.00
—Black label with rainbow			
❑ 5338	Poor Boy/Wail!	1958	25.00
—Dark blue label, silver print			
❑ 5362	Seesaw/Little Bo	1959	12.00
MALA			
❑ 473	Holy Smokes/Our Faded Love	1964	8.00
❑ 482	El Toro/Lonely World	1964	8.00
❑ 487	The Yea Yea Song/Misty Sea	1964	8.00
OLD TOWN			
❑ 1018	Crazy Love/Never Let Me Go	1956	100.00
PORT			
❑ 70037	Poor Boy/See Saw	1963	12.00

ROYCE, EARL, AND THE OLYMPICS British group; no relation to other Olympics groups.

Number	Title (A Side/B Side)	Yr	NM
45s			
TOWER			
❑ 137	Que Sera Sera Sera/I Really Do	1965	15.00

ROZZI, LITTLE SAMMY

Number	Title (A Side/B Side)	Yr	NM
45s			
PELHAM			
❑ 722	Christine/Over the Rainbow	1961	200.00

RUBBER BAND, THE (1)

Number	Title (A Side/B Side)	Yr	NM
45s			
ABC			
❑ 10849	Plastic Soul/Let's Sail Away	1966	10.00
COLUMBIA			
❑ 44013	In and Out of My Life/ Bring Your Love	1967	10.00
REPRISE			
❑ 0637	I'm Gonna Make It/Messin' Up the Mind of a Young Girl	1967	10.00

RUBBER BAND, THE (2)

Number	Title (A Side/B Side)	Yr	NM
45s			
GRT			
❑ 1	Sunshine of Your Love/ Deserted Cities of the Heart	1969	6.00
Albums			
GRT			
❑ 10000	Cream Songbook	1969	25.00
❑ 10007	Hendrix Songbook	1969	25.00
❑ 10015	Beatles Songbook	1969	25.00

RUBBER CITY REBELS

Number	Title (A Side/B Side)	Yr	NM
Albums			
CAPITOL			
❑ ST-12100	Rubber City Rebels	1980	40.00

RUBBER MEMORY

Number	Title (A Side/B Side)	Yr	NM
Albums			
R.P.C.			
❑ 69401	Welcome	196?	1000.

RUBEN AND THE JETS Also see FRANK ZAPPA.

Number	Title (A Side/B Side)	Yr	NM
45s			
MERCURY			
❑ 73381	If I Could Be Your Love Again/ Wedding Bells	1973	6.00
❑ 73411	Charlena/Mah Man Flash	1973	6.00
Albums			
MERCURY			
❑ SRM-1-659	For Real	1973	25.00
❑ SRM-1-694	Con Safos	1974	25.00

RUBETTES

Number	Title (A Side/B Side)	Yr	NM
45s			
POLYDOR			
❑ 15089	Sugar Baby Love/ You Could Have Told Me	1974	5.00
❑ 15092	Tonight/Silent Movie Queen	1974	4.00
❑ 15102	I Can Do It/If You've Got the Time	1975	4.00
STATE/MCA			
❑ 40549	Juke Box Jive/Put a Back Beat to That Music	1976	4.00
❑ 40632	Rock Is Dead/Dark Side of the World	1976	4.00
Albums			
STATE			
❑ MCA-2193	Rubettes	1976	12.00

RUBIN

Number	Title (A Side/B Side)	Yr	NM
45s			
KAPP			
❑ 869	You've Been Away/Baby, You're My Everything	1967	400.00

RUBY AND THE ROMANTICS

Number	Title (A Side/B Side)	Yr	NM
45s			
A&M			
❑ 1042	Hurting Each Other/Baby, I Could Be So Good at Loving You	1969	8.00
ABC			
❑ 10911	Twilight Time/Una Bella Brazilian Melody	1967	10.00
❑ 10941	Only Heaven Knows/ This Is No Laughing Matter	1967	10.00
❑ 11065	On a Clear Day You Can See Forever/More Than Yesterday, Less Than Tomorrow	1968	10.00
KAPP			
❑ 501	Our Day Will Come/ Moonlight and Music	1963	15.00
❑ 525	My Summer Love/Sweet Love and Sweet Forgiveness	1963	12.00
❑ 544	Hey There Lonely Boy/ Not a Moment Too Soon	1963	12.00
❑ 544 [PS]	Hey There Lonely Boy/ Not a Moment Too Soon	1963	15.00
❑ 557	Young Wings Can Fly (Higher Than You Know)/ Day Dreaming	1963	12.00
❑ 557 [PS]	Young Wings Can Fly (Higher Than You Know)/ Day Dreaming	1963	15.00
❑ 578	Our Everlasting Love/ Much Better Off Than I've Ever Been	1964	12.00
❑ 601	Baby Come Home/ Every Day's a Holiday	1964	12.00
❑ 615	When You're Young and In Love/I Cry Alone	1964	12.00
❑ 646	Does He Really Care for Me/ Nevertheless (I'm in Love with You)	1965	12.00
❑ 665	We'll Meet Again/Your Baby Doesn't Love You Anymore	1965	12.00
❑ 702	Nobody But My Baby/ Imagination	1965	12.00
❑ 759	We Can Make It/Remember Me	1966	10.00
❑ 773	Hey There Lonely Boy/Think	1966	10.00
❑ 839	I Know/We'll Love Again	1967	10.00
Albums			
ABC			
❑ S-638	More Than Yesterday	1968	20.00
KAPP			
❑ KL-1323 [M]	Our Day Will Come	1963	30.00
❑ KL-1341 [M]	Till Then	1963	25.00
❑ KL-1458 [M]	The Greatest Hits Album	1966	20.00
❑ KL-1526 [M]	Ruby and the Romantics	1967	25.00
❑ KS-3323 [S]	Our Day Will Come	1963	40.00
❑ KS-3341 [S]	Till Then	1963	30.00
❑ KS-3458 [S]	The Greatest Hits Album	1966	25.00
❑ KS-3526 [S]	Ruby and the Romantics	1967	25.00
MCA			
❑ 541	The Greatest Hits Album	197?	10.00

R

Except when noted otherwise, VG = 25% of NM, and VG+ = 50% of NM. (Example: VG = $2.00, VG+ = $4.00 and NM = $8.00.)

Number	Title (A Side/B Side)	Yr	NM
PICKWICK			
SPC-3519	Makin' Out	1977?	10.00

RUFFIN, DAVID Also see DARYL HALL AND JOHN OATES; JIMMY AND DAVID RUFFIN; THE TEMPTATIONS; THE VOICE MASTERS.

Number	Title (A Side/B Side)	Yr	NM
45s			
ANNA			
1127	I'm in Love/One of These Days	1961	60.00
CHECK MATE			
1003	You Can Get What I Got/Action Speaks Louder Than Words	1961	60.00
1010	Mr. Bus Driver — Hurry!/Knock You Out (With Love)	1962	60.00
MOTOWN			
1140	My Whole World Ended (The Moment You Left Me)/I've Got to Find Myself a Brand New Baby	1968	6.00
1149	I've Lost Everything I've Ever Loved/We'll Have a Good Thing Going On	1969	6.00
1158	I'm So Glad I Fell for You/I Pray Every Day You Won't Regret Loving Me	1969	6.00
1178	Each Day Is a Lifetime/Don't Stop Loving Me	1971	6.00
1187	You Can Come Right Back to Me/Dinah	1971	6.00
1204	A Day in the Life of a Working Man/A Little More Trust	1972	6.00
1223	Blood Donors Needed/Go On with Your Bad Self	1973	6.00
1259	Common Man/I'm Just a Mortal Man	1973	6.00
1327	Me and Rock and Roll (Are Here to Stay)/Smiling Faces Sometimes	1974	6.00
1332	Take Me Clear from Here/I Just Want to Celebrate	1975	—
—Unreleased			
1336	Superstar/No Matter Where	1975	5.00
1376	Walk Away from Love/Love Can Be Hazardous to Your Health	1975	5.00
1388	Heavy Love/Love Can Be Hazardous To Your Health	1976	5.00
1393	Everything's Coming Up Love/No Matter Where	1976	5.00
1405	On and Off/Statue of a Fool	1976	5.00
1420	Just Let Me Hold You for a Night/Rode by the Place (Where We Used to Stay)	1977	5.00
1435	You're My Peace of Mind/Rose By the Place (Where We Used to Stay)	1978	5.00
WARNER BROS.			
49030	Sexy Dancer/Break My Heart	1979	4.00
49123	I Get Excited/Chain on the Brain	1979	4.00
49277	Slow Dance/Don't You Go Home	1980	4.00
49577	Still in Love with You/I Wanna Be with You	1980	4.00
Albums			
MOTOWN			
M5-146V1	My Whole World Ended	1981	8.00
—Reissue			
M5-211V1	At His Best	1981	8.00
—Reissue			
MS-685	My Whole World Ended	1969	20.00
MS-696	Feelin' Good	1969	15.00
M 733	David Ruffin	1971	—
—Canceled			
M-762	David Ruffin	1973	12.00
M6-818	Me 'N' Rock 'N' Roll Are Here to Stay	1974	12.00
M6-849	Who I Am	1975	12.00
M6-866	Everything's Coming Up Love	1976	12.00
M6-885	In My Stride	1977	12.00
M7-895	At His Best	1978	12.00
WARNER BROS.			
BSK 3306	So Soon We Change	1979	10.00
BSK 3416	Gentleman Ruffin	1980	10.00

RUFFIN, DAVID, AND EDDIE KENDRICK Also see each artist's individual listings; DARYL HALL AND JOHN OATES; THE TEMPTATIONS.

Number	Title (A Side/B Side)	Yr	NM
45s			
RCA			
5313-7-R	I Couldn't Believe It/Don't Know Why You're Dreamin'	1987	3.00
6925-7-R	One More for the Lonely Hearts Club/Don't Know Why You're Dreaming	1988	3.00

RUFFIN, JIMMY

Number	Title (A Side/B Side)	Yr	NM
45s			
ATCO			
6926	Tears of Joy/Goin' Home	1973	8.00
CHESS			
2160	Tell Me What You Want/Do You Know Me	1974	5.00
2168	What You See (Ain't Always What You Get)/Boy from Mississippi	1975	5.00
EPIC			
50339	Fallin' in Love with You/Fallin' in Love with You	1977	5.00
50384	Fallin' in Love with You/Fallin' in Love with You	1977	5.00
MIRACLE			
1	Don't Feel Sorry for Me/Heart	1961	200.00
RSO			
1021	Hold On to My Love/(Instrumental)	1980	5.00
1042	Night of Love/Searchin'	1980	5.00
SOUL			
35002	Since I've Lost You/I Want Her Love	1964	40.00
35016	As Long As There Is L-O-V-E/How Can I Say I'm Sorry	1965	10.00
35022	What Becomes of the Brokenhearted/Baby I've Got It	1966	15.00
35027	I've Passed This Way Before/Tomorrow's Tears	1966	10.00
35032	Gonna Give Her All the Love I've Got/World So Wide (Nowhere to Hide from Your Heart)	1967	8.00
35035	Don't You Miss Me A Little Bit Baby/I Want Her Love	1967	8.00
35043	I'll Say Forever My Love/Everybody Needs Love	1968	8.00
35046	Don't Let Him Take Your Love from Me/Lonely, Lonely Man Am I	1968	8.00
35053	Sad and Lonesome Feeling/Gonna Keep On Trying Till I Win Your Love	1968	8.00
35060	Farewell Is a Lonely Sound/If You Will Let Me, I Know I Can	1969	8.00
35077	Maria (You Were the Only One)/Living in a World I Created For Myself	1970	8.00
35092	Our Favorite Melody/You Gave Me Love	1972	6.00
Albums			
RSO			
RS-1-3078	Sunrise	1980	10.00
SOUL			
704 [M]	Top Ten	1967	25.00
—Full-color cover			
704 [M]	Top Ten	1967	50.00
—One-color cover			
S-704 [S]	Top Ten	1967	25.00
S-708	Ruff'n Ready	1969	25.00
SS-727	The Groove Governor	1970	20.00

RUFFIN, JIMMY AND DAVID Also see DAVID RUFFIN; JIMMY RUFFIN.

Number	Title (A Side/B Side)	Yr	NM
45s			
SOUL			
35076	Stand By Me/Your Love Was Worth Waiting For	1970	5.00
35082	When My Love Hand Comes Do Down/Steppin' On a Dream	1971	5.00
35086	Lo and Behold/The Things We Have to Do	1971	5.00
Albums			
MOTOWN			
M5-108V1	Motown Superstar Series, Vol. 8	1981	10.00
SOUL			
SS-728	I Am My Brother's Keeper	1970	20.00

RUFUS Includes records as "Rufus Featuring Chaka Khan" and "Rufus and Chaka." Also see THE AMERICAN BREED.

Number	Title (A Side/B Side)	Yr	NM
45s			
ABC			
11356	Slip 'N Slide/I Finally Found You	1973	8.00
11376	Whoever's Thrilling You (Is Killing Me)/I Finally Found You	1973	6.00
11394	Feel Good/Keep It Coming	1973	6.00
11427	Tell Me Something Good/Smokin' Room	1974	6.00
12010	Tell Me Something Good/Smokin' Room	1974	5.00
12032	You Got the Love/Rags to Rufus	1974	5.00
12066	Once You Get Started/Rufusized	1975	5.00
12099	Please Pardon Me (You Remind Me of a Friend)/Somebody's Watching You	1975	5.00
12149	Sweet Thing/Circles	1975	5.00
12179	Dance Wit' Me/Everybody's Got an Aura	1976	5.00
12197	Jive Talkin'/On Time	1976	5.00
12239	At Midnight (My Love Will Lift You Up)/Better Days	1976	5.00
12269	Holywood/Earth Song	1977	5.00
12296	Everlasting Love/Close the Door	1977	5.00
12349	Stay/My Ship Will Sail	1978	5.00
12390	Blue Love/Turn	1978	5.00
12444	Keep It Together (Declaration of Love)/Red Hot Poker	1979	5.00
EPIC			
10691	Read All About It/Brand New Day	1971	12.00
10691 [PS]	Read All About It/Brand New Day	1971	20.00
10726	Follow the Lamb/Fire One, Fire Two, Fire Three	1971	12.00
MCA			
41025	Ain't Nobody Like You/You're to Blame	1979	4.00
41131	Do You Love What You Feel/Dancin' Mood	1979	4.00
41191	What Am I Missing/Any Love	1980	4.00
41230	I'm Dancing for Your Love/Walk the Rockway	1980	4.00
51070	Tonight We Love/Afterwards	1981	4.00
51125	Party 'Til You're Broke/Hold On to a Friend	1981	4.00
51203	Sharing the Love/We Got the Way	1981	4.00
52002	True Love/Better Together	1982	4.00
WARNER BROS.			
29406	One Million Kisses/Stay	1983	4.00
29555	Ain't Nobody/Sweet Thing	1983	4.00
29675	Blinded by the Boogie/You're Really Out of Line	1983	4.00
29790	Take It to the Hop/Distant Lover	1983	4.00
Albums			
ABC			
X-783	Rufus	1973	10.00
X-809	Rags to Rufus	1974	10.00
D-837	Rufusized	1974	10.00
D-909	Rufus Featuring Chaka Khan	1975	10.00
D-975	Ask Rufus	1977	10.00
AA-1049	Street Player	1978	10.00
AA-1049 [PD]	Street Player	1978	25.00
—Promo-only picture disc			
AA-1098	Numbers	1979	10.00
AA-1098 [PD]	Numbers	1979	20.00
—Promo-only picture disc			
COMMAND			
CQD-40023 [Q]	Rufusized	1974	20.00
CQD-40024 [Q]	Rags to Rufus	1974	20.00
MCA			
642	Rufus	1980	6.00
—Reissue of ABC 783			
5103	Masterjam	1979	10.00
5159	Party 'Til You're Broke	1981	10.00
5270	Camouflage	1982	10.00
5339	The Very Best of Rufus	1983	10.00
37034	Rags to Rufus	1980	6.00
—Reissue of ABC 809			
37035	Rufusized	1980	6.00
—Reissue of ABC 837			
37036	Rufus Featuring Chaka Khan	1980	6.00
—Reissue of ABC 909			
37037	Ask Rufus	1980	6.00
—Reissue of ABC 975			
37038	Street Player	1980	6.00
—Reissue of ABC 1049			
37039	Numbers	1980	6.00
—Reissue of ABC 1098			
37157	Masterjam	198?	6.00
—Reissue of 5103			
WARNER BROS.			
23679 [(2)]	Live: Stompin' at the Savoy	1983	12.00
23753	Seal in Red	1984	10.00

RUFUS AND CARLA Also see CARLA THOMAS; RUFUS THOMAS.

Number	Title (A Side/B Side)	Yr	NM
45s			
ATCO			
6177	Cause I Love You/Deep Down Inside	1960	25.00
—As "Carla and Rufus"			
6199	I Didn't Believe/Yeah, Yea-Ah	1961	25.00
—As "Rufus and Friend"			

R

Todd Rundgren, "I Love my Life," Warner Bros. 22868, 1989, $3.

Number	Title (A Side/B Side)	Yr	NM
SATELLITE			
❑ 102	Cause I Love You/ Deep Down Inside	1960	40.00
STAX			
❑ 151	That's Really Some Good/ Night Time Is the Right Time	1964	12.00
❑ 176	When You Move You Lose/ We're Tight	1965	12.00
❑ 184	Birds and Bees/ Never Let You Go	1966	12.00
Albums			
STAX			
❑ STX-4124	Chronicle	1979	15.00

RUGBYS, THE

Number	Title (A Side/B Side)	Yr	NM
45s			
AMAZON			
❑ 1	You, I/Stay with Me	1969	8.00
—Black vinyl			
❑ 1 [DJ]	You, I/Stay with Me	1969	20.00
—Colored vinyl			
❑ 4	The Light/Wendegahl Warlock	1970	8.00
❑ 6	Rockin' All Over/Juditha Gina	1970	8.00
SMASH			
❑ 1997	James Is the Name/ 'Til the Day I Die	1965	12.00
Albums			
AMAZON			
❑ 1000	Hot Cargo	1970	20.00

RUMBLERS, THE

Number	Title (A Side/B Side)	Yr	NM
45s			
DOT			
❑ 16421	Boss/I Don't Need You No More	1963	15.00
❑ 16455	Boss Strikes Back/Sorry	1963	15.00
❑ 16480	Angry Sea (Walmea)/Bugged	1963	15.00
❑ 16521	It's a Gas/Tootananny	1963	15.00
DOWNEY			
❑ 103	Boss/I Don't Need You No More	1962	30.00
❑ 106	Boss Strikes Back/Sorry	1963	30.00
❑ 107	Angry Sea (Walmea)/Bugged	1963	30.00
❑ 111	It's a Gas/Tootananny	1963	30.00
❑ 114	High Octane/Night Scene	1964	25.00
❑ 119	The Hustler/Riot in Cell Block #9	1964	25.00
❑ 127	Soulful Jerk/Hey-Did-a-Da-Do	1964	25.00
❑ 133	Boss Soul/Till Always	1965	25.00
HIGHLAND			
❑ 1026	Intersection/Stomping Theme	1962	50.00
Albums			
DOT			
❑ DLP-3509 [M]	Boss!	1963	50.00
❑ DLP-25509 [S]	Boss!	1963	60.00
DOWNEY			
❑ DLP-1001 [M]	Boss!	1963	180.00
❑ DLPS-1001 [S]	Boss!	1963	250.00

RUMOUR, THE GRAHAM PARKER's band.

Number	Title (A Side/B Side)	Yr	NM
45s			
ARISTA			
❑ 0451	Emotional Traffic/ Hard Enough to Show	1979	4.00
MERCURY			
❑ 73949	I'm So Glad/This Town	1977	4.00
Albums			
ARISTA			
❑ AL 4235	Frogs, Sprouts, Clogs & Krauts	1979	12.00
HANNIBAL			
❑ 1305	Purity of Essence	1981	15.00
MERCURY			
❑ SRM-1-1174	Max	1977	15.00

RUNAROUNDS, THE Probably more than one group.

Number	Title (A Side/B Side)	Yr	NM
45s			
CAPITOL			
❑ 5644	Perfect Woman/You're a Drag	1966	25.00
COUSINS			
❑ 1004	Mashed Potato Mary/ I'm All Alone	1964	20.00
FELSTED			
❑ 8704	Send Her Back/Carrie, You're An Angel	1964	30.00
KC			
❑ 116	Unbelievable/Hurray for Love	1963	25.00
❑ 116	Unbelievable/Hurray for Love	1963	40.00
—Brown vinyl			
MGM			
❑ 13763	My Little Girl/You Lied	1967	15.00
PIO			
❑ 107	The Nearest Thing to Heaven/ Lover's Lane	1961	150.00
TARHEEL			
❑ 065	Are You Looking for a Sweetheart/Let Them Talk	1963	20.00

RUNAWAYS, THE Also see LITA FORD; JOAN JETT AND THE BLACKHEARTS.

Number	Title (A Side/B Side)	Yr	NM
45s			
MERCURY			
❑ 73819	Cherry Bomb/Blackmail	1976	15.00
❑ 73890	Heartbeat/Neon Angels on the Road to Ruin	1977	14.00
Albums			
MARILYN			
❑ USM 1004	Born to Be Bad	1991	15.00
MERCURY			
❑ SRM-1-1090	The Runaways	1976	25.00
❑ SRM-1-1126	Queens of Noise	1977	25.00
❑ SRM-1-3705	Waiting for the Night	1977	25.00
❑ SRM-1-3740	Live in Japan	1978	50.00
RHINO			
❑ RNDF-250 [PD]	Little Lost Girls	1982	25.00
❑ RNEP-602 [EP]	Mama Weer All Crazee Now	1983	15.00
❑ RNLP-70861	Little Lost Girls	1987	12.00
—Reissue of Rhino 250 on regular vinyl			

RUNDGREN, TODD Also see NAZZ (1); UTOPIA.

Number	Title (A Side/B Side)	Yr	NM
12-Inch Singles			
FORWARD			
❑ 7008 [DJ]	Day Job (LP Version) (Radio Version) (Dub)	1993	15.00
WARNER BROS.			
❑ PRO-A-2371 [DJ]	Something to Fall Back On (same on both sides)	1985	10.00
45s			
AMPEX			
❑ 31001	We Gotta Get You a Woman/ Medley	1970	10.00
—As "Runt"			
BEARSVILLE			
❑ 0003	I Saw the Light/Marlene	1972	12.00
❑ 0003	I Saw the Light/Marlene	1972	12.00
—Blue vinyl			
❑ 0007	Couldn't I Just Tell You/ Wolfman Jack	1972	6.00
❑ 0009	Hello It's Me/Cold Morning Light	1973	6.00
❑ 0020	A Dream Goes On Forever/ Heavy Metal Kids	1974	6.00
❑ 0030	We Gotta Get You a Woman/ I Saw the Light	1973	4.00
—"Back to Back Hits" series			
❑ 0301	Breathless/Wolfman Jack	1974	6.00
❑ 0304	Real Man/Prana	1975	5.00
❑ 0309	Good Vibrations/When I Pray	1976	5.00
❑ 0310	Love of the Common Man/ Black and White	1976	5.00
❑ 0324	Can We Still Be Friends/ Determination	1978	5.00
❑ 0324	Can We Still Be Friends/ Out of Control	1978	5.00
❑ 0330	You Cried Wolf/Onomatopoeia	1978	5.00
❑ 0335	It Wouldn't Have Made Any Difference/Did You Ever Learn	1979	5.00
❑ 29686	Bang the Drum All Day/Chant	1983	6.00
❑ 29759	Emperor of the Highway/ Hideaway	1983	4.00
❑ 31002	Be Nice to Me/Broke Down and Busted	1971	8.00
—As "Runt-Todd Rundgren"			
❑ 31004	A Long Time, A Long Way to Go/ Parole	1971	8.00
—As "Runt-Todd Rundgren"			
❑ 49696	Time Heals/Tiny Demons	1981	4.00
❑ 49771	Compassion/Pulse	1981	5.00
COLUMBIA			
❑ 06151	Loving You's a Dirty Job (But Somebody's Gotta Do It)/ Before This Night Is Through	1986	4.00
—With Bonnie Tyler			

Number	Title (A Side/B Side)	Yr	NM

GUARDIAN

❑ S7-19726 Can We Still Be Friends/I Saw the Light 1997 3.00

RHINO

❑ 74426 Bang the Drum All Day/Can We Still Be Friends 1987 4.00

WARNER BROS.

❑ 22868 [PS] I Love My Life/Parallel Lines 1989 3.00
❑ 28821 Something to Fall Back On/Lockjaw 1986 4.00

7-Inch Extended Plays

BEARSVILLE

❑ SB 2066 I Saw the Light/You Left Me Sore/Hello It's Me//Piss Aaron/It Takes Two to Tango/Sweeter Memories 1972 12.00
—Jukebox issue; small hole, plays at 33 1/3 rpm
❑ SB 2066 [PS] Something/Anything? 1972 12.00
—Part of "Little LP" series (LLP #236)
❑ BHS 3522-EP Time Heals/Tiny Demons 1981 5.00
—33 1/3 rpm, small hole; bonus record included with the LP "Healing"

Albums

AMPEX

❑ A-10105 Runt 1970 50.00
—LP jacket and label list 10 tracks and album actually has 10
❑ A-10105 Runt 1970 100.00
—LP jacket and label list 10 tracks, but the album has 11
❑ A-10105 Runt 1970 150.00
—LP jacket and label list 10 tracks, but the album has 12

BEARSVILLE

❑ PRO 524 [DJ] The Todd Rundgren Radio Show 1972 110.00
❑ PRO 597 [DJ] Ikon/Todd Rundgren Interview 1974 100.00
❑ PRO-A-788 [DJ] Todd Rundgren Radio Sampler 1978 50.00
—Highlights of "Back to the Bars" plus interview of Todd by Patti Smith
❑ BR 2046 Runt 1972 15.00
—Another reissue, after switch from Ampex to Warner Bros. distribution
❑ BR 2047 The Ballad of Todd Rundgren 1972 15.00
—Reissue of 10116
❑ 2BX 2066 [(2)] Something/Anything? 1972 25.00
—Regular copy with black vinyl
❑ 2BX 2066 [(2)] Something/Anything? 1972 200.00
—White label with one record on red vinyl and the other on blue vinyl
❑ BR 2133 A Wizard/A True Star 1973 12.00
❑ BHS 3522 Healing 1981 10.00
—Add $5 if bonus 7-inch 33 1/3 single (Time Heals/Tiny Demons) is included
❑ 2BR 6952 [(2)] Todd 1974 15.00
❑ BR 6957 Initiation 1975 10.00
❑ BR 6963 Faithful 1976 10.00
❑ BRK 6981 Hermit of Mink Hollow 1978 10.00
❑ 2BRX 6986 [(2)] Back to the Bars 1978 12.00
❑ A-10105 Runt 1971 25.00
—Reissue with new label
❑ A-10116 The Ballad of Todd Rundgren 1971 80.00
❑ 23732 The Ever Popular Tortured Artist Effect 1983 10.00

MOBILE FIDELITY

❑ 2-225 Something/Anything? 1995 40.00
—Audiophile vinyl

RHINO

❑ RNLP 70862 Runt 1987 10.00
❑ RNLP 70863 The Ballad of Todd Rundgren 1987 10.00
❑ RNLP 70864 A Wizard/A True Star 1987 10.00
❑ RNLP 70866 Initiation 1987 10.00
❑ RNLP 70868 Faithful 1987 10.00
❑ RNLP 70871 Hermit of Mink Hollow 1988 10.00
❑ RNLP 70874 Healing 1987 10.00
❑ RNLP 70876 The Ever Popular Tortured Artist Effect 1988 10.00
❑ RNDA 71107 Something/Anything? 1987 12.00
❑ RNDA 71108 Todd 1987 12.00
❑ RNDA 71109 Back to the Bars 1987 12.00
❑ R1-71491 Anthology (1968-1985) 1989 20.00

WARNER BROS.

❑ 25128 A Cappella 1985 10.00
❑ 25881 Nearly Human 1989 15.00

RUSH

12-Inch Singles

MERCURY

❑ MK-75 [DJ] The Trees//Prelude/Circumstances 1978 40.00
❑ MK-125 [DJ] The Spirit of Radio/The Trees/Working Man 1980 60.00
❑ MK-137 [DJ] Entre Nous (4:37) (3:45) 1980 60.00
❑ MK-188 [DJ] A Passage to Bangkok (Live)/Freewill (Live) 1981 25.00
❑ MK-216 [DJ] New World Man/Vital Signs (Live) 1981 25.00
—Clear vinyl
❑ PRO 276-1 [DJ] Distant Early Warning/Between the Wheels 1984 15.00
❑ PRO 290-1 [DJ] The Body Electric (same on both sides) 1984 20.00
❑ PRO 320-1 [DJ] Red Sector A/The Enemy Within 1984 30.00
—Red vinyl
❑ PRO 382-1 [DJ] The Big Money (same on both sides) 1985 12.00
❑ PRO 400-1 [DJ] Mystic Rhythms (6:08) (same on both sides) 1985 25.00
❑ PRO 532-1 [DJ] Force Ten (same on both sides) 1987 15.00
❑ PRO 689-1 [DJ] Marathon (Live) (same on both sides) 1988 20.00

45s

MERCURY

❑ PRO 319-7 [DJ] Red Sector A (same on both sides) 1984 20.00
❑ PRO 383-7 [DJ] The Big Money (5:35)/(4:32) 1985 20.00
❑ DJ-407 (73623) [DJ] Finding My Way (mono/stereo) 1974 60.00
❑ DJ-417 (73647) [DJ] In the Mood (mono/stereo) 1974 60.00
❑ DJ-553 (73681) [DJ] Fly by Night/Anthem 1975 60.00
❑ 73623 Finding My Way/Need Some Love 1974 80.00
❑ 73647 In the Mood/What You're Doing 1974 80.00
❑ 73681 Fly by Night/Anthem 1975 80.00
❑ 73728 Return of the Prince/I Think I'm Going Bald 1975 80.00
❑ 73728 [DJ] Return of the Prince (3:01)/(2:54) 1975 60.00
❑ 73737 Lakeside Park/Bastille Day 1975 80.00
❑ 73737 [DJ] Lakeside Park (3:16) (mono/stereo) 1975 60.00
❑ 73803 The Twilight Zone/Lessons 1976 80.00
❑ 73803 [DJ] The Twilight Zone (mono/stereo) 1976 60.00
❑ 73873 Fly by Night-In the Mood/Something for Nothing 1976 10.00
❑ 73912 Making Memories/The Temples of Syrinx 1977 10.00
❑ 73958 Closer to the Heart/Madrigal 1977 10.00
❑ 73990 Fly by Night/Anthem 1978 10.00
❑ 74051 The Trees/Circumstances 1979 10.00
❑ 76044 The Spirit of Radio/Circumstances 1980 10.00
❑ 76060 Entre Nous/Different Strings 1980 10.00
❑ 76095 Limelight/XYZ 1981 10.00
❑ 76109 Tom Sawyer/Witch Hunt 1981 10.00
❑ 76109 [PS] Tom Sawyer/Witch Hunt 1981 25.00
❑ 76124 Closer to the Heart/Freewill 1981 8.00
❑ 76179 New World Man/Vital Signs 1982 8.00
❑ 76179 [PS] New World Man/Vital Signs 1982 10.00
❑ 76196 Subdivisions/Countdown 1982 10.00
❑ 880050-7 The Body Electric/Between the Wheels 1984 10.00
❑ 884191-7 The Big Money/Red Sector A 1985 5.00
❑ 884191-7 [PS] The Big Money/Red Sector A 1985 7.00
❑ 888891-7 Time Stand Still/High Water 1987 5.00
❑ 888891-7 [PS] Time Stand Still/High Water 1987 7.00

Albums

ATLANTIC

❑ 82040 Presto 1989 15.00
❑ 83531 [(2)] Vapor Trails 2002 25.00
❑ 83728 Feedback 2004 16.00

MERCURY

❑ MK-32 [DJ] Everything Your Listener Ever Wanted to Hear by Rush ... But You Were Afraid to Play 1977 150.00
❑ MK-185 [DJ] Rush 'N' Roulette 1981 120.00
—Promo-only six-track EP that has six grooves cut in it; the song it plays is based on where you place the stylus
❑ SRM-1-1011 Rush 1974 10.00
—Based on the LP's release date, original copies theoretically have red labels, rather than the common "Chicago skyline" labels; those would be worth at least twice this price
❑ SRM-1-1011 Rush 1983 8.00
—Black label
❑ SRM-1-1023 Fly by Night 1975 10.00
—"Chicago skyline" label
❑ SRM-1-1023 Fly by Night 1983 8.00
—Black label
❑ SRM-1-1046 Caress of Steel 1975 10.00
—"Chicago skyline" label
❑ SRM-1-1046 Caress of Steel 1983 8.00
—Black label
❑ SRM-1-1079 2112 1976 10.00
—"Chicago skyline" label
❑ SRM-1-1079 2112 1983 8.00
—Black label
❑ SRM-1-1184 A Farewell to Kings 1977 10.00
—"Chicago skyline" label
❑ SRM-1-1184 A Farewell to Kings 1983 8.00
—Black label
❑ SRP-1-1300 [PD] Hemispheres 1979 40.00
❑ SRM-1-3743 Hemispheres 1978 10.00
—"Chicago skyline" label; with poster
❑ SRM-1-3743 Hemispheres 1983 8.00
—Black label
❑ SRM-1-4001 Permanent Waves 1980 10.00
—Custom label
❑ SRM-1-4013 Moving Pictures 1981 10.00
—Custom label
❑ SRM-1-4063 Signals 1982 10.00
❑ SRM-2-7001 [(2)] Exit... Stage Left 1981 12.00
❑ SRM-2-7508 [(2)] All the World's a Stage 1976 12.00
—"Chicago skyline" labels
❑ SRM-2-7508 [(2)] All the World's a Stage 1983 10.00
—Black labels
❑ SRM-3-9200 [(3)] Archives 1978 20.00
—"Chicago skyline" labels
❑ SRM-3-9200 [(3)] Archives 1983 18.00
—Black labels
❑ 818476-1 Grace Under Pressure 1984 10.00
❑ 822541-1 Rush 1985 8.00
—Reissue with new number
❑ 822542-1 Fly by Night 1985 8.00
—Reissue with new number
❑ 822543-1 Caress of Steel 1985 8.00
—Reissue with new number
❑ 822545-1 2112 1985 8.00
—Reissue with new number
❑ 822546-1 A Farewell to Kings 1985 8.00
—Reissue with new number
❑ 822547-1 Hemispheres 1985 8.00
—Reissue with new number
❑ 822548-1 Permanent Waves 1985 8.00
—Reissue with new number
❑ 822549-1 Moving Pictures 1985 8.00
—Reissue with new number
❑ 822550-1 Signals 1985 8.00
—Reissue with new number
❑ 822551-1 [(2)] Exit...Stage Left 1985 10.00
—Reissue with new number
❑ 822552-1 [(2)] All the World's a Stage 1985 10.00
—Reissue with new number
❑ 822553-1 [(3)] Archives 1985 15.00
—Reissue with new number
❑ 826098-1 Power Windows 1985 10.00
❑ 832464-1 Hold Your Fire 1987 10.00
❑ 836346-1 [(2)] A Show of Hands 1988 12.00

RUSH, MERRILEE

45s

AGP

❑ 107 Reach Out/Love Street 1969 6.00
❑ 112 Your Loving Eyes Are Blind/Everyday Livin' Days 1969 6.00
❑ 121 Sign On for the Good Times/Robin McCarver 1969 6.00
❑ 126 Angel of the Morning/It's Worth It All 1970 6.00

BELL

❑ 705 Angel of the Morning/Reap What You Sow 1968 8.00
❑ 738 Sunshine and Roses/That Kind of Woman 1968 8.00

SCEPTER

❑ 12329 Child of Mine/Everything Has Got to Be Free 1971 6.00

UNITED ARTISTS

❑ XW930 Could It Be Love I Found Tonight/Be True to You 1976 4.00
❑ XW993 Save Me/Easy, Soft and Slow 1977 4.00
❑ XW1103 Mama/Rainstorm 1977 4.00
❑ XW1181 Angel of the Morning/Save 1978 4.00

Albums

BELL

❑ 6020 [M] Angel of the Morning 1968 40.00
—Mono is white label promo only with "Monaural" on label; sticker with "This is a monaural record for radio station play only" on cover
❑ 6020 [S] Angel of the Morning 1968 20.00

LIBERTY

❑ LN-10166 Merilee Rush 1981 8.00
—Budget-line reissue

UNITED ARTISTS

❑ UA-LA735-G Merilee Rush 1977 10.00

RUSH, RAY

45s

PARKWAY

❑ 846 So What/Can This Be Love 1962 15.00

RUSH, TOM

45s

COLUMBIA

❑ 10021 Ladies Love Outlaws/Maggie 1974 4.00
❑ 10087 No Regrets/Maggie 1975 4.00
❑ 4S-45149 Drop Down Mama/Child's Song 1970 6.00
❑ 45185 Old Man's Song/Lost My Drivin' Wheel 1970 5.00
❑ 45364 Wrong End of the Rainbow/Merrimac County 1971 5.00
❑ 45584 Wind on the Water/Mother Earth 1972 5.00
❑ 45669 Kids These Days/Seems the Songs 1972 5.00

R

Number	Title (A Side/B Side)	Yr	NM
ELEKTRA			
❑ 45604	Who Do You Love/On the Road Again	1966	8.00
❑ 45607	Sugar Babe/Urge for Going	1967	8.00
❑ 45630	No Regrets/Shadow Dream Song	1968	6.00
❑ 45718	Something in the Way She Moves/Who Do You Love	1971	6.00
PRESTIGE			
❑ 289	Diamond Joe/Every Day in the Week	1964	12.00
Albums			
COLUMBIA			
❑ CS 9972	Tom Rush	1970	12.00
—Orange label			
❑ CS 9972	Tom Rush	1970	15.00
—Red "360 Sound" label			
❑ C 30402	Wrong End of the Rainbow	1970	12.00
❑ KC 31306	Merrimack County	1972	12.00
❑ KC 33054	Ladies Love Outlaws	1974	12.00
❑ PC 33907	The Best of Tom Rush	1976	12.00
ELEKTRA			
❑ EKL-288 [M]	Tom Rush	1965	15.00
❑ EKL-308 [M]	Take a Little Walk with Me	1966	15.00
❑ EKS-7288 [S]	Tom Rush	1965	15.00
❑ EKS-7308 [S]	Take a Little Walk with Me	1966	15.00
❑ EKS-74018	The Circle Game	1968	15.00
❑ EKS-74062	Classic Rush	1971	15.00
FANTASY			
❑ 24709 [(2)]	Tom Rush	1973	15.00
—Reissue of Prestige/Folklore recordings			
FOLKLORE			
❑ FRLP-14003 [M]	Got a Mind to Ramble	1964	20.00
❑ FRST-14003 [S]	Got a Mind to Ramble	1964	25.00
LY CORNU			
❑ SA-70-2	Tom Rush at the Unicorn	1962	100.00
PRESTIGE			
❑ PR-7374 [M]	Blues — Songs — Ballads	1965	20.00
❑ PRST-7374 [S]	Blues — Songs — Ballads	1965	25.00
❑ PRST-7536	Got a Mind to Ramble	1968	15.00
—Reissue of Folklore LP			

RUSS, LONNIE

Number	Title (A Side/B Side)	Yr	NM
45s			
4J			
❑ 501	My Wife Can't Cook/Something Old, Something New	1962	15.00
❑ 504	Flip Flop/Tell Me Now	1963	25.00
❑ 507	We Belong Together (same on both sides)	1963	20.00
❑ 510	Lil' Evett/Them Greens	1963	20.00

RUSSELL, BOBBY

Number	Title (A Side/B Side)	Yr	NM
45s			
BUENA VISTA			
❑ 473	The Ballad of Smith & Gabriel Jimmy Boy/Summer Sweet	1969	10.00
❑ 474	The Ballad of Smith & Gabriel Billyboy/Summer Sweet	1969	10.00
COLUMBIA			
❑ 45901	Mid American Manufacturing Tycoon/Ships in the Night	1973	4.00
❑ 46045	The Night the Lights Went Out in Georgia/Go Chase Your Rainbow	1974	4.00
D			
❑ 1115	Not Even Friends/Shackled	1960	12.00
—With Sadie Russell			
ELF			
❑ 90014	Dusty/I Made You This Way	1968	6.00
❑ 90020	1432 Franklin Pike Circle Hero/Let's Talk About It	1968	6.00
❑ 90023	Carlie/Ain't Society Great	1969	6.00
❑ 90027	Then She's a Lover/He Wrote a Song	1969	6.00
❑ 90031	Better Homes and Gardens/Summer Sweet	1969	6.00
F&L			
❑ 518	Camp Getcha 'Losa Ya/Arm Chair Quarterback	1982	6.00
FELSTED			
❑ 8520	The Raven/She's Gonna Be Sorry	1958	15.00
HIT			
❑ 63	The Reverend Mr. Black/Little Band of Gold	1963	10.00
—With the Tennessee Three			
❑ 66	Still/Losing You	1963	10.00
—B-side by Katy Richards			
IMAGE			
❑ 1014	Goin' Steady Dream/To the Ones with Broken Hearts	1961	12.00
MONUMENT			
❑ 899	Once a Day/You Were Mine	1965	8.00
❑ 929	Friends and Memories/Wish I'd Say That	1966	8.00
NATIONAL GENERAL			
❑ 006	As Far As I'm Concerned/Traveling with a Star	1970	8.00
PRIVATE STOCK			
❑ 45,046	Little Boxes/(B-side unknown)	1975	5.00
RISING SONS			
❑ 700	Bluebird/Tears Tell	1967	8.00
UNITED ARTISTS			
❑ 50788	Saturday Morning Confusion/Little Ole Song About Love	1971	5.00
❑ 50853	Goodbye/It Hurts	1971	5.00
❑ 50888	Easy Made for Lovin'/The Bell	1972	5.00
❑ 50904	You Babe/Back to Sausalito	1972	5.00
❑ 50959	Welcome to the U.S. Army/This Is the Life	1972	5.00
Albums			
ELF			
❑ 9500 [M]	Words, Music, Laughter & Tears	1969	40.00
—Mono copies are white label promo only and say "Monaural" on the label			
❑ 9500 [S]	Words, Music, Laughter & Tears	1969	20.00
❑ 9501	Unlimited	1970	15.00
UNITED ARTISTS			
❑ UAS-5548	Saturday Morning Confusion	1971	12.00

RUSSELL, HAL

Number	Title (A Side/B Side)	Yr	NM
Albums			
NESSA			
❑ N-21	NRG Ensemble	1981	20.00
❑ N-25	Generation	1982	20.00

RUSSELL, KURT

Number	Title (A Side/B Side)	Yr	NM
45s			
CAPITOL			
❑ 2823	I Believe in Love/It Ain't Gonna Rain Anymore	1970	10.00
Albums			
CAPITOL			
❑ SKAO-492	Kurt Russell	1970	30.00

RUSSELL, LEE

See LEON RUSSELL.

RUSSELL, LEON

Includes records by his country-western alter ego, "Hank Wilson" and "Hank and Mary Wilson." Also see WILLIE NELSON.

Number	Title (A Side/B Side)	Yr	NM
45s			
A&M			
❑ 734	Cindy/Misty	1964	20.00
ARK 21			
❑ S7-58714	Daddy Sang Bass/He Stopped Loving Her Today	1998	3.00
DOT			
❑ 16771	Everybody's Talkin' 'Bout the Young/It's Alright with Me	1965	40.00
PARADISE			
❑ 628	Good Time Charlie's Got the Blues/Ain't No Love in the City	1984	4.00
❑ 629	Wabash Cannonball/Tennessee Waltz	1984	4.00
—As "Hank Wilson"; A-side with Willie Nelson			
❑ 631	Rescue My Heart/Lost Love	1985	4.00
❑ 631 [PS]	Rescue My Heart/Lost Love	1985	10.00
❑ 8208	Rainbow in Your Eyes/Love's Supposed to Be That Way	1976	4.00
—As "Leon and Mary Russell"			
❑ 8274	Satisfy You/Windsong	1976	4.00
—As "Leon and Mary Russell"			
❑ 8369	Love Crazy/Say You Will	1977	4.00
—As "Leon and Mary Russell"			
❑ 8438	Easy Love/Hold On to This Feeling	1977	4.00
—As "Leon and Mary Russell"			
❑ 8667	Elvis and Marilyn/Anita Bryant	1978	5.00
❑ 8667 [PS]	Elvis and Marilyn/Anita Bryant	1978	5.00
❑ 8719	Midnight Lover/From Maine to Mexico	1978	5.00
❑ 49662	Over the Rainbow/I've Just Seen a Face	1981	4.00
RCA VICTOR			
❑ 47-6884	(I Tasted) Tears on Your Lips/A Catchy Tune	1957	30.00
—As "Lee Russell"			
ROULETTE			
❑ 4049	Honky Tonk Woman/Rainbow at Midnight	1958	25.00
—As "Lee Russell"			
SHELTER			
❑ 301	Roll Away the Stone/Hummingbird	1970	6.00
❑ 7302	It Takes a Lot to Laugh, It Takes a Train to Cry/Home Sweet Oklahoma	1970	6.00
❑ 7305	A Hard Rain's A-Gonna Fall/Me and Baby Jane	1971	6.00
❑ 7316	A Song for You/A Hard Rain's A-Gonna Fall	1971	6.00
❑ 7325	Tight Rope/This Masquerade	1972	5.00
❑ 7328	Slipping Into Christmas/Christmas in Chicago	1972	5.00
❑ 7328 [PS]	Slipping Into Christmas/Christmas in Chicago	1972	25.00
❑ 7336	Roll in My Sweet Baby's Arms/I'm So Lonesome I Could Cry	1973	5.00
—As "Hank Wilson"			
❑ 7337	Queen of the Roller Derby/Roll Away the Stone	1973	5.00
❑ 7338	A Six Pack to Go/Uncle Pen	1973	5.00
—As "Hank Wilson"			
❑ 40210	If I Were a Carpenter/Wild Horses	1974	4.00
❑ 40210 [PS]	If I Were a Carpenter/Wild Horses	1974	8.00
❑ 40277	Time for Love/Leaving Whipporwhill	1974	4.00
❑ 40378	Lady Blue/Laying Right Here in Heaven	1975	4.00
❑ 40483	Back to the Island/Little Hideaway	1975	4.00
❑ 62004	Bluebird/Back to the Island	1976	4.00
❑ 65033	Slipping Into Christmas/Christmas in Chicago	1975	5.00
—Reissue of 7328			
Albums			
MCA			
❑ 682	Leon Russell	1979	8.00
—Reissue of Shelter 52007			
❑ 683	Leon Russell and the Shelter People	1979	8.00
—Reissue of Shelter 52008			
❑ 685	Carney	1979	8.00
—Reissue of Shelter 52011			
❑ 686	Will O' the Wisp	1979	8.00
—Reissue of Shelter 52020			
❑ 37114	Best of Leon	1980	8.00
—Reissue of Shelter 52004			
PARADISE			
❑ 0002	Hank Wilson Vol. II	1984	12.00
❑ PR 2943	Wedding Album	1976	12.00
—As "Leon and Mary Russell"			
❑ BSK 3066	Make Love to the Music	1977	12.00
—As "Leon and Mary Russell"			
❑ BSK 3172	Americana	1978	12.00
❑ BSK 3341	Life and Love	1979	12.00
❑ BSK 3532	The Live Album	1981	10.00
SHELTER			
❑ SHE-1001	Leon Russell	1968	20.00
❑ SR 2108	Stop All That Jazz	1974	15.00
❑ SR 2118	Leon Russell	1974	12.00
—Reissue of 8901			
❑ SR 2119	Leon Russell and the Shelter People	1974	12.00
—Reissue of 8903			
❑ SR 2121	Carney	1974	12.00
—Reissue of 8911			
❑ SR 2138	Will O' the Wisp	1975	15.00
❑ SW-8901	Leon Russell	1970	15.00
—Early reissue of 1001			
❑ SW-8903	Leon Russell and the Shelter People	1971	15.00
❑ SW-8911	Carney	1972	15.00
❑ STCO-8917 [(3)]	Leon Live	1973	20.00
❑ SW-8923	Hank Wilson's Back, Vol. 1	1973	15.00
—As "Hank Wilson"			
❑ 52004	Best of Leon	1976	10.00
❑ 52007	Leon Russell	1977	10.00
—Reissue of 2118			
❑ 52008	Leon Russell and the Shelter People	1977	10.00
—Reissue of 2119			
❑ 52011	Carney	1977	10.00
—Reissue of 2121			
❑ 52014	Hank Wilson's Back, Vol. 1	1977	10.00
—Reissue of 8923			
❑ 52016	Stop All That Jazz	1977	10.00
—Reissue of 2108			
❑ 52020	Will O' the Wisp	1977	10.00
—Reissue of 2138			

RUSSELL, LEON, AND MARC BENNO See ASYLUM CHOIR.

RUSTIX

45s

RARE EARTH

Number	Title (A Side/B Side)	Yr	NM
❑ 5011	Can't You Hear the Music Play/ I Guess This Is Goodbye	1969	6.00
❑ 5014	Come On People/Free Again	1970	6.00
❑ 5034	My Peace of Heaven/ Down, Down	1971	—
—Canceled			
❑ 5037	We All End Up in Boxes/ Down, Down	1971	6.00

Albums

RARE EARTH

Number	Title (A Side/B Side)	Yr	NM
❑ RS-508	Bedlam	1969	15.00
—Regular cover			
❑ RS-508	Bedlam	1969	30.00
—Rounded-top cover			
❑ RS-513	Come On, People	1970	12.00

RUSTY AND DOUG See RUSTY AND DOUG KERSHAW.

RUTLES, THE

45s

WARNER BROS.

Number	Title (A Side/B Side)	Yr	NM
❑ 8560	I Must Be in Love/ Doubleback Alley	1978	12.00

Albums

WARNER BROS.

Number	Title (A Side/B Side)	Yr	NM
❑ PRO-A-723 [DJ]	The Rutles	1978	25.00
—Yellow vinyl with five songs and "banana" label			
❑ HS 3151	The Rutles	1978	25.00
—With bound-in booklet			

RYAN, BARRY Also see PAUL AND BARRY RYAN.

45s

MGM

Number	Title (A Side/B Side)	Yr	NM
❑ 14010	Eloise/Love, I Almost Found You	1968	8.00

POLYDOR

Number	Title (A Side/B Side)	Yr	NM
❑ 14014	Look to the Right, Look to the Left/Oh For the Love of Me	1970	6.00
❑ 14035	Give Me a Sign/Kitsch	1970	6.00
❑ 14065	It Is Written/Annabelle	1970	—
—Canceled			
❑ 14108	Can't Let You Go/When I Was a Child	1971	6.00

PRIDE

Number	Title (A Side/B Side)	Yr	NM
❑ 1012	Alimony Money Blues/ From My Head to My Toe	1972	5.00
❑ 1032	Can't Let You Go/L.A. Woman	1973	5.00

RYAN, CATHY

45s

KING

Number	Title (A Side/B Side)	Yr	NM
❑ 4848	Come Home/The Cricket, the Dove, and the Goldfish	1955	30.00
❑ 4890	Only a Dream/High Falutin' Heart	1956	30.00
❑ 4916	Lazy River/Love You with All My Might	1956	30.00

RYAN, PAUL AND BARRY Also see BARRY RYAN.

45s

MGM

Number	Title (A Side/B Side)	Yr	NM
❑ 13442	Don't Bring Me Your Heartaches/ To Remind You of Our Love	1966	10.00
❑ 13472	Have Pity on the Boy/ There You Go	1966	10.00
❑ 13546	Silent Street/'Twas on a Night Like This	1966	10.00
❑ 13609	Have You Ever Loved Somebody/I'll Tell You Later	1966	10.00
❑ 13719	Keep It Out of Sight/ Who Told You	1967	8.00
❑ 13911	Madrigal/Pictures of Today	1968	8.00

RYDELL, BOBBY

45s

CAMEO

Number	Title (A Side/B Side)	Yr	NM
❑ (no #) [DJ]	Steel Pier	1963	25.00
—One-sided "Steel Pier Promotion"			
❑ 160	Please Don't Be Mad/ Makin' Time	1959	50.00
❑ 164	All I Want Is You/For You, For You	1959	20.00
❑ 167	Kissin' Time/You'll Never Tame Me	1959	15.00
❑ 167 [PS]	Kissin' Time/You'll Never Tame Me	1959	25.00
❑ 169	We Got Love/I Dig Girls	1959	15.00
❑ 169 [PS]	We Got Love/I Dig Girls	1959	25.00
❑ 171	Wild One/Little Bitty Girl	1960	15.00
❑ 171 [PS]	Wild One/Little Bitty Girl	1960	25.00
❑ 175	Swingin' School/Ding-a-Ling	1960	15.00

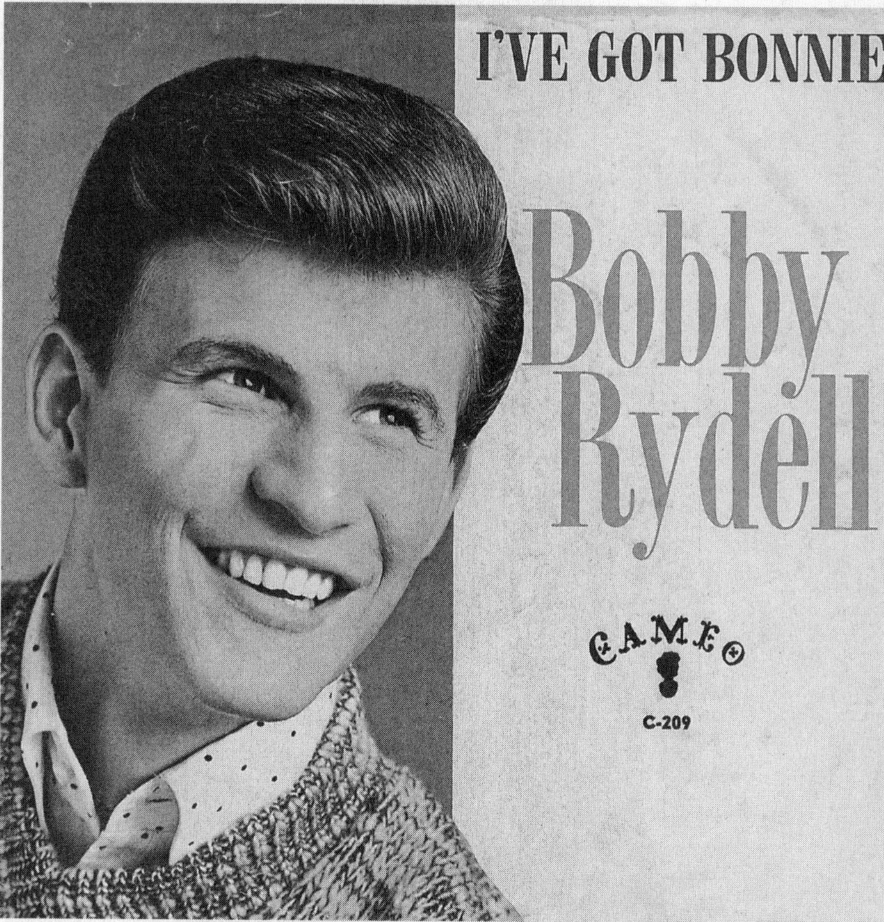

Bobby Rydell, "I've Got Bonnie," Cameo 209, 1962, **$20.**

Number	Title (A Side/B Side)	Yr	NM
❑ 175 [PS]	Swingin' School/Ding-a-Ling	1960	25.00
❑ 179	Volare/I'd Do It Again	1960	15.00
❑ 179 [PS]	Volare/I'd Do It Again	1960	25.00
❑ 182	Sway/Groovy Tonight	1961	15.00
❑ 182 [PS]	Sway/Groovy Tonight	1961	25.00
❑ 186	Good Time Baby/Cherie	1961	15.00
❑ 186 [PS]	Good Time Baby/Cherie	1961	25.00
❑ 190	That Old Black Magic/Don't Be Afraid (To Fall in Love)	1961	15.00
❑ 190 [PS]	That Old Black Magic/Don't Be Afraid (To Fall in Love)	1961	25.00
❑ 192	The Fish/The Third House	1961	15.00
❑ 192 [PS]	The Fish/The Third House	1961	25.00
❑ 201	I Wanna Thank You/ The Door to Paradise	1961	15.00
❑ 201 [PS]	I Wanna Thank You/ The Door to Paradise	1961	25.00
❑ 209	I've Got Bonnie/Lose Her	1962	12.00
❑ 209 [PS]	I've Got Bonnie/Lose Her	1962	20.00
❑ 217	I'll Never Dance Again/ Gee It's Wonderful	1962	12.00
❑ 217 [PS]	I'll Never Dance Again/ Gee It's Wonderful	1962	20.00
❑ 228	The Cha-Cha-Cha/ The Best Man Cried	1962	15.00
❑ 228 [PS]	The Cha-Cha-Cha/ The Best Man Cried	1962	25.00
❑ 242	Butterfly Baby/Love Is Blind	1963	15.00
❑ 242 [PS]	Butterfly Baby/Love Is Blind	1963	25.00
❑ 252	Wildwood Days/Will You Be My Baby	1963	12.00
❑ 252 [PS]	Wildwood Days/Will You Be My Baby	1963	20.00
❑ 265	Little Queenie/The Woodpecker Song	1963	15.00
❑ 265 [PS]	Little Queenie/The Woodpecker Song	1963	25.00
❑ 272	Let's Make Love Tonight/ Childhood Sweetheart	1963	12.00
❑ 272 [PS]	Let's Make Love Tonight/ Childhood Sweetheart	1963	20.00
❑ 280	Forget Him/Love, Love Go Away	1963	12.00
❑ 280 [PS]	Forget Him/Love, Love Go Away	1963	20.00
❑ 309	Make Me Forget/Little Girl, You've Had a Busy Day	1964	12.00
❑ 309 [PS]	Make Me Forget/Little Girl, You've Had a Busy Day	1964	20.00
❑ 320	A World Without Love/ Our Faded Love	1964	15.00
❑ 320 [PS]	A World Without Love/ Our Faded Love	1964	25.00
❑ 361	Ciao, Ciao Bambino/ Voce de la Notte	1965	15.00
❑ 1070	Forget Him/A Message from Bobby	1963	20.00
—Bonus single with Cameo LP C-1070, "Top Hits of 1963"			

CAPITOL

Number	Title (A Side/B Side)	Yr	NM
❑ 5305	I Just Can't Say Goodbye/ Two Is the Loneliest Number	1964	10.00
❑ 5305 [PS]	I Just Can't Say Goodbye/ Two Is the Loneliest Number	1964	15.00
❑ 5352	Diana/Stranger in the World	1965	10.00
❑ 5436	The Joker/Side Show	1965	10.00
❑ 5513	When I See That Girl of Mine/ It Takes Two	1965	10.00
❑ 5556	Roses in the Snow/ A Word for Today	1965	10.00
❑ 5696	She Was the Girl/Not You	1966	10.00
❑ 5780	Open for Business As Usual/ You Gotta Enjoy Joy	1966	10.00

P.I.P.

Number	Title (A Side/B Side)	Yr	NM
❑ 6515	Sway/Feels Good	1976	5.00
❑ 6521	You're Not the Only Girl for Me/ Give Me Your Answer	1976	4.00
❑ 6531	It's Getting Better/ The Singles Scene	1976	4.00

PERCEPTION

Number	Title (A Side/B Side)	Yr	NM
❑ 519	California Sunshine/Honey Buns	1973	5.00
❑ 552	Everything Seemed Better (When I Was Younger)/ Sunday Son	1974	5.00

RCA VICTOR

Number	Title (A Side/B Side)	Yr	NM
❑ 47-9892	Chapel on the Hill/It Must Be Love	1970	6.00

Except when noted otherwise, VG = 25% of NM, and VG+ = 50% of NM. (Example: VG = $2.00, VG+ = $4.00 and NM = $8.00.)

Bobby Rydell and Chubby Checker,
Bobby Rydell/Chubby Checker, Cameo C-1013, 1961, mono, **$30.**

Number	Title (A Side/B Side)	Yr	NM
REPRISE			
❑ 0656	The Lovin' Things/That's What I Call Lovin'	1968	8.00
❑ 0684	The River Is Wide/Absence Makes the Heart Grow Fonder	1968	8.00
❑ 0751	Every Little Bit Hurts/ Time and Changes	1968	8.00
VEKO			
❑ 730/1	Dream Age/Fatty Fatty	1958	120.00
VENISE			
❑ 201	Fatty, Fatty/Happy Happy	1961	30.00
7-Inch Extended Plays			
CAPITOL			
❑ SXA-2281	You're Nobody Till Somebody Loves You/Stranger in the World/Bellazza//Time Out for Tears/Dansero/It's a Sin to Tell a Lie	1965	10.00
—Jukebox issue; small hole, plays at 33 1/3 rpm			
❑ SXA-2281 [PS]	Somebody Loves You	1965	10.00
Albums			
CAMEO			
❑ C-1006 [M]	We Got Love	1959	60.00
❑ C-1007 [M]	Bobby Sings	1960	50.00
❑ C-1009 [M]	Bobby's Biggest Hits	1961	25.00
—Standard cover			
❑ C-1009 [M]	Bobby's Biggest Hits	1961	80.00
—Original with die-cut cover and textured inner sleeve			
❑ C-1010 [M]	Bobby Rydell Salutes "The Great Ones"	1961	25.00
❑ SC-1010 [S]	Bobby Rydell Salutes "The Great Ones"	1961	40.00
❑ C-1011 [M]	Rydell at the Copa	1961	25.00
❑ SC-1011 [S]	Rydell at the Copa	1961	40.00
❑ C-1019 [M]	All the Hits	1962	25.00
—Black vinyl			
❑ C-1019 [M]	All the Hits	1962	150.00
—Red vinyl			
❑ C-1028 [M]	Bobby Rydell's Biggest Hits, Vol. 2	1962	25.00
❑ C-1040 [M]	All the Hits, Vol. 2	1963	25.00

Number	Title (A Side/B Side)	Yr	NM
❑ SC-1040 [P]	All the Hits, Vol. 2	1963	40.00
❑ C-1043 [M]	Bye Bye Birdie	1963	25.00
❑ C-1055 [M]	Wild (Wood) Days	1963	20.00
❑ SC-1055 [S]	Wild (Wood) Days	1963	30.00
❑ C-1070 [M]	The Top Hits of 1963	1963	20.00
—Came with bonus single, also numbered 1070			
❑ SC-1070 [S]	The Top Hits of 1963	1963	30.00
—Came with bonus single, also numbered 1070			
❑ C-1080 [M]	Forget Him	1964	20.00
❑ SC-1080 [R]	Forget Him	1964	20.00
❑ C-2001 [M]	16 Golden Hits	1965	20.00
❑ SC-2001 [R]	16 Golden Hits	1965	20.00
CAPITOL			
❑ ST 2281 [S]	Somebody Loves You	1965	20.00
❑ T 2281 [M]	Somebody Loves You	1965	15.00
P.I.P.			
❑ 6818	Born with a Smile	1976	10.00
SPIN-O-RAMA			
❑ 143 [M]	Starring Bobby Rydell	196?	12.00
❑ S-143 [S]	Starring Bobby Rydell	196?	12.00
STRAND			
❑ SL-1120 [M]	Bobby Rydell Sings	196?	25.00
❑ SLS-1120 [R]	Bobby Rydell Sings	196?	20.00
VENISE			
❑ 10035 [M]	Twistin'	1962	25.00
—Also includes tracks by Barry Norman and Stephen Garrick			

RYDELL, BOBBY/CHUBBY CHECKER Also see each artist's individual listings.

Number	Title (A Side/B Side)	Yr	NM
45s			
CAMEO			
❑ 12E [DJ]	Chubby Sings Bobby-Bobby Sings Chubby	1962	40.00
—B-side blank, promo only			
❑ 13E [DJ]	What Are You Doing New Year's Eve?	1962	40.00
—B-side blank, promo only			
❑ 205	Jingle Bell Rock/ Jingle Bell Imitations	1961	15.00
❑ 205 [PS]	Jingle Bell Rock/ Jingle Bell Imitations	1961	25.00
❑ 214	Teach Me to Twist/ Swingin' Together	1962	15.00
❑ 214 [PS]	Teach Me to Twist/ Swingin' Together	1962	25.00
Albums			
CAMEO			
❑ C 1013 [M]	Bobby Rydell/Chubby Checker	1961	30.00
❑ C-1063 [M]	Chubby Checker and Bobby Rydell	1963	20.00

RYDER, MITCH Also see DETROIT; MITCH RYDER AND THE DETROIT WHEELS.

Number	Title (A Side/B Side)	Yr	NM
12-Inch Singles			
RIVA			
❑ MK 244 [DJ]	When You Were Mine (same on both sides)	1983	10.00
45s			
AVCO EMBASSY			
❑ 4550	Jenny Take a Ride/I Never Had It Better	1970	10.00
DOT			
❑ 17290	I Believe (There Must Be Someone)/Sugar Bee (We Three)	1970	6.00
❑ 17325	It's Been a Long, Long, Long Time/Direct Me	1970	6.00
DYNOVOICE			
❑ 901	What Now My Love/Blessing in Disguise	1967	8.00
❑ 905	Personality-Chantilly Lace/ I Make a Fool of Myself	1968	8.00
❑ 916	Lights of the Night/I Need Loving You	1968	8.00
❑ 934	Baby I Need Your Loving/ Ring Your Bell	1969	8.00
NEW VOICE			
❑ 824	Joy/I'd Rather Go to Jail	1967	8.00
❑ 826	You Are My Sunshine/Wild Child	1967	8.00
❑ 828	Come See About Me/ A Face in the Crowd	1968	8.00
❑ 830	Ruby Baby/You Get Your Kicks	1968	8.00
RIVA			
❑ 213	When You Were Mine/Stand	1983	5.00
Albums			
DYNO VOICE			
❑ 1901 [M]	What Now My Love	1967	20.00
❑ 31901 [S]	What Now My Love	1967	20.00
RIVA			
❑ RV 7503	Never Kick a Sleeping Dog	1983	10.00
SEEDS & STEMS			
❑ 7801	How I Spent My Summer Vacation	1978	12.00
❑ 7804	Naked But Not Dead	1980	12.00

RYDER, MITCH, AND THE DETROIT WHEELS Also see DETROIT; THE DETROIT WHEELS; BILLY LEE AND THE RIVIERAS; MITCH RYDER.

Number	Title (A Side/B Side)	Yr	NM
45s			
NEW VOICE			
❑ 801	I Need Help/I Hope	1965	10.00
❑ 806	Jenny Take a Ride!/ Baby Jane (Mo-Mo Jane)	1965	12.00
—Actual A-side title			
❑ 806	Jenny Takes a Ride!/ Baby Jane (Mo-Mo Jane)	1965	25.00
—Note slightly different A-side title			
❑ 808	Little Latin Lupe Lu/I Hope	1966	10.00
❑ 811	Break Out/I Need Help	1966	10.00
❑ 814	Takin' All I Can Get/ You Get Your Kicks	1966	10.00
❑ 817	Devil with a Blue Dress On & Good Golly Miss Molly/ I Had It Made	1966	12.00
❑ 820	Sock It To Me — Baby!/ I Never Had It Better	1967	10.00
—Version 2: With lyric "Hits me like a PUNCH!" with no doubt about the last word. The copies of this we've seen have a blue label, both "painted on" and "not "painted on," but we can't say yet that ALL copies with that label have this version.			
❑ 820	Sock It To Me — Baby!/ I Never Had It Better	1967	25.00
—Version 1: With lyric "Feels like a punch," mumbled to the point that it sounds obscene. The copy of this we've seen has a multicolor, concentric circle label, but we can't yet say that ALL copies with this label are this version.			
❑ 820 [PS]	Sock It To Me — Baby!/ I Never Had It Better	1967	20.00
—Black strip at the top with white and red print			
❑ 820 [PS]	Sock It To Me — Baby!/ I Never Had It Better	1967	30.00
—White strip at the top with black print			
❑ 822	Too Many Fish in the Sea & Three Little Fishes/ One Grain of Sand	1967	10.00

Except when noted otherwise, VG = 25% of NM, and VG+ = 50% of NM. (Example: VG = $2.00, VG+ = $4.00 and NM = $8.00.)

Number	Title (A Side/B Side)	Yr	NM
❑ 822 [PS]	Too Many Fish in the Sea & Three Little Fishes/ One Grain of Sand	1967	20.00
PHILCO-FORD			
❑ HP-4	Jenny Take a Ride/ Sock It To Me Baby	1967	15.00
—4-inch plastic "Hip Pocket Record" with color sleeve			
Albums			
CREWE			
❑ CR-1335	All Mitch Ryder Hits!	1969	15.00
—Reissue of New Voice 2004			
NEW VOICE			
❑ 2000 [M]	Take a Ride	1966	25.00
❑ S-2000 [S]	Take a Ride	1966	30.00
❑ 2002 [M]	Breakout…!!!	1966	20.00
—With "Devil with a Blue Dress On/Good Golly Miss Molly"			
❑ 2002 [M]	Breakout…!!!	1966	25.00
—Without "Devil with a Blue Dress On/Good Golly Miss Molly"			
❑ S-2002 [S]	Breakout…!!!	1966	25.00
—With "Devil with a Blue Dress On/Good Golly Miss Molly"			
❑ S-2002 [S]	Breakout…!!!	1966	30.00
—Without "Devil with a Blue Dress On/Good Golly Miss Molly"			
❑ 2003 [M]	Sock It To Me!	1967	25.00
❑ S-2003 [S]	Sock It To Me!	1967	30.00
❑ 2004 [M]	All Mitch Ryder Hits!	1967	30.00
❑ NVS-2004 [S]	All Mitch Ryder Hits!	1967	20.00
❑ S-2005	Mitch Ryder Sings the Hits	1968	20.00
RHINO			
❑ R1-70941	Rev Up: The Best of Mitch Ryder and the Detroit Wheels	1989	12.00
SUNDAZED			
❑ LP 5083	Breakout ... !!!	2001	12.00
—Reissue on 180-gram vinyl			
VIRGO			
❑ 12001	The Best of Mitch Ryder and the Detroit Wheels	1972	12.00

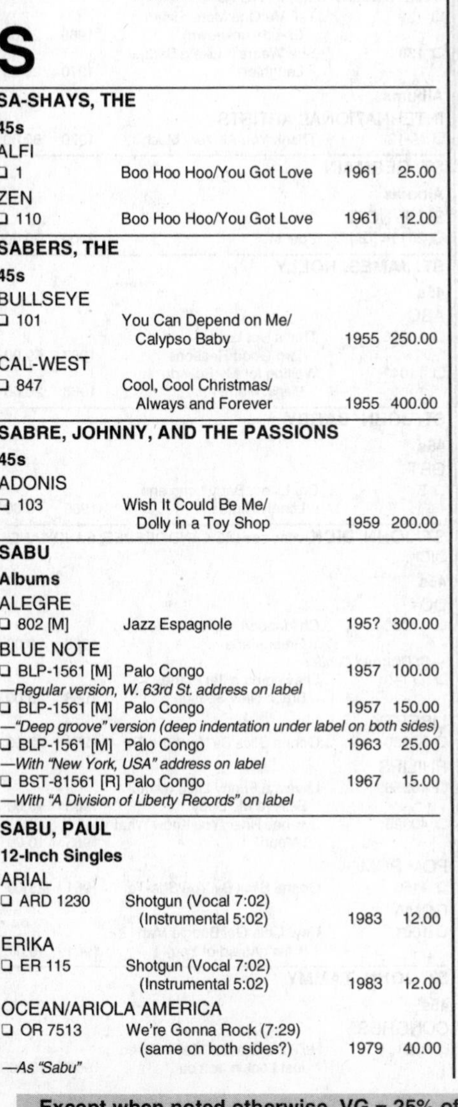

S

SA-SHAYS, THE

Number	Title (A Side/B Side)	Yr	NM
45s			
ALFI			
❑ 1	Boo Hoo Hoo/You Got Love	1961	25.00
ZEN			
❑ 110	Boo Hoo Hoo/You Got Love	1961	12.00

SABERS, THE

Number	Title (A Side/B Side)	Yr	NM
45s			
BULLSEYE			
❑ 101	You Can Depend on Me/ Calypso Baby	1955	250.00
CAL-WEST			
❑ 847	Cool, Cool Christmas/ Always and Forever	1955	400.00

SABRE, JOHNNY, AND THE PASSIONS

Number	Title (A Side/B Side)	Yr	NM
45s			
ADONIS			
❑ 103	Wish It Could Be Me/ Dolly in a Toy Shop	1959	200.00

SABU

Number	Title (A Side/B Side)	Yr	NM
Albums			
ALEGRE			
❑ 802 [M]	Jazz Espagnole	195?	300.00
BLUE NOTE			
❑ BLP-1561 [M]	Palo Congo	1957	100.00
—Regular version, W. 63rd St. address on label			
❑ BLP-1561 [M]	Palo Congo	1957	150.00
—"Deep groove" version (deep indentation under label on both sides)			
❑ BLP-1561 [M]	Palo Congo	1963	25.00
—With "New York, USA" address on label			
❑ BST-81561 [R]	Palo Congo	1967	15.00
—With "A Division of Liberty Records" on label			

SABU, PAUL

Number	Title (A Side/B Side)	Yr	NM
12-Inch Singles			
ARIAL			
❑ ARD 1230	Shotgun (Vocal 7:02) (Instrumental 5:02)	1983	12.00
ERIKA			
❑ ER 115	Shotgun (Vocal 7:02) (Instrumental 5:02)	1983	12.00
OCEAN/ARIOLA AMERICA			
❑ OR 7513	We're Gonna Rock (7:29) (same on both sides?)	1979	40.00
—As "Sabu"			

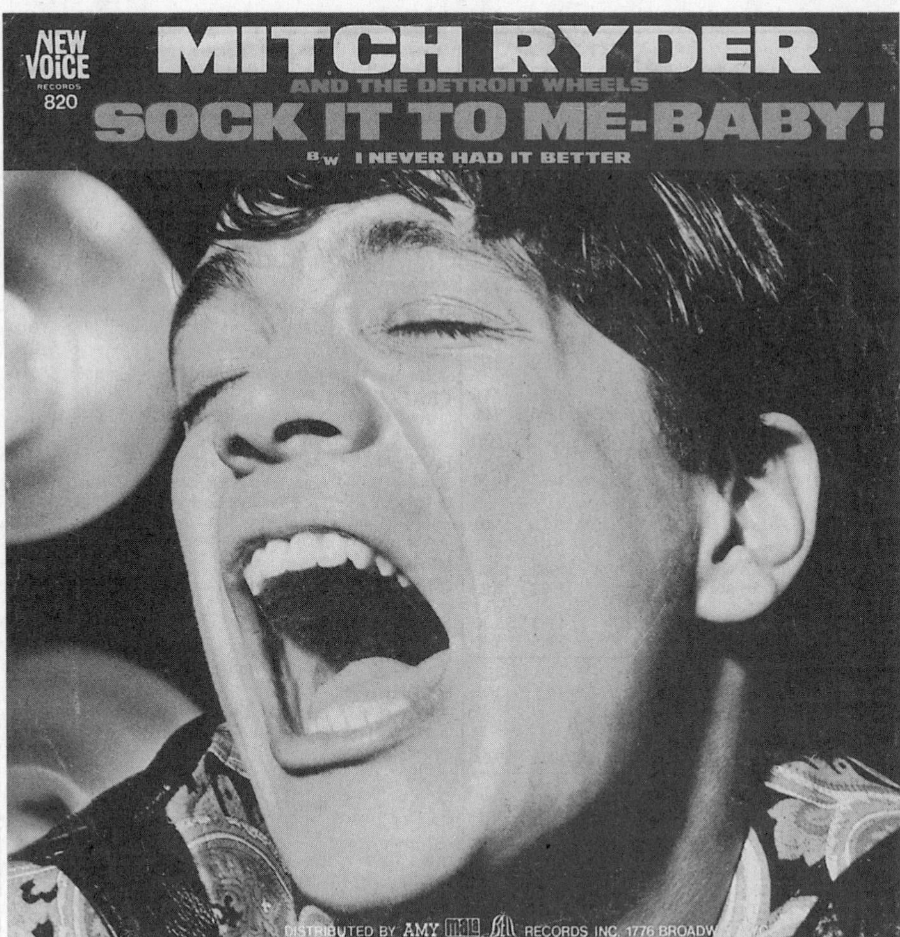

Mitch Ryder and the Detroit Wheels, "Sock It to Me – Baby!," New Voice 820, 1967, black strip at top, $20.

Number	Title (A Side/B Side)	Yr	NM
45s			
MCA			
❑ 41211	Rock Me Slowly/Streetheart	1980	8.00
—As "Sabu"			
OCEAN/ARIOLA AMERICA			
❑ 7510	Loose Lucy Is on the Loose/ You're Mine Forever	1979	15.00
—As "Sabu"			
Albums			
MCA			
❑ 3236	Sabu	1980	12.00
—As "Sabu"			
OCEAN/ARIOLA AMERICA			
❑ SW-49902	Sabu	1979	25.00
—As "Sabu"			

SACCO See LOU CHRISTIE.

SACRED MUSHROOM, THE Members of this group were later in POCO and PURE PRAIRIE LEAGUE.

Number	Title (A Side/B Side)	Yr	NM
Albums			
PARALLAX			
❑ P-4001	The Sacred Mushroom	1969	150.00

SAD SACKS, THE

Number	Title (A Side/B Side)	Yr	NM
45s			
IMPERIAL			
❑ 5517	Sack Dresses/Guard Your Heart	1958	15.00

SADLER, SSGT. BARRY

Number	Title (A Side/B Side)	Yr	NM
45s			
RCA VICTOR			
❑ 47-8739	The Ballad of the Green Berets/ Letter from Vietnam	1966	6.00
❑ 47-8739 [PS]	The Ballad of the Green Berets/ Letter from Vietnam	1966	8.00
❑ 47-8804	The "A" Team/An Empty Glass	1966	6.00
❑ 47-8804 [PS]	The "A" Team/An Empty Glass	1966	8.00
❑ 47-8966	Not Just Lonely/One Day Nearer Home	1966	6.00
❑ 47-9008	I Won't Be Home This Christmas/A Woman Is a Weepin' Willow Tree	1966	8.00
7-Inch Extended Plays			
RCA VICTOR			
❑ VLP 3547	The Ballad of the Green Berets/ I'm a Lucky One/Letter from Vietnam//I'm Watching the Raindrops Fall/Saigon/Garet Trooper	1966	10.00
—Jukebox issue; small hole, plays at 33 1/3 rpm			
❑ VLP 3547 [PS]	Ballads of the Green Berets	1966	10.00
Albums			
RCA VICTOR			
❑ LPM-3547 [M]	Ballads of the Green Berets	1966	15.00
❑ LSP-3547 [S]	Ballads of the Green Berets	1966	20.00
❑ LPM-3605 [M]	"A" Team, The	1966	15.00
❑ LSP-3605 [S]	"A" Team, The	1966	20.00
❑ LPM-3691 [M]	Back Home	1967	20.00
❑ LSP-3691 [S]	Back Home	1967	15.00

SAFARIS, THE

Number	Title (A Side/B Side)	Yr	NM
45s			
DEE JAY			
❑ 203	My Image of a Girl (Is You)/ C'mon Everybody	1989	4.00
—Red vinyl			
❑ 203 [PS]	My Image of a Girl (Is You)/ C'mon Everybody	1989	4.00
ELDO			
❑ 101	Image of a Girl/ Four Steps to Love	1960	25.00
❑ 105	The Girl with the Story in Her Eyes/Summer Nights	1960	25.00
❑ 110	In the Still of the Night/Shadows	1960	30.00
❑ 113	Garden of Love/ Soldier of Fortune	1961	30.00

Except when noted otherwise, VG = 25% of NM, and VG+ = 50% of NM. (Example: VG = $2.00, VG+ = $4.00 and NM = $8.00.)

Number	Title (A Side/B Side)	Yr	NM
VALIANT			
❑ 6036	Kick Out/Lonely Surf Guitar	1963	30.00
SAGA			
45s			
ATLANTIC			
❑ 89195	Only Time Will Tell/ The Way of the World	1987	3.00
PORTRAIT			
❑ 03359	On the Loose/Framed	1982	4.00
❑ RNR-03532	On the Loose/(B-side blank)	1983	6.00
—One-sided budget release			
❑ 03791	Wind Him Up/Amnesia	1983	4.00
❑ 04178	The Flyer/The Sounds of Strangers	1983	4.00
❑ 04178 [PS]	The Flyer/The Sounds of Strangers	1983	4.00
❑ 04361	Scratching the Surface/ The Sound of Strangers	1984	3.00
❑ 05463	What Do I Know/Easy Way Out	1985	3.00
Albums			
ATLANTIC			
❑ 81794	Wildest Dreams	1987	10.00
POLYDOR			
❑ PD-1-6209	Saga	1979	15.00
PORTRAIT			
❑ ARR 38246	Worlds Apart	1982	10.00
❑ FR 38246	Worlds Apart	1982	8.00
—Reissue with new prefix			
❑ FR 38999	Heads or Tales	1983	8.00
❑ BFR 40145	Behaviour	1985	8.00
SAGES, THE			
45s			
RCA VICTOR			
❑ 47-8760	In the Beginning/I'm Not Going to Cry	1965	25.00
SAGITTARIUS			
45s			
COLUMBIA			
❑ 44163	My World Fell Down/Libra	1967	10.00
❑ 44289	Hotel Indiscreeet/Virgo	1967	10.00
❑ 44398	Another Time/Pisces	1967	10.00
❑ 44503	The Truth Is Not Real/You Know I've Found a Way	1968	10.00
❑ 44613	Keeper of the Games/ I'm Not Living Here	1968	10.00
TOGETHER			
❑ 105	In My Room/Navajo Girl	1969	10.00
❑ 122	I Can Still See Your Face/ I Guess the Lord Must Be in New York City	1969	10.00
Albums			
COLUMBIA			
❑ CS 9644	Present Tense	1968	30.00
TOGETHER			
❑ STT-1002	The Blue Marble	1969	50.00
—With two bonus photos; deduct 25 percent if missing			
SAHL, MORT			
45s			
GNP CRESCENDO			
❑ 467	Nixon's Odyssey/Watergate	1973	5.00
REPRISE			
❑ 20038	About Women (Part 1)/ About Women (Part 2)	1961	10.00
Albums			
FANTASY			
❑ 7005 [M]	Mort Sahl at Sunset	196?	30.00
—Black vinyl			
❑ 7005 [M]	Mort Sahl at Sunset	196?	40.00
—Red vinyl			
GNP CRESCENDO			
❑ GNPS-2070	Sing a Song of Watergate	1973	15.00
MERCURY			
❑ MG-21112 [M]	Anyway...Onward	1967	20.00
❑ SR-61112 [S]	Anyway...Onward	1967	20.00
REPRISE			
❑ R-5002 [M]	The New Frontier	1961	20.00
❑ R9-5002 [S]	The New Frontier	1961	25.00
❑ R-5003 [M]	Mort Sahl On Relationships	1961	40.00
❑ R9-5003 [S]	Mort Sahl On Relationships	1961	50.00
—Joan Collins appears on the cover			
VERVE			
❑ MGV-15002 [M]	The Future Lies Ahead	1959	20.00
❑ MGV-15004 [M]	1960: Look Forward in Anger	1959	20.00
❑ MGV-15006 [M]	A Way of Life	1960	20.00
❑ MGV-15012 [M]	Mort Sahl at the Hungry I	1960	20.00
❑ MGVS-15012 [S]	Mort Sahl at the Hungry I	1960	25.00
❑ V-15021 [M]	The Next President	1961	20.00
❑ V6-15021 [S]	The Next President	1961	25.00
❑ V-15049 [M]	Great Moments of Comedy	1965	15.00
SAHM, DOUG Also see SIR DOUGLAS QUINTET.			
45s			
ABC DOT			
❑ 17656	Cowboy Peyton Place/ I Love the Way You Love (The Way I Love You)	1976	6.00
❑ 17674	Crying Inside Sometimes/ I'm Missing You	1976	6.00
ATLANTIC			
❑ 2946	Is Anybody Going to San Antone/Don't Turn Around	1973	8.00
COBRA			
❑ 116	Just a Moment/Sapphire	1961	50.00
CRAZY CAJUN			
❑ 2004	If You Really Want/ Not Tomato Man	1974	5.00
HARLEM			
❑ 108	Baby Tell Me/Sapphire	1960	50.00
❑ 108 [DJ]	Baby Tell Me/Sapphire	1960	100.00
—Gold vinyl promo			
❑ 113	More and More/Slow Down	1960	50.00
MERCURY			
❑ 73098	Be Real/I Don't Want to Go Home	1970	20.00
—As "Wayne Douglas"			
PERSONALITY			
❑ 260	Baby, What's On Your Mind/ Crazy, Crazy Feeling	1962	50.00
RENNER			
❑ 212	Big Hat/Makes No Difference	1961	40.00
❑ 212 [DJ]	Big Hat/Makes No Difference	1961	100.00
—Red vinyl promo			
❑ 215	Baby, What's On Your Mind/ Crazy, Crazy Feeling	1961	40.00
❑ 215 [DJ]	Baby, What's On Your Mind/ Crazy, Crazy Feeling	1961	100.00
—Red vinyl promo			
❑ 226	Two Hearts in Love/Just Because	1962	40.00
❑ 232	Little Angel/Cry	1963	40.00
❑ 240	Lucky Me/A Year Ago Tonight	1963	40.00
❑ 247	Mr. Kool/Bill Beatty	1964	50.00
SARG			
❑ 113	A Real American Joe/ Rolling Rolling	1958	100.00
—As "Little Doug"			
SATIN			
❑ 100	Crazy Daisy/I Can't Believe You Wanna Leave	1959	50.00
SOFT			
❑ 1031	Cry/Down the Pike	1965	30.00
SWINGIN'			
❑ 625	Why, Why, Why/If You Ever Need Me	1960	25.00
TEAR DROP			
❑ 3074	It's a Man Down There/4 A.M.	1966	25.00
—As "Him"			
TEARDROP			
❑ 3479	Who Were You Thinking Of/ Velma	1982	4.00
—With Augie Myers			
❑ 3481	I'm Not a Fool Anymore/ Don't Fight It	1982	4.00
—With Augie Myers			
WARNER BROS.			
❑ 7819	Girls Today/Groover's Paradise	1974	5.00
WARRIOR			
❑ 507	Crazy Daisy/If I Ever Need You	1958	80.00
Albums			
ABC DOT			
❑ DO-2057	Texas Rock for Country Rollers	1976	15.00
ANTONE'S			
❑ ANT-0008	Juke Box Music	1989	12.00
ATLANTIC			
❑ SD 7254	Doug Sahm and Band	1973	15.00
MERCURY			
❑ SRM-1-655	Rough Edges	1972	30.00
TAKOMA			
❑ TAK-7075	Hell of a Spell	1980	12.00
TEARDROP			
❑ TD-5000	The West Side Sound Rolls Again	1982	12.00
WARNER BROS.			
❑ BS 2810	Groovers Paradise	1974	20.00
SAIGONS, THE			
45s			
DOOTONE			
❑ 375	You're Heavenly/Honey Gee	1955	400.00
SAILCAT			
45s			
ELEKTRA			
❑ 45782	Motorcycle Mama/ Rainbow Road	1972	5.00
❑ 45817	Bee Bee Gunn/Baby Ruth	1972	5.00
❑ 45844	She Showed Me/ Sweet Little Jenny	1973	5.00
Albums			
ELEKTRA			
❑ EKS-75029	Sailcat	1972	15.00
SAINT, CATHY			
45s			
DAISY			
❑ 501	Big Bad World/Mr. Heartbreak	1963	50.00
ST. ANDREW'S FAIRWAY			
45s			
TMI			
❑ 75-0101	Pocketful of Pennies/Cross Over	1972	6.00
❑ ZS7 9009	Pocketful of Pennies/Cross Over	1972	7.00
ST. ANTHONY'S FIRE			
Albums			
ZONK			
❑ (# unknown)	St. Anthony's Fire	1968	400.00
ST. CLOUD, ENDLE			
45s			
INTERNATIONAL ARTISTS			
❑ 129	Tell Me One More Time/ (B-side unknown)	1969	20.00
❑ 139	She Wears It Like a Badge/ Laughter	1970	20.00
Albums			
INTERNATIONAL ARTISTS			
❑ IA-12	Thank You All Very Much	1970	60.00
ST. GERMAIN			
Albums			
BLUE NOTE			
❑ 25114 [(2)]	Tourist	2000	30.00
ST. JAMES, HOLLY			
45s			
ABC			
❑ 10996	That's Not Love/ Two Good Reasons	1967	60.00
❑ 11042	Waiting for My Friend/ Magic Moments	1968	20.00
ST. JOHN, BARRY			
45s			
GRT			
❑ 2	Cry Like a Baby/Long and Lonely Nights	1969	6.00
ST. JOHN, DICK Also see DICK AND DEEDEE; SANDY AND DICK.			
45s			
DOT			
❑ 17080	Childhood/Lady of the Burning Green-Jade	1968	8.00
—Of Dick and Deedee			
❑ 17140	Leaving on a Jet Plane/ Brand New Season	1968	8.00
LIBERTY			
❑ 55380	Gonna Stick By You/Sha-Ta	1961	12.00
PHILIPS			
❑ 40256	Love's a Funny Little Game/ Believe Me Baby	1965	10.00
❑ 40325	Swanee River/You Know What I Mean	1965	10.00
POM POM			
❑ 4156	Gonna Stick By You/Sha-Ta	1961	25.00
ROMA			
❑ 1001	Hey, Little Gal/Boogie Man (I Ain't Afraid of You)	1961	15.00
ST. JOHN, TAMMY			
45s			
CONGRESS			
❑ 236	He's the One for Me/I'm Tired Just Lookin' at You	1965	10.00

Except when noted otherwise, VG = 25% of NM, and VG+ = 50% of NM. (Example: VG = $2.00, VG+ = $4.00 and NM = $8.00.)

Number	Title (A Side/B Side)	Yr	NM
❑ 258	Dark Shadows and Empty Hallways/I Mustn't Cry	1965	10.00

ST. LOUIS JIMMY

45s

Number	Title (A Side/B Side)	Yr	NM
DUKE			
❑ 110	Drinkin' Woman/Why Work	1953	120.00
HERALD			
❑ 407	Hard Luck Boogie/Good Book Blues	1953	200.00
❑ 408	Your Evil Ways/Whiskey Drinkin' Woman	1953	200.00
PARROT			
❑ 823	Going Down Slow/Murder in the First Degree	1955	200.00

Albums

Number	Title (A Side/B Side)	Yr	NM
BLUESVILLE			
❑ BVLP-1028 [M]	Goin' Down Blues	1961	120.00
—Blue label, silver print			
❑ BVLP-1028 [M]	Goin' Down Blues	1964	25.00
—Blue label, trident logo at right			

ST. LOUIS UNION

45s

Number	Title (A Side/B Side)	Yr	NM
PARROT			
❑ 9812	Girl/Respect	1966	8.00

ST. PETERS, CRISPIAN

45s

Number	Title (A Side/B Side)	Yr	NM
JAMIE			
❑ 1302	At This Moment/You'll Forget Me, Goodbye	1965	15.00
❑ 1309	At This Moment/No No No	1966	10.00
❑ 1310	You Were On My Mind/What I'm Gonna Be	1966	10.00
❑ 1320	The Pied Piper/Sweet Dawn My True Love	1966	12.00
❑ 1324	Changes/My Little Brown Eyes	1966	10.00
❑ 1328	Your Ever Changin' Mind/But She's Untrue	1966	10.00
❑ 1334	Almost Persuaded/You Are Gone	1967	10.00
❑ 1344	Free Spirit/I'm Always Crying	1967	10.00
❑ 1359	Please Take Me Back/Look Into My Teardrops	1968	8.00

Albums

Number	Title (A Side/B Side)	Yr	NM
JAMIE			
❑ JLPM-3027 [M]	The Pied Piper	1966	30.00
❑ JLPS-3027 [R]	The Pied Piper	1966	20.00

ST. ROMAIN, KIRBY

45s

Number	Title (A Side/B Side)	Yr	NM
IMCO			
❑ 2103	Baby Doll/Summertime Fun	1964	10.00
INETTE			
❑ 103	Summer's Comin'/Miss You So	1963	12.00
❑ 104	Butterflies/Walk On Mr. Blue	1963	12.00
❑ 106	Love Is Magic/I Don't Wanna Fall in Love	1964	12.00
TEARDROP			
❑ 3036	Oh Baby Doll/Summertime Fun	1964	10.00

ST. SHAW, MIKE

45s

Number	Title (A Side/B Side)	Yr	NM
REPRISE			
❑ 0273	Take This Hammer/What's That I Hear	1964	10.00
❑ 0282	Mike's Mid-Nite Special/Summer Skies and Golden Sands	1964	10.00
❑ 0325	From the Bottom of My Heart/Send Me Some Lovin'	1964	12.00

Albums

Number	Title (A Side/B Side)	Yr	NM
REPRISE			
❑ R-6128 [M]	The Mike St. Shaw Trio	1964	20.00
❑ RS-6128 [S]	The Mike St. Shaw Trio	1964	25.00

SAINT STEVEN

45s

Number	Title (A Side/B Side)	Yr	NM
PROBE			
❑ 463	Louisiana Home/Aye Aye Poe Day	1969	20.00

Albums

Number	Title (A Side/B Side)	Yr	NM
PROBE			
❑ CPLP-4506	Over the Hills	1969	75.00

SAINTE-MARIE, BUFFY

45s

Number	Title (A Side/B Side)	Yr	NM
ABC			
❑ 12183	Starwalker/Free the Lady	1976	5.00
❑ 12203	Look at the Facts/(B-side unknown)	1976	5.00
MCA			
❑ 40193	Can't Believe the Feeling When You're Gone/Waves	1974	5.00
❑ 40216	Sweet Little Vera/Waves	1974	5.00
❑ 40286	I Can't Take It No More/Native North American Child: An Odyssey	1974	5.00
❑ 40347	Sweet, Fast Hooker Blues/Generation	1975	5.00
❑ 40368	Love's Got to Breathe and Fly/Nobody Will Ever Know It's Real But You	1975	5.00
VANGUARD			
❑ 35028	Until It's Time for You to Go/The Flower and the Apple Tree	1963	10.00
❑ 35050	Until It's Time for You to Go/Jusqu'au Jour Ou Tu Partiras	1967	8.00
❑ 35053	Circle Game/Until It's Time for You to Go	1967	8.00
❑ 35064	Soulful Shade of Blue/Piney Wood Hills	1968	8.00
❑ 35072	Better to Find Out for Yourself/Sometimes When I Get to Thinkin'	1968	8.00
❑ 35075	From the Bottom of My Heart/I'm Gonna Be a Country Girl Again	1969	8.00
❑ 35091	He's a Keeper of the Fire/Better to Find Out for Yourself	1970	6.00
❑ 35108	The Circle Game/Better to Find Out for Yourself	1970	6.00
❑ 35116	Soldier Blue/Until It's Time for You to Go	1970	6.00
❑ 35127	She Used to Wanna Be a Ballerina/Moratorium	1971	6.00
❑ 35135	Helpless/Now You've Been Gone a Long Time	1971	6.00
❑ 35143	I'm Gonna Be a Country Girl Again/Piney Wood Hills	1971	5.00
❑ 35151	Mister Can't You See/Moonshot	1972	5.00
❑ 35156	He's an Indian Cowboy in the Rodeo/Not the Lovin' Kind	1972	5.00
❑ 35172	I Wanna Hold Your Hand Forever/Jeremiah	1972	5.00
❑ 35180	Soldier Blue/(B-side unknown)	1973	5.00

Albums

Number	Title (A Side/B Side)	Yr	NM
ABC			
❑ D-929	Sweet America	1976	12.00
MCA			
❑ 405	Buffy	1974	12.00
❑ 451	Changing Woman	1975	12.00
VANGUARD			
❑ VSD 3/4 [(2)]	The Best of Buffy Sainte-Marie	1970	20.00
❑ VSD 33/34 [(2)]	The Best of Buffy Sainte-Marie, Vol. 2	1974	15.00
❑ VRS 9142 [M]	It's My Way	1964	15.00
❑ VRS 9171 [M]	Many a Mile	1965	15.00
❑ VRS 9211 [M]	Little Wheel Spin and Spin	1966	15.00
❑ VRS 9250 [M]	Fire & Fleet & Candlelight	1967	15.00
❑ VSQ 40003 [Q]	Moon Shot	1972	25.00
❑ VSQ 40020 [Q]	Quiet Places	1973	25.00
❑ VMS 73113	The Best of Buffy Sainte-Marie	1985	10.00
❑ VSD 79142 [S]	It's My Way	1964	20.00
❑ VSD 79171 [S]	Many a Mile	1965	20.00
❑ VSD 79211 [S]	Little Wheel Spin and Spin	1966	20.00
❑ VSD 79250 [S]	Fire & Fleet & Candlelight	1967	20.00
❑ VSD 79280	I'm Gonna Be a Country Girl Again	1968	15.00
❑ VSD 79300	Illuminations	1969	15.00
❑ VSD 79311	She Used to Wanna Be a Ballerina	1971	15.00
❑ VSD 79312	Moon Shot	1972	15.00
❑ VSD 79330	Quiet Places	1973	12.00
❑ VSD 79340	Native Child: Odyssey	1974	12.00

SAINTS, THE

12-Inch Singles

Number	Title (A Side/B Side)	Yr	NM
TVT			
❑ 2111 [DJ]	Just Like Fire Would (same on both sides)	1987	8.00
❑ 2123	The Music Goes 'Round My Head/Stay	1988	8.00

45s

Number	Title (A Side/B Side)	Yr	NM
SIRE			
❑ 1005	(I'm) Stranded/No Time	1977	15.00
—Promo copy worth 50% less			
❑ 1005 [PS]	(I'm) Stranded/No Time	1977	7.00

Albums

Number	Title (A Side/B Side)	Yr	NM
SIRE			
❑ SR 6039	(I'm) Stranded	1977	25.00
❑ SRK 6055	Eternally Yours	1978	25.00
TVT			
❑ 2111	All Fools Day	1987	10.00
❑ 2121	Prodigal Son	1988	10.00

SAKAMOTO, KYU

45s

Number	Title (A Side/B Side)	Yr	NM
CAPITOL			
❑ 4945	Sukiyaki/Anoko No Namaewa Nantenkana	1963	8.00
—Third pressing: A-side spelled correctly with no subtitle			
❑ 4945	Sukiyaki/Anoko No Namaewa Nantenkana	1963	10.00
—Second pressing: A-side spelled correctly, subtittled "Music of 'Ue O Muite Aruko' "			
❑ 4945	Sukiyaka/Anoko No Namaewa Nantenkana	1963	15.00
—First pressing: Misspelled A-side			
❑ 5016	China Nights (Shina No Yoru)/Benkyo No Cha Cha Cha	1963	8.00
❑ 5080	The Olympics Song/Tankobushi	1963	8.00
❑ 5262	Sayonara Tokyo/I Like You	1964	8.00
EMI			
❑ 4150	Why/Elimo	1975	5.00

Albums

Number	Title (A Side/B Side)	Yr	NM
CAPITOL			
❑ DT 10349 [R]	Sukiyaki and Other Japanese Hits	1963	15.00
❑ T 10349 [M]	Sukiyaki and Other Japanese Hits	1963	25.00

SALAS BROTHERS, THE

45s

Number	Title (A Side/B Side)	Yr	NM
FARO			
❑ 614	Leaving You/Darling, Please Bring Your Love	1964	10.00
❑ 619	The Return of Farmer John/Love Is Strange	1965	10.00
❑ 625	Donde Este Santa Claus/One Like Mine	1966	8.00

SALEM MASS

Albums

Number	Title (A Side/B Side)	Yr	NM
SALEM MASS			
❑ SM-101	Witch Burning	1972	250.00

SALEMS, THE

45s

Number	Title (A Side/B Side)	Yr	NM
EPIC			
❑ 9480	Ol' Man River/Maria	1961	15.00
MERCURY			
❑ 71754	My Precious Love/I'll Still Go On Loving You	1961	15.00

SALES, SOUPY

45s

Number	Title (A Side/B Side)	Yr	NM
ABC-PARAMOUNT			
❑ 10646	The Mouse/Pachalafaka	1965	12.00
❑ 10681	Speedy Gonzales/Hey, Pearl	1965	10.00
❑ 10747	I'm a Bird Watching Man/Where the Blue Folks Go	1965	10.00
BRUNSWICK			
❑ 55472	Break Your Back/Tom Jones (Push and Pull)	1972	10.00
CAPITOL			
❑ 5752	Spanish Flea/That Wasn't No Girl	1966	10.00
❑ 5752 [PS]	Spanish Flea/That Wasn't No Girl	1966	30.00
❑ 5766	Backwards Alphabet/Use Your Noggin	1966	10.00
MOTOWN			
❑ 1141	Muck-Arty Park/Green Grow the Lilacs	1968	40.00
REPRISE			
❑ 244	Santa Claus Is Surfin' to Town/Santa Claus Is Comin' to Town	1963	30.00
❑ 0368	Pie in the Face/Soupy Sez	1965	15.00
❑ 20041	Hippy's Cha Cha Hips/White Fang	1961	15.00
❑ 20064	Because of Black Tooth/Soupy's Theme	1962	15.00
❑ 20108	My Baby's Got a Crush on Frankenstein/Doggone Doggie	1962	15.00
❑ 20189	And That's a Shame/Hilly Billy Ding Dong Choo Choo	1963	15.00
WIZDOM			
❑ W1978	It's My Ego/It's My Ego	1978	10.00
—Promo only			

Albums

Number	Title (A Side/B Side)	Yr	NM
ABC-PARAMOUNT			
❑ 503 [M]	Spy with a Pie	1965	25.00
❑ S-503 [S]	Spy with a Pie	1965	30.00
❑ 517 [M]	Soupy Sales Sez Do the Mouse and Other Teen Hits	1965	25.00
❑ S-517 [S]	Soupy Sales Sez Do the Mouse and Other Teen Hits	1965	30.00

S

Number	Title (A Side/B Side)	Yr	NM
MCA			
5274	Still Soupy After All These Years	1981	12.00
MOTOWN			
MS 686	A Bag of Soup	1969	25.00
REPRISE			
R 6010 [M]	The Soupy Sales Show	1961	30.00
R9 6010 [S]	The Soupy Sales Show	1961	40.00
R 6052 [M]	Up in the Air	1962	30.00
R9 6052 [S]	Up in the Air	1962	40.00

SALLEE, VICKIE

Number	Title (A Side/B Side)	Yr	NM
45s			
DOT			
16651	Jimmy Darling/Wild Angel	1964	10.00
16710	Little Wishing Star/Oh My Love	1965	10.00
REPRISE			
20118	There Goes the Lucky One/Your Favorite Lie	1962	15.00

SALLYANGIE

Also see MIKE OLDFIELD.

Number	Title (A Side/B Side)	Yr	NM
Albums			
WARNER BROS.			
WS 1783	Children of the Sun	1969	15.00

SALSOUL ORCHESTRA, THE

Number	Title (A Side/B Side)	Yr	NM
12-Inch Singles			
SALSOUL			
358 [DJ]	Deck the Halls (7:29)/The Salsoul Christmas Suite (7:59)	1981	12.00
45s			
SALSOUL			
2002	Salsoul Hustle/Salsoul Hustle (Part 2)	1975	5.00
2004	Tangerine/Salsoul Hustle	1975	5.00
2007	You're Just the Right Size/Chicago Bus Stop (Ooh I Like It)	1976	5.00
2011	Nice 'n' Naasty/Nightcrawler	1976	5.00
2016	My Love Is Free/(B-side unknown)	1976	5.00
2018	Ritzy Mambo/Salsoul: 3001	1977	5.00
2037	Short Shorts/It's a New Day	1977	5.00
2038	Getaway/Magic Bird of Fire	1977	5.00
2052	We Wish You a Merry Christmas/Merry Christmas All	1976	5.00
2052 [PS]	We Wish You a Merry Christmas/Merry Christmas All	1976	6.00
2064	West Side Encounter — West Side Story (Medley)/Evergreen	1978	4.00
2072	Sgt. Pepper's Lonely Hearts Club Band/Ease On Down the Road	1978	4.00
2077	The Little Drummer Boy/Christmas Time	1978	5.00
2086	Somebody to Love/(B-side unknown)	1979	4.00
2093	Street Sense/Sun After the Rain	1979	4.00
2096	How High/Nothing Can Change This Love	1979	4.00
2155	Deck The Halls/The Salsoul Christmas Suite	1981	4.00
7026	Take Some Time Out (For Love)/(B-side unknown)	1982	3.00
7050	How I Love It So/(B-side unknown)	1983	3.00
Albums			
SALSOUL			
CA-1001	Christmas Jollies	198?	8.00
—Reissue			
CA-1004	Christmas Jollies II	198?	8.00
—Reissue			
SZS 5501	The Salsoul Orchestra	1975	10.00
SZS 5502	Nice 'n' Naasty	1976	10.00
SZS 5507	Christmas Jollies	1976	12.00
SZS 5515	Magic Journey	1977	10.00
SA-8500	Up the Yellow Brick Road	1978	10.00
SA-8508	Greatest Disco Hits/Music for Non-Stop Dancing	1978	10.00
SA-8516	Street Sense	1979	10.00
SA-8528	How High	1980	10.00
SA 8547	Christmas Jollies II	1981	12.00
SA-8552	Heat It Up	1982	10.00

SALT WATER TAFFY

Number	Title (A Side/B Side)	Yr	NM
45s			
BUDDAH			
37	Finders Keepers/He'll Pay	1968	8.00
57	Sticks and Stones/Suddenly I See	1968	8.00
METROMEDIA			
220	Summertime Girl/Spend the Sunshine	1971	8.00
UNITED ARTISTS			
50691	Summertime Girl/One Hand Washes the Other	1970	10.00
Albums			
BUDDAH			
BDS-5021	Finders Keepers	1968	20.00

SALVATION

Number	Title (A Side/B Side)	Yr	NM
45s			
ABC			
11025	Love Comes in Funny Packages/Think Twice	1967	8.00
UNITED ARTISTS			
50695	Tomorrow Is the First Day of the Rest of Your Life/Someday the Gray Will Come	1970	8.00
Albums			
ABC			
S-623	Salvation	1968	20.00
S-653	Gypsy Carnival Caravan	1968	20.00

SAM AND DAVE

Also see SAM MOORE.

Number	Title (A Side/B Side)	Yr	NM
45s			
ALSTON			
777	Never, Never/Lotta Lovin'	1964	20.00
ATLANTIC			
2517	You Don't Know What You Mean to Me/This Is Your World	1968	6.00
2540	Can't You Find Another Way (Of Doing It)/Still Is the Night	1968	6.00
2568	Everybody Got to Believe in Somebody/If I Didn't Have a Girl Like You	1968	6.00
2590	Soul Sister, Brown Sugar/Come On In	1968	6.00
2608	Born Again/Get It	1969	6.00
2668	Holdin' On/Ooh Ooh Ooh	1969	6.00
2714	I'm Not an Indian Giver/Baby-Baby Don't Stop Now	1970	6.00
2728	One Part Love, Two Parts Pain/When You Steal from Me	1970	6.00
2733	When You Steal from Me (You're Only Hurting Yourself)/You Easily Excite Me	1970	6.00
2839	Don't Pull Your Love/Jody Ryder Got Killed	1971	6.00
CONTEMPO			
7004	We Can Work It Out/Why Did You Do It	1977	5.00
MARLIN			
6100	I Need Love/Keep a-Walkin'	1961	40.00
6104	No More Pain/My Love Belongs to You	1961	40.00
ROULETTE			
4419	I Need Love/Keep a-Walkin'	1962	12.00
4445	No More Pain/My Love Belongs to You	1962	12.00
4461	She's Alright/It Feels So Nice	1962	12.00
4480	It Was So Nice While It Lasted/You Ain't No Big Thing, Baby	1963	12.00
4508	If She'll Still Have Me/Listening for My Name	1963	12.00
4533	I Found Out/I Got a Thing Going On	1963	12.00
4671	It Feels So Nice/It Was So Nice While It Lasted	1966	8.00
STAX			
168	Goodnight Baby/A Place Nobody Can Find	1965	15.00
175	I Take What I Want/Sweet Home	1965	12.00
180	You Don't Know Like I Know/Blame Me (Don't Blame My Heart)	1965	12.00
189	Hold On! I'm a-Comin'/I Got Everything I Need	1966	15.00
198	Said I Wasn't Gonna Tell Nobody/If You Got the Loving	1966	10.00
204	You Got Me Hummin'/Sleep Good Tonight	1967	10.00
210	When Something Is Wrong with My Baby/Small Portion of Your Love	1967	10.00
218	Soothe Me/I Can't Stand Up for Falling Down	1967	10.00
231	Soul Man/May I Baby	1967	12.00
242	I Thank You/Wrap It Up	1968	12.00
UNITED ARTISTS			
XW438	A Little Bit of Good (Cures a Whole Lot of Bad)/Blinded by Love	1974	6.00
XW531	Under the Boardwalk/Give It What You Can	1974	6.00
Albums			
ATLANTIC			
SD 8205	I Thank You	1968	25.00
SD 8218	The Best of Sam and Dave	1969	20.00
81279	The Best of Sam and Dave	1985	10.00
81718	Soul Men	1987	10.00
—Reissue of Stax 725			
GUSTO			
0045	Sweet and Funky Gold	197?	10.00
ROULETTE			
R-25323 [M]	Sam and Dave	1966	30.00
SR-25323 [S]	Sam and Dave	1966	40.00
STAX			
ST-708 [M]	Hold On, I'm Comin'	1966	40.00
STS-708 [S]	Hold On, I'm Comin'	1966	50.00
ST-712 [M]	Double Dynamite	1966	30.00
STS-712 [S]	Double Dynamite	1966	40.00
ST-725 [M]	Soul Men	1967	30.00
STS-725 [S]	Soul Men	1967	40.00
UNITED ARTISTS			
UA-LA524-G	Back At 'Cha!	1975	12.00

SAM THE SHAM AND THE PHARAOHS

Number	Title (A Side/B Side)	Yr	NM
45s			
ATLANTIC			
2767	Me and Bobby McGee/Key to the Highway	1970	5.00
—As "Sam Samudio"			
DINGO			
001	Haunted House/How Does a Cheating Woman Feel	1964	200.00
FRETONE			
048	Wookie (Part 1)/Wookie (Part 2)	1977	10.00
—As "Sam the Sham"			
049	Ain't No Lie/Baby You Got It	1977	10.00
—As "Sam the Sham"			
MGM			
13322	Wooly Bully/Ain't Gonna Move	1965	15.00
13364	Ju Ju Hand/Big City Lights	1965	12.00
13364 [PS]	Ju Ju Hand/Big City Lights	1965	20.00
13397	Ring Dang Doo/Don't Try It Again	1965	12.00
13397 [PS]	Ring Dang Doo/Don't Try It Again	1965	20.00
13452	Red Hot/Long Long Way	1966	12.00
13506	Lil' Red Riding Hood/Love Me Like Before	1966	15.00
13581	The Hair on My Chinny Chin Chin/(I'm In with the) Out Crowd	1966	12.00
13581 [PS]	The Hair on My Chinny Chin Chin/(I'm In with the) Out Crowd	1966	20.00
13649	How Do You Catch a Girl/Love You Left Behind	1966	12.00
13649 [PS]	How Do You Catch a Girl/Love You Left Behind	1966	20.00
13713	Oh That's Good, No That's Bad/Take What You Can Get	1967	10.00
13747	Black Sheep/My Day's Gonna Come	1967	10.00
13803	Banned in Boston/Money's My Problem	1967	10.00
—As "The Sam the Sham Revue"			
13863	Yakety Yak/Let Our Love Light Shine	1967	10.00
—As "The Sam the Sham Revue"			
13920	Old Mac Donald Has a Boogaloo Farm/I Never Was No One	1968	10.00
13972	I Couldn't Spell !!@!/Down Home Strut	1968	15.00
14021	Wolly Bully/Ain't Gonna Move	1968	10.00
14642	Fate/Oh Lo	1973	10.00
PHILCO-FORD			
HP-3	Ju Ju Hand/Wooly Bully	1967	30.00
—4-inch plastic "Hip Pocket Record" with color sleeve			
TUPELO			
2982	Betty and Dupree/Manchild	1963	60.00
XL			
905	The Signifyin' Monkey/Juimonos	1964	50.00
906	Wooly Bully/Ain't Gonna Move	1965	300.00
Albums			
ATLANTIC			
SD 8271	Hard and Heavy	1971	15.00
—As "Sam Samudio"			
MGM			
E-4297 [M]	Wooly Bully	1965	30.00
SE-4297 [S]	Wooly Bully	1965	40.00
E-4317 [M]	Their Second Album	1965	25.00
SE-4317 [S]	Their Second Album	1965	30.00
E-4347 [M]	On Tour	1966	25.00
SE-4347 [S]	On Tour	1966	30.00
E-4407 [M]	Lil' Red Riding Hood	1966	25.00
SE-4407 [S]	Lil' Red Riding Hood	1966	30.00
E-4422 [M]	The Best of Sam the Sham and the Pharoahs	1967	20.00

Number	Title (A Side/B Side)	Yr	NM
❑ SE-4422 [S]	The Best of Sam the Sham and the Pharoahs	1967	25.00
❑ E-4477 [M]	Nefertiti	1967	25.00
❑ SE-4477	The Sam The Sham Revue	1968	20.00
—Retitled reissue			
❑ SE-4477 [S]	Nefertiti	1967	25.00
❑ SE-4526	Ten of Pentacles	1968	20.00
❑ ST 90422 [S]	Wooly Bully	1965	50.00
—Capitol Record Club edition			
❑ T 90422 [M]	Wooly Bully	1965	40.00
—Capitol Record Club edition			
POLYDOR			
❑ 827917-1	The Best of Sam the Sham and the Pharoahs	1985	10.00
RHINO			
❑ RNLP-122	Pharoahization: The Best of Sam the Sham and the Pharoahs (1965-1967)	1986	10.00

SAMHAIN
Also see THE MISFITS; DANZIG.

Number	Title (A Side/B Side)	Yr	NM
7-Inch Extended Plays			
PLAN 9			
❑ PL9-05	Unholy Passion	1985	50.00
—Red vinyl			
❑ PL9-05	Unholy Passion	1985	60.00
—White vinyl			
❑ PL9-05 [PS]	Unholy Passion	1985	50.00
—Maroon cover			
❑ PL9-05 [PS]	Unholy Passion	1985	60.00
—Tan cover			
Albums			
PLAN 9			
❑ PL9-04	Initium	1984	50.00
—Black vinyl; "8-84" scrawled in trail-off wax			
❑ PL9-04	Initium	1984	100.00
—500 on red vinyl			
❑ PL9-04	Initium	1984	300.00
—100 on white vinyl			
❑ PL9-04	Initium	1984	300.00
—No more than 100 on marbled black and white vinyl			
❑ PL9-04	Initium	1984	400.00
—Pink vinyl "error" pressing			
❑ PL9-05 [EP]	Unholy Passion	1985	12.00
—Black vinyl, maroon cover			
❑ PL9-05 [EP]	Unholy Passion	1985	80.00
—Black vinyl, tan cover (original)			
❑ PL9-05 [EP]	Unholy Passion	1985	100.00
—Red vinyl, maroon cover			
❑ PL9-05 [EP]	Unholy Passion	1985	100.00
—White vinyl, tan cover			
❑ PL9-07	November Coming Fire	1986	30.00
—Regular issue on black vinyl			
❑ PL9-07	November Coming Fire	1986	150.00
—200 on orange vinyl			

SAMMY AND THE DEL-LARKS

Number	Title (A Side/B Side)	Yr	NM
45s			
EA-JAY			
❑ 100	Baby Come On/I Never Will Forget	1961	200.00

SAMMY AND THEODORE

Number	Title (A Side/B Side)	Yr	NM
45s			
HIT			
❑ 235	Sounds of Silence/ Flowers on the Wall	1966	8.00
—B-side by the Sheridan Brothers			
❑ 246	Homeward Bound/Woman	1966	8.00
—B-side by Bobby and Buddy			
❑ 259	I Am a Rock/Did You Ever Have to Make Up Your Mind	1966	8.00
—B-side by the Jalopy Five			
❑ 323	Scarborough Fair (/Canticle)/ (Theme from) Valley of the Dolls	1968	8.00
—B-side by Kathy Shannon			

SAMPLE, JOE

Number	Title (A Side/B Side)	Yr	NM
Albums			
ABC			
❑ AA-1050	Rainbow Seeker	1978	10.00
❑ AA-1126	Carmel	1979	12.00
CRUSADERS			
❑ 16001	Carmel	198?	20.00
—Audiophile vinyl			
MCA			
❑ AA-1050	Rainbow Seeker	1979	8.00
—Reissue of ABC 1050			
❑ AA-1126	Carmel	1979	10.00
—Reissue of ABC 1126			
❑ 5172	Voices in the Rain	1981	10.00
❑ 5397	The Hunter	1983	10.00
❑ 5481	Oasis	1985	10.00
❑ 5978	Roles	1987	10.00
❑ 27077	Voices in the Rain	198?	8.00
—Budget-line reissue			
❑ 37210	Carmel	198?	8.00
—Budget-line reissue			
MOBILE FIDELITY			
❑ 1-016	Rainbow Seeker	1979	20.00
—Audiophile vinyl			
STORYVILLE			
❑ 4000	Fancy Dance	1980	12.00
WARNER BROS.			
❑ 25781	Spellbound	1989	12.00
❑ 26318	Ashes to Ashes	1990	15.00

SAMPLE, JOE; RAY BROWN; SHELLY MANNE

Number	Title (A Side/B Side)	Yr	NM
Albums			
EAST WIND			
❑ 10001	The Three	1976	20.00
INNER CITY			
❑ IC-6007	The Three	197?	15.00

SAMPLE, JOE, AND DAVID T. WALKER

Number	Title (A Side/B Side)	Yr	NM
Albums			
CRUSADERS			
❑ 16004	Swing Street Café	198?	20.00
—Audiophile vinyl			
MCA			
❑ 5785	Swing Street Café	198?	10.00

SAMUDIO, SAM
See SAM THE SHAM AND THE PHARAOHS.

SAN SEBASTIAN STRINGS, THE

Number	Title (A Side/B Side)	Yr	NM
45s			
WARNER BROS.			
❑ 7012	Days of the Dancing/ Pushing the Clouds Away	1967	5.00
❑ 7084	Mud Kids/Tender Earth	1967	5.00
❑ 7754	And Every Day Was Christmas/ Sunset Colors	1973	5.00
Albums			
STANYAN			
❑ 10043	La Mer	1972	10.00
WARNER BROS.			
❑ W 1670 [M]	The Sea	1967	15.00
❑ WS 1670 [S]	The Sea	1967	12.00
❑ W 1705 [M]	The Earth	1967	15.00
❑ WS 1705 [S]	The Earth	1967	12.00
❑ WS 1720	The Sky	1968	12.00
❑ 3WS 1730 [(3)]	The Sea, The Earth, The Sky	1968	20.00
❑ WS 1764	Home to the Sea	1968	12.00
❑ WS 1795	For Lovers	1969	12.00
❑ 3WS 1827 [(3)]	The Complete Sea	1969	20.00
❑ WS 1839	The Soft Sea	1970	12.00
❑ BS 2622	Winter	1972	10.00
❑ BS 2707	Summer	1973	10.00
❑ BS4-2707 [Q]	Summer	1973	15.00
❑ 4WS 2754 [(4)]	Seasons	1973	20.00
❑ BS 2768	Bouquet — The Best of the San Sebastian Strings	1974	10.00
❑ BS 2837	With Love	1975	10.00
❑ ST-91618	Home to the Sea	1968	15.00
—Capitol Record Club edition			

SANCHEZ, JOE

Number	Title (A Side/B Side)	Yr	NM
45s			
IMPERIAL			
❑ 66190	Unlucky Me/Our Love Baby Is Running Down	1966	20.00

SANCTUARY
Morphed into NEVERMORE.

Number	Title (A Side/B Side)	Yr	NM
Albums			
COLUMBIA			
❑ BFE 40920	Refuge Denied	1987	10.00
❑ 45085	Into The Mirror Black	1990	16.00

SANDALS, THE

Number	Title (A Side/B Side)	Yr	NM
45s			
AURA			
❑ 4501	School's Out/Wild As the Sea	1964	25.00
—As "The Sandells"			
WORLD PACIFIC			
❑ 405	Scrambler/Out Front	1964	25.00
—As "The Sandells"			
❑ 415	Endless Summer/6-Pak	1964	25.00
❑ 421	All Over Again/Always	1965	15.00
❑ 77840	Theme from Endless Summer/ 6-Pak	1966	15.00
❑ 77852	Tell Us Dylan/Why Should I Cry	1966	15.00
❑ 77867	Cloudy/House of Painted Glass	1967	15.00
Albums			
WORLD PACIFIC			
❑ ST-1818 [S]	Scrambler	1964	100.00
—As "The Sandells"; black vinyl			
❑ ST-1818 [S]	Scrambler	1964	250.00
—As "The Sandells"; red vinyl			
❑ WP-1818 [M]	Scrambler	1964	80.00
—As "The Sandells"			
❑ ST-1832 [S]	The Endless Summer	1966	30.00
❑ WP-1832 [M]	The Endless Summer	1966	25.00
❑ ST-21884	The Last of the Ski Bums	1969	25.00
—With skiers' silhouettes on cover			
❑ ST-21884	The Last of the Ski Bums	1969	25.00
—With Volkswagon bus on cover			

SANDERS, BOBBY

Number	Title (A Side/B Side)	Yr	NM
45s			
KAYBO			
❑ 618	It Was You/I'm On My Way	1961	100.00
KENT			
❑ 382	Maybe I'm Wrong/ You've Forgotten Me	1962	300.00
PICK-A-HIT			
❑ 100	Lover/The Way I Feel	196?	10.00

SANDERS, ED

Number	Title (A Side/B Side)	Yr	NM
Albums			
REPRISE			
❑ MS 2105	Beer Cans on the Moon	1972	25.00
❑ RS-6374	Sanders' Truckstop	1969	25.00

SANDERS, NELSON

Number	Title (A Side/B Side)	Yr	NM
45s			
LA BEAT			
❑ 6608	This Love Is Here to Stay/ Tired of Being Your Fool	1966	100.00
RAMBLER			
❑ 3001	Mojo Man/I'm Lonely	196?	1000.
SOUL KING			
❑ 402	I Hold the Key/It's Real	1991	12.00

SANDERS, PHAROAH

Number	Title (A Side/B Side)	Yr	NM
45s			
ARISTA			
❑ 0329	As You Are/Pharomba	1978	5.00
❑ 0356	Got to Give It Up/ (B-side unknown)	1978	5.00
Albums			
ABC IMPULSE!			
❑ A-9138 [M]	Tauhid	1967	30.00
❑ AS-9138 [S]	Tauhid	1967	20.00
❑ AS-9181	Karma	1969	20.00
❑ AS-9190	Jewels of Thought	1970	20.00
❑ AS-9199	Summun Bukmun Umyum	1970	20.00
❑ AS-9206	Thembi	1971	15.00
❑ AQ-9219 [Q]	Black Unity	1974	18.00
❑ AS-9219	Black Unity	1972	15.00
❑ AQ-9227 [Q]	Live at the East	1974	18.00
❑ AS-9227	Live at the East	1973	15.00
❑ AS-9229 [(2)]	The Best of Pharoah Sanders	1973	20.00
❑ AS-9233	Wisdom Through Music	1973	15.00
❑ AQ-9254 [Q]	Village of the Pharoahs	1974	18.00
❑ AS-9254	Village of the Pharoahs	1974	12.00
❑ AQ-9261 [Q]	Elevation	1974	18.00
❑ AS-9261	Elevation	1974	12.00
❑ AQ-9280 [Q]	Love in Us All	1975	18.00
❑ ASD-9280	Love in Us All	1975	12.00
ARISTA			
❑ AL 4161	Love Will Find a Way	1978	12.00
ESP-DISK'			
❑ 1003 [M]	Pharoah's First	1965	25.00
❑ S-1003 [S]	Pharoah's First	1965	30.00
GRP/IMPULSE!			
❑ IMP-219	Black Unity	199?	15.00
—Reissue on audiophile vinyl			
INDIA NAVIGATION			
❑ IN-1027	Pharoah	1977	12.00
MCA			
❑ 4151 [(2)]	The Best of Pharoah Sanders	1981	12.00
—Reissue of Impulse 9229			
❑ 29056	Tauhid	1981	8.00
—Reissue of Impulse 9138			
❑ 29057	Karma	1981	8.00
—Reissue of Impulse 9181			
❑ 29058	Jewels of Thought	1981	8.00
—Reissue of Impulse 9190			
❑ 29059	Thembi	1981	8.00
—Reissue of Impulse 9206			
SIGNATURE			
❑ FA 40952	Oh Lord, Let Me Do No Wrong	1989	12.00
STRATA-EAST			
❑ 19733	Izipho Sam (My Gifts)	1973	15.00
THERESA			
❑ 108/9 [(2)]	Journey to the One	1980	15.00
❑ 112/13 [(2)]	Rejoice	1981	15.00

S

Number	Title (A Side/B Side)	Yr	NM
❑ 116	Pharoah Sanders Live	1985	10.00
❑ 118	Heart Is a Melody	1986	10.00
❑ 121	Shukuru	1986	10.00
TIMELESS			
❑ SJP-253	Africa	1990	12.00
UPFRONT			
❑ 150	Spotlight	1973	12.00

SANDFORD, CHRIS

Number	Title (A Side/B Side)	Yr	NM
45s			
FONTANA			
❑ 1534	(I Wish They Wouldn't Always Say) I Sound Like the Guy from USA Blues/Little Man-Nobody Cares	1965	12.00

SANDLER AND YOUNG

Also known as "Tony Sandler and Ralph Young."

Number	Title (A Side/B Side)	Yr	NM
45s			
CAPITOL			
❑ 2083	In the Sunshine Days/Seven Lonely Days	1968	6.00
❑ 2157	Cotton Fields/Can I Trust You	1968	6.00
❑ 2333	I Sing Noel/Santa Claus Is Coming to Town	1968	6.00
❑ 2362	Life Is/Something Is Happening	1968	6.00
❑ 2423	Cuando Sali De Cuba/Viva El Amor	1969	6.00
❑ 2578	Heather/Pretty Things Come in Twos	1969	5.00
❑ 2636	Brazilian Love Song/On Days Like This	1969	5.00
❑ 5590	Let It Be Now/When Summer Is Gone	1966	6.00
❑ 5795	Chicago/Dominique	1966	6.00
❑ 5873	C'est Si Bon/Walk an Autumn Day with Me	1967	6.00
❑ 5928	More and More/Imagine Me	1967	6.00
P.I.P.			
❑ 6514	Medley: I Believe-Ave Maria/(B-side unknown)	1975	4.00
Albums			
CAPITOL			
❑ ST-159	Together	1968	12.00
❑ ST-241	Pretty Things Come in Twos	1969	12.00
❑ ST-449	Honey Come Back	1970	12.00
❑ ST 2598 [S]	Side by Side	1966	15.00
❑ T 2598 [M]	Side by Side	1966	12.00
—also known as "Tony Sandler and Ralph Young"			
❑ ST 2686 [S]	On the Move	1967	15.00
❑ T 2686 [M]	On the Move	1967	12.00
❑ ST 2802 [S]	More and More	1967	12.00
❑ T 2802 [M]	More and More	1967	15.00
❑ ST 2967	The Christmas World of Sandler and Young	1968	12.00
HOLIDAY			
❑ HDY 1942	Happy Holidays!	1981	8.00
—Reissue of True Value 2 (almost identical front cover, different back cover)			
RALTON			
❑ SY 200	Re-Discover Christmas	19??	15.00
—Has same contents as "Happy Holidays, Vol. 11"; is this the original?			
TRUE VALUE			
❑ 1	Happy Holidays, Album Eleven	1975	10.00
—Sold only at True Value Hardware stores			
❑ 2	Happy Holidays! Album Twelve	1976	10.00
—Sold only at True Value Hardware stores			

SANDMEN, THE (1)

Number	Title (A Side/B Side)	Yr	NM
45s			
BLUE JAY			
❑ 5002	If You Want Me/Searching for a New Love	1965	25.00

SANDMEN, THE (2)

BROOK BENTON was in this group.

Number	Title (A Side/B Side)	Yr	NM
45s			
OKEH			
❑ 7052	When I Grow Too Old to Dream/Somebody to Love	1955	50.00

SANDPEBBLES, THE

Number	Title (A Side/B Side)	Yr	NM
45s			
CALLA			
❑ 134	Forget It/Psychedelic Technicolor Dream	1967	10.00
❑ 141	Love Power/Because of Love	1967	15.00
❑ 148	If You Didn't Hear Me the First Time (I'll Say It Again)/Flower Power	1968	20.00
❑ 153	Let It Be Me/Soul Keeps Rolling Along	1968	20.00
❑ 155	Never My Love/Who Knows What Will Be Tomorrow	1968	12.00
❑ 160	You Turn Me On/The Garden of Eden	1969	30.00

SANDPIPERS, THE

Number	Title (A Side/B Side)	Yr	NM
45s			
A&M			
❑ 806	Guantanamera/What Makes You Dream, Pretty Girl	1966	6.00
❑ 819	Louie Louie/Things We Said Today	1966	8.00
❑ 835	La Bamba/For Baby	1967	6.00
❑ 851	It's Over/Glass	1967	6.00
❑ 861	Woman/Bon Soir Dame	1967	6.00
❑ 880	Softly, As I Leave You/Cuando Sali De Cuba	1967	6.00
❑ 939	Wooden Heart/Quando M'annamoro	1968	6.00
❑ 968	Softly/Cancion de Amor	1968	6.00
❑ 997	Suzanne/Let Go!	1968	6.00
❑ 1044	The Wonder of You/That Night	1969	6.00
❑ 1085	Temptations/Wave	1969	6.00
❑ 1116	Kum-Ba-Ya/Yellow Days	1969	6.00
❑ 1134	Come Saturday Morning/Pretty Flamingo	1969	6.00
❑ 1185	Come Saturday Morning/To Put Up with You	1970	5.00
❑ 1208	Beyond the Valley of the Dolls/Santo Domingo	1970	5.00
❑ 1227	Free to Carry On/The Whole World in His Hands	1970	5.00
❑ 1249	Drifter/Sound of Love	1971	5.00
❑ 1280	Chotta Matte Kudasel/Free to Carry On	1971	5.00
❑ 1306	Never My Love/Leland Loftis	1971	5.00
❑ 1314	A Gift of Song/Never My Love	1971	5.00
❑ 1372	Old Fashioned Love Song/Never Can Say Goodbye	1972	5.00
❑ 1388	The World Is a Circle/(Baby I Could Be) So Good at Lovin' You	1972	5.00
Albums			
A&M			
❑ LP-117 [M]	Guantanamera	1966	12.00
❑ LP-125 [M]	The Sandpipers	1967	15.00
❑ SP-3525 [(2)]	Foursider	1973	12.00
❑ SP-4117 [S]	Guantanamera	1966	15.00
❑ SP-4125 [S]	The Sandpipers	1967	12.00
❑ SP-4135	Misty Roses	1967	12.00
❑ SP-4147	Softly	1968	12.00
❑ SP-4159	The Spanish Album	1969	12.00
❑ SP-4180	The Wonder of You	1969	12.00
❑ SP-4246	Greatest Hits	1970	12.00
❑ SP-4262	Come Saturday Morning	1970	12.00
❑ SP-4328	A Gift of Song	1972	12.00
❑ SP-6014 [(2)]	Foursider	198?	10.00
—Reissue of 3525			

SANDS, EVIE

Number	Title (A Side/B Side)	Yr	NM
12-Inch Singles			
RCA VICTOR			
❑ JT-11549 [DJ]	Keep My Lovelight Burnin' (7:10 Stereo) (7:10 Mono)	1979	15.00
❑ PD-11549	Keep My Lovelight Burnin' (7:10)/I Can't Wait for You	1979	20.00
45s			
A&M			
❑ 980	Shadow of the Evening/Until It's Time for You to Go	1968	12.00
❑ 1026	One Fine Summer Morning/I'll Hold Out My Hand	1969	10.00
❑ 1090	Any Way That You Want Me/I'll Never Be Alone Again	1969	10.00
❑ 1157	Crazy Annie/Maybe Tomorrow	1969	10.00
❑ 1175	But You Know I Love You/Maybe Tomorrow	1970	10.00
❑ 1192	Take Me for a Little While/It's This I Am, I Find	1970	12.00
ABC-PARAMOUNT			
❑ 10458	The Roll/My Dog	1963	15.00
BLUE CAT			
❑ 118	Take Me for a Little While/Run Home to Your Mama	1965	30.00
❑ 122	You've Got Me Up Tight/I Can't Let Go	1965	20.00
CAMEO			
❑ 413	Picture Me Gone/It Makes Me Laugh	1966	60.00
❑ 436	The Love of a Boy/We Know Better	1966	15.00
❑ 475	Angel of the Morning/Dear John	1967	20.00
❑ 2002	Billy Sunshine/It Makes Me Laugh	1968	30.00
GOLD			
❑ 215	Danny Boy, I Love You So/I Was Moved	1964	15.00
HAVEN			
❑ 806	The Way You Do the Things You Do/Love in the Afternoon	1976	10.00
❑ 7010	Early Morning Sunshine/You Brought the Woman Out of Me	1975	6.00
❑ 7013	I Love Makin' Love to You/One Thing on My Mind	1975	6.00
❑ 7020	Yesterday Can't Hurt Me/(B-side unknown)	1975	8.00
RCA VICTOR			
❑ PB-11541	Keep My Lovelight Burnin'/I Can't Wait for You	1979	8.00
❑ PB-11653	You Sho' Look Good to Me/Brain Damage	1979	6.00
Albums			
A&M			
❑ SP-4239	Any Way That You Want Me	1969	30.00
HAVEN			
❑ ST-9202	Estate of Mind	1975	20.00
RCA VICTOR			
❑ AFL1-2943	Suspended Animation	1979	15.00

SANDS, JODIE

Number	Title (A Side/B Side)	Yr	NM
45s			
ABC-PARAMOUNT			
❑ 10337	We Had Words/Uno Momento	1962	12.00
❑ 10376	Hello, Heartache/This Little Fool	1962	12.00
❑ 10451	Time to Love/Charming Little Barefoot	1963	12.00
BERNLO			
❑ 1003	Love Me Always/Everybody Needs Somebody	1957	25.00
CHANCELLOR			
❑ 1003	With All My Heart/More Than Only Friends	1957	25.00
❑ 1005	If You're Not Completely Satisfied/Sayonara	1957	20.00
❑ 1009	The Way I Love You/Tantalizin' Love	1957	20.00
❑ 1015	Love Me Again/All I Ask of You	1958	20.00
❑ 1023	Someday/Always in My Heart	1958	20.00
PARIS			
❑ 543	I'd Cry No Tears/Kiss By Kiss	1960	15.00
❑ 551	Love Me Forever/Give Me a Break	1960	15.00
SIGNATURE			
❑ 12015	Turnabout Heart/Solo A Te Mio Amor	1959	15.00
TEEN			
❑ 109	Love Me Always/Everybody Needs Somebody	1955	40.00
THOR			
❑ 101	Hold Me/What Does It Mean	1959	20.00

SANDS, TOMMY

Number	Title (A Side/B Side)	Yr	NM
45s			
(NO LABEL)			
❑ T 929 [DJ]	People in Love/That's All I Want from You	1957	50.00
—"Promotion Record" with no label name; used to promote the movie "Sing Boy Sing"; T 929 is catalog number of LP and the most prominent number on label			
ABC-PARAMOUNT			
❑ 10466	Connie/Young Man's Fancy	1963	10.00
❑ 10480	Cinderella/Only 'Cause I'm Lonely	1963	10.00
❑ 10539	Won't You Be My Girl/Ten Dollars and a Clean White Shirt	1964	10.00
❑ 10591	Something More/Kisses (Love Theme)	1964	10.00
CAPITOL			
❑ F3639	Teen-Age Crush/Hep Dee Hootie	1957	25.00
❑ F3690	Ring-A-Ding-A-Ding/My Love Song	1957	25.00
❑ F3723	Goin' Steady/Ring My Phone	1957	25.00
❑ F3743	Let Me Be Loved/Fantastically Foolish	1957	20.00
❑ F3810	A Swingin' Romance/Man, Like Wow!	1957	20.00
❑ F3867	Sing, Boy, Sing/Crazy 'Cause I Love You	1957	20.00
❑ F3953	Teenage Doll/Hawaiian Rock	1958	20.00
❑ F3985	Big Date/After the Senior Prom	1958	20.00
❑ F3985 [PS]	Big Date/After the Senior Prom	1958	30.00
❑ F4036	Blue Ribbon Baby/I Love You Because	1958	20.00
❑ F4082	Bigger Than Texas/The Worryin' Kind	1958	20.00
❑ F4160	Is It Ever Gonna Happen/I Ain't Gittin' Rid of You	1959	15.00
❑ F4231	Sinner Man/Bring Me Your Love	1959	15.00

Except when noted otherwise, VG = 25% of NM, and VG+ = 50% of NM. (Example: VG = $2.00, VG+ = $4.00 and NM = $8.00.)

Number	Title (A Side/B Side)	Yr	NM
❑ F4259	I'll Be Seeing You/That's the Way I Am	1959	15.00
❑ F4259 [PS]	I'll Be Seeing You/That's the Way I Am	1959	30.00
❑ 4316	You Hold the Future/I Gotta Have You	1959	15.00
❑ 4366	That's Love/Crossroads	1960	15.00
❑ 4405	The Old Oaken Bucket/These Are the Things You Are	1960	15.00
❑ 4470	Doctor Heartache/On and On	1960	15.00
❑ 4580	Love in a Goldfish Bowl/I Love My Baby	1961	12.00
❑ 4611	Rainbow/Remember Me to Jennie	1961	12.00
❑ 4660	Wrong Side of Love/Jimmy's Song	1961	12.00
IMPERIAL			
❑ 66174	As Long As I'm Travelin'/It's the Only One I've Got	1966	8.00
❑ 66229	Second Star to the Left/Candy Store Prophet	1967	8.00
LIBERTY			
❑ 55807	Love's Funny/One Rose Today, One Rose Tomorrow	1965	8.00
❑ 55842	The Statue/Little Rosita	1965	8.00
❑ 55864	Waitin' in Your Welfare Line/Don't Do It Darlin'	1966	—
—Unreleased			
RCA VICTOR			
❑ 47-5435	Love Pains/Transfer	1953	30.00
❑ 47-5510	Roses Speak Louder Than Words/Spanish Coquita	1953	30.00
❑ 47-5628	A Dime and a Dollar/Life Is So Lonesome	1954	30.00
❑ 47-5697	Never Let Me Go/I Know About the Bees	1954	30.00
❑ 47-5800	Don't Drop It/A Place for Girls Like You	1954	30.00
❑ 47-6007	Kissin' Ain't No Fun/Something's Bound to Go Wrong	1955	30.00
❑ 47-6868	Don't Drop It/Love Pains	1957	20.00
SUPERSCOPE			
❑ 007	Seasons in the Sun/Ain't No Big Thing	1969	6.00
7-Inch Extended Plays			
CAPITOL			
❑ PRO 351 [DJ]	Goin' Steady/I Don't Know Why (I Just Do)//Graduation Day/A-You're Adorable (The Alphabet Song)	1957	40.00
—Promotional sampler from "Steady Date" album			
❑ EAP 1-848	*Goin' Steady/Teach Me Tonight/Gonna Get a Girl/Somewhere Along the Way	1957	30.00
❑ EAP 1-848 [PS]	Steady Date with Tommy Sands, Part 1	1957	30.00
❑ EAP 2-848	Walkin' My Baby Back Home/Too Young to Go Steady//A-You're Adorable (The Alphabet Song)/Graduation Day	1957	30.00
❑ EAP 2-848 [PS]	Steady Date with Tommy Sands, Part 2	1957	30.00
❑ EAP 3-848	Ring My Phone/I Don't Know Why//Too Young/I Don't Care Who Knows It	1957	30.00
❑ EAP 3-848 [PS]	Steady Date with Tommy Sands, Part 3	1957	30.00
❑ EAP 1-851	*Teen-Age Crush/My Love Song/Hep Dee Hootie (Cutie Wootie)/Ring-a-Ding-a-Ding	1957	30.00
❑ EAP 1-851 [PS]	Teen-Age Crush	1957	30.00
❑ EAP 1-929	*I'm Gonna Walk and Talk with My Lord/Who Baby/Rock of Ages/Sing Boy Sing	1958	30.00
❑ EAP 1-929 [PS]	Sing Boy Sing, Part 1	1958	30.00
❑ EAP 2-929	*A Bundle of Dreams/Just a Little Bit More/Soda-Pop Pop/Would I Love You	1958	30.00
❑ EAP 2-929 [PS]	Sing Boy Sing, Part 2	1958	30.00
❑ EAP 3-929	People in Love/Crazy Cause I Love You//Your Daddy Wants to Do Right/That's All I Want from You	1958	30.00
❑ EAP 3-929 [PS]	Sing Boy Sing, Part 3	1958	30.00
Albums			
CAPITOL			
❑ T 848 [M]	Steady Date with Tommy Sands	1957	60.00
❑ T 929 [M]	Sing Boy Sing	1958	60.00
❑ T 1081 [M]	Sands Storm	1959	50.00
❑ ST 1123 [S]	This Thing Called Love	1959	40.00
❑ T 1123 [M]	This Thing Called Love	1959	30.00
❑ ST 1239 [S]	When I'm Thinking of You	1960	40.00
❑ T 1239 [M]	When I'm Thinking of You	1960	30.00
❑ ST 1364 [S]	Sands at the Sands	1960	40.00
❑ T 1364 [M]	Sands at the Sands	1960	30.00
❑ ST 1426 [S]	Dream with Me	1961	40.00
❑ T 1426 [M]	Dream with Me	1961	30.00
GREEN LINNET			
❑ SIF-3044	Singing of the Times	1989	12.00
SANDY, FRANK			
45s			
MARK			
❑ 138	Shamrock/Here She Comes	1959	40.00
MGM			
❑ 12626	Somebody Loves Me/Tarantella Rock	1958	50.00
❑ 12678	Let's Go Rock 'N' Roll/Midnight Stomp	1958	100.00
SANDY AND DICK Also see DICK ST. JOHN.			
45s			
CONGRESS			
❑ 6015	Groove With What You Got/Sing Along with Groove With What You Got	1970	8.00
❑ 6021	Sweet Sweet Lovin'/Quick Like a Bunny	1970	8.00
SANETTES, THE			
45s			
OHN-J			
❑ 1001	Merry Christmas/Blessings From Above	1964	10.00
SANG, SAMANTHA			
45s			
ATCO			
❑ 6705	Don't Let It Happen Again/Love of a Woman	1969	6.00
❑ 6875	Nothing in the World Like Love/Mia Bamba	1972	5.00
PRIVATE STOCK			
❑ 45,178	Emotion/When Love Is Gone	1977	4.00
—Originals have brown labels			
❑ 45,178	Emotion/When Love Is Gone	1978	3.00
—Second pressings have skyline labels			
❑ 45,188	You Keep Me Dancing/Change of Heart	1978	3.00
UNITED ARTISTS			
❑ XW1297	I'll Never Get Enough of You/From Dance to Love	1979	3.00
❑ 1313	In the Midnight Hour/Now	1979	3.00
Albums			
LIBERTY			
❑ LN-10017	From Dance to Love	1980	8.00
—Budget-line reissue			
PRIVATE STOCK			
❑ PS-7009	Emotion	1978	10.00
UNITED ARTISTS			
❑ UA-LA965-H	From Dance to Love	1979	10.00
SANS, PEGGY			
45s			
TOLLIE			
❑ 9018	Give Your Love/Snow Man	1964	10.00
SANTAMARIA, MONGO			
12-Inch Singles			
TAPPAN ZEE			
❑ 10912	A Mi No Me Enganan (You Better Believe It)/Watermelon Man	1979	8.00
45s			
ATLANTIC			
❑ 2689	Feeling Alright/I Can't Get Next to You	1969	5.00
❑ 2717	Sunshine of Your Love/Heighty-Ho	1970	5.00
❑ 2770	Windjammer/No' Do'	1970	5.00
❑ 2794	Hippo Walk/Tell It	1971	5.00
❑ 2862	Come Cardella/I Wanna Know	1972	5.00
BATTLE			
❑ 45909	Watermelon Man/Don't Bother Me No More	1963	10.00
❑ 45917	Yeh-Yeh!/Get the Money	1963	8.00
❑ 45924	Creole/Fatback	1963	8.00
COLUMBIA			
❑ 43171	El Pussy Cat/Black-Eyed Peas	1964	6.00
❑ 43310	La Bamba/Streak O' Lean	1965	6.00
❑ 43613	I Got You/Walk On By	1966	6.00
❑ 43698	Call Me/El Bikini	1966	6.00
❑ 43962	Mongo's Boogaloo/Old Clothes	1967	6.00
❑ 44109	I Want to Know/Bossa-Negra	1967	6.00
❑ 44303	Funny Man/There Is a Mountain	1967	6.00
❑ 44397	Bloodshot/Juan Jose	1967	6.00
❑ 44452	Bonita/Sugar Cane Hombre	1968	6.00
❑ 44502	Cold Sweat/(Sittin' On) The Dock of the Bay	1968	6.00
❑ 44653	Hot Dog/Chili Beans	1968	6.00
❑ 44740	Cloud Nine/Son of a Preacher Man	1969	6.00
❑ 44812	Where We Are/(B-side unknown)	1969	6.00
❑ 44886	Twenty-Five Miles/El Tres	1969	6.00
❑ 44998	We Got Latin Soul/Getting It Out of My System	1969	6.00
FANTASY			
❑ 555	Tuli Bamba Charanga/Que Maravilloso Pachanga	196?	10.00
❑ 557	Para-Ti/Mongo's Theme	196?	10.00
RIVERSIDE			
❑ 4532	Cha Cha Blues/Tumba Le Le	196?	8.00
❑ 4574	Besito Pa Ti/Montuneando	196?	8.00
❑ 4586	Hammerhead/Tacos	196?	8.00
❑ 4587	Fatback/Sweet Tater Pie	1966	8.00
TAPPAN ZEE			
❑ 10920	A Mi No Me Enganan (You Better Believe It)/Sambita	1979	4.00
Albums			
ATLANTIC			
❑ SD 1567	Mongo '70	1970	12.00
❑ SD 1581	Mongo's Way	1971	12.00
❑ SD 1593	Mongo at Montreux	1972	12.00
❑ 1621 [M]	Up from the Roots	1972	25.00
—Mono is white label promo only; "d/j copy monaural" sticker on stereo cover			
❑ SD 1621 [S]	Up from the Roots	1972	12.00
❑ SD 8252	Feelin' Alright	1970	12.00
BATTLE			
❑ B-6120 [M]	Watermelon Man!	1963	20.00
❑ B-6129 [M]	Mongo at the Village Gate	1964	20.00
❑ BS-96120 [S]	Watermelon Man!	1963	25.00
❑ BS-96129 [S]	Mongo at the Village Gate	1964	25.00
COLUMBIA			
❑ CS 1060	Mongo's Greatest Hits	1970	12.00
❑ PC 1060	Mongo's Greatest Hits	198?	8.00
—Reissue with new prefix			
❑ CL 2298 [M]	El Pussy Cat	1965	12.00
—With "360 Sound Mono" in white at bottom of red label			
❑ CL 2298 [M]	El Pussy Cat	1965	20.00
—With "Guaranteed High Fidelity" in black at bottom of red label			
❑ CL 2375 [M]	Mr. Watermelon Man	196?	12.00
—Retitled reissue			
❑ CL 2375 [M]	La Bamba	1965	15.00
❑ CL 2411 [M]	El Bravo	1966	12.00
❑ CL 2473 [M]	Hey! Let's Party	1966	12.00
❑ CL 2612 [M]	Mongomania	1967	15.00
❑ CL 2770 [M]	Mongo Santamaria Explodes at the Village Gate	1967	15.00
❑ CS 9098 [S]	El Pussy Cat	1965	15.00
—With "360 Sound Stereo" in white at bottom of red label			
❑ CS 9098 [S]	El Pussy Cat	1965	25.00
—With "360 Sound Stereo" in black at bottom of red label			
❑ CS 9175 [S]	Mr. Watermelon Man	196?	15.00
—Retitled reissue			
❑ CS 9175 [S]	La Bamba	1965	20.00
❑ CS 9211 [S]	El Bravo	1966	15.00
❑ CS 9273 [S]	Hey! Let's Party	1966	15.00
❑ CS 9412 [S]	Mongomania	1967	12.00
❑ CS 9570 [S]	Mongo Santamaria Explodes at the Village Gate	1967	12.00
❑ CS 9653	Soul Bag	1968	15.00
❑ CS 9780	Stone Soul	1969	15.00
❑ CS 9937	Workin' on a Groovy Thing	1969	15.00
❑ CS 9988	All Strung Out	1970	15.00
CONCORD JAZZ			
❑ CJ-387	Ole Ola	1989	12.00
CONCORD PICANTE			
❑ CJP-327	Soy Yo	1987	10.00
❑ CJP-362	Soca Me Nice	1988	10.00
FANTASY			
❑ OJC-276	Yambu	1987	10.00
—Reissue of 8012			
❑ OJC-281	Sabroso	1987	10.00
—Reissue of 8058			
❑ OJC-490	Mongo at the Village Gate	1991	12.00
—Reissue of Riverside 93529			
❑ OJC-626	Summertime	1991	12.00
—Reissue of Pablo 2308 229			
❑ 3267 [M]	Yambu	1959	30.00
—Black vinyl			
❑ 3267 [M]	Yambu	1959	40.00
—Red vinyl			
❑ 3291 [M]	Mongo	1959	30.00
—Black vinyl			
❑ 3291 [M]	Mongo	1959	40.00
—Red vinyl			
❑ 3302 [M]	Our Man in Havana	1960	30.00
—Black vinyl			
❑ 3302 [M]	Our Man in Havana	1960	40.00
—Red vinyl			
❑ 3311 [M]	Mongo in Havana	1960	30.00
—Black vinyl			

S

Number	Title (A Side/B Side)	Yr	NM
❑ 3311 [M]	Mongo in Havana	1960	40.00
—Red vinyl			
❑ 3314 [M]	Sabroso	1960	30.00
—Black vinyl			
❑ 3314 [M]	Sabroso	1960	40.00
—Red vinyl			
❑ 3324 [M]	Arriba!	1961	30.00
—Black vinyl			
❑ 3324 [M]	Arriba!	1961	40.00
—Red vinyl			
❑ 3328 [M]	Mas Sabroso	1962	30.00
—Black vinyl			
❑ 3328 [M]	Mas Sabroso	1962	40.00
—Red vinyl			
❑ 3335 [M]	Viva Mongo!	1962	30.00
—Black vinyl			
❑ 3335 [M]	Viva Mongo!	1962	40.00
—Red vinyl			
❑ 3351 [M]	Mighty Mongo	1963	15.00
❑ MPF-4529	Mongo Santamaria's Greatest Hits	198?	8.00
—Budget-line reissue			
❑ 8012 [S]	Yambu	1962	20.00
—Black vinyl			
❑ 8012 [S]	Yambu	1962	30.00
—Blue vinyl			
❑ 8032 [S]	Mongo	1962	20.00
—Black vinyl			
❑ 8032 [S]	Mongo	1962	30.00
—Blue vinyl			
❑ 8045 [S]	Our Man in Havana	1962	20.00
—Black vinyl			
❑ 8045 [S]	Our Man in Havana	1962	30.00
—Blue vinyl			
❑ 8055 [S]	Mongo in Havana	1962	20.00
—Black vinyl			
❑ 8055 [S]	Mongo in Havana	1962	30.00
—Blue vinyl			
❑ 8058 [S]	Sabroso	1962	20.00
—Black vinyl			
❑ 8058 [S]	Sabroso	1962	30.00
—Blue vinyl			
❑ 8067 [S]	Arriba!	1962	20.00
—Black vinyl			
❑ 8067 [S]	Arriba!	1962	30.00
—Blue vinyl			
❑ 8071 [S]	Mas Sabroso	1962	20.00
—Black vinyl			
❑ 8071 [S]	Mas Sabroso	1962	30.00
—Blue vinyl			
❑ 8087 [S]	Viva Mongo!	1962	20.00
—Black vinyl			
❑ 8087 [S]	Viva Mongo!	1962	30.00
—Blue vinyl			
❑ 8351 [S]	Mighty Mongo	1963	20.00
❑ 8373	Mongo Santamaria's Greatest Hits	1967	12.00
❑ 9431	Mongo Y La Lupe	1974	12.00
HARMONY			
❑ H 30291	The Dock of the Bay	1971	10.00
MILESTONE			
❑ 47012 [(2)]	Watermelon Man	1974	15.00
❑ 47038 [(2)]	Skins	1976	15.00
PABLO			
❑ 2308229	Summertime	1980	12.00
PRESTIGE			
❑ 24018 [(2)]	Afro Roots	1973	15.00
RIVERSIDE			
❑ RLP-423 [M]	Go, Mongo!	1962	25.00
❑ R-3008 [M]	Explosion	1967	25.00
❑ RM-3008 [M]	Explosion	1968	25.00
❑ RS-3008 [S]	Explosion	1968	15.00
❑ RS-3045	Mongo Soul	1969	15.00
❑ RM-3523 [M]	Mongo Introduces La Lupe	1963	20.00
❑ RM-3529 [M]	Mongo at the Village Gate	1963	20.00
❑ RM-3530 [M]	Mongo Santamaria Explodes!	1964	20.00
❑ RS-9423 [S]	Go, Mongo!	1962	30.00
❑ RS-93523 [S]	Mongo Introduces La Lupe	1963	25.00
❑ RS-93529 [S]	Mongo at the Village Gate	1963	25.00
❑ RS-93530 [S]	Mongo Santamaria Explodes!	1964	25.00
TICO			
❑ LP-137 [10]	Chango	1955	80.00
❑ LP-1037 [M]	Chango: Mongo Santamaria's Drums and Chants	1957	60.00
❑ LP-1149 [M]	Mongo Santamaria's Drums and Chants	1967	20.00

SANTANA Also see JOURNEY; CARLOS SANTANA; GREGG ROLIE.

12-Inch Singles

Number	Title (A Side/B Side)	Yr	NM
COLUMBIA			
❑ AS 383 [DJ]	She's Not There (4:08) (2:58) (stereo/mono)	1977	15.00
❑ AS 517 [DJ]	Well All Right (short) (long)	1978	12.00
❑ AS 585 [DJ]	One Chain (Don't Make No Prison) (Long) (Short) (both on each side)	1978	8.00
❑ AS 842 [DJ]	Love Theme from Spartacus/Song for My Brother/Swapan Tari	1980	12.00
❑ AS 937 [DJ]	Winning/E Papa Ne	1981	8.00
❑ AS 1266 [DJ]	Sensitive Kind/Sensitive Kind (Live)	1981	10.00
❑ AS 1998 [DJ]	Say It Again (same on both sides)	1985	6.00
❑ CAS 2068 [DJ]	I'm the One Who Loves You (same on both sides)	1985	6.00
❑ CAS 2630 [DJ]	Veracruz (same on both sides)	1987	6.00
❑ 06762	Vera Cruz (Cool Mix)/Vera Cruz (Cool Whip Mix)	1987	6.00
❑ 10957	One Chain (Don't Make No Prison)/Life Is a Lady Holiday	1978	10.00

45s

Number	Title (A Side/B Side)	Yr	NM
ARISTA			
❑ 13773	Maria Maria (featuring The Product G&B)/Smooth (featuring Rob Thomas)	2000	5.00
❑ 50980	The Game of Love/Nothing at All	2003	4.00
—A-side featuring Michelle Branch; B-side featuring Musiq			
COLUMBIA			
❑ 01050	Winning/The Brightest Star	1981	4.00
❑ AE7 1064 [DJ]	All the Love of the Universe/Just in Time to See the Sun	1972	10.00
❑ 02178	The Sensitive Kind/American Gypsy	1981	4.00
❑ 02178 [PS]	The Sensitive Kind/American Gypsy	1981	5.00
❑ 02519	Searchin'/Tales of Kilimanjaro	1981	4.00
❑ 03160	Hold On/Oxun	1982	4.00
❑ 03268	Hold On	1982	6.00
—One-sided budget release			
❑ 03376	Nowhere to Run/Nueva York	1982	4.00
❑ 04034	Havana Moon/Lightnin'	1983	4.00
❑ 04758	Say It Again/Touchdown Raiders	1985	3.00
❑ 04758 [PS]	Say It Again/Touchdown Raiders	1985	4.00
❑ 04912	I'm the One Who Loves You/Right Now	1985	3.00
❑ 05677	They All Went to Mexico/Slow Movin' Outlaw	1985	3.00
—A-side: Willie Nelson and Carlos Santana; B-side: Willie and Lacy J. Dalton			
❑ 06654	Vera Cruz/Manuela	1987	4.00
❑ 07038	Vera Cruz (Remix)/Manuela	1987	3.00
❑ 07140	Praise/Love Is You	1987	3.00
❑ 10073	Mirage/Flor de Canela	1974	5.00
❑ 10088	Give and Take/Love Is Anew	1975	5.00
❑ 10336	Let It Shine/Tell Me Are You Tired	1976	5.00
❑ 10353	Dance Sister Dance (Baila Mi Hermana)/Let Me	1976	5.00
❑ 10421	Take Me with You/Europa (Earth's Cry Heaven's Smile)	1976	5.00
❑ 10481	Let the Children Play/Carnival	1977	5.00
❑ 10524	Give Me Love/Revelations	1977	5.00
❑ 10616	She's Not There/Zulu	1977	5.00
❑ 10677	Black Magic Woman/I'll Be Waiting	1978	5.00
❑ 10839	Well, All Right/Jericho	1978	5.00
❑ 10873	Stormy/Move On	1978	5.00
❑ 10938	One Chain (Don't Make a Prison)/Life Is a Lady-Holiday	1979	4.00
❑ 11144	You Know That I Love You/Aqua Marine	1979	4.00
❑ 11218	All I Ever Wanted/Lightning in the Sky	1980	4.00
❑ 45010	Jin-Go-Lo-Ba/Persuasion	1969	6.00
—Same song, different A-side title			
❑ 45010	Jingo/Persuasion	1969	6.00
❑ 45069	Evil Ways/Waiting	1970	6.00
❑ 45270	Black Magic Woman/Hope You're Feeling Better	1970	6.00
❑ 45270 [PS]	Black Magic Woman/Hope You're Feeling Better	1970	12.00
❑ 45330	Oye Como Va/Samba Pa Ti	1971	5.00
❑ 45330 [PS]	Oye Como Va/Samba Pa Ti	1971	8.00
❑ 45472	Everybody's Everything/Guajira	1971	5.00
❑ 45552	No One to Depend On/Taboo	1972	5.00
—Gray label			
❑ 45552	No One to Depend On/Taboo	1973	4.00
—Orange label			
❑ 45552 [PS]	No One to Depend On/Taboo	1972	8.00
❑ 45753	Look Up/All the Love of the Universe	1973	5.00
❑ 45999	When I Look Into Your Eyes/Samba De Sausalito	1974	5.00
❑ 46067	Incident at Neshabur/Samba Pa Ti	1974	5.00

7-Inch Extended Plays

Number	Title (A Side/B Side)	Yr	NM
COLUMBIA			
❑ 7-30595	Taboo/Everything's Coming Our Way//Jungle Strut/Batuka	1971	10.00
—Jukebox issue; small hole, plays at 33 1/3 rpm			
❑ 7-30595 [PS]	The New Santana Album	1971	10.00
❑ 7-32445	Love, Devotion & Surrender/Light of Life//Yours Is the Light/Samba de Sausalito	1973	12.00
—Jukebox issue; small hole, plays at 33 1/3 rpm			
❑ 7-32445 [PS]	Welcome	1973	12.00

Albums

Number	Title (A Side/B Side)	Yr	NM
ARISTA			
❑ 19080 [(2)]	Supernatural	2000	40.00
—Classic Records audiophile vinyl issue in gatefold cover with booklet			
CICADELIC			
❑ 1004	Santana '68	1988	12.00
COLUMBIA			
❑ CS 9781	Santana	1969	15.00
—"360 Sound" on label			
❑ CS 9781	Santana	1970	10.00
—Orange label			
❑ PC 9781	Santana	198?	8.00
❑ CQ 30130 [Q]	Abraxas	1972	20.00
❑ JC 30130	Abraxas	1977	8.00
❑ KC 30130	Abraxas	197?	10.00
—With no poster			
❑ KC 30130	Abraxas	1970	15.00
—Original copies have a poster			
❑ PC 30130	Abraxas	1985	8.00
❑ CQ 30595 [Q]	Santana	1972	20.00
❑ KC 30595	Santana	1971	12.00
—Not the same album as CS 9781; this is often called "Santana III"			
❑ PC 30595	Santana	197?	8.00
❑ KC 31610	Caravanserai	1972	12.00
❑ PC 31610	Caravanserai	197?	8.00
❑ PCQ 31610 [Q]	Caravanserai	1974	20.00
❑ PC 32455	Welcome	1973	12.00
—No bar code on cover			
❑ PC 32455	Welcome	1979	8.00
—With bar code on cover			
❑ PCQ 32455 [Q]	Welcome	1974	20.00
❑ PCQ 32964 [Q]	Santana	1974	20.00
—Quadraphonic issue of their debut album (9781)			
❑ JC 33050	Santana's Greatest Hits	1977	8.00
❑ PC 33050	Santana's Greatest Hits	1974	12.00
—No bar code on cover			
❑ PCQ 33050 [Q]	Santana's Greatest Hits	1974	20.00
❑ PC 33135	Borboletta	1974	12.00
—No bar code on cover			
❑ PC 33135	Borboletta	1979	8.00
—With bar code on cover			
❑ PCQ 33135 [Q]	Borboletta	1974	20.00
❑ PC 33576	Amigos	1976	12.00
—No bar code on cover			
❑ PC 33576	Amigos	1979	8.00
—With bar code on cover			
❑ PCQ 33576 [Q]	Amigos	1976	20.00
❑ JC 34423	Festival	1977	12.00
❑ JCQ 34423 [Q]	Festival	1977	20.00
❑ PC 34423	Festival	198?	8.00
❑ C2 34914 [(2)]	Moonflower	1977	15.00
❑ FC 35600	Inner Secrets	1978	12.00
❑ PC 35600	Inner Secrets	198?	8.00
—Budget-line reissue			
❑ FC 36154	Marathon	1979	12.00
❑ PC 36154	Marathon	198?	8.00
—Budget-line reissue			
❑ C2 36590 [(2)]	Swing of Delight	1980	15.00
❑ FC 37158	Zebop!	1981	12.00
❑ PC 37158	Zebop!	198?	8.00
—Budget-line reissue			
❑ FC 38122	Shango	1982	12.00
❑ PC 38122	Shango	198?	8.00
—Budget-line reissue			
❑ FC 39527	Beyond Appearances	1985	10.00
❑ PC 39527	Beyond Appearances	198?	8.00
—Budget-line reissue			
❑ HC 40130	Abraxas	1981	80.00
—Half-speed mastered edition			
❑ FC 40272	Freedom	1987	10.00
❑ C3X 44344 [(3)]	Viva Santana	1988	20.00
❑ HC 47158	Zebop!	1981	40.00
—Half-speed mastered edition			

SANTANA, CARLOS Also see SANTANA.

45s

Number	Title (A Side/B Side)	Yr	NM
COLUMBIA			
❑ 03925	Tales of Kilimanjaro/Watch Your Step	1983	4.00

Albums

Number	Title (A Side/B Side)	Yr	NM
COLUMBIA			
❑ AS 573 [DJ]	The Solo Guitar of Devadip Carlos Santana	1979	15.00
❑ JC 35686	Oneness/Silver Dreams-Golden Reality	1979	10.00
❑ C2 36590 [(2)]	The Swing of Delight	1980	12.00
❑ FC 38642	Havana Moon	1983	10.00
❑ FC 40875	Blues for Salvador	1987	10.00

SANTANA, CARLOS, AND MAHAVISHNU JOHN MCLAUGHLIN

Albums

COLUMBIA

Number	Title (A Side/B Side)	Yr	NM
❑ KC 32034	Love Devotion Surrender	1973	10.00
❑ PC 32034	Love Devotion Surrender	197?	8.00

—Reissue with new prefix

SANTANA, CARLOS, AND BUDDY MILES

Also see each artist's individual listings.

45s

COLUMBIA

Number	Title (A Side/B Side)	Yr	NM
❑ 45666	Them Changes/Evil Ways	1972	5.00

Albums

COLUMBIA

Number	Title (A Side/B Side)	Yr	NM
❑ KC 31308	Carlos Santana and Buddy Miles! Live!	1972	12.00
❑ PC 31308	Carlos Santana and Buddy Miles! Live!	197?	8.00

—Reissue with new prefix

SANTO AND JOHNNY

45s

CANADIAN AMERICAN

Number	Title (A Side/B Side)	Yr	NM
❑ 103	Sleep Walk/All Night Diner	1959	25.00
❑ 107	Tear Drop/The Long Walk Home	1959	15.00
❑ 111	Caravan/Summertime	1960	15.00
❑ 115	The Breeze and I/Lazy Day	1960	15.00
❑ 118	Love Lost/Annie	1960	15.00
❑ 118 [PS]	Love Lost/Annie	1960	50.00
❑ 120	Twistin' Bells/Bullseye!	1960	16.00
❑ 120 [PS]	Twistin' Bells/Bullseye!	1960	40.00
❑ 124	Hop Scotch/Sea Shells	1961	15.00
❑ 128	Theme from Come September/The Long Walk Home	1961	15.00
❑ 131	The Mouse/Birmingham	1961	15.00
❑ 132	Twistin' Bells/Christmas Day	1961	20.00

—B-side by Linda Scott

Number	Title (A Side/B Side)	Yr	NM
❑ 137	Spanish Harlem/Stage to Cimarron	1962	12.00
❑ 141	Three Caballeros/Step Aside	1962	12.00
❑ 144	Misirlou/Tokyo Twilight	1962	12.00
❑ 148	Twistin' Bells/Manhattan	1962	12.00
❑ 151	On Your Mark/Manhattan	1963	12.00
❑ 155	The Wandering Sea/Manhattan Spiritual	1963	12.00
❑ 161	Love Letters in the Sand/Lido Beach	1963	12.00
❑ 164	I'll Remember (In the Still of the Night)/Song for Rosemary	1964	12.00
❑ 164 [PS]	I'll Remember (In the Still of the Night)/Song for Rosemary	1964	25.00
❑ 167	A Thousand Miles Away/Road Block	1964	12.00
❑ 167 [PS]	A Thousand Miles Away/Road Block	1964	25.00
❑ 174	Sugar Stroll/Rattler	1964	12.00
❑ 177	A Hard Day's Night/And I Love Her	1964	15.00
❑ 182	Goldfinger/Sleep Walk	1964	12.00
❑ 182 [PS]	Goldfinger/Sleep Walk	1964	25.00
❑ 189	Brazilian Summer/Off Tempo	1965	12.00
❑ 194	Watermelon Man/Return to Naples	1965	12.00
❑ 204	Come with Me/The Young World	1967	10.00

IMPERIAL

Number	Title (A Side/B Side)	Yr	NM
❑ 66269	Live for Life/See You in September	1968	10.00
❑ 66292	Sleep Walk '68/It Must Be Him	1968	10.00

PAUSA

Number	Title (A Side/B Side)	Yr	NM
❑ 703	Come Back Soldier/Flamingo	1976	5.00

UNITED ARTISTS

Number	Title (A Side/B Side)	Yr	NM
❑ 970	Thunderball/Mister Kiss Kiss Bang Bang	1966	10.00

7-Inch Extended Plays

CANADIAN AMERICAN

Number	Title (A Side/B Side)	Yr	NM
❑ 1001	(contents unknown)	1959	80.00
❑ 1001 [PS]	Santo and Johnny	1959	80.00

Albums

CANADIAN AMERICAN

Number	Title (A Side/B Side)	Yr	NM
❑ CALP-1001 [M]	Santo & Johnny	1959	60.00
❑ SCALP-1001 [S]	Santo & Johnny	1959	80.00
❑ CALP-1002 [M]	Encore	1960	40.00
❑ SCALP-1002 [S]	Encore	1960	50.00
❑ CALP-1004 [M]	Hawaii	1961	40.00
❑ SCALP-1004 [S]	Hawaii	1961	50.00
❑ CALP-1006 [M]	Come On In	1962	30.00
❑ SCALP-1006 [S]	Come On In	1962	40.00
❑ CALP-1008 [M]	Around the World with Santo and Johnny	1962	30.00
❑ SCALP-1008 [S]	Around the World with Santo and Johnny	1962	40.00
❑ CALP-1011 [M]	Off Shore	1963	30.00
❑ SCALP-1011 [S]	Off Shore	1963	40.00
❑ CALP-1014 [M]	In the Still of the Night	1963	30.00
❑ SCALP-1014 [S]	In the Still of the Night	1963	40.00
❑ CALP-1016 [M]	Wish You Love	1964	30.00
❑ SCALP-1016 [S]	Wish You Love	1964	40.00
❑ CALP-1017 [M]	The Beatles' Greatest Hits	1965	40.00
❑ SCALP-1017 [S]	The Beatles' Greatest Hits	1965	50.00
❑ CALP-1018 [M]	Mucho	1965	30.00
❑ SCALP-1018 [S]	Mucho	1965	40.00

IMPERIAL

Number	Title (A Side/B Side)	Yr	NM
❑ LP-9363 [M]	Brilliant Guitar Sounds	1967	15.00
❑ LP-12363 [S]	Brilliant Guitar Sounds	1967	20.00
❑ LP-12366	Golden Guitars	1968	15.00
❑ LP-12418	On the Road Again	1968	15.00

SANTOS, LARRY

45s

ATLANTIC

Number	Title (A Side/B Side)	Yr	NM
❑ 2250	Someday (When I'm Gone)/True	1964	20.00

—With the Four Seasons on backup

BIG TREE

Number	Title (A Side/B Side)	Yr	NM
❑ 136	Life Is Beautiful/Touchin' You	1972	5.00

CASABLANCA

Number	Title (A Side/B Side)	Yr	NM
❑ 844	Can't Get You Off My Mind/We Can't Hide It Anymore	1975	6.00

—With "Can't Get You Off My Mind" listed as "Side A"

Number	Title (A Side/B Side)	Yr	NM
❑ 844	We Can't Hide It Anymore/Can't Get You Off My Mind	1976	4.00

—With "We Can't Hide It Anymore" listed as "Side A"

Number	Title (A Side/B Side)	Yr	NM
❑ 869	You Are Everything I Need/Long, Long Time	1976	4.00
❑ 881	Magic Mountain/Don't Let the Music Stop	1977	4.00

EVOLUTION

Number	Title (A Side/B Side)	Yr	NM
❑ 1007	Tomorrow Without Love/You Got Me Where You Want Me	1969	6.00
❑ 1010	Subway Man/Woman-Child	1969	6.00
❑ 1018	Great Divide/Paper Chase	1970	6.00
❑ 1024	Mornin' Sun/Wandering Man	1970	6.00
❑ 1029	Now That I Have Found You/Wandering Man	1970	6.00
❑ 1039	Let It End/Little Bit of You	1971	6.00
❑ 1043	I Love You More Than Everything/Let It End	1971	6.00

Albums

CASABLANCA

Number	Title (A Side/B Side)	Yr	NM
❑ NBLP 7030	You Are Everything I Need	1976	12.00
❑ NBLP 7061	Don't Let the Music Stop	1977	12.00

EVOLUTION

Number	Title (A Side/B Side)	Yr	NM
❑ 2002	Just a Man	1969	20.00
❑ 2015	Morning Sun	1971	15.00

SAPIANS, THE

45s

MERCURY

Number	Title (A Side/B Side)	Yr	NM
❑ 72502	Ask Yourself Why Babe/Love Ain't Makin' It No More	1965	200.00

SAPODILLA PUNCH

Albums

PHILIPS

Number	Title (A Side/B Side)	Yr	NM
❑ PHS 600312	Sapodilla Punch	1969	20.00

SAPPHIRES, THE (1)

45s

ABC-PARAMOUNT

Number	Title (A Side/B Side)	Yr	NM
❑ 10559	Hearts Are Made to Be Broken/Let's Break Up for Awhile	1964	15.00
❑ 10590	Thank You for Loving Me/Our Love Is Everywhere	1964	15.00
❑ 10639	Gee I'm Sorry, Baby/Gotta Have Your Love	1965	15.00
❑ 10693	Evil One/How Could I Say Goodbye	1965	15.00
❑ 10753	You'll Never Stop Me from Loving You/Gonna Be a Big Thing	1965	15.00
❑ 10778	Our Love Is Everywhere/Slow Fizz	1966	15.00

ITZY

Number	Title (A Side/B Side)	Yr	NM
❑ 8	Who Do You Love/Oh So Soon	1963	40.00

LOST-NITE

Number	Title (A Side/B Side)	Yr	NM
❑ 260	Gee I'm Sorry, Baby/Gotta Have Your Love	196?	5.00

—Reissue

SWAN

Number	Title (A Side/B Side)	Yr	NM
❑ 4143	Your True Love/Where Is Johnny Now	1963	15.00
❑ 4162	Who Do You Love/Oh So Soon	1963	15.00
❑ 4177	I Found Out Too Late/I've Got Mine, You Better Get Yours	1964	15.00
❑ 4184	Gotta Be More Than Friends/Moulin Rouge	1964	15.00

Albums

COLLECTABLES

Number	Title (A Side/B Side)	Yr	NM
❑ COL-5007	Who Do You Love	198?	10.00

SWAN

Number	Title (A Side/B Side)	Yr	NM
❑ LP-513 [M]	Who Do You Love	1964	300.00

SAPPHIRES, THE (2)

45s

RCA VICTOR

Number	Title (A Side/B Side)	Yr	NM
❑ 47-7357	Everyone Knows/So Glad	1958	20.00

SARATOGAS, THE

45s

IMPERIAL

Number	Title (A Side/B Side)	Yr	NM
❑ 5738	I'll Be Loving You/Get It in a Minute	1961	30.00

SARDO, FRANKIE

45s

ABC-PARAMOUNT

Number	Title (A Side/B Side)	Yr	NM
❑ 9963	Class Room/Fake Out	1958	20.00
❑ 10003	No Love Like Mine/Oh Linda	1959	20.00

LIDO

Number	Title (A Side/B Side)	Yr	NM
❑ 602	Kiss and Make Up/The Girl I'm Gonna Dream About	1959	20.00

MGM

Number	Title (A Side/B Side)	Yr	NM
❑ 12621	May I/My Story of Love	1958	20.00

NEWTOWN

Number	Title (A Side/B Side)	Yr	NM
❑ 5005	I Got You Where I Want You/Mr. Make Believe	1962	25.00

RAYNA

Number	Title (A Side/B Side)	Yr	NM
❑ 5005	Ring of Love/She Taught Me How to Cry	1962	15.00

STUDIO

Number	Title (A Side/B Side)	Yr	NM
❑ 9910	Just You Watch Me/I'm Sittin' at Home	1961	50.00

20TH FOX

Number	Title (A Side/B Side)	Yr	NM
❑ 208	I Know Why and So Do You/When the Bells Stop Ringing	1960	20.00
❑ 221	Dream Lover/Bonnie, Bonnie	1960	25.00

SARDO, JOHNNY

45s

CHOCK FULL-O-HITS

Number	Title (A Side/B Side)	Yr	NM
❑ 104	(Hip Hop) Take a Ride with Me/Hollywood Sign	1958	100.00

WARNER BROS.

Number	Title (A Side/B Side)	Yr	NM
❑ 5014	I Wanna Rock/Used Heart	1958	25.00
❑ 5044	Late, Late, Late to School/New Kid in Town	1959	25.00

SARNE, MIKE

45s

ASCOT

Number	Title (A Side/B Side)	Yr	NM
❑ 2213	An Englishman Sings "America Swings"/Can't Wait for Spring	1966	10.00

CAMEO

Number	Title (A Side/B Side)	Yr	NM
❑ 220	Come On Outside/Fountain of Love	1962	12.00

STELLAR

Number	Title (A Side/B Side)	Yr	NM
❑ 1506	Come Outside/Fountain of Love	1962	12.00

SARSTEDT, PETER

45s

SIRE

Number	Title (A Side/B Side)	Yr	NM
❑ 1028	Beirut/The Hollywood Sign	1978	4.00

UNITED ARTISTS

Number	Title (A Side/B Side)	Yr	NM
❑ 50923	You're a Lady/What Makes One Man Feel	1972	5.00

WORLD PACIFIC

Number	Title (A Side/B Side)	Yr	NM
❑ 77906	I Am a Cathedral/Blagged	1969	6.00
❑ 77911	Where Do You Go To (My Lovely)/Morning Mountain	1969	8.00
❑ 77919	Frozen Orange Juice/Aretuza Loser	1969	6.00
❑ 77919 [PS]	Frozen Orange Juice/Aretuza Loser	1969	10.00

S

Number	Title (A Side/B Side)	Yr	NM
❑ 77933	Step Into the Battlefield/ I Thought It Was	1970	6.00
Albums			
UNITED ARTISTS			
❑ UAS-5558	Every Word You Say Is Written Down	1971	10.00
WORLD PACIFIC			
❑ WPS-21895	Where Do You Go To, My Lovely	1969	15.00
❑ WPS-21899	As Though It Were a Movie	1969	15.00

SATAN AND THE DISCIPLES Allegedly, this is FREDDY FENDER.

Number	Title (A Side/B Side)	Yr	NM
45s			
GOLDBAND			
❑ 1188	Mummies Curse/Cat's Meow	1969	25.00
Albums			
GOLDBAND			
❑ 7750	Underground	1969	40.00

SATANS, THE

Number	Title (A Side/B Side)	Yr	NM
Albums			
(NO LABEL)			
❑ (no #) [M]	Raisin' Hell	1962	300.00

SATAN'S FOUR

Number	Title (A Side/B Side)	Yr	NM
45s			
B.T. PUPPY			
❑ 515	I Can't Find the Girl on My Mind/ Oh Cathy	1966	15.00
Albums			
B.T. PUPPY			
❑ BTS-1010	Mixed Soul	1970	150.00
—With the Cinnamon Angels			

SATELLITES, THE More than one group.

Number	Title (A Side/B Side)	Yr	NM
45s			
ABC-PARAMOUNT			
❑ 10038	Linda Jean/Rockateen	1959	40.00
CLASS			
❑ 234	Heavenly Angel/You Ain't Sayin' Nothin'	1958	30.00
CUPID			
❑ (no #)	Linda Jean/Rockateen	1959	80.00
D-M-G			
❑ 4001	Each Night/Darktown Strutters Ball	1960	30.00
MALYNN			
❑ 231	Heavenly Angel/ You Ain't Sayin' Nothin'	1958	25.00
PALACE			
❑ 102	Buzz Buzz/We Like Birdland	1960	20.00
PARROT			
❑ 313	Bodacious/El San Juan	1966	25.00
UNITED ARTISTS			
❑ 141	I Found a Girl/My Piggie's Gotta Dance	1958	40.00

SATINTONES, THE

Number	Title (A Side/B Side)	Yr	NM
45s			
MOTOWN			
❑ 1000	Sugar Daddy/My Beloved	1960	400.00
—With strings. Matrix number of A-side is "1000 G-3"			
❑ 1000	Sugar Daddy/My Beloved	1960	400.00
—Without strings. Matrix number of A-side is "MNT 12345"			
❑ 1006	Tomorrow and Always/ A Love That Can Never Be	1961	250.00
—With strings			
❑ 1006	Tomorrow and Always/A Love That Can Never Be	1961	250.00
—Without strings			
❑ 1006	Angel/A Love That Can Never Be	1961	1500.
❑ 1010	I Know How It Feels/ My Kind of Love	1961	200.00
❑ 1020	Zing Went the Strings of My Heart/Faded Letter	1962	200.00
TAMLA			
❑ 54026	Motor City/Going to the Hop	1960	800.00

SATISFACTIONS, THE (1)

Number	Title (A Side/B Side)	Yr	NM
45s			
LIONEL			
❑ 3201	This Bitter Earth/Ol' Man River	1970	12.00
❑ 3205	One Light Two Lights/ Turn Back the Tears	1970	12.00
❑ 3214	God I'm Losing My Baby/ O-o-o La La	1971	15.00

SATISFACTIONS, THE (2)

Number	Title (A Side/B Side)	Yr	NM
45s			
CHESAPEKE			
❑ 610	We Will Walk Together/Oh Why	1962	30.00

SATISFACTIONS, THE (3)

Number	Title (A Side/B Side)	Yr	NM
45s			
IMPERIAL			
❑ 66170	Bring It All Down/Daddy, You Just Gotta Let Him In	1966	20.00
SMASH			
❑ 2059	Give Me Your Love/ Stop Following Me	1966	15.00
❑ 2098	Take It or Leave It/You Got to Share	1967	30.00

SATISFACTIONS, THE (U) These could be group (1) or (3).

Number	Title (A Side/B Side)	Yr	NM
45s			
1-2-3			
❑ 1716	Gonna Get Right Tonight/ Living on a Prayer, a Hope and a Hand-Me-Down	1969	12.00
TWIN TOWN			
❑ 714	Bad Times/Don't Tell Me	1966	25.00

SATISFIERS, THE

Number	Title (A Side/B Side)	Yr	NM
45s			
CORAL			
❑ 61727	Come Away, Love/Where'll I Be Tomorrow Night	1956	15.00
❑ 61788	Over the Rainbow/Solitude	1957	15.00
❑ 61945	Will o' the Wisp/Remember That Crazy Rock and Roll	1958	15.00
JUBILEE			
❑ 5205	All or Nothing at All/ Lies, Nothing But Lies	1955	20.00
VEGAS			
❑ 626	Ghost of a Chance/ Fair Exchange	1960	12.00

SATURDAY, PATTY

Number	Title (A Side/B Side)	Yr	NM
45s			
SWAN			
❑ 4022	Ladies Choice/Love Is a Beautiful Thing	1959	25.00

SATURDAY KNIGHTS, THE

Number	Title (A Side/B Side)	Yr	NM
45s			
NOCTURNE			
❑ 1030	Sea Mist/Queen of the Nile	1963	50.00
SWAN			
❑ 4075	Ticonderoga/Tiger Lily	1961	20.00
—As "The Saturday Knights"			
❑ 4075	Ticonderoga/Tiger Lily	1961	30.00
—As "The Saturday Nights"			
❑ 4081	Hawaiian Tears/Texas Tommy	1961	20.00

SATURDAY'S CHILDREN

Number	Title (A Side/B Side)	Yr	NM
45s			
ABC-PARAMOUNT			
❑ 10505	Raindrops/Cry Wind	1963	10.00
DUNWICH			
❑ 139	Born on Saturday/ You Don't Know Better	1966	15.00
❑ 144	The Christmas Song/Deck Five	1967	15.00
❑ 156	Leave That Baby Alone/ I Hardly Know Her	1967	15.00

SAUNDERS, LITTLE BUTCHIE

Number	Title (A Side/B Side)	Yr	NM
45s			
HERALD			
❑ 485	Lindy Lou/Rock 'N' Roll Indian Dance	1956	50.00
❑ 491	Great Big Heart/I Wanna Holler	1956	50.00

SAUNDERS, MERL

Number	Title (A Side/B Side)	Yr	NM
45s			
FANTASY			
❑ 600	High Heel Sneakers/ (B-side unknown)	1964	10.00
❑ 620	Five More/Julia	1969	8.00
❑ 668	Save Mother Earth (Part 1)/ Save Mother Earth (Part 2)	1971	6.00
❑ 678	My Problems Got Problems/ Welcome to the Basement	1972	6.00
GALAXY			
❑ 747	I Pity the Fool/Tighten Up	1966	8.00
❑ 755	Soul Grooving/Up-Up and Away	1967	8.00
❑ 776	Iron Horse/A Little Bit of Righteousness	1970	8.00
Albums			
CRYSTAL CLEAR			
❑ 5006	Do I Move You	1980	20.00
—Direct-to-disc recording			
FANTASY			
❑ MPF-4533	Keystone Encores, Vol. 1	1988	12.00
❑ MPF-4534	Keystone Encores, Vol. 2	1988	12.00
❑ MPF-4535	Live at the Keystone, Vol. 1	1988	12.00
❑ MPF-4536	Live at the Keystone, Vol. 2	1988	12.00
❑ 8421	Heavy Turbulence	1972	15.00
❑ 9421	Fire Up	1973	20.00
—With Jerry Garcia and Tom Fogerty			
❑ 9460	Saunders	1974	15.00
❑ 9503	Leave Your Hat On	1976	12.00
❑ 79002 [(2)]	Live at the Keystone	198?	20.00
GALAXY			
❑ 8209	Soul Grooving	197?	15.00

SAVAGE, BOB

Number	Title (A Side/B Side)	Yr	NM
45s			
ABC-PARAMOUNT			
❑ 9915	Rock Around the World/ Butterfingers	1958	20.00

SAVAGE, DUKE, AND THE ARRIBINS

Number	Title (A Side/B Side)	Yr	NM
45s			
ARGO			
❑ 5346	Your Love/Hey Baby	1959	40.00

SAVAGE GRACE

Number	Title (A Side/B Side)	Yr	NM
45s			
REPRISE			
❑ 0924	Hymn to Freedom/ Come On Down	1970	6.00
❑ 0952	Watchtower (All Alone)/		
❑ Come On Down		1970	6.00
❑ 0988	Ivy/Save It for Me	1971	6.00
❑ 1022	Friends/Yonder	1971	6.00
Albums			
REPRISE			
❑ RS 6399	Savage Grace	1970	25.00
❑ RS 6484	Savage Grace 2	1971	25.00

SAVAGE RESURRECTION

Number	Title (A Side/B Side)	Yr	NM
45s			
MERCURY			
❑ 72778	Thing in "E"/The Fox Is Sick	1968	20.00
❑ 72778 [PS]	Thing in "E"/The Fox Is Sick	1968	40.00
Albums			
MERCURY			
❑ MG-21156 [M]	Savage Resurrection	1968	200.00
❑ SR-61156 [S]	Savage Resurrection	1968	100.00

SAVALAS, TELLY

Number	Title (A Side/B Side)	Yr	NM
45s			
MCA			
❑ 40301	If/Rubber Bands and Bits of String	1974	4.00
❑ 40363	Help Me Make It Through the Night/You've Lost That Lovin' Feelin'	1975	4.00
❑ 40468	Who Loves Ya Baby/ Nevertheless (I'm in Love with You)	1975	4.00
Albums			
AUDIO FIDELITY			
❑ AFSD-6271	Telly Savalas	1975	15.00
MCA			
❑ 436	Telly	1974	15.00
❑ 2160	Who Loves Ya Baby	1976	15.00

SAVATAGE TRANS-SIBERIAN ORCHESTRA related.

Number	Title (A Side/B Side)	Yr	NM
Albums			
ATLANTIC			
❑ 81247	Power of the Night	1985	12.00
❑ 81634	Fight for the Rock	1986	10.00
❑ 81775	Hall of the Mountain King	1987	10.00
❑ 82008	Gutter Ballet	1990	15.00
COMBAT			
❑ MX 6016 [EP]	The Dungeons Are Calling	1985	15.00
❑ 8018	Sirens	1986	12.00
—Reissue of Par LP with new cover			
PAR			
❑ PAR-1050	Sirens	1983	200.00
—Black vinyl			
❑ PAR-1050	Sirens	1983	400.00
—Blue vinyl			

Except when noted otherwise, VG = 25% of NM, and VG+ = 50% of NM. (Example: VG = $2.00, VG+ = $4.00 and NM = $8.00.)

SAVITT, BUDDY

45s

Number	Title (A Side/B Side)	Yr	NM
PARKWAY			
857	Smoke Gets in Your Eyes/Come Blow Your Horn	1962	12.00

SAVOY, RONNIE

45s

Number	Title (A Side/B Side)	Yr	NM
EPIC			
9619	I Hear Violins/The Marriage	1963	8.00
9708	Little Rascals/Sally Blue	1964	8.00
GONE			
5079	Ooh, What a Girl/Love Me As I Love You	1959	12.00
MGM			
12950	And the Heavens Cried/Big Chain	1960	20.00
13001	Bewitched/It's Gotta Be Love	1961	15.00
13042	Jungle Love Call/Your Cheatin' Heart	1961	15.00
PHILIPS			
40032	A Fool, A Loser, A Clown/Big Hand, Little Hand	1962	8.00
40071	Moonlight to Sunlight/21,000 Happiness Street	1962	8.00
WINGATE			
001	Memories Linger/Loving You	1965	25.00

SAVOY BROWN

45s

Number	Title (A Side/B Side)	Yr	NM
LONDON			
206	Everybody Loves a Drinkin' Man/Ride On Babe	1974	5.00
234	Walkin' 'n' Talkin'/Stranger Blues	1976	5.00
PARROT			
40034	Shake 'Em On Down/(B-side unknown)	1968	15.00
40037	Grits Ain't Groceries/She's Got a Ring in His Nose and a Ring on Her Hand	1969	8.00
40039	Train to Nowhere/Made Up My Mind	1969	8.00
40042	I'm Tired/Stay with Me Baby	1969	8.00
40046	Hard Way to Go/The Incredible Gnome Meets Jaxman	1970	6.00
40057	Poor Girl/Mr. Hare	1970	6.00
40060	Sitting and Thinking/(B-side unknown)	1971	6.00
40066	Tell Mama/Rock and Roll on the Radio	1971	6.00
40075	Coming Down Your Way/Can't Find You	1973	6.00
TOWN HOUSE			
1054	Lay Back in the Arms of Someone/Don't Tell Me I Told You	1981	4.00
1054 [PS]	Lay Back in the Arms of Someone/Don't Tell Me I Told You	1981	4.00
1055	Run to Me/Georgie	1981	4.00

Albums

Number	Title	Yr	NM
GNP CRESCENDO			
GNPS-2193	Make Me Sweat	1988	10.00
GNPS-2196	Kings of Boogie	1989	10.00
LONDON			
APS 638	Boogie Brothers	1974	10.00
PS 659	Wire Fire	1975	10.00
PS 670	Skin 'n' Bone	1976	10.00
PS 718	Savage Return	1978	10.00
LC-50000	The Best of Savoy Brown	1977	10.00
PARROT			
PAS 71024	Getting to the Point	1968	25.00
PAS 71027	Blue Matter	1969	25.00
PAS 71029	A Step Further	1969	15.00
PAS 71036	Raw Sienna	1970	15.00
PAS 71042	Looking In	1970	15.00
PAS 71047	Street Corner Talking	1971	15.00
XPAS 71052	Hellbound Train	1972	15.00
XPAS 71057	Lion's Share	1972	15.00
XPAS 71059	Jack the Toad	1973	15.00
TOWN HOUSE			
ST-7002	Rock 'n' Roll Warriors	1981	12.00
SKBK-7003 [(2)]	Greatest Hits Live in Concert	1982	15.00

SAWBUCK

45s

Number	Title (A Side/B Side)	Yr	NM
FILLMORE			
ZS7 7007	There Will Be Love/Bible Burning	1972	8.00

Albums

Number	Title	Yr	NM
FILLMORE			
Z 31248	Sawbuck	1972	20.00

SAWYER, RAY

Also see DR. HOOK.

45s

Number	Title (A Side/B Side)	Yr	NM
CAPITOL			
4344	(One More Year of) Daddy's Little Girl/I Need That High (But I Can't Stand the Taste)	1976	4.00
4386	Red-Winged Blackbird/The One I'm Holding Now	1977	4.00
4416	Walls and Doors/I Need That HIgh (But I Can't Stand the Taste)	1977	4.00
4592	Dancing Fool/Rhythm Guitar	1978	4.00
4747	What I'm Holding/I Want Johnny's Job	1979	4.00
4820	Drinking Wine Alone/I Don't Feel Like Smilin'	1980	4.00
SANDY			
1030	Rockin' Satellite/Bells in My Heart	1961	40.00
1037	I'm Gonna Leave/You Gave Me the Right	1961	25.00

Albums

Number	Title	Yr	NM
CAPITOL			
ST-11591	Ray Sawyer	1976	10.00

SAXON, EDDIE, AND THE PARAMOUNTS

45s

Number	Title (A Side/B Side)	Yr	NM
EMPRESS			
106	Blues No More/If It's Meant to Be	1962	150.00
106 [DJ]	Blues No More	1962	200.00
—Single-sided promo			

SAXON, SKY

Later recorded with THE SEEDS. Also see RITCHIE MARSH.

45s

Number	Title (A Side/B Side)	Yr	NM
CONQUEST			
777	They Say/Go Ahead and Cry	1964	30.00

Albums

Number	Title	Yr	NM
GNP CRESCENDO			
GNP-2040 [M]	A Full Spoon of Seedy Blues	1967	40.00
GNPS-2040 [S]	A Full Spoon of Seedy Blues	1967	35.00

SCAFFOLD, THE

With Mike McGear, Paul McCartney's brother.

45s

Number	Title (A Side/B Side)	Yr	NM
BELL			
701	Thank U Very Much/Ide B the First	1968	16.00
724	Do You Remember/Carry On Krow	1968	16.00
747	Lily the Pink/Buttons of Your Mind	1968	16.00
821	Charity Bubbles/Goose	1969	16.00
849	Jelly Covered Cloud/Liver Birds	1969	12.00
WARNER BROS.			
8001	Liverpool Lou/Ten Years After on Strawberry Jam	1974	6.00

Albums

Number	Title	Yr	NM
BELL			
6018 [M]	Thank U Very Much	1968	50.00
—Mono copies are promo only			
6018 [S]	Thank U Very Much	1968	50.00

SCAGGS, BOZ

12-Inch Singles

Number	Title (A Side/B Side)	Yr	NM
COLUMBIA			
AS 380 [DJ]	Hard Times (same on both sides)	1977	8.00
11350	Look What You've Done to Me/Jojo	1980	10.00

45s

Number	Title (A Side/B Side)	Yr	NM
ATLANTIC			
2692	I'm Easy/I'll Be Long Gone	1969	10.00
COLUMBIA			
01023	You Can Have Me Anytime/Georgia	1981	4.00
02423	Jojo/Miss Sun	1981	3.00
—Reissue			
02424	Breakdown Dead Ahead/Look What You've Done to Me	1981	3.00
—Reissue			
07780	Heart of Mine/You'll Never Know	1988	3.00
07780 [PS]	Heart of Mine/You'll Never Know	1988	4.00
07981	Cool Running/You'll Never Know	1988	3.00
08068	What's Number 1/Claudia	1988	3.00
10027	Slow Dancer/Pain of Love	1974	6.00
10124	You Make It So Hard (To Say Goodbye)/There Is Something Else	1975	5.00
10319	It's Over/Harbor Lights	1976	5.00
10367	Lowdown/Harbor Lights	1976	5.00
10440	What Can I Say/We're All Alone	1976	5.00
10491	Lido Shuffle/We're All Alone	1977	5.00
10606	Hard Times/We're Waiting	1977	5.00
10606 [PS]	Hard Times/We're Waiting	1977	10.00
10679	Hollywood/A Clue	1978	5.00
11241	Breakdown Dead Ahead/Isn't It Time	1980	4.00
11281	Jojo/Do Like You Do in New York	1980	4.00
11349	Look What You've Done to Me/Simone	1980	4.00
11406	Miss Sun/Dinah Flo	1980	4.00
45353	We Were Always Sweethearts/Painted Bells	1971	6.00
45408	Near You/Downright Woman	1971	6.00
45540	Here to Stay/Runnin' Blue	1972	6.00
45670	Dinah Flo/He's a Fool for You	1972	6.00
46025	You Make It So Hard (To Say Goodbye)/There Is Someone Else	1974	6.00
FULL MOON			
49676	You Make It So Hard (To Say Goodbye)/Something's Missing in My Life	1981	4.00
—B-side by Lady Sylvia			
VIRGIN			
S7-18048	I'll Be the One/Time Change	1994	4.00
S7-19529	It All Went Down the Drain/I've Got Your Love	1997	3.00
S7-19651	Fly Like a Bird/Sick and Tired	1997	3.00

Albums

Number	Title	Yr	NM
ATLANTIC			
SD 8239	Boz Scaggs	1969	12.00
SD 19166	Boz Scaggs	1977	8.00
COLUMBIA			
A2S 71 [(2)DJ]	KSAN Live Concert	1974	50.00
—Promo-only set released in plain cardboard jacket			
AS 203 [DJ]	The Boz Scaggs Sampler	1976	20.00
KC 30454	Moments	1971	10.00
PC 30454	Moments	197?	8.00
KC 30976	Boz Scaggs & Band	1971	10.00
PC 30976	Boz Scaggs & Band	197?	8.00
KC 31384	My Time	1972	10.00
PC 31384	My Time	197?	8.00
KC 32760	Slow Dancer	1974	10.00
—Second cover has a male dancer who is not Boz Scaggs			
KC 32760	Slow Dancer	1974	12.00
—Original cover has Boz Scaggs on a beach in only a bathing suit			
PC 32760	Slow Dancer	197?	8.00
JC 33920	Silk Degrees	1977	10.00
—Early reissue with new prefix			
PC 33920	Silk Degrees	1976	12.00
—Original edition with "PC" prefix and no bar code on back cover			
PC 33920	Silk Degrees	1985	8.00
—Budget-line reissue; bar code on back cover			
FC 36106	Middle Man	1980	10.00
PC 36106	Middle Man	198?	8.00
—Budget-line reissue			
FC 36841	Hits!	1980	10.00
PC 36841	Hits!	198?	8.00
—Budget-line reissue			
PC 37249	Down Two Then Left	198?	8.00
—Budget-line reissue			
JC 37429	Down Two Then Left	1977	10.00
FC 40463	Other Roads	1988	10.00
HC 43920	Silk Degrees	1981	30.00
—Half-speed mastered edition			

SCANDAL

45s

Number	Title (A Side/B Side)	Yr	NM
COLUMBIA			
03234	Goodbye to You/All My Life	1982	4.00
03615	Love's Got a Line on You/Another Bad Love	1983	4.00
03615 [PS]	Love's Got a Line on You/Another Bad Love	1983	—
03987	Win Some, Lose Some/Another Bad Love	1983	4.00
38-04424	The Warrior/Less Than Half	1984	4.00
38-04424 [PS]	The Warrior/Less Than Half	1984	—
04650	Hands Tied/Maybe We Went Too Far	1984	4.00
04650 [PS]	Hands Tied/Maybe We Went Too Far	1984	—
04750	Beat of a Heart/Tonight	1985	4.00
04750 [PS]	Beat of a Heart/Tonight	1985	—

Albums

Number	Title	Yr	NM
COLUMBIA			
5C 38194 [EP]	Scandal	1983	10.00
PC 38194 [EP]	Scandal	198?	6.00
—Reissue with new prefix			
FC 39173	Warrior	1984	10.00
8C8 39905 [EP]	Scandal featuring Patty Smyth	1985	20.00
—Picture disc EP with four of the group's biggest hits			

SCARBURY, JOEY

45s

Number	Title (A Side/B Side)	Yr	NM
ABC-DUNHILL			
4209	House of the Rising Sun/Midnight Mail	1969	10.00

S

Number	Title (A Side/B Side)	Yr	NM
BELL			
❑ 45113	Albuquerque/Foresee the Future	1971	6.00
❑ 45146	I'm Home Again/ Foresee the Future	1971	6.00
❑ 45314	Memphis Nights/ (B-side unknown)	1973	6.00
BIG TREE			
❑ 16008	I'm Gonna Sit Right Down and Write Myself a Letter/ Pretending to Make Love	1973	6.00
COLUMBIA			
❑ 3-10538	There's No One Home at My House/Long Time Love	1977	5.00
❑ 3-10785	Again and Again/Chances	1978	5.00
❑ 3-10990	Turn the Light On/ Sunset Boulevard	1979	5.00
ELEKTRA			
❑ 47147	The Theme from "The Greatest American Hero" (Believe It or Not)/Little Bit of Us	1981	3.00
—Revised A-side title, with the added word "The"			
❑ 47147	Theme from "Greatest American Hero" (Believe It or Not)/Little Bit of Us	1981	5.00
—Original 45 has no "The" in the title			
❑ 47147 [PS]	The Theme from "The Greatest American Hero" (Believe It or Not)/Little Bit of Us	1981	5.00
—Most picture sleeves have records with the original title			
❑ 47201	When She Dances/Everything But Love	1981	4.00
LIONEL			
❑ 3208	Mixed-Up Guy/Loved You Darlin' from the Very Start	1971	6.00
PLAYBOY			
❑ 6002	California Free/(B-side unknown)	1974	6.00
RCA			
❑ PB-13913	The River's Song/Billy's Home	1984	4.00
REENA			
❑ 1004	I Love You As You Are/ I'll Never Set You Free	1968	10.00
Albums			
ELEKTRA			
❑ 5E-537	America's Greatest Hero	1981	10.00

SCARLETS, THE (1)

Number	Title (A Side/B Side)	Yr	NM
45s			
DOT			
❑ 16004	Stampede/Park Avenue	1959	25.00
PRINCE			
❑ 1207	Stampede/Park Avenue	1959	50.00

SCARLETS, THE (2)

Number	Title (A Side/B Side)	Yr	NM
45s			
EVENT			
❑ 4287	Dear One/I've Lost	1958	40.00
LOST-NITE			
❑ 189	True Love/Cry Baby	196?	6.00
—Reissue			
❑ 338	Dear One/I've Lost	197?	5.00
—Reissue			
❑ 343	Darling, I'm Yours/Love Doll	197?	5.00
—Reissue			
❑ 347	Kiss Me/Indian Fever	197?	5.00
—Reissue			
RED ROBIN			
❑ 128	Dear One/I've Lost	1954	500.00
❑ 133	Darling, I'm Yours/Love Doll	1954	500.00
❑ 135	True Love/Cry Baby	1955	500.00
❑ 138	Kiss Me/Indian Fever	1955	600.00

SCARLETS, THE (3)

Number	Title (A Side/B Side)	Yr	NM
45s			
TOWER			
❑ 144	I've Had It/You Don't Love Me	1965	10.00

SCARLETS, THE (U)

Could be group (1).

Number	Title (A Side/B Side)	Yr	NM
45s			
FURY			
❑ 1036	Truly Yours/East of the Sun	1960	30.00

SCARLING

Number	Title (A Side/B Side)	Yr	NM
45s			
SYMPATHY FOR THE RECORD INDUSTRY			
❑ SFTRI 738	Crispin Glover/Love Becomes a Ghost	2004	3.00
—Red vinyl; small hole			

SCARS ON BROADWAY

Number	Title (A Side/B Side)	Yr	NM
Albums			
INTERSCOPE			
❑ 1159201	Scars on Broadway	2008	20.00

SCAVENGERS, THE

Number	Title (A Side/B Side)	Yr	NM
45s			
FENTON			
❑ 987	Curfew/Oasis	1964	50.00
MOBILE FIDELITY			
❑ 1005	The Angels Listened In/My Love Waits for Me	1963	30.00
❑ 1212	Devil's Reef/Little Annie	1963	30.00
STARS OF HOLLYWOOD			
❑ 1210	Shot Gun/Cream Puff	1963	50.00
❑ 1211	Shot Gun/Zip Code	1963	50.00
—"Cream Puff" and "Zip Code" are different titles for the same recording			
❑ 1212	Devil's Reef/Little Annie	1963	50.00
SUEMI			
❑ 4552	Bogus/Ghost Riders '65	1965	25.00

SCENE, THE

Number	Title (A Side/B Side)	Yr	NM
45s			
B.T. PUPPY			
❑ 533	Scenes (From Another World)/ You're in a Bad Way	1967	10.00

SCHAFF, MURRAY, AND THE ARISTOCRATS

Number	Title (A Side/B Side)	Yr	NM
45s			
JOSIE			
❑ 788	The Unfinished Rock/ Ooh How I Love Ya	1956	30.00
KING			
❑ 4977	How Many Miles/Tombstone Number 9	1956	30.00

SCHIFRIN, LALO

Listings include many of his soundtrack LPs.

Number	Title (A Side/B Side)	Yr	NM
12-Inch Singles			
CTI			
❑ OJ-2	Flamingo/Quiet Village/Jaws	1976	15.00
PABLO			
❑ RD-11004	Unicorn/Free Ride	1977	12.00
—With Dizzy Gillespie			
TABU			
❑ 5520	No One Home/(Instrumental)	1979	12.00
45s			
A&M			
❑ 1756	Theme from "The Master Gunfighter"/Theme from "The Trial of Billy Jack"	1975	5.00
AUDIO FIDELITY			
❑ 084	The Ugly Duckling/ (B-side unknown)	196?	10.00
CTI			
❑ 29	Turning Point/Flamingo	1976	4.00
❑ 36	Roller Coaster (From the Universal Film)/Love Theme from "The Eagle Has Landed"	1977	6.00
DOT			
❑ 17059	Mission Impossible/ Jim on the Move	1967	10.00
MCA			
❑ 40748	Magic Carousel/ Merry-Go-Round	1977	4.00
❑ 52175	Heliotrope Bouquet/ The Entertainer	1983	4.00
—B-side by Marvin Hamlisch			
MGM			
❑ 13139	Broken Date/Good Life	1963	10.00
❑ 13151	Hud/Jive Orbit	1963	10.00
❑ 13163	Haunting/Theme from "Dime with a Halo"	1963	10.00
❑ 13224	Seven Faces of Dr. Lao/ The Wave	1964	10.00
❑ 13251	Theme from "Rhino"/ Rhino Bomp	1964	10.00
❑ 13425	The Cincinnati Kid/ So Many Times	1965	8.00
❑ 13670	Venice After Dark/ Our Venetian Affair	1967	8.00
❑ 14153	Burning Bridges/Kelly's Heroes	1970	6.00
❑ 14180	Theme from "Medical Center"/ (B-side unknown)	1970	6.00
PABLO			
❑ RB-11003	Unicorn/Free Ride	1977	4.00
—With Dizzy Gillespie			
PARAMOUNT			
❑ 0001	Self Destruct/The Getaway	1969	8.00
❑ 0002	Mannix/End Game	1969	8.00
TABU			
❑ 5509	Moonlight Gypsies/ Prophecy of Love	1978	4.00
❑ 5519	No One Home/Middle of the Night	1979	4.00
TETRAGRAMMATON			
❑ 1533	Theme from "Che"/Embo Scada	1969	8.00
20TH CENTURY			
❑ 2150	Ape Shuffle/Escape from Tomorrow	1974	5.00
❑ 2205	Bolero/Dona Donna	1975	5.00
UNITED ARTISTS			
❑ 50649	What's New Pussycat/Pussycat, Pussycat, I Love You	1970	5.00
VERVE			
❑ 10290	Broken Date/Good Life	1963	8.00
❑ 10331	New Fantasy/Bachianas Brasilerias #5	1964	8.00
❑ 10365	Man from Thrush/Blues-A-Go-Go	1965	10.00
❑ 10434	The Wig/Beneath a Weeping Willow Shade	1966	8.00
❑ 10663	Agnus Dei/Sanctus Benedictus	1971	6.00
❑ 10663	Theme from "Medical Center"/ All for the Love of Sunshine	1971	8.00
WARNER BROS.			
❑ 7173	Foxtail/That Night	1968	6.00
❑ 7263	Bullitt/That Night	1969	6.00
Albums			
AMERICAN INT'L.			
❑ AILP 3003	The Amityville Horror	1979	10.00
AUDIO FIDELITY			
❑ AFLP-1981 [M]	Bossa Nova — New Brazilian Jazz	1962	20.00
❑ AFLP-2117 [M]	Eso Es Latino Jazz	1963	20.00
❑ AFSD-5981 [S]	Bossa Nova — New Brazilian Jazz	1962	25.00
❑ AFSD-6117 [S]	Eso Es Latino Jazz	1963	25.00
❑ AFSD-6195	The Other Side of Lalo Schifrin	1968	15.00
COLGEMS			
❑ COMO-5003 [M]	Murderer's Row	1967	50.00
❑ COSO-5003 [S]	Murderer's Row	1967	100.00
CTI			
❑ 5000	Black Widow	1976	12.00
❑ 5003	Towering Toccata	1977	12.00
DOT			
❑ DLP-3831 [M]	Music from Mission: Impossible	1967	30.00
❑ DLP-3833 [M]	Cool Hand Luke	1968	50.00
❑ DLP-25831 [S]	Music from Mission: Impossible	1967	40.00
❑ DLP-25833 [S]	Cool Hand Luke	1968	50.00
❑ DLP-25852	There's a Whole Lot of Schifrin Goin' On	1968	20.00
DRG			
❑ SBL-12591	The Fourth Protocol	1987	15.00
ENTR'ACTE			
❑ ERS-6508	Voyage of the Damned	1977	25.00
❑ ERS-6510	The Eagle Has Landed/ The Four Musketeers	1980	12.00
MCA			
❑ 2284	Rollercoaster	1977	15.00
❑ 2374	Nunzio	1978	12.00
❑ 5185	The Competition	1980	10.00
❑ 25012	The Cincinnati Kid	1986	8.00
❑ 25137	Liquidator	1966	8.00
MGM			
❑ E-4110 [M]	Piano, Strings and Bossa Nova	1963	15.00
❑ SE-4110 [S]	Piano, Strings and Bossa Nova	1963	20.00
❑ E-4156 [M]	Between Broadway and Hollywood	1963	15.00
❑ SE-4156 [S]	Between Broadway and Hollywood	1963	20.00
❑ E-4313 [M]	The Cincinnati Kid	1965	20.00
❑ SE-4313 [S]	The Cincinnati Kid	1965	25.00
❑ E-4413 ST [M]	Liquidator	1966	20.00
❑ SE-4413 ST [S]	Liquidator	1966	25.00
❑ SE-4742	Medical Center and Other Great Themes	1971	20.00
NAUTILUS			
❑ NR-51	Ins and Outs	198?	40.00
—Audiophile vinyl			
PALO ALTO			
❑ 8055	Ins and Outs	1983	12.00
PARAMOUNT			
❑ PAS-5002	More Music from Mission: Impossible	1969	40.00
❑ PAS-5004	Mannix	1969	30.00
ROULETTE			
❑ SR-42013	"Lalole" — The Latin Sound	1968	15.00

Number	Title (A Side/B Side)	Yr	NM
❑ R 52088 [M]	Lalo Brilliance	1962	20.00
❑ SR 52088 [S]	Lalo Brilliance	1962	25.00
TABU			
❑ JZ 35436	Gypsies	1978	12.00
❑ JZ 36091	No One Home	1979	12.00
TETRAGRAMMATON			
❑ T-5006	Che!	1969	30.00
TICO			
❑ LP-1070 [M]	Piano Espanol	1960	25.00
❑ LPS-1070 [S]	Piano Espanol	1960	30.00
VARESE SARABANDE			
❑ STV-81198	The Osterman Weekend	1983	10.00
VERVE			
❑ V-8543 [M]	Samba Paros Dos	1963	15.00
—With Bob Brookmeyer			
❑ V6-8543 [S]	Samba Paros Dos	1963	20.00
—With Bob Brookmeyer			
❑ V-8601 [M]	New Fantasy	1964	15.00
❑ V6-8601 [S]	New Fantasy	1964	20.00
❑ V-8624 [M]	Once a Thief and Other Themes	1965	15.00
❑ V6-8624 [S]	Once a Thief and Other Themes	1965	20.00
❑ V-8654 [M]	The Dissection and Reconstruction of Music from the Past	1966	15.00
❑ V6-8654 [S]	The Dissection and Reconstruction of Music from the Past	1966	20.00
❑ V6-8785	Insensatez	1968	15.00
❑ V6-8801	Rock Requiem	1971	12.00
WARNER BROS.			
❑ WS 1777	Bullitt	1968	60.00
❑ BS 2727	Enter the Dragon	1973	60.00
❑ BSK 3328	Boulevard Nights	1979	10.00

SCHILLER, LAWRENCE

Albums

Number	Title (A Side/B Side)	Yr	NM
CAPITOL			
❑ TAO 2574 [M]	LSD	1966	100.00
❑ KAO 2630 [M]	Why Did Lenny Bruce Die?	1967	30.00
❑ KAO 2652 [M]	Homosexuality in the American Male	1967	30.00

SCHILLING, JOHNNY, AND THE SHERWOODS

45s

Number	Title (A Side/B Side)	Yr	NM
C&A			
❑ 507	King of the World/Marcelle	1963	100.00

SCHOLARS, THE Featuring a young KENNY ROGERS.

45s

Number	Title (A Side/B Side)	Yr	NM
CUE			
❑ 7927/8	The Poor Little Doggie/What Did I Do Wrong	1956	40.00
DOT			
❑ 15498	Rock Road/Spin the Wheel	1956	20.00
❑ 15519	If You Listen with Your Heart/Poor Little Doggie	1956	20.00
IMPERIAL			
❑ 5449	I Didn't Want to Do It/Beloved	1957	25.00
❑ 5459	Eternally Yours/Kan-Gu-Wa	1957	25.00

SCHOOLBOYS, THE

45s

Number	Title (A Side/B Side)	Yr	NM
JUANITA			
❑ 103	Angel of Love/The Slide	1958	150.00
OKEH			
❑ 7076	Shirley/Please Say You Want Me	1957	30.00
—"Shirley" was the hit, but "Please Say You Want Me" is the side that has lived on			
❑ 7085	I Am Old Enough/Mary	1957	25.00
❑ 7090	Pearl/Carol	1957	25.00

SCHORY, DICK

Albums

Number	Title (A Side/B Side)	Yr	NM
CONCERT DISC			
❑ SC-21 [M]	Re-Percussion	1957	60.00
RCA VICTOR			
❑ LPM-1866 [M]	Music for Bang, Barroom and Harp	1958	60.00
❑ LSP-1866 [S]	Music for Bang, Barroom and Harp	1958	200.00
❑ LPM-2125 [M]	Music to Break Any Mood	1960	30.00
❑ LSP-2125 [S]	Music to Break Any Mood	1960	100.00
❑ LPM-2289 [M]	Wild Percussion and Horns A-Plenty	1960	30.00
❑ LSP-2289 [S]	Wild Percussion and Horns A-Plenty	1960	60.00
❑ LSA-2306 [S]	Runnin' Wild	1960	40.00
❑ LSA-2382 [S]	Stereo Action Goes Broadway	1961	40.00
❑ LPM-2485 [M]	Holiday for Percussion	1962	30.00
❑ LSA-2485 [S]	Holiday for Percussion	1962	40.00
❑ LSP-2613 [S]	Supercussion	1963	40.00
❑ LPM-2738 [M]	Politely Percussive	1963	30.00

Scorpions, *Tokyo Tapes*, RCA Victor CPL2-3039, 1978, $15.

Number	Title (A Side/B Side)	Yr	NM
❑ LSP-2738 [S]	Politely Percussive	1963	40.00
❑ LPM-2806 [M]	Dick Schory on Tour	1964	20.00
❑ LSP-2806 [S]	Dick Schory on Tour	1964	25.00
❑ LPM-2926 [M]	The Happy Hits	1964	20.00
❑ LSP-2926 [S]	The Happy Hits	1964	25.00

SCHROEDER, JOHN

45s

Number	Title (A Side/B Side)	Yr	NM
CAMEO			
❑ 366	The Fugitive Theme/Don't Break the Heart of Kimble	1965	20.00
❑ 385	You've Lost That Lovin' Feelin'/Funny How Love Can Be	1965	12.00
❑ 389	Agent 00-Soul/Nightrider	1965	25.00

SCHUMACHER, CHRISTINE, SINGS WITH THE SUPREMES Also see THE SUPREMES.

45s

Number	Title (A Side/B Side)	Yr	NM
MOTOWN			
❑ L-294-MO5 [DJ]	Mother You, Smother You (same on both sides)	1968	300.00
—Schumacher won a "Record a Record with the Supremes" contest on WKNR of Detroit. This is the rare result.			

SCOOBY DOO

45s

Number	Title (A Side/B Side)	Yr	NM
ZEPHYR			
❑ 006	Moonglow/Ernie's Journey	195?	20.00

Albums

Number	Title (A Side/B Side)	Yr	NM
ZEPHYR			
❑ ZMP-12002 [M]	Jerry Leiber Presents Scooby Doo	1959	50.00

SCORPION

Albums

Number	Title (A Side/B Side)	Yr	NM
TOWER			
❑ ST 5171	Scorpion	1969	50.00

SCORPIONS Rudolph Schenker's brother Michael was briefly a member - twice.

12-Inch Singles

Number	Title (A Side/B Side)	Yr	NM
MERCURY			
❑ MK 212 [DJ]	You Give Me All I Need (same on both sides)	1982	8.00
❑ 265 [DJ]	Rock You Like a Hurricane (same on both sides)	1984	10.00
❑ 359 [DJ]	Big City Nights (Edit) (LP)/No One Like You (Live)	1985	8.00
❑ 378 [DJ]	Loving You Sunday Morning/No One Like You	1985	8.00
❑ 833 [DJ]	I'm Leaving You (Long) (Short)	1984	8.00

45s

Number	Title (A Side/B Side)	Yr	NM
MERCURY			
❑ 76008	Coast to Coast/Loving You Sunday Morning	1979	4.00
❑ 76070	Make It Real/(B-side unknown)	1980	4.00
❑ 76084	Lady Starlight/(B-side unknown)	1980	4.00
❑ 76153	No One Like You/Now	1982	4.00
❑ 818440-7	Rock You Like a Hurricane/Coming Home	1984	3.00
❑ 818440-7 [PS]	Rock You Like a Hurricane/Coming Home	1984	5.00
❑ 866236-7	Send Me an Angel/Wind of Change (Russian Version)	1991	4.00
❑ 868180-7	Wind of Change/Money and Fame	1991	4.00
❑ 870323-7	Rhythm of Love/We Let It Rock…We Let It Roll	1988	3.00
❑ 870323-7 [PS]	Rhythm of Love/We Let It Rock…We Let It Roll	1988	3.00
❑ 870559-7	Believe in Love/Love on the Run	1988	3.00
❑ 872372-7	Passion Rules the Game/Media Overkill	1988	3.00
❑ 880082-7	Still Loving You/Bad Boys Running Wild	1984	3.00
❑ 880319-7	I'm Leaving You/Same Thrill	1984	3.00

Number	Title (A Side/B Side)	Yr	NM
RCA VICTOR			
❑ PB-10574	Speedy's Gone/ They Need a Million	1976	6.00
❑ PB-10691	In Trance/Night Lights	1976	6.00
Albums			
BILLINGSGATE			
❑ 1004	Lonesome Crow	1974	30.00
MERCURY			
❑ SRM-1-3795	Lovedrive	1979	10.00
❑ SRM-1-3825	Animal Magnetism	1980	10.00
❑ SRM-1-4039	Blackout	1982	10.00
❑ 814981-1	Love at First Sting	1984	10.00
—With man and woman on cover			
❑ 818885-1	Blackout	198?	8.00
—Reissue of 4039			
❑ 822038-1	Love at First Sting	1984	12.00
—Reissue with band on cover			
❑ 822555-1	Lovedrive	198?	8.00
—Reissue of 3795			
❑ 822556-1	Animal Magnetism	198?	8.00
—Reissue of 3825			
❑ 824344-1 [(2)]	World Wide Live	1985	12.00
❑ 832963-1	Savage Amusement	1988	10.00
❑ 842002-1	Best of Rockers 'N' Ballads	1989	10.00
❑ 846908-1	Crazy World	1990	15.00
RCA VICTOR			
❑ AFL1-2628	Taken by Force	1978	12.00
❑ CPL2-3039 [(2)]	Toyko Tapes	1978	15.00
❑ AFL1-3516	Best of Scorpions	1979	10.00
❑ AYL1-3659	Virgin Killer	1980	8.00
—"Best Buy Series" reissue			
❑ AFL1-4025	Fly to the Rainbow	1977	10.00
—Reissue with new prefix			
❑ PPL1-4025	Fly to the Rainbow	1975	12.00
❑ AFL1-4128	In Trance	1977	10.00
—Reissue with new prefix			
❑ PPL1-4128	In Trance	1976	12.00
❑ PPL1-4225	Virgin Killer	1977	12.00
❑ AYL1-4657	In Trance	1983	8.00
—"Best Buy Series" reissue			
❑ AYL1-5057	Fly to the Rainbow	1984	8.00
—"Best Buy Series" reissue			
❑ AFL1-5085	Best of Scorpions, Vol. 2	1984	10.00

SCOTT, BETTY

Number	Title (A Side/B Side)	Yr	NM
45s			
HIT			
❑ 78	My Whole World Is Falling Down/ Twist It Up	1963	8.00
—B-side by Herbert Hunter			

SCOTT, BILLY

Number	Title (A Side/B Side)	Yr	NM
45s			
CAMEO			
❑ 121	You're the Greatest/ That's Why I Was Born	1957	25.00
❑ 143	A Million Boys/The Town of Never Worry	1958	20.00
EVEREST			
❑ 19315	Carole/Stairway to the Stars	1959	15.00
LAMON			
❑ 10114	Merry Christmas/ A Night to Remember	1983	4.00

SCOTT, BUDDY

Number	Title (A Side/B Side)	Yr	NM
45s			
HIT			
❑ 230	May the Bird of Paradise Fly Up Your Nose/Turn! Turn! Turn!	1965	10.00
—B-side by Jackie and the Giants			

SCOTT, CALVIN

Number	Title (A Side/B Side)	Yr	NM
45s			
ATCO			
❑ 6696	I'm Taking You Home to Mama/ Sonny Boy (Be a Man)	1969	12.00
❑ 6729	Cry Like a Baby/More Than You'll Ever Know	1970	12.00
STAX			
❑ 0094	Shame on the Family Name/ I've Made a Reservation	1971	10.00
❑ 0110	Goin' Back to Eden/The Sadness for Things	1971	10.00
Albums			
STAX			
❑ STS-2046	I'm Not Blind... I Just Can't See	1972	80.00

SCOTT, CHRISTOPHER

Number	Title (A Side/B Side)	Yr	NM
Albums			
DECCA			
❑ DL 75141	Switched-On Bacharach	1969	15.00
❑ DL 75243	More Switched-On Bacharach	1970	15.00
MCA			
❑ 282	Switched-On Bacharach	1973	12.00
—Reissue of Decca 75141			

SCOTT, FREDDIE

Also see THE SYMPHONICS (2).

Number	Title (A Side/B Side)	Yr	NM
45s			
COLPIX			
❑ 692	Hey Girl/The Slide	1963	12.00
❑ 709	I Got a Woman/Brand New World	1963	10.00
❑ 724	Where Does Love Go/Where Have All the Flowers Gone	1964	10.00
❑ 752	On Broadway/If I Had a Hammer	1964	10.00
COLUMBIA			
❑ 43112	Mr. Heartache/One Heartache Too Many	1964	10.00
❑ 43199	Lonely Man/I'll Try Again	1964	10.00
❑ 43316	Don't Let It End/Come Up Singing	1965	10.00
❑ 43623	One Iddy Biddy Needle/ Forget Me If You Can	1966	10.00
JOY			
❑ 250	Baby, You're a Long Time Dead/Lost the Right	1961	12.00
❑ 255	I Gotta Stand Tall/When the Wind Changes	1961	12.00
❑ 280	I Gotta Stand Tall/When the Wind Changes	1963	10.00
P.I.P.			
❑ 8932	Deep Is the Night/The Great If	1972	5.00
PROBE			
❑ 481	I Shall Be Released/ Girl I Love You	1970	6.00
SHOUT			
❑ 207	Are You Lonely for Me/ Where Were You	1966	8.00
❑ 211	Cry to Me/No One Could Ever Love You	1967	8.00
❑ 212	Am I Grooving You/ Never You Mind	1967	8.00
❑ 216	He Will Break Your Heart I'll Be Gone	1967	8.00
❑ 220	He Ain't Give You None/Run Joy	1967	8.00
❑ 227	Just Like a Flower/ Spanish Harlem	1968	8.00
❑ 233	(You) Got What I Need/ Powerful Love	1968	10.00
❑ 238	Loving You Is Killing Me/Eileen	1968	8.00
❑ 245	Forever My Darling/ (You) Got What I Need	1969	10.00
VANGUARD			
❑ 35137	I Guess God Wants It This Way/ Please Listen	1971	5.00
Albums			
COLPIX			
❑ CP-461 [M]	Freddie Scott Sings and Sings and Sings	1964	60.00
—Gold label			
❑ CP-461 [M]	Freddie Scott Sings and Sings and Sings	1965	40.00
—Blue label			
❑ SCP-461 [R]	Freddie Scott Sings and Sings and Sings	1965	30.00
—Blue label			
❑ SCP-461 [S]	Freddie Scott Sings and Sings and Sings	1964	120.00
—Gold label			
COLUMBIA			
❑ CL 2258 [M]	Everything I Have Is Yours	1964	20.00
❑ CL 2660 [M]	Lonely Man	1967	20.00
❑ CS 9058 [S]	Everything I Have Is Yours	1964	25.00
❑ CS 9460 [S]	Lonely Man	1967	25.00
PROBE			
❑ CPLP-4517	I Shall Be Released	1970	25.00
SHOUT			
❑ SLP-501 [M]	Are You Lonely for Me	1967	20.00
❑ SLPS-501 [S]	Are You Lonely for Me	1967	25.00

SCOTT, FREDDIE, AND THE CHIMES

Number	Title (A Side/B Side)	Yr	NM
45s			
ARROW			
❑ 724	Please Call/A Letter Came This Morning	1958	40.00
❑ 726	Lovin' Baby/A Faded Memory	1958	40.00

SCOTT, JACK

Number	Title (A Side/B Side)	Yr	NM
45s			
ABC			
❑ 10843	Before the Bird Flies/Insane	1966	20.00
ABC-PARAMOUNT			
❑ 9818	Baby She's Gone/You Can Bet Your Bottom Dollar	1957	150.00
❑ 9860	Two Timin' Woman/I Need Your Love	1957	150.00
CAPITOL			
❑ 4554	A Little Feeling (Called Love)/ Now That I	1961	25.00
❑ 4554 [PS]	A Little Feeling (Called Love)/ Now That I	1961	50.00
❑ 4597	My Dream Came True/ Strange Desire	1961	20.00
❑ 4597 [PS]	My Dream Came True/ Strange Desire	1961	50.00
❑ 4637	Steps 1 and 2/One of These Days	1961	20.00
❑ 4637 [PS]	Steps 1 and 2/One of These Days	1961	50.00
❑ 4689	Cry, Cry, Cry/Grizzly Bear	1962	20.00
❑ 4689 [PS]	Cry, Cry, Cry/Grizzly Bear	1962	50.00
❑ 4738	The Part Where I Cry/You Only See What You Wanna See	1962	20.00
❑ 4796	Sad Story/I Can't Hold Your Letters	1962	20.00
❑ 4855	If Only/Green, Green Valley	1962	20.00
❑ 4903	Strangers/Laugh and the World Laughs With You	1963	20.00
❑ 4955	All I See Is Blue/Meo Myo	1963	20.00
CARLTON			
❑ 462	My True Love/Leroy	1958	30.00
❑ 483	With Your Love/Geraldine	1958	30.00
❑ 483 [PS]	With Your Love/Geraldine	1958	60.00
❑ 493	Goodbye Baby/Save My Soul	1959	30.00
❑ 493 [PS]	Goodbye Baby/Save My Soul	1959	60.00
❑ 504	I Never Felt Like This/Bella	1959	30.00
❑ 514	The Way I Walk/Midgie	1959	30.00
❑ 519 [M]	There Comes a Time/ Baby Marie	1959	20.00
❑ ST-519 [S]	There Comes a Time/Baby Marie	1959	40.00
DOT			
❑ 17475	May You Never Be Alone/ Face to the Wall	1973	5.00
❑ 17504	You're Just Getting Better/ Walk Through My Mind	1974	5.00
GROOVE			
❑ 58-0027	There's Trouble Brewin'/ Jingle Bell Slide	1963	20.00
❑ 58-0031	Blue Skies (Moving In on Me)/ I Knew You First	1964	15.00
❑ 58-0037	Wiggle On Out/What a Wonderful Night Out	1964	20.00
❑ 58-0042	Thou Shalt Not Steal/I Prayed for an Angel	1964	15.00
❑ 58-0049	Flakey John/Tall Tales	1964	20.00
GRT			
❑ 35	Billy Jack/Mary, Marry Me	1971	5.00
GUARANTEED			
❑ 209	What Am I Living For/ Indiana Waltz	1960	30.00
❑ 211	No One Will Ever Know/ Go Wild Little Sadie	1960	30.00
JUBILEE			
❑ 5606	My Special Angel/I Keep Changin' My Mind	1967	20.00
PONIE			
❑ 7021-10	Geraldine/Midgie	197?	4.00
❑ 7021-11	There's Trouble Brewin'/ Jingle Bell Slide	197?	4.00
❑ 7021-12	Flakey John/Wiggle On Out	197?	4.00
❑ 5121-15	Baby She's Gone/ Two Timin' Woman	197?	4.00
❑ 6063-20	Leroy/Go Wild Little Sadie	197?	4.00
❑ 6083-20	Country Witch/Blues, Stay Away from Me-Stones	197?	4.00
❑ 4104-30	Spirit of '76/(Instrumental)	1976	4.00
RCA VICTOR			
❑ 47-8505	Separation's Now Granted/ I Don't Believe in Tea Leaves	1965	15.00
❑ 47-8685	Looking for Linda/ I Hope I Think I Wish	1965	15.00
❑ 47-8724	Don't Hush the Laughter/Let's Learn to Live and Love Again	1965	15.00
TOP RANK			
❑ 2028 [M]	What in the World's Come Over You/Baby Baby	1959	30.00
❑ 2028 [S]	What in the World's Come Over You/Baby Baby	1959	40.00
❑ 2041 [M]	Burning Bridges/Oh Little One	1960	25.00
❑ 2041 [PS]	Burning Bridges/Oh Little One	1960	60.00
❑ 2041 [S]	Burning Bridges/Oh Little One	1960	60.00
❑ 2055	It Only Happened Yesterday/ Cool Water	1960	20.00
❑ 2075	Patsy/Old Time Religion	1960	20.00
❑ 2093	Is There Something on Your Mind/Found a Woman	1960	20.00
❑ 2093 [PS]	Is There Something on Your Mind/Found a Woman	1960	60.00
7-Inch Extended Plays			
CARLTON			
❑ EP 7/1070	Save My Soul/I Can't Help It// Geraldine/With Your Love	1959	200.00

Except when noted otherwise, VG = 25% of NM, and VG+ = 50% of NM. (Example: VG = $2.00, VG+ = $4.00 and NM = $8.00.)

Number	Title (A Side/B Side)	Yr	NM
❑ EP 7/1070 [PS]	Presenting Jack Scott (Vol. 1)	1959	200.00
❑ EP 7/1071	Indiana Waltz,/Midgie//My True Love/Leroy	1959	200.00
❑ EP 7/1071 [PS]	Presenting Jack Scott (Vol. 2)	1959	200.00
❑ EP 7/1072	No One Will Ever Know/Goodbye Baby//I'm Dreaming Of You/ The Way I Walk	1959	200.00
❑ EP 7/1072 [PS]	Jack Scott Sings	1959	200.00

TOP RANK

Number	Title (A Side/B Side)	Yr	NM
❑ 1001	What in the World's Come Over You/My King//Burning Bridges/Oh, Little One	1960	200.00
❑ 1001 [PS]	What in the World's Come Over You	1960	200.00

Albums

CAPITOL

Number	Title (A Side/B Side)	Yr	NM
❑ ST 2035 [S]	Burning Bridges	1964	150.00
❑ ST-8-2035	Burning Bridges	196?	200.00
—Capitol Record Club edition			
❑ T 2035 [M]	Burning Bridges	1964	80.00

CARLTON

Number	Title (A Side/B Side)	Yr	NM
❑ LP-12-107 [M]	Jack Scott	1959	150.00
❑ STLP-12-107 [S]	Jack Scott	1959	200.00
—With "Stereo" printed across the top			
❑ STLP-12-107 [S]	Jack Scott	1959	300.00
—With "Stereo" in felt letters horizontally along the top of cover			
❑ STLP-12-107 [S]	Jack Scott	1959	400.00
—With "Stereo" in felt letters vertically along the left of cover			
❑ LP-12-122 [M]	What Am I Living For	1959	120.00
❑ STLP-12-122 [S]	What Am I Living For	1959	320.00

JADE

Number	Title (A Side/B Side)	Yr	NM
❑ J33-113	Jack Is Back	198?	15.00
❑ J33-114	The Way I Rock	198?	15.00

PONIE

Number	Title (A Side/B Side)	Yr	NM
❑ 563	Jack Scott	1974	15.00
❑ 7055	Jack Scott	1977	15.00

TOP RANK

Number	Title (A Side/B Side)	Yr	NM
❑ RM-319 [M]	I Remember Hank Williams	1960	150.00
❑ RM-326 [M]	What in the World's Come Over You	1960	150.00
❑ RM-348 [M]	The Spirit Moves Me	1961	150.00
❑ SM-619 [S]	I Remember Hank Williams	1960	250.00
❑ SM-626 [S]	What in the World's Come Over You	1960	250.00
❑ SM-648 [S]	The Spirit Moves Me	1961	250.00

SCOTT, JOEL

45s

PHILLES

Number	Title (A Side/B Side)	Yr	NM
❑ 101	Here I Stand/You're My Only Love	1962	25.00

SCOTT, LINDA

45s

CANADIAN AMERICAN

Number	Title (A Side/B Side)	Yr	NM
❑ 123	I've Told Every Little Star/ Three Guesses	1961	20.00
❑ 127	Don't Bet Money Honey/ Starlight, Starbright	1961	20.00
❑ 129	I Don't Know Why/It's All Because	1961	20.00
❑ 132	Christmas Day/Twistin' Bells	1961	20.00
—B-side by Santo and Johnny			
❑ 133	Count Every Star/Land of Stars	1962	15.00
❑ 134	Bermuda/Lonely for You	1962	15.00

CONGRESS

Number	Title (A Side/B Side)	Yr	NM
❑ 101	Yessiree/Town Crier	1962	15.00
❑ 103	Never in a Million Years/ Through the Summer	1962	15.00
❑ 106	I Left My Heart in the Balcony/ Lopsided Love Affair	1962	15.00
❑ 108	I'm So Afraid of Losing You/ The Loneliest Girl in Town	1962	15.00
❑ 110	I'm Gonna Sit Right Down and Write Myself a Letter/ Ain't That Fun	1963	15.00
❑ 200	Let's Fall in Love/ I Know It, You Know It	1963	15.00
❑ 204	Who's Been Sleeping in My Bed/My Baby	1963	15.00
❑ 206	Let's Fall in Love/I Know It, You Know It	1964	15.00
❑ 209	I Envy You/Everybody Stopped Laughing at Jane	1964	15.00

KAPP

Number	Title (A Side/B Side)	Yr	NM
❑ 610	That Old Feeling/ This Is My Prayer	1964	10.00
❑ 641	If I Love Again/Patch It Up	1965	10.00
❑ 677	Don't Lose Your Head/ I'll See You in My Dreams	1965	10.00
❑ 713	You Baby/I Can't Get Through to You	1965	10.00
❑ 762	Toys/Take a Walk Bobby	1966	10.00

RCA VICTOR

Number	Title (A Side/B Side)	Yr	NM
❑ 47-9424	They Don't Know You/ Three Miles High	1967	10.00

7-Inch Extended Plays

CANADIAN AMERICAN

Number	Title (A Side/B Side)	Yr	NM
❑ CAEP 1005	Count Every Star/Catch a Falling Star//Stars Fell on Alabama/ Blue Star	196?	50.00
❑ CAEP 1005 [PS]	(title unknown)	196?	50.00

Albums

CANADIAN AMERICAN

Number	Title (A Side/B Side)	Yr	NM
❑ CALP-1005 [M]	Starlight, Starbright	1961	100.00
❑ SCALP-1005 [S]	Starlight, Starbright	1961	150.00
❑ CALP-1007 [M]	Great Scott!! Her Greatest Hits	1962	100.00
❑ SCALP-1007 [S]	Great Scott!! Her Greatest Hits	1962	150.00

CONGRESS

Number	Title (A Side/B Side)	Yr	NM
❑ CGL-3001 [M]	Linda	1962	40.00
❑ CGS-3001 [S]	Linda	1962	50.00

KAPP

Number	Title (A Side/B Side)	Yr	NM
❑ KL-1424 [M]	Hey, Look at Me Now	1965	40.00
❑ KS-3424 [S]	Hey, Look at Me Now	1965	50.00

SCOTT, NEIL

Better known as Neil Bogart, the founder of the Casablanca and Boardwalk record labels.

45s

CAMEO

Number	Title (A Side/B Side)	Yr	NM
❑ 476	(I Don't Stand) A Ghost of a Chancez with You/ Let Me Think It Over	1967	20.00

COMET

Number	Title (A Side/B Side)	Yr	NM
❑ 2151	Tomboy/Run to Me	1962	30.00

HERALD

Number	Title (A Side/B Side)	Yr	NM
❑ 581	(Chantilly, Silly Sort of Daffy as a Dilly Little Fussy Little Frilly Little) One Piece Bathing Suit/ Little Girl	1963	25.00

PORTRAIT

Number	Title (A Side/B Side)	Yr	NM
❑ 102	Bobby/I Haven't Found It with Another	1961	25.00
❑ 106	It Happened All Over Again/ My Confession	1961	25.00

SCOTT, PEGGY, AND JO JO BENSON

45s

SSS INTERNATIONAL

Number	Title (A Side/B Side)	Yr	NM
❑ 736	Lover's Holiday/Here with Me	1968	8.00
❑ 748	Pickin' Wild Mountain Berries/ Pure Love and Pleasure	1968	8.00
❑ 761	Soulshake/We Were Made for Each Other	1969	8.00
❑ 769	I Want to Love You Baby/ We Got Our Bag	1969	8.00
❑ 781	Sugarmaker/Lover's Heaven	1969	8.00
❑ 805	Let's Spend a Day Out in the Country/Little Things That Count	1970	6.00

Albums

SSS INTERNATIONAL

Number	Title (A Side/B Side)	Yr	NM
❑ 1	Soulshake	1968	25.00
❑ 2	Lover's Heaven	1969	25.00

SCOTT, RICKY

45s

CUB

Number	Title (A Side/B Side)	Yr	NM
❑ 9079	I Didn't Mean It/Darlin' Darlin'	1960	20.00

X-CLUSIVE

Number	Title (A Side/B Side)	Yr	NM
❑ 1001	I Didn't Mean It/Darlin' Darlin'	1960	80.00

SCOTT, RODNEY

45s

CANON

Number	Title (A Side/B Side)	Yr	NM
❑ 225	Granny Went Rockin'/ Bitter Tears	1961	200.00
❑ 231	You're So Square (Baby I Don't Care)/He'll Be There	1961	200.00

MR. PEEKE

Number	Title (A Side/B Side)	Yr	NM
❑ 119	You're So Square (Baby I Don't Care)/He'll Be There	1962	80.00
❑ 126	That's the Way It Goes/ Bitter Tears	1963	30.00

SCOTT, SHERREE

45s

ROBBINS

Number	Title (A Side/B Side)	Yr	NM
❑ 105	Twinkle Toes (The Littlest Reindeer)/Our Christmas Day	1959	40.00
❑ 1036	Fascinating Baby/You and I	1957	150.00

ROCKET

Number	Title (A Side/B Side)	Yr	NM
❑ 101	Whole Lotta Shakin' Goin' On/ Unhappy Birthday	1958	150.00
❑ 101 [PS]	Whole Lotta Shakin' Goin' On/ Unhappy Birthday	1958	200.00

SCOTT, SIMON

45s

IMPERIAL

Number	Title (A Side/B Side)	Yr	NM
❑ 66089	My Baby's Got Soul/Midnight	1965	20.00

SCOTT, TERRY

45s

VALIANT

Number	Title (A Side/B Side)	Yr	NM
❑ 6016	Little Angel/Love Only Me	1962	12.00

SCOTT, TOM

12-Inch Singles

ATLANTIC

Number	Title (A Side/B Side)	Yr	NM
❑ 703 [DJ]	Got to Get Out of New York/ Aerobia	1983	6.00

COLUMBIA

Number	Title (A Side/B Side)	Yr	NM
❑ AS 1249 [DJ]	So White and So Funky (same on both sides)	1981	6.00

45s

A&M

Number	Title (A Side/B Side)	Yr	NM
❑ 1345	Boss Walk/Looking Out for Number 7	1972	5.00

ABC IMPULSE!

Number	Title (A Side/B Side)	Yr	NM
❑ 265	The Honeysuckle Breeze/ Baby I Love You	1967	8.00

ATLANTIC

Number	Title (A Side/B Side)	Yr	NM
❑ 89763	Lollipoppin'/Come Back to Me	1983	4.00

COLUMBIA

Number	Title (A Side/B Side)	Yr	NM
❑ 02496	So White and So Funky/ We Belong Together	1981	4.00
❑ 10914	Beautiful Music/Lost Inside the Love of You	1979	4.00

ODE

Number	Title (A Side/B Side)	Yr	NM
❑ 50433	Gotcha (Theme from Starsky & Hutch)/Smoothin' On Down	1977	4.00
❑ 66043	Strut Your Stuff/Sneaking in the Back	1974	4.00
❑ 66048	Jump Back/T.C.B. in E	1974	4.00
❑ 66105	Tom Cat/Keep On Doin' It	1975	4.00
❑ 66109	Refried/Rock Island Rocket	1975	4.00
❑ 66118	Uptown and Country/ Appolina (Foxtrata)	1976	4.00
❑ 66121	Time and Love/Dirty Old Man	1976	4.00

Albums

A&M

Number	Title (A Side/B Side)	Yr	NM
❑ SP-4330	Great Scott!	1972	15.00

ABC IMPULSE!

Number	Title (A Side/B Side)	Yr	NM
❑ A-9163 [M]	Honeysuckle Breeze	1967	40.00
❑ AS-9163 [S]	Honeysuckle Breeze	1967	25.00
❑ AS-9171	Rural Still Life	1968	25.00

ATLANTIC

Number	Title (A Side/B Side)	Yr	NM
❑ 80106	Target	1983	10.00

COLUMBIA

Number	Title (A Side/B Side)	Yr	NM
❑ JC 35557	Intimate Strangers	1978	10.00
❑ PC 35557	Intimate Strangers	198?	8.00
—Budget-line reissue			
❑ JC 36137	Street Beat	1979	10.00
❑ JC 36352	The Best of Tom Scott	1980	10.00
❑ FC 37419	Apple Juice	1981	10.00

ELEKTRA/MUSICIAN

Number	Title (A Side/B Side)	Yr	NM
❑ 60162	Desire	1982	10.00

FLYING DUTCHMAN

Number	Title (A Side/B Side)	Yr	NM
❑ 106	Hair	1969	20.00
❑ 114	Paint Your Wagon	1970	20.00
❑ BDL1-0833	Tom Scott in L.A.	1975	12.00
❑ BXL1-0833	Tom Scott in L.A.	197?	10.00
—Second edition; new prefix, "RE" on cover			
❑ AYL1-3875	Tom Scott in L.A.	1980	8.00
—"Best Buy Series" reissue			

GRP

Number	Title (A Side/B Side)	Yr	NM
❑ GR-1044	Streamlines	1987	10.00
❑ GR-9571	Flashpoint	1988	10.00

MCA

Number	Title (A Side/B Side)	Yr	NM
❑ 29060	Rural Still Life	198?	8.00
—Reissue of Impulse 9171			

ODE

Number	Title (A Side/B Side)	Yr	NM
❑ PE 34952	Tom Scott and the L.A. Express	1977	8.00
—Reissue of 77021			
❑ PE 34956	Tom Cat	1977	8.00
—Reissue of 77029			
❑ PE 34959	New York Connection	1977	8.00
—Reissue of 77033			
❑ PE 34966	Blow It Out	1977	10.00
❑ SP-77021	Tom Scott and the L.A. Express	1974	10.00

S

Number	Title (A Side/B Side)	Yr	NM
❑ SP-77029	Tom Cat	1975	10.00
❑ SP-77033	New York Connection	1976	10.00
SOUNDWINGS			
❑ SW-202	Tom Scott	1986	10.00

SCOTT, WALTER
Lead singer with BOB KUBAN AND THE IN-MEN.

Number	Title (A Side/B Side)	Yr	NM
45s			
MUSICLAND U.S.A.			
❑ 111	Just You Wait/Silly Girl	1967	20.00
❑ 20009	Watch Out/My Shadow Is Gone	1966	15.00
❑ 20014	It's Been a Long Time/Proud	1966	15.00
PZAZZ			
❑ 026	Soul Stew Recipe/Feeling Something New Inside	1969	10.00
WHITE WHALE			
❑ 259	Just You Wait/Silly Girl	1967	20.00
Albums			
MUSICLAND U.S.A.			
❑ LP-3502 [M]	Great Scott	1967	20.00
❑ SLP-3502 [S]	Great Scott	1967	25.00
WHITE WHALE			
❑ WWS-7131	Walter Scott	1970	20.00

SCOTT BROTHERS, THE

Number	Title (A Side/B Side)	Yr	NM
45s			
COMET			
❑ 2153	Welcome Me/Letter from My Baby	1963	15.00
❑ 2161	Love Me Tenderly/ It's Gonna Happen Soon	1963	15.00
FTP			
❑ 409	Mama's Little Baby/ Cindy, Oh Cindy	1960	15.00
❑ 415	Kingdom of Love/Lonely Bluebird	1961	15.00
❑ 418	On Again, Off Again/ Sometimes I Wonder	1961	15.00
RIBBON			
❑ 6905	Keep Laughin'/Stolen Angel	1960	25.00
❑ 6911	Lost Love/Only Then	1960	25.00
SMASH			
❑ 2139	Got to Get a Groove/ My Day Has Come	1967	15.00
TODDLIN' TOWN			
❑ 125	A Hunk o' Funk/They All Came Back	1969	15.00
❑ 131	I Don't Wanna Lose You/ (B-side unknown)	1969	15.00
❑ 134	Top of the Mountain/ (B-side unknown)	1969	15.00
ZACHRON			
❑ 602	Magic Wand/We Like Girls	196?	15.00

SCOTT RICHARD CASE
See SRC.

SCOTT-HERON, GIL
Includes records with Brian Jackson.

Number	Title (A Side/B Side)	Yr	NM
12-Inch Singles			
ARISTA			
❑ 9216	Re-Ron/Re-Ron (Special Mix)	1984	10.00
45s			
ARISTA			
❑ 0117	Superman/We Beg Your Pardon America	1975	5.00
❑ 0152	Johannesburg/Fell Together	1975	5.00
❑ 0225	The Bottle Part 1/ The Bottle Part 2	1976	5.00
❑ 0285	Hello Sunday! Hello Road!/ Song of the Wind	1977	5.00
❑ 0317	Under the Hammer/ Backtrack in France	1978	5.00
❑ 0366	Angel Dust/Third World Revolution	1978	4.00
❑ 0390	Show Bizness/ Better Days Ahead	1979	4.00
❑ 0488	Shut 'Um Down/Baltimore	1980	4.00
❑ 0583	Legend in His Own Mind/ (B-side unknown)	1980	4.00
❑ 0647	"B" Movie/(B-side unknown)	1981	4.00
❑ 1011	Blue Collar/Fast Lane	1982	4.00
❑ 9253	Re-Ron/Re-Ron (Special Mix)	1984	4.00
Albums			
ARISTA			
❑ AL 4030	The First Minute of a New Day	1975	10.00
❑ AL 4044	From South Africa to South Carolina	1975	10.00
❑ AL 4147	Bridges	1977	10.00
❑ AB 4189	Secrets	1978	10.00
❑ A2L 5001 [(2)]	It's Your World	1976	12.00
❑ AL 8248	The Best of Gil Scott-Heron	1984	10.00
❑ AL 8301	The Mind of Gil Scott-Heron	1980	15.00
❑ ALB6-8306	The Best of Gil Scott-Heron	1985	8.00
—Reissue of 8248			
❑ AL 9514	1980	1980	10.00
❑ AL 9540	Real Eyes	1980	10.00
❑ AL 9566	Reflections	1981	10.00
❑ AL 9606	Moving Target	1982	10.00
BLUEBIRD			
❑ 6994-1-RB	The Revolution Will Not Be Televised	1988	12.00
FLYING DUTCHMAN			
❑ BLD1-0613	The Revolution Will Not Be Televised	1974	20.00
❑ BXL1-0613	The Revolution Will Not Be Televised	1978	12.00
—Reissue with new prefix			
❑ BXL1-2834	Pieces of a Man	1978	12.00
—Reissue of 10143			
❑ AYL1-3818	The Revolution Will Not Be Televised	1980	8.00
—"Best Buy Series" reissue			
❑ AYL1-3819	Pieces of a Man	1980	8.00
—"Best Buy Series" reissue			
❑ FD-10143	Pieces of a Man	1971	20.00
❑ FD-10153	Free Will	1972	20.00
STRATA-EAST			
❑ SES-19742	Winter in America	1974	25.00

SCOTTIES, THE

Number	Title (A Side/B Side)	Yr	NM
45s			
HIT			
❑ 95	Popsicles and Icicles/Louie Louie	1963	8.00
—B-side by I Kadez			

SCOTTSVILLE SQUIRREL BARKERS, THE
Chris Hillman, later of THE BYRDS, makes his first appearance on record here.

Number	Title (A Side/B Side)	Yr	NM
Albums			
CROWN			
❑ CST-346 [S]	Bluegrass Favorites	1963	60.00
❑ CLP-5346 [M]	Bluegrass Favorites	1963	50.00

SCRAMBLERS, THE

Number	Title (A Side/B Side)	Yr	NM
45s			
ARVEE			
❑ 6502	Super Surfer U.S.A./ Go Getera Go	1963	25.00
DEL-FI			
❑ 4237	The Beatle Walk/ The Beatle Blues	1964	25.00
Albums			
CROWN			
❑ CST-384 [S]	Cycle Psychos	1964	25.00
❑ CLP-5384 [M]	Cycle Psychos	1964	20.00
DIPLOMAT			
❑ D-2316 [M]	Motorcycle Scramble	1964	20.00
❑ DS-2316 [S]	Motorcycle Scramble	1964	25.00
WYNCOTE			
❑ SW-9048 [S]	Little Honda	1964	25.00
❑ W-9048 [M]	Little Honda	1964	20.00

SCREAMING GYPSY BANDITS

Number	Title (A Side/B Side)	Yr	NM
Albums			
BAR-B-Q			
❑ 004	The Dancer Inside You	1974	80.00
❑ 22185	In the Eye	1973	80.00

SCREAMING TREES
Also see MARK LANEGAN.

Number	Title (A Side/B Side)	Yr	NM
12-Inch Singles			
EPIC			
❑ EAS 3092 [DJ]	Something About Today/ This Perfect Day/New Day Yesterday	1991	8.00
❑ 73539	Uncle Anesthesia/Who Lies in Darkness/Ocean of Confusion/ Something About Today	1990	8.00
45s			
EPIC SOUNDTRAX			
❑ 74419	Nearly Lost You/Dyslexic Heart	1992	5.00
—B-side by Paul Westerberg			
7-Inch Extended Plays			
SUB POP			
❑ 48	Change Has Come	1989	15.00
—Two 7-inch 45s, one black vinyl, one white			
❑ 48	Change Has Come	1989	60.00
—Second pressing of above: red vinyl			
❑ 48 [PS]	Change Has Come	1989	15.00
—Poster sleeve			
Albums			
EPIC			
❑ E 46800	Uncle Anesthesia	1991	12.00
❑ E 48996	Sweet Oblivion	1992	12.00
SST			
❑ 105 [EP]	Other Worlds	1986	10.00
—Reissue of Velvetone cassette-only release			
❑ 132	Even If and Especially When	1987	10.00
❑ 188	Invisible Lantern	1988	10.00
❑ 248	Buzz Factory	1989	10.00
❑ 260 [(2)]	Anthology	1991	12.00
VELVETONE			
❑ 86002	Clairvoyance	1986	40.00

SCREAMING TRIBESMEN

Number	Title (A Side/B Side)	Yr	NM
12-Inch Singles			
SURVIVAL			
❑ 656491-6	Ayla//Santa's Little Helper/ A Stand Alone	1990	20.00

SEA HAGS

Number	Title (A Side/B Side)	Yr	NM
Albums			
CHRYSALIS			
❑ FV 41665	Sea Hags	1989	10.00

SEA SHELLS, THE

Number	Title (A Side/B Side)	Yr	NM
45s			
GOLIATH			
❑ 1357	Love Those Beach Boys/ Close to Jimmy	1964	40.00
JUBILEE			
❑ 5587	Hit the Surf/Barefoot in the Sand	1967	20.00

SEAL

Number	Title (A Side/B Side)	Yr	NM
12-Inch Singles			
SIRE			
❑ PRO-A-5065 [(2)DJ]	The Beginning (10 versions)	1991	10.00
—Two-record promo-only release			
❑ PRO-A-7057 [DJ]	Prayer for the Dying (3 versions)	1994	20.00
❑ 40200	The Beginning (5 versions)/ Deep Water	1991	6.00
45s			
SIRE			
❑ 17896	I'm Alive/Kiss from a Rose	1995	3.00
❑ 18053	Newborn Friend/Blues in "E"	1994	3.00
❑ 18138	Prayer for the Dying/ Dreaming in Metaphors	1994	3.00
❑ 19119	Killer	1992	—
—Cassette only			
❑ 19298	Crazy/Sparkle	1991	3.00
WARNER BROS.			
❑ 7-16552	Love's Divine (Album Edit)/ Where There's Gold	2004	3.00
❑ 7-16574	Waiting for You/Kiss from a Rose (Album Edit)	2003	3.00
❑ 7-16575	Get It Together/Crazy (7" Version)	2003	3.00
❑ 17708	Don't Cry/Fast Changes	1996	3.00

SEALS, DAN

Number	Title (A Side/B Side)	Yr	NM
45s			
ATLANTIC			
❑ 3674	Late at Night/(B-side unknown)	1980	8.00
—As "England Dan Seals"			
❑ 3769	Stones (Dig a Little Deeper)/ Laugh or Cry	1980	8.00
—As "England Dan Seals"			
❑ 3786	Love Me Like the Last Time/ (B-side unknown)	1980	8.00
—As "England Dan Seals"			
❑ 4015	Can't Get You Off My Mind/ (B-side unknown)	1982	6.00
❑ 4042	I Could Be Lovin' You Right Now/(B-side unknown)	1982	6.00
CAPITOL			
❑ B-44077	One Friend/Bop	1987	4.00
❑ B-44077 [PS]	One Friend/Bop	1987	4.00
❑ B-44130	Addicted/Maybe I'm Missing You Now	1988	3.00
❑ B-44267	Big Wheels in the Moonlight/ Factory Town	1988	3.00
❑ B-44345	They Rage On/Factory Town	1989	3.00
❑ B-44435	Love on Arrival/Those	1989	5.00
CAPITOL NASHVILLE			
❑ 7PRO-79120	Good Times (same on both sides)	1990	8.00
—Vinyl is promo only			
❑ 7PRO-79320	Bordertown (same on both sides)	1990	6.00
—Vinyl is promo only			
EMI AMERICA			
❑ B-8220	(You Bring Out) The Wild Side of Me/One Friend	1984	3.00
❑ B-8245	My Baby's Got Good Timing/ She Thinks I Still Care	1984	3.00

Number	Title (A Side/B Side)	Yr	NM
❑ B-8261	My Old Yellow Car/ On These Nights	1985	3.00
❑ B-8289	Bop/In San Antone	1985	4.00
❑ B-8311	Everything That Glitters (Is Not Gold)/So Easy to Need	1986	3.00
❑ B-8311 [PS]	Everything That Glitters (Is Not Gold)/So Easy to Need	1986	4.00
❑ B-8343	You Still Move Me/I'm Still Strung Out on You	1986	3.00
❑ B-8377	I Will Be There/Gonna Be Easy Now	1987	3.00
❑ B-8377 [PS]	I Will Be There/Gonna Be Easy Now	1987	4.00
❑ B-43023	Three Time Loser/ On the Front Line	1987	3.00

LIBERTY

Number	Title (A Side/B Side)	Yr	NM
❑ B-1496	Everybody's Dream Girl/ The Banker	1983	4.00
❑ B-1504	After You/Candle in the Rain	1983	4.00
❑ B-1512	You Really Go for the Heart/ On a Night Like This	1983	4.00
❑ B-1515	God Must Be a Cowboy/Nothin' Else Left to Do But Cry	1984	4.00

WARNER BROS.

Number	Title (A Side/B Side)	Yr	NM
❑ 7-18058	Love Thing/A Good Place to Be	1994	3.00
❑ 7-18192	All Fired Up/Hillbilly Fever	1994	3.00
❑ 7-18710	We Are One/Sweet Little Shoe	1992	3.00
❑ 7-18813	When Love Comes Around the Bend/Sweet Little Shoe	1992	3.00
❑ 7-18968	Mason Dixon Line/Be My Angel	1992	3.00
❑ 7-19176	Sweet Little Shoe/ Your Blue Heart	1991	3.00

Albums

CAPITOL

Number	Title	Yr	NM
❑ 1P 7999	On Arrival	1990	20.00
—Only available on vinyl from Columbia House			
❑ C1-46976	Rage On	1988	8.00
❑ CLT-48308	The Best	1988	8.00

EMI AMERICA

Number	Title	Yr	NM
❑ ST-17131	San Antone	1984	8.00
❑ ST-17166	Won't Be Blue Anymore	1985	8.00
❑ PW-17231	On the Front Line	1986	8.00

LIBERTY

Number	Title	Yr	NM
❑ LT-51149	Rebel Heart	1983	10.00

SEALS, JIMMY Also see THE CHAMPS; SEALS AND CROFTS.

45s

CARLTON

Number	Title (A Side/B Side)	Yr	NM
❑ 470	Sneaky Pete/Benguela	1958	30.00

CHALLENGE

Number	Title (A Side/B Side)	Yr	NM
❑ 9153	Wish for You, Want for You, Wait for You/Runaway Heart	1962	30.00
❑ 9200	Lady Heartbreak/Grounded	1963	30.00
❑ 59270	Everybody's Doing the Jerk/ Wa-Hoo	1965	20.00
❑ 59299	She's Not a Bad Girl/ The Yesterday of Our Love	1965	20.00

WINSTON

Number	Title (A Side/B Side)	Yr	NM
❑ 1021	Sneaky Pete/Benguela	1958	50.00
❑ 1027	Biscayne Bay/Juarez	1958	50.00

SEALS AND CROFTS Also see THE CHAMPS; JIMMY SEALS.

12-Inch Singles

WARNER BROS.

Number	Title (A Side/B Side)	Yr	NM
❑ PRO-A-722 [DJ]	You're the Love (5:22) (stereo/mono)	1978	15.00

45s

T-A

Number	Title (A Side/B Side)	Yr	NM
❑ 188	In Tune/Seldom's Sister	1969	8.00
❑ 191	See My Life/(B-side unknown)	1969	8.00
❑ 206	See My Life/In Tune// Hollow Reed/Leave	1970	10.00
❑ 208	Ridin' Thumb/Leave	1970	8.00
❑ 210	Gabriel Go On Home/Robin	1971	8.00

WARNER BROS.

Number	Title (A Side/B Side)	Yr	NM
❑ 7536	When I Meet Them/Irish Linen	1971	6.00
❑ 7565	Sudan Village/ High on a Mountain	1972	6.00
❑ 7606	Summer Breeze/ East of Ginger Trees	1972	5.00
❑ 7671	Hummingbird/Say	1972	5.00
❑ 7697	We May Never Pass This Way (Again)/Intone My Servant	1973	—
—Unreleased?			
❑ 7708	Diamond Girl/Wisdom	1973	5.00
❑ 7740	We May Never Pass This Way (Again)/Jessica	1973	5.00
❑ 7771	Unborn Child/Ledges	1974	4.00
❑ 7810	King of Nothing/Follow Me	1974	4.00
❑ 8075	I'll Play for You/Truth Is But a Woman	1975	4.00
❑ 8130	Castles in the Sand/ Golden Rainbow	1975	4.00
❑ 8190	Get Closer/Don't Fail	1976	4.00
❑ 8190 [PS]	Get Closer/Don't Fail	1976	20.00
❑ 8277	Baby, I'll Give It to You/ Advance Guards	1976	4.00
❑ 8405	My Fair Share/ East of Ginger Trees	1977	4.00
❑ 8405 [PS]	My Fair Share/ East of Ginger Trees	1977	6.00
❑ 8551	You're the Love/Midnight Blue	1978	4.00
❑ 8639	Magnolia Moon/Takin' It Easy	1978	4.00
❑ 49522	First Love/Kite Dreams	1980	4.00

7-Inch Extended Plays

WARNER BROS.

Number	Title	Yr	NM
❑ S 2761 [DJ]	Rachel/King of Nothing/ Desert People//The Story of Her Love/Dance by the Light of the Moon	1974	8.00
—33 1/3 rpm, small hole jukebox edition			
❑ S 2761 [PS]	Unborn Child	1974	10.00

Albums

K-TEL

Number	Title	Yr	NM
❑ NU 9610	Collection: 16 of Their Greatest Hits	1979	12.00

NAUTILUS

Number	Title	Yr	NM
❑ NR-10	Summer Breeze	1980	30.00
—Audiophile vinyl			

T-A

Number	Title	Yr	NM
❑ 5001	Seals and Crofts	1969	25.00
❑ 5004	Down Home	1970	25.00

WARNER BROS.

Number	Title	Yr	NM
❑ BS 2568	Year of Sunday	1971	12.00
—Green "WB" label			
❑ BS 2568	Year of Sunday	1973	10.00
—"Burbank" palm-tree label			
❑ BS 2629	Summer Breeze	1972	12.00
—Green "WB" label			
❑ BS 2629	Summer Breeze	1973	10.00
—"Burbank" palm-tree label			
❑ BS 2629	Summer Breeze	1979	8.00
—White or tan label			
❑ BS4 2629 [Q]	Summer Breeze	1974	20.00
❑ BS 2699	Diamond Girl	1973	12.00
—"Burbank" palm-tree label			
❑ BS 2699	Diamond Girl	1979	8.00
—White or tan label			
❑ BS4 2699 [Q]	Diamond Girl	1974	20.00
❑ BS 2761	Unborn Child	1974	12.00
❑ BS4 2761 [Q]	Unborn Child	1974	20.00
❑ 2WS 2809 [(2)]	Seals & Crofts I and II	1974	15.00
—Reissue of the two T-A LPs in one package			
❑ BS 2848	I'll Play for You	1975	10.00
❑ BS4 2848 [Q]	I'll Play for You	1975	20.00
❑ BS 2886	Greatest Hits	1975	10.00
❑ BS 2907	Get Closer	1976	10.00
❑ BS 2976	Sudan Village	1976	10.00
❑ BSK 3109	Greatest Hits	1977	8.00
—Reissue; any label variation			
❑ BSK 3165	Takin' It Easy	1978	10.00
❑ BSK 3365	The Longest Road	1980	10.00

SEAN AND THE BRANDYWINES

45s

DECCA

Number	Title (A Side/B Side)	Yr	NM
❑ 31910	She Ain't No Good/Cod'ine	1966	20.00
—Produced by Gary Usher			

SEARCH PARTY, THE

Albums

CENTURY CUSTOM

Number	Title	Yr	NM
❑ 32013	Montgomery Chapel	1969	2000.

SEARCHERS, THE

45s

KAPP

Number	Title (A Side/B Side)	Yr	NM
❑ KJB-22	Needles and Pins/Ain't That Just Like Me	1964	8.00
—Orange label "Winners Circle Series"			
❑ KJB-27	Love Potion Number Nine/ Hi-Heel Sneakers	1964	10.00
—Orange label "Winners Circle Series"; no black label counterpart			
❑ KJB-29	Bumble Bee/Everything You Do	1964	10.00
—Orange label "Winners Circle Series"; no black label counterpart			
❑ KJB-49	Bumble Bee/Everything You Do	1964	12.00
—Orange label "Winners Circle Series"; no black label counterpart			
❑ KJB-49	Bumble Bee/A Tear Fell	1965	10.00
—Orange label "Winners Circle Series"; no black label counterpart			
❑ 577	Needles and Pins/ Saturday Night Out	1964	10.00
❑ 577	Needles and Pins/ Ain't That Just Like Me	1964	12.00
❑ 577 [PS]	Needles and Pins/ Ain't That Just Like Me	1964	50.00
—Promo-only version with red print			
❑ 577 [PS]	Needles and Pins/ Ain't That Just Like Me	1964	100.00
—Promo-only "Rush Release" version with black print			
❑ 577 [PS]	Needles and Pins/ Saturday Night Out	1964	30.00
—Photo sleeve with blue background			
❑ 584	Ain't That Just Like Me/ Ain't Gonna Kiss You	1964	10.00
❑ 584 [PS]	Ain't That Just Like Me (special promo sleeve)	1964	50.00
❑ 593	Don't Throw Your Love Away/ I Pretend I'm with You	1964	10.00
❑ 609	Someday We're Gonna Love Again/No One Else Could Love Me	1964	10.00
❑ 609 [PS]	Someday We're Gonna Love Again/No One Else Could Love Me	1964	30.00
❑ 618	When You Walk in the Room/ I'll Be Missing You	1964	10.00
❑ 644	What Have They Done to the Rain/This Feeling Inside	1965	10.00
❑ 658	Goodbye My Lover Goodbye/ 'Til I Met You	1965	10.00
❑ 686	He's Got No Love/So Far Away	1965	10.00
❑ 706	Don't You Know Why/ You Can't Lie to a Liar	1965	10.00
❑ 729	Take Me for What I'm Worth/ Too Many Miles	1966	10.00
❑ 783	Have You Ever Loved Somebody/It's Just the Way	1966	10.00
❑ 811	Lovers/Popcorn Double Feature	1966	10.00

LIBERTY

Number	Title (A Side/B Side)	Yr	NM
❑ 55646	Sugar and Spice/ Saints and Sinners	1963	25.00
❑ 55689	Sugar and Spice/ Saints and Sinners	1964	15.00

MERCURY

Number	Title (A Side/B Side)	Yr	NM
❑ 72172	Sweets for My Sweet/ It's All Been a Dream	1963	25.00
❑ 72390	(Ain't That) Just Like Me/ I Can Tell	1964	15.00

RCA VICTOR

Number	Title (A Side/B Side)	Yr	NM
❑ 74-0484	Desdemona/The World Is Waiting for Tomorrow	1971	15.00
❑ 74-0652	Love Is Everywhere/ And the Button	1972	15.00

SIRE

Number	Title (A Side/B Side)	Yr	NM
❑ 49175	It's Too Late/Don't Hang On	1980	4.00
❑ 49665	Love's Melody/ Little Bit of Heaven	1981	4.00

WORLD PACIFIC

Number	Title (A Side/B Side)	Yr	NM
❑ 77908	Umbrella Man/ Over the Weekend	1969	25.00

Albums

KAPP

Number	Title	Yr	NM
❑ KL-1363 [M]	Meet the Searchers	1964	25.00
—With black label			
❑ KL-1363 [M]	Meet the Searchers	1964	40.00
—With black and blue label			
❑ KL-1409 [M]	This Is Us	1964	25.00
—Version 2: With sticker on front cover referring to "Love Potion No. 9"			
❑ KL-1409 [M]	This Is Us	1964	25.00
—Version 1: No sticker on front cover			
❑ KL-1412 [M]	The New Searchers LP	1965	25.00
❑ KL-1449 [M]	The Searchers No. 4	1965	25.00
❑ KL-1477 [M]	Take Me for What I'm Worth	1966	25.00
❑ KS-3363 [S]	Meet the Searchers	1964	30.00
—With black label			
❑ KS-3363 [S]	Meet the Searchers	1964	50.00
—With black and blue label			
❑ KS-3409 [S]	This Is Us	1964	30.00
—Version 2: With sticker on front cover referring to "Love Potion No. 9"			
❑ KS-3409 [S]	This Is Us	1964	30.00
—Version 1: No sticker on front cover			
❑ KS-3412 [S]	The New Searchers LP	1965	30.00
❑ KS-3419 [S]	The Searchers No. 4	1965	30.00
❑ KS-3477 [S]	Take Me for What I'm Worth	1966	30.00

MERCURY

Number	Title	Yr	NM
❑ MG-20914 [M]	Hear! Hear!	1964	30.00
—Version 3: With "Live from the Star Club" imprinted on cover			
❑ MG-20914 [M]	Hear! Hear!	1964	40.00
—Version 2: With sticker "Live from the Star Club" on cover			
❑ MG-20914 [M]	Hear! Hear!	1964	50.00
—White label promo			
❑ MG-20914 [M]	Hear! Hear!	1964	50.00
—Version 1: With only the title on the front cover			
❑ MG-20994 [M]	The Searchers Meet the Rattles	1965	75.00
❑ SR-60914 [S]	Hear! Hear!	1964	25.00
—Version 3: With "Live from the Star Club" imprinted on cover			
❑ SR-60914 [S]	Hear! Hear!	1964	30.00
—Version 2: With sticker "Live from the Star Club" on cover			
❑ SR-60914 [S]	Hear! Hear!	1964	40.00
—Version 1: With only the title on the front cover			
❑ SR-60994 [S]	The Searchers Meet the Rattles	1965	50.00

S

Number	Title (A Side/B Side)	Yr	NM
PYE			
❑ 501	The Searchers	1977?	15.00
—Reissue of Kapp hits			
❑ 508	The Searchers, Vol. 2	1976	15.00
RHINO			
❑ RNLP 162	Greatest Hits	1985	10.00
❑ R1-70162	Greatest Hits	1988	8.00
—Reissue of RNLP 162			
SIRE			
❑ SRK 3523	Love's Melodies	1981	10.00
❑ SRK 6082	The Searchers	1980	10.00

SEARS, RICKY

45s

Number	Title (A Side/B Side)	Yr	NM
MUSICOR			
❑ 1193	Borrowed Love/Bring Me Some Water	1966	8.00
❑ 1231	I'm Gonna Roast Your Duck/ Where's My Love	1967	8.00
❑ 1255	Make Him Go/No One Will Know	1967	8.00
❑ 1281	Change of Heart/Faded Memory	1967	8.00

SEATRAIN

45s

Number	Title (A Side/B Side)	Yr	NM
A&M			
❑ 994	As I Lay Losing/ Let the Duchess Know	1968	8.00
—As "Sea Train"			
❑ 994 [PS]	As I Lay Losing/ Let the Duchess Know	1968	15.00
—As "Sea Train"			
CAPITOL			
❑ 3067	13 Questions/Oh My Love-Sally Goodin	1971	6.00
❑ 3140	Song of Job/Waiting for Elijah	1971	6.00
❑ 3201	Marblehead Messenger/ Despair Tire	1971	6.00
❑ 3275	Gramercy/How Sweet Thy Song	1972	6.00
WARNER BROS.			
❑ 7696	Flute Thing/Freedom Is the Reason	1973	5.00

Albums

Number	Title (A Side/B Side)	Yr	NM
A&M			
❑ SP-4171	Sea Train	1969	15.00
CAPITOL			
❑ SMAS-650	Seatrain	1970	15.00
❑ SMAS-829	Marblehead Messenger	1971	15.00
❑ SN-16102	Seatrain	1980	8.00
—Budget-line reissue			
❑ SN-16103	Marblehead Messenger	1980	8.00
—Budget-line reissue			
WARNER BROS.			
❑ BS 2692	Watch	1973	12.00

SEAY, JOHNNY See JOHNNY SEA.

SEBASTIAN, JOHN Also see THE LOVIN' SPOONFUL.

45s

Number	Title (A Side/B Side)	Yr	NM
KAMA SUTRA			
❑ 254	She's a Lady/The Room Nobody Lives In	1968	10.00
❑ 254 [PS]	She's a Lady/The Room Nobody Lives In	1968	15.00
❑ 505	Younger Generation/Boredom	1970	8.00
MGM			
❑ 14122	Rainbows All Over Your Blues/ You're a Big Boy Now	1970	6.00
REPRISE			
❑ 0902	Fa-Fana-Fa/Magical Connection	1970	6.00
❑ 0918	What She Thinks About/ Red-Eye Express	1970	6.00
❑ 1026	I Don't Want Nobody Else/ Sweet Muse	1971	6.00
❑ 1050	We'll See/Well, Well, Well	1971	6.00
❑ 1074	Give Us a Break/Music for People Who Don't Speak English	1972	6.00
❑ 1349	Welcome Back/Warm Baby	1976	4.00
—Revised A-side title			
❑ 1349	Welcome Back Kotter/ Warm Baby	1976	8.00
—Original A-side title			
❑ 1355	Hideaway/One Step Forward, Two Steps Back	1976	4.00

Albums

Number	Title (A Side/B Side)	Yr	NM
MGM			
❑ SE-4654	John B. Sebastian	1969	15.00
❑ SE-4720	John Sebastian Live	1970	15.00
REPRISE			
❑ MS 2036	Cheapo-Cheapo Productions Presents Real Live John Sebastian	1971	12.00
❑ MS 2041	The Four of Us	1971	12.00
❑ MS 2187	Tarzana Kid	1974	12.00
❑ MS 2249	Welcome Back	1976	12.00
❑ RS 6379	John B. Sebastian	1969	20.00
—Same album as MGM 4654, but a different mix			
RHINO			
❑ R1-70170	The Best of John Sebastian (1969-1976)	1989	12.00

SECOND TIME, THE

45s

Number	Title (A Side/B Side)	Yr	NM
TOWER			
❑ 432	Listen to the Music/Psychedelic Senate	1968	10.00

Albums

Number	Title (A Side/B Side)	Yr	NM
TOWER			
❑ ST 5146	Listen to the Music	1968	20.00

SECRET OYSTER

Albums

Number	Title (A Side/B Side)	Yr	NM
PETERS INT'L.			
❑ 9003	Furtive Pearl	1973	30.00
❑ 9009	Sea Son	1974	25.00

SECRETS, THE (1) Girl group.

45s

Number	Title (A Side/B Side)	Yr	NM
OMEN			
❑ 15	Here I Am/I Feel a Thrill Coming On	1966	12.00
PHILIPS			
❑ 40146	The Boy Next Door/ Learnin' to Forget	1963	15.00
❑ 40173	Hey Big Boy/The Other Side of Town	1964	12.00
❑ 40173 [PS]	Hey Big Boy/The Other Side of Town	1964	20.00
❑ 40196	Here He Comes Now!/Oh Donnie	1964	12.00
❑ 40222	He's the Boy/He Doesn't Want You	1964	12.00

SECRETS, THE (2)

45s

Number	Title (A Side/B Side)	Yr	NM
SWAN			
❑ 4097	Hot Toddy/Twin Exhaust	1962	25.00
❑ 4097 [PS]	Hot Toddy/Twin Exhaust	1962	50.00

SECRETS, THE (U) Could be group (1).

45s

Number	Title (A Side/B Side)	Yr	NM
RED BIRD			
❑ 10-076	Every Day/A Smile Upside Down	1966	10.00

SEDAKA, NEIL Also see THE TOKENS.

12-Inch Singles

Number	Title (A Side/B Side)	Yr	NM
ELEKTRA			
❑ AS-11396-C [DJ]	All You Need Is the Music (5:30) (same on both sides)	1978	20.00
MCA CURB			
❑ L33-1196 [DJ]	New Orleans (With Gary U.S. Bonds 5:00) (Instrumental 3:18)/Come See About Me (With Mary Wilson 4:33)	1984	12.00

45s

Number	Title (A Side/B Side)	Yr	NM
COLLECTABLES			
❑ 4945	Laughter in the Rain/ The Immigrant	1994	3.00
❑ 4946	Bad Blood/Breaking Up Is Hard to Do	1994	3.00
DECCA			
❑ 30520	Laura Lee/Snowtime	1957	60.00
ELEKTRA			
❑ 45406	Amarillo/The Leaving Game	1977	4.00
❑ 45421	Alone at Last/Sleazy Love	1977	4.00
❑ 45525	Candy Kisses/All You Need Is the Music	1978	4.00
❑ 46017	Sad, Sad Story/Tillie the Twirler	1979	4.00
❑ 46615	Should've Never Let You Go/ You're So Good for Me	1980	4.00
—With Dara Sedaka			
❑ 47017	Letting Go/It's Good to Be Alive Again	1980	6.00
❑ 47184	My World Keeps Slipping Away/Love Is Spreading Over the World	1981	4.00
GUYDEN			
❑ 2004	Ring-a-Rockin'/Fly, Don't Fly on Me	1958	50.00
KIRSHNER			
❑ SP-45-291 [DJ]	I'm a Song (Sing Me)/ Silent Movies	1971	8.00
—Promo only number (mono versions)			
❑ SP-45-370 [DJ]	Beautiful You (Long)/ Beautiful You (Short)	1972	8.00
—Promo only number			
❑ 63-5017	I'm a Song (Sing Me)/ Silent Movies	1971	5.00
—As "Sedaka"			
❑ 63-5020	Superbird/Rosemary Blue	1972	5.00
❑ 63-5024	Beautiful You/Anywhere You're Gonna Be (Leba's Song)	1972	6.00
LEGION			
❑ 133	Ring-a-Rockin'/Fly, Don't Fly on Me	1958	100.00
MCA			
❑ 60189	Laughter in the Rain/ The Immigrant	197?	3.00
—Reissue			
MCA CURB			
❑ 52307	Your Precious Love/Searchin'	1983	4.00
—With Dara Sedaka			
❑ 52400	New Orleans/Rhythm of the Rain	1984	4.00
—With Gary U.S. Bonds			
MGM			
❑ 14564	Standing on the Inside/ Let Daddy Know	1973	5.00
❑ 14661	Alone in New York in the Rain/ Suspicions	1973	5.00
PYRAMID			
❑ 623	Oh Delilah/Neil's Twist	1962	30.00
—B-side is an instrumental version of the A-side credited to The Marvels			
RCA VICTOR			
❑ 37-7829	Calendar Girl/The Same Old Fool	1960	50.00
—"Compact Single 33" (small hole, plays at LP speed)			
❑ 37-7874	Little Devil/I Must Be Dreaming	1961	50.00
—"Compact Single 33" (small hole, plays at LP speed)			
❑ 37-7922	Sweet Little You/I Found My World in You	1961	50.00
—"Compact Single 33" (small hole, plays at LP speed)			
❑ 37-7957	Happy Birthday Sweet Sixteen/ Don't Lead Me On	1961	50.00
—"Compact Single 33" (small hole, plays at LP speed)			
❑ 47-7408	The Diary/No Vacancy	1958	20.00
❑ 47-7408 [DJ]	The Diary/No Vacancy	1958	40.00
—White label promo with Sedaka's photo on label			
❑ 47-7473	I Go Ape/Moon of Gold	1959	20.00
❑ 47-7530	You Gotta Learn Your Rhythm and Blues/Crying My Heart Out for You	1959	25.00
❑ 47-7595	Oh! Carol/One Way Ticket (To the Blues)	1959	20.00
❑ 47-7709	Stairway to Heaven/ Forty Winks Away	1960	15.00
❑ 47-7781	You Mean Everything to Me/ Run Samson Run	1960	15.00
❑ 47-7781 [PS]	You Mean Everything to Me/ Run Samson Run	1960	25.00
❑ 47-7829	Calendar Girl/The Same Old Fool	1960	15.00
❑ 47-7829 [PS]	Calendar Girl/The Same Old Fool	1960	25.00
❑ 47-7874	Little Devil/I Must Be Dreaming	1961	15.00
❑ 47-7874 [PS]	Little Devil/I Must Be Dreaming	1961	25.00
❑ 47-7922	Sweet Little You/I Found My World in You	1961	15.00
❑ 47-7922 [PS]	Sweet Little You/I Found My World in You	1961	25.00
❑ 47-7957	Happy Birthday Sweet Sixteen/ Don't Lead Me On	1961	15.00
❑ 47-8007	King of Clowns/Walk with Me	1962	15.00
❑ 47-8007 [PS]	King of Clowns/Walk with Me	1962	25.00
❑ 47-8046	Breaking Up Is Hard to Do/ As Long As I Live	1962	15.00
❑ 47-8046 [PS]	Breaking Up Is Hard to Do/ As Long As I Live	1962	25.00
❑ 47-8086	Next Door to An Angel/ I Belong to You	1962	15.00
❑ 47-8086 [PS]	Next Door to An Angel/ I Belong to You	1962	25.00
❑ 47-8137	Alice in Wonderland/Circulate	1963	12.00
❑ 47-8137 [PS]	Alice in Wonderland/Circulate	1963	25.00
❑ 47-8169	Let's Go Steady Again/ Waiting for Never	1963	12.00
❑ 47-8169 [PS]	Let's Go Steady Again/ Waiting for Never	1963	25.00
❑ 47-8209	The Dreamer/Look Inside Your Heart	1963	12.00
❑ 47-8209 [PS]	The Dreamer/Look Inside Your Heart	1963	25.00
❑ 47-8254	Bad Girl/Wait 'Til You See My Baby	1963	12.00
❑ 47-8341	The Closest Thing to Heaven/ Without a Song	1964	10.00
❑ 47-8341 [PS]	The Closest Thing to Heaven/ Without a Song	1964	20.00
❑ 47-8382	Sunny/She'll Never Be You	1964	10.00
❑ 47-8453	I Hope He Breaks Your Heart/ Too Late	1964	10.00
❑ 47-8511	Let the People Talk/ In the Chapel with You	1965	10.00
❑ 47-8511 [PS]	Let the People Talk/ In the Chapel with You	1965	20.00

Except when noted otherwise, VG = 25% of NM, and VG+ = 50% of NM. (Example: VG = $2.00, VG+ = $4.00 and NM = $8.00.)

Number	Title (A Side/B Side)	Yr	NM
❑ 47-8637	The World Through a Tear/ High On a Mountain	1965	10.00
❑ 47-8637 [PS]	The World Through a Tear/ High On a Mountain	1965	20.00
❑ 47-8737	The Answer to My Prayer/ Blue Boy	1965	10.00
❑ 47-8844	The Answer Lies Within/ Grown-Up Games	1966	10.00
❑ 47-9004	We Can Make It If We Try/ Too Late	1966	10.00
❑ 61-7595 [S]	Oh! Carol/One Way Ticket (To the Blues)	1959	50.00
—"Living Stereo" (large hole, plays at 45 rpm)			
❑ 61-7709 [S]	Stairway to Heaven/Forty Winks Away	1960	50.00
—"Living Stereo" (large hole, plays at 45 rpm)			
❑ 61-7781 [S]	You Mean Everything to Me/ Run Samson Run	1960	50.00
—"Living Stereo" (large hole, plays at 45 rpm)			
❑ 61-7829 [S]	Calendar Girl/The Same Old Fool	1960	50.00
—"Living Stereo" (large hole, plays at 45 rpm)			
❑ 447-0575	Oh! Carol/Calendar Girl	196?	6.00
—Gold Standard Series; black label			
❑ 447-0575	Oh! Carol/Calendar Girl	197?	4.00
—Gold Standard Series; red label			
❑ 447-0597	The Diary/Happy Birthday Sweet Sixteen	196?	6.00
—Gold Standard Series; black label			
❑ 447-0597	The Diary/Happy Birthday Sweet Sixteen	197?	4.00
—Gold Standard Series; red label			
❑ 447-0701	Breaking Up Is Hard to Do/ Next Door to An Angel	196?	6.00
—Gold Standard Series; black label			
❑ 447-0701	Breaking Up Is Hard to Do/ Next Door to An Angel	197?	4.00
—Gold Standard Series; red label			
❑ 447-0939	Little Devil/Stairway to Heaven	196?	6.00
—Gold Standard Series; black label			
❑ SP-45-96 [DJ]	RCA Victor Special DJ Spots	1960	50.00
—White label promo only; Sedaka introduces six songs and promotes his current release			

ROCKET

Number	Title (A Side/B Side)	Yr	NM
❑ 40313	Laughter in the Rain/Endlessly	1974	4.00
❑ 40370	The Immigrant/ Hey Mister Sunshine	1975	4.00
—No mention of John Lennon on label			
❑ 40370	The Immigrant/ Hey Mister Sunshine	1975	10.00
—With "Dedicated to John Lennon" under title in bold			
❑ 40426	That's When the Music Takes Me/Standing on the Inside	1975	4.00
❑ 40460	Bad Blood/Your Favorite Entertainer	1975	4.00
❑ 40500	Breaking Up Is Hard to Do/ Nana's Song	1975	4.00
❑ 40543	Love in the Shadows/Baby Don't Let It Mess Your Mind	1976	4.00
❑ 40582	Steppin' Out/Let You Walk Away	1976	4.00
❑ 40614	You Gotta Make Your Own Sunshine/Perfect Strangers	1976	4.00

SGC

Number	Title (A Side/B Side)	Yr	NM
❑ 005	Star-Crossed Lovers/We Had a Good Thing Going	1969	6.00
❑ 008	Rainy Jane/Jeannine	1970	6.00

7-Inch Extended Plays

RCA VICTOR

Number	Title (A Side/B Side)	Yr	NM
❑ LPC-105	Oh! Carol/Stairway to Heaven// The Diary/Run Samson Run	1961	50.00
—"Compact Double 33" with small hole			
❑ LPC-105 [PS]	Neil's Best	1961	50.00
❑ LPC-135	Little Devil/Circulate//Calendar Girl/We Kiss in a Shadow	1961	50.00
—"Compact Double 33" with small hole			
❑ LPC-135 [PS]	Little Devil	1961	50.00
❑ EPA-4334	I Go Ape/All I Need Is You//Stop! You're Knocking Me Out/ I Belong to You	1959	60.00
❑ EPA-4334 [PS]	I Go Ape	1959	60.00
❑ EPA-4353	Oh! Carol/Going Home to Mary Lou//The Girl for Me/I Ain't Hurtin' No More	1959	60.00
❑ EPA-4353 [PS]	Oh! Carol	1959	60.00

Albums

ACCORD

Number	Title (A Side/B Side)	Yr	NM
❑ SN-7152	Singer, Songwriter, Melody Maker	1981	10.00

ELEKTRA

Number	Title (A Side/B Side)	Yr	NM
❑ 6E-102	A Song	1977	10.00
❑ 6E-161	All You Need Is Music	1978	10.00
❑ 6E-259	In the Pocket	1980	10.00
❑ 6E-348	Neil Sedaka Now	1981	10.00

51 WEST

Number	Title (A Side/B Side)	Yr	NM
❑ Q 16003	I'm a Song	1979	12.00

INTERMEDIA

Number	Title (A Side/B Side)	Yr	NM
❑ QS 5015	Superbird	1982	10.00

KIRSHNER

Number	Title (A Side/B Side)	Yr	NM
❑ KES-111	Emergence	1971	15.00
❑ KES-117	Solitaire	1972	15.00

MCA

Number	Title (A Side/B Side)	Yr	NM
❑ 2357	Sedaka's Back	1978	10.00
—Reissue of Rocket 463			
❑ 5466	Come See About Me	1984	10.00

ORBIT

Number	Title (A Side/B Side)	Yr	NM
❑ RB-17196	Bravo!	1983	10.00

PICKWICK

Number	Title (A Side/B Side)	Yr	NM
❑ ACL1-7006	Breaking Up Is Hard to Do	197?	8.00

POLYDOR

Number	Title (A Side/B Side)	Yr	NM
❑ 831235-1	My Friend	1986	10.00

RCA CAMDEN

Number	Title (A Side/B Side)	Yr	NM
❑ ACL1-7006	Breaking Up Is Hard to Do	197?	10.00

RCA SPECIAL PRODUCTS

Number	Title (A Side/B Side)	Yr	NM
❑ DPL2-0149 [(2)]	Original Hits	1975	20.00

RCA VICTOR

Number	Title (A Side/B Side)	Yr	NM
❑ ANL1-0879	Oh! Carol	1975	10.00
❑ AFL1-0928	Neil Sedaka Sings His Greatest Hits	1977	10.00
—Reissue with new prefix			
❑ APL1-0928	Neil Sedaka Sings His Greatest Hits	1975	12.00
—Reissue of LSP-2627			
❑ ANL1-1314	Pure Gold	1976	10.00
❑ VPL1-1540	Live in Australia	1976	12.00
❑ APL1-1789	Emergence	1976	12.00
—Reissue of Kirshner 111			
❑ APL1-1790	Solitaire	1976	12.00
—Reissue of Kirshner 117			
❑ LPM-2035 [M]	Neil Sedaka	1959	60.00
❑ LSP-2035 [S]	Neil Sedaka	1959	100.00
❑ AFL1-2254	Sedaka — The '50s and '60s	1977	10.00
❑ LPM-2317 [M]	Circulate	1960	50.00
❑ LSP-2317 [S]	Circulate	1960	60.00
❑ LPM-2421 [M]	"Little Devil" and His Other Hits	1961	50.00
❑ LSP-2421 [S]	"Little Devil" and His Other Hits	1961	60.00
❑ AFL1-2524	The Many Sides of Neil Sedaka	1978	10.00
❑ LPM-2627 [M]	Neil Sedaka Sings His Greatest Hits	1962	40.00
❑ LSP-2627 [S]	Neil Sedaka Sings His Greatest Hits	1962	50.00
—Black label, dog on top, "Living Stereo" at bottom			
❑ LSP-2627 [S]	Neil Sedaka Sings His Greatest Hits	1969	20.00
—Reissue; orange label			
❑ ANL1-3465	Neil Sedaka Sings His Greatest Hits	1979	8.00
—Reissue of AFL1-0928			
❑ R 133511	Let's Go Steady Again	1976	15.00
—RCA Record Club edition			

ROCKET

Number	Title (A Side/B Side)	Yr	NM
❑ MCA-463	Sedaka's Back	1974	12.00
❑ PIG-2157	The Hungry Years	1975	12.00
❑ PIG-2195	Steppin' Out	1976	12.00
❑ PIG-2297	Neil Sedaka's Greatest Hits	1977	12.00

ROLLER SKATE

Number	Title (A Side/B Side)	Yr	NM
❑ TLA-50172	Is Anybody Gonna Miss You	1982	15.00

SEDAKA, NEIL, AND THE TOKENS WITH THE COINS Also see each artist's individual listings.

Albums

CROWN

Number	Title (A Side/B Side)	Yr	NM
❑ CST-366 [R]	Neil Sedaka and the Tokens and the Coins	1963	20.00
❑ CLP-5366 [M]	Neil Sedaka and the Tokens and the Coins	1963	30.00

SEEDS, THE Also see RITCHIE MARSH; SKY SAXON. Also see SKY SAXON.

45s

GNP CRESCENDO

Number	Title (A Side/B Side)	Yr	NM
❑ 354	Can't Seem to Make You Mine/ Daisy Mae	1965	15.00
❑ 354	Can't Seem to Make You Mine/ I Tell Myself	1967	10.00
❑ 354 [PS]	Can't Seem to Make You Mine/ I Tell Myself	1967	50.00
❑ 364	You're Pushing Too Hard/ Out of the Question	1965	15.00
❑ 370	The Other Place/ Try to Understand	1966	15.00
❑ 372	Pushin' Too Hard/ Try to Understand	1966	12.00
—With "GNP Crescendo" in box at top of label			
❑ 372	Pushin' Too Hard/ Try to Understand	1966	15.00
—With "GNP Crescendo" standing alone at top of label (no box)			
❑ 383	Mr. Farmer/No Escape	1967	8.00
❑ 383	Mr. Farmer/Up in Her Room	1967	8.00
❑ 383 [PS]	Mr. Farmer/Up in Her Room	1967	50.00
❑ 394	A Thousand Shadows/ March of the Flower Children	1967	8.00
❑ 394 [PS]	A Thousand Shadows/ March of the Flower Children	1967	20.00
❑ 398	The Wind Blows Your Hair/ Six Dreams	1967	8.00
❑ 408	Satisfy You/900 Million People Daily	1968	8.00
❑ 422	Fallin' Off the Edge of My Mind/ Wild Blood	1969	10.00

MGM

Number	Title (A Side/B Side)	Yr	NM
❑ 14163	Wish Me Up/Bad Part of Town	1970	20.00
❑ 14190	Did He Die/Love in a Summer Blanket	1970	20.00

PHILCO-FORD

Number	Title (A Side/B Side)	Yr	NM
❑ HP-26	Pushin' Too Hard/Can't Seem to Make You Mine	1968	25.00
—4-inch plastic "Hip Pocket Record" with color sleeve			

Albums

GNP CRESCENDO

Number	Title (A Side/B Side)	Yr	NM
❑ GNP-2023 [M]	The Seeds	1966	60.00
❑ GNPS-2023 [S]	The Seeds	1966	40.00
❑ GNP-2033 [M]	A Web of Sound	1967	60.00
❑ GNPS-2033 [S]	A Web of Sound	1967	40.00
❑ GNP-2038 [M]	Future	1967	40.00
—Deduct 25% if two inserts are missing			
❑ GNPS-2038 [S]	Future	1967	30.00
—Deduct 25% if two inserts are missing			
❑ GNP-2040 [M]	A Full Spoon of Seedy Blues	1968	60.00
❑ GNPS-2040 [S]	A Full Spoon of Seedy Blues	1968	25.00
❑ GNPS-2043	Raw and Alive	1968	25.00
❑ GNPS-2107	Fallin' Off the Edge	1977	10.00
❑ ST-91224	A Web of Sound	1968	30.00
—Capitol Record Club edition			

SEEGER, PETE Also see THE WEAVERS.

45s

COLUMBIA

Number	Title (A Side/B Side)	Yr	NM
❑ 42940	Little Boxes/Mail Myself to You	1963	8.00
❑ 43349	Healing River/Johnny Give Me	1965	8.00
❑ 43699	Draft Dodger Rag/ Guantanamera	1966	8.00
❑ 44273	Waist Deep in the Big Muddy/ Down by the Riverside	1967	8.00

FOLKWAYS

Number	Title (A Side/B Side)	Yr	NM
❑ 45-201	The Battle of New Orleans/ My Home's Across the Smokey Mountains	1959	12.00

Albums

ARAVEL

Number	Title (A Side/B Side)	Yr	NM
❑ AB 1006 [M]	Live Hootenanny	1963	15.00

BROADSIDE

Number	Title (A Side/B Side)	Yr	NM
❑ 502 [(2)]	Pete Seeger Sings and Answers Questions	1970	15.00

BULLDOG

Number	Title (A Side/B Side)	Yr	NM
❑ BDL-2011	20 Golden Pieces of Pete Seeger	198?	10.00

CAPITOL

Number	Title (A Side/B Side)	Yr	NM
❑ DW 2172 [R]	Folk Songs	1964	12.00
❑ W 2172 [M]	Folk Songs	1964	20.00
❑ DT 2718 [R]	Freight Train	1967	12.00
❑ T 2718 [M]	Freight Train	1967	20.00

COLUMBIA

Number	Title (A Side/B Side)	Yr	NM
❑ CL 1668 [M]	Pete Seeger Story Songs	1961	25.00
❑ CL 1916 [M]	The Bitter and the Sweet	1962	25.00
❑ CL 1947 [M]	Children's Concert at Town Hall	1963	25.00
❑ CL 2101 [M]	We Shall Overcome	1963	15.00
❑ CL 2257 [M]	I Can See a New Day	1965	15.00
❑ CL 2334 [M]	Strangers and Cousins	1964	15.00
❑ CL 2432 [M]	God Bless the Grass	1966	15.00
❑ CL 2503 [M]	Dangerous Songs?	1966	15.00
❑ CL 2616 [M]	Pete Seeger's Greatest Hits	1967	20.00
❑ CL 2705 [M]	Waist Deep in the Big Muddy	1967	20.00
❑ CS 8468 [S]	Pete Seeger Story Songs	1961	30.00
❑ CS 8716 [S]	The Bitter and the Sweet	1962	30.00
❑ CS 8747 [S]	Children's Concert at Town Hall	1963	30.00
❑ CS 8901 [S]	We Shall Overcome	1963	20.00
❑ CS 9057 [S]	I Can See a New Day	1965	20.00
❑ CS 9134 [S]	Strangers and Cousins	1964	20.00
❑ CS 9232 [S]	God Bless the Grass	1966	20.00
❑ CS 9303 [S]	Dangerous Songs?	1966	20.00
❑ CS 9416 [S]	Pete Seeger's Greatest Hits	1967	15.00
❑ PC 9416	Pete Seeger's Greatest Hits	198?	8.00
—Reissue with new prefix			
❑ CS 9505 [S]	Waist Deep in the Big Muddy	1967	15.00
❑ CS 9717	Pete Seeger Now	1968	15.00
❑ CS 9873	Young vs. Old	1969	15.00
❑ C 30739	Rainbow Race	1971	12.00
❑ KG 31949 [(2)]	The World of Pete Seeger	1972	15.00

DISC

Number	Title (A Side/B Side)	Yr	NM
❑ D-101 [M]	Sing with Seeger	1964	20.00

EVEREST ARCHIVE OF FOLK & JAZZ

Number	Title (A Side/B Side)	Yr	NM
❑ 201	Pete Seeger	1966	12.00

S

Number	Title (A Side/B Side)	Yr	NM
FOLKWAYS			
FP-3 [10]	Darling Corey	1950	100.00
FP-10 [10]	Lonesome Valley	195?	100.00
FP-43 [10]	A Pete Seeger Sampler	195?	100.00
FP-45 [10]	Goofing Off Suite	195?	100.00
FP-701 [10]	American Folk Songs for Children	195?	100.00
FP-710 [10]	Birds, Beasts, Bugs and Little Fishes	1954	100.00
FP-911 [10]	Folk Songs of Four Continents	195?	100.00
FA-2003 [10]	Darling Corey	1950	80.00
FA-2010 [10]	Lonesome Valley	195?	80.00
FA-2043 [10]	A Pete Seeger Sampler	1954	80.00
FA-2045 [10]	Goofing Off Suite	1954	80.00
FA-2175 [10]	Frontier Ballads, Vol. 1	1954	80.00
FA-2176 [10]	Frontier Ballads, Vol. 2	1954	80.00
FA-2311 [M]	Traditional Christmas Carols	1956	30.00
FA-2319 [M]	American Ballads	1957	30.00
FA-2320 [M]	American Favorite Ballads, Vol. 1	1957	30.00
FA-2321 [M]	American Favorite Ballads, Vol. 2	1958	30.00
FA-2322 [M]	American Favorite Ballads, Vol. 3	1958	30.00
FA-2323 [M]	American Favorite Ballads, Vol. 4	1961	20.00
FA-2412 [M]	Pete Seeger and Sonny Terry	1958	30.00
FA-2439 [M]	Nonesuch	196?	20.00
FA-2445 [M]	American Favorite Ballads, Vol. 5: Tunes and Songs As Sung by Pete Seeger	1962	20.00
FA-2450 [M]	Highlights of Pete Seeger at the Village Gate with Memphis Slim and Willie Dixon	1960	30.00
FA-2451 [M]	Pete Seeger at the Village Gate — Vol. 2	1960	30.00
FA-2452 [M]	With Voices Together We Sing	1956	25.00
FA-2453 [M]	Love Songs for Friends and Foes	1956	25.00
FA-2454 [M]	Rainbow Quest	1960	25.00
FA-2455 [M]	Sing Out with Pete!	1961	20.00
FA-2456 [M]	Broadsides	1964	20.00
FA-2501 [M]	Gazette, Vol. 1	1958	25.00
FA-2502 [M]	Gazette, Vol. 2	1962	20.00
FN-2511 [M]	Hootenanny Tonight!	195?	25.00
FN-2513 [M]	Sing Out! Hootenanny	1963	20.00
FS-3851 [M]	Indian Summer	1960	25.00
—With Michael Seeger			
5003 [(2)]	Frontier Ballads	1954	100.00
FH-5210 [M]	Champlain Valley Songs	1960	25.00
FH-5233 [M]	Songs of Struggle and Protest 1930-50	1959	25.00
FH-5251 [M]	American Industrial Ballads	1956	30.00
FH-5257	Fifty Sail On Newburgh Bay	1976	12.00
FH-5302 [M]	Broadside Ballads, Vol. 2	1963	20.00
FH-5436 [M]	Songs of the Spanish Civil War, Vol. 1	1961	20.00
FH-5485 [M]	Ballads of Sacco and Vanzetti	1963	20.00
FH-5595 [M]	WNEW's Story of Selma	1965	20.00
FH-5702 [(2)]	Pete Seeger Sings and Answers Questions	1968	25.00
FW-6843 [10]	German Folk Songs	1954	80.00
FW-6911 [10]	Folk Songs of Four Continents	1955	80.00
FW-6912 [10]	Bantu Choral Folk Songs	1955	80.00
FC-7020 [10]	Songs to Grow On — Vol. 2	1951	80.00
FC-7027 [10]	Songs to Grow On — Vol. 3	1951	80.00
FC-7526 [M]	Song and Play Time	195?	50.00
7527	Zhitkov's How I Hunted the Little Fellows	1980	12.00
FC-7601 [10]	American Folk Songs for Children	1953	80.00
FC-7610 [10]	Birds, Beasts, Bugs and Little Fishes	1954	80.00
FC-7611 [M]	Birds, Beasts, Bugs and Bigger Fishes	1954	50.00
FC-7674 [M]	American Game and Activity Songs for Children	1962	20.00
FI-8303 [M]	How to Play the Five String Banjo	195?	25.00
FI-8354 [M]	Folksinger's Guitar Guide Vol. 1: An Instruction Record	1955	30.00
FQ-8354 [M]	The Folksinger's Guitar Gude	1955	25.00
FI-8371 [M]	12-String Guitar As Played by Leadbelly	1962	20.00
FTS-31002 [R]	Pete Seeger Sings Woody Guthrie	1968	12.00
FTS-31017 [R]	American Favorite Ballads	1968	12.00
FTS-31018 [R]	Wimoweh and Other Songs of Freedom and Protest	1968	12.00
FTS-31022 [R]	Pete Seeger Sings Leadbelly	1968	12.00
FTS-31040 [R]	Banks of Marble and Other Songs	1974	12.00
FTS-32311 [R]	Traditional Christmas Carols	1967	15.00
FT-35001 [(2)]	The Nativity: By Sholem Asch	1963	15.00
FXM-36055 [(2)]	Sing Along	1980	15.00
37232	God Bless the Grass	1982	12.00
HARMONY			
HS 11337	John Henry and Other Folk Favorites	1969	12.00
ODYSSEY			
32160266	3 Saints, 4 Sinners and 6 Other People	1968	15.00
OLYMPIC			
7102	America's Balladeer	1973	12.00
PAIR			
PDL2-1076 [(2)]	Clearwater Classics	1986	12.00
PHILIPS			
PHM 2-300 [(2)M]	The Story of the Nativity	1963	20.00
PHS 2-300 [(2)S]	The Story of the Nativity	1963	25.00
SMITHSONIAN FOLKWAYS			
SF-40024	Traditional Christmas Carols	1989	12.00
STINSON			
SLP-52 [10]	Lincoln Brigade	1953	100.00
SLP-57 [10]	A Pete Seeger Concert	1953	100.00
SLP-90 [M]	Pete	1963	25.00
TRADITION			
2107	Folk Music of the World	1973	12.00
VANGUARD			
VSD-97/98 [(2)]	The Essential Pete Seeger	1978	15.00
VSD-73111	The Essential Pete Seeger, Vol. 1	198?	8.00
VSD-73112	The Essential Pete Seeger, Vol. 2	198?	8.00
VERVE FOLKWAYS			
FV-9008 [M]	Pete Seeger and Big Bill Broonzy in Concert	1965	20.00
FVS-9008 [S]	Pete Seeger and Big Bill Broonzy in Concert	1965	25.00
FV-9009 [M]	Pete Seeger On Campus	1965	20.00
FVS-9009 [S]	Pete Seeger On Campus	1965	25.00
FV-9013 [M]	Folk Music Live at the Village Gate	1965	20.00
FVS-9013 [S]	Folk Music Live at the Village Gate	1965	25.00
FV-9020 [M]	Little Boxes and Other Broadsides	1965	20.00
FVS-9020 [S]	Little Boxes and Other Broadsides	1965	25.00
WARNER BROS.			
BSK 3329	Circles and Seasons	1979	12.00

SEEKERS, THE

Number	Title (A Side/B Side)	Yr	NM
45s			
ATMOS			
711	Myra (Shake Up the Party)/Wild Rover	1965	20.00
CAPITOL			
2013	When the Good Apples Fall/Myra (Shake Up the Party)	1967	10.00
2122	Love Is Kind, Love Is Wine/All I Can Remember	1968	10.00
5383	I'll Never Find Another You/Open Up Them Pearly Gates	1965	12.00
5430	A World of Our Own/Sinner Man	1965	12.00
5430 [PS]	A World of Our Own/Sinner Man	1965	20.00
5531	The Carnival Is Over/We Shall Not Be Moved	1965	10.00
5622	Some Day, One Day/Nobody Knows the Trouble I've Seen	1966	10.00
5756	Georgy Girl/When the Stars Begin to Fall	1966	12.00
5787	Morningtown Ride/Walk with Me	1967	10.00
5974	I Wish You Could Be Here/On the Other Side	1967	10.00
CAPITOL CREATIVE PRODUCTS			
50 [DJ]	Island of Dreams/Breaking My Back — Instead of Using My Mind	1966	15.00
—B-side by Lou Rawls			
50 [PS]	Island of Dreams/Breaking My Back — Instead of Using My Mind	1966	20.00
—Custom sleeve; no titles or artist, but "#50" is at right and "Capitol has specially produced this record for Frito-Lay" is under the center hole			
MARVEL			
1060	Chilly Winds/The Light from the Lighthouse	1965	15.00
Albums			
CAPITOL			
ST-135 [S]	The Seekers Live	1969	12.00
ST 2319 [S]	The New Seekers	1965	15.00
T 2319 [M]	The New Seekers	1965	12.00
DT 2369 [R]	A World of Our Own	1965	12.00
T 2369 [M]	A World of Our Own	1965	12.00
ST 2431 [S]	Georgy Girl	1966	15.00
T 2431 [M]	Georgy Girl	1966	12.00
SM-2746 [P]	The Best of the Seekers	197?	10.00
ST 2746 [P]	The Best of the Seekers	196?	10.00
—Red and white "star" Starline label			
ST 2746 [P]	The Best of the Seekers	1967	12.00
—Red and white "target" Starline label; though the cover has an "ST" prefix, the record and trail-off wax have a "DT" prefix; "Morningtown Ride," Turn, Turn, Turn," and "We're Moving On" are in stereo			
T 2746 [M]	The Best of the Seekers	1967	12.00
KAO 2821 [M]	The Seekers Seen in Green	1968	40.00
SKAO 2821 [S]	The Seekers Seen in Green	1968	15.00
SN-16104 [P]	The Best of the Seekers	1980	8.00
MARVEL			
2060 [M]	The Seekers	1965	12.00
3060 [R]	The Seekers	1965	10.00

SEGAL, GEORGE

Number	Title (A Side/B Side)	Yr	NM
45s			
PHILIPS			
40468	The Yama-Yama Man/Yes Sir, That's My Baby	1967	8.00
SIGNATURE			
SB-10099	If You Like-a Me/What You Goin' to Do When the Rent Comes Around	1974	6.00
Albums			
PHILIPS			
PHM 200242 [M]	The Yama-Yama Man	1967	20.00
PHS 600242 [S]	The Yama-Yama Man	1967	20.00
SIGNATURE			
BSL1-0654	A Touch of Ragtime	1976	15.00

SEGER, BOB

Includes records with The Last Heard, The Bob Seger System and The Silver Bullet Band. Also see THE BEACH BUMS.

Number	Title (A Side/B Side)	Yr	NM
12-Inch Singles			
CAPITOL			
SPRO-8987 [DJ]	We've Got Tonite (single)/We've Got Tonite (LP)	1978	12.00
SPRO-9085/6 [DJ]	Old Time Rock and Roll/Sunspot Baby	1979	15.00
SPRO-9641/2 [DJ]	American Storm (Edit)/American Storm (LP)	1986	6.00
SPRO-9687/8 [DJ]	Tryin' to Live My Life Without You (3:00)/(3:46)	1981	10.00
SPRO-9705 [DJ]	Like a Rock (Edit)/Like a Rock (LP)	1986	8.00
SPRO-9736 [DJ]	The Aftermath (remix)/The Aftermath (LP)	1986	6.00
SPRO-9778 [DJ]	It's You (45 remix)/The Aftermath (remix)	1986	6.00
SPRO-9866/74 [DJ]	Miami (Extended)/Miami (LP)	1986	6.00
45s			
ABKCO			
4015	East Side Story/East Side Sound	1973	6.00
4016	Chain Smokin'/Persecution Smith	1973	6.00
4017	Heavy Music - Pt. I/Heavy Music - Pt. II	1973	6.00
4031	Heavy Music - Pt. I/Heavy Music - Pt. II	1973	5.00
CAMEO			
438	East Side Story/East Side Sound	1966	25.00
444	Sock It To Me, Santa/Florida Time	1966	30.00
465	Chain Smokin'/Persecution Smith	1967	25.00
473	Vagrant Winter/Very Few	1967	25.00
494	Heavy Music/Heavy Music (Part 2)	1967	20.00
CAPITOL			
2143	2 + 2 = ?/Death Row	1968	15.00
2297	Ramblin' Gamblin' Man/Tales of Lucy Blue	1968	12.00
2480	Ivory/The Lost Song (Love Needs to Be Loved)	1969	8.00
2576	Noah/Lennie Johnson	1969	8.00
2640	Lonely Man/Innervenus Eyes	1970	8.00
2748	Lucifer/Big River	1970	8.00
3187	Lookin' Back/Highway Child	1971	8.00
4062	Beautiful Loser/Fine Memory	1975	5.00
4116	Katmandu/Black Night	1975	5.00
4183	Nutbush City Limits/Travelin' Man	1975	5.00
4269	Nutbush City Limits/Lookin' Back	1976	5.00
4300	Beautiful Loser/Travelin' Man	1976	5.00
4369	Night Moves/Ship of Fools	1976	4.00
4422	Mainstreet/Jody Girl	1977	4.00
4449	Rock and Roll Never Forgets/Fire Down Below	1977	4.00
4581	Still the Same/Feel Like a Number	1978	4.00
4618	Hollywood Nights/Brave Strangers	1978	4.00

Number	Title (A Side/B Side)	Yr	NM
❑ 4653	We've Got Tonite/Ain't Got No Money	1978	4.00
❑ 4653 [DJ]	We've Got Tonite (mono/stereo)	1978	10.00
—Silver vinyl			
❑ 4653 [PS]	We've Got Tonite/Ain't Got No Money	1978	6.00
❑ 4702	Old Time Rock and Roll/Sunspot Baby	1979	4.00
❑ 4702 [PS]	Old Time Rock and Roll/Sunspot Baby	1979	6.00
❑ 4836	Fire Lake/Long Twin Silver Line	1980	4.00
❑ 4836 [PS]	Fire Lake/Long Twin Silver Line	1980	6.00
❑ 4863	Against the Wind/No Man's Land	1980	4.00
❑ 4863 [PS]	Against the Wind/No Man's Land	1980	6.00
❑ 4904	You'll Accomp'ny Me/Betty Lou's Gettin' Out Tonight	1980	5.00
❑ 4904 [PS]	You'll Accomp'ny Me/Betty Lou's Gettin' Out Tonight	1980	6.00
❑ 4951	The Horizontal Bop/Her Strut	1980	5.00
❑ 4951 [PS]	The Horizontal Bop/Her Strut	1980	100.00
❑ A-5042	Tryin' to Live My Life Without You/Brave Strangers	1981	3.00
❑ A-5042 [PS]	Tryin' to Live My Life Without You/Brave Strangers	1981	4.00
❑ A-5077	Feel Like a Number/Hollywood Nights	1981	4.00
❑ A-5077 [PS]	Feel Like a Number/Hollywood Nights	1981	5.00
❑ B-5187	Shame on the Moon/House Behind a House	1982	3.00
❑ B-5187 [PS]	Shame on the Moon/House Behind a House	1982	4.00
❑ B-5213	Even Now/Little Victories	1983	3.00
❑ B-5213 [PS]	Even Now/Little Victories	1983	4.00
❑ B-5235	Roll Me Away/Boomtown Blues	1983	3.00
❑ B-5235 [PS]	Roll Me Away/Boomtown Blues	1983	4.00
❑ B-5276	Old Time Rock and Roll/Till It Shines	1983	3.00
❑ B-5276 [PS]	Old Time Rock and Roll/Till It Shines	1983	5.00
❑ B-5413	Understanding/East L.A.	1984	3.00
❑ B-5413 [PS]	Understanding/East L.A.	1984	4.00
❑ B-5532	American Storm/Fortunate Son	1986	3.00
❑ B-5532 [PS]	American Storm/Fortunate Son	1986	3.00
❑ B-5592	Like a Rock/Livin' Inside My Heart	1986	3.00
❑ B-5592 [PS]	Like a Rock/Livin' Inside My Heart	1986	3.00
❑ B-5623	It's You/The Aftermath (12" Remix)	1986	3.00
❑ B-5623 [PS]	It's You/The Aftermath (12" Remix)	1986	3.00
❑ B-5658	Miami/Somewhere Tonight	1986	3.00
❑ B-5658 [PS]	Miami/Somewhere Tonight	1986	25.00
—May only have been released in the New York metro area, as it quotes reviewers from four different New York newspapers			
❑ SPRO 8433 [DJ]	Travelin' Man/Beautiful Loser	1976	10.00
❑ S7-18298	C'est La Vie/Night Moves	1995	4.00
❑ NR-44761	The Real Love/Roll Me Away	1991	4.00
❑ NR-44793	The Fire Inside/New Coat of Paint	1991	4.00
❑ S7-56784	Like a Rock/Sunspot Baby	1992	4.00
❑ S7-57732	New Coat of Paint/Blind Love	1992	4.00
❑ S7-57742	Night Moves/Her Strut	1992	4.00
❑ S7-57797	Old TIme Rock and Roll/Turn the Page	1992	4.00

HIDEOUT

Number	Title (A Side/B Side)	Yr	NM
❑ 1013	East Side Story/East Side Sound	1966	50.00
❑ 1014	Chain Smokin'/Persecution Smith	1966	50.00

MCA

Number	Title (A Side/B Side)	Yr	NM
❑ 53094	Shakedown/The Aftermath	1987	3.00
❑ 53094 [PS]	Shakedown/The Aftermath	1987	4.00
—Picture of Bob Seger on front cover			
❑ 53094 [PS]	Shakedown/The Aftermath	1987	15.00
—Picture of Eddie Murphy as Axel Foley on front cover			

PALLADIUM

Number	Title (A Side/B Side)	Yr	NM
❑ 1079	If I Were a Carpenter/Jesse James	1972	10.00
❑ 1117	Turn On Your Love Light/Who Do You Love?	1972	10.00
❑ 1143	Rosalie/Neon Sky	1972	10.00
❑ 1171	Need Ya/Seen a Lot of Floors	1973	10.00
❑ 1205	Get Out of Denver/Long Song Comin'	1974	10.00
❑ 1316	This Ole House/U.M.C.	1974	15.00

REPRISE

Number	Title (A Side/B Side)	Yr	NM
❑ PRO 571 [DJ]	Midnight Rider (same on both sides)	1972	15.00

Albums

CAPITOL

Number	Title (A Side/B Side)	Yr	NM
❑ (no #) [PD]	Night Moves	1977	40.00
—Promo-only picture disc			
❑ SM-172	Ramblin' Gamblin' Man	1977	8.00
❑ ST-172	Ramblin' Gamblin' Man	1969	30.00
—Black label with colorband			
❑ ST-236	Noah	1969	80.00
❑ SKAO-499	Mongrel	1970	25.00
❑ SM-499	Mongrel	1977	8.00
❑ ST-731	Brand New Morning	1971	100.00
❑ SPRO-8433 [DJ]	Consensus Cuts Edited for Airplay from "Live Bullet"	1976	25.00
❑ ST-11378	Beautiful Loser	1975	10.00
—Originals have orange labels			
❑ ST-11378	Beautiful Loser	1978	8.00
—Purple label with large Capitol logo			
❑ SKBB-11523 [(2)]	Live Bullet	1976	15.00
—Originals have orange labels			
❑ SKBB-11523 [(2)]	Live Bullet	1978	12.00
—Purple label with large Capitol logo			
❑ SKBB-11523 [(2)]	Live Bullet	1983	12.00
—Black label, print in colorband			
❑ STBK-11523 [(2)]	Live Bullet	1988	12.00
—Purple label with smaller Capitol logo			
❑ ST-11557	Night Moves	1976	10.00
❑ SW-11698	Stranger in Town	1978	10.00
❑ ST-11746	Smokin' O.P.'s	1978	10.00
❑ ST-11748	Seven	1978	10.00
❑ SEAX-11904 [PD]	Stranger in Town	1978	25.00
❑ SOO-12041	Against the Wind	1980	10.00
❑ STBK-12182 [(2)]	Nine Tonight	1981	15.00
❑ ST-12254	The Distance	1983	10.00
❑ PT-12398	Like a Rock	1986	10.00
❑ SN-16105	Ramblin' Gamblin' Man	1980	8.00
❑ SN-16106	Mongrel	1980	8.00
❑ SN-16107	Smokin' O.P.'s	1980	8.00
❑ SN-16108	Seven	1980	8.00
❑ SN-16315	Beautiful Loser	1984	8.00
❑ C1-30334	Greatest Hits	1994	15.00
❑ C1-91134	The Fire Inside	1991	12.00
❑ C1-99774	It's a Mystery	1995	—
—Canceled			
❑ R124284	Ramblin' Gamblin' Man	197?	20.00
—Orange label, "Capitol"at bottom; RCA Music Service edition with B-side label error listing the title as "Ramblin' Bamblin' Man"			

MOBILE FIDELITY

Number	Title (A Side/B Side)	Yr	NM
❑ 1-034	Night Moves	1980	40.00
—Audiophile vinyl			
❑ 1-127	Against the Wind	1983	40.00
—Audiophile vinyl			

PALLADIUM

Number	Title (A Side/B Side)	Yr	NM
❑ P-1006	Smokin' O.P.'s	1972	25.00

REPRISE

Number	Title (A Side/B Side)	Yr	NM
❑ MS 2109	Smokin' O.P.'s	1972	15.00
❑ MS 2126	Back in '72	1973	60.00
❑ MS 2184	Seven	1974	20.00

SELECTIONS, THE

45s

ANTONE

Number	Title (A Side/B Side)	Yr	NM
❑ 101	Guardian Angel/Soft and Sweet	1958	250.00

MONA LEE

Number	Title (A Side/B Side)	Yr	NM
❑ 129	Guardian Angel/Soft and Sweet	1959	60.00

SPECIALTY

Number	Title (A Side/B Side)	Yr	NM
❑ 751	Guardian Angel/Soft and Sweet	197?	10.00

SELF, MACK

45s

PHILLIPS INT'L.

Number	Title (A Side/B Side)	Yr	NM
❑ 3548	Mad at You/Willie Brown	1959	25.00

SUN

Number	Title (A Side/B Side)	Yr	NM
❑ 273	Easy to Love/Every Day	1957	30.00

SELF, RONNIE

45s

ABC-PARAMOUNT

Number	Title (A Side/B Side)	Yr	NM
❑ 9714	Pretty Bad Blues/Three Hearts Later	1956	100.00
❑ 9768	Alone/Sweet Love	1956	100.00

AMY

Number	Title (A Side/B Side)	Yr	NM
❑ 11009	High on Life/The Road Keeps Winding	1968	10.00

COLUMBIA

Number	Title (A Side/B Side)	Yr	NM
❑ 40875	Big Fool/Flame of Love	1957	40.00
❑ 40989	Ain't I'm a Dog/Rocky Road Blues	1957	40.00
❑ 41101	Bop-A-Lena/I Ain't Going Nowhere	1958	30.00
❑ 41166	Big Blon' Baby/Date Bait	1958	30.00
❑ 41241	Petrified/You're So Right for Me	1958	80.00

DECCA

Number	Title (A Side/B Side)	Yr	NM
❑ 30958	Big Town/This Must Be the Place	1959	25.00
❑ 31131	I've Been There/So High	1960	25.00
❑ 31351	Instant Man/Some Things You Can't Change	1962	25.00
❑ 31431	Oh Me, Oh My/Past, Present and Future	1962	25.00

KAPP

Number	Title (A Side/B Side)	Yr	NM
❑ 546	Houdini/Bless My Broken Heart	1963	20.00

7-Inch Extended Plays

COLUMBIA

Number	Title (A Side/B Side)	Yr	NM
❑ B-2149	(contents unknown)	1957	200.00
❑ B-2149 [PS]	Ain't I'm a Dog	1957	200.00

SELLERS, PETER

45s

CAPITOL

Number	Title (A Side/B Side)	Yr	NM
❑ F4159	I'm So Ashamed/A Drop of the Hard Stuff	1959	12.00
❑ 5580	A Hard Day's Night/Help	1966	15.00

UNITED ARTISTS

Number	Title (A Side/B Side)	Yr	NM
❑ X1221	Thank Heaven for Little Girls/Singin' in the Rain	1978	10.00
—As "Inspector Clouseau"			

Albums

ACAPELLA

Number	Title (A Side/B Side)	Yr	NM
❑ 1	Fool Brittania	1963	25.00
—With Joan Collins and Anthony Newley			

ANGEL

Number	Title (A Side/B Side)	Yr	NM
❑ 35884 [M]	The Best of Sellers	1960	30.00
❑ S 35884 [S]	The Best of Sellers	1960	40.00

EMI AMERICA

Number	Title (A Side/B Side)	Yr	NM
❑ SN-16396	Songs for Swingin' Sellers	1986	20.00
—First American issue of 1959 U.K. LP			

SELLERS, PETER, AND SOPHIA LOREN

45s

CAPITOL

Number	Title (A Side/B Side)	Yr	NM
❑ 4505	Bangers and Mash/Goodness Gracious Me	1961	12.00

Albums

ANGEL

Number	Title (A Side/B Side)	Yr	NM
❑ 35910 [M]	Peter Sellers and Sophia Loren	1961	30.00
❑ S 35910 [S]	Peter Sellers and Sophia Loren	1961	40.00

SEMI-COLONS, THE
May be a pseudonym for ? (QUESTION MARK) AND THE MYSTERIANS.

45s

CAMEO

Number	Title (A Side/B Side)	Yr	NM
❑ 468	Beachcomber/Set Aside	1967	20.00

SENATOR BOBBY

45s

PARKWAY

Number	Title (A Side/B Side)	Yr	NM
❑ 127	Wild Thing/Wild Thing	1966	12.00
—B-side by "Senator McKinley"			
❑ 137	Mellow Yellow/White Christmas	1967	10.00
—A-side by "Senator Bobby & Senator McKinley"; B-side by "Bobby the Poet" (Dylan impersonation)			
❑ 150	The Congressional Record/The Hardly Worthit Melody	1967	10.00
—By The Hardly Worthit Players			

RCA VICTOR

Number	Title (A Side/B Side)	Yr	NM
❑ 47-9522	Sock It To Me, Bobby/Sock It To Me, Baby	1968	10.00
—B-side by the Bobby Sockers			

Albums

PARKWAY

Number	Title (A Side/B Side)	Yr	NM
❑ P 7057 [M]	Boston Soul with the Hardly-Worthit Players	1967	20.00
❑ SP 7057 [S]	Boston Soul with the Hardly-Worthit Players	1967	20.00

SENATORS, THE (1)

45s

ABC-PARAMOUNT

Number	Title (A Side/B Side)	Yr	NM
❑ 10178	There's a New Man in the White House/A Sing-Along Song	1961	15.00

SENATORS, THE (2)

45s

ABNER

Number	Title (A Side/B Side)	Yr	NM
❑ 1031	Julie/It Doesn't Matter	1959	120.00

GOLDEN CREST

Number	Title (A Side/B Side)	Yr	NM
❑ 514	Loretta/Poor Little Puppet	1958	150.00

SENATORS, THE (3)

45s

BRISTOL

Number	Title (A Side/B Side)	Yr	NM
❑ 1916	Scheming/Tafu	1959	400.00

WINN

Number	Title (A Side/B Side)	Yr	NM
❑ 1917	Wedding Bells/I Shouldn't Care	1962	250.00

SENIORS, THE (1)

45s

ABC-PARAMOUNT

Number	Title (A Side/B Side)	Yr	NM
❑ 10736	No Surfin' 'Round Here/Cindy	1965	30.00

S

SENIORS, THE (2)

Number	Title (A Side/B Side)	Yr	NM
45s			
DECCA			
❑ 31112	I've Lived Before/Hello Mr. Robin	1960	20.00
❑ 31244	When I Fall in Love/ Baby, Say the Word	1961	20.00

SENIORS, THE (3)

Number	Title (A Side/B Side)	Yr	NM
45s			
EXCELLO			
❑ 2130	Why Did You Leave Me/ Sloo Foot Soo	1958	40.00
LOST-NITE			
❑ 194	Evening Shadows Falling (I Think of You)/I've Got Plenty of Love	196?	6.00
—Reissue			
TETRA			
❑ 4446	Evening Shadows Falling (I Think of You)/I've Got Plenty of Love	1956	200.00

SENIORS, THE (U)

Number	Title (A Side/B Side)	Yr	NM
45s			
ESV			
❑ 1016	Ah Sweet Mystery of Love/ Rock and Rolly	1960	25.00
KENT			
❑ 342	Hully Gully Fever/ Pitter Patter Heart	1960	20.00
TAMPA			
❑ 163	Who's Gonna Know/ It's Been a Long Time	1959	40.00

SENORS, THE
Allegedly THE ISLEY BROTHERS in disguise.

Number	Title (A Side/B Side)	Yr	NM
45s			
SUE			
❑ 756	May I Have This Dance/ Searching for Olive Oil	1962	50.00

SENSATIONAL EPICS, THE

Number	Title (A Side/B Side)	Yr	NM
45s			
CAMEO			
❑ 450	I've Been Hurt/It's a Gas	1967	25.00
CAPITOL			
❑ 2381	All My Hard Times/Play It by Ear	1969	15.00
WARNER BROS.			
❑ 7168	Be Young, Be Foolish, Be Happy/ You Warp My Mind Girl	1968	15.00

SENSATIONS, THE
Also see YVONNE BAKER.

Number	Title (A Side/B Side)	Yr	NM
45s			
ARGO			
❑ 5391	Music, Music, Music/A Part of Me	1961	10.00
❑ 5405	Let Me In/Oh Yes I'll Be True	1961	12.00
—Brown label			
❑ 5405	Let Me In/Oh Yes I'll Be True	1961	20.00
—Black label			
❑ 5412	That's My Desire/Eyes	1962	10.00
—By "Yvonne Baker and the Sensations"			
❑ 5420	Party Across the Hall/ No Changes	1962	10.00
—By "Yvonne Baker and the Sensations"			
❑ 5446	When My Lover Comes Home/ Father Dear	1963	10.00
—By "Yvonne Baker and the Sensations"			
ATCO			
❑ 6056	Yes Sir, That's My Baby/ Sympathy	1955	40.00
❑ 6067	Please Mr. Disc Jockey/ Ain't He Sweet	1956	40.00
❑ 6075	Cry Baby Cry/My Heart Cries for You	1956	40.00
❑ 6083	Little Wallflower/Such a Love	1957	40.00
❑ 6090	My Debut to Love/ You Made Me Love You	1957	40.00
❑ 6115	Kiddy Car Love/ Romance in the Dark	1958	40.00
JUNIOR			
❑ 1002	We Were Meant to Be/It's Good Enough for Me	1963	12.00
❑ 1005	You Made a Fool of Me/ That's What You've Gotta Do	1963	20.00
❑ 1010	I Can't Change/ Mend the Torn Pieces	1964	12.00
❑ 1021	We Were Meant to Be /It's Good Enough for Me	1964	12.00
LOST-NITE			
❑ 255	Let Me In/Oh Yes I'll Be True	196?	5.00
—Reissue			
TOLLIE			
❑ 9009	You Made a Fool of Me/That's What You've Gotta Do	1964	10.00
Albums			
ARGO			
❑ LP-4022 [M]	Let Me In/Music, Music, Music	1963	500.00

SENSATIONS OF LONDON, THE

Number	Title (A Side/B Side)	Yr	NM
45s			
YORK			
❑ 406	Look at My Baby/ What a Wonderful Feeling	1966	15.00

SENTIMENTALS, THE

Number	Title (A Side/B Side)	Yr	NM
45s			
CHECKER			
❑ 875	I Want to Love You/ Teenie Teenager	1957	40.00
CORAL			
❑ 62100	We Three/Understanding Love	1959	25.00
❑ 62172	Deep Down in My Heart/ Two Different Worlds	1960	25.00
MINT			
❑ 801	I Want to Love You/ Tommie Teenager	1957	50.00
❑ 802	Sunday Kind of Love/ Wedding Bells	1957	40.00
❑ 803	I'm Your Fool, Always/ Rock Me, Mama	1958	40.00
❑ 805	You're Mine/Danny Boy	1958	40.00
❑ 807	Found a New Baby/ I'll Miss These Things	196?	12.00
❑ 808	This Time/I Want to Love You	196?	12.00
VANITY			
❑ 589	Love Is a Gamble/If It Isn't for You	1959	25.00

SENTINALS, THE

Number	Title (A Side/B Side)	Yr	NM
45s			
ADMIRAL			
❑ 900	Roughshod/Copy Cat Walk	1961	50.00
DEL-FI			
❑ 4197	Big Surf/Sunset Beach	1963	30.00
ERA			
❑ 3082	Torchula/Latin'ia	1962	30.00
❑ 3097	Christmas Eve/Latin Soul	1962	30.00
❑ 3117	Infinity/Encinada	1963	30.00
—As "The Sentinal Six"			
POINT			
❑ 5100	The Bee/Over You	1963	50.00
❑ 5101	Blue Booze/Bony Moronie	1962	50.00
WCEB			
❑ 23	Torchula/Latin'ia	1962	50.00
WESTCO			
❑ 12	I've Been Blue/Hit the Road	1964	30.00
❑ 14	Tell Me/Hit the Road	1964	30.00
Albums			
DEL-FI			
❑ DFLP-1232 [M]	Big Surf!	1963	100.00
❑ DFST-1232 [S]	Big Surf!	1963	150.00
❑ DLF 1232	Big Surf!	1997	12.00
❑ DFLP-1241 [M]	Surfer Girl	1963	70.00
❑ DFST-1241 [S]	Surfer Girl	1963	100.00
❑ DLF 1241	Surfer Girl	1997	12.00
SUTTON			
❑ SSU-338 [S]	Vegas Go-Go	1964	50.00
❑ SU-338 [M]	Vegas Go-Go	1964	40.00

SEQUINS, THE
More than one group.

Number	Title (A Side/B Side)	Yr	NM
45s			
A&M			
❑ 761	I'll Be Satisfied/Who Says You Can't Jerk to the Old Time Music	1965	12.00
ASCOT			
❑ 2140	You Can't Sit Still/Mr. Leader of the Band	1963	15.00
CAMEO			
❑ 161	To Be Young/The Mountains	1959	20.00
GOLD STAR			
❑ 101	Hey Romeo/I've Got to Overcome	1970	6.00
LOST-NITE			
❑ 344	Why Can't You Treat Me Right/ Don't Fall in Love	197?	5.00
—Reissue			
RED ROBIN			
❑ 140	Why Can't You Treat Me Right/ Don't Fall in Love	1956	400.00
TERRACE			
❑ 7511	Love Me Forever/You're Dancing Now	1962	15.00
❑ 7515	Hideaway/I Ain't Gonna Cry (No More)	1963	15.00

SERENADERS, THE (1)

Number	Title (A Side/B Side)	Yr	NM
45s			
CHOCK FULL O' HITS			
❑ 101	I Wrote a Letter/Never Let Me Go	1957	300.00
❑ 102	Dance Darling, Dance/ Give Me a Girl	1957	200.00
MGM			
❑ 12623	I Wrote a Letter/Never Let Me Go	1958	100.00
❑ 12666	Dance Darling, Dance/ Give Me a Girl	1958	120.00
MOTOWN			
❑ 1046	If Your Heart Says Yes/ I'll Cry Tomorrow	1963	2000.
—VG 1000; VG+ 1500			
RAE COX			
❑ 101	Gotta Go to School/ My Girl Flip-Flop	1959	60.00
RIVERSIDE			
❑ 4549	Adios, My Love/Two Lovers Make One Fool	1963	100.00
V.I.P.			
❑ 25002	If Your Heart Says Yes/ I'll Cry Tomorrow	1964	100.00

SERENADERS, THE (2)

Number	Title (A Side/B Side)	Yr	NM
45s			
CORAL			
❑ 60720	It's Funny/Confession Is Good for the Soul	1952	300.00
❑ 65093	Misery/But I Forgive You	1952	300.00
DELUXE			
❑ 6022	Please, Please Forgive Me/Baby	1953	500.00
JVB			
❑ 2001	Tomorrow Night/Why Don't You Do Right	1952	400.00
LOST-NITE			
❑ 334	Will She Know?/I Want to Love You Baby	197?	5.00
—Reissue			
RED ROBIN			
❑ 115	Will She Know?/I Want to Love You Baby	1953	1500.
SWING TIME			
❑ 347	M-A-Y-B-E-L-L/Ain't Gonna Cry No More	1954	1200.

SERENADERS, THE (3)

Number	Title (A Side/B Side)	Yr	NM
45s			
HANOVER			
❑ 4507	Honolulu/Summer Job	1959	15.00
❑ 4514	Alaska/Where Did You Go	1959	15.00

SERENADERS, THE (U)
Could be group (1) or (2).

Number	Title (A Side/B Side)	Yr	NM
45s			
STARFIRE			
❑ 115	Nite Owl/I'm Gonna Love You	1980	6.00
TEEN LIFE			
❑ 9	Love Me Now/Gates of Gold	1958	700.00

SERENADETTS, THE

Number	Title (A Side/B Side)	Yr	NM
45s			
ENRICA			
❑ 1008	Boyfriend/The Big Night	1961	12.00

SERPENT POWER

Number	Title (A Side/B Side)	Yr	NM
Albums			
VANGUARD			
❑ VRS-9252 [M]	Serpent Power	1967	120.00
❑ VSD-79252 [S]	Serpent Power	1967	60.00

SERRATT, HOWARD

Number	Title (A Side/B Side)	Yr	NM
45s			
SUN			
❑ 198	I Must Be Saved/ Troublesome Waters	1954	2000.

SETZER, BRIAN
Also see STRAY CATS. Also see STRAY CATS.

Number	Title (A Side/B Side)	Yr	NM
12-Inch Singles			
EMI AMERICA			
❑ SPRO-9576 [DJ]	The Knife Feels Like Justice (4:03) (same on both sides)	1985	12.00
❑ SPRO-9665 [DJ]	Boulevard of Broken Dreams (same on both sides)	1986	12.00

S

Except when noted otherwise, VG = 25% of NM, and VG+ = 50% of NM. (Example: VG = $2.00, VG+ = $4.00 and NM = $8.00.)

Number	Title (A Side/B Side)	Yr	NM
❑ SPRO-9719 [DJ]	Chains Around Your Heart (same on both sides)	1986	12.00

EMI MANHATTAN

Number	Title (A Side/B Side)	Yr	NM
❑ SPRO 04008 [DJ]	When the Sky Comes Tumblin' Down (same on both sides)	1988	8.00
❑ 4109 [DJ]	Rebelene (same on both sides)	1988	12.00
❑ SPRO 04109 [DJ]	Rebelene (same on both sides)	1988	12.00
❑ V-56097	When the Sky Comes Tumblin' Down (Extended Mix 5:45) (7" Version 4:13) (Dub Version 7:12) (Dub Instrumental 3:44)/Cross of Love	1988	10.00

45s

EMI AMERICA

Number	Title (A Side/B Side)	Yr	NM
❑ B-8301	The Knife Feels Like Justice/Barbwire Fence	1986	4.00
❑ B-8301 [PS]	The Knife Feels Like Justice/Barbwire Fence	1986	4.00
❑ B-8320	Boulevard of Broken Dreams/Keep Your Lovin' Strong	1986	4.00
❑ B-8320 [PS]	Boulevard of Broken Dreams/Keep Your Lovin' Strong	1986	4.00
❑ B-8336	Chains Around Your Heart/Three Guys	1986	8.00

INTERSCOPE

Number	Title (A Side/B Side)	Yr	NM
❑ 069 497406-7	Gettin' in the Mood (Talkin' Trash Version)/(with trumpet solo)	2000	6.00

—As "Brian Setzer Orchestra"

Albums

EMI AMERICA

Number	Title (A Side/B Side)	Yr	NM
❑ ST-17178	The Knife Feels Like Justice	1986	10.00
❑ ST-517178	The Knife Feels Like Justice	1986	12.00

—Columbia House edition

EMI MANHATTAN

Number	Title (A Side/B Side)	Yr	NM
❑ E1-46963	Live Nude Guitars	1988	12.00

INTERSCOPE

Number	Title (A Side/B Side)	Yr	NM
❑ 90183	The Dirty Boogie	1998	15.00

—As "The Brian Setzer Orchestra"

SURFDOG

Number	Title (A Side/B Side)	Yr	NM
❑ 67124	Ignition!	2001	15.00

—As "Brian Setzer '68 Comeback Special"; red vinyl

SEVEN BLENDS, THE

Albums

ROULETTE

Number	Title (A Side/B Side)	Yr	NM
❑ R-25172 [M]	Twistin' at the Miami Beach Peppermint Lounge	1962	20.00
❑ SR-25172 [S]	Twistin' at the Miami Beach Peppermint Lounge	1962	25.00

SEVEN OF US

45s

RED BIRD

Number	Title (A Side/B Side)	Yr	NM
❑ 10-069	The Way to Your Heart/How Could You	1966	30.00
❑ 10-080	Jamboree/It's Not Easy to Forget	1966	30.00

SEVEN SOULS, THE

45s

OKEH

Number	Title (A Side/B Side)	Yr	NM
❑ 4-7289	I Still Love You/I'm No Stranger	1967	500.00

VENTURE

Number	Title (A Side/B Side)	Yr	NM
❑ 614	Groovin' In/Got to Find a Way	1968	40.00

7TH AVENUE AVIATORS, THE See FRANKIE KARL.

SEVENTH SONS, THE

Albums

ESP-DISK'

Number	Title (A Side/B Side)	Yr	NM
❑ 1078	The Seventh Sons	1967	30.00

SEVENTH WAVE, THE

Albums

JANUS

Number	Title (A Side/B Side)	Yr	NM
❑ 7008	Things to Come	1974	20.00
❑ 7021	Psi-Fi	1975	20.00

SEVERINSON, DOC

45s

AMHERST

Number	Title (A Side/B Side)	Yr	NM
❑ 110	Tonight Show Theme/Skyliner	1986	5.00

COMMAND

Number	Title (A Side/B Side)	Yr	NM
❑ 4039	Cry Me a River/This Is All I Ask	1963	10.00
❑ 4065	It Ain't Necessarily So/Manha de Carnival	1965	8.00
❑ 4071	Phantom Trumpet/You Are My Sunshine	1965	8.00
❑ 4080	In a Little Spanish Town/Tennessee Waltz	1966	8.00
❑ 4084	If He Walked Into My Life/Mothers and Daughters	1966	8.00
❑ 4087	Sunday Morning/When the Saints Go Marching In	1967	8.00
❑ 4091	Is Paris Burning/Walk On By	1967	8.00
❑ 4098	Monday, Monday/Music to Think By	1967	8.00
❑ 4101	Canadian Sunset/One Step Above	1968	6.00
❑ 4117	Trumpets and Crumpets/Free Again	1968	6.00
❑ 4122	Lullaby from "Rosemary's Baby"/That's What Love's About	1968	6.00
❑ 4124	Summer's Coming Back/That's What Love's About	1969	6.00
❑ 4125	Barbarella/Knowing When to Leave	1969	6.00
❑ 4133	Come Together/Carry That Weight	1970	6.00
❑ 4137	Power to the People/Bottleneck	1971	6.00

EPIC

Number	Title (A Side/B Side)	Yr	NM
❑ 9311	Do You Know a Story/Oh, Mr. Dillon	1959	12.00
❑ 50220	I Wanna Be with You/The World's Gone Home	1976	4.00
❑ 50318	Little Tiny Feets/Melody (Aria)	1976	4.00

RCA VICTOR

Number	Title (A Side/B Side)	Yr	NM
❑ 74-0904	Last Tango in Paris/Alone Again	1973	4.00

Albums

ABC

Number	Title (A Side/B Side)	Yr	NM
❑ S-737	16 Great Performances	1971	10.00
❑ X-771	Trumpets, Crumpets	1973	10.00

AMHERST

Number	Title (A Side/B Side)	Yr	NM
❑ AMH-3311	The Tonight Show Band with Doc Severinson	1986	10.00
❑ AMH-3312	The Tonight Show Band with Doc Severinson, Vol. II	1987	10.00
❑ AMH-3319	Facets	1988	10.00

COMMAND

Number	Title (A Side/B Side)	Yr	NM
❑ RS 819 SD [S]	Tempestuous Trumpet	1961	20.00
❑ RS 33-819 [M]	Tempestuous Trumpet	1961	15.00
❑ RS 837 SD [S]	The Big Band's Back in Town	1962	20.00
❑ RS 33-837 [M]	The Big Band's Back in Town	1962	15.00
❑ RS 859 SD [S]	Torch Songs for Trumpet	1963	20.00
❑ RS 33-859 [M]	Torch Songs for Trumpet	1963	15.00
❑ RS 883 SD [S]	High, Wide and Wonderful	1965	20.00
❑ RS 33-883 [M]	High, Wide and Wonderful	1965	15.00
❑ RS 893 SD [S]	Fever!	1966	15.00
❑ RS 33-893 [M]	Fever!	1966	12.00
❑ RS 901 SD [S]	Live!	1966	15.00
❑ RS 33-901 [M]	Live!	1966	12.00
❑ RS 904 SD [S]	Command Performances	1966	15.00
❑ RS 33-904 [M]	Command Performances	1966	12.00
❑ RS 909 SD [S]	Swinging and Singing	1967	12.00
❑ RS 33-909 [M]	Swinging and Singing	1967	15.00
❑ RS 917 SD [S]	The New Sound	1967	12.00
❑ RS 33-917 [M]	The New Sound	1967	15.00
❑ RS 927 SD	The Great Arrival	1968	12.00
❑ RS 937 SD	Doc Severinson with Strings	1969	12.00
❑ RS 950 SD	The Closet	1970	12.00
❑ RS 952 SD	The Best of Doc Severinson	1970	12.00
❑ QD-40003 [Q]	Fever!	1972	15.00

EPIC

Number	Title (A Side/B Side)	Yr	NM
❑ PE 34078	Night Journey	1976	10.00
❑ PE 34925	A Brand New Thing	1977	10.00

EVEREST ARCHIVE OF FOLK & JAZZ

Number	Title (A Side/B Side)	Yr	NM
❑ 334	Doc Severinson and Friends	1978	10.00

FIRSTLINE

Number	Title (A Side/B Side)	Yr	NM
❑ FDLP 5001	London Sessions	1980	12.00

JUNO

Number	Title (A Side/B Side)	Yr	NM
❑ 1001	I Feel Good	1970	12.00

MCA

Number	Title (A Side/B Side)	Yr	NM
❑ 4168 [(2)]	The Best of Doc Severinson	198?	10.00

PICKWICK

Number	Title (A Side/B Side)	Yr	NM
❑ SPC-3608	Torch Songs for Trumpet	1978	8.00
❑ SPC 3627	Tempestuous Trumpet	1978	8.00

RCA VICTOR

Number	Title (A Side/B Side)	Yr	NM
❑ APL1-0273	Rhapsody for Now!	1973	12.00
❑ LSP-4522	Brass Roots	1971	12.00
❑ AFL1-4669	Doc	1977	10.00

—Reissue with new prefix

Number	Title (A Side/B Side)	Yr	NM
❑ LSP-4669	Doc	1972	12.00

SEVILLE, DAVID Also see ROSS BAGDASARIAN; THE CHIPMUNKS.

45s

LIBERTY

Number	Title (A Side/B Side)	Yr	NM
❑ 55041	Armen's Theme/Carousel in Rome	1956	25.00
❑ 55055	The Donkey and the Schoolboy/The Gift	1957	25.00
❑ 55079	Camel Rock/Gotta Get to Your House	1957	25.00
❑ 55079 [PS]	Camel Rock/Gotta Get to Your House	1957	50.00
❑ 55105	Pretty Dark Eyes/Cecelia	1957	25.00
❑ 55113	Bagdad Express/Starlight, Starbright	1957	25.00
❑ 55124	Bonjour Tristesse/Dance from Bonjour Tristesse	1958	25.00
❑ 55132	Witch Doctor/Don't Whistle at Me Baby	1958	30.00
❑ 55140	The Bird on My Head/Hey There Moon	1958	25.00
❑ 55153	Little Brass Band/Take Five	1958	25.00
❑ 55163	The Mountain/Mr. Grape	1958	25.00
❑ 55272	Witch Doctor/Swanee River	1960	20.00
❑ 55314	Oh Judge, Your Honor, Dear Sir, Sweetheart/Freddy, Freddy	1961	25.00

UNITED ARTISTS

Number	Title (A Side/B Side)	Yr	NM
❑ 0063	Witch Doctor/The Bird on My Head	1973	4.00

—"Silver Spotlight Series" reissue

7-Inch Extended Plays

LIBERTY

Number	Title (A Side/B Side)	Yr	NM
❑ LSX-1003	(contents unknown)	1958	40.00
❑ LSX-1003 [PS]	Witch Doctor	1958	40.00

Albums

LIBERTY

Number	Title (A Side/B Side)	Yr	NM
❑ LRP-3073 [M]	The Music of David Seville	1957	80.00
❑ LRP-3092 [M]	The Witch Doctor	1958	100.00

SEVILLE, DAVID, AND THE CHIPMUNKS See THE CHIPMUNKS.

SEVILLES, THE

45s

CAL-GOLD

Number	Title (A Side/B Side)	Yr	NM
❑ 172	Don't You Know I Care/(B-side unknown)	1962	20.00

GALAXY

Number	Title (A Side/B Side)	Yr	NM
❑ 717	Treat You Right/Hey, Hey, Hey	1963	15.00
❑ 721	Charlena/Loving You	1963	15.00
❑ 727	Creation/Baby	1964	15.00

JC

Number	Title (A Side/B Side)	Yr	NM
❑ 116	Charlena/Loving You (Is My Desire)	1960	30.00
❑ 118	Louella/Salt Mine	1961	25.00
❑ 120	Fat Sally/Working Hard	1961	20.00

SEWARD, ALEC

Albums

BLUESVILLE

Number	Title (A Side/B Side)	Yr	NM
❑ BVLP-1076 [M]	Creepin' Blues	1963	80.00

—Blue label, silver print

Number	Title (A Side/B Side)	Yr	NM
❑ BVLP-1076 [M]	Creepin' Blues	1964	25.00

—Blue label, trident logo at right

SEX CLARK FIVE

7-Inch Extended Plays

RECORDS TO RUSSIA

Number	Title (A Side/B Side)	Yr	NM
❑ RTR 916-59	Ketchup If You Can	1991	3.00

—All copies on red vinyl

Number	Title (A Side/B Side)	Yr	NM
❑ RTR 916-59 [PS]	Ketchup If You Can	1991	3.00
❑ RTR-01211	Neita Grew Up Last Night	1986	6.00
❑ RTR-01211 [PS]	Neita Grew Up Last Night	1986	6.00

WERNHER BROS.

Number	Title (A Side/B Side)	Yr	NM
❑ WBEP-001	Martinlutherkinks Hit Parade	1994	3.00

—Clear vinyl

Number	Title (A Side/B Side)	Yr	NM
❑ WBEP-001	Martinlutherkinks Hit Parade	1994	4.00

—Brown vinyl

Number	Title (A Side/B Side)	Yr	NM
❑ WBEP-001 [PS]	Martinlutherkinks Hit Parade	1994	3.00

—Three different covers exist, each of equal value.

Albums

BLOOD MONEY

Number	Title (A Side/B Side)	Yr	NM
❑ ERATO 59	Battle of Sex Clark Five	1989	18.00

RECORDS TO RUSSIA

Number	Title (A Side/B Side)	Yr	NM
❑ LP 408	Strum & Drum!	1986	120.00

—Test pressing with 24 tracks

Number	Title (A Side/B Side)	Yr	NM
❑ LP 408	Strum & Drum!	1987	15.00

—Second pressing: 20 tracks, no halftones, different back photo

Number	Title (A Side/B Side)	Yr	NM
❑ LP 408	Strum & Drum!	1987	20.00

—First pressing: 20 tracks, photos are halftones

SKYCLAD

Number	Title (A Side/B Side)	Yr	NM
❑ (NOT) BM 131	Antedium	1992	15.00

SEX PISTOLS Johnny Rotten would later join Public Image Ltd.

45s

WARNER BROS.

Number	Title (A Side/B Side)	Yr	NM
❑ 8516	Pretty Vacant/Sub-Mission	1978	20.00
❑ 8516 [DJ]	Pretty Vacant (mono/stereo)	1978	10.00
❑ 8516 [PS]	Pretty Vacant/Sub-Mission	1978	10.00

Number	Title (A Side/B Side)	Yr	NM
Albums			
RESTLESS			
❑ 72255	Better Live Than Dead	1988	12.00
❑ 72256 [EP]	The Mini-Album	1988	8.00
❑ 72257	The Ex-Pistols: The Swindle Continues	1988	12.00
❑ 72511	Live at Chelmsford Top Security Prison	1990	18.00
RHINO/WARNER BROS.			
❑ 3147	Never Mind the Bollocks Here's the Sex Pistols	2008	18.00
SKYCLAD			
❑ SEX 6	We've Cum For Your Children	1988	16.00
WARNER BROS.			
❑ BSK 3147	Never Mind the Bollocks Here's the Sex Pistols	1978	16.00
—With white WB label			
❑ BSK 3147	Never Mind the Bollocks Here's the Sex Pistols	1978	25.00
—Any other version with custom label			
❑ BSK 3147	Never Mind the Bollocks Here's the Sex Pistols	1978	30.00
—With sticker "Contains Sub-Mission"			

SEX PISTOLS, THE

Number	Title (A Side/B Side)	Yr	NM
45s			
WARNER BROS.			
❑ 8516 [DJ]	Pretty Vacant (mono/stereo)	1978	10.00

SH-BOOMS, THE
See THE CHORDS.

SHA NA NA

Number	Title (A Side/B Side)	Yr	NM
45s			
KAMA SUTRA			
❑ 503	Lovers Never Say Goodbye/Remember Then	1970	6.00
❑ 507	Pay Day/Rock and Roll Is Here to Stay	1970	6.00
❑ 522	Only One Song/Yakety Yak	1971	6.00
❑ 528	Top Forty of the Lord/I Wonder Why	1971	6.00
❑ 528 [PS]	Top Forty of the Lord/I Wonder Why	1971	10.00
❑ 555	Bounce in Your Buggy/Bless My Soul	1972	6.00
❑ 555 [PS]	Bounce in Your Buggy/Bless My Soul	1972	10.00
❑ 560	In the Still of the Night/Sea Cruise	1972	5.00
❑ 578 [DJ]	In the Still of the Night (mono/stereo)	1973	15.00
—As "Eddie and the Evergreens"; may be promo only			
❑ 592	Maybe I'm Old Fashioned/Stroll All Night	1974	5.00
❑ 592 [PS]	Maybe I'm Old Fashioned/Stroll All Night	1974	10.00
❑ 596	Too Chubby to Boogie/(B-side unknown)	1974	5.00
❑ 602	Just Like Romeo and Juliet/Circles of Love	1975	5.00
❑ 603	You're the Only Light on My Horizon Now	1975	5.00
❑ 604	Shanghied/Chills in My Spine	1975	5.00
RSO			
❑ 909	Rock and Roll Is Here to Stay/Greased Lightnin'	1978	4.00
—B-side by John Travolta			
❑ 930	Blue Moon/Sandy	1979	4.00
—B-side by John Travolta			
Albums			
ACCORD			
❑ SN-7115	Remember Then	1981	10.00
❑ SN-7146	Sh-Boom	1981	10.00
BUDDAH			
❑ BDM-5692	Rock & Roll Is Here to Stay!	1978	10.00
❑ BDM-5703	The Best of Sha Na Na	1978	10.00
EMUS			
❑ ES-12037	On Stage	1978	10.00
KAMA SUTRA			
❑ KSBS-2010	Rock & Roll Is Here to Stay!	1969	15.00
❑ KSBS-2034	Sha Na Na	1971	15.00
❑ KSBS-2050	The Night Is Still Young	1972	15.00
❑ KSBS-2073 [(2)]	The Golden Age of Rock 'n' Roll	1973	20.00
❑ KSBS-2075	From the Streets of New York	1973	15.00
❑ KSBS-2077	Rock & Roll Is Here to Stay!	1974	15.00
❑ KSBS-2600	Hot Sox	1974	15.00
❑ KSBS-2605	Sha Na Now	1975	15.00
❑ KSBS-2609 [(2)]	The Best...Sha Na Na	1976	15.00
NASHVILLE			
❑ NR-12348-122 [(2)]	Rockin' in the 80's	1980	12.00
REALM			
❑ 2V 8058 [(2)]	All-Time Greatest Rock 'n' Roll Hits	1977	15.00
❑ 1V 8059	Rock 'n' Roll Dance Party	1977	12.00

SHA-WEES, THE

Number	Title (A Side/B Side)	Yr	NM
45s			
ALADDIN			
❑ 3170	No One to Love Me/Early Sunday Morning	1953	4000.

SHADES, THE
More than one group.

Number	Title (A Side/B Side)	Yr	NM
45s			
ALADDIN			
❑ 3453	Dear Lori/One Touch of Heaven	1959	300.00
AOK			
❑ 1028	Ginger Bread Man/The Hip	1967	30.00
BIG TOP			
❑ 3003	Sun Glasses/Undivided Attention	1958	100.00
—B-side by The Knott Sisters			

SHADES OF BLUE

Number	Title (A Side/B Side)	Yr	NM
45s			
IMPACT			
❑ 1007	Oh, How Happy/Little Orphan Boy	1966	20.00
❑ 1014	Lonely Summer/With This Ring	1966	20.00
❑ 1015	Happiness/The Night	1966	20.00
❑ 1026	All I Want Is Love/How Do You Save a Dying Love	1967	20.00
❑ 1028	Penny Arcade/Funny Kind of Love	1967	20.00
Albums			
IMPACT			
❑ IM-101 [M]	Happiness Is the Shades of Blue	1966	50.00
❑ IM-1001 [S]	Happiness Is the Shades of Blue	1966	60.00

SHADES OF JOY

Number	Title (A Side/B Side)	Yr	NM
45s			
FONTANA			
❑ 1659	Soul Truth/I Do Like Rock	1969	10.00
Albums			
FONTANA			
❑ SRF-67592	Shades of Joy	1969	20.00

SHADOWS, THE (1)
Backing group for CLIFF RICHARD. Includes early records as "The Drifters" and "The Four Jets." Also see JET HARRIS AND TONY MEEHAN.

Number	Title (A Side/B Side)	Yr	NM
45s			
ABC-PARAMOUNT			
❑ 10073	Saturday Dance/Lonesome Fella	1960	30.00
❑ 10138	Apache/Quartermaster's Stores	1960	30.00
ATLANTIC			
❑ 2111	FBI/The Frightened City	1961	20.00
❑ 2135	Kon-Tiki/Man of Mystery	1962	20.00
❑ 2146	Wonderful Land/Stars Fell on Stockton	1962	20.00
❑ 2166	Guitar Tango/What a Lovely Thing	1962	20.00
❑ 2177	Dance On/The Rumble	1963	20.00
❑ 2235	Theme for Young Lovers/The Rise and Fall of Flingel Bunt	1964	20.00
❑ 2257	Rhythm and Greens/The Miracle	1964	20.00
CAPITOL			
❑ F-4220	Feelin' Fine/Don't Be a Fool	1959	40.00
—As "The Drifters"			
❑ F-4270	Driftin'/Jet Black	1959	40.00
—As "The Four Jets"			
EPIC			
❑ 9793	Mary Anne/Chu Chi	1965	20.00
❑ 9826	Stingray/Alice in Sunderland	1965	20.00
❑ 9848	Don't Make My Baby Blue/My Grandfather's Clock	1965	20.00
❑ 10020	I Met a Girl/Last Night Set	1966	20.00
Albums			
ATLANTIC			
❑ 8084 [M]	Out of the Shadows	1962	200.00
—Canada-only release?			
❑ 8089 [M]	Surfing with the Shadows	1963	150.00
❑ SD 8089 [S]	Surfing with the Shadows	1963	300.00
❑ 8097 [M]	The Shadows Know	1964	100.00
❑ SD 8097 [S]	The Shadows Know	1964	200.00

SHADOWS, THE (2)

Number	Title (A Side/B Side)	Yr	NM
45s			
DECCA			
❑ 28765	No Use/Stay	1953	250.00
❑ 48307	Tell Her/Don't Be Bashful	1954	300.00
❑ 48322	Big Mouth Mama/Better Than Gold	1954	300.00

SHADOWS, THE (3)

Number	Title (A Side/B Side)	Yr	NM
45s			
DEL-FI			
❑ 4109	Under the Stars of Love/Jungle Fever	1958	60.00

SHADOWS, THE (4)

Number	Title (A Side/B Side)	Yr	NM
45s			
DOTTIE			
❑ 1006	I Wonder Why/Tell This Lonely Heart Goodbye	1961	20.00

SHADOWS, THE (U)
Could be group (3) or an entirely different group.

Number	Title (A Side/B Side)	Yr	NM
45s			
DELTA			
❑ 1509	Bop-A-Lena/There Stands the Glass	1958	200.00

SHADOWS OF KNIGHT, THE

Number	Title (A Side/B Side)	Yr	NM
45s			
ATCO			
❑ 6634	Gloria '69/A Spaniard at My Door	1968	16.00
❑ 6776	I Am the Hunter/Warwick County Affair	1970	16.00
AURAVISION			
❑ (no #)	Potato Chip	196?	60.00
—One-sided cardboard disc, 5 inches wide with small hole			
DUNWICH			
❑ 116	Gloria/Dark Side	1966	15.00
—Dark pink and yellow label; other label variations may exist			
❑ 116	Gloria/Dark Side	1966	20.00
—Yellow label, "Distributed by Atco Record Sales Co."			
❑ 116	Gloria/Dark Side	1966	25.00
—Gold label, no mention of Atco Records			
❑ 122	Oh Yeah/Light Bulb Blues	1966	20.00
❑ 122 [PS]	Oh Yeah/Light Bulb Blues	1966	30.00
❑ 128	Bad Little Woman/Gospel Zone	1966	15.00
❑ 128 [PS]	Bad Little Woman/Gospel Zone	1966	200.00
❑ 141	I'm Gonna Make You Mine/I'll Make You Sorry	1966	25.00
❑ 151	The Behemoth/Willie Jean	1967	20.00
❑ 167	Someone Like Me/There for Love	1967	20.00
PHONOGRAPH			
❑ 1002/2001	Sweetness in Motion/Nikki-Hoki (No One Else Will Ever Do)	1986	8.00
SUPER K			
❑ 108	Taurus/My Fire Department Needs a Fireman	1969	10.00
❑ 110	Run, Run, Billy Porter/My Fire Department Needs a Fireman	1969	10.00
TEAM			
❑ 520	Shake/From Way Out to Way In	1968	16.00
Albums			
DUNWICH			
❑ 666 [M]	Gloria	1966	50.00
❑ S-666 [S]	Gloria	1966	80.00
❑ 667 [M]	Back Door Men	1966	50.00
❑ S-667 [S]	Back Door Men	1966	80.00
SUNDAZED			
❑ LP 5006	Raw and Live at the Cellar 1966	1992	10.00
❑ LP 5034	Gloria	1999	12.00
—Reissue on 180-gram vinyl			
❑ LP 5035	Back Door Men	1999	12.00
—Reissue on 180-gram vinyl			
SUPER K			
❑ SKS-6002	The Shadows of Knight	1969	50.00

SHADRACK

Number	Title (A Side/B Side)	Yr	NM
Albums			
IGL			
❑ 132	Chameleon	1971	300.00

SHAFTO, BOBBY

Number	Title (A Side/B Side)	Yr	NM
45s			
RUST			
❑ 5082	She's My Girl/Wonderful You	1964	10.00
❑ 5092	I'll Never Get Over You/Who Wouldn't Love a Girl Like That	1964	10.00
❑ 5096	Baby Then/How Could You Do a Thing Like That to Me	1965	10.00
❑ 5108	Lonely Is As Lonely Does/The Same Old Room	1966	12.00
❑ 5110	See Me Cry/A Little Like You	1966	10.00

SHAG, THE

Number	Title (A Side/B Side)	Yr	NM
45s			
CAPITOL			
❑ 5995	Stop and Listen/Melissa	1967	40.00

S

Except when noted otherwise, VG = 25% of NM, and VG+ = 50% of NM. (Example: VG = $2.00, VG+ = $4.00 and NM = $8.00.)

Number	Title (A Side/B Side)	Yr	NM

SHAGGS, THE (1)

45s

CAPITOL

❑ 2511	Mean Woman Blues/ She Makes Me Happy	1969	10.00

SHAGGS, THE (2) This all-male band comprised students at the University of Notre Dame.

Albums

MCM

❑ 1295	Wink	1967	250.00

—No number on label — this number is found in the trail-off wax on each side

SHAGGS, THE (3) This band comprised three sisters from New Hampshire attempting to sing and play.

45s

FLEETWOOD

❑ 4584	My Pal Foot-Foot/ Things I Wonder	1969	—

—Listed on a Fleetwood Records discography, but was it ever released?

Albums

ROUNDER

❑ 3032	Philosophy of the World	1980	25.00
❑ 3056	Shaggs' Own Thing	1982	25.00

THIRD WORLD

❑ 3001	Philosophy of the World	1969	2000.

SHAGGY BOYS, THE

45s

RED BIRD

❑ 10-074	Stop the Clock/In the Morning	1966	15.00

UNITED ARTISTS

❑ 50100	You and Me/Joy in the Morning	1966	15.00
❑ 50135	That's the Only Way/Behind These Stained Glass Windows	1967	15.00

SHAGS, THE Probably more than one group.

45s

CAMEO

❑ 470	Tell Me/As Long As I Have You	1967	20.00

GOLDEN VOICE

❑ 3112	What Am I to Do/It Ain't Easy	1967	25.00
❑ 3112 [PS]	What Am I to Do/It Ain't Easy	1967	75.00
❑ 3114	Talk to a Sidewalk/Did I Say (That I Love You)	1967	25.00
❑ 3114 [PS]	Talk to a Sidewalk/Did I Say (That I Love You)	1967	75.00

KAYDEN

❑ 407	Tell Me/As Long As I Have You	1966	40.00
❑ 408	Breathe in My Ear/Easy Street	1966	25.00

LAURIE

❑ 3353	I Call Your Name/Hide Away	1966	25.00

NUTTA

❑ 1018	Wait and See/It Hurts Me Bad	196?	20.00

TAURUS

❑ 1881	Don't Press Your Luck/ Hey Little Girl	1967	150.00

SHAKERS, THE

45s

ABC

❑ 10960	Love, Love, Love/One Wonderful Moment	1967	8.00

AUDIO FIDELITY

❑ 119	Break It All/Ticket to Ride	1966	10.00

Albums

AUDIO FIDELITY

❑ AFLP-2155 [M]	The Shakers Break It All	1966	40.00
❑ AFSD-6155 [S]	The Shakers Break It All	1966	50.00

SHAKEY JAKE

45s

BLUESVILLE

❑ 807	My Foolish Heart/Jake's Blues	1960	20.00

Albums

BLUESVILLE

❑ BVLP-1008 [M]	Good Times	1960	120.00
—Blue label, silver print			
❑ BVLP-1008 [M]	Good Times	1964	30.00
—Blue label, trident logo at right			
❑ BVLP-1027 [M]	Mouth Harp Blues	1961	120.00
—Blue label, silver print			
❑ BVLP-1027 [M]	Mouth Harp Blues	1964	30.00
—Blue label, trident logo at right			

WORLD PACIFIC

❑ WPS-21886	Blues Makers	196?	30.00

SHAKEY VICK

Albums

JANUS

❑ JLS-3000	Little Woman, You're So Sweet	1970	20.00

SHAM 69

Albums

SIRE

❑ SRK-6060	Tell Us the Truth	1978	15.00

SHAM-ETTES, THE

45s

MGM

❑ 13618	Big Bad Wolf (Hey There)/ I'd Rather Have You	1966	15.00
❑ 13798	He'll Come Back/You're Welcome Back	1967	12.00

SHANE, BOB Also see THE KINGSTON TRIO.

45s

DECCA

❑ 32239	Simple Gifts/Weeping Annaleah	1967	10.00
❑ 32275	Honey/I Don't Think of You Anymore	1968	10.00

SHANGRI-LAS, THE

45s

LANA

❑ 143	Leader of the Pack/What Is Love	196?	10.00

—Oldies reissue

MERCURY

❑ 72645	I'll Never Learn/Sweet Sounds of Summer	1966	20.00
❑ 72670	Footsteps on the Roof/ Take the Time	1967	20.00

RED BIRD

❑ 10-008	Remember (Walkin' in the Sand)/It's Easier to Cry	1964	25.00
❑ 10-014	Leader of the Pack/ What Is Love	1964	25.00
❑ 10-018	Give Him a Great Big Kiss/ Twist and Shout	1964	25.00
❑ 10-019	Maybe/Shout	1964	20.00
❑ 10-025	Out in the Streets/The Boy	1965	20.00
❑ 10-030	Give Us Your Blessings/ Heaven Only Knows	1965	20.00
❑ 10-036	Right Now and Not Later/ The Train from Kansas City	1965	20.00
❑ 10-043	I Can Never Go Home Anymore/Bull Dog	1965	20.00
❑ 10-043	I Can Never Go Home Anymore/Sophisticated Boom Boom	1965	30.00
❑ 10-048	Long Live Our Love/Bull Dog	1966	20.00
❑ 10-048	Long Live Our Love/ Sophisticated Boom Boom	1966	20.00
❑ 10-053	He Cried/Dressed in Black	1966	20.00
❑ 10-068	Past, Present and Future/Love You More Than Yesterday	1966	20.00
❑ 10-068	Past, Present and Future/ Paradise	1966	20.00

SCEPTER

❑ 1291	Wishing Well/Hate to Say I Told You So	1964	20.00

SMASH

❑ 1866	Simon Says/Simon Speaks	1963	40.00

SPOKANE

❑ 4006	Wishing Well/Hate to Say I Told You So	1964	30.00

Albums

COLLECTABLES

❑ COL-5011	Remember…Their Greatest Hits	198?	10.00

MERCURY

❑ MG-21099 [M]	The Shangri-Las' Golden Hits	1966	40.00
❑ SR-61099 [S]	The Shangri-Las' Golden Hits	1966	50.00

POLYDOR

❑ 824807-1	Golden Hits of the Shangri-Las	1985	10.00

POST

❑ 4000	The Shangri-Las Sing	196?	20.00

RED BIRD

❑ 20101 [M]	Leader of the Pack	1965	150.00
❑ 20104 [M]	Shangri-Las '65	1965	150.00
❑ 20104 [M]	I Can Never Go Home Anymore	1966	100.00

—Retitled version with title song added and "Sophisticated Boom Boom" dropped

SHANK AND MAYDIEA

45s

FLIP

❑ 361	Why Don't You Tell Me/ Bye Bye Baby (My Pride)	1962	10.00

SHANKAR, ANANDA

Albums

REPRISE

❑ RS-6398	Ananda Shankar	1970	20.00

SHANKAR, RAVI Also see GEORGE HARRISON AND FRIENDS.

45s

APPLE

❑ 1838	Joi Bangla-Oh Bhaugowan/ Raga Mishra-Jhinjhoti	1971	8.00
—By Ravi Shankar & Ali Akbar with Alla Rakah			
❑ 1838 [PS]	Joi Bangla-Oh Bhaugowan/ Raga Mishra-Jhinjhoti	1971	20.00

DARK HORSE

❑ 10001	I Am Missing You/Lost	1974	5.00

SPARK

❑ SP-07	Transmigration/ (B-side unknown)	1973	6.00

—As "R. Shankar"

WORLD PACIFIC

❑ 77871	Pather Panchali/Gat Kirawani	1967	8.00
❑ 77898	Charly Theme/Love Montage	1968	8.00

Albums

ANGEL

❑ 35468 [M]	Music of India	196?	25.00
❑ S 36026 [S]	West Meets East, Vol. 2	1968	15.00
❑ 36418 [M]	West Meets East	1967	25.00
—With Yahudi Menuhin			
❑ S 36418 [S]	West Meets East	1967	20.00
—With Yahudi Menuhin			
❑ S 36806	Concerto for Sitar and Orchestra	1972	12.00
❑ DS-37920	Raga Mishra Piloo	1982	10.00
❑ DS-37935	Raga-Mala (Sitar Concert No. 2)	1983	10.00

APPLE

❑ SWAO-3384	Raga	1971	25.00
❑ SVBB-3396 [(2)]	Ravi Shankar In Concert	1973	40.00

BLUESVILLE

❑ BVLP-1078 [M]	The Master Musician of India	1964	25.00

CAPITOL

❑ DT 2720 [R]	Three Ragas	1967	15.00
❑ T 2720 [M]	Three Ragas	1967	20.00
❑ ST 10482 [S]	Two Raga Moods	196?	25.00
❑ T 10482 [M]	Two Raga Moods	196?	20.00
❑ ST 10497 [S]	Exotic Sitar and Sarod	196?	25.00
❑ T 10497 [M]	Exotic Sitar and Sarod	196?	20.00
❑ ST 10504	Ravi	196?	15.00
❑ SP-10561	Raga Parameshwari	1972	12.00

COLUMBIA

❑ WL 119 [M]	The Sounds of India	196?	25.00
❑ CL 2496 [M]	Sounds of India	1966	15.00
❑ CL 2760 [M]	The Genius of Ravi Shankar	1967	20.00
❑ OS 3230	Chappaqua	1968	15.00
❑ CS 9296 [S]	Sounds of India	1966	20.00
❑ CS 9560 [S]	The Genius of Ravi Shankar	1967	15.00

DARK HORSE

❑ SP 22002	Shankar Family and Friends	1974	12.00
❑ SP 22007	Music Festival from India	1975	12.00

DEUTCHE GRAMMOPHON

❑ 2531 216	Ragas Hameer & Gara	198?	10.00
❑ 2531 280	Raga Jogeshwari	198?	10.00
❑ 2531 356	Homage to Mahatma Gandhi; Homage to Baba Allauddin	198?	10.00
❑ 2531 381	Pad Hasapa, for Koto; etc.	198?	10.00

FANTASY

❑ 24714 [(2)]	Ragas	1973	15.00

ORIENTAL

❑ BGRP-108	Raga Sanjh Kalyan	198?	10.00

PRIVATE MUSIC

❑ 2016-1-P	The Shankar Project: Tana Mana	1988	10.00
❑ 2044-1-P	Inside the Kremlin	1989	10.00

SPARK

❑ 06	Transmigration Macabre	1973	12.00

WORLD PACIFIC

❑ WP-1421 [M]	Ravi Shankar In Concert	1965	15.00
❑ WP-1422 [M]	India's Master Musician	1965	15.00
❑ WP-1430 [M]	Ravi Shankar In London	1966	15.00
❑ WP-1431 [M]	Ragas and Talas	1966	15.00
❑ WP-1432 [M]	Portrait of Genius	1966	15.00
❑ WP-1434 [M]	Sound of the Sitar	1967	15.00
❑ WP-1438 [M]	Three Ragas	1967	15.00
❑ WP-1441 [M]	Ravi Shankar in New York	1967	15.00
❑ WP-1442 [M]	Ravi Shankar at the Monterey International Pop Festival	1967	20.00
❑ ST-21421 [S]	Ravi Shankar In Concert	1965	20.00
❑ ST-21422 [S]	India's Master Musician	1965	20.00
❑ ST-21430 [S]	Ravi Shankar In London	1966	20.00
❑ ST-21431 [S]	Ragas and Talas	1966	20.00
❑ ST-21432 [S]	Portrait of Genius	1966	20.00

S

Number	Title (A Side/B Side)	Yr	NM
ST-21434 [S]	Sound of the Sitar	1967	20.00
ST-21438 [S]	Three Ragas	1967	20.00
ST-21441 [S]	Ravi Shankar in New York	1967	20.00
ST-21442 [S]	Ravi Shankar at the Monterey International Pop Festival	1967	20.00
ST-21449	Ravi Shankar in San Francisco	1968	20.00
ST-21454	Charly	1969	15.00
ST-21464	Morning Raga/Evening Raga	1970	15.00
ST-21467	Ravi Shankar at Woodstock	1970	15.00
WPS-26201 [(2)]	His Festival from India	1968	20.00

SHANNON See MARTY WILDE.

SHANNON, DEL

45s

ABC DUNHILL

Number	Title (A Side/B Side)	Yr	NM
4193	Sweet Mary Lou/Comin' Back to me	1969	15.00
4224	Sister Isabelle/Colorado Rain	1970	15.00
AMY			
897	Mary Jane/Stains on My Letter	1964	25.00
905	Handy Man/Give Her Lots of Lovin'	1964	15.00
911	Do You Want to Dance/This Is All I Have to Give	1964	15.00
915	Keep Searchin' (We'll Follow the Sun)/Broken Promises	1964	16.00
919	Stranger in Town/Over You	1965	16.00
925	Why Don't You Tell Him/Break Up	1965	15.00
937	Move It On Over/She Still Remembers Tony	1965	15.00
947	I Can't Believe My Ears/I Wish I Wasn't Me Tonight	1966	40.00
—Withdrawn shortly after release; promos worth about half these values			
BERLEE			
501	Sue's Gotta Be Mine/Now She's Gone	1963	15.00
502	That's the Way Love Is/Time of the Day	1964	15.00
BIG TOP			
3067	Runaway/Jody	1961	30.00
3075	Hats Off to Larry/Don't Gild the Lily, Lily	1961	25.00
3083	So Long Baby/The Answer to Everything	1961	25.00
3091	Hey! Little Girl/I Don't Care Anymore	1961	25.00
3098	Ginny in the Mirror/I Won't Be There	1962	25.00
3112	Cry Myself to Sleep/I'm Gonna Move On	1962	25.00
3117	The Swiss Maid/You Never Talked About Me	1962	25.00
3131	Little Town Flirt/The Wamboo	1962	25.00
3143	Two Kinds of Teardrops/Kelly	1963	25.00
3152	From Me to You/Two Silhouettes	1963	60.00
—A-side is the first American version of a Beatles song			
ERIC			
189 [S]	Runaway/Hats Off to Larry	1972	6.00
—Both sides of this reissue are the original recordings in true stereo!			
ISLAND			
021	Tell Her No/Restless	1975	15.00
038	Cry Baby Cry/In My Arms Again	1975	15.00
LANA			
141	Runaway/Jody	196?	8.00
—Oldies reissue			
142	Hats Off to Larry/Don't Gild the Lily, Lily	196?	8.00
—Oldies reissue			
LIBERTY			
55866	The Big Hurt/I Got It Bad	1966	12.00
55889	Hey Little Star/For a Little While	1966	12.00
55894	Show Me/Never Thought I Could	1966	12.00
55904	Under My Thumb/She Was Mine	1966	12.00
55939	She/What Makes You Run	1967	12.00
55961	Led Along/I Can't Be True	1967	12.00
55993	Runaway '67/He Cheated	1967	15.00
56018	Runnin' On Back/Thinkin' It Over	1968	10.00
56018 [PS]	Runnin' On Back/Thinkin' It Over	1968	30.00
56036	Magical Musical Box/Gemini	1968	10.00
56070	Raindrops/You Don't Love Me	1968	10.00
LOST-NITE			
220	Runaway/Hey Little Girl	196?	5.00
—Reissue			
222	Hats Off to Larry/Little Town Flirt	196?	5.00
—Reissue			
NETWORK			
47951	Sea of Love/Midnight Train	1981	5.00
48006	To Love Someone/Liar	1982	5.00
TWIRL			
4001	Runaway/Hey Little Girl	196?	6.00
4002	Hats Off to Larry/Little Town Flirt	196?	6.00
WARNER BROS.			
28853	Stranger on the Run/What You Gonna Do with That	1985	5.00
29098	In My Arms Again/You Can't Forgive Me	1985	5.00

Albums

AMY

Number	Title	Yr	NM
8003 [M]	Handy Man	1964	50.00
S-8003 [S]	Handy Man	1964	80.00
8004 [M]	Del Shannon Sings Hank Williams	1965	50.00
S-8004 [S]	Del Shannon Sings Hank Williams	1965	80.00
8006 [M]	1,661 Seconds with Del Shannon	1965	50.00
S-8006 [S]	1,661 Seconds with Del Shannon	1965	80.00
BIG TOP			
12-1303 [M]	Runaway	1961	300.00
12-1303 [S]	Runaway	1961	1600.
12-1308 [B]	Little Town Flirt	1963	1000.
—One side is mono, one side is stereo; should be played to identify			
12-1308 [M]	Little Town Flirt	1963	150.00
12-1308 [S]	Little Town Flirt	1963	1500.
—Stereo copies are not identified as such on either cover or label; some, but not all, copies have an "S" in the dead wax. Playing is the best way to identify.			
DOT			
DLP 3824 [M]	The Best of Del Shannon	1967	50.00
DLP 25824 [R]	The Best of Del Shannon	1967	40.00
ELEKTRA			
5E-568	Drop Down and Get Me	1981	10.00
LIBERTY			
LRP-3453 [M]	This Is My Bag	1966	30.00
LRP-3479 [M]	Total Commitment	1966	30.00
LRP-3539 [M]	The Further Adventures of Charles Westover	1967	50.00
LST-7453 [S]	This Is My Bag	1966	40.00
LST-7479 [S]	Total Commitment	1966	40.00
LST-7539 [S]	The Further Adventures of Charles Westover	1967	80.00
PICKWICK			
SPC-3595 [R]	The Best of Del Shannon	197?	10.00
POST			
9000 [R]	Del Shannon Sings	196?	40.00
RHINO			
RNLP-71056 [M]	Runaway Hits	1986	10.00
SIRE			
SASH-3708 [(2)P]	The Vintage Years	1975	25.00
TWIRL			
5001 [M]	Del Shannon's Greatest Hits	196?	200.00
—LP was never issued; price is for front cover slick, which is known to exist			
UNITED ARTISTS			
UA-LA151-E	Del Shannon Live in England	1973	25.00

SHANNON, JACKIE See JACKIE DeSHANNON.

SHANNON, KATHY

45s

HIT

Number	Title (A Side/B Side)	Yr	NM
290	Love Eyes/This Is My Song	1967	8.00
296	Don't Sleep in the Subway/Jackson	1967	8.00
—B-side by Jack and Sherry Young			
298	I Take It Back/Little Bit o' Soul	1967	8.00
—B-side by the Chellows			
303	Ode to Billie Joe/White Rabbit	1967	8.00
—B-side by the Chords (2)			
310	It Must Be Him/The Rain, the Park, and Other Things	1967	8.00
—B-side by the Flowers			
311	To Sir with Love/Even the Bad Times Are Good	1967	8.00
—B-side by the Jalopy Five			
323	(Theme from) Valley of the Dolls/Scarborough Fair (/Canticle)	1968	8.00
—B-side by Sammy and Theodore			
327	Do You Know the Way to San Jose/Cry Like a Baby	1968	8.00
—B-side by the Jalopy Five			
334	Angel of the Morning/Jumpin' Jack Flash	1968	8.00
—B-side by the Jalopy Five			
340	The House That Jack Built/1-2-3, Red Light	1968	8.00
—B-side by the Fantastics			
343	Harper Valley P.T.A./Hey Jude	1968	8.00
—B-side by the Jalopy Five			
346	Those Were the Days/Girl Watcher	1968	8.00
—B-side by the Chords (2)			
353	Son-of-a-Preacher-Man/Worst That Could Happen	1969	8.00
—B-side by the Chords (2)			

SHANNON, PAT

45s

AMOS

Number	Title (A Side/B Side)	Yr	NM
152	I Ain't Got Time Anymore/(B-side unknown)	1970	5.00
163	Liar/Something's Coming My Way	1971	5.00
CAPITOL			
3802	Eleanor Jones/102 Times a Day	1973	4.00
DECCA			
30545	Maybelle/Knock, Knock, Who's There	1958	12.00
30666	You're So Wild/Awaiting Love	1958	30.00
30751	Summer's Over/We Found Love	1958	12.00
30905	Summertime's Comin'/The Snake and the Bookworm	1959	12.00
31072	Everything But You/So Happy Now	1960	12.00
UNI			
55191	Back to Dreamin' Again/Moody	1969	5.00
55229	It's So Easy/102 Times a Day	1970	5.00
55229	It's So Easy/The Story of Your Life	1970	5.00
WARNER BROS.			
7210	Candy Apple, Cotton Candy/She Sleeps Alone	1968	6.00
7237	Here They Come Again/Run to Home	1968	6.00

SHANTONS, THE

45s

JAY-MAR

Number	Title (A Side/B Side)	Yr	NM
(# unknown)	Triangle Love/Lover's March	1959	400.00
241	To Be in Love with You/Lucille	1959	800.00
1292	The Christmas Song/Santa Claus Is Coming to Town	1960	200.00

SHANTY BOYS, THE

Albums

ELEKTRA

Number	Title	Yr	NM
EKL-142 [M]	Off-Beat Folk Songs	1958	30.00

SHAPIRO, HELEN

45s

CAPITOL

Number	Title (A Side/B Side)	Yr	NM
4561	Don't Treat Me Like a Child/When I'm With You	1961	12.00
4627	You Don't Know/A Marvelous Lie	1961	12.00
4662	Walkin' Back to Happiness/Kiss 'N' Run	1961	12.00
4735	Tell Me What He Said/I Apologize	1962	12.00
EPIC			
9549	Little Miss Lonely/Keep Away from Other Girls	1962	12.00
9599	Woe Is Me/No Trespassing	1963	12.00
JANUS			
120	A Glass of Wine/Waiting on the Shores of Nowhere	1970	6.00
MUSICOR			
1075	It Might As Well Rain Until September/Shop Around	1965	10.00
TOWER			
346	Make Me Belong to You/The Way of the World	1967	8.00

Albums

EPIC

Number	Title	Yr	NM
LN 24075 [M]	A Teenager in Love	1962	25.00
BN 26075 [S]	A Teenager in Love	1962	30.00

SHARKS

45s

MCA

Number	Title (A Side/B Side)	Yr	NM
40120	Follow Me/Ole Jelly Roll	1973	5.00
40246	Kung Fu/Elevator Dancing	1974	5.00

Albums

MCA

Number	Title	Yr	NM
351	First Water	1973	15.00
415	Jab It in Your Eye	1974	15.00

S

Except when noted otherwise, VG = 25% of NM, and VG+ = 50% of NM. (Example: VG = $2.00, VG+ = $4.00 and NM = $8.00.)

SHARMEERS, THE

Number	Title (A Side/B Side)	Yr	NM
45s			
RED TOP			
❑ 109	A School Girl in Love/You're My Love	1958	150.00

SHARMETTES, THE

Number	Title (A Side/B Side)	Yr	NM
45s			
KING			
❑ 5648	Answer Me/My Dream	1962	15.00
❑ 5686	I Want to Be Loved/Tell Me	1962	15.00

SHARON MARIE

Number	Title (A Side/B Side)	Yr	NM
45s			
CAPITOL			
❑ 5064	Run-Around Lover/Summertime	1963	250.00
❑ 5195	The Story of My Life/Thinkin' 'Bout You Baby	1964	200.00

—Both these records were produced by Brian Wilson

SHARP, DEE DEE
Includes records as "Dee Dee Sharp Gamble."

Number	Title (A Side/B Side)	Yr	NM
45s			
ATCO			
❑ 6445	Bye Bye Baby/My Best Friend's Man	1966	10.00
❑ 6502	Baby I Love You/What Am I Gonna Do	1967	8.00
❑ 6557	We Got a Thing Goin' On/What 'Cha Gonna Do About It	1968	8.00
—With Ben E. King			
❑ 6576	Woman Will Do Wrong/You're Just a Fool in Love	1968	8.00
❑ 6587	This Love Won't Run Out/Help Me Find My Glove	1968	8.00
CAMEO			
❑ 212	Mashed Potato Time/Set My Heart at Ease	1962	20.00
❑ 219	Gravy (For My Mashed Potatoes)/Baby Cakes	1962	15.00
❑ 219 [PS]	Gravy (For My Mashed Potatoes)/Baby Cakes	1962	25.00
❑ 230	Ride!/The Night	1962	15.00
❑ 230 [PS]	Ride!/The Night	1962	25.00
❑ 244	Do the Bird/Lover Boy	1963	15.00
❑ 244 [PS]	Do the Bird/Lover Boy	1963	25.00
❑ 260	Rock Me in the Cradle of Love/You'll Never Be Mine	1963	15.00
❑ 260 [PS]	Rock Me in the Cradle of Love/You'll Never Be Mine	1963	25.00
❑ 274	Wild!/Why Doncha Ask Me	1963	15.00
❑ 274 [PS]	Wild!/Why Doncha Ask Me	1963	25.00
❑ 296	Where Did I Go Wrong/Willyam, Willyam	1964	12.00
❑ 296 [PS]	Where Did I Go Wrong/Willyam, Willyam	1964	20.00
❑ 329	Never Pick a Pretty Boy/He's No Ordinary Guy	1964	12.00
❑ 335	Deep Dark Secret/Good	1964	500.00
❑ 347	To Know Him Is to Love Him/There Ain't Nothin' I Wouldn't Do for You	1965	10.00
❑ 357	Let's Twine/That's What My Mama Said	1965	10.00
❑ 375	I Really Love You/Standing in the Need of Love	1965	10.00
❑ 375 [PS]	I Really Love You/Standing in the Need of Love	1965	15.00
❑ 382	It's a Funny Situation/There Ain't Nothin' I Wouldn't Do for You	1965	10.00
FAIRMOUNT			
❑ 1004	(It's Wonderful) The Love I Feel for You/Willyam, Wilyam	1966	10.00
GAMBLE			
❑ 219	What Kind of Lady/You're Gonna Miss Me (When I'm Gone)	1968	20.00
❑ 4005	The Bottle or Me/You're Gonna Miss Me (When I'm Gone)	1969	15.00
PHILADELPHIA INT'L.			
❑ 02041	Breaking and Entering/I Love You Anyway	1981	4.00
❑ 3512	Conquer the World Together/We Gotta Good Thing Goin'	1971	6.00
—With Bunny Sigler			
❑ 3625	Flashback/Nobody Can Take Your Place	1977	5.00
❑ 3636	I'd Really Love to See You Tonight/What Color Is Love	1977	5.00
❑ 3638	I Believe in Love/Just As Long As I Know You're Mine	1978	5.00
❑ 3644	Tryin' to Get the Feeling Again/I Wanna Be Your Woman	1978	5.00
❑ 70058	I Love You Anyway/Easy Money	1981	4.00
—Philadelphia International records as "Dee Dee Sharp Gamble"			
TSOP			
❑ 4776	Happy 'Bout the Whole Thing/Touch My Life	1976	5.00
❑ 4778	I'm Not in Love/Make It Till Tomorrow	1976	5.00
Albums			
CAMEO			
❑ C-1018 [M]	It's Mashed Potato Time	1962	60.00
❑ C-1022 [M]	Songs of Faith	1962	40.00
❑ SC-1022 [S]	Songs of Faith	1962	50.00
❑ C-1027 [M]	All the Hits	1962	40.00
❑ SC-1027 [S]	All the Hits	1962	50.00
❑ C-1032 [M]	All the Hits, Vol. 2	1963	40.00
❑ SC-1032 [S]	All the Hits, Vol. 2	1963	50.00
❑ C-1050 [M]	Do the Bird	1963	40.00
❑ SC-1050 [S]	Do the Bird	1963	50.00
❑ C-1062 [M]	Biggest Hits	1963	40.00
❑ C-1074 [M]	Down Memory Lane	1963	40.00
❑ C-2002 [M]	18 Golden Hits	1964	40.00
❑ SC-2002 [S]	18 Golden Hits	1964	50.00
PHILADELPHIA INT'L.			
❑ PZ 33839	Happy 'Bout the Whole Thing	1976	10.00
❑ PZ 34437	What Color Is Love	1977	10.00
❑ JZ 36370	Dee Dee	1980	10.00

SHARP, DEE DEE, AND CHUBBY CHECKER
Also see each artist's individual listings.

Number	Title (A Side/B Side)	Yr	NM
45s			
CAMEO			
❑ 103 [DJ]	Do You Love Me?/One More Time	1962	40.00
—Yellow label, black print, promo only			
Albums			
CAMEO			
❑ C-1029 [M]	Down to Earth	1962	40.00
❑ SC-1029 [S]	Down to Earth	1962	50.00

SHARP, RANDY

Number	Title (A Side/B Side)	Yr	NM
Albums			
NAUTILUS			
❑ NR-1	First in Line	1980	40.00
—Standard cover			
❑ NR-1	First in Line	1980	50.00
—Styrofoam cover			

SHARP, ROSEMARY

Number	Title (A Side/B Side)	Yr	NM
45s			
CANYON CREEK			
❑ 0210	The Stairs/Until I Fall in Love Again	1988	5.00
❑ 0401	Real Good Heartache/(B-side unknown)	1987	6.00
❑ 0908	If You're Gonna Tell Me Lies (Tell Me Good Ones)/(B-side unknown)	1987	6.00
❑ 1226	Didn't You Go and Leave Me/(B-side unknown)	1986	6.00

SHARPE, RAY

Number	Title (A Side/B Side)	Yr	NM
45s			
A&M			
❑ 1297	Dream On, Donna/Another Piece of the Puzzle	1971	5.00
ATCO			
❑ 6402	Help Me (Get the Feeling) Part 1/Help Me (Get the Feeling) Part 2	1966	10.00
❑ 6437	I Can't Take It/Mary Jane	1966	10.00
DOT			
❑ 15788	Oh, My Baby's Gone/That's the Way I Feel	1958	15.00
❑ 15974	Oh, My Baby's Gone/That's the Way I Feel	1959	12.00
GREGMARK			
❑ 14	(The New) Linda Lu/The Bus Song	1963	12.00
HAMILTON			
❑ 50002	Oh, My Baby's Gone/That's the Way I Feel	1959	10.00
JAMIE			
❑ 1128	Linda Lu/Red Sails in the Sunset	1959	15.00
❑ 1128	Linda Lu/Monkey's Uncle	1959	25.00
❑ 1138	Long John/T.A. Blues	1959	15.00
❑ 1149	Bermuda/Gonna Let It Go This Time	1960	15.00
❑ 1155	For You My Love/Red Sails in the Sunset	1960	15.00
❑ 1164	Give'n Up/Kewpie Doll	1960	15.00
LHI			
❑ 1215	Linda Lu/Monkey's Uncle	1967	8.00
MONUMENT			
❑ 874	Let's Go, Let's Go, Let's Go/It's Too Cold	1965	10.00
PARK AVENUE			
❑ 4904	Do the Thaxton/Baby Ora	196?	10.00
❑ 4906	Almost Grown/(B-side unknown)	196?	10.00
TREY			
❑ 3011	Justine/On the Street Where You Live	1961	12.00
Albums			
AWARD			
❑ LMP-711 [M]	Welcome Back, Linda Lu	1964	120.00

SHARPS, THE
Possibly more than one group.

Number	Title (A Side/B Side)	Yr	NM
45s			
ALADDIN			
❑ 3401	What Will I Gain/Shufflin'	1957	50.00
❑ 3401	What Will I Gain/Shufflin'	1957	400.00
—Purple vinyl			
CHESS			
❑ 1690	6 Months, 3 Weeks, 2 Days/Cha-Cho Bop	1958	30.00
—B-side by Jack McVea			
COMBO			
❑ 146	All My Love/Look What You've Done to Me	1958	50.00
DOT			
❑ 15806	All My Love/Look What You've Done to Me	1958	15.00
JAMIE			
❑ 1040	Sweet Sweetheart/Come On	1957	40.00
❑ 1108	Have Love, Will Travel/Look at Me	1958	50.00
❑ 1114	Here's My Heart/Gig-A-Lene	1958	30.00
LAMP			
❑ 2007	Our Love Is Here to Stay/Lock My Heart	1957	30.00
STAR-HI			
❑ 10406	Double Clutch/If Love Is What You Want	1960	30.00
TAG			
❑ 2200	6 Months, 3 Weeks, 2 Days/Cha-Cho Bop	1957	100.00
—B-side by Jack McVea			
VIK			
❑ 0264	Sweet Sweetheart/Come On	1957	25.00
WIN			
❑ 702	Teenage Girl/We Three	1958	50.00

SHARPTONES, THE

Number	Title (A Side/B Side)	Yr	NM
45s			
POST			
❑ 2009	Since I Fell for You/Made to Love	1955	400.00

SHATNER, WILLIAM

Number	Title (A Side/B Side)	Yr	NM
45s			
DECCA			
❑ 32399	How Insensitive/Transformed Man	1969	20.00
Albums			
DECCA			
❑ DL 5043 [M]	The Transformed Man	1969	150.00
—Mono is white label promo only; in stereo cover with "Monaural" sticker			
❑ DL 75043 [S]	The Transformed Man	1969	60.00
K-TEL			
❑ NC 494 [(2)]	Captain of the Starship	1978	50.00
—Reissue of Lemli album			
LEMLI			
❑ 9400 [(2)]	William Shatner — Live!	1977	30.00

SHAW, ARTIE

Number	Title (A Side/B Side)	Yr	NM
Albums			
RCA VICTOR			
❑ VPM-6062 [(2)]	This Is Artie Shaw, Vol. 2	1976	12.00
—Black labels, dog near top			

SHAW, JIMMY

Number	Title (A Side/B Side)	Yr	NM
45s			
IMPERIAL			
❑ 5603	Take a Chance on Me/Big Chief Hug-Um An' Kiss-Um	1959	20.00

SHAW, JOHN, AND THE DELL-OS

Number	Title (A Side/B Side)	Yr	NM
45s			
U-C			
❑ 5002	Why Did You Leave Me/Why Does It Have to Be Her	1957	4000.
—VG 2,000; VG+ 3,000			

SHAW, MARLENA

12-Inch Singles

COLUMBIA

Number	Title (A Side/B Side)	Yr	NM
❑ 11025	Love Dancin'/No One Yet	1979	5.00

POLYDOR

Number	Title (A Side/B Side)	Yr	NM
❑ PRO 628 [DJ]	I Want to Know (same on both sides)	1988	8.00

SOUTH BAY

Number	Title (A Side/B Side)	Yr	NM
❑ 1004	More Room at the Top/At Last	1982	10.00
❑ 22004	Never Give Up on You/ (B-side unknown)	1983	8.00

45s

BLUE NOTE

Number	Title (A Side/B Side)	Yr	NM
❑ XW209	Last Tango in Paris/ (B-side unknown)	1973	5.00
❑ XW366	Easy Evil/Just Don't Want to Be Lonely	1973	5.00
❑ XW550	The Feeling's Good/But For Now	1974	5.00
❑ XW649	You/Loving You Is Like a Party	1975	5.00
❑ XW691	Feel Like Makin' Love/ You Taught Me How to Speak in Love	1975	5.00
❑ XW790	It's Better Than Walkin' Out/ Be for Real	1976	5.00
❑ XW844	Love Has Gone Away/This Time I'll Be Sweeter	1976	5.00
❑ 1981	Somewhere/You Must Believe	1972	6.00

CADET

Number	Title (A Side/B Side)	Yr	NM
❑ 5549	Let's Wade in the Water/ Show Time	1966	8.00
❑ 5557	Mercy, Mercy, Mercy/ Go Away Little Boy	1967	8.00
❑ 5571	Brother Where Are You/ Waiting for Charlie to Come Home	1967	8.00
❑ 5592	Matchmaker, Matchmaker/ A Couple of Losers	1968	6.00
❑ 5618	Looking Through the Eyes of Love/Anyone Can Move a Mountain	1968	6.00
❑ 5638	California Soul/The House That Jack Built	1969	6.00
❑ 5650	Woman of the Ghetto/ I'm Satisfied	1969	6.00
❑ 5656	Looking Through the Eyes of Love/California Soul	1969	6.00

COLUMBIA

Number	Title (A Side/B Side)	Yr	NM
❑ 10542	Yu-Ma/Go Away Little Boy// No Deposit, No Return	1977	5.00
❑ 10589	Johnny/Pictures and Memories	1977	5.00
❑ 10661	Don't Ask to Stay Until Tomorrow/ No Deposit, No Return	1978	5.00
❑ 10746	Dreamin'/Places	1978	5.00
❑ 11034	Love Dancin'/No One Yet	1979	12.00

POLYDOR

Number	Title (A Side/B Side)	Yr	NM
❑ 887776-7	I Want to Know/Love Is In Flight	1988	4.00

Albums

BLUE NOTE

Number	Title (A Side/B Side)	Yr	NM
❑ BN-LA143-F	From the Depths of My Soul	1974	15.00
❑ BN-LA397-G	Who Is This Bitch, Anyway?	1975	15.00
❑ BN-LA606-G	Just a Matter	1976	15.00
❑ BST-84422	Marlena	1972	15.00

CADET

Number	Title (A Side/B Side)	Yr	NM
❑ LPS-803	Different Bags	1968	20.00
❑ LPS-833	Spice of Life	1969	20.00

COLUMBIA

Number	Title (A Side/B Side)	Yr	NM
❑ PC 34458	Sweet Beginnings	1977	12.00
❑ JC 35073	Acting Up	1978	12.00
❑ JC 35632	Take a Bite	1979	12.00
❑ JC 36367	The Best of Marlena Shaw	1980	10.00

VERVE

Number	Title (A Side/B Side)	Yr	NM
❑ 831438-1	It Is Love	1987	10.00
❑ 837312-1	Love Is In Flight	1988	10.00

SHAW, SANDIE

45s

MERCURY

Number	Title (A Side/B Side)	Yr	NM
❑ 72315	Ya, Ya, Da, Da/As Long As You're Happy	1964	15.00

RCA VICTOR

Number	Title (A Side/B Side)	Yr	NM
❑ 47-9594	Together/One More Lie	1968	8.00
❑ 74-0118	Voice in the Crowd/Monsieur Dupont	1969	8.00
❑ 74-0370	Love Is For the Two of Us/ Wight Is Wight	1970	8.00

REPRISE

Number	Title (A Side/B Side)	Yr	NM
❑ 0320	(There's) Always Something There to Remind Me/ Don't You Know	1964	12.00
❑ 0342	Girl Don't Come/I'd Be Far Better Off Without You	1965	10.00
❑ 0365	I'll Stop at Nothing/ You Can't Blame Him	1965	10.00
❑ 0375	Long Live Love/I've Heard About Him	1965	10.00
❑ 0394	Stop Feeling Sorry for Yourself/ I'll Stop at Nothing	1965	10.00
❑ 0427	If Ever You Need Me/ How Can You Tell	1965	10.00
❑ 0449	Tomorrow/Hurting You	1966	10.00
❑ 0488	Nothing Comes Easy/ Stop Before You Start	1966	10.00
❑ 0546	Think Sometime About Me/ Hide All Emotion	1967	10.00
❑ 0575	Puppet on a String/I Had a Dream Last Night	1967	10.00
❑ 20191	Me/Now	1963	15.00
	—B-side by Bob Candee		

Albums

REPRISE

Number	Title (A Side/B Side)	Yr	NM
❑ R-6166 [M]	Sandie Shaw	1965	40.00
❑ RS-6166 [R]	Sandie Shaw	1965	50.00
❑ R-6191 [M]	Me	1966	30.00
❑ RS-6191 [S]	Me	1966	40.00

SHAW, SERENA

Albums

RAMA

Number	Title (A Side/B Side)	Yr	NM
❑ RLP-5001 [M]	Cry My Love	1956	400.00

SHEAN AND JENKYNS

45s

GNP CRESCENDO

Number	Title (A Side/B Side)	Yr	NM
❑ 198	Goofy-Footer Ho-Dad/ Do the Commercial	1963	25.00

SHEARING, GEORGE

45s

CAPITOL

Number	Title (A Side/B Side)	Yr	NM
❑ XE 1-1715 [S]	The Outlaw/When April Comes Again	1962	12.00
	—Small hole, plays at 33 1/3 rpm		
❑ XE 2-1715 [S]	Monophraseology/My New Mambo	1962	12.00
	—Small hole, plays at 33 1/3 rpm		
❑ XE 3-1715 [S]	Be-Bop Irishman/I'll Be Around	1962	12.00
	—Small hole, plays at 33 1/3 rpm		
❑ XE 4-1715 [S]	Jumpin' with Symphony Sid/ Cocktails for Two	1962	12.00
	—Small hole, plays at 33 1/3 rpm		
❑ XE 5-1715 [S]	Lullaby of Birdland (Part 1)/ (Part 2)	1962	12.00
	—Small hole, plays at 33 1/3 rpm		
❑ 4418	Blue Malibu/Honeysuckle Rose	1960	8.00
❑ 4922	The Stripper/Fairy Tales	1963	8.00
❑ 5850	On a Clear Day You Can See Forever/Call Me	1967	6.00

MGM

Number	Title (A Side/B Side)	Yr	NM
❑ 10647	In a Chinese Garden/ (B-side unknown)	1950	20.00
	—Note: Earlier George Shearing 45s on MGM may exist		
❑ 10687	I'll Remember April/Jumping with Symphony Sid	1950	20.00
❑ 10720	I Didn't Know What Time It Was/ How's Trix	1950	20.00
❑ 10763	When Your Lover Has Gone/ Carnegie Horizons	1950	20.00
❑ 10859	Roses of Picardy/ Pick Yourself Up	1950	20.00
❑ 10907	For You/Little White Lies	1951	15.00
❑ 10956	I'll Be Around/Quintessence	1951	15.00
❑ 10986	The Breeze and I/ I Remember You	1951	15.00
❑ 11046	Don't Blame Me/Brain Waves	1951	15.00
❑ 11153	Thine Alone/Geneva's Move	1952	15.00
❑ 11199	To a Wild Rose/Swedish Pastry	1952	15.00
❑ 11282	Simplicity/5 O'Clock Whistle	1952	15.00
❑ 11354	Lullaby of Birdland/When Lights Are Low	1952	15.00
❑ 11425	There's a Lull in My Life/ Midnight Belongs to You	1953	15.00
❑ 11493	Body and Soul/I Hear a Rhapsody	1953	15.00
❑ 11545	Indian Summer/Appreciation	1953	15.00
❑ 11600	Easy to Love/Wrap Your Troubles in Dreams	1953	15.00
❑ 11639	Tiempo de Concerro (Part 1)/ Tiempo de Concerro (Part 2)	1953	15.00
❑ 11677	A Sinner Kissed an Angel/ Mood for Milt	1954	12.00
❑ 11754	I've Never Been in Love Before/ Mambo Inn	1954	12.00
❑ 11833	Lullaby of Birdland/ Love Is Here to Stay	1954	12.00
❑ 11876	Adieu/Undecided	1954	12.00
❑ 11943	The Lady Is a Tramp/ Cool Mambo	1955	12.00
❑ 12038	Ill Wind/Drune Negrita	1955	12.00
❑ 12079	Get Off My Back/Love Is Just Around the Corner	1955	12.00
❑ 12132	Stranger in Paradise/ Point and Counterpoint	1955	12.00
❑ 12182	Hallelujah/Basso Profundo	1956	12.00
❑ 12227	Spring Is Here/Minor Trouble	1956	12.00
❑ 12309	Over the Rainbow/ Lonely Moments	1956	12.00
❑ 12349	My Silent Love/As Long As There's Music	1956	12.00

7-Inch Extended Plays

CAPITOL

Number	Title (A Side/B Side)	Yr	NM
❑ EAP 1-648	Autumn in New York/The Man I Love	195?	12.00
❑ EAP 1-648 [PS]	The Shearing Spell, Part 1	195?	12.00
❑ EAP 1-858	The Folks Who Live on the Hill// Moon Song/Medley: As Long As I Live-Let's Live Again	195?	12.00
❑ EAP 1-858 [PS]	Black Satin, Part 1	195?	12.00
❑ EAP 2-858	If I Should Lose You/Starlight Souvenirs//Nothing Ever Changes My Love for You	195?	12.00
❑ EAP 2-858 [PS]	Black Satin, Part 2	195?	12.00

MGM

Number	Title (A Side/B Side)	Yr	NM
❑ X1006	For You/I Remember You// Thine Alone/I'll Be Around	1953	15.00
❑ X1006 [PS]	For You	1953	15.00
❑ X1017	(contents unknown)	1953	15.00
❑ X1017 [PS]	In a Chinese Garden	1953	15.00

Albums

BASF

Number	Title (A Side/B Side)	Yr	NM
❑ 25340	Light, Airy and Swinging	1973	12.00
❑ 25351	The Way We Are	1974	12.00
❑ MC-25612	Continental Experience	1975	12.00

CAPITOL

Number	Title (A Side/B Side)	Yr	NM
❑ SKAO-139	The Best of George Shearing, Vol. 2	1969	12.00
❑ ST-181	Fool on the Hill	1969	12.00
❑ T 648 [M]	The Shearing Spell	1956	30.00
	—Turquoise label		
❑ T 648 [M]	The Shearing Spell	1959	20.00
	—Black label with colorband, logo on left		
❑ DT 720 [R]	Velvet Carpet	196?	12.00
❑ T 720 [M]	Velvet Carpet	1956	30.00
	—Turquoise label		
❑ T 720 [M]	Velvet Carpet	1959	20.00
	—Black label with colorband, logo on left		
❑ T 720 [M]	Velvet Carpet	1962	15.00
	—Black label with colorband, logo on top		
❑ DT 737 [R]	Latin Escapade	196?	12.00
❑ T 737 [M]	Latin Escapade	1957	30.00
	—Turquoise label		
❑ T 737 [M]	Latin Escapade	1959	20.00
	—Black label with colorband, logo on left		
❑ T 737 [M]	Latin Escapade	1962	15.00
	—Black label with colorband, logo on top		
❑ ST 858 [S]	Black Satin	1959	20.00
	—Black label with colorband, logo on left		
❑ ST 858 [S]	Black Satin	1962	15.00
	—Black label with colorband, logo on top		
❑ T 858 [M]	Black Satin	1957	30.00
	—Turquoise label		
❑ T 858 [M]	Black Satin	1959	20.00
	—Black label with colorband, logo on left		
❑ T 858 [M]	Black Satin	1962	15.00
	—Black label with colorband, logo on top		
❑ T 909 [M]	Shearing Piano	1957	30.00
	—Turquoise label		
❑ T 909 [M]	Shearing Piano	1959	20.00
	—Black label with colorband, logo on left		
❑ T 943 [M]	Night Mist	1957	30.00
	—Turquoise label		
❑ ST 1038 [S]	Burnished Brass	1959	25.00
	—Black label with colorband, logo on left		
❑ ST 1038 [S]	Burnished Brass	1962	20.00
	—Black label with colorband, logo on top		
❑ T 1038 [M]	Burnished Brass	1958	20.00
	—Black label with colorband, logo on left		
❑ T 1038 [M]	Burnished Brass	1962	15.00
	—Black label with colorband, logo on top		
❑ ST 1082 [S]	Latin Lace	1958	25.00
	—Black label with colorband, logo on left		
❑ ST 1082 [S]	Latin Lace	1962	20.00
	—Black label with colorband, logo on top		
❑ T 1082 [M]	Latin Lace	1958	20.00
	—Black label with colorband, logo on left		
❑ T 1082 [M]	Latin Lace	1962	15.00
	—Black label with colorband, logo on top		
❑ ST 1124 [S]	Blue Chiffon	1959	25.00
	—Black label with colorband, logo on left		
❑ ST 1124 [S]	Blue Chiffon	1962	20.00
	—Black label with colorband, logo on top		
❑ T 1124 [M]	Blue Chiffon	1959	20.00
	—Black label with colorband, logo on left		
❑ T 1124 [M]	Blue Chiffon	1962	15.00
	—Black label with colorband, logo on top		
❑ ST 1187 [S]	George Shearing On Stage	1959	25.00
	—Black label with colorband, logo on left		

Except when noted otherwise, VG = 25% of NM, and VG+ = 50% of NM. (Example: VG = $2.00, VG+ = $4.00 and NM = $8.00.)

Number	Title (A Side/B Side)	Yr	NM
❑ ST 1187 [S]	George Shearing On Stage	1962	20.00
—Black label with colorband, logo on top			
❑ T 1187 [M]	George Shearing On Stage	1959	20.00
—Black label with colorband, logo on left			
❑ T 1187 [M]	George Shearing On Stage	1962	15.00
—Black label with colorband, logo on top			
❑ ST 1275 [S]	Latin Affair	1960	25.00
—Black label with colorband, logo on left			
❑ ST 1275 [S]	Latin Affair	1962	20.00
—Black label with colorband, logo on top			
❑ T 1275 [M]	Latin Affair	1960	20.00
—Black label with colorband, logo on left			
❑ T 1275 [M]	Latin Affair	1962	15.00
—Black label with colorband, logo on top			
❑ ST 1334 [S]	White Satin	1960	25.00
—Black label with colorband, logo on left			
❑ ST 1334 [S]	White Satin	1962	20.00
—Black label with colorband, logo on top			
❑ T 1334 [M]	White Satin	1960	20.00
—Black label with colorband, logo on left			
❑ T 1334 [M]	White Satin	1962	15.00
—Black label with colorband, logo on top			
❑ ST 1416 [S]	On the Sunny Side of the Strip	1960	25.00
—Black label with colorband, logo on left			
❑ ST 1416 [S]	On the Sunny Side of the Strip	1962	20.00
—Black label with colorband, logo on top			
❑ T 1416 [M]	On the Sunny Side of the Strip	1960	20.00
—Black label with colorband, logo on left			
❑ T 1416 [M]	On the Sunny Side of the Strip	1962	15.00
—Black label with colorband, logo on top			
❑ SM-1472	The Shearing Touch	1977	10.00
—Reissue with new prefix			
❑ ST 1472 [S]	The Shearing Touch	1961	25.00
—Black label with colorband, logo on left			
❑ ST 1472 [S]	The Shearing Touch	1962	20.00
—Black label with colorband, logo on top			
❑ T 1472 [M]	The Shearing Touch	1961	20.00
—Black label with colorband, logo on left			
❑ T 1472 [M]	The Shearing Touch	1962	15.00
—Black label with colorband, logo on top			
❑ ST 1567 [S]	Mood Latino	1961	25.00
—Black label with colorband, logo on left			
❑ ST 1567 [S]	Mood Latino	1962	20.00
—Black label with colorband, logo on top			
❑ T 1567 [M]	Mood Latino	1961	20.00
—Black label with colorband, logo on left			
❑ T 1567 [M]	Mood Latino	1962	15.00
—Black label with colorband, logo on top			
❑ ST 1628 [S]	Satin Affair	1961	25.00
—Black label with colorband, logo on left			
❑ ST 1628 [S]	Satin Affair	1962	20.00
—Black label with colorband, logo on top			
❑ T 1628 [M]	Satin Affair	1961	20.00
—Black label with colorband, logo on left			
❑ T 1628 [M]	Satin Affair	1962	15.00
—Black label with colorband, logo on top			
❑ ST 1715 [S]	San Francisco Scene	1962	20.00
❑ T 1715 [M]	San Francisco Scene	1962	15.00
❑ ST 1755 [S]	Concerto for My Love	1962	20.00
❑ T 1755 [M]	Concerto for My Love	1962	15.00
❑ ST 1827 [S]	Jazz Moments	1963	20.00
❑ T 1827 [M]	Jazz Moments	1963	15.00
❑ ST 1873 [S]	Bossa Nova	1963	20.00
❑ T 1873 [M]	Bossa Nova	1963	15.00
❑ ST 1874 [S]	Touch Me Softly	1963	20.00
❑ T 1874 [M]	Touch Me Softly	1963	15.00
❑ ST 1992 [S]	Jazz Concert	1963	20.00
❑ T 1992 [M]	Jazz Concert	1963	15.00
❑ ST 2048 [S]	Old Gold and Ivory	1964	15.00
❑ T 2048 [M]	Old Gold and Ivory	1964	12.00
❑ SM-2104	The Best of George Shearing	1977	10.00
—Reissue with new prefix			
❑ ST 2104 [S]	The Best of George Shearing	1964	15.00
❑ T 2104 [M]	The Best of George Shearing	1964	12.00
❑ ST 2143 [S]	Deep Velvet	1964	15.00
❑ T 2143 [M]	Deep Velvet	1964	12.00
❑ ST 2272 [S]	Out of the Woods	1965	15.00
❑ T 2272 [M]	Out of the Woods	1965	12.00
❑ ST 2326 [S]	Latin Rendezvous	1965	15.00
❑ T 2326 [M]	Latin Rendezvous	1965	12.00
❑ ST 2372 [S]	Here and Now	1965	15.00
❑ T 2372 [M]	Here and Now	1965	12.00
❑ ST 2447 [S]	Rare Form	1965	15.00
❑ T 2447 [M]	Rare Form	1965	12.00
❑ ST 2567 [S]	That Fresh Feeling	1966	15.00
❑ T 2567 [M]	That Fresh Feeling	1966	12.00
❑ ST 2699 [S]	George Shearing Today	1967	12.00
❑ T 2699 [M]	George Shearing Today	1967	15.00
❑ SM-11454	Latin Escapade	197?	10.00
❑ SM-11800	Black Satin	1978	10.00
CONCORD CONCERTO			
❑ CC-2010	George Shearing and Barry Tuckwell Play the Music of Cole Porter	1986	10.00
CONCORD JAZZ			
❑ CJ-110	Blues Alley Jazz	1980	10.00
❑ CJ-132	On a Clear Day	1981	10.00
—With Brian Torff			
❑ CJ-171	Alone Together	1981	10.00
❑ CJ-177	First Edition	1982	10.00
❑ CJ-246	Live at the Café Carlyle	1984	10.00
❑ CJ-281	Grand Piano	1985	10.00
❑ CJ-318	More Grand Piano	1987	10.00
❑ CJ-335	Breakin' Out	1988	10.00
❑ CJ-346	Dexterity	1988	10.00
❑ CJ-357	A Perfect Match	1988	10.00
—With Ernestine Anderson			
❑ CJ-371	The Spirit of 176	1989	12.00
—With Hank Jones			
❑ CJ-388	George Shearing in Dixieland	1989	12.00
❑ CJ-400	Piano	1989	12.00
DISCOVERY			
❑ DL-3002 [10]	George Shearing Quintet	1950	60.00
EVEREST ARCHIVE OF FOLK & JAZZ			
❑ 223	Young George Shearing	1968	10.00
❑ 236	The Early Years, Vol. 2	1969	10.00
LONDON			
❑ LL 295 [10]	Souvenirs	1951	60.00
❑ LL 1343 [M]	By Request	1956	30.00
MGM			
❑ E-90 [10]	A Touch of Genius	1951	50.00
❑ GAS-143	You're Hearing George Shearing	1970	12.00
❑ E-155 [10]	I Hear Music	1952	50.00
❑ E-226 [10]	When Lights Are Low	1953	50.00
❑ E-252 [10]	An Evening with George Shearing	1954	50.00
❑ E-518 [10]	You're Hearing the George Shearing Quartet	1950	60.00
❑ E-3122 [M]	An Evening with Shearing	1955	30.00
❑ E-3175 [M]	Shearing Caravan	1955	30.00
❑ E-3216 [M]	You're Hearing George Shearing	1955	30.00
❑ E-3264 [M]	When Lights Are Low	1955	30.00
❑ E-3265 [M]	Touch of Genius	1955	30.00
❑ E-3266 [M]	I Hear Music	1955	30.00
❑ E-3293 [M]	Shearing in Hi-Fi	1955	30.00
❑ E-3796 [M]	You're Hearing the Best of George Shearing	1960	15.00
❑ E-4041 [M]	Satin Latin	1962	15.00
❑ SE-4041 [R]	Satin Latin	1962	12.00
❑ E-4042 [M]	Soft and Silky	1962	15.00
❑ SE-4042 [R]	Soft and Silky	1962	12.00
❑ E-4043 [M]	Smooth and Swinging	1962	15.00
❑ SE-4043 [R]	Smooth and Swinging	1962	12.00
❑ E-4169 [M]	The Very Best of George Shearing	1963	15.00
❑ SE-4169 [R]	The Very Best of George Shearing	1963	12.00
MOSAIC			
❑ MQ7-157 [(7)]	The Complete Capitol Live Recordings of George Shearing	199?	120.00
PAUSA			
❑ 7035	Light, Airy and Swinging	1977	10.00
❑ PR 7049	The Reunion	1977	10.00
—With Stephane Grappelli			
❑ 7072	500 Miles High	1979	10.00
❑ 7088	Getting in the Swing of Things	1981	10.00
❑ 7116	On Target	198?	10.00
❑ 9030	The Shearing Touch	198?	10.00
❑ 9036	Jazz Moments	1985	10.00
❑ 9065	Latin Affair	1986	10.00
PICKWICK			
❑ SPC-3039	Lullaby of Birdland	197?	10.00
❑ SPC-3100	You Stepped Out of a Dream	197?	10.00
SAVOY			
❑ MG-15003 [10]	Piano Solo	1951	60.00
SAVOY JAZZ			
❑ SJL-1117	So Rare	198?	10.00
SHEBA			
❑ 101	Out of This World	197?	12.00
❑ 103	George Shearing Trio	197?	12.00
❑ 104	George Shearing Quartet	197?	12.00
❑ 105	As Requested	197?	12.00
❑ 106	Music to Hear	197?	12.00
❑ 107	GAS	197?	12.00
VERVE			
❑ VSP-9 [M]	Classic Shearing	1966	15.00
❑ VSPS-9 [R]	Classic Shearing	1966	12.00
❑ 821664-1	My Ship	198?	10.00
❑ 827977-1 [(2)]	Lullaby of Birdland	1986	12.00

SHEARING, GEORGE, AND THE MONTGOMERY BROTHERS

Albums

Number	Title (A Side/B Side)	Yr	NM
FANTASY			
❑ OJC-040	George Shearing and the Montgomery Brothers	198?	10.00
JAZZLAND			
❑ JLP-55 [M]	Love Walked In	1961	30.00
—Cover has Shearing and the brothers			
❑ JLP-55 [M]	Love Walked In	1962	25.00
—Cover has a woman			
❑ JLP-955 [S]	Love Walked In	1961	40.00
—Cover has Shearing and the brothers			
❑ JLP-955 [S]	Love Walked In	1962	30.00
—Cover has a woman			
RIVERSIDE			
❑ 6087	George Shearing and the Montgomery Brothers	197?	10.00
—Reissue of Jazzland LP			

SHEARING, GEORGE, AND MEL TORME

Also see each artist's individual listings.

Albums

Number	Title (A Side/B Side)	Yr	NM
CONCORD JAZZ			
❑ CJ-190	An Evening with George Shearing and Mel Torme	1982	10.00
❑ CJ-219	Top Drawer	1983	10.00
❑ CJ-248	An Evening at Charlie's	1984	10.00
❑ CJ-294	An Elegant Evening	1985	10.00
❑ CJ-341	A Vintage Year	1988	10.00

SHEARS, BILLY, AND THE ALL AMERICANS

45s

Number	Title (A Side/B Side)	Yr	NM
SILVER FOX			
❑ 12+1	Brother Paul/Message to Seymour	1969	12.00

SHEEP, THE

By the same people who gave us THE STRANGELOVES.

45s

Number	Title (A Side/B Side)	Yr	NM
BOOM			
❑ 60000	Hide and Seek/Twelve Months Later	1966	20.00
❑ 60007	Dynamite/I Feel Good	1966	20.00

SHEFFIELDS, THE

45s

Number	Title (A Side/B Side)	Yr	NM
DESTINATION			
❑ 613	My Loving Days Are Through/Please Come Back	1966	15.00
❑ 621	Do You Still Love Me/Nothing I Can Do	1966	20.00
DOT			
❑ 16722	Plenty of Love/Bags Groove	1965	15.00
FENTON			
❑ 980	Nothing I Can Do/My Only Wish	1965	25.00
❑ 2118	Fool Minus a Heart/Blowin' in the Wind	1966	25.00

SHEIKS, THE

More than one group. Some of these were labeled "The Shieks."

45s

Number	Title (A Side/B Side)	Yr	NM
AMY			
❑ 807	Come On Back/Please Don't Take Away the Girl I Love	1960	200.00
CAT			
❑ 116	Walk That Walk/The Kissing Song (Sweetie Lover)	1955	40.00
EF-N-DE			
❑ 1000	Give Me Another Chance/Baby Don't You Cry	1955	600.00
FEDERAL			
❑ 12237	So Fine/Sentimental Heart	1955	150.00
JAMIE			
❑ 1147	Candlelight Cafe/The Song of Old Paree	1959	20.00
LEGRAND			
❑ 1013	What I'd Do for Your Love/Why Should I Dance	1961	100.00
❑ 1016	Cocoanut Woman/Twist That Twist	1962	25.00
MGM			
❑ 12876	Baghdad Rock (Part 1)/Baghdad Rock (Part 2)	1960	20.00

SHELDON, DOUG

45s

Number	Title (A Side/B Side)	Yr	NM
CONGRESS			
❑ 266	How Can I Tell Her/It's Because of You	1966	10.00
MGM			
❑ 13261	Lonely Boy/Hello There Lonely Baby	1964	12.00

SHELLS, THE

45s

Number	Title (A Side/B Side)	Yr	NM
END			
❑ 1022	Pretty Little Girl/Sippin' Soda	1958	150.00
❑ 1050	Whispering Wings/Shooma Dom Dom	1959	50.00
GONE			
❑ 5103	Pretty Little Girl/Sippin' Soda	1961	25.00

S

Number	Title (A Side/B Side)	Yr	NM
JOHNSON			
❑ 099	My Cherie/Explain It to Me	1972	6.00
❑ 104	Baby Oh Baby/Angel Eyes	1957	40.00
❑ 104	Baby Oh Baby/What's in An Angel's Eyes	1960	15.00
—Note lengthened B-side title			
❑ 106	Don't Say Goodbye/Pleading	1958	100.00
❑ 107	Explain It to Me/An Island Unknown	1961	25.00
❑ 109	Better Forget Him/Can't Take It	1961	25.00
❑ 110	In the Dim Light of the Dark/ O-Mi Yum-Mi Yum-Mi	1961	25.00
❑ 112	Sweetest One/Baby Walk On In	1961	30.00
❑ 119	Deep in My Heart/(It's a) Happy Holiday	1962	30.00
❑ 120	The Drive/A Toast to Your Birthday	1962	30.00
❑ 127	On My Honor/My Royal Love	1963	50.00
❑ 332	Explain It to Me/An Island Unknown	1961	15.00
JOSIE			
❑ 912	Deep in My Heart/ Our Wedding Day	1963	20.00
ROULETTE			
❑ 4156	The Thief/She Wasn't Meant for Me	1959	30.00
Albums			
CANDELITE			
❑ 1000	Accapella	197?	15.00
COLLECTABLES			
❑ COL-5077	Golden Classics	198?	10.00

SHELTON, GARY

45s

Number	Title (A Side/B Side)	Yr	NM
ALPINE			
❑ 56	Honey Bee/Till the End of the Line	1960	30.00
MARK			
❑ 145	Goodbye Little Darlin' Goodbye/Stop the World	1960	200.00
MERCURY			
❑ 71310	Kissin' at the Drive-In/ Yours Till I Die	1958	30.00

SHELTON, RICKY VAN

45s

Number	Title (A Side/B Side)	Yr	NM
COLUMBIA			
❑ 38-06542	Wild-Eyed Dream/Think It Over	1986	4.00
❑ 38-07025	Crime of Passion/Don't We All Have the Right	1987	3.00
❑ 38-07311	Somebody Lied/Working Man's Blues	1987	3.00
❑ 38-07672	Life Turned Her That Way/ I Don't Care	1987	3.00
❑ 38-07798	Don't We All Have the Right/ Baby, I'm Ready	1988	3.00
❑ 38-08022	I'll Leave This World Loving You/Sometimes I Cry in My Sleep	1988	4.00
❑ 13-08391	Wild-Eyed Dream/ Crime of Passion	1988	3.00
—"Hall of Fame" series; gray label			
❑ 38-08529	From a Jack to a King/ The Picture	1988	3.00
❑ 38-68694	Hole in My Pocket/Let Me Live with Love (And Die with You)	1989	3.00
❑ 38-68994	Living Proof/Somebody's Back in Town	1989	3.00
❑ 38-73077	Statue of a Fool/He's Got You	1989	3.00
❑ 38-73263	I've Cried My Last Tear for You/ I Still Love You	1990	3.00
❑ 38-73413	I Meant Every Word He Said/ Sometimes I Cry in My Sleep	1990	3.00
❑ 38-73587	Life's Little Ups and Downs/ Love Is Burnin'	1990	3.00
❑ 38-73780	I Am a Simple Man/Backroads	1991	4.00
❑ 38-73956	Keep It Between the Lines/ Weekend World	1991	4.00
❑ 38-74104	After the Lights Go Out/ Oh Heart of Mine	1991	3.00
❑ 38-74258	Backroads/Call Me Up	1992	3.00
❑ 38-74418	Wear My Ring Around Your Neck/Who'll Turn Out the Lights	1992	4.00
Albums			
COLUMBIA			
❑ B6C 40602	Wild-Eyed Dream	1987	8.00
❑ FC 44221	Loving Proof	1988	8.00
❑ C 45250	RVS III	1990	15.00
❑ FC 45269	Ricky Van Shelton Sings Christmas	1989	12.00
❑ C 46855	Backroads	1990	20.00
—Vinyl available only through Columbia House			

SHENANDOAH VALLEY BOYS

See JIM EANES.

SHEP AND THE LIMELITES

Also see THE HEARTBEATS; SHANE SHEPPARD.

45s

Number	Title (A Side/B Side)	Yr	NM
HULL			
❑ 740	Daddy's Home/This I Know	1961	20.00
—Tan label. Note: Any colored vinyl version is a counterfeit.			
❑ 740	Daddy's Home/This I Know	1961	25.00
—Red label			
❑ 740	Daddy's Home/This I Know	1961	40.00
—Pink label			
❑ 742	Ready for Your Love/ You'll Be Sorry	1961	20.00
❑ 747	Three Steps from the Altar/ Oh What a Feeling	1961	20.00
❑ 748	Our Anniversary/ Who Told the Sandman	1962	20.00
❑ 751	What Did Daddy Do/Teach Me, Teach Me How to Twist	1962	20.00
❑ 753	Gee Baby, What About You/ Everything Is Going to Be Alright	1962	20.00
❑ 756	Remember Baby/The Monkey	1963	20.00
❑ 757	Stick By Me (And I'll Stick By You)/It's All Over Now	1963	20.00
❑ 759	Steal Away (With Your Baby)/ For All My Love	1963	20.00
❑ 761	Easy to Remember (When You Want to Forget)/Why, Why Won't You Believe Me	1964	20.00
❑ 767	I'm All Alone/Why Did You Fall for Me	1964	20.00
❑ 770	Party for Two/You Better Believe	1965	30.00
❑ 772	In Case I Forget/ I'm a-Hurting Inside	1965	20.00
Albums			
HULL			
❑ 1001 [M]	Our Anniversary	1962	1200.
ROULETTE			
❑ R-25350 [M]	Our Anniversary	1967	80.00
❑ SR-25350 [R]	Our Anniversary	1967	50.00

SHEPARDS, THE

45s

Number	Title (A Side/B Side)	Yr	NM
ABC-PARAMOUNT			
❑ 10758	Little Girl Lost/Let Yourself Go	1965	25.00

SHEPHERD, CYBILL

45s

Number	Title (A Side/B Side)	Yr	NM
PARAMOUNT			
❑ 0299	My Heart Belongs to Daddy/ Anything Goes	1974	10.00
Albums			
PARAMOUNT			
❑ PAS-1018	Cybill Does It...to Cole Porter	1974	20.00
—With poster			

SHEPHERD SISTERS

Some of these spelled the name "Shepard," others "Sheppard," but they are all the same group.

45s

Number	Title (A Side/B Side)	Yr	NM
ATLANTIC			
❑ 2176	What Makes Little Girls Cry/ Don't Mention My Name	1963	10.00
❑ 2195	Talk Is Cheap/ The Greatest Lover	1963	10.00
BIG TOP			
❑ 3066	Hapsburg Serenade/ Schoen-A, Schoen-A	1961	15.00
LANCE			
❑ 125	Alone (Why Must I Be Alone)/ Congratulations to Someone	1957	25.00
MELBA			
❑ 100	Gone with the Wind/ Rock and Roll, Cha Cha	1956	25.00
❑ 108	Remember That Crazy Rock and Roll Turf/I Walked Beside the Sea	1957	25.00
MERCURY			
❑ 71244	Gettin' Ready for Freddie/ The Best Thing There Is	1957	25.00
❑ 71306	Eatin' Pizza/A Boy and a Girl	1958	20.00
❑ 71350	Dancing Baby/Is It a Crime	1958	20.00
MGM			
❑ 12766	Heart and Soul/(It's No) Sin	1959	20.00
PRIVATE STOCK			
❑ 45,063	Our Town/(B-side unknown)	1975	6.00
20TH CENTURY FOX			
❑ 468	I've Got a Secret/ Finders Keepers	1964	10.00
UNITED ARTISTS			
❑ 350	Deeply/I'm Still Dancin'	1961	12.00
❑ 456	Lolita Ya Ya/Marvin	1962	12.00
WARWICK			
❑ 511	Here Comes Heaven Again/ I Think It's Time	1959	15.00
❑ 530	Alone/Rocky	1960	15.00
❑ 548	Yea Yea Dixie/How Softly a Heart Breaks	1960	15.00
YORK			
❑ 50002	Alone (New Version)/ Alone (Original Version)	1965	10.00

SHEPPARD, BUDDY, AND THE HOLIDAYS

THE BELMONTS in disguise.

45s

Number	Title (A Side/B Side)	Yr	NM
SABINA			
❑ 506	My Love Is Real/Brahms' Lullaby (Time to Dream)	1962	50.00
❑ 510	Now It's All Over/That Background Sound	1963	50.00

SHEPPARD, NEIL

45s

Number	Title (A Side/B Side)	Yr	NM
ALMONT			
❑ 314	You Can't Go Far Without a Guitar (Unless You're Ringo Starr)/Betty Is the Girl for You	1964	30.00

SHEPPARD, SHANE

Also see SHEP AND THE LIMELITES.

45s

Number	Title (A Side/B Side)	Yr	NM
APT			
❑ 25039	Too Young to Wed/ Two Loving Hearts	1960	50.00
❑ 25046	One Week from Today/I'm So Lonely (What Can I Do)	1960	40.00

SHEPPARDS, THE

More than one group?

45s

Number	Title (A Side/B Side)	Yr	NM
ABNER			
❑ 7006	Elevator Operator/Loving You	1961	12.00
APEX			
❑ 7750	Loving You/Island of Love	1959	40.00
❑ 7752	Just Like You/Feel Like Lovin'	1959	25.00
❑ 7755	It's Crazy/Meant to Be	1960	25.00
❑ 7759	Just When I Need You Most/ Society Gal	1960	25.00
❑ 7760	Come Home, Come Home/ Just Like You	1960	25.00
❑ 7762	Tragic/Feel Like Lovin'	1961	25.00
BUNKY			
❑ 7764	Island of Love/Steal Away	1969	6.00
❑ 7766	I'm Not Wanted/Your Love (Has a Hole in It)	1969	6.00
CONSTELLATION			
❑ 123	Island of Love/Give a Hug to Me	1964	10.00
❑ 176	Island of Love/Give a Hug to Me	1966	8.00
IMPACT			
❑ 1018	Poor Man's Thing/When Johnny Comes Marching Home	1967	30.00
LOST-NITE			
❑ 223	Island of Love/Never Felt This Way Before	196?	5.00
—Reissue			
OKEH			
❑ 7173	Walkin'/Pretend You're Still Mine	1963	10.00
PAM			
❑ 1001	Never Let Me Go/Give a Hug to Me	1961	12.00
SHARP			
❑ 6039	What's the Name of the Game/ Glitter in Your Eyes	1961	12.00
UNITED			
❑ 198	Sherry/Mozelle	1957	250.00
VEE JAY			
❑ 406	Every Now and Then/ Glitter in Your Eyes	1961	12.00
❑ 441	Tragic/Come to Me	1962	20.00
Albums			
COLLECTABLES			
❑ COL-5078	Golden Classics	198?	10.00
CONSTELLATION			
❑ C-4 [M]	Collectors Showcase: The Sheppards	1964	80.00
❑ CS-4 [R]	Collectors Showcase: The Sheppards	1964	40.00
SOLID SMOKE			
❑ SS-8004	The Sheppards	1980	10.00
❑ SS-8028	18 Dusty Diamonds	1984	10.00

Except when noted otherwise, VG = 25% of NM, and VG+ = 50% of NM. (Example: VG = $2.00, VG+ = $4.00 and NM = $8.00.)

SHERIDAN, BOBBY

Number	Title (A Side/B Side)	Yr	NM
45s			
SUN			
❑ 354	Red Man/Sad News	1961	30.00

SHERIDAN, MIKE, AND THE NIGHTRIDERS

Number	Title (A Side/B Side)	Yr	NM
45s			
LIVERPOOL SOUND			
❑ 902	Please Mr. Postman/In Love	1964	120.00

SHERIDAN, TONY, AND THE BEAT BROTHERS

See THE BEATLES.

SHERIDAN BROTHERS, THE

Number	Title (A Side/B Side)	Yr	NM
45s			
HIT			
❑ 235	Flowers on the Wall/Sounds of Silence	1966	8.00
—B-side by Sammy and Theodore			

SHERIFF AND THE RAVELS

Number	Title (A Side/B Side)	Yr	NM
45s			
VEE JAY			
❑ 306	Shombalor/Lonely One	1959	40.00

SHERLOCKS, THE

Number	Title (A Side/B Side)	Yr	NM
45s			
DOT			
❑ 16890	Skin of My Teeth/Turn Her Down	1966	20.00
❑ 16953	Shades of Blue/Too Good to Be True	1966	12.00

SHERMAN, ALLAN

Number	Title (A Side/B Side)	Yr	NM
45s			
RCA VICTOR			
❑ 47-8412	The End of a Symphony (Part 1)/The End of a Symphony (Part 2)	1964	10.00
❑ 47-8412 [PS]	The End of a Symphony (Part 1)/The End of a Symphony (Part 2)	1964	30.00
❑ 47-9693	Fig Leaves Are Falling/Juggling	1968	6.00
WARNER BROS.			
❑ 5378	Hello Mudduh! Hello Fadduh! (A Letter from Camp)/Rat Fink	1963	12.00
❑ 5378	Hello Mudduh! Hello Fadduh! (A Letter from Camp)/Here's to the Crabgrass	1963	15.00
❑ 5378 [PS]	Hello Mudduh! Hello Fadduh! (A Letter from Camp)/Rat Fink	1963	20.00
❑ 5406	The Twelve Gifts of Christmas/You Went the Wrong Way, Old King Louie	1963	25.00
❑ 5419	My Son the Vampire/I Can't Dance	1964	12.00
❑ 5435	Skin (Heart)/The Drop-Outs March	1964	10.00
❑ 5449	Hello Mudduh! Hello Fadduh! New 1964 Version/Hello Mudduh! Hello Fadduh! Original Version	1964	12.00
❑ 5449 [PS]	Hello Mudduh! Hello Fadduh! New 1964 Version/Hello Mudduh! Hello Fadduh! Original Version	1964	20.00
❑ 5490	Pop Hates the Beatles/Grow Mrs. Goldfarb	1964	15.00
❑ 5614	Crazy Downtown/The Drop-Outs March	1965	10.00
❑ 5672	The Drinking Man's Diet/The Laarge Daark Aardvark Song	1965	10.00
❑ 5806	His Own Little Island/Odd Ball	1966	10.00
❑ 5896	Westchester Hadassah/Strange Things in My Soup	1967	10.00
❑ 7112	Hello Mudduh! Hello Fadduh! (A Letter from Camp)/Sarah Jackman	1968	6.00
—"Back to Back Hits" series — originals have green "W7" labels			
7-Inch Extended Plays			
WARNER BROS.			
❑ PRO 145 [DJ]	Sarah Jackman/Oh Boy//Jump Down, Spin Around/Shake Hands with Your Uncle Max	196?	20.00
—Promo-only EP from "My Son, the Folk Singer"; probably not issued with picture sleeve			
❑ S 1487	Won't You Come Home Disraeli?/Medley/The Let's All Call Up AT&T†March//Mexican Hat Dance/When I Was A Lad/Me	196?	15.00
—Jukebox issue; small hole, plays at 33 1/3 rpm			
❑ S 1487 [PS]	My Son, the Celebrity	196?	15.00
Albums			
JUBLIEE			
❑ JGM 5019 [M]	More Folk Songs by Allan Sherman	1963	20.00
—Two early Allan Sherman sides plus comedy bits by others			
RCA RED SEAL			
❑ LM-2773 [M]	Peter and the Commissar	1964	20.00
❑ LSC-2773 [S]	Peter and the Commissar	1964	25.00
—With Arthur Fiedler and the Boston Pops Orchestra			
RHINO			
❑ RNLP-005	The Best of Allan Sherman	198?	10.00
❑ RNLP 70818	A Gift of Laughter	1986	10.00
WARNER BROS.			
❑ W 1475 [M]	My Son, the Folk Singer	1962	15.00
❑ WS 1475 [S]	My Son, the Folk Singer	1962	20.00
—Gold label			
❑ W 1487 [M]	My Son, the Celebrity	1963	15.00
❑ WS 1487 [S]	My Son, the Celebrity	1963	20.00
—Gold label			
❑ W 1501 [M]	My Son, the Nut	1963	15.00
❑ WS 1501 [S]	My Son, the Nut	1963	20.00
—Gold label			
❑ W 1539 [M]	Allan in Wonderland	1964	12.00
❑ WS 1539 [S]	Allan in Wonderland	1964	15.00
—Gold label			
❑ W 1569 [M]	For Swingin' Livers Only!	1964	12.00
❑ WS 1569 [S]	For Swingin' Livers Only!	1964	15.00
❑ W 1604 [M]	My Name Is Allan	1965	12.00
❑ WS 1604 [S]	My Name Is Allan	1965	15.00
—Gold label			
❑ W 1649 [M]	Allan Sherman — Live	1966	12.00
❑ WS 1649 [S]	Allan Sherman — Live	1966	15.00
—Gold label			
❑ W 1684 [M]	Togetherness	1967	15.00
❑ WS 1684 [S]	Togetherness	1967	20.00
—Gold label			

SHERMAN, BOBBY

Number	Title (A Side/B Side)	Yr	NM
45s			
CAMEO			
❑ 403	Happiness Is/Can't Get Used to Loving You	1966	10.00
❑ 403 [DJ]	Happiness Is	1966	20.00
—One-sided promo			
CONDOR			
❑ 1002	I'll Never Tell You/Telegram	1969	10.00
DECCA			
❑ 31672	Man Overboard/You Make Me Happy	1964	15.00
❑ 31741	It Hurts Me/Give Me Your Word	1965	15.00
❑ 31741 [PS]	It Hurts Me/Give Me Your Word	1965	50.00
❑ 31779	Hey Little Girl/Well All Right	1965	15.00
DOT			
❑ 16566	I Want to Hear It From Her/Nobody's Sweetheart	1963	15.00
EPIC			
❑ 10181	Cold Girl/Think of Rain	1967	10.00
❑ 10181 [PS]	Cold Girl/Think of Rain	1967	20.00
JANUS			
❑ 246	Runaway/Mr. Success	1975	4.00
❑ 254	Our Last Song Together/Sunshine Rose	1975	4.00
METROMEDIA			
❑ 68-0100	Early in the Morning/Unborn Lullaby	1973	5.00
❑ 121	Little Woman/One Too Many Mornings	1969	5.00
❑ 121 [PS]	Little Woman/One Too Many Mornings	1969	5.00
❑ 150	La La La (If I Had You)/Time	1969	5.00
❑ 150 [PS]	La La La (If I Had You)/Time	1969	5.00
❑ 177	Easy Come, Easy Go/July Seventeen	1970	5.00
❑ 177	Easy Come, Easy Go/Sounds Along the Way	1970	5.00
❑ 177 [PS]	Easy Come, Easy Go/July Seventeen	1970	5.00
❑ 188	Hey, Mister Sun/Two Blind Mice	1970	5.00
❑ 188 [PS]	Hey, Mister Sun/Two Blind Mice	1970	5.00
❑ 194	Julie, Do Ya Love Me/Spend Some Time Lovin' Me	1970	5.00
❑ 194 [PS]	Julie, Do Ya Love Me/Spend Some Time Lovin' Me	1970	5.00
❑ 204	Goin' Home (Sing a Song of Christmas Cheer)/Love's What You're Gettin' for Christmas	1970	6.00
❑ 204 [PS]	Goin' Home (Sing a Song of Christmas Cheer)/Love's What You're Gettin' for Christmas	1970	8.00
❑ 206	Cried Like a Baby/Is Anybody There	1971	5.00
❑ 206 [PS]	Cried Like a Baby/Is Anybody There	1971	5.00
❑ 217	The Drum/Free Now to Roam	1971	5.00
❑ 217 [PS]	The Drum/Free Now to Roam	1971	5.00
❑ 222	Waiting at the Bus Stop/Run Away	1971	5.00
❑ 222 [PS]	Waiting at the Bus Stop/Run Away	1971	5.00
❑ 227	Jennifer/Getting Together	1971	5.00
❑ 227 [PS]	Jennifer/Getting Together	1971	5.00
❑ 240	Together Again/Picture a Little Girl	1972	5.00
❑ 240 [PS]	Together Again/Picture a Little Girl	1972	5.00
❑ 249	I Don't Believe in Magic/Just a Little While Longer	1972	5.00
PARKWAY			
❑ 967	Goody Galumshus/Anything Your Little Heart Desires	1966	10.00
STARCREST			
❑ 100	Judy, You'll Never Know/Telegram	1962	20.00
TROPHY SERIES			
❑ MTS 1	Little Woman/La La La (If I Had You)	197?	5.00
—Reissue on Metromedia's short-lived "oldies" label			
❑ MTS 3	Easy Come, Easy Go/Hey, Mister Sun	197?	5.00
—Reissue on Metromedia's short-lived "oldies" label			
❑ MTS 4	Julie, Do Ya Love Me/Spend Some Time Lovin' Me	197?	5.00
—Reissue on Metromedia's short-lived "oldies" label			
Albums			
METROMEDIA			
❑ MD 1014	Bobby Sherman	1969	15.00
❑ MD 1028	Here Comes Bobby	1970	15.00
❑ MD 1032	With Love, Bobby	1970	15.00
❑ MD 1038	Bobby Sherman Christmas Album	1970	15.00
❑ MD 1040	Portrait of Bobby	1971	15.00
❑ MD 1045	Getting Together	1971	15.00
❑ KMD 1048	Bobby Sherman's Greatest Hits	1972	12.00
❑ MD 1060	Just for You	1973	15.00

SHERRYS, THE

Number	Title (A Side/B Side)	Yr	NM
45s			
GUYDEN			
❑ 2068	Pop-Pop-Pop-Eye/Your Hand in Mine	1962	15.00
❑ 2077	Slop Time/Let's Stomp Again	1963	15.00
❑ 2084	Saturday Night/I've Got No One	1963	15.00
❑ 2094	Monk, Monk, Monkey/That Boy of Mine	1963	15.00
MERCURY			
❑ 72256	No No Baby/That Guy of Mine	1964	12.00
ROBERTS			
❑ 701	Slow Jerk/Confusion	1965	12.00
Albums			
GUYDEN			
❑ GLP 503 [M]	At the Hop with the Sherrys	1963	250.00

S

SHEVELLES, THE

Number	Title (A Side/B Side)	Yr	NM
45s			
WORLD ARTISTS			
❑ 1023	Oo Poo Pa Doo/Like I Love You	1964	12.00
❑ 1025	How Would You Like Me to Love You/I Could Conquer the World	1964	12.00

SHEVETON, TONY

Number	Title (A Side/B Side)	Yr	NM
45s			
PARROT			
❑ 10616	Dance with Me/A Million Drums	1964	15.00

SHIEKS, THE

See THE SHEIKS.

SHIELDS, BILLY

Pseudonym of TONY ORLANDO.

Number	Title (A Side/B Side)	Yr	NM
45s			
HARBOUR			
❑ 304	I Was a Boy/Moments from Now	1969	25.00

SHIELDS, BOBBY

Number	Title (A Side/B Side)	Yr	NM
45s			
MELBA			
❑ 105	Land of Rock and Roll/I Wouldn't Change You for the World	1956	60.00

SHIELDS, THE

Number	Title (A Side/B Side)	Yr	NM
45s			
ATCO			
❑ 7071	The Way I Feel Tonight/All Right by Me	1977	5.00
CONTINENTAL			
❑ 4072	You Told Another Lie/Barnyard Dance	1961	400.00

DOT

Number	Title (A Side/B Side)	Yr	NM
❑ 136	You Cheated/Nature Boy	196?	10.00
—Reissue; black label			
❑ 136	You Cheated/Nature Boy	197?	5.00
—Reissue; pink, orange and red "swirl" label			
❑ 15805	You Cheated/That's the Way It's Gonna Be	1958	25.00
❑ 15856	I'm Sorry Now/Nature Boy	1958	30.00
❑ 15940	Fare Thee Well/Play the Game Fair	1959	25.00

TENDER

Number	Title (A Side/B Side)	Yr	NM
❑ 513	You Cheated/That's the Way It's Gonna Be	1958	40.00
—With reference to Dot Records on label			
❑ 513	You Cheated/That's the Way It's Gonna Be	1958	150.00
—No reference to Dot Records on label			
❑ 518	I'm Sorry Now/Nature Boy	1958	60.00
❑ 521	Fare Thee Well/Play the Game Fair	1959	60.00

TRANSCONTINENTAL

Number	Title (A Side/B Side)	Yr	NM
❑ 1013	The Girl Around the Corner/Fare Thee Well, My Love	1960	100.00

SHILOH Don Henley, later of EAGLES, was in this group. The album was produced by KENNY ROGERS.

45s

AMOS

Number	Title (A Side/B Side)	Yr	NM
❑ 140	Jennifer/Tell Her to Get Out of Your Life	1970	12.00
❑ 162	Down on the Farm/Simple Little Down Home Rock & Roll Love Song for Rosie	1971	12.00

Albums

AMOS

Number	Title (A Side/B Side)	Yr	NM
❑ AAS-7015	Shiloh	1971	80.00

SHINDIGS, THE Also known as THE BOBBY FULLER FOUR.

45s

MUSTANG

Number	Title (A Side/B Side)	Yr	NM
❑ 3003	Thunder Reef/Wolfman	1965	40.00

SHIP, THE

Albums

ELEKTRA

Number	Title (A Side/B Side)	Yr	NM
❑ EKS-75036	The Ship	1972	20.00

SHIRELLES, THE

45s

BELL

Number	Title (A Side/B Side)	Yr	NM
❑ 760	A Most Unusual Boy/Look What You've Done to My Heart	1969	10.00
❑ 787	Looking Glass/Playthings	1969	10.00
❑ 815	Never Give You Up/Go Away and Find Yourself	1969	10.00

BLUE ROCK

Number	Title (A Side/B Side)	Yr	NM
❑ 4051	Don't Mess with Cupid/Sweet Sweet Lovin'	1968	10.00
❑ 4066	Call Me/There's a Storm Goin' Home in My Heart	1968	10.00

DECCA

Number	Title (A Side/B Side)	Yr	NM
❑ 25506	I Met Him on a Sunday/My Love Is a Charm	196?	15.00
—Early reissue			
❑ 30588	I Met Him on a Sunday/I Want You to Be My Boyfriend	1958	25.00
❑ 30669	My Love Is a Charm/Slop Time	1958	40.00
❑ 30761	Stop Me/I Got the Message	1958	40.00

PHILCO-FORD

Number	Title (A Side/B Side)	Yr	NM
❑ HP-30	Soldier Boy/My Heart Belongs to You	1968	20.00
—4-inch plastic "Hip Pocket Record" with color sleeve			

RCA VICTOR

Number	Title (A Side/B Side)	Yr	NM
❑ 47-0902	Let's Give Each Other Love/Deep in the Night	1973	8.00
❑ 48-1019	No Sugar Tonight/Strange, I Still Love You	1971	10.00
❑ 48-1032	Brother, Brother/Sunday Dreaming	1972	10.00
❑ APBO-0192	Touch the Wind (Eres Tu)/Do What You've a Mind To	1973	8.00

SCEPTER

Number	Title (A Side/B Side)	Yr	NM
❑ 1203	Dedicated to the One I Love/Look A Here Baby	1958	20.00
—Red label			
❑ 1203	Dedicated to the One I Love/Look A Here Baby	1958	40.00
—White label			
❑ 1205	A Teardrop and a Lollipop/Doin' the Ronde	1959	20.00
—Red label			
❑ 1205	A Teardrop and a Lollipop/Doin' the Ronde	1959	30.00
—White label			
❑ 1207	Please Be My Boyfriend/I Saw a Tear	1960	20.00
—Red label			
❑ 1207	Please Be My Boyfriend/I Saw a Tear	1960	30.00
—White label			
❑ 1208	Tonight's the Night/The Dance Is Over	1960	20.00
—Red label			
❑ 1208	Tonight's the Night/The Dance Is Over	1960	25.00
—Pink label			
❑ 1208	Tonight's the Night/The Dance Is Over	1960	30.00
—White label			
❑ 1211	Will You Love Me Tomorrow/Boys	1960	30.00
—Revised A-side title			
❑ 1211	Tomorrow/Boys	1960	40.00
—Original A-side title			
❑ 1217	Mama Said/Blue Holiday	1961	20.00
❑ 1220	A Thing of the Past/What a Sweet Thing That Was	1961	20.00
❑ 1223	Big John/Twenty-One	1961	20.00
❑ 1227	Baby It's You/Things I Want to Hear (Pretty Words)	1961	20.00
❑ 1228	Soldier Boy/Love Is a Swingin' Thing	1962	15.00
❑ 1234	Welcome Home Baby/Mama, Here Comes the Bride	1962	15.00
❑ 1237	Stop the Music/It's Love That Really Counts	1962	15.00
❑ 1243	Everybody Loves a Lover/I Don't Think So	1962	15.00
❑ 1248	Foolish Little Girl/Not for All the Money in the World	1963	15.00
❑ 1248 [PS]	Foolish Little Girl/Not for All the Money in the World	1963	40.00
❑ 1255	Don't Say Goodnight and Mean Goodbye/I Didn't Mean to Hurt You	1963	12.00
❑ 1255 [PS]	Don't Say Goodnight and Mean Goodbye/I Didn't Mean to Hurt You	1963	40.00
❑ 1259	What Does a Girl Do?/Don't Let It Happen to You	1963	12.00
❑ 1260	It's a Mad, Mad, Mad, Mad World/31 Flavors	1963	12.00
❑ 1264	Tonight You're Gonna Fall in Love with Me/20th Century Rock and Roll	1963	12.00
❑ 1267	Sha-La-La/His Lips Get In the Way	1964	12.00
❑ 1278	Thank You Baby/Doomsday	1964	12.00
❑ 1284	Maybe Tonight/Lost Love	1964	12.00
❑ 1292	Are You Still My Baby/I Saw a Tear	1964	12.00
❑ 1296	Shh, I'm Watching the Movies/A Plus B	1965	12.00
❑ 12101	March (You'll Be Sorry)/Everybody's Goin' Mad	1965	10.00
❑ 12114	My Heart Belongs to You/Love That Man	1965	10.00
❑ 12123	(Mama) My Soldier Boy Is Coming Home/Soldier Boy	1965	10.00
❑ 12132	I Met Him on a Sunday — '66/Love That Man	1966	10.00
❑ 12150	Till My Baby Comes Home/Que Sera, Sera	1966	10.00
❑ 12162	Shades of Blue/After Midnight	1966	10.00
❑ 12162	Shades of Blue/Looking Around	1966	10.00
❑ 12178	Teasin' Me/Look Away	1966	10.00
❑ 12185	Don't Go Home (My Little Baby)/Nobody Baby After You	1967	10.00
❑ 12192	Too Much of a Good Thing/Bright Shiny Colors	1967	10.00
❑ 12198	Last Minute Miracle/No Doubt About It	1967	10.00
❑ 12209	Wild and Sweet/Wait Till I Give the Signal	1968	10.00
❑ 12217	Hippie Walk (Part 1)/Hippie Walk (Part 2)	1968	10.00

TIARA

Number	Title (A Side/B Side)	Yr	NM
❑ 6112	I Met Him on a Sunday/I Want You to Be My Boyfriend	1958	800.00
—Note: Copies with any catalog number except 6112 are reproductions with little collector value			

UNITED ARTISTS

Number	Title (A Side/B Side)	Yr	NM
❑ 50648	There Goes My Baby-Be My Baby/Strange, I Still Love You	1970	8.00
❑ 50693	It's Gonna Take a Miracle/Lost	1970	8.00
❑ 50740	Take Me for a Little While/Dedicated to the One I Love	1971	8.00

Albums

RCA VICTOR

Number	Title (A Side/B Side)	Yr	NM
❑ LSP-4581	Happy and In Love	1971	15.00
❑ LSP-4698	The Shirelles	1972	15.00

RHINO

Number	Title (A Side/B Side)	Yr	NM
❑ RNDA-1101 [(2)]	Anthology (1959-1967)	1984	12.00

SCEPTER

Number	Title (A Side/B Side)	Yr	NM
❑ S-501 [M]	Tonight's the Night	1961	200.00
—"Scepter" in scroll at top of label			
❑ SPM-501 [M]	Tonight's the Night	1962	60.00
—"Scepter Records" at left of label			
❑ SPS-501 [S]	Tonight's the Night	1965	100.00
❑ S-502 [M]	The Shirelles Sing to Trumpets and Strings	1961	200.00
—"Scepter" in scroll at top of label			
❑ SPM-502 [M]	The Shirelles Sing to Trumpets and Strings	1962	60.00
—"Scepter Records" at left of label			
❑ SPS-502 [S]	The Shirelles Sing to Trumpets and Strings	1965	100.00
❑ SPM-504 [M]	Baby It's You	1962	100.00
❑ SPS-504 [S]	Baby It's You	1965	100.00
❑ SPM-505 [M]	A Twist Party	1962	80.00
❑ SPS-505 [S]	A Twist Party	1965	100.00
❑ SPM-507 [M]	The Shirelles' Greatest Hits	1962	40.00
❑ SPS-507 [S]	The Shirelles' Greatest Hits	1965	50.00
❑ SPM-511 [M]	Foolish Little Girl	1963	50.00
❑ SPS-511 [S]	Foolish Little Girl	1965	80.00
❑ SPM-514 [M]	It's a Mad, Mad, Mad, Mad World	1963	40.00
❑ SPS-514 [S]	It's a Mad, Mad, Mad, Mad World	1963	50.00
❑ SPM-516 [M]	The Shirelles Sing the Golden Oldies	1964	40.00
❑ SPS-516 [S]	The Shirelles Sing the Golden Oldies	1964	50.00
❑ SPM-560 [M]	The Shirelles' Greatest Hits, Vol. 2	1967	20.00
❑ SPS-560 [S]	The Shirelles' Greatest Hits, Vol. 2	1967	25.00
❑ SPM-562 [M]	Spontaneous Combustion	1967	40.00
❑ SPS-562 [S]	Spontaneous Combustion	1967	50.00
❑ SPS-569	Eternally Soul	1968	30.00
❑ SPS-2-599 [(2)]	Remember When	1972	20.00

SPRINGBOARD

Number	Title (A Side/B Side)	Yr	NM
❑ 4006	The Shirelles Sing Their Very Best	1973	8.00

UNITED ARTISTS

Number	Title (A Side/B Side)	Yr	NM
❑ UA-LA340-E	The Very Best of the Shirelles	1974	10.00

SHIRLEY (AND COMPANY) Shirley Goodman, earlier of SHIRLEY AND LEE.

45s

VIBRATION

Number	Title (A Side/B Side)	Yr	NM
❑ 532	Shame, Shame, Shame/(Instrumental)	1974	5.00
❑ 535	Cry, Cry, Cry/(Instrumental)	1975	5.00
❑ 539	Disco Shirley/Keep On Rolling On	1975	5.00
❑ 542	I Like to Dance/Jim Doc C'ain	1976	5.00
❑ 579	Revelations True/(Instrumental)	1978	5.00

Albums

VIBRATION

Number	Title (A Side/B Side)	Yr	NM
❑ 128	Shame Shame Shame	1975	10.00

SHIRLEY AND LEE Also see SHIRLEY (AND COMPANY).

45s

ALADDIN

Number	Title (A Side/B Side)	Yr	NM
❑ 3153	I'm Gone/Sweethearts	1952	100.00
❑ 3173	Baby/Shirley Come Back to Me	1953	120.00
❑ 3192	Shirley's Back/So In Love	1953	60.00
❑ 3205	Two Happy People/The Proposal	1953	50.00
❑ 3222	Why Did I/Lee Goofed	1954	50.00
❑ 3244	Confessin'/Keep On	1954	50.00
❑ 3258	Comin' Over/Takes Money	1954	50.00
❑ 3289	Feel So Good/You'd Be Thinking of Me	1955	40.00
❑ 3302	Let's Dream/I'll Do It	1955	40.00
❑ 3325	Let the Good Times Roll/Do You Mean to Hurt Me So	1956	60.00
❑ 3338	I Feel Good/Now That It's Over	1956	25.00
❑ 3362	When I Saw You/That's What I Want to Do	1957	20.00
❑ 3369	I Want to Dance/Marry Me	1957	20.00
❑ 3380	Rock All Night/Don't You Know I Love You	1957	20.00
❑ 3390	Rockin' with the Clock/The Flirt	1957	20.00
❑ 3405	Love No One But You (I Love You So)/I'll Thrill You	1958	20.00
❑ 3418	Everybody's Rocking/Don't Leave Me Here to Cry	1958	20.00
❑ 3432	Come On and Have Your Fun/All I Want to Do Is Cry	1958	20.00
❑ 3455	True Love/When Day Is Done	1959	20.00

IMPERIAL

Number	Title (A Side/B Side)	Yr	NM
❑ 013	Let the Good Times Roll/Feel So Good	196?	10.00
—"The Golden Series" reissue; gold label, Imperial logo at top			
❑ 5818	Together We Stand (Divided We Fall)/The Joker	1962	10.00
❑ 5854	My Last Letter/I'm Early Enough	1962	10.00

Except when noted otherwise, VG = 25% of NM, and VG+ = 50% of NM. (Example: VG = $2.00, VG+ = $4.00 and NM = $8.00.)

Number	Title (A Side/B Side)	Yr	NM
❑ 5868	Don't Stop Now/A Little Thing	1962	10.00
❑ 5922	The Golden Rule/Hey Little Boy	1963	10.00
❑ 5970	Dancing World/I'm Gone	1963	10.00
❑ 5979	Paper Doll/The Brink of Disaster	1963	10.00
❑ 66000	Somebody Put a Jukebox in the Study Hall/Never Let Me Go	1963	10.00
UNITED ARTISTS			
❑ 0087	Let the Good Times Roll/Feel So Good	1973	4.00
—"Silver Spotlight Series" reissue			
❑ XW274	Let the Good Times Roll/That's What I Wanna Do	1973	5.00
WARWICK			
❑ 581	Let the Good Times Roll/Keep Loving Me	1960	12.00
❑ 609	Two Peas in a Pod/Your Love Makes the Difference	1961	12.00
❑ 664	Well-a, Well-a/Our Kids	1961	12.00
❑ 679	Let's Live It Up/Girl, You're Married Now	1962	12.00
Albums			
ALADDIN			
❑ 807 [M]	Let the Good Times Roll	1956	1500.
IMPERIAL			
❑ LP-9179 [M]	Let the Good Times Roll	1962	300.00
—Reissue of Aladdin LP			
SCORE			
❑ SLP-4023 [M]	Let the Good Times Roll	1957	800.00
—Reissue of Aladdin LP			
WARWICK			
❑ W-2028 [M]	Let the Good Times Roll	1961	150.00
❑ W-2028ST [S]	Let the Good Times Roll	1961	300.00

SHIRTS, THE

Number	Title (A Side/B Side)	Yr	NM
45s			
CAPITOL			
❑ 4750	Can't Cry Anymore/I'm in Love Again	1979	4.00
❑ 4750 [PS]	Can't Cry Anymore/I'm in Love Again	1979	6.00
❑ 4783	Don't You Hesitate/Ground Zero	1979	4.00
❑ 4783 [PS]	Don't You Hesitate/Ground Zero	1979	6.00
Albums			
CAPITOL			
❑ SW-11791	The Shirts	1978	14.00
❑ ST-11944	Street Light Shine	1979	14.00
❑ SW-12085	Inner Sleeve	1980	12.00

SHOCKED, MICHELLE

Number	Title (A Side/B Side)	Yr	NM
12-Inch Singles			
MERCURY			
❑ 618 [DJ]	Anchorage (same on both sides)	1988	6.00
❑ PRO 701 [DJ]	When I Grow Up/Memories of East Texas/Yamboree Queen/Strawberry Jam	1988	15.00
❑ PRO701 [DJ]	When I Grow Up/Memories of East Texas/Yamboree Queen/Strawberry Jam	1988	15.00
❑ 757 [DJ]	On the Greener Side/Must Be Luff	1989	10.00
❑ 757 [DJ]	On the Greener Side/Must Be Luff	1989	10.00
45s			
MERCURY			
❑ 870611-7	Anchorage/Anchorage (Live Video Version)	1988	3.00
❑ 870611-7 [PS]	Anchorage/Anchorage (Live Video Version)	1988	3.00
❑ 872590-7	When I Grow Up/Fogtown	1989	3.00
❑ 872590-7 [PS]	When I Grow Up/Fogtown	1989	3.00
Albums			
MERCURY			
❑ PRO 797 [DJ]	Live	1990	20.00
—Five-song mini-LP for radio stations with custom jacket			
❑ PRO797 [DJ]	Live	1990	20.00
—Five-song mini-LP for radio stations with custom jacket			
❑ 834581-1	The Texas Campfire Tapes	1988	12.00
❑ 834924-1	Short Sharp Shocked	1988	10.00
❑ 838878-1	Captain Swing	1989	10.00

SHOCKING BLUE, THE

Number	Title (A Side/B Side)	Yr	NM
45s			
BUDDAH			
❑ 258	Sleepless at Midnight/Serenade	1971	6.00
COLOSSUS			
❑ 108	Venus/Hot Sand	1969	10.00
❑ 108 [PS]	Venus/Hot Sand	1969	15.00
❑ 111	Mighty Joe/I'm a Woman	1970	8.00
❑ 111 [PS]	Mighty Joe/I'm a Woman	1970	12.00
❑ 116	Long and Lonesome Road/Ackaragh	1970	8.00
❑ 123	Never Love a Railroad Man/Never Marry	1970	8.00
❑ 141	Boll Weevil/Long and Lonesome Road	1971	6.00
MGM			
❑ 14481	When I Was a Girl/Eve and the Apple	1973	6.00
❑ 14543	Oh Love/Inkpot	1973	6.00
21 RECORDS			
❑ 99517	Venus/Mighty Joe	1986	4.00
Albums			
COLOSSUS			
❑ CS-1000	The Shocking Blue	1970	25.00

SHOES

Number	Title (A Side/B Side)	Yr	NM
12-Inch Singles			
ELEKTRA			
❑ 11440 [DJ]	I Don't Wanna Hear It/Now and Then	1979	15.00
❑ 11440 [DJ]	I Don't Wanna Hear It/Now and Then	1979	15.00
45s			
BOMP!			
❑ 116	Okay/Tomorrow Night	1978	4.00
❑ 116 [PS]	Okay/Tomorrow Night	1978	4.00
ELEKTRA			
❑ 46557	Too Late/Now and Then	1979	4.00
❑ 46557 [PS]	Too Late/Now and Then	1979	4.00
❑ 46571	Tomorrow Night/Now and Then	1979	4.00
❑ 46598	I Don't Miss You/In My Arms Again	1980	4.00
❑ 47130	Karen/She Satisfies	1981	4.00
Albums			
(NO LABEL)			
❑ (no #)	One in Versailles	1976	120.00
BLACK VINYL			
❑ 51477	Black Vinyl Shoes	1977	80.00
ELEKTRA			
❑ 6E-244	Present Tense	1979	10.00
❑ 6E-303	Tongue Twister	1980	10.00
❑ AS11570 [DJ]	Shoes on Ice — Live	1982	40.00
—Promo-only 7-song live record; issued in generic jacket			
❑ AS 11570 [DJ]	Shoes on Ice — Live	1982	50.00
—Promo-only 7-song live record; issued in generic jacket			
❑ 60146	Boomerang	1982	10.00
PVC			
❑ 7904	Black Vinyl Shoes	1979	20.00

SHONDELL, TROY

Number	Title (A Side/B Side)	Yr	NM
45s			
AVM			
❑ 14	(I'm Looking for Some) New Blue Jeans/(B-side unknown)	1988	7.00
BEAR			
❑ 2002	No One Knows/Sweet Enough	1989	6.00
BRITE STAR			
❑ 2453	This Time/You're Nobody's Child	1973	8.00
❑ 2459	Still Loving You/Rip It Up	1973	8.00
❑ 4691	Deeper and Deeper in Love/Love Stuff	1974	8.00
DECCA			
❑ 31712	You Can't Catch Me/Walkin' in a Memory	1964	10.00
EVEREST			
❑ 2015	Gone/Some People Never Learn	1963	10.00
❑ 2018	I've Got a Woman/No Fool Like an Old Fool	1963	10.00
❑ 2041	Trouble/Little Miss Tease	1964	10.00
GAYE			
❑ 2010	This Time/I Catch Myself Crying	1961	80.00
GOLDCREST			
❑ 161-A	This Time/Girl After Girl	1961	25.00
—With "Distributed by Liberty Record Sales" on label			
❑ 161-A	This Time/Girl After Girl	1961	30.00
—With no "Distributed by Liberty" on label			
ITCO			
❑ 105	And We Made Love/Imitation Woman	198?	5.00
LIBERTY			
❑ 55353	This Time/Girl After Girl	1961	20.00
❑ 55398	Tears from an Angel/Island in the Sky	1961	16.00
❑ 55445	Just Because/Na-Ne-No	1962	16.00
RIC			
❑ 174	Just a Dream/Just Like Me	1965	10.00
❑ 184	Big Windy City/I Thought That You Were Mine	1966	10.00
STAR-FOX			
❑ 77	Still Loving You/Doctor Love	1979	8.00
TELESONIC			
❑ 804	(Sittin' Here) Lovin' You/(Here I Am) Single Again	1980	8.00
TRX			
❑ 5001	A Rose and a Baby Ruth/Here It Comes Again	1967	8.00
❑ 5003	Head Man/She's Got Everything She Needs	1967	8.00
❑ 5015	Let's Go All the Way/Let Me Love You	1968	8.00
❑ 5019	Something's Wrong in Indiana/A Rose and a Baby Ruth	1969	8.00
Albums			
EVEREST			
❑ 1206 [S]	The Many Sides of Troy Shondell	1963	80.00
❑ 5206 [M]	The Many Sides of Troy Shondell	1963	50.00
SUNSET			
❑ SUM-1174 [M]	This Time	1967	15.00
❑ SUS-5174 [S]	This Time	1967	15.00

SHONDELLES, THE

Number	Title (A Side/B Side)	Yr	NM
45s			
KING			
❑ 5597	Don't Cry My Soldier Boy/My Love	1962	20.00
❑ 5656	Wonderful One/I Gotta Tell It	1962	20.00
❑ 5705	Muscle Bound/Special Delivery	1963	20.00
❑ 5755	Watusi, One More/Ooo, Sometimes	1963	20.00

SHONDELLS, THE See TOMMY JAMES AND THE SHONDELLS.

SHOOTERS, THE
With OTIS REDDING.

Number	Title (A Side/B Side)	Yr	NM
45s			
TRANS WORLD			
❑ 6908	Tuff Enuff/She's All Right	1960	100.00

SHOOTING STAR

Number	Title (A Side/B Side)	Yr	NM
12-Inch Singles			
EPIC			
❑ AS 1739 [DJ]	Winner/Train Rolls On	1983	8.00
❑ AS1739 [DJ]	Winner/Train Rolls On	1983	8.00
GEFFEN			
❑ PRO2335 [DJ]	Summer Sun (same on both sides)	1985	8.00
❑ PRO2351 [DJ]	Heat of the Night (same on both sides)	1985	8.00
❑ PRO-A-2335 [DJ]	Summer Sun (same on both sides)	1985	8.00
❑ PRO-A-2351 [DJ]	Heat of the Night (same on both sides)	1985	8.00
PASHA			
❑ AS 1877 [DJ]	Take It/Get Ready Boy	1984	8.00
❑ AS1877 [DJ]	Take It/Get Ready Boy	1984	8.00
45s			
EPIC			
❑ 02516	Flesh and Blood/You've Got Love	1981	3.00
❑ 04025	Straight Ahead/Taken Enough	1983	3.00
GEFFEN			
❑ 28994	Summer Sun/Time	1985	3.00
❑ 28994 [PS]	Summer Sun/Time	1985	3.00
VIRGIN			
❑ 02755	Hang On for Your Life/Hollywood	1982	3.00
❑ 03028	Do You Feel Alright/Where You Gonna Run	1982	3.00
❑ 03285	Heartache/Let It Out	1982	3.00
❑ 67005	You've Got What I Need/Wild in the Streets	1980	3.00
❑ 67005 [PS]	You've Got What I Need/Wild in the Streets	1980	3.00
❑ 67010	Bring It On/(B-side unknown)	1980	3.00
Albums			
EPIC			
❑ NFE 37407	Hang On for Your Life	1981	10.00
❑ PE 37720	Shooting Star	1982	8.00
—Reissue of Virgin VA 13133			
❑ FE 38020	3 Wishes	1982	10.00
❑ BFE 38683	Burning	1983	10.00
GEFFEN			
❑ GHS 24056	Silent Scream	1985	10.00
VIRGIN			
❑ VA 13133	Shooting Star	1979	10.00

SHORT, BOBBY

Number	Title (A Side/B Side)	Yr	NM
45s			
ATLANTIC			
❑ 1157	Down in Mexico/ Sand in My Shoes	1957	12.00
Albums			
ATLANTIC			
❑ SD 2-606 [(2)]	Bobby Short Loves Cole Porter	1972	20.00
❑ SD 2-607 [(2)]	Mad About Noel Coward	1972	20.00
❑ SD 2-608 [(2)]	Bobby Short Is K-RA-Z-Y for Gershwin	1973	15.00
❑ SD 2-609 [(2)]	Live at the Café Carlyle	1974	15.00
❑ SD 2-610 [(2)]	Bobby Short Celebrates Rodgers and Hart	197?	15.00
❑ 1214 [M]	Songs by Bobby Short	1955	30.00
—Black label			
❑ 1214 [M]	Songs by Bobby Short	1961	20.00
—White "fan" logo at right of label			
❑ 1214 [M]	Songs by Bobby Short	1963	15.00
—Black "fan" logo at right of label			
❑ 1230 [M]	Bobby Short	1956	30.00
—Black label			
❑ 1230 [M]	Bobby Short	1961	20.00
—White "fan" logo at right of label			
❑ 1230 [M]	Bobby Short	1963	15.00
—Black "fan" logo at right of label			
❑ 1262 [M]	Speaking of Love	1958	30.00
—Black label			
❑ 1262 [M]	Speaking of Love	1961	20.00
—White "fan" logo at right of label			
❑ SD 1262 [S]	Speaking of Love	1959	40.00
—Green label			
❑ SD 1262 [S]	Speaking of Love	1961	25.00
—White "fan" logo at right of label			
❑ 1285 [M]	Sing Me a Swing Song	1958	30.00
—Black label			
❑ 1285 [M]	Sing Me a Swing Song	1961	20.00
—White "fan" logo at right of label			
❑ 1285 [M]	Sing Me a Swing Song	1963	15.00
—Black "fan" logo at right of label			
❑ 1302 [M]	The Mad Twenties	1959	30.00
—Black label			
❑ 1302 [M]	The Mad Twenties	1961	20.00
—White "fan" logo at right of label			
❑ 1302 [M]	The Mad Twenties	1963	15.00
—Black "fan" logo at right of label			
❑ SD 1302 [S]	The Mad Twenties	1959	40.00
—Green label			
❑ SD 1302 [S]	The Mad Twenties	1961	25.00
—White "fan" logo at right of label			
❑ SD 1302 [S]	The Mad Twenties	1963	20.00
—Black "fan" logo at right of label			
❑ 1321 [M]	On the East Side	1960	30.00
—Black label			
❑ 1321 [M]	On the East Side	1961	20.00
—White "fan" logo at right of label			
❑ 1321 [M]	On the East Side	1963	15.00
—Black "fan" logo at right of label			
❑ SD 1321 [S]	On the East Side	1960	40.00
—Green label			
❑ SD 1321 [S]	On the East Side	1961	25.00
—White "fan" logo at right of label			
❑ SD 1321 [S]	On the East Side	1963	20.00
—Black "fan" logo at right of label			
❑ SD 1535	Jump for Joy	1969	12.00
❑ SD 1574	Nobody Else But Me	1971	12.00
❑ SD 1620	The Very Best of Bobby Short	1973	12.00
❑ SD 1664	The Mad Twenties	1974	12.00
❑ SD 1689	Personal	1977	12.00
❑ 81715 [(4)]	50 from Bobby Short	1987	30.00
❑ 81778	Guess Who's in Town: The Lyrics of Andy Razaf	1988	10.00
ELEKTRA			
❑ E1-60002	Moments Like This	1982	10.00

SHORT CROSS

Number	Title (A Side/B Side)	Yr	NM
Albums			
GRIZZLY			
❑ S-16013	Arising	1970	250.00

SHORTER, WAYNE

Also see WEATHER REPORT.

Number	Title (A Side/B Side)	Yr	NM
12-Inch Singles			
COLUMBIA			
❑ CAS 2609	Remote Control (Extended) (LP)	1985	6.00
45s			
VEE JAY			
❑ 363	Black Diamond/ Harry's Last Stand	1960	12.00
Albums			
BLUE NOTE			
❑ BN-LA014-G	Moto Grosso Feio	1973	15.00
❑ LT-988	The Soothsayer	1979	12.00
❑ LT-1056	Etcetera	1980	12.00
❑ BLP-4173 [M]	Night Drreamer	1964	25.00
❑ BLP-4182 [M]	Juju	1965	25.00
❑ BLP-4194 [M]	Speak No Evil	1966	25.00
❑ BLP-4219 [M]	The All Seeing Eye	1966	25.00
❑ B1-29100	The All Seeing Eye	1994	15.00
❑ B1-32096	Schizophrenia	1995	15.00
❑ B1-33581	Etcetera	1995	15.00
❑ B1-46509	Speak No Evil	1997	15.00
—Reissue on 180-gram vinyl			
❑ BST-84173 [S]	Night Drreamer	1964	30.00
—With New York, USA address on label			
❑ BST-84173 [S]	Night Drreamer	1967	15.00
—With "A Division of Liberty Records" on label			
❑ BST-84182	Juju	198?	10.00
—"The Finest in Jazz Since 1939" reissue			
❑ BST-84182 [S]	Juju	1965	30.00
—With New York, USA address on label			
❑ BST-84182 [S]	Juju	1967	15.00
—With "A Division of Liberty Records" on label			
❑ BST-84194 [S]	Speak No Evil	1966	30.00
—With New York, USA address on label			
❑ BST-84194 [S]	Speak No Evil	1967	15.00
—With "A Division of Liberty Records" on label			
❑ BST-84219 [S]	The All Seeing Eye	1966	30.00
—With New York, USA address on label			
❑ BST-84219 [S]	The All Seeing Eye	1967	15.00
—With "A Division of Liberty Records" on label			
❑ BST-84232	Adam's Apple	1967	20.00
❑ BST-84232	Adam's Apple	1985	10.00
—"The Finest in Jazz Since 1939" reissue			
❑ BST-84297	Schizophrenia	1969	20.00
❑ BST-84332	Super Nova	1970	20.00
❑ BST-84363	The Odyssey of Iska	1971	15.00
❑ B1-91141	The Best of Wayne Shorter	1988	10.00
COLUMBIA			
❑ PC 33418	Native Dancer	1975	12.00
—Originals have no bar code			
❑ PC 33418	Native Dancer	198?	8.00
—Reissue with bar code			
❑ FC 40055	Atlantis	1985	10.00
❑ FC 40373	Phantom Navigator	1987	10.00
❑ FC 44110	Joy Ryder	1988	10.00
GNP CRESCENDO			
❑ GNPS-2075 [(2)]	Wayne Shorter	1973	15.00
TRIP			
❑ 5009 [(2)]	Shorter Moments	1974	12.00
VEE JAY			
❑ LP-3006 [M]	Introducing Wayne Shorter	1960	40.00
❑ SR-3006 [S]	Introducing Wayne Shorter	1960	50.00
❑ VJS-3006	Introducing Wayne Shorter	1986	12.00
—1980s reissue on thinner vinyl			
❑ LP-3029 [M]	Wayning Moments	1962	30.00
❑ SR-3029 [S]	Wayning Moments	1962	40.00
❑ VJS-3029	Wayning Moments	198?	12.00
—1980s reissue on thinner vinyl			
❑ LP-3057 [M]	Second Genesis	1963	30.00
❑ SR-3057 [S]	Second Genesis	1963	40.00
❑ VJS-3057	Second Genesis	198?	12.00
—1980s reissue on thinner vinyl			

SHOTGUN EXPRESS

With ROD STEWART.

Number	Title (A Side/B Side)	Yr	NM
45s			
UPTOWN			
❑ 747	I Could Feel the Whole World Turn/Curtains	1967	30.00

SHOTGUN LTD.

Number	Title (A Side/B Side)	Yr	NM
45s			
PROPHESY			
❑ 55004	River of Hope/(B-side unknown)	1971	8.00
Albums			
PROPHESY			
❑ 6050	Shotgun Ltd.	1971	20.00

SHOWMEN, THE

With General Johnson, later of CHAIRMEN OF THE BOARD.

Number	Title (A Side/B Side)	Yr	NM
45s			
AMY			
❑ 11036	Action/What Would It Take	1968	8.00
IMPERIAL			
❑ 66033	It Will Stand/Country Fool	1964	12.00
❑ 66071	Country Fool/Somebody Help Me	1964	12.00
LIBERTY			
❑ 56166	It Will Stand/Country Fool	1970	6.00
MINIT			
❑ 632	It Will Stand/Country Fool	1961	20.00
—Black label			
❑ 632	It Will Stand/Country Fool	1961	30.00
—Orange label			
❑ 643	The Wrong Girl/Fate Planned It This Way	1962	50.00
❑ 647	Com'n Home/I Love You, Can't You See	1962	25.00
❑ 654	True Fine Mama/ The Owl Sees You	1962	25.00
❑ 662	39-21-46/Swish Fish	1963	25.00
❑ 32007	39-21-46/Swish Fish	1966	10.00
SWAN			
❑ 4213	In Paradise/Take It Baby	1965	10.00
❑ 4219	Our Love Will Grow/ You're Everything	1965	10.00
❑ 4241	Please Try and Understand/ Honey House	1966	10.00
UNITED ARTISTS			
❑ 0100	It Will Stand/I'm a Happy Man	1973	5.00
—"Silver Spotlight Series" reissue; B-side by the Jive Five			
Albums			
COLLECTABLES			
❑ COL-5162	Golden Classics	198?	10.00

SHUFFLES, THE

Number	Title (A Side/B Side)	Yr	NM
45s			
RAYCO			
❑ 508	Do You Remember My Darling/ Dancin' Little Girl	1963	200.00

SHUT DOWNS, THE

Number	Title (A Side/B Side)	Yr	NM
45s			
DIMENSION			
❑ 1016	Four on the Floor/Beach Buggy	1963	25.00
KARSONG			
❑ 501	Four on the Floor/Straightaway	1963	50.00

SICKNICKS, THE

Number	Title (A Side/B Side)	Yr	NM
45s			
AMY			
❑ 824	The Presidential Press Conference (Part 1)/ The Presidential Press Conference (Part 2)	1961	15.00
❑ 824 [PS]	The Presidential Press Conference (Part 1)/ The Presidential Press Conference (Part 2)	1961	25.00
❑ 831	Wadja Say Mr. K (Part 1)/ Wadja Say Mr. K (Part 2)	1961	15.00
Albums			
AMY			
❑ 2 [M]	Sick #2	1961	30.00

SIDEKICKS, THE

Number	Title (A Side/B Side)	Yr	NM
45s			
RCA VICTOR			
❑ 47-8864	Suspicions/Up on the Roof	1966	10.00
❑ 47-8969	Fifi the Flea/Not Now	1966	10.00
❑ 47-9079	He's My Friend/Miss Charlotte	1967	10.00
❑ 47-9174	Sight and Sound/You Gave Me Somebody to Love	1967	10.00
Albums			
RCA VICTOR			
❑ LPM-3712 [M]	Fifi the Flea	1966	20.00
❑ LSP-3712 [S]	Fifi the Flea	1966	25.00

SIDEWALK SURFERS, THE

Number	Title (A Side/B Side)	Yr	NM
45s			
JUBILEE			
❑ 5496	Skate Board/Fun Last Summer	1965	50.00

SIDEWINDERS, THE

Number	Title (A Side/B Side)	Yr	NM
45s			
RCA VICTOR			
❑ 48-1033	Rendezvous/O Miss Mary	1972	8.00
Albums			
RCA VICTOR			
❑ LSP-4694	The Sidewinders	1972	20.00

SIERRAS, THE

Number	Title (A Side/B Side)	Yr	NM
45s			
DOT			
❑ 16569	Plan for Love/ Then I'll Still Love You	1963	12.00
GOLDISC			
❑ G-4	I Should Have Loved You/ I'll Believe It When I See It	1963	30.00
KNOX			
❑ 102	So Many Sleepless Nights/ Nearer My Heart	1962	100.00
MAIL CALL			
❑ 2333/4	Stormy Weather/Chance	1963	200.00

SIGLER, BUNNY

Number	Title (A Side/B Side)	Yr	NM
12-Inch Singles			
GOLD MIND			
❑ 501	Glad to Be Your Lover (8:48)/I'm Funkin' You Tonight (5:30)	1979	12.00

Except when noted otherwise, VG = 25% of NM, and VG+ = 50% of NM. (Example: VG = $2.00, VG+ = $4.00 and NM = $8.00.)

Number	Title (A Side/B Side)	Yr	NM
45s			
CRAIG			
❑ 501	I Won't Cry/Come On Home	1961	30.00
—As Bunny "Mr. Emotions" Sigler			
DECCA			
❑ 31880	Everything's Gonna Be All Right/For Cryin' Out Loud	1965	25.00
❑ 31947	Will You Love Me Tomorrow/Comparatively Speaking	1966	12.00
❑ 32183	Will You Love Me Tomorrow/Let Them Talk	1967	10.00
GOLD MIND			
❑ 4008	Let Me Party with You (Part 1) (Party, Party, Party)/Let Me Party with You (Part 2) (Party, Party, Party)	1977	5.00
❑ 4010	I Got What You Need/It's Time to Twist	1978	5.00
❑ 4012	Only You/Good Good Feeling	1978	6.00
—A-side with Loleatta Holloway; B-side is Holloway solo			
❑ 4014	Don't Even Try (Give It Up)/I'm a Fool	1978	5.00
❑ 4018	By the Way You Dance (I Knew It Was You)/Glad to Be Your Lover	1979	5.00
❑ 4020	I'm Funking You Tonight with My Music/Glad to Be Your Lover	1979	5.00
NEPTUNE			
❑ 14	Where Do the Lonely Go/Great Big Liar	1969	8.00
❑ 15	We're Only Human/Sure Didn't Take Long	1969	8.00
—With Cindy Scott			
❑ 24	Conquer the World Together/We're Only Human	1970	8.00
—With Cindy Scott			
❑ 25	Don't Stop Doing What You're Doing/Where Do the Lonely Go	1970	8.00
PARKWAY			
❑ 123	Girl Don't Make Me Wait/Always in the Wrong Place (At the Wrong Time)	1966	10.00
❑ 153	Let the Good Times Roll & Feel So Good/There's No Love Left (In This Old Heart of Mine)	1967	12.00
❑ 6000	Lovey Dovey & You're So Fine/Sunny Sunday	1967	10.00
❑ 6001	Follow Your Heart/Can You Dig It	1967	10.00
PHILADELPHIA INT'L.			
❑ 3505	Everybody Needs Good Lovin' (Part 1)/Everybody Needs Good Lovin' (Part 2)	1971	6.00
❑ 3512	Conquer the World Together/We Gotta Good Thing Goin'	1971	6.00
—With Dee Dee Sharp			
❑ 3519	Heaven Knows I've Changed/Regina	1972	6.00
❑ 3523	Tossin' and Turnin'/Picture Us	1972	6.00
❑ 3532	Theme from "Five Fingers of Death"/Regina	1973	6.00
❑ 3536	That's How Long I'll Be Loving You/Heaven Knows I've Changed	1973	6.00
❑ 3545	Love Train (Part 1)/Love Train (Part 2)	1974	6.00
❑ 3554	Keep Smilin'/Somebody Free	1974	6.00
❑ 3560	Shake Your Booty/Your Love Is Good	1975	6.00
❑ 3575	Somebody Free/That's How Long I'll Be Loving You	1975	6.00
❑ 3582	Jingle Bells (Part 1)/Jingle Bells (Part 2)	1975	5.00
❑ 3597	My Music/Can't Believe That You Love Me	1976	6.00
❑ 3608	Somebody Loves You/Woman, Woman	1976	6.00
SALSOUL			
❑ 2114	How Can I Tell Her (It's Over)/Since the Day I First Saw You	1980	4.00
❑ 2125	Super Duper Duper Superman/Kool Aid	1980	4.00
V-TONE			
❑ 500	Family Dance/Hold On	196?	20.00
Albums			
GOLD MIND			
❑ 7502	Let Me Party with You	1978	12.00
❑ 9503	I've Always Wanted to Sing... Not Just Write Songs	1979	12.00
PARKWAY			
❑ P-50000 [M]	Let the Good Times Roll	1967	40.00
❑ PS-50000 [S]	Let the Good Times Roll	1967	40.00
PHILADELPHIA INT'L.			
❑ KZ 32589	That's How Long I'll Be Loving You	1974	15.00
❑ KZ 33249	Keep Smilin'	1974	15.00
❑ PZ 34267	My Music	1976	15.00
SALSOUL			
❑ SA-8531	Let It Snow	1980	12.00

SIGNATURES, THE

Number	Title (A Side/B Side)	Yr	NM
45s			
NORMAN			
❑ 210	Julie Is Her Name/Someone in Love	1957	300.00
WHIPPET			
❑ 210	Julie Is Her Name/Someone in Love	1957	50.00
Albums			
WARNER BROS.			
❑ W 1250 [M]	The Signatures Sing In	1958	30.00
❑ WS 1250 [S]	The Signatures Sing In	1958	40.00
❑ W 1353 [M]	Prepare to Flip!	1959	30.00
❑ WS 1353 [S]	Prepare to Flip!	1959	40.00
WHIPPET			
❑ WLP-702 [M]	The Signatures — Their Voices and Instruments	1957	60.00

SILBERMAN, BENEDICT, ORCHESTRA AND CHORUS

Number	Title (A Side/B Side)	Yr	NM
45s			
PALETTE			
❑ 5037	The Chipmunk Song/Lovers of Paris	1959	10.00

SILHOUETTES, THE

Number	Title (A Side/B Side)	Yr	NM
45s			
ACE			
❑ 552	I Sold My Heart to the Junkman/What Would You Do	1958	20.00
❑ 562	Evelyn/Never Will Part	1959	20.00
—As "Bill Horton and the Silhouettes"			
EMBER			
❑ 1029	Get a Job/I Am Lonely	1958	30.00
—Red label			
❑ 1029	Get a Job/I Am Lonely	1958	40.00
—Orange label			
❑ 1029	Get a Job/I Am Lonely	1960	20.00
—Black label			
❑ 1032	Headin' for the Poorhouse/Miss Thing	1958	20.00
❑ 1037	Bing Bong/Voodoo Eyes	1958	20.00
GOODWAY			
❑ 101	Not Me Baby/Gaucho Serenade	1966	200.00
—As "The New Silhouettes"			
GRAND			
❑ 142	Wish I Could Be There/Move On Over	1956	200.00
IMPERIAL			
❑ 5899	The Push/Which Way Did She Go	1962	12.00
JUNIOR			
❑ 391	Get a Job/I Am Lonely	1957	600.00
—Blue label (second press)			
❑ 391	Get a Job/I Am Lonely	1957	800.00
—Brown label (first press)			
❑ 396	I Sold My Heart to the Junkman/What Would You Do	1958	100.00
❑ 400	Evelyn/Never Will Part	1959	200.00
❑ 993	Your Love/Rent Man	1963	30.00
LANA			
❑ 108	Get a Job/I Am Lonely	196?	8.00
—Oldies reissue			
LOST-NITE			
❑ 254	Get a Job/I Am Lonely	196?	5.00
—Reissue			
❑ 418	Bing Bong/Voodoo Eyes	197?	5.00
—Reissue			
UNITED ARTISTS			
❑ 147	I Sold My Heart to the Junkman/What Would You Do	1958	—
—Canceled			
Albums			
GOODWAY			
❑ GLP-100	The Silhouettes 1958-1968/Get a Job	1968	300.00

SILK Also see MICHAEL STANLEY BAND.

Number	Title (A Side/B Side)	Yr	NM
45s			
DECCA			
❑ 32829	Come Over Here/Falling in Love Isn't Easy	1971	8.00
Albums			
ABC			
❑ S-694	Smooth As Raw Silk	1969	25.00

SILKIE, THE

Number	Title (A Side/B Side)	Yr	NM
45s			
FONTANA			
❑ 1525	You've Got to Hide Your Love Away/City Winds	1965	15.00
—Light blue label; A-side was produced by John Lennon and Paul McCartney, with the two and George Harrison playing along			
❑ 1525	You've Got to Hide Your Love Away/City Wind	1965	20.00
—Dark blue label			
❑ 1536	The Keys to My Soul/Leave Me to Cry	1965	10.00
❑ 1551	Born to Be With You/I'm So Sorry	1966	10.00
Albums			
FONTANA			
❑ MGF 27548 [M]	You've Got to Hide Your Love Away	1965	40.00
—With purplish, black and white cover			
❑ MGF 27548 [M]	You've Got to Hide Your Love Away	1965	50.00
—With full-color cover			
❑ SRF 67548 [R]	You've Got to Hide Your Love Away	1965	30.00
—With purplish, black and white cover			
❑ SRF 67548 [R]	You've Got to Hide Your Love Away	1965	40.00
—With full-color cover			

SILLY SURFERS, THE

Number	Title (A Side/B Side)	Yr	NM
Albums			
MERCURY			
❑ MG-20977 [M]	The Sounds of the Silly Surfers	1965	80.00
❑ SR-60977 [S]	The Sounds of the Silly Surfers	1965	100.00

SILLY SURFERS, THE / THE WEIRD-OHS

Number	Title (A Side/B Side)	Yr	NM
Albums			
HAIRY			
❑ 101 [M]	The Sounds of the Silly Surfers/The Sounds of the Weird-Ohs	1964	150.00

SILVA TONES, THE

Number	Title (A Side/B Side)	Yr	NM
45s			
ARGO			
❑ 5281	Chi-Wa-Wa (That's All I Want from You)/Roses Are Blooming	1957	25.00
❑ 5281	That's All I Want from You/Roses Are Blooming	1957	30.00
MONARCH			
❑ 615	That's All I Want from You/Roses Are Blooming	1957	30.00
—Black label			
❑ 615	That's All I Want from You/Weepin' and a-Wailin'	1957	50.00
—Yellow label			

SILVER, HORACE

Number	Title (A Side/B Side)	Yr	NM
45s			
BLUE NOTE			
❑ XW325	Liberated Brother/Nothin' Can Stop Me Now	1973	5.00
❑ XW905	Slow Down (Tranquilizer Suite)/Time and Effort	1976	5.00
❑ XW1032	Togetherness/Out of the Night (Came You)	1977	5.00
❑ 1608	Safari/Thou Swell	195?	12.00
❑ 1625	Opus de Funk/Day In Day Out	195?	12.00
❑ 1630	Doodlin'/The Preacher	195?	12.00
❑ 1631	Room 608/Creepin' In	195?	12.00
❑ 1654	Enchantment/Camouflage	195?	12.00
❑ 1655	Senor Blues/Cool Eyes	195?	12.00
❑ 1672	Home Cookin'/The Back Beat	195?	12.00
❑ 1673	Soulsville/No Smokin'	195?	12.00
❑ 1705	The Outlaw/Safari	195?	12.00
❑ 1740	Finger Poppin'/Come On Home	1959	10.00
❑ 1741	Cookin' at the Continental/Juicy Lucy	1959	10.00
❑ 1742	Mellow D/Swingin' the Samba	1959	10.00
❑ 1750	Break City/Sister Sadie	1959	10.00
❑ 1751	Blowin' the Blues Away/The Baghdad Blues	1959	10.00
❑ 1784	Strollin'/Nica's Dream	1960	10.00
❑ 1785	Where Are You?/Me and My Baby	1960	10.00
❑ 1817	Filthy McNasty (Part 1)/Filthy McNasty (Part 2)	1961	10.00
❑ 1818	Doin' the Thing (Part 1)/Doin' the Thing (Part 2)	1961	10.00
❑ 1871	Tokyo Blues (Part 1)/Tokyo Blues (Part 2)	1962	10.00
❑ 1872	Sayonara Blues (Part 1)/Sayonara Blues (Part 2)	1962	10.00
❑ 1873	Too Much Sake (Part 1)/Too Much Sake (Part 2)	1962	10.00
❑ 1902	Let's Get to the Nitty Gritty/Silver's Serenade	1963	10.00

S

Number	Title (A Side/B Side)	Yr	NM
❑ 1903	Dragon Lady/ Sweet Sweetie Dee	1963	10.00
❑ 1912	Song for My Father (Part 1)/ Song for My Father (Part 2)	1964	8.00
❑ 1913	Que Pasa (Part 1)/ Que Pasa (Part 2)	1964	8.00
❑ 1923	The Cape Verdean Blues/ Pretty Eyes	1965	8.00
❑ 1924	The African Queen (Part 1)/ The African Queen (Part 2)	1965	8.00
❑ 1932	The Jody Grind (Part 1)/ The Jody Grind (Part 2)	1967	8.00
❑ 1939	Serenade to a Soul Sister/ Psychedelic Sally	1968	8.00
❑ 1946	Down and Out/Take a Little Love	1969	8.00
❑ 1963	The Show Has Begun/ There's Much to Be Done	197?	6.00
❑ 1975	Acid, Pot or Pills/I've Had a Little Talk	197?	6.00
❑ 1978	Cause and Effect/Horn of Life	197?	6.00

Albums

BLUE NOTE

Number	Title (A Side/B Side)	Yr	NM
❑ BN-LA054-F	The Pursuit of the 27th Man	1973	15.00
—Dark blue label with black stylized "b" at upper right			
❑ BN-LA402-H2 [(2)]	Horace Silver	1975	25.00
❑ BN-LA406-G	Silver 'n' Brass	1975	20.00
❑ BN-LA581-G	Silver 'n' Wood	1976	25.00
❑ BN-LA708-G	Silver 'n' Voices	1977	20.00
❑ BN-LA853-H	Silver 'n' Percussion	1978	15.00
❑ BN-LA945-H	Sterling Silver	1979	15.00
❑ LWB-1033 [(2)]	Silver and Strings Play Music of the Spheres	1980	30.00
❑ BLP-1518 [M]	Horace Silver and the Jazz Messengers	1956	300.00
—"Deep groove" edition, W. 63rd St. address on label			
❑ BLP-1518 [M]	Horace Silver and the Jazz Messengers	1956	600.00
—"Deep groove" version; Lexington Ave. address on label			
❑ BLP-1518 [M]	Horace Silver and the Jazz Messengers	1963	50.00
—"New York, USA" address on label			
❑ BLP-1520 [M]	Spotlight on Drums	1956	300.00
—"Deep groove" edition, W. 63rd St. address on label			
❑ BLP-1520 [M]	Spotlight on Drums	1956	600.00
—"Deep groove" version; Lexington Ave. address on label			
❑ BLP-1520 [M]	Spotlight on Drums	1963	50.00
—"New York, USA" address on label			
❑ BLP-1539 [M]	Six Pieces of Silver	1957	200.00
—"Deep groove" edition, W. 63rd St. address on label			
❑ BLP-1539 [M]	Six Pieces of Silver	1957	600.00
—"Deep groove" version; Lexington Ave. address on label			
❑ BLP-1539 [M]	Six Pieces of Silver	1963	50.00
—"New York, USA" address on label			
❑ BLP-1562 [M]	The Stylings of Silver	1957	120.00
—Regular edition, W. 63rd St. address on label			
❑ BLP-1562 [M]	The Stylings of Silver	1957	250.00
—"Deep groove" version; W. 63rd St. address on label			
❑ BLP-1562 [M]	The Stylings of Silver	1963	40.00
—"New York, USA" address on label			
❑ BST-1562 [S]	The Stylings of Silver	1959	100.00
—Regular edition, W. 63rd St. address on label			
❑ BST-1562 [S]	The Stylings of Silver	1959	200.00
—"Deep groove" version; W. 63rd St. address on label			
❑ BST-1562 [S]	The Stylings of Silver	1963	40.00
—"New York, USA" address on label			
❑ BLP-1589 [M]	Further Explorations	1958	120.00
—Regular edition, W. 63rd St. address on label			
❑ BLP-1589 [M]	Further Explorations	1958	200.00
—"Deep groove" version; W. 63rd St. address on label			
❑ BLP-1589 [M]	Further Explorations	1963	40.00
—"New York, USA" address on label			
❑ BST-1589 [S]	Further Explorations	1959	100.00
—Regular edition, W. 63rd St. address on label			
❑ BST-1589 [S]	Further Explorations	1959	150.00
—"Deep groove" version; W. 63rd St. address on label			
❑ BST-1589 [S]	Further Explorations	1963	40.00
—"New York, USA" address on label			
❑ BLP-4008 [M]	Finger Poppin'	1959	120.00
—Regular edition, W. 63rd St. address on label			
❑ BLP-4008 [M]	Finger Poppin'	1959	200.00
—"Deep groove" version; W. 63rd St. address on label			
❑ BLP-4008 [M]	Finger Poppin'	1963	40.00
—"New York, USA" address on label			
❑ BST-4008 [S]	Finger Poppin'	1959	100.00
—Regular edition, W. 63rd St. address on label			
❑ BST-4008 [S]	Finger Poppin'	1959	150.00
—"Deep groove" version; W. 63rd St. address on label			
❑ BST-4008 [S]	Finger Poppin'	1963	40.00
—"New York, USA" address on label			
❑ BLP-4017 [M]	Blowin' the Blues Away	1959	120.00
—Regular edition, W. 63rd St. address on label			
❑ BLP-4017 [M]	Blowin' the Blues Away	1959	200.00
—"Deep groove" version; W. 63rd St. address on label			
❑ BLP-4017 [M]	Blowin' the Blues Away	1963	40.00
—"New York, USA" address on label			
❑ BLP-4042 [M]	Horace-Scope	1960	120.00
—Regular edition, W. 63rd St. address on label			
❑ BLP-4042 [M]	Horace-Scope	1960	200.00
—"Deep groove" version; W. 63rd St. address on label			
❑ BLP-4042 [M]	Horace-Scope	1963	40.00
—"New York, USA" address on label			
❑ BLP-4076 [M]	Doin' the Thing at the Village Gate	1961	150.00
—W. 63rd St. address on label			
❑ BLP-4076 [M]	Doin' the Thing at the Village Gate	1963	80.00
—"New York, USA" address on label			
❑ BLP-4110 [M]	The Tokyo Blues	1962	100.00
—"New York, USA" on label			
❑ BLP-4131 [M]	Silver's Serenade	1963	100.00
—"New York, USA" on label			
❑ BLP-4185 [M]	Song for My Father (Cantiga Para Meu Pai)	1965	100.00
—"New York, USA" on label			
❑ BLP-4220 [M]	The Cape Verdean Blues	1965	100.00
❑ BLP-4250 [M]	The Jody Grind	1966	80.00
—"A Division of Liberty Records" on label			
❑ BLP-5018 [10]	New Faces	1953	800.00
❑ BLP-5034 [10]	Horace Silver Trio, Vol. 2	1954	800.00
❑ BLP-5058 [10]	Horace Silver Quintet	1955	700.00
❑ BLP-5062 [10]	Horace Silver Quintet	1955	700.00
❑ B1-46548	Song for My Father	1997	15.00
—Reissue on 180-gram vinyl			
❑ BST-81518	Horace Silver and the Jazz Messengers	1985	15.00
—"The Finest in Jazz Since 1939" reissue			
❑ BST-81518 [R]	Horace Silver and the Jazz Messengers	1967	25.00
—"A Division of Liberty Records" on label			
❑ B1-81520	The Horace Silver Trio	1989	12.00
—"The Finest in Jazz Since 1939" reissue			
❑ BST-81520 [R]	Spotlight on Drums	1967	20.00
—With "A Division of Liberty Records" on label			
❑ B1-81539	Six Pieces of Silver	1988	12.00
—"The Finest in Jazz Since 1939" reissue			
❑ BST-81539 [R]	Six Pieces of Silver	1967	20.00
—With "A Division of Liberty Records" on label			
❑ BST-81562 [S]	The Stylings of Silver	1967	20.00
—With "A Division of Liberty Records" on label			
❑ BST-81589 [S]	Further Explorations	1967	20.00
—With "A Division of Liberty Records" on label			
❑ B1-84008	Finger Poppin'	198?	12.00
—"The Finest in Jazz Since 1939" reissue			
❑ BST-84008 [S]	Finger Poppin'	1967	20.00
—With "A Division of Liberty Records" on label			
❑ BST-84017	Blowin' the Blues Away	1985	12.00
—"The Finest in Jazz Since 1939" reissue			
❑ BST-84017 [S]	Blowin' the Blues Away	1959	120.00
—W. 63rd St. address on label			
❑ BST-84017 [S]	Blowin' the Blues Away	1963	40.00
—"New York, USA" address on label			
❑ BST-84017 [S]	Blowin' the Blues Away	1967	25.00
—"A Division of Liberty Records" on label			
❑ BST-84042 [S]	Horace-Scope	1960	120.00
—W. 63rd St. address on label			
❑ BST-84042 [S]	Horace-Scope	1963	40.00
—"New York, USA" address on label			
❑ BST-84042 [S]	Horace-Scope	1967	25.00
—"A Division of Liberty Records" on label			
❑ B1-84076	Doin' the Thing at the Village Gate	1989	12.00
—"The Finest in Jazz Since 1939" reissue			
❑ BST-84076 [S]	Doin' the Thing at the Village Gate	1961	120.00
—W. 63rd St. address on label			
❑ BST-84076 [S]	Doin' the Thing at the Village Gate	1963	80.00
—"New York, USA" address on label			
❑ BST-84076 [S]	Doin' the Thing at the Village Gate	1967	25.00
—"A Division of Liberty Records" on label			
❑ BST-84110 [S]	The Tokyo Blues	1962	80.00
—"New York, USA" address on label			
❑ BST-84110 [S]	The Tokyo Blues	1967	25.00
—"A Division of Liberty Records" on label			
❑ BST-84131 [S]	Silver's Serenade	1963	80.00
—"New York, USA" address on label			
❑ BST-84131 [S]	Silver's Serenade	1967	25.00
—"A Division of Liberty Records" on label			
❑ BST-84185	Song for My Father (Cantiga Para Meu Pai)	1985	12.00
—"The Finest in Jazz Since 1939" reissue			
❑ BST-84185 [S]	Song for My Father (Cantiga Para Meu Pai)	1965	70.00
—"New York, USA" address on label			
❑ BST-84185 [S]	Song for My Father (Cantiga Para Meu Pai)	1967	25.00
—"A Division of Liberty Records" on label			
❑ BST-84220 [S]	The Cape Verdean Blues	1965	70.00
—"New York, USA" address on label			
❑ BST-84220 [S]	The Cape Verdean Blues	1967	25.00
—"A Division of Liberty Records" on label			
❑ BST-84250 [S]	The Jody Grind	1966	60.00
—"New York, USA" address on label			
❑ BST-84250 [S]	The Jody Grind	1967	25.00
—"A Division of Liberty Records" on label			
❑ BST-84277	Serenade to a Soul Sister	1968	80.00
—"A Division of Liberty Records" on label			
❑ BST-84309	You Gotta Take a Little Love	1969	50.00
—"A Division of Liberty Records" on label			
❑ BST-84325	The Best of Horace Silver	1970	30.00
—"A Division of Liberty Records" on label			
❑ BST-84352	That Healin' Feelin' (Phase 1)	1970	80.00
—"A Division of Liberty Records" on label			
❑ BST-84368	Total Response (Phase 2)	1971	100.00
❑ BST-84420	Phase Three "All"	1972	50.00
—"A Division of United Artists Records" on blue and white label			
❑ B1-91143	The Best of Horace Silver	1988	12.00
❑ B1-93206	The Best of Horace Silver, Vol. 2	1989	12.00

EPIC

Number	Title (A Side/B Side)	Yr	NM
❑ LN 3326 [M]	Silver's Blue	1956	120.00
❑ LA 16006 [M]	Silver's Blue	1959	60.00
—Reissue with new cover			
❑ BA 17006 [R]	Silver's Blue	196?	25.00

SILVER APPLES

45s

KAPP

Number	Title (A Side/B Side)	Yr	NM
❑ 923	Whirly Bird/Oscillations	1968	8.00

Albums

KAPP

Number	Title (A Side/B Side)	Yr	NM
❑ KS-3562	Silver Apples	1968	30.00
—Add 1/3 if poster is enclosed			
❑ KS-3584	Contact	1969	30.00

SILVER CONVENTION

12-Inch Singles

MIDSONG INT'L.

Number	Title (A Side/B Side)	Yr	NM
❑ L33-1977 [DJ]	Spend the Night with Me (9:27)/ Mission to Venus (8:45)	1978	15.00
❑ JD-11027 [DJ]	Hollywood Music/ (B-side unknown)	1976	15.00
❑ 13906	Spend the Night with Me (9:27)/ Mission to Venus (8:45)	1978	12.00

45s

MIDLAND INT'L.

Number	Title (A Side/B Side)	Yr	NM
❑ MB-10212	Save Me/Save Me Again	1975	4.00
❑ MB-10339	Fly, Robin, Fly/Chains of Love	1975	4.00
—Second pressing: "Fly, Robin, Fly" is 3:05, matrix number is 10339-Z			
❑ MB-10339	Fly, Robin, Fly/Chains of Love	1975	6.00
—First pressing: "Fly, Robin, Fly" is 3:45, matrix number is 10339-A			
❑ MB-10571	Get Up and Boogie (That's Right)/Son of a Gun	1976	4.00
—Second pressing: "Get Up and Boogie" is under three minutes long			
❑ MB-10571	Get Up and Boogie (That's Right)/Son of a Gun	1976	6.00
—First pressing: "Get Up and Boogie" is 4:05, matrix number is 10571-A			
❑ MB-10571 [PS]	Get Up and Boogie (That's Right)/ Son of a Gun	1976	6.00
❑ MB-10723	No, No Joe/Another Girl	1976	4.00
❑ MB-10849	Thank You Mr. D.J./Dancing in the Aisles (Take Me Higher)	1976	4.00

MIDSONG INT'L.

Number	Title (A Side/B Side)	Yr	NM
❑ GB-10939	Fly, Robin, Fly/Get Up and Boogie (That's Right)	1977	3.00
—Gold Standard Series			
❑ MB-10972	Telegram/(B-side unknown)	1977	4.00
❑ MB-11062	Save Me '77/Hotshot	1977	4.00
❑ 40896	Breakfast in Bed/Spend the Night with Me	1978	4.00

Albums

MIDLAND INT'L.

Number	Title (A Side/B Side)	Yr	NM
❑ BKL1-1129	Save Me	1975	10.00
❑ BKL1-1369	Silver Convention	1976	10.00
❑ BKL1-1824	Madhouse	1976	10.00

MIDSONG INT'L.

Number	Title (A Side/B Side)	Yr	NM
❑ BXL1-1129	Save Me	1978	8.00
—Reissue with new prefix			
❑ BXL1-1369	Silver Convention	1978	8.00
—Reissue with new prefix			
❑ BXL1-1824	Madhouse	1978	8.00
—Reissue with new prefix			
❑ BKL1-2296	Golden Girls	1977	10.00
❑ BXL1-2296	Golden Girls	1978	8.00
—Reissue with new prefix			

SILVER DUST

45s

SUN

Number	Title (A Side/B Side)	Yr	NM
❑ 1124	Father and Son/Castle in the Sun	1971	5.00

SILVER FLEET

A precursor to 10CC.

45s

UNI

Number	Title (A Side/B Side)	Yr	NM
❑ 55271	Look Out World/C'mon Plane	1971	25.00

SILVERSTEIN, SHEL

45s

COLUMBIA

Number	Title (A Side/B Side)	Yr	NM
❑ 10053	Everybody's Makin' It Big But Me/ The Man Who Got No Sign	1974	5.00
❑ 10153	Sahra Cynthia Sylvia Stout Would Not Take the Garbage Out/The Man Who Got No Sign	1975	5.00
❑ 45450	A Front Row Seat to Hear Ole Johnny Sing/26 Second Song	1971	6.00
❑ 45772	Sahra Cynthia Sylvia Stout Would Not Take the Garbage Out/Stacey Brown Got Two	1973	6.00
❑ 45885	All About You/Peace Proposal	1973	6.00

Except when noted otherwise, VG = 25% of NM, and VG+ = 50% of NM. (Example: VG = \$2.00, VG+ = \$4.00 and NM = \$8.00.)

Number	Title (A Side/B Side)	Yr	NM
RCA VICTOR			
❑ 47-9844	Policeman, Woman, Taxicab/ Three Legged Man	1970	8.00
❑ 74-0158	A Boy Named Sue/Somebody Stole My Rig	1969	8.00
Albums			
ATLANTIC			
❑ 8072 [M]	Inside Folk Songs	1962	30.00
❑ SD 8072 [S]	Inside Folk Songs	1962	40.00
CADET			
❑ LP 4052 [M]	I'm So Good I Don't Have to Brag!	1965	25.00
❑ LPS 4052 [S]	I'm So Good I Don't Have to Brag!	1965	30.00
❑ LP 4054 [M]	Drain My Brain	1966	25.00
❑ LPS 4054 [S]	Drain My Brain	1966	30.00
COLUMBIA			
❑ KC 31119	Freakin' at the Freakers' Ball	1972	15.00
❑ PC 31119	Freakin' at the Freakers' Ball	1979	8.00
—Budget-line reissue			
❑ FC 39412	Where the Sidewalk Ends	1984	10.00
❑ 9C9 39611 [PD]	Where the Sidewalk Ends	1984	25.00
—Picture disc			
❑ FC 40219	A Light in the Attic	1985	10.00
CRESTVIEW			
❑ CRV 804 [M]	Stag Party	1963	25.00
❑ CRS 7804 [S]	Stag Party	1963	30.00
ELEKTRA			
❑ EKL-176 [M]	Hairy Jazz	1961	100.00
❑ EKS-7176 [S]	Hairy Jazz	1961	150.00
FLYING FISH			
❑ FF-211	Conch Train Robbery	1980	12.00
JANUS			
❑ 2JLS 3052 [(2)]	Crouching on the Outside	1973	15.00
PARACHUTE			
❑ RRLP-9007	Songs and Stories	1978	12.00
❑ 20512 [DJ]	Selected Cuts from Songs and Stories	1978	20.00
—Promo-only EP			
RCA VICTOR			
❑ LSP-4192	A Boy Named Sue (And His Other Country Songs)	1969	20.00

SIMMONS, GENE

Number	Title (A Side/B Side)	Yr	NM
45s			
CASABLANCA			
❑ 951	Radioactive/See You in Your Dreams	1978	6.00
Albums			
CASABLANCA			
❑ NBLP 7120	Gene Simmons	1978	20.00
❑ NBPIX 7120 [PD]	Gene Simmons	1978	60.00

SIMMONS, "JUMPIN'" GENE

Number	Title (A Side/B Side)	Yr	NM
45s			
AGP			
❑ 119	Back Home Again/ Don't Worry About Me	1969	8.00
CHECKER			
❑ 948	Bad Boy Willie/Goin' Back to Memphis	1960	12.00
DELTUNE			
❑ 1201	Why Didn't I Think of That/ Tennessee Party Time	1977	8.00
—As "Gene Simmons"			
EPIC			
❑ 10601	She's There When I Come Home/Magnolia Street	1970	6.00
HI			
❑ 2034	Teddy Bear/Your True Love	1961	10.00
❑ 2050	Caldonia/Be Her Number One	1962	10.00
❑ 2076	Haunted House/ Hey, Hey Little Girl	1964	15.00
—As "Gene Simmons"			
❑ 2076	Haunted House/ Hey, Hey Little Girl	1964	15.00
—As "Jumpin' Gene Simmons"			
❑ 2080	The Dodo/The Jump	1964	10.00
❑ 2086	Skinnie Minnie/ I'm a Ramblin' Man	1965	10.00
❑ 2092	Mattie Rae/Folsom Prison Blues	1965	10.00
❑ 2102	The Batman/Bossy Boss	1966	15.00
❑ 2113	Go On Shoes/Keep That Meat in the Pan	1966	10.00
MALA			
❑ 12012	I'm Just a Loser/Lila	1968	10.00
SANDY			
❑ 1027	The Waiting Game/ Shenandoah Waltz	1959	20.00
—As "Morris Gene Simmons"			
SUN			
❑ 299	Drinkin' Wine/I Done Told You	1958	150.00
—As "Gene Simmons"			
Albums			
HI			
❑ HL 2018 [M]	Jumpin' Gene Simmons	1964	50.00
❑ SHL 32018 [S]	Jumpin' Gene Simmons	1964	70.00

SIMON, CARLY Also see THE SIMON SISTERS.

Number	Title (A Side/B Side)	Yr	NM
12-Inch Singles			
ELEKTRA			
❑ 11399 [DJ]	Tranquillo (same on both sides)	1978	10.00
EPIC			
❑ 05277	My New Boyfriend (3 versions)	1985	6.00
45s			
ARISTA			
❑ 2083	Better Not Tell Her/Happy Birthday	1990	3.00
❑ 2164	Life Is Eternal/We Just Got Here	1990	3.00
❑ 9525	Coming Around Again/Itsy Bitsy Spider	1986	3.00
❑ 9525 [PS]	Coming Around Again/Itsy Bitsy Spider	1986	4.00
—Black and white photo of Carly Simon			
❑ 9525 [PS]	Coming Around Again/ Itsy Bitsy Spider	1986	4.00
—Color photo of Carly Simon			
❑ 9525 [PS]	Coming Around Again/ Itsy Bitsy Spider	1986	8.00
—With "Heartburn" movie scenes			
❑ 9587	Give Me All Night/ Sleight of Hand	1987	3.00
❑ 9587 [PS]	Give Me All Night/ Sleight of Hand	1987	3.00
❑ 9619	The Stuff That Dreams Are Made Of/As Time Goes By	1987	3.00
❑ 9619 [PS]	The Stuff That Dreams Are Made Of/As Time Goes By	1987	3.00
❑ 9653	All I Want Is You/On a Hot Summer Night	1987	3.00
❑ 9653 [PS]	All I Want Is You/ On a Hot Summer Night	1987	3.00
❑ 9732 [DJ]	Do the Walls Come Down (same on both sides)	1988	5.00
—Not released as stock copy on this number			
❑ 9732 [PS]	Do the Walls Come Down (same on both sides)	1988	5.00
—Promo-only picture sleeve			
❑ 9754	You're So Vain/Do the Walls Come Down	1988	3.00
❑ 9754 [PS]	You're So Vain/Do the Walls Come Down	1988	3.00
❑ 9793	Let the River Run/ The Turn of the Tide	1988	3.00
❑ 9793 [PS]	Let the River Run/ The Turn of the Tide	1988	3.00
ELEKTRA			
❑ 45246	Attitude Dancing/ Are You Ticklish	1975	5.00
❑ 45248	Slave/Look Me in the Eyes	1975	—
—Unreleased?			
❑ 45263	Waterfall/After the Storm	1975	5.00
❑ 45278	More and More/Love Out in the Street	1975	5.00
❑ 45325	It Keeps You Runnin'/ Look Me in the Eyes	1976	4.00
❑ 45341	Half a Chance/Libby	1976	4.00
—Butterfly label			
❑ 45341	Half a Chance/Libby	1976	5.00
—Red label			
❑ 45413	Nobody Does It Better/ After the Storm	1977	4.00
❑ 45477	You Belong to Me/ In a Small Moment	1978	4.00
❑ 45477 [PS]	You Belong to Me/ In a Small Moment	1978	6.00
❑ 45506	Devoted to You/Boys in the Trees	1978	4.00
—A-side with James Taylor			
❑ 45544	Tranquillo (Melt My Heart)/ Back Down to Earth	1978	4.00
❑ 45724	That's the Way I've Always Heard It Should Be/Alone	1971	6.00
❑ 45748	Our First Day Together/ Share the Land	1971	—
—Unreleased			
❑ 45759	Anticipation/The Garden	1971	6.00
❑ 45774	Legend in Your Own Time/ Julie Through the Glass	1972	6.00
❑ 45796	The Girl You Think You Are/ Share the Land	1972	6.00
❑ 45824	You're So Vain/His Friends Are More Than Fond of Robin	1972	6.00
❑ 45843	The Right Thing to Do/ We Have No Secrets	1973	5.00
❑ 45880	Mockingbird/Grownup	1974	5.00
—A-side with James Taylor			
❑ 45887	Haven't Got Time for the Pain/ Mind on My Man	1974	5.00
❑ 46051	Vengeance/Love You by Heart	1979	4.00
❑ 46051 [PS]	Vengeance/Love You by Heart	1979	5.00
❑ 46514	Spy/Pure Sin	1979	4.00
❑ 69953	Hidin' Away/Fight for It	1982	4.00
—With Jesse Colin Young			
❑ 69953 [PS]	Hidin' Away/Fight for It	1982	6.00
—With Jesse Colin Young			
EPIC			
❑ 05419	Tired of Being Blonde/ Black Honeymoon	1985	3.00
❑ 05419 [PS]	Tired of Being Blonde/ Black Honeymoon	1985	4.00
❑ 05596	My New Boyfriend/The Wives Are in Connecticut	1985	3.00
MIRAGE			
❑ 4051	Why/Why	1982	4.00
—B-side by Chic			
❑ 4051 [PS]	Why/Why	1982	6.00
❑ 99963	Why/(Instrumental)	1982	4.00
PLANET			
❑ YB-13779	Someone Waits for You/ (B-side unknown)	1984	4.00
WARNER BROS.			
❑ 29428	Hello Big Man/Dawn You Get to Me	1983	4.00
❑ 29484	You Know What to Do/Orpheus	1983	4.00
❑ 29484 [PS]	You Know What to Do/Orpheus	1983	5.00
❑ 49518	Jesse/Stardust	1980	4.00
❑ 49518 [PS]	Jesse/Stardust	1980	5.00
❑ 49630	Take Me As I Am/James	1980	4.00
❑ 49689	Come Upstairs/Them	1981	4.00
❑ 49880	From the Heart/Hurt	1981	4.00
❑ 50027	Body and Soul/Get Along Without You Very Well	1982	4.00
Albums			
ARISTA			
❑ AL-8443	Coming Around Again	1987	8.00
❑ AL-8526	Greatest Hits Live	1988	8.00
❑ AL-8582	My Romance	1990	12.00
❑ AL-8650	Have You Seen Me Lately?	1990	12.00
DIRECT DISK			
❑ SD-16608	Boys in the Trees	1980	50.00
—Audiophile vinyl			
ELEKTRA			
❑ 6E-109	The Best of Carly Simon	1977	8.00
—Reissue of 7E-1048			
❑ 6E-128	Boys in the Trees	1978	10.00
❑ 5E-506	Spy	1979	10.00
❑ 7E-1002	Hotcakes	1974	10.00
❑ EQ-1002 [Q]	Hotcakes	1974	20.00
❑ 7E-1033	Playing Possum	1975	10.00
❑ EQ-1033 [Q]	Playing Possum	1975	20.00
❑ 7E-1048	The Best of Carly Simon	1975	10.00
❑ EQ-1048 [Q]	The Best of Carly Simon	1975	20.00
❑ 7E-1064	Another Passenger	1976	10.00
❑ EQ-1064 [Q]	Another Passenger	1976	—
—Not released			
❑ EQ-4082 [Q]	Carly Simon	1974	20.00
❑ EQ-5049 [Q]	No Secrets	1974	20.00
❑ EKS-74082	Carly Simon	1971	12.00
❑ EKS-75016	Anticipation	1971	12.00
❑ EKS-75049	No Secrets	1972	12.00
—With lyrics on innersleeve			
❑ EKS-75049	No Secrets	1973	10.00
—Without lyrics on innersleeve			
EPIC			
❑ FE 39970	Spoiled Girl	1985	10.00
WARNER BROS.			
❑ BSK 3443	Come Upstairs	1980	10.00
❑ BSK 3592	Torch	1981	10.00
❑ 23886	Hello Big Man	1983	10.00

SIMON, JOE

Number	Title (A Side/B Side)	Yr	NM
12-Inch Singles			
SPRING			
❑ 025 [DJ]	One Step at a Time (5:33) (3:39)	1977	15.00
❑ 057 [DJ]	Love Vibration (same on both sides)	1978	12.00
45s			
COMPLEAT			
❑ 140	It Turns Me Inside Out/ Morning, Noon and Night	1985	4.00
❑ 146	Mr. Right or Mr. Right Now/ Let Me Have My Way with You	1985	4.00
DOT			
❑ 16570	Just Like Yesterday/ Only a Dream	1964	8.00
HUSH			
❑ 103	It's a Miracle/Land of Love	1960	12.00
❑ 104	Call My Name/Everybody Needs Somebody	1961	12.00

S

Paul Simon, "Allergies," Warner Bros. 294537, 1983, **$4.**

Number	Title (A Side/B Side)	Yr	NM
❑ 106	Pledge of Love/It's All Over	1961	12.00
❑ 107	I See Your Face/Troubles	1961	12.00
❑ 108	Land of Love/I Keep Remembering	1962	12.00
POSSE			
❑ 5001	Baby, When Love Is In Your Heart (It's In Your Eyes)/ Are We Breaking Up	1980	5.00
❑ 5005	Glad You Came My Way/ I Don't Wanna Make Love	1980	5.00
❑ 5010	Are We Breaking Up/ We're Together	1981	5.00
❑ 5014	Fallin' in Love with You/Magnolia	1981	5.00
❑ 5018	You Give Life to Me/ (Instrumental)	1982	5.00
—With Clare Bathe			
❑ 5019	Go Sam/(Instrumental)	1982	5.00
❑ 5021	Get Down, Get Down "82"/It Be's That Way Sometime	1982	5.00
❑ 5038	Deeper Than Love/Step by Step	198?	5.00
SOUND STAGE 7			
❑ 1508	Misty Blue/That's the Way I Want Our Love	1972	5.00
❑ 1512	Who's Julie/The Girl's Alright with Me	1973	5.00
❑ 1514	Someone to Lean On/ I Got a Whole Lotta Lovin'	1974	5.00
❑ 1521	Funny How Time Slips Away/ Message from Maria	1976	5.00
❑ 2564	Teenager's Prayer/ Long Hot Summer	1966	8.00
❑ 2569	Too Many Teardrops/What Makes a Man Feel Good	1966	8.00
❑ 2577	My Special Prayer/Travelin' Man	1966	8.00
❑ 2583	Put Your Trust in Me (Depend on Me)/Just a Dream	1967	8.00
❑ 2589	Nine Pound Steel/The Girl's Alright with Me	1967	8.00
❑ 2602	No Sad Songs/Come On and Get It	1967	8.00
❑ 2608	(You Keep Me) Hangin' On/ Long Hot Summer	1968	8.00
❑ 2617	Message from Maria/ I Worry About You	1968	8.00
❑ 2622	Looking Back/Standing in the Safety Zone	1968	8.00
❑ 2628	The Chokin' Kind/ Come On and Get It	1969	6.00
❑ 2634	Baby, Don't Be Looking in My Mind/Don't Let Me Lose the Feeling	1969	6.00
❑ 2637	Oon-Guela (Part 1)/ Oon-Guela (Part 2)	1969	8.00
❑ 2641	It's Hard to Get Along/San Francisco Is a Lonely Town	1969	6.00
❑ 2651	Moon Walk Part 1/ Moon Walk Part 2	1969	6.00
❑ 2656	Farther On Down the Road/ Wounded Man	1970	6.00
❑ 2664	Yours Love/I Got a Whole Lotta Lovin'	1970	6.00
❑ 2667	That's the Way I Want Our Love/When	1970	6.00
SPRING			
❑ 108	Your Time to Cry/I Love You More (Than Anything)	1970	5.00
❑ 113	Help Me Make It Through the Night/To Lay Down Beside You	1971	5.00
❑ 113 [PS]	Help Me Make It Through the Night/To Lay Down Beside You	1971	6.00
❑ 115	You're the One for Me/ I Ain't Givin' Up	1971	5.00
❑ 118	Georgia Blues/All My Hard Times	1971	5.00
❑ 120	Drowning in the Sea of Love/ Let Me Be the One	1971	5.00
❑ 124	Pool of Bad Luck/ Glad to Be Your Lover	1972	5.00
❑ 128	Power of Love/ The Mirror Don't Lie	1972	5.00
❑ 130	Trouble in My Home/ I Found My Dad	1972	5.00
❑ 133	Step by Step/ Talk Don't Bother Me	1973	5.00
❑ 138	Theme from Cleopatra Jones/ Who Is That Lady	1973	5.00
❑ 138 [PS]	Theme from Cleopatra Jones/ Who Is That Lady	1973	6.00
❑ 141	River/Love Never Hurt Nobody	1973	5.00
❑ 145	Carry Me/Do You Know What It's Like to Be Lonesome	1974	5.00
❑ 149	The Best Time of My Life/ What We Gonna Do Now	1974	5.00
❑ 156	Get Down, Get Down (Get On the Floor)/In My Baby's Arms	1975	5.00
❑ 159	Music in My Bones/Fire Burning	1975	5.00
❑ 163	I Need You, You Need Me/ I'll Take Care (Of You)	1975	5.00
❑ 166	Come Get to This/Let the Good Times Roll	1976	5.00
❑ 169	Easy to Love/Can't Stand the Pain	1976	5.00
❑ 172	You Didn't Have to Play No Games/What's Left to Do	1977	5.00
❑ 176	One Step at a Time/ Track of Your Love	1977	5.00
❑ 178	For Your Love, Love, Love/ I've Got a Jones on You Baby	1977	5.00
❑ 184	I.O.U./It Must Be Love	1978	5.00
❑ 190	Love Vibration/(Instrumental)	1978	5.00
❑ 194	Going Through These Changes/I Can't Stand a Liar	1979	5.00
❑ 3003	I Wanna Taste Your Love/ Make Every Moment Count	1979	5.00
❑ 3006	Hooked on Disco Music/ I Still Love You	1980	5.00
VEE JAY			
❑ 609	My Adorable One/Say (That My Love Is True)	1964	8.00
❑ 663	When You're Near/ When I'm Gone	1965	8.00
❑ 694	Let's Do It Over/The Whoo Pee	1965	8.00
Albums			
BUDDAH			
❑ BDS-7512	Joe Simon	1969	25.00
COMPLEAT			
❑ 671015-1	Mr. Right	1985	12.00
POSSE			
❑ 10002	Glad You Came My Way	1981	12.00
❑ 10003	By Popular Demand	1982	12.00
SOUND STAGE 7			
❑ 5000 [(2)]	The World of Joe Simon	197?	12.00
—Reissue of 32536			
❑ SSM-5003 [M]	Pure Soul	1967	30.00
❑ SSS-15003 [S]	Pure Soul	1967	40.00
❑ SSS-15004	No Sad Songs	1968	40.00
❑ SSS-15005	Simon Sings	1968	40.00
❑ SSS-15006	The Chokin' Kind	1969	30.00
❑ SSS-15008	Joe Simon…Better Than Ever	1969	30.00
❑ SSS-15009	The Best of Joe Simon	1972	15.00
❑ KZ 31916	Greatest Hits	1972	12.00
❑ ZG 32536 [(2)]	The World of Joe Simon	1974	15.00
❑ ZG 33879 [(2)]	The Chokin' Kind/Joe Simon… Better Than Ever	1975	15.00
SPRING			
❑ SPR-4701	The Sounds of Simon	1971	25.00
❑ SPR-5702	Drowning in the Sea of Love	1972	25.00
❑ SPR-5704	The Power of Joe Simon	1973	25.00
❑ SPR-5705	Simon Country	1973	15.00
❑ SPR-6702	Mood, Heart and Soul	1974	15.00
❑ SPR-6706	Get Down	1975	15.00
❑ SPR-6710	Today	1975	15.00
❑ SPR-6713	Easy to Love	1976	15.00
❑ SPR-6716	Bad Case of Love	1977	15.00
❑ SPR-6720	Love Vibrations	1979	15.00

SIMON, PAUL Includes records under various pseudonyms, such as "Paul Kane," "Jerry Landis" and "True Taylor." Also see SIMON AND GARFUNKEL; TICO AND THE TRIUMPHS; TOM AND JERRY (1).

Number	Title (A Side/B Side)	Yr	NM
12-Inch Singles			
WARNER BROS.			
❑ PRO-A-889 [DJ]	Late in the Evening/ How the Heart Approaches What It Yearns	1980	10.00
❑ PRO-A-2100 [DJ]	Allergies (LP) (7" Version)	1983	8.00
❑ PRO-A-2610 [DJ]	Graceland (LP Version) (Edit)	1986	6.00
❑ PRO-A-2652 [DJ]	The Boy in the Bubble (LP Version) (Extended)	1987	6.00
❑ PRO-A-4480 [DJ]	The Obvious Child (The Single) (same on both sides)	1990	8.00
45s			
AMY			
❑ 875	The Lone Teen Ranger/Lisa	1962	60.00
—As "Jerry Landis"			
BIG			
❑ 614	True or False/Teenage Fool	1958	100.00
—As "True Taylor"			

Except when noted otherwise, VG = 25% of NM, and VG+ = 50% of NM. (Example: VG = $2.00, VG+ = $4.00 and NM = $8.00.)

Number	Title (A Side/B Side)	Yr	NM
CANADIAN AMERICAN			
❑ 130	I'm Lonely/I Wish I Weren't in Love	1961	100.00
—As "Jerry Landis"; the rarest of his pre-Columbia solo singles			
COLUMBIA			
❑ 10197	Gone at Last/Take Me to the Mardi Gras	1975	5.00
—A-side with Phoebe Snow and the Jesse Dixon Singers			
❑ 10270	50 Ways to Leave Your Lover/ Some Folks Lives Roll Easy	1975	5.00
❑ 10332	Still Crazy After All These Years/ I Do It for Your Love (Live)	1976	5.00
❑ 10630	Slip Slidin' Away/ Something So Right	1977	5.00
—Later pressings correct the LP title to "Greatest Hits, Etc." The Oak Ridge Boys are credited in the fine print.			
❑ 10630	Slip Slidin' Away/ Something So Right	1977	6.00
—First pressings claim the A-side came from the LP "Blatant Greatest Hits." The Oak Ridge Boys are not mentioned.			
❑ 10711	Stranded in a Limousine/ Have a Good Time	1978	6.00
❑ 45547	Mother and Child Reunion/ Paranoia Blues	1972	4.00
—Gray label			
❑ 45547	Mother and Child Reunion/ Paranoia Blues	1972	5.00
—Orange label			
❑ 45585	Me and Julio Down by the Schoolyard/Congratulations	1972	4.00
—Gray label			
❑ 45585	Me and Julio Down by the Schoolyard/Congratulations	1972	5.00
—Orange label			
❑ 45638	Duncan/Run That Body Down	1972	5.00
❑ 45859	Kodachrome/Tenderness	1973	5.00
—With printing on label: "Kodachrome is a registered trademark for color film."			
❑ 45859	Kodachrome/Tenderness	1973	6.00
—With sticker on label: "Kodachrome is a registered trademark for color film."			
❑ 45859	Kodachrome/Tenderness	1973	6.00
—With no trademark disclaimer on label			
❑ 45900	American Tune/One Man's Ceiling Is Another Man's Floor	1973	5.00
❑ 45900 [PS]	American Tune/One Man's Ceiling Is Another Man's Floor	1973	10.00
❑ 45907	Loves Me Like a Rock/ Learn How to Fall	1973	5.00
—With the Dixie Hummingbirds			
❑ 46038	The Sound of Silence/ Mother and Child Reunion	1974	8.00
MGM			
❑ 12822	Anna Belle/Loneliness	1959	50.00
—As "Jerry Landis"			
TRIBUTE			
❑ 128	Carlos Dominguez/He Was My Brother	1963	60.00
—As "Paul Kane"; authentic copies make no mention of Paul Simon on the label			
WARNER BROS.			
❑ 19464	Proof/The Coast	1991	3.00
❑ 27903	Graceland/Hearts and Bones	1988	5.00
❑ 28221	Under African Skies/ I Know What I Know	1987	3.00
—A-side with Linda Ronstadt			
❑ 28221 [PS]	Under African Skies/ I Know What I Know	1987	3.00
❑ 28389	Diamonds on the Soles of Her Shoes/All Around the World Or the Myth of Fingerprints	1987	3.00
❑ 28389 [PS]	Diamonds on the Soles of Her Shoes/All Around the World Or the Myth of Fingerprints	1987	3.00
❑ 28460	The Boy in the Bubble/ Crazy Love, Part 2	1987	3.00
❑ 28460 [PS]	The Boy in the Bubble/ Crazxy Love, Part 2	1987	3.00
❑ 28522	Graceland/Hearts and Bones	1986	3.00
❑ 28522 [PS]	Graceland/Hearts and Bones	1986	3.00
❑ 28667	You Can Call Me Al/Gumboots	1986	3.00
❑ 28667 [PS]	You Can Call Me Al/Gumboots	1986	3.00
❑ 29333	Think Too Much/Song About the Moon	1984	4.00
❑ 29453	Allergies/Think Too Much (ii)	1983	4.00
❑ 29453 [PS]	Allergies/Think Too Much (ii)	1983	4.00
❑ 49511	Late in the Evening/How the Heart Approaches What It Yearns	1980	4.00
❑ 49511 [PS]	Late in the Evening/How the Heart Approaches What It Yearns	1980	5.00
❑ 49601	One-Trick Pony/Long, Long Day	1980	4.00
❑ 49675	Oh, Marion/God Bless the Absentee	1981	4.00

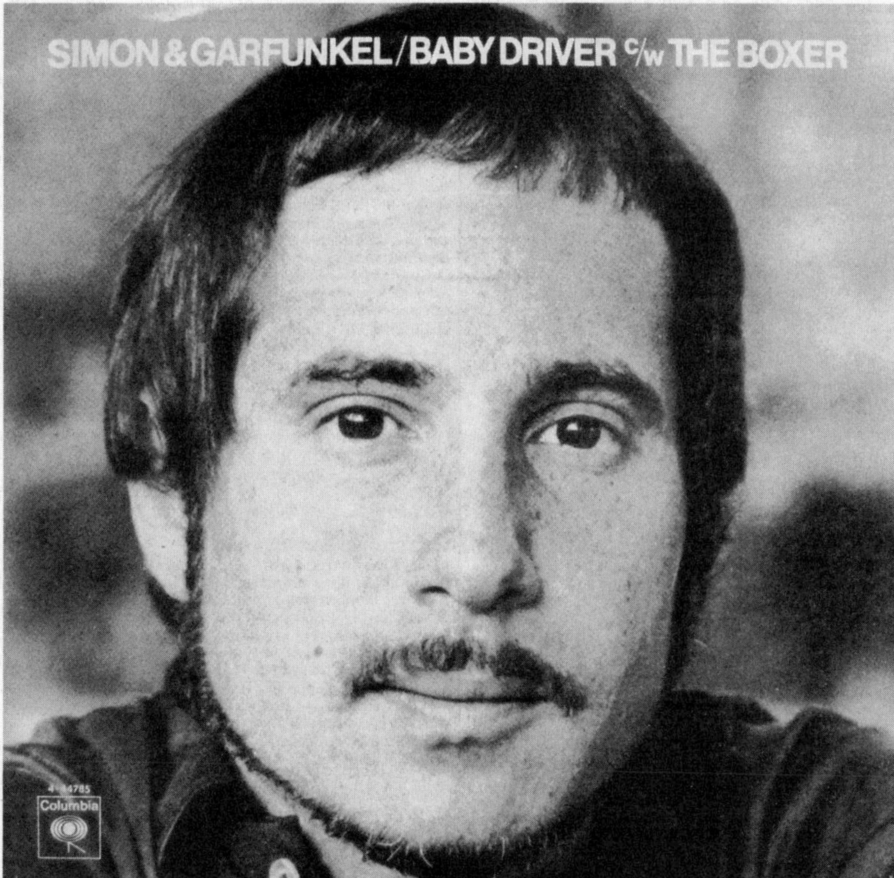

Simon and Garfunkel, "Baby Driver," Columbia 44785, 1969, **$8.**

Number	Title (A Side/B Side)	Yr	NM
WARWICK			
❑ 522	Swanee/Toot, Toot, Tootsie Goodbye	1960	50.00
—As "Jerry Landis"			
❑ 552	Shy/Just a Boy	1960	50.00
—As "Jerry Landis"			
❑ 588	I'd Like to Be/Just a Boy	1960	50.00
—As "Jerry Landis"			
❑ 619	Play Me a Sad Song/ It Means a Lot to Them	1961	50.00
—As "Jerry Landis"			
Albums			
COLUMBIA			
❑ CQ 30750 [Q]	Paul Simon	1974	20.00
❑ KC 30750	Paul Simon	1972	10.00
❑ CQ 32280 [Q]	There Goes Rhymin' Simon	1974	20.00
❑ KC 32280	There Goes Rhymin' Simon	1973	10.00
❑ PC 32280	There Goes Rhymin' Simon	1980	8.00
❑ PC 32855	Paul Simon in Concert — Live Rhymin'	1974	10.00
❑ PC 33540	Still Crazy After All These Years	1975	10.00
—Original release has no bar code on cover			
❑ PC 33540	Still Crazy After All These Years	1980	8.00
—With bar code on cover			
❑ PCQ 33540 [Q]	Still Crazy After All These Years	1975	20.00
❑ JC 35032	Greatest Hits, Etc.	1977	10.00
❑ C5X 37581 [(5)]	Collected Works	1981	40.00
—Contains his first four post-S&G solo albums plus the elusive "Paul Simon Songbook," otherwise unavailable in U.S.			
❑ HC 43540	Still Crazy After All These Years	1981	40.00
—Half-speed mastered edition			
❑ HC 45032	Greatest Hits, Etc.	1981	40.00
—Half-speed mastered edition			
DCC COMPACT CLASSICS			
❑ LPZ-2060	Paul Simon	1998	30.00
—Audiophile vinyl			
❑ LPZ-2062	There Goes Rhymin' Simon	1998	30.00
—Audiophile vinyl			

Number	Title (A Side/B Side)	Yr	NM
WARNER BROS.			
❑ WBMS-140 [(2)DJ]	The Paul Simon Interview Show	1986	50.00
—Promo-only "Graceland"-era program in the "Warner Bros. Music Show" series			
❑ HS 3472	One-Trick Pony	1980	10.00
❑ 23942	Hearts and Bones	1983	10.00
❑ 23942 [DJ]	Hearts and Bones	1983	20.00
—Promo only on Quiex II vinyl			
❑ 25447	Graceland	1986	10.00
❑ 25588	Paul Simon	1988	12.00
❑ 25589	There Goes Rhymin' Simon	1988	12.00
❑ 25590	Paul Simon in Concert — Live Rhymin'	1988	12.00
❑ 25591	Still Crazy After All These Years	1988	12.00
❑ 25789 [(2)]	Negotiations and Love Songs	1988	15.00
❑ 26098	The Rhythm of the Saints	1990	15.00
❑ 46814	Songs from The Capeman	1997	80.00
❑ 49982-1	Surprise	2006	15.00

SIMON AND GARFUNKEL Also see ART GARFUNKEL; PAUL SIMON; TOM AND JERRY (1).

Number	Title (A Side/B Side)	Yr	NM
45s			
ABC-PARAMOUNT			
❑ 10788	That's My Story/Tia-Juana Blues	1966	20.00
—Outtakes from Tom and Jerry days			
COLUMBIA			
❑ AE 43 [DJ]	Keep the Customer Satisfied/ America	1971	12.00
—Both sides are stereo			
❑ 10230	My Little Town//Art Garfunkel: Rag Doll/Paul Simon: You're Kind	1975	5.00
❑ 10230 [PS]	My Little Town//Art Garfunkel: Rag Doll/Paul Simon: You're Kind	1975	5.00
❑ 43396	The Sounds of Silence/We've Got a Groovey Thing Goin'	1965	10.00
—With the "folk-rock" hit version of the A-side			

Number | Title (A Side/B Side) | Yr | NM

❑ 43396 The Sounds of Silence/We've Got a Groovey Thing Goin' 1965 50.00
—With the original acoustic version of the A-side; a known stock copy is pressed on vinyl rather than styrene and has the number "ZSP 111384-1G" in the dead wax
❑ 43396 [DJ] The Sounds of Silence (Acoustic)/(Electric) 1965 50.00
—Red vinyl promo containing, possibly in error, the acoustic version on one side and the electric version on the other; the acoustic version has ZSP-111384-1D in the trail-off wax and the electric version has ZSP-111384-1C in the trail-off
❑ 43511 Homeward Bound/Leaves That Are Green 1966 10.00
❑ 43511 [DJ] Homeward Bound (same on both sides) 1966 50.00
—Red vinyl promo
❑ 43617 I Am a Rock/Flowers Never Bend with the Rainfall 1966 10.00
❑ 43617 [DJ] I Am a Rock (same on both sides) 1966 50.00
—Red vinyl promo
❑ 43728 The Dangling Conversation/The Big Bright Green Pleasure Machine 1966 10.00
❑ 43728 [DJ] The Dangling Conversation (same on both sides) 1966 50.00
—Red vinyl promo
❑ 43728 [PS] The Dangling Conversation/The Big Bright Green Pleasure Machine 1966 20.00
❑ 43873 A Hazy Shade of Winter/For Emily, Wherever I May Find Her 1966 10.00
❑ 44046 At the Zoo/The 59th Street Bridge Song (Feelin' Groovy) 1967 10.00
❑ 44046 [PS] At the Zoo/The 59th Street Bridge Song (Feelin' Groovy) 1967 40.00
❑ 44232 Fakin' It/You Don't Know Where Your Interest Lies 1967 10.00
—As far as we can tell, all copies have the A-side listed with a time of "2:74"
❑ 44465 Scarborough Fair (/Canticle)/April Come She Will 1968 10.00
❑ 44511 Mrs. Robinson/Old Friends-Bookends 1968 8.00
—Label says "From the Columbia Lp BOOKENDS," etc. with no reference to "The Graduate"
❑ 44511 Mrs. Robinson/Old Friends-Bookends 1968 10.00
—Label says "From the Motion Picture 'The Graduate'"
❑ 44785 The Boxer/Baby Driver 1969 6.00
—B-side mix (mono) is different than stereo LP version, especially near the end of the song
S
❑ 44785 [DJ] Baby Driver (mono/stereo) 1969 15.00
—Promo 45s exist promoting this song as the "hit"!
❑ 44785 [PS] The Boxer/Baby Driver 1969 8.00
❑ 45079 Bridge Over Troubled Water/Keep the Customer Satisfied 1970 6.00
❑ 45079 [PS] Bridge Over Troubled Water/Keep the Customer Satisfied 1970 8.00
❑ 45133 Cecilia/The Only Living Boy in New York 1970 6.00
—Red label, "Columbia" in black at top
❑ 45133 Cecilia/The Only Living Boy in New York 1970 10.00
—Red label, continuous "Columbia Records" in white along outer edge
❑ 45133 [PS] Cecilia/The Only Living Boy in New York 1970 8.00
❑ 45237 El Condor Pasa/Why Don't You Write Me 1970 6.00
❑ 45663 America/For Emily, Whenever I May Find Her 1972 6.00
❑ JZSP 116469 [DJ] 7 O'Clock News-Silent Night (same on both sides) 1966 25.00
—Promo-only Christmas release for radio stations

WARNER BROS.
❑ 50053 Wake Up Little Susie/Me and Julio Down by the Schoolyard 1982 4.00

7-Inch Extended Plays

COLUMBIA
❑ 7-9529 A Hazy Shade of Winter/Mrs. Robinson/Bookends Theme//At the Zoo/Old Friends/Fakin' It 1968 15.00
—Jukebox issue; small hole, plays at 33 1/3 rpm
❑ 7-9529 [PS] Bookends 1968 15.00
❑ 7-9914 Song for the Asking/So Long, Frank Lloyd Wright/El Condor Pasa//Keep the Customer Satisfied/Why Don't You Write Me/Bye Bye Love 1970 15.00
—Jukebox issue; small hole, plays at 33 1/3 rpm
❑ 7-9914 [PS] Bridge Over Troubled Water 1970 15.00

Albums

CBS
❑ KCS 9914 Bridge Over Troubled Water 1970 15.00
—"360 Sound Stereo" on label; pressed in U.S. for export

Number | Title (A Side/B Side) | Yr | NM

COLUMBIA
❑ CL 2249 [M] Wednesday Morning, 3 A.M. 1964 25.00
—"Guaranteed High Fidelity" on label
❑ CL 2249 [M] Wednesday Morning, 3 A.M. 1965 15.00
—"Mono" on label
❑ CL 2469 [M] Sounds of Silence 1966 15.00
—With "Simon and Garfunkel" and "Sounds of Silence" in large upper and lowercase letters on front cover with all song titles listed; "Tiger Beat" magazines on back cover are airbrushed out
❑ CL 2469 [M] Sounds of Silence 1966 20.00
—With "Simon and Garfunkel" and "Sounds of Silence" in large upper and lowercase letters on front cover with all song titles listed; "Tiger Beat" magazine is pictured twice on back cover
❑ CL 2469 [M] Sounds of Silence 1966 30.00
—With "Simon and Garfunkel" and "Sounds of Silence" in all capital letters on front cover with no list of songs
❑ CL 2563 [M] Parsley, Sage, Rosemary and Thyme 1966 20.00
❑ KCL 2729 [M] Bookends 1968 100.00
—Red label, "Mono" at bottom
❑ CS 9049 [S] Wednesday Morning, 3 A.M. 1964 25.00
—"360 Sound Stereo" in black on label
❑ CS 9049 [S] Wednesday Morning, 3 A.M. 1965 15.00
—"360 Sound Stereo" in white on label
❑ CS 9049 [S] Wednesday Morning, 3 A.M. 1970 10.00
—Orange label
❑ PC 9049 [S] Wednesday Morning, 3 A.M. 197? 8.00
—Budget-line reissue
❑ CS 9269 [S] Sounds of Silence 1966 12.00
—With "Simon and Garfunkel" and "Sounds of Silence" in large upper and lowercase letters on front cover with all song titles listed; "Tiger Beat" magazines on back cover are airbrushed out
❑ CS 9269 [S] Sounds of Silence 1966 20.00
—With "Simon and Garfunkel" and "Sounds of Silence" in large upper and lowercase letters on front cover with all song titles listed; "Tiger Beat" magazine is pictured twice on back cover
❑ CS 9269 [S] Sounds of Silence 1966 30.00
—With "Simon and Garfunkel" and "Sounds of Silence" in all capital letters on front cover with no list of songs
❑ CS 9269 [S] Sounds of Silence 1970 10.00
—Orange label
❑ JC 9269 Sounds of Silence 197? 8.00
—Reissue with new prefix
❑ PC 9269 [S] Sounds of Silence 198? 8.00
—Budget-line reissue
❑ CS 9363 [S] Parsley, Sage, Rosemary and Thyme 1966 15.00
—"360 Sound Stereo" on label
❑ CS 9363 [S] Parsley, Sage, Rosemary and Thyme 1970 10.00
—Orange label
❑ PC 9363 [S] Parsley, Sage, Rosemary and Thyme 197? 8.00
—Budget-line reissue
❑ KCS 9529 [M] Bookends 1968 30.00
—White label "Special Mono Radio Station Copy"
❑ KCS 9529 [S] Bookends 1968 12.00
—"360 Sound Stereo" on label; add 25% for poster
❑ KCS 9529 [S] Bookends 1970 10.00
—Orange label
❑ PC 9529 [S] Bookends 197? 8.00
—Budget-line reissue
❑ JC 9914 Bridge Over Troubled Water 197? 8.00
—Reissue with new prefix
❑ KCS 9914 Bridge Over Troubled Water 1970 10.00
—Orange label
❑ KCS 9914 Bridge Over Troubled Water 1970 12.00
—"360 Sound Stereo" on label
❑ KCS 9914 Bridge Over Troubled Water 2000 25.00
—Classic Records reissue on audiophile vinyl
❑ PC 9914 Bridge Over Troubled Water 198? 8.00
—Budget-line reissue
❑ CQ 30995 [Q] Bridge Over Troubled Water 1971 25.00
❑ PCQ 30995 [Q] Bridge Over Troubled Water 1974 20.00
—Reissue with new prefix; possibly the only difference between this and the original is a sticker on the cover with the new number
❑ JC 31350 Simon and Garfunkel's Greatest Hits 197? 8.00
—Reissue with new prefix
❑ KC 31350 Simon and Garfunkel's Greatest Hits 1972 12.00
—Original covers are slightly oversized
❑ C5X 37587 [(5)] Collected Works 1981 40.00
❑ HC 41350 Simon and Garfunkel's Greatest Hits 1982 30.00
—Half-speed mastered edition
❑ HC 49914 Bridge Over Troubled Water 1982 30.00
—Half-speed mastered edition

MOBILE FIDELITY
❑ 1-173 Bridge Over Troubled Water 198? 40.00
—Audiophile vinyl

PICKWICK
❑ PC-3059 [M] The Hit Sounds of Simon and Garfunkel 1966 60.00
❑ SPC-3059 [R] The Hit Sounds of Simon and Garfunkel 1966 30.00

SEARS
❑ SPS-435 Simon and Garfunkel 196? 30.00

Number | Title (A Side/B Side) | Yr | NM

TEE VEE
❑ TV-2002 [(5)] The Complete Collection 1980 50.00
—Alternate number is Columbia Special Products P5-15333; also contains solo material by both Paul Simon and Art Garfunkel, plus a rare true stereo mix of "You Don't Know Where Your Interest Lies"

WARNER BROS.
❑ 2BSK 3654 [(2)] The Concert in Central Park 1982 12.00

SIMON SISTERS, THE

CARLY SIMON and her sister Lucy.

45s

CHILDREN'S RECORDS OF AMERICA
❑ 100 My Love Is Like a Red, Red Rose/The Lamb 1968 20.00

COLUMBIA
❑ 02675 Maryanne/(B-side unknown) 1982 4.00
—As "Carly and Lucy Simon"
❑ 45840 Red, Red Rose/Lobster Quadrille 1973 6.00
—As "Carly and Lucy Simon"

KAPP
❑ 586 Winkin', Blinkin' and Nod/So Glad I'm Here 1964 15.00
❑ 624 Cuddlebug/No One to Talk My Troubles To 1964 15.00

Albums

COLUMBIA
❑ CR 21525 The Lobster Quadrille 1969 15.00
❑ CR 21539 The Simon Sisters Sing for Children 1972 15.00
❑ CC 24506 The Lobster Quadrille 1969 20.00
—Special edition with booklet

KAPP
❑ KL-1359 [M] Winkin', Blinkin' and Nod 1964 30.00
❑ KL-1397 [M] Cuddlebug 1964 40.00
❑ KS-3359 [S] Winkin', Blinkin' and Nod 1964 40.00
❑ KS-3397 [S] Cuddlebug 1964 50.00

SIMONE, NINA

45s

BETHLEHEM
❑ 3031 My Baby Just Cares for Me/He Needs Me 1962 8.00
❑ 3099 I Loves You Porgy/My Baby Just Cares for Me 1970 5.00
❑ 11021 I Loves You, Porgy/Love Me or Leave Me 1959 12.00
❑ 11052 Little Girl Blue/He Needs Me 1960 10.00
❑ 11055 Don't Smoke in Bed/African Mailman 1960 10.00
❑ 11057 Mood Indigo/Central Park Blues 1960 10.00
❑ 11087 For All We Know/Good Bait 1960 10.00
❑ 11088 You'll Never Walk Alone/Plain Gold Ring 1960 10.00
❑ 11089 He's Got the Whole World in His Hands/Central Park Blues 1960 10.00

COLPIX
❑ 116 Solitaire/Chilly Winds 1959 10.00
❑ 124 Children Go Where I Send Thee/Willow Weep for Me 1959 10.00
❑ 135 It Might As Well Be Spring/The Other Woman 1959 10.00
❑ 143 Summertime/Fine and Mellow 1960 10.00
❑ 151 Since My Love Has Gone/Tomorrow (We Shall Meet Once More) 1960 10.00
❑ 156 If Only for Tonight/(B-side unknown) 1960 10.00
❑ 158 Nobody Knows You When You're Down and Out/Black Is the Color of My True Love's Hair 1960 10.00
❑ 175 Trouble in Mind/Cotton-Eyed Joe 1960 10.00
❑ 197 The Work Song/Memphis in June 1961 10.00
❑ 608 You Can Have Him/Gin House Blues 1961 10.00
❑ 614 Come On Back, Jack/You've Been Gone Too Long 1961 10.00
❑ 635 In the Evening by the Moonlight/Chilly Winds Don't Blow 1962 8.00
❑ 647 I Got It Bad/I Want a Little Sugar in My Bowl 1962 8.00
❑ 703 Blackbird/Little Liza Jane 1963 8.00

CTI
❑ 44 Baltimore/The Family 1978 5.00
❑ 46 Forget/Baltimore 1978 5.00
❑ 49 The Family/That's All I Want from You 1978 5.00

PHILIPS
❑ 40194 I Loves You Porgy/Old Jim Crow 1964 8.00
❑ 40216 Mississippi Goddam/Sea Lion Woman 1964 8.00
❑ 40232 Don't Let Me Be Misunderstood/A Monster 1964 8.00
❑ 40254 I Am Blessed/How Can I 1965 8.00

Number	Title (A Side/B Side)	Yr	NM
❑ 40286	I Put a Spell on You/ Gimme Some	1965	8.00
❑ 40337	Either Way I Lose/Break Down and Let It All Out	1965	8.00
❑ 40359	Why Keep On Breaking My Heart/I Love Your Lovin' Ways	1966	6.00
❑ 40376	See-Line Woman/I Love Your Lovin' Ways	1966	6.00
❑ 40404	What More Can I Say/ Four Women	1966	6.00
❑ 40418	Don't Pay Them No Mind/ (B-side unknown)	1966	6.00
RCA VICTOR			
❑ 47-9120	Do I Move You/Day and Night	1967	6.00
❑ 47-9286	It Be's That Way Sometime/ You'll Go to Hell	1967	6.00
❑ 47-9375	Cherish/I Wish I Knew How It Would Feel to Be Free	1967	6.00
❑ 47-9447	To Love Somebody/ I Can't See Nobody	1968	6.00
❑ 47-9532	Why (Part 1)/Why (Part 2)	1968	6.00
❑ 47-9602	Do What You Gotta Do/ Peace of Mind	1968	6.00
❑ 47-9686	Ain't Got No; I Got Life/ Real, Real	1968	6.00
❑ 47-9730	Revolution (Part 1)/ Revolution (Part 2)	1969	6.00
❑ 47-9749	Suzanne/Turn, Turn, Turn (To Everything There Is a Season)	1969	6.00
❑ 74-0269	To Be Young, Gifted and Black/ Save Me	1969	6.00
❑ 74-0311	Who Knows Where the Time Goes/The Assignment Song	1970	6.00
❑ 74-0467	Here Comes the Sun/ New World Coming	1971	—
—Canceled			
❑ 74-0471	New World Coming/O-o-h Child	1971	6.00
❑ 74-0514	Here Comes the Sun/Angel of the Morning	1971	6.00
❑ 74-0871	My Sweet Lord-Today Is a Killer/Poppies	1973	6.00

Albums

Number	Title	Yr	NM
ACCORD			
❑ SN-7108	In Concert	1981	10.00
BETHLEHEM			
❑ BCP-6003	Nina Simone's Finest	197?	12.00
❑ BCP-6028 [M]	Jazz As Played in an Exclusive Side Street Club	1959	80.00
❑ BCP-6028 [M]	The Original Nina Simone	1961	30.00
—Retitled reissue			
❑ SBCP-6028 [S]	Jazz As Played in an Exclusive Side Street Club	1959	100.00
❑ SBCP-6028 [S]	The Original Nina Simone	1961	40.00
—Retitled reissue			
❑ BCP-6041 [M]	Nina Simone and Her Friends	1960	40.00
❑ SBCP-6041 [S]	Nina Simone and Her Friends	1960	50.00
—With Carmen McRae and Chris Connor			
CANYON			
❑ 7705	Gifted and Black	1971	15.00
COLPIX			
❑ CP-407 [M]	The Amazing Nina Simone	1959	25.00
❑ SCP-407 [S]	The Amazing Nina Simone	1959	30.00
❑ CP-409 [M]	Nina at Town Hall	1960	25.00
❑ SCP-409 [S]	Nina at Town Hall	1960	30.00
❑ CP-412 [M]	Nina at Newport	1960	25.00
❑ SCP-412 [S]	Nina at Newport	1960	30.00
❑ CP-419 [M]	Forbidden Fruit	1961	25.00
❑ SCP-419 [S]	Forbidden Fruit	1961	30.00
❑ CP-421 [M]	Nina Simone at the Village Gate	1961	25.00
❑ SCP-421 [S]	Nina Simone at the Village Gate	1961	30.00
❑ CP-425 [M]	Nina Sings Ellington	1962	25.00
❑ SCP-425 [S]	Nina Sings Ellington	1962	30.00
❑ CP-443 [M]	Nina's Choice	1963	25.00
❑ SCP-443 [S]	Nina's Choice	1963	30.00
❑ CP-455 [M]	Nina Simone at Carnegie Hall	1963	25.00
❑ SCP-455 [S]	Nina Simone at Carnegie Hall	1963	30.00
❑ CP-465 [M]	Folksy Nina	1964	25.00
❑ SCP-465 [S]	Folksy Nina	1964	30.00
❑ CP-496 [M]	Nina with Strings	1966	25.00
❑ SCP-496 [S]	Nina with Strings	1966	30.00
CTI			
❑ 7084	Baltimore	1978	12.00
PHILIPS			
❑ PHM 200135 [M]	Nina Simone In Concert	1964	15.00
❑ PHM 200148 [M]	Broadway...Blues...Ballads	1964	15.00
❑ PHM 200172 [M]	I Put a Spell on You	1965	15.00
❑ PHM 200187 [M]	Pastel Blues	1965	15.00
❑ PHM 200202 [M]	Let It All Out	1966	15.00

Simple Minds, "Alive & Kicking," A&M 2783, 1985, $3.

Number	Title (A Side/B Side)	Yr	NM
❑ PHM 200207 [M]	Wild Is the Wind	1966	15.00
❑ PHM 200219 [M]	The High Priestess of Soul	1967	15.00
❑ PHS 600135 [S]	Nina Simone In Concert	1964	20.00
❑ PHS 600148 [S]	Broadway...Blues...Ballads	1964	20.00
❑ PHS 600172 [S]	I Put a Spell on You	1965	20.00
❑ PHS 600187 [S]	Pastel Blues	1965	20.00
❑ PHS 600202 [S]	Let It All Out	1966	20.00
❑ PHS 600207 [S]	Wild Is the Wind	1966	20.00
❑ PHS 600219 [S]	The High Priestess of Soul	1967	20.00
❑ PHS 600298	The Best of Nina Simone	1969	20.00
❑ 822846-1	The Best of Nina Simone	198?	10.00
PM			
❑ 018	A Very Rare Evening	1979	12.00
QUINTESSENCE			
❑ 25421	Silk and Soul	1979	10.00
RCA VICTOR			
❑ AFL1-0241	It Is Finished — Nina 1974	1977	10.00
—Reissue with new prefix			
❑ APL1-0241	It Is Finished — Nina 1974	1974	12.00
❑ AFL1-1788	Poets	1977	10.00
—Reissue with new prefix			
❑ APL1-1788	Poets	1976	12.00
❑ LPM-3789 [M]	Nina Simone Sings the Blues	1967	25.00
❑ LSP-3789 [S]	Nina Simone Sings the Blues	1967	15.00
❑ LPM-3837 [M]	Silk and Soul	1967	25.00
❑ LSP-3837 [S]	Silk and Soul	1967	15.00
❑ LSP-4065	'Nuff Said	1968	15.00
❑ LSP-4102	Nina Simone and Piano	1968	15.00
❑ LSP-4152	To Love Somebody	1969	15.00
❑ LSP-4248	Black Gold	1970	15.00
❑ AFL1-4374	The Best of Nina Simone	1977	10.00
—Reissue with new prefix			
❑ LSP-4374	The Best of Nina Simone	1970	15.00
❑ AFL1-4536	Here Comes the Sun	1977	10.00
—Reissue with new prefix			
❑ LSP-4536	Here Comes the Sun	1971	15.00
❑ LSP-4757	Emergency Ward!	1972	15.00
SALSOUL			
❑ SA-8546	Little Girl Blue	1982	10.00
TRIP			
❑ 8020 [(2)]	Live in Europe	1973	12.00
❑ 8021 [(2)]	Black Is the Color	1973	12.00
❑ 9521	Portrait	197?	10.00
VERVE			
❑ 831437-1	Let It Be Me	1987	10.00

SIMPLE MINDS

12-Inch Singles

Number	Title (A Side/B Side)	Yr	NM
A&M			
❑ SP-12057	Promised You a Miarcle (Remix Version 5:56) (Dub Version 5:28)/The American (7:01)	1982	15.00
❑ SP-12086	Waterfront/The Hunter and the Hunted	1983	15.00
❑ SP-12125	Don't You (Forget About Me) (long)/A Brass Band in Africa	1985	12.00
❑ SP-12155	Alive & Kicking (5:24)/ Up on the Catwalk (Live)	1985	8.00
❑ SP-12172	Sanctify Yourself (Extended Version 7:10)/ (Dub Version 6:10)	1985	8.00
❑ SP-12177	All the Things She Said (Extended Version 5:06)/ Don't You (Forget About Me) (Live)	1986	8.00
❑ SP-12244	Promised You a Miracle/Book of Brilliant Things/Glittering Prize/Celebrate (all live)	1987	10.00
❑ 17223 [DJ]	Promised You a Miracle (Long)/ Promised You a Miracle (Short)	1982	10.00
❑ SP-17223 [DJ]	Promised You a Miracle (Extended Version 6:27) (Album Version 4:26)	1982	15.00
❑ SP-17267 [DJ]	Waterfront/Up on the Catwalk	1984	15.00

S

Number	Title (A Side/B Side)	Yr	NM
❑ 17277 [DJ]	Speed Your Love to Me/ Waterfront	1984	10.00
❑ SP-17277 [DJ]	Speed Your Love to Me/ Waterfront	1984	15.00
❑ SP-17304 [DJ]	Don't You (Forget About Me) (same on both sides)	1984	15.00
❑ SP-17355 [DJ]	Alive and Kicking (same on both sides)	1984	15.00
❑ 17363 [DJ]	Sanctify Yourself (same on both sides)	1985	8.00
❑ SP-17363 [DJ]	Sanctify Yourself (5:00) (same on both sides)	1985	10.00
❑ 17371 [DJ]	All the Things She Said (same on both sides)	1986	8.00
❑ SP-17371 [DJ]	All the Things She Said (same on both sides)	1986	12.00
❑ 17480 [DJ]	Alive & Kicking (Live)/Don't You (Forget About Me) (Live)/ Promised You a Miracle (Live)	1988	8.00
❑ SP-17480 [DJ]	Alive & Kicking (Live)/Don't You (Forget About Me) (Live)/ Promised You a Miracle (Live)	1988	10.00
❑ 17728 [DJ]	This Is Your Land (Edit)/This Is Your Land (LP)/Saturday Girl/Year of the Dragon	1989	8.00
❑ SP-17728 [DJ]	This Is Your Land (Edit) (LP Version)/Saturday Girl/ Year of the Dragon	1989	12.00

VIRGIN

Number	Title (A Side/B Side)	Yr	NM
❑ 12726 [DJ]	Hypnotised (4 versions)	1995	8.00
❑ SPRO-12726 [DJ]	Hypnotised (Extended Remix 6:19) (Malfunction Mix 5:45) (Extended Remix Instrumental 6:18) (LP Version 5:53)	1995	12.00

45s

A&M

Number	Title (A Side/B Side)	Yr	NM
❑ 1413	This Is Your Land/Saturday Girl	1989	6.00
❑ 2523	Promised You a Miracle/ The American	1983	5.00
❑ 2523 [PS]	Promised You a Miracle/ The American	1983	6.00
❑ 2556 [DJ]	Someone, Somewhere in Summertime (same on both sides)	1983	4.00
—No stock copy was issued			
❑ 2556 [DJ]	Someone, Somewhere in Summertime (same on both sides)	1983	10.00
—No stock copy was issued			
❑ 2629	Speed Your Love to Me/ Bass Line	1984	10.00
❑ 2703	Don't You (Forget About Me)/ A Brass Bed in Africa	1984	3.00
❑ 2703 [PS]	Don't You (Forget About Me)/ A Brass Bed in Africa	1984	3.00
—No LP cover pictured on front			
❑ 2703 [PS]	Don't You (Forget About Me)/ A Brass Bed in Africa	1984	4.00
—With "The Breakfast Club" LP cover pictured in full color on front			
❑ 2783	Alive & Kicking/Up on the Catwalk (Live)	1985	3.00
❑ 2783 [PS]	Alive & Kicking/Up on the Catwalk (Live)	1985	3.00
❑ 2810	Sanctify Yourself/Sanctify Yourself (Dub Version)	1986	2.00
❑ 2810 [PS]	Sanctify Yourself/Sanctify Yourself (Dub Version)	1986	2.00
❑ 2828	All the Things She Said/Don't You (Forget About Me) (Live)	1986	3.00
❑ 2828 [PS]	All the Things She Said/Don't You (Forget About Me) (Live)	1986	8.00
❑ 2954	Promised You a Miracle/ Book of Brilliant Things	1987	3.00
❑ 2954 [PS]	Promised You a Miracle/Book of Brilliant Things	1987	3.00
❑ 8662	Alive and Kicking/Don't You (Forget About Me)	198?	3.00
—"A&M Memories" reissue			

VIRGIN

Number	Title (A Side/B Side)	Yr	NM
❑ S7-18402	She's a River (Single Edit)/ Celtic Strings	1995	8.00
—Blue vinyl			
❑ S7-18558	Hypnotised/And the Band Played On	1995	6.00

Albums

A&M

Number	Title (A Side/B Side)	Yr	NM
❑ SP-3927	Street Fighting Years	1989	10.00
❑ SP-6-4928	New Gold Dream (81-82-83-84)	1982	12.00
—Originals have gold and purple marbled vinyl			
❑ SP-6-4981	Sparkle in the Rain	1984	10.00
❑ SP-5092	Once Upon a Time	1985	8.00
❑ SP-6850 [(2)]	Live in the City of Light	1987	15.00
❑ R 101142	Street Fighting Years	1989	12.00
—BMG Direct Marketing edition			
❑ R 142320	Once Upon a Time	1985	12.00
—RCA Music Service edition; has front and back covers reversed			
❑ R 209526 [(2)]	Live in the City of Light	1987	20.00
—BMG Direct Marketing edition			

PVC

Number	Title (A Side/B Side)	Yr	NM
❑ 7910	Life in a Day	1979	20.00

STIFF

Number	Title (A Side/B Side)	Yr	NM
❑ TEES-102	Themes for Great Cities	1982	15.00

VIRGIN

Number	Title (A Side/B Side)	Yr	NM
❑ 90610	Sister Feelings Call	1987	10.00
—First U.S. issue of LP originally released in 1981			
❑ 90858	Life in a Day	1988	10.00
—Reissue of PVC 7910			
❑ 90859	Real to Real Cacophony	1988	10.00
—First U.S. edition of early LP			

SIMPLY RED

12-Inch Singles

EASTWEST

Number	Title (A Side/B Side)	Yr	NM
❑ 1738 [DJ]	Something Got Me Started (3 mixes)	1991	10.00
❑ DMD 1738 [DJ]	Something Got Me Started (Hurley's House Remix 5:56) (Hurley's Dub 5:44) (E-Smoove's Late Nite Mix 5:00) (E-Smoove Dub 5:44)	1991	10.00
❑ ED 5841 [(2)DJ]	Remembering the First Time (6 versions)	1995	15.00
❑ ED 5888 [DJ]	Angel (Soundtrack Version) (Mousse T Soul Mix) (Smooth Soul Mix) (Club Mix) (Simply Red Mix) (Radio Remix)	1996	12.00
❑ ED 6012 [DJ]	Angel (Temple Dub 7.14) (Club Mix 6.06) (Instrumental 6.05)	1996	8.00
❑ ED 6089 [DJ]	The Air That I Breathe (3 versions)	1998	15.00
❑ ED 6111 [DJ]	Mellow My Mind (RH Factor Pop Mix) (RH Factor Radio Edit) (RH Factor Club Mix) (RH Factor Dub)	1998	10.00
❑ ED 6190 [(2)DJ]	Ain't That a Lot of Love (Phats 'n' Small Mutant Disco Mix) (Phats 'n' Small Mutant Disco Dub) (Club 39 Underground Club) (Club 39 Underground Dub) (Johnny Vicious Filter Factory Club) (Johnny Vicious Filter Factory Dub)	1999	15.00
❑ 96290	Something Got Me Started (4 versions)	1991	8.00

ELEKTRA

Number	Title (A Side/B Side)	Yr	NM
❑ 5088 [DJ]	Money$ Too Tight (To Mention) (3 versions)	1985	10.00
❑ ED 5088 [DJ]	Money$ Too Tight (To Mention) (Cutback Mix) (Dub Mix) (7" Version)	1985	8.00
❑ ED5112 [DJ]	Come to My Aid (2 mixes)/ Granma's Hands	1985	8.00
❑ ED 5112 [DJ]	Come to My Aid (Survival Mix) (Heavy Dub)/Granma's Hands	1985	8.00
❑ 5210 [DJ]	The Right Thing (3 versions)	1987	6.00
❑ ED 5210 [DJ]	The Right Thing (Extended Version) (LP Version) (Edit)	1987	6.00
❑ 5227 [DJ]	Infidelity/Infidelity (Stretch Mix)	1987	5.00
❑ ED 5227 [DJ]	Infidelity (LP Version) (Stretch Mix)	1987	6.00
❑ 5247 [DJ]	Maybe Someday ... (same on both sides)	1987	5.00
❑ ED 5247 [DJ]	Maybe Someday ... (LP Version) (same on both sides)	1987	6.00
❑ 5268 [DJ]	Suffer (Edit) (same on both sides)	1987	6.00
❑ ED 5268 [DJ]	Suffer (Edit of LP Version) (same on both sides)	1987	8.00
❑ 5358 [DJ]	It's Only Love (Valentine Mix)/ It's Only Love (Edit of Mix)	1989	5.00
❑ ED 5358 [DJ]	It's Only Love (Valentine Mix) (Valentine Mix Edit)	1989	7.00
❑ ED 5378 [DJ]	If You Don't Know Me By Now (same on both sides)	1989	8.00
❑ ED5378 [DJ]	If You Don't Know Me By Now (same on both sides)	1989	8.00
❑ 5407 [DJ]	You've Got It (same on both sides)	1989	7.00
❑ ED 5407 [DJ]	You've Got It (same on both sides)	1989	8.00
❑ 66703	If You Don't Know Me By Now/ Move On Out (Live)/ Shine (Live)	1989	8.00
❑ 66807	Infidelity (Stretch Mix)/Love Fire (Massive Red Mix)/ Lady Godiva's Room	1987	8.00
❑ 66816	The Right Thing/There's a Light/Every Time We Say Goodbye	1987	8.00
❑ 66872	Holding Back the Years/ Drowning in My Own Tears/ Picture Book	1986	10.00
❑ 66883	Money$ Too Tight (To Mention) (Cutback Mix) (Single Version) (Dub Version)	1985	8.00

45s

ELEKTRA

Number	Title (A Side/B Side)	Yr	NM
❑ 65939	If You Don't Know Me By Now/ You've Got It	199?	3.00
—"Spun Gold" reissue			
❑ 65979	Holding Back the Years/Money$ Too Tight (To Mention)	198?	3.00
—"Spun Gold" reissue			
❑ 69269	You've Got It/She'll Have to Go	1989	4.00
❑ 69297	If You Don't Know Me By Now/ Move On Out	1989	3.00
❑ 69297 [PS]	If You Don't Know Me By Now/ Move On Out	1989	3.00
❑ 69317	It's Only Love/Turn It Up	1989	3.00
❑ 69317 [PS]	It's Only Love/Turn It Up	1989	3.00
❑ 69428	Suffer/Let Me Have It All	1987	3.00
❑ 69448	Maybe Someday.../Broken Man	1987	3.00
❑ 69448 [PS]	Maybe Someday.../Broken Man	1987	3.00
❑ 69468	Infidelity/Lady Godiva's Room	1987	3.00
❑ 69468 [PS]	Infidelity/Lady Godiva's Room	1987	3.00
❑ 69487	The Right Thing/There's a Light	1987	3.00
❑ 69487 [PS]	The Right Thing/There's a Light	1987	3.00
❑ 69528	Money$ Too Tight (To Mention)/ Picture Book (Dub)	1986	3.00
❑ 69528 [PS]	Money$ Too Tight (To Mention)/ Picture Book (Dub)	1986	3.00
❑ 69564	Holding Back the Years/ I Won't Feel Bad	1986	3.00
❑ 69574	Come to My Aid (Remix)/ Look At You Now	1986	5.00
❑ 69574 [PS]	Come to My Aid (Remix)/ Look At You Now	1986	8.00
❑ 69607	Money$ Too Tight (To Mention)/ Open Up the Red Box	1985	5.00
❑ 69607 [PS]	Money$ Too Tight (To Mention)/ Open Up the Red Box	1985	5.00

Albums

ELEKTRA

Number	Title (A Side/B Side)	Yr	NM
❑ ED5236 [DJ]	Simply Red Interview	1989	30.00
—Nelson George interviews Mick Hucknall and Lamont Dozier; promo-only			
❑ ED 5236 [DJ]	Simply Red Billboard Interview	1989	40.00
—Nelson George interviews Mick Hucknall and Lamont Dozier; promo-only			
❑ 60452	Picture Book	1985	8.00
❑ 60727	Men and Women	1987	8.00
❑ 60828	A New Flame	1989	10.00
❑ R 101012	A New Flame	1989	12.00
—BMG Direct Marketing edition			
❑ R 152858	Men and Women	1987	10.00
—RCA Music Service edition			
❑ R 153936	Picture Book	1985	10.00
—RCA Music Service edition			

SIMPSON, VALERIE

Also see ASHFORD AND SIMPSON.

45s

TAMLA

Number	Title (A Side/B Side)	Yr	NM
❑ 54204	Back to Nowhere/Can't It Wait Until Tomorrow	1971	5.00
❑ 54224	Silly Wasn't I/I Believe I'm Gonna Take This Ride	1972	5.00
❑ 54231	Genius/One More Baby Child Born	1973	5.00

Albums

TAMLA

Number	Title (A Side/B Side)	Yr	NM
❑ T 311	Valerie Simpson Exposed	1971	15.00
❑ T 317	Valerie Simpson	1972	15.00
❑ T6-351	Keep It Comin'	1977	12.00

SIMPSONS, THE

45s

GEFFEN

Number	Title (A Side/B Side)	Yr	NM
❑ 19007	Deep, Deep Trouble/ Sibling Rivalry	1991	10.00

Albums

GEFFEN

Number	Title (A Side/B Side)	Yr	NM
❑ GHS 24308	The Simpsons Sing the Blues	1990	25.00

SIMS, BOBBY

45s

HIT

Number	Title (A Side/B Side)	Yr	NM
❑ 269	Poor Side of Town/If I Were a Carpenter	1966	8.00
—B-side by Bobby Brooks			
❑ 272	That's Life/Snoopy vs. the Red Baron	1966	8.00
—B-side by the Chords (2)			
❑ 276	Wild Thing/Music to Watch Girls By	1967	8.00
—B-side by the Jalopy Five			
❑ 287	I Think We're Alone Now/ Penny Lane	1967	10.00
—B-side by the Jalopy Five			

Number	Title (A Side/B Side)	Yr	NM
❑ 297	San Francisco (Be Sure to Wear Flowers in Your Hair)/ A Whiter Shade of Pale	1967	8.00
—B-side by the Fantastics			
❑ 309	Please Love Me Forever/ People Are Strange	1967	8.00
—B-side by the Fantastics			
❑ 312	An Open Letter to My Teenage Son/Keep the Ball Rollin'	1967	8.00
—B-side by Jimmy Lewis and the Elfs			
❑ 320	Honey/The Ballad of Bonnie and Clyde	1968	8.00
—B-side by Ed Hardin			
❑ 339	Dreams of the Everyday Housewife/Hello, I Love You	1968	8.00
—B-side by the Chords (2)			
❑ 348	Who's Making Love/White Room	1968	8.00
—B-side by the Fantastics			

SIMS, FRANKIE LEE

45s

ACE

Number	Title (A Side/B Side)	Yr	NM
❑ 524	What Will Lucy Do/Misery Blues	1957	40.00
❑ 527	Hey Little Girl/Walking with Frankie	1957	40.00
❑ 539	I Warned You Baby/My Talk Didn't Do No Good	1957	40.00
SPECIALTY			
❑ 459	Lucky Man Blues/Don't Take It Out on Me	1953	50.00
❑ 478	I'm Long, Long Gone/Yeh Baby	1953	40.00
❑ 487	I'll Get Along Somehow/ Rhumba My Boogie	1954	40.00
VIN			
❑ 1006	She Likes to Boogie Low/Well Goodbye Baby	1958	30.00

SIMS, MARVIN L.

45s

KAREN

Number	Title (A Side/B Side)	Yr	NM
❑ 1547	Sweet Thang/Your Love Is So Wonderful	1969	15.00
—As "Marvin Sims"			
MELLOW			
❑ 1002	What Can I Do?/Now I'm in Love with You	1966	100.00
❑ 1004	(Nina) Have You Seen My Baby (Part 1)/(Part 2)	1967	30.00
❑ 1005	Hurting Inside/Disillusioned	1967	50.00
MERCURY			
❑ 73288	Dream a Dream/I Can't Turn You Loose	1972	25.00
—As "Marvin Sims"			
❑ 73340	Love Is No Sin/You Gotta Go	1972	25.00
❑ 73364	It's Too Late/(B-side unknown)	1973	25.00
REVUE			
❑ 11024	Talkin' 'Bout Soul/Old Man Time	1968	30.00
❑ 11038	Danger/Get Off My Back	1969	50.00
RIVERTOWN			
❑ 498	Love Is on the Way/ Blow Away Breeze	1980	80.00
UNI			
❑ 55217	I Can't Understand It/ It's Your Love	1970	12.00

SIMS TWINS, THE

45s

KENT

Number	Title (A Side/B Side)	Yr	NM
❑ 4556	Bring It On Home Where You Belong/Under the Double Eagle	1971	6.00
PARKWAY			
❑ 6002	Together/Baby It's Real	1968	10.00
SAR			
❑ 117	Soothe Me/I'll Never Come Running Back to You	1961	15.00
❑ 125	The Smile/Right to Love	1962	12.00
❑ 130	Double Portion of Love/ You're Pickin' in the Right Cotton Patch	1962	12.00
❑ 136	I Gopher You/Good Good Lovin'	1963	12.00
❑ 138	That's Where It's At/ Movin' and a Groovin'	1963	12.00
SPECIALTY			
❑ 731	Make It On Up/Something Hanging on Your Mind	197?	6.00

SINATRA, FRANK Also see TOMMY DORSEY.

12-Inch Singles

QWEST

Number	Title (A Side/B Side)	Yr	NM
❑ PRO-A-2216 [DJ]	Mack the Knife (Remix 4:50) (same on both sides)	1984	12.00

Frank Sinatra, "I Believe I'm Gonna Love You," Reprise 1335, 1975, **$40.**

Number	Title (A Side/B Side)	Yr	NM
REPRISE			
❑ PRO-A-674 [DJ]	Night and Day/Everybody Ought to Be in Love	1977	80.00
❑ PRO-A-865 [DJ]	Theme from New York, New York (same on both sides)	1980	50.00
45s			
(NO LABEL)			
❑ KB-2077/8	High Hopes with Jack Kennedy/ Jack Kennedy All the Way	1960	300.00
—No artist or label shown, but Sinatra does sing the A-side			
CAPITOL			
❑ X1-1069 [S]	titles unknown	196?	20.00
—Stereo jukebox single, 33 1/3 rpm, small hole			
❑ X2-1069 [S]	titles unknown	196?	20.00
—Stereo jukebox single, 33 1/3 rpm, small hole			
❑ X3-1069 [S]	Day In — Day Out/Saturday Night	196?	20.00
—Stereo jukebox single, 33 1/3 rpm, small hole			
❑ X1-1417 [S]	That Old Feeling/How Deep Is the Ocean	1960	20.00
—Stereo jukebox single, 33 1/3 rpm, small hole			
❑ X2-1417 [S]	Fools Rush In/I've Got a Crush on You	1960	20.00
—Stereo jukebox single, 33 1/3 rpm, small hole			
❑ X1-1491 [S]	When You're Smiling/ It All Depends on You	1961	20.00
—Stereo jukebox single, 33 1/3 rpm, small hole			
❑ X2-1491 [S]	S'posin'/Blue Moon	1961	20.00
—Stereo jukebox single, 33 1/3 rpm, small hole			
❑ X3-1491 [S]	It's Only a Paper Moon/ My Blue Heaven	1961	20.00
—Stereo jukebox single, 33 1/3 rpm, small hole			
❑ X4-1491 [S]	I Concentrate on You/Should I	1961	20.00
—Stereo jukebox single, 33 1/3 rpm, small hole			
❑ X5-1491 [S]	September in the Rain/ You Do Something to Me	1961	20.00
—Stereo jukebox single, 33 1/3 rpm, small hole			
❑ X1-1594 [S]	titles unknown	1961	20.00
—Stereo jukebox single, 33 1/3 rpm, small hole			
❑ X2-1594 [S]	Five Minutes More/ Almost Like Being in Love	1961	20.00
—Stereo jukebox single, 33 1/3 rpm, small hole			

Number	Title (A Side/B Side)	Yr	NM
❑ X3-1594 [S]	Yes Indeed/American Beauty Rose	1961	20.00
—Stereo jukebox single, 33 1/3 rpm, small hole			
❑ XE 1-1676 [S]	September Song/When the World Was Young	1962	20.00
—Stereo jukebox single; 33 1/3 rpm, small hole			
❑ XE 2-1676 [S]	titles unknown	1962	20.00
—Stereo jukebox single, 33 1/3 rpm, small hole			
❑ XE 3-1676 [S]	There Will Never Be Another You/Somewhere Along the Way	1962	20.00
—Stereo jukebox single; 33 1/3 rpm, small hole			
❑ XE 4-1676 [S]	These Foolish Things (Remind Me of You)/It's a Blue World	1962	20.00
—Stereo jukebox single; 33 1/3 rpm, small hole			
❑ F1699	Young at Heart/I've Got the World on a String	1955	100.00
—Early reissue			
❑ PRO 1707/8 [DJ]	Mistletoe and Holly (with spoken intro)/Mistletoe and Holly	1960	100.00
—Christmas Seals record for 1960, with Sinatra introducing the song			
❑ XE-1729 [S]	They Came to Cordura/I Gotta Right to Sing the Blues	1962	20.00
—Stereo jukebox single, 33 1/3 rpm, small hole			
❑ F2450	I'm Walking Behind You/ Lean Baby	1953	25.00
—Add 50% for intact center			
❑ F2505	My One and Only Love/I've Got the World on a String	1953	20.00
—Add 50% for intact center			
❑ F2560	Anytime, Anywhere/From Here to Eternity	1953	20.00
❑ F2638	I Love You/South of the Border	1953	20.00
❑ F2703	Young at Heart/Take a Chance	1953	20.00
❑ F2787	Don't Worry 'Bout Me/I Could Have Told You	1954	20.00
❑ F2816	Three Coins in the Fountain/Rain	1954	20.00
❑ F2864	The Girl That Got Away/ Half as Lovely	1954	20.00
❑ F2922	It Worries Me/When I Stop Loving You	1954	20.00
❑ 2954	White Christmas/ The Christmas Waltz	1962	10.00
—Reissue without the "F" prefix on orange and yellow swirl label			

Number	Title (A Side/B Side)	Yr	NM
F2954	White Christmas/The Christmas Waltz	1954	20.00
F2993	You My Love/Someone to Watch Over Me	1954	20.00
F3018	Melody of Love/I'm Gonna Live Till I Die	1954	20.00
F3050	Why Should I Cry Over You?/Don't Change Your Mind About Me	1954	20.00
F3084	Two Hearts, Two Kisses/From the Bottom to the Top	1955	15.00
F3102	Learnin' the Blues/If I Had Three Wishes	1955	15.00
F3130	Not as a Stranger/How Could You Do a Thing Like That to Me?	1955	15.00
F3218	Same Old Saturday Night/Fairy Tale	1955	15.00
F3260	Love and Marriage/The Impatient Years	1955	20.00
F3290	(Love Is) The Tender Trap/Weep They Will	1955	15.00
F3350	Flowers Mean Forgiveness/You'll Get Yours	1956	15.00
F3423	(How Little It Maters) How Little We Know/Five Hundred Guys	1956	15.00
F3469	You're Sensational/Johnny Concho Theme (Wait for Me)	1956	15.00
F3507	Well, Did You Evah?/True Love	1956	15.00
—A-side by Bing Crosby and Frank Sinatra; B-side by Bing Crosby and Grace Kelly			
F3508	Who Wants to Be a Millionaire/Mind If I Make Love to You?	1956	15.00
F3552	Hey! Jealous Lover/You Forgot All the Words	1956	15.00
F3552	Jealous Lover/You Forgot All the Words	1956	25.00
—Original pressings contain this title			
F3608	Can I Steal a Little Love/Your Love for Me	1956	15.00
F3703	Crazy Love/So Long, My Love	1957	12.00
F3744	You're Cheatin' Yourself (If You're Cheatin' On Me)/Something Wonderful Happens in Summer	1957	12.00
F3793	All the Way/Chicago	1957	12.00
F3859	Witchcraft/Tell Her You Love Her	1957	12.00
F3900	Mistletoe and Holly/The Christmas Waltz	1957	15.00
—"The Christmas Waltz" here is a different version than that on Capitol 2954.			
F3952	How Are Ya' Fixed for Love?/Nothin' in Common	1958	12.00
—By Frank Sinatra and Keely Smith			
F4003	Same Old Song and Dance/Monique (Song from Kings Go Forth)	1958	12.00
F4070	Mr. Success/Sleep Warm	1958	12.00
F4103	Song from "Some Came Running"/No One Ever Tells You	1958	12.00
F4103	To Love and Be Loved/No One Ever Tells You	1958	12.00
F4103 [PS]	To Love and Be Loved/No One Ever Tells You	1958	100.00
—Promo-only sleeve			
F4155	French Foreign Legion/Time After Time	1959	12.00
F4214	High Hopes/All My Tomorrows	1959	15.00
F4214 [PS]	High Hopes/All My Tomorrows	1959	200.00
F4284	Talk to Me/They Came to Cordura	1959	12.00
4376	River, Stay 'Way from My Door/It's Over, It's Over, It's Over	1960	12.00
4408	Nice 'N' Easy/This Was My Love	1960	12.00
4466	Ol' MacDonald/You'll Always Be the One I Love	1960	12.00
4546	My Blue Heaven/Sentimental Baby	1960	12.00
4615	American Beauty Rose/Sentimental Journey	1961	12.00
4677	The Moon Was Yellow/I've Heard That Song Before	1962	12.00
4729	Five Minutes More/I'll Remember April	1962	12.00
4815	I Love Paris/Hidden Persuasion	1962	12.00
6019	Young at Heart/Learnin' the Blues	196?	6.00
—Starline reissue label			
6027	All the Way/High Hopes	196?	6.00
—Starline reissue label			
6078	Witchcraft/Chicago	1966	6.00
—Starline reissue label			
6193	One for My Baby/I've Got You Under My Skin	197?	6.00
6195	In the Wee Small Hours of the Morning/Night and Day	197?	6.00
S7-17704	I've Got You Under My Skin/Come Rain or Come Shine	1994	—
—A-side with Bono, B-side with Gloria Estefan; canceled			
S7-18204	Jingle Bells/I'll Be Home for Christmas	1994	5.00
—Red vinyl			
58741	Mistletoe and Holly/The Christmas Waltz	1998	3.00
77683	Witchcraft/When You're Smiling	2001	3.00
—B-side by Dean Martin			
COLUMBIA			
1-106	Sunflower/Once in Love with Amy	1948	60.00
—All records with a "1-" prefix are Microgroove 33 1/3 rpm 7-inch singles			
1-112	Why Can't You Behave/No Orchids for My Lady	1948	60.00
B-112 [(4)]	The Voice of Frank Sinatra	1950	150.00
—Includes records 36918, 36919, 36920 and 36921 plus box			
1-130	Comme Ci, Comme Ca/While the Angelus Was Ringing	1948	60.00
1-144	When Is Sometime/If You Stub Your Toe on the Moon	1949	60.00
1-154	Where Is the One/Bop Goes My Heart	1949	60.00
B-167 [(4)]	Christmas Songs by Sinatra	1950	150.00
—Includes records 38256, 38257, 38258 and 38259 plus box			
1-174	Bali Ha'i/Some Enchanted Evening	1949	60.00
1-191	The Right Girl for Me/Night After Night	1949	60.00
B-197 [(4)]	Dedicated to You	1950	150.00
—Includes records 38683, 38684, 38685 and 38686 plus box			
B-218 [(4)]	Sing and Dance with Frank Sinatra	1950	150.00
—Includes records 38996, 38997, 38998 and 38999 plus box			
1-222	It Happens Every Spring/The Hucklebuck	1949	60.00
1-260	Let's Take an Old-Fashioned Walk/Just One Way to Say I Love You	1949	60.00
—With Doris Day			
1-307	I Only Have Eyes for You/It All Depends on You	1949	60.00
1-315	Don't Cry Joe/The Wedding of Lili Marlene	1949	60.00
1-316	Just a Kiss Apart/Bye Bye Baby	1949	60.00
1-326	If I Ever Love Again/Every Man Should Marry	1949	60.00
1-372	Could'ja/That Lucky Old Sun	1949	60.00
1-380	On the Island of Stromboli/Mad About You	1949	60.00
1-427	The Old Master Painter/Lost in the Stars	1949	60.00
1-440	Sorry/Why Remind Me	1949	60.00
1-491	Sunshine Cake/We've Got a Sure Thing	1949	60.00
1-496	Chattanoogie Shoe Shine Boy/God's Country	1950	60.00
1-508	You'll Never Walk Alone/Begin the Beguine	1950	60.00
1-511	Among My Souvenirs/September Song	1950	60.00
1-611	Kisses and Tears/When the Sun Goes Down	1950	60.00
1-624	American Beauty Rose/Just an Old Stone House	1950	60.00
1-650	Poinciana/There's No Business Like Show Business	1950	60.00
1-669	Peachtree Street/This Is the Night	1950	60.00
1-718	Goodnight Irene/My Blue Heaven	1950	60.00
6-718	Goodnight Irene/My Blue Heaven	1950	30.00
1-780	Life Is So Peculiar/Dear Little Boy of Mine	1950	60.00
1-845	One Finger Melody/Accidents Will Happen	1950	60.00
1-888	Nevertheless/I Guess I'll Have to Dream the Rest	1950	60.00
6-888	Nevertheless/I Guess I'll Have to Dream the Rest	1950	30.00
1-924	Remember Me in Your Dreams/Let It Snow, Let It Snow, Let It Snow	1950	60.00
6-924	Remember Me in Your Dreams/Let It Snow, Let It Snow, Let It Snow	1950	30.00
1-936	I Am Loved/You Don't Remind Me	1950	60.00
6-936	I Am Loved/You Don't Remind Me	1950	30.00
13-33011	Nancy/Ol' Man River	1975	6.00
—Hall of Fame series; new prefix			
3-33011	Nancy/Ol' Man River	1961	50.00
—Hall of Fame series; Compact Single 33			
4-33011	Nancy/Ol' Man River	1960	10.00
33306	I've Got a Crush on You/The Birth of the Blues	1977	6.00
—Hall of Fame series			
33319	Among My Souvenirs/September Song	1977	6.00
—Hall of Fame series			
36814	If You Are But a Dream/Put Your Dreams Away	1950	20.00
—Most Columbia 45s from 36000-39000 are reissues of titles that first appeared on 78s			
36825	You'll Never Walk Alone/If I Loved You	1950	20.00
36918	You Go to My Head/I Don't Know Why	1950	20.00
36919	These Foolish Things/A Ghost of a Chance	1950	20.00
36920	Why Shouldn't I?/Try a Little Tenderness	1950	20.00
36921	Paradise/Someone to Watch Over Me	1950	20.00
—The above four comprise the box set The Voice of Frank Sinatra, B-112			
37161	Among My Souvenirs/September Song	1950	20.00
37257	That Old Black Magic/How Deep Is the Ocean?	1950	20.00
37259	She's Funny That Way/Embraceable You	1950	20.00
38151	I've Got a Crush on You/Ever Homeward	1950	20.00
38163	All of Me/I Went Down to Virginia	1950	20.00
38256	Silent Night/Adeste Fideles	1950	20.00
38257	Jingle Bells/White Christmas	1950	20.00
38258	O Little Town Of Bethlehem/It Came Upon A Midnight Clear	1950	20.00
38259	Have Yourself a Merry Little Christmas/Santa Claus Is Comin' to Town	1950	20.00
—The above four comprise the box set Christmas Songs by Sinatra, B-167			
38446	Bali Ha'i/Some Enchanted Evening	1950	20.00
38683	The Moon Was Yellow/The Music Stopped	1950	20.00
38684	Strange Music/I Love You	1950	20.00
38685	Where or When/None But the Lonely Heart	1950	20.00
38686	Always/Why Was I Born?	1950	20.00
—The above four comprise the box set Dedicated to You, B-197			
38829	Poinciana/There's No Business Like Show Business	1950	20.00
38892	Goodnight Irene/My Blue Heaven	1950	15.00
—Reissue of Columbia 6-718			
38996	Lover/When You're Smiling	1950	20.00
38997	The Continental/It's Only a Paper Moon	1950	20.00
38998	Should I?/My Blue Heaven	1950	20.00
38999	It All Depends on You/You Do Something to Me	1950	20.00
—The above four comprise the box set Sing and Dance with Frank Sinatra, B-218			
39044	Nevertheless/I Guess I'll Have to Dream the Rest	1950	15.00
—Reissue of Columbia 6-888			
39069	Remember Me in Your Dreams/Let It Snow, Let It Snow, Let It Snow	1950	15.00
—Reissue of Columbia 6-924			
39079	I Am Loved/You Don't Remind Me	1950	15.00
—Reissue of Columbia 6-936			
39118	Take My Love/Come Back to Sorrento	1950	15.00
3-39118	Take My Love/Come Back to Sorrento	1950	150.00
—Microgroove 33 1/3 rpm, 7-inch single			
39141	Love Means Love/Cherry Pies Ought to Be You	1951	25.00
3-39141	Love Means Love/Cherry Pies Ought to Be You	1951	600.00
—Microgroove 33 1/3 rpm, 7-inch single			
39213	Faithful/You're the One	1951	20.00
3-39213	Faithful/You're the One	1951	150.00
—Microgroove 33 1/3 rpm, 7-inch single			
39294	Hello, Young Lovers/We Kissed in a Shadow	1951	15.00
39346	I Whistle a Happy Tune/Love Me	1951	15.00
39425	Mama Will Bark/I'm a Fool to Want You	1951	40.00
—"Frank Sinatra & Dagmar"; the record Ol' Blue Eyes called his worst			
39493	I Fall in Love with You Everyday/It's a Long Way from Your House	1951	20.00
39498	It Never Entered My Mind/Try a Little Tenderness	1951	15.00
39527	Castle Rock/Deep Night	1951	20.00
39592	April in Paris/London by Night	1951	15.00
39652	I Hear a Rhapsody/I Could Write a Book	1952	15.00
39687	Feet of Clay/Don't Ever Be Afraid to Go Home	1952	20.00

Number	Title (A Side/B Side)	Yr	NM
❑ 39726	My Girl/Walkin' in the Sunshine	1952	20.00
❑ 39787	Luna Rosa/Tennessee Newsboy	1952	20.00
❑ 39819	Azure-Te/Bim Bam Baby	1952	15.00
❑ 39882	The Birth of the Blues/Why Try to Change Me Now?	1952	15.00
❑ 40229	I'm Glad There Is You/You Can Take My Word For It Baby	1954	20.00
❑ 40522	Dream/American Beauty Rose	1955	15.00
❑ 40565	Sheila/Day by Day	1955	30.00
❑ 41133	I'm a Fool to Want You/If I Forget You	1958	15.00
❑ 50003	Among My Souvenirs/September Song	1954	10.00
—Hall of Fame series			
❑ 50028	I've Got a Crush on You/The Birth of the Blues	1954	10.00
—Hall of Fame series			
❑ 50053	Nancy/The Girl That I Marry	1955	10.00
—Hall of Fame series			
❑ 50066	You'll Never Walk Alone/If I Loved You	1955	10.00
—Hall of Fame series			
❑ 50069	Saturday Night/Five Minutes More	1955	10.00
—Hall of Fame series			
❑ 50079	Silent Night/Adeste Fideles	1955	10.00
—Hall of Fame series			
❑ JZSP 116427/8 [DJ]	White Christmas/Have Yourself A Merry Little Christmas	1966	50.00
ISLAND/CAPITOL			
❑ 858076-7	I've Got You Under My Skin/Stay (Faraway, So Close!)	1994	4.00
—A-side: Frank Sinatra and Bono; B-side: U2			
❑ 858076-7 [PS]	I've Got You Under My Skin/Stay (Faraway, So Close!)	1994	4.00
—A-side: Frank Sinatra and Bono; B-side: U2			
MCA			
❑ 55127	Fly Me to the Moon/Check Yes or No	1995	4.00
—A-side with George Strait; B-side is George Strait solo			
QWEST			
❑ 28844	The Best of Everything/Teach Me Tonight	1985	4.00
❑ 29139	Mack the Knife/It's All Right with Me	1984	5.00
❑ 29223	L.A. Is My Lady/Until the Real Thing Comes Along	1984	5.00
❑ 29223 [PS]	L.A. Is My Lady/Until the Real Thing Comes Along	1984	15.00
RCA VICTOR			
❑ 27-0012	Night and Day/The Lamplighter's Serenade	1948	15.00
—All RCA and 45s are reissues of material first issued on 78s. Part of WPT-5			
❑ 27-0076	Stardust/(B-side unknown)	1949	15.00
—From WDT 15			
❑ 27-0077	I'll Never Smile Again/(B-side unknown)	1949	15.00
—From WDT 15			
❑ 27-0095	Somewhere A Voice Is Calling/(B-side unknown)	1949	15.00
—From WDT 20			
❑ 27-0151	Daybreak/There Are Such Things	1948	15.00
❑ 447-0116	I'll Never Smile Again/I'll Be Seeing You	1950	12.00
❑ 447-0123	Stardust/There Are Such Things	1950	12.00
❑ 447-0408	Night and Day/The Lamplighter's Serenade	1952	12.00
❑ 447-0445	Street of Dreams/East of the Sun	1952	12.00
❑ 447-0928	Night and Day/The Night We Called It a Day	1972	6.00
❑ 447-0929	The Song Is You/The Lamplighter's Serenade	1972	6.00
❑ DTAO-3001	Street of Dreams/Whispering	1973	12.00
❑ DTBO-3012	The One I Love/This Love of Mine	1973	12.00
REPRISE			
❑ 0053	I'll Be Seeing You/Without a Song	1962	200.00
—Released in Great Britain as 20,053; pressed in the United States later			
❑ GRE 0113	Bad, Bad Leroy Brown/Let Me Try Again	1975	20.00
—"Back to Back Hits" series			
❑ GRE 0122	Theme from New York, New York/You and Me (We Wanted It All)	1981	4.00
—"Back to Back Hits" series			
❑ S 168 [S]	Moon River/Days of Wine and Roses	1964	20.00
❑ S 169 [S]	Three Coins in the Fountain/The Way You Look Tonight	1964	20.00
❑ S 170 [S]	Secret Love/In the Cool, Cool, Cool of the Evening	1964	20.00
❑ S 171 [S]	It Might As Well Be Spring/Swinging on a Star	1964	20.00
❑ S 172 [S]	All the Way/The Continental	1964	20.00
—The above five are 33 1/3 rpm, small hole jukebox singles			

Number	Title (A Side/B Side)	Yr	NM
❑ 243	Have Yourself a Merry Little Christmas/How Shall I Send Thee?	1963	20.00
—B-side by Les Baxter			
❑ 0249	Stay with Me/Talk to Me Baby	1963	10.00
❑ 0279	My Kind of Town/I Like to Lead When I Dance	1964	10.00
❑ 0279 [PS]	My Kind of Town/I Like to Lead When I Dance	1964	150.00
—Sleeve issued with promo copies only			
❑ 0301	Softly, As I Leave You/Then Suddenly Love	1964	10.00
❑ 0314	I Heard the Bells on Christmas Day/The Little Drummer Boy	1964	20.00
❑ 0314 [PS]	I Heard the Bells on Christmas Day/The Little Drummer Boy	1964	50.00
❑ 0317	We Wish You the Merriest/Go Tell It on the Mountain	1964	40.00
—By Frank Sinatra/Bing Crosby/Fred Waring			
❑ 0317 [PS]	We Wish You the Merriest/Go Tell It on the Mountain	1964	60.00
—By Frank Sinatra/Bing Crosby/Fred Waring			
❑ 0332	Somewhere in Your Heart/Emily	1964	8.00
—From here through 0677, originals on dark brown & orange label			
❑ 0350	Anytime at All/Available	1964	8.00
❑ 0373	Tell Her (You Love Her Each Day)/Here's to the Losers	1965	8.00
❑ 0380	Forget Domani/I Can't Believe I'm Losing You	1965	8.00
❑ 0398	When Somebody Loves You/When I'm Not Near the Girl I Love	1965	8.00
❑ 0410	Everybody Has the Right to Be Wrong/I'll Only Miss Her When I Think of Her	1965	8.00
❑ 0429	It Was a Very Good Year/Moment to Moment	1965	8.00
❑ 0429 [PS]	It Was a Very Good Year/Moment to Moment	1965	25.00
❑ 0470	Strangers in the Night/Oh, You Crazy Moon	1966	10.00
❑ 0493	Frank Sinatra Reads from Gunga Din	1966	500.00
—300 pressed and given away to friends; no stock copies			
❑ 0509	Summer Wind/You Make Me Feel So Young	1966	10.00
❑ 0531	That's Life/The September of My Years	1966	10.00
❑ 0531 [PS]	That's Life/The September of My Years	1966	25.00
❑ 0561	Somethin' Stupid/I Will Wait for You	1967	8.00
—A-side: Nancy Sinatra and Frank Sinatra			
❑ 0561	Somethin' Stupid/Give Her Love	1967	10.00
—A-side: Nancy Sinatra and Frank Sinatra			
❑ 0610	The World We Knew (Over and Over)/You Are There	1967	8.00
❑ 0631	This Town/This Is My Love	1967	8.00
❑ 0677	I Can't Believe I'm Losing You/How Old Am I?	1967	8.00
❑ 0702	My Kind of Town/That's Life	1968	5.00
—"Back to Back Hits" series			
❑ 0706	September of My Years/Softly, As I Leave You	1968	5.00
—"Back to Back Hits" series			
❑ 0710	Strangers in the Night/Summer Wind	1968	5.00
—"Back to Back Hits" series			
❑ 0713	It Was a Very Good Year/Stay with Me	1968	5.00
—"Back to Back Hits" series			
❑ 0727	Somethin' Stupid/The World We Knew (Over and Over)	1968	5.00
—"Back to Back Hits" series; A-side with Nancy Sinatra			
❑ 0734	My Way/Cycles	1970	5.00
—"Back to Back Hits" series			
❑ 0764	Cycles/My Way of Life	1968	6.00
—From here though 0865, orange/tan label with "W7/:r" logo			
❑ 0790	Whatever Happened to Christmas?/I Wouldn't Trade Christmas	1968	12.00
—B-side by The Sinatra Family			
❑ 0798	Rain in My Heart/Star	1968	6.00
❑ 0817	My Way/Blue Lace	1969	10.00
❑ 0852	Love's Been Good to Me/A Man Alone	1969	8.00
❑ 0865	Goin' Out of My Head/Forget to Remember	1969	8.00
❑ 0895	I Would Be in Love (Anyway)/Watertown	1970	8.00
—From here through 29903, orange (or tan) label with ":r" logo in square			
❑ 0920	The Train/What's Now Is Now	1969	8.00
❑ 0970	Lady Day/Song of the Sabia	1969	8.00
❑ 0980	Feelin' Kinda Sunday/Kids	1970	8.00
—A-side by Nancy Sinatra and Frank Sinatra; B-side by Nancy Sinatra			
❑ 0981	Something/Bein' Green	1970	8.00
❑ PRO-S-1007	To Love a Child (mono/stereo)	1982	300.00
—Special pressing of 500 with small hole, given to Nancy Reagan for distributuion at a White House function.			

Number	Title (A Side/B Side)	Yr	NM
❑ 1010	Witchcraft/Young at Heart	1971	8.00
❑ 1011	Life's a Trippy Thing/I'm Not Afraid	1971	8.00
—A-side by Nancy Sinatra and Frank Sinatra			
❑ 1181	Let Me Try Again/Send In the Clowns	1973	8.00
❑ 1190	You Will Be My Music/Winners	1973	8.00
❑ 1196	Bad, Bad Leroy Brown/I'm Gonna Make It All the Way	1974	8.00
❑ 1208	You Turned My World Around/Satisfy Me One More Time	1974	8.00
❑ 1327	Anytime (I'll Be There)/The Hurt Doesn't Go Away	1975	8.00
❑ 1335	I Believe I'm Gonna Love You/The Only Couple on the Floor	1975	8.00
❑ 1335 [PS]	I Believe I'm Gonna Love You	1975	40.00
—Issued with promo copies only			
❑ 1342	A Baby Just Like You/Christmas Mem'ries	1975	10.00
❑ 1342 [PS]	A Baby Just Like You/Christmas Mem'ries	1975	20.00
—Red and black printing, released with stock copies			
❑ 1342 [PS]	A Baby Just Like You/Christmas Mem'ries	1975	40.00
—Blue printing, released with promo copies only			
❑ 1343	Empty Tables/The Saddest Thing of All	1976	8.00
❑ 1347	I Sing the Songs (I Write the Songs)/Empty Tables	1976	10.00
❑ 1364	Stargazer/The Best I Ever Had	1976	8.00
❑ 1364 [PS]	Stargazer/The Best I Ever Had	1976	15.00
—Special sleeve: "New Sinatra Single"			
❑ 1377	Dry Your Eyes/Like a Sad Song	1976	8.00
❑ 1382	I Love My Wife/Send In the Clowns	1976	10.00
❑ 1386	Night and Day/Everybody Ought to Be in Love	1977	8.00
❑ 15999	My Way/Cycles	199?	3.00
—"Back to Back Hits" series			
❑ 19355	Fly Me to the Moon/The Last Dance	1991	4.00
❑ 20001	The Second Time Around/Tina	1961	25.00
—Originals on light blue label			
❑ 20010	Granada/The Curse of an Aching Heart	1961	15.00
—From here through 0317, originals on peach label			
❑ 20010 [PS]	Granada/The Curse of an Aching Heart	1961	25.00
❑ 20023	I'll Be Seeing You/The One I Love	1961	15.00
❑ 20024	Imagination/It's Always You	1961	15.00
❑ 20025	I'm Getting Sentimental Over You/East of the Sun (And West of the Moon)	1961	15.00
❑ 20026	There Are Such Things/Polkadots and Moonbeams	1961	15.00
❑ 20027	Without a Song/It Started All Over Again	1961	15.00
❑ 20028	Take Me/Daybreak	1961	15.00
❑ 20040	Pocketful of Miracles/Name It and It's Yours	1961	15.00
❑ 20040 [PS]	Pocketful of Miracles/Name It and It's Yours	1961	60.00
❑ 20059	Stardust/Come Rain or Come Shine	1962	15.00
❑ 20063	Everybody's Twistin'/Nothin' But the Best	1962	15.00
❑ 20063 [PS]	Everybody's Twistin'/Nothin' But the Best	1962	30.00
❑ 20092	Goody, Goody/Love Is Just Around the Corner	1962	12.00
❑ 20107	The Look of Love/I Left My Heart in San Francisco	1962	50.00
❑ 20107	The Look of Love/Indiscreet	1962	50.00
❑ 20128	Me and My Shadow/Sam's Song	1962	15.00
—A-side by Frank Sinatra and Sammy Davis, Jr.; B-side by Sammy Davis Jr. and Dean Martin			
❑ 20128 [PS]	Me and My Shadow/Sam's Song	1962	50.00
—A-side by Frank Sinatra and Sammy Davis, Jr.; B-side by Sammy Davis Jr. and Dean Martin			
❑ 20151	Call Me Irresponsible/Tina	1963	10.00
—B-side changed for commercial release			
❑ 20151	Call Me Irresponsible/Come Blow Your Horn	1963	500.00
—One stock copy is known to exist!			
❑ 20151 [DJ]	Call Me Irresponsible/Come Blow Your Horn	1963	100.00
❑ 20151 [PS]	Call Me Irresponsible/Come Blow Your Horn	1963	200.00
—Sleeve accompanies promo copies only			
❑ 20157 [DJ]	California/America the Beautiful	1963	250.00
—No stock copies isssued			
❑ 20157 [DJ]	California/America the Beautiful	1978	200.00
—Private pressing of 1,000 for Sinatra's personal use			
❑ 20157 [PS]	California/America the Beautiful	1963	750.00
—No stock copies isssued			
❑ 20184	I Have Dreamed/Come Blow Your Horn	1963	10.00
❑ 20209	Love Isn't Just for the Young/You Brought a New Kind of Love to Me	1963	12.00

S

Number	Title (A Side/B Side)	Yr	NM
❑ 20209 [PS]	Love Isn't Just for the Young/You Brought a New Kind of Love to Me	1963	50.00
❑ 20217	Fugue for Tinhorns/The Oldest Established (Permanent Floating Crap Game in New York)	1963	15.00
—By Frank Sinatra/Bing Crosby/Dean Martin			
❑ 20217 [PS]	Fugue for Tinhorns/The Oldest Established (Permanent Floating Crap Game in New York)	1963	75.00
—By Frank Sinatra/Bing Crosby/Dean Martin			
❑ 20235	Tangerine/A New Kind of Love	1963	—
—Unreleased			
❑ 29677	Here's to the Band/It's Sunday	1983	8.00
❑ 29903	To Love a Child/That's What God Looks Like to Me	1982	8.00
❑ 29903 [PS]	To Love a Child/That's What God Looks Like to Me	1982	15.00
❑ 40003	I Never Knew/Don't Be That Way	196?	20.00
—Jukebox 33 1/3 rpm, small hole single			
❑ 40006	Imagination/It's Always You	196?	20.00
—Jukebox record; small hole, plays at 33 1/3 rpm			
❑ 40009	It Started All Over Again/Without a Song	196?	20.00
—Jukebox 33 1/3 rpm, small hole single			
❑ 40013	Come Rain or Come Shine/It Might As Well Be Spring	196?	20.00
—Jukebox 33 1/3 rpm, small hole single			
❑ 40036	Pennies from Heaven/Please Be Kind	1963	20.00
—Jukebox 33 1/3 rpm, small hole single			
❑ 40037	The Tender Trap/Looking at the World Thru Rose Colored Glasses	1963	20.00
—Jukebox 33 1/3 rpm, small hole single			
❑ 40038	My Kind of Girl/I Only Have Eyes for You	1963	20.00
—Jukebox 33 1/3 rpm, small hole single			
❑ 40039	Nice Work If You Can Get It/Learnin' the Blues	1963	20.00
—Jukebox 33 1/3 rpm, small hole single			
❑ 40040	I'm Gonna Sit Right Down and Write Myself a Letter/I Won't Dance	1963	20.00
—Jukebox 33 1/3 rpm, small hole single			
❑ 40050	Please Be Kind/My Kind of Girl	1963	20.00
—Jukebox 33 1/3 rpm, small hole single			
❑ 49233	Theme from New York, New York/That's What God Looks Like to Me	1980	10.00
❑ 49233 [PS]	Theme from New York, New York/That's What God Looks Like to Me	1980	15.00
❑ 49517	You and Me (We Wanted It All)/I've Been There	1980	8.00
❑ 49827	Say Hello/Good Thing Going	1981	8.00
—B-side listed on label as "RE-2"			
❑ 49827	Say Hello/Good Thing Going	1981	8.00
—B-side listed on label as "RE-1"			

7-Inch Extended Plays

CAPITOL

Number	Title (A Side/B Side)	Yr	NM
❑ EAP 1-488	My Funny Valentine/The Girl Next Door//They Can't Take That Away from Me/Violets for Your Furs	1954	20.00
❑ EAP 1-488 [PS]	Songs for Young Lovers, Vol. 1	1954	20.00
❑ EAP 2-488	A Foggy Day/Like Someone I Love//I Get a Kick Out of You/Little Girl Blue	1954	20.00
❑ EAP 2-488 [PS]	Songs for Young Lovers, Vol. 2	1954	20.00
❑ EBF 488 [PS]	Songs for Young Lovers	1954	50.00
—Both of above EPs in gatefold sleeve			
❑ EAP 1-510	Young at Heart/I've Got the World on a String//From Here to Eternity/South of the Border	1954	25.00
❑ EAP 1-510 [PS]	Young at Heart	1954	25.00
❑ EAP 1-528	Just One of Those Things/I'm Gonna Sit Right Down and Write Myself a Letter//Sunday/Wrap Your Troubles in Dreams	1954	20.00
❑ EAP 1-528 [PS]	Swing Easy, Part I	1954	20.00
❑ EAP 2-528	Taking a Chance on Love/Jeepers Creepers//Get Happy/All of Me	1954	20.00
❑ EAP 2-528 [PS]	Swing Easy, Part II	1954	20.00
❑ EBF 528 [PS]	Swing Easy	1954	50.00
—Both 1-528 and 2-528 EPs in gatefold sleeve			
❑ EAP 1-542	Three Coins in the Fountain/My One and Only Love//Don't Worry 'Bout Me/I Love You	1954	25.00
❑ EAP 1-542 [PS]	3 Coins in the Fountain	1954	25.00
❑ EAP 1-571	Young at Heart/Someone to Watch Over Me//Just One of Those Things/You, My Love	1954	25.00
❑ EAP 1-571 [PS]	Frank Sinatra Sings Songs from His Warner Bros. Picture "Young at Heart"	1954	25.00
❑ EAP 1-581	In the Wee Small Hours of the Morning/I See Your Face Before Me//I'll Never Be the Same/This Love of Mine	1954	20.00
❑ EAP 1-581 [PS]	In the Wee Small Hours, Part 1	1955	20.00
❑ EAP 2-581	I'll Be Around/I Get Along Without You Very Well//It Never Entered My Mind/Dancing on the Ceiling	1955	20.00
❑ EAP 2-581 [PS]	In the Wee Small Hours, Part 2	1955	20.00
❑ EAP 3-581	Deep in a Dream/Mood Indigo//Glad to Be Unhappy/Ill Wind	1955	20.00
❑ EAP 3-581 [PS]	In the Wee Small Hours, Part 3	1955	20.00
❑ EAP 4-581	Can't We Be Friends/When Your Lover Has Gone//What Is This Thing Called Love/Last Night When We Were Young	1955	20.00
❑ EAP 4-581 [PS]	In the Wee Small Hours, Part 4	1955	20.00
❑ EBF 1-581 [PS]	In the Wee Small Hours, Parts 1 and 2	1955	50.00
—Gatefold sleeve for some editions of EAP 1-581 and 2-581			
❑ EBF 2-581 [PS]	In the Wee Small Hours, Parts 3 and 4	1955	50.00
—Gatefold sleeve for some editions of EAP 3-581 and 4-581			
❑ SU-581	In the Wee Small Hours of the Morning/I Get Along Without You Very Well//What Is This Thing Called Love/Dancing on the Ceiling	196?	25.00
—Stereo jukebox issue; small hole, plays at 33 1/3 rpm			
❑ SU-581 [PS]	In the Wee Small Hours	196?	25.00
❑ EAP 1-590	I'm Gonna Live Till I Die/Day In—Day Out//Melody of Love/Ever Since You Went Away	1955	25.00
—Second song on B-side by The Skyliners with Ray Anthony (no Sinatra involvement)			
❑ EAP 1-590 [PS]	Melody of Love	1955	25.00
❑ EAP 1-629	Two Hearts, Two Kisses (Make One Love)/Don't Change Your Mind About Me//Learnin' the Blues/Why Should I Cry Over You?	1955	25.00
❑ EAP 1-629 [PS]	Session with Sinatra	1955	25.00
❑ DU-653	It Happened in Monterey/Too Marvelous for Words/Anything Goes//You Make Me Feel So Young/I've Got You Under My Skin	196?	25.00
—Jukebox EP, plays at 33 1/3 rpm, small hole			
❑ DU-653 [PS]	Songs for Swingin' Lovers	196?	25.00
❑ EAP 1-653	You Make Me Feel So Young/It Happened in Monterey//Anything Goes/How About You	1956	20.00
❑ EAP 1-653 [PS]	Songs for Swingin' Lovers, Part 1	1956	25.00
—With Sinatra facing away from the embracing couple			
❑ EAP 1-653 [PS]	Songs for Swingin' Lovers, Part 1	1957	20.00
—With Sinatra facing toward the embracing couple			
❑ EAP 2-653	You're Getting to Be a Habit with Me/You Brought a New Kind of Love to Me//Makin' Whoopee/Swingin' Down the Lane	1956	20.00
❑ EAP 2-653 [PS]	Songs for Swingin' Lovers, Part 2	1956	25.00
—With Sinatra facing away from the embracing couple			
❑ EAP 2-653 [PS]	Songs for Swingin' Lovers, Part 2	1957	20.00
—With Sinatra facing toward the embracing couple			
❑ EAP 3-653	Too Marvelous for Words/Old Devil Moon//We'll Be Together Again	1956	20.00
❑ EAP 3-653 [PS]	Songs for Swingin' Lovers, Part 3	1956	25.00
—With Sinatra facing away from the embracing couple			
❑ EAP 3-653 [PS]	Songs for Swingin' Lovers, Part 3	1957	20.00
—With Sinatra facing toward the embracing couple			
❑ EAP 4-653	Pennies from Heaven/Love Is Here to Stay//I've Got You Under My Skin/I Thought About You	1956	20.00
❑ EAP 4-653 [PS]	Songs for Swingin' Lovers, Part 4	1956	25.00
—With Sinatra facing away from the embracing couple			
❑ EAP 4-653 [PS]	Songs for Swingin' Lovers, Part 4	1957	20.00
—With Sinatra facing toward the embracing couple			
❑ EBF 1-653 [PS]	Songs for Swingin' Lovers, Parts 1 and 2	1956	60.00
—Gatefold sleeve for some editions of EAP 1-653 and 2-653; with Sinatra facing away from the embracing couple			
❑ EBF 1-653 [PS]	Songs for Swingin' Lovers, Parts 1 and 2	1957	50.00
—Gatefold sleeve for some editions of EAP 1-653 and 2-653; with Sinatra facing toward the embracing couple			
❑ EBF 2-653 [PS]	Songs for Swingin' Lovers, Parts 3 and 4	1956	60.00
—Gatefold sleeve for some editions of EAP 3-653 and 4-653; with Sinatra facing away from the embracing couple			
❑ EBF 2-653 [PS]	Songs for Swingin' Lovers, Parts 3 and 4	1957	50.00
—Gatefold sleeve for some editions of EAP 3-653 and 4-653; with Sinatra facing toward the embracing couple			
❑ EAP 1-673	Our Town/The Impatient Years//Love and Marriage/Look to Your Heart	1956	50.00
❑ EAP 1-673 [PS]	Our Town	1956	50.00
❑ DU-768	I've Got the World on a String/Three Coins in the Fountain/Love and Marriage//South of the Border/Young at Heart/The Tender Trap	196?	25.00
—Jukebox EP, plays at 33 1/3 rpm, small hole			
❑ DU-768 [PS]	This Is Sinatra	196?	25.00
❑ EAP 1-789	Close to You/Love Locked Out//The End of a Love Affair	1956	20.00
❑ EAP 1-789 [PS]	Close to You, Part 1	1956	20.00
❑ EAP 2-789	P.S. I Love You//With Every Breath I Take/I Couldn't Sleep a Wink Last Night	1956	20.00
❑ EAP 2-789 [PS]	Close to You, Part 2	1956	20.00
❑ EAP 3-789	Everything Happens to Me/It Could Happen to You//I've Had My Moments	1956	20.00
❑ EAP 3-789 [PS]	Close to You, Part 3	1956	20.00
❑ EAP 4-789	Don't Like Goodbyes//It's Easy to Remember/Blame It on My Youth	1956	20.00
❑ EAP 4-789 [PS]	Close to You, Part 4	1956	20.00
❑ EBF 1-789 [PS]	Close to You, Parts 1 and 2	1956	50.00
—Gatefold sleeve for some editions of EAP 1-789 and 2-789			
❑ EBF 2-789 [PS]	Close to You, Parts 3 and 4	1956	50.00
—Gatefold sleeve for some editions of EAP 3-789 and 4-789			
❑ EAP 1-800	How Little We Know/Flowers Mean Forgiveness//You Forgot All the Words/Hey! Jealous Lover	1956	30.00
❑ EAP 1-800 [PS]	Hey! Jealous Lover	1956	30.00
❑ EAP 1-803	The Lonesome Road/You'd Be So Nice to Come Home To//From This Moment On/Nice Work If You Can Get It	1957	20.00
❑ EAP 1-803 [PS]	A Swingin' Affair, Part 1	1957	20.00
❑ EAP 2-803	I Won't Dance/At Long Last Love//I Got It Bad and That Ain't Good/I Guess I'll Have to Change My Plan	1957	20.00
❑ EAP 2-803 [PS]	A Swingin' Affair, Part 2	1957	20.00
❑ EAP 3-803	No One Ever Tells You/If I Had You//I Wish I Were in Love Again/I Got Plenty o' Nuttin'	1957	20.00
❑ EAP 3-803 [PS]	A Swingin' Affair, Part 3	1957	20.00
❑ EAP 4-803	Oh! Look at Me Now/Stars Fell on Alabama//Night and Day	1957	20.00
❑ EAP 4-803 [PS]	A Swingin' Affair, Part 4	1957	20.00
❑ EBF 1-803 [PS]	A Swingin' Affair, Parts 1 and 2	1957	50.00
—Gatefold sleeve for some editions of EAP 1-803 and 2-803			
❑ EBF 2-803 [PS]	A Swingin' Affair, Parts 3 and 4	1957	50.00
—Gatefold sleeve for some editions of EAP 3-803 and 4-803			
❑ EAP 1-855	Where Are You?/Where Is the One//Baby Won't You Please Come Home	1957	20.00
❑ EAP 1-855 [PS]	Where Are You? Part 1	1957	20.00
❑ EAP 2-855	I'm a Fool to Want You//I Cover the Waterfront/Laura	1957	20.00
❑ EAP 2-855 [PS]	Where Are You? Part 2	1957	20.00
❑ EAP 3-855	Lonely Town//The Night We Called It a Day/Autumn Leaves	1957	20.00
❑ EAP 3-855 [PS]	Where Are You? Part 3	1957	20.00
❑ EAP 4-855	There's No You//I Think of You/Maybe You'll Be There	1957	20.00
❑ EAP 4-855 [PS]	Where Are You? Part 4	1957	20.00
❑ EBF 1-855 [PS]	Where Are You? Parts 1 and 2	1957	50.00
—Gatefold sleeve for some editions of EAP 1-855 and 2-855			
❑ EBF 2-855 [PS]	Where Are You? Parts 3 and 4	1957	50.00
—Gatefold sleeve for some editions of EAP 3-855 and 4-855			
❑ EAP 1-894	Jingle Bells/The Christmas Song//Mistletoe and Holly/I'll Be Home for Christmas	1957	12.00
❑ EAP 1-894 [PS]	A Jolly Christmas from Frank Sinatra, Part 1	1957	12.00
❑ EAP 2-894	O Little Town of Bethlehem/Adeste Fideles//It Came Upon a Midnight Clear/Silent Night	1957	12.00
❑ EAP 2-894 [PS]	A Jolly Christmas from Frank Sinatra, Part 2	1957	12.00
❑ EAP 3-894	The Christmas Waltz/Have Yourself a Merry Little Christmas//The First Noel/Hark the Herald Angels Sing	1957	12.00
❑ EAP 3-894 [PS]	A Jolly Christmas from Frank Sinatra, Part 3	1957	12.00
❑ EAP 1-920	Come Fly with Me/Isle of Capri//It's Nice to Go Trav'ling	1958	15.00
❑ EAP 1-920 [PS]	Come Fly with Me, Part 1	1958	15.00
❑ EAP 2-920	Autumn in New York//April in Paris/Around the World	1958	15.00

Except when noted otherwise, VG = 25% of NM, and VG+ = 50% of NM. (Example: VG = $2.00, VG+ = $4.00 and NM = $8.00.)

Number	Title (A Side/B Side)	Yr	NM
❑ EAP 2-920 [PS]	Come Fly with Me, Part 2	1958	15.00
❑ EAP 3-920	Moonlight in Vermont//London by Night/Let's Get Away from It All	1958	15.00
❑ EAP 3-920 [PS]	Come Fly with Me, Part 3	1958	15.00
❑ EAP 4-920	On the Road to Mandalay//Blue Hawaii/Brazil	1958	15.00
❑ EAP 4-920 [PS]	Come Fly with Me, Part 4	1958	15.00
❑ SU-920	Come Fly with Me/Moonlight in Vermont//April in Paris/On the Road to Mandalay	196?	25.00
—Jukebox EP, plays at 33 1/3 rpm, small hole			
❑ SU-920 [PS]	Come Fly with Me	196?	25.00
❑ EAP 1-982	Hey! Jealous Lover/Everybody Loves Somebody//I Believe/Put Your Dreams Away	1958	20.00
❑ EAP 1-982 [PS]	This Is Sinatra, Vol. Two, Part 1	1958	20.00
❑ EAP 2-982	Something Wonderful Happens in Summer/Half As Lovely//So Long My Love/It's the Same Old Dreams	1958	20.00
❑ EAP 2-982 [PS]	This Is Sinatra, Vol. Two, Part 2	1958	20.00
❑ EAP 3-982	You're Cheatin' Yourself/You'll Always Be the One I Love// Johnny Concho Theme (Wait for Me)/If You Are But a Dream	1958	20.00
❑ EAP 3-982 [PS]	This Is Sinatra, Vol. Two, Part 3	1958	20.00
❑ EAP 4-982	You Forgot All the Words/How Little We Know//Time After Time/Crazy Love	1958	20.00
❑ EAP 4-982 [PS]	This Is Sinatra, Vol. 2, Part 4	1958	20.00
❑ EAP 1-1013	The Lady Is a Tramp/Witchcraft// Come Fly with Me/Tell Her You Love Her	1958	30.00
❑ EAP 1-1013 [PS]	Frank Sinatra!	1958	30.00
❑ EAP 1-1053	Only the Lonely/Blues in the Night	1958	20.00
❑ EAP 1-1053 [PS]	Frank Sinatra Sings for Only the Lonely	1958	20.00
❑ EAP 1-1069	Come Dance with Me/ Something's Gotta Give//The Song Is You/The Last Dance	1958	15.00
❑ EAP 1-1069 [PS]	Come Dance with Me, Part 1	1958	15.00
❑ EAP 2-1069	Just in Time/Dancing in the Dark/ /Cheek to Cheek/Baubles, Bangles and Beads	1958	15.00
❑ EAP 2-1069 [PS]	Come Dance with Me, Part 2	1958	15.00
❑ EAP 3-1069	Saturday Night/Day In — Day Out//Too Close for Comfort/I Could Have Danced All Night	1958	15.00
❑ EAP 3-1069 [PS]	Come Dance with Me, Part 3	1958	15.00
❑ EAP 1-1159	Angel Eyes/Willow Weep for Me	1958	30.00
❑ EAP 1-1159 [PS]	Frank Sinatra Sings Angel Eyes	1958	30.00
❑ EAP 1-1221	When No One Cares/I'll Never Smile Again//A Cottage for Sale/None But the Lonely Heart	1959	15.00
❑ EAP 1-1221 [PS]	No One Cares, Part 1	1959	15.00
❑ EAP 2-1221	I Don't Stand a Ghost of a Chance with You/Here's That Rainy Day//I Can't Get Started	1959	15.00
❑ EAP 2-1221 [PS]	No One Cares, Part 2	1959	15.00
❑ EAP 3-1221	*Stormy Weather/Where Do You Go/Why Try to Change Me Now/Just Friends	1959	15.00
❑ EAP 3-1221 [PS]	No One Cares, Part 3	1959	15.00
❑ EAP 1-1224	High Hopes/All My Tomorrows// French Foreign Legion/ Mr. Success	1959	30.00
❑ EAP 1-1224 [PS]	High Hopes	1959	30.00
❑ SEP 1-1233 [PS]	French Foreign Legion	1959	50.00
❑ SEP 1-1233 [S]	French Foreign Legion/ Mr. Success//Come Dance with Me/The Last Dance	1959	50.00
❑ EAP 1-1348	Talk to Me/They Came to Cordura//When No One Cares/Where Do You Go?	1959	30.00
❑ EAP 1-1348 [PS]	Talk to Me	1959	30.00
❑ EAP 1-1417	*Nice 'n' Easy/That Old Feeling/She's Funny That Way/Dream	1960	20.00
❑ EAP 1-1417 [PS]	Nice 'n' Easy, Part 1	1960	20.00
❑ EAP 2-1417	How Deep Is the Ocean/ Mam'selle//Try a Little Tenderness/Embraceable You	1960	20.00
❑ EAP 2-1417 [PS]	Nice 'n' Easy, Part 2	1960	20.00
❑ EAP 3-1417	You Go to My Head/I've Got a Crush on You//Fools Rush In/ Nevertheless	1960	20.00
❑ EAP 3-1417 [PS]	Nice 'n' Easy, Part 3	1960	20.00
❑ EAP 1-1491	When You're Smiling (The Whole World Smiles With You)/Blue Moon//S'Posin'/It All Depends on You	1961	25.00
❑ EAP 1-1491 [PS]	Sinatra's Swingin' Session, Part 1	1961	25.00
❑ EAP 2-1491	Always/I Can't Believe You're in Love with Me//It's Only a Paper Moon/My Blue Heaven	1961	25.00
❑ EAP 2-1491 [PS]	Sinatra's Swingin' Session, Part 2	1961	25.00
❑ EAP 3-1491	Should I/September in the Rain//I Concentrate on You/ You Do Something to Me	1961	25.00
❑ EAP 3-1491 [PS]	Sinatra's Swingin' Session, Part 3	1961	25.00
❑ MA1-1583	Three Coins in the Fountain/ Learnin' the Blues//Young-at-Heart/Love and Marriage	1961	25.00
—"Capitol 33 Compact"; small hole, plays at 33 1/3 rpm			
❑ MA1-1583 [PS]	Frank Sinatra	1961	25.00
❑ EAP 1-1594	(contents unknown)	1961	25.00
❑ EAP 1-1594 [PS]	Come Swing with Me, Part 1	1961	25.00
❑ EAP 2-1594	(contents unknown)	1961	25.00
❑ EAP 2-1594 [PS]	Come Swing with Me, Part 2	1961	25.00
❑ EAP 3-1594	(contents unknown)	1961	25.00
❑ EAP 3-1594 [PS]	Come Swing with Me, Part 3	1961	25.00
❑ SU-1762	All the Way/Hey Jealous Lover/ Lean Baby//Witchcraft/ One for My Baby	196?	25.00
—Jukebox EP, plays at 33 1/3 rpm, small hole			
❑ SU-1762 [PS]	The Great Years	196?	25.00
❑ SXA-1762	(Love Is) The Tender Trap/It's Over, It's Over, It's Over/The Nearness of You//The Gal That Got Away/When Your Lover Has Gone/The Last Dance	196?	25.00
—Jukebox EP, plays at 33 1/3 rpm, small hole			
❑ SXA-1762 [PS]	The Great Years	196?	25.00
COLUMBIA			
❑ B-112 [PS]	The Voice of Frank Sinatra	1950	50.00
—Gatefold cover for 2-EP set (1115 and 1116)			
❑ B-167 [PS]	Christmas Songs by Sinatra	1952	50.00
—Gatefold cover for 2-EP set (1322 and 1323)			
❑ B-218 [PS]	Sing and Dance with Frank Sinatra	1950	50.00
—Gatefold sleeve for 2-EP set (1129 and 1130)			
❑ B-337 [PS]	Requested By You	1953	25.00
—Gatefold cover for 2-EP set (1559 and 1560)			
❑ B-419 [PS]	I've Got a Crush on You	1952	50.00
—Gatefold cover for 2-EP set (1907 and 1908)			
❑ 5-1115	You Go to My Head/Someone to Watch Over Me//A Ghost of a Chance/Paradise	1952	25.00
—One record of 2-EP version of B-112			
❑ 5-1116	These Foolish Things/Why Shouldn't I//I Don't Know Why/ Try a Little Tenderness	1952	25.00
—One record of 2-EP version of B-112			
❑ 5-1129	Lover/It's Only a Paper Moon// The Continental/When You're Smiling	1952	25.00
—One record of 2-EP version of B-218			
❑ 5-1130	My Blue Heaven/It All Depends on You//You Do Something to Me/Should I	1952	25.00
—One record of 2-EP version of B-218			
❑ 5-1193	Always/Blue Skies//How Deep Is the Ocean/They Say It's Wonderful	1952	25.00
—Record that goes with cover B-1524			
❑ 5-1322	White Christmas/Jingle Bells// Have Yourself a Merry Little Christmas/Have Yourself a Merry Little Christmas	1952	25.00
—One record of 2-EP version of B-167			
❑ 5-1323	Silent Night, Holy Night/Adeste Fideles//O Little Town of Bethlehem/It Came Upon a Midnight Clear	1952	25.00
—One record of 2-EP version of B-167			
❑ 5-1355	Some Enchanted Evening/Bali Ha'i//People Will Say We're in Love/Oh, What a Beautiful Morning	1952	30.00
—Record that goes with cover B-1608			
❑ 5-1389	Soliloquy//If I Loved You/You'll Never Walk Alone	1952	30.00
—Record that goes with cover B-1673			
❑ B-1524 [PS]	Frank Sinatra Sings Irving Berlin	1952	25.00
❑ 5-1555	Embraceable You/I've Got a Crush on You//Someone to Watch Over Me/Where Is My Bess?	1953	25.00
—Record that goes with cover B-1673			
❑ 5-1559	(contents unknown)	1953	25.00
—Side 1 and Side 4 of B-337			
❑ 5-1560	Deep Purple/Body and Soul// Begin the Beguine/Laura	1953	25.00
—Side 2 and Side 3 of B-337			
❑ B-1608 [PS]	Frank Sinatra Sings Hits from South Pacific and Oklahoma	1952	30.00
❑ B-1620 [PS]	Carousel Sung by Frank Sinatra	1952	30.00
❑ B-1673 [PS]	Frank Sinatra Sings George Gershwin	1953	25.00
❑ B-1702	Ol' Man River/All the Things You Are//Why Was I Born/ The Song Is You	1953	25.00
❑ B-1702 [PS]	Frank Sinatra Sings Jerome Kern	1953	25.00
❑ B-1815	I Concentrate on You/Why Can't You Behave//Why Shouldn't I/ You Do Something to Me	1954	25.00
❑ B-1815 [PS]	Frank Sinatra Sings Cole Porter	1954	25.00
❑ B-1872	(contents unknown)	1954	25.00
❑ B-1872 [PS]	Frank Sinatra Sings Rodgers and Hart	1954	25.00
❑ 5-1907	I've Got a Crush on You/They Say It's Wonderful//If I Loved You/You Do Something to Me	1952	25.00
—One record of 2-EP set B-419			
❑ 5-1908	I Only Have Eyes for You/The Girl That I Marry//I Hear a Rhapsody/April in Paris	1952	25.00
—One record of 2-EP set B-419			
❑ B-1984	Hello Young Lovers/I Only Have Eyes for You//Falling in Love with Love/You'll Never Know	1955	25.00
❑ B-1984 [PS]	Frankie, Vol. 1	1955	25.00
❑ B-1985	It All Depends on You/S'posin'//All of Me/Time After Time	1955	25.00
❑ B-1985 [PS]	Frankie, Vol. 2	1955	25.00
❑ B-1986	How Cute Can You Be/Almost Like Being in Love//Nancy/Oh! What It Seemed to Be	1955	25.00
❑ B-1986 [PS]	Frankie, Vol. 3	1955	25.00
❑ B-2515	I Couldn't Sleep a Wink Last Night/A Lovely Way to Spend an Evening//People Will Say We're in Love/Oh, What a Beautiful Momin'	1957	25.00
❑ B-2515 [PS]	Frank Sinatra (Hall of Fame Series)	1957	25.00
❑ B-2516	Nancy (With the Laughing Face)/Day by Day//They Say It's Wonderful/The Girl That I Marry	1957	25.00
❑ B-2516 [PS]	Frank Sinatra (Hall of Fame Series)	1957	25.00
❑ B-2517	The Birth of the Blues/I've Got a Crush on You//Five Minutes More/Someone to Watch Over Me	1957	25.00
❑ B-2517 [PS]	Frank Sinatra (Hall of Fame Series)	1957	25.00
❑ B-2542	Castle Rock/Farewell, Farewell to Love//A Little Learnin' Is a Dangerous Thing	1957	50.00
❑ B-2542 [PS]	Frank Sinatra with Harry James and Pearl Bailey	1957	50.00
❑ B-2559	I Could Write a Book/If You Are But a Dream//I'm a Fool to Want You/I Should Care	1958	25.00
❑ B-2559 [PS]	Frank Sinatra (Hall of Fame Series)	1958	25.00
❑ B-2564	Ol' Man River/You'll Never Walk Alone//Soliloquy	1958	25.00
❑ B-2564 [PS]	Frank Sinatra (Hall of Fame Series)	1958	25.00
❑ B-2589	September Song/Among My Souvenirs//The Things We Did Last Summer/Oh! What It Seemed to Be	1958	25.00
❑ B-2589 [PS]	Frank Sinatra (Hall of Fame Series)	1958	25.00
❑ B-2614	One for My Baby/If I Loved You/ /Put Your Dreams Away/ You'll Never Know	1958	25.00
❑ B-2614 [PS]	Frank Sinatra (Hall of Fame Series)	1958	25.00
❑ B-2626	Close to You/Embraceable You//The Charm of You/ I Dream of You	1958	25.00
❑ B-2626 [PS]	Frank Sinatra (Hall of Fame Series)	1958	25.00
❑ B-2638	Stormy Weather/Why Was I Born//The House I Live In/ How Deep Is the Ocean	1958	25.00

S

Number	Title (A Side/B Side)	Yr	NM
❑ B-2638 [PS]	Frank Sinatra (Hall of Fame Series)	1958	25.00
❑ B-2641	All or Nothing at All/You Go to My Head//Why Try to Change Me Now/I Concentrate on You	1958	25.00
❑ B-2641 [PS]	Frank Sinatra (Hall of Fame Series)	1958	25.00
❑ B-7431	I Don't Know Why (I Just Do)/Try a Little Tenderness//(I Don't Stand) A Ghost of a Chance/Paradise	1955	25.00
❑ B-7431 [PS]	The Voice, Vol. I	1955	25.00
❑ B-7432	(contents unknown)	1955	25.00
❑ B-7432 [PS]	The Voice, Vol. II	1955	25.00
❑ B-7433	Over the Rainbow/That Old Black Magic//Spring Is Here/Lover	1955	25.00
❑ B-7433 [PS]	The Voice, Vol. III	1955	25.00
❑ B-9021	That Old Feeling/Blue Skies//Autumn in New York/Don't Cry Joe	1956	25.00
❑ B-9021 [PS]	That Old Feeling	1956	25.00
❑ B-9022	The Nearness of You/That Lucky Old Sun//Full Moon and Empty Arms/Once in Love with Amy	1956	25.00
❑ B-9022 [PS]	The Nearness of You	1956	25.00
❑ B-9023	A Fellow Needs a Girl/Poinciana (Song of the Tree)//For Every Man There's a Woman/Mean to Me	1956	25.00
❑ B-9023 [PS]	A Fellow Needs a Girl	1956	25.00
❑ B-9531	I Guess I'll Have to Dream the Rest/If Only She'd Look My Way//Love Me/Nevertheless	1957	25.00
❑ B-9531 [PS]	Adventures of the Heart, Vol. I	1957	25.00
❑ B-9532	We Kiss in a Shadow/I Am Loved//Take My Love/I Could Write a Book	1957	25.00
❑ B-9532 [PS]	Adventures of the Heart, Vol. II	1957	25.00
❑ B-9533	Mad About You/Sorry//On the Island of Stromboli/It's Only a Paper Moon	1957	25.00
❑ B-9533 [PS]	Adventures of the Heart, Vol. III	1957	25.00
❑ B-10321	White Christmas/Jingle Bells//Have Yourself a Merry Little Christmas/Santa Claus Is Coming to Town	1957	30.00
❑ B-10321 [PS]	Christmas Dreaming, Vol. 1	1957	40.00
❑ B-10322	Silent Night, Holy Night/Adeste Fideles//O Little Town of Bethlehem/It Came Upon the Midnight Clear	1957	30.00
❑ B-10322 [PS]	Christmas Dreaming, Vol. 2	1957	40.00
❑ ZTEP 28595/6 [DJ]	Nancy/I'm a Fool to Want You//Full Moon and Empty Arms/The Birth of the Blues	1958	50.00
❑ ZTEP 28595/6 [PS]	Nancy	1958	50.00
—Limited edition EP for the B.T. Babbit Soap Co.			
RCA VICTOR			
❑ 947-0176	Night and Day/East of the Sun//Fools Rush In/The Lamplighter's Serenade	1954	30.00
—Part 1 of EPBT 3063			
❑ 947-0177	Everything Happens to Me/I'll Be Seeing You//This Is the Beginning of the End/Street of Dreams	1954	30.00
—Part 2 of EPBT 3063			
❑ EPBT-3063 [PS]	Fabulous Frankie	1954	40.00
—Cover for 947-0176 and 947-0177			
❑ EPA-5014	Oh! Look at Me Now/This Love of Mine//I Guess I'll Have to Dream the Rest/How Do You Do Without Me	1958	20.00
❑ EPA-5014 [PS]	Frankie and Tommy	1958	20.00
❑ EPA-5147	The Lamplighter's Serenade/The Night We Called It a Day//The Song Is You/Night and Day	1960	25.00
❑ EPA-5147 [PS]	Frank Sinatra	1960	25.00
REPRISE			
❑ SR 1011	Days of Wine and Roses/Moon River/In the Cool, Cool, Cool of the Evening//Swingin' on a Star/All the Way/The Way You Look Tonight	1964	20.00
—Stereo jukebox issue; small hole, plays at 33 1/3 rpm			
❑ SR 1011 [PS]	Days of Wine and Roses, Moon River and Other Academy Award Winners	1964	20.00
❑ SR 1012	Fly Me to the Moon/I Wanna Be Around/More//I Can't Stop Loving You/The Good Life/I Wish You Love	1965	20.00
—33 1/3 rpm, small hole, "Promotion"			

Number	Title (A Side/B Side)	Yr	NM
❑ SR 1012 [PS]	It Might As Well Be Swing	1965	20.00
❑ SR 1013	Dear Heart/Pass Me By/I Can't Believe I'm Losing You//Come Blow Your Horn/Softly As I Leave You/Then Suddenly Love	1965	20.00
—Jukebox issue; small hole, plays at 33 1/3 rpm			
❑ SR 1013 [PS]	Softly As I Leave You	1965	20.00
❑ SR 1018	Moon Love/Moonlight Serenade//Moonlight Becomes You/The Moon Got in My Eyes/I Wished on the Moon	1966	20.00
—Jukebox issue; 33 1/3 rpm, small hole			
❑ SR 1018 [PS]	Moonlight Sinatra	1966	20.00
❑ SR 1019	Come Fly with Me/Street of Dreams/You Make Me Feel So Young//Fly Me to the Moon/Where or When/My Kind of Town (reprise)	1966	20.00
—Stereo jukebox issue; small hole, plays at 33 1/3 rpm			
❑ SR 1019 [PS]	Sinatra at the Sands	1966	20.00
❑ SR 1022	The World We Knew (Over and Over)/Don't Sleep in the Subway/You Are There//Somethin' Stupid (Duet with Nancy Sinatra)/This Town/Drinking Again	1967	20.00
—Stereo jukebox issue; small hole, plays at 33 1/3 rpm			
❑ SR 1022 [PS]	Frank Sinatra (The World We Knew)	1967	20.00
❑ SR 1024	Follow Me/Sunny//Yellow Days/Indian Summer	1968	20.00
—As "Francis A. Sinatra & Edward K. Ellington"; jukebox issue; 33 1/3 rpm, small hole			
❑ SR 1024 [PS]	Francis A. and Edward K.	1968	20.00
❑ SR 1033	Drinking Water (Aqua de Beber)/Someone to Light Up My Life/Triste//Leaving on a Jet Plane/Bein' Green/One Note Samba	1971	15.00
—Stereo jukebox issue; small hole, plays at 33 1/3 rpm			
❑ SR 1033 [PS]	Sinatra and Company	1971	15.00
—Part of "Little LP" series (#178)			
❑ SR 1034	My Way/Love's Been Good to Me//Goin' Out of My Head/Star/The September of My Years	1972	15.00
—Jukebox issue; small hole, plays at 33 1/3 rpm			
❑ SR 1034 [PS]	Frank Sinatra's Greatest Hits, Vol. II	1972	15.00
—Part of "Little LP" series (#191)			
❑ PRO-S-2115 [DJ]	You'd Be So Easy to Love/Theme from New York, New York//Come Fly with Me/Summer Wind	1984	20.00
—Small hole, plays at 33 1/3 rpm			
❑ PRO-S-2115 [PS]	Stereo Review Salutes Frank Sinatra	1984	20.00
—Special promo available from "Stereo Review" magazine			
❑ SR 2155	Let Me Try Again/You Will Be My Music//Winners/You're So Right (For What's Wrong in My Life)	1973	20.00
—Jukebox issue; small hole, plays at 33 1/3 rpm			
❑ SR 2155 [PS]	Ol' Blue Eyes Is Back	1973	20.00
—Part of Little LP series (# LLP 233)			
❑ SR 2195	What Are You Doing the Rest of Your Life?/Bad, Bad Leroy Brown//You Are the Sunshine of My Life/The Summer Knows/Tie a Yellow Ribbon	1974	15.00
—Stereo jukebox issue; small hole, plays at 33 1/3 rpm			
❑ SR 2195 [PS]	Some Nice Things I've Missed	1974	15.00
—Part of "Little LP" series (#267)			
❑ R-40026	I Hadn't Anyone Till You/Misty/Stardust//Come Rain or Come Shine/All or Nothing at All	1962	25.00
—Jukebox issue; small hole, plays at 33 1/3 rpm			
❑ R-40026 [PS]	Sinatra and Strings	1962	25.00
❑ R-40027	Goody Goody/They Can't Take That Away from Me/I Get a Kick Out of You//Tangerine/Serenade in Blue/Pick Yourself Up	196?	25.00
—Stereo jukebox issue; small hole, plays at 33 1/3 rpm			
❑ R-40027 [PS]	Sinatra and Swingin' Brass	196?	25.00
❑ R-40043	(Love Is) The Tender Trap/Please Be Kind/Nice Work If You Can Get It//My Kind of Girl/Learnin' the Blues	1963	25.00
—Stereo jukebox issue; small hole, plays at 33 1/3 rpm			
❑ R-40043 [PS]	Sinatra-Basie	1963	25.00

Albums

Number	Title (A Side/B Side)	Yr	NM
ARTANIS			
❑ ARZ 101 [(2)]	Sinatra '57 In Concert	1999	—
—Canceled			
BOOK-OF-THE-MONTH			
❑ (# unknown) [(6)]	Tommy Dorsey/Frank Sinatra: The Complete Sessions	1983	100.00
CAPITOL			
❑ DWBB-254 [(2)R]	Close-Up	1969	20.00
—Reissue in one package of "This Is Sinatra" and "This Is Sinatra, Vol. Two"			
❑ DKAO-374 [R]	Frank Sinatra's Greatest Hits	1969	12.00
❑ H 488 [10]	Songs for Young Lovers	1954	60.00
❑ H 528 [10]	Swing Easy	1954	60.00
❑ STBB-529 [(2)]	What Is This Thing Called Love?/The Night We Called It a Day	1970	15.00
❑ DW 581 [R]	In the Wee Small Hours	196?	12.00
❑ H1-581 [10]	In the Wee Small Hours, Part 1	1955	100.00
❑ H2-581 [10]	In the Wee Small Hours, Part 2	1955	100.00
❑ SM-581	In the Wee Small Hours	197?	8.00
❑ W 581 [M]	In the Wee Small Hours	1955	40.00
—Gray label original			
❑ W 581 [M]	In the Wee Small Hours	1959	25.00
—Black label with colorband			
❑ W 587 [M]	Swing Easy/Songs for Young Lovers	1955	40.00
—Gray label original; 12-inch version of two 10-inch LPs			
❑ W 587 [M]	Swing Easy/Songs for Young Lovers	1959	25.00
—Black label with colorband			
❑ DW 653 [R]	Songs for Swingin' Lovers!	196?	12.00
❑ SM-653	Songs for Swingin' Lovers!	197?	8.00
❑ W 653 [M]	Songs for Swingin' Lovers!	1956	40.00
—Gray label; cover has Sinatra facing toward the embracing couple			
❑ W 653 [M]	Songs for Swingin' Lovers!	1956	50.00
—Gray label; cover has Sinatra facing away from the embracing couple			
❑ W 653 [M]	Songs for Swingin' Lovers!	1959	25.00
—Black label with colorband			
❑ STBB-724 [(2)]	My One and Only Love/Sentimental Journey	1971	15.00
❑ T 735 [M]	Frank Sinatra Conducts Tone Poems of Color	1956	60.00
—Turquoise label			
❑ T 735 [M]	Frank Sinatra Conducts Tone Poems of Color	1959	40.00
—Black label with colorband			
❑ DT 768 [R]	This Is Sinatra!	196?	12.00
❑ T 768 [M]	This Is Sinatra!	1956	30.00
—Turquoise label			
❑ T 768 [M]	This Is Sinatra!	196?	15.00
—Gold "Starline" label			
❑ T 768 [M]	This Is Sinatra!	196?	20.00
—Black "Starline" label			
❑ DW 789 [R]	Close to You	196?	12.00
❑ W 789 [M]	Close to You	1957	30.00
—Gray label			
❑ W 789 [M]	Close to You	1959	20.00
—Black label with colorband			
❑ DW 803 [R]	A Swingin' Affair!	196?	12.00
❑ W 803 [M]	A Swingin' Affair!	1957	20.00
—Black label with colorband			
❑ W 803 [M]	A Swingin' Affair!	1957	30.00
—Gray label			
❑ SW 855 [S]	Where Are You?	1959	40.00
—Originals do not include "I Cover the Waterfront"			
❑ SW 855 [S]	Where Are You?	196?	30.00
—Later releases restore "I Cover the Waterfront"			
❑ W 855 [M]	Where Are You?	1957	30.00
—Gray label			
❑ W 855 [M]	Where Are You?	1959	20.00
—Black label with colorband			
❑ DT 894 [R]	The Sinatra Christmas Album	196?	10.00
—Rechanneled reissue of A Jolly Christmas with Frank Sinatra with same contents; some copies have this cover and "A Jolly Christmas" labels			
❑ SM-894 [R]	The Sinatra Christmas Album	197?	8.00
—Reissue in rechanneled stereo; any color label			
❑ T 894 [M]	The Sinatra Christmas Album	196?	20.00
—Reissue of A Jolly Christmas with Frank Sinatra with same contents; some copies have this cover and "A Jolly Christmas" labels			
❑ W 894 [M]	A Jolly Christmas from Frank Sinatra	1957	40.00
—Original mono with gray label			
❑ W 894 [M]	A Jolly Christmas from Frank Sinatra	1958	30.00
—Black colorband label, logo at left			
❑ SM-920	Come Fly with Me	197?	8.00
❑ SW 920 [S]	Come Fly with Me	1959	30.00
❑ W 920 [M]	Come Fly with Me	1958	40.00
—Gray label			
❑ W 920 [M]	Come Fly with Me	1959	20.00
—Black label with colorband			
❑ DW 982 [R]	This Is Sinatra, Vol. Two	196?	12.00
❑ W 982 [M]	This Is Sinatra, Vol. Two	1958	40.00
—Gray label			
❑ W 982 [M]	This Is Sinatra, Vol. Two	1959	20.00
—Black label with colorband, logo at left			
❑ W 982 [M]	This Is Sinatra, Vol. Two	1963	15.00
—Black label with colorband, logo at top			
❑ SW 1053 [S]	Frank Sinatra Sings for Only the Lonely	1959	30.00
—Originals do not include "It's a Lonesome Old Town" and "Spring Is Here"			

Except when noted otherwise, VG = 25% of NM, and VG+ = 50% of NM. (Example: VG = $2.00, VG+ = $4.00 and NM = $8.00.)

Number	Title (A Side/B Side)	Yr	NM
❑ SW 1053 [S]	Frank Sinatra Sings for Only the Lonely	196?	25.00
—Later releases restore "It's a Lonesome Old Town" and "Spring Is Here"			
❑ W 1053 [M]	Frank Sinatra Sings for Only the Lonely	1958	40.00
—Gray label			
❑ W 1053 [M]	Frank Sinatra Sings for Only the Lonely	1959	20.00
—Black label with colorband			
❑ SW 1069 [S]	Come Dance with Me!	1959	30.00
❑ W 1069 [M]	Come Dance with Me!	1959	20.00
❑ DW 1164 [R]	Look to Your Heart	196?	12.00
❑ W 1164 [M]	Look to Your Heart	1959	30.00
❑ SM-1221	No One Cares	197?	8.00
❑ SW 1221 [S]	No One Cares	1959	30.00
❑ W 1221 [M]	No One Cares	1959	20.00
❑ SW 1417 [S]	Nice 'N' Easy	1960	25.00
❑ W 1417 [M]	Nice 'N' Easy	1960	20.00
❑ DW 1429 [R]	Swing Easy	1960	12.00
❑ W 1429 [M]	Swing Easy	1960	20.00
❑ DW 1432 [R]	Songs for Young Lovers	1960	12.00
❑ W 1432 [M]	Songs for Young Lovers	1960	20.00
❑ SM-1491	Sinatra's Swingin' Session!!!	197?	8.00
❑ SW 1491 [S]	Sinatra's Swingin' Session!!!	1961	25.00
❑ W 1491 [M]	Sinatra's Swingin' Session!!!	1961	20.00
❑ SW 1538 [S]	All the Way	1961	25.00
❑ W 1538 [M]	All the Way	1961	20.00
❑ SW 1594 [S]	Come Swing with Me!	1961	25.00
❑ W 1594 [M]	Come Swing with Me!	1961	20.00
❑ SM-1676	Point of No Return	197?	8.00
❑ SW 1676 [S]	Point of No Return	1962	25.00
❑ W 1676 [M]	Point of No Return	1962	20.00
❑ SW 1729 [P]	Sinatra Sings…Of Love and Things	1962	20.00
❑ W 1729 [M]	Sinatra Sings…Of Love and Things	1962	20.00
❑ SWCO 1762 [(3)P]	Sinatra, The Great Years	1962	40.00
❑ WCO 1762 [(3)M]	Sinatra, The Great Years	1962	30.00
❑ DW 1825 [R]	Sinatra Sings Rodgers and Hart	1963	12.00
❑ W 1825 [M]	Sinatra Sings Rodgers and Hart	1963	20.00
❑ DT 1919 [R]	Tell Her You Love Her	1963	12.00
❑ T 1919 [M]	Tell Her You Love Her	1963	20.00
❑ DW 1994 [R]	Sinatra Sings the Select Johnny Mercer	1963	12.00
❑ W 1994 [M]	Sinatra Sings the Select Johnny Mercer	1963	20.00
❑ DT 2036 [R]	The Greatest Hits of Frank Sinatra	1964	12.00
❑ T 2036 [M]	The Greatest Hits of Frank Sinatra	1964	20.00
❑ PRO-2163/4/5/6 [(2)DJ]	Selections from Sinatra, The Great Years	1962	40.00
❑ DW 2301 [R]	Sinatra Sings the Select Cole Porter	1965	12.00
❑ W 2301 [M]	Sinatra Sings the Select Cole Porter	1965	20.00
❑ DT 2602 [R]	Forever Frank	1966	12.00
❑ T 2602 [M]	Forever Frank	1966	20.00
❑ DT 2700 [R]	The Movie Songs	1967	12.00
❑ T 2700 [M]	The Movie Songs	1967	20.00
❑ STFL 2814 [(6)P]	The Frank Sinatra Deluxe Set	1968	60.00
❑ TFL 2814 [(6)M]	The Frank Sinatra Deluxe Set	1968	100.00
❑ DKAO 2900 [R]	The Best of Frank Sinatra	1968	15.00
❑ PRO-2974/5 [DJ]	Frank Sinatra Minute Masters	1965	40.00
—Edited version of 20 songs			
❑ SY-4528 [S]	Come Fly with Me	197?	10.00
—Reissue of SW 920 with orange label and "Capitol" at bottom			
❑ SY-4533 [S]	Frank Sinatra Sings for Only the Lonely	197?	10.00
—Reissue of SW-1053 on orange label with "Capitol" at bottom			
❑ DNFR 7630 [(6)P]	The Sinatra Touch	19??	60.00
❑ ST-11309	One More for the Road	1973	10.00
❑ SABB-11367 [(2)P]	Round #1	1974	15.00
❑ SM-11502	A Swingin' Affair!	1976	10.00
❑ SM-11801	Come Swing with Me	1978	10.00
❑ M-11883	This Is Sinatra!	1979	10.00
❑ SN-16109	The Best of Frank Sinatra	198?	8.00
—Budget-line reissue			
❑ DN-16110	What Is This Thing Called Love	198?	8.00
—Budget-line reissue			
❑ SN-16111	The Night We Called It a Day	198?	8.00
—Budget-line reissue			
❑ N-16112	My One and Only Love	198?	8.00
—Budget-line reissue			
❑ SN-16113	Sentimental Journey	198?	8.00
—Budget-line reissue			
❑ N-16148	Look to Your Heart	198?	8.00
—Budget-line reissue			
❑ SN-16149	Sinatra Sings…Of Love and Things	198?	8.00
—Budget-line reissue			
❑ SN-16202	Frank Sinatra Sings for Only the Lonely	198?	8.00
—Budget-line reissue			
❑ SN-16203	Come Dance with Me!	198?	8.00
—Budget-line reissue			
❑ SN-16204	Nice 'N' Easy	198?	8.00
—Budget-line reissue			
❑ SN-16205	All the Way	198?	8.00
—Budget-line reissue			
❑ SN-16267	Where Are You	198?	8.00
—Budget-line reissue			
❑ DN-16268	This Is Sinatra, Vol. Two	198?	8.00
—Budget-line reissue			
❑ C1-89611	Duets	1993	20.00
❑ DW 90986 [R]	Sentimental Journey	1966	15.00
—Capitol Record Club issue			
❑ W 90986 [M]	Sentimental Journey	1966	25.00
—Capitol Record Club issue			
❑ DQBO 91261 [(2)R]	Songs for the Young at Heart	196?	30.00
—Capitol Record Club issue			
❑ C1-94777 [(5)]	The Capitol Years	1990	100.00
—With book and wraparound banner. Only 5,000 were pressed			
❑ STBB-95191 [(2)]	Sinatra Sings the Great Ones	1973	20.00
—Longines Symphonette (formerly Capitol) Record Club issue			
❑ STBB-500724 [(2)]	My One and Only Love/ Sentimental Journey	197?	15.00
—Columbia Record Club edition of STBB-724			

CAPITOL PICKWICK SERIES

Number	Title (A Side/B Side)	Yr	NM
❑ PC-3450 [M]	The Nearness of You	196?	12.00
❑ SPC-3450 [R]	The Nearness of You	196?	10.00
❑ PC-3452 [M]	Try a Little Tenderness	196?	12.00
❑ SPC-3452 [R]	Try a Little Tenderness	196?	10.00
❑ PC-3456 [M]	Nevertheless	196?	12.00
❑ SPC-3456 [R]	Nevertheless	196?	10.00
❑ PC-3457 [M]	Just One of Those Things	196?	12.00
❑ SPC-3457 [R]	Just One of Those Things	196?	10.00
❑ PC-3458 [M]	This Love of Mine	196?	12.00
❑ SPC-3458 [R]	This Love of Mine	196?	10.00
❑ PC-3463 [M]	My Cole Porter	196?	12.00
❑ SPC-3463 [R]	My Cole Porter	196?	10.00

COLUMBIA

Number	Title (A Side/B Side)	Yr	NM
❑ C2L 6 [(2)M]	The Frank Sinatra Story	1958	30.00
❑ S3L 42 [(3)M]	The Essential Frank Sinatra	1966	100.00
❑ S3S 42 [(3)R]	The Essential Frank Sinatra	1966	50.00
❑ CL 606 [M]	Frankie	1955	25.00
—Cover has Frank with Debbie Reynolds			
❑ CL 606 [M]	Frankie	1955	30.00
—Cover has drawing of Frank Sinatra wearing a hat			
❑ CL 743 [M]	The Voice	1956	25.00
❑ CL 743 [M]	The Voice	1999	25.00
—Classic Records reissue on audiophile vinyl			
❑ CL 884 [M]	Frank Sinatra Conducts Music of Alec Wilder	1956	40.00
—Reissue of Columbia Masterworks ML 4271			
❑ CL 902 [M]	That Old Feeling	1956	25.00
❑ CL 953 [M]	Adventures of the Heart	1957	25.00
❑ CL 1032 [M]	Christmas Dreaming	1957	80.00
❑ CL 1136 [M]	Put Your Dreams Away	1958	25.00
❑ CL 1241 [M]	Love Is a Kick	1958	25.00
❑ CL 1297 [M]	The Broadway Kick	1958	25.00
❑ CL 1359 [M]	Come Back to Sorrento	1959	25.00
❑ CL 1448 [M]	Reflections	1959	60.00
❑ CL 2474 [M]	Greatest Hits, The Early Years, Vol. 1	1966	15.00
❑ CAS 2475 [DJ]	The Voice: The Columbia Years Sampler	1986	40.00
❑ CL 2521 [10]	Get Happy	1955	60.00
—"House Party Series" release			
❑ CL 2539 [10]	I've Got a Crush on You	1955	60.00
—"House Party Series" release; different contents from CL 6290			
❑ CL 2542 [10]	Christmas with Sinatra	1955	60.00
—"House Party Series" release			
❑ CL 2572 [M]	Greatest Hits, The Early Years, Vol. 2	1966	15.00
❑ CL 2739 [M]	The Essential Frank Sinatra, Vol. 1	1967	25.00
❑ CL 2740 [M]	The Essential Frank Sinatra, Vol. 2	1967	25.00
❑ CL 2741 [M]	The Essential Frank Sinatra, Vol. 3	1967	25.00
❑ CL 2913 [M]	Frank Sinatra in Hollywood	1968	80.00
❑ CL 6001 [10]	The Voice of Frank Sinatra	1949	70.00
—Original in pink paper cover			
❑ CL 6001 [10]	The Voice of Frank Sinatra	1950	60.00
—Blue cardboard cover			
❑ CL 6019 [10]	Christmas Songs by Sinatra	1948	100.00
—With "gingerbread man" cover			
❑ CL 6019 [10]	Christmas Songs by Sinatra	1949	80.00
—With green vinylite cover			
❑ CL 6059 [10]	Frankly Sentimental	1951	60.00
❑ CL 6087 [10]	Songs by Sinatra, Vol. 1	1952	60.00
❑ CL 6096 [10]	Dedicated to You	1952	100.00
—Three of the tracks on this LP are alternate takes unavailable on vinyl anywhere else			
❑ CL 6143 [10]	Sing and Dance with Frank Sinatra	1953	60.00
❑ CL 6290 [10]	I've Got a Crush on You	1954	60.00
❑ CS 9274 [R]	Greatest Hits, The Early Years, Vol. 1	1966	10.00
❑ PC 9274	Greatest Hits, The Early Years, Vol. 1	197?	8.00
❑ CS 9372 [R]	Greatest Hits, The Early Years, Vol. 2	1966	10.00
❑ PC 9372	Greatest Hits, The Early Years, Vol. 2	197?	8.00
❑ CS 9539 [R]	The Essential Frank Sinatra, Vol. 1	1967	12.00
❑ CS 9540 [R]	The Essential Frank Sinatra, Vol. 2	1967	12.00
❑ CS 9541 [R]	The Essential Frank Sinatra, Vol. 3	1967	12.00
❑ CS 9713 [R]	Frank Sinatra in Hollywood	1968	12.00
❑ KG 31358 [(2)]	In the Beginning	1971	40.00
—Original edition; titles of songs at left on front cover			
❑ PG 31358 [(2)]	In the Beginning	197?	12.00
—Revised version; titles of songs at right on front cover			
❑ C6X 40343 [(6)]	The Voice: The Columbia Years 1943-1952	1986	80.00
❑ PC 40707	Christmas Dreaming	1987	30.00
—Reissue of CL 1032 with an extra track			
❑ C2X 40897 [(2)]	Hello Young Lovers	1988	30.00
❑ PC 44238 [M]	Sinatra Rarities	1989	40.00

COLUMBIA MASTERWORKS

Number	Title (A Side/B Side)	Yr	NM
❑ ML 4271 [M]	Frank Sinatra Conducts Music of Alec Wilder	1955	100.00

HARMONY

Number	Title (A Side/B Side)	Yr	NM
❑ HL 7400 [M]	Have Yourself a Merry Little Christmas	1967	30.00
❑ HL 7405 [M]	Romantic Scenes from the Early Years	1967	30.00
❑ HS 11200 [R]	Have Yourself a Merry Little Christmas	1967	20.00
—At least two different cover designs exist			
❑ HS 11205 [R]	Romantic Scenes from the Early Years	1967	12.00
❑ HS 11277 [R]	Someone to Watch Over Me	1968	15.00
❑ HS 11390 [R]	Frank Sinatra	1969	15.00
❑ KH 30318 [R]	Greatest Hits, Early Years	1971	15.00

LONGINES SYMPHONETTE

Number	Title (A Side/B Side)	Yr	NM
❑ LS-308A [(10)]	Sinatra: The Works	1972	75.00
❑ LS-309A [(6)]	Sinatra: The Works	1973	40.00
—Abridged version of LS-308A			
❑ SYS-5637	Sinatra Like Never Before	1972	25.00
—Bonus LP with purchase of LS-308A			

MOBILE FIDELITY

Number	Title (A Side/B Side)	Yr	NM
❑ SC-1 [(16)]	Sinatra	1983	600.00
—Audiophile vinyl; only two of the 16 records in this box were released individually			
❑ 1-086	Nice 'N' Easy	1981	40.00
—Audiophile vinyl			
❑ 1-135 [M]	A Jolly Christmas from Frank Sinatra	1984	40.00
—Audiophile vinyl using the original title			

PAIR

Number	Title (A Side/B Side)	Yr	NM
❑ PDL2-1027 [(2)]	All-Time Classics	1986	12.00
❑ PDL2-1028 [(2)]	Timeless	1986	12.00
❑ PDL2-1122 [(2)]	Classic Performances	1986	12.00

QWEST

Number	Title (A Side/B Side)	Yr	NM
❑ 25145	L.A. Is My Lady	1984	12.00

RCA VICTOR

Number	Title (A Side/B Side)	Yr	NM
❑ APL1-0497 [R]	What'll I Do	1974	12.00
❑ LPV-583 [M]	This Love of Mine	1971	40.00
❑ ANL1-1050 [R]	What'll I Do	1976	10.00
❑ LPM-1569 [M]	Tommy Plays, Frankie Sings	1957	40.00
—Second issue with new title			
❑ LPM-1569 [M]	Frankie and Tommy	1957	60.00
—First issue of this LP			
❑ LPM-1632 [M]	We Three	1958	40.00
—Second issue, "RE" on cover			
❑ LPM-1632 [M]	We Three	1958	60.00
—First issue			
❑ LPT-3063 [10]	Fabulous Frankie	1953	60.00
❑ CPL2-4334 [(2)]	The Sinatra/Dorsey Sessions, Vol. 1	1982	25.00
❑ CPL2-4335 [(2)]	The Sinatra/Dorsey Sessions, Vol. 2	1982	25.00
❑ CPL2-4336 [(2)]	The Sinatra/Dorsey Sessions, Vol. 3	1982	25.00
❑ AFL1-4741 [R]	Radio Years (Sinatra/Dorsey/Stordahl)	1983	15.00

REPRISE

Number	Title (A Side/B Side)	Yr	NM
❑ F 1001 [M]	Ring-a-Ding-Ding!	1961	20.00
❑ R9 1001 [S]	Ring-a-Ding-Ding!	1961	25.00
❑ F 1002 [M]	Sinatra Swings	1961	20.00
—Retitled version of "Swing Along with Me"; Capitol threatened legal action because of its "Come Swing With Me!" collection			

S

Number	Title (A Side/B Side)	Yr	NM
❑ F 1002 [M]	Swing Along with Me	1961	40.00
—Original title			
❑ R9 1002 [S]	Sinatra Swings	1961	25.00
—Retitled version of "Swing Along with Me"; Capitol threatened legal action because of its "Come Swing With Me!" collection			
❑ R9 1002 [S]	Swing Along with Me	1961	50.00
—Original title			
❑ F 1003 [M]	I Remember Tommy	1961	20.00
❑ R9 1003 [S]	I Remember Tommy	1961	25.00
❑ F 1004 [M]	Sinatra & Strings	1962	15.00
❑ R9 1004 [S]	Sinatra & Strings	1962	20.00
❑ F 1005 [M]	Sinatra and Swingin' Brass	1962	15.00
❑ R9 1005 [S]	Sinatra and Swingin' Brass	1962	20.00
❑ F 1006 [M]	Great Songs from Great Britain	1962	80.00
—Only released in the UK			
❑ R9 1006 [S]	Great Songs from Great Britain	1962	100.00
—Only released in the UK			
❑ F 1007 [M]	All Alone	1962	15.00
❑ R9 1007 [S]	All Alone	1962	20.00
❑ F 1008 [M]	Sinatra-Basie	1963	15.00
❑ R9 1008 [S]	Sinatra-Basie	1963	20.00
❑ F 1009 [M]	The Concert Sinatra	1963	15.00
❑ R9 1009 [S]	The Concert Sinatra	196?	20.00
—Without cover reference to "35mm Stereo"			
❑ R9 1009 [S]	The Concert Sinatra	1963	25.00
—Original pressings declare this was recorded in "35mm Stereo"			
❑ R-1010 [M]	Sinatra's Sinatra	1963	15.00
—Gatefold jacket; some copies have eight photos of previous Frank Sinatra Reprise LPs at the right side of the inside gatefold; we don't yet know the relative rarity of these variations, or which came first, or whether they also exist on stereo copies			
❑ R-1010 [M]	Sinatra's Sinatra	1963	15.00
—Gatefold jacket; some copies have a large photo of Sinatra holding a pack of Lucky Strikes at the right side of the inside gatefold; we don't yet know the relative rarity of these variations, or which came first, or whether they also exist on stereo copies			
❑ R9 1010 [S]	Sinatra's Sinatra	1963	20.00
❑ F 1011 [M]	Days of Wine and Roses, Moon River, and Other Academy Award Winners	1964	15.00
❑ FS 1011 [S]	Days of Wine and Roses, Moon River, and Other Academy Award Winners	1964	20.00
❑ F 1012 [M]	It Might As Well Be Swing	1964	15.00
❑ FS 1012 [S]	It Might As Well Be Swing	1964	20.00
❑ F 1013 [M]	Softly, As I Leave You	1964	15.00
❑ FS 1013 [S]	Softly, As I Leave You	1964	20.00
❑ F 1014 [M]	September of My Years	1965	15.00
❑ FS 1014 [S]	September of My Years	1965	20.00
❑ F 1015 [M]	My Kind of Broadway	1965	15.00
❑ FS 1015 [S]	My Kind of Broadway	1965	20.00
❑ 2F 1016 [(2)M]	A Man and His Music	1965	20.00
❑ 2F/2FS 1016	A Man and His Music Special Box	1965	200.00
—Blue slipcase with embossed silver front, raised letters, plus 4-page booklet and a signed card (deduct 50% if card missing). Add this to LP value.			
❑ 2FS 1016 [(2)S]	A Man and His Music	1965	25.00
❑ F 1017 [M]	Strangers in the Night	1966	12.00
❑ FS 1017 [S]	Strangers in the Night	1966	15.00
❑ F 1018 [M]	Moonlight Sinatra	1966	15.00
❑ FS 1018 [S]	Moonlight Sinatra	1966	20.00
❑ 2F 1019 [(2)M]	Sinatra at the Sands	1966	20.00
❑ 2FS 1019 [(2)S]	Sinatra at the Sands	1966	25.00
❑ F 1020 [M]	That's Life	1966	12.00
❑ FS 1020 [S]	That's Life	1966	15.00
❑ F 1021 [M]	Francis Albert Sinatra & Antonio Carlos Jobim	1967	12.00
❑ FS 1021 [S]	Francis Albert Sinatra & Antonio Carlos Jobim	1967	15.00
❑ F 1022 [M]	Frank Sinatra (The World We Knew)	1967	15.00
❑ FS 1022 [S]	Frank Sinatra (The World We Knew)	1967	15.00
❑ FS 1023	The Sinatra Christmas Album	1967	100.00
—Album never released; value is for cover slick			
❑ FS 1024	Francis A. and Edward K.	1968	20.00
❑ FS 1025	Frank Sinatra's Greatest Hits	1968	15.00
❑ FS 1027	Cycles	1969	15.00
❑ FS 1028	SinatraJobim	1969	4000.
—Unreleased; test pressings exist (value is for one of these). 8-track tapes also exist and are 10% of this value; VG value 1000; VG+ value 1000			
❑ FS 1029	My Way	1969	15.00
❑ FS4 1029 [Q]	My Way	1974	25.00
❑ FS 1030	A Man Alone & Other Songs of Rod McKuen	1969	15.00
❑ FS 1030	A Man Alone & Other Songs of Rod McKuen	1969	400.00
—Signed copies with gatefold cover and hardbound book; 400 made			
❑ FS 1031	Watertown	1970	25.00
—With gatefold and poster			
❑ FS 1032	Frank Sinatra's Greatest Hits, Vol. 2	1970	—
—Canceled?			
❑ FS 1033	Sinatra and Company	1971	15.00
❑ FS 1034	Frank Sinatra's Greatest Hits, Vol. 2	1972	15.00
❑ FS4-1034 [Q]	Frank Sinatra's Greatest Hits, Vol. 2	1974	25.00
❑ FS 2155	Ol' Blue Eyes Is Back	1973	12.00
❑ FS4 2155 [Q]	Ol' Blue Eyes Is Back	1974	25.00
❑ FS4 2194 [Q]	Some Nice Things I've Missed	1974	25.00
❑ FS 2195	Some Nice Things I've Missed	1974	12.00
❑ FS 2207	Sinatra — The Main Event Live	1974	12.00
❑ 3FS 2300 [(3)]	Trilogy: Past, Present, Future	1980	20.00
❑ FS 2305	She Shot Me Down	1981	12.00
❑ 5004 [DJ]	A Man and His Music, Part II	1966	300.00
—Promotional album for use by Budweiser			
❑ 5230 [DJ]	Songbook, Vol. 1	1971	50.00
❑ 5267 [(2)DJ]	Songbook, Vol. 2	1972	100.00
❑ 5409 [DJ]	I Sing the Songs	1976	50.00
❑ F 6045 [M]	Sinatra Conducts Music from Pictures and Plays	1962	30.00
❑ R9 6045 [S]	Sinatra Conducts Music from Pictures and Plays	1962	40.00
❑ R 6167 [M]	Sinatra '65	1965	15.00
❑ RS 6167 [S]	Sinatra '65	1965	20.00
❑ R1 73798 [S]	Francis Albert Sinatra & Antonio Carlos Jobim	2004	15.00
—180-gram reissue			
❑ R1 73799 [S]	September of My Years	2004	15.00
—180-gram reissue			
❑ SMAS-92081	A Man Alone & Other Songs of Rod McKuen	1969	20.00
—Capitol Record Club edition			
❑ SMAS-93119	Watertown	1970	25.00
—Capitol Record Club edition; does not contain poster			

TIME-LIFE

Number	Title (A Side/B Side)	Yr	NM
❑ SLGD-02 [(2)]	Legendary Singers: Frank Sinatra	1985	25.00

SINATRA, FRANK; DEAN MARTIN; SAMMY DAVIS, JR.

Albums

ARTANIS

Number	Title (A Side/B Side)	Yr	NM
❑ ARZ 102 [(2)]	The Summit	1999	—
—Canceled			

SINATRA, NANCY

Includes duets with Lee Hazlewood. Also see MEL TILLIS.

45s

ELEKTRA

Number	Title (A Side/B Side)	Yr	NM
❑ 46659	Let's Keep It That Way/One Jump Ahead of the Storm	1979	5.00

PRIVATE STOCK

Number	Title (A Side/B Side)	Yr	NM
❑ 45,022	Annabel of Mobile/(B-side unknown)	1975	5.00
❑ 45,075	Kinky Love/She Played the Piano and He Beat the Drum	1976	5.00
❑ 45,108	Indian Summer/Holly and Hawkeye	1976	5.00
—With Lee Hazelwood			
❑ 45,158	It's For My Dad/A Gentle Man Like You	1977	5.00

RCA VICTOR

Number	Title (A Side/B Side)	Yr	NM
❑ 47-0864	It's the Love/Kind of a Woman	1973	8.00
❑ 74-0614	Paris Summer/Down from Dover	1971	8.00
—With Lee Hazlewood			
❑ APBO-0029	Ain't No Sunshine/Sugar Me	1973	5.00

REPRISE

Number	Title (A Side/B Side)	Yr	NM
❑ 0238	Tammy/Thanks to You	1963	20.00
❑ 0263	Where Do the Lonely Go/Just Think About the Good Times	1964	20.00
❑ 0292	This Love of Mine/There Goes the Bride	1964	20.00
❑ 0335	The Answer to Everything/True Love	1965	15.00
❑ 0407	So Long Babe/If He'd Love Me	1965	15.00
❑ 0432	These Boots Are Made for Walkin'/The City Never Sleeps at Night	1965	12.00
❑ 0461	How Does That Grab You, Darlin'?/The Last of the Secret Agents	1966	10.00
❑ 0491	Friday's Child/Hutchinson Jail	1966	10.00
❑ 0514	In Our Time/Leave My Dog Alone	1966	10.00
❑ 0527	Sugar Town/Summer Wine	1966	12.00
❑ 0559	Love Eyes/Coastin'	1967	10.00
❑ 0561	Somethin' Stupid/I Will Wait for You	1967	8.00
—A-side: Nancy Sinatra and Frank Sinatra; B-side: Frank Sinatra			
❑ 0561	Somethin' Stupid/Give Her Love	1967	10.00
—A-side: Nancy Sinatra and Frank Sinatra; B-side: Frank Sinatra			
❑ 0595	Jackson/You Only Live Twice	1967	10.00
—A-side: With Lee Hazlewood			
❑ 0620	Lightning's Girl/Until It's Time for You to Go	1967	10.00
❑ 0620 [PS]	Lightning's Girl/Until It's Time for You to Go	1967	20.00
❑ 0629	Lady Bird/Sand	1967	8.00
—With Lee Hazlewood			
❑ 0636	Tony Rome/This Town	1967	8.00
❑ 0651	Some Velvet Morning/Oh Lonesome Me	1967	8.00
—With Lee Hazlewood			
❑ 0670	100 Years/See the Little Children	1968	8.00
❑ 0701	These Boots Are Made for Walkin'/Love Eyes	1968	5.00
—"Back to Back Hits" series			
❑ 0721	Sugar Town/Summer Wine	1968	5.00
—"Back to Back Hits" series			
❑ 0726	Jackson/Summer Wine	1968	5.00
—With Lee Hazlewood; "Back to Back Hits" series			
❑ 0729	Lightning's Girl/One Velvet Morning	1968	5.00
—B-side with Lee Hazlewood; "Back to Back Hits" series			
❑ 0756	Happy/Nice 'N' Easy	1968	8.00
❑ 0789	Good Time Girl/Old Devil Moon	1968	8.00
❑ 0813	God Knows I Love You/Just Plain Old Me	1969	8.00
❑ 0821	Here We Go Again/Memories	1969	8.00
❑ 0851	Drummer Man/Home	1969	8.00
❑ 0880	It's Such a Lonely Time of the Year/Kids	1969	10.00
❑ 0890	I Love Them All/Home	1970	8.00
❑ 0932	Hello L.A., Bye Bye Birmingham/White Tattoo	1970	8.00
❑ 0968	I'm Not a Girl Anymore/How Are Things in California	1970	8.00
❑ 0980	Feelin' Kinda Sunday/Kids	1970	8.00
—A-side by Nancy Sinatra and Frank Sinatra			
❑ 0991	Is Anybody Goin' to San Antone/Hook and Ladder	1971	8.00
❑ 0991 [PS]	Is Anybody Goin' to San Antone/Hook and Ladder	1971	15.00
❑ 1011	Life's a Trippy Thing/I'm Not Afraid	1971	8.00
—A-side by Nancy Sinatra and Frank Sinatra; B-side by Frank Sinatra solo			
❑ 1021	Did You Ever/Back on the Road	1971	8.00
—As "Nancy and Lee" (Hazlewood)			
❑ 1034	Glory Road/Is Anybody Goin' to San Antone	1971	8.00
❑ 20017	Not Just Your Friend/Cuff Links and a Tie Clip	1961	20.00
❑ 20017 [PS]	Not Just Your Friend/Cuff Links and a Tie Clip	1961	60.00
❑ 20045	To Know Him Is to Love Him/Like I Do	1962	20.00
❑ 20097	June, July and August/Think of Me	1962	20.00
❑ 20127	Tonight You Belong to Me/You Can Have Any Boy	1962	20.00
❑ 20144	Put Your Head on My Shoulder/I See the Moon	1963	20.00
❑ 20188	The Cruel War/One Way	1963	20.00

7-Inch Extended Plays

REPRISE

Number	Title (A Side/B Side)	Yr	NM
❑ SR 6251	It's Such a Pretty World/Jackson/When It's Over//Oh Lonesome Me/End of the World/Lay Some Happiness on Me	1967	15.00
—Jukebox issue; small hole, plays at 33 1/3 rpm			
❑ SR 6251 [PS]	Country My Way	1967	15.00
❑ SR 6277	I Gotta Get Out of This Town/Younger Than Springtime/Things//See the Little Children/Up, Up and Away/This Town	1967	15.00
—Jukebox issue; small hole, plays at 33 1/3 rpm			
❑ SR 6277 [PS]	Movin' with Nancy	1967	15.00

Albums

RCA VICTOR

Number	Title (A Side/B Side)	Yr	NM
❑ LSP-4645	Nancy and Lee Again	1972	30.00
—With Lee Hazlewood			
❑ LSP-4774	Woman	1973	25.00
❑ VPS-6078 [(2)]	This Is Nancy Sinatra	1972	50.00

REPRISE

Number	Title (A Side/B Side)	Yr	NM
❑ R-6202 [M]	Boots	1966	25.00
❑ RS-6202 [S]	Boots	1966	30.00
❑ R-6207 [M]	How Does That Grab You?	1966	20.00
❑ RS-6207 [S]	How Does That Grab You?	1966	25.00
❑ R-6221 [M]	Nancy in London	1966	20.00
❑ RS-6221 [S]	Nancy in London	1966	25.00
❑ R-6239 [M]	Sugar	1967	25.00
❑ RS-6239 [S]	Sugar	1967	20.00
❑ R-6251 [M]	Country, My Way	1967	25.00
❑ RS-6251 [S]	Country, My Way	1967	20.00
❑ RS-6273	Nancy and Lee	1968	20.00
—With Lee Hazlewood			
❑ R-6277 [M]	Movin' with Nancy	1967	25.00
❑ RS-6277 [S]	Movin' with Nancy	1967	20.00
❑ RS-6333	Nancy	1969	20.00
❑ RS-6409	Nancy's Greatest Hits	1970	20.00
❑ ST-91341 [S]	Boots	1967	40.00
—Capitol Record Club edition			
❑ ST-91349 [S]	Movin' with Nancy	1967	30.00
—Capitol Record Club edition			

RHINO

Number	Title (A Side/B Side)	Yr	NM
❑ R1-70166	Fairy Tales and Fantasies: The Best of Nancy and Lee	1989	10.00
—With Lee Hazlewood			

S

Except when noted otherwise, VG = 25% of NM, and VG+ = 50% of NM. (Example: VG = $2.00, VG+ = $4.00 and NM = $8.00.)

Number	Title (A Side/B Side)	Yr	NM
❑ RNLP-70227	Boots: Nancy Sinatra's All-Time Hits (1966-1970)	1987	10.00

SINATRA FAMILY, THE See VARIOUS ARTISTS COMPILATIONS in back.

SINCERELY, SAN JOSE These are recordings by a band otherwise called Fritz, featuring vocals by Lindsey Buckingham and Stevie Nicks, later of FLEETWOOD MAC.

45s

KARMA

Number	Title (A Side/B Side)	Yr	NM
❑ 301	What the World Needs Now/ You Don't Get Young Anymore	1968	1500.

SINCERES, THE (1)

45s

Number	Title (A Side/B Side)	Yr	NM
COLUMBIA			
❑ 43110	Sincerely/Snap Your Fingers	1964	15.00
EPIC			
❑ 9583	Kookie Ookie/Our Winter Love	1963	15.00
TAURUS			
❑ 377	The Magic of Love/Tell Her	1966	30.00

SINCERES, THE (2)

45s

Number	Title (A Side/B Side)	Yr	NM
JORDAN			
❑ 117	You're Too Young/ Forbidden Love	1960	250.00
RICHIE			
❑ 545	Please Don't Cheat on Me/ If You Should Leave Me	1961	100.00
—With Roulette Records distribution mentioned on label			
❑ 545	Please Don't Cheat on Me/ If You Should Leave Me	1961	700.00
—No mention of Roulette Records on label			
SIGMA			
❑ 1003/4	Darling/Do You Remember	1960	400.00

SINFIELD, PETE Also see KING CRIMSON.

Albums

MANTICORE

Number	Title (A Side/B Side)	Yr	NM
❑ MC 66667	Still	1973	20.00

SING A SONG WITH THE BEATLES

Albums

TOWER

Number	Title (A Side/B Side)	Yr	NM
❑ DKAO 5000 [R]	Sing a Song with the Beatles	1965	200.00
❑ KAO 5000 [M]	Sing a Song with the Beatles	1965	150.00
—No artist listed on label			

SINGER, JOHNNY

45s

HIT

Number	Title (A Side/B Side)	Yr	NM
❑ 178	Ode to the Little Brown Shack Out Back/Do-Wacka-Do	1965	8.00
—B-side by Charlie Bare			
❑ 233	Make the World Go Away/Fever	1965	8.00
—B-side by the Chords (2)			

SINGING DOGS, THE, DON CHARLES PRESENTS

45s

Number	Title (A Side/B Side)	Yr	NM
RCA			
❑ PA-10129	Jingle Bells/Oh! Susanna	1976	4.00
—Black label, dog near top			
RCA VICTOR			
❑ 47-6344	Oh! Susannah//Pat-a-Cake/ Three Blind Mice/Jingle Bells	1955	15.00
—"Jingle Bells" is part of a medley and lasts 1:15			
❑ 47-6344 [PS]	Oh! Susannah//Pat-a-Cake/ Three Blind Mice/Jingle Bells	1955	25.00
❑ 47-6432	Hot Dog Rock and Roll/ Hot Dog Boogie	1956	12.00
❑ 48-1020	Jingle Bells/Oh! Susannah	1971	5.00
—First reissue; "Jingle Bells" lengthened to 1:47 on this and future issues			
❑ 48-1021	Hot Dog Rock and Roll/ Hot Dog Boogie	1971	5.00
❑ F2NW-7846/7 [DJ]	Pearl's Jingle Bells/Caesar's Pat-A-Cake/King's Three Blind Mice//Dolly's Oh! Susanna (Fast)/ Dolly's Oh! Susanna (Slow)	1955	40.00
—Banded version for radio use ("Jingle Bells" is 1:15)			
❑ PA-10129	Jingle Bells/Oh! Susannah	1974	8.00
—First issue of PA-10129 has tan or brown (also possibly orange) labels			

Siouxsie and the Banshees, *Dear Prudence*, Geffen 29358, 1984, $5.

SINGING MCENTIRES, THE (PAKE, REBA AND SUSIE)

45s

BOSS

Number	Title (A Side/B Side)	Yr	NM
❑ SPS-194	The Ballad of John McEntire/ Interview by the Grandchildren	1969	500.00
—Supposedly only 25 copies were pressed			

SINGING NUN, THE

45s

PHILIPS

Number	Title (A Side/B Side)	Yr	NM
❑ 40152	Dominique/Entres Les Etoiles (Among the Stars)	1963	6.00
❑ 40152 [PS]	Dominique/Entres Les Etoiles (Among the Stars)	1963	12.00
❑ 40163	Dominique/Les Pieds de Missionaires	1963	6.00
❑ 40163 [PS]	Dominique/Les Pieds de Missionaires	1963	15.00
—Almost identical to the 40152 sleeve			
❑ 40165	Tous Les Chemins/ Frere "Tout Le" Monde	1964	5.00
❑ 40165 [PS]	Tous Les Chemins/ Frere "Tout Le" Monde	1964	12.00
❑ 40195	Une Fleur (A Flower)/ Avec Toi (With You)	1964	5.00

Albums

PHILIPS

Number	Title (A Side/B Side)	Yr	NM
❑ PCC 203 [M]	Soeur Sourire: The Singing Nun	1963	15.00
❑ PCC 209 [M]	Her Joy, Her Songs	1964	15.00
❑ PCC 603 [S]	Soeur Sourire: The Singing Nun	1963	15.00
❑ PCC 609 [S]	Her Joy, Her Songs	1964	15.00

SINGING REINDEER, THE See DANCER, PRANCER, AND NERVOUS.

SINGLETON, MARGIE Also see LEON ASHLEY; GEORGE JONES.

45s

Number	Title (A Side/B Side)	Yr	NM
ASHLEY			
❑ 200	The Little Girl I Didn't Have the Courage to Keep/Seemed You'd Never Been Good	197?	8.00
❑ 2000	Sooner or Later/Angel Hands	1967	10.00
❑ 2011	Ode to Billie Joe/Big Boys Don't Need Mamas	1967	10.00
❑ 2050	Wandering Mind/Your Conscience Sends Me Flowers	1968	10.00
❑ 2090	Chill Winds/Little Darlin'	1968	10.00
❑ 5000	Harper Valley P.T.A./ (B-side unknown)	1968	10.00
❑ 7500	Jesus Is My Pusher/ Lord Take Me Right Now	1969	10.00
❑ 35002	All That Love Is Gone/ Blindness of the Wife	197?	6.00
❑ 35006	Enough of a Woman/Dreaming Bigger Than You	197?	6.00
❑ 35012	I Guess I've Just Loved You Too Long/The Well's Not Dry	197?	6.00
D			
❑ 1007	I Want to Be Where You're Gonna Be/Shattered Kingdom	1958	30.00
MERCURY			
❑ 71359	Oo-Wee, You're the One for Me/Teddy	1958	20.00
❑ 71672	Destination Love/Toss a Pebble	1960	15.00
❑ 71733	She Will Break Your Heart/ Voices of Love	1960	15.00
❑ 71814	Your Old Love Letters/ Are You Ever Too Young	1961	12.00
❑ 71928	I'll Just Walk On By/Her Image Keeps Getting in the Way	1962	12.00
❑ 72002	Chained to a Promise/ Living in the Danger Zone	1962	12.00

Number	Title (A Side/B Side)	Yr	NM
❑ 72079	Magic Star (Telstar)/Only Your Shadow Knows	1963	12.00
❑ 72124	I Don't Have to Look Pretty/Walkin' Back to Happiness	1963	12.00
❑ 72213	Old Records/How Do You Say Goodbye	1963	12.00
❑ 72268	Forget Me Not/I Don't Want You This Way	1964	12.00
❑ 72363	Don't Be Good to Me/It's Too Much	1964	12.00
STARDAY			
❑ 287	One Step Nearer to You/Not What He's Got	1957	25.00
❑ 309	My Picture of You/Love Is a Treasure	1957	25.00
❑ 323	Beautiful Dawn/Take Time Out for Love	1957	25.00
❑ 443	Nothin' But True Love/It's Better to Know	1959	20.00
❑ 472	The Eyes of Love/Angel Hands	1959	20.00
❑ 502	For the Love of Jim/My Special Dream	1960	20.00
UNITED ARTISTS			
❑ 896	What Could I Do/You Shake My Hand and Kiss Me on the Cheek	1965	10.00
❑ 939	I'm Guilty This Time/You Took the Easy Way Out	1965	10.00

Albums

Number	Title	Yr	NM
ASHLEY			
❑ 3003	Margie Singleton Sings Country Music with Soul	1968	15.00
PICKWICK			
❑ SPC-3133	Harper Valley P.T.A.	197?	10.00
UNITED ARTISTS			
❑ UAL-3459 [M]	Crying Time	1965	15.00
❑ UAS-6459 [S]	Crying Time	1965	20.00

SINGLETON, MARGIE, AND FARON YOUNG

Also see each artist's individual listings.

45s

Number	Title (A Side/B Side)	Yr	NM
MERCURY			
❑ 72237	Keeping Up with the Joneses/No Thanks, I Just Had One	1964	12.00
❑ 72237 [PS]	Keeping Up with the Joneses/No Thanks, I Just Had One	1964	20.00
❑ 72312	Another Woman's Man — Another Man's Woman/Honky Tonk Happy	1964	12.00

SIOUXSIE AND THE BANSHEES

12-Inch Singles

Number	Title (A Side/B Side)	Yr	NM
GEFFEN			
❑ PRO2114 [DJ]	Dear Prudence/Dazzle	1984	20.00
❑ PRO2478 [DJ]	Cities in Dust (Remix)/Cities in Dust (LP Version)	1986	20.00
❑ PRO2648 [DJ]	This Wheel's on Fire (7")/This Wheel's on Fire (LP Version)	1987	8.00
❑ PRO2731 [DJ]	The Passenger (3 versions)	1987	15.00
❑ PRO3195 [DJ]	Peek-a-Boo (3 versions)	1988	10.00
❑ PRO-A-2114 [DJ]	Dear Prudence/Dazzle	1984	20.00
❑ PRO-A-2478 [DJ]	Cities in Dust (Remix)/Cities in Dust (LP Version)	1986	20.00
❑ PRO-A-2648 [DJ]	This Wheel's on Fire (7")/This Wheel's on Fire (LP Version)	1987	8.00
❑ PRO-A-2731 [DJ]	The Passenger (3 versions)	1987	15.00
❑ PRO-A-3195 [DJ]	Peek-a-Boo (3 versions)	1988	10.00
❑ 4281 [DJ]	Kiss Them for Me (4 versions)	1991	10.00
❑ 4281 [DJ]	Kiss Them for Me (4 versions)	1991	10.00
❑ 4361 [DJ]	Fear (Of the Unknown) (6 versions)	1991	12.00
❑ 4361 [DJ]	Fear (Of the Unknown) (6 versions)	1991	12.00
❑ 4368 [DJ]	Fear (Of the Unknown) (Techno-Vertigo Mix)/Fear (Of the Unknown) (Dub)	1991	10.00
❑ 4368 [DJ]	Fear (Of the Unknown) (Techno-Vertigo Mix)/Fear (Of the Unknown) (Dub)	1991	10.00
❑ 20399	Cities in Dust (2 versions)/An Execution/Quarter Drawing of the Dog	1986	12.00
❑ 20609	Wheels on Fire (Remix)/Shooting Sun/Sleepwalking	1987	6.00
❑ 20977	Peek-a-Boo (2 versions)/False Face/Catwalk	1988	8.00
❑ 21100	The Killing Jar (3 mixes)/Something Wicked/A re You Still Dying, Darling?	1988	12.00
❑ 21383	Standing There (2 mixes)/Divided/Solar Choir	1989	12.00
PVC			
❑ 4902	Arabian Knights/Supernatural Thing//Conga Conga/Slap Dash Snap	1981	15.00

45s

Number	Title (A Side/B Side)	Yr	NM
GEFFEN			
❑ 19031	Kiss Them for Me	1991	—
—Cassette only			
❑ 19111	Fear (Of the Unknown)	1991	—
—Cassette only			
❑ 27760	Peek-A-Boo/False Face	1988	3.00
❑ 27760 [PS]	Peek-A-Boo/False Face	1988	5.00
❑ 28813	Cities in Dust/An Execution	1986	3.00
❑ 28813 [PS]	Cities in Dust/An Execution	1986	5.00
❑ 29358	Dear Prudence/Tattoo	1984	3.00
❑ 29358 [PS]	Dear Prudence/Tattoo	1984	5.00
POLYDOR			
❑ 14561	Hong Kong Garden/Overground	1979	40.00
PVC			
❑ 1001	Israel/Red Over White	1980	6.00
❑ 1001 [PS]	Israel/Red Over White	1980	8.00
WARNER BROS.			
❑ 18825	Face to Face	1993	—
—Cassette only			

Albums

Number	Title	Yr	NM
GEFFEN			
❑ GHS 24030	Hyaena	1984	10.00
❑ GHS 24046	The Scream	1984	10.00
—Reissue of Polydor PD1-6207			
❑ GHS 24047	Join Hands	1984	10.00
❑ GHS 24048	Kaleidoscope	1984	10.00
—Reissue of PVC 7921			
❑ GHS 24049	A Kiss in the Dream House	1984	10.00
❑ GHS 24050	Juju	1984	10.00
—Reissue of PVC 8903			
❑ GHS 24051	Once Upon a Time: The Singles	1984	10.00
—Reissue of PVC 8906			
❑ GHS 24052 [(2)]	Nocturne	1984	10.00
❑ GHS 24092	Tinderbox	1986	10.00
❑ GHS 24134	Through the Looking Glass	1987	10.00
❑ GHS 24205	Peepshow	1988	10.00
❑ GEF 24387	Superstition	1991	15.00
❑ GEF 24630	The Rapture	1995	15.00
POLYDOR			
❑ PD1-6207	The Scream	1978	30.00
PVC			
❑ 7921	Kaleidoscope	1980	25.00
❑ 8903	Ju Ju	1981	25.00
—Original copies include bonus single "Israel"/"Red Over White"			
❑ 8906	Once Upon a Time: The Singles	1981	20.00
—With poster and inner sleeve			
WARNER BROS.			
❑ WBMS-138 [DJ]	The Tinderbox Interview	1986	25.00
—Part of "The Warner Bros. Music Show"			

SIR DOUGLAS QUINTET

Also see THE DEVONS; DOUG SAHM.

45s

Number	Title (A Side/B Side)	Yr	NM
ATLANTIC			
❑ 2965	The Nitty Gritty/I'm Just Tired of Getting Burned	1973	8.00
❑ 2985	Texas Tornado/Blue Horizon	1973	8.00
—As "Sir Douglas Band"			
CASABLANCA			
❑ 828	Roll With the Punches/I'm Not That Kat Anymore	1975	25.00
MERCURY			
❑ 73257	Michoacan/Westside Blues Again	1971	6.00
PACEMAKER			
❑ 280	Sugar Bee/Blue Norther	1964	20.00
PHILIPS			
❑ 40676	What About Tomorrow/A Nice Song	1970	8.00
❑ 40676 [PS]	What About Tomorrow/A Nice Song	1970	15.00
❑ 40687	Pretty Flower/Catch the Man on the Fly	1970	8.00
❑ 40708	Wasted Days, Wasted Nights/Me and My Destiny	1971	8.00
SMASH			
❑ 2169	Are Inlaws Really Outlaws/Sell a Song	1968	8.00
❑ 2191	Mendocino/I Wanna Be Your Mama Again	1968	8.00
❑ 2222	Lawd, I'm Just a Country Boy in This Great Big Freaky City/It Didn't Even Bring Me Down	1969	8.00
❑ 2233	Dynamite Woman/Too Many Dociled Minds	1969	8.00
❑ 2253	At the Crossroads/Texas Me	1969	8.00
❑ 2259	Nuevo Laredo/I Don't Wanna Go Home	1970	8.00
TRIBE			
❑ 8308	She's About a Mover/We'll Take Our Last Walk Tonight	1965	12.00
—Gray label with Indian head			
❑ 8308	She's About a Mover/We'll Take Our Last Walk Tonight	1965	15.00
—White label (not marked as a promo)			
❑ 8310	The Tracker/Blue Brother	1965	10.00
—Gray label with Indian head			
❑ 8310	The Tracker/Blue Brother	1965	12.00
—White label (not marked as a promo)			
❑ 8312	In Time/The Story of John Hardy	1965	10.00
❑ 8314	The Rains Came/Bacon Fat	1966	10.00
❑ 8317	She's Gotta Be Boss/Quarter to Three	1966	10.00
❑ 8318	Beginning of the End/Love Don't Treat Me Fair	1966	10.00
❑ 8321	She Digs My Love/When I Sing the Blues	1966	10.00
❑ 8323	Hang Loose/I'm Sorry	1967	10.00

Albums

Number	Title	Yr	NM
ABC DOT			
❑ DO-2057	Texas Rock for Country Rollers	1976	15.00
—As "Sir Doug and the Texas Tornadoes"			
ATLANTIC			
❑ SD 7287	Texas Tornado	1974	15.00
—As "Sir Douglas Band"			
BEAT ROCKET			
❑ BR 123	The Best of the Sir Douglas Quintet	2000	12.00
—Reissue of Tribe LP on 180-gram vinyl			
❑ BR 124	The Sir Douglas Quintet Is Back!	2000	12.00
—New compilation of Tribe material on 180-gram vinyl			
PHILIPS			
❑ PHS 600344	1 + 1 + 1 = 4	1970	25.00
❑ PHS 600353	The Return of Doug Saldana	1971	25.00
R&M			
❑ UDL-2343	The Tracker	1981	20.00
SMASH			
❑ SRS-67108	Sir Douglas Quintet + 2 = Honkey Blues	1968	30.00
❑ SRS-67115	Mendocino	1969	25.00
❑ SRS-67130	Together After Five	1970	25.00
TAKOMA			
❑ TAK-7086	The Best of the Sir Douglas Quintet	1980	12.00
❑ TAK-7088	Border Wave	1981	12.00
❑ TAK-7095	Sir Douglas Quintet Live	1985	12.00
TRIBE			
❑ TR 37001 [M]	The Best of the Sir Douglas Quintet	1966	70.00
❑ TRS 47001 [R]	The Best of the Sir Douglas Quintet	1966	50.00
VARRICK			
❑ 004	Quintessence	1983	12.00

SIR LORD BALTIMORE

45s

Number	Title (A Side/B Side)	Yr	NM
MERCURY			
❑ 73181	I Got a Woman/Master Headache	1970	8.00

Albums

Number	Title	Yr	NM
MERCURY			
❑ SRM-1-613	Sir Lord Baltimore	1971	25.00
❑ SR-61328	Kingdom Come	1970	25.00

SIR WALTER RALEIGH AND THE COUPONS

45s

Number	Title (A Side/B Side)	Yr	NM
A&M			
❑ 757	White Cliffs of Dover/Something or Other	1965	10.00
❑ 764	While I Wait/Somethin'	1965	10.00
JERDEN			
❑ 760	Tomorrow's Gonna Be Another Day/Whitcomb St.	1965	12.00
—As "Sir Raleigh and the Coupons"			
TOWER			
❑ 156	Tell Her Tonight/If You Need Me	1965	10.00
❑ 220	I Don't Want to Cry/Always	1966	10.00

SISK, SHIRLEY

45s

Number	Title (A Side/B Side)	Yr	NM
SUN			
❑ 365	I Forgot to Remember to Forget/The Other Side	1961	25.00

Number	Title (A Side/B Side)	Yr	NM

SISTER DOUBLE HAPPINESS

45s

SUB POP

❑ 77 Don't Worry/Wheels a-Spinnin' 1990 2.00
❑ 77 Don't Worry/Wheels a-Spinnin' 1990 6.00
—First 2,000 on green vinyl
❑ 77 [PS] Don't Worry/Wheels a-Spinnin' 1990 2.00
—Still in print as of the end of 1995

Albums

REPRISE

❑ PRO5010 [DJ] Heart and Mind 1991 40.00
—Available as stock copy on cassette and CD only
❑ PRO-A-5010 [DJ]Heart and Mind 1991 40.00
—Vinyl is promo only

SST

❑ 162 Sister Double Happiness 1988 10.00

SISTER SLEDGE

12-Inch Singles

ATLANTIC

❑ DSKO97 [DJ] As (same on both sides) 1977 15.00
❑ 850 [DJ] Frankie (Club Mix) (Dub Mix)/Hold Out Poppy 1985 6.00
❑ DMD 850 [DJ] Frankie (Club Mix 6:18) (Dub Mix 5:09)/Hold Out Poppy (LP Version 3;57) 1985 10.00
❑ 868 [DJ] Dancing on the Jagged Edge/(Dub) 1985 6.00
❑ DMD 868 [DJ] Dancing on the Jagged Edge (LP Version) (Dub) 1985 10.00
❑ 979 [DJ] Here to Stay (2 mixes)/Make a Wish 1986 6.00
—B-side by Joe Cruz
❑ DMD 979 [DJ] Here to Stay (Extended Version 7:38) (LP Version 3:50)/Make a Wish 1986 8.00
—"Make a Wish" by Joe Cruz
❑ 86769 Here to Stay (Extended Version 7:38) (LP Version 3:50)/Make a Wish 1986 10.00
—"Make a Wish" by Joe Cruz
❑ 86862 Dancing on the Jagged Edge (LP Version) (Dub) 1985 10.00
❑ 86882 Frankie (Club Mix 6:18) (Dub Mix 5:09)/Hold Out Poppy (LP Version 3;57) 1985 10.00

COTILLION

❑ DSKO 97 [DJ] As (same on both sides) 1977 30.00
❑ DSKO 144 [DJ] He's the Greatest Dancer (6:04)/We Are Family (8:06) 1979 30.00
❑ DSKO 212 [DJ] Got to Love Somebody (6:50) (same on both sides) 1979 20.00
❑ DMD 229 [DJ] Reach Your Peak (5:26) (same on both sides) 1980 12.00
❑ DMD 256 [DJ] All American Girls (same on both sides?) 1981 30.00
❑ DMD 277 [DJ] He's Just a Runaway (A Tribute to Bob Marley) (6:05) (3:57) 1981 15.00
❑ DMD 645 [DJ] B.Y.O.B. (Bring Your Own Baby) (Special Disco Mix 6:43) (Short Version 3:50) 1983 40.00
❑ DK 4710 He's the Greatest Dancer (6:04)/We Are Family (8:06) 1979 30.00
❑ DM 4814 He's Just a Runaway (A Tribute to Bob Marley) (6:05)/Ooh, You Caught My Heart 1981 20.00

RHINO

❑ 76019 We Are Family (Sure Is Pure Mix) (Original Mix)/Lost in Music (Sure Is Pure Mix) (Original Mix) 1993 12.00

45s

ATCO

❑ 6924 The Weatherman/Have You Met My Friend 1973 40.00
❑ 6940 Mama Never Told Me/Neither One of Us (Wants to Be the First to Say Goodbye) 1973 60.00
❑ 7008 Love Don't You Go Through No Changes on Me/Don't You Miss Him 1974 12.00
❑ 7020 Circle of Love (Caught in the Middle)/Cross My Heart 1975 12.00
❑ 7035 Love Has Found Me/Love Ain't Easy 1975 12.00

ATLANTIC

❑ 7-89357 Here to Stay/Make a Wish 1986 4.00
—B-side by Joe Cruz
❑ 7-89466 You're Fine/(B-side unknown) 1985 6.00
❑ 7-89520 Dancing on the Jagged Edge/You Need Me 1985 4.00
❑ 7-89547 Frankie/Peer Pressure 1985 4.00
❑ 7-89547 [PS] Frankie/Peer Pressure 1985 5.00

COTILLION

❑ 44202 Thank You for Today/Have Love Will Travel 1976 5.00
❑ 44208 Cream of the Crop/Love Ain't Easy 1976 8.00
❑ 44220 Blockbuster Boy/Moondancer 1977 6.00
❑ 44226 Baby, It's the Rain/Hold Onto This Feeling 1977 6.00
❑ 44234 I've Seen Better Days/Do It to the Max 1978 6.00
❑ 44245 He's the Greatest Dancer/Somebody Loves Me 1978 5.00
❑ 44251 We Are Family/Easier to Love 1979 5.00
❑ 45001 Lost in Music/Thinking of You 1979 5.00
❑ 45007 Got to Love Somebody/Good Girl Now 1979 5.00
❑ 45013 Reach Your Peak/You Fooled Around 1980 5.00
❑ 45020 Let's Go on Vacation/Easy Street 1980 5.00
❑ 46007 All American Girls/Happy Feeling 1981 5.00
❑ 46012 Next Time You'll Know/If You Really Want Me 1981 5.00
❑ 46017 He's Just a Runaway (A Tribute to Bob Marley)/(Long Version) 1981 5.00
❑ 47000 My Guy/Il Macquillage Lady 1982 7.00
❑ 47007 All the Man That I Need/Light Footin' 1982 5.00
❑ 7-99834 Gotta Get Back to Love/Lifetime Lover 1983 5.00
❑ 7-99885 B.Y.O.B. (Bring Your Own Baby)/(B-side unknown) 1983 5.00

Albums

ATCO

❑ SD 36-105 Circle of Love 1975 20.00

ATLANTIC

❑ 81255 When the Boys Meet the Girls 1985 10.00

COTILLION

❑ SD 5209 We Are Family 1979 10.00
❑ SD 5231 The Sisters 1982 10.00
❑ SD 9919 Together 1976 20.00
❑ SD 16012 Love Somebody Today 1980 10.00
❑ SD 16027 All American Girls 1981 10.00
❑ 90069 Bet Cha Say That to All the Girls 1983 10.00

SISTERS OF MERCY

12-Inch Singles

ELEKTRA

❑ ED 5263 [DJ] This Corrosion (2 mixes) 1987 10.00
❑ ED5263 [DJ] This Corrosion (2 mixes) 1987 10.00
❑ 5294 [DJ] Dominion/Dominion Mother Russia 1987 8.00
❑ 5294 [DJ] Dominion/Dominion Mother Russia 1987 8.00
❑ ED 5321 [DJ] Lucretia My Reflection (3 versions) 1987 10.00
❑ ED5321 [DJ] Lucretia My Reflection (3 versions) 1987 10.00
❑ 66790 This Corrosion/Torch/Colours 1987 10.00

45s

ELEKTRA

❑ 69378 Lucretia My Reflection/Long Train 1988 3.00
❑ 69378 [PS] Lucretia My Reflection/Long Train 1988 6.00
❑ 69434 This Corrosion/Torch 1987 3.00
❑ 69434 [PS] This Corrosion/Torch 1987 6.00

Albums

ELEKTRA

❑ 60405 First and Last and Always 1985 14.00
❑ 60762 Floodland 1987 14.00

SIX PENTZ, THE

45s

BRENT

❑ 7062 Imitation Situation/Please Come Home 1967 20.00
❑ 7064 Don't Say You're Sorry/Tinkle Talk 1967 20.00

SIX TEENS, THE

45s

FLIP

❑ 315 A Casual Look/Teenage Promise 1956 20.00
❑ 317 Send Me Flowers/Afar Into the Night 1956 15.00
❑ 320 My Special Guy/Only Jim 1956 15.00
❑ 322 Arrow of Love/Was It a Dream of Mine 1957 15.00
❑ 326 Baby You're Dynamite/My Surprise 1957 15.00
❑ 329 My Secret/Stop Playing Ping Pong 1958 15.00
❑ 333 Danny/Love's Funny That Way 1958 15.00
❑ 338 Baby-O/Oh, It's Crazy 1958 20.00
❑ 346 Why Do I Go to School/Heaven Knows I Love You 1959 25.00
❑ 350 So Happy/That Wonderful Secret of Love 1960 15.00
❑ 351 A Little Prayer/Suddenly in Love 1960 15.00

SIXPENCE, THE

45s

ALL AMERICAN

❑ 313 Fortune Teller/My Flash on You 1966 40.00
❑ 333 Hey Joe/(B-side unknown) 1967 30.00
❑ 353 Fortune Teller/My Flash on You 1967 30.00

DOT

❑ 16959 Fortune Teller/My Flash on You 1966 25.00

IMPACT

❑ 1025 What to Do/You're the Love 1967 25.00

SKA KINGS, THE

45s

ATLANTIC

❑ 2232 Jamaica Ska/Oil in My Lamp 1964 10.00
❑ 2236 Last Night Ska/Watermelon Man Ska 1964 10.00

SKAGGS, RICKY

45s

EPIC

❑ 19-02034 Don't Get Above Your Raising/Low and Lonely 1981 4.00
❑ 14-02499 You May See Me Walkin'/So Round, So Firm, So Fully Packed 1981 4.00
❑ 14-02692 Crying My Heart Out Over You/Lost to a Stranger 1982 4.00
❑ 14-02931 I Don't Care/If That's the Way You Feel 1982 4.00
❑ 15-03096 Don't Get Above Your Raising/You May See Me Walkin' 1982 3.00
—Gray label reissue
❑ 34-03212 Heartbroke/Don't Think I'll Cry 1982 4.00
❑ ENR-03265 Heartbroke 1982 7.00
—One-sided budget release
❑ 34-03482 I Wouldn't Change You If I Could/One Way Rider 1982 4.00
❑ ENR-03491 I Wouldn't Change You If I Could 1982 7.00
—One-sided budget release
❑ 34-03812 Highway 40 Blues/Don't Let Your Sweet Love Die 1983 4.00
❑ 34-04044 You've Got a Lover/Let's Love the Bad Times Away 1983 4.00
❑ 34-04668 Something in My Heart/Baby, I'm in Love with You 1984 4.00
❑ 34-04831 Country Boy/Wheel Hoss 1985 4.00
❑ 34-05585 You Make Me Feel Like a Man/Rendezvous 1985 4.00
❑ 34-05748 Cajun Moon/Rockin' the Boat 1985 4.00
❑ 34-05898 I've Got a New Heartache/She Didn't Say Why 1986 4.00
❑ 34-06327 Love's Gonna Get You Someday/Walkin' in Jerusalem 1986 4.00
❑ 34-06650 I Wonder If I Care As Much/Raisin' the Dickens 1987 4.00
❑ 34-07060 Love Can't Ever Get Better Than This/Daddy Was a Hardworking, Honest Man 1987 4.00
—With Sharon White
❑ 34-07416 I'm Tired/San Antonio Rose 1987 4.00
❑ 34-07721 (Angel on My Mind) That's Why I'm Walkin'/Lord, She Sure Is Good at Lovin' Me 1988 4.00
❑ 34-07924 Thanks Again/If You Don't Believe the Bible 1988 4.00
❑ 34-08063 Old Kind of Love/Woman You Won't Break Mine 1988 4.00
❑ 15-08454 Cajun Moon/Love's Gonna Get You Someday 1988 3.00
—Gray label reissue
❑ 15-08459 I've Got a New Heartache /Love Can't Ever Get Better Than This 1988 3.00
—Gray label reissue
❑ 15-08464 Country Boy/You Make Me Feel Like a Man 1988 3.00
—Gray label reissue
❑ 34-68693 Lovin' Only Me/Home Is Wherever You Are 1989 4.00
—B-side with Sharon White
❑ 34-68995 Let It Be You/The Fields of Home 1989 4.00
❑ 34-73078 Heartbreak Hurricane/Casting My Shadows in the Road 1989 4.00
❑ 34-73312 Hummingbird/Kentucky Thunder 1990 4.00
❑ 34-73496 He Was On to Somethin' (So He Made You)/When I Love 1990 4.00
❑ 34-73947 Life's Too Long (To Live Like This)/Lonesome for You 1991 4.00

Number | Title (A Side/B Side) | Yr | NM

❑ 34-74147 Same Ol' Love/My Father's Son 1991 4.00
❑ 34-74311 From the Word Love/You Can't Take It With You When You Go 1992 4.00

SUGAR HILL
❑ 3706 I'll Take the Blame/Could You Love Me One More Time 1980 10.00

SUGAR HILL/EPIC
❑ 34-04245 Don't Cheat in Our Hometown/Children Go 1983 4.00
❑ 34-04394 Honey (Open That Door)/She's More to Be Pitied 1984 4.00
❑ 34-04527 Uncle Pen/I'm Head Over Heels in Love 1984 4.00

Albums

ATLANTIC
❑ 82834 Solid Ground 1995 15.00

EPIC
❑ EAS 2022 [DJ] The Ricky Skaggs Story 1990 30.00
—Promo-only interview record
❑ FE 37193 Waitin' for the Sun to Shine 1981 10.00
❑ FE 37996 Highways and Heartaches 1982 10.00
❑ FE 39409 Favorite Country Songs 1985 10.00
❑ FE 39410 Country Boy 1984 10.00
❑ FE 40103 Live in London 1985 10.00
❑ FE 40309 Love's Gonna Get Ya! 1986 8.00
❑ FE 40623 Comin' Home to Stay 1988 8.00
❑ FE 45027 Kentucky Thunder 1989 10.00

ROUNDER
❑ 0151 Family and Friends 1982 12.00

SUGAR HILL
❑ SH-3706 Sweet Temptation 1979 12.00
❑ SH-3711 Skaggs and Rice 1980 12.00

SUGAR HILL/EPIC
❑ FE 38954 Don't Cheat in Our Hometown 1983 10.00

SKAGGS, RICKY, AND JAMES TAYLOR

45s

EPIC
❑ AE72569 [DJ] New Star Shining (same on both sides) 1986 3.00
❑ AE7 2569 [DJ] New Star Shining (same on both sides) 1986 4.00
❑ AE7 2569 [PS] New Star Shining 1986 4.00

SKAGGS, RICKY, AND KEITH WHITLEY

Albums

REBEL
❑ 1504 Second Generation Bluegrass 1972 20.00
❑ 1550 That's It 1975 20.00

SKARLETTONES, THE

45s

EMBER
❑ 1053 Do You Remember/Will You Dream 1959 120.00

SKEE BROTHERS, THE

45s

EPIC
❑ 9275 Big Deal/While I'm Away 1958 100.00

OKEH
❑ 7108 That's All She Wrote/Four Aces 1959 50.00

ROULETTE
❑ 4164 Romeo Joe/Lu Ann 1959 20.00

SKELLERN, PETER

45s

LONDON
❑ 20075 You're a Lady/Manifesto 1972 5.00

PRIVATE STOCK
❑ 45,028 Hold On to Love/(B-side unknown) 1975 4.00
❑ 45,054 Hard Times/And Then You'll Fall 1975 4.00

SKELTON, EDDIE

45s

DIXIE
❑ 2011 Keep It Swinging/Without You 1958 1500.

STARDAY
❑ 294 My Heart Gets Lonely/Let Me Be With You Forever 1957 150.00

SKID ROW (1)
Cream-like band featuring GARY MOORE.

Albums

EPIC
❑ E 30404 Skid Row 1971 25.00
❑ E 30913 34 Hours 1971 25.00

Number | Title (A Side/B Side) | Yr | NM

SKID ROW (2)
New Jersey hard rockers featuring SEBASTIAN BACH.

45s

ATLANTIC
❑ 88883 18 and Life//Midnight/Tornado 1989 3.00
❑ 88883 [PS] 18 and Life//Midnight/Tornado 1989 3.00
❑ 88886 I Remember You/Makin' a Mess 1989 3.00
❑ 88886 [PS] I Remember You/Makin' a Mess 1989 3.00
❑ 88935 Youth Gone Wild/Sweet Little Sister 1989 3.00
❑ 88935 [PS] Youth Gone Wild/Sweet Little Sister 1989 3.00

Albums

ATLANTIC
❑ 1P-8136 Slave to the Grind 1991 30.00
—U.S. vinyl version available only from Columbia House; all copies are the censored version with "Beggars Day"
❑ 81936 Skid Row 1989 10.00

SKIP AND FLIP
Also see GARY PAXTON.

45s

BRENT
❑ 7002 It Was I/Lunch Hour 1959 25.00
❑ 7005 Fancy Nancy/It Could Be 1959 25.00
❑ 7010 Cherry Pie/I'll Quit Cryin' Over You 1960 25.00
❑ 7013 Teenage Honeymoon/Hully Gully Cha Cha Cha 1960 20.00
❑ 7017 The Green Door/Willow Tree 1960 20.00
❑ 7028 Over the Mountain/One More Drink for Julie 1962 20.00

CALIFORNIA
❑ 2325 Tossin' and Turnin'/Everyday I Have to Cry 1963 15.00

REV
❑ 3523 Why Not Confess/Johnny Risk 1959 25.00
—As "Gary and Clyde"

TIME
❑ 1007 Why Not Confess/Johnny Risk 1959 —
—May not exist; we know of a different record using the number 1007 on Time
❑ 1031 Betty Jean/Doubt 1961 20.00

SKIP AND THE CREATIONS

Albums

JUSTICE
❑ (# unknown) Mobam 196? 400.00

SKY
Doug Fieger, later of The Knack, was in this group.

45s

RCA VICTOR
❑ 74-0419 Goodie Two Shoes/Make It in Time 1971 6.00
❑ 74-0611 Let It Lie Low/Taking the Long Way Home 1971 6.00

Albums

RCA VICTOR
❑ LSP-4457 Sky 1970 15.00
❑ LSP-4514 Sailor's Delight 1971 15.00

SKYLARK

45s

CAPITOL
❑ 3378 What Would I Do Without You/Suites for My Lady 1972 4.00
❑ 3511 Wildflower/The Writings on the Wall 1973 5.00
❑ 3661 I'll Have to Go Away/Twenty-Six Years 1973 4.00
❑ 3773 Virgin Green/If That's the Way You Want It 1973 4.00

Albums

CAPITOL
❑ ST-11048 Skylark 1972 15.00
❑ ST-11256 Skylark 2 1973 12.00

SKYLARKS, THE (1)

45s

ADMIRAL
❑ 500 I'll Surf Around the World/How Many Times 1963 30.00

SKYLARKS, THE (2)

45s

DECCA
❑ 48241 The Glory of Love/You and I 1951 500.00

Number | Title (A Side/B Side) | Yr | NM

SKYLARKS, THE (3)

45s

EVERLAST
❑ 5022 Everybody's Got Somebody/Jeannie 1963 30.00

SKYLARKS, THE (4)

45s

RCA VICTOR
❑ 47-5257 Home in Pasadena/I Had the Craziest Dream 1953 25.00

SKYLARKS, THE (5)

45s

VERVE
❑ 10082 Ol' Man River/There's a Boat Dat's Leavin' for New York 1957 20.00

SKYLARKS, THE (U)

45s

THUNDERBIRD
❑ 102 Do You Know?/Here Comes the Fool 196? 12.00

SKYLINERS, THE

45s

ATCO
❑ 6270 Since I Fell for You/I'd Die 1963 40.00

CALICO
❑ 103/4 Since I Don't Have You/One Night, One Night 1959 50.00
❑ 106 This I Swear/Tomorrow 1959 30.00
❑ 109 It Happened Today/Lonely Way 1959 30.00
❑ 114 How Much/Lorraine from Spain 1960 25.00
❑ 117 Pennies from Heaven/I'll Be Seeing You 1960 25.00
❑ 120 Believe Me/Happy Time 1960 25.00

CAMEO
❑ 215 Three Coins in the Fountain/Everyone But You 1962 40.00

CAPITOL
❑ 3979 Where Have They Gone/I Could Have Loved You So Well 1974 25.00
—As "Jimmy Beaumont and the Skyliners"

CLASSIC ARTISTS
❑ 123 You're My Christmas Present/Another Lonely New Year's Eve 1990 5.00

COLPIX
❑ 188 I'll Close My Eyes/The Door Is Still Open 1961 40.00
❑ 607 Ba'ion Rhythms/The End of a Story 196? 40.00
—As "Jimmy Beaumont and the Skyliners"
❑ 613 Close Your Eyes/Our Love Will Last 1961 40.00

DRIVE
❑ 6250 Our Day Is Here/The Day the Clown Cried 1976 8.00

JUBILEE
❑ 5506 The Loser/Everything Is Fine 1965 15.00
❑ 5512 Who Do You Love/Get Yourself a Baby 1965 15.00
❑ 5520 I Run to You/Don't Hurt Me Baby 1965 15.00

MOTOWN
❑ 1046 [DJ] Since I Fell for You/I'd Die 1963 2000.
—Record never got beyond the test pressing stage (2 known copies). VG 1000 ; VG+ 1500

ORIGINAL SOUND
❑ 35 Since I Don't Have You/One Night, One Night 1963 15.00
❑ 36 Pennies from Heaven/I'll Be Seeing You 1963 15.00
❑ 37 This I Swear/It Happened Today 1963 15.00

TORTOISE INT'L.
❑ PB-11243 Oh How Happy/We've Got Love on Our Side 1978 8.00
❑ PB-11312 Smile On Me/Love Bug (Done Bit Me Again) 1978 8.00

VISCOUNT
❑ 104 Comes Love/Tell Me 1962 20.00

Albums

CALICO
❑ LP-3000 [M] The Skyliners 1959 600.00
—Yellow and blue label
❑ LP-3000 [M] The Skyliners 196? 200.00
—Blue label

KAMA SUTRA
❑ KSBS-2026 Once Upon a Time 1971 25.00

Number	Title (A Side/B Side)	Yr	NM

ORIGINAL SOUND

OS-5010 [M]	Since I Don't Have You	1963	50.00
OSS-8873 [S]	Since I Don't Have You	1963	70.00
OSS-8873 [S]	Since I Don't Have You	197?	15.00

—Reissue on thinner vinyl

SLADE
Includes early releases as "Ambrose Slade." Also see THE IN-BE-TWEENS.

45s
CBS ASSOCIATED

04398	Run Runaway/Can't Tame a Hurricane	1984	4.00
04528	My Oh My/High and Dry	1984	4.00
04865	Little Sheila/Lock Up Your Daughters	1985	4.00

COTILLION

44128	Get Down and Get With It/The Gospel According to Rasputin	1971	25.00
44139	Cos I Love You/Gotta Keep a-Rockin'	1971	25.00
44150	Look Wot You Dun/Candidate	1972	25.00

POLYDOR

15041	Look Wot You Dun/Candidate	1972	10.00
15044	Cuz I Love You/My Life Is Natural	1972	10.00
15046	Take Me Back 'Ome/Wondering Why	1972	10.00
15053	Mama Weer All Crazee Now/Man Who Speeks Evil	1972	10.00
15060	Gudbuy T' Jane/I Won't Let It 'Appen Again	1973	10.00
15069	Cum On Feel the Noize/I'm Mee, I'm Now, An' That's Orl	1973	15.00
15080	Let the Good Times Roll/Feel So Fine-I Don' Mind	1973	10.00

REPRISE

1182	Skweeze Me Pleeze Me/My Town	1973	8.00

WARNER BROS.

7759	Merry Christmas Everybody/Don't Blame Me	1973	10.00
7777	Good Time Gals/We're Really Gonna Raise the Roof	1974	8.00
7808	How Can It Be/When the Lights Are Out	1974	8.00
8134	How Does It Feel/OK, Yesterday Was Yesterday	1975	8.00
8185	Nobody's Fool/When the Chips Are Down	1976	8.00

Albums
CBS ASSOCIATED

FZ 39336	Keep Your Hands Off My Power Supply	1984	10.00
PZ 39336	Keep Your Hands Off My Power Supply	1985	8.00

—Budget-line reissue

FZ 39976	Rogues Gallery	1985	12.00
BFZ 40908	You Boyz Make Big Noize	1986	12.00

COTILLION

SD 9035	Play It Loud	1970	50.00

FONTANA

SRF-67598	Ballzy	1969	150.00
SRF-67598 [DJ]	Ballzy	1969	100.00

—White label promo

POLYDOR

PD-5508	Slade Alive!	1972	15.00
PD-5524	Slayed?	1973	15.00

REPRISE

MS 2173	Sladest	1973	15.00

WARNER BROS.

BS 2770	Stomp Your Hands, Clap Your Feet	1974	15.00
BS 2865	Slade in Flame	1975	15.00
BS 2936	Nobody's Fools	1976	20.00

SLADES, THE

45s
DOMINO

500	You Cheated/The Waddle	1958	40.00
800	You Gambled/No Time	1959	40.00
901	Just You/It's Better to Love	1959	30.00
906	It's Your Turn/Take My Heart	1961	40.00
1000	Summertime/You Must Try	1961	30.00

LIBERTY

55118	Baby/You Mean Everything to Me	1957	25.00
55118	Baby/You Mean Everything to Me	1957	50.00

—As "The Spades," in error

SLAUGHTER

Albums
CHRYSALIS

F1-21702 [DJ]	Stick It To Ya	1990	30.00

—Black generic sleeve with hole; numbered edition of 500 with sticker that says "Limited Edition Special Vinyl Pressing Metal Radio Only"

F1-21911	The Wild Life	1992	20.00

—Vinyl version available only through Columbia House

R 120666 [EP]	Stick It Live	1990	20.00

—Vinyl version available only through BMG Direct Marketing

SLAVIN, SLICK

45s
IMPERIAL

5540	Speed Crazy/She Says She's Mine	1958	30.00

SLAYER

Albums
AMERICAN

C2 69192 [(2)]	Diabolus in Musica	1998	30.00

COMBAT

MX 8020	Hell Awaits	1985	20.00

DEF AMERICAN

DFS 24307	Seasons in the Abyss	1990	18.00

DEF JAM

GHS 24131	Reign in Blood	1986	18.00
GHS 24203	South of Heaven	1988	14.00

METAL BLADE

E 1034	Show No Mercy	1983	20.00
MBR 1037 [PD]	Live Undead	1984	30.00

—Limited edition picture disc

71034	Show No Mercy	198?	12.00

—Early reissue of 1034

72214 [PD]	Show No Mercy	1987	25.00

—Picture disc in plastic sleeve

72217	Live Undead	1987	20.00
72297	Hell Awaits	1988	16.00

—Reissue of Combat LP

SLED, BOB, AND THE TOBOGGANS

45s
CAMEO

400	Here We Go (Surfer Boys Are Going Skiing)/Sea and Ski	1966	50.00

SLEDGE, PERCY

12-Inch Singles
CAPRICORN

PRO 672 [DJ]	When She's Touching Me (same on both sides)	1977	12.00

45s
ATLANTIC

2326	When a Man Loves a Woman/Love Me Like You Mean It	1966	15.00
2342	Warm and Tender Love/Sugar Puddin'	1966	12.00
2358	It Tears Me Up/Heart of a Child	1966	10.00
2383	Baby, Help Me/You Got That Something Wonderful	1967	20.00
2396	Out of Left Field/It Can't Be Stopped	1967	12.00
2414	Love Me Tender/What Am I Living For	1967	12.00
2434	Just Out of Reach (Of My Two Empty Arms)/Hard to Believe	1967	12.00
2453	Cover Me/Behind Every Great Man There Is a Woman	1967	12.00
2490	Take Time to Know Her/It's All Wrong But It's Alright	1968	12.00
2539	Sudden Stop/Between These Arms	1968	15.00
2563	You're All Around Me/Self-Preservation	1968	10.00
2594	My Special Prayer/Bless Your Little Sweet Soul	1969	12.00
2616	Any Day Now/The Angels Listened In	1969	25.00
2646	Woman of the Night/Kind Woman	1969	12.00
2679	Faithful and True/True Love Travels on a Gravel Road	1969	15.00
2719	Too Many Rivers to Cross/Push Mr. Pride Aside	1970	12.00
2754	Help Me Make It Through the Night/Thief in the Night	1970	8.00
2826	Stop the World Tonight/That's the Way I Want to Live My Life	1971	8.00
2848	Rainbow Road/Standing on the Mountain	1971	12.00
2886	Sunday Brother/Everything You'll Ever Need	1972	8.00
2963	Sunshine/Unchanging Love	1973	10.00
7-88802	When a Man Loves a Woman/Twentieth Century Fox	1989	10.00

—B-side by the Escape Club

7-89262	When a Man Loves a Woman/Cover Me	1987	3.00
7-89262 [PS]	When a Man Loves a Woman/Cover Me	1987	4.00

ATLANTIC OLDIES SERIES

OS 13021	When a Man Loves a Woman/Cover Me	197?	5.00

—Gold label

OS 13021	When a Man Loves a Woman/Cover Me	198?	3.00

—Silver, black and red label

OS 13022	Take Time to Know Her/Warm and Tender Love	197?	5.00

—Gold label

OS 13022	Take Time to Know Her/Warm and Tender Love	198?	3.00

—Silver, black and red label

CAPRICORN

0209	I'll Be Your Everything/Blue Water	1974	8.00
0220	If This Is the Last Time/Behind Closed Doors	1975	10.00
0273	When She's Touching Me/When a Boy Becomes a Man	1977	8.00

ERIC

4014	When a Man Loves a Woman/Goodnight My Love	197?	4.00

—Reissue; B-side by Jesse Belvin

MONUMENT

WS4 03612	You Had to Be There/Hard Lovin' Woman	1983	10.00
WS4 03878	She's Too Pretty to Cry/Home Type Thing	1983	10.00

PHILCO-FORD

HP-12	When a Man Loves a Woman/Baby Help Me	1967	25.00

—4-inch plastic "Hip Pocket Record" with color sleeve

TRIP

129	When a Man Loves a Woman/Any Day Now	197?	5.00

—Reissue; B-side by Chuck Jackson

7-Inch Extended Plays
ATLANTIC

SD 78180	Take Time to Know Her/Feed the Flame/Out of Left Field//Cover Me/Baby Help Me/I Love Everything About You	1968	20.00

—Jukebox issue; small hole, plays at 33 1/3 rpm

SD 78180 [PS]	Take Time to Know Her	1968	20.00

Albums
ATLANTIC

8125 [M]	When a Man Loves a Woman	1966	50.00
SD 8125 [R]	When a Man Loves a Woman	1966	30.00
8132 [M]	Warm and Tender Soul	1966	50.00
SD 8132 [R]	Warm and Tender Soul	1966	30.00
8146 [M]	The Percy Sledge Way	1967	50.00
SD 8146 [S]	The Percy Sledge Way	1967	50.00
SD 8180	Take Time to Know Her	1968	50.00
SD 8210	The Best of Percy Sledge	1969	25.00
80212	The Ultimate Collection: When a Man Loves a Woman	1983	12.00

CAPRICORN

CP 0147	I'll Be Your Everything	1974	15.00

MONUMENT

FW 38532	Percy!	1983	12.00

SLICK, GRACE
Also see THE GREAT SOCIETY; JEFFERSON AIRPLANE; JEFFERSON STARSHIP; PAUL KANTNER AND GRACE SLICK.

12-Inch Singles
RCA

JD-13708 [DJ]	All the Machines (Long)/All the Machines (Short)	1984	6.00

45s
GRUNT

BFBO-0183	Theme from "Manhole"/Come Again, Toucan	1973	6.00

RCA

PB-11939	Seasons/Angel of Night	1980	4.00
PB-11939 [PS]	Seasons/Angel of Night	1980	5.00
PB-12041	Dreams/Do It the Hard Way	1980	4.00
PB-12171	Sea of Love/Full Moon Man	1981	4.00
PB-12172	Mistreater/Full Moon Man	1981	—

—Canceled

PB-12186	Round and Round/Full Moon Man	1981	—

—Canceled

PB-13764	Through the Window/Habits	1984	4.00

Albums

GRUNT

Number	Title (A Side/B Side)	Yr	NM
❑ BFL1-0347	Manhole	1974	12.00
❑ AYL1-3736	Manhole	1981	8.00

—"Best Buy Series" reissue

RCA VICTOR

Number	Title (A Side/B Side)	Yr	NM
❑ AFL1-3544	Dreams	1980	10.00
❑ AQL1-3851	Welcome to the Wrecking Ball	1981	10.00
❑ DJL1-3922 [DJ]	Welcome to the Wrecking Ball Interview	1981	20.00
❑ DJL1-3923 [DJ]	RCA Special Radio Series	1981	20.00

SLICKEE BOYS

45s

DACOIT

Number	Title (A Side/B Side)	Yr	NM
❑ 004	The Brain That Refused to Die/Love In	1980	6.00
❑ 004 [PS]	The Brain That Refused to Die/Love In	1980	6.00
❑ 005	Here to Stay/Porcelain Butter Kitchen	1981	6.00
❑ 005 [PS]	Here to Stay/Porcelain Butter Kitchen	1981	6.00
❑ 011	When I Go to the Beach/Invisible People	1983	8.00

—3,000 copies were pressed

Number	Title (A Side/B Side)	Yr	NM
❑ 011 [PS]	When I Go to the Beach/Invisible People	1983	8.00

DECEASED

Number	Title (A Side/B Side)	Yr	NM
❑ 005	Long Way to Go/Control (Live)	1995	3.00

—Limited edition of 500

Number	Title (A Side/B Side)	Yr	NM
❑ 005 [PS]	Long Way to Go/Control (Live)	1995	3.00

TWIN/TONE

Number	Title (A Side/B Side)	Yr	NM
❑ TTR 8336	When I Go to the Beach/Invisible People	1984	3.00

—3,000 copies were pressed

Number	Title (A Side/B Side)	Yr	NM
❑ TTR 8336 [PS]	When I Go to the Beach/Invisible People	1984	3.00

7-Inch Extended Plays

DACOIT

Number	Title (A Side/B Side)	Yr	NM
❑ 001	Hot and Cool	1976	8.00
❑ 001 [PS]	Hot and Cool	1976	16.00

—Gatefold full-color picture sleeve (not every copy of this EP has a picture sleeve)

DSI

Number	Title (A Side/B Side)	Yr	NM
❑ 8	10th Anniversary EP	1988	5.00

—First pressing of 500 on black vinyl

Number	Title (A Side/B Side)	Yr	NM
❑ 8	10th Anniversary EP	1988	5.00

—Second pressing of 500 on white vinyl

Number	Title (A Side/B Side)	Yr	NM
❑ 8 [PS]	10th Anniversary EP	1988	5.00

—First pressing of sleeve is beige

Number	Title (A Side/B Side)	Yr	NM
❑ 8 [PS]	10th Anniversary EP	1988	5.00

—Second pressing of sleeve is green

LIMP

Number	Title (A Side/B Side)	Yr	NM
❑ 001	Mersey Mersey Me	1978	8.00

—Blue labels

Number	Title (A Side/B Side)	Yr	NM
❑ 001	Mersey Mersey Me	1978	12.00

—Yellow labels

Number	Title (A Side/B Side)	Yr	NM
❑ 001 [PS]	Mersey Mersey Me	1978	8.00

—Pink sleeve

Number	Title (A Side/B Side)	Yr	NM
❑ 001 [PS]	Mersey Mersey Me	1978	12.00

—Blue sleeve

Number	Title (A Side/B Side)	Yr	NM
❑ 005	3rd EP	1979	10.00
❑ 005 [PS]	3rd EP	1979	10.00

—Includes decal, lyrics and fan club insert

Albums

DACOIT

Number	Title (A Side/B Side)	Yr	NM
❑ 1001	Separated Vegetables	1977	80.00

—Limited edition of 100 copies

GIANT

Number	Title (A Side/B Side)	Yr	NM
❑ GR 16037-1	Live at Last	1989	10.00

LIMP

Number	Title (A Side/B Side)	Yr	NM
❑ 1003	Separated Vegetables	1980	25.00

—Limited edition of 300 copies; reissue with new cover

TWIN/TONE

Number	Title (A Side/B Side)	Yr	NM
❑ TTR 8337	Cybernetic Dreams of Pi	1983	15.00
❑ TTR 8544	Uh Oh, No Breaks	1985	12.00

SLITS, THE

12-Inch Singles

EPIC

Number	Title (A Side/B Side)	Yr	NM
❑ 02576	Earthbeat & Earthdub//Or What Is It	1981	10.00

45s

ANTILLES

Number	Title (A Side/B Side)	Yr	NM
❑ ANS-102	Typical Girls/I Heard It Through the Grapevine	1980	10.00

—Presumably an American release

Number	Title (A Side/B Side)	Yr	NM
❑ ANS-102 [PS]	Typical Girls/I Heard It Through the Grapevine	1980	15.00

—Fold-out poster sleeve

Albums

ANTILLES

Number	Title (A Side/B Side)	Yr	NM
❑ AN-7077	Cut	1979	40.00

SLLEDNATS, THE

See THE STANDELLS.

SLOAN, P.F.

Cohort of STEVE BARRI. Also see THE FANTASTIC BAGGYS; THE GRASS ROOTS; THE IMAGINATIONS (2); THE INNER CIRCLE; THE LIFEGUARDS (2); PHILIP AND STEPHAN; THE RALLY PACKS; THE RINCON SURFSIDE BAND; THE STREET CLEANERS; THEMES INC.; WILLIE AND THE WHEELS.

45s

ALADDIN

Number	Title (A Side/B Side)	Yr	NM
❑ 3461	All I Want Is Lovin'/Little Girl in the Cabin	1959	25.00

—As "Flip Sloan"

ATCO

Number	Title (A Side/B Side)	Yr	NM
❑ 6663	Star Gazin'/New Design	1969	20.00

DUNHILL

Number	Title (A Side/B Side)	Yr	NM
❑ 4007	Sins of the Family/This Mornin'	1965	15.00
❑ 4016	Halloween Mary/I'd Have to Be Out of My Mind	1965	15.00
❑ 4016 [PS]	Halloween Mary/I'd Have to Be Out of My Mind	1965	25.00

—Sleeve is promo only

Number	Title (A Side/B Side)	Yr	NM
❑ 4024	From a Distance/Patterns	1966	25.00
❑ 4037	City Women/Top of a Fence	1966	15.00
❑ 4054	I Found a Girl/A Melody for You	1966	15.00
❑ 4064	Sunflower, Sunflower/The Man Behind the Red Balloon	1967	25.00
❑ 4064 [PS]	Sunflower, Sunflower/The Man Behind the Red Balloon	1967	30.00
❑ 4106	Karma (Study of Divination)/I Can't Help But Wonder, Elizabeth	1967	25.00

—As "Philip Sloan"

MART

Number	Title (A Side/B Side)	Yr	NM
❑ 802	She's My Girl/If You Believe in Me	1960	80.00

MUMS

Number	Title (A Side/B Side)	Yr	NM
❑ 6010	Let Me Be/Springtime	1972	20.00

Albums

ATCO

Number	Title (A Side/B Side)	Yr	NM
❑ SD 33-268	Measure of Pleasure	1968	25.00

DUNHILL

Number	Title (A Side/B Side)	Yr	NM
❑ D-50004 [M]	Songs of Our Times	1965	25.00
❑ DS-50004 [S]	Songs of Our Times	1965	30.00
❑ D-50007 [M]	Twelve More Times	1966	25.00
❑ DS-50007 [S]	Twelve More Times	1966	30.00

MUMS

Number	Title (A Side/B Side)	Yr	NM
❑ KZ 31260	Raised on Records	1972	20.00

RHINO

Number	Title (A Side/B Side)	Yr	NM
❑ RNLP-70133	Precious Times: The Best of P.F. Sloan	1986	10.00

SLY

See SLY STEWART.

SLY AND THE FAMILY STONE

Also see GRAHAM CENTRAL STATION; SLY STEWART.

45s

EPIC

Number	Title (A Side/B Side)	Yr	NM
❑ 10229	Higher/Underdog	1967	10.00
❑ 10256	Dance to the Music/Let Me Hear It from You	1967	10.00
❑ 10353	Life/M'Lady	1968	8.00
❑ 10407	Everyday People/Sing a Simple Song	1968	10.00
❑ 10407 [PS]	Everyday People/Sing a Simple Song	1968	12.00
❑ 10450	Stand!/I Want to Take You Higher	1969	10.00
❑ 10450 [PS]	Stand!/I Want to Take You Higher	1969	12.00
❑ 10497	Hot Fun in the Summertime/Fun	1969	10.00
❑ 10555	Thank You Falettinme Be Mice Elf Agin/Everybody Is a Star	1969	6.00
❑ 10555 [PS]	Thank You Falettinme Be Mice Elf Agin/Everybody Is a Star	1969	10.00
❑ 10805	Family Affair/Luv N' Haight	1971	6.00
❑ 10829	Runnin' Away/Brave & Strong	1972	6.00
❑ 10850	Smilin'/Luv N' Haight	1972	6.00
❑ 11017	If You Want Me to Stay/Babies Makin' Babies	1973	6.00
❑ 11017	If You Want Me to Stay/Thankful N' Thoughtful	1973	6.00
❑ 11060	Frisky/If It Were Left Up to Me	1973	6.00
❑ 11140	Time for Livin'/Small Talk	1974	6.00
❑ 8-50033	Loose Booty/Can't Strain My Brain	1974	6.00
❑ 50119	Hot Fun in the Summertime/Fun	1975	8.00
❑ 50135	I Get High on You/That's Lovin' You	1975	5.00
❑ 50175	Li Lo Li/Who Do You Love	1975	5.00
❑ 50201	Greed/Crossword Puzzle	1976	5.00
❑ 50331	Family Again/Nothing Less Than Happiness	1977	5.00

LOADSTONE

Number	Title (A Side/B Side)	Yr	NM
❑ 3951	I Ain't Got Nobody/I Can't Turn You Loose	1967	20.00

WARNER BROS.

Number	Title (A Side/B Side)	Yr	NM
❑ 29682	High Y'All/Ha Ha He He	1983	4.00
❑ 49062	Sheer Energy/Remember Who You Are	1979	4.00
❑ 49132	Who's to Say/Same Thing	1979	4.00

7-Inch Extended Plays

EPIC

Number	Title (A Side/B Side)	Yr	NM
❑ 7-30986	You Caught Me Smilin'/Runnin' Away/Space Cowboy//Just Like a Baby/P.O.E.T.	1971	15.00

—Jukebox issue; small hole, plays at 33 1/3 rpm

Number	Title (A Side/B Side)	Yr	NM
❑ 7-30986 [PS]	There's a Riot Goin' On	1971	15.00

Albums

EPIC

Number	Title (A Side/B Side)	Yr	NM
❑ AS 264 [DJ]	Everything You Always Wanted to Hear by Sly and the Family Stone But Were Afraid to Ask For	1976	25.00

—Promo-only compilation

Number	Title (A Side/B Side)	Yr	NM
❑ LN 24324 [M]	A Whole New Thing	1967	20.00
❑ LN 24371 [M]	Dance to the Music	1968	40.00
❑ BN 26324 [S]	A Whole New Thing	1967	20.00
❑ BN 26371 [S]	Dance to the Music	1968	15.00
❑ BN 26397	Life	1968	15.00
❑ BN 26456	Stand!	1969	15.00
❑ PE 26456	Stand!	1986	8.00

—Budget-line reissue

Number	Title (A Side/B Side)	Yr	NM
❑ EQ 30325 [Q]	Sly and the Family Stone's Greatest Hits	1971	100.00

—Has alternate mixes of "Hot Fun in the Summertime," "Thank You" and "Everybody Is a Star," which are not rechanneled stereo as they are on other LPs

Number	Title (A Side/B Side)	Yr	NM
❑ KE 30325	Sly and the Family Stone's Greatest Hits	1970	12.00

—Yellow label, gatefold cover

Number	Title (A Side/B Side)	Yr	NM
❑ PE 30325	Sly and the Family Stone's Greatest Hits	1979	8.00

—Budget-line reissue

Number	Title (A Side/B Side)	Yr	NM
❑ E 30333	Life	1971	12.00

—Reissue of 26397

Number	Title (A Side/B Side)	Yr	NM
❑ E 30334	Dance to the Music	1971	12.00

—Reissue of 26371

Number	Title (A Side/B Side)	Yr	NM
❑ E 30335	A Whole New Thing	1971	12.00

—Reissue of 26324

Number	Title (A Side/B Side)	Yr	NM
❑ KE 30986	There's a Riot Goin' On	1971	12.00

—Yellow label, gatefold cover

Number	Title (A Side/B Side)	Yr	NM
❑ KE 32134	Fresh	1973	10.00

—Orange label

Number	Title (A Side/B Side)	Yr	NM
❑ PE 32930	Small Talk	1974	10.00

—Orange label

Number	Title (A Side/B Side)	Yr	NM
❑ PEQ 32930 [Q]	Small Talk	1974	25.00
❑ PE 33835	High on You	1975	10.00

—Orange label

Number	Title (A Side/B Side)	Yr	NM
❑ PEQ 33835 [Q]	High on You	1975	25.00
❑ PE 34348	Heard Ya Missed Me, Well I'm Back	1976	10.00

—Orange label

Number	Title (A Side/B Side)	Yr	NM
❑ JE 35974	Ten Years Too Soon	1979	10.00
❑ E2 37071 [(2)]	Anthology	1981	15.00

WARNER BROS.

Number	Title (A Side/B Side)	Yr	NM
❑ BSK 3303	Back on the Right Track	1979	10.00
❑ 23700	Ain't But the Right Way	1983	10.00

SMACK, THE

Albums

AUDIO HOUSE

Number	Title (A Side/B Side)	Yr	NM
❑ (# unknown)	The Smack	1968	2000.

SMALL, MILLIE

45s

ATCO

Number	Title (A Side/B Side)	Yr	NM
❑ 6384	Tongue Tied/Blood Shot Eyes	1965	10.00

ATLANTIC

Number	Title (A Side/B Side)	Yr	NM
❑ 2266	Bring It On Home to Me/I've Fallen in Love with a Snowman	1965	10.00

BRIT

Number	Title (A Side/B Side)	Yr	NM
❑ 7002	My Street/Mixed-Up, Lonely, Self-Centered, Spoiled Kind of Boy	1965	12.00

SMASH

Number	Title (A Side/B Side)	Yr	NM
❑ 1893	My Boy Lollipop/Something's Gotta Be Done	1964	15.00
❑ 1920	Sweet William/What Am I Living For	1964	12.00
❑ 1940	I Love the Way You Love/Bring It On Home to Me	1964	12.00
❑ 1946	Don't You Know/Tom Hark	1964	12.00

S

Number	Title (A Side/B Side)	Yr	NM
Albums			
SMASH			
❑ MGS-27055 [M]	My Boy Lollipop	1964	50.00
❑ SRS-67055 [R]	My Boy Lollipop	1964	40.00

SMALL FACES Also see FACES.

Number	Title (A Side/B Side)	Yr	NM
45s			
IMMEDIATE			
❑ 501	Itchykoo Park/I'm Only Dreaming	1967	12.00
❑ 1902	Here Come the Nice/Talk to You	1967	10.00
❑ 5003	Tin Soldier/I Feel Much Better	1968	10.00
❑ 5003 [PS]	Tin Soldier/I Feel Much Better	1968	25.00
❑ 5007	Lazy Sunday/Rollin' Over	1968	10.00
❑ 5009	The Universal/Donkey Rides A Penny A Glass	1968	15.00
❑ 5012	Mad John/The Journey	1969	15.00
❑ 5014	Afterglow of Your Love/Wham, Bam, Thank You Ma'am	1969	15.00
PRESS			
❑ 5007	Almost Grown/Hey Girl	1969	20.00
❑ 9794	What 'Cha Gonna Do About It/ What's a Matter	1965	25.00
❑ 9826	Sha-La-La-La-Lee/ Grow Your Own	1966	15.00
PRIDE			
❑ 1006	Runaway/Shake	1972	12.00
RCA VICTOR			
❑ 47-8949	Understanding/All or Nothing	1966	20.00
❑ 47-8949 [PS]	Understanding/All or Nothing	1966	30.00
❑ 47-9055	My Mind's Eye/ I Can't Dance with You	1966	20.00
Albums			
ACCORD			
❑ AN-7157	By Appointment	1982	10.00
ATLANTIC			
❑ SD 19113	Playmates	1977	10.00
❑ SD 19171	78 in the Shade	1978	10.00
COMPLEAT			
❑ 67-2004 [(2)]	Big Music	1985	12.00
❑ 67-5003	Ogden's Nut Gone Flake	1985	10.00
—Reissue			
IMMEDIATE			
❑ 4225	Ogden's Nut Gone Flake	1973	15.00
—Reissue has a standard square cover			
❑ Z12 52002 [S]	There Are But Four Small Faces	1967	50.00
—Color cover (counterfeits have either black and white or black and green covers)			
❑ Z12 52008 [S]	Ogden's Nut Gone Flake	1968	50.00
—Originals have a round cover			
MGM			
❑ M3F-4955	Archetypes	1974	12.00
PRIDE			
❑ PRD 0001 [R]	Early Faces	1972	15.00
❑ PRD 0014 [P]	The History of the Small Faces	1973	12.00
SIRE			
❑ SASH-3709 [(2)]	The Vintage Years	1976	15.00

SMALLEY, LEROY

Number	Title (A Side/B Side)	Yr	NM
45s			
GOLDEN WORLD			
❑ 7	Girls Are Sentimental/ Ain't It a Shame	1964	80.00

SMART TONES, THE

Number	Title (A Side/B Side)	Yr	NM
45s			
HERALD			
❑ 529	Bob-O-Link/Ginny	1958	100.00

SMASHING PUMPKINS Featuring Billy Corgan.

Number	Title (A Side/B Side)	Yr	NM
45s			
LIMITED POTENTIAL			
❑ LIMP 006	I Am One/Not Worth Asking	1990	120.00
❑ LIMP 006 [PS]	I Am One/Not Worth Asking	1990	120.00
SUB POP			
❑ 90	Tristessa/La Dolly Vita	1991	25.00
—Pink vinyl (4,000 pressed)			
❑ 90	Tristessa/La Dolly Vita	1991	30.00
—Black vinyl (3,000 pressed)			
❑ 90	Tristessa/La Dolly Vita	1991	500.00
—Red vinyl (5 pressed)			
❑ 90 [PS]	Tristessa/La Dolly Vita	1991	25.00
❑ 90	Tristessa/La Dolly Vita	1991	120.00
—Gray vinyl (50 pressed)			
VIRGIN			
❑ 38522	1979/Bullet with Butterfly Wings	1996	5.00
❑ 38522 [PS]	1979/Bullet with Butterfly Wings	1996	5.00
❑ 38825	1979/Bullet with Butterfly Wings	2002	4.00
—Reissue in the "For Jukeboxes Only!" series			

The Small Faces, "Tin Soldier," Immediate 5003, 1968, $25.

Number	Title (A Side/B Side)	Yr	NM
Albums			
CAROLINE			
❑ 1705	Gish	199?	18.00
—With "Remastered" under the bar code			
❑ 1705	Gish	1991	60.00
—Originals do not have the word "Remastered" under the bar code			
❑ 1740 [(2)]	Siamese Dream	199?	50.00
—Pink marbled vinyl			
❑ 1740 [(2)]	Siamese Dream	1993	80.00
—Originals have dark red vinyl			
❑ 1767	Pisces Iscariot	1994	100.00
—Regular pressing on colored vinyl, not numbered, no bonus 7-inch single			
❑ 1767	Pisces Iscariot	1994	300.00
—First 2,000 copies, hand-numbered on back cover, came with a bonus 7-inch single			
❑ 45879 [(2)]	Adore	1998	30.00
—Different cover than CD version, and the entire LP was remixed into mono			
❑ 48936 [(2)]	Machina/ The Machines of God	2000	30.00
—With bound-in booklet			
CONSTANTINOPLE			
❑ CR 01-04 [(5)]	Machina II/The Friends and Enemies of Modern Music	2000	3000.
—Exactly 25 copies were pressed as two 12-inch and three 10-inch records, with the presumption that at least some of them would be bootlegged onto CDs and into downloadable files via the Internet. (This has indeed happened, so many fans have heard the music.) It's not known whether any of the 25 copies have left the hands of their original recipients, so the price above is highly speculative and probably conservative; VG value 1000; VG+ value 2000			

SMILE (1) Brian May and Roger Taylor, later of QUEEN, were in this group.

Number	Title (A Side/B Side)	Yr	NM
45s			
MERCURY			
❑ 72977	Earth/Step on Me	1968	200.00

SMILE (2)

Number	Title (A Side/B Side)	Yr	NM
45s			
UNI			
❑ 55313	A Year Every Night/Southbound	1972	6.00
❑ 55336	Tonight/One Night Stand	1972	6.00

SMITH Also see GAYLE McCORMACK.

Number	Title (A Side/B Side)	Yr	NM
45s			
ABC DUNHILL			
❑ 4206	Baby It's You/I Don't Believe (I Believe)	1969	8.00
❑ 4206 [PS]	Baby It's You/I Don't Believe (I Believe)	1969	12.00
❑ 4228	Take a Look Around/ Mojalesky Ridge	1970	6.00
❑ 4238	What Am I Gonna Do/ Born in Boston	1970	6.00
❑ 4238 [PS]	What Am I Gonna Do/ Born in Boston	1970	10.00
❑ 4246	Comin' Back to Me (Ooh Baby)/ Minus-Plus	1970	6.00
Albums			
ABC DUNHILL			
❑ DS-50056	A Group Called Smith	1969	15.00
❑ DS-50081	Minus-Plus	1970	15.00

SMITH, ARLENE Also see THE CHANTELS.

Number	Title (A Side/B Side)	Yr	NM
45s			
BIG TOP			
❑ 3073	Love, Love, Love/He Knows I Love Him Too Much	1961	30.00
SPECTORIOUS			
❑ 150	Good Girls/Everything	196?	100.00

SMITH, BETTY, GROUP

Number	Title (A Side/B Side)	Yr	NM
45s			
LONDON			
❑ 1763	Virginia/Double Shuffle	1958	12.00
❑ 1787	Bewitched/Hand Jive	1958	12.00

Number	Title (A Side/B Side)	Yr	NM
❑ 1819	My Foolsih Heart/Betty's Blues	1958	12.00

SMITH, BOB

Albums

KENT

Number	Title (A Side/B Side)	Yr	NM
❑ KST-551 [(2)]	The Visit	1970	100.00

—Deduct 25 percent if poster is missing

SMITH, BOBBIE, AND THE DREAM GIRLS

See THE DREAM GIRLS.

SMITH, CARL

45s

ABC HICKORY

Number	Title (A Side/B Side)	Yr	NM
❑ 54004	A Way with Words/Till I Stop Meeting You	1976	5.00
❑ 54009	Show Me a Brick Wall/It's Teardrop Time	1977	5.00
❑ 54016	This Kinda Love Ain't Meant for Sunday School/There Stands the Glass	1977	5.00
❑ 54022	This Lady Loving Me/Loose Talk	1978	5.00
❑ 54030	Remembered by Someone (Remembered by Me)/It Takes Four Feet to Make a Yard	1978	5.00
❑ 54037	I Can't Get the Last Memory Down/Silver Tongued Cowboy	1978	5.00

COLUMBIA

Number	Title (A Side/B Side)	Yr	NM
❑ 4-20712	Guilty Conscience/Washing My Dreams in Tears	1950	30.00
❑ 4-20741	I Overlooked an Orchid/I Betcha My Heart I Love You	1950	30.00
❑ 4-20765	This Side of Heaven/I Won't Be at Home	1950	30.00
❑ 4-20796	Let's Live a Little/There's Nothing As Sweet As My Baby	1951	25.00
❑ 4-20825	Mr. Moon/If Teardrops Were Pennies	1951	25.00
❑ 4-20862	Let Old Mother Nature Have Her Way/Me and My Broken Heart	1951	25.00
❑ 4-20893	(When You Feel Like You're in Love) Don't Just Stand There/The Little Girl in My Home Town	1952	25.00
❑ 4-20922	Are You Teasing Me/It's a Lovely, Lovely World	1952	25.00
❑ 4-20942	It's a Lovely, Lovely World/(When You Feel Like You're in Love) Don't Just Stand There	1952	25.00
❑ 4-21008	Our Honeymoon/Sing Her a Love Song	1952	25.00
❑ 4-21040	The Blood That Stained the Old Rugged Cross/Gethsemane	1951	30.00
—With the Carters			
❑ 4-21051	That's the Kind of Love I'm Looking For/My Lonely Heart's Runnin' Wild	1952	20.00
❑ 4-21087	Orchids Mean Goodbye/Just Wait 'Til I Get You Alone	1953	20.00
❑ 4-21110	Nail Scarred Hand/We Shall Meet Someday	1953	25.00
❑ 4-21119	Trademark/Do I Like It?	1953	20.00
❑ 4-21129	Hey Joe!/Darling Am I the One	1953	20.00
❑ 4-21166	Satisfaction Guaranteed/Who'll Buy My Heartaches	1953	20.00
❑ 4-21192	How About You/I'll Be Listening	1953	20.00
❑ 4-21197	Dog-Gone It, Baby, I'm in Love/What Am I Going to Do	1954	20.00
❑ 4-21226	Back Up Buddy/If You Tried As Hard to Love Me	1954	20.00
❑ 4-21266	Go, Boy, Go/If You Saw Her Through My Eyes	1954	20.00
❑ 4-21317	Loose Talk/More Than Anything Else in the World	1954	20.00
❑ 4-21340	Kisses Don't Lie/No, I Don't Believe I Will	1955	20.00
❑ 4-21368	Wait a Little Longer Please, Jesus/Works of the Lord	1955	25.00
❑ 4-21382	There She Goes/Old Lonesome Times	1955	20.00
❑ 4-21411	Baby I'm Ready/I Just Don't Care Anymore	1955	20.00
❑ 4-21429	Don't Tease Me/I Just Dropped In to Say Goodbye	1955	20.00
❑ 4-21462	You're Free to Go/I Feel Like Cryin'	1955	20.00
❑ 4-21493	I've Changed/If You Do Dear	1956	20.00
❑ 4-21507	Answers/My Dream of the Old Rugged Cross	1956	25.00
❑ 4-21522	You Are the One/Doorstep to Heaven	1956	20.00
❑ 4-21552	Before I Met You/Wicked Lies	1956	20.00
❑ 30848 [S]	(titles unknown)	1960	15.00
❑ 30849 [S]	(titles unknown)	1960	15.00
❑ 30850 [S]	(titles unknown)	1960	15.00
❑ 30851 [S]	(titles unknown)	1960	15.00
❑ 31473 [S]	(titles unknown)	1962	15.00
❑ 31474 [S]	(titles unknown)	1962	15.00
❑ 31475 [S]	(titles unknown)	1962	15.00
❑ 31476 [S]	(titles unknown)	1962	15.00
❑ 31477 [S]	(titles unknown)	1962	15.00
—The above 10 are "Stereo Seven" 7-inch 33 1/3 rpm singles with small holes			
❑ 4-40823	You Can't Hurt Me Anymore/That's the Way I Like You the Best	1957	15.00
❑ 4-40918	Mr. Lost/Try to Take It Like a Man	1957	15.00
❑ 4-40970	No Trespassing/Happy Street	1957	—
—Canceled			
❑ 4-40984	Why, Why/Emotions	1957	15.00
❑ 4-41092	Your Name Is Beautiful/You're So Easy to Love	1958	15.00
❑ 4-41170	Guess I've Been Around Too Long/Goodnight Mr. Sun	1958	15.00
❑ 4-41243	Walking the Slow Walk/A Love Was Born	1958	15.00
❑ 4-41290	The Best Years of Your Life/Mr. Moon	1958	15.00
❑ 4-41344	It's All My Heartache/I'll Kiss the Past Goodbye	1959	12.00
❑ 4-41417	Ten Thousand Drums/The Tall, Tall Gentleman	1959	12.00
❑ 4-41417 [PS]	Ten Thousand Drums/The Tall, Tall Gentleman	1959	25.00
❑ 4-41489	Tomorrow Night/I'll Walk with You	1959	12.00
❑ 4-41557	Make the Waterwheel Roll/Past	1960	12.00
❑ 4-41610	A Pain a Pill Can't Locate/If I Had You (I'd Live for You Only)	1962	12.00
❑ 4-41642	Cut Across Shorty/Why Did You Come My Way	1960	12.00
❑ 4-41729	If the World Don't End Tomorrow/Lonely Old Room	1960	12.00
❑ 4-41819	You Make Me Live Again/I Don't Know How	1960	12.00
❑ 4-41948	Are You True to Me/More Habit Than Desire	1961	12.00
❑ 4-42042	Kisses Never Lie/Why Can't You Be Satisfied with Me	1961	12.00
❑ 4-42222	Air Mail to Heaven/Things That Mean the Most	1961	12.00
❑ 4-42349	The Best Dressed Beggar (In Town)/I Used to Be	1962	12.00
❑ 4-42490	Gettin' Even/I Volunteer	1962	12.00
❑ 4-42610	A Pain a Pill Can't Locate/If I Had You (I'd Live for You Only)	1962	12.00
❑ 4-42686	Live for Tomorrow/Let's Talk This Thing Over	1963	12.00
❑ 4-42768	In the Back Room Tonight/Take My Love with You, Too	1963	12.00
❑ 4-42858	Triangle/I Almost Forgot Her Today	1963	12.00
❑ 4-42949	The Pillow That Whispers/Sweet Little Country Girl	1964	12.00
❑ 4-43033	Take My Ring Off Your Finger/The Ballad of Hershel Lawson	1964	12.00
❑ 4-43124	Lonely Girl/When It's Over	1964	12.00
❑ 4-43200	She Called Me Baby/My Friends Are Gonna Be Strangers	1965	10.00
❑ 4-43266	Be Good to Her/Keep Me Fooled	1965	10.00
❑ 4-43361	Let's Walk Away Strangers/Ain't Love a Hurting Thing	1965	10.00
❑ 4-43485	Why Do I Keep Doing This to Us/Why Can't You Feel Sorry for Me	1966	10.00
❑ 4-43599	Sweet Temptation/(Is My) Ring on Your Finger	1966	10.00
❑ 4-43753	Man with a Plan/You Mean Ol' Moon	1966	10.00
❑ 4-43866	You Better Be Better to Me/It's Only a Matter of Time	1966	10.00
❑ 4-44034	I Should Get Away for Awhile (From You)/Mighty Day	1967	8.00
❑ 4-44233	Deep Water/I Really Don't Want to Know	1967	8.00
❑ 4-44396	Foggy River/When Will the Rainbow Follow the Rain	1967	8.00
❑ 4-44486	You Ought to Hear Me Cry/I Used Up My Last Chance Last Night	1968	8.00
❑ 4-44620	There's No More Love/Remember Me (I'm the One Who Loves You)	1968	8.00
❑ 4-44702	Faded Love and Winter Roses/Until I Looked at You	1968	8.00
❑ 4-44816	Good Deal, Lucille/Never Gonna Cry No More	1969	8.00
❑ 4-44939	I Love You Because/Mister, Come and Get Your Wife	1969	8.00
❑ 4-45031	Heartbreak Avenue/It's Nice to See You Once Again	1969	8.00
❑ 4-45086	Pull My String and Wind Me Up/It's All Right	1970	8.00
❑ 4-45177	Pick Me Up on Your Way Down/Bonaparte's Retreat	1970	8.00
❑ 4-45225	How I Love Them Old Songs/Little Crop of Cotton Tops	1970	8.00
❑ 4-45262	Big Murph/My Mother's Eyes	1970	8.00
❑ 4-45293	Don't Worry 'Bout the Mule (Just Load the Wagon)/Darling Days	1970	8.00
❑ 4-45382	Lost It on the Road/I'm Wound Up Tight	1971	8.00
❑ 4-45436	Red Door/You Walked in My Sleep Last Night	1971	8.00
❑ 4-45497	Don't Say You're Mine/Country Soul Man	1971	8.00
❑ 4-45558	Mama Bear/Before My Time	1972	8.00
❑ 4-45648	If This Is Goodbye/If You Saw Her	1972	8.00
❑ 4-45832	What a Difference Your Love Would Make/When You're Gone (There Will Be Nothing Left)	1973	8.00
❑ 4-45923	I Need Help/Yesterday Is Gone	1973	8.00

HICKORY/MGM

Number	Title (A Side/B Side)	Yr	NM
❑ 329	Dreaming Again/I Ain't Getting Nowhere with You	1974	6.00
❑ 337	The Way I Lose My Mind/Happy Birthday My Darlin'	1975	5.00
❑ 347	Everything I Touch Turns to Sugar/Lost Highway	1975	5.00
❑ 352	The Girl I Love/Me and My Broken Heart	1975	5.00
❑ 357	Roly Poly/Remembered by Someone (Remembered by Me)	1975	5.00
❑ 363	She Is/I Can't Go On Like This	1976	5.00
❑ 371	If You Don't, Somebody Else Will/It's Gonna Be One of Those Days	1976	5.00

7-Inch Extended Plays

COLUMBIA

Number	Title (A Side/B Side)	Yr	NM
❑ B-2131	*You Are the One/You Can't Hurt Me Anymore/That's the Way I Like You Best/Before I Met You	1957	25.00
❑ B-2131 [PS]	Four Hits by Carl Smith	1957	25.00
❑ B-2801	*Let Old Mother Nature Have Her Way/Me and My Broken Heart/If Teardrops Were Pennies/I Overlooked an Orchid	1959	20.00
❑ B-2801 [PS]	Carl Smith (Hall of Fame Series)	1959	20.00
❑ B-10221	San Antonio Rose/Time Changes Everything//Lovin' Is Livin'/Oh, No!	1957	20.00
❑ B-10221 [PS]	Smith's the Name, Vol. I	1957	20.00
❑ B-10222	If I Could Hold Back the Dawn/That's What You Think//Live and Let Live/If You Want It, I've Got It	1957	20.00
❑ B-10222 [PS]	Smith's the Name, Vol. II	1957	20.00
❑ B-10223	Please Come Back Home/Look What Thoughts Done to Me//The House That Love Built/Come Back to Me	1957	20.00
❑ B-10223 [PS]	Smith's the Name, Vol. III	1957	20.00

Albums

ABC HICKORY

Number	Title (A Side/B Side)	Yr	NM
❑ HB-44005	This Lady Loves Me	1977	12.00
❑ HB-44015	The Silver-Tongued Cowboy	1978	12.00

COLUMBIA

Number	Title (A Side/B Side)	Yr	NM
❑ GP 31 [(2)]	The Carl Smith Anniversary Album/20 Years of Hits	1970	25.00
❑ CL 959 [M]	Sunday Down South	1957	50.00
❑ CL 1022 [M]	Smith's the Name	1957	50.00
❑ CL 1172 [M]	Let's Live a Little	1958	50.00
❑ CL 1532 [M]	The Carl Smith Touch	1960	25.00
❑ CL 1740 [M]	Easy to Please	1961	25.00
❑ CL 1937 [M]	Carl Smith's Greatest Hits	1962	20.00
❑ CL 2091 [M]	The Tall, Tall Gentleman	1963	20.00
❑ CL 2173 [M]	There Stands the Glass	1964	20.00
❑ CL 2293 [M]	I Want to Live and Love	1965	20.00
❑ CL 2358 [M]	Kisses Don't Lie	1965	20.00
❑ CL 2501 [M]	Man with a Plan	1966	20.00
❑ CL 2579 [10]	Carl Smith	1955	100.00
❑ CL 2610 [M]	The Country Gentleman	1967	20.00
❑ CL 2687 [M]	The Country Gentleman Sings His Favorites	1967	25.00
❑ CL 2822 [M]	Deep Water	1968	30.00
❑ CL 2888 [M]	Country on My Mind	1968	50.00
❑ CS 8352 [S]	The Carl Smith Touch	1960	30.00
❑ CS 8540 [S]	Easy to Please	1961	30.00
❑ CS 8737 [S]	Carl Smith's Greatest Hits	1962	25.00
❑ CS 8891 [S]	The Tall, Tall Gentleman	1963	25.00
❑ CS 8973 [S]	There Stands the Glass	1964	25.00
❑ CL 9023 [10]	Sentimental Songs	195?	100.00
❑ CL 9026 [10]	Softly and Tenderly	195?	80.00
❑ CS 9093 [S]	I Want to Live and Love	1965	25.00
❑ CS 9158 [S]	Kisses Don't Lie	1965	25.00
❑ CS 9301 [S]	Man with a Plan	1966	25.00
❑ CS 9410 [S]	The Country Gentleman	1967	25.00
❑ CS 9487 [S]	The Country Gentleman Sings His Favorites	1967	20.00
❑ CS 9622 [S]	Deep Water	1968	20.00
❑ CS 9688 [S]	Country on My Mind	1968	20.00

Except when noted otherwise, VG = 25% of NM, and VG+ = 50% of NM. (Example: VG = $2.00, VG+ = $4.00 and NM = $8.00.)

Number	Title (A Side/B Side)	Yr	NM
❑ CS 9786	Faded Love and Winter Roses	1969	20.00
❑ CS 9807	Carl Smith's Greatest Hits, Vol. 2	1969	20.00
❑ CS 9870	Carl Smith Sings a Tribute to Roy Acuff	1969	20.00
❑ CS 9898	I Love You Because	1970	20.00
❑ C 30215	Carl Smith with the Tunesmiths	1970	20.00
❑ C 30548	Bluegrass	1971	20.00
❑ C 31277	Don't Say You're Mine	1972	20.00
❑ KC 31606	If This Is Goodbye	1972	20.00
❑ FC 38906	Carl Smith	198?	10.00

HICKORY/MGM

Number	Title (A Side/B Side)	Yr	NM
❑ H3G 4518	The Way I Lose My Mind	1975	12.00
❑ H3G 4522	The Girl I Love	1975	12.00

ROUNDER

Number	Title (A Side/B Side)	Yr	NM
❑ SS-25	Old Lonesome Times	1988	10.00

SMITH, CARL; LEFTY FRIZZELL; MARTY ROBBINS

Albums

COLUMBIA

Number	Title (A Side/B Side)	Yr	NM
❑ CL 2544 [10]	Carl, Lefty and Marty	1955	400.00

SMITH, HUEY "PIANO"

45s

ACE

Number	Title (A Side/B Side)	Yr	NM
❑ 521	Everybody's Wailin'/Little Liza Jane	1956	25.00
❑ 530	Rockin' Pneumonia and the Boogie Woogie Flu (Part 1/Part 2)	1957	30.00
❑ 538	Free, Single and Disengaged/Just a Lonely Clown	1957	25.00
❑ 545	Don't You Just Know It/High Blood Pressure	1958	25.00
❑ 548	Havin' a Good Time/We Like Birdland	1958	25.00
❑ 553	Don't You Know Yockomo/Well, I'll Be John Brown	1958	25.00
❑ 562	Would You Believe It (I Have a Cold)/Genevieve	1959	20.00
❑ 571	Tu-Ber-Cu-Lucas and the Sinus Blues/Dearest Darling	1959	20.00
❑ 584	Beatnik Blues/For Cryin' Out Loud	1960	15.00
❑ 638	She Got Low Down/Mean, Mean, Mean	1961	15.00
❑ 639	She Got Low Down/Mean, Mean, Mean//Little Liza Jane/Rockin' Pnuemonia	1961	25.00
❑ 649	Pop-Eye/Scald Dog	1962	15.00
❑ 672	Every Once in a While/Somebody Told It	1962	12.00
❑ 8002	Talk to Me Baby/If It Ain't One Thing, It's Another	1962	12.00
❑ 8008	Let's Bring 'Em Back Again/Quiet as It's Kept	1963	15.00

CONSTELLATION

Number	Title (A Side/B Side)	Yr	NM
❑ 102	He's Back Again/Quiet As It's Kept	1963	10.00

COTILLION

Number	Title (A Side/B Side)	Yr	NM
❑ 44142	Rockin' Pneumonia and the Boogie Woogie Flu (Part 1/Part 2)	1971	6.00

IMPERIAL

Number	Title (A Side/B Side)	Yr	NM
❑ 5721	The Little Moron/Someone to Love	1961	12.00
❑ 5747	Behind the Wheel — Part 1/Behind the Wheel — Part 2	1961	12.00
❑ 5772	More Girls/Sassy Sara	1961	12.00
❑ 5789	Don't Knock It/Shag-a-Tooth	1961	12.00

INSTANT

Number	Title (A Side/B Side)	Yr	NM
❑ 3287	I'll Never Forget/Bury Me Dead	1967	8.00
❑ 3297	Two Way Pockaway (Part 1)/Two Way Pockaway (Part 2)	1969	8.00
❑ 3301	Epitaph of Uncle Tom/Eight Bars of Amen	1969	8.00
❑ 3303	You Got Too (Part 1)/You Got Too (Part 2)	1969	8.00
❑ 3305	Ballad of a Black Man/The Whatcha Call 'Em	1970	8.00

SAVOY

Number	Title (A Side/B Side)	Yr	NM
❑ 1113	You Made Me Cry/You're Down with Me	1953	100.00

VIN

Number	Title (A Side/B Side)	Yr	NM
❑ 1024	I Didn't Do It/They Kept On	1960	15.00

Albums

ACE

Number	Title (A Side/B Side)	Yr	NM
❑ LP-1004 [M]	Having a Good Time	1959	400.00
❑ LP-1015 [M]	For Dancing	1961	250.00
❑ LP-1027 [M]	'Twas the Night Before Christmas	1962	250.00
❑ LP-1027 [M]	'Twas the Night Before Christmas	198?	15.00
—Reissue with "Dr. John Band" credited on front cover and label			
❑ LP-2021	Rock 'N' Roll Revival	197?	30.00
❑ 2038	Good Old Rock & Roll	198?	15.00

GRAND PRIX

Number	Title (A Side/B Side)	Yr	NM
❑ K-418 [M]	Huey "Piano" Smith	196?	20.00
❑ KS-418 [R]	Huey "Piano" Smith	196?	12.00

RHINO

Number	Title (A Side/B Side)	Yr	NM
❑ RNLP-70222	Serious Clownin': The History of Huey "Piano" Smith and the Clowns	1986	12.00

SMITH, HURRICANE

45s

CAPITOL

Number	Title (A Side/B Side)	Yr	NM
❑ 3148	Don't Let It Die/The Writer Sings His Song	1971	5.00
❑ 3383	Oh Babe, What Would You Say?/Getting to Know You	1972	4.00
—Orange label with "Capitol" at bottom			
❑ 3383	Oh Babe, What Would You Say?/Getting to Know You	1972	6.00
—Red and orange "target" label			
❑ 3455	Who Was It?/Take Suki Home	1972	4.00

EMI

Number	Title (A Side/B Side)	Yr	NM
❑ 3809	Beautiful Day-Beautiful Night/Sam	1973	4.00

Albums

CAPITOL

Number	Title (A Side/B Side)	Yr	NM
❑ ST-11139	Hurricane Smith	1972	10.00

SMITH, JIMMY

45s

BLUE NOTE

Number	Title (A Side/B Side)	Yr	NM
❑ 1635	High and Mighty/You Get Cha	195?	12.00
❑ 1636	The Preacher/Midnight Sun	195?	12.00
❑ 1637	Tenderly/Joy	195?	12.00
❑ 1641	The Champ (Part 1)/The Champ (Part 2)	195?	12.00
❑ 1642	Bubbis/Bayou	195?	12.00
❑ 1643	Judo Mambo/Autumn Leaves	195?	12.00
❑ 1644	Willow Weep for Me/Fiddlin' the Minors	195?	12.00
❑ 1652	I Cover the Waterfront/I Can't Give You Anything	195?	12.00
❑ 1660	New Preacher (Part 1)/New Preacher (Part 2)	195?	12.00
❑ 1665	Where or When (Part 1)/Where or When (Part 2)	195?	12.00
❑ 1666	Love Is a Many-Splendored Thing (Part 1)/Love Is a Many-Splendored Thing (Part 2)	195?	12.00
❑ 1667	How High the Moon/Summertime	195?	12.00
❑ 1668	Plum Nellie/I'm Getting Sentimental	195?	12.00
❑ 1676	All Day Long (Part 1)/All Day Long (Part 2)	195?	12.00
❑ 1677	Funk's Oasis (Part 1)/Funk's Oasis (Part 2)	195?	12.00
❑ 1682	I Can't Get Started/Penthouse Serenade	195?	12.00
❑ 1683	East of the Sun/The Very Thought of You	195?	12.00
❑ 1685	Blue Moon (Part 1)/Blue Moon (Part 2)	195?	12.00
❑ 1686	There'll Never Be Another You/Jitterbug Waltz	195?	12.00
❑ 1703	After Hours (Part 1)/After Hours (Part 2)	195?	12.00
❑ 1704	Just Friends/Lover Man	195?	12.00
❑ 1711	The Swingin' Shepherd Blues/Cha Cha J.	195?	12.00
❑ 1727	Ain't No Use/Angel Eyes	195?	12.00
—With Bill Henderson			
❑ 1728	Ain't That Love/Willow Weep for Me	195?	12.00
—With Bill Henderson			
❑ 1765	Makin' Whoopee/What's New	196?	10.00
❑ 1766	Mack the Knife/When Johnny Comes Marching Home	196?	10.00
❑ 1767	Alfredo/I Got a Woman	196?	10.00
❑ 1768	Come On Baby/See See Rider	196?	10.00
❑ 1769	Since I Fell for You/Motorin' Along	196?	10.00
—With Kenny Burrell			
❑ 1819	Midnight Special (Part 1)/Midnight Special (Part 2)	1962	10.00
❑ 1820	Jumpin' the Blues/One O'Clock Blues	1962	10.00
❑ 1851	Ain't She Sweet/Everybody Loves My Baby	1962	10.00
❑ 1852	Honeysuckle Rose/Lulu's Back in Town	1962	10.00
❑ 1877	Back at the Chicken Shack (Part 1)/Back at the Chicken Shack (Part 2)	1963	10.00
❑ 1878	Minor Chant (Part 1)/Minor Chant (Part 2)	1963	10.00
❑ 1879	Sermon (Part 1)/Sermon (Part 2)	1963	10.00
❑ 1904	When My Dreamboat Comes Home (Part 1)/When My Dreamboat Comes Home (Part 2)	1964	10.00
❑ 1905	Matilda, Matilda/Can Heat	1964	10.00
❑ 1906	Pork Chop (Part 1)/Pork Chop (Part 2)	1964	10.00
❑ 1909	Prayer Meetin' (Part 1)/Prayer Meetin' (Part 2)	1964	10.00
❑ 1910	Red Top (Part 1)/Red Top (Part 2)	1964	10.00
❑ 1925	I Cover the Waterfront/I Can't Give You Anything But Love	1966	8.00
❑ 1927	Bucket!/Sassy Mae	1966	8.00

MERCURY

Number	Title (A Side/B Side)	Yr	NM
❑ 73895	Can't Hide Love/No Place in Space	1977	4.00
❑ 73972	I've Got Love on My Mind/Side Mouthin'	1977	4.00

PRIDE

Number	Title (A Side/B Side)	Yr	NM
❑ 7602	Groovin'/Why Can't We Live Together	1974	5.00

VERVE

Number	Title (A Side/B Side)	Yr	NM
❑ CS6-5 [(5)]	Celebrity Scene: Jimmy Smith	1967	60.00
—Box set of five singles (10502-10506). Price includes box, all 5 singles, jukebox title strips, bio. Records are sometimes found by themselves, so they are also listed separately.			
❑ 10255	Walk on the Wild Side (Part 1)/Walk on the Wild Side (Part 2)	1962	8.00
❑ 10262	Ol' Man River/Bashin'	1962	8.00
❑ 10278	Step Right Up (Part 1)/Step Right Up (Part 2)	1963	8.00
❑ 10283	Hobo Flats (Part 1)/Hobo Flats (Part 2)	1963	8.00
❑ 10298	Blueberry Hill/Walk Right In	1963	8.00
❑ 10299	Theme from "Any Number Can Win"/What'd I Say	1963	8.00
❑ 10314	Who's Afraid of Virginia Woolf?/Who's Afraid of Virginia Woolf? (Part 2)	1964	8.00
❑ 10330	The Cat/Basin Street Blues	1964	8.00
❑ 10346	Goldfinger (Part 1)/Goldfinger (Part 2)	1965	8.00
❑ 10363	The Organ Grinder's Swing/I'll Close My Eyes	1965	8.00
—With Kenny Burrell and Grady Tate			
❑ 10382	Theme from "Where the Spies Are"/Slow Theme from "Where the Spies Are"	1966	8.00
❑ 10393	Got My Mojo Working (Part 1)/Got My Mojo Working (Part 2)	1966	8.00
❑ 10424	Who Do You Love (Part 1)/Who Do You Love (Part 2)	1966	8.00
❑ 10467	Cat in a Tree (Part 1)/Cat in a Tree (Part 2)	1966	8.00
❑ 10502 [DJ]	Walk on the Wild Side (Part 1)/Walk on the Wild Side (Part 2)	1967	10.00
❑ 10503 [DJ]	The Cat/Basin Street Blues	1967	10.00
❑ 10504 [DJ]	Got My Mojo Working (Part 1)/Got My Mojo Working (Part 2)	1967	10.00
❑ 10504 [DJ]	Got My Mojo Working (Part 1)/Got My Mojo Working (Part 2)	1967	10.00
❑ 10505 [DJ]	I'm Your Hoochie Coochie Man (Part 1)/I'm Your Hoochie Coochie Man (Part 2)	1967	10.00
❑ 10506 [DJ]	Cat in a Tree (Part 1)/Cat in a Tree (Part 2)	1967	10.00
❑ 10506 [DJ]	Cat in a Tree (Part 1)/Cat in a Tree (Part 2)	1967	10.00
❑ 10536	Respect/Funky Broadway	1967	8.00
❑ 10583	Chain of Fools (Part 1)/Chain of Fools (Part 2)	1968	8.00
❑ 10623	Mission: Impossible/Gentle Rain	1968	8.00
❑ 10652	Groove Drops/By the Time I Get to Phoenix	1970	6.00
❑ 10660	One Bad Apple/Theme from "The Night Visitor"	1971	6.00
❑ 10668	Jimmy Smith Is a Midnight Cowboy/Recession or Depression	1971	6.00
❑ 10672	For Everyone Under the Sun/Sag' Shootin' His Arrow	1972	6.00
❑ 10695	Lolita/Straight Ahead	1972	6.00
❑ 10724	And I Love You So/Ritual (Funky 5/4)	1973	6.00

Albums

BLUE NOTE

Number	Title (A Side/B Side)	Yr	NM
❑ BN-LA400-H2 [(2)]	Jimmy Smith	1975	15.00
❑ LT-992	Confirmation	1979	10.00
❑ LT-1054	Cool Blues	1980	10.00
❑ LT-1092	On the Sunny Side	1981	10.00
❑ BLP-1512 [M]	Jimmy Smith at the Organ, Vol. 1	1956	100.00
—Regular edition, Lexington Ave. address on label			
❑ BLP-1512 [M]	Jimmy Smith at the Organ, Vol. 1	1956	150.00
—"Deep groove" version (deep indentation under label on both sides)			
❑ BLP-1512 [M]	Jimmy Smith at the Organ, Vol. 1	1963	25.00
—With New York, USA address on label			

S

Number	Title (A Side/B Side)	Yr	NM
❑ BLP-1514 [M]	Jimmy Smith at the Organ, Vol. 2	1956	100.00
—Regular edition, Lexington Ave. address on label			
❑ BLP-1514 [M]	Jimmy Smith at the Organ, Vol. 2	1956	150.00
—"Deep groove" version (deep indentation under label on both sides)			
❑ BLP-1514 [M]	Jimmy Smith at the Organ, Vol. 2	1963	25.00
—With New York, USA address on label			
❑ BLP-1525 [M]	The Incredible Jimmy Smith at the Organ, Vol. 3	1956	100.00
—Regular edition, Lexington Ave. address on label			
❑ BLP-1525 [M]	The Incredible Jimmy Smith at the Organ, Vol. 3	1956	150.00
—"Deep groove" version (deep indentation under label on both sides)			
❑ BLP-1525 [M]	The Incredible Jimmy Smith at the Organ, Vol. 3	1963	25.00
—With New York, USA address on label			
❑ BLP-1528 [M]	The Incredible Jimmy Smith at Club Baby Grand, Wilmington, Delaware, Vol. 1	1956	100.00
—Regular edition, Lexington Ave. address on label			
❑ BLP-1528 [M]	The Incredible Jimmy Smith at Club Baby Grand, Wilmington, Delaware, Vol. 1	1956	150.00
—"Deep groove" version (deep indentation under label on both sides)			
❑ BLP-1528 [M]	The Incredible Jimmy Smith at Club Baby Grand, Wilmington, Delaware, Vol. 1	1963	25.00
—With New York, USA address on label			
❑ BLP-1529 [M]	The Incredible Jimmy Smith at Club Baby Grand, Wilmington, Delaware, Vol. 2	1956	100.00
—Regular edition, Lexington Ave. address on label			
❑ BLP-1529 [M]	The Incredible Jimmy Smith at Club Baby Grand, Wilmington, Delaware, Vol. 2	1956	150.00
—"Deep groove" version (deep indentation under label on both sides)			
❑ BLP-1529 [M]	The Incredible Jimmy Smith at Club Baby Grand, Wilmington, Delaware, Vol. 2	1963	25.00
—With New York, USA address on label			
❑ BLP-1547 [M]	A Date with Jimmy Smith, Vol. 1	1957	80.00
—Regular edition, W. 63rd St. address on label			
❑ BLP-1547 [M]	A Date with Jimmy Smith, Vol. 1	1957	120.00
—"Deep groove" version (deep indentation under label on both sides)			
❑ BLP-1547 [M]	A Date with Jimmy Smith, Vol. 1	1963	25.00
—With New York, USA address on label			
❑ BLP-1548 [M]	A Date with Jimmy Smith, Vol. 2	1957	80.00
—Regular edition, W. 63rd St. address on label			
❑ BLP-1548 [M]	A Date with Jimmy Smith, Vol. 2	1957	120.00
—"Deep groove" version (deep indentation under label on both sides)			
❑ BLP-1548 [M]	A Date with Jimmy Smith, Vol. 2	1963	25.00
—With New York, USA address on label			
❑ BLP-1551 [M]	Jimmy Smith at the Organ, Vol. 1	1957	80.00
—Regular edition, W. 63rd St. address on label			
❑ BLP-1551 [M]	Jimmy Smith at the Organ, Vol. 1	1957	120.00
—"Deep groove" version (deep indentation under label on both sides)			
❑ BLP-1551 [M]	Jimmy Smith at the Organ, Vol. 1	1963	25.00
—With New York, USA address on label			
❑ BLP-1552 [M]	Jimmy Smith at the Organ, Vol. 2	1957	80.00
—Regular edition, W. 63rd St. address on label			
❑ BLP-1552 [M]	Jimmy Smith at the Organ, Vol. 2	1957	120.00
—"Deep groove" version (deep indentation under label on both sides)			
❑ BLP-1552 [M]	Jimmy Smith at the Organ, Vol. 2	1963	25.00
—With New York, USA address on label			
❑ BLP-1556 [M]	The Sounds of Jimmy Smith	1957	80.00
—Regular edition, W. 63rd St. address on label			
❑ BLP-1556 [M]	The Sounds of Jimmy Smith	1957	120.00
—"Deep groove" version (deep indentation under label on both sides)			
❑ BLP-1556 [M]	The Sounds of Jimmy Smith	1963	25.00
—With New York, USA address on label			
❑ BLP-1563 [M]	Jimmy Smith Plays Pretty Just for You	1957	80.00
—Regular edition, W. 63rd St. address on label			
❑ BLP-1563 [M]	Jimmy Smith Plays Pretty Just for You	1957	120.00
—"Deep groove" version (deep indentation under label on both sides)			
❑ BLP-1563 [M]	Jimmy Smith Plays Pretty Just for You	1963	25.00
—With New York, USA address on label			
❑ BST-1563 [S]	Jimmy Smith Plays Pretty Just for You	1959	50.00
—Regular edition, W. 63rd St. address on label			
❑ BST-1563 [S]	Jimmy Smith Plays Pretty Just for You	1959	80.00
—"Deep groove" version (deep indentation under label on both sides)			
❑ BST-1563 [S]	Jimmy Smith Plays Pretty Just for You	1963	20.00
—With New York, USA address on label			
❑ BLP-1585 [M]	Groovin' at Small's Paradise, Vol. 1	1958	80.00
—Regular edition, W. 63rd St. address on label			
❑ BLP-1585 [M]	Groovin' at Small's Paradise, Vol. 1	1958	120.00
—"Deep groove" version (deep indentation under label on both sides)			
❑ BLP-1585 [M]	Groovin' at Small's Paradise, Vol. 1	1963	25.00
—With New York, USA address on label			
❑ BST-1585 [S]	Groovin' at Small's Paradise, Vol. 1	1959	50.00
—Regular edition, W. 63rd St. address on label			
❑ BST-1585 [S]	Groovin' at Small's Paradise, Vol. 1	1959	80.00
—"Deep groove" version (deep indentation under label on both sides)			
❑ BST-1585 [S]	Groovin' at Small's Paradise, Vol. 1	1963	20.00
—With New York, USA address on label			
❑ BLP-1586 [M]	Groovin' at Small's Paradise, Vol. 2	1958	80.00
—Regular edition, W. 63rd St. address on label			
❑ BLP-1586 [M]	Groovin' at Small's Paradise, Vol. 2	1958	120.00
—"Deep groove" version (deep indentation under label on both sides)			
❑ BLP-1586 [M]	Groovin' at Small's Paradise, Vol. 2	1963	25.00
—With New York, USA address on label			
❑ BST-1586 [S]	Groovin' at Small's Paradise, Vol. 2	1959	50.00
—Regular edition, W. 63rd St. address on label			
❑ BST-1586 [S]	Groovin' at Small's Paradise, Vol. 2	1959	80.00
—"Deep groove" version (deep indentation under label on both sides)			
❑ BST-1586 [S]	Groovin' at Small's Paradise, Vol. 2	1963	20.00
—With New York, USA address on label			
❑ BLP-4002 [M]	House Party	1959	80.00
—Regular edition, W. 63rd St. address on label			
❑ BLP-4002 [M]	House Party	1959	120.00
—"Deep groove" version (deep indentation under label on both sides)			
❑ BLP-4002 [M]	House Party	1963	25.00
—With New York, USA address on label			
❑ BST-4002 [S]	House Party	1959	50.00
—Regular edition, W. 63rd St. address on label			
❑ BST-4002 [S]	House Party	1959	80.00
—"Deep groove" version (deep indentation under label on both sides)			
❑ BST-4002 [S]	House Party	1963	20.00
—With New York, USA address on label			
❑ BLP-4011 [M]	The Sermon	1959	80.00
—Regular edition, W. 63rd St. address on label			
❑ BLP-4011 [M]	The Sermon	1959	120.00
—"Deep groove" version (deep indentation under label on both sides)			
❑ BLP-4011 [M]	The Sermon	1963	25.00
—With New York, USA address on label			
❑ BST-4011 [S]	The Sermon	1959	50.00
—Regular edition, W. 63rd St. address on label			
❑ BST-4011 [S]	The Sermon	1959	80.00
—"Deep groove" version (deep indentation under label on both sides)			
❑ BST-4011 [S]	The Sermon	1963	20.00
—With New York, USA address on label			
❑ BLP-4030 [M]	Crazy Baby	1960	80.00
—Regular edition, W. 63rd St. address on label			
❑ BLP-4030 [M]	Crazy Baby	1960	120.00
—"Deep groove" version (deep indentation under label on both sides)			
❑ BLP-4030 [M]	Crazy Baby	1963	25.00
—With New York, USA address on label			
❑ BLP-4050 [M]	Home Cookin'	1961	50.00
—With W. 63rd St. address on label			
❑ BLP-4050 [M]	Home Cookin'	1963	20.00
—With New York, USA address on label			
❑ BLP-4078 [M]	Midnight Special	1961	50.00
—With 61st St. address on label			
❑ BLP-4078 [M]	Midnight Special	1963	20.00
—With New York, USA address on label			
❑ BLP-4100 [M]	Jimmy Smith Plays Fats Waller	1962	50.00
—With 61st St. address on label			
❑ BLP-4100 [M]	Jimmy Smith Plays Fats Waller	1963	20.00
—With New York, USA address on label			
❑ BLP-4117 [M]	Back at the Chicken Shack	1963	25.00
❑ BLP-4141 [M]	Rockin' the Boat	1963	25.00
❑ BLP-4164 [M]	Prayer Meetin'	1964	25.00
❑ BLP-4200 [M]	Softly as a Summer Breeze	1965	25.00
❑ BLP-4235 [M]	Bucket!	1966	25.00
❑ BLP-4255 [M]	I'm Movin' On	1967	30.00
❑ BST-81512 [R]	Jimmy Smith at the Organ, Vol. 1	1967	12.00
❑ BST-81514 [R]	Jimmy Smith at the Organ, Vol. 2	1967	12.00
❑ BST-81525 [R]	The Incredible Jimmy Smith at the Organ, Vol. 3	1967	12.00
❑ BST-81528 [R]	The Incredible Jimmy Smith at Club Baby Grand, Wilmington, Delaware, Vol. 1	1967	12.00
❑ BST-81529 [R]	The Incredible Jimmy Smith at Club Baby Grand, Wilmington, Delaware, Vol. 2	1967	12.00
❑ BST-81547 [R]	A Date with Jimmy Smith, Vol. 1	1967	12.00
❑ BST-81548 [R]	A Date with Jimmy Smith, Vol. 2	1967	12.00
❑ BST-81551 [R]	Jimmy Smith at the Organ, Vol. 1	1967	12.00
❑ BST-81552 [R]	Jimmy Smith at the Organ, Vol. 2	1967	12.00
❑ BST-81556 [R]	The Sounds of Jimmy Smith	1967	12.00
❑ BST-81563 [S]	Jimmy Smith Plays Pretty Just for You	1967	15.00
❑ BST-81585 [S]	Groovin' at Small's Paradise, Vol. 1	1967	15.00
❑ BST-81586 [S]	Groovin' at Small's Paradise, Vol. 1	1967	15.00
❑ BST-84002	House Party	1985	10.00
—"The Finest in Jazz Since 1939" reissue			
❑ BST-84002 [S]	House Party	1967	15.00
❑ BST-84011 [S]	The Sermon	1967	15.00
❑ B1-84030	Crazy Baby	1988	10.00
—"The Finest in Jazz Since 1939" reissue			
❑ BST-84030 [S]	Crazy Baby	1960	50.00
—With W. 63rd St. address on label			
❑ BST-84030 [S]	Crazy Baby	1963	20.00
—With New York, USA address on label			
❑ BST-84030 [S]	Crazy Baby	1967	15.00
—With "A Division of Liberty Records" on label			
❑ BST-84050 [S]	Home Cookin'	1961	50.00
—With W. 63rd St. address on label			
❑ BST-84050 [S]	Home Cookin'	1963	20.00
—With New York, USA address on label			
❑ BST-84050 [S]	Home Cookin'	1967	15.00
—With "A Division of Liberty Records" on label			
❑ B1-84078	Midnight Special	1989	10.00
—"The Finest in Jazz Since 1939" reissue			
❑ BST-84078 [S]	Midnight Special	1961	50.00
—With 61st St. address on label			
❑ BST-84078 [S]	Midnight Special	1963	20.00
—With New York, USA address on label			
❑ BST-84078 [S]	Midnight Special	1967	15.00
—With "A Division of Liberty Records" on label			
❑ BST-84100 [S]	Jimmy Smith Plays Fats Waller	1962	50.00
—With 61st St. address on label			
❑ BST-84100 [S]	Jimmy Smith Plays Fats Waller	1963	20.00
—With New York, USA address on label			
❑ BST-84100 [S]	Jimmy Smith Plays Fats Waller	1967	15.00
—With "A Division of Liberty Records" on label			
❑ BST-84117	Back at the Chicken Shack	1985	10.00
—"The Finest in Jazz Since 1939" reissue			
❑ BST-84117 [S]	Back at the Chicken Shack	1963	30.00
—With New York, USA address on label			
❑ BST-84117 [S]	Back at the Chicken Shack	1967	15.00
—With "A Division of Liberty Records" on label			
❑ BST-84141 [S]	Rockin' the Boat	1963	30.00
—With New York, USA address on label			
❑ BST-84141 [S]	Rockin' the Boat	1967	15.00
—With "A Division of Liberty Records" on label			
❑ B1-84164	Prayer Meetin'	1988	10.00
—"The Finest in Jazz Since 1939" reissue			
❑ BST-84164 [S]	Prayer Meetin'	1964	30.00
—With New York, USA address on label			
❑ BST-84164 [S]	Prayer Meetin'	1967	15.00
—With "A Division of Liberty Records" on label			
❑ BST-84200 [S]	Softly as a Summer Breeze	1965	30.00
—With New York, USA address on label			
❑ BST-84200 [S]	Softly as a Summer Breeze	1967	15.00
—With "A Division of Liberty Records" on label			
❑ BST-84235 [S]	Bucket!	1966	30.00
—With New York, USA address on label			
❑ BST-84235 [S]	Bucket!	1967	15.00
—With "A Division of Liberty Records" on label			
❑ BST-84255 [S]	I'm Movin' On	1967	20.00
❑ BST-84269	Open House	1968	20.00
❑ BST-84296	Plain Talk	1969	20.00
❑ B1-85125	Go For Whatcha Know	198?	10.00
❑ BST-89901 [(2)]	Jimmy Smith's Greatest Hits!	1969	25.00
❑ LWB-89901 [(2)]	Jimmy Smith's Greatest Hits!	198?	15.00
❑ B1-91140	The Best of Jimmy Smith	1988	10.00
ELEKTRA/MUSICIAN			
❑ 60175	Off the Top	1983	10.00
❑ 60301	Keep On Comin'	1984	10.00
GUEST STAR			
❑ 1344 [M]	Jimmy Smith	196?	12.00
❑ G 1914 [M]	Jimmy Smith	196?	12.00
INNER CITY			
❑ 1121	The Cat Strikes Again	1981	10.00
MERCURY			
❑ SRM-1-1127	Sit On It!	1976	10.00
❑ SRM-1-1189	It's Necessary	1977	10.00
❑ SRM-1-3716	Unfinished Business	1978	10.00
METRO			
❑ M-521 [M]	Jimmy Smith at the Village Gate	1965	12.00
❑ MS-521 [S]	Jimmy Smith at the Village Gate	1965	12.00
❑ M-568 [M]	Live In Concert/The Incredible Jimmy Smith	196?	12.00
❑ M-568 [S]	Live In Concert/The Incredible Jimmy Smith	196?	12.00
MGM			
❑ GAS-107	Jimmy Smith (Golden Archive Series)	1970	15.00
❑ SE-4709	The Other Side	1970	12.00
❑ SE-4751	I'm Gon' Git Myself Together	1971	12.00
MILESTONE			
❑ M-9176	Prime Time	198?	10.00
MOSAIC			
❑ MQ5-154 [(5)]	The Complete February 1957 Jimmy Smith Blue Note Sessions	199?	80.00
PICKWICK			
❑ SPC-3023	Stranger in Paradise	196?	10.00
PRIDE			
❑ 6011	Black Smith	1974	12.00
SUNSET			
❑ SUM-1175 [M]	Jimmy Smith Plays the Standards	1967	15.00
❑ SUS-5175 [S]	Jimmy Smith Plays the Standards	1967	12.00
❑ SUS-5316	Just Friends	1971	12.00

S

Except when noted otherwise, VG = 25% of NM, and VG+ = 50% of NM. (Example: VG = \$2.00, VG+ = \$4.00 and NM = \$8.00.)

VERVE

Number	Title (A Side/B Side)	Yr	NM
❑ V6-652-2 [(2)]	24 Karat Hits	196?	15.00
❑ UMV-2073	Organ Grinder Swing	198?	10.00
—Reissue of 8628			
❑ V-8474 [M]	Bashin'	1962	20.00
❑ V6-8474 [S]	Bashin'	1962	25.00
❑ V-8544 [M]	Hobo Flats	1963	20.00
❑ V6-8544 [S]	Hobo Flats	1963	25.00
❑ V-8552 [M]	Any Number Can Win	1963	20.00
❑ V6-8552 [S]	Any Number Can Win	1963	25.00
❑ V-8583 [M]	Who's Afraid of Virginia Woolf?	1964	20.00
❑ V6-8583 [S]	Who's Afraid of Virginia Woolf?	1964	25.00
❑ V-8587 [M]	The Cat	1964	20.00
❑ V6-8587 [S]	The Cat	1964	25.00
❑ V-8604 [M]	Christmas '64	1964	20.00
❑ V6-8604 [S]	Christmas '64	1964	25.00
❑ V-8618 [M]	The Monster	1965	15.00
❑ V6-8618 [S]	The Monster	1965	20.00
❑ V-8628 [M]	Organ Grinder Swing	1965	15.00
❑ V6-8628 [S]	Organ Grinder Swing	1965	20.00
❑ V-8641 [M]	Got My Mojo Workin'	1966	15.00
❑ V6-8641 [S]	Got My Mojo Workin'	1966	20.00
❑ V-8652 [M]	Peter and the Wolf	1966	20.00
❑ V6-8652 [S]	Peter and the Wolf	1966	25.00
❑ V-8666 [M]	Christmas Cookin'	1966	20.00
❑ V6-8666 [S]	Christmas Cookin'	1966	25.00
❑ V-8667 [M]	Hoochie Coochie Man	1966	15.00
❑ V6-8667 [S]	Hoochie Coochie Man	1966	20.00
❑ V-8705 [M]	Respect	1967	20.00
❑ V6-8705 [S]	Respect	1967	15.00
❑ V-8721 [M]	The Best of Jimmy Smith	1967	20.00
❑ V6-8721 [S]	The Best of Jimmy Smith	1967	15.00
❑ V6-8745 [S]	Stay Loose	1968	15.00
❑ V6-8750	Livin' It Up!	1968	15.00
❑ V6-8770	The Boss	1969	15.00
❑ V6-8794	Groove Drops	1970	15.00
❑ V6-8800	Plain Brown Wrapper	1971	12.00
❑ V6-8806	Root Down	1972	12.00
❑ V6-8809	Bluesmith	1973	12.00
❑ V6-8814 [(2)]	History of Jimmy Smith	1973	15.00
❑ V6-8832	Portuguese Soul	1974	12.00
❑ SMAS-90643 [S]	The Monster	1965	25.00
—Capitol Record Club edition			
❑ MAS-90751 [M]	Got My Mojo Workin'	1966	20.00
—Capitol Record Club edition			
❑ SMAS-90751 [S]	Got My Mojo Workin'	1966	25.00
❑ 823308-1	Bashin'	1986	10.00
—Reissue of 8474			

SMITH, JIMMY, AND WES MONTGOMERY

Albums

VERVE

Number	Title (A Side/B Side)	Yr	NM
❑ UMV-2069	Jimmy and Wes, The Dynamic Duo	198?	10.00
—Reissue of 8678			
❑ V-8678 [M]	Jimmy and Wes, The Dynamic Duo	1967	20.00
❑ V6-8678 [S]	Jimmy and Wes, The Dynamic Duo	1967	15.00
❑ V6-8766	The Further Adventures of Jimmy Smith and Wes Montgomery	1969	15.00

SMITH, JOHNNY "HAMMOND" See JOHNNY HAMMOND.

SMITH, LENDON, AND THE JESTERS

45s

METEOR

Number	Title (A Side/B Side)	Yr	NM
❑ 5030	Women/Lost Love	1956	150.00

SMITH, LEON

45s

EPIC

Number	Title (A Side/B Side)	Yr	NM
❑ 9326	Little 40 Ford/Cry All the Time	1959	40.00

LAVENDER

Number	Title (A Side/B Side)	Yr	NM
❑ 1851	Basic Surf/Jailer, Bring Me Water	196?	30.00

WILLIAMETTE

Number	Title (A Side/B Side)	Yr	NM
❑ 101	Little 40 Ford/Once I Had a Heart	1959	120.00
❑ 105	Honey Honey/That's the Way	1959	30.00
❑ 109	Flip, Flop and Fly/Sweet Love	1960	30.00

SMITH, LONNIE

12-Inch Singles

T.K. DISCO

Number	Title (A Side/B Side)	Yr	NM
❑ TKD-78	For the Love of It (7:03)/ Funk Reaction (5:50)	1978	12.00

45s

BLUE NOTE

Number	Title (A Side/B Side)	Yr	NM
❑ 1945	Think/Son of Ice Bag	1969	6.00
❑ 1955	Soul Talk (Part 1)/ Soul Talk (Part 2)	1969	6.00

GROOVE MERCHANT

Number	Title (A Side/B Side)	Yr	NM
❑ 1034	Afro-Desia (Part 1)/ Afro-Desia (Part 2)	1975	4.00
❑ 1037	Keep On Lovin'/Lean Meat	1976	4.00

Albums

BLUE NOTE

Number	Title (A Side/B Side)	Yr	NM
❑ B1-28266	Drives	1994	15.00
❑ B1-31249	Move Your Hand	1996	15.00
❑ B1-31880	Live at Club Mozambique	1995	15.00
❑ BST-84290	Think!	1968	20.00
❑ BST-84313	Turning Point	1969	20.00
❑ BST-84326	Move Your Hand	1970	15.00
❑ BST-84351	Drives	1971	15.00

CHIAROSCURO

Number	Title (A Side/B Side)	Yr	NM
❑ 2019	When the Night Is Right	1979	12.00

COLUMBIA

Number	Title (A Side/B Side)	Yr	NM
❑ CL 2696 [M]	Finger-Lickin' Good Soul Organ	1967	25.00
❑ CS 9496 [S]	Finger-Lickin' Good Soul Organ	1967	20.00

GROOVE MERCHANT

Number	Title (A Side/B Side)	Yr	NM
❑ 3308	Afro-Desia	1975	12.00
❑ 3312	Keep On Lovin'	1976	12.00

KUDU

Number	Title (A Side/B Side)	Yr	NM
❑ 02	Mama Wailer	1972	12.00

SMITH, LONNIE LISTON

12-Inch Singles

COLUMBIA

Number	Title (A Side/B Side)	Yr	NM
❑ 01882	Space Princess (7:01)/ Quiet Moments	1979	10.00

DOCTOR JAZZ

Number	Title (A Side/B Side)	Yr	NM
❑ 04624	If You Take Care of Me (2 versions)/Silhouettes	1984	6.00

STARTRAK

Number	Title (A Side/B Side)	Yr	NM
❑ P-044	Obsession (# of versions unknown)	1990	6.00
—With Phyllis Hyman			
❑ P-050	Dance Floor (3 versions)	199?	6.00
❑ P-056	Star Flower (3 versions)	199?	6.00

45s

COLUMBIA

Number	Title (A Side/B Side)	Yr	NM
❑ 10747	Journey Into Love/Sunburst	1978	4.00
❑ 10810	Bright Moments/We Can Dream	1978	4.00
❑ 10903	Space Princess/Quiet Moments	1979	4.00
❑ 11057	A Song for the Children/ A Gift of Love	1979	4.00
❑ 11217	Give Peace a Chance (Make Love Not War)/Free and Easy	1980	4.00
❑ 11269	Love Is the Answer/Bridge Through Time	1980	4.00

DOCTOR JAZZ

Number	Title (A Side/B Side)	Yr	NM
❑ 03836	Never Too Late/Divine Light	1983	3.00
❑ 03996	Mystic Woman/A Lonely Way to Be	1983	3.00
❑ 04623	If You Take Care of Me/ Silhouettes	1984	3.00

FLYING DUTCHMAN

Number	Title (A Side/B Side)	Yr	NM
❑ DB-10214	Expansions — Part 1/ Expansions — Part 2	1975	5.00
❑ DB-10392	A Chance for Peace/Sunset	1975	5.00
❑ DB-10616	Goddess of Love/Get Down Everybody (It's Time for World Peace)	1976	5.00
❑ DB-10702	Peace and Love/Quiet Down	1976	5.00

RCA

Number	Title (A Side/B Side)	Yr	NM
❑ PB-10920	Renaissance/Space Lady	1977	5.00

Albums

BLUEBIRD

Number	Title (A Side/B Side)	Yr	NM
❑ 6996-1-RB	Golden Dreams	1988	10.00

COLUMBIA

Number	Title (A Side/B Side)	Yr	NM
❑ JC 35332	Loveland	1978	10.00
❑ JC 35654	Exotic Mysteries	1979	10.00
❑ JC 36141	Song for the Children	1979	10.00
❑ JC 36366	The Best of Lonnie Liston Smith	1980	10.00
❑ JC 36373	Love Is the Answer	1980	10.00

DOCTOR JAZZ

Number	Title (A Side/B Side)	Yr	NM
❑ FW 38447	Dreams of Tomorrow	1983	10.00
❑ FW 39420	Silhouettes	1984	10.00
❑ FW 40063	Rejuvenation	1985	10.00

FLYING DUTCHMAN

Number	Title (A Side/B Side)	Yr	NM
❑ BDL1-0591	Cosmic Funk	1974	12.00
❑ BXL1-0591	Cosmic Funk	1978	8.00
—Reissue with new prefix			
❑ BDL1-0934	Expressions	1975	12.00
❑ BXL1-0934	Expressions	1978	8.00
—Reissue with new prefix			
❑ BDL1-1196	Visions of a New World	1975	12.00
❑ BXL1-1196	Visions of a New World	1978	8.00
—Reissue with new prefix			
❑ BDL1-1460	Reflections of a Golden Dream	1976	12.00
❑ BXL1-1460	Reflections of a Golden Dream	1978	8.00
—Reissue with new prefix			
❑ 10163	Astral Travelling	1973	12.00

RCA VICTOR

Number	Title (A Side/B Side)	Yr	NM
❑ AFL1-1822	Renaissance	1978	8.00
—Reissue with new prefix			
❑ APL1-1822	Renaissance	1976	10.00
❑ AFL1-2433	Live!	1978	8.00
—Reissue with new prefix			
❑ APL1-2433	Live!	1977	10.00
❑ AFL1-2897	The Best of Lonnie Liston Smith	1978	10.00

STARTRAK

Number	Title (A Side/B Side)	Yr	NM
❑ STA-4021	Love Goddess	198?	10.00

SMITH, MARTHA

45s

CAMEO

Number	Title (A Side/B Side)	Yr	NM
❑ 359	As I Watch You Walk Away/It Always Seems Like Summer	1965	40.00

SMITH, O.C.

12-Inch Singles

SHADY BROOK

Number	Title (A Side/B Side)	Yr	NM
❑ SD 12-008	You Thrill Me (5:53)/ Everything's Changed (5:53)	1979	12.00

45s

BIG TOP

Number	Title (A Side/B Side)	Yr	NM
❑ 3039	You Are My Sunshine/ Well I'm Dancin'	1960	12.00
—As "Ocie Smith"			

CADENCE

Number	Title (A Side/B Side)	Yr	NM
❑ 1304	Slow Walk/Forbidden Fruit	1956	15.00
—As "Ocie Smith"			
❑ 1312	If You Don't Love Me/ Bad Man of Missouri	1957	15.00
—As "Ocie Smith"			
❑ 1329	Lighthouse/Too Many	1957	15.00
—As "Ocie Smith"			

CARIBOU

Number	Title (A Side/B Side)	Yr	NM
❑ 9017	Together/Just Couldn't Help Myself	1976	20.00
❑ 9021	Simple Life/Come with Me	1977	5.00

CITATION

Number	Title (A Side/B Side)	Yr	NM
❑ 1034	Try a Little Tenderness/ How Times Have Changed	1958	20.00
—As "Ocie Smith"			

COLUMBIA

Number	Title (A Side/B Side)	Yr	NM
❑ 3-10031	La La Peace Song/ When Morning Comes	1974	6.00
❑ 4-43525	That's Life/I'm Your Man	1966	40.00
❑ 4-43809	On Easy Street/Beyond the Next Hill	1966	200.00
❑ 4-44151	Double Life/The Season	1967	30.00
❑ 4-44425	The Son of Hickory Holler's Tramp/The Best Man	1968	8.00
❑ 4-44555	Main Street Mission/ Gas Food Lodging	1968	8.00
❑ 4-44616	Little Green Apples/Long Black Limousine	1968	8.00
❑ 4-44705	Isn't It Lonely Together/ I Ain't the Worryin' Kind	1968	6.00
❑ 4-44751	Honey (I Miss You)/ Keep On Keepin' On	1969	6.00
❑ 4-44859	Friend, Lover, Woman, Wife/ I Taught Her Everything She Knows	1969	6.00
❑ 4-44948	Daddy's Little Man/ If I Leave You Now	1969	6.00
❑ 4-44948 [PS]	Daddy's Little Man/ If I Leave You Now	1969	8.00
❑ 4-45038	Me and You/Can't Take My Eyes Off You	1969	6.00
❑ 4-45098	Isn't Life Beautiful/Moody	1970	6.00
❑ 4-45160	Primrose Lane/Melodee	1970	6.00
❑ 4-45206	Baby I Need Your Loving/San Francisco Is a Lonely Town	1970	20.00
❑ 4-45301	Downtown U.S.A./That's What Life Is All About	1971	10.00
❑ 4-45343	Clean Up Your Own Back Yard/ I've Been There	1971	6.00
❑ 4-45435	Help Me Make It Through the Night/Diamond in the Rough	1971	6.00
❑ 4-45655	Don't Misunderstand/ If You Touch Me	1972	6.00
❑ 4-45863	La La Peace Song/ When Morning Comes	1973	8.00

FAMILY

Number	Title (A Side/B Side)	Yr	NM
❑ 5000	Dreams Come True/ (B-side unknown)	1980	6.00

MGM

Number	Title (A Side/B Side)	Yr	NM
❑ K12233	Lost Horizon and Shangri-La/ Going, Going, Gone	1956	15.00
—As "Ocie Smith"			
❑ 12321	Just Kiss Me/At Last My Baby's Coming Home	1956	15.00
—As "Ocie Smith"			

S

Number	Title (A Side/B Side)	Yr	NM
MOTOWN			
1623	Love Changes/Got to Know	1982	20.00
1636	I Betcha/That's One for Love	1982	30.00
RENDEZVOUS			
101	What'cha Gonna Do/ Nothing But the Best	1986	5.00
102	You're the First, the Last, My Everything/You Saved Me	1986	10.00
103	Brenda/(Instrumental)	1986	6.00
SHADY BROOK			
1045	Love to Burn/Give Me Time	1978	12.00
1049	Living Without Your Love/Can't Be the One to Say It's Over	1978	6.00
45012	Love Is Forever/(B-side unknown)	197?	5.00
SOUTH BAY			
1003	Love Changes/Got to Know	1982	30.00
TRIUNE			
93-625	After All Is Said and Done/Brenda	1993	8.00

7-Inch Extended Plays

Number	Title (A Side/B Side)	Yr	NM
COLUMBIA			
7-9680	The Son of Hickory Holler's Tramp/Little Green Apples//By the Time I Get to Phoenix/Sitting on the Dock of the Bay	1968	12.00
—Jukebox issue; small hole, plays at 33 1/3 rpm			
7-9680 [PS]	Hickory Holler Revisited	1968	12.00

Albums

Number	Title (A Side/B Side)	Yr	NM
CARIBOU			
PZ 34471	Together	1977	25.00
COLUMBIA			
CL 2714 [M]	The Dynamic O.C. Smith	1967	50.00
CS 9514 [S]	The Dynamic O.C. Smith	1967	30.00
CS 9680 [M]	Hickory Holler Revisited	1968	25.00
—White label promo "Special Mono Radio Station Copy" with stereo number			
CS 9680 [S]	Hickory Holler Revisited	1968	12.00
CS 9756	For Once in My Life	1969	12.00
CS 9908	O.C. Smith at Home	1969	12.00
C 30227	O.C. Smith's Greatest Hits	1970	12.00
C 30664	Help Me Make It Through the Night	1971	20.00
KC 33247	La La Peace Song	1974	20.00
FAMILY			
1000	Dreams Come True	1980	15.00
HARMONY			
KH 30317	O.C. Smith	1971	10.00
MOTOWN			
6019 ML	Love Changes	1982	25.00
RENDEZVOUS			
50006	What'cha Gonna Do	1986	15.00
SHADY BROOK			
SB-012	Love Is Forever	1978	12.00
SOUTH BAY			
SB 1001	Love Changes	1982	30.00

SMITH, OCIE

See O.C. SMITH.

SMITH, PATTI, GROUP

12-Inch Singles

Number	Title (A Side/B Side)	Yr	NM
ARISTA			
SP-62 [DJ]	Frederick (Studio)/Frederick (Live)	1977	15.00
9688	People Have the Power/ Where Duty Calls/Wild Leaves	1988	6.00

45s

Number	Title (A Side/B Side)	Yr	NM
ARISTA			
SP-2 [DJ]	Pissing in the River (mono/stereo)	1976	25.00
SP-4 [DJ]	Ask the Angels (mono/stereo)	1977	25.00
—With lyric insert (deduct 20% if missing)			
0171	Gloria/My Generation	1976	10.00
0171 [PS]	Gloria/My Generation	1976	10.00
0318	Because the Night/God Speed	1978	4.00
—A-side co-written by Bruce Springsteen			
0318 [PS]	Because the Night/God Speed	1978	10.00
0427	Frederick/Frederick (Live)	1979	5.00
0427 [PS]	Frederick/Frederick (Live)	1979	10.00
0453	So You Want to Be a Rock and Roll Star//5-4-3-2-1/A Fire of Unknown Origin	1979	4.00
0453 [PS]	So You Want to Be a Rock and Roll Star//5-4-3-2-1/A Fire of Unknown Origin	1979	20.00
9173	Because the Night/So You Want to Be a Rock 'n' Roll Star	198?	3.00
—"Flashback" reissue			
9689	People Have the Power/ Wild Leaves	1988	3.00
9689 [PS]	People Have the Power/ Wild Leaves	1988	4.00
9762	I Was (Looking for You)/ Up There Down There	1988	3.00
MER			
601	Hey Joe/Piss Factory	1974	80.00
SIRE			
1009	Hey Joe/Piss Factory	1977	10.00
1009 [PS]	Hey Joe/Piss Factory	1977	15.00

Albums

Number	Title (A Side/B Side)	Yr	NM
ARISTA			
AL 4066	Horses	1975	12.00
—With the word "Horses" in white letters on the front cover			
AL 4066	Horses	1975	15.00
—With the word "Horses" in black letters on the front cover			
AL 4097	Radio Ethiopia	1977	12.00
AB 4171	Easter	1978	12.00
AB 4221	Wave	1979	10.00
ALB6-8349	Easter	198?	8.00
—Reissue			
ALB6-8362	Horses	198?	8.00
—Reissue			
ALB6-8379	Radio Ethiopia	198?	8.00
—Reissue			
AL 8453	Dreams of Life	1988	10.00
AL 8546	Wave	1990	8.00
—Reissue			
R 100469	Dreams of Life	1988	12.00
—BMG Music Service edition			
COLUMBIA			
C2 90330 [(2)]	Trampin'	2004	15.00

SMITH, RAY

45s

Number	Title (A Side/B Side)	Yr	NM
CELEBRITY CIRCLE			
6901	I Walk the Line/Fool #1	1964	15.00
CINNAMON			
755	Tiilted Cup of Love/I'd Traded Better for Worse	1973	5.00
760	It Wasn't Easy/It's Just Not the Same	1973	5.00
773	The First Lonely Weekend/ A Handful of Friends	1973	5.00
795	Ten Steps Out in Front/ Because of Losing You	1974	5.00
COLUMBIA			
2-225 (?)	Rainbow/Waltz of the Alamo	1949	40.00
—Microgroove 33 1/3 rpm single, small hole			
2-290 (?)	Snowdeer/Roll Along Kentucky Moon	1949	40.00
—Microgroove 33 1/3 rpm single, small hole			
2-300 (?)	An Old Christmas Card/ Jolly Old St. Nicholas	1949	40.00
—Microgroove 33 1/3 rpm single, small hole			
2-305 (?)	Wedding Bells/I'm Throwing Rice (At the Girl I Love)	1949	40.00
—Microgroove 33 1/3 rpm single, small hole			
2-310 (?)	Pretty Little Eyes of Blue/ Tennessee Polka	1949	40.00
—Microgroove 33 1/3 rpm single, small hole			
2-531	Unfaithful One/Daddy's Little Girl	1950	40.00
—Microgroove 33 1/3 rpm single, small hole			
2-534 (?)	I'm Saving Mother's Wedding Ring for You/Mommy Can I Take My Doll	1950	40.00
—Microgroove 33 1/3 rpm single, small hole			
2-590 (?)	No Trespassing/The Sun Has Gone Down	1950	40.00
—Microgroove 33 1/3 rpm single, small hole			
DIAMOND			
193	Everybody's Goin' Somewhere/Au-Go-Go-Go	1965	15.00
ERA BACK TO BACK HITS			
048	Rockin' Little Angel/ Robbin' the Cradle	197?	5.00
—B-side by Tony Bellus			
HEART			
250	Gone, Baby, Gone/ (B-side unknown)	195?	2000.
—VG 1000; VG+ 1500			
INFINITY			
003	After This Night Is Through/ Turn On the Moonlight	1961	15.00
007	Let Yourself Go/ Johnny the Hummer	1961	15.00
JUDD			
1016	Rockin' Little Angel/ That's All Right	1959	30.00
1017	Maria Elena/Put Your Arms Around Me Honey	1960	30.00
1019	One Wonderful Love/ Makes Me Feel Good	1960	30.00
1021	Blonde Hair, Blue Eyes/ You Don't Want Me	1960	30.00
NU-TONE			
1182	Deep in My Heart/She's Mine	1964	15.00
SHI-RAY			
101	Sleepy Eyed Woman/ Pretty Juke Box	197?	6.00
SMASH			
1787	Room 503/These Four Precious Years	1962	15.00
SUN			
298	So Right/Right Behind You Baby	1958	30.00
308	Why, Why, Why/You Made a Hit	1958	30.00
319	Rockin' Bandit/Sail Away	1959	30.00
372	Travelin' Salesman/I Won't Miss You ('Til You're Gone)	1961	30.00
375	Hey Boss Man/Candy Doll	1962	30.00
TOLLIE			
9029	Here Comes My Baby Back Again/Did We Have a Party	1964	20.00
TOPPA			
1071	Almost Alone/A Place Within My Heart	1962	20.00
VEE JAY			
579	Rockin' Robin/Robbin' the Cradle	1964	15.00
WARNER BROS.			
5371	I'm Snowed/Turn Over a New Leaf	1963	15.00
ZIRKON			
1055	After This Night Is Through/ Turn On the Moonlight	1961	20.00

Albums

Number	Title (A Side/B Side)	Yr	NM
COLUMBIA			
CL 1937 [M]	Ray Smith's Greatest Hits	1963	25.00
CS 8737 [S]	Ray Smith's Greatest Hits	1963	30.00
JUDD			
JLPA-701 [M]	Travelin' with Ray	1960	700.00
STOMP OFF			
SOS-1012	Jungle Blues	198?	12.00
"T"			
56062 [M]	The Best of Ray Smith	196?	100.00
WIX			
1000	I'm Gonna Rock Some More	197?	15.00

SMITH, ROBERT CURTIS

45s

Number	Title (A Side/B Side)	Yr	NM
ARHOOLIE			
502	Love Each Other/Please Don't Drive Me Away	1961	20.00

Albums

Number	Title (A Side/B Side)	Yr	NM
BLUESVILLE			
BVLP-1064 [M]	Clarksdale Blues	1963	80.00
—Blue label, silver print			
BVLP-1064 [M]	Clarksdale Blues	1964	25.00
—Blue label, trident logo at right			

SMITH, RONNIE

45s

Number	Title (A Side/B Side)	Yr	NM
BRUNSWICK			
55137	Lookie, Lookie, Lookie/ Tiny Kisses	1959	40.00
HAMILTON			
50003	My Babe/I've Got a Love	1959	25.00
IMPERIAL			
5667	It Hurts Me So/Long Time No Love	1960	30.00
5679	I Hear You Knocking/ I Started Out Walkin'	1960	30.00

SMITH, SAMMI

45s

Number	Title (A Side/B Side)	Yr	NM
COLUMBIA			
44212	He Went a Little Bit Farther/ Foxy Dan	1967	10.00
44370	So Long, Charlie Brown, Don't Look for Me Around/ Turn Around	1967	8.00
44523	Why Do You Do Me Like You Do/22 Road Markers to a Mile	1968	8.00
4-44663	Sand Covered Angels/ It's Not Time Now	1968	8.00
44905	Brownsville Lumberyard/ Shadows of Your Mind	1969	8.00
CYCLONE			
100	What a Lie/It's Not My Way	1979	4.00
104	The Letter/It's a Day for Sad Songs	1979	4.00
ELEKTRA			
45292	Huckleberry Pie/I Won't Sing No Love Songs Anymore	1975	5.00
—With Even Stevens			
45300	As Long As There's a Sunday/ Children	1976	4.00

Number	Title (A Side/B Side)	Yr	NM
❑ 45320	Rabbit Tracks/I'll Get Better	1976	4.00
❑ 45334	Sunday School to Broadway/ Goodmornin', Sunshine, Goodbye	1976	4.00
❑ 45374	Loving Arms/I Just Wanted to Sing	1977	4.00
❑ 45398	I Can't Stop Loving You/ De Grazia's Song	1977	4.00
❑ 45429	Days That End in "Y"/ Hallelujah for Beer	1977	4.00
❑ 45476	It Just Won't Feel Like Cheating (With You)/I Ain't Got Time to Rock No Babies	1978	4.00
❑ 45504	Norma Jean/Lookin' for Lovin'	1978	4.00
MEGA			
❑ 0001	He's Everywhere/This Room for Rent	1970	5.00
❑ 0015	Help Me Make It Through the Night/When Michael Calls	1970	6.00
❑ 0026	Then You Walk In/Willie	1971	5.00
❑ 0039	For the Kids/Saunder's Ferry Lane	1971	5.00
❑ 0056	Kentucky/The Marionette	1971	5.00
❑ 0068	Girl in New Orleans/Isn't It Sad	1972	5.00
❑ 0079	I've Got to Have You/ Jimmy's in Georgia	1972	5.00
❑ 0097	The Toast of '45/Tony	1972	5.00
❑ 0109	I Miss You Most When You're Here/Billy Jacks	1973	5.00
❑ 0118	City of New Orleans/Don't Blow No Smoke on Me	1973	5.00
❑ 204	The Rainbow in Daddy's Eyes/ Birmingham Mistake	1974	5.00
❑ 210	Never Been to Spain/ It's Not Easy	1974	5.00
❑ 212	Help Me Make It Through the Night/When Michael Calls	1974	4.00
—Reissue of 0015			
❑ 1214	Long Black Veil/Paste Me On Some Feathers`	1974	5.00
❑ 1222	Cover Me/He Makes It Hard to Say Goodbye	1975	5.00
❑ 1233	She's in Love with a Rodeo Man/ Fool for Something Years	1975	5.00
❑ 1236	Today I Started Loving You Again/Fine As Wine	1975	5.00
❑ 1246	My Window Faces the South/ Before the Next Teardrop Falls	1976	5.00
PLAYBACK			
❑ 1340	Gonna Lay Me Down Beside My Memories/I'd Do It All Over Again	1989	5.00
❑ 1354	Cloudy Days/(B-side unknown)	1989	5.00
SOUND FACTORY			
❑ 425	I Just Want to Be with You/ I've Never Loved You More Than I Do Now	1980	4.00
❑ 427	Cheatin's a Two-Way Street/The Legend of Wooley Swamp	1981	4.00
❑ 432	Waltz Across Texas/I Need Thatr Shoulder After All	1981	6.00
—With Ernest Tubb			
❑ 433	Gypsy and Joe/(B-side unknown)	1982	4.00
❑ 446	Sometimes I Cry When I'm Alone/Once or Twice	1981	4.00
STEP ONE			
❑ 342	You Just Hurt My Last Feeling/ Lying in My Arms	1985	4.00
❑ 347	An Offer I Couldn't Refuse/One Away from One Too Many	1985	4.00
❑ 351	Love Me All Over/Don't Let It Happen Again	1986	4.00
ZODIAC			
❑ 1000	Help Me Make It Through the Night/Saunder's Ferry Drive	1976	4.00
❑ 1005	Just You 'n' Me/Walking in the Sunshine	1976	4.00
❑ 1013	Rings for Sale/You Don't Want My Love	1976	4.00
Albums			
ELEKTRA			
❑ 7E-1058	As Long As There's a Sunday	1976	10.00
❑ 7E-1108	Mixed Emotions	1977	10.00
HARMONY			
❑ H 30616	The World of Sammi Smith	1971	10.00
MEGA			
❑ MLPS-601	Rainbow in Daddy's Eyes	1974	12.00
❑ MLPS-604	Sammi's Greatest Hits	1974	12.00
❑ MLPS-612	Today I Started Loving You Again	1975	12.00
❑ 31-1000	Help Me Make It Through the Night	1971	12.00
❑ 31-1007	Lonesome	1971	12.00
❑ 31-1011	Something Old, Something New, Something Blue	1972	12.00
❑ 31-1019	The Best of Sammi Smith	1973	12.00

The Smiths, "What Difference Does it Make?," Sire 29239, 1984, **$20.**

Number	Title (A Side/B Side)	Yr	NM
❑ 31-1021	The Toast of '45	1973	12.00
PICKWICK			
❑ 6167	Help Me Make It Through the Night	197?	10.00
ZODIAC			
❑ 5004	Her Way	1976	10.00

SMITH, SHELBY

45s

Number	Title (A Side/B Side)	Yr	NM
REBEL			
❑ 728	Rockin' Mama/Since My Baby Said Goodbye	1962	400.00

SMITH, SOMETHIN', AND THE REDHEADS

45s

Number	Title (A Side/B Side)	Yr	NM
EPIC			
❑ 5-9025	Gee/Just in Case You Change Your Mind	1954	12.00
—As "Somethin' Smith and the Skylarks"			
❑ 5-9048	If I Could Be with You/Oh Jane	1954	10.00
❑ 5-9093	It's a Sin to Tell a Lie/ My Baby Just Cares for Me	1955	10.00
❑ 5-9106	The Ace in the Hole/ Charley, My Boy	1955	10.00
❑ 5-9119	When All the Streets Are Dark/ Pretty Baby	1955	10.00
❑ 5-9140	Red Head/Pinch Me (I Must Be Dreamin')	1956	10.00
❑ 5-9168	In a Shanty in Old Shanty Town/ Coal Dust on the Fiddle	1956	10.00
❑ 5-9179	Heartaches/Cecelia	1956	10.00
❑ 5-9188	When I Grow Too Old to Dream/ We'll Build a Bungalow	1956	10.00
❑ 5-9197	Sweet Stuff/I Hope You Know What You're Doin'	1957	10.00
❑ 5-9208	Ma (She's Makin' Eyes at Me)/ Mambo, Tango, Samba, Chalypso Rhumba Blues	1957	10.00
❑ 5-9221	You Always Hurt the One You Love/My Melancholy Baby	1957	10.00
❑ 5-9247	Ev'ry Night at 9 O'Clock/ I'm Gonna Wrap Up All My Heartaches	1957	10.00
❑ 5-9264	School Bus Rock/I Thank You, Mr. Moon	1958	12.00
❑ 5-9269	My Secret Inspiration/ The Brush Off	1958	10.00
❑ 5-9280	I Don't Want to Set the World on Fire/You Made Me Love You	1958	10.00
❑ 5-9313	Mr. D.J. (Please Play a Song for Me)/That's Togetherness	1959	10.00
❑ 5-9340	Poor Butterfly/Ten Chaperones	1959	10.00
❑ 5-9389	Ballin' the Jack/It's a Sin to Tell a Lie	1960	8.00
MGM			
❑ 13023	Ain't We Got Fun/We'll Meet Again	1961	8.00
7-Inch Extended Plays			
EPIC			
❑ EG 7117	There's a Little Bit of Corn Born in All of Us-California Here I Come/It's a Sin to Tell a Lie// Pretty Baby/Back in Your Own Back Yard	195?	20.00
❑ EG 7117 [PS]	It's a Sin to Tell a Lie	195?	20.00
Albums			
EPIC			
❑ LN 3138 [M]	Somethin' Smith and the Redheads	1959	30.00
❑ LN 3373 [M]	Put the Blame on Mame	196?	25.00
MGM			
❑ E-3941 [M]	Ain't We Got Fun Kinda Songs	1961	20.00
❑ SE-3941 [S]	Ain't We Got Fun Kinda Songs	1961	25.00

SMITH, WARREN

45s

Number	Title (A Side/B Side)	Yr	NM
LIBERTY			
❑ 55248	I Don't Believe I'll Fall in Love Today/Cave-In	1960	20.00

Number	Title (A Side/B Side)	Yr	NM
❑ 55302	Odds and Ends (Bits and Pieces)/ A Whole Lot of Nothin'	1961	20.00
❑ 55336	Call of the Wild/ Old Lonesome Feeling	1961	20.00
❑ 55361	Why Baby Why/Why I'm Walking	1961	20.00
—With Shirley Collie			
❑ 55409	Bad News Gets Around/Five Minutes of the Latest Blues	1962	20.00
❑ 55475	Book of Broken Hearts/ 160 Pounds of Hurt	1962	20.00
❑ 55615	Big City Ways/That's Why I Sing in a Honky Tonk	1963	15.00
❑ 55699	Blue Smoke/Judge and Jury	1964	15.00
MERCURY			
❑ 72825	Lie to Me/When the Heartaches Get to Me	1968	10.00
SUN			
❑ 239	Rock and Roll Ruby/I'd Rather Be Safe Than Sorry	1956	80.00
❑ 250	Ubangi Stomp/Black Jack David	1956	60.00
❑ 268	Miss Froggie/So Long, I'm Gone	1957	40.00
❑ 286	I Fell in Love/I've Got Love If You Want It	1958	30.00
❑ 314	Goodbye Mr. Love/Sweet Sweet Girl	1959	40.00
WARNER BROS.			
❑ 5125	Dear Santa/The Meaning of Christmas	1959	25.00
Albums			
LIBERTY			
❑ LRP-3199 [M]	The First Country Collection of Warren Smith	1961	50.00
❑ LST-7199 [S]	The First Country Collection of Warren Smith	1961	70.00

SMITH, WHISTLING JACK

Number	Title (A Side/B Side)	Yr	NM
45s			
DERAM			
❑ 85005	I Was Kaiser Bill's Batman/ The British Grin 'N' Bear	1967	8.00
❑ 85041	Only When I Laff/Early One Morning	1969	6.00
Albums			
DERAM			
❑ DE 16006 [M]	I Was Kaiser Bill's Batman	1967	25.00
❑ DES 18006 [S]	I Was Kaiser Bill's Batman	1967	20.00

SMITHS, THE
Also see MORRISSEY. Also see MORRISSEY.

Number	Title (A Side/B Side)	Yr	NM
12-Inch Singles			
SIRE			
❑ PRO2843 [DJ]	Girlfriend in a Coma (same on both sides)	1987	20.00
❑ PRO2893 [DJ]	Stop Me If You've Heard This One Before (same on both sides)	1987	15.00
❑ PRO-A-2843 [DJ]	Girlfriend in a Coma (same on both sides)	1987	20.00
❑ PRO-A-2893 [DJ]	Stop Me If You've Heard This One Before (same on both sides)	1987	15.00
❑ 20284	How Soon Is Now? (long 6:43) (edit)/Girl Afraid	1984	12.00
❑ 20392	The Boy with the Thorn in His Side/Rubber Ring/Asleep	1986	12.00
❑ 20544	Panic/Vicar in a Tutu/ The Draize Train	1986	15.00
❑ 20591	Ask/Cemetery Gates/ Golden Lights	1986	10.00
❑ 40583	This Charming Man (7 versions)/ Wonderful Woman	1990	18.00
45s			
SIRE			
❑ 28136	Stop Me If You Think You've Heard This One Before/ I Keep Mine Hidden	1987	5.00
❑ 28136 [PS]	Stop Me If You Think You've Heard This One Before/ I Keep Mine Hidden	1987	10.00
❑ 29007	How Soon Is Now?/ Shakespear's Sister/ Headmaster Ritual	1985	15.00
❑ 29007 [PS]	How Soon Is Now?/ Shakespear's Sister/ Headmaster Ritual	1985	20.00
❑ 29239	What Difference Does It Make/ Back to the Old Home	1984	10.00
❑ 29239 [PS]	What Difference Does It Make/ Back to the Old Home	1984	20.00
Albums			
SIRE			
❑ 25065	The Smiths	1984	15.00
❑ 25269	Meat Is Murder	1985	15.00
❑ 25426	The Queen Is Dead	1986	15.00
❑ 25649	Strangeways, Here We Come	1987	14.00
❑ 25669 [(2)]	Louder Than Bombs	1987	15.00
❑ 25786	"Rank"	1988	12.00
WARNER BROS.			
❑ WBMS-130 [DJ]	The Warner Bros. Music Show	1985	14.00
—One side: The Smiths; the other side: The Blasters			
❑ WBMS-130 [DJ]	Music and Interviews	1985	40.00
—Part of "The Warner Bros. Music Show" series; one side is The Smiths; the other side is The Blasters			

SMITHSONIAN JAZZ REPERTORY ENSEMBLE, THE

Number	Title (A Side/B Side)	Yr	NM
Albums			
SMITHSONIAN			
❑ N-021	The Music of Fats Waller and James P. Johnson	1988	15.00

SMOKE, THE (1)
California group. Jimmy Greenspoon, later a member of THREE DOG NIGHT, appears on the LP cover, but not on the record itself.

Number	Title (A Side/B Side)	Yr	NM
Albums			
SIDEWALK			
❑ ST 5912	The Smoke	1968	40.00

SMOKE, THE (2)
Houston-based group.

Number	Title (A Side/B Side)	Yr	NM
45s			
ORBIT			
❑ 1126	Mainstream/Church House Blues	1968	50.00
UNI			
❑ 55154	Choose It (Part 1)/ Choose It (Part 2)	1969	10.00
Albums			
UNI			
❑ 73052	The Smoke	1969	25.00
❑ 73065	The Smoke at George's Coffee Shop	1970	25.00

SMOKE RINGS, THE

Number	Title (A Side/B Side)	Yr	NM
45s			
DOT			
❑ 16975	Love's the Thing/ She Gives Me Love	1966	20.00
PROSPECT			
❑ 101	Love's the Thing/ She Gives Me Love	1966	40.00

SMOKE RISE, THE

Number	Title (A Side/B Side)	Yr	NM
45s			
PARAMOUNT			
❑ 0113	I'm Here (Love Me)/Survival	1971	8.00
Albums			
PARAMOUNT			
❑ PAS-9000 [(2)]	The Survival of St. Joan	1971	20.00
—With booklet			

SMOKESTACK LIGHTNIN'

Number	Title (A Side/B Side)	Yr	NM
45s			
BELL			
❑ 755	Light in My Window/ Long Stemmed Eyes	1968	6.00
❑ 777	I Idolize You/Something's Got a Hold on You	1969	6.00
❑ 836	Baby Don't Get Crazy/ The Blue Albino Shuffle	1969	6.00
❑ 861	Hello L.A., Bye-Bye Birmingham/Well Tuesday	1970	6.00
WHITE WHALE			
❑ 243	Nadine/Crossroadds Blues	1967	8.00
❑ 256	Look What You've Done/ Got a Good Love	1967	8.00
Albums			
BELL			
❑ 6026	Off the Wall	1969	20.00

SMOKEY JOE

Number	Title (A Side/B Side)	Yr	NM
45s			
FLIP			
❑ 228	The Signifying Monkey/ Listen to Me Baby	1955	500.00
SUN			
❑ 228	The Signifying Monkey/ Listen to Me Baby	1956	300.00
❑ 393	The Signifying Monkey/ Listen to Me Baby	1964	200.00

SMOKIE

Number	Title (A Side/B Side)	Yr	NM
45s			
MCA			
❑ 40429	If You Think You Know How to Love Me/'Tis Me	1975	5.00
—As "Smokey"			
❑ 40471	Don't Play Your Rock 'N' Roll to Me/Talking Her 'Round	1975	5.00
—As "Smokey"			
RSO			
❑ 860	Living Next Door to Alice/When My Back Was Against the Wall	1976	5.00
❑ 874	If You Think You Know How to Love Me/Make Ya Boogie	1977	4.00
❑ 881	Needles and Pins/No One Could Ever Love You More	1977	4.00
❑ 900	For a Few Dollars More/ I Can't Stay Here Tonight	1978	4.00
❑ 934	No More Letters/Oh Carol	1979	4.00
Albums			
MCA			
❑ 2152	Smokey	1975	12.00
—As "Smokey"			
RSO			
❑ RS-1-3005	Midnight Café	1976	10.00
❑ RS-1-3029	Bright Lights and Back Alleys	1978	10.00

SMOOTHIES, THE
With JOHN PHILLIPS and SCOTT McKENZIE.

Number	Title (A Side/B Side)	Yr	NM
45s			
DECCA			
❑ 31105	Softly/Joanie	1960	20.00
❑ 31159	Ride, Ride, Ride/Lonely Boy and Pretty Girl	1960	20.00

SMOTHERS, DICK
Also see THE SMOTHERS BROTHERS.

Number	Title (A Side/B Side)	Yr	NM
45s			
MERCURY			
❑ 72717	Saturday Night at the World/ They Are Gone	1967	20.00
❑ 72717 [PS]	Saturday Night at the World/ They Are Gone	1967	25.00

SMOTHERS BROTHERS, THE
Also see DICK SMOTHERS.

Number	Title (A Side/B Side)	Yr	NM
45s			
MERCURY			
❑ 72027	Fly Ezekiel/They Call the Wind Maria	1962	10.00
❑ 72182	Jenny Brown/You Go This-a-Way	1963	10.00
❑ 72323	Coo Coo/Slithery Dee	1964	10.00
❑ 72483	The Three Song/The World I Used to Know	1965	8.00
❑ 72483 [PS]	The Three Song/The World I Used to Know	1965	15.00
❑ 72519	The Toy Song/Little Sacha Sugar	1966	8.00
❑ 72519 [PS]	The Toy Song/Little Sacha Sugar	1966	15.00
❑ 72573	Writer of Songs/Lark Day	1966	8.00
SMOTHERS INC.			
❑ 79151	The Christmas Bunny Part 1/ The Christmas Bunny Part 2	1969	25.00
❑ 79151 [PS]	The Christmas Bunny Part 1/ The Christmas Bunny Part 2	1969	50.00
Albums			
MERCURY			
❑ MGDJ-20 [DJ]	Best of the Smothers Brothers	1964	40.00
❑ MGDJ-25 [DJ]	It's Smothers Brothers Month	1964	40.00
❑ MG-20611 [M]	The Songs and Comedy of the Smothers Brothers!	1962	15.00
❑ MG-20675 [M]	The Two Sides of the Smothers Brothers	1962	15.00
❑ MG-20777 [M]	(Think Ethnic!)	1963	15.00
❑ MG-20862 [M]	Curb Your Tongue, Knave!	1963	15.00
❑ MG-20904 [M]	It Must Have Been Something I Said!	1964	15.00
❑ MG-20948 [M]	Tour De Farce American History and Other Unrelated Subjects	1964	15.00
❑ MG-20989 [M]	Aesop's Fables the Smothers Brothers Way	1965	15.00
❑ MG-21051 [M]	Mom Always Liked You Best!	1965	15.00
❑ MG-21064 [M]	The Smothers Brothers Play It Straight	1966	15.00
❑ MG-21089 [M]	Golden Hits of the Smothers Brothers, Vol. 2	1966	15.00
❑ SR-60611 [S]	The Songs and Comedy of the Smothers Brothers!	1962	20.00
❑ SR-60675 [S]	The Two Sides of the Smothers Brothers	1962	20.00
❑ SR-60777 [S]	(Think Ethnic!)	1963	20.00
❑ SR-60862 [S]	Curb Your Tongue, Knave!	1963	20.00
❑ SR-60904 [S]	It Must Have Been Something I Said!	1964	20.00

Except when noted otherwise, VG = 25% of NM, and VG+ = 50% of NM. (Example: VG = $2.00, VG+ = $4.00 and NM = $8.00.)

Number	Title (A Side/B Side)	Yr	NM
❑ SR-60948 [S]	Tour De Farce American History and Other Unrelated Subjects	1964	20.00
❑ SR-60989 [S]	Aesop's Fables the Smothers Brothers Way	1965	20.00
❑ SR-61051 [S]	Mom Always Liked You Best!	1965	20.00
❑ SR-61064 [S]	The Smothers Brothers Play It Straight	1966	20.00
❑ SR-61089 [S]	Golden Hits of the Smothers Brothers, Vol. 2	1966	20.00
❑ SR-61193	Smothers Comedy Brothers Hour	1968	20.00
RHINO			
❑ R1-70188	Sibling Revelry: The Best of the Smothers Brothers	1988	10.00

SNEAKY PETE

Albums

Number	Title (A Side/B Side)	Yr	NM
SHILO			
❑ 4086	Sneaky Pete	1979	30.00

SNOOP DOGG

Albums

Number	Title (A Side/B Side)	Yr	NM
DEATH ROW/INTERSCOPE			
❑ INT2-90038 [(2)]	Tha Doggfather	1996	50.00
—As "Snoop Doggy Dogg"			

SNOW

Albums

Number	Title (A Side/B Side)	Yr	NM
EPIC			
❑ BN 26435	Snow	1969	25.00

SNOW, EDDIE

45s

Number	Title (A Side/B Side)	Yr	NM
SUN			
❑ 226	Ain't That Right/Bring Your Love Back Home	1955	200.00

SNOW, HANK

45s

Number	Title (A Side/B Side)	Yr	NM
RCA			
❑ 2721-7-R	I've Been Everywhere/Ancient History	1990	3.00
—"Gold Standard Series" reissue			
❑ PB-10804	You're Wondering Why/Somewhere Someone Is Waiting for You	1976	5.00
❑ PB-11021	Trouble in Mind/Trying to Get My Baby Off My Mind	1977	5.00
❑ PB-11080	I'm Still Movin' On/I'm Gonna Bid My Blues Goodbye	1977	5.00
❑ PB-11153	Breakfast with the Blues/I've Done At Least One Thing	1977	5.00
❑ PB-11192	That Heart Belongs to Me/Love Is So Elusive	1978	5.00
❑ PB-11276	Nevertheless/Don't Rock the Boat	1978	5.00
❑ PB-11377	Ramblin' Rose/Red Roses	1978	5.00
❑ PB-11487	The Mysterious Lady from St. Martinique/Get On My Love Train	1979	5.00
❑ PB-11622	A Good Gal Is Hard to Find/I Wish My Heart Could Talk	1979	5.00
❑ PB-11734	It Takes Too Long/6 String Tennessee Flattop	1979	5.00
RCA VICTOR			
❑ 37-7869	Beggar to a King/Poor Little Jimmie	1961	25.00
—"Compact Single 33" with small hole			
❑ 47-4095	Hobo Bill's Last Ride/Wreck of the Old 97	1951	20.00
❑ 47-4096	Ben Dewberry's Final Run/Engineer's Child	1951	20.00
❑ 47-4097	The Mystery of Number Five/One More Ride	1951	20.00
—The above three comprise a box set			
❑ 47-4346	Music Makin' Mama from Memphis/The Highest Bidder	1951	25.00
❑ 47-4398	Pray/These Things Shall Pass	1951	25.00
❑ 47-4522	The Gold Rush Is Over/Why Do You Promise Me	1952	25.00
❑ 47-4593	I'm Movin' On/Marriage Vow	1952	20.00
❑ 47-4594	Music Makin' Mama from Memphis/Down the Trail of Aching Hearts	1952	20.00
❑ 47-4595	Unwanted Sign Upon Your Heart/The Rhumba Boogie	1952	20.00
❑ 47-4596	The Golden Rocket/Bluebird Island	1952	20.00
—The above four comprise a box set			
❑ 47-4632	My Mother/I Just Telephone Upstairs	1952	25.00
❑ 47-4733	Lady's Man/Married by the Bible, Divorced by the Law	1952	25.00
❑ 47-4856	Jesus Wept/I'm in the Mood for Love	1952	25.00
❑ 47-4909	I Went to Your Wedding/Boogie Woogie Flying Cloud	1952	25.00
❑ 47-4973	Zeb Turney's Gal/Golden River	1952	20.00
❑ 47-4974	Moanin'/I Knew That We'd Meet Again	1952	20.00
❑ 47-4975	My Little Golden Horseshoe/The Yodeling Cowboy	1952	20.00
❑ 47-4976	Confused with the Blues/On That Old Hawaiian Shore	1952	20.00
—The above four comprise a box set			
❑ 47-5006	Broken Hearted/I Wonder Where You Are Tonight	1952	20.00
❑ 47-5026	Love Entered the Iron Door/I Cried But My Tears Were Too Late	1952	20.00
❑ 47-5034	(Now and Then, There's) A Fool Such As I/The Gal Who Invented Kissin'	1952	20.00
❑ 47-5155	Honeymoon on a Rocket Ship/There Wasn't an Organ at Our Wedding	1953	20.00
❑ 47-5220	Jimmie the Kid/My Blue Eyed Jane	1953	15.00
❑ 47-5221	When Jimmie Rodgers Said Goodbye/Treasure Untold	1953	15.00
❑ 47-5222	Southern Cannonball/Anniversary Blue Yodel	1953	15.00
❑ 47-5223	Why Did You Give Me Your Love/Mississippi River Blues	1953	15.00
—The above four comprise a box set			
❑ 47-5249	Glory Land March/In Daddy's Footsteps	1953	20.00
❑ 47-5296	Spanish Fire Ball/Between Fire and Water	1953	20.00
❑ 47-5340	Christmas Roses/Reindeer Boogie	1953	25.00
❑ 47-5380	For Now and Always/A Message from the Tradewinds	1953	20.00
❑ 47-5490	When Mexican Joe Met Jole Blon/No Longer a Prisoner	1953	20.00
❑ 47-5548	I'm Glad I'm On the Inside/Invisible Hands	1953	20.00
❑ 47-5592	Panamama/Act 1, Act 2, Act 3	1954	20.00
❑ 47-5648	My Religion's Not Old Fashioned/Old Rattler	1954	25.00
—With Grandpa Jones			
❑ 47-5698	I Don't Hurt Anymore/My Arabian Baby	1954	20.00
❑ 47-5794	The Alphabet/My Religion's Not Old Fashioned	1954	20.00
❑ 47-5912	That Crazy Mambo Thing/The Next Voice You Hear	1954	20.00
❑ 47-5960	Let Me Go, Lover!/I've Forgotten You	1954	20.00
❑ 47-6057	Yellow Roses/Would You Mind	1955	15.00
❑ 47-6154	Cryin', Prayin', Waitin', Hopin'/I'm Glad I Got to See You Once Again	1955	15.00
❑ 47-6269	Born to Be Happy/Mainliner (The Hawk with Silver Wings)	1955	15.00
❑ 47-6326	In an Eighteenth Century Drawing Room/La Cucaracha	1955	15.00
❑ 47-6379	These Hands/I'm Moving In	1956	15.00
❑ 47-6578	Conscience I'm Guilty/Hula Rock	1956	25.00
❑ 47-6715	Stolen Moments/Two Won't Care	1956	15.00
❑ 47-6772	Oh, Wonderful World/Carnival of Venice	1957	15.00
❑ 47-6831	Calypso Sweethearts/Marriage and Divorce	1957	15.00
❑ 47-6955	Tangled Mind/My Arms Are a House	1957	15.00
❑ 47-7060	Unfaithful/Intro to Listeners-Squid Giggin' Ground	1957	15.00
❑ 47-7121	The Blue Danube Waltz/Under the Double Eagle	1957	15.00
❑ 47-7154	Whispering Rain/I Wish I Was the Moon	1958	15.00
❑ 47-7233	Big Wheels/I'm Hurting All Over	1958	15.00
❑ 47-7325	A Woman Captured Me/My Lucky Friend	1958	15.00
❑ 47-7448	Doggone That Train/Father Time and Mother Love	1959	15.00
❑ 47-7524	Chasin' a Rainbow/I Heard My Heart Break Last Night	1959	15.00
❑ 47-7586	The Last Ride/The Party of the Second Part	1959	15.00
❑ 47-7702	Rockin', Rollin' Ocean/Walkin' and Talkin'	1960	15.00
❑ 47-7748	Miller's Cave/The Change of the Tide	1960	15.00
❑ 47-7803	The Man Behind the Gun/I'm Asking for a Friend	1960	15.00
❑ 47-7869	Beggar to a King/Poor Little Jimmie	1961	12.00
❑ 47-7933	The Restless One/I Know	1961	12.00
❑ 47-8009	You Take the Future (And I'll Take the Past)/Dog Bone	1962	12.00
❑ 47-8072	I've Been Everywhere/Ancient History	1962	12.00
❑ 47-8151	The Man Who Robbed the Bank at Santa Fe/You're Losing Your Baby	1963	12.00
❑ 47-8151 [PS]	The Man Who Robbed the Bank at Santa Fe/You're Losing Your Baby	1963	25.00
❑ 47-8239	Ninety Miles an Hour (Down a Dead End Street)/Blue Roses	1963	12.00
❑ 47-8334	Breakfast with the Blues/I Stepped Over the Line	1964	12.00
❑ 47-8437	My Memories of You/Ninety Days	1964	12.00
❑ 47-8488	The Wishing Well (Down in the Well)/Human	1964	12.00
❑ 47-8548	Trouble in Mind/In the Misty Moonlight	1965	10.00
❑ 47-8655	The Queen of Draw Poker Town/Tears in the Trade Winds	1965	10.00
❑ 47-8713	I've Cried a Mile/Crazy Little Train (Of Love)	1965	10.00
❑ 47-8808	The Count Down/Isle of Sicily	1966	10.00
❑ 47-9012	Hula Love/Letter from Vietnam	1966	10.00
❑ 47-9030	Christmas Cannonball/God Is My Santa Claus	1966	12.00
❑ 47-9188	Down at the Pawn Shop/Listen	1967	10.00
❑ 47-9300	Learnin' a New Way of Life/Wild Flower	1967	10.00
❑ 47-9433	Who Will Answer? (Aleluya No. 1)/I Just Wanted to Know (How the Wind Was Blowing)	1968	10.00
❑ 47-9523	The Late and Great Love (Of My Life)/Born for You	1968	10.00
❑ 47-9685	The Name of the Game Was Love/The Gypsy and Me	1968	8.00
❑ 47-9856	Vanishing Breed/What More Can I Say	1970	8.00
❑ 47-9907	Come the Morning/Francesca	1970	8.00
❑ 47-9964	Duquesne, Pennsylvania/So Goes My Heart	1971	8.00
❑ 48-0056	Marriage Vow/The Star Spangled Waltz	1949	40.00
—Originals on green vinyl			
❑ 48-0056	Marriage Vow/The Star Spangled Waltz	195?	25.00
—Reissues on black vinyl			
❑ 48-0088	The Blind Boy's Dog/Anniversary of My Broken Heart	1949	40.00
—Originals on green vinyl			
❑ 48-0104	My Filipino Rose/The Law of Love	1949	40.00
—Originals on green vinyl			
❑ 48-0147	Nobody's Child/The Only Rose	1950	40.00
—Originals on green vinyl			
❑ 48-0214	Blue Ranger/Only a Rose from My Mother's Grave	1950	30.00
—Originals on green vinyl			
❑ 48-0224	Brand on My Heart/I'll Not Forget My Mother's Prayers	1950	30.00
—Originals on green vinyl			
❑ 48-0303	The Drunkard's Son/I Wonder Where You Are Tonight	1950	30.00
—Originals on green vinyl			
❑ 48-0328	I'm Movin' On/With This Ring I Thee Wed	1950	20.00
—Reissues on black vinyl			
❑ 48-0328	I'm Movin' On/With This Ring I Thee Wed	1950	40.00
—Originals on green vinyl			
❑ 48-0356	The Night I Stole Sammy Morgan's Gin/I Cried But My Tears Were Too Late	1950	30.00
—Originals on green vinyl			
❑ 48-0362	No Golden Tomorrow Ahead/You Broke the Chain That Held Our Hearts	1950	25.00
—Originals on green vinyl			
❑ 48-0363	Wasted Love/My Two Timin' Woman	1950	25.00
—Originals on green vinyl			
❑ 48-0364	Somewhere Along Life's Highway/Within This Broken Heart of Mine	1950	25.00
—Originals on green vinyl			
❑ 48-0400	The Golden Rocket/Paving the Highway with Tears	1950	30.00
—Originals on green vinyl			
❑ 48-0431	The Rhumba Boogie/You Pass Me By	1951	25.00
❑ 48-0498	Unwanted Sign Upon Your Heart/Your Locket Is My Broken Heart	1951	25.00
❑ 74-0151	Rome Wasn't Built in a Day/Like a Bird	1969	8.00
❑ 74-0251	That's When the Hurtin' Sets In/I'm Movin'	1969	8.00

Number	Title (A Side/B Side)	Yr	NM
❑ 74-0459	Blue Christmas/Nestor, The Long Eared Christmas Donkey	1971	—
—Unreleased			
❑ 74-0544	No One Will Ever Know/Seashores of Old Mexico	1971	8.00
❑ 74-0676	Canadian Pacific/My Way	1972	7.00
❑ 74-0818	The Governor's Hand/Rolling Thunder in My Mind	1972	7.00
❑ 74-0915	North to Chicago/Friend	1973	7.00
❑ APBO-0215	Hello Love/Until the End of Time	1974	7.00
❑ APBO-0307	That's You and Me/Brand on My Heart	1974	7.00
❑ PB-10108	Easy to Love/Just a Faded Petal from a Beautiful Bouquet	1974	6.00
❑ PB-10136	A Letter to Santa Claus/Christmas Roses	1974	7.00
❑ PB-10225	Merry-Go-Round of Love/My Filipino Love	1975	6.00
❑ PB-10338	Hijack/The Last Ride	1975	6.00
❑ PB-10439	Colorado Country Morning/I Keep Dreaming of You All the Time	1975	6.00
❑ PB-10459	Blue Christmas/Nestor, The Long Eared Christmas Donkey	1975	7.00
❑ GB-10513	Hello Love/Until the End of Time	1976	4.00
—"Gold Standard Series" reissue			
❑ PB-10681	Who's Been Here Since I've Been Gone/That's When He Dropped the World in My Hands	1976	6.00

7-Inch Extended Plays

RCA VICTOR

Number	Title (A Side/B Side)	Yr	NM
❑ 547-0097	I'm Movin' On/Down the Trail of Achin' Hearts//The Rhumba Boogie/Bluebird Island	195?	20.00
—One record of 2-EP set EPB 3026			
❑ 547-0098	The Golden Rocket/Unwanted Sign Upon Your Heart//Music Makin' Mama from Memphis/Marriage Vow	195?	20.00
—One record of 2-EP set EPB 3026			
❑ EPA 295	You Broke the Chain That Held Our Hearts/Wasted Love//No Golden Tomorrows Ahead/My Two Timin' Woman	195?	20.00
❑ EPA 295 [PS]	Hank Snow Favorites	195?	20.00
❑ EPA 310	"The Wreck of the Old '97/One More Ride/The Mystery of Number Five/Hobo Bill's Last Ride	195?	20.00
❑ EPA 310 [PS]	Hank Snow Sings Famous Railroading Songs	195?	20.00
❑ EPA 472	Frosty the Snowman/Silent Night//Christmas Roses/The Reindeer Boogie	1953	20.00
❑ EPA 472 [PS]	A Country Christmas with Hank Snow	1953	20.00
❑ EPA 503	These Things Shall Pass/He'll Understand and Say "Well Done"//Jesus Wept/The Glory Land March	195?	20.00
❑ EPA 503 [PS]	These Things Shall Pass	195?	20.00
❑ EPA 582	Twelfth Street Rag/Rainbow Boogie//Vaya Con Dios (May God Be with You)/Madison Madness	1954	20.00
❑ EPA 582 [PS]	Hank Snow's Country Guitar	1954	20.00
❑ 547-0606	Just Keep a-Movin'/The Bill Is Falling Due//Caribbean/Blue Sea Blues	1955	20.00
—One record of 2-EP set EPB-1113			
❑ 547-0607	Can't Have You Blues/A Scale to Measure Love//Cuba Rhumba/Blossoms in the Springtime	1955	20.00
—One record of 2-EP set EPB-1113			
❑ EPA 794	Country Classics	1956	20.00
❑ EPA 794	I'm Movin' On/THe Rhumba Boogie//The Golden Rocket/Music Making Mama from Memphis	1956	20.00
❑ EPB-1113 [PS]	Just Keep a-Movin'	1955	20.00
—Gatefold cover for 547-0606 and 547-0607			
❑ VLP-2812	Stolen Moments/Miller's Cave/Just a Faded Petal from a Beautiful Bouquet//Let Me Go Lover/The Gal Who Invented Kissing/Tangled Mind	196?	15.00
❑ VLP-2812 [PS]	More Hank Snow Souvenirs	196?	15.00
❑ EPB 3026 [PS]	Country Classics	195?	20.00
—Gatefold cover for 547-0097 and 547-0098			
❑ EPA-5062	I'm Moving On/Marriage Vow//The Rhumba Boogie/With This Ring I Thee Wed	1958	15.00
❑ EPA-5062 [PS]	Hank Snow (Gold Standard Series)	1958	15.00
❑ EPA-5086	(Now and Then, There's) A Fool Such As I/The Golden Rocket//I Don't Hurt Anymore/The Star Spangled Waltz	195?	15.00
❑ EPA-5086 [PS]	The Golden Rocket (Gold Standard Series)	195?	15.00

Albums

PAIR

Number	Title (A Side/B Side)	Yr	NM
❑ PDL2-1004 [(2)]	I'm Movin' On	1986	12.00

RCA CAMDEN

Number	Title (A Side/B Side)	Yr	NM
❑ ACL1-0124	Snowbird	1973	10.00
❑ ACL2-0337 [(2)]	When My Blue Moon Turns to Gold Again	197?	15.00
❑ CAL-514 [M]	The Singing Ranger	1959	20.00
❑ CAS-514 [R]	The Singing Ranger	196?	12.00
❑ ACL1-0540	I'm Movin' On	1974	10.00
❑ CAL-680 [M]	The Southern Cannonball	1961	20.00
❑ CAS-680 [R]	The Southern Cannonball	196?	12.00
❑ CAL-722 [M]	The One and Only Hank Snow	1962	20.00
❑ CAS-722 [R]	The One and Only Hank Snow	1962	12.00
❑ CAL-782 [M]	The Last Ride	1963	20.00
❑ CAS-782 [R]	The Last Ride	1963	12.00
❑ CAL-836 [M]	Old and Great Songs	1964	15.00
❑ CAS-836 [S]	Old and Great Songs	1964	12.00
❑ CAL-910 [M]	The Highest Bidder	1965	12.00
❑ CAS-910 [S]	The Highest Bidder	1965	15.00
❑ CAL-964 [M]	Travelin' Blues	1966	12.00
❑ CAS-964 [S]	Travelin' Blues	1966	15.00
❑ CAL-2160 [M]	My Early Favorites	1967	15.00
❑ CAS-2160 [S]	My Early Favorites	1967	12.00
❑ CAS-2235	Somewhere Along Life's Highway	1968	12.00
❑ CAS-2257	My Nova Scotia Home	1968	12.00
❑ CAS-2348	I Went to Your Wedding	1969	12.00
❑ CAS-2443	Memories Are Made of This	1970	12.00
❑ CAS-2513	Lonesome Whistle	1972	12.00
❑ CAS-2560	The Legend of Old Doc Brown	1972	12.00
❑ CXS-9009 [(2)]	The Wreck of the 97	197?	15.00

RCA VICTOR

Number	Title (A Side/B Side)	Yr	NM
❑ DPL2-0134 [(2)]	The Living Legend	197?	100.00
—RCA Special Products release			
❑ APL1-0162	Grand Ole Opry Favorites	1973	15.00
❑ APL1-0441	Hello Love	1974	15.00
❑ APL1-0608	That's You and Me	1974	15.00
❑ APL1-0908	You're Easy to Love	1975	15.00
❑ LPM-1113 [M]	Just Keep a-Movin'	1955	100.00
❑ LPM-1156 [M]	Old Doc Brown and Other Narrations	1955	100.00
❑ ANL1-1207	Grand Ole Opry Favorites	1975	10.00
—Reissue of APL1-0162			
❑ LPM-1233 [M]	Country Classics	1956	80.00
❑ APL1-1361	Live from Evangel Temple	1976	12.00
—With Jimmy Snow			
❑ LPM-1419 [M]	Country and Western Jamboree	1957	80.00
❑ LPM-1435 [M]	Hank Snow's Country Guitar	1957	80.00
❑ LPM-1638 [M]	Hank Snow Sings Sacred Songs	1958	60.00
❑ LPM-2043 [M]	Hank Snow Sings Jimmie Rodgers Songs	1959	50.00
❑ LSP-2043 [S]	Hank Snow Sings Jimmie Rodgers Songs	1959	80.00
❑ ANL1-2194	The Jimmie Rodgers Story	1977	10.00
—Reissue of 4708			
❑ LPM-2285 [M]	Hank Snow Souvenirs	1961	30.00
❑ LSP-2285 [S]	Hank Snow Souvenirs	1961	40.00
❑ APL1-2400	#104 — Still Movin' On	1977	12.00
❑ LPM-2458 [M]	Big Country Hits	1961	30.00
❑ LSP-2458 [S]	Big Country Hits	1961	40.00
❑ LPM-2675 [M]	I've Been Everywhere	1963	30.00
❑ LSP-2675 [S]	I've Been Everywhere	1963	40.00
❑ LPM-2705 [M]	Railroad Man	1963	30.00
❑ LSP-2705 [S]	Railroad Man	1963	40.00
❑ LPM-2812 [M]	More Hank Snow Souvenirs	1964	25.00
❑ LSP-2812 [S]	More Hank Snow Souvenirs	1964	30.00
❑ LPM-2901 [M]	Songs of Tragedy	1964	25.00
❑ LSP-2901 [S]	Songs of Tragedy	1964	30.00
❑ LPM-3026 [10]	Country Classics	1952	200.00
❑ LPM-3070 [10]	Hank Snow Sings	1952	180.00
❑ LPM-3131 [10]	Hank Snow Salutes Jimmie Rodgers	1953	180.00
❑ AHL1-3208	Mysterious Lady	1979	12.00
❑ LPM-3267 [10]	Hank Snow's Country Guitar	1954	180.00
❑ LPM-3317 [M]	Your Favorite Country Hits	1965	25.00
❑ LSP-3317 [S]	Your Favorite Country Hits	1965	30.00
❑ LPM-3378 [M]	Gloryland March	1965	25.00
❑ LSP-3378 [S]	Gloryland March	1965	30.00
❑ ANL1-3470	The Best of Hank Snow	1980	8.00
❑ LPM-3471 [M]	Heartbreak Trail - A Tribute to the Sons of the Pioneers	1966	25.00
❑ LSP-3471 [S]	Heartbreak Trail - A Tribute to the Sons of the Pioneers	1966	30.00
❑ LPM-3478 [M]	The Best of Hank Snow	1966	20.00
❑ LSP-3478 [S]	The Best of Hank Snow	1966	25.00
❑ AHL1-3511	Instrumentally Yours	1980	12.00
❑ LPM-3548 [M]	Guitar Stylings of Hank Snow	1966	25.00
❑ LSP-3548 [S]	Guitar Stylings of Hank Snow	1966	30.00
❑ LPM-3595 [M]	Gospel Train	1966	30.00
❑ LSP-3595 [S]	Gospel Train	1966	40.00
❑ LPM-3737 [M]	Snow in Hawaii	1967	30.00
❑ LSP-3737 [S]	Snow in Hawaii	1967	25.00
❑ LPM-3826 [M]	Christmas with Hank Snow	1967	30.00
❑ LSP-3826 [S]	Christmas with Hank Snow	1967	25.00
❑ LPM-3857 [M]	Spanish Fire Ball and Other Great Hank Snow Stylings	1967	30.00
❑ LSP-3857 [S]	Spanish Fire Ball and Other Great Hank Snow Stylings	1967	25.00
❑ LPM-3965 [M]	Hits, Hits and More Hits	1968	100.00
❑ LSP-3965 [S]	Hits, Hits and More Hits	1968	25.00
❑ LSP-4032	Tales of the Yukon	1968	25.00
❑ LSP-4122	Snow in All Seasons	1969	25.00
❑ LSP-4306	Hank Snow Sings in Memory of Jimmie Rodgers	1970	20.00
❑ LSP-4379	Cure for the Blues	1970	20.00
❑ LSP-4501	Tracks and Trains	1971	20.00
❑ LSP-4601	Award Winners	1971	20.00
❑ LSP-4708	The Jimmie Rodgers Story	1972	15.00
❑ LSP-4798	The Best of Hank Snow, Vol. 2	1972	15.00
❑ AHL1-5497	Collector's Series	1986	10.00
❑ LPM-6014 [(2)M]	This Is My Story	1966	40.00
❑ LSP-6014 [(2)S]	This Is My Story	1966	50.00

READER'S DIGEST

Number	Title (A Side/B Side)	Yr	NM
❑ RDA-216 [(6)]	I'm Movin' On	197?	120.00

SCHOOL OF MUSIC

Number	Title (A Side/B Side)	Yr	NM
❑ 1149 [M]	The Guitar	1958	250.00
—Deduct 20 percent if instruction book is missing			

SNOW, HANK, AND CHET ATKINS

Albums

RCA VICTOR

Number	Title (A Side/B Side)	Yr	NM
❑ LPM-2952 [M]	Reminiscing	1964	25.00
❑ LSP-2952 [S]	Reminiscing	1964	30.00
❑ LSP-4254	By Special Request - C.B. Atkins and C.E. Snow	1970	20.00

SNOW, HANK, AND ANITA CARTER

45s

RCA VICTOR

Number	Title (A Side/B Side)	Yr	NM
❑ 47-6500	Keep Your Promise, Willie Thomas/It's You, Only You, That I Love	1956	15.00
❑ 48-0441	Down the Trail of Achin' Hearts/Bluebird Island	1951	25.00

Albums

RCA VICTOR

Number	Title (A Side/B Side)	Yr	NM
❑ LPM-2580 [M]	Together Again	1962	30.00
❑ LSP-2580 [S]	Together Again	1962	40.00

SNOW, HANK, AND KELLY FOXTON

45s

RCA

Number	Title (A Side/B Side)	Yr	NM
❑ PB-11891	Hasn't It Been Good Together/It Was Love	1980	5.00
❑ PB-11967	There's Something About You/All I Want to Do Is Touch You	1980	5.00
❑ PB-12102	Pain Didn't Shout/Check	1980	5.00
❑ PB-12235	Things/Forbidden Lovers	1981	5.00

Albums

RCA VICTOR

Number	Title (A Side/B Side)	Yr	NM
❑ AHL1-3496	Lovingly Yours	1980	10.00
❑ AYL1-3987	Win Some, Lose Some, Lonesome	1981	10.00

SNOW, HANK; PORTER WAGONER; HANK LOCKLIN

Albums

RCA VICTOR

Number	Title (A Side/B Side)	Yr	NM
❑ LPM-2723 [M]	Three Country Gentlemen	1963	30.00
❑ LSP-2723 [S]	Three Country Gentlemen	1963	40.00

SNOW MEN, THE

Early version of THE SUNRAYS.

45s

CHALLENGE

Number	Title (A Side/B Side)	Yr	NM
❑ 59227	Ski Storm (Part 1)/Ski Storm (Part 2)	1964	30.00

SNYDER, TERRY, AND THE ALL-STARS

See ENOCH LIGHT.

SOCIAL DISTORTION

12-Inch Singles

EPIC

Number	Title (A Side/B Side)	Yr	NM
❑ EAS 2120 [DJ]	Ring of Fire/Lonesome Train	1990	15.00
❑ EAS2120 [DJ]	Ring of Fire/Lonesome Train	1990	15.00
❑ EAS 4348 [DJ]	Bad Luck (same on both sides)	1992	15.00
❑ EAS4348 [DJ]	Bad Luck (same on both sides)	1992	15.00

13TH STORY

Number	Title (A Side/B Side)	Yr	NM
❑ SD 4501	1945/Under My Thumb/Playpen	1985	15.00

Number	Title (A Side/B Side)	Yr	NM
45s			
(NO LABEL)			
❑ (no #)	Ball & Chain (Skeletal Mix) (same on both sides)	1990	8.00
—KROQ (Los Angeles)-related promo dated 12-21-90			
EPIC			
❑ ES7 4568 [DJ]	Cold Feelings/Bad Luck (Live Acoustic)	1992	4.00
❑ ES74568 [DJ]	Cold Feelings/Bad Luck (Live Acoustic)	1992	4.00
❑ 74229	Bad Luck/Bye Bye Baby	1992	3.00
POSH BOY			
❑ PBS 11	Mainliner/Playpen	1981	12.50
❑ PBS 11 [PS]	Mainliner/Playpen	1981	12.50
SOCIAL DISTORTION			
❑ (# unknown)	1945/Under My Thumb/ Playpen	1982	30.00
❑ (# unknown) [PS]	1945/Under My Thumb/Playpen	1982	30.00
—Sleeve notes distribution by Faulty Products			
❑ 4502	Mommy's Little Monster/ Another State of Mind	1983	16.00
❑ 4502 [PS]	Mommy's Little Monster/ Another State of Mind	1983	16.00
TRIPLE X			
❑ 51023-7	Another State of Mind/ Mommy's Little Monster	1989	5.00
—Clear vinyl			
❑ 51023-7 [PS]	Another State of Mind/ Mommy's Little Monster	1989	5.00
Albums			
EPIC			
❑ E 46055	Social Distortion	1990	20.00
❑ E 47948	Somewhere Between Heaven and Hell	1992	20.00
EPIC/550 MUSIC			
❑ E 64380	White Light, White Heat, White Trash	1996	12.00
RESTLESS			
❑ 72251	Prison Bound	1988	20.00
13TH FLOOR			
❑ SD 1301	Mommy's Little Monster	1983	40.00
—Standard cover with lyric sheet			
❑ SD 1301	Mommy's Little Monster	1983	60.00
—Gatefold cover			
TIME BOMB			
❑ 43500	Mommy's Little Monster	1995	15.00
❑ 43501	Prison Bound	1995	15.00
❑ 43502	Mainliner (Wreckage from the Past)	1995	15.00
❑ 43516 [(2)]	Live at the Roxy	1998	18.00
TRIPLE X			
❑ 51019	Mommy's Little Monster	1989	20.00
—Clear vinyl			
SOCIALITES, THE			
45s			
ARRAWAK			
❑ 1004	Jimmy/The Click	1962	20.00
WARNER BROS.			
❑ 5476	You're Losing Your Touch/ Jive Jimmy	1964	12.00
SOCIETY'S CHILDREN			
45s			
ATCO			
❑ 6538	White Christmas/ I'll Let You Know	1967	12.00
❑ 6553	Count the Ways/Golden Child	1968	10.00
❑ 6597	Live for Today/I'll Let You Know	1968	10.00
❑ 6618	A Tribute to the Four Seasons/ Golden Child	1968	20.00
SOF-TONES, THE			
45s			
CEE BEE			
❑ 1062	Oh Why/(B-side unknown)	195?	8000.
—VG 4000; VG+ 6000			
SOFT CELL			
12-Inch Singles			
AMNESIA			
❑ 62201	It's a Mug's Game (7" and 12" mixes)/Sex Dwarf	1981	20.00
SIRE			
❑ PRO1037 [DJ]	What!/Insecure Me	1982	15.00
❑ PRO1096 [DJ]	Loving You, Hating Me (2 versions)/Heat	1983	12.00
❑ PRO-A-1037 [DJ]	What!/Insecure Me	1982	15.00

Soft Cell, *What!*, Sire 29976, 1982, $4.

Number	Title (A Side/B Side)	Yr	NM
❑ PRO-A-1096 [DJ]	Loving You, Hating Me (2 versions)/Heat	1983	12.00
❑ 49856	Tainted Love-Where Did Our Love Go/Memorabilia/ Tainted Dub	1981	8.00
45s			
SIRE			
❑ PRO1028 [DJ]	Tainted Love/Where Did Our Love Go (Long)//Tainted Love/ Where Did Our Love Go (Short)	1982	10.00
❑ GSRE 0435	Tainted Love/Where Did Our Love Go//What	1983	4.00
—Back to Back Hits series; First release of medley on U.S. stock 45			
❑ PRO-S-1028 [DJ]	Tainted Love/Where Did Our Love Go (Long)//Tainted Love/ Where Did Our Love Go (Short)	1982	10.00
❑ 29641	Heat/It's a Mugs Game	1983	4.00
❑ 29812	Loving You Hating Me/ It's a Mugs Game	1983	9.00
❑ 29812 [DJ]	Loving You Hating Me (mono/stereo)	1983	3.00
❑ 29812 [DJ]	Loving You Hating Me (mono/stereo)	1983	3.00
❑ 29812 [PS]	Loving You Hating Me/ It's a Mugs Game	1983	3.00
❑ 29976	What!/A Man Could Get Lost	1982	4.00
❑ 49855	Tainted Love/Memorabilia	1981	3.00
❑ 49855 [PS]	Tainted Love/Memorabilia	1981	6.00
Albums			
SIRE			
❑ BSK 3647	Non-Stop Erotic Cabaret	1981	12.00
❑ 23694 [EP]	Non-Stop Ecstatic Dancing	1982	10.00
❑ 23769	The Art of Falling Apart	1983	12.00
—With limited 12-inch EP			
❑ 23989 [EP]	Soul Inside	1983	10.00
❑ 25096	This Last Night	1984	10.00

Number	Title (A Side/B Side)	Yr	NM
SOFT MACHINE, THE			
45s			
PROBE			
❑ 452	Joy of a Toy/Why Are We Sleeping	1969	10.00
Albums			
ACCORD			
❑ SN-7178	Memories	1981	10.00
COLUMBIA			
❑ G 30339 [(2)]	Third	1970	15.00
❑ C 30754	Fourth	1971	12.00
❑ KC 31604	5	1972	12.00
❑ KG 32260 [(2)]	Six	1973	15.00
❑ KC 32716	Seven	1974	12.00
COMMAND			
❑ 964 SD [(2)]	Soft Machine	1973	15.00
—Reissue of Probe LPs in one package			
PROBE			
❑ CPLP-4500	The Soft Machine	1968	40.00
—Cover with moving parts			
❑ CPLP-4500	The Soft Machine	1969	20.00
—Regular cover			
❑ CPLP-4505	The Soft Machine, Vol. 2	1969	25.00
SOLDIER BOYS, THE Also see DON COVAY.			
45s			
SCEPTER			
❑ 1230	I'm Your Soldier Boy/ You Picked Me	1962	60.00
SOLITAIRES, THE			
45s			
ARGO			
❑ 5316	Walking Along/Please Kiss This Letter	1958	30.00
MGM			
❑ 13221	Fool That I Am/Fair Weather Lover	1964	30.00

S

Number	Title (A Side/B Side)	Yr	NM
OLD TOWN			
❑ 1000	Blue Valentine/Wonder Boy	1954	400.00
—Black vinyl			
❑ 1000	Blue Valentine/Wonder Boy	1954	1500.
—Red vinyl			
❑ 1003	Chapel of St. Clair/If I Loved You	1954	—
—Unreleased?			
❑ 1006/7	Please Remember My Heart/ South of the Border	1954	700.00
—Black vinyl			
❑ 1006/7	Please Remember My Heart/ South of the Border	1954	3000.
—Red vinyl			
❑ 1006/8	Please Remember My Heart/ Chances I've Taken	1954	150.00
❑ 1008	Chances I've Taken/Lonely	1954	700.00
❑ 1008	Please Remember My Heart/ Chances I've Taken	196?	25.00
—Blue label			
❑ 1010	I Don't Stand a Ghost of a Chance/Girl of Mine	1955	500.00
❑ 1012	My Dear/What Did She Say	1955	400.00
—Logo in Old English style			
❑ 1012	My Dear/What Did She Say	1956	75.00
—Logo in block letters			
❑ 1014	The Wedding/Don't Fall in Love	1955	100.00
❑ 1015	Magic Rose/Later for You Baby	1955	100.00
❑ 1019	The Honeymoon/Fine Little Girl	1956	100.00
❑ 1026	You've Sinned/The Angels Sang	1956	100.00
❑ 1026	You've Sinned/You're Back with Me	1956	300.00
❑ 1032	Give Me One More Chance/ Nothing Like a Little Love	1956	200.00
❑ 1034	Walking Along/Please Kiss This Letter	1957	75.00
—Yellow label			
❑ 1034	Walking Along/Please Kiss This Letter	196?	25.00
—Blue label			
❑ 1044	I Really Love You So/ Thrill of Love	1957	400.00
❑ 1049	Walkin' and Talkin'/ No More Sorrows	1958	100.00
❑ 1059	Please Remember My Heart/ Big Mary's House	1958	40.00
❑ 1066	Embraceable You/ Round Goes My Heart	1959	40.00
❑ 1071	Light a Candle in the Chapel/ Helpless	1959	40.00
❑ 1096	Lonesome Lover/Pretty Thing	1961	40.00
❑ 1139	The Time Is Here/Honey Babe	1963	30.00

S

SOME OF CHET'S FRIENDS
Also see CHET ATKINS.

Number	Title (A Side/B Side)	Yr	NM
45s			
RCA VICTOR			
❑ 47-9229	Chet's Tune/Country Gentleman	1967	10.00
❑ 47-9229 [PS]	Chet's Tune/Country Gentleman	1967	15.00
❑ 74-0799	Chet's Tune (Part 1)/ Chet's Tune (Part 2)	1972	6.00

SOMETHING WILD

Number	Title (A Side/B Side)	Yr	NM
45s			
PSYCHEDELIC			
❑ 1691	Trippin' Out/She's Kinda Weird	1966	300.00

SOMETHING YOUNG

Number	Title (A Side/B Side)	Yr	NM
45s			
FONTANA			
❑ 1556	Oh, Don't Come Crying/ The Words I'm Seeking	1966	25.00

SOMMERS, RONNY
See SONNY.

SONIC YOUTH

Number	Title (A Side/B Side)	Yr	NM
12-Inch Singles			
BLAST FIRST			
❑ BFUS 34	Teenage Riot (edit)/ Silver Rocket/Kissability	1988	10.00
DGC			
❑ 4123 [DJ]	Kool Thing/Kool Thing (8-track demo)	1990	12.00
❑ 4172 [DJ]	Disappear (3 versions)	1991	8.00
ENIGMA			
❑ EPRO 182 [DJ]	Candle (Edit)/Hey Joni (Live)/ Flower (Live)/Ghost Bitch (Live)	1989	25.00
❑ EPRO182 [DJ]	Candle (Edit)/Hey Joni (Live)/ Flower (Live)/Ghost Bitch (Live)	1989	25.00
HOMESTEAD			
❑ HMS 047	Flower/Halloween	1986	25.00
45s			
DGC			
❑ 19664	Personality Crisis/Dirty Boots	1990	15.00
—Given away with copies of Sassy magazine			
❑ 106610 [DJ]	Goo	1990	10.00
—Promo flexi-disc with backing card			
FORCED EXPOSURE			
❑ 001	Making the Nature Scene/I Killed Christgau with My Big Fuckin' Dick	1984	50.00
❑ 001	Making the Nature Scene/I Killed Christgau with My Big Fuckin' Dick	1984	150.00
—Test pressing (25 made with special sleeve)			
❑ 001 [PS]	Making the Nature Scene/ I Killed Christgau with My Big Fuckin' Dick	1984	50.00
—Black and white sleeve			
❑ 001 [PS]	Making the Nature Scene/ I Killed Christgau with My Big Fuckin' Dick	1984	150.00
—Special multi-color sleeve with live band shot on rear; only released with test pressings (25 made)			
❑ 012	Silver Rocket/You Pose You Lose/Non-Metal Dude Wearing Metal Tee	1988	25.00
❑ 012 [PS]	Silver Rocket/You Pose You Lose/Non-Metal Dude Wearing Metal Tee	1988	25.00
IRIDESCENCE			
❑ 12	Death Valley 69/Brave Men Run	1984	12.50
—With Lydia Lunch			
❑ 12 [PS]	Death Valley 69/Brave Men Run	1984	12.50
NEW ALLIANCE			
❑ 030	Burnin' Up/Tuff Titty Rap/ Into the Groovey	1986	10.00
—As "Ciccone Youth"			
❑ 030 [PS]	Burnin' Up/Tuff Titty Rap/ Into the Groovey	1986	10.00
SUB POP			
❑ 26	Touch Me I'm Sick/Halloween	1988	15.00
—B-side by Mudhoney; black vinyl			
❑ 26	Touch Me I'm Sick/Halloween	1988	30.00
—B-side by Mudhoney; clear vinyl			
❑ 26 [PS]	Touch Me I'm Sick/Halloween	1988	20.00
—#2 in Sub Pop Singles Club series			
Albums			
DGC			
❑ 24297	Goo	1990	30.00
❑ 24485	Dirty	1992	25.00
❑ 24632	Experimental Jet Set, Trash and No Star	1994	40.00
❑ 24825 [(2)]	Washing Machine	1995	40.00
ENIGMA			
❑ 75403 [(2)]	Daydream Nation	1988	30.00
GEFFEN			
❑ 490650-1	NYC Ghosts and Flowers	2000	15.00
GOOFIN'			
❑ GOO 04	Murray Street	2002	12.00
❑ GOO 05 [(4)]	Dirty (Deluxe Edition)	2003	30.00
❑ GOO 06 [(2)]	Sonic Nurse	2004	15.00
❑ GOO 07 [(4)]	Goo (Deluxe Edition)	2005	30.00
❑ GOO 08 [(2)]	Sonic Youth	2006	20.00
—Reissue of 1982 debut album with a second record of bonus tracks			
❑ GOO 11	Rather Ripped	2006	12.00
HOMESTEAD			
❑ HMS 016	Bad Moon Rising	1985	25.00
❑ HMS 021 [EP]	Death Valley '69	1985	25.00
—With Lydia Lunch			
KONKURRENT			
❑ FISH-9	In the Fishtank	2002	15.00
—With I.C.P. and The Ex; U.S. editions are distributed by Touch and Go Records			
MOBILE FIDELITY			
❑ 1-257	Goo	1996	100.00
—Audiophile vinyl			
MY SO-CALLED RECORDS			
❑ 3 [(2)]	A Thousand Leaves	1998	15.00
NEUTRAL			
❑ 001 [EP]	Sonic Youth	1982	80.00
❑ N-1 [EP]	Sonic Youth	1982	80.00
❑ 9	Confusion Is Sex	1983	70.00
RHINO			
❑ R1 71591	Made in U.S.A. (Soundtrack)	1995	15.00
—Clear vinyl record and sleeve; music recorded in 1986			
SST			
❑ 059	Evol	1986	40.00
❑ 080 [EP]	Starpower	1986	30.00
❑ 096	Confusion Is Sex	1987	40.00
—Reissue of Neutral 9			
❑ 097 [EP]	Sonic Youth	1987	25.00
❑ 134	Sister	1987	25.00
❑ 155 [EP]	Master Dik	1988	25.00
SYR			
❑ 1	Anagrama	1997	10.00
—Red vinyl			
❑ 2	Slaapkamers Met Slagroom	1997	10.00
—Teal vinyl			
❑ 3	Invito Al Cielo	1998	10.00
—With Jim O'Rourke; clear vinyl			
❑ 4 [(2)]	Goodbye 20th Century	1999	15.00
❑ 5 [(2)]	Kim Gordon - DJ Olive - Ikue Mori	2000	12.00

SONICS, THE (1)
Male vocal group.

Number	Title (A Side/B Side)	Yr	NM
45s			
AMCO			
❑ 001	It's You/Preacher Man	1962	200.00
CHECKER			
❑ 922	This Broken Heart/ You Made Me Cry	1959	25.00
HARVARD			
❑ 801	This Broken Heart/ You Made Me Cry	1959	400.00
❑ 922	This Broken Heart/ You Made Me Cry	1959	50.00
JAMIE			
❑ 1235	Sugaree/Beautiful Brown Eyes	1962	20.00
X-TRA			
❑ 107	Once in a Lifetime/It Ain't True	1958	2000.

SONICS, THE (2)
Rock band from the Pacific Northwest.

Number	Title (A Side/B Side)	Yr	NM
45s			
BURDETTE			
❑ 106	Dirty Old Man/Bama Lama Bama Loo	1975	8.00
ETIQUETTE			
❑ 11	Keep a-Knockin'/The Witch	1965	30.00
❑ 16	The Hustler/Boss Hoss	1965	30.00
❑ 18	Don't Be Afraid of the Dark /Shot Down	1965	30.00
❑ 22	Don't Believe in Christmas/ Christmas Spirit	1965	30.00
—B-side by the Wailers			
❑ 23	Louie Louie/Cinderella	1966	30.00
GREAT NORTHWEST			
❑ 702	The Witch/Bama Lama Bama Loo	1979	5.00
JERDEN			
❑ 809	Love Lights/You Got Your Head On Backwards	1966	15.00
❑ 810	The Witch/Like No Other	1966	15.00
❑ 811	Psycho/Maintaining My Cool	1966	15.00
NORTON			
❑ 45-066	Don't Believe in Christmas/ Santa Claus	1997	2.00
—A-side is reissue of Etiquette 22			
❑ 45-066 [PS]	Don't Believe in Christmas/ Santa Claus	1997	2.00
PICCADILLY			
❑ 244	Anyway the Wind Blows/ Lost Love	1967	20.00
—A-side written by Frank Zappa			
UNI			
❑ 55039	Anyway the Wind Blows/ Lost Love	1967	15.00
—A-side written by Frank Zappa			
Albums			
BEAT ROCKET			
❑ BR 114	Introducing the Sonics	199?	12.00
BOMP!			
❑ 4011	Sinderella	1980	15.00
BUCKSHOT			
❑ 001	Explosives	1973	200.00
ETIQUETTE			
❑ ETALB-024 [M]	Here Are the Sonics!!!	1965	200.00
—Purple label			
❑ ETALB-024 [M]	Here Are the Sonics!!!	1965	250.00
—Red label			
❑ ETLPS-024	Here Are the Sonics!!!	1984	16.00
—Purple label, flimsier vinyl, with date on back cover			
❑ ETLPS-024 [S]	Here Are the Sonics!!!	1965	300.00
—Purple label			
❑ ETLPS-024 [S]	Here Are the Sonics!!!	1965	400.00
—Red label			
❑ ETALB-027 [M]	The Sonics Boom	1966	300.00
❑ ETLPS-027	The Sonics Boom	1984	10.00
—Flimsier vinyl, with date on back cover			
❑ ETLPS-027 [R]	The Sonics Boom	1966	200.00
FIRST AMERICAN			
❑ FA-7715	Original Northwest Punk	1978	20.00
❑ FA-7719	Unreleased	1980	20.00
❑ FA-7779	Fire and Ice	1983	20.00

Except when noted otherwise, VG = 25% of NM, and VG+ = 50% of NM. (Example: VG = $2.00, VG+ = $4.00 and NM = $8.00.)

Number	Title (A Side/B Side)	Yr	NM
JERDEN			
❑ JRL-7007 [M]	Introducing the Sonics	1967	200.00
❑ JRS-7007 [R]	Introducing the Sonics	1967	150.00

SONICS, THE (2); THE WAILERS; THE GALAXIES

Albums

Number	Title (A Side/B Side)	Yr	NM
ETIQUETTE			
❑ ETALB-025	Merry Christmas	1984	10.00
—Flimsier vinyl, with date on back cover			
❑ ETALB-025 [M]	Merry Christmas	1965	500.00

SONICS, THE (U)
Some of these could be group (1); none of these are group (2).

45s

Number	Title (A Side/B Side)	Yr	NM
ARMONIA			
❑ 102	Funny/I Get That Feeling	1962	150.00
GAITY			
❑ 114	Marlene/(B-side unknown)	1959	2000.
—VG 1000; VG+ 1500			
GROOVE			
❑ 0112	Bumble Bee/As I Live On	1955	200.00
NOCTURNE			
❑ 110	Triangle Love/Evil Eye	1959	80.00
RKO UNIQUE			
❑ 411	Triangle Love/Evil Eye	1957	60.00

SONNETS, THE

45s

Number	Title (A Side/B Side)	Yr	NM
GUYDEN			
❑ 2112	I Can't Get Sentimental/ Forever for You	1964	15.00
HERALD			
❑ 477	Please Won't You Call Me/Why Should We Break Up	1956	60.00

SONNY
Contains many records he made under aliases. Also see SONNY AND CHER.

45s

Number	Title (A Side/B Side)	Yr	NM
ATCO			
❑ 6369	Laugh at Me/Tony	1965	12.00
—B-side credited to "Sonny's Group"			
❑ 6386	The Revolution Kind/Georgia and John Quetzal	1965	12.00
❑ 6505	Misty Roses/I Told My Girl to Go Away	1967	10.00
❑ 6531	Pammie's on a Bummer/My Best Friend's Girl Is Out of Sight	1967	10.00
FIDELITY			
❑ 3020	Wearing Black/Don't Have to Tell Me	1960	25.00
—As "Don Christy"			
GO			
❑ 1001	As Long As You Love Me/ I'll Always Be Grateful	1960	25.00
—As "Don Christy"			
HIGHLAND			
❑ 1160	I'll Change/Try It Out on Me	1963	30.00
—As "Sonny Bono"			
MCA			
❑ 40139	Rub Your Nose/Laugh at Me	1973	4.00
—As "Sonny Bono"			
❑ 40271	Our Last Show/Classified 1A	1974	4.00
—As "Sonny Bono"			
NAME			
❑ 3	As Long As You Love Me /I'll Always Be Grateful	1960	25.00
—As "Don Christy"			
SPECIALTY			
❑ 672	Wearing Black/One Little Answer	1959	25.00
—As "Don Christy"			
❑ 733	One Little Answer/Comin' Down the Chimney	1974	6.00
—As "Sonny Bono and Little Tootsie"			
SWAMI			
❑ 1001	Don't Shake My Tree/(Mama) Come Get Your Baby Boy	1961	25.00
—As "Ronny Sommers"			
VEE JAY			
❑ 710	Midnight Surf/Ride the Wild Quetzal	1966	25.00
—As "Sonny Bono"			

Albums

Number	Title (A Side/B Side)	Yr	NM
ATCO			
❑ 33-229 [M]	Inner Views	1967	20.00
❑ SD 33-229 [S]	Inner Views	1967	20.00

SONNY AND CHER
Includes early records as "Caesar and Cleo." Also see CHER; SONNY.

45s

Number	Title (A Side/B Side)	Yr	NM
ATCO			
❑ 6345	Just You/Sing C'est La Vie	1965	10.00
❑ 6359	I Got You Babe/It's Gonna Rain	1965	12.00
❑ 6381	But You're Mine/Hello	1965	12.00
❑ 6395	What Now My Love/ I Look for You	1965	12.00
❑ 6420	Have I Stayed Too Long/ Leave Me Be	1966	10.00
❑ 6440	Little Man/Monday	1966	10.00
❑ 6449	Living for You/Love Don't Come	1966	10.00
❑ 6461	The Beat Goes On/ Love Don't Come	1967	12.00
❑ 6480	A Beautiful Story/Podunk	1967	10.00
❑ 6486	Plastic Man/It's the Little Things	1967	10.00
❑ 6507	It's the Little Things/ Don't Talk to Strangers	1967	10.00
❑ 6541	Good Combination/You and Me	1968	10.00
❑ 6555	Circus/I Would Marry You Today	1968	10.00
❑ 6605	You Gotta Have a Thing of Your Own/I Got You Babe	1968	10.00
❑ 6684	You're a Friend of Mine/ I Would Marry You Today	1969	10.00
❑ 6758	Get It Together/Hold Me Tighter	1970	8.00
KAPP			
❑ 2141	Real People/Somebody	1971	4.00
❑ 2151	All I Ever Need Is You/ I Got You Babe	1971	5.00
❑ 2163	A Cowboy's Work Is Never Done/Somebody	1972	5.00
❑ 2176	When You Say Love/Crystal Clear and Muddy Waters	1972	4.00
MCA			
❑ 40026	Mama Was a Rock and Roll Singer, Papa Used to Write All Her Songs (Parts 1 & 2)	1973	4.00
❑ 40083	The Greatest Show on Earth/ You Know Darn Well	1973	4.00
PHILCO-FORD			
❑ HP-8	I Got You Babe/ The Beat Goes On	1967	25.00
—4-inch plastic "Hip Pocket Record" with color sleeve			
REPRISE			
❑ 0308	Love Is Strange/Do You Want to Dance	1964	20.00
—As "Caesar and Cleo"			
❑ 0309	Baby Don't Go/ Walkin' the Quetzal	1964	20.00
❑ 0392	Baby Don't Go/ Walkin' the Quetzal	1965	15.00
❑ 0419	Love Is Strange/Let the Good Times Roll	1965	20.00
—As "Caesar and Cleo"			
❑ 0419 [PS]	Love Is Strange/Let the Good Times Roll	1965	40.00
—As "Caesar and Cleo"			
❑ 0723	Baby Don't Go/Love Is Strange	1968	5.00
—"Back to Back Hits" series — originals have both "r:" and "W7" logos			
VAULT			
❑ 909	The Letter/Spring Fever	1964	30.00
—As "Caesar and Cleo"			
❑ 916	The Letter/Spring Fever	1965	12.00
❑ 916 [PS]	The Letter/Spring Fever	1965	50.00
WARNER BROS.			
❑ 8341	You're Not Right for Me/ Wrong Number	1977	5.00

7-Inch Extended Plays

Number	Title (A Side/B Side)	Yr	NM
ATCO			
❑ LSD 33-177	It's Gonna Rain/You've Really Got a Hold on Me//I Got You Babe/The Letter/Why Don't They Let Us Fall in Love	1965	25.00
—Jukebox issue; small hole, plays at 33 1/3 rpm			
❑ LSD 33-177 [PS]	Look At Us	1965	25.00
KAPP			
❑ 34875	More Today Than Yesterday/ I Love What You Did With The Love I Gave You/Here Comes That Rainy Day Feeling//Crystal Clear-Muddy Waters/United We Stand/All I Ever Need Is You	1972	10.00
—Jukebox issue; small hole, plays at 33 1/3 rpm			
❑ 34875 [PS]	All I Ever Need Is You	1972	10.00
—Part of "Little LP" series (LLP #184)			

Albums

Number	Title (A Side/B Side)	Yr	NM
ATCO			
❑ 33-177 [M]	Look At Us	1965	15.00
—With white box that says "Includes Their Big Hit 'I Got You Babe'" (second edition)			
❑ 33-177 [M]	Look At Us	1965	20.00
—Without white box that says "Includes Their Big Hit 'I Got You Babe'" (original)			
❑ SD 33-177 [S]	Look At Us	1965	15.00
—With white box that says "Includes Their Big Hit 'I Got You Babe'" (second edition)			
❑ SD 33-177 [S]	Look At Us	1965	25.00
—Without white box that says "Includes Their Big Hit 'I Got You Babe'" (original)			
❑ 33-183 [M]	The Wondrous World of Sonny and Cher	1966	15.00
❑ SD 33-183 [S]	The Wondrous World of Sonny and Cher	1966	20.00
❑ 33-203 [M]	In Case You're in Love	1967	15.00
❑ SD 33-203 [S]	In Case You're in Love	1967	20.00
❑ 33-214 [M]	Good Times	1967	15.00
❑ SD 33-214 [S]	Good Times	1967	20.00
❑ 33-219 [M]	The Best of Sonny and Cher	1967	15.00
❑ SD 33-219 [P]	The Best of Sonny and Cher	1967	20.00
—"What Now My Love," "A Beautiful Story," "But You're Mine" and "Laugh at Me" are rechanneled			
❑ SD 2-804 [(2)]	The Two of Us	1972	20.00
—Combines "Look at Us" and "In Case You're in Love"			
❑ A2M 5177 [(2)M]	Sonny & Cher's Greatest Hits	1967	30.00
—Columbia Record Club exclusive			
❑ A2S 5178 [(2)S]	Sonny & Cher's Greatest Hits	1967	30.00
—Columbia Record Club exclusive			
❑ SD 11000	The Beat Goes On	1975	15.00
KAPP			
❑ KS-3654	Sonny & Cher Live	1971	15.00
❑ KS-3660	All I Ever Need Is You	1972	15.00
—Orange and red swirl label			
❑ KS-3660	All I Ever Need Is You	1972	20.00
—Black label with red "Kapp" cap at top			
❑ KS-3660	All I Ever Need Is You	1972	30.00
—Red label with red "Kapp" cap at top			
❑ KRS-5560	All I Ever Need Is You	1972	12.00
—Reissue; orange and red swirl label; some of these have a sticker on the front cover with the new number with no difference in value			
❑ ST-94312	All I Ever Need Is You	1972	20.00
—Capitol Record Club edition			
MCA			
❑ 2009	Sonny & Cher Live	1973	12.00
—Reissue of Kapp 3654			
❑ 2021	All I Ever Need Is You	1973	12.00
—Reissue of Kapp 3660			
❑ 2101	Mama Was a Rock & Roll Singer Papa Used to Write All Her Songs	1973	12.00
❑ 2117	Greatest Hits	1974	12.00
❑ 2-8004 [(2)]	Sonny & Cher Live in Las Vegas, Vol. 2	1973	15.00
PAIR			
❑ PDL2-1140 [(2)]	Sonny & Cher At Their Best	1986	12.00
REPRISE			
❑ R 6177 [M]	Baby Don't Go	1965	30.00
❑ RS 6177 [P]	Baby Don't Go	1965	30.00
—By "Sonny & Cher & Friends" (also includes The Lettermen, Bill Medley and The Blendells)			
TVP			
❑ TVP-1021	The Hits of Sonny & Cher	1977	12.00

SONNY AND THE DEMONS

Albums

Number	Title (A Side/B Side)	Yr	NM
UNITED ARTISTS			
❑ UAL-3316 [M]	Drag Kings	1964	50.00
❑ UAS-6316 [S]	Drag Kings	1964	60.00

SONS OF CHAMPLIN, THE
With Bill Champlin, later of CHICAGO.

45s

Number	Title (A Side/B Side)	Yr	NM
ARIOLA AMERICA			
❑ 7606	Look Out/Queen of the Rain	1975	4.00
❑ 7627	Hold On/Still in Love with You	1976	4.00
❑ 7633	You/Imagination's Sake	1976	4.00
❑ 7653	Follow Your Heart/Here Is Where Your Love Belongs	1976	4.00
❑ 7664	Saved by the Grace of Your Love/ West End	1977	4.00
CAPITOL			
❑ 2437	1982-A/Black and Blue Rainbow	1969	8.00
❑ 2534	Freedom/Hello Sunlight	1969	8.00
❑ 2663	It's Time/Why Do People Run	1969	8.00
❑ 2786	You Can Fly/Terry's Tune	1970	6.00
❑ SPRO4668	Jesus is Coming/Part II	1968	20.00
—Distributed by request from Capitol mail order; small hole			
❑ SPRO4668 [PS]	Jesus is Coming/Part II	1968	40.00
—Distributed by request from Capitol mail order; small hole			
COLUMBIA			
❑ 45872	Welcome to the Dance/Swim	1973	5.00
GOLDMINE			
❑ 101	Look Out/Queen of the Rain	1975	5.00

S

Number	Title (A Side/B Side)	Yr	NM
VERVE			
❑ 10500	Sing Me a Lullaby/Fat City	1967	25.00

Albums

Number	Title (A Side/B Side)	Yr	NM
ARIOLA AMERICA			
❑ SW-50002	The Sons of Champlin	1975	10.00
❑ ST-50007	A Circle Filled with Love	1976	10.00
❑ SW-50017	Loving Is Why	1977	10.00
CAPITOL			
❑ SWBB-200 [(2)]	Loosen Up Naturally	1969	20.00
—With the F-word airbrushed off the cover artwork			
❑ SWBB-200 [(2)]	Loosen Up Naturally	1969	25.00
—With the F-word scratched off the cover artwork			
❑ SWBB-200 [(2)]	Loosen Up Naturally	1969	50.00
—With the F-word clearly visible as part of the cover artwork			
❑ SKAO-322	The Sons	1969	25.00
❑ ST-675	Follow Your Heart	1971	20.00
COLUMBIA			
❑ KC 32341	Welcome to the Dance	1973	15.00
GOLDMINE			
❑ GM 94930	The Sons of Champlin	1975	20.00
SONS OF CHAMPLIN			
❑ (no #)	Minus Seeds and Stems	1969	500.00

SONS OF HEROES

Albums

Number	Title (A Side/B Side)	Yr	NM
MCA			
❑ 39010	Sons of Heroes	1983	20.00

SONS OF ROBIN STONE

12-Inch Singles

Number	Title (A Side/B Side)	Yr	NM
PEZZA			
❑ P-11	I Need It Bad (Club 4:28) (Radio Mix) (Instrumental)	1982	25.00

45s

Number	Title (A Side/B Side)	Yr	NM
ATCO			
❑ 6929	Got to Get You Back/Love Is Just Around the Corner	1974	80.00
EPIC			
❑ 8-50257	Let's Do It Now/It Only Happens in the Movies	1976	70.00

SONS OF THE PIONEERS

45s

Number	Title (A Side/B Side)	Yr	NM
CORAL			
❑ 9-61186	River of No Return/The Lilies Grow High	1954	20.00
❑ 9-61316	Montana/Lonely Little Room	1954	20.00
❑ 9-64172	Sierra Nevada/If You Would Only Be Mine	1954	20.00
DECCA			
❑ 9-29814	Cool Water/Tumbling Tumbleweeds	1956	15.00
GRANITE			
❑ 550	Cool Water/Pretty Painted Ladies	1976	6.00
❑ 551	Indian Woman/(B-side unknown)	1977	6.00
RCA VICTOR			
❑ 47-2836	Cool Water/Chant of the Wanderer	1949	30.00
❑ 47-2837	Tumbling Tumbleweeds/The Everlasting Hills of Oklahoma	1949	30.00
❑ 47-2838	Trees/The Timber Trail	1949	30.00
—The above three comprise a box set; quickly reissued as 48-0004, 0005 and 0006			
❑ 47-3983	America Forever/Little White Cross	1950	25.00
❑ 47-4071	Roses/Mexicali Rose	1951	20.00
❑ 47-4072	Moonlight and Roses/Bring Your Roses to Her Now	1951	20.00
❑ 47-4073	San Antonio Rose/Room Full of Roses	1951	20.00
—The above three comprise a box set			
❑ 47-4131	Daddy's Little Cowboy/Baby I Ain't Gonna Cry No More	1951	20.00
❑ 47-4264	Heart Break Hill/The Wind	1951	20.00
❑ 47-4347	The Lord's Prayer/Resurectus	1951	20.00
❑ 47-4431	Outlaws/I Still Do	1951	20.00
❑ 47-4459	I Told Them All About You/Ho-Le-O	1952	20.00
❑ 47-4571	Land Beyond the Sun/Waltz of the Roses	1952	20.00
❑ 47-4639	Diesel Smoke/Almost	1952	20.00
❑ 47-4937	Let's Pretend/The Everlasting Hills of Oklahoma	1952	20.00
❑ 47-6055	The Ballad of Davy Crockett/Graveyard Filler of the West	1955	25.00
❑ 47-6109	I Wonder When We'll Ever Know/The King's Highway	1955	15.00
❑ 47-6123	The Tennessee Rock 'n' Roll/The Three of Us	1955	25.00
❑ 47-6184	Be What You Want to Be/Epidemic	1955	15.00
❑ 47-6276	Yaller Yaller Gold/King of the River	1955	20.00
❑ 47-6376	How Great Thou Art/The Last Frontier	1956	15.00
❑ 47-6507	The Searchers/Song of the Prodigal Son	1956	15.00
❑ 47-6655	For the Love of You/Timmy's Tune	1956	15.00
❑ 47-6890	One More Time/Hasta La Vista	1957	15.00
❑ 47-7024	Ballad of the Cowboy Sailor/The Piney Woods	1957	15.00
❑ 47-7079	High Ridin' Woman/God Has His Arms Around Me	1957	15.00
❑ 47-7392	A Fiddle, a Rifle, an Ax and a Bible/My Last Goodbye	1958	12.00
❑ 47-8310	Crazy Arms/Cattle Call Rondolet	1963	10.00
❑ 47-8575	Destiny/Green Ice and Mountain Men	1965	10.00
❑ 47-9509	Gringo's Guitar/Margretta	1968	8.00
❑ 48-0004	Cool Water/Chant of the Wanderer	1949	30.00
—Green vinyl original			
❑ 48-0004	Cool Water/Chant of the Wanderer	1951	20.00
—Black vinyl reissue			
❑ 48-0005	Tumbling Tumbleweeds/Everlasting Hills of Oklahoma	1949	20.00
—Black vinyl reissue			
❑ 48-0005	Tumbling Tumbleweeds/Everlasting Hills of Oklahoma	1949	30.00
—Green vinyl original			
❑ 48-0006	Trees/The Timber Trail	1949	20.00
—Black vinyl reissue			
❑ 48-0006	Trees/The Timber Trail	1949	30.00
—Green vinyl original			
❑ 48-0007	Blue Prairie/Cowboy Camp Meetin'	1949	20.00
—Black vinyl reissue			
❑ 48-0007	Blue Prairie/Cowboy Camp Meetin'	1949	30.00
—Green vinyl original			
❑ 48-0060	Room Full of Roses/Riders in the Sky	1949	30.00
—Green vinyl original			
❑ 48-0094	Rounded Up in Glory/Too High, Too Wide, Too Low	1949	30.00
—Green vinyl original			
❑ 48-0095	Lead Me Gently Home Father/Power in the Blood	1949	30.00
—Green vinyl original			
❑ 48-0096	The Old Rugged Cross/Read the Bible Every Day	1949	30.00
—Green vinyl original			
❑ 48-0101	Lie Low Little Doggies/Bar None Ranch	1949	30.00
—Green vinyl original			
❑ 48-0141	Red River Valley/Santa Fe, New Mexico	1950	30.00
—Green vinyl original			
❑ 48-0171	Wedding Bells/Love at the County Fair	1950	30.00
—With Dale Evans; green vinyl original			
❑ 48-0183	Cigareets, Whusky and Wild, Wild Women/My Best to You	1950	30.00
—Green vinyl; reissue of hit 78 rpm from 1947			
❑ 48-0184	Let's Go West Again/Let Me Share Your Name	1950	30.00
—Green vinyl original			
❑ 48-0220	Teardrops in My Heart/You Don't Know What Lonesome Is	1950	30.00
—Green vinyl; reissue of hit 78 from 1947			
❑ 48-0221	The Sea Walker/The Touch of God's Hand	1950	30.00
—Green vinyl original			
❑ 48-0306	Roses/The Eagle's Heart	1950	25.00
—Green vinyl original			
❑ 48-0315	Rollin' Dust/Wagons West	1950	25.00
—Green vinyl original			
❑ 48-0345	Song of the Wagonmaster/Chuckawalla Swing	1950	25.00
—Green vinyl original			
❑ 48-0366	Land Beyond the Sun/I Told Them All About You	1950	25.00
—Green vinyl original			
❑ 48-0368	Old Man Atom/What This Country Needs	1950	25.00
—Green vinyl original			
❑ 48-0388	Where Are You/What This Country Needs	1950	25.00
—Green vinyl original			
❑ 48-0486	Lonesome/The Wondrous Word	1951	20.00
❑ 74-0199	Talli Wind/Hawaiian Lullaby	1969	8.00
❑ WBY-25	The Ballad of Davy Crockett/The Graveyard Filler of the West	1955	30.00
❑ WBY-25 [PS]	The Ballad of Davy Crockett/The Graveyard Filler of the West	1955	50.00
❑ WBY-27	A Whale of a Tale/Old Betsy	1955	25.00
❑ WBY-46	Home on the Range/Cheyenne	1957	20.00
❑ WBY-46 [PS]	Home on the Range/Cheyenne	1957	30.00
❑ WBY-68	Wagon Train/Lie Low Little Doggies	195?	20.00
❑ WBY-71	The Restless Gun/Bunkhouse Bugle Boy	1957	20.00
❑ WBY-71 [PS]	The Restless Gun/Bunkhouse Bugle Boy	1957	30.00
❑ VP-3-2668 [S]	El Paso/Your Cheatin' Heart	196?	15.00
—B-side by Skeeter Davis; jukebox issue; small hole, plays at 33 1/3 rpm			

7-Inch Extended Plays

Number	Title (A Side/B Side)	Yr	NM
RCA VICTOR			
❑ 547-0029	Cool Water/Chant of the Wanderer//Tumbling Tumbleweeds/The Everlasting Hills of Oklahoma	195?	20.00
—One record of 2-EP set EPB 3032			
❑ 547-0030	Cowboy Camp Meetin'/Blue Prairie//The Timber Trail/Trees	195?	20.00
—One record of 2-EP set EPB 3032			
❑ EPA 422	Empty Saddles/There's a Gold Mine in the Sky//Home on the Range/Old Pioneer	1952	25.00
❑ EPA 422 [PS]	Sons of the Pioneers Sing Western Favorites	1952	25.00
❑ EPA 650	Tumbling Tumbleweeds/Press Along to the Big Corral/Wind/Bunkhouse Bugle Boy//Home on the Range/La Borachita/Timber Trail/Happy Cowboy	1955	20.00
❑ EPA 650 [PS]	Favorite Cowboy Songs Vol. I	1955	20.00
❑ EPA 651	Cowboy Lament/Pajarillo Barrenquero/So Long to the Red River Valley/Come and Get It//Cool Water/Curly Joe from Idaho/Cowboy's Dream/Along the Santa Fe Trail	1955	20.00
❑ EPA 651 [PS]	Favorite Cowboy Songs Vol. 2	1955	20.00
❑ EPB 3032 [PS]	Cowboy Classics	195?	20.00
—Gatefold cover for 547-0029 and 547-0030			

Albums

Number	Title (A Side/B Side)	Yr	NM
COLUMBIA			
❑ FC 37439	The Sons of the Pioneers: Columbia Historical Edition	1981	10.00
MCA			
❑ 730	Tumbleweed Trails	198?	10.00
RCA CAMDEN			
❑ CAL-413 [M]	Wagons West	1958	20.00
❑ CAS-413 [R]	Wagons West	1963	12.00
❑ CAL-587 [M]	Room Full of Roses	1960	20.00
RCA VICTOR			
❑ PRM-104 [M]	Westward Ho!	1961	25.00
—Special-products issue			
❑ LPM-1130 [M]	Favorite Cowboy Songs	1955	50.00
❑ LPM-1431 [M]	How Great Thou Art	1957	50.00
❑ LPM-1483 [M]	One Man's Songs	1957	50.00
❑ LPM-2118 [M]	Cool Water	1960	25.00
❑ LSP-2118 [S]	Cool Water	1960	30.00
❑ ANL1-2332	A Country-Western Songbook	1977	15.00
❑ LPM-2356 [M]	Lure of the West	1961	25.00
❑ LSP-2356 [S]	Lure of the West	1961	30.00
❑ LPM-2456 [M]	Tumbleweed Trails	1962	25.00
❑ LSP-2456 [S]	Tumbleweed Trails	1962	30.00
❑ LPM-2603 [M]	Our Men Out West	1963	20.00
❑ LSP-2603 [S]	Our Men Out West	1963	25.00
❑ LPM-2652 [M]	Hymns of the Cowboy	1963	20.00
❑ LSP-2652 [S]	Hymns of the Cowboy	1963	25.00
❑ LPM-2737 [M]	Trail Dust	1963	20.00
❑ LSP-2737 [S]	Trail Dust	1963	25.00
❑ LPM-2855 [M]	Country Fare	1964	20.00
❑ LSP-2855 [S]	Country Fare	1964	25.00
❑ LPM-2957 [M]	Down Memory Trail	1964	20.00
❑ LSP-2957 [S]	Down Memory Trail	1964	25.00
❑ LPM-3032 [10]	Cowboy Classics	1952	100.00
❑ LPM-3095 [10]	Cowboy Hymns and Spirituals	1952	100.00
❑ LPM-3162 [10]	Western Classics	1953	100.00
❑ LPM-3351 [M]	Legends of the West	1965	15.00
❑ LSP-3351 [S]	Legends of the West	1965	20.00
❑ ANL1-3468	The Best of the Sons of the Pioneers	1980	10.00
❑ LPM-3476 [M]	The Best of Sons of the Pioneers	1966	15.00
❑ LSP-3476 [S]	The Best of Sons of the Pioneers	1966	20.00
❑ LPM-3554 [M]	The Songs of Bob Nolan	1966	15.00
❑ LSP-3554 [S]	The Songs of Bob Nolan	1966	20.00
❑ AYL1-3679	Cool Water	1980	10.00
❑ LPM-3714 [M]	Campfire Favorites	1967	25.00
❑ LSP-3714 [S]	Campfire Favorites	1967	20.00
❑ LPM-3964 [M]	South of the Border	1968	80.00
❑ LSP-3964 [S]	South of the Border	1968	20.00
❑ AYM1-4092	Let's Go West Again	1981	10.00
READER'S DIGEST			
❑ RBA-135-A [(7)]	Down Memory Trail with the Sons of the Pioneers	1981	60.00

SILVER SPUR

Number	Title (A Side/B Side)	Yr	NM
❑ S 581 [(2)]	Celebration: Commemorating 50 Years of the Sons of the Pioneers	1982	15.00

SOOTZ, MANNY

45s

PIRATE

Number	Title (A Side/B Side)	Yr	NM
❑ 841	Cape Canaveral (Part 1)/Cape Canaveral (Part 2)	1957	25.00

SOPHISTICATES, THE

45s

VIVA

Number	Title (A Side/B Side)	Yr	NM
❑ 61	When Elvis Comes Marching Home/Woody's Place	1960	50.00

SOPHOMORES, THE (1)

45s

CHORD

Number	Title (A Side/B Side)	Yr	NM
❑ 1302	Charades/What Can I Do	1957	40.00

DAWN

Number	Title (A Side/B Side)	Yr	NM
❑ 216	Cool, Cool Baby/Every Night About This Time	1956	25.00
❑ 218	Linda/I Get a Thrill	1956	25.00
❑ 223	Ocean Blue/I Left My Sugar	1956	25.00
❑ 225	Is There Someone for Me/Everybody Loves Me	1957	25.00
❑ 228	I Just Can't Keep the Tears from Tumblin' Down/If I Should Lose Your Love	1957	25.00
❑ 237	Checkers/Each Time I Hold You	1958	25.00

EPIC

Number	Title (A Side/B Side)	Yr	NM
❑ 9259	Charades/What Can I Do	1957	20.00

SOPHOMORES, THE (2)

45s

SOUND STAGE 7

Number	Title (A Side/B Side)	Yr	NM
❑ 2533	Summer of '64/I Know I Should (Every Night)	1964	10.00

SOPWITH "CAMEL," THE

45s

KAMA SUTRA

Number	Title (A Side/B Side)	Yr	NM
❑ 217	Hello Hello/Treadin'	1966	12.00
❑ 224	Postcard from Jamaica/Little Orphan Annie	1967	12.00
❑ 224 [PS]	Postcard from Jamaica/Little Orphan Annie	1967	20.00
❑ 236	Great Morpheum/Saga of the Lowdown Letdown	1967	12.00
❑ 236 [PS]	Great Morpheum/Saga of the Lowdown Letdown	1967	12.00

REPRISE

Number	Title (A Side/B Side)	Yr	NM
❑ 1179	Sleazy Love/Fazon	1973	8.00

Albums

KAMA SUTRA

Number	Title (A Side/B Side)	Yr	NM
❑ KSBS-2063	Hello Hello	1973	20.00
❑ KLP-8060 [M]	The Sopwith Camel	1967	30.00
❑ KLPS-8060 [S]	The Sopwith Camel	1967	30.00

REPRISE

Number	Title (A Side/B Side)	Yr	NM
❑ MS 2108	The Miraculous Hump Returns	1973	25.00

SORENSON BROTHERS, THE

45s

MARLINDA

Number	Title (A Side/B Side)	Yr	NM
❑ 7507/8	They've Landed/Stowaway	196?	50.00

SORROWS, THE

45s

WARNER BROS.

Number	Title (A Side/B Side)	Yr	NM
❑ 5662	Take a Heart/We Should Get Along Fine	1965	25.00

SOUL, DAVID

45s

MGM

Number	Title (A Side/B Side)	Yr	NM
❑ 13510	The Covered Man/I Will Warm Your Heart	1966	10.00
❑ 13589	Was I Ever So Wrong/Before	1966	10.00
❑ 13842	No One's Gonna Cry/Quiet Kind of Hate	1967	10.00

PRIVATE STOCK

Number	Title (A Side/B Side)	Yr	NM
❑ 45,129	Don't Give Up on Us/Black Bean Soup	1976	4.00
❑ 45,150	Going In with My Eyes Open/Topanga	1977	4.00
❑ 45,163	Silver Lady/The Rider	1977	4.00

Albums

PRIVATE STOCK

Number	Title (A Side/B Side)	Yr	NM
❑ PS-2019	David Soul	1977	10.00
❑ PS-7001	Playing to an Audience of One	1977	10.00

SOUL, JIMMY

45s

SPQR

Number	Title (A Side/B Side)	Yr	NM
❑ 3221	My Little Room/Ella Is Yella	1964	10.00
❑ 3300	Twistin' Matilda/I Can't Hold Out Any Longer	1962	12.00
❑ 3302	When Matilda Comes Back/Some Kinda Nut	1962	12.00
❑ 3304	Guess Things Happen That Way/My Baby Loves to Bowl	1963	12.00
❑ 3305	If You Wanna Be Happy/Don't Release Me	1963	15.00
❑ 3305 [PS]	If You Wanna Be Happy/Don't Release Me	1963	30.00
❑ 3310	Treat 'Em Tough/Church Street in the Summertime	1963	12.00
❑ 3312	Go 'Way Christina/Everybody's Gone Ape	1963	12.00
❑ 3314	Change Partners/I Hate You Baby	1963	12.00
❑ 3315	My Girl-She Sure Can Cook/A Woman Is Smarter in Every Kinda Way	1964	10.00
❑ 3318	You Can't Have Your Cake/Take Me to Los Angeles	1964	10.00
❑ 3319	Twistin' Matilda/Treat 'Em Tough	1964	10.00

20TH FOX

Number	Title (A Side/B Side)	Yr	NM
❑ 413	Respectable/I Wish I Could Dance	1963	10.00

Albums

SPQR

Number	Title (A Side/B Side)	Yr	NM
❑ E 16001	If You Wanna Be Happy	1963	150.00

SOUL, JOHNNY

45s

FEDERAL

Number	Title (A Side/B Side)	Yr	NM
❑ 12557	I Want Some/Darling, Darling, I Love You	1970	20.00

SSS INTERNATIONAL

Number	Title (A Side/B Side)	Yr	NM
❑ 763	I Almost Called Your Name/Take Me Where the Sun Never Shines	1969	40.00
❑ 785	Lonely Man/Come and Get It	1970	30.00

SOUL AGENTS, THE

45s

CAMEO

Number	Title (A Side/B Side)	Yr	NM
❑ 350	Let's Make It Pretty Baby/The Seventh Son	1965	35.00

INTERPHON

Number	Title (A Side/B Side)	Yr	NM
❑ 7702	I Just Want to Make Love to You/Mean Woman Blues	1964	20.00

SOUL ASYLUM

12-Inch Singles

A&M

Number	Title (A Side/B Side)	Yr	NM
❑ 750211 [DJ]	Easy Street/One Way Conversation	1991	10.00
❑ 750217401 [DJ]	Spinning/All the King's Friends	1990	6.00
❑ 75021 7401 1 [DJ]	Spinning/All the King's Friends	1990	6.00
❑ 75021 7410 1 [DJ]	Easy Street/One Way Conversation	1991	10.00
❑ 75021 7503 1 [DJ]	Something Out of Nothing/Freaks (Live)/To Sir with Love (Live)/Marionette (Live)	1990	20.00
❑ 7502175031 [DJ]	Something Out of Nothing/Freaks (Live)/To Sir with Love (Live)/Marionette (Live)	1990	20.00
❑ 17552 [DJ]	Sometime to Return (same on both sides)	1988	6.00
❑ 17552 [DJ]	Sometime to Return (same on both sides)	1988	6.00
❑ 17610 [DJ]	Standing in the Doorway/James at 16 medley	1988	8.00
❑ 17610 [DJ]	Standing in the Doorway/James at 16 medley	1988	8.00

45s

COLUMBIA

Number	Title (A Side/B Side)	Yr	NM
❑ 74966	Runaway Train/Never Really Been (Live)	1993	—
—Cassette only			
❑ 77959	Misery/Hope	1995	3.00
❑ 77959 [PS]	Misery/Hope	1995	4.00
❑ 78215	Promises Broken/Can't Even Tell (Live)	1996	2.00
❑ 78215 [PS]	Promises Broken/Can't Even Tell (Live)	1996	3.00

TWIN/TONE

Number	Title (A Side/B Side)	Yr	NM
❑ TTR 8560	Tied to the Tracks/Long Way Home	1985	12.00
❑ TTR 8560 [PS]	Tied to the Tracks/Long Way Home	1985	12.00

Albums

A&M

Number	Title (A Side/B Side)	Yr	NM
❑ SP-5197	Hang Time	1988	15.00
❑ 75031 5318 1	...And the Horse They Rode In On	1990	16.00
—Blue vinyl			

COLUMBIA

Number	Title (A Side/B Side)	Yr	NM
❑ C 48898	Grave Dancers Union	1993	15.00
❑ C 57616	Let Your Dim Light Shine	1995	12.00
❑ C 67618	Candy From a Stranger	1998	12.00

TWIN/TONE

Number	Title (A Side/B Side)	Yr	NM
❑ TTR 8439	Say What You Will, Clarence... Karl Sold the Truck	1984	20.00
❑ TTR 8666	Made to Be Broken	1986	15.00
❑ TTR 8691	While You Were Out	1986	15.00
❑ TTR 88144 [EP]	Clam Dip & Other Delights	1988	20.00

SOUL BROTHERS SIX

45s

ATLANTIC

Number	Title (A Side/B Side)	Yr	NM
❑ 2406	Some Kind of Wonderful/I'll Be Loving You	1967	15.00
❑ 2456	You Better Check Yourself/What Can You Do When You Ain't Got Nobody	1967	12.00
❑ 2535	Your Love Is Such a Wonderful Love/I Can't Live Without You	1968	12.00
❑ 2592	Somebody Else Is Loving My Baby/Thank You Baby for Loving Me	1969	12.00
❑ 2645	What You Got (Is So Good for Me)/Drive	1969	12.00

PHIL-L.A. OF SOUL

Number	Title (A Side/B Side)	Yr	NM
❑ 355	Funky Funky Way of Making Love/Let Me Be the One	1972	6.00
❑ 360	You're My World/You Gotta Come a Little Closer	1973	6.00
❑ 365	Let Me Do What We Ain't Doin'/Lost the Will to Live	1974	6.00

SOUL CHILDREN, THE

45s

EPIC

Number	Title (A Side/B Side)	Yr	NM
❑ 50178	Finders Keepers/Midnight Sunshine	1976	5.00
❑ 50236	If You Move I'll Fall/Little Understanding	1976	5.00
❑ 50345	Where Is Your Woman Tonight?/Merry-Go-Round	1977	5.00
❑ 50405	There Always/You Don't Need a Ring	1977	5.00

STAX

Number	Title (A Side/B Side)	Yr	NM
❑ 0008	Give 'Em Love/Move Over	1968	8.00
❑ 0018	I'll Understand/Doin' Our Thing	1969	8.00
❑ 0030	Tighten Up My Thang/Take Up the Slack	1969	8.00
❑ 0050	The Sweeter He Is — Part 1/The Sweeter He Is — Part 2	1969	8.00
❑ 0062	Hold On, I'm Coming/Make It Good	1970	7.00
❑ 0075	Give Me One Good Reason Why/Finish Me Off	1970	7.00
❑ 0086	Let's Make a Sweet Thing Sweeter/Finish Me Off	1971	7.00
❑ 0119	Hearsay/Don't Take My Sunshine	1972	7.00
❑ 0132	Don't Take My Kindness for Weakness/Just the One	1972	7.00
❑ 0152	It Ain't Always What You Do (It's Who You Let See You Do It)/All That Shines Ain't Gold	1973	7.00
❑ 0170	Love Is a Hurtin' Thing/Poem on the School House Door	1973	7.00
❑ 0182	I'll Be the Other Woman/Come Back Kind of Love	1973	6.00
❑ 0218	Love Makes It Right/Love Makes It Right — Part 2	1974	6.00
❑ 0230	What's Happening Baby/What's Happening Baby — Part 2	1974	6.00
❑ 3206	Can't Give Up a Good Thing/Signed, Sealed and Delivered	1978	5.00
❑ 3211	Summer in the Shade/Hard Living with a Woman	1978	5.00
❑ 3214	Who You Used to Be/Believing	1978	5.00

Albums

EPIC

Number	Title (A Side/B Side)	Yr	NM
❑ PE 33902	Finders Keepers	1976	15.00
❑ PE 34455	Where Is Your Woman Tonight	1977	15.00

STAX

Number	Title (A Side/B Side)	Yr	NM
❑ STS-2018	Soul Children	1969	30.00
❑ STS-2043	The Best of Two Worlds	1971	30.00
❑ STS-3003	Genesis	1972	30.00

S

Number	Title (A Side/B Side)	Yr	NM
❑ STX-4105	Open Door Policy	1978	15.00
❑ STX-4120	Chronicle	1979	12.00
❑ STS-5507	Friction	1974	30.00

SOUL CLAN, THE SOLOMON BURKE, ARTHUR CONLEY, DON COVAY, BEN E. KING and JOE TEX.

45s

ATLANTIC

Number	Title (A Side/B Side)	Yr	NM
❑ 2530	Soul Meeting/That's How It Feels	1968	10.00
❑ 2530 [PS]	Soul Meeting/That's How It Feels	1968	15.00

SOUL COMFORTERS, THE

45s

HOLLYWOOD

Number	Title (A Side/B Side)	Yr	NM
❑ 1042	White Christmas/Silent Night	1955	30.00

SOUL FINDERS, THE

Albums

RCA CAMDEN

Number	Title (A Side/B Side)	Yr	NM
❑ CAL-2170 [M]	Sweet Soul Music	1967	30.00
❑ CAS-2170 [S]	Sweet Soul Music	1967	30.00
❑ CAL-2239 [M]	An Explosive Album of Soul	1968	30.00
❑ CAS-2239 [S]	An Explosive Album of Soul	1968	30.00

SOUL GENERATION, THE

45s

EBONY SOUNDS

Number	Title (A Side/B Side)	Yr	NM
❑ 175	That's the Way It's Got to Be (Body and Soul)/ Mandingo Woman	1972	10.00
❑ 176	Million Dollars/Super Fine	1973	10.00
❑ 177	A Ray of Hope/Young Bird	1973	10.00
❑ 181	I Wonder What She's Doin'/ Key to Your Heart	1973	12.00
❑ 181	Praying for a Miracle/In Your Way	1974	15.00

Albums

EBONY SOUNDS

Number	Title (A Side/B Side)	Yr	NM
❑ 2000	Beyond Body and Soul	1972	20.00

SOUL SISTERS, THE

45s

GUYDEN

Number	Title (A Side/B Side)	Yr	NM
❑ 2066	The Warm-Up/ Because I Love You	1962	25.00

KAYO

Number	Title (A Side/B Side)	Yr	NM
❑ 5101	I Can't Let Him Go/ (B-side unknown)	1963	25.00

SUE

Number	Title (A Side/B Side)	Yr	NM
❑ 10-005	Good Time Tonight/ Foolish Dreamer	1964	15.00
❑ 107	Loop de Loop/Long Gone	1964	15.00
❑ 111	Just a Moment Ago/I Won't Be Your Fool Anymore	1964	15.00
❑ 130	Think About the Good Times/ The Right Time	1965	15.00
❑ 140	Flashback/Give Me Some Satisfaction	1966	15.00
❑ 799	I Can't Stand It/Blueberry Hill	1964	15.00

VEEP

Number	Title (A Side/B Side)	Yr	NM
❑ 1291	A Thousand Mountains/ You Got 'Em Beat	1968	12.00

Albums

SUE

Number	Title (A Side/B Side)	Yr	NM
❑ LP-1022 [M]	I Can't Stand It	1964	200.00
❑ STLP-1022 [S]	I Can't Stand It	1964	400.00

SOUL SOCIETY, THE

45s

DOT

Number	Title (A Side/B Side)	Yr	NM
❑ 17136	Sidewinder/Afro-Desia	1968	10.00

Albums

DOT

Number	Title (A Side/B Side)	Yr	NM
❑ DLP-25842	Satisfaction	1969	25.00

SOUL SURFERS, THE

45s

CHALLENGE

Number	Title (A Side/B Side)	Yr	NM
❑ 9209	Cannonball/Home from Camp	1963	40.00
❑ 59249	Cannonball/In the Misty Moonlight	1964	15.00
—B-side by Jerry Wallace			

SOUL SURVIVORS

45s

ATCO

Number	Title (A Side/B Side)	Yr	NM
❑ 6627	Turn Out the Fire/Go Out Walking	1968	8.00
❑ 6650	Tell Daddy/Mama Soul	1969	8.00
❑ 6735	Still Got My Head/Tempting 'Bout to Get Me	1970	8.00

CRIMSON

Number	Title (A Side/B Side)	Yr	NM
❑ 1010	Expressway to Your Heart/ Hey Gyp	1967	12.00
❑ 1012	Explosion (In My Soul)/ Dathon's Theme	1967	10.00
❑ 1016	Poor Man's Dream /Impossible Mission	1968	10.00

DECCA

Number	Title (A Side/B Side)	Yr	NM
❑ 32080	Devil with a Blue Dress On/ Shakin' with Linda	1967	15.00

DOT

Number	Title (A Side/B Side)	Yr	NM
❑ 16793	Look at Me/Can't Stand to Be in Love with You	1965	20.00
❑ 16830	Hung Up on Losin'/Snow Man	1966	12.00

LOST-NITE

Number	Title (A Side/B Side)	Yr	NM
❑ 331	Expressway to Your Heart/ Hey Gyp	197?	5.00
—Reissue			

PHILADELPHIA INT'L.

Number	Title (A Side/B Side)	Yr	NM
❑ 3595	Happy Birthday America (Part 1)/ Happy Birthday America (Part 2)	1976	5.00
❑ 3595 [PS]	Happy Birthday America (Part 1)/ Happy Birthday America (Part 2)	1976	8.00

TSOP

Number	Title (A Side/B Side)	Yr	NM
❑ 4756	City of Brotherly Love/The Best Time Was the Last Time	1974	6.00
❑ 4760	What It Takes/Virgin Girl	1974	6.00
❑ 4768	Your Love/Lover to Me	1975	6.00

Albums

ATCO

Number	Title (A Side/B Side)	Yr	NM
❑ SD 33-277	Take Another Look	1969	25.00

CRIMSON

Number	Title (A Side/B Side)	Yr	NM
❑ CR-502 [M]	When the Whistle Blows Anything Goes	1967	50.00
❑ CR-502 S [S]	When the Whistle Blows Anything Goes	1967	30.00

TSOP

Number	Title (A Side/B Side)	Yr	NM
❑ KZ 33186	The Soul Survivors	1975	12.00

SOULFUL STRINGS, THE

45s

CADET

Number	Title (A Side/B Side)	Yr	NM
❑ 5559	Paint It Black/Love Is a Hurtin' Thing	1967	6.00
❑ 5576	Burning Spear/Within You Without You	1968	6.00
❑ 5607	(Sittin' On) The Dock of the Bay/ The Stripper	1968	6.00
❑ 5617	The Who Who Song/Jericho	1968	6.00
❑ 5633	I Wish It Would Rain/Listen Here	1969	6.00
❑ 5654	A Love Song/Zabezi	1969	6.00

Albums

CADET

Number	Title (A Side/B Side)	Yr	NM
❑ LP-776 [M]	Paint It Black	1967	15.00
❑ LPS-776 [S]	Paint It Black	1967	12.00
❑ LPS-796	Groovin' with the Soulful Strings	1967	12.00
❑ LPS-805	Another Exposure	1968	12.00
❑ LPS-814	The Magic of Christmas	1968	12.00
❑ LPS-820	In Concert/Back by Demand	1969	12.00
❑ LPS-834	String Fever	1969	12.00
❑ LPS-846	Gamble-Huff	1971	10.00
❑ 50022 [(2)]	Best of the Soulful Strings	1973	12.00

SOUND SYMPOSIUM, THE

45s

DOT

Number	Title (A Side/B Side)	Yr	NM
❑ 17296	The Mighty Quinn/ I'll Be Your Baby Tonight	1969	10.00

Albums

DOT

Number	Title (A Side/B Side)	Yr	NM
❑ DLP-3871 [M]	Paul Simon Interpreted	1968	30.00
—Stereo cover with white "Monaural" sticker; label is regular stock copy			
❑ DLP-25871 [S]	Paul Simon Interpreted	1968	20.00
❑ DLP-25952	Bob Dylan Interpreted	1969	20.00

SOUNDGARDEN Also see SOUNDGARDEN. Also see SOUNDGARDEN.

12-Inch Singles

A&M

Number	Title (A Side/B Side)	Yr	NM
❑ SP-17933 [DJ]	Loud Love (same on both sides)	1989	20.00
❑ SP-17896 [DJ]	Hands All Over (same on both sides)	1989	20.00
❑ 75021 7290 1 [DJ]	Jesus Christ Pose/ Drawing Flies	1992	8.00
❑ 7502172901 [DJ]	Jesus Christ Pose/ Drawing Flies	1992	8.00
❑ 75021 7338 1 [DJ]	Rusty Cage (2 versions)/ Girl U Want/Shwo Me/ Into the Void	1991	15.00
❑ 7502173381 [DJ]	Rusty Cage (2 versions)/ Girl U Want/Shwo Me/ Into the Void	1991	15.00
❑ SP-17896 [DJ]	Hands All Over (same on both sides)	1989	20.00
❑ SP-17933 [DJ]	Loud Love (same on both sides)	1989	20.00

45s

A&M

Number	Title (A Side/B Side)	Yr	NM
❑ 31458 0766 7	Black Hole Sun/Spoonman	1994	6.00
❑ 31458 0974 7	Fell On Black Days/My Wave	1995	6.00

SUB POP

Number	Title (A Side/B Side)	Yr	NM
❑ 12a	Hunted Down/Nothing to Say	1987	50.00
—500 copies pressed, all on blue vinyl			
❑ 12a [PS]	Hunted Down/Nothing to Say	1987	50.00
—Special blue sleeve (not a PS) with above			
❑ 83	Room a Thousand Years Wide/ H.I.V. Baby	1990	15.00
—Black vinyl; bonus in Sub Pop Singles Club series			
❑ 83	Room a Thousand Years Wide/ H.I.V. Baby	1990	30.00
—Grape vinyl			
❑ 83 [PS]	Room a Thousand Years Wide/ H.I.V. Baby	1990	20.00

Albums

A&M

Number	Title (A Side/B Side)	Yr	NM
❑ SP-17951 [DJ]	Louder Than Live	1990	50.00
—Promo-only live album on blue vinyl			
❑ 31454 0198 1 [(2)]	Superunknown	1994	30.00
—Blue vinyl			
❑ 31454 0198 1 [(2)]	Superunknown	1994	30.00
—Clear vinyl			
❑ 31454 0198 1 [(2)]	Superunknown	1994	30.00
—Gold vinyl			
❑ 31454 0526-1 [(2)]	Down on the Upside	1996	20.00
❑ SP-5252	Louder Than Love	1989	20.00
—Black vinyl			
❑ SP-5252	Louder Than Love	1989	40.00
—Red vinyl			
❑ SP-5252	Louder Than Love	1989	60.00
—Green vinyl			
❑ 75021 5374 1	Badmotorfinger	1991	40.00
—Limited edition on yellow vinyl			
❑ SP-17951 [DJ]	Louder Than Live	1990	80.00
—Promo-only live album on blue vinyl			

SST

Number	Title (A Side/B Side)	Yr	NM
❑ 201	Ultramega OK	1988	20.00
❑ 231 [EP]	Flower	1988	15.00
❑ 911 [10]	Flower	1988	12.00

SUB POP

Number	Title (A Side/B Side)	Yr	NM
❑ 12 [EP]	Screaming Life	1987	150.00
—First 500 copies on orange vinyl			
❑ 12 [EP]	Screaming Life	1987	18.00
—Reissues on any color vinyl except black or orange			
❑ 12 [EP]	Screaming Life	1987	20.00
—Black vinyl			
❑ 17 [EP]	Fopp	1988	50.00

SOUNDS, INC.

45s

LIBERTY

Number	Title (A Side/B Side)	Yr	NM
❑ 55709	The Spartans/Detroit	1964	8.00
❑ 55729	Rinky Dink/Spanish Harlem	1964	8.00
❑ 55789	In the Hall of the Mountain King/ Time for You	1965	8.00
❑ 55844	On the Brink/I Am Comin' Thru	1965	8.00

SOUNDS LIKE US

45s

FONTANA

Number	Title (A Side/B Side)	Yr	NM
❑ 1570	Outside Chance/ Clock on the Wall	1967	40.00

JILL ANN

Number	Title (A Side/B Side)	Yr	NM
❑ 101	Outside Chance/ Clock on the Wall	1966	60.00

SOMA

Number	Title (A Side/B Side)	Yr	NM
❑ 8108	It Was a Very Good Year/ The Other Side of the Record	1967	50.00

SOUNDS OF OUR TIMES, THE

45s

CAPITOL

Number	Title (A Side/B Side)	Yr	NM
❑ 2109	The Look of Love/A Whiter Shade of Pale	1968	8.00

Except when noted otherwise, VG = 25% of NM, and VG+ = 50% of NM. (Example: VG = $2.00, VG+ = $4.00 and NM = $8.00.)

Number	Title (A Side/B Side)	Yr	NM
❑ 2291	Hey Jude/Harper Valley P.T.A.	1968	15.00

—Collectible for its inexplicable error in composer's credit on "Hey Jude," claiming the song was written by "Paul Lennon" and "John McCartney"!

Albums

CAPITOL

Number	Title (A Side/B Side)	Yr	NM
❑ ST-117	Hey Jude	1969	12.00
❑ ST-8-0117	Hey Jude	1969	15.00

—Capitol Record Club edition

Number	Title (A Side/B Side)	Yr	NM
❑ ST-182	Galveston	1969	12.00
❑ ST 2817 [S]	Music of the Flower Children	1968	12.00
❑ T 2817 [M]	Music of the Flower Children	1968	20.00
❑ ST 2892 [S]	The Sounds of Our Time Play "Love Is Blue"	1968	12.00
❑ T 2892 [M]	The Sounds of Our Time Play "Love Is Blue"	1968	25.00

SOUNDS OF SUNSHINE

45s

P.I.P.

Number	Title (A Side/B Side)	Yr	NM
❑ 6527	Nadia's Theme (Vocal)/Nadia's Theme (Instrumental)	1976	4.00

RANWOOD

Number	Title (A Side/B Side)	Yr	NM
❑ 896	Love Means (You Never Have to Say You're Sorry)/Linda, the Untouchable	1971	5.00
❑ 912	It's Hard to Say Goodbye Forever/I Do All My Crying in the Rain	1971	4.00
❑ 913	Yesterday Keeps Getting in the Way/Anything Can Happen	1971	4.00
❑ 921	Make It Happy/Nature Boy	1972	4.00
❑ 925	Today Is the First Day (Of the Rest of Your Life)/Make Believe Saturday Night	1972	4.00
❑ 932	The End of the World/Over and Over	1972	4.00
❑ 940	Sea Gull/She Takes Care of Me	1973	4.00

Albums

P.I.P.

Number	Title (A Side/B Side)	Yr	NM
❑ 6823	Nadia's Theme	1976	10.00

RANWOOD

Number	Title (A Side/B Side)	Yr	NM
❑ 8089	Love Means You Never Have to Say You're Sorry	1971	10.00
❑ 8095	Today Is the First Day (Of the Rest of Your Life)	1972	10.00

SOUNDS ORCHESTRAL

45s

JANUS

Number	Title (A Side/B Side)	Yr	NM
❑ 124	Love in the Shadows/Louie, Louie	1970	6.00

PARKWAY

Number	Title (A Side/B Side)	Yr	NM
❑ 120	Pretty Flamingo/Sounds Like Jacques	1966	8.00
❑ 155	A Man and a Woman/West of Carnaby	1967	8.00
❑ 942	Cast Your Fate to the Wind/To Wendy With Love	1965	10.00
❑ 958	Canadian Sunset/Have Faith in Your Love	1965	8.00
❑ 968	A Boy and a Girl/Go Home Girl	1966	8.00
❑ 973	Thunderball/Mr. Kiss Kiss Bang Bang	1966	8.00

Albums

JANUS

Number	Title (A Side/B Side)	Yr	NM
❑ JLS-3014	One More Time	197?	15.00

PARKWAY

Number	Title (A Side/B Side)	Yr	NM
❑ P 7046 [M]	Cast Your Fate to the Wind	1965	15.00
❑ SP 7046 [S]	Cast Your Fate to the Wind	1965	20.00
❑ P 7047 [M]	The Soul of Sounds Orchestral	1965	15.00
❑ SP 7047 [S]	The Soul of Sounds Orchestral	1965	20.00
❑ P 7050 [M]	Impressions of James Bond	1966	20.00
❑ SP 7050 [S]	Impressions of James Bond	1966	30.00

SOUNDS UNLIMITED

45s

ABC

Number	Title (A Side/B Side)	Yr	NM
❑ 10803	Nobody But Me/Why Doesn't She Believe Me	1966	20.00

DUNWICH

Number	Title (A Side/B Side)	Yr	NM
❑ 157	A Girl As Sweet As You/Little Brother	1967	25.00

SOUP

Albums

ARF ARM

Number	Title (A Side/B Side)	Yr	NM
❑ 1	Soup	1970	120.00

BIG TREE

Number	Title (A Side/B Side)	Yr	NM
❑ BTS 2007	The Album Soup	1971	35.00

SOUTH, JOE

45s

ALLWOOD

Number	Title (A Side/B Side)	Yr	NM
❑ 402	Just Remember You're Mine/Silly Me	1962	12.00

APT

Number	Title (A Side/B Side)	Yr	NM
❑ 25084	Deep Inside Me/I Want to Be Somebody	1965	10.00

CAPITOL

Number	Title (A Side/B Side)	Yr	NM
❑ 2060	Birds of a Feather/It Got Away	1967	8.00
❑ 2169	How Can I Unlove You/She's Almost You	1968	8.00
❑ 2248	Games People Play/Mirror of Your Mind	1968	8.00
❑ 2284	Redneck/Don't Throw Your Love to the Wind	1968	8.00
❑ 2491	Leanin' On You/Don't You Be Ashamed	1969	6.00
❑ 2532	Birds of a Feather/These Are Not My People	1969	6.00
❑ 2592	Don't It Make You Want to Go Home/Heart's Desire	1969	6.00
❑ 2704	Walk a Mile in My Shoes/Sheltered	1969	6.00
❑ 2755	Children/The Clock Up On the Wall	1970	5.00
❑ 2916	Why Does a Man Do What He Has to Do/Be a Believer	1970	5.00
❑ 3008	Rose Garden/Mirror of Your Mind	1971	6.00
❑ 3053	United We Stand/So the Seeds Are Growing	1971	5.00
❑ 3204	Fool Me/Devil May Care	1971	5.00
❑ 3450	One Man Band/Coming Down All Alone	1972	5.00
❑ 3487	I'm a Star/Misunderstanding	1972	5.00
❑ 3554	Real Thing/Save Your Best	1973	5.00
❑ 3717	Riverdog/It Hurts Me Too	1973	5.00

COLUMBIA

Number	Title (A Side/B Side)	Yr	NM
❑ 43983	Backfield in Motion/I'll Come Back to You	1967	12.00
❑ 44218	A Fool in Love/Great Day	1967	12.00

FAIRLANE

Number	Title (A Side/B Side)	Yr	NM
❑ 21006	You're the Reason/Jukebox	1961	20.00
❑ 21010	Masquerade/I'm Sorry for You	1961	15.00
❑ 21015	Slippin' Around/Just to Be with You Again	1962	15.00

ISLAND

Number	Title (A Side/B Side)	Yr	NM
❑ 034	To Have, to Hold and Let Go/Midnight Rainbows	1975	4.00

MGM

Number	Title (A Side/B Side)	Yr	NM
❑ 13145	Same Old Song/Standing Invitation	1963	10.00
❑ 13196	Concrete Jungle/The Last One to Know	1963	10.00
❑ 13276	Naughty Claudie/Little Queenie	1964	10.00

NRC

Number	Title (A Side/B Side)	Yr	NM
❑ 002	I'm Snowed/It's Only You	1958	40.00
❑ 022	Chills/What a Night	1959	15.00
❑ 041	Little Bluebird/Play It Cool	1959	15.00
❑ 053	Tell the Truth/If You Only Knew Her	1960	15.00
❑ 065	Let's Talk It Over/Formality	1961	15.00
❑ 5000	The Purple People Eater Meets the Witch Doctor/My Fondest Memories	1958	15.00
❑ 5001	One Fool to Another/Texas Ain't the Biggest Anymore	1958	15.00

Albums

ACCORD

Number	Title (A Side/B Side)	Yr	NM
❑ SN-7119	Party People	1981	10.00

CAPITOL

Number	Title (A Side/B Side)	Yr	NM
❑ ST-108	Introspect	1968	20.00
❑ ST-235	Games People Play	1969	15.00
❑ ST-392	Don't It Make You Want to Go Home	1969	15.00
❑ SM-450	Joe South's Greatest Hits	1977	8.00

—Reissue with new prefix

Number	Title (A Side/B Side)	Yr	NM
❑ ST-450	Joe South's Greatest Hits	1970	15.00
❑ ST-637	So the Seeds Are Growing	1971	12.00
❑ ST-845	Joe South	1972	12.00
❑ ST-11074	A Look Inside	1972	12.00

ISLAND

Number	Title (A Side/B Side)	Yr	NM
❑ ILPS-9328	Midnight Rainbows	1975	10.00

MINE

Number	Title (A Side/B Side)	Yr	NM
❑ MSG-1100	Walkin' Shoes	1971	12.00

—Reissue with new title

Number	Title (A Side/B Side)	Yr	NM
❑ MSG-1100	The Joe South Story	1971	15.00

NASHVILLE

Number	Title (A Side/B Side)	Yr	NM
❑ 2092	You're the Reason	1970	12.00

PICKWICK

Number	Title (A Side/B Side)	Yr	NM
❑ SPC-3314	Games People Play	197?	10.00

SOUTH 40

45s

METROBEAT

Number	Title (A Side/B Side)	Yr	NM
❑ 4450	The Penny Song/Good Lovin'	1967	12.00
❑ 4457	I Want Sunshine/Goin' Someplace Else	1968	12.00

Albums

METROBEAT

Number	Title (A Side/B Side)	Yr	NM
❑ MBS-1000	Live at the Someplace Else	1968	25.00

SOUTH STREET MISSION BAND

45s

CAMEO

Number	Title (A Side/B Side)	Yr	NM
❑ 415	Theme from The Young Ones/Hooka Tooka	1966	10.00

SOUTHSIDE JOHNNY AND THE ASBURY JUKES

12-Inch Singles

ATLANTIC

Number	Title (A Side/B Side)	Yr	NM
❑ 907 [DJ]	Walk Away Renee (same on both sides)	1986	6.00
❑ 907 [DJ]	Walk Away Renee (same on both sides)	1986	6.00
❑ 954 [DJ]	Tell Me (same on both sides)	1986	6.00
❑ 954 [DJ]	Tell Me (same on both sides)	1986	6.00

MIRAGE

Number	Title (A Side/B Side)	Yr	NM
❑ 652 [DJ]	Love Is the Drug (same on both sides)	1983	6.00
❑ 652 [DJ]	Love Is the Drug (same on both sides)	1983	6.00
❑ 666 [DJ]	Trash It Up (Remix)/Ms. Park Ave.	1983	6.00
❑ 666 [DJ]	Trash It Up (Remix)/Ms. Park Ave.	1983	6.00
❑ 683 [DJ]	Get Your Body on the Job (same on both sides)	1983	6.00
❑ 683 [DJ]	Get Your Body on the Job (same on both sides)	1983	6.00
❑ 96973	Get Your Body on the Job/Slow Burn	1983	8.00

45s

ATLANTIC

Number	Title (A Side/B Side)	Yr	NM
❑ 89356	Tell Me/I Can't Wait	1986	3.00
❑ 89394	Walk Away Renee/I Can't Wait	1986	3.00

EPIC

Number	Title (A Side/B Side)	Yr	NM
❑ 50238	The Fever/I Don't Want to Go Home	1976	5.00
❑ 50393	First Night/Without Love	1977	5.00
❑ 50466	Love on the Wrong Side of Town/Some Things You Don't Change	1977	5.00
❑ 50646	Trapped Again/This Time Baby's Gone for Good	1979	4.00

MERCURY

Number	Title (A Side/B Side)	Yr	NM
❑ 76007	I'm So Anxious/Your Reply	1979	4.00
❑ 76023	Wait in Vain/Living in the Real World	1979	4.00
❑ 76074	On the Beach/Goodbye Love	1980	4.00
❑ 76081	Restless Heart/(B-side unknown)	1980	4.00

MIRAGE

Number	Title (A Side/B Side)	Yr	NM
❑ 99698	Actions Speak Louder Than Words/Love Is the Drug	1984	4.00
❑ 99732	New Romeo/Tell Me Lies	1984	4.00
❑ 99802	Get Your Body on the Job/Slow Burn	1983	4.00
❑ 99839	Ms. Park Ave./Trash It Up	1983	4.00

Albums

ATLANTIC

Number	Title (A Side/B Side)	Yr	NM
❑ 81654	At Least We Got Shoes	1986	8.00

CYPRESS

Number	Title (A Side/B Side)	Yr	NM
❑ YL-0115	Slow Dance	1988	10.00

EPIC

Number	Title (A Side/B Side)	Yr	NM
❑ AS 275 [DJ]	Jukes Live at the Bottom Line	1976	30.00
❑ PE 34180	I Don't Want to Go Home	1976	10.00

—Orange label, no bar code

Number	Title (A Side/B Side)	Yr	NM
❑ PE 34180	I Don't Want to Go Home	1979	8.00

—Dark blue label, most have bar codes on back cover

Number	Title (A Side/B Side)	Yr	NM
❑ PE 34668	This Time It's for Real	1977	10.00

—Orange label, no bar code

Number	Title (A Side/B Side)	Yr	NM
❑ PE 34668	This Time It's for Real	198?	8.00

—Dark blue label, bar code on back cover

Number	Title (A Side/B Side)	Yr	NM
❑ JE 35488	Hearts of Stone	1978	10.00

—Orange label, no bar code

Number	Title (A Side/B Side)	Yr	NM
❑ PE 35488	Hearts of Stone	198?	8.00

—Dark blue label, bar code on back cover

Number	Title (A Side/B Side)	Yr	NM
❑ JE 36246	Havin' a Party with Southside Johnny	1979	10.00
❑ PE 36246	Havin' a Party with Southside Johnny	198?	8.00

—Budget-line reissue with new prefix

MERCURY

Number	Title (A Side/B Side)	Yr	NM
❑ SRM-1-3793	The Jukes	1979	10.00

S

Number	Title (A Side/B Side)	Yr	NM
❑ SRM-1-3836	Love Is a Sacrifice	1980	10.00
❑ SRM-2-8602 [(2)]	Live — Reach Out and Touch the Sky	1981	12.00
❑ 826285-1 [(2)]	Live — Reach Out and Touch the Sky	198?	10.00
—Reissue of 8602			
MIRAGE			
❑ 90113	Trash It Up!	1983	10.00
❑ 90186	In the Heat	1984	10.00

SOUTHWEST F.O.B.
ENGLAND DAN AND JOHN FORD COLEY were in this group.

Number	Title (A Side/B Side)	Yr	NM
45s			
GPC			
❑ 1945	Smell of Incense/Green Skies	1968	20.00
HIP			
❑ 8002	Smell of Incense/Green Skies	1968	10.00
❑ 8009	Nadine/All One Big Game	1969	10.00
❑ 8015	Independent Me/As I Look at You	1969	10.00
❑ 8022	Feelin' Groovy/Beggar Man	1969	10.00
Albums			
HIP			
❑ 7001	Smell of Incense	1969	30.00

SOUVENIRS, THE
May be three different groups.

Number	Title (A Side/B Side)	Yr	NM
45s			
DOOTO			
❑ 412	So Long Daddy/Arlene, Sweet Little Texas Queen	1957	50.00
INFERNO			
❑ 2001	I Could Have Danced All Night/It's Too Bad	1967	50.00
REPRISE			
❑ 20065	The Worm/The Bump	1962	15.00
❑ 20066	The Real McCoy/The Watusi	1962	15.00

SPACEMEN, THE

Number	Title (A Side/B Side)	Yr	NM
45s			
ALTON			
❑ 254	The Clouds/The Lonely Jet Pilot	1959	20.00

SPADES, THE (1)
Nashville studio group.

Number	Title (A Side/B Side)	Yr	NM
45s			
HIT			
❑ 226	You've Got Your Troubles/Everybody Loves a Clown	1965	8.00
—B-side by Jason Allen			

SPADES, THE (2)
For records on Liberty, see THE SLADES.

SPADES, THE (3)

Number	Title (A Side/B Side)	Yr	NM
45s			
MAJOR			
❑ 1007	Close to You/I'm on Fire	1959	60.00

SPADES, THE (4)
Evolved into THE THIRTEENTH FLOOR ELEVATORS. Zero 10001 was recorded before Roky Erickson joined the group.

Number	Title (A Side/B Side)	Yr	NM
45s			
ZERO			
❑ 10001	I Need a Girl/Do You Want to Dance	1965	60.00
❑ 10002	You're Gonna Miss Me/We Sell Soul	1966	400.00
—Beware counterfeits			

SPANDAU BALLET

Number	Title (A Side/B Side)	Yr	NM
12-Inch Singles			
CHRYSALIS			
❑ AS1630 [DJ]	Lifeline (same on both sides)	1983	6.00
❑ AS 1630 [DJ]	Lifeline (same on both sides)	1983	10.00
❑ AS 1760 [DJ]	Gold (Live 5:04) (LP Version 4:49)	1983	12.00
❑ AS 1885 [DJ]	Only When You Leave (Extended Version 6:45) (Album Version 4:48)	1984	12.00
❑ CDS-2528	Chant No. 1 (I Don't Need This Pressure On)/Feel the Chant/To Cut a Long Story Short	1981	10.00
❑ CDS-2598	Instinction (Special 12" Version)/Glow	1982	8.00
❑ 4V9 42668	Communication (Club Mix) (Single Version)	1983	8.00
❑ 4V9 42681	Lifeline (Special Club Mix) (Dub Version) (A Cappella)	1983	10.00
❑ 4V9 42740	Gold (Extended Remix 7:12) (Instrumental 2:40)	1983	10.00
❑ 4V9 42805	Only When You Leave (Extended Version) (Album Version)/Paint Me Down (Live)	1984	8.00
EPIC			
❑ EAS2664 [DJ]	How Many Lies (same on both sides)	1986	7.00
❑ EAS 02664 [DJ]	How Many Lies (same on both sides)	1986	8.00
45s			
CHRYSALIS			
❑ 2473	To Cut a Long Story Short/(Dub Version)	1981	6.00
❑ 2528	Chant No. 1/Feel the Chant	1981	6.00
❑ VS4 42686	Lifeline/Live and Let Live	1983	6.00
❑ VS4 42720	True/Gently	1983	3.00
❑ VS4 42720 [PS]	True/Gently	1983	3.00
❑ VS4 42743	Gold/(Live)	1983	3.00
❑ VS4 42743 [PS]	Gold/(Live)	1983	3.00
❑ VS4 42770	Communication/Code of Love	1984	4.00
❑ VS4 42792	Only When You Leave/Paint Me Down (Live)	1984	3.00
❑ VS4 42792 [PS]	Only When You Leave/Paint Me Down (Live)	1984	3.00
❑ VS8 42950	Chant No. 1/Lifeline	1985	3.00
—Silver label reissue			
❑ VS8 42951	True/Gold	1985	3.00
—Silver label reissue			
❑ VS8 42952	Communication/Only When You Leave	1985	3.00
—Silver label reissue			
EPIC			
❑ 34-06664	How Many Lies/Snakes and Lovers	1987	3.00
❑ 34-06664 [PS]	How Many Lies/Snakes and Lovers	1987	10.00
❑ 34-07190	Through the Barricades/Snakes and Lovers	1987	6.00
Albums			
CHRYSALIS			
❑ CHR 1331	Journeys to Glory	1981	12.00
❑ CHR 1353	Diamond	1982	10.00
❑ FV 41331	Journeys to Glory	1983	8.00
—Reissue			
❑ FV 41353	Diamond	1983	8.00
—Reissue of CHR 1353			
❑ PV 41353	Diamond	1986	8.00
—Reissue of FV 41353 with new prefix			
❑ B6V 41403	True	1983	12.00
—Original prefix			
❑ FV 41403	True	1983	8.00
—Reissue with new prefix			
❑ FV 41473	Parade	1984	10.00
❑ FV 41498	The Singles Collection	1985	10.00
EPIC			
❑ FE 40642	Through the Barricades	1987	12.00
MOBILE FIDELITY			
❑ 1-152	True	1984	20.00
—Audiophile vinyl			

SPANIELS, THE
Also see POOKIE HUDSON.

Number	Title (A Side/B Side)	Yr	NM
45s			
BUDDAH			
❑ 153	Goodnight Sweetheart/Maybe	1969	8.00
CALLA			
❑ 172	Fairy Tales/Jealous Heart	1970	6.00
CANTERBURY			
❑ 101	Peace of Mind/She Sang to Me/Danny Boy	1974	5.00
CHANCE			
❑ 1141	Baby It's You/Bounce	1953	500.00
❑ 1141	Baby It's You/Bounce	1953	2000.
—Red vinyl			
LOST-NITE			
❑ 262	Baby It's You/Bounce	197?	4.00
❑ 265	The Bells Ring Out/House Cleaning	197?	4.00
❑ 268	Goodnite, Sweetheart, Goodnite/You Don't Move Me	197?	4.00
❑ 271	Do-Wah/Don'cha Go	197?	4.00
❑ 274	Play It Cool/Let's Make Up	197?	4.00
❑ 277	False Love/Do You Really	197?	4.00
❑ 280	You Painted Pictures/Hey, Sister Lizzie	197?	4.00
❑ 283	Dear Heart/Why Won't You Dance	197?	4.00
❑ 286	Everyone's Laughing/I.O.U.	197?	4.00
❑ 289	I Lost You/Crazy Baby	197?	4.00
❑ 292	You Gave Me Peace of Mind/Please Don't Tease	197?	4.00
❑ 295	You're Gonna Cry/I Like It Like That	197?	4.00
❑ 298	Stormy Weather/Here Is Why I Love You	197?	4.00
❑ 301	Tina/Great Googley Moo	197?	4.00
❑ 304	Since I Fell for You/Baby Come Along with Me	197?	4.00
❑ 307	This Is a Lovely Way to Spend an Evening/Red Sails in the Sunset	197?	4.00
❑ 446	I Know/Bus Fare Home	197?	4.00
NEPTUNE			
❑ 124	I Love You For Sentimental Reasons/Meek Man	1961	20.00
—As "Pookie Hudson and the Spaniels"			
NORTH AMERICAN			
❑ 001	Fairy Tales/Jealous Heart	1970	5.00
❑ 002	Stand in Line/Lonely Man	1970	5.00
❑ 1114	Come Back to These Arms/Money Blues	1970	5.00
OWL			
❑ 328	Little Goe/The Posse	1973	5.00
VEE JAY			
❑ 101	Baby It's You/Bounce	1953	800.00
—Black vinyl, maroon label			
❑ 101	Baby It's You/Bounce	1953	4500.
—Red vinyl			
❑ 101	Baby It's You/Bounce	1961	40.00
—Black vinyl, black label			
❑ 103	The Bells Ring Out/House Cleaning	1953	300.00
❑ 103	The Bells Ring Out/House Cleaning	1953	600.00
—Red vinyl			
❑ 107	Goodnite, Sweetheart, Goodnite/You Don't Move Me	1953	200.00
—Black vinyl, correct spelling			
❑ 107	Goodnite, Sweetheart, Goodnite/You Don't Move Me	1953	300.00
—Black vinyl; as "Spanials"			
❑ 107	Goodnite, Sweetheart, Goodnite/You Don't Move Me	1953	800.00
—Red vinyl; no "Trade Mark Reg" on label			
❑ 107	Goodnite, Sweetheart, Goodnite/You Don't Move Me	1993	8.00
—Red vinyl; "Trade Mark Reg" on label; included in Vee-Jay CD box set			
❑ 116	Play It Cool/Let's Make Up	1954	100.00
❑ 116	Play It Cool/Let's Make Up	1954	500.00
—Red vinyl			
❑ 131	Do-Wah/Don'cha Go	1955	80.00
❑ 131	Do-Wah/Don'cha Go	1955	500.00
—Red vinyl			
❑ 154	You Painted P ictures/Hey, Sister Lizzie	1955	50.00
—As "Spanials"			
❑ 154	You Painted Pictures/Hey, Sister Lizzie	1955	60.00
❑ 178	False Love/Do You Really	1956	150.00
❑ 189	Dear Heart/Why Won't You Dance	1956	150.00
❑ 202	Since I Fell for You/Baby Come Along with Me	1956	150.00
❑ 229	Please Don't Tease/You Gave Me Peace of Mind	1956	60.00
❑ 246	Everyone's Laughing/I.O.U.	1957	60.00
❑ 257	You're Gonna Cry/I Need Your Kisses	1957	60.00
❑ 264	I Love You/Crazee Babee	1958	60.00
❑ 278	Tina/Great Googly Moo	1958	60.00
❑ 290	Stormy Weather/Here Is Why I Love You	1958	60.00
❑ 301	Baby It's You/Heart and Soul	1958	60.00
❑ 310	Trees/I Like It Like That	1959	60.00
❑ 328	These Three Words/100 Years from Today	1959	60.00
❑ 342	People Will Say We're in Love/The Bells Ring Out	1960	100.00
❑ 350	I Know/Bus Fare Home	1960	40.00
Albums			
LOST-NITE			
❑ LLP-19 [10]	The Spaniels	1981	12.00
—Red vinyl			
VEE JAY			
❑ LP-1002 [M]	Goodnite, It's Time to Go	1958	600.00
—Maroon label; group pictured on cover			
❑ LP-1002 [M]	Goodnite, It's Time to Go	1961	200.00
—Black label; dogs on cover			
❑ VJLP-1002 [M]	Goodnite, It's Time to Go	198?	12.00
—Legitimate reissue on flimsier vinyl than originals			
❑ LP-1024 [M]	The Spaniels	1960	300.00

SPANKY AND OUR GANG

Number	Title (A Side/B Side)	Yr	NM
45s			
EPIC			
❑ 50170	When I Wanna/I Won't Brand You	1975	5.00
❑ 50206	L.A. Freeway/Standing Room Only	1976	5.00
MERCURY			
❑ DJ-101 [DJ]	Give a Damn (mono/stereo)	1968	12.00
—Special promo for the New York Urban Coalition			

Number	Title (A Side/B Side)	Yr	NM
❑ DJ-101 [PS]	Give a Damn (mono/stereo)	1968	20.00
—Fold-open sleeve with insert letter			
❑ DJ-106 [DJ]	Yesterday's Rain/ Yesterday's Rain	1968	15.00
❑ 72598	And Your Bird Can Sing/ Sealed with a Kiss	1966	20.00
❑ 72679	Sunday Will Never Be the Same/Distance	1967	8.00
❑ 72714	Making Every Minute Count/ If You Could Only Be Me	1967	8.00
❑ 72714 [PS]	Making Every Minute Count/ If You Could Only Be Me	1967	10.00
❑ 72732	Lazy Day/(It Ain't Necessarily) Byrd Avenue	1967	8.00
❑ 72732 [PS]	Lazy Day/(It Ain't Necessarily) Byrd Avenue	1967	10.00
❑ 72765	Sunday Morning/Echoes	1968	8.00
❑ 72765 [PS]	Sunday Morning/Echoes	1968	10.00
❑ 72795	Like to Get to Know You/ Three Ways from Tomorrow	1968	8.00
—Orange and tan swirl label			
❑ 72795	Like to Get to Know You/ Three Ways from Tomorrow	1968	10.00
—Red label with white "Mercury" in all caps across top of label			
❑ 72795 [PS]	Like to Get to Know You/Three Ways from Tomorrow	1968	10.00
❑ 72831	Give a Damn/Swinging Gate	1968	8.00
❑ 72871	Yesterday's Rain/Without Rhyme or Reason	1968	8.00
❑ 72890	Anything You Choose/ Mecca Flat Blues	1969	8.00
❑ 72926	And She's Mine/Leopard Skinned Phones	1969	8.00
❑ 72982	Everybody's Talkin'/ (B-side unknown)	1969	8.00

PHILCO-FORD

Number	Title (A Side/B Side)	Yr	NM
❑ HP-19	Making Every Minute Count/ Byrd Avenue	1968	15.00
—4-inch plastic "Hip Pocket Record" with color sleeve			

Albums

EPIC

Number	Title (A Side/B Side)	Yr	NM
❑ PE 33580	Change	1975	12.00

MERCURY

Number	Title (A Side/B Side)	Yr	NM
❑ MG-21124 [M]	Spanky and Our Gang	1967	30.00
❑ SR-61124 [S]	Spanky and Our Gang	1967	20.00
❑ SR-61161	Like to Get to Know You	1968	20.00
❑ SR-61183	Anything You Choose/ Without Rhyme or Reason	1969	20.00
❑ SR-61227	Spanky's Greatest Hit(s)	1969	20.00
❑ SR-61326	Live	1971	15.00

RHINO

Number	Title (A Side/B Side)	Yr	NM
❑ RNLP-70131	The Best of Spanky and Our Gang (1967-1969)	1986	12.00

SPARKLETONES, THE (1) Also see JOE BENNETT AND THE SPARKLETONES.

45s

ABC-PARAMOUNT

Number	Title (A Side/B Side)	Yr	NM
❑ 10659	Run Rabbit Run/ Well Dressed Man	1965	15.00

SPARKLETONES, THE (2)

45s

PAGEANT

Number	Title (A Side/B Side)	Yr	NM
❑ 604	Just One Chance/Dear Little Boy	196?	50.00

SPARKS Includes records as "Halfnelson." This group did not use the article "The" before its name. Includes records as "Halfnelson." This group did not use the article "The" before its name.

12-Inch Singles

ATLANTIC

Number	Title (A Side/B Side)	Yr	NM
❑ 325 [DJ]	I Predict (6:19) (2:55)	1982	10.00
❑ 325 [DJ]	I Predict (6:19) (2:55)	1982	10.00
❑ 753 [DJ]	Progress (Extended Club)/ Sparks in the Dark (Extended Club)/With All My Might	1984	6.00
❑ 753 [DJ]	Progress (Extended Club)/ Sparks in the Dark (Extended Club)/With All My Might	1984	6.00

ELEKTRA

Number	Title (A Side/B Side)	Yr	NM
❑ 11412 [DJ]	Beat the Clock (7:44)/Tryouts for the Human Race (7:54)	1979	10.00
❑ 11412 [DJ]	Beat the Clock (7:44)/Tryouts for the Human Race (7:54)	1979	10.00
❑ 11412 [DJ]	Tryouts for the Human Race (7:54) (4:00)	1979	12.00
❑ 11412 [DJ]	Tryouts for the Human Race (7:54) (4:00)	1979	12.00

MCA CURB

Number	Title (A Side/B Side)	Yr	NM
❑ L33-17143 [DJ]	Music That You Can Dance To (same on both sides)	1986	6.00
❑ L33-17143 [DJ]	Music That You Can Dance To (same on both sides)	1986	6.00
❑ 23640	Music That You Can Dance To (3 versions)	1986	5.00
❑ 23684	Fingertips (2 versions)/ The Scene (Edit)	1986	5.00

RHINO

Number	Title (A Side/B Side)	Yr	NM
❑ RNTW 70410	So Important (3 versions)	1988	6.00
❑ RNTW 70412	Just Got Back from Heaven (5 versions)	1989	6.00

45s

ATLANTIC

Number	Title (A Side/B Side)	Yr	NM
❑ 4030	I Predict/Moustache	1982	3.00
❑ 4030 [PS]	I Predict/Moustache	1982	4.00
❑ 4065	Eaten by the Monster of Love/ Mickey Mouse	1982	3.00
❑ 89616	Pretending to Be Drunk/ Kiss Me Quick	1984	3.00
❑ 89797	All You Ever Think About Is Sex/ I Wish I Looked a Little Better	1983	3.00
❑ 89866	Cool Places/Sports	1983	3.00
—A-side: Sparks and Jane Wiedlin			
❑ 89866 [PS]	Cool Places/Sports	1983	4.00

BEARSVILLE

Number	Title (A Side/B Side)	Yr	NM
❑ 0006	Wonder Girl/(No More) Mr. Nice Guys	1972	10.00

COLUMBIA

Number	Title (A Side/B Side)	Yr	NM
❑ 10579	Forever Young/ Over the Summer	1977	15.00

ELEKTRA

Number	Title (A Side/B Side)	Yr	NM
❑ 46045	Tryouts for the Human Race/ No. 1 in Heaven	1979	5.00

ISLAND

Number	Title (A Side/B Side)	Yr	NM
❑ 001	This Town Ain't Big Enough for Both of Us/Barbecutie	1974	5.00
❑ 009	Talent Is an Asset/ Lost and Found	1974	5.00
❑ 023	Something for the Girl with Everything/Achoo	1975	5.00
❑ 043	Looks, Looks, Looks/ The Wedding of Jackie	1975	15.00

MCA CURB

Number	Title (A Side/B Side)	Yr	NM
❑ 52879	Shopping Mall of Love/Music That You Can Dance To	1986	3.00

PRIVATE I

Number	Title (A Side/B Side)	Yr	NM
❑ 05627	Armies of the Night/Give It Up	1985	3.00
—B-side by Evelyn "Champagne" King			

RCA

Number	Title (A Side/B Side)	Yr	NM
❑ PD-12252	Tips for Teens/Don't Shoot Me	1981	—
—Unreleased			

Albums

ANTILLES

Number	Title (A Side/B Side)	Yr	NM
❑ ANT-7044	Kimono My House	198?	10.00
—Reissue of Island 9272			

ATLANTIC

Number	Title (A Side/B Side)	Yr	NM
❑ SD 19347	Angst in My Pants	1982	10.00
❑ 80055	Sparks in Outer Space	1983	10.00
❑ 80160	Pulling Rabbits Out of a Hat	1984	10.00

BEARSVILLE

Number	Title (A Side/B Side)	Yr	NM
❑ BV 2048	Halfnelson	1971	25.00
—Original issue of "Sparks" as "Halfnelson"			
❑ BV 2048	Sparks	1972	12.00
—Reissue under the group's new name			
❑ BR 2110	A Woofer in Tweeter's Clothing	1973	12.00

COLUMBIA

Number	Title (A Side/B Side)	Yr	NM
❑ PC 34359	Big Beat	1976	10.00
—Originals have no bar code			
❑ PC 34901	Introducing Sparks	1977	10.00
—Originals have no bar code			

ELEKTRA

Number	Title (A Side/B Side)	Yr	NM
❑ 6E-186	No. 1 in Heaven	1979	10.00

IN THE RED

Number	Title (A Side/B Side)	Yr	NM
❑ ITR 131	Hello Young Lovers	2006	12.00

ISLAND

Number	Title (A Side/B Side)	Yr	NM
❑ ILPS-9272	Kimono My House	1974	12.00
—Originals have multicolor island-scene label			
❑ ILPS-9312	Propaganda	1975	12.00
—Originals have multicolor island-scene label			
❑ ILPS-9345	Indiscreet	1975	12.00
—Originals have black label and no Warner Bros. distribution			
❑ 5318093	Kimono My House	2009	20.00

MCA CURB

Number	Title (A Side/B Side)	Yr	NM
❑ 5780	Music That You Can Dance To	1986	10.00

RCA VICTOR

Number	Title (A Side/B Side)	Yr	NM
❑ AFL1-4091	Whomp That Sucker	1981	10.00

RHINO

Number	Title (A Side/B Side)	Yr	NM
❑ R1-70841	Interior Design	1988	10.00

SPARKS, THE Possibly more than one group.

45s

ARWIN

Number	Title (A Side/B Side)	Yr	NM
❑ 114	Something's Happened/ Robin Redbreast	1958	20.00

CARLTON

Number	Title (A Side/B Side)	Yr	NM
❑ 522	The Genie/Gee, That's Bad	1959	20.00

CUB

Number	Title (A Side/B Side)	Yr	NM
❑ 9151	Woe, Woe/Cool It	1967	10.00

DECCA

Number	Title (A Side/B Side)	Yr	NM
❑ 30378	Ol' Man River/Merry, Merry Lou	1957	12.00
❑ 30509	Roamin' Candle/ A Cuddle and a Kiss	1957	12.00
❑ 30974	Why Did You Leave/La Macerena	1959	10.00

HULL

Number	Title (A Side/B Side)	Yr	NM
❑ 723	Danny Boy/Run Run Run	1957	400.00
❑ 724	Adreann/Finger	1957	150.00

SPARKS OF RHYTHM, THE

45s

APOLLO

Number	Title (A Side/B Side)	Yr	NM
❑ 479	Women, Women, Women/ Don't Love You Anymore	1955	300.00
❑ 481	Hurry Home/Stars Are in the Sky	1955	300.00
❑ 541	Handy Man/Everybody Rock and Roll	1959	50.00

SPARROW, THE Evolved into STEPPENWOLF. Also see MARS BONFIRE.

45s

COLUMBIA

Number	Title (A Side/B Side)	Yr	NM
❑ 10234	Eli's Coming/Oh Doctor	1975	10.00
❑ 43755	Tomorrow's Ship/Isn't It Strange	1966	25.00
—As "The Sparrows"			
❑ 43755 [PS]	Tomorrow's Ship/Isn't It Strange	1966	100.00
—As "The Sparrows"			
❑ 43960	Green Bottle Lover/Down Goes Your Love Life	1967	25.00
—As "The Sparrows"			

Albums

COLUMBIA

Number	Title (A Side/B Side)	Yr	NM
❑ CS 9758	John Kay and Sparrow	1969	40.00
—Red "360 Sound" label			

SPARROWS, THE Probably three different groups.

45s

DAVIS

Number	Title (A Side/B Side)	Yr	NM
❑ 456	Love Me Tender/ Come Back to Me	1957	300.00

JAY DEE

Number	Title (A Side/B Side)	Yr	NM
❑ 783	Tell Me Baby/Why Did You Leave Me	1953	500.00
❑ 790	I'll Be Loving You/Hey!	1954	500.00

Albums

ELKAY

Number	Title (A Side/B Side)	Yr	NM
❑ 3009 [M]	That Mersey Sound	1964	40.00

SPARTAS, THE

45s

HIT

Number	Title (A Side/B Side)	Yr	NM
❑ 137	House of the Rising Sun/ Bread and Butter	1964	15.00
—B-side by Danny and Deanie			
❑ 154	I'm Crying/Have I the Right	1964	15.00
❑ 158	Dance, Dance, Dance/ Everything's Alright	1964	12.00
—B-side by the Roamers			
❑ 181	Sha La La/Midnight Special	1965	12.00
—B-side by Harvey Frolic			
❑ 251	Good Lovin'/Soul and Inspiration	1966	12.00
—B-side by John Brooks			

SPATS, THE

45s

ABC-PARAMOUNT

Number	Title (A Side/B Side)	Yr	NM
❑ 10585	Gator Tails and Monkey Ribs/ The Roach	1964	10.00
❑ 10600	She Kissed Me Last Night/ There's a Party in the Pad Down Below	1964	15.00
❑ 10640	Billy, the Blue Grasshoper/Gotta Tell Ya All About It, Baby	1965	45.00
❑ 10711	Go Go Yamaha/Have You Ever Seen Me Crying	1965	30.00
❑ 10790	Scoobee Doo/She Done Moved	1966	50.00

ENITH

Number	Title (A Side/B Side)	Yr	NM
❑ 1268	Gator Tails and Monkey Ribs/ The Roach	1964	40.00

Number | Title (A Side/B Side) | Yr | NM

Albums
ABC-PARAMOUNT
❑ 502 [M] Cookin' with the Spats 1965 20.00
❑ S-502 [S] Cookin' with the Spats 1965 30.00

SPECIALS, THE

12-Inch Singles
CHRYSALIS
❑ 42793 Free Nelson Mandela (3 mixes) 1984 10.00
—As "The Special AKA"
CHRYSALIS/2 TONE
❑ CDS-2525 Ghost Town/Why/Friday Night, Saturday Morning 1981 10.00

45s
CHRYSALIS
❑ 42794 Free Nelson Mandela/ Break Down the Door 1984 10.00
—As "The Special AKA"
CHRYSALIS/2 TONE
❑ 2374 Gangsters/The Selecter 1979 4.00
—B-side by The Selecter
❑ 2374 [PS] Gangsters/The Selecter 1979 8.00
—Sleeve says "The Specials," theoretically for use with any Specials single

Albums
CHRYSALIS
❑ CHR 1265 The Specials 1979 15.00
❑ CHR 1303 More Specials 1980 12.00
❑ PV 41265 The Specials 1986 10.00
—Reissue
❑ PV 41303 More Specials 1983 8.00
—Reissue

SPECTOR, PHIL Also see THE TEDDY BEARS; THE RIGHTEOUS BROTHERS.

45s
PAVILLION
❑ AE7 1354 [DJ] Phil Spector's Christmas Medley (same on both sides) 1981 15.00
—Promo-only sampler from the Pavillion reissue of Phil Spector's Christmas Album
PHILLES
❑ (no #) [DJ] Thanks for Giving Me the Right Time! (same on both sides) 1965 1000.
—Has Phil's picture on label; actually plays "Ebb Tide" by the Righteous Brothers

SPECTOR, RONNIE Also see THE RONETTES; VERONICA.

12-Inch Singles
COLUMBIA
❑ CAS 2701 [DJ] Who Can Sleep (same on both sides) 1987 8.00
EPIC
❑ ASF 350 [DJ] Say Goodbye to Hollywood/ Baby Please Don't Go 1977 40.00
TOM CAT
❑ JD-10380 [DJ] You'd Be Good for Me (same on both sides) 197? 30.00
—Promo only on red vinyl

45s
ALSTON
❑ 3738 It's a Heartache/ I Wanna Come Over 1978 8.00
APPLE
❑ 1832 Try Some, Buy Some/ Tandoori Chicken 1971 7.00
❑ 1832 Try Some, Buy Some/ Tandoori Chicken 1971 8.00
—With star on A-side label
❑ 1832 [PS] Try Some, Buy Some/ Tandoori Chicken 1971 10.00
COLUMBIA
❑ 07082 Who Can Sleep/ When We Danced 1987 4.00
❑ 07082 [PS] Who Can Sleep/ When We Danced 1987 4.00
❑ 07300 Love on a Rooftop/ Good Love Is Hard to Find 1987 4.00
EPIC
❑ 50374 Say Goodbye to Hollywood/ Baby Please Don't Go 1977 10.00
❑ 50374 [PS] Say Goodbye to Hollywood/ Baby Please Don't Go 1977 25.00
POLISH
❑ 202 Darlin'/Tonight 1980 5.00
TOM CAT
❑ JB-10380 [DJ] You'd Be Good for Me/ Something Tells Me 1975 10.00
—Promo only on blue vinyl
❑ PB-10380 You'd Be Good for Me/ Something Tells Me 1975 5.00
WARNER/SPECTOR
❑ 0409 Paradise/When I Saw You 1976 10.00

Albums
COLUMBIA
❑ C 40620 Unfinished Business 1987 10.00
POLISH
❑ PRG-808 Siren 1980 12.00

SPECTORS THREE, THE

45s
TREY
❑ 3001 I Really Do/I Know Why 1959 25.00
❑ 3005 My Heart Stood Still/Mr. Robin 1960 25.00

SPEEDO AND THE IMPALAS See THE IMPALAS.

SPEEDY AND THE REVERBS

45s
REVERB
❑ 51 100 Proof/Gas Chamber 196? 50.00

SPELLMAN, BENNY

45s
ACE
❑ 630 That's All I Ask of You/ Roll On Big Wheel 1961 20.00
ALON
❑ 9018 Tain't the Truth/No Don't Stop 1965 10.00
❑ 9024 The Word Game/I Feel Good 1965 20.00
❑ 9027 It Must Be Love/ Spirit of Loneliness 1965 10.00
❑ 9031 It's for You/This Is My Love 1966 10.00
ATLANTIC
❑ 2291 The Word Game/I Feel Good 1965 10.00
MINIT
❑ 606 Life Is Too Short/Ammerette 1960 15.00
❑ 613 Darling No Matter Where/ I Didn't Know 1960 15.00
❑ 644 Lipstick Traces (On a Cigarette)/ Fortune Teller 1962 12.00
❑ 652 Every Now and Then/I'm in Love 1962 12.00
❑ 659 Stickin' Whicha' Baby/You Got to Get It 1963 12.00
❑ 664 Ammerette/Talk About Love 1963 12.00
SANSU
❑ 462 But If You Love Her/Sinner Girl 1967 8.00
WATCH
❑ 6336 Slow Down Baby (You Drive Too Fast)/Someday They'll Understand 1964 10.00

SPELLMAN, JIMMY

45s
DOT
❑ 15564 Here I Am/Make Up Your Mind 1957 30.00
❑ 15607 Doggonit/I'll Never Smile Again 1957 30.00

SPENCE, ALEXANDER "SKIP" Also see MOBY GRAPE.

Albums
COLUMBIA
❑ CS 9831 Oar 1969 60.00
SUNDAZED
❑ LP 5030 Oar 2000 20.00
—Reissue on 180-gram vinyl

SPENCER, JEREMY Also see FLEETWOOD MAC.

45s
ATLANTIC
❑ 3588 Cool Breeze/You Got the Right 1979 5.00
❑ 3601 Cool Breeze/You Got the Right 1979 5.00
❑ 3624 [DJ] Travelin' (same on both sides) 1979 5.00
—May be promo-only
COLUMBIA
❑ 45854 Can You Hear the Song/ The World in Her Heart 1973 5.00

Albums
ATLANTIC
❑ SD 19236 Flee 1979 10.00
COLUMBIA
❑ KC 31990 Jeremy Spencer and the Children of God 1972 15.00

SPENCER AND SPENCER DICKIE GOODMAN and Mickey Shorr.

45s
ARGO
❑ 5331 Russian Bandstand/Brass Wail 1959 25.00
GONE
❑ 5053 Stagger Lawrence/ Strogonoff Cha Cha 1959 25.00

SPHEERIS, JIMMY

45s
COLUMBIA
❑ 45646 I Am the Mercury/The Nest 1972 5.00
❑ 45875 The Original Tap Dancing Kid/ Beautiful News 1973 5.00
EPIC
❑ 50159 Tequila Moonlight/Sunken Skies 1975 4.00
❑ 50286 It's All in the Game/The Captain Comes Cold 1976 4.00

Albums
COLUMBIA
❑ C 30988 The Isle of View 1972 15.00
❑ KC 32157 The Original Tap Dancing Kid 1973 15.00
EPIC
❑ PE 33565 The Dragon Is Dancing 1975 12.00
❑ PE 34276 Ports of the Heart 1976 12.00

SPICES, THE

45s
CARLTON
❑ 480 Tell Me Little Girl/Money, Fortune and Fame 1958 300.00

SPIDELLS, THE

45s
CORAL
❑ 62508 Pushed Out of the Picture/ With You in Mind 1966 50.00
❑ 62531 Don't You Forget That You're My Baby/If It Ain't One Thing (It's Another) 1967 20.00

SPIDER-MAN

Albums
LIFESONG
❑ LS 6001 Rock Reflections of a Superhero 1976 25.00

SPIDERS, THE (1)

45s
IMPERIAL
❑ 5265 I Didn't Want to Do It/ You're the One 1954 100.00
❑ 5280 Tears Begin to Flow/ I'll Stop Cryin' 1954 100.00
❑ 5291 I'm Searching/I'm Slippin' In 1954 250.00
❑ 5305 The Real Thing/Mm Mm Baby 1954 100.00
❑ 5318 She Keeps Me Wondering/ (3 x 7) = "21" 1954 100.00
❑ 5331 That's Enough/ Lost and Bewildered 1955 75.00
❑ 5344 Am I the One/ Sukey, Sukey, Sukey 1955 75.00
❑ 5354 Bells in My Heart/For a Thrill 1955 100.00
—Red label
❑ 5354 Bells in My Heart/For a Thrill 1957 30.00
—Black label
❑ 5366 Is It True/Witchcraft 1955 40.00
—Red label
❑ 5366 Is It True/Witchcraft 1955 100.00
—Blue label
❑ 5376 Don't Pity Me/How I Feel 1956 40.00
—Featuring Chuck Carbo
❑ 5393 A-1 in My Heart/Dear Mary 1956 30.00
—As "The Spiders with Chuck Carbo"
❑ 5618 I Didn't Want to Do It/ You're the One 1959 30.00
❑ 5714 You're the One/Tennessee Slim 1960 30.00
❑ 5739 Witchcraft/(True) You Don't Love Me 1961 30.00

Albums
IMPERIAL
❑ LP-9142 [M] I Didn't Wanna Do It 1961 600.00

SPIDERS, THE (2) Early ALICE COOPER.

45s
MASCOT
❑ 112 Why Don't You Love Me/ Hitch Hike 1965 1500.
SANTA CRUZ
❑ 003 Don't Blow Your Mind/ No Price Tag 1966 1000.

SPIDERS, THE (U) Definitely not group (2); could be group (1).

45s
LAWN
❑ 234 Run Boy Run/Baby Doll 1964 12.00

Except when noted otherwise, VG = 25% of NM, and VG+ = 50% of NM. (Example: VG = $2.00, VG+ = $4.00 and NM = $8.00.)

Number	Title (A Side/B Side)	Yr	NM
PHILIPS			
❑ 40363	No No Boy/How Could I Fall in Love	1966	8.00

SPIKE DRIVERS, THE

45s

Number	Title (A Side/B Side)	Yr	NM
OM 1000			
❑ 1676	High Time/Baby Won't You Let Me Tell You How I Lost My Mind	1966	30.00
REPRISE			
❑ 0535	High Time/Baby Won't You Let Me Tell You How I Lost My Mind	1966	20.00
❑ 0558	Strange Mysterious Sounds/ Break Out the Wine	1967	20.00

SPINAL TAP

45s

Number	Title (A Side/B Side)	Yr	NM
ENIGMA			
❑ 1143	Christmas With The Devil/ Christmas With The Devil (Scratch Mix)	1984	6.00
❑ 1143 [PS]	Christmas With The Devil/ Christmas With The Devil (Scratch Mix)	1984	10.00

Albums

Number	Title (A Side/B Side)	Yr	NM
MCA			
❑ 10514 [PD]	Break Like the Wind	1992	15.00
—Picture disc (only U.S. vinyl version of this LP)			

SPINDLES, THE

45s

Number	Title (A Side/B Side)	Yr	NM
ABC			
❑ 10802	To Make You Mine/And the Band Played On	1966	20.00
❑ 10850	No One Loves You (The Way I Do)/Ten Shades of Blue	1966	25.00

SPINDRIFTS, THE

45s

Number	Title (A Side/B Side)	Yr	NM
ABC-PARAMOUNT			
❑ 9904	Belinda/Cha Cha Doo	1958	25.00

SPINNERS Many, though not all, of these did not use the article "The" before the name. These are all by the group known as "The Detroit Spinners" in the U.K.

45s

Number	Title (A Side/B Side)	Yr	NM
ATLANTIC			
❑ 2904	I'll Be Around/How Could I Let You Get Away	1972	5.00
❑ 2927	Could It Be I'm Falling in Love/ Just You and Me Baby	1972	5.00
❑ 2962	One of a Kind (Love Affair)/ Don't Let the Green Grass Fool You	1973	5.00
❑ 2973	Ghetto Child/We Belong Together	1973	5.00
❑ 3006	Mighty Love — Pt. 1/ Mighty Love — Pt. 2	1974	5.00
❑ 3027	I'm Coming Home/He'll Never Love You Like I Do	1974	5.00
❑ 3029	Then Came You/Just As Long As We Have Love	1974	6.00
—With Dionne Warwicke			
❑ 3202	Then Came You/Just As Long As We Have Love	1974	5.00
—With Dionne Warwicke			
❑ 3206	Love Don't Love Nobody (Part 1)/Love Don't Love Nobody (Part 2)	1974	5.00
❑ 3252	Living a Little, Loving a Little/ Smile, We Have Each Other	1975	5.00
❑ 3268	Sadie/Lazy Susan	1975	5.00
❑ 3284	They Just Can't Stop it the (Games People Play)/ I Don't Want to Lose You	1975	5.00
—Same A-side, altered title			
❑ 3284	Games People Play/ I Don't Want to Lose You	1975	10.00
❑ 3309	Love Or Leave/You Made a Promise to Me	1975	5.00
❑ 3341	Wake Up Susan/ If You Can't Be in Love	1976	5.00
❑ 3355	The Rubberband Man/ Now That We're Together	1976	5.00
❑ 3382	You're Throwing a Good Love Away/You're All I Need in Life	1977	5.00
❑ 3400	Me and My Music/ I'm Riding Your Shadow	1977	5.00
❑ 3425	Heaven on Earth (So Fine)/ I'm Tired of Giving	1977	5.00
❑ 3462	Easy Come, Easy Go/ Love Is One Step Away	1978	5.00
❑ 3483	If You Wanna Do a Dance/ One in a Life Proposal	1978	5.00
❑ 3546	Are You Ready for Love/ Once You Fall in Love	1978	5.00

Spinal Tap, "Christmas with the Devil," Enigma 1143, 1984, **$10.**

Number	Title (A Side/B Side)	Yr	NM
❑ 3590	Don't Let the Man Get You/ I Love the Music	1979	5.00
❑ 3619	Body Language/With My Eyes	1979	5.00
❑ 3637	Working My Way Back to You-Forgive Me, Girl/Disco Ride	1979	4.00
❑ 3637	Working My Way Back to You/ Disco Ride	1979	8.00
—Original pressings mention only one song on the A-side			
❑ 3664	Cupid-I've Loved You for a Long Time/Pipedreams	1980	4.00
❑ 3757	Love Trippin'/Now That You're Mine Again	1980	4.00
❑ 3765	I Just Want to Fall in Love/ Heavy on the Sunshine	1980	4.00
❑ 3798	Yesterday Once More-Nothing Remains the Same/ Be My Love	1981	4.00
❑ 3814	Long Live Soul Music/Give Your Lady What She Wants	1981	4.00
❑ 3827	Winter of Our Love/The Deacon	1981	4.00
❑ 3848	What You Feel Is Real/ Street Talk	1981	4.00
—With Gino Soccio			
❑ 3865	You Go Your Way (I'll Go Mine)/ Got to Be Love	1981	4.00
❑ 3882 [DJ]	Love Connection (same on both sides)	1981	5.00
—May be promo only			
❑ 4007	Never Thought I'd Fall in Love/ Send a Little Love	1982	4.00
❑ 89226	Spaceballs/Spaceballs (Dub Version)	1987	3.00
❑ 89648	(We Have Come Into) Our Time for All/All Your Love	1984	4.00
❑ 89689	Right or Wrong/Love Is In Season	1984	4.00
❑ 89862	City Full of Memories/ No Other Love	1983	4.00
❑ 89922	Funny How Time Slips Away/ I'm Calling You Now	1982	4.00
❑ 89962	Magic in the Moonlight/ So Far Away	1982	4.00
MIRAGE			
❑ 99580	She Does/(B-side unknown)	1986	3.00
❑ 99604	Put Us Together Again/ Show Us Your Magic	1985	3.00
MOTOWN			
❑ 1067	Sweet Thing/How Can I	1964	15.00
❑ 1078	I'll Always Love You/ Tomorrow May Never Come	1965	15.00
❑ 1093	Truly Yours/Where Is That Girl	1966	15.00
❑ 1109	For All We Know/Cross My Heart	1967	15.00
❑ 1136	I Just Can't Help But Feel the Pain/Bad, Bad Weather	1968	15.00
❑ 1155	In My Diary/(She's Gonna Love Me) At Sundown	1969	1500.
❑ 1235	Together We Can Make Such Sweet Music/ Bad, Bad Weather	1973	8.00
TRI-PHI			
❑ 1001	That's What Girls Are Made For/Heebie-Jeebies	1961	25.00
❑ 1004	Love (I'm So Glad I Found You)/ Sudbuster	1961	25.00
❑ 1007	What Did She Use/Itching for My Baby, I Know Where to Scratch	1962	25.00
❑ 1010	She Loves Me So/ Whistling About You	1962	25.00
❑ 1013	I've Been Hurt/I Got Your Water Boiling Baby (I'm Gonna Cook Your Goose)	1962	25.00
❑ 1018	She Don't Love Me/Too Young, Too Much, Too Soon	1962	30.00
V.I.P.			
❑ 25050	In My Diary/(She's Gonna Love Me) At Sundown	1969	25.00
❑ 25054	Message from a Black Man/ (She's Gonna Love Me) At Sundown	1970	12.00
❑ 25057	It's a Shame/Together We Can Make Such Sweet Music	1970	12.00
❑ 25060	We'll Have It Made/ My Whole World Ended (The Moment You Left Me)	1971	12.00

Spirit, *Future Games*, Mercury SRM-1-1122, 1977, **$12.**

Number	Title (A Side/B Side)	Yr	NM
7-Inch Extended Plays			
ATLANTIC			
❑ SD 7-7256	One Of A Kind (Love Affair)/ Just You and Me Baby/ I'll Be Around//Just Can't Get You Out of My Mind/Could It Be I'm Falling in Love	1973	12.00
—Jukebox issue; small hole, plays at 33 1/3 rpm			
❑ SD 7-7256	Spinners	1973	12.00
—Part of "Little LP" series (LLP #216)			
❑ SD 7-7296	Since I Been Gone/Love Has Gone Away//Ain't No Price on Happiness/I'm Glad You Walked Into My Life	1974	10.00
—Jukebox issue; small hole, plays at 33 1/3 rpm			
❑ SD 7-7296 [PS]	Mighty Love	1974	10.00
Albums			
ATLANTIC			
❑ SD 2-910 [(2)]	Spinners Live!	1975	15.00
❑ QD 7256 [Q]	Spinners	1974	20.00
❑ SD 7256	Spinners	1973	12.00
❑ SD 7296	Mighty Love	1974	12.00
❑ SD 16032	Labor of Love	1981	10.00
❑ QD 18118 [Q]	New and Improved	1974	20.00
❑ SD 18118	New and Improved	1974	12.00
❑ QD 18141 [Q]	Pick of the Litter	1975	20.00
❑ SD 18141	Pick of the Litter	1975	12.00
❑ SD 18181	Happiness is Being with the Spinners	1976	12.00
❑ SD 19100	Yesterday, Today & Tomorrow	1977	12.00
❑ SD 19146	Spinners/8	1977	12.00
❑ SD 19179	The Best of the Spinners	1978	12.00
❑ SD 19219	From Here to Eternally	1979	12.00
❑ SD 19256	Dancin' and Lovin'	1980	10.00
❑ SD 19270	Love Trippin'	1980	10.00
❑ SD 19318	Can't Shake This Feelin'	1981	10.00
❑ 80020	Grand Slam	1982	10.00
MIRAGE			
❑ 90456	Lovin' Feelings	1985	10.00
MOTOWN			
❑ M5-109V1	Motown Superstar Series, Vol. 9	1982	8.00
❑ M5-132V1	The Original Spinners	1981	12.00
—Reissue of Motown 639			
❑ M5-199V1	The Best of the Spinners	1981	12.00
—Reissue of Motown 769			
❑ M 639 [M]	The Original Spinners	1967	25.00
❑ MS 639 [P]	The Original Spinners	1967	30.00
❑ M 769	The Best of the Spinners	1973	15.00
V.I.P.			
❑ 405	2nd Time Around	1970	40.00
VOLT			
❑ V-3403	Down to Business	1989	12.00

SPINNERS, THE None of these are the popular soul group. Also see THE LIVERPOOL SPINNERS.

Number	Title (A Side/B Side)	Yr	NM
45s			
CAPITOL			
❑ F3955	Love's Prayer/Goofin'	1958	40.00
CRYSTALETTE			
❑ 736	Boomerang/Slave Chain	1960	50.00
—Reissued under different titles and on different labels credited to the Crestriders and Duke Mitchell			
END			
❑ 1045	Bird Watcher/Richard Pry, Private Eye	1959	40.00
—Multicolor label			
❑ 1045	Bird Watcher/Richard Pry, Private Eye	1959	100.00
—Gray label			
LAWSON			
❑ 324	Surfing Monkey/Beatle Mania	1964	30.00
LIBERTY			
❑ 55339	Till the End of Time/Dream	1961	10.00
RCA VICTOR			
❑ 47-8427	All I Want/It Must Be Love	1964	10.00
RHYTHM			
❑ 125	Marvella/My Love and Your Love	1958	400.00
SMASH			
❑ 1845	Happy Hootenanny/Nothin'	1963	10.00
WARNER BROS.			
❑ 5084	Little Otis/Rag Mop	1959	12.00
Albums			
TIME			
❑ S-2092 [S]	Party — My Pad After Surfin'	1963	30.00
❑ 52092 [M]	Party — My Pad After Surfin'	1963	25.00

SPINNEY, CARROLL

Number	Title (A Side/B Side)	Yr	NM
45s			
COLUMBIA			
❑ 4-45247	I Love Trash/Up and Down	1970	8.00
—As "Oscar (Carroll Spinney)"; B-side by Jim Henson and Frank Oz as "Two Monsters"			

SPIRAL STARECASE

Number	Title (A Side/B Side)	Yr	NM
45s			
COLUMBIA			
❑ 44442	Makin' My Mind Up/ Baby What I Mean	1968	6.00
❑ 44566	Inside, Outside, Upside Down/ I'll Run	1968	6.00
❑ 44741	More Today Than Yesterday/ Broken Hearted Man	1969	8.00
❑ 44924	Sweet Little Thing/ No One for Me to Turn To	1969	5.00
❑ 45048	She's Ready/Judas to the Love We Know	1969	5.00
Albums			
COLUMBIA			
❑ CS 9852	More Today Than Yesterday	1969	25.00
—"360 Sound" label			

SPIRALS, THE

Number	Title (A Side/B Side)	Yr	NM
45s			
CAPITOL			
❑ F4084	Rockin' Cow/Everybody Knows	1958	50.00
SMASH			
❑ 1719	Please Be My Love/ Forever and a Day	1961	100.00

SPIRES, BIG BOY

Number	Title (A Side/B Side)	Yr	NM
45s			
CHANCE			
❑ 1137	About to Lose My Mind/ Which One Do I Love	1953	2500.

SPIRIT Also see RANDY CALIFORNIA.

Number	Title (A Side/B Side)	Yr	NM
12-Inch Singles			
MERCURY			
❑ 301 [DJ]	I Got a Line on You (Edit)/ Black Satin Nights	1984	6.00
45s			
EPIC			
❑ 10648	Animal Zoo/Red Light Roll On	1970	6.00
❑ 10685	Soldier/Mr. Skin	1970	6.00
❑ 10701	Mr. Skin/Nature's Way	1971	5.00
❑ 10849	Darkness/Cadillac Cowboys	1972	5.00
❑ 10849 [PS]	Darkness/Cadillac Cowboys	1972	15.00
❑ 11020	Mr. Skin/Nature's Way	1973	4.00
MERCURY			
❑ 73697	America the Beautiful-The Times They Are a-Changin'/ Lady of the Lakes	1975	5.00
❑ 73722	Holy Man/Looking Into Darkness	1975	5.00
❑ 73837	Atomic Boogie/Farther Along	1976	4.00
ODE			
❑ 108	Mechanical World/Uncle Jack	1967	10.00
❑ 115	I Got a Line on You/She Smiles	1968	10.00
❑ 122	Dark Eyed Woman/ New Dope in Town	1969	8.00
❑ 128	1984/Sweet Stella Baby	1969	8.00
POTATO			
❑ 1722	Nature's Way/Rock and Roll Planet	1978	5.00
❑ 1722 [PS]	Nature's Way/Rock and Roll Planet	1978	5.00
RHINO			
❑ 008	Turn to the Right/Potato Land Theme Song	1980	5.00
Albums			
EPIC			
❑ E 30267	Twelve Dreams of Dr. Sardonicus	1970	20.00
—Yellow label			
❑ KE 30267	Twelve Dreams of Dr. Sardonicus	1973	10.00
—Orange label			
❑ PE 30267	Twelve Dreams of Dr. Sardonicus	197?	8.00
—Orange or dark blue label, with or without bar code			

 Except when noted otherwise, VG = 25% of NM, and VG+ = 50% of NM. (Example: VG = $2.00, VG+ = $4.00 and NM = $8.00.)

Number	Title (A Side/B Side)	Yr	NM
❑ KE 31175	Feedback	1972	20.00
—Yellow label			
❑ KE 31175	Feedback	1973	10.00
—Orange label			
❑ KEG 31457 [(2)]	Spirit	1972	15.00
—Reissue of Ode 44004 and 44016 in one package; yellow labels			
❑ PEG 31457 [(2)]	Spirit	197?	12.00
—Reissue with new prefix and orange labels			
❑ KE 31461	The Family That Plays Together	1972	12.00
—Reissue of Ode 44014 with slightly different cover; yellow label			
❑ KE 31461	The Family That Plays Together	1973	10.00
—Orange label			
❑ KE 32271	The Best of Spirit	1973	12.00
❑ PE 32271	The Best of Spirit	1979	8.00
—Dark blue label; bar code on cover			
❑ BG 33761 [(2)]	The Family That Plays Together/Feedback	1976	12.00
I.R.S.			
❑ 82007	Rapture in the Chambers	1989	12.00
MERCURY			
❑ SRM-2-804 [(2)]	Spirit of '76	1975	15.00
❑ SRM-1-1053	Son of Spirit	1975	12.00
❑ SRM-1-1094	Farther Along	1976	12.00
❑ SRM-1-1122	Future Games	1977	12.00
❑ 818514-1	Spirit of '84	1984	10.00
ODE			
❑ Z12 44003 [M]	Spirit	1968	40.00
❑ Z12 44004 [S]	Spirit	1968	25.00
❑ Z12 44014	The Family That Plays Together	1968	25.00
❑ Z12 44016	Clear Spirit	1969	25.00
POTATO			
❑ 2001	Live	1978	10.00
RHINO			
❑ RNSP-303	Potatoland	1981	10.00
SUNDAZED			
❑ LP 5067	Now or Anywhere	2000	16.00
❑ LP 5068	Eventide	2000	16.00
❑ LP 5082	Clear	2001	16.00
❑ LP 5085	The Family That Plays Together	2001	16.00

SPIRITS AND WORM

45s

Number	Title (A Side/B Side)	Yr	NM
A&M			
❑ 1104	Fanny Firecracker/You and I Together	1969	40.00

Albums

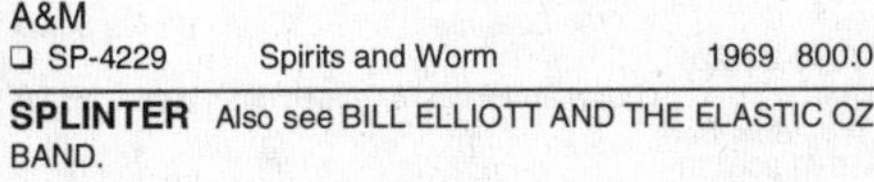

Number	Title (A Side/B Side)	Yr	NM
A&M			
❑ SP-4229	Spirits and Worm	1969	800.00

SPLINTER Also see BILL ELLIOTT AND THE ELASTIC OZ BAND.

45s

Number	Title (A Side/B Side)	Yr	NM
DARK HORSE			
❑ 8439	Round and Round/I'll Bend for You	1977	4.00
❑ 8523	I Need Your Love/Motions of Love	1978	4.00
❑ 10002	Costafine Town/Elly-Mae	1974	6.00
❑ 10002 [PS]	Costafine Town/Elly-Mae	1974	8.00
❑ 10003	China Light/Haven't Got Time	1975	6.00
❑ 10007	Which Way Will I Get Home/What Is It (If You Never Tried It Yourself)	1975	6.00
❑ 10010	After Five Years/Halfway There	1976	5.00

Albums

Number	Title (A Side/B Side)	Yr	NM
DARK HORSE			
❑ DH 3073	Two Man Band	1977	25.00
❑ SP-22001	The Place I Love	1974	20.00
❑ SP-22006	Harder to Live	1975	20.00

SPLIT ENZ Featuring the Finn brothers. Featuring the Finn brothers.

12-Inch Singles

Number	Title (A Side/B Side)	Yr	NM
A&M			
❑ SP-17157 [DJ]	I Don't Wanna Dance/Hard Act to Follow/History Never Repeats	1981	25.00
—Promo-only picture disc in plastic sleeve; used as a teaser for the "Waiata" LP			
❑ 17192 [DJ]	Six Months in a Leaky Boat/Hello Sandy Allen/Never Ceases to Amaze	1982	8.00
❑ SP-17192 [DJ]	Six Months in a Leaky Boat/Hello Sandy Allen/Never Ceases to Amaze	1982	10.00
❑ 17483 [DJ]	Message to My Girl/I Got You	1987	8.00
❑ SP-17483 [DJ]	Message to My Girl/I Got You	1987	10.00

45s

Number	Title (A Side/B Side)	Yr	NM
A&M			
❑ 2252	I Got You/Double Happy	1980	5.00
❑ 2252 [PS]	I Got You/Double Happy	1980	8.00
❑ 2285	I Hope I Never/Choral Sea	1980	8.00
❑ 2285 [PS]	I Hope I Never/Choral Sea	1980	8.00

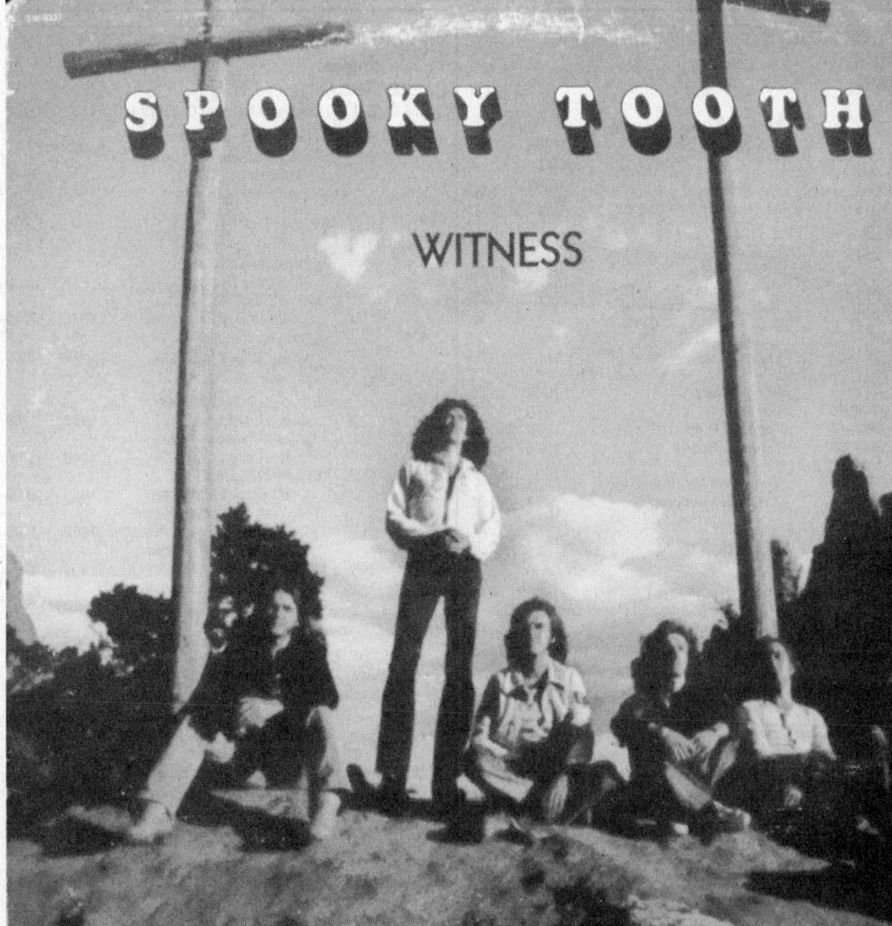

Spooky Tooth, *Witness*, Island, SW-9255, 1973, **$12.**

Number	Title (A Side/B Side)	Yr	NM
❑ 2293	What's the Matter with You/Nobody Takes Me Seriously	1980	5.00
❑ 2339	One Step Ahead/In the Wars	1981	4.00
—Regular release with no laser etching			
❑ 2339	One Step Ahead/In the Wars	1981	5.00
—First pressing: Laser-etched design on record			
❑ 2339 [PS]	One Step Ahead/In the Wars	1981	4.00
—No reference to laser-etched single on sleeve			
❑ 2339 [PS]	One Step Ahead/In the Wars	1981	5.00
—Special picture sleeve for laser-etched single			
❑ 2351	Iris/Clumsy	1981	8.00
❑ 2411	Six Months in a Leaky Boat/Make Sense of It	1982	3.00
❑ 2411 [PS]	Six Months in a Leaky Boat/Make Sense of It	1982	3.00
❑ 2430	Dirty Creature/Make Sense of It	1982	—
—Unreleased			
❑ 2430 [DJ]	Dirty Creature (same on both sides)	1982	5.00
❑ 2430 [DJ]	Dirty Creature (same on both sides)	1982	8.00
❑ 2652	Message to My Girl/Kia Kaha	1984	6.00
❑ 2958	I Got You/(B-side unknown)	1987	10.00
❑ 8742	I Got You/Six Months in a Leaky Boat	1996	3.00
—"A&M Memories" reissue with "Collectables" logo			
FAN CLUB			
❑ (no #) [DJ]	Merry Christmas from Split Enz	1982	20.00
—Green vinyl for members of fan club			
❑ (no [DJ]	Merry Christmas from Split Enz	1982	10.00
—Green vinyl for members of fan club			

Albums

Number	Title (A Side/B Side)	Yr	NM
A&M			
❑ SP-3153	Frenzy	1981	12.00
—First U.S. issue of 1979 recordings			
❑ SP-3235	True Colours	1984	20.00
—Reissue; record is NOT laser etched			
❑ SP-3255	Waiata	1984	8.00
—Reissue			
❑ SP-3256	Time & Tide	1984	8.00
—Reissue			
❑ SP-3289	History Never Repeats: The Best of Split Enz	1987	12.00
❑ SP-4822	True Colours	1980	10.00
—All copies are laser etched on one side; mostly blue cover with orange triangles			
❑ SP-4822	True Colours	1980	10.00
—All copies are laser etched on one side; mostly purple cover with yellow triangles			
❑ SP-4822	True Colours	1980	10.00
—All copies are laser etched on one side; mostly red cover with green triangles			
❑ SP-4822	True Colours	1980	10.00
—All copies are laser etched on one side; mostly yellow cover with blue triangles			
❑ SP-4848	Waiata	1981	10.00
❑ SP-4894	Time & Tide	1982	12.00
❑ SP-4963	Conflicting Emotions	1984	10.00
CHRYSALIS			
❑ CHR 1131	Mental Notes	1976	12.00
❑ CHR 1145	Disrythmia	1977	12.00
❑ PV 41131	Mental Notes	198?	8.00
—Budget-line reissue of CHR 1131			
❑ PV 41145	Disrythmia	198?	8.00
—Budget-line reissue of CHR 1145			

SPOKESMEN, THE

45s

Number	Title (A Side/B Side)	Yr	NM
DECCA			
❑ 31844	The Dawn of Correction/For You Babe	1965	12.00
❑ 31874	It Ain't Fair/Have Courage, Be Careful	1965	10.00
❑ 31895	Michelle/Better Days Are Yet to Come	1966	10.00
❑ 31949	Today's the Day/Enchante	1966	10.00
❑ 32049	I Love How You Love Me/Beautiful Girl	1966	10.00
WINCHESTER			
❑ 1001	Mary Jane/Flashback	1967	12.00

Albums

Number	Title (A Side/B Side)	Yr	NM
DECCA			
❑ DL 4712 [M]	The Dawn of Correction	1965	25.00
❑ DL 74712 [S]	The Dawn of Correction	1965	30.00

S

SPOOKY TOOTH Also see PATTO; GARY WRIGHT; FOREIGNER.

Number	Title (A Side/B Side)	Yr	NM
45s			
A&M			
1144	That Was Only Yesterday/ Waitin' for the Wind	1969	8.00
ISLAND			
004	The Mirror/Hell or High Water	1974	5.00
1219	All Sewn Up/Things Change	1973	6.00
MALA			
12013	Love Really Changed Me/ Spooky Blow	1968	10.00
12022	The Weight/Do Right People	1968	10.00
Albums			
A&M			
SP-3124	Spooky Two	198?	8.00
—Budget-line reissue			
SP-4194	Spooky Two	1969	20.00
SP-4225	Ceremony	1970	20.00
SP-4266	The Last Puff	1970	20.00
SP-4300	Tobacco Road	1971	15.00
—Reissue of Bell LP			
SP-4385	You Broke My Heart So I Busted Your Jaw	1973	15.00
ACCORD			
SN-7168	Hell or High Water	1982	10.00
BELL			
6019 [M]	Spooky Tooth	1968	60.00
—Mono is white label promo only; record in stereo cover			
6019 [S]	Spooky Tooth	1968	25.00
ISLAND			
SW-9255	Witness	1973	12.00
SW-9292	The Mirror	1974	12.00
ILPS-9337	Witness	1974	10.00

SPORTONES, THE

Number	Title (A Side/B Side)	Yr	NM
45s			
MUNICH			
101	In My Dreams/So Sincere	1959	500.00

SPOTLIGHTERS, THE Two different groups?

Number	Title (A Side/B Side)	Yr	NM
45s			
ALADDIN			
3436	Please Be My Girlfriend/Whisper	1958	100.00
3441	This Is My Story/Preaching	1959	100.00
IMPERIAL			
5342	It's Cold/Bam Jingle Jingle	1955	125.00
5342	It's Cold/Bam Jingle Jingle	1955	250.00
—Red vinyl			

SPOTNICKS, THE

Number	Title (A Side/B Side)	Yr	NM
45s			
ATCO			
6261	Orange Blossom Special/ Hava Nagila	1963	12.00
FELSTED			
8649	Spotnick/Old Spinning Wheel	1962	12.00
LAURIE			
3241	I'm Goin' Home/Orange Blossom Special	1964	10.00
3260	Summer in Sweden/ Endless Sleep	1964	10.00
3297	Just Listen to My Heart/ Pony Express	1965	10.00
3333	Drum Didley/Orange Blossom Special	1966	10.00

SPOTSWOOD, KENDRA

Number	Title (A Side/B Side)	Yr	NM
45s			
TUFF			
407	Stickin' with My Baby/Jive Guy	1965	10.00

SPRING Also see AMERICAN SPRING.

Number	Title (A Side/B Side)	Yr	NM
45s			
UNITED ARTISTS			
50848	Now Everything's Been Said/ Awake	1971	30.00
50907	Good Times/Sweet Mountain	1972	80.00
Albums			
UNITED ARTISTS			
UAS-5571	Spring	1972	25.00
UAS-5571 [DJ]	Spring	1972	100.00
—Special promo package in 12x12 folder; includes LP, press kit and a packet of seeds			

SPRINGERS, THE

Number	Title (A Side/B Side)	Yr	NM
45s			
WALES			
428	Nothing's Too Good for My Baby/ (B-side unknown)	196?	1500.

SPRINGFIELD, DUSTY Also see THE SPRINGFIELDS.

Number	Title (A Side/B Side)	Yr	NM
12-Inch Singles			
CASABLANCA			
20245 [DJ]	Donnez-Moi/I Am Curious + 1	1982	15.00
UNITED ARTISTS			
SP-178 [DJ]	That's the Kind of Love I've Got for You (7:06) (same on both sides)	1978	20.00
45s			
ABC DUNHILL			
4341	Who Gets Your Love/ Of All the Things	1973	6.00
4344	Mama's Little Girl/ Learn to Say Goodbye	1973	6.00
4357	Mama's Little Girl/ Learn to Say Goodbye	1973	8.00
ATLANTIC			
2580	Son-of-a-Preacher-Man/ Just a Little Lovin'	1968	10.00
2580 [PS]	Son-of-a-Preacher-Man/ Just a Little Lovin'	1968	15.00
2606	Breakfast in Bed/ Don't Forget About Me	1969	8.00
2623	The Windmills of Your Mind/I Don't Want to Hear It Anymore	1969	8.00
2647	Willie & Laura May Jones/ That Old Sweet Roll	1969	6.00
2673	In the Land of Make Believe/ So Much Love	1969	6.00
2685	A Brand New Me/ Bad Case of the Blues	1969	6.00
2705	Silly, Silly, Fool/Joe	1970	6.00
2729	I Wanna Be a Free Girl/ Let Me In Your Way	1970	6.00
2739	Never Love Again/Lost	1970	6.00
2771	What Good Is I Love You/What Do You Do When Love Dies	1970	6.00
2825	Nothing Is Forever/Haunted	1971	6.00
2841	I Believe in You/ Someone Who Cared	1971	6.00
CASABLANCA			
2356	I Am Curious/Donnez-Moi	1981	4.00
ENIGMA			
75042	Nothing Has Been Proved/ (Instrumental)	1989	5.00
PHILIPS			
40162	I Only Want to Be with You/ Once Upon a Time	1963	12.00
40180	Stay Awhile/Something Special	1964	10.00
40180 [PS]	Stay Awhile/Something Special	1964	20.00
40207	Wishin' and Hopin'/Do Re Mi (Forget About the Do and Think About Me)	1964	12.00
40229	All Cried Out/I Wish I'd Never Loved You	1964	10.00
40229 [PS]	All Cried Out/I Wish I'd Never Loved You	1964	20.00
40245	Guess Who/Live It Up	1964	10.00
40245 [PS]	Guess Who/Live It Up	1964	20.00
40270	Losing You/Here She Comes	1965	10.00
40270 [PS]	Losing You/Here She Comes	1965	20.00
40303	In the Middle of Nowhere/ Baby, Don't You Know	1965	10.00
40303 [PS]	In the Middle of Nowhere/ Baby, Don't You Know	1965	20.00
40319	I Just Don't Know What to Do with Myself/Some of Your Lovin'	1965	10.00
40319 [PS]	I Just Don't Know What to Do with Myself/Some of Your Lovin'	1965	20.00
40371	You Don't Have to Say You Love Me/Little by Little	1966	10.00
40371 [PS]	You Don't Have to Say You Love Me/Little by Little	1966	20.00
40396	All I See Is You/ I'm Gonna Leave You	1966	10.00
40396 [PS]	All I See Is You/ I'm Gonna Leave You	1966	20.00
40439	I'll Try Anything/ The Corrupt Ones	1967	10.00
40439 [PS]	I'll Try Anything/ The Corrupt Ones	1967	20.00
40465	The Look of Love/Give Me Time	1967	10.00
40498	What's It Gonna Be/ Small Town Girl	1967	10.00
40498 [PS]	What's It Gonna Be/ Small Town Girl	1967	16.00
40547	Sweet Ride/No Stranger Am I	1968	10.00
40553	La Bamba/I Close My Eyes and Count to Ten	1968	10.00
20TH CENTURY			
2457	It Goes Like It Goes/I Wish That Love Would Last	1980	5.00
UNITED ARTISTS			
XW1006	Let Me Love You Once Before You Go/I'm Your Child	1977	5.00
XW1205	Checkmate/Sandra	1978	5.00
XW1225	Give Me the Night/Checkmate	1978	5.00
XW1255	Living Without Your Love/ Get Yourself to Love	1978	5.00
7-Inch Extended Plays			
PHILIPS			
PL-2700 [PS]	The Look of Love	196?	20.00
PL-2700 [S]	The Look of Love/Give Me Time/Chained to a Memory// Sunny/What's It Gonna Be/ If You Go Away	196?	20.00
—Jukebox issue; small hole, plays at 33 1/3 rpm			
Albums			
ABC DUNHILL			
DSX-50128	Cameo	1973	15.00
DSX-50186	Longings	1974	—
—Unreleased			
ATLANTIC			
SD 8214	Dusty in Memphis	1969	15.00
—Second pressings have green and red labels			
SD 8214	Dusty in Memphis	1969	30.00
—Originals have purple and brown labels			
8249 [DJ]	A Brand New Me	1970	40.00
—Mono white label promo			
SD 8249	A Brand New Me	1970	15.00
CASABLANCA			
NBLP-7271	White Heat	1982	12.00
4 MEN WITH BEARDS			
4M 112	Dusty in Memphis	2002	15.00
—Reissue on 180-gram vinyl			
LIBERTY			
LN-10024	It Begins Again	1980	8.00
—Budget-line reissue of United Artists LP of same name			
LN-10026	Living Without Your Love	1980	8.00
—Budget-line reissue of United Artists LP of same name			
PHILIPS			
PHM-200133 [M]	Stay Awhile	1964	30.00
PHM-200156 [M]	Dusty	1964	30.00
PHM-200174 [M]	Oooooo Weeeee!	1965	40.00
PHM-200210 [M]	You Don't Have to Say You Love Me	1966	30.00
PHM-200220 [M]	Dusty Springfield's Golden Hits	1966	25.00
—With "Goin' Back"			
PHM-200220 [M]	Dusty Springfield's Golden Hits	1967	20.00
—Without "Goin' Back"			
PHM-200256 [M]	The Look of Love	1967	25.00
PHM-200303 [M]	Everything's Coming Up Dusty	1967	25.00
PHS-600133 [P]	Stay Awhile	1964	40.00
PHS-600156 [P]	Dusty	1964	40.00
PHS-600174 [S]	Oooooo Weeeee!	1965	50.00
PHS-600210 [S]	You Don't Have to Say You Love Me	1966	40.00
PHS-600220 [P]	Dusty Springfield's Golden Hits	1966	35.00
—With "Goin' Back"			
PHS-600220 [P]	Dusty Springfield's Golden Hits	1967	25.00
—Without "Goin' Back"			
PHS-600256 [S]	The Look of Love	1967	30.00
PHS-600303 [S]	Everything's Coming Up Dusty	1967	30.00
POLYDOR			
824467-1	Dusty Springfield's Golden Hits	1985	10.00
UNITED ARTISTS			
UA-LA791	It Begins Again	1978	15.00
UA-LA936	Living Without Your Love	1979	15.00
WING			
PKW-2-120 [(2)]	Something Special	196?	20.00
SRW-16380	Just Dusty	196?	12.00

SPRINGFIELD, RICK

Number	Title (A Side/B Side)	Yr	NM
12-Inch Singles			
RCA			
8393-1-R	Honeymoon in Beirut/ Tear It All Down	1988	6.00
PD-12273	I've Done Everything for You/ Love Is Alright Tonite	1981	8.00

Number	Title (A Side/B Side)	Yr	NM
❑ PD-13009	Love Is Alright Tonite/ Everybody's Girl	1981	8.00
❑ PD-13075	Don't Talk to Strangers/ Calling All Girls	1982	8.00
❑ JD-13509 [DJ]	Affair of the Heart (Long) (Short)	1983	8.00
❑ JR-13577 [DJ]	Human Touch (same on both sides)	1983	8.00
❑ PD-13617	Human Touch (Vocal)/ (Instrumental)	1983	10.00
❑ PD-13651	Souls/Souls (Live)	1983	8.00
❑ JR-13747 [DJ]	Love Somebody (same on both sides)	1984	8.00
❑ JD-13815 [DJ]	Don't Walk Away (3:38) (4:00)	1984	8.00
❑ PD-13868	Bop 'Til You Drop/Taxi Dancing	1984	8.00
❑ JR-13882 [DJ]	Bop 'Til You Drop (same on both sides)	1984	8.00
❑ JR-14051 [DJ]	Celebrate Youth (same on both sides)	1985	6.00
❑ PD-14052	Celebrate Youth (Long) (Short)	1985	6.00
❑ JR-14119 [DJ]	State of the Heart (Special Rock Radio Edited Version) (same on both sides)	1985	8.00
45s			
CAPITOL			
❑ 3340	Speak to the Sky/Why	1972	8.00
❑ 3340 [PS]	Speak to the Sky/Why	1972	15.00
❑ 3466	What Would the Children Think/ Come On Everybody	1972	8.00
❑ 3466 [PS]	What Would the Children Think/ Come On Everybody	1972	15.00
❑ 3637	I'm Your Superman/ Why Are You Waiting	1973	8.00
❑ 3713	Believe in Me/The Liar	1973	12.00
CHELSEA			
❑ 3051	Take a Hand/Archangel	1976	5.00
❑ 3055	Million Dollar Face/ (B-side unknown)	1976	5.00
❑ 3056	Jessica/Archangel	1976	5.00
COLUMBIA			
❑ 45935	Believe in Me/The Liar	1973	6.00
❑ 46032	Streakin' Across the U.S.A./ Music to Streak By	1974	6.00
❑ 46057	American Girls/Weep No More	1974	5.00
MERCURY			
❑ 880405-7	Bruce/Guenevere	1984	4.00
❑ 880405-7 [PS]	Bruce/Guenevere	1984	5.00
RCA			
❑ 6853-7-R	Rock of Life/The Language of Love	1988	3.00
❑ 6853-7-R [PS]	Rock of Life/The Language of Love	1988	3.00
❑ 8391-7-R	Honeymoon in Beirut/ My Father's Chair	1988	3.00
❑ 8391-7-R [PS]	Honeymoon in Beirut/ My Father's Chair	1988	3.00
❑ PB-12166	I've Done Everything for You/ Red Hot and Blue Love	1981	4.00
❑ PB-12166 [PS]	I've Done Everything for You/ Red Hot and Blue Love	1981	4.00
❑ PB-12201	Jessie's Girl/Carry Me Away	1981	4.00
❑ PB-12201 [PS]	Jessie's Girl/Carry Me Away	1981	5.00
❑ PB-13008	Love Is Alright Tonite/ Everybody's Girl	1981	4.00
❑ PB-13008 [PS]	Love Is Alright Tonite/ Everybody's Girl	1981	4.00
❑ PB-13070	Don't Talk to Strangers/Tonight	1982	4.00
❑ PB-13070 [PS]	Don't Talk to Strangers/Tonight	1982	4.00
❑ PB-13245	What Kind of Fool Am I/ How Do You Talk to Girls	1982	4.00
❑ PB-13303	I Get Excited/Kristina	1982	4.00
❑ PB-13303 [PS]	I Get Excited/Kristina	1982	4.00
❑ GB-13482	Jessie's Girl/I've Done Everything for You	1983	3.00
—Gold Standard Series			
❑ GB-13483	Don't Talk to Strangers/ What Kind of Fool Am I	1983	3.00
—Gold Standard Series			
❑ PB-13497	Affair of the Heart/ Like Father, Like Son	1983	3.00
❑ PB-13497 [PS]	Affair of the Heart/ Like Father, Like Son	1983	4.00
❑ PB-13576	Human Touch/Alyson	1983	3.00
❑ PB-13650	Souls/Souls (Live)	1983	3.00
❑ PB-13650 [PS]	Souls/Souls (Live)	1983	4.00
❑ PB-13738	Love Somebody/The Great Lost Art of Conversation	1984	3.00
❑ PB-13738 [PS]	Love Somebody/The Great Lost Art of Conversation	1984	3.00
—Without sticker on sleeve			
❑ PB-13738 [PS]	Love Somebody/The Great Lost Art of Conversation	1984	6.00
—With "Special Dollar Refund Offer" sticker on sleeve and $1 off coupon for the purchase of the LP "Hard to Hold" inside			
❑ GB-13794	Affair of the Heart/Human Touch	1984	3.00
—Gold Standard Series			
❑ PB-13813	Don't Walk Away/S.F.O.	1984	3.00
❑ PB-13813 [PS]	Don't Walk Away/S.F.O.	1984	3.00

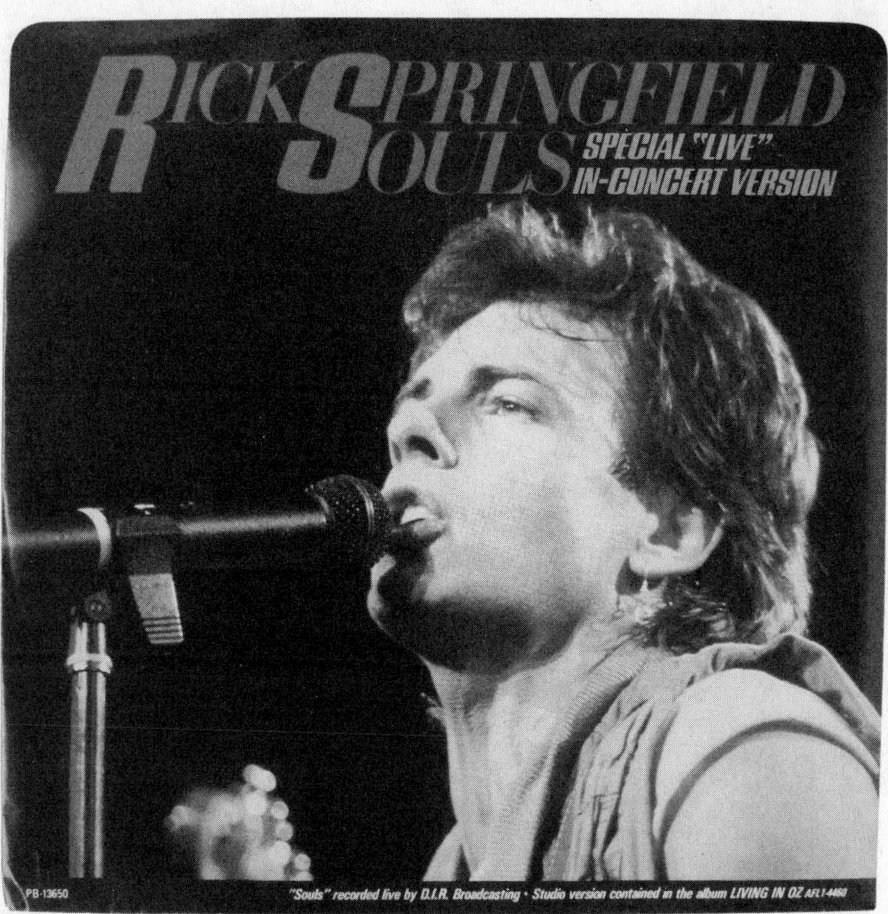

Rick Springfield, "Souls," RCA 13650, 1983, **$4.**

Number	Title (A Side/B Side)	Yr	NM
❑ PB-13861	Bop 'Til You Drop/Taxi Dancing	1984	3.00
—B-side: With Randy Crawford			
❑ PB-13861 [PS]	Bop 'Til You Drop/Taxi Dancing	1984	3.00
❑ PB-14047	Celebrate Youth/ Stranger in the House	1985	3.00
❑ PB-14047 [PS]	Celebrate Youth/ Stranger in the House	1985	3.00
❑ PB-14120	State of the Heart/The Power of Love (The Tao of Love)	1985	3.00
❑ PB-14120 [PS]	State of the Heart/The Power of Love (The Tao of Love)	1985	3.00
Albums			
CAPITOL			
❑ SMAS-11047	Beginnings	1972	20.00
❑ SMAS-11206	Comic Book Heroes	1973	40.00
—Withdrawn and reissued on Columbia			
❑ SN-16251	Beginnings	1981	8.00
—Budget-line reissue			
CHELSEA			
❑ 515	Wait for Night	1976	15.00
COLUMBIA			
❑ KC 32704	Comic Book Heroes	1973	15.00
❑ PC 32704	Comic Book Heroes	1981	8.00
—Budget-line reissue			
MERCURY			
❑ 824107-1	Beautiful Feelings	1984	10.00
RCA			
❑ 6620-1-R	Rock of Life	1988	8.00
❑ 9817-1-R	Rick Springfield's Greatest Hits	1989	12.00
RCA VICTOR			
❑ ARL1-3697	Working Class Dog	1981	10.00
❑ AFL1-4125	Success Hasn't Spoiled Me Yet	1982	10.00
❑ AFL1-4235	Wait for Night	1982	10.00
—Reissue of Chelsea LP			
❑ AFL1-4660	Living in Oz	1983	10.00
❑ AYL1-4766	Working Class Dog	1983	8.00
—"Best Buy Series" reissue			
❑ AYL1-4767	Success Hasn't Spoiled Me Yet	1983	8.00
—"Best Buy Series" reissue			
❑ ABL1-4935	Hard to Hold	1984	10.00

Number	Title (A Side/B Side)	Yr	NM
❑ AJL1-5370	Tao	1985	10.00

SPRINGFIELD RIFLE, THE

Number	Title (A Side/B Side)	Yr	NM
45s			
❑ ABC❑ 10878	The Bears/There Is Life on Mars	1966	10.00
JERDEN			
❑ 812	Stop and Take a Look Around/ 100 or Two	1967	12.00
❑ 815	All She Said/It Ain't Happened	1967	12.00
❑ 901	I'll Be Standing There/ Will You Love Me Tomorrow	196?	12.00
❑ 902	Left of Nowhere/ I Must Go for a Walk	196?	12.00
❑ 905	I Love You/That's All I Really Need	196?	12.00
TOWER			
❑ 455	I Love Her/That's All I Really Need	1968	10.00
Albums			
BURDETTE			
❑ ST-5159	The Springfield Rifle	1969	25.00

SPRINGFIELDS, THE

Also see DUSTY SPRINGFIELD.

Number	Title (A Side/B Side)	Yr	NM
45s			
PHILIPS			
❑ 40038	Silver Threads and Golden Needles/Aunt Rhody	1962	15.00
❑ 40072	Dear Hearts and Gentle People/Gotta Travel On	1962	12.00
❑ 40092	Little By Little/Waf-Woof	1963	12.00
❑ 40099	Foggy Mountain Top/ Island of Dreams	1963	12.00
❑ 40121	Say I Won't Be There/Little Boat	1963	12.00
Albums			
PHILIPS			
❑ PHM 200052 [M]	Silver Threads and Golden Needles	1962	30.00

Bruce Springsteen, "Dancing in the Dark," Columbia 04463, 1984, **$5.**

Number	Title (A Side/B Side)	Yr	NM
❑ PHM 200076 [M]	Folksongs from the Hills	1963	30.00
❑ PHS 600052 [S]	Silver Threads and Golden Needles	1962	40.00
❑ PHS 600076 [S]	Folksongs from the Hills	1963	40.00

SPRINGSTEEN, BRUCE

12-Inch Singles

ASYLUM

Number	Title (A Side/B Side)	Yr	NM
❑ 11442 [DJ]	Devil with a Blue Dress Medley/ Before the Deluge	1979	40.00
—B-side by Jackson Browne			

COLUMBIA

Number	Title (A Side/B Side)	Yr	NM
❑ AS 928 [DJ]	Fade Away/Be True/ Held Up Without a Gun	1981	50.00
❑ AS 1329 [DJ]	Santa Claus Is Comin' to Town (same on both sides)	1981	40.00
—White label promo			
❑ AS1329 [DJ]	Santa Claus Is Comin' to Town (same on both sides)	1981	40.00
—White label promo			
❑ AS 1862 [DJ]	Dancing in the Dark (same on both sides)	1984	20.00
—Red label, black and white cover			
❑ AS1862 [DJ]	Dancing in the Dark (same on both sides)	1984	20.00
—Red label, black and white cover			
❑ AS 1959 [DJ]	Born in the U.S.A. (same on both sides)	1984	20.00
—Red label, black and white cover			
❑ AS1959 [DJ]	Born in the U.S.A. (same on both sides)	1984	20.00
—Red label, black and white cover			
❑ AS 2007 [DJ]	I'm on Fire (same on both sides)	1985	20.00
—Red label, black and white cover			
❑ AS2007 [DJ]	I'm on Fire (same on both sides)	1985	20.00
—Red label, black and white cover			
❑ AS 2082 [DJ]	Glory Days (same on both sides)	1985	20.00
—Red label, black and white cover			
❑ AS2082 [DJ]	Glory Days (same on both sides)	1985	20.00
—Red label, black and white cover			
❑ CAS 2147 [DJ]	I'm Goin' Down (same on both sides)	1985	20.00
—Red label, black and white cover			
❑ CAS2147 [DJ]	I'm Goin' Down (same on both sides)	1985	20.00
—Red label, black and white cover			
❑ CAS 2223 [DJ]	My Hometown (same on both sides)	1985	20.00
—Red label, black and white cover			
❑ CAS2223 [DJ]	My Hometown (same on both sides)	1985	20.00
—Red label, black and white cover			
❑ CAS 2636 [DJ]	Fire/Because the Night/Seeds	1986	25.00
❑ CAS2636 [DJ]	Fire/Because the Night/Seeds	1986	25.00
❑ CAS 2806 [DJ]	Brilliant Disguise (same on both sides)	1987	15.00
❑ CAS2806 [DJ]	Brilliant Disguise (same on both sides)	1987	15.00
❑ 05028	Dancing in the Dark (Blaster Mix)/(Radio) (Dub)	1984	12.00
❑ 05087	Cover Me (Undercover Mix) (Dub 1)/(Dub 2) (Radio)	1984	12.00
❑ 05147	Born in the U.S.A. (Freedom Mix)/ (Dub) (Radio)	1984	12.00
❑ 74416	57 Channels (And Nothin' On) (Little Steven Remix 1 & 2)// There's a Riot Goin' On/ Part Man Part Monkey	1992	15.00

45s

COLUMBIA

Number	Title (A Side/B Side)	Yr	NM
❑ AE7 1088 [DJ]	Rosalita (Come Out Tonight)// Spirit in the Night/Growin' Up	1974	300.00
—Small hole, plays at 33 1/3 RPM			
❑ AE7 1332 [DJ]	Santa Claus Is Coming to Town (same on both sides)	1981	20.00
❑ AE7 1332 [PS]	Santa Claus Is Coming to Town (same on both sides)	1981	25.00
❑ 03243	Hungry Heart/Fade Away	198?	3.00
—"Columbia Hall of Fame" series; gray label			
❑ 03243	Hungry Heart/Fade Away	1983	4.00
—"Columbia Hall of Fame" series; red label			
❑ 04463	Dancing in the Dark/Pink Cadillac	1984	4.00
❑ 04463 [PS]	Dancing in the Dark/Pink Cadillac	1984	5.00
❑ 04561	Cover Me/Jersey Girl	1984	4.00
—Spoken intro to "Jersey Girl" is deleted. Dead wax has matrix number followed by "-2" and a letter.			
❑ 04561	Cover Me/Jersey Girl	1984	10.00
—First pressings have a spoken intro to "Jersey Girl." Dead wax has matrix number followed by "-1" and a letter.			
❑ 04561 [PS]	Cover Me/Jersey Girl	1984	5.00
❑ 04680	Born in the U.S.A./ Shut Out the Light	1984	4.00
❑ 04680 [PS]	Born in the U.S.A./ Shut Out the Light	1984	5.00
❑ 04772	I'm on Fire/Johnny Bye Bye	1985	4.00
❑ 04772 [PS]	I'm on Fire/Johnny Bye Bye	1985	5.00
❑ 04924	Glory Days/Stand On It	1985	4.00
❑ 04924 [PS]	Glory Days/Stand On It	1985	5.00
❑ 05603	I'm Goin' Down/Janey, Don't You Lose Heart	1985	4.00
❑ 05603 [PS]	I'm Goin' Down/Janey, Don't You Lose Heart	1985	5.00
❑ 05728	My Hometown/Santa Claus Is Coming to Town	1985	4.00
❑ 05728 [PS]	My Hometown/Santa Claus Is Coming to Town	1985	4.00
❑ 06432	War/Merry Christmas Baby	1986	4.00
❑ 06432 [PS]	War/Merry Christmas Baby	1986	4.00
❑ 06657	Fire/Incident on 57th Street	1987	5.00
❑ 06657 [PS]	Fire/Incident on 57th Street	1987	5.00
❑ 07595	Brilliant Disguise/Lucky Man	1987	4.00
❑ 07595 [PS]	Brilliant Disguise/Lucky Man	1987	4.00
❑ 07663	Tunnel of Love/Two for the Road	1987	4.00
❑ 07663 [PS]	Tunnel of Love/Two for the Road	1987	4.00
❑ 07726	One Step Up/Roulette	1988	4.00
❑ 07726 [PS]	One Step Up/Roulette	1988	4.00
❑ 08408	Dancing in the Dark/Pink Cadillac	1984	3.00
—Gray label reissue			
❑ 08409	Cover Me/Jersey Girl	1984	3.00
—Gray label reissue			
❑ 08410	Born in the U.S.A./ Shut Out the Light	1984	3.00
—Gray label reissue			
❑ 08411	I'm on Fire/Johnny Bye Bye	1985	3.00
—Gray label reissue			
❑ 08412	Glory Days/Stand On It	1985	3.00
—Gray label reissue			
❑ 08413	I'm Goin' Down/Janey, Don't You Lose Heart	1985	3.00
—Gray label reissue			
❑ 08414	My Hometown/Santa Claus Is Coming to Town	1985	3.00
—Gray label reissue; many copies of this were issued with Columbia 05728 picture sleeves			
❑ 10209	Born to Run/Meeting Across the River	1975	20.00
❑ 10274	Tenth Avenue Freeze-Out/ She's the One	1976	15.00
❑ 10763	Prove It All Night/Factory	1978	12.00
❑ 10801	Badlands/Streets of Fire	1978	12.00
❑ 11391	Hungry Heart/Held Up Without a Gun	1980	4.00
❑ 11391 [PS]	Hungry Heart/Held Up Without a Gun	1980	6.00
❑ 11431	Fade Away/Be True	1981	4.00
—Corrected second pressing			
❑ 11431	Fade Away/To Be True	1981	25.00
—Erroneous first pressing			
❑ 11431 [PS]	Fade Away/Be True	1981	6.00
❑ 33323	Born to Run/Spirit in the Night	1976	4.00
—"Columbia Hall of Fame" series; red label			
❑ 33323	Born to Run/Spirit in the Night	198?	3.00
—"Columbia Hall of Fame" series; gray label			
❑ 45805	Blinded by the Light/The Angel	1972	500.00
❑ 45805 [DJ]	Blinded by the Light (mono/stereo)	1972	50.00
❑ 45805 [DJ]	Blinded by the Light (mono/stereo)	1972	60.00
❑ 45805 [PS]	Blinded by the Light/The Angel	1972	400.00
❑ 45864	Spirit in the Night/For You	1973	1500.
❑ 45864 [DJ]	Spirit in the Night (mono/stereo)	1973	50.00
❑ 45864 [DJ]	Spirit in the Night (mono/stereo)	1973	50.00
❑ 73796	Tunnel of Love/Two for the Road	1991	3.00
—Reissue			
❑ 73943	One Step Up/Roulette	1991	3.00
—Reissue			
❑ 74273	Human Touch/Better Days	1992	4.00
❑ 74354	57 Channels (And Nothin' On)/ Part Man Part Monkey	1992	4.00
❑ 77384	Streets of Philadelphia/ If I Should Fall Behind	1994	4.00
❑ 77847	Secret Garden/Thunder Road (Live)	1995	3.00
❑ 77847 [PS]	Secret Garden/Thunder Road (Live)	1995	3.00

Albums

COLUMBIA

Number	Title (A Side/B Side)	Yr	NM
❑ (# unknown) [PD]	Darkness on the Edge of Town	1978	150.00
—Promo-only picture disc			
❑ AS 978 [DJ]	As Requested Around the World	1981	50.00
❑ AS978 [DJ]	As Requested Around the World	1981	50.00

 Except when noted otherwise, VG = 25% of NM, and VG+ = 50% of NM. (Example: VG = $2.00, VG+ = $4.00 and NM = $8.00.)

Number	Title (A Side/B Side)	Yr	NM
❑ AS 1957 [DJ]	Bruce Springsteen	1985	30.00
—Five-song mini-LP with five B-sides of singles from Born in the U.S.A.			
❑ AS1957 [DJ]	Bruce Springsteen	1985	30.00
—Five-song mini-LP with five B-sides of singles from Born in the U.S.A.			
❑ AS 1957 [DJ]	Bruce Springsteen	1987	20.00
—Five-song mini-LP with five B-sides of singles from Born in the U.S.A.; second pressings say so on the label			
❑ AS1957 [DJ]	Bruce Springsteen	1987	20.00
—Five-song mini-LP with five B-sides of singles from Born in the U.S.A.; second pressings say so on the label			
❑ AS2543 [DJ]	Bruce Springsteen and the E Street Band: Live 1975-1985	1986	30.00
—Sampler from 5-LP live set			
❑ CAS 2543 [DJ]	Bruce Springsteen and the E Street Band: Live 1975-1985	1986	30.00
—Sampler from 5-LP live set			
❑ 88697-17060-1	Magic	2007	15.00
❑ JC 31903	Greetings from Asbury Park, N.J.	1977	8.00
—Reissue of the first PC-prefix version			
❑ KC 31903	Greetings from Asbury Park, N.J.	1973	20.00
❑ KC 31903 [DJ]	Greetings from Asbury Park, N.J.	1973	200.00
—Promotional copy with timing strip and "Bruce Springsteen Fact Sheet" attached to back cover. Authentic fact sheets are on glossy stock			
❑ KC31903 [DJ]	Greetings from Asbury Park, N.J.	1973	200.00
—Promotional copy with timing strip and "Bruce Springsteen Fact Sheet" attached to back cover. Authentic fact sheets are on glossy stock			
❑ PC 31903	Greetings from Asbury Park, N.J.	1975	10.00
—Without bar code on cover			
❑ PC 31903	Greetings from Asbury Park, N.J.	1979	8.00
—With bar code on cover			
❑ JC 32432	The Wild, the Innocent & the E Street Shuffle	1977	8.00
—Reissue of the first PC-prefix version			
❑ KC 32432	The Wild, the Innocent & the E Street Shuffle	1973	20.00
❑ PC 32432	The Wild, the Innocent & the E Street Shuffle	1975	10.00
—Without bar code on cover			
❑ PC 32432	The Wild, the Innocent & the E Street Shuffle	1979	8.00
—With bar code on cover			
❑ HC 33795	Born to Run	1981	50.00
—Half-speed mastered edition (original)			
❑ JC 33795	Born to Run	1977	8.00
❑ PC 33795	Born to Run	1975	10.00
—Jon Landau's name is correct on the back cover			
❑ PC 33795	Born to Run	1975	15.00
—Sticker with the correct spelling of Jon Landau is on the back cover			
❑ PC 33795	Born to Run	1975	25.00
—Jon Landau's name is misspelled "John" on the back cover			
❑ PC 33795	Born to Run	1999	25.00
—Classic Records reissue, identified as such on back cover; corrected pressing with gatefold			
❑ PC 33795	Born to Run	1999	40.00
—Classic Records reissue, identified as such on back cover; "error" first pressing with no gatefold			
❑ PC 33795 [DJ]	Born to Run	1975	100.00
—White label promo			
❑ PC33795 [DJ]	Born to Run	1975	100.00
—White label promo			
❑ PC 33795 [DJ]	Born to Run	1975	1200.
—Test pressing with "Bruce Springsteen -- Born to Run" in script print. Also includes mailing envelope, letter from CBS and orange patch; VG value 400; VG+ value 800			
❑ PC33795 [DJ]	Born to Run	1975	1200.
—Test pressing with "Bruce Springsteen -- Born to Run" in script print. Also includes mailing envelope, letter from CBS and orange patch			
❑ JC 35318	Darkness on the Edge of Town	1978	10.00
—Original pressings have thick paper innersleeves and small titles on back cover			
❑ JC 35318	Darkness on the Edge of Town	198?	8.00
—Later pressings have thin paper innersleeves and larger titles on back cover			
❑ JC 35318 [DJ]	Darkness on the Edge of Town	1978	100.00
—White label promo			
❑ JC35318 [DJ]	Darkness on the Edge of Town	1978	100.00
—White label promo			
❑ PC2 36854 [(2)]	The River	1980	12.00
❑ PC2 36854 [(2)DJ]	The River	1980	40.00
—White label promo, without letter			
❑ PC236854 [(2)DJ]	The River	1980	40.00
—White label promo, without letter			
❑ PC2 36854 [(2)DJ]	The River	1980	75.00
—White label promo, with photocopied letter from CBS			
❑ PC236854 [(2)DJ]	The River	1980	75.00
—White label promo, with photocopied letter from CBS			
❑ TC 38358	Nebraska	1982	10.00
❑ QC 38653	Born in the U.S.A.	1984	10.00
❑ C5X 40558 [(5)]	Bruce Springsteen and the E Street Band: Live 1975-1985	1986	40.00
❑ OC 40999	Tunnel of Love	1987	10.00
❑ HC 43795	Born to Run	1982	40.00
—Half-speed mastered edition (reissue)			
❑ 3C 44445 [EP]	Chimes of Freedom	1988	10.00
❑ HC 45318	Darkness on the Edge of Town	1981	40.00
—Half-speed mastered edition			

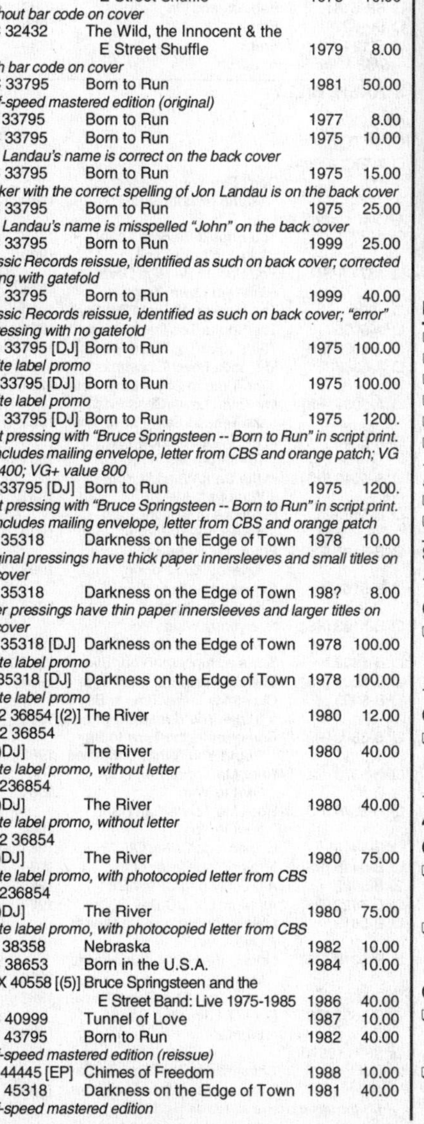

Bruce Springsteen, *The Ghost of Tom Joad*, Columbia C 67484, 1995, **$12.**

Number	Title (A Side/B Side)	Yr	NM
❑ C 53000	Human Touch	1992	12.00
❑ C 53001	Lucky Town	1992	12.00
❑ C2 67060 [(2)]	Greatest Hits	1995	15.00
❑ C 67484	The Ghost of Tom Joad	1995	20.00
❑ C2 69746 [(2)]	18 Tracks	1999	15.00
❑ C3 85490 [(3)]	Live in New York City	2001	20.00
—As of press date, all known copies contain "Born to Run," but the song is not listed on either the record jacket or label			
❑ C2 86600 [(2)]	The Rising	2002	18.00
❑ C2 93900 [(2)]	Devils and Dust	2005	18.00

SPRINGSTONE, BRUCE

12-Inch Singles

CLEAN CUTS

Number	Title (A Side/B Side)	Yr	NM
❑ CC-1202	Bedrock Rap/(Meet the) Flintstones//Take Me Out to the Ballgame	1982	12.00
—With cardboard cover that calls this "Live at Bedrock"			

COLD CUTS

Number	Title (A Side/B Side)	Yr	NM
❑ CC-1202	Bedrock Rap/(Meet the) Flintstones//Take Me Out to the Ballgame	1982	25.00
—With cardboard cover that calls this "Live at Bedrock"			

45s

CLEAN CUTS

Number	Title (A Side/B Side)	Yr	NM
❑ CC-902	Bedrock Rap/(Meet the) Flintstones//Take Me Out to the Ballgame	1982	5.00
❑ CC-902 [PS]	Bedrock Rap/(Meet the) Flintstones//Take Me Out to the Ballgame	1982	5.00

COLD CUTS

Number	Title (A Side/B Side)	Yr	NM
❑ CC-902	Bedrock Rap/(Meet the) Flintstones//Take Me Out to the Ballgame	1982	8.00
❑ CC-902 [PS]	Bedrock Rap/(Meet the) Flintstones//Take Me Out to the Ballgame	1982	8.00

SPUR

Albums

CINEMA

Number	Title (A Side/B Side)	Yr	NM
❑ CSLP-1500	Spur of the Moment	196?	80.00

SPUTNIKS, THE

45s

CLASS

Number	Title (A Side/B Side)	Yr	NM
❑ 217	My Love Is Gone/Hey Maryann	1958	50.00
❑ 222	Wait a Little While/ Johnny's Little Lamb	1958	40.00

PAM MAR

Number	Title (A Side/B Side)	Yr	NM
❑ 601	My Love Is Gone/Hey Maryann	1957	250.00

SPYRO GYRA

Albums

AMHERST

Number	Title (A Side/B Side)	Yr	NM
❑ AMH-1014	Spyro Gyra	1978	15.00

GRP

Number	Title (A Side/B Side)	Yr	NM
❑ GR-9608	Fast Forward	1990	15.00

INFINITY

Number	Title (A Side/B Side)	Yr	NM
❑ INF-9004	Morning Dance	1979	12.00

MCA

Number	Title (A Side/B Side)	Yr	NM
❑ 1445	City Kids	1986	8.00
—Budget-line reissue			
❑ 5108	Catching the Sun	1980	10.00
❑ 5149	Carnaval	1981	10.00
❑ 5238	Freetime	1981	10.00
❑ 5368	Incognito	1982	10.00
❑ 5431	City Kids	1983	10.00
❑ 5606	Alternating Currents	1985	10.00
❑ 5753	Breakout	1986	10.00
❑ 6235	Rites of Summer	1988	10.00
❑ 6309	Point of View	1989	12.00
❑ 6893 [(2)]	Access All Areas	1984	12.00
❑ 16010	Catching the Sun	1982	40.00
—Audiophile vinyl			
❑ 37148	Morning Dance	198?	8.00
—Reissue of Infinity LP			

S

Squeeze, "Black Coffee in Bed," A&M 8219, 1982, **$10.**

Number	Title (A Side/B Side)	Yr	NM
❑ 37149	Spyro Gyra	198?	8.00
—Reissue of Amherst LP			
❑ 37176	Carnaval	198?	8.00
—Budget-line reissue			
❑ 42046	Stories Without Words	1987	10.00
NAUTILUS			
❑ NR-9	Morning Dance	1979	40.00
—Audiophile vinyl			

SQUEEZE

12-Inch Singles

Number	Title (A Side/B Side)	Yr	NM
A&M			
❑ 17158 [DJ]	Tempted/Is That Love/ Messed Around	1981	8.00
❑ 17158 [DJ]	Tempted/Is That Love/ Messed Around	1981	8.00
❑ 17349 [DJ]	Hits of the Year/By Your Time/ Last Time Forever	1985	8.00
❑ 17349 [DJ]	Hits of the Year/By Your Time/ Last Time Forever	1985	8.00
❑ 17489 [DJ]	Hourglass (same on both sides)	1987	8.00
❑ 17489 [DJ]	Hourglass (same on both sides)	1987	8.00

45s

Number	Title (A Side/B Side)	Yr	NM
A&M			
❑ 1457	If It's Love/Frank's Bag	1989	—
—May be cassette-only			
❑ 1616	If I Didn't Love You/ Another Nail in My Heart	1980	10.00
—5-inch single with small hole, plays at 33 1/3 RPM			
❑ 1616 [PS]	If I Didn't Love You/ Another Nail in My Heart	1980	10.00
—Special "Tiny Collector's Edition" sleeve with above single			
❑ 2033	Take Me, I'm Yours/Night Nurse	1978	—
—Label credit: U.K. Squeeze; the existence of this record as a stock copy has not been confirmed			
❑ 2033 [DJ]	Take Me, I'm Yours (mono)/ Take Me, I'm Yours (stereo)	1978	4.00
—Label credit: U.K. Squeeze			
❑ 2033 [DJ]	Take Me, I'm Yours (mono)/ Take Me, I'm Yours (stereo)	1978	4.00
—Label credit: U.K. Squeeze			
❑ 2146	Cool for Cats/Model	1979	4.00
❑ 2146 [PS]	Cool for Cats/Model	1979	4.00
❑ 2168	Goodbye Girl/Slightly Drunk	1979	4.00
❑ 2168 [PS]	Goodbye Girl/Slightly Drunk	1979	4.00
❑ 2229	If I Didn't Love You/Pretty One	1980	4.00
❑ 2229 [PS]	If I Didn't Love You/Pretty One	1980	6.00
❑ 2247	Pulling Mussels (From the Shell)/ Pretty One	1980	4.00
❑ 2247 [PS]	Pulling Mussels (From the Shell)/ Pretty One	1980	4.00
❑ 2263	Another Nail in My Heart//Going Crazy/What the Butler Saw	1980	4.00
❑ 2263 [PS]	Another Nail in My Heart//Going Crazy/What the Butler Saw	1980	8.00
❑ 2345	Tempted/Trust	1981	3.00
❑ 2345 [PS]	Tempted/Trust	1981	6.00
❑ 2377	Messed Around/Yap, Yap, Yap	1981	3.00
❑ 2413	I've Returned/When the Hangover Strikes	1982	3.00
❑ 2424	Black Coffee in Bed/The Hunt	1982	3.00
❑ 2424 [PS]	Black Coffee in Bed/The Hunt	1982	10.00
❑ 2518	Annie Get Your Gun/ Spanish Guitar	1983	3.00
❑ 2534	Another Nail in My Heart//Going Crazy/What the Butler Saw	1983	3.00
❑ 2776	Hits of the Year/Fortnight Saga	1985	3.00
❑ 2776 [PS]	Hits of the Year/Fortnight Saga	1985	3.00
❑ 2967	Hourglass/Wedding Bells	1987	3.00
❑ 2967 [PS]	Hourglass/Wedding Bells	1987	3.00
❑ 2994	853-5937/Take Me I'm Yours (Live)	1987	3.00
❑ 2994 [PS]	853-5937/Take Me I'm Yours (Live)	1987	8.00
—A tough sleeve to find			
❑ 3021	Footprints/Black Coffee in Bed (Live)	1988	3.00
❑ 3021 [PS]	Footprints/Black Coffee in Bed (Live)	1988	—
❑ AMS 7495	Christmas Day/Going Crazy	1979	8.00
—Black vinyl			
❑ AMS 7495	Christmas Day/Going Crazy	1979	12.00
—White vinyl			
❑ AMS 7495 [PS]	Christmas Day/Going Crazy	1979	8.00
—Both record and sleeve are U.K. imports			
❑ 8683	Tempted/Black Coffee in Bed	198?	3.00
—Reissue			
RCA			
❑ 62800	Tempted/My Sharona	1994	4.00
—B-side by The Knack			
❑ 62800 [PS]	Tempted/My Sharona	1994	4.00
—B-side by The Knack			

Albums

Number	Title (A Side/B Side)	Yr	NM
A&M			
❑ SP-3185	U.K. Squeeze	198?	8.00
—Reissue			
❑ SP-3231	Cool for Cats	198?	8.00
—Reissue			
❑ SP-3232	Argybargy	198?	8.00
—Reissue			
❑ SP-3253	East Side Story	198?	8.00
—Reissue			
❑ SP-3254	Sweets from a Stranger	198?	8.00
—Reissue; none of these have 2-inch flap			
❑ SP-3413 [EP]	Six Squeeze Songs Crammed Into One 10-Inch Record	1979	10.00
—10-inch EP in 12-inch "squeezed" jacket			
❑ SP-4687	U.K. Squeeze	1978	12.00
—Later pressings on black vinyl			
❑ SP-4687	U.K. Squeeze	1978	20.00
—First pressing on red vinyl			
❑ SP-4759	Cool for Cats	1979	12.00
❑ SP-4802	Argybargy	1980	12.00
❑ SP-4854	East Side Story	1981	10.00
❑ SP-4899	Sweets from a Stranger	1982	10.00
—With flap removed or never there			
❑ SP-4899	Sweets from a Stranger	1982	12.00
—Original pressings have a 2-inch flap on the right side of the front cover with critics' raves			
❑ SP-4922	Singles 45's and Under	1983	10.00
❑ SP-5085	Cosi Fan Tutti Frutti	1985	10.00
❑ SP-5161	Babylon and On	1987	10.00
❑ SP-5278	Frank	1989	10.00
❑ R 124200	Frank	1989	12.00
—BMG Music Service edition			

SQUIER, BILLY

45s

Number	Title (A Side/B Side)	Yr	NM
CAPITOL			
❑ 7PRO-79694 [DJ]	Don't Say You Love Me (same on both sides)	1989	10.00
—Vinyl is promo only			
❑ 4877	You Should Be High Love/ Like I'm Lovin' You	1980	5.00
❑ 4877 [PS]	You Should Be High Love/ Like I'm Lovin' You	1980	5.00
❑ 4901	The Music's All Right/Big Beat	1980	5.00
❑ A-5005	The Stroke/Too Daze Gone	1981	4.00
❑ A-5005 [PS]	The Stroke/Too Daze Gone	1981	5.00
❑ A-5037	My Kinda Lover/Christmas Is the Time to Say "I Love You"	1981	4.00
❑ A-5037 [PS]	My Kinda Lover/Christmas Is the Time to Say "I Love You"	1981	5.00
❑ A-5040	In the Dark/Whadda You Want from Me	1981	4.00
❑ A-5040 [PS]	In the Dark/Whadda You Want from Me	1981	5.00
❑ B-5135	Emotions in Motion/ It Keeps You Rockin'	1982	4.00
❑ B-5135 [PS]	Emotions in Motion/ It Keeps You Rockin'	1982	5.00
❑ B-5163	Everybody Wants You/ Keep Me Satisfied	1982	4.00
❑ B-5163 [PS]	Everybody Wants You/ Keep Me Satisfied	1982	5.00
❑ B-5202	She's a Runner/In Your Eyes	1983	4.00
❑ B-5202 [PS]	She's a Runner/In Your Eyes	1983	5.00
❑ B-5303	Christmas Is the Time to Say "I Love You"/White Christmas	1983	5.00
❑ B-5303 [PS]	Christmas Is the Time to Say "I Love You"/White Christmas	1983	6.00
❑ B-5370	Rock Me Tonite/Can't Get Next to You	1984	3.00
❑ B-5370 [PS]	Rock Me Tonite/Can't Get Next to You	1984	4.00
❑ B-5416	Eye on You/Calley Oh	1984	3.00
❑ B-5416 [PS]	Eye on You/Calley Oh	1984	4.00
❑ B-5422	All Night Long/Calley Oh	1984	3.00
❑ B-5422 [PS]	All Night Long/Calley Oh	1984	4.00
❑ B-5619	Love Is the Hero/Learn How to Live (Live)	1986	3.00
❑ B-5619 [PS]	Love Is the Hero/Learn How to Live (Live)	1986	3.00
❑ B-5657	Shot O' Love/One Good Woman	1986	3.00
❑ B-5657 [PS]	Shot O' Love/One Good Woman	1986	3.00
❑ SPRO 9870 [DJ]	Christmas Is The Time To Say I Love You/White Christmas	1983	8.00
—Has the same picture sleeve as B-5303			

Except when noted otherwise, VG = 25% of NM, and VG+ = 50% of NM. (Example: VG = $2.00, VG+ = $4.00 and NM = $8.00.)

Number	Title (A Side/B Side)	Yr	NM
❑ SPRO9870 [DJ]	Christmas Is The Time To Say I Love You/White Christmas	1983	8.00
—Has the same picture sleeve as B-5303			
❑ S7-17395	Rhythm (A Bridge So Far)/ Lovin' You Ain't So Hard	1993	4.00
❑ S7-18207	Christmas Is the Time to Say "I Love You"/Everybody Wants You	1994	4.00
—Green vinyl			
❑ S7-57890	Christmas Is the Time to Say "I Love You"/Christmas Blues	1992	5.00
—B-side by Canned Heat			
❑ 58749	Christmas Is the Time to Say "I Love You"/White Christmas	1998	3.00
❑ 7PRO-79694 [DJ]	Don't Say You Love Me (same on both sides)	1989	10.00
—Vinyl is promo only			

SQUIRES, THE (1)

Number	Title (A Side/B Side)	Yr	NM
45s			
ALADDIN			
❑ 3360	Dreamy Eyes/Danglin' with My Heart	1957	100.00
KICKS			
❑ 1	Dream Come True/Lucy Lou	1954	800.00
MAMBO			
❑ 105	Sindy/Do-Be-Do-Be-Wop-Wop	1955	150.00
VITA			
❑ 105	Sindy/Do-Be-Do-Be-Wop-Wop	1960	100.00
❑ 113	Sweet Girl/Me and My Deal	1955	100.00
❑ 116	Heavenly Angel/Sweet Girl	1955	100.00

SQUIRES, THE (2)

Number	Title (A Side/B Side)	Yr	NM
45s			
ATCO			
❑ 6442	Go Ahead/Going All the Way	1966	150.00

SQUIRES, THE (3)

Number	Title (A Side/B Side)	Yr	NM
45s			
CHAN			
❑ 102	Movin' Out/Our Theme	1961	30.00
❑ 105	Mean Misery/Chattanooga Choo Choo	1962	30.00
MGM			
❑ 13044	Movin' Out/Our Theme	1961	15.00

SQUIRES, THE (4)

Number	Title (A Side/B Side)	Yr	NM
45s			
COMBO			
❑ 35	Let's Give Love a Try/Whop	1952	500.00
❑ 42	Oh Darling/My Little Girl	1953	600.00

SQUIRES, THE (U)

We can't conclusively place any of these with the above groups. Of course, they may not be any of the above groups.

Number	Title (A Side/B Side)	Yr	NM
45s			
CONGRESS			
❑ 223	Joyce/Can't Believe That You've Grown Up	1964	60.00
FLAIR			
❑ 1030	Sayonara/Mia Bella Donna	1954	30.00
GEE			
❑ 1082	Don't Accuse Me/ So Many Tears Ago	1962	50.00
HERALD			
❑ 580	Why Should I Suffer/Walkin'	1963	30.00
STARLITE			
❑ 1/2	Movin'/Night Road	1964	50.00
V			
❑ 109	The Sultan/Aurora	1961	3000.
—Canadian release only; with a very early Neil Young. VG 1000; VG+ 2000			

SQUIRRELS, THE

Number	Title (A Side/B Side)	Yr	NM
45s			
CAMEO			
❑ 284	Grandma's House/ The Girl That I'll Adore	1963	10.00
—B-side by the Philadelphia Minstrels			

SRC

As in Scott Richard Case.

Number	Title (A Side/B Side)	Yr	NM
45s			
A-SQUARE			
❑ 301	I'm So Glad/Who Is That Girl	1967	25.00
—As "Scott Richard Case"			
❑ 402	Get the Picture/I Need You	1967	25.00
—B-side by the Rationals			
CAPITOL			
❑ 2327	Black Sheep/Morning Hood	1968	10.00
❑ 2457	Turn Into Love/Up All Night	1969	10.00
❑ 2726	Never Before Now/My Fortune's Coming True	1970	10.00
Albums			
CAPITOL			
❑ ST-134	Milestones	1969	40.00
❑ SKAO-273	Travellers Tale	1970	40.00
❑ ST 2991	SRC	1968	60.00

ST. PARADISE

Also see TED NUGENT; MONTROSE.

Number	Title (A Side/B Side)	Yr	NM
Albums			
WARNER BROS.			
❑ BSK 3281	St. Paradise	1979	12.00

STACKRIDGE

Number	Title (A Side/B Side)	Yr	NM
45s			
DECCA			
❑ 32923	Dora the Female Explorer/ (B-side unknown)	1972	10.00
SIRE			
❑ 717	The Last Plimsoul/ Spin Around the Room	1974	5.00
Albums			
DECCA			
❑ DL 75317	Stackridge	1971	25.00
MCA			
❑ 308	Friendliness	1973	10.00
SIRE			
❑ SASD-7503	Pinafore Days	1974	10.00
❑ SASD-7509	Extravaganza	1975	10.00

STAFFORD, TERRY

Number	Title (A Side/B Side)	Yr	NM
45s			
A&M			
❑ 707	Heartaches on the Way/ You Left Me Here to Cry	1963	12.00
ATLANTIC			
❑ CY-4006	Amarillo by Morning/ Say, Has Anybody Seen My Sweet Gypsy Rose	1973	8.00
❑ 4015	Captured/It Sure Is Bad to Love Her	1974	6.00
❑ 4026	Stop If You Love Me/ We've Grown Close	1974	6.00
CASINO			
❑ 113	It Sure Is Bad to Love Her/ (B-side unknown)	1977	6.00
CRUSADER			
❑ 101	Suspicion/Judy	1964	15.00
❑ 105	I'll Touch a Star/Playing with Fire	1964	12.00
❑ 109	Follow the Rainbow/ Are You a Fool Like Me	1964	12.00
❑ 110	A Little Bit Better/Hoping	1964	12.00
EASTLAND			
❑ 101	Back Together/Life's Railway to Heaven	198?	5.00
LANA			
❑ 139	Suspicion/Judy	196?	8.00
—Oldies reissue			
MELODYLAND			
❑ 6009	Darling, Think It Over/ I Can't Find It	1975	5.00
MERCURY			
❑ 72538	Out of the Picture/Forbidden	1966	10.00
MGM			
❑ 14232	Mean Woman Blues-Candy Man/Chilly Chicago	1971	6.00
❑ 14271	California Dancer/The Walk	1971	6.00
PLAYER			
❑ 134	Lonestar Lonesome/ (B-side unknown)	1989	6.00
SIDEWALK			
❑ 902	Soldier Boy/When Sin Stops, Love Begins	1966	10.00
❑ 914	A Step or Two Behind You/ The Joke's on Me	1967	10.00
WARNER BROS.			
❑ 7286	Big in Dallas/Will a Man Ever Learn	1969	6.00
Albums			
ATLANTIC			
❑ SD 7282	Say, Has Anybody Seen My Sweet Gypsy Rose	1974	12.00
CRUSADER			
❑ CLP-1001 [M]	Suspicion!	1964	40.00
❑ CLP-1001S [S]	Suspicion!	1964	60.00

STAIRSTEPS, THE

See THE FIVE STAIRSTEPS.

STALK-FORREST GROUP, THE

Early version of BLUE OYSTER CULT.

Number	Title (A Side/B Side)	Yr	NM
45s			
ELEKTRA			
❑ 45693	What Is Quicksand/ Arthur Comics	1970	50.00

STAMPEDERS

Number	Title (A Side/B Side)	Yr	NM
45s			
BELL			
❑ 45120	Sweet City Woman/Gator Road	1971	6.00
❑ 45154	Devil You/Giant in the Streets	1971	5.00
❑ 45188	Monday Morning Choo-Choo/ Then Came the White Man	1972	6.00
❑ 45226	Wild Eyes/Carryin' On	1972	6.00
❑ 45331	Oh My Lady/No Destination	1973	6.00
CAPITOL			
❑ 3868	Goodbye Goodbye/ Me and My Stone	1974	4.00
❑ 3964	Running Out of Time/Ramona	1974	4.00
MGM			
❑ 13970	Be a Woman/I Don't Believe	1968	12.00
POLYDOR			
❑ 14060	Carry Me/I Didn't Need You Anyhow	1970	10.00
QUALITY			
❑ 501	Hard Lovin' Woman/ Hit the Road Jack	1976	4.00
❑ 505	Sweet Love Bandit/Let It Begin	1976	4.00
Albums			
BELL			
❑ 6068	Sweet City Woman	1971	15.00
CAPITOL			
❑ ST-11288	From the Fire	1973	12.00
❑ ST-11328	New Day	1974	12.00
QUALITY			
❑ 1001	Hit the Road	1976	12.00

STANDARDS, THE

The record on Amos may be by a different group than the others.

Number	Title (A Side/B Side)	Yr	NM
45s			
AMOS			
❑ 134	When You Wish Upon a Star/ (Instrumental)	1969	10.00
CHESS			
❑ 1869	My Heart Belongs to You/ Hello Love	1963	40.00
DEBRO			
❑ 3178	Tears Bring Heartaches/ No, No, No	1963	200.00
GLENDEN			
❑ 1315	It Isn't Fair/Everybody Knows	1964	20.00
MAGNA			
❑ 1314	My Heart Belongs to You/ Hello Love	1963	80.00
❑ 1315	It Isn't Fair/Everybody Knows	1963	50.00
ROULETTE			
❑ 4487	Tears Bring Heartaches/ No, No, No	1963	30.00

STANDELLS, THE

Also see DICK DODD.

Number	Title (A Side/B Side)	Yr	NM
45s			
LIBERTY			
❑ 55680	The Peppermint Beatle/ The Shake	1964	25.00
❑ 55722	Help Yourself/I'll Go Crazy	1964	20.00
❑ 55743	So Fine/Linda Lou	1964	20.00
MGM			
❑ 13350	Someday You'll Cry/ Zebra in the Kitchen	1965	30.00
SUNSET			
❑ 61000	Ooh Poo Pah Doo/Help Yourself	1966	20.00
TOWER			
❑ 185	Dirty Water/Rari	1966	20.00
❑ 257	Sometimes Good Guys Don't Wear White/ Why Did You Hurt Me	1966	15.00
❑ 282	Why Pick on Me/Mr. Nobody	1966	15.00
❑ 310	Try It/Poor Shell of a Man	1967	15.00
❑ 310 [PS]	Try It/Poor Shell of a Man	1967	50.00
❑ 312	Don't Tell Me What to Do/ When I Was a Cowboy	1967	80.00
—By "The Sllednats" (Standells backwards)			
❑ 314	Riot on Sunset Strip/ Black Hearted Woman	1967	15.00
❑ 314 [PS]	Riot on Sunset Strip/Black Hearted Woman	1967	80.00

S

Number	Title (A Side/B Side)	Yr	NM
348	Can't Help But Love You/Ninety-Nine and One Half	1967	15.00
398	Animal Girl/Soul Drippin'	1968	15.00
VEE JAY			
643	The Boy Next Door/B.J. Quetzal	1965	20.00
643 [PS]	The Boy Next Door/B.J. Quetzal	1965	200.00
679	Big Boss Man/Don't Say Goodbye	1965	20.00
Albums			
LIBERTY			
LRP-3384 [M]	The Standells In Person at P.J.'s	1964	80.00
LST-7384 [S]	The Standells In Person at P.J.'s	1964	100.00
RHINO			
RNLP-107	The Best of the Standells	1983	10.00
RNLP-115	Rarities	1983	10.00
RNLP-70176	The Best of the Standells (Golden Archive Series)	1987	10.00
SUNSET			
SUM-1136 [M]	Live and Out of Sight	1966	25.00
SUS-5136 [S]	Live and Out of Sight	1966	30.00
TOWER			
ST 5027 [R]	Dirty Water	1966	50.00
T 5027 [M]	Dirty Water	1966	60.00
ST 5044 [S]	Why Pick on Me	1966	60.00
T 5044 [M]	Why Pick on Me	1966	50.00
ST 5049 [S]	The Hot Ones	1966	60.00
T 5049 [M]	The Hot Ones	1966	50.00
ST 5098 [S]	Try It	1967	60.00
T 5098 [M]	Try It	1967	50.00

STANDLEY, JOHNNY

Number	Title (A Side/B Side)	Yr	NM
45s			
CAPITOL			
F2249	It's In the Book (Part 1)/(Part 2)	1952	25.00
F2569	Proud New Father/Clap Your Hands	1953	25.00
F3544	Get Out and Vote! (Part 1)/(Part 2)	1956	20.00

STANLEY, MICHAEL, BAND

Number	Title (A Side/B Side)	Yr	NM
45s			
ARISTA			
0348	Why Should Love Be This Way/Late Show	1978	4.00
0368	Baby If You Wanna Dance/Fool's Parade	1978	4.00
0436	Last Night/Down to the Wire	1979	4.00
EMI AMERICA			
8063	He Can't Love You/Carolyn	1980	3.00
8064	Lover/Save a Little Piece for Me	1981	3.00
8090	Falling in Love Again/Does It Hurt	1981	3.00
8097	Victim of Circumstance/When Your Heart Says It's Right	1981	3.00
8130	When I'm Holding You Tight/In Between the Lines	1982	3.00
8146	Take the Time/Just a Little Bit Longer	1982	3.00
8178	My Town/Just How Good	1983	3.00
8189	Someone Like You/Highlife	1983	3.00
EPIC			
50116	I'm Gonna Love You/Step the Way	1975	4.00
50151	Face the Music/Song for My Children	1975	4.00
50242	Ladies' Choice/Sweet Refrain	1976	4.00
50416	Love Hasn't Been Here/Nothing's Gonna Change My Mind	1977	4.00
MCA			
40177	Roll On/Yours for a Song	1974	5.00
TUMBLEWEED			
TWA-1010	Rock and Roll Man/Denver Rain	1972	10.00
—As "Michael Stanley"			
Albums			
ARISTA			
AL 4182	Cabin Fever	1978	10.00
AL 4236	Greatest Hints	1979	10.00
EMI AMERICA			
SN-16352	Heartland	1985	8.00
—Budget-line reissue			
SN-16353	You Can't Fight Fashion	1985	8.00
—Budget-line reissue			
SN-16392	MSB	1986	8.00
—Budget-line reissue			
SW-17040	Heartland	1980	10.00
SW-17056	North Coast	1981	10.00
ST-17071	MSB	1982	10.00
ST-17100	You Can't Fight Fashion	1983	10.00
EPIC			
PE 33492	You Break It…You Bought It!	1975	12.00
—Original with orange label and no bar code			
PE 33492	You Break It…You Bought It!	198?	8.00
—Reissue with dark blue label and bar code			
PE 33917	Ladies' Choice	1976	12.00
—Original with orange label and no bar code			
PE 33917	Ladies' Choice	198?	8.00
—Reissue with dark blue label and bar code			
PEG 34661 [(2)]	Stagepass	1977	15.00
MCA			
372	Friends and Legends	1973	12.00
TUMBLEWEED			
TWS 106	Michael Stanley	1972	20.00
—Blue textured cover			

STANLEY, PAUL

Number	Title (A Side/B Side)	Yr	NM
45s			
CASABLANCA			
940	Hold Me, Touch Me/Goodbye	1978	6.00
—"Casablanca Record and FilmWorks" label			
940	Hold Me, Touch Me/Goodbye	1978	12.00
—Tan label with camel			
Albums			
CASABLANCA			
NBLP-7123	Paul Stanley	1978	25.00
NBPIX-7123 [PD]	Paul Stanley	1978	60.00

STANSHALL, VIVIAN Also see THE BONZO DOG BAND.

Number	Title (A Side/B Side)	Yr	NM
45s			
LIBERTY			
56171	Labio-Dental Fricative/Paper-Round	1970	20.00

STAPLE SINGERS, THE Also see MAVIS STAPLES.

Number	Title (A Side/B Side)	Yr	NM
12-Inch Singles			
PRIVATE I			
05078	Slippery People (5:30)/(Instrumental)	1984	5.00
05266	Are You Ready? (Extended)/(Dub)	1985	5.00
45s			
CURTOM			
0109	Let's Do It Again/After Sex	1975	4.00
0113	New Orleans/A Whole Lot of Love	1976	4.00
EPIC			
9748	Be Careful of Stones That You Throw/More Than a Hammer and Nail	1964	10.00
9776	Do Something for Yourself/Samson and Delilah	1965	10.00
9825	Freedom Highway/The Funeral	1965	10.00
9880	Why/What Are They Doing	1965	10.00
10054	King of Kings/Step Aside	1966	10.00
10104	Pray On/It's Been a Change	1966	10.00
10158	Why (Am I Treated So Bad)/What Are They Doing (In Heaven Today)	1967	8.00
10220	For What It's Worth/Are You Sure	1967	8.00
10264	Deliver Me/He	1967	8.00
10294	Let's Get Together/Power of Love	1968	8.00
10339	Crying in the Chapel/Nothing Lasts Forever	1968	8.00
10742	For What It's Worth/Why	1971	6.00
PRIVATE I			
04384	H-A-T-E (Don't Live Here Anymore)/Can You Hang	1984	4.00
04583	Slippery People/On My Own Again	1984	4.00
04711	This Is Our Night/Turning Point	1984	4.00
05565	Are You Ready/Love Wowks in Strange Ways	1985	4.00
05565 [PS]	Are You Ready/Love Wowks in Strange Ways	1985	6.00
05727	Nobody Can Make It on Their Own/Reasons to Love	1985	4.00
RIVERSIDE			
4518	Gloryland/Hammer and Nails	1962	12.00
4531	Gambling Man/Use What You Got	1962	12.00
4540	There Was a Star/The Virgin Mary Had One Son	1962	12.00
4553	I Can't Help from Cryin'/Let That Liar Again	1963	12.00
4563	Cotton Fields/This Land	1963	12.00
4568	Blowing in the Wind/Wish I Had Answered	1963	12.00
SHARP			
603	This May Be the Last Time/This Same Jesus	1960	15.00
STAX			
0007	Long Walk to D.C./Stay with Us	1968	6.00
0019	The Ghetto/Got to Be Some Changes Made	1968	6.00
0031	(Sittin' On) The Dock of the Bay/Top of the Mountain	1969	6.00
0039	The Gardener/The Challenge	1969	6.00
0052	When Will We Be Paid/Tend to Your Own Business	1969	6.00
0066	Give a Damn/God Bless the Children	1970	6.00
0074	Brand New Day/God Bless the Children	1970	6.00
0083	Heavy Makes You Happy (Sha-Na-Boom-Boom)/Love Is Plentiful	1970	6.00
0084	Who Took the Merry Out of Christmas/(Instrumental)	1970	8.00
0093	You've Got to Earn It/I'm a Lover	1971	5.00
0104	Respect Yourself/You're Gonna Make Me Cry	1971	5.00
0125	I'll Take You There/I'm Just Another Soldier	1972	5.00
0137	This World/Are You Sure	1972	5.00
0156	Oh La De Da/We the People	1973	5.00
0164	Be What You Are/I Like the Things About Me	1973	5.00
—B-side by Cal Starr			
0179	If You're Ready (Come Go with Me)/Love Comes in All Colors	1973	5.00
0196	Touch a Hand, Make a Friend/Tellin' Lies	1974	5.00
0213	What's Your Thing/Whicha Way Did It Go	1974	5.00
—B-side by Pops Staples			
0215	City in the Sky/That's What Friends Are For	1974	5.00
0227	My Main Man/Who Made the Man	1974	5.00
0248	Back Road Into Town/My Main Man	1975	5.00
20TH CENTURY			
2508	Hold On to Your Dreams/Cold and Windy Night	1981	4.00
UNITED			
165	It Rained Children/Won't You Sit Down	1955	400.00
VEE JAY			
169	God's Wonderful Love/If I Could Hear My Mother	1956	20.00
224	Uncloudy Day/I Know I Got Religion	1956	20.00
846	Let Me Ride/I'm Coming Home	1957	20.00
856	I Had a Dream/Help Me Jesus	1958	15.00
866	Love Is the Way/On My Way to Heaven	1959	15.00
870	I'm Leaving/Going Away	1959	15.00
881	Downward Road/So Soon	1959	15.00
893	Pray On/Too Close	1960	12.00
902	I've Been Scorned/Don't Knock	1961	12.00
912	Sit Down Servant/Swing Low	1962	12.00
930	Swing Low Sweet Chariot/I'm So Glad	1963	12.00
WARNER BROS.			
8279	Love Me, Love Me, Love Me/Pass It On	1976	4.00
8317	Sweeter Than the Sweet/Making Love	1977	4.00
8460	See a Little Further (Than My Bed)/Let's Go to the Disco	1977	4.00
8510	I Honestly Love You/Family Tree	1978	4.00
8669	Unlock Your Mind/Mystery Train	1978	4.00
8748	Chica Boom/Handwriting on the Wall	1979	4.00
49598	God Can/Unlock Your Mind	1980	4.00
—Warner Bros. titles as "The Staples"			
Albums			
ARCHIVE OF GOSPEL MUSIC			
62	The Staple Singers	1968	12.00
72	The Staple Singers, Vol. 2	1969	12.00
BUDDAH			
BDS-2009	The Best of the Staple Singers	1969	20.00
BDS-7508	Will the Circle Be Unbroken	1969	20.00
CURTOM			
CU 5005	Let's Do It Again	1975	12.00
EPIC			
LN 24132 [M]	Amen	1965	20.00
LN 24163 [M]	Freedom Highway	1965	20.00
LN 24196 [M]	Why	1966	20.00
LN 24237 [M]	Pray On	1967	25.00
LN 24332 [M]	For What It's Worth	1967	25.00
BN 26132 [S]	Amen	1965	25.00
BN 26163 [S]	Freedom Highway	1965	25.00
BN 26196 [S]	Why	1966	25.00
BN 26237 [S]	Pray On	1967	20.00
BN 26332 [S]	For What It's Worth	1967	20.00

Except when noted otherwise, VG = 25% of NM, and VG+ = 50% of NM. (Example: VG = $2.00, VG+ = $4.00 and NM = $8.00.)

Number	Title (A Side/B Side)	Yr	NM
❑ BN 26373	What the World Needs Now Is Love	1968	20.00
❑ EG 30635 [(2)]	The Staple Singers Make You Happy	1971	20.00
FANTASY			
❑ 9423	Use What You Got	1973	15.00
❑ 9442	The 25th Day of December	1973	15.00
HARMONY			
❑ KH 31775	Tell It Like It Is	1972	12.00
MILESTONE			
❑ 47028 [(2)]	A Great Day	197?	15.00
PICKWICK			
❑ 7001	The Staple Singers	197?	10.00
PRIVATE I			
❑ FZ 39460	The Turning Point	1984	10.00
❑ BFZ 40109	The Staple Singers	1985	10.00
STAX			
❑ STS-2004	Soul Folk in Action	1968	25.00
❑ STS-2016	We'll Get Over	1969	20.00
❑ STS-2034	The Staple Swingers	1971	20.00
❑ STS-3002	Be Altitude: Respect Yourself	1972	15.00
❑ STS-3015	Be What You Are	1973	15.00
❑ STX-4116	Be Altitude: Respect Yourself	198?	10.00
—Reissue of 3002			
❑ STX-4119	Chronicle	198?	10.00
❑ STS-5515	City in the Sky	1974	15.00
❑ STS-5523	The Best of the Staple Singers	1975	15.00
❑ MPS-8511	This Time Around	198?	10.00
❑ MPS-8532	We'll Get Over	198?	10.00
—Reissue of 2016			
❑ MPS-8553	Be What You Are	1990	12.00
—Reissue of 3015			
TRIP			
❑ 7000	Uncloudy Day	197?	10.00
❑ 7014	Swing Low	197?	10.00
❑ 7019	The Best of the Staple Singers	197?	10.00
❑ 8014	The Other Side of the Staple Singers	1972	10.00
20TH CENTURY			
❑ T-636	Hold On to Your Dream	1981	10.00
VEE JAY			
❑ LP-5000 [M]	Uncloudy Day	1959	30.00
❑ LP-5008 [M]	Will the Circle Be Unbroken	1960	30.00
❑ LP-5014 [M]	Swing Low	1961	30.00
❑ LP-5019 [M]	Best of the Staple Singers	1962	30.00
❑ LP-5030 [M]	Swing Low Sweet Chariot	1963	30.00
VEE JAY/CHAMELEON			
❑ D1-74782 [(2)]	The Best of the Staple Singers	1988	15.00
WARNER BROS.			
❑ BS 2945	Pass It On	1976	12.00
—As "The Staples"			
❑ BS 3084	Family Tree	1977	12.00
—As "The Staples"			
❑ BSK 3192	Unlock Your Mind	1978	12.00
—As "The Staples"			

STAPLES, GORDON, AND THE MOTOWN STRINGS

45s

Number	Title (A Side/B Side)	Yr	NM
MOTOWN			
❑ 1180	Strung Out/Sounds of the Zodiac	1971	30.00
❑ 1180 [DJ]	Strung Out (same on both sides)	1971	30.00
—Red vinyl promo			

STAPLES, MAVIS

Also see THE STAPLE SINGERS.

12-Inch Singles

Number	Title (A Side/B Side)	Yr	NM
PAISLEY PARK			
❑ PRO-A-4397 [DJ]	Melody Cool (Edit) (LP)	1990	8.00
❑ PRO-A-5991 [DJ]	The Voice (same on both sides)	1993	10.00
❑ 21287	Jaguar (4 versions)	1989	8.00
❑ 21748	Melody Cool (4 versions)/Time Waits for No One (Edit)	1990	8.00
WARNER BROS.			
❑ PRO-A-2444 [DJ]	Show Me How It Works (same on both sides)	1986	6.00
❑ 8837	Tonight I Feel Like Dancing/If I Can't Have You	1979	12.00

45s

Number	Title (A Side/B Side)	Yr	NM
CURTOM			
❑ 0132	A Piece of the Action/Till Blossoms Bloom	1977	4.00
PAISLEY PARK			
❑ 22968	20th Century Express/All the Discomforts of Home	1989	3.00
PHONO			
❑ 1051	Love Gone Bad/(B-side unknown)	1984	5.00
VOLT			
❑ 4044	I Have Learned to Do Without You/Since I Fell for You	1970	5.00
❑ 4086	Endlessly/Don't Change Me Now	1972	5.00
WARNER BROS.			
❑ PRO-S-3878 [DJ]	Christmas Vacation (same on both sides)	1989	5.00
❑ 8838	Tonight I Feel Like Dancing/If I Can't Have You	1979	4.00
❑ 28765	Show Me How It Works/Half Time	1986	3.00
❑ 49054	Oh What a Feeling/If I Can't Have You	1979	4.00

Albums

Number	Title (A Side/B Side)	Yr	NM
CURTOM			
❑ CU 5019	A Piece of the Action	1977	12.00
PAISLEY PARK			
❑ 25798	Time Waits for No One	1989	12.00
STAX			
❑ STX-4118	Mavis Staples	198?	10.00
—Reissue of Volt 6007			
❑ MPS-8539	Only for the Lonely	1987	10.00
—Reissue of Volt 6010			
VOLT			
❑ VOS-6007	Mavis Staples	1969	20.00
❑ VOS-6010	Only for the Lonely	1970	20.00
WARNER BROS.			
❑ BSK 3319	Oh What a Feeling	1979	12.00

STAR FIRES, THE

45s

Number	Title (A Side/B Side)	Yr	NM
HARAL			
❑ 777	Each Night at Nine/What Good Is Money	1962	100.00
LAURIE			
❑ 3332	You Done Me Wrong/Like Socks and Shoes	1966	20.00

STARCASTLE

Albums

Number	Title (A Side/B Side)	Yr	NM
EPIC			
❑ AS 296 [DJ]	Fountains of Light Banded for Airplay	1977	40.00
—White label, promo-only version with separations between tracks			
❑ PE 33914	Starcastle	1976	12.00
—Orange label			
❑ PE 34375	Fountains of Light	1977	12.00
—Orange label			
❑ 34935 [PD]	Citadel	1978	50.00
—Picture disc, possibly promo only			
❑ PE 34935	Citadel	1977	12.00
—Orange label			
❑ JE 35441	Real to Reel	1978	12.00
—Orange label			

STARCHER, BUDDY

45s

Number	Title (A Side/B Side)	Yr	NM
BOONE			
❑ 1038	History Repeats Itself/Sniper's Hill	1966	10.00
COLUMBIA			
❑ 2-380 (?)	I Planted a Rose/Isn't He Wonderful	1949	40.00
—Microgroove 33 1/3 rpm 7-inch single, small hole			
❑ 2-400 (?)	New Wildwood Flower/Walk Lightly, You're Stepping on My Heart	1949	40.00
—Microgroove 33 1/3 rpm 7-inch single, small hole			
❑ 2-490 (?)	Beyond the Sunset/Are You Facing the World All Alone	1949	40.00
—Microgroove 33 1/3 rpm 7-inch single, small hole			
❑ 2-580 (?)	Colored Child's Funeral/Oh Leave One Token of Your Love	1950	50.00
—Microgroove 33 1/3 rpm 7-inch single, small hole			
❑ 4-20723	I'll Forgive Dear But Never Forget/My Old Pal of Yesterday	1950	30.00
DECCA			
❑ 31975	Tax Payer's Lament/Day of Decision	1966	8.00
❑ 32012	Fall of a Nation/The Last Supper	1966	8.00
HEART WARMING			
❑ 5069	When Payday Comes/What Then?	1967	8.00
STARDAY			
❑ 439	The Battle of New Orleans/Pale Wildwood Flower	1959	15.00
❑ 460	Billy the Kid/Running Away from the Blues	1959	15.00
❑ 471	Ace of Hearts/Cryin'	1959	15.00
❑ 763	Little Red Riding Hood/Ace of Hearts	1966	8.00

Albums

Number	Title (A Side/B Side)	Yr	NM
DECCA			
❑ DL 4796 [M]	History Repeats Itself	1966	20.00
❑ DL 74796 [S]	History Repeats Itself	1966	25.00
STARDAY			
❑ SLP-211 [M]	Buddy Starcher and His Mountain Guitar	1962	30.00
❑ SLP-382 [M]	History Repeats Itself	1966	30.00

STARFIRES, THE (1)

45s

Number	Title (A Side/B Side)	Yr	NM
APT			
❑ 25030	Fender Bender/Camel Walk	1959	20.00
PACE			
❑ 101	Fender Bender/Camel Walk	1959	40.00

STARFIRES, THE (2)

45s

Number	Title (A Side/B Side)	Yr	NM
ATOMIC			
❑ A-1912	Love Will Break Your Heart/The Dances	1961	80.00
BARGAIN			
❑ 5001	You're the One/So Much	1961	60.00
❑ 5003	Love Will Break Your Heart/The Dances	1961	60.00
D&H			
❑ 200	These Foolish Things/Let's Do the Pony	1961	120.00

STARFIRES, THE (3)

45s

Number	Title (A Side/B Side)	Yr	NM
BERNICE			
❑ 201	Yearning for You/Do-Ko-Icki-No	1958	150.00
DECCA			
❑ 30730	Three Roses/I Have Someone	1958	40.00
❑ 30916	Love Is Here to Stay/Tomorrow	1959	50.00

STARFIRES, THE (4)

45s

Number	Title (A Side/B Side)	Yr	NM
DUEL			
❑ 518	Fools Fall in Love/Under the Stars	1962	50.00
TRIUMPH			
❑ 61	Fink/Work Out Fine	1965	20.00

Albums

Number	Title (A Side/B Side)	Yr	NM
OHIO RECORDING SERVICE			
❑ 34 [M]	The Starfires Play	1964	50.00

STARFIRES, THE (5)

45s

Number	Title (A Side/B Side)	Yr	NM
G.I.			
❑ 4001	I Never Loved Her/Linda	1965	2500.
❑ 4002	Rockin' Dixie/(B-side unknown)	1965	100.00
❑ 4004	Cry for Freedom/(B-side unknown)	1965	100.00

Albums

Number	Title (A Side/B Side)	Yr	NM
LABREA			
❑ LS-8018 [M]	Teenbeat A-Go-Go	1965	50.00

STARFIRES, THE (6)

Early version of THE OUTSIDERS.

45s

Number	Title (A Side/B Side)	Yr	NM
PAMA			
❑ 115	Ring of Love/Cheating Game	196?	40.00
❑ 117	Chartreuse Caboose/Billy's Blues	196?	40.00

STARFIRES, THE (7)

45s

Number	Title (A Side/B Side)	Yr	NM
ROUND			
❑ 1016	Space Needle/The Jordan Stomp	1962	40.00
❑ 1016 [PS]	Space Needle/The Jordan Stomp	1962	60.00

STARFIRES, THE (8)

45s

Number	Title (A Side/B Side)	Yr	NM
SONIC			
❑ 7163	Re-Entry/Hand Full of Blood	1963	30.00

STARLAND VOCAL BAND

45s

Number	Title (A Side/B Side)	Yr	NM
WINDSONG			
❑ CB-10588	Afternoon Delight/Starland	1976	4.00
❑ CB-10785	California Day/War Surplus Baby	1976	4.00
❑ CB-10855	Hail, Hail, Rock and Roll/Ain't It the Fall	1976	4.00
❑ GB-10943	Afternoon Delight/California Day	1977	3.00
—"Gold Standard Series" reissue			
❑ CB-11067	Light of My Life/Prism	1977	4.00
❑ CB-11168	Mr. Wrong/Too Long a Journey	1977	4.00

S

Except when noted otherwise, VG = 25% of NM, and VG+ = 50% of NM. (Example: VG = $2.00, VG+ = $4.00 and NM = $8.00.)

Number	Title (A Side/B Side)	Yr	NM
❑ CB-11261	Late Nite Radio/ Please Mrs. Newslady	1978	4.00
❑ CB-11899	Loving You with My Eyes/ Apartment for Rent	1980	4.00
❑ CB-12011	Thought I Would Never Find Love/Love Stuff	1980	4.00

Albums

WINDSONG

Number	Title (A Side/B Side)	Yr	NM
❑ BHL1-1351	Starland Vocal Band	1976	12.00
❑ BHL1-2239	Rear View Mirror	1977	12.00
❑ BXL1-2598	Late Nite Radio	1978	12.00
❑ BXL1-3536	4 x 4	1980	12.00

STARLETS, THE (1)

Later recorded as THE ANGELS (1).

45s

ASTRO

Number	Title (A Side/B Side)	Yr	NM
❑ 202/3	P.S. I Love You/Where Is My Love Tonight	1960	30.00
❑ 204	Romeo and Juliet/Listen for a Lonely Tambourine	1960	25.00

STARLETS, THE (2)

45s

CHESS

Number	Title (A Side/B Side)	Yr	NM
❑ 1997	My Baby's Real/Loving You Is Something New	1967	25.00
❑ 2038	I Wanna Be Good to You/ Watered Down	1968	20.00

STARLETS, THE (3)

This is the same group that, as THE BLUE-BELLES, recorded "I Sold My Heart to the Junkman."

45s

LUTE

Number	Title (A Side/B Side)	Yr	NM
❑ 5909	I'm So Young/He's Got It	1960	25.00

PAM

Number	Title (A Side/B Side)	Yr	NM
❑ 1003	Better Tell Him No/ You Are the One	1961	20.00
❑ 1004	My Last Cry/Money Hungry	1961	20.00

STARLETTES, THE

45s

CHECKER

Number	Title (A Side/B Side)	Yr	NM
❑ 895	Please Ring My Phone/Jungle Love	1958	150.00

STARLIGHTERS, THE

45s

CAPITOL

Number	Title (A Side/B Side)	Yr	NM
❑ F844	Rag Mop/It's Not Bad	1950	30.00

CRYSTALETTE

Number	Title (A Side/B Side)	Yr	NM
❑ 661	Sweetheart of Sigma Chi/Don't Call Me Coach, Call Me George	1952	25.00
❑ 662	Christmas Won't Be the Same (With You Away)/La Pinata (Mexican Christmas Song)	1952	30.00

END

Number	Title (A Side/B Side)	Yr	NM
❑ 1031	It's Twelve O'Clock/The Birdland	1958	500.00
❑ 1049	I Cried/You're the One to Blame	1959	80.00
❑ 1072	A Story of Love/Let's Take a Stroll	1960	120.00

IRMA

Number	Title (A Side/B Side)	Yr	NM
❑ 101	Love Cry/Last Night	1956	400.00

LAMP

Number	Title (A Side/B Side)	Yr	NM
❑ 2014	Slipping Out/Rocking Too Much	1958	50.00

SUN COAST

Number	Title (A Side/B Side)	Yr	NM
❑ 1001	Until You Return/Whomp, Whomp	1956	250.00

WHEEL

Number	Title (A Side/B Side)	Yr	NM
❑ 1004	Hot Licks/Creepin'	1960	15.00

STARLINGS, THE (1)

45s

DAWN

Number	Title (A Side/B Side)	Yr	NM
❑ 212	I'm Just a Crying Fool/ Hokey-Smokey Mama	1955	600.00
❑ 213	A-Loo, A-Loo/I Gotta Go Now	1955	400.00

JOSIE

Number	Title (A Side/B Side)	Yr	NM
❑ 760	My Plea for Love/Music, Maestro, Please	1954	500.00

STARLINGS, THE (2)

45s

WORLD PACIFIC

Number	Title (A Side/B Side)	Yr	NM
❑ 809	All I Want/That's Me	1959	40.00

STARLITES, THE (2)

For records on Everlast, Fury and Sphere Sound, see JACKIE AND THE STARLITES.

STARR, ANDY

45s

KAPP

Number	Title (A Side/B Side)	Yr	NM
❑ 190	Do It Right Now/I Waited for You to Remember	1957	25.00

MGM

Number	Title (A Side/B Side)	Yr	NM
❑ 12263	Rockin' Rollin' Stone/ I Wanna Go South	1956	150.00
❑ 12315	She's a-Going, Jessie/ Old Deacon Jones	1956	150.00
❑ 12364	Round and Round/ Give Me a Woman	1957	150.00
❑ 12421	No Room for Your Kind/ One More Time	1957	150.00

STARR, EDWIN

12-Inch Singles

A.S.K.

Number	Title (A Side/B Side)	Yr	NM
❑ S-29116	Hit Me with Your Love/ Over and Over	198?	8.00

20TH CENTURY

Number	Title (A Side/B Side)	Yr	NM
❑ TCD-62	I Just Wanna Do My Thing/ Mr. Davenport and Mr. James	1977	15.00
❑ TCD-107 [DJ]	Tell a Star (same on both sides)	1980	10.00
❑ TCD-128 [DJ]	Real Live #10 (stereo/mono)	1981	10.00

45s

GORDY

Number	Title (A Side/B Side)	Yr	NM
❑ 7066	Gonna Keep On Tryin' Til I Win Your Love/I Want My Baby Back	1967	6.00
❑ 7071	I Am the Man for You Baby/ My Weakness Is You	1968	6.00
❑ 7078	Way Over There/If My Heart Could Tell the Story	1968	6.00
❑ 7083	Twenty-Five Miles/ Love Is the Destination	1969	6.00
❑ 7083 [DJ]	Twenty-Five Miles (same on both sides)	1969	20.00
—Promo only on red vinyl			
❑ 7087	I'm Still a Struggling Man/ Pretty Little Angel	1969	6.00
❑ 7090	Oh How Happy/Ooh Baby Baby	1969	6.00
—With Blinky			
❑ 7097	Time/Running Back and Forth	1970	6.00
❑ 7101	War/He Who Picks a Rose	1970	6.00
❑ 7104	Stop the War Now/Gonna Keep On Tryin' Til I Win Your Love	1970	6.00
❑ 7107	Funky Music Sho Nuff Turns Me On/Cloud Nine	1971	6.00

GRANITE

Number	Title (A Side/B Side)	Yr	NM
❑ 522	Pain/I'll Never Forget You	1975	5.00
❑ 528	Stay with Me/Party	1975	5.00
❑ 532	Abyssinia Jones/Beginning	1975	5.00

MONTAGE

Number	Title (A Side/B Side)	Yr	NM
❑ 1216	Tired of It/(B-side unknown)	1982	4.00

MOTOWN

Number	Title (A Side/B Side)	Yr	NM
❑ 1276	You've Got My Soul on Fire/Love (The Lonely People's Prayer)	1973	5.00
❑ 1284	Ain't It Hell Up in Harlem/Don't It Feel Good to Be Free	1973	5.00
❑ 1300	Big Papa/Like We Used to Do	1974	5.00
❑ 1326	Who's Right or Wrong/Lonely Rainy Days in San Diego	1974	5.00

RIC-TIC

Number	Title (A Side/B Side)	Yr	NM
❑ 103	Agent Double-O-Soul/ (Instrumental)	1965	15.00
❑ 107	Back Street/(Instrumental)	1965	15.00
❑ 109	Stop Her on Sight (S.O.S.)/ I Have Faith in You	1966	15.00
❑ 109X [DJ]	Scott's On Swingers (S.O.S.)/ I Have Faith in You	1966	50.00
❑ 114	Headline News/Harlem	1966	15.00
❑ 118	It's My Turn Now/Girls Are Getting Prettier	1967	15.00
❑ 120	You're My Mellow/ My Kind of Woman	1967	60.00

SOUL

Number	Title (A Side/B Side)	Yr	NM
❑ 35096	Take Me Clear from Here/ Ball of Confusion	1972	6.00
❑ 35100	Who Is the Leader of the People/ Don't Tell Me I'm Crazy	1972	6.00
❑ 35103	There You Go/(Instrumental)	1973	6.00

20TH CENTURY

Number	Title (A Side/B Side)	Yr	NM
❑ 2338	I Just Wanna Do My Thing/ Mr. Davenport and Mr. James	1977	4.00
❑ 2389	I'm So Into You/ Don't Waste Your Time	1978	4.00
❑ 2396	Contact/Don't Waste Your Time	1978	4.00
❑ 2408	H.A.P.P.Y. Radio/My Friend	1979	4.00
❑ 2420	It's Called the Rock/Patiently	1979	4.00
❑ 2423	It's Called the Rock/ H.A.P.P.Y. Radio	1979	4.00
❑ 2441	It's Called the Rock/ H.A.P.P.Y. Radio	1980	4.00
❑ 2445	Stronger Than You Think I Am/ (Instrumental)	1980	4.00
❑ 2450	Tell-A-Star/Boop Boop Song	1980	4.00
❑ 2455	Get Up-Whirlpool/ Better and Better	1980	4.00
❑ 2477	Twenty-Five Miles/Never Turn My Back on You	1980	4.00
❑ 2496	Real Live #10/Sweat	1981	4.00

Albums

GORDY

Number	Title (A Side/B Side)	Yr	NM
❑ GS-931	Soul Master	1968	25.00
❑ GS-940	25 Miles	1969	25.00
❑ GS-945	Just We Two	1969	20.00
—With Blinky			
❑ GS-948	War & Peace	1970	20.00
❑ GS-956	Involved	1971	20.00

GRANITE

Number	Title (A Side/B Side)	Yr	NM
❑ 1005	Free to Be Myself	1975	12.00

MOTOWN

Number	Title (A Side/B Side)	Yr	NM
❑ M5-103V1	Superstar Series, Vol. 3	1981	10.00
❑ M5-170V1	War & Peace	1981	10.00

PICKWICK

Number	Title (A Side/B Side)	Yr	NM
❑ SPC-3387	25 Miles	197?	10.00

20TH CENTURY

Number	Title (A Side/B Side)	Yr	NM
❑ T-538	Edwin Starr	1977	10.00
❑ T-559	Clean	1978	10.00
❑ T-591	Happy Radio	1979	10.00
❑ T-615	Stronger Than You	1980	10.00
❑ T-634	The Best of Edwin Starr	1981	10.00

STARR, RAY

45s

KING

Number	Title (A Side/B Side)	Yr	NM
❑ 5652	I Have to Laugh to Keep from Crying/In the Middle of Two Hearts	1962	10.00

STARR, RICHARD

45s

CAMEO

Number	Title (A Side/B Side)	Yr	NM
❑ 340	Witchcraft Love/ Singing the Blues	1965	15.00

STAGE

Number	Title (A Side/B Side)	Yr	NM
❑ 100	Love Is Not a Game/ Groovy Thing	196?	40.00

STARR, RINGO

Also see THE BEATLES; GEORGE HARRISON AND FRIENDS.

12-Inch Singles

ATLANTIC

Number	Title (A Side/B Side)	Yr	NM
❑ DSKO 93 [DJ]	Drowning in the Sea of Love (5:08) (same on both sides)	1977	30.00

45s

APPLE

Number	Title (A Side/B Side)	Yr	NM
❑ 1826 [PS]	Beaucoups of Blues/ Coochy-Coochy	1970	40.00
—Sleeve with wrong catalog number (actually 2969)			
❑ 1831	It Don't Come Easy/Early 1970	1971	8.00
❑ 1831	It Don't Come Easy/Early 1970	1971	12.00
—With star on A-side label			
❑ 1831	It Don't Come Easy/Early 1970	1975	30.00
—With "All Rights Reserved" on label			
❑ 1831 [PS]	It Don't Come Easy/Early 1970	1971	30.00
❑ 1849	Back Off Boogaloo/Blindman	1972	8.00
—Green-background label			
❑ 1849	Back Off Boogaloo/Blindman	1972	75.00
—Blue-background label			
❑ 1849 [DJ]	Back Off Boogaloo/Blindman	1972	150.00
—White label			
❑ 1849 [PS]	Back Off Boogaloo/Blindman	1972	15.00
—Black paper with flat finish			
❑ 1849 [PS]	Back Off Boogaloo/Blindman	1972	40.00
—Glossy black on one side, gray on the other			
❑ 1849 [PS]	Back Off Boogaloo/Blindman	1972	40.00
—Glossy black paper on both sides			
❑ 1865	Photograph/Down and Out	1973	6.00
—Custom star label			
❑ 1865 [PS]	Photograph/Down and Out	1973	20.00
❑ P-1865 [DJ]	Photograph (mono/stereo)	1973	50.00
❑ 1870	You're Sixteen/Devil Woman	1973	6.00
—Custom star label			
❑ 1870	You're Sixteen/Devil Woman	1973	25.00
—Regular Apple label			
❑ 1870 [PS]	You're Sixteen/Devil Woman	1973	25.00
❑ P-1870 [DJ]	You're Sixteen (mono/stereo)	1973	50.00
❑ 1872	Oh My My/Step Lightly	1974	6.00
—Custom star label			
❑ 1872	Oh My My/Step Lightly	1974	8.00
—Regular Apple label			
❑ P-1872 [DJ]	Oh My My (Edited Mono)/ Oh My My (Long Stereo)	1974	50.00

Except when noted otherwise, VG = 25% of NM, and VG+ = 50% of NM. (Example: VG = $2.00, VG+ = $4.00 and NM = $8.00.)

Number	Title (A Side/B Side)	Yr	NM
❑ 1876	Only You/Call Me	1974	6.00
—Custom nebula label			
❑ 1876	Only You/Call Me	1974	8.00
—Regular Apple label			
❑ 1876 [PS]	Only You/Call Me	1974	20.00
❑ P-1876 [DJ]	Only You (mono/stereo)	1974	40.00
❑ 1880	No No Song/Snookeroo	1975	6.00
—Custom nebula label			
❑ P-1880 [DJ]	No No Song/Snookeroo (both mono)	1975	40.00
❑ P-1880 [DJ]	No No Song/Snookeroo (both stereo)	1975	40.00
❑ 1882	It's All Down to Goodnight Vienna/Oo-Wee	1975	6.00
—Custom nebula label			
❑ 1882 [PS]	It's All Down to Goodnight Vienna/Oo-Wee	1975	20.00
❑ P-1882 [DJ]	It's All Down to Goodnight Vienna (mono/stereo)	1975	40.00
❑ P-1882 [DJ]	Oo-Wee/Oo-Wee	1975	70.00
❑ 2969	Beaucoups of Blues/ Coochy-Coochy	1970	8.00
—With "Mfd. by Apple" on label and no star on A-side label			
❑ 2969	Beaucoups of Blues/ Coochy-Coochy	1970	25.00
—With small Capitol logo on bottom of B-side label and star on A-side label			
❑ 2969	Beaucoups of Blues/ Coochy-Coochy	1970	40.00
—With "Mfd. by Apple" on label and star on A-side label			
❑ 2969 [PS]	Beaucoups of Blues/ Coochy-Coochy	1970	50.00
—Sleeve with correct catalog number			
ATLANTIC			
❑ 3361	A Dose of Rock 'N' Roll/Cryin'	1976	10.00
❑ 3361 [DJ]	A Dose of Rock 'N' Roll (With Intro)/(Without Intro)	1976	15.00
—Light blue label with Atlantic logo at top			
❑ 3361 [DJ]	A Dose of Rock 'N' Roll (With Intro)/(Without Intro)	1976	100.00
—All-white label with no Atlantic logo at top			
❑ 3371	Hey Baby/Lady Gaye	1976	30.00
❑ 3371 [DJ]	Hey Baby (mono/stereo)	1976	15.00
—Red and white label on mono side, light blue label on stereo side			
❑ 3371 [DJ]	Hey Baby (mono/stereo)	1976	100.00
—All-white label with no Atlantic logo at top			
❑ 3371 [DJ]	Hey Baby/(B-side blank)	1976	300.00
—Light blue label			
❑ 3412	Drowning in the Sea of Love/ Just a Dream	1977	120.00
❑ 3412 [DJ]	Drowning in the Sea of Love (mono/stereo)	1977	25.00
❑ 3429	Wings/Just a Dream	1977	30.00
❑ 3429 [DJ]	Wings (mono/stereo)	1977	15.00
—Red and white label on mono side, light blue label on stereo side			
❑ 3429 [DJ]	Wings (mono/stereo)	1977	100.00
—All-white label with no Atlantic logo at top			
BOARDWALK			
❑ NB7-11-130	Wrack My Brain/Drumming Is My Madness	1981	5.00
❑ NB7-11-130 [DJ]	Wrack My Brain (mono/stereo)	1981	15.00
❑ NB7-11-130 [PS]	Wrack My Brain/ Drumming Is My Madness	1981	5.00
❑ NB7-11-134	Private Property/Stop and Take the Time to Smell the Roses	1982	12.00
❑ NB7-11-134 [DJ]	Private Property (same on both sides)	1982	15.00
CAPITOL			
❑ 1831	It Don't Come Easy/Early 1970	1976	25.00
—Orange label			
❑ 1831	It Don't Come Easy/Early 1970	1978	6.00
—Purple late-1970s label			
❑ 1831	It Don't Come Easy/Early 1970	1983	6.00
—Black colorband label			
❑ 1831	It Don't Come Easy/Early 1970	1988	5.00
—Purple late-1980s label (wider)			
❑ 1849	Back Off Boogaloo/Blindman	1976	30.00
—Orange label			
❑ 1849	Back Off Boogaloo/Blindman	1978	8.00
—Purple late-1970s label			
❑ 1865	Photograph/Down and Out	1978	8.00
—Purple late-1970s label			
❑ 1865	Photograph/Down and Out	1983	8.00
—Black colorband label			
❑ 1865	Photograph/Down and Out	1988	6.00
—Purple late-1980s label (wider)			
❑ 1870	You're Sixteen/Devil Woman	1976	60.00
—Orange label			
❑ 1870	You're Sixteen/Devil Woman	1978	8.00
—Purple late-1970s label			
❑ 1870	You're Sixteen/Devil Woman	1983	8.00
—Black colorband label			
❑ 1870	You're Sixteen/Devil Woman	1988	5.00
—Purple late-1980s label (wider)			
❑ 1876	Only You/Call Me	1978	8.00
—Purple late-1970s label			

Ringo Starr, *Stop and Smell the Roses*, Boardwalk NB1-33246, 1981, **$10.**

Number	Title (A Side/B Side)	Yr	NM
❑ 1876	Only You/Call Me	1983	100.00
—Black colorband label			
❑ 1880	No No Song/Snookeroo	1978	8.00
—Purple late-1970s label			
❑ 1880	No No Song/Snookeroo	1983	8.00
—Black colorband label			
❑ 1880	No No Song/Snookeroo	1988	30.00
—Purple late-1980s label (wider)			
❑ 1882	It's All Down to Goodnight Vienna/Oo-Wee	1978	8.00
—Purple late-1970s label			
❑ 2969	Beaucoups of Blues/ Coochy-Coochy	1976	40.00
—Orange label			
❑ B-44409	Act Naturally/Key's in the Mailbox	1989	15.00
—A-side with Buck Owens; B-side is Owens solo			
❑ P-B-44409 [DJ]	Act Naturally (same on both sides)	1989	30.00
—With Buck Owens			
MERCURY			
❑ MELP-195 [DJ]	La De Da/Everyday	1998	15.00
—Number only in the dead wax			
❑ MELP-195 [PS]	La De Da/Everyday	1998	15.00
—The above record and sleeve were a giveaway from Beatlefest and J&R's Music World with advance purchase of the CD "Vertical Man" and later from Beatlefest with any Ringo Starr Mercury CD.			
PORTRAIT			
❑ 6-70015	Lipstick Traces (On a Cigarette)/ Old Time Relovin'	1978	15.00
❑ 6-70015 [DJ]	Lipstick Traces (On a Cigarette) (mono/stereo)	1978	20.00
❑ 6-70018	Heart on My Sleeve/ Who Needs a Heart	1978	15.00
❑ 6-70018 [DJ]	Heart on My Sleeve (mono/stereo)	1978	20.00
THE RIGHT STUFF			
❑ S7-18178	In My Car/She's About a Mover	1994	8.00
—Gold/orange vinyl			
❑ S7-18179	Wrack My Brain/Private Property	1994	8.00
—Red vinyl			

Number	Title (A Side/B Side)	Yr	NM
Albums			
APPLE			
❑ SW-3365	Sentimental Journey	1970	20.00
❑ SMAS-3368	Beaucoups of Blues	1970	20.00
❑ SWAL-3413	Ringo	1973	20.00
—Standard issue with booklet; Side 1, Song 2 identified on cover as "Hold On"			
❑ SWAL-3413	Ringo	1973	400.00
—With a 5:26 version of "Six O'Clock." On later copies, the song is shortened to 4:05 though the label still says 5:26. All known copies have a promo punch-hole in top corner of jacket; on Side 2 record, "Six O'Clock" will be the widest track.			
❑ SWAL-3413	Ringo	1974	25.00
—Later issue with booklet; Side 1, Song 2 identified on cover as "Have You Seen My Baby"			
❑ SW-3417	Goodnight Vienna	1974	12.00
❑ SW-3422	Blast from Your Past	1975	15.00
ATLANTIC			
❑ SD 18193	Ringo's Rotogravure	1976	15.00
—Deduct 2/3 for cut-outs			
❑ SD 18193 [DJ]	Ringo's Rotogravure	1976	30.00
—With "DJ Only" scrawled into trail-off area			
❑ SD 19108	Ringo the 4th	1977	15.00
—Deduct 1/2 for cut-outs			
❑ SD 19108 [DJ]	Ringo the 4th	1977	30.00
—With "DJ Only" scrawled into trail-off area			
BOARDWALK			
❑ NB1-33246	Stop and Smell the Roses	1981	10.00
—Deduct 1/2 for cut-outs			
CAPITOL			
❑ SW-3365	Sentimental Journey	197?	40.00
—Purple label, large Capitol logo			
❑ SN-16114	Ringo	198?	15.00
—Green label budget-line reissue with all errors corrected			
❑ SN-16218	Sentimental Journey	198?	25.00
—Green label budget-line reissue			
❑ SN-16219	Goodnight Vienna	198?	25.00
—Green label budget-line reissue			
❑ SN-16235	Beaucoups of Blues	198?	20.00
—Green label budget-line reissue			
❑ SN-16236	Blast from Your Past	198?	15.00
—Green label budget-line reissue			

Starz, *Violation*, Capitol SW-11617, 1977, **$10.**

Number	Title (A Side/B Side)	Yr	NM
PORTRAIT			
❑ JR 35378	Bad Boy	1978	15.00

—Deduct 1/3 for cut-outs

Number	Title (A Side/B Side)	Yr	NM
❑ JR 35378 [DJ]	Bad Boy	1978	30.00

—Regular white-label promo in standard jacket

Number	Title (A Side/B Side)	Yr	NM
❑ JR 35378 [DJ]	Bad Boy	1978	100.00

—White label promo with "Advance Promotion" on label; in plain white cover

Number	Title (A Side/B Side)	Yr	NM
RHINO			
❑ R1 70199	Starr Struck: Ringo's Best 1976-1983	1989	25.00
RYKODISC			
❑ RALP 0190	Ringo Starr and His All-Starr Band	1990	30.00

—With limited, numbered obi (deduct $5 if missing)

STARR, SALLY Philadelphia TV star backed by members of BILL HALEY AND HIS COMETS.

45s

Number	Title (A Side/B Side)	Yr	NM
ARCADE			
❑ 157	Rocky the Rockin' Rabbit/ Sing a Song of Happiness	1960	30.00
CLYMAX			
❑ 301	Rockin' in the Nursery/ Little Pedro	1959	40.00

7-Inch Extended Plays

Number	Title (A Side/B Side)	Yr	NM
CLYMAX			
❑ EP-1001	Cuckoo in the Clock/Sing a Song of Happiness// TV Pal/A.B.C. Rock	1959	30.00

—Second record of 3-EP set; master numbers are JB 142/JB 143

Number	Title (A Side/B Side)	Yr	NM
❑ EP-1001	Rockin' in the Nursery/Little Pedro//Rockin' Horse Cowgirl/ Good Night Dear Lord	1959	30.00

—Third record of 3-EP set; master numbers are JB-144/JB-145

Number	Title (A Side/B Side)	Yr	NM
❑ EP-1001	Toy Shop in the Town/ Happy Birthday//Candy Red/ Blue Ranger	1959	30.00

—First record of 3-EP set; master numbers are JB-140/JB-141

Number	Title (A Side/B Side)	Yr	NM
❑ EP-1001/2/3 [PS]	Our Gal Sal	1959	40.00

—Triple gatefold cover for all three EP-1001 records (despite what the cover says, the records are each numbered 1001)

Albums

Number	Title (A Side/B Side)	Yr	NM
ARCADE			
❑ 1001 [M]	Our Gal Sal	1960	80.00
CLYMAX			
❑ 1001 [M]	Our Gal Sal	1959	200.00

STARSHIP (2) No relation to the 1980s Starship, this features MICKEY DOLENZ.

45s

Number	Title (A Side/B Side)	Yr	NM
LION			
❑ 132	Johnny B. Goode/ It's Amazing to Me	1973	25.00

STARZ

45s

Number	Title (A Side/B Side)	Yr	NM
CAPITOL			
❑ 4343	Monkey Business/(She's Just A) Fallen Angel	1976	5.00
❑ 4343 [PS]	Monkey Business/(She's Just A) Fallen Angel	1976	7.00
❑ 4399	Cherry Baby/Rock Six Times	1977	4.00
❑ 4399 [PS]	Cherry Baby/Rock Six Times	1977	6.00
❑ 4399	Cherry Baby/Rock Six Times	1977	10.00

—Originals on yellow vinyl

Number	Title (A Side/B Side)	Yr	NM
❑ 4434	Sing It, Shout It/Subway Terror	1977	4.00
❑ 4434 [PS]	Sing It, Shout It/Subway Terror	1977	6.00
❑ 4434	Sing It, Shout It/Subway Terror	1977	10.00

—Originals on yellow vinyl

Number	Title (A Side/B Side)	Yr	NM
❑ 4546	(Any Way That You Want It) I'll Be There/Texas	1978	4.00
❑ 4546 [PS]	(Any Way That You Want It) I'll Be There/Texas	1978	5.00
❑ 4566	Hold On to the Night/Texas	1978	4.00
❑ 4637	So Young, So Bad/ Coliseum Rock	1978	4.00
❑ 4637 [PS]	So Young, So Bad/ Coliseum Rock	1978	5.00
❑ 4671	Last Night I Wrote a Letter/ Coliseum Rock	1979	5.00

Albums

Number	Title (A Side/B Side)	Yr	NM
CAPITOL			
❑ SPRO-8657/8 [DJ]	Live at Municipal Auditorium, Louisville, March 30, 1978	1978	30.00

—Promo-only "Superstars Radio Network Presents" album

Number	Title (A Side/B Side)	Yr	NM
❑ ST-11539	Starz	1976	10.00
❑ SW-11617	Violation	1977	10.00

—Black vinyl

Number	Title (A Side/B Side)	Yr	NM
❑ SW-11617	Violation	1977	20.00

—Gold vinyl

Number	Title (A Side/B Side)	Yr	NM
❑ ST-11730	Attention Shoppers!	1978	10.00
❑ ST-11861	Coliseum Rock	1978	10.00
METAL BLADE			
❑ 73430	Live in Action	1989	12.00
VIOLATION			
❑ 0001	Live in America	1983	15.00

STATENS, THE

45s

Number	Title (A Side/B Side)	Yr	NM
MARK-X			
❑ 8011	Summertime Is the Time for Love/That Certain Kind	1961	80.00

STATLERS, THE

45s

Number	Title (A Side/B Side)	Yr	NM
LITTLE STAR			
❑ 108	Vicky/Gone	1962	150.00

STATON, CANDI

12-Inch Singles

Number	Title (A Side/B Side)	Yr	NM
LA			
❑ 8012	Without You I Cry (4:47)/ (B-side unknown)	1981	10.00
SUGAR HILL			
❑ 568	Count On Me/(Instrumental)	1981	10.00
❑ 571	Suspicious Minds/ Love and Be Free	1982	10.00
WARNER BROS.			
❑ PRO-A-772 [DJ]	Honest I Do Love You (6:31) (same on both sides)	1978	12.00
❑ PRO-A-827 [DJ]	Chance (5:34)/Rock (7:16)	1979	12.00
❑ PRO-A-867 [DJ]	Looking for Love (same on both sides)	1980	12.00
❑ 8820	When You Wake Up Tomorrow/ Rough Times	1979	12.00

45s

Number	Title (A Side/B Side)	Yr	NM
FAME			
❑ XW256	Something's Burning/ It's Not Love	1973	5.00
❑ XW328	Love Chain/I'm Gonna Hold On	1973	5.00
❑ 1456	I'd Rather Be an Old Man's Sweetheart (Than a Young Man's Fool)/For You	1969	6.00
❑ 1459	Never in Public/You Don't Love Me No More	1969	6.00
❑ 1460	I'm Just a Prisoner (Of Your Good Lovin')/ Heart on a String	1969	6.00
❑ 1466	Sweet Feeling/Evidence	1970	6.00
❑ 1472	Stand By Your Man/How Can I Put Out the Flame (When You Keep the Fire Burning)	1970	6.00
❑ 1476	He Called Me Baby/What Would Become of Me	1970	6.00
❑ 1478	Mr. and Mrs. Untrue/ Too Hurt to Cry	1971	6.00
❑ 91000	In the Ghetto/Sure As Sin	1972	5.00
❑ 91005	Lovin' You, Lovin' Me/ You Don't Love Me No More	1972	5.00
❑ 91009	Do It in the Name of Love/The Thanks I Get for Loving You	1972	5.00
LA			
❑ 0080	Without You I Cry/ (B-side unknown)	1981	5.00
SUGAR HILL			
❑ 770	Count on Me/(B-side unknown)	1981	5.00
❑ 776	Suspicious Minds/ (B-side unknown)	1982	5.00
❑ 784	Hurry Sundown/Count on Me	1982	5.00
UNITY			
❑ 711	Now That You Have the Upper Hand/(B-side unknown)	196?	150.00
WARNER BROS.			
❑ 8038	As Long As He Takes Care of Business/Little Taste of Love	1974	4.00
❑ 8078	Here I Am Again/ Your Opening Night	1975	4.00

Except when noted otherwise, VG = 25% of NM, and VG+ = 50% of NM. (Example: VG = $2.00, VG+ = $4.00 and NM = $8.00.)

Number	Title (A Side/B Side)	Yr	NM
❑ 8112	Six Nights and a Day/ We Can Work It Out	1975	4.00
❑ 8181	Young Hearts Run Free/I Know	1976	4.00
❑ 8249	Run to Me/What a Feeling	1976	4.00
❑ 8320	A Dreamer of a Dream/ When You Want Love	1977	4.00
❑ 8387	Nights on Broadway/You Are	1977	4.00
❑ 8461	Music Speaks Louder Than Words/Cotton Candi	1977	4.00
❑ 8477	Listen to the Music/Music Speaks Louder Than Words	1977	4.00
❑ 8582	Victim/So Blue	1978	4.00
❑ 8691	Honest I Do Love You/I'm Gonna Make Me Love You	1978	4.00
❑ 8821	When You Wake Up Tomorrow/ Rough Times	1979	4.00
❑ 49061	Chance/I Live	1979	4.00
❑ 49240	Looking for Love/It's Real	1980	4.00
❑ 49240 [PS]	Looking for Love/It's Real	1980	6.00
❑ 49536	The Hunter Gets Captured by the Game/If You Feel the Need	1980	4.00

Albums

FAME

Number	Title	Yr	NM
❑ 1800	Candi Staton	1972	20.00
❑ ST-4201	I'm a Prisoner	1970	20.00
❑ ST-4202	Stand By Your Man	1971	20.00

WARNER BROS.

Number	Title	Yr	NM
❑ BS 2830	Candi	1974	12.00
❑ BS 2948	Young Hearts Run Free	1976	12.00
❑ BS 3040	Music Speaks Louder Than Words	1977	12.00
❑ BSK 3207	House of Love	1978	12.00
❑ BSK 3333	Chance	1979	12.00
❑ BSK 3428	Candi Staton	1980	12.00

STATON, DAKOTA

45s

CAPITOL

Number	Title (A Side/B Side)	Yr	NM
❑ PRO 408/9 [DJ]	Trust in Me/The Late, Late Show	1957	20.00
—White label "Special DJ Album Highlights"			
❑ F3010	My Heart's Delight/What Do You Know About Love	1955	12.00
❑ F3059	For the Rest of My Life/ No Mama, No Papa	1955	12.00
❑ F3128	Don't Leave Me Now/Little You	1955	12.00
❑ F3181	Abracadabra/I Never Dreamt	1955	12.00
❑ F3293	It Feels So Nice/Dangerous Age	1955	12.00
❑ F3361	How High the Moon/ Weak for the Man	1956	12.00
❑ F3489	My Friend/Don't Mean Maybe	1956	12.00
❑ F3546	You Know I Do/I Told You So	1956	12.00
❑ F3876	The Late Late Show/Trust in Me	1958	10.00
❑ F3958	Invitation/The Party's Over	1958	10.00
❑ F4012	Confessin' the Blues/ Blues in My Heart	1958	10.00
❑ F4299	Where Did You Go?/Avalon	1959	10.00
❑ 4372	My Babe/Romance in the Dark	1960	10.00
❑ 4465	First Things First/I Don't Worry	1960	10.00
❑ 4512	All in My Mind/Hey Lawdy Mama	1961	10.00
❑ 4673	When I Grow Too Old to Dream/ Mean and Evil Blues	1961	10.00
❑ 4790	Porgy/On Chapel Hill	1962	10.00
❑ 4910	Once There Lived a Fool/ You'd Better Go Now	1963	10.00

GROOVE MERCHANT

Number	Title (A Side/B Side)	Yr	NM
❑ 1011	Let It Be Me/Losing Battle	1972	5.00
❑ 1017	(I Want a) Country Man/ I Love You More Than You'll Ever Know	1973	5.00
❑ 1019	How Did He Look/Girl Talk	1973	5.00

UNITED ARTISTS

Number	Title (A Side/B Side)	Yr	NM
❑ 611	When It's Sleepy Time Down South/Massachusetts	1963	8.00

7-Inch Extended Plays

CAPITOL

Number	Title	Yr	NM
❑ EAP 1-876	*Broadway/Trust in Me/ Moonray/Ain't No Use	1958	15.00
❑ EAP 1-876 [PS]	The Late, Late Show, Part 1	1958	15.00
❑ EAP 2-876	Summertime/Misty//Give Me the Simple Life/You Showed Me the Way	1958	15.00
❑ EAP 2-876 [PS]	The Late, Late Show, Part 2	1958	15.00
❑ EAP 1-1170	*Crazy He Calls Me/Idaho/ How Does It Feel?/ How High the Moon	1959	15.00
❑ EAP 1-1170 [PS]	Crazy He Calls Me, Part 1	1959	15.00
❑ EAP 2-1170	(contents unknown)	1959	15.00
❑ EAP 2-1170 [PS]	Crazy He Calls Me, Part 2	1959	15.00

Albums

CAPITOL

Number	Title	Yr	NM
❑ DT 876 [R]	The Late, Late Show	196?	12.00
❑ SM-876	The Late, Late Show	1977	10.00
—Reissue with new prefix			
❑ T 876 [M]	The Late, Late Show	1957	50.00
—Turquoise or gray label			
❑ T 876 [M]	The Late, Late Show	1959	30.00
—Black label with colorband, Capitol logo at left			
❑ T 876 [M]	The Late, Late Show	1962	15.00
—Black label with colorband, Capitol logo at top			
❑ M-1003	In the Night	1976	10.00
—Reissue with new prefix			
❑ T 1003 [M]	In the Night	1958	50.00
—Turquoise or gray label			
❑ T 1003 [M]	In the Night	1959	30.00
—Black label with colorband, Capitol logo at left			
❑ ST 1054 [S]	Dynamic!	1959	40.00
—Black label with colorband, Capitol logo at left			
❑ ST 1054 [S]	Dynamic!	1962	20.00
—Black label with colorband, Capitol logo at top			
❑ T 1054 [M]	Dynamic!	1958	30.00
—Black label with colorband, Capitol logo at left			
❑ T 1054 [M]	Dynamic!	1962	15.00
—Black label with colorband, Capitol logo at top			
❑ ST 1170 [S]	Crazy He Calls Me	1959	40.00
—Black label with colorband, Capitol logo at left			
❑ ST 1170 [S]	Crazy He Calls Me	1962	20.00
—Black label with colorband, Capitol logo at top			
❑ T 1170 [M]	Crazy He Calls Me	1959	30.00
—Black label with colorband, Capitol logo at left			
❑ T 1170 [M]	Crazy He Calls Me	1962	15.00
—Black label with colorband, Capitol logo at top			
❑ ST 1241 [S]	Time to Swing	1959	40.00
—Black label with colorband, Capitol logo at left			
❑ ST 1241 [S]	Time to Swing	1962	20.00
—Black label with colorband, Capitol logo at top			
❑ T 1241 [M]	Time to Swing	1959	30.00
—Black label with colorband, Capitol logo at left			
❑ T 1241 [M]	Time to Swing	1962	15.00
—Black label with colorband, Capitol logo at top			
❑ ST 1325 [S]	More Than the Most	1960	40.00
—Black label with colorband, Capitol logo at left			
❑ ST 1325 [S]	More Than the Most	1962	20.00
—Black label with colorband, Capitol logo at top			
❑ T 1325 [M]	More Than the Most	1960	30.00
—Black label with colorband, Capitol logo at left			
❑ T 1325 [M]	More Than the Most	1962	15.00
—Black label with colorband, Capitol logo at top			
❑ ST 1387 [S]	Ballads and the Blues	1960	40.00
—Black label with colorband, Capitol logo at left			
❑ ST 1387 [S]	Ballads and the Blues	1962	20.00
—Black label with colorband, Capitol logo at top			
❑ T 1387 [M]	Ballads and the Blues	1960	30.00
—Black label with colorband, Capitol logo at left			
❑ T 1387 [M]	Ballads and the Blues	1962	15.00
—Black label with colorband, Capitol logo at top			
❑ ST 1427 [S]	Softly	1961	40.00
—Black label with colorband, Capitol logo at left			
❑ ST 1427 [S]	Softly	1962	20.00
—Black label with colorband, Capitol logo at top			
❑ T 1427 [M]	Softly	1961	30.00
—Black label with colorband, Capitol logo at left			
❑ T 1427 [M]	Softly	1962	15.00
—Black label with colorband, Capitol logo at top			
❑ ST 1490 [S]	Dakota	1961	40.00
—Black label with colorband, Capitol logo at left			
❑ ST 1490 [S]	Dakota	1962	20.00
—Black label with colorband, Capitol logo at top			
❑ T 1490 [M]	Dakota	1961	30.00
—Black label with colorband, Capitol logo at left			
❑ T 1490 [M]	Dakota	1962	15.00
—Black label with colorband, Capitol logo at top			
❑ ST 1597 [S]	'Round Midnight	1961	40.00
—Black label with colorband, Capitol logo at left			
❑ ST 1597 [S]	'Round Midnight	1962	20.00
—Black label with colorband, Capitol logo at top			
❑ T 1597 [M]	'Round Midnight	1961	30.00
—Black label with colorband, Capitol logo at left			
❑ T 1597 [M]	'Round Midnight	1962	15.00
—Black label with colorband, Capitol logo at top			
❑ ST 1649 [S]	Dakota at Storyville	1962	25.00
❑ T 1649 [M]	Dakota at Storyville	1962	20.00

GROOVE MERCHANT

Number	Title	Yr	NM
❑ 510	Madame Foo-Foo	1972	12.00
❑ 521	I Want a Country Man	1973	12.00
❑ 532	Ms. Soul	1974	12.00
❑ 4410 [(2)]	Confessin'	197?	15.00

LONDON

Number	Title	Yr	NM
❑ PS 495 [S]	Dakota '67	1967	15.00
❑ LL 3495 [M]	Dakota '67	1967	20.00

Status Quo, *Quo*, A&M SP-3649, 1974, **$12.**

S

Number	Title (A Side/B Side)	Yr	NM
MUSE			
❑ MR-5401	Dakota Staton	1991	15.00
UNITED ARTISTS			
❑ UAL-3292 [M]	From Dakota with Love	1963	20.00
❑ UAL-3312 [M]	Live and Swinging	1963	20.00
❑ UAL-3355 [M]	Dakota Staton with Strings	1964	20.00
❑ UAS-6292 [S]	From Dakota with Love	1963	25.00
❑ UAS-6316 [S]	Live and Swinging	1963	25.00
❑ UAS-6355 [S]	Dakota Staton with Strings	1964	25.00
VERVE			
❑ V6-8799	I've Been There	1971	15.00

STATUES, THE

Number	Title (A Side/B Side)	Yr	NM
45s			
HOLIDAY			
❑ 1026 [DJ]	White Christmas/Get Off My Roof	197?	12.00
—B-side by Jerry and the Landsliders			
LIBERTY			
❑ 55245	Blue Velvet/Keep the Hall Light Burning	1959	20.00
❑ 55292	White Christmas/Jeannie with the Light Brown Hair	1960	25.00
❑ 55363	Ten Commandments of Love/Love at First Sight	1961	20.00

STATUS CYMBAL, THE

Number	Title (A Side/B Side)	Yr	NM
45s			
RCA VICTOR			
❑ 47-9344	Blang-Dang (Yesterday and Tomorrow)/Takin' My Time	1967	10.00
❑ 47-9419	In the Morning/Having Fun Again	1967	10.00
❑ 47-9598	From My Swing/With a Little Love	1968	10.00
Albums			
RCA VICTOR			
❑ LPM-3993 [M]	In the Morning	1968	40.00
❑ LSP-3993 [S]	In the Morning	1968	20.00

STATUS QUO

Number	Title (A Side/B Side)	Yr	NM
45s			
A&M			
❑ 1425	Don't Waste My TIme/All the Reasons	1973	5.00
❑ 1445	Paper Plane/All the Reasons	1973	5.00
❑ 1510	Carolina/Softer Ride	1974	5.00
BELL			
❑ 45417	Gerdundula/(B-side unknown)	1973	5.00
CADET CONCEPT			
❑ 7001	Pictures of Matchstick Men/Gentleman Joe's Sidewalk Café	1968	10.00
❑ 7006	Ice in the Sun/When My Mind Is Not Live	1968	8.00
❑ 7010	Technicolor Dreams/Spicks and Specks	1969	8.00
❑ 7015	Black Veils of Melancholy/To Be Free	1969	8.00
❑ 7017	The Price of Love/Little Miss Nothing	1969	8.00
CAPITOL			
❑ 4039	Nightride/Down Down	1975	4.00
❑ 4125	Bye Bye Johnny/Down Down	1975	4.00
❑ 4407	Wild Side of Life/All Through the Night	1977	4.00
JANUS			
❑ 127	Down the Dustpipe/Face Without a Soul	1970	6.00
❑ 141	Gerdundula/In My Chair	1970	6.00
PYE			
❑ 65000	Good Thinking/Tuned to the Music	1971	6.00
❑ 65017	Mean Girl/Everything	1971	6.00
RIVA			
❑ 206 [DJ]	Living on an Island/(B-side unknown)	1980	12.00
Albums			
A&M			
❑ SP-3615	Hello!	1974	12.00
❑ SP-3649	Quo	1974	12.00
❑ SP-4381	Piledriver	1973	12.00
CADET CONCEPT			
❑ LPS-315	Messages from the Status Quo	1968	50.00
CAPITOL			
❑ ST-11381	On the Level	1975	10.00
❑ ST-11509	Status Quo	1976	10.00
❑ SKBB-11623 [(2)]	Status Quo Live	1977	12.00
❑ ST-11749	Rockin' All Over the World	1978	10.00
JANUS			
❑ JLS-3018	Ma Kelly's Greasy Spoon	1970	22.00
MERCURY			
❑ 836651-1	Status Quo	1989	12.00
PYE			
❑ 3301	Dog of Two Head	1971	22.00
RIVA			
❑ 7402	Now Here This	1980	12.00

STEALERS WHEEL Also see GERRY RAFFERTY.

Number	Title (A Side/B Side)	Yr	NM
45s			
A&M			
❑ 1416	Stuck in the Middle with You/Jose	1973	5.00
❑ 1450	Everyone's Agreed That Everything Will Turn Out Fine/Next to Me	1973	4.00
❑ 1483	Star/What More Could You Want	1973	4.00
❑ 1483 [PS]	Star/What More Could You Want	1973	6.00
❑ 1529	You Put Something Better Inside of Me/Wheelin'	1974	4.00
❑ 1675	This Morning/Found My Way to You	1975	4.00
❑ 2075	(Everyone's Agreed That) Everything Will Turn Out Fine/Who Cares	1978	5.00
Albums			
A&M			
❑ SP-4377	Stealers Wheel	1973	12.00
❑ SP-4419	Ferguslie Park	1974	12.00
❑ SP-4517	Right or Wrong	1974	12.00
❑ SP-4708	Stuck in the Middle with You — The Best of Stealers Wheel	1978	10.00

STEAM

Number	Title (A Side/B Side)	Yr	NM
45s			
FONTANA			
❑ 1667	Na Na Hey Hey Kiss Him Goodbye/It's the Magic in You Girl	1969	8.00
MERCURY			
❑ 30160	Na Na Hey Hey Kiss Him Goodbye/Don't Stop Lovin' Me	1976	4.00
—Reissue			
❑ 30160 [PS]	Na Na Hey Hey Kiss Him Goodbye/Don't Stop Lovin' Me	1976	20.00
—Special Chicago White Sox sleeve, available only in that area			
❑ 73020	I've Gotta Make You Love Me/One Good Woman	1970	6.00
❑ 73053	What I'm Saying Is True/I'm the One Who Loves You	1970	6.00
❑ 73117	Don't Stop Lovin' Me/Do Unto Others	1970	6.00
Albums			
MERCURY			
❑ SR 61254	Steam	1969	20.00

STEAMHAMMER

Number	Title (A Side/B Side)	Yr	NM
Albums			
EPIC			
❑ BN 26490	Reflection	1969	30.00
❑ BN 26552	Steamhammer	1970	30.00

STEEL

Number	Title (A Side/B Side)	Yr	NM
45s			
EPIC			
❑ 5-10753	Never on a Monday/Rosie Lee	1971	8.00
Albums			
EPIC			
❑ E 30875	Steel	1971	20.00

STEELE, DON Former disc jockey known as "The Real Don Steele."

Number	Title (A Side/B Side)	Yr	NM
45s			
CAMEO			
❑ 399	Tina Delgado Is Alive/Hole in My Soul	1966	25.00
PATCHES			
❑ 102	Cecil, the Unwanted French Fry/(B-side unknown)	1969	20.00

STEELEYE SPAN

Number	Title (A Side/B Side)	Yr	NM
45s			
CHRYSALIS			
❑ 2008	Gaudete/Royal Forester	1972	6.00
❑ 2102	Gaudete/Royal Forester	1974	5.00
❑ 2262	Rag Doll/Hunting the Wren	1978	4.00
Albums			
BIG TREE			
❑ BTS 2004	Please to See the King	1971	30.00
CHRYSALIS			
❑ CHR 1008	Below the Salt	1972	15.00
—Green label, "3300 Warner Blvd." address			
❑ CHR 1008	Below the Salt	1977	12.00
—Blue label, New York address			
❑ CHR 1046	Parcel of Rogues	1973	15.00
—Green label, "3300 Warner Blvd." address			
❑ CHR 1046	Parcel of Rogues	1977	12.00
—Blue label, New York address			
❑ CHR 1053	Now We Are Six	1974	15.00
—Green label, "3300 Warner Blvd." address			
❑ CHR 1053	Now We Are Six	1977	12.00
—Blue label, New York address			
❑ CHR 1071	Commoners Crown	1975	15.00
—Green label, "3300 Warner Blvd." address			
❑ CHR 1071	Commoners Crown	1977	12.00
—Blue label, New York address			
❑ CHR 1091	All Around My Hat	1975	15.00
—Green label, "3300 Warner Blvd." address			
❑ CHR 1091	All Around My Hat	1977	12.00
—Blue label, New York address			
❑ CHR 1119	Please to See the King	1976	15.00
—Reissue of Big Tree LP; green label, "3300 Warner Blvd." address			
❑ CHR 1119	Please to See the King	1977	12.00
—Blue label, New York address			
❑ CHR 1120	Hark the Village Wait	1976	15.00
—First US issue of debut LP; green label, "3300 Warner Blvd." address			
❑ CHR 1120	Hark the Village Wait	1977	12.00
—Blue label, New York address			
❑ CHR 1121	Ten Man Mop	1976	15.00
—First US issue of third UK LP; green label, "3300 Warner Blvd." address			
❑ CHR 1121	Ten Man Mop	1977	12.00
—Blue label, New York address			
❑ CHR 1123	Rocket Cottage	1976	15.00
—Green label, "3300 Warner Blvd." address			
❑ CHR 1123	Rocket Cottage	1977	12.00
—Blue label, New York address			
❑ CHR2 1136 [(2)]	The Steeleye Span Story: Original Masters	1977	15.00
❑ CHR 1151	Storm Force Ten	1978	12.00
❑ CHR 1199	Live at Last	1978	12.00
❑ V2X 41136 [(2)]	The Steeleye Span Story: Original Masters	1984	12.00
—Reissue of 1136			
MOBILE FIDELITY			
❑ 1-027	All Around My Hat	1980	40.00
—Audiophile vinyl			
PAIR			
❑ CRPDL-2-1021 [(2)]	Dogs and Ferrets	1983	15.00
SHANACHIE			
❑ 64020	Tempted and Tried	1989	12.00
❑ 79039	Below the Salt	1989	12.00
❑ 79045	Parcel of Rogues	1989	12.00
❑ 79049	Ten Man Mop	1989	12.00
❑ 79052	Hark the Village Wait	1989	12.00
❑ 79059	All Around My Hat	1989	12.00
❑ 79060	Now We Are Six	1989	12.00
❑ 79063	Back in Line	1989	12.00
❑ 79071/2 [(2)]	Portfolio	1990	20.00
TAKOMA			
❑ TAK-7097	Sails of Silver	1981	10.00

STEELY DAN

Number	Title (A Side/B Side)	Yr	NM
12-Inch Singles			
ABC			
❑ SPDJ-26 [DJ]	Aja (same on both sides)	1977	20.00
❑ SPDJ-32 [DJ]	Deacon Blues (same on both sides)	1978	20.00
❑ SPDJ-36 [DJ]	Josie (same on both sides)	1978	20.00
❑ SPDJ-47 [DJ]	Here at the Western World (same on both sides)	1978	15.00
45s			
ABC			
❑ 11323	Dallas/Sail the Waterway	1972	30.00
—Neither of these songs has appeared on a U.S. Steely Dan album – not even the "complete" CD box set!			
❑ 11338	Do It Again/Fire in the Hole	1972	4.00
❑ 11352	Reeling In the Years/Only a Fool Would Say That	1973	4.00
—Later pressings have "abc" in a rainbow box			
❑ 11352	Reeling In the Years/Only a Fool Would Say That	1973	5.00
—Original pressings have "abc" children's blocks in a white triangle			
❑ 11382	Show Biz Kids/Razor Boy	1973	4.00
❑ 11396	My Old School/of the Quarter	1973	4.00
❑ 11439	Rikki Don't Lose That Number/Any Major Dude Will Tell You	1974	4.00
❑ 12014	Rikki Don't Lose That Number/Any Major Dude Will Tell You	1974	6.00
❑ 12033	Pretzel Logic/Through with Buzz	1974	4.00
❑ 12101	Black Friday/Throw Back the Little Ones	1975	4.00
❑ 12128	Chain Lightning/Bad Sneakers	1975	4.00
❑ 12195	Kid Charlemagne/Green Earrings	1976	4.00
❑ 12222	The Fez/Sign In Stranger	1976	4.00

S

Number	Title (A Side/B Side)	Yr	NM
❑ 12320	Peg/I Got the News	1977	4.00
❑ 12355	Deacon Blues/Home at Last	1978	4.00
❑ 12404	Josie/Black Cow	1978	4.00
MCA			
❑ 40894	FM (No Static at All)/ (Instrumental)	1978	4.00
❑ 51036	Hey Nineteen/Bodhisattva	1980	4.00
❑ 51082	Time Out of Mind/Bodhisattva	1981	4.00
7-Inch Extended Plays			
ABC			
❑ PRO-779	My Old School//Pearl of the Quarter/King of the World	1973	15.00
—Stereo jukebox issue; small hole, plays at 33 1/3 rpm			
❑ PRO-779 [PS]	Countdown to Ecstasy	1973	15.00
—Part of "Little LP" series (#225)			
❑ PRO-40015	With a Gun/Rikki Don't Lose That Number//Barrytown/ Pretzel Logic	1974	20.00
—Quadraphonic jukebox issue; small hole, plays at 33 1/3 rpm			
❑ PRO-40015 [PS]	Pretzel Logic	1974	20.00
—Part of "Little LP" series (#QD 255)			
Albums			
ABC			
❑ 758	Can't Buy a Thrill	1972	12.00
—Black label			
❑ 758	Can't Buy a Thrill	1974	10.00
—Multicolor label			
❑ 779	Countdown to Ecstasy	1973	12.00
—Black label			
❑ 779	Countdown to Ecstasy	1974	10.00
—Multicolor label			
❑ 806	Pretzel Logic	1974	10.00
—Multicolor label			
❑ 806	Pretzel Logic	1974	12.00
—Black label			
❑ 846	Katy Lied	1975	12.00
❑ 931	The Royal Scam	1976	12.00
❑ AA-1006	Aja	1977	12.00
❑ AK-1107 [(2)]	Greatest Hits	1978	15.00
ABC DUNHILL			
❑ SMAS-94976	Can't Buy a Thrill	1973	25.00
—Capitol Record Club edition pressed on the wrong label			
COMMAND			
❑ QD-40009 [Q]	Can't Buy a Thrill	1974	20.00
—Second issue with no border around the cover			
❑ QD-40009 [Q]	Can't Buy a Thrill	1974	25.00
—First issue with wide border around outside of cover			
❑ QD-40010 [Q]	Countdown to Ecstasy	1974	20.00
❑ QD-40015 [Q]	Pretzel Logic	1974	20.00
GEFFEN			
❑ MCA 1693	Gaucho	2008	20.00
MCA			
❑ AA-1006	Aja	1980	10.00
❑ 1591	Can't Buy a Thrill	1987	6.00
❑ 1592	Countdown to Ecstasy	1987	6.00
❑ 1593	Pretzel Logic	1987	6.00
❑ 1594	Katy Lied	1987	6.00
❑ 1595	The Royal Scam	1987	6.00
❑ 1688	Aja	1987	6.00
❑ 1693	Gaucho	1987	6.00
—Many in the 1500 and 1600 series have a gold stamp with the new number on the cover			
❑ 5324	Gold	1982	10.00
❑ 2-6008 [(2)]	Greatest Hits	1980	12.00
❑ 6102	Gaucho	1980	10.00
❑ 16009	Gaucho	1981	50.00
—Audiophile pressing			
❑ 16016	Gold	1982	50.00
—Audiophile pressing			
❑ 37040	Can't Buy a Thrill	1980	8.00
❑ 37041	Countdown to Ecstasy	1980	8.00
❑ 37042	Pretzel Logic	1980	8.00
❑ 37043	Katy Lied	1980	8.00
❑ 37044	The Royal Scam	1980	8.00
❑ 37243	Gold	1984	8.00
MOBILE FIDELITY			
❑ 1-007	Katy Lied	1979	80.00
—Audiophile vinyl			
❑ 1-033	Aja	1980	50.00
—Audiophile vinyl			

STEIN, FRANK N., AND THE TOMBSTONES

Number	Title (A Side/B Side)	Yr	NM
45s			
MARCO			
❑ 003	Mess Around/Graveyard Giggle	1962	40.00

STEIN, FRANKIE, AND THE GHOULS

Number	Title (A Side/B Side)	Yr	NM
45s			
KING			
❑ 6414	Franken Boogie/All She Wants to Do Is Boogie	1972	10.00
POWER			
❑ 338	Goon River/Weerdo the Wolf	1964	25.00
❑ 338 [PS]	Goon River/Weerdo the Wolf	1964	30.00

STEIN, LOU

Number	Title (A Side/B Side)	Yr	NM
45s			
BRUNSWICK			
❑ 9-80229	Poinciana/Tenderly	1952	15.00
EPIC			
❑ 5-9134	Butterfly Cha-Cha-Cha/ Lou's Tune	1955	15.00
❑ 5-9156	The Phonograph Song/There'll Be Some Changes Made	1956	15.00
MERCURY			
❑ 71328	Got a Match?/Who Slammed the Door	1958	10.00
❑ 71368	I'm Looking Over a Four Leaf Clover/I'll Be With You in Apple Blossom Time	1958	10.00
MURBO			
❑ 1033	That Old Time Flavour/ Winds of Change	1969	8.00
RKO UNIQUE			
❑ 385	Almost Paradise/Soft Sands	1957	12.00
❑ 403	The Little Spinet/Song of the East	1957	12.00
7-Inch Extended Plays			
EPIC			
❑ EG 7078	(contents unknown)	195?	10.00
❑ EG 7078 [PS]	House Hop	195?	10.00
Albums			
AUDIOPHILE			
❑ AP-198	Solo Piano	1984	10.00
BRUNSWICK			
❑ BL 58053 [10]	Lou Stein	1953	50.00
CHIAROSCURO			
❑ 140	Tribute to Tatum	197?	12.00
❑ CR-2027	Temple of the Gods	1979	15.00
CORAL			
❑ CRL 57003 [M]	Sweet and Lovely	195?	25.00
❑ CRL 57201 [M]	Sing Around the Piano	1958	20.00
DREAMSTREET			
❑ DR-106	Lou Stein Trio Live at the Dome	1986	10.00
EPIC			
❑ LG 3101 [M]	House Top	1955	40.00
❑ LN 3148 [M]	Three, Four and Five	1955	40.00
❑ LN 3186 [M]	From Broadway to Paris	1955	40.00
JUBILEE			
❑ JLP-8 [10]	Six for Kicks	1954	50.00
❑ JLP-1019 [M]	Eight for Kicks, Four for Laughs	1956	40.00
MASTERSEAL			
❑ MS33-1812 [M]	Mood Music for Beer and Pretzels	1957	15.00
MERCURY			
❑ MG-20159 [M]	Honky Tonk Piano	195?	20.00
❑ MG-20271 [M]	Saloon Favorites	195?	15.00
❑ MG-20364 [M]	Honky Tonk Piano	195?	15.00
❑ MG-20469 [M]	Honky Tonk Piano and a Hot Banjo	1960	12.00
❑ SR-60054 [S]	Honky Tonk Piano	1959	20.00
❑ SR-60151 [S]	Honky Tonk Piano and a Hot Banjo	1960	15.00
MUSICOR			
❑ MM-2057 [M]	Hey Louie! Play Melancholy Baby!	1967	15.00
❑ MS-3057 [S]	Hey Louie! Play Melancholy Baby!	1967	12.00
WING			
❑ MGW-12219 [M]	The Lou Stein-Way of Piano Pleasure	196?	12.00
❑ SRW-16219 [S]	The Lou Stein-Way of Piano Pleasure	196?	15.00
WORLD JAZZ			
❑ WJLPS-17	Lou Stein and Friends	1980	12.00

STEINBERG, DAVID

Number	Title (A Side/B Side)	Yr	NM
45s			
COLUMBIA			
❑ 46075	The Nixon Tapes/The Exam	1974	5.00
Albums			
COLUMBIA			
❑ KC 32563	Booga Booga	1974	10.00
❑ PC 33390	Goodbye to the Seventies	1975	10.00
ELEKTRA			
❑ EKS-74063	Disguised as a Normal Person	1970	12.00
UNI			
❑ 73013	The Incredible Shrinking God	1968	15.00

STEPHENS, LEIGH

BLUE CHEER guitarist.

Number	Title (A Side/B Side)	Yr	NM
45s			
PHILIPS			
❑ 40628	Red Weather/Saki Swadoo	1969	12.00
Albums			
PHILIPS			
❑ PHS 600294	Red Weather	1969	80.00

STEPPENWOLF

Also see JOHN KAY; SPARROW.

Number	Title (A Side/B Side)	Yr	NM
45s			
ABC			
❑ 1436	The Pusher/Born to Be Wild	1970	4.00
—"Goldies 45" series			
❑ 1436 [PS]	The Pusher/Born to Be Wild	1970	6.00
ABC DUNHILL			
❑ 4138	Born to Be Wild/ Everybody's Next One	1968	8.00
❑ 4161	Magic Carpet Ride/ Sookie Sookie	1968	8.00
❑ 4182	Rock Me/Jupiter Child	1969	8.00
❑ 4192	It's Never Too Late/ Happy Birthday	1969	6.00
❑ 4205	Move Over/Power Play	1969	6.00
❑ 4221	Monster/Berry Rides Again	1969	6.00
❑ 4234	Hey Lawdy Mama/Twisted	1970	6.00
❑ 4248	Screaming Night Hog/ Spiritual Fantasy	1970	6.00
❑ 4261	Who Needs Ya/ Earschplittenloudenboomer	1970	6.00
❑ 4269	Snow Blind Friend/Hippo Stomp	1971	5.00
❑ 4283	Ride with Me/For Madmen Only	1971	5.00
❑ 4283	Ride with Me/Black Pit	1971	40.00
—This is much rarer than the version with the other flip side			
❑ 4283 [PS]	Ride with Me/For Madmen Only	1971	6.00
❑ 4292	For Ladies Only/Sparkle Eyes	1971	5.00
ALLEGIANCE			
❑ 3909	Hot Night in a Cold Town/Every Man for Himself	1983	4.00
—As "John Kay and Steppenwolf"			
DUNHILL			
❑ 4109	The Ostrich/A Girl I Know	1967	10.00
❑ 4123	Sookie Sookie/ Take What You Need	1968	10.00
MUMS			
❑ 6031	Straight Shootin' Woman/ Justice, Don't Be Slow	1974	4.00
❑ 6031 [PS]	Straight Shootin' Woman/ Justice, Don't Be Slow	1974	6.00
❑ 6034	Get Into the Wind/Morning Blue	1974	4.00
❑ 6036	Fool's Fantasy/Smokey Factory Blues	1975	4.00
❑ 6040	Caroline (Are You Ready for the Outlaw)/Angel Drawers	1975	4.00
Albums			
ABC			
❑ AC-30008	The ABC Collection	1976	15.00
ABC DUNHILL			
❑ DS-50029 [S]	Steppenwolf	1968	20.00
❑ DS-50037	The Second	1968	25.00
—With chrome border on cover			
❑ DS-50037	The Second	1968	30.00
—With white border on cover			
❑ DSX-50053	At Your Birthday Party	1969	20.00
❑ DS-50060	Early Steppenwolf	1969	20.00
—Actually a 1967 concert by Sparrow (pre-Steppenwolf)			
❑ DS-50066	Monster	1969	20.00
❑ DSD-50075 [(2)]	Steppenwolf 'Live'	1970	25.00
❑ DSX-50090	Steppenwolf 7	1970	20.00
❑ DSX-50099	Steppenwolf Gold/ Their Great Hits	1971	20.00
❑ DSX-50110	For Ladies Only	1971	20.00
❑ DSX-50124	Rest in Peace	1972	20.00
❑ DSX-50135	16 Greatest Hits	1973	20.00
DUNHILL			
❑ D-50029 [M]	Steppenwolf	1968	150.00
❑ DS-50029 [S]	Steppenwolf	1968	40.00
❑ ST-91487	Steppenwolf	1968	25.00
—Capitol Record Club edition			
❑ SKAO-93083	Monster	1969	25.00
—Capitol Record Club edition on old-style Dunhill label			
EPIC			
❑ PE 33583	Hour of the Wolf	1975	12.00
❑ PE 34120	Skullduggery	1976	12.00
❑ JE 34382	Reborn to Be Wild	1977	12.00
MCA			
❑ 1599	16 Greatest Hits	198?	8.00
—Reissue of 37049			
❑ 2-6013 [(2)]	Steppenwolf 'Live'	198?	10.00
❑ 37045	Steppenwolf	1979	8.00
❑ 37046	The Second	1979	8.00
❑ 37047	Steppenwolf 7	1979	8.00

S

Number	Title (A Side/B Side)	Yr	NM
❑ 37049	16 Greatest Hits	1979	8.00
❑ DSX-50099	Steppenwolf Gold/ Their Great Hits	1980	12.00
—Columbia House edition on blue rainbow label, but retaining the original ABC Dunhill catalog number			
MUMS			
❑ PZ 33093	Slow Flux	1974	15.00
NAUTILUS			
❑ NR-53	Wolftracks	198?	50.00
—As "John Kay and Steppenwolf"; audiophile vinyl			
PICKWICK			
❑ SPC-3603	Best of Steppenwolf	1978	10.00

STEVE & EYDIE See STEVE LAWRENCE AND EYDIE GORME.

STEVENS, CAT

Number	Title (A Side/B Side)	Yr	NM
12-Inch Singles			
A&M			
❑ 8440 [DJ]	Was Dog a Doughnut (Remix) (same on both sides)	1977	15.00
45s			
A&M			
❑ 1211	Lady D'Arbanville/Time — Fill My Eyes	1970	5.00
❑ 1231	Wild World/Miles from Nowhere	1970	5.00
❑ 1265	Moon Shadow/I Think I See the Light	1971	4.00
❑ 1265 [PS]	Moon Shadow/I Think I See the Light	1971	6.00
❑ 1291	Peace Train/Where Do the Children Play	1971	4.00
❑ 1291 [PS]	Peace Train/Where Do the Children Play	1971	6.00
❑ 1335	Morning Has Broken/ I Want to Live in a Wigwam	1972	4.00
❑ 1335 [PS]	Morning Has Broken/ I Want to Live in a Wigwam	1972	6.00
❑ 1396	Sitting/Crab Dance	1972	4.00
❑ 1396 [PS]	Sitting/Crab Dance	1972	6.00
❑ 1418	The Hurt/Silent Sunlight	1973	4.00
❑ 1418 [PS]	The Hurt/Silent Sunlight	1973	6.00
❑ 1503	Oh Very Young/100 I Dream	1974	4.00
❑ 1503 [PS]	Oh Very Young/100 I Dream	1974	6.00
❑ 1549	Another Saturday Night/ Home in the Sky	1974	—
—Unreleased?			
❑ 1602	Another Saturday Night/ Home in the Sky	1974	4.00
❑ 1602 [PS]	Another Saturday Night/ Home in the Sky	1974	6.00
❑ 1645	Ready/I Think I See the Light	1974	4.00
❑ 1700	Two Fine People/Bad Penny	1975	4.00
❑ 1785	Banapple Gas/Ghost Town	1976	4.00
❑ 1785 [PS]	Banapple Gas/Ghost Town	1976	12.00
❑ 1924	(I Never Wanted) To Be a Star/ Land O' Freelove and Goodbye	1977	4.00
❑ 1948	(Remember the Days of the) Old School Yard/Land O' Freelove and Goodbye	1977	4.00
❑ 1948 [PS]	(Remember the Days of the) Old School Yard/Land O' Freelove and Goodbye	1977	6.00
❑ 1971	Was Dog a Doughnut/ Sweet Jamaica	1977	4.00
❑ 2109	Bad Brakes/Nascimento	1979	4.00
❑ 2126	Randy/Nascimento	1979	4.00
❑ 2683	If You Want to Sing Out, Sing Out/ I Want to Live in a Wigwam	1984	4.00
❑ 2711 [DJ]	Father and Son (same on both sides)	1985	10.00
—No stock copies issued			
DERAM			
❑ 7501	I Love My Dog/Portobello Road	1966	10.00
❑ 7505	Matthew and Son/Granny	1967	10.00
❑ 7518	Kitty/The Blackness of the Night	1968	8.00
❑ 85006	I'm Gonna Get Me a Gun/ School Is Out	1967	10.00
❑ 85015	Laughing Apple/Bad Night	1967	10.00
❑ 85079	Kitty/Where Are You	1972	6.00
7-Inch Extended Plays			
A&M			
❑ LLP-4391	Foreigner Suite (Part 1)/(Part 2)	1973	8.00
—Jukebox issue; small hole, plays at 33 1/3 rpm			
❑ LLP-4391 [PS]	Foreigner	1973	8.00
—Part of "Little LP" series (LLP #227)			
Albums			
A&M			
❑ SP-3160	Mona Bone Jakon	198?	8.00
—Reissue of 4260			
❑ SP-3285	Footsteps in the Dark — Greatest Hits, Vol. Two	1986	8.00
—Reissue of 3736			
❑ SP-3623	Buddha and the Chocolate Box	1974	12.00
❑ SP-3736	Footsteps in the Dark — Greatest Hits, Vol. Two	1984	10.00
❑ SP-4260	Mona Bone Jakon	1970	12.00
—Brown label			
❑ SP-4260	Mona Bone Jakon	1974	10.00
—Mostly silver label with gradually fading "A&M"			
❑ SP-4280	Tea for the Tillerman	1971	12.00
—Brown label			
❑ SP-4280	Tea for the Tillerman	1974	10.00
—Mostly silver label with gradually fading "A&M"			
❑ SP-4313	Teaser and the Firecat	1971	12.00
—Brown label			
❑ SP-4313	Teaser and the Firecat	1974	10.00
—Mostly silver label with gradually fading "A&M"			
❑ SP-4365	Catch Bull at Four	1972	12.00
❑ SP-4391	Foreigner	1973	12.00
❑ SP-4519	Greatest Hits	1975	12.00
❑ SP-4555	Numbers	1975	12.00
❑ SP-4702	Izitso	1977	12.00
❑ SP-4735	Back to Earth	1978	12.00
❑ QU-53623 [Q]	Buddha and the Chocolate Box	1974	20.00
❑ QU-54280 [Q]	Tea for the Tillerman	1974	—
—Not released			
❑ QU-54313 [Q]	Teaser and the Firecat	1974	—
—Not released			
❑ QU-54365 [Q]	Catch Bull at Four	1974	—
—Not released			
❑ QU-54391 [Q]	Foreigner	1974	20.00
❑ QU-54519 [Q]	Greatest Hits	1975	20.00
DERAM			
❑ DE 16005 [M]	Matthew and Son	1967	20.00
❑ DES 18005 [P]	Matthew and Son	1967	15.00
❑ DES 18005/10 [(2)P]	Matthew and Son/New Masters	1971	15.00
❑ DES 18010 [S]	New Masters	1968	15.00
❑ DES 18061 [P]	Very Young and Early Songs	1972	12.00
LONDON			
❑ LC-50010	Cat's Cradle	1977	12.00
❑ 820321-1	Cat's Cradle	1985	8.00
MOBILE FIDELITY			
❑ 1-035	Tea for the Tillerman	1979	40.00
—Audiophile vinyl			
❑ MFQR-035	Tea for the Tillerman	1984	120.00
—Ultra High Quality Recording in a box			
❑ 1-244	Teaser and the Firecat	1996	40.00
—Audiophile vinyl			
❑ 1-254	Izitso	1996	25.00
—Audiophile vinyl			

STEVENS, CONNIE

Also see EDD BYRNES.

Number	Title (A Side/B Side)	Yr	NM
45s			
BELL			
❑ 866	She'll Never Understand Him/ 5:30 Plane	1970	5.00
❑ 922	Keep Growing Strong/Tick-Tock	1970	5.00
❑ 992	Keep Growing Strong/ (B-side unknown)	1971	5.00
❑ 45234	Simple Girl/(B-side unknown)	1972	5.00
MGM			
❑ 13906	Cinderella Could Have Saved Us All/Wouldn't It Be Nice (To Have Wings and Fly)	1968	6.00
WARNER BROS.			
❑ 5092	Apollo/Why Do I Cry for Joey	1959	20.00
❑ 5137	Sixteen Reasons/Little Sister	1960	12.00
—Second pressing has red label with arrows			
❑ 5137	Sixteen Reasons/Little Sister	1960	15.00
—First pressing has pink labels			
❑ 5159	Too Young to Go Steady/ A Little Kiss Is a Kiss Is a Kiss	1960	12.00
❑ 5159 [PS]	Too Young to Go Steady/ A Little Kiss Is a Kiss Is a Kiss	1960	30.00
❑ 5217	Make Believe Lover/ And This Is Mine	1961	12.00
❑ 5232	If You Don't, Somebody Else Will/Greenwood Tree	1961	12.00
❑ 5265	Why'd You Wanna Make Me Cry/Just One Kiss	1962	12.00
❑ 5289	Mr. Songwriter/I Couldn't Say No	1962	12.00
❑ 5318	Hey, Good Lookin'/ Nobody's Lonesome for Me	1962	12.00
❑ 5380	Little Miss Understood/ There Goes Your Guy	1963	10.00
❑ 5425	A Girl Never Knows/ They're Jealous of Me	1964	10.00
❑ 5610	Now That You've Gone/ Lost in Wonderland	1965	12.00
❑ 5656	In the Deep of Night/ Something Beautiful	1965	10.00
❑ 5691	Don't You Want to Love Me/ In My Room (El Amor)	1966	10.00
❑ 5804	All of My Life/That's All I Want from You	1966	10.00
❑ 5834	How Bitter the Taste of Love/ Most of All	1966	10.00
❑ 5872	It'll Never Happen Again/ What Will I Tell Him	1966	10.00
❑ 7128	Sixteen Reasons/ Make Believe Lover	1968	5.00
—"Back to Back Hits" series — originals have green labels with "W7" logo			
Albums			
HARMONY			
❑ HS 11312	The Hank Williams Songbook	1969	15.00
WARNER BROS.			
❑ W 1208 [M]	Conchetta	1958	50.00
❑ WS 1208 [S]	Conchetta	1958	60.00
❑ W 1382 [M]	Connie Stevens from "Hawaiian Eye"	1960	30.00
❑ WS 1382 [S]	Connie Stevens from "Hawaiian Eye"	1960	40.00
❑ W 1431 [M]	From Me to You	1962	30.00
❑ WS 1431 [S]	From Me to You	1962	40.00
❑ W 1432 [M]	Connie	1962	30.00
❑ WS 1432 [S]	Connie	1962	40.00
❑ W 1460 [M]	The Hank Williams Songbook	1962	30.00
❑ WS 1460 [S]	The Hank Williams Songbook	1962	40.00

STEVENS, DEBBIE

Number	Title (A Side/B Side)	Yr	NM
45s			
ABC-PARAMOUNT			
❑ 10034	Billy Boy's Theme/I Sit and Cry	1959	15.00
APT			
❑ 25027	If You Can't Rock Me/ What Will I Tell My Heart	1959	25.00

STEVENS, DODIE

Number	Title (A Side/B Side)	Yr	NM
45s			
CRYSTALETTE			
❑ 724	Pink Shoe Laces/Coming of Age	1959	20.00
❑ 728	Yes-Sir-Ee/The Five Pennies	1959	20.00
DOLTON			
❑ 83	You Don't Have to Prove a Thing to Me/I Wore Out Our Record	1963	12.00
❑ 88	Sailor Boy/Does Goodnight Mean Goodbye	1964	12.00
DOT			
❑ 15975	Miss Lonely Heart/Poor Butterfly	1959	20.00
❑ 16002	Steady Date/Mairzy Doats	1959	20.00
❑ 16067	Candy Store Blues/ Gringo's Guitar	1960	15.00
❑ 16103	No/A Tisket, A Tasket	1960	15.00
❑ 16139	Am I Too Young/So Let's Dance	1960	15.00
❑ 16166	Merry Christmas Baby/ Jingle Bells	1960	20.00
❑ 16167	Yes, I'm Lonesome Tonight/ Too Young	1960	20.00
❑ 16200	I Fall to Pieces/Turn Around	1961	15.00
❑ 16259	Let Me Tell You About Johnny/ You Are the Only One	1961	15.00
❑ 16279	The In-Between Years/ Trade Winds	1961	15.00
❑ 16339	I Cried/Dancing on My Ceiling	1962	15.00
❑ 16389	Pink Shoelaces/Yes-Sir-Ee	1962	15.00
IMPERIAL			
❑ 5908	Don't Send Me No Roses/Daddy Could Get Me One of These	1963	15.00
❑ 5930	Hello Stranger/For a Little While	1963	15.00
Albums			
DOT			
❑ DLP-3212 [M]	Dodie Stevens	1960	30.00
❑ DLP-3323 [M]	Over the Rainbow	1960	30.00
❑ DLP-3371 [M]	Pink Shoelaces	1961	30.00
❑ DLP-25212 [S]	Dodie Stevens	1960	40.00
❑ DLP-25323 [S]	Over the Rainbow	1960	40.00
❑ DLP-25371 [S]	Pink Shoelaces	1961	40.00

STEVENS, JOHNNY

Number	Title (A Side/B Side)	Yr	NM
45s			
FORD			
❑ 123	Oh Yeah/Last Chicken in the Shack	1963	30.00
PARKWAY			
❑ 805	Apple Taffy/Mm, Baby, Mm	1959	25.00

STEVENS, MARK, AND THE CHARMERS

Number	Title (A Side/B Side)	Yr	NM
45s			
ALLISON			
❑ 921	Magic Rose/Come Back to My Heart	1962	60.00

STEVENS, NEIL

Number	Title (A Side/B Side)	Yr	NM
45s			
BRUNSWICK			
❑ 55095	More and More/ What Could Be Better	1958	30.00
—With the Dee-Vines			

S

Except when noted otherwise, VG = 25% of NM, and VG+ = 50% of NM. (Example: VG = $2.00, VG+ = $4.00 and NM = $8.00.)

GOLDISC

Number	Title (A Side/B Side)	Yr	NM
❑ 3019	Ballad of Love/Tonight My Heart She Is Crying	1961	20.00
—With the Temptations			

GONE

Number	Title (A Side/B Side)	Yr	NM
❑ 5067	Ballad of Love/Gambler's Game	1959	50.00

STEVENS, TARI

45s

FAIRMOUNT

Number	Title (A Side/B Side)	Yr	NM
❑ 1001	(Your Love Was Just a) False Alarm/Bad Boy	1966	150.00
—Counterfeits exist; they are on all-green labels			

STEVENS, TERRI

45s

RCA VICTOR

Number	Title (A Side/B Side)	Yr	NM
❑ 47-6165	Why Am I to Blame/What Am I Trying to Forget	1955	20.00
❑ 47-6300	All I Want Is You/I've Always Loved You	1955	20.00
❑ 47-6393	Dood-ly Dood-ly/I'll Come When You Call	1956	20.00
❑ 47-6633	Sweet World/That's How I Cried Over You	1956	20.00
❑ 47-7014	Pick-Up Girl/Untouched Heart	1957	20.00

STEVENSON, B.W.

45s

MCA

Number	Title (A Side/B Side)	Yr	NM
❑ 41151	A Special Wish/Holding a Special Place for You	1979	4.00
❑ 41166	Headin' Home/Holding a Special Place for You	1980	4.00

PRIVATE STOCK

Number	Title (A Side/B Side)	Yr	NM
❑ 45,208	Holdin' On for Dear Love/I'm a Better Man for Lovin' You	1979	4.00

RCA VICTOR

Number	Title (A Side/B Side)	Yr	NM
❑ 47-0728	Say What I Feel/Lonesome Song	1972	5.00
❑ 47-0778	On My Own/Highway One	1972	5.00
❑ 47-0840	Minuet for My Lady/Don't Go to Mexico	1972	5.00
❑ 47-0952	Shambala/My Feet Are So Weary	1973	6.00
❑ APBO-0030	My Maria/August Evening Lady	1973	6.00
❑ APBO-0171	River of Love/Lucky Touch	1973	5.00
❑ APBO-0242	Song for Katy/Look for the Light	1974	4.00
❑ APBO-0279	Remember Me/Roll On	1974	4.00
❑ PB-10012	Here We Go Again/Little Bit of Understanding	1974	4.00
❑ GB-10158	My Maria/Shambala	1975	3.00
—Gold Standard Series			

WARNER BROS.

Number	Title (A Side/B Side)	Yr	NM
❑ 8184	Jerrry's Bar and Grill/Way Down by the Ocean	1976	4.00
❑ 8247	Dream Baby/Wastin' Time	1976	4.00
❑ 8343	Down to the Station/May You Find Yourself in Heaven	1977	4.00

Albums

MCA

Number	Title (A Side/B Side)	Yr	NM
❑ 3215	Lifeline	1980	10.00

RCA VICTOR

Number	Title (A Side/B Side)	Yr	NM
❑ APL1-0088	My Maria	1973	12.00
❑ APD1-0410 [Q]	Calabasas	1974	20.00
❑ APL1-0410	Calabasas	1974	12.00
❑ APL1-2394	The Best of B.W. Stevenson	1977	10.00
❑ LSP-4685	B.W. Stevenson	1972	15.00
❑ LSP-4794	Lead Free	1972	15.00

WARNER BROS.

Number	Title (A Side/B Side)	Yr	NM
❑ BS 2901	We Be Sailin'	1976	10.00
❑ BS 3012	Lost	1977	10.00

STEWART, AL

45s

ARISTA

Number	Title (A Side/B Side)	Yr	NM
❑ 0362	Time Passages/Almost Lucy	1978	4.00
❑ 0389	Song on the Radio/A Man for All Seasons	1979	4.00
❑ 0552	Midnight Rocks/Constantinople	1980	4.00
❑ 0576	Paint by Numbers/Optical Illusion	1980	4.00
❑ 0585	Running Man/Merlin's Theme	1981	4.00
❑ 0639	Indian Summer/Soko (Needless to Say)	1981	4.00

JANUS

Number	Title (A Side/B Side)	Yr	NM
❑ 243	Nostradamus/Terminal Eyes	1974	5.00
❑ 250	Carol/Sirens of Titan	1975	5.00
❑ 266	Year of the Cat/Broadway Hotel	1976	5.00
❑ 267	On the Border/Flying Sorcery	1977	5.00

Albums

ARISTA

Number	Title (A Side/B Side)	Yr	NM
❑ AL 4190	Time Passages	1978	10.00
❑ AL6-8326	Year of the Cat	198?	8.00
—Reissue of Arista 9503			
❑ AL6-8342	Time Passages	198?	8.00
—Reissue of 4190			
❑ AL6-8359	Past, Present and Future	198?	8.00
—Reissue of Arista 9524			
❑ A2L 8607 [(2)]	Live/Indian Summer	1981	12.00
❑ AL 9503	Year of the Cat	1979	10.00
—Reissue of Janus 7022			
❑ AL 9520	24 Carrots	1980	10.00
❑ AL 9524	Past, Present and Future	1980	10.00
—Reissue of Janus 3063			
❑ AL 9525	Modern Times	1980	10.00
—Reissue of Janus 7012			

ENIGMA

Number	Title (A Side/B Side)	Yr	NM
❑ D1-73316	Last Days of the Century	1988	12.00

EPIC

Number	Title (A Side/B Side)	Yr	NM
❑ BN 26564	Love Chronicles	1970	20.00

JANUS

Number	Title (A Side/B Side)	Yr	NM
❑ 3063	Past, Present and Future	1974	15.00
❑ 7012	Modern Times	1975	12.00
❑ 7022	Year of the Cat	1976	12.00
❑ 7026 [(2)]	The Early Years	1977	15.00
❑ 7026 [DJ]	The Early Years	1977	30.00
—Promo-only condensation of 2-LP set with rubber-stamp cover			

MOBILE FIDELITY

Number	Title (A Side/B Side)	Yr	NM
❑ 1-009	Year of the Cat	1979	40.00
—Audiophile vinyl			
❑ 1-082	Time Passages	1981	30.00
—Audiophile vinyl			

NAUTILUS

Number	Title (A Side/B Side)	Yr	NM
❑ NR-34	24 Carrots	198?	30.00
—Audiophile vinyl			

PASSPORT

Number	Title (A Side/B Side)	Yr	NM
❑ PB-6042	Russians and Americans	1986	12.00

STEWART, BILLY

45s

ARGO

Number	Title (A Side/B Side)	Yr	NM
❑ 5256	Billy's Blues (Part 1)/Billy's Blues (Part 2)	1956	40.00

CHESS

Number	Title (A Side/B Side)	Yr	NM
❑ 1625	Billy's Blues (Part 1)/Billy's Blues (Part 2)	1956	60.00
❑ 1820	Reap What You Sow/Fat Boy	1962	12.00
❑ 1835	True Fine Lovin'/Wedding Bells	1962	12.00
❑ 1852	Scramble/Oh What Can the Matter Be	1963	12.00
❑ 1868	Strange Feeling/Sugar and Spice	1963	12.00
❑ 1888	Count Me Out/A Fat Boy Can Cry	1964	10.00
❑ 1905	Tell It Like It Is/My Sweet Senorita	1964	10.00
❑ 1922	I Do Love You/Keep Loving	1965	10.00
❑ 1932	Sitting in the Park/Once Again	1965	10.00
❑ 1941	How Nice It Is/No Girl	1965	10.00
❑ 1948	Because I Love You/Mountain of Love	1965	10.00
❑ 1960	Love Me/Why Am I Lonely	1966	10.00
❑ 1966	Summertime/To Love, To Love	1966	12.00
—Blueish label			
❑ 1966	Summertime/To Love, To Love	1966	15.00
—Black label			
❑ 1978	Secret Love/Look Back and Smile	1966	10.00
❑ 1991	Every Day I Have the Blues/Ol' Man River	1967	10.00
❑ 2002	Cross My Heart/Why (Do I Love You So)	1967	10.00
❑ 2053	Tell Me the Truth/What Have I Done	1968	10.00
❑ 2063	I'm in Love (Oh Yes I Am)/Crazy 'Bout You Baby	1969	10.00
❑ 2080	By the Time I Get to Phoenix/We'll Always Be Together	1969	10.00

OKEH

Number	Title (A Side/B Side)	Yr	NM
❑ 7095	Baby, You're My Only Love/Billy's Heartache	1957	300.00

UNITED ARTISTS

Number	Title (A Side/B Side)	Yr	NM
❑ 340	This Is a Fine Time/Young in Years	1961	15.00

Albums

CHESS

Number	Title (A Side/B Side)	Yr	NM
❑ LP-1496 [M]	I Do Love You	196?	30.00
—Green "woman" cover			
❑ LP-1496 [M]	I Do Love You	1965	80.00
—Red cover, black "wheel"			
❑ LPS-1496 [S]	I Do Love You	196?	40.00
—Green "woman" cover			
❑ LPS-1496 [S]	I Do Love You	1965	100.00
—Red cover, black "wheel"			
❑ LP-1499 [M]	Unbelievable	1966	30.00
❑ LPS-1499 [S]	Unbelievable	1966	40.00
❑ LP-1513 [M]	Billy Stewart Teaches Old Standards New Tricks	1967	30.00
❑ LPS-1513 [S]	Billy Stewart Teaches Old Standards New Tricks	1967	40.00
❑ LPS-1547	Billy Stewart Remembered	1970	25.00
❑ CH-9104	The Greatest Sides	198?	10.00
❑ CH-50059	Cross My Heart	1974	15.00

STEWART, DANNY See SLY STEWART.

STEWART, JOHN Also see THE KINGSTON TRIO.

45s

ALLEGIANCE

Number	Title (A Side/B Side)	Yr	NM
❑ 3900	The Queen of Hollywood High/Judy in G Major	198?	4.00

CAPITOL

Number	Title (A Side/B Side)	Yr	NM
❑ 2469	Mother Country/Shackles and Chains	1969	6.00
❑ 2538	July, You're a Woman/She Believes in Me	1969	6.00
❑ 2605	Armstrong/Anna on a Memory	1969	6.00
❑ 2711	Earth Rider/The Lady and the Outlaw	1969	6.00
❑ 2712	World of No Return/Wild Is Love	1969	8.00
—B-side by Patti Drew			
❑ 2842	Clack Clack/Marshall Wind	1970	6.00

RCA VICTOR

Number	Title (A Side/B Side)	Yr	NM
❑ 74-0970	Chilly Winds/Durango	1973	5.00
❑ APBO-0109	Anna on a Memory/Wheatfield	1973	5.00
❑ PB-10003	July, You're a Woman/Runaway Fool of Love	1974	5.00
❑ PB-10227	Survivors/Josie	1975	5.00
❑ PB-10268	Survivors/Josie	1975	5.00

RSO

Number	Title (A Side/B Side)	Yr	NM
❑ 894	Promise the Wind/Morning Thunder	1978	4.00
❑ 931	Gold/Comin' Out of Nowhere	1979	4.00
❑ 1000	Midnight Wind/Somewhere Down the Line	1979	4.00
❑ 1016	Lost Her in the Sun/Heart of the Dream	1979	4.00
❑ 1031	(Odin) Spirit of the Water/Love Has Tied My Wings	1980	4.00

VITA

Number	Title (A Side/B Side)	Yr	NM
❑ 169	Rockin' Anna/Lorraine	1958	250.00
—As "Johnny Stewart"			

WARNER BROS.

Number	Title (A Side/B Side)	Yr	NM
❑ PRO504 [PS]	The Bad Old Daysr/Just an Old Love Song	1971	15.00
—Promo only			
❑ 7525	Daydream Believer/Sweet Lizard	1971	5.00
❑ 7552	Light Come Shine/A Little Road and a Stone to Roll	1972	5.00
❑ 7592	An Accent of Halley's Comet/Arkansas Breakout	1972	5.00

Albums

AFFORDABLE DREAMS

Number	Title (A Side/B Side)	Yr	NM
❑ AD-01	Trancas	1984	10.00

ALLEGIANCE

Number	Title (A Side/B Side)	Yr	NM
❑ AV-431	Blondes	1982	10.00

CAPITOL

Number	Title (A Side/B Side)	Yr	NM
❑ ST-203	California Bloodlines	1969	15.00
❑ ST-540	Willard	1970	15.00
❑ SM-2975	Signals Through the Glass	1977	10.00
—Reissue with new prefix			
❑ ST 2975	Signals Through the Glass	1968	20.00
❑ SN-16150	California Bloodlines	198?	8.00
—Budget-line reissue			
❑ SN-16151	Willard	198?	8.00
—Budget-line reissue			

CYPRESS

Number	Title (A Side/B Side)	Yr	NM
❑ 661117-1	Punch the Big Guy	1987	10.00

HOMECOMING

Number	Title (A Side/B Side)	Yr	NM
❑ HC-0200	Centennial	1984	10.00
❑ HC-0300	The Last Campaign	1985	10.00
❑ HC-0500	The Trio Years	1986	10.00

RCA VICTOR

Number	Title (A Side/B Side)	Yr	NM
❑ CPL2-0265 [(2)]	The Phoenix Concerts — Live	1974	15.00
❑ APL1-0816	Wingless Angels	1975	12.00
❑ AFL1-3513	John Stewart in Concert	1980	10.00
❑ AYL1-3731	Cannons in the Rain	1981	8.00
—"Best Buy Series" reissue			
❑ LSP-4827	Cannons in the Rain	1973	12.00

RSO

Number	Title (A Side/B Side)	Yr	NM
❑ RS-1-3027	Fire in the Wind	1977	10.00
❑ RS-1-3051	Bombs Away Dream Babies	1979	10.00
❑ RS-1-3074	Dream Babies Go Hollywood	1980	10.00

WARNER BROS.

Number	Title (A Side/B Side)	Yr	NM
❑ WS 1948	The Lonesome Picker Rides Again	1971	12.00
❑ BS 2611	Sunstorm	1972	12.00

S

STEWART, ROD Also see JEFF BECK; FACES; PYTHON LEE JACKSON; SHOTGUN EXPRESS.

12-Inch Singles

GEFFEN

Number	Title (A Side/B Side)	Yr	NM
❑ PRO-A-2787 [DJ]	Twistin' the Night Away (same on both sides)	1987	8.00

WARNER BROS.

Number	Title (A Side/B Side)	Yr	NM
❑ PRO 680 [DJ]	The Killing of Georgie (6:31) (same on both sides)	1977	25.00
—Promo only on blue vinyl			
❑ PRO 680 [DJ]	The Killing of Georgie (6:31) (same on both sides)	1977	100.00
—Promo only on red vinyl			
❑ PRO-A-921 [DJ]	Passion (Long Version 7:30) (LP Version 5:35)	1980	12.00
❑ PRO-A-989 [DJ]	Young Turks (Edit) (LP Version)	1981	12.00
❑ PRO-A-1078 [DJ]	Guess I'll Always Love You (same on both sides)	1982	10.00
❑ PRO-A-2032 [DJ]	Baby Jane (same on both sides?)	1983	10.00
❑ PRO-A-2063 [DJ]	Dancin' Alone/Ghetto Blaster/ What Am I Gonna Do	1983	8.00
❑ PRO-A-2148 [DJ]	Infatuation (Edit 4:03) (LP Version 5:12)	1984	8.00
❑ PRO-A-2184 [DJ]	Some Guys Have All the Luck (Edit)/Bad for You	1984	8.00
❑ PRO-A-2505 [DJ]	Love Touch (Edit) (LP Version)	1986	8.00
❑ PRO-A-2538 [DJ]	A Night Like This (same on both sides)	1986	8.00
❑ PRO-A-2559 [DJ]	Another Heartache (LP Version) (Edit)	1986	10.00
❑ PRO-A-2618 [DJ]	Every Beat of My Heart (English Edit) (LP Version)	1986	8.00
❑ PRO-A-3837 [DJ]	This Old Heart of Mine (2 versions?)	1990	10.00
❑ WBSD 8727	Da Ya Think I'm Sexy?/Scarred and Scared	1978	12.00
❑ 21268	Crazy About Her (Just a Crazy Sure! Mix 6:29) (Crazy Dub 6:05) (Kyle Wyld West Edit 4:08) (Acca Dub 4:12)/ Dynamite (LP Version 4:16)	1989	6.00

45s

COLLECTABLES

Number	Title (A Side/B Side)	Yr	NM
❑ 4947	Your Song/Twisting the Night Away	199?	3.00
—This is the first appearance of "Your Song" on a U.S. 45			

GEFFEN

Number	Title (A Side/B Side)	Yr	NM
❑ 28303	Twistin' the Night Away/ Let's Get Small	1987	4.00
—B-side by Steve Martin			
❑ 28303 [PS]	Twistin' the Night Away/ Let's Get Small	1987	4.00

J

Number	Title (A Side/B Side)	Yr	NM
❑ 21249	These Foolish Things/ It Had to Be You	2002	3.00
❑ 65772	What a Wonderful World/ For Sentimental Reasons	2004	3.00
—A-side with Stevie Wonder			

MERCURY

Number	Title (A Side/B Side)	Yr	NM
❑ 73009	Handbags and Gladrags/ An Old Raincoat Won't Ever Let You Down	1970	10.00
❑ 73031	Handbags and Gladrags/ Man of Constant Sorrow	1970	8.00
❑ 73095	It's All Over Now/Joe's Lament	1970	10.00
❑ 73115	Only a Hero/Gasoline Alley	1970	10.00
❑ 73156	Cut Across Shorty/Gasoline Alley	1970	10.00
❑ 73175	My Way of Giving/Lady Day	1971	6.00
❑ 73196	Country Comfort/Gasoline Alley	1971	6.00
❑ 73224	Maggie May/Reason to Believe	1971	6.00
❑ 73244	(I Know) I'm Losing You/ Mandolin Wind	1971	5.00
❑ 73330	You Wear It Well/True Blue	1972	5.00
❑ 73330 [PS]	You Wear It Well/True Blue	1972	15.00
❑ 73344	Angel/Lost Paraguayos	1972	5.00
❑ 73412	Twistin' the Night Away// True Blue-Lady Day	1973	5.00
❑ 73412 [PS]	Twistin' the Night Away// True Blue-Lady Day	1973	6.00
❑ 73426	Oh No Not My Baby/Jodie	1973	5.00
❑ 73426 [PS]	Oh No Not My Baby/Jodie	1973	6.00
❑ 73636	Mine for Me/Farewell	1974	5.00
❑ 73660	Let Me Be Your Car/Sailor	1974	6.00
❑ 73802	Every Picture Tells a Story/ What's Made Milwaukee Famous (Has Made a Loser Out of Me)	1976	5.00

PRESS

Number	Title (A Side/B Side)	Yr	NM
❑ 9722	Good Morning Little Schoolgirl/ I'm Gonna Move to the Outskirts of Town	1965	40.00

PRIVATE STOCK

Number	Title (A Side/B Side)	Yr	NM
❑ 45,130	Shake/Bright Lights, Big City	1976	6.00

WARNER BROS.

Number	Title (A Side/B Side)	Yr	NM
❑ GWB 0349	Tonight's the Night (Gonna Be Alright)/ The First Cut Is the Deepest	1978	3.00
—"Back to Back Hits" series			
❑ GWB 0359	You're In My Heart (The Final Acclaim)/Hot Legs	1979	3.00
—"Back to Back Hits" series			
❑ GWB 0371	I Was Only Joking/The Killing of Georgie (Part 1 and 2)	1979	3.00
—"Back to Back Hits" series			
❑ GWB 0382	Da Ya Think I'm Sexy?/ Ain't Love a Bitch	1980	3.00
—"Back to Back Hits" series			
❑ GWB 0404	Passion/Somebody Special	1981	3.00
—"Back to Back Hits" series			
❑ GWB 0427	Young Turks/Tonight I'm Yours (Don't Hurt Me)	1982	3.00
—"Back to Back Hits" series			
❑ GWB 0469	Baby Jane/What Am I Gonna Do (I'm So in Love with You)	1984	3.00
—"Back to Back Hits" series			
❑ GWB 0522	Infatuation/Some Guys Have All the Luck	1985	3.00
—"Back to Back Hits" series			
❑ 8066	As Long As You Tell Him/ You Can Make Me Dance, Sing or Anything	1975	5.00
—As "Rod Stewart and Faces"			
❑ 8102	As Long As You Tell Him/ You Can Make Me Dance, Sing or Anything	1975	4.00
—As "Rod Stewart and Faces"			
❑ 8146	Sailing/All in the Name of Rock and Roll	1975	4.00
❑ 8170	This Old Heart of Mine/ Still Love Again	1975	5.00
❑ 8262	Tonight's the Night (Gonna Be Alright)/Fool for You	1976	4.00
❑ 8321	The First Cut Is the Deepest/ Ball Trap	1977	4.00
❑ 8396	The Killing of Georgie (Part 1 and 2)/Rosie	1977	4.00
❑ 8475	You're In My Heart (The Final Acclaim)/You Got a Nerve	1977	4.00
❑ 8535	Hot Legs/You're Insane	1978	4.00
❑ 8535 [PS]	Hot Legs/You're Insane	1978	5.00
❑ 8568	I Was Only Joking/Born Loose	1978	4.00
❑ 8568 [PS]	I Was Only Joking/Born Loose	1978	5.00
❑ 8724 [DJ]	Da Ya Think I'm Sexy? (Edited Version 4:16)/ (Full Version 5:21)	1978	6.00
❑ 8724 [PS]	Da Ya Think I'm Sexy?/ Scarred and Scared	1978	5.00
❑ 8724	Da Ya Think I'm Sexy?/ Scarred and Scared	1978	4.00
—Off-white label			
❑ 8724	Da Ya Think I'm Sexy?/ Scarred and Scared	1978	10.00
—"Burbank" palm trees label			
❑ 8810	Ain't Love a Bitch/Last Summer	1979	4.00
❑ 8810 [PS]	Ain't Love a Bitch/Last Summer	1979	5.00
❑ 15995	Broken Arrow/Downtown Train	1993	3.00
—"Back to Back Hits" series; only U.S. 45 release of A-side			
❑ 17195	Ooh La La/A Night Like This	1998	3.00
❑ 17459	If We Fall in Love Tonight/ Tom Traubert's Blues (Waltzing Matilda)	1996	3.00
❑ 17847	Leave Virginia Alone/ Shock to the System	1995	3.00
❑ 17854	This/The Groom's Still Waiting at the Altar	1995	3.00
❑ 18424	Having a Party/Sweet Little Rock and Roller	1993	3.00
❑ 18427	Reason to Believe/ It's All Over Now	1993	3.00
❑ 18511	Have I Told You Lately/ Gasoline Alley	1993	4.00
❑ 19322	The Motown Song/ Sweet Soul Marie	1991	3.00
❑ 19366	Rhythm of My Heart/ Moment of Glory	1991	3.00
❑ 19983	This Old Heart of Mine/ You're In My Heart	1990	3.00
❑ 21976	Love Touch (Love Theme from Legal Eagles)/Hot Legs	1988	3.00
—"Back to Back Hits" series			
❑ 22685	Downtown Train/The Killing of Georgie (Part 1 and 2)	1989	3.00
❑ 22685 [PS]	Downtown Train/The Killing of Georgie (Part 1 and 2)	1989	8.00
❑ 27657	Crazy About Her/Dynamite	1989	3.00
❑ 27729	My Heart Can't Tell You No/ The Wild Horse	1988	3.00
❑ 27729 [PS]	My Heart Can't Tell You No/ The Wild Horse	1988	3.00
❑ 27796	Forever Young/Days of Rage	1988	3.00
❑ 27796 [PS]	Forever Young/Days of Rage	1988	3.00
❑ 27927	Lost in You/Almost Illegal	1988	3.00
❑ 27927 [PS]	Lost in You/Almost Illegal	1988	3.00
❑ 28625	Every Beat of My Heart/Trouble	1986	3.00
❑ 28625 [PS]	Every Beat of My Heart/Trouble	1986	3.00
❑ 28631	Another Heartache/You're In My Heart (The Final Acclaim)	1986	3.00
❑ 28631 [PS]	Another Heartache/You're In My Heart (The Final Acclaim)	1986	3.00
❑ 28668	Love Touch (Love Theme from Legal Eagles)/ Heart Is on the Line	1986	3.00
❑ 28668 [PS]	Love Touch (Love Theme from Legal Eagles)/ Heart Is on the Line	1986	3.00
❑ 29122	All Right Now/Dancin' Alone	1984	4.00
❑ 29215	Some Guys Have All the Luck/ I Was Only Joking	1984	4.00
❑ 29215 [PS]	Some Guys Have All the Luck/ I Was Only Joking	1984	4.00
❑ 29256	Infatuation/She Won't Dance with Me	1984	4.00
❑ 29256 [PS]	Infatuation/She Won't Dance with Me	1984	4.00
❑ 29256	Infatuation/Three Time Loser	1984	4.00
❑ 29564	What Am I Gonna Do (I'm So in Love with You)/Dancin' Alone	1983	4.00
❑ 29564 [PS]	What Am I Gonna Do (I'm So in Love with You)/Dancin' Alone	1983	4.00
❑ 29608	Baby Jane/Ready Now	1983	4.00
❑ 29874	Guess I'll Always Love You/ Rock My Plimsoul	1982	4.00
❑ 29874 [PS]	Guess I'll Always Love You/ Rock My Plimsoul	1982	5.00
❑ 49138	I Don't Want to Talk About It/ Best Days of My Life	1979	4.00
❑ 49138 [PS]	I Don't Want to Talk About It/ Best Days of My Life	1979	5.00
❑ 49617	Passion/Better Off Dead	1980	4.00
❑ 49617 [DJ]	Passion (Edit 4:45) (Full Version 5:29)	1980	6.00
❑ 49617 [PS]	Passion/Better Off Dead	1980	5.00
❑ 49686	Somebody Special/ She Won't Dance with Me	1981	4.00
❑ 49843	Young Turks/Sonny	1981	4.00
❑ 49843 [PS]	Young Turks/Sonny	1981	5.00
❑ 49886	Tonight I'm Yours (Don't Hurt Me)/Tora, Tora, Tora	1981	4.00
❑ 49886 [PS]	Tonight I'm Yours (Don't Hurt Me)/Tora, Tora, Tora	1981	5.00
❑ 50051	How Long/Jealous	1982	4.00
❑ 50051 [PS]	How Long/Jealous	1982	5.00
❑ 50051 [DJ]	How Long (Edit 3:48)/ (LP Version 4:12)	1982	6.00

7-Inch Extended Plays

MERCURY

Number	Title (A Side/B Side)	Yr	NM
❑ MEPL-28 [DJ]	I'd Rather Go Blind/What's Made Milwaukee Famous//Italian Girls/Twistin' the Night Away	1972	10.00
❑ MEPL-28 [PS]	A Rod Stewart Promotion Special	1972	10.00

Albums

ACCORD

Number	Title (A Side/B Side)	Yr	NM
❑ SN-7142	Rod the Mod	1981	12.00

DCC COMPACT CLASSICS

Number	Title (A Side/B Side)	Yr	NM
❑ LPZ-2010	Never a Dull Moment	1995	30.00
—Audiophile vinyl			

J

Number	Title (A Side/B Side)	Yr	NM
❑ 55710	As Time Goes By... The Great American Songbook Vol. 2	2003	15.00
❑ 62182	Stardust... The Great American Songbook Vol. III	2004	15.00

MERCURY

Number	Title (A Side/B Side)	Yr	NM
❑ SRM-1-609	Every Picture Tells a Story	1971	10.00
—With poster missing; red label			
❑ SRM-1-609	Every Picture Tells a Story	1971	15.00
—Original cover has an attached, perforated poster			
❑ SRM-1-646	Never a Dull Moment	1972	12.00
—Red label			
❑ SRM-1-680	Sing It Again Rod	1973	12.00
—Red label			
❑ SRM-1-697	Rod Stewart/Faces Live: Coast to Coast Overtures and Beginners	1973	15.00
—By "Rod Stewart/Faces"			
❑ SRM-1-1017	Smiler	1974	12.00
—Chicago skyline label			

S

Number	Title (A Side/B Side)	Yr	NM
❑ SRM-2-7507 [(2)]	The Best of Rod Stewart	1976	15.00
❑ SRM-2-7509 [(2)]	The Best of Rod Stewart, Vol. 2	1977	15.00
❑ SR-61237	The Rod Stewart Album	1969	25.00
—Cover is yellow with no black border			
❑ SR-61237	The Rod Stewart Album	1971	15.00
—Cover is yellow with black border; red label			
❑ SR-61264	Gasoline Alley	1970	20.00
—Cover is textured, most noticeably on the pebbles			
❑ SR-61264	Gasoline Alley	1971	15.00
—Cover is not textured; red label			
❑ 822385-1	Every Picture Tells a Story	1984	8.00
❑ 822791-1 [(2)]	The Best of Rod Stewart, Vol. 2	1985	12.00
❑ 824881-1	Gasoline Alley	1985	8.00
❑ 824882-1	Sing It Again Rod	1985	8.00
❑ 826287-1 [(2)]	The Best of Rod Stewart	1985	12.00
MOBILE FIDELITY			
❑ 1-054	Blondes Have More Fun	1980	25.00
—Audiophile vinyl			
PRIVATE STOCK			
❑ PS-2021	A Shot of Rhythm and Blues	1976	15.00
SPRINGBOARD			
❑ SPB-4030	Rod Stewart and The Faces	197?	12.00
❑ SPB-4063	Rod Stewart and Steampacket	197?	12.00
TRIP			
❑ TOP-16-31	Looking Back/16 Early Hits	1974	12.00
UNITED DISTRIBUTORS			
❑ UDL-2391	The Day Will Come	1981	20.00
WARNER BROS.			
❑ BS 2875	Atlantic Crossing	1975	10.00
❑ BS 2938	A Night on the Town	1976	10.00
❑ BSK 3092	Foot Loose and Fancy Free	1977	10.00
❑ BSK 3108	Atlantic Crossing	1977	8.00
—Reissue of 2875			
❑ BSK 3116	A Night on the Town	1977	8.00
—Reissue of 2938			
❑ BSK 3261	Blondes Have More Fun	1978	10.00
❑ BSP 3276 [PD]	Blondes Have More Fun	1978	20.00
❑ HS 3373	Rod Stewart Greatest Hits	1979	10.00
❑ HS 3485	Foolish Behaviour	1980	10.00
❑ BSK 3602	Tonight I'm Yours	1981	10.00
❑ 23743 [(2)]	Absolutely Live	1982	12.00
❑ 23743 [(2)DJ]	Absolutely Live	1982	25.00
—Promo only on Quiex II vinyl			
❑ 23877	Body Wishes	1983	8.00
❑ 23877 [DJ]	Body Wishes	1983	15.00
—Promo only on Quiex II vinyl			
❑ 25095	Camouflage	1984	8.00
—Issued with 16 different back covers, all of equal value, that, when assembled, form a giant poster			
❑ 25446	Rod Stewart	1986	8.00
❑ 25884	Out of Order	1988	8.00
❑ 26158	Downtown Train: Selections from the Storyteller Anthology	1990	12.00

STEWART, SANDY

Number	Title (A Side/B Side)	Yr	NM
45s			
ATCO			
❑ 6137	Playmates/Heavenly Father	1959	10.00
COLPIX			
❑ 669	My Coloring Book/I Heard You Cried Last Night	1962	8.00
❑ 669 [PS]	My Coloring Book/I Heard You Cried Last Night	1962	15.00
❑ 669	My Coloring Book (Without Verse)/(With Verse)	1962	10.00
❑ 681	My Favorite Song/Promise of Love	1963	8.00
❑ 704	I Know He Needs Her/Please Don't Fall in Love with Me Again	1963	8.00
DCP			
❑ 1004	Draw Me a Circle/Little Child (Mommy Dear)	1964	8.00
❑ 1122	Yellow and Green Make Me Blue/I'll Never Go There Anymore	1964	8.00
EASTWEST			
❑ 122	To My Love/Music, Music, Music	1958	10.00
EPIC			
❑ 9070	No One Came to My Party/Mama, Mama	1954	12.00
OKEH			
❑ 6941	Since You Went Away from Me/Before	1953	12.00
❑ 6967	If My Heart Had a Window/Punch Brother Punch	1953	12.00
❑ 6991	Loved and Lost/Please Come Home	1953	12.00
20TH CENTURY			
❑ 5007	The Game of Love/Do Ya Do Ya	1954	12.00
❑ 5014	I'm Goin' Home/Saturday Night	1954	12.00
UNITED ARTISTS			
❑ 232	Indoor Sports/Time Waits for No One	1960	10.00
❑ 287	Past the Age of Innocence/Richest Girl in the World	1961	10.00
❑ 332	Nice Guy/Lord and Master	1961	10.00
"X"			
❑ 0126	Johnny Darling/No More Love	1955	12.00
❑ 0156	Puddin' 'n' Pie/In Nuevo Laredo	1955	12.00
❑ 0176	Could It Be?/I'll Take Care of You	1955	12.00
Albums			
AUDIOPHILE			
❑ AP-205	Sandy Stewart Sings Songs of Jerome Kern	1985	10.00
—Accompanied by Dick Hyman on piano			
COLPIX			
❑ CP-441 [M]	My Coloring Book	1963	25.00
❑ SCP-441 [S]	My Coloring Book	1963	30.00

STEWART, SLY

Sylvester Stewart, later "Sly" of SLY AND THE FAMILY STONE.

Number	Title (A Side/B Side)	Yr	NM
12-Inch Singles			
EPIC			
❑ 50794	Dance to the Music/Sing a Simple Song	1979	15.00
—As "Sly Stone"			
45s			
A&M			
❑ 2890	Eek-Ah-Bo-Static Automatic/Black Girls	1986	3.00
—B-side by Rae Dawn Chong			
❑ 2896	Love and Affection/Black Girls	1986	3.00
—A-side as "Sly Stone and Martha Davis"; B-side by Rae Dawn Chong			
AUTUMN			
❑ 3	I Just Learned How to Swim/Scat Swim	1964	20.00
—Sylvester Stewart, later "Sly" of The Family Stone			
❑ 14	Buttermilk — Part 1/Buttermilk — Part 2	1965	20.00
—As "Sly"			
❑ 26	Temptation Walk/Temptation Walk — Part 2	1966	20.00
EPIC			
❑ 50795	Dance to the Music/Sing a Simple Song	1979	5.00
—As "Sly Stone"			
G&P			
❑ 901	Help Me With My Heart/A Long Time Away	1962	250.00
—As "Sylvester Stewart"			
LUKE			
❑ 1008	A Long Time Alone/I'm Just a Fool	1961	250.00
—As "Danny Stewart"			
Albums			
SCULPTURE			
❑ SCP-2001	San Francisco Recordings 1964-1967	197?	20.00
—As "Sly Stone"			

STEWART BROTHERS, THE

With Sylvester "SLY" STEWART, later of SLY AND THE FAMILY STONE.

Number	Title (A Side/B Side)	Yr	NM
45s			
ENSIGN			
❑ 4032	The Rat/Ra Ra Roo	1959	100.00
KEEN			
❑ 2113	Sleep on the Porch/Yum Yum	1960	100.00

STIFF LITTLE FINGERS

Number	Title (A Side/B Side)	Yr	NM
45s			
CHRYSALIS			
❑ 2405	At the Edge//Running Bear/White Christmas	1979	6.00
—Tracks 1 and 2 are not Christmas songs			
❑ 2405	At the Edge//Silly Encores	1979	6.00
—Sleeve and record are U.K. imports			
❑ 2406	White Christmas/	1979	—
—U.K. import			
Albums			
CAROLINE			
❑ 1377	See You Up There	1990	12.00
CHRYSALIS			
❑ CHR 1270	Nobody's Heroes	1980	20.00
❑ CHR 1300	Hanx	1980	20.00
❑ CHR 1339	Go For It	1981	20.00
ROUGH TRADE			
❑ ROUGH US 5	Inflammable Material	1980	25.00
—Released in U.K. in 1979			

STILLROVEN, THE

Number	Title (A Side/B Side)	Yr	NM
45s			
AUGUST			
❑ 101	Little Picture Playhouse/Cast Thy Burden Upon the Stone	1968	50.00
❑ 102	Necessary Person/Come in the Morning	1968	40.00
❑ 102	Necessary Person/Have You Ever Seen Me	1968	40.00
FALCON			
❑ 69	Hey Joe/Sunny Day	1967	75.00
❑ 7296	She's Your Woman/I'm Not Your Steppin' Stone	1966	150.00
ROULETTE			
❑ 4748	Hey Joe/Sunny Day	1967	25.00

STILLS, STEPHEN

Also see BUFFALO SPRINGFIELD; CROSBY, STILLS AND NASH; CROSBY, STILLS, NASH AND YOUNG; THE STILLS-YOUNG BAND.

Number	Title (A Side/B Side)	Yr	NM
12-Inch Singles			
ATLANTIC			
❑ PR 623 [DJ]	Stranger (same on both sides)	1984	6.00
❑ PR 650 [DJ]	Can't Let Go (same on both sides)	1984	6.00
45s			
ATLANTIC			
❑ 2778	Love the One You're With/To a Flame	1970	6.00
❑ 2790	Sit Yourself Down/We Are Not Helpless	1971	5.00
❑ 2806	Change Partners/Relaxing Town	1971	5.00
❑ 2806 [PS]	Change Partners/Relaxing Town	1971	6.00
❑ 2820	Marianne/Nothin' to Do But Today	1971	5.00
❑ 2876	It Doesn't Matter/Rock & Roll's Crazy Medley	1972	5.00
❑ 2888	Rock and Roll Crazies/Colorado	1972	5.00
—With Manassas			
❑ 2917	Down the Road/Guaguanco De Vero	1972	5.00
—With Manassas			
❑ 2959	So Many Times/Isn't It About Time	1973	5.00
❑ 89597	Only Love Can Break Your Heart/Love Again	1984	4.00
❑ 89611	Can't Let Go/Grey to Green	1984	4.00
—With Walter Finnegan			
❑ 89633	Stranger/No Hiding Place	1984	4.00
❑ 89633 [PS]	Stranger/No Hiding Place	1984	4.00
COLUMBIA			
❑ 10179	Turn Back the Pages/Shuffle Just as Bad	1975	5.00
❑ 10369	Buyin' Time/Soldier	1976	5.00
❑ 10804	Lowdown/Can't Get No Booty	1978	5.00
❑ 10872	Thoroughfare Gap/Lowdown	1978	5.00
7-Inch Extended Plays			
ATLANTIC			
❑ SD 7-7206	Bluebird Revisited/Ecology Song//Sugar Babe/Marianne/Relaxing Town	1971	12.00
—Jukebox issue; small hole, plays at 33 1/3 rpm			
❑ SD 7-7206 [PS]	Stephen Stills 2	1971	12.00
—Part of "Little LP" series (LLP #157)			
Albums			
ATLANTIC			
❑ SD 2-903 [(2)]	Manassas	1972	15.00
❑ SD 7202	Stephen Stills	1970	12.00
❑ SD 7206	Stephen Stills 2	1971	12.00
❑ SD 7250	Down the Road	1973	12.00
❑ SD 18156	Stephen Stills Live	1975	12.00
❑ SD 18201	Still Stills — The Best of Stephen Stills	1976	10.00
❑ 80177	Right By You	1984	8.00
COLUMBIA			
❑ PC 33575	Stills	1975	10.00
—No bar code on cover			
❑ PC 33575	Stills	198?	8.00
—Bar code on cover			
❑ PCQ 33575 [Q]	Stills	1975	20.00
❑ PC 34348	Illegal Stills	1976	10.00
❑ JC 35380	Thoroughfare Gap	1978	10.00

STILLS-YOUNG BAND, THE

STEPHEN STILLS and NEIL YOUNG.

Number	Title (A Side/B Side)	Yr	NM
45s			
REPRISE			
❑ 1365	Long May You Run//12/8 Blues (All the Same)	1976	6.00
❑ 1378	Midnight on the Bay/Black Coral	1976	5.00
Albums			
REPRISE			
❑ MS 2253	Long May You Run	1976	10.00

S

Except when noted otherwise, VG = 25% of NM, and VG+ = 50% of NM. (Example: VG = $2.00, VG+ = $4.00 and NM = $8.00.)

Sting, "Englishman in New York," A&M 1200, 1987, $3.

STING

12-Inch Singles

A&M

Number	Title (A Side/B Side)	Yr	NM
❑ 31458 0465 1	Demolition Man (6 versions)	1993	8.00
❑ 31458 8380 1 [(2)DJ]	When We Dance (3 versions)/ If You Love Somebody Set Them Free (8 versions)/ Demolition Man	1994	25.00
❑ 3145883801 [(2)DJ]	When We Dance (3 versions)/ If You Love Somebody Set Them Free (8 versions)/Demolition Man	1994	25.00
❑ 12132	If You Love Somebody Set Them Free (3 versions)/ Another Day	1985	8.00
—Original copies have an insert			
❑ 12153	Love Is the Seventh Wave (2 versions)	1985	6.00
❑ 12164	Russians/Gabriel's Message/ I Burn for You (Live)	1985	6.00
❑ 12251	We'll Be Together (4 versions)/ Conversation with a Dog	1987	8.00
❑ 17216 [DJ]	I Burn for You/Only You	1982	10.00
❑ 17216 [DJ]	I Burn for You/Only You	1982	10.00
❑ 17324 [DJ]	If You Love Somebody Set Them Free (same on both sides)	1985	6.00
❑ 17324 [DJ]	If You Love Somebody Set Them Free (same on both sides)	1985	6.00
❑ 17339 [DJ]	Fortress Around Your Heart/ Consider Me Gone (Live)	1985	6.00
❑ 17339 [DJ]	Fortress Around Your Heart/ Consider Me Gone (Live)	1985	6.00
❑ 17526 [DJ]	Be Still My Beating Heart (2 versions)	1987	6.00
❑ 17526 [DJ]	Be Still My Beating Heart (2 versions)	1987	6.00

45s

A&M

Number	Title (A Side/B Side)	Yr	NM
❑ 31458 0530 7	Shape of My Heart/If I Ever Lose My Faith in You	1994	3.00
❑ 31458 0838 7	When We Dance/Fields of Gold	1994	3.00
❑ 1200	Englishman in New York/ If You're There	1988	3.00
❑ 1200 [PS]	Englishman in New York/ If You're There	1988	3.00
❑ 1211	Fragile/Gragilidad	1988	3.00
❑ 1242	They Dance Alone (Gueca Solo)/ They Dance Alone (Gueca Solo)	1988	3.00
❑ 75021 1541 7	All This Time/I Miss You Kate	1991	4.00
❑ 31458 1582 7	You Still Touch Me/Let Your Soul Be Your Pilot	1996	2.00
❑ 31458 1582 7 [PS]	You Still Touch Me/ Let Your Soul Be Your Pilot	1996	2.00
❑ 31458 1982 7	I'm So Happy I Can't Stop Crying/ This Was Never Meant to Be	1996	3.00
❑ 2501	Spread a Little Happiness/ Only You	1982	4.00
❑ 2738	If You Love Somebody Set Them Free/Another Day	1985	3.00
—Normal red and black label			
❑ 2738	If You Love Somebody Set Them Free/Another Day	1985	4.00
—Blue custom label			
❑ 2738 [PS]	If You Love Somebody Set Them Free/Another Day	1985	3.00
❑ 2765	If You Love Somebody Set Them Free/Another Day	1985	5.00
❑ 2765 [PS]	If You Love Somebody Set Them Free/Another Day	1985	5.00
❑ 2767	Fortress Around Your Heart/ Consider Me Gone	1985	3.00
❑ 2767 [PS]	Fortress Around Your Heart/ Consider Me Gone	1985	3.00
❑ 2787	Love Is the Seventh Wave/ The Dream of the Blue Turtles	1985	3.00
❑ 2787 [PS]	Love Is the Seventh Wave/ The Dream of the Blue Turtles	1985	3.00
❑ 2799	Russians/Gabriel's Message	1985	3.00
❑ 2799 [PS]	Russians/Gabriel's Message	1985	3.00
❑ 2983	We'll Be Together/ Conversation with a Dog	1987	3.00
❑ 2983 [PS]	We'll Be Together/ Conversation with a Dog	1987	3.00
❑ 2992	Be Still My Beating Heart/ Ghost in the Strand	1987	3.00
❑ 2992 [PS]	Be Still My Beating Heart/ Ghost in the Strand	1987	3.00
❑ 8655	If You Love Somebody Set Them Free/Fortress Around Your Heart	198?	3.00
—Reissue			
❑ 8656	Love Is the Seventh Wave/ Russians	198?	3.00
—Reissue			
❑ 8722	All This Time/Be Still My Beating Heart	199?	3.00
—Reissue			
❑ 8723	The Soul Cages/Why Should I Cry for You?	199?	3.00
—Reissue series; first appearance on U.S. 45 for both sides			
❑ 8740	Shape of My Heart/If I Ever Lose My Faith in You	1996	3.00
—Reissue			
❑ 069 497214 7	Brand New Day/I'm So Happy I Can't Stop Crying	1999	3.00
❑ 069 497404 7	Desert Rose/After the Rain Has Fallen	2000	3.00

ARK 21

Number	Title (A Side/B Side)	Yr	NM
❑ S7-19939	This Was Never Meant to Be/ This Was Never Meant to Be (Shellac Mix)	1998	4.00
—B-side by Anne Dudley			

Albums

A&M

Number	Title	Yr	NM
❑ SP-3295 [EP]	...Nada Como El Sol	1988	20.00
—Spanish versions of songs from "...Nothing Like the Sun"			
❑ SP-3750	The Dream of the Blue Turtles	1985	10.00
❑ SP-6402 [(2)]	...Nothing Like the Sun	1987	12.00
❑ 75021 6405-1	The Soul Cages	1991	12.00
❑ R 150266	The Dream of the Blue Turtles	1985	12.00
—RCA Music Service edition			
❑ R 273965 [(2)]	...Nothing Like the Sun	1987	14.00
—BMG Direct Marketing edition			

MOBILE FIDELITY

Number	Title	Yr	NM
❑ 1-185	The Dream of the Blue Turtles	1985	20.00
—Audiophile vinyl			

STINGERS, THE

Albums

CROWN

Number	Title	Yr	NM
❑ CST-476 [S]	Guitars A Go Go	196?	40.00
❑ CLP-5476 [M]	Guitars A Go Go	196?	30.00

STINIT, DANE

45s

SUN

Number	Title (A Side/B Side)	Yr	NM
❑ 402	Always on the Go/Don't Knock What You Don't Understand	1966	15.00
❑ 405	Sweet Country Girl/That Muddy Ole River	1967	15.00

STITES, GARY

45s

CARLTON

Number	Title (A Side/B Side)	Yr	NM
❑ 508	Lonely for You/Shine That Ring	1959	20.00
❑ 516	A Girl Like You/Hey Little Girl	1959	20.00
❑ 521	Starry Eyed/Without Your Love	1959	20.00
❑ 525	Lawdy Miss Clawdy/ Don't Wanna Say Goodbye	1960	20.00
❑ 529	Gloria Lee/Hey, Hey	1960	20.00

EPIC

Number	Title (A Side/B Side)	Yr	NM
❑ 10064	Hurting/Thinking of You	1966	12.00

MADISON

Number	Title (A Side/B Side)	Yr	NM
❑ 138	Young Love/Little Tear	1960	15.00
❑ 155	Honey Girl/Little Lonely One	1961	15.00

MR. PEEKE

Number	Title (A Side/B Side)	Yr	NM
❑ 122	You Doubted Me/ Only a Fool Would Say	1962	15.00

Albums

CARLTON

Number	Title	Yr	NM
❑ LP-120 [M]	Lonely for You	1960	80.00
❑ STLP-120 [S]	Lonely for You	1960	120.00

STITT, SONNY

45s

ARGO

Number	Title (A Side/B Side)	Yr	NM
❑ 5403	It All Depends on You (Part 1)/ It All Depends on You (Part 2)	1961	10.00
❑ 5433	Rearin' Back (Part 1)/ Rearin' Back (Part 2)	1963	8.00
❑ 5493	Flame and Frost/My Main Man	1965	8.00
—With Bennie Green			

Except when noted otherwise, VG = 25% of NM, and VG+ = 50% of NM. (Example: VG = $2.00, VG+ = $4.00 and NM = $8.00.)

Number	Title (A Side/B Side)	Yr	NM
CADET			
❑ 5701	Mr. Bojangles/Blue Monsoon	1974	4.00
❑ 5705	Will You Love Me Tomorrow/ Satan	1974	4.00
❑ 5708	Theme from The Godfather Part II/Ocho Nos	1974	5.00
ENTERPRISE			
❑ 9001	Private Number/Heads or Tails	1969	6.00
IMPULSE!			
❑ 230	Salt and Pepper (Part 1)/ Salt and Pepper (Part 2)	1964	8.00
—With Paul Gonsalves			
PRESTIGE			
❑ 239	'Nuther Fu'ther (Part 1)/ 'Nuther Fu'ther (Part 2)	1963	10.00
❑ 263	Ringin' In/Pam Ain't Blue	1963	10.00
❑ 282	Thirty-Three Ninety-Six (Part 1)/Thirty-Three Ninety-Six (Part 2)	1963	10.00
❑ 304	Shangri-La/Soul Shack	1964	10.00
❑ 392	Night Crawler/Answering Service	1965	8.00
❑ 404	Star Eyes/Who Can I Turn To	196?	8.00
❑ 438	Blue Lights/Up and Over	196?	8.00
❑ 710	Candy/Lover Man	1969	6.00
ROULETTE			
❑ 4701	What's New/Morgan's Song	1966	8.00
❑ 4713	Stardust (Part 1)/Stardust (Part 2)	1966	8.00
WINGATE			
❑ 006	The Double-O-Soul of Sonny Stitt (Part 1 and 2)	1965	8.00
❑ 010	Just Dust/Concerto for Jazz Lovers	1966	8.00
❑ 011	Stitt's Groove/Marr's Groove	1966	8.00
—With Hank Marr			
WORLD PACIFIC			
❑ 398	My Mother's Eyes/ Summer Special	1963	10.00

Albums

Number	Title (A Side/B Side)	Yr	NM
ABC IMPULSE!			
❑ AS-43 [S]	Sonny Stitt Now!	1968	20.00
—Black label with red ring			
❑ AS-43 [S]	Sonny Stitt Now!	1975	12.00
—Green, purple, blue "target" label			
❑ AS-52 [S]	Salt and Pepper	1968	20.00
—With Paul Gonsalves; black label with red ring			
ARGO			
❑ LP-629 [M]	Sonny Stitt	1958	50.00
❑ LP-661 [M]	Burnin'	1960	40.00
❑ LPS-661 [S]	Burnin'	1960	50.00
❑ LP-683 [M]	Sonny Stitt at the D.J. Lounge	1961	40.00
❑ LPS-683 [S]	Sonny Stitt at the D.J. Lounge	1961	50.00
❑ LP-709 [M]	Rearin' Back	1962	40.00
❑ LPS-709 [S]	Rearin' Back	1962	50.00
❑ LP-730 [M]	Move On Over	1964	40.00
❑ LPS-730 [S]	Move On Over	1964	50.00
❑ LP-744 [M]	My Main Man	1965	40.00
❑ LPS-744 [S]	My Main Man	1965	50.00
ATLANTIC			
❑ 1395 [M]	Sonny Stitt and the Top Brass	1962	25.00
❑ SD 1395 [S]	Sonny Stitt and the Top Brass	1962	30.00
❑ 1418 [M]	Stitt Plays Bird	1964	30.00
❑ SD 1418 [S]	Stitt Plays Bird	1964	40.00
❑ SD 3008	Deuces Wild	1970	20.00
❑ 90139	Sonny Stitt and the Top Brass	198?	12.00
BLACK LION			
❑ 307	Night Work	197?	12.00
BLACKHAWK			
❑ 528	Good Life	1982	12.00
CADET			
❑ CA-629 [R]	Sonny Stitt	197?	10.00
—Yellow and pink label			
❑ LP-629 [M]	Sonny Stitt	1966	20.00
—Fading blue label			
❑ CA-661	Burnin'	197?	12.00
—Yellow and pink label			
❑ LP-661 [M]	Burnin'	1966	20.00
—Fading blue label			
❑ LPS-661 [S]	Burnin'	1966	25.00
—Fading blue label			
❑ CA-683	Sonny Stitt at the D.J. Lounge	197?	12.00
—Yellow and pink label			
❑ LP-683 [M]	Sonny Stitt at the D.J. Lounge	1966	20.00
—Fading blue label			
❑ LPS-683 [S]	Sonny Stitt at the D.J. Lounge	1966	25.00
—Fading blue label			
❑ CA-709	Rearin' Back	197?	12.00
—Yellow and pink label			
❑ LP-709 [M]	Rearin' Back	1966	20.00
—Fading blue label			
❑ LPS-709 [S]	Rearin' Back	1966	25.00
—Fading blue label			
❑ CA-730 [S]	Move On Over	197?	12.00
—Yellow and pink label			
❑ LP-730 [M]	Move On Over	1966	20.00
—Fading blue label			
❑ LPS-730 [S]	Move On Over	1966	25.00
—Fading blue label			
❑ LP-744 [M]	My Main Man	1966	20.00
—Fading blue label			
❑ LPS-744 [S]	My Main Man	1966	25.00
—Fading blue label			
❑ LP-760 [M]	Inter-Action	1966	30.00
—Fading blue label			
❑ LPS-760 [S]	Inter-Action	1966	40.00
—Fading blue label			
❑ LP-770 [M]	Soul In the Night	1966	30.00
—Fading blue label			
❑ LPS-770 [S]	Soul In the Night	1966	40.00
—Fading blue label			
❑ CA-50026	Mr. Bojangles	1973	40.00
❑ 2CA-50039 [(2)]	I Cover the Waterfront	1974	30.00
❑ CA-50060	Satan	1974	20.00
❑ CA-60040	Never Can Say Goodbye	1975	20.00
CATALYST			
❑ 7608	Forecast	1976	20.00
—With Red Holloway			
❑ 7616	I Remember Bird	1977	20.00
❑ 7620	Tribute to Duke Ellington	1977	15.00
CHESS			
❑ 2ACMJ-405 [(2)]	Interaction	197?	20.00
—With Zoot Sims			
❑ CH-9317	Sonny Stitt	1990	12.00
❑ CH-91523	Sonny Stitt at the D.J. Lounge	198?	12.00
COBBLESTONE			
❑ CST-9013	Tune-Up	1972	25.00
❑ CST-9021	Constellation	1973	20.00
COLPIX			
❑ CP-499 [M]	Broadway Soul	1964	30.00
❑ SCP-499 [S]	Broadway Soul	1964	40.00
DELMARK			
❑ DS-426	Made for Each Other	1972	20.00
FANTASY			
❑ OJC-009	Sonny Stitt/Bud Powell/J.J. Johnson	198?	12.00
❑ OJC-060	Kaleidoscope	198?	12.00
FLYING DUTCHMAN			
❑ BDL1-1197	Dumpy Mama	1975	25.00
❑ BDL1-1538	Stomp Off Let's Go	1976	20.00
GALAXY			
❑ 8204	In the Beginning	197?	20.00
GRP/IMPULSE!			
❑ IMP-210	Salt and Pepper	1997	15.00
—Reissue on audiophile vinyl			
IMPULSE!			
❑ A-43 [M]	Sonny Stitt Now!	1963	50.00
❑ AS-43 [S]	Sonny Stitt Now!	1963	60.00
❑ A-52 [M]	Salt and Pepper	1964	40.00
❑ AS-52 [S]	Salt and Pepper	1964	50.00
—With Paul Gonsalves			
JAZZ MAN			
❑ 5040	Night Work	198?	12.00
—Reissue of Black Lion LP			
JAZZLAND			
❑ JLP-71 [M]	Low Flame	1962	40.00
❑ JLP-971 [S]	Low Flame	1962	50.00
JAZZTONE			
❑ J-1231 [M]	Early Modern	1956	80.00
❑ J-1263 [M]	Early Modern	1957	60.00
MUSE			
❑ MR-5006	12!	1973	15.00
❑ MR-5023	The Champ	1974	15.00
❑ MR-5067	Mellow	1975	20.00
❑ MR-5091	My Buddy: Sonny Stitt Plays for Gene Ammons	1976	15.00
❑ MR-5129	Blues for Duke	1978	12.00
❑ MR-5204	Sonny's Back	1981	15.00
❑ MR-5228	In Style	1982	12.00
❑ MR-5269	The Last Stitt Sessions, Vol. 1	1983	15.00
❑ MR-5280	The Last Stitt Sessions, Vol. 2	1984	15.00
❑ MR-5323	Constellation	1986	15.00
—Reissue of Cobblestone 9021			
❑ MR-5334	Tune-Up	1987	15.00
—Reissue of Cobblestone 9013			
NEW JAZZ			
❑ NJLP-103 [10]	Sonny Stitt and Bud Powell	1950	500.00
PACIFIC JAZZ			
❑ PJ-71 [M]	My Mother's Eyes	1963	80.00
❑ ST-71 [S]	My Mother's Eyes	1963	80.00
PAULA			
❑ 4004	Soul Girl	1974	12.00
PHOENIX			
❑ 15	Superstitt	197?	10.00
❑ 19	Battles	197?	10.00
PRESTIGE			
❑ PRLP-103 [10]	Sonny Stitt Plays	1951	400.00
❑ PRLP-111 [10]	Mr. Saxophone	1951	400.00
❑ PRLP-126 [10]	Favorites, Vol. 1	1952	400.00
❑ PRLP-148 [10]	Favorites, Vol. 2	1953	400.00
❑ PRLP-7024 [M]	Sonny Stitt with Bud Powell and J.J. Johnson	1956	150.00
❑ PRLP-7077 [M]	Kaleidoscope	1957	120.00
—Yellow label with W. 50th St address			
❑ PRLP-7133 [M]	Stitt's Bits	1958	120.00
❑ PRLP-7244 [M]	Stitt Meets Brother Jack	1962	80.00
—Yellow label with Bergenfield, N.J. address			
❑ PRLP-7244 [M]	Stitt Meets Brother Jack	1964	40.00
—Blue label with trident logo			
❑ PRST-7244 [S]	Stitt Meets Brother Jack	1962	70.00
❑ PRLP-7248 [M]	All God's Chillun Got Rhythm	1962	80.00
—Yellow label with Bergenfield, N.J. address			
❑ PRLP-7248 [M]	All God's Chillun Got Rhythm	1964	40.00
—Blue label with trident logo			
❑ PRST-7248 [R]	All God's Chillun Got Rhythm	1962	30.00
❑ PRLP-7297 [M]	Soul Shack	1964	80.00
—Yellow label with Bergenfield, N.J. address			
❑ PRLP-7297 [M]	Soul Shack	1965	40.00
—Blue label with trident logo			
❑ PRST-7297 [S]	Soul Shack	1964	70.00
—Silver label with Bergenfield, N.J. address			
❑ PRST-7297 [S]	Soul Shack	1965	40.00
—Blue label with trident logo			
❑ PRLP-7302 [M]	Primitive Soul!	1964	80.00
—Yellow label with Bergenfield, N.J. address			
❑ PRLP-7302 [M]	Primitive Soul!	1965	40.00
—Blue label with trident logo			
❑ PRST-7302 [S]	Primitive Soul!	1964	70.00
—Silver label			
❑ PRST-7302 [S]	Primitive Soul!	1965	40.00
—Blue label with trident logo			
❑ PRLP-7332 [M]	Shangri-La	1964	40.00
—Blue label, trident logo at right			
❑ PRST-7332 [S]	Shangri-La	1964	50.00
—Blue label, trident logo at right			
❑ PRLP-7372 [M]	Soul People	1965	40.00
—Blue label, trident logo at right			
❑ PRST-7372 [S]	Soul People	1965	50.00
—Blue label, trident logo at right			
❑ PRST-7372 [S]	Soul People	197?	25.00
—Green label			
❑ PRLP-7436 [M]	Night Crawler	1966	40.00
—Blue label, trident logo at right			
❑ PRST-7436 [S]	Night Crawler	1966	50.00
—Blue label, trident logo at right			
❑ PRLP-7452 [M]	'Nuther Fu'ther	1966	40.00
—Blue label, trident logo at right			
❑ PRST-7452 [S]	'Nuther Fu'ther	1966	50.00
—Blue label, trident logo at right			
❑ PRST-7452 [S]	'Nuther Fu'ther	197?	25.00
—Green label			
❑ PRLP-7459 [M]	Pow!	1967	50.00
—Blue label, trident logo at right			
❑ PRST-7459 [S]	Pow!	1967	40.00
—Blue label, trident logo at right			
❑ PRST-7585	Stitt's Bits, Vol. 1	1968	30.00
❑ PRST-7612	Stitt's Bits, Vol. 2	1969	30.00
❑ PRST-7635	Soul Electricity	1969	30.00
❑ PRST-7701	The Best of Sonny Stitt with Brother Jack McDuff	1969	25.00
❑ PRST-7759	Night Letter	1970	20.00
❑ PRST-7769	Best for Lovers	1970	25.00
❑ PRST-7839	Bud's Blues	1974	20.00
❑ P-10012	Turn It On	1971	30.00
❑ P-10032	Black Vibrations	1972	30.00
❑ 10048	Goin' Down Slow	1973	25.00
❑ P-10074	So Doggone Good	1974	15.00
❑ P-24044 [(2)]	Genesis	1974	20.00
PROGRESSIVE			
❑ PRO-7034	Sonny Stitt Meets Sadik Hakim	1978	25.00
ROOST			
❑ LP-415 [10]	Sonny Stitt Plays Arrangements from the Pen of Johnny Richards	1952	400.00
❑ LP-418 [10]	Jazz at the Hi-Hat	1954	400.00
❑ LP-1203 [M]	Battle of Birdland	1955	120.00
❑ LP-1208 [M]	Sonny Stitt	1956	120.00
❑ LP-2204 [M]	Sonny Stitt Plays Arrangements of Quincy Jones	1957	150.00
❑ LP-2208 [M]	Sonny Stitt	1957	120.00
❑ LP-2219 [M]	37 Minutes and 48 Seconds with Sonny Stitt	1957	80.00
❑ LP-2226 [M]	Sonny Stitt with the New Yorkers	1958	80.00
❑ LP-2230 [M]	The Saxophone of Sonny Stitt	1959	70.00
❑ SLP-2230 [S]	The Saxophone of Sonny Stitt	1959	60.00
❑ LP-2235 [M]	A Little Bit of Stitt	1959	70.00
❑ SLP-2235 [S]	A Little Bit of Stitt	1959	60.00
❑ LP-2240 [M]	The Sonny Side of Stitt	1960	70.00
❑ SLP-2240 [S]	The Sonny Side of Stitt	1960	60.00
❑ LP-2244 [M]	Stittsville	1960	70.00
❑ SLP-2244 [S]	Stittsville	1960	80.00
❑ LP-2245 [M]	Sonny Side Up	1960	80.00
❑ SLP-2245 [S]	Sonny Side Up	1960	80.00
❑ LP-2247 [M]	Feelin's	1962	60.00

Number	Title (A Side/B Side)	Yr	NM
❑ SLP-2247 [S]	Feelin's	1962	60.00
❑ LP-2252 [M]	Sonny Stitt in Orbit	1963	50.00
❑ SLP-2252 [S]	Sonny Stitt in Orbit	1963	50.00
❑ LP-2253 [M]	Sonny Stitt Goes Latin	1963	50.00
❑ SLP-2253 [S]	Sonny Stitt Goes Latin	1963	50.00

ROULETTE

Number	Title (A Side/B Side)	Yr	NM
❑ SR-5002	Stardust	197?	15.00
—Reissue of 42048			
❑ R-25339 [M]	The Matadors Meet the Bull	1965	40.00
❑ SR-25339 [S]	The Matadors Meet the Bull	1965	50.00
❑ R-25343 [M]	What's New?	1966	30.00
❑ SR-25343 [S]	What's New?	1966	40.00
❑ R-25348 [M]	I Keep Comin' Back	1967	40.00
❑ SR-25348 [S]	I Keep Comin' Back	1967	30.00
❑ R-25354 [M]	Parallel-O-Stitt	1968	50.00
❑ SR-25354 [S]	Parallel-O-Stitt	1968	25.00
❑ SR-42035	Make Someone Happy	1969	20.00
❑ SR-42048	Stardust	1970	20.00

SAVOY

Number	Title (A Side/B Side)	Yr	NM
❑ MG-9006 [10]	All Star Series: Sonny Stitt	1953	300.00
❑ MG-9012 [10]	New Sounds in Modern Music	1953	300.00
❑ MG-9014 [10]	New Trends Of Jazz	1953	300.00

SAVOY JAZZ

Number	Title (A Side/B Side)	Yr	NM
❑ SJL-1165	Symphony Hall Swing	1986	15.00

SOLID STATE

Number	Title (A Side/B Side)	Yr	NM
❑ SS-18047	Little Green Apples	1968	20.00
❑ SS-18057	Come Hither	1969	20.00

TRIP

Number	Title (A Side/B Side)	Yr	NM
❑ TLX-5008 [(2)]	Two Sides of Sonny Stitt	1974	15.00

UPFRONT

Number	Title (A Side/B Side)	Yr	NM
❑ UPF-196	Sonny's Blues	197?	12.00

VERVE

Number	Title (A Side/B Side)	Yr	NM
❑ UMV-2558	New York Jazz	198?	12.00
❑ UMV-2634	Only the Blues	198?	12.00
❑ MGVS-6038 [S]	The Hard Swing	1960	40.00
❑ MGVS-6041 [S]	Sonny Stitt Plays Jimmy Giuffre Arrangements	1960	40.00
❑ MGVS-6108 [S]	Sonny Stitt Sits In with the Oscar Peterson Trio	1960	40.00
❑ MGVS-6149	Sonny Stitt Blows the Blues	1996	40.00
—Audiophile reissue by Classic Records			
❑ MGVS-6149 [S]	Sonny Stitt Blows the Blues	1960	40.00
❑ MGVS-6149-45 [(4)]	Sonny Stitt Blows the Blues	1999	40.00
—Audiophile reissue by Classic Records; plays at 45 rpm			
❑ MGVS-6154 [S]	Saxophone Supremacy	1960	—
—Canceled			
❑ MGVS-6162 [S]	Sonny Stitt Swings the Most	1960	—
—Canceled			
❑ MGV-8219 [M]	New York Jazz	1957	50.00
❑ V-8219 [M]	New York Jazz	1961	25.00
❑ MGV-8250 [M]	Only the Blues	1958	50.00
❑ V-8250 [M]	Only the Blues	1961	25.00
❑ MGV-8262 [M]	Sonny Side Up	1958	60.00
❑ V-8262 [M]	Sonny Side Up	1961	30.00
❑ MGV-8306 [M]	The Hard Swing	1959	50.00
❑ V-8306 [M]	The Hard Swing	1961	25.00
❑ V6-8306 [S]	The Hard Swing	1961	20.00
❑ MGV-8309 [M]	Sonny Stitt Plays Jimmy Giuffre Arrangements	1959	50.00
❑ V-8309 [M]	Sonny Stitt Plays Jimmy Giuffre Arrangements	1961	25.00
❑ V6-8309 [S]	Sonny Stitt Plays Jimmy Giuffre Arrangements	1961	20.00
❑ MGV-8324 [M]	Personal Appearance	1959	50.00
❑ V-8324 [M]	Personal Appearance	1961	25.00
❑ MGV-8344 [M]	Sonny Stitt Sits In with the Oscar Peterson Trio	1959	50.00
❑ V-8344 [M]	Sonny Stitt Sits In with the Oscar Peterson Trio	1961	25.00
❑ V6-8344 [S]	Sonny Stitt Sits In with the Oscar Peterson Trio	1961	20.00
❑ MGV-8374 [M]	Sonny Stitt Blows the Blues	1960	50.00
❑ V-8374 [M]	Sonny Stitt Blows the Blues	1961	25.00
❑ V6-8374 [S]	Sonny Stitt Blows the Blues	1961	20.00
❑ MGV-8377 [M]	Saxophone Supremacy	1960	50.00
❑ V-8377 [M]	Saxophone Supremacy	1961	25.00
❑ MGV-8380 [M]	Sonny Stitt Swings the Most	1960	50.00
❑ V-8380 [M]	Sommy Stitt Swings the Most	1961	25.00
❑ MGV-8403 [M]	Sonny Stitt	1960	—
—Canceled			
❑ V-8451 [M]	The Sensual Sound of Sonny Stitt	1962	20.00
❑ V6-8451 [S]	The Sensual Sound of Sonny Stitt	1962	25.00
❑ V6-8837	Previously Unreleased Recordings	1974	12.00

WHO'S WHO IN JAZZ

Number	Title (A Side/B Side)	Yr	NM
❑ 21022	Sonny, Sweets and Jaws	1981	15.00
❑ 21025	The Bubba's Sessions	1982	15.00

STITT, SONNY, AND GENE AMMONS

Albums

Number	Title (A Side/B Side)	Yr	NM
❑			—

STOECKLEIN, VAL

45s

DOT

Number	Title (A Side/B Side)	Yr	NM
❑ 17200	Sounds of Yesterday/ Say It's Not Over	1969	15.00
❑ 17234	All the Way Home/I Wonder Who I'll Be Tomorrow	1969	15.00

Albums

DOT

Number	Title (A Side/B Side)	Yr	NM
❑ DLP-3904 [M]	Grey Life	1968	100.00
—Label is black, as if stock copy, but record is found inside stereo (25904) cover with "Monaural Promotion Not for Sale" sticker on front			
❑ DLP-25904 [S]	Grey Life	1968	40.00

STOLOFF, MORRIS

45s

COLPIX

Number	Title (A Side/B Side)	Yr	NM
❑ 103	Wild One/Bell, Book and Candle	1959	8.00

DECCA

Number	Title (A Side/B Side)	Yr	NM
❑ 9-29888	Moonglow and Theme from "Picnic"/Theme from "Picnic"	1956	10.00
—B-side by George Duning			
❑ 9-30030	Manhattan Romance & Sweet Sue, Just You/The Solid Gold Cadillac	1956	10.00
❑ 9-30064	Exactly Like You & Wanna Go Back to You/You Can't Run Away from It	1956	10.00
❑ 9-30167	Nightfall/Theme from "Full of Life"	1956	10.00
❑ 9-30388	Harmonica Theme from "Fire Down Below"/Half of My Heart	1957	10.00

MERCURY

Number	Title (A Side/B Side)	Yr	NM
❑ 70428X45	Memphis Blues/Wagon Wheels	1954	20.00
❑ 70472X45	Stars Fell Over Alabama/ By the Waters of Minnetonka	1954	20.00

REPRISE

Number	Title (A Side/B Side)	Yr	NM
❑ 0339	Sylvia/None But the Brave	1965	8.00

WARNER BROS.

Number	Title (A Side/B Side)	Yr	NM
❑ 5227	Fanny/Panisse and Son	1961	8.00

Albums

DECCA

Number	Title (A Side/B Side)	Yr	NM
❑ DL 8574 [M]	This Is Kim	1957	60.00
—Black label, silver print; Kim Novak is the cover model			

STOMPERS, THE

45s

GONE

Number	Title (A Side/B Side)	Yr	NM
❑ 5120	Stompin' Round the Christmas Tree/Forgive Me	1961	150.00

LANDA

Number	Title (A Side/B Side)	Yr	NM
❑ 684	Foolish One/ Quarter to Four Stomp	1962	25.00
❑ 684	Foolish One/Surf Stompin'	1962	25.00

MERCURY

Number	Title (A Side/B Side)	Yr	NM
❑ 72111	Frump/Blacksmith Blues	1963	15.00
—As "The Ski Stompers"			

SOUVENIR

Number	Title (A Side/B Side)	Yr	NM
❑ 1003	I Miss You So/Blue Moon of Kentucky	1960	100.00

STONE, JIMMY

45s

CROSS COUNTRY

Number	Title (A Side/B Side)	Yr	NM
❑ 523	Found/Mine	1956	300.00

GONE

Number	Title (A Side/B Side)	Yr	NM
❑ 5001	Found/Mine	1957	200.00

STONE, JUDY

45s

CAMEO

Number	Title (A Side/B Side)	Yr	NM
❑ 330	4,003,221 Tears from Now/ Hello Faithless	1964	20.00

STONE, SLY

See SLY STEWART.

STONE CIRCUS, THE

45s

MAINSTREAM

Number	Title (A Side/B Side)	Yr	NM
❑ 694	Mister Grey/(B-side unknown)	1969	20.00

Albums

MAINSTREAM

Number	Title (A Side/B Side)	Yr	NM
❑ S-6119	The Stone Circus	1969	80.00

STONE COUNTRY

45s

RCA VICTOR

Number	Title (A Side/B Side)	Yr	NM
❑ 47-9534	Wheels on Fire/ Million Dollar Bash	1968	8.00

Albums

RCA VICTOR

Number	Title (A Side/B Side)	Yr	NM
❑ LSP-3958	Stone Country	1968	20.00

STONE PONEYS

Also see LINDA RONSTADT.

45s

CAPITOL

Number	Title (A Side/B Side)	Yr	NM
❑ 2004	Different Drum/I've Got to Know	1967	15.00
❑ 2110	Up to My Neck in High Muddy Water/Carnival Bear	1968	10.00
❑ 2110 [PS]	Up to My Neck in High Muddy Water/Carnival Bear	1968	40.00
—By "Linda Ronstadt and the Stone Poneys"			
❑ 2195	Hobo (Mornin' Glory)/Some of Shelly's Blues	1968	10.00
❑ 5838	All the Beautiful Things/Sweet Summer Blue and Gold	1967	10.00
❑ 5910	One for One/Evergreen	1967	10.00

SIDEWALK

Number	Title (A Side/B Side)	Yr	NM
❑ 937	So Fine/Everyone Has Their Own Ideas	1968	200.00

Albums

CAPITOL

Number	Title (A Side/B Side)	Yr	NM
❑ ST 2666 [S]	The Stone Poneys	1967	30.00
❑ T 2666 [M]	The Stone Poneys	1967	25.00
❑ ST 2763 [S]	Evergreen, Vol. 2	1967	30.00
❑ T 2763 [M]	Evergreen, Vol. 2	1967	40.00
❑ ST 2863	Linda Ronstadt/Stone Poneys and Friends Vol. III	1968	50.00
❑ ST-11383	The Stone Poneys Featuring Linda Ronstadt	1974	10.00

PICKWICK

Number	Title (A Side/B Side)	Yr	NM
❑ SPC-3298	Stoney End	1976	12.00

STONE ROSES, THE

12-Inch Singles

SILVERTONE

Number	Title (A Side/B Side)	Yr	NM
❑ 1301	I Wanna Be Adored (2 versions)/ Going Down/Simeone	1989	8.00
❑ 1315-1	Fool's Gold (9:53)/Fool's Gold (4:15)/What the World Is Waiting For	1990	10.00
—Gold vinyl			
❑ 1399-1	One Love (7:45)/One Love (3:35)/Something's Burning	1990	8.00

Albums

SILVERTONE

Number	Title (A Side/B Side)	Yr	NM
❑ 1184-1-J	The Stone Roses	1989	12.00

STONE THE CROWS

45s

POLYDOR

Number	Title (A Side/B Side)	Yr	NM
❑ 14033	Fool on the Hill/ Raining in My Heart	1969	—
—Canceled			

Albums

POLYDOR

Number	Title (A Side/B Side)	Yr	NM
❑ 24-4019	Stone the Crows	1970	20.00
❑ PD-5020	Teenage Licks	1972	20.00
❑ PD-5037	Continuous Performance	1972	20.00

STONEGROUND

Albums

WARNER BROS.

Number	Title (A Side/B Side)	Yr	NM
❑ WS 1895	Stoneground	1971	15.00
❑ 2WS 1956 [(2)]	Family Album	1971	20.00
❑ BS 2645	Stoneground 3	1972	14.00

STONES, THE

45s

SULLY

Number	Title (A Side/B Side)	Yr	NM
❑ 928	She Said Yeah/Watch Me	1966	75.00
—Reissued with group renamed "The Tracers"			

STONEY AND MEATLOAF

Also see MEAT LOAF.

45s

RARE EARTH

Number	Title (A Side/B Side)	Yr	NM
❑ 5027	What You See Is What You Get/ Lady Be Mine	1971	6.00
❑ 5033	The Way You Do the Things You Do/It Takes All Kinds of People	1971	6.00

Albums

PRODIGAL

Number	Title (A Side/B Side)	Yr	NM
❑ 10	Stoney and Meatloaf	1978	12.00

RARE EARTH

Number	Title (A Side/B Side)	Yr	NM
❑ R 528	Stoney and Meatloaf	1971	20.00

STOOGES, THE See IGGY AND THE STOOGES.

STOOKEY, PAUL Also see PETER, PAUL AND MARY.

45s

BENSON

Number	Title (A Side/B Side)	Yr	NM
❑ 5616 [DJ]	For Christmas (same on both sides)	198?	4.00

—As "Noel Paul Stookey and the Bodyworks Band"

Number	Title (A Side/B Side)	Yr	NM
❑ 5616 [PS]	For Christmas (same on both sides)	198?	4.00

WARNER BROS.

Number	Title (A Side/B Side)	Yr	NM
❑ 7511	Wedding Song (There Is Love)/Give a Damn	1971	6.00
❑ 7602	Hey, Sad Sack/Sebastian	1972	5.00
❑ 7683	Funky Monkey (Part 1)/Blessed	1973	5.00

—As "Noel Paul Stookey"

Albums

WARNER BROS.

Number	Title (A Side/B Side)	Yr	NM
❑ WS 1912	Paul and...	1971	10.00
❑ BS 2674	One Night Stand	1973	10.00

—As "Noel Paul Stookey"

STORIES

45s

KAMA SUTRA

Number	Title (A Side/B Side)	Yr	NM
❑ 545	I'm Coming Home/You Told Me	1972	4.00
❑ 558	Top of the City/Stepback	1972	4.00
❑ 566	Darling/Take Cover	1972	4.00
❑ 574	Love in Motion/Changes Have Begun	1973	4.00
❑ 577	Brother Louie/What Comes After	1973	5.00
❑ 577	Brother Louie/Changes Have Begun	1973	6.00
❑ 584	Mammy Blue/Travelling Underground	1973	4.00
❑ 588	Circles/If It Feels Good	1974	4.00
❑ 594	Another Love/Love Is In Motion	1974	4.00

Albums

KAMA SUTRA

Number	Title (A Side/B Side)	Yr	NM
❑ KSBS-2051	Stories	1972	12.00
❑ KSBS-2068	About Us	1973	12.00

—Regular cover; "Brother Louie" added as the last song on side 2

Number	Title (A Side/B Side)	Yr	NM
❑ KSBS-2068	About Us	1973	15.00

—Gatefold cover; "Brother Louie" added as the last song on side 2

Number	Title (A Side/B Side)	Yr	NM
❑ KSBS-2068	About Us	1973	30.00

—Gatefold; does NOT contain "Brother Louie"

Number	Title (A Side/B Side)	Yr	NM
❑ KSBS-2078	Traveling Underground	1974	12.00

STORM, BILLY

45s

ATLANTIC

Number	Title (A Side/B Side)	Yr	NM
❑ 2076	In the Chapel in the Moonlight/Sure As You're Born	1960	12.00
❑ 2098	When You Dance/Dear One	1961	12.00
❑ 2112	Honey Love/A Kiss from Your Lips	1961	12.00

BUENA VISTA

Number	Title (A Side/B Side)	Yr	NM
❑ 403	Puppy Love Is Here to Stay/Push Over	1962	15.00
❑ 413	Love Theme from El Cid/Cee Cee Rider	1962	15.00
❑ 415	Double Date/Good Girl	1963	15.00
❑ 418	'Deed I Do/Lonely People Do Foolish Things	1963	15.00
❑ 424	He Knows How Much We Can Bear/Motherless Child	1963	20.00
❑ 429	Since I Fell for You/Body and Soul	1964	20.00

COLUMBIA

Number	Title (A Side/B Side)	Yr	NM
❑ 4-41356	This Is Always/I've Come of Age	1959	15.00
❑ 41431	Easy Chair/You Just Can't Plan These Things	1959	15.00
❑ 41494	I Can't Stop Crying for You/Emotion	1959	15.00
❑ 41545	Enchanted/When the Whole World Smiles Again	1959	15.00

GREGMARK

Number	Title (A Side/B Side)	Yr	NM
❑ 9	3000 Tears/Who'll Keep an Eye on Jane	1961	12.00

HANNA-BARBERA

Number	Title (A Side/B Side)	Yr	NM
❑ 474	Please Don't Mention Her Name/The Warmest Love	1966	20.00
❑ 474 [PS]	Please Don't Mention Her Name/The Warmest Love	1966	25.00

INFINITY

Number	Title (A Side/B Side)	Yr	NM
❑ 013	Love Theme from El Cid/Don't Let Go	1962	12.00
❑ 018	Since I Fell for You/A Million Miles from Nowhere	1963	12.00
❑ 023	I Can't Help It/Educated Fool	1963	12.00

LOMA

Number	Title (A Side/B Side)	Yr	NM
❑ 2001	Baby, Don't Look Down/I Never Want to Dream Again	1964	10.00
❑ 2009	Goldfinger Theme/Debbie and Mitch	1965	10.00

ODE

Number	Title (A Side/B Side)	Yr	NM
❑ 120	Coal Mine/Tonight I'll Be Staying Here with You	1968	8.00

Albums

BUENA VISTA

Number	Title (A Side/B Side)	Yr	NM
❑ BV-3315 [M]	Billy Storm	1963	100.00
❑ STER-3315 [S]	Billy Storm	1963	120.00

FAMOUS

Number	Title (A Side/B Side)	Yr	NM
❑ F-504	This Is the Night	1969	100.00

STORM, RORY, AND THE HURRICANES The group that Ringo Starr drummed for before joining the Beatles. He is not on this record.

45s

COLUMBIA

Number	Title (A Side/B Side)	Yr	NM
❑ 43018	I Can Tell/Let's Stomp	1964	25.00

—B-side by Faron's Flamingos

STORM, TOM, AND THE PEPS

45s

GE GE

Number	Title (A Side/B Side)	Yr	NM
❑ 501	I Love You/That's the Way Love Is	1965	30.00

STORME, ROBB

45s

AURORA

Number	Title (A Side/B Side)	Yr	NM
❑ 162	Here Today/Don't Cry	1966	12.00

CAPITOL

Number	Title (A Side/B Side)	Yr	NM
❑ 5452	Love Is Strange/Shy Guy	1965	10.00

STORMS, THE Also see JODY REYNOLDS.

45s

SUNDOWN

Number	Title (A Side/B Side)	Yr	NM
❑ 114	Thunder/Tarantula	1959	50.00

—This was re-recorded on Indigo 127

STORYTELLERS, THE

45s

CAPITOL

Number	Title (A Side/B Side)	Yr	NM
❑ 5042	I Don't Want an Angel/Down in the Valley	1964	25.00

CLASSIC ARTISTS

Number	Title (A Side/B Side)	Yr	NM
❑ 137	Christmas Time Is Coming/White Christmas	1990	5.00

—B-side by The Storytellers and Vicky Tafoya

DIMENSION

Number	Title (A Side/B Side)	Yr	NM
❑ 1014	When Two People/Time Will Tell	1963	20.00

RAMARCA

Number	Title (A Side/B Side)	Yr	NM
❑ 501	When Two People/Time Will Tell	1963	30.00

STACK

Number	Title (A Side/B Side)	Yr	NM
❑ 500	Hey Baby/You Played Me for a Fool	1959	200.00

STOWAWAYS, THE

Albums

JUSTICE

Number	Title (A Side/B Side)	Yr	NM
❑ JLP-148	The Stowaways	1968	500.00

STRANGE, BILLY

45s

BUENA VISTA

Number	Title (A Side/B Side)	Yr	NM
❑ 406	I'll Remember April/The Mooncussors	1962	10.00
❑ 417	Johnny Shiloh/Day by Day	1963	10.00

COLISEUM

Number	Title (A Side/B Side)	Yr	NM
❑ 605	A Lotta Limbo (Part 1)/A Lotta Limbo (Part 2)	1963	12.00

GNP CRESCENDO

Number	Title (A Side/B Side)	Yr	NM
❑ 308	Wildwood Flower/Wabash Cannonball	1964	8.00
❑ 309	Charade/Where's Baby Gone	1964	8.00
❑ 320	The James Bond Theme/007 Theme	1964	8.00
❑ 334	Goldfinger/(Theme from) The Munsters	1965	8.00
❑ 341	The Man with the Golden Arm/Raunchy	1965	8.00
❑ 360	Remember Me (I'm the One Who Loves You)/Trains and Boats and Planes	1965	8.00
❑ 367	Our Man Flint/Run, Spy, Run	1966	8.00
❑ 374	Caliente/Have Tequila	1966	8.00
❑ 390	Go Ahead and Cry/Yours Is a World I Can't Live In	1967	6.00
❑ 395	You Only Live Twice/For a Few Dollars More	1967	6.00
❑ 413	Hang 'Em High/Five Card Stud	1968	6.00
❑ 417	The High Chaparral/Gunsmoke	1968	6.00
❑ 477	Chattanooga Choo Choo/Track Walkin'	1974	4.00
❑ 800	Star Trek/Theme from "Jaws"	1975	5.00

LIBERTY

Number	Title (A Side/B Side)	Yr	NM
❑ 55362	Long Steel Road/Soft Chains of Love	1961	10.00
❑ 55414	A Life of Pretend/I'm Still Crying	1962	10.00

TOWER

Number	Title (A Side/B Side)	Yr	NM
❑ 515	De Sade/Nocturne Permission	1969	8.00

Albums

CHESS

Number	Title (A Side/B Side)	Yr	NM
❑ CH2-6027 [(2)]	One More Time	1988	12.00

COLISEUM

Number	Title (A Side/B Side)	Yr	NM
❑ CM-1001 [M]	Limbo Rock	1962	40.00

GNP CRESCENDO

Number	Title (A Side/B Side)	Yr	NM
❑ GNP-94 [M]	Twelve String Guitar	1963	12.00
❑ GNPS-94 [S]	Twelve String Guitar	1963	15.00
❑ GNP-97 [M]	Mr. Guitar	1963	12.00
❑ GNPS-97 [S]	Mr. Guitar	1963	15.00
❑ GNP-98 [M]	Five String Banjo	1964	12.00
❑ GNPS-98 [S]	Five String Banjo	1964	15.00
❑ GNP-2004 [M]	The James Bond Theme	1964	12.00
❑ GNPS-2004 [S]	The James Bond Theme	1964	15.00
❑ GNP-2006 [M]	Goldfinger	1965	12.00
❑ GNPS-2006 [S]	Goldfinger	1965	15.00
❑ GNP-2009 [M]	English Hits of '65	1965	12.00
❑ GNPS-2009 [S]	English Hits of '65	1965	15.00
❑ GNP-2012 [M]	Billy Strange Plays the Hits	1965	12.00
❑ GNPS-2012 [S]	Billy Strange Plays the Hits	1965	15.00
❑ GNP-2016 [M]	Folk Rock Hits	1965	12.00
❑ GNPS-2016 [S]	Folk Rock Hits	1965	15.00
❑ GNP-2019 [M]	Secret Agent File	1966	12.00
❑ GNPS-2019 [S]	Secret Agent File	1966	15.00
❑ GNP-2022 [M]	In the Mexican Bag	1966	12.00
❑ GNPS-2022 [S]	In the Mexican Bag	1966	15.00
❑ GNP-2024 [M]	Billy Strange Plays Roger Miller Hits	1966	12.00
❑ GNPS-2024 [S]	Billy Strange Plays Roger Miller Hits	1966	15.00
❑ GNP-2030 [M]	Billy Strange with the Challengers	1966	15.00
❑ GNPS-2030 [S]	Billy Strange with the Challengers	1966	20.00
❑ GNP-2037 [M]	The Best of Billy Strange	1967	12.00
❑ GNPS-2037 [S]	The Best of Billy Strange	1967	12.00
❑ GNPS-2039	A James Bond Double Feature	1967	12.00
❑ GNPS-2041	Railroad Man	1968	12.00
❑ GNPS-2046	Great Western Themes	1969	12.00
❑ GNPS-2094	Dyn-o-mite Guitar	197?	10.00

SUNSET

Number	Title (A Side/B Side)	Yr	NM
❑ SUS-5209	Mr. Guitar	1968	10.00

SURREY

Number	Title (A Side/B Side)	Yr	NM
❑ SS-1002	The Best of Billy Strange	1965	15.00

TRADITION

Number	Title (A Side/B Side)	Yr	NM
❑ 2080	Strange Country	1969	10.00

STRANGE, TOMMY

45s

ERA

Number	Title (A Side/B Side)	Yr	NM
❑ 3157	Don't Bug Me Baby/Two Steps Forward	1965	8.00

RAMCO

Number	Title (A Side/B Side)	Yr	NM
❑ 1986	Piano Man from Louisiana/My Mind Just Don't Fit My Head	1967	8.00
❑ 1995	She Was Never Mine to Lose/One More Time	1967	8.00

ROCKO

Number	Title (A Side/B Side)	Yr	NM
❑ 504	Nervous and Shakin' All Over/What Am I to Do	1958	200.00

STRANGEBREW

45s

ABC

Number	Title (A Side/B Side)	Yr	NM
❑ 11217	Union Man/I Can Hardly Wait to Live	1969	12.00

Albums

ABC

Number	Title (A Side/B Side)	Yr	NM
❑ ABCS-672	Very Strangebrew	1969	20.00

STRANGELOVES, THE Also see THE SHEEP.

45s

BANG

Number	Title (A Side/B Side)	Yr	NM
❑ 501	I Want Candy/It's About My Baby	1965	15.00
❑ 508	Cara-Lin/(Roll On) Mississippi	1965	12.00
❑ 514	Night Time/Rhythm of Love	1965	12.00
❑ 524	Hand Jive/I Gotta Dance	1966	12.00
❑ 544	Just the Way You Are/Quarter to Three	1967	12.00

SIRE

Number	Title (A Side/B Side)	Yr	NM
❑ 4102	I Wanna Do It/Honey Do	1968	10.00

S

Strawberry Alarm Clock, *The World in a Sea Shell*, Uni 73035, 1968, **$40.**

Number	Title (A Side/B Side)	Yr	NM
SWAN			
❑ 4192	Love Love (That's All I Want from You)/I'm on Fire	1964	20.00
Albums			
BANG			
❑ BLP-211 [M]	I Want Candy	1965	80.00
❑ BLPS-211 [S]	I Want Candy	1965	100.00

STRANGERS, THE

Number	Title (A Side/B Side)	Yr	NM
45s			
CAPITOL			
❑ 3144	Song from Sleepwalk/ Slow 'n Easy	1971	8.00
—By "Merle Haggard's Strangers"			
❑ 3376	I'm a Light Boy/ Shoulder to Cry On	1972	10.00

STRANGERS, THE (1) Instrumental group; the only Strangers that made the charts.

Number	Title (A Side/B Side)	Yr	NM
45s			
TITAN			
❑ 1701	The Caterpillar Crawl/ Rockin' Rebel	1959	30.00
❑ 1702	Hill Stomp/A Lost Soul	1959	25.00
❑ 1704	Boogie Man/Young Maggie	1960	25.00
❑ 1711	Navajo/Dance of the Ants	1960	25.00

STRANGERS, THE (2)

Number	Title (A Side/B Side)	Yr	NM
45s			
CHATTAHOOCHIE			
❑ 710	Like a Stranger/Can't Get the Water from My Eye	1966	12.00
JUBILEE			
❑ 5514	Plan On Someone New/ What's the Matter Baby	1965	12.00

STRANGERS, THE (3)

Number	Title (A Side/B Side)	Yr	NM
45s			
CHECKER			
❑ 1010	Darlin'/Pa and Billie	1962	15.00

STRANGERS, THE (4)

Number	Title (A Side/B Side)	Yr	NM
45s			
CHOICE			
❑ 5	"Bart" Maverick/"Bret" Maverick	1960	20.00

STRANGERS, THE (5)

Number	Title (A Side/B Side)	Yr	NM
45s			
CHRISTY			
❑ 107	We're in Love, We're in Love, We're in Love/Crab Louie	1959	30.00
❑ 108	J-U-D-Y/The Lord Will Welcome You	1959	25.00

STRANGERS, THE (6) Group that backed BOBBY VEE on some of his later records, most notably "Come Back When You Grow Up."

Number	Title (A Side/B Side)	Yr	NM
45s			
CUCA			
❑ 1172	Runaway/John Henry	1960	200.00
LIBERTY			
❑ 55481	Toy Soldier/Loco	1962	20.00
❑ 55550	Card Shark/Mindreader	1963	20.00

STRANGERS, THE (7)

Number	Title (A Side/B Side)	Yr	NM
45s			
KING			
❑ 4697	My Friends/I've Got Eyes	1954	400.00
❑ 4709	Blue Flowers/Beg and Steal	1954	500.00
❑ 4728	Hoping You'll Understand/ Just Don't Care	1954	400.00
❑ 4745	Drop Down to My Place/ Get It One More Time	1954	300.00
❑ 4766	How Long Must I Wait/ Dreams Came True	1955	250.00
❑ 4821	Without a Friend/Think Again	1955	60.00
—With "High Fidelity" on label			
❑ 4821	Without a Friend/Think Again	1955	250.00
—Without "High Fidelity" on label (original)			

STRANGERS, THE (8)

Number	Title (A Side/B Side)	Yr	NM
45s			
LINDA			
❑ 118	Easy Livin'/Tell Me	1965	30.00
WARNER BROS.			
❑ 5438	Night Winds/These Are the Things I Love	1964	20.00

STRANGERS, THE (9)

Number	Title (A Side/B Side)	Yr	NM
45s			
MGM			
❑ 11980	Strange Lady in Town/North Dakota	1955	40.00

STRANGLERS, THE

Number	Title (A Side/B Side)	Yr	NM
12-Inch Singles			
EPIC			
❑ EAS 1022 [DJ]	All Day and All of the Night (short)/All Day and All of the Night (Long)	1988	6.00
❑ EAS1022 [DJ]	All Day and All of the Night (short)/All Day and All of the Night (Long)	1988	6.00
❑ EAS 2067 [DJ]	Sweet Smell of Success (4 versions)/Instead of This/ Poisonality	1990	12.00
❑ EAS2067 [DJ]	Sweet Smell of Success (4 versions)/Instead of This/ Poisonality	1990	12.00
❑ EAS 2160 [DJ]	Someone Like You/Motorbike/ Something	1990	10.00
❑ EAS2160 [DJ]	Someone Like You/Motorbike/ Something	1990	10.00
❑ EAS2573 [DJ]	Always the Sun (3 mixes)	1986	6.00
❑ EAS 02573 [DJ]	Always the Sun (3 mixes)	1986	6.00
❑ EAS2711 [DJ]	Dreamtime/Shakin' Like a Leaf (Jelly Mix)	1986	6.00
❑ EAS 02711 [DJ]	Dreamtime/Shakin' Like a Leaf (Jelly Mix)	1986	6.00
❑ 03564	Midnight Summer Dream/ Paradise	1983	8.00
❑ 05144	Skin Deep/Here and There/ Vladimir and the Beast	1985	8.00
45s			
A&M			
❑ 1973	Hanging Around/Grip (Get a Grip on Yourself)/Something Better Change/Straighten Out	1977	5.00
—With pink and white marbled vinyl			
❑ 1973 [DJ]	Hanging Around/Grip (Get a Grip on Yourself)/Something Better Change/Straighten Out	1977	4.00
—With pink and white marbled vinyl; "totally safe" promo versions			
❑ 1973 [DJ]	Hanging Around/Grip (Get a Grip on Yourself)/Something Better Change/Straighten Out	1977	4.00
—With pink and white marbled vinyl; "totally safe" promo versions			
❑ 1973 [PS]	Hanging Around/Grip (Get a Grip on Yourself)/Something Better Change/Straighten Out	1977	4.00
—Promo sleeve accompanying the "totally safe" 45			
❑ 1973 [PS]	Hanging Around/Grip (Get a Grip on Yourself)/Something Better Change/Straighten Out	1977	5.00
❑ 2054	Nice 'N' Sleazy/Shut Up	1978	4.00
EPIC			
❑ 06990	Always the Sun/Mayan Skies	1987	3.00
❑ 07205	Dreamtime/Ghost Train	1987	3.00
I.R.S.			
❑ 9018	The Raven/Duchess	1980	4.00
❑ 9018 [PS]	The Raven/Duchess	1980	4.00
7-Inch Extended Plays			
I.R.S.			
❑ SP-70952	White Room/Straighten Out// Do the European/Choosey Suzie	1980	6.00
—Bonus with early copies of LP "Stranglers IV"; no picture sleeve			
Albums			
A&M			
❑ SP-4648	Rattus Norvegicus	1977	16.00
—With bonus single "Peasant in the Big Shitty"/"Choosie Suzie" (FREE-3)			
❑ SP-4659	No More Heroes	1977	16.00
❑ SP-4706	Black and White	1978	12.00
—Black vinyl without bonus single			
❑ SP-4706	Black and White	1978	16.00
—Grey marbled wax; first 75,000 released with white-vinyl EP (FREE-9)			

Except when noted otherwise, VG = 25% of NM, and VG+ = 50% of NM. (Example: VG = $2.00, VG+ = $4.00 and NM = $8.00.)

EMI AMERICA

Number	Title (A Side/B Side)	Yr	NM
❑ ST-17189	The Men in Black	1986	15.00
—Reissue			
❑ SQ-17207	La Folie	1986	15.00
—U.S. issue of 1981 U.K. release			

EPIC

Number	Title (A Side/B Side)	Yr	NM
❑ BFE 38542	Feline	1983	12.00
❑ BFE 39959	Aural Sculpture	1985	12.00
❑ BFE 40607	Dreamtime	1986	10.00
❑ FE 44209	All Live and All of the Night	1988	10.00
❑ E 46120	Stranglers 10	1990	10.00
❑ E 47081	The Stranglers Greatest Hits 1977-1990	1990	12.00

I.R.S.

Number	Title (A Side/B Side)	Yr	NM
❑ SP-70011	Stranglers IV	1980	15.00
—First pressings with bonus 7-inch EP (SP-70952)			

STIFF AMERICA

Number	Title (A Side/B Side)	Yr	NM
❑ USE-10	The Men in Black	1981	15.00

STRASSMAN, MARCIA

45s

UNI

Number	Title (A Side/B Side)	Yr	NM
❑ 55006	The Flower Children/ Out of the Picture	1967	10.00
❑ 55023	The Groovy World of Jack and Jill/The Flower Shop	1967	10.00
❑ 55023 [PS]	The Groovy World of Jack and Jill/The Flower Shop	1967	15.00
❑ 55056	Star Gazer/Self-Analysis	1968	10.00

STRAWBERRY ALARM CLOCK

45s

ALL AMERICAN

Number	Title (A Side/B Side)	Yr	NM
❑ 373	Incense and Peppermints/ The Birdman of Alcatrash	1967	200.00

UNI

Number	Title (A Side/B Side)	Yr	NM
❑ 55018	Incense and Peppermints/ The Birdman of Alcatrash	1967	12.00
❑ 55046	Tomorrow/Birds in My Tree	1967	10.00
❑ 55055	Pretty Song from Psych-Out/Sit with the Guru	1968	10.00
❑ 55076	Barefoot in Baltimore/Angry Young Man	1968	10.00
❑ 55093	Paxton's Back Street Carnival/ Sea Shell	1968	10.00
❑ 55113	Stand By/Miss Attraction	1969	8.00
❑ 55125	Good Morning Starshine/ Me and the Township	1969	8.00
❑ 55158	Desiree/Changes	1969	8.00
❑ 55185	Small Package/ Starting Out the Day	1969	8.00
❑ 55190	I Climbed the Mountain/Three	1969	8.00
❑ 55218	California Day/Three	1970	20.00
❑ 55241	Girl from the City/Three	1970	20.00

Albums

UNI

Number	Title (A Side/B Side)	Yr	NM
❑ 3014 [M]	Incense and Peppermints	1967	50.00
❑ 73014 [S]	Incense and Peppermints	1967	40.00
❑ 73025	Wake Up It's Tomorrow	1968	40.00
❑ 73035	The World in a Sea Shell	1968	40.00
❑ 73054	Good Morning Starshine	1969	40.00
❑ 73074	The Best of the Strawberry Alarm Clock	1970	40.00

VOCALION

Number	Title (A Side/B Side)	Yr	NM
❑ VL 73915	Changes	1971	50.00

STRAWBERRY CHILDREN

45s

SOUL CITY

Number	Title (A Side/B Side)	Yr	NM
❑ 758	Love Years Coming/ One Stands Here	1967	20.00

STRAWBS, THE

45s

A&M

Number	Title (A Side/B Side)	Yr	NM
❑ 944	Oh How She Changed/ Or Am I Dreaming	1968	5.00
❑ 998	Poor Jimmy Wilson/The Man Who Called Himself Jesus	1968	5.00
❑ 1242 [DJ]	Where Is This Dream of Your Youth (mono/stereo)	1971	6.00
—No stock copies known			
❑ 1364	Heavy Disguise/Benedictus	1972	5.00
❑ 1419	Part of the Union/Tomorrow	1973	5.00
❑ 1451	Lay Down/The Winter and the Summer	1973	5.00
❑ 1476	Shine On Silver Sun/ And Wherefore	1973	5.00
❑ 1519	Round and Round/ The Heroine's Theme	1974	5.00
❑ 1687	Where Do You Go/Lemon Pie	1975	4.00
❑ 1747	Little Sleepy/Golden Salamander	1975	4.00

ARISTA

Number	Title (A Side/B Side)	Yr	NM
❑ 0327	I Don't Want to Talk About It/ Words of Wisdom	1978	4.00

OYSTER

Number	Title (A Side/B Side)	Yr	NM
❑ 702	I Only Want My Love to Grow on You/(Wasting My Time) Thinking of You	1976	4.00
❑ 704	So Close and Yet So Far Away/ (B-side unknown)	1977	4.00
❑ 705	Burning for Me/Heartbreaker	1977	4.00

Albums

A&M

Number	Title (A Side/B Side)	Yr	NM
❑ SP-3607	Hero and Heroine	1974	15.00
❑ SP-4288	Just a Collection of Antiques and Curios	1971	15.00
❑ SP-4304	From the Witchwood	1971	15.00
❑ SP-4344	Grave New World	1972	15.00
❑ SP-4383	Bursting at the Seams	1973	15.00
❑ SP-4506	Ghosts	1975	15.00
❑ SP-4544	Nomadness	1975	15.00
❑ SP-6005 [(2)]	Best of the Strawbs	1978	12.00

ARISTA

Number	Title (A Side/B Side)	Yr	NM
❑ AB 4172	Deadlines	1978	10.00

OYSTER

Number	Title (A Side/B Side)	Yr	NM
❑ OY-1603	Deep Cuts	1976	12.00
❑ OY-1604	Burning for You	1977	12.00

STRAY CATS

Also see BRIAN SETZER. Also see BRIAN SETZER.

12-Inch Singles

EMI AMERICA

Number	Title (A Side/B Side)	Yr	NM
❑ SPRO-9868 [DJ]	Reckless (same on both sides)	1986	12.00
❑ SPRO [DJ]	(She's) Sexy + 17 (3:13)/ (She's) Sexy + 17 (3:28)	1983	12.00
❑ SPRO-9868 [DJ]	Reckless (same on both sides)	1986	15.00
❑ SPRO-9959/65 [DJ]	(She's) Sexy + 17 (3:13) (3:28)	1983	12.00

45s

EMI AMERICA

Number	Title (A Side/B Side)	Yr	NM
❑ B-8122	Stray Cat Strut/ You Don't Believe Me	1982	3.00
❑ B-8122 [PS]	Stray Cat Strut/ You Don't Believe Me	1982	8.00
❑ B-8132	Rock This Town/ You Can't Hurry Love	1982	3.00
❑ B-8132 [PS]	Rock This Town/ You Can't Hurry Love	1982	4.00
❑ B-8168	(She's) Sexy + 17/ Lookin' Better Every Beer	1983	3.00
❑ B-8168 [PS]	(She's) Sexy + 17/ Lookin' Better Every Beer	1983	3.00
❑ BB-8169-1	(She's) Sexy + 17/ Lookin' Better Every Beer	1983	5.00
—Paired with 8169-2			
❑ BB-8169-1/2 [PS]	(She's) Sexy + 17/Lookin' Better Every Beer/Cruisin'/ Lucky Charm	1983	5.00
—Gatefold sleeve for two-record set			
❑ BB-8169-2	Cruisin'/Lucky Charm	1983	5.00
—Paired with 8169-1			
❑ B-8185	I Won't Stand In Your Way/ (Acappella Version)	1983	3.00
❑ B-8194	Look at That Cadillac/ Lucky Charm	1984	5.00
❑ B-8194 [PS]	Look at That Cadillac/ Lucky Charm	1984	5.00

Albums

EMI

Number	Title (A Side/B Side)	Yr	NM
❑ R 101178	Blast Off	1989	15.00
—BMG Music Service edition			

EMI AMERICA

Number	Title (A Side/B Side)	Yr	NM
❑ SN-16354	Rant 'n' Rave with the Stray Cats	1985	8.00
—Budget-line reissue			
❑ ST-17070	Built for Speed	1982	10.00
❑ SO-17102	Rant 'n' Rave with the Stray Cats	1983	10.00
❑ ST-17226	Rock Therapy	1986	15.00
❑ ST-517070	Built for Speed	1982	10.00
—Columbia House edition			

MOBILE FIDELITY

Number	Title (A Side/B Side)	Yr	NM
❑ 1-125	Built for Speed	1983	—
—Released only on cassette			

STREAMERS, THE

45s

DOT

Number	Title (A Side/B Side)	Yr	NM
❑ 16648	Slip-Stream/Blue Mountain	1964	30.00

STREET CLEANERS, THE

Yet another incarnation of P.F. SLOAN and STEVE BARRI.

45s

AMY

Number	Title (A Side/B Side)	Yr	NM
❑ 914	Garbage City/That's Cool, That's Trash	1964	30.00

STREET CORNERS, THE

45s

PARKWAY

Number	Title (A Side/B Side)	Yr	NM
❑ 997	My Generation/I Don't Care	1966	10.00

STREET NOISE

45s

EVOLUTION

Number	Title (A Side/B Side)	Yr	NM
❑ 1014	Run or Die/Six Days on the Road	1969	8.00

Albums

EVOLUTION

Number	Title (A Side/B Side)	Yr	NM
❑ 2010	Street Noise	1970	20.00

STREISAND, BARBRA

Also see BARBRA AND NEIL.

12-Inch Singles

CASABLANCA

Number	Title (A Side/B Side)	Yr	NM
❑ NBD 20199	No More Tears (Enough Is Enough) (11:40)/(B-side blank)	1979	10.00
—With Donna Summer			

COLUMBIA

Number	Title (A Side/B Side)	Yr	NM
❑ AS 217 [DJ]	Shake Me, Wake Me, When It's Over (same on both sides)	1975	100.00
❑ AS 625 [DJ]	The Main Event/Fight (11:42) (same on both sides)	1979	25.00
❑ AS 1610 [DJ]	Memory (same on both sides)	1981	40.00
❑ AS99 1791 [DJ]	The Way He Makes Me Feel (same on both sides?)	1983	50.00
—Promo-only picture disc in plastic sleeve with sticker			
❑ 43-02089	Promises (5:55)/ Make It Like a Memory	1981	25.00
❑ 44-05167	Emotion (Vocal Dance Version 6:34) (Instrumental 4:44)	1985	20.00

45s

ARISTA

Number	Title (A Side/B Side)	Yr	NM
❑ 0123	How Lucky Can You Get/ More Than You Know	1975	6.00

COLUMBIA

Number	Title (A Side/B Side)	Yr	NM
❑ 11-02065	Promises/Make It Like a Memory	1981	4.00
❑ 18-02621	Comin' In and Out of Your Life/ Lost Inside of You	1981	4.00
❑ 18-02717	Memory/Evergreen (Love Theme from "A Star Is Born")	1982	4.00
❑ 38-04177	The Way He Makes Me Feel (Studio)/(Film Version)	1983	3.00
❑ 38-04177 [PS]	The Way He Makes Me Feel (Studio)/(Film Version)	1983	4.00
❑ 38-04357	Papa Can You Hear Me?/ Will Someone Ever Look at Me That Way	1984	3.00
❑ 38-04357 [PS]	Papa Can You Hear Me?/ Will Someone Ever Look at Me That Way	1984	4.00
❑ 38-04605	Left in the Dark/Here We Are at Last	1984	3.00
❑ 38-04605 [PS]	Left in the Dark/Here We Are at Last	1984	4.00
❑ 38-04695	Make No Mistake, He's Mine/ Clear Sailing	1984	3.00
—A-side with Kim Carnes			
❑ 38-04695 [PS]	Make No Mistake, He's Mine/ Clear Sailing	1984	4.00
❑ 38-04707	Emotion/Here We Are at Last	1984	3.00
❑ 38-04707 [PS]	Emotion/Here We Are at Last	1984	4.00
❑ 38-05680	Somewhere/Not While I'm Around	1985	3.00
❑ 38-05680 [PS]	Somewhere/Not While I'm Around	1985	4.00
❑ 38-05837	Send In the Clowns/Being Alive	1986	4.00
❑ 38-05837 [PS]	Send In the Clowns/Being Alive	1986	8.00
❑ 38-08026	All I Ask of You/On My Way to You	1988	4.00
❑ 38-08026 [PS]	All I Ask of You/On My Way to You	1988	4.00
❑ 38-08062	Till I Loved You/Two People	1988	3.00
—A-side with Don Johnson			
❑ 38-08062 [PS]	Till I Loved You/Two People	1988	4.00
❑ 10075	Love in the Afternoon/ Guava Jelly	1974	5.00
❑ 10130	Let the Good Times Roll/ Jubilation	1975	5.00
❑ 10198	My Father's Song/By the Way	1975	5.00
❑ 10272	Shake Me, Wake Me, When It's Over/Widescreen	1975	5.00
❑ 3-10450	Love Theme from "A Star Is Born" (Evergreen)/ I Believe in Love	1976	5.00
❑ 3-10450 [PS]	Love Theme from "A Star Is Born" (Evergreen)/ I Believe in Love	1976	6.00

Number	Title (A Side/B Side)	Yr	NM
3-10555	My Heart Belongs to Me/Answer Me	1977	5.00
3-10756	Songbird/Honey Can I Put On Your Clothes	1978	4.00
3-10777	Love Theme from "Eyes of Laura Mars" (Prisoner)/Laura and Nevil	1978	4.00
3-10931	Superman/A Man I Loved	1979	4.00
3-11008	The Main Event/Fight//(Instrumental)	1979	4.00
1-11125	No More Tears (Enough Is Enough)/Wet	1979	4.00
—A-side with Donna Summer			
1-11125 [PS]	No More Tears (Enough Is Enough)/Wet	1979	5.00
1-11179	Kiss Me in the Rain/I Ain't Gonna Cry Tonight	1980	4.00
1-11364	Woman in Love/Run Wild	1980	4.00
11-11390	Guilty/Life Story	1980	4.00
—A-side with Barry Gibb			
11-11430	What Kind of Fool/The Love Inside	1981	4.00
—A-side with Barry Gibb			
42631	Happy Days Are Here Again/When the Sun Comes Out	1962	20.00
42648	My Coloring Book/Lover Come Back to Me	1962	15.00
42937	Gotta Move/Make Believe	1964	15.00
42965	People/I Am Woman	1964	10.00
43127	Funny Girl/Absent Minded Me	1964	10.00
43248	Why Did I Choose You/My Love	1965	8.00
43323	My Man/Where Is the Wonder	1965	8.00
43403	He Touched Me/I Like Him	1965	8.00
43469	Second Hand Rose/The Kind of Man a Woman Needs	1965	8.00
43518	Where Am I Going?/You Wanna Bet	1966	6.00
43612	Sam, You Made the Pants Too Long/The Minute Waltz	1966	6.00
43739	La Mer/C'est Rien	1966	8.00
43808	Free Again/I've Been Here	1966	6.00
43896	Sleep in Heavenly Peace (Silent Night)/Gounod's Ave Maria	1966	10.00
43896 [PS]	Sleep in Heavenly Peace (Silent Night)/Gounod's Ave Maria	1966	20.00
44225	Stout-Hearted Men/Look	1967	6.00
44331	Lover Man (Oh, Where Can You Be)/My Funny Valentine	1967	6.00
44350	Jingle Bells?/White Christmas	1967	30.00
44350 [PS]	Jingle Bells?/White Christmas	1967	40.00
44351	Have Yourself a Merry Little Christmas/The Best Gift	1967	10.00
44351 [PS]	Have Yourself a Merry Little Christmas/The Best Gift	1967	20.00
44352	My Favorite Things/The Christmas Song	1967	30.00
44352 [PS]	My Favorite Things/The Christmas Song	1967	40.00
44354	I Wonder As I Wander/The Lord's Prayer	1967	30.00
44474	Our Corner of the Night/He Could Show Me	1968	5.00
44532	Morning After/Where Is the Wonder	1968	5.00
44622	Funny Girl/I'd Rather Be Blue Over You	1968	5.00
44704	Don't Rain on My Parade/My Man	1968	6.00
44775	Punky's Dilemma/Frank Mills	1969	5.00
44921	Honey Pie/Little Tin Soldier	1969	5.00
45040	What About Today/What Are You Doing the Rest of Your Life	1969	5.00
45072	Love Is Only Love/Before the Parade Passes By	1970	5.00
45147	The Best Thing You've Ever Done/Summer Me, Winter Me	1970	5.00
45236	Stoney End/I'll Be Home	1970	5.00
45341	Time and Love/No Easy Way Down	1971	5.00
45384	Flim Flam Man/Maybe	1971	5.00
45414	Where You Lead/Since I Fell for You	1971	5.00
45471	Mother/The Summer Knows	1971	5.00
45511	One Less Bell to Answer-A House Is Not a Home/Space Captain	1971	5.00
45626	Sweet Inspiration-Where You Lead/Didn't We	1972	5.00
45686	Sing a Song-Make Your Own Kind of Music/Starting Here-Starting Now	1972	5.00
45739	Didn't We/On a Clear Day	1972	5.00
45780	If I Close My Eyes/(Instrumental)	1973	5.00
45944	The Way We Were/What Are You Doing the Rest of Your Life	1973	5.00
—A-side contains a different vocal than most of the album versions			
46024	All in Love Is Fair/My Buddy-How About Me	1974	5.00
68691	What Were We Thinking Of/Why Let It Go	1989	3.00
73016	We're Not Makin' Love Anymore/Here We Are at Last	1989	3.00
73794	Till I Loved You/Two People	1991	3.00
—Reissue			
38-73944	All I Ask of You/On My Way to You	1991	3.00
—Reissue			
38-77533	Ordinary Miracles/(Live)	1994	4.00
JZSP 79183/4 [DJ]	I'm All Smiles/Autumn	1964	30.00
—White label promo only			

7-Inch Extended Plays

COLUMBIA

Number	Title (A Side/B Side)	Yr	NM
7-30378	Stoney End/Just a Little Lovin' (Early in the Mornin')/Maybe//I Don't Know Where I Stand/If You Could Read My Mind	1971	12.00
—Jukebox issue; small hole, plays at 33 1/3 rpm			
7-30378 [PS]	Stoney End	1971	12.00

COLUMBIA MASTERWORKS

Number	Title (A Side/B Side)	Yr	NM
7-3220	Funny Girl/My Man/People//Roller Skate Rag/I'd Rather Be Blue Over You/Don't Rain on My Parade	1964	15.00
—Jukebox issue; small hole, plays at 33 1/3 rpm			
7-3220 [PS]	Funny Girl	1964	15.00

Albums

COLUMBIA

Number	Title	Yr	NM
A2S 1779 [(2)DJ]	The Legend of Barbra Streisand	1983	80.00
—Promo-only interview LP for "Yentl"			
CL 2007 [M]	The Barbra Streisand Album	1963	20.00
—"Guaranteed High Fidelity" on label			
CL 2007 [M]	The Barbra Streisand Album	1966	12.00
—"360 Sound Mono" on label			
CL 2054 [M]	The Second Barbra Streisand Album	1963	20.00
—"Guaranteed High Fidelity" on label			
CL 2054 [M]	The Second Barbra Streisand Album	1963	200.00
—Promo only on blue vinyl (white label)			
CL 2054 [M]	The Second Barbra Streisand Album	1966	12.00
—"360 Sound Mono" on label			
CL 2154 [M]	The Third Album	1964	20.00
—"Guaranteed High Fidelity" on label			
CL 2154 [M]	The Third Album	1966	12.00
—"360 Sound Mono" on label			
CL 2215 [M]	People	1964	20.00
—"Guaranteed High Fidelity" on label			
CL 2215 [M]	People	1966	12.00
—"360 Sound Mono" on label			
CL 2336 [M]	My Name Is Barbra	1965	20.00
—"Guaranteed High Fidelity" on label			
CL 2336 [M]	My Name Is Barbra	1966	12.00
—"360 Sound Mono" on label			
CL 2409 [M]	My Name Is Barbra, Two	1965	15.00
CL 2478 [M]	Color Me Barbra	1966	15.00
CL 2478 [M]	Color Me Barbra	1966	200.00
—Promo only on red vinyl (white label)			
CL 2547 [M]	Je M'Appelle Barbra	1966	15.00
CL 2682 [M]	Simply Streisand	1967	30.00
CL 2757 [M]	A Christmas Album	1967	25.00
CS 8807 [S]	The Barbra Streisand Album	1963	25.00
—"360 Sound Stereo" in black on label			
CS 8807 [S]	The Barbra Streisand Album	1966	15.00
—"360 Sound Stereo" in white on label			
CS 8807 [S]	The Barbra Streisand Album	1970	10.00
—Orange label			
PC 8807	The Barbra Streisand Album	197?	8.00
—Reissue with new prefix			
CS 8854 [S]	The Second Barbra Streisand Album	1963	25.00
—"360 Sound Stereo" in black on label			
CS 8854 [S]	The Second Barbra Streisand Album	1963	200.00
—Promo only on blue vinyl (white label)			
CS 8854 [S]	The Second Barbra Streisand Album	1966	15.00
—"360 Sound Stereo" in white on label			
CS 8854 [S]	The Second Barbra Streisand Album	1970	10.00
—Orange label			
PC 8854	The Second Barbra Streisand Album	197?	8.00
—Reissue with new prefix			
CS 8954 [S]	The Third Album	1964	25.00
—"360 Sound Stereo" in black on label			
CS 8954 [S]	The Third Album	1966	15.00
—"360 Sound Stereo" in white on label			
CS 8954 [S]	The Third Album	1970	10.00
—Orange label			
PC 8954	The Third Album	197?	8.00
—Reissue with new prefix			
CS 9015 [S]	People	1964	25.00
—"360 Sound Stereo" in black on label			
CS 9015 [S]	People	1966	15.00
—"360 Sound Stereo" in white on label			
CS 9015 [S]	People	1970	10.00
—Orange label			
PC 9015	People	197?	8.00
—Reissue with new prefix			
CS 9136 [S]	My Name Is Barbra	1965	25.00
—"360 Sound Stereo" in black on label			
CS 9136 [S]	My Name Is Barbra	1966	15.00
—"360 Sound Stereo" in white on label			
CS 9136 [S]	My Name Is Barbra	1970	10.00
—Orange label			
PC 9136	My Name Is Barbra	197?	8.00
—Reissue with new prefix			
CS 9209 [S]	My Name Is Barbra, Two	1965	20.00
—Red "360 Sound Stereo" label			
CS 9209 [S]	My Name Is Barbra, Two	1970	10.00
—Orange label			
PC 9209	My Name Is Barbra, Two	197?	8.00
—Reissue with new prefix			
CS 9278 [S]	Color Me Barbra	1966	20.00
—Red "360 Sound Stereo" label			
CS 9278 [S]	Color Me Barbra	1966	200.00
—Promo only on red vinyl (white label)			
CS 9278 [S]	Color Me Barbra	1970	10.00
—Orange label			
PC 9278	Color Me Barbra	197?	8.00
—Reissue with new prefix			
CS 9347 [S]	Je M'Appelle Barbra	1966	20.00
—Red "360 Sound Stereo" label			
CS 9347 [S]	Je M'Appelle Barbra	1970	10.00
—Orange label			
PC 9347	Je M'Appelle Barbra	197?	8.00
—Reissue with new prefix			
CS 9482 [S]	Simply Streisand	1967	20.00
—Red "360 Sound Stereo" label			
CS 9482 [S]	Simply Streisand	1970	10.00
—Orange label			
PC 9482	Simply Streisand	197?	8.00
—Reissue with new prefix			
CS 9557 [S]	A Christmas Album	1967	20.00
—Red "360 Sound Stereo" label			
CS 9557 [S]	A Christmas Album	1970	8.00
—Orange label			
PC 9557	A Christmas Album	198?	6.00
—Reissue with new prefix and bar code			
CS 9710	A Happening in Central Park	1968	15.00
—Red "360 Sound Stereo" label			
CS 9710	A Happening in Central Park	1970	10.00
—Orange label			
PC 9710	A Happening in Central Park	197?	8.00
—Reissue with new prefix			
CS 9816	What About Today?	1969	15.00
—Red "360 Sound Stereo" label			
CS 9816	What About Today?	1970	10.00
—Orange label			
PC 9816	What About Today?	197?	8.00
—Reissue with new prefix			
JC 9968	Barbra Streisand's Greatest Hits	197?	6.00
—Another reissue with a new prefix (postdates PC)			
KCS 9968	Barbra Streisand's Greatest Hits	1970	10.00
—Orange label			
KCS 9968	Barbra Streisand's Greatest Hits	1970	15.00
—Red "360 Sound Stereo" label			
PC 9968	Barbra Streisand's Greatest Hits	197?	8.00
—Reissue with new prefix			
CQ 30378 [Q]	Stoney End	1972	25.00
KC 30378	Stoney End	1971	15.00
PC 30378	Stoney End	197?	8.00
—Reissue with new prefix			
CQ 30792 [Q]	Barbra Joan Streisand	1972	25.00
KC 30792	Barbra Joan Streisand	1971	15.00
PC 30792	Barbra Joan Streisand	197?	8.00
—Reissue with new prefix			
CQ 31760 [Q]	Live Concert at the Forum	1972	25.00
KC 31760	Live Concert at the Forum	1972	15.00
PC 31760	Live Concert at the Forum	197?	8.00
—Reissue with new prefix			
KC 32655	Barbra Streisand...And Other Musical Instruments	1973	12.00
PC 32655	Barbra Streisand...And Other Musical Instruments	197?	8.00
—Reissue with new prefix			
JC 32801	The Way We Were	197?	8.00
—Reissue with new prefix			
PC 32801	The Way We Were	1974	12.00
—Revised version; has this title on spine, label and front cover			
PC 32801	Barbra Streisand Featuring The Way We Were and All In Love Is Fair	1974	20.00
—Original version with this title on spine and label, and no title on front cover			
PCQ 32801 [Q]	The Way We Were	1974	25.00
PC 33095	Butterfly	1974	12.00
—Original with no bar code			
PC 33095	Butterfly	198?	8.00
—Reissue with bar code			
PCQ 33095 [Q]	Butterfly	1974	20.00
PC 33815	Lazy Afternoon	1975	12.00
—Original with no bar code			
PC 33815	Lazy Afternoon	198?	8.00
—Reissue with bar code			

Number	Title (A Side/B Side)	Yr	NM
❑ PCQ 33815 [Q]	Lazy Afternoon	1975	25.00
❑ JS 34403	A Star Is Born	1976	12.00
—With Kris Kristofferson			
❑ JC 34830	Streisand Superman	1977	12.00
❑ PC 34830	Streisand Superman	198?	8.00
—Budget-line reissue			
❑ PC 35275	Songbird	198?	8.00
—Budget-line reissue			
❑ JC 35375	Songbird	1978	12.00
❑ FC 35679	Barbra Streisand's Greatest Hits, Vol. 2	1978	12.00
❑ FC 36258	Wet	1979	10.00
❑ FC 36750	Guilty	1980	10.00
❑ TC 37678	Memories	1981	10.00
❑ JS 39152	Yentl	1983	10.00
❑ QC 39480	Emotion	1984	10.00
❑ OC 40092	The Broadway Album	1985	10.00
❑ OC 40788	One Voice	1987	10.00
❑ OC 40880	Till I Loved You	1988	10.00
❑ HC 42801	The Way We Were	1982	30.00
—Half-speed mastered edition			
❑ OC 45369	A Collection: Greatest Hits.. And More	1989	15.00
❑ HC 45679	Barbra Streisand's Greatest Hits, Vol. 2	1980	30.00
—Half-speed mastered edition			
❑ HC 46750	Guilty	1982	30.00
—Half-speed mastered edition			
❑ HC 47678	Memories	1982	30.00
—Half-speed mastered edition			

COLUMBIA MASTERWORKS

Number	Title (A Side/B Side)	Yr	NM
❑ M 33452	Classical Barbra	1976	12.00

STRENGTH, "TEXAS" BILL

45s

SUN

Number	Title (A Side/B Side)	Yr	NM
❑ 346	Guess I'd Better Go/Senorita	1960	25.00
—As "Bill Strength"			

STRIDER

Albums

WARNER BROS.

Number	Title (A Side/B Side)	Yr	NM
❑ BS 2722	Exposed	1973	24.00

STRIDERS, THE (1)

45s

APOLLO

Number	Title (A Side/B Side)	Yr	NM
❑ 480	I Wonder/Hesitating Fool	1955	300.00

DERBY

Number	Title (A Side/B Side)	Yr	NM
❑ 857	Come Back to Me Tomorrow/ Rollin'	1954	200.00

STRIDERS, THE (2)

45s

COLUMBIA

Number	Title (A Side/B Side)	Yr	NM
❑ 43738	Sorrow/Say You Love Me	1966	20.00
❑ 43948	Am I On Your Mind/ There's a Storm Comin'	1966	20.00
❑ 44143	When You Walk In the Room/ Do It Now	1967	15.00

DELTA

Number	Title (A Side/B Side)	Yr	NM
❑ 2137	Give Me a Break/ Say You Love Me	196?	50.00

LAVETTE

Number	Title (A Side/B Side)	Yr	NM
❑ 5008	Sorrow/When You Walk in the Room	1966	40.00

STRIKES, THE

45s

IMPERIAL

Number	Title (A Side/B Side)	Yr	NM
❑ 5433	Baby I'm Sorry/If You Can't Rock Me	1957	50.00
❑ 5446	Rockin'/I Don't Want to Cry Over You	1957	50.00

LIN

Number	Title (A Side/B Side)	Yr	NM
❑ 5006	Baby I'm Sorry/If You Can't Rock Me	1957	75.00

STRING CHEESE

Albums

WOODEN NICKEL

Number	Title (A Side/B Side)	Yr	NM
❑ WNS-1001	String Cheese	1971	20.00

STRONG, BARRETT

45s

ANNA

Number	Title (A Side/B Side)	Yr	NM
❑ 1111	Money (That's What I Want)/ Oh I Apologize	1960	30.00
❑ 1116	You Know What to Do/ Yes, No, Maybe So	1960	25.00

ATCO

Number	Title (A Side/B Side)	Yr	NM
❑ 6225	Seven Sins/What Went Wrong	1962	40.00

CAPITOL

Number	Title (A Side/B Side)	Yr	NM
❑ 4052	Is It True/Anywhere	1975	5.00
❑ 4120	Surrender/There's Something About You	1975	5.00
❑ 4223	Gonna Make It Right/The Man Up in the Sky	1976	5.00

EPIC

Number	Title (A Side/B Side)	Yr	NM
❑ 11011	Stand Up and Cheer for the Preacher (Part 1)/Stand Up and Cheer for the Preacher (Part 2)	1973	5.00

PHASE II

Number	Title (A Side/B Side)	Yr	NM
❑ 02048	Rock It Easy/Love Will Make It Right	1981	4.00

TAMLA

Number	Title (A Side/B Side)	Yr	NM
❑ B0003631-21	Money (That's What I Want)/ Oh I Apologize	2005	10.00
—Bonus 45 included with the 6-CD box set "The Complete Motown Singles Vol. 1: 1959-1961"			
❑ 54022	Let's Rock/Do the Very Best You Can	1960	2000.
—VG 1000; VG+ 1500			
❑ 54027	Money (That's What I Want)/ Oh I Apologize	1960	120.00
—Horizontal lines label			
❑ 54027	Money (That's What I Want)/ Oh I Apologize	1962	50.00
—Globe label			
❑ 54029	You Know What to Do/ Yes, No, Maybe So	1960	50.00
❑ 54033	I'm Gonna Cry/Whirl Wind	1960	50.00
❑ 54035	You Got What It Takes/ Money and Me	1961	50.00
❑ 54043	Two Wrongs Don't Make a Right/ Misery	1961	50.00

TOLLIE

Number	Title (A Side/B Side)	Yr	NM
❑ 9023	Make Up Your Mind/I Better Run	1964	30.00

Albums

CAPITOL

Number	Title (A Side/B Side)	Yr	NM
❑ ST-11376	Stronghold	1975	12.00

STRONG, NOLAN, AND THE DIABLOS

Some of these refer only to "The Diablos," others only to "Nolan Strong."

45s

FORTUNE

Number	Title (A Side/B Side)	Yr	NM
❑ 509/10	Adios, My Desert Love/(I Want) An Old Fashioned Girl	1954	100.00
❑ 511	The Wind/Baby, Be Mine	1954	100.00
❑ 511	The Wind/Baby, Be Mine	196?	20.00
—Later pressing adds reference to LP on which it appears			
❑ 514	Hold Me Until Eternity/Route 16	1955	100.00
❑ 516	Daddy Rockin' Strong/ Do You Remember What You Did Last Night	1955	100.00
❑ 518	The Way You Dog Me Around/ Jump, Shake and Move	1955	100.00
❑ 519	You're the Only Girl, Dolores/ You Are	1956	80.00
❑ 522	Teardrop from Heaven/ Try Me One More Time	1956	80.00
❑ 525	Can't We Talk This Over/ The Mambo of Love	1957	80.00
❑ 529	For Old Times' Sake/My Heart Will Always Belong to You	1959	40.00
❑ 531	I Am With You/Goodbye Matilda	1959	40.00
❑ 532	If I Could Be with You Tonite/ I Wanna Know	1959	40.00
❑ 536	Since You're Gone/ What You Gonna Do	1960	30.00
❑ 544	Blue Moon/I Don't Care	1962	20.00
❑ 546	Mind Over Matter (I'm Gonna Make You Mine)/Beside You	1962	20.00
❑ 553	I Really Love You/ You're My Love	1963	20.00
❑ 556	(Yeah, Baby) It's Because of You/ You're Every Beat of My Heart	1963	20.00
❑ 564	Are You Making a Fool Out of Me/You're My Happiness	1964	15.00
❑ 569	(What Did That Genie Mean When He Said) Ali-Coochie/ (You're Not Good Looking But) You're Presentable	1964	15.00
❑ 574	The Way You Dog Me Around/ Jump with Me	1980	15.00

PYRAMID

Number	Title (A Side/B Side)	Yr	NM
❑ 159	White Christmas/Danny Boy	19??	15.00

Albums

FORTUNE

Number	Title (A Side/B Side)	Yr	NM
❑ LP-8010 [M]	Fortune of Hits	196?	50.00
—Yellow label			
❑ LP-8010 [M]	Fortune of Hits	1961	220.00
—Purple label, thick vinyl			
❑ LP-8010 [M]	Fortune of Hits	197?	15.00
—Purple label, thinner, more flexible vinyl			
❑ LP-8012 [M]	Fortune of Hits, Vol. 2	196?	50.00
—Yellow label			
❑ LP-8012 [M]	Fortune of Hits, Vol. 2	1962	220.00
—Purple label, thick vinyl			
❑ LP-8012 [M]	Fortune of Hits, Vol. 2	197?	15.00
—Purple label, thinner, more flexible vinyl			
❑ LP-8015 [M]	Mind Over Matter	196?	60.00
—Yellow label			
❑ LP-8015 [M]	Mind Over Matter	1963	250.00
—Purple label, thick vinyl			
❑ LP-8015 [M]	Mind Over Matter	197?	20.00
—Purple label, thinner, more flexible vinyl			

STRUMMER, JOE

12-Inch Singles

EPIC

Number	Title (A Side/B Side)	Yr	NM
❑ EAS1103 [DJ]	Trash City (same on both sides)	1988	5.00
❑ EAS 01103 [DJ]	Trash City (same on both sides)	1988	5.00

MCA

Number	Title (A Side/B Side)	Yr	NM
❑ 23655	Love Kills (3 versions)	1986	8.00

VIRGIN

Number	Title (A Side/B Side)	Yr	NM
❑ 1125 [DJ]	Filibustero (3 versions)	1987	6.00
❑ 1125 [DJ]	Filibustero (3 versions)	1987	6.00
❑ 96725	Filibustero (2 versions)/ Brooding Six	1987	6.00

45s

VIRGIN

Number	Title (A Side/B Side)	Yr	NM
❑ 99381	Filibustero/Straight Shooter	1988	4.00

Albums

EPIC

Number	Title (A Side/B Side)	Yr	NM
❑ E 45372	Earthquake Weather	1989	12.00

STRUNK, JUD

45s

AD-MEDIA

Number	Title (A Side/B Side)	Yr	NM
❑ 6416	The Santa Song/A Special Christmas Tree	1969	10.00
❑ 6416 [PS]	The Santa Song/A Special Christmas Tree	1969	15.00

CAPITOL

Number	Title (A Side/B Side)	Yr	NM
❑ 3960	My Country/The Will	1974	6.00

COLUMBIA

Number	Title (A Side/B Side)	Yr	NM
❑ 4-45121	David's Place/Lion in the Park	1970	8.00
❑ 4-45189	Self-Eating Watermelon/ Children at Play	1970	8.00

MCA

Number	Title (A Side/B Side)	Yr	NM
❑ 40872	Tell Me Where I Am Tonight/ Fool on My Shoulder	1978	4.00

MELODYLAND

Number	Title (A Side/B Side)	Yr	NM
❑ 6015	The Biggest Parakeets in Town/ I Wasn't Wrong About You	1975	5.00
❑ 6027	Pamela Brown/They're Tearing Down a Town	1975	5.00

MGM

Number	Title (A Side/B Side)	Yr	NM
❑ 14388	Jacob Brown/Long Ride Home	1972	6.00
❑ 14463	Daisy a Day/The Searchers	1972	7.00
❑ 14572	Next Door Neighbor's Kid/ I'd Prefer to Do It All Again	1973	6.00

Albums

COLUMBIA

Number	Title (A Side/B Side)	Yr	NM
❑ CS 9990	Downeast Viewpoint	1970	15.00

HARMONY

Number	Title (A Side/B Side)	Yr	NM
❑ KH 32344	Mr. Bojangles and Other Favorites	1973	10.00

MCA

Number	Title (A Side/B Side)	Yr	NM
❑ 2309	A Semi-Reformed Tequila Crazed Gypsy	1977	10.00

MGM

Number	Title (A Side/B Side)	Yr	NM
❑ SE-4790	Jones General Store	1972	12.00
❑ SE-4898	Daisy a Day	1973	12.00

STRYPER

Christian metal pioneers.

45s

ENIGMA

Number	Title (A Side/B Side)	Yr	NM
❑ 061	Winter Wonderland/ Reason For The Season	1984	8.00
❑ B-75009	Honestly/Sing-Along-Song	1986	3.00
❑ B-75009 [PS]	Honestly/Sing-Along-Song	1986	8.00

Albums

ENIGMA

Number	Title (A Side/B Side)	Yr	NM
❑ E-1064	The Yellow and Black Attack	1984	40.00
—Original with six tracks; yellow vinyl			
❑ 71064	The Yellow and Black Attack	1984	20.00
—Original with six tracks; black vinyl			
❑ 72077	Soldiers Under Command	1985	12.00
—Black vinyl			
❑ 72077	Soldiers Under Command	1985	20.00
—White vinyl			
❑ ST-73207	The Yellow and Black Attack	1985	10.00
—Reissue with eight tracks; black vinyl, square sleeve			

Number	Title (A Side/B Side)	Yr	NM
❑ ST-73207	The Yellow and Black Attack	1985	20.00
—Reissue with eight tracks; blue vinyl, round sleeve			
❑ ST-73217	Soldiers Under Command	1985	10.00
—Reissue with new number			
❑ PJAS-73237	To Hell with the Devil	1986	10.00
—Cover is black			
❑ PJAS-73237	To Hell with the Devil	1986	20.00
—Cover has band as winged angels in battle			
❑ SEAX-73277	To Hell with the Devil	1986	25.00
—Picture disc in plastic sleeve			
❑ D1-73317	In God We Trust	1988	10.00

STUART, CHAD Also see CHAD AND JEREMY.

45s

SIDEWALK

Number	Title (A Side/B Side)	Yr	NM
❑ 944	Good Morning Sunrise/Paxton's Song	1968	8.00
❑ 944 [PS]	Good Morning Sunrise/Paxton's Song	1968	15.00

STUART, CHAD AND JILL Also see CHAD STUART.

45s

COLUMBIA

Number	Title (A Side/B Side)	Yr	NM
❑ 43467	The Cruel War/I Can't Talk to You	1965	8.00
❑ 43467 [PS]	The Cruel War/I Can't Talk to You	1965	15.00

STUART, CHAD, AND JEREMY CLYDE

See CHAD AND JEREMY.

STUART, MARTY

45s

COLUMBIA

Number	Title (A Side/B Side)	Yr	NM
❑ 38-05724	Arlene/Midnight Moonlight	1985	4.00
❑ 38-05724 [PS]	Arlene/Midnight Moonlight	1985	8.00
❑ 38-05897	Honky Tonker/Anyhow I Love You	1986	4.00
❑ 38-06230	All Because of You/Maria (Love to See You Again)	1986	4.00
❑ 38-06425	Do You Really Want My Lovin'/Heart of Stone	1986	4.00
❑ 38-07729	Mirrors Don't Lie/Freight Train Boogie	1988	4.00
❑ 38-07914	Matches/Old Hat	1988	4.00

MCA

Number	Title (A Side/B Side)	Yr	NM
❑ 53687	Cry Cry Cry/The Wild One	1989	3.00
❑ 53751	Don't Leave Her Lonely Too Long/The Coal Mine Blues	1989	3.00
❑ 53975	Little Things/Paint the Town Tonight	1990	4.00
❑ 54065	Till I Found You/Half a Heart	1991	4.00
❑ 54145	Tempted/I'm Blue, I'm Lonesome	1991	5.00
❑ 54253	Burn Me Down/Blue Train	1992	4.00
❑ 54477	Now That's Country/Me & Hank & Jumpin' Jack Flash	1992	4.00
❑ 54538	High on a Mountain Top/Just Between You and Me	1992	4.00
❑ 54607	Hey Baby/Down Home	1993	3.00
❑ 54777	Kiss Me, I'm Gone/Marty Stuart Visits the Moon	1994	4.00
❑ 54840	Love and Luck/Oh What a Silent Night	1994	4.00
❑ 54915	That's What Love's About/Shake Your Hips	1994	3.00
❑ 55010	The Likes of Me/You Can Walk All Over Me	1995	3.00
❑ 55069	If I Ain't Got You/Wheels	1995	3.00
❑ 55226	Thanks to You/Country Girls	1996	3.00
❑ 55270	You Can't Stop Love/The Mississippi Mudcat and Sister Cheryl Crow	1996	3.00
❑ 79001	Hillbilly Rock/Western Girls	1990	6.00
❑ 79068	Western Girls/Me and Billy the Kid	1990	4.00

MCA NASHVILLE

Number	Title (A Side/B Side)	Yr	NM
❑ 72096	Red, Red Wine and Cheatin' Songs/Goin' Nowhere Fast	1999	3.00

Albums

COLUMBIA

Number	Title (A Side/B Side)	Yr	NM
❑ B6C 40302	Marty Stuart	1986	30.00

MCA

Number	Title (A Side/B Side)	Yr	NM
❑ 42312	Hillbilly Rock	1989	15.00
❑ R 170076	Tempted	1990	25.00
—Vinyl version available only through BMG Direct Marketing			

RIDGE RUNNER

Number	Title (A Side/B Side)	Yr	NM
❑ RRR 0013	Marty	1978	30.00

SUGAR HILL

Number	Title (A Side/B Side)	Yr	NM
❑ 3726	Busy Bee Café	1981	30.00

STUART, MARTY, AND STEVE EARLE

45s

DECCA

Number	Title (A Side/B Side)	Yr	NM
❑ 55206	Crying, Waiting, Hoping/Maybe Baby	1996	3.00
—B-side by Nitty Gritty Dirt Band			

STUART, MARTY, AND TRAVIS TRITT

45s

MCA

Number	Title (A Side/B Side)	Yr	NM
❑ 54405	This One's Gonna Hurt You (For a Long, Long Time)/The King of Dixie	1992	5.00
❑ 55197	Honky Tonkin's What I Do Best/Me & Hank & Jumpin' Jack Flash	1996	4.00

STUBBS, JOE

45s

LU-PINE

Number	Title (A Side/B Side)	Yr	NM
❑ 120	Keep On Loving Me/What's My Destiny	1964	200.00

STUDENT NURSES, THE

45s

RCA VICTOR

Number	Title (A Side/B Side)	Yr	NM
❑ 47-8482	Kiss Me Goodnight/Simply	1964	25.00

STUDENTS, THE

45s

ARGO

Number	Title (A Side/B Side)	Yr	NM
❑ 5386	I'm So Young/Every Day of the Week	1961	20.00

CHECKER

Number	Title (A Side/B Side)	Yr	NM
❑ 902	I'm So Young/Every Day of the Week	1958	40.00
❑ 1004	My Vow to You/That's How I Feel	1962	15.00

NOTE

Number	Title (A Side/B Side)	Yr	NM
❑ 10012	I'm So Young/Every Day of the Week	1958	500.00
❑ 10019	My Vow to You/That's How I Feel	1959	400.00

RED TOP

Number	Title (A Side/B Side)	Yr	NM
❑ 100	My Heart Is an Open Door/Mommy and Daddy	1958	40.00
—Red label			
❑ 100	My Heart Is an Open Door/Mommy and Daddy	1958	200.00
—Blue label			

STUFFY AND HIS FROZEN PARACHUTE BAND

Albums

PARAMOUNT

Number	Title (A Side/B Side)	Yr	NM
❑ PAS-6070	Stuffy and His Frozen Parachute Band	1974	25.00
—Reissue of Water Street 1002			

WATER STREET

Number	Title (A Side/B Side)	Yr	NM
❑ WST 1002	Stuffy and His Frozen Parachute Band	1974	50.00

STYLERS, THE (1)

45s

GOLDEN CREST

Number	Title (A Side/B Side)	Yr	NM
❑ 117	You Tell Me/Blues in the Night	1957	40.00
❑ 117 [PS]	You Tell Me/Blues in the Night	1957	100.00
❑ 129	Kiss and Run Lover/Girlie, Girlie, Girlie	1957	40.00

JUBILEE

Number	Title (A Side/B Side)	Yr	NM
❑ 5168	Believe It or Not/The World Is Yours	1954	40.00
❑ 5188	Shoo Shoo Sha La La/I Love Ya Like Crazy	1955	40.00
❑ 5246	Lost John/Huffin' and Puffin'	1956	40.00
❑ 5253	Confession of a Sinner/Gonna Tell 'Em	1956	40.00
❑ 5279	Breaker of Hearts/Miracle in Milan	1957	30.00

STYLERS, THE (U) These could both be by group (1), or they may be different groups.

45s

GORDY

Number	Title (A Side/B Side)	Yr	NM
❑ 7018	Going Steady Anniversary/Pushing Up Daisies	1963	60.00

KICKS

Number	Title (A Side/B Side)	Yr	NM
❑ 2	Gentle as a Teardrop/There Were Others	1954	500.00

STYLES, THE (1)

45s

JOSIE

Number	Title (A Side/B Side)	Yr	NM
❑ 920	I Love You for Sentimental Reasons/School Bells to Chapel Bells	1964	60.00

SERENE

Number	Title (A Side/B Side)	Yr	NM
❑ 1501	Scarlet Angel/Gotta Go, Go, Go	1961	150.00

STYLES, THE (2)

45s

MODERN

Number	Title (A Side/B Side)	Yr	NM
❑ 1048	I Know You Know That I Know/Baby You're Alive	1967	12.00

SWAN

Number	Title (A Side/B Side)	Yr	NM
❑ 4258	I Do Love You/Hush Little Girl	1966	12.00

STYLETTES, THE

45s

CAMEO

Number	Title (A Side/B Side)	Yr	NM
❑ 337	On Fire/Packing Up My Memories	1964	60.00
❑ 353	You'll Go First/My Boy	1965	40.00

SAN-DEE

Number	Title (A Side/B Side)	Yr	NM
❑ 1010/1	On Fire/Packing Up My Memories	1964	120.00

STYLISTICS, THE

12-Inch Singles

H&L

Number	Title (A Side/B Side)	Yr	NM
❑ 2008	The Lion Sleeps Tonight (5:29)/Fly! (6:09)	1977	15.00

STREETWISE

Number	Title (A Side/B Side)	Yr	NM
❑ 2236	Give a Little Love/Give a Little Love (Sing Along Version)	1984	8.00
❑ 2237	Some Things Never Change/Row Your Love	1985	8.00
❑ 2238	Special/(B-side unknown)	1985	8.00
❑ 2241	Let's Go Rockin' (Tonight)/(B-side unknown)	1986	8.00

45s

AMHERST

Number	Title (A Side/B Side)	Yr	NM
❑ 301	Because I Love You Girl/My Love, Come Live With Me	1985	4.00

AVCO

Number	Title (A Side/B Side)	Yr	NM
❑ 4581	You Are Everything/Country Living	1971	5.00
❑ 4591	Betcha by Golly, Wow/Ebony Eyes	1972	5.00
❑ 4595	People Make the World Go Round/Point of No Return	1972	5.00
❑ 4603	I'm Stone in Love with You/Make It Last	1972	5.00
❑ 4611	Break Up to Make Up/You and Me	1973	5.00
❑ 4618	You'll Never Get to Heaven (If You Break My Heart)/If You Don't Watch Out	1973	5.00
❑ 4625	Rockin' Roll Baby/Pieces	1973	5.00
❑ 4634	You Make Me Feel Brand New/Only for the Children	1974	5.00
❑ 4640	Let's Put It All Together/I Take It Out on You	1974	5.00
❑ 4647	Heavy Fallin' Out/Go Now	1974	5.00
❑ 4649	Star on a TV Show/Hey Girl, Come and Get It	1975	5.00
❑ 4652	Thank You Baby/Sing, Baby, Sing	1975	5.00
❑ 4656	Can't Give You Anything (But My Love)/I'd Rather Be Hurt by You	1975	5.00
❑ 4661	Funky Weekend/If You Are There	1975	5.00
❑ 4664	You Are Beautiful/Michael and Me	1976	5.00
❑ 4664 [PS]	You Are Beautiful/Michael and Me	1976	10.00

AVCO EMBASSY

Number	Title (A Side/B Side)	Yr	NM
❑ 4555	You're a Big Girl Now/Let the Junkie Beat the Pusher	1970	6.00
❑ 4572	Stop, Look, Listen (To Your Heart)/If I Love You	1971	6.00

H&L

Number	Title (A Side/B Side)	Yr	NM
❑ 4669	Can't Help Falling in Love/Jenny	1976	4.00
❑ 4674	Because I Love You, Girl/You Are	1976	4.00
❑ 4676	Only You/What Goes Around Comes Around	1976	4.00
❑ 4678	I Got a Letter/Satin Doll	1977	4.00
❑ 4681	Shame and Scandal in the Family/That Don't Shake Me	1977	4.00
❑ 4686	I'm Coming Home/I Run to You	1977	4.00
❑ 4695	Fool of the Year/Good Thing Goin'	1978	4.00

MERCURY

Number	Title (A Side/B Side)	Yr	NM
❑ 74005	First Impressions/Your Love's Too Good to Be Forgotten	1978	4.00
❑ 74022	I Can't Stop Livin'/You're the Best Thing in My Life	1978	4.00
❑ 74042	Love at First Sight/Broken Wing	1979	4.00
❑ 74057	Don't Know Where I'm Going/You Make Me Feel So Doggone Good	1979	4.00

Except when noted otherwise, VG = 25% of NM, and VG+ = 50% of NM. (Example: VG = $2.00, VG+ = $4.00 and NM = $8.00.)

Number	Title (A Side/B Side)	Yr	NM
PHILADELPHIA INT'L.			
❑ 02901	Callin' You/Don't Come Telling Me Lies	1982	4.00
❑ 03085	Lighten Up/We Should Be Lovers	1982	4.00
SEBRING			
❑ 8370	You're a Big Girl Now/Let the Junkie Beat the Pusher	1970	30.00
STREETWISE			
❑ 1136	Give a Little Love/Give a Little Love (Sing Along Version)	1984	4.00
❑ 1137	Some Things Never Change/Row Your Love	1985	4.00
❑ 1138	Special/(B-side unknown)	1985	4.00
TSOP			
❑ 02195	What's Your Name/Almost There	1981	4.00
❑ 02588	Mine All Mine/Closer Than Close	1981	4.00
❑ 02702	Habit/I've Got This Feeling	1982	4.00
❑ 4789	Hurry Up This Way Again/It Started Out	1980	4.00
❑ 4798	And I'll See You No More/Driving Me Wild	1980	4.00

Albums

Number	Title	Yr	NM
AMHERST			
❑ AMH-743	The Best of the Stylistics	1986	10.00
❑ AMH-744	All-Time Classics	1986	10.00
❑ AMH-745	The Best of the Stylistics, Vol. 2	1986	10.00
❑ AMH-746	Greatest Love Hits	1986	10.00
AVCO			
❑ 11006	Round 2: The Stylistics	1972	20.00
❑ 11010	Rockin' Roll Baby	1973	20.00
❑ AV-33023	The Stylistics	1971	20.00
❑ AV-69001	Let's Put It All Together	1974	15.00
❑ AV-69004	Heavy	1974	15.00
❑ AV-69005	The Best of the Stylistics	1975	15.00
❑ 69008	Thank You Baby	1975	15.00
❑ 69010	You Are Beautiful	1975	15.00
H&L			
❑ 69013	Fabulous	1976	12.00
❑ 69032	Wonder Woman	1978	12.00
MERCURY			
❑ SRM-1-3727	In Fashion	1978	12.00
❑ SRM-1-3753	Love Spell	1979	12.00
PHILADELPHIA INT'L.			
❑ FZ 37955	1982	1982	10.00
TSOP			
❑ JZ 36470	Hurry Up This Way Again	1980	10.00
❑ FZ 37458	Closer Than Close	1981	10.00

STYLISTS, THE

45s

Number	Title (A Side/B Side)	Yr	NM
V.I.P.			
❑ 25066	What Is Love/Where Did the Children Go	1970	25.00

STYX

12-Inch Singles

Number	Title (A Side/B Side)	Yr	NM
A&M			
❑ SP-17021 [DJ]	The Grand Illusion (same on both sides)	1977	15.00

45s

Number	Title (A Side/B Side)	Yr	NM
A&M			
❑ 1786	Lorelei/Midnight Ride	1976	4.00
❑ 1818	Born for Adventure/Light Up	1976	5.00
❑ 1877	Mademoiselle/Light Up	1976	5.00
❑ 1900	Jennifer/Shooz	1976	5.00
❑ 1931	Crystal Ball/Put Me On	1977	5.00
❑ 1977	Come Sail Away/Put Me On	1977	4.00
❑ 1977 [PS]	Come Sail Away/Put Me On	1977	6.00
❑ 2007	Fooling Yourself (The Angry Young Man)/The Grand Finale	1978	4.00
❑ 2007 [PS]	Fooling Yourself (The Angry Young Man)/The Grand Finale	1978	6.00
❑ 2087	Blue Collar Man (Long Nights)/Superstars	1978	4.00
❑ 2087 [PS]	Blue Collar Man (Long Nights)/Superstars	1978	6.00
❑ 2110	Renegade/Sing for the Day	1979	4.00
❑ 2110	Sing for the Day/Queen of Spades	1979	5.00
❑ 2110 [PS]	Renegade/Sing for the Day	1979	5.00
❑ 2188	Babe/I'm O.K.	1979	4.00
❑ 2206	Why Me/Lights	1979	4.00
❑ 2228	Borrowed Time/Eddie	1980	4.00
❑ 2294	The Best of Times/Lights	1980	—
—Unreleased?			
❑ 2300	The Best of Times/Lights	1981	4.00
❑ 2300 [PS]	The Best of Times/Lights	1981	4.00
❑ 2323	Too Much Time on My Hands/Queen of Spades	1981	4.00
❑ 2348	Nothing Ever Goes As Planned/Never Say Never	1981	4.00
❑ 2525	Mr. Roboto/Snowblind	1983	3.00
❑ 2525 [PS]	Mr. Roboto/Snowblind	1983	3.00
❑ 2543	Don't Let It End/Rockin' the Paradise	1983	3.00
❑ 2543 [PS]	Don't Let It End/Rockin' the Paradise	1983	3.00
❑ 2560	Double Life/Haven't We Been Here Before	1983	3.00
❑ 2568	High Time/Double Life	1983	3.00
❑ 2625	Music Time/Heavy Metal Poisoning	1984	3.00
❑ 2625 [PS]	Music Time/Heavy Metal Poisoning	1984	3.00
❑ 8696	Show Me the Way/Love at First Sight	1993	4.00
—Reissue series; both songs were unreleased on 45 until this record			
WOODEN NICKEL			
❑ BWBO-0065	You Need Love/Winner Take All	1973	5.00
❑ 65-0106	Best Thing/What Has Come Between	1972	5.00
❑ 65-0111	I'm Gonna Make You Feel It/Quick Is the Beat of My Heart	1972	5.00
❑ 65-0116	Lady/You Better Ask	1973	10.00
❑ BWBO-0252	Young Man/Unfinished Song	1974	5.00
❑ WB-10027	Lies/22 Years	1974	5.00
❑ WB-10102	Lady/Children of the Land	1974	5.00
❑ WB-10272	You Need Love/You Better Ask	1975	5.00
❑ WB-10329	Best Thing/Havin' a Ball	1975	5.00
❑ GB-10492	Lady/Children of the Land	1975	4.00
—Gold Standard Series			
❑ WB-11205	Winner Take All/Best Thing	1978	5.00

Albums

Number	Title	Yr	NM
A&M			
❑ SP-3217	Equinox	1984	8.00
❑ SP-3218	Crystal Ball	1984	8.00
❑ SP-3223	The Grand Illusion	1984	8.00
❑ SP-3224	Pieces of Eight	1984	8.00
❑ SP-3239	Cornerstone	1984	8.00
❑ SP-3240	Paradise Theater	1984	8.00
—3200 series LPs are reissues			
❑ SP-3711	Cornerstone	1979	10.00
❑ SP-3711	Cornerstone	1979	30.00
—Silver vinyl pressing, reportedly for fan club members			
❑ SP-3719	Paradise Theater	1981	10.00
❑ SP-3734	Kilroy Was Here	1983	10.00
❑ SP-4559	Equinox	1975	10.00
❑ SP-4604	Crystal Ball	1976	10.00
❑ SP-4637	The Grand Illusion	1977	10.00
❑ PR-4724 [PD]	Pieces of Eight	1978	25.00
❑ SP-4724	Pieces of Eight	1978	10.00
❑ 75021 5327 1	Edge of the Century	1990	20.00
❑ SP-6514 [(2)]	Caught in the Act	1984	12.00
❑ SP-8431 [(2)DJ]	The Styx Radio Special	1977	25.00
—Promo only; green cover			
❑ SP-17053 [(3)DJ]	Styx Radio Special	1978	40.00
—Promo-only box set			
❑ SP-17222 [(2)DJ]	Radio Sampler and Interview Album	1983	25.00
—Promo only; with "Kilroy Was Here" album graphic on cover			
MOBILE FIDELITY			
❑ 1-026	The Grand Illusion	1979	30.00
—Audiophile vinyl			
NAUTILUS			
❑ NR-15	Pieces of Eight	1981	25.00
—Audiophile vinyl			
❑ NR-27	Cornerstone	1982	20.00
—Audiophile vinyl			
❑ NR-45	Paradise Theater	198?	30.00
—Audiophile vinyl			
RCA VICTOR			
❑ AFL1-3593	Styx	1979	10.00
❑ AFL1-3594	Lady	1979	10.00
—Retitled version of "Styx II"			
❑ AFL1-3595	Serpent	1979	10.00
—Retitled version of "The Serpent Is Rising"			
❑ AFL1-3596	Miracles	1979	10.00
—Retitled version of "Man of Miracles"			
❑ AFL1-3597	Best of Styx	1979	10.00
❑ AYL1-3888	Styx	1980	8.00
❑ AYL1-4233	Lady	1981	8.00
—Retitled version of "Styx II"			
❑ AYL1-4756	Best of Styx	1982	8.00
WOODEN NICKEL			
❑ BWL1-0287	The Serpent Is Rising	1974	20.00
❑ BWL1-0638	Man of Miracles	1974	20.00
—Second version contains "Best Thing"			
❑ BWL1-0638	Man of Miracles	1974	30.00
—Original version contains "Lies"			
❑ BWL1-1008	Styx	1975	15.00
❑ WNS-1008	Styx	1972	20.00
❑ BWL1-1012	Styx II	1975	15.00
❑ WNS-1012	Styx II	1973	20.00
—With die-cut cover			
❑ BWL1-2250	Best of Styx	1977	12.00

STYX (2)

45s

Number	Title (A Side/B Side)	Yr	NM
ABC			
❑ 10848	Don't Bring Me Down/MacDougal Street	1966	12.00

STYX (U)

Definitely not the more famous Styx; could be group (2), though.

45s

Number	Title (A Side/B Side)	Yr	NM
ONYX			
❑ 2200	Puppetmaster/Hey, I'm Lost	1966	25.00
PARAMOUNT			
❑ 0104	Promised Land/Soul Flow	1971	6.00

SUDDENS, THE

Also recorded as THE SAFARIS.

45s

Number	Title (A Side/B Side)	Yr	NM
SUDDEN			
❑ 103	Garden of Love/Childish Ways	1961	100.00

SUGAR BEARS, THE

KIM CARNES was in this group.

45s

Number	Title (A Side/B Side)	Yr	NM
BIG TREE			
❑ 122	Someone Like You/You Are the One	1971	6.00
❑ 143	Right On/Happiness Train	1972	6.00
❑ 151	Some Kind of a Summer/Put Some Love Into It	1972	6.00

Albums

Number	Title	Yr	NM
BIG TREE			
❑ BTS-2009	Introducing the Sugar Bears	1972	20.00

SUGAR CANES, THE

45s

Number	Title (A Side/B Side)	Yr	NM
KING			
❑ 5157	Poor Boy/Sioux Rock	1958	25.00

SUGAR CREEK

Albums

Number	Title	Yr	NM
METROMEDIA			
❑ MD 1020	Please Tell a Friend	1969	60.00

SUGARLOAF

45s

Number	Title (A Side/B Side)	Yr	NM
BRUT			
❑ 805	Round and Round/Colorado Jones	1973	5.00
❑ 815	I Got a Song/Myra, Myra	1973	5.00
❑ 815 [PS]	I Got a Song/Myra, Myra	1973	6.00
CLARIDGE			
❑ 402	Don't Call Us, We'll Call You/Texas Two-Lane	1974	5.00
❑ 405	Stars in My Eyes/Myra, Myra	1975	5.00
❑ 408	Boogie Man/I Got a Song	1975	5.00
❑ 415	Have a Good Time/You Set My Dreams to Music	1976	5.00
❑ 422	Last Dance, Take a Chance/Satisfaction Guaranteed	1976	5.00
LIBERTY			
❑ 56183	Green-Eyed Lady/West of Tomorrow	1970	6.00
❑ 56218	Tongue in Cheek/Woman	1970	5.00
❑ 56218 [PS]	Tongue in Cheek/Woman	1970	10.00
UNITED ARTISTS			
❑ 0062	Green-Eyed Lady/Tongue in Cheek	1973	4.00
—"Silver Spotlight Series" reissue			
❑ 50757	Woman/Tongue in Cheek	1971	—
—Unreleased			
❑ 50784	Chest Fever/Mother Nature's Wine	1971	5.00

Albums

Number	Title	Yr	NM
BRUT			
❑ 6006	I Got a Song	1973	15.00
CLARIDGE			
❑ 1000	Don't Call Us, We'll Call You	1975	12.00
LIBERTY			
❑ LST-7640	Sugarloaf	1970	20.00
❑ LST-11010	Spaceship Earth	1971	20.00

SUGGS, BRAD

45s

Number	Title (A Side/B Side)	Yr	NM
METEOR			
❑ 5034	Charcoal Suit/Bop Baby Bop	1956	400.00
PHILLIPS INT'L.			
❑ 3545	Low Outside/706 Union	1959	25.00
❑ 3549	I Walk the Line/Ooh-Wee	1959	25.00
❑ 3554	Cloudy/Partly Cloudy	1960	25.00
❑ 3563	My Gypsy/Sam's Tune	1960	25.00
❑ 3571	Elephant Walk/Catching Up	1961	25.00

S

SUICIDAL TENDENCIES

12-Inch Singles

CAROLINE

Number	Title (A Side/B Side)	Yr	NM
❑ 1453	Possessed to Skate/ Human Guinea Pig/ + 1	198?	12.00

EPIC

Number	Title (A Side/B Side)	Yr	NM
❑ AS 1386 [DJ]	Surf and Slam/Pledge Your Allegiance	1988	12.00
❑ 07873	Trip at the Brain/Sulcyco Mania	1988	12.00

45s

EPIC

Number	Title (A Side/B Side)	Yr	NM
❑ 74868	I'll Hate You Better/Mandatory Love Songs//Just Another Love Song/Won't Fall in Love Today	1993	8.00

—Heart-shaped purple vinyl in plastic sleeve

Albums

CAROLINE

Number	Title (A Side/B Side)	Yr	NM
❑ CAROL 1336	Join the Army	1987	15.00

EPIC

Number	Title (A Side/B Side)	Yr	NM
❑ FE 44288	How Will I Laugh Tomorrow When I Can't Even Smile Today	1988	12.00
❑ 6E 45244	Controlled by Hatred/ Feel Like Shit...Deja Vu	1989	12.00
❑ E 45389	Lights...Camera...Revolution	1990	12.00

FRONTIER

Number	Title (A Side/B Side)	Yr	NM
❑ 1011	Suicidal Tendencies	1983	15.00
❑ 4604-1-L	Suicidal Tendencies	198?	15.00

SUICIDE

Albums

ANTILLES

Number	Title (A Side/B Side)	Yr	NM
❑ AN-7080	Alan Vega-Martin Rev	1980	12.00

RED STAR

Number	Title (A Side/B Side)	Yr	NM
❑ RS-1	Suicide	1977	20.00
❑ RED-800	Suicide	1980	14.00

—Reissue of RS-1

WAX TRAX!

Number	Title (A Side/B Side)	Yr	NM
❑ 7072	A Way of Life	1989	10.00

SUICIDE COMMANDOS

45s

P.S.

Number	Title (A Side/B Side)	Yr	NM
❑ (# unknown)	Emisson Control/Cliche Ole/ Monster Au Go Go	1976	15.00
❑ (# unknown)	Match Mismatch/ Mark He's a Terror	1977	5.00
❑ (# unknown) [PS]	Emisson Control/Cliche Ole/ Monster Au Go Go	1976	15.00
❑ (# unknown) [PS]	Match Mismatch/ Mark He's a Terror	1977	5.00

Albums

BLANK

Number	Title (A Side/B Side)	Yr	NM
❑ 002	The Suicide Commandos Make a Record	1977	30.00

TWIN/TONE

Number	Title (A Side/B Side)	Yr	NM
❑ TTR 7906	The Commandos Commit Suicide Dance Concert	1979	75.00

—Limited edition of 1,000 copies

SULLIVAN, JIM

45s

LONDON

Number	Title (A Side/B Side)	Yr	NM
❑ 9585	Back and Forth/Toad Stool	1963	12.00

SULLIVAN, NIKI

Also see THE CRICKETS (1).

45s

DOT

Number	Title (A Side/B Side)	Yr	NM
❑ 15751	Three Steps to Heaven/ It's All Over	1958	100.00

JOLI

Number	Title (A Side/B Side)	Yr	NM
❑ 073	Do the Dive/My Lost Dream	196?	60.00
❑ 075	It Really Doesn't Matter/ You Better Get a Move On	196?	75.00

SULTANS, THE (1)

45s

ASCOT

Number	Title (A Side/B Side)	Yr	NM
❑ 2228	I Wanna Know/Gloria	1967	20.00

SULTANS, THE (2)

45s

DUKE

Number	Title (A Side/B Side)	Yr	NM
❑ 125	Good Thing Baby/ How Deep Is the Ocean	1954	100.00
❑ 133	I Cried My Heart Out/Baby Don't Put Me Down	1954	100.00
❑ 135	Boppin' with the Mambo/What Makes Me Feel This Way	1954	100.00
❑ 178	My Love Is So High/If I Could Tell	1957	50.00

SULTANS, THE (3)

45s

GUYDEN

Number	Title (A Side/B Side)	Yr	NM
❑ 2079	Someone You Can Trust/ Christina	1963	15.00

JAM

Number	Title (A Side/B Side)	Yr	NM
❑ 103	Toss in My Sleep/I Feel Your Love Growing Cold	1962	30.00
❑ 107	Mary, Mary/How Far Does a Friendship Go	1963	30.00
❑ 113	Poor Boy/Don't Tie Me Down	1964	30.00

TILT

Number	Title (A Side/B Side)	Yr	NM
❑ 782	It'll Be Easy/You Got Me Goin'	1961	40.00

—Black label

Number	Title (A Side/B Side)	Yr	NM
❑ 782	It'll Be Easy/You Got Me Goin'	1961	100.00

—Yellow label

SULTANS, THE (4)

45s

JUBILEE

Number	Title (A Side/B Side)	Yr	NM
❑ 5054	Lemon Squeezing Daddy/ You Captured My Heart	1951	250.00
❑ 5077	Blues at Dawn/Don't Be Angry	1952	800.00

SUMAC, YMA

45s

CAPITOL

Number	Title (A Side/B Side)	Yr	NM
❑ CDF 244 [PS]	Voice of the Xtabay	195?	15.00

—Box for 15647, 15648, 15649 and 19650 (listed separately)

Number	Title (A Side/B Side)	Yr	NM
❑ F1717	Virgin of the Sun God/ Lure of the Unknown Love	1951	20.00
❑ F1819	Birds/Najalas Lament	1951	20.00
❑ F1819 [PS]	Birds/Najalas Lament	1951	40.00
❑ F2079	Babalu/Wimoweh	1952	20.00
❑ F15647	Virgin of the Sun God/ Lure of the Unknown Love	195?	15.00
❑ F15648	Monkeys/High Andes	195?	15.00
❑ F15649	Dance of the Winds/Chant of the Chosen Maidens	195?	15.00
❑ F15650	Dance of the Moon Festival/ Earthquake	195?	15.00

—The above four comprise box set CDF-244, "Voice of the Xtabay"

CORAL

Number	Title (A Side/B Side)	Yr	NM
❑ 60741	The Sun Maidens/Beautiful Eyes	1952	20.00
❑ 60742	Cholitas Punenas/ The Hummingbird	1952	20.00
❑ 60743	One Love/Indian Love	1952	20.00
❑ 60744	La Benita/I Love Only You	1952	20.00

—The above four comprise a box set

7-Inch Extended Plays

CAPITOL

Number	Title (A Side/B Side)	Yr	NM
❑ EAP 1-299	(contents unknown)	1955	25.00
❑ EAP 1-299 [PS]	Legend of the Sun Virgin, Part 1	1955	25.00
❑ EAP 2-299	(contents unknown)	1955	25.00
❑ EAP 2-299 [PS]	Legend of the Sun Virgin, Part 2	1955	25.00
❑ EAP 1-564	(contents unknown)	1955	25.00
❑ EAP 1-564 [PS]	Mambo!	1955	25.00
❑ EAP 2-564	(contents unknown)	1955	25.00
❑ EAP 2-564 [PS]	Mambo!	1955	25.00
❑ EAP 1-770	(contents unknown)	1956	20.00
❑ EAP 1-770 [PS]	Legend of the Jivaro, Part 1	1956	20.00
❑ EAP 2-770	(contents unknown)	1956	20.00
❑ EAP 2-770 [PS]	Legend of the Jivaro, Part 2	1956	20.00
❑ EAP 3-770	(contents unknown)	1956	20.00
❑ EAP 3-770 [PS]	Legend of the Jivaro, Part 3	1956	20.00

CORAL

Number	Title (A Side/B Side)	Yr	NM
❑ EC 81050	(contents unknown)	1954	50.00
❑ EC 81050 [PS]	Presenting Yma Sumac	1954	50.00
❑ EC 81051	(contents unknown)	1954	50.00
❑ EC 81051 [PS]	Presenting Yma Sumac	1954	50.00

Albums

CAPITOL

Number	Title (A Side/B Side)	Yr	NM
❑ H 244 [10]	Voice of the Xtabay	1952	100.00
❑ L 299 [10]	Legend of the Sun Virgin	1952	120.00
❑ SM-299 [M]	Legend of the Sun Virgin	197?	12.00
❑ T 299 [M]	Legend of the Sun Virgin	1955	50.00
❑ L 423 [10]	Inca Taqui	1953	100.00
❑ H 564 [10]	Mambo!	1954	100.00
❑ T 564 [M]	Mambo!	1955	50.00
❑ DW 684 [R]	Voice of the Xtabay and Inca Taqui	1963	15.00
❑ SM-684	Voice of the Xtabay and Inca Taqui	197?	12.00

—On this reissue, Side 1 is in mono

Number	Title (A Side/B Side)	Yr	NM
❑ W 684 [M]	Voice of the Xtabay and Inca Taqui	1955	50.00

—Gray label

Number	Title (A Side/B Side)	Yr	NM
❑ W 684 [M]	Voice of the Xtabay and Inca Taqui	1963	20.00

—Black colorband label, "Capitol" at top

Number	Title (A Side/B Side)	Yr	NM
❑ T 770 [M]	Legend of the Jivaro	1956	50.00

—Turquoise label

Number	Title (A Side/B Side)	Yr	NM
❑ T 770 [M]	Legend of the Jivaro	1963	20.00

—Black colorband label, "Capitol" at top

Number	Title (A Side/B Side)	Yr	NM
❑ ST 1169 [S]	Fuego del Andes	1959	50.00
❑ T 1169 [M]	Fuego del Andes	1959	40.00
❑ M-11892	Mambo!	1979	12.00

CORAL

Number	Title (A Side/B Side)	Yr	NM
❑ CRL 56058 [10]	Presenting Yma Sumac	1952	120.00

LONDON

Number	Title (A Side/B Side)	Yr	NM
❑ XPS 608	Miracles	1972	20.00

SUMMER, DONNA

12-Inch Singles

ATLANTIC

Number	Title (A Side/B Side)	Yr	NM
❑ DMD 1333 [DJ]	This Time I Know It's for Real (Extended Remix 7:21) (Instrumental 3:34)/ If It Makes You Feel Good	1989	15.00
❑ DMD 1382 [DJ]	Love's About to Change My Heart (PWL 12" Mix) (PWL 7" Mix) (Clivilles & Cole 12" Mix) (Dub 2) (Clivilles & Cole 7" Mix)	1989	10.00
❑ DMD 1431 [DJ]	Breakaway (Extended Mix 6:08) (Power Radio Mix 4:02)/I Don't Wanna Get Hurt (12" Mix)	1989	15.00
❑ DMD 1709 [DJ]	When Love Cries (Vocal Club Dub) (Radio Mix) (Club Mix) (Instrumental)	1991	10.00
❑ DMD 1758 [DJ]	Work That Magic (4:34) (6:20) (5:00)/Let There Be Peace	1991	12.00
❑ DMD 2574 [(2)DJ]	The Power of One (Johnathan Peters Club Mix) (Johnathan Peters Radio Mix) (Tommy Musto Vocal Mix) (Musto Beats) (Gel Dub) (JP Sound Factory Dub) (Sound Factory Club Mix) (Drum-a-Pella)	2000	30.00
❑ 85021	The Power of One (4 versions)	2000	12.00
❑ 85961	When Love Cries (4 versions)	1991	8.00
❑ 86255	Breakaway (Extended Mix) (Power Radio Mix)/I Don't Wanna Get Hurt (12" Mix)	1989	10.00
❑ 86309	Love's About to Change My Heart (5 versions)	1989	10.00
❑ 86415	This Time I Know It's for Real (Extended) (Instrumental) (LP Version)	1989	10.00

CASABLANCA

Number	Title (A Side/B Side)	Yr	NM
❑ NBD 100	Winter Melody/Spring Affair	1977	15.00
❑ PRO 1148 [DJ]	Love to Love You Baby (16:49)/ Flash Light (10:43)	1994	20.00

—B-side by Parliament; promo-only reissue

Number	Title (A Side/B Side)	Yr	NM
❑ NBLP 7041	Love to Love You Baby (16:50)/ Try Me, I Know We Can Make It (17:55)	1976	20.00

—One song on each side, yet it has an LP catalog number

Number	Title (A Side/B Side)	Yr	NM
❑ NBD 20104	I Feel Love (8:15)/Theme from "The Deep" (Down, Deep Inside) (6:06)//(B-side blank)	1977	20.00
❑ NBD 20112 [DJ]	Rumour Has It/I Love You// (B-side blank)	1978	15.00
❑ NBD 20148 [DJ]	Mac Arthur Park Suite (17:33)/ (B-side blank)	1978	15.00
❑ NBD 20159 [DJ]	Hot Stuff (Long Version)/ (B-side blank)	1979	12.00
❑ NBD 20167	Hot Stuff/Bad Girls//(B-side blank)	1979	15.00
❑ NBD 20193 [DJ]	Dim All the Lights (7:10)/ (B-side blank)	1979	25.00
❑ NBD 20199	No More Tears (Enough Is Enough) (11:40)/(B-side blank)	1979	10.00

—With Barbra Streisand

Number	Title (A Side/B Side)	Yr	NM
❑ NBD 20226 [DJ]	Walk Away (Disco Mix 7:15)/ (B-side blank)	1979	15.00
❑ 856357-1	Melody of Love (Classic Club Mix) (Boss Mix) (Epris Mix) (Mijango's Powertools Trip #1)	1994	10.00

EPIC

Number	Title (A Side/B Side)	Yr	NM
❑ EAS 42153 [DJ]	I Will Go with You (Con Te Partiro) (Club 69 Future Mix) (Rosabel Dark Dub) (Rosabel Main Vox 12") (Hex Hector Extended Vocal Mix)	1999	10.00
❑ EAS 42547 [DJ]	I Will Go with You (Con Te Partiro) (Club 69 Underground Anthem) (Welcome Summer-time Fun Extended Mix) (Warren Rigg Summer Dub) (Club 69 Underground Dub)	1999	12.00
❑ EAS 42676 [DJ]	I Will Go with You (Con Te Partiro) (Skill Masters Remix 5:08) (Messy Boys Jazz Dub 6:37) (Welcome Downtempo Extended Remix 4:46)		

Except when noted otherwise, VG = 25% of NM, and VG+ = 50% of NM. (Example: VG = $2.00, VG+ = $4.00 and NM = $8.00.)

Number	Title (A Side/B Side)	Yr	NM
	(Trouser Enthusiasts Twisted Kiss Mix 10:18) (Johnny Newman Drifting Mix 5:59)	1999	15.00
❑ EAS 42892 [DJ]	Love Is the Healer (Thunderpuss 2000 Club Mix 8:58) (Eric Kupper's I Feel Healed 7" Mix) (JP's Sound Factory Mix 9:27) (Thunderpuss 2000 Radio Mix 3:19)	1999	12.00
❑ EAS 46473 [DJ]	Love Is the Healer (4 versions)	1999	15.00
❑ 49-79202	I Will Go with You (Con Te Partiro) (4 versions)	1999	10.00
❑ 49-79226	I Will Go with You (Con Te Partiro) (Club 69 Underground Anthem) (Rosabel Dark Dub) (Warren Rigg Summer Dub) (Club 69 Trippy Dub)	1999	8.00

GEFFEN

Number	Title (A Side/B Side)	Yr	NM
❑ PRO-A-910 [DJ]	The Wanderer (stereo/mono)	1980	15.00
❑ PRO-A-925 [DJ]	Cold Love/Looking Up/Who Do You Think You're Foolin'	1980	10.00
❑ PRO-A-1041 [DJ]	Love Is In Control (Edit) (LP)	1982	10.00
❑ PRO-A-2180 [DJ]	There Goes My Baby (same on both sides)	1984	10.00
❑ PRO-A-2802 [DJ]	Dinner with Gershwin (7:43) (same on both sides)	1987	10.00
❑ PRO-A-3036 [DJ]	All Systems Go (Dance Mix)/ Fascination	1987	10.00
❑ 20273	Supernatural Love (Extended Dance Remix 6:12)/Face the Music (4:14)	1984	8.00
❑ 20635	Dinner with Gershwin (Extended) (Instrumental)	1987	8.00
❑ 29938	Love Is In Control (Dance Remix 7:03)/(Instrumental)	1982	8.00

INTERHIT

Number	Title (A Side/B Side)	Yr	NM
❑ 10164	Carry On (Outta Control Mix) (Hot Tracks Mix) (Slammin' Cox Mix) (Hysteria Mix)	1997	10.00

—With Giorgio Moroder

MERCURY

Number	Title (A Side/B Side)	Yr	NM
❑ PRO 226-1 [DJ]	Unconditional Love (Club Mix 5:20)/(Instrumental 4:40)	1983	12.00
❑ 812370-1	She Works Hard for the Money (Special Long Version) (Instrumental)	1983	10.00
❑ 814592-1	Unconditional Love (Remix)/ She Works Hard for the Money (Remix)	1983	10.00

UNIVERSAL

Number	Title (A Side/B Side)	Yr	NM
❑ U8P-1130 [DJ]	Whenever There Is Love (Club Mix) (Club Dub) (Riff Dub) (Tribal Beats) (Instrumental) (7" Mix)	1998	40.00

45s

ATLANTIC

Number	Title (A Side/B Side)	Yr	NM
❑ 88792	Breakaway/Thinkin' Bout My Baby	1989	4.00
❑ 88840	Love's About to Change My Heart (PWL 7" Mix)/ (Clivilles & Cole 7" Mix)	1989	3.00
❑ 88899	This Time I Know It's for Real/ If It Makes You Feel Good	1989	3.00
❑ 88899 [PS]	This Time I Know It's for Real/ If It Makes You Feel Good	1989	4.00

CASABLANCA

Number	Title (A Side/B Side)	Yr	NM
❑ 872	Spring Affair/Come with Me	1976	5.00
❑ 874	Winter Melody/Spring Affair	1977	5.00
❑ 884	I Feel Love/Can't We Just Sit Down (And Talk It Over)	1977	5.00
—Second pressings have "I Feel Love" listed as "Side A"			
❑ 884	Can't We Just Sit Down (And Talk It Over)/I Feel Love	1977	6.00
—Original copies have "Can't We Just Sit Down" labeled as "Side A"			
❑ 884 [DJ]	I Feel Love (stereo/mono)	1977	8.00
—Both sides are shorter than the version on the stock 45			
❑ 884 [DJ]	Can't We Just Sit Down (And Talk It Over) (stereo/mono)	1977	10.00
❑ 907	I Love You/Once Upon a Time	1977	5.00
❑ 916	Rumour Has It/ Once Upon a Time	1978	5.00
❑ 926	Last Dance/With Your Love	1978	4.00
❑ 939	Mac Arthur Park/ Once Upon a Time	1978	4.00
❑ 959	Heaven Knows/Only One Love	1979	4.00
—A-side with Brooklyn Dreams			
❑ 978	Hot Stuff/Journey to the Center of Your Heart	1979	4.00
❑ 988	Bad Girls/On My Honor	1979	4.00
❑ 2201	Dim All the Lights/There Will Always Be a You	1979	4.00
❑ 2236	On the Radio/There Will Always Be a You	1980	4.00
❑ 2273	Our Love/Sunset People	1980	5.00
❑ 2300	Walk Away/Could It Be Magic	1980	4.00
❑ 858366-7	Melody of Love/ The Christmas Song	1994	3.00
❑ 858366-7 [PS]	Melody of Love/ The Christmas Song	1994	3.00

EPIC

Number	Title (A Side/B Side)	Yr	NM
❑ 38-79201	I Will Go with You (Con Te Partiro)/Love On & On	1999	3.00

GEFFEN

Number	Title (A Side/B Side)	Yr	NM
❑ 27939	Fascination/All Systems Go	1988	4.00
❑ 28165	Only the Fool Survives/ Love Shock	1987	4.00
—A-side with Mickey Thomas			
❑ 28165 [PS]	Only the Fool Survives/ Love Shock	1987	4.00
—A-side with Mickey Thomas			
❑ 28418	Dinner with Gershwin/ (Instrumental)	1987	4.00
❑ 28418 [PS]	Dinner with Gershwin/ (Instrumental)	1987	4.00
❑ 29142	Supernatural Love/ Face the Music	1984	4.00
❑ 29142 [PS]	Supernatural Love/ Face the Music	1984	4.00
❑ 29291	There Goes My Baby/ Maybe It's Over	1984	4.00
❑ 29291 [PS]	There Goes My Baby/ Maybe It's Over	1984	4.00
❑ 29805	The Woman in Me/ Livin' in America	1982	4.00
❑ 29805 [PS]	The Woman in Me/ Livin' in America	1982	4.00
❑ 29895	State of Independence/ Love Is Just a Breath Away	1982	4.00
❑ 29895 [PS]	State of Independence/ Love Is Just a Breath Away	1982	4.00
❑ 29982	Love Is In Control (Finger on the Trigger)/ Sometimes Like Butterflies	1982	4.00
❑ 29982 [PS]	Love Is In Control (Finger on the Trigger)/ Sometimes Like Butterflies	1982	5.00
❑ 49563	The Wanderer/Stop Me	1980	4.00
—Second pressings have WB logo replaced by Geffen logo			
❑ 49563 [PS]	The Wanderer/Stop Me	1980	5.00
❑ 49634	Cold Love/Grand Illusion	1980	4.00
❑ 49634 [PS]	Cold Love/Grand Illusion	1980	5.00
❑ 49664	Who Do You Think You're Foolin'/Runnin' for Cover	1981	4.00

MERCURY

Number	Title (A Side/B Side)	Yr	NM
❑ 812370-7	She Works Hard for the Money/ I Do Believe (I'll Fall in Love)	1983	4.00
❑ 812370-7 [PS]	She Works Hard for the Money/ I Do Believe (I'll Fall in Love)	1983	5.00
❑ 814088-7	Unconditional Love/Woman	1983	4.00
❑ 814088-7 [PS]	Unconditional Love/Woman	1983	5.00
❑ 814922-7	Love Has a Mind of Its Own/ Stop, Look and Listen	1983	4.00
—A-side with Matthew Ward			

OASIS

Number	Title (A Side/B Side)	Yr	NM
❑ 401 A /B	Love to Love You Baby/ Need-A-Man Blues	1975	12.00
—"Love to Love You Baby" has a radically different mix on the above first pressing			
❑ 401 AA/BB	Love to Love You Baby (4:55)/ Love to Love You Baby (3:24)	1975	6.00
—Both sides are remixed compared to the original 45 mix			
❑ 405	Could It Be Magic/ Whispering Waves	1976	6.00
❑ 406	Try Me, I Know We Can Make It/ Wasted	1976	6.00
❑ 406 [PS]	Try Me, I Know We Can Make It/ Wasted	1976	8.00

WARNER BROS./GEFFEN

Number	Title (A Side/B Side)	Yr	NM
❑ 49563	The Wanderer/Stop Me	1980	6.00
—Original pressings have a WB logo on the left side and "Geffen Records" in a box at the top of the label			

Albums

ATLANTIC

Number	Title (A Side/B Side)	Yr	NM
❑ 81987	Another Place and Time	1989	12.00

CASABLANCA

Number	Title (A Side/B Side)	Yr	NM
❑ NBLP 7038	Four Seasons of Love	1976	10.00
❑ NBLP 7056	I Remember Yesterday	1977	10.00
❑ NBLP 7078 [(2)]	Once Upon a Time...	1977	12.00
❑ NBLP 7119 [(2)]	Live and More	1978	12.00
❑ NBPIX 7119 [PD]	The Best of Live and More	1979	20.00
❑ NBLP 7150 [(2)]	Bad Girls	1979	12.00
❑ NBLP 7191 [(2)]	On the Radio — Greatest Hits Vols. 1 and 2	1979	12.00
❑ NBLP 7201	Greatest Hits, Vol. 1	1979	8.00
❑ NBLP 7202	Greatest Hits, Vol. 2	1979	8.00
❑ NBLP 7244	Walk Away — Collector's Edition (The Best of 1977-1980)	1980	10.00
❑ 811123-1 [(2)]	Live and More	1985	10.00
❑ 822557-1 [(2)]	Bad Girls	1984	10.00
❑ 822558-1 [(2)]	On the Radio — Greatest Hits Vols. 1 and 2	1984	10.00
❑ 822559-1	Greatest Hits, Vol. 2	1984	8.00
❑ 822560-1	Walk Away	1984	8.00

EPIC

Number	Title (A Side/B Side)	Yr	NM
❑ E2 69910 [(2)]	Live and More Encore	1999	15.00

GEFFEN

Number	Title (A Side/B Side)	Yr	NM
❑ GHS 2000	The Wanderer	1980	10.00
❑ GHS 2005	Donna Summer	1982	10.00
❑ GHS 24040	Cats Without Claws	1984	10.00
❑ GHS 24040 [DJ]	Cats Without Claws	1984	15.00
—Promo only on Quiex II vinyl			
❑ GHS 24102	All Systems Go	1987	10.00

MERCURY

Number	Title (A Side/B Side)	Yr	NM
❑ 812265-1	She Works Hard for the Money	1983	10.00
❑ 826144-1	The Summer Collection	1985	10.00

OASIS

Number	Title (A Side/B Side)	Yr	NM
❑ OCLP 5003	Love to Love You Baby	1975	12.00
—Add 50% if poster is included			
❑ OCLP 5004	A Love Trilogy	1976	12.00
❑ 822792-1	Love to Love You Baby	1985	8.00

SUMMER SOUNDS, THE

Albums

LAUREL

Number	Title (A Side/B Side)	Yr	NM
❑ 90973	Up Down	196?	1000.

SUMMERHILL

45s

TETRAGRAMMATON

Number	Title (A Side/B Side)	Yr	NM
❑ 1528	Soft Voice/The Last Day	1969	10.00

Albums

TETRAGRAMMATON

Number	Title (A Side/B Side)	Yr	NM
❑ T-114	Summerhill	1969	30.00

SUMMERS, ANDY

12-Inch Singles

A&M

Number	Title (A Side/B Side)	Yr	NM
❑ 12119	2010/To Hal and Back	1984	8.00

45s

A&M

Number	Title (A Side/B Side)	Yr	NM
❑ 2513 [DJ]	I Advance Masked (same on both sides)	1982	4.00
—With Robert Fripp; no stock copy was issued			
❑ 2513 [DJ]	I Advance Masked (same on both sides)	1982	4.00
—With Robert Fripp; no stock copy was issued			
❑ 2699	Parade/Train	1984	3.00
—With Robert Fripp			
❑ 2704	2010/To Hal and Back	1984	3.00
❑ 2704 [PS]	2010/To Hal and Back	1984	4.00

MCA

Number	Title (A Side/B Side)	Yr	NM
❑ 53112	Love Is the Strangest Way/XYZ	1987	3.00

Albums

MCA

Number	Title (A Side/B Side)	Yr	NM
❑ 42007	XYZ	1987	10.00

PRIVATE MUSIC

Number	Title (A Side/B Side)	Yr	NM
❑ 2039-1-P	Mysterious Barricades	1988	10.00

SUMMERS, ANDY, AND ROBERT FRIPP

12-Inch Singles

A&M

Number	Title (A Side/B Side)	Yr	NM
❑ 17219 [DJ]	I Advance Masked (same on both sides)	1982	10.00
❑ 17219 [DJ]	I Advance Masked (same on both sides)	1982	10.00

Albums

A&M

Number	Title (A Side/B Side)	Yr	NM
❑ SP-17299 [DJ]	Speak Out Interview	1982	25.00
—Issued in generic cover with sticker			
❑ SP-4913	I Advance Masked	1982	10.00
❑ SP9-5011	Bewitched	1984	10.00
❑ SP-17299 [DJ]	Speak Out Interview	1982	25.00
—Issued in generic cover with sticker			

SUMMERS, DAVEY, AND THE SINGING ANTS

45s

DORE

Number	Title (A Side/B Side)	Yr	NM
❑ 684	Gonna Climb That Big Ole Hill/ Doin' the Davey Drag	1963	40.00

SUMMERS, GENE

45s

CAPRI

Number	Title (A Side/B Side)	Yr	NM
❑ 502	Blue Diamond/You Said You Loved Me	196?	20.00
❑ 507	Alabama Shake/Just Because	1964	60.00

S

Number	Title (A Side/B Side)	Yr	NM
JAMIE			
❑ 1273	Blue Diamond/You Said You Loved Me	1964	15.00
JAN			
❑ 100	School of Rock 'N' Roll/ Straight Skirt	1958	60.00
❑ 102	Nervous/Gotta Love That	1959	60.00
❑ 106	Twixteen/I'll Never Be Lonely	1959	60.00
MERCURY			
❑ 72606	Green-Eyed Monster/The Clown	1966	15.00
TEARDROP			
❑ 3405	Goodbye Priscilla (Bye Bye Baby Blue)/Down on the Farm	1977	8.00
❑ 3405 [DJ]	Goodbye Priscilla (Bye Bye Blue Baby)	1977	12.00

—Single-sided promo copies have erroneous subtitle

SUMMERS, JOHNNY

45s

Number	Title (A Side/B Side)	Yr	NM
YORKTOWN			
❑ 1007	Prove It to Me/(B-side unknown)	196?	500.00
❑ 1009	I Can't Let Go/(B-side unknown)	196?	1200.

SUN-RAYS, THE

45s

Number	Title (A Side/B Side)	Yr	NM
SUN			
❑ 293	Love Is a Stranger/ The Lonely Hours	1958	40.00

SUNBEAMS, THE (1)

45s

Number	Title (A Side/B Side)	Yr	NM
ACME			
❑ 109	Please Say You'll Be Mine/ You've Got to Rock and Roll	1957	3000.
HERALD			
❑ 451	Tell Me Why/Come Back Baby	1955	300.00
LOST-NITE			
❑ 427	Tell Me Why/Come Back Baby	197?	5.00

—Reissue

SUNBEAMS, THE (2)

45s

Number	Title (A Side/B Side)	Yr	NM
DOT			
❑ 1271	I'm Gonna Go Home to Mama/ Blue Mountain Waltz	1955	30.00
❑ 1280	How About It/ Wrap It Up and Save It	1956	30.00

SUNBEAMS, THE (3)

45s

Number	Title (A Side/B Side)	Yr	NM
TOLLIE			
❑ 9022	Sing a Song/Good Old Days	1964	12.00

SUNDAY FUNNIES, THE

45s

Number	Title (A Side/B Side)	Yr	NM
CAPITOL			
❑ 5614	Another Time, Another Place/ Headlines	1966	12.00
HIDEOUT			
❑ 1070	Heavy Music/Path of Freedom	196?	30.00
MERCURY			
❑ 72571	Wonder Woman/ She's Not at All Like You	1966	12.00
RARE EARTH			
❑ 5035	Walk Down the Path of Freedom/It's Just a Dream	1971	8.00
UNI			
❑ 55157	Baby, I Could Be So Good at Loving You/See Things My Way	1969	10.00

Albums

Number	Title (A Side/B Side)	Yr	NM
RARE EARTH			
❑ RS-526	The Sunday Funnies	1971	12.00
❑ RS-538	Benediction	1972	12.00

SUNDIALS, THE

45s

Number	Title (A Side/B Side)	Yr	NM
GUYDEN			
❑ 2065	Chapel of Love/ Whether to Resist	1962	200.00

SUNDOWN PLAYBOYS, THE

45s

Number	Title (A Side/B Side)	Yr	NM
APPLE			
❑ 1852	Saturday Night Special/ Valse De Soleil Coucher	1972	15.00
GOLDBAND			
❑ 1073	Sundown Waltz/River Two Step	195?	30.00

SUNDOWNERS, THE

45s

Number	Title (A Side/B Side)	Yr	NM
JAMIE			
❑ 1271	A Shot of Rhythm 'N' Blues/ Come On In	1964	12.00

Albums

Number	Title (A Side/B Side)	Yr	NM
LIBERTY			
❑ LRP-3269 [M]	Folk Songs for the Rich	1962	20.00
❑ LST-7269 [S]	Folk Songs for the Rich	1962	25.00

SUNGLOWS, THE

See SUNNY AND THE SUNLINERS.

SUNLINERS, THE

45s

Number	Title (A Side/B Side)	Yr	NM
GOLDEN WORLD			
❑ 31	The Swingin' Kind/All Alone	1965	150.00
MGM			
❑ 13809	Land of Nod/Well One	1967	25.00

SUNLOVERS, THE

45s

Number	Title (A Side/B Side)	Yr	NM
BREAKTHROUGH			
❑ 1002	My Poor Heart/This Love of Ours	1967	300.00
MUTT & JEFF			
❑ 17	My Poor Heart/This Love of Ours	1967	200.00
❑ 18	You'll Never Make the Grade/ This Love of Ours	1967	200.00
❑ 21	I'll Treat You Right/ (B-side unknown)	1967	200.00
REVUE			
❑ 11045	Main Street/Main Street Shuffle	1969	150.00

SUNNY AND THE HORIZONS

45s

Number	Title (A Side/B Side)	Yr	NM
LUXOR			
❑ 1013	Nature's Creation/ Because They Tell Me	1962	75.00
—Red label			
❑ 1013	Nature's Creation/ Because They Tell Me	1962	200.00
—Yellow label			

SUNNY AND THE SUNGLOWS

See SUNNY AND THE SUNLINERS.

SUNNY AND THE SUNLINERS

45s

Number	Title (A Side/B Side)	Yr	NM
DISCO GRANDE			
❑ 1021	Peanuts (La Cacahuata)/ Fallaste Corazon	1965	20.00
—A later issue than first pressings of Sunglow 107			
KEY-LOC			
❑ 1010	I Want to Come Home for Christmas Part 1/Part 2	1966	8.00
OKEH			
❑ 7143	Golly Gee/Touring	1962	12.00
—As "Sunny and the Sunglows"			
SUNGLOW			
❑ 102	Sylvia/(B-side unknown)	1961	15.00
❑ 103	A Dream/The Lasso	1961	15.00
❑ 104	Golly Gee/Touring	1961	15.00
❑ 105	Once in a While/Ho Ho Ha Ha	1962	15.00
❑ 106	Won't You Tell Me/ (B-side unknown)	1962	15.00
❑ 107	Peanuts (La Cacahuata)/ Fallaste Corazon	1962	20.00
❑ 107	La Cacahuata/Fallaste Corazon	1962	30.00
—Original issue of this record; no mention of "Peanuts" on label; composer listed as "Desconocido" (Spanish for "Unknown")			
❑ 107	Peanuts (La Cacahuata)/ Happy Hippo	1963	15.00
❑ 107	Peanuts (La Cacahuata)/ Love Me (All My Love Belongs to You)	1965	12.00
❑ 109	Close Your Eyes/ Ooo Poo Pa Doo	1963	15.00
❑ 110	Talk to Me/Pony Time	1963	20.00
❑ 111	Rags to Riches/It Won't Be Me	1963	18.00
❑ 112	The Dog/You Can Make It If You Try	1963	15.00
❑ 115	Till the End of Time/La Bamba	1964	15.00
❑ 116	Guess Who/Just as I Thought	1964	15.00
❑ 117	Love Me/Honey Child	1964	15.00
❑ 118	Popcorn/The Circus	1964	15.00
❑ 118	Popcorn/All Night Worker	1965	15.00
❑ 119	Baby I Apologize/ Cut Across Shorty	1965	15.00
❑ 120	Oh Heart/Latin Trumpet	1965	15.00
❑ 122	Fly Me to the Moon/La Macarena	1966	15.00
❑ 123	If You Don't Love Me/ (B-side unknown)	1966	15.00
❑ 124	Just a Game/Maria Elena	1966	15.00
❑ 125	Again/Roly Poly	1967	15.00
❑ 127	It's Okay/99 + 1	1968	15.00
—All Sunglow releases as "The Sunglows"			
TEAR DROP			
❑ 3014	Talk to Me/Every Week, Every Month, Every Year	1963	10.00
—A-side as "Sunny and the Sunglows"			
❑ 3016	Carino Nuevo/(B-side unknown)	1963	12.00
❑ 3022	Rags to Riches/Not Even Judgment Day	1963	10.00
❑ 3025	Cuando El Destino/ (B-side unknown)	1963	12.00
❑ 3027	Out of Sight, Out of Mind/ No One Else Will Do	1964	10.00
❑ 3031	Pa Que Sientas, Lo Que Sientex Que Tal Te Sientes/ De Mi Nada Mas, Usted	1964	12.00
—As "Sunny Ozuna"			
❑ 3035	It's Too Late/You Gave Me a True Love	1964	10.00
❑ 3037	Tu Nueva Viva/ Dime Como Le Haces	1964	12.00
❑ 3040	You Send Me/ His Greatest Creation	1964	10.00
❑ 3045	Something's Got a Hold on Me/ Teenage Promise-I'm Not a Fool Anymore	1964	10.00
❑ 3056	Token of Love/ Little Dancing Girl	1965	10.00
—As "Sunny Ozuna"			
❑ 3066	El Ta Conazo/La Diudades	1965	12.00
❑ 3067	Hitch Hike/That Night in San Antonio	1965	10.00
❑ 3071	Too Young/The Very Thought of You	1965	10.00
❑ 3079	Trick Bag/Cheatin' Traces	1965	10.00
❑ 3094	Fly Me to the Moon/ Short Short Shorty	1966	8.00
❑ 3096	Tristie Y Lastimado/ (B-side unknown)	1966	12.00
❑ 3123	No One Else Will Do/ Cheatin' Traces	1966	8.00
❑ 3183	Wonderful Girl/Talk That Trash	1966	8.00
WHITE WHALE			
❑ 324	It's Okay/99 + 1	1969	8.00
—As "The Sunglows"			

Albums

Number	Title (A Side/B Side)	Yr	NM
KEY-LOC			
❑ 3001 [M]	Smile Now, Cry Later	196?	25.00
❑ 3002 [M]	No Te Chifles	196?	25.00
❑ 3003 [M]	Sunny and the Sunliners Live in Hollywood	196?	25.00
❑ 3004 [M]	Canta Sunny	196?	25.00
❑ 3005 [M]	A Little Brown-Eyed Soul	196?	25.00
❑ 3006 [M]	This Is My Band	196?	25.00
❑ 3007 [M]	Versatile	196?	25.00
❑ 3008 [M]	Adelante	196?	25.00
❑ 3009 [M]	Sky High	196?	25.00
❑ 3010 [M]	The Missing Link	196?	25.00
SUNGLOW			
❑ SLP-101 [M]	Sunny Ozuna and the Sunglows	1963	100.00
—As "The Sunglows"			
❑ SLP-102 [M]	The Fabulous Sunglows	1964	100.00
—As "The Sunglows"			
❑ SLP-103 [M]	The Original Peanuts	1965	80.00
—As "The Sunglows"			
❑ SLP-103S [S]	The Original Peanuts	1965	100.00
—As "The Sunglows"			
TEAR DROP			
❑ LPM-2000 [M]	Talk to Me	1963	100.00
❑ LPM-2001 [M]	Las Vegas Welcomes Sunny and the Sunliners	1964	40.00
❑ LPM-2008 [M]	Teardrop Presents Sunny and the Sunliners	196?	40.00

SUNRAYS, THE

Also see THE SNOW MEN.

45s

Number	Title (A Side/B Side)	Yr	NM
TOWER			
❑ 101	Outta Gas/Car Party	1964	20.00
❑ 148	I Live for the Sun/Bye Baby Bye	1965	12.00
❑ 191	Andrea/You Don't Phase Me	1966	12.00
❑ 224	Still/When You're Not There	1966	12.00
❑ 256	Don't Take Yourself Too Seriously/I Look Baby, I Can't See	1966	12.00
❑ 256 [PS]	Don't Take Yourself Too Seriously/I Look Baby, I Can't See	1966	25.00
❑ 290	Hi, How Are You/Just 'Round the River Bend	1966	15.00
❑ 340	Loaded with Love/Time (A Special Thing)	1967	15.00
WARNER BROS.			
❑ 5253	Talk to Him/Gideon	1962	15.00

S

Except when noted otherwise, VG = 25% of NM, and VG+ = 50% of NM. (Example: VG = $2.00, VG+ = $4.00 and NM = $8.00.)

Number	Title (A Side/B Side)	Yr	NM
Albums			
TOWER			
❑ ST 5017 [S]	Andrea	1966	60.00
❑ T 5017 [M]	Andrea	1966	50.00
SUNSET DRAGSTERS, THE			
Albums			
PALACE			
❑ M-775 [M]	Hot Rod Rally	196?	60.00
❑ PST-775 [S]	Hot Rod Rally	196?	80.00
SUNSETS, THE (1)			
45s			
CHALLENGE			
❑ 9186	C.C. Rider/The Chug-a-Lug	1963	40.00
❑ 9198	Lonely Surfer Boy/ Playmate of the Year	1963	40.00
❑ 9208	My Little Beach Bunny/ My Little Surfin' Woody	1963	50.00
PETAL			
❑ 1040	Lydia/Only You, Only Me	1963	50.00
Albums			
PALACE			
❑ M-752 [M]	Surfing with the Sunsets	1963	40.00
❑ PST-752 [S]	Surfing with the Sunsets	1963	50.00
SUNSETS, THE (2)			
45s			
RAE COX			
❑ 102	How Will I Remember/ Sittin' and Cryin'	1959	40.00
SUPER K GENERATION, THE			
45s			
LAURIE			
❑ 3413	Heartful O'Soul (Part 1)/ Heartful O'Soul (Part 2)	1967	10.00
SUPER STOCKS, THE			
45s			
CAPITOL			
❑ 5153	Thunder Road/Wheel Stands	1964	25.00
Albums			
CAPITOL			
❑ ST 1997 [S]	Hot Rod Rally	1963	70.00
❑ T 1997 [M]	Hot Rod Rally	1963	50.00
❑ (S)T 2060	Thunder Road Bonus Poster	1964	50.00
❑ ST 2060 [S]	Thunder Road	1964	125.00
❑ T 2060 [M]	Thunder Road	1964	100.00
❑ ST 2113 [S]	Surf Route 101	1964	125.00
—Without bonus single			
❑ ST 2113 [S]	Surf Route 101	1964	150.00
—With bonus single, "Doin' the Surfink"/"Finksville, U.S.A." by Mr. Gasser and the Weirdos, in special pocket on front cover			
❑ T 2113 [M]	Surf Route 101	1964	100.00
—Without bonus single			
❑ T 2113 [M]	Surf Route 101	1964	125.00
—With bonus single, "Doin' the Surfink"/"Finksville, U.S.A." by Mr. Gasser and the Weirdos, in special pocket on front cover			
❑ ST 2190 [S]	School Is a Drag	1964	120.00
❑ T 2190 [M]	School Is a Drag	1964	100.00
SUPERFINE DANDELION, THE			
45s			
MAINSTREAM			
❑ 672	People in the Street/ (B-side unknown)	1967	12.00
❑ 673	Crazy Town/Janie's Tomb	1967	12.00
Albums			
MAINSTREAM			
❑ S-6102 [S]	The Superfine Dandelion	1967	40.00
❑ 56102 [M]	The Superfine Dandelion	1967	40.00
SUPERIORS, THE (1)			
45s			
ATCO			
❑ 6106	Lost Love/Don't Say Goodbye	1957	70.00
LOST-NITE			
❑ 177	Lost Love/Don't Say Goodbye	196?	6.00
—Reissue			
MAIN LINE			
❑ 104	Lost Love/Don't Say Goodbye	1958	600.00
—With Fairmount Ave., Philadelphia street address on label			
❑ 104	Lost Love/Don't Say Goodbye	1962	40.00
—No address on label or only "Philadelphia, Pennsylvania" address on label			
SUPERIORS, THE (2)			
45s			
FAL			
❑ 301	What Is Love/Flee the Scene	1961	80.00

Supertramp, "Cannonball," A&M 2731, 1985, $3.

Number	Title (A Side/B Side)	Yr	NM
FEDERAL			
❑ 12436	I'm Sorry Baby (I Didn't Mean to Do You Wrong)/Dance of Love	1961	30.00
SUPERIORS, THE (3)			
45s			
MGM			
❑ 13503	Can't Make It Without You/ Let Me Make You Happy	1966	12.00
SUE			
❑ 12	Heavenly Angel/I'd Rather Die	1969	8.00
VERVE			
❑ 10370	Tell Me to Go/What Would I Do	1965	20.00
SUPERSAX			
Albums			
CAPITOL			
❑ ST-11177	Supersax Plays Bird	1973	10.00
❑ ST-11271	Supersax Plays Bird, Vol. 2/ Salt Peanuts	1974	10.00
❑ ST-11371	Supersax Plays Bird with Strings	1975	10.00
COLUMBIA			
❑ FC 39140	Supersax and L.A. Voices	1984	10.00
❑ FC 39925	Supersax and L.A. Voices, Vol. 2	1985	10.00
❑ FC 40547	Supersax and L.A. Voices Vol. 3: Straighten Up and Fly Right	1986	10.00
❑ FC 44436	Stone Bird	1989	12.00
MOBILE FIDELITY			
❑ 1-511	Supersax Plays Bird	1981	40.00
—Audiophile vinyl			
PAUSA			
❑ 7038	Chasin' the Bird	1977	10.00
❑ 7082	Dynamite!	1979	10.00
❑ 9028	Supersax Plays Bird, Vol. 2/ Salt Peanuts	198?	8.00

Number	Title (A Side/B Side)	Yr	NM
SUPERTRAMP			
12-Inch Singles			
A&M			
❑ SP-12130	Cannonball (Direct to Disc Version) (Instrumental)	1985	30.00
❑ SP-12254	I'm Beggin' You (3 remixes)	1987	8.00
❑ SP-17320 [DJ]	Cannonball (Edit) (Single Version) (Direct-to-Disc Version)	1985	15.00
45s			
A&M			
❑ 1305	Forever/Your Poppa Don't Mind	1971	6.00
❑ 1660	Bloody Well Right/Dreamer	1975	5.00
❑ 1766	Lady/You Started Laughing When I Held You in My Arms	1975	—
—Unreleased?			
❑ 1793	Lady/You Started Laughing When I Held You in My Arms	1976	5.00
❑ 1814	Sister Moonshine/ Ain't Nobody But Me	1976	5.00
❑ 1938	Give a Little Bit/Downstream	1977	4.00
❑ 1938 [PS]	Give a Little Bit/Downstream	1977	6.00
❑ 1981	Dreamer/From Now On	1977	5.00
❑ 1981 [PS]	Dreamer/From Now On	1977	6.00
❑ 2128	The Logical Song/Just Another Nervous Wreck	1979	4.00
❑ 2128 [PS]	The Logical Song/Just Another Nervous Wreck	1979	5.00
❑ 2162	Goodbye Stranger/Even in the Quietest Moments	1979	4.00
❑ 2162 [PS]	Goodbye Stranger/Even in the Quietest Moments	1979	5.00
❑ 2193	Take the Long Way Home/Ruby	1979	4.00
❑ 2193 [PS]	Take the Long Way Home/Ruby	1979	4.00
—With yellow maze			
❑ 2193 [PS]	Take the Long Way Home/Ruby	1979	5.00
—With green maze			
❑ 2193 [PS]	Take the Long Way Home/Ruby	1979	5.00
—With red maze. Other colors may exist as well.			
❑ 2269	Dreamer/From Now On	1980	4.00
❑ 2269 [PS]	Dreamer/From Now On	1980	5.00

S

Number	Title (A Side/B Side)	Yr	NM
❑ 2292	Breakfast in America/ You Started Laughing	1980	4.00
❑ 2502	It's Raining Again/Bonnie	1982	4.00
❑ 2502 [PS]	It's Raining Again/Bonnie	1982	4.00
❑ 2517	My Kind of Lady/ Know Who You Are	1983	4.00
❑ 2517 [PS]	My Kind of Lady/ Know Who You Are	1983	4.00
❑ 2720 [DJ]	Still in Love with You (same on both sides)	1985	—
—Unreleased?			
❑ 2731	Cannonball/Every Open Door	1985	3.00
❑ 2731 [PS]	Cannonball/Every Open Door	1985	3.00
❑ 2760	Better Days/No In-Between	1985	3.00
❑ 2985	I'm Beggin' You/No Inbetween	1987	3.00
❑ 2985 [PS]	I'm Beggin' You/No Inbetween	1987	3.00
❑ 2996	Free as a Bird/Thing for You	1987	3.00
❑ 8663	Cannonball/Better Days	198?	3.00
—"A&M Memories" reissue			

Albums

A&M

Number	Title	Yr	NM
❑ SP-3129	Indelibly Stamped	198?	8.00
—Budget-line reissue			
❑ SP-3149	Supertramp	198?	8.00
—Budget-line reissue			
❑ SP-3214	Crisis? What Crisis?	1982	8.00
—Budget-line reissue			
❑ SP-3215	Even in the Quietest Moments	1982	8.00
—Budget-line reissue			
❑ SP-3284	...Famous Last Words...	1986	8.00
—Budget-line reissue			
❑ SP-3647	Crime of the Century	1974	12.00
❑ SP-3708	Breakfast in America	1979	8.00
❑ SP-3730 [PD]	Breakfast in America	1979	500.00
—In-house picture discs featuring A&M staff members posing with the cover model			
❑ SP-3732	...Famous Last Words...	1982	10.00
❑ SP-4274	Supertramp	197?	10.00
—Second edition with silverish label			
❑ SP-4274	Supertramp	1970	20.00
—First edition with brown label			
❑ SP-4311	Indelibly Stamped	197?	10.00
—Second edition with silverish label			
❑ SP-4311	Indelibly Stamped	1971	20.00
—First edition with brown label			
❑ SP-4560	Crisis? What Crisis?	1975	12.00
❑ SP-4634	Even in the Quietest Moments...	1977	12.00
❑ SP-4665	Supertramp	1978	12.00
—Reissue of 4274			
❑ SP-5013	Brother Where You Bound	1985	10.00
❑ SP-5181	Free as a Bird	1987	10.00
❑ SP-6702 [(2)]	Paris	1980	12.00
❑ 2136471	Crime of the Century	2008	20.00
❑ 2137081	Breakfast in America	2008	20.00

MOBILE FIDELITY

Number	Title	Yr	NM
❑ 1-005	Crime of the Century	1979	40.00
—Audiophile vinyl			
❑ MFQR-005	Crime of the Century	1983	120.00
—Ultra High Quality Recording; in box			
❑ 1-045	Breakfast in America	1980	50.00
—Audiophile vinyl			

SWEET THUNDER

Number	Title	Yr	NM
❑ 5	Even in the Quietest Moments...	198?	40.00
—Audiophile vinyl			

SUPREMES, THE Motown girl group. Also see FLORENCE BALLARD; THE PRIMETTES; DIANA ROSS.

12-Inch Singles

MOTOWN

Number	Title	Yr	NM
❑ 37463 1157 1 [DJ]	Someday We'll Be Together (Sound Factory Mix 6:57) (Def Mix 8:42) (Radio Edit Mix 3:03)	1994	15.00
—As "Diana Ross and the Supremes"; remixes of the 1969 hit			

45s

EEOC

Number	Title	Yr	NM
❑ SL4M-3114 [DJ]	Things Are Changing (same on both sides)	1965	150.00
❑ SL4M-3114 [PS]	Things Are Changing (same on both sides)	1965	150.00
—Promotional item for the Equal Employment Opportunity Commission (number not on sleeve)			

GEORGE ALEXANDER INC.

Number	Title	Yr	NM
❑ 1079 [DJ]	The Only Time I'm Happy/ Supremes Interview	1965	60.00

MOTOWN

Number	Title (A Side/B Side)	Yr	NM
❑ 1008	I Want a Guy/Never Again	1961	300.00
❑ 1027	Your Heart Belongs to Me/ (He's) Seventeen	1962	25.00
❑ 1027 [PS]	Your Heart Belongs to Me/ (He's) Seventeen	1962	400.00
❑ 1034	Let Me Go the Right Way/ Time Changes Things	1962	50.00
❑ 1040	My Heart Can't Take It No More/ You Bring Back Memories	1963	40.00
❑ 1044	A Breath Taking Guy/ Rock and Roll Banjo Band	1963	25.00
❑ 1044	A Breath Taking, First Sight Soul Shaking, One Night Love Making, Next Day Heart Breaking Guy/Rock and Roll Banjo Band	1963	100.00
—Original pressing with long title. This does exist on stock copies as well as on promos.			
❑ 1051	When the Lovelight Starts Shining Through His Eyes/ Standing at the Crossroads of Love	1963	20.00
❑ 1054	Run, Run, Run/I'm Giving You Your Freedom	1964	25.00
❑ 1060	Where Did Our Love Go/ He Means the World to Me	1964	20.00
❑ 1060 [PS]	Where Did Our Love Go/ He Means the World to Me	1964	30.00
❑ 1066	Baby Love/Ask Any Girl	1964	20.00
❑ 1066 [PS]	Baby Love/Ask Any Girl	1964	30.00
❑ 1068	Come See About Me/ Always in My Heart	1964	20.00
❑ 1074	Stop! In the Name of Love/ I'm in Love Again	1965	15.00
❑ 1074 [PS]	Stop! In the Name of Love/ I'm in Love Again	1965	30.00
❑ 1075	Back in My Arms Again/ Whisper You Love Me Boy	1965	15.00
❑ 1075 [PS]	Back in My Arms Again/ Whisper You Love Me Boy	1965	30.00
❑ 1080	Nothing But Heartaches/ He Holds His Own	1965	15.00
❑ 1080 [PS]	Nothing But Heartaches/ He Holds His Own	1965	30.00
❑ 1083	I Hear a Symphony/Who Could Ever Doubt My Love	1965	15.00
❑ 1085	Children's Christmas Song/ Twinkle, Twinkle Little Me	1965	20.00
❑ 1085 [DJ]	Children's Christmas Song/ Twinkle, Twinkle Little Me	1965	25.00
—Promo only on red vinyl			
❑ 1085 [PS]	Children's Christmas Song/ Twinkle, Twinkle Little Me	1965	35.00
❑ 1089	My World Is Empty Without You/ Everything Is Good About You	1966	15.00
❑ 1094	Love Is Like an Itching in My Heart/He's All I Got	1966	15.00
❑ 1097	You Can't Hurry Love/ Put Yourself in My Place	1966	15.00
❑ 1097 [PS]	You Can't Hurry Love/ Put Yourself in My Place	1966	30.00
❑ 1101	You Keep Me Hangin' On/ Remove This Doubt	1966	15.00
❑ 1101 [PS]	You Keep Me Hangin' On/ Remove This Doubt	1966	30.00
❑ 1103	Love Is Here and Now You're Gone/There's No Stopping Us Now	1967	12.00
❑ 1107	The Happening/ All I Know About You	1967	12.00
❑ 1111	Reflections/Going Down for the Third Time	1967	8.00
—Starting here, through 1156, as "Diana Ross and the Supremes"			
❑ 1116	In and Out of Love/I Guess I'll Always Love You	1967	8.00
❑ 1122	Forever Came Today/ Time Changes Things	1968	8.00
❑ 1125	What the World Needs Now/ Your Kiss of Fire	1968	—
—Unreleased			
❑ 1126	Some Things You Never Get Used To/You've Been So Wonderful to Me	1968	8.00
❑ 1135	Love Child/Will This Be the Day	1968	8.00
❑ 1139	I'm Livin' in Shame/I'm So Glad I Got Somebody	1969	8.00
❑ 1146	The Composer/The Beginning of the End	1969	8.00
❑ 1148	No Matter What Sign You Are/ The Young Folks	1969	8.00
❑ 1156	Someday We'll Be Together/ He's My Sunny Boy	1969	8.00
❑ 1162	Up the Ladder to the Roof/Bill, When Are You Coming Home	1970	6.00
—Starting here, name reverts to "The Supremes" (unless noted)			
❑ 1167	Everybody's Got the Right to Love/But I Love You More	1970	6.00
❑ 1172	Stoned Love/Shine on Me	1970	6.00
❑ 1182	Nathan Jones/Happy (Is a Bumpy Road)	1971	6.00
❑ 1190	Touch/It's So Hard for Me to Say Goodbye	1971	6.00
❑ 1195	Floy Joy/This Is the Story	1972	5.00
❑ 1200	Automatically Sunshine/ Precious Little Things	1972	5.00
❑ 1206	Your Wonderful, Sweet Sweet Love/The Wisdom of Time	1972	5.00
❑ 1213	I Guess I'll Miss the Man/ Over and Over	1972	5.00
❑ 1225	Bad Weather/Oh Be My Love	1973	5.00
❑ 1350	It's All Been Said Before/ (B-side unassigned)	1975	—
—Unreleased			
❑ 1357	He's My Man/Give Out But Don't Give Up	1975	5.00
❑ 1374	Where Do I Go from Here/Give Out But Don't Give Up	1975	5.00
❑ 1391	I'm Gonna Let My Heart Do the Walking/Early Morning Love	1976	5.00
❑ 1407	You're My Driving Wheel/You're What's Missing in My Life	1976	5.00
❑ 1415	Let Yourself Go/You Are the Heart of Me	1977	5.00
❑ 1488	Medley of Hits/Where Did We Go Wrong	1980	4.00
—As "Diana Ross and the Supremes"			
❑ 1523	Medley of Hits/Where Did We Go Wrong	1981	4.00
—As "Diana Ross and the Supremes"			

TAMLA

Number	Title	Yr	NM
❑ 54038	I Want a Guy/Never Again	1961	60.00
—Globes label			
❑ 54038	I Want a Guy/Never Again	1961	125.00
—Lines label			
❑ 54045	Buttered Popcorn/ Who's Lovin' You	1961	60.00
—Globes label			
❑ 54045	Buttered Popcorn/ Who's Lovin' You	1961	125.00
—Lines label			

TOPPS/MOTOWN

Number	Title	Yr	NM
❑ 1	Baby Love	1967	75.00
—Cardboard record			
❑ 2	Stop in the Name of Love	1967	75.00
—Cardboard record			
❑ 3	Where Did Our Love Go	1967	75.00
—Cardboard record			
❑ 15	Come See About Me	1967	75.00
—Cardboard record			
❑ 16	My World Is Empty Without You	1967	75.00
—Cardboard record			

7-Inch Extended Plays

MOTOWN

Number	Title	Yr	NM
❑ S 621 [PS]	Where Did Our Love Go	1965	25.00
❑ S 621 [S]	He Means the World to Me/Baby Love/Ask Any Girl//Where Did Our Love Go/Come See About Me/Run, Run, Run	1965	25.00
—33 1/3 rpm, small hole			

Albums

DORAL

Number	Title	Yr	NM
❑ DRL 104	Doral Presents Diana Ross and the Supremes	1971	50.00
—Available through Doral cigarettes			

MOTOWN

Number	Title	Yr	NM
❑ M5-101V1	Superstar Series, Vol. 1	1981	12.00
—By "Diana Ross and the Supremes"			
❑ PR-102 [DJ]	Touch Interview	1971	25.00
❑ M5-138V1	The Supremes A' Go-Go	1981	12.00
—Reissue of Motown 649			
❑ M5-147V1	I Hear a Symphony	1981	12.00
—Reissue of Motown 643			
❑ M5-158V1	The Supremes Sing Country Western and Pop	1981	8.00
—Reissue of Motown 625			
❑ M5-162V1	The Supremes at the Copa	1981	12.00
—Reissue of Motown 636			
❑ M5-182V1	The Supremes Sing Holland-Dozier-Holland	1981	12.00
—Reissue of Motown 650			
❑ M5-203V1	Diana Ross and the Supremes Greatest Hits, Vol. 3	1981	12.00
—Reissue of Motown 702			
❑ M5-223V1	Meet the Supremes	1982	8.00
—Reissue of Motown 606			
❑ M5-237V1	Greatest Hits	1982	10.00
—Reissue (unknown if it's the complete 2-record set or an edited version)			
❑ M 606 [M]	Meet the Supremes	1963	30.00
—With close-up of group's faces			
❑ M 606 [M]	Meet the Supremes	1963	900.00
—With group sitting on stools			
❑ MS 606 [S]	Meet the Supremes	1964	40.00
—With close-up of group's faces			
❑ MT/MS 610	The Supremes Sing Ballads and Blues	1963	—
—Unreleased			
❑ M 621 [M]	Where Did Our Love Go	1964	30.00
❑ MS 621 [S]	Where Did Our Love Go	1964	40.00
❑ M 623 [M]	A Bit of Liverpool	1964	40.00
❑ MS 623 [S]	A Bit of Liverpool	1964	50.00
❑ MS 625 [S]	The Supremes Sing Country, Western & Pop	1965	30.00

Except when noted otherwise, VG = 25% of NM, and VG+ = 50% of NM. (Example: VG = $2.00, VG+ = $4.00 and NM = $8.00.)

Number	Title (A Side/B Side)	Yr	NM
❑ MT-625 [M]	The Supremes Sing Country, Western & Pop	1965	25.00
❑ MT/MS 626	The Supremes Live! Live! Live!	1965	—
—Unreleased			
❑ M 627 [M]	More Hits by the Supremes	1965	25.00
❑ MS 627 [S]	More Hits by the Supremes	1965	30.00
❑ MT/MS 628	There's a Place for Us	1965	—
—Unreleased			
❑ M 629 [M]	We Remember Sam Cooke	1965	25.00
❑ MS 629 [S]	We Remember Sam Cooke	1965	30.00
—The above LP came out before Motown 627			
❑ M 636 [M]	The Supremes at the Copa	1965	25.00
❑ MS 636 [S]	The Supremes at the Copa	1965	30.00
❑ MT/MS 637	A Tribute to the Girls	1965	—
—Unreleased			
❑ MS 638 [S]	Merry Christmas	1965	40.00
—Same as above, but in stereo			
❑ MT 638 [M]	Merry Christmas	1965	30.00
❑ M 643 [M]	I Hear a Symphony	1966	25.00
❑ MS 643 [S]	I Hear a Symphony	1966	30.00
❑ MTMS 648	Pure Gold	1966	—
—Unreleased			
❑ M 649 [M]	The Supremes A' Go-Go	1966	25.00
❑ MS 649 [S]	The Supremes A' Go-Go	1966	30.00
❑ M 650 [M]	The Supremes Sing Holland-Dozier-Holland	1967	25.00
❑ MS 650 [S]	The Supremes Sing Holland-Dozier-Holland	1967	30.00
❑ M 659 [M]	The Supremes Sing Rodgers & Hart	1967	25.00
❑ MS 659 [S]	The Supremes Sing Rodgers & Hart	1967	30.00
❑ M 663 [(2)M]	Diana Ross and the Supremes Greatest Hits	1967	30.00
❑ MS 663 [(2)S]	Diana Ross and the Supremes Greatest Hits	1967	40.00
❑ MT/MS 663	Diana Ross and the Supremes Greatest Hits Poster	1967	10.00
❑ M 665 [M]	Reflections	1968	30.00
❑ MS 665 [S]	Reflections	1968	20.00
❑ MS 670	Love Child	1968	20.00
❑ M 672 [M]	Funny Girl	1968	30.00
—Mono appears to be promo only			
❑ MS 672 [S]	Funny Girl	1968	20.00
—The above LP came out before Motown 670			
❑ M 676 [M]	Live at London's Talk of the Town	1968	30.00
—Mono is promo only			
❑ MS 676 [S]	Live at London's Talk of the Town	1968	20.00
—The above LP came out before Motown 670 and 672			
❑ MS 689	Let the Sunshine In	1969	20.00
❑ MS 694	Cream of the Crop	1969	20.00
❑ MS 702	Diana Ross and the Supremes Greatest Hits, Vol. 3	1970	20.00
❑ MS 705	Right On	1970	15.00
—By "The Supremes"; the first LP after Diana Ross left			
❑ MS 708 [(2)]	Farewell	1970	25.00
—By "Diana Ross and the Supremes"			
❑ MS 720	New Ways But Love Stays	1970	15.00
❑ MS 737	Touch	1971	15.00
❑ MS 746	Promises Kept	1972	—
—Unreleased			
❑ M 751L	Floy Joy	1972	15.00
❑ M 756L	The Supremes	1972	15.00
❑ M9-794L3 [(3)]	Anthology (1962-1969)	1974	25.00
—By "Diana Ross and the Supremes"			
❑ M6-828	The Supremes	1975	15.00
❑ M6-863S1	High Energy	1976	15.00
❑ M6-873S1	Mary, Scherrie and Susaye	1976	15.00
❑ M7-904R1	The Supremes at Their Best	1978	15.00
❑ 5245 ML	Love Child	1982	8.00
—Reissue of MS 670			
❑ 5252 ML	Merry Christmas	1982	10.00
—Reissue of MS 638			
❑ 5270 ML	Where Did Our Love Go	1982	8.00
—Reissue of MS 621			
❑ 5278 ML	Captured Live on Stage	1982	8.00
—Reissue?			
❑ 5305 ML	Let the Sunshine In	1983	8.00
—Reissue of MS 689			
❑ 5313 ML	Great Songs and Performances That Inspired the Motown 25th Anniversary TV Special	1983	10.00
❑ 5361 ML	Motown Legends	1985	10.00
❑ 5371 ML	Diana Ross and the Supremes Sing Motown	1985	10.00
❑ 5381 ML3 [(3)]	25th Anniversary	1986	20.00
—By "Diana Ross and the Supremes"			

NATURAL RESOURCES

Number	Title (A Side/B Side)	Yr	NM
❑ NR 4006T1	Where Did Our Love Go	1978	12.00
—Reissue of Motown 621			
❑ NR 4010	Merry Christmas	1978	12.00
—Reissue of Motown 638			

PICKWICK

Number	Title (A Side/B Side)	Yr	NM
❑ SPC-3383	Baby Love	197?	12.00
—Edited reissue of Motown 621			

UNIVERSAL MOTOWN

Number	Title (A Side/B Side)	Yr	NM
❑ 5315839	I Hear a Symphony	2009	20.00

SUPREMES, THE (2)

45s

ACE

Number	Title (A Side/B Side)	Yr	NM
❑ 534	Just for You and I/Don't Leave Me Here to Cry	1957	80.00

SUPREMES, THE (3)

45s

APT

Number	Title (A Side/B Side)	Yr	NM
❑ 25055	Another Chance to Love/Fidgety	1961	40.00

SUPREMES, THE (4)

45s

KITTEN

Number	Title (A Side/B Side)	Yr	NM
❑ 6969	Could This Be You/Margie	1956	500.00

SUPREMES, THE (5)

45s

MARK

Number	Title (A Side/B Side)	Yr	NM
❑ 129	Nobody Can Love You/Snap, Crackle and Pop	1958	800.00

SUPREMES, THE (6)

45s

MASCOT

Number	Title (A Side/B Side)	Yr	NM
❑ 126	Little Sally Walker/Just Yell	1960	100.00

SUPREMES, THE (7)

45s

OLD TOWN

Number	Title (A Side/B Side)	Yr	NM
❑ 1024	Tonight/My Babe	1956	100.00
❑ 1024	Tonight/She Don't Want Me No More	1956	150.00

SUPREMES, THE, AND THE FOUR TOPS

Also see each artist's individual listings.

45s

MOTOWN

Number	Title (A Side/B Side)	Yr	NM
❑ 1173	River Deep-Mountain High/Together We Can Make Such Sweet Music	1970	6.00
❑ 1181	You Gotta Have Love in Your Heart/I'm Glad About It	1971	6.00

Albums

MOTOWN

Number	Title (A Side/B Side)	Yr	NM
❑ M5-123V1A	The Magnificent Seven	1981	12.00
—Reissue of Motown 717			
❑ MS 717	The Magnificent Seven	1970	15.00
❑ MS 736	The Return of the Magnificent Seven	1971	15.00
❑ MS 745	Dynamite	1971	15.00

SUPREMES, THE, DIANA ROSS AND, AND THE TEMPTATIONS

Also see each artist's individual listings.

45s

MOTOWN

Number	Title (A Side/B Side)	Yr	NM
❑ 1137	I'm Gonna Make You Love Me/A Place in the Sun	1968	7.00
❑ 1137 [PS]	I'm Gonna Make You Love Me/A Place in the Sun	1968	20.00
❑ 1142	I'll Try Something New/The Way You Do the Things You Do	1969	7.00
❑ 1150	Stubborn Kind of Fellow/Try It Baby	1969	7.00
❑ 1153	The Weight/For Better or Worse	1969	7.00

Albums

MOTOWN

Number	Title (A Side/B Side)	Yr	NM
❑ M5-139V1	Diana Ross and the Supremes Join the Temptations	1981	12.00
—Reissue of Motown 679			
❑ M5-171V1	TCB	1981	12.00
—Reissue of Motown 682			
❑ M 679 [M]	Diana Ross and the Supremes Join the Temptations	1968	30.00
❑ MS 679 [S]	Diana Ross and the Supremes Join the Temptations	1968	20.00
❑ MS 682	TCB	1968	20.00
❑ MS 692	Together	1969	20.00
❑ MS 699	On Broadway	1969	20.00

SUPREMES FOUR, THE

45s

SARA

Number	Title (A Side/B Side)	Yr	NM
❑ 1032	I Lost My Job/I Love You Patricia	1958	2000.

SURE CURE, THE

45s

PARKWAY

Number	Title (A Side/B Side)	Yr	NM
❑ 145	Anything You Want/I Wanna Do It	1967	10.00

SURF BOYS, THE

45s

KARATE

Number	Title (A Side/B Side)	Yr	NM
❑ 526	Da Doo Ron Ron/Hurt	1966	25.00

SCEPTER

Number	Title (A Side/B Side)	Yr	NM
❑ 12180	Stuck in the Chimney/I Told Santa Claus I Want You	1966	25.00

SURF BREAKERS, THE

45s

MERCURY

Number	Title (A Side/B Side)	Yr	NM
❑ 72174	Hang Ten/Ridin' In #9	1963	50.00

SURF BUNNIES, THE

45s

DOT

Number	Title (A Side/B Side)	Yr	NM
❑ 16523	Our Surfer Boys/Surf Bunny Beach	1963	30.00

GOLIATH

Number	Title (A Side/B Side)	Yr	NM
❑ 1352	Our Surfer Boys/Surf Bunny Beach	1963	50.00
❑ 1353	Surf City High/Met the Boy I Adore	1963	50.00

SURF RIDERS, THE

45s

DECCA

Number	Title (A Side/B Side)	Yr	NM
❑ 31477	The Birds/Blues for the Birds	1963	30.00

NASCO

Number	Title (A Side/B Side)	Yr	NM
❑ 6008	I'm Out/Rocko Socko	1958	60.00

SURF STOMPERS, THE

Also see BRUCE JOHNSTON.

Albums

DEL-FI

Number	Title (A Side/B Side)	Yr	NM
❑ DFLP-1236 [M]	The Original Surfer Stomp	1963	60.00
❑ DFST-1236 [S]	The Original Surfer Stomp	1963	80.00
❑ DLF-1236	The Original Surfer Stomp	1997	12.00

SURF TEENS, THE

Albums

SUTTON

Number	Title (A Side/B Side)	Yr	NM
❑ SSU-339 [S]	Surf Mania	1963	60.00
❑ SU-339 [M]	Surf Mania	1963	50.00

SURFARIS, THE (1)

45s

DECCA

Number	Title (A Side/B Side)	Yr	NM
❑ 31538	Point Panic/Waikiki Run	1963	15.00
❑ 31561	A Surfer's Christmas List/Santa's Speed Shop	1963	30.00
❑ 31581	I Wanna Take a trip to the Islands/Scatter Shield	1964	20.00
❑ 31605	Murphy the Surfie/Go Go Go For Louie's Place	1964	15.00
❑ 31641	Bossa Barracuda/Dune Buggy	1964	15.00
❑ 31682	Hot Rod High/Karen	1964	15.00
❑ 31731	Beat 65/Black Denim	1965	20.00
❑ 31784	Theme of the Battle Maiden/Somethin' Else	1965	20.00
❑ 31835	Catch a Little Ride with Me/Don't Hurt My Little Sister	1965	20.00
❑ 31954	Hey Joe Where Are You Going/So Get Out	1966	20.00
❑ 32003	Wipe Out/I'm a Hog for You	1966	10.00

DFS

Number	Title (A Side/B Side)	Yr	NM
❑ 11/12	Wipe Out/Surfer Joe	1963	3000.
—VG 1500; VG+ 2250			

DOT

Number	Title (A Side/B Side)	Yr	NM
❑ 144	Wipe Out/Surfer Joe	1966	10.00
—Black label, script "Dot" in multicolor letters			
❑ 144	Wipe Out/Surfer Joe	1969	6.00
—Muilticolor label, "DOT" in all capital letters in box at top			
❑ 144 [DJ]	Wipe Out (same on both sides)	1966	100.00
—Red vinyl			
❑ 144 [DJ]	Wipe Out (same on both sides)	1966	150.00
—Red vinyl; error pressing with "Surfer Joe" on both sides			
❑ 16479	Wipe Out/Surfer Joe	1963	15.00
❑ 16757	Surfer Joe/Can't Sit Down	1965	30.00
—B-side by the Challengers, but credited to the Surfaris			
❑ 16757	Surfer Joe/Can't Sit Down	1965	50.00
—B-side by the Challengers, and credited correctly			
❑ 16966	Show Biz/Chicago Green	1966	10.00
❑ 17008	Shake/The Search	1967	10.00

PRINCESS

Number	Title (A Side/B Side)	Yr	NM
❑ 50	Wipe Out/Surfer Joe	1963	150.00
—With short versions of both songs. "RE-1" is in the trail-off area.			
❑ 50	Wipe Out/Surfer Joe	1963	400.00
—With long versions of both songs. No "RE-1" is in the trail-off area.			
❑ 52	Spanish Moon/She's Got the Blues	1963	100.00
—Reissued on Vault 911 credited to THE TRAVELERS; we don't know if Princess 52 exists credited to the Travelers, but we know this version exists			

Number	Title (A Side/B Side)	Yr	NM
Albums			
DECCA			
❑ DL 4470 [M]	The Surfaris Play Wipe Out	1963	25.00
❑ DL 4487 [M]	Hit City '64	1964	40.00
❑ DL 4560 [M]	Fun City, U.S.A.	1964	40.00
❑ DL 4614 [M]	Hit City '65	1965	40.00
❑ DL 4663 [M]	It Ain't Me, Babe	1965	40.00
❑ DL 74470 [S]	The Surfaris Play Wipe Out	1963	30.00
❑ DL 74487 [S]	Hit City '64	1964	50.00
❑ DL 74560 [S]	Fun City, U.S.A.	1964	50.00
❑ DL 74614 [S]	Hit City '65	1965	50.00
❑ DL 74663 [S]	It Ain't Me, Babe	1965	50.00
DOT			
❑ DLP-3535 [M]	Wipe Out	1963	30.00
—With no back cover photo of the Surfaris			
❑ DLP-3535 [M]	Wipe Out	1963	40.00
—With back cover photo featuring four Surfaris			
❑ DLP-3535 [M]	Wipe Out	1963	50.00
—With back cover photo featuring five Surfaris			
❑ DLP-25535 [S]	Wipe Out	1963	40.00
—With no back cover photo of the Surfaris			
❑ DLP-25535 [S]	Wipe Out	1963	50.00
—With back cover photo featuring four Surfaris			
❑ DLP-25535 [S]	Wipe Out	1963	80.00
—With back cover photo featuring five Surfaris			
PICKWICK			
❑ SPC-3636	Wipe Out and Surfer Joe	1978	15.00

SURFARIS, THE (2) This group was forced to change its name to "The Original Surfaris."

Number	Title (A Side/B Side)	Yr	NM
45s			
CHANCELLOR			
❑ 1142	The Midnight Surf/Psyche-Out	1963	50.00
DEL-FI			
❑ 4219	Surfari/Bombora	1963	100.00
FELSTED			
❑ 8688	Tor-Chula/Psyche-Out	1964	50.00
NORTHRIDGE			
❑ 1001	Moment of Truth/Church Key	1963	60.00
—B-side by the Biscaynes			
REGANO			
❑ 1062	Surfin' '63/Boss Beat	1963	50.00
—As "The Original Surfaris"			
REPRISE			
❑ 20180	Moment of Truth/Church Key	1963	30.00
—B-side by the Biscaynes			
SURFARI			
❑ 301	Gum Dipped Slicks/High Time	1964	100.00
—As "The Original Surfaris"			
Albums			
DIPLOMAT			
❑ D-2309 [M]	Wheels-Shorts-Hot Rods	1963	25.00
—As "The Original Surfaris"			
❑ DS-2309 [S]	Wheels-Shorts-Hot Rods	1963	30.00
—As "The Original Surfaris"			
SUNDAZED			
❑ LP-5014	Bombora!	199?	10.00
—As "The Original Surfaris"			

SURFRIDERS, THE

Number	Title (A Side/B Side)	Yr	NM
Albums			
VAULT			
❑ LP-105 [M]	Surfbeat, Vol. 2	1963	30.00
❑ VS-105 [S]	Surfbeat, Vol. 2	1963	40.00

SURFSIDERS, THE

Number	Title (A Side/B Side)	Yr	NM
Albums			
DESIGN			
❑ DLP-208 [M]	The Beach Boys Songbook	1965	15.00
❑ DLPS-208 [S]	The Beach Boys Songbook	1965	20.00

SURVIVOR

Number	Title (A Side/B Side)	Yr	NM
12-Inch Singles			
CASABLANCA			
❑ PRO 287-1 [DJ]	Moment of Truth (same on both sides)	1984	8.00
SCOTTI BROS.			
❑ ZAS 1291 [DJ]	Didn't Know It Was Love (2 versions)	1988	6.00
❑ AS 1740 [DJ]	Caught in the Game (Long Version 4:46) (Short Version 4:10)	1983	6.00
❑ ZAS 2046 [DJ]	The Search Is Over (4:13) (same on both sides)	1985	8.00
45s			
CASABLANCA			
❑ 880053-7	Moment of Truth/It Doesn't Have to Be This Way	1984	4.00
SCOTTI BROS.			
❑ 511	Somwhere in America/Freelance	1980	5.00
❑ 517	Rebel Girl/Freelance	1980	5.00
❑ ZS5 02435	Summer Nights/Love Is On My Side	1981	5.00
❑ ZS5 02435 [DJ]	Summer Nights (3:07)/(3:23)	1981	6.00
❑ ZS5 02560	Poor Man's Son/Love Is On My Side	1981	4.00
❑ ZS5 02700	Summer Nights/Take You on a Saturday	1982	4.00
❑ ZS5 02912	Eye of the Tiger/Take You on a Saturday	1982	4.00
❑ ZS5 02912 [PS]	Eye of the Tiger/Take You on a Saturday	1982	6.00
❑ ZS4 03213	American Heartbeat/Silver Girl	1982	4.00
❑ ZS4 03213 [PS]	American Heartbeat/Silver Girl	1982	5.00
❑ ZS4 03485	The One That Really Matters/Hesitation Dance	1983	4.00
❑ ZS4 04074	Caught in the Game/Slander	1983	4.00
❑ ZS4 04074 [PS]	Caught in the Game/Slander	1983	5.00
❑ ZS4 04347	I Never Stopped Loving You/Ready for the Real Thing	1984	4.00
❑ ZS4 04603	I Can't Hold Back/I See You in Everyone	1984	3.00
❑ ZS4 04603 [PS]	I Can't Hold Back/I See You in Everyone	1984	4.00
❑ ZS4 04685	High on You/Broken Promises	1984	3.00
❑ ZS4 04685 [PS]	High on You/Broken Promises	1984	4.00
❑ ZS4 04871	The Search Is Over/It's the Singer, Not the Song	1985	3.00
❑ ZS4 04871 [PS]	The Search Is Over/It's the Singer, Not the Song	1985	4.00
❑ ZS4 05579	First Night/Feels Like Love	1985	3.00
❑ ZS4 05579 [PS]	First Night/Feels Like Love	1985	4.00
❑ ZS4 05663	Burning Heart/Feels Like Love	1985	3.00
❑ ZS4 05663 [PS]	Burning Heart/Feels Like Love	1985	4.00
❑ ZS4 06381	Is This Love/Can't Let You Go	1986	3.00
❑ ZS4 06381 [PS]	Is This Love/Can't Let You Go	1986	4.00
❑ ZS4 06705	How Much Love/Backstreet Love Affair	1987	3.00
❑ ZS4 07070	Man Against the World/Oceans	1987	3.00
❑ ZS4 07070 [PS]	Man Against the World/Oceans	1987	4.00
❑ ZS4 08067	Didn't Know It Was Love/Rhythm of the City	1988	3.00
❑ ZS4 68526	Across the Miles/Burning Bridges	1989	4.00
Albums			
SCOTTI BROTHERS			
❑ SB 7107	Survivor	1980	12.00
❑ ARZ 37549	Premonition	1981	10.00
❑ PZ 37549	Premonition	198?	6.00
—Budget-line reissue with new prefix			
❑ FZ 38062	Eye of the Tiger	1982	8.00
❑ PZ 38062	Eye of the Tiger	198?	6.00
—Budget-line reissue with new prefix			
❑ QZ 38791	Caught in the Game	1983	8.00
❑ FZ 39578	Vital Signs	1984	8.00
❑ FZ 40457	When Seconds Count	1986	8.00
❑ OZ 44282	Too Hot to Sleep	1988	8.00

SURVIVORS, THE Dave Nowlen, Bob Norberg and friends with help from BRIAN WILSON. This record is NOT by the Beach Boys.

Number	Title (A Side/B Side)	Yr	NM
45s			
CAPITOL			
❑ 5102	Pamela Jean/After the Game	1963	1000.

SUSIE AND THE FOUR TRUMPETS

Number	Title (A Side/B Side)	Yr	NM
45s			
UNITED ARTISTS			
❑ 471	Starry Eyes/Blue Little Girl	1962	60.00

SUTCH, SCREAMING LORD

Number	Title (A Side/B Side)	Yr	NM
45s			
CAMEO			
❑ 341	She's Fallen in Love with the Monster Man/Bye Bye Baby	1964	15.00
COTILLION			
❑ 44149	Gotta Keep a-Rocking/Country Club	1972	10.00
—As "Lord Sutch"			
Albums			
COTILLION			
❑ SD 9015	Lord Sutch and Heavy Friends	1970	30.00
—With Jimmy Page, John Bonham and Jeff Beck			
❑ SD 9049	Hands of Jack the Ripper	1972	30.00

SUTHERLAND BROTHERS Also see SUTHERLAND BROTHERS AND QUIVER.

Number	Title (A Side/B Side)	Yr	NM
45s			
COLUMBIA			
❑ 10758	One More Night with You/When I Say I Love You (The Pie)	1978	4.00
❑ 11003	On the Rocks/As Long As I've Got You	1979	4.00
ISLAND			
❑ 1203	Long Long Day/The Pie	1972	5.00
❑ 1209	Sailing/Hallelujah	1972	5.00
Albums			
COLUMBIA			
❑ JC 35293	Down to Earth	1978	10.00
❑ JC 35703	When the Night Comes Down	1979	10.00
ISLAND			
❑ SW-9315	The Sutherland Brothers Band	1972	12.00

SUTHERLAND BROTHERS AND QUIVER
Also see each artist's individual listings.

Number	Title (A Side/B Side)	Yr	NM
45s			
COLUMBIA			
❑ 10284	Arms of Mary/Love on the Moon	1976	5.00
❑ 10362	When the Train Comes/Mad Trail	1976	5.00
❑ 10460	Secrets/Something's Burning	1976	5.00
ISLAND			
❑ 1217	(I Don't Want to Love You But) You Got Me Anyway/Rock and Roll Show	1973	4.00
❑ 1220	Dream Kid/Silver Sister	1974	4.00
Albums			
COLUMBIA			
❑ PC 33982	Reach for the Sky	1976	10.00
❑ PC 34376	Slipstream	1977	10.00
ISLAND			
❑ SW-9326	Lifeboat	1973	10.00
❑ SW-9341	Dream Kid	1974	10.00

SUZY AND THE RED STRIPES Actually Linda McCartney with Wings. Also see PAUL McCARTNEY.

Number	Title (A Side/B Side)	Yr	NM
12-Inch Singles			
CAPITOL			
❑ V-15244	Seaside Woman/B-Side to Seaside	1986	40.00
EPIC			
❑ ASF 361 [DJ]	Seaside Woman (same on both sides)	1977	30.00
45s			
CAPITOL			
❑ B-5608	Seaside Woman/B-Side to Seaside	1986	30.00
EPIC			
❑ 50403	Seaside Woman/B-Side to Seaside	1977	10.00
❑ 50403 [DJ]	Seaside Woman (mono/stereo)	1977	25.00
—Red vinyl, orange label on one side, white on the other			
❑ 50403 [DJ]	Seaside Woman (mono/stereo)	1977	100.00
—"Advance Promotion" label, black vinyl			
❑ 50403 [DJ]	Seaside Woman (mono/stereo)	1977	100.00
—Black vinyl, orange label on one side, white on the other			

SVEN AND CHARLOTTE Former members of THE HEP STARS.

Number	Title (A Side/B Side)	Yr	NM
45s			
MORNINGSTAR			
❑ 507	Bang-a-Boomerang/Roly Poly Girl	1974	10.00
—As "Svenne and Lotta"			

SWAGMEN, THE

Number	Title (A Side/B Side)	Yr	NM
45s			
PARKWAY			
❑ 854	By the Yonder Tree/East Virginia	1962	12.00
Albums			
PARKWAY			
❑ SP-7015 [S]	Meet the Swagmen	1962	50.00

SWALLOWS, THE

Number	Title (A Side/B Side)	Yr	NM
45s			
AFTER HOURS			
❑ 104	My Baby/Good Time Girls	1954	2400.
—VG 800; VG+ 1600			
FEDERAL			
❑ 12319	Oh Lonesome Me/Angel Baby	1958	40.00
❑ 12328	We Want to Rock/Rock-a-Bye-Baby Rock	1958	40.00
❑ 12329	Beside You/Laughing Boy	1958	40.00
❑ 12333	Itchy Twitchy Feeling/Who Knows, Do You?	1958	40.00
KING			
❑ 4458	Will You Be Mine/Dearest	1951	1500.
❑ 4466	Since You've Been Away/Wishing for You	1951	—
—Unconfirmed on 45 rpm			
❑ 4501	Eternally/It Ain't the Meat	1952	800.00
—Black vinyl			
❑ 4501	Eternally/It Ain't the Meat	1952	2500.
—Blue vinyl			
❑ 4501	Eternally/It Ain't the Meat	1952	2500.
—Green vinyl			

S

Except when noted otherwise, VG = 25% of NM, and VG+ = 50% of NM. (Example: VG = $2.00, VG+ = $4.00 and NM = $8.00.)

Number	Title (A Side/B Side)	Yr	NM
❑ 4515	Tell Me Why/Roll, Roll, Pretty Baby	1952	2000.
—VG 1000; VG+ 1500			
❑ 4525	Beside You/You Left Me	1952	400.00
❑ 4533	You Walked In/I Only Have Eyes for You	1952	800.00
❑ 4579	Where Do I Go from Here/Please, Baby, Please	1952	800.00
❑ 4612	Laugh (Though You Want to Cry)/Our Love Is Dying	1953	500.00
❑ 4632	Nobody's Lovin' Me/Bicycle Tillie	1953	500.00
❑ 4656	Trust Me/Pleading Blues	1953	400.00
❑ 4676	I'll Be Waiting/It Feels So Good	1953	400.00

SWALLOWS, THE (2)

Number	Title (A Side/B Side)	Yr	NM
45s			
GUYDEN			
❑ 2023	How Long Must a Fool Go On/You Must Try	1959	50.00
—Reissued credited to "The Guides"			

SWAMP RATS, THE

Number	Title (A Side/B Side)	Yr	NM
45s			
CO & CE			
❑ 245	In the Midnight Hour/It's Not Easy	1967	20.00
ST. CLAIR			
❑ 69	Louie Louie/Hey Joe	1966	50.00
❑ 2222	Psycho/Here, There and Everywhere	1966	200.00
❑ 3333	Two Tymes Two/(B-side unknown)	1966	50.00
❑ 711711	It's Not Easy/No Friend of Mine	1966	50.00

SWAN, BILLY

Number	Title (A Side/B Side)	Yr	NM
45s			
A&M			
❑ 2046	Hello! Remember Me/Never Go Lookin' Again	1978	4.00
❑ 2103	No Way Around It (It's Love)/Forever in Your Love	1978	4.00
COLUMBIA			
❑ 10443	Shake, Rattle and Roll/I Got It for You	1976	4.00
❑ 10486	Swept Away/California Song (For Malibu)	1977	4.00
EPIC			
❑ 02196	I'm Into Lovin' You/Not Far from Forty	1981	3.00
❑ 02601	Stuck Right in the Middle of Your Love/Soft Touch	1981	3.00
❑ 02841	With Their Kind of Money and Our Kind of Love/Lay Down and Love Me Tonight	1982	3.00
❑ 03226	Your Picture Still Loves Me (And I Still Love You)/Give Your Lovin' to Me	1982	3.00
❑ 03505	Rainbows and Butterflies/Only Be You	1982	3.00
❑ 03917	Yes/I Can't Stop Writing L ove Songs	1983	3.00
❑ 51000	Do I Have to Draw a Picture/I Want to Change Your Life	1981	3.00
MERCURY			
❑ 884668-7	You Must Be Lookin' for Me/Three Chord Rock & Roll	1986	3.00
❑ 888320-7	I'm Gonna Get You/Three Chord Rock & Roll	1987	3.00
MGM			
❑ 14008	El Paso/The Sweet Sound of Your Name	1968	10.00
MONUMENT			
❑ 45-275	Don't Be Cruel/Vanessa	1979	4.00
❑ 940	Breakin' Up/Out of Her System	1966	12.00
❑ 988	I've Got to Have You/Below Average Everyday Girl	1966	12.00
❑ 8597	Wedding Bells/P.M.S.	1974	5.00
❑ 8621	I Can Help/The Ways of a Woman in Love	1974	5.00
❑ 8641	I'm Her Fool/I'd Like to Work for You	1975	4.00
❑ 8651	Come By/Woman Handled My Mind	1975	4.00
❑ 8661	Everything's the Same (Ain't Nothing Changed)/Overnite Thing (Usually)	1975	4.00
❑ 8682	Just Want to Taste Your Wine/Love You Baby to the Bone	1976	4.00
❑ 8697	Vanessa/Number 1	1976	4.00
❑ 8706	You're the One/Mr. Misery	1976	4.00
RISING SONS			
❑ 702	Friendship/You Got Me Laughing	1967	10.00
Albums			
A&M			
❑ SP-4686	You're OK, I'm OK	1978	10.00
COLUMBIA			
❑ PZ 33279	I Can Help	1977	8.00
—Reissue of Monument 33279			
❑ PZ 33805	Rock 'n' Roll Moon	1977	8.00
—Reissue of Monument 33805			
❑ PZ 34183	Billy Swan	1977	8.00
—Reissue of Monument 34183			
❑ PC 34473	Four	1977	10.00
EPIC			
❑ FE 37079	I'm Into Lovin' You	1981	10.00
MONUMENT			
❑ 7629	Billy Swan At His Best	1978	10.00
❑ KZ 33279	I Can Help	1974	10.00
❑ PZ 33805	Rock 'n' Roll Moon	1975	10.00
❑ PZ 34183	Billy Swan	1976	10.00

SWANN, BETTYE

Number	Title (A Side/B Side)	Yr	NM
45s			
ABET			
❑ 9450	Make Me Yours/I Will Not Cry	1973	10.00
❑ 9453	Don't Wait Too Long/I Can't Stop Loving You	1973	10.00
❑ 9455	The Heartache Is Gone/Fall in Love with Me	1973	10.00
ATLANTIC			
❑ 2869	Victim of a Foolish Heart/Cold Day (In Hell)	1972	15.00
❑ 2921	Today I Started Loving You Again/I'd Rather Go Blind	1972	20.00
❑ 2950	Till I Get It Right/Yours Until Tomorrow	1973	12.00
❑ 3019	The Boy Next Door/Kiss My Love Goodbye	1974	250.00
❑ 3019 [DJ]	The Boy Next Door (stereo/mono)	1974	20.00
❑ 3211	Time to Say Goodbye/When the Game Is Played on You	1974	20.00
❑ 3262	All the Way In or All the Way Out/Doing for the One I Love	1975	12.00
❑ 3352	Heading in the Right Direction/Be Strong Enough to Hold On	1976	15.00
BIG TREE			
❑ 16054	Storybook Children/Just As Sure	1976	100.00
—With Sam Dees			
CAPITOL			
❑ 2263	I'm Lonely for You/(My Heart Is) Closed for the Season	1968	30.00
❑ 2382	Don't Touch Me/(My Heart Is) Closed for the Season	1969	30.00
❑ 2382 [PS]	Don't Touch Me/(My Heart Is) Closed for the Season	1969	30.00
❑ 2515	Angel of the Morning/No Faith No Love	1969	20.00
❑ 2606	Don't You Ever Get Tired (Of Hurting Me)/Willie and Laura Mae Jones	1969	12.00
❑ 2723	Little Things Mean a Lot/Just Because You Can't Be Mine	1970	20.00
❑ 2850	Ain't That Peculiar/Don't Let It Happen to Us	1970	15.00
FAME			
❑ 1479	I Can't Let You Break My Heart/I'm Just Living a Lie	1971	40.00
MONEY			
❑ 108	Don't Wait Too Long/What Is My Life Coming To	1965	30.00
❑ 113	What Can It Be/The Man That Said No	1965	30.00
❑ 118	The Heartache Is Gone/Our Love	1966	30.00
❑ 126	Make Me Yours/I Will Not Cry	1967	30.00
❑ 129	Fall in Love with Me/Lonely Love	1967	20.00
❑ 135	You Gave Me Love/Don't Look Back	1968	40.00
❑ 136	I Think I'm Falling in Love/Don't Take My Mind	1968	20.00
Albums			
ABET			
❑ LP 405	Make Me Yours	197?	20.00
CAPITOL			
❑ ST-190	The Soul View Now!	1969	100.00
❑ ST-270	Don't You Ever Get Tired of Hurting Me	1969	50.00
COLLECTABLES			
❑ COL-5177	Make Me Yours	198?	10.00
MONEY			
❑ 1103 [M]	Make Me Yours	1967	25.00
❑ S-1103 [S]	Make Me Yours	1967	25.00

SWANS, THE (1)

Number	Title (A Side/B Side)	Yr	NM
45s			
BALLAD			
❑ 1003/6	It's a Must/Night Train	1954	600.00
❑ 1007	Happy/The Santa Claus Boogie	1955	600.00
FORTUNE			
❑ 822	I'll Forever Love You/Mister Cool Breeze	1955	800.00
LOST-NITE			
❑ 134	No More/My True Love	196?	8.00
—Reissue			
RAINBOW			
❑ 233	No More/My True Love	1954	1500.
—Red vinyl			
STEAMBOAT			
❑ 101	Believe in Me/In the Morning	1956	2500.

SWANS, THE (2)

Number	Title (A Side/B Side)	Yr	NM
45s			
CAMEO			
❑ 302	The Boy with the Beatle Hair/Please Hurry Home	1964	40.00
PARKWAY			
❑ 881	Daydreamin' of You/The Promise	1963	30.00
SWAN			
❑ 4151	He's Mine/You Better Be a Good Girl Now	1963	30.00

SWANS, THE (3)

Number	Title (A Side/B Side)	Yr	NM
45s			
ROULETTE			
❑ 4213	He Wasn't On the Air Again Today/If I Could Stop Every Clock	1959	25.00

SWANSON, BOBBY

Number	Title (A Side/B Side)	Yr	NM
45s			
DONNA			
❑ 1326	Tom and Susie/China Doll	1960	25.00
❑ 1336	Janie's Face/Peggy's Last Birthday	1961	25.00
❑ 1356	Twisting at the Top/Hello There Lover Doll	1962	25.00
IGLOO			
❑ 1003	Rockin' Little Eskimo/Ballad of an Angel	1959	400.00

SWATLEY, HANK

Number	Title (A Side/B Side)	Yr	NM
45s			
AARON			
❑ 101	Oakie Boogie/I Can't Help It	1957	500.00

SWEATHOG

Number	Title (A Side/B Side)	Yr	NM
45s			
COLUMBIA			
❑ 45416	Things Yet to Come/Runneth Over	1971	5.00
❑ 45492	Hallelujah/Still on the Road	1971	5.00
❑ 45575	Things Yet to Come/Rejoice, Rejoice, Rejoice	1972	5.00
❑ 45609	Rock and Roll Revival/Ride Louise Ride	1972	5.00
Albums			
COLUMBIA			
❑ C 30601	Sweathog	1971	12.00
❑ KC 31144	Hallelujah	1972	12.00

SWEET, MATTHEW

Number	Title (A Side/B Side)	Yr	NM
12-Inch Singles			
A&M			
❑ 17691 [DJ]	Vertigo (2 versions)/You Gotta/Silent City	1989	6.00
COLUMBIA			
❑ CAS 2484 [DJ]	Save Time for Me (same on both sides)	1986	5.00
45s			
COLUMBIA			
❑ 06286	Save Time for Me/Watch You Walking	1986	3.00
❑ 06640	Blue Fools/Anyone Would Say You're Wrong	1987	3.00
Albums			
A&M			
❑ SP-5233	Earth	1989	15.00
COLUMBIA			
❑ BFC 40417	Inside	1986	15.00

Number	Title (A Side/B Side)	Yr	NM
ZOO			
❑ 31130	Blue Sky on Mars	1997	15.00
—All copies autographed by Matthew Steel on the label			
ZOO/CLASSIC			
❑ 11015	Girlfriend	1995	50.00
—Audiophile vinyl pressing; released on CD in 1991			
❑ 11050	Altered Beast	1995	20.00
—Audiophile vinyl pressing; released on CD in 1993			
❑ 11081	100% Fun	1995	20.00

SWEET, THE (1) British glam band.

Number	Title (A Side/B Side)	Yr	NM
45s			
BELL			
❑ 45106	Funny, Funny/You're Not Wrong for Loving Me	1971	8.00
❑ 45126	Co-Co/You're Not Wrong for Loving Me	1971	6.00
❑ 45184	Poppa Joe/Jeanie	1972	6.00
❑ 45251	Little Willy/Man from Mecca	1972	6.00
❑ 45361	Blockbuster/Need a Lot of Lovin'	1973	5.00
❑ 45408	Wig-Wam Bam/New York Connection	1973	5.00
CAPITOL			
❑ 4055	Ballroom Blitz/Restless	1975	5.00
❑ 4157	Fox on the Run/ Burn On the Flame	1975	5.00
❑ 4220	Action/Medussa	1976	5.00
❑ 4429	Fever of Love/Heartbreak Today	1977	5.00
❑ 4454	Funk It Up (David's Song)/ Stairway to the Stars	1977	5.00
❑ 4549	Love Is Like Oxygen/Cover Girl	1978	5.00
❑ 4610	California Nights/Dream On	1978	5.00
❑ 4730	Mother Earth/Why Don't You	1979	4.00
❑ 4908	Sixties Man/Water's Edge	1980	4.00
PARAMOUNT			
❑ 0044	All You'll Ever Get from Me/ The Juicer	1970	20.00
20TH CENTURY			
❑ 2033	It's Lonely Out There/ I'm On My Way	1973	10.00
—U.S. issue of 1968 material that was on Fontana in the U.K.			
Albums			
BEAT ROCKET			
❑ BR 125	Hell Raisers!	2000	12.00
BELL			
❑ 1125	The Sweet	1973	25.00
CAPITOL			
❑ SPRO-8371/2 [DJ]	For A.O.R. Radio Only	1976	25.00
❑ SPRO-8849 [DJ]	Short and Sweet	1978	30.00
❑ ST-11395	Desolation Boulevard	1975	12.00
❑ ST-11496	Give Us a Wink	1976	12.00
❑ STAO-11636	Off the Record	1977	12.00
❑ SKAO-11744	Level Headed	1978	12.00
❑ PRO-11929 [DJ]	Cut Above the Rest	1979	50.00
—Special promo box contains record, cassette, 8-track, photo, bio			
❑ ST-11929	Cut Above the Rest	1979	12.00
❑ ST-12106	Sweet VI	1980	12.00
❑ SN-16115	Give Us a Wink	1980	8.00
—Budget-line reissue			
❑ SN-16116	Off the Record	1980	8.00
—Budget-line reissue			
❑ SN-16117	Level Headed	1980	8.00
—Budget-line reissue			
❑ SN-16118	Cut Above the Rest	1980	8.00
—Budget-line reissue			
❑ SN-16287	Desolation Boulevard	1981	8.00
—Budget-line reissue			
KORY			
❑ 3009	The Sweet	1977	12.00
—Reissue of Bell LP			

SWEET, THE (2)

Number	Title (A Side/B Side)	Yr	NM
45s			
SMASH			
❑ 2116	Got to Have More Love/ You Can't Win at Love	1967	15.00
❑ 2136	Broken Heart Attack/Don't Do It	1967	15.00

SWEET INSPIRATIONS, THE Also see CISSY HOUSTON.

Number	Title (A Side/B Side)	Yr	NM
12-Inch Singles			
CARIBOU			
❑ ASD 333 [DJ]	Black Sunday Parts 1 and 2 (same on both sides)	1977	15.00
RSO			
❑ 304 [DJ]	Love Is On the Way (6:10)/ (Instrumental)	1979	12.00
45s			
ATLANTIC			
❑ 2410	Why (Am I Treated So Bad)/ I Don't Want to Go On Without You	1967	8.00
❑ 2418	Let It Be Me/When Something Is Wrong with My Baby	1967	8.00
❑ 2436	I've Been Loving You Too Long (To Stop Now)/That's How Strong My Love Is	1967	8.00
❑ 2449	O' What a Fool I've Been/ Don't Fight It	1967	8.00
❑ 2465	Reach Out for Me/Do Right Woman — Do Right Man	1967	8.00
❑ 2476	Sweet Inspiration/I'm Blue	1968	8.00
❑ 2529	To Love Somebody/ Where Did It Go	1968	8.00
❑ 2551	Unchained Melody/Am I Ever Gonna See My Baby Again	1968	8.00
❑ 2571	What the World Needs Now Is Love/You Really Didn't Mean It	1968	8.00
❑ 2620	Crying in the Rain/Everyday Will Be Like a Holiday	1969	8.00
❑ 2638	Sweets for My Sweet/ Get a Little Order	1969	8.00
❑ 2653	Don't Go/Chained	1969	8.00
❑ 2686	(Gotta Find) A Brand New Lover — Part I/(Gotta Find) A Brand New Lover — Part II	1969	8.00
❑ 2720	At Last I Found a Love/ That's the Way My Baby Is	1970	6.00
❑ 2732	Them Boys/Flash in the Pan	1970	6.00
❑ 2750	This World/A Light Sings	1970	6.00
❑ 2779	Evidence/Change Me Not	1970	6.00
CARIBOU			
❑ 9022	Black Sunday/(Instrumental)	1977	4.00
RSO			
❑ 932	Love Is On the Way/ (Instrumental)	1979	5.00
❑ 1013	Love Is On the Way/ (Instrumental)	1979	4.00
STAX			
❑ 0178	Emercury/Slipped and Tripped	1973	5.00
❑ 0203	Try a Little Tenderness/ Dirty Tricks	1974	5.00
Albums			
ATLANTIC			
❑ SD 8155	The Sweet Inspirations	1968	20.00
❑ SD 8182	Songs of Faith and Inspiration	1968	20.00
❑ 8201 [M]	What the World Needs Now Is Love	1969	50.00
—Mono is white label promo only; "d/j copy monaural" sticker on stereo cover			
❑ SD 8201 [S]	What the World Needs Now Is Love	1969	20.00
❑ SD 8225	Sweets for My Sweet	1969	20.00
❑ SD 8253	Sweet, Sweet Soul	1970	20.00
RSO			
❑ RS-1-3058	Hot Butterfly	1979	10.00
STAX			
❑ STS-3017	Estelle, Myrna and Sylvia	1973	20.00

SWEET MARQUEES, THE

Number	Title (A Side/B Side)	Yr	NM
45s			
APACHE			
❑ 1516	You Lied/I Love My Baby	1961	300.00

SWEET PANTS

Number	Title (A Side/B Side)	Yr	NM
Albums			
BARKLEY			
❑ 1141	Fat Peter Presents Sweet Pants	1969	200.00

SWEET SENSATION (1)

Number	Title (A Side/B Side)	Yr	NM
45s			
PYE			
❑ 71002	Sad Sweet Dreamer/ Surething, Yes I Do	1974	4.00
❑ 71026	Ride Away from the Sun/ (B-side unknown)	1975	4.00
❑ 71049	Mr. Cool/(B-side unknown)	1975	4.00
Albums			
PYE			
❑ 12110	Sweet Sensation	1975	10.00

SWEET SICK TEENS, THE

Number	Title (A Side/B Side)	Yr	NM
45s			
RCA VICTOR			
❑ 37-7940	The Pretzel/Agnes, the Teenage Russian Spy	1961	80.00
—"Compact Single 33" (small hole, plays at LP speed)			
❑ 47-7940	The Pretzel/Agnes, the Teenage Russian Spy	1961	40.00

SWEET TEENS, THE

Number	Title (A Side/B Side)	Yr	NM
45s			
FLIP			
❑ 311	Forever More/Don't Worry About a Thing	1955	60.00
GEE			
❑ 1030	My Valentine/With This Ring	1957	60.00

SWEET THREE, THE

Number	Title (A Side/B Side)	Yr	NM
45s			
CAMEO			
❑ 463	Don't Leave Me Now/ I Would If I Could	1967	15.00
DECCA			
❑ 31938	Spring Fever (Part 1)/(Part 2)	1966	20.00
❑ 32005	Big Lovers Come in Small Packages/That's the Way It Is (When a Girl's in Love)	1966	50.00

SWEET TOOTHE

Number	Title (A Side/B Side)	Yr	NM
Albums			
DOMINION			
❑ NR-7360	Testing	1974	300.00

SWEETIES, THE

Number	Title (A Side/B Side)	Yr	NM
45s			
END			
❑ 1110	After You/Paul's Love	1962	20.00

SWEETWATER

Number	Title (A Side/B Side)	Yr	NM
45s			
REPRISE			
❑ 0787	My Crystal Spiker/What's Wrong	1968	8.00
❑ 0816	Motherless Child/Why Oh Why	1969	8.00
❑ 0835	For Pete's Sake/Bondeau	1969	8.00
❑ 0987	Just for You/Look Out	1971	6.00
❑ 1002	Day Song/Without Me	1971	6.00
❑ 1076	Join the Band (Part 1)/ Join the Band (Part 2)	1972	6.00
Albums			
REPRISE			
❑ RS 6313	Sweetwater	1968	15.00
❑ RS 6417	Just for You	1970	15.00
❑ RS 6473	Melon	1971	15.00

SWENSONS, THE

Number	Title (A Side/B Side)	Yr	NM
45s			
X-TRA			
❑ 100	Remember Me to My Darling/ Golly Boo	1957	200.00

SWIFT, BASIL, AND THE SEEGRAMS Also see DANNY HUTTON.

Number	Title (A Side/B Side)	Yr	NM
45s			
MERCURY			
❑ 72386	Farmer's Daughter/Shambles	1965	200.00

SWIFT, DICK

Number	Title (A Side/B Side)	Yr	NM
45s			
HIT			
❑ 21	Sealed with a Kiss/Breaking Up Is Hard to Do	1962	8.00
—B-side by Bill Arndt			

SWIFT RAIN

Number	Title (A Side/B Side)	Yr	NM
Albums			
HI			
❑ SHL-32064	Coming Down	1971	25.00

SWINGIN' MEDALLIONS

Number	Title (A Side/B Side)	Yr	NM
45s			
CAPITOL			
❑ 2338	Sun, Sand and Sea/ Hey, Hey Baby	1968	8.00
DOT			
❑ 16721	Bye Bye, Silly Girl/ I Want to Be Your Guy	1965	12.00
4 SALE			
❑ 002	Double Shot (Of My Baby's Love)/Here It Comes Again	1966	100.00
1-2-3			
❑ 1723	We're Gonna Hate Ourselves in the Morning/It's Alright	1970	8.00
❑ 1732	Rollin' Rovin' River/Don't Let Your Feet Touch the Ground	1971	8.00
SMASH			
❑ 2033	Double Shot (Of My Baby's Love)/Here It Comes Again	1966	15.00
❑ 2050	She Drives Me Out of My Mind/ You Gotta Have Faith	1966	12.00

S

Number	Title (A Side/B Side)	Yr	NM
❑ 2075	I Don't Want to Lose It for You Baby/Night Owl	1966	12.00
❑ 2084	Don't Cry No More/ I Found a Rainbow	1967	10.00
❑ 2107	Turn On the Music/Summer's Not the Same This Year	1967	10.00
❑ 2129	Bow and Arrow/Where Can I Go to Get Soul	1967	10.00

Albums

SMASH

Number	Title	Yr	NM
❑ MGS-27083 [M]	Double Shot (Of My Baby's Love)	1966	30.00
—Later pressings contain a "censored" version of the title song			
❑ MGS-27083 [M]	Double Shot (Of My Baby's Love)	1966	40.00
—First pressing contains the original 45 version of the title song			
❑ SRS-67083 [S]	Double Shot (Of My Baby's Love)	1966	40.00
—Later pressings contain a "censored" version of the title song			
❑ SRS-67083 [S]	Double Shot (Of My Baby's Love)	1966	50.00
—First pressing contains the original 45 version of the title song			

SWINGING BLUE JEANS, THE
Also see TERRY SYLVESTER.

45s

IMPERIAL

Number	Title	Yr	NM
❑ 66021	Hippy Hippy Shake/ Now I Must Go	1964	15.00
❑ 66030	Good Golly Miss Molly/ Shaking Feeling	1964	12.00
❑ 66049	Shake, Rattle and Roll/ You're No Good	1964	12.00
❑ 66059	Tutti Frutti/Promise You'll Tell Her	1964	12.00
❑ 66090	It Isn't There/One of These Days	1965	12.00
❑ 66154	Don't Make Me Over/ What Can I Do Today	1966	12.00
❑ 66225	Now the Summer's Gone/ Rumors, Gossip, Words Untrue	1967	10.00
❑ 66255	Something's Coming Along/ Tremblin'	1967	10.00

Albums

IMPERIAL

Number	Title	Yr	NM
❑ LP-9261 [M]	Hippy Hippy Shake	1964	80.00
❑ LP-12261 [R]	Hippy Hippy Shake	1964	80.00

SWINGING TIGERS

45s

TAMLA

Number	Title	Yr	NM
❑ 54024	Snake Walk (Part 1)/ Snake Walk (Part 2)	1960	300.00

SWINGLE SINGERS, THE

45s

PHILIPS

Number	Title	Yr	NM
❑ 40157	Fugue in D Minor/ Prelude in F Minor	1963	6.00

Albums

COLUMBIA

Number	Title	Yr	NM
❑ PC 34194	Rags and All That Jazz	1976	10.00

COLUMBIA MASTERWORKS

Number	Title	Yr	NM
❑ M 33013	Love Songs for Madrigals and Madriguys	1976	10.00

MMG

Number	Title	Yr	NM
❑ 1115	Swingle Skyliner	198?	8.00
❑ 1125	Folio	198?	8.00

PHILIPS

Number	Title	Yr	NM
❑ PHS 2-5400 [(2)]	Bachanalia	1972	12.00
—Reissue of 600-197 and 600-126 in same package			
❑ PHM 200097 [M]	Bach's Greatest Hits	1963	10.00
❑ PHM 200126 [M]	Going Baroque	1964	10.00
❑ PHM 200149 [M]	Anyone for Mozart?	1965	10.00
❑ PHM 200191 [M]	Getting Romantic	1965	10.00
❑ PHM 200214 [M]	Rococo A-Go-Go	1966	10.00
❑ PHM 200225 [M]	Encounter	1966	12.00
—With the Modern Jazz Quartet			
❑ PHM 200261 [M]	Spanish Masters	1967	10.00
❑ PHS 600097 [S]	Bach's Greatest Hits	1963	12.00
❑ PHS 600126 [S]	Going Baroque	1964	12.00
❑ PHS 600149 [S]	Anyone for Mozart?	1965	12.00
❑ PHS 600191 [S]	Getting Romantic	1965	12.00
❑ PHS 600214 [S]	Rococo A-Go-Go	1966	12.00
❑ PHS 600225 [S]	Encounter	1966	15.00
—With the Modern Jazz Quartet			
❑ PHS 600261 [S]	Spanish Masters	1967	12.00
❑ PHS 600288	Back to Bach	1968	10.00
❑ PHS 700004	The Joy of Singing	1973	10.00
❑ 824544-1	Jazz Sebastian Bach	1985	8.00
❑ 824545-1	Place Vendome	1985	8.00
—With the Modern Jazz Quartet; reissue of 600-225			

SWISHER, DEBRA

45s

BOOM

Number	Title	Yr	NM
❑ 60001	You're So Good to Me/ Thank You and Goodnight	1966	12.00

SYCAMORES, THE

45s

GROOVE

Number	Title	Yr	NM
❑ 0121	I'll Be Waiting/Darling, Is It True	1955	200.00

SYDELLS, THE

45s

BELTONE

Number	Title	Yr	NM
❑ 2032	In the Night/The Hokey Pokey	1963	15.00

SYLVAIN SYLVAIN
NEY YORK DOLLS guitarist.

45s

RCA

Number	Title	Yr	NM
❑ PB-11937	Every Boy and Every Girl/ Deeper and Deeper	1980	5.00
❑ PB-11937 [PS]	Every Boy and Every Girl/ Deeper and Deeper	1980	5.00
❑ JJ-12010	14th Street Beat/Tonight	1980	—
—Unreleased			

Albums

RCA VICTOR

Number	Title	Yr	NM
❑ AFL1-3475	Sylvain Sylvain	1980	12.00
❑ AFL1-3913	Syl Sylvain and the Teardrops	1982	12.00
❑ DJL1-4062 [DJ]	RCA Special Radio Series XII	1981	20.00
—Promo-only interviews and music			

SYLVERS, FOSTER
Also see THE SYLVERS.

45s

A&M

Number	Title	Yr	NM
❑ 1480	I'll Do It/Pretty Baby	1990	5.00
—As "Foster Sylvers & Hy-Tech"			

CAPITOL

Number	Title	Yr	NM
❑ 4553	Don't Let Me Go for Someone Else/Super Scoop	1978	4.00

MGM

Number	Title	Yr	NM
❑ 14580	Misdemeanor/So Close	1973	5.00
❑ 14630	Hey Little Girl/I'll Get You in the End	1973	5.00

PRIDE

Number	Title	Yr	NM
❑ 1031	Misdemeanor/So Close	1973	10.00

Albums

PRIDE

Number	Title	Yr	NM
❑ 0027	Foster Sylvers	1973	12.00

SYLVERS, THE
Also see FOSTER SYLVERS.

12-Inch Singles

GEFFEN

Number	Title	Yr	NM
❑ 20258	In One Love and Out the Other (Extended)/(Instrumental)	1984	6.00

45s

CAPITOL

Number	Title	Yr	NM
❑ 4179	Boogie Fever/Free Style	1975	4.00
❑ 4255	Cotton Candy/I Can Be for Real	1976	4.00
❑ 4336	Hot Line/That's What Love Is Made Of	1976	4.00
❑ 4405	High School Dance/Lovin' You Is Like Lovin' the Wind	1977	4.00
❑ 4493	Any Way You Want Me/ Lovin' Me Back	1977	4.00
❑ 4532	New Horizon/Charisma	1978	4.00

CASABLANCA

Number	Title	Yr	NM
❑ 938	Don't Stop, Get Off/ Love Won't Let Me Go	1978	4.00
❑ 953	Forever Yours/ Diamonds Are Rare	1978	4.00
❑ 992	I Feel So Good Tonight/ Hoochie Coochie Dancin'	1979	4.00
❑ 2207	I Feels So Good Tonight/ Mahogany	1979	4.00

GEFFEN

Number	Title	Yr	NM
❑ 29061	Falling for Your Love/ (Instrumental)	1985	3.00
❑ 29293	In One Love and Out the Other/ Falling for Your Love	1984	3.00
❑ 29293 [PS]	In One Love and Out the Other/ Falling for Your Love	1984	3.00

MGM

Number	Title	Yr	NM
❑ 14352	You Got What It Takes/ Time to Ride	1972	6.00
❑ 14579	Stay Away from Me/ I'll Never Be Ashamed	1973	6.00
❑ 14678	Through the Love in My Heart/ Cry of a Dreamer	1973	4.00
❑ 14698	Hang On Sloopy/Na Na Hey Hey Kiss Him Goodbye	1974	4.00
—As "Foster, Pat & Angie Sylvers"			
❑ 14721	I Aim to Please/ Wish You Were Here	1974	4.00

PRIDE

Number	Title	Yr	NM
❑ 1001	Fool's Paradise/I'm Truly Happy	1972	5.00
❑ 1019	Wish That I Could Talk to You/ How Love Hurts	1972	5.00
❑ 1029	Stay Away from Me/ I'll Never Be Ashamed	1973	5.00
❑ 1029 [PS]	Stay Away from Me/ I'll Never Be Ashamed	1973	6.00

SOLAR

Number	Title	Yr	NM
❑ 47949	Come Back, Lover, Come Back/There's a Place	1981	4.00
❑ 48002	Take It to the Top/ I'm Getting Over	1982	4.00

VERVE

Number	Title	Yr	NM
❑ 10664	Come On Give Me a Chance/ I'm Just a Lonely Soul	1971	10.00

Albums

CAPITOL

Number	Title	Yr	NM
❑ ST-11465	Showcase	1976	10.00
❑ ST-11580	Something Special	1976	10.00
❑ ST-11705	New Horizons	1977	10.00
❑ ST-11868	Best of the Sylvers	1978	10.00

CASABLANCA

Number	Title	Yr	NM
❑ NBLP 7103	Forever Yours	1978	10.00
❑ NBLP 7151	Disco Fever	1979	10.00

GEFFEN

Number	Title	Yr	NM
❑ GHS 24039	Bizarre	1984	10.00

MGM

Number	Title	Yr	NM
❑ SE-4930	The Sylvers III	1974	10.00

PRIDE

Number	Title	Yr	NM
❑ 0007	The Sylvers	1972	12.00
❑ 0026	The Sylvers II	1973	12.00

SOLAR

Number	Title	Yr	NM
❑ 22	Concept	1981	10.00

SYLVESTER, TERRY
Also see THE HOLLIES; THE SWINGING BLUE JEANS.

45s

EPIC

Number	Title	Yr	NM
❑ 20002	It's Better Off This Way/For the Peace of All Mankind	1974	4.00
❑ 20002 [PS]	It's Better Off This Way/For the Peace of All Mankind	1974	5.00
❑ 50017	It's Better Off This Way/ For the Peace of All Mankind	1974	4.00
❑ 50532	Silver and Gold/ Realistic Situation	1978	4.00

Albums

EPIC

Number	Title	Yr	NM
❑ KE 33076	Terry Sylvester	1974	12.00

SYLVESTER, TONY, AND THE NEW INGREDIENT
See THE MAIN INGREDIENT.

SYLVIA, MARGO
See TUNE WEAVERS.

SYLVIA (1)
R&B singer and record company mogul (All Platinum/Stang/Vibration, Sugar Hill). Also see MICKEY AND SYLVIA.

45s

ALL PLATINUM

Number	Title	Yr	NM
❑ 2303	I Can't Help It/It's a Good Life	1969	8.00
❑ 2350	Sho Nuff Boogie (Part 1)/ Sho Nuff Boogie (Part 2)	1974	5.00
—With the Moments			

JUBILEE

Number	Title	Yr	NM
❑ 5093	Drive, Daddy, Drive/I Found Somebody to Love	1952	50.00
—As "Little Sylvia"			

STANG

Number	Title	Yr	NM
❑ 5015	Have You Had Any Lately/ Anytime	1970	6.00

SUGAR HILL

Number	Title	Yr	NM
❑ 781	It's Good to Be the Queen/ (B-side unknown)	1982	4.00

VIBRATION

Number	Title	Yr	NM
❑ 512	Next Time I See You/ Gimme a Little Action	1972	6.00
❑ 521	Pillow Talk/My Thing	1973	6.00
❑ 524	Didn't I/Had Any Lately	1973	5.00
❑ 525	Soul Je T'Aime/Sunday	1973	5.00
—With Ralfi Pagan			
❑ 527	Alfredo/Lay It On Me	1973	5.00

S

Number	Title (A Side/B Side)	Yr	NM
❑ 528	Private Performance/ If You Get the Notion	1974	5.00
❑ 529	Sweet Stuff/Had Any Lately	1974	5.00
❑ 530	Easy Evil/Give It Up in Vain	1974	5.00
❑ 536	Pussy Cat (Part 1)/ Pussy Cat (Part 2)	1975	5.00
❑ 567	L.A. Sunshine/Taxi	1976	5.00
❑ 570	Lay It On Me (Vocal)/ (Instrumental)	1977	5.00
❑ 572	Lollipop Man/Lay It On Me	1977	5.00
❑ 576	Automatic Lover/Stop Boy	1978	5.00
Albums			
STANG			
❑ 1010	Sylvia	197?	20.00
SUGAR HILL			
❑ 258	Sylvia I	1981	10.00
VIBRATION			
❑ 126	Pillow Talk	1973	15.00
❑ 131	Lay It On Me	1977	12.00
❑ 143	Brand New Funk	197?	12.00

SYLVIAN, DAVID Also see JAPAN.

Number	Title (A Side/B Side)	Yr	NM
Albums			
VIRGIN			
❑ 2167 [DJ]	Ink in the Well — A Conversation	1987	20.00
—Promo-only interview album			
❑ 90677	Secrets of the Beehive	1987	10.00
❑ 90904	Plight and Premonition	1988	10.00
—With Holger Czukay			

SYLVIAN, DAVID, AND ROBERT FRIPP

Number	Title (A Side/B Side)	Yr	NM
12-Inch Singles			
VIRGIN			
❑ 14125 [DJ]	Darshan (3 versions)	1994	12.00

SYMBOLS, THE (1)

Number	Title (A Side/B Side)	Yr	NM
45s			
DORE			
❑ 666	Last Year About This Time/Better Get Your Own One Buddy	1963	15.00

SYMBOLS, THE (2)

Number	Title (A Side/B Side)	Yr	NM
45s			
IMPERIAL			
❑ 66382	I Will Still Be There/ The Wrong Girl	1969	8.00

SYMBOLS, THE (3)

Number	Title (A Side/B Side)	Yr	NM
45s			
MGM			
❑ 13348	One Fine Girl/Don't Go	1965	10.00
❑ 13463	Don't Go/Oo Wee Baby	1966	10.00

SYMBOLS, THE (4)

Number	Title (A Side/B Side)	Yr	NM
45s			
VINTAGE			
❑ 1007	Bye Bye/I Love You	1973	5.00

SYMBOLS, THE (U)

Number	Title (A Side/B Side)	Yr	NM
45s			
LAURIE			
❑ 3401	Bye Bye Baby/The Things You Do to Me	1967	10.00
❑ 3435	The Best Part of Breaking Up/ Again	1968	10.00
PRESIDENT			
❑ 102	Canadian Sunset/ The Gentle Art of Loving	1966	10.00

SYMPHONICS, THE (1)

Number	Title (A Side/B Side)	Yr	NM
45s			
ABC			
❑ 11068	Boy (Please Help Me)/ It's Gonna Be Real Hard	1968	8.00
BRUNSWICK			
❑ 55303	Don't Fail Me Now/ Silent Kind of Guy	1966	10.00
❑ 55313	No More/(She's Just a) Sad Girl	1967	10.00

SYMPHONICS, THE (2) This Symphonics features FREDDIE SCOTT.

Number	Title (A Side/B Side)	Yr	NM
45s			
ENRICA			
❑ 1002	Come On Honey/ A Blessing to You	1959	20.00

SYNDICATE, THE

Number	Title (A Side/B Side)	Yr	NM
45s			
DORE			
❑ 743	My Baby Is Barefoot/ Love Will Take Away	1965	200.00
DOT			
❑ 16807	Egyptian Thing/She Haunts You	1965	40.00

SYNDICATE OF SOUND

Number	Title (A Side/B Side)	Yr	NM
45s			
BELL			
❑ 640	Little Girl/You	1966	20.00
❑ 646	Rumors/Upper Hand	1966	15.00
❑ 655	Goodtime Music/Keep It Up	1966	15.00
❑ 666	Mary/That Kind of Man	1967	15.00
BUDDAH			
❑ 156	Brown Paper Bag/Reverb Beat	1970	10.00
❑ 183	Mexico/First to Love You	1970	10.00
CAPITOL			
❑ 2426	You're Looking Fine/ Change the World	1969	10.00
DEL-FI			
❑ 4304	Prepare for Love/Tell the World	1965	75.00
HUSH			
❑ 228	Little Girl/You	1966	150.00
PHILCO-FORD			
❑ HP-29	Little Girl/Rumors	1968	20.00
—4-inch plastic "Hip Pocket Record" with color sleeve			
SCARLET			
❑ 503	Prepare for Love/Tell the World	1965	75.00
Albums			
BELL			
❑ 6001 [M]	Little Girl	1966	50.00
❑ S-6001 [S]	Little Girl	1966	80.00
SUNDAZED			
❑ LP 5051	Little Girl	2001	12.00
—Reissue on 180-gram vinyl			

SYNERGY

Number	Title (A Side/B Side)	Yr	NM
12-Inch Singles			
AUDION			
❑ 12204 [DJ]	Redstone/Metropolitan Theme	1987	12.00
PASSPORT			
❑ SP-30 [DJ]	Phobos and Deimos Go to Mars (Edit) (LP)	1978	15.00
45s			
PASSPORT			
❑ 7907	Classical Gas/Cybersports	1976	8.00
Albums			
AUDION			
❑ SYN 204	Metropolitan Suite	1987	10.00
PASSPORT			
❑ PG-1	Computer Experiments Vol. One	1981	15.00
❑ PB 6000	Cords	1978	10.00
—Later pressings on black vinyl			
❑ PB 6000	Cords	1978	15.00
—First pressing on clear vinyl			
❑ PB 6001	Electronic Realizations for Rock Orchestra	1979	10.00
—Reissue of 98009			
❑ PB 6002	Sequencer	1979	10.00
—Reissue of 98014			
❑ PB 6003	Games	1979	10.00
❑ PB 6005	Audion	1981	10.00
❑ P2B 11002 [(2)]	Semi-Conductor	1984	12.00
❑ PPSD-98009	Electronic Realizations for Rock Orchestra	1975	12.00
❑ PPSD-98014	Sequencer	1976	12.00

SZABO, GABOR

Number	Title (A Side/B Side)	Yr	NM
45s			
BLUE THUMB			
❑ 200	Breezin'/Azure Blue	1971	5.00
—With Bobby Womack			
❑ 7118	Close to You/Love Theme from "Spartacus"	1971	5.00
BUDDAH			
❑ 215	That's What Happens/ Rocky Raccoon	1971	6.00
—With Lena Horne			
CTI			
❑ 14	It's Going to Take Some Time/ (B-side unknown)	1973	5.00
IMPULSE!			
❑ 244	Yesterday/Walk On By	1966	8.00
❑ 248	Gypsy Queen/Bang Bang	1966	8.00
❑ 254	Spellbinder/Witchcraft	1966	8.00
❑ 257	Paint It Black/ Sophisticated Wheels	1967	8.00
❑ 263	The Beat Goes On/Space	1967	8.00
❑ 268	Twelve Thirty (Young Girls Are Coming to the Canyon)/ Saigon Bride	1968	8.00
MERCURY			
❑ 73840	Keep Smilin'/Baby Rattle Shake	1976	4.00
❑ 73957	Alicia/The Biz	1977	4.00
SKYE			
❑ 451	Theme from "Valley of the Dolls"/ Sunshine Superman	1968	6.00
❑ 454	Bacchanal/The Look of Love	1968	6.00
❑ 459	Fire Dance/Ferris Wheel	1969	6.00
❑ 4515	Dear Prudence/Stormy	1969	6.00
Albums			
ABC IMPULSE!			
❑ AS-9105	Gypsy 66	1968	12.00
❑ AS-9123	Spellbinder	1968	12.00
❑ AS-9128	Jazz Raga	1968	12.00
❑ AS-9146	The Sorcerer	1968	12.00
❑ AS-9151	Wind, Sky and Diamonds	1968	15.00
❑ AS-9159	Light My Fire	1968	15.00
❑ AS-9167	More Sorcery	1968	15.00
❑ AS-9173	The Best of Gabor Szabo	1968	15.00
❑ AS-9204 [(2)]	His Great Hits	1971	15.00
BLUE THUMB			
❑ BTS-28	High Contrast	1972	12.00
—With Bobby Womack			
❑ 6014	Live	1974	12.00
❑ BTS-8823	Magical Connection	1971	12.00
BUDDAH			
❑ 18-SK	Watch What Happens	1970	12.00
❑ 20-SK	Blowin' Some Old Smoke	1971	12.00
CTI			
❑ 6026	Mizrab	1973	12.00
❑ 6035	Rambler	1974	12.00
GRP/IMPULSE!			
❑ IMP-211	The Sorcerer	199?	15.00
—Reissue on audiophile vinyl			
IMPULSE!			
❑ A-9105 [M]	Gypsy 66	1966	20.00
❑ AS-9105 [S]	Gypsy 66	1966	25.00
❑ A-9123 [M]	Spellbinder	1966	20.00
❑ AS-9123 [S]	Spellbinder	1966	25.00
❑ A-9128 [M]	Jazz Raga	1967	25.00
❑ AS-9128 [S]	Jazz Raga	1967	20.00
❑ A-9146 [M]	The Sorcerer	1967	25.00
❑ AS-9146 [S]	The Sorcerer	1967	20.00
❑ AS-9151	Wind, Sky and Diamonds	1968	25.00
—This exists on the pre-ABC Impulse! label, though theoretically it shouldn't. Other titles may exist on that label also.			
MCA			
❑ 4155 [(2)]	His Great Hits	198?	12.00
MERCURY			
❑ SRM-1-1091	Nightflight	1976	10.00
❑ SRM-1-1141	Faces	1977	10.00
PEPITA			
❑ 707	Femme Fatalo	198?	10.00
SALVATION			
❑ 704	Macho	1975	12.00
SKYE			
❑ MK-3 [M]	Bacchanal	1968	40.00
—Mono is promo only; "Monaural Promotion Copy" sticker on stereo cover			
❑ SK-3 [S]	Bacchanal	1968	15.00
❑ SK-7	Dreams	1969	15.00
❑ SK-9	Gabor Szabo 1969	1969	15.00
❑ SK-15	Lena & Gabor	1970	15.00
—With Lena Horne			

SZIGETI, SANDY

Number	Title (A Side/B Side)	Yr	NM
45s			
DECCA			
❑ 32862	America's Sweetheart/ My Steady Diet	1971	10.00
—Produced by Rick Nelson			

T

T.C. ATLANTIC

Number	Title (A Side/B Side)	Yr	NM
45s			
AESOP'S LABEL			
❑ 6044	Once Upon a Melody/ I Love You So, Little Girl	1965	25.00
B. SHARP			
❑ 272	Mona/My Babe	1966	40.00
CANDY FLOSS			
❑ 101	I'm So Glad/Twenty Years Ago	1968	40.00
PARAMOUNT			
❑ 0098	Judgment Train/Shine the Light	1971	15.00
PARROT			
❑ 330	I'm So Glad/Twenty Years Ago	1968	25.00
❑ 338	Love Is Just/Faces	1969	20.00
TURTLE			
❑ 1103	Faces/Baby, Please Don't Go	1966	150.00

Except when noted otherwise, VG = 25% of NM, and VG+ = 50% of NM. (Example: VG = \$2.00, VG+ = \$4.00 and NM = \$8.00.)

Number	Title (A Side/B Side)	Yr	NM
❑ 1105	Shake/Spanish Harlem	1967	40.00
Albums			
DOVE			
❑ LP-4459	T.C. Atlantic	1966	100.00
T.I.M.E.			
45s			
LIBERTY			
❑ 56020	Take Me Along/Make It Right	1968	10.00
❑ 56020 [PS]	Take Me Along/Make It Right	1968	15.00
❑ 56060	Tripping Into Sunshine/What Would Life Be Without You	1968	10.00
Albums			
LIBERTY			
❑ LST-7558	T.I.M.E.	1968	25.00
❑ LST-7605	Smooth Ball	1969	25.00
T. REX Featuring Marc Bolan.			
45s			
A&M			
❑ 955	Child Star/Debora	1968	12.00
—As "Tyrannosaurus Rex"			
BLUE THUMB			
❑ 212	By the Light of the Magical Moon/Find a Little Wood	1971	6.00
❑ SP-6115/6 [DJ]	Ride a White Swan/Is It Love	1970	12.00
—As "Tyrannosaurus Rex"; LP bonus disc			
❑ 7121	Ride a White Swan/ Summertime Blues	1970	8.00
—As "Tyrannosaurus Rex"			
CASABLANCA			
❑ 810	Precious Star/(B-side unknown)	1974	6.00
REPRISE			
❑ 1006	Hot Love//One Inch Rock/ Seagull Woman	1971	6.00
❑ 1032	Bang a Gong (Get It On)/ Raw Ramp	1971	8.00
❑ 1056	Jeepster/Rip Off	1971	6.00
❑ 1078	Telegram Sam/Cadillac	1972	6.00
❑ 1095	Metal Guru/Lady	1972	6.00
❑ 1122	The Slider/Rock On	1972	6.00
❑ 1150	Bang a Gong (Get It On)/ Telegram Sam	1972	4.00
—"Back to Back Hits" series			
❑ 1151	Jeepster/Metal Guru	1972	4.00
—"Back to Back Hits" series			
❑ 1161	Born to Boogie/The Groover	1973	5.00
❑ 1161 [PS]	Born to Boogie/The Groover	1973	25.00
❑ 1170	Hot Love/Rip Off	1973	5.00
Albums			
A&M			
❑ SP-3514 [(2)]	Tyrannosaurus Rex (A Beginning)	1972	15.00
—Compilation of early LPs Prophets, Seers & Sages and My People Were Fair and Had Sky in Their Hair But Now They're Content to Wear Stars on Their Brows			
BLUE THUMB			
❑ BTS 7	Unicorn	1969	20.00
❑ BTS 18	A Beard of Stars	1970	20.00
—Add $5 for bonus single SP-6115/6, "Ride a White Swan"/"Is It Love." For reasons unknown, the single seems to be much more readily available than the LP			
CASABLANCA			
❑ NBLP 7005	Light of Love	1974	12.00
—Reissue of 9006			
❑ NB 9006	Light of Love	1974	15.00
—Original, distributed by Warner Bros.			
MARC ON WAX/RELATIVITY			
❑ 8249	Bolan's Zip Gun	198?	10.00
❑ 8250	Zinc Alloy & The Hidden Riders of Tomorrow	198?	10.00
❑ 8251	Dandy in the Underworld	198?	10.00
❑ 8252	Futuristic Dragon	198?	10.00
❑ 8253	The Slider	198?	10.00
❑ 8254	Tanx	198?	10.00
REPRISE			
❑ PRO 511 [DJ]	An Interview with Marc Bolan	1971	100.00
❑ MS 2095	The Slider	1972	16.00
❑ MS 2132	Tanx	1973	16.00
❑ RS 6440	T. Rex	1971	16.00
❑ RS 6466	Electric Warrior	1971	16.00
RHINO			
❑ R1-76111	Electric Warrior	2003	15.00
—Reissue on 180-gram vinyl			
WARNER BROS.			
❑ 25333	T. Rextasy: The Best of T. Rex, 1970-1973	1985	10.00

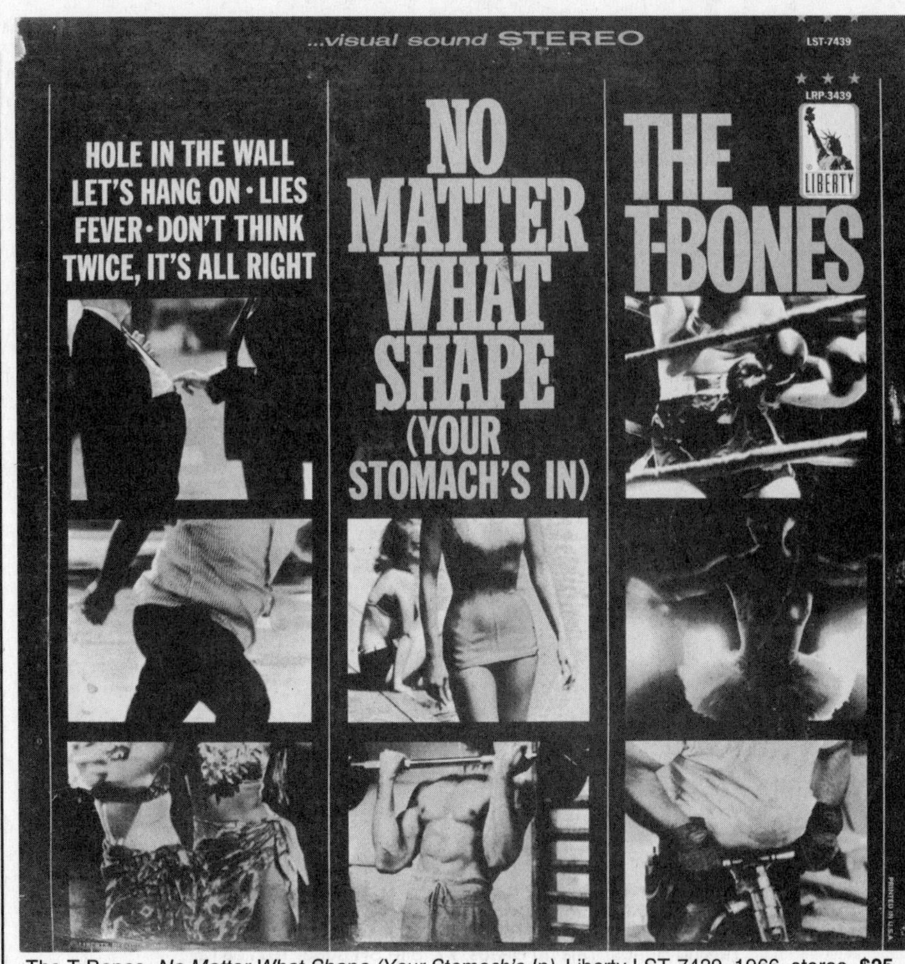

The T-Bones, *No Matter What Shape (Your Stomach's In)*, Liberty LST-7439, 1966, stereo, **$25.**

Number	Title (A Side/B Side)	Yr	NM
T.S.U. TORONADOES, THE			
45s			
ATLANTIC			
❑ 2579	Getting the Corners/ What Good Am I!	1968	8.00
❑ 2614	Got to Get Through to You/ The Goose	1969	8.00
VOLT			
❑ 4030	My Thing Is a Moving Thing/ Still Love You	1969	6.00
❑ 4038	One Flight Too Many/ Play the Music Toronadoes	1970	6.00
T2			
Albums			
LONDON			
❑ PS 583	It'll All Work Out in Boomland	1971	80.00
T.V. AND THE TRIBESMEN			
Albums			
HANNA-BARBERA			
❑ HLP-9507 [S]	Barefootin'	1966	25.00
T-BIRDS, THE			
45s			
CHESS			
❑ 1778	Green Stamps/Come On Dance with Me	1961	25.00
❑ 1792	Hog Wild/Taco Harry	1961	25.00
GONE			
❑ 5141	Wild Stomp/Soft Smoke	1962	20.00
T-BIRD			
❑ 101	Green Stamps/Come On Dance with Me	1961	40.00
VEGAS			
❑ 720	Nobody But You/Have You Ever Been in Love Before	1968	60.00

Number	Title (A Side/B Side)	Yr	NM
T-BONES, THE Members of this group later formed HAMILTON, JOE FRANK AND REYNOLDS.			
45s			
LIBERTY			
❑ 55677	Draggin'/Rail-Vette	1964	20.00
❑ 55814	That's Where It's At/Pearlin'	1965	15.00
❑ 55836	No Matter What Shape (Your Stomach's In)/Feelin' Fine	1965	12.00
❑ 55867	Sippin' & Chippin'/ Moment of Softness	1966	10.00
❑ 55885	Wherever You Look, Wherever You Go/Underwater	1966	10.00
❑ 55906	Let's Go Get Stoned/ Farre Thee Well	1966	10.00
❑ 55925	Balboa Blues/Walkin' My Cat Named Dog	1966	10.00
❑ 55951	Tee Hee Hee (My Life Seems Different Now)/ Proper Thing to Do	1967	10.00
UNITED ARTISTS			
❑ 0068	No Matter What Shape (Your Stomach's In)/ Sippin' N Chippin'	1973	5.00
—"Silver Spotlight Series" reissue			
7-Inch Extended Plays			
LIBERTY			
❑ LST-4-7439	*Hole in the Wall/Let's Hang On/Lies/Fever/Don't Think Twice, It's Alright	1966	20.00
—Jukebox issue; small hole, plays at 33 1/3 rpm			
❑ LST-4-7439 [PS]	No Matter What Shape (Your Stomach's In)	1966	20.00
Albums			
LIBERTY			
❑ LRP-3346 [M]	Boss Drag	1963	60.00
❑ LRP-3363 [M]	Boss Drag at the Beach	1964	60.00
❑ LRP-3404 [M]	Doin' the Jerk	1965	40.00
❑ LRP-3439 [M]	No Matter What Shape (Your Stomach's In)	1966	20.00
❑ LRP-3446 [M]	Sippin' and Chippin'	1966	20.00

Talking Heads, *Talking Heads: 77*, Sire SR 6036, 1977, **$12.**

Number	Title (A Side/B Side)	Yr	NM
❑ LRP-3471 [M]	Everyone's Gone to the Moon	1966	20.00
❑ LST-7346 [S]	Boss Drag	1963	100.00
❑ LST-7363 [S]	Boss Drag at the Beach	1964	100.00
❑ LST-7404 [S]	Doin' the Jerk	1965	60.00
❑ LST-7439 [S]	No Matter What Shape (Your Stomach's In)	1966	25.00
❑ LST-7446 [S]	Sippin' and Chippin'	1966	25.00
❑ LST-7471 [S]	Everyone's Gone to the Moon	1966	25.00
SUNSET			
❑ SUM-1119 [M]	Shapin' Things Up	196?	12.00
❑ SUS-5119 [S]	Shapin' Things Up	196?	15.00

TABBYS, THE

45s

Number	Title (A Side/B Side)	Yr	NM
TIME			
❑ 1008	Yes I Do/My Darling	1959	25.00
—Red label			
❑ 1008	Yes I Do/My Darling	1959	50.00
—Blue label			

TABS, THE

45s

Number	Title (A Side/B Side)	Yr	NM
DOT			
❑ 15887	Avenue of Tears/The First Star	1959	30.00
GARDENA			
❑ 110	Never Forget/Rock and Roll Holiday	1960	50.00
NASCO			
❑ 6016	Will We Meet Again/ Still Love You Baby	1958	30.00
NOBLE			
❑ 719	Never Forget/Rock and Roll Holiday	1959	150.00
❑ 720	Oops/My Girl Is Gone	1959	400.00
VEE JAY			
❑ 418	Dance All By Myself/Dance Party	1961	20.00
❑ 446	Mash Dem Taters/ But You're My Baby	1962	20.00
WAND			
❑ 130	Two Stupid Feet/Footsteps	1962	15.00
❑ 139	I'm with You/Take My Love Along with You	1963	15.00

TAD

45s

Number	Title (A Side/B Side)	Yr	NM
SUB POP			
❑ 19	Ritual Device/Daisy	1988	37.50
—964 on clear vinyl			
❑ 19	Ritual Device/Daisy	1988	62.50
—70 on gold vinyl			
❑ 19 [PS]	Ritual Device/Daisy	1988	37.50
—Plastic sleeve			
❑ 37	Damaged 1/Damaged 2	1989	15.00
—B-side by Pussy Galore			
❑ 37 [PS]	Damaged 1/Damaged 2	1989	15.00
—B-side by Pussy Galore; #8 in Sub Pop Singles Club series			
❑ 55	Loser/Cooking with Gas	1990	7.50
❑ 55	Loser/Cooking with Gas	1990	22.50
—First 3,000 on green vinyl			
❑ 55 [PS]	Loser/Cooking with Gas	1990	7.50
❑ 80	Jinx/Pig Iron	1990	5.00
—Black vinyl			
❑ 80	Jinx/Pig Iron	1990	20.00
—2,000 on yellow vinyl			
❑ 80	Jinx/Pig Iron	1990	30.00
—Some on "glacial white vinyl"			
❑ 80 [PS]	Jinx/Pig Iron	1990	5.00
❑ 182	Salem/Welt	1993	2.00
❑ 182 [PS]	Salem/Welt	1993	2.00
❑ 1000	Jack Pepsi/Plague Years	1991	25.00
—No picture sleeve; bonus in Sub Pop Singles Club series			

Albums

Number	Title (A Side/B Side)	Yr	NM
SUB POP			
❑ 27	God's Balls	1989	20.00
—First 2,000 with gatefold cover			
❑ 27	God's Balls	1989	12.00
—Others in standard cover			
❑ 27	God's Balls	1989	15.00
—Next 500 with "Manzine"			
❑ 49 [EP]	Salt Lick	1990	10.00
❑ 89	8-Way Santa	1991	12.00

TADS, THE

45s

Number	Title (A Side/B Side)	Yr	NM
DOT			
❑ 15518	Your Reason/The Pink Panther	1956	25.00
LIBERTY BELL			
❑ 9010	Your Reason/The Pink Panther	1956	50.00
REV			
❑ 3513	Wolf Call/She Is My Dream	1958	50.00

TAFFYS, THE

45s

Number	Title (A Side/B Side)	Yr	NM
AMY			
❑ 933	Bongo Man/The Game Called Love	1965	15.00
FAIRMOUNT			
❑ 610	Everybody South Street/ Key to My Heart	1963	10.00
PAGEANT			
❑ 608	Can't We Just Be Friends/ Peter Cottontail	1963	10.00
PARKWAY			
❑ 872	Everybody South Street/ Can't We Just Be Friends	1963	15.00

TAGES, THE With PETER FRAMPTON.

45s

Number	Title (A Side/B Side)	Yr	NM
VERVE			
❑ 10626	Halcyon Days/I Read You Like an Open Book	1968	20.00

TAKERS, THE

45s

Number	Title (A Side/B Side)	Yr	NM
INTERPHON			
❑ 7709	Think/If You Don't Come Back	1964	10.00

TALAS Features bassist Billy Sheehan of DAVID LEE ROTH and MR. BIG fame.

Albums

Number	Title (A Side/B Side)	Yr	NM
COMBAT			
❑ 8005	Live Speed On Ice	1984	15.00
EVENFALL			
❑ EF 401	Talas	1979	28.00
RELATIVITY			
❑ EMCL 8001	Sink Your Teeth Into That	1982	16.00

TALKING HEADS

12-Inch Singles

Number	Title (A Side/B Side)	Yr	NM
SIRE			
❑ PRO2046 [DJ]	Burning Down the House/Pull Up the Roots/Slippery People (Cassette Version)	1983	8.00
❑ PRO2057 [DJ]	Burning Down the House (same on both sides)	1983	8.00
❑ PRO2101 [DJ]	This Must Be the Place (Naive Melody)/This Must Be the Place (Naive Melody) (Edit)	1983	8.00
❑ PRO2207 [DJ]	Once in a Lifetime (Edit) (same on both sides)	1984	6.00
❑ PRO2305 [DJ]	Road to Nowhere (LP version)/ Road to Nowhere (Edit)	1985	6.00
❑ PRO2348 [DJ]	And She Was (same on both sides)	1985	6.00
❑ PRO2376 [DJ]	Stay Up Late (same on both sides)	1985	6.00
❑ PRO2556 [DJ]	Wild Wild Life (same on both sides)	1986	6.00
❑ PRO2593 [DJ]	Puzzlin' Evidence (same on both sides)	1986	8.00
❑ PRO2638 [DJ]	Love for Sale (same on both sides)	1986	5.00
❑ PRO2947 [DJ]	(Nothing But) Flowers (Radio Edit)/(Nothing But) Flowers (LP Version)	1988	5.00
❑ PRO3182 [DJ]	Blind (Extended Remix) (same on both sides)	1988	5.00
❑ PRO846 [DJ]	Life During Wartime/I Zimbra/Air	1979	16.00
❑ PRO903 [DJ]	Crosseyed and Painless (long)/ Crosseyed and Painless (Short)	1980	16.00
❑ PRO-A-846 [DJ]	Life During Wartime/I Zimbra/Air	1979	16.00
❑ PRO-A-903 [DJ]	Crosseyed and Painless (long)/ Crosseyed and Painless (Short)	1980	16.00
❑ PRO-A-2046 [DJ]	Burning Down the House/ Pull Up the Roots/Slippery People (Cassette Version)	1983	8.00
❑ PRO-A-2057 [DJ]	Burning Down the House (same on both sides)	1983	8.00

Except when noted otherwise, VG = 25% of NM, and VG+ = 50% of NM. (Example: VG = $2.00, VG+ = $4.00 and NM = $8.00.)

Number	Title (A Side/B Side)	Yr	NM
❑ PRO-A-2101 [DJ]	This Must Be the Place (Naive Melody)/This Must Be the Place (Naive Melody) (Edit)	1983	8.00
❑ PRO-A-2207 [DJ]	Once in a Lifetime (Edit) (same on both sides)	1984	6.00
❑ PRO-A-2305 [DJ]	Road to Nowhere (LP version)/Road to Nowhere (Edit)	1985	6.00
❑ PRO-A-2348 [DJ]	And She Was (same on both sides)	1985	6.00
❑ PRO-A-2376 [DJ]	Stay Up Late (same on both sides)	1985	6.00
❑ PRO-A-2556 [DJ]	Wild Wild Life (same on both sides)	1986	6.00
❑ PRO-A-2593 [DJ]	Puzzlin' Evidence (same on both sides)	1986	8.00
❑ PRO-A-2638 [DJ]	Love for Sale (same on both sides)	1986	5.00
❑ PRO-A-2947 [DJ]	(Nothing But) Flowers (Radio Edit)/(Nothing But) Flowers (LP Version)	1988	5.00
❑ PRO-A-3182 [DJ]	Blind (Extended Remix) (same on both sides)	1988	5.00
❑ 20143	Slippery People/Making Flippy Floppy	1983	7.00
❑ 20171	Swamp (2 mixes)/Slippery People	1983	7.00
❑ 20378	And She Was (Extended)/Television Man (Remix)	1985	6.00
❑ 20593	Wild Wild Life (2 mixes)/People Like Us (Movie Version)	1986	10.00
❑ 20620	Love for Sale (3 mixes)/Hey Now (Kids Mix)	1987	10.00
❑ 20732	Radio Head (2 versions)/Hey Now (2 versions)	1988	6.00
❑ 20892	Blind (4 mixes)/Bill	1988	6.00

45s

SIRE

Number	Title (A Side/B Side)	Yr	NM
❑ GSRE 0452	Take Me to the River/Life During Wartime	198?	3.00
—"Back to Back Hits" reissue			
❑ GSRE 0479	Burning Down the House/This Must Be the Place	198?	3.00
—"Back to Back Hits" reissue			
❑ 737	Love Goes to Bulding on Fire/New Feeling	1977	10.00
❑ 737 [PS]	Love Goes to Bulding on Fire/New Feeling	1977	10.00
❑ 1002	Uh-Oh, Love Comes to Town/I Wish You Wouldn't Say That	1977	6.00
❑ 1002 [PS]	Uh-Oh, Love Comes to Town/I Wish You Wouldn't Say That	1977	6.00
❑ 1013	Psycho Killer/Psycho Killer (Acoustic)	1978	8.00
❑ 1013 [PS]	Psycho Killer/Psycho Killer (Acoustic)	1978	8.00
❑ 1032	Take Me to the River/Thank You for Sending Me an Angel (Version)	1978	4.00
❑ 1032 [PS]	Take Me to the River/Thank You for Sending Me an Angel (Version)	1978	4.00
❑ 21975	Wild, Wild Life/And She Was	198?	3.00
—"Back to Back Hits" reissue			
❑ 27948	Blind/Still	1988	2.00
❑ 27948 [PS]	Blind/Still	1988	4.00
❑ 27992	(Nothing But) Flowers/Ruby Dear	1988	2.00
❑ 27992 [PS]	(Nothing But) Flowers/Ruby Dear	1988	4.00
❑ 28497	Love for Sale/Hey Now	1987	2.00
❑ 28497 [PS]	Love for Sale/Hey Now	1987	2.00
❑ 28629	Wild Wild Life/People Like Us (Movie Version)	1986	2.00
❑ 28629 [PS]	Wild Wild Life/People Like Us (Movie Version)	1986	4.00
❑ 28917	And She Was/And She Was (Dub)	1985	2.00
❑ 28917 [PS]	And She Was/And She Was (Dub)	1985	4.00
❑ 28987	Road to Nowhere/Give Me Back My Name	1985	3.00
❑ 28987 [PS]	Road to Nowhere/Give Me Back My Name	1985	4.00
❑ 29080	Stop Making Sense (Girlfriend Is Better)/Heaven	1985	3.00
❑ 29080 [PS]	Stop Making Sense (Girlfriend Is Better)/Heaven	1985	4.00
❑ 29163	Once in a Lifetime/This Must Be the Place (Naive Melody)	1984	3.00
❑ 29163 [PS]	Once in a Lifetime/This Must Be the Place (Naive Melody)	1984	3.00
❑ 29451	This Must Be the Place (Naive Melody)/Moon Rocks	1983	3.00
❑ 29451 [PS]	This Must Be the Place (Naive Melody)/Moon Rocks	1983	4.00
❑ 29565	Burning Down the House/I Get Wild-Wild Gravity	1983	3.00
❑ 29565 [PS]	Burning Down the House/I Get Wild-Wild Gravity	1983	4.00
❑ 49075	Life During Wartime (This Ain't No Party...This Ain't No Disco...This Ain't No Foolin' Around)/Electric Guitar	1979	4.00
❑ 49649	Once in a Lifetime/Seen and Not Seen	1981	4.00
❑ 49734	Houses in Motion/The Overload	1981	4.00

Albums

RHINO VINYL

Number	Title	Yr	NM
❑ R1-70802	Remain in Light	2006	15.00
—Reissue on 180-gram vinyl			

SIRE

Number	Title	Yr	NM
❑ PRO1033 [DJ]	Psycho Killer/Life During Wartime/Take Me to the River/Houses in Motion	1982	15.00
—Promo-only 4-song sampler			
❑ PRO930 [DJ]	Talking Heads	1980	15.00
—Promo-only 4-song sampler from "Remain in Light"			
❑ PRO-A-930 [DJ]	Talking Heads	1980	15.00
—Promo-only 4-song sampler from "Remain in Light"			
❑ PRO-A-1033 [DJ]	The Name of This Band Is Talking Heads Sampler	1982	15.00
—Promo only			
❑ 2SR 3590 [(2)]	The Name of This Band Is Talking Heads	1982	20.00
❑ SR 6036	Talking Heads '77	1977	12.00
❑ SR 6058	More Songs About Buildings and Food	1978	12.00
❑ SRK 6058	More Songs About Buildings and Food	1979	8.00
—Reissue with new prefix			
❑ SRK 6076	Fear of Music	1979	10.00
❑ SRK 6095	Remain in Light	1981	10.00
❑ 23771	Speaking in Tongues	1983	20.00
—Clear vinyl in oversize plastic container with Robert Rauschenberg artwork			
❑ 23883	Speaking in Tongues	1983	10.00
—Standard issue			
❑ 25121	Stop Making Sense (Soundtrack)	1984	15.00
—First issue with booklet and black & white cover			
❑ 25186	Stop Making Sense (Soundtrack)	1984	10.00
—Second issue: No booklet, color cover			
❑ 25305	Little Creatures	1985	10.00
❑ 25512	True Stories	1986	10.00
❑ 25654	Naked	1988	10.00
❑ R 124560	Stop Making Sense	1984	12.00
—RCA Music Service edition			
❑ R 150102	Speaking in Tongues	1983	12.00
—BMG Direct Marketing edition			
❑ R 153810	Naked	1988	12.00
—BMG Direct Marketing edition			
❑ R 153839	Little Creatures	1985	12.00
—RCA Music Service edition			

WARNER BROS.

Number	Title	Yr	NM
❑ WBMS-104 [DJ]	The Warner Bros. Music Show—Talking Heads Live on Tour	1979	25.00
—Promo-only radio show (has been counterfeited)			
❑ WBMS-104 [DJ]	Talking Heads Live on Tour	1979	25.00
—Part of "The Warner Bros. Music Show" series (has been counterfeited)			

TALLEY, JOHNNY T.

45s

MERCURY

Number	Title (A Side/B Side)	Yr	NM
❑ 70902	Lonesome Train/(I've Changed My) Wild Mind	1956	300.00

TALLYSMEN, THE

45s

TALLY

Number	Title (A Side/B Side)	Yr	NM
❑ 200688	Little By Little/You Don't Care About Me	1966	60.00

TAMANEERS, THE

45s

BRAMLEY

Number	Title (A Side/B Side)	Yr	NM
❑ 102	Searching/Be Anything (But Be Mine)	1960	400.00

TAMBLYN, LARRY

45s

FARO

Number	Title (A Side/B Side)	Yr	NM
❑ 601	Patty Ann/Dearest	1960	20.00
❑ 603	The Lie/My Bride-to-Be	1960	20.00
❑ 612	This Is the Night/Destiny	1961	25.00

LINDA

Number	Title (A Side/B Side)	Yr	NM
❑ 112	You'll Be Mine Someday/The Girl in My Heart	1963	20.00
—With the Standells			

TAMMI AND THE BACHELORS

45s

BANGAR

Number	Title (A Side/B Side)	Yr	NM
❑ 00610	My Summer Love/My Love	1964	25.00

TAMMYS, THE

45s

UNITED ARTISTS

Number	Title (A Side/B Side)	Yr	NM
❑ 632	Take Back Your Ring/Part of Growing Up	1963	12.00
❑ 678	Egyptian Shamba/What's So Sweet About Sweet Sixteen	1963	12.00

VEEP

Number	Title (A Side/B Side)	Yr	NM
❑ 1210	Gypsy/Hold Back the Light of Dawn	1965	12.00
❑ 1220	His Actions Speak Louder Than Words/Blues Sixteen	1965	12.00

TAMPA RED

45s

RCA VICTOR

Number	Title (A Side/B Side)	Yr	NM
❑ 47-4275	Boogie Woogie Women/I Won't Let Her Do It	1951	50.00
❑ 47-4399	She's a Cool Operator/Green and Lucky Blues	1951	50.00
❑ 47-4722	But I Forgive You/I'm Gonna Put You Down	1952	50.00
❑ 47-4898	True Love/Look-a There, Look-a There	1952	50.00
❑ 47-5134	All Mixed Up Over You/Too Late Too Long	1953	40.00
❑ 47-5273	I'll Never Let You Go/Got a Mind to Leave This Town	1953	40.00
❑ 47-5523	So Craazy About You Baby/So Much Trouble	1953	40.00
❑ 47-5594	If She Don't Come Back/Big Stars Falling	1954	40.00
❑ 50-0002	If You Ever Change Your Ways/Chicago Breakdown	1949	120.00
—Gray label, orange vinyl; With Big Maceo			
❑ 50-0019	Come On If You're Coming/When Things Go Wrong with You	1950	120.00
—Gray label, orange vinyl			
❑ 50-0027	It's a Brand New Boogie/Put Your Money Where Your Mouth Is	1950	120.00
—Gray label, orange vinyl			
❑ 50-0041	I'll Find My Way/That's Her Own Business	1950	120.00
—Gray label, orange vinyl			
❑ 50-0071	It's Too Late Now/Please Try to See It My Way	1950	100.00
—Gray label, orange vinyl			
❑ 50-0084	1950 Blues/Love Her with a Feelin'	1950	100.00
—Gray label, orange vinyl			
❑ 50-0094	It's Good Like That/New Deal Blues	1950	100.00
—Gray label, orange vinyl			
❑ 50-0107	Sweet Little Angel/Don't Blame Shorty for That	1951	80.00
❑ 50-0112	Midnight Boogie/I Miss My Lovin' Blues	1951	80.00
❑ 50-0123	She's Dynamite/Early in the Morning	1951	80.00
❑ 50-0136	Pretty Baby Blues/Since My Baby's Been Gone	1951	80.00

Albums

BLUEBIRD

Number	Title	Yr	NM
❑ AXM2-5501 [(2)]	Guitar Wizard	1975	15.00

BLUES CLASSICS

Number	Title	Yr	NM
❑ 25	Guitar Wizard (1935-53)	197?	12.00

BLUESVILLE

Number	Title	Yr	NM
❑ BVLP-1030 [M]	Don't Tampa with the Blues	1961	120.00
—Blue label, silver print			
❑ BVLP-1030 [M]	Don't Tampa with the Blues	1963	30.00
—Blue label, trident logo at right			
❑ BVLP-1043 [M]	Don't Jive Me	1962	120.00
—Blue label, silver print			
❑ BVLP-1043 [M]	Don't Jive Me	1963	30.00
—Blue label, trident logo at right			

FANTASY

Number	Title	Yr	NM
❑ OBC-516	Don't Tampa with the Blues	198?	10.00

YAZOO

Number	Title	Yr	NM
❑ 1039	Bottleneck Guitar	197?	12.00

T

TAMS, THE

45s

Number	Title (A Side/B Side)	Yr	NM
ABC			
10825	Holding On/Is It Better to Have Loved a Little	1966	8.00
10885	Shelter/Get Away (Leave Me Alone)	1966	8.00
10929	Breaking Up/How 'Bout It	1967	8.00
10956	Everything Else Is Gone/Mary, Mary, Row Your Boat	1967	8.00
11019	All My Heard Times/A Little More Soul	1967	8.00
11066	Be Young, Be Foolish, Be Happy/That Same Old Song	1968	8.00
11128	Laugh at the World/Trouble Maker	1968	8.00
11183	Sunshine, Rainbow, Blue Sky, Brown Eyed Girl/There's a Great Big Change in Me	1969	8.00
11228	Be Young, Be Foolish, Be Happy/Love, Love, Love	1969	8.00
11358	Don't You Just Know It/Making Music	1973	5.00
ABC DUNHILL			
4290	Hey Girl Don't Bother Me/Weep Little Girl	1971	6.00
4290 [PS]	Hey Girl Don't Bother Me/Weep Little Girl	1971	10.00
—Title sleeve with "#1 in England"			
ABC-PARAMOUNT			
10502	What Kind of Fool (Do You Think I Am)/Laugh It Off	1963	15.00
10533	It's All Right (You're Just in Love)/You Lied to Your Daddy	1964	12.00
10573	Hey Girl Don't Bother Me/Take Away	1964	12.00
10601	Silly Little Girl/Weep Little Girl	1964	12.00
10614	The Truth Hurts/Why Did My Little Girl Cry	1965	10.00
10635	What Do You Do/Unlove You	1965	10.00
10702	Concrete Jungle/Till the End of Time	1965	10.00
10741	Carryin' On/I've Been Hurt	1965	10.00
10779	Got to Get Used to a Broken Heart/Riding for a Fall	1966	10.00
APT			
26010	Long Distance Operator/Numbers	1970	6.00
ARLEN			
711	Untie Me/Disillusioned	1962	12.00
717	Deep Inside Me/If You're So Smart (Why Do You Have a Broken Heart)	1962	12.00
720	You'll Never Know/Blue Shadows	1963	12.00
729	Don't Ever Go/Find Another Love	1963	12.00
CAPITOL			
3050	The Tams Medley/Wire Help	1971	6.00
COMPLEAT			
109	My Baby Sure Can Shag/Making True Love	1983	4.00
GENERAL AMERICAN			
714	My Baby Loves Me/Find Another Love	1962	15.00
HERITAGE			
101	Vacation Time/If Love Were Like Rivers	1961	300.00
KING			
6012	Untie Me/Find Another Love	1965	10.00
1-2-3			
1726	How Long Love/Too Much Foolin' Around	1970	6.00
SWAN			
4055	Sorry/Valley of Love	1960	15.00

Albums

Number	Title	Yr	NM
ABC			
ABCS-481 [R]	Presenting the Tams	1968	20.00
—Reissue of ABC-Paramount 481			
ABCS-499 [S]	Hey Girl, Don't Bother Me	1964	20.00
—Reissue of ABC-Paramount 499			
ABC-596 [M]	Time for the Tams	1967	30.00
ABCS-596 [S]	Time for the Tams	1967	30.00
ABCS-627	A Little More Soul	1968	25.00
ABCS-673	A Portrait of the Tams	1969	25.00
ABC-PARAMOUNT			
ABC-481 [M]	Presenting the Tams	1964	50.00
ABCS-481 [R]	Presenting the Tams	1964	30.00
ABC-499 [M]	Hey Girl, Don't Bother Me	1964	30.00
ABCS-499 [S]	Hey Girl, Don't Bother Me	1964	40.00
CAPITOL			
SM-11839	The Best of the Tams	1979	12.00
COMPLEAT			
CMLP-5001 [EP]	Beach Music from the Tams	198?	8.00
1-2-3			
ST-567	The Best of the Tams	1970	20.00
SOUNDS SOUTH			
SO-16010	The Mighty, Mighty Tams	1977	15.00

TAMS, THE (2)

45s

Number	Title (A Side/B Side)	Yr	NM
MINK			
22	Memory Lane/Teenage Kids	1959	40.00
—Originally issued as "The Stereos"			
PARKWAY			
863	Memory Lane/A Lovely Piano	1963	20.00
—The same record was reissued as "The Hippies"			

TAN GEERS

45s

Number	Title (A Side/B Side)	Yr	NM
OKEH			
4-7319	Let My Heart and Soul Be Free/What's the Use of Me Trying	1968	400.00

TANEGA, NORMA

45s

Number	Title (A Side/B Side)	Yr	NM
NEW VOICE			
807	Walkin' My Cat Named Dog/I'm the Sky	1966	12.00
810	A Street That Rhymes at 6 A.M./Treat Me Right	1966	10.00
815	Bread/Waves	1966	10.00
821	No Stranger Am I/Run on the Run	1967	10.00

Albums

Number	Title	Yr	NM
NEW VOICE			
NV-2001 [M]	Walkin' My Cat Named Dog	1966	40.00
NVS-2001 [S]	Walkin' My Cat Named Dog	1966	80.00

TANGERINE DREAM

12-Inch Singles

Number	Title (A Side/B Side)	Yr	NM
RELATIVITY			
EMC 8044	Streethawk (2 versions)/Tiergarten	1985	20.00

45s

Number	Title (A Side/B Side)	Yr	NM
MCA			
40740	Betrayal (Sorcerer's Theme)/Grind	1977	10.00
VIRGIN			
9516	Moonlight (Part 2)/Coldwater Canyon (Part 2)	1977	10.00
9516 [DJ]	Moonlight (Part 2) (mono/stereo)	1977	10.00
9516 [DJ]	Moonlight/Cherokee Lane	1977	10.00
9516 [DJ]	Moonlight/Desert Dream	1977	10.00

Albums

Number	Title	Yr	NM
CAROLINE			
CAROL 1349	Livemiles	1988	12.00
ELEKTRA			
5E-521	Thief	1981	10.00
5E-557	Exit	1981	10.00
EMI AMERICA			
ST-17141	Flashpoint	1984	10.00
MCA			
2277	Sorcerer	1977	12.00
6165	Legend	1986	8.00
PRIVATE MUSIC			
2042-1-P	Optical Race	1988	15.00
2047-1-P	Miracle Mile	1989	15.00
2057-1-P	Lily on the Beach	1989	15.00
RELATIVITY			
EMC 8043	Le Parc	198?	12.00
EMC 8045 [(2)]	Poland	198?	15.00
86561 8068	Electronic Meditation	1986	12.00
86561 8069	Alpha Centauri	1986	12.00
86561 8070 [(2)]	Zeit	1986	15.00
86561 8071	Atam	1986	12.00
86561 8072	Green Desert	1986	12.00
86561 8113	Underwater Sunlight	1986	12.00
VIRGIN			
VR 13-108	Phaedra	1974	15.00
VR 13-116	Rubycon	1975	15.00
PZ 34427	Stratosfear	1976	15.00
PZG 35014 [(2)]	Encore	1977	20.00
VIRGIN INTERNATIONAL			
VI 2010	Phaedra	1979	10.00
—Reissue			
VI 2025	Rubycon	1979	10.00
—Reissue			
VI 2044	Ricochet	1975	15.00
VI 2068	Stratosfear	1979	12.00
—Reissue of 34427			
VI 2097	Cyclone	1979	10.00
—Reissue			
VI 2111	Force Majeure	1979	12.00

TANGERINE ZOO, THE

45s

Number	Title (A Side/B Side)	Yr	NM
MAINSTREAM			
682	A Trip to the Zoo/One More Heartache	1968	20.00
690	Like People/(B-side unknown)	1968	20.00

Albums

Number	Title	Yr	NM
MAINSTREAM			
S-6107	Tangerine Zoo	1968	50.00
S-6118	Outside Looking In	1969	70.00

TANGIERS, THE

Possibly more than one group. Also see THE HOLLYWOOD FLAMES.

45s

Number	Title (A Side/B Side)	Yr	NM
A-J			
905	The Plea/The Waddle	1962	25.00
CLASS			
224	School Days Will Be Over/Don't Try	1958	30.00
DECCA			
29603	I Won't Be Around/Tabarin	1955	150.00
29971	Remember Me/Oh, Baby!	1956	150.00
STRAND			
25039	Ping Pong/Don't Stop the Music	1961	30.00

TANTONES, THE

45s

Number	Title (A Side/B Side)	Yr	NM
LAMP			
2002	No Matter/I Love You, Really I Do	1957	150.00
2008	So Afraid/Tell Me	1957	150.00

TARANTULA

45s

Number	Title (A Side/B Side)	Yr	NM
A&M			
1156	Billy the Birdman/Love Is for Peace	1969	8.00

Albums

Number	Title	Yr	NM
A&M			
SP-4202	Tarantula	1969	24.00

TARANTULAS, THE

45s

Number	Title (A Side/B Side)	Yr	NM
ATLANTIC			
2102	Tarantula/Black Widow	1961	25.00
STOP			
102	Herky Jerky/Vera Brown	1964	10.00

TARGETS, THE

45s

Number	Title (A Side/B Side)	Yr	NM
KING			
5538	It Doesn't Matter/Girls, Girls, Girls	1961	40.00

TARRIERS, THE

Also see VINCE MARTIN.

45s

Number	Title (A Side/B Side)	Yr	NM
DECCA			
31387	Last Night I Had the Strangest Dream/Lonesome Traveler	1962	10.00
31470	Casey Jones/Mary Ann	1963	10.00
31524	Lonesome Traveller/Seven Daffodils	1963	10.00
31631	San Francisco Bay Blues/Guantanamera	1964	10.00
GLORY			
246	Wishing Well Song/East Virginia	1956	15.00
249	The Banana Boat Song/No Hidin' Place	1956	20.00
254	Those Brown Eyes/Chaucon	1957	15.00
255	I Know Where I'm Going/Pretty Boy	1957	15.00
264	Dunya/Quinto	1957	15.00
271	Lonesome Traveler/East Virginia	1958	15.00
286	Tom Dooley/Everybody Loves Saturday Night	1958	15.00
UNITED ARTISTS			
168	Hard Travelin'/Times Are Getting Hard	1959	12.00

Albums

Number	Title	Yr	NM
ATLANTIC			
8042 [M]	Tell the World	1960	30.00
SD 8042 [S]	Tell the World	1960	40.00
DECCA			
DL 4342 [M]	The Tarriers	1962	25.00
DL 4538 [M]	Gather 'Round	1964	25.00
DL 74342 [S]	The Tarriers	1962	30.00
DL 74538 [S]	Gather 'Round	1964	30.00

Number	Title (A Side/B Side)	Yr	NM
GLORY			
❑ PG-1200 [M]	The Tarriers	1958	60.00
KAPP			
❑ KL 1349 [M]	The Original Tarriers	1963	25.00
❑ KS 3349 [S]	The Original Tarriers	1963	30.00
UNITED ARTISTS			
❑ UAL-4033 [M]	Hard Travelin'	1959	30.00
❑ UAS-5033 [S]	Hard Travelin'	1959	40.00
TARRYTONS, THE			
45s			
DOT			
❑ 16537	Rough Surfin'/Mansion on the Hill	1963	25.00
EXCLUSIVE			
❑ 2270	Rough Surfin'/Mansion on the Hill	1963	40.00
TASSELS, THE			
45s			
AMY			
❑ 946	To a Soldier Boy/The Boy for Me	1966	10.00
MADISON			
❑ 117	To a Soldier Boy/The Boy for Me	1959	25.00
❑ 121	To a Young Lover/My Guy and I	1959	20.00
TASTE RORY GALLAGHER was in this group.			
Albums			
ATCO			
❑ SD 33-296	Taste	1969	25.00
❑ SD 33-322	On the Boards	1970	25.00
TATE, BILLY			
45s			
IMPERIAL			
❑ 5337 *—Script logo*	Single Life/You Told Me	1955	200.00
PEACOCK			
❑ 1671	Don't Call My Name/Right from Wrong	1957	30.00
TATE, HOWARD			
45s			
ATLANTIC			
❑ 2836	Keep Cool (Don't Be a Fool)/Strugglin'	1971	6.00
❑ 2860	She's a Burglar/You Don't Know Nothing About Love	1972	6.00
❑ 2894	Eight Days on the Road/Girl of the North Country	1972	6.00
EPIC			
❑ 11118	Can You Top This/Ain't Got Nobody to Give It To	1974	5.00
TURNTABLE			
❑ 505	These Are the Things That Make Me Know You're Gone/That's What Happens	1969	8.00
❑ 1018	My Soul's Got a Hole In It/It's Too Late	1970	8.00
UTOPIA			
❑ 510	Half a Man/(B-side unknown)	1966	25.00
VERVE			
❑ 10420	Ain't Nobody Home/How Come My Bull Dog Don't Bark	1966	8.00
❑ 10464	Look at Granny Run, Run/Half a Man	1966	8.00
❑ 10496	Get It While You Can/Glad I Knew Better	1967	8.00
❑ 10525	Baby I Love You/How Blue Can You Get	1967	8.00
❑ 10547	I Learned It All the Hard Way/Part-Time Love	1967	8.00
❑ 10573	Stop/Shoot 'Em All Down	1967	8.00
❑ 10604	Night Owl/Everyday I Have the Blues	1968	8.00
❑ 10625	I'm Your Servant/Sweet Love Child	1968	8.00
Albums			
ATLANTIC			
❑ SD 8303	Howard Tate	1971	20.00
TURNTABLE			
❑ 5002	Reaction	1969	20.00
VERVE			
❑ V-5022 [M]	Get It While You Can	1967	20.00
❑ V6-5022 [S]	Get It While You Can	1967	25.00
TATE, LAURIE			
45s			
ATLANTIC			
❑ 965	Rock Me Daddy/You Can't Stop My Crying	1952	100.00

Number	Title (A Side/B Side)	Yr	NM
TATE, TOMMY			
45s			
ABC-PARAMOUNT			
❑ 10626	What's the Matter/Ordinarily	1965	25.00
KOKO			
❑ 722	Hardtimes S.O.S./Always	1976	6.00
❑ 723	If You Ain't Man Enough/Revelations	1976	6.00
❑ 727	I'm So Satisfied/If You Ain't Man Enough	1977	6.00
❑ 2109	I Remember/Help Me Love	1971	6.00
❑ 2112	School of Life/I Remember	1972	6.00
❑ 2114	I Ain't Gonna Worry/More Power To You	1972	6.00
OKEH			
❑ 7242	Are You From Heaven/I'm Taking On Pain	1966	20.00
❑ 7253	Big Blue Diamonds/Lover's Reward	1967	20.00
TAUPIN, BERNIE ELTON JOHN's songwriting partner.			
45s			
RCA			
❑ 5162-7-R	Friend of the Flag/Backbone	1987	3.00
❑ 5162-7-R [PS]	Friend of the Flag/Backbone	1987	3.00
❑ 5216-7-R	Citizen Jane/White Boys in Chains	1987	3.00
❑ 5216-7-R [PS]	Citizen Jane/White Boys in Chains	1987	3.00
Albums			
ASYLUM			
❑ 6E-263	He Who Rides the Tiger	1980	12.00
ELEKTRA			
❑ EKS-75020	Bernie Taupin	1972	15.00
RCA			
❑ 5922-1-R	Tribe	1987	10.00
❑ 6420-1-RAB [(2)DJ]	Interview Album	1987	20.00
TAVENER, JOHN			
Albums			
APPLE			
❑ SMAS-3369	The Whale	1972	20.00
TAX FREE			
Albums			
POLYDOR			
❑ 24-4053	Tax Free	1971	20.00
TAYLOR, ALEX			
45s			
BANG			
❑ 739	Don't Look at Me That Way/Sunny Day to Rain	1978	4.00
CAPRICORN			
❑ 0004	Comin' Back to You/Who Will the Next Fool Be	1972	5.00
❑ 0018	Lizzie and the Rainman/Change Your Sexy Ways	1973	5.00
❑ 8013	Highway Song/C Song	1971	5.00
❑ 8016	Baby Ruth/All in Line	1971	5.00
❑ 8019	Night Owl/Southern Kids	1971	5.00
Albums			
CAPRICORN			
❑ CP 0101	Dinnertime	1972	10.00
❑ 860	With Friends and Neighbors	1971	10.00
TAYLOR, ANDREW			
45s			
GONE			
❑ 5109	That's How I Feel About You/Never Bite Off More Than You Could Chew	1961	200.00
TAYLOR, AUSTIN			
TAYLOR, BILL, AND SMOKEY JO			
45s			
FLIP			
❑ 502	Split Personality/Lonely Sweetheart	1955	1500.
TAYLOR, BILLY			
45s			
CITATION			
❑ 5002	Income Taxes and You/Lullaby to Carolyn	1962	15.00
FAME			
❑ 502	Little Jewel/Study Hall Romance	196?	300.00

Number	Title (A Side/B Side)	Yr	NM
FELCO			
❑ 101	Wombie Zombie/I'm Young	1959	20.00
FELSTED			
❑ 8564	Bandstand Baby/Cat with No Future	1959	20.00
TOWER			
❑ 421	Sunny/I Wish I Knew How I Would Feel to Be Free	1968	8.00
Albums			
ABC IMPULSE!			
❑ AS-71 [S]	My Fair Lady Loves Jazz	1968	15.00
ABC-PARAMOUNT			
❑ ABC-112 [M]	Evergreens	1956	50.00
❑ ABC-134 [M]	Billy Taylor At the London House	1956	50.00
❑ ABC-162 [M]	Billy Taylor Introduces Ira Sullivan	1957	50.00
❑ ABC-177 [M]	My Fair Lady Loves Jazz	1957	50.00
❑ ABC-226 [M]	The New Trio	1958	50.00
❑ ABCS-226 [S]	The New Trio	1958	40.00
ARGO			
❑ LP-650 [M]	Taylor Made Flute	1959	50.00
❑ LPS-650 [S]	Taylor Made Flute	1959	40.00
ATLANTIC			
❑ ALR-113 [10]	Piano Panorama	1951	150.00
❑ 1277 [M] *—Black label*	The Billy Taylor Touch	1958	50.00
❑ 1277 [M] *—Multicolor label, white "fan" logo at right*	The Billy Taylor Touch	1961	25.00
❑ 1329 [M] *—Black label*	One for Fun	1960	50.00
❑ SD 1329 [S] *—Green label*	One for Fun	1960	50.00
BELL			
❑ S-6049	OK Billy!	1970	15.00
CAPITOL			
❑ ST 2039 [S]	Right Here, Right Now	1963	25.00
❑ T 2039 [M]	Right Here, Right Now	1963	20.00
❑ ST 2302 [S]	Midnight Piano	1965	25.00
❑ T 2302 [M]	Midnight Piano	1965	20.00
CONCORD JAZZ			
❑ CJ-145	Where've You Been	1981	10.00
FANTASY			
❑ OJC-015	The Billy Taylor Trio with Candido	1982	10.00
❑ OJC-1730	Cross Section	198?	10.00
IMPULSE!			
❑ A-71 [M]	My Fair Lady Loves Jazz	1965	20.00
❑ AS-71 [S]	My Fair Lady Loves Jazz	1965	25.00
MERCURY			
❑ MG-20722 [M]	Impromptu	1962	20.00
❑ SR-60722 [S]	Impromptu	1962	25.00
MONMOUTH-EVERGREEN			
❑ 7089	Jazz Alive	1978	12.00
MOODSVILLE			
❑ MVLP-16 [M] *—Green label*	Interlude	1961	50.00
❑ MVLP-16 [M] *—Blue label, trident logo at right*	Interlude	1965	25.00
NEW JAZZ			
❑ NJLP-8313 [M] *—Canceled; reassigned to Status*	Live! At Town Hall	1963	—
PAUSA			
❑ 7096	Sleeping Bee	198?	10.00
PRESTIGE			
❑ 16-2 [M] *—This album plays at 16 2/3 rpm and is marked as such; white label*	Let's Get Away from It All	1957	500.00
❑ PRLP-139 [10]	Billy Taylor Trio, Vol. 1	1953	220.00
❑ PRLP-165 [10]	Billy Taylor Trio, Vol. 2	1953	250.00
❑ PRLP-168 [10]	Billy Taylor Trio, Vol. 3	1953	220.00
❑ PRLP-184 [10]	Billy Taylor Trio	1954	200.00
❑ PRLP-188 [10]	Billy Taylor Trio	1954	200.00
❑ PRLP-194 [10]	Billy Taylor Trio In Concert at Town Hall, December 17, 1954	1955	200.00
❑ PRLP-7001 [M]	A Touch of Taylor	1955	80.00
❑ PRLP-7015 [M]	Billy Taylor Trio, Vol. 1	1956	80.00
❑ PRLP-7016 [M]	Billy Taylor Trio, Vol. 2	1956	100.00
❑ PRLP-7051 [M]	The Billy Taylor Trio with Candido	1956	80.00
❑ PRLP-7071 [M]	Cross Section	1956	80.00
❑ PRLP-7093 [M]	Billy Taylor Trio at Town Hall	1957	80.00
❑ PRST-7664 [R]	A Touch of Taylor	1969	15.00
❑ PRST-7762	Today!	1970	15.00
RIVERSIDE			
❑ RLP 12-306 [M]	Billy Taylor with Four Flutes	1959	50.00
❑ RLP 12-319 [M]	Billy Taylor Trio Uptown	1960	50.00
❑ RLP 12-339 [M]	Warming Up	1960	50.00
❑ RLP-1151 [S]	Billy Taylor with Four Flutes	1959	40.00
❑ RLP-1168 [S]	Billy Taylor Trio Uptown	1960	40.00
❑ RLP-1195 [S]	Warming Up	1960	40.00
ROOST			
❑ R-406 [10]	Jazz at Storyville	1952	120.00
❑ R-409 [10]	Taylor Made Jazz	1952	120.00

T

Number	Title (A Side/B Side)	Yr	NM
SAVOY			
❑ MG-9035 [10]	Billy Taylor Piano	1953	120.00
SESAC			
❑ N-3001 [M]	Custom Taylored	1959	60.00
❑ SN-3001 [S]	Custom Taylored	1959	50.00
STATUS			
❑ ST-8313 [M]	Live! At Town Hall	1965	40.00
SURREY			
❑ S-1033 [M]	Easy Life	1966	25.00
❑ SS-1033 [S]	Easy Life	1966	30.00
TOWER			
❑ ST-5111 [S]	I Wish I Knew	1968	25.00
WEST 54			
❑ 8008	Live at Storyville	198?	12.00

TAYLOR, BOBBY, AND THE VANCOUVERS

45s

Number	Title (A Side/B Side)	Yr	NM
GORDY			
❑ 7069	Does Your Mama Know About Me/Fading Away	1968	20.00
❑ 7073	I Am Your Man/If You Love Her	1968	20.00
❑ 7079	Malinda/It's Growing	1968	20.00
❑ 7088	Oh I've Been Blessed/It Should Have Been Me Loving Her	1969	600.00
❑ 7092	My Girl Is Gone/It Should Have Been Me Loving Her	1969	20.00
INTEGRA			
❑ 103	This Is My Woman/(B-side unknown)	1968	100.00
MOWEST			
❑ 5006	Hey Lordy/Just a Little Bit Closer	1971	15.00
PLAYBOY			
❑ 6046	Why Play Games/Don't Wonder Why	1975	5.00
SUNFLOWER			
❑ 126	There Are Roses Somewhere in the World/It Was a Good Time	1972	25.00
V.I.P.			
❑ 25053	Oh I've Been Blessed/Blackmail	1969	25.00

Albums

Number	Title (A Side/B Side)	Yr	NM
GORDY			
❑ G-930 [M]	Bobby Taylor and the Vancouvers	1968	80.00
—Mono is promo only			
❑ GS-930 [S]	Bobby Taylor and the Vancouvers	1968	60.00
❑ GS-942	Taylor Made Soul	1969	60.00

TAYLOR, CARMEN

45s

Number	Title (A Side/B Side)	Yr	NM
APOLLO			
❑ 489	Oh Please/Teen Age Ball	1956	60.00
ATLANTIC			
❑ 1002	Lovin' Daddy/Ding Dong	1953	50.00
❑ 1015	Big Mamou Daddy/Mamma Me and Johnny Free	1953	50.00
❑ 1041	Freddie/Ooh I	1954	120.00
GUYDEN			
❑ 100	Let Me Go Lover/No More, No Less	1954	40.00
KAMA SUTRA			
❑ 206	My Son/You're Puttin' Me On	1966	12.00
KING			
❑ 5085	So What/Why Did You Leave Me Alone	1957	50.00

TAYLOR, CHIP

45s

Number	Title (A Side/B Side)	Yr	NM
BUDDAH			
❑ 325	Angel of the Morning/(B-side unknown)	1972	6.00
❑ 344	Londonderry Company/(B-side unknown)	1973	6.00
CAPITOL			
❑ 4692	Saint Sebastian/One Night Out with the Boys	1979	4.00
❑ 4840	Stealin' Each Other Blind/He Ain't Makin' Music Anymore	1980	4.00
COLUMBIA			
❑ 10446	Hello Atlanta/Farmer's Daughter	1976	4.00
❑ 10520	Three Younger Bandits/Nothing Like You Girl	1977	4.00
❑ 44736	It's Such a Lonely Time of Year/(Instrumental)	1968	12.00
EPIC			
❑ 10567	It's Such a Lonely Time of Year/(Instrumental)	1969	10.00
MALA			
❑ 476	On My World/Joanie's Blues	1964	12.00
❑ 489	Suzannah (Comin' Home to Louisiana)/(B-side unknown)	1964	12.00
❑ 507	Young Love/Betty Ann	1965	10.00
MGM			
❑ 12993	Foolin' Around/Innocent Eyes	1961	20.00
❑ 13040	If You Don't Want Me Now/Sad Songs	1961	20.00
WARNER BROS.			
❑ 5314	Here I Am/I Love You But I Know	1962	15.00
❑ 5333	Lucky Star/A Guy Don't Need a Lot of Time	1963	15.00
❑ 8050	Me As I Am/Comin' From Behind	1974	4.00
❑ 8090	Early Sunday Morning/Shickshinny	1975	4.00
❑ 8128	Big River/John Tucker's On the Wagon Again	1975	4.00
❑ 8159	Circle of Tears/You're Alright, Charlie	1975	4.00

Albums

Number	Title (A Side/B Side)	Yr	NM
BUDDAH			
❑ BDS-5118	Gasoline	1972	12.00
CAPITOL			
❑ ST-11909	Saint Sebastian	1979	10.00
COLUMBIA			
❑ KC 34345	Somebody Shoot Out the Jukebox	1977	10.00
WARNER BROS.			
❑ BS 2718	Last Chance	1973	12.00
❑ BS 2824	Some of Us	1974	12.00

TAYLOR, DEBBIE

45s

Number	Title (A Side/B Side)	Yr	NM
ARISTA			
❑ 0144	I Don't Wanna Leave You/Just Don't Pay	1975	10.00
DECCA			
❑ 32259	Check Yourself/Wait Until I'm Gone	1968	15.00
GWP			
❑ 501	Never Gonna Let Him Know/Let's Prove Them Wrong	1969	15.00
❑ 510	Don't let It End/How Long Can This Last	1969	15.00
❑ 512	Momma Look Sharp/No Brag, Just Fact	1969	15.00
GWP'S GRAPEVINE			
❑ 202	Don't Nobody Mess with My Baby/Stop	1970	15.00
POLYDOR			
❑ 14219	I Have Learned to Do Without You/Cheaper in the Long Run	1974	30.00
❑ 14252	Superstar/A Good Woman Don't Grow on Trees	1974	—
—Canceled			
TODAY			
❑ TLP-1007	Comin' Down on You	1972	50.00
❑ 1510	No Deposit, No Return/Too Sad to Tell	1972	12.00

TAYLOR, EDDIE

45s

Number	Title (A Side/B Side)	Yr	NM
VEE JAY			
❑ 149	Bad Boy/E.T. Blues	1955	120.00
❑ 185	Big Town Playboy/Ride 'Em On Down	1956	80.00
❑ 206	You'll Always Have a Home/Don't Knock at My Door	1956	60.00
❑ 267	I'm Gonna Love You/Looking for Trouble	1958	40.00
VIVID			
❑ 104	I'm Sitting Here/Do You Want Me to Cry	1964	20.00

TAYLOR, FAITH, AND THE SWEET TEENS

45s

Number	Title (A Side/B Side)	Yr	NM
BEA & BABY			
❑ 104	I Need Him to Love Me/I Love You Darling	1959	50.00
FEDERAL			
❑ 12334	Your Candy Kisses/Won't Someone Tell Me Why?	1958	50.00

TAYLOR, FELICE

45s

Number	Title (A Side/B Side)	Yr	NM
KENT			
❑ 483	Good Luck/I Can Feel Your Love	1967	15.00
❑ 488	Captured by Your Love/New Love	1968	15.00
MUSTANG			
❑ 3024	It May Be Winter Outside (But In My Heart It's Spring)/Winter Again	1966	15.00
❑ 3026	I'm Under the Influence of Love/Love Theme	1967	20.00

TAYLOR, FRANK

45s

Number	Title (A Side/B Side)	Yr	NM
BRACK			
❑ 106	When Two Worlds Collide/Talk Back Trembling Lips	196?	10.00
❑ 118	Oh Lonesome Me/Somewhere in Kentucky	196?	10.00
❑ 124	Lovesick Blues/Indifferent Bartenders	196?	10.00
❑ 129	Bayou Pon Pon/Talk Back Trembling Lips	196?	10.00
CHART			
❑ 502	Bubbles in the Glass/A Part of You	1963	15.00
❑ 1055	From Brown to Blue/You Didn't Leave Me Much to Live For	1964	12.00
❑ 1095	Lost, Strayed or Stolen/She Used to Be My Girl	1964	12.00
❑ 1150	Blue Part of the Blues/Tears and Tears to Pay	1964	12.00
❑ 1235	Forty Winks/I Can't Stand This Living Alone	1965	12.00
❑ 1495	Judas Feet/Life of Reilly	1967	10.00
CHART ACTION			
❑ 113	If You Were on Trial for Loving Me/Nobody's Darlin' But Mine	196?	20.00
❑ 117	Countryfied/Most of All	196?	20.00
❑ 801	Diesel on My Tail/Live and Let Live	196?	15.00

TAYLOR, GLORIA

45s

Number	Title (A Side/B Side)	Yr	NM
COLUMBIA			
❑ 4-45986	Deep Inside You/World That's Not Real	1974	12.00
GLO-WHIZ			
❑ 1	You Got to Pay the Price/Loving You and Being Loved By You	1969	25.00
KING SOUL			
❑ 493	Poor Unfortunate Me/You Might Need Me Another Day	1968	60.00
❑ 865	Do Your Duty/Born a Woman	196?	40.00
MERCURY			
❑ 73137	Yesterday Will Never Come Again/Unyielding	1970	20.00
❑ 73186	Don't Want to Be a Girl That Cries/Total Disaster	1970	60.00
SELECTOR SOUND			
❑ 1976	Had It All the Time/What's Your World	197?	40.00
SILVER FOX			
❑ 14	You Got to Pay the Price/Loving You and Being Loved By You	1969	12.00
❑ 19	Grounded Part 1/Part 2	1970	15.00

TAYLOR, JAMES

12-Inch Singles

Number	Title (A Side/B Side)	Yr	NM
COLUMBIA			
❑ ASF 358 [DJ]	Handy Man (mono/stereo)	1977	15.00
❑ AS 1240 [DJ]	Summer's Here/Hard Times	1981	8.00

45s

Number	Title (A Side/B Side)	Yr	NM
APPLE			
❑ 1805	Carolina in My Mind/Taking It In	1969	300.00
❑ 1805	Carolina in My Mind/Something's Wrong	1970	8.00
—Without star on A-side label			
❑ 1805	Carolina in My Mind/Something's Wrong	1970	10.00
—With star on A-side label			
❑ 1805 [DJ]	Carolina on My Mind/Something's Wrong	1970	30.00
—Promo with error in title on A-side			
COLUMBIA			
❑ 02093	Hard Times/Summer's Here	1981	3.00
❑ 02093 [PS]	Hard Times/Summer's Here	1981	4.00
❑ 05681	Everyday/Limousine Driver	1985	3.00
❑ 05681 [PS]	Everyday/Limousine Driver	1985	4.00
❑ 05785	Only One/Mona	1986	3.00
❑ 05785 [PS]	Only One/Mona	1986	3.00
❑ 05884	That's Why I'm Here/Going Around One More Time	1986	3.00
❑ 06278	Only a Dream in Rio/Turn Away	1986	3.00
❑ 07616	Never Die Young/Valentine's Day	1987	3.00

Except when noted otherwise, VG = 25% of NM, and VG+ = 50% of NM. (Example: VG = $2.00, VG+ = $4.00 and NM = $8.00.)

Number	Title (A Side/B Side)	Yr	NM
❑ 07616 [PS]	Never Die Young/Valentine's Day	1987	4.00
❑ 07948	Baby Boom Baby/Letter in the Mail	1988	3.00
❑ 08493	Sweet Potato Pie/First of May	1988	3.00
❑ 10557	Handy Man/Bartender's Blues	1977	4.00
❑ 10602	Your Smiling Face/If I Keep My Heart Out of Sight	1977	4.00
❑ 10676	(What a) Wonderful World/Wooden Planes	1978	6.00
—By Art Garfunkel with Paul Simon and James Taylor; B-side is Garfunkel solo			
❑ 10689	Honey Don't Leave L.A./Another Grey Morning	1978	4.00
❑ 11005	Up on the Roof/Chanson Francaise	1979	4.00
❑ 60514	Her Town Too/Believe It or Not	1981	4.00
—A-side: James Taylor and J.D. Souther			

WARNER BROS.

Number	Title (A Side/B Side)	Yr	NM
❑ 7387	Sweet Baby James/Suite for 20G	1970	8.00
❑ 7423	Fire and Rain/Anywhere Like Heaven	1970	8.00
❑ 7460	Country Road/Sunny Skies	1970	6.00
❑ 7498	You've Got a Friend/You Can Close Your Eyes	1971	6.00
❑ 7521	Long Ago and Far Away/Let Me Ride	1971	5.00
❑ 7655	Don't Let Me Be Lonely Tonight/Wow, Don't You Know	1972	5.00
❑ 7682	One Man Parade/Nobody But You	1973	5.00
❑ 7695	Hymn/Fanfare	1973	5.00
❑ 8015	Let It All Fall Down/Daddy's Baby	1974	5.00
❑ 8028	Walking Man/Daddy's Baby	1974	5.00
❑ 8109	How Sweet It Is (To Be Loved By You)/Sarah Maria	1975	5.00
❑ 8137	Mexico/Gorilla	1975	5.00
❑ 8222	Shower the People/I Can Dream of You	1976	5.00
❑ 8278	Woman's Gotta Have It/You Make It Easy	1976	5.00

7-Inch Extended Plays

WARNER BROS.

Number	Title (A Side/B Side)	Yr	NM
❑ S 2561	Places in My Past/Love Has Brought Me Around/Hey Mister, That's Me Up on the Jukebox//Mud Slide Slim/Isn't It Nice to Be Home Again/Riding on a Railroad	1971	10.00
—Jukebox issue; small hole, plays at 33 1/3 rpm			
❑ S 2561 [PS]	Mud Slide Slim	1971	10.00
—Part of "Little LP" series (LLP #150)			

Albums

APPLE

Number	Title (A Side/B Side)	Yr	NM
❑ SKAO 3352	James Taylor	1969	25.00
—With title in black print			
❑ SKAO 3352	James Taylor	1970	20.00
—With title in orange print			

COLUMBIA

Number	Title (A Side/B Side)	Yr	NM
❑ JC 34811	JT	1977	10.00
❑ PC 34811	JT	198?	8.00
❑ FC 36058	Flag	1979	10.00
❑ PC 36058	Flag	198?	8.00
❑ PC 37009	Dad Loves His Work	198?	8.00
❑ TC 37009	Dad Loves His Work	1981	10.00
❑ FC 40052	That's Why I'm Here	1985	10.00
❑ FC 40851	Never Die Young	1988	10.00
❑ HC 47009	Dad Loves His Work	1983	40.00
—Half-speed mastered edition			

EUPHORIA

Number	Title (A Side/B Side)	Yr	NM
❑ EST-2	James Taylor and the Original Flying Machine 1967	1971	12.00

NAUTILUS

Number	Title (A Side/B Side)	Yr	NM
❑ NR-29	Gorilla	1981	40.00
—Audiophile pressing			

TRIP

Number	Title (A Side/B Side)	Yr	NM
❑ TLP-9513	Rainy Day Man	197?	10.00
—Reissue of Euphoria album			

WARNER BROS.

Number	Title (A Side/B Side)	Yr	NM
❑ WS 1843	Sweet Baby James	1970	10.00
—Green "WB" label with "Contains Fire and Rain and Country Road" added to front cover			
❑ WS 1843	Sweet Baby James	1970	15.00
—Green "WB" label with no reference to other songs on front cover			
❑ WS 1843	Sweet Baby James	1970	25.00
—Very early pressings have green label with "W7" logo			
❑ WS 1843	Sweet Baby James	1973	8.00
—"Burbank" label or cream label			
❑ BS 2561	Mud Slide Slim and the Blue Horizon	1971	10.00
—Green "WB" label			
❑ BS 2561	Mud Slide Slim and the Blue Horizon	1973	8.00
—"Burbank" label or cream label			
❑ BS 2660	One Man Dog	1972	10.00
—Green "WB" label			
❑ BS 2660	One Man Dog	1973	8.00
—"Burbank" label or cream label			
❑ BS4 2660 [Q]	One Man Dog	1975	15.00
❑ BS 2794	Walking Man	1973	10.00
—"Burbank" label			
❑ BS 2794	Walking Man	1979	8.00
—Cream label			
❑ BS 2866	Gorilla	1975	10.00
—"Burbank" label			
❑ BS 2866	Gorilla	1979	8.00
—Cream label			
❑ BS4 2866 [Q]	Gorilla	1975	15.00
❑ BS 2912	In the Pocket	1976	10.00
—"Burbank" label			
❑ BS 2912	In the Pocket	1979	8.00
—Cream label			
❑ BS 2979	Greatest Hits	1976	12.00
—This and other variations of this title have re-recorded versions of "Carolina in My Mind" and "Something in the Way She Moves."			
❑ BSK 3113	Greatest Hits	1977	10.00
—"Burbank" label			
❑ BSK 3113	Greatest Hits	1979	8.00
—Cream label			
❑ ST-93138	Sweet Baby James	1970	20.00
—Capitol Record Club edition			
❑ 274300	Sweet Baby James	2007	25.00
—Reissue on 180-gram vinyl with replica of original green "WB" label and lyric poster			

TAYLOR, JOHNNIE

12-Inch Singles

BEVERLY GLEN

Number	Title (A Side/B Side)	Yr	NM
❑ BG 2002	What About My Love/Reaganomics	1982	10.00

45s

BEVERLY GLEN

Number	Title (A Side/B Side)	Yr	NM
❑ 2003	What About My Love/Reaganomics	1982	4.00
❑ 2004	I'm So Proud/I Need a Freak	1982	4.00
❑ 2007	Just Ain't Good Enough/Don't Wait	1983	4.00
❑ 2016	Seconds of Your Love/Shoot for the Stars	1983	4.00

COLUMBIA

Number	Title (A Side/B Side)	Yr	NM
❑ AE7 1153 [DJ]	God Is Standing By/God Is Amazing	1977	8.00
—B-side by Deniece Williams; promo with "Suggested Christmas Programming" on label			
❑ 10281	Disco Lady/You're the Best in the World	1976	5.00
❑ 10334	Somebody's Gettin' It/Please Don't Stop (That Song from Playing)	1976	5.00
❑ 10478	Love Is Better in the A.M. (Part 1)/Love Is Better in the A.M. (Part 2)	1977	5.00
❑ 10541	Your Love Is Rated X/Here I Go (Through These Chains Again)	1977	5.00
❑ 10610	Disco 9000/Right Now	1977	4.00
❑ 10709	Keep On Dancing/I Love to Make Love When It's Raining	1978	4.00
❑ 10776	Give Me My Baby/Ever Ready	1978	4.00
❑ 11084	(Ooh-Wee) She's Killing Me/Play Something Pretty	1979	4.00
❑ 11315	I Got This Thing for Your Love/Signing Off with Love	1980	4.00
❑ 11373	I Wanna Get Into You/Baby Don't Hesitate	1980	4.00

DERBY

Number	Title (A Side/B Side)	Yr	NM
❑ 101	Shine, Shine, Shine/Dance What You Wanna	1963	15.00
❑ 1006	Baby, We've Got Love/In Love with You	1963	15.00
❑ 1010	I Need Lots of Love/Getting Married Soon	1964	15.00

MALACO

Number	Title (A Side/B Side)	Yr	NM
❑ 2107	Lady, My Whole World Is You/L-O-V-E	1984	3.00
❑ 2111	Good with My Hips/This Is Your Night	1985	3.00
❑ 2118	Still Called the Blues/She's Cheatin' on Me	1985	3.00
❑ 2125	Wall to Wall/(B-side unknown)	1986	3.00
❑ 2128	Can I Love You/There's Nothing I Wouldn't Do	1986	3.00
❑ 2132	Just Because/When She Stops Asking	1987	3.00
❑ 2135	Don't Make Me Late/Happy Time	1987	3.00
❑ 2140	If I Lose Your Love/Something Is Going Wrong	1987	3.00
❑ 2143	Everything's Out in the Open/Got to Leave This Woman	1988	3.00
❑ 2153	In Control/I Found a Love	1989	3.00
❑ 2159	Still Crazy for You/(B-side unknown)	1989	3.00

RCA

Number	Title (A Side/B Side)	Yr	NM
❑ PB-11137	I Want You Back Again/Heaven Bless This Home	1977	5.00

SAR

Number	Title (A Side/B Side)	Yr	NM
❑ 114	A Whole Lotta Woman/Why Oh Why	1961	20.00
❑ 131	Never Never/Rome (Wasn't Built in a Day)	1962	40.00
❑ 156	Oh, How I Love You/Run, But You Can't Hide	1964	15.00

STAX

Number	Title (A Side/B Side)	Yr	NM
❑ 0009	Who's Making Love/I'm Trying	1968	8.00
❑ 0023	Take Care of Your Homework/Hold On This Time	1969	8.00
❑ 0033	Testify (I Wanna)/I Had a Fight with Love	1969	8.00
❑ 0042	Just Keep On Loving Me/My Life	1969	8.00
—With Carla Thomas			
❑ 0046	I Could Never Be President/It's Amazing	1969	8.00
❑ 0055	Love Bones/Mr. Nobody Is Somebody	1969	8.00
❑ 0068	Steal Away/Friday Night	1970	6.00
❑ 0078	I Am Somebody (Part 1)/I Am Somebody (Part 2)	1970	6.00
❑ 0085	Jody's Got Your Girl and Gone/A Fool Like Me	1970	6.00
❑ 0089	I Don't Wanna Lose You/Party Life	1971	6.00
❑ 0096	Hijackin' Love/Love in the Streets	1971	6.00
❑ 0114	Standing In for Jody/Shackin' Up	1972	6.00
❑ 0122	Doing My Own Thing (Part 1)/Doing My Own Thing (Part 2)	1972	6.00
❑ 0142	Stop Doggin' Me/Stop Teasin' Me	1972	6.00
❑ 0155	Don't You Fool with My Soul (Part 1)/Don't You Fool with My Soul (Part 2)	1973	6.00
❑ 0161	I Believe in You (You Believe in Me)/Love Depression	1973	6.00
—With A-side time listed at 4:37			
❑ 0161	I Believe in You (You Believe in Me)/Love Depression	1973	6.00
—With A-side time listed at 3:58			
❑ 0176	Cheaper to Keep Her/I Can Read Between the Lines	1973	6.00
❑ 186	I Had a Dream/Changes	1966	10.00
❑ 193	I Got to Love Somebody's Baby/Just the One I've Been Looking For	1966	10.00
❑ 0193	We're Getting Careless with Our Love/Poor Make Believer	1974	6.00
❑ 202	Little Bluebird/Toe Hold	1967	10.00
❑ 0208	I've Been Born Again/At Night Time	1974	6.00
❑ 209	Ain't That Loving You/Outside Love	1967	10.00
❑ 226	If I Had It to Do Over/You Can't Get Away from It	1967	10.00
❑ 0226	It's September/Just One Moment	1974	6.00
❑ 235	Somebody's Sleeping in My Bed/Strange Thing	1967	10.00
❑ 0241	Try Me Tonight/Free	1975	6.00
❑ 247	Next Time/Sundown	1968	10.00
❑ 253	I Ain't Particular/Where There's Smoke There's Fire	1968	10.00
❑ 3201	It Don't Pay to Get Up in the Mornin'/Just Keep On Loving Me	1977	5.00

Albums

BEVERLY GLEN

Number	Title (A Side/B Side)	Yr	NM
❑ 10001	Just Ain't Good Enough	1982	12.00

COLUMBIA

Number	Title (A Side/B Side)	Yr	NM
❑ PC 33951	Eargasm	1976	12.00
—Originals have no bar code			
❑ PC 33951	Eargasm	1986	8.00
—Budget-line reissue with bar code			
❑ PCQ 33951 [Q]	Eargasm	1976	20.00
❑ PC 34401	Rated Extraordinaire	1977	12.00
❑ PCQ 34401 [Q]	Rated Extraordinaire	1977	20.00
❑ JC 35340	Ever Ready	1978	12.00
❑ JC 36061	She's Killing Me	1979	12.00
❑ JC 36548	A New Day	1980	12.00
❑ JC 37127	The Best of Johnnie Taylor	1981	12.00

ICHIBAN

Number	Title (A Side/B Side)	Yr	NM
❑ ICH-1022	Stuck in the Mud	198?	10.00
❑ ICH-1042	Ugly Man	198?	10.00

MALACO

Number	Title (A Side/B Side)	Yr	NM
❑ MAL-7421	This Is Your Night	198?	10.00
❑ MAL-7431	Wall to Wall	198?	10.00
❑ MAL-7440	Lover Boy	198?	10.00
❑ MAL-7446	In Control	198?	10.00
❑ MAL-7452	Crazy 'Bout You	1989	10.00
❑ MAL-7460	Just Can't Do Right	1991	10.00
❑ MAL-7463	The Best of Johnnie Taylor on Malaco, Vol. 1	1992	10.00

T

Number	Title (A Side/B Side)	Yr	NM
STAX			
❑ ST-715 [M]	Wanted: One Soul Singer	1967	50.00
❑ STS-715 [S]	Wanted: One Soul Singer	1967	60.00
❑ STS-2005	Who's Making Love	1968	40.00
❑ STS-2008	Raw Blues	1969	25.00
❑ STS-2012	Rare Stamps	1969	25.00
❑ STS-2023	The Johnnie Taylor Philosophy Continues	1969	25.00
❑ STS-2030	One Step Beyond	1971	25.00
❑ STS-2032	Johnnie Taylor's Greatest Hits	1970	25.00
❑ STS-3014	Taylored in Silk	1973	20.00
❑ STX-4115	Who's Making Love	198?	10.00
—Reissue of 2005			
❑ STS-5509	Super Taylor	1974	20.00
❑ STS-5521	The Best of Johnnie Taylor	1975	20.00
❑ MPS-8508	Raw Blues	1982	10.00
❑ MPS-8520	Super Hits	1983	10.00
❑ MPS-8537	Taylored in Silk	1987	10.00
—Reissue of 3014			
❑ MPS-8558	Little Bluebird	1988	10.00
❑ 88001 [(2)]	Chronicle	1977	20.00

TAYLOR, KATE

Number	Title (A Side/B Side)	Yr	NM
45s			
COLUMBIA			
❑ 10596	It's In His Kiss (The Shoop Shoop Song)/Jason and Ida	1977	4.00
❑ 10787	It's Growin'/Slow and Steady	1978	4.00
❑ 11017	It's the Same Old Song/Champagne and Wine	1979	4.00
COTILLION			
❑ 44112	Handbags and Gladrags/You Can Close Your Eyes	1971	5.00
❑ 44124	Lo and Behold-Jesus Is Just Alright/Home Again	1971	5.00
Albums			
COLUMBIA			
❑ JC 35089	Kate Taylor	1978	10.00
❑ JC 36034	It's In There and It's Got to Come Out	1979	10.00
COTILLION			
❑ SD 9045	Sister Kate	1971	10.00

TAYLOR, KATHY

Number	Title (A Side/B Side)	Yr	NM
45s			
HIT			
❑ 55	The End of the World/Our Day Will Come	1963	8.00
—B-side by Clara and the Cleftones			
❑ 86	I Can't Stay Mad at You/Wonderful! Wonderful!	1963	8.00
—B-side by Wayne Harris			

TAYLOR, KINGSIZE, AND THE DOMINOES

Number	Title (A Side/B Side)	Yr	NM
Albums			
MIDNIGHT			
❑ HLP-2101 [M]	Real Gonk Man	1965	50.00
❑ HST-2101 [S]	Real Gonk Man	1965	100.00

TAYLOR, KOKO

Number	Title (A Side/B Side)	Yr	NM
45s			
CHECKER			
❑ 1092	I Got What It Takes/What Kind of Man Is This	1964	15.00
❑ 1106	Don't Mess with the Messer/Whatever I Am You Made Me	1965	15.00
❑ 1135	Wang Dang Doodle/Blues Heaven	1966	15.00
❑ 1140	Good Advice/When I Think of My Baby	1966	15.00
❑ 1148	Good Advice/Tell Me the Truth	1966	15.00
❑ 1166	Just Love Me/Egg on the Run	1967	15.00
❑ 1174	(I Got) All You Need/All Money Spent (On Feeling Good)	1967	15.00
❑ 1191	Fire/Insane Asylum	1968	15.00
❑ 1230	Separate or Integrate/I Don't Care	1968	15.00
U.S.A.			
❑ 745	Like Heaven to Me/Honky Tonky	1963	25.00
YAMBO			
❑ 107/108	A Mighty Love/Instant Everything	197?	20.00
Albums			
ALLIGATOR			
❑ AL 4711	The Earthshaker	1978	12.00
❑ AL 4724	From the Heart of a Woman	1981	10.00
❑ AL 4740	Queen of the Blues	1985	10.00
❑ AL 4754	An Audience with the Queen	1987	10.00
❑ AL 4784	Junp for Joy	1990	15.00
CHESS			
❑ CH-9263	Koko Taylor	1987	12.00
—Reissue of 1532			

TAYLOR, LEROY

Number	Title (A Side/B Side)	Yr	NM
45s			
BRUNSWICK			
❑ 55345	Oh Linda/Nobody Can Love You	1967	60.00
COLPIX			
❑ 739	Dr. Fix-It/Time (Brings About a Change)	1964	25.00
COLUMBIA			
❑ 4-42258	Dooley Walk/Hey, I Like It	1962	20.00
SHRINE			
❑ 0101	Takin' My Time/I'll Understand	1965	300.00
—As "Leroy Taylor and the Four Kays"			

TAYLOR, LITTLE JOHNNY

Number	Title (A Side/B Side)	Yr	NM
45s			
GALAXY			
❑ 718	You'll Need Another Favor/What You Need Is a Ball	1963	12.00
❑ 722	Part Time Love/Somewhere Down the Line	1963	20.00
❑ 725	Since I Found a New Love/My Heart Is Filled with Pain	1963	12.00
❑ 729	First Class Love/If You Love Me	1964	10.00
❑ 731	You Win, I Lose/Nightingale Melody	1964	10.00
❑ 733	True Love/I Smell Trouble	1964	10.00
❑ 735	For Your Precious Love/I've Never Had a Woman Like You Before	1965	8.00
❑ 736	Help Yourself/Somebody's Got to Pay	1965	8.00
❑ 739	One More Chance/Looking at the Future	1965	8.00
❑ 743	Please Come Home For Christmas/Miracle Maker	1965	8.00
❑ 745	My Love Is Real/All I Want Is You	1966	8.00
❑ 748	Zig Zag Lightning/The Things I Used to Do	1966	8.00
❑ 752	I Know You Hear Me Calling/Big Blue Diamonds	1967	8.00
❑ 756	Driving Wheel/Darling Believe in Me	1967	8.00
❑ 764	Double or Nothing/Sometimey Woman	1968	8.00
ICHIBAN			
❑ 169	Christmas Is Here Again/Ugly Man	1988	6.00
❑ 174	Christmas Is Here Again/I Enjoy You	1989	6.00
RONN			
❑ 43	Make Love to Me Baby/Sweet Soul Woman	1970	6.00
❑ 48	How Can a Broke Man Survive/Make Love to Me Baby	1970	6.00
❑ 51	How Are You Fixed for Love/Keep On Keepin' On	1971	6.00
❑ 55	Everybody Knows About My Good Thing Pt. 1/Pt. 2	1971	6.00
❑ 59	It's My Fault Darling/There Is Something On Your Mind	1972	6.00
❑ 64	Open House at My House (Part 1)/Open House at My House (Part 2)	1972	6.00
❑ 66	As Long As I Don't See You/Strange Bed with a Bad Head	1972	6.00
❑ 69	I'll Make It Worth Your While/You're Not the Only One	1973	6.00
❑ 73	My Special Rose/A Thousand Miles Away	1973	6.00
❑ 78	You're Savin' Your Best Lovin' for Me/What Would I Do Without You	1974	6.00
❑ 83	I Don't Want It All/I Can't See Myself As a One-Woman Man	1974	6.00
❑ 85	Found a New Love/Oh, How I Love My Baby	1975	6.00
❑ 87	True Love/When Are You Coming Home	1975	6.00
❑ 88	A Hard Head Makes a Sore Behind/The Future	1976	6.00
❑ 92	L.J.T./I Should Have Known	197?	6.00
❑ 98	Just One More Chance/New Song	197?	6.00
Albums			
FANTASY			
❑ MPF-4510	Little Johnny Taylor's Greatest Hits	1982	10.00
GALAXY			
❑ 203 [M]	Little Johnny Taylor	1963	100.00
❑ 207 [M]	Little Johnny Taylor's Greatest Hits	1964	100.00
❑ 8203 [S]	Little Johnny Taylor	1963	150.00
❑ 8207 [S]	Little Johnny Taylor's Greatest Hits	1964	150.00
RONN			
❑ LPS-7530	Everybody Knows About My Good Thing	1972	25.00
❑ LSP-7532	Open House at My House	1973	25.00
❑ LSP-7535	L.J.T.	1975	20.00

TAYLOR, LITTLE JOHNNY, AND TED TAYLOR

Number	Title (A Side/B Side)	Yr	NM
45s			
RONN			
❑ 75	Walking the Floor/Cry It Out Baby	1973	6.00
❑ 89	Pretending Love/Funky Ghetto	1976	6.00
Albums			
RONN			
❑ LSP-7533	The Super Taylors	1973	20.00

TAYLOR, LIVINGSTON

Number	Title (A Side/B Side)	Yr	NM
45s			
CAPRICORN			
❑ 0032	Somewhere Over the Rainbow/Lady Tomorrow	1973	4.00
❑ 0045	I Can Dream of You/Loving Be My New Horizon	1974	4.00
❑ 8012	Carolina Day/Sit On Back	1971	5.00
❑ 8025	Get Out of Bed/Mom, Dad	1971	5.00
CRITIQUE			
❑ 99255	City Lights/Louie	1989	3.00
EPIC			
❑ 50604	I Will Be in Love with You/How Much Your Sweet Love Means to Me	1978	4.00
❑ 50667	I'll Come Running/No Thank You Skycap	1979	4.00
❑ 50894	First Time Love/Pajamas	1980	4.00
Albums			
ATCO			
❑ SD 33-334	Livingston Taylor	1970	12.00
CAPRICORN			
❑ CP 0114	Over the Rainbow	1973	10.00
❑ 863	Liv	1971	10.00
EPIC			
❑ JE 36153	Man's Best Friend	1979	10.00

TAYLOR, MAD MAN

Number	Title (A Side/B Side)	Yr	NM
45s			
EASTWEST			
❑ 117	Rumble Tumble/Rock and Roll Espanola	1958	75.00

TAYLOR, R. DEAN

Number	Title (A Side/B Side)	Yr	NM
45s			
AUDIO MASTER			
❑ 1	At the High School Dance/How Wrong Can You Be?	1960	200.00
FARR			
❑ 001	We'll Show Them All/Magdalena	1976	5.00
MALA			
❑ 444	I'll Remember/It's a Long Way to St. Louis	1962	100.00
RARE EARTH			
❑ 5013	Indiana Wants Me/Love's Your Name	1970	6.00
❑ 5023	Ain't It a Sad Thing/Back Street	1970	5.00
❑ 5023 [PS]	Ain't It a Sad Thing/Back Street	1970	10.00
❑ 5026	Gotta See Jane/Back Street	1971	5.00
❑ 5030	Candy Apple Red/Woman Alive	1971	5.00
❑ 5041	Taos New Mexico/Shadow	1972	5.00
STRUMMER			
❑ 3748	Let's Talk It Over/(B-side unknown)	1982	6.00
20TH CENTURY			
❑ 2510	Let's Talk It Over/Add Up the Score	1981	4.00
V.I.P.			
❑ 25042	Don't Fool Around/There's a Ghost in My House	1966	25.00
❑ 25045	Gotta See Jane/Don't Fool Around	1967	25.00
Albums			
RARE EARTH			
❑ RS-522	I Think, Therefore I Am	1971	15.00

TAYLOR, RENEE

Number	Title (A Side/B Side)	Yr	NM
45s			
FELSTED			
❑ 8620	His Pigs/I'm in Love with Jack	1961	12.00

TAYLOR, SHEILA

45s

MELODYLAND

Number	Title (A Side/B Side)	Yr	NM
❑ 6013	How Important Can It Be/ She Satisfies	1975	5.00

TAYLOR, SHERRI

45s

GLORECO

Number	Title (A Side/B Side)	Yr	NM
❑ 1002	I've Got a Crush/ (B-side unknown)	196?	60.00

MOTOWN

Number	Title (A Side/B Side)	Yr	NM
❑ 1004	Lover/That's Why I Love You So Much	1960	40.00

—With Singin' Sammy Ward

TAYLOR, TED

12-Inch Singles

MCA

Number	Title (A Side/B Side)	Yr	NM
❑ L33-1985 [DJ]	Keepin' My Head Above Water (6:58) (3:17)	1978	15.00

T.K. DISCO

Number	Title (A Side/B Side)	Yr	NM
❑ TKD 31	Ghetto Disco (7:03)/(Part 2)	1977	25.00

45s

ALARM

Number	Title (A Side/B Side)	Yr	NM
❑ 110	Everybody's Stealing/Caught Up in a Good Woman's Love	1975	8.00
❑ 112	Steal Away/Somebody's Gettin' It	1976	8.00
❑ 114	Gonna Hate Myself/Stick By Me	1976	8.00
❑ 117	Ghetto Disco/You Can Make It If You Try	1977	8.00
❑ 2119	Paying for My Love Mistakes/ Two Minute Warning	1977	8.00
❑ 2123	Talk to Me/You Made Loving You Easy	1978	8.00
❑ 2124	Spanish Harlem/Paying for My Love Mistakes	1978	8.00

APT

Number	Title (A Side/B Side)	Yr	NM
❑ 25063	Little Things Mean a Lot/ My Days and Nights	1962	25.00

ATCO

Number	Title (A Side/B Side)	Yr	NM
❑ 6388	Dancing Annie/Try Me Again	1965	15.00
❑ 6408	Long Distance Love/ River's Invitation	1966	10.00
❑ 6434	Help the Bear/Thank You for Helping Me See the Light	1966	15.00
❑ 6481	Baby Come Back to Me/ Feed the Flame	1967	15.00

DADE

Number	Title (A Side/B Side)	Yr	NM
❑ 5000	I Lost the Best Thing I Ever Had/ Darling If You Must Leave	1963	40.00

DUKE

Number	Title (A Side/B Side)	Yr	NM
❑ 304	Be Ever Wonderful/ Since You're Home	1959	25.00
❑ 308	Count the Stars/Hold Me Tight	1959	25.00

EBB

Number	Title (A Side/B Side)	Yr	NM
❑ 113	Days Are Dark/Everywhere I Go	1957	30.00
❑ 132	If I Don't See You Again/ Keep Walking On	1958	30.00
❑ 151	Very Truly Yours/Wrapped Up in a Dream	1958	40.00

GOLD EAGLE

Number	Title (A Side/B Side)	Yr	NM
❑ 1805	My Darling/She's a Winner	196?	20.00
❑ 1808	Bandstand Drag/Rockin' Hoss	196?	15.00
—As "Ted Taylor Combo"; these are instrumentals			
❑ 1810	That Happy Day/I Don't Care	196?	20.00
❑ 1812	No Matter What You Do/ Never in My Life	196?	20.00

JEWEL

Number	Title (A Side/B Side)	Yr	NM
❑ 748	Days Are Dark/Very Truly Yours	1965	10.00
❑ 759	You've Been Crying/ Close Your Eyes	1966	10.00
❑ 774	Keep Walking On/ Everywhere I Go	1966	10.00

LAURIE

Number	Title (A Side/B Side)	Yr	NM
❑ 3067	Push Push/A Heart That's True	1960	15.00
—As "Austin Taylor"			
❑ 3076	You've Been Crying/ Little Boy How Old Are You	1960	15.00
❑ 3082	I Don't Want to Love You/ Lovin' Hands	1961	15.00
—As "Austin Taylor"			
❑ 3095	I Love Being Loved by You/ Together Forever	1961	15.00
—As "Austin Taylor"			

MCA

Number	Title (A Side/B Side)	Yr	NM
❑ 40937	Keepin' My Head Above Water/ I Can't Fake It Anymore	1978	10.00
❑ 40977	Chase the World Away/ Double My Money Bag	1978	15.00

OKEH

Number	Title (A Side/B Side)	Yr	NM
❑ 4-7154	Don't Lie/Pretending Love	1962	20.00
❑ 4-7159	You Must Have Been Meant for Me/Time Has a Way	1962	15.00
❑ 4-7165	I'll Release You/ Can't Take No More	1962	15.00
❑ 4-7171	Be Ever Wonderful/ That's Life I Guess	1963	20.00
❑ 4-7176	You Give Me Nothing to Go On/ Him Instead of Me	1963	20.00
❑ 4-7179	It Ain't Like That No More/ I'll Make It Up to You	1963	20.00
❑ 4-7190	So Hard/Need You Home	1964	15.00
❑ 4-7198	Somebody's Always Trying/ Top of the World	1964	60.00
❑ 4-7206	Don't Deceive Me (Please Don't Go)/If It Wasn't for You	1964	20.00
❑ 4-7214	So Long, Bye Bye/ I Love You, Yes I Do	1965	20.00
❑ 4-7222	(Love Is Like a) Ramblin' Rose/ I'm So Satisfied	1965	20.00
❑ 4-7231	Stay Away from My Baby/ Walking Out of Your Life	1965	15.00
❑ 4-7240	Daddy's Baby/Mercy Have Pity	1966	15.00
❑ 4-7252	Big Wheel/No One But You	1966	15.00

RONN

Number	Title (A Side/B Side)	Yr	NM
❑ 15	Miss You So/ I'm Gonna Get Tough	1967	10.00
❑ 21	Ollie Mae/I Need Your Love So Bad	1968	10.00
❑ 25	Honey Lou/Without a Woman	1968	10.00
❑ 29	Strangest Feeling/ You Got to Feel It	1969	10.00
❑ 33	Long Ago/I'm Gonna Send You Back to Oklahoma	1969	10.00
❑ 34	It's Too Late/The Road of Love	1969	10.00
❑ 37	I'm Lonely Tonight/If I Thought You Needed Me	1969	10.00
❑ 40	Loving Physician/I Feel a Chill	1970	10.00
❑ 44	Something Strange Is Goin' On in My House/Funky Thing	1970	10.00
❑ 46	It's a Funky Situation/ I'm Glad You're Home	1970	10.00
❑ 49	Can't Take No More/Singing Man	1971	10.00
❑ 52	How's Your Love Life Baby/ (This Is a) Troubled World	1971	10.00
❑ 57	How Do You Walk Away from Fear/Only the Lonely Knows	1971	10.00
❑ 63	Houston Town/I'm Just a Crumb in Your Breadbox	1972	10.00
❑ 65	I Want to Be Part of You Girl/ Going in the Hole	1972	10.00
❑ 72	What a Fool/Make Up for Lost Time	1973	8.00
❑ 74	Break of Day/ Fair Weather Woman	1973	8.00
❑ 77	She Loves to Do It As Well As You/Ready for the Heartbreak	1974	8.00
❑ 82	For All the Days in My Life/I've Got to Find Somebody New	1974	8.00
❑ 106	Cummin's Prison Farm/ Houston Town	1984	6.00
❑ 112	Be Ever Wonderful/ I Love You Just the Same	198?	6.00
❑ 114	Little Red Rooster/ Stay Away from My Baby	198?	6.00
❑ 116	Steal Away/My Key Jump Back in My Hand	198?	6.00

SOLPUGIDS

Number	Title (A Side/B Side)	Yr	NM
❑ 101	I Let You Hurt Me Too Long/ Pleading for Love	198?	8.00
❑ 102	You're Tippin', She's Rippin'/ Little Red Rooster	198?	8.00

TOP RANK

Number	Title (A Side/B Side)	Yr	NM
❑ 2011	I'm Saving My Love/ Chanta-Lula	1959	25.00
❑ 2048	I Need You So/Has My Love Grown Cold	1960	25.00
❑ 2076	Darling Take Me Back/ Look Out	1960	30.00
❑ 3001	You Know I Do/Someday (I Know, I Know)	1961	30.00

WARWICK

Number	Title (A Side/B Side)	Yr	NM
❑ 628	You Know I Do/Someday (I Know, I Know)	1961	20.00

Albums

ALARM

Number	Title (A Side/B Side)	Yr	NM
❑ 1000	1976	1976	30.00

MCA

Number	Title (A Side/B Side)	Yr	NM
❑ 3059	Keepin' My Head Above Water	1978	12.00

OKEH

Number	Title (A Side/B Side)	Yr	NM
❑ OKM-12104 [M]	Be Ever Wonderful	1963	30.00
❑ OKM-12109 [M]	Blues and Soul	1965	30.00
❑ OKM-12113 [M]	Ted Taylor's Greatest Hits	1966	25.00
❑ OKS-14104 [S]	Be Ever Wonderful	1963	40.00
❑ OKS-14109 [S]	Blues and Soul	1965	40.00
❑ OKS-14113 [S]	Ted Taylor's Greatest Hits	1966	30.00

RONN

Number	Title (A Side/B Side)	Yr	NM
❑ LPS-7528	Shades of Blue	1969	12.00
❑ LPS-7529	You Can Dig It!	197?	12.00
❑ LPS-7531	Taylor Made	1972	12.00
❑ LP-8003	Be Ever Wonderful	198?	10.00
❑ LP-8004	Steal Away	198?	10.00

SOLPUGIDS

Number	Title (A Side/B Side)	Yr	NM
❑ 1001	Be Ever Wonderful	198?	15.00
❑ 1002	Taylor Made for You	198?	15.00

TAYLOR, TRUE

See PAUL SIMON.

TAYLOR, VERNON

45s

DOT

Number	Title (A Side/B Side)	Yr	NM
❑ 15632	I've Got the Blues/ The Losing Game	1957	100.00
❑ 15697	Satisfaction Guaranteed/ Why Must You Leave Me	1958	50.00

SUN

Number	Title (A Side/B Side)	Yr	NM
❑ 310	Breeze/Today Is a Blue Day	1958	25.00
❑ 325	Sweet and Easy to Love/ Mystery Train	1959	35.00

TAYLOR, VINCE

45s

PALETTE

Number	Title (A Side/B Side)	Yr	NM
❑ 5065	I'll Be Your Hero/ Jet Black Machine	1960	12.00
❑ 5084	Move Over Tiger/ What Cha Gonna Do	1961	12.00

TAYLOR, ZOLA

45s

RPM

Number	Title (A Side/B Side)	Yr	NM
❑ 405	Make Love to Me/Oh My Dear	1954	300.00

TAZMEN, THE

45s

ABC-PARAMOUNT

Number	Title (A Side/B Side)	Yr	NM
❑ 9812	Easy Pickin'/The Chicken	1957	15.00

TEA COMPANY, THE

45s

SMASH

Number	Title (A Side/B Side)	Yr	NM
❑ 2176	Come and Have Some Tea with Me/Flowers	1968	15.00

Albums

SMASH

Number	Title (A Side/B Side)	Yr	NM
❑ SRS-67105	Come and Have Some Tea	1968	50.00

TEAM MATES, THE

45s

ABC-PARAMOUNT

Number	Title (A Side/B Side)	Yr	NM
❑ 10760	If Only I Had Known/ You Must Pay	1965	12.00

LE CAM

Number	Title (A Side/B Side)	Yr	NM
❑ 701	I Just Might/Sooner or Later	196?	25.00
❑ 706	If Only I Had Known/ You Must Pay	196?	25.00
❑ 707	Once There Was a Time/ Come On Baby	1962	25.00

PAULA

Number	Title (A Side/B Side)	Yr	NM
❑ 220	Most of All/Please Believe Me	1965	30.00

PHILIPS

Number	Title (A Side/B Side)	Yr	NM
❑ 40029	Once There Was a Time/ Never Believed in Love	1962	12.00

TEARDROP EXPLODES, THE

12-Inch Singles

MERCURY

Number	Title (A Side/B Side)	Yr	NM
❑ 172 [DJ]	When I Dream/Ha Ha I'm Drowning/Reward	1980	20.00

Albums

MERCURY

Number	Title (A Side/B Side)	Yr	NM
❑ SRM-1-4016	Kilimanjaro	1981	12.00
❑ SRM-1-4035	Wilder	1981	12.00

TEARDROPS, THE (1)

45s

DORE

Number	Title (A Side/B Side)	Yr	NM
❑ 679	Little Orphan Boy/ (Instrumental)	1963	12.00

TEARDROPS, THE (2)

45s

DOT

Number	Title (A Side/B Side)	Yr	NM
❑ 15669	Bridge of Love/Jellyfish	1957	25.00

RENDEZVOUS

Number	Title (A Side/B Side)	Yr	NM
102	Catch Me, I'm Falling Again/Sugar Baby	1958	30.00

TEARDROPS, THE (3)

45s

JOSIE

Number	Title (A Side/B Side)	Yr	NM
766	The Stars Are Out Tonight/Oh Stop It	1954	300.00
771	My Heart/Ooh Baby	1954	500.00

PORT

Number	Title (A Side/B Side)	Yr	NM
70019	The Stars Are Out Tonight/Oh Stop It	1960	25.00

TEARDROPS, THE (4)

Even though on the same label as group (3), this is a different group.

45s

JOSIE

Number	Title (A Side/B Side)	Yr	NM
856	We Won't Tell/Al Chiar Di Luna (Porto Fortuna)	1959	25.00
862	Cry No More/You're My Hollywood Star	1959	25.00
873	Daddy's Little Girl/Always You	1960	25.00

TEARDROPS, THE (5)

45s

KING

Number	Title (A Side/B Side)	Yr	NM
5004	My Inspiration/I Prayed for Love	1956	25.00
5037	After School/Don't Be Afraid to Love	1957	25.00

TEARDROPS, THE (6)

Girl group.

45s

MUSICOR

Number	Title (A Side/B Side)	Yr	NM
1139	Tears Come Tumbling/You Won't Be There	1965	15.00
1218	I Will Love You Dear Forever/Bubblegummers	1966	15.00

SAXONY

Number	Title (A Side/B Side)	Yr	NM
1007	Tonight I'm Gonna Fall in Love Again/That's Why I'll Get By	1964	80.00
1008	I'm Gonna Steal Your Boyfriend/Call Me and I'll Be Happy	1965	25.00
1009	Tears Come Tumbling/You Won't Be There	1965	20.00

TEARDROPS, THE (7)

45s

SAMPSON

Number	Title (A Side/B Side)	Yr	NM
634	Come Back to Me/Sweet Lovin' Daddy-O	1952	400.00

TEARDROPS, THE (U)

Albums

20TH CENTURY FOX

Number	Title (A Side/B Side)	Yr	NM
FXG-5011 [M]	The Teardrops at Trinchi's	1963	25.00

TEARS FOR FEARS

12-Inch Singles

FONTANA

Number	Title (A Side/B Side)	Yr	NM
874711-1	Sowing the Seeds of Love (Full Version 6:50)/Tears Roll Down (3:14)/Shout (US Remix 8:00)	1989	12.00
876249-1	Woman in Chains (5:29) (Instrumental 5;00)/My Life in the Suicide Ranks (4:35)/Always in the Past (4:31)	1990	12.00
876897-1	Advice for the Young at Heart (4:49)/Johnny Panic and the Bible of Dreams (4:17)/Music for Tables (3:33)	1990	12.00

MERCURY

Number	Title (A Side/B Side)	Yr	NM
PRO 363-1 [DJ]	Shout (Edit)/Shout (LP version)	1985	12.00
PRO 393-1 [DJ]	Head Over Heels (Live)/Broken-Head-Broken (Live)	1985	15.00
234 [DJ]	Pale Shelter (same on both sides)	1983	8.00
PRO 234-1 [DJ]	Pale Shelter (same on both sides)	1983	12.00
238 [DJ]	Mad World (same on both sides)	1983	12.00
MK 238 [DJ]	Mad World (3:32) (same on both sides)	1983	12.00
MK 245 [DJ]	Change (Special Club Mix) (Special AOR Mix)	1983	25.00
PRO 340-1 [DJ]	Everybody Wants to Rule the World (same on both sides)	1985	15.00
PRO 363-1 [DJ]	Shout (Edit 4:24) (Album Version Edit 5:58)	1985	12.00
PRO 366-1 [DJ]	Shout (US Remix 8:00) (Dub 6:49) (Acapella 5:49)	1985	15.00
374 [DJ]	Head Over Heels (Remix 45 Version)/Broken Head Over Heels Broken	1985	8.00
PRO 374-1 [DJ]	Head Over Heels (Remix 45 Version 4:15)/Broken/Head Over Heels/Broken (7:10)	1985	12.00
PRO 393-1 [DJ]	Head Over Heels (Live 4:15)//Broken/Head Over Heels/Broken (Live 7:36)	1985	15.00
410 [DJ]	Mothers Talk (same on both sides)	1986	6.00
PRO 410-1 [DJ]	Mothers Talk (4:14) (same on both sides)	1986	8.00
880659-1	Everybody Wants to Rule the World (Extended Version 5:40) (LP Version 4:10)/Pharaohs	1985	10.00
880899-1	Head Over Heels (Preacher Mix 8:04) (Remix 4:14)/When in Love with a Blind Man (2:22)	1985	10.00
880929-1	Shout (US Remix 8:00) (UK Remix 7:40)/The Big Chair (3:20)	1985	10.00
884638-1	Mothers Talk (Beat of the Drum Mix 8:54) (Long Version 6:18) (LP Version 4:14)	1986	10.00

45s

FONTANA

Number	Title (A Side/B Side)	Yr	NM
874710-7	Sowing the Seeds of Love/Tears Roll Down	1989	3.00
874710-7 [PS]	Sowing the Seeds of Love/Tears Roll Down	1989	3.00
876248-7	Woman in Chains/Always in the Past	1990	3.00
876248-7 [PS]	Woman in Chains/Always in the Past	1990	3.00

MERCURY

Number	Title (A Side/B Side)	Yr	NM
-7 [DJ]	Head Over Heels (Live) (same on both sides)	1985	10.00
PRO 342-7 DJ [DJ]	Everybody Wants to Rule the World (same on both sides)	1985	10.00
PRO 392-7 DJ [DJ]	Head Over Heels (Live) (same on both sides)	1985	10.00
812213-7	Mad World/Ideas As Opiates	1983	8.00
812213-7 [PS]	Mad World/Ideas As Opiates	1983	8.00
812677-7	Change/The Conflict	1983	8.00
862240-7	Break It Down Again/Bloodletting Go	1993	5.00
862804-7	Goodnight Song/New Star	1993	5.00
880294-7	Shout/The Big Chair	1985	3.00
880294-7 [PS]	Shout/The Big Chair	1985	4.00
880659-7	Everybody Wants to Rule the World/Pharaohs	1985	3.00
880899-7	Head Over Heels/When in Love with a Blind Man	1985	3.00
880899-7 [PS]	Head Over Heels/When in Love with a Blind Man	1985	3.00
884636-7	Mothers Talk/Sea Song	1986	3.00
884636-7 [PS]	Mothers Talk/Sea Song	1986	3.00

Albums

FONTANA

Number	Title (A Side/B Side)	Yr	NM
R 133653	The Seeds of Love	1989	12.00
—BMG Direct Marketing edition			
838730-1	The Seeds of Love	1989	10.00

MERCURY

Number	Title (A Side/B Side)	Yr	NM
R 143666	Songs from the Big Chair	1985	12.00
—BMG Direct Marketing edition			
811039-1	The Hurting	1983	10.00
—Photo of group next to duck pond on cover (reissue)			
811039-1	The Hurting	1983	15.00
—Child on cover (original)			
824300-1	Songs from the Big Chair	1985	10.00

TEASERS, THE

45s

CHECKER

Number	Title (A Side/B Side)	Yr	NM
800	I Was a Fool to Love You/How Could You Hurt One So	1954	600.00
800	I Was a Fool to Love You/How Could You Hurt One So	1954	1200.
—Red vinyl			

TECHNICS, THE

45s

CHEX

Number	Title (A Side/B Side)	Yr	NM
1010	Has He Told You/Workout With a Pretty Girl	1963	30.00
—As "Tony and the Technics"			
1012	Because I Really Love You/A Man's Confusion	1963	30.00
1013	Hey Girl Don't Leave Me/I Met Her on the First of September	1963	40.00

TECHNIQUES, THE (1)

45s

ROULETTE

Number	Title (A Side/B Side)	Yr	NM
4030	Hey! Little Girl/In a Round-About Way	1957	25.00
4048	(Why Did I Ever) Let Her Go/Marindy	1958	25.00
4097	The Wisest Man You Know/Moon Tan	1958	25.00

STARS

Number	Title (A Side/B Side)	Yr	NM
551	Hey Little Girl/In a Round-About Way	1957	40.00

TECHNIQUES, THE (2)

Unrelated to the above, this group evidently is from the Lubbock, Texas area.

45s

VENUS

Number	Title (A Side/B Side)	Yr	NM
RK4M-8540/1	Dream Theme/Autumn Rain	1964	20.00

TECHNOTRONIC

12-Inch Singles

SBK

Number	Title (A Side/B Side)	Yr	NM
SPRO-05470 [DJ]	Move This (LP Version)/Pump Up the Jam (Terry Dome Mix)	1992	10.00
V-19701	Pump Up the Jam (Vocal Attack 5:00) (Jam Edit Mix 5:00) (Original Mix 5:00) (7" Version 3:36)	1989	10.00
—As "Technotronic featuring Felly"			
V-19704	Get Up (Before the Night Is Over) (Def Mix 8:12) (Album Version 4:47) (7" Edit 3:30) (Far East Mix 5:58)/Pump Up the Jam (Techno Mix 4:48)	1990	8.00
V-19709	This Beat Is Technotronic (Get On It Club Mix) (Radio Edit) (7" Mix) (This Dub Is Technotronic)/Pump Up the Jam (Punami Mix)/Tough	1990	8.00
V-19723	Techno Medley (Pettibone Mix 8:30) (Pettibone Instrumental 7:20)/Rockin' Over the Beat (Hacienda Mix 7:05)	1990	7.00
Y-19765	Move This (LP Version)/Pump Up the Jam (Terry Dome Mix)	1992	8.00
VV-58359 [(2)]	Move It to the Rhythm (Club Mix 6:02) (Tronic Groove 8:11) (MCT 12" Mix 8:11) (Massive Remix 5:26) (Technophobic Dub) (Koen's Dub Remix) (Harvard Dub) (Dangerous Remix) (Trope Remix)	1995	15.00
—As "Technotronic featuring Ya Kid K"; two-record version			
Y-58359	Move It to the Rhythm (Club Mix 6:02) (Tronic Groove 8:11) (MCT 12" Mix 8:11) (Massive Remix 5:26)	1995	8.00
—As "Technotronic featuring Ya Kid K"; one-record version			

45s

SBK

Number	Title (A Side/B Side)	Yr	NM
B-07311	Pump Up the Jam/(Instrumental)	1989	10.00
—As "Technotronic featuring Felly"			
B-07311 [PS]	Pump Up the Jam/(Instrumental)	1989	15.00
—Both the record and sleeve received limited distribution			
B-07315	Get Up (Before the Night Is Over)/Raw	1990	4.00
S7-17320	Rockin' Over the Beat/Tarzan Boy	1993	5.00
—B-side by Baltimora; green vinyl			
S7-18481	Move It to the Rhythm/Recall	1995	5.00
—As "Technotronic featuring Ya Kid K"			
S7-57878	Move This/Pump Up the Jam	1992	5.00

Albums

SBK

Number	Title (A Side/B Side)	Yr	NM
K1-93422	Pump Up the Jam — The Album	1989	20.00
K1-95028	Trip On This — The Remixes	1990	20.00

TEDDY AND HIS PATCHES

45s

CHANCE

Number	Title (A Side/B Side)	Yr	NM
100	Suzy Creamcheese/From Day to Day	1967	150.00
668	Suzy Creamcheese/It Ain't Nothin'	1967	150.00
669	Haight Ashbury/It Ain't Nothin'	1967	100.00

TEDDY AND THE CONTINENTALS

45s

PIK

Number	Title (A Side/B Side)	Yr	NM
235	Tick Tick Tock/Everybody Pony	1961	25.00

RAGO

Number	Title (A Side/B Side)	Yr	NM
201	Tick Tick Tock/Wild Christening Party	1962	25.00
—B-side by the Teen Kings			

RICHIE

Number	Title (A Side/B Side)	Yr	NM
445	Do You/Tighten Up	1961	40.00
—With Roulette Records distribution mentioned on label			

Except when noted otherwise, VG = 25% of NM, and VG+ = 50% of NM. (Example: VG = $2.00, VG+ = $4.00 and NM = $8.00.)

Number	Title (A Side/B Side)	Yr	NM
❑ 445	Do You/Tighten Up	1961	100.00
—With no mention of Roulette distribution on label			
❑ 453	Crying Over You/ Crossfire With Me Baby	1963	50.00
❑ 1001	Tick Tick Tock/Everybody Pony	1961	60.00

TEDDY AND THE TWILIGHTS

Number	Title (A Side/B Side)	Yr	NM
45s			
SWAN			
❑ 4102	Woman Is a Man's Best Friend/ Goodbye to Love	1962	25.00
❑ 4115	You Gotta Be Alone to Cry/ Running Around	1962	20.00
❑ 4126	I'm Just Your Clown/ Bimini Bimbo	1962	20.00

TEDDY BEARS, THE

With PHIL SPECTOR and Annette Kleinbard (a.k.a. Carol Connors).

Number	Title (A Side/B Side)	Yr	NM
45s			
DORE			
❑ 503	To Know Him, Is to Love Him/ Don't You Worry My Little Pet	1958	30.00
❑ 520	Wonderful Loveable You/Till You'll Be Mine	1959	20.00
IMPERIAL			
❑ 5562	Oh Why/I Don't Need You Anymore	1959	30.00
❑ 5581	You Said Goodbye/ If You Only Knew	1959	30.00
❑ 5594	Seven Lonely Days/ Don't Go Away	1959	30.00
Albums			
IMPERIAL			
❑ LP-9067 [M]	The Teddy Bears Sing!	1959	300.00
❑ LP-12010 [S]	The Teddy Bears Sing!	1959	1200.

TEDDY BOYS, THE

Number	Title (A Side/B Side)	Yr	NM
45s			
CAMEO			
❑ 433	Where Have All the Good Times Gone/La La	1966	20.00
❑ 448	Mona/Good Morning Blues	1966	20.00
MGM			
❑ 13515	Jezebel/It's You	1966	20.00

TEE, WILLIE

Number	Title (A Side/B Side)	Yr	NM
45s			
A.F.O.			
❑ 307	All for One/Always Accused	1962	15.00
❑ 311	Why Lie/I Found Out You Are My Cousin	1963	15.00
ATLANTIC			
❑ 2273	Teasin' You/Walkin' Up a One-Way Street	1965	10.00
❑ 2287	Thank You John/ Dedicated to You	1965	10.00
❑ 2302	I Want Somebody/ You Better Say Yes	1965	10.00
CAPITOL			
❑ 2369	Walk Tall (Baby, That's What I Need)/I'm Only a Man	1968	8.00
❑ 2892	Reach Out for Me/The Love of a Married Man	1970	8.00
CINDERELLA			
❑ 1202	Foolish Girl/(B-side unknown)	196?	40.00
GATOR			
❑ 701	She Really Did Surprise Me/ (B-side unknown)	196?	30.00
HOT LINE			
❑ 910	Close Your Eyes/I Heard Everything You Said	196?	8.00
NOLA			
❑ 708	Teasin' You/Walkin' Up a One-Way Street	1964	250.00
UNITED ARTISTS			
❑ XW910	I'd Give It to You/Look Out World	1976	5.00
Albums			
CAPITOL			
❑ ST-199	I'm Only a Man	1969	15.00
UNITED ARTISTS			
❑ UA-LA655-G	Anticipation	1976	12.00

TEE SET, THE

Number	Title (A Side/B Side)	Yr	NM
45s			
COLOSSUS			
❑ 107	Ma Belle Amie/Angels Coming in the Holy Night	1969	7.00
❑ 107 [PS]	Ma Belle Amie/Angels Coming in the Holy Night	1969	8.00
❑ 114	If You Do Believe in Love/ Charmaine	1970	6.00
❑ 139	She Likes Weeds/A Country Ride	1971	6.00
Albums			
COLOSSUS			
❑ CCS-1001	Ma Belle Amie	1970	15.00

TEEGARDEN AND VAN WINKLE

Number	Title (A Side/B Side)	Yr	NM
45s			
PLUMM			
❑ 68102	God, Love, and Rock & Roll (We Believe)/Work Me Tomorrow	1970	15.00
WESTBOUND			
❑ 170	God, Love and Rock & Roll/ Work Me Tomorrow	1970	5.00
❑ 170 [PS]	God, Love and Rock & Roll/ Work Me Tomorrow	1970	6.00
❑ 171	Everything Is Going to Be All Right/You Do	1970	5.00
❑ 187	Stoned on the Love for Jesus/ I Need You	1971	5.00
❑ 200	Passing Gas/Ride Away with Me	1971	5.00
❑ 210	Carry On/Ride Away with Me	1972	5.00
Albums			
ATCO			
❑ 33-272 [M]	An Evening at Home with Teegarden and Van Winkle	1968	40.00
—Mono is white label promo only			
❑ SD 33-272 [S]	An Evening at Home with Teegarden and Van Winkle	1968	15.00
WESTBOUND			
❑ 2003	But Anyhow	1969	15.00
❑ 2010	On Our Way	1971	15.00

TEEMATES, THE

Number	Title (A Side/B Side)	Yr	NM
45s			
AUDIO FIDELITY			
❑ 104	Dream On Little Girl/Moving Out	1964	15.00
❑ 105	Night Fall/No More Tomorrows	1964	15.00
Albums			
AUDIO FIDELITY			
❑ AFLP-3042 [M]	Jet Set Dance Discotheque	1964	40.00
❑ AFSD-7042 [S]	Jet Set Dance Discotheque	1964	50.00

TEEN ANGELS, THE

Number	Title (A Side/B Side)	Yr	NM
45s			
SUN			
❑ 388	Ain't Gonna Let You (Break My Heart)/Tell Me My Love	1964	30.00

TEEN CLEFS, THE

Number	Title (A Side/B Side)	Yr	NM
45s			
DICE			
❑ 98/99	Sputnik/Hiding My Tears with a Smile	1959	150.00

TEEN KINGS, THE

See ROY ORBISON.

TEEN-KINGS, THE

Number	Title (A Side/B Side)	Yr	NM
45s			
BEE			
❑ 1114/5	That's a Teen-Age Love/ Tell Me If You Know	1959	1500.
—Legitimate original copies are on black vinyl			
WILLETT			
❑ 118	Don't Just Stand There/ My Greatest Wish	1959	250.00

TEEN QUEENS, THE

Number	Title (A Side/B Side)	Yr	NM
45s			
ANTLER			
❑ 4014	There's Nothing on My Mind (Part 1)/There's Nothing on My Mind (Part 2)	1959	15.00
❑ 4015	Politician/I'm a Fool	1959	15.00
❑ 4016	Donny (Part 1)/Donny (Part 2)	1960	15.00
❑ 4017	I Hear Violins/Magoo Can See	1960	15.00
KENT			
❑ 359	Eddie My Love/Just Goofed	1961	12.00
RCA VICTOR			
❑ 47-7206	Dear Tommy/You Good Boy-You Get Cookie	1958	16.00
❑ 47-7396	Movie Star/First Crush	1958	16.00
RPM			
❑ 453	Eddie My Love/Just Goofed	1956	30.00
—Black label			
❑ 453	Eddie My Love/Just Goofed	1956	120.00
—Red label			
❑ 460	So All Alone/Baby Mine	1956	25.00
❑ 464	Billy Boy/Until the Day I Die	1956	25.00
❑ 470	Red Top/Love Sweet Love	1956	25.00
❑ 480	My First Love/(B-side unknown)	1956	25.00
❑ 484	Rock Everybody/ My Heart's Desire	1957	20.00
❑ 500	I Miss You/Two Loves and Two Lives	1957	20.00
Albums			
CROWN			
❑ CST-373 [R]	The Teen Queens	1963	30.00
❑ CLP-5022 [M]	Eddie My Love	1956	250.00
—Black label, all silver print			
❑ CLP-5022 [M]	Eddie My Love	196?	100.00
—Black label, "CROWN" in alternating colored letters			
❑ CLP-5373 [M]	The Teen Queens	1963	50.00
RPM			
❑ LRP-3007 [M]	Eddie My Love	1956	—
—Canceled			

TEEN TONES, THE

More than one group. Some may be listed as "Teen-Tones."

Number	Title (A Side/B Side)	Yr	NM
45s			
DANDY DAN			
❑ 2	Darling I Love You/My Sweet	1958	80.00
DECCA			
❑ 30895	Don't Call Me Baby, I'll Call You/ Yes You May	1959	30.00
GONE			
❑ 5061	The Rockin' Rumble/ Latino Part 2	1959	30.00
SWAN			
❑ 4040	My Little Baby/Head Strong Baby	1959	30.00
TRI-DISC			
❑ 102	I'm So Happy/Shoutin' Twist	1961	15.00
WYNNE			
❑ 107	Faded Love/Gypsy Boogie	1958	25.00

TEENAGE JESUS AND THE JERKS

Number	Title (A Side/B Side)	Yr	NM
45s			
MIGRAINE/LUST UNLUST			
❑ CC-333	Orphans/Less of Me	1978	12.50
❑ CC-333 [PS]	Orphans/Less of Me	1978	12.50
❑ CC-334	Baby Doll/Freud in Flop/ Race Mixing	1979	12.50
❑ CC-334 [PS]	Baby Doll/Freud in Flop/ Race Mixing	1979	12.50
Albums			
MIGRANE/LUST UNLUST			
❑ CC-336 [EP]	Teenage Jesus and the Jerks	1979	30.00
—Black vinyl			
❑ CC-336 [EP]	Teenage Jesus and the Jerks	1979	40.00
—Pink vinyl			

TEENAGE MOONLIGHTERS

Number	Title (A Side/B Side)	Yr	NM
45s			
MARK			
❑ 134	Sorry Sorry/I Want to Cry	1960	2000.
—VG 1000; VG+ 1500			

TEENAGERS, THE

These are records by the original group without FRANKIE LYMON. Also see FRANKIE LYMON AND THE TEENAGERS.

Number	Title (A Side/B Side)	Yr	NM
45s			
END			
❑ 1071	Crying/Tonight's the Night	1960	60.00
❑ 1076	Can You Tell Me/ A Little Wiser Now	1960	40.00
GEE			
❑ 1046	Flip Flop/Everything to Me	1957	30.00
ROULETTE			
❑ 4086	My Broken Heart/ Momma Wanna Rock	1958	80.00

TEENBEATS, THE

Number	Title (A Side/B Side)	Yr	NM
45s			
TEENBEAT			
❑ (No #)	Surfbound/Mr. Moto	1963	80.00

TEENETTES, THE

Number	Title (A Side/B Side)	Yr	NM
45s			
BRUNSWICK			
❑ 55125	I Want a Boy with a Hi-Fi Supersonic Stereophonic Bloop Bleep/From the Word Go	1959	25.00
JOSIE			
❑ 830	My Lucky Star/Too Young to Fall in Love	1958	60.00

TELSTARS, THE

Number	Title (A Side/B Side)	Yr	NM
45s			
COLUMBIA			
❑ 44141	Keep On Running/Hold Tight	1967	20.00
IMPERIAL			
❑ 5903	Continental Mash/Stomp Happy	1962	25.00

Number	Title (A Side/B Side)	Yr	NM
TEEN			
❑ 510	Continental Mash/Stomp Happy	1962	40.00
❑ 513	Pow Wow/Lovina	1963	35.00
❑ 516	Topless/Spaghetti Strap	1964	35.00
❑ 517	Tough George/ 'Cause I Really Do	1964	35.00

TEMPEST

Albums

Number	Title (A Side/B Side)	Yr	NM
WARNER BROS.			
❑ BS 2682	Tempest	1973	25.00

TEMPLE, BOB

45s

Number	Title (A Side/B Side)	Yr	NM
KING			
❑ 4958	Come Back, Come Back/ Vam Vam Varoose	1956	30.00

TEMPO-TONES, THE

45s

Number	Title (A Side/B Side)	Yr	NM
ACME			
❑ 713	Get Yourself Another Fool/ Ride Along	1957	150.00
❑ 715	In My Dreams/ My Boy Sleep Pete	1957	500.00
❑ 718	Come Into My Heart/Somewhere There Is Sunshine	1957	500.00
❑ 722	The Day I Met You/ Wishing All the Time	1957	400.00

TEMPOS, THE

Probably more than one group.

45s

Number	Title (A Side/B Side)	Yr	NM
ASCOT			
❑ 2167	When You Loved Me/ My Barbara Ann	1965	25.00
❑ 2173	I Wish It Were Summer/ My Barbara Ann	1965	25.00
CANTERBURY			
❑ 504	Here I Come (Countdown) Part 1/ Here I Come (Countdown) Part 2	1967	15.00
CLIMAX			
❑ 102	See You in September/ Bless You My Love	1959	20.00
❑ 105	The Crossroads of Love/ Whatever Happens	1959	20.00
FAIRMOUNT			
❑ 611	Oh Play That Thing/Monkey Doo	1963	12.00
HI-Q			
❑ 100	It's Tough/Sham-Rock	1959	40.00
KAPP			
❑ 178	Kingdom of Love/That's What You Do to Me	1957	25.00
❑ 199	Prettiest Girl in School/ Never You Mind	1957	25.00
❑ 213	I Got a Job/Strollin' with My Baby	1958	25.00
MONTEL			
❑ 955	I Gotta Make a Move/It Was You	1966	15.00
PARIS			
❑ 550	Look Homeward, Angel/ Under Ten Flags	1960	20.00
RHYTHM			
❑ 121	Promise Me/Never Let Me Go	1958	500.00
RILEY'S			
❑ 8781	Don't Leave Me/I Need You	1966	30.00
U.S.A.			
❑ 810	Why Don't You Write Me/ A Thief in the Night	1965	25.00

Albums

Number	Title (A Side/B Side)	Yr	NM
JUSTICE			
❑ JLP-104	Speaking of the Tempos	1966	500.00

TEMPREES

45s

Number	Title (A Side/B Side)	Yr	NM
EPIC			
❑ 50192	I Found Love on a Disco Floor/ There Ain't a Dream Been Dreamed	1976	5.00
WE PRODUCE			
❑ 1801	I'm for You, You for Me/ Rules and Regulations	1971	8.00
❑ 1803	(Girl) I Love You/I Love You, You Love Me	1971	8.00
❑ 1805	My Baby Love/If I Could Say What's On My Mind	1972	8.00
❑ 1807	Explain It to Her Mama/ Love Can Be So Wonderful	1972	8.00
❑ 1808	Dedicated to the One I Love/ I Love You, You Love Me	1972	8.00
❑ 1810	A Thousand Miles Away/ Chalk It Up to Experience	1973	8.00
❑ 1811	Love's Maze/Wrap Me in Love	1973	8.00
❑ 1812	At Last/Love Can Be So Wonderful	1974	7.00
❑ 1813	You Make Me Love You/ You Make the Sunshine	1974	7.00
❑ 1814	Mr. Cool That Ain't Cool/ Lovin' You Is So Easy	1974	7.00
❑ 1815	I Love, I Love/Your Love	1975	7.00
❑ 1816	Come and Get Your Love/ I'll Live Her Life	1975	7.00

Albums

Number	Title (A Side/B Side)	Yr	NM
WE PRODUCE			
❑ 1901	Love Men	1972	60.00
❑ 1903	Love Maze	1973	60.00
❑ 1905	Temprees 3	1974	60.00

TEMPTATIONS, THE

The famous Detroit/Motown male vocal group. Also see EDDIE KENDRICKS; DAVID RUFFIN; THE SUPREMES AND THE TEMPTATIONS.

12-Inch Singles

Number	Title (A Side/B Side)	Yr	NM
GORDY			
❑ PR-68 [DJ]	Power (6:06)/Behind the Groove (6:04)	1980	25.00
—B-side by Teena Marie			
❑ PR-131 [DJ]	Miss Busy Body (Get Your Body Busy) (5:28) (Instrumental Part 2 5:32)	1983	10.00
—No label name mentioned; listed here as the 45 was on Gordy			
❑ PR-163 [DJ]	Treat Her Like a Lady (Club Mix 6:10) (Dub Reprise 3:45)/ Let It All Blow (Club Mix 6:10) (Blowy's Reprise Instrumental 4:48) (Radio Edit of Club Mix 3:40)	1984	30.00
—B-side by Dazz Band; it also may have a "Motown" promo label			
❑ 4550GG	Do You Really Love Your Baby (Club Mix 6:36) (Radio Edit of Club Mix 4:17) (Dub Mix 5:04)/I'll Keep My Light in Your Window	1985	8.00
MOTOWN			
❑ PR-180 [DJ]	A Fine Mess (same on both sides)	1986	8.00
❑ 37463 1025 1 [DJ]	Hoops on Fire (3 versions)	1992	8.00
❑ 1132 [DJ]	Get Ready 1990 (4 versions)	1990	10.00
❑ 1604 [DJ]	The Jones' (4 versions)	1991	10.00
❑ 4590MG	Papa Was a Rollin' Stone (Vocal 8:57) (Instrumental 7:15)	1987	—
—Canceled			
❑ 4598MG	Look What You Started (12-Inch Vocal 7:00) (Radio Edit 4:40)//(12-Inch Piano Dub 7:03) (12-Inch Beat Acapella 4:35)/More Love, Your Love	1987	10.00
❑ MOT-4649	All I Want from You/ (Instrumental)	1989	8.00
❑ MOT-4679	Special/O.A.O. Lover	1989	8.00
❑ MOT-4698	Soul to Soul (unknown versions)	1990	8.00
❑ L33-17880 [DJ]	All I Want from You (Club Mix)/ (Debbie Favorite Mix)	1989	8.00
❑ L33-18149 [DJ]	Soul to Soul (3 versions)	1990	10.00
❑ L33-18206 [DJ]	One Step at a Time (3 versions)	1990	10.00
❑ 20073 [DJ]	I'm Here (Radio Edit) (Instrumental) (LP Version) (Acappella)	2000	15.00
❑ 53954	Get Ready 1990 (4 versions)	1990	10.00

45s

Number	Title (A Side/B Side)	Yr	NM
ATLANTIC			
❑ 3436	In a Lifetime/I Could Never Stop Loving You	1977	4.00
❑ 3461	Think for Yourself/ Let's Live in Place	1978	4.00
❑ 3517	Bare Back/I See My Child	1978	4.00
❑ 3538	Ever Ready Love/ Touch Me Again	1978	4.00
❑ 3567	Mystic Woman/I Just Don't Know How to Let You Go	1979	4.00
GORDY			
❑ 1616	Standing on the Top-Part 1/Part 2	1982	4.00
—With Rick James			
❑ 1631	More on the Inside/ Money's Hard to Get	1982	4.00
❑ 1654	Silent Night/Everything for Christmas	1982	6.00
❑ 1666	Love on My Mind Tonight/Bring Your Body Here	1983	4.00
❑ 1683	Made in America/Surface Thrills	1983	4.00
❑ 1707	Miss Busy Body (Get Your Body Busy)/(Instrumental)	1983	4.00
❑ 1713	Silent Night/Everything for Christmas	1983	5.00
❑ 1720	Sail Away/Isn't the Night Fantastic	1984	4.00
❑ 1765	Treat Her Like a Lady/ Isn't the Night Fantastic	1984	4.00
❑ 1781	My Love Is True (Truly for You)/ Set Your Love Right	1985	4.00
❑ 1789	How Can You Say That It's Over/I'll Keep My Light in My Window	1985	4.00
❑ 1818	Do You Really Love Your Baby/ I'll Keep My Light in My Window	1985	4.00
❑ 1834	Touch Me/Set Your Love Right	1986	4.00
❑ 1856	Lady Soul/Put Us Together Again	1986	4.00
❑ 1871	To Be Continued/You're the One	1986	4.00
❑ 1871 [PS]	To Be Continued/You're the One	1986	6.00
❑ 1881	Someone/Love Me Right	1987	4.00
❑ 7001	Dream Come True/ Isn't She Pretty	1962	40.00
❑ 7010	Paradise/Slow Down Heart	1962	30.00
❑ 7015	I Want a Love I Can See/ The Further You Look, The Less You See	1963	25.00
❑ 7020	May I Have This Dance?/ Farewell, My Love	1963	25.00
❑ 7028	The Way You Do the Things You Do/Just Let Me Know	1964	15.00
❑ 7032	I'll Be in Trouble/The Girl's Alright with Me	1964	15.00
❑ 7035	Girl (Why You Wanna Make Me Blue)/Baby, Baby I Need You	1964	15.00
❑ 7038	My Girl/Nobody But My Baby	1965	15.00
❑ 7038 [PS]	My Girl/Nobody But My Baby	1965	120.00
❑ 7040	It's Growing/What Love Has Joined Together	1965	15.00
❑ 7043	Since I Lost My Baby/ You've Got to Earn It	1965	15.00
❑ 7047	My Baby/Don't Look Back	1965	15.00
❑ 7049	Get Ready/Fading Away	1966	15.00
❑ 7054	Ain't Too Proud to Beg/ You'll Lose a Precious Love	1966	15.00
❑ 7055	Beauty Is Only Skin Deep/ You're Not an Ordinary Girl	1966	15.00
❑ 7055 [PS]	Beauty Is Only Skin Deep/ You're Not an Ordinary Girl	1966	40.00
❑ 7057	(I Know) I'm Losing You/I Couldn't Cry If I Wanted To	1966	15.00
❑ 7061	All I Need/Sorry Is a Sorry Word	1967	10.00
❑ 7063	You're My Everything/ I've Been Good to You	1967	10.00
—"Gordy" on left			
❑ 7063	You're My Everything/I've Been Good to You	1967	15.00
—"Gordy" on top			
❑ 7065	(Loneliness Made Me Realize) It's You That I Need/Don't Send Me Away	1967	10.00
❑ 7068	I Wish It Would Rain/I Truly, Truly Believe	1967	10.00
❑ 7072	I Could Never Love Another (After Loving You)/Gonna Give Her All the Love I've Got	1968	10.00
❑ 7074	Please Return Your Love to Me/ How Can I Forget	1968	10.00
❑ 7081	Cloud Nine/Why Did She Have to Leave Me	1968	8.00
❑ 7082	Silent Night/Rudolph, the Red-Nosed Reindeer	1968	12.00
❑ 7084	Run Away Child, Running Wild/ I Need Your Love	1969	8.00
❑ 7086	Don't Let the Joneses Get You Down/Since I've Lost You	1969	8.00
❑ 7093	I Can't Get Next to You/ Running Away (Ain't Gonna Help You)	1969	8.00
❑ 7096	Psychedelic Shack/ That's the Way Love Is	1970	6.00
❑ 7099	Ball of Confusion (That's What the World Is Today)/ It's Summer	1970	6.00
❑ 7099 [PS]	Ball of Confusion (That's What the World Is Today)/ It's Summer	1970	20.00
❑ 7102	Ungena Za Ulimwengu (Unite the World)/ Hum Along and Dance	1970	6.00
❑ 7105	Just My Imagination (Running Away with Me)/You Make Your Own Heaven and Hell Right Here on Earth	1971	6.00
❑ 7109	It's Summer/I'm the Exception to the Rule	1971	6.00
❑ 7111	Superstar (Remember How You Got Where You Are)/ Gonna Keep On Tryin' Till I Win Your Love	1971	6.00
❑ 7115	Take a Look Around/Smooth Sailing (From Now On)	1972	6.00
❑ 7119	Mother Nature/Funky Music Sho Nuff Turns Me On	1972	6.00
❑ 7121	Papa Was a Rollin' Stone/ (Instrumental)	1972	6.00
❑ 7126	Masterpiece/(Instrumental)	1973	6.00
❑ 7129	Plastic Man/Hurry Tomorrow	1973	6.00

Except when noted otherwise, VG = 25% of NM, and VG+ = 50% of NM. (Example: VG = $2.00, VG+ = $4.00 and NM = $8.00.)

Number	Title (A Side/B Side)	Yr	NM
❑ 7131	Hey Girl (I Like Your Style)/Ma	1973	6.00
❑ 7133	Let Your Hair Down/ Ain't No Justice	1973	6.00
❑ 7135	Heavenly/Zoom	1974	6.00
❑ 7136	You've Got My Soul on Fire/ I Need You	1974	6.00
❑ 7138	Happy People/(Instrumental)	1974	6.00
❑ 7142	Shakey Ground/I'm a Bachelor	1975	6.00
❑ 7144	Glasshouse/The Prophet	1975	6.00
❑ 7146	Keep Holding On/What You Need Most (I Do Best of All)	1975	6.00
❑ 7150	Up the Creek (Without a Paddle)/Darling Stand By Me (Song for a Woman)	1976	6.00
❑ 7151	Who Are You (And What Are You Doing the Rest of Your Life)/Darling Stand By Me (Song for a Woman)	1976	—
—Unreleased			
❑ 7152	Let Me Count the Ways (I Love You)/Who Are You (And What Are You Doing the Rest of Your Life)	1976	6.00
❑ 7183	Power/Power (Part 2)	1980	4.00
❑ 7183 [DJ]	Power (same on both sides)	1980	20.00
—Promo only on red vinyl			
❑ 7188	Struck by Lightning Twice/ I'm Coming Home	1980	4.00
❑ 7208	Aiming at Your Heart/ Life of a Cowboy	1981	40.00
❑ 7213	Oh What a Night/Isn't the Night Fantastic	1981	4.00

MIRACLE

Number	Title (A Side/B Side)	Yr	NM
❑ 5	Oh, Mother of Mine/ Romance Without Finance	1961	100.00
❑ 12	Check Yourself/Your Wonderful Love	1961	100.00

MOTOWN

Number	Title (A Side/B Side)	Yr	NM
❑ 903	One Step at a Time/ (Instrumental)	1990	4.00
❑ 1501	Take Me Away/There's More Where That Came From	1980	4.00
❑ 1837	A Fine Mess/Wishful Thinking	1986	4.00
❑ 1837 [PS]	A Fine Mess/Wishful Thinking	1986	6.00
❑ 1908	I Wonder Who She's Seeing Now/Girls (They Like It)	1987	3.00
❑ 1908 [PS]	I Wonder Who She's Seeing Now/Girls (They Like It)	1987	4.00
❑ 1920	Look What You Started/ More Love, Your Love	1987	3.00
❑ 1933	Do You Wanna Go with Me/ Put Your Foot Down	1988	3.00
❑ 1974	All I Want from You/ (Instrumental)	1989	3.00
❑ 2004	Special/O.A.O. Lover	1989	4.00
❑ 2023	Soul to Soul (same on both sides?)	1990	4.00
❑ 860862-7	Stay/My Girl	1998	3.00

MOTOWN YESTERYEAR

Number	Title (A Side/B Side)	Yr	NM
❑ Y-690F	Silent Night/Give Love at Christmas	1985	4.00

TOPPS/MOTOWN

Number	Title (A Side/B Side)	Yr	NM
❑ 4	My Girl	1967	75.00
—Cardboard record			
❑ 13	The Way You Do the Things You Do	1967	75.00
—Cardboard record			

7-Inch Extended Plays

GORDY

Number	Title (A Side/B Side)	Yr	NM
❑ G-60914	My Baby/Since I Lost My Baby/ Girl (Why You Wanna Make Me So Blue)//The Girl's Alright with Me/Just Another Lonely Night/Don't Look Back	1966	50.00
—Stereo jukebox issue; small hole, plays at 33 1/3 rpm			
❑ G-60914 [PS]	The Temptin' Temptations	1966	50.00

Albums

ATLANTIC

Number	Title (A Side/B Side)	Yr	NM
❑ SD 19143	Hear to Tempt You	1977	12.00
❑ SD 19188	Bare Back	1978	12.00

GORDY

Number	Title (A Side/B Side)	Yr	NM
❑ G 911 [M]	Meet the Temptations	1964	30.00
❑ GS 911 [S]	Meet the Temptations	1964	40.00
—Script "Gordy" at top of label			
❑ GS 911 [S]	Meet the Temptations	1967	20.00
—Block "Gordy" inside "G" on left of label			
❑ G 912 [M]	The Temptations Sing Smokey	1965	30.00
❑ GS 912 [S]	The Temptations Sing Smokey	1965	40.00
—Script "Gordy" at top of label			
❑ GS 912 [S]	The Temptations Sing Smokey	1967	20.00
—Block "Gordy" inside "G" on left of label			
❑ G 914 [M]	Temptin' Temptations	1965	25.00
❑ GS 914 [S]	Temptin' Temptations	1965	30.00
—Script "Gordy" at top of label			
❑ GS 914 [S]	Temptin' Temptations	1967	20.00
—Block "Gordy" inside "G" on left of label			

The Temptations, *With a Lot o' Soul*, Gordy GS-922, 1967, stereo, **$20.**

Number	Title (A Side/B Side)	Yr	NM
❑ G 918 [M]	Gettin' Ready	1966	25.00
❑ GS 918 [S]	Gettin' Ready	1966	30.00
—Script "Gordy" at top of label			
❑ GS 918 [S]	Gettin' Ready	1967	20.00
—Block "Gordy" inside "G" on left of label			
❑ G 919 [M]	The Temptations' Greatest Hits	1966	25.00
❑ GS 919 [S]	The Temptations' Greatest Hits	1966	30.00
—Script "Gordy" at top of label			
❑ GS 919 [S]	The Temptations' Greatest Hits	1967	20.00
—Block "Gordy" inside "G" on left of label			
❑ G 921 [M]	Temptations Live!	1967	25.00
❑ GS 921 [S]	Temptations Live!	1967	20.00
—Block "Gordy" inside "G" on left of label			
❑ GS 921 [S]	Temptations Live!	1967	30.00
—Script "Gordy" at top of label			
❑ G 922 [M]	With a Lot o' Soul	1967	25.00
❑ GS 922 [S]	With a Lot o' Soul	1967	20.00
—Block "Gordy" inside "G" on left of label			
❑ GS 922 [S]	With a Lot o' Soul	1967	25.00
—Script "Gordy" at top of label			
❑ G 924 [M]	The Temptations in a Mellow Mood	1967	25.00
❑ GS 924 [S]	The Temptations in a Mellow Mood	1967	25.00
❑ G 927 [M]	The Temptations Wish It Would Rain	1968	40.00
—Mono is white-label promo only			
❑ GS 927 [S]	The Temptations Wish It Would Rain	1968	20.00
❑ GS 933	The Temptations Show	1969	20.00
❑ GS 938	Live at the Copa	1968	20.00
❑ GS 939	Cloud Nine	1969	20.00
❑ GS 947	Psychedelic Shack	1970	20.00
❑ GS 949	Puzzle People	1969	20.00
❑ GS 951	The Temptations' Christmas Card	1969	25.00
❑ GS 953	Live at London's Talk of the Town	1970	20.00
❑ GS 954	Temptations Greatest Hits II	1970	20.00
❑ GS 957	Sky's the Limit	1971	20.00
❑ G 961L	Solid Rock	1972	20.00
❑ G 962L	All Directions	1972	20.00
❑ G 965L	Masterpiece	1973	20.00
❑ G 966V1	1990	1973	15.00
❑ G6-969S1	A Song for You	1975	15.00
❑ G6-971S1	Wings of Love	1976	15.00
❑ G6-973S1	House Party	1975	15.00
❑ G7-975S1	The Temptations Do the Temptations	1976	15.00
❑ G8-994M1	Power	1980	12.00
❑ G8-998M1	Give Love at Christmas	1980	15.00
❑ G8-1006M1	The Temptations	1981	12.00
❑ 6008 GL	Reunion	1982	12.00
❑ 6032 GL	Surface Thrills	1983	12.00
❑ 6085 GL	Back to Basics	1984	12.00
❑ 6119 GL	Truly for You	1984	12.00
❑ 6164 GL	Touch Me	1986	12.00
❑ 6207 GL	To Be Continued	1986	12.00

MOTOWN

Number	Title (A Side/B Side)	Yr	NM
❑ M5-140V1	Meet the Temptations	1981	12.00
—Reissue of Gordy 911			
❑ M5-144V1	Masterpiece	1981	12.00
—Reissue of Gordy 965			
❑ M5-164V1	Psychedelic Shack	1981	12.00
—Reissue of Gordy 947			
❑ M5-172V1	Puzzle People	1981	12.00
—Reissue of Gordy 949			
❑ M5-205V1	The Temptations Sing Smokey	1981	12.00
—Reissue of Gordy 912			
❑ M5-212V1	All the Million Sellers	1982	12.00
❑ M 782 [(3)]	Anthology	1973	25.00
❑ 5251 ML	The Temptations Christmas Card	1982	10.00
—Reissue of Gordy 951			
❑ 5279 ML	Give Love at Christmas	1983	10.00
—Reissue of Gordy 998			
❑ 5389 ML [(2)]	25th Anniversary	1986	15.00
❑ 6246 ML	Together Again	1987	12.00
❑ MOT-6275	Special	1989	12.00

NATURAL RESOURCES

Number	Title (A Side/B Side)	Yr	NM
❑ NR 4005T1	The Temptations in a Mellow Mood	1978	12.00
—Reissue of Gordy 924			

PICKWICK

Number	Title (A Side/B Side)	Yr	NM
❑ SPC-3540	Psychedelic Shack	197?	12.00
—Reissue of Gordy 947			

Ten Years After, *Watt*, Deram XDES-18050, 1970, large "Deram" at top of label, **$15.**

Number	Title (A Side/B Side)	Yr	NM
UNIVERSAL MOTOWN			
❑ 5316011	Cloud Nine	2009	20.00
—Reissue of Gordy 939			

TEMPTATIONS, THE (2) White doo-wop group.

Number	Title (A Side/B Side)	Yr	NM
45s			
GOLDISC			
❑ 3001	Barbara/Someday	1960	20.00
—Multicolor (black, red, gold) label			
❑ 3001	Barbara/Someday	1960	30.00
—All-black label			
❑ 3007	Letter of Devotion/Fickle Little Girl	1960	25.00

TEMPTATIONS, THE (3)

Number	Title (A Side/B Side)	Yr	NM
45s			
KING			
❑ 5118	Standing Alone/Roaches Rock	1958	300.00

TEMPTATIONS, THE (4)

Number	Title (A Side/B Side)	Yr	NM
45s			
PARKWAY			
❑ 803	Temptations/Birds N' Bees	1959	30.00

TEMPTATIONS, THE (5)

Number	Title (A Side/B Side)	Yr	NM
45s			
P&L			
❑ 1001	Blue Surf/Egyptian Surf	1963	60.00

TEMPTATIONS, THE (6)

Number	Title (A Side/B Side)	Yr	NM
45s			
SAVOY			
❑ 1532	Mister Juke Box/Mad at Love	1958	20.00
❑ 1550	I Love You/Don't You Know	1958	20.00

TEMPTONES, THE DARYL HALL was in this group.

Number	Title (A Side/B Side)	Yr	NM
45s			
ARCTIC			
❑ 130	Girl, I Love You/Good-Bye	1967	40.00
❑ 136	Say These Words of Love/ This Could Be the Start of Something Good	1967	40.00

TEN BROKEN HEARTS Allegedly, NEIL DIAMOND appears on this record.

Number	Title (A Side/B Side)	Yr	NM
45s			
DIAMOND			
❑ 123	Ten Lonely Guys/Shining Star	1962	40.00

10CC Also see GRAHAM GOULDMAN; HOTLEGS.

Number	Title (A Side/B Side)	Yr	NM
45s			
MERCURY			
❑ 73678	I'm Not in Love/ Channel Swimmer	1975	5.00
❑ 73725	Art for Art's Sake/ Get It While You Can	1975	5.00
❑ 73725 [PS]	Art for Art's Sake/ Get It While You Can	1975	8.00
❑ 73779	I'm Mandy Fly Me/ How Dare You	1976	5.00
❑ 73875	The Things We Do for Love/ Hot to Trot	1976	5.00
❑ 73917	People in Love/Don't Squeeze Me Like Toothpaste	1977	5.00
❑ 73943	Good Morning Judge/I'm So Laid Back I'm Laid Out	1977	5.00
❑ 73980	You've Got a Cold/ The Wall Street Shuffle	1977	5.00
POLYDOR			
❑ 14511	Dreadlock Holiday/ Nothing Can Move Me	1978	5.00
❑ 14528	For You and I/Take These Chains	1978	5.00
UK			
❑ 49005	Donna/Hot Sun Rock	1972	6.00
❑ 49015	Ruber Bullets/Waterfall	1973	6.00
❑ 49019	Headline Hustler/Speed Kills	1973	6.00
❑ 49023	The Wall Street Shuffle/ Gismo My Way	1974	6.00
WARNER BROS.			
❑ 29973	Power of Love/Action Man in Motown Suit	1982	5.00
❑ 49266	It Doesn't Matter Anymore/ Strange Lover	1980	5.00

Number	Title (A Side/B Side)	Yr	NM
Albums			
MERCURY			
❑ SRM-1-1029	The Original Soundtrack	1975	12.00
❑ SRM-1-1061	How Dare You!	1976	12.00
❑ SRM-1-3702	Deceptive Bends	1977	12.00
❑ SRM-2-8600 [(2)]	Live and Let Live	1977	15.00
POLYDOR			
❑ PD-1-6161	Bloody Tourists	1978	10.00
❑ PD-1-6244	Greatest Hits 1972-1978	1979	10.00
U.K.			
❑ 53105	10cc	1973	15.00
❑ AUKS 53107	Sheet Music	1974	15.00
❑ 53110	100cc	1975	15.00
WARNER BROS.			
❑ BSK 3442	Look Hear?	1980	10.00
❑ BSK 3575	Ten Out of Ten	1981	10.00

10,000 MANIACS

Number	Title (A Side/B Side)	Yr	NM
12-Inch Singles			
ELEKTRA			
❑ ED 5239 [DJ]	Peace Train (3:26) (same on both sides)	1987	10.00
❑ ED 5258 [DJ]	Don't Talk (LP Version) (Edit of LP Version)	1987	12.00
❑ ED 5278 [DJ]	Like the Weather (3:57) (same on both sides)	1987	10.00
❑ ED 5312 [DJ]	What's the Matter Here (Edit 4:04) (LP Version 4:51)	1987	12.00
❑ ED 5376 [DJ]	Trouble Me (same on both sides)	1989	12.00
❑ ED 5399 [DJ]	Eat for Two (same on both sides)	1989	10.00
❑ ED 5416 [DJ]	You Happy Puppet (same on both sides)	1989	12.00
❑ ED 5499 [DJ]	My Mother the War (same on both sides)	1990	12.00
GEFFEN			
❑ PRO-A-1117 [DJ]	More Than This (Hard Club Mix 7:14) (Tee's In House Dub 6:53) (Tee's Frozen Dub 6:47) (TNT Extended Mix 5:54)	1997	10.00
45s			
ELEKTRA			
❑ 64595	Because the Night/Eat for Two	1993	4.00
❑ 65962	Like the Weather/Peace Train	198?	3.00
—"Spun Gold" reissue			
❑ 69253	You Happy Puppet/Gunshy	1989	8.00
❑ 69279	Eat for Two/The Big Parade	1989	5.00
❑ 69298	Trouble Me/The Lion's Share	1989	4.00
❑ 69298 [PS]	Trouble Me/The Lion's Share	1989	4.00
❑ 69388	What's the Matter Here?/ Cherry Tree	1988	4.00
❑ 69388 [PS]	What's the Matter Here?/ Cherry Tree	1988	4.00
❑ 69418	Like the Weather/ A Campfire Song	1988	4.00
❑ 69418 [PS]	Like the Weather/ A Campfire Song	1988	4.00
❑ 69439	Don't Talk/City of Angels	1987	4.00
❑ 69439 [PS]	Don't Talk/City of Angels	1987	4.00
❑ 69457	Peace Train/Painted Desert	1987	4.00
❑ 69457 [PS]	Peace Train/Painted Desert	1987	4.00
Albums			
CHRISTIAN BURIAL			
❑ P-2010 [EP]	Human Conflict #5	1983	80.00
❑ P-3001	Secrets of the I Ching	1984	120.00
ELEKTRA			
❑ ED 5270 [DJ]	Interview	1987	30.00
—Lenny Kaye interviews Natalie Merchant; promo only			
❑ 60428	The Wishing Chair	1985	12.00
❑ 60738	In My Tribe	1987	10.00
❑ 60738 [DJ]	In My Tribe	1987	15.00
—Promo-only audiophile pressing			
❑ 60815	Blind Man's Zoo	1989	12.00
❑ 60815 [DJ]	Blind Man's Zoo	1989	15.00
—Promo-only audiophile pressing (white labels)			
❑ R 100481	In My Tribe	1987	12.00
—BMG Direct Marketing edition			
❑ R 130236	Blind Man's Zoo	1989	12.00
—BMG Direct Marketing edition			

TEN WHEEL DRIVE Featuring Genya Ravan.

Number	Title (A Side/B Side)	Yr	NM
45s			
CAPITOL			
❑ 3700	Monsoon Rain/Close Up the Cheese	1973	5.00
POLYDOR			
❑ 14015	Tightrope/Lapidary	1969	5.00
❑ 14024	Eye of the Needle/I Am a Want Ad	1970	5.00
❑ 14037	Morning Much Better/ Stay with Me	1970	5.00
❑ 14052	Don't Blame Me/ 20 Miles from Home	1971	5.00

Except when noted otherwise, VG = 25% of NM, and VG+ = 50% of NM. (Example: VG = $2.00, VG+ = $4.00 and NM = $8.00.)

Number	Title (A Side/B Side)	Yr	NM
Albums			
CAPITOL			
❑ ST-11199	Ten Wheel Drive	1973	10.00
POLYDOR			
❑ 24-4008	Construction #1	1969	12.00
❑ 24-4024	Brief Replies	1970	12.00
❑ 24-4062	Peculiar Friends	1971	12.00

TEN YEARS AFTER

Number	Title (A Side/B Side)	Yr	NM
45s			
COLUMBIA			
❑ 45457	I'd Love to Change the World/ Let the Sky Fall	1971	5.00
❑ 45530	Baby Won't You Let Me Rock 'N' Roll You/Once There Was a Time	1972	5.00
❑ 45736	You Can't Win Them All/ Choo Choo Mama	1972	5.00
❑ 45787	Tomorrow, I'll Be Out of Town/ Convention Prevention	1973	5.00
❑ 45915	I'm Going Home/ You Give Me Loving	1973	5.00
❑ 46061	It's Getting Harder/ I Wanted to Boogie	1974	5.00
DERAM			
❑ 7529	If You Should Love Me/ Love Like a Man	1970	8.00
❑ 85027	Portable People/The Sounds	1968	8.00
❑ 85035	Hear Me Calling/I'm Going Home	1968	8.00
Albums			
CHRYSALIS			
❑ CHS 1083	Ssssh	1975	10.00
❑ CHS 1084	Cricklewood Green	1975	10.00
❑ CHS 1085	Watt	1975	10.00
❑ F1-21001	A Space in Time	1989	8.00
❑ F1-21009	Rock and Roll Music to the World	1989	8.00
❑ F1-21083	Ssssh	1989	8.00
❑ F1-21084	Cricklewood Green	1989	8.00
❑ F1-21085	Watt	1989	8.00
❑ F1-21573	Positive Vibrations	1989	8.00
❑ F1-21580	Universal	1989	8.00
❑ F1-21722	About Time	1989	12.00
❑ PV 41001	A Space in Time	1987	8.00
❑ PV 41009	Rock and Roll Music to the World	1987	8.00
❑ FV 41049 [(2)]	Recorded Live	1987	10.00
❑ PV 41083	Ssssh	1983	8.00
❑ PV 41084	Cricklewood Green	1983	8.00
❑ PV 41085	Watt	1983	8.00
❑ PV 41573	Positive Vibrations	1987	8.00
❑ FV 41580	Universal	1988	10.00
COLUMBIA			
❑ CQ 30801 [Q]	A Space in Time	1973	16.00
❑ KC 30801	A Space in Time	1971	12.00
❑ PC 30801	A Space in Time	1979	8.00
❑ C 31779	Rock and Roll Music to the World	197?	10.00
—Reissue with new prefix			
❑ KC 31779	Rock and Roll Music to the World	1972	12.00
❑ C2X 32288 [(2)]	Recorded Live	1973	15.00
❑ PC 32851	Positive Vibrations	1974	10.00
❑ PC 34366	Classic Performances of Ten Years After	1976	10.00
DERAM			
❑ DE 16009 [M]	Ten Years After	1968	50.00
❑ DES 18009 [S]	Ten Years After	1968	20.00
❑ DES 18016	Undead	1968	15.00
❑ DES 18021	Stonedhenge	1969	15.00
❑ DES 18029	Ssssh	1969	15.00
❑ DES 18038	Cricklewood Green	1970	15.00
❑ XDES 18050	Watt	1970	15.00
—With large "DERAM" on top half of label			
❑ XDES 18050	Watt	1970	25.00
—With "LONDON" under smaller "DERAM" at top of label			
❑ XDES 18064	Alvin Lee and Company	1972	12.00
❑ DES 18072	Goin' Home! Their Greatest Hits	1975	12.00
❑ SMAS-93428	Watt	1970	20.00
—Capitol Record Club edition			
LONDON			
❑ LC 50008	Greatest Hits	1977	10.00
❑ 820324-1	Greatest Hits	1986	8.00

TENDER SLIM

Number	Title (A Side/B Side)	Yr	NM
45s			
GREY CLIFF			
❑ 723	Teenage Hayride/Hey Joe!	1959	15.00
HERALD			
❑ 571	Don't Cut Out on Me/ I'm Checkin' Up	1962	15.00

TENDER TONES, THE

Number	Title (A Side/B Side)	Yr	NM
45s			
DUCKY			
❑ 713	I Love You So/Just for a Little While	1959	800.00

TENDERFOOTS, THE

Number	Title (A Side/B Side)	Yr	NM
45s			
FEDERAL			
❑ 12214	Kissing Bug/Watussi Wussi Wo	1955	60.00
❑ 12219	My Confession/ Save Me Some Kisses	1955	60.00
❑ 12225	Those Golden Bells/ I'm Yours Anyhow	1955	80.00
❑ 12228	Sindy/Sugar Ways	1955	120.00

TENNESSEE DRIFTERS, THE

Number	Title (A Side/B Side)	Yr	NM
45s			
DOT			
❑ 1166	Boogie Woogie Baby/ Drive Those Blues Away	1953	30.00
❑ 1187	Corrine, Corrina/ Somebody Loves You	1954	30.00

TENNESSEE ERNIE
See TENNESSEE ERNIE FORD.

TENNESSEE GUITARS, THE

Number	Title (A Side/B Side)	Yr	NM
45s			
SUN			
❑ 1102	Tennessee Toddy/Trophy Run	1969	6.00

TENNESSEE SIX AND FOUR MORE, THE

Number	Title (A Side/B Side)	Yr	NM
45s			
HIT			
❑ 89	Down at Papa Joe's/I'm Leaving It Up to You	1963	8.00
—B-side by Dotty and Dan			

TERMITES, THE

Number	Title (A Side/B Side)	Yr	NM
45s			
BEE			
❑ 1825	Give Me Your Heart/Carrie Lou	1964	50.00

TERRACETONES, THE

Number	Title (A Side/B Side)	Yr	NM
45s			
APT			
❑ 25016	Words of Wisdom/ Ride of Paul Revere	1958	100.00

TERRELL, ERNIE

Number	Title (A Side/B Side)	Yr	NM
45s			
ARGO			
❑ 5511	Dear Abbie/I Can't Wait	1965	12.00

TERRELL, TAMMI
Also see MARVIN GAYE AND TAMMI TERRELL; TAMMY MONTGOMERY.

Number	Title (A Side/B Side)	Yr	NM
45s			
MOTOWN			
❑ 1086	I Can't Believe You Love Me/ Hold Me Oh My Darling	1965	10.00
❑ 1095	Come On and See Me/ Baby Don'tcha Worry	1966	10.00
❑ 1115	What a Good Man He Is/ There Are Things	1967	10.00
❑ 1138	This Old Heart of Mine (Is Weak for You)/ Just Too Much to Hope For	1968	10.00
Albums			
MOTOWN			
❑ M5-231V1	Irresistible Tammi	1982	10.00
❑ MS-652	Irresistible Tammi	1969	50.00

TERRI AND THE KITTENS

Number	Title (A Side/B Side)	Yr	NM
45s			
IMPERIAL			
❑ 5728	Wedding Bells/You Cheated	1961	20.00

TERRI AND THE VELVETEENS

Number	Title (A Side/B Side)	Yr	NM
45s			
KERWOOD			
❑ 711	Bells of Love/You've Broken My Heart	1962	40.00

TERRI-TONES, THE

Number	Title (A Side/B Side)	Yr	NM
45s			
CORTLAND			
❑ 105	Go/The Sinner	1962	50.00
REGENCY			
❑ 929	Go/The Sinner	1962	30.00

TERRY, DON

Number	Title (A Side/B Side)	Yr	NM
45s			
LIN			
❑ 5018	Knees Shakin'/She Giggles	1959	150.00

TERRY, DOSSIE

Number	Title (A Side/B Side)	Yr	NM
45s			
KING			
❑ 5072	Thunderbird/I Got a Watch Dog	1957	50.00
❑ 5890	Thunderbird/Be-Bop Wino	1964	15.00
—B-side by the Lamplighters			
RCA VICTOR			
❑ 47-4474	Didn't Satisfy You/24 Years	1952	60.00
❑ 47-4648	When I Hit the Number/ My Love Is Gone	1952	60.00
❑ 47-4864	Lost My Head/Sad, Sad Affair	1952	60.00

TERRY, GENE

Number	Title (A Side/B Side)	Yr	NM
45s			
GOLDBAND			
❑ 1066	Cindy Lou/Teardrops in My Eyes	1958	120.00
❑ 1081	Never Let Her Go/No Mail Today	1958	40.00
❑ 1088	Cinderella, Cinderella/ Guy with a Million Dreams	1959	30.00
SAVOY			
❑ 1559	This Should Go On Forever/ Fine, Fine, Fine	1959	20.00

TERRY, LARRY

Number	Title (A Side/B Side)	Yr	NM
45s			
TESTA			
❑ 006	Hep Cat/Why Did She Go	1960	1200.

TERRY, NAT

Number	Title (A Side/B Side)	Yr	NM
45s			
IMPERIAL			
❑ 5150	Take It Easy/I Don't Know Why	1951	100.00

TERRY, SONNY

Number	Title (A Side/B Side)	Yr	NM
45s			
CAPITOL			
❑ F931	Telephone Blues/Dirty Mistreater Don't You Know	1950	120.00
CHESS			
❑ 1860	Dangerous Woman/ Hootenanny Blues	1963	20.00
CHOICE			
❑ 15	Hootin'/Dupre	1961	20.00
GOTHAM			
❑ 517	Baby Let's Have Some Fun/ Four O'Clock Blues	1951	40.00
❑ 518	Harmonica Rhumba/ Lonesome Room	1951	40.00
GRAMERCY			
❑ 1004	Hootin' Blues/(B-side unknown)	1952	50.00
—Black vinyl			
❑ 1004	Hootin' Blues/(B-side unknown)	1952	100.00
—Colored vinyl			
GROOVE			
❑ 0015	Lost Jawbone/Louise	1954	30.00
❑ 0135	Ride and Roll/Hootin' Blues #2	1956	30.00
HARLEM			
❑ 2327	Dangerous Woman/ I Love You Baby	1954	300.00
JAX			
❑ 305	I Don't Worry (Sittin' on Top of the World)/Man Ain't Nothin' But a Fool	195?	400.00
—Colored vinyl			
OLD TOWN			
❑ 1023	Uncle Bud/Climbing on Top of the Hill	1956	25.00
RCA VICTOR			
❑ 47-5492	Hootin' and Jumpin'/ Hooray, Hooray	1953	100.00
❑ 47-5577	Sonny Is Drinking/I'm Gonna Rock My Wig	1954	100.00
RED ROBIN			
❑ 110	Harmonica Hop/Doggin' My Heart Around	1952	300.00
Albums			
ALLIGATOR			
❑ AL-4734	Whoopin'	198?	12.00
—With Johnny Winter, Willie Dixon and others			
BLUE LABOR			
❑ 101	Robbin' the Grave	197?	12.00
BLUESVILLE			
❑ BVLP-1025 [M]	Sonny's Story	1961	80.00
—Bright blue label, no trident logo			
❑ BVLP-1025 [M]	Sonny's Story	1964	25.00
—Blue label with trident logo on right			
❑ BVLP-1069 [M]	Sonny Is King	1963	80.00
—Bright blue label, no trident logo			

Number	Title (A Side/B Side)	Yr	NM
❑ BVLP-1069 [M]	Sonny Is King	1964	25.00
—Blue label with trident logo on right			
COLLECTABLES			
❑ COL-5195	Chain Gang Blues	198?	10.00
❑ COL-5307	Sonny Terry	198?	10.00
ELEKTRA			
❑ EKL-14 [10]	Folk Blues	1954	150.00
❑ EKL-15 [10]	City Blues	1954	150.00
—With Alec Stewart			
FANTASY			
❑ OBC-521	Sonny Is King	198?	10.00
FOLKWAYS			
❑ FP-35 [10]	Harmonica and Vocal Solos	1952	150.00
❑ FA-2006 [10]	Sonny Terry's Washboard Band	195?	100.00
—Black and white cover (reissue)			
❑ FP-2006 [10]	Sonny Terry's Washboard Band	1950	150.00
—Blue and white cover			
❑ FA-2035 [10]	Harmonica and Vocal Solos	1952	100.00
❑ FS-2369	On the Road	196?	15.00
❑ 3821	A New Sound	198?	12.00
PRESTIGE			
❑ PRST-7802	Sonny Is King	1970	15.00
RIVERSIDE			
❑ RLP-644 [M]	Sonny Terry and His Mouth Harp	195?	80.00
STINSON			
❑ 55	Sonny Terry and His Mouth Harp	197?	12.00
—Reissue of 10-inch LP			
❑ SLP-55 [10]	Sonny Terry and His Mouth Harp	1950	150.00
TERRY, SONNY, AND BROWNIE MCGHEE Also see each artist's individual listings.			
45s			
BLUESVILLE			
❑ 802	Let Me Be Your Big Dig/ Stranger Here	196?	20.00
❑ 809	Pawnshop/Too Nicey Mama	196?	20.00
❑ 818	Freight Train/Beggin' and Tryin'	196?	20.00
CHOICE			
❑ 1	John Henry/Oh Lawdy Pick a Bale of Cotton	196?	20.00
—As "Brownie & Sonny"			
❑ 7	Study War No More/ I'm Gonna Tell God	196?	20.00
—As "Brownie & Sonny"			
Albums			
A&M			
❑ SP-4379	Sonny & Brownie	1973	12.00
ARCHIVE OF FOLK MUSIC			
❑ 242	Brownie & Sonny	198?	12.00
BLUESVILLE			
❑ BVLP-1002 [M]	Down Home Blues	1960	80.00
—Bright blue label, no trident logo			
❑ BVLP-1002 [M]	Down Home Blues	1964	25.00
—Blue label with trident logo on right			
❑ BVLP-1005 [M]	Blues and Folk	1960	80.00
—Bright blue label, no trident logo			
❑ BVLP-1005 [M]	Blues and Folk	1964	25.00
—Blue label with trident logo on right			
❑ BVLP-1020 [M]	Blues All Around My Head	1961	80.00
—Bright blue label, no trident logo			
❑ BVLP-1020 [M]	Blues All Around My Head	1964	25.00
—Blue label with trident logo on right			
❑ BVLP-1033 [M]	Blues in My Soul	1961	80.00
—Bright blue label, no trident logo			
❑ BVLP-1033 [M]	Blues in My Soul	1964	25.00
—Blue label with trident logo on right			
❑ BVLP-1058 [M]	Live at the Second Fret	1962	80.00
—Bright blue label, no trident logo			
❑ BVLP-1058 [M]	Live at the Second Fret	1964	25.00
—Blue label with trident logo on right			
BLUESWAY			
❑ BLS-6028	Long Way from Home	1969	15.00
❑ BLS-6059	Couldn't Believe My Eyes	1970	15.00
COLLECTABLES			
❑ COL-5198	Golden Classics: Blowin' the Fuses	198?	10.00
EVEREST			
❑ 206	Sonny Terry	1968	25.00
❑ 242	Brownie McGhee and Sonny Terry	1969	25.00
FANTASY			
❑ OBC-503	Sonny's Story	1984	10.00
❑ OBC-505	Brownie's Blues	1984	10.00
❑ F-3254 [M]	Sonny Terry & Brownie McGhee	1961	40.00
—Black vinyl			
❑ F-3254 [M]	Sonny Terry & Brownie McGhee	1961	150.00
—Red vinyl			
❑ F-3296 [M]	Just a Closer Walk with Thee	1962	40.00
—Black vinyl			
❑ F-3296 [M]	Just a Closer Walk with Thee	1962	150.00
—Red vinyl			

Number	Title (A Side/B Side)	Yr	NM
❑ F-3317 [M]	Blues and Shouts	1962	40.00
—Black vinyl			
❑ F-3317 [M]	Blues and Shouts	1962	150.00
—Red vinyl			
❑ F-3340 [M]	Sonny and Brownie at Sugar Hill	1962	40.00
—Black vinyl			
❑ F-3340 [M]	Sonny and Brownie at Sugar Hill	1962	150.00
—Red vinyl			
❑ FS-8091 [S]	Sonny and Brownie at Sugar Hill	1962	40.00
—Black vinyl			
❑ FS-8091 [S]	Sonny and Brownie at Sugar Hill	1962	150.00
—Blue vinyl			
❑ 24708 [(2)]	Back to New Orleans	1972	15.00
❑ 24721 [(2)]	Midnight Special	1977	15.00
❑ 24723 [(2)]	California Blues	1981	15.00
FOLKLORE			
❑ FRLP-14013 [M]	Down Home Blues	1964	40.00
❑ FRST-14013 [S]	Down Home Blues	1964	50.00
FOLKWAYS			
❑ FA-2327 [M]	Blues and Folk Songs	1960	30.00
❑ F-2421 [M]	Traditional Blues, Vol. 1	1961	30.00
❑ FS-2421 [S]	Traditional Blues, Vol. 1	1961	40.00
❑ F-2422 [M]	Traditional Blues, Vol. 2	1961	30.00
❑ FS-2422 [S]	Traditional Blues, Vol. 2	1961	40.00
FONTANA			
❑ SGF-67599	Where the Blues Begin	1969	25.00
KIMBERLEY			
❑ 2017 [M]	Southern Meetin'	1963	20.00
❑ 11017 [S]	Southern Meetin'	1963	25.00
MAINSTREAM			
❑ M-6049 [M]	Hometown Blues	1966	20.00
❑ MS-6049 [S]	Hometown Blues	1966	25.00
MOBILE FIDELITY			
❑ 1-233	Sonny and Brownie	1996	20.00
—Audiophile vinyl			
MUSE			
❑ 5117	Hootin'	198?	12.00
❑ 5131	You Hear Me Talkin'	198?	12.00
OLYMPIC			
❑ 7108	Hootin' & Hollerin'	1972	12.00
PRESTIGE			
❑ PRLP-7715	Best of Sonny Terry and Brownie McGhee	1969	15.00
❑ PRLP-7803	Live at the Second Fret	1970	15.00
ROULETTE			
❑ R-25074 [M]	The Folk Songs of Sonny & Brownie	1959	50.00
❑ RS-25074 [S]	The Folk Songs of Sonny & Brownie	1959	80.00
SAVOY			
❑ SJL-1137	Climbin' Up	1984	10.00
❑ 12218	Down Home Blues	1973	12.00
SHARP			
❑ 2003 [M]	Down Home Blues	195?	150.00
SMASH			
❑ MGS-27067 [M]	Brownie McGhee at the Bunkhouse	1965	30.00
❑ SRS-67067 [S]	Brownie McGhee at the Bunkhouse	1965	40.00
SMITHSONIAN/FOLKWAYS			
❑ SF-40011	Sing	198?	10.00
STORYVILLE			
❑ 4007	Brownie & Sonny	1972	12.00
TOPIC			
❑ T-29 [M]	Songs	1958	50.00
VEE JAY			
❑ VJLP-1138	Coffee House Blues	198?	10.00
—With Lightnin' Hopkins			
VERVE			
❑ MGV 3008 [M]	Blues Is My Companion	1961	80.00
VERVE FOLKWAYS			
❑ FV 9010 [M]	Get Together	1965	25.00
❑ FVS 9010 [S]	Get Together	1965	30.00
❑ FV 9019 [M]	Guitar Highway	1965	25.00
❑ FVS 9019 [S]	Guitar Highway	1965	30.00
WASHINGTON			
❑ W-702 [M]	Talkin' 'Bout the Blues	1961	50.00
WORLD PACIFIC			
❑ ST-1294 [S]	Blues Is a Story	1960	80.00
❑ WP-1294 [M]	Blues Is a Story	1960	50.00
❑ ST-1296 [S]	Down South Summit Meetin'	1960	80.00
❑ WP-1296 [M]	Down South Summit Meetin'	1960	50.00

Number	Title (A Side/B Side)	Yr	NM
TERRY AND THE MACS			
45s			
ABC-PARAMOUNT			
❑ 9668	Baby-O-Mine/Love Is a Beautiful Thing	1956	20.00
❑ 9721	You Don't Have to Explain/ Spinning, Spinning, Spinning	1956	20.00
❑ 9753	Please Don't Tease/ The Mystery of Love	1956	20.00
TERRY AND THE PIRATES			
45s			
CHESS			
❑ 1696	Talk About the Girl/ What Did He Say	1958	40.00
TERRY AND THE TAGS			
45s			
SYLVESTER			
❑ 100	Rampage/The Twomp	1962	50.00
TEX, JOE			
12-Inch Singles			
EPIC			
❑ 50352	Ain't Gonna Bump No More (With No Big Fat Woman)/Be Cool (Willie Is Dancing with a Sissy)	1977	20.00
45s			
ACE			
❑ 544	Cut It Out/Just for You and Me	1958	60.00
❑ 550	Mother's Advice/You Little Baby Face Thing	1958	80.00
❑ 559	Charlie Brown Got Expelled/ Blessed Are These Tears	1959	60.00
❑ 572	Don't Hold It Against Me/ Yum, Yum, Yum	1959	60.00
❑ 591	Boys Will Be Boys/ Grannie Stole the Show	1960	40.00
❑ 674	Boys Will Be Boys/ Baby You're Right	1963	15.00
ANNA			
❑ 1119	All I Could Do Was Cry (Part 1)/ All I Could Do Was Cry (Part 2)	1960	40.00
❑ 1124	I'll Never Break Your Heart (Part 1)/I'll Never Break Your Heart (Part 2)	1960	40.00
❑ 1128	Baby, You're Right/Ain't It a Mess	1961	40.00
ATLANTIC			
❑ 2874	I'll Never Fall in Love Again (Part 1)/I'll Never Fall in Love Again (Part 2)	1972	6.00
CHECKER			
❑ 1104	Baby, You're Right/All I Could Do Was Cry (Part 2)	1965	12.00
DIAL			
❑ 1001	Bad Feet/I Know Him	1971	6.00
❑ 1003	Papa's Dream/I'm Comin' Home	1971	6.00
❑ 1006 [DJ]	King Thaddeus (mono/stereo)	1971	7.00
—May be promo only			
❑ 1008	Give the Baby Anything the Baby Wants/Takin' a Chance	1971	6.00
❑ 1010	I Gotcha/A Mother's Prayer	1972	6.00
❑ 1012	You Said a Bad Word/ It Ain't Gonna Work Baby	1972	6.00
❑ 1018	Rain Go Away/King Thaddeus	1973	6.00
❑ 1020	Woman Stealer/ Cat's Got Her Tongue	1973	6.00
❑ 1020 [PS]	Woman Stealer/ Cat's Got Her Tongue	1973	8.00
❑ 1021	All the Heaven a Man Really Needs/Let's Go Somewhere and Talk	1973	6.00
❑ 1024	Trying to Win Your Love/ I've Seen Enough	1973	6.00
❑ 1154	Sassy Sexy Wiggle/ Under Your Powerful Love	1975	6.00
❑ 1155	I'm Goin' Back Again/ My Body Wants You	1975	6.00
❑ 1156	Baby, It's Rainin'/Have You Ever	1975	6.00
❑ 1157	Mama Red/Love Shortage	1975	6.00
❑ 2800	Loose Caboose/Music Ain't Got No Color	1979	5.00
❑ 2801	Who Gave Birth to the Funk/ If You Don't Want the Man	1979	5.00
❑ 2802	Discomania/Fat People	1979	5.00
❑ 3000	What Should I Do/The Only Girl I've Ever Loved	1961	12.00
❑ 3002	One Giant Step/The Rib	1961	12.00
❑ 3003	Popeye Johnny/Hand Shakin', Love Makin', Girl Talkin', Son-of-a-Gun From Next Door	1962	12.00
❑ 3007	Meet Me in Church/ Be Your Own Judge	1962	12.00
❑ 3009	I Let Her Get Away/The Peck	1963	12.00

Except when noted otherwise, VG = 25% of NM, and VG+ = 50% of NM. (Example: VG = $2.00, VG+ = $4.00 and NM = $8.00.)

Number	Title (A Side/B Side)	Yr	NM
❑ 3013	Someone to Take Your Place/I Should Have Kissed You More	1963	12.00
❑ 3016	I Wanna Be Free/Blood's Thicker Than Water	1963	150.00
❑ 3019	Looking for My Pig/Say Thank You	1964	12.00
❑ 3020	I'd Rather Have You/Old Time Lover	1964	12.00
❑ 3023	I Had a Good Thing But I Left (Part 1)/I Had a Good Thing But I Left (Part 2)	1964	12.00
❑ 4001	Hold What You've Got/Fresh Out of Tears	1964	15.00
❑ 4003	You Better Get It/You Got What It Takes	1965	10.00
❑ 4006	A Woman Can Change a Man/Don't Let Your Left Hand Know	1965	10.00
❑ 4011	One Monkey Don't Stop No Show/Build Your Love on a Solid Foundation	1965	10.00
❑ 4016	I Want To (Do Everything For You)/Funny Bone	1965	10.00
❑ 4022	A Sweet Woman Like You/Close the Door	1965	10.00
❑ 4026	The Love You Save (May Be Your Own)/If Sugar Was As Sweet As You	1966	10.00
❑ 4028	S.Y.S.L.J.F.M. (Letter Song)/I'm a Man	1966	10.00
❑ 4033	I Believe I'm Gonna Make It/Better Believe It, Baby	1966	10.00
❑ 4045	I've Got to Do a Little Bit Better/What in the World	1966	10.00
❑ 4051	Papa Was Too/Truest Woman in the World	1966	10.00
❑ 4055	Show Me/A Woman Sees a Hard Time (When Her Man Is Gone)	1967	8.00
❑ 4059	Woman Like That, Yeah/I'm Going and Get It	1967	8.00
❑ 4061	A Woman's Hands/See See Rider	1967	8.00
❑ 4063	Skinny Legs and All/Watch the One	1967	10.00
❑ 4068	I'll Make Every Day Christmas (For My Woman)/Don't Give Up	1967	12.00
❑ 4069	Men Are Gettin' Scarce/You're Gonna Thank Me, Woman	1968	8.00
❑ 4076	I'll Never Do You Wrong/Wooden Spoon	1968	8.00
❑ 4079	Chocolate Cherry/Betwixt and Between	1968	8.00
❑ 4083	Keep the One You Got/Go Home and Do It	1968	8.00
❑ 4086	You Need Me, Baby/Baby, Be Good	1968	8.00
❑ 4089	That's Your Baby/Sweet, Sweet Woman	1968	8.00
❑ 4090	Buying a Book/Chicken Crazy	1969	8.00
❑ 4093	That's the Way/Anything You Wanna Know	1969	8.00
❑ 4094	We Can't Sit Down Now/It Ain't Sanitary	1969	8.00
❑ 4095	I Can't See You No More (When Johnny Comes Marching Home Again)/Sure Is Good	1969	8.00
❑ 4096	Everything Happens on Time/You're Right, Ray Charles	1970	8.00
❑ 4098	I'll Never Fall in Love Again/The Only Way I Know to Love You	1970	8.00
EPIC			
❑ 50313	Ain't Gonna Bump No More (With No Big Fat Woman)/I Mess Up Everything I Get My Hands On	1976	5.00
❑ 50426	Hungry for Your Love/I Almost Got to Heaven Once	1977	5.00
❑ 50494	Rub Down/Be Kind to Old People	1977	5.00
❑ 50530	Get Back, Leroy/You Can Be My Star	1978	5.00
HANDSHAKE			
❑ 02565	Don't Do Da Do/Here Comes No. 34 (Do the Earl Campbell)	1981	4.00
KING			
❑ 4840	Come In This House/Davy, You Upset My Home	1955	60.00
❑ 4884	My Biggest Mistake/Right Back to My Arms	1956	50.00
❑ 4911	She's Mine/I Had to Come Back to You	1956	50.00
❑ 4980	Get Way Back/Pneumonia	1956	50.00
❑ 5064	I Want to Have a Talk with You/Ain't Nobody's Business	1957	50.00
❑ 5981	Come In This House/I Want to Have a Talk with You	1965	10.00

Albums

Number	Title (A Side/B Side)	Yr	NM
ACCORD			
❑ SN-7174	J.T.'s Funk	1982	10.00
ATLANTIC			
❑ 8106 [M]	Hold What You've Got	1965	40.00
❑ SD 8106 [P]	Hold What You've Got	1965	50.00
❑ 8115 [M]	The New Boss	1965	40.00
❑ SD 8115 [S]	The New Boss	1965	50.00
❑ 8124 [M]	The Love You Save	1966	40.00
❑ SD 8124 [S]	The Love You Save	1966	50.00
❑ 8133 [M]	I've Got to Do a Little Better	1966	40.00
❑ SD 8133 [S]	I've Got to Do a Little Better	1966	50.00
❑ 8144 [M]	The Best of Joe Tex	1967	20.00
❑ SD 8144 [P]	The Best of Joe Tex	1967	25.00
❑ SD 8156	Live and Lively	1968	20.00
❑ 8187 [M]	Soul Country	1968	40.00
—Mono is white label promo only; "d/j copy monaural" sticker on cover			
❑ SD 8187 [S]	Soul Country	1968	20.00
❑ SD 8211	Happy Soul	1969	20.00
❑ SD 8231	Buying a Book	1969	20.00
❑ SD 8254	Joe Tex Sings with Strings and Things	1970	15.00
❑ SD 8292	From the Roots Came the Rapper	1972	15.00
❑ 81278	The Best of Joe Tex	1985	10.00
CHECKER			
❑ LP-2993 [M]	Hold On	1965	150.00
DIAL			
❑ DL 6002	I Gotcha	1972	15.00
❑ DL 6004	Joe Tex Spills the Beans	1973	15.00
❑ DL 6100	He Who Is Without Funk Cast the First Stone	1979	10.00
EPIC			
❑ PE 34666	Bumps and Bruises	1977	12.00
KING			
❑ 935 [M]	The Best of Joe Tex	1965	100.00
❑ KS-935 [R]	The Best of Joe Tex	1965	75.00
LONDON			
❑ LC-50017	Super Soul	1977	10.00
PARROT			
❑ PA 61002 [M]	The Best of Joe Tex	1965	50.00
❑ PAS 71002 [R]	The Best of Joe Tex	1965	30.00
PRIDE			
❑ PRD-0020	The History of Joe Tex	1973	10.00
RHINO			
❑ RNLP-70191	I Believe I'm Gonna Make It: The Best of Joe Tex 1964-1972	1988	10.00

TEX AND THE CHEX

45s

Number	Title (A Side/B Side)	Yr	NM
ATLANTIC			
❑ 2116	I Do Love You/My Love	1961	60.00
NEWTOWN			
❑ 5010	Watching Willie Wobble/Be on the Lookout for My Girl	1963	20.00
20TH FOX			
❑ 411	Beach Party/Now (Love Me)	1963	30.00

TEXANS, THE

Also see JOHNNY AND DORSEY BURNETTE.

45s

Number	Title (A Side/B Side)	Yr	NM
GOTHIC			
❑ 001	Old Reb/Rockin' Johnny Home	1961	30.00
INFINITY			
❑ 001	Green Grass of Texas/Bloody River	1961	30.00
JOX			
❑ 001	Old Reb/Rockin' Johnny Home	1965	30.00
VEE JAY			
❑ 658	Green Grass of Texas/Bloody River	1965	20.00

THARP, CHUCK, AND THE FIREBALLS

See THE FIREBALLS.

THEE MIDNITERS

45s

Number	Title (A Side/B Side)	Yr	NM
CHATTAHOOCHIE			
❑ 666	Land of a Thousand Dances (Part 1)/Land of a Thousand Dances (Part 2)	1965	15.00
❑ 666-2	Land of a Thousand Dances (Part 1)/Ball O' Twine	1965	15.00
❑ 674	Sad Girl/Heat Wave	1965	16.00
❑ 675	Sad Girl/Heat Wave	1965	15.00
❑ 684	Whittier Blvd./Evil Love	1965	15.00
❑ 693	I Need Someone/Empty Heart	1965	20.00
❑ 695	Brother, Where Are You/Heat Wave	1966	15.00
❑ 706	Are You Angry/I Found a Peanut	1966	15.00
UNI			
❑ 55170	She Only Wants What She Can't Get/I've Come Alive	1969	10.00
WHITTIER			
❑ 201	That's All/To Be with You	196?	12.00
❑ 500	Love, Special Delivery/Don't Go Away	1966	20.00
❑ 500 [PS]	Love, Special Delivery/Don't Go Away	1966	50.00
❑ 501	The Midnite Feeling/It'll Never Be Over for Me	1966	20.00
❑ 501 [PS]	The Midnite Feeling/It'll Never Be Over for Me	1966	50.00
❑ 503	Dragon Fly/The Big Ranch	1966	20.00
❑ 504	Never Knew I Had It So Bad/The Walking Song	1967	20.00
❑ 504	Never Knew I Had It So Bad/Everybody Needs Somebody	1967	30.00
❑ 507	Jump Five and Harmonize/Looking Out a Window	1967	20.00
❑ 508	Chile Con Soul/Tu Despedida	1967	20.00
❑ 509	Breakfast on the Grass/Dreaming Casually	1967	20.00
❑ 511	You're Gonna Make Me Cry/Make Ends Meet	1968	200.00
❑ 512	The Ballad of Cesar Chavez/The Ballad of Cesar Chavez (Spanish)	1968	20.00
❑ 513	Chicano Power/Never Goin' to Give You Up	1968	20.00
❑ 674	Sad Girl/Heat Wave	1968	12.00
❑ 694	It's Not Unusual/It's Not Unusual	1969	12.00

Albums

Number	Title (A Side/B Side)	Yr	NM
CHATTAHOOCHIE			
❑ C-1001 [M]	Thee Midniters	1965	60.00
❑ CS-1001 [S]	Thee Midniters	1965	80.00
WHITTIER			
❑ W-5000 [M]	Bring You Love Special Delivery	1966	40.00
❑ WS-5000 [S]	Bring You Love Special Delivery	1966	50.00
❑ W-5001 [M]	Unlimited	1966	40.00
❑ WS-5001 [S]	Unlimited	1966	50.00
❑ W-5002 [M]	Giants	1967	40.00
❑ WS-5002 [S]	Giants	1967	50.00
ZYANYA/RHINO			
❑ RNLP-063	The Best of Thee Midniters	1983	12.00

THEE MUFFINS

Albums

Number	Title (A Side/B Side)	Yr	NM
(NO LABEL)			
❑ (no #)	Thee Muffins Pop Up!	1967	200.00

THEE PROPHETS

45s

Number	Title (A Side/B Side)	Yr	NM
KAPP			
❑ 962	Playgirl/Patricia Ann	1969	10.00
❑ 997	Some Kind of Wonderful/They Call Her Sorrow	1969	10.00
❑ 2038	Rag Doll Boy/It Isn't So Easy	1969	10.00
❑ 2087	Little Bit of Love/Come to Me Girl	1970	10.00

Albums

Number	Title (A Side/B Side)	Yr	NM
KAPP			
❑ KS-3596	Playgirl	1969	20.00

THEM

Also see BELFAST GYPSIES; VAN MORRISON.

45s

Number	Title (A Side/B Side)	Yr	NM
A&M			
❑ 1201	Baby Please Don't Go/Danger Heartbreak Dead Ahead	1988	4.00
—B-side by the Marvelettes			
❑ 1201 [PS]	Danger Heartbreak Dead Ahead/Baby Please Don't Go	1988	4.00
—"Good Morning Vietnam" sleeve			
HAPPY TIGER			
❑ 525	Lonely Weekends/I Am Waiting	1969	15.00
❑ 534	Memphis Lady/Nobody Cares	1970	12.00
PARROT			
❑ 365	Gloria/Bring 'Em On In	1971	10.00
❑ 3003	Richard Cory/Don't You Know	1966	15.00
❑ 3006	Don't Start Crying Now/I Can Only Give You Everything	1966	15.00
❑ 9702	Don't Start Crying Now/One, Two Brown Eyes	1964	20.00
❑ 9727	Gloria/Baby, Please Don't Go	1965	16.00
❑ 9749	Here Comes the Night/All By Myself	1965	15.00
❑ 9784	Gonna Dress in Black/Half As Much	1965	15.00
❑ 9796	Mystic Eyes/If You and I Could Be As Two	1965	15.00
❑ 9819	Call My Name/Bring 'Em On In	1966	15.00

T

Number	Title (A Side/B Side)	Yr	NM
RUFF			
❑ 1088	Walking in the Queen's Garden/I Happen to Love You	1967	25.00
TOWER			
❑ 384	Walking in the Queen's Garden/I Happen to Love You	1967	12.00
❑ 384 [PS]	Walking in the Queen's Garden/I Happen to Love You	1967	30.00
❑ 407	But It's Alright/Square Room	1968	12.00
❑ 461	Waltz of the Flies/We've All Agreed to Help	1969	12.00
❑ 461 [PS]	Waltz of the Flies/We've All Agreed to Help	1969	25.00
—Promo only picture sleeve			
❑ 493	Corina/Dark Are the Shadows	1969	12.00
Albums			
HAPPY TIGER			
❑ HT-1004	Them	1969	50.00
❑ HT-1012	Them In Reality	1971	120.00
LONDON			
❑ PS 639 [P]	Backtrackin'	1974	10.00
❑ LC-50001 [R]	The Story of Them	1977	10.00
❑ 820326-1	Them Featuring Van Morrison	1985	10.00
PARROT			
❑ PA 61005 [M]	Them Featuring "Here Comes the Night"	1965	80.00
❑ PA 61005 [M]	Them Featuring "Gloria"	1966	50.00
—Same album as above, but with slightly different title			
❑ PA 61008 [M]	Them Again	1966	80.00
❑ PAS 71005 [R]	Them Featuring "Here Comes the Night"	1965	70.00
❑ PAS 71005 [R]	Them Featuring "Gloria"	1966	40.00
—Same album as above, but with slightly different title			
❑ PAS 71008 [R]	Them Again	1966	50.00
❑ BP 71053 [(2)P]	Them Featuring Van Morrison	1972	12.00
—"Gloria," "Here Comes the Night," "If You and I Could Be as Two," "One More Time" and "One Two Brown Eyes" are true stereo.			
TOWER			
❑ ST 5104 [S]	Now and Them	1967	80.00
❑ T 5104 [M]	Now and Them	1967	50.00
❑ ST 5116 [S]	Time Out! Time In for Them	1968	100.00

THEM (2)

Number	Title (A Side/B Side)	Yr	NM
45s			
KING			
❑ 5967	Don't Look Now/A Girl Like You	1964	15.00

THEMES, INC.

Yet another creation of STEVE BARRI and P.F. SLOAN.

Number	Title (A Side/B Side)	Yr	NM
45s			
VEE JAY			
❑ 635	Theme from Petyon Place/Paula's Percussion	1964	15.00

THERRIEN, JOE, JR.

Number	Title (A Side/B Side)	Yr	NM
45s			
BRUNSWICK			
❑ 9-55005	Hey Babe, Let's Go Downtown/Come Back to Me Darling	1957	40.00
❑ 9-55017	Wheels/You're Long Gone	1957	80.00
JAT			
❑ 101	I Ain't Gonna Be Around/Play Me a Blue Song	1958	80.00
LIDO			
❑ 505	Hey Babe, Let's Go Downtown/Come Back to Me Darling	1957	120.00

THESE TRAILS

Legendary psychedelic folk from Hawaii.

Number	Title (A Side/B Side)	Yr	NM
Albums			
SINERGIA			
❑ SR 4059	These Trails	1973	180.00

THEY MIGHT BE GIANTS

Number	Title (A Side/B Side)	Yr	NM
12-Inch Singles			
BAR NONE			
❑ EPRO 130 [DJ]	Ana Ng (same on both sides)	1988	10.00
❑ EPRO 167 [DJ]	They'll Need a Crane (same on both sides)	1989	10.00
ELEKTRA			
❑ ED 5427 [DJ]	Birdhouse in Your Soul (same on both sides)	1989	8.00
❑ ED 5453 [DJ]	Twisting (same on both sides)	1990	8.00
❑ ED 5458 [DJ]	Twisting/James K. Polk/Ant	1990	8.00
❑ ED 5460 [DJ]	Istanbul (Not Constantinople) (Album Version) (Brownsville Mix)	1990	8.00
❑ ED 5463 [DJ]	Istanbul (Not Constantinople) (Brownsville Mix 5:15) (Bedford-Stuyvesant Mix 2:30) (Park Slope Mix 2:45) (Willamsburg Mix 2:34)	1990	10.00
❑ ED 5496 [DJ]	Your Racist Friend (Album Version) (Sampla-Delic Remix)	1990	8.00
❑ ED 5891 [DJ]	S-E-X-X-Y (Warren Rigg Microwave Mix 7:52) (Warren Rigg Instrumental 7:52) (Tee's Freeze Mix 5:21) (Tee's In House Dub 5:58) (Tee's Cappella 4:55)	1996	10.00
❑ 63995	S-E-X-X-Y (Warren Rigg Microwave Mix 7:52) (Warren Rigg Instrumental 7:52) (Tee's Freeze Mix 5:21) (Tee's In House Dub 5:58) (Tee's Cappella 4:55)	1996	8.00
45s			
ELEKTRA			
❑ 64578	O Tannenbaum/Christmas Cards	1993	3.00
—Green vinyl			
❑ 64578 [PS]	O Tannenbaum/Christmas Cards	1993	3.00
❑ 64602	Why Does the Sun Shine? (The Sun Is a Mass of Incandescent Gas)/Jessica	1993	2.00
❑ 64602 [PS]	Why Does the Sun Shine? (The Sun Is a Mass of Incandescent Gas)/Jessica	1993	2.00
❑ 64998	Birdhouse in Your Soul/Hot Cha	1990	8.00
EVA-TONE			
❑ 8506475	Everything Right Is Wrong/You'll Miss Me	1985	8.00
—Flexidisc			
❑ 8506475 [PS]	Everything Right Is Wrong/You'll Miss Me	1985	8.00
—Also known as "Wiggle Diskette"; sleeve is two pieces of paper wrapped around a piece of cardboard, with a woman at a loom on the front			
Albums			
BAR NONE			
❑ A-HAON 002	They Might Be Giants	1986	20.00
—Original edition contains lyric sheet and no mention of Restless Records			
❑ A-HAON 004 [EP]	Don't Let's Start	1987	20.00
❑ A-HAON 005 [EP]	(She Was a) Hotel Detective	1988	20.00
BAR NONE/RESTLESS			
❑ A-HAON 002	They Might Be Giants	1988	15.00
—With mention of Restless Records			
❑ 72600	Lincoln	1988	15.00
❑ 72605 [EP]	Don't Let's Start	1988	15.00
—Reissue of A-HAON 004			
❑ 72611 [EP]	They'll Need a Crane	1989	10.00
ELEKTRA			
❑ 60907	Flood	1990	15.00
❑ E1-60907	Flood	1990	15.00
—Columbia House edition			
❑ R 114772	Flood	1990	15.00
—BMG Music Service edition			

THIN LIZZY

Also see PHIL LYNOTT; MOTORHEAD; WHITESNAKE.

Number	Title (A Side/B Side)	Yr	NM
12-Inch Singles			
WARNER BROS.			
❑ PRO-A-754 [DJ]	Cowboy Song/The Boys Are Back in Town/Rosalie	1978	20.00
45s			
LONDON			
❑ 20076	Whiskey in the Jar/Black Boys on the Corner	1972	15.00
❑ 20078	Broken Dreams/Randolph's Tango	1973	15.00
❑ 20082	Little Darling/The Rocket	1973	15.00
MERCURY			
❑ 73786	The Boys Are Back in Town/Jailbreak	1976	5.00
❑ 73841	Cowboy Song/Angel from the Coast	1976	5.00
❑ 73867	Rocky/Half-Caste	1976	6.00
❑ 73882	Old Flame/Johnny the Fox Meets Jimmy the Weed	1977	5.00
❑ 73892	Don't Believe a Word/Boogie Woogie Dance	1977	5.00
❑ 73945	Bad Reputation/Dancing in the Moonlight (It's Caught Me in the Spotlight)	1977	5.00
VERTIGO			
❑ 202	Night Life/Showdown	1974	10.00
❑ 205	Wild One/Freedom Song	1975	10.00
WARNER BROS.			
❑ 8648	Cowboy Song/Johnny the Fox Meets Jimmy the Weed	1978	5.00
❑ 49019	S & M/Do Anything You Want To	1979	5.00
❑ 49078	Got to Give It Up/With Love	1979	5.00
❑ 49643	Killer on the Loose/Sugar Blues	1980	4.00
❑ 49679	We Will Be Strong/Sweetheart	1981	5.00
❑ 50056	Hollywood/Pressure Will Blow	1982	4.00
Albums			
LONDON			
❑ PS 594	Thin Lizzy	1971	40.00
❑ PS 636	Vagabonds of the Western World	1973	30.00
❑ LC-50004	The Rocker (1971-1974)	1977	14.00
MERCURY			
❑ SRM-1-1081	Jailbreak	1976	12.00
❑ SRM-1-1107	Night Life	1976	12.00
—Reissue of Vertigo 2002			
❑ SRM-1-1108	Fighting	1976	12.00
—Reissue of Vertigo 2005			
❑ SRM-1-1119	Johnny the Fox	1976	12.00
❑ SRM-1-1186	Bad Reputation	1977	12.00
❑ 5310376	Jailbreak	2008	20.00
❑ 5313416	Black Rose/A Rock Legend	2009	20.00
VERTIGO			
❑ VEL-2002	Night Life	1974	15.00
❑ VEL-2005	Fighting	1975	15.00
VH1 CLASSICS			
❑ VH 132	Still Dangerous	2009	20.00
WARNER BROS.			
❑ BS2 3213 [(2)]	Live and Dangerous	1978	12.00
❑ BSK 3338	Black Rose/A Rock Legend	1979	10.00
❑ BSK 3496	Chinatown	1980	10.00
❑ BSK 3622	Renegade	1982	10.00
❑ 23831	Thunder and Lightning	1983	10.00
❑ 23986 [(2)]	"Life" — Live	1984	15.00

THIN MEN, THE

Number	Title (A Side/B Side)	Yr	NM
45s			
PARKWAY			
❑ 916	Indian Love Call/Guitar Blues	1964	15.00

THINGS TO COME

Number	Title (A Side/B Side)	Yr	NM
45s			
DUNWICH			
❑ 124	I'm Not Talkin'/'Til the End	1966	50.00
STARFIRE			
❑ 103	Sweet Gina/(B-side unknown)	1966	40.00
WARNER BROS.			
❑ 7164	Come Alive/Dancer	1968	15.00
❑ 7228	Cool Day/Hello	1968	15.00

THINK

Number	Title (A Side/B Side)	Yr	NM
45s			
BIG TREE			
❑ 15000	Once You Understand/Gather	1974	4.00
COLUMBIA			
❑ 44627	Faster Faster/Stop Runnin' Away	1968	6.00
❑ 44848	California (Is Getting So Heavy)/It's a Good Thing	1969	6.00
LAURIE			
❑ 3583	Once You Understand/Gather	1972	5.00
❑ 3594	It's Not the World — It's the People/Who Are You to Tell Me What to Do?	1972	5.00
Albums			
LAURIE			
❑ SLLP-2052	Encounter	1972	12.00

THIRD ESTATE, THE

Number	Title (A Side/B Side)	Yr	NM
Albums			
THIRD ESTATE			
❑ LP-1000	Years Before the Wine	1976	200.00

THIRD POWER

Number	Title (A Side/B Side)	Yr	NM
Albums			
VANGUARD			
❑ VSD-6554	Believe	1970	30.00

THIRD RAIL, THE

Number	Title (A Side/B Side)	Yr	NM
45s			
CAMEO			
❑ 445	The Subway Train That Came to Life/Train Rush Hour Stomp	1966	15.00
EPIC			
❑ 10191	Run, Run, Run/No Return	1967	10.00
❑ 10240	Boppa Do Down Down/Invisible Man	1967	8.00
❑ 10285	Overdose of Love/It's Time to Say Goodbye	1968	8.00
❑ 10323	Shape of Things to Come/She Ain't No Choir Girl	1968	8.00
❑ 10457	The Ballad of General Humpty/Beggin' Me to Stay	1969	8.00

Number	Title (A Side/B Side)	Yr	NM
Albums			
EPIC			
LN 24327 [M]	Id Music	1967	30.00
BN 26327 [S]	Id Music	1967	40.00

THIRTEENTH FLOOR ELEVATORS, THE

Number	Title (A Side/B Side)	Yr	NM
45s			
CONTACT			
5269	You're Gonna Miss Me/Tried to Hide	1966	150.00
HANNA-BARBERA			
492	You're Gonna Miss Me/Tried to Hide	1966	300.00
INTERNATIONAL ARTISTS			
107	You're Gonna Miss Me/Tried to Hide	1967	20.00
—Yellow label			
107	You're Gonna Miss Me/Tried to Hide	1967	40.00
—Blue label			
111	Reverberation (Doubt)/Fire Engine	1967	40.00
113	Before You Accuse Me/Levitation	1968	40.00
121	Baby Blue/She Lives	1968	40.00
122	Slip Inside This House/Splash 1	1968	40.00
126	May the Circle Remain Unbroken/I'm Gonna Love You Too	1968	40.00
130	Livin' On/Scarlet and Gold	1969	40.00
Albums			
INTERNATIONAL ARTISTS			
1 [M]	Psychedelic Sounds	1967	250.00
—Green and yellow label			
1 [M]	Psychedelic Sounds	1968	150.00
—All-yellow label			
1 [S]	Psychedelic Sounds	1968	150.00
—All-yellow label			
1 [S]	Psychedelic Sounds	1968	200.00
—Aqua-blue label			
1 [S]	Psychedelic Sounds	1979	30.00
—Repressing with "Masterfonics" in dead wax			
5 [M]	Easter Everywhere	1968	400.00
—Mono is promo only			
5 [S]	Easter Everywhere	1968	150.00
—With custom inner sleeve			
5 [S]	Easter Everywhere	1968	150.00
—Without custom inner sleeve			
5 [S]	Easter Everywhere	1979	30.00
—Repressing with "Masterfonics" in dead wax			
8	13th Floor Elevators Live	1968	100.00
8	13th Floor Elevators Live	1979	25.00
—Repressing with "Masterfonics" in dead wax			
9	Bull of the Woods	1968	80.00
9	Bull of the Woods	1979	25.00
—Repressing with "Masterfonics" in dead wax			

.38 SPECIAL

Number	Title (A Side/B Side)	Yr	NM
45s			
A&M			
1246	Rock and Roll Strategy/Love Strikes	1988	3.00
1246 [PS]	Rock and Roll Strategy/Love Strikes	1988	3.00
1273	Second Chance/Comin' Down Tonight	1989	3.00
1424	Comin' Down Tonight/Chauahoocie	1989	3.00
1946	Long Time Gone/Four Wheels	1977	4.00
1964	Tell Everybody/Play a Simple Song	1977	4.00
2051	I'm a Fool for You/Travelin' Man	1978	4.00
2205	Rockin' Into the Night/Robin Hood	1979	4.00
2242	Stone Cold Believer/Stone Cold Believer (Part 2)	1980	4.00
2316	Hold On Loosely/Throw Out the Line	1981	4.00
2330	Fantasy Girl/Honky Tonk Dancer	1981	4.00
2330 [PS]	Fantasy Girl/Honky Tonk Dancer	1981	4.00
2412	Caught Up in You/Firestarter	1982	4.00
2412 [PS]	Caught Up in You/Firestarter	1982	4.00
2431	You Keep Runnin' Away/Prisoners of Rock and Roll	1982	4.00
2431 [PS]	You Keep Runnin' Away/Prisoners of Rock and Roll	1982	4.00
2505	Chain Lightnin'/Back on the Track	1982	4.00
2594	If I'd Been the One/Twentieth Century Fox	1983	3.00
2594 [PS]	If I'd Been the One/Twentieth Century Fox	1983	3.00
2615	Back Where You Belong/Undercover Lover	1984	3.00
2615 [PS]	Back Where You Belong/Undercover Lover	1984	3.00
2633	Long Distance Affair/One Time for Old Times	1984	3.00
2831	Like No Other Night/Hearts on Fire	1986	3.00
2831 [PS]	Like No Other Night/Hearts on Fire	1986	3.00
2854	Somebody Like You/Against the Night	1986	3.00
2854 [PS]	Somebody Like You/Against the Night	1986	3.00
2873	One in a Million/Last Time	1986	3.00
2955	Back to Paradise/Hold On Loosely	1987	3.00
2955 [PS]	Back to Paradise/Hold On Loosely	1987	3.00
CAPITOL			
B-5405	Teacher Teacher/Twentieth Century Fox	1984	3.00
B-5405 [PS]	Teacher Teacher/Twentieth Century Fox	1984	3.00
Albums			
A&M			
SP-3164	.38 Special	198?	8.00
—Budget-line reissue of 4638			
SP-3165	Special Delivery	198?	8.00
—Budget-line reissue of 4684			
SP-3216	Rockin' Into the Night	198?	8.00
—Budget-line reissue of 4782			
SP-3298	Wild-Eyed Southern Boys	198?	8.00
—Budget-line reissue of 4835			
SP-3299	Special Forces	198?	8.00
—Budget-line reissue of 4888			
SP-3310	Tour de Force	198?	8.00
—Budget-line reissue of 4971			
SP-3910	Flashback	1987	10.00
—Includes bonus 7-inch 33 1/3 rpm small hole single "Flashback Live EP"; deduct 40 percent if missing			
SP-4638	.38 Special	1977	12.00
SP-4684	Special Delivery	1978	12.00
SP-4782	Rockin' Into the Night	1979	12.00
SP-4835	Wild-Eyed Southern Boys	1981	10.00
SP-4888	Special Forces	1982	10.00
SP-4971	Tour de Force	1983	10.00
SP-5115	Strength in Numbers	1986	10.00
SP-5218	Rock & Roll Strategy	1988	10.00
SP-17402 [DJ]	10 From 38	1986	15.00
—Promo-only compilation			

31ST OF FEBRUARY, THE

Number	Title (A Side/B Side)	Yr	NM
45s			
VANGUARD			
35066	Sandcastles/Pick a Gripe	1968	10.00
35087	In the Morning When I'm Real/Porcelain Mirrors	1969	10.00
Albums			
VANGUARD			
VSD-6503	The 31st of February	1969	40.00

31 FLAVORS, THE

Number	Title (A Side/B Side)	Yr	NM
Albums			
CROWN			
CST-592	Hair	1968	50.00

THOMAS, BUELL

Number	Title (A Side/B Side)	Yr	NM
45s			
DALTON			
102	Shepherds & Kings/My Christmas Star	19??	4.00
—B-side by Jean Doran			
DOOTONE			
316	Santa Claus Walks Just Like Daddy/You're My Christmas	1953	30.00
—B-side by Gerri Goodley			
318	Green Christmas/For My Bride At Christmas Time	1953	30.00

THOMAS, CARLA

Also see OTIS AND CARLA; RUFUS AND CARLA.

Number	Title (A Side/B Side)	Yr	NM
45s			
ATLANTIC			
2086	Gee Whiz (Look at His Eyes)/For You	1960	15.00
2101	A Love of My Own/Promises	1961	12.00
2113	Wish Me Good Luck/In Your Spare Time	1961	12.00
2132	The Masquerade Is Over/I Kinda Think He Does	1962	12.00
2163	I'll Bring It On Home to You/I Can't Take It	1962	12.00
2189	What a Fool I've Been/The Life I Live	1963	12.00
2212	Gee Whiz, It's Christmas/All I Want for Christmas Is You	1963	15.00
2238	I've Got No Time to Lose/A Boy Named Tom	1964	12.00
2258	A Woman's Love/Don't Let the Love Light Leave	1964	12.00
2272	How Do You Quit (Someone You Love)/The Puppet	1965	12.00
GUSTO			
816	All I Want for Christmas Is You/Gee Whiz, It's Christmas	1979	10.00
—A Canadian import ($5) from 1986 exists on King			
SATELLITE			
104	Gee Whiz (Look at His Eyes)/For You	1960	500.00
STAX			
0011	I've Fallen in Love/Where Do I Go	1968	8.00
0024	I Like What You're Doing (To Me)/Strung Out	1969	8.00
0042	Just Keep On Loving Me/My Love	1969	8.00
—With Johnnie Taylor			
0044	I Can't Stop/I Need You Woman	1969	5.00
—With William Bell			
0056	Guide Me Well/Some Other Man (Is Beating Your Time)	1970	8.00
0061	The Time for Love Is Anytime/Living in the City	1970	6.00
0067	All I Have to Do Is Dream/Leave the Girl Alone	1970	5.00
—With William Bell			
0080	Hi De Ho (That Old Sweet Roll)/I Loved You Like I Love My Very Life	1970	6.00
0113	You've Got a Cushion to Fall On/Love Means (You Never Have to Say You're Sorry)	1972	6.00
0133	Sugar/You've Got a Cushion to Fall On	1972	6.00
0149	I May Not Be All You Want/Sugar	1972	6.00
172	Stop! Look What You're Doing/Every Ounce of Strength	1965	12.00
0173	I Have a God Who Loves/Love Among People	1973	6.00
183	Comfort Me/I'm for You	1966	12.00
188	Let Me Be Good to You/Another Night Without My Man	1966	12.00
188 [PS]	Let Me Be Good to You/Another Night Without My Man	1966	100.00
195	B-A-B-Y/What Have You Got to Offer Me	1966	15.00
206	All I Want for Christmas Is You/Winter Snow	1966	12.00
207	Something Good (Is Going to Happen to You)/It's Starting to Grow	1967	10.00
214	Unchanging Love/When Tomorrow Comes	1967	10.00
222	I'll Always Have Faith in You/Stop Thief	1967	10.00
239	Pick Up the Pieces/Separation	1967	10.00
251	A Dime a Dozen/I Want You Back	1968	10.00
Albums			
ATLANTIC			
8057 [M]	Gee Whiz	1961	100.00
—With white "fan" logo			
8057 [M]	Gee Whiz	1963	40.00
—With black "fan" logo			
SD 8057 [S]	Gee Whiz	1961	150.00
—With white "fan" logo			
SD 8057 [S]	Gee Whiz	1963	50.00
—With black "fan" logo			
SD 8232	The Best of Carla Thomas	1969	25.00
STAX			
706 [M]	Comfort Me	1966	35.00
706 [P]	Comfort Me	1966	50.00
709 [M]	Carla	1966	35.00
709 [S]	Carla	1966	50.00
718 [M]	The Queen Alone	1967	35.00
718 [S]	The Queen Alone	1967	50.00
STS-2019	Memphis Queen	1969	35.00
STS-2044	Love Means Carla Thomas	1971	35.00
MPS-8538	Memphis Queen	1987	10.00
—Budget-line reissue			

THOMAS, CARLA, AND RUFUS THOMAS

See RUFUS AND CARLA.

THOMAS, DANNY

Number	Title (A Side/B Side)	Yr	NM
45s			
DECCA			
9-29641	Bring Back Our Beale Street/It's Wonderful When	1955	12.00
9-29842	Nobody Knows But the Lord/Little Miss Tippy Toes	1956	12.00
MYRRH			
120	People We've Grown to Love/Little Boy Tracks	1973	7.00

Number	Title (A Side/B Side)	Yr	NM
131	I'll Still Be Loving You/Jesus Is My Kind of People	197?	7.00
134	I'll Still Be Loving You/(B-side unknown)	1974	7.00
RCA VICTOR			
47-5142	Oh Moon/Hush-a-Bye	1952	15.00

THOMAS, GENE

Also see GENE AND DEBBE.

45s

Number	Title (A Side/B Side)	Yr	NM
CIMARRON			
103	First Times/Goldrush Can Do the Waltz and Rhumba Too	197?	7.00
104	Minnowhauling Man/I Taught You So Many Things	197?	7.00
HICKORY			
1592	Babe, I Wish You Well/Listen Buddy	1971	7.00
1608	Lay It Down/Remembered by Someone	1971	7.00
1631	Touch Something Good/Watching It Go	1972	7.00
PICTURE			
6971	Only Me/What Will My Mary Say	196?	30.00
SAN			
1516	It Hurts/My Baby's in Love with Another Guy	196?	20.00
1517	Long Black Limousine/Play That Lonely Record	196?	20.00
1518	I Took You for Granted Too Long/Blame It on the Moon	196?	20.00
TRX			
5023	Destiny's Children/The More I Think	1969	7.00
5025	The Nature of a Man/Reasons	1969	7.00
UNITED ARTISTS			
338	Sometime/Everyday	1961	12.00
501	It's Make Believe/So Wrong	1962	12.00
583	Peace of Mind/The Puppet	1963	12.00
584	Baby's Gone/Stand By Love	1963	—
—Canceled			
640	Baby's Gone/Stand By Love	1963	12.00
725	The Last Song/Bobby and the Boys	1964	10.00
771	Playing Those Old Records/Together Again	1964	10.00
799	Half the Time/I'd Rather Not Talk About It	1964	10.00
871	Down the Road/It's a Sad World	1965	10.00
VENUS			
1439	Sometime/Every Night	1961	30.00
1441	Lamp of Love/Two Lips	1961	20.00
1443	Mysteries of Love/That's What You Are to Me	1962	20.00
1444	Down the Road/(B-side unknown)	1962	80.00
1445	It's Make Believe/So Wrong	1962	60.00

THOMAS, IAN

12-Inch Singles

Number	Title (A Side/B Side)	Yr	NM
CHRYSALIS			
CHS-2-PDJ [DJ]	Goodnight Mrs. Calabash (same on both sides?)	1976	10.00
MERCURY			
PRO 300-1 [DJ]	Do You Right (same on both sides)	1984	10.00
PRO 402-1 [DJ]	Harmony (same on both sides)	1985	10.00

45s

Number	Title (A Side/B Side)	Yr	NM
ATLANTIC			
3470	Coming Home/Clear Sailing	1978	5.00
3505	Sally/(B-side unknown)	1978	5.00
CHRYSALIS			
2116	Liars/(B-side unknown)	1976	6.00
JANUS			
224	Painted Ladies/Will You Still Love Me	1973	6.00
242	Long Long Way/Count Your Blessings	1974	7.00

Albums

Number	Title (A Side/B Side)	Yr	NM
ATLANTIC			
SD 19167	Still Here	1978	10.00
CHRYSALIS			
CHR 1126	Goodnight Mrs. Calabash	1976	12.00
JANUS			
JLS-3058	Ian Thomas	1973	12.00
JXS-7005	Long Long Way	1974	12.00
MERCURY			
822319-1	Riders on Dark Horses	1984	10.00
826030-1	Add Water	1985	12.00

THOMAS, IRMA

45s

Number	Title (A Side/B Side)	Yr	NM
CANYON			
21	Save a Little Bit for Me/That's How I Feel About You	1970	6.00
31	I'll Do It All Over You/We Won't Be In Your Way Anymore	1970	6.00
CHESS			
2010	Cheater Man/Somewhere Crying	1967	8.00
2017	A Woman Will Do Wrong/I Gave You Everything	1967	8.00
2036	Good to Me/We Got Something Good	1968	8.00
COTILLION			
44144	Full Time Woman/She's Taken My Part	1972	6.00
IMPERIAL			
66013	Wish Someone Would Care/Break-A-Way	1964	12.00
66041	Time Is On My Side/Anyone Who Knows What Love Is (Will Understand)	1964	12.00
66069	Times Have Changed/Moments to Remember	1964	10.00
66080	He's My Guy/(I Want a) True, True Love	1964	10.00
66095	Some Things You Better Get Used To/You Don't Miss a Good Thing	1965	10.00
66106	Nobody Wants to Hear Nobody's Troubles/I'm Gonna Cry Till My Tears Run Dry	1965	10.00
66120	Hurts All Over/It's Starting to Get Me Now	1965	10.00
66137	Take a Look/What Are You Trying to Do	1965	10.00
66178	It's a Man-Woman's World (Part 1)/It's a Man-Woman's World (Part 2)	1966	10.00
MINIT			
625	Cry On/Girl Needs Boy	1961	12.00
633	It's Too Soon to Know/That's All I Ask	1961	12.00
642	Gone/Done Got Over It	1962	12.00
653	It's Raining/I Did My Part	1962	12.00
660	Somebody Told Me/Two Winters Long	1963	12.00
666	Ruler of My Heart/Hitting on Nothing	1963	12.00
RON			
328	Don't Mess with My Man/Set Me Free	1960	15.00
330	Good Man/I May Be Wrong	1960	15.00
UNITED ARTISTS			
0088	Wish Someone Would Care/Take a Look	1973	4.00
—"Silver Spotlight Series" reissue			

Albums

Number	Title (A Side/B Side)	Yr	NM
BANDY			
70003	Irma Thomas Sings	197?	30.00
FUNGUS			
FB-25150	In Between Tears	1973	40.00
IMPERIAL			
LP-9266 [M]	Wish Someone Would Care	1964	50.00
LP-9302 [M]	Take a Look	1966	50.00
LP-12266 [S]	Wish Someone Would Care	1964	60.00
LP-12302 [S]	Take a Look	1966	60.00
RCS			
1004	Safe with Me	1980	30.00

THOMAS, JAMO

45s

Number	Title (A Side/B Side)	Yr	NM
CHESS			
1971	Must I Holler/I'll Be Your Fool	1966	15.00
DECCA			
32293	Education Is Where It's At (Part 1)/(Part 2)	1968	15.00
32406	Bahama Mama (Part I)/(Part II)	1968	15.00
SOUND STAGE 7			
2584	Nassau Daddy/Jive Mother-in-Law	1967	20.00
2596	Bahama Mama (Part I)/(Part II)	1967	15.00
THOMAS			
303	I Spy (For the FBI)/Snake Hip Mama	1966	15.00
303 [PS]	I Spy (For the FBI)/Snake Hip Mama	1966	30.00
304	Arrest Me/Jamo's Soul	1966	25.00
304 [PS]	Arrest Me/Jamo's Soul	1966	50.00

THOMAS, MILLIE

45s

Number	Title (A Side/B Side)	Yr	NM
CAMEO			
358	All Over Again/Take Me Home	1965	15.00

THOMAS, PAT

45s

Number	Title (A Side/B Side)	Yr	NM
MGM			
K13102	Desafinado (Slightly Out of Tune)/One Note Samba	1962	8.00
K13102 [PS]	Desafinado (Slightly Out of Tune)/One Note Samba	1962	12.00
K13124	Home in the Meadow/Where There's Love, There's Hope	1963	20.00
K13171	I'm in the Mood for Love/Just Say Auf Wiederseh'n	1963	10.00
VERVE			
10269	Desafinado (Slightly Out of Tune)/One Note Samba	1962	10.00
10269 [PS]	Desafinado (Slightly Out of Tune)/One Note Samba	1962	12.00
10333	Long Long Night/I Can't Wait Until I See My Baby's Face	1964	10.00

Albums

Number	Title (A Side/B Side)	Yr	NM
MGM			
E-4103 [M]	Desafinado	1962	15.00
SE-4103 [S]	Desafinado	1962	20.00
E-4206 [M]	Moody's Mood	1964	20.00
SE-4206 [S]	Moody's Mood	1964	25.00
STRAND			
SL-1015 [M]	Jazz Patterns	1961	40.00
SLS-1015 [S]	Jazz Patterns	1961	50.00

THOMAS, RAY

Also see THE MOODY BLUES.

45s

Number	Title (A Side/B Side)	Yr	NM
THRESHOLD			
67020	High Above My Head/Love Is the Key	1975	5.00
67023	One Night Stand/Carousel	1975	5.00

Albums

Number	Title (A Side/B Side)	Yr	NM
THRESHOLD			
THS 16	From Mighty Oaks	1975	15.00
THS 17	Hopes Wishes & Dreams	1976	15.00
THSX-102 [DJ]	Ray Thomas Discusses The Recording of His First Solo Album From Mighty Oaks	1975	50.00

THOMAS, RUFUS

Also see RUFUS AND CARLA.

12-Inch Singles

Number	Title (A Side/B Side)	Yr	NM
ICHIBAN			
12-103	Rappin' Rufus (3 versions)	1985	8.00

45s

Number	Title (A Side/B Side)	Yr	NM
ARTISTS OF AMERICA			
126	If There Were No Music/Blues in the Basement	1976	5.00
AVI			
149	Who's Makin' Love to Your Old Lady/Hot Grits	1977	4.00
178	I Ain't Gettin' Older, I'm Gettin' Better (Part 1)/I Ain't Gettin' Older, I'm Gettin' Better (Part 2)	1977	4.00
HI			
78520	Fried Chicken/I Ain't Got Time	1978	4.00
HIGH STACKS			
9801	Hey Rufus!/Body Fine	1999	3.00
—B-side by the Barkays			
ICHIBAN			
85-103	Rappin' Rufus/(Instrumental)	1985	4.00
METEOR			
5039	I'm Steady Holdin' On/The Easy Livin' Plan	1956	150.00
STAX			
0010	Funky Mississippi/So Hard to Get Along With	1968	6.00
0022	Funky Way/I Want to Hold You	1969	6.00
0059	Do the Funky Chicken/Turn Your Damper Down	1969	6.00
0071	Sixty Minute Man/The Preacher and the Bear	1970	6.00
0079	(Do the) Push and Pull Part I/(Do the) Push and Pull Part II	1970	6.00
0090	The World Is Round/(I Love You) For Sentimental Reasons	1971	6.00
0098	The Breakdown (Part 1)/The Breakdown (Part 2)	1971	6.00
0112	Do the Funky Penguin (Part 1)/Do the Funky Penguin (Part 2)	1971	6.00
126	It's Aw-Rite/Can't Ever Let You Go	1962	15.00
0129	Love Trap/6-3-8	1972	6.00

Except when noted otherwise, VG = 25% of NM, and VG+ = 50% of NM. (Example: VG = $2.00, VG+ = $4.00 and NM = $8.00.)

Number	Title (A Side/B Side)	Yr	NM
❑ 130	The Dog/Did You Ever Love a Woman	1963	15.00
❑ 140	Walking the Dog/You Said	1963	12.00
❑ 140	Walking the Dog/Fine and Mellow	1963	30.00
❑ 0140	Itch and Scratch (Part 1)/Itch and Scratch (Part 2)	1972	6.00
❑ 144	Can Your Monkey Do the Dog/ I Want to Get Married	1964	12.00
❑ 149	Somebody Stole My Dog/ I Want to Be Loved	1964	12.00
❑ 0153	Funky Robot (Part 1)/ Funky Robot (Part 2)	1973	6.00
❑ 157	Jump Back/All Night Worker	1964	12.00
❑ 167	Baby Walk/Little Sally Walker	1965	8.00
❑ 173	Willy Nilly/Sho' Gonna Mess Him Up	1965	8.00
❑ 0177	I Know You Don't Want Me No More/I'm Still in Love with You	1973	6.00
❑ 178	Chicken Scratch/The World Is Round	1965	8.00
❑ 0187	I'll Be Your Santa Baby/ That Makes Christmas Day	1973	6.00
❑ 0192	The Funky Bird/Steal a Little	1974	6.00
❑ 200	Talkin' 'Bout True Love/ Sister's Got a Boyfriend	1967	8.00
❑ 0219	Boogie Ain't Nothin' (But Gettin' Down) (Part 1)/Boogie Ain't Nothin' (But Gettin' Down) (Part 2)	1974	6.00
❑ 221	Sophisticated Sissy/ Grasy Spoon	1967	8.00
❑ 0236	Do the Double Bump/ Do the Double Bump	1975	6.00
❑ 240	Down Ta My House/ Steady Holding On	1968	8.00
❑ 250	The Memphis Train/I Think I Made a Boo-Boo	1968	8.00
❑ 0254	Jump Back '75 (Part 1)/ Jump Back '75 (Part 2)	1975	6.00
❑ 1073	I'll Be Your Santa Claus/ Christmas Comes Once A Year	197?	5.00

—B-side by Albert King; reissue

SUN

Number	Title (A Side/B Side)	Yr	NM
❑ 181	Bear Cat/Walking in the Rain	1953	200.00

—No subtitle on A-side

Number	Title (A Side/B Side)	Yr	NM
❑ 181	Bear Cat (The Answer to Hound Dog)/Walking in the Rain	1953	350.00

—With subtitle on A-side

Number	Title (A Side/B Side)	Yr	NM
❑ 188	Tiger Man (King of the Jungle)/ Save Your Money	1953	500.00

Albums

A.V.I.

Number	Title (A Side/B Side)	Yr	NM
❑ 6015	If There Were No Music	1977	15.00
❑ 6046	I Ain't Gettin' Older, I'm Gettin' Better	1978	15.00

ALLIGATOR

Number	Title (A Side/B Side)	Yr	NM
❑ AV-4769	That Woman Is Poison	1988	10.00

GUSTO

Number	Title (A Side/B Side)	Yr	NM
❑ 0064	Rufus Thomas	1980	10.00

STAX

Number	Title (A Side/B Side)	Yr	NM
❑ ST-704 [M]	Walking the Dog	1963	150.00
❑ STS-2028	Do the Funky Chicken	1970	25.00
❑ STS-2039	Rufus Thomas Live/Doing the Push and Pull at P.J.'s	1971	25.00
❑ STS-3004	Did You Hear Me	1972	25.00
❑ STS-3008	Crown Prince of Dance	1973	25.00

THOMAS, TIMMY

12-Inch Singles

GOLD MOUNTAIN

Number	Title (A Side/B Side)	Yr	NM
❑ 81203	Gotta Give a Little Love/ Gotta Give a Little Love (Dub)	1984	6.00
❑ 81203 [DJ]	Gotta Give a Little Love (5:26) (4:35)	1984	8.00

45s

GLADES

Number	Title (A Side/B Side)	Yr	NM
❑ 1703	Why Can't We Live Together/ Funky Me	1972	6.00
❑ 1709	People Are Changin'/ Rainbow Power	1973	6.00
❑ 1712	Let Me Be Your Eyes/Cold Cold People	1973	6.00
❑ 1717	What Can I Tell Her/Opportunity	1973	6.00
❑ 1719	One Brief Moment/Rio Girl	1974	6.00
❑ 1721	Deep in You/Spread Us Around	1974	5.00
❑ 1723	I've Got to See You Tonight/ You're the Song (I've Always Wanted to Sing)	1974	5.00
❑ 1727	Sexy Woman/ Sweet Brown Sugar	1975	5.00
❑ 1730	Ebony Affair/It's What They Can't See	1975	5.00
❑ 1735	Love Shine/Running Out of Time	1976	5.00
❑ 1740	Stone to the Bone/Watch It! Watch It!	1977	5.00
❑ 1748	Touch to Touch/When a House Got Music	1978	5.00
❑ 1749	Freak In, Freak Out/ Say Love, Can You Chase	1978	5.00
❑ 1758	Drown in My Own Tears (Part 1)/ Drown in My Own Tears (Part 2)	1980	5.00

GOLD MOUNTAIN

Number	Title (A Side/B Side)	Yr	NM
❑ 82004	Gotta Give a Little Love (Ten Years After)/Same Old Song	1984	4.00
❑ 82008	Love Is Never Too Late/ Let It Flow	1984	4.00

GOLDWAX

Number	Title (A Side/B Side)	Yr	NM
❑ 320	Have Some Boogaloo/ Liquid Mood	1967	15.00
❑ 327	It's My Life/Whole Lotta Shakin' Goin' On	1967	15.00

MARLIN

Number	Title (A Side/B Side)	Yr	NM
❑ 3348	Are You Crazy??? (Pt. 1)/ Are You Crazy??? (Pt. 2)	1981	4.00

Albums

GLADES

Number	Title (A Side/B Side)	Yr	NM
❑ 33-6501	Why Can't We Live Together	1973	15.00

GOLD MOUNTAIN

Number	Title (A Side/B Side)	Yr	NM
❑ GM-80006	Gotta Give a Little Love	1984	10.00

THOMAS, VIC

45s

PHILIPS

Number	Title (A Side/B Side)	Yr	NM
❑ 40183	Napoleon Bonaparte/Marianne	1964	75.00
❑ 40228	Village of Love/There Stands An Empty Man	1964	75.00

THOMPSON, BILLY

45s

COLUMBUS

Number	Title (A Side/B Side)	Yr	NM
❑ 1043	Black Eyed Girl/Kiss Tomorrow Goodbye	1965	200.00

WAND

Number	Title (A Side/B Side)	Yr	NM
❑ 1108	Black Eyed Girl/Kiss Tomorrow Goodbye	1966	60.00

THOMPSON, JUNIOR

45s

ATCO

Number	Title (A Side/B Side)	Yr	NM
❑ 6500	You're the One/Jungle Girl	1967	12.00

METEOR

Number	Title (A Side/B Side)	Yr	NM
❑ 5029	Mama's Little Baby/Raw Deal	1956	400.00

THOMPSON, LORETTA

45s

SKOOP

Number	Title (A Side/B Side)	Yr	NM
❑ 1050	Buddy-Big Bopper-Ritchie/ Square from Nowhere	1959	50.00

UNITED

Number	Title (A Side/B Side)	Yr	NM
❑ 214	He Do Ho Rock 'N' Roll/ Let's Change the Alphabet	1958	40.00

THOMPSON, PEGGY

45s

HIT

Number	Title (A Side/B Side)	Yr	NM
❑ 04	Love Letters/Soldier Boy	1962	8.00
❑ 07	Mashed Potato Time/ (B-side unknown)	1962	8.00
❑ 15	I Sold My Heart to the Junkman/ Snap Your Fingers	1962	8.00

—B-side by Benny Lattimore

THOMPSON, RICHARD

Also see FAIRPORT CONVENTION; RICHARD AND LINDA THOMPSON.

45s

CAPITOL

Number	Title (A Side/B Side)	Yr	NM
❑ S7-18043	I Can't Wake Up to Save My Life/Easy There	1994	5.00
❑ 58810	Crawl Back (Under My Stone)/ Bathsheba Smiles	1999	3.00

Albums

BONG LOAD

Number	Title (A Side/B Side)	Yr	NM
❑ BL 44 [(2)]	Mock Tudor	1999	15.00
❑ BL 52 [(2)]	Action Packed	2001	15.00

—1,000 copies pressed on "Coke-bottle green" vinyl

CAPITOL

Number	Title (A Side/B Side)	Yr	NM
❑ C1-48845	Amnesia	1988	8.00
❑ C1-95713	Rumor & Sigh	1991	12.00

CARTHAGE

Number	Title (A Side/B Side)	Yr	NM
❑ CGLP-4405	Henry the Human Fly	1983	8.00

—Reissue of Reprise LP

Number	Title (A Side/B Side)	Yr	NM
❑ CGLP-4409	Strict Tempo	1983	8.00
❑ CGLP-4413 [(2)]	Richard Thompson (Guitar/Vocal)	1983	10.00

—Reissue of Island 9421 with original UK title

DIVERSE

Number	Title (A Side/B Side)	Yr	NM
❑ DIV 009	Front Parlour Ballads	2005	25.00

HANNIBAL

Number	Title (A Side/B Side)	Yr	NM
❑ HNLP-1313	Heart of Kindness	1983	10.00
❑ HNLP-1316	Small Town Romance	1984	10.00

POLYDOR

Number	Title (A Side/B Side)	Yr	NM
❑ 825421-1	Across a Crowded Room	1985	8.00
❑ 829728-1	Daring Adventures	1986	8.00

REPRISE

Number	Title (A Side/B Side)	Yr	NM
❑ MS 2112	Henry the Human Fly	1972	20.00

THOMPSON, RICHARD AND LINDA

Albums

CARTHAGE

Number	Title (A Side/B Side)	Yr	NM
❑ CGLP-4403	Sunnyvista	1983	10.00

—First U.S. issue of this LP

Number	Title (A Side/B Side)	Yr	NM
❑ CGLP-4404	Pour Down Like Silver	1983	8.00

—Reissue of Island 9348

Number	Title (A Side/B Side)	Yr	NM
❑ CGLP-4407	I Want to See the Bright Lights Tonight	1983	10.00

—Reissue of Island 9266 (UK)

Number	Title (A Side/B Side)	Yr	NM
❑ CGLP-4408	Hokey Pokey	1983	8.00

—Reissue of Island 9305

Number	Title (A Side/B Side)	Yr	NM
❑ CGLP-4412	First Light	1983	8.00

—Reissue of Chrysalis 1177

CHRYSALIS

Number	Title (A Side/B Side)	Yr	NM
❑ CHR 1177	First Light	1978	15.00
❑ CHR 1247	Sunnyvista	1979	—

—Unreleased in U.S.

HANNIBAL

Number	Title (A Side/B Side)	Yr	NM
❑ HNBL 1303	Shoot Out the Lights	1982	10.00

ISLAND

Number	Title (A Side/B Side)	Yr	NM
❑ ILPS 9266	I Want to See the Bright Lights Tonight	1974	—

—Unreleased in U.S. on this number

Number	Title (A Side/B Side)	Yr	NM
❑ ILPS 9305	Hokey Pokey	1974	15.00
❑ ILPS 9348	Pour Down Like Silver	1975	15.00
❑ ISLA 9421 [(2)]	Bright Lights and Live! More or Less	1977	20.00

—First U.S. issue of "I Want to See the Bright Lights Tonight" plus an LP of unreleased material

THOR-ABLES, THE

45s

TITANIC

Number	Title (A Side/B Side)	Yr	NM
❑ 1001	Our Love Song/Get That Bread	1962	300.00
❑ 1002	My Reckless Heart/Batman and Robin	1962	300.00

THORINSHIELD

45s

PHILIPS

Number	Title (A Side/B Side)	Yr	NM
❑ 40492	The Best of All/Life Is a Dream	1967	8.00
❑ 40521	Family of Man/ Lonely Mountain Again	1968	8.00

Albums

PHILIPS

Number	Title (A Side/B Side)	Yr	NM
❑ PHS 600251	Thorinshield	1968	20.00

THORNE, DAVID

45s

ADMIRAL

Number	Title (A Side/B Side)	Yr	NM
❑ 750	Time Out for Tears/ Since You Went Away	1964	15.00
❑ 756	I Love You, Yes I Do/ Send a Little My Way	1964	15.00
❑ 761	You're Next/Talkin' to Myself	1965	15.00
❑ 768	If You Were Mine Again/ Where'll I Be Tomorrow Night	1965	15.00
❑ 772	Dearest/Turning Point	1965	15.00

CHOICE

Number	Title (A Side/B Side)	Yr	NM
❑ 10	Night-Time Baby/Annie Doesn't Live Here Any More	1960	20.00

—As "David Throne"

RIVERSIDE

Number	Title (A Side/B Side)	Yr	NM
❑ 4520	I'll Be There/If You Should Ever Need Me	1962	12.00
❑ 4530	The Alley Cat Song/ The Moon Was Yellow	1962	12.00
❑ 4552	Don't Let It Get Away/One More Fool, One More Broken Heart	1963	12.00

SAVOY

Number	Title (A Side/B Side)	Yr	NM
❑ 1577	You Can't Do Me This Way/ These Are the Things	1959	20.00

T

THORNTON, BIG MAMA

Number	Title (A Side/B Side)	Yr	NM
45s			
ARHOOLIE			
❑ 512	Swing It On Home/ My Heavy Load	1968	8.00
❑ 520	Ball and Chain/ Wade in the Water	1968	8.00
BAYTONE			
❑ 107	You Did Me Wrong/ Big Mama's Blues	1961	15.00
GALAXY			
❑ 749	Life Goes On/Because It's Love	1966	10.00
KENT			
❑ 424	Before Day/Me and My Chauffeur	1965	10.00
MERCURY			
❑ 72981	Hound Dog/Let's Go Get Started	1969	8.00
PEACOCK			
❑ 1603	Everytime I Think of You/ Mischievous Boogie	1952	100.00
❑ 1612	Hound Dog/Nightmare	1953	180.00
❑ 1612	Hound Dog/Rock-a-Bye Baby	1953	200.00
❑ 1621	They Call Me Big Mama/ Cotton Pickin' Blues	1953	100.00
❑ 1626	Big Change/I Ain't No Fool Either	1953	100.00
❑ 1632	I've Searched the Whole World/ I Smell a Rat	1954	60.00
❑ 1642	Stop Hoppin' on Me/ Story of My Blues	1954	60.00
❑ 1647	Walking Blues/Rock-a-Bye Baby	1955	60.00
❑ 1650	The Fish/Laugh, Laugh, Laugh	1955	60.00
❑ 1681	Just Like a Dog/ My Man Called Me	1957	40.00
SOTOPLAY			
❑ SO-0033/34	Summer Time/The Truth'll Come to the Light	1965	15.00
Albums			
ARHOOLIE			
❑ F-1028 [M]	Big Mama Thornton in Europe	1966	30.00
❑ F-1032 [M]	Chicago Blues: The Queen at Monterey	1967	30.00
❑ F-1039 [M]	Ball and Chain	1968	30.00
BACK BEAT			
❑ BLP-68	She's Back	1970	25.00
MERCURY			
❑ SR-61225	Stronger Than Dirt	1969	25.00
❑ SR-61249	The Way It Is	1970	25.00
PENTAGRAM			
❑ PE-10005	Saved	1971	20.00
VANGUARD			
❑ VSD-79351	Jail	1974	15.00
❑ VSD-79354	Sassy Mama	1975	15.00

THORNTON, FRADKIN AND UNGER

Number	Title (A Side/B Side)	Yr	NM
45s			
ESP-DISK			
❑ 63019	God Bless California/Sometimes	1972	15.00

—Paul McCartney appears on this record

THORPE, BILLY

Number	Title (A Side/B Side)	Yr	NM
45s			
PASHA			
❑ 02562	No Rules on the Road/ You Touched Me	1981	4.00
❑ 03153	East of Eden's Gate/ Hold On to Your Dream	1982	4.00
❑ 03351	No Show Tonight/ East of Eden's Gate	1982	4.00
POLYDOR			
❑ 2018	Children of the Sun/Wrapped in the Chains of Your Love	1979	5.00
❑ 2025	Dream-Maker/The Beginning	1980	4.00
Albums			
CAPRICORN			
❑ CPN 0221	Children of the Sun	1979	20.00
ELEKTRA			
❑ 6E-294	21st Century Man	1980	10.00
PASHA			
❑ ARZ 37499	Stimulation	1981	10.00
❑ FZ 38179	East of Eden's Gate	1982	10.00
❑ BFZ 40682	Children of the Sun... Revisited	1987	10.00
POLYDOR			
❑ PD-1-6228	Children of the Sun	1979	12.00

3 1/2

Number	Title (A Side/B Side)	Yr	NM
45s			
CAMEO			
❑ 425	Don't Cry to Me Babe/R&B in C	1966	15.00
❑ 442	Problem Child/Hey Mom, Hey Dad	1966	15.00
❑ 451	Hey Gyp/Hey Kitty, Cool Kitty	1967	15.00
❑ 485	Angel Baby (Don't You Ever Leave Me)/You Turned Your Back on Love	1967	20.00

THREE BELLS, THE

Number	Title (A Side/B Side)	Yr	NM
45s			
LAWN			
❑ 251	He Doesn't Love Me/ Softly in the Night	1965	12.00

THREE BLONDE MICE

Number	Title (A Side/B Side)	Yr	NM
45s			
ATCO			
❑ 6324	Ringo Bells/The 12 Days of Christmas	1964	30.00
❑ 6353	Alley Cat/What Did I Say	1965	10.00

THREE CHUCKLES, THE Also see TEDDY RANDAZZO.

Number	Title (A Side/B Side)	Yr	NM
45s			
BOULEVARD			
❑ 100	Runaround/At Last You Understand	1954	80.00
VIK			
❑ 0186	Anyway/The Funny Little Things We Used to Do	1956	20.00
❑ 0194	Tell Me/And the Angels Sing	1956	20.00
❑ 0216	Gypsy in My Soul/We're Still Holding Hands	1956	20.00
❑ 0232	Fallen Out of Love/ Midnight 'Til Dawn	1956	20.00
❑ 0244	Won't You Give Me a Chance/ We're Gonna Rock Tonight	1956	20.00
"X"			
❑ 0066	Runaround/At Last You Understand	1954	25.00
❑ 0095	Foolishly/ If I Should Love Again	1955	25.00
❑ 0134	So Long/You Should Have Told Me	1955	25.00
❑ 0150	Blue Lover/Realize	1955	25.00
❑ 0162	Times Two, I Love You/ Still Thinking of You	1955	25.00
❑ 0186	Anyway/The Funny Little Things We Used to Do	1956	25.00
❑ 0194	Tell Me/And the Angels Sing	1956	25.00
❑ 0216	Gypsy in My Soul/We're Still Holding Hands	1956	25.00
7-Inch Extended Plays			
"X"			
❑ EXA-192	To Each His Own/Solitude// In the Still of the Night/ It's Been a Long, Long Time	1955	40.00
❑ EXA-192 [PS]	The Three Chuckles (Vol. 1)	1955	40.00
❑ EXA-193	(contents unknown)	1955	40.00
❑ EXA-193 [PS]	The Three Chuckles (Vol. 2)	1955	40.00
❑ EXA-194	(contents unknown)	1955	40.00
❑ EXA-194 [PS]	The Three Chuckles (Vol. 3)	1955	40.00
Albums			
VIK			
❑ LX-1067 [M]	The Three Chuckles	1956	250.00

THREE D'S, THE (1)

Number	Title (A Side/B Side)	Yr	NM
45s			
BRUNSWICK			
❑ 55152	Nothing to Wear/The Happiest Boy and Girl	1959	25.00
PARIS			
❑ 503	Little Billy Boy/Let Me Know	1957	20.00
❑ 508	Never Let You Go/ Birth of An Angel	1957	20.00
❑ 511	Baby Doll/Crazy Little Woman	1958	20.00
❑ 514	Jumpin' Jack/I Never Saw My Pretty Little Baby Alone	1958	20.00
PILGRIM			
❑ 719	Broken Dreams/Tell Me That You Love Me	1956	25.00
SQUARE			
❑ 502	Squeeze/Graveyard Cha-Cha	1959	80.00

THREE D'S, THE (2)

Number	Title (A Side/B Side)	Yr	NM
45s			
CAPITOL			
❑ 5188	Sinner Man/Give, Said the Little Stream	1964	10.00
❑ 5249	Chim Chim Cheree/Crayon Box	1964	10.00
Albums			
CAPITOL			
❑ ST 2171 [S]	New Dimensions in Folk Songs	1964	25.00
❑ T 2171 [M]	New Dimensions in Folk Songs	1964	20.00
❑ ST 2314 [S]	I Won't Be Worried Long	1965	25.00
❑ T 2314 [M]	I Won't Be Worried Long	1965	20.00

THREE D'S, THE (U)

Number	Title (A Side/B Side)	Yr	NM
45s			
DEAN			
❑ 521	Broken Hearted/I Love You So	1961	20.00

THREE DEGREES, THE

Number	Title (A Side/B Side)	Yr	NM
45s			
ARIOLA AMERICA			
❑ 801	My Simple Heart/ Hot Summer Night	1980	4.00
❑ 7721	Giving Up, Giving In/ Woman in Love	1978	4.00
❑ 7742	Woman in Love/ Out of Love Again	1979	4.00
❑ 7746	The Runner/Out of Love Again	1979	4.00
EPIC			
❑ 50283	What I Did for Love/ Macaronie Man	1976	4.00
❑ 50330	In Love We Grow/ Standing Up for Love	1977	4.00
ICHIBAN			
❑ 89-167	Tie U Up/(B-side unknown)	1989	5.00
METROMEDIA			
❑ 109	Down in the Boondocks/ Warm Weather Music	1969	8.00
❑ 128	Feeling of Love/ Warm Weather Music	1969	8.00
NEPTUNE			
❑ 23	Reflections of Yesterday What I See	1970	6.00
PHILADELPHIA INT'L.			
❑ 3534	Dirty Ol Man/Can't You See What You're Doing to Me	1973	6.00
❑ 3539	Year of Decision/A Woman Needs a Good Man	1974	5.00
❑ 3550	When Will I See You Again/ Year of Decision	1974	5.00
❑ 3561	I Didn't Know/Dirty Ol Man	1975	5.00
❑ 3568	Take Good Care of Yourself/ Here I Am	1975	5.00
❑ 3585	Free Ride/Loving Cup	1976	5.00
ROULETTE			
❑ 7072	Melting Pot/The Grass Will Sing for You	1970	6.00
❑ 7079	Maybe/Collage	1970	6.00
❑ 7079	Maybe/Sugar on Sunday	1970	6.00
❑ 7088	I Do Take You/You're the Fool	1970	6.00
❑ 7097	You're the One/Stardust	1971	6.00
❑ 7102	There's So Much Love All Around/Yours	1971	6.00
❑ 7105	Ebb Tide/Low Down	1971	6.00
❑ 7117	Trade Winds/I Turn to You	1972	6.00
❑ 7125	Find My Way/I Wanna Be Your Baby	1972	6.00
❑ 7137	I Won't Let You Go/ Through Misty Eyes	1972	6.00
SWAN			
❑ 4197	Gee Baby (I'm Sorry)/Do What You're Supposed to Do	1965	12.00
❑ 4214	I'm Gonna Need You/ Just Right for Love	1965	12.00
❑ 4224	Close Your Eyes/ Gotta Draw the Line	1965	12.00
❑ 4235	Look in My Eyes/Drivin' Me Mad	1965	12.00
❑ 4245	Maybe/Yours	1966	12.00
❑ 4253	I Wanna Be Your Baby/ Tales Are True	1966	12.00
❑ 4267	Love of My Life/Are You Satisfied	1967	12.00
WARNER BROS.			
❑ 7198	Contact/Oh No Not Again	1968	10.00
Albums			
ARIOLA AMERICA			
❑ OL 1501	Three D	1980	10.00
❑ SW-50044	New Dimensions	1978	10.00
EPIC			
❑ PE 34385	Standing Up for Love	1977	12.00
ICHIBAN			
❑ ICH-1041	Three Degrees...And Holding	198?	10.00
PHILADELPHIA INT'L.			
❑ KZ 32406	The Three Degrees	1974	12.00
❑ KZ 33162	International	1975	12.00
❑ PZ 33840	The Three Degrees Live	1975	12.00
ROULETTE			
❑ 3015	So Much Love	1975	10.00
❑ SR-42050	Maybe	1970	40.00

THREE DOG NIGHT Also see DANNY HUTTON; CORY WELLS AND THE ENEMYS.

45s

Number	Title (A Side/B Side)	Yr	NM
ABC			
❑ 12114	'Til the World Ends/Yo Te Quiero Hablo (Take You Down)	1975	4.00
❑ 12192	Everybody Is a Masterpiece/ Drive On, Ride On	1976	4.00
ABC DUNHILL			
❑ 4168	Nobody/It's for You	1968	12.00
❑ 4168 [PS]	Nobody/It's for You	1968	30.00
—Sleeve is promo only			
❑ 4177	Try a Little Tenderness/That No One Ever Hurt So Bad	1969	8.00
❑ 4191	One/Chest Fever	1969	8.00
❑ 4203	Easy to Be Hard/Dreaming Isn't Good for You	1969	8.00
❑ 4215	Eli's Coming/Circle for a Landing	1969	8.00
❑ 4229	Celebrate/Feeling Alright	1970	6.00
❑ 4239	Mama Told Me (Not to Come)/ Rock and Roll Widow	1970	6.00
❑ 4239 [PS]	Mama Told Me (Not to Come)/ Rock and Roll Widow	1970	12.00
❑ 4250	Out in the Country/ Good Time Living	1970	6.00
❑ 4262	One Man Band/It Ain't Easy	1970	6.00
❑ 4272	Joy to the World/I Can Hear You Calling	1971	5.00
❑ 4282	Liar/Can't Get Enough of It	1971	5.00
❑ 4294	An Old Fashioned Love Song/ Jam	1971	5.00
❑ 4299	Never Been to Spain/ Peace of Mind	1972	5.00
❑ 4299	Never Been to Spain//Intro Poem: Mistakes and Illusions/Peace of Mind	1972	6.00
❑ 4306	The Family of Man/ Going in Circles	1972	5.00
❑ 4317	Black and White/Freedom for the Stallion	1972	5.00
❑ 4331	Pieces of April/The Writings on the Wall	1972	5.00
❑ 4352	Shambala/Our "B" Side	1973	4.00
—Later pressings have "Dunhill" in a box on both labels (1968-72 style)			
❑ 4352	Shambala/Our "B" Side	1973	5.00
—Transitional pressings have "Dunhill" in children's blocks on one label and "Dunhill" in a box on the other label			
❑ 4352	Shambala/Our "B" Side	1973	5.00
—First pressings have "Dunhill" spelled out in children's blocks			
❑ 4370	Let Me Serenade You/ Storybook Feeling	1973	4.00
❑ 4382	The Show Must Go On/ On the Way Back Home	1974	4.00
❑ 15001	Sure As I'm Sittin' Here/ Anytime Babe	1974	4.00
❑ 15010	The Show Must Go On/ On the Way Back Home	1974	8.00
❑ 15013	Play Something Sweet (Brickyard Blues)/ I'd Be So Happy	1974	4.00
PASSPORT			
❑ 7921	It's a Jungle Out There/ Somebody's Gonna Get Hurt	1983	5.00

7-Inch Extended Plays

Number	Title (A Side/B Side)	Yr	NM
ABC			
❑ PRO-40014	The Show Must Go On/Sure As I'm Sitting Here//Anytime Babe/Put Out the Light	1974	20.00
—Quadraphonic jukebox issue; small hole, plays at 33 1/3 rpm			
❑ PRO-40014 [PS]	Hard Labor	1974	20.00
—Part of "Little LP" series (#QD 257)			
ABC DUNHILL			
❑ LLP-231	Happy Song/Play Children Play//Storybook Feeling/ Ridin' Thumb	1973	12.00
—Jukebox issue; small hole, plays at 33 1/3 rpm			
❑ LLP-231 [PS]	Cyan	1973	12.00
❑ PRO-50108	My Impersonal Life/An Old Fashioned Love Song//Never Dreamed You'd Leave in Summer/Jam	1971	12.00
—Jukebox issue; small hole, plays at 33 1/3 rpm			
❑ PRO-50108 [PS]	Harmony	1971	12.00

Albums

Number	Title (A Side/B Side)	Yr	NM
ABC			
❑ 888	Coming Down Your Way	1975	10.00
❑ 928	American Pastime	1976	10.00
ABC COMMAND			
❑ CQD-40014 [Q]	Hard Labor	1974	20.00
❑ CQD-40018 [Q]	Coming Down Your Way	1975	20.00
ABC DUNHILL			
❑ DS-50048	Three Dog Night	1968	15.00
❑ DS-50048	Three Dog Night "One"	1969	12.00
—Same album as above, but with revised title on cover			
❑ DS-50058	Suitable for Framing	1969	12.00
❑ DS-50068	Three Dog Night Was Captured Live at the Forum	1969	12.00
❑ DS-50078	It Ain't Easy	1970	12.00
—Regular front cover with gatefold			
❑ DS-50078	It Ain't Easy	1970	100.00
—Original cover with band members in the nude			
❑ DSX-50088	Naturally	1970	12.00
—With detachable cardboard poster intact			
❑ DSX-50098	Golden Bisquits	1971	12.00
—With detachable cardboard poster intact; interestingly, the label spells the LP title "Golden Biscuits"			
❑ DSX-50108	Harmony	1971	12.00
❑ DSD-50118	Seven Separate Fools	1972	12.00
—With seven oversize playing cards included			
❑ DSY-50138 [(2)]	Around the World with Three Dog Night	1973	15.00
❑ DSX-50158	Cyan	1973	12.00
❑ DSD-50168	Hard Labor	1974	10.00
—With huge Band-Aid as part of the LP artwork			
❑ DSD-50168	Hard Labor	1974	15.00
—With huge Band-Aid attached to jacket, covering the "childbirth"			
❑ DSD-50168	Hard Labor	1974	30.00
—With uncensored "childbirth" front cover			
❑ DSD-50178	Joy to the World: Their Greatest Hits	1974	12.00
—With gatefold cover			
❑ DSD-50178	Joy to the World: Their Greatest Hits	1975	10.00
—With standard cover			
❑ SKAO-92057	Suitable for Framing	1969	15.00
—Capitol Record Club edition			
❑ SKAO-93211	It Ain't Easy	1970	15.00
—Capitol Record Club edition			
❑ SMAS-93422	Naturally	1970	15.00
—Capitol Record Club edition			
❑ SVAS-94772	Seven Separate Fools	1972	15.00
—Capitol Record Club edition			
AT EASE			
❑ MD 11109	Three Dog Night: Their Greatest Recordings	1978	20.00
—"This Album Compiled Exclusively for Military Personnel" by ABC			
COLUMBIA SPECIAL PRODUCTS			
❑ P 14769	Three Dog Night	1978	15.00
MCA			
❑ 6018 [(2)]	The Best of Three Dog Night	1982	12.00
❑ 37120	Joy to the World: Their Greatest Hits	1980	8.00
PASSPORT			
❑ PB 5001 [EP]	It's a Jungle	1983	8.00
PICKWICK			
❑ SPC-3664	Golden Greats of Three Dog Night	1979	10.00
SESSIONS			
❑ ARI-1004 [(2)]	Sessions Presents Three Dog Night	1977	12.00

Three Dog Night, *Seven Separate Fools*, ABC-Dunhill DSD-50118, 1972, with oversize playing cards, **$12.**

THREE DOTS AND A DASH With JESSE BELVIN.

45s

Number	Title (A Side/B Side)	Yr	NM
IMPERIAL			
❑ 5164	I'll Never Love Again/Let's Do It	1951	500.00

THREE FRIENDS, THE (1)

45s

Number	Title (A Side/B Side)	Yr	NM
CAL-GOLD			
❑ 169	Walkin' Shoes/Blue Ribbon Baby	1961	200.00
IMPERIAL			
❑ 5763	Dedicated (To the Songs I Love)/ Happy as a Man Can Be	1961	30.00
❑ 5773	You're a Square/Go On to School	1961	20.00

THREE FRIENDS, THE (2)

45s

Number	Title (A Side/B Side)	Yr	NM
BRUNSWICK			
❑ 55032	Jinx/Chinese Tearoom	1957	30.00
LIDO			
❑ 500	Baby I'll Cry/Blanche	1956	40.00
—Blue label			
❑ 500	Baby I'll Cry/Blanche	1956	60.00
—Gray label			
❑ 502	I'm Only a Boy/Jinx	1957	50.00

Number	Title (A Side/B Side)	Yr	NM
❑ 504	Now That You've Gone/Chinese Tea Room	1957	50.00

LOST-NITE

Number	Title (A Side/B Side)	Yr	NM
❑ 398	Baby I'll Cry/Blanche	197?	5.00

—Reissue

THREE G'S, THE

45s

COLUMBIA

Number	Title (A Side/B Side)	Yr	NM
❑ 4-41175	Let's Go Steady for the Summer/Wild Man	1958	20.00
❑ 4-41256	I'll Wait Forever/Sweet Thing	1958	15.00
❑ 4-41292	These Are the Little Things/Wonder	1958	15.00
❑ 4-41383	When It's Summer Again/Oh, Suzette	1959	15.00
❑ 4-41513	Barbara/Don't Cry Kathy	1959	15.00
❑ 4-41584	Eeny-Meeny-Miny-Moe/Take That Step	1960	15.00
❑ 4-41678	Let's Go Steady for the Summer/Love Call	1960	15.00
❑ 4-41868	She's Mine/Take My Love	1960	15.00
❑ 4-41955	Foolish Tears/Blueberry Hill	1961	15.00

RIP

Number	Title (A Side/B Side)	Yr	NM
❑ 138	Toy Telephone/Going Steady	1958	30.00

THREE MAN ARMY, THE

Albums

KAMA SUTRA

Number	Title (A Side/B Side)	Yr	NM
❑ KSBS-2044	A Third of a Lifetime	1971	30.00

—Pink label, gatefold cover

REPRISE

Number	Title (A Side/B Side)	Yr	NM
❑ MS 2150	Three Man Army	1973	20.00
❑ MS 2182	Three Man Army Two	1974	20.00

THREE PENNIES, THE

45s

B.T. PUPPY

Number	Title (A Side/B Side)	Yr	NM
❑ 501	A Penny for Your Thoughts/Why Am I So Shy	1964	12.00
❑ 511	A Penny for Your Thoughts/Why Am I So Shy	1965	15.00

—As "The English Muffins"; these are the same recordings as on 501

THREE PLAYMATES, THE

45s

SAVOY

Number	Title (A Side/B Side)	Yr	NM
❑ 1523	Giddy-Up-a-Ding-Dong/It Must Be Love	1957	25.00
❑ 1528	Sugah Wooga/Lovey Dovey Pair	1958	25.00
❑ 1537	(Do-oo, Do-oo) I Dreamer/Give Your Love to Me	1958	25.00

T

THREE SOULS, THE

45s

ARGO

Number	Title (A Side/B Side)	Yr	NM
❑ 5369	The Horse/Madisonville	1960	20.00
❑ 5472	Hi-Heel Sneakers/Dangerous Dan Express	1964	15.00
❑ 5514	You're No Good/Chitterlins Con Carne	1965	12.00

NOTE

Number	Title (A Side/B Side)	Yr	NM
❑ 10015	Night Time/Smorgasbord	1959	20.00

Albums

ARGO

Number	Title (A Side/B Side)	Yr	NM
❑ LP-4005 [M]	Almost Like Being In Love	1960	—
—Canceled			
❑ LPS-4005 [S]	Almost Like Being In Love	1960	—
—Canceled			
❑ LP-4036 [M]	Dangerous Dan Express	1964	20.00
❑ LPS-4036 [S]	Dangerous Dan Express	1964	25.00
❑ LP-4044 [M]	Soul Sounds	1965	20.00
❑ LPS-4044 [S]	Soul Sounds	1965	25.00

THREE SUNS, THE

45s

RCA VICTOR

Number	Title (A Side/B Side)	Yr	NM
❑ 47-2756	Dancing Tambourine/Stumbling	1949	10.00
❑ 47-2757	Dizzy Fingers/Eccentric	1949	10.00
❑ 47-2758	Nola/The Doll Dance	1949	10.00
❑ 47-2759	Canadian Capers/The Wedding of the Painted Doll	1949	10.00
—The above four comprise a box set			
❑ 47-2842	I'll Never Wish for More Than This/The Breeze and I	1949	10.00
—The above four comprise a box set			
❑ 47-2898	Hurry! Hurry! Hurry!/Ballin' the Jack	1949	12.00
❑ 47-2924	Ting-a-Ling/Everybody Kiss the Bride	1949	12.00
❑ 47-2964	Lover's Gold/In a Shady Nook by a Babbling Brook	1949	12.00
❑ 47-2996	Hop Scotch Polka/The Windmill's Turning	1949	12.00
❑ 47-3025	Soft Lips/Give Me Some Sugar, Sugar Baby	1949	12.00
❑ 47-3057	Adeste Fideles/Santa Claus Is Coming to Town	1949	10.00
❑ 47-3058	Winter Wonderland/White Christmas	1949	10.00
❑ 47-3059	Jingle Bells/Silent Night	1949	10.00
—The above three comprise box set WP 250, "The Three Suns Present Your Christmas Favorites"			
❑ 47-3079	Close Your Eyes and Dream/Merry Maiden Polka	1949	12.00
❑ 47-3094	The Donkey Serenade/Serenade	1949	10.00
❑ 47-3095	Penthouse Serenade/Frasquita Serenade	1949	10.00
❑ 47-3096	Serenade from the Student Prince/Serenade in the Night	1949	10.00
—The above three comprise a box set			
❑ 47-3105	Beyond the Sunset/The Game of Broken Hearts	1949	30.00
—With Rosalie Allen and Elton Britt			
❑ 47-3202	Sugar Blues/The French Can-Can Song	1949	12.00
❑ 47-3230	Goofus/Ragging the Scale	1949	10.00
❑ 47-3231	Josephine/Parade of the Wooden Soldiers	1949	10.00
❑ 47-3232	The Darktown Strutters' Ball/The Glow-Worm	1949	10.00
—The above three comprise a box set			
❑ 47-3272	Cruising Down the River/Allah's Holiday	1949	12.00
❑ 47-3722	Blue Prelude/I May Hate Myself in the Morning	1950	12.00
❑ 47-3768	The Flying Red Horse Polka/Leicester Square Rag	1950	12.00
❑ 47-3786	Abide with Me/Ave Maria	1950	10.00
❑ 47-3787	Lead Kindly Light/Whispering Hope	1950	10.00
❑ 47-3817	Miaianne/When the Saints Go Marching In	1950	12.00
❑ 47-3824	Gone Fishin'/So Tall a Tree	1950	12.00
❑ 47-3843	Jalousie (Jealousy)/Fiddle Faddle	1950	12.00
❑ 47-3844	Ritual Fire Dance/Malaguena	1950	12.00
❑ 47-3924	Sleigh Ride/I'll Find You	1949	15.00
❑ 47-3976	It Is No Secret (What God Can Do)/To Think You've Chosen Me	1950	12.00
❑ 47-4010	After You've Gone/Remember Me in Your Dreams	1950	12.00
❑ 47-4090	The Syncopated Clock/March of Cards	1951	12.00
❑ 47-4122	What Will I Tell My Heart/I Whistle a Happy Tune	1951	12.00
❑ 47-4150	Tom's Tune/These Things I Offer You	1951	12.00
❑ 47-4199	Come On-a My House/Hula Blues	1951	10.00
❑ 47-4200	Auf Wiedersehn/Hands Across the Table	1951	10.00
❑ 47-4201	Autumn Leaves/La Vie En Rose	1951	10.00
❑ 47-4202	You and the Night and the Music/Yours Is My Heart Alone	1951	10.00
—The above four comprise a box set			
❑ 47-4221	The Bird of Happiness/At the End of Day	1951	12.00
❑ 47-4258	Kol Nidre/Eili Eili	1951	12.00
❑ 47-4287	Little Jumping Jack/Painting Clouds with Sunshine	1951	12.00
❑ 47-4323	Sleigh Ride/Uncle Mistletoe	1951	15.00
❑ 47-4385	Sunshower/Sleepy Serenade	1951	12.00
❑ 47-4463	Laura/My Reverie	1952	10.00
❑ 47-4464	April in Paris/Moonglow	1952	10.00
❑ 47-4465	Intermezzo/Moonlight Sonata	1952	10.00
❑ 47-4466	My Silent Love/Smoke Rings	1952	10.00
—The above four comprise a box set			
❑ 47-4510	Cool, Cool Kisses/Stolen Love	1952	12.00
❑ 47-4562	You're Not Worth My Tears/Two Wrongs Never Make a Right	1952	12.00
❑ 47-4677	Delicado/Plink, Plank, Plunk	1952	12.00
❑ 47-4790	Birds 'n' Bees/Sky-High	1952	12.00
❑ 47-5082	Twilight Boogie/Junga-Junga	1952	12.00
❑ 47-5185	Waggashoe/Ecstacy Tango	1953	12.00
❑ 47-5246	Anna/Little Red Monkey	1953	12.00
❑ 47-5347	Under Paris Skies/Don't Take Love from Me	1953	12.00
❑ 47-5417	Invisible Hands/One Step	1953	12.00
❑ 47-5463	Peg o' My Heart/Jealous	1953	12.00
❑ 47-5553	The Creep/Just One More Chance	1953	12.00
❑ 47-5711	Under a Blanket of Blue/Gimme a Little Kiss	1954	12.00
❑ 47-5768	Moonlight and Roses (Bring Mem'ries of You)/Crazy Legs	1954	12.00
❑ 47-5874	Touch/Southern Star	1954	12.00
❑ 47-5961	For You/Perdido	1954	12.00
❑ 47-6084	I Wonder, I Wonder, I Wonder/Dancing with Tears in My Eyes	1955	10.00
❑ 47-6202	Satan Takes a Holiday/You and You Alone	1955	10.00
❑ 47-6273	Arrividerci Roma/Cha Cha Joe	1955	10.00
❑ 47-6461	The Beautiful Girls of Vienna/Petite Papillon	1956	10.00
❑ 47-6574	Theme from The Proud Ones/Haunted Guitar	1956	10.00
❑ 47-6713	Postmark: Vienna/Wind River Valley	1956	10.00
❑ 47-6881	The Lovers/Wailin' Guitar	1957	10.00
❑ 47-7072	Tumbling Tumbleweeds/Sentimental Journey	1957	10.00
❑ 47-7187	Rainbow/Tweety	1958	10.00
❑ 47-7416	Volcano/Cha Cha Charleston	1958	10.00
❑ 47-7970	Honey Bee/Fun in the Sun	1961	8.00
❑ 47-8373	My Man/Happy Wedding Song	1964	8.00
❑ 47-2839	Twilight Time/Hindustan	1949	10.00
❑ 47-2840	Deep Purple/Dardanella	1949	10.00
❑ 47-2841	Sunrise Serenade/When Day Is Done	1949	10.00
—The above three comprise box set WP 185, "The Three Suns Present"			
❑ 47-3788	Beautiful Isle of Somewhere/In the Garden	1950	10.00
—The above three comprise box set WP-285, "The Three Suns Present Your Favorite Hymns"			
❑ 47-4128	Waltz Serenade/Waltz in A-Flat	1951	10.00
❑ 47-4129	Rosenkavalier - Waltz/Two Hearts in Three-Quarter Time	1951	10.00
❑ 47-4130	The Sleeping Beauty Waltz/Coppelia Waltz	1951	10.00
—The above three comprise box set WP 313, "3/4 Time"			
❑ WP 185 [PS]	The Three Suns Present	1949	10.00
—Box for three-record set (47-2839, 47-2840, 47-2841)			
❑ WP 250 [PS]	Your Christmas Favorites	1949	10.00
—Box for three-record set (47-3057, 47-3058, 47-3059)			
❑ WP-285 [PS]	The Three Suns Present Your Favorite Hymns	1950	10.00
—Box for set containing 47-3786, 47-3787, 47-3788			
❑ WP 313 [PS]	3/4 Time	1951	10.00
—Box for 3-record set (47-4128, 47-4129, 47-4130)			

7-Inch Extended Plays

RCA VICTOR

Number	Title (A Side/B Side)	Yr	NM
❑ 547-0031	Twilight Time/Dardamella//When Day Is Done/The Breeze and I	1952	12.00
—One record of 2-EP set EPB 3034			
❑ 547-0032	Sunrise Serenade/I'll Never Wish for More Than This//Deep Purple/Hindustan	1952	12.00
—One record of 2-EP set EPB 3034			
❑ 547-0087	My Reverie/Moon Glow//Intermezzo/Smoke Rings	1952	12.00
—One record of 2-EP set EPB 3012			
❑ 547-0088	My Silent Love/Moonlight Sonata//April in Paris/Laura	1952	12.00
—One record of 2-EP set EPB 3012			
❑ LPC-110	Twilight Time/Don't Take Your Love from Me//Peg o' My Heart/Arrivederci Roma	1961	10.00
—"Compact 33 Double"; small hole, plays at 33 1/3 rpm			
❑ LPC-110 [PS]	Twilight Time	1961	10.00
❑ 547-0208	Sweet & Low/Out of Nowhere//Someone to Watch Over Me/My Prayer	195?	12.00
—One record of 2-EP set EPB 3075			
❑ 547-0209	Because/Yesterdays//Lullaby of the Leaves/Deep Night	195?	12.00
—One record of 2-EP set EPB 3075			
❑ EPA-241	The Donkey Serenade/Serenade (Schubert)//Serenade (From The Student Prince)/Serenade in the Night	195?	12.00
❑ EPA-241 [PS]	The Three Suns Serenade	195?	12.00
❑ EPA 250	White Christmas/Winter Wonderland//Silent Night/Jingle Bells	195?	12.00
❑ EPA 250 [PS]	The Three Suns Present Your Christmas Favorites	195?	12.00
❑ EPA-278	Ragging the Scale/Goofus//Josephine/Parade of the Wooden Soldiers	195?	12.00
❑ EPA-278 [PS]	Raggin' the Scales	195?	12.00
❑ EPA-292	Jalousie/Fiddle Faddle//In a Persian Market/Hora Staccato	195?	12.00
❑ EPA-292 [PS]	The Three Suns Present Pop Concert Favorites	195?	12.00
❑ EPA-313	Rosenkavalier Waltz/Two Hearts in Three-Quarter Time//The Sleeping Beauty Waltz/Coppelia Waltz	195?	12.00
❑ EPA-313 [PS]	The Three Suns in Three-Quarter Time	195?	12.00
❑ EPA 330	Hands Across the Table/Auf Wiedersehen//You and the Night and the Music/Yours Is My Heart Alone	195?	12.00
❑ EPA 330 [PS]	Hands Across the Table	195?	12.00

Except when noted otherwise, VG = 25% of NM, and VG+ = 50% of NM. (Example: VG = $2.00, VG+ = $4.00 and NM = $8.00.)

Number	Title (A Side/B Side)	Yr	NM
❑ EPA-400	Ritual Fire Dance/Malaguena//The Syncopated Clock/Delicado	195?	12.00
❑ EPA-400 [PS]	The Three Suns Present Pop Concert Favorites, Vol. II	195?	12.00
❑ EPA-414	The Legend of the Glass Mountain/Tenderly//Jet/Petite Waltz	195?	12.00
❑ EPA-414 [PS]	The Three Suns Moods	195?	12.00
❑ EPA-442	Peg o' My Heart/Ballin' the Jack//The Glow-Worm/The Darktown Strutters Ball	195?	12.00
❑ EPA-442 [PS]	Three Suns Party	195?	12.00
❑ EPA-454	Till I Waltz Again with You/Keep it a Secret//Tell Me You're Mine/Oh, Happy Day	195?	12.00
❑ EPA-454 [PS]	Top Pops Vol. I	195?	12.00
❑ EPA-460	Even Now/Wild Horses//Your Cheatin' Heart/Have You Heard	195?	12.00
❑ EPA-460 [PS]	Top Pops Vol. II	195?	12.00
❑ EPA-618	Autumn Leaves/Waltz Serenade//La Vie En Rose/Waltz in A Flat	1955	12.00
❑ EPA-618 [PS]	Autumn Leaves	1955	12.00
❑ EPA 653	Jingle Bells/Adeste Fideles/Joy to the World//Deck the Halls with Boughs of Holly/The Monastery Bells/Hark the Herald Angels Sing	1955	12.00
❑ EPA 653 [PS]	The Sounds of Christmas	1955	12.00
❑ EPA 655	White Christmas/Santa Claus Is Coming to Town/Der Tannenbaum//It Came Upon a Midnight Clear/Greensleeves/God Rest Ye Merry Gentlemen	1955	12.00
❑ EPA 655 [PS]	White Christmas	1955	12.00
❑ EPA 736	My Reverie/Intermezzo//Tenderly/Laura	1956	10.00
❑ EPA 736 [PS]	(title unknown)	1956	10.00
❑ 547-1040	There Is No Greater Love/A Sinner Kissed an Angel//Autumn Nocturne/Blue Orchids	1954	10.00
—One record of 2-EP set EPB 1041			
❑ 547-1041	Stars Fell on Alabama/The Touch of Your Lips//Moonlight in Vermont/Flamingo	1954	10.00
—One record of 2-EP set EPB 1041			
❑ EPB 1041 [PS]	Soft and Sweet	1954	10.00
❑ EPB 3012 [PS]	Twilight Moods	1952	12.00
—Two-pocket jacket for two-EP set			
❑ EPB 3034 [PS]	The Three Suns Present	1952	12.00
—Two-pocket jacket for two-EP set			
❑ EPB 3075 [PS]	Slumber Time	195?	12.00
❑ EPA-5021	Twilight Time/Hindustan//Peg o' My Heart/Canadian Capers	1958	10.00
❑ EPA-5021 [PS]	The Three Suns (Gold Standard Series)	1958	10.00
ROYALE			
❑ EP 121	Twilight Time/It's Dawn Again//Star Dust/Barcarolle	195?	10.00
❑ EP 121 [PS]	The Three Suns	195?	10.00
Albums			
GOLDEN TONE			
❑ 14094	In Orbit	195?	12.00
PICKWICK			
❑ SPC-3037	Twilight Time	197?	10.00
RCA CAMDEN			
❑ CAL-633 [M]	The Sound of Christmas	1964	12.00
❑ CAS-633(e) [R]	The Sound of Christmas	1964	12.00
RCA VICTOR			
❑ LPM-3 [10]	Three-Quarter Time	1951	50.00
❑ LPM-28 [10]	Hands Across the Table	1951	50.00
❑ LPM-52 [10]	Christmas Favorites	1951	50.00
❑ LPM-1041 [M]	Soft and Sweet	1955	30.00
❑ LPM-1132 [M]	Sounds of Christmas	1955	30.00
❑ LPM-1171 [M]	Twilight Time	1956	30.00
❑ LPM-1173 [M]	My Reverie	1956	30.00
❑ LPM-1219 [M]	Slumber Time	1956	30.00
❑ LPM-1220 [M]	Malaguena	1956	30.00
❑ LPM-1249 [M]	High Fi and Wide	1956	30.00
❑ LPM-1316 [M]	Easy Listening	1956	30.00
❑ LPM-1333 [M]	Midnight for Two	1957	30.00
❑ LPM-1543 [M]	The Things in Love in Hi-Fi	1958	20.00
❑ LSP-1543 [S]	The Things in Love in Hi-Fi	1958	30.00
❑ LPM-1578 [M]	Let's Dance with the Three Suns	1958	20.00
❑ LSP-1578 [S]	Let's Dance with the Three Suns	1958	30.00
❑ LPM-1669 [M]	Love in the Afternoon	1959	20.00
❑ LSP-1669 [S]	Love in the Afternoon	1959	30.00
❑ LPM-1734 [M]	Having a Ball with the Three Suns	1959	20.00
❑ LSP-1734 [S]	Having a Ball with the Three Suns	1959	30.00
❑ ANL1-1779(e)	Pure Gold	1974	10.00
❑ LPM-1964 [M]	Swingin' on a Star	1959	20.00
❑ LSP-1964 [S]	Swingin' on a Star	1959	30.00
❑ LPM-2054 [M]	A Ding Dong Dandy Christmas!	1959	20.00
❑ LSP-2054 [S]	A Ding Dong Dandy Christmas!	1959	30.00
❑ LPM-2120 [M]	Twilight Memories	1960	20.00
❑ LSP-2120 [S]	Twilight Memories	1960	25.00
❑ LPM-2235 [M]	On a Magic Carpet	1960	20.00
❑ LSP-2235 [S]	On a Magic Carpet	1960	25.00
❑ LPM-2307 [M]	Dancing on a Cloud	1961	20.00
❑ LSP-2307 [S]	Dancing on a Cloud	1961	25.00
❑ LPM-2310 [M]	Fever and Smoke	1961	20.00
❑ LSP-2310 [S]	Fever and Smoke	1961	25.00
❑ LPM-2437 [M]	Fun in the Sun	1961	20.00
❑ LSP-2437 [S]	Fun in the Sun	1961	25.00
❑ LPM-2532 [M]	Movin' 'N' Groovin'	1962	20.00
❑ LSP-2532 [S]	Movin' 'N' Groovin'	1962	25.00
❑ LPM-2617 [M]	Warm and Tender	1962	20.00
❑ LSP-2617 [S]	Warm and Tender	1962	25.00
❑ LPM-2715 [M]	Everything Under the Sun	1963	15.00
❑ LSP-2715 [S]	Everything Under the Sun	1963	20.00
❑ LPM-2904 [M]	One Enchanted Evening	1964	15.00
❑ LSP-2904 [S]	One Enchanted Evening	1964	20.00
❑ LPM-2963 [M]	A Swingin' Thing	1964	15.00
❑ LSP-2963 [S]	A Swingin' Thing	1964	20.00
❑ LPM-3012 [10]	Twilight Moods	1952	50.00
❑ LPM-3034 [10]	The Three Suns Present	1952	50.00
❑ LPM-3040 [10]	Busy Fingers	1952	50.00
❑ LPM-3056 [10]	Christmas Party	1952	50.00
❑ LPM-3075 [10]	Slumbertime	1953	50.00
❑ LPM-3113 [10]	Pops Concert Favorites	1953	50.00
❑ LPM-3125 [10]	Mods	1953	50.00
❑ LPM-3130 [10]	Top Pops	1953	50.00
❑ LPM-3146 [10]	Polka Time	1954	50.00
❑ LPM-3174 [10]	Sacred Hymns	1954	50.00
❑ LPM-3354 [M]	Country Music Shindig	1965	15.00
❑ LSP-3354 [S]	Country Music Shindig	1965	20.00
❑ LPM-3447 [M]	The Best of the Three Suns	1965	15.00
❑ LSP-3447 [S]	The Best of the Three Suns	1965	20.00
❑ VPS-6075 [(2)]	This Is the Three Suns	1972	15.00
ROYALE			
❑ 1 [10]	Twilight Time	1951	50.00
❑ 29 [10]	Midnight Time	1951	50.00
SEARS			
❑ SPS-437	Twilight Time	1969	12.00
VARSITY			
❑ VLP-6001 [10]	Twilight Time	1950	50.00
❑ VLP-6048 [10]	Midnight Time	1950	50.00

THREE VALES, THE

Number	Title (A Side/B Side)	Yr	NM
45s			
CINDY			
❑ 3007	Blue Lights/Ay, Ay, Ay	1957	120.00

THREETEENS, THE

Number	Title (A Side/B Side)	Yr	NM
45s			
REV			
❑ 3516	Dear 53310761/Doowaddie	1958	40.00
❑ 3522	X + Y = Z/For the Love of Mike	1959	25.00
TODD			
❑ 1021	X + Y = Z/For the Love of Mike	1959	20.00

THRILLERS, THE (1)

Number	Title (A Side/B Side)	Yr	NM
45s			
BIG TOWN			
❑ 109	The Drunkard/Mattie, Leave Me Alone	1953	400.00
HERALD			
❑ 432	Lizabeth/Please Talk to Me	1954	400.00
THRILLER			
❑ 3530	Lessie Mae/I'm Going to Live My Life Alone	1953	1000.

THRILLERS, THE (2)

Number	Title (A Side/B Side)	Yr	NM
45s			
UPTOWN			
❑ 715	Come What May/This I Know Little Girl	1965	12.00

THRILLINGTON, PERCY "THRILLS"

See PAUL McCARTNEY.

THRILLS, THE

Number	Title (A Side/B Side)	Yr	NM
45s			
CAPITOL			
❑ 5631	What Can Go Wrong/No One	1966	20.00
❑ 5719	Here's a Heart/Bring It On Home to Me	1966	20.00
❑ 5871	Show the World Where It's At/Underneath My Make-Up	1967	20.00

THUDPUCKER, JIMMY

Number	Title (A Side/B Side)	Yr	NM
45s			
WARNER BROS.			
❑ 8245	Ginny's Song (Part 1)/Ginny's Song (Part 2)	1976	6.00
❑ 8245 [PS]	Ginny's Song (Part 1)/Ginny's Song (Part 2)	1976	6.00
WINDSONG			
❑ CB-11230	You Can't Fight It/Take Your Life	1978	5.00
❑ CB-11230 [PS]	You Can't Fight It/Take Your Life	1978	5.00
Albums			
WINDSONG			
❑ BXL1-2589	Greatest Hits	1977	20.00

THUNDER, JOHNNY

Number	Title (A Side/B Side)	Yr	NM
45s			
CALLA			
❑ 161	I'm Alive/Verbal Expressions of T.V.	1969	6.00
DIAMOND			
❑ 129	Loop De Loop/Don't Be Ashamed	1962	15.00
❑ 132	Rock-a-Bye My Darling/The Rosy Dance	1963	10.00
❑ 132 [PS]	Rock-a-Bye My Darling/The Rosy Dance	1963	20.00
❑ 137	The Outlaw/Jailer, Bring Me Water	1963	10.00
❑ 148	Hey Child/Darling Je Vous Aime Beaucoup	1963	10.00
❑ 152	Constitution of Love/Good Morning Sadness	1964	8.00
❑ 155	Everybody Likes to Dance with Johnny/Zoo-Lee-Oh	1964	8.00
❑ 169	More, More More Love, Love, Love/Shout It to the World	1964	8.00
❑ 175	Send Her to Me/Shout It to the World	1964	8.00
❑ 185	Suzie-Q/Dear John, I'm Going to Leave You	1965	8.00
❑ 192	Everybody Do the Sloopy/Beautiful	1965	8.00
❑ 196	My Prayer/A Broken Heart	1966	8.00
❑ 206	Bewildered/Just Me and You	1966	8.00
❑ 218	Make Love to Me/Teach Me Tonight	1967	8.00
—With Ruby Winters			
❑ 222	Am I Right or Am I Wrong/You Send Me	1967	8.00
❑ 238	We Only Have One Life (Let's Live It Together)/❑ \Teach Me Tonight	1968	8.00
—With Ruby Winters			
❑ 246	Put It in Motion/Groovy Two Shoes	1968	8.00
EPIC			
❑ 9329	Ever Your Man/Horror Show	1959	15.00
UNITED ARTISTS			
❑ 50736	Power to the People/Love Trip	1971	6.00
Albums			
DIAMOND			
❑ D-5001 [M]	Loop De Loop	1963	100.00
❑ DS-5001 [S]	Loop De Loop	1963	150.00
REAL			
❑ RR-1	So Alone	196?	15.00

THUNDER AND ROSES

Number	Title (A Side/B Side)	Yr	NM
45s			
UNITED ARTISTS			
❑ 50536	Country Life/I Love a Woman	1969	12.00
Albums			
UNITED ARTISTS			
❑ UAS-6709	King of the Black Sunrise	1969	30.00

THUNDER BOLTS, THE

Number	Title (A Side/B Side)	Yr	NM
45s			
RONDACK			
❑ 7546	Thunder Head/Blending	196?	50.00

THUNDER HEADS, THE

Number	Title (A Side/B Side)	Yr	NM
45s			
CARTWHEEL			
❑ 100	Thunder Head/Unemployment	1966	30.00

THUNDERBOLTS, THE

Number	Title (A Side/B Side)	Yr	NM
45s			
DOT			
❑ 16496	Lost Planets/March of the Spacemen	1963	20.00

THUNDERCLAP NEWMAN

Jimmy McCulloch, later of WINGS, was in this group.

Number	Title (A Side/B Side)	Yr	NM
45s			
TRACK			
❑ 2656	Something in the Air/Wilhelmina	1969	10.00

Number | Title (A Side/B Side) | Yr | NM

❑ 2769 Something in the Air/Wilhelmina 1970 6.00

Albums

MCA

❑ 354 Hollywood Dream 1974 10.00

—Reissue of Track 354

TRACK

❑ 354 Hollywood Dream 1973 12.00

—Reissue of Track 8264

❑ SD 8264 Hollywood Dream 1970 25.00

THUNDERGRIN

45s

EPIC

❑ 10215 Women in the Street/Mr. Simms 1967 10.00

THUNDERKLOUD, BILLY, AND THE CHIEFTONES

45s

POLYDOR

❑ 14321 Indian Nation (The Lament of the Cherokee Reservation Indian)/I'm Going Right to Where I Do Wrong 1976 5.00

❑ 14338 Try a Little Tenderness/A Natural Feelin' for You 1976 5.00

❑ 14362 It's Alright/The Wanderer 1976 5.00

❑ 14383 Let Me Be Your Man/A Hundred Years from Now 1977 5.00

❑ 14412 Oklahoma Wind/The Trouble with Angels 1977 5.00

❑ 14449 Let Me Love You/My Lady 1977 5.00

20TH CENTURY

❑ 2116 You Touched My Life/When Love Is Right 1974 6.00

❑ 2164 Kick the Can/I'm Havin' a Party 1975 5.00

❑ 2181 What Time of Day/When Love Is Right 1975 5.00

❑ 2239 Pledging My Love/I Will Love You Until I Die 1975 5.00

Albums

SUPERIOR

❑ SR-103 All Through the Night 197? 15.00

❑ S-2010 Where Do I Begin to Tell the Story 1975 15.00

20TH CENTURY

❑ T-452 Off the Reservation 1974 12.00

❑ T-471 What Time of Day 1975 12.00

THUNDERPUSSY

Albums

M.R.T.

❑ 31748 Documents of Captivity 1973 150.00

THUNDERTONES, THE

45s

DONNA

❑ 1343 Thunder Rhythm/Pay Day 1961 30.00

DOT

❑ 16137 Jungle Fever/Hot Ice 1960 30.00

❑ 16177 The Street Beat/Happy Little Jug 1961 30.00

—As "Lenny and the Thundertones"

THUNDERTREE

Albums

ROULETTE

❑ SR-42038 Thundertree 1970 30.00

THURMOND, DUFF

45s

NEW VOICE

❑ 816 If You Love Me Baby/Now That You Left Me 1966 60.00

THURSDAY'S CHILDREN

45s

INTERNATIONAL ARTISTS

❑ 110 Air Conditioned Man/Sominoes 1967 150.00

❑ 115 Help, Murder, Police/You Can't Forget About That 1967 150.00

N-JOY

❑ 1019 Running Around on Me/I Don't Need Your Love 1967 15.00

PARADISE

❑ 1022 You'll Never Be My Girl/Try, Girl 1966 1000.

THYME

45s

A-SQUARE

❑ 201 Somehow/Shame, Shame 1969 40.00

❑ 202 Time of the Season/I Found a Love 1969 40.00

Number | Title (A Side/B Side) | Yr | NM

BANG

❑ 546 Love to Love/Very Last Day 1967 20.00

TIATT, LYNN, AND THE COMETS

45s

PUSSYCAT

❑ 1 Dad Is Home/Vilma's Jump-Up 195? 300.00

TICO AND THE TRIUMPHS

PAUL SIMON was a member.

45s

AMY

❑ 835 Motorcycle/I Don't Believe Them 1961 100.00

❑ 845 Wildflower/Express Train 1962 100.00

❑ 860 Cry, Lil' Boy, Cry/Get Up and Do the Wobble 1962 100.00

❑ 876 Cards of Love/Noise 1963 200.00

MADISON

❑ 169 Motorcycle/I Don't Believe Them 1961 200.00

TIDES, THE

45s

HIT

❑ 42 Telstar/The Lonely Bull 1962 10.00

—B-side by the Dan Rubin Orchestra

TIEKEN, FREDDIE, AND THE ROCKERS

Albums

I.T.

❑ 2301 [M] By Popular Demand 1957 50.00

❑ 2304 [M] Freddie Tieken and the Rockers 1958 50.00

TIFFANY SHADE, THE

45s

MAINSTREAM

❑ 677 One Good Reason/Would You Take My Mind Out for a Walk 1968 15.00

❑ 680 An Older Man/Sam 1968 15.00

Albums

MAINSTREAM

❑ S-6105 The Tiffany Shade 1968 100.00

TIFFANYS, THE

Probably not all the same group.

45s

ARCTIC

❑ 101 Love Me/Happiest Girl in the World 1964 20.00

ATLANTIC

❑ 2240 Please Tell Me/Gossip 1964 20.00

JOSIE

❑ 942 I Feel the Same Way Too/I Just Wanna Be a Girl 1965 12.00

❑ 952 Heaven on Earth/Take Another Look at Me 1966 12.00

KR

❑ 120 He's Good for Me/It's Got to Be a Great Song 1967 20.00

—As "The Tiffanies"

MRS

❑ 777 Please Tell Me/Gossip 1964 80.00

RKO

❑ 120 He's Good for Me/It's Got to Be a Great Song 1967 10.00

—Are the KR and RKO releases one and the same? We don't know

ROCKIN' ROBIN

❑ 1 I've Got a Girl/I Don't Dig Western Movies 1963 300.00

SWAN

❑ 4104 Atlanta/The Pleasure of Love 1962 20.00

TIGERS, THE

45s

COLPIX

❑ 773 GeeTO Tiger/The Prowl 1965 50.00

❑ SPEC-773 GeeTO Tiger/The Big Sounds of the GeeTO Tiger 1965 80.00

—Special promotional issue

❑ SPEC-773 [PS] GeeTO Tiger/The Big Sounds of the GeeTO Tiger 1965 200.00

—Sleeve appears to have been available only with the promotional B-side

TIKIS, THE

45s

ASCOT

❑ 2186 Stop-Look-Listen/Cream in My Coffee 1965 10.00

❑ 2204 High School Dropout Blues/Whole Lotta Soul 1966 10.00

Number | Title (A Side/B Side) | Yr | NM

AUTUMN

❑ 18 If I've Been Dreaming/Pay Attention to Me 1965 10.00

—As "The Other Tikis"

❑ 28 Bye Bye Bye/Lost My Love Today 1966 10.00

—As "The Other Tikis"

DIAL

❑ 4048 Somebody's Sun/Little Miss Lovelight 1966 10.00

MINARET

❑ 115 Big Feet/One More Chance 196? 12.00

❑ 116 Popsicle/All That Talk 196? 12.00

❑ 118 Traveling Shoes/Valley of Tears 196? 12.00

WARNER BROS.

❑ 5818 Bye Bye Bye/Lost My Love Today 1966 10.00

Albums

MINARET

❑ TLP-7001 [M] The Tikis 196? 100.00

PHILIPS

❑ PHM 200043 [M] The Tikis 1962 25.00

❑ PHS 600043 [S] The Tikis 1962 30.00

TIKIS, THE, AND THE FABULONS

45s

PANORAMA

❑ 13 Take a Look/For Your Love 1965 20.00

TOWER

❑ 181 Take a Look/Cherry Pie 1965 12.00

TIL, SONNY

Also see THE ORIOLES.

45s

JUBILEE

❑ 5060 I Never Knew (I Could Love Anybody)/My Prayer 1951 300.00

❑ 5066 Fool's World/For All We Know 1951 300.00

—Black vinyl

❑ 5066 Fool's World/For All We Know 1951 800.00

—Red vinyl

❑ 5090 Once in Awhile/I Only Have Eyes for You 1952 50.00

—With Edna McGriff

❑ 5099 Good/Picadilly 1952 80.00

—With Edna McGriff

❑ 5112 Have You Heard/Lonely Wine 1953 200.00

❑ 5118 (Danger) Soft Shoulders/Congratulations to Someone 1953 200.00

❑ 5394 Night and Day/Shimmy Time 1960 20.00

RCA VICTOR

❑ 47-9733 You're All I Need/After You 1969 8.00

❑ 47-9759 Tears and Misery/I Better Leave Love Alone 1969 8.00

❑ 74-0390 Don't Feel No Pain/One Big Happy Family 1970 8.00

❑ 74-0432 Colours/Love Is What It's All About 1971 8.00

❑ 74-0529 'Til Then/Love or Desire 1971 8.00

❑ 74-0606 Crying in the Chapel/What Are You Doing New Year's Eve 1971 8.00

ROULETTE

❑ 4079 Shy/First Blush 1958 20.00

Albums

DOBRE

❑ 1026 Back to the Chapel 1978 12.00

RCA VICTOR

❑ LSP-4451 Sonny Til Returns 1970 20.00

❑ LSP-4538 Old Gold/New Gold 1971 15.00

TILLER, FLOYD

45s

HIT

❑ 275 Born Free/Winchester Cathedral 1966 8.00

—B-side by the New Orleans Band

TILLMAN, BERTHA

45s

BRENT

❑ 7029 Oh My Angel/Lovin' Time 1962 30.00

❑ 7032 I Wish/(I Believe) Something Funny Is Going On 1962 40.00

JOCKO

❑ 599 What Am I Trying to Prove?/(B-side unknown) 196? 20.00

TILLOTSON, JOHNNY

45s

AMOS

❑ 117 Tears on My Pillow/Remember When 1969 6.00

Except when noted otherwise, VG = 25% of NM, and VG+ = 50% of NM. (Example: VG = $2.00, VG+ = $4.00 and NM = $8.00.)

Number	Title (A Side/B Side)	Yr	NM
❑ 125	What Am I Living For/ Joy to the World	1969	6.00
❑ 128	Raining in My Heart/Today I Started Loving You Again	1969	6.00
❑ 136	Susan/Love Waits for Me	1970	6.00
❑ 146	I Don't Believe In It Anymore/ Kansas City, Kansas	1970	6.00

ATLANTIC

Number	Title (A Side/B Side)	Yr	NM
❑ 87978	Bim Bam Boom/ (B-side unknown)	1990	4.00

BUDDAH

Number	Title (A Side/B Side)	Yr	NM
❑ 232	Star Spangled Bus/Apple Bend	1971	5.00
❑ 256	Welfare Hero/The Flower Kissed the Shoes That Jesus Wore	1971	5.00
❑ 279	Make Me Believe/The Flower Kissed the Shoes That Jesus Wore	1972	5.00
❑ 311	Your Love's Been a Long Time Comin'/Apple Bend	1972	5.00

CADENCE

Number	Title (A Side/B Side)	Yr	NM
❑ 1353	Dreamy Eyes/Well, I'm Your Man	1958	20.00
❑ 1354	I'm Never Gonna Kiss You/ Cherie, Cherie	1958	25.00
—With Genevieve			
❑ 1365	True True Happiness/ Love Is Blind	1959	20.00
❑ 1372	Why Do I Love You So/ Never Let Me Go	1959	20.00
❑ 1377	Earth Angel/Pledging My Love	1960	20.00
❑ 1377 [PS]	Earth Angel/Pledging My Love	1960	30.00
❑ 1384	Poetry in Motion/ Princess, Princess	1960	20.00
❑ 1391	Jimmy's Girl/His True Love Said Godbye	1960	15.00
❑ 1391 [PS]	Jimmy's Girl/His True Love Said Godbye	1960	30.00
❑ 1404	Without You/Cutie Pie	1961	15.00
❑ 1409	Dreamy Eyes/Well, I'm Your Man	1961	15.00
❑ 1418	It Keeps Right On a-Hurtin'/ She Gave Sweet Love to Me	1962	15.00
❑ 1424	Send Me the Pillow You Dream On/What'll I Do	1962	15.00
❑ 1432	I Can't Help It (If I'm Still in Love with You)/I'm So Lonesome I Could Cry	1962	15.00
❑ 1434	Out of My Mind/Empty Feelin'	1963	15.00
❑ 1437	You Can Never Stop Me Loving You/Judy, Judy, Judy	1963	15.00
❑ 1441	Funny How Time Slips Away/ A Very Good Year for Girls	1963	15.00

COLUMBIA

Number	Title (A Side/B Side)	Yr	NM
❑ 10125	Big Ole Jean/Mississippi Lady	1975	5.00
❑ 10199	Right Here in Your Arms/ Willow County Request Live	1975	5.00
❑ 45842	Sunshine of My Life/If You Wouldn't Be My Lady	1973	5.00
❑ 45984	So Much of My Life/I Love How She Needs Me	1973	5.00
❑ 46065	Till I Can't Take It Anymore/ Sunday Kind of Woman	1974	5.00

MGM

Number	Title (A Side/B Side)	Yr	NM
❑ 13181	Talk Back Trembling Lips/ Another You	1963	12.00
❑ 13181 [PS]	Talk Back Trembling Lips/ Another You	1963	20.00
❑ 13193	Worried Guy/Please Don't Go Away	1963	10.00
❑ 13193 [PS]	Worried Guy/Please Don't Go Away	1963	20.00
❑ 13232	I Rise, I Fall/I'm Watching My Watch	1964	10.00
❑ 13232 [PS]	I Rise, I Fall/I'm Watching My Watch	1964	20.00
❑ 13255	Worry/Sufferin' from a Heartache	1964	10.00
❑ 13255 [PS]	Worry/Sufferin' from a Heartache	1964	20.00
❑ 13284	She Understands Me/Tomorrow	1964	10.00
❑ 13284 [PS]	She Understands Me/Tomorrow	1964	20.00
❑ 13316	Angel/Little Boy	1965	10.00
❑ 13316 [PS]	Angel/Little Boy	1965	20.00
❑ 13344	Then I'll Count Again/ One's Yours, One's Mine	1965	10.00
❑ 13344 [PS]	Then I'll Count Again/ One's Yours, One's Mine	1965	20.00
❑ 13376	Heartaches by the Number/ Your Mem'ry Comes Along	1965	10.00
❑ 13376 [PS]	Heartaches by the Number/ Your Mem'ry Comes Along	1965	20.00
❑ 13408	Our World/(Wait 'Till You See) My Gidget	1965	10.00
❑ 13445	Hello Enemy/I Never Loved You Anyway	1966	10.00
❑ 13499	Me, Myself and I/Country Boy, Country Boy	1966	10.00
❑ 13519	No Love at All/What Am I Gonna Do	1966	10.00
❑ 13598	More Than Before/Baby's Gone	1966	10.00
❑ 13598	More Than Before/ Open Up Your Heart	1966	10.00
❑ 13633	Christmas Country Style/ Christmas Is the Best of All	1966	10.00
❑ 13684	Strange Things Happen/ Tommy Jones	1967	10.00
❑ 13738	Don't Tell Me It's Raining/ Takin' It Easy	1967	10.00
❑ 13829	You're the Reason/ Countin' My Teardrops	1967	10.00
❑ 13888	I Can Spot a Cheater/ It Keeps Right On a-Hurtin'	1968	8.00
❑ 13924	I Haven't Begun to Love You Yet/Why So Lonely	1968	8.00
❑ 13977	Letter to Emily/Your Mem'ry Comes Along	1968	8.00

Johnny Tillotson, "Talk Back Trembling Lips," MGM K13181, 1963, **$20.**

REWARD

Number	Title (A Side/B Side)	Yr	NM
❑ 03327	Baby You Do It for Me (And I'll Do It for You)/She's Not As Married As She Used to Be	1982	4.00
❑ 03901	Crying/You're a Beautiful Place to Be	1983	4.00
❑ 04123	Burnin'/What's Another Year	1983	4.00
❑ 04346	Lay Back (In the Arms of Somebody)/What's Another Year	1984	4.00

SCEPTER

Number	Title (A Side/B Side)	Yr	NM
❑ 12389	Song for Hank Williams (mono/stereo)	1973	8.00
—With John Edward Beland; may be promo-only			

UNITED ARTISTS

Number	Title (A Side/B Side)	Yr	NM
❑ XW860	It Could've Been Nashville/ Summertime Lovin'	1976	5.00
❑ XW986	Toy Hearts/Just An Ordinary Man	1977	5.00

7-Inch Extended Plays

CADENCE

Number	Title (A Side/B Side)	Yr	NM
❑ CLLP 33-1	Poetry in Motion/Jimmy's Girl/ True, True Happiness//Earth Angel/Why Do I Love You So/ Pledging My Love	1961	20.00
—Jukebox issue; small hole, plays at 33 1/3 rpm			
❑ CLLP 33-1 [PS]	This Is Johnny Tillotson	1961	30.00
—Cardboard insert in heavy vinyl envelope			
❑ CLLP 33-2	Without You/Much Beyond Compare/Well I'm Your Man/ /Princess Princess/Dreamy Eyes/Cutie Pie	1961	20.00
—Jukebox issue; small hole, plays at 33 1/3 rpm			
❑ CLLP 33-2 [PS]	Words and Music by Johnny Tillotson	1961	30.00
—Cardboard insert in heavy vinyl envelope			
❑ CEP-114	True True Happiness/Love Is Blind//Dreamy Eyes/Well I'm Your Man	1960	25.00
❑ CEP-114 [PS]	Johnny Tillotson	1960	25.00

Albums

ACCORD

Number	Title (A Side/B Side)	Yr	NM
❑ SN-7194	Scrapbook	1982	10.00

AMOS

Number	Title (A Side/B Side)	Yr	NM
❑ AAS 7006	Tears on My Pillow	1969	20.00

BARNABY

Number	Title (A Side/B Side)	Yr	NM
❑ BR-4007	Johnny Tillotson's Greatest	1977	12.00

BUDDAH

Number	Title (A Side/B Side)	Yr	NM
❑ BDS-5112	Johnny Tillotson	1972	15.00

CADENCE

Number	Title (A Side/B Side)	Yr	NM
❑ CLP-3052 [M]	Johnny Tillotson's Best	1961	40.00
—Maroon and silver label			
❑ CLP-3052 [M]	Johnny Tillotson's Best	1962	25.00
—Red and black label			
❑ CLP-3058 [M]	It Keeps Right On a-Hurtin'	1962	30.00
❑ CLP-3067 [M]	You Can Never Stop Me Loving You	1963	30.00
❑ CLP-25052 [P]	Johnny Tillotson's Best	1961	50.00
—Maroon and silver label			
❑ CLP-25052 [P]	Johnny Tillotson's Best	1962	30.00
—Red and black label			
❑ CLP-25058 [S]	It Keeps Right On a-Hurtin'	1962	40.00
❑ CLP-25067 [P]	You Can Never Stop Me Loving You	1963	40.00

EVEREST

Number	Title (A Side/B Side)	Yr	NM
❑ 4113	Johnny Tillotson's Greatest Hits	1982	10.00

METRO

Number	Title (A Side/B Side)	Yr	NM
❑ M-561 [M]	Johnny Tillotson Sings Tillotson	1967	15.00
❑ MS-561 [S]	Johnny Tillotson Sings Tillotson	1967	20.00

MGM

Number	Title (A Side/B Side)	Yr	NM
❑ E-4188 [M]	Talk Back Trembling Lips	1964	20.00
❑ SE-4188 [S]	Talk Back Trembling Lips	1964	25.00
❑ E-4224 [M]	The Tillotson Touch	1964	20.00
❑ SE-4224 [S]	The Tillotson Touch	1964	25.00
❑ E-4270 [M]	She Understands Me	1965	20.00
❑ SE-4270 [S]	She Understands Me	1965	25.00
❑ E-4302 [M]	That's My Style	1965	20.00
❑ SE-4302 [S]	That's My Style	1965	25.00
❑ E-4328 [M]	Our World	1965	20.00
❑ SE-4328 [S]	Our World	1965	25.00
❑ E-4395 [M]	No Love at All	1966	20.00
❑ SE-4395 [S]	No Love at All	1966	25.00
❑ E-4402 [M]	The Christmas Touch	1966	20.00
❑ SE-4402 [S]	The Christmas Touch	1966	25.00
❑ E-4452 [M]	Here I Am	1967	20.00
❑ SE-4452 [S]	Here I Am	1967	25.00
❑ E-4532 [M]	The Best of Johnny Tillotson	1968	30.00
—May be promo only (yellow label)			
❑ SE-4532 [S]	The Best of Johnny Tillotson	1968	20.00
❑ SE-4814	The Very Best of Johnny Tillotson	1971	12.00
❑ ST 90410 [S]	The Tillotson Touch	1965	30.00
—Capitol Record Club edition			
❑ T 90410 [M]	The Tillotson Touch	1965	30.00
—Capitol Record Club edition			

UNITED ARTISTS

Number	Title (A Side/B Side)	Yr	NM
❑ UA-LA759-G	Johnny Tillotson	1977	10.00

TIM TAM AND THE TURN-ONS

45s

PALMER

Number	Title (A Side/B Side)	Yr	NM
❑ 5002	Wait a Minute/Ophelia	1965	25.00
❑ 5003	Cheryl Ann/Sealed with a Kiss	1966	30.00
❑ 5006	Kimberly/I Leave You in Tears	1966	40.00
❑ 5014	Don't Say Hi/(Instrumental)	1967	25.00

TIMBER CREEK

Albums

RENEGADE

Number	Title (A Side/B Side)	Yr	NM
❑ 95014	Hellbound Highway	1975	150.00

TIMERS, THE

With GARY USHER and BRIAN WILSON.

45s

REPRISE

Number	Title (A Side/B Side)	Yr	NM
❑ 20231	No-Go Showboat/Competition Coupe	1963	100.00

TIMMOTHY

Albums

PEAR

Number	Title (A Side/B Side)	Yr	NM
❑ (# unknown)	Strange But True	1972	200.00

TIN HOUSE

45s

EPIC

Number	Title (A Side/B Side)	Yr	NM
❑ 10739	I Want Your Baby/Be Good and Be Kind	1971	8.00

Albums

EPIC

Number	Title (A Side/B Side)	Yr	NM
❑ E 30511	Tin House	1971	20.00

TIN MACHINE

12-Inch Singles

EMI

Number	Title (A Side/B Side)	Yr	NM
❑ SPRO4282 [DJ]	Under the God (same on both sides)	1989	15.00
❑ SPRO 04282 [DJ]	Under the God (same on both sides)	1989	15.00
❑ SPRO4374 [DJ]	Heaven's In Here/Heaven's In Here (Edit)	1989	15.00
❑ SPRO 04374 [DJ]	Heaven's In Here/Heaven's In Here (Edit)	1989	15.00

Albums

EMI

Number	Title (A Side/B Side)	Yr	NM
❑ E1-91990	Tin Machine	1989	12.00
—Featuring David Bowie			
❑ R 164054	Tin Machine	1989	14.00
—BMG Direct Marketing edition			

TIN TIN

45s

ATCO

Number	Title (A Side/B Side)	Yr	NM
❑ 6794	Toast and Marmalade for Tea/Manhattan Woman	1971	8.00
❑ 6821	Is That the Way/Swans on the Canal	1971	6.00
❑ 6853	Set Sail for England/The Cavalry Is Coming	1971	6.00

POLYDOR

Number	Title (A Side/B Side)	Yr	NM
❑ 15055	Talking Turkey/The Cavalry Is Coming	1972	6.00

SIRE

Number	Title (A Side/B Side)	Yr	NM
❑ 29750	Kiss Me/Kiss Me	1983	5.00

Albums

ATCO

Number	Title (A Side/B Side)	Yr	NM
❑ SD 33-350	Tin Tin	1970	15.00
❑ SD 33-370	Astral Taxi	1971	15.00

TINA WITH DADDY AND MOMMY

"Mommy and Daddy" are TAMMY WYNETTE and GEORGE JONES; Tina is their stepdaughter.

45s

EPIC

Number	Title (A Side/B Side)	Yr	NM
❑ 11099	Telephone Call/No Charge	1974	5.00

TINDLEY, GEORGE

45s

EMBER

Number	Title (A Side/B Side)	Yr	NM
❑ 1058	The Gypsy/I Wish	1960	15.00
❑ 1060	Wedding Bells/No Lonely Nights	1960	15.00

HERALD

Number	Title (A Side/B Side)	Yr	NM
❑ 558	Close Your Eyes/Heart of Gold	1961	12.00

PARKWAY

Number	Title (A Side/B Side)	Yr	NM
❑ 834	Fairy Tales/Just For You	1962	12.00

WAND

Number	Title (A Side/B Side)	Yr	NM
❑ 11205	Ain't That Peculiar/It's All Over But the Shouting	1969	8.00
❑ 11208	Honky Tonk Women/So Help Me Woman	1969	8.00
❑ 11215	Wan-Tu-Wah-Zuree/Pity the Poor Man	1970	8.00

TINGLING MOTHER'S CIRCUS

45s

MUSICOR

Number	Title (A Side/B Side)	Yr	NM
❑ 1335	Positively Negative/Sunday Kind of Feeling	1968	10.00
❑ 1359	I Found a New Love/Happy Bubble	1969	10.00

ROULETTE

Number	Title (A Side/B Side)	Yr	NM
❑ 4758	Face in My Mind/Isn't It Strange	1967	15.00

Albums

MUSICOR

Number	Title (A Side/B Side)	Yr	NM
❑ MS-3167	Circus of the Mind	1968	25.00

TINY TIM

45s

BLUE CAT

Number	Title (A Side/B Side)	Yr	NM
❑ 127	April Showers/Little Girl	1966	12.00

BOUQUET

Number	Title (A Side/B Side)	Yr	NM
❑ B-101	Be My Love/Oh How I Miss You Tonight	1968	20.00
❑ B-102	On the Good Ship Lollipop/Don't Take Your Love From Me	1968	20.00

BROKEN

Number	Title (A Side/B Side)	Yr	NM
❑ 101 [PS]	Mr. Ed/Memory	1984	10.00
—Black vinyl			
❑ 101 [PS]	Mr. Ed/Memory	1984	20.00
—Colored vinyl			

CLONE

Number	Title (A Side/B Side)	Yr	NM
❑ CRI111	I'm Just a Lonesome Clone/I'm the One (That They're Crazy About)	1984	10.00

CLOUDS

Number	Title (A Side/B Side)	Yr	NM
❑ 17 [PS]	Tip-Toe to the Gas Pumps/The Hicky (On Your Neck)	1979	10.00

FRESH SQUEEZED

Number	Title (A Side/B Side)	Yr	NM
❑ 4507	Dick Tracy Rides Again/Ready for Love	1990	10.00

GAS 'ER UP

Number	Title (A Side/B Side)	Yr	NM
❑ -1001T [B]	Tip-Toe to the Gas Pumps (stereo)/Tip-Toe to the Gas Pumps (mono)	1979	15.00
—This 45 was given away by a gas station chain for filling your tank			

KAMA

Number	Title (A Side/B Side)	Yr	NM
❑ OV567	Howard Cosell (We Think You're Swell)/The Bi-Centennial Song (I Believe in America)	1976	15.00

RA JO

Number	Title (A Side/B Side)	Yr	NM
❑ SLP30	Zoot Zoot Zoot Here Comes Santa in His New Space Suit/Unknown	1981	15.00

REPETE

Number	Title (A Side/B Side)	Yr	NM
❑ R45-277	Tip-Toe Through the Tulips With Me/Cinnamon	1990	8.00

REPRISE

Number	Title (A Side/B Side)	Yr	NM
❑ PRO-276	Tiny Tim Radio Spots	1968	25.00
—Plays four ads for "God Bless Tiny Tim" album; sent to radio stations only			
❑ 0679	Tip-Toe Thru' the Tulips with Me/Fill Your Heart	1968	8.00
❑ 0740	Tip-Toe Thru' the Tulips with Me/Don't Bite the Hand That's Feeding You	1971	4.00
—"Back to Back Hits" series			
❑ 0760	Bring Back Those Rock-A-Bye Baby Days/Hello, Hello	1968	6.00
❑ 0760	Bring Back Those Rock-A-Bye Baby Days/This Is All I Ask	1968	6.00
❑ 0769	Hello, Hello/The Other Side	1968	6.00
❑ 0802	Great Balls of Fire/As Time Goes By	1969	6.00
❑ 0802 [S]	Great Balls of Fire/As Time Goes By	1968	20.00
❑ 0837	On the Good Ship Lollipop/America I Love You	1969	6.00
❑ 0855	Mickey the Monkey/Neighborhood Children	1969	6.00
❑ 0867	I'm a Lonesome Little Raindrop/What the World Needs Now Is Love	1969	6.00
❑ 0939	Don't Bite the Hand That's Feeding You/What Kind of American Are You	1970	6.00
❑ 0985	Why/Spaceship Song	1971	15.00
—The label on the A-side label has a heart with arrow through it and "TINY TIM & MISS VICKI" written inside			
❑ 20174	Bring Back Rockabye Baby Days/Just Say I Love Her	1963	12.00
—B-side by Johnny Prophet			

SCEPTER

Number	Title (A Side/B Side)	Yr	NM
❑ 12351	Am I Just Another Pretty Face/The Movies	1972	10.00

SOLID BRASS

Number	Title (A Side/B Side)	Yr	NM
❑ 101	Comic Strip Man/Tell Me That You Love Me (My Sweetheart)	1981	10.00
—With insert; a printed insert note from Tiny was included in some copies; the record has no promo markings, but the picture sleeve has "special promotional copy" on it; the picture sleeve also lists two album titles (Tell Me That You Love Me and I Won't Dance), but neither of these albums was ever released			
❑ 101	Comic Strip Man/Tell Me That You Love Me (My Sweetheart)	1981	10.00
—Without insert			
❑ 103 [PS]	Telll Me That You Love Me/Honest, Dear Honest	1981	10.00

STARDUST

Number	Title (A Side/B Side)	Yr	NM
❑ URC1225	Tip-Toe Through the Tulips With Me/Alley Oop	1988	8.00

TCC

Number	Title (A Side/B Side)	Yr	NM
❑ 2343	Tip-Toe Disco (Part I)/Tip-Toe Disco (Part 2 Instrumental)	1977	10.00

TOILET

Number	Title (A Side/B Side)	Yr	NM
❑ RB101	I Ain't Got No Money/Alice Blue Gown	1973	15.00

TOP BILLING

Number	Title (A Side/B Side)	Yr	NM
❑ TBR20	Yummy Yummy Pizza/Oh, Oh, Those Landlords	1981	15.00
—A New York pizza company gave these away			

TRUE

Number	Title (A Side/B Side)	Yr	NM
❑ 109 [PS]	I'm Gonna Be a Country Queen/I Ain't No Cowboy (I Just Found This Hat)	1977	10.00
❑ 109 [PS]	I'm Gonna Be a Country Queen/I Ain't No Cowboy (I Just Found This Hat)	1977	10.00
—This 45 was given away by a gas station chain when you filled your tank			

20TH CENTURY

Number	Title (A Side/B Side)	Yr	NM
❑ 88-1	I Saw Mr. Presley Tip-Toeing Through the Tulips/Sam	1988	25.00
—Came with Tiny's picture on promo envelope			
❑ U-30528M	I'll Never Get Married Again/The Chicken Dance	1988	10.00

VIC TIM

Number	Title (A Side/B Side)	Yr	NM
❑ 100?	Maggie May/When You and I Were Young, Maggie	1972	20.00
❑ 777	Why Did They Have to Die So Young/Letter Edged in Black	1971	20.00
—Vic Tim was a label that Tiny Tim started after leaving Reprise Records in 1971; the A-side is dedicated to Jimi Hendrix, Janis Joplin, and Jim Morrison			
❑ 778	The Ballad of Attica Prison/The Prisoners Song	1971	20.00
❑ 1001	Rudolph The Red-Nosed Reindeer/White Christmas	1971	15.00
❑ 1007	Delilah/Sunshine	1972	20.00

Albums

BOUQUET

Number	Title (A Side/B Side)	Yr	NM
❑ SLP-711	Love and Kisses from Tiny Tim	1968	12.00

Except when noted otherwise, VG = 25% of NM, and VG+ = 50% of NM. (Example: VG = $2.00, VG+ = $4.00 and NM = $8.00.)

Number	Title (A Side/B Side)	Yr	NM

REPRISE

Number	Title (A Side/B Side)	Yr	NM
❑ R 6292 [M]	God Bless Tiny Tim	1968	40.00
—Mono copies may all be white label promos			
❑ RS 6292 [S]	God Bless Tiny Tim	1968	15.00
❑ RS 6323	Tiny Tim's Second Album	1969	15.00
❑ RS 6351	For All My Little Friends	1969	15.00

TINY TIM AND THE HITS

45s

ROULETTE

Number	Title (A Side/B Side)	Yr	NM
❑ 4123	Wedding Bells/Doll Baby	1958	50.00

TIP TOPS, THE

45s

PARKWAY

Number	Title (A Side/B Side)	Yr	NM
❑ 868	Oo-Kook-a-Boo/He's a Braggin'	1963	12.00

ROULETTE

Number	Title (A Side/B Side)	Yr	NM
❑ 4684	Meetcha at the Cheetah/ A Little Bit More	1966	120.00

TIPTON, JOHN

45s

DATE

Number	Title (A Side/B Side)	Yr	NM
❑ 2-1641	Spring/Two Lonely Lips	1969	8.00
❑ 2-1663	Game of Promise/Sleepy Eyes	1969	8.00

TIPTON, LESTER

45s

LA BEAT

Number	Title (A Side/B Side)	Yr	NM
❑ P 6607	This Won't Change/Go On	196?	4000.

TITANS, THE

More than one group.

45s

BANGAR

Number	Title (A Side/B Side)	Yr	NM
❑ 00611	Surfer's Lullaby/Motivation	1964	25.00

CLASS

Number	Title (A Side/B Side)	Yr	NM
❑ 244	No Time/The Tootin' Tutor	1959	25.00

DUFF'S

Number	Title (A Side/B Side)	Yr	NM
❑ 111	Little Girl/Pretty Young Thing	1969	12.00
❑ 112	Ode to Billy Martin/ Please Don't Be Angry	1970	12.00

FIDELITY

Number	Title (A Side/B Side)	Yr	NM
❑ 3016	What Have I Done/ Everybody Happy?	1960	30.00

METROBEAT

Number	Title (A Side/B Side)	Yr	NM
❑ 4452	To Covet the Turf/ Mountain of Love	196?	20.00

MGM

Number	Title (A Side/B Side)	Yr	NM
❑ 13207	Yojimbo/Midnight in Tokyo	1964	12.00
—B-side by the Tokyo Boys			

NOLTA

Number	Title (A Side/B Side)	Yr	NM
❑ 351	A-Rab/Marquette	1961	25.00

SOMA

Number	Title (A Side/B Side)	Yr	NM
❑ 1402	A Summer Place/ Tchaikovsky Rides Again	1963	20.00
❑ 1411	The No Place Special/ Reveille Rock	1964	20.00

SOUND OF MUSIC

Number	Title (A Side/B Side)	Yr	NM
❑ 12186	Need You/Fun Seekers	196?	12.00
❑ 12186 [PS]	Need You/Fun Seekers	196?	50.00

SPECIALTY

Number	Title (A Side/B Side)	Yr	NM
❑ 614	Sweet Peach/Free and Easy	1957	25.00
❑ 625	Don't You Just Know It/Can It Be	1958	25.00
❑ 632	Arlene/Love Is a Wonderful Thing	1958	25.00

STUDIO CITY

Number	Title (A Side/B Side)	Yr	NM
❑ 1008	The No Place Special/ Reveille Rock	1964	40.00

VITA

Number	Title (A Side/B Side)	Yr	NM
❑ 148	Rhythm and Blues/So Hard to Laugh, So Easy to Cry	1957	75.00
❑ 158	G'Wan Home Calypso/Look What You're Doing Baby	1957	60.00

Albums

MGM

Number	Title (A Side/B Side)	Yr	NM
❑ E-3992 [M]	Today's Teen Beat	1961	30.00
❑ SE-3992 [S]	Today's Teen Beat	1961	40.00

TITONES, THE

45s

SCEPTER

Number	Title (A Side/B Side)	Yr	NM
❑ 1206	Symbol of Love/The Movies	1960	25.00
—Red label			
❑ 1206	Symbol of Love/The Movies	1960	50.00
—White label			

WAND

Number	Title (A Side/B Side)	Yr	NM
❑ 105	Symbol of Love/My Movie Queen	1960	20.00

TITUS GROAN

Albums

JANUS

Number	Title (A Side/B Side)	Yr	NM
❑ JLS-3024	Titus Groan	1971	30.00

TITUS OATES

Albums

LIPS

Number	Title (A Side/B Side)	Yr	NM
❑ (no #)	Jungle Lady	1974	200.00

TJADER, CAL

45s

FANTASY

Number	Title (A Side/B Side)	Yr	NM
❑ 531	Yesterdays/Bei Mir Bist Du Schoen	195?	15.00
—Red vinyl			
❑ 532	Fascinatin' Rhythm/ I Concentrate on You	195?	15.00
—Red vinyl			
❑ 533	Wachi Wara/For Heaven's Sake	195?	15.00
—Red vinyl			
❑ 534	It Ain't Necessarily So/ Mambo Macumba	195?	15.00
—Red vinyl; the above four comprise a box set			
❑ 536	Lucero/Chloe	195?	15.00
❑ 538	Sonny Boy/Mamblues	195?	15.00
❑ 540	As I Love You/I've Waited So Long	195?	15.00
❑ 544	Black Orchid/Afro Blue	195?	15.00
❑ 547	Doxie (Part 1)/Doxie (Part 2)	195?	15.00
❑ 552	Cool/Maria	1960	10.00
—Black vinyl			
❑ 552	Cool/Maria	1960	15.00
—Red vinyl (possibly promo only)			
❑ 562	The Continental/ (B-side unknown)	196?	10.00
❑ 605	Dixie/Mamblues	196?	10.00
❑ 659	Evil Ways/First There Is a Mountain	1971	6.00

SAVOY

Number	Title (A Side/B Side)	Yr	NM
❑ 1117	Love Me or Leave Me/Tangerine	1953	20.00
❑ 1120	I Want to Be Happy/Minority	1954	20.00

SKYE

Number	Title (A Side/B Side)	Yr	NM
❑ 452	Ode to Billie Joe/Solar Heat	1968	8.00
❑ 4510	My Little Red Book/Moneypenny	1968	8.00

VERVE

Number	Title (A Side/B Side)	Yr	NM
❑ 10275	Weeping Bossa Nova/Silenciosa	1962	10.00
❑ 10300	The Fakir/China Nights	1963	10.00
❑ 10315	Sake and Greens/Shoji	1964	10.00
❑ 10325	People/Poor Butterfly	1964	10.00
❑ 10345	Soul Sauce (Guacha Guaro)/ Somewhere in the Night	1965	8.00
❑ 10364	Soul Bird/The Whiffenpoof Song	1965	8.00
❑ 10397	Soul Burst/Cuchy Frito Man	1966	8.00
❑ 10431	Guajira en Azul/Modesty	1966	8.00
❑ 10552	Trick or Treat/Quando Quando Que Sera	1967	8.00

Albums

CONCORD JAZZ

Number	Title (A Side/B Side)	Yr	NM
❑ CJ-159	The Shining Sea	1981	10.00

CONCORD PICANTE

Number	Title (A Side/B Side)	Yr	NM
❑ CJP-113	La Onda Va Bien	1979	12.00
❑ CJP-133	Gozame! Pero Ya...	1980	12.00
❑ CJP-176	A Fuego Vivo	1981	10.00
❑ CJP-247	Good Vibes	1983	10.00

CRYSTAL CLEAR

Number	Title (A Side/B Side)	Yr	NM
❑ 8003	Huracan	1978	25.00
—Direct-to-disc recording			

FANTASY

Number	Title (A Side/B Side)	Yr	NM
❑ 3-9 [10]	The Cal Tjader Trio	1953	100.00
—Black vinyl			
❑ 3-9 [10]	The Cal Tjader Trio	1953	150.00
—Any of various non-black vinyl pressings			
❑ 3-17 [10]	Ritmo Caliente	1954	100.00
—Black vinyl			
❑ 3-17 [10]	Ritmo Caliente	1954	150.00
—Any of various non-black vinyl pressings			
❑ 3-18 [10]	Tjader Plays Mambo	1954	150.00
—Red vinyl			
❑ OJC-271	Mambo with Tjader	1987	10.00
—Reissue of 3202			
❑ OJC-274	Tjader Plays Mambo	1987	10.00
—Reissue of 3221			
❑ OJC-277	San Francisco Moods	1987	10.00
—Reissue of 8017			
❑ OJC-278	A Night at the Blackhawk	1987	10.00
—Reissue of 8026			
❑ OJC-279	Concert on the Campus	1987	10.00
—Reissue of 8044			
❑ OJC-285	Cal Tjader Plays the Harold Arlen Songbook	1987	10.00
—Reissue of 8072			
❑ OJC-436	Jazz at the Blackhawk	1990	10.00
—Reissue of 8096			
❑ OJC-642	Latin Kick	1991	12.00
—Reissue of 8033			
❑ OJC-643	Cal Tjader's Latin Concert	1991	12.00
—Reissue of 8014			
❑ 3202 [M]	Mambo with Tjader	1955	100.00
—Red vinyl			
❑ 3202 [M]	Mambo with Tjader	1956	50.00
—Black vinyl, red label, non-flexible vinyl			
❑ 3202 [M]	Mambo with Tjader	196?	25.00
—Black vinyl, red label, flexible vinyl			
❑ 3211 [M]	Tjader Plays Tjazz	1956	50.00
—Black vinyl, red label, non-flexible vinyl			
❑ 3211 [M]	Tjader Plays Tjazz	1956	100.00
—Red vinyl			
❑ 3216 [M]	Ritmo Caliente	1956	50.00
—Black vinyl, red label, non-flexible vinyl			
❑ 3216 [M]	Ritmo Caliente	1956	100.00
—Red vinyl			
❑ 3216 [M]	Ritmo Caliente	196?	25.00
—Black vinyl, red label, flexible vinyl			
❑ 3221 [M]	Tjader Plays Mambo	1956	50.00
—Black vinyl, red label, non-flexible vinyl			
❑ 3221 [M]	Tjader Plays Mambo	1956	100.00
—Red vinyl			
❑ 3221 [M]	Tjader Plays Mambo	196?	25.00
—Black vinyl, red label, flexible vinyl			
❑ 3227 [M]	Cal Tjader Quartet	1956	100.00
—Red vinyl			
❑ 3232 [M]	The Cal Tjader Quintet	1956	50.00
—Black vinyl, red label, non-flexible vinyl			
❑ 3232 [M]	The Cal Tjader Quintet	1956	100.00
—Red vinyl			
❑ 3232 [M]	The Cal Tjader Quintet	196?	25.00
—Black vinyl, red label, flexible vinyl			
❑ 3241 [M]	Jazz at the Blackhawk	1957	30.00
—Black vinyl, red label, non-flexible vinyl			
❑ 3241 [M]	Jazz at the Blackhawk	1957	50.00
—Red vinyl			
❑ 3241 [M]	Jazz at the Blackhawk	196?	15.00
—Black vinyl, red label, flexible vinyl			
❑ 3250 [M]	Latin Kick	1957	30.00
—Black vinyl, red label, non-flexible vinyl			
❑ 3250 [M]	Latin Kick	1957	50.00
—Red vinyl			
❑ 3250 [M]	Latin Kick	196?	15.00
—Black vinyl, red label, flexible vinyl			
❑ 3253 [M]	Cal Tjader	1958	40.00
—Black vinyl, non-flexible vinyl			
❑ 3253 [M]	Cal Tjader	1958	60.00
—Red vinyl			
❑ 3262 [M]	Mas Ritmo Caliente	1958	30.00
—Black vinyl, red label, non-flexible vinyl			
❑ 3262 [M]	Mas Ritmo Caliente	1958	50.00
—Red vinyl			
❑ 3262 [M]	Mas Ritmo Caliente	196?	15.00
—Black vinyl, red label, flexible vinyl			
❑ 3271 [M]	San Francisco Moods	1958	30.00
—Black vinyl, red label, non-flexible vinyl			
❑ 3271 [M]	San Francisco Moods	1958	50.00
—Red vinyl			
❑ 3271 [M]	San Francisco Moods	196?	15.00
—Black vinyl, red label, flexible vinyl			
❑ 3275 [M]	Cal Tjader's Latin Concert	1958	30.00
—Black vinyl, red label, non-flexible vinyl			
❑ 3275 [M]	Cal Tjader's Latin Concert	1958	50.00
—Red vinyl			
❑ 3275 [M]	Cal Tjader's Latin Concert	196?	15.00
—Black vinyl, red label, flexible vinyl			
❑ 3278 [M]	Tjader Plays Tjazz	1958	30.00
—Black vinyl, red label, non-flexible vinyl			
❑ 3278 [M]	Tjader Plays Tjazz	1958	50.00
—Red vinyl; reissue of 3211			
❑ 3278 [M]	Tjader Plays Tjazz	196?	15.00
—Black vinyl, red label, flexible vinyl			
❑ 3279 [M]	Latin for Lovers	1958	30.00
—Black vinyl, red label, non-flexible vinyl			
❑ 3279 [M]	Latin for Lovers	1958	50.00
—Red vinyl			
❑ 3279 [M]	Latin for Lovers	196?	15.00
—Black vinyl, red label, flexible vinyl			
❑ 3283 [M]	A Night at the Blackhawk	1959	30.00
—Black vinyl, red label, non-flexible vinyl			
❑ 3283 [M]	A Night at the Blackhawk	1959	50.00
—Red vinyl			
❑ 3283 [M]	A Night at the Blackhawk	196?	15.00
—Black vinyl, red label, flexible vinyl			
❑ 3289 [M]	Tjader Goes Latin	1959	30.00
—Black vinyl, red label, non-flexible vinyl			
❑ 3289 [M]	Tjader Goes Latin	1959	50.00
—Red vinyl			
❑ 3289 [M]	Tjader Goes Latin	196?	15.00
—Black vinyl, red label, flexible vinyl			
❑ 3295 [M]	Concert by the Sea	1959	30.00
—Black vinyl, red label, non-flexible vinyl			
❑ 3295 [M]	Concert by the Sea	1959	50.00
—Red vinyl			
❑ 3295 [M]	Concert by the Sea	196?	15.00
—Black vinyl, red label, flexible vinyl			
❑ 3299 [M]	Concert on the Campus	196?	15.00
—Black vinyl, red label, flexible vinyl			
❑ 3299 [M]	Concert on the Campus	1960	25.00
—Black vinyl, red label, non-flexible vinyl			

T

Number	Title (A Side/B Side)	Yr	NM
❑ 3299 [M]	Concert on the Campus	1960	40.00
—Red vinyl			
❑ 3307 [M]	Cal Tjader Quartet	196?	15.00
—Black vinyl, red label, flexible vinyl			
❑ 3307 [M]	Cal Tjader Quartet	1960	25.00
—Black vinyl, red label, non-flexible vinyl			
❑ 3307 [M]	Cal Tjader Quartet	1960	40.00
—Red vinyl			
❑ 3309 [M]	Demasiado Caliente	196?	15.00
—Black vinyl, red label, flexible vinyl			
❑ 3309 [M]	Demasiado Caliente	1960	25.00
—Black vinyl, red label, non-flexible vinyl			
❑ 3309 [M]	Demasiado Caliente	1960	40.00
—Red vinyl			
❑ 3310 [M]	West Side Story	196?	15.00
—Black vinyl, red label, flexible vinyl			
❑ 3310 [M]	West Side Story	1960	25.00
—Black vinyl, red label, non-flexible vinyl			
❑ 3310 [M]	West Side Story	1960	40.00
—Red vinyl			
❑ 3313 [M]	Cal Tjader Quintet	196?	15.00
—Black vinyl, red label, flexible vinyl			
❑ 3313 [M]	Cal Tjader Quintet	1961	25.00
—Black vinyl, red label, non-flexible vinyl			
❑ 3313 [M]	Cal Tjader Quintet	1961	40.00
—Red vinyl; evidently a different album than 3232			
❑ 3315 [M]	Cal Tjader Live and Direct	196?	15.00
—Black vinyl, red label, flexible vinyl			
❑ 3315 [M]	Cal Tjader Live and Direct	1961	25.00
—Black vinyl, red label, non-flexible vinyl			
❑ 3315 [M]	Cal Tjader Live and Direct	1961	40.00
—Red vinyl			
❑ 3326 [M]	Mambo	196?	15.00
—Black vinyl, red label, flexible vinyl			
❑ 3326 [M]	Mambo	1961	25.00
—Black vinyl, red label, non-flexible vinyl			
❑ 3326 [M]	Mambo	1961	40.00
—Red vinyl			
❑ 3330 [M]	Cal Tjader Plays the Harold Arlen Songbook	196?	15.00
—Black vinyl, red label, flexible vinyl			
❑ 3330 [M]	Cal Tjader Plays the Harold Arlen Songbook	1961	25.00
—Black vinyl, red label, non-flexible vinyl			
❑ 3330 [M]	Cal Tjader Plays the Harold Arlen Songbook	1961	40.00
—Red vinyl			
❑ 3339 [M]	Latino	196?	15.00
—Black vinyl, red label, flexible vinyl			
❑ 3339 [M]	Latino	1962	25.00
—Black vinyl, red label, non-flexible vinyl			
❑ 3339 [M]	Latino	1962	40.00
—Red vinyl			
❑ 3341 [M]	Concert by the Sea, Vol. 2	196?	15.00
—Black vinyl, red label, flexible vinyl			
❑ 3341 [M]	Concert by the Sea, Vol. 2	1962	25.00
—Black vinyl, red label, non-flexible vinyl			
❑ 3341 [M]	Concert by the Sea, Vol. 2	1962	40.00
—Red vinyl			
❑ 3366 [M]	Cal Tjader's Greatest Hits	1965	15.00
❑ 3374 [M]	Cal Tjader's Greatest Hits, Volume 2	1966	15.00
❑ MPF-4527	Cal Tjader's Greatest Hits	1987	10.00
—Reissue of 8366			
❑ MPF-4530	Cal Tjader's Greatest Hits, Vol. 2	1987	10.00
—Reissue of 8374			
❑ 8003 [S]	Mas Ritmo Caliente	196?	12.00
—Black vinyl, blue label, flexible vinyl			
❑ 8003 [S]	Mas Ritmo Caliente	196?	20.00
—Black vinyl, blue label, non-flexible vinyl			
❑ 8003 [S]	Mas Ritmo Caliente	196?	30.00
—Blue vinyl			
❑ 8014 [S]	Cal Tjader's Latin Concert	196?	12.00
—Black vinyl, blue label, flexible vinyl			
❑ 8014 [S]	Cal Tjader's Latin Concert	196?	20.00
—Black vinyl, blue label, non-flexible vinyl			
❑ 8014 [S]	Cal Tjader's Latin Concert	196?	30.00
—Blue vinyl			
❑ 8016 [S]	Latin for Lovers	196?	12.00
—Black vinyl, blue label, flexible vinyl			
❑ 8016 [S]	Latin for Lovers	196?	20.00
—Black vinyl, blue label, non-flexible vinyl			
❑ 8016 [S]	Latin for Lovers	196?	30.00
—Blue vinyl			
❑ 8017 [S]	San Francisco Moods	196?	12.00
—Black vinyl, blue label, flexible vinyl			
❑ 8017 [S]	San Francisco Moods	196?	20.00
—Black vinyl, blue label, non-flexible vinyl			
❑ 8017 [S]	San Francisco Moods	196?	30.00
—Blue vinyl			
❑ 8019 [S]	Latin for Dancers	196?	100.00
—Blue vinyl; the existence of this has been confirmed. Black vinyl copies of 8019 are unknown.			
❑ 8019 [S]	Latin for Dancers	196?	120.00
—A red vinyl copy with this number is known to exist also, probably pressed in error			
❑ 8026 [S]	A Night at the Blackhawk	196?	12.00
—Black vinyl, blue label, flexible vinyl			
❑ 8026 [S]	A Night at the Blackhawk	196?	20.00
—Black vinyl, blue label, non-flexible vinyl			
❑ 8026 [S]	A Night at the Blackhawk	196?	30.00
—Blue vinyl			
❑ 8030 [S]	Tjader Goes Latin	196?	12.00
—Black vinyl, blue label, flexible vinyl			
❑ 8030 [S]	Tjader Goes Latin	196?	20.00
—Black vinyl, blue label, non-flexible vinyl			
❑ 8030 [S]	Tjader Goes Latin	196?	30.00
—Blue vinyl			
❑ 8033 [S]	Latin Kick	196?	12.00
—Black vinyl, blue label, flexible vinyl			
❑ 8033 [S]	Latin Kick	196?	20.00
—Black vinyl, blue label, non-flexible vinyl			
❑ 8033 [S]	Latin Kick	196?	30.00
—Blue vinyl			
❑ 8038 [S]	Concert by the Sea	196?	12.00
—Black vinyl, blue label, flexible vinyl			
❑ 8038 [S]	Concert by the Sea	196?	20.00
—Black vinyl, blue label, non-flexible vinyl			
❑ 8038 [S]	Concert by the Sea	196?	30.00
—Blue vinyl			
❑ 8044 [S]	Concert on the Campus	196?	12.00
—Black vinyl, blue label, flexible vinyl			
❑ 8044 [S]	Concert on the Campus	196?	20.00
—Black vinyl, blue label, non-flexible vinyl			
❑ 8044 [S]	Concert on the Campus	196?	30.00
—Blue vinyl			
❑ 8053 [S]	Demasiado Caliente	196?	12.00
—Black vinyl, blue label, flexible vinyl			
❑ 8053 [S]	Demasiado Caliente	196?	20.00
—Black vinyl, blue label, non-flexible vinyl			
❑ 8053 [S]	Demasiado Caliente	196?	30.00
—Blue vinyl			
❑ 8054 [S]	West Side Story	196?	12.00
—Black vinyl, blue label, flexible vinyl			
❑ 8054 [S]	West Side Story	196?	20.00
—Black vinyl, blue label, non-flexible vinyl			
❑ 8054 [S]	West Side Story	196?	30.00
—Blue vinyl			
❑ 8057 [S]	Mambo	196?	12.00
—Black vinyl, blue label, flexible vinyl			
❑ 8057 [S]	Mambo	1962	20.00
—Black vinyl, blue label, non-flexible vinyl			
❑ 8057 [S]	Mambo	1962	30.00
—Blue vinyl			
❑ 8059 [S]	Cal Tjader Live and Direct	196?	12.00
—Black vinyl, blue label, flexible vinyl			
❑ 8059 [S]	Cal Tjader Live and Direct	1962	20.00
—Black vinyl, blue label, non-flexible vinyl			
❑ 8059 [S]	Cal Tjader Live and Direct	1962	30.00
—Blue vinyl			
❑ 8072 [S]	Cal Tjader Plays the Harold Arlen Songbook	196?	12.00
—Black vinyl, blue label, flexible vinyl			
❑ 8072 [S]	Cal Tjader Plays the Harold Arlen Songbook	1962	20.00
—Black vinyl, blue label, non-flexible vinyl			
❑ 8072 [S]	Cal Tjader Plays the Harold Arlen Songbook	1962	30.00
—Blue vinyl			
❑ 8077 [R]	Ritmo Caliente	196?	12.00
—Black vinyl, blue label, flexible vinyl			
❑ 8077 [R]	Ritmo Caliente	1962	20.00
—Black vinyl, blue label, non-flexible vinyl			
❑ 8077 [R]	Ritmo Caliente	1962	30.00
—Blue vinyl			
❑ 8079 [S]	Latino	196?	12.00
—Black vinyl, blue label, flexible vinyl			
❑ 8079 [S]	Latino	1962	20.00
—Black vinyl, blue label, non-flexible vinyl			
❑ 8079 [S]	Latino	1962	30.00
—Blue vinyl			
❑ 8083 [R]	Cal Tjader Quartet	1962	12.00
—Black vinyl, blue label, flexible vinyl			
❑ 8083 [R]	Cal Tjader Quartet	1962	20.00
—Black vinyl, blue label, non-flexible vinyl			
❑ 8083 [R]	Cal Tjader Quartet	1962	30.00
—Blue vinyl			
❑ 8084 [S]	Cal Tjader Quintet	1962	12.00
—Black vinyl, blue label, flexible vinyl			
❑ 8084 [S]	Cal Tjader Quintet	1962	20.00
—Black vinyl, blue label, non-flexible vinyl			
❑ 8084 [S]	Cal Tjader Quintet	1962	30.00
—Blue vinyl; stereo version of 3313			
❑ 8085 [R]	The Cal Tjader Quintet	196?	12.00
—Black vinyl, blue label, flexible vinyl			
❑ 8085 [R]	The Cal Tjader Quintet	196?	20.00
—Black vinyl, blue label, non-flexible vinyl			
❑ 8085 [R]	The Cal Tjader Quintet	196?	30.00
—Blue vinyl; stereo version of 3232			
❑ 8096 [R]	Jazz at the Blackhawk	196?	12.00
—Black vinyl, blue label, flexible vinyl			
❑ 8096 [R]	Jazz at the Blackhawk	1962	20.00
—Black vinyl, blue label, non-flexible vinyl			
❑ 8096 [R]	Jazz at the Blackhawk	1962	30.00
—Blue vinyl			
❑ 8097 [R]	Tjader Plays Tjazz	196?	12.00
—Black vinyl, blue label, flexible vinyl			
❑ 8097 [R]	Tjader Plays Tjazz	1962	20.00
—Black vinyl, blue label, non-flexible vinyl			
❑ 8097 [R]	Tjader Plays Tjazz	1962	30.00
—Blue vinyl			
❑ 8098 [S]	Concert by the Sea, Vol. 2	196?	12.00
—Black vinyl, blue label, flexible vinyl			
❑ 8098 [S]	Concert by the Sea, Vol. 2	1962	20.00
—Black vinyl, blue label, non-flexible vinyl			
❑ 8098 [S]	Concert by the Sea, Vol. 2	1962	30.00
—Blue vinyl			
❑ 8366 [S]	Cal Tjader's Greatest Hits	1965	12.00
❑ 8374 [S]	Cal Tjader's Greatest Hits, Vol. 2	1966	12.00
❑ 8379	West Side Story	1967	12.00
—Reissue of 8054			
❑ 8406	Tjader	1970	12.00
❑ 8416	Agua Dulce	1971	12.00
❑ 9409	Live at the Funky Quarters	1970	12.00
❑ 9422	Primo	1972	12.00
❑ 9424	Mambo with Tjader	1973	12.00
❑ 9446	Last Bolero in Berkeley	1974	12.00
❑ 9463	Puttin' It Together	1974	12.00
❑ 9482	Last Night When We Were Young	1975	12.00
❑ 9502	Amazonas	1975	12.00
❑ 9521	At Grace Cathedral	1977	12.00
❑ 9533	Guarabe	1977	12.00
❑ 24712 [(2)]	Los Ritmos Caliente	197?	15.00

GALAXY

Number	Title (A Side/B Side)	Yr	NM
❑ 5107	Breathe Easy	1977	12.00
❑ 5121	Here	1978	12.00

MGM

Number	Title (A Side/B Side)	Yr	NM
❑ 10008	Sonido Nuevo	197?	15.00

PRESTIGE

Number	Title (A Side/B Side)	Yr	NM
❑ 24026 [(2)]	The Monterey Concerts	1973	15.00

SAVOY

Number	Title (A Side/B Side)	Yr	NM
❑ MG-9036 [10]	Cal Tjader — Vibist	1954	100.00

SKYE

Number	Title (A Side/B Side)	Yr	NM
❑ SK-1	Solar Heat	1968	20.00
❑ SK-10	Cal Tjader Plugs In	1969	20.00
❑ SK-19	Tjader-Ade	1970	15.00

VERVE

Number	Title (A Side/B Side)	Yr	NM
❑ V-8419 [M]	In a Latin Bag	1961	20.00
❑ V6-8419 [S]	In a Latin Bag	1961	25.00
❑ V-8459 [M]	Saturday Night...Sunday Night at the Blackhawk	1962	20.00
❑ V6-8459 [S]	Saturday Night...Sunday Night at the Blackhawk	1962	25.00
❑ V-8470 [M]	The Contemporary Music of Mexico and Brazil	1962	20.00
❑ V6-8470 [S]	The Contemporary Music of Mexico and Brazil	1962	25.00
❑ V-8507 [M]	Several Shades of Jade	1963	20.00
❑ V6-8507 [S]	Several Shades of Jade	1963	25.00
❑ V-8531 [M]	Sona Libre	1963	20.00
❑ V6-8531 [S]	Sona Libre	1963	25.00
❑ V-8575 [M]	Breeze from the East	1964	20.00
❑ V6-8575 [S]	Breeze from the East	1964	25.00
❑ V-8585 [M]	Warm Wave	1964	20.00
❑ V6-8585 [S]	Warm Wave	1964	25.00
❑ V-8614 [M]	Soul Sauce	1965	20.00
❑ V6-8614 [S]	Soul Sauce	1965	25.00
❑ V-8626 [M]	Soul Bird: Whippenpoof	1965	20.00
❑ V6-8626 [S]	Soul Bird: Whippenpoof	1965	25.00
❑ V-8637 [M]	Soul Burst	1965	20.00
❑ V6-8637 [S]	Soul Burst	1965	25.00
❑ V-8651 [M]	El Soni Do Nuevo — The New Soul Sound	1966	15.00
❑ V6-8651 [S]	El Soni Do Nuevo — The New Soul Sound	1966	20.00
❑ V-8671 [M]	Along Comes Cal	1966	15.00
❑ V6-8671 [S]	Along Comes Cal	1966	20.00
❑ V-8725 [M]	The Best of Cal Tjader	1967	15.00
❑ V6-8725 [S]	The Best of Cal Tjader	1967	20.00
❑ V-8730 [M]	Hip Vibrations	1967	20.00
❑ V6-8730 [S]	Hip Vibrations	1967	15.00
❑ V6-8769	The Prophet	1969	15.00
❑ 827756-1	Soul Sauce	1986	10.00
—Reissue of 8614			

TJADER, CAL, AND CHARLIE BYRD

Albums

FANTASY

Number	Title (A Side/B Side)	Yr	NM
❑ 9453	Tambu	1974	12.00

TJADER, CAL/DON ELLIOTT

Albums

SAVOY

Number	Title (A Side/B Side)	Yr	NM
❑ MG-12054 [M]	Vib-Rations	1956	40.00
—Reissue of 9036 and 9033			

TJADER, CAL, AND STAN GETZ

45s

FANTASY

Number	Title (A Side/B Side)	Yr	NM
❑ 566	For All We Know/Ginza Samba	196?	10.00

Albums

FANTASY

Number	Title (A Side/B Side)	Yr	NM
❑ 3266 [M]	Cal Tjader-Stan Getz Sextet	1958	30.00
—Black vinyl, red label, non-flexible vinyl			
❑ 3266 [M]	Cal Tjader-Stan Getz Sextet	1958	50.00
—Red vinyl			

Except when noted otherwise, VG = 25% of NM, and VG+ = 50% of NM. (Example: VG = $2.00, VG+ = $4.00 and NM = $8.00.)

Number	Title (A Side/B Side)	Yr	NM
❑ 3266 [M]	Cal Tjader-Stan Getz Sextet	196?	15.00
—Black vinyl, red label, flexible vinyl			
❑ 3348 [M]	Cal Tjader-Stan Getz Sextet	1963	15.00
—Reissue of 3266			
❑ 8005 [S]	Cal Tjader-Stan Getz Sextet	196?	12.00
—Black vinyl, blue label, flexible vinyl			
❑ 8005 [S]	Cal Tjader-Stan Getz Sextet	196?	20.00
—Black vinyl, blue label, non-flexible vinyl			
❑ 8005 [S]	Cal Tjader-Stan Getz Sextet	196?	30.00
—Blue vinyl			
❑ 8348 [S]	Cal Tjader-Stan Getz Quartet	1963	12.00
—Reissue of 8005			

TJADER, CAL, AND CARMEN MCRAE

Albums

CONCORD JAZZ

Number	Title (A Side/B Side)	Yr	NM
❑ CJ-189	Heat Wave	1982	10.00

TOAD HALL

45s

BARNABY

Number	Title (A Side/B Side)	Yr	NM
❑ ZS7 2052	Hallelujah! I'm a Bum/I'm Leaving You Louisiana	1971	8.00

Albums

LIBERTY

Number	Title (A Side/B Side)	Yr	NM
❑ LST-7580	Toad Hall	1968	25.00

TOAD THE WET SPROCKET

45s

COLUMBIA

Number	Title (A Side/B Side)	Yr	NM
❑ 74706	All I Want/Walk on the Ocean	1992	3.00
❑ 74892	I Will Not Take These/So Alive	1993	—
—Cassette only			
❑ 77474	Fall Down/All Right	1994	3.00

Albums

COLUMBIA

Number	Title (A Side/B Side)	Yr	NM
❑ FC 45326	Bread and Circus	1989	12.00
❑ C 46060	Pale	1990	30.00
—Marbled white (almost greenish) vinyl			
❑ C 47309	Fear	1991	20.00

TODAY AND TOMORROW

45s

NOOSE

Number	Title (A Side/B Side)	Yr	NM
❑ 812	Dooley Swings (Part 1)/Dooley Swings (Part 2)	1959	40.00

TODAY'S PEOPLE

45s

20TH CENTURY

Number	Title (A Side/B Side)	Yr	NM
❑ 2032	He/I Didn't Know	1973	6.00
❑ 2079	I Belong/Come Back to Save Us	1974	6.00

TODD, DYLAN

45s

RCA VICTOR

Number	Title (A Side/B Side)	Yr	NM
❑ 47-6463	The Ballad of James Dean/More Precious Than Gold	1956	30.00
❑ 47-6463 [PS]	The Ballad of James Dean/More Precious Than Gold	1956	50.00
❑ 47-6711	Timber/Golden Spurs and a Silver Saddle	1956	20.00

TODD, FULLER

45s

KING

Number	Title (A Side/B Side)	Yr	NM
❑ 5048	Old Fashioned/Proud Lady Heart Stealer	1957	25.00
❑ 5075	Real True Love/Young Hearts Are True	1957	25.00
❑ 5111	Top Ten Rock/Jeannie Marie	1958	25.00

TODD, JOHNNY

45s

MODERN

Number	Title (A Side/B Side)	Yr	NM
❑ 1003	Pink Cadillac/What's Up	1956	120.00

TODD, NICK

45s

DOT

Number	Title (A Side/B Side)	Yr	NM
❑ 15643	Plaything/The Honey Song	1957	20.00
❑ 15675	At the Hop/I Do	1957	20.00
❑ 15688	Teen-Age Cutie/Ever Since I Met Lucy	1958	20.00
❑ 15772	Forever and a Day/Too Much Rosita	1958	20.00
❑ 15860	My Little Girl/Does Your Heart Beat for Me?	1958	20.00
❑ 15893	Red Roses for a Blue Lady/Little Rosey Red	1959	15.00
❑ 15951	Tiger/Twice As Nice	1959	15.00
❑ 15981	Invisible Man/Sayin' Something	1959	15.00
❑ 16109	Each Moment/Your Love's Gotta Grip on Me	1960	15.00

TOE FAT

45s

RARE EARTH

Number	Title (A Side/B Side)	Yr	NM
❑ 5019	Bad Side of the Moon/Just Like Me	1970	6.00

Albums

RARE EARTH

Number	Title (A Side/B Side)	Yr	NM
❑ RS-511	Toe Fat	1970	25.00
❑ RS-525	Toe Fat Two	1971	25.00

TOGGERY FIVE, THE

Also see FREDDIE AND THE DREAMERS.

45s

TOWER

Number	Title (A Side/B Side)	Yr	NM
❑ 119	I'm Gonna Jump/Bye Bye Bird	1965	15.00

TOKAYS, THE

45s

BONNIE

Number	Title (A Side/B Side)	Yr	NM
❑ 102	Lost and Found/Fatty-Boom Bi Laddy	1962	100.00

BRUTE

Number	Title (A Side/B Side)	Yr	NM
❑ 001	Hey Senorita/Baby Baby Baby	1967	120.00

SCORPIO

Number	Title (A Side/B Side)	Yr	NM
❑ 403	Now/Ask Me No Questions	1966	20.00

TOKENS, THE

NEIL SEDAKA was (very) briefly a member. Also see THE COEDS; CROSS COUNTRY; THE FOUR WINDS (1); JOHNNY AND THE TOKENS; UNITED STATES DOUBLE QUARTET.

45s

ATCO

Number	Title (A Side/B Side)	Yr	NM
❑ 7009	The Lord Can't Sing a Solo/Penny Whistle Band	1974	6.00

B.T. PUPPY

Number	Title (A Side/B Side)	Yr	NM
❑ 500	A Girl Named Arlene/Swing	1964	12.00
❑ 502	He's in Town/Oh Cathy	1964	12.00
❑ 504	You're My Girl/Havin' Fun	1964	12.00
❑ 505	Nobody But You/Mr. Cupid	1965	10.00
❑ 507	A Message to the World/Sylvie Sleepin'	1965	10.00
❑ 512	Only My Friend/Cattle Call	1965	10.00
❑ 513	The Bells of St. Mary/Just One Smile	1966	10.00
❑ 515	The Three Bells/Message to the World	1966	10.00
❑ 518	I Hear Trumpets Blow/Don't Cry, Sing Along with the Music	1966	10.00
❑ 519	Breezy/Greatest Moments of a Girl's Life	1966	10.00
❑ 519 [PS]	Breezy/Greatest Moments of a Girl's Life	1966	25.00
❑ 525	Green Plant/Saloogy	1967	10.00
❑ 552	Please Say You Want Me/Get a Job	1969	10.00

BELL

Number	Title (A Side/B Side)	Yr	NM
❑ 45190	You and Me/I Like to Throw My Head Back and Sing	1972	6.00

BUDDAH

Number	Title (A Side/B Side)	Yr	NM
❑ 151	She Lets Her Hair Down (Early in the Morning)/Oh to Get Away	1970	6.00
❑ 159	Don't Worry Baby/If the Shoe Fits Ya Baby	1970	5.00
❑ 159	Don't Worry Baby/Some People Sleep	1970	5.00
❑ 174	Both Sides Now/I Could See Me (Dancin' with You)	1970	5.00
❑ 187	Listen to the Words (Listen to the Music)/Groovin' On the Sunshine	1970	5.00

DATE

Number	Title (A Side/B Side)	Yr	NM
❑ 2737	Oh What a Night/(Hey Hey) Juanita	1961	50.00

GARY

Number	Title (A Side/B Side)	Yr	NM
❑ 1006	Doom-Lang/Come Dance with Me	1961	100.00

LAURIE

Number	Title (A Side/B Side)	Yr	NM
❑ 3180	I'll Always Love You/Please Write	1963	20.00

MELBA

Number	Title (A Side/B Side)	Yr	NM
❑ 104	While I Dream/I Love My Baby	1956	50.00

RCA

Number	Title (A Side/B Side)	Yr	NM
❑ 8749-7-R	Re-Doo-Wopp/I'm Through with You	1988	4.00
❑ 8836-7-R	Re-Doo-Wopp (Edit)/I'm Through with You	1988	4.00

RCA VICTOR

Number	Title (A Side/B Side)	Yr	NM
❑ 37-7896	When I Go to Sleep at Night/Dry Your Eyes	1961	40.00
—"Compact Single 33" (small hole, plays at LP speed)			
❑ 37-7925	Sincerely/When the Summer Is Through	1961	40.00
—"Compact Single 33" (small hole, plays at LP speed)			
❑ 37-7954	The Lion Sleeps Tonight/Tina	1961	50.00
—"Compact Single 33" (small hole, plays at LP speed)			
❑ 37-7991	B'wa Nina/Weeping River	1962	40.00
—"Compact Single 33" (small hole, plays at LP speed)			
❑ 37-8018	The Riddle/Big Boat	1962	40.00
—"Compact Single 33" (small hole, plays at LP speed)			
❑ 47-7896	When I Go to Sleep at Night/Dry Your Eyes	1961	20.00
❑ 47-7896 [PS]	When I Go to Sleep at Night/Dry Your Eyes	1961	40.00
❑ 47-7925	Sincerely/When the Summer Is Through	1961	20.00
❑ 47-7954	The Lion Sleeps Tonight/Tina	1961	25.00
❑ 47-7991	B'wa Nina/Weeping River	1962	20.00
❑ 47-7991 [PS]	B'wa Nina/Weeping River	1962	30.00
—"The Lion Sleeps Tonight" LP mentioned on sleeve			
❑ 47-7991 [PS]	B'wa Nina/Weeping River	1962	50.00
—No mention of "The Lion Sleeps Tonight" LP on sleeve			
❑ 47-8018	The Riddle/Big Boat	1962	20.00
❑ 47-8018 [PS]	The Riddle/Big Boat	1962	40.00
❑ 47-8052	La Bomba/A Token of Love	1962	20.00
❑ 47-8052 [PS]	La Bomba/A Token of Love	1962	40.00
❑ 47-8089	I'll Do My Crying Tomorrow/Dream Angel Goodnight	1962	20.00
❑ 47-8089 [PS]	I'll Do My Crying Tomorrow/Dream Angel Goodnight	1962	40.00
❑ 47-8114	A Bird Flies Out of Sight/Wishing	1962	20.00
❑ 47-8114 [PS]	A Bird Flies Out of Sight/Wishing	1962	40.00
❑ 47-8148	Tonight I Met An Angel/Hindi Lullabye	1963	15.00
❑ 47-8148 [PS]	Tonight I Met An Angel/Hindi Lullabye	1963	30.00
❑ 47-8210	Hear the Bells/ABC 1-2-3	1963	15.00
❑ 47-8210 [PS]	Hear the Bells/ABC 1-2-3	1963	30.00
❑ 47-8309	Two Cars/Let's Go to the Drag Strip	1963	15.00
❑ 47-8309 [PS]	Two Cars/Let's Go to the Drag Strip	1963	80.00

ROULETTE

Number	Title (A Side/B Side)	Yr	NM
❑ 4174	Roses Are Red/Pictures in My Wallet	1959	30.00
—As "Darrell and the Oxfords"			
❑ 4230	Can't You Tell/Your Mother Said So	1960	30.00
—As "Darrell and the Oxfords"			

RUST

Number	Title (A Side/B Side)	Yr	NM
❑ 5094	Arlene/Rumble in the Park	1965	10.00

WARNER BROS.

Number	Title (A Side/B Side)	Yr	NM
❑ 5900	Portrait of My Love/She Comes and Goes	1967	8.00
❑ 5900 [PS]	Portrait of My Love/She Comes and Goes	1967	20.00
❑ 7056	It's a Happening World/How Nice	1967	6.00
❑ 7099	Ain't That Peculiar/Bye, Bye, Bye	1967	6.00
❑ 7118	Portrait of My Love/It's a Happening World	1968	5.00
—"Back to Back Hits" series — originals have green labels with "W7" logo			
❑ 7169	Till/Poor Man	1968	6.00
❑ 7183	Mister Swail/Needles of Evergreen	1968	10.00
—As "Margo, Margo, Medress and Siegel"			
❑ 7202	Animal/Bathroom Wall	1968	6.00
❑ 7233	Grandfather/The Banana Boat Song	1968	6.00
❑ 7255	The World Is Full of Wonderful Things/Some People Sleep	1968	6.00
❑ 7280	Go Away Little Girl-Young Girl/I Want to Make Love to You	1969	6.00
❑ 7323	I Could Be/End of the World	1969	6.00

WARWICK

Number	Title (A Side/B Side)	Yr	NM
❑ 615	Tonight I Fell in Love/I'll Always Love You	1961	30.00

Albums

B.T. PUPPY

Number	Title (A Side/B Side)	Yr	NM
❑ BTP-1000 [M]	I Hear Trumpets Blow	1966	20.00
❑ BTPS-1000 [P]	I Hear Trumpets Blow	1966	25.00
❑ BTPS-1006	Tokens of Gold	1969	25.00
❑ BTPS-1012	Greatest Moments	1970	25.00
❑ BTPS-1014	December 5th	1971	200.00
❑ BTPS-1027	Intercourse	1971	600.00

BUDDAH

Number	Title (A Side/B Side)	Yr	NM
❑ BDS-5059	Both Sides Now	1971	15.00

DIPLOMAT

Number	Title (A Side/B Side)	Yr	NM
❑ D-2308 [M]	Kings of the Hot Rods	196?	25.00
❑ DS-2308 [S]	Kings of the Hot Rods	196?	30.00

RCA

Number	Title (A Side/B Side)	Yr	NM
❑ 8534-1-R	Re-Doo-Wopp	1988	10.00

T

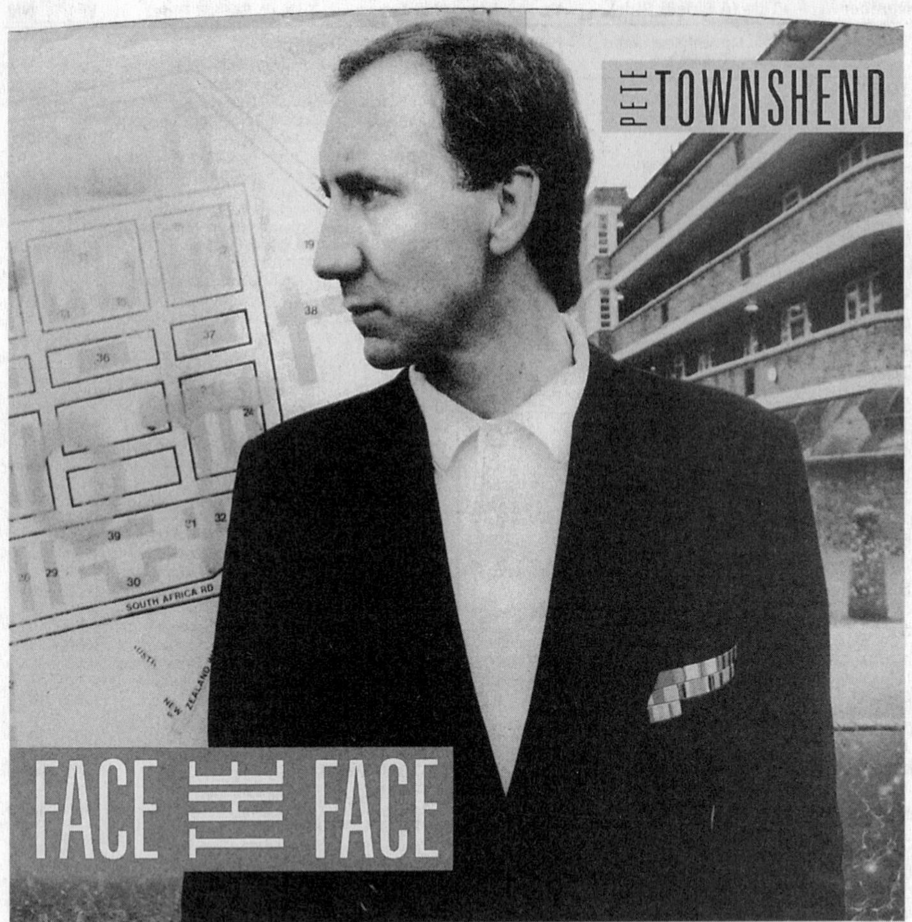

Pete Townshend, "Face the Face," Atco 7-99590, 1985, **$3.**

Number	Title (A Side/B Side)	Yr	NM
RCA VICTOR			
❑ LPM-2514 [M]	The Lion Sleeps Tonight	1961	80.00
❑ LSP-2514 [S]	The Lion Sleeps Tonight	1961	150.00
❑ LPM-2631 [M]	We, The Tokens, Sing Folk	1962	40.00
❑ LSP-2631 [S]	We, The Tokens, Sing Folk	1962	50.00
❑ LPM-2886 [M]	Wheels	1964	80.00
❑ LSP-2886 [S]	Wheels	1964	100.00
❑ LPM-3685 [M]	The Tokens Again	1966	40.00
❑ LSP-3685 [S]	The Tokens Again	1966	50.00
WARNER BROS.			
❑ W 1685 [M]	It's a Happening World	1967	25.00
❑ WS 1685 [S]	It's a Happening World	1967	20.00

TOKENS, THE AND THE HAPPENINGS Also see each artist's individual listings.

Albums

Number	Title (A Side/B Side)	Yr	NM
B.T. PUPPY			
❑ BTP-1002 [M]	Back to Back	1967	20.00
—Half this LP is by the Tokens, the other half by the Happenings			
❑ BTPS-1002 [S]	Back to Back	1967	25.00

TOLBERT, ISRAEL

45s

Number	Title (A Side/B Side)	Yr	NM
WARREN/STAX			
❑ 106	Big Leg Woman (With a Short Short Mini Skirt)/I Got Love	1970	8.00
❑ 107	Shake Your Big Hips/Lost Love	1971	10.00

TOLLIVER, MICKEY, AND THE CAPITOLS

45s

Number	Title (A Side/B Side)	Yr	NM
CINDY			
❑ 3002	Rose Marie/Millie	1957	200.00

TOM AND JERRIO

45s

Number	Title (A Side/B Side)	Yr	NM
ABC-PARAMOUNT			
❑ 10638	Boo-Ga-Loo/Boomerang	1965	12.00
❑ 10704	Great Goo-Ga Moo-Ga/Come On and Love Me	1965	12.00
❑ 10787	Oolya-Coo/Bacardi	1966	12.00
LOST-NITE			
❑ 248	Boo-Ga-Loo/Boomerang	196?	5.00
—Reissue			

TOM TOM CLUB

12-Inch Singles

Number	Title (A Side/B Side)	Yr	NM
SIRE			
❑ PRO-A-996 [DJ]	Genius of Love/Lorelei	1981	20.00
❑ PRO-A-2096 [DJ]	Pleasure of Love (Album Version 6:33) (Instrumental Version 5:27)	1983	10.00
❑ 20132	The Man with the 4-Way Hips (Extended Version 7:20) (Edited Version 3:30) (Dub Version 7:12)	1983	6.00
❑ 20164	Pleasure of Love (Long Version) (Instrumental)	1983	8.00
❑ 21198	Suboceana (12" Dance Mix 7:48) (Jacking Deep and High Mix 6:20) (12" Club Mix 8:01) (Magic Juan Mix 5:25)/Devil Does Your Dog Bite (LP Version 3:40)	1989	7.00
❑ 21285	Call of the Wild (12" Remix 6:53) (12" Club Mix 7:38)/Genius of Love (Live 6:01)/Wordy Rappinghood (Live 6:16)	1989	8.00
❑ 29930	Under the Boardwalk (Version 4:12)/On, On, On (3:44)/ Lorelei (6:20)	1982	8.00
❑ 40444	Sunshine and Ecstasy (XTC Mix) (XTC Dub) (Tom Tom Dub) (Sunshine and Sensi Mix) (Sunshine Mix) (Lovepump Dub)/As the Disco Ball Turns (Album Version)	1992	8.00
❑ 40600	You Sexy Thing (Extended Album Version) (Dub) (Lost in Bass) (Sexy Remix) (Deep Bass)/Who Wants an Ugly Girl? (Extended Album Version)	1992	8.00
❑ DSRE 49817	Wordy Rappinghood (Special 12" Version 6:40)/Spooks (6:30)	1981	50.00
❑ 50057	Wordy Rappinghood	1982	—
—Canceled on this number?			
TIP TOP			
❑ RA 12-0607 [DJ]	Happiness Can't Buy Money (Automator's Handsome Boy Modeling School Main Remix 6:19) (Automator's Handsome Boy Modeling School Instrumental Remix 6:19) (Automator's Handsome Boy Modeling School Vocal Mutes Remix 6:19) (Tom Tom Club Album Version 6:05)	2000	8.00

45s

Number	Title (A Side/B Side)	Yr	NM
SIRE			
❑ GSRE 0430	Genius of Love/Wordy Rappinghood	198?	3.00
—"Back to Back Hits" reissue			
❑ 18695	You Sexy Thing	1993	—
—Cassette only			
❑ 18862	Sunshine and Ecstasy	1992	—
—Cassette only			
❑ 7-22998	Suboceana/Devil Does Your Dog Bite	1989	5.00
❑ 7-29437	Pleasure of Love/ Never Took a Penny	1983	4.00
❑ 7-29437 [PS]	Pleasure of Love/ Never Took a Penny	1983	4.00
❑ 7-29549	The Man with the 4-Way Hips/ (Dub)	1983	4.00
❑ 7-29549 [PS]	The Man with the 4-Way Hips/ (Dub)	1983	4.00
❑ 49813	Wordy Rappinghood (edit)/ (You Don't Stop) Wordy Rappinghood	1981	5.00
❑ 49882	Genius of Love/Lorelei	1981	4.00
❑ DSRE 50067	Wordy Rappinghood (edit)/ (You Don't Stop) Wordy Rappinghood	1982	4.00

Albums

Number	Title (A Side/B Side)	Yr	NM
SIRE			
❑ SRK 3628	Tom Tom Club	1981	10.00
❑ 23916	Close to the Bone	1983	10.00
❑ 25888	Boom Boom Chi Boom Boom	1989	10.00
WARNER BROS.			
❑ WBMS-120 [DJ]	Wordy Rapping with the Tom Tom Club	1986	20.00
—Part of "The Warner Bros. Music Show"; promo only			

TOMBOYS, THE

45s

Number	Title (A Side/B Side)	Yr	NM
SWAN			
❑ 4181	I'd Rather Fight Than Switch/ Mary Had a Little Kiss	1964	10.00

TOMBSTONES, THE

45s

Number	Title (A Side/B Side)	Yr	NM
CAPITOL			
❑ 5997	Times Will Be Hard/Mary Jane	1967	10.00

TOMITA

45s

Number	Title (A Side/B Side)	Yr	NM
RCA			
❑ PB-10819	Planet Mars/Planet Venus	1976	4.00
RCA VICTOR			
❑ APBO-0308	Golliwog's Cakewalk/ Clair de Lune	1974	5.00
❑ APBO-0308 [PS]	Golliwog's Cakewalk/ Clair de Lune	1974	8.00
❑ PB-10296	The Great Gate of Kiev/ Baba Yaya	1975	5.00
❑ PB-10683	Firebird Suite: Infernal Dance/ Firebird Suite: Finale	1976	5.00

Albums

Number	Title (A Side/B Side)	Yr	NM
RCA RED SEAL			
❑ ARD1-0488 [Q]	Snowflakes Are Dancing	1974	15.00
❑ ARL1-0488	Snowflakes Are Dancing	1974	10.00
❑ ARD1-0838 [Q]	Moussorgsky: Pictures at an Exhibition	1975	15.00
❑ ARL1-0838	Moussorgsky: Pictures at an Exhibition	1975	10.00
❑ ARD1-1312 [Q]	Firebird	1976	15.00
❑ ARL1-1312	Firebird	1976	10.00
❑ ARL1-1919	Holst: The Planets	1976	10.00
❑ ARL1-2616	Kosmos	1978	10.00
❑ ARL1-2885	The Bermuda Triangle	1979	10.00
❑ ARL1-3412	Ravel: Bolero	1980	10.00
❑ ARL1-3439	Greatest Hits	1980	10.00
❑ ARL1-4019	A Voyage Through His Greatest Hits, Vol. 2	1981	10.00
❑ ARL1-4317	Grand Canyon Suite	1982	10.00

Except when noted otherwise, VG = 25% of NM, and VG+ = 50% of NM. (Example: VG = $2.00, VG+ = $4.00 and NM = $8.00.)

Number | Title (A Side/B Side) | Yr | NM

❑ ATL1-4332 Snowflakes Are Dancing 1982 12.00
—Reissue with die-cut cover and custom innersleeve
❑ ARL1-5037 Spacewalk — Impressions of an Astronaut 1984 10.00
❑ ARL1-5184 Canon of the 3 Stars 1984 10.00
❑ ARL1-5461 Live at Linz, 1984 — The Mind of the Universe 1985 10.00

TOMLIN, LILY
45s
POLYDOR
❑ 14180 20th Century Blues/Blues 1973 5.00
❑ 14283 Edith Ann/Detroit City 1975 5.00
Albums
ARISTA
❑ AB 4142 Lily Tomlin On Stage 1977 12.00
POLYDOR
❑ 24-4055 This Is a Recording 1971 10.00
❑ PD 5023 And That's the Truth 1972 10.00
❑ PD 6051 Modern Scream 1976 12.00

TOMMY AND THE HUSTLERS
45s
FANTASY
❑ 573 Diggin' Out/The Right Size 1963 25.00
❑ 573 Diggin' Out/The Right Size 1963 40.00
—Green vinyl

TOMMY AND THE RIVIERAS
45s
CAMEO
❑ 461 Messin' with the Kid/(Make It to) Detroit City 1967 25.00

TOMMY AND THE TWISTERS
45s
REGENT
❑ 205 Mr. Twist/Hucklebuck Twist 1962 12.00
Albums
REGENT
❑ MG-6104 [M] Let's All Do the Twist 1961 40.00

TOMS, GARY, EMPIRE
45s
MCA
❑ 40770 Turn It Out (Tear This Building Down)/Hurricane 1977 4.00
MERCURY
❑ 74012 1-2-3-4/Feelin' Good Again 1978 4.00
❑ 74023 Welcome to Harlem/ (B-side unknown) 1978 4.00
P.I.P.
❑ 6504 7-6-5-4-3-2-1 (Blow Your Whistle)/7-6-5-4-3-2-1 (Blow Your Whistle) (Long Version) 1975 5.00
❑ 6509 Drive My Car/The New Empire 1975 5.00
❑ 6517 Love Me Right (Short Version)/ Love Me Right (Long Version) 1976 5.00
❑ 6524 Stand Up and Shout/Party Hardy 1976 5.00
Albums
MCA
❑ 2289 Turn It Out 1977 10.00
MERCURY
❑ SRM-1-3731 Do It Again 1978 10.00
P.I.P.
❑ 6814 7-6-5-4-3-2-1 Blow Your Whistle 1975 10.00

TONETTES, THE Two different groups?
45s
ABC-PARAMOUNT
❑ 9905 Oh What a Baby/Howie 1958 20.00
DOE
❑ 101 Oh What a Baby/Howie 1958 80.00
❑ 103 Uh Oh/He Loves Me, He Loves Me Not 1958 60.00
MODERN
❑ 997 Tonight You Belong to Me/ Don't Fall in Love Too Soon 1956 25.00
VOLT
❑ 101 Please Don't Go/No Tears 1962 20.00
❑ 104 Stolen Angel/Teardrop Sea 1963 20.00

TONEY, OSCAR, JR.
45s
BELL
❑ 672 For Your Precious Love/ Ain't That True Love 1967 10.00
❑ 681 Turn On Your Love Light/ Any Day Now 1967 10.00
❑ 688 Unlucky Guy/You Can Lead Your Woman to the Altar 1967 10.00
❑ 699 Without Love (There Is Nothing)/Love That Never Grows Old 1968 10.00
❑ 714 Never Get Enough of Your Love/ Love That Never Grows Old 1968 10.00
CAPRICORN
❑ 0005 I Do What You Wish/ Thank You, Honey Chile 1972 6.00
❑ 8005 Down on My Knees/ Seven Days Tomorrow 1970 8.00
❑ 8010 I Wouldn't Be a Poor Boy/ Person to Person 1970 8.00
❑ 8018 Workin' Together/Baby Is Mine 1971 8.00
KING
❑ 5906 Can It All Be Love/You Are Going to Need Me 1964 20.00
❑ 6108 Keep On Loving Me/I've Found a True Love 1967 12.00
Albums
BELL
❑ 6006 [M] For Your Precious Love 1967 25.00
❑ S-6006 [S] For Your Precious Love 1967 30.00

TONGUE AND GROOVE
45s
FONTANA
❑ 1640 Cherry Ball/Devil 1969 8.00
❑ 1653 Come On in My Kitchen/ Mailman's Sack 1969 8.00
Albums
FONTANA
❑ SRF-67593 Tongue and Groove 1968 20.00

TONTO'S EXPANDING HEAD BAND
Albums
EMBRYO
❑ SD 732 Zero Time 1971 20.00

TONY AND JOE
45s
DORE
❑ 619 Twist and Freeze/Long Black Stockings 1961 15.00
❑ 688 The Freeze/Gonna Get a Little Kissin' Tonight 1963 15.00
ERA
❑ 1075 The Freeze/Gonna Get a Little Kissin' Tonight 1958 20.00
❑ 1083 Play Something Sentimental Mr. D.J./Where Can You Be? 1958 25.00
FLYTE
❑ 106 Fairytale Love/(B-side unknown) 1959 15.00
GARDENA
❑ 103 Instant Love/The Duck Walk 1960 15.00

TONY AND THE DAYDREAMS
45s
PLANET
❑ 1008 Why Don't You Be Nice/I'll Never Tell 1958 100.00
❑ 1054 Christmas Lullaby/Handin' Hand 1961 200.00

TONY AND THE HOLIDAYS
45s
ABC-PARAMOUNT
❑ 10295 There Goes My Heart Again/ My Love Is Real 1962 200.00

TONY AND THE MASQUINS
45s
RUTHIE
❑ 1000 My Angel Eyes/Fugi Womma 1961 100.00

TONY AND THE RAINDROPS
45s
CHESAPEKE
❑ 609 While Walking/Our Love Is Over 1961 60.00
CROSLEY
❑ 340 Tina/My Heart Cried 1962 200.00

TONY AND THE TECHNICS See THE TECHNICS.

TONY AND THE TWILIGHTERS Early version of ANTHONY AND THE SOPHOMORES.
45s
JALYNNE
❑ 106 Be My Girl/Did You Make Up Your Mind 1960 80.00

RED TOP
❑ 127 Key to My Heart/Yes or No 1960 200.00

TONY AND TYRONE
45s
ATLANTIC
❑ 2458 Please Operator/ Apple of My Eye 1967 30.00
COLUMBIA
❑ 43432 Turn It On/Talkin' About the People 1965 15.00

TOO MUCH JOY
12-Inch Singles
GIANT
❑ PRO-A-4352 [DJ] That's a Lie (Remix)/Seasons in the Sun/IF I Was a Mekon 1990 8.00
45s
DISCOVERY
❑ 74526 The Kids Don't Understand/ Get Me Out of Here 1996 2.00
—Pink marbled vinyl
❑ 74526 [PS] The Kids Don't Understand/ Get Me Out of Here 1996 2.00
7-Inch Extended Plays
JOYBUZZER
❑ JB-001 Dr. Seuss Is Dead 1994 15.00
—Giveaway for people who join Too Much Joy's fan club
WARNER BROS.
❑ PRO-S-5034 [DJ] Rap Like Mine/G.I. Jesus// No Good for You (Live)/ Lucifer Chicken 1991 15.00
—"Soil X Samples 5"; clear yellow vinyl, purple label; B-side by Sister Double Happiness
Albums
ALIAS
❑ A-003 Son of Sam I Am 1988 10.00
GIANT
❑ PRO-A-5054 [DJ] Besides 1991 12.00
—Promo-only collection
STONEGARDEN
❑ SGN-901 Green Eggs and Crack 1987 200.00

TOOMORROW OLIVIA NEWTON-JOHN was in this group.
45s
KIRSHNER
❑ 63-5005 Goin' Back/You're My Baby Now 1970 60.00

TOONE, GENE
45s
ANNETTE
❑ 1001 You're My Baby/Jose 1964 200.00
—Produced by Phil Spector
SIMCO
❑ 30000 What More Do You Want/ (B-side unknown) 196? 1200.
❑ 30002 A Love Triangle/Turn to Be 196? 100.00
❑ 30003 So Glad Trouble Don't Last/ Every Now and Then 196? 100.00
WAND
❑ 11293 Baby Boy (Part 1)/Baby Boy (Part 2) 1975 6.00

TOOTIE AND THE BOUQUETS
45s
PARKWAY
❑ 887 The Conqueror/ You Done Me Wrong 1963 25.00

TOOTS AND THE MAYTALS
Albums
ISLAND
❑ ILPS 9330 Funky Kingston 1975 12.00
MANGO
❑ MLPS 9330 Funky Kingston 197? 10.00
—Reissue of Island 9330
❑ MLPS 9374 Reggae Got Soul 1976 12.00
❑ MLPS 9534 Pass the Pipe 198? 10.00
❑ MLPS 9590 Just Like That 1980 10.00
❑ MLPS 9647 Live 1980 12.00
❑ MLPS 9670 Knock Out 1982 10.00
❑ 9781 Reggae Greats 198? 10.00

TOP DRAWER
Albums
WISH BONE
❑ 721207 Solid Oak 1969 400.00

T

TOP HITS, THE

Number	Title (A Side/B Side)	Yr	NM
45s			
NORMAN			
❑ 504	Love No One/Thum-A-Lum-A	1961	200.00

TOP NOTES, THE

Number	Title (A Side/B Side)	Yr	NM
45s			
ABC-PARAMOUNT			
❑ 10399	I Love You So Much/It's Alright	1963	10.00
ATLANTIC			
❑ 2066	A Wonderful Time/ Walkin' with Love	1960	15.00
❑ 2080	Say Man/Warm Your Heart	1960	15.00
❑ 2097	Hearts of Stone/ The Basic Things	1961	15.00
❑ 2115	Twist and Shout/Always Late (Why Lead Me On)	1961	25.00

TOPICS, THE (1) R&B group.

Number	Title (A Side/B Side)	Yr	NM
45s			
CARNIVAL			
❑ 520	She's So Fine/I Don't Have to Cry	1966	100.00
—Counterfeit identification: Run-out groove is extremely wide; sound quality is poor; "clown" logo is incomplete and blurry			
CASTLE			
❑ 1002	Women's Liberation/ I'll Understand	197?	30.00
CHADWICK			
❑ 102	Hey Girl (Where Are You Going)/ If Love Comes Knocking	1967	800.00
DREAM			
❑ 1	Have Your Fun/A Man Ain't Supposed to Cry	196?	4000.
—VG 2000; VG+ 3000			
HEAVY DUTY			
❑ 3	Try a Little Love/All Good Things Must End	1972	40.00
MERCURY			
❑ 73447	Booking Up Baby/Giving Up	1974	500.00

TOPICS, THE (2) Also see THE FOUR SEASONS.

Number	Title (A Side/B Side)	Yr	NM
45s			
PERRI			
❑ 1007	The Girl in My Dreams/ (B-side blank)	1961	150.00
—One-sided record			

TOPPERS, THE More than one group.

Number	Title (A Side/B Side)	Yr	NM
45s			
ABC-PARAMOUNT			
❑ 9667	George Washington/ Honey, Honey	1956	20.00
❑ 9699	God Bless Kids and Little Animals/Tornado	1956	20.00
❑ 9759	Three Roads/Lonely	1956	20.00
AVALON			
❑ 63707	I Love You, I Love You/ Bow-Legged Boy	1954	40.00
DECCA			
❑ 30209	The Purple Hills/ Stashu Pandowski	1957	15.00
❑ 30297	Pots and Pans/It Was Twice As Big As I Thought It Was	1957	15.00
JUBILEE			
❑ 5136	Let Me Bang Your Box/You're Laughing 'Cause I'm Crying	1954	150.00
STACY			
❑ 927	Tell Me Why/All Around	1962	12.00

TOPPS, THE

Number	Title (A Side/B Side)	Yr	NM
45s			
RED ROBIN			
❑ 126	What Do You Do (To Make Me Love You So)/Tippin'	1954	300.00
❑ 131	I've Got a Feeling/Won't You Come Home Baby	1954	300.00

TOPS, THE

Number	Title (A Side/B Side)	Yr	NM
45s			
SINGULAR			
❑ 712	An Innocent Kiss/Walkin' with My Baby	1957	120.00

TOPSIDERS, THE

Number	Title (A Side/B Side)	Yr	NM
45s			
JOSIE			
❑ 907	Heartbreak Hotel/Let the Good Times Roll	1963	12.00
Albums			
JOSIE			
❑ JOZ-4000 [M]	Rock Goes Folk	1963	25.00

TORNADOES, THE (1) British band.

Number	Title (A Side/B Side)	Yr	NM
45s			
DATE			
❑ 1519	Hey Baby!/Next Stop Kansas City	1966	12.00
LONDON			
❑ 9561	Telstar/Jungle Fever	1962	25.00
❑ 9579	Globetrottin'/Like Locomotion	1963	20.00
❑ 9581	Ridin' the Wind/The Breeze and I	1963	20.00
❑ 9599	Life on Venus (Telstar II)/Robot	1963	20.00
❑ 9614	Theme from "The Scales of Justice"/The Ice Cream Man	1963	20.00
❑ 11003	Telestar/Jungle Fever	1964	20.00
—Gold label "Demand Performance" with misspelled A-side			
TOWER			
❑ 152	Stompin' Through the Rye/ Early Bird	1965	15.00
❑ 171	Stingray/Aqua Marina	1965	15.00
Albums			
LONDON			
❑ LL 3279 [M]	Telstar	1963	200.00
❑ LL 3293 [M]	The Sounds of the Tornadoes	1963	200.00
—Basically the same album as above, but with a new cover, one different track and the song order shuffled.			

TORNADOES, THE (2) California surf band, also called "Hollywood Tornadoes."

Number	Title (A Side/B Side)	Yr	NM
45s			
AERTAUN			
❑ 100	Bustin' Surfboards/ Beyond the Surf	1962	40.00
❑ 101	The Gremmie (Part 1)/ The Gremmie (Part 2)	1963	25.00
—As "The Hollywood Tornadoes"			
❑ 102	Inebriated Surfer/Moon Dawg	1963	30.00
—As "The Hollywood Tornadoes"			
❑ 103	Phantom Surfer/ Shootin' Beavers	1963	30.00
❑ 103	Phantom Surfer/Lightnin'	1964	25.00
—B-side is same recording as "Shootin' Beavers" but retitled			
Albums			
JOSIE			
❑ J-4005 [M]	Bustin' Surfboards	1963	200.00
❑ JS-4005 [S]	Bustin' Surfboards	1963	300.00
SUNDAZED			
❑ LP-5024	Bustin' Surfboards	1996	10.00

TORNADOES, THE (3)

Number	Title (A Side/B Side)	Yr	NM
45s			
ABC-PARAMOUNT			
❑ 10174	Cora/Like a Frog	1960	20.00

TORNADOES, THE (4)

Number	Title (A Side/B Side)	Yr	NM
45s			
CUCA			
❑ 1092	Scalping Party/7-0-7	1962	40.00
❑ 1099	Loneliest Guy in the World/ It Always Makes Me Cry	1962	30.00
❑ 1104	Hey There/Standing Watch	1963	30.00

TORQUAYS, THE

Number	Title (A Side/B Side)	Yr	NM
45s			
AERTAUN			
❑ 1020	Turmoil/Crying in the Chapel	1964	30.00
COLPIX			
❑ 782	Image of a Girl/Stolen Moments	1965	20.00
GEE CEE			
❑ 8163	Escondido/Surfer's City	1963	50.00
GYPSY			
❑ 265	Busting Point/The Other Side	1965	50.00
ORIGINAL SOUND			
❑ 66	Harmonica Man/ Our Teenage Love	1967	20.00
PUNCH			
❑ 1007	Shake a Tail Feather/Temptation	196?	20.00
ROCK-IT			
❑ 1004	Image of a Girl/Stolen Moments	1965	30.00
❑ 1005	Hooked on Her/Harmonica Man	1965	30.00

TORQUES, THE

Number	Title (A Side/B Side)	Yr	NM
45s			
DIAL			
❑ 4060	Merry Maker/You Make Me Feel So Good	1967	20.00
LEMCO			
❑ 880	Tidal Wave/Harlem Nocturne	1965	30.00
❑ 890	Mercy Mercy/Bumpin'	1966	30.00
❑ 1001	Linden Walk/Deep Blue, At Dusk	196?	30.00
❑ 1007	I've Been Hurt/Bumpin'	1966	25.00
Albums			
LEMCO			
❑ 604	The Torques Live	1966	200.00
WIGGINS			
❑ 64010	Zoom!	1967	200.00

TORQUETTS, THE

Number	Title (A Side/B Side)	Yr	NM
45s			
SANTA CRUZ			
❑ 10002	Any More/(Who's Got The) Tortillas	196?	50.00
TORQUETT			
❑ 005/6	Feedback/Bacardi	196?	50.00
❑ 007/8	Side Swiped/Blue Corral	196?	25.00

TORRANCE, RICHARD

Number	Title (A Side/B Side)	Yr	NM
45s			
CAPITOL			
❑ 4417	Leave My Love Behind/ Rio De Janeiro Blue	1977	4.00
❑ 4554	Long Lonely Nights/I Can't Ask for Anymore Than You	1978	4.00
❑ 4644	Be Bop 'n Holla/ Let's Call It a Night	1978	4.00
SHELTER			
❑ 40374	Don't Let Me Down Again/Hard Heavy Road	1975	4.00
❑ 40419	Lady/Southern Belles	1975	4.00
Albums			
CAPITOL			
❑ SW-11610	Bareback	1977	10.00
❑ SW-11660	Anything's Possible	1978	10.00
❑ SW-11699	Double Take	1978	10.00
SHELTER			
❑ 2112	Eureka	1974	12.00
❑ 2134	Belle of the Ball	1975	10.00

TORRENCE, GEORGE

Number	Title (A Side/B Side)	Yr	NM
45s			
DUO DISC			
❑ 117	Together at Last/ Fine Foxy Frame	1965	20.00
EPIC			
❑ 5-9453	Such a Fool Was I/ Way Over Yonder	1961	20.00
KING			
❑ 5376	Go Away/So Good to Me	1960	20.00
SHOUT			
❑ 224	(Mama Come Quick and Bring Your) Licking Stick/ So Long Goodbye	1968	12.00

TORRENCE, JOHNNY

Number	Title (A Side/B Side)	Yr	NM
45s			
IMPERIAL			
❑ 5230	Sad Day/Bad Habit	1953	120.00
❑ 5897	Rat Race/Your Lover Man	1962	15.00
R&B			
❑ 1306	Rosalie/Living from Day to Day	1954	200.00
—With the Jewels			

TOTO

Number	Title (A Side/B Side)	Yr	NM
12-Inch Singles			
COLUMBIA			
❑ AS 637 [DJ]	Georgy Porgy (5:07) (3:48)	1979	30.00
❑ AS 904 [DJ]	Goodbye Elenore (same on both sides)	1981	20.00
❑ AS 1953 [DJ]	Stranger in Town (Edited Version) (Album Version)	1984	12.00
❑ AS 1995 [DJ]	Holyanna (Single Edited Version) (Album Version)	1985	12.00
❑ 43-11040	Georgy Porgy/Child's Anthem	1979	15.00
45s			
COLUMBIA			
❑ (no #)	Hold the Line/Takin' It Back	1978	15.00
—Picture disc in plastic sleeve; made for Licorice Pizza; price includes insert			
❑ 11-01056	It's the Last Night/Turn Back	1981	6.00
❑ 18-02811	Rosanna/It's a Feeling	1982	4.00
❑ 18-03143	Make Believe/We Made It	1982	4.00
❑ 18-03143 [PS]	Make Believe/We Made It	1982	5.00
❑ CNR-03267	Make Believe/(B-side blank)	1982	6.00
—One-sided budget release			
❑ 38-03335	Africa/Good for You	1982	4.00
❑ CNR-03399	Africa/(B-side blank)	1982	6.00
—One-sided budget release			
❑ 38-03597	I Won't Hold You Back/ Afraid of Love	1983	3.00

Except when noted otherwise, VG = 25% of NM, and VG+ = 50% of NM. (Example: VG = $2.00, VG+ = $4.00 and NM = $8.00.)

Number	Title (A Side/B Side)	Yr	NM
❑ 38-03597 [PS]	I Won't Hold You Back/Afraid of Love	1983	4.00
❑ 38-03981	Waiting for Your Love/Lovers in the Night	1983	3.00
❑ 38-04672	Stranger in Town/Change of Heart	1984	3.00
❑ 38-04672 [PS]	Stranger in Town/Change of Heart	1984	4.00
❑ 38-04752	Holyanna/Mr. Friendly	1985	3.00
❑ 38-04752 [PS]	Holyanna/Mr. Friendly	1985	4.00
❑ 38-04844	How Does It Feel/Mr. Friendly	1985	3.00
❑ 38-06280	I'll Be Over You/In a Word	1986	3.00
❑ 38-06280 [PS]	I'll Be Over You/In a Word	1986	3.00
❑ 38-06570	Without Your Love/Can't Stand It Any Longer	1987	3.00
❑ 38-06570 [PS]	Without Your Love/Can't Stand It Any Longer	1987	3.00
❑ 38-07030	Till the End/Don't Stop Me Now	1987	4.00
❑ 38-07030 [DJ]	Till the End (Edited Version)/(Long Version)	1987	5.00
❑ 38-07715	Pamela/The Seventh One	1988	3.00
❑ 38-07715 [PS]	Pamela/The Seventh One	1988	3.00
❑ 38-07945	Straight for the Heart/The Seventh One	1988	3.00
❑ 38-07945 [PS]	Straight for the Heart/The Seventh One	1988	3.00
❑ 38-08010	Anna/The Seventh One	1988	8.00

—Scarce as stock copy

Number	Title (A Side/B Side)	Yr	NM
❑ 38-08010 [DJ]	Anna (4:03)/(4:55)	1988	5.00
❑ 3-10830	Hold the Line/Takin' It Back	1978	5.00
❑ 3-10898	I'll Supply the Love/You Are the Flower	1979	5.00
❑ 3-10944	Georgy Porgy/Child's Anthem	1979	5.00
❑ 1-11173	99/Hydra	1980	4.00
❑ 1-11238	All Us Boys/Hydra	1980	5.00
❑ 11-11437	Goodbye Elenore/Turn Back	1981	6.00

POLYDOR

Number	Title (A Side/B Side)	Yr	NM
❑ 881628-7	Dune (Desert Theme)/Theme from Dune	1985	5.00

Albums

COLUMBIA

Number	Title	Yr	NM
❑ AS 577 [DJ]	Special Radio Interview	1979	20.00
❑ JC 35317	Toto	1978	10.00
❑ PC 35317	Toto	198?	8.00

—Budget-line reissue with new prefix

Number	Title	Yr	NM
❑ FC 36229	Hydra	1979	10.00
❑ PC 36229	Hydra	198?	8.00

—Budget-line reissue with new prefix

Number	Title	Yr	NM
❑ FC 36813	Turn Back	1981	10.00
❑ PC 36813	Turn Back	1984	8.00

—Budget-line reissue with new prefix

Number	Title	Yr	NM
❑ PD 36813 [PD]	Turn Back	1981	25.00

—Promo-only picture disc

Number	Title	Yr	NM
❑ FC 37728	Toto IV	1982	10.00
❑ 8C8 38685 [EP]	Africa/Rosanna	1983	20.00

—Africa-shaped picture disc; numbered like an LP although it has only these two songs on it and is (approximately) 7 inches

Number	Title	Yr	NM
❑ QC 38962	Isolation	1984	10.00
❑ 9C9 39911 [PD]	Isolation	1984	20.00
❑ FC 40273	Fahrenheit	1986	10.00
❑ FC 40873	The Seventh One	1988	10.00
❑ C 45369	Past to Present 1977-1990	1990	25.00

—Vinyl available only from Columbia House

Number	Title	Yr	NM
❑ HC 47728	Toto IV	198?	40.00

—Half-speed mastered edition

MOBILE FIDELITY

Number	Title	Yr	NM
❑ 1-250	Toto IV	1996	40.00

—Audiophile vinyl

TOUCH

Albums

GEAR FAB

Number	Title	Yr	NM
❑ GF 105 [(2)]	Street Suite	1999	25.00

—Reissue of rare album plus bonus tracks

MAINLINE

Number	Title	Yr	NM
❑ 2001	Street Suite	1969	2000.

—VG value 1000; VG+ value 1500

TOUCHSTONE

Albums

UNITED ARTISTS

Number	Title	Yr	NM
❑ UAS-5563	Tarot	1972	30.00

TOUSAN, AL

See ALLEN TOUSSAINT.

TOUSSAINT, ALLEN

45s

ALON

Number	Title (A Side/B Side)	Yr	NM
❑ 9021	Go Back Home/Poor Boy, Got to Move	1965	10.00

BELL

Number	Title (A Side/B Side)	Yr	NM
❑ 732	Get Out of My Life, Woman/Gotta Travel On	1968	8.00
❑ 748	Hans Christian Anderson/I've Got That Feeling Now	1968	8.00
❑ 782	Tequila/We the People	1969	8.00

RCA VICTOR

Number	Title (A Side/B Side)	Yr	NM
❑ 47-7192	Whirlaway/Happy Times	1958	25.00

—As "Al Tousan"

REPRISE

Number	Title (A Side/B Side)	Yr	NM
❑ 1109	Soul Sister/She Once Belonged to Me	1972	5.00
❑ 1132	Am I Expecting Too Much/Out of the City	1972	5.00
❑ 1334	Country John/When the Party's Over	1975	4.00

SCEPTER

Number	Title (A Side/B Side)	Yr	NM
❑ 12317	From a Whisper to a Scream/Secret Touch of Love	1971	6.00
❑ 12334	Working in a Coal Mine/What Is Success	1971	6.00

SEVILLE

Number	Title (A Side/B Side)	Yr	NM
❑ 103	Chico/Sweetie-Pie	1960	15.00

—All Seville releases as "Al Tousan"

Number	Title (A Side/B Side)	Yr	NM
❑ 110	Back Home in Indiana/Naomi	1960	15.00
❑ 113	A Blue Mood/Moo Moo	1961	15.00
❑ 124	Twenty Years Later/Real Churchy	1962	15.00

WARNER BROS.

Number	Title (A Side/B Side)	Yr	NM
❑ 8561	Night People/Optimism Blues	1978	4.00
❑ 8609	Happiness/Lover of Love	1978	4.00

Albums

RCA VICTOR

Number	Title	Yr	NM
❑ LPM-1767 [M]	The Wild Sounds of New Orleans	1958	300.00

—As "Al Tousan"

REPRISE

Number	Title	Yr	NM
❑ MS 2062	Life, Love and Faith	1972	25.00

SCEPTER

Number	Title	Yr	NM
❑ 24003	Toussaint	1971	25.00

WARNER BROS.

Number	Title	Yr	NM
❑ BSK 3142	Motion	1978	12.00

TOWER OF POWER

12-Inch Singles

COLUMBIA

Number	Title (A Side/B Side)	Yr	NM
❑ 10738	Lovin' You Is Gonna See Me Through/Yin-Yang Thang	1978	10.00

45s

COLUMBIA

Number	Title (A Side/B Side)	Yr	NM
❑ 10409	You Ought to Be Havin' Fun/While We Went to the Moon	1976	5.00
❑ 10461	Ain't Nothin' Stoppin' Us Now/Because I Think the World of You	1976	5.00
❑ 10718	Lovin' You Is Gonna See Me Through/I Am a Fool	1978	4.00
❑ 10780	Love Bug/We Came to Play	1978	4.00
❑ 11012	Rock Baby/Heaven Must Have Made You	1979	4.00
❑ 11157	In Due Time/And You Know It	1979	4.00

WARNER BROS.

Number	Title (A Side/B Side)	Yr	NM
❑ 7612	You're Still a Young Man/Skating on Thin Ice	1972	6.00
❑ 7635	Down to the Nightclub/What Happened to the World That Day	1972	6.00
❑ 7687	So Very Hard to Go/Clean Slate	1973	6.00
❑ 7733	This Time It's Real/Soul Vaccination	1973	6.00
❑ 7748	What is Hip?/Clever Girl	1973	6.00
❑ 7796	Time Will Tell/Oakland Stroke	1974	6.00
❑ 7828	Don't Change Horses (In the Middle of a Stream)/I Got the Chop	1974	6.00
❑ 8055	Only So Much Oil in the Ground/Give Me the Proof	1974	6.00
❑ 8083	Willing to Learn/Walkin' Up Hip Street	1975	5.00
❑ 8121	You're So Wonderful, So Marvelous/Stroke '75	1975	5.00
❑ 8151	Soul of a Child/Treat Me Like Your Man	1975	5.00

Albums

COLUMBIA

Number	Title	Yr	NM
❑ PC 34302	Ain't Nothin' Stoppin' Us Now	1976	10.00

—No bar code on cover

Number	Title	Yr	NM
❑ PC 34302	Ain't Nothin' Stoppin' Us Now	198?	8.00

—Budget-line reissue with bar code

Number	Title	Yr	NM
❑ PCQ 34302 [Q]	Ain't Nothin' Stoppin' Us Now	1976	15.00
❑ JC 34906	We Came to Play!	1978	10.00
❑ JC 35784	Back on the Streets	1979	10.00

DIRECT DISC

Number	Title	Yr	NM
❑ SD 16601	Back to Oakland	1980	25.00

—Audiophile vinyl

SAN FRANCISCO

Number	Title	Yr	NM
❑ SD 204	East Bay Grease	1971	50.00

SHEFFIELD LABS

Number	Title	Yr	NM
❑ 17	Direct	1982	25.00

—Direct-to-disc recording

WARNER BROS.

Number	Title	Yr	NM
❑ BS 2616	Bump City	1972	15.00

—Green "WB" label

Number	Title	Yr	NM
❑ BS 2681	Tower of Power	1973	12.00

—"Burbank" palm trees label

Number	Title	Yr	NM
❑ BS 2681	Tower of Power	1973	15.00

—Green "WB" label

Number	Title	Yr	NM
❑ BS 2681	Tower of Power	1979	8.00

—White or tan label

Number	Title	Yr	NM
❑ BS 2749	Back to Oakland	1974	15.00

—"Burbank" palm trees label

Number	Title	Yr	NM
❑ BS 2749	Back to Oakland	1979	8.00

—White or tan label

Number	Title	Yr	NM
❑ BS 2834	Urban Renewal	1975	15.00

—"Burbank" palm trees label

Number	Title	Yr	NM
❑ BS 2880	In the Slot	1975	15.00

—"Burbank" palm trees label

Number	Title	Yr	NM
❑ BS 2924	Live and In Living Color	1976	15.00

—"Burbank" palm trees label

Number	Title	Yr	NM
❑ BS 2924	Live and In Living Color	1979	8.00

—White or tan label

TOWNS, CHRIS, AND THE TOWNSMEN

45s

CEE TEE

Number	Title (A Side/B Side)	Yr	NM
❑ 1001	Va Va Voom/Funky Sunday	196?	25.00

COTILLION

Number	Title (A Side/B Side)	Yr	NM
❑ 44016	Soul of My Sister/Sop It Up	1968	20.00
❑ 44027	Stuff/Earthy	1969	15.00

PORT

Number	Title (A Side/B Side)	Yr	NM
❑ 3021	Turn to Me/You Don't Know What You're Getting (Till You've Got It)	196?	50.00

—As "Chris Towns Unit"

TOWNSEND, BOB

45s

MINARET

Number	Title (A Side/B Side)	Yr	NM
❑ 106	Christmas Message From Space/The Night Before New Year's	1962	10.00

TOWNSEND, HENRY

Albums

BLUESVILLE

Number	Title	Yr	NM
❑ BVLP-1041 [M]	Tired Bein' Mistreated	1962	120.00

—Blue label, silver print

Number	Title	Yr	NM
❑ BVLP-1041 [M]	Tired Bein' Mistreated	1964	30.00

—Blue label, trident logo at side

TOWNSEND, SHERRELL

45s

GONE

Number	Title (A Side/B Side)	Yr	NM
❑ 5135	He Thinks I Still Care/Glass of Tears	1962	20.00

LITTLE STAR

Number	Title (A Side/B Side)	Yr	NM
❑ 115	I Love You Alone/Summer Days Are Here	1962	40.00

LUTE

Number	Title (A Side/B Side)	Yr	NM
❑ 6015	I Love You Alone/Summer Days Are Here	1961	30.00

TOWNSHEND, PETE

Also see THE WHO.

12-Inch Singles

ATCO

Number	Title (A Side/B Side)	Yr	NM
❑ PR 804 [DJ]	Face the Face (long and short)/Hiding Out	1985	15.00
❑ PR 863 [DJ]	Secondhand Love (same on both sides)	1985	8.00
❑ PR 1009 [DJ]	Ask Yourself/Brooklyn Kids	1987	8.00
❑ 96833	Face the Face (6:08)/Won't Get Fooled Again (Live)	1985	7.00

45s

ATCO

Number	Title (A Side/B Side)	Yr	NM
❑ 7217	Let My Love Open the Door/And I Moved	1980	4.00
❑ 7312	A Little Is Enough/Cat's in a Cupboard	1980	4.00
❑ 7318	Rough Boys/Jools and Jim	1980	4.00
❑ 99499	Barefootin'/Behind Blue Eyes	1986	3.00
❑ 99499 [PS]	Barefootin'/Behind Blue Eyes	1986	4.00
❑ 99553	Secondhand Love/White City Fighting	1986	3.00
❑ 99577	Give Blood/Magic Bus	1986	3.00
❑ 99577 [PS]	Give Blood/Magic Bus	1986	4.00
❑ 99590	Face the Face/Hiding Out	1985	3.00
❑ 99590 [PS]	Face the Face/Hiding Out	1985	4.00
❑ 99884	Bargain/Dirty Water	1983	4.00
❑ 99884 [PS]	Bargain/Dirty Water	1983	4.00
❑ 99973	Slit Skirts/Uniforms	1982	4.00

T

Number	Title (A Side/B Side)	Yr	NM
❑ 99989	Face Dances Part Two/ Man Watching	1982	4.00
❑ 99989 [PS]	Face Dances Part Two/ Man Watching	1982	4.00

ATLANTIC

Number	Title (A Side/B Side)	Yr	NM
❑ 88875	A Friend Is a Friend/ Man Machines	1989	3.00
❑ 88875 [PS]	A Friend Is a Friend/ Man Machines	1989	4.00

Albums

ATCO

Number	Title (A Side/B Side)	Yr	NM
❑ SD 32-100	Empty Glass	1980	10.00
❑ SD 38-149	All the Best Cowboys Have Chinese Eyes	1982	10.00
❑ PR 940 [EP]	Deep End Sampler	1986	20.00

—Promo-only sampler from Deep End Live

Number	Title (A Side/B Side)	Yr	NM
❑ 90063 [(2)]	Scoop	1983	12.00
❑ 90473	White City — A Novel	1985	10.00
❑ 90539 [(2)]	Another Scoop	1987	12.00
❑ 90553	Pete Townshend's Deep End Live!	1986	10.00

ATLANTIC

Number	Title (A Side/B Side)	Yr	NM
❑ 81996	The Iron Man: The Musical by Pete Townshend	1989	10.00

—Also includes tracks by John Lee Hooker, Simon Townshend, Nina Simone, The Who

DECCA

Number	Title (A Side/B Side)	Yr	NM
❑ 79189	Who Came First	1972	20.00

—With poster (deduct 50% if missing). Evidently a near-simultaneous release with Track 79189

EEL PIE

Number	Title (A Side/B Side)	Yr	NM
❑ EPR-0007 [(2)]	Another Scoop	2002	40.00

—Classic Records edition on "Quiex SV" vinyl

Number	Title (A Side/B Side)	Yr	NM
❑ EPR-0013 [(3)]	Scoop 3	2001	50.00

—Classic Records edition on "Quiex SV" vinyl

MCA

Number	Title (A Side/B Side)	Yr	NM
❑ 2026	Who Came First	1973	12.00

—Reissue of 79189

TRACK

Number	Title (A Side/B Side)	Yr	NM
❑ PR-A-160 [DJ]	Pete Townshend Talks To and About Thunderclap Newman	1970	100.00

—One-sided promo-only interview record

Number	Title (A Side/B Side)	Yr	NM
❑ 79189	Who Came First	1972	20.00

—With poster (deduct 50% if missing)

TOWNSHEND, PETE, AND RONNIE LANE

Also see each artist's individual listings.

45s

MCA

Number	Title (A Side/B Side)	Yr	NM
❑ 40818	My Baby Gives It Away/ April Fool	1977	4.00
❑ 40878	Nowhere to Run/ Keep Me Turning	1978	4.00

Albums

ATCO

Number	Title (A Side/B Side)	Yr	NM
❑ 90097	Rough Mix	1983	8.00

—Reissue of MCA LP

MCA

Number	Title (A Side/B Side)	Yr	NM
❑ 2295	Rough Mix	1977	10.00

TOWNSMEN, THE

45s

CARDINAL

Number	Title (A Side/B Side)	Yr	NM
❑ 1022	Pretty Patricia/My Memories	195?	15.00

COLUMBIA

Number	Title (A Side/B Side)	Yr	NM
❑ 43207	Please Don't Say Goodbye/ Gotta Get Moving	1965	10.00

EVENT

Number	Title (A Side/B Side)	Yr	NM
❑ 503	(Gloria's Theme) From "Burrerfield 8"/ (B-side unknown)	196?	20.00

HERALD

Number	Title (A Side/B Side)	Yr	NM
❑ 585	Is It All Over/Just a Little Bit	1963	15.00

JOEY

Number	Title (A Side/B Side)	Yr	NM
❑ 6202	Moonlight Was Made for Lovers/ I'm in the Mood for Love	1963	25.00

PJ

Number	Title (A Side/B Side)	Yr	NM
❑ 1341	That's All I'll Ever Need/ I Can't Let Go	1963	200.00

VANITY

Number	Title (A Side/B Side)	Yr	NM
❑ 579/80	It's Time/Little Jeanie	1960	20.00

WARNER BROS.

Number	Title (A Side/B Side)	Yr	NM
❑ 5190	You're Having the Last Dance with Me/Gloria's Theme from "Butterfield-8"	1960	12.00

TOY DOLLS, THE

45s

ERA

Number	Title (A Side/B Side)	Yr	NM
❑ 3093	Little Tin Soldier/Fly Away	1962	15.00

TOYS, THE

45s

DYNO VOICE

Number	Title (A Side/B Side)	Yr	NM
❑ 209	A Lover's Concerto/This Night	1965	12.00
❑ 214	Attack/See How They Run	1965	10.00
❑ 218	My My Heart Be Cast Into Stone/On Backstreet	1966	10.00
❑ 219	Can't Get Enough of You Baby/ Silver Spoon	1966	10.00
❑ 222	Baby Toys/Happy Birthday Broken Heart	1966	10.00

DYNO VOX

Number	Title (A Side/B Side)	Yr	NM
❑ 209	A Lover's Concerto/This Night	1965	25.00

MUSICOR

Number	Title (A Side/B Side)	Yr	NM
❑ 1300	You Got It Baby/You've Got to Give Her Love	1968	8.00
❑ 1319	Sealed with a Kiss/I Got My Heart Set on You	1968	8.00

PHILIPS

Number	Title (A Side/B Side)	Yr	NM
❑ 40432	Ciao Baby/I Got Carried Away	1967	10.00
❑ 40456	My Love Sonata/I Close My Eyes	1967	10.00

Albums

DYNOVOICE

Number	Title (A Side/B Side)	Yr	NM
❑ 9002 [M]	The Toys Sing "A Lover's Concerto" and "Attack!"	1966	40.00
❑ S-9002 [P]	The Toys Sing "A Lover's Concerto" and "Attack!"	1966	50.00

TRACERS, THE

45s

SULLY

Number	Title (A Side/B Side)	Yr	NM
❑ 928	She Said Yeah/Watch Me	1966	50.00

—Originally released under the name "The Stones;" produced with both blue and white labels

TRACEY, WREG

45s

ANNA

Number	Title (A Side/B Side)	Yr	NM
❑ 1105	All I Want Is You/Take Me Back	1959	40.00
❑ 1126	All I Want for Christmas (Is Your Love)/Take Me Back	1960	40.00

TRACEY TWINS, THE

45s

EASTWEST

Number	Title (A Side/B Side)	Yr	NM
❑ 108	Heartbreak Hill/Don't Mean Maybe Baby	1958	20.00

EPIC

Number	Title (A Side/B Side)	Yr	NM
❑ 9230	Kissin' Diploma/Because We Are Young	1957	20.00

RESERVE

Number	Title (A Side/B Side)	Yr	NM
❑ 110	Tonight You Belong to Me/ (B-side unknown)	1956	25.00
❑ 114	Do You Ever Think of Me/ (B-side unknown)	195?	25.00

TRACY, BILL

45s

DEL-FI

Number	Title (A Side/B Side)	Yr	NM
❑ 4124	You're My Girl/Tops to Summer	1959	20.00
❑ 4132	I'm So Happy/January Love	1959	20.00

DOT

Number	Title (A Side/B Side)	Yr	NM
❑ 15797	One Chance/Hold Me, Thrill Me, Kiss Me	1958	60.00
❑ 15868	Flame Out/Disappointed	1958	40.00

RADIANT

Number	Title (A Side/B Side)	Yr	NM
❑ 1504	High School Hero/Lost Love	1961	15.00

RPM

Number	Title (A Side/B Side)	Yr	NM
❑ 489	Kiss at Daybreak/ No One But You	1957	40.00

TRADE WINDS, THE

45s

KAMA SUTRA

Number	Title (A Side/B Side)	Yr	NM
❑ 212	Mind Excursion/Little Susan's Dreamin'	1966	12.00
❑ 218	I Believe in Her/Catch Me in the Meadow	1966	12.00
❑ 234	Mind Excursion/Only When I'm Dreamin'	1967	12.00

RED BIRD

Number	Title (A Side/B Side)	Yr	NM
❑ 10-020	New York's a Lonely Town/ Club Seventeen	1965	20.00
❑ 10-028	Girl from Greenwich Village/ There's a Rock and Roll Show in Town	1965	20.00
❑ 10-033	Summertime Girl/ The Party Starts at Nine	1965	40.00

Albums

KAMA SUTRA

Number	Title (A Side/B Side)	Yr	NM
❑ KLP-8057 [M]	Excursions	1967	25.00
❑ KLPS-8057 [S]	Excursions	1967	30.00

TRADER HORNE

Albums

JANUS

Number	Title (A Side/B Side)	Yr	NM
❑ JLS-3012	Morning Way	1970	55.00

TRADEWINDS, THE

45s

DAWN CORY

Number	Title (A Side/B Side)	Yr	NM
❑ 1005	Surfin' Thunder/Gotcha	196?	80.00

RCA VICTOR

Number	Title (A Side/B Side)	Yr	NM
❑ 47-7511	Toni/Twins	1959	20.00
❑ 47-7553	Furry Murray/Crossroads	1959	20.00

TRADITIONS, THE

45s

ABET

Number	Title (A Side/B Side)	Yr	NM
❑ 9435	Ruby Tuesday/Twinkle Little Star	1969	200.00

ARTCO

Number	Title (A Side/B Side)	Yr	NM
❑ 45-102	On Fire/My Heart	1966	2000.

BAR CLAY

Number	Title (A Side/B Side)	Yr	NM
❑ 19671	Oh My Love/Girls	1967	60.00
❑ 19678	My Life with You/ Something Gone Wrong	1967	70.00

TRAFFIC

Also see JIM CAPALDI; DAVE MASON; STEVE WINWOOD.

45s

ASYLUM

Number	Title (A Side/B Side)	Yr	NM
❑ 45207	Walking in the Wind/ (Instrumental)	1974	5.00

ISLAND

Number	Title (A Side/B Side)	Yr	NM
❑ 1201	Rock and Roll Stew (Part 1)/ Rock and Roll Stew (Part 2)	1972	5.00

UNITED ARTISTS

Number	Title (A Side/B Side)	Yr	NM
❑ 0129	Paper Sun/Empty Pages	1973	4.00

—"Silver Spotlight Series" reissue

Number	Title (A Side/B Side)	Yr	NM
❑ 1694	Feelin' Alright?/You Can All Join In	197?	5.00

—"Silver Spotlight Series" reissue

Number	Title (A Side/B Side)	Yr	NM
❑ 50195	Paper Sun/Giving to You	1967	10.00
❑ 50218	Hole in My Shoe/Smiling Phases	1967	10.00
❑ 50232	Here We Go 'Round the Mulberry Bush/Coloured Rain	1967	10.00
❑ 50261	Heaven Is In Your Mind/No Face, No Name and No Number	1968	8.00
❑ 50460	Feelin' Alright?/Withering Tree	1968	8.00
❑ 50500	Medicated Goo/Pearly Queen	1969	6.00
❑ 50692	Empty Pages/ Stranger to Himself	1970	6.00
❑ 50841	Gimme Some Lovin' (Part 1)/ Gimme Some Lovin' (Part 2)	1971	6.00

—By "Traffic, Etc."

Number	Title (A Side/B Side)	Yr	NM
❑ 50883	Glad (Part 1)/Glad (Part 2)	1972	6.00

VIRGIN

Number	Title (A Side/B Side)	Yr	NM
❑ S7-17971	Here Comes a Man (Rock Mix)/ Glad (Live)	1994	4.00
❑ S7-18134	Some Kinda Woman/Forty Thousand Headmen (Live)	1994	4.00

Albums

ASYLUM

Number	Title (A Side/B Side)	Yr	NM
❑ 7E-1020	When the Eagle Flies	1974	12.00

ISLAND

Number	Title (A Side/B Side)	Yr	NM
❑ ILSD 2 [(2)]	Traffic — On the Road	197?	15.00

—Reissue

Number	Title (A Side/B Side)	Yr	NM
❑ ILPS 9180	The Low Spark of High Heeled Boys	197?	12.00

—Reissue

Number	Title (A Side/B Side)	Yr	NM
❑ ILPS 9224	Shoot Out at the Fantasy Factory	197?	12.00

—Reissue

Number	Title (A Side/B Side)	Yr	NM
❑ SW-9306	The Low Spark of High Heeled Boys	1971	15.00
❑ SW-9323	Shoot Out at the Fantasy Factory	1973	15.00
❑ SMAS-9336 [(2)]	Traffic — On the Road	1973	20.00
❑ 90026	The Low Spark of High Heeled Boys	1983	8.00

—Reissue

Number	Title (A Side/B Side)	Yr	NM
❑ 90027	Shoot Out at the Fantasy Factory	1983	8.00

—Reissue

Number	Title (A Side/B Side)	Yr	NM
❑ 90028 [(2)]	Traffic — On the Road	1983	12.00

—Reissue

Number	Title (A Side/B Side)	Yr	NM
❑ 90058	John Barleycorn Must Die	1983	8.00

—Reissue

Number	Title (A Side/B Side)	Yr	NM
❑ 90059	Traffic	1983	8.00

—Reissue

Number	Title (A Side/B Side)	Yr	NM
❑ 90060	Mr. Fantasy	1983	8.00
—Reissue			
❑ 8427791	The Low Spark of High Heeled Boys	2008	20.00
❑ 8427801	John Barleycorn Must Die	2008	20.00
MOBILE FIDELITY			
❑ 1-209	The Low Spark of High Heeled Boys	1994	50.00
—Audiophile vinyl			
UNITED ARTISTS			
❑ UA-LA421-G	Heavy Traffic	1975	15.00
❑ UA-LA526-G	More Heavy Traffic	1975	15.00
❑ UAL-3651 [M]	Heaven Is In Your Mind	1967	60.00
❑ UAS-5500	Best of Traffic	1969	20.00
—Originals have pink and orange labels			
❑ UAS-5504	John Barleycorn Must Die	1970	20.00
—Originals have black and orange labels			
❑ UAS-5550	Welcome to the Canteen	1971	15.00
❑ UAS-6651 [S]	Heaven Is In Your Mind	1967	50.00
❑ UAS-6651 [S]	Mr. Fantasy	1968	25.00
—Retitled version of "Heaven Is In Your Mind" with green strip across top of back with song titles			
❑ UAS-6651 [S]	Mr. Fantasy	1968	35.00
—Retitled version of "Heaven Is In Your Mind" with old title still on back cover			
❑ UAS-6676	Traffic	1968	20.00
—Originals have purple and orange labels			
❑ UAS-6702	Last Exit	1969	20.00
—Originals have purple and orange labels			
❑ ST-92018	Last Exit	1969	30.00
—Capitol Record Club edition; label is the old-style black with circles at the top!			

TRAILER, REX, AND THE PLAYBOYS

Albums

Number	Title (A Side/B Side)	Yr	NM
CROWN			
❑ CLP-5158 [M]	Country & Western	1958	25.00

TRAITS, THE Also see ROY HEAD.

45s

Number	Title (A Side/B Side)	Yr	NM
ASCOT			
❑ 2108	Linda Lou/Little Mama	1962	30.00
PACEMAKER			
❑ 254	Too Good to Be True/ Gotta Keep Cool	1967	20.00
RENNER			
❑ 221	Linda Lou/Little Mama	1962	40.00
❑ 229	Got My Mojo Working/Woe Woe	1962	25.00
—Black vinyl			
❑ 229 [DJ]	Got My Mojo Working/Woe Woe	1962	40.00
—Promo only on colored vinyl			
SCEPTER			
❑ 12169	Harlem Shuffle/Strange Lips Start Old Memories	1966	8.00
❑ 12169	Harlem Shuffle/Somewhere	1966	10.00
TNT			
❑ 164	One More Time/Don't Be Blue	1959	20.00
—Later reissued on TNT 194 credited to "Roy Head"			
❑ 175	Live It Up/Yes I Do	1960	20.00
❑ 177	My Baby's Fine/Here I Am in Love Again	1960	20.00
❑ 181	Summer Time Love/ Your Turn to Cry	1960	20.00
❑ 185	Night Time Blues/Walking All Day	1961	20.00
UNIVERSAL			
❑ 30494	Harlem Shuffle/Somewhere	1966	30.00

TRAMLINE

Albums

Number	Title (A Side/B Side)	Yr	NM
A&M			
❑ SP-4208	Somewhere Down the Line	1969	20.00

TRAMMPS, THE Also see THE VOLCANOS.

12-Inch Singles

Number	Title (A Side/B Side)	Yr	NM
ATLANTIC			
❑ PR 102 [DJ]	The Night the Lights Went Out (same on both sides)	1977	12.00
❑ PR 139 [DJ]	Soul Bones/Love Magnet	1978	12.00
❑ PR 170 [DJ]	Teaser/Life Insurance Policy	1979	12.00
❑ DSKO 173	The Night the Lights Went Out (7:06)/Hooked for Life (4:40)	1977	15.00
❑ PR 224 [DJ]	Hard Rock and Disco (same on both sides)	1980	12.00
❑ PR 251 [DJ]	Looking for You/Mellow Out	1980	12.00
VENTURE			
❑ 5024	Up on the Hill (Mt. U)	1983	7.00

45s

Number	Title (A Side/B Side)	Yr	NM
ATLANTIC			
❑ 3286	Hooked for Life/I'm Alright	1975	5.00
❑ 3306	That's Where the Happy People Go (Short)/That's Where the Happy People Go (Long)	1975	5.00

Traffic, *The Low Spark of High Heeled Boys*, Island SW-9306, 1971, **$15.**

Number	Title (A Side/B Side)	Yr	NM
❑ 3345	Soul Searchin' Time/ Love Is a Funky Thing	1976	5.00
❑ 3365	Ninety-Nine and a Half (Won't Do)/Can We Come Together	1976	5.00
❑ 3389	Disco Inferno/You Touch My Hot Line	1977	6.00
❑ 3389	Disco Inferno/That's Where the Happy People Go	1978	5.00
—Reissue in conjunction with the success of "Saturday Night Fever"			
❑ 3389 [PS]	Disco Inferno/You Touch My Hot Line	1977	8.00
❑ 3403	I Feel Like I've Been Livin' (On the Dark Side of the Moon)/Don't Burn Bridges	1977	5.00
❑ 3442	The Night the Lights Went Out/ I'm So Glad You Came Along	1977	5.00
❑ 3460	Seasons for Girls/ Body Contact Contract	1978	5.00
❑ 3460	Seasons for Girls/ Love Ain't Been Easy	1978	5.00
❑ 3537	Soul Bones/Love Magnet	1978	5.00
❑ 3573	More Good Times to Remember/Teaser	1979	5.00
❑ 3654	Dance Contest/ Hard Rock and Disco	1980	4.00
❑ 3669	Music Freek/V.I.P.	1980	4.00
❑ 3777	Mellow Out/Looking for You	1980	4.00
❑ 3797	I Don't Want to Ever Lose Your Love/Breathtaking View	1981	4.00
BUDDAH			
❑ 306	Zing Went the Strings of My Heart/Penguin at the Big Apple	1972	6.00
—As "Trammps"			
❑ 306	Zing Went the Strings of My Heart/Penguin at the Big Apple	1972	10.00
—As "Tramps"			
❑ 321	Sixty Minute Man/Scrub Board	1972	6.00
❑ 339	Rubber Band/Pray All You Sinners	1973	6.00
❑ 507	Hold Back the Night/Tom's Song	1975	5.00
GOLDEN FLEECE			
❑ 3251	Love Epidemic/I Know That Feeling	1973	6.00
❑ 3253	Where Do We Go from Here/ Shout	1974	6.00
❑ 3255	Trusting Heart/Down These Dark Streets	1974	6.00

Albums

Number	Title (A Side/B Side)	Yr	NM
ATLANTIC			
❑ SD 18172	Where the Happy People Go	1976	10.00
❑ SD 18211	Disco Inferno	1977	10.00
❑ SD 19148	The Trammps III	1977	10.00
❑ SD 19194	The Best of the Trammps	1978	10.00
❑ SD 19210	The Whole World's Dancing	1979	10.00
❑ SD 19267	Mixin' It Up	1980	10.00
❑ SD 19290	Slipping Out	1981	10.00
BUDDAH			
❑ BDS-5641	The Legendary Zing Album Featuring the Fabulous Trammps	1975	12.00
GOLDEN FLEECE			
❑ KZ 33163	Trammps	1975	10.00
PHILADELPHIA INT'L.			
❑ PZ 33163	Disco Champs	1977	8.00
—Reissue of Golden Fleece LP			

TRANQUILS, THE

45s

Number	Title (A Side/B Side)	Yr	NM
HAMILTON			
❑ 50005	You're Such a Much/One Billion, Seven Million and Thirty-Three	1959	30.00

TRANSIENTS, THE

Albums

Number	Title (A Side/B Side)	Yr	NM
HORIZON			
❑ WP-1633 [M]	The Funky 12 String Guitar	1963	20.00
❑ WPS-1633 [S]	The Funky 12 String Guitar	1963	25.00

TRAPEZE

Includes future JUDAS PRIEST drummer Dave Holland plus multi-band bassist/vocalist GLENN HUGHES.

45s

Number	Title (A Side/B Side)	Yr	NM
THRESHOLD			
❑ 67001	Send Me No More Letters/Another Day	1970	8.00
❑ 67005 [DJ]	Black Cloud (mono/stereo)	1971	10.00
❑ 67011	Coast to Coast/Your Love Is Alright	1972	8.00

Albums

Number	Title (A Side/B Side)	Yr	NM
PAID			
❑ 2003	Hold On	1981	10.00
THRESHOLD			
❑ THS 2	Trapeze	1970	40.00
❑ THS 4	Medusa	1971	80.00
❑ THS 8	You Are the Music, We're Just the Band	1972	40.00
❑ THS 11	The Final Swing	1974	40.00
WARNER BROS.			
❑ BS 2828	Hot Wire	1974	12.00
❑ BS 2887	Trapeze	1975	12.00

TRAPP, SANDY

45s

Number	Title (A Side/B Side)	Yr	NM
PARKWAY			
❑ 840	Love Sickness/I Don't Know	1962	10.00

TRASH

45s

Number	Title (A Side/B Side)	Yr	NM
APPLE			
❑ 1804	Road to Nowhere/Illusions	1969	50.00
—Without star on A-side label			
❑ 1804	Road to Nowhere/Illusions	1969	100.00
—With star on A-side label			
❑ 1811	Golden Slumbers-Carry That Weight/Trash Can	1969	15.00
—A-side listed as "Golden Slumbers/Carry That Weight"			
❑ 1811	Golden Slumbers-Carry That Weight/Trash Can	1969	20.00
—A-side listed as "Golden Slumbers and Carry That Weight"			
❑ 1811	Golden Slumbers-Carry That Weight/Trash Can	1969	20.00
—A-side listed as "Golden Slumbers Carry That Weight"			
❑ PRO-4671/2	Road to Nowhere (Edit)/Road to Nowhere	1969	80.00

TRASHMEN, THE

45s

Number	Title (A Side/B Side)	Yr	NM
ARGO			
❑ 5516	Bird '65/Ubangi Stomp	1965	50.00
BEAR			
❑ 1966	Keep Your Hands Off My Baby/Lost Angel	1965	20.00
ERA BACK TO BACK HITS			
❑ 016	Liar, Liar/Surfin' Bird	197?	5.00
—B-side by the Castaways			
ERIC			
❑ 247	Surfin' Bird/Liar, Liar	197?	5.00
—B-side by the Castaways; reissue			
GARRETT			
❑ 4002	Surfin' Bird/King of the Surf	1963	30.00
❑ 4003	Bird Dance Beat/A-Bone	1964	20.00
❑ 4005	Bad News/On the Move	1964	20.00
❑ 4010	Peppermint Man/New Generation	1964	20.00
❑ 4012	Whoa Dad/Walkin' My Baby	1964	20.00
❑ 4012 [PS]	Whoa Dad/Walkin' My Baby	1964	250.00
❑ 4013	Dancing with Santa/Real Live Doll	1964	25.00
❑ 4013 [PS]	Dancing with Santa/Real Live Doll	1964	250.00
GET HIP			
❑ 2	Well All Right/That's What They Say	1994	4.00
LANA			
❑ 136	Surfin' Bird/King of the Surf	196?	10.00
—Oldies reissue			
METROBEAT			
❑ 7927	Green, Green Backs of Home/Address Enclosed	1968	15.00
OLDIES 45			
❑ 301	Surfin' Bird/King of the Surf	1965	12.00
—Early reissue			
SOMA			
❑ 1469	Surfin' Bird/Liar, Liar	1966	12.00
—B-side by the Castaways			
SUNDAZED			
❑ 102	Henrietta/Rumble	1995	2.00
❑ 102 [PS]	Henrietta/Rumble	1995	2.00
❑ 103	Lucille/Green Onions	1995	2.00
❑ 103 [PS]	Lucille/Green Onions	1995	2.00
❑ 104	Roll Over Beethoven/Betty Jean	1995	2.00
❑ 104 [PS]	Roll Over Beethoven/Betty Jean	1995	2.00
❑ 112	Dancing with Santa/Real Live Doll	1996	2.00
—Red vinyl			
❑ 112 [PS]	Dancing with Santa/Real Live Doll	1996	2.00
TERRIFIC			
❑ 5003	Surfin' Bird/Bird Dance Beat	196?	10.00
—Early reissue			
TRIBE			
❑ 8315	Hanging On Me/Some Lies	1966	40.00

Albums

Number	Title (A Side/B Side)	Yr	NM
BEAT ROCKET			
❑ BR 107	Surfin' Bird	1999	12.00
—Reissue on 180-gram vinyl			
GARRETT			
❑ GA-200 [M]	Surfin' Bird	1964	220.00
❑ GAS-200 [R]	Surfin' Bird	1964	350.00
SUNDAZED			
❑ LP 5002	Live Bird '65-'67	1991	10.00
❑ LP 5003	Great Lost Album	1991	10.00

TRAVELERS, THE

Probably more than one group.

45s

Number	Title (A Side/B Side)	Yr	NM
ABC-PARAMOUNT			
❑ 10119	June, July, August and September/What a Weekend	1960	20.00
ANDEX			
❑ 2011	I'll Be Home for Christmas/Katie the Kangaroo	1958	30.00
❑ 4033	I Go for You/I'll Always Be in Love with You	1959	30.00
❑ 34006	Why/Teenage Machine Age	1957	30.00
❑ 34012	He's Got the Whole World in His Hands/Green Town Girl	1957	30.00
DECCA			
❑ 31215	Ivy on the Old School Wall/Cadwallader 0002	1961	40.00
❑ 31282	White Rose/Oh My Love (Love Me)	1961	40.00
DON RAY			
❑ 5965	Traveler/Seven Minutes Till Four	1963	50.00
MAGIC LAMP			
❑ 516	Big House/Goin' Home	1964	12.00
VAULT			
❑ 911	Spanish Moon/She's Got the Blues	1964	15.00
YELLOW SAND			
❑ 2	Windy and Warm/Last Date	1963	50.00
❑ 451	Groovy/(B-side unknown)	1965	30.00
❑ 452	Malibu Sunset/Hang On	1965	30.00

TRAVELING SALESMEN

45s

Number	Title (A Side/B Side)	Yr	NM
RCA VICTOR			
❑ 47-9167	I'm Alive/Days of My Years	1967	20.00

TRAVELING WILBURYS

45s

Number	Title (A Side/B Side)	Yr	NM
WARNER BROS.			
❑ 19443	Wilbury Twist/New Blue Moon	1991	10.00
—Issued only in Europe			
❑ 19443 [PS]	Wilbury Twist/New Blue Moon	1991	10.00
❑ 19523	She's My Baby/New Blue Moon	1990	10.00
—"Wilbury" logo on label; issued only in Europe			
❑ 19523 [PS]	She's My Baby/New Blue Moon	1990	10.00
❑ 19773	Nobody's Child/Lumiere	1990	10.00
—B-side by Dave Stewart and the Spiritual Cowboys; "Wilbury" logo on label; issued only in Europe			
❑ 19773 [PS]	Nobody's Child/Lumiere	1989	10.00
WILBURY			
❑ 21867	Handle with Care/End of the Line	1990	15.00
—"Back to Back Hits" series			
❑ 27637	End of the Line/Congratulations	1989	15.00
❑ 27637 [DJ]	End of the Line (same on both sides)	1989	20.00
❑ 27637 [DJ]	End of the Line (same on both sides)	1989	20.00
❑ 27637 [PS]	End of the Line/Congratulations	1989	20.00
❑ 27732	Handle with Care/Margarita	1988	8.00
❑ 27732 [DJ]	Handle with Care (same on both sides)	1988	15.00
❑ 27732 [DJ]	Handle with Care (same on both sides)	1988	15.00
❑ 27732 [PS]	Handle with Care/Margarita	1988	8.00

Albums

Number	Title (A Side/B Side)	Yr	NM
WILBURY			
❑ 25796	Traveling Wilburys (Vol. One)	1988	20.00
❑ 26324	Traveling Wilburys, Vol. 3	1990	20.00

TRAVELLERS, THE

45s

Number	Title (A Side/B Side)	Yr	NM
GASS			
❑ 1000	Tie Me Surfer Board Down, Sport/In the Pines	1963	40.00

TRAVERS, MARY

Also see PETER, PAUL AND MARY.

45s

Number	Title (A Side/B Side)	Yr	NM
CHRYSALIS			
❑ 2202	The Air That I Breathe/You Turn Me Around	1977	5.00
❑ 2367	Freedom/(B-side unknown)	1979	4.00
WARNER BROS.			
❑ 7481	Follow Me/I Guess He'd Rather Be in Colorado	1971	5.00
❑ 7517	The Song Is Love/Ericka with the Windy Yellow Hair	1971	5.00
❑ 7588	Morning Glory/That's Enough for Me	1972	5.00
❑ 7675	Too Many Mondays/That Year There Was No Winter	1972	5.00
❑ 7731	Five Hundred Miles/Oh, What a Feeling	1973	5.00
❑ 7790	Circles/I'll Have to Say I Love You in a Song	1974	5.00

Albums

Number	Title (A Side/B Side)	Yr	NM
CHRYSALIS			
❑ CHR 1168	It's In Everyone of Us	1978	10.00
WARNER BROS.			
❑ WS 1907	Mary	1971	12.00
—Green "WB" label			
❑ BS 2609	Morning Glory	1972	12.00
—Green "WB" label			
❑ BS 2677	All My Choices	1973	12.00
—Green "WB" label			
❑ BS 2795	Circles	1974	12.00
—"Burbank" palm-trees label			

TRAVIS AND BOB

45s

Number	Title (A Side/B Side)	Yr	NM
BIG TOP			
❑ 3054	Pocahontas/Day Dreams	1960	15.00
MERCURY			
❑ 71797	Give Your Love to Me/Stay Close to Me	1961	15.00
❑ 71866	The Spider and the Fly/What a Change	1961	15.00
SANDY			
❑ 1017	Tell Him No/We're Too Young	1959	20.00
—With Dot Records distribution mentioned on label			
❑ 1017	Tell Him No/We're Too Young	1959	25.00
—With no mention of Dot Records on label			
❑ 1019	Teenage Vision/Little Bitty Johnny	1959	20.00
❑ 1024	Lover's Rendezvous/Oh Yeah	1959	20.00
❑ 1029	That's How Long/Wake Up and Cry	1960	20.00

TRAYNOR, JAY

Also see JAY AND THE AMERICANS.

45s

Number	Title (A Side/B Side)	Yr	NM
ABC			
❑ 10809	Come On/The Merry-Go-Round Is Slowing You Down	1966	15.00
❑ 10845	Up and Over/Don't Let the End Begin	1966	30.00
CORAL			
❑ 62396	How Sweet It Is/I Rise, I Fall	1964	12.00
—As "JAY, formerly of Jay & the Americans"			
❑ 62420	I've Known You All My Life/Little Sister	1964	12.00

TREADWELL, IRENE

45s

Number	Title (A Side/B Side)	Yr	NM
JAY DEE			
❑ 782	Church Bells Are Ringing on Christmas Morning/Dear Santa Bring Back My Daddy to Me	1953	20.00

TREASURERS, THE

45s

Number	Title (A Side/B Side)	Yr	NM
CROWN			
❑ 005	Story of Love/I Walk with An Angel	1961	300.00

TREASURES, THE

45s

Number	Title (A Side/B Side)	Yr	NM
SHIRLEY			
❑ 500	Hold Me Tight/Pete Meets Vinnie	1964	30.00

Except when noted otherwise, VG = 25% of NM, and VG+ = 50% of NM. (Example: VG = \$2.00, VG+ = \$4.00 and NM = \$8.00.)

Number	Title (A Side/B Side)	Yr	NM
VALOR			
❑ (# unknown)	Minor Chaos/Valley of the Broken Hearts	1964	100.00
—Sources differ as to what the number of this record is, and we've never seen a copy, so we haven't listed one.			
❑ (# unknown)	Minor Chaos/Valley of the Broken Hearts	1964	200.00
—Green vinyl			
❑ (# unknown)	Minor Chaos/Valley of the Broken Hearts	1964	400.00
—Marbled vinyl			

TREBELAIRES, THE

Number	Title (A Side/B Side)	Yr	NM
45s			
NESTOR			
❑ 16	There Goes That Train/I Gotta	1954	100.00

TREBLE CHORDS, THE

Number	Title (A Side/B Side)	Yr	NM
45s			
DECCA			
❑ 31015	Teresa/My Little Girl	1959	100.00

TREE

Number	Title (A Side/B Side)	Yr	NM
Albums			
GOAT FARM			
❑ 580	Tree	1970	70.00

TREE SWINGERS, THE

Number	Title (A Side/B Side)	Yr	NM
45s			
BIG TOP			
❑ 3058	Only Forever/Kissin' and Cookin'	1960	15.00
GUYDEN			
❑ 2036	Kookie Little Paradise/Teaching the Natives to Sing	1960	15.00

TREMAINES, THE

Number	Title (A Side/B Side)	Yr	NM
45s			
CASH			
❑ 100/1	Jingle, Jingle/Moon Shining Bright	1958	400.00
KANE			
❑ 008	Heavenly/Wonderful, Marvelous	1959	50.00
OLD TOWN			
❑ 1051	Jingle, Jingle/Moon Shining Bright	1958	50.00
V-TONE			
❑ 507	Heavenly/Wonderful, Marvelous	1959	25.00
VAL			
❑ 100/1	Jingle, Jingle/Moon Shining Bright	1958	250.00

TREMELOES, THE Also see BRIAN POOLE AND THE TREMELOES.

Number	Title (A Side/B Side)	Yr	NM
45s			
DJM			
❑ 1008	Hard Woman/My Friend Delaney	1976	5.00
❑ 1016	September, November, December/(B-side unknown)	1976	5.00
EPIC			
❑ 10075	Good Day Sunshine/What a State I'm In	1966	12.00
❑ 10139	Here Comes My Baby/Gentlemen of Pleasure	1967	10.00
❑ 10184	Silence Is Golden/Let Your Hair Hang Down	1967	10.00
❑ 10184 [PS]	Silence Is Golden/Let Your Hair Hang Down	1967	15.00
❑ 10233	Even the Bad Times Are Good/Jenny's All Right	1967	8.00
❑ 10233 [PS]	Even the Bad Times Are Good/Jenny's All Right	1967	15.00
❑ 10293	Suddenly You Love Me/Suddenly Winter	1968	8.00
❑ 10328	Girl from Nowhere/Helule, Helule	1968	8.00
❑ 10376	My Little Lady/All the World to Me	1968	8.00
❑ 10437	I Shall Be Released/I Miss My Baby	1969	8.00
❑ 10467	Up, Down, All Around/Hello World	1969	8.00
❑ 10548	(Call Me) Number One/Instant Whip	1969	8.00
❑ 10621	Breakheart Motel/By the Way	1970	10.00
❑ 10682	Me and My Life/Try Me	1970	8.00
❑ 10807	My Woman/Hello Buddy	1971	6.00
❑ 10996	Yodelay/Blue Suede Tie	1973	6.00
7-Inch Extended Plays			
EPIC			
❑ 5-26388	Peggy Sue/The Lion Sleeps Tonight/Willy and the Hand Jive//Everyday/Rag Doll/Ain't Nothing But a House Party	1968	15.00
—Jukebox issue; small hole, plays at 33 1/3 rpm			
❑ 5-26388 [PS]	World Explosion	1968	15.00

The Tremeloes, *Suddenly You Love Me*, Epic LN 24363, 1968, mono, **$30.**

Number	Title (A Side/B Side)	Yr	NM
Albums			
DJM			
❑ 2	Shiner	1974	12.00
EPIC			
❑ LN 24310 [M]	Here Comes My Baby	1967	30.00
❑ LN 24326 [M]	Even the Bad Times Are Good	1967	25.00
❑ LN 24363 [M]	Suddenly You Love Me	1968	30.00
❑ LN 24388 [M]	World Explosion '58/'68	1968	60.00
—White label promo only			
❑ BN 26310 [R]	Here Comes My Baby	1967	20.00
❑ BN 26326 [P]	Even the Bad Times Are Good	1967	30.00
❑ BN 26363 [R]	Suddenly You Love Me	1968	20.00
❑ BN 26388 [S]	World Explosion '58/'68	1968	30.00

TREMELOES, THE/THE HOLLIES

Number	Title (A Side/B Side)	Yr	NM
45s			
EPIC			
❑ 10184/0 [DJ]	Silence Is Golden/Carrie-Anne	1967	100.00
—Promo only on red vinyl			
❑ 10184/0 [PS]	Silence Is Golden/Carrie-Anne	1967	300.00
—"There's Room for Two at the Top!" across top of sleeve; has photos of both bands; all the print is in red			

TREMELOS, THE

Number	Title (A Side/B Side)	Yr	NM
45s			
ROCKLAND			
❑ 102	Jaguar/Fly	196?	50.00

TREMONTS, THE

Number	Title (A Side/B Side)	Yr	NM
45s			
BRUNSWICK			
❑ 55217	Believe My Heart/Legend of Love	1961	30.00
PAT RICCIO			
❑ 101	Believe My Heart/Legend of Love	1961	100.00

TREN-DELLS, THE

Number	Title (A Side/B Side)	Yr	NM
45s			
CAPITOL			
❑ 4852	Nite Owl/Hully Gully Jones	1962	12.00
JAM			
❑ 101	Nite Owl/Hully Gully Jones	1962	25.00
❑ 111	Hey Da-Da Dow/Tough Little Buggy	1962	25.00
SOUND STAGE 7			
❑ 2508	Mr. Doughnut Man/Ain't That Funny	1963	12.00
TILT			
❑ 779	I'm So Young/Don't You Hear Me Calling Baby	1961	30.00
—As "The Trend-Els"			
❑ 788	Moments Like This/I Miss You So	1962	30.00

TREN-TEENS, THE

Number	Title (A Side/B Side)	Yr	NM
45s			
CARNIVAL			
❑ 501	My Baby's Gone/Your Yah Yah Is Gone	1964	100.00

TRENDS, THE (1)

Number	Title (A Side/B Side)	Yr	NM
45s			
ABC			
❑ 10817	A Night for Love/Gonna Have to Show You	1966	25.00
❑ 10881	No One There/That's How I Like It	1966	25.00
❑ 10944	Check My Tears/Don't Drop Out of School	1967	20.00
❑ 10993	Thanks for a Little Lovin'/I Never Knew How Good I Had It	1967	20.00
❑ 11091	Soul Clap/Big Parade	1968	20.00
❑ 11150	Not Another Day/You Sure Know How to Hurt a Guy	1968	40.00
ABC-PARAMOUNT			
❑ 10731	Not Too Old to Cry/If You Don't Dig the Blues	1965	40.00
SMASH			
❑ 1914	Dance with My Baby/To Be Happy Enough	1964	25.00
❑ 1933	Get Something Going/That's the Way the Story Goes	1964	25.00

TRENDS, THE (2)

Number	Title (A Side/B Side)	Yr	NM
45s			
ARGO			
❑ 5341	I'll Be True/Class Ring	1959	30.00
SCOPE			
❑ 102	Gone Again/Silly Grin	1959	80.00

TRENDS, THE (U)

Definitely not group (1), but it may not be group (2), either.

Number	Title (A Side/B Side)	Yr	NM
45s			
RCA VICTOR			
❑ 47-7733	The Beard/Chug-a-Lug	1960	15.00

TRENIERS, THE

Number	Title (A Side/B Side)	Yr	NM
45s			
BRUNSWICK			
❑ 55014	Holy Mackerel Andy/Rock Calypso Joe	1957	20.00
❑ 55033	Pennies from Heaven/Ooh-La-La	1957	20.00
❑ 55047	Goodnight Irene/Rubbing Noses in the Midnight Sun	1958	20.00
DOM			
❑ 410	Gotta Travel On/Let It All Hang Out	1968	8.00
DOT			
❑ 15882	Never Never/When Your Hair Has Turned to Silver	1958	20.00
EPIC			
❑ 9127	Go! Go! Go!/Doin' 'Em Up	1955	25.00
❑ 9144	Rock'n Roll Call/Day-Old Bread and Canned Beans	1956	25.00
❑ 9162	Boodie Green/Good Rockin' Tonight	1956	25.00
OKEH			
❑ 6804	Go! Go! Go!/Plenty of Money	1951	50.00
❑ 6826	Hey, Little Girl/Old Woman Blues	1951	40.00
❑ 6853	It Rocks, It Rolls, It Swings/Taxi Blues	1952	40.00
❑ 6876	Hadacol, That's All/Long Distance Blues	1952	40.00
❑ 6904	Rockin' on Sunday Night/Cheatin' On Me	1952	40.00
❑ 6932	Hi-Yo Silver/Poon-Tang!	1953	40.00
❑ 6937	The Moondog/Poon-Tang!	1953	50.00
❑ 6960	Rockin' Is Our Bizness/Sugar Doo	1953	40.00
❑ 6984	I'd Do Nothin' But Grieve/This Is It	1953	40.00
❑ 7012	You Know, Yeah! Tiger/Bug Dance	1953	40.00
❑ 7023	Rock-a-Beatin' Boogie/Trapped	1954	40.00
❑ 7035	Bald Head/Come On Let's Face It	1954	40.00
❑ 7050	Who Put the "Ungh" in the Mambo/Get Out of the Car	1955	30.00
❑ 7057	Devil's Mambo/Do, Do, Do (Do-Be-Oo-Be-Oo)	1955	30.00
VIK			
❑ 0214	Lover Come Back to Me/Sorrento	1956	25.00
❑ 0227	Rock and Roll President/Cool It Baby	1956	25.00
7-Inch Extended Plays			
EPIC			
❑ EG-7014	(contents unknown)	1955	50.00
❑ EG-7014 [PS]	Go! Go! Go!	1955	50.00
❑ EG-7114	(contents unknown)	195?	50.00
❑ EG-7114 [PS]	Those Crazy Treniers	195?	50.00
Albums			
DOT			
❑ DLP-3257 [M]	Souvenir Album	1960	100.00
EPIC			
❑ LG 3125 [M]	The Treniers on TV	1955	200.00

TRENT, JACKIE

The record on Nasco may be by a different singer than the others.

Number	Title (A Side/B Side)	Yr	NM
45s			
A&M			
❑ 1022	Hollywood/Don't Send Me Away	1969	6.00
KAPP			
❑ 583	Only One Such As You/If You Love Me, Really Love Me	1964	12.00
❑ 630	Somewhere in the World/I Heard Someone Say	1964	12.00
NASCO			
❑ 6012	Little Andy/What's He Got	1958	25.00
PARKWAY			
❑ 941	Don't Stand in My Way/How Soon	1965	12.00
❑ 955	Where Are You Now My Love/On the Other Side of the Tracks	1965	12.00
❑ 963	To Show I Love Him/When Summertime Is Over	1965	12.00
WARNER BROS.			
❑ 5683	It's All in the Way You Look at Life/Time After Time	1965	10.00
❑ 5865	If You Ever Leave Me/Take Me Away	1966	10.00
❑ 7022	Hummingbird/I'll Be with You	1967	8.00
❑ 7070	It's Not Easy Loving You/Your Love Is Everywhere	1967	8.00
❑ 7178	7:10 to Suburbia/Stop Me and Buy One	1968	8.00
❑ 7189	I'll Be With You/Two of Us	1968	8.00

TRENTONS, THE

Number	Title (A Side/B Side)	Yr	NM
45s			
SHEPHERD			
❑ 2204	All Alone/Star Bright	1962	80.00

TREVOR, VAN

Number	Title (A Side/B Side)	Yr	NM
45s			
ATLANTIC			
❑ 2175	Tuesday Girl/I Want to Cry	1963	10.00
BAND BOX			
❑ 367	Born to Be in Love with You/It's So Good to Be Loved	1966	8.00
❑ 371	Our Side/When You've Lost Your Baby	1966	8.00
❑ 373 [DJ]	Christmas In The Country/Holiday Driving (PSA Announcements)	1966	10.00
❑ 374	He's Losing His Mind/A Fool Called Me	1967	8.00
CANADIAN AMERICAN			
❑ 181	Louisiana Hot Sauce/Satisfaction Is Guaranteed	1964	20.00
❑ 188	The Girl from the Main Street Diner/For This Girl	1965	15.00
CLARIDGE			
❑ 305	Christmas in Washington Square/Melting Snow	1965	15.00
DATE			
❑ 1565	You've Been So Good to Me/Sunday Morning	1967	8.00
❑ 1594	Take Me Along with You/Guitar	1968	8.00
ROYAL AMERICAN			
❑ 3	Mercy Hospital/Something Missing in Me	1970	5.00
❑ 9	Luziana River/Sweet Diana	1970	5.00
❑ 23	Wish I Was Home Instead/Did I Have a Good Time	1970	5.00
❑ 31	Lonely Looking Woman/Johnnie and Annie	1971	5.00
❑ 67	Shiny New Penny/You and Only You	1972	5.00
❑ 280	The Things That Matter/Band of Gold	1969	6.00
❑ 283	A Man Away from Home/I've Got Today to Live For	1969	6.00
❑ 289	Funny Familiar Forgotten Feelings/Daddy's Little Man	1969	6.00
VIVID			
❑ 1004	C'mon Now Baby/A Fling of the Past	1963	30.00
—Backing group is The Four Seasons			
Albums			
BAND BOX			
❑ (# unknown)	Come On Over to Our Side	1967	20.00
DATE			
❑ DES-4008	You've Been So Good to Me	1967	15.00
ROYAL AMERICAN			
❑ 2800	Funny Familiar Forgotten Feelings	1969	15.00

TREXLER, GARY

Number	Title (A Side/B Side)	Yr	NM
45s			
RCA VICTOR			
❑ 47-7258	I Flipped/Turn About	1958	15.00
❑ 47-7420	The Look/You Made Up for Everything	1958	15.00
REV			
❑ 3507	Teen Baby/Cloud Full of Tears	1957	20.00

TRIANGLE, THE

Number	Title (A Side/B Side)	Yr	NM
45s			
AMARET			
❑ 108	Music, Music, Music/Magic Touch	1969	10.00
❑ 113	Ninety Nine and a Half/Lucille	1969	10.00
Albums			
AMARET			
❑ 5000	How Now Brown Cow	1969	25.00

TRIANGLES, THE

Number	Title (A Side/B Side)	Yr	NM
45s			
FARGO			
❑ 1023	Dance the Magoo/Step-Up-and-Go	1962	15.00
FIFO			
❑ 107	My Oh My/Really I Do	1964	200.00
HERALD			
❑ 549	Savin' My Love/'Tis a Pity	1960	40.00

TRIBULATIONS, THE

Number	Title (A Side/B Side)	Yr	NM
45s			
IMPERIAL			
❑ 66416	Mama's Love/You Gave Me Up for Promises	1969	30.00

TRICKELS, THE

Number	Title (A Side/B Side)	Yr	NM
45s			
GONE			
❑ 5078	With Each Step a Tear/Outside the Chapel Door	1959	100.00
POWER			
❑ 250	With Each Step a Tear/When I Fall in Love	1958	200.00

TRICYCLE

Number	Title (A Side/B Side)	Yr	NM
Albums			
ABC			
❑ S-674	Tricycle	1969	20.00

TRIDELS, THE

Number	Title (A Side/B Side)	Yr	NM
45s			
SAN-DEE			
❑ 1009	Land of Love/Image of My Love	1963	50.00

TRIGGER, VIC

Number	Title (A Side/B Side)	Yr	NM
Albums			
SANCTUARY			
❑ 12103	Electronic Wizard	1977	100.00

TRIMBLE, BOBB

Number	Title (A Side/B Side)	Yr	NM
Albums			
(NO LABEL)			
❑ (no #)	Harvest of Dreams	1982	150.00
VENGEANCE			
❑ BT-8458	Iron Curtain Dream	1980	800.00

TRINA, MARGUERITE

Number	Title (A Side/B Side)	Yr	NM
45s			
BELLA			
❑ 19	The Rocking Tree/The Brat	1959	12.00

TRINIDADS, THE

Number	Title (A Side/B Side)	Yr	NM
45s			
FORMAL			
❑ 1005	Don't Say Goodbye/On My Happy Way	1959	200.00
❑ 1006	One Lonely Night/When We're Together	1959	200.00

TRIO

Number	Title (A Side/B Side)	Yr	NM
Albums			
MERCURY			
❑ MX-1-509 [EP]	Trio (Contains the Hit Da Da Da)	1982	15.00
❑ 814320-1	Trio and Error	1983	20.00

TRIOLO, FRANK

Number	Title (A Side/B Side)	Yr	NM
45s			
FLAGSHIP			
❑ 106	Ice Cream Baby/Pretty Little Woman	1958	400.00

TRIPP, PAUL

Number	Title (A Side/B Side)	Yr	NM
45s			
MUSICOR			
❑ 1125	An Old-Fashioned Christmas/I've Got a Date with Santa	1965	12.00

TRIPP, TOM

Number	Title (A Side/B Side)	Yr	NM
45s			
HIT			
❑ 93	Since I Fell for You/Dominique	1963	8.00
—B-side by Betty Coleson			

Except when noted otherwise, VG = 25% of NM, and VG+ = 50% of NM. (Example: VG = $2.00, VG+ = $4.00 and NM = $8.00.)

TRIPSICHORD MUSIC BOX, THE

Albums

Number	Title (A Side/B Side)	Yr	NM
JANUS			
❑ JLS-3016	The Tripsichord Music Box	1971	200.00

TRIUMVIRAT

45s

Number	Title (A Side/B Side)	Yr	NM
CAPITOL			
❑ 4700	Waterfall/Jo Ann Walker	1979	5.00

Albums

Number	Title (A Side/B Side)	Yr	NM
CAPITOL			
❑ ST-11392	Spartacus	1975	12.00
❑ ST-11551	Old Loves Die Hard	1976	12.00
❑ ST-11697	Pompeii	1977	12.00
❑ ST-11862	A La Carte	1978	12.00
❑ SN-16119	Illusions on a Double Dimple	1980	8.00
—Budget-line reissue			
❑ SN-16120	Pompeii	1980	8.00
—Budget-line reissue			
❑ SN-16121	Spartacus	1980	8.00
—Budget-line reissue			
❑ SN-16122	Old Loves Die Hard	1980	8.00
—Budget-line reissue			
❑ SN-16123	A La Carte	1980	8.00
—Budget-line reissue			
HARVEST			
❑ ST-11311	Illusions on a Double Dimple	1974	15.00

TROGGS, THE

45s

Number	Title (A Side/B Side)	Yr	NM
ATCO			
❑ 6415	Wild Thing/I Want You	1966	20.00
❑ 6415	Wild Thing/With a Girl Like You	1966	20.00
—"Wild Thing" writer is correctly credited as "Taylor."			
❑ 6415	Wild Thing/With a Girl Like You	1966	25.00
—"Wild Thing" writer is incorrectly credited as "Presley."			
❑ 6444	I Can't Control Myself/Gonna Make You	1966	15.00
BELL			
❑ 45405	Listen to the Man/Queen of Sorrow	1973	8.00
❑ 45426	Strange Movies/I'm on Fire	1973	8.00
FONTANA			
❑ 1548	Wild Thing/From Home	1966	10.00
❑ 1552	With a Girl Like You/I Want You	1966	10.00
❑ 1557	I Can't Control Myself/Gonna Make You	1966	10.00
❑ 1576	You're Lying/Give It To Me	1967	8.00
❑ 1585	6-5-4-3-2-1/Anyway That You Want Me	1967	8.00
❑ 1593	Night of the Long Grass/Girl in Black	1967	8.00
❑ 1607	Love Is All Around/When Will the Rain Come	1967	10.00
❑ 1622	You Can Cry If You Want To/There's Something About You	1968	8.00
❑ 1630	Surprise, Surprise/Cousin Jane	1968	8.00
❑ 1634	Hip Hip Hooray/Say Darlin'	1968	8.00
PAGE ONE			
❑ 21026	Evil Woman/Heads Or Tails	1969	6.00
❑ 21030	Easy Lovin'/Give Me Something	1970	6.00
❑ 21032	Come Now/Lover	1970	6.00
❑ 21035	The Raver/You	1970	6.00
PRIVATE STOCK			
❑ 45,102	Rolling Stone/(B-side unknown)	1976	5.00
PYE			
❑ 65011	Feels Like a Woman/Everything's Funny	1972	8.00
❑ 71015	Good Vibrations/Push It Up to Me	1975	5.00
❑ 71035	Summertime/Jerry Come Down	1975	5.00
❑ 71054	Satisfaction/(B-side unknown)	1975	5.00

Albums

Number	Title (A Side/B Side)	Yr	NM
ATCO			
❑ 33-193 [M]	Wild Thing	1966	50.00
❑ SD 33-193 [R]	Wild Thing	1966	40.00
FONTANA			
❑ MGF 27556 [M]	Wild Thing/With a Girl Like You	1966	40.00
—Contents identical to the Atco LP; two slightly different cover variations are known; record has mono number and plays mono; number "27556" in trail-off			
❑ MGF 27556 [R]	Wild Thing/With a Girl Like You	1966	30.00
—Contents identical to the Atco LP; two slightly different cover variations are known; record has mono number but plays in rechanneled stereo; number "2/67556" in trail-off			
❑ SRF 67556 [R]	Wild Thing/With a Girl Like You	1966	30.00
—Contents identical to the Atco LP; two slightly different cover variations are known			
❑ SRF 67576 [R]	Love Is All Around	1968	30.00
MKC			
❑ 214	Live at Max's Kansas City	1980	12.00
PRIVATE STOCK			
❑ PS-2008	The Troggs Tapes	1976	12.00
PYE			
❑ 12112	The Troggs	1975	12.00
RHINO			
❑ RNLP-118	The Best of the Troggs	1985	10.00
❑ R1 70118	The Best of the Troggs	1988	8.00
SIRE			
❑ SASH-3714 [(2)]	The Vintage Years	1976	15.00

TROLL, THE

45s

Number	Title (A Side/B Side)	Yr	NM
SMASH			
❑ 2208	Satin City News/Professor Potts' Pornographic Projector	1969	12.00

Albums

Number	Title (A Side/B Side)	Yr	NM
SMASH			
❑ SRS-67114	Animated Music	1969	50.00

TROLLS, THE

45s

Number	Title (A Side/B Side)	Yr	NM
ABC			
❑ 10823	Every Day and Every Night/Are You the One	1966	12.00
❑ 10884	Laughing All the Way/Someone Here Inside	1966	10.00
❑ 10916	They Don't Know/There Was a Time	1967	10.00
❑ 10952	Baby. What You Ain't Got (I Ain't in Need)/Who Was That Boy	1967	10.00
RUFF			
❑ 1010	Into My Arms/That's the Way My Love Is	1966	300.00
U.S.A.			
❑ 905	I Got to Have You/Don't Come Around	1968	25.00
WARRIOR			
❑ 173	Stupid Girl/I Don't Recall	1967	50.00
❑ 173 [PS]	Stupid Girl/I Don't Recall	1967	75.00

TROPHIES, THE More than one group?

45s

Number	Title (A Side/B Side)	Yr	NM
CHALLENGE			
❑ 9133	Desire/Doggone It	1962	60.00
❑ 9149	Peg O' My Heart/I Laughed So Hard I Cried	1962	15.00
❑ 9170	That's All I Want from You/Felicia	1962	15.00
KAPP			
❑ 714	Everywhere I Go/Baby Don't Live Here Anymore	1965	15.00
❑ 750	Leave My Girl Alone/You're the Queen	1966	15.00
NORK			
❑ 79907	Walkin' the Dog/Somethin' Blue	196?	20.00

TROUBADOURS DE ROI BAUDOUIN

Albums

Number	Title (A Side/B Side)	Yr	NM
PHILIPS			
❑ PCC 206 [M]	Missa Luba	1963	15.00
❑ PCC 606 [S]	Missa Luba	1963	15.00
—Released in '63, this didn't chart until 1969			

TROWER, ROBIN Also see JACK BRUCE/ROBIN TROWER; PROCOL HARUM.

12-Inch Singles

Number	Title (A Side/B Side)	Yr	NM
ATLANTIC			
❑ PR 2251 [DJ]	Shattered (LP version)/Shattered (Live Version)	1988	8.00
❑ PR 2374 [DJ]	Love Won't Wait Forever (same on both sides)	1988	6.00
GNP CRESCENDO			
❑ PRO-1 [DJ]	Secret Doors (same on both sides)	1986	8.00
❑ PRO-2 [DJ]	No Time (same on both sides)	1987	8.00
❑ PRO-3 [DJ]	Caroline (same on both sides)	1987	8.00

45s

Number	Title (A Side/B Side)	Yr	NM
CHRYSALIS			
❑ 2009	Man of the World/Take a Fast Train	1973	6.00
❑ 2113	Too Rolling Stoned (Part 1)/Too Rolling Stoned (Part 2)	1976	6.00
❑ 2122	Caledonia/Messin' the Blues	1976	6.00
❑ 2172	Sweet Wine of Love/In City Dreams	1977	4.00
❑ 2206	Somebody Calling/Bluebird	1978	4.00
❑ 2238	My Love (Burning Love)/(B-side unknown)	1978	4.00
❑ 2272	It's for You/Birthday Boy	1979	4.00

Albums

Number	Title (A Side/B Side)	Yr	NM
ATLANTIC			
❑ 81838	Take What You Need	1988	10.00
❑ 82080	In the Line of Fire	1990	12.00
CHRYSALIS			
❑ CHR 1039	Twice Removed from Yesterday	1973	12.00
—Green label, "3300 Warner Blvd." address			
❑ CHR 1039	Twice Removed from Yesterday	1977	10.00
—Blue label, New York address			
❑ CHR 1057	Bridge of Sighs	1974	12.00
—Green label, "3300 Warner Blvd." address			
❑ CHR 1057	Bridge of Sighs	1977	10.00
—Blue label, New York address			
❑ CHR 1073	For Earth Below	1975	12.00
—Green label, "3300 Warner Blvd." address			
❑ CHR 1073	For Earth Below	1977	10.00
—Blue label, New York address			
❑ CHR 1089	Robin Trower Live!	1976	12.00
—Green label, "3300 Warner Blvd." address			
❑ CHR 1089	Robin Trower Live!	1977	10.00
—Blue label, New York address			
❑ CHR 1107	Long Misty Days	1976	12.00
—Green label, "3300 Warner Blvd." address			
❑ CHR 1107	Long Misty Days	1977	10.00
—Blue label, New York address			
❑ CHR 1148	In City Dreams	1977	12.00
❑ CHR 1189	Caravan to Midnight	1978	12.00
❑ CHR 1215	Victims of the Fury	1980	12.00
❑ CHR 1324	B.L.T.	1981	10.00
❑ PV 41039	Twice Removed from Yesterday	1983	8.00
—Reissue			
❑ FV 41057	Bridge of Sighs	1984	8.00
—Reissue			
❑ PV 41057	Bridge of Sighs	1986	8.00
—Reissue			
❑ PV 41073	For Earth Below	1984	8.00
—Reissue			
❑ PV 41089	Robin Trower Live!	1983	8.00
—Reissue			
❑ PV 41107	Long Misty Days	1983	8.00
—Reissue			
❑ PV 41148	In City Dreams	1984	8.00
—Reissue			
❑ PV 41189	Caravan to Midnight	1984	8.00
—Reissue			
❑ PV 41215	Victims of the Fury	1983	8.00
—Reissue			
❑ PV 41324	B.L.T.	1984	8.00
—Reissue			
❑ FV 41420	Back It Up	1983	10.00
❑ PV 41420	Back It Up	1986	10.00
—Reissue			
GNP CRESCENDO			
❑ 2187	Passion	1986	10.00
PASSPORT			
❑ PB-6049	Beyond the Mist	1985	10.00

TROY, BILLY

45s

Number	Title (A Side/B Side)	Yr	NM
BARNABY			
❑ ZS7 2035	Longer Than Awhile/My Nancy's Love	1971	8.00
❑ ZS7 2054	Isn't It Lonely Together/Sally's Sayin' Somethin'	1971	8.00

TROY, DORIS

45s

Number	Title (A Side/B Side)	Yr	NM
APPLE			
❑ 1820	Ain't That Cute/Vaya Con Dios	1970	8.00
❑ 1824	Jacob's Ladder/Get Back	1970	8.00
ATLANTIC			
❑ 2188	Just One Look/Bossa Nova Blues	1963	20.00
❑ 2206	Tomorrow Is Another Day/What'cha Gonna Do About It	1963	12.00
❑ 2222	One More Chance/Please Little Angel	1964	12.00
❑ 2269	Hurry/He Don't Belong to Me	1965	12.00
CALLA			
❑ 114	Heartaches/I'll Do Anything	1966	20.00
CAPITOL			
❑ 2043	Face Up to the Truth/He's Qualified	1967	8.00
MIDLAND INT'L.			
❑ MB-10806	Lyin' Eyes/Give God Glory	1976	5.00
❑ MB-11082	Can't Hold On/Another Look	1977	5.00

Albums

Number	Title (A Side/B Side)	Yr	NM
APPLE			
❑ ST-3371	Doris Troy	1970	25.00
ATLANTIC			
❑ 8088 [M]	Just One Look	1964	30.00

Number	Title (A Side/B Side)	Yr	NM
❑ SD 8088 [P]	Just One Look	1964	50.00
—The title song is rechanneled			

TROYKA

Albums

Number	Title (A Side/B Side)	Yr	NM
COTILLION			
❑ SD 9020	Troyka	1970	35.00

TRU-TONES, THE

45s

Number	Title (A Side/B Side)	Yr	NM
CHART			
❑ 634	Tears in My Eyes/Magic	1957	800.00
DEN RIC			
❑ 4527	I'm the Guy/(B-side unknown)	196?	40.00
KEB			
❑ 6037	Soldier's Last Letter/(B-side unknown)	196?	40.00

TRUELEERS, THE

45s

Number	Title (A Side/B Side)	Yr	NM
CHECKER			
❑ 1026	Forget About Him/Waiting for You	1962	12.00

TRUMPETEERS, THE (1)

Gospel group. Also known as "The CBS Trumpeteers."

45s

Number	Title (A Side/B Side)	Yr	NM
IMPERIAL			
❑ 5972	Milky White Way/Leave That Lie Alone	1963	15.00
❑ 5994	Seven Angels/Just a Little Walk with Jesus	1963	15.00
JUBILEE			
❑ 5654	Milky White Way/Prayer for Today	1969	10.00
—As "The CBS Trumpeteers"			
NASHBORO			
❑ 788	God Is Coming/One Day I Was Walking	1963	15.00
—As "The CBS Trumpeteers"			
❑ 805	Everything Moves/My Heart Bubbles Over	1964	15.00
—As "The CBS Trumpeteers"			
❑ 887	Little Wooden Church/Lord, Ease My Weary Mind	1966	15.00
—As "The CBS Trumpeteers"			
OKEH			
❑ 6871	Don't Miss That Train/Home Don't Seem Like Home	1952	100.00
❑ 6890	I'll Fly Away/Leave It in His Hands	1953	100.00

TRUMPETEERS, THE (2)

For records on Splash, see BILLY MURE.

TRYTHALL, GIL

45s

Number	Title (A Side/B Side)	Yr	NM
ATHENA			
❑ 5013	Yakety Moog/Foggy Mountain Breakdown	1970	6.00

Albums

Number	Title (A Side/B Side)	Yr	NM
ATHENA			
❑ 6003	Switched On Nashville/Country Moog	1970	12.00
❑ 6004	Nashville Gold	1970	12.00

TUBES, THE

12-Inch Singles

Number	Title (A Side/B Side)	Yr	NM
A&M			
❑ SP-17068 [DJ]	Prime Time/No Way Out	1979	10.00
CAPITOL			
❑ SPRO 9012 [DJ]	The Monkey Time (same on both sides)	1983	10.00
❑ SPRO 9332 [DJ]	Piece by Piece (same on both sides)	1985	6.00
❑ SPRO 9728 [DJ]	Gonna Get It Next Time (same on both sides)	1982	8.00

45s

Number	Title (A Side/B Side)	Yr	NM
A&M			
❑ 1733	White Punks on Dope (Part 1)/White Punks on Dope (Part 2)	1975	8.00
❑ 1733 [PS]	White Punks on Dope (Part 1)/White Punks on Dope (Part 2)	1975	12.00
❑ 1755	What Do You Want from Life/Space Baby	1975	7.00
❑ 1826	Don't Touch Me There/Proud to Be an American	1976	6.00
❑ 1956	This Town/I'm Just a Mess	1977	6.00
❑ 2037	Show Me a Reason/I Saw Her Standing There	1978	6.00
❑ 2120	Prime Time/No Way Out	1979	6.00
❑ 2149	Love's a Mystery (I Don't Understand)/Telecide	1979	6.00
❑ 8591	White Punks on Dope/What Do You Want from Life?	198?	3.00
—Reissue			
CAPITOL			
❑ A-5007	Don't Want to Wait Anymore/Think About Me	1981	3.00
❑ A-5007 [PS]	Don't Want to Wait Anymore/Think About Me	1981	4.00
❑ A-5016	Talk To Ya Later/Power Tools	1981	6.00
❑ B-5091	Gonna Get It Next Time/Sports Fans	1982	6.00
❑ B-5217	She's a Beauty/When You're Ready to Come	1983	3.00
—Second pressing has a black label with colorband			
❑ B-5217	She's a Beauty/When You're Ready to Come	1983	4.00
—First pressing has a purple label			
❑ B-5217 [PS]	She's a Beauty/When You're Ready to Come	1983	8.00
❑ B-5254	The Monkey Time/Sports Fans	1983	3.00
❑ B-5254 [PS]	The Monkey Time/Sports Fans	1983	4.00
❑ B-5258	Tip of My Tongue/Keyboard Kids	1983	4.00
❑ B-5443	Piece by Piece/Night People	1985	3.00
❑ B-5443 [PS]	Piece by Piece/Night People	1985	4.00
❑ SPRO-9740 [DJ]	Sports Fans (same on both sides)	1982	5.00
❑ SPRO-9909 [DJ]	She's a Beauty (same on both sides)	1983	12.00
CAPITOL STARLINE			
❑ X-6328	Don't Want to Wait Anymore/Talk To Ya Later	198?	3.00
TUBES			
❑ 12682XS	Tubular Holiday	1982	50.00
—Fan club flexidisc			
❑ 833502XS	Happy Holidaze	1983	50.00
—Fan club flexidisc			

Albums

Number	Title (A Side/B Side)	Yr	NM
A&M			
❑ SP-3161	The Tubes	198?	8.00
—Reissue of SP-4534			
❑ SP-3222	Young and Rich	198?	8.00
—Reissue of SP-4580			
❑ SP-3242	Remote Control	198?	8.00
—Reissue of SP-4751			
❑ SP-3243	Now	198?	10.00
—Reissue of SP-4632			
❑ SP-3244	T.R.A.S.H. (Tubes Rarities And Smash Hits)	198?	8.00
—Reissue of SP-4870			
❑ SP-4534	The Tubes	1975	12.00
❑ SP-4580	Young and Rich	1976	12.00
❑ SP-4632	Now	1977	12.00
❑ SP-4751	Remote Control	1979	12.00
❑ SP-4870	T.R.A.S.H. (Tubes Rarities And Smash Hits)	1981	10.00
❑ SP-6003 [(2)]	What Do You Want From Live!	1978	15.00
❑ SP-17012 [DJ]	Tubes Live/Edited for Trouble-Free Airplay (The First "Clean" Tubes Album)	1978	20.00
—Generic cover with sticker; promo only			
CAPITOL			
❑ SOO-12151	The Completion Backward Principle	1981	10.00
❑ ST-12260	Outside/Inside	1983	10.00
❑ ST-12381	Love Bomb	1985	10.00
❑ SN-16360	Outside/Inside	1985	8.00
—Reissue of ST-12260			
❑ SN-16378	The Completion Backward Principle	1986	8.00
—Reissue of SOO-12151			
❑ SN-16446	Love Bomb	1987	8.00
—Reissue of ST-12381			

TUCKER, BILLY JOE

45s

Number	Title (A Side/B Side)	Yr	NM
DOT			
❑ 16240	Boogie Woogie Bill/Mail Train	1961	100.00
MAHA			
❑ 103	Boogie Woogie Bill/Mail Train	1961	300.00

TUCKER, MAUREEN

Albums

Number	Title (A Side/B Side)	Yr	NM
50 SKIDILLION WATTS			
❑ MOE 1 [EP]	Moejadkatebarry	1987	14.00
❑ MOE 7	Life in Exile After Abdication	1989	12.00
TRASH			
❑ TLP-1001	Playin' Possum	1981	30.00

TUCKER, MICKEY

Albums

Number	Title (A Side/B Side)	Yr	NM
MUSE			
❑ MR-5174	Mister Mysterious	1978	12.00
❑ MR-5223	The Crawl	1979	12.00
XANADU			
❑ 128	Triplicity	1976	12.00
❑ 143	Sojourn	1977	12.00

TUCKER, RICK

45s

Number	Title (A Side/B Side)	Yr	NM
COLUMBIA			
❑ 4-41041	Patty Baby/Don't Do Me This Way	1957	100.00
HITSVILLE			
❑ 6035	I Heard a Song/Plans That We Made	1976	6.00
OAK			
❑ 1066	Honey I'm Just Walking Out the Door/(B-side unknown)	1989	5.00

TUCKY BUZZARD

45s

Number	Title (A Side/B Side)	Yr	NM
CAPITOL			
❑ 3171	Pisces Apple Lady/Time Will Be Your Doctor	1971	6.00
PASSPORT			
❑ 7901	Gold Medallions/Fast Bluesy Woman	1974	5.00

Albums

Number	Title (A Side/B Side)	Yr	NM
CAPITOL			
❑ ST-787	Tucky Buzzard	1971	16.00
❑ ST-864	Warm Slash	1972	18.00
PASSPORT			
❑ 97001	Alright in the Night	1973	15.00
❑ 98002	Tucky Buzzard	1974	15.00

TUDOR MINSTRELS, THE

45s

Number	Title (A Side/B Side)	Yr	NM
LONDON			
❑ 1012	Love in the Open Air/A Theme from "The Family Way"	1966	50.00

TUFF DARTS

45s

Number	Title (A Side/B Side)	Yr	NM
SIRE			
❑ 1015	(I Wanna Know) Who's Been Sleeping Here?/Rats	1978	4.00
❑ 1015 [PS]	(I Wanna Know) Who's Been Sleeping Here?/Rats	1978	4.00

Albums

Number	Title (A Side/B Side)	Yr	NM
SIRE			
❑ SRK 6048	Tuff Darts!	1978	12.00

TUFFS, THE

45s

Number	Title (A Side/B Side)	Yr	NM
DORE			
❑ 757	I Only Cry Once a Day Now/The Moon Out There	1966	25.00
DOT			
❑ 16304	Surfer Stomp (Part 1)/Surfer Stomp (Part 2)	1962	25.00

TULLY, LEE, AND MILT MOSS

45s

Number	Title (A Side/B Side)	Yr	NM
FLAIR-X			
❑ 3007	Around the World with Elwood Pretzel (Part 1)/Around the World with Elwood Pretzel (Part 2)	1956	50.00

TUNE ROCKERS, THE

45s

Number	Title (A Side/B Side)	Yr	NM
UNITED ARTISTS			
❑ 139	The Green Mosquito/Warm Up	1958	20.00
❑ 0145	The Green Mosquito/Bust Out	1973	4.00
—"Silver Spotlight Series" reissue; B-side by the Busters			

TUNEDROPS, THE

45s

Number	Title (A Side/B Side)	Yr	NM
GONE			
❑ 5003	Rosie Lee/Speak for Yourself	1957	40.00
❑ 5072	Smoothie/Jumpin' Jellybeans	1959	25.00
METRO			
❑ 20028	Smoothie/Jumpin' Jelly Beans	1959	40.00

TUNEMASTERS, THE

45s

Number	Title (A Side/B Side)	Yr	NM
MARK			
❑ 7002	Sending This Letter/It's All Over	1957	300.00

TURBANS, THE
Also see THE TURKS/THE TURBANS.

45s

HERALD

Number	Title (A Side/B Side)	Yr	NM
❑ 458	When You Dance/Let Me Show You (Around My Heart)	195?	20.00
	—Yellow label, block print inside flag		
❑ 458	When You Dance/Let Me Show You (Around My Heart)	1955	50.00
	—Yellow label, script print inside flag		
❑ 469	Sister Sookey/I'll Always Watch Over You	1956	30.00
❑ 478	B-I-N-G-O (Bingo)/I'm Nobody's	1956	30.00
❑ 486	It Was a Nite Like This/All of My Love	1956	30.00
❑ 495	Valley of Love/Bye and Bye	1957	30.00
❑ 510	Congratulations/The Wadda-Do	1957	25.00

IMPERIAL

Number	Title (A Side/B Side)	Yr	NM
❑ 5807	Six Questions/The Lament of Silver Gulch	1962	40.00
❑ 5828	This Is My Story/Clicky Clicky Clack	1962	25.00
❑ 5847	I Wonder (I Wanna Know)/The Damage Is Done	1962	20.00

LOST-NITE

Number	Title (A Side/B Side)	Yr	NM
❑ 414	When You Dance/Let Me Show You (Around My Heart)	197?	5.00
	—Reissue		
❑ 432	Congratulations/The Wadda-Do	197?	5.00
	—Reissue		
❑ 433	Sister Sookey/I'll Always Watch Over You	197?	5.00
	—Reissue		

MONEY

Number	Title (A Side/B Side)	Yr	NM
❑ 209	Tick Tock Awoo/Nest Is Warm	1955	200.00
❑ 209	Tick Tock Awoo/No No Cherry	1955	200.00

PARKWAY

Number	Title (A Side/B Side)	Yr	NM
❑ 820	When You Dance/Golden Rings	1961	25.00

RED TOP

Number	Title (A Side/B Side)	Yr	NM
❑ 115	I Promise You Love/Curfew Time	1959	50.00

ROULETTE

Number	Title (A Side/B Side)	Yr	NM
❑ 4281	Diamonds and Pearls/Bad Man	1960	20.00
❑ 4326	Three Friends (Two Lovers)/I'm Not Your Fool Anymore	1961	20.00

Albums

HERALD

Number	Title (A Side/B Side)	Yr	NM
❑ 5009	Presenting the Turbans	197?	20.00
	—No such album was released in the 1950s; this is a bootleg that has some collector value.		

LOST-NITE

Number	Title (A Side/B Side)	Yr	NM
❑ LLP-25 [10]	The Turbans	1981	10.00
	—Red vinyl		

RELIC

Number	Title (A Side/B Side)	Yr	NM
❑ 5009	The Turbans' Greatest Hits	198?	12.00

TURBINES, THE

45s

CENCO

Number	Title (A Side/B Side)	Yr	NM
❑ 116	We Got to Start Over/(B-side unknown)	196?	1200.

TURKS, THE
More than one group.

45s

BALLY

Number	Title (A Side/B Side)	Yr	NM
❑ 1017	This Heart of Mine/Why Did You	1956	30.00

CASH

Number	Title (A Side/B Side)	Yr	NM
❑ 1042	It Can't Be True/Wagon Wheels	1956	30.00
	—As "The Original Turks"		

CLASS

Number	Title (A Side/B Side)	Yr	NM
❑ 256	Hully Gully/Rockville U.S.A.	1959	20.00

IMPERIAL

Number	Title (A Side/B Side)	Yr	NM
❑ 5783	I'm a Fool/It Can't Be True	1961	12.00

KEEN

Number	Title (A Side/B Side)	Yr	NM
❑ 3-4016	Father Time/Okay	1958	20.00

KNIGHT

Number	Title (A Side/B Side)	Yr	NM
❑ 2005	I'm a Fool/It Can't Be True	1958	20.00

MONEY

Number	Title (A Side/B Side)	Yr	NM
❑ 215	I'm a Fool/I've Been Accused	1956	40.00

P.B.D.

Number	Title (A Side/B Side)	Yr	NM
❑ 112	Baja/Dianne	196?	30.00
❑ 113	Wipeout/Hideaway	196?	30.00

TURKS, THE / THE TURBANS
Also see each artist's individual listings.

45s

MONEY

Number	Title (A Side/B Side)	Yr	NM
❑ 211	Emily/When I Return	1955	60.00

TURLEY, RICHARD

45s

DOT

Number	Title (A Side/B Side)	Yr	NM
❑ 16231	I Wanna Dance/Since I Met You	1961	40.00

FRATERNITY

Number	Title (A Side/B Side)	Yr	NM
❑ 845	Makin' Love with My Baby/All About Ann	1959	40.00

TURNER, IKE
Also see IKE AND TINA TURNER.

45s

ARTISTIC

Number	Title (A Side/B Side)	Yr	NM
❑ 1504	(I Know) You Don't Love Me/Down and Out	1958	30.00

COBRA

Number	Title (A Side/B Side)	Yr	NM
❑ 5033	Box Top/Walking Down the Aisle	1959	30.00

FEDERAL

Number	Title (A Side/B Side)	Yr	NM
❑ 12297	Do You Mean It/She Made My Blood Run Cold	1957	100.00
❑ 12304	Rock a Bucket/The Big Question	1957	50.00
❑ 12307	You've Changed My Love/Trail Blazer	1957	40.00

FLAIR

Number	Title (A Side/B Side)	Yr	NM
❑ 1040	Cubano Jump/Loosely	1954	60.00
❑ 1059	Cuban Getaway/Go To It	1955	60.00

KING

Number	Title (A Side/B Side)	Yr	NM
❑ 5553	The Big Question/She Made My Blood Run Cold	1961	15.00

LIBERTY

Number	Title (A Side/B Side)	Yr	NM
❑ 56194	Takin' Back My Name/Love Is a Game	1970	5.00

RPM

Number	Title (A Side/B Side)	Yr	NM
❑ 356	You're Driving Me Insane/Trouble and Heartaches	1952	400.00
❑ 362	My Heart Belongs to You/Lookin' for My Baby	1952	60.00
	—As "Bonnie and Ike Turner"		
❑ 446	As Long As I Have You/I Wanna Make Love to You	1955	40.00

SUE

Number	Title (A Side/B Side)	Yr	NM
❑ 722	My Love/That's All I Need	1959	20.00

UNITED ARTISTS

Number	Title (A Side/B Side)	Yr	NM
❑ XW460	Take My Hand, Precious Lord/Father Alone	1974	5.00
❑ 50865	River Deep Mountain High/Na Na	1971	5.00
❑ 50900	Right On/Tacks in My Shoes	1972	5.00
❑ 50930	Lawdy Miss Clawdy/Tacks in My Shoes	1972	5.00
❑ 51102	Dust My Broom/You Won't Let Me Go	1973	5.00

Albums

CROWN

Number	Title (A Side/B Side)	Yr	NM
❑ CST-367 [R]	Ike Turner Rocks the Blues	1963	100.00
❑ CLP-5367 [M]	Ike Turner Rocks the Blues	1963	200.00

FANTASY

Number	Title (A Side/B Side)	Yr	NM
❑ F-9597	The Edge	1980	10.00

POMPEII

Number	Title (A Side/B Side)	Yr	NM
❑ SD 6003	A Black Man's Soul	1969	15.00

UNITED ARTISTS

Number	Title (A Side/B Side)	Yr	NM
❑ UA-LA087-F	Bad Dreams	1973	15.00
❑ UAS-5576	Blues Roots	1972	15.00

TURNER, IKE AND TINA
Also see IKE TURNER; TINA TURNER.

12-Inch Singles

STRIPED HORSE

Number	Title (A Side/B Side)	Yr	NM
❑ 1201	Living for the City (5:02)/Bootsy Whitelaw (4:01)	1985	15.00

45s

A&M

Number	Title (A Side/B Side)	Yr	NM
❑ 1118	River Deep, Mountain High/I'll Keep You Happy	1969	10.00
❑ 1170	A Love Like Yours/Save the Last Dance for Me	1970	10.00

BLUE THUMB

Number	Title (A Side/B Side)	Yr	NM
❑ 101	I've Been Loving You Too Long/Grumbling	1969	6.00
❑ 102	The Hunter/Crazy 'Bout You Baby	1969	6.00
❑ 104	Bold Soul Sister/I Know	1969	6.00
❑ 202	I've Been Loving You Too Long/Crazy 'Bout You Baby	1971	25.00

CENCO

Number	Title (A Side/B Side)	Yr	NM
❑ 112	Get It-Get It/You Weren't Ready (For My Love)	1967	15.00

INNIS

Number	Title (A Side/B Side)	Yr	NM
❑ 6666	Betcha Can't Kiss Me/Don't Lie to Me	1968	10.00
❑ 6667	So Fine/So Blue Over You	1968	10.00

KENT

Number	Title (A Side/B Side)	Yr	NM
❑ 402	I Can't Believe What You Say (For Seeing What You Do)/My Baby Now	1964	10.00
❑ 409	Am I a Fool in Love/Please, Please, Please	1964	10.00
❑ 418	Chicken Shack/He's the One	1965	10.00
❑ 4514	Plaese, Please, Please (Part 1)/Please, Please, Please (Part 2)	1970	6.00

LIBERTY

Number	Title (A Side/B Side)	Yr	NM
❑ 56177	I Want to Take You Higher/Contact High	1970	6.00
❑ 56207	Workin' Together/The Way You Love Me	1970	6.00
❑ 56216	Proud Mary/Funkier Than a Mosquito's Tweeter	1970	6.00

LOMA

Number	Title (A Side/B Side)	Yr	NM
❑ 2011	I'm Thru with Love/Tell Her I'm Not Home	1965	10.00
❑ 2015	Somebody Needs You/Just to Be with You	1965	10.00

MINIT

Number	Title (A Side/B Side)	Yr	NM
❑ 32060	I'm Gonna Do All I Can (To Do Right By My Man)/You've Got Too Many Ties That Bind	1969	6.00
❑ 32068	I Wish It Would Rain/With a Little Help from My Friends	1969	6.00
❑ 32077	I Wanna Jump/Treating Us Funky	1969	6.00
❑ 32087	Come Together/Honky Tonk Women	1970	6.00

MODERN

Number	Title (A Side/B Side)	Yr	NM
❑ 1007	Good Bye, So Long/Hurt Is All You Gave Me	1965	10.00
❑ 1012	I Don't Need/Gonna Have Fun	1965	10.00

PHILLES

Number	Title (A Side/B Side)	Yr	NM
❑ 131	River Deep — Mountain High/I'll Keep You Happy	1966	20.00
❑ 134	Two to Tango/A Man Is a Man Is a Man	1966	15.00
❑ 135	I'll Never Need More Love Than This/The Cash Box Blues Or (Oops We Printed the Wrong Story Again)	1967	15.00
❑ 136	I Idolize You/A Love Like Yours	1967	15.00

POMPEII

Number	Title (A Side/B Side)	Yr	NM
❑ 7003	Betcha Can't Kiss Me/Cussin', Cryin', and Carryin' On	1969	8.00
❑ 66675	It Sho' Ain't Me/We Need An Understanding	1968	8.00
❑ 66700	Shake a Tail Feather/Cussin', Cryin', and Carryin' On	1969	8.00

SONJA

Number	Title (A Side/B Side)	Yr	NM
❑ 2001	If I Can't Be First/I'm Going Back Home	1968	12.00
❑ 2005	You Can't Miss Nothing That You Never Had/God Gave Me You	1968	12.00

SUE

Number	Title (A Side/B Side)	Yr	NM
❑ 135	Two Is a Couple/Tin Top House	1965	15.00
❑ 138	The New Breed (Part 1)/The New Breed (Part 2)	1965	15.00
❑ 139	Stagger Lee and Billy/Can't Chance a Breakup	1965	15.00
❑ 146	Dear John/I Made a Promise Up Above	1966	12.00
❑ 730	A Fool in Love/The Way You Love Me	1960	30.00
❑ 734	You're My Baby/A Fool Too Long	1960	25.00
❑ 735	I Idolize You/Letter from Tina	1960	25.00
❑ 740	I'm Jealous/You're My Baby	1961	25.00
❑ 749	It's Gonna Work Out Fine/Won't You Forgive Me	1961	30.00
	—With correct A-side title		
❑ 749	Gonna Work Out Fine/Won't You Forgive Me	1961	50.00
	—With erroneous A-side title		
❑ 753	Poor Fool/You Can't Blame Me	1961	20.00
❑ 757	Tra La La La La/Puppy Love	1962	15.00
❑ 760	Prancing/It's Gonna Work Out Fine	1962	15.00
❑ 765	You Shoulda Treated Me Right/Sleepless	1962	15.00
❑ 768	Tina's Dilemma/I Idolize You	1962	15.00
❑ 772	The Argument/Mind in a Whirl	1962	15.00
❑ 774	Please Don't Hurt Me/Worried and Hurtin' Inside	1962	15.00
❑ 784	Don't Play Me Cheap/Wake Up	1963	15.00

TANGERINE

Number	Title (A Side/B Side)	Yr	NM
❑ 963	Beauty Is Only Skin Deep/Anything You Wasn't Born With	1966	10.00
❑ 967	Dust My Broom/I'm Hooked	1966	10.00

T

Number	Title (A Side/B Side)	Yr	NM
UNITED ARTISTS			
SP-48 [DJ]	I Want to Take You Higher/Ooh Poo Pah Doo	1971	10.00
0119	A Fool in Love/I Idolize You	1973	4.00
0120	It's Gonna Work Out Fine/Poor Fool	1973	4.00
0121	I Want to Take You Higher/Come Together	1973	4.00
0122	Proud Mary/Tra La La La La	1973	4.00
—0119 through 0122 are "Silver Spotlight Series" reissues			
XW174	With a Little Help from My Friends/Early One Morning	1973	5.00
XW257	Work On Me/Born Free	1973	5.00
XW298	Nutbosh City Limits/Help Him	1973	6.00
XW409	Get it Out of Your Mind/Sweet Rhode Island Red	1974	5.00
XW524	Nutbush City Limits/Ooh Poo Pah Doo	1974	4.00
—Reissue			
XW528	Sexy Ida (Part 1)/Sexy Ida (Part 2)	1974	5.00
XW598X	Baby, Get It On/Baby, Get It On (Disco Version)	1975	5.00
50782	Ooh Poo Pah Doo/I Wanna Jump	1971	5.00
50837	I'm Yours/Doin' It	1971	5.00
50881	Do Wah Ditty (Got to Get Ya)/Up in Heah	1972	5.00
50913	Outrageous/Feel Good	1972	5.00
50939	Games People Play/Pick Me Up	1972	5.00
50955	Let Me Touch Your Mind/Chopper	1972	5.00
WARNER BROS.			
5433	A Fool for a Fool/No Tears to Cry	1964	12.00
5433 [PS]	A Fool for a Fool/No Tears to Cry	1964	40.00
5461	It's All Over/Finger Poppin'	1964	12.00
5493	Ooh Poop A Doo/Merry Christmas Baby	1964	12.00

Albums

Number	Title (A Side/B Side)	Yr	NM
A&M			
SP-3179	River Deep — Mountain High	1982	10.00
—Budget-line reissue			
SP-4178	River Deep — Mountain High	1969	25.00
—Official release of Philles 4011			
ABC			
4014	16 Great Performances	1975	12.00
ACCORD			
SN-7147	Hot and Sassy	1981	10.00
BLUE THUMB			
BTS 5	Outta Season	1968	15.00
BTS 11	The Hunter	1969	15.00
BTS 49	The Best of Ike & Tina Turner	1973	12.00
BTS-8805	Outta Season	1971	12.00
—Early reissue of Blue Thumb 5			
CAPITOL			
ST-571	Her Man, His Woman	1971	15.00
COLLECTABLES			
COL-5107	Golden Classics	198?	10.00
COL-5137	It's Gonna Work Out Fine	198?	10.00
EMI AMERICA			
ST-17212	It's Gonna Work Out Fine	1986	10.00
SQ-17216	Workin' Together	1986	10.00
HARMONY			
HS 11360	Ooh Poo Pah Doo	1969	15.00
H 30567	Something's Got a Hold on Me	1971	15.00
KENT			
KST-514 [S]	The Ike and Tina Turner Revue Live	1964	40.00
KST-519 [S]	The Soul of Ike and Tina	1966	40.00
KST-538	Festival of Live Performances	1969	30.00
KST-550	Please Please Please	1971	30.00
K-5014 [M]	The Ike and Tina Turner Revue Live	1964	30.00
K-5019 [M]	The Soul of Ike and Tina	1966	30.00
LIBERTY			
LT-917	Airwaves	1981	8.00
LST-7637	Come Together	1970	15.00
LST-7650	Workin' Together	1970	15.00
LO-51156	Get Back!	1985	10.00
LOMA			
L 5904 [M]	Live! The Ike & Tina Turner Show Vol. 2	1966	25.00
LS 5904 [S]	Live! The Ike & Tina Turner Show, Vol. 2	1966	30.00
—Reissue of Warner Bros. 1579?			
MINIT			
24018	In Person	1969	20.00
PHILLES			
PHLP 4011 [M]	River Deep — Mountain High	1967	8000.
—Value is for record alone; covers were not printed			
PICKWICK			
SPC-3284	Too Hot to Hold	197?	10.00
POMPEII			
6000 [M]	So Fine	1968	60.00
—Mono is white label promo only; fromt cover has "d/j copy monaural" sticker on it			
SD 6000 [S]	So Fine	1968	25.00
SD 6004	Cussin', Cryin' and Carryin' On	1969	25.00
SD 6006	Get It Together	1969	25.00
STRIPED HORSE			
SHL-2001	Golden Empire	1986	10.00
SUE			
LP 1038 [M]	The Greatest Hits of Ike and Tina Turner	1965	300.00
LP 2001 [M]	The Soul of Ike and Tina Turner	1961	400.00
LP 2003 [M]	Ike and Tina Turner's Kings of Rhythm Dance	1962	400.00
—Despite the title, this is an all-instrumental album (Tina's vocals do not appear)			
LP 2004 [M]	Dynamite	1963	400.00
LP 2005 [M]	Don't Play Me Cheap	1963	400.00
LP 2007 [M]	It's Gonna Work Out Fine	1963	400.00
SUNSET			
SUS-5265	The Fantastic Ike & Tina Turner	1969	15.00
SUS-5286	Ike & Tima Turner's Greatest Hits	1969	15.00
UNART			
S 21021	Greatest Hits	197?	10.00
UNITED ARTISTS			
UA-LA064-G [(2)]	The World of Ike & Tina Live	1973	15.00
UA-LA180-F	Nutbush City Limits	1973	12.00
UA-LA203-G	The Gospel According to Ike & Tina Turner	1974	12.00
UA-LA312-G	Sweet Rhode Island Red	1974	12.00
UA-LA592-G	Greatest Hits	1976	12.00
UA-LA707-G	Delilah's Power	1977	12.00
UA-LA917-H	Airwaves	1978	12.00
UAS-5530	'Nuff Said	1971	12.00
UAS-5598	Feel Good	1972	12.00
UAS-5660	Let Me Touch Your Mind	1972	12.00
UAS-5667	Ike & Tina Turner's Greatest Hits	1972	12.00
UAS-9953 [(2)]	Live at Carnegie Hall/What You Hear Is What You Get	1971	15.00
WARNER BROS.			
W 1579 [M]	Live! The Ike & Tina Turner Show	1965	30.00
WS 1579 [S]	Live! The Ike & Tina Turner Show	1965	40.00
WS 1810	Ike & Tina Turner's Greatest Hits	1969	25.00

TURNER, JESSE LEE

45s

Number	Title (A Side/B Side)	Yr	NM
CARLTON			
496	The Little Space Girl/Shake, Baby, Shake	1959	20.00
509	Baby Please Don't Tease/Thinkin'	1959	20.00
509 [PS]	Baby Please Don't Tease/Thinkin'	1959	40.00
FRATERNITY			
855	Teen-Age Misery/That's My Girl	1959	20.00
855 [PS]	Teen-Age Misery/That's My Girl	1959	40.00
GNP CRESCENDO			
184	All You Gotta Do (Is Ask Me To)/Voice Changing Song	1962	12.00
188	Shotgun Boogie/Ballad of Billy Sol Estes	1962	60.00
IMPERIAL			
5635	Slippin' Around/Early in the Morning	1960	15.00
5649	I'm the Little Space Girl's Father/Valley of Lost Soldiers	1960	20.00
TOP RANK			
2064	Do I Worry/All Right, Be That Way	1960	20.00

TURNER, JOE

45s

Number	Title (A Side/B Side)	Yr	NM
ATLANTIC			
939	Chains of Love/After My Laughter Came Tears	1951	500.00
949	The Chill Is On/Bump Miss Suzie	1951	800.00
960	Sweet Sixteen/I'll Never Stop Loving You	1952	120.00
970	Don't You Cry/Poor Lover's Blues	1952	100.00
982	Still in Love/Baby I Still Want You	1953	100.00
1001	Honey Hush/Crawdad Hole	1953	200.00
1016	TV Mama/Oke-She-Moke-She-Pop	1954	120.00
1026	Shake, Rattle, and Roll/You Know I Love You	1954	80.00
1040	Well All Right/Married Woman	1954	70.00
1053	Flip, Flop, and Fly/Ti-Ri-Lee	1955	50.00
1069	Hide and Seek/Midnight Cannonball	1955	50.00
1080	Morning, Noon and Night/The Chicken and the Hawk	1956	50.00
1088	Corinne, Corinna/Boogie Woogie Country Girl	1956	30.00
1100	Rock a While/Lipstick, Powder, and Paint	1956	30.00
1122	Midnight Special Train/Feeling Happy	1957	30.00
1131	Red Sails in the Sunset/After a While	1957	30.00
1146	Love Roller Coaster/A World of Trouble	1957	30.00
1155	I Need a Girl/Trouble in Mind	1957	30.00
1167	Teen-Age Letter/Wee Baby Blues	1957	30.00
1184	Blues in the Night/Jump for Joy	1958	30.00
2034	Got You On My Mind/Love, Oh Careless Love	1959	20.00
2044	Tomorrow Night/Honey Hush	1959	20.00
2054	Chains of Love/My Little Honey Dripper	1960	20.00
2072	My Reason for Living/Sweet Sue	1960	20.00
BAYOU			
015	The Blues Jumped the Rabbit/The Sun Is Shining	1951	300.00
BLUESTIME			
45001	Two Loves Have I/Shake, Rattle and Roll	195?	40.00
BLUESWAY			
61009	Big Wheel/Bluer Than Blue	1967	8.00
CORAL			
62408	I Walk a Lonely Mile/I'm Packin' Up	1964	15.00
62429	Shake, Rattle and Roll/There'll Be Some Tears Falling	1964	15.00
DECCA			
29711	Piney Brown Blues/I Got a Gal for Every Day of the Week	1955	40.00
29924	Corrine, Corrina/It's the Same Old Story	1956	40.00
KENT			
512	Love Ain't Nothin'/10-20-25-30	1969	6.00
4561	Chains of Love/Battle Hymn of the Republic	1971	6.00
4569	One Hour in Your Garden/You've Been Squeezin' My Lemons	1972	6.00
MGM			
10719	Moody Baby/Feeling So Sad	1951	300.00
OKEH			
6829	Cherry Red/Joe Turner Blues	1951	200.00
RONN			
28	Up on the Mountain/I Love You Baby	1969	6.00
35	Morning Glory/Night-Time Is the Right Time	1969	6.00
RPM			
345	Riding Blues/Playful Baby	1952	200.00
—With Pete Johnson			

7-Inch Extended Plays

Number	Title (A Side/B Side)	Yr	NM
ATLANTIC			
EP 536	Honey Hush/Sweet Sixteen//Chains of Love/T.V. Mama	1955	150.00
EP 536 [PS]	Joe Turner Sings	1955	150.00
EP 565	Shake, Rattle and Roll/Flip, Flop and Fly//In the Evenin'/When the Sun Goes Down	1956	150.00
EP 565 [PS]	Joe Turner	1956	150.00
EP 586	*Corrine Corrina/The Chicken and the Hawk/Feeling Happy/Hide and Seek	195?	150.00
EP 586 [PS]	Joe Turner	195?	150.00
EP 606	*Crawdad Hole/The Chicken and the Hawk/Boogie Woogie Country Girl/Midnight Special Train	195?	120.00
EP 606 [PS]	Rock with Joe Turner	195?	120.00
EMARCY			
EP-1-6132	(contents unknown)	195?	100.00
EP-1-6132 [PS]	Joe Turner	195?	100.00

Albums

Number	Title (A Side/B Side)	Yr	NM
ARHOOLIE			
2004 [M]	Jumpin' the Blues	1962	20.00
ATCO			
33-376 [M]	Joe Turner — His Greatest Recordings	1971	15.00
ATLANTIC			
1234 [M]	The Boss of the Blues	1956	120.00
—Black label			
1234 [M]	The Boss of the Blues	1960	100.00
—White "bullseye" label			
1234 [M]	The Boss of the Blues	1961	40.00
—White "fan" logo on label			
1234 [M]	The Boss of the Blues	1963	15.00
—Black "fan" logo on label			

Except when noted otherwise, VG = 25% of NM, and VG+ = 50% of NM. (Example: VG = $2.00, VG+ = $4.00 and NM = $8.00.)

Number	Title (A Side/B Side)	Yr	NM
❑ SD 1234 [S]	The Boss of the Blues	1959	180.00
—Green label			
❑ SD 1234 [S]	The Boss of the Blues	1960	150.00
—White "bullseye" label			
❑ SD 1234 [S]	The Boss of the Blues	1961	50.00
—White "fan" logo on label			
❑ SD 1234 [S]	The Boss of the Blues	1963	20.00
—Black "fan" logo on label			
❑ 1332 [M]	Big Joe Rides Again	1959	150.00
—Black label			
❑ 1332 [M]	Big Joe Rides Again	1960	40.00
—White "fan" logo on label			
❑ 1332 [M]	Big Joe Rides Again	1963	15.00
—Black "fan" logo on label			
❑ SD 1332 [S]	Big Joe Rides Again	1959	200.00
—Green label			
❑ SD 1332 [S]	Big Joe Rides Again	1960	50.00
—White "fan" logo on label			
❑ SD 1332 [S]	Big Joe Rides Again	1963	20.00
—Black "fan" logo on label			
❑ 8005 [M]	Joe Turner	1957	150.00
—Black label			
❑ 8005 [M]	Joe Turner	1961	40.00
—White "fan" logo on label			
❑ 8005 [M]	Joe Turner	1963	15.00
—Black "fan" logo on label			
❑ 8023 [M]	Rockin' the Blues	1958	120.00
—Black label			
❑ 8023 [M]	Rockin' the Blues	1960	40.00
—White "fan" logo on label			
❑ 8023 [M]	Rockin' the Blues	1963	15.00
—Black "fan" logo on label			
❑ 8033 [M]	Big Joe Is Here	1959	120.00
—Black label			
❑ 8033 [M]	Big Joe Is Here	1960	40.00
—White "fan" logo on label			
❑ 8033 [M]	Big Joe Is Here	1960	100.00
—White "bullseye" label			
❑ 8033 [M]	Big Joe Is Here	1963	15.00
—Black "fan" logo on label			
❑ 8081 [M]	The Best of Joe Turner	1963	50.00
❑ SD 8812	Boss of the Blues	1981	10.00
—Reissue of 1234			
❑ 81752	Greatest Hits	1987	10.00
BLUES SPECTRUM			
❑ BS-104	Great Rhythm and Blues Oldies Vol. 4	197?	15.00
BLUESTIME			
❑ 9002 [M]	The Real Boss of the Blues	196?	40.00
❑ 29002 [S]	The Real Boss of the Blues	196?	30.00
BLUESWAY			
❑ BL 6006 [M]	Singing the Blues	1967	20.00
❑ BLS-6006 [S]	Singing the Blues	1967	25.00
❑ S-6060	Roll 'Em	1973	15.00
DECCA			
❑ DL 8044 [M]	Joe Turner Sings Kansas City Jazz	1953	250.00
FANTASY			
❑ OJC-497	Trumpet Kings Meet Joe Turner	1991	12.00
INTERMEDIA			
❑ QS-5008	Rock This Joint	198?	10.00
❑ QS-5026	The Very Best of Joe Turner — Live	198?	10.00
❑ QS-5030	The Blues Boss — Live	198?	10.00
❑ QS-5036	Everyday I Have the Blues	198?	10.00
❑ QS-5043	Roll Me Baby	198?	10.00
KENT			
❑ KST-542	Joe Turner Turns On the Blues	1973	15.00
MCA			
❑ 1325	Early Big Joe	198?	10.00
MUSE			
❑ MR-5293	Blues Train	198?	10.00
—With Roomful of Blues and Dr. John			
PABLO			
❑ 2310717	Trumpet Kings Meet Joe Turner	197?	12.00
❑ 2310760	Nobody in Mind	197?	12.00
❑ 2310776	In the Evening	197?	12.00
❑ 2310800	Things That I Used to Do	197?	12.00
❑ 2310818	Every Day I Have the Blues	198?	12.00
❑ 2310848	The Best of Joe Turner	1980	12.00
❑ 2310863	Have No Fear, Joe Turner Is Here	1983	12.00
❑ 2310883	Singing the Same, Sad, Happy, Forever Blues	1983	12.00
❑ 2310913	Patcha, Patcha, All Night Long	198?	12.00
❑ 2310937	Flip, Flop and Fly	1989	12.00
❑ 2405404	The Best of "Big" Joe Turner	198?	12.00
SAVOY			
❑ MG-14012 [M]	Blues'll Make You Happy	1958	150.00
❑ MG-14106 [M]	Careless Love	1963	80.00
SAVOY JAZZ			
❑ SJC-406	Blues'll Make You Happy	1985	10.00
—Reissue of Savoy 14012			
❑ SJL-2223 [(2)]	Have No Fear	197?	15.00

TURNER, JOE (2)

Number	Title (A Side/B Side)	Yr	NM
Albums			
CHIAROSCURO			
❑ 147	King of Stride	1976	15.00
CLASSIC JAZZ			
❑ 138	Effervescent	1976	15.00
PABLO			
❑ 2310763	Another Epoch Stride Piano	197?	12.00

TURNER, JOE, AND PETE JOHNSON

Number	Title (A Side/B Side)	Yr	NM
Albums			
EMARCY			
❑ MG-36014 [M]	Joe Turner and Pete Johnson	1955	200.00

TURNER, ODELLE

Number	Title (A Side/B Side)	Yr	NM
45s			
ATLANTIC			
❑ 964	Alarm Clock Boogie/ Draggin' Hours	1952	150.00

TURNER, SAMMY

Number	Title (A Side/B Side)	Yr	NM
45s			
BIG TOP			
❑ 3007	Thunderbolt/Sweet Annie Laurie	1959	25.00
❑ 3016 [M]	Lavender-Blue/Wrapped Up in a Dream	1959	20.00
❑ 3016 [S]	Lavender-Blue/Wrapped Up in a Dream	1959	60.00
❑ 3029 [M]	Always/Symphony	1959	20.00
❑ 3029 [S]	Always/Symphony	1959	50.00
❑ 3032	Paradise/I'd Be a Fool Again	1960	20.00
❑ 3038	Goodnight Irene/I Want to Be Loved	1960	20.00
❑ 3049	Fools Fall in Love/Stay My Love	1960	20.00
❑ 3061	Falling/The Things I Love	1961	15.00
❑ 3065	Little Sir Echo/ Love Keeps Calling	1961	15.00
❑ 3070	Starlight, Starbright/ Let's Donkey On Down	1961	15.00
❑ 3082	Pour It On/The Fool of the Year	1961	15.00
❑ 3089	Falling/Raincoat in the River	1961	25.00
—B-side produced by Phil Spector			
MILLENNIUM			
❑ 616	Do You Know (What Life Is All About)/Nothing Can Separate Me (From Your Love)	1978	5.00
MOTOWN			
❑ 1055	Only You/Right Now	1964	30.00
PACIFIC			
❑ 3016	Lavender-Blue/Wrapped Up in a Dream	1959	40.00
—Despite label name, Pacific Records was in North Carolina!			
20TH FOX			
❑ 6610	For Your Love I'll Die/ The House I Live In	1965	10.00
VERVE			
❑ 10465	A Child Was Born/Come to Me Comf'tably	1966	30.00
Albums			
BIG TOP			
❑ 12-1301 [M]	Lavender Blue Moods	1959	300.00
—May not exist in stereo			

TURNER, SPYDER

Number	Title (A Side/B Side)	Yr	NM
45s			
KWANZA			
❑ 7688	Since I Don't Have You/ Happy Days	1973	6.00
MGM			
❑ 13617	Stand By Me/You're Good Enough for Me	1966	10.00
❑ 13692	Don't Hold Back/I Can't Take It Anymore	1967	8.00
❑ 13739	For Your Precious Love/I Can't Wait to See My Baby's Face	1967	8.00
❑ 14263	I Can't Make It Anymore/I'm Alive with a Lovin' Feeling	1971	6.00
WHITFIELD			
❑ 8526	I've Been Waiting/ Tomorrow's Only Yesterday	1978	4.00
❑ 8596	Get Down/Is It Love You're After	1978	4.00
❑ 49190	You're So Fine/Only Love	1980	4.00
Albums			
MGM			
❑ E-4450 [M]	Stand By Me	1967	25.00
❑ SE-4450 [S]	Stand By Me	1967	30.00
WHITFIELD			
❑ BSK 3124	Music Web	1978	10.00
❑ BSK 3397	Only Love	1979	10.00

TURNER, TINA

Also see IKE AND TINA TURNER.

Number	Title (A Side/B Side)	Yr	NM
12-Inch Singles			
CAPITOL			
❑ V-8579	Let's Stay Together (5:14)/ I Wrote a Letter	1983	8.00
❑ V-8597	What's Love Got to Do with It/ Rock 'N' Roll Widow	1984	8.00
❑ V-8609	Better Be Good to Me (7:40)/ When I Was Young	1984	8.00
❑ V-8620	Private Dancer/Nutbush City Limits	1985	10.00
❑ V-8635	Show Some Respect (Remix 5:42)/Let's Pretend We're Married	1985	8.00
❑ V-8655	We Don't Need Another Hero/ (Instrumental)	1985	8.00
❑ SPRO-9140 [DJ]	I Might Have Been Queen/ Better Be Good to Me// Steel Claw/Private Dancer	1984	15.00
—With "legs" cover			
❑ SPRO-9146 [DJ]	What's Love Got to Do with It (LP Version 3:49) (same on both sides)	1984	12.00
❑ SPRO-9196 [DJ]	What's Love Got to Do with It (Extended) (same on both sides)	1984	12.00
❑ SPRO-9224/34 [DJ]	Better Be Good to Me (LP Version) (Single Version)	1985	10.00
❑ SPRO-9238 [DJ]	Better Be Good to Me (3 versions)	1985	10.00
❑ SPRO-9264 [DJ]	Better Be Good to Me (Live) (same on both sides)	1984	10.00
❑ SPRO-9425/6 [DJ]	We Don't Need Another Hero (Remix) (Instrumental)	1985	6.00
❑ SPRO-9493/4 [DJ]	One of the Living (Club Version) (Single Version)	1985	10.00
❑ SPRO-9826 [DJ]	Back Where You Started (same on both sides)	1986	8.00
❑ SPRO-9867 [DJ]	Overnight Sensation (same on both sides)	1987	10.00
❑ V-15205	One of the Living (Special Club Version) (Dub) (Instrumental)	1985	8.00
❑ V-15249	Typical Male (Dance Mix) (Single Version) (Dub Mix)/ Don't Turn Around	1986	8.00
❑ V-15261	Two People (Dance Mix) (Dub Mix) (Single Mix)/ Havin' a Party	1986	8.00
❑ V-15273	What You Get Is What You See (4 versions)	1987	8.00
❑ V-15296	Break Every Rule (3 versions)/ Take Me to the River	1987	8.00
❑ V-15349	Afterglow (12" Vocal Dance Mix) (7" Mix) (Glowing Dub) (Tina's House Mix)	1987	7.00
❑ V-15543	Steamy Windows (Vocal Mix) (House Mix) (12" Dub Mix) (12" House Dub Mix)	1989	7.00
❑ SPRO-79168/92 [DJ]	Afterglow (4 versions)	1987	8.00
FANTASY			
❑ D-161	Party Vibes (8:11)/Shame, Shame, Shame (5:06)	1980	12.00
VIRGIN			
❑ SPRO 11056 [DJ]	Goldeneye (Morales Club Mix 10:00) (LP Version 4:47)/ (Morales 007 Dub 9:37) (Morales Dub of Bond 5:36)	1995	7.00
❑ SPRO-12716 [DJ]	On Silent Wings (Soul Solutions' Club Mix) (Instrumental) (Percappella) (Radio Edit)	1996	15.00
❑ SPRO 14918 [DJ]	When the Heartache Is Over (Hex Hector 12" Vocal Mix 8:45) (Hex Hector 7" Vocal Mix 3:30) (Hex Hector 12" Just Drums Mix 5:01)	1999	12.00
❑ SPRO 14951 [(2)DJ]	When the Heartache Is Over (Hex Hector 12" Vocal Mix 8:45) (Hex Hector 7" Vocal Mix 3:30) (Hex Hector 12" Instrumental 8:45) (Hex Hector Acapella 4:02) (Metro Mix 5:45) (7th District Mix		

T

Number	Title (A Side/B Side)	Yr	NM
	5:11) (Hex Hector 12" Just Drums Mix 5:01) (LP Version 3:46)	1999	20.00
❑ SPRO 14964 [DJ]	When the Heartache Is Over (Superchumbo Mix) (same on both sides)	1999	40.00
❑ Y-38578	In Your Wildest Dreams (Pink Noise Club Mix) (Deep Dish Paradise Mix) (Pleasant Instrumental) (Joe Extended Remix) (Antonio Banderas Crossover Mix) (Crossover Dub)	1996	10.00
—With Barry White			
❑ Y-38691	When the Heartache Is Over (Hex Hector 12" Vocal Mix 8:45) (Hex Hector 7" Vocal Mix 3:30) (Hex Hector 12" Instrumental 8:45) (Metro Mix 5:45) (7th District Mix 5:11) (Hex Hector Acapella 4:02)	1999	8.00
45s			
CAPITOL			
❑ B-5322	Let's Stay Together/ I Wrote a Letter	1984	3.00
❑ B-5322 [PS]	Let's Stay Together/ I Wrote a Letter	1984	5.00
❑ B-5354	What's Love Got to Do with It/ Rock 'N' Roll Widow	1984	3.00
❑ B-5354 [PS]	What's Love Got to Do with It/ Rock 'N' Roll Widow	1984	4.00
❑ B-5387	Better Be Good to Me/When I Was Young	1984	3.00
❑ B-5387 [PS]	Better Be Good to Me/ When I Was Young	1984	4.00
❑ B-5433	Private Dancer/ Nutbush City Limits	1984	3.00
❑ B-5433 [PS]	Private Dancer/ Nutbush City Limits	1984	4.00
❑ B-5461	Show Some Respect/Let's Pretend We're Married	1985	3.00
❑ B-5461 [PS]	Show Some Respect/Let's Pretend We're Married	1985	4.00
❑ B-5491	We Don't Need Another Hero (Thunderdome)/ (Instrumental)	1985	3.00
❑ B-5491 [PS]	We Don't Need Another Hero (Thunderdome)/ (Instrumental)	1985	4.00
❑ B-5518	One of the Living/ One of the Living (Dub)	1985	3.00
❑ B-5518 [PS]	One of the Living/ One of the Living (Dub)	1985	4.00
❑ B-5615	Typical Male/Don't Turn Around	1986	3.00
❑ B-5615 [PS]	Typical Male/Don't Turn Around	1986	3.00
❑ B-5644	Two People/Havin' a Party	1986	3.00
❑ B-5644 [PS]	Two People/Havin' a Party	1986	3.00
❑ B-5668	What You Get Is What You See/ What You Get Is What You See (Live)	1987	3.00
❑ B-5668 [PS]	What You Get Is What You See/ What You Get Is What You See (Live)	1987	3.00
❑ B-44003	Break Every Rule/ Take Me to the River	1987	3.00
❑ B-44003 [PS]	Break Every Rule/ Take Me to the River	1987	3.00
❑ B-44111	Afterglow/(B-side unknown)	1987	4.00
❑ B-44442	The Best/Undercover Agent for the Blues	1989	3.00
❑ B-44442 [PS]	The Best/Undercover Agent for the Blues	1989	3.00
❑ B-44473	Steamy Windows/The Best	1989	3.00
❑ B-44473 [PS]	Steamy Windows/The Best	1989	3.00
❑ NR-44510	Look Me in the Heart/ Stronger Than the Wind	1990	3.00
❑ S7-57702	Way of the World/You Know Who	1992	3.00
FANTASY			
❑ 948	Lean On Me/ Shame, Shame, Shame	1984	4.00
POLYDOR			
❑ PRO-002 [DJ]	Acid Queen/Pinball Wizard	1975	40.00
—B-side by Elton John; promo-only			
POMPEII			
❑ 66682	Too Hot to Hold/You Got What You Wanted	1968	10.00
UNITED ARTISTS			
❑ XW 724	Whole Lotta Love/ Rockin' 'N' Rollin'	1975	6.00
❑ XW 730	Delilah's Power/That's My Power	1975	6.00
❑ XW 920	Come Together/I Want to Take You Higher	1977	6.00
❑ XW 1265	Fire Down Below/Viva La Money	1979	5.00
VIRGIN			
❑ S7-17401	I Don't Wanna Fight/Tina's Wish	1993	3.00
❑ S7-17498	Why Must We Wait Until Tonight/Shake a Tail Feather	1993	3.00
❑ S7-18047	Proud Mary (Edit Live Version)/ The Best (Live)	1994	5.00
—Red vinyl			
❑ S7-19217	Missing You/Do Something	1996	3.00
❑ 38691	When the Heartache Is Over/ On Silent Wings	2000	3.00
Albums			
CAPITOL			
❑ 1P 8192 [(2)]	Simply the Best	1991	20.00
—Columbia House edition (only US vinyl version)			
❑ ST-12330	Private Dancer	1984	8.00
❑ PJ-12530	Break Every Rule	1986	8.00
❑ C1-90126 [(2)]	Tina Live in Europe	1988	12.00
❑ C1-91873	Foreign Affair	1989	8.00
FANTASY			
❑ MFP-4520 [EP]	Mini	1984	8.00
SPRINGBOARD			
❑ SPB-4033	The Queen	1972	10.00
UNITED ARTISTS			
❑ UA-LA200-F	Tina Turns the Country On	1973	15.00
❑ UA-LA495-G	Acid Queen	1975	12.00
❑ UA-LA919-G	Rough	1978	12.00
WAGNER			
❑ 14108	Good Hearted Woman	1979	12.00

TURNER, TITUS

Number	Title (A Side/B Side)	Yr	NM
45s			
ATCO			
❑ 6310	Baby Girl (Part 1)/Baby Girl (Part 2)	1964	8.00
ATLANTIC			
❑ 1127	A-Knockin' at My Baby's Door/ Hungry Man	1957	20.00
COLUMBIA			
❑ 42873	Young Wings Can Fly/ Goodbye Rose	1963	10.00
❑ 42947	Make Someone Love You/I'm a Fool About My Mama	1964	10.00
ENJOY			
❑ 1005	People Sure Act Funny/My Darkest Hour	1962	10.00
❑ 1015	Soulville/My Darkest Hour	1963	10.00
❑ 2010	Bow Wow/I Love You Baby	1963	10.00
GLOVER			
❑ 201	We Told You Not to Marry/ Taking Care of Business	1959	25.00
❑ 202	When the Sergeant Comes Marching Home/Up Jumps the Devil	1960	25.00
JAMIE			
❑ 1174	Sound-Off/Me and My Lonely Telephone	1960	15.00
❑ 1177	Pony Train/Bla, Bla, Cha Cha Cha	1961	12.00
❑ 1184	Hey Doll Baby/I Want a Steady Girl	1961	12.00
❑ 1189	Horsin' Around/ Chances Go Around	1961	12.00
❑ 1202	Shake the Hand of a Fool/ Beautiful Stranger	1961	12.00
❑ 1213	Walk on the Wild Twist/ Twistin' Train	1962	10.00
JOSIE			
❑ 990	I Just Can't Keep It to Myself/ People Sure Are Funny	1968	6.00
❑ 1012	His Funeral, My Trial/ Do You Dig It	1969	6.00
KING			
❑ 5067	Have Mercy Baby/You Turned Lamps Too	1957	12.00
❑ 5095	Hold Your Loving/Stop the Rain	1957	12.00
❑ 5129	Follow Me/Way Down Yonder	1958	12.00
❑ 5140	Coralee/Tears of Joy Fill My Eyes	1958	12.00
❑ 5186	The Return of Staggolee/ Answer Me	1959	12.00
❑ 5213 [M]	Tarzan/Fall Guy	1959	12.00
❑ S-5213 [S]	Tarzan/Fall Guy	1959	30.00
❑ 5243	Bonnie Baby/ Miss Rubberneck Jones	1959	12.00
❑ 5465	Way Down Yonder/ Miss Rubberneck Jones	1961	10.00
MURBO			
❑ 1001	Huckle Buckle Beanstalk/Hoop Hoop Hoop a Hoopa Doo	1965	8.00
OKEH			
❑ 6844	Same Old Feeling/Don't Take Everybody to Be Your Friend	1951	30.00
❑ 6883	What'cha Gonna Do for Me/ Got So Much Trouble	1952	25.00
❑ 6907	Jambalaya/Please Baby	1952	25.00
❑ 6929	Christmas Morning/ Be Sure You Know	1952	30.00
❑ 6938	My Plea/It's Too Late Now	1953	25.00
❑ 6961	Big Mary's/Living in Misery	1953	25.00
❑ 7027	Over the Rainbow/ My Lonely Room	1954	25.00
❑ 7038	Hello Stranger/Devilish Woman	1954	25.00
❑ 7244	Eye to Eye/What Kinda Deal Is This	1966	8.00
PHILIPS			
❑ 40445	(I'm Afraid the) Masquerade Is Over/Mary Mack	1967	8.00
WING			
❑ 90006	All Around the World/ Do You Know	1955	20.00
❑ 90033	Sweet and Low/Big John	1955	20.00
❑ 90058	Get on the Right Track, Baby/ I'll Wait Forever	1956	20.00
Albums			
JAMIE			
❑ JLP-3018 [M]	Sound Off	1961	20.00
❑ JLPS-3018 [S]	Sound Off	1961	30.00

TURNER, VELVERT, GROUP

Number	Title (A Side/B Side)	Yr	NM
Albums			
FAMILY PRODUCTIONS			
❑ FPS-2704	Velvert Turner Group	1972	50.00

TURNER, ZEB

Number	Title (A Side/B Side)	Yr	NM
Albums			
AUDIO LAB			
❑ AL-1537 [M]	Country Music in the Turner Style	1959	150.00

TURNPIKES, THE

Number	Title (A Side/B Side)	Yr	NM
45s			
CAPITOL			
❑ 2234	Cast a Spell/ Nothing But Promises	1968	25.00

TURNQUIST REMEDY

Number	Title (A Side/B Side)	Yr	NM
Albums			
PENTAGRAM			
❑ PE-10004	Turnquist Remedy	1970	25.00

TURRENTINE, STANLEY

Number	Title (A Side/B Side)	Yr	NM
12-Inch Singles			
BLUE NOTE			
❑ SPRO-79031 [DJ]	Boogie On Reggae Woman (2 versions)/Creepin'	1987	6.00
❑ SPRO-79031 [DJ]	Boogie On Reggae Woman (2 versions)/Creepin'	1987	6.00
ELEKTRA			
❑ 11472 [DJ]	Deja Vu (mono/stereo)	1980	10.00
❑ 11472 [DJ]	Deja Vu (mono/stereo)	1980	10.00
FANTASY			
❑ D-108	Disco Dancing (7:58)// Heritage/Feed the Fire	1978	10.00
45s			
BLUE NOTE			
❑ 1780	Look Out/Journey Into Melody	196?	10.00
❑ 1781	Little Cheri/Minor Chant	196?	10.00
❑ 1845	Smile, Stacy (Part 1)/Smile, Stacy (Part 2)	196?	8.00
❑ 1846	Soft Pedal Blues (Part 1)/Soft Pedal Blues (Part 2)	196?	8.00
❑ 1847	Pia/Dorene, Don't Cry	196?	8.00
❑ 1848	We'll See You After Awhile, Ya Hear? (Part 1/Part 2)	196?	8.00
❑ 1893	Trouble #2 (Part 1)/Trouble #2 (Part 2)	196?	8.00
❑ 1894	Never Let Me Go/Major's Minor	196?	8.00
❑ 1917	River's Invitation (Part 1)/ River's Invitation (Part 2)	196?	8.00
❑ 1929	Walk On By/And Satisfy	196?	8.00
❑ 1933	Feeling Good/What Could I Do Without You	196?	8.00
❑ 1936	Love Is Blue/Spooky	1969	6.00
❑ 1940	The Look of Love/This Guy's in Love with You	1969	6.00
❑ 1948	Always Something There (To Remind Me)/When I Look Into Your Eyes	1970	6.00
CTI			
❑ 1	Sugar (Part 1)/Sugar (Part 2)	1971	5.00
❑ 10	I Told Jesus/(B-side unknown)	1972	5.00
ELEKTRA			
❑ 46509	Take Me Home/Long Time Gone	1979	4.00
❑ 46533	Concentrate on You/ Together Again	1979	4.00
❑ 46576	Betcha/Hamlet (So Peaceful)	1980	4.00

T

Except when noted otherwise, VG = 25% of NM, and VG+ = 50% of NM. (Example: VG = $2.00, VG+ = $4.00 and NM = $8.00.)

Number	Title (A Side/B Side)	Yr	NM
❑ 47008	Is It You/Inflation	1980	4.00
❑ 47074	Deja Vu/Don't Misunderstand	1981	4.00
❑ 47156	Having Fun with Mr. T/ World Chimes	1981	4.00
❑ 47245	After the Love Is Gone/ I'll Give You My Love	1981	4.00
FANTASY			
❑ 745	Spaced/Naked as the Day I Was Born	1975	5.00
❑ 772	All By Myself/There Is a Place	1976	5.00
❑ 778	Hope That We Can Be Together Soon/There Is a Place	1976	5.00
❑ 782	You'll Never Find Another Love Like Mine/The Man with the Sad Face	1976	5.00
❑ 790	Evil Ways/Love Hangover	1977	5.00
❑ 804	Papa "T" (Part 1)/Papa "T" (Part 2)	1977	5.00
❑ 816	Walkin'/Ann, Wonderful One	1977	5.00
❑ 834	Disco Dancing/Heritage	1978	5.00
IMPULSE!			
❑ 256	Let It Go/Good Looking Out	1967	8.00
Albums			
BAINBRIDGE			
❑ BT-1038	Stan the Man	1981	12.00
BLUE NOTE			
❑ BN-LA394-H2 [(2)]	Stanley Turrentine	1975	20.00
❑ BN-LA883-J2 [(2)]	Jubilee Shout!!	1977	30.00
❑ LT-993	New Time Shuffle	1979	15.00
❑ LT-1037	In Memory Of...	1980	25.00
❑ LT-1075	Mr. Natural	1980	15.00
❑ LT-1095	Ain't No Way	1981	15.00
❑ BLP-4039 [M]	Look Out!	1960	150.00
—Regular version with W. 63rd St. address on label			
❑ BLP-4039 [M]	Look Out!	1960	200.00
—"Deep groove" version; W. 63rd St. address on label			
❑ BLP-4039 [M]	Look Out!	1963	40.00
—With New York, USA address on label			
❑ BLP-4057 [M]	Blue Hour	1961	150.00
—With W. 63rd St. addresss on label			
❑ BLP-4057 [M]	Blue Hour	1963	40.00
—With New York, USA address on label			
❑ BLP-4065 [M]	Comin' Your Way	1961	—
—Canceled			
❑ BLP-4069 [M]	Up at Minton's, Vol. 1	1961	120.00
—With W. 63rd St. addresss on label			
❑ BLP-4069 [M]	Up at Minton's, Vol. 1	1963	40.00
—With New York, USA address on label			
❑ BLP-4070 [M]	Up at Minton's, Vol. 2	1961	120.00
—With W. 63rd St. addresss on label			
❑ BLP-4070 [M]	Up at Minton's, Vol. 2	1963	40.00
—With New York, USA address on label			
❑ BLP-4081 [M]	Dearly Beloved	1961	120.00
—With W. 63rd St. address on label			
❑ BLP-4081 [M]	Dearly Beloved	1963	40.00
—With New York, USA address on label			
❑ BLP-4096 [M]	That's Where It's At	1962	120.00
—With W. 63rd St. address on label			
❑ BLP-4096 [M]	That's Where It's At	1963	60.00
—With New York, USA address on label			
❑ BLP-4122 [M]	Jubilee Shout!!!	1963	—
—Canceled			
❑ BLP-4129 [M]	Never Let Me Go	1963	60.00
❑ BLP-4150 [M]	A Chip Off the Old Block	1963	60.00
❑ BLP-4162 [M]	Hustlin'	1964	60.00
❑ BLP-4201 [M]	Joyride	1965	50.00
❑ BLP-4234 [M]	Stanley Turrentine	1965	—
—Canceled			
❑ BLP-4240 [M]	Rough 'n Tumble	1966	50.00
❑ BLP-4256 [M]	The Spoiler	1967	80.00
—"A Division of Liberty Records" on label			
❑ BLP-4268 [M]	Easy Walker	1967	100.00
—"A Division of Liberty Records" on label			
❑ BST-84039 [S]	Look Out!	1960	60.00
—With W. 63rd St. addresss on label			
❑ BST-84039 [S]	Look Out!	1963	40.00
—With New York, USA address on label			
❑ BST-84039 [S]	Look Out!	1967	25.00
—With "A Division of Liberty Records" on label			
❑ BST-84057	Blue Hour	1986	12.00
—"The Finest in Jazz Since 1939" label reissue			
❑ BST-84057 [S]	Blue Hour	1961	120.00
—With W. 63rd St. address on label			
❑ BST-84057 [S]	Blue Hour	1963	40.00
—With New York, USA address on label			
❑ BST-84057 [S]	Blue Hour	1967	25.00
—With "A Division of Liberty Records" on label			
❑ BST-84057 [S]	Blue Hour	1971	20.00
—With "A Division of United Artists" on label			
❑ B1-84065	Comin' Your Way	1988	15.00
—"The Finest in Jazz Since 1939" label; first issue of LP			
❑ BST-84065 [S]	Comin' Your Way	1961	—
—Canceled			
❑ BST-84069 [S]	Up at Minton's, Vol. 1	1961	120.00
—With W. 63rd St. address on label			

Number	Title (A Side/B Side)	Yr	NM
❑ BST-84069 [S]	Up at Minton's, Vol. 1	1963	40.00
—With New York, USA address on label			
❑ BST-84069 [S]	Up at Minton's, Vol. 1	1967	25.00
—With "A Division of Liberty Records" on label			
❑ BST-84070 [S]	Up at Minton's, Vol. 2	1961	120.00
—With W. 63rd St. addresss on label			
❑ BST-84070 [S]	Up at Minton's, Vol. 2	1963	40.00
—With New York, USA address on label			
❑ BST-84070 [S]	Up at Minton's, Vol. 2	1967	25.00
—With "A Division of Liberty Records" on label			
❑ BST-84081 [S]	Dearly Beloved	1961	120.00
—With W. 63rd St. address on label			
❑ BST-84081 [S]	Dearly Beloved	1963	50.00
—With New York, USA address on label			
❑ BST-84081 [S]	Dearly Beloved	1967	25.00
—With "A Division of Liberty Records" on label			
❑ BST-84096	That's Where It's At	1986	12.00
—"The Finest in Jazz Since 1939" reissue			
❑ BST-84096 [S]	That's Where It's At	1962	120.00
—With W. 63rd St. address on label			
❑ BST-84096 [S]	That's Where It's At	1963	50.00
—With New York, USA address on label			
❑ BST-84096 [S]	That's Where It's At	1967	25.00
—With "A Division of Liberty Records" on label			
❑ BST-84122	Jubilee Shout!!	1986	15.00
—"The Finest in Jazz Since 1939" label; first issue of LP			
❑ BST-84129 [S]	Never Let Me Go	1963	60.00
—With New York, USA address on label			
❑ BST-84129 [S]	Never Let Me Go	1967	25.00
—With "A Division of Liberty Records" on label			
❑ BST-84150 [S]	A Chip Off the Old Block	1963	60.00
—With New York, USA address on label			
❑ BST-84150 [S]	A Chip Off the Old Block	1967	25.00
—With "A Division of Liberty Records" on label			
❑ BST-84162 [S]	Hustlin'	1964	60.00
—With New York, USA address on label			
❑ BST-84162 [S]	Hustlin'	1967	25.00
—With "A Division of Liberty Records" on label			
❑ BST-84162 [S]	Hustlin'	1970	15.00
—With "A Division of United Artists" on label			
❑ BST-84201	Joyride	1984	12.00
—"The Finest in Jazz Since 1939" label reissue			
❑ BST-84201 [S]	Joyride	1964	60.00
—With New York, USA address on label			
❑ BST-84201 [S]	Joyride	1967	25.00
—With "A Division of Liberty Records" on label			
❑ BST-84234 [S]	Stanley Turrentine	1965	—
—Canceled			
❑ BST-84240 [S]	Rough 'n Tumble	1966	50.00
—With New York, USA address on label			
❑ BST-84240 [S]	Rough 'n Tumble	1967	25.00
—With "A Division of Liberty Records" on label			
❑ BST-84256 [S]	The Spoiler	1967	40.00
—"A Division of Liberty Records" on label			
❑ BST-84268 [S]	Easy Walker	1967	50.00
—"A Division of Liberty Records" on label			
❑ BST-84286	The Look of Love	1968	30.00
—With "A Division of Liberty Records" on label			
❑ BST-84286	The Look of Love	1971	20.00
—With "A Division of United Artists" on label			
❑ BST-84298	Always Something There	1968	40.00
—"A Division of Liberty Records" on label			
❑ BST-84315	Common Touch!	1969	30.00
—"A Division of Liberty Records" on label			
❑ BST-84336	Another Story	1969	40.00
—"A Division of Liberty Records" on label			
❑ BST-84424	Z.T.'s Blues	1985	12.00
—"The Finest in Jazz Since 1939" on label			
❑ BT-85105	Straight Ahead	1984	12.00
—"The Finest in Jazz Since 1939" on label			
❑ BT-85140	Wonderland	1987	12.00
—"The Finest in Jazz Since 1939" on label			
❑ B1-90261	La Place	1989	15.00
—"The Finest in Jazz Since 1939" on label			
❑ B1-93201	The Best of Stanley Turrentine	1989	15.00
—"The Finest in Jazz Since 1939" on label			
CTI			
❑ 6005	Sugar	1971	20.00
❑ 6010	Salt Song	1971	20.00
❑ 6017	Cherry	1972	20.00
❑ 6030	Don't Mess with Mister T.	1973	15.00
❑ CTSQ-6030 [Q]	Don't Mess with Mister T.	1973	80.00
❑ 6048	The Baddest Turrentine	1974	15.00
❑ 6052	The Sugar Man	1975	20.00
❑ 8006	Sugar	1981	12.00
—Reissue of 6005			
❑ 8008	Salt Song	1981	12.00
—Reissue of 6010			
❑ 8010	Cherry	1981	12.00
—Reissue of 6017			
❑ 8011	Don't Mess with Mister T.	1981	12.00
—Reissue of 6030			
ELEKTRA			
❑ 6E-217	Betcha	1979	10.00
❑ 6E-269	Inflation	1980	10.00
❑ 5E-534	Tender Togetherness	1981	12.00
❑ 60201	Home Again	1982	12.00
FANTASY			
❑ FPM-4002 [Q]	Pieces of Dreams	1974	25.00
❑ F-9465	Pieces of Dreams	1974	15.00

Number	Title (A Side/B Side)	Yr	NM
❑ F-9478	In the Pocket	1975	15.00
❑ F-9493	Have You Ever Seen the Rain	1975	15.00
❑ F-9508	Everybody Come On Out	1976	15.00
❑ F-9519	The Man with the Sad Face	1976	15.00
❑ F-9534	Nightwings	1977	15.00
❑ F-9548	West Side Highway	1978	15.00
❑ F-9563	What About You!	1978	12.00
❑ F-9604	Use the Stairs	1980	12.00
IMPULSE!			
❑ AS-9115	Let It Go	1967	25.00
MAINSTREAM			
❑ S-6041 [S]	Tiger Tail	1965	50.00
❑ 56041 [M]	Tiger Tail	1965	40.00
PHOENIX 10			
❑ PHX-317 [(2)]	Yester-Me, Yester-You	198?	12.00
SUNSET			
❑ SUS-5255	The Soul of Stanley Turrentine	196?	12.00
TIME			
❑ S-2086 [S]	Stan the Man	1962	120.00
❑ 52086 [M]	Stan the Man	1962	100.00
TRIP			
❑ TLX-5006 [(2)]	Yester-Me, Yester-You	197?	15.00
UPFRONT			
❑ UPF-147	Stanley Turrentine	197?	12.00

TURTLES, THE

Also see FLO AND EDDIE.

Number	Title (A Side/B Side)	Yr	NM
45s			
LOST-NITE			
❑ 435	Elenore/Is It Any Wonder	197?	5.00
❑ 436	Happy Together/ The Walking Song	197?	5.00
❑ 437	It Ain't Me, Babe/Almost There	197?	5.00
—Reissue			
❑ 438	Let Me Be/Your Maw Said You Cried	197?	5.00
—Reissue			
❑ 439	She'd Rather Be with Me/ Rugs of Woods & Flowers	197?	5.00
❑ 440	She's My Girl/Chicken Little Was Right	197?	5.00
—Reissue			
❑ 441	You Baby/Wanderin' Kind	197?	5.00
—Reissue			
❑ 442	You Showed Me/Buzz Saw	197?	5.00
—Reissue			
RHINO			
❑ RNOR 4504	You Know What I Mean/ She's My Girl	1984	4.00
❑ RNOR 74406	Happy Together/ There You Sit Lonely	1987	4.00
❑ RNOR 74406 [PS]	Happy Together/ There You Sit Lonely	1987	4.00
WHITE WHALE			
❑ 222	It Ain't Me, Babe/Almost There	1965	12.00
❑ 224	Let Me Be/Your Maw Said You Cried	1965	10.00
❑ 227	You Baby/Wanderin' Kind	1966	10.00
❑ 231	Grim Reaper of Love/Come Back	1966	20.00
❑ 234	We'll Meet Again/ Outside Chance	1966	15.00
❑ 237	Outside Chance/ Making My Mind Up	1966	10.00
❑ 238	Can I Get to Know You Better?/ Like the Seasons	1966	10.00
❑ 244	Happy Together/ Like the Seasons	1967	8.00
❑ 244 [PS]	Happy Together/ Like the Seasons	1967	40.00
❑ 249	She'd Rather Be with Me/ The Walking Song	1967	8.00
❑ 249 [PS]	She'd Rather Be with Me/ The Walking Song	1967	25.00
❑ 251	Guide for the Married Man/ Think I'll Run Away	1967	40.00
—Withdrawn shortly after release			
❑ 254	You Know What I Mean/Rugs of Woods and Flowers	1967	8.00
❑ 254 [PS]	You Know What I Mean/Rugs of Woods and Flowers	1967	15.00
❑ 260	She's My Girl/Chicken Little Was Right	1967	8.00
—White concentric circles on mostly blue label			
❑ 260	She's My Girl/Chicken Little Was Right	1967	10.00
—All-blue label			
❑ 260 [PS]	She's My Girl/Chicken Little Was Right	1967	20.00
❑ 264	Sound Asleep/ Umbassa the Dragon	1968	8.00
❑ 264 [PS]	Sound Asleep/ Umbassa the Dragon	1968	15.00
❑ 273	The Story of Rock and Roll/ Can't You Hear the Cows	1968	8.00

Number	Title (A Side/B Side)	Yr	NM
❑ 273 [PS]	The Story of Rock and Roll/ Can't You Hear the Cows	1968	50.00
❑ 276	Elenore/Surfer Dan	1968	8.00
❑ 276 [PS]	Elenore/Surfer Dan	1968	12.00
❑ 292	You Showed Me/Buzz Saw	1969	8.00
❑ 292 [PS]	You Showed Me/Buzz Saw	1969	12.00
❑ 306	House on the Hill/Come Over	1969	20.00
❑ 308	You Don't Have to Walk in the Rain/Come Over	1969	8.00
❑ 308 [PS]	You Don't Have to Walk in the Rain/Come Over	1969	10.00
❑ 326	Love in the City/Bachelor Mother	1969	8.00
❑ 326 [PS]	Love in the City/Bachelor Mother	1969	10.00
❑ 334	Lady-O/Somewhere Friday Nite	1969	8.00
❑ 341	Who Would Ever Think That I Would Marry Margaret?/We Ain't Gonna Party No More	1970	15.00
❑ 350	Is It Any Wonder?/ Wanderin' Kind	1970	8.00
❑ 355	Eve of Destruction/ Wanderin' Kind	1970	8.00
❑ 364	Me About You/ Think I'll Run Away	1970	8.00

Albums

Number	Title (A Side/B Side)	Yr	NM
RHINO			
❑ RNLP 151	It Ain't Me Babe	1983	10.00
❑ RNLP 152	Happy Together	1983	10.00
❑ RNLP 153	You Baby	1983	10.00
❑ RNLP 154	Wooden Head	1983	10.00
❑ RNLP 160	Greatest Hits	1983	10.00
❑ RNDF 280 [EP]	Turtle-Sized	1984	12.00
—Green vinyl turtle-shaped EP			
❑ RNPD 900	1968	1984	8.00
❑ RNPD 901 [PD]	1968	1984	12.00
❑ RNLP 70155	Chalon Road	1986	10.00
❑ RNLP 70156	The Turtles Present the Battle of the Bands	1986	10.00
❑ RNLP 70157	Turtle Soup	1986	10.00
❑ RNLP 70158	Shell Shock	1986	10.00
❑ RNLP 70159	Turtle Wax: The Best of the Turtles, Vol. 2	1988	10.00
❑ RNLP 70177	The Best of the Turtles (Golden Archives Series)	1987	10.00
SIRE			
❑ SASH-3703 [(2)]	The Turtles' Greatest Hits/Happy Together Again	1974	20.00
WHITE WHALE			
❑ WW 111 [M]	It Ain't Me Babe	1965	30.00
❑ WW 112 [M]	You Baby	1966	30.00
❑ WW 114 [M]	Happy Together	1967	20.00
❑ WW 115 [M]	The Turtles! Golden Hits	1967	25.00
❑ WWS 7111 [S]	It Ain't Me Babe	1965	40.00
❑ WWS 7112 [S]	You Baby	1966	40.00
❑ WWS 7114 [S]	Happy Together	1967	25.00
❑ WWS 7115 [S]	The Turtles! Golden Hits	1967	20.00
❑ WWS 7118	The Turtles Present the Battle of the Bands	1968	25.00
❑ WW 7124	Turtle Soup	1969	25.00
❑ WW 7127	The Turtles! More Golden Hits	1970	20.00
❑ WW 7133	Wooden Head	1970	20.00

TURTLES, THE (2)

45s

Number	Title (A Side/B Side)	Yr	NM
RCA VICTOR			
❑ 47-6356	Mystery Train/Say You Care	1955	25.00

TUXEDOMOON

12-Inch Singles

Number	Title (A Side/B Side)	Yr	NM
RALPH			
❑ TX 8204	What Use? (Remix)/Crash!	1982	22.00

45s

Number	Title (A Side/B Side)	Yr	NM
RALPH			
❑ TX 8003	What Use?/Crash	1980	4.00
❑ TX 8003 [PS]	What Use?/Crash	1980	4.00
❑ TX 8054	Dark Companion/59 to 1 Remix	1980	4.00
❑ TX 8054 [PS]	Dark Companion/59 to 1 Remix	1980	4.00
TIDAL WAVE			
❑ TWR 101	Joeboy (The Electronic Ghost)/ Pinheads on the Move	1978	15.00
❑ TWR 101 [PS]	Joeboy (The Electronic Ghost)/ Pinheads on the Move	1978	15.00
TIME RELEASE			
❑ TRR 101	Joeboy (The Electronic Ghost)/ Pinheads on the Move	1979	7.50
❑ TRR 101 [PS]	Joeboy (The Electronic Ghost)/ Pinheads on the Move	1979	7.50
❑ TRR 102	Stranger/Love/No Hope	1979	7.50
❑ TRR 102 [PS]	Stranger/Love/No Hope	1979	7.50

Albums

Number	Title (A Side/B Side)	Yr	NM
RALPH			
❑ TX 8004-L	Half-Mute	1980	12.00
❑ TX 8104	Desire	1981	12.00
❑ TX 8354	A Thousand Lives by Picture	1983	12.00
TUXEDOMOON			
❑ EP 45 [EP]	Tuxedomoon	1978	20.00
❑ EP 79 [EP]	Scream with a View	1979	20.00

TV ON THE RADIO

Albums

Number	Title (A Side/B Side)	Yr	NM
DGC			
❑ 1188201	Dear Science	2008	20.00

TWEEDS, THE

45s

Number	Title (A Side/B Side)	Yr	NM
CAMEO			
❑ 367	A Walk in the Black Forest/ 3 O'Clock in the Morning	1965	12.00
CORAL			
❑ 62542	What's Your Name/ A Thing of the Past	1967	10.00
❑ 62551	We Got Time/I Want Her to Know	1968	10.00

TWEETERS, THE

45s

Number	Title (A Side/B Side)	Yr	NM
DECCA			
❑ 30725	Mascara Mama/ The Campus Rock	1958	30.00

TWENTIETH CENTURY ZOO, THE

45s

Number	Title (A Side/B Side)	Yr	NM
CAZ			
❑ 103	You Don't Remember/ Love in Your Face	1967	25.00
VAULT			
❑ 948	Rainbow/Bullfrog	1969	12.00

7-Inch Extended Plays

Number	Title (A Side/B Side)	Yr	NM
SUNDAZED			
❑ SEP 145	You Don't Remember//Love in Your Face/Tossin' and Turnin'	1999	2.00
❑ SEP 145 [PS]	You Don't Remember	1999	2.00

Albums

Number	Title (A Side/B Side)	Yr	NM
VAULT			
❑ LPS-122	Thunder on a Clear Day	1968	60.00

21ST CENTURY, THE

45s

Number	Title (A Side/B Side)	Yr	NM
GOSPEL TRUTH			
❑ 1209	Who's Supposed to Be Raising Who/If the Shoe Fits, Wear It	1973	15.00
RCA VICTOR			
❑ PB-10201	Remember the Rain/You're My Only World	1975	8.00
❑ PB-10364	Child/See My Love Growin' Old	1975	6.00

Albums

Number	Title (A Side/B Side)	Yr	NM
RCA VICTOR			
❑ APL1-1189	Ahead of Our Time	1975	30.00

23 SKIDOO

45s

Number	Title (A Side/B Side)	Yr	NM
MERCURY			
❑ 72874	The New Year's Song/Courtesy	1968	10.00

TWICE AS MUCH

45s

Number	Title (A Side/B Side)	Yr	NM
MGM			
❑ 13530	Sittin' on a Fence/ Baby I Want You	1966	15.00
—A-side is a Mick Jagger-Keith Richards song that only later was released by the Rolling Stones.			
❑ 13530 [PS]	Sittin' on a Fence/ Baby I Want You	1966	30.00
❑ 13600	Step Out of Line/Simplified	1966	10.00

TWIGGY

45s

Number	Title (A Side/B Side)	Yr	NM
BELL			
❑ 45115	Zoo De Zoo Zong/ Zoo De Zoo Zong	1971	10.00
—Might be promo only			
CAPITOL			
❑ 5903 [PS]	Over and Over/ When I Think of You	1967	30.00
❑ 5903	Over and Over/ When I Think of You	1967	10.00
MERCURY			
❑ 73863	Rain on the Roof/Vanilla Olay	1976	6.00
❑ 73923	I Lie Awake and Dream of You/ Woman in Love	1977	6.00

Albums

Number	Title (A Side/B Side)	Yr	NM
MERCURY			
❑ SRM-1-1093	Twiggy	1976	12.00
❑ SRM-1-1138	Please Get My Name Right	1977	12.00

TWILIGHTERS, THE (1)

45s

Number	Title (A Side/B Side)	Yr	NM
BELL			
❑ 624	Be Faithful/Thumper	1965	20.00

TWILIGHTERS, THE (2)

45s

Number	Title (A Side/B Side)	Yr	NM
BUBBLE			
❑ 1334	My Silent Prayer/ Little Bitty Bed Bug	1962	40.00
CHESS			
❑ 1803	Scratchin'/Tears	1961	25.00
CHOLLY			
❑ 712	Let There Be Love/Eternally	1957	1000.
DOT			
❑ 15526	Eternally/I Believe	1957	40.00
EBB			
❑ 117	Pride and Joy/Live Like a King	1957	40.00
ELDO			
❑ 115	Nothin'/Do You Believe	1961	25.00
IMPERIAL			
❑ 66201	Shake a Tail Feather/ Road to Fortune	1966	12.00
❑ 66238	I Still Love You/Meat Ball	1967	12.00
JVB			
❑ 83	How Many Times/Water-Water	1957	800.00
MGM			
❑ 55011	Little Did I Dream/ Gotta Get On the Train	1955	300.00
❑ 55014	Lovely Lady/Half Angel	1955	400.00
PICO			
❑ 2801	Eternally/I Believe	1957	80.00

TWILIGHTERS, THE (3)

45s

Number	Title (A Side/B Side)	Yr	NM
CADDY			
❑ 103	Eternally/I Believe	1955	250.00

TWILIGHTERS, THE (4)

45s

Number	Title (A Side/B Side)	Yr	NM
FRATERNITY			
❑ 889	To Love in Vain/ The Beginning of Love	1961	25.00
—As "The Twi-Lighters"			

TWILIGHTERS, THE (5)

45s

Number	Title (A Side/B Side)	Yr	NM
MARSHALL			
❑ 702	Please Tell Me You're Mine/ Wondering	1953	200.00
—Black vinyl			
❑ 702	Please Tell Me You're Mine/ Wondering	1953	1000.
—Red vinyl			

TWILIGHTERS, THE (6)

45s

Number	Title (A Side/B Side)	Yr	NM
SPECIALTY			
❑ 548	It's True/Wha-Bop-Sh-Wah	1955	60.00

TWILIGHTERS, THE (7)

45s

Number	Title (A Side/B Side)	Yr	NM
SPIN			
❑ 0001	Yes You Are/A Possibility	1960	200.00

TWILIGHTERS, THE (U)

45s

Number	Title (A Side/B Side)	Yr	NM
GROOVE			
❑ 0154	Sittin' in a Corner/It's a Cold, Cold, Rainy Day	1956	60.00
—As "The Twi-Lighters"			
RICKI			
❑ 907	Help Me/Rockin' Mule	1961	40.00
SARA			
❑ 1048	Restless Love/Can't You Stay a Little Longer	1961	60.00
VANCO			
❑ 204	Out of My Mind/ I Need Your Lovin'	1968	10.00

TWILLEY, DWIGHT

12-Inch Singles

Number	Title (A Side/B Side)	Yr	NM
ARISTA			
❑ SP-79 [DJ]	Somebody to Love/Money	1979	12.00
CBS ASSOCIATED			
❑ ZAS 2360 [DJ]	Sexual (same on both sides)	1986	10.00

Except when noted otherwise, VG = 25% of NM, and VG+ = 50% of NM. (Example: VG = $2.00, VG+ = $4.00 and NM = $8.00.)

Number	Title (A Side/B Side)	Yr	NM
EMI AMERICA			
❑ SPRO-9104 [DJ]	Little Bit of Love (Edit)/Little Bit of Love (LP)	1984	8.00
45s			
ARISTA			
❑ 0278	Rock and Roll 47/Twilley Don't Mind	1977	5.00
❑ 0278 [n/a]	Rock and Roll 47/Twilley Don't Mind	1977	5.00
❑ 0299	Trying to Find My Baby/Here She Comes	1977	5.00
❑ 0311	Looking for the Magic/Invasion	1978	5.00
❑ 0415	Out of My Hands/Nothing's Ever Gonna Change So Fast	1979	4.00
❑ 0433	Runaway/Burnin' Sand	1979	4.00
❑ 0478	Somebody to Love/Money (That's What I Want)	1979	4.00
CBS ASSOCIATED			
❑ 06050	Sexual/Wild Dogs	1986	3.00
❑ 06050 [PS]	Sexual/Wild Dogs	1986	3.00
EMI AMERICA			
❑ 8109	Later That Night/Somebody to Love	1982	4.00
❑ 8115	I Found the Magic/I'm Back Again	1982	4.00
❑ 8196	Girls/To Get to You	1984	3.00
❑ 8196 [PS]	Girls/To Get to You	1984	4.00
❑ 8206	Little Bit of Love/Mad Dog	1984	3.00
❑ 8206 [PS]	Little Bit of Love/Mad Dog	1984	4.00
❑ 8235	Why You Wanna Break My Heart/Chilly D's Theme	1984	3.00
❑ 8235 [PS]	Why You Wanna Break My Heart/Chilly D's Theme	1984	3.00
PRIVATE I			
❑ 04820	Keep On Working/(Instrumental)	1985	3.00
SHELTER			
❑ 40380	I'm on Fire/Did You See What Happened	1975	5.00
❑ 40380 [PS]	I'm on Fire/Did You See What Happened	1975	10.00
❑ 40450	Sincerely/You Were So Warm	1975	5.00
❑ 40450 [PS]	Sincerely/You Were So Warm	1975	5.00
❑ 62003	Could Be Love/Feeling in the Dark	1976	5.00
❑ 62003 [PS]	Could Be Love/Feeling in the Dark	1976	8.00
THE RIGHT STUFF			
❑ S7-19563	I'm on Fire/Looking for the Magic	1997	3.00
Albums			
ARISTA			
❑ AB 4140	Twilley Don't Mind	1977	10.00
❑ AB 4214	Twilley	1979	10.00
❑ AB 4251	Blueprint	1980	—
—Unreleased			
CBS ASSOCIATED			
❑ BFZ 40266	Wild Dogs	1986	8.00
EMI AMERICA			
❑ ST-17064	Scuba Divers	1982	10.00
❑ ST-17107	Jungle	1984	10.00
MCA			
❑ 688	Sincerely	1981	8.00
—Reissue of Shelter LP			
SHELTER			
❑ SA-52001	Sincerely	1976	10.00

TWIN-TONES, THE

See THE TWINS.

TWINK

Number	Title (A Side/B Side)	Yr	NM
Albums			
SIRE			
❑ SES-97022	Think Pink	1970	100.00

TWINKLE

Number	Title (A Side/B Side)	Yr	NM
45s			
AURORA			
❑ 163	The End of the World/What Am I Doing Here with You	1966	10.00
TOLLIE			
❑ 9040	The Boy of My Dreams/Terry	1965	15.00
❑ 9047	Ain't Nobody Home But Me/Golden Lights	1965	12.00

TWINS, THE

Number	Title (A Side/B Side)	Yr	NM
45s			
LANCER			
❑ 106	Heart of Gold/Buttercup	1959	15.00
❑ 106 [PS]	Heart of Gold/Buttercup	1959	30.00
—Number not on sleeve			
RCA VICTOR			
❑ 47-7148	My Dear/The Flip Skip	1958	20.00
—As "The Twin-Tones"			
❑ 47-7235	Jo-Ann's Sister/Who Knows the Secret	1958	20.00
❑ 47-7382	Classroom Rock/Gee Whiz	1958	20.00
7-Inch Extended Plays			
RCA VICTOR			
❑ EPA-4107	Jo-Ann/Before You Go//My Dancing Lady/One Mail a Day	1957	20.00
—As "The Twin-Tones"			
❑ EPA-4107 [PS]	Jim and John The Twin-Tones	1957	20.00
❑ EPA-4237	My Dear/The Flip Skip//I Want a Girl/Together Forever	1958	20.00
❑ EPA-4237 [PS]	Teenagers Love the Twins	1958	20.00
Albums			
RCA VICTOR			
❑ LPM-1708 [M]	Teenagers Love the Twins	1958	50.00

TWISTED SISTER

Number	Title (A Side/B Side)	Yr	NM
12-Inch Singles			
ATLANTIC			
❑ PR 844 [DJ]	You Want What We Got (3:45) (same on both sides)	1985	12.00
45s			
(NO LABEL)			
❑ (no #)	Bad Boys (Of Rock 'n' Roll)/Ladys Boy	1980	12.00
❑ (no #) [PS]	Bad Boys (Of Rock 'n' Roll)/Ladys Boy	1980	12.00
ATLANTIC			
❑ 89215	Hot Love/Tonight	1987	3.00
❑ 89445	You Want What We Got/Shoot 'Em Dead	1986	3.00
❑ 89478	Leader of the Pack/I Wanna Rock	1985	3.00
❑ 89478 [PS]	Leader of the Pack/I Wanna Rock	1985	3.00
❑ 89591	The Price/S.M.F.	1985	3.00
❑ 89617	I Wanna Rock/The Kids Are Back	1984	3.00
❑ 89617 [PS]	I Wanna Rock/The Kids Are Back	1984	3.00
❑ 89641	We're Not Gonna Take It/You Can't Stop Rock 'N' Roll	1984	3.00
❑ 89641 [PS]	We're Not Gonna Take It/You Can't Stop Rock 'N' Roll	1984	3.00
Albums			
ATLANTIC			
❑ 80074	You Can't Stop Rock 'n' Roll	1983	8.00
❑ 80156	Stay Hungry	1984	8.00
❑ 81256	Under the Blade	1985	8.00
❑ 81275	Come Out and Play	1985	8.00
❑ 81772	Love Is for Suckers	1987	8.00
SECRET			
❑ SECX 9	Under the Blade	1982	12.00
—UK import			
❑ SECXP 9 [PD]	Under the Blade	1982	20.00
—UK import			
❑ SHH 13712 [EP]	Ruff Cutts	1981	15.00
—UK import			

TWISTERS, THE

Number	Title (A Side/B Side)	Yr	NM
45s			
APT			
❑ 25045	Come Go with Me/Pretty Little Girl Next Door	1960	20.00
CAMPUS			
❑ 125	Elvis Leaves Sorrento/Street Dance	1961	30.00
CAPITOL			
❑ 4451	Turn the Page/Dancing Little Clown	1960	20.00
DUAL			
❑ 502	Silly Chilli/Peppermint Twist Time	1962	12.00
FELCO			
❑ 103	Count Down 1-2-3/Speed Limit	1959	25.00
SUN-SET			
❑ 501	Please Come Back/This Is the End	1961	600.00
Albums			
TREASURE			
❑ TLP-890 [M]	Doin' the Twist	1962	30.00

TWISTIN' KINGS

Number	Title (A Side/B Side)	Yr	NM
45s			
MOTOWN			
❑ 1022	Xmas Twist/White House Twist	1961	40.00
❑ 1023	Congo (Part 1)/Congo (Part 2)	1962	40.00
Albums			
MOTOWN			
❑ M-601 [M]	Twistin' the World Around	1961	300.00

TWO CHAPS, THE

With JAY BLACK, later of JAY AND THE AMERICANS.

Number	Title (A Side/B Side)	Yr	NM
45s			
ATLANTIC			
❑ 1195	Forgive Me/No More	1958	30.00

2 LIVE CREW, THE

Number	Title (A Side/B Side)	Yr	NM
12-Inch Singles			
FRESH BEAT			
❑ FBR-001	The Revelation/2 Live "It's Gotta Be Fresh!"	1985	50.00
❑ FBR-002	What I Like (unknown versions)	1985	50.00
LIL' JOE			
❑ LJR 890	Shake a Lil' Somethin' (4 versions)	1996	7.00
❑ LJRX 891	Shake a Lil' Somethin' (7 versions)	1996	10.00
❑ LJR 893	Do the Damn Thing (4 versions)/You Should Be Dancing (Clean)/Puff Puff Give (Clean)/Stallion Strip (Clean)	1997	6.00
❑ LJR 893	Do the Wild Thing (4 versions)/(same on both sides)	1997	6.00
❑ LJR 895	Be My Private Dancer (Radio Version) (Album Version (Accapella For You Mix) (Instrumental)/Table Dance (Radio Version) (Album Version) (Accapella For You Mix) (Instrumental)	1997	8.00
❑ LJR 897	2 Live Party (7 versions)	1998	6.00
❑ LJR 899	The Real One (Explicit Version) (Clean Remix) (Extra Clean Version) (Instrumental)/Shake Your Pants (Explicit) (Clean) (Instrumental)/Album Snippets	1998	6.00
—As "The 2 Live Crew Featuring Ice-T"			
❑ LJR 902	2 Live Is Here (4 versions)/Ay Papi (4 versions)	1999	10.00
LUKE			
❑ GR 462	We Like to Chill (2 versions)/Greatest Hits Megamix	1993	6.00
❑ GR 476	Yeah, Yeah (4 versions)/Hell, Yeah (4 versions)	1994	7.00
—As "The New 2 Live Crew"			
❑ GR 481	You Go, Girl (10 versions)	1994	10.00
—As "The New 2 Live Crew"			
❑ GR 483	2 Live Freestyle (4 versions)	1994	6.00
—As "The New 2 Live Crew"			
❑ DMD 1671 [DJ]	Hangin' with the Homeboys and Dr. Feelgood (2 versions)/Vacate the Premises	1991	6.00
—As "2 Live Crew & Triple XXX"; with Vince Neil			
❑ DMD 1716 [DJ]	Pop That Pussy (4 versions)	1991	7.00
❑ DMD 1773 [DJ]	Who's Doin' Who (Clean Version) (X Rated Version)/The Caper	1991	10.00
❑ PR 3484 [DJ]	Banned in the U.S.A. (Radio Mix) (Radio Instrumental) (Black Mix) (Percapella)	1990	8.00
—As "Luke Featuring the 2 Live Crew"			
❑ PR 4389 [DJ]	Who's Doin' Who (same on both sides?)	1991	10.00
—As "Luke Featuring the 2 Live Crew"			
❑ 96216	Who's Doin' Who (2 versions)/The Caper	1991	10.00
❑ 96291	Pop That Pussy (LP Version Explicit)/Pop That Coochie (Clean) (Remix)/Mega Mix V	1991	6.00
❑ 96398	Do the Bart (Clean LP) (Clean Remix) (Explicit)/Face Down A— Up/Face Down A—Up (Live in Concert)	1990	10.00
—As "Luke Featuring The 2 Live Crew"			
❑ 96416	Mama Juanita (5 versions)	1990	10.00
—As "Luke Featuring The 2 Live Crew"			
❑ 96440	Banned in the U.S.A. (Radio Mix) (Radio Instrumental) (Black Mix) (Percapella)	1990	10.00
—As "Luke Featuring The 2 Live Crew"			
LUKE SKYYWALKER			
❑ GR 105	Get It Girl (2 versions)/Cut It Up	1988	15.00
❑ GR 112	Move Somethin' (Clean Version) (XXX-Rated Mix)	1988	15.00
❑ GR 113	We Want Some P*ssy (3 versions)	1988	15.00
❑ GR 117	Do Wah Diddy (Remix Radio)/I Can't Go for That	1988	8.00
❑ GR 125	The Bomb Has Dropped/One and One	1989	12.00
—With Trouble Funk			
❑ GR 127	Me So Horny (Clean Version) (Nasty Version)/Get the F**k Out of My House (Nasty Acid Mix) (Nasty Piano Mix) (Nasty LP Version)	1989	12.00

T

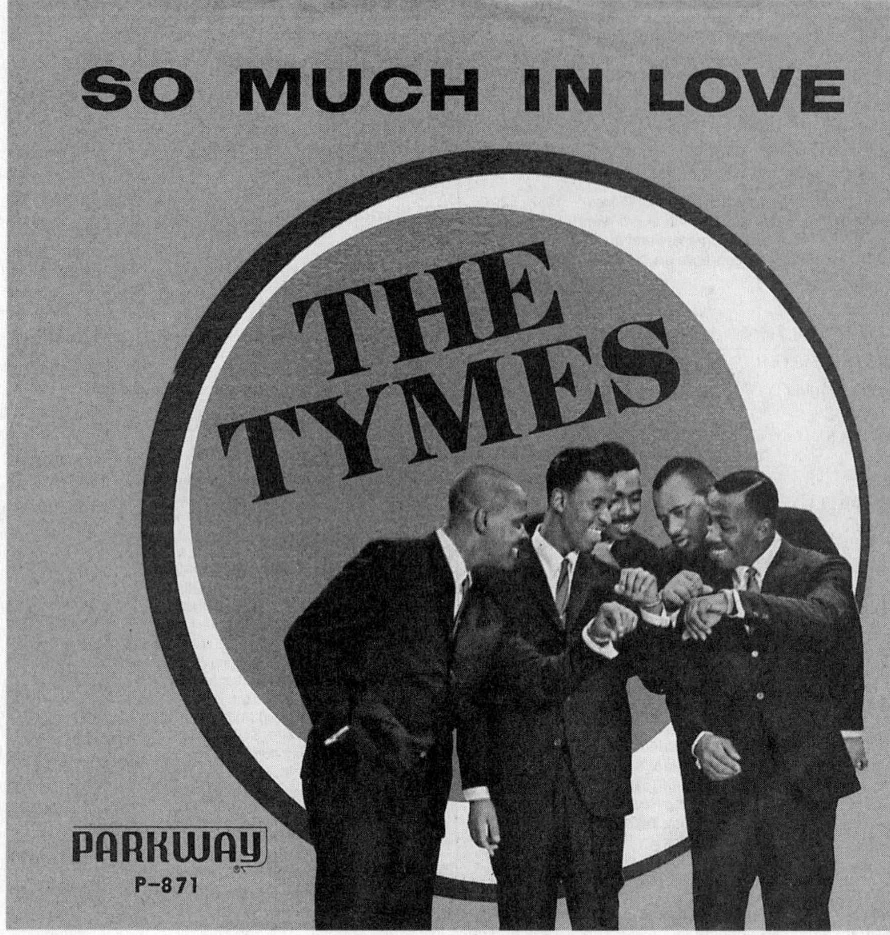

The Tymes, "So Much in Love," Parkway 871, 1963, **$30.**

Number	Title (A Side/B Side)	Yr	NM
❑ GR 133	We Want Some Pussy ('89 House Mix 6:34) (Classic Dance Mix 2:53) (Liberty City Long Hard Mix 6:40) (Live In Concert Version 3:00)	1990	15.00
MACOLA			
❑ MRC-1014	The Revelation/What I Like	1985	30.00
SKYYWALKER			
❑ GR 137	C'mon Babe (Radio Mix) (Extended Bass Mix) (Doodoo Brown Mix)/If You Believe In Having Sex	1990	10.00
❑ GR 144	European Ultimix (10:32)/The Funk Shop (Radio)/The F*ck Shop (Nasty)	1990	12.00
WTG			
❑ PAS 1462 [DJ]	Yakety Yak (Dirty House Mix) (7" Radio Mix) (House Version) (Street Mix) (Bass Mix) (Bonus Beats)	1988	8.00
❑ 45-68168	Yakety Yak (Bass Mix) (Dirty House Mix) (House Version) (7" Radio Mix)	1988	10.00
45s			
LUKE			
❑ 98915	Banned in the U.S.A./ (Instrumental)	1990	5.00
—As "Luke Featuring The 2 Live Crew"			
LUKE SKYYWALKER			
❑ LS-104 [DJ]	Move Somethin'/(Dirty Version)	1988	10.00
❑ LS-110 [DJ]	The Bomb Has Dropped (same on both sides)	1989	10.00
❑ LS-113 [DJ]	Me So Horny (same on both sides)	1989	15.00
WTG			
❑ 31-68491	Yakety Yak/(B-side unknown)	1988	4.00
Albums			
EFFECT			
❑ E 3003	Live in Concert	1990	10.00
LIL' JOE			
❑ XR-215 [(2)]	Shake a Lil' Somethin'	1996	15.00
❑ XR-227 [(2)]	The 2 Live Crew Goes to the Movies — A Decade of Hits	1997	12.00
❑ XR-231 [(2)]	The Real One	1998	12.00
❑ XR-238 [(2)]	Greatest Hits Vol. 2	1999	15.00
❑ XR- 239 [(2)]	Greatest Hits Vol. 2/Edit	1999	15.00
❑ 264 [(2)]	Private Personal Parts	2000	12.00
❑ 286 [(2)]	Essential DJ 12" and Mega Mixes	2002	10.00
LUKE			
❑ 122 [(2)]	Greatest Hits	1992	20.00
❑ 123 [(2)]	Greatest Hits/Edit	1992	20.00
❑ 207 [(2)]	Back at Your Ass for the Nine-4	1994	20.00
—As "The New 2 Live Crew"			
❑ 208 [(2)]	Back At You for '94	1994	20.00
—As "The New 2 Live Crew"; edited version			
❑ DMD 1760 [(2)]	Sports Weekend (As Nasty As They Wanna Be Part II)	1991	15.00
—Promo-only vinyl issue in generic black cardboard sleeve			
❑ 91424	Banned in the U.S.A.	1990	15.00
—As "Luke Featuring The 2 Live Crew"			
LUKE SKYYWALKER			
❑ XR-100	The 2 Live Crew "Is What We Are"	1987	15.00
❑ XR-101	Move Somethin'	1988	12.00
❑ XR-107 [(2)]	As Nasty As They Wanna Be	1989	15.00
❑ XR- 108	As Clean As They Wanna Be	1989	15.00

2 OF CLUBS

Number	Title (A Side/B Side)	Yr	NM
45s			
FRATERNITY			
❑ F972	Heart/My First Heartbreak	1966	10.00
❑ F975	Walk Tall/So Blue Is Fall	1966	12.00
❑ F975	Walk Tall Like a Man/ So Blue Is Fall	1966	15.00
❑ F990	Let Me Walk with You/ You Love Me	1967	10.00
❑ F994	River Deep — Mountain High/ You Love Me	1967	15.00
❑ F999	Look Away/(B-side unknown)	1967	15.00

TWO OF US, THE

Number	Title (A Side/B Side)	Yr	NM
45s			
CAMEO			
❑ 390	We'll Build a New World/ Get Together	1965	12.00

TWO PEOPLE

Number	Title (A Side/B Side)	Yr	NM
45s			
A&M			
❑ 776	Barbara/Everybody's Talkin'	1965	15.00
LIBERTY			
❑ 55841	Knock on Wood/Two of Us	1965	15.00
❑ 55870	Me and My Shadow/Uphill Climb to the Bottom	1966	15.00
❑ 55896	Love Isn't Tears Only/ We Don't Do That Anymore	1966	15.00
❑ 55916	I Really Don't Want to Know/ You're Gonna Hurt Me	1966	15.00
REVUE			
❑ 11033	Stop, Leave My Heart Alone/ Love Dust	1969	150.00

TYLER, FRANKIE See FRANKIE VALLI.

TYLER, JOEY

Number	Title (A Side/B Side)	Yr	NM
45s			
REPRISE			
❑ 0269	All the Good Times Are Over/ When You Got Nothin' Else, You Got the Blues	1964	10.00

TYLER, KIP

Number	Title (A Side/B Side)	Yr	NM
45s			
CHALLENGE			
❑ 1014	She Got Eyes/Shadow Street	1957	30.00
❑ 59008	Jungle Hop/Ooh Yeah Baby	1958	40.00
EBB			
❑ 154	She's My Witch/Rumble Rock	1959	50.00
❑ 156	Oh Linda/Kali Lou	1959	50.00
GYRO DISC			
❑ 711	Surfer's Lament (Eternity)/ Toledo	1963	50.00
❑ 711 [PS]	Surfer's Lament (Eternity)/ Toledo	1963	100.00
IMPERIAL			
❑ 5641	Rocket 'Round the Universe/ The Goblin Trot	1960	30.00

TYLER, WILLIE, AND LESTER

Number	Title (A Side/B Side)	Yr	NM
Albums			
TAMLA			
❑ TM-265 [M]	Hello Dummy	1965	200.00

TYMES, THE

Number	Title (A Side/B Side)	Yr	NM
12-Inch Singles			
RCA			
❑ PD-11068	How Am I to Know/ I'll Take You There	1977	12.00
45s			
CAPITOL			
❑ 3440	When I Look Around Me/ Smile a Tender Smile	1972	6.00
COLUMBIA			
❑ 44630	People/For Love of Ivy	1968	8.00
❑ 44799	God Bless the Child/The Love That You're Looking For	1969	6.00
❑ 44917	Find My Way/If You Love Me Baby	1969	6.00
❑ 45078	Love Child/Most Beautiful Married Lady	1970	6.00
❑ 45336	She's Gone/Someone to Watch Over Me	1971	6.00
MGM			
❑ 13536	Pretend/Street Talk	1966	20.00
❑ 13631	(Touch of) Baby/What Would I Do	1966	20.00
PARKWAY			
❑ 871	So Much in Love/Roscoe James McClain	1963	15.00
❑ 871	So in Love/Roscoe James McClain	1963	25.00
—Original title of A-side			
❑ 871 [PS]	So Much in Love/Roscoe James McClain	1963	30.00
❑ 884	Wonderful! Wonderful!/ Come with Me to the Sea	1963	15.00
❑ 884 [PS]	Wonderful! Wonderful!/ Come with Me to the Sea	1963	25.00
❑ 891	Somewhere/View from My Window	1963	15.00
❑ 891 [PS]	Somewhere/View from My Window	1963	25.00

 Except when noted otherwise, VG = 25% of NM, and VG+ = 50% of NM. (Example: VG = $2.00, VG+ = $4.00 and NM = $8.00.)

Number	Title (A Side/B Side)	Yr	NM
❑ 908	To Each His Own/Wonderland of Love	1964	15.00
❑ 908 [PS]	To Each His Own/Wonderland of Love	1964	25.00
❑ 919	The Magic of Our Summer Love/With All My Heart	1964	15.00
❑ 919 [PS]	The Magic of Our Summer Love/With All My Heart	1964	25.00
❑ 924	Here She Comes/Malibu	1964	15.00
❑ 924 [PS]	Here She Comes/Malibu	1964	25.00
❑ 933	The Twelfth of Never/Here She Comes	1964	15.00
❑ 7039	Isle of Love/I'm Always Chasing Rainbows	1964	15.00
—Included as a bonus with album 7039			
RCA			
❑ PB-10862	Love's Illusion/Savannah Sunny Sunday	1976	4.00
❑ PB-11136	I'll Take You There/How Am I to Know (The Things a Girl in Love Should Know)	1977	4.00
❑ GB-12082	You Little Trustmaker/Ms. Grace	1980	—
—Unreleased?			
RCA VICTOR			
❑ PB-10022	You Little Trustmaker/The North Hills	1974	5.00
❑ PB-10128	Ms. Grace/The Crutch	1974	4.00
❑ PB-10244	Interloop/Someday, Somehow I'm Keeping You	1975	4.00
❑ PB-10422	God's Gonna Punish You/If I Can't Make You Smile	1975	4.00
❑ GB-10493	You Little Trustmaker/The North Hills	1975	4.00
—Gold Standard Series			
❑ PB-10561	Good Morning Dear Lord/It's Cool	1976	4.00
❑ PB-10713	Goin' Through the Motions/Only Your Love	1976	4.00
WINCHESTER			
❑ 1002	These Foolish Things (Remind Me of You)/This Time It's Love	1967	10.00
Albums			
ABKCO			
❑ 4228	The Best of Tymes	1973	12.00
COLUMBIA			
❑ CS 9778	People	1969	15.00
PARKWAY			
❑ P 7032 [M]	So Much in Love	1963	40.00
—With group standing in front-cover photo			
❑ P 7032 [M]	So Much in Love	1963	200.00
—With head-and-shoulders group photo on front cover			
❑ P 7038 [M]	The Sound of the Wonderful Tymes	1963	40.00
❑ SP 7038 [S]	The Sound of the Wonderful Tymes	1963	50.00
❑ P 7039 [M]	Somewhere	1964	50.00
—Includes bonus single 7039 (deduct 20 percent if missing)			
❑ P 7049 [M]	18 Greatest Hits	1964	40.00
RCA VICTOR			
❑ APL1-0727	Trustmaker	1974	12.00
❑ APL1-1835	Turning Point	1976	12.00
❑ APL1-2406	Diggin' Their Roots	1977	12.00

TYNER, MCCOY

Number	Title (A Side/B Side)	Yr	NM
45s			
COLUMBIA			
❑ 03151	Island Birdie/Love Surrounds Us Everywhere	1982	4.00
IMPULSE!			
❑ 240	Duke's Place/Searchin'	1965	8.00
MILESTONE			
❑ 304	Rotunda/For Tomorrow	197?	5.00
Albums			
ABC IMPULSE!			
❑ AS-18	Inception	1968	12.00
❑ AS-33	Reaching Fourth	1968	12.00
❑ AS-39	Nights of Ballads and Blues	1968	12.00
❑ AS-48	McCoy Tyner Live at Newport	1968	12.00
❑ AS-63	Today and Tomorrow	1968	12.00
❑ AS-79	McCoy Tyner Plays Duke Ellington	1968	12.00
❑ IA-9235 [(2)]	Reevaluation: The Impulse! Years	197?	15.00
❑ IA-9338 [(2)]	Early Trios	1978	15.00
BLUE NOTE			
❑ BN-LA022-F	Extensions	1973	15.00
❑ BN-LA223-G	Asante	1974	15.00
❑ BLP-4264 [M]	The Real McCoy	1967	25.00
❑ BLP-84264	The Real McCoy	1987	10.00
—"The Finest in Jazz Since 1939" label			
❑ BST-84264	The Real McCoy	1970	12.00
—With United Artists distribution			
❑ BST-84264 [S]	The Real McCoy	1967	20.00
—With "A Division of Liberty Records" on label			
❑ BST-84275	Tender Moments	1968	20.00
—With "A Division of Liberty Records" on label			
❑ BST-84275	Tender Moments	1970	12.00
—With United Artists distribution			
❑ BST-84275	Tender Moments	1985	10.00
—"The Finest in Jazz Since 1939" label			
❑ BLP-84307	Time for Tyner	1987	10.00
—"The Finest in Jazz Since 1939" label			
❑ BST-84307	Time for Tyner	1969	20.00
—With "A Division of Liberty Records" on label			
❑ BST-84338	Expansions	1969	20.00
—With "A Division of Liberty Records" on label			
❑ BST-84338	Expansions	1970	12.00
—With United Artists distribution			
❑ BST-84338	Expansions	1984	10.00
—"The Finest in Jazz Since 1939" label			
❑ B1-91651	Revelations	1989	12.00
COLUMBIA			
❑ FC 37375	La Leyenda de la Hora (The Legend of the Hour)	1981	10.00
❑ FC 38053	Looking Out	1982	10.00
ELEKTRA/MUSICIAN			
❑ 60350	Dimensions	1984	10.00
FANTASY			
❑ OJC-311	Sahara	1988	10.00
—Reissue of Milestone 9039			
❑ OJC-313	Song for My Lady	1988	10.00
—Reissue of Milestone 9044			
❑ OJC-618	Song of the New World	1991	10.00
—Reissue of Milestone 9049			
❑ OJC-650	Echoes of a Friend	1991	10.00
—Reissue of Milestone 9055			
GRP/IMPULSE!			
❑ 216	McCoy Tyner Plays Duke Ellington	1997	20.00
—Reissue on audiophile vinyl			
❑ 220	Inception	1997	20.00
—Reissue on audiophile vinyl			
❑ 221	Nights of Ballads and Blues	1997	20.00
—Reissue on audiophile vinyl			
IMPULSE!			
❑ A-18 [M]	Inception	1962	25.00
❑ AS-18 [S]	Inception	1962	25.00
❑ A-33 [M]	Reaching Fourth	1963	25.00
❑ AS-33 [S]	Reaching Fourth	1963	25.00
❑ A-39 [M]	Nights of Ballads and Blues	1963	25.00
❑ AS-39 [S]	Nights of Ballads and Blues	1963	25.00
❑ A-48 [M]	McCoy Tyner Live at Newport	1963	25.00
❑ AS-48 [S]	McCoy Tyner Live at Newport	1963	25.00
❑ A-63 [M]	Today and Tomorrow	1964	25.00
❑ AS-63 [S]	Today and Tomorrow	1964	25.00
❑ A-79 [M]	McCoy Tyner Plays Duke Ellington	1965	25.00
❑ AS-79 [S]	McCoy Tyner Plays Duke Ellington	1965	25.00
MCA			
❑ 4126 [(2)]	Great Moments with McCoy Tyner	1981	12.00
❑ 4156 [(2)]	Reevaluation: The Impulse Years	1981	12.00
—Reissue of Impulse! 9235			
❑ 4157 [(2)]	Early Trios	1981	12.00
—Reissue of Impulse! 9338			
MILESTONE			
❑ FPM-4006 [Q]	Song of the New World	197?	20.00
❑ 9039	Sahara	197?	10.00
❑ 9044	Song for My Lady	197?	10.00
❑ 9049	Song of the New World	197?	10.00
❑ 9055	Echoes of a Friend	1974	10.00
❑ 9056	Sama Layuca	1974	10.00
❑ 9063	Trident	1975	10.00
❑ 9067	Fly with the Wind	1976	10.00
❑ 9072	Focal Point	1977	10.00
❑ 9079	Inner Voices	1978	10.00
❑ 9085	The Greeting	1978	10.00
❑ 9087	Together	1979	10.00
❑ 9091	Passion Dance	1979	10.00
❑ 9094	Horizon	1980	10.00
❑ 9102	13th House	1981	10.00
❑ 9167	Uptown/Downtown	1988	10.00
❑ M-47062	Reflections	1981	10.00
❑ 55001 [(2)]	Enlightenment	1973	12.00
❑ 55002 [(2)]	Atlantis	1975	12.00
❑ 55003 [(2)]	Supertrios	1977	12.00
❑ 55007 [(2)]	4 x 4	1980	12.00
PALO ALTO			
❑ PA-8083	Just Feelin'	1985	10.00
PAUSA			
❑ 9007	Time for Tyner	198?	8.00
—Reissue of Blue Note 84307			
QUICKSILVER			
❑ QS-4010	Just Feelin'	1990	10.00
—Reissue of Palo Alto LP			
TIMELESS			
❑ SJP-260	Bon Voyage	1990	10.00

TYRANNOSAURUS REX

See T. REX.

TYRELL, DANNY, AND THE CLEESHAYS

Number	Title (A Side/B Side)	Yr	NM
45s			
EASTMAN			
❑ 784	You're Only Seventeen/Let's Walk, Let's Talk	1958	40.00

TYSON, ROY

Number	Title (A Side/B Side)	Yr	NM
45s			
DOUBLE L			
❑ 723	Oh What a Night for Love/Not Too Young	1963	80.00
❑ 733	The Girl I Love/I Want to Be Your Boyfriend	1964	100.00

U

U.K.

Prog rock supergroup.

Number	Title (A Side/B Side)	Yr	NM
45s			
POLYDOR			
❑ 2028	Rendenvous/When Will You Realize	1980	5.00
❑ 14491	In the Dead of Night/Mental Medication	1978	5.00
❑ 14551	Nothing to Lose/In the Dead of Night	1979	5.00
Albums			
POLYDOR			
❑ PD-1-6146	U.K.	1978	10.00
❑ PD-1-6194	Danger Money	1979	10.00
❑ PD-1-6234	Night After Night	1979	10.00

U.K.'S, THE

Number	Title (A Side/B Side)	Yr	NM
45s			
CAMEO			
❑ 342	Ever Faithful Ever True/Your Love Is All I Want	1965	20.00

U-MEN

Number	Title (A Side/B Side)	Yr	NM
45s			
AMPHETAMINE REPTILE			
❑ Scale 8	Freezebomb/That's Wild About Jack	1988	25.00
❑ Scale 8 [PS]	Freezebomb/That's Wild About Jack	1988	20.00
—Second sleeve has white heavy paper			
❑ Scale 8 [PS]	Freezebomb/That's Wild About Jack	1988	25.00
—First sleeve has gray heavy paper			
BLACK LABEL			
❑ BLR 001	Solid Action/Dig It a Hole	1987	8.00
❑ BLR 001 [PS]	Solid Action/Dig It a Hole	1987	8.00
—Second sleeve has black title			
❑ BLR 001 [PS]	Solid Action/Dig It a Hole	1987	20.00
—First sleeve has silver title			
7-Inch Extended Plays			
BOMBSHELTER			
❑ SPY 007	Blight/Flowers DGIH//Shoot 'Em Down/Gila	1984	50.00
❑ SPY 007 [PS]	Blight/Flowers DGIH//Shoot 'Em Down/Gila	1984	50.00
Albums			
BLACK LABEL			
❑ BLR 002	Step on a Bug The Red Toad Speaks	1988	12.00
HOMESTEAD			
❑ HMS 024 [EP]	Stop Spinning	1985	12.00

U.S. 1

Number	Title (A Side/B Side)	Yr	NM
45s			
PRIVATE STOCK			
❑ 45,045	Bye Bye Baby/Creation	1975	6.00

U2

Number	Title (A Side/B Side)	Yr	NM
10-Inch Singles			
ISLAND			
❑ PR12 6804 [DJ]	Lemon (Bad Yard Club 8:35)/Lemon (Serious Def Dub 6:33)	1993	50.00
—Promo-only 10-inch single on yellow vinyl			
❑ PR126804 [DJ]	Lemon (Bad Yard Dub)/Lemon (Serious Def Dub)	1993	50.00
—Promo-only 10-inch single on yellow vinyl			

U.K., *U.K.*, Polydor PD-1-6146, 1978, **$10.**

Number	Title (A Side/B Side)	Yr	NM
12-Inch Singles			
INTERSCOPE			
❑ INTR-10254-1 [DJ]	Beautiful Day (Perfecto Vocal Mix) (Quincey & Sonance Mix)	2000	20.00
❑ INTR-10428-1 [DJ]	Elevation (Escalation Mix 7:04) (Influx Mix 4:02) (Quincey & Sonance Mix 6:53)	2001	20.00
❑ 562972-1	Beautiful Day (same on both sides)	2000	20.00
ISLAND			
❑ PR 582 [DJ]	I Will Follow (Live) (same on both sides)	1983	80.00
❑ DMD 604 [DJ]	New Year's Day (same on both sides)	1983	25.00
—This version has a few extra beats in the long instrumental break that aren't on any other known version of the song			
❑ PR 635 [DJ]	(Pride) In the Name of Love (same on both sides)	1984	20.00
—Note that the parentheses in the title are in the wrong place			
❑ DMD 643 [DJ]	Two Hearts Beat As One (5:57)/ /(Album Version) (Edit)	1983	25.00
❑ PR 675 [DJ]	Wire (same on both sides)	1984	50.00
❑ PR 701 [DJ]	A Sort of Homecoming (same on both sides)	1984	40.00
❑ PR 774 [DJ]	Bad (Live) (same on both sides)	1985	100.00
❑ PRO-A2-940 RE-1 [DJ]	I Will Follow/Night Train	1980	100.00
—B-side by Steve Winwood			
❑ PR 1021 [DJ]	With or Without You (same on both sides)	1987	20.00
❑ DMD 1258 [DJ]	Desire (2:59) (The Hollywood Remix 5:58)/Hallelujah Here She Comes	1988	20.00
❑ DMD 1269 [DJ]	Angel of Harlem/A Room at the Heartbreak Hotel/Love Rescue Me (Live)	1988	20.00
❑ DMD 1310 [DJ]	When Love Comes to Town (7:30) (3:30)/God Part II/ Dancing Barefoot	1989	20.00
❑ DMD 1324 [DJ]	When Love Comes to Town (Live from the Kingdom Club Mix) (same on both sides)	1989	30.00
❑ DMD 1349 [DJ]	All I Want Is You/Unchained Melody/Everlasting Love	1989	15.00
❑ 2499 [DJ]	Desire (same on both sides)	1988	10.00
❑ PR 2499 [DJ]	Desire (same on both sides)	1988	15.00
❑ PR12 6701 [DJ]	Mysterious Ways (The Perfecto Mix) (Ultimatum Mix) (Apollo 440 Magic Hour Remix) (Solar Plexus Extended Club Mix) (Tabla Motown Remix)	1991	25.00
❑ PR12 6715 [DJ]	Zoo Station/Lady with the Spinning Head (LP Version) (Extended Dance Mix)	1992	100.00
—Promo-only picture disc in plastic sleeve			
❑ PR12 6784 [DJ]	Numb (same on both sides)	1993	40.00
—Test pressing; no label name on label, but the number is there			
❑ PR126784 [DJ]	Numb (same on both sides)	1993	40.00
—No label name on label			
❑ PR12 7345 [(3)DJ]	Discotheque (Album Version?) (David Holmes Mix) (DM Deep Extended Club Mix) (DM Deep Beats Mix) (DM TEC Radio Mix) (DM Deep Instrumental Mix) (Howie B, Hairy B Mix) (Hexidecimal Mix)	1997	30.00
❑ PR12 7398 [DJ]	Discotheque (DM Deep Club Mix 6:58) (DM Tec Club Mix 7:20)	1997	60.00
❑ PR12 7463 [DJ]	Staring at the Sun (Monster Truck Mix) (Lab Rat Mix) (Sad Bastards Mix)	1997	20.00
❑ PR12 7822 [DJ]	Mofo (Mother's Mix) (House Flavor Mix)/If God Will Send His Angels (Big Yam)	1997	20.00
❑ 96550	All I Want Is You//Unchained Melody/Everlasting Love	1988	10.00
❑ 96570	When Love Comes to Town/ Dancing Barefoot/When Love Comes to Town (Live from the Kingdom Mix)/God Part II (The Hard Metal Dance Mix)	1989	20.00
❑ 96590	Angel of Harlem/A Room at the Heartbreak Hotel/Love Rescue Me (Live)	1988	10.00
❑ 96600	Desire (2:59) (The Hollywood Remix 5:58)/Hallelujah Here She Comes	1988	10.00
❑ 96740	Where the Streets Have No Name/Race Against Time/ Silver and Gold/ Sweetest Thing	1987	15.00
❑ 96757	I Still Haven't Found What I'm Looking For//Spanish Eyes/ Deep in the Heart	1987	12.00
❑ 96786	With or Without You//Luminous Times (Hold On to Love)/ Walk to the Water	1987	15.00
❑ 854789-1	Discotheque (DM Deep Club Mix) (Hexidecimal Mix) (DM Deep Instrumental Mix) (Radio Edit)	1997	8.00
❑ 862957-1	Lemon (Bad Yard Club 10:13) (Version Dub 6:35) (Momo's Reprise 4:08) (Perfecto Mix 8:56) (Jeep Mix 5:30)	1993	30.00
—Yellow vinyl			
❑ 864281-1	Even Better Than the Real Thing (The Perfecto Mix) (Sexy Dub Mix)/(Apollo 440 Stealth Sonic Remix) (V16 Exit Wound Remix) (A440 vs. U2 Instrumental Remix)	1992	12.00
❑ 864521-1	Who's Gonna Ride Your Wild Horses (The Temple Bar Edit) (The Temple Bar Remix)/ Paint It, Black/Fortunate Son	1992	15.00
❑ 866189-1	Mysterious Ways (LP Version) (Solar Plexus Extended Club Mix) (Apollo 440 Magic Hour Remix) (Tabla Motown Remix) (Solar Plexus Club Mix)	1991	8.00
❑ 866533-1	One//Lady with the Spinning Head/Satellite of Love	1992	15.00
❑ 866977-1	Even Better Than the Real Thing/Salome/Where Did It All Go Wrong (Demo)/Lady with the Spinning Head (Extended Dance Mix)	1992	10.00
❑ 868885-1	The Fly/Alex Descends Into Hell for a Glass of Milk-Korova 1/The Lounge Fly Mix	1991	10.00
45s			
INTERSCOPE			
❑ B0003580-21	Vertigo (same on both sides)	2004	5.00
—Approximately 1,000 were made; both sides have custom labels			
ISLAND			
❑ PR 564 [DJ]	I Will Follow (Mini LP Cut)/ (Special Remix for Radio)	1983	50.00
❑ 49716	I Will Follow/Out of Control (Live)	1980	20.00
❑ 49716 [PS]	I Will Follow/Out of Control (Live)	1980	25.00
❑ 49716 [PS]	I Will Follow/Out of Control (Live)	1980	60.00
—Promo-only poster sleeve with tour dates			
❑ 94961	With or Without You/ In God's Country	1988	5.00
—Gold label "Revival of the Fittest: series			
❑ 94974	Gloria/Sunday Bloody Sunday	1987	6.00
—Gold label "Revival of the Fittest: series; only U.S. 45 release for either track; "Sunday Bloody Sunday" has a unique edit			
❑ 94975	New Year's Day/Two Hearts Beat As One	1987	6.00
—Gold label "Revival of the Fittest" series			
❑ 94976	I Will Follow/Pride" (In the Name of Love)	1987	6.00
—Gold label "Revival of the Fittest: series			
❑ 99199	All I Want Is You/ Unchained Melody	1989	4.00
❑ 99199 [PS]	All I Want Is You/ Unchained Melody	1989	4.00
❑ 99225	When Love Comes to Town/ Dancing Barefoot	1989	3.00
—A-side with B.B. King			
❑ 99225 [PS]	When Love Comes to Town/ Dancing Barefoot	1989	3.00
❑ 99250	Desire/Hallelujah Here She Comes	1988	3.00
❑ 99250 [PS]	Desire/Hallelujah Here She Comes	1988	3.00
—Standard paper sleeve			
❑ 99250 [PS]	Desire/Hallelujah Here She Comes	1988	6.00
—Cardboard gatefold sleeve			
❑ 99254	Angel of Harlem/A Room at the Heartbreak Hotel	1988	3.00
❑ 99254 [PS]	Angel of Harlem/A Room at the Heartbreak Hotel	1988	3.00
❑ 99384	In God's Country/ Bullet the Blue Sky	1988	5.00
—Black label jukebox pressing; both sides play at 45 rpm			

Except when noted otherwise, VG = 25% of NM, and VG+ = 50% of NM. (Example: VG = $2.00, VG+ = $4.00 and NM = $8.00.)

Number	Title (A Side/B Side)	Yr	NM
❑ 99385	In God's Country//Bullet the Blue Sky/Running to Stand Still	1988	4.00
—A-side plays at 45 rpm, B-side at 33 1/3 rpm			
❑ 99385 [PS]	In God's Country//Bullet the Blue Sky/Running to Stand Still	1988	4.00
—Cardboard sleeve			
❑ 99385 [PS]	In God's Country//Bullet the Blue Sky/Running to Stand Still	1988	4.00
—Paper sleeve			
❑ 99407	Where the Streets Have No Name/Silver and Gold	1987	6.00
—Black label jukebox pressing; both sides play at 45 rpm			
❑ 99408	Where the Streets Have No Name//Silver and Gold/Sweetest Thing	1987	3.00
—A-side plays at 45 rpm, B-side at 33 1/3 rpm			
❑ 99408 [PS]	Where the Streets Have No Name//Silver and Gold/Sweetest Thing	1987	3.00
—Paper sleeve			
❑ 99408 [PS]	Where the Streets Have No Name//Silver and Gold/Sweetest Thing	1987	4.00
—Cardboard sleeve			
❑ 99430	I Still Haven't Found What I'm Looking For//Spanish Eyes/Deep in the Heart	1987	3.00
—A-side plays at 45 rpm, B-side at 33 1/3 rpm			
❑ 99430 [PS]	I Still Haven't Found What I'm Looking For//Spanish Eyes/Deep in the Heart	1987	3.00
—Paper sleeve			
❑ 99430 [PS]	I Still Haven't Found What I'm Looking For//Spanish Eyes/Deep in the Heart	1987	4.00
—Cardboard sleeve			
❑ 99431	I Still Haven't Found What I'm Looking For/Spanish Eyes	1987	12.00
—Black label jukebox pressing; both sides play at 45 rpm			
❑ 99453	With or Without You/Walk on the Water	1987	20.00
—White label jukebox pressing, both sides play at 45 rpm			
❑ 99469	With or Without You//Luminous Times (Hold On to Love)/Walk on the Water	1987	3.00
—A-side plays at 45 rpm, B-side at 33 1/3 rpm			
❑ 99469 [PS]	With or Without You//Luminous Times (Hold On to Love)/Walk on the Water	1987	3.00
—Paper sleeve			
❑ 99469 [PS]	With or Without You//Luminous Times (Hold On to Love)/Walk on the Water	1987	4.00
—Cardboard sleeve			
❑ 99704	Pride (In the Name of Love)/Boomerang II	1984	5.00
❑ 99704 [PS]	Pride (In the Name of Love)/Boomerang	1984	5.00
❑ 99789	I Will Follow (Live)/Two Hearts Beat as One (Live)	1983	6.00
❑ 99861	Two Hearts Beat as One/Endless Deep	1983	8.00
❑ 99861 [PS]	Two Hearts Beat as One/Endless Deep	1983	8.00
❑ 99915	New Year's Day/Treasure (Whatever Happened to Pete the Chop?)	1983	8.00
❑ 854774-7	Discotheque/Holy Joe (Garage Mix)	1997	5.00
❑ 854972-7	Staring at the Sun/North and South of the River	1997	4.00
ISLAND/CAPITOL			
❑ 858076-7	Stay (Faraway, So Close!)/I've Got You Under My Skin	1994	5.00
—B-side: Frank Sinatra and Bono			
❑ 858076-7 [PS]	Stay (Faraway, So Close!)/I've Got You Under My Skin	1994	6.00
—B-side: Frank Sinatra and Bono			
Albums			
INTERSCOPE			
❑ 1263001	No Line on the Horizon	2009	30.00
ISLAND			
❑ PR 2049 [DJ]	The Joshua Tree Interview... Their Words and Music	1987	40.00
❑ PR12 7545-1 [(2)]	PopMart Sampler	1997	50.00
—Promo-only 8-song collection of old and new U2 material			
❑ ILPS 9646	Boy	1980	15.00
❑ ILPS 9680	October	1981	12.00
—Back cover has engineering credits, etc., in upper left			
❑ ILPS 9680	October	1981	15.00
—Back cover is blank (no engineering credits, etc.) in upper left			
❑ 90040	Boy	1983	8.00
—Third pressings have black labels			
❑ 90040	Boy	1983	12.00
—Reissue; first pressings have dark purple labels			
❑ 90040	Boy	1983	10.00
—Second pressings have light blue labels			

U2, *The Unforgettable Fire*, Island 90231, 1984, **$10.**

Number	Title (A Side/B Side)	Yr	NM
❑ 90067	War	1983	8.00
—Third pressings have black labels			
❑ 90067	War	1983	10.00
—Second pressings have light blue labels			
❑ 90067	War	1983	12.00
—Original pressings have dark purple labels			
❑ 90092	October	1983	8.00
—Third pressings have black labels			
❑ 90092	October	1983	10.00
—Second pressings have light blue labels			
❑ 90092	October	1983	10.00
—Reissue; first pressings have dark purple labels			
❑ 90127-1-B [EP]	Under a Blood Red Sky	1983	15.00
—White labels with "Mini LP" logo; with version of "The Electric Co." in which Bono sings snippets of "A-Me-Ri-Ca" from West Side Story and "Send In The Clowns" during the instrumental break.			
❑ 90127-1-B [EP]	Under a Blood Red Sky	1983	10.00
—White labels with "Mini LP" logo; edited version of "The Electric Co."			
❑ 90231	The Unforgettable Fire	1984	10.00
❑ 90279-1-A [EP]	Wide Awake in America	1985	10.00
❑ 90581	The Joshua Tree	1987	10.00
—With lyric sheet			
❑ 91003 [(2)]	Rattle and Hum	1988	15.00
❑ R 114632	October	1983	12.00
—RCA Music Service edition			
❑ R 124619	War	1983	12.00
—BMG Direct Marketing edition			
❑ R 140642 [EP]	Wide Awake in America	1985	12.00
—RCA Music Service edition			
❑ R 144636	Boy	1983	12.00
—RCA Music Service edition			
❑ R 153501	The Joshua Tree	1987	12.00
—RCA Music Service edition; no lyric sheet			
❑ R 153598 [EP]	Under a Blood Red Sky	1983	10.00
—BMG Direct Marketing edition			
❑ R 154515	The Unforgettable Fire	1985	12.00
—RCA Music Service edition			
❑ R 200596 [(2)]	Rattle and Hum	1988	15.00
—BMG Direct Marketing edition			
❑ 510347-1	Achtung Baby	1991	40.00
—U.S. LP covers are uncensored (Adam Clayton appears naked without any "X" or shamrock over his appendage)			
❑ 518047-1	Zooropa	1993	25.00
—All "U.S." copies actually are British imports			
❑ 524334-1 [(2)]	Pop	1997	20.00
❑ 811148-1	War	1990	8.00
—Reissue; sticker with new number placed over bar code of leftover 90067 pressings			
❑ 818008-1 [EP]	Under a Blood Red Sky	1990	8.00
—Reissue; sticker with new number placed over bar code of leftover 90127 pressings			
❑ 822898-1	The Unforgettable Fire	1990	8.00
—Reissue; new sticker placed on leftover Island/Atco pressings			
❑ 842296-1	Boy	1990	8.00
—Reissue; sticker with new number placed over bar code of leftover 90040 pressings			
❑ 842297-1	October	1990	8.00
—Reissue; sticker with new number placed over bar code of leftover 90092 pressings			
❑ 842298-1	The Joshua Tree	1990	8.00
—Reissue; sticker with new number placed over bar code of leftover 90581 pressings			
❑ 842299-1 [(2)]	Rattle and Hum	1990	12.00
—Reissue; sticker with new number placed over bar code of leftover 91003 pressings			
❑ 842479-1 [EP]	Wide Awake in America	1990	8.00
—Reissue; sticker with new number placed over bar code of leftover 90279 pressings			
❑ 1082901	October	2008	20.00
❑ 1083201	War	2008	20.00
❑ 1084301	Boy	2008	20.00
❑ 1095001 [EP]	Under a Blood Red Sky	2008	20.00
MOBILE FIDELITY			
❑ 1-207	The Unforgettable Fire	1994	60.00
—Audiophile vinyl			
WARNER BROS.			
❑ WBMS-117 [DJ]	Two Sides Live	1981	120.00
—Promo only, part of "The Warner Bros. Music Show"; legitimate copies are on black vinyl			

UBANS, THE

45s

Number	Title (A Side/B Side)	Yr	NM
RADIANT			
❑ 102	Gloria/On the Bridge	1964	200.00

U

UFO, *Misdemeanor*, Chrysalis BFV 41518, 1986, **$10.**

Number	Title (A Side/B Side)	Yr	NM
UFO LONE STAR, MICHAEL SCHENKER GROUP, WAYSTED, GARY MOORE related.			
12-Inch Singles			
CHRYSALIS			
❑ CHS-5-PDJ [DJ]	Try Me (3:25) (4:52)	1977	20.00
❑ CHS-28-PDJ [DJ]	Lonely Heart (same on both sides)	1981	10.00
❑ VAS 2266 [DJ]	This Time//Too Hot to Handle/ Lights Out	1986	10.00
❑ VAS 2363 [DJ]	Night Run/Blue	1986	12.00
45s			
CHRYSALIS			
❑ 2040	Doctor Doctor/Lipstick Traces	197?	6.00
❑ 2157	Too Hot to Handle/Electric Phase	1977	8.00
—Red vinyl			
❑ 2157 [PS]	Too Hot to Handle/Electric Phase	1977	10.00
❑ 2178	Try Me/Gettin' Ready	1977	5.00
❑ 2239	Cherry/You Don't Fool Me	1978	5.00
❑ 2263	Only You Can Rock Me/ Ain't No Baby	1978	5.00
❑ 2308	Doctor Doctor/Lights Out	1979	5.00
❑ 2590	Back in My Life/You'll Get Love	1981	5.00
Albums			
CHRYSALIS			
❑ CHR 1059	Phenomenon	1974	15.00
—Green label			
❑ CHR 1059	Phenomenon	1977	12.00
—Fading blue label			
❑ CHR 1074	Force It	1975	12.00
❑ CHR 1103	No Heavy Petting	1976	12.00
❑ CHR 1127	Lights Out	1977	12.00
❑ CHR 1182	Obsession	1978	12.00
❑ CHR 1209 [(2)]	Strangers in the Night	1979	15.00
❑ CHR 1239	No Place to Run	1980	12.00
❑ CHR 1307	The Wild, the Willing and the Innocent	1981	12.00
❑ CHR 1360	Mechanix	1982	12.00
❑ PV 41059	Phenomenon	1983	8.00
❑ PV 41074	Force It	1983	8.00
❑ PV 41103	No Heavy Petting	1983	8.00
❑ FV 41127	Lights Out	1983	8.00
❑ PV 41127	Lights Out	1986	8.00
—Reissue of FV 41127			
❑ PV 41182	Obsession	1983	8.00
❑ V2X 41209 [(2)]	Strangers in the Night	1983	14.00
❑ PV 41239	No Place to Run	1983	8.00
❑ PV 41307	The Wild, the Willing and the Innocent	1983	8.00
❑ PV 41360	Mechanix	1983	8.00
❑ FV 41402	Making Contact	1983	10.00
❑ PV 41402	Making Contact	1986	8.00
—Reissue of FV 41402			
❑ BFV 41518	Misdemeanor	1986	10.00
❑ FV 41644	The Best of the Rest	1988	12.00
METAL BLADE/ENIGMA			
❑ 7 73404 1 [EP]	Ain't Misbehavin'	1989	10.00
RARE EARTH			
❑ RS 624	UFO 1	1971	30.00
UGLYS, THE			
45s			
ABC-PARAMOUNT			
❑ 10707	Wake Up My Mind/Ugly Blues	1965	40.00
❑ 10748	It's Alright/A Friend	1965	12.00
❑ 10773	Quiet Explosion/A Good Idea	1966	12.00
ULMER, JAMES "BLOOD"			
Albums			
ARTISTS HOUSE			
❑ 13	Are You Glad to Be in America?	1980	20.00
❑ AH 9407	Tales of Captain Black	1979	20.00
BLUE NOTE			
❑ BT-85136	America — Do You Remember the Love?	1987	12.00
CARAVAN OF DREAMS			
❑ CDP 85004	Live at the Caravan of Dreams	1986	15.00
COLUMBIA			
❑ ARC 37493	Free Lancing	1981	20.00
❑ ARC 38285	Black Rock	1982	20.00
❑ BFC 38900	Odyssey	1983	12.00
IN+OUT			
❑ 7007	Revealing	1990	12.00
ULTIMATE SPINACH			
45s			
MGM			
❑ 14023	(Just Like) Romeo and Juliet/ Some Days You Just Can't Win	1969	12.00
Albums			
MGM			
❑ E-4518 [M]	Ultimate Spinach	1968	30.00
❑ SE-4518 [S]	Ultimate Spinach	1968	25.00
❑ E-4570 [M]	Behold & See	1968	50.00
—Mono is promo only (yellow label)			
❑ SE-4570 [S]	Behold & See	1968	25.00
❑ SE-4600	Ultimate Spinach	1969	25.00
ULTRA VIOLET			
45s			
CAPITOL			
❑ 3743	Shanghai Bill/La Vie En Rose	1973	6.00
Albums			
CAPITOL			
❑ ST-11244	Ultra Violet	1973	25.00
ULTRAVOX			
12-Inch Singles			
CHRYSALIS			
❑ CHSPDJ [DJ]	Sleepwalk (same on both sides)	1980	10.00
❑ CHS-22-PDJ [DJ]	Sleepwalk (same on both sides)	1980	10.00
❑ CHS35PDJ [DJ]	The Voice (same on both sides)	1981	8.00
❑ CHS-35-PDJ [DJ]	The Voice (same on both sides)	1981	8.00
❑ CHS51PDJ [DJ]	Reap the Wind Wind/Hosanna	1982	15.00
❑ CHS-51-PDJ [DJ]	Reap the Wind Wind/Hosanna	1982	12.00
❑ AS1662 [DJ]	Hymn (2 versions)/ Reap the Wild Wind	1983	8.00
❑ AS 1662 [DJ]	Hymn (2 versions)/ Reap the Wild Wind	1983	10.00
❑ VAS1840 [DJ]	One Small Day (same on both sides)	1984	6.00
❑ VAS 1840 [DJ]	One Small Day (same on both sides)	1984	8.00
❑ VAS2028 [DJ]	Love's Great Adventure/ One Small Day (Edit)	1985	7.00
❑ VAS 2028 [DJ]	Love's Great Adventure/ One Small Day (Edit)	1985	8.00
❑ CHS-2522	All Stood Still (Remix)// Alles Klar/Keep Talking	1981	12.00
❑ 4V9-42783	Dancing with Tears in My Eyes/ One Small Day	1984	10.00
45s			
CHRYSALIS			
❑ CHS-2515	Vienna/Passing Strangers	1981	5.00
❑ VS4-42682	Reap the Wild Wind/ Hosanna (In Excelsis Deo)	1983	5.00
❑ VS4-42781	Dancing with Tears in My Eyes/ Building	1984	4.00
❑ VS4-42781 [PS]	Dancing with Tears in My Eyes/ Building	1984	5.00
Albums			
ANTILLES			
❑ AN 7069	Systems of Romance	1978	15.00
❑ AN 7079	Three Into One	1980	15.00
CHRYSALIS			
❑ CHR 1296	Vienna	1980	10.00
❑ CHR 1338	Rage in Eden	1981	10.00
❑ FV 41296	Vienna	198?	8.00
—Reissue			
❑ B6V 41394	Quartet	1983	10.00
❑ FV 41459	Lament	1984	10.00
❑ FV 41490	The Collection	1984	10.00
ISLAND			
❑ ILPS 9449	Ultravox!	1977	15.00
UMILIANI, PIERO			
45s			
ARIEL			
❑ 500	Mah-Na Mah-Na/You Tried to Warn Me	1969	12.00
—From the movie "Swedish Heaven and Hell"; Umiliani's name is only in parentheses on the label, making it appear as if he is merely the composer			
UNBEATABLES, THE			
45s			
DAWN			
❑ 552	I Love Paris/What I Say	1964	40.00

Except when noted otherwise, VG = 25% of NM, and VG+ = 50% of NM. (Example: VG = $2.00, VG+ = $4.00 and NM = $8.00.)

Number	Title (A Side/B Side)	Yr	NM
Albums			
DAWN			
❑ 5050 [M]	Live at Palisades Park	1964	150.00
UNCHAINED MYNDS, THE			
45s			
BUDDAH			
❑ 111	We Can't Go On This Way/ Going Back to Miami	1969	15.00
❑ 119	Every Day/(B-side unknown)	1969	15.00
❑ 140	You, Me, and My Yo-Yo/ Every Day	1970	15.00
TEEN TOWN			
❑ 106	We Can't Go On This Way/ Going Back to Miami	1969	40.00
TRANSACTION			
❑ 705	We Can't Go On This Way/ Going Back to Miami	1968	15.00
❑ 705	Hole in My Shoe/Warm Smoke	1969	25.00
❑ 705	Hole in My Shoe/Warm Smoke	1969	25.00
—As The Takers			
❑ 705 [PS]	We Can't Go On This Way/ Going Back to Miami	1968	40.00
UNCLE DOG			
45s			
MCA			
❑ 40005	River Road/Boogie with Me	1973	5.00
Albums			
MCA			
❑ 302	Old Hat	1973	20.00
UNCLE TUPELO			
45s			
ROCKVILLE			
❑ 6055	I Got Drunk/Sin City	1990	6.00
❑ 6055 [PS]	I Got Drunk/Sin City	1990	6.00
❑ 6069	Gun/I Wanna Destroy You	1991	5.00
❑ 6069 [PS]	Gun/I Wanna Destroy You	1991	5.00
❑ 6089	Sauget Wind/ Looking for a Way Out	1992	8.00
—Clear vinyl			
❑ 6089 [PS]	Sauget Wind/ Looking for a Way Out	1992	8.00
—Clear vinyl			
Albums			
ROCKVILLE			
❑ 6050-1	No Depression	1990	60.00
❑ 6110-1 [(2)]	Still Feel Gone/March 16-20, 1992	1992	150.00
SUNDAZED			
❑ LP-5153 [(2)]	89/93: An Anthology	2002	25.00
UNDERBEATS, THE			
45s			
BANGAR			
❑ 00632	Annie Do the Dog/ Sweet Words of Love	1964	15.00
—Blue label			
❑ 00632	Annie Do the Dog/ Sweet Words of Love	1964	20.00
—Red label			
❑ 00657 [DJ]	Broken Arrow/Little Romance	1964	40.00
GARRETT			
❑ 4004	Foot Stompin'/Route 66	1964	25.00
METROBEAT			
❑ 4449	Sweetest Girl in the World/ It's Gonna Rain Today	1967	25.00
SOMA			
❑ 1449	Book of Love/Darling Lorraine	1966	15.00
❑ 1458	I Can't Stand It/Shake It for Me	1966	50.00
TWIN-TOWN			
❑ 706	Jo Jo Gunne/Our Love	1965	40.00
UNDERDOGS, THE			
45s			
HIDEOUT			
❑ 1001	The Man in the Glass/Friday at the Hideout (Judy Be Mine)	1965	40.00
❑ 1004	Little Girl/Don't Pretend	1965	40.00
❑ 1011	Surprise Surprise/ Get Down on Your Knees	1966	40.00
REPRISE			
❑ 0422	The Man in the Glass/Friday at the Hideout (Judy Be Mine)	1965	20.00
❑ 0446	Little Girl/Don't Pretend	1966	20.00
V.I.P.			
❑ 25040	Love's Gone Bad/Mo Jo Hanna	1966	20.00

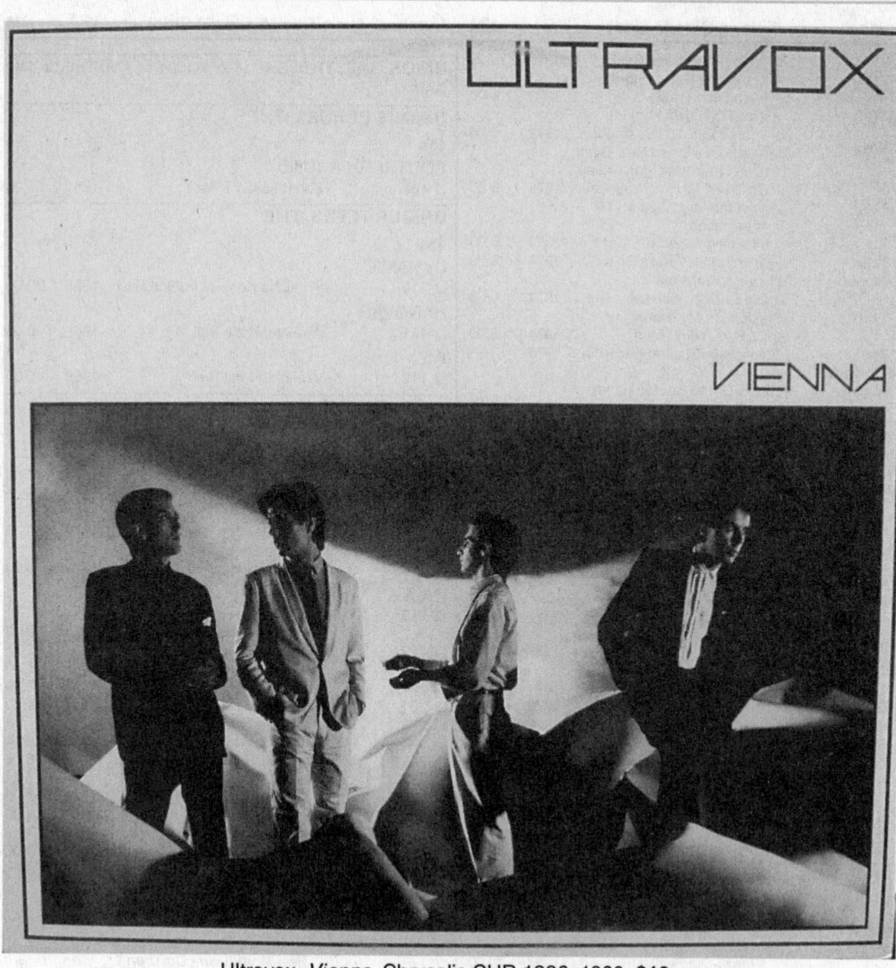

Ultravox, *Vienna*, Chrysalis CHR 1296, 1980, **$10.**

Number	Title (A Side/B Side)	Yr	NM
UNDERGRADS, THE			
Albums			
SOMERSET			
❑ P-21600 [M]	Bluegrass Hoot on Campus	1963	10.00
❑ SF-21600 [S]	Bluegrass Hoot on Campus	1963	12.00
UNDERGROUND, THE			
45s			
MAINSTREAM			
❑ 660	Easy/Satisfy'n Sunday	1967	25.00
❑ 667	Get Him Out of Your Mind/ Take Me Back	1967	25.00
UNDERGROUND SUNSHINE Also see THE CHALLENGERS (4).			
45s			
INTREPID			
❑ ITDJ-3 [DJ]	Don't Shut Me Out (mono/stereo)	1969	12.00
—Promo issue of 75012			
❑ 75002	Birthday/All I Want Is You	1969	12.00
❑ 75012	Don't Shut Me Out/ Take Me, Break Me	1969	10.00
❑ 75019	Nine to Five (Ain't My Bag)/ Rotten Woman Blues	1969	10.00
❑ 75029	Jesus Is Just Alright/ Six O'Clock	1970	10.00
Albums			
INTREPID			
❑ IT-74003	Let There Be Light	1969	30.00
UNDERTAKERS, THE			
45s			
BLACK WATCH			
❑ BW5545/6	I Fell in Love (For the Very First Time)/Throw Your Love Away Girl	1965	150.00
—As The Takers			

Number	Title (A Side/B Side)	Yr	NM
INTERPHON			
❑ IN-7709/6	Think/If You Don't Come Back	1964	25.00
PARKWAY			
❑ 909	Just a Little Bit/Stupidity	1964	20.00
UNDERTONES, THE			
45s			
HARVEST			
❑ A-5027	It's Going to Happen/ Fairly in the Money Now	1981	6.00
SIRE			
❑ 49195	Teenage Kicks/Smarter Than U	1980	6.00
❑ 49283	Wednesday Week/Told You So	1980	6.00
Albums			
CAPITOL			
❑ ST-12358	All Wrapped Up	1983	15.00
HARVEST			
❑ ST-12159	Positive Touch	1981	15.00
SIRE			
❑ SRK 6071	The Undertones	1979	12.00
❑ SRK 6088	Hypnotised	1980	12.00
UNDISPUTED TRUTH, THE			
12-Inch Singles			
WHITFIELD			
❑ 8306	Let's Go Down to the Disco (9:10)/You + Me = Love	1976	20.00
❑ 8783	Show Time (8:59)/ Misunderstood	1979	15.00
45s			
GORDY			
❑ 7106	Save My Love for a Rainy Day/ Since I've Lost You	1971	8.00
❑ 7108	Smiling Faces Sometimes/ You Got the Love I Need	1971	6.00
❑ 7112	You Make Your Own Heaven and Hell Right Here on Earth/ Ball of Confusion (That's What the World Is Today)	1971	6.00

U

Number | Title (A Side/B Side) | Yr | NM

❑ 7114 What It Is/California Soul 1972 6.00
❑ 7117 Papa Was a Rollin' Stone/Friendship Train 1972 6.00
❑ 7122 With a Little Help from My Friends/Girl You're Alright 1972 6.00
❑ 7124 Mama I Got a Brand New Thing (Don't Say No)/Gonna Keep On Tryin' Till I Win Your Love 1973 6.00
❑ 7130 Law of the Land/Just My Imagination (Running Away with Me) 1973 6.00
❑ 7134 Help Yourself/What's Going On 1974 6.00
❑ 7139 I'm a Fool for You/Girl's Alright with Me 1974 6.00
❑ 7140 Big John Is My Name/L'il Red Ridin' Hood 1974 6.00
❑ 7141 Earthquake Shake/Spaced Out 1975 —
—Unreleased
❑ 7143 UFO's/Got to Get My Hands on Some Lovin' 1975 6.00
❑ 7145 Higher Than High/Spaced Out 1975 6.00
❑ 7147 Boogie Bump Boogie/I Saw Her When You Met Her 1975 6.00

WHITFIELD
❑ 8231 You + Me = Love/(Instrumental) 1976 6.00
❑ 8295 Let's Get Down to the Disco/Loose 1977 6.00
❑ 8362 Hole in the Wall/Sunshine 1977 6.00
❑ 8781 Show Time (Part 1)/(Part 2) 1979 6.00
❑ 8873 I Can't Get Enough of Your Love/Misunderstood 1979 6.00

Albums

GORDY
❑ G 955L The Undisputed Truth 1971 25.00
❑ G5-959 Face to Face with the Truth 1972 20.00
❑ G5-963 Law of the Land 1973 20.00
❑ G6-968 Down to Earth 1974 20.00
❑ G6-970 Cosmic Truth 1975 20.00
❑ G6-972 Higher Than High 1975 20.00

WHITFIELD
❑ BS 2967 Method to the Madness 1977 20.00
❑ BSK 3202 Smokin' 1979 15.00

UNFOLDING

Albums

AUDIO FIDELITY
❑ AFLP-2184 [M] How to Blow Your Mind and Have a Freak-Out Party 1967 70.00
❑ AFSD-6184 [S] How to Blow Your Mind and Have a Freak-Out Party 1967 100.00

UNFORGETTABLES, THE

45s

COLPIX
❑ 192 It Hurts/Was It All Right 1961 30.00

PAMELA
❑ 204 Oh Wishing Well/Daddy Must Be a Man 1961 300.00
❑ 204 Oh Wishing Well/Daddy Must Be a Man 1961 500.00
—Blue vinyl

TITANIC
❑ 5012 He'll Be Sorry/Oh There He Goes 1963 40.00

UNICORN

45s

CAPITOL
❑ 3954 Bog Trotter/Ooh, Mother 1974 5.00
❑ 3993 Blue Pine Trees/Electric Night 1974 5.00

Albums

CAPITOL
❑ ST-11334 Blue Pine Trees 1974 10.00
—Produced by David Gilmour (Pink Floyd)
❑ ST-11453 Unicorn 2 1976 10.00
❑ ST-11692 One More Tomorrow 1977 10.00

UNIFICS, THE

45s

KAPP
❑ 935 Court of Love/Which One Should I Choose 1968 12.00
❑ 957 The Beginning of My End/Sentimental Man 1968 12.00
❑ 957 [PS] The Beginning of My End/Sentimental Man 1968 15.00
❑ 985 It's a Groovy World!/Memories 1969 12.00
❑ 985 [PS] It's a Groovy World!/Memories 1969 15.00
❑ 2026 Toshisumasu/It's All Over 1969 12.00
❑ 2058 Got to Get You/Memories 1969 12.00

Albums

KAPP
❑ KS-3582 Sittin' In at the Court of Love 1968 25.00

UNION GAP, THE

See GARY PUCKETT AND THE UNION GAP.

UNIQUE ECHOES, THE

45s

SOUTHERN SOUND
❑ 108 Zoom/Italian Twist 1962 50.00

UNIQUE TEENS, THE

45s

DYNAMIC
❑ 110 Whatcha Know Now/Run Fast 1959 30.00

HANOVER
❑ 4510 Jeannie/At the Ball 1959 40.00

IVY
❑ 112 Jeannie/At the Ball 1958 40.00

UNIQUES, THE (1)

Country singer Joe Stampley was a member of this group.

45s

PARAMOUNT
❑ 0017 Eunice/No One But You 1970 5.00
❑ 0058 Shadow of Love/Lazy Afternoon 1970 5.00
❑ 0116 Lucille/One Night with You 1971 5.00
❑ 0172 Will You Love Me Tomorrow/I Am a Gemini 1972 5.00

PAULA
❑ 219 Not Too Long Ago/Fast Way of Living 1965 10.00
❑ 222 Too Good to Be True/Never Been in Love 1965 8.00
❑ 227 Lady's Man/Bolivar 1965 8.00
❑ 231 Strange/You Ain't Tuff 1966 8.00
❑ 238 All These Things/Tell Me What to Do 1966 8.00
❑ 245 Goodbye, So Long/Run and Hide 1966 8.00
❑ 255 Please Come Home for Christmas/(Instrumental) 1966 12.00
❑ 264 Groovin' Out/Areba 1967 8.00
❑ 275 Every Now and Then (I Cry)/Love Is a Precious Thing 1967 8.00
❑ 289 Go On and Leave/I'll Do Anything 1967 8.00
—B-side by University of Utah Chamber Choir
❑ 299 It's All Over Now/All I Took Was Love 1968 6.00
❑ 307 It Hurts Me to Remember/I Sure Feel More (Like I Do Then I Did When I Got Here) 1968 6.00
❑ 313 How Lucky Can One Man Be/You Don't Miss Your Water 1968 6.00
❑ 320 Sha-La Love/You Know (That I Love You) 1970 5.00
❑ 324 My Babe/Toys Are Made for Children 1970 5.00
❑ 332 All These Things/You Know That I Love You 1970 5.00

Albums

PAULA
❑ LP-2190 [M] Uniquely Yours 1966 25.00
❑ LPS-2190 [S] Uniquely Yours 1966 30.00
❑ LP-2194 [M] Happening Now 1967 25.00
❑ LPS-2194 [S] Happening Now 1967 30.00
❑ LP-2199 [M] Playtime 1968 25.00
❑ LPS-2199 [S] Playtime 1968 25.00
❑ LPS-2204 The Uniques 1969 25.00
❑ LPS-2208 Golden Hits 1970 25.00

UNIQUES, THE (2)

45s

AMBER
❑ 2004 Taboo/Ghost Riders in the Sky 1961 50.00

UNITED SOUTHERN
❑ 104 Renegade/Malaguena 1961 30.00

UNIQUES, THE (3)

45s

BANGAR
❑ 00609 Baby Don't Cry/Little Angel 1967 20.00

UNIQUES, THE (4)

45s

BLISS
❑ 1004 I'm So Unhappy/I'm Confessin' 1961 500.00

END
❑ 1012 Tell the Angels/Hey, Little Cupid 1958 250.00

FLIPPIN'
❑ 202 Come Marry Me/Do You Remember 1959 50.00

GONE
❑ 5113 I'm So Unhappy/It's Got to Come 1961 70.00
❑ 5113 I'm So Unhappy/I'm Confessin' 1961 200.00

MR. CEE
❑ 100 Look at Me/Bossa Nova Cha Cha 1960 300.00

PRIDE
❑ 1018 I'm So Unhappy/It's Got to Come 1960 250.00

TEE KAY
❑ 112 One Million Miles Away/All at Once 1962 50.00

UNIQUES, THE (5)

45s

CAPITOL
❑ 4949 Loving You/Blue Skies 1963 12.00

ROULETTE
❑ 4528 Send Him to Me/This Little Boy of Mine 1963 20.00

UNIQUES, THE (6)

45s

DEMAND
❑ 1994 Merry Christmas, Darling/I Wanna Chance 198? 8.00
—B-side by the Vows; green vinyl "collector's issue"
❑ 2490 Times Change/Alright, OK, You Win 1964 50.00
❑ 2936 Merry Christmas Darling/Rockin' Rudolph 1963 80.00
❑ 3950 Merry Christmas Darling (And A Happy New Year Too)/Times Change 1963 50.00

DOT
❑ 16533 Merry Christmas Darling/Times Change 1963 40.00

UNIQUES, THE (7)

45s

PEACOCK
❑ 1677 Right Now/Somewhere 1957 30.00
❑ 1695 Mysterious/Picture of My Baby 1960 25.00

UNIQUES, THE (U)

45s

CLIFTON
❑ 62 After New Year's Eve/Kiss, Kiss, Kiss 19?? 8.00

LUCKY FOUR
❑ 1024 Silvery Moon/Chocolate Bar 1962 200.00

UNIT FOUR PLUS TWO

45s

LONDON
❑ 1009 I Was Only Playing Games/I Won't Let You Down 1966 15.00
❑ 9732 Sorrow and Pain/Woman from Liberia 1965 15.00
❑ 9751 Concrete and Clay/When I Fall in Love 1965 15.00
❑ 9751 Concrete and Clay/Wild as the Wind 1965 25.00
❑ 9761 You've Never Been in Love Like This Before/Tell Somebody You Know 1965 15.00
❑ 9790 Stop Wasting Your Time/Hark 1965 15.00

Albums

LONDON
❑ PS 427 [P] Unit Four Plus Two #1 1965 50.00
❑ LL 3427 [M] Unit Four Plus Two #1 1965 40.00

UNITED FRUIT CO.

45s

LAURIE
❑ 3408 On the Good Ship Lollipop/Sunshine Street 1967 10.00

UNITED STATES DOUBLE QUARTET

THE TOKENS and The Kirby Stone Four.

45s

B.T. PUPPY
❑ 524 Life Is Groovy/Split 1966 10.00
❑ 547 Walking Along-Happy Wanderer/When I Lock My Door 1968 10.00
❑ 551 Do Re Mi/When I Lock My Door 1969 10.00

Albums

B.T. PUPPY
❑ BTS-1005 Life Is Groovy 1969 50.00

UNITED STATES OF AMERICA, THE

Albums

COLUMBIA
❑ CL 2814 [M] The United States of America 1968 100.00
—Mono is promo only
❑ CS 9614 [S] The United States of America 1968 40.00
—Without outer bag

Except when noted otherwise, VG = 25% of NM, and VG+ = 50% of NM. (Example: VG = $2.00, VG+ = $4.00 and NM = $8.00.)

Number	Title (A Side/B Side)	Yr	NM
❑ CS 9614 [S]	The United States of America	1968	80.00
—With outer bag			
UNIVERSALS, THE Probably more than one group.			
45s			
ASCOT			
❑ 2124	Dear Ruth/Gotta Little Girl	1963	60.00
CORA-LEE			
❑ 501	The Picture/He's So Right	1958	40.00
FESTIVAL			
❑ 1601	Dreaming/Love Bound	1961	60.00
—No subtitle on A-side			
❑ 25001	Dreaming/Love Bound	1961	25.00
MARK-X			
❑ 7004	Teenage Love/Again	1957	200.00
MODERN			
❑ 1057	New Lease on Life/ Without Friends	1968	10.00
SHEPHERD			
❑ 2200	A Love Only You Can Give/ I'm in Love	1962	50.00
SOUTHERN			
❑ 102	Dear Ruth/Prayer of Love	1963	50.00
Albums			
RELIC			
❑ 5006	Acapella Showcase	197?	10.00
UNKNOWN, THE			
45s			
AUTOGRAPH			
❑ 206	I Have Returned/Keep Talking, Baby	1960	40.00
UNKNOWNS, THE (1) Also see STEVE ALAIMO; MARK LINDSAY.			
45s			
PARROT			
❑ 307	Melody for an Unknown Girl/ Keith's Song	1966	25.00
UNKNOWNS, THE (2)			
45s			
SHIELD			
❑ 7101	One More Chance/You and Me	196?	200.00
X-TRA			
❑ 102	One More Chance/You and Me	1957	1000.
UNKNOWNS, THE (U)			
45s			
MARLIN			
❑ 16008	Tighter/Young Enough to Cry	1966	25.00
UNLUV'D, THE			
45s			
MGM			
❑ K13903	I Got It Bad/Steadfastly	1968	12.00
PARKWAY			
❑ 138	Ain't Gonna Do You No Harm/ An Exception to the Rule	1967	25.00
TRUE LOVE			
❑ 1000	Ain't Gonna Do You No Harm/ An Exception to the Rule	1967	50.00
UNRELATED SEGMENTS, THE			
45s			
HANNA-BARBERA			
❑ 514	It's Unfair/Story of My Life	1967	40.00
LIBERTY			
❑ 55992	It's Gonna Rain/ Where You Gonna Go	1967	15.00
❑ 56052	Cry, Cry, Cry/It's Not Fair	1968	100.00
UNTAMED, THE			
45s			
PLANET			
❑ 117	It's Not True/Gimme Gimme Some Shade	1966	40.00
—Also reported to be Planet 103			
UNTOUCHABLES, THE At least two different groups.			
45s			
ALAN K			
❑ 6901	Little Mary/Funny What a Little Kiss Can Do	1962	200.00
DOT			
❑ 16306	Blues in the Night/Bondaru	1962	15.00
LIBERTY			
❑ 55335	You're on Top/Lovely Dee	1961	20.00
❑ 55423	Papa/Medicine Man	1962	20.00

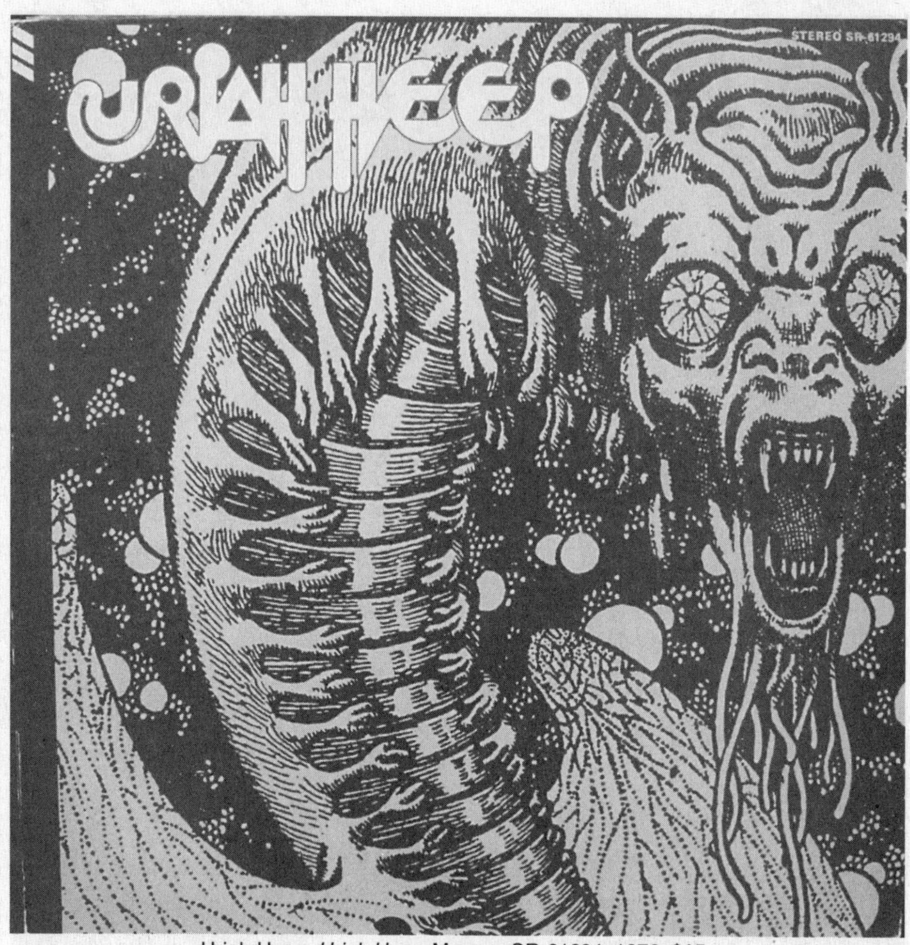

Uriah Heep, *Uriah Heep*, Mercury SR-61294, 1970, **$15.**

Number	Title (A Side/B Side)	Yr	NM
MADISON			
❑ 128	Poor Boy Need a Preacher/ New Fad	1960	25.00
❑ 134	Goodnight Sweetheart Goodnight/Vickie Lee	1960	25.00
❑ 139	Sixty Minute Man/ Everybody's Laughin'	1960	25.00
❑ 147	Do Your Best/Raisin' Cain	1961	25.00
MCA/STIFF			
❑ 52725	I Spy (For the F.B.I.)/ Freak in the Street	1985	4.00
❑ 52725 [PS]	I Spy (For the F.B.I.)/ Freak in the Street	1985	4.00
NAU VOO			
❑ 809	Blue Chip Bounce (Part 1)/ Blue Chip Bounce (Part 2)	1960	15.00
WASP			
❑ 105	Don't Go, I'm Beggin'/ Baby, Let's Wait	1967	25.00
UNUSUAL WE			
Albums			
PULSAR			
❑ 10608	Unusual We	1969	30.00
UPBEATS, THE			
45s			
JOY			
❑ 223	Oh What It Seemed to Be/The Night We Both Said Goodbye	1958	25.00
❑ 227	Keep Cool Crazy Heart/ You're the One I Care For	1959	25.00
❑ 229	Satin Shoes/Teenie Weenie Bikini	1959	25.00
❑ 233	To Me You're a Song/ Unbelievable Love	1959	25.00
PREP			
❑ 119	Never in My Life/I Don't Know	1957	30.00
❑ 131	Will You Be Mine?/ My Last Frontier	1958	30.00

Number	Title (A Side/B Side)	Yr	NM
SWAN			
❑ 4010	Just Like in the Movies/ My Foolish Heart	1958	25.00
UPCHURCH, PHIL			
45s			
BOYD			
❑ 3398	You Can't Sit Down Part 2/ You Can't Sit Down Part 1	1961	12.00
CADET			
❑ 5661	You Don't Know the Reason/ I Don't Know	1970	6.00
KUDU			
❑ 926	You Got Style/Ave Maria	1975	5.00
—With Tennyson Stephens			
MARLIN			
❑ 3325	Strawberry Letter 23/ (B-side unknown)	1978	4.00
UNITED ARTISTS			
❑ 329	You Can't Sit Down Part 2/ You Can't Sit Down Part 1	1961	10.00
❑ 355	Pink Lollipop/Straw Hat	1961	10.00
❑ 385	The Hog/That's Where It Is	1961	10.00
❑ 417	Organ Grinder's Swing/ The Persian	1962	10.00
❑ 488	The Stonewall/Flap Jack	1962	10.00
Albums			
BLUE THUMB			
❑ BTS-59	Lovin' Feelin'	1973	12.00
❑ BTS-6005 [(2)]	Darkness, Darkness	1971	20.00
BOYD			
❑ B-398 [M]	You Can't Sit Down	1961	80.00
❑ BS-398 [S]	You Can't Sit Down	1961	100.00
CADET			
❑ LPS-826	Upchurch	1969	15.00
❑ LPS-840	The Way I Feel	1970	15.00
JAM			
❑ 007	Free and Easy	198?	12.00

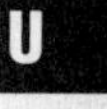

Utopia, *Oops! Wrong Planet*, Bearsville BRK 6970, 1977, **$12.**

Number	Title (A Side/B Side)	Yr	NM
KUDU			
❑ 22	Phil Upchurch and Tennyson Stevens	1975	12.00
MARLIN			
❑ 2209	Phil Upchurch	1978	12.00
MILESTONE			
❑ MSP-9010	Feeling Blue	1968	15.00
UNITED ARTISTS			
❑ UAL-3162 [M]	You Can't Sit Down, Part 2	1961	30.00
❑ UAL-3175 [M]	Big Hit Dances	1962	25.00
❑ UAS-6162 [S]	You Can't Sit Down, Part 2	1961	40.00
❑ UAS-6175 [S]	Big Hit Dances	1962	30.00

UPFRONTS, THE

Number	Title (A Side/B Side)	Yr	NM
45s			
LUMMTONE			
❑ 103	It Took Time/Betty Lou and the Lions	1960	50.00
❑ 104	Too Far to Turn Around/ Married Jive	1960	40.00
❑ 106	Why You Kiss Me/Little Girl	1961	50.00
❑ 107	Send Me Someone to Love Who Will Love Me/ Baby For Your Love	1961	30.00
—Black label			
❑ 107	Send Me Someone to Love Who Will Love Me/ Baby For Your Love	1961	50.00
—White label			
❑ 108	It Took Time/Baby For Your Love	1962	25.00
❑ 114	Do the Beetle/Most of the Pretty Girls	1964	60.00

UPSETTERS, THE

Number	Title (A Side/B Side)	Yr	NM
45s			
ABC			
❑ 11081	Tossin' and Turnin'/Always in the Wrong Place at the Wrong Time	1968	10.00
❑ 11120	Don't Be Cruel/Down Home	1968	10.00
AUTUMN			
❑ 4	Autumn's Here/Draggin' the Main	1964	25.00
FALCON			
❑ 1010	The Upsetter/The Strip	1958	20.00
FIRE			
❑ 1029	Jaywalking/Steppin' Out	1960	20.00
GEE			
❑ 1055	The Blues/Rollin' On	1960	20.00
HIT			
❑ 237	No Matter What Shape (Your Stomach's In)/Barbara Ann	1966	8.00
—B-side by the Chellows			
LITTLE STAR			
❑ 123	Yes, It's Me/Every Night About This Time	1962	50.00
—With Little Richard			

UPTONES, THE

Number	Title (A Side/B Side)	Yr	NM
45s			
LUTE			
❑ 6225	No More/I'll Be There	1962	20.00
—Multicolor label			
❑ 6225	No More/I'll Be There	1962	30.00
—Black label			
❑ 6229	Be Mine/Dreamin'	1962	40.00
MAGNUM			
❑ 714	Dreaming/Wear My Ring	1963	20.00
WATTS			
❑ 1080	Dreaming/Wear My Ring	1963	30.00

URIAH HEEP

Number	Title (A Side/B Side)	Yr	NM
45s			
CHRYSALIS			
❑ 2274	Come Back to Me/ Love or Nothing	1978	4.00
MERCURY			
❑ 73103	Gypsy/Real Turned On	1970	8.00
❑ 73145	Come Away Melinda/Wake Up	1970	8.00
❑ 73154	I Wanna Be Free/ What Should Be Done	1971	8.00
❑ 73174	High Priestess/(B-side unknown)	1970	10.00
❑ 73243	Look at Yourself/Love Machine	1971	8.00
❑ 73271	Why/The Wizard	1971	8.00
❑ 73307	Easy Livin'/All My Life	1972	8.00
❑ 73349	Sweet Lorraine/Blind Eye	1972	6.00
❑ 73406	Tears in My Eyes/July Morning	1973	6.00
❑ 76177	That's the Way It Is/Son of a Bitch	1982	4.00
❑ 76177 [PS]	That's the Way It Is/Son of a Bitch	1982	5.00
WARNER BROS.			
❑ 7738	Stealin'/Sunshine	1973	5.00
❑ 7836	Something or Nothing/ What Can I Do	1974	—
—Unreleased?			
❑ 8013	Something or Nothing/ What Can I Do	1974	5.00
❑ 8132	Prima Dance/Stealin'	1975	5.00
❑ 8581	Masquerade/Free Me	1978	5.00
7-Inch Extended Plays			
WARNER BROS.			
❑ S 2724	Dreamer/One Day//If I Had the Time/Circus	1974	10.00
—Jukebox issue; small hole, plays at 33 1/3 rpm			
❑ S 2724 [PS]	Sweet Freedom	1974	10.00
—Part of "Little LP" series (LLP #230)			
Albums			
CHRYSALIS			
❑ CHR 1204	Fallen Angel	1978	10.00
COLUMBIA			
❑ BFC 40132	Equator	1985	8.00
MERCURY			
❑ SRM-1-614	Look at Yourself	1971	10.00
❑ SRM-1-630	Demons and Wizards	1972	12.00
❑ SRM-1-652	The Magician's Birthday	1972	10.00
❑ SRM-1-1070	The Best of Uriah Heep	1976	8.00
❑ SRM-1-4057	Abominog	1982	8.00
❑ SRM-2-7503 [(2)]	Uriah Heep Live	1973	12.00
❑ SR-61294	Uriah Heep	1970	15.00
❑ SR-61319	Salisbury	1970	12.00
❑ 812313-1	Head First	1983	8.00
❑ 822476-1	The Best of Uriah Heep	1986	8.00
—Reissue of Mercury 1070			
WARNER BROS.			
❑ BS 2724	Sweet Freedom	1973	10.00
❑ W 2800	Wonderworld	1974	10.00
❑ BS 2869	Return to Fantasy	1975	10.00
❑ BS 2949	High and Mighty	1976	10.00
❑ BS 3013	Firefly	1977	10.00
❑ BSK 3145	Innocent Victim	1978	10.00

USHER, GARY   Also see THE TIMERS.

Number	Title (A Side/B Side)	Yr	NM
45s			
CAPITOL			
❑ 5128	The Beetle/Jody	1964	50.00
❑ 5193	Sacramento/That's the Way I Feel	1964	80.00
—Produced by Brian Wilson			
❑ 5403	It's a Lie/Jody	1965	50.00
DOT			
❑ 16518	Three Surfer Boys/Milky Way	1963	400.00
LAN-CET			
❑ 144	Tomorrow/Lies	1961	60.00
TITAN			
❑ 1716	Driven Insane/You're the Girl	1961	150.00

UTMOSTS, THE

Number	Title (A Side/B Side)	Yr	NM
45s			
PAN-OR			
❑ 1123	I Need You/Big Man	1962	120.00

UTOPIA   Also see TODD RUNDGREN.

Number	Title (A Side/B Side)	Yr	NM
12-Inch Singles			
NETWORK			
❑ 67935	Hammer in My Heart (same on both sides)	1983	15.00
—Probably promo only			
PASSPORT			
❑ 4004 [DJ]	Cry Baby +2	1984	10.00
WAX TRAX!			
❑ WAX-9099 [DJ]	Greater Than One (same on both sides)	1989	10.00
45s			
BEARSVILLE			
❑ 0317	Sunburst Finish/ Communion with the Sun	1977	4.00
❑ 0321	Love Is the Answer/Marriage of Heaven and Hell	1977	4.00
❑ 29947	Junk Rock/Lysistrata	1982	5.00
❑ 49180	Set Me Free/Umbrella Man	1980	5.00
❑ 49247	Love Alone/Very Last Time	1980	4.00

Except when noted otherwise, VG = 25% of NM, and VG+ = 50% of NM. (Example: VG = $2.00, VG+ = $4.00 and NM = $8.00.)

Number	Title (A Side/B Side)	Yr	NM
❑ 49545	Second Nature/You Make Me Crazy	1980	4.00
❑ 49579	Always Late/I Just Want to Touch You	1980	4.00
❑ 50062	One World/Special Interest	1982	5.00

NETWORK

Number	Title (A Side/B Side)	Yr	NM
❑ 69830	Hammer in My Heart/I'm Looking at You But I'm Talking to Myself	1983	4.00
❑ 69859	Feet Don't Fail Me Now/There Goes My Inspiration	1982	4.00

PASSPORT

Number	Title (A Side/B Side)	Yr	NM
❑ 7923	Cry Baby/Winston Smith Takes It on the Jaw	1984	4.00
❑ 7923 [PS]	Cry Baby/Winston Smith Takes It on the Jaw	1984	5.00
❑ 7927	Stand for Something/Mated	1985	4.00

Albums

BEARSVILLE

Number	Title (A Side/B Side)	Yr	NM
❑ BRK 3487	Deface the Music	1980	12.00
❑ BRK 3666	Swing to the Right	1982	12.00
❑ BR 6954	Todd Rundgren's Utopia	1974	12.00
❑ BR 6961	Todd Rundgren's Utopia/Another Live	1975	12.00
❑ BR 6965	RA	1977	12.00
❑ BRK 6970	Oops! Wrong Planet	1977	12.00
❑ BRK 6991	Adventures in Utopia	1979	12.00

NETWORK

Number	Title (A Side/B Side)	Yr	NM
❑ 60183 [(2)]	Utopia	1982	15.00

—The second record has the same five songs on both sides

PASSPORT

Number	Title (A Side/B Side)	Yr	NM
❑ PB 6029	Oblivion	1984	10.00
❑ PB 6044	POV	1985	10.00
❑ PB 6053	Trivia	1986	10.00

RHINO

Number	Title (A Side/B Side)	Yr	NM
❑ RNLP 70865	Todd Rundgren's Utopia	1987	8.00
❑ RNLP 70867	Todd Rundgren's Utopia/Another Live	1987	8.00
❑ RNLP 70869	RA	1987	8.00
❑ RNLP 70870	Oops! Wrong Planet	1987	8.00
❑ RNLP 70872	Adventures in Utopia	1987	8.00
❑ RNLP 70873	Deface the Music	1987	8.00
❑ RNLP 70875	Swing to the Right	1987	8.00
❑ R1-70892	Anthology (1974-1985)	1989	10.00

UTOPIANS, THE

45s

IMPERIAL

Number	Title (A Side/B Side)	Yr	NM
❑ 5861	Dutch Treat/Ain't No Such Thing	1962	30.00
❑ 5876	Along My Lonely Way/Hurry to Your Date	1962	400.00
❑ 5921	Let Love Come Later/Opera vs. the Blues	1963	25.00

UTOPIAS, THE

45s

LASALLE

Number	Title (A Side/B Side)	Yr	NM
❑ 0072	Girls Are Against Me/(B-side unknown)	196?	1200.

V

V.I.P.'S

45s

BIG TOP

Number	Title (A Side/B Side)	Yr	NM
❑ 100	Don't Pass Me By/You Ain't Good for Nothing	1965	12.00
❑ 518	You Pulled a Fast One/Flashback	1964	12.00
❑ 521	I'm On to You Baby/If He Wants Me	1964	12.00

CONGRESS

Number	Title (A Side/B Side)	Yr	NM
❑ 211	My Girl Cried/Strange Little Girl	1964	15.00

V-EIGHTS, THE

45s

ABC-PARAMOUNT

Number	Title (A Side/B Side)	Yr	NM
❑ 10201	Papa's Yellow Tie/My Heart	1961	20.00

MOST

Number	Title (A Side/B Side)	Yr	NM
❑ 711/3	Pretty Girl/Please Come Back	1959	100.00

VIBRO

Number	Title (A Side/B Side)	Yr	NM
❑ 4005	Papa's Yellow Tie/My Heart	1960	30.00
❑ 4007	Let's Take a Chance/Hot Water	1961	30.00

VACELS, THE Also see RICKY AND THE VACELS.

45s

KAMA SUTRA

Number	Title (A Side/B Side)	Yr	NM
❑ 200	You're My Baby (And Don't You Forget It)/Hey Girl, Stop Leading Me On	1965	20.00
❑ 204	Can You Please Crawl Out Your Window/I'm Just a Poor Boy	1965	20.00

VAGRANTS, THE

45s

ATCO

Number	Title (A Side/B Side)	Yr	NM
❑ 6473	Respect/I Love You Yes I Do	1967	15.00
❑ 6513	Beside the Sea/Sunny Summer Rain	1967	15.00
❑ 6552	And When It's Over/I Don't Need Your Lovin'	1968	15.00

SOUTHERN SOUND

Number	Title (A Side/B Side)	Yr	NM
❑ 204	Oh, Those Eyes/You're Too Young	1966	25.00

VANGUARD

Number	Title (A Side/B Side)	Yr	NM
❑ 35038	I Can't Make a Friend/Young Blues	1966	50.00
❑ 35038 [PS]	I Can't Make a Friend/Young Blues	1966	100.00
❑ 35042	Final Hour/Your Hasty Heart	1966	20.00

Albums

ARISTA

Number	Title (A Side/B Side)	Yr	NM
❑ AL-8459	The Great Lost Vagrants Album	1987	20.00

VAL-AIRES, THE Forerunner to THE VOGUES.

45s

CORAL

Number	Title (A Side/B Side)	Yr	NM
❑ 62177	Laurie My Love/Which One Will It Be	1960	80.00

WILLETTE

Number	Title (A Side/B Side)	Yr	NM
❑ 114	Laurie My Love/Which One Will It Be	1959	400.00

VAL-CHORDS, THE

45s

GAME TIME

Number	Title (A Side/B Side)	Yr	NM
❑ 104	Candy Store Love/You're Laughing at Me	1957	100.00

—With sword logo

Number	Title (A Side/B Side)	Yr	NM
❑ 104	Candy Store Love/You're Laughing at Me	1957	300.00

—With no sword logo

VAL-TONES, THE

45s

DELUXE

Number	Title (A Side/B Side)	Yr	NM
❑ 6084	Tender Darling/Siam Sam	1955	150.00

VALADIERS, THE

45s

GORDY

Number	Title (A Side/B Side)	Yr	NM
❑ 7003	While I'm Away/Because I Love Her	1962	60.00
❑ 7013	I Found a Girl/You'll Be Sorry Someday	1963	60.00

MIRACLE

Number	Title (A Side/B Side)	Yr	NM
❑ 6	Greeting (This Is Uncle Sam)/Take a Chance	1961	50.00

—With subtitle on A-side and 2:15 version of B-side

Number	Title (A Side/B Side)	Yr	NM
❑ 6	Greetings/Take a Chance	1961	80.00

—With no subtitle on A-side and 2:23 version of B-side

VALAQUONS, THE

45s

LAGUNA

Number	Title (A Side/B Side)	Yr	NM
❑ 102	Teardrops/Madeleine	1964	200.00

RAYCO

Number	Title (A Side/B Side)	Yr	NM
❑ 516	Jolly Green Giant/Diddy Bop	1965	30.00

TANGERINE

Number	Title (A Side/B Side)	Yr	NM
❑ 951	I Wanna Woman/Window Shopping on Girl's Avenue	1965	25.00

VALE, RICKY, AND THE SURFERS

Albums

STRAND

Number	Title (A Side/B Side)	Yr	NM
❑ SL-1104 [M]	Everybody's Surfin'	1963	40.00
❑ SLS-1104 [S]	Everybody's Surfin'	1963	50.00

VALENS, RITCHIE

45s

DEL-FI

Number	Title (A Side/B Side)	Yr	NM
❑ 1287	La Bamba '87/La Bamba	1987	5.00
❑ 4106	Come On, Let's Go/Framed	1958	80.00
❑ 4110	Donna/La Bamba	1958	30.00

—Light blue label

Number	Title (A Side/B Side)	Yr	NM
❑ 4110	Donna/La Bamba	1958	40.00

—Green label

Number	Title (A Side/B Side)	Yr	NM
❑ 4110	Donna/La Bamba	1958	70.00

—Blue/green/black label with circles

Number	Title (A Side/B Side)	Yr	NM
❑ 4110	Donna/La Bamba	196?	15.00

—Black label with light blue sawtooth border

Number	Title (A Side/B Side)	Yr	NM
❑ 4110	Donna/La Bamba	196?	25.00

—Light blue label with black sawtooth border

Number	Title (A Side/B Side)	Yr	NM
❑ 4110	Donna/La Bamba	1958	40.00

—White label, similar in style to the green and light blue labels (probably not a promo)

Number	Title (A Side/B Side)	Yr	NM
❑ 4111	Fast Freight/Big Baby Blues	1959	40.00

—As "Ritchie Valens"

Number	Title (A Side/B Side)	Yr	NM
❑ 4111	Fast Freight/Big Baby Blues	1959	50.00

—As "Arvee Allens"

Number	Title (A Side/B Side)	Yr	NM
❑ 4114	That's My Little Susie/In a Turkish Town	1959	40.00
❑ 4114 [PS]	That's My Little Susie/In a Turkish Town	1959	—

—Rumored to exist, but without conclusive evidence, we will delete this from future editions

Number	Title (A Side/B Side)	Yr	NM
❑ 4117	Little Girl/We Belong Together	1959	30.00
❑ 4117 [PS]	Little Girl/We Belong Together	1959	100.00
❑ 4128	Stay Beside Me/Big Baby Blues	1959	25.00
❑ 4133	The Paddiwack Song/Cry, Cry, Cry	1960	25.00
❑ 51341 [DJ]	Come On Let's Go/La Bamba	1998	5.00
❑ 51341 [PS]	Come On Let's Go/La Bamba	1998	5.00

—Promotional issue in advance of box set; number is not on sleeve, but is on record

LANA

Number	Title (A Side/B Side)	Yr	NM
❑ 153	Donna/La Bamba	196?	8.00

—Oldies reissue

LOST-NITE

Number	Title (A Side/B Side)	Yr	NM
❑ 201	Donna/La Bamba	196?	6.00

—Reissue

Number	Title (A Side/B Side)	Yr	NM
❑ 212	Come On Let's Go/Framed	196?	6.00

—Reissue

7-Inch Extended Plays

DEL-FI

Number	Title (A Side/B Side)	Yr	NM
❑ PR-1 [DJ]	La Bamba/We Belong Together//Donna/Framed	1960	150.00
❑ PR-1 [PS]	Ritchie Valens (Limited Valens Memorial Series)	1960	200.00

—Sleeve accompanying promo-only EP states "February Is Ritchie Valens Memorial Month"

Number	Title (A Side/B Side)	Yr	NM
❑ DFEP-101	(contents unknown)	1959	150.00
❑ DFEP-101 [PS]	Ritchie Valens	1959	150.00

—Cardboard sleeve

Number	Title (A Side/B Side)	Yr	NM
❑ DFEP-101 [PS]	Ritchie Valens	1959	150.00

—Paper sleeve

Number	Title (A Side/B Side)	Yr	NM
❑ DFEP-111	(contents unknown)	1960	150.00
❑ DFEP-111 [PS]	Ritchie Valens	1960	150.00

Albums

DEL-FI

Number	Title (A Side/B Side)	Yr	NM
❑ DFLP 1201 [M]	Ritchie Valens	1959	150.00

—Black label with "diamonds" border

Number	Title (A Side/B Side)	Yr	NM
❑ DFLP 1201 [M]	Ritchie Valens	1959	250.00

—Blue label with black border

Number	Title (A Side/B Side)	Yr	NM
❑ DFLP 1206 [M]	Ritchie	1959	150.00
❑ DFLP 1214 [M]	In Concert at Pacoima Jr. High	1960	250.00
❑ DFLP 1225 [M]	His Greatest Hits	1963	150.00

—White cover

Number	Title (A Side/B Side)	Yr	NM
❑ DFLP 1225 [M]	His Greatest Hits	1963	350.00

—Black cover

Number	Title (A Side/B Side)	Yr	NM
❑ DFLP 1247 [M]	His Greatest Hits, Vol. 2	1965	150.00

GUEST STAR

Number	Title (A Side/B Side)	Yr	NM
❑ GS-1469 [M]	The Original Ritchie Valens	1963	30.00
❑ GSS-1469 [R]	The Original Ritchie Valens	1963	20.00
❑ GS-1484 [M]	The Original La Bamba	1963	30.00
❑ GSS-1484 [R]	The Original La Bamba	1963	20.00

MGM

Number	Title (A Side/B Side)	Yr	NM
❑ GAS-117	Ritchie Valens (Golden Archive Series)	1970	30.00

RHINO

Number	Title (A Side/B Side)	Yr	NM
❑ RNDF-200	The Best of Ritchie Valens	1981	12.00
❑ RNBC-2798 [(3)]	The History of Ritchie Valens	198?	25.00
❑ RNLP-70178	The Best of Ritchie Valens (Golden Archive Series)	1987	10.00
❑ RNLP-70231	Ritchie Valens	1987	10.00
❑ RNLP-70232	Ritchie	1987	10.00
❑ RNLP-70233	In Concert at Pacoima Jr. High	1987	10.00

VALENS, RITCHIE / JERRY KOLE

Albums

CROWN

Number	Title (A Side/B Side)	Yr	NM
❑ CLP-5336 [M]	Ritchie Valens and Jerry Kole	1963	30.00

VALENTI, DINO Also see QUICKSILVER MESSENGER SERVICE.

45s

ELEKTRA

Number	Title (A Side/B Side)	Yr	NM
❑ 45012	Birdses/Don't Let It Down	1964	15.00

Albums

EPIC

Number	Title (A Side/B Side)	Yr	NM
❑ LN 24335 [M]	Dino Valenti	1967	20.00
❑ BN 26335 [S]	Dino Valenti	1967	20.00

V

VALENTI, JOHN

45s

Number	Title (A Side/B Side)	Yr	NM
ARIOLA AMERICA			
❑ 7625	Anything You Want/ That's the Way Life Goes	1976	6.00
❑ 7656	I Wrote This Song for You/ Morning Song	1977	6.00
❑ 7663	I Love Her Too/Morning Song	1977	6.00
RAINTREE			
❑ 2204	Machines/Driving Back to You	1975	6.00
—As "John LiVigni"			
RCA VICTOR			
❑ PB-12160	That's the Way Love Goes/ Who Will It Be	1981	5.00
❑ PB-12237	I Won't Change/Stephanie	1981	6.00

VALENTINE, HILTON

Former member of THE ANIMALS.

Albums

Number	Title (A Side/B Side)	Yr	NM
CAPITOL			
❑ ST-330	All in Your Head	1969	30.00

VALENTINE, JOE

45s

Number	Title (A Side/B Side)	Yr	NM
RACHAN			
❑ 311	She's Gone Again/ Coming On Home	196?	300.00
RONN			
❑ 14	I Can't Stand to See You Go/ One Night of Satisfaction	1967	30.00
❑ 30	A Woman's Love/ Hands On, Hands Off	1969	20.00
TEE-JAY			
❑ 17379	All the Love I Have for You Is Gone/One Night Stand	197?	30.00
❑ 17380	True Love/Sharing Your Love	197?	40.00
VAL			
❑ 7225	I Lost the Only Love I Had/Surely, I'll Never Do You Wrong	196?	1200.
VALERIE			
❑ 67119	I Can't Stand to See You Go/ One Night of Satisfaction	1967	200.00

VALENTINE, PENNY

45s

Number	Title (A Side/B Side)	Yr	NM
LIBERTY			
❑ 55774	I Want to Kiss Ringo Goodbye/ Show Me the Way to Love You	1964	30.00

VALENTINES, THE (1)

45s

Number	Title (A Side/B Side)	Yr	NM
BETHLEHEM			
❑ 3055	I'll Forget You/Yes, You Made It That Way	1962	25.00
KING			
❑ 5338	Please Don't Leave, Please Don't Go/That's It Man	1960	25.00
❑ 5433	That's How I Feel/Hey Ruby	1960	25.00
❑ 5830	I Have Two Loves/Camping Out	1963	20.00
UNITED ARTISTS			
❑ 764	Alone in the Night/Mink Coats and Sneakers	1964	15.00

VALENTINES, THE (2)

45s

Number	Title (A Side/B Side)	Yr	NM
OLD TOWN			
❑ 1009	Tonight Kathleen/Summer Love	1954	800.00
RAMA			
❑ 171	Lily Maebelle/Falling for You	1955	50.00
—Red label			
❑ 171	Lily Maebelle/Falling for You	1955	200.00
—Blue label			
❑ 181	I Love You Darling/Hand Me Down Love	1955	150.00
❑ 186	Christmas Prayer/K-I-S-S Me	1955	50.00
—Red label			
❑ 186	Christmas Prayer/K-I-S-S Me	1955	500.00
—Blue label			
❑ 196	Why/The Woo Woo Train	1956	50.00
—Red label			
❑ 196	Why/The Woo Woo Train	1956	100.00
—Blue label			
❑ 201	Twenty Minutes (Before the Hour)/I'll Never Let You Go	1956	100.00
❑ 208	Nature's Creation/ My Story of Love	1956	100.00
❑ 228	Don't Say Goodnight/ I Cried Oh, Oh	1957	200.00
ROULETTE			
❑ 58	Christmas Prayer/ Nature's Creation	196?	10.00
—"Golden Goodies Series"			

VALENTINES, THE (3)

45s

Number	Title (A Side/B Side)	Yr	NM
SOUND STAGE 7			
❑ 2646	I'm Alright Now/Gotta Get Yourself Together	1969	15.00
❑ 2663	If You Love Me/Breakaway	1970	12.00

VALENTINES, THE (U)

45s

Number	Title (A Side/B Side)	Yr	NM
IONA			
❑ 1003	The Sock/Sixteen Senoritas	196?	15.00
LUDIX			
❑ 102	Johnny One Heart/Mama I Have Come Home	1962	20.00

VALENTINO, DANNY

45s

Number	Title (A Side/B Side)	Yr	NM
MGM			
❑ K12835	Stampede/(You Gotta Be a) Music Man	1959	20.00
❑ K12881	Biology/A Million Tears	1960	15.00
❑ K12952	Pictures from the Past/ Till the End of Forever	1960	15.00

VALENTINO, MARK

45s

Number	Title (A Side/B Side)	Yr	NM
SWAN			
❑ 4121	The Push and Kick/ Walking Alone	1962	15.00
❑ 4135	Hey You're Lookin' Good/Do It	1963	12.00
❑ 4142	Jivin' at the Drive-In/ Part Time Job	1963	12.00

Albums

Number	Title (A Side/B Side)	Yr	NM
SWAN			
❑ SLP-508 [M]	Mark Valentino	1963	50.00

VALENTINO, SAL

Of THE BEAU BRUMMELS.

45s

Number	Title (A Side/B Side)	Yr	NM
FALCO			
❑ 306	Lisa Marie/I Wanna Twist	1962	75.00
WARNER BROS.			
❑ 7268	An Added Attraction (Come and See Me)/Alligator Man	1969	10.00
❑ 7289	Friends and Lovers/ Alligator Man	1969	10.00
❑ 7368	Silkie/Going for Rochelle	1970	10.00

VALENTINO AND THE LOVERS

45s

Number	Title (A Side/B Side)	Yr	NM
DONNA			
❑ 1345	One Teardrop Too Late/ I'm Gonna Love	1961	40.00

VALENTINOS, THE

Also see BOBBY WOMACK.

45s

Number	Title (A Side/B Side)	Yr	NM
ABKCO			
❑ 4044	It's All Over Now/ Lookin' for a Love	197?	8.00
ASTRA			
❑ 1026	Lookin' for a Love/ Somewhere There's a Girl	196?	10.00
—Reissue of Sar 132			
CHESS			
❑ 1952	Do It Right/What About Me	1966	12.00
❑ 1977	Let's Get Together/Sweeter Than the Day Before	1966	12.00
JUBILEE			
❑ 5636	Death of Love/Tired of Being Nobody	1968	10.00
❑ 5650	Two Lovers' History/You've Got the Kind of Love That's for Real	1969	10.00
SAR			
❑ 132	Lookin' for a Love/Somewhere There's a Girl	1962	20.00
❑ 137	I'll Make It Alright/Darling Come Back Home	1963	20.00
❑ 144	Baby, Lots of Luck/She's So Good to Me	1963	20.00
❑ 152	It's All Over Now/Tired of Living in the Country	1964	20.00
❑ 155	Bitter Dreams/Everybody Wants to Fall in Love	1964	15.00

VALENTYNE, RUDY

45s

Number	Title (A Side/B Side)	Yr	NM
ROULETTE			
❑ 4610	Don't Ever Leave Me/ I Won't Cry Anymore	1965	10.00
❑ 4618	When I Fall in Love/ When I Was a Child	1965	8.00
❑ 4619	And Now/Ev'rything Beautiful	1965	8.00
❑ 4620	Who Can I Turn To/More Than This I Cannot Give	1965	8.00

Albums

Number	Title (A Side/B Side)	Yr	NM
ROULETTE			
❑ R-25299 [M]	And Now... Rudy Valentyne	1965	20.00
❑ SR-25299 [S]	And Now... Rudy Valentyne	1965	25.00

VALERY, DANA

45s

Number	Title (A Side/B Side)	Yr	NM
ABC			
❑ 11138	The Lamplighter's Psalm/Didn't I	1968	12.00
❑ 11161	A Girl Without Love/Happy Birthday to Me	1968	12.00
❑ 11214	Surround Yourself with Sorrow/ Breakfast in Bed	1969	12.00
COLUMBIA			
❑ 44004	Having You Around/ You Don't Know Where Your Interest Lies	1967	25.00
—With Paul Simon			
❑ 44301	Imagine/You	1967	12.00
❑ 44389	Zabadak/Having You Around	1967	12.00
LIBERTY			
❑ 56156	Clinging Vine/Get In Line Girl	1970	8.00
❑ 56209	Point of No Return/Put Your Hand in the Hand	1970	8.00
PHANTOM			
❑ HB-10566	Will You Love Me Tomorrow/ I Never Had It So Good	1975	5.00
SCOTTI BROS.			
❑ 509	I Don't Want to Be Lonely/ Rainbow Connection	1979	4.00
❑ 612	I Gave You My Love/ Roses and Rainbows	1980	4.00

VALETS, THE

45s

Number	Title (A Side/B Side)	Yr	NM
JON			
❑ 4025	I Need Someone/When I Met You	1958	100.00
❑ 4219	Sherry/You and You Alone	1959	30.00
VULCAN			
❑ 135	Sherry/You and You Alone	1959	200.00

VALHALLA

Albums

Number	Title (A Side/B Side)	Yr	NM
UNITED ARTISTS			
❑ UAS-6730	Valhalla	1969	25.00

VALIANTS, THE (1)

45s

Number	Title (A Side/B Side)	Yr	NM
ANDEX			
❑ 4026	Please Wait My Love/ Freida, Freida	1958	120.00
—Some copies were pressed with this label in error (Keen 4026 is the "correct" issue)			
KEEN			
❑ 4008	Temptation of My Heart/ Freida, Freida	1958	50.00
❑ 4026	Please Wait My Love/ Freida, Freida	1958	60.00
❑ 34004	This Is the Nite/ Good Golly Miss Molly	1957	40.00
❑ 34007	Lover Lover/Walkin' Girl	1958	40.00
❑ 82120	This Is the Nite/Walkin' Girl	1960	20.00
SHAR-DEE			
❑ 703	Dear Cindy/Surprise	1959	40.00
—With London distribution credit on label			
❑ 703	Dear Cindy/Surprise	1959	120.00
—No mention of London distribution on label			

VALIANTS, THE (2)

45s

Number	Title (A Side/B Side)	Yr	NM
ALLSTAR			
❑ 3677	Jack the Ripper/ (B-side unknown)	196?	20.00

VALIANTS, THE (3)

45s

Number	Title (A Side/B Side)	Yr	NM
DOT			
❑ 16884	I'll Return to You/Don't Make the Same Mistake	1966	12.00

VALIANTS, THE (4)

45s

Number	Title (A Side/B Side)	Yr	NM
FAIRLANE			
❑ 21007	Blue Jeans and a Pony Tail/ See Saw	1961	20.00
IMPERIAL			
❑ 5843	Love Comes in Many Ways/ You Are Sweeter Than Wine	1962	15.00

Except when noted otherwise, VG = 25% of NM, and VG+ = 50% of NM. (Example: VG = $2.00, VG+ = $4.00 and NM = $8.00.)

Number	Title (A Side/B Side)	Yr	NM
❑ 5915	Living in Paradise/I'm in a World of My Own	1963	15.00
KC			
❑ 108	Frankie's Angel/Are You Ready	1962	15.00

VALIANTS, THE (5)

45s

Number	Title (A Side/B Side)	Yr	NM
SPECK			
❑ 1001	Wedding Bells/Velma	1958	2500.

VALIANTS, THE (U)

45s

Number	Title (A Side/B Side)	Yr	NM
JOY			
❑ 235	Let Me Go Lover/Let Me Ride	1960	20.00
ROULETTE			
❑ 4510	Johnny Lonely/Eternal Triangle	1963	20.00

VALLEY, JIM

Of PAUL REVERE AND THE RAIDERS.

45s

Number	Title (A Side/B Side)	Yr	NM
DUNHILL			
❑ 4096	Try, Try, Try/Invitations	1967	12.00
❑ 4096 [PS]	Try, Try, Try/Invitations	1967	20.00
❑ 4103	Go-Go Round/Maintain	1967	12.00
JERDEN			
❑ 814	I'm Real/There Is Love	1967	20.00
❑ 814 [DJ]	I'm Real/There Is Love	1967	25.00

VALLI

45s

Number	Title (A Side/B Side)	Yr	NM
SCEPTER			
❑ 1233	Hurry Home to Me (Soldier Boy)/Jimmy's in a Hurry	1962	15.00
—With the Shirelles backing up			

VALLI, FRANKIE

Includes records under numerous pseudonyms. Also see THE FOUR LOVERS; THE FOUR SEASONS.

45s

Number	Title (A Side/B Side)	Yr	NM
ATLANTIC			
❑ 89720	American Pop/Why	1983	4.00
—With Manhattan Transfer			
CAPITOL			
❑ B-5115	Can't Say No to You/You Make It Beautiful	1982	4.00
—With Cheryl Ladd			
❑ B-5115 [PS]	Can't Say No to You/You Make It Beautiful	1982	5.00
CINDY			
❑ 3012	Come Si Bella/Real (This Is Real)	1958	200.00
—As "Franke Valli and the Romans"			
CORONA			
❑ 1234	My Mother's Eyes/The Laugh's on Me	1953	1500.
—As "Frank Valley"			
DECCA			
❑ 30994	It May Be Wrong/Please Take a Chance	1959	200.00
—As "Frankie Vally"			
MCA			
❑ 41253	Doctor Dance/Where Did We Go Wrong	1980	5.00
—With Chris Forde			
MERCURY			
❑ 70381	Forgive and Forget/Somebody Else Took Her Home	1954	200.00
—As "Frankie Valley"; black label			
❑ 70381	Forgive and Forget/Somebody Else Took Her Home	1954	300.00
—As "Frankie Valley"; maroon label			
MOTOWN			
❑ 1251	You've Got Your Troubles/Listen to Yesterday	1973	12.00
❑ 1279	The Scalawag Song (And I Will Love You)/Listen to Yesterday	1973	12.00
MOWEST			
❑ 5011	Love Isn't Here/Poor Fool	1972	12.00
❑ 5025	The Night (mono/stereo)	1972	10.00
—Evidently, stock copies do not exist			
OKEH			
❑ 7103	I Go Ape/If You Care	1958	300.00
—As "Frankie Tyler"			
PHILIPS			
❑ DJP-16 [DJ]	My Mother's Eyes (mono/stereo)	1967	50.00
—Only issued as a promo; alternate number is 40460, but actual issue of 40460 is "C'mon Marianne" by the Four Seasons			
❑ 40407	The Proud One/Ivy	1966	10.00
❑ 40407 [PS]	The Proud One/Ivy	1966	15.00
❑ 40446	Can't Take My Eyes Off You/The Trouble with Me	1967	10.00
❑ 40446 [PS]	Can't Take My Eyes Off You/The Trouble with Me	1967	15.00
❑ 40484	I Make a Fool of Myself/September Rain (Here Comes the Rain)	1967	10.00
❑ 40484 [PS]	I Make a Fool of Myself/September Rain (Here Comes the Rain)	1967	15.00
❑ 40510	To Give (The Reason I Live)/Watch Where You Walk	1967	10.00
❑ 40510 [PS]	To Give (The Reason I Live)/Watch Where You Walk	1967	15.00
❑ 40622	The Girl I'll Never Know (Angels Never Fly This Low)/A Face Without a Name	1969	10.00
❑ 40622 [PS]	The Girl I'll Never Know (Angels Never Fly This Low)/A Face Without a Name	1969	15.00
❑ 40661	You've Got Your Troubles/A Dream of Kings	1970	12.00
❑ 40680	Circles in the Sand/My Mother's Eyes	1970	10.00
PRIVATE STOCK			
❑ 45,003	My Eyes Adored You/Watch Where You Walk	1974	5.00
❑ 45,021	Swearin' to God/Why	1975	5.00
❑ 45,043	Our Day Will Come/You Can Bet	1975	5.00
❑ 45,074	Fallen Angel/Carrie (I Would Marry You)	1976	5.00
❑ 45,098	We're All Alone/You to Me Are Everything	1976	5.00
❑ 45,109	Boomerang/Look at the World, It's Changing	1976	5.00
❑ 45,140	Easily/What Good Am I Without You	1977	5.00
❑ 45,154	Second Thoughts/So She Says	1977	5.00
❑ 45,169	I Need You/I'm Gonna Love You	1977	5.00
❑ 45,180	I Could Have Loved You/Rainstorm	1978	5.00
RSO			
❑ 897	Grease/Grease (Instrumental)	1978	6.00
SMASH			
❑ 1995	The Sun Ain't Gonna Shine (Anymore)/This Is Goodbye	1965	10.00
❑ 2015	(You're Gonna) Hurt Yourself/Night Hawk	1965	15.00
—B-side by the Valli Boys			
❑ 2037	You're Ready Now/Cry for Me	1966	10.00
WARNER BROS.			
❑ 8670	No Love at All/Save Me, Save Me	1978	5.00
❑ 8734	Fancy Dancer/Needing You	1979	5.00

Albums

Number	Title	Yr	NM
MCA			
❑ 743	Heaven Above Me	1982	8.00
—Reissue of 5134			
❑ 756	The Very Best of Frankie Valli	1982	8.00
—Reissue of 3198			
❑ 3198	The Very Best of Frankie Valli	1980	10.00
❑ 5134	Heaven Above Me	1979	10.00
MOTOWN			
❑ M5-104V1	Motown Superstar Series, Vol. 4	1981	10.00
❑ M6-852	Inside You	1975	15.00
PHILIPS			
❑ PHM 200247 [M]	Frankie Valli — Solo	1967	40.00
❑ PHS 600247 [S]	Frankie Valli — Solo	1967	30.00
❑ PHS 600274	Timeless	1968	25.00
PRIVATE STOCK			
❑ PS-2000	Closeup	1975	12.00
❑ PS-2001	Frankie Valli Gold	1975	12.00
❑ PS-2006	Our Day Will Come	1975	12.00
❑ PS-2017	Valli	1976	12.00
❑ PS-7002	Lady Put the Light Out	1977	12.00
❑ PS-7012	Hits	1978	12.00
WARNER BROS.			
❑ BSK 3233	Frankie Valli...Is the Word	1978	10.00

VALLI, FRANKIE, AND THE FOUR SEASONS

See THE FOUR SEASONS.

VALLI, JUNE

45s

Number	Title (A Side/B Side)	Yr	NM
ABC-PARAMOUNT			
❑ 10442	You Say You Wanna Be Around/Gather Your Dreams	1963	8.00
❑ 10467	Catch Myself Crying/Silly Girl	1963	8.00
DCP			
❑ 1120	Empty Rooms/I'm Made for Love (Not for Hurtin')	1964	8.00
MERCURY			
❑ 10029X45 [S]	Apple Green/Oh Why	1960	20.00
❑ 71332X45	Dance with Me/La Santa Venuta	1958	10.00
❑ 71382X45	The Wedding/Lunch Hour	1958	10.00
❑ 71422X45	The Answer to a Maiden's Prayer/In His Arms	1959	10.00
❑ 71461X45	An Anonymous Letter/Bygones	1959	10.00
❑ 71480X45	I Love You Truly/You Were Meant for Me	1959	10.00
❑ 71520X45	My Darling, My Darling/Shadows	1959	10.00
❑ 71588X45 [M]	Apple Green/Oh Why	1960	10.00
❑ 71653	I'll Step Aside/Looking at the World	1960	10.00
❑ 71688	Love in Bloom/Flittin' and a Flirtin'	1960	10.00
❑ 71729	Weep for Me Lover/Borrowed Kisses	1960	10.00
❑ 71750	Guess Things Happen That Way/Tell Him for Me	1961	10.00
❑ 71800	Come Back to Sorrento/The World We Love In	1961	10.00
❑ 71882	Everlastin'/So Long Loser	1961	10.00
RCA VICTOR			
❑ 47-4298	Always, Always/Now, Now, Now	1951	15.00
❑ 47-4388	Cry/The Three Bells	1951	15.00
❑ 47-4759	Strange Sensation/So Madly in Love	1952	15.00
❑ 47-4900	Taboo/Mighty Lonesome Feeling	1952	15.00
❑ 47-5017	Why Don't You Believe Me/A Shoulder to Weep On	1952	15.00
❑ 47-5177	Congratulations to Someone/Love and Hate	1953	15.00
❑ 47-5298	Brass Ring Love/Many Are the Times	1953	15.00
❑ 47-5368	Crying in the Chapel/Love Every Moment You Live	1953	15.00
❑ 47-5488	Mystery Street/Don't Forget to Write	1953	15.00
❑ 47-5653	The Gypsy Was Wrong/Old Shoes and a Bag of Rice	1954	15.00
❑ 47-5740	I Understand/Love, Tears and Kisses	1954	15.00
❑ 47-5837	Tell Me, Tell Me/Boy Wanted	1954	15.00
❑ 47-5924	Ole Pappy Time/Wrong, Wrong, Wrong	1954	15.00
❑ 47-5988	Young and Foolish/Tell It to Me Again	1955	15.00
❑ 47-6078	Unchained Melody/Tomorrow	1955	15.00
❑ 47-6215	Oh! My Love/A Kiss Like Yours	1955	15.00
❑ 47-6258	The Things They Say/Por Favor	1955	15.00
❑ 47-6331	Don't Tell Me Not to Love You/Oh! What a Day	1955	15.00
❑ 47-6402	Madonna in Blue/While There's Time	1956	12.00
❑ 47-6464	Sleepy Head/From the Wrong Side of Town	1956	12.00
❑ 47-6552	Shangri-La/I've Got Something in My Eye	1956	12.00
❑ 47-6662	Beauty Isn't Everything/Now	1956	12.00
❑ 47-6852	Will You Love Me Still/Strictly Sentimental	1957	12.00
❑ 47-7032	Baby Come Home/Open Your Arms	1957	12.00
UNITED ARTISTS			
❑ 466	Hush Little Baby/I'm Afraid	1962	8.00
❑ 490	I Forgot More Than You'll Ever Know/Is It Right or Wrong	1962	8.00

7-Inch Extended Plays

Number	Title	Yr	NM
RCA VICTOR			
❑ EPA-667	Body and Soul/Don't Take Your Love from Me//Can't Help Lovin' Dat Man/But Not for Me	195?	12.00
❑ EPA-667 [PS]	Body and Soul	195?	12.00

Albums

Number	Title	Yr	NM
AUDIO FIDELITY			
❑ AFSD-6214 [S]	June Valli Today	1969	20.00
MERCURY			
❑ MG-20463 [M]	Do-It-Yourself Wedding Album	1959	20.00
❑ SR-60145 [S]	Do-It-Yourself Wedding Album	1959	25.00
RCA VICTOR			
❑ LPM-1120 [M]	The Torch	1955	40.00

VALOR, TONY

45s

Number	Title (A Side/B Side)	Yr	NM
MUSICTONE			
❑ 1119	There's a Story in My Heart/So Tenderly	1963	150.00

VALQUINS, THE

45s

Number	Title (A Side/B Side)	Yr	NM
GAITY			
❑ 161/2	My Dear/Falling Star	1959	800.00
❑ 161/2	My Dear/Falling Star	1959	1500.
—Red vinyl			

VALRAYS, THE

45s

Number	Title (A Side/B Side)	Yr	NM
PARKWAY			
❑ 880	Get A Board/Pee Wee	1963	30.00
❑ 904	Yo Me Pregunto/Tonky	1964	20.00

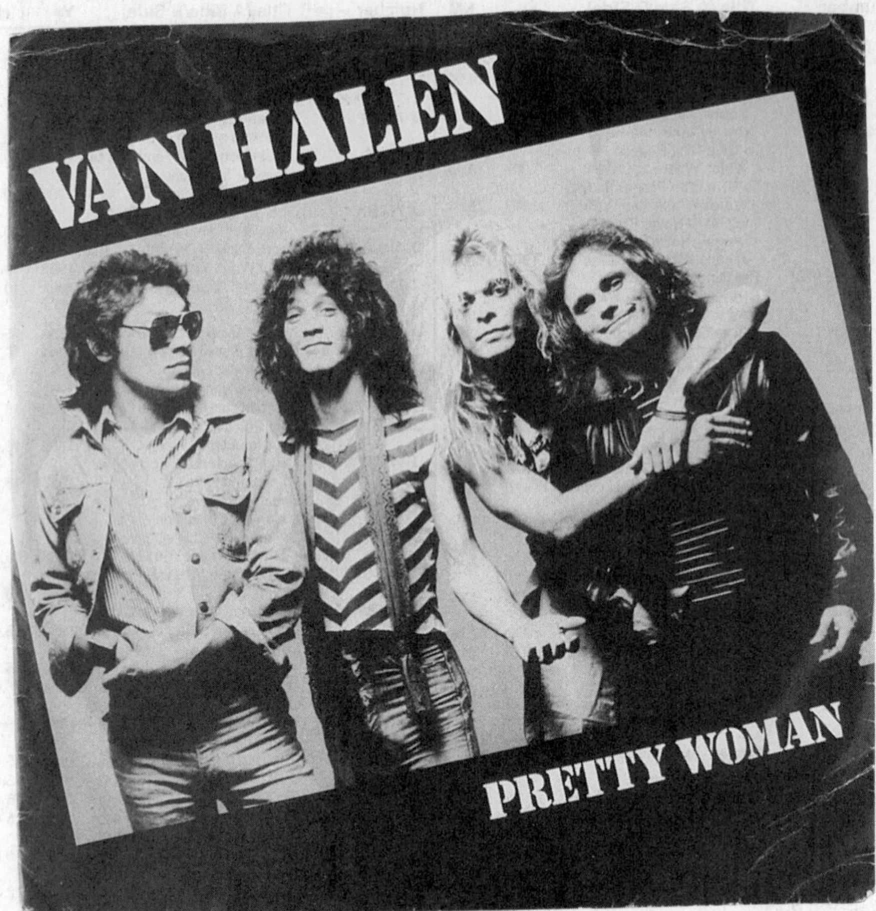

Van Halen, "Pretty Woman," Warner Bros. 50003, 1982, $5.

Number	Title (A Side/B Side)	Yr	NM
VALS, THE			
45s			
ASCOT			
❑ 2163	Too Late/I'm Stepping Out with My Memories	1964	30.00
UNIQUE LABORATORIES			
❑ (no #)	The Song of a Lover/ Compensation Blues	1962	1000.
VALTONES, THE			
45s			
GEE			
❑ 1004	You Belong to My Heart/Have You Ever Met an Angel	1956	300.00
VALUMES, THE See THE VOLUMES.			
VAMPIRES, THE			
45s			
CARROLL			
❑ 104	Why Didn't I Listen to Mother/ Did Anybody Lose a Tear	1962	150.00
Albums			
UNITED ARTISTS			
❑ UAL-3378 [M]	The Vampires at the Monster Ball	1964	25.00
❑ UAS-6378 [S]	The Vampires at the Monster Ball	1964	30.00
VAN, HARVIE JUNE			
45s			
BRIAR			
❑ 121	Natividad (Nativity)/Dasher (With the Light Upon His Tail)	1961	20.00
KING			
❑ 1369	Can Can Skirt/My Sins of Yesterday	1954	25.00
❑ 1387	The Lights Are Growing Dim/ I'm Jut Not That Kind	1954	20.00
❑ 1482	Don't Offer Me the Stars/Mama Don't Chase My Love Away	1955	20.00

Number	Title (A Side/B Side)	Yr	NM
❑ 1497	False or True/I Found Out	1955	20.00
RCA VICTOR			
❑ 47-7548	Butcher Boy/Leaving Woman Blues	1959	12.00
❑ 47-7668	When You Are Here/ Poor Wildwood Flower	1960	12.00
❑ 47-7778	Johnny Darling/ Little Wooden Man	1960	12.00
TODD			
❑ 1078	Biggest Broken Heart in Town/ Good Morning Mr. Echo	1962	12.00
VAN DER GRAAF GENERATOR Featuring Peter Hammill.			
45s			
MERCURY			
❑ 72979	Necromancer/Afterwards	1969	20.00
Albums			
ABC DUNHILL			
❑ DS 50097	H to He Who Am the Only One	1971	30.00
CHARISMA			
❑ CAS-1051	Pawn Hearts	1971	30.00
MERCURY			
❑ SRM-1-1069	Godbluff	1975	18.00
❑ SRM-1-1096	Still Life	1976	18.00
❑ SRM-1-1116	World Record	1976	18.00
❑ SR-61238	The Aerosol Grey Machine	1969	100.00
PROBE			
❑ CPLP-4515	The Least We Can Do Is Wave to Each Other	1970	30.00
PVC			
❑ 9901 [(2)]	Vital	1979	15.00
VAN DERBUR, MARILYN			
Albums			
DECCA			
❑ DL 8770 [M]	Miss America	1958	40.00

Number	Title (A Side/B Side)	Yr	NM
VAN DYKE, CONNIE			
45s			
MOTOWN			
❑ 1041	Oh Freddie/It Hurt Me Too	1963	50.00
WHEELSVILLE			
❑ 112	Don't Do Nothin' I Wouldn't Do/ The Words Won't Come	196?	150.00
VAN DYKE, EARL, AND THE SOUL BROTHERS			
45s			
RENAISSANCE			
❑ 5000	September Song/ (B-side unknown)	196?	75.00
SOUL			
❑ 35006	Soul Stomp/Hot 'N' Tot	1964	20.00
❑ 35009	All for You/Too Many Fish in the Sea	1965	800.00
❑ 35014	I Can't Help Myself/How Sweet It Is To Be Loved By You	1965	20.00
❑ 35018	The Flick (Part 1)/ The Flick (Part 2)	1966	20.00
❑ 35028	6 x 6/There Is No Greater Love	1967	20.00
—By Earl Van Dyke and the Motown Brass			
❑ 35059	Runaway Child, Running Wild/ Gonna Give Her All the Love I've Got	1969	20.00
Albums			
MOTOWN			
❑ M-631 [M]	The Motown Sound	1965	40.00
❑ MS-631 [S]	The Motown Sound	1965	50.00
SOUL			
❑ SS-715	The Earl of Funk	1970	40.00
VAN DYKE, REGGIE			
45s			
PARKWAY			
❑ 829	Sweetness/Happy Music	1961	15.00
VAN DYKES, THE (1)			
45s			
DELUXE			
❑ 6193	The Bells Are Ringing/ The Meaning of Love	1960	25.00
DONNA			
❑ 1333	Gift of Love/Guardian Angel	1961	40.00
FELSTED			
❑ 8565	Once Upon a Dream/ Dame Tu Corazon	1959	25.00
KING			
❑ 5158	The Bells Are Ringing/ The Meaning of Love	1958	70.00
SPRING			
❑ 1113	Gift of Love/Guardian Angel	1961	120.00
VAN DYKES, THE (2)			
45s			
HUE			
❑ 6501	No Man Is an Island/I Won't Hold It Against You	1965	30.00
MALA			
❑ 520	No Man Is an Island/I Won't Hold It Against You	1965	15.00
❑ 530	I've Got to Go On Without You/ What Will I Do If I Lose You	1966	12.00
❑ 539	Never Let Me Go/I've Got to Find a Love	1966	12.00
❑ 549	You Need Confidence/ You're Shakin' Me Up	1966	12.00
❑ 566	A Sunday Kind of Love/ I'm So Happy	1967	20.00
❑ 584	Tears of Joy/Save My Love for a Rainy Day	1967	40.00
Albums			
BELL			
❑ 6004 [M]	Tellin' It Like It Is	1967	50.00
❑ S-6004 [S]	Tellin' It Like It Is	1967	60.00
VAN DYKES, THE (3)			
45s			
CO-OP			
❑ 515	Rich Girl/Miracle After Miracle	1967	20.00
❑ 516	Rock-a-Bye Girl/I'll Be By	1967	20.00
GREEN SEA			
❑ 101	Rich Girl/Again and Again	1965	40.00
❑ 105	Rock-a-Bye Girl/I'll Be By	1966	50.00
❑ 108	Miracle After Miracle/ How Can I Forget Her	1966	40.00

Except when noted otherwise, VG = 25% of NM, and VG+ = 50% of NM. (Example: VG = $2.00, VG+ = $4.00 and NM = $8.00.)

Number	Title (A Side/B Side)	Yr	NM

VAN DYKES, THE (4)

45s

DECCA

Number	Title (A Side/B Side)	Yr	NM
❑ 30654	The Fixer/Run Betty, Run	1958	40.00
❑ 30762	Come On Baby/Lambie Baby	1958	40.00
❑ 31036	Better Come Back to Me/ I Don't Know What to Do	1959	60.00

VAN DYKES, THE (U)

45s

ATLANTIC

Number	Title (A Side/B Side)	Yr	NM
❑ 2161	King of Fools/Stupidity	1962	15.00

VAN EATEN, LON AND DERREK

45s

A&M

Number	Title (A Side/B Side)	Yr	NM
❑ 1643	Wildfire/Music Lover	1974	5.00
—All A&M records as "Lon and Derrek"			
❑ 1662	Who Do You Outdo/All You're Hungry For Is Love	1975	5.00
❑ 1696	The Harder You Pull... The Tighter It Gets/Dancing in the Dark	1975	5.00
❑ 1845	Loving You/Baby It's You	1976	4.00

APPLE

Number	Title (A Side/B Side)	Yr	NM
❑ 1845	Sweet Music/Song of Songs	1972	8.00
❑ 1845 [PS]	Sweet Music/Song of Songs	1972	10.00

Albums

A&M

Number	Title (A Side/B Side)	Yr	NM
❑ SP-4507	Who Do You Outdo	1975	10.00

APPLE

Number	Title (A Side/B Side)	Yr	NM
❑ SMAS-3390	Brother	1972	15.00

VAN HALEN Also see SAMMY HAGAR; DAVID LEE ROTH; CHICKENFOOT.

12-Inch Singles

WARNER BROS.

Number	Title (A Side/B Side)	Yr	NM
❑ PRO-A-1006 [DJ]	Pretty Woman/Happy Trails	1982	15.00
❑ PRO-A-2105 [DJ]	Jump (same on both sides)	1984	12.00
❑ PRO-A-2126 [DJ]	I'll Wait (Edit)/Drop Dead Legs	1984	12.00
❑ PRO-A-2162 [DJ]	Panama (same on both sides)	1984	10.00
❑ PRO-A-2177 [DJ]	Hot for Teacher (Edit) (LP Version)	1984	15.00
❑ PRO-A-2453 [DJ]	Why Can't This Be Love (same on both sides)	1986	10.00
❑ PRO-A-2477 [DJ]	Best of Both Worlds (same on both sides)	1986	10.00
❑ PRO-A-2483 [DJ]	Dreams (Edit 4:24) (LP Version 4:54)	1986	12.00
❑ PRO-A-2523 [DJ]	Summer Nights (same on both sides)	1986	10.00
❑ PRO-A-2542 [DJ]	Love Walks In (same on both sides)	1986	10.00
❑ PRO-A-2586 [DJ]	5150 (same on both sides)	1986	15.00
❑ PRO-A-2622 [DJ]	Best of Both Worlds (Live)/ Rock and Roll (Live)	1986	15.00

45s

WARNER BROS.

Number	Title (A Side/B Side)	Yr	NM
❑ 8515	You Really Got Me/Atomic Punk	1978	7.00
❑ 8556	Runnin' with the Devil/Eruption	1978	10.00
❑ 8556 [PS]	Runnin' with the Devil/Eruption	1978	30.00
❑ 8631	Jamie's Cryin'/I'm the One	1978	10.00
❑ 8707	Feel Your Love Tonight/ Ain't Talkin' 'Bout Love	1978	10.00
❑ 8823 [PS]	Dance the Night Away/ Outta Love Again	1979	12.00
❑ 8823	Dance the Night Away/ Outta Love Again	1979	6.00
❑ 17810	Not Enough/Amsterdam	1995	5.00
❑ 17909	Can't Stop Lovin' You/ Crossing Over	1995	5.00
❑ 18592	Judgment Day/Dreams	1993	5.00
❑ 19151	Top of the World/Poundcake	1992	5.00
❑ 27565	Feels So Good/ Sucker in a 3-Piece	1989	5.00
❑ 27746	Finish What Ya Started/ Sucker in a 3-Piece	1988	3.00
❑ 27746 [PS]	Finish What Ya Started/ Sucker in a 3-Piece	1988	3.00
❑ 27827	When It's Love/Cabo Wabo	1988	3.00
❑ 27827 [PS]	When It's Love/Cabo Wabo	1988	3.00
❑ 27891	Black and Blue/Apolitical Blues	1988	3.00

Van Halen, "Love Walks In," Warner Bros. 28626, 1986, **$3.**

Number	Title (A Side/B Side)	Yr	NM
❑ 27891 [PS]	Black and Blue/Apolitical Blues	1988	5.00
❑ 28505	Best of Both Worlds/ Best of Both Worlds (Live)	1986	3.00
❑ 28505 [PS]	Best of Both Worlds/ Best of Both Worlds (Live)	1986	3.00
❑ 28626	Love Walks In/Summer Nights	1986	3.00
❑ 28626 [PS]	Love Walks In/Summer Nights	1986	3.00
❑ 28702	Dreams/Inside	1986	3.00
❑ 28740	Why Can't This Be Love/Get Up	1986	3.00
❑ 28740 [PS]	Why Can't This Be Love/Get Up	1986	3.00
❑ 29199	Hot for Teacher/Little Dreamer	1984	3.00
❑ 29199 [PS]	Hot for Teacher/Little Dreamer	1984	4.00
—Regular picture sleeve			
❑ 29199 [PS]	Hot for Teacher/Little Dreamer	1984	8.00
—Special plastic sleeve with inserts			
❑ 29250	Panama/Drop Dead Legs	1984	3.00
❑ 29250 [PS]	Panama/Drop Dead Legs	1984	3.00
❑ 29307	I'll Wait/Girl Gone Bad	1984	3.00
❑ 29307 [PS]	I'll Wait/Girl Gone Bad	1984	4.00
❑ 29384	Jump/House of Pain	1984	3.00
❑ 29384 [PS]	Jump/House of Pain	1984	3.00
❑ 29929	Secrets/Big Bad Bill	1982	6.00
❑ 29986	Dancing in the Street/Full Bug	1982	4.00
❑ 49035	Beautiful Girls/D.O.A.	1979	5.00
❑ 49501	And the Cradle Will Rock.../ Could This Be Magic	1980	5.00
❑ 49751	So This Is Love/ Read About It Later	1981	5.00
❑ 49751 [PS]	So This Is Love/ Read About It Later	1981	8.00
❑ 50003	(Oh) Pretty Woman/Happy Trails	1982	4.00
❑ 50003	Pretty Woman/Happy Trails	1982	5.00
❑ 50003 [PS]	(Oh) Pretty Woman/Happy Trails	1982	4.00
❑ 50003 [PS]	Pretty Woman/Happy Trails	1982	5.00
—Original copies of both record and sleeve have no subtitles			

Albums

DCC COMPACT CLASSICS

Number	Title (A Side/B Side)	Yr	NM
❑ LPZ-2066	Van Halen	1998	40.00
—Audiophile vinyl			

WARNER BROS.

Number	Title (A Side/B Side)	Yr	NM
❑ PRO 705 [DJ]	Looney Tunes	1978	75.00
—Promo-only EP on red vinyl			
❑ BSK 3075	Van Halen	1978	12.00
—Early pressings have "Burbank" labels			
❑ BSK 3075	Van Halen	1979	10.00
—White/cream labels			
❑ HS 3312	Van Halen II	1979	10.00
❑ HS 3415	Women and Children First	1980	10.00
❑ HS 3540	Fair Warning	1981	10.00
❑ BSK 3677	Diver Down	1982	10.00
❑ 23985	1984	1984	10.00
❑ 23985 [DJ]	1984	1984	25.00
—Promo on Quiex II vinyl			
❑ 25394	5150	1986	10.00
❑ 25732	OU812	1988	10.00
❑ W1-26594	For Unlawful Carnal Knowledge	1991	25.00
—The only U.S. vinyl version was released through Columbia House			
❑ 45760	Balance	1995	25.00

VAN LOAN, JOE

45s

FORD

Number	Title (A Side/B Side)	Yr	NM
❑ 122	Autumn Leaves/Love Divided	1963	20.00

V-TONE

Number	Title (A Side/B Side)	Yr	NM
❑ 200	Forever/Give Me Your Heart	1958	150.00

VAN ZANDT, ED

45s

HIT

Number	Title (A Side/B Side)	Yr	NM
❑ 28	Little Diane/Devil Woman	1962	8.00
—B-side by Bill Murphy			

VAN ZANDT, TOWNES

45s

POPPY

Number	Title (A Side/B Side)	Yr	NM
❑ XW170	Fraulein/Don't Let the Sunshine Fool You	1973	6.00
❑ XW238	Pancho and Lefty /(B-side unknown)	1973	10.00
❑ 506	Talking Karate Blues/ Waiting Around to Die	1968	8.00
❑ 510	Second Lovers/ (B-side unknown)	1968	8.00

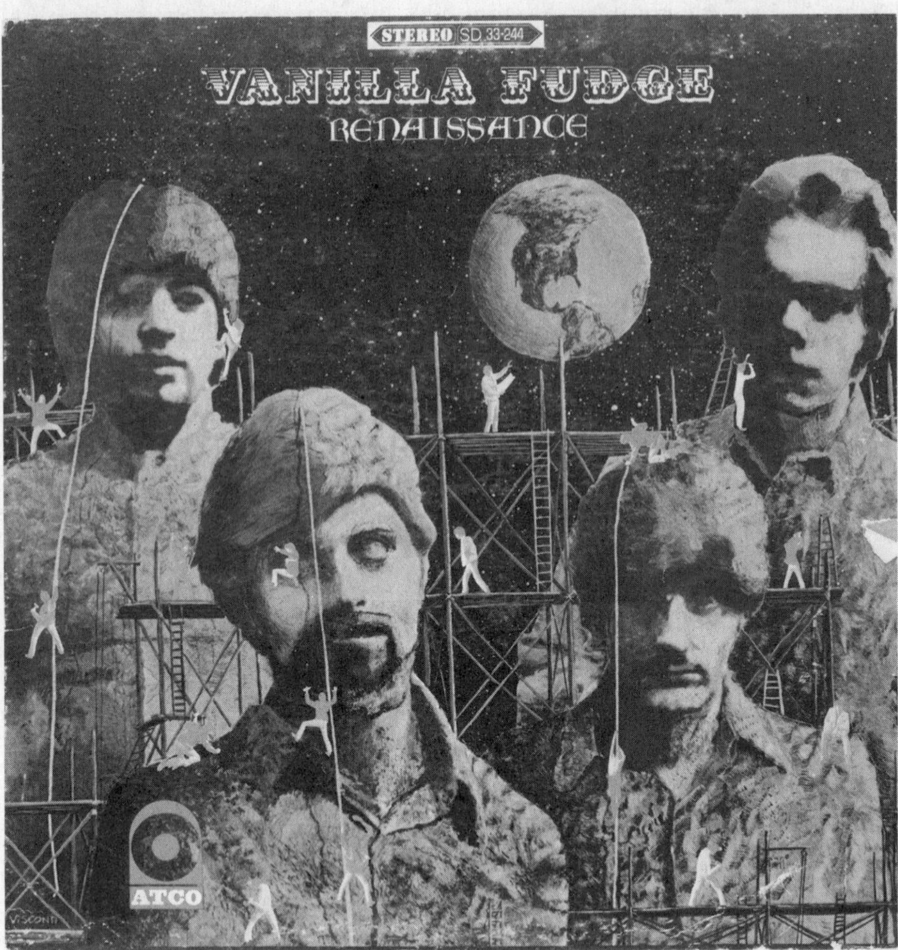

Vanilla Fudge, *Renaissance*, Atco SD 33-244, 1968, purple and brown label, **$20.**

Number	Title (A Side/B Side)	Yr	NM
❑ 90104	Come Tomorrow/ Delta Momma Blues	1970	8.00
❑ 90108	Greensboro Woman/Stand-In	1971	8.00
❑ 90113	If I Needed You/Sunshine Boy	1971	8.00
❑ 90116	Honky Tonkin'/Snow Don't Fall	1972	8.00

TOMATO

Number	Title (A Side/B Side)	Yr	NM
❑ 10003	Who Do You Love/ (B-side unknown)	1977	5.00
❑ 10005	When She Don't Need Me/ No Place to Fall	1978	5.00

Albums

POPPY

Number	Title (A Side/B Side)	Yr	NM
❑ PP-LA004-F	The Late Great Townes Van Zandt	1973	15.00
❑ PYS-5700	High, Low and In Between	1972	15.00
❑ PYS-40001	For the Sake of a Song	1968	25.00
❑ PYS-40004	Our Mother, The Mountain	1969	15.00
❑ PYS-40007	Townes Van Zandt	1969	15.00
❑ PYS-40012	Delta Momma Blues	1970	15.00

SUGAR HILL

Number	Title (A Side/B Side)	Yr	NM
❑ SH-1020	At My Window	1987	10.00
❑ SH-1026	Live and Obscure	1989	10.00

TOMATO

Number	Title (A Side/B Side)	Yr	NM
❑ 7001 [(2)]	Live at the Old Quarter, Houston, Texas	1977	15.00
❑ 7011	The Late Great Townes Van Zandt	1978	12.00
—Reissue of Poppy 004			
❑ 7012	High, Low and In Between	1978	12.00
—Reissue of Poppy 5700			
❑ 7013	Delta Momma Blues	1978	12.00
—Reissue of Poppy 40012			
❑ 7014	Townes Van Zandt	1978	12.00
—Reissue of Poppy 40007			
❑ 7015	Our Mother, The Mountain	1978	12.00
—Reissue of Poppy 40004			
❑ 7017	Flyin' Shoes	1978	12.00

VANCE, FRANKIE

45s

REVUE

Number	Title (A Side/B Side)	Yr	NM
❑ 11048	Do You Hear Me Baby/Can't Break the Habit (Of Your Love)	1969	40.00
❑ 11062	You Are My Solution/ Somewhere in Your Life (You've Been Hurt)	1970	25.00

VANGELIS

12-Inch Singles

POLYDOR

Number	Title (A Side/B Side)	Yr	NM
❑ PRO 459-1 [DJ]	Hymne (same on both sides)	1986	20.00

45s

POLYDOR

Number	Title (A Side/B Side)	Yr	NM
❑ PRO 204 [DJ]	L'Enfant (same on both sides)	1979	10.00
❑ PRO 458-7 [DJ]	Hymne (same on both sides)	1986	10.00
❑ 2189	Titles/Eric's Theme	1981	20.00
—Original issue of this single			
❑ 2189	Chariots of Fire — Titles/ Eric's Theme	1982	4.00
❑ 2189 [DJ]	Titles (same on both sides)	1981	10.00
—Promo; red label			
❑ 2189 [DJ]	Titles (same on both sides)	1981	12.00
—Promo; white label; "Special Edition for Adult Contemporary Radio" on label			
❑ 2189 [DJ]	Chariots of Fire — Titles (same on both sides)	1982	5.00
—White label promo			
❑ 2189 [PS]	Chariots of Fire — Titles/ Eric's Theme	1982	8.00
❑ 873550-7	Chariots of Fire/Hymne	1989	4.00
—"Timepieces" reissue			

RCA

Number	Title (A Side/B Side)	Yr	NM
❑ JB-10733 [DJ]	So Long Ago, So Clear/ Heaven and Hell Theme	1976	12.00
—May not exist as a stock copy; if it does, it would fetch at least twice this amount			
❑ JH-10882 [DJ]	Pulstar (stereo/mono)	1977	8.00
❑ PB-10882	Pulstar/Alpha	1977	15.00
❑ PB-13402	To the Unknown Man Part I/Part II	1982	8.00

Albums

ARISTA

Number	Title (A Side/B Side)	Yr	NM
❑ AL-8545	Direct	1988	10.00

DEUTSCHE GRAMMAPHON

Number	Title (A Side/B Side)	Yr	NM
❑ 415196-1	Invisible Connections	1985	15.00
—All copies for U.S. distribution were pressed in West Germany			

POLYDOR

Number	Title (A Side/B Side)	Yr	NM
❑ PD-1-6199	China	1979	10.00
❑ PD-1-6335	Chariots of Fire	1981	10.00
❑ 815732-1	Antarctica	198?	15.00
—Most copies may be imports			
❑ 823396-1	Soil Festivities	1984	10.00
❑ 825245-1	Mask	1985	10.00
❑ 825384-1	Chariots of Fire	1985	8.00
—Reissue			
❑ 829663-1	Opera Sauvage	1986	8.00
—Reissue			
❑ 839518-1	Themes	1989	15.00

RCA VICTOR

Number	Title (A Side/B Side)	Yr	NM
❑ DJL1-1849 [DJ]	The Vangelis Radio Special	1976	100.00
—Promo only music and interviews			
❑ AFL1-2627	Spiral	1977	10.00
❑ AFL1-3020	Beaubourg	1978	12.00
❑ AYL1-4387	Beaubourg	1982	8.00
—"Best Buy Series" reissue			
❑ AFL1-4397	To the Unknown Man	1982	8.00
❑ AFL1-5110	Heaven and Hell	197?	8.00
—Reissue prefix; black label, dog near top			
❑ LPL1-5110	Heaven and Hell	1976	10.00
—Original prefix; tan label			
❑ AFL1-5136	Albedo 0.39	197?	8.00
—Reissue prefix			
❑ LPL1-5136	Albedo 0.39	1976	10.00
—Original prefix			

VERTIGO

Number	Title (A Side/B Side)	Yr	NM
❑ VEL-1019	Earth	1974	50.00
—As "Vangelis O."			

VANGUARDS, THE (1)

45s

LAMP

Number	Title (A Side/B Side)	Yr	NM
❑ 652	It's To Late for Love/The Thought of Losing Your Love	1970	12.00
—Yes, the label misspelled the A-side			
❑ 653	Girl Go Away/Man Without Knowledge	1970	12.00

WHIZ

Number	Title (A Side/B Side)	Yr	NM
❑ 612	Somebody Please/I Can't Use You Girl	1969	10.00

VANGUARDS, THE (2)

45s

DERBY

Number	Title (A Side/B Side)	Yr	NM
❑ 854	Don't Let It Happen Again/So Live	1954	400.00

VANGUARDS, THE (3)

45s

IVY

Number	Title (A Side/B Side)	Yr	NM
❑ 103	Moonlight/I'm Movin'	1958	40.00
—No mention of "Billy Butler's Orchestra"			
❑ 103	Moonlight/I'm Movin'	1958	120.00
—With mention of "Billy Butler's Orchestra"			

VANGUARDS, THE (4)

45s

WARNER BROS.

Number	Title (A Side/B Side)	Yr	NM
❑ 5800	Girl/A Stranger in Your Town	1966	12.00

VANGUARDS, THE (U)

45s

DOT

Number	Title (A Side/B Side)	Yr	NM
❑ 15791	Baby Doll/My Friend Mary Ann	1958	25.00

VANILLA FUDGE

Also see CACTUS, BECK, BOGERT & APPICE.

45s

ATCO

Number	Title (A Side/B Side)	Yr	NM
❑ 6495	You Keep Me Hangin' On/ Take Me for a Little While	1967	12.00
❑ 6554	The Look of Love/ Where Is My Mind	1968	8.00
❑ 6590	You Keep Me Hangin' On/ Come by Day, Come by Night	1968	10.00
❑ 6616	Take Me for a Little While/ Thoughts	1968	8.00
❑ 6632	Season of the Witch (Part 1)/ Season of the Witch (Part 2)	1968	8.00
❑ 6655	Good Good Lovin'/Shot Gun	1969	8.00
❑ 6679	People/Some Velvet Morning	1969	8.00
❑ 6703	Need Love/I Can't Make It Alone	1969	8.00
❑ 6728	Windmills of Your Mind/Lord in the Country	1970	6.00
❑ 99729	Mystery/The Stranger	1984	4.00

Except when noted otherwise, VG = 25% of NM, and VG+ = 50% of NM. (Example: VG = $2.00, VG+ = $4.00 and NM = $8.00.)

Number	Title (A Side/B Side)	Yr	NM

7-Inch Extended Plays

ATCO

Number	Title (A Side/B Side)	Yr	NM
❑ SP-4516 [DJ]	Eleanor Rigby-Part 1/You Keep Me Hanging On//Eleanor Rigby-Part 2/Ticket to Ride	1968	20.00
—Promo only, white label			
❑ SP-4516 [PS]	(title unknown)	1968	20.00
—Paper sleeve with above EP			

Albums

ATCO

Number	Title (A Side/B Side)	Yr	NM
❑ 33-224 [M]	Vanilla Fudge	1967	25.00
❑ SD 33-224	Vanilla Fudge	197?	8.00
—Any later label			
❑ SD 33-224 [S]	Vanilla Fudge	1967	20.00
—Purple and brown label			
❑ SD 33-224 [S]	Vanilla Fudge	1969	12.00
—Yellow label			
❑ 33-237 [M]	The Beat Goes On	1968	40.00
❑ SD 33-237	The Beat Goes On	1968	20.00
—Purple and brown label			
❑ SD 33-237	The Beat Goes On	1969	12.00
—Yellow label			
❑ SD 33-244	Renaissance	1968	20.00
—Purple and brown label			
❑ SD 33-244	Renaissance	1969	12.00
—Yellow label			
❑ SD 33-278	Near the Beginning	1969	15.00
❑ SD 33-303	Rock 'N' Roll	1969	15.00
❑ 90006	The Best of Vanilla Fudge	1982	10.00
❑ 90149	Mystery	1984	12.00

SUNDAZED

Number	Title (A Side/B Side)	Yr	NM
❑ LP 5168 [M]	Vanilla Fudge	2004	15.00
—Reissue on 180-gram vinyl			

VANILLA ICE

12-Inch Singles

SBK

Number	Title (A Side/B Side)	Yr	NM
❑ V-19724	Ice Ice Baby (4 versions)/Play That Funky Music (3 versions)	1990	8.00
❑ V-19726	Play That Funky Music (Short Radio Funk) (Long Radio Funk) (Sky King's Medley) (Sky King's Funky Club Jam) (Sky King's Short & Sweet Funk) (Sky King's Groove Icestrumental)	1990	8.00
❑ V-19730	I Love You (Short Version 4:21) (Long Version 5:10) (Instrumental Version 5:10)/ Stop That Train (Short Version 3:54) (Long Version 4:28)	1991	8.00
❑ V-19746	Cool As Ice (Everybody Get Loose Mix 5:31) (Naomi Gets Loose Mix 5:31) (Radio Edit 3:38) (Instrumental 5:30)	1991	8.00
❑ Y-58096	Roll 'Em Up (Album Version) (Instrumental) (Ice-capella)/ (same on both sides)	1994	7.00

45s

COLLECTABLES

Number	Title (A Side/B Side)	Yr	NM
❑ 6119	Play That Funky Music/ Ice Ice Baby	199?	3.00
—Reissue			

SBK

Number	Title (A Side/B Side)	Yr	NM
❑ LS-57394	Play That Funky Music/ Ice Ice Baby	1991	5.00

—"For Jukebox Use Only" on label; this was the prototype for the successful Capitol "For Jukeboxes Only!" 7-inch single series that began in 1992

Albums

ULTRA

Number	Title (A Side/B Side)	Yr	NM
❑ ULT 4019	Hooked	1990	40.00

—Basically the same album as "To the Extreme," which was not issued on vinyl in the United States

VANITY FARE

45s

BRENT

Number	Title (A Side/B Side)	Yr	NM
❑ 7067	Peter Who (Peter Pan)/ Salt Water Babies	1967	8.00

DJM

Number	Title (A Side/B Side)	Yr	NM
❑ 70024	Where Did All the Good Times Go/Stand	1971	5.00
❑ 70029	Big Parade/Nowhere to Go	1971	5.00

PAGE ONE

Number	Title (A Side/B Side)	Yr	NM
❑ 21007	I Live for the Sun/ On the Other Side of Life	1969	6.00
❑ 21020	Highway of Dreams/ Waiting for the Nightfall	1969	6.00
❑ 21027	Early in the Morning/ You Made Me Love You	1969	8.00
❑ 21029	Hitchin' a Ride/Man Child	1970	8.00
❑ 21033	(I Remember) Summer Morning/Megowd (Something Tells Me)	1970	6.00
❑ 21036	Where Did All the Good Times Go/Stand	1970	7.00

SOMA

Number	Title (A Side/B Side)	Yr	NM
❑ 5000	Hitchin' a Ride/ Early in the Morning	197?	5.00
—Reissue			

20TH CENTURY

Number	Title (A Side/B Side)	Yr	NM
❑ 2012	Rock and Roll Is Back/ Making for the Sun	1973	5.00
❑ 2036	Down Home/Take It, Shake It, Break My Heart	1973	5.00

Albums

PAGE ONE

Number	Title (A Side/B Side)	Yr	NM
❑ 2502	Early in the Morning	1970	20.00

VANN, TEDDY

45s

CAPITOL

Number	Title (A Side/B Side)	Yr	NM
❑ 5878	Theme from Coloredman/ Introduction to the Adventures of Coloredman	1967	40.00

COLUMBIA

Number	Title (A Side/B Side)	Yr	NM
❑ 4-41996	Lonely Crowd/I Was Born to Love You	1961	15.00
❑ 4-42145	The Rhythm & Blues Song/ Soon One Morning	1961	15.00

END

Number	Title (A Side/B Side)	Yr	NM
❑ 1059	There Is Someone/Sweetheart	1959	20.00

JUBILEE

Number	Title (A Side/B Side)	Yr	NM
❑ 5424	River Keep Moving/Who Knows What Will Be Tomorrow	1962	15.00

ROULETTE

Number	Title (A Side/B Side)	Yr	NM
❑ 4300	Do You Love Me/Young and Pretty Woman	1960	20.00

TRIPLE-X

Number	Title (A Side/B Side)	Yr	NM
❑ 101	Cindy/I'm Waiting	1960	20.00

VAPORS, THE

45s

EMI

Number	Title (A Side/B Side)	Yr	NM
❑ S7-18919	Turning Japanese/It's My Life	1995	3.00
—Reissue; B-side by Talk Talk			

LIBERTY

Number	Title (A Side/B Side)	Yr	NM
❑ 1364	Turning Japanese/Talk Talk	1980	3.00
❑ 1411	Jimmie Jones/Silver Machine	1981	3.00

UNITED ARTISTS

Number	Title (A Side/B Side)	Yr	NM
❑ 1364	Turning Japanese/Talk Talk	1980	4.00
❑ 1364	Turning Japanese	1980	15.00
—Oblong white vinyl with custom sleeve			

Albums

LIBERTY

Number	Title (A Side/B Side)	Yr	NM
❑ LT-1049	New Clear Days	1981	10.00
—Reissue			
❑ LT-1090	Magnets	1981	10.00

UNITED ARTISTS

Number	Title (A Side/B Side)	Yr	NM
❑ LT-1049	New Clear Days	1980	15.00

VAQUEROS, THE

45s

AUDITION

Number	Title (A Side/B Side)	Yr	NM
❑ 6102	Desert Wind/Echo	1964	50.00

BANGAR

Number	Title (A Side/B Side)	Yr	NM
❑ 00647	Birds and Bees/80-Foot Wave	1964	40.00

VARE, RONNIE, AND THE INSPIRATIONS

45s

DELL

Number	Title (A Side/B Side)	Yr	NM
❑ 5203	Let's Rock, Little Girl/ Love Is Just for Two	1959	50.00

VAREEATIONS, THE

45s

DIONN

Number	Title (A Side/B Side)	Yr	NM
❑ 506	The Time/Ssab-Bbrom	1968	15.00
❑ 510	Foolish One/It's the Loving Season	1969	15.00

VARISCO, PAUL, AND THE MILESTONES

45s

DATE

Number	Title (A Side/B Side)	Yr	NM
❑ 2-1650	Gotta Have Love/Look Around You People	1969	8.00

VARNER, DON

45s

QUINCY

Number	Title (A Side/B Side)	Yr	NM
❑ 8002	Tear Stained Face/ Meet Me in the Church	1969	250.00

VEEP

Number	Title (A Side/B Side)	Yr	NM
❑ 1296	Tear Stained Face/ Meet Me in the Church	1969	200.00

VASEL, MARIANNE, AND ERICH STORZ

45s

MERCURY

Number	Title (A Side/B Side)	Yr	NM
❑ 71286X45	The Little Train (Die Kleine Bimmelbahn)/Sunny Lake Walk	1958	15.00

VAUGHAN, DENNY

Also includes records as "Denny Vaughn."

45s

CORAL

Number	Title (A Side/B Side)	Yr	NM
❑ 9-60316	Autumn Leaves/Patricia	1950	20.00
❑ 9-60321	A Marshmallow World/ So Long, Sally	1950	20.00
❑ 9-60334	I Guess I'll Have to Dream the Rest/Gee, But I'm Lonesome Tonight	1950	20.00
❑ 9-60355	If/Wait for Me	1951	20.00
❑ 9-60393	Too Young/I Love the Way You Say Goodnight	1951	20.00
❑ 9-60432	Love Tales/Mellow Mood	1951	20.00
❑ 9-60524	Do You Really Love Me?/ I Want to Remember	1951	20.00
❑ 9-60531	Moonlight and Roses/Moonglow	1951	15.00
❑ 9-60532	Roses of Picardy/ Moon Over Miami	1951	15.00
❑ 9-60533	Rose Room/ The Moon Was Yellow	1951	15.00
❑ 9-60534	By the Light of the Silvery Moon/ I'm Bringing a Red, Red Rose	1951	15.00
—The above four comprise a box set			

GLORY

Number	Title (A Side/B Side)	Yr	NM
❑ 251	If You Believe/C'est Ca	1957	15.00
❑ 256	Wonderful, Wonderful!/ Since You Went Away	1957	15.00
❑ 261	Heart Beats/Once Again	1957	15.00
❑ 278	My Lost Love/Thoughts of You	1958	15.00
❑ 293	Lover's Lament/Ma Vleur D'Amor	1959	15.00

KAPP

Number	Title (A Side/B Side)	Yr	NM
❑ 143	Walk Hand in Hand/ Just Sing a Song	1956	15.00
—As "Denny Vaughn"			

Albums

BEVERLY HILLS

Number	Title (A Side/B Side)	Yr	NM
❑ BHS-19	Aberga-Denny	1969	15.00

CORAL

Number	Title (A Side/B Side)	Yr	NM
❑ CRL 56038 [10]	Moonlight and Roses	1951	50.00

VAUGHAN, FRANKIE

45s

COLUMBIA

Number	Title (A Side/B Side)	Yr	NM
❑ 41279	One Thing Led to Another/ So Happy in Love	1958	15.00
❑ 41406	Honey Bunny Baby/Big Deal	1959	15.00
❑ 41480	Ain't Gonna Lead This Life No More/Heart of a Man	1959	15.00
❑ 41537	The Very Very Young/ If You Ever Fall in Love	1959	15.00
❑ 41638	Hey You with the Crazy Eyes/ The Key	1960	15.00
❑ 41859	Do You Still Love Me/Milord	1960	15.00

EPIC

Number	Title (A Side/B Side)	Yr	NM
❑ 9238	Pebble on the Beach/Isn't This a Lovely Evening	1957	15.00
❑ 9265	We're Not Alone/Can't Get Along Without You	1958	15.00
❑ 9273	Judy/Am I Wasting My Time with You	1958	16.00

MALA

Number	Title (A Side/B Side)	Yr	NM
❑ 588	If I Didn't Care/So Tired	1968	6.00
❑ 12004	Nevertheless/Girl Talk	1968	6.00

PHILIPS

Number	Title (A Side/B Side)	Yr	NM
❑ 40070	Hercules/I'm Gonna Clip Your Wings	1962	12.00
❑ 40349	Forgotten Man/Wait	1965	8.00

Albums

PHILIPS

Number	Title (A Side/B Side)	Yr	NM
❑ PHM 200006 [M]	Singin' Happy	1962	20.00
❑ PHS 600006 [S]	Singin' Happy	1962	25.00

VAUGHAN, SARAH

45s

ATLANTIC

Number	Title (A Side/B Side)	Yr	NM
❑ 1012	It Might As Well Be Spring/ You Go to My Head	1953	100.00
❑ 3835	Fool on the Hill/Get Back	1981	5.00

V

Number	Title (A Side/B Side)	Yr	NM
COLUMBIA			
❑ 1-199	Black Coffee/As You Desire Me	1949	40.00
—Microgroove 33 1/3 rpm single			
❑ 1-258 (?)	Tonight I Shall Sleep (With a Smile on My Face)/ While You're Gone	1949	40.00
—Microgroove 33 1/3 rpm single			
❑ 1-321	That Lucky Old Sun (Just Rolls Around Heaven All Day)/ Make Believe (You Are Glad When You're Sorry)	1949	40.00
—Microgroove 33 1/3 rpm single			
❑ 1-385 (?)	Fool's Paradise/Lonely Girl	1949	40.00
—Microgroove 33 1/3 rpm single			
❑ 1-395 (?)	I Cried for You/You Say You Care	1950	40.00
—Microgroove 33 1/3 rpm single			
❑ 1-485	I'm Crazy to Love You/ Summertime	1950	40.00
—Microgroove 33 1/3 rpm single			
❑ 1-625 (?)	Just Friends/You Taught Me to Love Again	1950	40.00
—Microgroove 33 1/3 rpm single			
❑ 1-679	Our Very Own/Don't Be Afraid	1950	40.00
—Microgroove 33 1/3 rpm single			
❑ 1-757 (?)	(I Love the Girl) I Love the Guy/ Thinking of You	1950	40.00
—Microgroove 33 1/3 rpm single			
❑ 6-757 (?)	(I Love the Girl) I Love the Guy/ Thinking of You	1950	30.00
❑ 1-830 (?)	Perdido/Whippa Whippa Woo	1950	40.00
—Microgroove 33 1/3 rpm single			
❑ 6-830 (?)	Perdido/Whippa Whippa Woo	1950	30.00
❑ 1-926	The Nearness of You/ You're Mine You	1950	40.00
—Microgroove 33 1/3 rpm single			
❑ 6-926	The Nearness of You/ You're Mine You	1950	30.00
❑ 4-38925	(I Love the Girl) I Love the Guy/ Thinking of You	1950	25.00
❑ 4-39001	Perdido/Whippa Whippa Woo	1950	25.00
❑ 4-39071	The Nearness of You/ You're Mine You	1950	25.00
❑ 4-39124	I'll Know/Gas Pipe Leaking	1950	25.00
❑ 4-39207	Ave Maria/A City Called Heaven	1951	25.00
❑ 4-39370	These Things I Offer You (For a Lifetime)/Deep Purple	1951	25.00
❑ 4-39446	Vanity/My Reverie	1951	25.00
❑ 4-39494	After Hours/Out of Breath	1951	25.00
❑ 4-39576	I Ran All the Way Home/ Just a Moment More	1951	25.00
❑ 4-39634	Pinky/A Miracle Happened	1952	20.00
❑ 4-39719	If Someone Had Told Me/ Corner to Corner	1952	20.00
❑ 4-39789	Time to Go/Street of Dreams	1952	20.00
❑ 4-39839	Say You'll Wait for Me/My Tormented Heart	1952	20.00
❑ 4-39873	Sinner or Saint/Mighty Lonesome Feeling	1952	20.00
❑ 4-39932	Lovers' Quarrel/I Confess	1953	20.00
❑ 4-39963	Spring Will Be a Little Late This Year/A Blues Serenade	1953	20.00
❑ 4-40041	Time/Linger Awhile	1953	20.00
MAINSTREAM			
❑ 5517	Imagine/Sweet Gingerbread Man	1971	5.00
❑ 5521	Pieces of Dreams/Once You've Been in Love	1972	5.00
❑ 5522	What Are You Doing the Rest of Your Life/The Summer Knows	1972	5.00
❑ 5523	Summer Me, Winter Me/The Story of a Frasier	1972	5.00
❑ 5527	And the Feeling's Good/Deep in the Night	1972	5.00
❑ 5533	Rainy Days and Mondays/Just a Little Lovin'	1973	5.00
❑ 5541	Send In the Clowns/(B-side unknown)	1973	5.00
❑ 5544	Alone Again (Naturally)/Run to Me	1973	5.00
❑ 5553	Do Away with April/I Need You More	1974	5.00
MERCURY			
❑ 10020 [S]	Smooth Operator/Maybe It's Because (I Love You Too Much)	1959	20.00
❑ 70299x45	And This Is My Beloved/Easy Come, Easy Go Lover	1954	15.00
❑ 70331x45	It's Easy to Remember/Come Along with Me	1954	15.00
❑ 70423x45	Ol' Devil Moon/Saturday	1954	15.00
❑ 70469x45	Make Yourself Comfortable/ Idle Gossip	1954	15.00
❑ 70534x45	How Important Can It Be/ Waltzing Down the Aisle	1955	15.00
❑ 70595x45	Whatever Lola Wants/Oh Yeah	1955	15.00
❑ 70646x45	Experience Unnecessary/ Slowly, With Feeling	1955	15.00
❑ 70693x45	Johnny, Be Smart/Hey Naughty Papa	1955	15.00
❑ 70727x45	C'est La Vie/Never	1955	15.00
❑ 70777x45	Mr. Wonderful/You Ought to Have a Wife	1956	12.00
❑ 70846x45	Hot and Cold Running Tears/ That's Not the Kind of Love I Want	1956	12.00
❑ 70885x45	Fabulous Character/The Other Woman	1956	12.00
❑ 70947x45	It Happened Again/I Wanna Play House	1956	12.00
❑ 71020x45	The Banana Boat Song/I've Got a New Heartache	1956	12.00
❑ 71030x45	Leave It to Love/The Bashful Matador	1957	12.00
❑ 71085x45	Poor Butterfly/April Give Me One More Day	1957	12.00
❑ 71157x45	Band of Angels/Please Mr. Brown	1957	12.00
❑ 71235x45	Gone Train/Next Time Around	1957	12.00
❑ 71303	Padre/Spin the Bottle	1958	12.00
❑ 71326	What's So Bad About It/Too Much Too Soon	1958	12.00
❑ 71380	I Ain't Hurtin'/Everything I Do	1958	12.00
❑ 71407	Are You Certain/Cool Baby	1959	12.00
❑ 71433	Separate Ways/Careless	1959	12.00
❑ 71477	Broken-Hearted Melody/Misty	1959	12.00
❑ 71519 [M]	Smooth Operator/Maybe It's Because (I Love You Too Much)	1959	12.00
❑ 71562	Eternally/You're My Baby	1960	12.00
❑ 71610	Some Other Spring/Our Waltz	1960	12.00
❑ 71642	Maybe You'll Be There/Doodlin'	1960	12.00
❑ 71669	For All We Know/ The Rough Years	1960	12.00
❑ 71702	Close to You/Out of This World	1960	12.00
❑ 71742	If You Are But a Dream/ Mary Contrary	1960	12.00
❑ 72249	Bluesette/You Got It Made	1964	10.00
❑ 72300	How's the World Treating You/ Sole, Sole, Sole	1964	10.00
❑ 72381	The Other Side of Me/ We Almost Made It	1965	8.00
❑ 72417	Pawn Broker/Bye Bye (Theme from Peter Gunn)	1965	8.00
❑ 72510	Darling/I'll Never Be Lonely Again	1965	8.00
❑ 72543	A Lover's Concerto/First Thing Every Morning	1966	8.00
❑ 72588	Everybody Loves Somebody/ 1-2-3	1966	8.00
MGM			
❑ K10705	Tenderly/I'll Wait and Pray	1950	30.00
❑ K10762	What a Difference A Day Made/ I Can't Get Started	1950	30.00
❑ K10819	I Cover the Waterfront/Don't Worry 'Bout Me	1950	30.00
❑ K10890	I'm Gonna Sit Right Down and Write Myself a Letter/I'm Through with Love	1951	25.00
❑ K11068	Don't Blame Me/If You Could See Me Now	1951	25.00
REMINGTON			
❑ R-45-1067	Interlude/Signing Off	195?	10.00
ROULETTE			
❑ 4285	Serenata/Let's	1960	10.00
❑ 4325	True Believer/What's the Use	1961	10.00
❑ 4359	April/Oh Lover	1961	10.00
❑ 4378	Untouchable/The Hills of Assisi	1961	10.00
❑ 4397	If Love Is Good to Me/ A Great Day	1961	10.00
❑ 4413	One Mint Julep/Mama (He Treats Your Daughter Mean)	1962	10.00
❑ 4482	Call Me Irresponsible/ There'll Be Other Times	1963	8.00
❑ 4497	Once Upon a Summertime/ Snowbound	1963	8.00
❑ 4516	What'll I Do/I Believe in You	1963	8.00
❑ 4547	The Wallflower Waltz/Only	1964	8.00
❑ 4604	A Taste of Honey/The Good Life	1965	8.00
❑ SSR-33-8047 [S]	When Your Lover Has Gone/ I'm Gonna Laugh You Out of My Life	196?	15.00
—Small hole, plays at 33 1/3 rpm			
WARNER BROS.			
❑ 49890	Theme from "Sharkey's Machine"/Sharkey's Theme	1981	4.00
—B-side by Eddie Harris			

7-Inch Extended Plays

Number	Title (A Side/B Side)	Yr	NM
COLUMBIA			
❑ 5-1407	Deep Purple/Just Friends// Street of Dreams/You Taught Me to Love Again	195?	25.00
—Alternate numbers are "B-1631-1" and "B-1631-2"			
❑ B-1631 [PS]	Deep Purple	195?	25.00
❑ B-2551	*Deep Purple/You're Mine, You/Street of Dreams/ The Nearness of You	195?	20.00
❑ B-2551 [PS]	Sarah Vaughan (Hall of Fame Series)	195?	20.00
❑ B-2588	*Perdido/Linger Awhile/Time/ Corner to Corner	1959	20.00
❑ B-2588 [PS]	Sarah Vaughan (Hall of Fame Series)	1959	20.00
❑ B-7452	Come Rain or Come Shine/ Mean to Me//It Might As Well Be Spring/Can't Get Out of This Mood	195?	25.00
❑ B-7452 [PS]	Sarah Vaughan in Hi-Fi	195?	25.00
MERCURY			
❑ EP-1-3305	I'm in the Mood for Love/ I Don't Know Why//Honey/ Let's Put Out the Lights	195?	12.00
❑ EP-1-3305 [PS]	Songs by Sarah Vaughan	195?	12.00
❑ EP-1-3396	Smooth Operator/You're My Baby//Eternally/Broken-Hearted Melody	195?	12.00
❑ EP-1-3396 [PS]	The Divine Sarah Vaughan	195?	12.00
MGM			
❑ X1019	(contents unknown)	1953	15.00
❑ X1019 [PS]	I've Got a Crush on You	1953	15.00
❑ X1020	The Man I Love/Body and Soul// I Can Make You Love Me/Once in a While	1953	15.00
❑ X1020 [PS]	The Man I Love	1953	15.00

Albums

Number	Title	Yr	NM
ACCORD			
❑ SN-7195	Simply Divine	1981	10.00
ALLEGRO			
❑ 1592 [M]	Sarah Vaughan	1955	50.00
❑ 1608 [M]	Sarah Vaughan	1955	50.00
❑ 3080 [10]	Early Sarah	195?	80.00
ALLEGRO ELITE			
❑ 4106 [10]	Sarah Vaughan Sings	195?	30.00
ATLANTIC			
❑ SD 16037	Songs of the Beatles	1981	12.00
BRYLEN			
❑ BN 4411	Desires	198?	10.00
—Last name is misspelled "Vaughn"			
CBS MASTERWORKS			
❑ FM 37277	Gershwin Live!	1982	10.00
—With the Los Angeles Philharmonic Orchestra			
❑ FM 42519	Brazilian Romance	1987	10.00
COLUMBIA			
❑ CL 660 [M]	After Hours with Sarah Vaughan	1955	50.00
❑ CL 745 [M]	Sarah Vaughan in Hi-Fi	1956	50.00
❑ CL 914 [M]	Linger Awhile	1956	50.00
❑ CL 6133 [10]	Sarah Vaughan	1950	120.00
COLUMBIA SPECIAL PRODUCTS			
❑ P 13084	Sarah Vaughan in Hi-Fi	1976	10.00
—Reissue of Columbia 745			
❑ P 14364	Linger Awhile	1978	10.00
—Reissue of Columbia 914			
CONCORD			
❑ 3018 [M]	Sarah Vaughan Concert	1957	30.00
CORONET			
❑ 277	Sarah Vaughan Belts the Hits	196?	15.00
EMARCY			
❑ EMS-2-412 [(2)]	Sarah Vaughan Live	197?	12.00
❑ MG-26005 [10]	Images	1954	80.00
❑ MG-36004 [M]	Sarah Vaughan	1955	80.00
❑ MG-36058 [M]	In the Land of Hi-Fi	1956	80.00
❑ MG-36089 [M]	Sassy	1956	50.00
❑ MG-36109 [M]	Swingin' Easy	1957	50.00
❑ 814187-1 [(2)]	The George Gershwin Songbook	1983	12.00
❑ 824864-1	The Rodgers & Hart Songbook	1985	10.00
❑ 826454-1	In the Land of Hi-Fi	1986	10.00
—Reissue of 36058			
EVEREST ARCHIVE OF FOLK & JAZZ			
❑ 250	Sarah Vaughan	197?	10.00
❑ 271	Sarah Vaughan, Vol. 2	1973	10.00
❑ 325	Sarah Vaughan, Vol. 3	197?	10.00
FORUM			
❑ F-9034 [M]	Dreamy	196?	12.00
❑ SF-9034 [S]	Dreamy	196?	15.00
HARMONY			
❑ HL 7158 [M]	The Great Sarah Vaughan	196?	12.00
LION			
❑ L 70052 [M]	Tenderly	1958	25.00

V

Except when noted otherwise, VG = 25% of NM, and VG+ = 50% of NM. (Example: VG = $2.00, VG+ = $4.00 and NM = $8.00.)

Number	Title (A Side/B Side)	Yr	NM
MAINSTREAM			
❑ MRL 340	Time in My Life	1972	15.00
❑ MRL 361	Sarah Vaughan/Michel Legrand	1972	15.00
❑ MRL 379	Feelin' Good	1973	15.00
❑ MRL 404	Sarah Vaughan and the Jimmy Rowles Quintet	1974	15.00
❑ MRL 412	Send In the Clowns	1974	15.00
❑ MRL 419	More Sarah Vaughan from Japan	1974	15.00
❑ MRL 2401 [(2)]	Sarah Vaughan "Live" In Japan	1973	20.00
MASTERSEAL			
❑ MS-55 [M]	Sarah Vaughan Sings	195?	25.00
MERCURY			
❑ MGP-2-100 [(2)M]	Great Songs from Hit Shows	1957	60.00
❑ MGP-2-101 [(2)M]	Sarah Vaughan Sings George Gershwin	1957	60.00
❑ MG-20094 [M]	Sarah Vaughan at the Blue Note	1956	40.00
❑ MG-20219 [M]	Wonderful Sarah	1957	40.00
❑ MG-20223 [M]	In a Romantic Mood	1957	40.00
❑ MG-20244 [M]	Great Songs from Hit Shows, Vol. 1	1958	30.00
❑ MG-20245 [M]	Great Songs from Hit Shows, Vol. 2	1958	30.00
❑ MG-20310 [M]	Sarah Vaughan Sings George Gershwin, Vol. 1	1958	30.00
❑ MG-20311 [M]	Sarah Vaughan Sings George Gershwin, Vol. 2	1958	30.00
❑ MG-20326 [M]	Sarah Vaughan and Her Trio at Mr. Kelly's	1958	40.00
❑ MG-20370 [M]	Vaughan and Violins	1958	40.00
❑ MG-20383 [M]	After Hours at the London House	1958	40.00
❑ MG-20438 [M]	The Magic of Sarah Vaughan	1959	30.00
❑ MG-20441 [M]	No 'Count Sarah	1959	30.00
❑ MG-20540 [M]	The Divine Sarah Vaughan	1960	25.00
❑ MG-20580 [M]	Close to You	1960	25.00
❑ MG-20617 [M]	My Heart Sings	1961	25.00
❑ MG-20645 [M]	Sarah Vaughan's Golden Hits	1961	20.00
❑ MG-20831 [M]	Sassy Swings the Tivoli	1962	20.00
❑ MG-20882 [M]	Vaughan with Voices	1963	20.00
❑ MG-20941 [M]	Viva Vaughan	1964	15.00
❑ MG-21009 [M]	Sarah Vaughan Sings the Mancini Songbook	1965	15.00
❑ MG-21069 [M]	Pop Artistry	1966	15.00
❑ MG-21079 [M]	The New Scene	1966	15.00
❑ MG-21116 [M]	Sassy Swings Again	1967	15.00
❑ MG-21122 [M]	It's a Man's World	1967	15.00
❑ MG-25188 [10]	Divine Sarah	1955	100.00
❑ MG-25213 [10]	The Divine Sarah Sings	1955	100.00
❑ SR-60020 [S]	After Hours at the London House	1959	40.00
❑ SR-60038 [S]	Vaughan and Violins	1959	40.00
❑ SR-60041 [S]	Great Songs from Hit Shows, Vol. 1	1959	40.00
❑ SR-60045 [S]	Sarah Vaughan Sings George Gershwin, Vol. 1	1959	40.00
❑ SR-60046 [S]	Sarah Vaughan Sings George Gershwin, Vol. 2	1959	40.00
❑ SR-60078 [S]	Great Songs from Hit Shows, Vol. 2	1959	40.00
❑ SR-60110 [S]	The Magic of Sarah Vaughan	1959	40.00
❑ SR-60116 [S]	No 'Count Sarah	1959	40.00
❑ SR-60240 [S]	Close to You	1960	30.00
❑ SR-60255 [S]	The Divine Sarah Vaughan	1960	30.00
❑ SR-60617 [S]	My Heart Sings	1961	30.00
❑ SR-60645 [S]	Sarah Vaughan's Golden Hits	1961	25.00
—Original black label version			
❑ SR-60645 [S]	Sarah Vaughan's Golden Hits	1965	15.00
—Red label version with white "MERCURY" alone at top			
❑ SR-60645 [S]	Sarah Vaughan's Golden Hits	1968	12.00
—Red label with multiple Mercury logos along the label edge			
❑ SR-60831 [S]	Sassy Swings the Tivoli	1962	25.00
❑ SR-60882 [S]	Vaughan with Voices	1963	25.00
❑ SR-60941 [S]	Viva Vaughan	1964	20.00
❑ SR-61009 [S]	Sarah Vaughan Sings the Mancini Songbook	1965	20.00
❑ SR-61069 [S]	Pop Artistry	1966	20.00
❑ SR-61079 [S]	The New Scene	1966	20.00
❑ SR-61116 [S]	Sassy Swings Again	1967	20.00
❑ SR-61122 [S]	It's a Man's World	1967	20.00
❑ 826320-1 [(6)]	The Complete Sarah Vaughan on Mercury Vol. 1: Great Jazz years (1954-56)	1986	40.00
❑ 826327-1 [(5)]	The Complete Sarah Vaughan on Mercury Vol. 2: Great American Songs (1956-57)	1986	40.00
❑ 826333-1 [(6)]	The Complete Sarah Vaughan on Mercury Vol. 3: Great Show on Stage (1954-56)	1986	40.00
❑ 830721-1 [(4)]	The Complete Sarah Vaughan on Mercury Vol. 4 Part 1: Live in Europe (1963-64)	1987	40.00
❑ 830726-1 [(5)]	The Complete Sarah Vaughan on Mercury Vol. 4 Part 2: Sassy Swings Again	1987	40.00
METRO			
❑ M-539 [M]	Tenderly	1965	12.00
❑ MS-539 [S]	Tenderly	1965	15.00

Number	Title (A Side/B Side)	Yr	NM
MGM			
❑ E-165 [10]	Tenderly	1950	120.00
❑ E-544 [10]	Sarah Vaughan Sings	1951	120.00
❑ E-3274 [M]	My Kinda Love	1955	50.00
—Combination of two 10-inch LPs on one 12-inch LP			
MUSICRAFT			
❑ 504	Divine Sarah	197?	10.00
❑ MVS-2002	The Man I Love	1986	10.00
❑ MVS-2006	Lover Man	1986	10.00
PABLO			
❑ 2310821	How Long	1978	10.00
❑ 2310885	The Best of Sarah Vaughan	1983	10.00
❑ 2312101	I Love Brazil	1978	10.00
❑ 2312111	The Duke Ellington Songbook One	1979	10.00
❑ 2312116	The Duke Ellington Songbook Two	1980	10.00
❑ 2312125	Copacabana	1981	10.00
❑ 2405416	The Best of Sarah Vaughan	1990	10.00
PABLO TODAY			
❑ 2312137	Crazy and Mixed Up	1982	10.00
PALACE			
❑ 5191 [M]	Sarah Vaughan Sings	195?	25.00
PICKWICK			
❑ PCS-3035	Fabulous Sarah Vaughan	197?	10.00
REMINGTON			
❑ RLP-1024 [10]	Hot Jazz	1953	200.00
RIVERSIDE			
❑ RLP 2511 [10]	Sarah Vaughan Sings with John Kirby	1955	100.00
RONDO-LETTE			
❑ A-35 [M]	Songs of Broadway	1958	25.00
❑ A-53 [M]	Sarah Vaughan Sings	1959	25.00
ROULETTE			
❑ RE-103 [(2)]	Echoes of an Era: The Sarah Vaughan Years	197?	15.00
❑ K-105 [(2)M]	The Sarah Vaughan Years	196?	20.00
❑ SK-105 [(2)S]	The Sarah Vaughan Years	196?	30.00
❑ R 52046 [M]	Dreamy	1960	30.00
❑ SR 52046 [S]	Dreamy	1960	40.00
❑ R 52060 [M]	Divine One	1960	25.00
❑ SR 52060 [S]	Divine One	1960	30.00
❑ R 52070 [M]	After Hours	1961	25.00
❑ SR 52070 [S]	After Hours	1961	30.00
❑ R 52082 [M]	You're Mine	1962	25.00
❑ SR 52082 [S]	You're Mine	1962	30.00
—Black vinyl			
❑ SR 52082 [S]	You're Mine	1962	60.00
—Red vinyl			
❑ R 52091 [M]	Snowbound	1962	20.00
❑ SR 52091 [S]	Snowbound	1962	25.00
❑ R 52092 [M]	The Explosive Side of Sarah	1962	20.00
❑ SR 52092 [S]	The Explosive Side of Sarah	1962	25.00
❑ R 52100 [M]	Star Eyes	1963	15.00
❑ SR 52100 [S]	Star Eyes	1963	20.00
❑ R 52104 [M]	Lonely Hours	1963	15.00
❑ SR 52104 [S]	Lonely Hours	1963	20.00
❑ R 52109 [M]	The World of Sarah Vaughan	1964	15.00
❑ SR 52109 [S]	The World of Sarah Vaughan	1964	20.00
❑ R 52112 [M]	Sweet 'N Sassy	1964	15.00
❑ SR 52112 [S]	Sweet 'N Sassy	1964	20.00
❑ R 52116 [M]	Sarah Sings Soulfully	1965	15.00
❑ SR 52116 [S]	Sarah Sings Soulfully	1965	20.00
❑ R 52118 [M]	Sarah Plus Two	1965	15.00
❑ SR 52118 [S]	Sarah Plus Two	1965	20.00
❑ R 52123 [M]	Sarah Slightly Classical	1966	15.00
❑ SR 52123 [S]	Sarah Slightly Classical	1966	20.00
ROYALE			
❑ 18129 [10]	Sarah Vaughan and Orchestra	195?	30.00
❑ 18149 [10]	Sarah Vaughan and Orchestra	195?	30.00
—Includes recordings made on the Musicraft label in the 1940s			
SCEPTER CITATION			
❑ CTN-18029	The Best of Sarah Vaughan	1972	12.00
SPIN-O-RAMA			
❑ 73 [M]	Sweet, Sultry and Swinging	196?	40.00
❑ S-73 [S]	Sweet, Sultry and Swinging	196?	50.00
❑ 114 [M]	The Divine Sarah Vaughan	196?	40.00
❑ S-114 [S]	The Divine Sarah Vaughan	196?	50.00
TIME-LIFE			
❑ SLGD-09 [(2)]	Legendary Singers: Sarah Vaughan	1985	15.00
TRIP			
❑ 5501	Sarah Vaughan	197?	10.00
❑ 5517	Sassy	197?	10.00
❑ 5523	In the Land of Hi-Fi	197?	10.00
❑ 5551	Swingin' Easy	197?	10.00
WING			
❑ MGW-12123 [M]	All Time Favorites	1963	12.00
❑ MGW-12280 [M]	The Magic of Sarah Vaughan	1964	12.00
❑ SRW-16123 [S]	All Time Favorites	1963	15.00
❑ SRW-16280 [S]	The Magic of Sarah Vaughan	1964	15.00

Number	Title (A Side/B Side)	Yr	NM
VAUGHAN, SARAH, AND COUNT BASIE			
Albums			
PABLO			
❑ 2312130	Send In the Clowns	1980	10.00
ROULETTE			
❑ SR 42018	Count Basie and Sarah Vaughan	1968	15.00
❑ R 52061 [M]	Count Basie and Sarah Vaughan	1960	25.00
❑ SR 52061 [S]	Count Basie and Sarah Vaughan	1960	30.00
VAUGHAN, SARAH, AND BILLY ECKSTINE			
Also see each artist's individual listings.			
45s			
MERCURY			
❑ 71122	Passing Strangers/The Door Is Open	1957	12.00
❑ 71393	Alexander's Ragtime Band/No Limit	1959	12.00
7-Inch Extended Plays			
MGM			
❑ X1002	Dedicated to You/You're All I Need//Ev'ry Day/I Love You	195?	20.00
❑ X1002 [PS]	Dedicated to You	195?	20.00
Albums			
EMARCY			
❑ 822526-1	The Irving Berlin Songbook	1984	10.00
LION			
❑ L-70088 [M]	Billy and Sarah	195?	25.00
MERCURY			
❑ MG-20316 [M]	Sarah Vaughan and Billy Eckstine Sing the Best of Irving Berlin	1959	30.00
❑ SR-60002 [S]	Sarah Vaughan and Billy Eckstine Sing the Best of Irving Berlin	1959	40.00
VAUGHAN, SARAH; DINAH WASHINGTON; JOE WILLIAMS			
Albums			
ROULETTE			
❑ R 52108 [M]	We Three	1964	15.00
❑ SR 52108 [S]	We Three	1964	20.00
VAUGHAN, STEVIE RAY			
45s			
EPIC			
❑ 04031	Pride and Joy/Rude Mood	1983	5.00
❑ 05731	Change It/Look at Little Sister	1985	4.00
❑ 06601	Superstition/Pride and Joy	1987	4.00
❑ 06696	Willie the Wimp/Superstition	1987	4.00
❑ 06696 [DJ]	Willie the Wimp (LP Version)/Willie the Wimp (Edit)	1987	8.00
❑ 07340	Pipeline/Love Struck Baby	1987	4.00
—With Dick Dale			
❑ 07340 [PS]	Pipeline/Love Struck Baby	1987	7.00
—With Dick Dale			
❑ 69025	Double Crossfire/Travis Walk	1989	4.00
❑ 73212	This House Is Rockin'/Tightrope	1990	4.00
❑ 74142	The Sky Is Crying/Chitlins Con Carne	1991	4.00
❑ 74198	Empty Arms/Wham	1992	4.00
❑ 78205	Taxman/The House Is Rockin'	1995	4.00
Albums			
EPIC			
❑ BFE 38734	Texas Flood	1983	10.00
❑ FE 39304	Couldn't Stand the Weather	1984	10.00
❑ 8E8 39609 [PD]	Couldn't Stand the Weather	1984	150.00
❑ FE 40036	Soul to Soul	1985	10.00
❑ E2 40511 [(2)]	Live Alive	1986	12.00
❑ FE 45024	In Step	1989	10.00
❑ E 47390	The Sky Is Crying	1991	30.00
❑ E 66217	Greatest Hits	1995	15.00
VAUGHN, DENNY See DENNY VAUGHAN.			
VAUGHN, YVONNE Later recorded as DONNA FARGO.			
45s			
DOT			
❑ 16751	Lonely Little Girl/When You Gonna Tell Her About Me	1965	150.00
VEE, BOBBY			
45s			
COGNITO			
❑ 010	Tremble On/Always Be Each Other's Best Friend	1981	5.00
LIBERTY			
❑ 54510	Devil or Angel/Rubber Ball	196?	6.00
❑ 54511	More Than I Can Say/Stayin' In	196?	6.00
❑ 54523	Take Good Care of My Baby/Please Don't Ask About Barbara	196?	6.00
❑ 54524	Run to Him/Sharing You	196?	6.00

The Zombies, *Odessey & Oracle*, Date TES 4013, 1968, **$30.**

Number	Title (A Side/B Side)	Yr	NM
❑ 54536	The Night Has a Thousand Eyes/ Charms	196?	6.00
❑ 54559	Come Back When You Grow Up/Beautiful People	196?	6.00
—Records in the 54500s are from a reissue series			
❑ 55208	Suzie Baby/Flyin' High	1959	25.00
❑ 55234	What Do You Want/ My Love Loves Me	1959	20.00
❑ 55251	Laurie/One Last Kiss	1960	15.00
❑ 55270	Devil or Angel/Since I Met You Baby	1960	20.00
❑ 55270 [PS]	Devil or Angel/Since I Met You Baby	1960	30.00
❑ 55287	Rubber Ball/Everyday	1960	20.00
❑ 55287 [PS]	Rubber Ball/Everyday	1960	30.00
❑ 55296	More Than I Can Say/Stayin' In	1961	15.00
❑ 55296 [PS]	More Than I Can Say/Stayin' In	1961	30.00
❑ 55325	How Many Tears/Baby Face	1961	15.00
❑ 55325 [PS]	How Many Tears/Baby Face	1961	30.00
❑ 55354	Take Good Care of My Baby/ Bashful Bob	1961	15.00
❑ 55388	Run to Him/Walkin' with My Angel	1961	20.00
❑ 55419	Please Don't Ask About Barbara/I Can't Say Goodbye	1962	15.00
❑ 55419 [PS]	Please Don't Ask About Barbara/I Can't Say Goodbye	1962	25.00
❑ 55451	Sharing You/In My Baby's Eyes	1962	15.00
❑ 55479	Punish Her/Someday (When I'm Gone from You)	1962	20.00
❑ 55479 [PS]	Punish Her/Someday (When I'm Gone from You)	1962	30.00
—With the Crickets			
❑ 55517	A Not-So-Merry Christmas/ Christmas Vacation	1962	30.00
—This record's existence has been questioned			
❑ 55521	The Night Has a Thousand Eyes/Anonymous Phone Call	1962	12.00
❑ 55530	Charms/Bobby Tomorrow	1963	12.00
❑ 55530 [PS]	Charms/Bobby Tomorrow	1963	20.00
❑ 55581	Be True to Yourself/ A Letter from Betty	1963	10.00
❑ 55581 [PS]	Be True to Yourself/ A Letter from Betty	1963	20.00

Number	Title (A Side/B Side)	Yr	NM
❑ 55636	Yesterday and You (Armen's Theme)/Never Love a Robin	1963	10.00
❑ 55654	Stranger in Your Arms/1963	1963	10.00
❑ 55654 [PS]	Stranger in Your Arms/1963	1963	20.00
❑ 55670	I'll Make You Mine/She's Sorry	1964	10.00
❑ 55700	Hickory, Dick and Doc/I Wish You Were Mine Again	1964	10.00
❑ 55726	Where Is She/How to Make a Farewell	1964	10.00
❑ 55751	(There'll Come a Day When) Ev'ry Little Bit Hurts/ Pretend You Don't See Her	1964	10.00
❑ 55761	Cross My Heart/This Is the End	1965	8.00
❑ 55790	Keep On Trying/You Won't Forget Me	1965	8.00
❑ 55828	Run Like the Devil/Take a Look Around Us	1965	8.00
❑ 55843	The Story of My Life/High Coin	1965	8.00
❑ 55854	A Girl I Used to Know/Gone	1965	8.00
❑ 55877	Butterfly/Save a Love	1966	—
—Canceled?			
❑ 55877	Look at Me Girl/Save a Love	1966	8.00
❑ 55921	Before You Go/Here Today	1966	8.00
❑ 55964	Come Back When You Grow Up/Swahili Serenade	1967	8.00
❑ 55964	Come Back When You Grow Up/That's All There Is to That	1967	8.00
❑ S-55964 [S]	Come Back When You Grow Up/Swahili Serenade	1967	20.00
—Small hole, plays at 33 1/3 rpm; promo "Audition Record" only			
❑ 56009	Beautiful People/I May Be Gone	1967	8.00
❑ 56014	Maybe Just Today/ You're a Big Girl Now	1968	6.00
❑ 56014 [PS]	Maybe Just Today/ You're a Big Girl Now	1968	12.00
❑ 56033	Medley: My Girl-Hey Girl/ Just Keep It Up	1968	6.00
❑ 56057	Do What You Gotta Do/ Thank You	1968	6.00
❑ 56080	I'm Into Lookin' for Someone to Love Me/Thank You	1968	6.00
❑ 56096	Jenny Come to Me/Santa Cruz	1969	6.00

Number	Title (A Side/B Side)	Yr	NM
❑ 56124	Let's Call It a Day Girl/I'm Gonna Make It Up to You	1969	6.00
❑ 56149	Electric Trains and You/ In and Out of Love	1969	6.00
❑ 56178	The Woman in My Life/ No Obligations	1970	6.00
❑ 56208	Sweet Sweetheart/Rock and Roll Music and You	1970	6.00
SHADY BROOK			
❑ 45013	Saying Goodbye/(I'm) Lovin' You	1975	5.00
❑ 45026	You're Never Gonna Find Someone Like Me (Long Version)/You're Never Gonna Find Someone Like Me (Short Version)	1976	5.00
❑ 45030	It's Good to Be Here/ If I Needed You	1976	5.00
SOMA			
❑ 1110	Suzie Baby/Flyin' High	1959	60.00
UNITED ARTISTS			
❑ 0020	Devil or Angel/Stayin' In	1973	4.00
❑ 0021	Rubber Ball/Punish Her	1973	4.00
❑ 0022	Take Good Care of My Baby/ Please Don't Ask About Barbara	1973	4.00
❑ 0023	Run to Him/Sharing You	1973	4.00
❑ 0024	The Night Has a Thousand Eyes/Charms	1973	4.00
❑ 0025	Come Back When You Grow Up/Beautiful People	1973	4.00
—0020 through 0025 are "Silver Spotlight Series" reissues			
❑ XW199	Take Good Care of My Baby/ Every Opportunity	1973	5.00
—As "Robert Thomas Velline"			
❑ XW1142	Well All Right/Something Has Come Between Us	1978	5.00
❑ 50755	Signs/Something to Say	1971	5.00
❑ 50875	Sweet Sweetheart/ Electric Trains and You	1972	5.00

7-Inch Extended Plays

Number	Title (A Side/B Side)	Yr	NM
LIBERTY			
❑ LSX-1006	Devil or Angel/One Last Kiss// What Do You Want/My Love Loves Me	1960	50.00
❑ LSX-1006 [PS]	Devil or Angel	1960	50.00
❑ LSX-1010	(contents unknown)	1960	50.00
❑ LSX-1010 [PS]	Bobby Vee's Hits	1960	50.00
❑ LSX-1013	*Run to Him/Take Good Care of My Baby/Walkin' with My Angel/How Many Tears	1961	50.00
❑ LSX-1013 [PS]	Bobby Vee	1961	50.00

Albums

Number	Title	Yr	NM
LIBERTY			
❑ LRP-3165 [M]	Bobby Vee Sings Your Favorites	1960	50.00
❑ LRP-3181 [M]	Bobby Vee	1961	40.00
❑ LRP-3186 [M]	Bobby Vee With Strings and Things	1961	40.00
❑ LRP-3205 [M]	Bobby Vee Sings Hits of the Rockin' 50's	1961	40.00
❑ LRP-3211 [M]	Take Good Care of My Baby	1962	30.00
❑ LRP-3228 [M]	Bobby Vee Meets the Crickets	1962	40.00
❑ LRP-3232 [M]	A Bobby Vee Recording Session	1962	30.00
❑ LRP-3245 [M]	Bobby Vee's Golden Greats	1962	30.00
❑ LRP-3267 [M]	Merry Christmas from Bobby Vee	1962	30.00
❑ LRP-3285 [M]	The Night Has a Thousand Eyes	1963	30.00
❑ LRP-3289 [M]	Bobby Vee Meets the Ventures	1963	40.00
❑ LRP-3336 [M]	I Remember Buddy Holly	1963	40.00
❑ LRP-3352 [M]	Bobby Vee Sings the New Sound from England!	1964	25.00
❑ LRP-3385 [M]	30 Big Hits From the 60's	1964	25.00
❑ LRP-3393 [M]	Bobby Vee Live on Tour	1965	25.00
❑ LRP-3448 [M]	30 Big Hits From the 60's, Vol. 2	1966	25.00
❑ LRP-3464 [M]	Bobby Vee's Golden Greats, Vol. 2	1966	20.00
❑ LRP-3480 [M]	Look at Me Girl	1966	20.00
❑ LRP-3534 [M]	Come Back When You Grow Up	1967	20.00
❑ LST-3554 [M]	Just Today	1968	40.00
—Cover is stereo with "Audition Mono Not for Sale" sticker, but the label is regular stock mono			
❑ LST-7165 [S]	Bobby Vee Sings Your Favorites	1960	80.00
❑ LST-7181 [S]	Bobby Vee	1961	50.00
❑ LST-7186 [S]	Bobby Vee With Strings and Things	1961	50.00
❑ LST-7205 [S]	Bobby Vee Sings Hits of the Rockin' 50's	1961	50.00
❑ LST-7211 [S]	Take Good Care of My Baby	1962	40.00
❑ LST-7228 [S]	Bobby Vee Meets the Crickets	1962	50.00
❑ LST-7232 [S]	A Bobby Vee Recording Session	1962	40.00
❑ LST-7245 [S]	Bobby Vee's Golden Greats	1962	40.00
❑ LST-7267 [S]	Merry Christmas from Bobby Vee	1962	40.00
❑ LST-7285 [S]	The Night Has a Thousand Eyes	1963	40.00
❑ LST-7289 [S]	Bobby Vee Meets the Ventures	1963	50.00
❑ LST-7336 [S]	I Remember Buddy Holly	1963	50.00
❑ LST-7352 [S]	Bobby Vee Sings the New Sound from England!	1964	30.00
❑ LST-7385 [S]	30 Big Hits From the 60's	1964	30.00

Number	Title (A Side/B Side)	Yr	NM
❑ LST-7393 [S]	Bobby Vee Live on Tour	1965	30.00
❑ LST-7448 [S]	30 Big Hits From the 60's, Vol. 2	1966	30.00
❑ LST-7464 [S]	Bobby Vee's Golden Greats, Vol. 2	1966	25.00
❑ LST-7480 [S]	Look at Me Girl	1966	25.00
❑ LST-7534 [S]	Come Back When You Grow Up	1967	25.00
❑ LST-7554 [S]	Just Today	1968	25.00
❑ LST-7592	Do What You Gotta Do	1968	30.00
❑ LST-7612	Gates, Grills and Railings	1969	30.00
❑ LN-10223	I Remember Buddy Holly	198?	8.00
❑ LM-51008	Bobby Vee's Golden Greats	198?	8.00
SUNSET			
❑ SUM-1111 [M]	Bobby Vee	1966	10.00
❑ SUM-1162 [M]	A Forever Kind of Love	1967	10.00
❑ SUM-1186 [M]	The Christmas Album	1967	12.00
—Reissue of Liberty album with two fewer tracks			
❑ SUS-5111 [S]	Bobby Vee	1966	12.00
❑ SUS-5162 [S]	A Forever Kind of Love	1967	12.00
❑ SUS-5186 [S]	The Christmas Album	1967	12.00
UNITED ARTISTS			
❑ UA-LA025-G2 [(2)]	Legendary Masters Series	1973	300.00
—Withdrawn before release, but a few copies survived			
❑ UA-LA085-G	Robert Thomas Velline	1973	20.00
❑ UA-LA332-E	The Very Best of Bobby Vee	1975	12.00
❑ LT-1008	Bobby Vee's Golden Greats	1980	10.00
❑ UAS-5656	Nothin' Like a Sunny Day	1972	12.00

VEERS, RUSS

45s

Number	Title (A Side/B Side)	Yr	NM
TREND			
❑ 30010	Warm As Toast/The Answer	1958	500.00

VEGA, SUZANNE

45s

Number	Title (A Side/B Side)	Yr	NM
A&M			
❑ 2759	Neighborhood Girls/Marlene on the Wall	1985	3.00
❑ 2834	Left of Center/Small Blue Thing	1986	3.00
❑ 2937	Luka/Night Vision	1987	3.00
❑ 2937 [PS]	Luka/Night Vision	1987	4.00
❑ 2960	Solitude Standing/Tom's Diner	1987	3.00
❑ 2960 [PS]	Solitude Standing/Tom's Diner	1987	4.00
❑ 2988	Gypsy/Left of Center	1987	3.00
❑ 2988 [PS]	Gypsy/Left of Center	1987	50.00

Albums

Number	Title (A Side/B Side)	Yr	NM
A&M			
❑ SP-6-5072	Suzanne Vega	1985	10.00
❑ SP-5136	Solitude Standing	1987	8.00
❑ 75021 5293 1	Days of Open Hand	1990	12.00
❑ SP-17472 [DJ]	Portrait of an Artist	1987	15.00
—Promo-only 7-song sampler			

VEGA, TATA

12-Inch Singles

Number	Title (A Side/B Side)	Yr	NM
MOTOWN			
❑ M00021-D1	I Just Keep Thinking About You Baby (6:01)/Get It Up for Love (5:58)	1979	15.00

45s

Number	Title (A Side/B Side)	Yr	NM
QWEST			
❑ 7-28754	Miss Celie's Blues (Sister)// Celie Shaves Mr./ Scarification Contest	1986	5.00
❑ 7-28754 [PS]	Miss Celie's Blues (Sister)// Celie Shaves Mr./ Scarification Contest	1986	6.00
—"The Color Purple" picture sleeve			
TAMLA			
❑ 54271	Full Speed Ahead/Just As Long As There Is You	1976	6.00
❑ 54282	You'll Never Rock Alone/Just When Things Are Getting Good	1977	10.00
❑ 54299	I Just Keep Thinking About You Baby/Music in My Heart	1979	6.00
❑ 54304	I Need You Now/In the Morning	1979	25.00
❑ 54316	You Keep Me Hangin' On/You Better Watch Out	1980	6.00

Albums

Number	Title (A Side/B Side)	Yr	NM
TAMLA			
❑ T6-347S1	Full Speed Ahead	1976	15.00
❑ T6-353S1	Totally Tata	1977	15.00
❑ T7-360R1	Try My Love	1978	15.00
❑ T8-370M1	Givin' All My Love	1980	25.00

VEGAS, PAT AND LOLLY Also see REDBONE.

45s

Number	Title (A Side/B Side)	Yr	NM
APOGEE			
❑ 101	Don't You Remember/ The Robot Walk	1964	15.00
MERCURY			
❑ 72509	Walk On (Right Out of My Life)/ Let's Get It On	1965	12.00

Suzanne Vega, "Solitude Standing," A&M 2960, 1987, $4.

Number	Title (A Side/B Side)	Yr	NM
REPRISE			
❑ 20199	Boom Boom/Two Figures (On the Wedding Cake)	1963	20.00

Albums

Number	Title (A Side/B Side)	Yr	NM
MERCURY			
❑ MG-21059 [M]	At the Haunted House	1966	30.00
❑ SR-61059 [S]	At the Haunted House	1966	40.00

VEJTABLES, THE

45s

Number	Title (A Side/B Side)	Yr	NM
AUTUMN			
❑ 15	I Still Love You/Anything	1965	12.00
❑ 23	The Last Thing on My Mind/ Mansion of Texas	1965	12.00
UPTOWN			
❑ 741	Feel the Music/Shadows	1967	10.00

VEL-TONES, THE More than one group.

45s

Number	Title (A Side/B Side)	Yr	NM
COY			
❑ 101	Cal's Tune/Playboy	1959	2000.
—VG 1000; VG+ 1500			
GOLDWAX			
❑ 301	Darling/I Do	1966	15.00
JIN			
❑ 107	Lover Blues/Take a Ride	1959	40.00
❑ 115	Jailbird/I'm Yours Now	1959	40.00
KAPP			
❑ 268	Cal's Tune/Playboy	1959	100.00
LOST-NITE			
❑ 103	Now/I Need You So	1961	100.00
MERCURY			
❑ 71526	Fool in Love/Someday	1959	30.00
SATELLITE			
❑ 100	Fool in Love/Someday	1959	100.00
VEL			
❑ 9178	Broken Heart/Please Say You'll Be True	1960	1500.
WEDGE			
❑ 1013	My Dear/I Want to Know	1964	200.00
ZARA			
❑ 901	Now/I Need You So	1960	80.00

VELAIRES, THE

45s

Number	Title (A Side/B Side)	Yr	NM
JAMIE			
❑ 1198	Roll Over Beethoven/Brazil	1961	20.00
❑ 1203	Sticks and Stones/Dream	1961	15.00
❑ 1211	It's Almost Tomorrow/ Ubangi Stomp	1962	15.00
❑ 1223	Memory Tree/Don't Wake Me Up	1962	15.00
PALMS			
❑ 726	Roll Over Beethoven/Brazil	1961	50.00
—As "The Flairs"			

VELEZ, MARTHA

45s

Number	Title (A Side/B Side)	Yr	NM
MCA			
❑ 41244	What Becomes of the Broken-hearted/Wild Night in Paradise	1980	4.00
POLYDOR			
❑ 14158	Magic in His Hands/Black Rose	1973	6.00
SIRE			
❑ 722	Mockingbird/Aggravation	1975	5.00
—With Pete Wingfield			
❑ 727	Disco Night/Come On In	1976	5.00
❑ 735	Money Man/There You Are	1976	5.00
❑ 1010	When You Were Beautiful/ Up to You	1977	5.00
❑ 4111	Tell Mama/Swamp Man	1969	10.00

Albums

Number	Title (A Side/B Side)	Yr	NM
POLYDOR			
❑ PD 5034	Hypnotized	1972	15.00
SIRE			
❑ SR 6040	American Heartbeat	1977	10.00
❑ SES-7409	Matinee Weepers	1973	15.00

The Velvet Underground, *The Velvet Underground*, MGM SE-4617, 1969, stock copy, **$40-$50** (see listings).

Number	Title (A Side/B Side)	Yr	NM
❑ SASD-7515	Escape from Babylon	1976	10.00
—Produced by Bob Marley			
❑ SES-97008	Fiends and Angels	1969	30.00

VELLS, THE Later recorded as MARTHA AND THE VANDELLAS.

45s

Number	Title (A Side/B Side)	Yr	NM
MEL-O-DY			
❑ 103	There He Is At My Door/You'll Never Cherish a Love So True	1962	100.00

VELONS, THE

45s

Number	Title (A Side/B Side)	Yr	NM
BJM			
❑ 6568	Summer Love/ Why Don't You Write	1965	20.00
❑ 6569	That's What Love Can Do/ That's All Right	1965	20.00
BLAST			
❑ 216	Shelly/From the Chapel	1964	100.00

VELOURS, THE

45s

Number	Title (A Side/B Side)	Yr	NM
CLIFTON			
❑ 1987	Old Fashion Christmas/ I Wish You Love	19??	6.00
CUB			
❑ 9014	Crazy Love/I'll Never Smile Again	1958	25.00
❑ 9029	Blue Velvet/Tired of Your Rock and Rollin'	1959	25.00
END			
❑ 1090	Lover Come Back/ The Lonely One	1961	20.00
GOLDISC			
❑ 3012	Daddy Warbucks/Sweet Sixteen	1960	25.00
GONE			
❑ 5092	Can I Come Over Tonight/Where There's a Will (There's a Way)	1960	20.00
LOST-NITE			
❑ 391	My Love Come Back/ Honey Drop	197?	5.00
—Reissue			
❑ 394	Can I Come Over Tonight/Where There's a Will (There's a Way)	197?	5.00
—Reissue			
❑ 400	This Could Be the Night/ Hands Across the Table	197?	5.00
—Reissue			
❑ 402	What You Do to Me/Romeo	197?	5.00
—Reissue			
MGM			
❑ 13780	Don't Pity Me/I'm Gonna Change	1967	30.00
ONYX			
❑ 501	My Love Come Back/ Honey Drop	1956	200.00
❑ 508	What You Do to Me/Romeo	1957	800.00
❑ 512	Can I Come Over Tonight/Where There's a Will (There's a Way)	1957	200.00
❑ 515	This Could Be the Night/ Hands Across the Table	1957	120.00
❑ 520	Remember/Can I Walk You Home	1958	60.00
ORBIT			
❑ 9001	Remember/Can I Walk You Home	1958	50.00
RONA			
❑ 010	Woman for Me/(B-side unknown)	1966	25.00
STUDO			
❑ 9902	I Promise/Little Sweetheart	1959	50.00

VELVATONES, THE

45s

Number	Title (A Side/B Side)	Yr	NM
METEOR			
❑ 5042	Real Gone Baby/ Feeling Kinda Lonely	1957	200.00
NU KAT			
❑ 110	Impossible/I'm Leaving Home	1959	50.00

VELVELETTES, THE

45s

Number	Title (A Side/B Side)	Yr	NM
I.P.G.			
❑ 1002	There He Goes/That's the Reason Why	1963	100.00
SOUL			
❑ 35025	These Things Will Keep Me Loving You/Since You've Been Loving Me	1966	20.00
V.I.P.			
❑ 25007	Needle in a Haystack/ Should I Tell Them	1964	25.00
❑ 25013	He Was Realy Sayin' Somethin'/ Throw a Farewell Kiss	1965	25.00
❑ 25017	I'm the Exception to the Rule/ Lonely, Lonely Girl Am I	1965	20.00
❑ 25021	A Bird in the Hand (Is Worth Two in the Bush)/(B-side unknown)	1965	800.00
❑ 25030	A Bird in the Hand (Is Worth Two in the Bush)/Since You've Been Loving Me	1965	20.00
❑ 25034	These Things Will Keep Me Loving You/Since You've Been Loving Me	1966	30.00

VELVET, JIMMY Two different singers, both of whom also recorded as "Jimmy Velvit"! If someone can help us tell who's who, we'd really appreciate it.

45s

Number	Title (A Side/B Side)	Yr	NM
ABC-PARAMOUNT			
❑ 10488	We Belong Together/ History of Love	1963	20.00
❑ 10528	To the Aisle/Lonely, Lonely Night	1964	20.00
BELL			
❑ 692	Let Me Keep Your Love/ Woman in Bloom	1967	8.00
CAMEO			
❑ 464	Take Me Tonight/Young Hearts	1967	25.00
❑ 488	Roses Are Blue/ A Touch of Velvet	1967	25.00
CORREC-TONE			
❑ 102	When I Needed You/ Bouquet of Flowers	1962	100.00
—As "James Velvet"; the Supremes sing backup			
CUB			
❑ 9100	Sometimes at Night/Look at Me	1961	15.00
❑ 9111	When I Needed You/ Bouquet of Flowers	1962	15.00
DIVISION			
❑ 102	Sometimes at Night/Look at Me	1961	20.00
PHILIPS			
❑ 40285	It's Almost Tomorrow/Blue Eyes (Don't Run Away)	1965	20.00
❑ 40314	I Won't Be Back This Year/ Young Hearts	1965	20.00
ROYAL AMERICAN			
❑ 286	It's You/A Woman	1968	8.00
❑ 291	Blue Velvet/Missing You	1969	8.00
STARTIME			
❑ 103	Wisdom of a Fool/ Want to Be Loved	196?	12.00
TEAR DROP			
❑ 3353	Don't Go Near a Woman/ Hey Nashville	196?	12.00
❑ 3395	Oh Lonesome Me-Detroit City/ Crazy Arms	196?	12.00
—As "James Velvit"			
TOLLIE			
❑ 9037	Teen Angel/Mission Bell	1964	15.00
UNITED ARTISTS			
❑ 50272	Good Good Lovin'/ Heart Breakin' Misery	1968	20.00
VELVET			
❑ 201	We Belong Together/ You're Mine	1963	100.00
—As "Jimmy Velvit"			
VELVET TONE			
❑ 102	It's Almost Tomorrow/ Young Hearts	1965	30.00

Albums

Number	Title (A Side/B Side)	Yr	NM
UNITED ARTISTS			
❑ UAS-6653	A Touch of Velvet	1968	25.00
VELVET TONE			
❑ 501	A Touch of Velvet	1968	60.00

Except when noted otherwise, VG = 25% of NM, and VG+ = 50% of NM. (Example: VG = $2.00, VG+ = $4.00 and NM = $8.00.)

VELVET KEYS, THE

45s

KING

Number	Title (A Side/B Side)	Yr	NM
❑ 5090	My Baby's Gone/Let's Stay After School	1957	80.00
❑ 5109	Don't Take My Picture, Take Me/The Truth About Youth	1958	80.00

VELVET NIGHT

45s

METROMEDIA

Number	Title (A Side/B Side)	Yr	NM
❑ 110	Velvet Night/I'm Sure He'll Come Most Anytime	1969	8.00

Albums

METROMEDIA

Number	Title (A Side/B Side)	Yr	NM
❑ MD-1028	Velvet Night	1970	30.00

VELVET SOUNDS, THE

45s

COSMOPOLITAN

Number	Title (A Side/B Side)	Yr	NM
❑ 100/101	Silver Star/The Devil and the Stocker	1953	600.00
❑ 105/106	Pretty Darling/Who'll Take My Place	1953	400.00
❑ 530/531	Hanging Up Christmas Stockings/Sing A Song Of Christmas Cheer	1953	500.00

VELVET UNDERGROUND, THE

Also see JOHN CALE; LOU REED; MAUREEN TUCKER; NICO. Includes releases with NICO. Also see JOHN CALE; LOU REED.

12-Inch Singles

VERVE

Number	Title (A Side/B Side)	Yr	NM
❑ PRO 349-1 [DJ]	Foggy Notion/I Can't Stand It	1985	15.00

45s

COTILLION

Number	Title (A Side/B Side)	Yr	NM
❑ 44107	Who Loves the Sun/Oh, Sweet Nothin'	1971	1200.
—Stock copy; red--orange label			
❑ 44107 [DJ]	Who Loves the Sun (mono/stereo)	1971	100.00
—Promo copy; white label; three different label variations exist, each of equal value			

MGM

Number	Title (A Side/B Side)	Yr	NM
❑ VU-1 [DJ]	The Velvet Underground	1969	500.00
—Yellow label; radio ad for the third album with three song excerpts			
❑ VU-1 [PS]	The Velvet Underground	1969	1500.
❑ 14057	What Goes On/Jesus	1969	—
—Existence of a stock copy of this record has been questioned; if it exists, it would have a blue and gold label			
❑ 14057 [DJ]	What Goes On/Jesus	1969	200.00
—Promo copy; yellow label			

VERVE

Number	Title (A Side/B Side)	Yr	NM
❑ 10427	All Tomorrow's Parties/I'll Be Your Mirror	1966	600.00
—Stock copy; dark blue label			
❑ 10427 [DJ]	All Tomorrow's Parties/I'll Be Your Mirror	1966	300.00
—Promo copy; light blue label			
❑ 10427 [PS]	All Tomorrow's Parties/I'll Be Your Mirror	1966	8000.
❑ 10466	Femme Fatale/Sunday Morning	1966	400.00
—Stock copy; dark blue label			
❑ 10466 [DJ]	Femme Fatale/Sunday Morning	1966	300.00
—Promo copy; light blue label			
❑ 10560	White Light/White Heat//Here She Comes Now	1967	300.00
—Stock copy; dark blue label			
❑ 10560 [DJ]	White Light/White Heat//I Heard Her Call My Name	1967	200.00
—Promo copy; light blue label			

Albums

COTILLION

Number	Title (A Side/B Side)	Yr	NM
❑ 9034 [M]	Loaded	1970	250.00
—Mono is white label promo only; "d/j copy monaural" sticker on front cover; no "SD" prefix on label			
❑ SD 9034 [S]	Loaded	197?	15.00
—Reissue with purplish label			
❑ SD 9034 [S]	Loaded	1970	150.00
—White label promo; not the monaural version, this one has no sticker on the cover and has the "SD" prefix on the label			
❑ SD 9034 [S]	Loaded	1970	20.00
—Original pressing has a light blue label			
❑ SD 9034 [S]	Loaded	198?	12.00
—Reissue with purplish label and bar code on back cover			
❑ SD 9034 [S]	Loaded	2001	10.00
—Rhino/Scorpio reissue; purplish label			
❑ SD 9500	Live at Max's Kansas City	197?	15.00
—Reissue with purplish label			
❑ SD 9500	Live at Max's Kansas City	1972	20.00
—Original pressing has a light blue label			
❑ SD 9500	Live at Max's Kansas City	198?	12.00
—Reissue with purplish label and bar code on back cover			
❑ SD 9500	Live at Max's Kansas City	2001	10.00
—Rhino/Scorpio reissue; light blue label			
❑ SD 9500 [DJ]	Live at Max's Kansas City	1972	75.00
—White label promo with "d/j copy monaural" sticker on front cover, which in this case is odd because all copies are mono!			

MERCURY

Number	Title (A Side/B Side)	Yr	NM
❑ SRM-2-7504 [(2)]	1969 (Live)	1974	15.00
—Reissues with Chicago skyline labels			
❑ SRM-2-7504 [(2)]	1969 (Live)	1974	50.00
—Originals with red labels			
❑ SRM-2-7504 [(2)]	1969 (Live)	1983	20.00
—Reissue with black labels; non-gatefold cover; no bar code on back			
❑ SRM-2-7504 [(2)DJ]	1969 (Live)	1974	100.00
—White label promo			

MGM

Number	Title (A Side/B Side)	Yr	NM
❑ GAS-131	The Velvet Underground (Golden Archive Series)	1970	40.00
—Blue and gold label stock copy			
❑ GAS-131 [DJ]	The Velvet Underground (Golden Archive Series)	1970	100.00
—White label promo			
❑ GAS-131 [DJ]	The Velvet Underground (Golden Archive Series)	1970	100.00
—Yellow label promo			
❑ SE-4617	The Velvet Underground	1969	50.00
—With "BMI" publishing credit			
❑ SE-4617	The Velvet Underground	1971	40.00
—With "ASCAP" publishing credit			
❑ SE-4617 [DJ]	The Velvet Underground	1969	250.00
—White label promo			
❑ SE-4617 [DJ]	The Velvet Underground	1969	250.00
—Yellow label promo			
❑ M3G 4950	Archetypes	1974	20.00
❑ M3G 4950 [DJ]	Archetypes	1974	40.00
—White label promo			
❑ SW-95722	Archetypes	1974	30.00
—Longines Symphonette edition			

POLYDOR

Number	Title (A Side/B Side)	Yr	NM
❑ 8232901 [S]	The Velvet Underground and Nico	2008	20.00

PRIDE

Number	Title (A Side/B Side)	Yr	NM
❑ 0022	Lou Reed and the Velvet Underground	1973	15.00
—Tan label; label calls this "That's the Story of My Life"			
❑ 0022 [DJ]	Lou Reed and the Velvet Underground	1973	50.00
—White label; label calls this "That's the Story of My Life"			

VERVE

Number	Title (A Side/B Side)	Yr	NM
❑ V-5008 [M]	The Velvet Underground and Nico	1967	200.00
—Version 3: With peel-off banana peel, torso is airbrushed off the cover (deduct 50% if banana sticker removed)			
❑ V-5008 [M]	The Velvet Underground and Nico	1967	300.00
—Version 1: With peel-off banana peel, photo of band framed by a male torso (deduct 50% if banana sticker is gone)			
❑ V-5008 [M]	The Velvet Underground and Nico	1967	300.00
—Version 2: With peel-off banana peel, photo of torso obscured by a large black sticker (deduct 50% if stickers removed)			
❑ V-5008 [M]	The Velvet Underground and Nico	1967	400.00
—Promo copy; white label			
❑ V-5008 [M]	The Velvet Underground and Nico	1967	400.00
—Promo copy; yellow label			
❑ V6-5008 [S]	The Velvet Underground and Nico	1967	150.00
—Version 3: With peel-off banana peel, torso is airbrushed off the cover, publishing on label is credited to "Three Prong Music" (deduct 50% if banana sticker removed)			
❑ V6-5008 [S]	The Velvet Underground and Nico	1967	200.00
—Version 1: With peel-off banana peel, photo of band framed by a male torso (deduct 50% if banana sticker is gone)			
❑ V6-5008 [S]	The Velvet Underground and Nico	1967	200.00
—Version 2: With peel-off banana peel, photo of torso obscured by a sticker (deduct 50% if stickers removed)			
❑ V6-5008 [S]	The Velvet Underground and Nico	1968	100.00
—Version 4: With peel-off banana peel, torso is airbrushed off the cover, publishing on label is credited to "Oakfield Avenue Music," Side 2 trail-off wax has an "RE-1" (deduct 50% if banana sticker removed)			
❑ V6-5008 [S]	The Velvet Underground and Nico	1970	80.00
—Version 5: With unpeelable banana; blue label with silver "T" shape on it; publishing on the label is credited to "Oakfield Avenue Music"			
❑ V6-5008 [S]	The Velvet Underground and Nico	1973	70.00
—Version 6: Same as Version 5 except the label is now white with "MGM" at left and "Verve" at right			
❑ V6-5008 [S]	The Velvet Underground and Nico	1975	50.00
—Version 7: Same as Version 5, but the label is now black with silver T-shape			
❑ V6-5008 [S]	The Velvet Underground and Nico	1978	25.00
—Version 8; The cover is no longer a gatefold			
❑ V-5046 [M]	White Light/White Heat	1967	300.00
—White label promo			
❑ V-5046 [M]	White Light/White Heat	1967	300.00
—Yellow label promo			
❑ V-5046 [M]	White Light/White Heat	1967	700.00
—Version 2: No "skeleton" on cover			
❑ V-5046 [M]	White Light/White Heat	1967	800.00
—Version 1: "Skeleton" cover — a black-on-black skeleton is visible when cover is viewed at an angle			
❑ V6-5046 [S]	White Light/White Heat	1967	40.00
—Version 2: No "skeleton" on cover; publishing on label is credited to "Three Prong Music"			
❑ V6-5046 [S]	White Light/White Heat	1967	80.00
—Version 1: "Skeleton" cover — a black-on-black skeleton is visible when cover is viewed at an angle			
❑ V6-5046 [S]	White Light/White Heat	1967	250.00
—Yellow label promo			
❑ V6-5046 [S]	White Light/White Heat	1968	30.00
—Version 3: No "skeleton" on cover; publishing on label is credited to "Oakfield Avenue Music"			
❑ 815454-1	The Velvet Underground	1985	12.00
—Reissue of MGM SE-4617			
❑ 823290-1	The Velvet Underground and Nico	1985	12.00
—Reissue of Verve V6-5008			
❑ 823721-1	VU	1985	12.00
❑ 825119-1	White Light/White Heat	1985	12.00
—Reissue of Verve V6-5046			
❑ 826284-1 [(2)]	1969 (Live)	1985	12.00
—Reissue of Mercury SRM-2-7504			
❑ 829405-1	Another View	1986	12.00

VELVETEENS, THE

45s

GOLDEN ARTISTS

Number	Title (A Side/B Side)	Yr	NM
❑ 614	I Feel Sorry for You Baby/Ching Bam Bah	1965	10.00

LAURIE

Number	Title (A Side/B Side)	Yr	NM
❑ 3126	I Thank You/Meant to Be	1962	15.00

STARK

Number	Title (A Side/B Side)	Yr	NM
❑ 101	Teen Prayer/Baby Baby	1961	20.00
—Slightly altered A-side title			
❑ 101	The Teen Prayer/Baby Baby	1961	30.00
—New A-side title			
❑ 101	Please Holy Father/Baby Baby	1961	50.00
—Original title of A-side			
❑ 105	I Thank You/Meant to Be	1962	25.00

VELVETEERS, THE

45s

SPITFIRE

Number	Title (A Side/B Side)	Yr	NM
❑ 15	Tell Me You're Mine/Boo Wacka Boo	1956	4000.
—VG 2000; VG+ 3000			

VELVETIERS, THE

45s

RIC

Number	Title (A Side/B Side)	Yr	NM
❑ 958	Oh Baby/Feelin' Right Saturday Night	1958	300.00

VELVETONES, THE (1)

45s

ALADDIN

Number	Title (A Side/B Side)	Yr	NM
❑ 3372	Glory of Love/I Love Her So	1957	200.00
❑ 3391	I Found My Love/Melody of Love	1957	200.00
❑ 3463	My Every Thought/Little Girl I Love You So	1960	300.00

D

Number	Title (A Side/B Side)	Yr	NM
❑ 1049	Come Back/Penalty of Love	1959	150.00
❑ 1072	Worried Over You/Space Man	1959	100.00

DEB

Number	Title (A Side/B Side)	Yr	NM
❑ 1008	Stars of Wonder/Who Took My Girl	1959	150.00

IMPERIAL

Number	Title (A Side/B Side)	Yr	NM
❑ 5878	The Glory of Love/I Love Her So	1962	30.00
❑ 66020	The Glory of Love/I Found My Love	1964	15.00

VELVETONES, THE (2)

Girl group.

45s

ASCOT

Number	Title (A Side/B Side)	Yr	NM
❑ 2117	I Want Him So Bad/Yes I Will	1962	15.00
❑ 2126	Starry Eyed/I'm Ashamed	1963	15.00

VELVETONES, THE (3)

45s

GARP

Number	Title (A Side/B Side)	Yr	NM
❑ 102	Mister X/(B-side unknown)	1965	60.00
—Black vinyl			
❑ 102	Mister X/(B-side unknown)	1965	120.00
—Red vinyl			

V

The Ventures, *Play Guitar with the Ventures*, Volume 2, Dolton BLP-16502, 1960s, mono, **$25.**

Number	Title (A Side/B Side)	Yr	NM
VELVETONES, THE (4)			
45s			
VERVE			
❑ 10514	What Can the Matter Be/ Hairy Lumpty Bump	1967	12.00
VELVETONES, THE (U) Could be group (3); could be someone completely different.			
45s			
GLENN			
❑ 309	Doheny Run/Static	1965	30.00
VELVET			
❑ 101	Doheny Run/Static	1965	70.00
VELVETS, THE (1)			
45s			
MONUMENT			
❑ 435	That Lucky Old Sun/ Time and Again	1961	30.00
❑ 441	Tonight (Could Be the Night)/ Spring Fever	1961	30.00
❑ 448	Lana/Laugh	1961	30.00
❑ 458	The Love Express/Don't Let Him Take My Baby	1962	25.00
❑ 464	Let the Good Times Roll/ The Lights Go On, The Lights Go Off	1962	25.00
❑ 810	Crying in the Chapel/Dawn	1963	20.00
❑ 836	Nightmare/Here Comes That Song Again	1964	20.00
❑ 861	If/Let the Fool Kiss You	1964	20.00
❑ 961	Baby the Magic Is Gone/ Let the Fool Kiss You	1966	15.00
❑ 8917	Tonight (Could Be the Night)/ That Lucky Old Sun (Just Rolls Around Heaven)	197?	5.00
—"Golden Series" reissue			

Number	Title (A Side/B Side)	Yr	NM
VELVETS, THE (2)			
45s			
EVENT			
❑ 4285	I/At Last	197?	8.00
FURY			
❑ 1012	I-I-I (Love You So-So-So)/ Dance Honey Dance	1958	50.00
LOST-NITE			
❑ 335	They Tried/She's Gotta Grin	197?	5.00
❑ 341	I/At Last	197?	5.00
—Reissue			
❑ 345	Tell Her/I Cried	197?	5.00
—Reissue			
PILGRIM			
❑ 706	I/At Last	1956	50.00
❑ 710	Tell Her/I Cried	1956	50.00
RED ROBIN			
❑ 120	They Tried/She's Gotta Grin	1953	200.00
❑ 122	I/At Last	1953	150.00
❑ 127	Tell Her/I Cried	1954	150.00
VELVETS, THE (U) These could be by group (1).			
45s			
PLAID			
❑ 101	Everybody Knows/ Hand Jivin' Baby	1959	80.00
20TH FOX			
❑ 165	Happy Days Are Here Again/ If I Could Be with You	1959	25.00
VENEERS, THE			
45s			
PRINCETON			
❑ 102	Believe Me (My Angel)/I	1960	40.00
TREYCO			
❑ 402	With All My Love/Recipe of Love	1963	15.00

Number	Title (A Side/B Side)	Yr	NM
VENET, NICK			
45s			
DECCA			
❑ 31939	Theme from "Out of Sight"/ Camp Side	1966	10.00
IMPERIAL			
❑ 5522	Love In Be-Bop Time/ Honey Baby	1958	20.00
VENTRILLS, THE			
45s			
PARKWAY			
❑ 141	Alone in the Night/Confusion	1967	12.00
VENTURES, THE			
12-Inch Singles			
TRIDEX			
❑ 1245	Surfin' and Spyin'/Showdown at Newport	1981	20.00
45s			
BLUE HORIZON			
❑ 100	The Real McCoy/ Cookies and Coke	1960	600.00
❑ 101	Walk-Don't Run/Home	1960	2500.
❑ 102	Hold Me, Thrill Me, Kiss Me/ No Next Time	1960	200.00
—As "Scott Douglas and the Venture Quintet"			
DOLTON			
❑ 25	Walk — Don't Run/Home	1960	25.00
❑ 25X	Walk — Don't Run/The McCoy	1960	20.00
❑ 28	Perfidia/No Trespassing	1960	20.00
❑ 28 [PS]	Perfidia/No Trespassing	1960	50.00
❑ 32	Ram-Bunk-Shush/Lonely Heart	1961	20.00
❑ 41	Lullaby of the Leaves/Ginchy	1961	20.00
❑ 44	(Theme from) Silver City/ Bluer Than Blue	1961	20.00
❑ 47	Blue Moon/Lady of Spain	1961	20.00
❑ 50	Yellow Jacket/Genesis	1962	20.00
❑ 55	Instant Mashed/My Bonnie	1962	20.00
❑ 60	Lolita Ya-Ya/Lucille	1962	20.00
❑ 67	The 2,000 Pound Bee (Part 1)/ The 2,000 Pound Bee (Part 2)	1962	20.00
❑ 68	El Cumbanchero/ Skip To M'Limbo	1963	15.00
❑ 78	The Ninth Wave/ Damaged Goods	1963	15.00
❑ 85	The Savage/The Chase	1963	15.00
❑ 91	Journey to the Stars/ Walkin' with Pluto	1964	15.00
❑ 94	Fugitive/Scratchin'	1964	15.00
❑ 96	Walk... Don't Run '64/ The Cruel Sea	1964	15.00
❑ 96 [PS]	Walk... Don't Run '64/ The Cruel Sea	1964	30.00
❑ 300	Slaughter on Tenth Avenue/ Rap City	1964	12.00
❑ 300 [PS]	Slaughter on Tenth Avenue/ Rap City	1964	25.00
❑ 303	Diamond Head/Lonely Girl	1965	12.00
❑ 306	Pedal Pusher/The Swingin' Creeper	1965	12.00
❑ 308	Ten Seconds to Heaven/ Bird Rockers	1965	12.00
❑ 311	La Bomba/Gemini	1965	12.00
❑ 312	Sleigh Ride/Snow Flakes	1965	15.00
❑ 316	Secret Agent Man/00-711	1966	12.00
❑ 320	Blue Star/Comin' Home Baby	1966	12.00
❑ 320 [PS]	Blue Star/Comin' Home Baby	1966	25.00
❑ 321	Arabesque/Ginza Lights	1966	12.00
❑ 323	Green Hornet Theme/ Fuzzy and Wild	1966	12.00
❑ 323 [PS]	Green Hornet Theme/ Fuzzy and Wild	1966	30.00
❑ 325	Penetration/Wild Thing	1966	12.00
❑ 325 [PS]	Penetration/Wild Thing	1966	25.00
❑ 327	Theme from "The Wild Angels"/ Kickstand	1967	12.00
❑ S7-19770	Rudolph the Red-Nosed Reindeer/Frosty (The Snow Man)	1997	3.00
—B-side by Jan and Dean on Liberty			
EMI			
❑ S7-18212	Jingle Bell Rock/Jingle Bells	1994	5.00
—Red vinyl			
❑ SPRO 19949 [DJ]	Rudolf The Red-Nosed Reindeer/Depression	1994	5.00
—B-side by Johnny and the Dwellers			
❑ SPRO 19949 [PS]	Rudolf The Red-Nosed Reindeer/Depression	1994	5.00
LIBERTY			
❑ 54518	Walk — Don't Run/ Ram-Bunk-Shush	196?	6.00

Except when noted otherwise, VG = 25% of NM, and VG+ = 50% of NM. (Example: VG = $2.00, VG+ = $4.00 and NM = $8.00.)

Number	Title (A Side/B Side)	Yr	NM
❑ 54519	Perfidia/Blue Moon	196?	6.00
❑ 54557	Wipe Out/Secret Agent Man	196?	7.00

—Records in the 54500s are from a reissue series

Number	Title (A Side/B Side)	Yr	NM
❑ 55967	Strawberry Fields Forever/ Endless Dream	1967	8.00
❑ 55977	Theme from "Endless Summer"/ Strawberry Fields Forever	1967	8.00
❑ 56007	On the Road/ Mirrors and Shadows	1967	8.00
❑ 56019	Flights of Fantasy/Vibrations	1968	6.00
❑ 56044	Walk Don't Run-Land of 1000 Dances/Too Young to Know My Mind	1968	6.00
❑ 56068	Hawaii Five-O/Soul Breeze	1968	8.00
❑ 56115	Theme from A Summer Place/ A Summer Love	1969	6.00
❑ 56153	Expo Seven-O/Swan Lake	1970	6.00
❑ 56169	The Wanderer/The Mercenary	1970	6.00
❑ 56189	Storefront Lawyers (Theme)/ Kern County Line	1970	6.00

TRIDEX

Number	Title (A Side/B Side)	Yr	NM
❑ 501	Surfin' and Spyin'/ Rumble at Newport	1981	5.00

—A-side with Charlotte Caffey and Jane Wiedlin of the Go-Go's, who did their own version on an early single

Number	Title (A Side/B Side)	Yr	NM
❑ 501 [PS]	Surfin' and Spyin'/ Rumble at Newport	1981	5.00

UNITED ARTISTS

Number	Title (A Side/B Side)	Yr	NM
❑ 0050	Walk—Don't Run/ Ram-Bunk-Shush	1973	4.00

—0050, 0051 and 0052 are "Silver Spotlight Series" reissues

Number	Title (A Side/B Side)	Yr	NM
❑ 0051	Perfidia/Telstar	1973	4.00
❑ 0052	Hawaii Five-O/Walk— Don't Run '64	1973	4.00
❑ XW207	Last Tango in Paris/Prima Vera	1973	6.00
❑ XW277	Skylab/The Little People	1973	6.00
❑ XW333	Also Sprach Zarathustra (2001)/ The Cisco Kid	1973	6.00
❑ XW369	Main Theme from The Young and the Restless/Eloise	1973	6.00
❑ XW392	Main Theme from The Young and the Restless/Eloise	1974	6.00
❑ XW392 [PS]	Main Theme from The Young and the Restless/Eloise	1974	8.00
❑ XW578	Theme from "Airport 1975"/The Man with the Golden Gun	1974	6.00
❑ XW687	Superstar Revue (Part 1)/ Superstar Revue (Part 2)	1975	6.00
❑ XW784	Moonlight Serenade (Part 1)/ Moonlight Serenade (Part 2)	1976	8.00

—As "The New Ventures"

Number	Title (A Side/B Side)	Yr	NM
❑ XW942	Theme from "Charlie's Angels"/ Theme from "Starsky and Hutch"	1977	8.00
❑ XW1100	Walk Don't Run '77/ Amanda's Theme	1977	6.00
❑ XW1161	Wipe Out/Nadia's Theme	1978	4.00

—Reissue

Number	Title (A Side/B Side)	Yr	NM
❑ 50800	Indian Sun/Squaw Man	1971	6.00
❑ 50800 [PS]	Indian Sun/Squaw Man	1971	8.00
❑ 50851	Theme from "Shaft"/Tight Fit	1971	6.00
❑ 50872	Joy/Cherries Jubilee	1972	6.00
❑ 50903	Beethoven's Sonata in C# Minor/Peter and the Wolf	1972	6.00
❑ 50925	Honky Tonk (Part 1)/ Honky Tonk (Part 2)	1972	6.00
❑ 50989	Last Night/Ram-Bunk-Shush	1972	6.00

7-Inch Extended Plays

DOLTON

Number	Title (A Side/B Side)	Yr	NM
❑ BEP-503	Walk — Don't Run/The McCoy// Honky Tonk/Raunchy	1960	80.00
❑ BEP-503 [PS]	Walk — Don't Run	1960	80.00
❑ 4-8031	House of the Rising Sun/Night Train/Rap City//Walk Don't Run '64/One Mint Julep/The Creeper	1964	15.00

—Jukebox single, small hole, plays at 33 1/3 rpm

Number	Title (A Side/B Side)	Yr	NM
❑ 4-8031 [PS]	Walk Don't Run '64	1964	15.00

Albums

COMPLEAT

Number	Title (A Side/B Side)	Yr	NM
❑ 672013-1	The Best of the Ventures	1986	10.00

DOLTON

Number	Title (A Side/B Side)	Yr	NM
❑ BLP 2003 [M]	Walk Don't Run	1960	50.00

—Pale blue label with dolphins on top

Number	Title (A Side/B Side)	Yr	NM
❑ BLP 2003 [M]	Walk Don't Run	1963	20.00

—Dark label, logo on left

Number	Title (A Side/B Side)	Yr	NM
❑ BLP 2004 [M]	The Ventures	1961	50.00

—Pale blue label with dolphins on top

Number	Title (A Side/B Side)	Yr	NM
❑ BLP 2004 [M]	The Ventures	1963	20.00

—Dark label, logo on left

Number	Title (A Side/B Side)	Yr	NM
❑ BLP 2006 [M]	Another Smash!!!	1961	50.00

—Pale blue label with dolphins on top

Number	Title (A Side/B Side)	Yr	NM
❑ BLP 2006 [M]	Another Smash!!!	1963	20.00

—Dark label, logo on left

Number	Title (A Side/B Side)	Yr	NM
❑ BLP 2008 [M]	The Colorful Ventures	1961	50.00

—Pale blue label with dolphins on top

Number	Title (A Side/B Side)	Yr	NM
❑ BLP 2008 [M]	The Colorful Ventures	1963	20.00

—Dark label, logo on left

Number	Title (A Side/B Side)	Yr	NM
❑ BLP 2010 [M]	Twist with the Ventures	1962	50.00

—Pale blue label with dolphins on top

Number	Title (A Side/B Side)	Yr	NM
❑ BLP 2010 [M]	Dance!	1963	20.00

—Dark label, logo on left; retitled version of "Twist with the Ventures"

Number	Title (A Side/B Side)	Yr	NM
❑ BLP 2014 [M]	The Ventures' Twist Party, Vol. 2	1962	50.00

—Pale blue label with dolphins on top

Number	Title (A Side/B Side)	Yr	NM
❑ BLP 2014 [M]	Dance with the Ventures	1963	20.00

—Dark label, logo on left' retitled version of "The Ventures' Twist Party, Vol. 2"

Number	Title (A Side/B Side)	Yr	NM
❑ BLP 2016 [M]	Mashed Potatoes and Gravy	1962	30.00
❑ BLP 2016 [M]	Beach Party	1963	20.00

—Retitled version of "Mashed Potatoes and Gravy"

Number	Title (A Side/B Side)	Yr	NM
❑ BLP 2017 [M]	Going to the Ventures Dance Party!	1962	30.00
❑ BLP 2019 [M]	The Ventures Play Telstar, The Lonely Bull	1962	30.00
❑ BLP 2022 [M]	Surfing	1963	25.00
❑ BLP 2023 [M]	The Ventures Play the Country Classics	1963	25.00
❑ BLP 2024 [M]	Let's Go!	1963	25.00
❑ BLP 2027 [M]	(The) Ventures in Space	1964	40.00
❑ BLP 2029 [M]	The Fabulous Ventures	1964	25.00
❑ BLP 2031 [M]	Walk, Don't Run, Vol. 2	1964	25.00
❑ BLP 2033 [M]	The Ventures Knock Me Out!	1965	25.00
❑ BLP 2035 [M]	The Ventures on Stage	1965	25.00
❑ BLP 2037 [M]	The Ventures A-Go-Go	1965	25.00
❑ BLP-2038 [M]	The Ventures' Christmas Album	1965	30.00
❑ BLP 2040 [M]	Where the Action Is	1966	20.00
❑ BLP 2042 [M]	The Ventures/Batman Theme	1966	30.00
❑ BLP 2045 [M]	Go with the Ventures!	1966	20.00
❑ BLP 2047 [M]	Wild Things!	1966	20.00
❑ BLP 2050 [M]	Guitar Freakout	1967	20.00
❑ BST 8003 [S]	Walk Don't Run	1960	60.00

—Pale blue label with dolphins on top

Number	Title (A Side/B Side)	Yr	NM
❑ BST 8003 [S]	Walk Don't Run	1963	25.00

—Dark label, logo on left

Number	Title (A Side/B Side)	Yr	NM
❑ BST 8004 [S]	The Ventures	1961	60.00

—Pale blue label with dolphins on top

Number	Title (A Side/B Side)	Yr	NM
❑ BST 8004 [S]	The Ventures	1963	25.00

—Dark label, logo on left

Number	Title (A Side/B Side)	Yr	NM
❑ BST 8006 [S]	Another Smash!!!	1961	60.00

—Pale blue label with dolphins on top

Number	Title (A Side/B Side)	Yr	NM
❑ BST 8006 [S]	Another Smash!!!	1963	25.00

—Dark label, logo on left

Number	Title (A Side/B Side)	Yr	NM
❑ BST 8008 [S]	The Colorful Ventures	1961	60.00

—Pale blue label with dolphins on top

Number	Title (A Side/B Side)	Yr	NM
❑ BST 8008 [S]	The Colorful Ventures	1963	25.00

—Dark label, logo on left

Number	Title (A Side/B Side)	Yr	NM
❑ BST 8010 [S]	Twist with the Ventures	1962	60.00

—Pale blue label with dolphins on top

Number	Title (A Side/B Side)	Yr	NM
❑ BST 8010 [S]	Dance!	1963	25.00

—Dark label, logo on left; retitled version of "Twist with the Ventures"

Number	Title (A Side/B Side)	Yr	NM
❑ BST 8014 [S]	The Ventures' Twist Party, Vol. 2	1962	60.00

—Pale blue label with dolphins on top

Number	Title (A Side/B Side)	Yr	NM
❑ BST 8014 [S]	Dance with the Ventures	1963	25.00

—Dark label, logo on left' retitled version of "The Ventures' Twist Party, Vol. 2"

Number	Title (A Side/B Side)	Yr	NM
❑ BST 8016 [S]	Mashed Potatoes and Gravy	1962	40.00
❑ BST 8016 [S]	Beach Party	1963	25.00

—Retitled version of "Mashed Potatoes and Gravy"

Number	Title (A Side/B Side)	Yr	NM
❑ BST 8017 [S]	Going to the Ventures Dance Party!	1962	40.00
❑ BST 8019 [S]	The Ventures Play Telstar, The Lonely Bull	1962	40.00
❑ BST 8022 [S]	Surfing	1963	30.00
❑ BST 8023 [S]	The Ventures Play the Country Classics	1963	30.00
❑ BST 8024 [S]	Let's Go!	1963	30.00
❑ BST 8027 [S]	(The) Ventures in Space	1964	50.00
❑ BST 8029 [S]	The Fabulous Ventures	1964	30.00
❑ BST 8031 [S]	Walk, Don't Run, Vol. 2	1964	30.00
❑ BST 8033 [S]	The Ventures Knock Me Out!	1965	30.00
❑ BST 8035 [S]	The Ventures on Stage	1965	30.00
❑ BST 8037 [S]	The Ventures A-Go-Go	1965	30.00
❑ BST-8038 [S]	The Ventures' Christmas Album	1965	20.00
❑ BST 8040 [S]	Where the Action Is	1966	25.00
❑ BST 8042 [S]	The Ventures/Batman Theme	1966	40.00
❑ BST 8045 [S]	Go with the Ventures!	1966	25.00
❑ BST 8047 [S]	Wild Things!	1966	25.00
❑ BST 8050 [S]	Guitar Freakout	1967	25.00
❑ BLP 16501 [M]	Play Guitar with the Ventures	1965	25.00
❑ BLP 16502 [M]	Play Guitar with the Ventures, Vol. 2	196?	25.00
❑ BLP 16503 [M]	Play Guitar with the Ventures, Vol. 3	196?	25.00
❑ BLP 16504 [M]	Play Guitar with the Ventures, Vol. 4	196?	25.00
❑ BST 16504 [S]	Play Guitar with the Ventures, Vol. 4	196?	30.00
❑ BST 17501 [S]	Play Guitar with the Ventures	1965	30.00
❑ BST 17502 [S]	Play Guitar with the Ventures, Vol. 2	196?	30.00
❑ BST 17503 [S]	Play Guitar with the Ventures, Vol. 3	196?	30.00

LIBERTY

Number	Title (A Side/B Side)	Yr	NM
❑ LRP-2052 [M]	Super Psychedelics	1967	20.00
❑ LRP-2053 [M]	Golden Greats by the Ventures	1967	20.00
❑ LRP-2054 [M]	$1,000,000.00 Weekend	1967	20.00
❑ LRP-2055 [M]	Flights of Fancy	1968	30.00
❑ LST-8003	Walk Don't Run	1970	15.00

—Reissue of Dolton 8003 with new front cover, original back cover

Number	Title (A Side/B Side)	Yr	NM
❑ LST-8003	Walk Don't Run	1970	20.00

—Reissue of Dolton 8003 with new front and back covers

Number	Title (A Side/B Side)	Yr	NM
❑ LT-8003	Walk Don't Run	1981	8.00
❑ LST-8023	I Walk the Line and Other Giant Hits	1970	20.00

—Reissue of "The Ventures Play the Country Classics"

Number	Title (A Side/B Side)	Yr	NM
❑ LST-8031	Walk, Don't Run, Vol. 2	1970	25.00

—Reissue of Dolton 8031 with new cover

Number	Title (A Side/B Side)	Yr	NM
❑ LST-8050	Revolving Sounds	1970	30.00

—Reissue of "Guitar Freakout"

Number	Title (A Side/B Side)	Yr	NM
❑ LST-8052 [S]	Super Psychedelics	1967	25.00
❑ LST-8052 [S]	Changing Times	1970	40.00

—Reissue of "Super Psychedelics"

Number	Title (A Side/B Side)	Yr	NM
❑ LST-8053 [S]	Golden Greats by the Ventures	1967	20.00
❑ LTAO-8053	Golden Greats by the Ventures	1981	8.00
❑ LST-8054 [S]	$1,000,000.00 Weekend	1967	20.00
❑ LST-8055 [S]	Flights of Fancy	1968	20.00
❑ LST-8057	The Horse	1968	20.00
❑ LST-8057	On the Scene	1970	15.00

—Reissue of "The Horse"

Number	Title (A Side/B Side)	Yr	NM
❑ LST-8059	Underground Fire	1969	20.00
❑ LST-8060	More Golden Greats	1970	15.00
❑ LST-8061	Hawaii Five-O	1969	15.00
❑ LST-8062	Swamp Rock	1969	15.00
❑ LN-10122	The Very Best of the Ventures	1981	8.00
❑ LN-10155	The Ventures Play Telstar, The Lonely Bull	1981	8.00
❑ LN-10156	The Ventures Play the Country Classics	1981	8.00
❑ LN-10188	Walk, Don't Run, Vol. 2	1984	8.00
❑ LN-10190	(The) Ventures in Space	1984	8.00
❑ LN-10203	The Ventures	1984	8.00
❑ LN-10224	TV Themes	1984	8.00
❑ LST-35000 [(2)]	The Ventures 10th Anniversary Album	1970	20.00

SUNSET

Number	Title (A Side/B Side)	Yr	NM
❑ SUM-1160 [M]	The Guitar Genius of the Ventures	1967	12.00
❑ SUS-5160 [S]	The Guitar Genius of the Ventures	1967	15.00
❑ SUS-5270	Super Group	1969	12.00
❑ SUS-5317	A Decade with the Ventures	1970	12.00

UNITED ARTISTS

Number	Title (A Side/B Side)	Yr	NM
❑ UXS-80 [(2)]	The Ventures	1971	15.00
❑ UA-LA147-G [(2)]	Only Hits	1973	15.00
❑ UA-LA217-E	The Jim Croce Songbook	1973	12.00
❑ UA-LA331-E	The Very Best of the Ventures	1974	12.00
❑ UA-LA586-F	Rocky Road	1976	12.00
❑ UA-LA717-F	TV Themes	1977	25.00
❑ UAS-5547	Theme from Shaft	1971	12.00
❑ UAS-5575	Joy/The Ventures Play the Classics	1972	12.00
❑ UAS-5649	Rock and Roll Forever	1972	12.00
❑ UAS-6796	New Testament	1971	12.00

VENUS, VIK

45s

BUDDAH

Number	Title (A Side/B Side)	Yr	NM
❑ 118	Moonflight/Everybody's On Strike	1969	10.00
❑ 138	Moon Jack/Moon Welcome	1969	8.00

VER PLANCK, MARLENE

45s

MOUNTED

Number	Title (A Side/B Side)	Yr	NM
❑ 112	Someday Boy/(B-side unknown)	197?	6.00
❑ 115	Red and Yellow Flowers and Me/I Still Feel You Lovin' Me	197?	6.00

Albums

AUDIOPHILE

Number	Title (A Side/B Side)	Yr	NM
❑ AP-121	You'd Better Love Me	197?	10.00
❑ AP-138	Marlene Ver Planck Loves Johnny Mercer	197?	10.00
❑ AP-160	A New York Singer	1980	10.00
❑ AP-169	A Warmer Place	1981	10.00
❑ AP-186	I Like to Sing	1984	10.00
❑ AP-218	Marlene Ver Planck Sings Alec Wilder	1986	10.00
❑ AP-235	Pure and Natural	1988	10.00

MOUNTED

Number	Title (A Side/B Side)	Yr	NM
❑ 108	A Breath of Fresh Air	1968	15.00
❑ 114	This Happy Feeling	197?	15.00

SAVOY

Number	Title (A Side/B Side)	Yr	NM
❑ MG-12058 [M]	I Think of You with Every Breath I Take	1956	50.00

—As "Marlene"

Number	Title (A Side/B Side)	Yr	NM

VERA, BILLY Includes records as "Billy and the Beaters."

45s

ALFA

Number	Title (A Side/B Side)	Yr	NM
❑ 7002	I Can Take Care of Myself/Corner of the Night	1981	4.00
—As "Billy and the Beaters"			
❑ 7005	At This Moment/Someone Will School You, Someone Will Cool You	1981	5.00
❑ 7005 [PS]	At This Moment/Someone Will School You, Someone Will Cool You	1981	5.00
—As "Billy and the Beaters"			
❑ 7012	Millie, Make Me Some Chili/Someone Will School You, Someone Will Cool You	1981	4.00
—As "Billy and the Beaters"			
❑ 7020	We Got It All/You Own It	1982	4.00

ATLANTIC

Number	Title (A Side/B Side)	Yr	NM
❑ 2526	With Pen in Hand/Good Morning Blues	1968	8.00
❑ 2555	I've Been Loving You Too Long/Are You Coming to My Party	1968	8.00
❑ 2586	Julie/Time Doesn't Matter Anymore	1968	8.00
❑ 2628	Bible Salesman/Are You Coming to My Party	1969	6.00
❑ 2700	I've Never Been Loved Like This Before/J.W.'s Dream	1970	6.00

CAPITOL

Number	Title (A Side/B Side)	Yr	NM
❑ B-44149	Between Like and Love/Heart Be Still	1988	3.00
❑ B-44149 [PS]	Between Like and Love/Heart Be Still	1988	3.00
❑ B-44200	Ronnie's Song/Between Like and Love	1988	3.00

MACOLA

Number	Title (A Side/B Side)	Yr	NM
❑ 8912	She Ain't Johnnie/My Girl Josephine	1987	4.00

MIDLAND INT'L.

Number	Title (A Side/B Side)	Yr	NM
❑ MB-10639	Back Door Man/Run and Tell the People	1976	5.00
❑ MB-10909	Private Clown/Billy, Meet Your Son	1977	5.00
❑ MB-11042	I've Had Enough/Something Like Nothing Before	1977	5.00
❑ 72014	She Ain't Johnnie/I've Had Enough	1977	5.00

RHINO

Number	Title (A Side/B Side)	Yr	NM
❑ 74403	At This Moment/Peanut Butter	1986	3.00
❑ 74403	At This Moment/I Can Take Care of Myself	1986	5.00
❑ 74404	I Can Take Care of Myself/Millie, Make Some Chili	1987	3.00
❑ 74404 [PS]	I Can Take Care of Myself/Millie, Make Some Chili	1987	5.00
❑ 74407	Hopeless Romantic/(B-side unknown)	1987	3.00

V

RUST

Number	Title (A Side/B Side)	Yr	NM
❑ 5051	My Heart Cries/All My Love	1962	20.00

Albums

ALFA

Number	Title (A Side/B Side)	Yr	NM
❑ 10001	Billy and the Beaters	1981	15.00
❑ 10012	Billy Vera	1982	12.00

ATLANTIC

Number	Title (A Side/B Side)	Yr	NM
❑ 8197 [M]	With Pen in Hand	1968	40.00
❑ SD 8197 [S]	With Pen in Hand	1968	25.00

CAPITOL

Number	Title (A Side/B Side)	Yr	NM
❑ C1-46948	Retro Nuevo	1988	10.00

MACOLA

Number	Title (A Side/B Side)	Yr	NM
❑ 0961	The Billy Vera Album	1987	10.00
—Reissue of Midsong Int'l. LP			

MIDSONG INT'L.

Number	Title (A Side/B Side)	Yr	NM
❑ BKL1-2219	Out of the Darkness	1977	12.00

RHINO

Number	Title (A Side/B Side)	Yr	NM
❑ RNLP 70185	The Atlantic Years	1987	10.00
❑ RNLP 70858	By Request — The Best of Billy Vera and the Beaters	1986	12.00

THUNDER

Number	Title (A Side/B Side)	Yr	NM
❑ TVLP 0018	The Hollywood Sessions	1987	10.00

VERA, BILLY, AND JUDY CLAY

45s

ATLANTIC

Number	Title (A Side/B Side)	Yr	NM
❑ 2445	Storybook Children/Really Together	1967	8.00
❑ 2480	Country Girl — City Man/So Good	1968	8.00
❑ 2515	Ever Since/When Do We Go	1968	8.00
❑ 2654	Tell It Like It Is/Reaching for the Moon	1969	6.00

Albums

ATLANTIC

Number	Title (A Side/B Side)	Yr	NM
❑ 8174 [M]	Storybook Children	1967	25.00
❑ SD 8174 [S]	Storybook Children	1967	30.00

VERA, RICKY, AND STEVE ALLEN

45s

CORAL

Number	Title (A Side/B Side)	Yr	NM
❑ 61098	How Can Santa Come to Puerto Rico/Can I Wait Up for Santa Claus	1953	30.00

VERITY, JOHN, BAND

Albums

ABC DUNHILL

Number	Title (A Side/B Side)	Yr	NM
❑ DSX-50170	The John Verity Band	1974	20.00

VERLAINE, TOM Also see TELEVISION.

12-Inch Singles

I.R.S.

Number	Title (A Side/B Side)	Yr	NM
❑ 17369 [DJ]	A Town Called Walker/Marquee Moon (Live)	1987	10.00

Albums

ELEKTRA

Number	Title (A Side/B Side)	Yr	NM
❑ 6E-216	Tom Verlaine	1979	15.00

I.R.S.

Number	Title (A Side/B Side)	Yr	NM
❑ 42050	Flash Light	1987	10.00

WARNER BROS.

Number	Title (A Side/B Side)	Yr	NM
❑ BSK 3539	Dreamtime	1981	10.00
❑ BSK 3685	Words from the Front	1982	10.00
❑ 25144	Cover	1984	10.00

VERNE, LARRY

45s

ERA

Number	Title (A Side/B Side)	Yr	NM
❑ 3024	Mr. Custer/Okefenokee Two-Step	1960	15.00
❑ 3034	Mister Livingston/Roller Coaster	1960	12.00
❑ 3034 [PS]	Mister Livingston/Roller Coaster	1960	25.00
❑ 3044	Abdul's Party/Tubby Tilly	1961	12.00
❑ 3051	Charlie at the Bat/Pow, Right in the Kisser	1961	12.00
❑ 3065	Beatnik/Speck	1961	12.00
❑ 3075	Hoo-Ha/I'm a Brave Little Soldier	1962	12.00
❑ 3091	The Coward Who Won the West/The Porcupine Patrol	1962	12.00
❑ 3139	Return of Mr. Custer/Running Through the Forest	1964	12.00

Albums

ERA

Number	Title (A Side/B Side)	Yr	NM
❑ 104 [M]	Mister Larry Verne	1961	60.00

VERNON, MARIE

45s

ALLIED

Number	Title (A Side/B Side)	Yr	NM
❑ 5012	I Want You For Christmas/Christmas Tree Waltz	195?	15.00

VERNON GIRLS, THE

45s

CHALLENGE

Number	Title (A Side/B Side)	Yr	NM
❑ 59234	We Love the Beatles/Hey Lover Boy	1964	30.00
❑ 59261	Only You Can Do It/Stupid Little Girl	1964	10.00

VERONICA Also see THE RONETTES; RONNIE SPECTOR.

45s

PHIL SPECTOR

Number	Title (A Side/B Side)	Yr	NM
❑ 1	So Young/Larry L.	1964	200.00
❑ 2	Why Don't They Let Us Fall in Love/Chubby Danny D	1964	200.00
❑ 2	Why Can't They Let Us Fall in Love/Chubby Danny D	1964	600.00
—Note slightly different A-side title			

VERSATILES, THE More than one group.

45s

ATLANTIC

Number	Title (A Side/B Side)	Yr	NM
❑ 2004	Passing By/Crying	1958	40.00

PEACOCK

Number	Title (A Side/B Side)	Yr	NM
❑ 1910	White Cliffs of Dover/Just Words	1963	30.00

RAMCO

Number	Title (A Side/B Side)	Yr	NM
❑ 3717	Blue Feeling/Just Pretending	1962	200.00

RO-CAL

Number	Title (A Side/B Side)	Yr	NM
❑ 1002	I'll Whisper in Your Ear/Lundee Dundee	1960	100.00

SEA CREST

Number	Title (A Side/B Side)	Yr	NM
❑ 6001	Lonely Boy/Moon Dawg	1964	25.00

VERSATONES, THE Probably more than one group.

45s

ALL STAR

Number	Title (A Side/B Side)	Yr	NM
❑ 501	Tight Skirt and Sweater/Bila	1958	40.00

ATLANTIC

Number	Title (A Side/B Side)	Yr	NM
❑ 2211	Tight Skirt and Sweater/Bila	1963	20.00

FENWAY

Number	Title (A Side/B Side)	Yr	NM
❑ 7001	Tight Skirt and Sweater/Bila	1960	25.00

LOST-NITE

Number	Title (A Side/B Side)	Yr	NM
❑ 115	Tight Skirt and Sweater/Bila	196?	8.00

RCA VICTOR

Number	Title (A Side/B Side)	Yr	NM
❑ 47-6917	Wait for Me/De Obeah Man	1957	15.00
❑ 47-6976	Lovely Teenage Girl/Bikini Baby	1957	15.00

Albums

RCA VICTOR

Number	Title (A Side/B Side)	Yr	NM
❑ LPM-1538 [M]	The Versatones	1957	100.00

VERTUES FOUR, THE

45s

SEA SEVEN

Number	Title (A Side/B Side)	Yr	NM
❑ 22	Angel Baby/Uphill, Downhill	1963	40.00

VESPE, LITTLE JOE

45s

PARKWAY

Number	Title (A Side/B Side)	Yr	NM
❑ 877	Caravan/Conservative Twist	1963	10.00

VESPERS, THE

45s

SWAN

Number	Title (A Side/B Side)	Yr	NM
❑ 4156	Cupid/When I Walk with My Angel	1963	40.00

VESTELLES, THE

45s

DECCA

Number	Title (A Side/B Side)	Yr	NM
❑ 9-30733	Come Home/Ditta Wa Do	1958	30.00

VETTES, THE With BRUCE JOHNSTON.

45s

MGM

Number	Title (A Side/B Side)	Yr	NM
❑ 13186	Little Ford Ragtop/Happy Hodaddy (With Ragtop Caddy)	1963	50.00

Albums

MGM

Number	Title (A Side/B Side)	Yr	NM
❑ E-4193 [M]	Rev-Up	1963	100.00
❑ SE-4193 [S]	Rev-Up	1963	120.00

VIBES, THE (1)

45s

ABC-PARAMOUNT

Number	Title (A Side/B Side)	Yr	NM
❑ 9810	Darling/Come Back Baby	1957	50.00

VIBES, THE (2) Probably the same group as THE VIBRANAIRES.

45s

AFTER HOURS

Number	Title (A Side/B Side)	Yr	NM
❑ 105	Stop Torturing Me/Stop Jibing, Baby	1954	2000.

CHARIOT

Number	Title (A Side/B Side)	Yr	NM
❑ 105	Stop Torturing Me/Stop Jibing, Baby	1954	1500.

VIBES, THE (3)

45s

ALLIED

Number	Title (A Side/B Side)	Yr	NM
❑ 10006	What's Her Name/You Are	1958	60.00
❑ 10007	Misunderstood/Let the Old Folks Talk	1959	40.00

VIBES, THE (4)

45s

PERSPECTIVE

Number	Title (A Side/B Side)	Yr	NM
❑ 5858	Pretty Baby (I Saw You Last Night)/Crying for You	1960	100.00

VIBES, THE (5)

45s

RAYNA

Number	Title (A Side/B Side)	Yr	NM
❑ 103	You Got Me Crying/A Killer Came to Town	196?	40.00

VIBRA-SONICS, THE

45s

IDEAL

Number	Title (A Side/B Side)	Yr	NM
❑ 94874	Thunder Storm/Drag Race	1964	50.00

Except when noted otherwise, VG = 25% of NM, and VG+ = 50% of NM. (Example: VG = \$2.00, VG+ = \$4.00 and NM = \$8.00.)

VIBRANAIRES, THE Probably the same group as THE VIBES (2).

45s

Number	Title (A Side/B Side)	Yr	NM
AFTER HOURS			
❑ 103	Doll Face/Ooh, I Feel So Good	1954	2500.
CHARIOT			
❑ 103	Doll Face/Ooh, I Feel So Good	1954	2000.

VIBRATIONS, THE Also see THE JAYHAWKS; THE MARATHONS (1).

45s

Number	Title (A Side/B Side)	Yr	NM
ATLANTIC			
❑ 2204	Between Hello and Goodbye/Lonesome Little Lonely Girl	1963	12.00
❑ 2221	My Girl Sloopy/Daddy Woo-Woo	1964	12.00
BET			
❑ 1	So Blue/Love Me Like You Should	1960	100.00
CHECKER			
❑ 954	So Blue/Love Me Like You Should	1960	30.00
❑ 961	Feel So Bad/Cave Man	1960	20.00
❑ 967	Doing the Slop/So Little Time	1961	20.00
❑ 969	The Watusi/Wallflower	1961	20.00
❑ 974	The Continental/The Junkeroo	1961	20.00
❑ 982	Don't Say Goodbye/Stranded in the Jungle	1961	20.00
❑ 987	All My Love Belongs to You/Stop Right Now	1961	40.00
❑ 990	Let's Pony Again/What Made You Change Your Mind	1961	20.00
❑ 1002	Over the Rainbow/Oh, Cindy	1962	15.00
❑ 1011	The New Hully Gully/Anytime	1962	15.00
❑ 1022	Hamburgers on a Bun/If He Don't	1962	15.00
❑ 1038	Since I Fell for You/May the Best Man Win	1963	15.00
❑ 1061	Dancing Danny/(Instrumental)	1963	15.00
CHESS			
❑ 2151	Shake It Up/Make It Last	1974	6.00
EPIC			
❑ 10418	I Took an Overdose/Because You're Mine	1968	20.00
MANDALA			
❑ 2511	Ain't No Greens in Harlem/Wind-Up Toy	1972	6.00
❑ 2514	Man Overboard/(B-side unknown)	1972	6.00
NEPTUNE			
❑ 19	Expressway to Your Heart/Who's Gonna Help Me Now	1969	8.00
❑ 21	Smoke Signals/Who's Gonna Help Me Now	1970	8.00
❑ 28	Right On Brothers, Right On/Surprise Party for Baby	1970	8.00
OKEH			
❑ 7205	Sloop Dance/Watusi Time	1964	12.00
❑ 7212	Hello Happiness/Keep On Keeping On	1965	12.00
❑ 7220	End Up Crying/Ain't Love That Way	1965	12.00
❑ 7228	Talkin' 'Bout Love/If You Only Knew	1965	12.00
❑ 7230	Misty/Finding Out the Hard Way	1965	12.00
❑ 7238	Gina/The Story of a Starry Night	1966	—
—Unreleased			
❑ 7241	Canadian Sunset/The Story of a Starry Night	1966	10.00
❑ 7249	Forgive and Forget/Gonna Get Along Without You Now	1966	10.00
❑ 7257	And I Love Her/Soul a-Go-Go	1966	10.00
❑ 7276	Pick Me/You Better Beware	1967	10.00
❑ 7297	Together/Come To Yourself	1967	10.00
❑ 7311	Love in Them There Hills/Remember the Rain	1968	10.00

Albums

Number	Title	Yr	NM
CHECKER			
❑ LP-2978 [M]	The Watusi	1961	200.00
MANDALA			
❑ 3006	Taking a New Step	1972	20.00
OKEH			
❑ OKM-12111 [M]	Shout	1965	30.00
❑ OKM-12112 [M]	Misty	1966	30.00
❑ OKM-12114 [M]	New Vibrations	1967	30.00
❑ OKS-14111 [S]	Shout	1965	40.00
❑ OKS-14112 [S]	Misty	1966	40.00
❑ OKS-14114 [S]	New Vibrations	1967	40.00
❑ OKS-14129	The Vibrations' Greatest Hits	1969	30.00

VIC, PAUL AND BRUCE See THE CANADIAN BEADLES.

VICEROYS, THE (1)

45s

Number	Title (A Side/B Side)	Yr	NM
ALADDIN			
❑ 3273	Please, Baby, Please/I'm Yours As Long As I Live	1955	400.00

VICEROYS, THE (2)

45s

Number	Title (A Side/B Side)	Yr	NM
BETHLEHEM			
❑ 3045	Sea Green/Moasin'	1962	20.00
❑ 3045	Seagrams/Moasin'	1962	25.00
—Original A-side title			
❑ 3070	Joshin'/Buzz Bomb	1963	20.00
❑ 3070	The Fox/Buzz Bomb	1963	25.00
—Original A-side title			
❑ 3088	Not Too Much Twist/Tears on My Pillow	1965	20.00

VICEROYS, THE (3)

45s

Number	Title (A Side/B Side)	Yr	NM
BOLO			
❑ 736	Granny's Pad/Blues Bouquet	1962	12.00
❑ 739	Goin' Back to Granny's/Get Set	1963	12.00
❑ 743	Dartell Stomp/Granny's Medley	1964	10.00
❑ 749	Please, Please, Please/Tiger Shark	1964	10.00
❑ 750	Bacon Fat/Until	1965	10.00
❑ 754	That Sound/Tired of Waiting for You	1965	10.00
DOT			
❑ 16456	Granny's Pad/Blues Bouquet	1963	8.00

Albums

Number	Title	Yr	NM
BOLO			
❑ BLP-8000 [M]	The Viceroys at Granny's Pad	1963	40.00

VICEROYS, THE (4)

45s

Number	Title (A Side/B Side)	Yr	NM
LITTLE STAR			
❑ 107	I'm So Sorry (It's Ending with You)/Uncle Sam Needs You	1961	150.00
ORIGINAL SOUND			
❑ 15	Dreamy Eyes/Ball 'N' Chain	1961	40.00
RAMCO			
❑ 3715	My Heart/I Need Your Love So Bad	1962	4000.
—VG 2000; VG+ 3000			
SMASH			
❑ 1716	I'm So Sorry (It's Ending with You)/Uncle Sam Needs You	1961	20.00

VICEROYS, THE (U)

45s

Number	Title (A Side/B Side)	Yr	NM
E'DEN			
❑ 9001	Don't Let Go/Down Beat Blues	1962	12.00
IMPERIAL			
❑ 66058	Death of an Angel/Earth Angel	1964	12.00

VICTIMS, THE

45s

Number	Title (A Side/B Side)	Yr	NM
BRG			
❑ 101	You Got the Magic/Destination Undecided/Don't Come Knockin'/Help Me Baby	1977	35.00
❑ 101 [PS]	You Got the Magic/Destination Undecided/Don't Come Knockin'/Help Me Baby	1977	35.00
PLAN 9			
❑ PL 1005	Annette/I Want Head/Behind the Times/Nervous	1978	70.00
❑ PL 1005 [PS]	Annette/I Want Head/Behind the Times/Nervous	1978	60.00
—Black and white sleeve			
❑ PL 1005 [PS]	Annette/I Want Head/Behind the Times/Nervous	1978	70.00
—Red and white sleeve			

VICTORIA, C.B.

Albums

Number	Title	Yr	NM
JANUS			
❑ JXS-7029	Dawning Day	1976	12.00

VICTORIALS, THE

45s

Number	Title (A Side/B Side)	Yr	NM
IMPERIAL			
❑ 5398	I Get That Feeling/The Prettiest Girl in the World	1956	50.00

VICTORIANS, THE More than one group.

45s

Number	Title (A Side/B Side)	Yr	NM
ARNOLD			
❑ 571	Move In a Little Closer/Lovin'	1963	20.00
BANG			
❑ 550	Merry-Go-Round/Wasn't the Summer Short	1967	15.00
LIBERTY			
❑ 55574	Climb Every Mountain/What Makes Little Girls Cry	1963	20.00
❑ 55656	The Monkey Stroll/You're Invited to a Party	1964	15.00
❑ 55693	Happy Birthday Blues/Oh What a Night for Love	1964	15.00
❑ 55728	If I Loved You/The Monkey Stroll	1964	15.00
REPRISE			
❑ 0434	I Saw My Girl/Baby Toys	1965	15.00
SAXONY			
❑ 103	Heartbreaking Moon/I'm Rollin'	1956	500.00
SELMA			
❑ 1002	Wedding Bells/Please Say You Do	1956	300.00

VICTORY FIVE, THE

45s

Number	Title (A Side/B Side)	Yr	NM
TERP			
❑ 101	I Never Knew/Swing Low	1958	600.00
—All copies on colored vinyl			

VIDALTONES, THE

45s

Number	Title (A Side/B Side)	Yr	NM
JOSIE			
❑ 900	Forever/Someone to Love	1962	40.00

VIDELS, THE

45s

Number	Title (A Side/B Side)	Yr	NM
EARLY			
❑ 702	I Wish/Blow, Winds, Blow	1960	400.00
JDS			
❑ 5004	Mr. Lonely/I'll Forget You	1960	20.00
—Multicolor label			
❑ 5004	Mr. Lonely/I'll Forget You	1960	30.00
—Gray label			
❑ 5005	She's Not Coming Home/Now That Summer Is Here	1960	20.00
—Multicolor label			
❑ 5005	She's Not Coming Home/Now That Summer Is Here	1960	30.00
—Gray label			
KAPP			
❑ 361	Streets of Love/I'll Keep On Waiting	1960	20.00
❑ 405	A Letter from Ann/This Year's Mister New	1961	40.00
MEDIEVAL			
❑ 203	Be My Girl/A Place in Your Heart	1961	15.00
MUSICNOTE			
❑ 117	We Belong Together/It's All Over	1963	50.00
RHODY			
❑ 2000	Be My Girl/A Place in Your Heart	1959	50.00
TIC TAC TOE			
❑ 5005	She's Not Coming Home/Now That Summer Is Here	1962	50.00

VIDEOS, THE

45s

Number	Title (A Side/B Side)	Yr	NM
CASINO			
❑ 102	Trickle, Trickle/Moonglow You Know	1958	20.00
—With playing cards on label			
❑ 102	Trickle, Trickle/Moonglow You Know	1958	30.00
—"Casino" in normal print; no playing cards; no mention of distribution by Gone			
❑ 102	Trickle, Trickle/Moonglow You Know	1958	50.00
—"Casino" in shadow print; no playing cards; no mention of distribution by Gone			
❑ 102	Trickle, Trickle/Moonglow You Know	1961	25.00
—No playing cards; with distribution by Gone			
❑ 105	Love or Infatuation/Shoo-Be-Doo-Be Cha Cha Cha	1959	300.00
LOST-NITE			
❑ 218	Trickle, Trickle/Moonglow You Know	196?	5.00
—Reissue			

V

VIGRASS AND OSBORNE

With Gary Osborne, later a collaborator with Elton John.

45s

EPIC

Number	Title (A Side/B Side)	Yr	NM
❑ 50044	Gypsy Woman/Haystacks	1974	5.00

UNI

Number	Title (A Side/B Side)	Yr	NM
❑ 55330	Men of Learning/Forever Autumn	1972	6.00
❑ 55344	Virginia/Ballerina	1972	5.00
❑ 55355	Remember Pearl Harbor/ Mister Deadline	1972	5.00

Albums

EPIC

Number	Title (A Side/B Side)	Yr	NM
❑ KE 33077	Steppin' Out	1975	12.00

UNI

Number	Title (A Side/B Side)	Yr	NM
❑ 73129	Queues	1971	15.00

VILLAGE PEOPLE

12-Inch Singles

CASABLANCA

Number	Title (A Side/B Side)	Yr	NM
❑ NBD 20144	Y.M.C.A. (6:47)/Macho Man (5:18)/(B-side blank)	1978	20.00
❑ NBD 20155 [DJ]	In the Navy (6:21)/Manhattan Woman (6:35)/(B-side blank)	1979	40.00
❑ NBD 20165	In the Navy (6:21)/Go West (6:38)	1979	15.00
❑ NBD 20166	Go West (6:38)/Citizens of the World (6:38)	1979	15.00
❑ NBD 20194	Sleazy (7:58)/Save Me (Up Tempo) (5:07)	1979	20.00
❑ NBD 20203 [DJ]	Ready for the 80's (6:53) (same on both sides)	1979	20.00
❑ NBD 20221	Can't Stop the Music (7:52)/ Liberation (4:57)	1980	20.00
❑ NBD 20224	Magic Night (5:57)/ I Love You to Death	1980	15.00

MEGA

Number	Title (A Side/B Side)	Yr	NM
❑ 2280	Medley (In the Navy/Macho Man/Y.M.C.A.) (8:48)/Sex Over the Phone (6:56)	1985	15.00
❑ 2292	New York City (Vocal) (Dub)	1985	15.00

RCA

Number	Title (A Side/B Side)	Yr	NM
❑ JD-12259 [DJ]	5 O'Clock in the Morning/Do You Wanna Spend the Night	1981	12.00

45s

CASABLANCA

Number	Title (A Side/B Side)	Yr	NM
❑ 896	San Francisco (You've Got Me)/ Village People	1977	8.00
❑ 922	Macho Man/Key West	1978	5.00
❑ 945	Y.M.C.A./The Women	1978	5.00
❑ 973	In the Navy/Manhattan Woman	1979	5.00
❑ 973 [PS]	In the Navy/Manhattan Woman	1979	30.00

—Picture sleeve is promo only

Number	Title (A Side/B Side)	Yr	NM
❑ 984	Go West/Citizens of the World	1979	5.00
❑ 2213	Sleazy/Save Me (Uptempo)	1979	4.00
❑ 2220	Ready for the 80's/Sleazy	1979	5.00
❑ 2261	Can't Stop the Music/Milkshake	1980	4.00
❑ 2261 [PS]	Can't Stop the Music/Milkshake	1980	8.00
❑ 2291	Magic Night/I Love You to Death	1980	4.00

RCA

Number	Title (A Side/B Side)	Yr	NM
❑ PB-12258	5 O'Clock in the Morning/ Food Fight	1981	5.00
❑ PB-12258 [PS]	5 O'Clock in the Morning/ Food Fight	1981	6.00
❑ PB-12331	Action Man/Jungle City	1981	8.00

Albums

CASABLANCA

Number	Title (A Side/B Side)	Yr	NM
❑ NBLP-7064	Village People	1977	10.00
❑ NBPIX-7064 [PD]	Village People	1978	20.00
❑ NBLP-7096	Macho Man	1978	10.00
❑ NBPIX-7096 [PD]	Macho Man	1978	20.00
❑ NBLP-7118	Cruisin'	1978	10.00
❑ NBPIX-7118 [PD]	Cruisin'	1978	20.00
❑ NBLP-7144	Go West	1979	10.00
❑ NBLP-7183 [(2)]	Live and Sleazy	1979	12.00
❑ NBLP-7220	Can't Stop the Music (Soundtrack)	1980	10.00

—Also includes one song by the Ritchie Family and one song by David London

RCA VICTOR

Number	Title (A Side/B Side)	Yr	NM
❑ AFL1-4105	Renaissance	1981	12.00

RHINO

Number	Title (A Side/B Side)	Yr	NM
❑ R1-70167	Greatest Hits	1988	15.00

VILLAGE SOUL CHOIR, THE

45s

ABBOTT

Number	Title (A Side/B Side)	Yr	NM
❑ 2010	The Cat Walk/The Country Walk	1970	10.00
❑ 2013	Love Everyday, Love Every Night/(B-side unknown)	1970	10.00
❑ 2028	Sissy Football (Pt. 1)/(Pt. 2)	197?	15.00

VILLAGE STOMPERS, THE

45s

CAMEO

Number	Title (A Side/B Side)	Yr	NM
❑ 2000	Sing All Together/ (B-side unknown)	1967	8.00

EPIC

Number	Title (A Side/B Side)	Yr	NM
❑ 9617	Washington Square/ Turkish Delight	1963	8.00
❑ 9617 [PS]	Washington Square/ Turkish Delight	1963	10.00
❑ 9655	Blue Grass/The La-Dee-La Song	1964	6.00
❑ 9655 [PS]	Blue Grass/The La-Dee-La Song	1964	8.00
❑ 9674	From Russia with Love/ The Bridges of Budapest	1964	6.00
❑ 9702	Haunted House/Mozambique	1964	6.00
❑ 9718	Oh, Marie/Limehouse Blues	1964	6.00
❑ 9740	Fiddler on the Roof/ Moonlight on the Ganges	1964	6.00
❑ 9785	Brother, Can You Spare a Dime/ Magic Horn	1965	6.00
❑ 9785 [PS]	Brother, Can You Spare a Dime/ Magic Horn	1965	8.00
❑ 9824	Those Magnificant Men in Their Flying Machines/ Sweetwater Bay	1965	6.00
❑ 9868	The Bride of Bleecker Street/ Call Me	1965	6.00
❑ 10017	Second Hand Rose/ The Poet and the Prophet	1966	6.00
❑ 10106	Chopsticks/Wilkommen	1966	6.00
❑ 10142	Rose of Washington Square/ When I Tell You That I Love You	1967	6.00

Albums

EPIC

Number	Title (A Side/B Side)	Yr	NM
❑ LN 24078 [M]	Washington Square	1963	15.00
❑ LN 24090 [M]	More Sounds of Washington Square	1964	15.00
❑ LN 24109 [M]	Around the World with the Village Stompers	1964	12.00
❑ LN 24129 [M]	New Beat on Broadway!	1964	12.00
❑ LN 24161 [M]	Some Folk, a Bit of Country and a Whole Lot of Dixie	1965	12.00
❑ LN 24180 [M]	A Taste of Honey	1965	12.00
❑ LN 24235 [M]	One More Time	1966	12.00
❑ LN 24318 [M]	The Village Stompers' Greatest Hits	1967	12.00
❑ BN 26078 [S]	Washington Square	1963	20.00
❑ BN 26090 [S]	More Sounds of Washington Square	1964	20.00
❑ BN 26109 [S]	Around the World with the Village Stompers	1964	15.00
❑ BN 26129 [S]	New Beat on Broadway!	1964	15.00
❑ BN 26161 [S]	Some Folk, a Bit of Country and a Whole Lot of Dixie	1965	15.00
❑ BN 26180 [S]	A Taste of Honey	1965	15.00
❑ BN 26235 [S]	One More Time	1966	15.00
❑ BN 26318 [S]	The Village Stompers' Greatest Hits	1967	15.00

VILLAGE VOICES, THE

See THE FOUR SEASONS.

VINCE AND THE WAIKIKI RUMBLERS

45s

BIG BEN

Number	Title (A Side/B Side)	Yr	NM
❑ 1003	Waikiki Rumble/Pacifica	1965	50.00

ZODIAC

Number	Title (A Side/B Side)	Yr	NM
❑ 1004	Waikiki Rumble/Pacifica	1965	80.00

VINCENT, GENE

45s

CAPITOL

Number	Title (A Side/B Side)	Yr	NM
❑ F3450	Be-Bop-a-Lula/Woman Love	1956	50.00

—With small Capitol logo; counterfeits exist on a white label with blue vinyl

Number	Title (A Side/B Side)	Yr	NM
❑ F3450	Be-Bop-a-Lula/Woman Love	1956	70.00

—With large Capitol logo

Number	Title (A Side/B Side)	Yr	NM
❑ F3530	Race with the Devil/ Gonna Back Up, Baby	1956	40.00
❑ F3558	Bluejean Bop/Who Slapped John	1956	40.00
❑ F3617	Crazy Legs/Important Words	1956	50.00
❑ F3678	B-I-Bickey-Bi-Bo-Bo-Go/Five Days, Five Days	1957	50.00
❑ F3763	Lotta Lovin'/Wear My Ring	1957	50.00
❑ F3839	Dance to the Bop/I Got It	1957	30.00
❑ 3871	Be-Bop-a-Lula/Lotta Lovin'	1974	15.00
❑ F3874	Walkin' Home from School/ I Gotta Baby	1958	40.00
❑ F3959	Baby Blue/True to You	1958	50.00
❑ F4010	Yes I Love You Baby/ Rocky Road Blues	1958	40.00
❑ F4051	Little Lover/Git It	1958	40.00
❑ F4105	Say Mama/Be-Bop Boogie Boy	1958	50.00
❑ F4153	Over the Rainbow/Who's Pushin' Your Swing	1959	50.00
❑ F4237	The Night Is So Lonely/Right Now	1959	50.00
❑ F4237 [PS]	The Night Is So Lonely/Right Now	1959	2000.
❑ 4313	Wild Cat/Right Here on Earth	1959	50.00
❑ 4442	Pistol Packin' Mama/ Anna Annabella	1960	40.00
❑ 4525	Mister Loneliness/ If You Want My Lovin'	1961	25.00
❑ 4665	Lucy Star/Baby Don't Believe Him	1961	25.00

CHALLENGE

Number	Title (A Side/B Side)	Yr	NM
❑ 59337	Bird Doggin'/Ain't That Too Much	1966	20.00
❑ 59347	Lonely Street/I've Got My Eyes on You	1966	20.00
❑ 59365	Born to Be a Rolling Stone/ Pickin' Poppies	1967	20.00

FOREVER

Number	Title (A Side/B Side)	Yr	NM
❑ 6001	Story of the Rockers/ Pickin' Poppies	1969	50.00

KAMA SUTRA

Number	Title (A Side/B Side)	Yr	NM
❑ 514	Sunshine/Geese	1970	12.00
❑ 518	High On Life/The Day the World Turned Blue	1971	12.00

PLAYGROUND

Number	Title (A Side/B Side)	Yr	NM
❑ 100	Story of the Rockers/ Pickin' Poppies	1968	200.00

7-Inch Extended Plays

CAPITOL

Number	Title (A Side/B Side)	Yr	NM
❑ EAP 1-764	Bluejean Bop/Jezebel//Jumps, Giggles and Shouts/Ain't She Sweet	1957	150.00
❑ EAP 1-764 [PS]	Bluejean Bop! Part 1	1957	150.00
❑ EAP 2-764	*Who Slapped John/Wedding Bells/Up a Lazy River/Bop Street	1957	150.00
❑ EAP 2-764 [PS]	Bluejean Bop! Part 2	1957	150.00
❑ EAP 3-764	*Jump Back, Honey, Jump Back/Waltz of the Wind/I Flipped/Peg o' My Heart	1957	150.00
❑ EAP 3-764 [PS]	Bluejean Bop! Part 3	1957	150.00
❑ EAP 1-811	Red Blue Jeans and a Ponytail/ You Told a Fib//Hold Me, Hug Me, Rock Me/Unchained Melody	1957	150.00
❑ EAP 1-811 [PS]	Gene Vincent and the Blue Caps, Part 1	1957	150.00
❑ EAP 2-811	*Cruisin'/You Better Believe/ Double Talkin' Baby/Blues Stay Away from Me	1957	150.00
❑ EAP 2-811 [PS]	Gene Vincent and the Blue Caps, Part 2	1957	150.00
❑ EAP 3-811	*Pink Thunderbird/Pretty, Pretty Baby/Cat Man/I Sure Miss You	1957	150.00
❑ EAP 3-811 [PS]	Gene Vincent and the Blue Caps, Part 3	1957	150.00
❑ EAP 1-970	*Frankie and Johnnie/In My Dreams/You'll Never Walk Alone/Brand New Beat	1958	150.00
❑ EAP 1-970 [PS]	Gene Vincent Rocks! And the Blue Caps Roll, Part 1	1958	150.00
❑ EAP 2-970	*By the Light of the Silvery Moon/Flea Brain/Rollin' Danny/Your Cheatin' Heart	1958	150.00
❑ EAP 2-970 [PS]	Gene Vincent Rocks! And the Blue Caps Roll, Part 2	1958	150.00
❑ EAP 3-970	You Belong to Me/Time Will Bring You Everything//Should I Ever Love Again/It's No Lie	1958	150.00
❑ EAP 3-970 [PS]	Gene Vincent Rocks! And the Blue Caps Roll, Part 3	1958	150.00
❑ EAP 1-985	Lovely Loretta/Dance to the Bop//Dance in the Street/ Baby Blue	1958	200.00
❑ EAP 1-985 [PS]	Hot Rod Gang	1958	200.00
❑ EAP 1-1059	*Five Feet of Lovin'/The Wayward Wind/Somebody Help Me/Keep It a Secret	1958	150.00
❑ EAP 1-1059 [PS]	A Gene Vincent Record Date, Part 1	1958	150.00
❑ EAP 2-1059	Git It/Teenage Partner//Hey, Good Lookin'/I Can't Help It	1958	150.00
❑ EAP 2-1059 [PS]	A Gene Vincent Record Date, Part 2	1958	150.00
❑ EAP 3-1059	I Love You/Peace of Mind// Summertime/Look What You Gone and Done to Me	1958	150.00
❑ EAP 3-1059 [PS]	A Gene Vincent Record Date, Part 3	1958	150.00

NORTON

Number	Title (A Side/B Side)	Yr	NM
❑ EP-076	My Love (In Love Again)/ Lonesome Boy//The Night Is So Lonely/In My Dreams	1999	2.00
❑ EP-076 [PS]	Blue Gene	1999	2.00

Number	Title (A Side/B Side)	Yr	NM
Albums			
CAPITOL			
❑ DKAO-380 [R]	Gene Vincent's Greatest	1969	50.00
❑ SM-380 [R]	Gene Vincent's Greatest	197?	15.00
—Abridged reissue of DKAO-380			
❑ T 764 [M]	Bluejean Bop!	1957	400.00
—Turquoise label stock copy			
❑ T 764 [M]	Bluejean Bop!	1957	1000.
—Black label promo			
❑ T 764 [M]	Bluejean Bop!	1957	1000.
—Yellow label promo			
❑ T 811 [M]	Gene Vincent and the Blue Caps	1957	400.00
—Turquoise label stock copy			
❑ T 811 [M]	Gene Vincent and the Blue Caps	1957	1000.
—Black label promo			
❑ T 811 [M]	Gene Vincent and the Blue Caps	1957	1000.
—Yellow label promo			
❑ T 970 [M]	Gene Vincent Rocks! And the Blue Caps Roll	1958	400.00
—Turquoise label stock copy			
❑ T 970 [M]	Gene Vincent Rocks! And the Blue Caps Roll	1958	1000.
—Black label promo			
❑ T 970 [M]	Gene Vincent Rocks! And the Blue Caps Roll	1958	1000.
—Yellow label promo			
❑ T 1059 [M]	A Gene Vincent Record Date	1958	400.00
—Turquoise label stock copy			
❑ T 1059 [M]	A Gene Vincent Record Date	1958	1000.
—Black label promo			
❑ T 1059 [M]	A Gene Vincent Record Date	1958	1000.
—Yellow label promo			
❑ T 1207 [M]	Sounds Like Gene Vincent	1959	300.00
—Black label with colorband, Capitol logo at left			
❑ ST 1342 [S]	Crazy Times	1960	500.00
—Black label with colorband, Capitol logo at left			
❑ T 1342 [M]	Crazy Times	1960	300.00
—Black label with colorband, Capitol logo at left			
❑ SM-11287	The Bop That Just Won't Stop	1974	15.00
❑ N-16208	Gene Vincent's Greatest	198?	12.00
—Budget-line reissue			
❑ N-16209	The Bop That Just Won't Stop	198?	12.00
—Budget-line reissue			
DANDELION			
❑ 9-102	I'm Back and I'm Proud	1970	50.00
INTERMEDIA			
❑ QS-5074	Rockabilly Fever	198?	12.00
KAMA SUTRA			
❑ KSBS 2019	Gene Vincent	1970	50.00
❑ KSBS 2027	The Day the World Turned Blue	1971	50.00
ROLLIN' ROCK			
❑ 022	Forever	1981	15.00

VINCENT & PESCI The "Pesci" is future movie star Joe Pesci.

Number	Title (A Side/B Side)	Yr	NM
45s			
MAINSTREAM			
❑ 5531	Can You Fix The Way I Talk For Christmas?/Little People Blues	1972	10.00

VINEGAR JOE ROBERT PALMER was in this group.

Number	Title (A Side/B Side)	Yr	NM
45s			
ATCO			
❑ 6912	See the World/Circles	1973	8.00
❑ 6922	Whole Lotta Shakin' Goin' On/Rock 'n Roll Gypsies	1973	8.00
Albums			
ATCO			
❑ SD 7007	Vinegar Joe	1972	15.00
❑ SD 7016	Rock 'n Roll Gypsies	1973	15.00

VINSON, EDDIE "CLEANHEAD"

Number	Title (A Side/B Side)	Yr	NM
45s			
BETHLEHEM			
❑ 11097	Cherry Red/Kidney Stew	1961	20.00
BLUESWAY			
❑ 61005	Cadillac Blues/Old Maid Got Married	1967	12.00
KING			
❑ 4563	Good Bread Alley/I Need You Tonight	1952	60.00
❑ 4582	Lonesome Train/Person to Person	1952	60.00
❑ 6305	Person to Person/Cherry Red Blues	1970	6.00
MERCURY			
❑ 70334	Old Man Boogie/You Can't Have My Love No More	1954	200.00
❑ 70525	Anxious Heart/Suffer Fool	1954	120.00
❑ 70621	Tomorrow May Never Come/Big Chief Rain in the Face	1955	100.00
RIVERSIDE			
❑ 4512	Back Door Blues/Hold It	1962	20.00
Albums			
AAMCO			
❑ 312 [M]	Cleanhead's Back in Town	196?	40.00
BETHLEHEM			
❑ BCP-5005 [M]	Eddie "Cleanhead" Vinson Sings	1957	100.00
❑ BCP-6036	Back in Town	1978	15.00
BLUESWAY			
❑ BL-6007 [M]	Cherry Red	1967	25.00
❑ BLS-6007 [S]	Cherry Red	1967	25.00
CIRCLE			
❑ CLP-57	Kidney Stew	1983	12.00
DELMARK			
❑ 631	Old Kidney Stew Is Fine	1980	12.00
FLYING DUTCHMAN			
❑ 31-1012	You Can't Make Love Alone	197?	15.00
KING			
❑ KS-1087	Cherry Red	1969	25.00
MUSE			
❑ MR-5116	The Clean Machine	1978	15.00
❑ MR-5208	Eddie "Cleanhead" Vinson and the Muse All-Stars: Live at Sandy's	1979	12.00
❑ MR-5243	Eddie "Cleanhead" Vinson and the Muse All-Stars: Hold It Right There	198?	12.00
❑ MR-5282	Cleanhead and Roomful of Blues	1982	12.00
❑ MR-5310	Eddie "Cleanhead" Vinson Sings the Blues	198?	12.00
PABLO			
❑ 2310866	I Want a Little Girl	198?	12.00
REGGIES			
❑ 1000	Rollin' Over the Devil	1981	12.00
RIVERSIDE			
❑ RLP-502 [M]	Back Door Blues	1965	40.00
❑ RLS-9502 [S]	Back Door Blues	1965	40.00

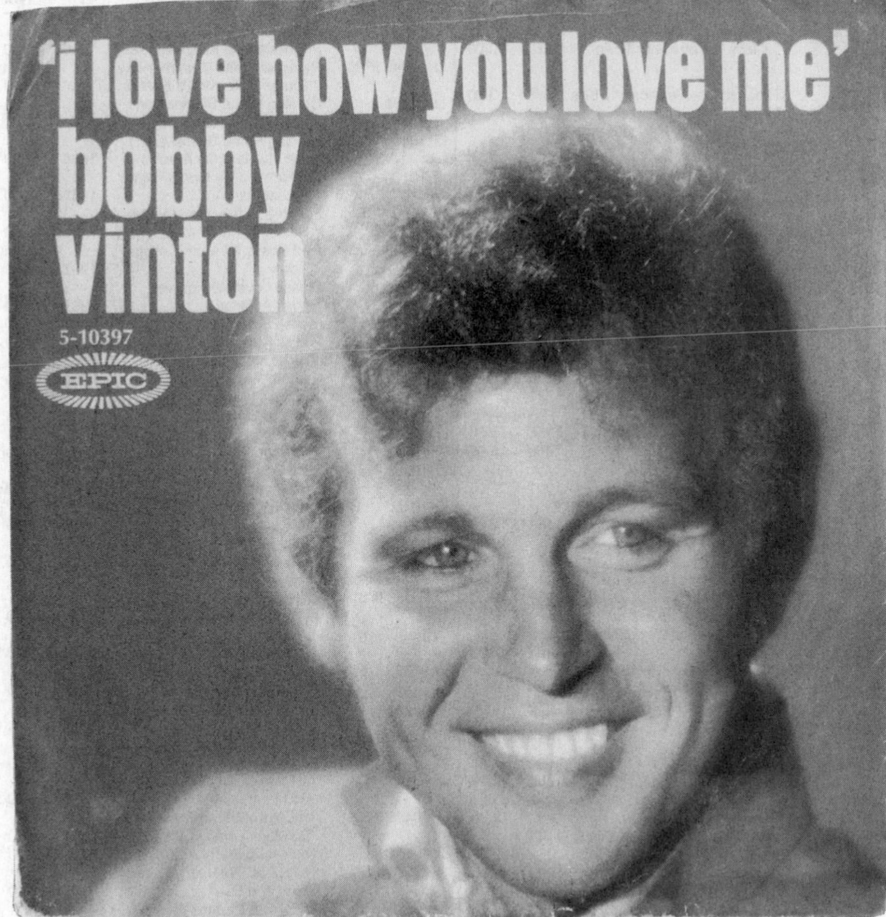

Bobby Vinton, "I Love How You Love Me," Epic 10397, 1968, $10.

VINSON, EDDIE "CLEANHEAD"/JIMMY WITHERSPOON Also see each artist's individual listings.

Number	Title (A Side/B Side)	Yr	NM
Albums			
KING			
❑ 634 [M]	Battle of the Blues, Vol. 3	1960	1500.

VINTON, BOBBY

Number	Title (A Side/B Side)	Yr	NM
45s			
ABC			
❑ 12022	My Melody of Love/I'll Be Loving You	1974	4.00
—Multi-colored label			
❑ 12022	My Melody of Love/I'll Be Loving You	1974	5.00
—Black label			
❑ 12056	Beer Barrel Polka/Dick and Jane	1974	4.00
❑ 12100	Wooden Heart/Polka Pose	1975	4.00
❑ 12131	My Gypsy Love/Midnight Show	1975	4.00
❑ 12178	Moonight Serenade/Why Can't I Get Over You	1976	4.00
❑ 12186	Save Your Kisses for Me/Love Shine	1976	4.00
❑ 12229	Love Is the Reason/Nobody But Me	1976	4.00
❑ 12265	Only Love Can Break a Heart/Once More with Feeling	1977	4.00
❑ 12293	Hold Me, Thrill Me, Kiss Me/Her Name Is Love	1977	4.00
❑ 12308	All My Todays/Strike Up the Band for Love	1977	4.00
ALPINE			
❑ 50	First Impression/You'll Never Forget	1959	30.00
❑ 59	The Sheik/A Freshman and a Sophomore	1960	25.00
BOBBY VINTON			
❑ 100	Santa Must Be Polish/Santa Claus Is Coming to Town	1987	3.00

Number	Title (A Side/B Side)	Yr	NM
100 [PS]	Santa Must Be Polish/Santa Claus Is Coming to Town	1987	3.00

CURB

Number	Title (A Side/B Side)	Yr	NM
10512	The Last Rose/Sealed with a Kiss	1988	3.00
10541	Please Tell Her That I Said Hello/Getting Used to Being Loved Again	1989	3.00
10560	It's Been One of Those Days/(Now and Then There's) A Fool Such As I	1989	3.00
76751	The Only Fire That Burns/What Did You Do with Your Old 45's	1990	4.00

DIAMOND

Number	Title (A Side/B Side)	Yr	NM
121	I Love You the Way You Are/You're My Girl	1962	20.00
—B-side by Chuck and Johnny			

ELEKTRA

Number	Title (A Side/B Side)	Yr	NM
45503	My First, My Only Love/Summerlove Sensation	1978	4.00

EPIC

Number	Title (A Side/B Side)	Yr	NM
34-06537	Blue Velvet/Blue on Blue	1986	5.00
9417	Posin'/Tornado	1960	15.00
9440	Corrina, Corrina/Little Lonely One	1961	15.00
9469	Hip-Swinging, High-Stepping, Drum Majorette/Will I Ask Ya	1961	15.00
9509	Roses Are Red (My Love)/You and I	1962	12.00
9509 [PS]	Roses Are Red (My Love)/You and I	1962	15.00
—Bobby Vinton looks straight ahead, chin in hand			
9509 [PS]	Roses Are Red (My Love)/You and I	1962	15.00
—Bobby Vinton looks toward the lower right corner			
9532	Rain, Rain Go Away/Over and Over	1962	12.00
9532 [PS]	Rain, Rain Go Away/Over and Over	1962	15.00
3-9550 [S]	Please Help Me, I'm Falling/Sentimental Me	1962	12.00
—Jukebox issue, but unlike most, it has a large hole and plays at 45			
9551	Excerpts from "Roses Are Red"	1962	12.00
9552	Excerpts from "Roses Are Red"	1962	12.00
9553	Excerpts from "Roses Are Red"	1962	12.00
9554	Excerpts from "Roses Are Red"	1962	12.00
9561	Trouble Is My Middle Name/Let's Kiss and Make Up	1962	10.00
9561 [PS]	Trouble Is My Middle Name/Let's Kiss and Make Up	1962	15.00
9577	Over the Mountain (Across the Sea)/Faded Pictures	1963	10.00
9577 [PS]	Over the Mountain (Across the Sea)/Faded Pictures	1963	15.00
9593	Blue on Blue/Those Little Things	1963	12.00
9593 [PS]	Blue on Blue/Those Little Things	1963	15.00
9593 [DJ]	Blue on Blue/Those Little Things	1963	30.00
—Promo only on blue vinyl			
9614	Blue Velvet/Is There a Place (Where I Can Go)	1963	12.00
9614 [PS]	Blue Velvet/Is There a Place (Where I Can Go)	1963	15.00
9638	There! I've Said It Again/The Girl with the Bow in Her Hair	1963	12.00
9638 [PS]	There! I've Said It Again/The Girl with the Bow in Her Hair	1963	15.00
9662	My Heart Belongs to Only You/Warm and Tender	1964	10.00
9662 [PS]	My Heart Belongs to Only You/Warm and Tender	1964	15.00
9687	Tell Me Why/Remembering	1964	8.00
9687 [PS]	Tell Me Why/Remembering	1964	15.00
9705	Clinging Vine/Imagination Is a Magic Dream	1964	8.00
9705 [PS]	Clinging Vine/Imagination Is a Magic Dream	1964	12.00
9730	Mr. Lonely/It's Better to Have Loved	1964	10.00
9730 [PS]	Mr. Lonely/It's Better to Have Loved	1964	12.00
9741	The Bell That Couldn't Jingle/Dearest Santa	1964	10.00
9768	Long Lonely Nights/Satin	1965	8.00
9768 [PS]	Long Lonely Nights/Satin	1965	12.00
9791	L-O-N-E-L-Y/Graduation Tears	1965	8.00
9791 [PS]	L-O-N-E-L-Y/Graduation Tears	1965	12.00
9814	Theme from "Harlow" (Lonely Girl)/If I Should Lose Your Love	1965	8.00
9814 [PS]	Theme from "Harlow" (Lonely Girl)/If I Should Lose Your Love	1965	12.00
9846	What Color (Is a Man)/Love or Infatuation	1965	8.00
9869	Satin Pillows/Careless	1965	8.00
9869 [PS]	Satin Pillows/Careless	1965	12.00
9894	Tears/Go Away Pain	1966	6.00
10014	Dum-De-Da/Blue Clarinet	1966	6.00
10014 [PS]	Dum-De-Da/Blue Clarinet	1966	10.00
10048	Petticoat White (Summer Sky Blue)/All the King's Horses	1966	6.00
10048 [PS]	Petticoat White (Summer Sky Blue)/All the King's Horses	1966	10.00
10090	Coming Home Soldier/Don't Let My Mary Go Around	1966	6.00
10090 [PS]	Coming Home Soldier/Don't Let My Mary Go Around	1966	10.00
10136	For He's a Jolly Good Fellow/Sweet Maria	1967	6.00
10136 [PS]	For He's a Jolly Good Fellow/Sweet Maria	1967	10.00
10168	Red Roses for Mom/College Town	1967	6.00
10228	Please Love Me Forever/Miss America	1967	8.00
10228 [PS]	Please Love Me Forever/Miss America	1967	10.00
10266	Just As Much As Ever/Another Memory	1967	6.00
10266 [PS]	Just As Much As Ever/Another Memory	1967	10.00
10305	Take Good Care of My Baby/Strange Sensations	1968	6.00
10305 [PS]	Take Good Care of My Baby/Strange Sensations	1968	10.00
10350	Halfway to Paradise/(My Little) Christie	1968	6.00
10350	Halfway to Paradise/(My Little) Kristie	1968	10.00
—Note variation in B-side spelling			
10350 [PS]	Halfway to Paradise/(My Little) Christie	1968	10.00
10397	I Love How You Love Me/Little Barefoot Boy	1968	6.00
10397 [PS]	I Love How You Love Me/Little Barefoot Boy	1968	10.00
10461	To Know You Is to Love You/The Beat of My Heart	1969	5.00
10461 [PS]	To Know You Is to Love You/The Beat of My Heart	1969	10.00
10485	The Days of Sand and Shovels/So Many Lonely Girls	1969	5.00
10485 [PS]	The Days of Sand and Shovels/So Many Lonely Girls	1969	10.00
10554	Where Is Love/For All We Know	1969	5.00
10576	My Elusive Dreams/Over and Over	1970	5.00
10576 [PS]	My Elusive Dreams/Over and Over	1970	10.00
10629	No Arms Can Ever Hold You/I've Got That Lovin' Feelin'	1970	5.00
10629 [PS]	No Arms Can Ever Hold You/I've Got That Lovin' Feelin'	1970	8.00
10651	Why Don't They Understand/Where Is Love	1970	5.00
10651 [PS]	Why Don't They Understand/Where Is Love	1970	8.00
10689	Christmas Eve in My Home Town/The Christmas Angel	1970	6.00
10711	She Loves Me/I'll Make You My Baby	1971	5.00
10736	And I Love You So/She Loves Me	1971	5.00
10790	A Little Bit of You/God Bless America	1971	5.00
10822	Every Day of My Life/You Can Do It to Me Anytime	1972	5.00
10822 [PS]	Every Day of My Life/You Can Do It to Me Anytime	1972	8.00
10861	Sealed with a Kiss/All My Life	1972	5.00
10861 [PS]	Sealed with a Kiss/All My Life	1972	8.00
10936	But I Do/When You Love	1972	5.00
10936 [PS]	But I Do/When You Love	1972	8.00
10980	I Love You the Way You Are/Hurt	1973	5.00
11038	Where Are the Children/I Can't Believe That It's All Over	1973	5.00
50080	Clinging Vine/I Can't Believe That It's All Over	1975	5.00
50169	Christmas Eve in My Home Town/The Christmas Angel	1975	5.00

LARC

Number	Title (A Side/B Side)	Yr	NM
81019	You Are Love/Ghost of Another Man	1983	5.00

MELODY

Number	Title (A Side/B Side)	Yr	NM
5001/2	Always in My Heart/Harlem Nocturne	1960	25.00

TAPESTRY

Number	Title (A Side/B Side)	Yr	NM
001	Disco Polka (Pennsylvania Polka)/I Could Have Danced All Night	1979	4.00
002	Make Believe It's Your First Time/I Remember Loving You	1979	4.00
003	He/My First and Only Love	1980	4.00
005	It Was Nice to Know You John/Ain't That Lovin' You	1981	5.00
006	Let Me Love You, Goodbye/You Are Love	1981	4.00
007	Forever and Ever/Ain't That Lovin' You	1982	4.00
008	She Will Survive (Poland)/Love Is the Reason	1982	4.00
008 [PS]	She Will Survive (Poland)/Love Is the Reason	1982	5.00
010	It Hurts to Be in Love/Love Makes Everything Better	1985	4.00
013	What Did You Do with Your Old 45s/(B-side unknown)	1986	4.00
1986	Sweet Lady of Liberty (same on both sides)	1986	4.00
4009	Bed of Roses/I Know a Goodbye	1984	4.00

7-Inch Extended Plays

ABC

Number	Title (A Side/B Side)	Yr	NM
LLP-271	The Most Beautiful Girl/My Melody of Love/Never Ending Song of Love//You'll Never Know/Am I Losing You/Here in My Heart	1974	10.00
—Jukebox issue; small hole, plays at 33 1/3 rpm			
LLP-271 [PS]	Melodies of Love	1974	10.00

EPIC

Number	Title (A Side/B Side)	Yr	NM
EG 7215	Silver Bells/White Christmas//O Holy Night/The Christmas Song	1963	10.00
EG 7215 [PS]	Songs of Christmas	1963	10.00
7-26081	You're Nobody 'Til Somebody Loves You/Trying/Unchained Melody//To Each His Own/I Can Dream, Can't I/My Foolish Heart	1964	12.00
—Jukebox issue; small hole, plays at 33 1/3 rpm; original edition			
7-26081 [PS]	There! I've Said It Again	1964	12.00
—Slightly different cover than on N7-26081			
N7-26081	To Each His Own/You're Nobody 'Til Somebody Loves You/There! I've Said It Again//I Can Dream, Can't I?/Too Young/My Heart Belongs to Only You	196?	10.00
—Jukebox issue; small hole, plays at 33 1/3 rpm; revised edition			
N7-26081 [PS]	There! I've Said It Again	196?	10.00
—Slightly different cover than on 7-26081			
5-26341	Please Love Me Forever/It's All in the Game/Love Me with All Your Heart//Just As Much As Ever/P.S. I Love You/My Song of Love	1967	10.00
—Stereo jukebox issue; small hole, plays at 33 1/3 rpm			
5-26341 [PS]	Please Love Me Forever	1967	10.00
5-26382	Take Good Care of My Baby/I Apologize/To Think You've Chosen Me//Sentimental Me/Serenade of the Bells/Forget Me Not	1968	10.00
—Jukebox issue; small hole, plays at 33 1/3 rpm			
5-26382 [PS]	Take Good Care of My Baby	1968	10.00
5-26437	If I Didn't Care/Shangri-La/It's No Sin//Why Don't You Believe Me/Together/Save the Last Dance for Me	1968	10.00
—Jukebox issue; small hole, plays at 33 1/3 rpm			
5-26437 [PS]	I Love How You Love Me	1968	10.00
7-31642	Our Day Will Come/Song Sung Blue/Come Softly to Me//Some Kind of Wonderful/Somebody's Breaking My Heart/I'm Leaving It Up to You	1972	10.00
—Jukebox issue; small hole, plays at 33 1/3 rpm			
7-31642 [PS]	Sealed with a Kiss	1972	10.00

Albums

ABC

Number	Title	Yr	NM
X-851	Melodies of Love	1974	10.00
D-891	Heart of Hearts	1975	10.00
D-924	The Bobby Vinton Show	1975	10.00
D-957	Serenades of Love	1976	10.00
AB-981	The Name Is Love	1977	10.00

COLUMBIA LIMITED EDITION

Number	Title	Yr	NM
LE 10016	Big Ones	197?	10.00
LE 10052	Please Love Me Forever	197?	10.00
LE 10139	Roses Are Red	197?	10.00
LE 10140	Blue Velvet	197?	10.00
—Reissue of Epic 26068			

COLUMBIA MUSICAL TREASURY

Number	Title	Yr	NM
6P 6035 [(6)]	The Bobby Vinton Treasury	197?	30.00
—"Columbia House" logo on upper right back cover			

EPIC

Number	Title	Yr	NM
BN 579 [S]	Dancing at the Hop	1961	50.00
BN 597 [S]	Young Man with a Big Band	1961	50.00
LN 3727 [M]	Dancing at the Hop	1961	30.00
LN 3780 [M]	Young Man with a Big Band	1961	30.00
LN 24020 [M]	Roses Are Red	1962	15.00
LN 24035 [M]	Bobby Vinton Sings the Big Ones	1962	15.00

Number	Title (A Side/B Side)	Yr	NM
LN 24049 [M]	The Greatest Hits of the Greatest Groups	1963	15.00
LN 24068 [M]	Blue Velvet	1963	15.00
—Retitled version of "Blue On Blue"			
LN 24068 [M]	Blue On Blue	1963	25.00
—Stock copy on black vinyl			
LN 24068 [M]	Blue On Blue	1963	150.00
—Promo only on blue vinyl			
LN 24081 [M]	There! I've Said It Again	1964	15.00
LN 24098 [M]	Bobby Vinton's Greatest Hits	1964	12.00
—Despite lower number, this came out after "Tell Me Why"			
LN 24113 [M]	Tell Me Why	1964	12.00
LN 24122 [M]	A Very Merry Christmas	1964	12.00
LN 24136 [M]	Mr. Lonely	1965	12.00
LN 24154 [M]	Bobby Vinton Sings for Lonely Nights	1965	12.00
LN 24170 [M]	Drive-In Movie Time	1965	12.00
LN 24182 [M]	Satin Pillows and Careless	1966	12.00
LN 24187 [M]	More of Bobby Vinton's Greatest Hits	1966	12.00
LN 24188 [M]	Country Boy	1966	12.00
LN 24203 [M]	Live at the Copa	1967	12.00
LN 24245 [M]	Bobby Vinton's Newest Hits	1967	12.00
LN 24341 [M]	Please Love Me Forever	1967	15.00
BN 26020 [S]	Roses Are Red	1962	20.00
BN 26035 [S]	Bobby Vinton Sings the Big Ones	1962	20.00
BN 26049 [S]	The Greatest Hits of the Greatest Groups	1963	20.00
BN 26068 [S]	Blue Velvet	1963	20.00
—Retitled version of "Blue On Blue"			
BN 26068 [S]	Blue On Blue	1963	30.00
BN 26081 [S]	There! I've Said It Again	1964	20.00
BN 26098 [S]	Bobby Vinton's Greatest Hits	1964	15.00
—Despite lower number, this came out after "Tell Me Why"			
PE 26098	Bobby Vinton's Greatest Hits	198?	8.00
—Budget-line reissue			
BN 26113 [S]	Tell Me Why	1964	15.00
BN 26122 [S]	A Very Merry Christmas	1964	15.00
BN 26136 [S]	Mr. Lonely	1965	15.00
BN 26154 [S]	Bobby Vinton Sings for Lonely Nights	1965	15.00
BN 26170 [S]	Drive-In Movie Time	1965	15.00
BN 26182 [S]	Satin Pillows and Careless	1966	15.00
BN 26187 [S]	More of Bobby Vinton's Greatest Hits	1966	15.00
BN 26188 [S]	Country Boy	1966	15.00
BN 26203 [S]	Live at the Copa	1967	15.00
BN 26245 [S]	Bobby Vinton's Newest Hits	1967	15.00
BN 26341 [S]	Please Love Me Forever	1967	15.00
BN 26382	Take Good Care of My Baby	1968	15.00
BN 26437	I Love How You Love Me	1968	15.00
BN 26471	Vinton	1969	15.00
BN 26517	Bobby Vinton's Greatest Hits of Love	1970	15.00
BN 26540	My Elusive Dreams	1970	15.00
KE 31286	Ev'ry Day of My Life	1972	12.00
KEG 31487 [(2)]	Bobby Vinton's All-Time Greatest Hits	1972	15.00
PEG 31487 [(2)]	Bobby Vinton's All-Time Greatest Hits	197?	12.00
—Reissue			
KE 31642	Sealed with a Kiss	1972	12.00
PE 32921	With Love	1974	10.00
KEG 33468 [(2)]	Bobby Vinton Sings the Golden Decade of Love	1975	12.00
KEG 33767 [(2)]	Greatest Hits/Greatest Hits of Love	1976	12.00
JE 35605	Autumn Memories	1979	10.00
JE 35998	Spring Sensations	1979	10.00
JE 35999	Summer Serenade	1979	10.00
HARMONY			
KH 11402	Vinton Sings Vinton	197?	10.00
PICKWICK			
SPC-3353	Melodies of Love	197?	8.00
TAPESTRY			
TRS-1001 [EP]	Santa Must Be Polish	1987	10.00

VIOLENT FEMMES

Number	Title (A Side/B Side)	Yr	NM
12-Inch Singles			
SLASH			
PRO-A-2422 [DJ]	Children of the Revolution/Children of the Revolution (Edit)	1986	6.00
PRO-A-3411 [DJ]	Nightmares/World We're Living In	1989	10.00
WARNER BROS.			
PRO-A-2422 [DJ]	Children of the Revolution (edit) (LP)	1986	20.00
45s			
SLASH			
28683	Chidren of the Revolution/World Without Mercy	1986	4.00
29521	Gone Daddy Gone/Good Feeling	1983	4.00
Albums			
RHINO			
R1-79951	Violent Femmes	2003	15.00
—Reissue on 180-gram vinyl			
SLASH			
23845	Violent Femmes	1983	15.00
25094	Hallowed Ground	1984	12.00
25340	The Blind Leading the Naked	1986	10.00
25819	3	1988	10.00
WARNER BROS.			
PRO-A-3519 [DJ]	3 On 3	1989	25.00
—Promo-only interviews and music			

VIPERS SKIFFLE GROUP, THE

Number	Title (A Side/B Side)	Yr	NM
45s			
CAPITOL			
F3673	Don't You Rock Me Daddy-O/10,000 Years Ago	1957	20.00
F3711	Cumberland Gap/Maggie Mae	1957	15.00

VIRGIN INSANITY

Number	Title (A Side/B Side)	Yr	NM
Albums			
FUNKY			
71411	Illusions of the Maintenance Man	1970	200.00

VIRTUES, THE

Includes records by "Frank Virtue" and "Frank Virtuoso."

Number	Title (A Side/B Side)	Yr	NM
45s			
ABC-PARAMOUNT			
10071	Blues in the Cellar/Vaya Con Dios	1959	15.00
ARCADE			
135	Ooh You Gotta/I Make a Mistake	1955	30.00
—As "Frank Virtue"			
FAYETTE			
1626	Guitar Boogie Shuffle '65/Moon Maid	1965	15.00
HIGHLAND			
2505	Bye Bye Blues/Happy Guitar	1960	25.00
2505X	Bye Bye Blues/Strollin' Again	1960	25.00
HUNT			
324 [M]	Guitar Boogie Shuffle/Guitar in Orbit	1959	25.00
S-324 [S]	Guitar Boogie Shuffle/Guitar in Orbit	1959	50.00
327	Flippin' In/Shufflin' Along	1959	20.00
328	Pickin' the Stroll/Virtue's Boogie Woogie	1959	20.00
329	Pony Walk/Virtue's Boogie Woogie	1959	20.00
331	Blues in the Cellar/Vaya Con Dios	1960	20.00
LIBERTY			
55706	Dream World/Move On	1964	12.00
—As "Frank Virtuoso"			
SURE			
501	Guitar Boogie Shuffle/Guitar in Orbit	1959	80.00
1733	Guitar Boogie Shuffle Twist/Guitar Boogie Stomp	1962	15.00
1779	Tel-Star Guitar/Jersey Bounce	1962	15.00
VIRNON			
603	Guitar Boogie Twist/Guitar Shimmy	1960	15.00
VIRTUE			
190	Cotton Candy/Love You	1966	10.00
2503	Guitar on the Wild Side/Meditation of the Soul	1970	6.00
WYNNE			
123	Highland Guitar/Pickin' Plankin' Boogie	1960	15.00
Albums			
FAYETTE			
1816 [M]	Frank Virtue and the Virtues	1964	40.00
—White cover			
1816 [M]	Frank Virtue and the Virtues	1964	60.00
—Blue cover			
STRAND			
L-1061 [M]	Guitar Boogie Shuffle	1960	30.00
SL-1061 [S]	Guitar Boogie Shuffle	1960	40.00
WYNNE			
WLP-111 [M]	Guitar Boogie Shuffle	1960	120.00
WLP-711 [S]	Guitar Boogie Shuffle	1960	180.00

VISCAYNES, THE

Sylvester Stewart [Sly Stone] was a member.

Number	Title (A Side/B Side)	Yr	NM
45s			
TROPO			
101	I Guess I'll Be/Stop What You're Doing	1958	150.00
VPM			
1006	Yellow Moon/Heavenly Angel	1961	40.00

VISCOUNTS, THE (1)

Number	Title (A Side/B Side)	Yr	NM
45s			
AMY			
940	Harlem Nocturne/Dig	1965	12.00
949	Night Train/When the Saints Go Marching In	1966	12.00
CORAL			
62490	Come, Come On Back/Off Shore	1966	10.00
62520	Moonlight in Vermont/Sweet Georgia Brown	1967	10.00
MADISON			
123	Harlem Nocturne/Dig	1959	25.00
129	The Touch/Chug-a-Lug	1960	15.00
133	Night Train/Summertime	1960	15.00
140	Wabash Blues/So Slow	1960	15.00
152	Shadrack/This Place	1961	15.00
159	Little Brown Jug/Opus One	1961	15.00
165	Drag Race/Sophisticated Lady	1961	15.00
MR. PEACOCK			
101	When Johnny Comes Marching Home/Mark's Mood	1961	12.00
107	The Continental Walk/Hully Gully	1962	12.00
112	Night Flight/A Girl Like You	1962	12.00
MR. PEEKE			
125	Night for Love/Ballin' the Jack	1963	12.00
Albums			
AMY			
8008 [M]	Harlem Nocturne	1965	40.00
S-8008 [S]	Harlem Nocturne	1965	50.00
MADISON			
1001 [M]	The Viscounts	1960	200.00

VISCOUNTS, THE (2)

Number	Title (A Side/B Side)	Yr	NM
45s			
MERCURY			
71073	My Girl/Raindrop	1957	40.00

VISION OF SUNSHINE

Number	Title (A Side/B Side)	Yr	NM
Albums			
AVCO EMBASSY			
33007	Vision of Sunshine	1970	30.00

VISIONS, THE

Several different groups.

Number	Title (A Side/B Side)	Yr	NM
45s			
BIG TOP			
3092	Tell Me You're Mine/All Through the Night	1961	20.00
3119	Secret Worlds of Tears/Swingin' Wedding	1962	20.00
BRUNSWICK			
55206	So Close/There'll Be No Next Time	1961	25.00
COED			
598	Down in My Heart/Tell Her Now	1964	12.00
ELGEY			
1003	Teenager's Life/Little Moon	1960	40.00
LOST-NITE			
102	Teenager's Life/Little Moon	196?	6.00
—Yellow label with "street lamp" logo			
102	Teenager's Life/Little Moon	1961	25.00
—Original pressing on pink label with no "street lamp" logo			
MERCURY			
72188	Oh Boy What a Girl/Tommy's Girl	1963	15.00
ORIGINAL SOUND			
32	Look at Me Now/Cigarette	1963	15.00
UNI			
55031	How Can I Be Down/Threshold of Love	1967	12.00
55042	Keepin' Your Eyes on the Sun/Small Town Commotion	1967	12.00
WARNER BROS.			
5898	Black and White Rainbow/Bulldog Cadillac	1967	10.00

VISITORS, THE (1)

Number	Title (A Side/B Side)	Yr	NM
45s			
DAKAR			
603	I'm in Danger/Until You Came Along	1969	8.00
613	I'm Gonna Stay/Lonely One, Only Son	1969	8.00
TANGERINE			
1003	My Love Is Ready and Waiting/What About Me	1970	8.00
1010	Anytime Is the Right Time/Nevertheless	1970	8.00

Number	Title (A Side/B Side)	Yr	NM
VISITORS, THE (2)			
45s			
TOWER			
❑ 268	Theme from The Wild Angels/ Is It Them or Me	1966	15.00
VISTAS, THE			
45s			
REBEL			
❑ 77755	Ghost Wave/Surfer's Minuet	1963	50.00
VENPRO			
❑ 1000	Ghost Wave/Surfer's Minuet	1963	80.00
VISUALS, THE			
45s			
POPLAR			
❑ 115	The Submarine Race/ Maybe You	1962	40.00
❑ 117	My Juanita/A Boy, a Girl, and a Dream	1963	50.00
❑ 121	Please Don't Be Mad at Me/ Blue Enough to Cry	1963	300.00
VITALE, JOE			
45s			
ASYLUM			
❑ 47169	Never Gonna Leave You Alone/ Theme from Cabin Weirdos	1981	4.00
❑ 47210	The Lady on the Rock (It's America)/Plantation Harbor	1981	4.00
❑ 47251	Man Gonna Love You/I'm Flyin'	1981	4.00
ATLANTIC			
❑ 3204	Roller Coaster Weekend/Take a Chance on Love	1974	4.00
❑ 3260	Two of Us/Shot 'Em Up	1975	4.00
Albums			
ASYLUM			
❑ 5E-529	Plantation Harbor	1981	10.00
ATLANTIC			
❑ SD 18114	Rollercoaster Weekend	1975	10.00
VITELLS, THE			
45s			
DECCA			
❑ 31362	Shirley/The Dip	1962	30.00
VITO, SONNY			
45s			
ABC-PARAMOUNT			
❑ 9958	Cameo Ring/Teen-Age Blues	1958	12.00
STRAND			
❑ 25045	An Angel Cries/Mister Groovy	1961	12.00
VITO AND THE SALUTATIONS			
45s			
APT			
❑ 25079	High Noon/Walkin'	1965	50.00
BOOM			
❑ 60020	Bring Back Yesterday/I Want You to Be My Baby	1966	20.00
CRYSTAL BALL			
❑ 105	Unchained Melody/So Much	1978	5.00
HAROLD			
❑ 5009	Gloria/Let's Untwist the Twist	1962	50.00
HERALD			
❑ 583	Unchained Melody/ Hey Hey Baby	1963	30.00
❑ 586	Eenie Meenie/Extraordinary Girl	1964	25.00
KRAM			
❑ 5002	Your Way/Hey, Hey Baby	1962	50.00
LOST-NITE			
❑ 429	Unchained Melody/ Hey Hey Baby	197?	5.00
—Reissue			
RAYNA			
❑ 5009	Gloria/Let's Untwist the Twist	1962	50.00
RED BOY			
❑ 1001	So Wonderful (My Love)/ I'd Best Be Going	1966	25.00
❑ 5009	Gloria/Let's Untwist the Twist	1962	30.00
REGINA			
❑ 1320	Get a Job/Girls I Know	1964	30.00
RUST			
❑ 5106	Can I Depend on You/Hello Dolly	1966	20.00
SANDBAG			
❑ 103	So Wonderful (My Love)/ I'd Best Be Going	1966	20.00
WELLS			
❑ 1008	Can I Depend on You/ Liverpool Bound	1964	25.00
❑ 1008	Can I Depend on You/ Liverpool Bound	1964	50.00
—Yellow vinyl			
❑ 1010	The Banana Boat Song (Day-O)/Don't Count on Me	1964	25.00
VOCALEERS, THE Possibly more than one group.			
45s			
LOST-NITE			
❑ 333	Be True/Oh! Where	197?	5.00
—Reissue			
❑ 336	Is It a Dream/Hurry Home	197?	5.00
—Reissue			
❑ 339	I Walk Alone/How Soon	197?	5.00
—Reissue			
❑ 342	Will You Be True/Love You	197?	5.00
—Reissue			
❑ 346	Angel Face/Lovin' Baby	197?	5.00
—Reissue			
OLD TOWN			
❑ 1089	This Is the Night/ Love and Devotion	1960	25.00
PARADISE			
❑ 113	I Need Your Love So Bad/Have You Ever Loved Someone	1959	40.00
RED ROBIN			
❑ 113	Be True/Oh! Where	1953	600.00
❑ 114	Is It a Dream/Hurry Home	1953	300.00
❑ 119	I Walk Alone/How Soon	1953	400.00
❑ 125	Will You Be True/Love You	1954	300.00
❑ 132	Angel Face/Lovin' Baby	1954	300.00
TWISTIME			
❑ 11	Cootie Snap/A Golden Tear	1962	30.00
VEST			
❑ 832	Hear My Plea/The Night Is Quiet	1960	80.00
VOGUES, THE Also see THE VAL-AIRES.			
45s			
ABC-PARAMOUNT			
❑ 10672	Big Man/Golden Locket	1965	20.00
ASTRA			
❑ 1029	You're the One/ Goodnight My Love	1973	5.00
❑ 1030	Five O'Clock World/Land of Milk and Honey	1973	5.00
BELL			
❑ 991	Love Song/We're On Our Way	1971	5.00
❑ 45127	Take Time to Tell Her/ I'll Be with You	1971	5.00
❑ 45158	An American Family/ Gotta Have You Back	1971	5.00
BLUE STAR			
❑ 229	You're the One/Some Words	1965	25.00
CO & CE			
❑ 229	You're the One/Some Words	1965	12.00
❑ 232	Five O'Clock World/ Nothing to Offer You	1965	12.00
❑ 234	Magic Town/Humpty Dumpty	1966	10.00
❑ 238	The Land of Milk and Honey/ True Lovers	1966	10.00
❑ 240	Please Mr. Sun/ Don't Blame the Rain	1966	10.00
❑ 242	That's the Tune/ Midnight Dreams	1966	10.00
❑ 244	Take a Chance on My Heart/ Summer Afternoon	1967	10.00
❑ 246	Brighter Days/Lovers of the World Unite	1967	10.00
MAINSTREAM			
❑ 5524	Need You/(B-side unknown)	1972	5.00
MGM			
❑ 13813	Brighter Days/Lovers of the World Unite	1967	8.00
REPRISE			
❑ 0663	I've Got You on My Mind/Just What I've Been Looking For	1968	10.00
❑ 0686	Turn Around, Look at Me/Then	1968	8.00
❑ 0731	Turn Around, Look at Me/ My Special Angel	1969	5.00
—"Back to Back Hits" series			
❑ 0736	No, Not Much/Earth Angel (Will You Be Mine)	1970	5.00
—"Back to Back Hits" series			
❑ 0741	Five O'Clock World/Magic Town	1970	6.00
—"Back to Back Hits" series; "Five O'Clock World" has overdubbed strings			
❑ 0766	My Special Angel/I Keep It Hid	1968	8.00
❑ 0788	Till/I Will	1968	8.00
❑ 0803	Woman Helping Man/ No, Not Much	1969	6.00
❑ 0803	Woman Helping Man/ I'll Know My Love	1969	8.00
❑ 0820	Earth Angel (Will You Be Mine)/ P.S. I Love You	1969	6.00
❑ 0831	Moments to Remember/ Once in a While	1969	6.00
❑ 0844	Green Fields/Easy to Say	1969	6.00
❑ 0856	See That Girl/If We Only Have Love	1969	6.00
❑ 0887	God Only Knows/Moody	1970	6.00
❑ 0909	Over the Rainbow/Hey, That's No Way to Say Goodbye	1970	6.00
❑ 0931	50's Medley/Come Into My Arms	1970	6.00
❑ 0969	Since I Don't Have You/I Know You as a Woman	1970	6.00
20TH CENTURY			
❑ 2041	My Prayer/I've Got to Learn to Live Without You	1973	5.00
❑ 2060	Wonderful Summer/Guess Who	1973	5.00
❑ 2085	As Time Goes By/ Prisoner of Love	1974	5.00
Albums			
CO & CE			
❑ LP-1229 [M]	Meet the Vogues	1965	50.00
❑ LP-1230 [M]	Five O'Clock World	1966	50.00
—Stereo pressings of these two albums are not known to exist!			
PICKWICK			
❑ SPC-3188 [R]	Five O'Clock World	1971	10.00
❑ SPC-3214 [R]	A Lover's Concerto	1971	10.00
REPRISE			
❑ RS 6314	Turn Around, Look at Me	1968	15.00
—With "W7" and "r:" logos on two-tone orange label			
❑ RS 6326	Till	1969	15.00
—With "W7" and "r:" logos on two-tone orange label			
❑ RS 6347	Memories	1969	15.00
—With "W7" and "r:" logos on two-tone orange label			
❑ RS 6371	The Vogues' Greatest Hits	1969	15.00
—With "W7" and "r:" logos on two-tone orange label			
❑ RS 6395	The Vogues Sing the Good Old Songs	1970	12.00
❑ ST-91559	Turn Around, Look at Me	1968	20.00
—Capitol Record Club edition			
❑ SW-93040	The Vogues' Greatest Hits	1970	20.00
—Capitol Record Club edition			
SSS INTERNATIONAL			
❑ 34	The Vogues' Greatest Hits	1977	10.00
VOGUES, THE (2) No relation to the more famous group above.			
45s			
DOT			
❑ 15798	Love Is a Funny Little Game/ Which Witch Doctor	1958	25.00
❑ 15859	Try, Baby. Try/Falling Star	1958	25.00
VOGUES, THE (U) Definitely not group (1); could be group (2).			
45s			
CASCADE			
❑ 5908	Ev'ry Day, Ev'ry Night/Now I Lay Me Down to Cry	1959	20.00
VOICE MASTERS, THE LAMONT DOZIER and DAVID RUFFIN were originally in this group, though they did not appear on the later sides.			
45s			
ANNA			
❑ 101	Hope and Pray/Oop's I'm Sorry	1959	200.00
❑ 102	Needed/Needed (For Lovers Only)	1959	200.00
BAMBOO			
❑ 103	You've Hurt Me Baby/If a Woman Catches a Fool	1968	25.00
❑ 105	Never Gonna Leave You/ If a Woman Catches a Fool	1969	15.00
❑ 113	Dance Right Into My Heart/ If a Woman Catches a Fool	1970	15.00
FRISCO			
❑ 15235	In Love in Vain/Two Lovers	196?	100.00
VOICE OF THE BEEHIVE			
12-Inch Singles			
LONDON			
❑ 886370-1	I Say Nothing/The Things You See When You Don't Have Your Gun (Live)/In the Flesh	1988	10.00
45s			
LONDON			
❑ 886334-7	I Say Nothing/The Things You See When You Don't Have Your Gun	1988	8.00
❑ 886334-7 [PS]	I Say Nothing/The Things You See When You Don't Have Your Gun	1988	8.00

Except when noted otherwise, VG = 25% of NM, and VG+ = 50% of NM. (Example: VG = $2.00, VG+ = $4.00 and NM = $8.00.)

Number	Title (A Side/B Side)	Yr	NM
❑ 886500-7	Don't Call Me Baby/There's a Barbarian in the Back of My Car	1989	8.00
❑ 886500-7 [PS]	Don't Call Me Baby/There's a Barbarian in the Back of My Car	1989	8.00

Albums

LONDON

Number	Title (A Side/B Side)	Yr	NM
❑ 828100-1	Let It Bee	1988	15.00

VOICES, THE

45s

CASH

Number	Title (A Side/B Side)	Yr	NM
❑ 1011	Why/Two Things I Love	1955	60.00
❑ 1014	Hey Now/My Love Grows Stronger	1955	60.00
❑ 1015	I Want to Be Ready/Takes Two to Make a Home	1955	60.00
❑ 1016	Santa Claus Boogie/Santa Claus Baby	1955	80.00
❑ 1016	Santa Claus Boogie/Santa Claus Baby	197?	5.00

—Reproduction

SPECIALTY

Number	Title (A Side/B Side)	Yr	NM
❑ 754	Santa Claus Boogie/Santa Claus Baby	197?	15.00

—Red vinyl

VOICES OF EAST HARLEM, THE

45s

ELEKTRA

Number	Title (A Side/B Side)	Yr	NM
❑ 45753	Sit Yourself Down/Oxford Town	1971	6.00
❑ 45775	Angry/New York Lightning	1972	6.00

JUST SUNSHINE

Number	Title (A Side/B Side)	Yr	NM
❑ 504	Giving Love/New Vibrations	1973	5.00
❑ 510	I Like Having You Around/Cashing In	1973	5.00
❑ 517	Can You Feel It/Wanted Dead or Alive	1974	5.00

Albums

ELEKTRA

Number	Title (A Side/B Side)	Yr	NM
❑ EKS-74080	Right On Be Free	1970	10.00

JUST SUNSHINE

Number	Title (A Side/B Side)	Yr	NM
❑ 7	Voices of East Harlem	1973	10.00
❑ 3504	Can You Feel It?	1974	10.00

VOIGHT, WES

45s

DELUXE

Number	Title (A Side/B Side)	Yr	NM
❑ 6176	Midnight Blues/Another Guy's Line	1958	100.00
❑ 6180	I Want a Lover/Little Joan	1958	40.00

KING

Number	Title (A Side/B Side)	Yr	NM
❑ 5211 [M]	I'm Loving It/Everything's the Same	1959	60.00
❑ S-5211 [S]	I'm Loving It/Everything's the Same	1959	200.00
❑ 5231 [M]	I'm Ready to Go Steady/The Wind and the Cold Black Night	1959	40.00
❑ S-5231 [S]	I'm Ready to Go Steady/The Wind and the Cold Black Night	1959	100.00

VOLCANICS, THE

45s

PARKWAY

Number	Title (A Side/B Side)	Yr	NM
❑ 149	Your Kind of Loving/But I Love Her	1967	15.00

VOLCANOES, THE

45s

EPIC

Number	Title (A Side/B Side)	Yr	NM
❑ 9490	Shotgun/Stardust	1962	12.00

VOLCANOS, THE

Early version of THE TRAMMPS.

45s

ARCTIC

Number	Title (A Side/B Side)	Yr	NM
❑ 103	Make Your Move/Baby	1965	12.00
❑ 106	Storm Warning/Baby	1965	12.00
❑ 111	Help Wanted/Make Your Move	1965	12.00
❑ 115	(It's Against the) Laws of Love/(Instrumental)	1965	12.00

—With correct song title as above

Number	Title (A Side/B Side)	Yr	NM
❑ 115	(It's Against the) Rules of Love/(Instrumental)	1965	300.00

—With erroneous song title as above

Number	Title (A Side/B Side)	Yr	NM
❑ 125	Lady's Man/Help Wanted	1966	10.00
❑ 128	You're Number 1/Make Your Move	1967	10.00

VOLK, VAL, AND THE MATCHED ACES

45s

ROCKET

Number	Title (A Side/B Side)	Yr	NM
❑ 1050	A Rockin' Party Tonight/Spring Time Rock	195?	200.00

VOLTAGE BROTHERS, THE

12-Inch Singles

MTM

Number	Title (A Side/B Side)	Yr	NM
❑ SPRO-9647 [DJ]	Love's a Criminal (unknown versions)	1986	20.00
❑ V-73051	Love's a Criminal (unknown versions)	1986	8.00

45s

LIFESONG

Number	Title (A Side/B Side)	Yr	NM
❑ ZS8 1762	Feeling Good/Gone Too Far to Turn Around	1978	6.00
❑ ZS8 1766	Happening in the Streets/Working Together	1978	6.00
❑ ZS8 1780	Throw Down/The Prophet	1978	6.00

MTM

Number	Title (A Side/B Side)	Yr	NM
❑ B-72060	I Think I Miss You (After All)/Don't Jump the Gun	1985	5.00
❑ B-72067	Love's a Criminal/(B-side unknown)	1986	5.00
❑ B-72077	Insecure/(B-side unknown)	1986	5.00

Albums

LIFESONG

Number	Title (A Side/B Side)	Yr	NM
❑ JZ 35042	The Voltage Brothers	1978	20.00
❑ JZ 35653	Throw Down	1978	20.00

MTM

Number	Title (A Side/B Side)	Yr	NM
❑ ST-71055	The Voltage Brothers	1986	15.00

VOL.S, THE

45s

AMERICAN ARTS

Number	Title (A Side/B Side)	Yr	NM
❑ 6	Gotta Give Her Love/I Can't Live Without You	1964	30.00
❑ 18	I Just Can't Help Myself/One Way Lover	1965	30.00

CHEX

Number	Title (A Side/B Side)	Yr	NM
❑ 1002	I Love You/Dreams	1962	25.00

—With "Nationally Dist. by Jay-Gee Rec. Co. Inc." on label

Number	Title (A Side/B Side)	Yr	NM
❑ 1002	I Love You/Dreams	1962	40.00

—With no reference to Jay-Gee Records on label

Number	Title (A Side/B Side)	Yr	NM
❑ 1002	I Love You/Dreams	1962	300.00

—With typographical error crediting "The Valumes"

Number	Title (A Side/B Side)	Yr	NM
❑ 1005	Come Back Into My Heart/The Bell	1962	40.00

IMPACT

Number	Title (A Side/B Side)	Yr	NM
❑ 1017	That Same Old Feeling/The Trouble I've Seen	1966	50.00

INFERNO

Number	Title (A Side/B Side)	Yr	NM
❑ 2001	A Way to Love You/You Got It Baby	1967	20.00
❑ 2004	My Road Is the Right Road/My Kind of Girl	1967	20.00
❑ 5001	Ain't That Lovin' You/I Love You Baby	1968	20.00

JUBILEE

Number	Title (A Side/B Side)	Yr	NM
❑ 5446	Sandra/Teenage Paradise	1963	20.00
❑ 5454	Our Song/Oh My Mother-in-Law	1963	20.00

KAREN

Number	Title (A Side/B Side)	Yr	NM
❑ 1551	Am I Losing You/Ain't Gonna Give You Up	1970	8.00

OLD TOWN

Number	Title (A Side/B Side)	Yr	NM
❑ 1154	Why/Monkey Hop	1964	25.00

VONDELLS, THE

45s

AIRTOWN CUSTOM

Number	Title (A Side/B Side)	Yr	NM
❑ (# unknown)	Hey Girl You've Changed/(B-side unknown)	196?	1500.

VONNS, THE

45s

KING

Number	Title (A Side/B Side)	Yr	NM
❑ 5793	Leave Us Alone/So Many Days	1963	20.00

VONTASTICS, THE

45s

CHESS

Number	Title (A Side/B Side)	Yr	NM
❑ 2024	Why Must We Part/I Will Always Love You	1967	15.00

MOON SHOT

Number	Title (A Side/B Side)	Yr	NM
❑ 4702	Lady Love/When My Baby Comes Back Home	1967	30.00

ST. LAWRENCE

Number	Title (A Side/B Side)	Yr	NM
❑ 1007	Peace of Mind/No Love for Me	1966	15.00
❑ 1009	I Need You/Keep On Rolling	1966	20.00
❑ 1014	Day Tripper/My Baby	1966	20.00
❑ 1023	You Can Work It Out/Never Let Your Love Grow Cold	1967	15.00

SATELLITE

Number	Title (A Side/B Side)	Yr	NM
❑ 2002	I'll Never Say Goodbye/Don't Mess Around	1965	120.00

TODDLIN' TOWN

Number	Title (A Side/B Side)	Yr	NM
❑ 115	Let Me Down Easy/I'm the One You Need	1968	25.00

VOWS, THE

45s

MARKAY

Number	Title (A Side/B Side)	Yr	NM
❑ 103	I Wanna Chance/Have You Heard	1962	40.00

—Black label

Number	Title (A Side/B Side)	Yr	NM
❑ 103	I Wanna Chance/Have You Heard	1962	400.00

—Orange label

RAN-DEE

Number	Title (A Side/B Side)	Yr	NM
❑ 112	Girl in Red/Born with the Rhythm	196?	60.00

STA-SET

Number	Title (A Side/B Side)	Yr	NM
❑ 402	Say You'll Be Mine/When a Boy Loves a Girl	1963	60.00

TAMARA

Number	Title (A Side/B Side)	Yr	NM
❑ 506	The Things You Do to Me/Dottie	1963	40.00
❑ 760	Say You'll Be Mine/When a Boy Loves a Girl	1964	25.00

V.I.P.

Number	Title (A Side/B Side)	Yr	NM
❑ 25016	Buttered Popcorn/Tell Me	1965	40.00

VOXPOPPERS, THE

45s

AMP 3

Number	Title (A Side/B Side)	Yr	NM
❑ 1004	Wishing for Your Love/The Last Drag	1958	40.00

MERCURY

Number	Title (A Side/B Side)	Yr	NM
❑ 71282	Wishing for Your Love/The Last Drag	1958	20.00
❑ 71315	Pony Tail/Ping Pong Baby	1958	20.00

POPLAR

Number	Title (A Side/B Side)	Yr	NM
❑ 107	Come Back Little Girl/A Love to Last a Lifetime	1959	20.00

VERSAILLES

Number	Title (A Side/B Side)	Yr	NM
❑ 200	Can't Understand It/A Blessing After All	1959	30.00

WARWICK

Number	Title (A Side/B Side)	Yr	NM
❑ 589	Lonely for You/Helen Isn't Tellin'	1960	12.00

—As "Freddie and the Voxpoppers"

7-Inch Extended Plays

MERCURY

Number	Title (A Side/B Side)	Yr	NM
❑ EP 1-3391	Wishing for Your Love/The Last Drag//Stroll Roll/Guitar Stroll	1958	100.00
❑ EP 1-3391 [PS]	The Voxpoppers	1958	100.00

VY-DELLS, THE

45s

GARNET

Number	Title (A Side/B Side)	Yr	NM
❑ 101	What I'm Gonna Do/Unknown	196?	100.00

W

WADE, BILLY, AND THE 3 DEGREES

45s

ABC

Number	Title (A Side/B Side)	Yr	NM
❑ 45-10991	Tear It Up (Part 1)/Tear It Up (Part 2)	1967	10.00

WADE, DON

45s

SAN

Number	Title (A Side/B Side)	Yr	NM
❑ 206	Gone, Gone, Gone/(B-side unknown)	1958	300.00
❑ 207	Forever Yours/Oh Love	1958	30.00

WADE, RONNY

45s

KING

Number	Title (A Side/B Side)	Yr	NM
❑ 5061	Gotta Make Her Mine/Let Me Cry	1957	80.00
❑ 5078	I Know But I'll Never Tell/I Never Fall in Love Again	1957	50.00
❑ 5099	Annie Don't Work/I'll Sail My Ship Alone	1958	50.00
❑ 5112	All I Want/A King and a Vow	1958	50.00

WADE AND DICK

45s

SUN

Number	Title (A Side/B Side)	Yr	NM
❑ 269	Bop Bop Baby/Don't Need Your Lovin' Baby	1957	30.00

Tom Waits, *Rain Dogs*, Island 90299, 1985, $10.

Number	Title (A Side/B Side)	Yr	NM
WADSWORTH MANSION			
45s			
SUSSEX			
❑ 209	Sweet Mary/What's On Tonight	1970	6.00
—Later pressings have a short version of A-side			
❑ 209	Sweet Mary/What's On Tonight	1970	8.00
—First pressings have a much longer version of A-side			
❑ 215	Havin' Such a Good Time/ Michigan Harry Slaughter	1971	5.00
❑ 221	Nine on the Line/Queenie Dew	1971	5.00
Albums			
SUSSEX			
❑ SXBS-7008	Wadsworth Mansion	1971	20.00
❑ SXBS-7008	Wadsworth Manison	1971	25.00
—Some copies of this LP have the above typographical error			
WAGNER, DANNY, AND KINDRED SOUL			
45s			
IMPERIAL			
❑ 66305	I Lost a True Love/My Buddy	1968	30.00
❑ 66327	Harlem Shuffle/When Johnny Comes Marching Home	1968	20.00
Albums			
IMPERIAL			
❑ LP-12405	The Kindred Soul of Danny Wagner	1968	30.00
WAGNER, DAVID See CROW.			
WAGNER, DICK, AND THE FROSTS See THE FROST.			
WAIKIKIS, THE			
45s			
KAPP			
❑ KJB-30	Hawaii Tattoo/Tahiti Tamoure	1964	8.00
❑ KJB-52	Hawaii Honeymoon/ Remember Boa-Boa	1965	8.00
❑ 891	Pearly Shells/Tiny Bubbles	1968	5.00
PALETTE			
❑ 5091	Hawaii Tattoo/Aloha Parade	1962	12.00

Number	Title (A Side/B Side)	Yr	NM
❑ 5109	Tikitiki Puki/Tanita Tamoure	1963	10.00
Albums			
KAPP			
❑ KL-1366 [M]	Hawaii Tattoo	1964	15.00
❑ KL-1432 [M]	Hawaii Honeymoon	1965	15.00
❑ KL-1437 [M]	Beach Party	1965	15.00
❑ KL-1473 [M]	Lollipops and Roses	1966	15.00
❑ KL-1484 [M]	A Taste of Hawaii	1966	15.00
❑ KL-1555 [M]	Pearly Shells from Hawaii	1968	30.00
—White label promo in stereo cover, "Mono" sticker on front			
❑ KS-3366 [S]	Hawaii Tattoo	1964	20.00
❑ KS-3432 [S]	Hawaii Honeymoon	1965	20.00
❑ KS-3437 [S]	Beach Party	1965	20.00
❑ KS-3473 [S]	Lollipops and Roses	1966	20.00
❑ KS-3484 [S]	A Taste of Hawaii	1966	20.00
❑ KS-3555 [S]	Pearly Shells from Hawaii	1968	15.00
❑ KS-3575	Midnight Luau	1969	15.00
❑ KS-3593	Moonlight on Diamond Head	1969	15.00
❑ KS-3612	Greatest Hits	1970	12.00
MCA			
❑ 544	Pearly Shells from Hawaii	197?	10.00
❑ 547	Greatest Hits	197?	10.00
WAILERS, THE			
45s			
BELL			
❑ 694	Thinking Out Loud/You Can't Fly	1967	10.00
ETIQUETTE			
❑ 2	Mashi/Velva	1962	15.00
❑ 4	Stompin' Willie/Doin' the Seaside	1963	15.00
❑ 6	We're Goin' Surfin'/Shakedown	1963	15.00
❑ 7	Seattle/Party Time U.S.A.	1963	15.00
❑ 9	Tall Cool One/Frenzy	1964	15.00
❑ 12	You Better Believe It/ Don't Take It So Hard	1965	40.00
❑ 15	You Weren't Using Your Head/ Back to You	1965	40.00
❑ 19	Hang Up/Dirty Robber	1965	40.00
❑ 21	Out of Our Tree/I Got Me	1966	40.00

Number	Title (A Side/B Side)	Yr	NM
❑ 22	Christmas Spirit/Don't Believe in Christmas	1965	30.00
—B-side by the Sonics			
❑ 24	It's You Alone/Tears	1966	40.00
GOLDEN CREST			
❑ 375	Beat Guitar/Driftwood	19??	10.00
❑ 518	Tall Cool One/Roadrunner	1959	30.00
—Photo of group on label			
❑ 518	Tall Cool One/Roadrunner	1964	15.00
—No photo on label			
❑ 526	Mau-Mau/Dirty Robber	1959	25.00
—Photo of group on label			
❑ 526	Mau-Mau/Dirty Robber	1964	12.00
—No photo on label			
❑ 532	Wailin'/Shanghai'd	1960	25.00
—Photo of group on label			
❑ 532	Wailin'/Shanghai'd	1964	12.00
—No photo on label			
❑ 545	Lucille/Scratchin'	1960	25.00
—Photo of group on label			
❑ 545	Lucille/Scratchin'	1964	12.00
—No photo of group			
❑ 591	Mau-Mau/Beat Guitar	1964	10.00
IMPERIAL			
❑ 66028	Tall Cool One/Frenzy	1964	—
—Unreleased			
❑ 66045	Mashi/On the Rocks	1964	15.00
UNITED ARTISTS			
❑ 50026	Tears/It's You Alone	1966	10.00
❑ 50065	End of the Summer/ Think Kindly Baby	1966	10.00
❑ 50110	Tears (Don't Have to Fall)/ You Won't Lead Me On	1967	10.00
VIVA			
❑ 614	I'm Determined/I Don't Want to Follow You	1967	20.00
7-Inch Extended Plays			
NORTON			
❑ EP-085	Scotch on the Rocks/Snake Pit// Dirty Robber/High Wall	1999	2.00
❑ EP-085 [PS]	Scotch on the Rocks/Snake Pit// Dirty Robber/High Wall	1999	2.00
—Custom yellow sleeve with center hole			
Albums			
BELL			
❑ 6016	Walk Thru the People	1969	30.00
ETIQUETTE			
❑ ALB-01 [M]	The Fabulous Wailers at the Castle	196?	100.00
❑ ALB-022 [M]	The Wailers and Company	196?	80.00
❑ ALB-023 [M]	Wailers, Wailers, Everywhere	196?	100.00
❑ ALB-026 [M]	Out of Our Tree	1966	100.00
❑ 22296/7 [(2)]	The Wailers and Their Greatest Hits	1979	25.00
GOLDEN CREST			
❑ CR-3075 [M]	Fabulous Wailers	1959	250.00
—Full-color photo on cover			
❑ CR-3075 [M]	Fabulous Wailers	196?	50.00
—Title, no photo, on cover			
❑ CR-3075 [M]	Fabulous Wailers	1962	100.00
—Black and white photo on cover			
IMPERIAL			
❑ LP-9262 [M]	Tall Cool One	1964	50.00
❑ LP-12262 [S]	Tall Cool One	1964	80.00
UNITED ARTISTS			
❑ UAL-3557 [M]	Outburst!	1966	50.00
❑ UAS-6557 [S]	Outburst!	1966	80.00
WAILERS, THE (2)			
45s			
COLUMBIA			
❑ 40288	Hot Love/Stop the Clock	1954	120.00
WAINWRIGHT, LOUDON, III			
45s			
ARISTA			
❑ 0174	Bicentennial/ Talking Big Apple '75	1976	5.00
❑ 0340	Final Exam/(B-side unknown)	1978	5.00
COLUMBIA			
❑ 45726	Dead Skunk/Needless to Say	1972	8.00
—Gray label			
❑ 45726	Dead Skunk/Needless to Say	1973	6.00
—Orange label			
❑ 45849	New Paint/Say That You Love Me	1973	5.00
❑ 45949	Down Drinking at the Bar/ I Am the Way	1973	5.00
❑ 46064	Swimming Song/ Bell Bottom Pants	1974	5.00
Albums			
ARISTA			
❑ AL 4063	T Shirt	1976	12.00

Except when noted otherwise, VG = 25% of NM, and VG+ = 50% of NM. (Example: VG = $2.00, VG+ = $4.00 and NM = $8.00.)

Number	Title (A Side/B Side)	Yr	NM
❑ AB 4173	Final Exam	1978	12.00

ATLANTIC

Number	Title (A Side/B Side)	Yr	NM
❑ SD 8260	Loudon Wainwright III	1970	20.00
❑ SD 8291	Album II	1971	20.00

COLUMBIA

Number	Title (A Side/B Side)	Yr	NM
❑ KC 31462	Album III	1972	15.00
❑ PC 31462	Album III	198?	8.00
—Budget-line reissue			
❑ KC 32710	Attempted Mustache	1973	15.00
❑ PC 32710	Attempted Mustache	198?	8.00
—Budget-line reissue			
❑ PC 33369	Unrequited	1975	12.00
—No bar code on cover			
❑ PC 33369	Unrequited	198?	8.00
—Budget-line reissue with bar code			

ROUNDER

Number	Title (A Side/B Side)	Yr	NM
❑ 3050	A Live One	1979	12.00
❑ 3076	Fame and Wealth	1983	12.00
❑ 3096	I'm Alright	1986	10.00
❑ 3106	More Love Songs	1987	10.00

SILVERTONE

Number	Title (A Side/B Side)	Yr	NM
❑ 1203-1-J	Therapy	1989	12.00

WAITE, GENEVIEVE

Albums

PARAMOUR

Number	Title (A Side/B Side)	Yr	NM
❑ 5088	Romance Is on the Rise	1974	25.00

WAITRESSES, THE

12-Inch Singles

POLYDOR

Number	Title (A Side/B Side)	Yr	NM
❑ PRO 179 [DJ]	I Know What Boys Like/No Guilt	1982	8.00
❑ PRO 196 [DJ]	Bread and Butter (Remix)/ Bread and Butter (Dub)	1983	7.00
❑ 203 [DJ]	Bruiseology/Make the Weather	1983	7.00

45s

ANTILLES

Number	Title (A Side/B Side)	Yr	NM
❑ ANS-105	I Know What Boys Like/No Guilt	1980	5.00
—Small center hole			
❑ ANS-105 [PS]	I Know What Boys Like/No Guilt	1980	5.00
❑ ANS-4504	I Know What Boys Like/No Guilt	1980	5.00

COLLECTABLES

Number	Title (A Side/B Side)	Yr	NM
❑ 4949	Christmas Wrapping/ I Know What Boys Like	1994	3.00
—First U.S. stock 45 release			

POLYDOR

Number	Title (A Side/B Side)	Yr	NM
❑ PRO 193 [DJ]	Christmas Wrapping (same on both sides)	1981	10.00
❑ 2196	I Know What Boys Like/ It's My Car	1982	4.00
❑ 2214	No Guilt/Go On	1982	4.00
❑ 2225	Square Pegs/The Smartest Person I Know	1982	4.00
❑ 813394-7	Pleasure/Make the Weather	1983	4.00

ZE

Number	Title (A Side/B Side)	Yr	NM
❑ WIP 6763	Christmas Wrapping/ Christmas Fever	1981	20.00
—B-side by Charlelie Couture; U.K. import			
❑ WIP 6821	Christmas Wrapping/Hangover 1-1-83	1982	10.00
—U.K. pressing with punch-out center intact			
❑ WIP 6821 [PS]	Christmas Wrapping/Hangover 1-1-83	1982	10.00

Albums

POLYDOR

Number	Title (A Side/B Side)	Yr	NM
❑ PX-1-507 [EP]	I Could Rule the World If I Could Only Get the Parts	1982	10.00
❑ PD-1-6346	Wasn't Tomorrow Wonderful?	1982	10.00
❑ 810980-1	Bruiseology	1983	10.00
❑ 810980-1 [DJ]	Bruiseology	1983	25.00
—Promo only on purpleish vinyl			

WAITS, TOM

12-Inch Singles

ISLAND

Number	Title (A Side/B Side)	Yr	NM
❑ 96750	Hang On St. Christopher (Extended Remix)/ (Instrumental)	1987	15.00

45s

ASYLUM

Number	Title (A Side/B Side)	Yr	NM
❑ 11014	Ol' 55/(B-side unknown)	1973	6.00
❑ 45213	San Diego Serenade/ Diamonds on My Windshield	1974	5.00
❑ 45233	New Coat of Paint/Blue Skies	1975	5.00
❑ 45371	Step Right Up/The Piano Has Been Drinking	1976	5.00
❑ 45539	Red Shoes by the Drugstore/ Somewhere	1978	5.00
❑ 47077	Jersey Girl/Heartattack and Vine	1980	8.00

Albums

ASYLUM

Number	Title (A Side/B Side)	Yr	NM
❑ 6E-162	Blue Valentine	1978	10.00
❑ 6E-295	Heartattack and Vine	1980	10.00
❑ 7E-1015	The Heart of Saturday Night	1974	12.00
—Original "clouds" label, no Warner Communications logo			
❑ 7E-1015	The Heart of Saturday Night	1984	8.00
—Reissue with black and yellow label			
❑ 7E-1078	Small Change	1976	10.00
❑ 7E-1117	Foreign Affairs	1977	10.00
❑ 7E-2008 [(2)]	Nighthawks at the Diner	1975	12.00
❑ SD 5061	Closing Time	1973	12.00

Rick Wakeman, *The Myths and Legends of King Arthur and the Knights of the Round Table*, A&M SP-4515, 1975, **$12.**

ELEKTRA

Number	Title (A Side/B Side)	Yr	NM
❑ 60416	Anthology of Tom Waits	1985	10.00

EPITAPH

Number	Title (A Side/B Side)	Yr	NM
❑ 86547	Mule Variations	1999	12.00

ISLAND

Number	Title (A Side/B Side)	Yr	NM
❑ 90095	Swordfishtrombones	1983	12.00
❑ 90299	Rain Dogs	1985	10.00
❑ 90572	Franks Wild Years	1987	10.00
❑ 90987	Big Time	1988	10.00
❑ 424691	Swordfishtrombones	2009	20.00

WAKEFIELD SUN

45s

MGM

Number	Title (A Side/B Side)	Yr	NM
❑ 14028	When I See You/Get Out	1969	20.00
❑ 14072	Tryst on Love/ Sing a Simple Song	1969	30.00

Albums

MGM

Number	Title (A Side/B Side)	Yr	NM
❑ SE-4626	Wakefield Sun	1969	25.00

WAKEMAN, RICK Also see YES.

45s

A&M

Number	Title (A Side/B Side)	Yr	NM
❑ 1430	Catherine/Anne	1973	6.00
❑ 1627	The Journey/The Return	1974	5.00
❑ 1635	The Battle/And Now a Word from Our Sponsor	1974	5.00
❑ 1708	Merlin the Magician/Sir Galahad	1975	5.00
❑ 1937	White Rock/After the Ball	1977	5.00
❑ 2010	The Birdman of Alcatraz/And Now a Word from Our Sponsor	1978	8.00

Albums

A&M

Number	Title (A Side/B Side)	Yr	NM
❑ SP-3156	Journey to the Centre of the Earth	198?	8.00
—Budget-line reissue of 3621			
❑ SP-3229	The Six Wives of Henry VIII	1984	8.00
—Budget-line reissue of 4361			
❑ SP-3230	The Myths and Legends of King Arthur and the Knights of the Round Table	1984	8.00
—Budget-line reissue of 4515			
❑ SP-3621	Journey to the Centre of the Earth	1974	12.00
❑ SP-4361	The Six Wives of Henry VIII	1973	12.00
—Originals have brown labels			
❑ SP-4361	The Six Wives of Henry VIII	1974	10.00
—Silver label with "fading" A&M logo			
❑ SP-4515	The Myths and Legends of King Arthur and the Knights of the Round Table	1975	12.00
❑ SP-4583	No Earthly Connection	1976	12.00
❑ SP-4614	White Rock	1977	12.00
❑ SP-4660	Rick Wakeman's Criminal Record	1977	12.00
❑ SP-6501 [(2)]	Rhapsodies	1979	15.00
❑ QU-53621 [Q]	Journey to the Centre of the Earth	1974	25.00
❑ QU-54361 [Q]	The Six Wives of Henry VIII	1974	25.00
❑ QU-54515 [Q]	The Myths and Legends of King Arthur and the Knights of the Round Table	1975	25.00

MOBILE FIDELITY

Number	Title (A Side/B Side)	Yr	NM
❑ 1-230	Journey to the Centre of the Earth	1995	20.00
—Audiophile vinyl			

SWEET THUNDER

Number	Title (A Side/B Side)	Yr	NM
❑ 1	Journey to the Centre of the Earth	1981	50.00
—Audiophile vinyl			

VARESE SARABANDE

Number	Title (A Side/B Side)	Yr	NM
❑ STV-81162	The Burning (Soundtrack)	1982	20.00

W

Number	Title (A Side/B Side)	Yr	NM
WALCOS, THE			
45s			
DRUM			
❑ 011	Tell Me Why/Moonlight Rock	1959	100.00
WALES, HOWARD, AND JERRY GARCIA Also see JERRY GARCIA.			
45s			
DOUGLAS 7			
❑ ZS7 6501	South Side Strut/Uncle Martin's	1971	15.00
Albums			
DOUGLAS			
❑ Z 30589	Hooteroll	1971	40.00
WALKER, DAVID T.			
45s			
ODE			
❑ 66025	Hot Fun in the Summertime/I Want to Talk to You	1972	5.00
❑ 66037	Press On/Brother, Brother	1973	5.00
❑ 66042	I Got Work to Do/The Real T.	1974	5.00
❑ 66045	Loving You Is Sweeter Than Ever/Didn't I Blow Your Mind This Time	1974	5.00
❑ 66125	I Wish You Love/Oh Love	1976	5.00
REVUE			
❑ 11032	Reach Out for Me/Sidewalk	1969	10.00
❑ 11060	My Baby Loves Me/Can I Change My Mind	1969	6.00
❑ 11070	Watch Out Dynamite/Baby I Need Your Loving	1970	6.00
ZEA			
❑ 50005	Love Vibrations/(B-side unknown)	1970	5.00
Albums			
ODE			
❑ SP-77011	David T. Walker	1971	10.00
❑ SP-77020	Press On	1974	10.00
❑ SP-77035	On Love	1976	10.00
ZEA			
❑ 1000	Plum Happy	1970	15.00
WALKER, JERRY JEFF			
45s			
ATCO			
❑ 6594	Mr. Bojangles/Round and Round	1968	10.00
❑ 6767	I'm Gonna Tell on You/But For the Time	1970	6.00
ELEKTRA			
❑ 46016	Comfort and Crazy/Eastern Ave. River Railway Blues	1979	4.00
MCA			
❑ 40054	L.A. Freeway/Charlie Dunn	1973	4.00
❑ 40167	Desperadoes Waitin' for a Train/Gettin' By	1973	4.00
❑ 40250	Sangria Wine/Hill Country Rain	1974	4.00
❑ 40389	Goodbye Easy Street/Salvation Army Band	1975	4.00
❑ 40487	Jaded Lover/I Love You	1975	4.00
❑ 40570	Dear John Letter Lounge/It's a Good Night for Singing	1976	4.00
❑ 40622	(Looking for the) Heart of Saturday Night/Stoney	1976	4.00
❑ 40760	Mr. Bojangles/Don't It Make You Wanna Dance	1977	4.00
❑ 40822	Ro-Deo-Deo Cowboy/Leavin' Texas	1977	4.00
SOUTH COAST			
❑ 51146	Got Lucky Last Night/Maybe Mexico	1981	4.00
❑ 51215	Take It As It Comes/She Knows Her Daddy Sings	1981	4.00
❑ 52122	Don't Think Twice, It's Alright/Laying My Life on the Line	1982	4.00
TRIED & TRUE			
❑ 1690	I Feel Like Hank Williams Tonight/Mr. Bojangles	1989	5.00
❑ 1695	The Pickup Truck Song/The Pickup Truck Song (Long Version)	1989	5.00
❑ 1698	Trashy Women/I Feel Like Hank Williams Tonight	1989	5.00
Albums			
ATCO			
❑ SD 33-259	Mr. Bojangles	1968	25.00
❑ SD 33-297	Five Years Gone	1969	30.00
❑ SD 33-336	Bein' Free	1970	20.00
BAINBRIDGE			
❑ 6222	Mr. Bojangles	198?	10.00
DECCA			
❑ DL 75384	Jerry Jeff Walker	1972	15.00
ELEKTRA			
❑ 6E-163	Jerry Jeff	1978	10.00
❑ 6E-239	Too Old to Change	1980	10.00
MCA			
❑ 382	Viva Terlingua!	1973	10.00
❑ 450	Walker's Collectibles	1974	10.00
❑ 510	Jerry Jeff Walker	1975	10.00
—Reissue of Decca LP			
❑ 2156	Ridin' High	1975	10.00
❑ 2202	It's a Good Night for Singin'	1976	10.00
❑ 2350	Viva Terlingua!	1977	8.00
—Reissue of MCA 382			
❑ 2355	Walker's Collectibles	1977	8.00
—Reissue of MCA 450			
❑ 2358	Jerry Jeff Walker	1977	8.00
—Reissue of MCA 510			
❑ 3041	Contrary to Ordinary	1978	10.00
❑ 5128	The Best of Jerry Jeff Walker	1980	10.00
❑ 5355	Cowjazz	1983	10.00
❑ 6003 [(2)]	A Man Must Carry On	198?	10.00
—Budget-line reissue			
❑ 8013 [(2)]	A Man Must Carry On	1977	12.00
❑ 27026	It's a Good Night for Singin'	198?	8.00
—Budget-line reissue			
❑ 27027	Walker's Collectibles	198?	6.00
—Budget-line reissue			
❑ 37004	Jerry Jeff Walker	198?	6.00
—Budget-line reissue			
❑ 37005	Viva Terlingua!	198?	6.00
—Budget-line reissue			
❑ 37006	Ridin' High	198?	8.00
—Budget-line reissue			
❑ 37162	Contrary to Ordinary	198?	8.00
—Budget-line reissue			
SOUTHCOAST			
❑ 5199	Reunion	1981	10.00
VANGUARD			
❑ VSD-6521	Driftin' Way of Life	1969	20.00
❑ VMS-73124	Driftin' Way of Life	1985	8.00
—Reissue of 6521			
WALKER, JIMMIE			
Albums			
BUDDAH			
❑ BDS 5635	Dyn-O-Mite	1975	10.00
WALKER, JR., AND THE ALL STARS			
45s			
HARVEY			
❑ 113	Willie's Blues/Twist Lackawanna	1962	25.00
❑ 117	Cleo's Mood/Brain Washer	1963	20.00
❑ 119	Good Rockin'/Brain Washer	1963	20.00
MOTOWN			
❑ 1352	Country Boy/What Does It Take (To Win Your Love)	1975	5.00
❑ 1380	I'm So Glad/Hot Shot	1976	—
—Unreleased			
❑ 1689	Blow the House Down/Ball Baby	1983	4.00
SOUL			
❑ 35003	Monkey Jump/Satan's Blues	1964	15.00
❑ 35008	Shotgun/Hot Cha	1965	15.00
❑ 35008	Shot Gun/Hot Cha	1965	100.00
—Not only is the A-side title listed as two words, but the record is credited to "Jr. Walker and All The Stars"!			
❑ 35008 [PS]	Shotgun/Hot Cha	1965	25.00
❑ 35012	Do the Boomerang/Tune Up	1965	10.00
❑ 35013	Shake and Fingerpop/Cleo's Back	1965	10.00
❑ 35015	(I'm a) Road Runner/Shoot Your Shot	1965	10.00
❑ 35017	Cleo's Mood/Baby You Know It Ain't Right	1966	8.00
❑ 35024	How Sweet It Is (To Be Loved By You)/Nothing But Soul	1966	8.00
❑ 35024 [PS]	How Sweet It Is (To Be Loved By You)/Nothing But Soul	1966	20.00
❑ 35026	Money (That's What I Want) Part I/Money (That's What I Want) Part II	1966	8.00
❑ 35030	Pucker Up Buttercup/Anyway You Wanna	1967	8.00
❑ 35036	Shoot Your Shot/Ain't That the Truth	1967	8.00
❑ 35041	Come See About Me/Sweet Soul	1967	8.00
❑ 35048	Hip City — Part 1/Hip City — Part 2	1968	8.00
❑ 35055	Home Cookin'/Mutiny	1969	8.00
❑ 35062	What Does It Take (To Win Your Love)/Brainwasher — Part 1	1969	8.00
❑ 35067	These Eyes/Got to Find a Way to Win Maria Back	1969	6.00
❑ 35070	Gotta Hold On to This Feeling/Clinging to the Theory That She's Coming Back	1970	6.00
❑ 35073	Do You See My Love (For You Growing)/Groove and More	1970	6.00
❑ 35081	Holly Holy/Carry Your Own Load	1970	6.00
❑ 35084	Take Me Girl, I'm Ready/Right On Brothers and Sisters	1971	6.00
❑ 35090	Way Back Home/(Instrumental)	1971	6.00
❑ 35095	Walk in the Night/I Don't Want to Do Wrong	1972	6.00
❑ 35097	Groove Thang/Me and My Family	1972	6.00
❑ 35104	Gimme That Beat (Part 1)/Gimme That Beat (Part 2)	1973	6.00
❑ 35106	I Don't Need No Reason/Country Boy	1973	6.00
❑ 35108	Peace and Understanding (Is Hard to Find)/Soul Clappin'	1973	6.00
❑ 35110	Dancing Like They Do on Soul Train/I Ain't That Easy to Love	1973	6.00
❑ 35114 [DJ]	You Are the Sunshine of My Life/Until You Come Back to Me	1974	—
—Unreleased			
❑ 35116	I'm So Glad/Soul Clappin'	1975	5.00
❑ 35118	Hot Shot/You're No Ordinary Woman	1976	5.00
❑ 35122	Whopper Bopper Show Stopper/Hard Love	1977	5.00
WHITFIELD			
❑ 8861	Back Street Boogie/Don't Let Me Go Away	1979	4.00
❑ 49052	Wishing on a Star/Hole in the Wall	1979	4.00
Albums			
MOTOWN			
❑ M5-105V1	Motown Superstar Series, Vol. 5	1981	10.00
❑ M5-141V1	Shotgun	1981	10.00
—Reissue of Soul 701			
❑ M5-208V1	Greatest Hits	1981	10.00
—Reissue of Soul 718			
❑ M7-786 [(2)]	Anthology	1974	20.00
❑ 5297 ML	All the Great Hits of Jr. Walker and the All Stars	1984	10.00
❑ 6053 ML	Blow the House Down	1983	10.00
PICKWICK			
❑ SPC-3391	Shotgun	197?	12.00
SOUL			
❑ 701 [M]	Shotgun	1965	20.00
—Purple swirl label with "Soul" at top			
❑ 701 [M]	Shotgun	1965	60.00
—Mostly white label with vertical "Soul" at left			
❑ SS-701 [S]	Shotgun	1965	30.00
❑ 702 [M]	Soul Session	1966	20.00
—Purple swirl label with "Soul" at top			
❑ 702 [M]	Soul Session	1966	60.00
—Mostly white label with vertical "Soul" at left			
❑ SS-702 [S]	Soul Session	1966	30.00
❑ 703 [M]	Road Runner	1966	20.00
❑ SS-703 [S]	Road Runner	1966	30.00
❑ 705 [M]	"Live"	1967	20.00
❑ SS-705 [S]	"Live"	1967	30.00
❑ SS-710	Home Cookin'	1969	20.00
❑ SS-718	Greatest Hits	1969	20.00
❑ SS-721	Gotta Hold on to This Feeling	1969	25.00
❑ SS-721	What Does It Take to Win Your Love	1970	20.00
—Retitled version of above			
❑ SS-726	A Gassssss	1970	15.00
❑ S-732L	Rainbow Funk	1971	15.00
❑ SS-733	Moody Jr.	1971	15.00
❑ SS-738	Peace and Understanding Is Hard to Find	1973	15.00
❑ S6-742	Jr. Walker and the All Stars	1973	—
—Canceled			
❑ S6-745	Hot Shot	1976	15.00
❑ S6-747	Sax Appeal	1976	15.00
❑ S6-748	Whopper Bopper Show Stopper	1977	15.00
❑ S7-750	Smooth	1978	15.00
WHITFIELD			
❑ WHK 3331	Back Street Boogie	1980	12.00
WALKER, STEVE, AND THE BOLD See BOLD.			
WALKER, T-BONE			
45s			
ATLANTIC			
❑ 1045	Papa Ain't Salty/T-Bone Shuffle	1955	50.00
❑ 1074	Why Not/Play On Little Girl	1955	40.00
BLUESWAY			
❑ 61008	Confusion Blues/Every Night I Have to Cry	1967	8.00
CAPITOL			
❑ F799	Go Back to the One You Love/On Your Way Blues	1950	150.00

Number	Title (A Side/B Side)	Yr	NM
❑ F944	Too Much Trouble Blues/She's My Old Time Used to Be	1950	150.00

IMPERIAL

Number	Title (A Side/B Side)	Yr	NM
❑ 5202	Street Walkin' Woman/The Blues Is a Woman	1952	400.00

—Note: T-Bone Walker records on Imperial before 5202 are unconfirmed on 45 rpm.

Number	Title (A Side/B Side)	Yr	NM
❑ 5216	Blue Mood/Got No Use for You	1953	200.00
❑ 5228	Railroad Station Blues/Long Distance Blues	1953	200.00
❑ 5239	Party Girl/You're Here in the Dark	1953	300.00
❑ 5247	Everytime/Tell Me What's the Reason	1953	150.00
❑ 5261	I'm About to Lose My Mind/I Miss You Baby	1954	100.00
❑ 5264	Pony Tail/When the Sun Goes Down	1954	80.00
❑ 5274	Vida Lee/My Baby Is Now on My Mind	1954	80.00
❑ 5284	Bye Bye Baby/Wanderin' Heart	1954	80.00
❑ 5299	Teenage Baby/Strugglin' Blues	1954	80.00
❑ 5311	Love Is Just a Gamble/High Society	1954	80.00
❑ 5330	I'll Understand/The Hard Way	1955	50.00
❑ 5384	You Don't Understand/Say! Pretty Baby	1956	50.00
❑ 5695	Travelin' Blues/Strollin' with Bones	1960	15.00
❑ 5832	Evil Hearted Woman/Life Is Too Short	1962	15.00
❑ 5962	Doin' Time/Cold, Cold Water	1963	12.00

JETSTREAM

Number	Title (A Side/B Side)	Yr	NM
❑ 726	Reconsider Baby/I'm Not Your Fool Anymore	1966	10.00
❑ 730	T-Bone's Back/She's a Hit	1967	10.00

MODERN

Number	Title (A Side/B Side)	Yr	NM
❑ 1004	Should I Let Her Go/Hey Hey Baby	1965	10.00

POST

Number	Title (A Side/B Side)	Yr	NM
❑ 2002	I Get So Weary/Tell Me What's the Reason	1955	60.00

7-Inch Extended Plays

CAPITOL

Number	Title (A Side/B Side)	Yr	NM
❑ EAP 1-370	(contents unknown)	1953	200.00
❑ EAP 1-370 [PS]	Classics in Jazz	1953	200.00

Albums

ATLANTIC

Number	Title (A Side/B Side)	Yr	NM
❑ 8020 [M]	T-Bone Blues	1959	220.00
—Black label			
❑ 8020 [M]	T-Bone Blues	1960	70.00
—Red and purple label			
❑ SD 8256	T-Bone Blues	1970	20.00

BLUE NOTE

Number	Title (A Side/B Side)	Yr	NM
❑ BN-LA533-H2 [(2)]	Classics	1975	20.00

BLUESTIME

Number	Title (A Side/B Side)	Yr	NM
❑ 29004	Everyday I Have the Blues	1968	30.00
❑ 29010	Blue Rocks	1969	30.00

BLUESWAY

Number	Title (A Side/B Side)	Yr	NM
❑ BLS-6008	Stormy Monday Blues	1968	30.00
—Reissue of Wet Soul LP?			
❑ BLS-6014	Funky Town	1968	30.00
❑ BLS-6058	Dirty Mistreater	1973	15.00

BRUNSWICK

Number	Title (A Side/B Side)	Yr	NM
❑ BL 754126	The Truth	1968	30.00

CAPITOL

Number	Title (A Side/B Side)	Yr	NM
❑ H 370 [10]	Classics in Jazz	1953	1000.
❑ T 370 [M]	Classics in Jazz	1953	300.00
❑ T 1958 [M]	Great Blues Vocal and Guitar	1963	150.00

—Black "The Star Line" label (existence of black colorband label not confirmed)

DELMARK

Number	Title (A Side/B Side)	Yr	NM
❑ D-633 [M]	I Want a Little Girl	1967	40.00
❑ DS-633 [S]	I Want a Little Girl	1967	50.00

IMPERIAL

Number	Title (A Side/B Side)	Yr	NM
❑ LP-9098 [M]	T-Bone Walker Sings the Blues	1959	300.00
❑ LP-9116 [M]	Singing the Blues	1960	250.00
❑ LP-9146 [M]	I Get So Weary	1961	300.00

MOSAIC

Number	Title (A Side/B Side)	Yr	NM
❑ MR9-130 [(9)]	The Complete Recordings of T-Bone Walker 1940-1954	199?	300.00
—Limited edition of 7,500			

POLYDOR

Number	Title (A Side/B Side)	Yr	NM
❑ 24-4502	Good Feelin'	1972	15.00
❑ PD-5521	Fly Walker Airlines	1973	15.00

REPRISE

Number	Title (A Side/B Side)	Yr	NM
❑ 2RS 6483 [(2)]	Very Rare	1973	20.00

WET SOUL

Number	Title (A Side/B Side)	Yr	NM
❑ 1002	Stormy Monday Blues	1967	50.00

WALKER, WAYNE

45s

ABC-PARAMOUNT

Number	Title (A Side/B Side)	Yr	NM
❑ 9735	It's My Way/All I Can Do Is Cry	1956	60.00

BRUNSWICK

Number	Title (A Side/B Side)	Yr	NM
❑ 55133	Little Ole You/What Kind of God Do You Think You Are	1959	40.00

COLUMBIA

Number	Title (A Side/B Side)	Yr	NM
❑ 40905	A Teenage Love Affair/Whatever You Desire	1957	25.00
❑ 40979	Just a-Walkin' Around/Sands of Gold	1957	25.00
❑ 41042	Bo-Bo Sha Diddle Diddle/Come Away from His Arms	1957	25.00
❑ 41130	I'm Finally Free/It's Written in Your Arms	1958	25.00

CORAL

Number	Title (A Side/B Side)	Yr	NM
❑ 62328	Battle of the Bulge/Reaching for the Impossible	1962	15.00

EVEREST

Number	Title (A Side/B Side)	Yr	NM
❑ 19380	Love, Love, Love/Sweet Chains of Love	1960	15.00

WALKER BROTHERS, THE

Also see SCOTT ENGEL.

45s

KAY-Y

Number	Title (A Side/B Side)	Yr	NM
❑ 66785	Beautiful Brown Eyes/Ninety-Seven	1960	50.00

SMASH

Number	Title (A Side/B Side)	Yr	NM
❑ 1952	Doin' the Jerk/Pretty Girls Everywhere	1964	12.00
❑ 1976	Love Her/Seventh Dawn	1965	12.00
❑ 2000	Make It Easy on Yourself/But I Do	1965	15.00
❑ 2009	Make It Easy on Yourself/Doin' the Jerk	1965	12.00
❑ 2009 [PS]	Make It Easy on Yourself/Doin' the Jerk	1965	20.00
❑ 2016	My Ship Is Comin' In/You're All Around Me	1966	12.00
❑ 2016 [PS]	My Ship Is Comin' In/You're All Around Me	1966	20.00
❑ 2032	The Sun Ain't Gonna Shine (Anymore)/After the Lights Go Out	1966	12.00
❑ 2048	(Baby) You Don't Have to Tell Me/Young Man Cried	1966	12.00
❑ 2063	Another Tear Falls/Saddest Night in the World	1966	12.00

TOWER

Number	Title (A Side/B Side)	Yr	NM
❑ 218	I Only Came to Dance with You/Greens	1966	12.00

Albums

SMASH

Number	Title (A Side/B Side)	Yr	NM
❑ MGS-27076 [M]	Introducing the Walker Brothers	1965	50.00
❑ MGS-27082 [M]	The Sun Ain't Gonna Shine (Anymore)	1966	40.00
❑ SRS-67076 [R]	Introducing the Walker Brothers	1965	40.00
❑ SRS-67082 [P]	The Sun Ain't Gonna Shine (Anymore)	1966	50.00

—"The Sun Ain't Gonna Shine (Anymore)" and "When the Lights Go Out" are rechanneled.

TOWER

Number	Title (A Side/B Side)	Yr	NM
❑ ST 5026 [S]	I Only Came to Dance with You	1966	20.00
—As "Scott Engel and John Stewart"			
❑ T 5026 [M]	I Only Came to Dance with You	1966	15.00
—As "Scott Engel and John Stewart"			

WALLACE, BILLY

45s

DEB

Number	Title (A Side/B Side)	Yr	NM
❑ 883	Wolf Call/(B-side unknown)	1957	150.00
❑ 1003	Don't Flirt with My Baby/You'll Never Cheat Me Anymore	1958	150.00

MERCURY

Number	Title (A Side/B Side)	Yr	NM
❑ 70876	What'll I Do/That's My Reward	1956	200.00
❑ 70957	Mean Mistrteating Baby/Burning the Wind	1956	300.00

WALLACE, JIMMY

45s

ALPHA

Number	Title (A Side/B Side)	Yr	NM
❑ 006	I'll Be Back/(B-side unknown)	196?	1000.

WALLACE, SONNY

45s

YUCCA

Number	Title (A Side/B Side)	Yr	NM
❑ 127	Black Cadillac/If a Man Could See	1961	100.00

WALLER, GORDON

Also see PETER AND GORDON.

45s

BELL

Number	Title (A Side/B Side)	Yr	NM
❑ 794	The Lady in the Window/I Was a Boy When You Needed a Man	1969	8.00
❑ 882	Sunshine/You Gonna Hurt Yourself	1970	6.00

CAPITOL

Number	Title (A Side/B Side)	Yr	NM
❑ 2346	Everyday/Because of a Woman	1968	8.00
❑ 5886	Speak for Me/Little Nonie	1967	8.00

Albums

ABC

Number	Title (A Side/B Side)	Yr	NM
❑ X-749	And Gordon	1972	15.00

WALLS, TOM

45s

HIT

Number	Title (A Side/B Side)	Yr	NM
❑ 10	Funny Way of Laughin'/PT 109	1962	8.00
—B-side by Johnny Keaton			
❑ 20	Speedy Gonzales/The Stripper	1962	8.00
—B-side by the Music City Orchestra			

WALLS, VAN

45s

ATLANTIC

Number	Title (A Side/B Side)	Yr	NM
❑ 980	After Midnight/Blue Sender	1952	100.00

WALSH, JOE

Also see EAGLES; THE JAMES GANG (1).

12-Inch Singles

ABC

Number	Title (A Side/B Side)	Yr	NM
❑ SPDJ-46 [DJ]	Turn to Stone (same on both sides)	1978	20.00

FULL MOON

Number	Title (A Side/B Side)	Yr	NM
❑ PRO-A-2038 [DJ]	Space Age Whiz Kids (same on both sides)	1983	6.00

WARNER BROS.

Number	Title (A Side/B Side)	Yr	NM
❑ PRO-A-2340 [DJ]	Good Man Down (same on both sides)	1985	5.00
❑ PRO-A-2756 [DJ]	Radio Song (same on both sides)	1985	5.00
❑ PRO-A-2833 [DJ]	Malibu (same on both sides)	1985	5.00

45s

ABC

Number	Title (A Side/B Side)	Yr	NM
❑ 12115	Time Out/Help Me Through the Night	1975	5.00
❑ 12187	Walk Away/Help Me Through the Night	1976	5.00
❑ 12426	Rocky Mountain Way/Turn to Stone	1978	4.00

ABC DUNHILL

Number	Title (A Side/B Side)	Yr	NM
❑ 4327	I'll Tell the World About You/Mother Says	1972	5.00
❑ 4361	Rocky Mountain Way/Prayer	1973	5.00
❑ 4373	Meadows/Bookends	1973	5.00
❑ 15026	Turn to Stone/All Night Laundromat Blues	1974	5.00

ASYLUM

Number	Title (A Side/B Side)	Yr	NM
❑ 45493	Life's Been Good/Theme from Boat Weirdos	1978	4.00
❑ 45536	At the Station/Over and Over	1978	4.00
❑ 47144	A Life of Illusion/Rockets	1981	4.00
❑ 47197	Made Your Mind Up/Things	1981	4.00

EPIC

Number	Title (A Side/B Side)	Yr	NM
❑ 73843	Ordinary Average Guy/Alphabetical Order	1991	3.00

FULL MOON

Number	Title (A Side/B Side)	Yr	NM
❑ 69951	Waffle Stomp/Things	1982	4.00
❑ 69951 [PS]	Waffle Stomp/Things	1982	4.00

FULL MOON/ASYLUM

Number	Title (A Side/B Side)	Yr	NM
❑ 46639	All Night Long/Orange Blossom Special	1980	4.00
—B-side by Gilley's Urban Cowboy Band			
❑ 46639 [PS]	All Night Long/Orange Blossom Special	1980	5.00

WARNER BROS.

Number	Title (A Side/B Side)	Yr	NM
❑ 28225	In My Car/How Ya Doin'?	1987	3.00
❑ 28304	The Radio Song/How Ya Doin'?	1987	3.00
❑ 28304 [PS]	The Radio Song/How Ya Doin'?	1987	3.00
❑ 28910	Good Man Down/I Broke My Leg	1985	4.00
❑ 29454	I.L.B.T.'s/Love Letters	1983	4.00
❑ 29519	Here We Are Now/I Can Play That Rock and Roll	1983	4.00
❑ 29611	Space Age Whiz Kids/Theme from Island Weirdos	1983	4.00
❑ 29611 [PS]	Space Age Whiz Kids/Theme from Island Weirdos	1983	5.00

Joe Walsh, *But Seriously, Folks...*, Asylum 6E-141, 1978, **$10.**

Number	Title (A Side/B Side)	Yr	NM
Albums			
ABC			
❑ ABCD-932	You Can't Argue with a Sick Mind	1976	10.00
❑ AA-1083	The Best of Joe Walsh	1978	10.00
—Also contains two James Gang tracks			
ABC COMMAND			
❑ QD-40016 [Q]	The Smoker You Drink, the Player You Get	1974	20.00
❑ QD-40017 [Q]	So What	1975	—
—Not released			
ABC DUNHILL			
❑ DS-50130	Barnstorm	1972	10.00
—Of the James Gang and the Eagles			
❑ DS-50140	The Smoker You Drink, the Player You Get	1973	10.00
❑ DS-51071	So What	1974	10.00
ASYLUM			
❑ 6E-141	But Seriously, Folks...	1978	10.00
❑ 5E-523	There Goes the Neighborhood	1981	8.00
MCA			
❑ 37051	You Can't Argue with a Sick Mind	1979	8.00
—Reissue of ABC 932			
❑ 37052	The Best of Joe Walsh	1979	8.00
—Reissue of ABC 1083			
❑ 37053	Barnstorm	1979	8.00
—Reissue of ABC Dunhill 50130			
❑ 37054	The Smoker You Drink, the Player You Get	1979	8.00
—Reissue of ABC Dunhill 50140			
❑ 37055	So What	1979	8.00
—Reissue of ABC Dunhill 50171			
WARNER BROS.			
❑ 23884	You Bought It — You Name It	1983	8.00
❑ 25281	The Confessor	1985	8.00
❑ 25281 [DJ]	The Confessor	1985	15.00
—Promo only on Quiex II vinyl			
❑ 25606	Got Any Gum?	1987	8.00

Number	Title (A Side/B Side)	Yr	NM
WALSTON, RAY			
Albums			
VEE JAY			
❑ LP-1110 [M]	My Favorite Songs from "Mary Poppins" and Other Songs to Delight	1965	25.00
❑ SR-1110 [S]	My Favorite Songs from "Mary Poppins" and Other Songs to Delight	1965	30.00
WANDERERS, THE (1)			
45s			
CUB			
❑ 9003	A Teenage Quarrel/ My Shining Hour	1958	30.00
❑ 9019	Collecting Hearts/Two Hearts on a Window Pane	1958	40.00
❑ 9023	Please/Shadrack, Meshack, and Abednego	1959	30.00
❑ 9035	Only When You're Lonely/ I'm Not Ashamed	1959	30.00
❑ 9054	I Walked Through a Forest/I'm Waiting for Green Pastures	1959	30.00
❑ 9075	I Need You More/I Could Make You Mine	1960	30.00
❑ 9089	For Your Love/Sally Goodheart	1961	30.00
❑ 9094	I'll Never Smile Again/ A Little Too Long	1961	30.00
❑ 9099	She Wears My Ring/Somebody Else's Sweetheart	1961	50.00
❑ 9109	There Is No Greater Love/ As Time Goes By	1962	30.00
MGM			
❑ 13082	There Is No Greater Love/ As Time Goes By	1962	20.00
ONYX			
❑ 518	Thinking of You/Great Jumpin' Catfish	1957	60.00

Number	Title (A Side/B Side)	Yr	NM
ORBIT			
❑ 9003	A Teenage Quarrel/ My Shining Hour	1958	60.00
SAVOY			
❑ 1109	We Could Find Happiness/ Holy Mae Ethel	1953	500.00
UNITED ARTISTS			
❑ 570	After He Breaks Your Heart/ Run, Run Senorita	1963	15.00
❑ 648	I'll Know/You Can't Run Away from Me	1963	30.00
WANDERERS, THE (2)			
45s			
PANAMA			
❑ 3900	Quiet Night/One Look	1960	15.00
WANDERERS, THE (U) May be by group (1).			
45s			
GONE			
❑ 5005	Mask Off/My Lady Chocaonine	1957	30.00
WANDERERS THREE, THE			
45s			
DOLTON			
❑ 59	Cry I Do/Toro	1962	12.00
❑ 66	My Glory Land/Turn Around	1962	12.00
❑ 82	Wanderin'/Hi-De-Ink-Tum	1963	10.00
MGM			
❑ K13257	Gimmie Some/Long Time Man	1964	15.00
Albums			
DOLTON			
❑ BLP 2021 [M]	We Sing Folk Songs	1963	20.00
❑ BST 8021 [S]	We Sing Folk Songs	1963	25.00
WANDERLEY, WALTER			
45s			
A&M			
❑ 1023	Surfboard/When It Was Done	1969	6.00
GNP CRESCENDO			
❑ 824	Perpetual Motion Love/Monica	197?	4.00
TOWER			
❑ 296	You and I/What Do You Know About Me	1966	8.00
❑ 334	Brazilian Samba/Murmurio	1967	8.00
VERVE			
❑ 10421	Summer Samba (So Nice)/ Call Me	1966	8.00
❑ 10456	Chaganca/Amanha	1966	8.00
❑ 10539	On the South Side of Chicago/ Minha Saudade	1967	8.00
❑ 10579	Sensuous/Kee-Ka-Roo	1968	8.00
WORLD PACIFIC			
❑ 77861	Jet Samba (Samba Do Aviao)/ Sad Samba (Samba Triste)	1966	8.00
Albums			
A&M			
❑ SP-3018	When It Was Done	1969	12.00
❑ SP-3022	Moondreams	1969	12.00
CANYON			
❑ 7711	Return of the Original Sound	196?	12.00
GNP CRESCENDO			
❑ GNPS-2137	Brazil's Greatest Hits	197?	10.00
❑ GNPS-2142	Perpetual Motion Love	197?	10.00
MGM LATINO SERIES			
❑ LAT 10010 [S]	Cheganca	197?	15.00
—Reissue of Verve V6-8676			
PHILIPS			
❑ PHM 200227 [M]	Brazilian Blend	1967	12.00
❑ PHM 200233 [M]	Organ-ized	1967	12.00
❑ PHS 600227 [S]	Brazilian Blend	1967	15.00
❑ PHS 600233 [S]	Organ-ized	1967	15.00
TOWER			
❑ ST 5047 [S]	From Rio with Love	1966	15.00
❑ T 5047 [M]	From Rio with Love	1966	15.00
❑ ST 5058 [S]	Murmurio	1967	15.00
❑ T 5058 [M]	Murmurio	1967	15.00
VERVE			
❑ V-8658 [M]	Rain Forest	1966	15.00
❑ V6-8658 [S]	Rain Forest	1966	20.00
❑ V-8676 [M]	Cheganca	1966	15.00
❑ V6-8676 [S]	Cheganca	1966	20.00
❑ V-8706 [M]	Batucada	1967	20.00
❑ V6-8706 [S]	Batucada	1967	15.00
❑ V-8739 [M]	Kee-Ka-Roo	1967	20.00
❑ V6-8739 [S]	Kee-Ka-Roo	1967	15.00
WORLD PACIFIC			
❑ WP-1856 [M]	Samba So!	1967	20.00
❑ WP-1866 [M]	Quarteto Bossamba	1967	25.00

Except when noted otherwise, VG = 25% of NM, and VG+ = 50% of NM. (Example: VG = $2.00, VG+ = $4.00 and NM = $8.00.)

Number	Title (A Side/B Side)	Yr	NM
❑ ST-21856 [S]	Samba So!	1967	15.00
❑ ST-21866 [S]	Quarteto Bossamba	1967	15.00

WAR

Also see ERIC BURDON AND WAR.

12-Inch Singles

Number	Title (A Side/B Side)	Yr	NM
AVENUE			
❑ 76028	Da Roof (3 versions)	1994	8.00
LAX			
❑ 02122	Cinco de Mayo (7:29) (3:59)	1981	10.00
PRIORITY			
❑ VL-9364	Low Rider '87 (Extended Version 7:45) (Radio Edit) (Instrumental)	1987	15.00
❑ VL-9502	Livin' in the Red (versions unknown)	1987	12.00
RCA			
❑ PD-13062	You Got the Power/ Cinco de Mayo	1982	10.00
❑ PD-13239	Outlaw/I'm About Somebody	1982	10.00
❑ JD-13323 [DJ]	Just Because (same on both sides)	1982	8.00
❑ PD-13323	Just Because (Long Version)/ The Jungle (Medley)	1982	10.00
SISAPA			
❑ 76707	Truth Be Known (4 versions)	1991	8.00
UNITED ARTISTS			
❑ SP-184 [DJ]	Youngblood (Livin' in the Streets) (9:07)/Keep On Doin'	1978	15.00

45s

Number	Title (A Side/B Side)	Yr	NM
BLUE NOTE			
❑ 1009	L.A. Sunshine/Slowly We Walk Together	1977	5.00
COCO PLUM			
❑ 2002	Groovin'/(Instrumental)	1985	4.00
LAX			
❑ 02120	Cinco de Mayo/Don't Let No One Get You Down	1981	5.00
MCA			
❑ 40820	Galaxy (Part 1)/Galaxy (Part 2)	1977	5.00
❑ 40820 [PS]	Galaxy (Part 1)/Galaxy (Part 2)	1977	6.00
❑ 40883	Hey Senorita/ Sweet Fighting Lady	1978	5.00
❑ 40995	Good, Good Feelin'/Baby Face (She Said Do Do Do Do)	1979	5.00
❑ 41061	I'm the One Who Understands/ Corns & Callouses	1979	5.00
❑ 41158	Don't Take It Away/ The Music Band 2 (We Are the Music Band)	1979	5.00
❑ 41209	I'll Be Around/The Music Band 2 (We Are the Music Band)	1980	5.00
RCA			
❑ PB-13061	You Got the Power/ Cinco de Mayo	1982	4.00
❑ PB-13239	Outlaw/I'm About Somebody	1982	4.00
❑ PB-13322	Just Because/The Jungle (Medley)	1982	4.00
❑ JH-13426 [DJ]	Baby, It's Cold Outside (same on both sides)	1982	5.00
❑ PB-13544	Life (Is So Strange)/W.W. III	1983	4.00
UNITED ARTISTS			
❑ XW163	The Cisco Kid/Beetles in the Bog	1973	5.00
❑ XW281	Gypsy Man/Deliver the Word	1973	5.00
❑ XW350	Me and Baby Brother/ In Your Eyes	1973	5.00
❑ XW432	Ballero/Slippin' Into Darkness	1974	5.00
❑ XW629	Why Can't We Be Friends?/ In Mazatlin	1975	5.00
❑ XW629 [PS]	Why Can't We Be Friends?/ In Mazatlin	1975	6.00
❑ XW706	Low Rider/So	1975	5.00
❑ XW706 [PS]	Low Rider/So	1975	6.00
❑ XW834	Summer/All Day Music	1976	5.00
❑ XW1213	Youngblood/(Instrumental)	1978	5.00
❑ XW1247	Sing a Happy Song/This Funky Music Makes You Feel Good	1978	5.00
❑ 50746	Lonely Feelin'/Sun Oh Sun	1971	8.00
❑ 50746 [PS]	Lonely Feelin'/Sun Oh Sun	1971	12.00
❑ 50815	All Day Music/Get Down	1971	8.00
❑ 50867	Slippin' Into Darkness/ Happy Head	1971	6.00
❑ 50975	The World Is a Ghetto/ Four Cornered Room	1972	6.00

7-Inch Extended Plays

Number	Title (A Side/B Side)	Yr	NM
UNITED ARTISTS			
❑ SP-92 [DJ]	Where Was You At/City, Country, City//Beetles in the Bog/Four Cornered Room	1972	10.00
❑ SP-92 [PS]	Edited Versions from The World Is a Ghetto	1972	10.00

Albums

Number	Title (A Side/B Side)	Yr	NM
AVENUE			
❑ R1 71706	Peace Sign	1994	15.00
BLUE NOTE			
❑ BN-LA690-G [(2)]	Platinum Jazz	1977	12.00
LAX			
❑ PW 37111	All Day Music	1981	10.00
—Reissue of United Artists 5546			
❑ PW 37112	The World Is a Ghetto	1981	10.00
—Reissue of United Artists 5652			
❑ PW 37113	Why Can't We Be Friends?	1981	10.00
—Reissue of United Artists 441			
MCA			
❑ 745	Galaxy	1983	8.00
—Reissue of MCA 3030			
❑ 747	The Music Band	1983	8.00
—Reissue of MCA 3085			
❑ 751	The Music Band 2	1983	8.00
—Reissue of MCA 3193			
❑ 3030	Galaxy	1977	10.00
❑ 3085	The Music Band	1979	10.00
❑ 3193	The Music Band 2	1979	10.00
❑ 5156	The Music Band Live	1980	10.00
❑ 5362	Best of the Music Band	1982	10.00
❑ 5411	Music Band Jazz	1983	10.00
PRIORITY			
❑ SL 9467	The Best of War...And More	1987	10.00
RCA VICTOR			
❑ AFL1-4208	Outlaw	1982	10.00
❑ AFL1-4598	Life (Is So Strange)	1983	10.00
UNITED ARTISTS			
❑ SP-103 [DJ]	Radio Free War	1974	25.00
—Promo only on blue vinyl			
❑ UA-LA128-F	Deliver the Word	1973	12.00
❑ UA-LA193-J [(2)]	War Live!	1974	15.00
❑ UA-LA441-G	Why Can't We Be Friends?	1975	10.00
❑ UA-LA648-G	Greatest Hits	1976	10.00
❑ UAS-5508	War	1971	15.00
❑ UAS-5546	All Day Music	1971	15.00
❑ UAS-5652	The World Is a Ghetto	1972	12.00

WAR BABIES, THE

45s

Number	Title (A Side/B Side)	Yr	NM
UNI			
❑ 55164	War Baby/Together Forever	1969	8.00

WARD, BILLY, AND THE DOMINOES

Also includes "The Dominoes."

45s

Number	Title (A Side/B Side)	Yr	NM
ABC-PARAMOUNT			
❑ 10128	You're Mine/The World Is Waiting for the Sunrise	1960	20.00
❑ 10156	You/Gypsy	1960	20.00
DECCA			
❑ 29933	St. Therese of the Roses/Home Is Where You Hang Your Hat	1956	30.00
❑ 30043	Come On, Shake, Let's Crawl/ Will You Remember	1956	30.00
❑ 30149	Half a Love (Is Better Than None)/Evermore	1956	30.00
❑ 30199	Rock, Plymouth Rock/ Till Kingdom Come	1957	30.00
❑ 30420	To Each His Own/I Don't Stand a Ghost of a Chance	1957	30.00
❑ 30514	September Song/When the Saints Go Marching In	1957	30.00
FEDERAL			
❑ 12001	Do Something For Me/ Chicken Blues	1951	800.00
—Note: Federal 12010 and 12016 were issued only on 78s			
❑ 12022AA	Sixty Minute Man/I Can't Escape from You	1951	500.00
❑ 12022	Sixty Minute Man/I Can't Escape from You	195?	200.00
—Gold top, no "AA" on label; though this version has been counterfeited, there are legitimate copies without the "AA" on the label; the best way to confirm it is to, if possible, compare it to an "AA" pressing, as they will be exactly the same in every way except for the absence of the "AA"			
❑ 12036	Heart to Heart/Looking for a Man to Satisfy My Soul	1951	500.00
—With Little Esther			
❑ 12039	I Am with You/ Weeping Willow Blues	1951	400.00
❑ 12059	That's What You're Doing to Me/When the Swallows Come Back to Capistrano	1952	400.00
❑ 12068AA	Have Mercy Baby/ Deep Sea Blues	1952	250.00
❑ 12072	Love, Love, Love/That's What You're Doing to Me	1952	200.00
❑ 12105	I'd Be Satisfied/No Room	1952	180.00
❑ 12106	I'm Lonely/Yours Forever	1952	180.00
❑ 12114	The Bells/Pedal Pushin' Papa	1952	200.00
❑ 12129	These Foolish Things Remind Me of You/Don't Leave Me This Way	1953	300.00
—Green label, gold top			
❑ 12129	These Foolish Things Remind Me of You/Don't Leave Me This Way	1954	100.00
—Green label, silver top			
❑ 12129	These Foolish Things Remind Me of You/Don't Leave Me This Way	1955	30.00
—All-green label			
❑ 12139	You Can't Keep a Good Man Down/Where Now Little Heart	1953	100.00
❑ 12162	Until the Real Thing Comes Along/My Baby's 3 D	1954	100.00
❑ 12178	Tootsie Roll/Move to the Outskirts of Town	1954	100.00
❑ 12184	Handwriting on the Wall/ One Moment with You	1954	200.00
❑ 12193	Above Jacob's Ladder/ Little Black Train	1954	50.00
❑ 12209	Can't Do Sixty No More/ If I Never Get to Heaven	1955	100.00
❑ 12218	Love Me Now or Let Me Go/ Cave Man	1955	50.00
❑ 12263	Bobby Sox Baby/How Long, How Long Blues	1956	50.00
❑ 12301	St. Louis Blues/ One Moment with You	1957	50.00
❑ 12308	Have Mercy Baby/ Love, Love, Love	1957	40.00
JUBILEE			
❑ 5163	Gimme, Gimme, Gimme/ Come to Me, Baby	1954	30.00
❑ 5213	Sweethearts on Parade/ Take Me Back to Heaven	1955	30.00
KING			
❑ 1280	Rags to Riches/Don't Ask Me	1953	50.00
❑ 1281	Christmas in Heaven/Ringing In a Brand New Year	1953	100.00
❑ 1342	Tenderly/Little Lie	1954	50.00
❑ 1364	Three Coins in the Fountain/ Lonesome Road	1954	50.00
❑ 1368	Little Things Mean a Lot/ I Really Don't Want to Know	1954	40.00
❑ 1492	Learnin' the Blues/ May I Never Love	1955	40.00
❑ 1502	Over the Rainbow/Give Me You	1955	40.00
❑ 5322	Sixty Minute Man/ Have Mercy Baby	1960	20.00
❑ 5463	Lay It on the Line/That's How You Know You're Growing Old	1961	20.00
❑ 6002	I'm Walking Behind You/ This Love of Mine	1965	20.00
❑ 6016	O Holy Night/What Are You Doin' New Year's Eve	1965	20.00
LIBERTY			
❑ 55071	Star Dust/Lucinda	1957	25.00
❑ 55071 [PS]	Star Dust/Lucinda	1957	100.00
❑ 55099	Deep Purple/Do It Again	1957	25.00
❑ 55111	My Proudest Possession/ Someone Greater Than I	1957	25.00
❑ 55126	Solitude/You Grow Sweeter As the Years Go By	1958	25.00
❑ 55136	Jennie Lee/Music, Maestro, Please	1958	25.00
❑ 55181	Please Don't Say No/ Behave, Hula Girl	1959	25.00
RO-ZAN			
❑ 10001	Man in the Stain Glass Window/ My Fair Weather Friend	1961	20.00
UNITED ARTISTS			
❑ 0017	Stardust/These Foolish Things	1973	5.00
—"Silver Spotlight Series" reissue			

7-Inch Extended Plays

Number	Title (A Side/B Side)	Yr	NM
DECCA			
❑ ED 2549	(contents unknown)	1958	200.00
❑ ED 2549 [PS]	Billy Ward and His Dominoes	1958	200.00
FEDERAL			
❑ 212	Sixty Minute Man/Do Something for Me//Have Mercy Baby/ Don't Leave Me This Way	1956	100.00
—All-green label			
❑ 212	Sixty Minute Man/Do Something for Me//Have Mercy Baby/ Don't Leave Me This Way	1956	400.00
—Green label, silver top			
❑ 212 [PS]	Billy Ward and His Dominoes, Vol. 1	1956	100.00

W

Number	Title (A Side/B Side)	Yr	NM
❑ 262	*The Bells/Pedal Pushin' Papa/I'd Be Satisfied/That's What You're Doing to Me	1957	100.00
—All-green label			
❑ 262	*The Bells/Pedal Pushin' Papa/I'd Be Satisfied/That's What You're Doing to Me	1957	400.00
—Green label, silver top			
❑ 262 [PS]	Billy Ward and His Dominoes, Vol. 2	1957	100.00
❑ 269	*These Foolish Things Remind Me of You/Rags to Riches/When the Swallows Come Back to Capistrano/Harbor Lights	1957	100.00
—All-green label			
❑ 269	*These Foolish Things Remind Me of You/Rags to Riches/When the Swallows Come Back to Capistrano/Harbor Lights	1957	400.00
—Green label, silver top			
❑ 269 [PS]	Billy Ward and His Dominoes Singing the All Time Hit Standards	1957	100.00
LIBERTY			
❑ LEP-1-3056	(contents unknown)	1959	100.00
❑ LEP-1-3056 [PS]	Sea of Glass (Part One)	1959	100.00
❑ LEP-2-3056	Deep River/By and By//The House of the Lord/The Lullaby Divine	1959	100.00
❑ LEP-2-3056 [PS]	Sea of Glass (Part 2)	1959	100.00
❑ LEP-3-3056	(contents unknown)	1959	100.00
❑ LEP-3-3056 [PS]	Sea of Glass (Part 3)	1959	100.00
❑ LEP-1-3083	Stardust/Eatin' and Sleepin'//Music, Maestro, Please/I'll Never Ask for More Than This	1959	100.00
❑ LEP-1-3083 [PS]	Yours Forever (Part One)	1959	100.00
❑ LEP-2-3083	Deep Purple/Lucinda//These Foolish Things/Don't Say I Love You	1959	100.00
❑ LEP-2-3083 [PS]	Yours Forever (Part Two)	1959	100.00
❑ LEP-3-3083	Smoke Gets in Your Eyes/Do It Again//If You Please/Yours Forever	1959	100.00
❑ LEP-3-3083 [PS]	Yours Forever (Part Three)	1959	100.00
Albums			
DECCA			
❑ DL 8621 [M]	Billy Ward and the Dominoes	1958	200.00
FEDERAL			
❑ 295-94 [10]	Billy Ward and His Dominoes	1955	13000.
—VG value 6000; VG+ value 9500			
❑ 548 [M]	Billy Ward and His Dominoes	1958	1500.
❑ 559 [M]	Clyde McPhatter with Billy Ward and His Dominoes	1958	1200.
KING			
❑ 548 [M]	Billy Ward and His Dominoes	1958	—
—Unknown			
❑ 559 [M]	Clyde McPhatter with Billy Ward and His Dominoes	1958	600.00
—Yellow cover			
❑ 559 [M]	Clyde McPhatter with Billy Ward and His Dominoes	196?	300.00
—Pink cover			
❑ 733 [M]	Billy Ward and His Dominoes Featuring Clyde McPhatter and Jackie Wilson	1961	600.00
❑ 952 [M]	24 Songs	1966	50.00
❑ 5005	14 Hits	197?	12.00
❑ 5008	21 Hits	197?	12.00
LIBERTY			
❑ LRP-3056 [M]	Sea of Glass	1957	60.00
❑ LRP-3083 [M]	Yours Forever	1958	60.00
❑ LRP-3113 [M]	Pagan Love Song	1959	60.00
❑ LST-7113 [S]	Pagan Love Song	1959	100.00

WARD, BURT

Number	Title (A Side/B Side)	Yr	NM
45s			
MGM			
❑ 13632	Boy Wonder I Love You/Orange Colored Sky	1966	200.00
—Written and produced by Frank Zappa			

WARD, HERB

Number	Title (A Side/B Side)	Yr	NM
45s			
ARGO			
❑ 5510	Strange Change/Why Do You Want to Leave	1965	80.00
RCA VICTOR			
❑ 47-9688	Honest to Goodness/If You Got to Leave Me	1968	60.00

WARD, JOE

Number	Title (A Side/B Side)	Yr	NM
45s			
GUSTO			
❑ 814	Nuttin' For Christmas/Christmas Time's A Coming	1979	4.00
—B-side by Mac Wiseman			
KING			
❑ 4854	Nuttin' for Xmas/Christmas Questions	1955	12.00
❑ 4897	Upsy Down Town/Mama Darling	1956	20.00
❑ 4931	Rock and Roll Merry-Go-Round/Freckle Face	1956	20.00

WARD, ROBIN

Number	Title (A Side/B Side)	Yr	NM
45s			
DOT			
❑ 16530	Wonderful Summer/Dream Boy	1963	12.00
❑ 16578	Winter's Here/Bobby	1963	10.00
❑ 16599	Johnny Come and Get Me/Where the Blue of the Night Meets the Gold of the Day	1964	20.00
❑ 16624	In His Car/Wishing	1964	25.00
Albums			
DOT			
❑ DLP 3555 [M]	Wonderful Summer	1963	200.00
❑ DLP 25555 [S]	Wonderful Summer	1963	300.00

WARD, SINGIN' SAMMY

Number	Title (A Side/B Side)	Yr	NM
45s			
MOTOWN			
❑ 1004	Lover/That's Why I Love You So Much	1960	40.00
—With Sherri Taylor			
SOUL			
❑ 35004	Bread Winner/You've Got to Change	1964	50.00
TAMLA			
❑ 54030	What Makes You Love Him/The Child Is Really Wild	1960	75.00
—With globe label			
❑ 54030	What Makes You Love Him/The Child Is Really Wild	1960	200.00
—With lines label			
❑ 54049	What Makes You Love Him/Don't Take It Away	1961	50.00
❑ 54057	Everybody Knew It/Big Joe Moe	1962	50.00
❑ 54071	Part Time Love/Someday Pretty Baby	1962	50.00

WARD, WALTER, AND THE CHALLENGERS

Later recorded as THE OLYMPICS.

Number	Title (A Side/B Side)	Yr	NM
45s			
MELATONE			
❑ 1002	I Can Tell/The Mambo Beat	1957	400.00

WARDELL AND THE SULTANS

Number	Title (A Side/B Side)	Yr	NM
45s			
IMPERIAL			
❑ 5812	The Original Popeye/Dance Time	1962	20.00
❑ 5886	I Need Your Love/I'm Broke	1962	15.00

WARE, CURTIS, AND THE FOUR DO-MATICS

Number	Title (A Side/B Side)	Yr	NM
45s			
KAYBEE			
❑ 101	Flame in My Heart/Am I in Love	1961	500.00

WARE, EDDIE

Number	Title (A Side/B Side)	Yr	NM
45s			
STATES			
❑ 130	That's the Stuff I Like/Lonely Broken Heart	1954	120.00

WARLOCKS, THE (1)

Members of this group later joined ZZ TOP.

Number	Title (A Side/B Side)	Yr	NM
45s			
ARA			
❑ 1017	If You Really Want Me to Stay/Good Time Trippin'	1968	150.00

WARLOCKS, THE (2)

Number	Title (A Side/B Side)	Yr	NM
45s			
DECCA			
❑ 31806	I'll Go Crazy/Temper Tantrum	1965	20.00
WASHINGTON SQUARE			
❑ 2023	Hey Joe/Girl	1966	20.00

WARMEST SPRING, THE

Number	Title (A Side/B Side)	Yr	NM
45s			
PARKWAY			
❑ 985	Younger Girl/It Doesn't Matter Now	1966	10.00
❑ 985 [DJ]	Younger Girl	1966	20.00
—One-sided white label promo			
❑ 990	Suddenly (You Find Love)/Hard, Hard Girl	1966	10.00

WARNER, PETE

Number	Title (A Side/B Side)	Yr	NM
45s			
POLYDOR			
❑ 14278	I Just Want to Spend My Life with You/Hands	1975	200.00

WARNES, JENNIFER

Number	Title (A Side/B Side)	Yr	NM
45s			
ARISTA			
❑ 0223	Right Time of the Night/Daddy Don't Go	1976	5.00
❑ 0252	I'm Dreaming/Don't Lead Me On	1977	5.00
❑ 0430	I Know a Heartache When I See One/Frankie in the Rain	1979	4.00
❑ 0455	Don't Make Me Over/I'm Restless	1979	4.00
❑ 0497	When the Feeling Comes Around/Shot Through the Heart	1980	4.00
❑ 0611	Could It Be Love/I'm Restless	1982	4.00
❑ 0670	Come to Me/I'm Restless	1982	4.00
CASABLANCA			
❑ 814603-7	All the Right Moves/Theme — All the Right Moves	1983	4.00
—A-side with Chris Thompson; B-side by David Campbell			
CYPRESS			
❑ 661111-7	Ain't No Cure for Love/Famous Blue Raincoat	1986	4.00
❑ 661111-7 [PS]	Ain't No Cure for Love/Famous Blue Raincoat	1986	5.00
❑ 661115-7	First We Take Manhattan/Famous Blue Raincoat	1987	4.00
❑ 661115-7 [PS]	First We Take Manhattan/Famous Blue Raincoat	1987	4.00
PARROT			
❑ 324	Here, There and Everywhere/Sunny Day Blue	1968	12.00
❑ 328	Chelsea Morning/The Park	1969	10.00
❑ 333	I Am Waiting/The Leaves	1969	10.00
❑ 336	Easy to Be Hard/Let the Sunshine In	1969	10.00
❑ 343	We're Not Gonna Take It/The Weather's Better	1970	8.00
❑ 346	Old Folks/Cajun Train	1970	8.00
—All of the above as "Jennifer"			
REPRISE			
❑ 1070	Last Song/These Days	1972	8.00
—As "Jennifer"			
WARNER BROS.			
❑ 29593	Nights Are Forever/Kick the Can	1983	4.00
Albums			
ARISTA			
❑ AL 4062	Jennifer Warnes	1977	10.00
❑ AB 4217	Shot Through the Heart	1979	10.00
❑ AL 9560	The Best of Jennifer Warnes	1982	8.00
CYPRESS			
❑ 661111-1	Famous Blue Raincoat	1987	30.00
PARROT			
❑ PAS-71020	I Can Remember Anything	1968	20.00
—As "Jennifer"			
❑ PAS-71034	See Me	1970	20.00
—As "Jennifer"			
ROCK THE HOUSE			
❑ RTH 5052	Famous Blue Raincoat	1996	50.00
—Classic Records reissue			

WARRANT

Number	Title (A Side/B Side)	Yr	NM
45s			
COLUMBIA			
❑ 38-68606	Down Boys/Cold Sweat	1989	4.00
❑ 38-68985	Heaven/In the Sticks	1989	4.00
❑ 38-73035	Big Talk/D.R.F.S.R.	1989	4.00
❑ 38-73300	Sometimes She Cries/32 Pennies	1990	4.00
❑ 38-73510	Cherry Pie/Thin Disguise	1990	4.00
❑ 38-73597	I Saw Red/(Acoustic Version)	1990	4.00
❑ 38-73598	Blind Faith/Mr. Rainmaker	1991	4.00
❑ 38-73644	Uncle Tom's Cabin/Sure Feels Good to Me	1991	4.00
❑ 38-74445	Machine Gun/Inside Out	1992	5.00
❑ 38-74781	The Bitter Pill/Quicksand	1992	5.00

Albums

Number	Title (A Side/B Side)	Yr	NM
COLUMBIA			
❑ FC 44383	Dirty Rotten Filthy Stinking Rich	1988	8.00
❑ C 45487	Cherry Pie	1990	15.00

WARREN, BEVERLY

45s

Number	Title (A Side/B Side)	Yr	NM
B.T. PUPPY			
❑ 521	Would You Believe/ So Glad You're My Baby	1966	10.00
❑ 526	He's So Fine/March	1967	10.00
RUST			
❑ 5098	Baby Hullabaloo/Let Me Get Close to You	1964	12.00
UNITED ARTISTS			
❑ 543	It Was Me Yesterday/ Like a Million Years	1963	15.00

WARREN, BOBBY, FIVE

45s

Number	Title (A Side/B Side)	Yr	NM
JORDAN			
❑ 119	Nite-Beat/Medicine Man	1960	40.00

WARREN, DOUG

45s

Number	Title (A Side/B Side)	Yr	NM
IMAGE			
❑ 1011	Around Midnight/If the World Don't End Tomorrow	1960	40.00
❑ 1013	Ain't Gonna Wait No Longer/ Ain't That Love	1960	30.00

WARREN, RUSTY

45s

Number	Title (A Side/B Side)	Yr	NM
JUBILEE			
❑ 5473	Lil' Lizzy Beth/Life Is Really Worth Living	1964	12.00

7-Inch Extended Plays

Number	Title (A Side/B Side)	Yr	NM
JUBILEE			
❑ EP-45-2049	Roll Me Over//Do It Now/ Twist Blues	1963	15.00
❑ EP-45-2049 [PS]	Rusty Warren Sings	1963	15.00

Albums

Number	Title (A Side/B Side)	Yr	NM
GNP CRESCENDO			
❑ 2079 [(2)]	Knockers Up!/Songs for Sinners	1975	15.00
❑ 2080 [(2)]	Rusty Warren Bounces Back/ Sin-Sational	1975	15.00
❑ 2081	Rusty Warren Lays It on the Line	1975	12.00
❑ 2088	Knockers Up! '76	1976	12.00
❑ 2103	Bottoms Up!	1976	12.00
❑ 2114	Sexplosion	1977	12.00
JUBILEE			
❑ JGM-2024 [M]	Songs for Sinners	1960	25.00
❑ JGM-2029 [M]	Knockers Up!	1960	25.00
❑ JLP 2034 [M]	Sin-Sational	1961	25.00
❑ JGM 2039 [M]	Rusty Warren Bounces Back	1961	25.00
❑ JGM 2044 [M]	Rusty Warren in Orbit	1962	25.00
❑ JLP 2049 [M]	Banned in Boston?	1963	25.00
❑ JGM-2054 [M]	Sex-X-Ponent	1964	25.00
—Cover has JGM prefix; label has JG prefix			
❑ JGM-2059 [M]	More Knockers Up!	1965	25.00
❑ JGM-2064 [M]	Rusty Rides Again	1966	25.00
❑ JGM 2069 [M]	Bottoms Up!	1967	20.00
❑ JGS 2069 [S]	Bottoms Up!	1967	20.00
❑ JGM 2074	Look What I've Got for You	1967	20.00
❑ JLP 5025 [M]	Portrait of Life	196?	20.00
❑ JLPS 5025 [S]	Portrait of Life	196?	20.00

WARWICK, DEE DEE

45s

Number	Title (A Side/B Side)	Yr	NM
ATCO			
❑ 6754	Make Love to Me/She Didn't Know (She Kept On Talkin')	1970	6.00
❑ 6769	I'm Only Human/If This Was the Last Song	1970	6.00
❑ 6796	Cold Night in Georgia/ Searchin'	1971	6.00
❑ 6810	Suspicious Minds/I'm Glad I'm a Woman	1971	6.00
❑ 6840	Everybody's Got to Believe in Somebody/Signed, Dee Dee	1971	6.00
BLUE ROCK			
❑ 4008	Do It with All Your Heart/ Happiness	1965	15.00
❑ 4027	We're Doing Fine/I Want to Be with You	1965	15.00
❑ 4032	Baby I'm Yours/Gotta Get a Hold of Myself	1965	15.00
JUBILEE			
❑ 5459	You're No Good/Don't Call Me	1963	25.00
MERCURY			
❑ 72584	I Want to Be with You/ Lover's Chant	1966	8.00
❑ 72638	I'm Gonna Make You Love Me/ Yours Until Tomorrow	1966	8.00
❑ 72667	When Love Slips Away/ House of Gold	1967	8.00
❑ 72710	Locked in Your Love/Alfie	1967	8.00
❑ 72738	Don't You Ever Give Up on Me/ We've Got Everything Going for Us	1967	8.00
❑ 72788	Girls Need Love/It's Not Fair	1968	8.00
❑ 72834	I'll Be Better Off (Without You)/ Monday, Monday	1968	8.00
❑ 72880	Foolish Fool/Thank You Girl	1969	8.00
❑ 72927	That's Not Love/It's Not Fair	1969	8.00
❑ 72940	Next Time (You Fall in Love)/ Ring of Bright Water	1969	8.00
❑ 72966	I (Who Have Nothing)/ Where Is That Rainbow	1969	8.00
❑ 73397	I Haven't Got Anything Better to Do/All That Love Went to Waste	1973	8.00
PRIVATE STOCK			
❑ 45,011	Get Out of My Life/Funny How We Change Places	1975	5.00
❑ 45,033	This Time May Be My Last/Funny How We Change Places	1975	5.00
SUTRA			
❑ 134	Move with the World/The Way We Used to Be	1984	4.00
❑ 134 [PS]	Move with the World/The Way We Used to Be	1984	4.00

Albums

Number	Title (A Side/B Side)	Yr	NM
ATCO			
❑ SD 33-337	Turnin' Around	1970	25.00
MERCURY			
❑ MG-21100 [M]	I Want to Be with You	1967	25.00
❑ SR-61100 [S]	I Want to Be with You	1967	25.00
❑ SR-61221	Foolish Fool	1968	25.00

WARWICK, DIONNE

12-Inch Singles

Number	Title (A Side/B Side)	Yr	NM
ARISTA			
❑ ADP 9145 [DJ]	Got a Date (7:04) (4:07)	1983	8.00
RIVER NORTH			
❑ 51416 4686 1	What the World Needs Now Is Love (6 versions)	1998	10.00
—With the Hip-Hop Nation United			

45s

Number	Title (A Side/B Side)	Yr	NM
ARISTA			
❑ 0419	I'll Never Love This Way Again/ In Your Eyes	1979	4.00
❑ 0459	Deja Vu/All the Time	1979	4.00
❑ 0498	After You/Out of My Hands	1980	4.00
❑ 0527	No Night So Long/ Reaching for the Sky	1980	4.00
❑ 0572	Easy Love/You Never Said Goodbye	1980	4.00
❑ 0602	Some Changes Are For Good/ This Time Is Ours	1981	4.00
❑ 0630	There's a Long Road Ahead of Me/Medley of Hits	1981	4.00
❑ 0673	Friends in Love/What Is This	1982	4.00
—A-side with Johnny Mathis			
❑ 0701	For You/What Is This	1982	4.00
❑ 1015	Heartbreaker/I Can't See Anything But You	1982	4.00
❑ 1040	Take the Short Way Home/ Just One More Night	1983	4.00
❑ 1067	All the Love in the World/ You Are My Love	1983	—
—Unreleased?			
❑ 9032	All the Love in the World/ You Are My Love	1983	4.00
❑ 9073	How Many Times Can We Say Goodbye/What Can a Miracle Do	1983	4.00
—With Luther Vandross			
❑ 9145	Got a Date/Two Ships Passing in the Night	1984	4.00
❑ 9281	Finder of Lost Loves/It's Love	1984	4.00
—A-side with Glen Jones			
❑ 9341	Run to Me/No Love in Sight	1985	3.00
—A-side with Barry Manilow			
❑ 9460	Whisper in the Dark/ Extravagant Gestures	1986	3.00
❑ 9460 [PS]	Whisper in the Dark/ Extravagant Gestures	1986	3.00
❑ 9567	Love Power/In a World Such As This	1987	3.00
—A-side with Jeffrey Osborne			
❑ 9567 [PS]	Love Power/In a World Such As This	1987	3.00
❑ 9638	Reservations for Two/ For Everything You Are	1987	3.00
—A-side with Kashif			
❑ 9638 [PS]	Reservations for Two/ For Everything You Are	1987	3.00
❑ 9652	Another Chance for Love/ Cry on Me	1987	3.00
—A-side with Howard Hewett			
❑ 9652 [PS]	Another Chance for Love/ Cry on Me	1987	3.00
❑ 9901	Take Good Care of You and Me/Heartbreak of Love	1989	3.00
—A-side with Jeffrey Osborne; B-side with June Pointer			
❑ 9940	I Don't Need Another Love/ Hertbreaker	1990	3.00
—A-side with the Spinners			
❑ 9940 [PS]	I Don't Need Another Love/ Hertbreaker	1990	3.00
ATLANTIC			
❑ 3029	Then Came You/Just As Long As We Have Love	1974	6.00
—With the Spinners			
❑ 3202	Then Came You/Just As Long As We Have Love	1974	5.00
—With the Spinners			
MUSICOR			
❑ 6303	If I Ruled the World/Only Love Can Break a Heart	1977	5.00
RIVER NORTH			
❑ 163024-7	What the World Needs Now Is Love (same on both sides)	1998	4.00
—With the Hip-Hop Nation United			
SCEPTER			
❑ 1239	Don't Make Me Over/ I Smiled Yesterday	1962	12.00
❑ 1247	This Empty Place/ Wishin' and Hopin'	1963	12.00
❑ 1247 [PS]	This Empty Place/ Wishin' and Hopin'	1963	20.00
❑ 1253	Make the Music Play/ Please Make Him Love Me	1963	12.00
❑ 1262	Anyone Who Had a Heart/ The Love of a Boy	1963	12.00
❑ 1274	Walk On By/Any Old Time of Day	1964	12.00
❑ 1282	You'll Never Get to Heaven (If You Break My Heart)/ A House Is Not a Home	1964	10.00
❑ 1285	Reach Out for Me/How Many Days of Sadness	1964	10.00
❑ 1294	You Can Have Him/Is There Another Way to Love Him	1965	10.00
❑ 1298	Who Can I Turn To/Don't Say I Didn't Tell You Something	1965	10.00
❑ 12104	Here I Am/They Long to Be Close to You	1965	10.00
❑ 12111	Looking with My Eyes/Only the Strong, Only the Brave	1965	10.00
❑ 12122	Are You There (With Another Girl)/If I Ever Make You Cry	1965	10.00
❑ 12133	Message to Michael/Here Where There Is Love	1966	8.00
❑ 12153	Trains and Boats and Planes/ Don't Go Breaking My Heart	1966	8.00
❑ 12167	I Just Don't Know What to Do with Myself/In Between the Heartaches	1966	8.00
❑ 12181	Another Night/Go with Love	1966	8.00
❑ 12187	Alfie/The Beginning of Loneliness	1967	8.00
❑ 12196	The Windows of the World/ Walk Little Dolly	1967	8.00
❑ 12203	I Say a Little Prayer/(Theme from) Valley of the Dolls	1967	8.00
❑ 12216	Do You Know the Way to San Jose?/Let Me Be Lonely	1968	8.00
❑ 12226	Who Is Gonna Love Me?/ (There's) Always Something There to Remind Me	1968	8.00
❑ 12231	Promises, Promises/Whoever You Are, I Love You	1968	7.00
❑ 12241	This Girl's In Love with You/ Dream Sweet Dreamer	1969	7.00
❑ 12249	The April Fools/Slaves	1969	7.00
❑ 12256	Odds and Ends/As Long As There's an Apple Tree	1969	7.00
❑ 12262	You've Lost That Lovin' Feeling/Window Wishing	1969	7.00
❑ 12273	I'll Never Fall in Love Again/ What the World Needs Now Is Love	1970	7.00
❑ 12276	Let Me Go to Him/Loneliness Remembers What Happiness Forgets	1970	6.00
❑ 12285	Paper Mache/The Wine Is Young	1970	6.00
❑ 12294	Make It Easy on Yourself/ Knowing When to Leave	1970	6.00
❑ 12300	The Green Grass Starts to Grow/ They Don't Give Medals to Yesterday's Heroes	1970	6.00
❑ 12309	Who Gets the Guy/ Walk the Way You Talk	1971	6.00

W

Number	Title (A Side/B Side)	Yr	NM
12326	Amanda/He's Moving On	1971	6.00
12336	The Love of My Man/Hurts So Bad	1971	6.00
12346	Raindrops Keep Falling on My Head/Is There Another Way to Love You	1972	6.00
12352	I'm Your Puppet/Don't Make Me Over	1972	6.00
12383	Medley: Reach Out and Touch (Somebody's Hand)-All Kinds of People/The Good Life	1973	6.00
WARNER BROS.			
7560	If We Only Have Love/Close to You	1972	5.00
7669	Don't Let My Teardrops Bother TYou/I Think You Need Love	1973	5.00
7693	(I'm) Just Being Myself/You're Gonna Need Me	1973	5.00
8026	Sure Thing/Who Knows	1974	5.00
8088	Take it from Me/It's Magic	1975	5.00
8154	Once You Hit the Road/World of My Dreams	1975	5.00
8183	His House and Me/Ronnie Lee	1976	5.00
8280	I Didn't Mean to Love You/He's Not for You	1976	5.00
8419	Do You Believe in Love at First Sight/Do I Have to Cry	1977	5.00
8501	Keepin' My Head Above Water/Livin' It Up Is Startin' to Get Me Down	1977	5.00
8530	Don't Ever Take Your Love Away/Do I Have to Cry	1978	4.00

7-Inch Extended Plays

Number	Title (A Side/B Side)	Yr	NM
SCEPTER			
SGS-523	Walk On By/People/You'll Never Get to Heaven//Reach Out for Me/A House Is Not a Home/I Smiled Yesterday	196?	15.00
—Jukebox issue; small hole, plays at 33 1/3 rpm			
SGS-523 [PS]	Make Way for Dionne Warwick	196?	15.00
SGS 565	Don't Make Me Over/Anyone Who Had a Heart/Wishin' and Hopin'//This Empty Place/(There's) Always Something There to Remind Me/Any Old Time of Day	1968	12.00
—Jukebox issue; small hole, plays at 33 1/3 rpm			
SGS 565 [PS]	Dionne Warwick's Golden Hits, Part One	1968	12.00
SGS 568	Do You Know the Way to San Jose/Let Me Be Lonely/As Long As There's an Apple Tree//(Theme from) Valley of the Dolls/Up, Up and Away/Where Would I Go	1968	12.00
—Jukebox issue; small hole, plays at 33 1/3 rpm			
SGS 568 [PS]	Valley of the Dolls	1968	12.00

Albums

Number	Title	Yr	NM
ARISTA			
AB 4230	Dionne	1979	10.00
AL 8104	How Many Times Can We Say Goodbye	1983	10.00
A2L 8111 [(2)]	Hot! Live and Otherwise	1983	10.00
—Budget-line reissue			
AL 8262	Finder of Lost Loves	1985	10.00
AL 8295	Dionne	1985	8.00
—Budget-line reissue			
AL 8338	Heartbreaker	1985	8.00
—Budget-line reissue			
AL 8358	Friends in Love	1985	8.00
—Budget-line reissue			
AL 8398	Friends	1985	10.00
AL 8446	Reservations for Two	1987	10.00
AL 8540	Greatest Hits 1979-1990	1989	12.00
AL 8573	Dionne Warwick Sings Cole Porter	1990	12.00
A2L 8605 [(2)]	Hot! Live and Otherwise	1981	12.00
AL 9526	No Night So Long	1980	10.00
AL 9585	Friends in Love	1982	10.00
AL 9609	Heartbreaker	1982	10.00
EVEREST			
4103	Dionne Warwick	1981	10.00
MOBILE FIDELITY			
2-098 [(2)]	Hot! Live and Otherwise	1982	30.00
—Audiophile vinyl			
MUSICOR			
2501	Only Love Can Break a Heart	1977	12.00
PAIR			
PDL2-1043 [(2)]	The Dynamic Dionne Warwick	1986	12.00
PDL2-1098 [(2)]	Masterpieces	1986	12.00
PICKWICK			
PTP-2056 [(2)]	Alfie	1973	12.00
—As "Dionne Warwicke"			
RHINO			
RNDA-1100 [(2)]	Anthology 1962-1971	1985	15.00
SCEPTER			
S-508 [M]	Presenting Dionne Warwick	1963	15.00
SS-508 [S]	Presenting Dionne Warwick	1963	20.00
S-517 [M]	Anyone Who Had a Heart	1964	15.00
SS-517 [S]	Anyone Who Had a Heart	1964	20.00
LP-523 [M]	Make Way for Dionne Warwick	1964	15.00
SPS-523 [S]	Make Way for Dionne Warwick	1964	20.00
LP-528 [M]	The Sensitive Sound of Dionne Warwick	1965	15.00
SPS-528 [S]	The Sensitive Sound of Dionne Warwick	1965	20.00
SPS-531 [S]	Here I Am	1965	20.00
SRM-531 [M]	Here I Am	1965	15.00
SPS-534 [S]	Dionne Warwick in Paris	1966	15.00
SRM-534 [M]	Dionne Warwick in Paris	1966	12.00
SPS-555 [S]	Here Where There Is Love	1966	15.00
SRM-555 [M]	Here Where There Is Love	1966	12.00
SPS-559 [S]	On Stage and in the Movies	1967	15.00
SRM-559 [M]	On Stage and in the Movies	1967	12.00
SPS-563 [S]	The Windows of the World	1967	15.00
SRM-563 [M]	The Windows of the World	1967	12.00
SPS-565 [S]	Dionne Warwick's Golden Hits, Part One	1967	15.00
SRM-565 [M]	Dionne Warwick's Golden Hits, Part One	1967	20.00
SPS-567 [S]	The Magic of Believing	1968	20.00
SRM-567 [M]	The Magic of Believing	1968	30.00
SPS-568 [S]	Valley of the Dolls	1968	15.00
SRM-568 [M]	Valley of the Dolls	1968	50.00
—May only exist as a white label promo			
SPS-571	Promises, Promises	1968	15.00
SPS-573	Soulful	1969	15.00
SPS-575	Dionne Warwick's Greatest Motion Picture Hits	1969	15.00
SPS-577	Dionne Warwick's Golden Hits, Part 2	1969	15.00
SPS-581	I'll Never Fall in Love Again	1970	15.00
SPS-587	Very Dionne	1970	15.00
SPS 2-596 [(2)]	The Dionne Warwicke Story	1971	20.00
—As "Dionne Warwicke"			
SPS-598 [(2)]	From Within	1972	20.00
—As "Dionne Warwicke"			
P2M 5139 [(2)M]	Dionne!	1967	20.00
—Columbia Record Club exclusive			
P2S 5140 [(2)S]	Dionne!	1967	20.00
—Columbia Record Club exclusive			
ST-91010 [S]	Here Where There Is Love	1966	20.00
—Capitol Record Club edition			
ST-91099 [S]	On Stage and in the Movies	1967	20.00
—Capitol Record Club edition			
SPRINGBOARD			
SPS-4001	The Golden Voice of Dionne Warwick	1972	10.00
—As "Dionne Warwicke"			
SPS-4002	Dionne Warwicke Sings Her Very Best	1972	10.00
—As "Dionne Warwicke"			
SPS-4003	One Hit After Another	1972	10.00
—As "Dionne Warwicke"			
SPS-4032	Greatest Hits, Vol. 2	197?	10.00
TIME-LIFE			
SLGD-18 [(2)]	Legendary Singers: Dionne Warwick	1987	15.00
UNITED ARTISTS			
UA-LA337-G	The Very Best of Dionne Warwicke	1974	12.00
—As "Dionne Warwicke"			
WARNER BROS.			
BS 2585	Dionne	1971	12.00
—As "Dionne Warwicke"			
BS 2658	Just Being Myself	1973	12.00
—As "Dionne Warwicke"			
BS 2846	Then Came You	1975	12.00
—As "Dionne Warwicke"			
BS4 2846 [Q]	Then Came You	1975	20.00
—As "Dionne Warwicke"			
BS 2893	Track of the Cat	1975	12.00
BS 3119	Love at First Sight	1976	12.00

WASHINGTON, BABY

Also includes records as "Justine Washington."

45s

Number	Title (A Side/B Side)	Yr	NM
ABC-PARAMOUNT			
10223	My Time to Cry/Let Love Go By	1961	15.00
—As Jeanette "Baby" Washington			
10245	There You Go Again/Don't Cry, Foolish Heart	1961	15.00
AVI			
253	I Wanna Dance/I Can't Get Over Losing You	1978	5.00
—As Jeanette "Baby" Washington			
CHECKER			
918	I Hate to See You Go/Knock Yourself Out	1959	25.00
CHESS			
2099	Happy Birthday/Is It Worth It	1970	6.00
COTILLION			
44047	I Don't Know/I Can't Afford to Lose Him	1969	6.00
44065	Let Them Talk/I Love You Brother	1970	6.00
44086	Don't Let Me Lose This Dream/I'm Good Enough for You	1970	6.00
J&S			
1604	There Must Be a Reason/Congratulations Honey	1957	50.00
1632	I Hate to See You Go/Knock Yourself Out	1958	30.00
1656	Every Day/Smitty's Rock	1961	60.00
LIBERTY			
1393	Silent Night/Merry Christmas Baby	1980	5.00
—B-side by Charles Brown			
LOST-NITE			
256	That's How Heartaches Are Made/There He Is	196?	5.00
—Reissue			
MASTER 5			
3500	Can't Get Over Losing You/(B-side unknown)	1974	6.00
9103	Forever/(B-side unknown)	1973	6.00
—With Don Gardner			
9104	Just Can't Get You Out of My Mind/(B-side unknown)	1973	6.00
9107	I've Got to Break Away/You (Just a Dream)	1973	6.00
NEPTUNE			
101	The Time/You Never Could Be Mine	1959	30.00
104	The Bells (On Our Wedding Day)/(B-side unknown)	1959	30.00
107	Work Out/Let's Love in the Midnight	1960	30.00
120	Medicine Man/Tears Fall	1961	25.00
—As "Jeanette B. Washington"			
122	Nobody Cares (About Me)/(B-side unknown)	1961	25.00
—As "Jeanette (Baby) Washington"			
SUE			
104	The Clock/Standing on the Pier	1964	8.00
114	It'll Never Be Over for Me/Move On Drifter	1964	8.00
119	Your Fool/Run My Heart	1965	8.00
124	I Can't Wait Until I See My Baby/Who's Going to Take Care of Me	1965	8.00
—As Justine Washington			
129	Only Those in Love/The Ballad of Bobby Dawn	1965	8.00
149	Silent Night/White Christmas	1967	20.00
150	Either You're With Me (Or Either You're Not)/You Are What You Are	1967	15.00
764	Hey Lonely One/No Tears	1962	12.00
767	Handful of Memories/Careless Hands	1962	10.00
769	Hush Heart/I've Got a Feeling	1962	10.00
783	That's How Heartaches Are Made/There He Is	1963	10.00
790	Leave Me Alone/You and the Night and the Music	1963	80.00
794	Hey Lonely One/Doodlin'	1963	10.00
797	I Can't Wait Until I See My Baby/Who's Going to Take Care of Me	1964	10.00
—As Justine Washington			
UNITED ARTISTS			
0143	That's How Heartaches Are Made/Leave Me Alone	1973	5.00
—"Silver Spotlight Series" reissue			
VEEP			
1274	Silent Night/White Christmas	1967	20.00
1297	Think About the Good Times/Hold Back the Dawn	1969	8.00

Albums

Number	Title	Yr	NM
AVI			
AV-6038	I Wanna Dance	1978	10.00
COLLECTABLES			
COL-5040	The Best of Baby Washington	198?	10.00
COL-5108	Only Those in Love	198?	10.00
COL-5124	That's How Heartaches Are Made	198?	10.00

Except when noted otherwise, VG = 25% of NM, and VG+ = 50% of NM. (Example: VG = $2.00, VG+ = $4.00 and NM = $8.00.)

Number	Title (A Side/B Side)	Yr	NM
SUE			
❑ LP-1014 [M]	That's How Heartaches Are Made	1963	150.00
❑ LP-1042 [M]	Only Those in Love	1965	150.00
❑ LPS-1042 [S]	Only Those in Love	1965	300.00
TRIP			
❑ 8009	The One and Only Baby Washington	1971	15.00
VEEP			
❑ VPS-16528	With You in Mind	1968	25.00

WASHINGTON, DINAH

45s

Number	Title (A Side/B Side)	Yr	NM
MERCURY			
❑ 5488	Harbor Lights/I Cross My Fingers	1950	25.00
❑ 5503	Time Out for Tears/Only a Moment Ago	1950	25.00
❑ 5510	How Deep Is the Ocean/Harbor Lights	1950	25.00
❑ 5665	I'm a Fool/If You Don't Believe I'm Leaving	1951	25.00
❑ 5728	Cold, Cold Heart/Mixed Emotions	1951	25.00
❑ 5736	Just One More Chance/Baby Did You Hear	1951	25.00
❑ 5804	No Time for Blues/(B-side unknown)	1952	25.00
❑ 5842	I Can't Face the Music/Mad About the Boy	1952	25.00
❑ 5906	Stormy Weather/Make Believe Dreams	1952	25.00
❑ 8181	I Wanna Be Loved/Love with Misery	1950	40.00
—Note: Earlier Dinah Washington 45s in the Mercury 8000 series may exist			
❑ 8187	I'll Never Be Free/Big Deal	1950	25.00
❑ 8192	How Deep Is the Ocean/Why Don't You Think Things Over	1950	25.00
❑ 8194	My Kind of Man/I Wanna Be Loved by You	1950	25.00
❑ 8195	It Isn't Fair/I'll Never Be Free	1950	25.00
❑ 8206	If I Loved You/My Kind of Man	1950	25.00
❑ 8207	Fast Movin' Mama/Juice Head Man of Mine	1950	25.00
❑ 8209	My Heart Cries for You/I Apologize	1951	25.00
❑ 8211	I Won't Cry Anymore/Don't Say You're Sorry Again	1951	25.00
❑ 8231	Ain't Nobody's Bizness If I Do/Please Send Me Someone to Love	1951	25.00
❑ 8232	I'm So Lonely I Could Cry/Fine Fine Daddy	1951	25.00
❑ 8249	Saturday Night/Be Fair to Me	1951	25.00
❑ 8257	Hey Good Lookin'/Out in the Cold Again	1951	80.00
—With The Ravens			
❑ 8267	Wheel of Fortune/Tell Me Why	1952	25.00
❑ 8269	Trouble in Mind/New Blowtop Blues	1952	25.00
❑ 8292	Pillow Blues/Double Dealin' Daddy	1952	25.00
❑ 8294	My Song/Half As Much	1952	25.00
❑ 10008 [S]	What a Diff'rence a Day Made/Come On Home	1959	25.00
—The A-side title is listed differently on the stereo 45 than on the mono 45 (71435)			
❑ 70046	I Cried for You/Gambler's Blues	1953	25.00
❑ 70125	Ain't Nothing Good/You Let My Love Grow Old	1953	25.00
❑ 70175	My Lean Baby/Never Never	1953	25.00
❑ 70214	TV Is the Thing (This Year)/Fat Daddy	1953	25.00
❑ 70263	Silent Night/The Lord's Prayer	1953	25.00
❑ 70284	Since My Man Has Gone and Went/My Man's an Undertaker	1953	25.00
❑ 70329	Short John/Feel Like I Wanna Cry	1954	20.00
❑ 70336	Such a Night/Until Sunrise	1954	20.00
❑ 70392	(No, No, No) You Can't Love Two/Big Long Slidin' Thing	1954	40.00
❑ 70439	I Don't Hurt Anymore/Dream	1954	20.00
❑ 70497	Teach Me Tonight/Wishing Well	1954	20.00
❑ 70537	That's All I Want from You/You Stay on My Mind	1955	20.00
❑ 70600	If It's the Last Thing I Do/I Diddie	1955	20.00
❑ 70653	I Hear Those Bells/The Cheat	1955	20.00
❑ 70694	I Concentrate on You/Not Without You	1955	20.00
❑ 70728	I'm Lost Without You Tonight/You Might Have Told Me	1955	20.00
❑ 70776	The Show Must Go On/I Just Couldn't Stand It No More	1956	15.00
❑ 70833	Let's Get Busy Too/Let's Go Around Together	1956	15.00
❑ 70868	Cat on a Hot Tin Roof/The First Time	1956	15.00
❑ 70906	Soft Winds/Tears to Burn	1956	15.00
❑ 70968	Relax, Max/The Kissing Way Home	1956	15.00
❑ 71018	All Because of You/To Love and Be Loved	1956	15.00
❑ 71043	You Let My Love Grow Old/I Know	1957	15.00
❑ 71087	Ain't Nobody Home/I'm Gonna Keep My Eyes on You	1957	15.00
❑ 71220	Everybody Loves My Baby/Blues Down Home	1957	15.00
❑ 71317	Ring-a My Phone/Never Again	1958	15.00
❑ 71377	Make Me a Present of You/All of Me	1958	15.00
❑ 71435	What a Diff'rence a Day Makes/Come On Home	1959	15.00
❑ 71508	Unforgettable/Nothing in the World	1959	10.00
❑ 71557	Ol' Santa/The Light	1959	12.00
❑ 71560	It Could Happen to You/Age of Miracles	1960	10.00
❑ 71635	This Bitter Earth/I Understand	1960	10.00
❑ 71696	Love Walked In/I'm in Heaven Tonight	1960	10.00
❑ 71744	We Have Love/Looking Back	1960	10.00
❑ 71744 [PS]	We Have Love/Looking Back	1960	15.00
❑ 71778	Early Every Morning (Early Every Evening Too)/Do You Want It That Way	1961	10.00
❑ 71778 [PS]	Early Every Morning (Early Every Evening Too)/Do You Want It That Way	1961	15.00
❑ 71812	Our Love Is Here to Stay/Congratulations to Someone	1961	10.00
❑ 71812 [PS]	Our Love Is Here to Stay/Congratulations to Someone	1961	15.00
❑ 71876	September in the Rain/Wake the Town and Tell the People	1961	10.00
❑ 71876 [PS]	September in the Rain/Wake the Town and Tell the People	1961	15.00
❑ 71922	Tears and Laughter/If I Should Lose You	1962	10.00
❑ 71922 [PS]	Tears and Laughter/If I Should Lose You	1962	15.00
❑ 71958	Dream/Such a Night	1962	10.00
❑ 71958 [PS]	Dream/Such a Night	1962	15.00
❑ 72015	I Want to Be Loved/Am I Blue	1962	8.00
❑ 72015 [PS]	I Want to Be Loved/Am I Blue	1962	15.00
❑ 72040	Cold, Cold Heart/I Don't Hurt Anymore	1962	8.00
❑ 72040 [PS]	Cold, Cold Heart/I Don't Hurt Anymore	1962	15.00
ROULETTE			
❑ 4424	Where Are You/You're Nobody 'Til Somebody Loves You	1962	8.00
❑ 4444	For All We Know/I Wouldn't Know (What to Do)	1962	8.00
❑ 4455	You're a Sweetheart/It's a Mean Old Man's World	1962	8.00
❑ 4476	Romance in the Dark/No Hard Feelings	1963	8.00
❑ 4490	Soulsville/Let Me Be the First to Know	1963	8.00
❑ 4520	The Show Must Go On/I'll Drown in My Own Tears	1963	8.00
❑ 4534	That Sunday (That Summer)/A Stranger on Earth	1963	8.00
❑ 4538	Call Me Irresponsible/Funny Thing	1963	8.00

7-Inch Extended Plays

Number	Title (A Side/B Side)	Yr	NM
EMARCY			
❑ EP 1-6054	(contents unknown)	195?	25.00
❑ EP 1-6054 [PS]	After Hours with Miss "D"	195?	25.00
❑ EP-1-6080	*Lover Come Back to Me/I've Got You Under My Skin/There Is No Greater Love	1955	25.00
❑ EP-1-6080 [PS]	Dinah Jams	1955	25.00
❑ EP-1-6082	You Go to My Head (Beginning)/(Conclusion)	1955	25.00
❑ EP-1-6082 [PS]	Jammin' with Dinah	1955	25.00
❑ EP-1-6119	You Don't Know What Love Is/My Old Flame//Make the Man Love Me	1956	25.00
❑ EP-1-6119 [PS]	For Those in Love — Vol. II	1956	25.00
MERCURY			
❑ EP 1-3395	(contents unknown)	195?	20.00
❑ EP 1-3395 [PS]	Dinah Washington	195?	20.00
❑ EP 1-4035	(contents unknown)	195?	20.00
❑ EP 1-4035 [PS]	Dinah Washington	195?	20.00
❑ EP 1-4041	(contents unknown)	195?	20.00
❑ EP 1-4041 [PS]	For Lonely Lovers	195?	20.00
ROULETTE			
❑ SBG 269 [PS]	Dinah Washington	196?	15.00
❑ SBG 269 [S]	What's New/Somebody Else Is Taking My Place/I'll Never Stop Loving You//He's My Guy/To Forget About You/That Old Feeling	196?	15.00
—Jukebox issue; smal hole, plays at 33 1/3 rpm			

Albums

Number	Title (A Side/B Side)	Yr	NM
ACCORD			
❑ SN-7207	Retrospective	1982	10.00
COLLECTABLES			
❑ COL-5200	Golden Classics	1989	10.00
DELMARK			
❑ DL-451	Mellow Mama	1992	20.00
EMARCY			
❑ EMS-2-401 [(2)]	Jazz Sides	197?	15.00
❑ MG-26032 [10]	After Hours with Miss D	1954	150.00
❑ MG-36000 [M]	Dinah Jams	1955	80.00
❑ MG-36011 [M]	For Those in Love	1955	70.00
❑ MG-36028 [M]	After Hours with Miss D	1955	70.00
—Reissue of 26032			
❑ MG-36065 [M]	Dinah	1956	70.00
❑ MG-36073 [M]	In the Land of Hi-Fi	1956	60.00
❑ MG-36104 [M]	The Swingin' Miss "D"	1956	60.00
❑ MG-36119 [M]	Dinah Washington Sings Fats Waller	1957	60.00
❑ MG-36130 [M]	Dinah Washington Sings Bessie Smith	1957	60.00
❑ MG-36141 [M]	Newport '58	1958	50.00
❑ 814184-1 [(2)]	Slick Chick (On the Mellow Side)	1983	12.00
❑ 824883-1 [(2)]	Jazz Sides	198?	12.00
—Reissue of 401			
❑ 826453-1	In the Land of Hi-Fi	1986	10.00
EVEREST ARCHIVE OF FOLK & JAZZ			
❑ FS-297	Dinah Washington	197?	12.00
GRAND AWARD			
❑ GA 33-318 [M]	Dinah Washington Sings the Blues	1955	50.00
—Add 50% if removable wrap-around cover is still there			
HARLEM HIT PARADE			
❑ 8002	Finer Dinah	197?	10.00
MERCURY			
❑ MGP-2-103 [(2)M]	This Is My Story	1963	25.00
—Combines 20788 and 20789 in one package			
❑ MGP-2-603 [(2)S]	This Is My Story	1963	30.00
—Combines 60788 and 60789 in one package			
❑ MG-20119 [M]	Music for a First Love	1957	50.00
❑ MG-20120 [M]	Music for Late Hours	1957	50.00
❑ MG-20247 [M]	The Best in Blues	1958	50.00
❑ MG-20439 [M]	The Queen	1959	30.00
❑ MG-20479 [M]	What a Diff'rence a Day Makes!	1960	30.00
❑ MG-20523 [M]	Newport '58	1960	30.00
—Reissue of EmArcy 36141			
❑ MG-20525 [M]	Dinah Washington Sings Fats Waller	1960	30.00
—Reissue of EmArcy 36119			
❑ MG-20572 [M]	Unforgettable	1961	25.00
❑ MG-20604 [M]	I Concentrate on You	1961	25.00
❑ MG-20614 [M]	For Lonely Lovers	1961	25.00
❑ MG-20638 [M]	September in the Rain	1961	25.00
❑ MG-20661 [M]	Tears and Laughter	1962	25.00
❑ MG-20729 [M]	I Wanna Be Loved	1962	25.00
❑ MG-20788 [M]	This Is My Story — Dinah Washington's Golden Hits, Vol. 1	1963	15.00
❑ MG-20789 [M]	This Is My Story — Dinah Washington's Golden Hits, Vol. 2	1963	15.00
❑ MG-20829 [M]	The Good Old Days	1963	15.00
❑ MG-20928 [M]	The Queen and Quincy	1965	15.00
❑ MG-21119 [M]	Dinah Discovered	1967	20.00
❑ MG-25060 [10]	Dinah Washington	1950	150.00
❑ MG-25138 [10]	Dynamic Dinah	1952	150.00
❑ MG-25140 [10]	Blazing Ballads	1952	150.00
❑ SR-60111 [S]	The Queen	1959	40.00
❑ SR-60158 [S]	What a Diff'rence a Day Makes!	1960	40.00
❑ SR-60200 [S]	Newport '58	1960	40.00
❑ SR-60202 [S]	Dinah Washington Sings Fats Waller	1960	40.00
❑ SR-60232 [S]	Unforgettable	1961	30.00
❑ SR-60604 [S]	I Concentrate on You	1961	30.00
❑ SR-60614 [S]	For Lonely Lovers	1961	30.00
❑ SR-60638 [S]	September in the Rain	1961	30.00
❑ SR-60661 [S]	Tears and Laughter	1962	30.00
❑ SR-60729 [S]	I Wanna Be Loved	1962	30.00
❑ SR-60788 [S]	This Is My Story — Dinah Washington's Golden Hits, Vol. 1	1963	20.00
❑ SR-60789 [S]	This Is My Story — Dinah Washington's Golden Hits, Vol. 2	1963	20.00
❑ SR-60829 [S]	The Good Old Days	1963	20.00
❑ SR-60928 [S]	The Queen and Quincy	1965	20.00
❑ SR-61119 [S]	Dinah Discovered	1967	15.00

Number	Title (A Side/B Side)	Yr	NM
❑ 818815-1	What a Diff'rence a Day Makes!	198?	8.00
—Reissue			
❑ 822867-1	This Is My Story — Dinah Washington's Golden Hits, Vol. 1	1985	8.00
—Reissue			
PICKWICK			
❑ SPC-3043	Dinah Washington	196?	10.00
❑ SPC-3230	I Don't Hurt Anymore	197?	10.00
❑ SPC-3536	Greatest Hits	197?	10.00
ROULETTE			
❑ RE 104 [(2)]	Echoes of an Era	196?	15.00
❑ RE 117 [(2)]	Queen of the Blues	1971	15.00
❑ RE 125 [(2)]	The Immortal Dinah Washington	1973	15.00
❑ R 25170 [M]	Dinah '62	1962	15.00
❑ SR 25170 [S]	Dinah '62	1962	20.00
❑ R 25180 [M]	In Love	1962	15.00
❑ SR 25180 [S]	In Love	1962	20.00
❑ R 25183 [M]	Drinking Again	1962	15.00
❑ SR 25183 [S]	Drinking Again	1962	20.00
❑ R 25189 [M]	Back to the Blues	1963	15.00
❑ SR 25189 [S]	Back to the Blues	1963	20.00
❑ R 25220 [M]	Dinah '63	1963	15.00
❑ SR 25220 [S]	Dinah '63	1963	20.00
❑ R 25244 [M]	In Tribute	1963	15.00
❑ SR 25244 [S]	In Tribute	1963	20.00
❑ R 25253 [M]	A Stranger on Earth	1964	15.00
❑ SR 25253 [S]	A Stranger on Earth	1964	20.00
❑ R 25269 [M]	Dinah Washington	1964	15.00
❑ SR 25269 [S]	Dinah Washington	1964	20.00
❑ R 25289 [M]	The Best of Dinah Washington	1965	15.00
❑ SR 25289 [S]	The Best of Dinah Washington	1965	20.00
❑ 42014	The Best of Dinah Washington	1968	12.00
—Reissue of 25289			
TRIP			
❑ 5500	Dinah Jams	1973	10.00
❑ 5516	After Hours	1973	10.00
❑ 5524	Tears and Laughter	1974	10.00
❑ 5556	Dinah Washington Sings Bessie Smith	197?	10.00
❑ 5565	The Swingin' Miss D	197?	10.00
❑ TLX 9505 [(2)]	Sad Songs — Blue Songs	197?	12.00
VERVE			
❑ 818930-1	The Fats Waller Songbook	1984	10.00
WING			
❑ PKW-2-121 [(2)]	The Original Queen of Soul	1969	20.00
❑ MGW-12140 [M]	The Late Late Show	1963	12.00
❑ MGW-12271 [M]	Dinah Washington Sings Fats Waller	1964	12.00
❑ SRW-16140 [S]	The Late Late Show	1963	12.00
❑ SRW-16271 [S]	Dinah Washington Sings Fats Waller	1964	12.00
❑ SRW-16386	The Original Soul Sister	196?	12.00

WASHINGTON, DINAH, AND BROOK BENTON

Also see each artist's individual listings.

45s

Number	Title (A Side/B Side)	Yr	NM
MERCURY			
❑ 71565	Baby (You Got What It Takes)/I Do	1960	15.00
❑ 71629	A Rockin' Good Way (To Mess Around and Fall in Love)/I Believe	1960	15.00
❑ 71629 [PS]	A Rockin' Good Way (To Mess Around and Fall in Love)/I Believe	1960	25.00

Albums

Number	Title (A Side/B Side)	Yr	NM
MERCURY			
❑ MG-20588 [M]	The Two of Us	1960	25.00
❑ SR-60244 [S]	The Two of Us	1960	30.00
❑ 824823-1	The Two of Us	1985	8.00
—Reissue			

WASHINGTON, GINO

45s

Number	Title (A Side/B Side)	Yr	NM
ATAC			
❑ 101	Doin' the Popcorn/What Can a Man Do	1969	30.00
❑ 102	I'll Be Around/(B-side unknown)	1969	40.00
❑ 2830	Rat Race/(B-side unknown)	1969	30.00
❑ 7823	Like My Baby/(B-side unknown)	1969	40.00
CONGRESS			
❑ 269	Understanding/Water	1966	12.00
❑ 273	Beach Bash/Hi Hi Hazel	1966	12.00
CORREC-TONE			
❑ 503	Gino Is a Coward/Puppet on a String	1962	60.00
DJM			
❑ 1011	You Lovely Witch/Love Me, Love Me	1976	6.00
KAPP			
❑ 796	All I Need/Whatever Will Be, Will Be	1966	10.00
MALA			
❑ 12029	Like My Baby/I'll Be Around When You Want Me	1968	40.00
RIC-TIC			
❑ 100	Gino Is a Coward/Puppet on a String	1964	20.00
SIDRA			
❑ 9005	Romeo/Now You're Lonely	196?	25.00
SONBERT			
❑ 3770	Gino Is a Coward/Puppet on a String	1963	25.00
WAND			
❑ 147	Out of This World/Come Monkey with Me	1964	20.00

Albums

Number	Title (A Side/B Side)	Yr	NM
ATAC			
❑ 2730	Gino Washington's Golden Hits	1969	30.00
KAPP			
❑ KL-1415 [M]	Gino Washington's Ram Jam Band	1967	20.00
❑ KS-3415 [S]	Gino Washington's Ram Jam Band	1967	25.00

WASHINGTON, GROVER, JR.

12-Inch Singles

Number	Title (A Side/B Side)	Yr	NM
COLUMBIA			
❑ 44-06863	Summer Nights (Extended Version)/Strawberry Moon (Extended Version)	1987	15.00
ELEKTRA			
❑ ED 4903 [DJ]	Brazilian Memories (6:03)/I'll Be with You	1983	8.00
❑ ED 5004 [DJ]	Inside Moves (Edit) (LP Version)	1984	8.00
❑ AS 11470 [DJ]	Let It Flow (For Dr. J) (5:52)/Winelight	1980	12.00
❑ 67938	The Best Is Yet to Come (5:58)/More Than Meets the Eye	1982	12.00
—With Patti LaBelle			

45s

Number	Title (A Side/B Side)	Yr	NM
COLUMBIA			
❑ 38-07240	Summer Nights/Strawberry Moon	1987	5.00
❑ 38-07621	The Look of Love/Shwaree Ride	1987	5.00
❑ 38-73040	Jamaica/Split Second (Act II, The Bar Scene)	1989	6.00
ELEKTRA			
❑ 46060	Tell Me About It Now/Feel It Comin'	1979	5.00
❑ 47071	Let It Flow (For Dr. J.)/Winelight	1980	5.00
❑ 47103	Just the Two of Us/Make Me a Memory (Sad Samba)	1981	4.00
—Bill Withers sings on A-side, but is not credited on the record			
❑ 47103 [PS]	Just the Two of Us/Make Me a Memory (Sad Samba)	1981	5.00
❑ 47140	Winelight/Take Me There	1981	5.00
❑ 47246	Be Mine (Tonight)/Reaching Out	1981	4.00
❑ 47246 [PS]	Be Mine (Tonight)/Reaching Out	1981	5.00
❑ 47425	Jamming/East River Drive	1982	5.00
❑ 7-69680	When I Look at You/Secret Sounds	1984	4.00
❑ 7-69708	Inside Moves/Sassy Stew	1984	4.00
❑ 7-69834	Brazilian Memories/I'll Be with You	1983	5.00
❑ 7-69887	The Best Is Yet to Come/More Than Meets the Eye	1982	4.00
—With Patti LaBelle			
KUDU			
❑ 902	Inner City Blues/Ain't No Sunshine	1972	8.00
❑ 903	Mercy Mercy Me (Part 1)/Mercy Mercy Me (Part 2)	1972	8.00
❑ 909	No Tears in the End/Body and Soul	1972	8.00
❑ 912	Where Is the Love (Part 1)/Where Is the Love (Part 2)	1973	8.00
❑ 916	Masterpiece (Part 1)/Masterpiece (Part 2)	1973	8.00
❑ 924	Mister Magic/Black Frost	1975	8.00
❑ 930	Knuckle Head (Part 1)/Knuckle Head (Part 2)	1976	8.00
❑ 937	A Secret Place (Part 1)/A Secret Place (Part 2)	1977	8.00
❑ 942	Summer Song/Juffere	1978	8.00
MOTOWN			
❑ 1454	Do Dat/Reed Seed (Trio Tune)	1978	6.00
❑ 1454 [DJ]	Do Dat (stereo/mono)	1978	12.00
—Promo only on yellow vinyl			
❑ 1486	Snake Eyes/Love	1979	4.00

Albums

Number	Title (A Side/B Side)	Yr	NM
COLUMBIA			
❑ FC 40510	Strawberry Moon	1987	10.00
❑ OC 44256	Then and Now	1988	10.00
❑ OC 45253	Time Out of Mind	1989	10.00
❑ C 48530	Next Exit	1992	20.00
ELEKTRA			
❑ 6E-182	Paradise	1979	10.00
❑ 6E-305	Winelight	1980	10.00
❑ 5E-562	Come Morning	1981	10.00
❑ 60215	The Best Is Yet to Come	1982	10.00
❑ 60318	Inside Moves	1984	10.00
❑ 60415	Anthology of Grover Washington, Jr.	1985	10.00
KUDU			
❑ KU-03	Inner City Blues	1971	12.00
❑ KU-07	All the King's Horses	1972	12.00
❑ KU-12	Soul Box, Vol. 1	1973	12.00
❑ KU-13	Soul Box, Vol. 2	1973	12.00
❑ KU-20	Mister Magic	1975	12.00
❑ KU-24	Feels So Good	1975	12.00
❑ KU-32	A Secret Place	1976	12.00
❑ KSQX-1213 [(2)Q]	Soul Box	1973	25.00
❑ KUX-1213 [(2)]	Soul Box	1973	15.00
—The two records also were issued separately			
❑ KUX-3637 [(2)]	Live at the Bijou	1977	15.00
MOTOWN			
❑ M5-165V1	A Secret Place	1981	8.00
—Reissue of Kudu 32			
❑ M5-175V1	Mister Magic	1981	8.00
—Reissue of Kudu 20			
❑ M5-177V1	Feels So Good	1981	8.00
—Reissue of Kudu 24			
❑ M5-184V1	Soul Box, Vol. 1	1981	8.00
—Reissue of half of Kudu 1213			
❑ M5-186V1	All the King's Horses	1981	8.00
—Reissue of Kudu 07			
❑ M5-187V1	Soul Box, Vol. 2	1981	8.00
—Reissue of half of Kudu 1213			
❑ M5-189V1	Inner City Blues	1981	8.00
—Reissue of Kudu 03			
❑ M8-239 [(2)]	Live at the Bijou	1982	12.00
—Reissue			
❑ M7-910	Reed Seed	1978	10.00
❑ M7-933	Skylarkin'	1980	10.00
❑ M9-940 [(2)]	Baddest	1980	15.00
❑ M9-961A2 [(2)]	Anthology	1981	15.00
❑ 5232 ML	Skylarkin'	1982	8.00
—Reissue of 933			
❑ 5236 ML	Reed Seed	1982	8.00
—Reissue of 910			
❑ 5307 ML	Greatest Performances	1983	10.00
❑ 6126 ML	Grover Washington Jr. at His Best	198?	10.00
NAUTILUS			
❑ NR-39	Winelight	1981	50.00
—Audiophile vinyl			

WATCHPOCKET

45s

Number	Title (A Side/B Side)	Yr	NM
TMI			
❑ 75-0100	Love Will Be the Answer/People All Around Me	1972	6.00
❑ ZS7 9005	Mammy Blue/(B-side unknown)	1971	7.00

WATERBOYS, THE

12-Inch Singles

Number	Title (A Side/B Side)	Yr	NM
ENSIGN			
❑ 201	December (long) (edit)	1983	15.00
ISLAND			
❑ 661 [DJ]	Church Not Made with Hands (Edit) (same on both sides)	1984	8.00
❑ 840 [DJ]	Don't Bang the Drum (same on both sides)	1985	6.00

45s

Number	Title (A Side/B Side)	Yr	NM
CHRYSALIS			
❑ S7-17527	Fisherman's Blues/Sweet Thing	1993	3.00
❑ S7-18398	The Whole of the Moon/Medicine Bow	1995	3.00

Albums

Number	Title (A Side/B Side)	Yr	NM
CHRYSALIS			
❑ PV 41541	The Waterboys	1986	8.00
—Reissue of first U.K. LP			
❑ PV 41542	A Pagan Place	1986	8.00
—Reissue			
❑ FV 41543	This Is the Sea	1986	10.00
—Reissue			
❑ FV 41589	Fisherman's Blues	1988	10.00
ISLAND			
❑ 90147 [EP]	The Waterboys	1983	10.00
❑ 90190	A Pagan Place	1984	15.00
❑ 90457	This Is the Sea	1985	12.00

Except when noted otherwise, VG = 25% of NM, and VG+ = 50% of NM. (Example: VG = $2.00, VG+ = $4.00 and NM = $8.00.)

WATERS, MUDDY

45s

CHESS

Number	Title (A Side/B Side)	Yr	NM
❑ 1509	All Night Long/Country Boy	1952	2500.
—Note: Muddy Waters records on Chess before 1509 are unconfirmed on 45 rpm			
❑ 1514	Please Have Mercy/ Looking for My Baby	1952	800.00
❑ 1526	Standing Around Crying/ Gone to Main St.	1952	700.00
❑ 1537	She's All Right/Sad, Sad Day	1953	400.00
❑ 1542	Who's Gonna Be Your Sweet Man/Turn the Lamp Down Low	1953	300.00
❑ 1550	Mad Love/Blow, Wind, Blow	1953	120.00
❑ 1560	I'm Your Hoochie Coochie Man/ You're So Pretty	1954	100.00
❑ 1571	Just Make Love to Me/Oh Yeh!	1954	60.00
❑ 1579	I'm Ready/I Don't Know Why	1954	60.00
❑ 1585	Lovin' Man/I'm a Natural Born Lover	1955	50.00
❑ 1596	I Want to Be Loved/My Eyes Keep Me in Trouble	1955	50.00
❑ 1602	Manish Boy/ Young Fashion Ways	1955	70.00
❑ 1612	Trouble, No More/Sugar Sweet	1955	80.00
❑ 1620	Forty Days and Forty Nights/ All Aboard	1956	40.00
❑ 1630	Don't Go No Farther/ Diamonds at Your Feet	1956	50.00
❑ 1644	I Got to Find My Baby/ Just to Be with You	1956	40.00
❑ 1652	Got My Mojo Working/Rock Me	1957	50.00
❑ 1667	Good News/Come Home Baby	1957	30.00
❑ 1680	I Live the Life I Love/Evil	1958	30.00
❑ 1692	I Won't Go/She's Got It	1958	30.00
❑ 1704	Close to You/She's Nineteen Years Old	1958	30.00
❑ 1718	Mean Mistreater/ Walking Thru the Park	1959	25.00
❑ 1724	Ooh Wee/Clouds in My Heart	1959	25.00
❑ 1733	Take the Bitter with the Sweet/ She's Into Somethin'	1959	25.00
❑ 1739	Recipe for Love/Tell Me Baby	1959	25.00
❑ 1748	I Feel So Good/When I Get to Thinking	1960	25.00
❑ 1752	I'm Your Doctor/ Ready Way Back	1960	25.00
❑ 1758	Love Affair/Look What You've Done	1960	25.00
❑ 1765	Tiger in Your Tank/ Meanest Woman	1960	25.00
❑ 1774	Got My Mojo Working/ Woman Wanted	1960	25.00
❑ 1796	Messin' with the Man/ Lonesome Room Blues	1961	20.00
❑ 1819	Going Home/Tough Times	1962	20.00
❑ 1827	Muddy Waters Twist/ You Shook Me	1962	25.00
❑ 1839	You Need Love/ Little Brown Bird	1962	25.00
❑ 1862	Five Long Years/ Twenty-Four Hours	1963	15.00
❑ 1895	The Same Thing/You Can't Lose What You Never Had	1964	15.00
❑ 1914	Short Dress Woman/ My John the Conqueror	1964	15.00
❑ 1921	Put Me in Your Lay-A-Way/ Still a Fool	1965	12.00
❑ 1937	My Dog Can't Bark/I Got a Rich Man's Woman	1965	12.00
❑ 1973	I'm Your Hoochie Coochie Man/ Corrina, Corrina	1966	12.00
❑ 2018	When the Eagle Flies/ Birdnest on the Ground	1967	10.00
❑ 2085	Going Home/I Feel So Good	1970	8.00
❑ 2107	Making Friends/ Two Steps Forward	1971	8.00
❑ 2143	Garbage Man/Can't Get No Grindin'	1973	6.00

Albums

BLUE SKY

Number	Title (A Side/B Side)	Yr	NM
❑ PZ 34449	Hard Again	1977	12.00
—No bar code on cover			
❑ PZ 34449	Hard Again	198?	8.00
—Budget-line reissue with bar code			
❑ JZ 34928	I'm Ready	1978	12.00
❑ PZ 34928	I'm Ready	198?	8.00
—Budget-line reissue			
❑ JZ 35712	Muddy "Mississippi" Waters Live	1980	12.00
❑ PZ 35712	Muddy "Mississippi" Waters Live	198?	8.00
—Budget-line reissue			
❑ JZ 37064	King Bee	1981	12.00
❑ PZ 37064	King Bee	198?	8.00
—Budget-line reissue			

CADET CONCEPT

Number	Title (A Side/B Side)	Yr	NM
❑ CS-314	Electric Mud	1968	25.00
❑ CS-320	After the Rain	1969	25.00

CHESS

Number	Title (A Side/B Side)	Yr	NM
❑ 127 [(2)]	Fathers and Sons	1969	25.00
❑ LP-1427 [DJ]	The Best of Muddy Waters	1957	1500.
—White label promo; VG value 500; VG+ value 1000			
❑ LP-1427 [M]	The Best of Muddy Waters	1957	500.00
—Black label			
❑ LPS-1427 [R]	The Best of Muddy Waters	196?	12.00
—Black label			
❑ LP-1444 [DJ]	Muddy Waters Sings Big Bill	1960	1000.
—White label promo			
❑ LP-1444 [M]	Muddy Waters Sings Big Bill	1960	300.00
❑ LPS-1444 [R]	Muddy Waters Sings Big Bill	196?	15.00
—Rechanneled stereo reissue			
❑ LP-1449 [M]	Muddy Waters at Newport	1962	120.00
❑ LP-1483 [M]	Folk Singer	1964	120.00
❑ LP-1501 [M]	The Real Folk Blues of Muddy Waters	1965	60.00
❑ LP-1507 [M]	Muddy, Brass and Blues	1966	40.00
❑ LPS-1507 [S]	Muddy, Brass and Blues	1966	50.00
❑ LP-1511 [M]	More Real Folk Blues	1967	50.00
❑ LPS-1511 [S]	More Real Folk Blues	1967	40.00
❑ LP-1533 [M]	Blues from Big Bill's Copacabana	1968	50.00
❑ LPS-1539	Sail On	1969	25.00
❑ LPS-1553	They Call Me Muddy Waters	1971	20.00
❑ CH-9101	Rolling Stone	1985	12.00
❑ CH-9180	Rare and Unissued	1986	12.00
❑ CH-9197	Muddy Waters Sings Big Bill	1986	10.00
—Reissue of 1444			
❑ CH-9198	Muddy Waters at Newport	1986	10.00
—Reissue of 1449			
❑ CH-9255	The Best of Muddy Waters	1987	10.00
—Reissue of 1427			
❑ CH-9261	Folk Singer	1987	10.00
—Reissue of 1483			
❑ CH-9274	The Real Folk Blues of Muddy Waters	1987	10.00
—Reissue of 1501			
❑ CH-9278	More Real Folk Blues	1988	10.00
—Reissue of 1511			
❑ CH-9286	Muddy, Brass and the Blues	1989	10.00
—Reissue of 1507			
❑ CH-9291	Trouble No More: Singles 1955-1959	1989	12.00
❑ CH-9298	The London Muddy Waters Sessions	1989	10.00
—Reissue of 60013			
❑ CH-9299	They Call Me Muddy Waters	1989	10.00
—Reissue of 1553			
❑ CH-9319	Can't Get No Grindin'	1990	10.00
—Reissue of 50023			
❑ CH-50012	Muddy Waters Live	1972	20.00
❑ CH-50023	Can't Get No Grindin'	1973	20.00
❑ 2CH-50033 [(2)]	Fathers and Sons	1974	20.00
—Reissue of 127			
❑ CH-50035	The Muddy Waters Woodstock Album	1976	15.00
❑ 2CH-60006 [(2)]	McKinley Morganfield, A.K.A. Muddy Waters	1971	25.00
❑ CH-60013	The London Muddy Waters Sessions	1972	20.00
❑ CH-60026	London Revisited	1974	15.00
❑ CH-60031	"Unk" in Funk	1975	15.00
❑ CH6-80002 [(6)]	The Chess Box	1990	50.00

INTERMEDIA

Number	Title (A Side/B Side)	Yr	NM
❑ QS-5071	Sweet Home Chicago	198?	10.00

MOBILE FIDELITY

Number	Title (A Side/B Side)	Yr	NM
❑ 1-201	Folk Singer	1994	50.00
—Audiophile vinyl			

MUSE

Number	Title (A Side/B Side)	Yr	NM
❑ MR-5008	Mud in Your Ear	198?	12.00

TESTAMENT

Number	Title (A Side/B Side)	Yr	NM
❑ 2210	Stovall's Plantation	197?	12.00

WATERS, MUDDY, AND HOWLIN' WOLF

Also see each artist's individual listings.

Albums

CHESS

Number	Title (A Side/B Side)	Yr	NM
❑ CH-9100	Muddy and The Wolf	1985	12.00

WATERS, ROGER

45s

COLUMBIA

Number	Title (A Side/B Side)	Yr	NM
❑ 38-04455	5:01 A.M. (The Pros and Cons of Hitch Hiking)/4:30 A.M. (Apparently They Were Travelling Abroad)	1984	3.00
❑ 38-04566	5:06 A.M. (Every Stranger's Eyes)/4:56 A.M. (For the First Time Today, Part 1)	1984	3.00
❑ 38-07180	Radio Waves/ Going to Live in L.A.	1987	3.00
❑ 38-07180 [PS]	Radio Waves/ Going to Live in L.A.	1987	3.00
❑ 38-07364	Sunset Strip/Money	1987	3.00
❑ 38-07364 [PS]	Sunset Strip/Money	1987	3.00
❑ 38-07617	Who Needs Information/ Molly's Song	1987	3.00
❑ 38-74363	What God Wants, Part 1 (Long)/What God Wants, Part 1 (Short)	1992	3.00

Albums

COLUMBIA

Number	Title (A Side/B Side)	Yr	NM
❑ FC 39290	The Pros and Cons of Hitch Hiking	1984	10.00
—Revised cover with black rectangle over woman's naked rear end			
❑ FC 39290	The Pros and Cons of Hitch Hiking	1984	20.00
—Original nude cover			
❑ PC 39290	The Pros and Cons of Hitch Hiking	1986	10.00
—Budget-line reissue with new prefix			
❑ FC 40795	Radio K.A.O.S.	1987	10.00

MERCURY

Number	Title (A Side/B Side)	Yr	NM
❑ R 209833 [(2)]	The Wall — Live in Berlin	1990	28.00
—BMG Direct Marketing version			
❑ 846611-1 [(2)]	The Wall — Live in Berlin	1990	30.00

WATKINS, LOVELACE

45s

GROOVE

Number	Title (A Side/B Side)	Yr	NM
❑ 58-0016	Tender Love/ Ma Cherie Au Revoir	1963	30.00
❑ 58-0016 [PS]	Tender Love/ Ma Cherie Au Revoir	1963	80.00
❑ 58-0023	I Won't Believe It/He'[s Lookin' Out for the World	1963	30.00

MGM

Number	Title (A Side/B Side)	Yr	NM
❑ 12875	Hello Young Lovers/When I Fall in Love	1960	15.00

SUE

Number	Title (A Side/B Side)	Yr	NM
❑ 10-003	Who Am I/Dreams	1968	12.00

UNI

Number	Title (A Side/B Side)	Yr	NM
❑ 55211	Fool on the Hill/Je Vous Aime Beaucoup	1970	12.00

Albums

MGM

Number	Title (A Side/B Side)	Yr	NM
❑ E-3831 [M]	The Voice of Lovelace Watkins	1960	25.00
❑ SE-3831 [S]	The Voice of Lovelace Watkins	1960	40.00

WATSON, CLAYTON

45s

LAVENDER

Number	Title (A Side/B Side)	Yr	NM
❑ 2454	Everybody's Boppin'/ Tall Skinny Annie	1958	400.00

WATSON, JOHN L., AND THE HUMMELFUGS

45s

PARKWAY

Number	Title (A Side/B Side)	Yr	NM
❑ 946	Lookin' for Love/I Only Came to Dance with You	1965	12.00

WATSON, JOHNNY "GUITAR"

45s

A&M

Number	Title (A Side/B Side)	Yr	NM
❑ 2383	Planet Funk/First Timothy Six	1981	4.00
❑ 2398	That's What Time It Is/ First Timothy Six	1982	4.00

ARVEE

Number	Title (A Side/B Side)	Yr	NM
❑ 5016	Untouchable/Johnny Guitar	1960	25.00
—As "Johnny Watson"			

CACTUS

Number	Title (A Side/B Side)	Yr	NM
❑ 118	Let's Rock/(B-side unknown)	1959	150.00

CLASS

Number	Title (A Side/B Side)	Yr	NM
❑ 246	The Bear/One More Kiss	1959	30.00
—As "Johnny Watson"			

DJM

Number	Title (A Side/B Side)	Yr	NM
❑ 1013	I Need It/Since I Met You Baby	1976	5.00
❑ 1019	Superman Lover/We're No Exception	1976	5.00
❑ 1020	Ain't That a Bitch/Won't You Forgive Me Baby	1977	6.00
❑ 1020 [PS]	Ain't That a Bitch/Won't You Forgive Me Baby	1977	8.00
❑ 1024	A Real Mother For Ya/ Nothing Left to Be Desired	1977	5.00
❑ 1029	Lover Jones/Tarzan	1977	5.00
❑ 1034	Love That Will Not Die/ A Damn Shame	1978	5.00
❑ 1100	Virginia's Pretty Funky/ The Institute	1978	5.00
—As "Watsonian Institute"			
❑ 1101	Gangster of Love/Guitar Disco	1978	5.00
❑ 1106	What the Hell Is This?/ Can You Handle It	1979	5.00
❑ 1304	Love Jones/(B-side unknown)	1980	5.00
❑ 1305	Telephone Bill/(B-side unknown)	1980	5.00

FANTASY

Number	Title (A Side/B Side)	Yr	NM
❑ 721	Like I'm Not Your Man/ You Bring Love	1974	6.00

W

Number	Title (A Side/B Side)	Yr	NM
❑ 739	I Don't Want to Be a Lone Ranger/You Can Stay But the Noise Must Go	1975	6.00
❑ 752	It's Too Late/Tripping	1975	6.00
FEDERAL			
❑ 12120	Highway 60/No I Can't	1953	150.00
❑ 12131	Motor Head Baby/Sad Fool	1953	150.00
❑ 12143	I Got Eyes/Walkin' to My Baby	1953	150.00
❑ 12157	What's Going On/Thinking	1953	150.00
❑ 12175	Half Pint of Whiskey/Space Guitar	1954	250.00
❑ 12183	Gettin' Drunk/You Can't Take It With You	1954	200.00
—All Federal 45s as "Young John Watson"			
KEEN			
❑ 3-4005	Gangster of Love/One Room Country Shack	1957	30.00
❑ 3-4023	Deana Baby/Honey	1957	30.00
KENT			
❑ 328	Those Lonely, Lonely Nights/(B-side unknown)	1959	20.00
KING			
❑ 5536	Posin'/Embraceable You	1961	20.00
❑ 5579	Broke and Lonely/Cuttin' In	1961	25.00
❑ 5607	The Nearness of You/I Just Want Me Some Love	1962	15.00
❑ 5666	What You Do to Me/Sweet Lovin' Mama	1962	15.00
❑ 5716	Cold, Cold Heart/That's the Chance You've Got to Take	1963	15.00
❑ 5774	Gangster of Love/In the Evening	1963	15.00
❑ 5833	I Say, I Love You/You Better Love Me	1964	15.00
OKEH			
❑ 7263	Keep On Lovin' You/South Like West	1966	12.00
❑ 7270	Hold On, I'm Comin'/Wolfman	1967	12.00
RPM			
❑ 423	Hot Little Mama/I Love to Love You	1955	50.00
❑ 431	Too Tired/Don't Touch Me	1955	50.00
❑ 436	Those Lonely, Lonely Nights/Someone Cares for Me	1955	40.00
❑ 447	Oh Baby/Give a Little	1955	40.00
❑ 455	Three Hours Past Midnight/Ruben	1956	40.00
❑ 471	She Moves Me/Love Me Baby	1956	40.00
VALLEY VUE			
❑ 769	Strike On Computers/(B-side unknown)	1984	5.00
Albums			
A&M			
❑ SP-4880	That's What Time It Is	1981	10.00
CADET			
❑ LP-4056 [M]	I Cried for You	1967	25.00
❑ LPS-4056 [S]	I Cried for You	1967	30.00
CHESS			
❑ LP-1490 [M]	Blues Soul	1965	70.00
❑ LPS-1490 [S]	Blues Soul	1965	80.00
DJM			
❑ 3	Ain't That a Bitch	1976	10.00
❑ 7	A Real Mother for Ya	1977	10.00
❑ 13	Master Funk	1978	10.00
—As "Watsonian Institute"			
❑ 19	Giant	1978	10.00
❑ 24	What the Hell Is This?	1979	10.00
❑ 27	E.D.P. Extra Disco Perception	1979	10.00
—As "Watsonian Institute"			
❑ 31	Love Jones	1980	10.00
❑ 501	Johnny "Guitar" Watson and the Family Clone	1981	10.00
❑ 714	Funk Beyond the Call of Duty	1977	10.00
FANTASY			
❑ MPF-4503	Greatest Hits	1981	10.00
❑ 9437	Listen	1973	12.00
❑ 9484	I Don't Want to Be Alone Stranger	1975	12.00
KING			
❑ 857 [M]	Johnny Guitar Watson	1963	400.00
MCA			
❑ 5273	The Very Best of Johnny "Guitar" Watson	1981	10.00
OKEH			
❑ OKM 12118 [M]	Bad	1967	30.00
❑ OKM 12124 [M]	In the Fats Bag	1967	30.00
❑ OKS 14118 [S]	Bad	1967	40.00
❑ OKS 14124 [S]	In the Fats Bag	1967	40.00
POWER PAK			
❑ 306	Gangster of Love	1978	10.00

WATSON, JOHNNY "GUITAR", AND LARRY WILLIAMS

Also see each artist's individual listings.

Number	Title (A Side/B Side)	Yr	NM
45s			
OKEH			
❑ 7274	Mercy, Mercy, Mercy/A Quitter Never Wins	1967	10.00
❑ 7281	Two for the Price of One/Too Late	1967	10.00
❑ 7281 [PS]	Two for the Price of One/Too Late	1967	25.00
❑ 7300	Find Yourself Someone to Love/Nobody	1967	25.00
—Backed by Kaleidoscope			
Albums			
OKEH			
❑ OKM 12122 [M]	Two for the Price of One	1967	40.00
❑ OKS 14122 [S]	Two for the Price of One	1967	60.00

WATSONIAN INSTITUTE

See JOHNNY "GUITAR" WATSON.

WATTS, ALAN

Number	Title (A Side/B Side)	Yr	NM
Albums			
ASCENSION			
❑ (# unknown)	Dhyana: of the Art of Meditation, Vol. 1	1970	30.00
❑ (# unknown)	Dhyana: of the Art of Meditation, Vol. 2	1970	30.00
MEA			
❑ LP-1001 [M]	Haiku Poems	1962	50.00
❑ LP-1002 [M]	Zen and Senryu	1962	50.00
❑ LP-1007 [M]	This Is It	1962	60.00
TOGETHER			
❑ 1025	Why Not Now	1970	25.00
WARNER BROS.			
❑ W 1923	The Sounds of Hinduism	1968	25.00

WATTS, CHARLIE

Number	Title (A Side/B Side)	Yr	NM
Albums			
COLUMBIA			
❑ FC 40570	The Charlie Watts Orchestra Live Fulham Town Hall	1986	15.00
CONTINUUM			
❑ 19308	From One Charlie	1990	25.00
—Box set with LP, book ("Ode to a High Flying Bird") and photo of Charlie Parker			

WATTS, NOBLE

Number	Title (A Side/B Side)	Yr	NM
45s			
BATON			
❑ 246	Easy Going (Part 1)/Easy Going (Part 2)	1957	25.00
❑ 249	Hard Times (The Slop)/Midnite Flight	1957	15.00
❑ 249	The Slop/Midnite Flight	1957	25.00
❑ 251	Rickey Tick/Blast Off	1958	15.00
❑ 254	The Slide/Shakin'	1958	15.00
❑ 257	Great Times/The Creep	1958	15.00
❑ 266	Flap Jack/Hot Tamales	1959	15.00
BRUNSWICK			
❑ 55382	Thingamajig/F.L.A.	1968	8.00
CUB			
❑ 9078	The Beaver/Frog Hop	1960	12.00
DELUXE			
❑ 6066	Mashing Potatoes/Pig Ears and Rice	1954	30.00
ENJOY			
❑ 1008	Jookin'/What Ya Gonna Do	1963	12.00
SIR			
❑ 273	Boogie Woogie/Mashed Potatoes	1959	15.00
VEE JAY			
❑ 268	South Shore Drive/Big Two Four	1956	30.00

WATTS 103RD STREET RHYTHM BAND, THE

See CHARLES WRIGHT AND THE WATTS 103RD STREET RHYTHM BAND.

❑ WAYLON AND JESSI

Also see JESSI COLTER; WAYLON JENNINGS.

Number	Title (A Side/B Side)	Yr	NM
45s			
RCA			
❑ PB-12176	Storms Never Last/I Ain't the One	1982	4.00
❑ PB-12245	Wild Side of Life/It Wasn't God Who Made Honky Tonk Angels	1982	4.00
RCA VICTOR			
❑ 47-9920	Suspicious Minds/I Ain't the One	1970	6.00
❑ 47-9992	Under Your Spell Again/Bridge Over Troubled Water	1971	6.00
❑ PB-10653	Suspicious Minds/I Ain't the One	1976	5.00
Albums			
RCA VICTOR			
❑ AAL1-3931	Leather and Lace	1981	10.00

WAYLON AND WILLIE

For convenience's sake, we've listed all the variations of their credits here, including "Willie Nelson and Waylon Jennings." Also see WAYLON JENNINGS; WILLIE NELSON.

Number	Title (A Side/B Side)	Yr	NM
45s			
COLUMBIA			
❑ 04131	Take It to the Limit/Till I Gain Control Again	1983	4.00
❑ 04131 [PS]	Take It to the Limit/Till I Gain Control Again	1983	5.00
EPIC			
❑ 73832	If I Can Find a Clean Shirt/Put Me on a Train Back to Texas	1991	3.00
❑ 74024	Tryin' to Outrun the Wind/The Makin's of a Song	1991	3.00
RCA			
❑ PB-11198	Mammas Don't Let Your Babies Grow Up to Be Cowboys/I Can Get Off on You	1978	4.00
❑ GB-11499	Mammas Don't Let Your Babies Grow Up to Be Cowboys/Luckenbach, Texas (Back to the Basics of Love)	1979	4.00
—Gold Standard Series			
❑ GB-11996	Mammas Don't Let Your Babies Grow Up to Be Cowboys/I Can Get Off on You	1980	3.00
—Gold Standard Series			
❑ PB-13073	Just to Satisfy You/Get Naked With You	1982	4.00
❑ PB-13319	(Sittin' On) The Dock of the Bay/Luckenbach, Texas	1982	4.00
RCA VICTOR			
❑ PB-10529	Good Hearted Woman/Heaven or Hell	1975	5.00
Albums			
COLUMBIA			
❑ FC 38562	Take It to the Limit	1983	10.00
RCA VICTOR			
❑ AAL1-2686	Waylon and Willie	198?	8.00
—Reissue with new prefix			
❑ AFL1-2686	Waylon and Willie	1978	10.00
❑ AFL1-2686 [DJ]	Waylon and Willie	1978	25.00
—Promo only on gold vinyl			
❑ AHL1-4455	WW II	1982	10.00
❑ AYL1-5134	Waylon and Willie	198?	8.00
—"Best Buy Series" reissue			
❑ AYL1-5138	WW II	198?	8.00
—"Best Buy Series" reissue			

WAYLON AND WILLIE/WAYLON AND JESSI

Number	Title (A Side/B Side)	Yr	NM
45s			
RCA			
❑ GB-10928	Good Hearted Woman/Suspicious Minds	1977	3.00
—Gold Standard Series			

WAYNE, ALVIS

Number	Title (A Side/B Side)	Yr	NM
45s			
ROLLIN' ROCK			
❑ 32	I Wanna Eat Your Pudding/It's Your Last Chance to Dance Tonight	1975	15.00
WESTPORT			
❑ 132	Swing Bop Boogie/Sleep, Rock-a-Roll Rock-a-Baby	1956	200.00
❑ 138	Don't Mean Maybe Baby/I'd Rather Be with You	1957	150.00
—As "Tony Wayne"			
❑ 138	Don't Mean Maybe Baby/I'd Rather Be with You	1958	100.00
—As "Alvis Wayne"			

WAYNE, BERNIE

Number	Title (A Side/B Side)	Yr	NM
45s			
ABC-PARAMOUNT			
❑ 9664	Vanessa/Piff, Paff, Puff	1956	20.00
❑ 9679	You're Kinda Cute/The Night Was Made for Dreamers	1956	20.00
❑ 9727	Shalimar/South of Saigon	1956	20.00
❑ 9752	Flirtango/Maracaibo	1956	20.00
❑ 9815	Leaky Faucet/Theme from "Abner the Baseball"	1957	20.00
❑ 9967	The Telegraph Operator and the Chorus Girl/Cool Caballero	1958	20.00
HANOVER			
❑ 4528	Now/Chickie	1960	20.00

W

Except when noted otherwise, VG = 25% of NM, and VG+ = 50% of NM. (Example: VG = $2.00, VG+ = $4.00 and NM = $8.00.)

Number	Title (A Side/B Side)	Yr	NM
IMPERIAL			
❑ 5575	The Whistling Pixie/Soft Shoe Rock	1959	15.00
RUST			
❑ 5063	38-24-38/Martinique	1963	12.00
20TH CENTURY FOX			
❑ 559	Christmas Is Over/Christmas Is Over	1964	8.00
—B-side by the Hushtones			

WAYNE, BILLY

Number	Title (A Side/B Side)	Yr	NM
45s			
FEDORA			
❑ 1008	Telegram/Heartbreak and Blues	1962	25.00
HILLCREST			
❑ 778	I Love My Baby/Walkin' n' Strollin'	1960	800.00

WAYNE, CARL, AND THE VIKINGS

Number	Title (A Side/B Side)	Yr	NM
45s			
ABC-PARAMOUNT			
❑ 10752	Shimmy Shammy Jingle/My Girl	1965	35.00

WAYNE, FARLEY

Number	Title (A Side/B Side)	Yr	NM
45s			
HIT			
❑ 18	That's Old Fashioned/Wolverton Mountain	1962	8.00

WAYNE, JOHN

Number	Title (A Side/B Side)	Yr	NM
45s			
CASABLANCA			
❑ 1002	I Have Faith/The Prayer	1979	6.00
LIBERTY			
❑ 55389	I Have Faith/Walk with Him	1961	12.00
Albums			
RCA VICTOR			
❑ AFL1-3484	America, Why I Love Her	1979	10.00
—Reissue of 4828			
❑ AYL1-3959	America, Why I Love Her	1981	8.00
—"Best Buy Series" reissue			
❑ LSP-4828	America, Why I Love Her	1973	25.00

WAYNE, THOMAS

Number	Title (A Side/B Side)	Yr	NM
45s			
CAPEHART			
❑ 5009	Tragedy/No More, No More	1961	30.00
CHALET			
❑ 1054	No One/You're Tearin' Down My Mind	1969	6.00
FERNWOOD			
❑ 106	You're the One That Done It/This Time	1958	300.00
❑ 109	Tragedy/Saturday Date	1959	30.00
❑ 111	Eternally/Scandalizing My Name	1959	30.00
❑ 113	Gonna Be Waitin'/Just Beyond	1959	30.00
❑ 120	Guilty of Love/Pancho Villa	1960	30.00
❑ 122	Girl Next Door/Because of You	1960	30.00
❑ 128	Tragedy/No More, No More	1961	30.00
MERCURY			
❑ 71287	You're the One That Done It/This Time	1958	80.00
❑ 71454	You're the One That Done It/This Time	1959	40.00
PHILLIPS INT'L.			
❑ 3577	I've Got It Made/The Quiet Look	1962	25.00
SANTO			
❑ 9053	Stop the River/Eighth Wonder of the World	1962	25.00
❑ 9057	Tragedy/Gonna Be Waiting	1962	25.00

WAYNE AND DEE

Number	Title (A Side/B Side)	Yr	NM
45s			
HIT			
❑ 221	I Got You Babe/Eve of Destruction	1965	12.00
—B-side by the Roamers			

WE FIVE

Number	Title (A Side/B Side)	Yr	NM
45s			
A&M			
❑ XMAS 1 [DJ]	My Favorite Things/The 12 Days Of Christmas	1968	12.00
—B-side by the Baja Marimba Band			
❑ XMAS 1 [PS]	My Favorite Things/The 12 Days Of Christmas	1968	15.00
—B-side by the Baja Marimba Band			
❑ 770	You Were On My Mind/Small World	1965	12.00
❑ 784	Let's Get Together/Cast Your Fate to the Wind	1965	8.00
❑ 793	You Let a Love Burn Out/Somewhere Beyond the Sea	1966	15.00
❑ 800	Somewhere/There Stands the Door	1966	15.00
❑ 820	What's Goin' On/The First Time	1966	8.00
❑ 894	High Flying Bird/What Do I Do	1967	6.00
❑ 1072	Walk On By/It Really Doesn't Matter	1969	6.00
MGM			
❑ 14618	Seven Day Change/Natural Way	1973	5.00
VAULT			
❑ 964	Never Goin' Back/Here Comes the Sun	1970	6.00
❑ 969	Catch the Wind/Oh, Lonesome Me	1970	6.00
VERVE			
❑ 10716	Bandstand Dancer/Rejoice	1973	5.00
7-Inch Extended Plays			
A&M			
❑ SP 411	You Were On My Mind/Softly, As I Leave You/Small World/ /Love Me Not Tomorrow/I Can Never Go Home Again/I Got Plenty o' Nuttin'	1965	15.00
—Stereo jukebox issue; small hole, plays at 33 1/3 rpm			
❑ SP 411 [PS]	You Were On My Mind	1965	15.00
❑ SP 438	Let's Get Together/Make Someone Happy/Somewhere/ /The First Time/Our Day Will Come/The Inch Worm	1966	15.00
—Stereo jukebox issue; small hole, plays at 33 1/3 rpm			
❑ SP 438 [PS]	Make Someone Happy	1966	15.00
Albums			
A&M			
❑ SP-111 [M]	You Were On My Mind	1965	15.00
❑ SP-138 [M]	Make Someone Happy	1967	20.00
❑ SP-4111 [S]	You Were On My Mind	1965	20.00
❑ SP-4138 [S]	Make Someone Happy	1967	15.00
❑ SP-4168	The Return of We Five	1969	15.00
VAULT			
❑ 136	Catch the Wind	1970	15.00

WE THE PEOPLE (1) Rock band from Florida.

Number	Title (A Side/B Side)	Yr	NM
45s			
CHALLENGE			
❑ 59333	Mirror of Your Mind/The Color of Love	1966	100.00
❑ 59340	You Burn Me Up and Down/He Doesn't Go About It Right	1966	100.00
❑ 59351	In the Past/St. John's Shop	1966	100.00
HOTLINE			
❑ 3680	My Brother, The Man/Proceed with Caution	1966	200.00
RCA VICTOR			
❑ 47-9292	Follow Me Back to Louisville/Fluorescent Hearts	1967	25.00
❑ 47-9393	Love Is a Beautiful Thing/The Day She Dies	1967	25.00
❑ 47-9498	When I Arrive/Ain't Gonna Find Nobody (Better Than You)	1968	75.00
REENA			
❑ 105	For No One to See/Feelings of My Emptiness	1967	50.00
❑ 116	Back Street Thoughts/Who Am I?	1967	50.00

WE THE PEOPLE (2) R&B group from New York.

Number	Title (A Side/B Side)	Yr	NM
45s			
LION			
❑ 122	You Made Me (A Brand New World)/Right Now	1972	15.00
❑ 148	Forgotten Man/Left in the Lost & Found	1973	20.00
❑ 164	Making My Daydream Real/Whatcha Done for Me, I'm Gonna Do for You	1974	200.00
MAP CITY			
❑ 305	Cat and Mouse (Round and Round)/We Can Survive	1969	12.00
VERVE			
❑ 10665	We Done Threw It Away/Right Now	1971	20.00

WE THE PEOPLE (U) Probably not (1), but it might be (2).

Number	Title (A Side/B Side)	Yr	NM
45s			
IMPERIAL			
❑ 66404	Moonstep/Earthrise	1969	15.00

WE TWO

Number	Title (A Side/B Side)	Yr	NM
45s			
ABC			
❑ 10930	Magic Moments/Way Down Deep Inside	1967	25.00

WEASELS, THE

Number	Title (A Side/B Side)	Yr	NM
Albums			
WING			
❑ MGW-12282 [M]	The Liverpool Beat	1964	25.00
❑ SRW-16282 [S]	The Liverpool Beat	1964	30.00

WEATHER REPORT Also see WAYNE SHORTER.

Number	Title (A Side/B Side)	Yr	NM
45s			
ARC			
❑ 10861	River People/Pursuit of the Woman with the Feathered Hat	1978	4.00
❑ 11166	Birdland/Brown Street	1979	4.00
❑ 11422	Rockin' in Rhythm/(B-side unknown)	1981	4.00
COLUMBIA			
❑ 10004	American Tango/(B-side unknown)	1974	5.00
❑ 10215	Between the Thighs/Lusitano	1975	5.00
❑ 10532	Birdland/Palladium	1977	5.00
❑ 45883	Adios/Boogie Woogie Waltz	1973	5.00
❑ 45964	125th Street Congress/Will	1973	5.00
Albums			
ARC			
❑ JC 35358	Mr. Gone	1978	10.00
—Original issue; no bar code on cover			
❑ PC 35358	Mr. Gone	1980	8.00
—Budget-line reissue; bar code on back cover			
❑ PC2 36030 [(2)]	8:30	1979	15.00
❑ JC 36793	Night Passage	1980	10.00
❑ PC 36793	Night Passage	198?	8.00
—Budget-line reissue			
❑ FC 37616	Weather Report	1982	10.00
❑ PC 37616	Weather Report	198?	8.00
—Budget-line reissue			
❑ HC 47616	Weather Report	1982	40.00
—"Half Speed Mastered" on cover			
COLUMBIA			
❑ C 30661	Weather Report	1971	12.00
—Original edition; no bar code on cover			
❑ KC 30661	Weather Report	1974	10.00
—Reissue of C 30661			
❑ PC 30661	Weather Report	1977	8.00
—Reissue; with or without bar code on cover			
❑ KC 31352	I Sing the Body Electric	1972	12.00
—Original edition; no bar code on cover			
❑ PC 31352	I Sing the Body Electric	1977	8.00
—Reissue; with or without bar code on cover			
❑ KC 32210	Sweetnighter	1973	12.00
—Original edition; no bar code on back cover			
❑ PC 32210	Sweetnighter	1977	8.00
—Reissue with new prefix; with or without bar code on cover			
❑ CQ 32494 [Q]	Mysterious Traveller	1974	30.00
❑ KC 32494	Mysterious Traveller	1974	12.00
—Original issue; no bar code on cover			
❑ PC 32494	Mysterious Traveller	1977	8.00
—Reissue; with or without bar code on cover			
❑ PC 33417	Tale Spinnin'	1975	12.00
—Original edition; no bar code on cover			
❑ PC 33417	Tale Spinnin'	1977	8.00
—Budget-line reissue; with or without bar code			
❑ PCQ 33417 [Q]	Tale Spinnin'	1975	30.00
❑ PC 34099	Black Market	1976	12.00
—No bar code on cover			
❑ PC 34099	Black Market	1980	8.00
—With bar code on cover			
❑ PC 34418	Heavy Weather	1977	10.00
—No bar code on cover			
❑ PC 34418	Heavy Weather	198?	8.00
—Budget-line reissue; bar code on back cover			
❑ FC 38427	Procession	1983	10.00
❑ FC 39147	Domino Theory	1984	10.00
❑ FC 39908	Sportin' Life	1985	10.00
❑ FC 40280	This Is This	1986	12.00
❑ HC 44418	Heavy Weather	198?	40.00
—"Half-Speed Mastered" on cover			

WEATHERLY, JIM

Number	Title (A Side/B Side)	Yr	NM
45s			
ABC			
❑ 12193	(Apples Won't Grow In) Colorado Snow/To a Gentler Time	1976	5.00
❑ 12213	Gonna Shine It On Again/People Some People Choose to Love	1976	5.00
❑ 12252	Storms of Troubled Times/(B-side unknown)	1977	5.00
❑ 12288	All That Keeps Me Going/I Hope It Never Rains Like That Again	1977	5.00

W

Number	Title (A Side/B Side)	Yr	NM
BUDDAH			
❑ 420	The Need to Be/Like Old Times Again	1974	5.00
❑ 420 [PS]	The Need to Be/Like Old Times Again	1974	6.00
❑ 444	I'll Still Love You/My First Day Without Her	1974	5.00
❑ 467	It Must Have Been the Rain/Mississippi	1975	5.00
❑ 505	What's One More Time/How'd We Ever Get This Way	1975	5.00
ELEKTRA			
❑ 46547	Smooth Sailin'/Let Me Love It Away	1979	4.00
❑ 46592	Gift from Missouri/All I Need to Know	1980	4.00
❑ 47027	Safe in the Arms of Your Love (Cold in the Streets)/All I Need to Know	1980	4.00
❑ 47096	Love That Went Away/(B-side unknown)	1980	4.00
RCA VICTOR			
❑ 74-0822	Loving You Is Just an Old Habit/Between His Goodbye and My Hello	1972	6.00
❑ 74-0897	Old Kentucky Moon/Until Your Ship Comes In	1973	6.00
❑ 74-0949	Where Peaceful Waters Flow/Like a First Time Thing	1973	6.00
❑ APBO-0020	Leavin' Dallas/It Must Be Love This Time	1973	5.00
❑ APBO-0153	Rebel Keeps On Rollin'/Same Old Song and Dance	1973	5.00
❑ PB-10134	High on Love/Like a First Time Thing	1974	5.00
20TH CENTURY FOX			
❑ 565	I'm Gonna Make It/Wise Men Never Speak	1965	15.00

Albums

Number	Title	Yr	NM
ABC			
❑ ABCD-937	The People Some People Choose to Love	1976	10.00
❑ ABCD-982	Pictures and Rhymes	1977	10.00
BUDDAH			
❑ BDS-5608	The Songs of Jim Weatherly	1974	10.00
❑ BDS-5637	Magnolias & Misfits	1975	10.00
RCA VICTOR			
❑ APL1-0090	A Simpler Time	1973	12.00
❑ APL1-0267	Jim Weatherly	1974	12.00
❑ LSP-4747	Weatherly	1972	12.00

WEAVER, DENNIS

45s

Number	Title (A Side/B Side)	Yr	NM
CASCADE			
❑ 5906	Girls (Wuz Made to Be Loved)/Michael Finnigan	1959	20.00
CENTURY CITY			
❑ 701	Days Like These/Cobwebs of Your Mind	1969	8.00
EVA			
❑ 103	The Apes/Chicken Mash	1963	12.00
IM'PRESS			
❑ 716	20th Century Man/No Name	1973	6.00
OVATION			
❑ 1056	Hubbardville Store/Prairie Dog Blues	1975	4.00
❑ 1056 [PS]	Hubbardville Store/Prairie Dog Blues	1975	5.00
WARNER BROS.			
❑ 5352	The Sinking of the Reuben James/Genesis Through Exodus	1963	15.00

Albums

Number	Title	Yr	NM
ABC			
❑ DP-847	People Songs	1974	12.00
IM'PRESS			
❑ 1614	Dennis Weaver	1972	15.00
OVATION			
❑ OVOD-1440	One More Road	1975	12.00

WEAVERS, THE Also see PETE SEEGER.

45s

Number	Title (A Side/B Side)	Yr	NM
DECCA			
❑ 9-284 [PS]	We Wish You a Merry Christmas	1951	15.00
—Empty box for 27783, 27817, 27818, 27819			
❑ 9-27053	Tzena, Tzena, Tzena/Around the World	1950	25.00
❑ 9-27077	Goodnight Irene/Tzena, Tzena, Tzena	1950	20.00
—Co-credited with Gordon Jenkins and His Orchestra			
❑ 27332	The Roving Kind/(The Wreck of the) John B	1950	15.00
❑ 27376	So Long (It's Been Good to Know Yuh)/Lonesome Traveller	1951	15.00
❑ 9-27515	On Top of Old Smoky/Across the Wide Missouri	1951	20.00
—With Terry Gilkyson			
❑ 27670	Kisses Sweeter Than Wine/When the Saints Go Marching In	1951	15.00
❑ 27726	The Frozen Logger/Darling Corey	1951	15.00
❑ 27727	I Know Where I'm Going-Hush Little Baby/Suliram	1951	15.00
❑ 27728	Drinking Gourd/Easy Rider Blues	1951	15.00
❑ 27783	We Wish You a Merry Christmas/One for the Little Bitty Baby	1951	15.00
—Sides 1 and 2 of "Album No. 9-284"			
❑ 27817	The Seven Blessings of Mary/The Twelve Days of Christmas	1951	15.00
—Sides 3 and 4 of "Album No. 9-284"			
❑ 27818	Go Tell It on the Mountain/Poor Little Jesus	1951	15.00
—Sides 5 and 6 of "Album No. 9-284"			
❑ 27819	Lulloo Lullay-It's Almost Day/Burgundian Carol-God Rest Ye Merry Gentlemen	1951	15.00
—Sides 7 and 8 of "Album No. 9-284"			
❑ 27928	Wimoweh/Old Paint	1952	15.00
❑ 28054	Around the Corner (Beneath the Berry Tree)/The Gandy Dancer's Ball	1952	15.00
❑ 28228	Run Home to Ma-Ma/Hard Ain't It Hard	1952	15.00
❑ 28272	Goodnight Irene/Midnight Special	1952	15.00
❑ 28434	Clementine/True Love	1952	15.00
❑ 28542	Down in the Valley/The Bay of Mexico	1953	15.00
❑ 28637	Taking It Easy/Benoni	1953	15.00
❑ 28919	Rock Island Shuffle/Sylvia	1953	15.00
VANGUARD			
❑ 35001	Done Laid Around/Take This Letter	196?	12.00
❑ 35005	Aunt Rhodie/Bury Me Beneath the Willows	196?	12.00
❑ 35009	This Land Is Your Land/Aweigh, Santy Ano	196?	12.00
❑ 35010	On My Journey/The Sinking of the Reuben James	196?	12.00
❑ 35014	The Keeper/Twelve Gates to the City	196?	12.00
❑ 35015	Fight On/Rally Round the Flag	196?	12.00

7-Inch Extended Plays

Number	Title	Yr	NM
DECCA			
❑ ED 2015	*Goodnight Irene/Tzena, Tzena, Tzena/On Top of Old Smoky/So Long (It's Been Good to Know Yuh)	195?	50.00
❑ ED 2015 [PS]	The Weavers, Vol. 1	195?	50.00

Albums

Number	Title	Yr	NM
ANALOGUE PRODUCTIONS			
❑ 005	Reunion at Carnegie Hall, 1963	199?	30.00
—Audiophile vinyl			
DECCA			
❑ DXB 173 [(2)M]	The Best of the Weavers	1965	25.00
❑ DL 4277 [M]	Weavers' Gold	1962	20.00
❑ DL 5285 [10]	Folk Songs of America and Other Lands	1951	100.00
❑ DL-5373 [10]	We Wish You a Merry Christmas	1952	100.00
❑ DXSB 7173 [(2)R]	The Best of the Weavers	1965	20.00
❑ DL 8893 [M]	The Best of the Weavers	1959	40.00
—Black label, silver print			
❑ DL 8893 [M]	Folk Songs Made Famous by the Weavers	196?	20.00
❑ DL 8909 [M]	Folk Songs Around the World	1959	40.00
❑ DL 74277 [R]	Weavers' Gold	1962	15.00
❑ DL 75169 [R]	The Weavers' Greatest Hits	1971	12.00
❑ DL 78893 [R]	Folk Songs Made Famous by the Weavers	196?	15.00
MCA			
❑ 4052 [(2)]	The Best of the Weavers	197?	15.00
—Reissue of Decca 7173; black rainbow labels			
❑ 4052 [(2)]	The Best of the Weavers	1980	12.00
—Blue rainbow labels			
VANGUARD			
❑ VSD-15/16 [(2)]	The Weavers' Greatest Hits	1971	15.00
❑ VSD 2022 [S]	Travelling on with the Weavers	1959	40.00
❑ VSD 2030 [S]	The Weavers at Home	1959	40.00
❑ VSD 2069 [S]	The Weavers at Carnegie Hall, Vol. 2	1960	40.00
❑ VSD 2101 [S]	Almanac	1961	40.00
❑ VSD 2150 [S]	Reunion at Carnegie Hall, 1963	1963	30.00
❑ SRV-3001 [(2)M]	The Weavers Song Bag	1967	20.00
❑ VRS-6533 [R]	The Weavers at Carnegie Hall	1970	12.00
❑ VRS-6537 [R]	The Weavers on Tour	1970	12.00
❑ VRS 9010 [M]	The Weavers at Carnegie Hall	1957	40.00
❑ VRS 9013 [M]	The Weavers on Tour	1957	40.00
❑ VRS 9024 [M]	The Weavers at Home	1959	30.00
❑ VRS 9043 [M]	Travelling on with the Weavers	1959	30.00
❑ VRS 9075 [M]	The Weavers at Carnegie Hall, Vol. 2	1960	30.00
❑ VRS 9100 [M]	Almanac	1961	30.00
❑ VRS 9130 [M]	Reunion at Carnegie Hall, 1963	1963	20.00
❑ VRS 9161 [M]	Reunion at Carnegie Hall, Part 2	1965	20.00
❑ SRV-73001 [(2)S]	The Weavers Song Bag	1967	25.00
❑ VMS-73101	The Weavers at Carnegie Hall	1984	8.00
—Reissue of 6533			
❑ VMS-73116	The Weavers on Tour	1985	8.00
—Reissue of 6537			
❑ VMS-73122	Classics	1985	10.00
❑ VSD 79161 [S]	Reunion at Carnegie Hall, Part 2	1965	30.00

WEB, THE

Albums

Number	Title	Yr	NM
DERAM			
❑ DES 18018	Fully Interlocking	1968	25.00

WEBB, BOOGIE BILL

45s

Number	Title (A Side/B Side)	Yr	NM
IMPERIAL			
❑ 5257	Bad Dog/I Ain't For It	1953	250.00

WEBB, JACK

45s

Number	Title (A Side/B Side)	Yr	NM
WARNER BROS.			
❑ 5003	Try a Little Tenderness/You'd Never Know the Old Place Now	1958	20.00

7-Inch Extended Plays

Number	Title	Yr	NM
RCA VICTOR			
❑ 547-0342	The Christmas Story (Part 1)/The Christmas Story (Part 4)	1953	30.00
❑ 547-0343	The Christmas Story (Part 2)/The Christmas Story (Part 3)	1953	30.00
❑ EPB 3199 [PS]	The Christmas Story	1953	40.00
—Cover for 2-EP set			

Albums

Number	Title	Yr	NM
RCA VICTOR			
❑ LPM-1126 [M]	Pete Kelly's Blues	1955	50.00
—Webb narrates; jazz combo plays			
❑ LPM-2053 [M]	Pete Kelly's Blues	1959	30.00
—Reissue of 1126			
❑ LSP-2053(e) [R]	Pete Kelly's Blues	1959	20.00
❑ LPM-3199 [10]	Dragnet — The Christmas Story	1954	150.00
WARNER BROS.			
❑ W 1207 [M]	You're My Girl	1958	30.00
❑ WS 1207 [S]	You're My Girl	1958	40.00
❑ WS 1207 [S]	You're My Girl	1958	40.00

WEBB, MORTI

45s

Number	Title (A Side/B Side)	Yr	NM
HIT			
❑ 122	People/I Don't Want to Be Hurt Anymore	1964	8.00
—B-side by Leroy Jones			

WEBER, JOAN

45s

Number	Title (A Side/B Side)	Yr	NM
COLUMBIA			
❑ 4-40366	Let Me Go, Lover!/Marionette	1954	12.00
❑ 4-40440	Call Me Careless/It May Sound Silly	1955	10.00
❑ 4-40474	Lover, Lover, Why Must We Part/Tell the Lord	1955	10.00
❑ 4-40535	Anything, Everything for Love/Don't Throw My Love Away	1955	10.00
❑ 4-40709	What Should a Teen Heart Do/Goodbye Lollipops, Hello Lipstick	1956	10.00
❑ 4-40852	Gone/A Love That's a Lie	1957	10.00
❑ 4-40898	Saturday Lover, Sunday Stranger/Who'll Be My Love	1957	10.00
MAPLE			
❑ 102	I Love My Baby/I Tried to Love You	196?	10.00

WEBS, THE (1) R&B group.

45s

Number	Title (A Side/B Side)	Yr	NM
ATLANTIC			
❑ 2415	Let's Party/Keep Your Love Strong	1967	12.00
MGM			
❑ 13602	People Sure Act Funny/You Pretty Fool	1966	12.00

Except when noted otherwise, VG = 25% of NM, and VG+ = 50% of NM. (Example: VG = $2.00, VG+ = $4.00 and NM = $8.00.)

Number	Title (A Side/B Side)	Yr	NM
POPSIDE			
❑ 4593	This Thing Called Love/Tomorrow	1967	10.00
❑ 4595	Give In/It's So Hard to Break a Habit	1968	10.00
VERVE			
❑ 10610	We Belong Together/I Want You Back	1968	10.00

WEBS, THE (2)
BOBBY GOLDSBORO was in this group.

Number	Title (A Side/B Side)	Yr	NM
45s			
HEART			
❑ 333	Blue Skies/Lost (Cricket in My Ear)	1962	40.00
LITE			
❑ 9004	Blue Skies/Lost (Cricket in My Ear)	1962	20.00

WEBTONES, THE

Number	Title (A Side/B Side)	Yr	NM
45s			
MGM			
❑ 12724	My Lost Love/Walk, Talk and Kiss	1958	25.00

WECHTER, JULIUS
See BAJA MARIMBA BAND.

WEDGES, THE

Number	Title (A Side/B Side)	Yr	NM
Albums			
TIME			
❑ S-2090 [S]	Hang Ten (For Surfers Only)	1963	70.00
❑ 52090 [M]	Hang Ten (For Surfers Only)	1963	50.00

WEIGAND, JACK

Number	Title (A Side/B Side)	Yr	NM
45s			
CAMEO			
❑ 178	Stairway to the Stars/Shangri-La	1960	8.00
❑ 185	Sixteen Candles/Prisoner of Love	1961	10.00
❑ 315	Stairway to the Stars/Prisoner of Love	1964	7.00
Albums			
CAMEO			
❑ C-1012 [M]	Stairway to the Stars	1961	12.00
❑ SC-1012 [S]	Stairway to the Stars	1961	15.00
WYNCOTE			
❑ SW-9017 [S]	Shangri-La and Other Favorites	1964	12.00
❑ W-9017 [M]	Shangri-La and Other Favorites	1964	10.00

WEIR, BOB
Also see THE GRATEFUL DEAD.

Number	Title (A Side/B Side)	Yr	NM
45s			
ARISTA			
❑ 0315	Bombs Away/Easy to Slip	1978	6.00
❑ 0336	I'll Be Doggone/Shade of Grey	1978	12.00
—May be promo only			
WARNER BROS.			
❑ 7611	One More Saturday Night/Cassidy	1972	12.00
Albums			
ARISTA			
❑ AL 4155	Heaven Help the Fool	1978	10.00
❑ AL 8366	Heaven Help the Fool	1985	8.00
—Budget-line reissue			
❑ AL 8367	Bobby and the Midnites	1985	8.00
—Budget-line reissue			
❑ AL 9568	Bobby and the Midnites	1981	10.00
WARNER BROS.			
❑ BS 2627	Ace	1972	30.00
—Black and white photo on back cover			
❑ BS 2627	Ace	1972	40.00
—Color photo on back cover			

WEIRD-OHS, THE

Number	Title (A Side/B Side)	Yr	NM
Albums			
MERCURY			
❑ MG-20976 [M]	The Sounds of the Weird-Ohs	1964	150.00
❑ SR-60976 [S]	The Sounds of the Weird-Ohs	1964	200.00

WEIRDOS

Number	Title (A Side/B Side)	Yr	NM
45s			
(NO LABEL)			
❑ (no #)	Skateboards to Hell/Adult Hood	1979	12.50
❑ (no #) [PS]	Skateboards to Hell/Adult Hood	1979	12.50
BOMP!			
❑ 112	Destroy All Music/Why Do You Exist?/A Life of Crime	1977	9.00
—White label, pressed on vinyl			
❑ 112	Destroy All Music/Why Do You Exist?/A Life of Crime	1977	20.00
—White label, pressed on styrene			
❑ 112	Destroy All Music/Why Do You Exist?/A Life of Crime	1977	40.00
—Black label, pressed on styrene			
❑ 112 [PS]	Destroy All Music/Why Do You Exist?/A Life of Crime	1977	9.00
DANGERHOUSE			
❑ 1063	We Got the Neutron Bomb/Solitary Confinement	1978	20.00
❑ 1063 [PS]	We Got the Neutron Bomb/Solitary Confinement	1978	20.00
Albums			
BOMP!			
❑ 4007 [EP]	Who? What? When? Where? Why?	1979	15.00
FRONTIER			
❑ 4623-1-L	Condor	1990	12.00
❑ 4630-1-L	Weird World	1991	12.00
OUT OF DARKNESS			
❑ OTD 001 [DJ]	Message from the Underworld	198?	40.00
—Promo-only release			
RHINO			
❑ RNEP 508 [EP]	Action Design	1980	20.00

WEISBERG, TIM
Also see DAN FOGELBERG.

Number	Title (A Side/B Side)	Yr	NM
45s			
A&M			
❑ 1318	Long Ago and Far Away/Hard Way to Go	1971	5.00
❑ 1330	Fog and Spice/For Those Who Never Dream	1972	5.00
❑ 1397	Our Thing/Tyme Cube	1972	5.00
❑ 1427	Killing Me Softly with His Song/Tibetan Silver	1973	5.00
❑ 1493	Do Dah/A Night for Crying	1973	5.00
❑ 1520	Streak-Out/A Night for Crying	1974	5.00
❑ 1680	Dion Blue/The Visit	1975	4.00
MCA			
❑ 41036	Midsummer's Dream/Moonchild	1979	4.00
❑ 41307	I'm the Lucky One/Magic Lady	1980	4.00
❑ 51042	What's Going On/Page One	1981	4.00
❑ 51163	Sleep Walk/Paula	1981	4.00
UNITED ARTISTS			
❑ XW933	Gonna Fly Now (Theme from "Rocky")/Just for Fun	1976	4.00
❑ XW1083	Cascade/Gene, Jean	1977	4.00
❑ 1227	Every Time I See Your Smile/So Good to Me	1978	4.00
Albums			
A&M			
❑ SP-3039	Tim Weisberg	1971	12.00
❑ SP-3045	Dreamspeaker	1973	10.00
❑ SP-3121	Tim Weisberg 4	198?	8.00
—Budget-line reissue			
❑ SP-3261	Smile/The Best of Tim Weisberg	198?	8.00
—Budget-line reissue			
❑ SP-3658	Tim Weisberg 4	1974	10.00
❑ SP-4352	Hurtwood Edge	1972	12.00
❑ SP-4545	Listen to the City	1975	10.00
❑ SP-4600	Live at Last!	1976	10.00
❑ SP-4749	Smile/The Best of Tim Weisberg	1979	10.00
CYPRESS			
❑ YL-0123	Outrageous Temptations	1989	12.00
❑ 661112-1	High Risk	1986	10.00
DESERT ROCK			
❑ DR-001	High Risk	1985	15.00
LIBERTY			
❑ LN-10029	Rotations	198?	8.00
—Budget-line reissue			
❑ LN-10031	The Tim Weisberg Band	198?	8.00
—Budget-line reissue			
MCA			
❑ 3084	Night-Rider!	1979	10.00
❑ 5125	Party of One	1980	10.00
❑ 5245	Travelin' Light	1981	10.00
NAUTILUS			
❑ NR-7	Tip of the Weisberg	1980	30.00
—Audiophile vinyl			
UNITED ARTISTS			
❑ UA-LA773-G	The Tim Weisberg Band	1977	10.00
❑ UA-LA857-H	Rotations	1978	10.00

WEISSBERG, ERIC, AND MARSHALL BRICKMAN

Number	Title (A Side/B Side)	Yr	NM
Albums			
ELEKTRA			
❑ EKL-238 [M]	New Dimensions in Banjo and Bluegrass	1963	20.00
❑ EKS-7238 [S]	New Dimensions in Banjo and Bluegrass	1963	25.00
—Mandolin-player label			
❑ EKS-7238 [S]	New Dimensions in Banjo and Bluegrass	1967	20.00
—Tan label with large stylized "E" at top			
❑ EKS-7238 [S]	New Dimensions in Banjo and Bluegrass	1969	15.00
—Red label with large stylized "E" at top			
❑ EKS-7238 [S]	New Dimensions in Banjo and Bluegrass	1971	12.00
—Butterfly label			
❑ EKS-7238 [S]	New Dimensions in Banjo and Bluegrass	1980	10.00
—Red label with Warner Communications logo in lower right			

WEISSBERG, ERIC, AND DELIVERANCE

Number	Title (A Side/B Side)	Yr	NM
45s			
EPIC			
❑ 50072	Yakety Yak/Meadow Muffins	1975	4.00
WARNER BROS.			
❑ 7718	Reuben's Train/Scalded Cat	1973	4.00
❑ 7756	Opening Day/Concrete Canyon Boogie	1973	4.00
Albums			
WARNER BROS.			
❑ BS 2720	Rural Free Delivery	1973	10.00

WEISSBERG, ERIC, AND STEVE MANDELL

Number	Title (A Side/B Side)	Yr	NM
45s			
WARNER BROS.			
❑ 7659	Dueling Banjos/End of a Dream	1972	4.00
—Later pressings credit the musicians; "Dueling Banjos" time is 2:12			
❑ 7659	Dueling Banjos/End of a Dream	1972	10.00
—A-side listed as "from the Warner Bros. motion picture Deliverance" with no artist mentioned on the B-side; "Dueling Banjos" time is 3:17			
❑ 7659	Dueling Banjos/End of a Dream	1973	6.00
—A-side listed as "from the Warner Bros. motion picture Deliverance" with no artist mentioned on the B-side; "Dueling Banjos" time is 2:12			
7-Inch Extended Plays			
WARNER BROS.			
❑ S 2683	Eight More Miles to Louisville/Dueling Banjos/Little Maggie//Pony Express/Buffalo Gals/Eighth of January	1973	10.00
—Jukebox issue; small hole, plays at 33 1/3 rpm			
❑ S 2683 [PS]	Dueling Banjos	1973	10.00
—Part of "Little LP" series (LLP #210)			
Albums			
WARNER BROS.			
❑ BS 2683	Dueling Banjos from Deliverance	1973	8.00
—"Burbank" palm trees label			
❑ BS 2683	Dueling Banjos from Deliverance	1973	10.00
—Except for the title song and "End of a Dream," this is actually a reissue of Elektra 7238; green label			
❑ BS 2683	Dueling Banjos from Deliverance	1979	6.00
—Tan or white label			

WELK, LAWRENCE
Also see DICK KESNER; THE LENNON SISTERS. Because we've been asked about it, we'll note that the Dick Dale who sometimes appears in the credits of Welk records (45s, EPs and LPs) is a saxophone player and vocalist and not the surf guitarist.

Number	Title (A Side/B Side)	Yr	NM
45s			
(NO LABEL)			
❑ (no #)	Season's Greetings From Your Dodge Dealer	196?	8.00
—Cardboard record			
CORAL			
❑ 60405	Shenandoah Waltz/Metro Polka	1951	12.00
—Note: Earlier Lawrence Welk 45s on Coral may exist			
❑ 60444	Moonlight Bay/Boomp! Pa-Deedle Doodle	1951	12.00
❑ 60514	Sad and Lonely/Irving	1951	12.00
❑ 60516	Slow Drive/Moonlight Bay	1951	12.00
❑ 60517	Tell Me/Cuddle Up a Little Closer, Lovey Mine	1951	12.00
❑ 60518	Yoo Hoo/I'm Forever Blowing Bubbles	1951	12.00
❑ 60519	Every Little Moment/Till We Meet Again	1951	12.00
❑ 60575	Sweetheart Waltz/I Wanna Say Hello	1951	12.00
❑ 60618	My Extraordinary Gal/Irene	1952	10.00
❑ 60619	Dolores/Emaline	1952	10.00
❑ 60620	Mary Lou/Annabelle	1952	10.00
❑ 60621	Louise/Sweet Eloise	1952	10.00
❑ 60630	Swingin' Down the Lane/You're Somebody	1952	10.00
❑ 60677	The Gandy Dancer's Ball/Ivory Rag	1952	10.00
❑ 60689	Bubbles in the Wine/Josephine	1952	15.00
❑ 60752	Dream House/Small Talk	1952	10.00
❑ 60784	Watermelon Weather/Busybody	1952	10.00
❑ 60806	Padam Padam (How It Echoes the Beat of My Heart)/Your Eyes So Lovely	1952	10.00
❑ 60813	Rustic Dance/Cocoanut Grove	1952	10.00
❑ 60828	Meet Mister Callaghan/Flirtation Waltz	1952	10.00

W

Number	Title (A Side/B Side)	Yr	NM
60893	Oh Happy Day/Your Mother and Mine	1952	10.00
60905	She Looked Down from Her Window/I'm Gonna Ring the Bell Tonight	1953	10.00
—Vocalist: Jack Smith			
60947	Minnie the Mermaid/Say It Isn't So	1953	10.00
60973	Ohio/It's Love	1953	10.00
60974	Canadian Capers/Did I Remember	1953	10.00
60975	Good Morning, Mr. Zip Zip Zip/Just Once Again	1953	10.00
60976	I'll See You in My Dreams/Peggy O'Neill	1953	10.00
60998	Bubbling Over/The La-De-Da Song	1953	10.00
61003	High Life Polka/Town and Country Polka	1953	10.00
61017	Hallejulah Brother/"O"	1953	10.00
61075	Ebb Tide/Beautiful Ohio	1953	10.00
61081	Angel on the Christmas Tree/Are My Ears On Straight	1953	15.00
—With Sara Berner			
61095	Christmas Carols (Part 1)/Christmas Carols (Part 2)	1953	12.00
61100	Joey's Theme/Coney Island	1953	10.00
61135	The Darktown Strutter's Ball/In the Mood	1954	10.00
61174	The Man with the Banjo/Until Sunrise	1954	10.00
61207	Nimble Fingers/Doll Dance	1954	10.00
—With Sara Berner			
61240	The Greatest Feeling in the World/Luxembourg Polka	1954	10.00
61318	At the Junior Prom/Home Again Blues	1954	10.00
61372	Elephant's Tango/Lazy Gondolier	1955	8.00
61387	I See God/Pray for Me	1955	8.00
61408	Hey, Mr. Banjo/Love Me or Leave Me	1955	8.00
61442	Ball of Fire/Go 'Way, Go 'Way	1955	8.00
61477	Wake the Town and Tell the People/I Hear Those Bells	1955	8.00
61508	Champagne Waltz/Musette	1955	8.00
61515	Bonnie Blue Gal/Sam the Old Accordian Man	1955	8.00
61524	It's Almost Tomorrow/Rice	1955	8.00
61574	Moritat (A Theme from the Threepenny Opera)/Stompin' at the Savoy	1956	8.00
61592	The Poor People of Paris/Nobody Knows But the Lord	1956	8.00
61595	Lisbon Antigua/Chain Gang	1956	8.00
61597	Mickey Mouse Mambo/Hi! to You	1956	12.00
61621	Practice, Practice What You Preach/What a Heavenly Night for Love	1956	8.00
61629	Helena Polka/Hot Pretzels	1956	8.00
61630	Jenny Lind/The Jolly Coppersmith	1956	8.00
61644	On the Street Where You Live/I Could Have Danced All Night	1956	8.00
61645	With a Little Bit of Luck/I've Grown Accustomed to Her Face	1956	8.00
61670	Weary Blues/In the Alps	1956	10.00
—With the McGuire Sisters			
61670 [PS]	Weary Blues/In the Alps	1956	15.00
61701	Tonight You Belong to Me/When the White Lilacs Bloom Again	1956	10.00
—With the Lennon Sisters			
61741	Around the World/Champagne Time	1956	8.00
61745	Ring Those Christmas Bells/Let's Have an Old-Fashioned Christmas	1956	10.00
61746	Christmas Waltz/Santa from Santa Fe	1956	12.00
—With the Lennon Sisters			
61765	Cinco Robles/Whispering Heart	1956	8.00
61783	McNamara's Band/Wild Colonial Boy	1957	8.00
61784	Dance Around a Stack of Barley/When Irish Eyes Are Smiling	1957	8.00
61786	Falling Star/It Was That Kiss	1957	8.00
61806	Ten Little Trees/The Bridge of Saint Lo	1957	8.00
61849	By the Bend of the River/Keyboard Serenade	1957	8.00
61870	Ricky-Dicky-Doo/To Be with You	1957	8.00
61893	Moon Love/We'll Be There	1957	8.00
61894	My Reverie/Fool Moon and Empty Arms	1957	8.00
61900	Lichtenstein Polka/You Know Too Much	1957	8.00
61914	Merry Christmas from Our House to Your House/Santa Claus Is Here Again	1957	12.00
—With the Lennon Sisters			
61937	One Note Polka/The Lovers on the Park Bench	1958	8.00
61958	I Want a Girl/When My Baby Smiles at Me	1958	8.00
62018	Walk with Me/Be Thankful	1958	8.00
62031	Mary Ann/Indiana Holiday	1958	8.00
62053	Outer Space Santa/All Around The Merry Christmas Tree	1958	12.00
—As "Lawrence Welk's Little Band"			
62056	Cha Cha Polka/I Never Should Have Let You Go	1958	8.00
62091	Gunsmoke/The Ballad of Paladin	1959	12.00
65511	Bubbles in the Wine/Josephine	196?	6.00
65517	Cocoanut Grove/Rustic Dance	196?	6.00
65523	Ave Maria/He'll Be There	196?	6.00
65541	Gold and Silver/Lichtenstein Polka	196?	6.00
65574	Pony Tail/The Wreck of the Old '88	196?	6.00
65604	I'll See You in My Dreams/Till We Meet Again	1966	5.00
98054 [DJ]	Christmas Carols (Part 1)/Christmas Carols (Part 2)	19??	8.00
—"Merry Christmas from Lawrence Welk" custom label			

DECCA

Number	Title (A Side/B Side)	Yr	NM
23855	Beer Barrel Polka/Pennsylvania Polka	1950	10.00
—Reissue of 78; part of "Album No. 9-24"			
23857	Clarinet Polka/Pound Your Table Polka	1950	10.00
—Reissue of 78; part of "Album No. 9-24"			
23858	Barbara Polka/Friendly Tavern Polka	1950	10.00
—Reissue of 78; part of "Album No. 9-24"			
24442	Bubbles in the Wine/Kentucky Waltz	1950	20.00
—78 originally released in 1948; original 45 has black label with "rays" on either side of the word "Decca"			
24442	Bubbles in the Wine/Kentucky Waltz	1955	12.00
—Second 45 has star under "Decca"			
24442	Bubbles in the Wine/Kentucky Waltz	1960	8.00
—Third 45 has color bars on label			

DOT

Number	Title (A Side/B Side)	Yr	NM
15924	The Swingin' Burglar/Bell Boogie	1959	8.00
—By "Lawrence Welk's Little Band;			
15967	Goodnight Sweetheart/This Night Is Young and You're So Beautiful	1959	8.00
—By "The Lawrence Welk Glee Club"			
15995	Every Night When You Say a Prayer/Thank the Lord for This Thanksgiving	1959	10.00
—With the Lennon Sisters			
16017	Christmas Moon/Peppy the Peppermint Bear	1959	12.00
—With the Lennon Sisters			
16062	Just Because/Tick-Tock Polka	1960	8.00
—With Myron Floren			
16063	Hour of Parting/Summer Set	1960	8.00
16065	Just Because/Tick-Tock Polka	1960	8.00
16114	It Started in Naples/I Get So Lonely (Oh Baby Mine)	1960	8.00
16145	Last Date/Remember Lolita	1960	6.00
16153	The Cradle to the Cross/Laura-Jean	1960	6.00
16161	Calcutta/My Grandfather's Clock	1960	8.00
16198	Theme from My Three Sons/Out of a Clear Blue Sky	1961	10.00
16222	Yellow Bird/Cruising Down the River	1961	6.00
16237	Riders in the Sky/My Love for You	1961	6.00
16285	You Gave Me Wings/A-One, a-Two, a-Cha Cha Cha	1961	6.00
16336	Runaway/Happy Love	1962	6.00
16364	Baby Elephant Walk/Theme from the Brothers Grimm	1962	8.00
16420	Zero-Zero/Night Theme	1962	6.00
16488	Scarlett O'Hara/Breakwater	1963	6.00
16526	Blue Velvet/Fiesta	1963	6.00
16582	Stockholm/Girl from Barbados	1964	6.00
16603	Hello, Dolly/Clair de Lune	1964	6.00
16620	Poodle Walk/Do I Need You	1964	6.00
16680	Sixteen Reasons/Little Things Mean a Lot	1964	6.00
16697	Apples and Bananas/Theme from "The Addams Family"	1965	8.00
16741	There's No One Like You/Schatzie	1965	6.00
16764	Down, Down, Down, Down/Jenny Dear	1965	6.00
16778	Summer Nights/La Bamba	1965	6.00
16794	Moonlight and Roses/Send Me the Pillow You Dream On	1965	6.00
16810	Currier and Ives/Tia-Juana	1965	6.00
16885	Wabash Cannonball/Tennessee Waltz	1966	5.00
16943	Family Affair/Tarzan (Tarzan's March)	1966	8.00
16981	Born Free/Winchester Cathedral	1966	5.00
17001	The Beat Goes On/Then You Can Tell Me Goodbye	1967	5.00

MERCURY

Number	Title (A Side/B Side)	Yr	NM
5411	Doo-Wacka-Doo/Pizzacata	1950	15.00
—Note: Earlier Lawrence Welk 45s on Mercury may exist			
5419	Hoop-De-Dee/If You Can Get a Drum with a Boom, Boom, Boom	1950	15.00
5434	Dakota Polka/Windy River	1950	15.00
5440	Deep Freezer Dinah/Fancy Free	1950	15.00
5469	Mama's Samba/Skaters Waltz in Springtime	1950	15.00
—Vocalist: Roberta Linn			
5487	Petite Waltz/The Middle of a Riddle	1950	15.00
5518	Emilia Polka/Tinker Polka	1950	15.00
5519	Julida Polka/Laughing Polka	1950	15.00
5529	Tiger Rag/Military Polka	1950	15.00
5666	Bubbles in the Wine/Back Home in Illinois	1951	20.00
5735	Merry Christmas Polka/Julida Polka	1951	15.00
70065	Julinda Polka/Swiss Lullaby	1953	12.00
70149	Fiddle-Dee-Dee/Dancing Doll	1953	12.00
70734	Hoop-De-Dee/Bar Room Polka	1955	10.00
70735	Amilia Polka/Tinker Polka	1955	10.00
70736	Julida Polka/Military Polka	1955	10.00
70737	Dakota Polka/Kit Kat Polka	1955	10.00
70738	Merry Christmas Polka/Laughing Polka	1955	12.00
70739	Tiger Rag/Chopsticks Polka	1955	10.00

RANWOOD

Number	Title (A Side/B Side)	Yr	NM
801	Green Tambourine/Watch What Happens	1968	4.00
814	Let's Make America What It Used to Be/To America with Love	1968	4.00
842	Galveston/Gentle on My Mind	1969	4.00
845	Land of Dreams/Chee Chee Kookaroo	1969	4.00
860	Jean/Spinning Wheel	1970	4.00
865	Hello Dolly/Southtown U.S.A.	1970	4.00
874	Applause/Smiles	1970	4.00
888	Candida/Endlessly	1971	4.00
905	No, No, Nanette/Too Many Rings Around Rosie	1971	4.00
915	Theme from Summer of '42/Adios, Au Revoir, Auf Wiedersehn	1971	4.00
920	Melody of Love (Parody)/Melody of Love	1972	8.00
—With Bob Hudson (of Hudson and Landry) on A-side			
1039	Fantastic, That's You/Oh Harry	1975	3.00
—With Henry Questa			
1068	Nadia's Theme (The Young and the Restless)/Johnny's Theme	1976	3.00
1073	Keep Your Eyes on the Sparrow/Paloma Blanca	1977	3.00
1091	Christmas In Los Angeles/Carol Of The Bells	1980	4.00
—By "The Lawrence Welk Christmas Chorale"			

7-Inch Extended Plays

CORAL

Number	Title (A Side/B Side)	Yr	NM
EC 81007	Bubbles in the Wine/Josephine//12th Street Rag/Ivory Rag	195?	12.00
EC 81007 [PS]	Dance Time	195?	12.00
EC 81101	The Girl Friend/Margie//Marie/Sweet Sue, Just You	195?	10.00
EC 81101 [PS]	(title unknown)	195?	10.00
EC 81109	Liebesfreud/Liebeslied (Love's Sorrow)//Schon Rosmarin (Fair Rosemary)/Caprice Viennois	195?	10.00
EC 81109 [PS]	Viennese Waltzes for Dancing, Vol. 1	195?	10.00
EC 81120	Malaguena/Lazy Gondolier//Blue Mirage/The Elephants Tango	195?	10.00
EC 81120 [PS]	Yours for Dancing	195?	10.00
EC 81133	I Could Have Danced All Night/I've Grown Accustomed to Her Face//On the Street Where You Live/With a Little Bit of Luck	1956	10.00
EC 81133 [PS]	My Fair Lady	1956	10.00
EC 81134	(contents unknown)	195?	10.00
EC 81134 [PS]	Champagne Medley Time	195?	10.00
EC 81134 [PS]	Say It With Music	195?	10.00
EC 81146	*Clarinet Polka/Champagne Polka/Pennsylvania Polka/Beer Barrel Polka	195?	10.00
EC 81146 [PS]	Pick-a-Polka	195?	10.00
EC 81148	(contents unknown)	195?	10.00

Except when noted otherwise, VG = 25% of NM, and VG+ = 50% of NM. (Example: VG = $2.00, VG+ = $4.00 and NM = $8.00.)

Number	Title (A Side/B Side)	Yr	NM
❑ EC 81148 [PS]	Moments to Remember	195?	10.00
❑ EC 81154	(contents unknown)	195?	10.00
❑ EC 81154 [PS]	The Stars Visit Lawrence Welk	195?	10.00
❑ EC 81157	(a) Tenderly (b) When Your Hair Has Turned to Silver/(a) Cuban Love Song (b) Honolulu Eyes//(a) Alice Blue Gown (b) Ramona/(a) Three O'Clock in the Morning (b) Sleep	195?	10.00
❑ EC 81157 [PS]	Waltz with Lawrence Welk	195?	10.00
❑ EC 81160	*Champagne and Roses/Room Full of Roses/Moonlight and Roses/Blue Champagne	195?	10.00
❑ EC 81160 [PS]	Champagne and Roses	195?	10.00
❑ EC 81171	*Alexander's Ragtime band/All Alone/When My Baby Smiles at Me/Row, Row, Row	195?	10.00
❑ EC 81171 [PS]	Champagne Dancing Party, Vol. I	195?	10.00
❑ EC 81172	(contents unknown)	195?	10.00
❑ EC 81172 [PS]	Champagne Dancing Party, Vol. II	195?	10.00
❑ EC 81180	All Around the Merry Christmas Tree/Merry Christmas from Our House to Your House//Outer Space Santa/Santa from Santa Fe	195?	10.00
❑ EC 81180 [PS]	Merry Christmas	195?	10.00
❑ EC 781181	Gunsmoke/Maverick//Ballad of Paladin/The Legend of Wyatt Earp	1959	15.00
—Stereo			
❑ EC 781181 [PS]	TV Western Theme Songs	1959	15.00
❑ EC 81502	Bubbles in the Wine/Cocoanut Grove//Metro Polka/Oh Happy Day	195?	10.00
❑ EC 81502 [PS]	Lawrence Welk	195?	10.00
❑ EC 82001 [PS]	Souvenir Album (Actually Recorded at the Aragon Ballroom)	195?	12.00
—Cover for 2-EP set (83000 and 83001)			
❑ EC 82005 [PS]	Nimble Fingers	195?	10.00
—Cover for 2-EP set (83006 and 83007)			
❑ EC 82026 [PS]	(title unknown)	195?	12.00
—Cover for 2-EP set (83056 and 83057)			
❑ EC 82027 [PS]	Say It With Music	1956	10.00
—Cover for 2-EP set (83058 and 83059)			
❑ EC 82032 [PS]	Jingle Bells	1956	12.00
—Cover for 2-EP set			
❑ 83000	Say It Isn't So/Minnie the Mermaid//Did I Remember/Canadian Capers	195?	10.00
—Part of 2-EP set EC 82001			
❑ 83001	Good Morning, Mr. Zip, Zip, Zip/Just Once Again//Peggy O'Neil/I'll See You in My Dreams	195?	10.00
—Part of 2-EP set EC 82001			
❑ 83006	Nimble Fingers/Flapperette//Nola/Dainty Miss	195?	10.00
—Part of 2-EP set EC 82005			
❑ 83007	Rag Doll/Doll Dance//The Wedding of the Painted Doll/Dancing Tambourine	195?	10.00
—Part of 2-EP set EC 82005			
❑ 83056	When Irish Eyes Are Smiling/My Heart Danced an Irish Jig//Irish Alphabet/McNamara's Band	1956	10.00
—Part of 2-EP set EC 82026			
❑ 83057	A Little Bit of Heaven (Shure They Call It Ireland)/Ireland Must Be Heaven For My Mother Came from There//Shamrocks, Shillelaghs and Shenanigans/Dance Aroun' a Stack of Barley	1956	10.00
—Part of 2-EP set EC 82026			
❑ 83058	Say It with Music/Tea for Two/Thou Swell/I Found a Million Dollar Baby in a Five and Ten Cent Store/Pretty Baby/Yes Sir, That's My Baby//Oh Lady Be Good/Somebody Loves Me/S'Wonderful/Sleepy Time Gal/My Blue Heaven/Doodle Doo Doo	1956	10.00
—Part of 2-EP set EC 82027			
❑ 83059	The Gypsy in My Soul/Exactly Like You/Anything Goes/Was That the Human Thing to Do/Cecilia/I Can't Believe It's True//Wabash Blues/September Song/Mood Indigo/Sympathy/L'Amour Toujours L'Amour (Love Everlasting)/Giannina Mia	1956	10.00
—Part of 2-EP set EC 82027			
❑ 83068	(contents unknown)	1956	10.00
—Part of 2-EP set EC 82032			
❑ 83069	Santa Claus Is Comin' To Town/Winter Wonderland//Christmas Dreaming (A Little Early This Year)/The Twelve Gifts Of Christmas	1956	10.00
—Part of 2-EP set EC 82032			
DECCA			
❑ ED 2023	Bubbles in the Wine/Josephine//Kentucky Waltz/Canadian Capers	195?	12.00
❑ ED 2023 [PS]	Lawrence Welk, Vol. 1	195?	12.00
❑ ED 2568	(contents unknown)	195?	12.00
❑ ED 2568 [PS]	Polkas and Champagne	195?	12.00
Albums			
CORAL			
❑ 7CXSB 5 [(2)S]	The Best of Lawrence Welk	196?	15.00
❑ CXB 5 [(2)M]	The Best of Lawrence Welk	196?	20.00
❑ CRL 56043 [10]	On Moonlight Bay	195?	30.00
❑ CRL 56045 [10]	Songs About My Extraordinary Gal and Her Friends	195?	30.00
❑ CRL 56088 [10]	Souvenir Album	195?	30.00
❑ CRL 56101 [10]	Nimble Fingers	195?	30.00
❑ CRL 56120 [10]	Viennese Waltzes for Dancing	1954	30.00
❑ CRL 57011 [M]	Lawrence Welk and His Sparkling Strings	1955	20.00
❑ CRL 57023 [M]	Lawrence Welk Introduces the Girl Friends	1955	25.00
❑ CRL 57025 [M]	TV Favorites	1955	20.00
❑ CRL 57036 [M]	Shamrocks and Champagne	1955	20.00
❑ CRL 57038 [M]	Bubbles in the Wine	1956	20.00
❑ CRL 57041 [M]	Say It With Music	1956	20.00
❑ CRL 57066 [M]	Lawrence Welk at Madison Square Garden	1956	20.00
❑ CRL 57067 [M]	Pick-A-Polka!	1956	20.00
❑ CRL 57068 [M]	Moments to Remember	1956	20.00
❑ CRL 57078 [M]	Champagne Pops Parade	1956	20.00
❑ CRL 57093 [M]	Merry Christmas from Lawrence Welk	1956	20.00
❑ CRL 57111 [M]	Show Time	1957	20.00
❑ CRL 57113 [M]	The World's Finest Music	1957	20.00
❑ CRL 57119 [M]	Waltz with Lawrence Welk	1957	20.00
❑ CRL 57146 [M]	Lawrence Welk Plays Dixieland	1957	20.00
❑ CRL 57178 [M]	Nimble Fingers	1957	20.00
❑ CRL 57186 [M]	Jingle Bells	1957	20.00
❑ CRL 57191 [M]	Songs of Faith	1958	15.00
❑ CRL 57214 [M]	Lawrence Welk Presents Keyboard Kapers	1958	15.00
❑ CRL 57226 [M]	Champagne Dancing Party	1958	15.00
❑ CRL 57260 [M]	Lawrence Welk Featuring the Lennon Sisters	1959	15.00
❑ CRL 57262 [M]	Lawrence Welk Featuring Larry Hooper	1959	15.00
❑ CRL 57267 [M]	TV Western Theme Songs	1959	15.00
❑ CRL 57353 [M]	My Golden Favorites	1961	12.00
❑ CRL 57383 [M]	Lawrence Welk Showcase	1962	12.00
❑ CRL 57439 [M]	Songs Everybody Knows	1964	12.00
❑ CRL 757036 [R]	Shamrocks and Champagne	196?	12.00
❑ CRL 757041 [R]	Say It With Music	196?	12.00
❑ CRL 757067 [R]	Pick-A-Polka!	1959	12.00
❑ CRL 757093 [R]	Merry Christmas from Lawrence Welk	196?	12.00
❑ CRL 757113 [R]	The World's Finest Music	196?	12.00
❑ CRL 757186 [R]	Jingle Bells	196?	12.00
❑ CRL 757226 [S]	Champagne Dancing Party	1958	20.00
❑ CRL 757267 [S]	TV Western Theme Songs	1959	20.00
❑ CRL 757353 [S]	My Golden Favorites	1961	12.00
❑ CRL 757383 [S]	Lawrence Welk Showcase	1962	12.00
❑ CRL 757439 [S]	Songs Everybody Knows	1964	12.00
CORONET			
❑ 275	Lawrence Welk and His Orchestra	196?	10.00
DECCA			
❑ DL 8213 [M]	Lawrence Welk's Polka Party	1956	15.00
❑ DL 8323 [M]	Around We Go	1956	15.00
❑ DL 8324 [M]	Welktime	1956	15.00
DESIGN			
❑ 200	Champagne Time	196?	10.00
❑ 912	Three of a Kind	196?	10.00
DOT			
❑ DLP 3164 [M]	Mr. Music Maker	1959	12.00
❑ DLP 3200 [M]	The Voices and Strings of Lawrence Welk	1959	12.00
❑ DLP 3218 [M]	The Lawrence Welk Glee Club	1959	12.00
❑ DLP 3224 [M]	Dance with Lawrence Welk	1959	12.00
❑ DLP 3238 [M]	Lawrence Welk Presents Great American Composers	1960	10.00
❑ DLP 3247 [M]	Lawrence Welk Presents Great Overtures in Dance Time	1960	10.00
❑ DLP 3248 [M]	I'm Forever Blowing Bubbles	1960	10.00
❑ DLP 3251 [M]	Songs of the Islands	1960	10.00
❑ DLP 3274 [M]	Strictly for Dancing	1960	10.00
❑ DLP 3284 [M]	To Mother	1960	10.00
❑ DLP 3296 [M]	Sweet and Lovely	1960	10.00
❑ DLP 3302 [M]	Polkas	1960	10.00
❑ DLP 3317 [M]	Lawrence in Dixieland	1960	10.00
❑ DLP 3318 [M]	Double Shuffle	1960	10.00
❑ DLP 3342 [M]	The Champagne Music of Lawrence Welk	1960	10.00
❑ DLP 3350 [M]	Last Date	1960	10.00
❑ DLP 3359 [M]	Calcutta!	1961	10.00
❑ DLP 3389 [M]	Yellow Bird	1961	10.00
❑ DLP 3395 [M]	Diamond Jubilee	1961	10.00
❑ DLP 3397 [M]	Silent Night and 13 Other Best-Loved Christmas Songs	1961	12.00
❑ DLP 3412 [M]	Moon River	1961	10.00
❑ DLP 3428 [M]	Young World	1962	10.00
❑ DLP 3432 [M]	Sing-a-Long Party	1962	10.00
❑ DLP 3457 [M]	Baby Elephant Walk and Theme from The Brothers Grimm	1962	10.00
❑ DLP 3489 [M]	Bubbles in the Wine	1962	10.00
❑ DLP 3499 [M]	Waltz Time	1963	10.00
❑ DLP 3510 [M]	1963's Early Hits	1963	10.00
❑ DLP 3528 [M]	Scarlett O'Hara	1963	10.00
❑ DLP 3544 [M]	A Tribute to the All-Time Greats	1963	10.00
❑ DLP 3552 [M]	Wonderful! Wonderful!	1963	10.00
❑ DLP 3572 [M]	Early Hits of 1964	1964	10.00
❑ DLP 3591 [M]	The Lawrence Welk Television Show 10th Anniversary	1964	10.00
❑ DLP 3611 [M]	The Golden Millions	1964	10.00
❑ DLP 3616 [M]	My First of 1965	1965	10.00
❑ DLP 3629 [M]	Apples and Bananas	1965	10.00
❑ DLP 3653 [M]	The Happy Wanderer	1966	10.00
❑ DLP 3663 [M]	Today's Great Hits	1966	10.00
❑ DLP 3688 [M]	Champagne on Broadway	1966	10.00
❑ DLP 3774 [M]	Winchester Cathedral	1966	10.00
❑ DLP 3779 [M]	Hymns We Love	1967	10.00
❑ DLP 3790 [M]	Lawrence Welk's "Hits of Our Time"	1967	10.00
❑ DLP 3812 [M]	Golden Hits/The Best of Lawrence Welk	1967	12.00
❑ DLP 25164 [S]	Mr. Music Maker	1959	15.00
❑ DLP 25200 [S]	Voices and Strings	1959	15.00
❑ DLP 25218 [S]	The Lawrence Welk Glee Club	1959	15.00
❑ DLP 25224 [S]	Dance with Lawrence Welk	1959	15.00
❑ DLP 25238 [S]	Lawrence Welk Presents Great American Composers	1960	12.00
❑ DLP 25247 [S]	Lawrence Welk Presents Great Overtures in Dance Time	1960	12.00
❑ DLP 25248 [S]	I'm Forever Blowing Bubbles	1960	12.00
❑ DLP 25251 [S]	Songs of the Islands	1960	12.00
❑ DLP 25274 [S]	Strictly for Dancing	1960	12.00
❑ DLP 25284 [S]	To Mother	1960	12.00
❑ DLP 25296 [S]	Sweet and Lovely	1960	12.00
❑ DLP 25302 [S]	Polkas	1960	12.00
❑ DLP 25317 [S]	Lawrence in Dixieland	1960	12.00
❑ DLP 25318 [S]	Double Shuffle	1960	12.00
❑ DLP 25342 [S]	The Champagne Music of Lawrence Welk	1960	12.00
❑ DLP 25350 [S]	Last Date	1960	12.00
❑ DLP 25359 [S]	Calcutta!	1961	12.00
❑ DLP 25389 [S]	Yellow Bird	1961	12.00
❑ DLP 25395 [S]	Diamond Jubilee	1961	12.00
❑ DLP 25397 [S]	Silent Night and 13 Other Best-Loved Christmas Songs	1961	15.00
❑ DLP 25412 [S]	Moon River	1961	12.00
❑ DLP 25428 [S]	Young World	1962	12.00
❑ DLP 25432 [S]	Sing-a-Long Party	1962	12.00
❑ DLP 25457 [S]	Baby Elephant Walk and Theme from The Brothers Grimm	1962	12.00
❑ DLP 25489 [S]	Bubbles in the Wine	1962	12.00
❑ DLP 25499 [S]	Waltz Time	1963	12.00
❑ DLP 25510 [S]	1963's Early Hits	1963	12.00
❑ DLP 25528 [S]	Scarlett O'Hara	1963	12.00
❑ DLP 25544 [S]	A Tribute to the All-Time Greats	1963	12.00
❑ DLP 25552 [S]	Wonderful! Wonderful!	1963	12.00
❑ DLP 25572 [S]	Early Hits of 1964	1964	12.00
❑ DLP 25591 [S]	The Lawrence Welk Television Show 10th Anniversary	1964	12.00
❑ DLP 25611 [S]	The Golden Millions	1964	12.00
❑ DLP 25616 [S]	My First of 1965	1965	12.00
❑ DLP 25629 [S]	Apples and Bananas	1965	12.00
❑ DLP 25653 [S]	The Happy Wanderer	1966	12.00
❑ DLP 25663 [S]	Today's Great Hits	1966	12.00
❑ DLP 25688 [S]	Champagne on Broadway	1966	12.00
❑ DLP 25774 [S]	Winchester Cathedral	1966	12.00
❑ DLP 25779 [S]	Hymns We Love	1967	12.00
❑ DLP 25790 [S]	Lawrence Welk's "Hits of Our Time"	1967	12.00
❑ DLP 25812 [S]	Golden Hits/The Best of Lawrence Welk	1967	10.00
HAMILTON			
❑ HLP 152 [M]	Mary Poppins	1965	10.00
❑ HLP 12152 [S]	Mary Poppins	1965	12.00
HARMONY			
❑ HL 7394 [M]	Vintage Champagne	1966	12.00
❑ HS 11194 [S]	Vintage Champagne	1966	12.00
❑ HS 11301	Champagne Dance Party	1969	10.00
HEARTLAND			
❑ 1006	Musical Family Reunion	198?	10.00
MCA			
❑ 733	Polka and Waltz Time	197?	8.00
—Reissue of Vocalion 73670			

Number	Title (A Side/B Side)	Yr	NM
❑ 4026 [(2)]	The Best of Lawrence Welk, Vol. 2	197?	12.00
❑ 4044 [(2)]	The Best of Lawrence Welk	197?	12.00
❑ 4104 [(2)]	The Best Polkas	197?	12.00
MCA CORAL			
❑ 20100	Champagne Music	197?	8.00
MERCURY			
❑ MG-20092 [M]	Dance Party	1956	15.00
MISTLETOE			
❑ MLP-1215	Christmas with Lawrence Welk	197?	10.00
PICKWICK			
❑ SPC-1019	The Christmas Song	197?	10.00
—Reissue of Coral LP "Jingle Bells" with shuffled running order			
❑ SPC-3070	Save the Last Dance for Me	196?	10.00
❑ SPC-3092	I'll See You Again	196?	10.00
❑ SPC-3116	You'll Never Walk Alone	196?	10.00
❑ SPC-3143	If You Were the Only One	196?	10.00
❑ SPC-3157	As Time Goes By	196?	10.00
❑ SPC-3196	Love Is a Many-Splendored Thing	197?	10.00
❑ SPC-3212	Blue Hawaii	197?	10.00
❑ SPC-3252	Polkas!	197?	10.00
PREMIER			
❑ 9043	Lawrence Welk	196?	10.00
RANWOOD			
❑ 2000	Merry Christmas	197?	10.00
❑ 2004	Polkas	197?	8.00
—With Myron Floren			
❑ 2005	Moon River	197?	6.00
—Reissue of Ranwood 8016			
❑ 2006	Yellow Bird	197?	6.00
—Reissue of Ranwood 8021			
❑ 2007	Songs of the Islands	197?	6.00
—Reissue of Ranwood 8022			
❑ 2008	Waltz Time	197?	6.00
—Reissue of Ranwood 8025			
❑ 2009	Hymns We Love	197?	6.00
—Reissue of Ranwood 8042			
❑ 2010	Memories	197?	6.00
—Reissue of Ranwood 8044			
❑ 4100	On Tour, Vol. 1	198?	8.00
❑ 4101	On Tour, Vol. 2	198?	8.00
❑ 5001 [(2)]	Reminiscing	1972	12.00
❑ 5005 [(2)]	24 of the World's Greatest Polkas	197?	12.00
—With Myron Floren			
❑ 6001 [(2)]	Lawrence Welk and His Musical Family in Concert	1973	12.00
❑ 6002	Lawrence Welk and His Musical Family Celebrate 50 Years in Music	1974	10.00
❑ 7002 [(2)]	200 Years of American Music	1976	12.00
❑ 7004 [(2)]	22 Great Waltzes	1977	12.00
❑ 7009 [(2)]	22 Great Songs for Dancing	1978	12.00
❑ 7016 [(2)]	22 Great Songs for Easy Listening	198?	12.00
❑ 7023 [(2)]	22 All-Time Big Band Favorites	1983	12.00
❑ 7028 [(2)]	22 All-Time Favorite Waltzes	198?	12.00
❑ 7029 [(2)]	22 Merry Christmas Favorites	198?	12.00
❑ 8003	Love Is Blue	1968	10.00
❑ 8016	Moon River	1968	8.00
—Reissue of Dot 25412			
❑ 8017	Winchester Cathedral	1968	8.00
—Reissue of Dot 25774			
❑ 8020	Silent Night and 13 Other Best-Loved Christmas Songs	1968	8.00
—Reissue of Dot 25397			
❑ 8021	Yellow Bird	1968	8.00
—Reissue of Dot 25389			
❑ 8022	Songs of the Islands	1968	8.00
—Reissue of Dot 25251			
❑ 8023	The Champagne Music of Lawrence Welk	1968	8.00
—Reissue of Dot 25342			
❑ 8024	Calcutta!	1968	8.00
—Reissue of Dot 25359			
❑ 8025	Waltz Time	1968	8.00
—Reissue of Dot 25499			
❑ 8026	The Lawrence Welk Television Show	1968	8.00
—Reissue of Dot 25591			
❑ 8027	Country Music's Great Hits	1968	10.00
❑ 8028	Golden Hits/The Best of Lawrence Welk	1968	8.00
—Reissue of Dot 25812			
❑ 8030	To America with Love	1968	10.00
❑ 8034	The Lawrence Welk Singers and Orchestra	1968	10.00
❑ 8042	Hymns We Love	1968	8.00
—Reissue of Dot 25779			
❑ 8044	Memories	1969	10.00
❑ 8049	Galveston	1969	10.00
❑ 8053	Lawrence Welk Plays I Love You Truly and Other Songs of Love	1969	10.00
❑ 8060	Jean	1969	10.00
❑ 8068	The Golden 60's	1970	10.00
❑ 8077	The Big Band Sound	1970	10.00
❑ 8079	Champagne Strings	1970	10.00
❑ 8083	Candida	1970	10.00
❑ 8087	No, No, Nanette	1971	10.00
❑ 8091	Go Away Little Girl	1971	10.00
❑ 8109	(More of) The Big Band Sound	1972	10.00
❑ 8114	The Good Life	1973	10.00
❑ 8130	Lawrence Welk Plays From That's Entertainment	1974	10.00
❑ 8140	Most Requested TV Favorites	1974	10.00
❑ 8145	25 Years on Television	1975	10.00
❑ 8162	The Best of Lawrence Welk: 20 Great Hits	1976	10.00
❑ 8165	Nadia's Theme	1976	10.00
❑ 8183	My Personal Favorites	1978	10.00
❑ 8184	Hallelujah!	1978	10.00
❑ 8191	Remembering the Sweet and Swing Band Era, Vol. 1	1979	10.00
❑ 8192	Remembering the Sweet and Swing Band Era, Vol. 2	1979	10.00
❑ 8194	Lawrence Welk Plays Dixieland	1980	10.00
❑ 8195 [(2)]	Reminiscing, Vol. 2	1980	12.00
❑ 8201	Lawrence Welk Presents Anacani	1982	10.00
❑ 8210	Musical Memories with Lawrence Welk	1984	8.00
❑ 8211	Come Waltz with Me	1984	8.00
❑ 10001 [(2)]	Live at Lake Tahoe	1978	12.00
❑ 10002 [(2)]	The Sweet and Swing Band Era	1979	12.00
READER'S DIGEST			
❑ RDA-07-A [(4)]	Merry Christmas from Lawrence Welk and His Champagne Music Makers	1970	25.00
❑ RDA 95 [(6)]	Champagne Music Varieties	196?	25.00
❑ RDA 156	Champagne Dance Time with Lawrence Welk	196?	10.00
SUNNYVALE			
❑ SVL-1015	Silent Night and 13 Other Best-Loved Christmas Songs	1978	8.00
—Same contents as Dot 25397			
THOMAS			
❑ 20052	The Magic of Color-Glo	196?	12.00
VOCALION			
❑ VL 3670 [M]	Polka and Waltz Time	196?	10.00
❑ VL 3671 [M]	Lawrence Welk and His Champagne Music	196?	10.00
❑ VL 3783 [M]	Lawrence Welk and His Champagne Music Makers Play for You	1967	12.00
❑ VL 73670 [R]	Polka and Waltz Time	196?	10.00
❑ VL 73671 [R]	Lawrence Welk and His Champagne Music	196?	10.00
❑ VL 73783 [R]	Lawrence Welk and His Champagne Music Makers Play for You	1967	10.00
❑ VL 73865	Champagne Polkas	1969	10.00
❑ VL 73888	Til the End of Time	1969	10.00
❑ VL 73921	Wonderful Music	1970	10.00
WING			
❑ PKW-2-114 [(2)]	With a-One and a-Two	1969	15.00
❑ MGW-12119 [M]	Dance Party	196?	12.00
❑ MGW-12210 [M]	Music for Polka Lovers	196?	12.00
❑ MGW-12214 [M]	Aragon Trianon Memories	196?	12.00
❑ SRW-16210 [S]	Music for Polka Lovers	196?	10.00
❑ SRW-16214 [R]	Aragon Trianon Memories	196?	10.00
❑ SRW-16379	The Best of Welk	196?	10.00

WELLER, FREDDY

Also see PAUL REVERE AND THE RAIDERS.

45s

Number	Title (A Side/B Side)	Yr	NM
ABC DOT			
❑ 17554	Love You Back to Georgia/Show Me the Way to Your Love	1975	5.00
❑ 17577	Stone Crazy/Still Making Love to You	1975	5.00
APT			
❑ 25096	Walk Away Slowly/You Better Go Join the Campfire	1966	10.00
COLUMBIA			
❑ 10016	You're Not Getting Older (You're Getting Better)/Are We Makin' Love	1974	4.00
❑ 10300	Ask Any Old Cheater Who Knows/A Legend in My Home	1976	4.00
❑ 10352	Liquor, Love and Life/Celia Brown	1976	4.00
❑ 10411	Room 269/I Drank Myself Sober	1976	4.00
❑ 10482	Strawberry Curls/When You Were Mine	1977	4.00
❑ 10539	Merry-Go-Round/One Man Show	1977	4.00
❑ 10598	Nobody Cares But You/Love Door	1977	4.00
❑ 10682	Let Me Fall Back in Your Arms/Snuff Queens	1978	4.00
❑ 10769	Bar Wars/One of the Mysteries of Love	1978	4.00
❑ 10837	Love Got in the Way/You Win Again	1978	4.00
❑ 10890	Fantasy Island/Take a Little Bit	1979	4.00
❑ 10973	Nadine/Too Many Memories	1979	4.00
❑ 11044	That Run-Away Woman of Mine/Atlanta	1979	4.00
❑ 11149	Go for the Night/Two Makes One Wonderful	1979	4.00
❑ 11221	A Million Old Goodbyes/Sleep with Me	1980	4.00
❑ 11266	Lost in Austin/Explosion!	1980	4.00
❑ 11394	Still Your Fool/Tonight I'm Drinkin'	1980	4.00
❑ 44800	Games People Play/Home	1969	5.00
❑ 44916	These Are Not My People/Never Knew Julie	1969	5.00
❑ 45026	Down in the Boondocks/Amarillo, Texas	1969	5.00
❑ 45087	I Shook the Hand/We Gotta All Get Together	1970	5.00
❑ 45138	Listen to the Young Folks/That Little Boy	1970	6.00
❑ 45276	The Promised Land/Goodnight Sandy	1970	5.00
❑ 45388	Indian Lake/Over You	1971	5.00
❑ 45451	Another Night of Love/Always Something Special	1971	5.00
❑ 45542	Ballad of a Hillbilly Singer/Good Old-Fashioned Music	1972	5.00
❑ 45624	The Roadmaster/Who Do You Love	1972	5.00
❑ 45723	She Loves Me (Right Out of My Mind)/Angel on My Shoulder	1972	5.00
❑ 45827	Too Much Monkey Business/It Sure Feels Good	1973	5.00
❑ 45902	The Perfect Stranger/Betty Ann and Shirley Cole	1973	5.00
❑ 45968	I've Just Got to Know (How Loving You Would Be)/Georgia Girl	1973	5.00
❑ 46040	Sexy Lady/Bobby Crabtree's Grave	1974	5.00
DORE			
❑ 595	No One to Love/Mary, I'm Glad to See You	1961	15.00

Albums

Number	Title	Yr	NM
ABC DOT			
❑ DOSD-2026	Love You Back to Georgia	1975	12.00
COLUMBIA			
❑ CS 1036	Listen to the Young Folks	1970	15.00
❑ CS 9904	Games People Play/These Are Not My People	1969	15.00
❑ C 30638	Promised Land	1971	12.00
❑ KC 31769	Roadmaster	1972	12.00
❑ KC 32218	Too Much Monkey Business	1973	12.00
❑ KC 32958	Sexy Lady	1974	12.00
❑ KC 33883	Greatest Hits	1975	12.00
❑ KC 34244	Liquor, Love and Life	1976	10.00
❑ PC 34709	One Man Show	1977	10.00
❑ KC 35658	Love Got in the Way	1979	10.00
HARMONY			
❑ KH 31784	Country Collection	1972	10.00

WELLES, ORSON

12-Inch Singles

Number	Title	Yr	NM
GNP CRESCENDO			
❑ 1206	I Know What It Is to Be Young/Love Is a Lovely Word	1984	15.00

45s

Number	Title	Yr	NM
GNP CRESCENDO			
❑ 8345	I Know What It Is to Be Young/Love Is a Lovely Word	1984	8.00

Albums

Number	Title	Yr	NM
AUDIO FIDELITY			
❑ W-90366	War of the Worlds	1964	15.00
—Capitol Record Club edition; same edited version as Audio Rarities LPA 2355			
AUDIO RARITIES			
❑ LPA 2355	War of the Worlds	1955	15.00
—Edited version of the October 30, 1938 Mercury Theatre radio broadcast			
EVOLUTION			
❑ 2 LPS 4001 [(2)]	War of the Worlds	1971	15.00
—Complete version of the October 30, 1938 Mercury Theatre radio broadcast			
LONGINES SYMPHONETTE			
❑ SY-5251	War of the Worlds	197?	15.00
—Complete version of the October 30, 1938 Mercury Theatre radio broadcast, but on one record			
MEDIARTS			
❑ 41-2	The Begatting of the President	1970	15.00

W

Except when noted otherwise, VG = 25% of NM, and VG+ = 50% of NM. (Example: VG = $2.00, VG+ = $4.00 and NM = $8.00.)

MURRAY HILL

Number	Title (A Side/B Side)	Yr	NM
❑ S 44217 [(2)]	War of the Worlds	197?	12.00

—Complete version of the October 30, 1938 Mercury Theatre radio broadcast; reissue of Evolution LP

UNITED ARTISTS

Number	Title (A Side/B Side)	Yr	NM
❑ UAS-5521	The Begatting of the President	1971	12.00

—Reissue of Mediarts LP

WELLINGTON, MARY SUE

45s

TUFF

Number	Title (A Side/B Side)	Yr	NM
❑ 400	Spoiled/Save a Little Monkey	1964	8.00

WELLINGTON, RUSTY

45s

ARCADE

Number	Title (A Side/B Side)	Yr	NM
❑ 116	Dog-Gone It Baby, I'm in Love/Every Precious Memory	1953	40.00
❑ 124	I Want a Little Lovin'/Slowly But Surely	1954	40.00
❑ 140	Blues from Tennessee/Jump Jump Honey	1955	40.00
❑ 144	The Convict and the Rose/I Ain't A-Movin' On No More	1957	40.00
❑ 184	The Allegash/I've Been Away from You So Long	1965	15.00
❑ 185	Soft Shoulders/The Old Man	1966	15.00
❑ 191	Lonely Lips/Isle of Wild Roses	1967	15.00

MGM

Number	Title (A Side/B Side)	Yr	NM
❑ 12581	Rocking Chair on the Moon/I Lost My Someone	1957	300.00

WELLS, BILLY, AND THE CRESCENTS

45s

RESERVE

Number	Title (A Side/B Side)	Yr	NM
❑ 105	I Love Only You/Julie	1956	600.00

WELLS, DONNIE

45s

SCEPTER

Number	Title (A Side/B Side)	Yr	NM
❑ 12119	Real Love/You've Got My Love	1965	25.00

WELLS, KITTY

45s

CAPRICORN

Number	Title (A Side/B Side)	Yr	NM
❑ 0208	Too Much Love Between Us/What About You	1974	6.00
❑ 0226	I've Been Loving You Too Long/Too Stubborn	1975	6.00
❑ 0240	Anybody Out There Wanna Be a Daddy/Somewhere Down the Road (There's a Country Girl)	1975	6.00
❑ 0264	Mary Hartman, Mary Hartman/Nickel Candy Bar	1976	6.00

DECCA

Number	Title (A Side/B Side)	Yr	NM
❑ 9-28232	It Wasn't God Who Made Honky Tonk Angels/I Don't Want Your Money, I Want Your Time	1952	30.00
❑ 9-28432	I Heard the Juke Box Playing/A Wedding Ring Ago	1952	25.00
❑ 9-28525	Divided by Two/The Things I Might Have Been	1953	25.00
❑ 9-28578	Paying for That Back Street Affair/Crying Steel Guitar Waltz	1953	25.00
❑ 9-28666	You Said You Could Do Without Me/Honky Tonk Waltz	1953	25.00
❑ 9-28753	I Don't Claim to Be an Angel/The Life They Live in Songs	1953	25.00
❑ 9-28797	Hey Joe/My Cold Cold Heart Is Melted Now	1953	25.00
❑ 9-28931	Cheatin's a Sin/I Gave My Wedding Dress Away	1953	25.00
❑ 9-29023	Release Me/After Dark	1954	25.00
❑ 9-29134	You're Not Easy to Forget/He's Married to Me	1954	25.00
❑ 9-29313	Thou Shalt Not Steal/I Hope My Divorce Is Never Granted	1954	25.00
❑ 9-29419	Makin' Believe/Whose Shoulder Will You Cry On	1955	20.00
❑ 9-29577	There's Poison in Your Heart/I'm in Love with You	1955	20.00
❑ 9-29728	Lonely Side of Town/I've Kissed You My Last Time	1955	20.00
❑ 9-29823	How Far Is Heaven/Dust on the Bible	1956	20.00

—A-side with Carol Sue

Number	Title (A Side/B Side)	Yr	NM
❑ 9-29956	Searching (For Someone Like You)/I'd Rather Stay Home	1956	20.00
❑ 9-30094	Repenting/I'm Counting on You	1956	20.00
❑ 9-30288	Three Ways (To Love You)/A Change of Heart	1957	15.00
❑ 9-30415	(I'll Always Be Your) Fraulein/What I Believe	1957	15.00
❑ 9-30551	I Can't Stop Loving You/She's No Angel	1958	15.00
❑ 9-30662	Jealousy/I Can't Help Wondering	1958	15.00
❑ 9-30736	Touch and Go Heart/He's Lost His Love for Me	1958	15.00
❑ 9-30804	Mommy for a Day/All the Time	1959	15.00
❑ 9-30890	Your Wild Life's Gonna Get You Down/You'll Never Be Mine Again	1959	15.00
❑ 9-30987	Amigo's Guitar/Lonely Is a Word	1959	15.00
❑ 31065	Left to Right/Memory of Love	1960	15.00
❑ 31123	Carmel by the Sea/The Man I Used to Know	1960	12.00
❑ 31192	The Other Cheek/Fickle Fun	1961	12.00
❑ 31246	Heartbreak U.S.A./There Must Be Another Way to Live	1961	12.00
❑ 31313	Day Into Night/Our Mansion Is a Prison Now	1961	12.00
❑ 31349	Unloved Unwanted/Au Revoir (Goodbye)	1962	12.00
❑ 31392	Will Your Lawyer Talk to God/The Big Let Down	1962	12.00
❑ 31422	We Missed You/Wicked World	1962	12.00
❑ 31441	Christmas Ain't Like Christmas Anymore/Dancer (With the Light Upon His Tail)	1962	15.00
❑ 31457	Cold and Lonely (Is the Forecast for Tonight)/Is It Asking Too Much	1963	10.00
❑ 31501	I Gave My Wedding Dress Away/A Heartache for a Keepsake	1963	10.00
❑ 31580	This White Circle on My Finger/(I Didn't Have to) Break Up Someone's Home	1964	10.00
❑ 31622	Password/I've Thought of Leaving You	1964	10.00
❑ 31705	I'll Repossess My Heart/Kill Him with Kindness	1964	10.00
❑ 31749	You Don't Hear/Six Lonely Hours	1965	10.00
❑ 31817	Meanwhile, Down at Joe's/Leavin' Town Tonight	1965	10.00
❑ 31881	A Woman Half My Age/When Your Little High Horse Runs Down	1966	10.00
❑ 31957	It's All Over (But the Crying)/You Left Your Mark on Me	1966	10.00
❑ 32024	Only Me and My Hairdresser Know/A Woman Never Forgets	1966	10.00
❑ 32088	Love Makes the World Go Around/I'm Just Not Smart	1967	8.00
❑ 32163	Queen of Honky Tonk Street/Wasting My Time	1967	8.00
❑ 32247	My Big Truck Drivin' Man/You Want Her Not Me	1967	8.00
❑ 32343	Gypsy King/When Hearts Grow Hard and Cold	1968	8.00
❑ 32389	Happiness Hill/You're No Angel Yourself	1968	8.00
❑ 32455	Guilty Street/Shape Up or Get Out	1969	8.00
❑ 32455 [PS]	Guilty Street/Shape Up or Get Out	1969	20.00

—Her only known Decca picture sleeve

Number	Title (A Side/B Side)	Yr	NM
❑ 32535	Just a Cheap Affair/Don't Call Me Your Darling	1969	8.00
❑ 32629	I Don't See What I Say/Gonna Find Me a Bluebird	1970	8.00
❑ 32700	Your Love Is the Way/It's Written All Over Your Face	1970	8.00
❑ 32763	I Love You/That Ain't a Woman's Way	1970	8.00
❑ 32795	They're Stepping All Over My Heart/Your Old Love Letters	1971	8.00
❑ 32840	Pledging My Love/Thank You for Loving Me	1971	8.00
❑ 32889	I'm the Wreck of Number Two/Reno Airport Nashville Plane	1971	8.00
❑ 32931	Sincerely/J.J. Sneed	1972	8.00
❑ 32976	A Bridge I Just Can't Burn/Love Is the Answer	1972	8.00
❑ 33016	I've Got Yesterday/Less Than a Lady	1972	8.00
❑ 33047	Full Grown Man/Every Step of the Way	1973	8.00
❑ 7-34185 [S]	Dasher (With the Light Upon His Tail)/C-H-R-I-S-T-M-A-S	1962	20.00

—Small hole, plays at 33 1/3 rpm

Number	Title (A Side/B Side)	Yr	NM
❑ 7-34186 [S]	Santa's On His Way/(B-side unknown)	1962	20.00

—Small hole, plays at 33 1/3 rpm

Number	Title (A Side/B Side)	Yr	NM
❑ 7-34187 [S]	titles unknown	1962	20.00

—Small hole, plays at 33 1/3 rpm

Number	Title (A Side/B Side)	Yr	NM
❑ 7-34188 [S]	Rudolph the Red-Nosed Reindeer/Blue Christmas	1962	20.00

—Small hole, plays at 33 1/3 rpm

Number	Title (A Side/B Side)	Yr	NM
❑ 7-34189 [S]	Ole Kris Kringle/(B-side unknown)	1962	20.00

—Small hole, plays at 33 1/3 rpm

Number	Title (A Side/B Side)	Yr	NM
❑ 9-46409	Precious Memories/Gloryland March	1952	40.00

MCA

Number	Title (A Side/B Side)	Yr	NM
❑ 40057	Easily Persuaded/It Doesn't Say	1973	6.00
❑ 40123	If I Was a Bottle/Mississippi Missus	1973	6.00

RCA VICTOR

Number	Title (A Side/B Side)	Yr	NM
❑ 47-5539	Gathering Flowers for the Master's Banquet/Don't Wait for the Last Minute to Pray	1953	25.00
❑ 47-5686	Kiss Me/Why Fall So Slowly	1954	25.00
❑ 48-0084	Love or Hate/Don't Wait for the Last Minute to Pray	1949	60.00

—Originals on green vinyl

Number	Title (A Side/B Side)	Yr	NM
❑ 48-0333	Make Up Your Mind/All Smiles Tonight	1950	50.00

—Originals on green vinyl

Number	Title (A Side/B Side)	Yr	NM
❑ 48-0384	How Far Is Heaven/My Mother	1950	50.00

—Originals on green vinyl

RUBOCA

Number	Title (A Side/B Side)	Yr	NM
❑ 122	Thank You for the Roses/Loving You Was All I Ever Needed	1979	8.00
❑ 123	Old Milwaukee Talking/I Never Told Him I Loved Him	1979	8.00
❑ 124	I Can't Help It/I'll Hold You in My Heart	1980	8.00

7-Inch Extended Plays

DECCA

Number	Title (A Side/B Side)	Yr	NM
❑ ED 2163	It Wasn't God Who Made Honky Tonk Angels/The Things I Might Have Been//Paying for That Back Street Affair/I Don't Claim to Be an Angel	1955	25.00
❑ ED 2163 [PS]	Kitty Wells Sings	1955	25.00
❑ ED 2361	Makin' Believe/Release Me//I'm Too Lonely to Smile/Searching for a Soldier's Grave	1956	20.00
❑ ED 2361 [PS]	Kitty Wells' Country Hit Parade, Part 1	1956	20.00
❑ ED 2362	There's Poison in Your Heart/Whose Shoulder Will You Cry On//Cheatin's a Sin/I've Kissed You My Last Time	1956	20.00
❑ ED 2362 [PS]	Kitty Wells' Country Hit Parade, Vol. 2	1956	20.00
❑ ED 2363	(contents unknown)	1956	20.00
❑ ED 2363 [PS]	Kitty Wells' Country Hit Parade, Vol. 3	1956	20.00
❑ ED 2518	*Winner of Your Heart/Right or Wrong/Pace That Kills/Dancing with a Stranger	1957	20.00
❑ ED 2518 [PS]	Winner of Your Heart, Vol. 1	1957	20.00
❑ ED 2519	*Each Day/She's No Angel/Broken Marriage Vows/Change of Heart	1957	20.00
❑ ED 2519 [PS]	Winner of Your Heart, Vol. 2 (Change of Heart)	1957	20.00
❑ ED 2520	*Mansion on the Hill/Standing Room Only/I Guess I'll Go On Dreaming/Stubborn Heart	1957	20.00
❑ ED 2520 [PS]	Winner of Your Heart, Vol. 3 (Stubborn Heart)	1957	20.00
❑ ED 2584	That's Me Without You/Waltz of the Angels//Lonely Street/Love Me to Pieces	1958	20.00
❑ ED 2584 [PS]	Lonely Street	1958	20.00
❑ ED 2646 [M]	*Dust on the Bible/I Dreamed I Searched Heaven for You/Lonesome Valley/My Loved Ones Are Waiting for Me	1959	20.00
❑ ED 2646 [PS]	Dust on the Bible	1959	20.00
❑ ED 7-2646 [PS]	Dust on the Bible	1959	30.00
❑ ED 7-2646 [S]	Dust on the Bible/I Dreamed I Searched Heaven for You//Lonesome Valley/My Loved Ones Are Waiting for Me	1959	30.00
❑ ED 2677	*Sugartime/Dark Moon/Bonaparte's Retreat/When the Moon Comes Over the Mountain	1960	20.00
❑ ED 2677 [PS]	Kitty's Choice	1960	20.00
❑ ED 2684	*Seasons of My Heart/Lonely Is a Word/Send Me the Pillow You Dream On/Amigo's Guitar	1960	20.00
❑ ED 2684 [PS]	Seasons of My Heart	1960	20.00
❑ ED 2692	(contents unknown)	1961	20.00
❑ ED 2692 [PS]	Kitty Wells	1961	20.00
❑ ED 2699	*Heartbreak U.S.A./Heart to Heart Talk/This Old Heart/Cold, Cold Heart	1961	20.00
❑ ED 2699 [PS]	Heartbreak U.S.A.	1961	20.00
❑ ED 2710	(contents unknown)	1962	20.00
❑ ED 2710 [PS]	Kitty Wells	1962	20.00
❑ ED 2717	(contents unknown)	1962	20.00
❑ ED 2717 [PS]	Kitty Wells	1962	20.00
❑ ED 2732	*Will Your Lawyer Talk to God/The Big Let Down/I'm Couting on You/I've Got a New Heartache	1962	20.00

W

Number	Title (A Side/B Side)	Yr	NM
❑ ED 2732 [PS]	Kitty Wells	1962	20.00
❑ ED 2737	*Wicked World/We Missed You/ Your Old Love Letters/Slowly	1963	20.00
❑ ED 2737 [PS]	Wicked World	1963	20.00
❑ ED 2749	*I Can't Stop Loving You/All the Time/Your Wild Life's Gonna Get You Down/Hey Joe	1963	20.00
❑ ED 2749 [PS]	All the Time	1963	20.00
❑ ED 2763	*I Gave My Wedding Dress Away/A Heartache for a Keepsake/Cold and Lonely/ Is It Asking Too Much	1963	20.00
❑ ED 2763 [PS]	Kitty Wells	1963	20.00
❑ ED 2777	*Talk Back Trembling Lips/ Busted/Ring of Fire/Guilty	1964	25.00
❑ ED 2777 [PS]	Talk Back Trembling Lips	1964	25.00
❑ ED 2780	*Password/B.J. the D.J./Old Records/As Usual	1964	25.00
❑ ED 2780 [PS]	Password	1964	30.00
❑ ED 2781	(contents unknown)	1965	30.00
❑ ED 2781 [PS]	This White Circle	1965	30.00
❑ ED 2804	(contents unknown)	1965	30.00
❑ ED 2804 [PS]	Burning Memories	1965	30.00
❑ 7-34043	Dark Moon/Your Cheatin' Heart/Beautiful Brown Eyes// Jambalaya/Jealous Heart/ My Happiness	196?	15.00
—Stereo jukebox issue; small hole, plays at 33 1/3 rpm			
❑ 7-34043 [PS]	Kitty's Choice	196?	15.00
❑ 7-34255	I've Thought of Leaving Too/As Usual/Begging to You// Password/This White Circle/ Gonna Find Me a Bluebird	196?	15.00
—Stereo jukebox issue; small hole, plays at 33 1/3 rpm			
❑ 7-34255 [PS]	Country Music Time	196?	15.00

Albums

DECCA

Number	Title (A Side/B Side)	Yr	NM
❑ DXB 174 [(2)M]	The Kitty Wells Story	1963	30.00
❑ DL 4075 [M]	Seasons of My Heart	1961	30.00
❑ DL 4108 [M]	Kitty Wells' Golden Favorites	1961	30.00
❑ DL 4141 [M]	Heartbreak U.S.A.	1961	30.00
❑ DL 4197 [M]	Queen of Country Music	1962	30.00
❑ DL 4270 [M]	Singing on Sunday	1962	30.00
❑ DL 4349 [M]	Christmas Day with Kitty Wells	1962	25.00
❑ DL 4493 [M]	Especially for You	1964	25.00
❑ DL 4554 [M]	Country Music Time	1964	25.00
❑ DL 4612 [M]	Burning Memories	1965	25.00
❑ DL 4658 [M]	Lonesome Sad and Blue	1965	25.00
❑ DL 4679 [M]	Family Gospel Sing	1965	25.00
❑ DL 4741 [M]	Kitty Wells Sings Songs Made Famous by Jim Reeves	1966	25.00
❑ DL 4776 [M]	Country All the Way	1966	25.00
❑ DL 4831 [M]	The Kitty Wells Show	1966	25.00
❑ DL 4857 [M]	Love Makes the World Go Around	1967	30.00
❑ DL 4929 [M]	Queen of Honky Tonk Street	1967	40.00
❑ DL 5001 [M]	Kitty Wells' Greatest Hits	1968	50.00
—White label promo only			
❑ DXSB 7174 [(2)P]	The Kitty Wells Story	1963	40.00
❑ DL 8293 [M]	Kitty Wells' Country Hit Parade	1956	60.00
—Black label, silver print			
❑ DL 8293 [M]	Kitty Wells' Country Hit Parade	1961	30.00
—Black label with color bars			
❑ DL 8552 [M]	Winner of Your Heart	1957	60.00
—Black label, silver print			
❑ DL 8552 [M]	Winner of Your Heart	1961	30.00
—Black label with color bars			
❑ DL 8732 [M]	Lonely Street	1958	60.00
—Black label, silver print			
❑ DL 8732 [M]	Lonely Street	1961	30.00
—Black label with color bars			
❑ DL 8858 [M]	Dust on the Bible	1959	60.00
—Black label, silver print			
❑ DL 8858 [M]	Dust on the Bible	1961	30.00
—Black label with color bars			
❑ DL 8888 [M]	After Dark	1959	60.00
—Black label, silver print			
❑ DL 8888 [M]	After Dark	1961	30.00
—Black label with color bars			
❑ DL 8979 [M]	Kitty's Choice	1960	50.00
—Black label, silver print			
❑ DL 8979 [M]	Kitty's Choice	1961	25.00
—Black label with color bars			
❑ DL 74075 [S]	Seasons of My Heart	1961	40.00
❑ DL 74108 [R]	Kitty Wells' Golden Favorites	196?	20.00
❑ DL 74141 [S]	Heartbreak U.S.A.	1961	40.00
❑ DL 74197 [S]	Queen of Country Music	1962	40.00
❑ DL 74270 [S]	Singing on Sunday	1962	40.00
❑ DL 74349 [S]	Christmas Day with Kitty Wells	1962	30.00
❑ DL 74493 [S]	Especially for You	1964	30.00
❑ DL 74554 [S]	Country Music Time	1964	30.00
❑ DL 74612 [S]	Burning Memories	1965	30.00
❑ DL 74658 [S]	Lonesome Sad and Blue	1965	30.00
❑ DL 74679 [S]	Family Gospel Sing	1965	30.00
❑ DL 74741 [S]	Kitty Wells Sings Songs Made Famous by Jim Reeves	1966	30.00
❑ DL 74776 [S]	Country All the Way	1966	30.00
❑ DL 74831 [S]	The Kitty Wells Show	1966	30.00
❑ DL 74857 [S]	Love Makes the World Go Around	1967	30.00
❑ DL 74929 [S]	Queen of Honky Tonk Street	1967	25.00
❑ DL 74961	Kitty Wells Showcase	1968	25.00
❑ DL 75001 [S]	Kitty Wells' Greatest Hits	1968	25.00
❑ DL 75067	Cream of Country Hits	1968	25.00
❑ DL 75098	Guilty Street	1969	25.00
❑ DL 75164	Bouquet of Country Hits	1969	20.00
❑ DL 75221	Singin' 'Em Country	1970	20.00
❑ DL 75245	Your Love Is the Way	1970	20.00
❑ DL 75277	They're Stepping All Over My Heart	1971	20.00
❑ DL 75313	Pledging My Love	1971	20.00
❑ DL 75325	Heartwarming Gospel Songs	1972	20.00
❑ DL 75350	Sincerely	1972	20.00
❑ DL 75382	I've Got Yesterday	1972	20.00
❑ DL 78293 [R]	Kitty Wells' Country Hit Parade	196?	20.00
❑ DL 78552 [R]	Winner of Your Heart	196?	20.00
❑ DL 78732 [R]	Lonely Street	196?	20.00
❑ DL 78858 [R]	Dust on the Bible	196?	20.00
❑ DL 78979 [S]	Kitty's Choice	1960	60.00
—Maroon label, silver print			
❑ DL 78979 [S]	Kitty's Choice	1961	30.00
—Black label with color bars			
❑ SW-94491	Sincerely	1972	25.00
—Capitol Record Club edition			

WELLS, KITTY, AND ROY DRUSKY

45s

DECCA

Number	Title (A Side/B Side)	Yr	NM
❑ 31164	I Can't Tell My Heart That/ When Do You Love Me	1960	12.00
❑ 31523	Another Chance to Fall in Love/ My World's Losing You	1963	10.00

WELLS, KITTY, AND RED FOLEY

Also see each artist's individual listings.

45s

DECCA

Number	Title (A Side/B Side)	Yr	NM
❑ 9-29065	One by One/I'm a Stranger in My Home	1954	25.00
❑ 9-29228	Skinnie Minnie (Fishtart)/ Thank You for Calling	1954	25.00
❑ 9-29390	As Long As I Live/Make Believe ('Til We Can Make It Come True)	1955	20.00
❑ 9-29740	You and Me/No One But You	1955	20.00
❑ 32126	Happiness Means You/ Hello Number One	1967	8.00
❑ 32223	Living as Strangers/ Loved and Wanted	1967	8.00
❑ 32427	Have I Told You Lately That I Love You?/We Need One More Chance	1968	8.00

7-Inch Extended Plays

DECCA

Number	Title (A Side/B Side)	Yr	NM
❑ ED 2667	I'm a Stranger in My Home/One by One//As Long As I Live/ Make Believe (Till We Can Make It Come True)	1959	25.00
❑ ED 2667 [PS]	Kitty Wells and Red Foley	1959	25.00
❑ 7-34297	One by One/Make Believe/As Long As I Live//You and Me/ I'm a Stranger in My Home/ No One But You	196?	25.00
—Jukebox issue; small hole, plays at 33 1/3 rpm			
❑ 7-34297 [PS]	Golden Favorites	196?	25.00

Albums

DECCA

Number	Title (A Side/B Side)	Yr	NM
❑ DL 4109 [M]	Golden Favorites	1961	30.00
❑ DL 4906 [M]	Together Again	1967	30.00
❑ DL 74109 [S]	Golden Favorites	1961	40.00
❑ DL 74906 [S]	Together Again	1967	25.00

WELLS, KITTY, AND WEBB PIERCE

Also see each artist's individual listings.

45s

DECCA

Number	Title (A Side/B Side)	Yr	NM
❑ 9-30183	Oh So Many Years/Can You Find It in Your Heart	1957	15.00
❑ 9-30489	One Week Later/ When I'm with You	1957	15.00
❑ 31663	Finally/He Made You for Me	1964	10.00

7-Inch Extended Plays

DECCA

Number	Title (A Side/B Side)	Yr	NM
❑ ED 2666	*Oh So Many Years/One Week Later/When I'm With You/ Can You FInd It in Your Heart	1959	25.00
❑ ED 2666 [PS]	Kitty Wells and Webb Pierce	1959	25.00

WELLS, KITTY, AND JOHNNY WRIGHT

45s

DECCA

Number	Title (A Side/B Side)	Yr	NM
❑ 32294	We'll Stick Together/ Heartbreak Waltz	1968	8.00
❑ 32604	There Won't Be Any Tree This Christmas/White Christmas	1969	8.00

Albums

DECCA

Number	Title (A Side/B Side)	Yr	NM
❑ DL 5028 [M]	We'll Stick Together	1968	50.00
—Mono appears to be white label promo only			
❑ DL 75028 [S]	We'll Stick Together	1968	25.00

WELLS, MARY

Also see MARVIN GAYE AND MARY WELLS.

45s

ATCO

Number	Title (A Side/B Side)	Yr	NM
❑ 6392	Dear Lover/Can't You See	1965	12.00
❑ 6423	Keep Me in Suspense/ Such a Sweet Thing	1966	12.00
❑ 6436	Fancy Free/Me and My Baby	1966	12.00
❑ 6469	Coming Home/Hey You Set My Soul on Fire	1967	12.00

EPIC

Number	Title (A Side/B Side)	Yr	NM
❑ 02664	Gigolo/I'm Changing My Ways	1982	4.00
❑ 02855	These Arms/Spend the Night With Me	1982	4.00

JUBILEE

Number	Title (A Side/B Side)	Yr	NM
❑ 5621	The Doctor/Two Lovers' History	1968	15.00
❑ 5629	Can't Get Away From Your Love/A Woman in Love	1968	15.00
❑ 5639	Don't Look Back/500 Miles	1968	15.00
❑ 5676	Mind Reader/Never Give a Man the World	1969	12.00
❑ 5684	Dig the Way I Feel/Love Shooting Bandit	1969	12.00
❑ 5695	Sweet Love/It Must Be	1970	12.00
❑ 5718	Mr. Tough/Never Give a Man the World	1971	12.00

MOTOWN

Number	Title (A Side/B Side)	Yr	NM
❑ 1003	Bye Bye Baby/ Please Forgive Me	1960	50.00
❑ 1011	I Don't Want to Take a Chance/ I'm Sorry	1961	20.00
—Blue "map" label			
❑ 1011	I Don't Want to Take a Chance/ I'm Sorry	1961	30.00
—Pink "lines" label			
❑ 1011 [PS]	I Don't Want to Take a Chance/ I'm Sorry	1961	80.00
❑ 1016	Strange Love/Come to Me	1961	20.00
❑ 1016 [PS]	Strange Love/Come to Me	1961	80.00
❑ 1024	The One Who Really Loves You/I'm Gonna Stay	1962	20.00
❑ 1024 [PS]	The One Who Really Loves You/I'm Gonna Stay	1962	80.00
❑ 1032	You Beat Me to the Punch/ Old Love (Let's Try It Again)	1962	20.00
❑ 1032 [PS]	You Beat Me to the Punch/ Old Love (Let's Try It Again)	1962	120.00
❑ 1035	Two Lovers/Operator	1962	20.00
❑ 1039	Laughing Boy/Two Wrongs Don't Make a Right	1963	20.00
❑ 1042	Your Old Stand By/What Love Has Joined Together	1963	20.00
❑ 1048	You Lost the Sweetest Boy/ What's Easy for Two Is So Hard for One	1963	20.00
❑ 1056	My Guy/Oh Little Boy (What Did You Do to Me)	1964	20.00
❑ 1061	When I'm Gone/Guarantee for a Lifetime	1964	600.00
❑ 1065	Whisper You Love Me/ I'll Be Available	1964	—
—Unreleased?			

REPRISE

Number	Title (A Side/B Side)	Yr	NM
❑ 1031	I Found What I Wanted/ I See a Future in You	1971	10.00
❑ 1308	If You Can't Give Her Love (Give Her Up)/Cancel My Subscription	1974	10.00

20TH CENTURY FOX

Number	Title (A Side/B Side)	Yr	NM
❑ 544	Ain't It the Truth/Stop Takin' Me for Granted	1964	15.00
❑ 555	Use Your Head/Everlovin' Boy	1965	15.00
❑ 570	Never, Never Leave Me?Why Don't You Let Yourself Go	1965	15.00
❑ 590	He's a Lover/I'm Learnin'	1965	15.00
❑ 590 [PS]	He's a Lover/I'm Learnin'	1965	30.00
❑ 6606	Me Without You/I'm Sorry	1965	15.00
❑ 6619	I Should Have Known Better/ Please Please Me	1965	20.00

Albums

ALLEGIANCE

Number	Title (A Side/B Side)	Yr	NM
❑ AV-444	The Old, the New, and the Best of Mary Wells	1984	10.00

ATCO

Number	Title (A Side/B Side)	Yr	NM
❑ 33-199 [M]	Two Sides of Mary Wells	1966	25.00
❑ SD 33-199 [S]	Two Sides of Mary Wells	1966	30.00

W

Except when noted otherwise, VG = 25% of NM, and VG+ = 50% of NM. (Example: VG = $2.00, VG+ = $4.00 and NM = $8.00.)

Number	Title (A Side/B Side)	Yr	NM
EPIC			
❑ ARE 37540	In and Out of Love	1981	15.00
JUBILEE			
❑ JGS-8018	Servin' Up Some Soul	1968	25.00
MOTOWN			
❑ M5-161V1	Bye Bye Baby/I Don't Want to Take a Chance	1981	10.00
❑ M5-167V1	Mary Wells Sings My Guy	1981	10.00
❑ M5-221V1	Two Lovers	1981	10.00
❑ MLP-600 [M]	Bye Bye Baby/I Don't Want to Take a Chance	1961	300.00
—White label stock copy			
❑ MLP-600 [M]	Bye Bye Baby/I Don't Want to Take a Chance	1962	250.00
—With map; label address above the center hole			
❑ M 605 [M]	The One Who Really Loves You	1962	160.00
—With map; label address above the center hole			
❑ M 605 [M]	The One Who Really Loves You	1964	40.00
—With map; label address around lower part of label			
❑ M 607 [M]	Two Lovers and Other Great Hits	1963	120.00
—With map; label address above the center hole			
❑ M 607 [M]	Two Lovers and Other Great Hits	1964	40.00
—With map; label address around lower part of label			
❑ M 611 [M]	Recorded Live on Stage	1963	120.00
—With map; label address above the center hole			
❑ M 611 [M]	Recorded Live on Stage	1964	40.00
—With map; label address around lower part of label			
❑ M 612	Second Time Around	1963	—
—Canceled			
❑ M 616 [M]	Greatest Hits	1964	40.00
❑ MS 616 [S]	Greatest Hits	1964	40.00
❑ M 617 [M]	Mary Wells Sings My Guy	1964	50.00
❑ M 653 [M]	Vintage Stock	1967	50.00
❑ MS 653 [S]	Vintage Stock	1967	50.00
❑ 5233 ML	Greatest Hits	1982	10.00
MOVIETONE			
❑ 71010 [M]	Ooh	1966	25.00
❑ 72010 [S]	Ooh	1966	30.00
20TH FOX			
❑ TFM 3171 [M]	Mary Wells	1965	40.00
❑ TFM 3178 [M]	Love Songs to the Beatles	1965	80.00
❑ TFS 4171 [S]	Mary Wells	1965	60.00
❑ TFS 4178 [S]	Love Songs to the Beatles	1965	100.00
❑ ST-90790 [S]	Love Songs to the Beatles	1965	150.00
—Capitol Record Club edition			

WENDIGO

Number	Title (A Side/B Side)	Yr	NM
45s			
SCEPTER			
❑ 12211	Gimmie Some Lovin' (Part 1)/Gimmie Some Lovin' (Part 2)	1968	12.00

WESLEY, FRED

Also includes the J.B.'s.

Number	Title (A Side/B Side)	Yr	NM
45s			
ATLANTIC			
❑ 3408	Up for the Down Stroke/When In Doubt	1977	5.00
KING			
❑ 6317	The Grunt (Part 1)/The Grunt (Part 2)	1970	10.00
—As "The J.B.'s"			
❑ 6333	These Are the J.B.'s (Part 1)/These Are the J.B.'s (Part 2)	1970	10.00
—As "The J.B.'s"			
PEOPLE			
❑ 602	Gimme Some More/The Rabbit Got the Gun	1972	6.00
—As "The J.B.'s"			
❑ 607	Pass the Peas/Hot Pants Road	1972	6.00
—As "The J.B.'s"			
❑ 610	Givin' Up Food for Funk (Part 1)/Givin' Up Food for Funk (Part 2)	1972	6.00
—As "The J.B.'s"			
❑ 614	Backstabbers/J.B. Shout	1972	6.00
❑ 616	If You Don't Get It the First Time/You Can Have Her Boogie	1973	6.00
❑ 617	Alone Again (Naturally)/Watermelon Man	1973	6.00
❑ 619	Sportin' Life/Dirty Harri	1973	6.00
❑ 621	Doing It to Death/Everybody Got Soul	1973	6.00
❑ 627	If You Don't Get It the First Time, Back Up and Try It Again, Party/You Can Have Watergate, Just Give Me Some Bucks and I'll Be Straight	1973	6.00
❑ 632	Same Beat - Part 1/Same Beat - Part 2	1974	6.00
❑ 638	Damn Right I Am Somebody-Part 1/Damn Right I Am Somebody-Part 2	1974	6.00
❑ 643	Rockin' Funky Watergate (Part 1)/Rockin' Funky Watergate (Part 2)	1974	6.00
❑ 646	Little Boy Black/Rockin' Funky Watergate (Part 2)	1974	6.00
❑ 648	Breakin' Bread/Funky Music Is My Style	1974	5.00
❑ 651	Makin' Love/Rice and Ribs	1975	5.00
❑ 654	Thank You for Lettin' Me Be Myself and Be Yours (Part 1)/Thank You for Lettin' Me Be Myself and Be Yours (Part 2)	1975	5.00
❑ 655	(It's Not the Express) It's the J.B.'s Monaurail, Part 1/(It's Not the Express) It's the J.B.'s Monaurail, Part 2	1975	5.00
❑ 660	Thank You for Lettin' Me Be Myself (Part 1)/Thank You for Lettin' Me Be Myself (Part 2)	1975	5.00
❑ 663	All Aboard the Funky Soul Train/Thank You for Lettin' Me Be Myself and You Be Yourself	1976	5.00
❑ 2502	My Brother (Part 1)/My Brother (Part 2)	1971	6.00
—As "The J.B.'s"			
RSO/CURTOM			
❑ 1037	House Party/I Make Music	1980	4.00
Albums			
ATLANTIC			
❑ SD 18214	A Blow for Me, A Toot to You	1977	12.00
❑ SD 19254	Say Blow by Blow Backwards	1979	12.00
PEOPLE			
❑ PE-5601	Food for Thought	1972	80.00
❑ PE-5603	Doing It to Death	1973	80.00
❑ PE-6602	Damn Right I Am Somebody	1974	20.00
❑ PE-6604	Breakin' Bread	1974	20.00

WESLEY, GATE

Number	Title (A Side/B Side)	Yr	NM
45s			
ATLANTIC			
❑ 2319	Do the Batman/Do the Thing	1966	25.00

WEST

Number	Title (A Side/B Side)	Yr	NM
45s			
EPIC			
❑ 5-10335	Just Like Tom Thumb's Blues/Baby You Been On My Mind	1968	10.00
❑ 5-10378	Step by Step/Summer Flower	1968	8.00
❑ 5-10449	Peaceful Times/You Only Think You've Come Home	1969	8.00
Albums			
EPIC			
❑ BN 26380	West	1968	20.00
❑ BN 26433	Bridges	1969	20.00

WEST, LESLIE

Also see MOUNTAIN; WEST, BRUCE & LAING.

Number	Title (A Side/B Side)	Yr	NM
12-Inch Singles			
PASSPORT			
❑ 6061 [DJ]	Love Is Forever (same on both sides)	1987	6.00
45s			
PHANTOM			
❑ ?B-10301	E.S.P./Don't Burn Me	1975	4.00
WINDFALL			
❑ 530	This Wheel's On Fire/Dreams of Milk and Honey	1969	5.00
❑ 531	Blood of the Sun/Long Red	1969	5.00
7-Inch Extended Plays			
PHANTOM			
❑ JF-10424 [DJ]	Honey/Dear Prudence//Get It Up/The Setting Sun	1975	10.00
Albums			
I.R.S.			
❑ 82016	Alligator	1989	15.00
PASSPORT			
❑ PB-6061	Theme	1987	12.00
PHANTOM			
❑ BPL1-0954	The Great Fatsby	1975	12.00
❑ BPL1-1258	The Leslie West Band	1976	12.00
WINDFALL			
❑ 4500	Mountain	1969	15.00

WEST, MAE

Number	Title (A Side/B Side)	Yr	NM
45s			
DAGONET			
❑ 6	Put the Loot in the Boot, Santa/With Love from Me to You	1966	15.00
DECCA			
❑ 29452	Love Is the Greatest Thing/All of Me	1955	15.00
❑ 32738	The Sayings of Mae West/More Sayings of Mae West	1970	10.00
MGM			
❑ 14491	Great Balls of Fire/Naked Ape	1973	8.00
PLAZA			
❑ 506	Am I Too Young/He's Good for Me	1962	12.00
TOWER			
❑ 260	Day Tripper/Treat Him Right	1966	10.00
❑ 260 [PS]	Day Tripper/Treat Him Right	1966	20.00
❑ 261	Shakin' All Over/If You Gotta Go	1966	10.00
❑ 261 [PS]	Shakin' All Over/If You Gotta Go	1966	20.00
20TH CENTURY FOX			
❑ 6718	Hard to Handle/You Gotta Taste All the Fruit	1968	10.00
❑ 6718 [PS]	Hard to Handle/You Gotta Taste All the Fruit	1968	25.00
Albums			
DAGONET			
❑ DG-4 [M]	Wild Christmas	1966	30.00
❑ DGS-4 [S]	Wild Christmas	1966	40.00
DECCA			
❑ DL 9016 [M]	The Fabulous Mae West	1955	60.00
—All-black label with silver print			
❑ DL 9016 [M]	The Fabulous Mae West	1960	30.00
—Black label with colorband			
❑ DL 79016 [R]	The Fabulous Mae West	1960	15.00
❑ DL 79176	The Original Voice Tracks from Her Greatest Movies	1970	15.00
MCA			
❑ 2053	The Fabulous Mae West	1974	12.00
—Reissue of Decca LP			
MEZZOTONE			
❑ 1 [10]	Mae West Songs, Vol. 1	1952	100.00
❑ 2 [10]	Mae West Songs, Vol. 2	1952	100.00
MGM			
❑ SE-4869	Great Balls of Fire	1972	20.00
ROUND			
❑ RS-100	Under the Mistletoe with Mae West	1977	20.00
TOWER			
❑ ST 5028 [S]	Way Out West	1966	40.00
❑ T 5028 [M]	Way Out West	1966	30.00

WEST, MARSHALL

Number	Title (A Side/B Side)	Yr	NM
45s			
PARKWAY			
❑ 878	This House Is Gonna Live/I Hurt Myself	1963	12.00

WEST, RED

Number	Title (A Side/B Side)	Yr	NM
45s			
DOT			
❑ 16268	Midnight Ride/Unforgiven	1961	20.00
JARO			
❑ 77031	FBI Story/What Must I Do	1960	50.00
SANTO			
❑ 9006	Bossa Nova Mamza/My Babe	1963	15.00

WEST, SONNY

Number	Title (A Side/B Side)	Yr	NM
45s			
ATLANTIC			
❑ 1174	Rave On!/Call On Cupid	1958	40.00
NOR VA JAK			
❑ 1956	Rock-Ola Ruby/Sweet Rockin' Baby	1959	100.00
—As "Sonee West"			

WEST, BRUCE & LAING

Also see JACK BRUCE; LESLIE WEST; MOUNTAIN.

Number	Title (A Side/B Side)	Yr	NM
45s			
WINDFALL			
❑ 45751	Shake Ma Thing (Rollin' Jack)/The Doctor	1973	5.00
❑ 45829	Why Don'tcha/Mississippi Queen	1973	5.00
Albums			
WINDFALL			
❑ CQ 31929 [Q]	Why Dontcha	1972	20.00
❑ KC 31929	Why Dontcha	1972	12.00
❑ CQ 32216 [Q]	Whatever Turns You On	1973	20.00
❑ KC 32216	Whatever Turns You On	1973	12.00
❑ KC 32899	Live 'N' Kickin'	1974	12.00

WEST COAST POP ART EXPERIMENTAL BAND, THE

Number	Title (A Side/B Side)	Yr	NM
45s			
AMOS			
❑ 119	Free As a Bird/Where's My Daddy	1969	15.00
REPRISE			
❑ 0552	Shifting Sands/1906	1967	25.00
❑ 0582	Help, I'm a Rock/Transparent Day	1967	25.00
❑ 0776	Smell of Incense/Unfree Child	1968	25.00

W

Number	Title (A Side/B Side)	Yr	NM
Albums			
AMOS			
❑ AAS-7004	Where's My Daddy	1969	50.00
FIFO			
❑ M 101	West Coast Pop Art Experimental Band	1966	500.00
—With plain cardboard cover			
❑ M 101	West Coast Pop Art Experimental Band	1966	2000.
—With regular cover; VG value 1000; VG+ value 1500			
RAZZBERRY SAWFLY			
❑ 800	West Coast Pop Art Experimental Band	1980	100.00
—Reissue of Fifo LP			
REPRISE			
❑ R 6247 [M]	The West Coast Pop Art Experimental Band, Part One	1967	80.00
❑ RS 6247 [S]	The West Coast Pop Art Experimental Band, Part One	1967	100.00
❑ R 6270 [M]	The West Coast Pop Art Experimental Band, Vol. 2	1967	80.00
❑ RS 6270 [S]	The West Coast Pop Art Experimental Band, Vol. 2	1967	100.00
❑ R 6298 [M]	Vol. 3: A Child's Guide to Good and Evil	1968	200.00
—May exist only as a white label promo			
❑ RS 6298 [S]	Vol. 3: A Child's Guide to Good and Evil	1968	100.00
SUNDAZED			
❑ LP 5036 [(2)]	West Coast Pop Art Experimental Band, Vol. One	1997	15.00

WEST, KANYE

Number	Title (A Side/B Side)	Yr	NM
Albums			
DEF JAM			
❑ 1219801	808s & Heartbreak	2008	30.00

WESTON, KIM Also see MARVIN GAYE AND KIM WESTON.

Number	Title (A Side/B Side)	Yr	NM
45s			
AURA			
❑ 7193	God Bless America/So Glad	197?	20.00
ENTERPRISE			
❑ 9101	Beautiful People/Goodness Gracious	1974	5.00
GORDY			
❑ 7041	I'll Never See My Love Again/A Thrill a Moment	1965	20.00
❑ 7046	Take Me in Your Arms (Rock Me A Little While)/Don't Compare Me to Her	1965	20.00
❑ 7050	Helpless/A Love Like Yours (Don't Come Knocking Every Day)	1966	20.00
MGM			
❑ 13720	I Got What You Need/Someone Like You	1967	20.00
❑ 13720 [PS]	I Got What You Need/Someone Like You	1967	40.00
❑ 13804	That's Groovy/Land of Tomorrow	1967	20.00
❑ 13881	Nobody/You're Just the Kind of Guy	1967	20.00
❑ 13927	Lift Every Voice and Sing/This Is America	1968	20.00
❑ 13928	The Impossible Dream/When Johnny Comes Marching Home	1968	15.00
❑ 13992	I Will Understand/Thankful	1968	15.00
PEOPLE			
❑ 1001	Danger, Heartbreak Ahead/I'll Be Thinkin'	1970	10.00
PRIDE			
❑ 1	Lift Every Voice and Sing/This Is America	1970	10.00
TAMLA			
❑ 54076	It Should Have Been Me/Love Me All the Way	1963	50.00
❑ 54085	Just Loving You/Another Train Coming	1963	50.00
❑ 54100	Looking for the Right Guy/Feel Alright Tonight	1964	50.00
❑ 54100 [DJ]	Looking for the Right Guy	1964	75.00
—One-sided white-label promo (B-side blank)			
❑ 54106	A Little More Love/Go Ahead and Laugh	1964	100.00
❑ 54110	I'm Still Loving You/Go Ahead and Laugh	1964	60.00
VOLT			
❑ 1502	If I Had My Way/Gonna Be Alright	1971	15.00
❑ 1503	Little By Little, Bit By Bit/(B-side unknown)	1971	15.00
Albums			
MGM			
❑ E-4477 [M]	For the First Time	1967	30.00
❑ SE-4477 [S]	For the First Time	1967	40.00
❑ SE-4561	This Is America	1968	40.00
VOLT			
❑ VOS-6014	Kim, Kim, Kim	1971	25.00

WET WILLIE

Number	Title (A Side/B Side)	Yr	NM
45s			
CAPRICORN			
❑ 0008	Shout Bamalama/Airport	1972	6.00
❑ 0022	Shout Bamalama/Airport	1973	6.00
❑ 0031	Country Side of Life/In Our Hearts	1973	6.00
❑ 0043	Keep On Smilin'/Soul Jones	1974	6.00
❑ 0052	Keep On Smilin'/Country Side of Life	1975	4.00
—"Back to Back Hits" reissue			
❑ 0206	Keep On Smilin'/Soul Jones	1974	4.00
❑ 0212	Country Side of Life/Don't Wait Too Long	1974	4.00
❑ 0224	Leona/Ain't He a Mess	1975	4.00
❑ 0231	Dixie Rock/She's My Lady	1975	4.00
❑ 0254	Everything That 'Cha Do (Will Come Back to You)/Walkin' By Myself	1976	4.00
❑ 0260	Comic Book Hero/Baby Fat	1976	4.00
❑ 8020	Rock and Roll Band/Dirty Leg	1971	8.00
EPIC			
❑ 50478	Street Corner Serenade/We Got Lovin'	1977	4.00
❑ 50528	Let It Shine/Make You Feel Love Again	1978	4.00
❑ 50714	Weekend/Mr. Streamline	1979	4.00
❑ 50760	The Hard Way/Ramona	1979	4.00
Albums			
CAPRICORN			
❑ CP 0109	Wet Willie II	1972	12.00
❑ CP 0113	Drippin' Wet/Live	1973	12.00
❑ CP 0128	Keep on Smilin'	1974	10.00
❑ CP 0138	Wet Willie	1974	10.00
—Reissue of 861			
❑ CP 0149	Dixie Rock	1975	10.00
❑ CP 0166	The Wetter the Better	1976	10.00
❑ CP 0182	Left Coast Live	1977	10.00
❑ CP 0200	Greatest Hits	1978	10.00
❑ SD 861	Wet Willie	1971	15.00
EPIC			
❑ JE 34983	Manorisms	1977	10.00
❑ JE 35794	Which One's Willie?	1979	10.00

WHALEFEATHERS, THE

Number	Title (A Side/B Side)	Yr	NM
Albums			
NASCO			
❑ 9003	The Whalefeathers Declare	1969	100.00
❑ 9005	The Whalefeathers	1970	100.00

WHAM! Also see GEORGE MICHAEL.

Number	Title (A Side/B Side)	Yr	NM
12-Inch Singles			
COLUMBIA			
❑ AS 1980 [DJ]	Careless Whisper (same on both sides)	1984	15.00
—As "Wham! featuring George Michael"			
❑ CAS 2122 [DJ]	Freedom (Album Version) (Single Remix)	1985	25.00
❑ 44-03177	Enjoy What You Do (Wham Rap) (Vocal) (Instrumental)	1982	25.00
—As "Wham! U.K."			
❑ 44-03501	Young Guns (Go For It) (6:53)/Going For It (4:49)	1983	12.00
—As "Wham! U.K."			
❑ 44-03933	Bad Boys/(Instrumental)	1983	7.00
—As "Wham!"			
❑ 44-03933	Bad Boys/(Instrumental)	1983	10.00
—As "Wham! U.K."			
❑ 44-05049	Wake Me Up Before You Go-Go/(Instrumental)	1984	10.00
❑ 44-05170	Careless Whisper (Extended Mix 6:20)/(Instrumental 4:52)	1984	10.00
—As "Wham! featuring George Michael"			
❑ 44-05180	Everything She Wants (Remix Long Version)/Like a Baby	1985	10.00
❑ 44-05238	Freedom (Extended Version 6:16) (Instrumental)/Heartbeat	1985	8.00
❑ 44-05322	I'm Your Man (Extended Stimulation Mix) (Acappella)/Do It Right (Instrumental)	1985	8.00
❑ 44H-07557	Young Guns (Go for It)/Bad Boys	1987	7.00
—"Mixed Masters" reissue			
EPIC			
❑ TA 4949	Last Christmas (Pudding Mix)/Everything She Wants	1984	20.00
—U.K. import			
45s			
COLUMBIA			
❑ CS7 2591 [DJ]	Last Christmas (4:24)/(6:43)	1986	15.00
❑ 38-03611	Young Guns (Go For It)/Going For It	1983	5.00
—As "Wham! U.K."			
❑ 38-03611 [PS]	Young Guns (Go For It)/Going For It	1983	5.00
—As "Wham! U.K."			
❑ 38-03611 [PS]	Young Guns (Go For It)	1983	8.00
—As "Wham! U.K."; "Demonstration — Not for Sale" on rear			
❑ 38-03932	Bad Boys/(Instrumental)	1983	4.00
—As "Wham!"			
❑ 38-03932	Bad Boys/(Instrumental)	1983	6.00
—As "Wham! U.K."			
❑ 38-04552	Wake Me Up Before You Go-Go/(Instrumental)	1984	3.00
❑ 38-04552 [PS]	Wake Me Up Before You Go-Go/(Instrumental)	1984	8.00
❑ 38-04691	Careless Whisper/(Instrumental)	1984	3.00
—As "Wham! featuring George Michael"			
❑ 38-04691 [PS]	Careless Whisper/(Instrumental)	1984	5.00
—As "Wham! featuring George Michael"; black & white sleeve			
❑ 38-04691 [PS]	Careless Whisper/(Instrumental)	1984	8.00
—As "Wham! featuring George Michael"; color sleeve			
❑ 38-04691 [PS]	Careless Whisper	1984	10.00
—As "Wham! featuring George Michael"; color sleeve; "Demonstration — Not for Sale" on rear			
❑ 38-04840	Everything She Wants/Like a Baby	1985	3.00
❑ 38-04840 [PS]	Everything She Wants/Like a Baby	1985	3.00
❑ 38-05409	Freedom/Heartbeat	1985	3.00
❑ 38-05409 [PS]	Freedom/Heartbeat	1985	3.00
❑ 38-05721	I'm Your Man/Do It Right	1985	3.00
❑ 38-05721 [PS]	I'm Your Man/Do It Right	1985	3.00
❑ 38-05721 [PS]	I'm Your Man/Do It Right	1985	6.00
—"Demonstration — Not for Sale" on rear			
❑ 38-06182	The Edge of Heaven/Blue (Live in China)	1986	3.00
❑ 38-06182 [PS]	The Edge of Heaven/Blue (Live in China)	1986	3.00
❑ 38-06294	Where Did Your Heart Go?/Wham! Rap '86	1986	3.00
❑ 38-06294 [PS]	Where Did Your Heart Go?/Wham! Rap '86	1986	3.00
❑ 38-68712	Wake Me Up Before You Go-Go/(Instrumental)	1988	3.00
—Reissue			
❑ 38-68713	Careless Whisper/(Instrumental)	1988	3.00
—Reissue			
❑ 38-68715	Everything She Wants/Like a Baby	1988	3.00
—Reissue			
EPIC			
❑ (no #)	Merry Xmas from Wham!	1984	20.00
—Fan club single, no sleeve; U.K. import			
❑ GA 4949	Last Christmas/Everything She Wants	1984	5.00
❑ GA 4949 [PS]	Last Christmas/Everything She Wants	1984	8.00
—Gatefold sleeve; sleeve and record are U.K. imports			
Albums			
COLUMBIA			
❑ BFC 38911	Fantastic	1983	15.00
—Cover and label list artist as "Wham! U.K."			
❑ FC 38911	Fantastic	1985	10.00
—Reissue; cover and label list artist as "Wham!"			
❑ FC 39595	Make It Big	1984	10.00
❑ 9C9 40062 [PD]	Make It Big	1985	25.00
—Picture disc			
❑ OC 40285	Music from the Edge of Heaven	1986	10.00
—With "removable sticker" list of song titles still on front cover			

WHAT FOUR, THE

Number	Title (A Side/B Side)	Yr	NM
45s			
CAPITOL			
❑ 5449	Anything for a Laugh/Baby Can't You Hear Me Call Your Name	1965	12.00
COLUMBIA			
❑ 43711	Baby, I Dig Love/It's Hard to Live on Promises	1966	12.00
❑ 43711 [PS]	Baby, I Dig Love/It's Hard to Live on Promises	1966	25.00
DESTINATION			
❑ 633	We Could Be Happy/Where Love Can Go	1967	12.00
—As "What For"			
ESP-DISK'			
❑ 109	Our Love Should Last Forever/(B-side unknown)	1966	30.00
MERCURY			
❑ 72716	Dandelion Wine/You're Wishin' I Was Someone Else	1967	25.00
—As "Whatt Four"			

Except when noted otherwise, VG = 25% of NM, and VG+ = 50% of NM. (Example: VG = $2.00, VG+ = $4.00 and NM = $8.00.)

Number	Title (A Side/B Side)	Yr	NM
REPRISE			
❑ 0387	Gemini 4/Night Surf	1965	25.00
TOWER			
❑ 404	Asparagus/Stop in the Name of Love	1968	12.00

WHAT-KNOTS, THE

Number	Title (A Side/B Side)	Yr	NM
45s			
DIAL			
❑ 4067	I Ain't Dead Yet/Talkin' 'Bout Our Breakup	1967	25.00

WHEEL MEN, THE

GARY USHER was in this group.

Number	Title (A Side/B Side)	Yr	NM
45s			
WARNER BROS.			
❑ 5480	Hon-Da Beach/School Is a Gas	1964	50.00

WHEELER, CLARENCE

Number	Title (A Side/B Side)	Yr	NM
Albums			
ATLANTIC			
❑ SD 1551	Doin' What We Wanna	1970	50.00
❑ SD 1585	The Love I've Been Looking For	1971	30.00
❑ SD 1636	New Chicago Blues	1973	18.00

WHEELER, MARY, AND THE KNIGHTS

Number	Title (A Side/B Side)	Yr	NM
45s			
ATOM			
❑ 701	A Falling Tear/I Feel in My Heart	196?	40.00

WHEELER, ONIE

Number	Title (A Side/B Side)	Yr	NM
45s			
CHARTA			
❑ 122	I Don't Believe We're Through/Pick Up the Pieces	1978	6.00
❑ 129	Lucie Ann's Song/I Don't Believe We're Through	1978	6.00
❑ 148	Onie's Bop/I'd Rather Scratch with the Chickens	1979	6.00
COLUMBIA			
❑ 4-21371	Little Mama/She Wiggled and Giggled	1955	20.00
❑ 4-21418	My Home Is Not a Home at All/That's What I Like	1955	20.00
❑ 4-21454	Cut It Out/I'm Satisfied with My Dreams	1955	20.00
❑ 4-21500	No I Don't Guess I Will/I Tried and I Tried	1956	20.00
❑ 4-21523	Onie's Bop/I Wanna Hold My Baby	1956	60.00
❑ 4-40787	A Beggar for Your Love/A Booger Gonna Getcha	1956	50.00
❑ 4-40911	Steppin' Out/Going Back to the City	1957	15.00
EPIC			
❑ 9540	What About Tomorrow/Sunnyland Farmer	1962	10.00
JAB			
❑ 9003	Just Leave Her to Me/Water Your Flower	1967	8.00
❑ 9013	Dirt Behind My Years/Burn Another Honky Tonk Down	1968	8.00
K-ARK			
❑ 606	Too Hot to Handle/I Need to Go Home	196?	15.00
❑ 617	You're Getting All Over Me/All Day, All Night, Always	196?	15.00
❑ 620	Go Home/I Saw Mother with God Last Night	196?	15.00
❑ 626	White Lightning Cherokee/Stubborn Heart	196?	15.00
❑ 671	Too Hot to Handle/I Need to Go Home	1966	10.00
❑ 856	Please Don't Plant Pretty Flowers/Which-A-Way, That-A-Way	197?	8.00
MUSICOR			
❑ 1096	I'm Gonna Hang My Britches Up/You're Too Good for Me	1965	10.00
❑ 1121	Her Porch Came Up to My Knees/Pretty Little Tomboy	1965	10.00
OKEH			
❑ 18022	When We All Get There/Run 'Em Off	1952	30.00
❑ 18026	Mother Prayed Loud in Her Sleep/A Million Years in Glory	195?	25.00
❑ 18037	Closing Time/I'll Swear You Don't Love Me	195?	25.00
❑ 18049	Love Me Like You Used to Do/Little Mama	195?	30.00
❑ 18058	Would You Like to Wear a Crown/I Saw Mother with God Last Night	1954	25.00
RANWOOD			
❑ 1025	EIO (The Sawmill Man)/Train to Louisville	1975	6.00
ROYAL AMERICAN			
❑ 76	John's Been Shucking My Corn/Make 'Em All Go Home	1973	5.00
❑ 85	Shuckin' My Way to the Hall of Fame/I Can't Pass an Orchard	1973	5.00
STARDAY			
❑ 767	Mr. Free/Dancing	1966	10.00
❑ 785	Playing Tricks/I Closed My Book Last Night	1966	10.00
SUN			
❑ 315	Jump Right Out of This Jukebox/Tell 'Em Off	1959	30.00
UNITED ARTISTS			
❑ 716	Wanted for Robbery/Who Put Out the Fire	1964	12.00

WHEELERS, THE

Number	Title (A Side/B Side)	Yr	NM
45s			
CENCO			
❑ 107	Once I Had a Girl/Shine 'Em On	196?	60.00

WHEELS, BURT, AND THE SPEEDSTERS

Number	Title (A Side/B Side)	Yr	NM
Albums			
CORONET			
❑ CX-216 [M]	Sounds of the Big Racers	1964	25.00
❑ CXS-216 [S]	Sounds of the Big Racers	1964	30.00

WHEELS, THE (1)

British group.

Number	Title (A Side/B Side)	Yr	NM
45s			
AURORA			
❑ 157	Bad Little Woman/Don't You Know	1966	25.00

WHEELS, THE (2)

Number	Title (A Side/B Side)	Yr	NM
45s			
FOLLY			
❑ 800	Clap Your Hands (Part 1)/Clap Your Hands (Part 2)	1959	15.00

WHEELS, THE (3)

Number	Title (A Side/B Side)	Yr	NM
45s			
IMPACT			
❑ 1029	Dancing in the Streets/A Taste of Money	1967	25.00

WHEELS, THE (4)

Number	Title (A Side/B Side)	Yr	NM
45s			
LOST-NITE			
❑ 109	My Heart's Desire/Let's Have a Ball	196?	8.00
PREMIUM			
❑ 405	My Heart's Desire/Let's Have a Ball	1956	60.00
❑ 408	Teasin' Heart/Loco	1956	80.00
❑ 410	I Can't Forget/How Could I Ever Leave Me	1956	150.00

WHEELS, THE (5)

Number	Title (A Side/B Side)	Yr	NM
45s			
ROULETTE			
❑ 4271	No One But You/I've Waited for a Lifetime	1960	20.00

WHEELS, THE (U)

Number	Title (A Side/B Side)	Yr	NM
45s			
TIME			
❑ 1003	Where Were You/So Young and So In Love	1958	80.00

WHIPPOORWILLS, THE

Number	Title (A Side/B Side)	Yr	NM
45s			
JOSIE			
❑ 892	Deep Within/Going to a Party	1961	60.00
VITA			
❑ 1005	Blue Raindrops/I Must Have Holes in My Head	195?	100.00

WHIPS, THE

More than one group.

Number	Title (A Side/B Side)	Yr	NM
45s			
DORE			
❑ 502	Yes, Master/Rosie's Blues	1958	20.00
FLAIR			
❑ 1025	Pleadin' Heart/She Done Me Wrong	1954	800.00
MGM			
❑ 13401	Whip It on Me, Baby/First Dance Fear	1965	12.00

WHIRLERS, THE

Number	Title (A Side/B Side)	Yr	NM
45s			
PORT			
❑ 70025	Tonight and Forever/Magic Mirror	1961	20.00
WHIRLIN' DISC			
❑ 108	Tonight and Forever/Magic Mirror	1956	80.00

WHIRLWINDS, THE

Number	Title (A Side/B Side)	Yr	NM
45s			
GUYDEN			
❑ 2052	Angel Love/The Mountain	1961	30.00
PHILIPS			
❑ 40139	Heartbeat/At the Party	1963	125.00

WHISPERS, THE

Well-known male R&B vocal group.

Number	Title (A Side/B Side)	Yr	NM
12-Inch Singles			
CAPITOL			
❑ SPRO 10230 [DJ]	Come On Home (Album Version) (Heavy D Remix)	1995	8.00
❑ V-15598	Innocent (Extended Mix) (Heat of the Heat Mix) (Midnight & You Mix) (Instrumental) (Whispers Groove)	1990	7.00
❑ V-15637	Is It Good to You (Fel the Heat Remix) (Feel the Heat Instrumental) (Midnight and You Remix) (Midnight and You Dub) (Whispers Jazzy Remix)	1990	7.00
❑ SPRO-79803 [DJ]	I Want 2B the 14U (same on both sides)	1991	8.00
SOLAR			
❑ ED 5017 [DJ]	Contagious (LP Version) (Edit Version)/Keep Your Love Around	1984	8.00
❑ ED 5036 [DJ]	Some Kinda Lover (same on both sides)	1984	8.00
❑ ED 5055 [DJ]	Don't Keep Me Waiting (4:08) (4:36)	1985	10.00
❑ AS-11565 [DJ]	Emergency (4:18 stereo/4:18 mono)	1982	12.00
❑ YD-11591	Can't Do Without Love (5:22) (same on both sides?)	1979	12.00
❑ YD-11895	And the Beat Goes On (7:30)/Can You Do the Boogie (6:07)	1979	20.00
❑ YD-12052	Out the Box/Welcome Into My Dream	1980	12.00
❑ YD-12155	It's a Love Thing (unknown versions)	1980	15.00
❑ YD-12233	I Can Make It Better/Say You (Would Love for Me Too)	1980	12.00
❑ YD-12299	This Kind of Lovin'/What Will I Do	1981	12.00
❑ 67930	Tonight (6:10)/Small Talkin' (4:06)	1983	10.00
❑ 67980	Love Is Where You Find It (5:20)/Say Yes	1982	10.00
❑ V-71153	Rock Steady (Vocal) (Instrumental)/Are You Going My Way	1987	8.00
❑ V-71163	No Pain No Gain (7 versions)	1988	8.00
SOUL TRAIN			
❑ SD-10997	Make It with You/You Are Number One	1977	15.00
45s			
CANADIAN AMERICAN			
❑ 179	It's Rainin', It's Pourin'/Tomorrow's On Your Side	1964	30.00
CAPITOL			
❑ S7-18394	Make Sweet Love to Me/My Funny Valentine	1995	3.00
❑ S7-18727	Come On Home/Better Watch Your Heart	1995	3.00
❑ 7PRO-79170/215	Innocent (7" Edit)/(Club Edit)	1990	8.00
—Vinyl is promo only			
DORE			
❑ 724	It Only Hurts for a Little While/The Happy One	1964	25.00
❑ 729	Slow Jerk/Never Again	1965	20.00
❑ 735	The Dip/Weirdo	1965	20.00
❑ 740	As I Sit Here/Shake It, Shake It	1965	20.00
❑ 751	Doctor Love/Lonely Avenue	1966	20.00
❑ 758	Walkin' the Fat Man/I Was Born When You Kissed Me	1966	20.00
❑ 768	Take a Lesson from the Teacher/Claire De Looney	1966	20.00
❑ 792	You Got a Man on Your Hands/You Can't Fight What's Right	1967	15.00

Number	Title (A Side/B Side)	Yr	NM
❑ 794	Needle in a Haystack/ Waltz for You	1967	15.00
❑ 833	Never Again/I Was Born When You Kissed Me	1969	12.00
❑ 842	The Dip/It Only Hurts for a Little While	1970	10.00

FONTANA

Number	Title (A Side/B Side)	Yr	NM
❑ 1564	My Long and Sleepless Night/ Knowin'	1966	20.00

JANUS

Number	Title (A Side/B Side)	Yr	NM
❑ 140	There's a Love for Everyone/ It Sure Ain't Pretty	1970	6.00
❑ 150	Your Love Is So Doggone Good/Cracker Jack	1971	6.00
❑ 174	Can't Help But Love You/ A Hopeless Situation	1971	6.00
❑ 184	I Only Meant to Wet My Feet/ You Fill My Life with Music	1972	6.00
❑ 200	Somebody Loves You/ Can We Love Forever	1972	6.00
❑ 212	POW-MIA/Does She Care	1973	6.00
❑ 222	Feel Like Comin' Home/I Love the Way You Make Me Feel	1973	6.00
❑ 231	A Mother for My Children/What More Can a Girl Ask For	1973	6.00
❑ 238	Bingo/Once More with Feeling	1974	6.00
❑ 244	What More Can a Girl Ask For/ Broken Home	1974	6.00
❑ 247	All I Ever Do (Is Dream of You)/ Here Comes Tomorrow	1975	6.00
❑ 253	You're What's Been Missing in My Life/Given a Little Love	1975	6.00

SOLAR

Number	Title (A Side/B Side)	Yr	NM
❑ YB-11246	(Let's Go) All the Way/ Chocolate Girl	1978	4.00
❑ GB-11328	Living Together (In Sin)/ One for the Money	1978	3.00
—Gold Standard Series			
❑ YB-11353	(Olivia) Lost and Turned Out/ Try and Make It Better	1978	4.00
❑ YB-11449	Happy Holidays to You/ Try and Make It Better	1978	6.00
❑ YB-11590	Can't Do Without Love/ Headlights	1979	4.00
❑ YB-11685	Homemade Lovin'/ You'll Never Get Away	1979	4.00
❑ YB-11739	A Song for Donny/ (Instrumental)	1979	4.00
❑ YB-11739 [PS]	A Song for Donny/ (Instrumental)	1979	6.00
❑ YB-11894	And the Beat Goes On/ Can You Do the Boogie	1980	4.00
❑ YB-11928	Lady/I Love You	1980	4.00
❑ GB-11977	(Let's Go) All the Way/ Lost and Turned Out	1980	3.00
—Gold Standard Series			
❑ YB-12050	Out the Box/Welcome Into My Dream	1980	4.00
❑ YB-12154	It's a Love Thing/Girl I Need You	1981	4.00
❑ GB-12230	And the Beat Goes On/Lady	1981	3.00
—Gold Standard Series			
❑ YB-12232	I Can Make It Better/Say You (Would Love for Me Too)	1981	4.00
❑ YB-12295	This Kind of Lovin'/What Will I Do	1981	4.00
❑ YB-13005	I'm the One for You/ I'm Gonna Love You More	1981	4.00
❑ GB-13486	It's a Love Thing/ Make That Move	1983	3.00
—Gold Standard Series; B-side by Shalamar			
❑ 47961	In the Raw/Small Talkin'	1982	4.00
❑ 48008	Emergency/Only You	1982	4.00
❑ 48008 [PS]	Emergency/Only You	1982	6.00
❑ 69639	Don't Keep Me Waiting/Suddenly	1985	4.00
❑ 69658	Some Kinda Lover/ Never Too Late	1985	4.00
❑ 69683	Contagious/(B-side unknown)	1984	4.00
❑ 69809	This Time/Love for Real	1983	4.00
❑ 69827	Keep On Lovin' Me/Try It Again	1983	4.00
❑ 69842	Tonight/Small Talkin'	1983	4.00
❑ 69965	Love Is Where You Find It/ Say Yes	1982	4.00
❑ B-70006	Rock Steady/Are You Going My Way	1987	3.00
❑ B-70012	Just Gets Better with Time/Say Yes	1987	3.00
❑ B-70017	In the Mood/(Instrumental)	1987	3.00
❑ B-70020	No Pain, No Gain/(Instrumental)	1988	3.00

SOUL CLOCK

Number	Title (A Side/B Side)	Yr	NM
❑ 104	Great Day/I Can't See Myself Leaving	1969	10.00
❑ 107	The Time Will Come/ Flying High	1969	10.00
❑ 109	What Will I Do/Remember	1969	10.00
❑ 1001	I Can Remember/ Planets of Life	1970	8.00
❑ 1004	Seems Like I Gotta Do Wrong/ Needle in a Haystack	1970	8.00
❑ 1005	I'm the One/You Must Be Doing All Right	1970	8.00

SOUL TRAIN

Number	Title (A Side/B Side)	Yr	NM
❑ SB-10430	In Love Forever/Fairytale	1975	5.00
❑ SB-10628	(You're a) Special Part of My Life/Grove Street	1976	5.00
❑ SB-10700	One for the Money (Part 1)/ One for the Money (Part 2)	1976	5.00
❑ SB-10773	Living Together (In Sin)/ I've Got a Feeling	1976	5.00
❑ SB-10878	You're Only As Good As You Think You Are/Sounds Like a Love Song	1977	5.00
❑ SB-10996	Make It with You/You Are Number One	1977	5.00
❑ SB-11139	I'm Gonna Make You My Wife/ You Never Miss Your Water	1977	5.00

Albums

ACCORD

Number	Title (A Side/B Side)	Yr	NM
❑ SN-7100	I Can Remember	1981	10.00

ALLEGIANCE

Number	Title (A Side/B Side)	Yr	NM
❑ AV-5004	Excellence	1985	10.00

CAPITOL

Number	Title (A Side/B Side)	Yr	NM
❑ C1-92957	More of the Night	1990	12.00

DORE

Number	Title (A Side/B Side)	Yr	NM
❑ 338	Shhh	197?	12.00

INTERMEDIA

Number	Title (A Side/B Side)	Yr	NM
❑ QS-5075	Doctor Love	198?	10.00

JANUS

Number	Title (A Side/B Side)	Yr	NM
❑ JLS-3041	The Whispers' Love Story	1972	50.00
❑ JLS-3046	Life and Breath	1973	40.00
❑ 7006	Bingo	1974	40.00
❑ 7013	Greatest Hits	1975	30.00

SOLAR

Number	Title (A Side/B Side)	Yr	NM
❑ S-27	Love Is Where You Find It	1982	10.00
❑ BXL1-2270	Open Up Your Love	1978	12.00
—Reissue of Soul Train 2270			
❑ BXL1-2774	Headlights	1978	12.00
❑ BXL1-3105	Whisper in Your Ear	1979	12.00
❑ BXL1-3521	The Whspers	1979	12.00
❑ BXL1-3578	Imagination	1980	12.00
❑ AYL1-3839	Open Up Your Love	1981	8.00
—"Best Buy Series" reissue			
❑ BXL1-3976	This Kind of Lovin'	1981	12.00
❑ BXL1-4242	The Best of the Whispers	1982	12.00
❑ 60216	Love for Love	1983	10.00
❑ 60356	So Good	1984	10.00
❑ 60451	Happy Holidays to You	1985	12.00
❑ ST-72554	Just Gets Better with Time	1987	10.00
❑ PZ 75306	Vintage Whispers	1989	12.00

SOUL CLOCK

Number	Title (A Side/B Side)	Yr	NM
❑ 22001	Planets of Life	1969	100.00

SOUL TRAIN

Number	Title (A Side/B Side)	Yr	NM
❑ BVL1-1450	One for the Money	1976	15.00
❑ BVL1-2270	Open Up Your Love	1977	15.00

WHISPERS, THE (2)

45s

GOTHAM

Number	Title (A Side/B Side)	Yr	NM
❑ 309	Fool Heart/Don't Fool with Lizzie	1953	250.00
❑ 312	Are You Sorry/We're Getting Married	1953	1500.

WHISPERS, THE (3)

45s

LAURIE

Number	Title (A Side/B Side)	Yr	NM
❑ 3344	Here Comes Summer/ If You Don't Care	1966	20.00

WHITCOMB, IAN

45s

JERDEN

Number	Title (A Side/B Side)	Yr	NM
❑ 735	Soho/Bony Moronie	1964	15.00
❑ 747	This Sporting Life/Soho	1964	15.00

TOWER

Number	Title (A Side/B Side)	Yr	NM
❑ 120	This Sporting Life/Fizz	1965	10.00
❑ 134	You Turn Me On (Turn On Song)/Poor But Honest	1965	15.00
❑ 134	Turn On Song/Poor But Honest	1965	25.00
❑ 155	N-E-R-V-O-U-S!/The End	1965	10.00
❑ 170	18 Whitcomb St./Fizz	1965	10.00
❑ 189	No Tears for Johnny/Be My Baby	1966	10.00
❑ 192	High Blood Pressure/ Good Hard Rock	1966	10.00
❑ 212	Lover's Prayer/Your Baby Has Gone Down the Plug Hole	1966	10.00
❑ 251	You Won't See Me/Please Don't Put Me on the Shelf	1966	10.00
❑ 274	Where Did Robinson Crusoe Go (With Friday on Saturday Night)/Poor Little Bird	1966	12.00
❑ 274 [PS]	Where Did Robinson Crusoe Go (With Friday on Saturday Night)/Poor Little Bird	1966	25.00
❑ 336	You Really Bent Me Out of Shape/Rolling Home Georgeanne	1967	10.00
❑ 355	You Really Bent Me Out of Shape/Rolling Home Georgeanne	1967	10.00
❑ 385	Groovy Day/Sally Sails the Sky	1967	10.00
❑ 385 [PS]	Groovy Day/Sally Sails the Sky	1967	40.00

UNITED ARTISTS

Number	Title (A Side/B Side)	Yr	NM
❑ XW162	They Go Wild, Simply Wild Over Me/Yaaka Hula Hickey Dula	1973	6.00

Albums

AUDIOPHILE

Number	Title (A Side/B Side)	Yr	NM
❑ AP-115	Treasures of Tin Pan Alley	197?	12.00
❑ AP-147	At the Ragtime Ball	1983	12.00

FIRST AMERICAN

Number	Title (A Side/B Side)	Yr	NM
❑ 7704	Crooner Tunes	1979	10.00
❑ 7725	Red Hot "Blue Heaven"	1980	10.00
❑ 7729	The Rock and Roll Years	1981	10.00
❑ 7751	Instrumentals	1981	10.00
❑ 7789	In Hollywood	1982	10.00

RHINO

Number	Title (A Side/B Side)	Yr	NM
❑ RNLP-127	The Best of Ian Whitcomb (1964-1968)	1986	8.00

SIERRA

Number	Title (A Side/B Side)	Yr	NM
❑ 8708	Pianomelt	1980	10.00

TOWER

Number	Title (A Side/B Side)	Yr	NM
❑ DT 5004 [R]	You Turn Me On	1965	20.00
❑ T 5004 [M]	You Turn Me On	1965	25.00
❑ ST 5042 [S]	Mod, Mod Music Hall	1966	20.00
❑ T 5042 [M]	Mod, Mod Music Hall	1966	15.00
❑ ST 5071 [S]	Yellow Underground	1967	20.00
❑ T 5071 [M]	Yellow Underground	1967	15.00
❑ ST 5100	Sock Me Some Rock	1968	20.00

UNITED ARTISTS

Number	Title (A Side/B Side)	Yr	NM
❑ UA-LA021-F	Under the Ragtime Moon	1972	10.00

WHITCOMB, IAN, AND DICK ZIMMERMAN

Albums

AUDIOPHILE

Number	Title (A Side/B Side)	Yr	NM
❑ AP-225	Steppin' Out	1987	10.00

STOMP OFF

Number	Title (A Side/B Side)	Yr	NM
❑ SOS-1017	Don't Say Goodbye Miss Ragtime	198?	12.00
❑ SOS-1049	My Wife Is Dancing Mad	198?	12.00

WHITE, ANDREW

Albums

ANDREW'S MUSIC

Number	Title (A Side/B Side)	Yr	NM
❑ AM-1	Andrew Nathaniel White III	197?	20.00
❑ AM-2 [(2)]	Live at the "New Thing"	197?	25.00
❑ AM-3	Live in Bucharest	197?	20.00
❑ AM-4	Who Got Da Funk?	197?	20.00
❑ AM-5	Passion Flower	197?	20.00
❑ AM-6	Songs for a French Lady	197?	20.00
❑ AM-7	Theme	1975	20.00
❑ AM-8	Live at the Foolery, Vol. 1	1975	15.00
❑ AM-9	Live at the Foolery, Vol. 2	1975	15.00
❑ AM-10	Live at the Foolery, Vol. 3	1975	15.00
❑ AM-11	Live at the Foolery, Vol. 4	1975	15.00
❑ AM-12	Live at the Foolery, Vol. 5	1975	15.00
❑ AM-13	Live at the Foolery, Vol. 6	1975	15.00
❑ AM-14	Collage	1975	15.00
❑ AM-15	Marathon' 75, Vol. 1	1976	15.00
❑ AM-16	Marathon' 75, Vol. 2	1976	15.00
❑ AM-17	Marathon' 75, Vol. 3	1976	15.00
❑ AM-18	Marathon' 75, Vol. 4	1976	15.00
❑ AM-19	Marathon' 75, Vol. 5	1976	15.00
❑ AM-20	Marathon' 75, Vol. 6	1976	15.00
❑ AM-21	Marathon' 75, Vol. 7	1976	15.00
❑ AM-22	Marathon' 75, Vol. 8	1976	15.00
❑ AM-23	Marathon' 75, Vol. 9	1976	15.00
❑ AM-24	Spotts, Maxine and Brown	1976	15.00
❑ AM-25	Countdown	1976	15.00
❑ AM-26	Red Top	1977	12.00
❑ AM-27	Trinkle, Trinkle	1977	12.00
❑ AM-28	Ebony Glaze	1977	12.00
❑ AM-29	Miss Ann	1977	12.00
❑ AM-30	Seven Giant Steps for Coltrane	1977	15.00
❑ AM-31	Live in New York Vol. 1	1977	12.00
❑ AM-32	Live in New York Vol. 2	1977	12.00
❑ AM-33	Bionic Saxophone	1978	12.00
❑ AM-36	Saxophonitis	1979	12.00
❑ AM-37	Weekend at One Step, Vol. 1: Fonk Update	1980	12.00
❑ AM-38	Weekend at One Step, Vol. 2: I Love Japan	1980	12.00
❑ AM-39	Weekend at One Step, Vol. 3: Have Band Will Travel	1980	12.00
❑ AM-42	Profile: White	1983	12.00

W

Except when noted otherwise, VG = 25% of NM, and VG+ = 50% of NM. (Example: VG = $2.00, VG+ = $4.00 and NM = $8.00.)

WHITE, BARRY

12-Inch Singles

A&M

Number	Title (A Side/B Side)	Yr	NM
❑ 31458 1027 1	Come On (6 versions)	1995	8.00
❑ 31458 8375 1 [DJ]	Practice What You Preach (7 versions)	1994	8.00
❑ SP-12237	Sho You Right (Remix) (Instrumental)	1987	6.00
—Black vinyl			
❑ SP-12237 [DJ]	Sho You Right (Remix) (Instrumental)	1987	12.00
—White vinyl			
❑ SP-12317	Super Lover (3 versions)	1989	6.00
❑ SP-12327	I Wanna Do It Good to Ya (3 versions)	1989	8.00
❑ 18026 [DJ]	I Wanna Do It Good to Ya (5 versions)	1989	6.00

20TH CENTURY

Number	Title (A Side/B Side)	Yr	NM
❑ TCD-88	I Love to Sing the Songs I Sing/(B-side unknown)	1979	12.00
❑ TCD-102	How Did You Know It Was Me?/(B-side unknown)	1979	12.00

UNLIMITED GOLD

Number	Title (A Side/B Side)	Yr	NM
❑ AS 864 [DJ]	I Believe in Love (3:26) (8:01)	1980	10.00
❑ 1403	It Ain't Love, Baby (Until You Give It)/Hung Up in Your Love	1979	12.00
❑ AS 1509 [DJ]	Change (4:22) (7:04)	1982	10.00
❑ 02429	Louie Louie/Ghetto Letto	1981	10.00
❑ 03051	Change/I Like You, You Like Me	1982	10.00
❑ 03381	Passion (Long)/Passion (Short)	1982	10.00
❑ 03958	America/Life	1983	10.00
❑ 04099	Don't Let 'Em Blow Your Mind/Dreams	1983	10.00
❑ 70075	Mi Nueva Cancion (Love Makin' Music)/Ella Es Todo Para Mi (She's Everything to Me)	1981	20.00

45s

A&M

Number	Title (A Side/B Side)	Yr	NM
❑ 31458 0924 7	Practice What You Preach/Come On	1995	3.00
—Second pressing indeed contains these two songs			
❑ 31458 0924 7	Practice What You Preach/Come On	1995	5.00
—First pressing actually contains Lo-Key?'s "I Got a Thang 4 Ya!"/"Sweet On U," which are otherwise unavailable on 45. Can be identified without playing by checking the trail-off vinyl for a different number than that on the record.			
❑ 1203	Right Night/There's a Place (Where Love Never Ends)	1988	3.00
❑ 1459	Super Lover/I Wanna Do It Good to Ya	1989	3.00
❑ 75021 1511 7	When Will I See You Again/Goodnight My Love	1990	3.00
❑ 2943	Sho' You Right/You're What's On My Mind	1987	3.00
❑ 2943 [PS]	Sho' You Right/You're What's On My Mind	1987	3.00
❑ 3000	For Your Love (I'd Do Most Anything)/I'm Ready for Love	1987	3.00
❑ 3000 [PS]	For Your Love (I'd Do Most Anything)/I'm Ready for Love	1987	3.00

FARO

Number	Title (A Side/B Side)	Yr	NM
❑ 613	Tracy/Flame of Love	1964	15.00
—B-side by the Atlantics			

20TH CENTURY

Number	Title (A Side/B Side)	Yr	NM
❑ (no #) [PS]	"With Love from Barry White"	1975	20.00
—Pink and white sleeve issued with some stock copies of "What Am I Gonna Do with You"			
❑ 2018	I'm Gonna Love You Just a Little More Baby/Just a Little More Baby	1973	5.00
❑ 2042	I've Got So Much to Give/I've Got So Much to Give	1973	5.00
❑ 2058	Never Never Gonna Give Ya Up/No, I'm Never Gonna Give Ya Up	1973	5.00
❑ 2077	Honey Please Can't You See/Honey Please Can't You See	1974	5.00
❑ 2120	Can't Get Enough of Your Love, Babe/Just Not Enough	1974	5.00
❑ 2133	You're the First, the Last, My Everything/More Than Anything, You're My Everything	1974	5.00
❑ 2177	What Am I Gonna Do with You/What Am I Gonna Do with You, Baby	1975	5.00
❑ 2208	I'll Do for You Anything You Want Me To/Anything You Want Me To	1975	5.00
❑ 2265	Let the Music Play/(Instrumental)	1975	5.00
❑ 2277	You See the Trouble with Me/I'm So Blue When You Are Too	1976	5.00
❑ 2298	Baby, We Better Try to Get It Together/If You Know, Won't You Tell Me	1976	5.00
❑ 2309	Don't Make Me Wait Too Long/Can't You See It's Only You I Want	1976	5.00
❑ 2328	I'm Qualified to Satisfy You/(Instrumental)	1977	5.00
❑ 2350	It's Ecstasy When You Lay Down Next to Me/I Never Thought I'd Fall in Love with You	1977	5.00
❑ 2361	Playing Your Game, Baby/Of All the Guys in the World	1977	5.00
❑ 2365	Oh What a Night for Dancing/You're So Good You're Bad	1978	5.00
❑ 2380	Your Sweetness Is My Weakness/It's Only Love Doing Its Thing	1978	5.00
❑ 2395	Just the Way You Are/Now I'm Gonna Make Love to You	1979	5.00
❑ 2416	I Love to Sing the Songs I Sing/Oh Me Oh My	1979	5.00
❑ 2433	How Did You Know It Was Me?/Oh Me Oh My	1979	5.00

UNLIMITED GOLD

Number	Title (A Side/B Side)	Yr	NM
❑ 1401	Any Fool Could See (You Were Meant for Me)/You're the One I Need	1979	4.00
❑ 1404	It Ain't Love, Babe (Until You Give It)/Hung Up in Your Love	1979	4.00
❑ 1411	Love Ain't Easy/I Found Love	1980	4.00
❑ 1415	Sheet Music/(Instrumental)	1980	4.00
❑ 1418	Love Makin' Music/Ella Es Todo Mi (She's Everything to Me)	1980	4.00
❑ 1420	I Believe in Love/You're the One I Need	1980	4.00
❑ 02425	Louie Louie/Ghetto Letto	1981	4.00
❑ 02580	Beware/Tell Me Who Do You Love	1981	4.00
❑ 02956	Change/I Like You, You Like Me	1982	4.00
❑ 03379	Passion/It's All About Love	1982	4.00
❑ 03957	America/Life	1983	4.00
❑ 04098	Don't Let 'Em Blow Your Mind/Dreams	1983	4.00

Albums

A&M

Number	Title	Yr	NM
❑ SP-5154	The Right Night and Barry White	1987	10.00
❑ SP-5256	The Man Is Back!	1990	10.00
❑ 75021 5377 1	Put Me in Your Mix	1991	12.00

CASABLANCA

Number	Title	Yr	NM
❑ 822782-1	Barry White's Greatest Hits	1984	8.00
❑ 822783-1	Barry White's Greatest Hits, Vol. 2	1984	8.00

SUPREMACY

Number	Title	Yr	NM
❑ SUP-8002	No Limit on Love	1974	12.00
—Compilation of older material			

20TH CENTURY

Number	Title	Yr	NM
❑ T-407	I've Got So Much to Give	1973	10.00
❑ T-423	Stone Gon'	1973	10.00
❑ T-444	Can't Get Enough	1974	10.00
❑ T-466	Just Another Way to Say I Love You	1975	10.00
❑ T-493	Barry White's Greatest Hits	1975	10.00
❑ T-502	Let the Music Play	1976	10.00
❑ T-516	Is This Whatcha Wont?	1976	10.00
❑ T-543	Barry White Sings for Someone You Love	1977	10.00
❑ T-571	Barry White The Man	1978	10.00
❑ T-590	I Love to Sing the Songs I Sing	1979	10.00
❑ T-599	Barry White's Greatest Hits, Vol. 2	1981	10.00

UNLIMITED GOLD

Number	Title	Yr	NM
❑ JZ 35763	The Message Is Love	1979	10.00
❑ FZ 36208	Barry White's Sheet Music	1980	10.00
❑ Z2X 36957 [(2)]	The Best of Our Love	1981	12.00
❑ FZ 37176	Beware	1982	10.00
❑ FZ 38048	Change	1982	10.00
❑ FZ 38711	Dedicated	1983	10.00

WHITE, BARRY AND GLODEAN

45s

UNLIMITED GOLD

Number	Title (A Side/B Side)	Yr	NM
❑ 02087	I Want You/Our Theme (Part 1)	1981	4.00
❑ 02419	You're the Only One for Me/This Love	1981	4.00
❑ 70064	Didn't We Make It Happen, Baby/Our Theme (Part 2)	1981	4.00

Albums

UNLIMITED GOLD

Number	Title	Yr	NM
❑ FZ 37054	Barry and Glodean White	1981	10.00

WHITE, BEN, AND THE DARCHAES

45s

ALJON

Number	Title (A Side/B Side)	Yr	NM
❑ 1247/8	Jocko Sent Me/Nationwide Stamps	1962	400.00

WHITE, JACK

45s

HIT

Number	Title (A Side/B Side)	Yr	NM
❑ 197	I've Got a Tiger by the Tail/Whisper Tell Me Sweetly	1965	8.00
—B-side by Connie Dee			
❑ 208	10 Little Bottles/Lonely Girl	1965	8.00
—B-side by Fred York			

WHITE, LENNY

45s

NEMPEROR

Number	Title (A Side/B Side)	Yr	NM
❑ 003	Chicken Fried Steak/(B-side unknown)	1975	4.00
❑ 012	Sweet Dreamer/(B-side unknown)	1976	4.00

Albums

ELEKTRA

Number	Title	Yr	NM
❑ 6E-121	Adventures of Astral Pirates	1978	10.00
❑ 6E-164	Streamline	1978	10.00
❑ 6E-223	Best of Friends	1979	10.00
❑ 6E-304	Twennynine with Lenny White	1980	10.00
❑ 5E-551	Just Like Dreamin'	1981	10.00

NEMPEROR

Number	Title	Yr	NM
❑ SD 435	Venusian Summer	1975	12.00
❑ SD 441	Big City	1977	12.00

WHITE, TONY JOE

12-Inch Singles

CASABLANCA

Number	Title (A Side/B Side)	Yr	NM
❑ NBD 20218	I Get Off On It	1980	12.00
—B-side is blank			

45s

ARISTA

Number	Title (A Side/B Side)	Yr	NM
❑ 0376	We'll Live on Love/You and Me Baby	1978	4.00
❑ 0395	It Must Be Love/We'll Live on Love	1979	4.00

CASABLANCA

Number	Title (A Side/B Side)	Yr	NM
❑ 2279	I Get Off on It/Feelin' Loose	1980	5.00
❑ 2304	Mamas Don't Let Your Cowboys Grow Up to Be Babies/Disco Blues	1980	5.00

COLUMBIA

Number	Title (A Side/B Side)	Yr	NM
❑ 38-03967	Swamp Rap/Living in the River City	1983	4.00
❑ 38-04134	The Lady in My Life/We Belong Together	1983	4.00
❑ 38-04356	We Belong Together/Naughty Lady	1984	4.00
❑ 38-04476	You Just Get Better All the Time/Do You Have a Garter Belt	1984	4.00
❑ 38-04683	Nobody's Baby Tonight/Down by the Border	1984	4.00

MONUMENT

Number	Title (A Side/B Side)	Yr	NM
❑ 1003	Georgia Pines/Ten More Miles to Louisiana	1967	8.00
❑ 1053	Watching the Trains Go By/Old Man Willie	1968	8.00
❑ 1070	I Protest/Man Can Only Stand So Much Pain	1968	8.00
❑ 1086	Soul Francisco/Whompt Out on You	1968	8.00
❑ 1104	Polk Salad Annie/Aspen Colorado	1968	10.00
❑ 1169	Roosevelt and Ira Lee (Night of the Mossacin)/The Migrant	1969	6.00
—Some, if not all, of these have "Moccasin" misspelled as above			
❑ 1193	High Sheriff/Groupy Girl	1970	6.00
❑ 1206	Save Your Sugar for Me/My Friend	1970	6.00
❑ 1227	Old Man Willis/Scratch My Back	1970	6.00

20TH CENTURY

Number	Title (A Side/B Side)	Yr	NM
❑ 2276	It Must Be Love/Susie-Q	1976	4.00
❑ 2322	Texas Woman/Hold On to Your Hiney	1976	4.00

WARNER BROS.

Number	Title (A Side/B Side)	Yr	NM
❑ 7468	The Daddy/Voodoo Village	1971	5.00
❑ 7477	My Kind of Woman/I Just Walked Away	1971	5.00
❑ 7505	Lustful Earl and the Married Woman/I Just Walked Away	1971	5.00
❑ 7523	Delta Love/That On the Road Look	1971	5.00

W

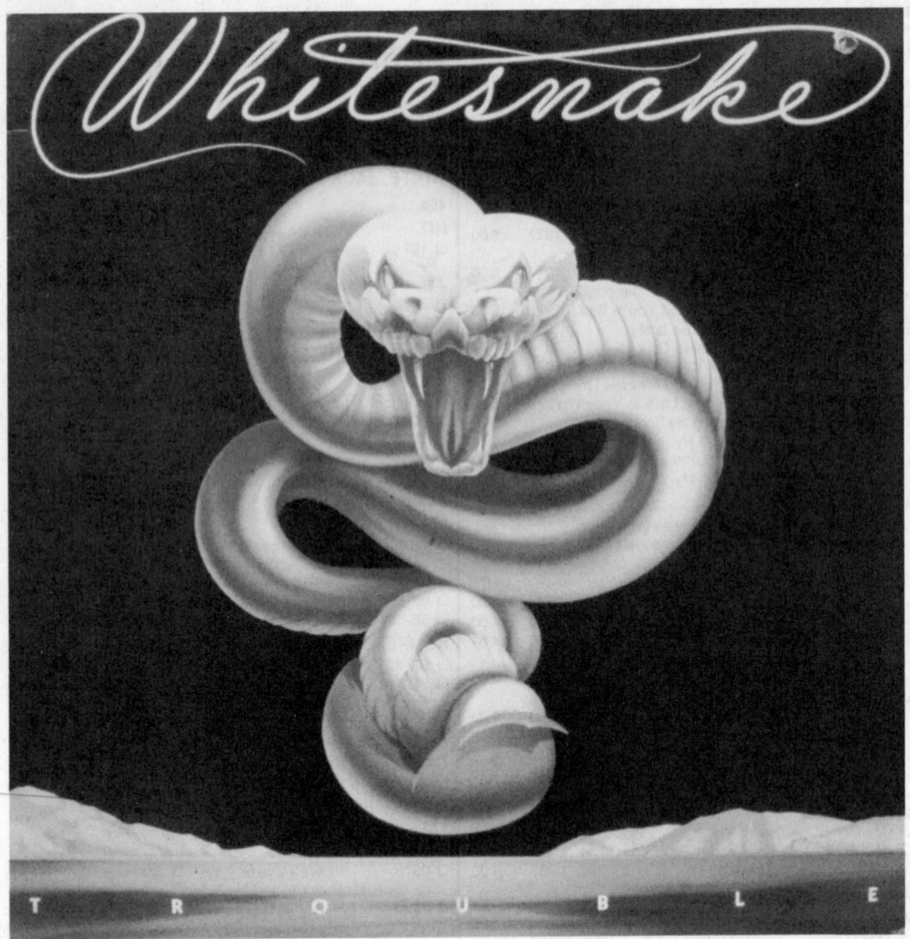

Whitesnake, *Trouble*, United Artists UA-LA937-H, 1978, **$12.**

Number	Title (A Side/B Side)	Yr	NM
❑ 7591	Even Trolls Love Rock and Roll/ If I Ever Saw a Good Thing	1972	5.00
❑ 7607	I've Got a Thing About You, Baby/Gospel Singer	1972	5.00
❑ 7712	Backwoods Preacher Man/ Saturday Night in Oak Grove, La.	1973	5.00
❑ 7780	Love 'Tween You and Me/ Sign of the Lion	1974	5.00
❑ 8042	Wishful Thinking/ Don't Let the Door	1974	5.00

Albums

CASABLANCA

Number	Title (A Side/B Side)	Yr	NM
❑ NBLP 7233	Real Thang	1980	10.00

COLUMBIA

Number	Title (A Side/B Side)	Yr	NM
❑ FC 38817	Dangerous	1983	10.00

MONUMENT

Number	Title (A Side/B Side)	Yr	NM
❑ SLP-18114	Black and White	1969	15.00
❑ SLP-18133	...Continued	1969	15.00
❑ SLP-18142	Tony Joe	1970	15.00

20TH CENTURY

Number	Title (A Side/B Side)	Yr	NM
❑ T-523	Eyes	1977	12.00

WARNER BROS.

Number	Title (A Side/B Side)	Yr	NM
❑ WS 1900	Tony Joe White	1971	12.00
❑ BS 2580	The Train I'm On	1972	12.00
❑ BS 2708	Homemade Ice Cream	1973	12.00

WHITE BOY

Albums

TRADEWIND

Number	Title (A Side/B Side)	Yr	NM
❑ MM-11761	The Average Rat Band	1976	150.00

WHITE LIGHT

Albums

CENTURY

Number	Title (A Side/B Side)	Yr	NM
❑ 39955	White Light	1968	300.00

WHITE PLAINS

45s

DERAM

Number	Title (A Side/B Side)	Yr	NM
❑ 85058	My Baby Loves Lovin'/ Show Me Your Hand	1970	8.00
❑ 85066	Lovin' You Baby/Noises (In My Head)	1970	6.00
❑ 85072	Carolina's Coming Home/ Every Little Move She Makes	1971	6.00
❑ 85076	When You Are a King/The World Gets Better with Love	1971	6.00
❑ 85080	I Can't Stop/Julie Anne	1972	6.00
❑ 85086	Step Into a Dream/Look to See	1973	6.00
❑ 85089	Does Anybody Know Where My Baby Is/Just for a Change	1973	6.00

Albums

DERAM

Number	Title (A Side/B Side)	Yr	NM
❑ DES 18045	My Baby Loves Lovin'	1970	15.00

WHITE TIGER

Albums

E.M.C.

Number	Title (A Side/B Side)	Yr	NM
❑ EMC-3653	White Tiger	1986	20.00

WHITE WITCH

45s

CAPRICORN

Number	Title (A Side/B Side)	Yr	NM
❑ 0012	And I'm Leaving/Parabrahm Greeting-Dweller of the Threshold	1972	6.00
❑ 0016	Don't Close Your Mind/ You're the One	1973	6.00
❑ 0023	Home Grown Girl/It's So Nice to Be Stoned	1973	6.00
❑ 0025	Home Grown Girl/Help Me Lord	1973	6.00
❑ 0080	Showdown/Walk On	1974	6.00

Albums

CAPRICORN

Number	Title (A Side/B Side)	Yr	NM
❑ CP 0107	White Witch	1973	25.00
❑ CP 0129	A Spiritual Greeting	1974	25.00

WHITE ZOMBIE Featuring Rob Zombie.

Albums

CAROLINE

Number	Title (A Side/B Side)	Yr	NM
❑ 1350	Soul Crusher	1988	20.00
❑ 1362	Make Them Die Slowly	1989	20.00

GEFFEN

Number	Title (A Side/B Side)	Yr	NM
❑ GEF 24806	Astro-Creep: 2000	1995	15.00

SILENT EXPLOSION

Number	Title (A Side/B Side)	Yr	NM
❑ (# unknown) [EP]	Psycho-Head Blowout	1986	60.00
❑ SE 002	Soul Crusher	1987	60.00

WHITEHEAD, EDDIE

45s

BLACK JACK

Number	Title (A Side/B Side)	Yr	NM
❑ 711	Just Your Fool/Give This Fool Another Chance	196?	4000.

—VG 2000; VG+ 3000

WHITESNAKE Also see DEEP PURPLE; THIN LIZZY.

12-Inch Singles

GEFFEN

Number	Title (A Side/B Side)	Yr	NM
❑ PRO-A-2155 [DJ]	Slow an' Easy (Edit) (LP Version)	1984	8.00
❑ PRO-A-2178 [DJ]	Love Ain't No Stranger (Edit) (LP Version)	1984	10.00
❑ PRO-A-2650 [DJ]	Still of the Night (same on both sides?)	1987	10.00
❑ PRO-A-2810 [DJ]	Is This Love (Edit 3:38) (LP Version 4:42)	1987	10.00
❑ 20694	Still of the Night (6:38)/ Don't Turn Away	1987	10.00
❑ 20695	Here I Go Again (Edit Remix)/ You're Gonna Break My Heart Again/Children of the Night	1987	10.00
❑ 20754	Is This Love/Bad Boys/Standing in the Shadow (Remix)/Need Your Love So Bad	1987	10.00

45s

GEFFEN

Number	Title (A Side/B Side)	Yr	NM
❑ 7-19951	The Deeper the Love/ Slip of the Tongue	1990	4.00
❑ 7-21902	Is This Love/Give Me All Your Love (1988 Mix)	199?	3.00
—"Back to Back Hits" reissue			
❑ 7-28103	Give Me All Your Love/ Straight for the Heart	1988	3.00
❑ 7-28103 [PS]	Give Me All Your Love/ Straight for the Heart	1988	3.00
❑ 7-28233	Is This Love/Bad Boys	1987	3.00
❑ 7-28233 [PS]	Is This Love/Bad Boys	1987	3.00
❑ 7-28331	Still of the Night/Don't Turn Away	1987	4.00
❑ 7-28339	Here I Go Again/ Children of the Night	1987	4.00
—A radically different version than that on the LP			
❑ 7-28339 [PS]	Here I Go Again/ Children of the Night	1987	4.00
❑ 7-29171	Love Ain't No Stranger/ Guilty of Love	1984	4.00
❑ 7-29171 [PS]	Love Ain't No Stranger/ Guilty of Love	1984	5.00

MIRAGE

Number	Title (A Side/B Side)	Yr	NM
❑ 3672	Fool for Your Loving/ Black and Blue	1980	7.00
❑ 3672 [DJ]	Fool for Your Loving (Long Version)/(Short Version)	1980	7.00
❑ 3672 [PS]	Fool for Your Loving/ Black and Blue	1980	8.00
❑ 3766	Ain't Gonna Cry No More/ Sweet Talker	1980	7.00
❑ 3794 [DJ]	Ain't No Love in the Heart of the City (same on both sides)	1981	10.00
—May be promo only			
❑ 3844	Don't Break My Heart Again/ Lonely Days, Lonely Nights	1981	10.00

UNITED ARTISTS

Number	Title (A Side/B Side)	Yr	NM
❑ UA-X1240-Y [DJ]	Ain't No Love in the Heart of the City (mono/stereo)	1978	12.00
—May be promo only; as "David Coverdale's Whitesnake"			
❑ UA-X1291-Y	The Time Is Right for Love/ Belgian Tom's Hot Trick	1979	10.00
❑ 1323	Long Way from Home/ We Wish You Well	1979	10.00

Albums

GEFFEN

Number	Title (A Side/B Side)	Yr	NM
❑ GHS 4018	Slide It In	1984	10.00
❑ GHS 24099	Whitesnake	1987	10.00
❑ GHS 24167	Come an' Get It	1987	10.00

—Reissue of Mirage 16043

Except when noted otherwise, VG = 25% of NM, and VG+ = 50% of NM. (Example: VG = $2.00, VG+ = $4.00 and NM = $8.00.)

Number	Title (A Side/B Side)	Yr	NM
❑ GHS 24168	Live... In the Heart of the City	1987	10.00
—Reissue of Mirage 19292			
❑ GHS 24173	Saints & Sinners	1988	10.00
—First U.S. issue of 1982 U.K. LP			
❑ GHS 24174	Snakebite	1988	10.00
—Reissue of United Artists 915			
❑ GHS24175	Trouble	1988	10.00
—Reissue of United Artists 937			
❑ GHS 24176	Lovehunter	1988	10.00
—Reissue of United Artists 981			
❑ GHS 24249	Slip of the Tongue	1989	10.00
❑ R 163629	Whitesnake	1987	12.00
—BMG Direct Marketing version			

MIRAGE

Number	Title (A Side/B Side)	Yr	NM
❑ WTG 16043	Come an' Get It	1981	12.00
❑ WTG 19276	Ready an' Willing	1980	12.00
❑ WTG 19292	Live... In the Heart of the City	1980	12.00

UNITED ARTISTS

Number	Title (A Side/B Side)	Yr	NM
❑ UA-LA915-H	Snakebite	1978	12.00
—As "David Coverdale's Whitesnake"			
❑ UA-LA937-H	Trouble	1978	12.00
❑ LT-981	Lovehunter	1979	12.00

WHITING, MARGARET

45s

CAPITOL

Number	Title (A Side/B Side)	Yr	NM
❑ 54-546	A Wonderful Guy/Younger Than Springtime	1949	25.00
—Note: Earlier Margaret Whiting 45s on Capitol may exist			
❑ 54-709	Dime a Dozen/Whirlwind	1949	25.00
❑ 54-724	It's a Most Unusual Day/St. Louis Blues	1949	25.00
❑ 54-748	Three Rivers/(It Happened at the) Festival of Roses	1949	25.00
❑ 54-776	The Sun Is Always Shining/Sorry	1949	25.00
❑ F809	You're An Old Smoothie/He's Funny That Way	1950	20.00
❑ F841	I Said My Pajamas (And Put On My Pray'rs)/Be Mine	1950	20.00
❑ F851	Solid As a Rock/Sure Thing	1950	20.00
❑ F874	It Might As Well Be Spring/How Deep Is the Ocean	1950	20.00
❑ F879	Come Rain or Come Shine/Dream Peddler's Serenade	1950	20.00
❑ F934	My Foolish Heart/Stay with the Happy People	1950	20.00
❑ F1027	Razza-Ma-Tazz/I Gotta Get Out of the Habit	1950	20.00
❑ F1041	Shawl of Galway Gray/If You Were Only Mine	1950	20.00
❑ F1042	Blind Date/Home Cookin'	1950	30.00
—With Bob Hope			
❑ F1103	I Didn't Know What Time It Was/This Can't Be Love	1950	20.00
❑ F1123	You're Mine You/I've Forgotten You	1950	20.00
❑ F1132	Let's Do It Again/Friendly Star	1950	20.00
❑ F1160	Don't Rock the Boat/I'm in Love with You	1950	15.00
—With Dean Martin			
❑ F1213	I've Never Been in Love Before/The Best Things for You	1950	15.00
❑ F1309	Once You Find Your Guy/Man Ain't Nothin' But a Nothin'	1950	15.00
❑ F1343	Over and Over and Over/The Moon Was Yellow	1950	15.00
❑ F1391	Faithful/Lonesome Gal	1951	15.00
❑ F1417	You Are One/Sing You Sinners	1951	15.00
❑ F1469	We Kiss in a Shadow/Make Man Love Me	1951	15.00
❑ F1491	Something Wonderful/Hello Young Lovers	1951	15.00
❑ F1566	Happy, Topper and Me/This Little Pig	1951	15.00
❑ F1585	Everlasting/The End of a Love Affair	1951	15.00
❑ F1645	It Might As Well Be Spring/How Deep Is the Ocean	1951	15.00
—Reissue of 78 rpm hit of 1945			
❑ F1671	Moonlight in Vermont/My Ideal	1951	15.00
—Reissue			
❑ F1702	Good Morning, Mr. Echo/River Road Two-Step	1951	15.00
❑ F1784	And So to Sleep/Beer Barrel Polka	1951	15.00
❑ F1801	Bill/More More More	1951	15.00
❑ F1845	That's For Sure/If I Can Love You	1951	15.00
❑ F1939	Round and Round/Oops	1952	15.00
❑ F1984	Foggy River/Try Me One More Time	1952	15.00
❑ F2000	I'll Walk Alone/I Could Write a Book	1952	15.00
❑ F2177	Till We Meet Again/The Gods Were Angry with Me	1952	15.00
❑ F2217	Alone Together/Outside of Heaven	1952	15.00
❑ F2292	Why Don't You Believe Me/Come Back to Me Johnny	1952	15.00
❑ F2331	Singing Bells/Take Care My Love	1953	15.00
❑ F2489	Something Wonderful Happens/Where Did He Go	1953	15.00
❑ F2550	Waltz to the Blues/C.O.D.	1953	15.00
❑ F2599	I Just Love You/The Night Holds No Fear	1953	15.00
❑ F2681	Kiss or Get Off the Spot/In the Still of the Night	1953	15.00
❑ F2717	I Speak to the Stars/It's Nice to Have You Home	1954	15.00
❑ F2853	Joey/Ask Me	1954	15.00
❑ F2869	How Long Has It Been/Affair of the Heart	1954	15.00
❑ F2913	All I Want Is All There Is And Then Some/Can This Be Mine	1954	15.00
❑ F2996	My Son, My Son/My Own True Love	1954	15.00
❑ F3067	Stowaway/Allah Be Praised	1955	12.00
❑ F3189	Mama's Pearls/Man	1955	12.00
❑ F3232	Lover Lover/I Kiss You a Million Times	1955	12.00
❑ F3314	I Love a Mystery/Bidin' My Time	1956	12.00
❑ F3412	Second Time in Love/Old Enough	1956	12.00
❑ F3473	True Love/Haunting Love	1956	12.00
❑ F3509	Hello Young Lovers/We Kiss in a Shadow	1956	12.00
❑ F3586	The Money Tree/Maybe I Love Him	1956	12.00
❑ F3666	Tippy Toe/Spring in Maine	1957	12.00
❑ 4638	On Second Thought/Who Can You Can	1961	10.00

DOT

Number	Title (A Side/B Side)	Yr	NM
❑ 15583	Kill Me with Kisses/Speak for Yourself, John	1957	10.00
❑ 15680	I Can't Help It (If I'm Still in Love with You)/That's Why I Was Born	1957	10.00
❑ 15742	I'm So Lonely I Could Cry/Hot Spell	1958	10.00
❑ 15804	Just a Dream/Pretty-Eyed Baby	1958	10.00
❑ 15826	I Love You Because/The Waiting Game	1958	10.00
❑ 15931	I'm Alone Because I Love You/Top of the Moon	1959	10.00
❑ 15973	Half As Much/My Ideal	1959	10.00

LONDON

Number	Title (A Side/B Side)	Yr	NM
❑ 101	The Wheel of Hurt/Nothing Lasts Forever	1966	6.00
❑ 106	Just Like a Man/World Inside Your Arms	1967	6.00
❑ 108	Only Love Can Break a Heart/Where Do I Stand	1967	6.00
❑ 115	I Almost Called Your Name/Let's Pretend	1968	6.00
❑ 119	I Hate to See Me Go/It Keeps Right On a Hurtin'	1968	6.00
❑ 122	Faithfully/Am I Losing You	1968	6.00
❑ 124	Maybe Just One More/Can't Get You Out of My Mind	1968	6.00
❑ 126	Love's the Only Answer/Where Was I	1969	6.00
❑ 128	Love Has a Way/At the End of the Ocean	1969	6.00
❑ 132	Theme from Z/Life Goes On	1970	5.00
❑ 137	Until It's Time for You to Go/I'll Tell Him Today	1970	5.00

VERVE

Number	Title (A Side/B Side)	Yr	NM
❑ 10212	Why Was I Born/You Couldn't Be Cuter	1960	10.00
❑ 10230	Hey, Look Me Over/What's New at the Zoo	1960	10.00
—With Mel Torme			

7-Inch Extended Plays

CAPITOL

Number	Title (A Side/B Side)	Yr	NM
❑ EAP 1-410	*My Ideal/Moonlight in Vermont/A Tree in the Meadow/It Might As Well Be Spring	195?	15.00
❑ EAP 1-410 [PS]	Love Songs	195?	15.00

Albums

AUDIOPHILE

Number	Title (A Side/B Side)	Yr	NM
❑ AP-152	Too Marvelous for Words	198?	10.00
❑ AP-173	Come a Little Closer	198?	10.00
❑ AP-207	This Lady's in Love with You	1986	10.00

CAPITOL

Number	Title (A Side/B Side)	Yr	NM
❑ H 163 [10]	South Pacific	1950	50.00
❑ H 209 [10]	Margaret Whiting Sings Rodgers and Hart	1950	50.00
❑ H 234 [10]	Songs	1950	50.00
❑ T 410 [M]	Love Songs	1954	40.00
❑ T 685 [M]	For the Starry-Eyed	1955	40.00

DOT

Number	Title (A Side/B Side)	Yr	NM
❑ DLP 3072 [M]	Goin' Places	1957	25.00
❑ DLP 3113 [M]	Margaret	1958	15.00
❑ DLP 3176 [M]	Margaret Whiting's Great Hits	1959	15.00
❑ DLP 3235 [M]	Ten Top Hits	1960	15.00
❑ DLP 3337 [M]	Just a Dream	1960	15.00
❑ DLP 25113 [S]	Margaret	1958	20.00
❑ DLP 25176 [S]	Margaret Whiting's Great Hits	1959	20.00
❑ DLP 25235 [S]	Ten Top Hits	1960	20.00
❑ DLP 25337 [S]	Just a Dream	1960	20.00

HAMILTON

Number	Title (A Side/B Side)	Yr	NM
❑ HLP 143 [M]	My Ideal	196?	12.00
❑ HLP 12143 [S]	My Ideal	196?	15.00

LONDON

Number	Title (A Side/B Side)	Yr	NM
❑ PS 497 [S]	The Wheel of Hurt	1967	15.00
❑ PS 510 [S]	Maggie Isn't Margaret Anymore	1967	15.00
❑ PS 527	Pop Country	1968	15.00
❑ LL 3497 [M]	The Wheel of Hurt	1967	20.00
❑ LL 3510 [M]	Maggie Isn't Margaret Anymore	1967	20.00

MGM

Number	Title (A Side/B Side)	Yr	NM
❑ E-4006 [M]	Past Midnight	1961	15.00
❑ SE-4006 [S]	Past Midnight	1961	20.00

VERVE

Number	Title (A Side/B Side)	Yr	NM
❑ V-4038 [M]	The Jerome Kern Song Book	1960	15.00
❑ V6-4038 [S]	The Jerome Kern Song Book	1960	20.00

WHITING, MARGARET, AND JIMMY WAKELY

45s

CAPITOL

Number	Title (A Side/B Side)	Yr	NM
❑ F800	Broken Down Merry-Go-Round/The Gods Were Angry with Me	1950	20.00
❑ F960	Let's Go to Church (Next Sunday Morning)/Why Do You Say Those Things	1950	20.00
❑ F1065	Close Your Pretty Eyes/Fools' Paradise	1950	20.00
❑ F1234	A Bushel and a Peck/Beyond the Reef	1950	15.00
❑ F1255	Silver Bells/Christmas Candy	1950	20.00
❑ F1382	Easter Parade/Let's Go to Church	1951	20.00
❑ F1500	When You and I Were Young Maggie Blues/Till We Meet Again	1951	15.00
❑ F1555	Star of Hope/Why Am I Losing You	1951	15.00
❑ F1634	Slipping Around/Wedding Bells	1951	15.00
—Reissue of 78 rpm hits from 1948			
❑ F1816	Let's Live a Little/I Don't Want to Be Free	1951	15.00
❑ F1965	Give Me More, More, More/Let Old Mother Nature Have Her	1952	15.00
❑ F2402	Gomen Nasai/I Learned to Love You Too Late	1953	15.00
❑ F2528	My Heart Knows/When Love Goes Wrong	1953	15.00
❑ F2689	Tennessee Church Bells/There's a Silver Moon on Golden Gate	1953	15.00
❑ F3905	Silver Bells/Christmas Candy	1958	12.00
❑ 54-40224	Slipping Around/Wedding Bells	1949	40.00
❑ 54-40246	I'll Never Slip Around Again/Six Times a Week and Twice on Sunday	1949	30.00

7-Inch Extended Plays

CAPITOL

Number	Title (A Side/B Side)	Yr	NM
❑ EAP 1-403	Slipping Around/Wedding Bells//I'll Never Slip Around Again/Six Times a Week and Twice on Sundays	195?	20.00
❑ EAP 1-403 [PS]	Margaret Whiting and Jimmy Wakely Sing	195?	20.00

Albums

HILLTOP

Number	Title (A Side/B Side)	Yr	NM
❑ JM-6053 [M]	I'll Never Slip Around Again	196?	12.00
❑ JS-6053 [R]	I'll Never Slip Around Again	196?	12.00

WHITLEY, RAY (1)

Cowboy singer; co-wrote "Back in the Saddle Again."

45s

ARZEE

Number	Title (A Side/B Side)	Yr	NM
❑ 128	Slightly on the Angel Side/Worlds Apart	197?	7.00

WHITLEY, RAY (2)

Best known as a composer; wrote "What Kind of Fool (Do You Think I Am)" for the Tams, among many others.

45s

APT

Number	Title (A Side/B Side)	Yr	NM
❑ 25086	I'll Tell the Robin/Runaway	1965	12.00

ATTARACK

Number	Title (A Side/B Side)	Yr	NM
❑ 103	Hey Girl Don't Bother Me/Everybody	196?	15.00

COLUMBIA

Number	Title (A Side/B Side)	Yr	NM
❑ 4-43607	Just a Boy in Love/The End of My World	1966	10.00

W

Number	Title (A Side/B Side)	Yr	NM
❑ 4-43980	Here Today, Gone Tomorrow/Take Back Your Mind	1967	10.00

1-2-3

Number	Title (A Side/B Side)	Yr	NM
❑ 1707	Don't Throw Your Love to the Wind/Underdose of Faith	1969	10.00

TRX

Number	Title (A Side/B Side)	Yr	NM
❑ 5007	Gotta Go There/1983	1968	10.00

VEE JAY

Number	Title (A Side/B Side)	Yr	NM
❑ 414	There Goes a Teardrop/I Wasn't Sure	1961	15.00
❑ 433	Yessiree, Yessiree/A Love We Can Have and Hold	1962	25.00
❑ 448	It Hurts/Deeper in Love	1962	15.00
❑ 521	Teenage Crush/Your Heartaches	1963	15.00

WHITLOCK, BOBBY

45s

ABC DUNHILL

Number	Title (A Side/B Side)	Yr	NM
❑ 4312	Song for Paula/Where There's a Will, There's a Way	1972	5.00
❑ 4318	Ease Your Pain/Satisfied	1972	5.00
❑ 4326	Hello L.A., Bye Bye Birmingham/Start All Over	1972	5.00
❑ 4332	Tell the Truth/You Came Along	1972	5.00

Albums

ABC DUNHILL

Number	Title (A Side/B Side)	Yr	NM
❑ DS-50121	Bobby Whitlock	1972	12.00
❑ DSX-50131	Raw Velvet	1972	12.00

CAPRICORN

Number	Title (A Side/B Side)	Yr	NM
❑ CP 0160	One of a Kind	1975	10.00
❑ CP 0168	Rock Your Sox Off	1976	10.00

WHITNEY SUNDAY

Albums

DECCA

Number	Title (A Side/B Side)	Yr	NM
❑ DL 75239	Whitney Sunday	1970	20.00

WHITTAKER, ROGER

45s

CAPITOL NASHVILLE

Number	Title (A Side/B Side)	Yr	NM
❑ 7PRO-79035	I'd Fall in Love Tonight (same on both sides)	1990	6.00
—Vinyl is promo only			
❑ 7PRO-79036	But She Loves Me (same on both sides)	1990	6.00
—Vinyl is promo only			
❑ 7PRO-79397	Take Away My Pain (same on both sides)	1990	6.00
—Vinyl is promo only			

MAIN STREET

Number	Title (A Side/B Side)	Yr	NM
❑ 93016	I Love You Because/Eternally	1983	5.00
❑ 93018	There Goes My Everything/(B-side unknown)	1984	5.00

RCA

Number	Title (A Side/B Side)	Yr	NM
❑ PB-10874	Here We Stand/Before She Breaks My Heart	1976	4.00
❑ PB-11218	Last Song/Sea Gull	1978	4.00
❑ PB-11300	Love Last Forever/If I Knew Just What to Say	1978	4.00
❑ PB-11760	You Are My Miracle/Blow Gentle Breeze	1979	4.00
❑ PB-11941	You Are My Miracle/Blow Gentle Breeze	1980	3.00
❑ PB-11966	Wishes/I Was Born	1980	3.00
❑ PB-12096	River Lady/Lighthouse	1980	—
—Unreleased			
❑ PB-12110	A Man Without Love/I Am But a Small Voice	1980	3.00
❑ PB-12165	Tall Dark Stranger/Goodbye	1981	3.00
❑ PB-12330	How Does It Feel/Moonshine	1981	3.00
❑ PB-13030	River Lady/Smooth Sailing	1981	3.00
❑ JB-13379 [DJ]	Too Beautiful to Cry/Together	1982	5.00
❑ PB-14043	Take a Little-Give a Little/Dover to Calais	1985	3.00
❑ PB-14147	My Silver Eagle/Chicago Girl	1985	3.00
❑ PB-14333	The Genius of Love/Everybody's Got a Lonely Heart	1986	3.00

RCA VICTOR

Number	Title (A Side/B Side)	Yr	NM
❑ 74-0320	New World in the Morning/Durham Town	1970	8.00
❑ 74-0355	I Don't Believe in It Anymore/I Should Have Taken My Time	1970	6.00
❑ 74-0442	Why/Moonshine	1971	6.00
❑ 74-0501	The Mexican Whistler/What Love Is	1971	6.00
❑ PB-10356	I Don't Believe In It Anymore/New World in the Morning	1975	4.00
❑ PB-10447	Durham Town (The Leaving)/Mexican Whistler	1975	4.00
❑ GB-10494	The Last Farewell/Paradise	1975	3.00
—Gold Standard Series			
❑ PB-10732	Summer Days/The First Hello, The Last Goodbye	1976	4.00
❑ PB-50030	The Last Farewell/Paradise	1975	4.00
—Canadian number, but pressed and released in the U.S. as well			

UNIVERSAL

Number	Title (A Side/B Side)	Yr	NM
❑ UVL-66010	Have I Told You Lately That I Love You/Just Across the Rio Grande	1989	4.00
❑ UVL-66030	There Goes My Everything/Love Still Means You to Me	1989	4.00

Albums

CAPITOL NASHVILLE

Number	Title (A Side/B Side)	Yr	NM
❑ C1 594058	World's Most Beautiful Christmas Songs	1990	15.00
—Available on vinyl through Columbia House only			

PAIR

Number	Title (A Side/B Side)	Yr	NM
❑ PDL2-1039 [(2)]	Golden Tones	1986	12.00
❑ PDL2-1111 [(2)]	Fire and Rain	1986	12.00

RCA VICTOR

Number	Title (A Side/B Side)	Yr	NM
❑ AFL1-0078	Traveling with Roger Whittaker	1978	10.00
—Reissue of APL1-0078			
❑ APL1-0078	Traveling with Roger Whittaker	1973	15.00
❑ AFL1-0855	Last Farewell" and Other Hits, The	1978	10.00
—Reissue of APL1-0855			
❑ APL1-0855	Last Farewell" and Other Hits, The	1975	12.00
❑ AQL1-0855	Last Farewell" and Other Hits, The	198?	8.00
—Reissue of AFL1-0855			
❑ AFL1-1313	The Magical World of Roger Whittaker	1978	10.00
—Reissue of APL1-1313			
❑ APL1-1313	The Magical World of Roger Whittaker	1976	12.00
❑ ANL1-1405	Roger Whittaker	1976	12.00
❑ AFL1-1853	Reflections of Love	1978	10.00
—Reissue of APL1-1853			
❑ APL1-1853	Reflections of Love	1976	12.00
❑ AFL1-2255	The Best of Roger Whittaker	1978	10.00
—Reissue of APL1-2255			
❑ APL1-2255	The Best of Roger Whittaker	1977	12.00
❑ AQL1-2255	The Best of Roger Whittaker	198?	8.00
—Reissue of AFL1-2255			
❑ AFL1-2525	Folk Songs	1978	12.00
❑ AQL1-2525	Folk Songs	198?	10.00
—Reissue of AFL1-2525			
❑ ANL1-2933	The Roger Whittaker Christmas Album	1978	12.00
❑ AFL1-3077	Imagine	1978	12.00
❑ AQL1-3077	Imagine	198?	8.00
—Reissue of AFL1-3077			
❑ AFL1-3355	When I Need You	1979	10.00
❑ AFL1-3501	Mirrors of My Mind	1979	10.00
❑ AQL1-3501	Mirrors of My Mind	198?	8.00
—Reissue of AFL1-3501			
❑ AFL1-3518	Voyager	1980	10.00
❑ AQL1-3518	Voyager	198?	8.00
—Reissue of AFL1-3518			
❑ AYL1-3670	The Magical World of Roger Whittaker	1980	8.00
—"Best Buy Series" reissue			
❑ AFL1-3778	With Love	1980	10.00
❑ AYL1-3911	When I Need You	1981	8.00
—"Best Buy Series" reissue			
❑ AYL1-3946	A Special Kind of Man	1981	8.00
—"Best Buy Series" reissue			
❑ CPL2-4057 [(2)]	Live in Concert	1981	12.00
❑ AFL1-4129	Changes	1982	10.00
❑ AYL1-4177	I Don't Believe in It Any More	1982	8.00
—"Best Buy Series" reissue			
❑ AYL1-4178	New World in the Morning	1982	8.00
—"Best Buy Series" reissue			
❑ AFL1-4321	The Wind Beneath My Wings	1983	10.00
❑ AFL1-4340	New World in the Morning	1978	10.00
—Reissue of LSP-4340			
❑ LSP-4340	New World in the Morning	1970	15.00
❑ AFL1-4405	I Don't Believe in It Any More	1978	10.00
—Reissue of LSP-4405			
❑ LSP-4405	I Don't Believe in It Any More	1970	15.00
❑ AFL1-4505	A Special Kind of Man	1978	10.00
—Reissue of LSP-4505			
❑ LSP-4505	A Special Kind of Man	1971	15.00
❑ LSP-4652	Loose and Fiery	1972	15.00
❑ AYL1-5166	The Best of Roger Whittaker	1985	6.00
—"Best Buy Series" reissue			
❑ AFL1-5803	The Genius of Love	1986	10.00
❑ NFL1-8047	Take a Little — Give a Little	1985	10.00

WHO, THE

Also see ROGER DALTREY; JOHN ENTWISTLE; KEITH MOON; PETE TOWNSHEND.

12-Inch Singles

MCA

Number	Title (A Side/B Side)	Yr	NM
❑ L33-1257 [DJ]	Twist and Shout/I Can't Explain/My Generation	1984	10.00

WARNER BROS.

Number	Title (A Side/B Side)	Yr	NM
❑ PRO-A-938 [DJ]	You Better You Bet (LP Version) (Edited Version)	1981	10.00
❑ PRO-A-1065 [DJ]	Athena (same on both sides)	1982	8.00
❑ PRO-A-1087 [DJ]	Eminence Front (LP Version) (Edited Version)	1982	10.00

45s

ATCO

Number	Title (A Side/B Side)	Yr	NM
❑ 6409	Substitute/Waltz for a Pig	1966	50.00
❑ 6509	Substitute/Waltz for a Pig	1967	20.00

DECCA

Number	Title (A Side/B Side)	Yr	NM
❑ 31725	I Can't Explain/Bald Headed Woman	1965	30.00
❑ 31801	Anyway, Anyhow, Anywhere/Anytime You Want Me	1965	50.00
❑ 31877	My Generation/Out in the Street (You're Going to Know Me)	1965	30.00
❑ 31988	The Kids Are Alright/A Legal Matter	1966	30.00
❑ 32058	I'm a Boy/In the City	1966	30.00
❑ 32114	Happy Jack/Whiskey Man	1967	30.00
❑ 32114 [PS]	Happy Jack/Whiskey Man	1967	50.00
❑ 32156	Pictures of Lily/Doctor, Doctor	1967	20.00
❑ 32206	I Can See for Miles/Mary-Anne with the Shaky Hands	1967	20.00
❑ 32288	Call Me Lightning/Dr. Jeckyll & Mr. Hyde	1968	25.00
❑ 32362	Magic Bus/Someone's Coming	1968	15.00
❑ 732465	Pinball Wizard/Dogs Part Two	1969	10.00
❑ 732465 [PS]	Pinball Wizard/Dogs Part Two	1969	20.00
❑ 32519	I'm Free/We're Not Gonna Take It	1969	10.00
❑ 32670	The Seeker/Here for More	1970	12.00
❑ 32708	Summertime Blues/Heaven and Hell	1970	12.00
❑ 732729	See Me, Feel Me/Overture from Tommy	1970	12.00
—With custom gold label			
❑ 732729 [PS]	See Me, Feel Me/Overture from Tommy	1970	20.00
❑ 32737	Young Man (Blues)/Substitute	1970	250.00
—Stock copies do exist			
❑ 32737 [DJ]	Young Man (Blues)/Substitute	1970	150.00
❑ 32737 [PS]	Young Man (Blues)/Substitute	1970	500.00
❑ 32846	Won't Get Fooled Again/I Don't Even Know Myself	1971	10.00
❑ 32888	Behind Blue Eyes/My Wife	1971	10.00
❑ 32983	Join Together/Baby, Don't You Do It	1972	10.00
❑ 34444 [DJ]	Happy Jack (same on both sides)	1967	40.00
—Promo-only number, pink label			
❑ 34470 [DJ]	Pictures of Lily (same on both sides)	1967	40.00
—Promo-only number, pink label			
❑ 734610 [DJ]	Amazing Journey/The Acid Queen	1970	25.00
❑ 734610/3 [DJ]	Excerpts from Tommy	1970	200.00
—Promo-only four-record box set with box and 4-page insert. As the records are sometimes found separately, they are also priced individually below.			
❑ 734611 [DJ]	Go to the Mirror Boy/Tommy Can You Hear Me	1970	25.00
❑ 734612 [DJ]	Smash the Mirror/Sensation	1970	25.00
❑ 734613 [DJ]	Sally Simpson/I'm Free	1970	25.00

MCA

Number	Title (A Side/B Side)	Yr	NM
❑ L45-1809 [DJ]	Had Enough (same on both sides)	1978	10.00
❑ 40475	Squeeze Box/Success Story	1975	5.00
❑ 40475 [PS]	Squeeze Box/Success Story	1975	30.00
—Sleeve is promo only			
❑ 40603	Slip Kid/Dreaming from the Waist	1976	5.00
❑ 40948	Who Are You/Had Enough	1978	5.00
❑ 40948 [DJ]	Who Are You (Short 3:22)/(Long 6:11)	1978	10.00
—Promo only; the long version has two lines deleted from the LP version			
❑ 40978	Trick of the Light/9:05	1978	5.00
❑ 41053	Long Live Rock/My Wife	1979	5.00
❑ 60106	See Me, Feel Me/Overture from Tommy	1973	5.00
—Reissue; black label with rainbow			
❑ 60110	I Can't Explain/Bald Headed Woman	1973	5.00
—Reissue; black label with rainbow			
❑ 60174	Pinball Wizard/Dogs Part Two	1974	5.00
—Reissue; black label with rainbow			
❑ 60174	Pinball Wizard/Dogs Part Two	1980	3.00
—Reissue; blue label with rainbow			

MERCURY

Number	Title (A Side/B Side)	Yr	NM
❑ DJ-570 [DJ]	I'm the Face/Zoot Suit	1980	5.00
❑ DJ-570 [PS]	I'm the Face/Zoot Suit	1980	6.00
—As "The High Numbers"			

POLYDOR

Number	Title (A Side/B Side)	Yr	NM
❑ 2022	5:15/I'm One	1979	4.00
❑ 2022 [PS]	5:15/I'm One	1979	6.00

Except when noted otherwise, VG = 25% of NM, and VG+ = 50% of NM. (Example: VG = $2.00, VG+ = $4.00 and NM = $8.00.)

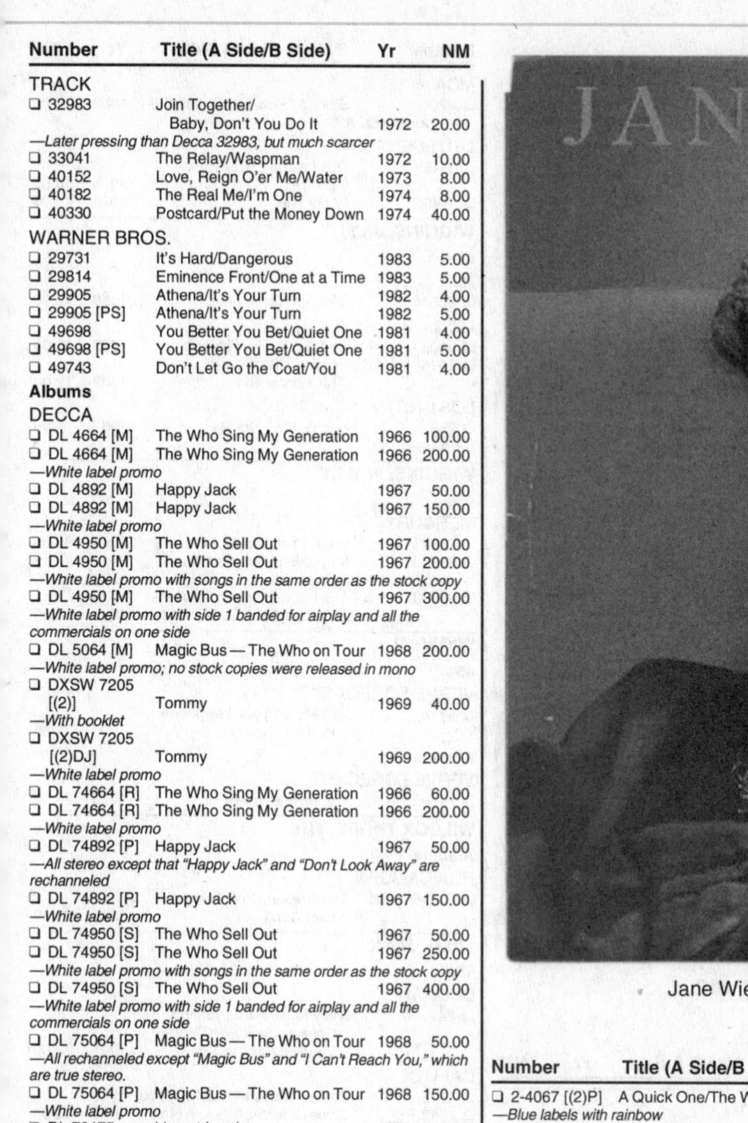

Number	Title (A Side/B Side)	Yr	NM
TRACK			
❑ 32983	Join Together/ Baby, Don't You Do It	1972	20.00
—Later pressing than Decca 32983, but much scarcer			
❑ 33041	The Relay/Waspman	1972	10.00
❑ 40152	Love, Reign O'er Me/Water	1973	8.00
❑ 40182	The Real Me/I'm One	1974	8.00
❑ 40330	Postcard/Put the Money Down	1974	40.00
WARNER BROS.			
❑ 29731	It's Hard/Dangerous	1983	5.00
❑ 29814	Eminence Front/One at a Time	1983	5.00
❑ 29905	Athena/It's Your Turn	1982	4.00
❑ 29905 [PS]	Athena/It's Your Turn	1982	5.00
❑ 49698	You Better You Bet/Quiet One	1981	4.00
❑ 49698 [PS]	You Better You Bet/Quiet One	1981	5.00
❑ 49743	Don't Let Go the Coat/You	1981	4.00
Albums			
DECCA			
❑ DL 4664 [M]	The Who Sing My Generation	1966	100.00
❑ DL 4664 [M]	The Who Sing My Generation	1966	200.00
—White label promo			
❑ DL 4892 [M]	Happy Jack	1967	50.00
❑ DL 4892 [M]	Happy Jack	1967	150.00
—White label promo			
❑ DL 4950 [M]	The Who Sell Out	1967	100.00
❑ DL 4950 [M]	The Who Sell Out	1967	200.00
—White label promo with songs in the same order as the stock copy			
❑ DL 4950 [M]	The Who Sell Out	1967	300.00
—White label promo with side 1 banded for airplay and all the commercials on one side			
❑ DL 5064 [M]	Magic Bus — The Who on Tour	1968	200.00
—White label promo; no stock copies were released in mono			
❑ DXSW 7205 [(2)]	Tommy	1969	40.00
—With booklet			
❑ DXSW 7205 [(2)DJ]	Tommy	1969	200.00
—White label promo			
❑ DL 74664 [R]	The Who Sing My Generation	1966	60.00
❑ DL 74664 [R]	The Who Sing My Generation	1966	200.00
—White label promo			
❑ DL 74892 [P]	Happy Jack	1967	50.00
—All stereo except that "Happy Jack" and "Don't Look Away" are rechanneled			
❑ DL 74892 [P]	Happy Jack	1967	150.00
—White label promo			
❑ DL 74950 [S]	The Who Sell Out	1967	50.00
❑ DL 74950 [S]	The Who Sell Out	1967	250.00
—White label promo with songs in the same order as the stock copy			
❑ DL 74950 [S]	The Who Sell Out	1967	400.00
—White label promo with side 1 banded for airplay and all the commercials on one side			
❑ DL 75064 [P]	Magic Bus — The Who on Tour	1968	50.00
—All rechanneled except "Magic Bus" and "I Can't Reach You," which are true stereo.			
❑ DL 75064 [P]	Magic Bus — The Who on Tour	1968	150.00
—White label promo			
❑ DL 79175	Live at Leeds	1970	40.00
—With gatefold cover and numerous inserts			
❑ DL 79182	Who's Next	1971	25.00
❑ DL 79184	Meaty Beaty Big and Bouncy	1971	30.00
—With poster (deduct 1/3 if missing)			
❑ DL 734586	The Who/The Strawberry Alarm Clock	1969	100.00
—Special Products release for Philco. One side has Who songs, the other, Strawberry Alarm Clock songs			
DIRECT DISC			
❑ SD 16610	Who Are You	1980	30.00
—Audiophile vinyl			
GEFFEN			
❑ 8136511	Who's Next	2008	20.00
LIFE			
❑ DL 74664 [R]	The Who Sing My Generation	1967	150.00
MCA			
❑ 1496	Who's Greatest Hits	1987	8.00
❑ 1577	Live at Leeds	1988	8.00
❑ 1578	Meaty Beaty Big and Bouncy	1988	8.00
❑ 1579	The Who By Numbers	1988	8.00
❑ 1580	Who Are You	1988	8.00
❑ L33-1987 [DJ]	Who Are You	1978	25.00
—White label promo with sticker "Who Are You Edited for Broadcast" on cover — the line "Who the fuck are you?" is deleted twice.			
❑ 2022	Live at Leeds	1973	12.00
❑ 2023	Who's Next	1973	12.00
❑ 2025	Meaty Beaty Big and Bouncy	1973	12.00
❑ 2044 [R]	The Who Sing My Generation	1974	50.00
❑ 2045 [P]	Happy Jack	1974	50.00
❑ 2161	The Who By Numbers	1975	12.00
❑ 3023	Live at Leeds	1977	10.00
❑ 3024	Who's Next	1977	10.00
❑ 3025	Meaty Beaty Big and Bouncy	1977	10.00
❑ 3026	The Who By Numbers	1977	10.00
❑ 3050	Who Are You	1978	10.00
❑ 2-4067 [(2)P]	A Quick One/The Who Sell Out	1976	20.00
—Black labels with rainbow			
❑ 2-4067 [(2)P]	A Quick One/The Who Sell Out	1978	15.00
—Tan labels			

Jane Wiedlin, "Blue Kiss," EMI Manhattan, 52674, 1985, **$3.**

Number	Title (A Side/B Side)	Yr	NM
❑ 2-4067 [(2)P]	A Quick One/The Who Sell Out	1980	12.00
—Blue labels with rainbow			
❑ 2-4068 [(2)P]	Magic Bus/The Who Sing My Generation	1976	20.00
—Black labels with rainbow			
❑ 2-4068 [(2)P]	Magic Bus/The Who Sing My Generation	1978	15.00
—Tan labels			
❑ 2-4068 [(2)P]	Magic Bus/The Who Sing My Generation	1980	12.00
—Blue labels with rainbow			
❑ 5220	Who's Next	1979	8.00
❑ 5408	Who's Greatest Hits	1983	8.00
❑ 5641	Who's Missing	1986	10.00
❑ 5712	Two's Missing	1987	10.00
❑ 6895 [(2)]	Quadrophenia	1980	10.00
❑ 6899 [(2)]	The Kids Are Alright	1980	10.00
—Early versions have number stamped in gold on cover with 11005 records. No difference in value.			
❑ 8018 [(2)]	Who's Last	1984	10.00
❑ 8031 [(2)]	Who's Better, Who's Best	1989	15.00
❑ 2-10004 [(2)]	Quadrophenia	1973	15.00
—Black labels with rainbow			
❑ 2-10005 [(2)]	Tommy	1973	15.00
—Black labels with rainbow			
❑ 2-10005 [(2)]	Tommy	1978	12.00
—Tan labels			
❑ 2-10005 [(2)]	Tommy	1980	10.00
—Blue labels with rainbow			
❑ 2-11005 [(2)]	The Kids Are Alright	1979	12.00
❑ 11164	Who's Next	1995	25.00
—"Heavy Vinyl" reissue on 180-gram vinyl with gatefold cover			
❑ 2-12001 [(2)]	Hooligans	1981	10.00
❑ 14950 [PD]	Who Are You	1978	15.00
—Picture disc			
❑ 3-19501 [(3)]	Join Together	1990	20.00
—Box set with booklet			
❑ 25986	It's Hard	1989	8.00
❑ 25987	Face Dances	1989	8.00
❑ 37000	Live at Leeds	1979	8.00
❑ 37001	Meaty Beaty Big and Bouncy	1979	8.00
❑ 37002	The Who By Numbers	1979	8.00
❑ 37003	Who Are You	1979	8.00
❑ 37169	Odds and Sods	1980	8.00

Number	Title (A Side/B Side)	Yr	NM
❑ 8310741 [(2)]	Quadrophenia	2008	30.00
—Tan labels			
MOBILE FIDELITY			
❑ 1-115	Face Dances	1984	50.00
—Audiophile vinyl			
TRACK			
❑ 2126	Odds and Sods	1974	25.00
❑ 2-4067 [(2)P]	A Quick One/The Who Sell Out	1974	25.00
❑ 2-4068 [(2)P]	Magic Bus/The Who Sing My Generation	1974	25.00
❑ 2-10004 [(2)]	Quadrophenia	1973	20.00
WARNER BROS.			
❑ WBMS-116 [DJ]	Filling In the Gaps	1981	50.00
—With generic "Warner Bros. Music Show" cover			
❑ WBMS-116 [DJ]	Filling In the Gaps	1981	80.00
—With drawing on cover			
❑ HS 3516	Face Dances	1981	8.00
❑ 23731	It's Hard	1982	8.00
❑ 23731 [DJ]	It's Hard	1982	30.00
—Promo version on Quiex II vinyl			

WHOLE OATS See DARYL HALL AND JOHN OATES.

WHYTE BOOTS, THE

45s

Number	Title (A Side/B Side)	Yr	NM
PHILIPS			
❑ 40422	Nightmare/Let No One Come Between Us	1967	80.00

WICHITA TRAIN WHISTLE, THE Produced by MICHAEL NESMITH.

45s

Number	Title (A Side/B Side)	Yr	NM
DOT			
❑ 17152	Tapioca Tundra/Don't Cry Now	1968	15.00
Albums			
DOT			
❑ DLP-25861	Mike Nesmith Presents/The Wichita Train Whistle Sings	1968	30.00

W

Wild Turkey, *Battle Hymn*, Reprise MS 2070, 1972, **$12.**

WIEDLIN, JANE

12-Inch Singles

Number	Title (A Side/B Side)	Yr	NM
EMI			
❑ 56179	World on Fire (4 versions)/ Flowers on the Battlefield	1990	6.00
EMI MANHATTAN			
❑ 56085	Rush Hour (4 versions)/ End of Love	1988	8.00
❑ 56105	Inside a Dream (5 mixes)/ Song of the Factory	1988	8.00
I.R.S.			
❑ 23585	Blue Kiss (3 versions)	1985	8.00

45s

Number	Title (A Side/B Side)	Yr	NM
EMI MANHATTAN			
❑ 50118	Rush Hour/The End of Love	1988	2.00
❑ 50118 [PS]	Rush Hour/The End of Love	1988	4.00
❑ 50145	Inside a Dream/ Song of the Factory	1988	2.00
❑ 50145 [PS]	Inside a Dream/ Song of the Factory	1988	2.00
I.R.S.			
❑ 52674	Blue Kiss/My Traveling Heart	1985	3.00
❑ 52674 [PS]	Blue Kiss/My Traveling Heart	1985	3.00
❑ 52674 [PS]	Blue Kiss/Somebody's Going to Get Into This House	1985	25.00

—Copies of the picture sleeve were printed, but the B-side was not pressed onto vinyl; a few were used as WLP, but not on stock copies with official B-side "My Traveling Heart"

Albums

Number	Title (A Side/B Side)	Yr	NM
EMI MANHATTAN			
❑ E1-48683	Fur	1988	10.00
❑ R 152262	Fur	1988	12.00
—BMG Direct Marketing edition			
I.R.S.			
❑ 5638	Jane Wiedlin	1985	10.00

WIER, RUSTY

45s

Number	Title (A Side/B Side)	Yr	NM
ABC			
❑ 12019	Stoned, Slow and Rugged/ Jeremiah Black	1974	6.00
BLACK HAT			
❑ 102	Close Your Eyes/ Kum-Back Bar and Grill	1987	6.00
❑ 103	(Lover of the) Other Side of the Hill/I Kept Thinkin' About You	1987	6.00
COLUMBIA			
❑ 3-10445	I Think It's Time (I Learned How to Let Her Go)/Me and Daisy on the Run	1976	4.00
COMPLEAT			
❑ 107	Don't It Make You Wanna Dance/ You Gave Me a Reason	1983	5.00
❑ 121	Lone Star Lady/I Still Believe in You	1984	5.00
LONGHORN			
❑ 101	(Lover of the) Other Side of the Hill/(B-side unknown)	1965	15.00
20TH CENTURY			
❑ 2188	I Heard You Been Layin' My Old Lady (Apologies to Susie)/ Aqua Dulce	1975	5.00
❑ 2219	Don't It Make You Wanna Dance/I Believe in the Way That You Love Me	1975	5.00
❑ 2273	I Don't Want to Lay This Guitar Down/Long and Lonesome Highway Blues	1976	5.00

Albums

Number	Title (A Side/B Side)	Yr	NM
ABC			
❑ D-820	Stoned, Slow and Rugged	1974	12.00
COLUMBIA			
❑ KC 34319	Black Hat Saloon	1976	10.00
❑ PC 34775	Stacked Deck	1977	10.00
MCA			
❑ 820	Stoned, Slow and Rugged	1980	8.00
—Reissue of ABC 820			
20TH CENTURY			
❑ T-469	Don't It Make You Wanna Dance?	1975	10.00
❑ T-495	Rusty Wier	1975	10.00

WIGGINS, JAY

45s

Number	Title (A Side/B Side)	Yr	NM
AMY			
❑ 955	Sad Girl/No, Not Me	1966	10.00
I.P.G.			
❑ 1008	Sad Girl/No, Not Me	196?	15.00
❑ 1015	Forgive Then Forget/ My Lonely Girl	196?	12.00
LOST-NITE			
❑ 258	Sad Girl/No, Not Me	196?	5.00
—Reissue			

WIGGINS, WALLY

45s

Number	Title (A Side/B Side)	Yr	NM
MERCURY			
❑ 71645	I Need You/Maybe Someday	1960	80.00
❑ 71713	Maybellene/Sweeter Than Sweet	1960	20.00
❑ 71953	The Habit of Loving You/Little Old Lady Who Lives in a Shoe	1962	30.00

WIGWAM

45s

Number	Title (A Side/B Side)	Yr	NM
VERVE FORECAST			
❑ 5114	Call Me on Your Telephone/ Wishful Thinker	1970	8.00

Albums

Number	Title (A Side/B Side)	Yr	NM
VERVE FORECAST			
❑ FTS-3089	Tombstone Valentine	1970	20.00

WILCOX THREE, THE

Albums

Number	Title (A Side/B Side)	Yr	NM
RCA CAMDEN			
❑ CAL-669 [M]	The Greatest Folk Songs Ever Sung	1961	20.00

WILD, JACK

45s

Number	Title (A Side/B Side)	Yr	NM
BUDDAH			
❑ 241	(Holy Moses) Everything's Coming Up Roses/Bring Yourself Back to Me	1971	8.00
CAPITOL			
❑ 2742	Some Beautiful/A Picture of You	1970	6.00
❑ 2742 [PS]	Some Beautiful/A Picture of You	1970	12.00
❑ 2868	Wait for Summer/Melody	1970	6.00

Albums

Number	Title (A Side/B Side)	Yr	NM
BUDDAH			
❑ BDS-5083	Everything's Coming Up Roses	1971	25.00
❑ BDS-5110	A Beautiful World	1972	25.00
CAPITOL			
❑ SKAO-545	The Jack Wild Album	1970	25.00

WILD BEES, THE

45s

Number	Title (A Side/B Side)	Yr	NM
RCA VICTOR			
❑ 47-7275	Doctor Rock/Bamboozled	1958	30.00

WILD BUTTER

45s

Number	Title (A Side/B Side)	Yr	NM
UNITED ARTISTS			
❑ 50688	Roxanna/Terribly Blind	1970	6.00

Albums

Number	Title (A Side/B Side)	Yr	NM
UNITED ARTISTS			
❑ UAS-6766	Wild Butter	1970	25.00

WILD-CATS, THE

45s

Number	Title (A Side/B Side)	Yr	NM
UNITED ARTISTS			
❑ 154	Gazachstahagen/ Billy's Cha Cha	1958	25.00
❑ 169	Dancing Elephants/ King Size Guitar	1959	25.00

Albums

Number	Title (A Side/B Side)	Yr	NM
UNITED ARTISTS			
❑ UAL-3031 [M]	Bandstand Record Hop	1958	50.00

WILD CHERRY

45s

Number	Title (A Side/B Side)	Yr	NM
A&M			
❑ 1656	Voodoo Doll/Because Your Love Is Mine	1974	5.00

Except when noted otherwise, VG = 25% of NM, and VG+ = 50% of NM. (Example: VG = \$2.00, VG+ = \$4.00 and NM = \$8.00.)

EPIC

Number	Title (A Side/B Side)	Yr	NM
❑ 50225	Play That Funky Music/The Lady Wants Your Money	1976	5.00
❑ 50306	Get It Up/Baby Don't You Know	1976	4.00
❑ 50362	Hot to Trot/Put Yourself in My Shoes	1977	4.00
❑ 50401	Are You Boogieing Around on Your Daddy/Hold On (With Strings)	1977	4.00
❑ 50500	Don't Stop, Get Off/ I Love My Music	1978	4.00
❑ 50551	1-2-3 Kind of Love/ Fools Fall in Love	1978	4.00
❑ 50619	This Old Heart of Mine (Is Weak for You)/Lana	1978	4.00
❑ 50702	Try a Piece of My Love/ Take Me Back	1979	4.00

UNITED ARTISTS

Number	Title (A Side/B Side)	Yr	NM
❑ XW217 [DJ]	Get Down (mono/stereo)	1973	5.00

—Stock copy not known to exist

Albums

EPIC

Number	Title	Yr	NM
❑ PE 34195	Wild Cherry	1976	12.00
❑ PE 34462	Electrified Funk	1977	10.00
❑ JE 35011	I Love My Music	1978	10.00
❑ JE 35760	Only the Wild	1979	10.00

WILD COUNTRY See ALABAMA.

WILD MAN STEVE

Albums

DEALER'S CHOICE

Number	Title	Yr	NM
❑ 777	Is It Good Baby	198?	15.00
❑ 780	Did He Really Say That	198?	15.00

DICK-ER

Number	Title	Yr	NM
❑ D 70	Do Not Disturb	1972	20.00

LAFF

Number	Title	Yr	NM
❑ 181	Eatin' Ain't Cheatin'	1973	12.00
❑ 191	When You're Hot You're Hot	1976	12.00

RAW

Number	Title	Yr	NM
❑ 7000	My Man! Wild Man!	1969	15.00
❑ 7001	Wild! Wild! Wild! Wild!	1970	15.00
❑ 7002	King of Them All	1971	15.00

WILD ONES, THE (1)

45s

MAINLINE

Number	Title (A Side/B Side)	Yr	NM
❑ 500	Caught in the Cookie Jar/ Super Fox	1965	10.00

MALA

Number	Title (A Side/B Side)	Yr	NM
❑ 564	High-Ho/Valerie	1967	8.00

UNITED ARTISTS

Number	Title (A Side/B Side)	Yr	NM
❑ 947	Wild Thing/Just Can't Cry Anymore	1965	12.00
❑ 971	My Love/Lord Love a Duck	1966	10.00
❑ 971 [PS]	My Love/Lord Love a Duck	1966	15.00
❑ 50043	For Your Love (I Would Do Almost Anything)/Never Givin' Up (On Your Love)	1966	10.00

Albums

UNITED ARTISTS

Number	Title	Yr	NM
❑ UAL-3450 [M]	The Arthur Sound	1965	25.00
❑ UAS-6450 [S]	The Arthur Sound	1965	30.00

WILD ONES, THE (2)

45s

SEARS

Number	Title (A Side/B Side)	Yr	NM
❑ 2180	Come On Back/(Instrumental)	1966	10.00
❑ 2180 [PS]	Come On Back/(Instrumental)	1966	30.00

WILD ONES, THE (3)

45s

S.P.Q.R.

Number	Title (A Side/B Side)	Yr	NM
❑ 3316	A Little Bit o' Soul/ I've Been Crying	1964	25.00

WILD TURKEY

Albums

CHRYSALIS

Number	Title	Yr	NM
❑ CHR 1010	Turkey	1973	10.00

REPRISE

Number	Title	Yr	NM
❑ MS 2070	Battle Hymn	1972	12.00

WILDCATS, THE (1)

45s

RCA VICTOR

Number	Title (A Side/B Side)	Yr	NM
❑ 47-6386	Keep Talkin'/Beatin' on a Rug	1956	40.00

WILDCATS, THE (2) Actually THE BLOSSOMS.

45s

REPRISE

Number	Title (A Side/B Side)	Yr	NM
❑ 0253	3625 Groovy Street/What Are We Gonna Do in '64	1964	20.00

WILDE, MARTY

45s

BELL

Number	Title (A Side/B Side)	Yr	NM
❑ 45603	All Night Girl/(B-side unknown)	1974	5.00

EPIC

Number	Title (A Side/B Side)	Yr	NM
❑ 9291	My Lucky Love/Misery's Child	1958	15.00
❑ 9356	Bad Boy/Teenage Years	1960	12.00
❑ 9392	Little Girl/Your Seventeenth Spring	1960	12.00
❑ 9400	Angry/My Baby Is Gone (Stop This World)	1960	12.00
❑ 9424	The Part of a Fool/ Forgotten Dreams	1960	—

—Unreleased?

HERITAGE

Number	Title (A Side/B Side)	Yr	NM
❑ 814 *—As "Shannon"*	Abergavenny/Alice in Blue	1969	6.00
❑ 814 [PS] *—As "Shannon"*	Abergavenny/Alice in Blue	1969	10.00
❑ 819 *—As "Shannon"*	Jesamine/Lullaby	1969	6.00

JAMIE

Number	Title (A Side/B Side)	Yr	NM
❑ 1282	Kiss Me/My, What a Woman	1964	10.00

Albums

EPIC

Number	Title	Yr	NM
❑ BN 575 [S]	Wilde About Marty	1960	100.00
❑ LN 3686 [M]	Bad Boy	1960	80.00
❑ LN 3711 [M]	Wilde About Marty	1960	80.00

WILDERNESS ROAD

45s

COLUMBIA

Number	Title (A Side/B Side)	Yr	NM
❑ 4-45565	Bounty Man/Dr. Morpho's Revenge	1972	8.00

Albums

COLUMBIA

Number	Title	Yr	NM
❑ C 31118	Wilderness Road	1972	20.00

REPRISE

Number	Title	Yr	NM
❑ MS 2125	Sold for the Prevention of Disease Only	1973	20.00

WILDING, BOBBY

45s

ABC-PARAMOUNT

Number	Title (A Side/B Side)	Yr	NM
❑ 10275	Mama/You Give Me No Choice	1961	12.00

DCP

Number	Title (A Side/B Side)	Yr	NM
❑ 1009	I Want to Be a Beatle/Since I've Been Wearing My Hair Like a Beatle	1964	20.00
❑ 1106	I Want You/Too Young to Fall in Love	1964	12.00

MAY

Number	Title (A Side/B Side)	Yr	NM
❑ 125	Slide (Part 1)/Slide (Part 2)	1962	12.00

WILDWOODS, THE Actually THE FIVE SATINS.

45s

CAPRICE

Number	Title (A Side/B Side)	Yr	NM
❑ 101	When the Swallows Come Back to Capistrano/Heart of Mine	1961	150.00

MAY

Number	Title (A Side/B Side)	Yr	NM
❑ 106	Golden Sunset/Here Comes Big Ed	1961	30.00

WILEY, CHUCK

45s

JAX

Number	Title (A Side/B Side)	Yr	NM
❑ 1004	I Love You So Much/ I Begin to Miss You	1959	100.00

UNITED ARTISTS

Number	Title (A Side/B Side)	Yr	NM
❑ 113	Tear It Up/Shake Up the Dance	1958	75.00
❑ 120	By My Side/Door to Door	1958	—

—Unreleased

WILKENS, ARTIE, AND THE PALMS

45s

STATES

Number	Title (A Side/B Side)	Yr	NM
❑ 157	Darling Patricia/ Please Come Back	1956	600.00

WILKINSON TRI-CYCLE

Albums

DATE

Number	Title	Yr	NM
❑ TES 4016	Wilkinson Tri-Cycle	1969	40.00

WILLIAMS, ALAINE

45s

PARKWAY

Number	Title (A Side/B Side)	Yr	NM
❑ 923	When Are We Getting Married/ So This Is Goodbye	1964	20.00

WILLIAMS, ANDRE

45s

AVIN

Number	Title (A Side/B Side)	Yr	NM
❑ 103	Rib Tips (Part 1)/Rib Tips (Part 2)	1965	12.00

CHECKER

Number	Title (A Side/B Side)	Yr	NM
❑ 1187	The Stroke/Humpin' Bumpin' and Trumpin'	1967	12.00
❑ 1205	Cadillac Jack/Mrs. Mother USA	1968	12.00
❑ 1214	Do the Popcorn/It's Gonna Be Fine in '69	1969	12.00
❑ 1219	Girdle Up/(Instrumental)	1969	12.00

EPIC

Number	Title (A Side/B Side)	Yr	NM
❑ 9196	Bacon Fat/Just Because of a Kiss	1956	25.00

FORTUNE

Number	Title (A Side/B Side)	Yr	NM
❑ 824	Pulling Time/Going Down to Tia-Juana	1955	80.00
❑ 827	Mozelle/Just Want a Little Lovin'	1956	40.00
❑ 828	Bobby Jean/It's All Over	1956	40.00
❑ 831	Bacon Fat/Just Because of a Kiss	1956	30.00
❑ 834	Mean Jean/You Are My Sunshine	1957	30.00
❑ 837	Jail Bait/My Tears	1957	80.00
❑ 839 *—With Gino Park*	Come On Baby/ The Greasy Chicken	1957	30.00
❑ 839 *—With Gino Park*	The Greasy Chicken/ Please Pass the Biscuits	1957	60.00
❑ 839 *—With Gino Park*	Don't Touch/Please Pass the Biscuits	1957	80.00
❑ 842	My Last Dance with You/ Hey! Country Girl	1958	30.00
❑ 847	Put a Chain on It/I'm All For You	1959	30.00
❑ 851 *—With Gino Park*	(Georgia May Is) Movin'/(Mmmm — Andre Williams Is) Movin'	1960	60.00
❑ 856	Jail House Blues/I Still Love You	1960	30.00

MIRACLE

Number	Title (A Side/B Side)	Yr	NM
❑ 4	Rosa Lee/Shoo Shoo	1960	1200.

NORTON

Number	Title (A Side/B Side)	Yr	NM
❑ 45-069	Poor Mr. Santa (N-N-Naughty!)/ Poor Mr. Santa (N-n-nice!)	1997	2.00
❑ 45-069 [PS]	Poor Mr. Santa (N-N-Naughty!)/ Poor Mr. Santa (N-n-nice!)	1997	2.00

RIC-TIC

Number	Title (A Side/B Side)	Yr	NM
❑ 124	You Got It And I Want It/ I Can't Stop Crying	1967	25.00

RONALD

Number	Title (A Side/B Side)	Yr	NM
❑ 1001	Please Give Me a Chance/ (B-side unknown)	196?	25.00

SPORT

Number	Title (A Side/B Side)	Yr	NM
❑ 105	Pearl Time/Soul Groove	1967	25.00

WINGATE

Number	Title (A Side/B Side)	Yr	NM
❑ 014	Loose Juice/Sweet Little Pussycat	1966	15.00
❑ 021	Do It! (Part 1)/Do It! (Part 2)	1966	20.00

Albums

SDEG

Number	Title	Yr	NM
❑ 4020	Directly from the Streets	198?	10.00

WILLIAMS, BARRY "Greg Brady" of THE BRADY BUNCH.

45s

PARAMOUNT

Number	Title (A Side/B Side)	Yr	NM
❑ 0122	Sweet Sweetheart/Sunny	1971	15.00
❑ 0122 [PS]	Sweet Sweetheart/Sunny	1971	20.00

WILLIAMS, BERNIE

45s

BELL

Number	Title (A Side/B Side)	Yr	NM
❑ 768	Ever Again/Next to You	1969	1200.

WILLIAMS, BETTY

45s

HIT

Number	Title (A Side/B Side)	Yr	NM
❑ 101	As Usual/The Boy Next Door	1964	8.00

—B-side by the Belles

WILLIAMS, BIG JOE

Albums

BLUESVILLE

Number	Title	Yr	NM
❑ BVLP-1056 [M]	Blues for 9 Strings	1962	100.00
❑ BVLP-1056 [M]	Blues for 9 Strings	1964	25.00

—Blue label, silver print (first entry); *—Blue label with trident logo* (second entry)

W

Number | Title (A Side/B Side) | Yr | NM

❑ BVLP-1067 [M] Big Joe Williams at Folk City 1963 100.00
—Blue label, silver print
❑ BVLP-1067 [M] Big Joe Williams at Folk City 1964 25.00
—Blue label with trident logo
❑ BVLP-1083 [M] Studio Blues 1964 25.00
—Blue label with trident logo
❑ BVLP-1083 [M] Studio Blues 1964 100.00
—Blue label, silver print

DELMARK
❑ DL-604 [M] Blues on Highway 49 1962 60.00
❑ DL-609 [M] Starvin' Chain Blues 1966 25.00

FOLKWAYS
❑ FA-3820 [M] Mississippi's Big Joe Williams 1962 30.00
❑ FAS-3820 [R] Mississippi's Big Joe Williams 1962 20.00

MILESTONE
❑ 3001 [M] Classic Delta Blues 1966 25.00

WILLIAMS, BILLY Also see THE CHARIOTEERS.

45s

CORAL
❑ 61212 Sh-Boom (Life Could Be a Dream)/Whenever Wherever 1954 12.00
❑ 61264 Love Me/The Honeydripper 1954 12.00
❑ 61346 Fools Rush In/He Follows She 1955 12.00
❑ 61462 Glory of Love/Wonderful, Wonderful One 1955 12.00
❑ 61498 Just a Little Bit More/Learning to Love 1955 12.00
❑ 61576 Cry Baby/A Crazy Little Place 1956 10.00
❑ 61639 Pray/You'll Reach Your Star 1956 10.00
❑ 61684 This Planet Earth/I Guess I'll Be On My Way 1956 10.00
❑ 61730 Shame, Shame, Shame/Don't Cry on My Shoulder 1956 10.00
❑ 61751 Stormy/Follow Me 1956 10.00
❑ 61795 Butterfly/The Pied Piper 1957 10.00
❑ 61830 I'm Gonna Sit Right Down and Write Myself a Letter/Date with the Blues 1957 12.00
❑ 61886 Got a Date with an Angel/The Lord Will Understand 1957 10.00
❑ 61932 Don't Let Go/Baby, Baby 1958 10.00
❑ 61961 There! I've Said It Again/Steppin' Out Tonight 1958 10.00
❑ 61999 I'll Get By/It's Prayin' Time 1958 10.00
❑ 62029 It Hurts So Much/So Long 1958 10.00
❑ 62069 Nola/Tied to the Strings of Your Heart 1959 10.00
❑ 62101 Goodnight Irene/Red Hot Love 1959 10.00
❑ 62131 Go to Sleep, Go to Sleep, Go to Sleep/Telephone Conversation 1959 8.00
—With Barbara McNair
❑ 62140 Smack Dab in the Middle/I Wonder 1959 8.00
❑ 62218 I Cried for You/The Lover of All Lovers 1960 8.00
❑ 62230 Begin the Beguine/For You 1960 8.00
❑ 62438 Why Do I Love You So/Raise Your Hand 1964 6.00
❑ 62438 Why Do I Love You So/The Honeydripper 1964 6.00

MERCURY
❑ 5866 Stay/Azure-Te (Paris Blues) 1952 15.00
❑ 5884 Who Knows/It's Best We Say Goodbye 1952 15.00
❑ 5902 That's What I'm Here For/Some Folks Do, Some Folks Don't 1952 15.00
❑ 70012 I Don't Know Why/Mad About 'Cha 1952 15.00
❑ 70094 Pour Me a Glass of Teardrops/It's a Miracle 1953 15.00
❑ 70180 This Side of Heaven/You're the One for Me 1953 15.00
❑ 70210 Why Do You Have to Go?/Cattle Call 1953 15.00
❑ 70271 If I Ever Get to Heaven/Ask Me No Questions 1953 15.00
❑ 70324 Invitation to Dance/I'll Close My Eyes 1954 15.00
❑ 70376 Go Home, Joe/You're the Only One I Adore 1954 15.00

MGM
❑ 10764 Longing/I Didn't Slip 1950 20.00
❑ 10857 The Room I'm Sleeping In/Music by Angels 1950 20.00
❑ 10928 Gaucho Serenade/I Won't Cry Anymore 1951 15.00
❑ 10967 Pretty Eyed Baby/You Made Me Love You 1951 15.00
❑ 10998 Shang-Hai/A Wondrous Word 1951 15.00
❑ 11066 Sin/It's Over 1951 15.00
❑ 11117 I'll Never Find You/Busy Line 1951 15.00
❑ 11145 No Other Love/Callaway Went That-A-Way 1952 15.00
❑ 11172 Wheel of Fortune/What Can I Say 1952 15.00
❑ 11184 Confetti/Don't Grieve 1952 15.00
❑ 12537 Shang-Hai/Gaucho Serenade 1957 10.00

7-Inch Extended Plays

CORAL
❑ EC 81164 "I'm Gonna Sit Right Down and Write Myself A Letter/Lucy Lou/The Lord Will Understand (And Say "Well Done")/The Honeydripper 1957 12.00
❑ EC 81164 [PS] (title unknown) 1957 12.00

MERCURY
❑ EP-1-3365 (title unknown) 195? 15.00
❑ EP-1-3365 If I Never Get to Heaven/Cattle Call//A Smile for Suzette/Azure-Te 195? 15.00

Albums

CORAL
❑ CRL 57184 [M] Billy Williams 1957 60.00
❑ CRL 57251 [M] Half Sweet, Half Beat 1959 50.00
❑ CRL 57343 [M] The Billy Williams Revue 1960 50.00
❑ CRL 757251 [S] Half Sweet, Half Beat 1959 80.00
❑ CRL 757343 [S] The Billy Williams Revue 1960 60.00

MERCURY
❑ MG 20317 [M] Oh Yeah! 1958 60.00

MGM
❑ E-3400 [M] The Billy Williams Quartet 1957 60.00

WING
❑ MGW-12131 [M] Vote for Billy Williams 1959 40.00

WILLIAMS, BILLY DEE

Albums

PRESTIGE LIVELY ARTS
❑ 30001 [M] Let's Misbehave 1962 40.00

WILLIAMS, CORA/SHIRLEY HAVEN AND THE FOUR JACKS

45s

FEDERAL
❑ 12079 I Ain't Coming Back Anymore/Sure Cure for the Blues 1952 600.00

WILLIAMS, DENIECE

12-Inch Singles

ARC
❑ AS 669 [DJ] I Found Love/Are You Thinking? 1979 25.00
❑ 23-10991 I've Got the Next Dance (6:21)/When Love Comes Calling 1979 15.00
❑ 43-11141 I Found Love (6:36)/Are You Thinking? (4:16) 1979 25.00

COLUMBIA
❑ AS 1838 [DJ] Let's Hear It for the Boy (6:00) (3:34) 1984 15.00
❑ CAS 2688 [DJ] Never Say Never (Extended 12" Mix 7:35) (Dance Mix 5:02) (7" Mix 3:42) 1987 10.00
❑ 44-04946 Heaven in Your Eyes (Extended Dance Version)/Love, Peace and Unity 1983 10.00
❑ 44-04988 Let's Hear It for the Boy (6:00) (Instrumental 4:13) 1984 8.00
❑ 44-05043 Next Love (7:07)/(Instrumental) 1984 8.00
❑ 44-05918 Wiser and Weaker (6:15) (5:50 Instrumental) 1986 8.00
❑ 44-06761 Never Say Never (Extended 12" Mix 7:35) (Dance Mix 5:02) (7" Mix 3:42) 1987 8.00
❑ 44-06929 I Confess (Dance Mix) (Dub Mix) (7" Mix) 1987 8.00
❑ 44-07889 I Can't Wait (12" Version 5:33) (7" Version 4:15) (Deniece-a-Dub 4:45) (7" Instrumental 4:15) 1988 8.00
❑ 23-10513 Free/It's Important to Me 1977 100.00
—Original pressing on red label with "Columbia" encircling the label edge
❑ 23-10513 Free/It's Important to Me 199? 8.00
—Repressing on red label with one "Columbia" in white at top

MCA
❑ 23975 Every Moment (Special Remix)/Do You Hear What I Hear? 1989 8.00

SPARROW
❑ SGL-11214 [DJ] They Say (same on both sides) 1986 12.00
—With Sandi Patti
❑ SGL-11742 [DJ] His Eye Is on the Sparrow (same on both sides) 1989 10.00

45s

ARC
❑ 11-02108 It's Your Conscience/Sweet Surrender 1981 5.00
❑ 18-02406 Silly/My Melody 1981 4.00
❑ 18-02812 It's Gonna Take a Miracle/A Part of Love 1982 4.00
❑ 18-03015 Waiting by the Hotline/Love Notes 1982 5.00
❑ 13-03242 It's Gonna Take a Miracle/Silly 1982 3.00
—Reissue
❑ 18-03261 Waiting/How Does It Feel 1982 6.00
❑ 3-10971 I've Got the Next Dance/When Love Comes Calling 1979 5.00
❑ 3-11063 I Found Love/Are You Thinking? 1979 5.00
❑ 11-60504 What Two Can Do/Suspicious 1981 4.00

COLUMBIA
❑ AE7 1153 [DJ] God Is Amazing/God Is Standing By 1977 8.00
—B-side by Johnnie Taylor; promo with "Suggested Christmas Programming" on label
❑ 38-03807 Do What You Feel/Love, Peace and Unity 1983 4.00
❑ 38-03807 [PS] Do What You Feel/Love, Peace and Unity 1983 4.00
❑ 38-04037 I'm So Proud/It's Okay 1983 4.00
❑ 38-04218 Heaven in Your Eyes/Love, Peace and Unity 1983 4.00
❑ 38-04417 Let's Hear It for the Boy/(Instrumental) 1984 3.00
❑ 38-04417 [PS] Let's Hear It for the Boy/(Instrumental) 1984 4.00
❑ 38-04537 Next Love/Picking Up the Pieces 1984 4.00
❑ 38-04537 [PS] Next Love/Picking Up the Pieces 1984 4.00
❑ 38-04641 Black Butterfly/Blind Dating 1984 5.00
❑ 38-06157 Wiser and Weaker/(Instrumental) 1986 3.00
❑ 38-06157 [PS] Wiser and Weaker/(Instrumental) 1986 3.00
❑ 38-06318 Healing/I Feel the Night 1986 4.00
❑ 38-07021 Never Say Never/Love Finds You 1987 3.00
❑ 38-07021 [PS] Never Say Never/Love Finds You 1987 3.00
❑ 38-07357 I Confess/(Instrumental) 1987 3.00
❑ 38-07633 Water Under the Bridge/Love Finds You 1987 4.00
❑ 38-07704 I Believe in You/(Instrumental) 1988 5.00
❑ 38-08014 I Can't Wait/(Instrumental) 1988 3.00
❑ 38-08014 [PS] I Can't Wait/(Instrumental) 1988 3.00
❑ 13-08425 Let's Hear It for the Boy/(Instrumental) 1988 3.00
—Reissue
❑ 38-08507 This Is As Good As It Gets/Don't Stop the Love 1988 4.00
❑ 3-10429 Free/Cause You Love Me Baby 1976 5.00
❑ 3-10556 That's What Friends Are For/It's Important to Me 1977 5.00
❑ 3-10648 Baby, Baby My Love's All for You/Be Good to Me 1977 5.00
❑ 3-10770 God Is Amazing/Season 1978 5.00

LOCK
❑ 600 Mama I Wish I'd Stayed at Home/I'd Believe Him 196? 80.00
—As "Denise Chandler"
❑ 752 Love Is Tears/I'm Walking Away 196? 40.00
—As "Denise Chandler"
❑ 753 You Hurt Me Now/Yes I'm Ready 196? 100.00
—As "Denise Chandler"

MCA
❑ 53707 Every Moment/Do You Hear What I Hear? 1989 5.00

SPARROW
❑ SGL-11211 [DJ] My Soul Desire/Personal Testimony 1986 5.00
❑ SGL-11211 [PS] My Soul Desire/Personal Testimony 1986 5.00
❑ SGL-11212 [DJ] I Surrender All/Personal Testimony 1986 5.00
❑ SGL-11213 [DJ] So Glad I Know/I Surrender All 1986 5.00
❑ SGL-11215 [DJ] Wings of an Eagle (same on both sides) 1986 8.00
—Pink vinyl
❑ SGL-11215 [PS] Wings of an Eagle (same on both sides) 1986 8.00
❑ SGL-11741 [DJ] Healing (same on both sides) 1986 5.00
❑ SGL-11741 [PS] Healing (same on both sides) 1986 5.00
❑ S7-18215 Do You Hear What I Hear/Silent Night 1994 6.00
—B-side by Bebe and Cece Winans; green vinyl

TODDLIN' TOWN
❑ 107 Love Is Tears/I'm Walkin' Away 1968 40.00
—As "Deniece Chandler"
❑ 113 Hey Baby/Glorious Feeling 1968 40.00
—As "Deniece Chandler"; with Lee Sain
❑ 118 I Don't Wanna Cry/Goodbye Cruel World 1969 40.00
—As "Deniece Chandler"
❑ 127 Shy Boy/Come On Home to My Baby 1969 30.00
—As "Deniece Chandler"

Number	Title (A Side/B Side)	Yr	NM
Albums			
ARC			
❑ AS 1432 [DJ]	Niecy	1982	25.00
—Promo-only picture disc			
❑ JC 35568	When Love Comes Calling	1979	12.00
❑ FC 37048	My Melody	1981	10.00
❑ PC 37048	My Melody	198?	8.00
—Budget-line reissue			
❑ FC 37952	Niecy	1982	10.00
❑ PC 37952	Niecy	198?	8.00
—Budget-line reissue			
❑ HC 47952	Niecy	1983	50.00
—Half-speed mastered edition			
COLUMBIA			
❑ PC 34242	This Is Niecy	1976	12.00
—No bar code on cover			
❑ PC 34242	This Is Niecy	198?	8.00
—Reissue with bar code on cover			
❑ JC 34911	Song Bird	1977	10.00
❑ PC 34911	Song Bird	198?	8.00
—Budget-line reissue			
❑ FC 38622	I'm So Proud	1983	10.00
❑ PC 38622	I'm So Proud	198?	8.00
—Budget-line reissue			
❑ FC 39366	Let's Hear It for the Boy	1984	10.00
❑ FC 40084	Hot on the Trail	1986	10.00
❑ FC 40486	Water Under the Bridge	1987	10.00
❑ FC 44322	As Good As It Gets	1989	10.00
MCA			
❑ 6338	Special Love	1989	10.00
SPARROW			
❑ SPR-1121	So Glad I Know	1986	12.00
❑ SPR-1174	Special Love	1989	12.00
❑ SPR-1256	From the Beginning	1990	15.00
❑ ST-41039	So Glad I Know	198?	12.00
—Reissue of 1121?			

WILLIAMS, HANK

Number	Title (A Side/B Side)	Yr	NM
45s			
MGM			
❑ KGC-107	Lovesick Blues/ Your Cheatin' Heart	196?	10.00
❑ KGC-108	Hey Good Lookin'/ Why Don't You Love Me	196?	10.00
❑ KGC-109	Honky Tonk Blues/Half as Much	196?	10.00
❑ KGC-110	Jambalaya/I'll Never Get Out of This World Alive	196?	10.00
❑ KGC-111	Kaw-Liga/Ramblin' Man	196?	10.00
❑ KGC-112	You Win Again/Moanin' the Blues	196?	10.00
❑ KGC-113	Cold, Cold Heart/I'm So Lonesome I Could Cry	196?	10.00
❑ KGC-127	My Bucket's Got a Hole in It/We Live in Two Different Worlds	196?	10.00
❑ KGC-128	I Can't Help It (If I'm Still in Love with You)/House of Gold	196?	10.00
❑ KGC-134	Long Gone Lonesome Blues/My Son Calls Another Man Daddy	196?	10.00
❑ KGC-142	Roly Poly/Just Waitin'	196?	10.00
—All of the above "KGC" singles are "Golden Circle Series" reissues; original editions have gold labels; later editions go for less			
❑ 8010	Lovesick Blues/Never Again (Will I Knock on Your Door)	1949	70.00
❑ K10033	Move It On Over/(Last Night) I Heard You Cryin' in Your Sleep	1950	50.00
—Yellow label; 78 first issued in 1947			
❑ K10171	Honky Tonkin'/I'll Be a Bachelor 'Til I Die	1950	50.00
—Yellow label; 78 first issued in 1948			
❑ K10328	Mansion on the Hill/I Can't Get You Off of My Mind	1950	50.00
—Yellow label; 78 first issued in 1949			
❑ K10352	Lovesick Blues/Never Again (Will I Knock on Your Door)	1950	50.00
—Reissue has original 45 rpm number in parentheses under this number			
❑ K10401	Wedding Bells/I've Just Told Mama Goodbye	1949	60.00
❑ 10434	Dear Brother/Lost on the River	1949	60.00
❑ 10461	Mind Your Own Business/ There'll Be No Teardrops Tonight	1949	60.00
❑ 10506	You're Gonna Change (Or I'm Gonna Leave)/Lost Highway	1949	60.00
❑ 10560	My Bucket's Got a Hole In It/I'm So Lonesome I Could Cry	1949	60.00
❑ 10609	I Just Don't Like This Kind of Lovin'/May You Never Be Alone	1950	40.00
❑ 10630	Beyond the Sunset/The Funeral	1950	60.00
—As "Luke the Drifter"			
❑ 10645	Long Gone Lonesome Blues/ My Son Calls Another Man Daddy	1950	40.00
❑ 10696	Why Don't You Love Me/ A House Without Love	1950	40.00

Hank Williams, *On Stage Volume II*, MGM SE-4109, 1963, stereo, black label, **$20.**

Number	Title (A Side/B Side)	Yr	NM
❑ 10718	Everything's OK/ Too Many Parties	1950	60.00
—As "Luke the Drifter"			
❑ 10760	They'll Never Take Her Love from Me/Why Should We Try Anymore	1950	40.00
❑ 10806	No, No, Joe/Help Me Understand	1950	60.00
—As "Luke the Drifter"			
❑ 10813	I Heard My Mother Praying for Me/Jesus Remembered Me	1950	50.00
❑ 10832	Moanin' the Blues/Nobody's Lonesome for Me	1950	40.00
❑ 10904	Cold, Cold Heart/Dear John	1951	30.00
❑ 10932	Just Waitin'/Men with Broken Hearts	1951	50.00
—As "Luke the Drifter"			
❑ 10961	I Can't Help It (If I'm Still in Love with You)/Howlin' at the Moon	1951	30.00
❑ 11000	Hey, Good Lookin'/ My Heart Would Know	1951	30.00
❑ 11017	I Dreamed About Mama Last Night/I've Been Down That Road Before	1951	50.00
—As "Luke the Drifter"			
❑ 11054	Crazy Heart/Lonesome Whistle	1951	30.00
❑ 11083	Leave Us Women Alone/ If You See My Baby	1951	40.00
❑ 11100	Baby, We're Really in Love I'd Still Want You	1951	30.00
❑ 11120	Ramblin' Man/A Picture from Life's Other Side	1952	40.00
—As "Luke the Drifter"			
❑ 11160	Honky Tonk Blues/I'm Sorry for You My Friend	1952	30.00
❑ 11202	Half As Much/Let's Turn Back the Years	1952	30.00
❑ 11283	Jambalaya (On the Bayou)/ Window Shopping	1952	30.00
❑ 11309	Be Careful of Stones That You Throw/Why Don't You Make Up Your Mind	1952	40.00
—As "Luke the Drifter"			
❑ 11318	Settin' the Woods On Fire/You Win Again	1952	30.00
❑ 11366	I'll Never Get Out of This World Alive/I Could Never Be Ashamed	1952	30.00
❑ 11416	Kaw-Liga/Your Cheatin' Heart	1953	30.00
❑ 11479	Take These Chains from My Heart/Ramblin' Man	1953	25.00
❑ 11533	I Won't Be Home No More/ My Love for You	1953	25.00
❑ 11574	Weary Blues from Waitin'/ I Can't Escape from You	1953	25.00
❑ 11628	Calling You/When God Comes and Gathers His Jewels	1953	25.00
❑ 11675	You Better Keep It on Your Mind/Low Down Blues	1954	25.00
❑ 11707	How Can You Refuse Him Now/ A House of Gold	1954	25.00
❑ 11768	I Ain't Got Nothin' But Time/ I'm Satisfied with You	1954	25.00
❑ 11861	Angel of Death/(I'm Gonna) Sing, Sing, Sing	1954	25.00
❑ 11928	Please Don't Let Me Love You/ Faded Love and Winter's Roses	1955	25.00
❑ 11975	Message to My Mother/ Mother Is Gone	1955	25.00
❑ 12029	A Teardrop on a Rose/ Alone and Forsaken	1955	25.00
❑ 12077	Someday You'll Call My Name/ The First Fall of Snow	1955	25.00
❑ 12127	The Battle of Armageddon/ Thank God	1955	25.00
❑ 12185	California Zephyr/Thy Burdens Are Greater Than Mine	1956	25.00
❑ 12244	I Wish I Had a Nickel/There's No Room in My Heart	1956	25.00
❑ 12332	Blue Love (In My Heart)/ Singing Waterfall	1956	25.00
❑ 12394	The Pale Horse and His Rider/ A Home in Heaven	1956	20.00
—As "Hank and Audrey Williams"			

W

Number	Title (A Side/B Side)	Yr	NM
❑ 12438	Ready to Go Home/We're Getting Closer	1957	20.00
❑ 12484	Leave Me Alone with the Blues/With Tears in My Eyes	1957	20.00
❑ 12535	No One Will Ever Know/The Waltz of the Wind	1957	20.00
❑ 12611	Why Don't You Love Me/I Can't Help It (If I'm Still in Love with You)	1958	20.00
❑ 12635	We Live in Two Different Worlds/My Bucket's Got a Hole In It	1958	20.00
❑ 12727	Just Waitin'/Roly-Poly	1958	20.00
❑ 13305	Your Cheatin' Heart/Lovesick Blues	1964	12.00
❑ 13305 [PS]	Your Cheatin' Heart/Lovesick Blues	1964	20.00
❑ 13359	Cold, Cold Heart/Pale Horse and His Rider	1965	12.00
❑ 13489	I'm So Lonesome I Could Cry/You Win Again	1966	12.00
❑ 13542	Kaw-Liga/Let's Turn Back the Years	1966	12.00
❑ 13630	There'll Be No Teardrops Tonight/They'll Never Take Her Love from Me	1966	12.00
❑ 13717	Long Gone Lonesome Blues/Hang On the Bell, Nellie	1967	12.00
❑ 14849	Why Don't You Love Me/Ramblin' Man	1976	6.00

7-Inch Extended Plays

MGM

Number	Title (A Side/B Side)	Yr	NM
❑ X-168 [PS]	Moanin' the Blues	1953	40.00
—Cover with X-4041 and X-4042			
❑ X-202 [PS]	The Hank Williams Memorial Album	1953	40.00
—Cover with X-4102 and X-4103			
❑ X-242 [PS]	Honky Tonkin'	1954	40.00
—Cover for X4108 and X4109			
❑ X-243 [PS]	I Saw the Light	195?	40.00
—Cover with X-4110 and X-4111			
❑ X-1014	Crazy Heart/Baby We're Really in Love//My Heart Would Know/I Can't Help It (If I'm Still in Love with You)	1953	80.00
—Yellow label			
❑ X-1014	Crazy Heart/Baby We're Really in Love//My Heart Would Know/I Can't Help It (If I'm Still in Love with You)	1960	20.00
—Black label			
❑ X-1014 [PS]	Crazy Heart	1953	20.00
❑ X-1047	Pictures from Life's Other Side/Men with Broken Hearts//Help Me Understand/Too Many Parties (And Too Many Pals)	1954	60.00
—Yellow label			
❑ X-1047	Pictures from Life's Other Side/Men with Broken Hearts//Help Me Understand/Too Many Parties (And Too Many Pals)	1960	20.00
—Black label			
❑ X-1047 [PS]	Hank Williams as Luke the Drifter	1954	20.00
❑ X-1076	Move It On Over/Fly Trouble//Window Shopping/Pan American	1954	60.00
—Yellow label			
❑ X-1076	Move It On Over/Fly Trouble//Window Shopping/Pan American	1960	20.00
—Black label			
❑ X-1076 [PS]	Move It On Over	1954	20.00
❑ X-1082	There'll Be No Tear-Drops Tonight/You're Gonna Change (Or I'm Gonna Leave)//Nobody's Lonesome for Me/Mind Your Own Business	1954	60.00
❑ X-1082	There'll Be No Tear-Drops Tonight/You're Gonna Change (Or I'm Gonna Leave)//Nobody's Lonesome for Me/Mind Your Own Business	1960	20.00
—Black label			
❑ X-1082 [PS]	There'll Be No Teardrops Tonight	1954	20.00
❑ X-1101	I Saw the Light/Mansion on the Hill//Six More Miles/Wedding Bells	1955	60.00
—Yellow label			
❑ X-1101	I Saw the Light/Mansion on the Hill//Six More Miles/Wedding Bells	1960	20.00
—Black label			
❑ X-1101 [PS]	Hank Williams Sings	1955	20.00
❑ X-1102	Lost Highway/I've Just Told Mama Goodbye//Wealth Won't Save Your Soul/A House Without Love	1955	60.00
—Yellow label			
❑ X-1102	Lost Highway/I've Just Told Mama Goodbye//Wealth Won't Save Your Soul/A House Without Love	1960	20.00
—Black label			
❑ X-1102 [PS]	Hank Williams Sings Vol. 2	1955	20.00
❑ X-1135	Ramblin' Man/My Son Calls Another Man Daddy//I Can't Escape from You/Nobody's Lonesome for Me	1955	40.00
—Yellow label			
❑ X-1135	Ramblin' Man/My Son Calls Another Man Daddy//I Can't Escape from You/Nobody's Lonesome for Me	1960	15.00
—Black label			
❑ X-1135 [PS]	Ramblin' Man Vol. 1	1955	15.00
❑ X-1136	Lonesome Whistle/I Jus' Don't Like This Kind of Livin'//Take These Chains from My Heart/Why Don't You Love Me?	1955	40.00
—Yellow label			
❑ X-1136	Lonesome Whistle/I Jus' Don't Like This Kind of Livin'//Take These Chains from My Heart/Why Don't You Love Me?	1960	15.00
—Black label			
❑ X-1136 [PS]	Ramblin' Man Vol. 2	1955	15.00
❑ X-1165	Why Don't You Make Up Your Mind/I've Been Down That Road Before//Just Waitin'/Everything's Okay	1955	40.00
—Yellow label			
❑ X-1165	Why Don't You Make Up Your Mind/I've Been Down That Road Before//Just Waitin'/Everything's Okay	1960	15.00
—Black label			
❑ X-1165 [PS]	Luke the Drifter	1955	15.00
❑ X-1215	Low Down Blues/Someday You'll Call My Name//Alone and Forsaken/Weary Blues From Waitin'	1956	40.00
—Yellow label			
❑ X-1215	Low Down Blues/Someday You'll Call My Name//Alone and Forsaken/Weary Blues From Waitin'	1960	15.00
—Black label			
❑ X-1215 [PS]	Moanin' the Blues Vol. 1	1956	15.00
❑ X-1216	Moanin' the Blues/I'm So Lonesome I Could Cry//My Sweet Love Ain't Around/Honky Tonk Blues	1956	40.00
—Yellow label			
❑ X-1216	Moanin' the Blues/I'm So Lonesome I Could Cry//My Sweet Love Ain't Around/Honky Tonk Blues	1960	15.00
—Black label			
❑ X-1216 [PS]	Moanin' the Blues Vol. 2	1956	15.00
❑ X-1217	Lovesick Blues/The Blues Come Around//I'm a Long Gone Daddy/Long Gone Lonesome Blues	1956	40.00
—Yellow label			
❑ X-1217	Lovesick Blues/The Blues Come Around//I'm a Long Gone Daddy/Long Gone Lonesome Blues	1960	15.00
—Black label			
❑ X-1217 [PS]	Moanin' the Blues Vol. 3	1956	15.00
❑ X-1218	I'm Gonna Sing/Message to My Mother//Thank God/The Angel of Death	1956	40.00
—Yellow label			
❑ X-1218	I'm Gonna Sing/Message to My Mother//Thank God/The Angel of Death	1960	15.00
—Black label			
❑ X-1218 [PS]	I Saw the Light	1956	15.00
❑ X-1235	*Honky Tonkin'/Mind Your Own Business/Rootie Tootie/I Ain't Got Nothing But Time	1956	40.00
—Yellow label			
❑ X-1235	*Honky Tonkin'/Mind Your Own Business/Rootie Tootie/I Ain't Got Nothing But Time	1960	15.00
—Black label			
❑ X-1235 [PS]	Honky Tonkin'	1956	15.00
❑ X-1317	Jambalaya (On the Bayou)/I Won't Be Home No More//Honky Tonk Blues/I'll Never Get Out of This World Alive	1957	40.00
—Yellow label			
❑ X-1317	Jambalaya (On the Bayou)/I Won't Be Home No More//Honky Tonk Blues/I'll Never Get Out of This World Alive	1960	15.00
—Black label			
❑ X-1317 [PS]	Honky Tonkin' Vol. 1	1957	15.00
❑ X-1318	Honky Tonkin'/Howlin' at the Moon//My Bucket's Got a Hole in It/Baby, We're Really in Love	1957	40.00
—Yellow label			
❑ X-1318	Honky Tonkin'/Howlin' at the Moon//My Bucket's Got a Hole in It/Baby, We're Really in Love	1960	15.00
—Black label			
❑ X-1318 [PS]	Honky Tonkin' Vol. 2	1957	15.00
❑ X-1319	Mind Your Own Business/Rootie Tootie//I Ain't Got Nothin' But Time/You Better Keep It on Your Mind	1957	40.00
—Yellow label			
❑ X-1319	Mind Your Own Business/Rootie Tootie//I Ain't Got Nothin' But Time/You Better Keep It on Your Mind	1960	15.00
—Black label			
❑ X-1319 [PS]	Honky Tonkin' Vol. 3	1957	15.00
❑ X-1491	Wedding Bells/May You Never Be Alone//Lost Highway/Why Should We Try Anymore	1958	30.00
—Yellow label			
❑ X-1491	Wedding Bells/May You Never Be Alone//Lost Highway/Why Should We Try Anymore	1960	15.00
—Black label			
❑ X-1491 [PS]	Sing Me a Blue Song Vol. 1	1958	15.00
❑ X-1492	I Heard You Crying in Your Sleep/Blue Love//Mansion on the Hill/They'll Never Take Her Love from Me	1958	30.00
—Yellow label			
❑ X-1492	I Heard You Crying in Your Sleep/Blue Love//Mansion on the Hill/They'll Never Take Her Love from Me	1960	15.00
—Black label			
❑ X-1492 [PS]	Sing Me a Blue Song Vol. 2	1958	15.00
❑ X-1493	I've Just Told Mama Goodbye/House Without Love//Six More Miles/Singing Waterfall	1958	30.00
—Yellow label			
❑ X-1493	I've Just Told Mama Goodbye/House Without Love//Six More Miles/Singing Waterfall	1960	15.00
—Black label			
❑ X-1493 [PS]	Sing Me a Blue Song Vol. 3	1958	15.00
❑ X-1554	There's No Room in My Heart/Waltz of the Wind//Pan American/With Tears in My Eyes	1958	30.00
—Yellow label			
❑ X-1554	There's No Room in My Heart/Waltz of the Wind//Pan American/With Tears in My Eyes	1960	15.00
—Black label			
❑ X-1554 [PS]	The Immortal Hank Williams Vol. 1	1958	15.00
❑ X-1555	I Wish I Had a Nickel/Fly Trouble//Please Don't Let Me Love You/I'm Satisfied with You	1958	30.00
—Yellow label			
❑ X-1555	I Wish I Had a Nickel/Fly Trouble//Please Don't Let Me Love You/I'm Satisfied with You	1960	15.00
—Black label			
❑ X-1555 [PS]	The Immortal Hank Williams Vol. 2	1958	15.00
❑ X-1556	No One Will Ever Know/Faded Love and Winter Roses//First Fall of Snow/California Zephyr	1958	30.00
—Yellow label			
❑ X-1556	No One Will Ever Know/Faded Love and Winter Roses//First Fall of Snow/California Zephyr	1960	15.00
—Black label			
❑ X-1556 [PS]	The Immortal Hank Williams Vol. 3	1958	15.00
❑ X-1612	Your Cheatin' Heart/Settin' the Woods on Fire//You Win Again/Hey, Good Lookin'	1959	30.00
—Yellow label			
❑ X-1612	Your Cheatin' Heart/Settin' the Woods on Fire//You Win Again/Hey, Good Lookin'	1960	15.00
—Black label			
❑ X-1612 [PS]	Hank Williams Memorial Album Vol. 1	1959	15.00
❑ X-1613	Cold, Cold Heart/Kaw-Liga//I Could Never Be Ashamed of You/Half As Much	1959	30.00
—Yellow label			
❑ X-1613	Cold, Cold Heart/Kaw-Liga//I Could Never Be Ashamed of You/Half As Much	1960	15.00
—Black label			

W

Except when noted otherwise, VG = 25% of NM, and VG+ = 50% of NM. (Example: VG = $2.00, VG+ = $4.00 and NM = $8.00.)

Number	Title (A Side/B Side)	Yr	NM
❑ X-1613 [PS]	Hank Williams Memorial Album Vol. 2	1959	15.00
❑ X-1636	Crazy Heart/Move It On Over//My Heart Would Know/I'm Sorry for You My Friend	1959	30.00
—Yellow label			
❑ X-1636	Crazy Heart/Move It On Over//My Heart Would Know/I'm Sorry for You My Friend	1960	15.00
—Black label			
❑ X-1636 [PS]	Hank Williams Memorial Album Vol. 3	1959	15.00
❑ X-1637	*I Can't Get You Off My Mind/I Don't Care (If Tomorrow Never Comes)/Dear John/My Love for You (Has Turned to Hate)	1959	15.00
—Black label			
❑ X-1637	*I Can't Get You Off My Mind/I Don't Care (If Tomorrow Never Comes)/Dear John/My Love for You (Has Turned to Hate)	1959	30.00
—Yellow label			
❑ X-1637 [PS]	The Unforgettable Hank Williams, Vol. 1	1959	15.00
❑ X-1638	On the Banks of the Old Ponchartrain/We Live in Two Different Worlds//I'll Be a Bachelor 'Til I Die/Let's Turn Back the Years	1959	30.00
—Yellow label			
❑ X-1638	On the Banks of the Old Ponchartrain/We Live in Two Different Worlds//I'll Be a Bachelor 'Til I Die/Let's Turn Back the Years	1960	15.00
—Black label			
❑ X-1638 [PS]	The Unforgettable Hank Williams, Vol. 2	1959	15.00
❑ X-1643	Pictures from Life's Other Side/Men with Broken Hearts//Help Me Understand/Too Many Parties and Too Many Pals	1959	30.00
—Yellow label			
❑ X-1643	Pictures from Life's Other Side/Men with Broken Hearts//Help Me Understand/Too Many Parties and Too Many Pals	1960	15.00
—Black label			
❑ X-1643 [PS]	Hank Williams as Luke the Drifter	1959	15.00
❑ X-1644	Be Careful of Stones That You Throw/I Dreamed About Mama Last Night//Funeral/Beyond the Sunset	1959	30.00
—Yellow label			
❑ X-1644	Be Careful of Stones That You Throw/I Dreamed About Mama Last Night//Funeral/Beyond the Sunset	1960	15.00
—Black label			
❑ X-1644 [PS]	Hank Williams as Luke the Drifter	1959	15.00
❑ X-1698	(contents unknown)	1960	15.00
❑ X-1698 [PS]	The Lonesome Sound of Hank Williams Vol. 1	1960	15.00
❑ X-1699	I'm Free at Last/Roly Poly//The Old Home/Rock My Cradle (Once Again)	1960	15.00
❑ X-1699 [PS]	The Lonesome Sound of Hank Williams Vol. 2	1960	15.00
❑ X-1700	(contents unknown)	1960	15.00
❑ X-1700 [PS]	The Lonesome Sound of Hank Williams Vol. 3	1960	15.00
❑ X-4041	Moanin' the Blues/I'm So Lonesome I Could Cry//My Sweet Love Ain't Around/Honky Tonk Blues	1953	40.00
—One record of "X168"			
❑ X-4042	Lovesick Blues/The Blues Come Around//I'm a Long Gone Daddy/Long Gone Lonesome Blues	1953	40.00
—One record of "X168"			
❑ X-4102	Your Cheatin' Heart/Settin' the Woods on Fire//You Win Again/Hey, Good Lookin'	1953	40.00
—One record of "X202"			
❑ X-4103	Cold, Cold Heart/Kaw-Liga//I Could Never Be Ashamed of You/Half As Much	1953	40.00
—One record of "X202"			
❑ X-4108	Honky Tonkin'/Howlin' at the Moon//My Bucket's Got a Hole in It/Baby, We're Really in Love	1954	40.00
—One record of "X242"			
❑ X-4109	Jambalaya (On the Bayou)/I Won't Be Home No More//Honky Tonk Blues/I'll Never Get Out of This World Alive	1954	40.00
—One record of "X242"			

Number	Title (A Side/B Side)	Yr	NM
❑ X-4110	I Saw the Light/Calling You//Dear Brother/Wealth Won't Save Your Soul	195?	40.00
—One record of "X243"			
❑ X-4111	How Can You Refuse Him Now/When God Comes and Gathers His Jewels//Just Remember Me/House of God	195?	40.00
—One record of "X243"			
❑ SLM-4377	I'm So Lonesome I Could Cry/You Win Again/Kaw-Liga//Lovesick Blues/Let's Turn Back the Years/I'm Sorry for You, My Friend	1966	25.00
—Jukebox issue; small hole, plays at 33 1/3 rpm			
❑ SLM-4377 [PS]	The Legend Lives Anew — Hank Williams with Strings	1966	25.00
Albums			
CANDELITE MUSIC			
❑ CMI-1951/2 [(2)]	The Golden Dream of Hank Williams	1976	15.00
COUNTRY MUSIC FOUNDATION			
❑ CMF-006	Just Me and My Guitar	198?	10.00
❑ CMF-007	The First Recordings	198?	10.00
METRO			
❑ M-509 [M]	Hank Williams	1966	20.00
❑ MS-509 [R]	Hank Williams	1966	12.00
❑ M-547 [M]	Mr. and Mrs. Hank Williams	1966	20.00
❑ MS-547 [R]	Mr. and Mrs. Hank Williams	1966	12.00
❑ M-602 [M]	The Immortal Hank Williams	1967	20.00
❑ MS-602 [R]	The Immortal Hank Williams	1967	12.00
MGM			
❑ 3E-2 [(3)M]	36 of His Greatest Hits	1957	200.00
—Yellow labels			
❑ 3E-2 [(3)M]	36 of His Greatest Hits	1960	100.00
—Black labels			
❑ 3E-4 [(3)M]	Hank Williams Sings 36 More of His Greatest Hits	1958	200.00
—Yellow labels			
❑ 3E-4 [(3)M]	Hank Williams Sings 36 More of His Greatest Hits	1960	100.00
—Black labels			
❑ E-107 [10]	Hank Williams Sings	1952	400.00
❑ E-168 [10]	Moanin' the Blues	1952	400.00
❑ E-202 [10]	Memorial Album	1953	400.00
❑ E-203 [10]	Hank Williams as Luke the Drifter	1953	400.00
❑ SE 240-2 [(2)]	24 Karat Hits	1969	25.00
❑ E-242 [10]	Honky Tonkin'	1954	400.00
❑ E-243 [10]	I Saw the Light	1954	400.00
❑ E-291 [10]	Ramblin' Man	1954	400.00
❑ PRO-912 [(3)DJ]	Reflections of Those Who Loved Him	1975	250.00
—Promo-only box set			
❑ E-3219 [M]	Ramblin' Man	1955	100.00
—Yellow label			
❑ E-3219 [M]	Ramblin' Man	1960	40.00
—Black label			
❑ E-3267 [M]	Hank Williams as Luke the Drifter	1955	100.00
—Yellow label			
❑ E-3267 [M]	Hank Williams as Luke the Drifter	1960	40.00
—Black label			
❑ E-3272 [M]	Memorial Album	1955	100.00
—Yellow label			
❑ E-3272 [M]	Memorial Album	1960	40.00
—Black label			
❑ E-3272 [M]	Memorial Album	1968	20.00
—Blue and gold label			
❑ E-3330 [M]	Moanin' the Blues	1956	100.00
—Yellow label			
❑ E-3330 [M]	Moanin' the Blues	1960	40.00
—Black label			
❑ E-3331 [M]	I Saw the Light	1956	200.00
—Yellow label; green cover			
❑ E-3331 [M]	I Saw the Light	1959	100.00
—Yellow label; church on cover			
❑ E-3331 [M]	I Saw the Light	1960	40.00
—Black label			
❑ SE-3331 [R]	I Saw the Light	1968	12.00
—Blue and gold label			
❑ E-3412 [M]	Honky Tonkin'	1957	100.00
—Yellow label			
❑ E-3412 [M]	Honky Tonkin'	1960	40.00
—Black label			
❑ E-3560 [M]	Sing Me a Blue Song	1957	100.00
—Yellow label			
❑ E-3560 [M]	Sing Me a Blue Song	1960	40.00
—Black label			
❑ E-3605 [M]	The Immortal Hank Williams	1958	100.00
—Yellow label			
❑ E-3605 [M]	The Immortal Hank Williams	1960	40.00
—Black label			
❑ E-3733 [M]	The Unforgettable Hank Williams	1959	100.00
—Yellow label			
❑ E-3733 [M]	The Unforgettable Hank Williams	1960	40.00
—Black label			
❑ SE-3733 [R]	The Unforgettable Hank Williams	1968	12.00
—Blue and gold label			

Number	Title (A Side/B Side)	Yr	NM
❑ E-3803 [M]	The Lonesome Sound of Hank Williams	1960	40.00
❑ E-3850 [M]	Wait for the Light to Shine	1960	40.00
❑ SE-3850 [R]	Wait for the Light to Shine	1968	12.00
—Blue and gold label			
❑ E-3918 [M]	Hank Williams' Greatest Hits	1961	40.00
❑ SE-3918 [R]	Hank Williams' Greatest Hits	1963	20.00
—Black label			
❑ SE-3918 [R]	Hank Williams' Greatest Hits	1968	12.00
—Blue and gold label			
❑ E-3923 [M]	Hank Williams Lives Again	1961	40.00
—Reissue of E-3272 with new title			
❑ SE-3923 [R]	Hank Williams Lives Again	1968	12.00
—Blue and gold label			
❑ E-3924 [M]	Let Me Sing a Blue Song	1961	40.00
—Reissue of E-3560			
❑ SE-3924 [R]	Let Me Sing a Blue Song	1968	12.00
—Blue and gold label			
❑ E-3925 [M]	Wanderin' Around	1961	40.00
—Reissue of E-3219			
❑ SE-3925 [R]	Wanderin' Around	1968	12.00
—Blue and gold label			
❑ E-3926 [M]	I'm Blue Inside	1961	40.00
—Reissue of E-3330			
❑ SE-3926 [R]	I'm Blue Inside	1968	12.00
—Blue and gold label			
❑ E-3927 [M]	Hank Williams as Luke the Drifter	1961	40.00
—Reissue of E-3267			
❑ SE-3927 [R]	Hank Williams as Luke the Drifter	1968	12.00
—Blue and gold label			
❑ E-3928 [M]	First, Last and Always	1961	40.00
—Reissue of E-3605			
❑ SE-3928 [R]	First, Last and Always	1968	12.00
—Blue and gold label			
❑ E-3955 [M]	The Spirit of Hank Williams	1961	40.00
❑ SE-3955 [R]	The Spirit of Hank Williams	1968	12.00
—Blue and gold label			
❑ E-3999 [M]	Hank Williams on Stage Recorded Live	1962	40.00
—Note revised title			
❑ E-3999 [M]	On Stage! Hank Williams Recorded Live	1962	60.00
❑ SE-3999 [R]	On Stage! Hank Williams Recorded Live	196?	20.00
—Black label			
❑ SE-3999 [R]	Hank Williams on Stage Recorded Live	1968	12.00
—Blue and gold label			
❑ E-4040 [M]	14 More of Hank Williams' Greatest Hits — Vol. II	1962	40.00
❑ SE-4040 [R]	14 More of Hank Williams' Greatest Hits — Vol. II	1963	15.00
—Black label			
❑ SE-4040 [R]	Hank Williams' Greatest Hits, Vol. 2	1968	12.00
—Blue and gold label			
❑ E-4109 [M]	On Stage Vol. II/Hank Williams	1963	40.00
❑ SE-4109 [R]	On Stage Vol. II/Hank Williams	1963	20.00
—Black label			
❑ SE-4109 [R]	On Stage Vol. II/Hank Williams	1968	12.00
—Blue and gold label			
❑ E-4138 [M]	Beyond the Sunset	1963	30.00
❑ SE-4138 [R]	Beyond the Sunset	1963	15.00
—Black label			
❑ E-4140 [M]	14 More of Hank Williams' Greatest Hits (Vol. 3)	1963	30.00
❑ SE-4140 [R]	14 More of Hank Williams' Greatest Hits (Vol. 3)	1963	15.00
—Black label			
❑ SE-4140 [R]	14 More of Hank Williams' Greatest Hits (Vol. 3)	1968	12.00
—Blue and gold label			
❑ E-4168 [M]	The Very Best of Hank Williams	1963	30.00
❑ SE-4168 [R]	The Very Best of Hank Williams	1963	15.00
—Black label			
❑ SE-4168 [R]	The Very Best of Hank Williams	1968	12.00
—Blue and gold label			
❑ E-4227 [M]	The Very Best of Hank Williams, Vol. 2	1964	30.00
❑ SE-4227 [R]	The Very Best of Hank Williams, Vol. 2	1964	15.00
—Black label			
❑ SE-4227 [R]	The Very Best of Hank Williams, Vol. 2	1968	12.00
—Blue and gold label			
❑ E-4254 [M]	Lost Highway (and Other Folk Ballads)	1964	40.00
❑ SE-4254 [R]	Lost Highway (and Other Folk Ballads)	1964	20.00
—Black label			
❑ SE-4254 [R]	Lost Highway (and Other Folk Ballads)	1968	12.00
—Blue and gold label			
❑ E-4267-4 [(4)M]	The Hank Williams Story	1965	60.00
❑ E-4300 [M]	Kaw-Liga and Other Humorous Songs	1965	30.00
❑ SE-4300 [R]	Kaw-Liga and Other Humorous Songs	1965	15.00
—Black label			

Number	Title (A Side/B Side)	Yr	NM
❑ SE-4300 [R]	Kaw-Liga and Other Humorous Songs	1968	12.00
—Blue and gold label			
❑ E-4377 [M]	The Legend Lives Anew — Hank Williams with Strings	1966	20.00
❑ SE-4377 [S]	The Legend Lives Anew — Hank Williams with Strings	1966	25.00
—Black label			
❑ SE-4377 [S]	The Legend Lives Anew — Hank Williams with Strings	1968	15.00
—Blue and gold label			
❑ E-4380 [M]	Movin' on — Luke the Drifter	1966	30.00
❑ SE-4380 [R]	Movin' on — Luke the Drifter	1968	12.00
—Blue and gold label			
❑ E-4429 [M]	More Hank Williams and Strings	1966	20.00
❑ SE-4429 [S]	More Hank Williams and Strings	1966	25.00
—Black label			
❑ SE-4429 [S]	More Hank Williams and Strings	1968	15.00
—Blue and gold label			
❑ E-4481 [M]	I Won't Be Home No More	1967	30.00
❑ SE-4481 [S]	I Won't Be Home No More	1967	20.00
—Black label			
❑ SE-4481 [S]	I Won't Be Home No More	1968	15.00
—Blue and gold label			
❑ E-4529 [M]	Hank Williams and Strings, Vol. 3	1968	40.00
❑ SE-4529 [S]	Hank Williams and Strings, Vol. 3	1968	20.00
❑ E-4576 [M]	Hank Williams in the Beginning	1968	40.00
❑ SE-4576 [R]	Hank Williams in the Beginning	1968	15.00
❑ SE-4651	Essential Hank Williams	1969	12.00
❑ SE-4680	Life to Legend	1970	12.00
❑ SE-4755-2 [(2)]	24 Greatest Hits	1971	15.00
❑ M3G-4954	Archetypes	1974	12.00
❑ MG-1-5019	Hank Williams, Sr., Live at the Grand Old Opry	1976	12.00
❑ MG-2-5401 [(2)]	24 Greatest Hits, Vol. 2	197?	15.00
❑ ST-90511 [R]	The Very Best of Hank Williams	1965	20.00
—Capitol Record Club edition			
❑ T-90511 [M]	The Very Best of Hank Williams	1965	40.00
—Capitol Record Club edition			
❑ ST-90884 [R]	Movin' on — Luke the Drifter	1968	15.00
—Capitol Record Club edition; blue and gold label			
❑ ST-91115 [S]	The Legend Lives Anew — Hank Williams with Strings	1968	20.00
—Capitol Record Club edition; blue and gold label			

POLYDOR

Number	Title (A Side/B Side)	Yr	NM
❑ SE-4168	The Very Best of Hank Williams	1976	8.00
—Reissue of MGM SE-4168			
❑ 821233-1 [(2)]	40 Greatest Hits	1984	15.00
❑ 823291-1	Hank Williams' Greatest Hits	1984	8.00
❑ 823292-1	The Very Best of Hank Williams	1984	8.00
❑ 823293-1 [(2)]	24 Greatest Hits	1984	12.00
❑ 823294-1 [(2)]	24 Greatest Hits, Vol. 2	1984	12.00
❑ 823695-1	Rare Takes and Radio Cuts	1984	10.00
❑ 825531-1	On the Air	1985	10.00
❑ 825548-1	I Ain't Got Nothin' But Time	1985	10.00
❑ 825551-1	Lovesick Blues	1985	10.00
❑ 825554-1	Lost Highway	1986	10.00
❑ 825557-1	I'm So Lonesome I Could Cry	1986	10.00
❑ 831574-1	Beyond the Sunset	1987	10.00
❑ 831633-1	Long Gone Lonesome Blues	1987	10.00
❑ 831634-1	Hey, Good Lookin'	1987	10.00
❑ 833749-1	Let's Turn Back the Years	1988	10.00
❑ 833752-1	I Won't Be Home No More	1988	10.00

TIME-LIFE

Number	Title (A Side/B Side)	Yr	NM
❑ TLCW-01 [(3)]	Country and Western Classics	1981	25.00
❑ STW-118	Country Music	1981	10.00

WILLIAMS, HANK /ROY ACUFF

Albums

LAMB AND LION

Number	Title (A Side/B Side)	Yr	NM
❑ LL-706 [(3)]	Hank Williams, Sr./Roy Acuff "Collector's Item!"	197?	40.00
—Sides 1-4 are reissues of Hank Williams; side 5-6 are Roy Acuff			

WILLIAMS, HANK, AND HANK WILLIAMS, JR.

Also see each artist's individual listings.

Albums

MGM

Number	Title (A Side/B Side)	Yr	NM
❑ E-4276 [M]	Father and Son	1965	20.00
❑ SE-4276 [S]	Father and Son	1965	25.00
❑ E-4378 [M]	Again	1966	20.00
❑ SE-4378 [S]	Again	1966	25.00
❑ 2SES-4865 [(2)]	Hank Williams: The Legend in Story and Song	1973	15.00
❑ M3HB 4975 [(2)]	Insights Into Hank Williams in Song and Story	1974	15.00

WILLIAMS, HANK, JR.

12-Inch Singles

WARNER BROS.

Number	Title (A Side/B Side)	Yr	NM
❑ PRO-A-2088 [DJ]	Woman on the Run (same on both sides)	1983	8.00
❑ PRO-A-2662 [DJ]	My Name Is Bocephus (same on both sides)	1987	8.00

45s

CAPRICORN

Number	Title (A Side/B Side)	Yr	NM
❑ 18486	Diamond Mine/Dirty Mind	1993	3.00
❑ 18614	Everything Comes Down to Money and Love/S.O.B. I'm Tired	1993	3.00
❑ 18800	Lyin' Jukebox/Fax Me a Beer	1992	3.00
❑ 18923	Come On Over to the Country/Wild Weekend	1992	3.00
❑ 19023	Hotel Whiskey/The Count Song	1992	3.00

ELEKTRA

Number	Title (A Side/B Side)	Yr	NM
❑ 46018	To Love Somebody/We Can Work It All Out	1979	5.00
❑ 46046	Family Tradition/Paying On Time	1979	5.00
❑ 46535	Whiskey Bent and Hell Bound/O.D.'d in Denver	1979	5.00
❑ 46593	Women I've Never Had/Tired of Being Johnny B. Goode	1980	5.00
❑ 46636	Kaw-Liga/The American Way	1980	5.00
❑ 47012	If You Don't Like Hank Williams/Outlaw Women	1980	6.00
❑ 47016	Old Habits/Won't It Be Nice	1980	5.00
❑ 47102	Texas Women/You Can't Find Many Kisses	1981	5.00
❑ 47137	Dixie on My Mind/Ramblin' Man	1981	5.00
❑ 47191	All My Rowdy Friends (Have Settled Down)/Everytime I Hear That Song	1981	5.00
❑ 47231 [DJ]	Little Drummer Boy/The Christmas Song	1981	8.00
—B-side by Sonny Curtis			
❑ 47257	A Country Boy Can Survive/Weatherman	1982	5.00
❑ 47462	Honky Tonkin'/High and Pressurized	1982	5.00
❑ 69846	Gonna Go Huntin' Tonight/Twodot, Montana	1983	4.00
❑ 69960	The American Dream/If Heaven Ain't a Lot Like Dixie	1982	4.00

MCG CURB

Number	Title (A Side/B Side)	Yr	NM
❑ 76932	I Ain't Goin' Peacefully/Greeted in Enid	1995	4.00
❑ 76948	Hog Wild/Wild Thing	1995	4.00

MGM

Number	Title (A Side/B Side)	Yr	NM
❑ 13208	Long Gone Lonesome Blues/Doesn't Anybody Know My Name	1964	12.00
❑ 13208 [PS]	Long Gone Lonesome Blues/Doesn't Anybody Know My Name	1964	20.00
❑ 13253	Guess What, That's Right, She's Gone/Goin' Steady with the Blues	1964	12.00
❑ 13253 [PS]	Guess What, That's Right, She's Gone/Goin' Steady with the Blues	1964	25.00
❑ 13278	Endless Sleep/My Bucket's Got a Hole In It	1964	12.00
❑ 13318	I'm So Lonesome I Could Cry/Is It That Much Fun to Hurt Someone	1965	12.00
❑ 13318 [PS]	I'm So Lonesome I Could Cry/Is It That Much Fun to Hurt Someone	1965	20.00
❑ 13353	I Went to All That Trouble for Nothin'/Mule Skinner Blues	1965	12.00
❑ 13392	Pecos Jail/You're Ruinin' My Life	1965	12.00
❑ 13392 [PS]	Pecos Jail/You're Ruinin' My Life	1965	25.00
❑ 13443	Rainmaker/The River	1966	12.00
❑ 13504	Standing in the Shadows/It's Written All Over Your Face	1966	12.00
❑ 13640	I Can't Take It No Longer/You Can Hear a Tear Drop	1966	12.00
❑ 13730	I'm In No Condition/I'm Gonna Break Your Heart	1967	12.00
❑ 13782	Nobody's Child/The Next Best Thing to Nothing	1967	12.00
❑ 13857	I Wouldn't Change a Thing About You (But Your Name)/No Meaning and No End	1967	12.00
❑ 13922	The Old Ryman/I Wonder Where You Are Tonight	1968	10.00
❑ 13968	It's All Over But the Crying/Rock in My Shoes	1968	10.00
❑ 14002	I Was With Red Foley (The Night He Passed Away)/On Trial	1968	12.00
—As "Luke the Drifter, Jr."			
❑ 14020	Custody/My Home Town Circle "R"	1968	12.00
—As "Luke the Drifter, Jr."			
❑ 14024	A Baby Again/Swim Across a Tear	1969	10.00
❑ 14047	Cajun Baby/My Heart Won't Let Me Go	1969	10.00
❑ 14062	Be Careful of Stones That You Throw/Book of Memories	1969	10.00
—As "Luke the Drifter, Jr."			
❑ 14077	I'd Rather Be Gone/Try, Try Again	1969	10.00
❑ 14095	Something to Think About/(There Must Be) A Better Way to Love	1969	10.00
—As "Luke the Drifter, Jr."			
❑ 14107	I Walked Out on Heaven/Your Love's One Thing	1970	8.00
❑ 14120	It Don't Take But One Mistake/Goin' Home	1970	8.00
—As "Luke the Drifter, Jr."			
❑ 14152	All for the Love of Sunshine/Ballad of the Moonshine	1970	8.00
❑ 14194	Rainin' in My Heart/A-Eee	1970	8.00
❑ 14240	I've Got a Right to Cry/Jesus Loved the Devil Out of Me	1971	8.00
❑ 14277	After All They All Used to Belong to Me/Happy Kind of Sadness	1971	8.00
❑ 14317	Ain't That a Shame/End of a Bad Day	1971	8.00
❑ 14371	Eleven Roses/Richmond Valley Breeze	1972	8.00
❑ 14421	Pride's Not Hard to Swallow/Hamburger Steak, Holiday Inn	1972	8.00
❑ 14486	After You/Knoxville Courthouse Blues	1973	6.00
❑ 14550	Hank/Hank (Part 2)	1973	6.00
❑ 14656	The Last Love Song/Those Tear Jerking Songs	1973	6.00
❑ 14700	Rainy Night in Georgia/Country Music in My Soul	1974	6.00
❑ 14731	I'll Think of Something/Country Music Lover	1974	6.00
❑ 14755	Angels Are Hard to Find/Getting Over You	1974	6.00
❑ 14794	Where He's Going, I've Already Gone/The Kind of Woman I've Got	1975	6.00
❑ 14813	The Same Old Story/Country Love	1975	6.00
❑ 14833	Stoned at the Jukebox/The Devil in the Bottle	1975	6.00
❑ 14845	Living Proof/Brothers of the Road	1976	6.00

VERVE

Number	Title (A Side/B Side)	Yr	NM
❑ 10540	Meter Reader Maid/Just a Dream	1967	50.00
—As "Bocephus"			
❑ 10572	Mental Revenge/Splish Splash	1967	40.00
—As "Bocephus"			

WARNER BROS.

Number	Title (A Side/B Side)	Yr	NM
❑ PRO-S-3838 [DJ]	All My Rowdy Friends (Are Here on Monday Night) (same on both sides)	1989	15.00
❑ PRO-S-4492 [DJ]	Don't Give Us a Reason (same on both sides)	1990	8.00
❑ 8345	She's the Star (On the Stage of My Mind)/Call Me, Honey, Won't You	1977	5.00
❑ 8361	Mobile Boogie/She's the Star (On the Stage of My Mind)	1977	5.00
❑ 8410	I'm Not Responsible/(Honey, Won't You) Call Me	1977	5.00
❑ 8451	One Night Stands/I'm Not Responsible	1977	5.00
❑ 8507	Feelin' Better/Once and For All	1977	5.00
❑ 8549	The New South/Storms Never Last	1978	6.00
❑ 8564	You Love the Thunder/I Just Ain't Been Able	1978	5.00
❑ 8641	I Fought the Law/It's Different with You	1978	5.00
❑ 8715	Old Flame, New Fire/Payin' On Time	1978	5.00
❑ 19193	Angels Are Hard to Find/Hollywood Honeys	1991	3.00
❑ 19352	If It Will It Will/Won't It Be Nice	1991	3.00
❑ 19463	I Mean I Love You/Stoned at the Jukebox	1990	3.00
❑ 19542	Don't Give Us a Reason/U.S.A. Today	1990	3.00
❑ 19818	Man to Man/Whiskey Bent and Hell Bound	1990	3.00
❑ 19872	Good Friends, Good Whiskey, Good Lovin'/Family Tradition	1990	3.00
❑ 19957	Ain't Nobody's Business/Big Mamou	1990	3.00
❑ 22945	Finders Are Keepers/What You Don't Know (Won't Hurt You)	1989	3.00
❑ 27584	There's a Tear in My Beer/You Brought Me Down to Earth	1989	4.00
—A-side with Hank Williams Sr.			
❑ 27584 [PS]	There's a Tear in My Beer/You Brought Me Down to Earth	1989	4.00
❑ 27722	Early in the Morning and Late at Night/I'm Just a Man	1988	3.00
❑ 27722 [PS]	Early in the Morning and Late at Night/I'm Just a Man	1988	4.00

W

Except when noted otherwise, VG = 25% of NM, and VG+ = 50% of NM. (Example: VG = $2.00, VG+ = $4.00 and NM = $8.00.)

Number	Title (A Side/B Side)	Yr	NM
❑ 27862	If the South Woulda Won/ Wild Streak	1988	3.00
❑ 27862 [PS]	If the South Woulda Won/ Wild Streak	1988	4.00
❑ 28120	Young Country/Buck Naked	1988	3.00
❑ 28120 [PS]	Young Country/Buck Naked	1988	4.00
❑ 28227	Heaven Can't Be Found/ Doctor's Song	1987	3.00
❑ 28227 [PS]	Heaven Can't Be Found/ Doctor's Song	1987	4.00
❑ 28369	Born to Boogie/What It Boils Down To	1987	3.00
❑ 28452	When Something Is Good (Why Does It Change)/ Loving Instructor	1987	3.00
❑ 28581	Mind Your Own Business/ My Name Is Bocephus	1986	4.00
❑ 28691	Country State of Mind/ Fat Friends	1986	4.00
❑ 28794	Ain't Misbehavin'/ I've Been Around	1986	4.00
❑ 28912	This Ain't Dallas/ I Really Like Girls	1985	4.00
❑ 29022	I'm for Love/Lawyers, Guns and Money	1985	4.00
❑ 29095	Major Moves/Mr. Lincoln	1985	4.00
❑ 29184	All My Rowdy Friends Are Coming Over Tonight/ Video Blues	1984	4.00
❑ 29253	Attitude Adjustment/ Knoxville Courthouse Blues	1984	4.00
❑ 29382	Man of Steel/Now I Know How George Feels	1984	4.00
❑ 29500	Queen of My Heart/She Had Me	1983	4.00
❑ 29633	Leave Them Boys Alone/The Girl in the Front Row at Fort Worth	1983	4.00

7-Inch Extended Plays

MGM

Number	Title (A Side/B Side)	Yr	NM
❑ SLM-4316	Cowpoke/Big Twenty/The Blizzard//Streets of Laredo/ The River†	1966	15.00
—Jukebox issue; small hole, plays at 33 1/3 rpm			
❑ SLM-4316 [PS]	Ballads of the Hills and Plains	1966	15.00

Albums

CAPRICORN

Number	Title (A Side/B Side)	Yr	NM
❑ W1-26806	Maverick	1992	20.00
—Columbia House edition (only U.S. vinyl release)			

ELEKTRA

Number	Title (A Side/B Side)	Yr	NM
❑ 6E-194	Family Tradition	1979	12.00
❑ 6E-237	Whiskey Bent and Hell Bound	1979	10.00
❑ 6E-278	Habits Old and New	1980	10.00
❑ 6E-330	Rowdy	1981	10.00
❑ 5E-535	The Pressure Is On	1981	10.00
❑ 5E-538	One Night Stands	1982	10.00
—Reissue			
❑ 5E-539	The New South	1982	10.00
—Reissue			
❑ 60100	High Notes	1982	10.00
❑ 60193	Hank Williams, Jr.'s, Greatest Hits	1982	10.00
❑ 60223	Strong Stuff	1983	15.00

MGM

Number	Title (A Side/B Side)	Yr	NM
❑ GAS-119	Hank Williams, Jr. (Golden Archive Series)	1970	15.00
❑ E-4213 [M]	Sings the Songs of Hank Williams	1964	20.00
❑ SE-4213 [S]	Sings the Songs of Hank Williams	1964	25.00
❑ E-4260 [M]	Your Cheatin' Heart	1964	20.00
❑ SE-4260 [S]	Your Cheatin' Heart	1964	25.00
❑ E-4316 [M]	Ballads of the Hills and Plains	1965	20.00
❑ SE-4316 [S]	Ballads of the Hills and Plains	1965	25.00
❑ E-4344 [M]	Blues My Name	1966	20.00
❑ SE-4344 [S]	Blues My Name	1966	25.00
❑ E-4391 [M]	Country Shadows	1966	20.00
❑ SE-4391 [S]	Country Shadows	1966	25.00
❑ E-4428 [M]	My Own Way	1967	20.00
❑ SE-4428 [S]	My Own Way	1967	25.00
❑ E-4513 [M]	The Best of Hank Williams, Jr.	1967	20.00
❑ SE-4513 [S]	The Best of Hank Williams, Jr.	1967	25.00
❑ E-4527 [M]	My Songs	1968	40.00
❑ SE-4527 [S]	My Songs	1968	25.00
❑ SE-4540	A Time to Sing	1968	25.00
❑ SE-4559	Luke the Drifter, Jr.	1969	20.00
❑ SE-4621	Songs My Father Left Me	1969	20.00
❑ SE-4632	Luke the Drifter, Jr. (Vol. 2)	1969	20.00
❑ SE-4644	Live at Cobo Hall, Detroit	1969	20.00
❑ SE-4656	Hank Williams, Jr.'s Greatest Hits	1970	15.00
❑ SE-4657	Sunday Morning	1970	15.00
❑ SE-4673	Luke the Drifter, Jr. (Vol. 3)	1970	15.00
❑ SE-4675	Hank Williams, Jr., Singing My Songs (Johnny Cash)	1970	15.00
❑ SE-4774	I've Got a Right to Cry/They All Used to Belong to Me	1971	15.00
❑ SE-4798	Sweet Dreams	1972	12.00
—With the Mike Curb Congregation			
❑ SE-4822	Hank Williams, Jr.'s Greatest Hits, Vol. 2	1972	12.00
❑ SE-4843	Eleven Roses	1972	12.00
❑ SE-4862	After You/Pride's Not Hard to Swallow	1973	12.00
❑ SE-4906	Just Pickin' — No Singin'	1973	12.00
❑ SE-4936	The Last Love Song	1973	12.00
❑ M3G-4971	Living Proof	1974	12.00
❑ M3G-4988	Bocephus	1974	12.00
❑ MG-1-5009	Hank Williams, Jr., and Friends	1975	40.00
❑ MG-1-5020	14 Greatest Hits	1976	12.00
❑ ST-90695 [S]	Blues My Name	1966	30.00
—Capitol Record Club edition			
❑ T-90695 [M]	Blues My Name	1966	25.00
—Capitol Record Club edition			
❑ T-90925 [M]	Country Shadows	1966	25.00
—Capitol Record Club edition			

PAIR

Number	Title (A Side/B Side)	Yr	NM
❑ PDL2-1164 [(2)]	I'm Walkin'	1987	12.00

POLYDOR

Number	Title (A Side/B Side)	Yr	NM
❑ 811902-1	Live at Cobo Hall, Detroit	1983	8.00
—Reissue			
❑ 811903-1	Hank Williams, Jr.'s Greatest Hits	1983	8.00
❑ 811906-1	Hank Williams, Jr.'s Greatest Hits, Vol. 2	1983	8.00
❑ 825091-1	14 Greatest Hits	1985	8.00
❑ 831575-1	Hank Williams, Jr., and Friends	1987	12.00
❑ 833069-1	Blues My Name	1987	8.00
❑ 833070-1	Eleven Roses	1987	8.00
❑ 835132-1	Standing in the Shadows	1988	8.00

WARNER BROS.

Number	Title (A Side/B Side)	Yr	NM
❑ 6E-194	Family Tradition	1983	8.00
❑ 6E-237	Whiskey Bent and Hell Bound	1983	8.00
❑ 6E-278	Habits Old and New	1983	8.00
❑ 6E-330	Rowdy	1983	8.00
❑ 5E-535	The Pressure Is On	1983	8.00
❑ 5E-538	One Night Stands	1983	8.00
❑ 5E-539	The New South	1983	8.00
❑ PRO-A-2092 [DJ]	The Hank Williams, Jr., Interview	1983	25.00
❑ BS 2988	One Night Stands	1977	12.00
❑ BS 3127	The New South	1977	12.00
❑ 23924	Man of Steel	1983	10.00
❑ 25088	Major Moves	1984	10.00
❑ 25267	Five-O	1985	10.00
❑ 25328	Greatest Hits — Vol. 2	1985	8.00
❑ 25412	Montana Café	1986	8.00
❑ 25514 [(2)]	The Early Years	1984	12.00
❑ 25538	Hank "Live"	1987	8.00
❑ 25593	Born to Boogie	1987	8.00
❑ 25725	Wild Streak	1988	8.00
❑ 25834	Greatest Hits III	1989	8.00
❑ 26090	Lone Wolf	1990	12.00
❑ 60100	High Notes	1983	8.00
❑ 60193	Hank Williams, Jr.'s, Greatest Hits	1983	8.00
❑ 60223	Strong Stuff	1983	10.00
❑ R 120612	America (The Way I See It)	1990	20.00
—BMG Music Service edition (no regular vinyl release)			
❑ R 160351	Pure Hank	1991	20.00
—BMG Music Service edition (no regular vinyl release)			

WILLIAMS, HANK, JR., AND LOIS JOHNSON

45s

MGM

Number	Title (A Side/B Side)	Yr	NM
❑ 14136	Removing the Shadow/ Party People	1970	8.00
❑ 14164	So Sad (To Watch Good Love Go Bad)/Let's Talk It Over Again	1970	8.00
❑ 14356	Send Me Some Lovin'/What We Used to Hang On To	1972	8.00
❑ 14443	Whole Lotta Loving/Why Should We Try Anymore	1972	8.00

Albums

MGM

Number	Title (A Side/B Side)	Yr	NM
❑ SE-4721	Removing the Shadow	1971	15.00
—The label has the word "Shadows" instead of "Shadow"			
❑ SE-4750	All for the Love of Sunshine	1971	20.00
❑ SE-4857	Send Me Some Lovin'/ Whole Lotta Lovin'	1972	20.00

WILLIAMS, HERB

45s

MGM

Number	Title (A Side/B Side)	Yr	NM
❑ 12431	Alimony Blues/Because You've Been Away	1957	20.00
—This record was erroneously listed in the past as a HANK Williams record			

WILLIAMS, JIM

45s

SUN

Number	Title (A Side/B Side)	Yr	NM
❑ 270	Please Don't Cry Over Me/ That Depends on You	1957	30.00

WILLIAMS, JIMMY

45s

ABC-PARAMOUNT

Number	Title (A Side/B Side)	Yr	NM
❑ 10471	I Gave My Love a Cherry/ Half Man	1963	12.00
❑ 10523	Green Pastures (23rd Psalm)/I'm Strung Out Over You, Baby	1964	12.00

ATLANTIC

Number	Title (A Side/B Side)	Yr	NM
❑ 2296	Walking on Air/I'm So Lost	1965	10.00

CUB

Number	Title (A Side/B Side)	Yr	NM
❑ 9031	My Pledge and My Promise/ Keep Me with You	1959	15.00
❑ 9039	C'mon Baby (What's Your Name)/Don't Put It Off (Do It Now)	1959	15.00

DUB

Number	Title (A Side/B Side)	Yr	NM
❑ 2842	You're Always Late/ I Belong to You	1958	100.00

DYNO VOICE

Number	Title (A Side/B Side)	Yr	NM
❑ 931	Mushroom City/Standing There	1969	8.00

HULL

Number	Title (A Side/B Side)	Yr	NM
❑ 765	I Can't Help Falling in Love/Smile	1964	10.00

LIMELIGHT

Number	Title (A Side/B Side)	Yr	NM
❑ 3038	Mrs. Cherry/Keoto'To	1964	10.00

MGM

Number	Title (A Side/B Side)	Yr	NM
❑ 11938	No One Knows/These Blues Are Over You	1955	20.00
❑ 12262	Alpha and Omega/Where Will I Shelter My Sheep	1956	20.00
❑ 12362	Throwing My Life Away/We're Drifting Further Apart	1956	20.00
❑ 12596	You're the One/I'll Only Give My Love	1957	25.00

ORBIT

Number	Title (A Side/B Side)	Yr	NM
❑ 9002	You're the One/I'll Only Give My Love	1958	15.00

ROULETTE

Number	Title (A Side/B Side)	Yr	NM
❑ 4303	There Is No Doubt/What a Change	1960	15.00

WILLIAMS, JUANITA

45s

GOLDEN WORLD

Number	Title (A Side/B Side)	Yr	NM
❑ 18	Baby Boy/You Knew What You Was Gettin'	1964	30.00

WINGATE

Number	Title (A Side/B Side)	Yr	NM
❑ 008	Some Things You Never Get Used To/You Knew What You Were Gettin'	1965	30.00

WILLIAMS, LARRY

Also see JOHNNY "GUITAR" WATSON AND LARRY WILLIAMS.

45s

BELL

Number	Title (A Side/B Side)	Yr	NM
❑ 813	I Could Love You Baby/Can't Find No Substitute for Love	1969	10.00
—With Johnny Watson			

CHESS

Number	Title (A Side/B Side)	Yr	NM
❑ 1736	My Baby's Got Soul/ Every Day I Wonder	1959	20.00
❑ 1745	Get Ready/Baby, Baby	1959	20.00
❑ 1761	I Wanna Know/Like a Gentle Man	1960	20.00
❑ 1764	Oh Baby/I Hear My Baby	1960	20.00
❑ 1805	Lawdy Mama/Fresh Out of Tears	1961	20.00

EL BAM

Number	Title (A Side/B Side)	Yr	NM
❑ 69	Call on Me/Boss Lovin'	1965	12.00

FANTASY

Number	Title (A Side/B Side)	Yr	NM
❑ 806	Doing the Best I Can (With What I Got)/Gimme Some	1977	5.00
❑ 810	One Thing or the Other (Part 1)/ One Thing or the Other (Part 2)	1977	5.00
❑ 841	The Resurrection of Funk/ (B-side unknown)	1978	5.00

MERCURY

Number	Title (A Side/B Side)	Yr	NM
❑ 72147	Woman/Can't Help Myself	1963	15.00

OKEH

Number	Title (A Side/B Side)	Yr	NM
❑ 7259	This Old Heart (Is So Lonely)/ I'd Rather Fight Than Switch	1966	10.00
❑ 7280	I Am the One/You Ask for One Good Reason	1967	10.00
❑ 7294	Just Because/Boss Lovin'	1967	10.00

SMASH

Number	Title (A Side/B Side)	Yr	NM
❑ 2035	Call on Me/Boss Lovin'	1966	12.00

SPECIALTY

Number	Title (A Side/B Side)	Yr	NM
❑ 597	Just Because/Let Me Tell You Baby	1957	30.00
❑ 608	Short Fat Fannie/High School Dance	1957	40.00

W

Number	Title (A Side/B Side)	Yr	NM
❑ 608	Short Fat Fannie/High School Dance	1984	4.00
—Gold vinyl			
❑ 615	Bony Moronie/You Bug Me, Baby	1957	40.00
❑ 615	Bony Moronie/You Bug Me, Baby	1984	4.00
—Red vinyl			
❑ 626	Dizzy, Miss Lizzy/Slow Down	1958	40.00
❑ 626	Dizzy, Miss Lizzy/Slow Down	1984	4.00
—Blue vinyl			
❑ 626 [PS]	Dizzy, Miss Lizzy/Slow Down	1958	80.00
❑ 634	Hootchy-Koo/The Dummy	1958	25.00
❑ 634	Hootchy-Koo/The Dummy	1984	4.00
—Green vinyl			
❑ 647	I Was a Fool/Peaches and Cream	1958	25.00
❑ 658	Bad Boy/She Said "Yeah"	1959	30.00
❑ 658	Bad Boy/She Said "Yeah"	1984	4.00
—Orange vinyl			
❑ 665	Steal a Little Kiss/I Can't Stop Loving You	1959	25.00
❑ 677	Give Me Your Love/Teardrops	1959	25.00
❑ 682	Ting-a-Ling/Little Schoolgirl	1960	25.00
❑ 682	Ting-a-Ling/Little Schoolgirl	1984	4.00
—Gold vinyl			
VENTURE			
❑ 622	Shake Your Body Girl/Love I Can't Seem to Find It	1968	10.00
❑ 627	Wake Up (Nothing Comes to a Sleeper But a Dream)/Love I Can't Seem to Find It	1968	10.00
Albums			
CHESS			
❑ LP-1457 [M]	Larry Williams	1961	200.00
OKEH			
❑ OKM-12123 [M]	Larry Williams' Greatest Hits	1967	30.00
❑ OKS-14123 [S]	Larry Williams' Greatest Hits	1967	40.00
SPECIALTY			
❑ SP-2109 [M]	Here's Larry Williams	1959	200.00
—Original pressing on thick vinyl with no copyright information on back cover			
❑ SP-2109 [M]	Here's Larry Williams	198?	10.00
—Reissue with thinner vinyl and copyright information on back			
❑ SP-7002 [(2)]	Bad Boy	1990	20.00

WILLIAMS, LENNY

Number	Title (A Side/B Side)	Yr	NM
Albums			
ABC			
❑ AB-1023	Choosing You	1977	10.00
❑ AA-1073	Spark of Love	1978	10.00
MCA			
❑ 3155	Love Current	1979	10.00
❑ 5147	Let's Do It Today	1980	10.00
❑ 5253	Taking Chances	1982	10.00
MOTOWN			
❑ M6-843	Rise Sleeping Beauty	1975	12.00

WILLIAMS, LEONA

Number	Title (A Side/B Side)	Yr	NM
45s			
ELEKTRA			
❑ 47114	I'm Almost Ready/The End of the World	1981	4.00
❑ 47162	You Can't Find Many Kisses/Guitar Pickin' Man	1981	4.00
❑ 47217	Always Late with Your Kisses/Startin' Today	1981	4.00
HICKORY			
❑ 1501	A Woman's Man/Ten Minutes Till Heartaches	1968	8.00
❑ 1511	Broadminded/Papa's Medicine Show	1968	8.00
❑ 1523	I Want Some More of This/They'll Never Take His Love from Me	1968	8.00
❑ 1532	Once More/I Narrowed This Triangle (Down to Two)	1969	8.00
❑ 1544	Baby, We're Really in Love/Circle of Love	1969	8.00
❑ 1555	Just Because of You/When I Stop Dreaming	1969	8.00
❑ 1565	This Ain't a Home No More/Yes Ma'am (He Found Me in a Honky Tonk)	1970	8.00
❑ 1578	If I'd Only Listened to Mama and Dad/Watch Her Go	1970	8.00
❑ 1590	Somewhere Inside/He's Just You Made Over	1971	8.00
❑ 1606	Country Girl with Hot Pants On/Babe, Just for You	1971	8.00
❑ 1619	Country Music in My Soul/The Boys and Lucy Brown	1972	7.00
❑ 1635	Happy Anniversary, Baby/The Old Place Is Gone	1972	7.00
❑ 1650	Out of Hand/Gentleman on My Mind	1972	7.00
❑ 1662	A Woman's Life Is More Than Just a Man/I'd Rather Die	1973	7.00
❑ 1670	Papa's Medicine Show/I Can't Tell My Heart That	1973	7.00
HICKORY/MGM			
❑ 304	Your Shoeshine Girl/Since I'm Not with the One I Love (I'll Love the One I'm With)	1973	6.00
❑ 310	Anything Goes/I Spent a Week There Last Night	1973	6.00
❑ 315	I'm Not Supposed to Love You Anymore/Once More	1974	6.00
MCA			
❑ 40515	If Anyone Ought to Know/I Wonder Where I'll Find You At Tonight	1976	5.00
❑ 40557	Cotton-Eyed Joe/San Quentin	1976	5.00
❑ 40856	Mama I've Got to Go to Memphis/That Lonely Unloved Wife Look	1978	5.00
❑ 40926	Rockin' Rollin' Stoned/Bright Morning Light	1978	5.00
❑ 40988	The Baby Song/Call Me Crazy Lady	1979	5.00
❑ 41006	Yes Ma'am (He Found Me in a Honky Tonk)/Good Nights Make Good Mornings	1979	5.00
❑ 41196	Catchin' Crawfish/Any Port in a Storm	1980	5.00
MERCURY			
❑ 818946-7	Midnight Love/My First Night Away from Home	1984	4.00
RCA VICTOR			
❑ PB-10097	Just Like a Prayer/A Lifetime to Forget	1974	6.00
❑ PB-10300	Shape Up or Ship Out/You Don't Love Me Like You Mean It	1975	6.00
Albums			
HICKORY			
❑ LPS-151	That Williams Girl	1971	15.00
❑ LPS-165	The Best of Leona Williams	1972	15.00
MCA			
❑ 2212	San Quentin's First Lady	1976	12.00
MERCURY			
❑ 822424-1	Someday When Things Are Good	1984	8.00

WILLIAMS, LESTER

Number	Title (A Side/B Side)	Yr	NM
45s			
DUKE			
❑ 123	Let's Do It/Good Lovin' Baby	1954	50.00
❑ 131	Crazy 'Bout You Baby/Don't Take Your Love from Me	1954	40.00
IMPERIAL			
❑ 5402	McDonald's Daughter/Daddy Loves You	1956	50.00
SPECIALTY			
❑ 422	I Can't Lose with the Stuff I Use/My Home Ain't Here	1952	100.00
❑ 431	Let Me Tell You a Thing or Two/Tryin' to Forget	1952	150.00
❑ 437	Sweet Lovin' Daddy/Lost Gal	1952	150.00
❑ 450	Brand New Baby/If I Knew How Much I Loved You	1953	100.00

WILLIAMS, LEW

Number	Title (A Side/B Side)	Yr	NM
45s			
IMPERIAL			
❑ 5394	Cat Talk/Gone Ape Man	1956	120.00
❑ 5411	Bop Bop Ba Doo Bop/Something I Said	1956	120.00
❑ 5429	Centipede/Abra Cadabra	1957	120.00
❑ 8306	Don't Mention My Name/I'll Play Your Game	1956	150.00

WILLIAMS, LUCINDA

Number	Title (A Side/B Side)	Yr	NM
Albums			
FOLKWAYS			
❑ 31066	Ramblin' on My Mind	1979	200.00
—As "Lucinda"			
❑ 31067	Happy Woman Blues	1980	150.00
—As "Lucinda"			
LOST HIGHWAY			
❑ B0002368-01 [(3)]	Live @ the Fillmore	2005	20.00
❑ B0006398-01 [(2)]	West	2007	15.00
❑ 088 170255-1	World Without Tears	2003	15.00
ROUGH TRADE			
❑ 66 [EP]	Passionate Kisses	1989	10.00
SMITHSONIAN/FOLKWAYS			
❑ 40003	Happy Woman Blues	1990	12.00
—Reissue			

WILLIAMS, MASON

Number	Title (A Side/B Side)	Yr	NM
45s			
MERCURY			
❑ 72603	Exciting Accident/Love Our Wine	1966	10.00
WARNER BROS.			
❑ 7190	Classical Gas/Long Time Blues	1968	6.00
❑ 7235	Baroque-a-Nova/Wanderlove	1968	5.00
❑ 7245	Cinderella Rockafella/Generatah-Oscillath	1968	5.00
❑ 7248	Saturday Night at the World/One Minute Commercial	1968	5.00
❑ 7272	Greensleeves/13 Dollar Stella	1969	5.00
❑ 7301	Gift of Song/Major Thang	1969	5.00
❑ 7402	Find a Reason to Believe/Jose's Piece	1970	5.00
❑ 7513	Here I Am Again/Train Ride in G	1971	5.00
7-Inch Extended Plays			
WARNER BROS.			
❑ S 1729	Overture/All the Time/Baroque-a-Nova//She's Gone Away/The Prince's Panties/Long Time Blues	1968	10.00
—Jukebox issue; small hole, plays at 33 1/3 rpm			
❑ S 1729 [PS]	The Mason Williams' Phonograph Record	1968	10.00
Albums			
AMERICAN GRAMAPHONE			
❑ AG-800	Classical Gas	1987	10.00
—With Mannheim Steamroller			
EVEREST			
❑ 3265	Listening Matter	1969	12.00
FLYING FISH			
❑ FF-059	Fresh Fish	1978	10.00
VEE JAY			
❑ VJ-1103 [M]	Them Poems and Things	1964	20.00
❑ VJS-1103 [S]	Them Poems and Things	1964	25.00
WARNER BROS.			
❑ W 1729 [M]	The Mason Williams Phonograph Record	1968	25.00
—Mono is white label promo only			
❑ WS 1729	The Mason Williams Phonograph Record	1970	10.00
—Green label with "WB" logo			
❑ WS 1729	The Mason Williams Phonograph Record	1973	8.00
—"Burbank" palm trees label			
❑ WS 1729	The Mason Williams Phonograph Record	1979	6.00
—White or tan label			
❑ WS 1729 [S]	The Mason Williams Phonograph Record	1968	12.00
—Green label with "W7" logo			
❑ WS 1776	The Mason Williams Ear Show	1968	12.00
❑ WS 1788	Music by Mason Williams	1969	12.00
❑ WS 1838	Hand Made	1970	12.00
❑ WS 1941	Sharepickers	1971	12.00

WILLIAMS, MAURICE, AND THE ZODIACS Also see THE GLADIOLAS.

Number	Title (A Side/B Side)	Yr	NM
45s			
ATLANTIC			
❑ 2199	Funny/Loneliness	1963	15.00
—As "The Zodiacs"			
❑ 2741	Sweetness/Whirlpool	1970	5.00
COLE			
❑ 100	Golly Gee/"I" Town	1959	50.00
❑ 101	Lover (Where Are You)/She's Mine	1959	40.00
DEESU			
❑ 302	Baby Baby/Being Without You	1967	20.00
❑ 304	May I/This Feeling	1967	20.00
❑ 307	Ooh Poo Pa Doo (Part 1)/Ooh Poo Pa Doo (Part 2)	1967	20.00
❑ 309	Don't Ever Leave Me/Surely	1967	20.00
❑ 311	Don't Be Half Safe/How to Pick a Winner	1967	20.00
❑ 318	Stay '68 (Live Version)/Dance, Dance, Dance	1968	15.00
HERALD			
❑ 552	Stay/Do You Believe	1960	20.00
❑ 556	Always/I Remember	1961	15.00
❑ 559	Do I/Come Along	1961	15.00
❑ 563	Someday/Come and Get It	1961	15.00
❑ 565	Please/High Blood Pressure	1961	15.00
❑ 572	It's Alright/Here I Stand	1962	15.00
LOST-NITE			
❑ 413	Stay/Do You Believe	197?	5.00
—Reissue			

Except when noted otherwise, VG = 25% of NM, and VG+ = 50% of NM. (Example: VG = $2.00, VG+ = $4.00 and NM = $8.00.)

Number	Title (A Side/B Side)	Yr	NM
❑ 443	May I/Lollipop	197?	5.00
—Reissue			
RCA			
❑ 5363-7-R	Stay/She's Like the Wind	1987	3.00
—B-side by Patrick Swayze			
SCEPTER			
❑ 12113	Nobody Knows/I Know	1965	15.00
SEA HORN			
❑ 503	My Baby's Gone/Return	1964	15.00
SELWYN			
❑ 5121	Say Yeah/College Girl	1959	50.00
SPHERE SOUND			
❑ 707	So Fine/The Winds	1965	12.00
VEE JAY			
❑ 678	May I/Lollipop	1965	20.00
VEEP			
❑ 1294	My Reason for Living/The Four Corners	1969	8.00
Albums			
COLLECTABLES			
❑ COL-5021	The Best of Maurice Williams and the Zodiacs	198?	10.00
HERALD			
❑ HLP-1014 [M]	Stay	1961	500.00
RELIC			
❑ 5017	Greatest Hits	197?	15.00
SNYDER			
❑ 5586 [M]	At the Beach	196?	100.00
SPHERE SOUND			
❑ SR-7007 [M]	Stay	1965	120.00
❑ SSR-7007 [R]	Stay	1965	80.00

WILLIAMS, OTIS, AND HIS CHARMS

Also see THE CHARMS.

Number	Title (A Side/B Side)	Yr	NM
45s			
DELUXE			
❑ 6088	Miss the Love/Tell Me Now	1955	30.00
—As "Otis Williams and His New Group"			
❑ 6090	Gum Drop/Save Me, Save Me	1955	30.00
—As "Otis Williams and His New Group"			
❑ 6091	That's Your Mistake/Too Late I Learned	1955	30.00
❑ 6092	Rolling Home/Do Be You	1956	30.00
❑ 6093	Ivory Tower/In Paradise	1956	30.00
❑ 6095	One Night Only/It's All Over	1956	30.00
❑ 6097	I'd Like to Thank You Mr. D.J./Whirlwind	1956	30.00
❑ 6098	Gypsy Lady/I'll Remember You	1956	30.00
❑ 6105	Blues Stay Away from Me/Pardon Me	1957	25.00
❑ 6115	Walkin' After Midnight/I'm Waiting Just for You	1957	25.00
❑ 6130	Nowhere on Earth/No Got De Woman	1957	25.00
❑ 6137	Talking to Myself/One Kind Word from You	1957	25.00
❑ 6138	United/Don't Deny Me	1957	25.00
❑ 6149	Dynamite Darling/Well Oh Well	1957	25.00
❑ 6158	Could This Be Magic/Oh Julie	1958	25.00
❑ 6160	Let Some Love in Your Heart/Baby-O	1958	25.00
❑ 6165	Burnin' Lips/Red Hot Love (Do This Love)	1958	25.00
❑ 6174	Don't Wake Up the Kids/You'll Remain Forever	1958	25.00
❑ 6178	My Friends/The Secret	1958	25.00
❑ 6181	Pretty Little Things Called Girls/Welcome Home	1959	25.00
❑ 6183	My Prayer Tonight/Watch Dog	1959	25.00
❑ 6185	I Knew It All the Time/Tears of Happiness	1959	25.00
❑ 6186	In Paradise/Who Knows	1959	25.00
❑ 6187	Blues Stay Away from Me/Funny What True Love Can Do	1959	25.00
KING			
❑ 5323	Chief Um (Take It Easy)/It's a Treat	1960	20.00
❑ 5332	Silver Star/Rickety Rickshaw Man	1960	20.00
❑ 5372	Image of a Girl/Wait a Minute Baby	1960	50.00
❑ 5389	The First Sign of Love/So Be It	1960	20.00
❑ 5421	Wait/And Take My Love	1960	20.00
❑ 5455	Little Turtle Dove/So Can I	1961	20.00
❑ 5497	Just Forget About Me/You Know How Much I Care	1961	20.00
❑ 5527	Pardon Me/Panic	1961	20.00
❑ 5558	Two Hearts/The Secret	1961	20.00
❑ 5682	When We Get Together/Only Young Once	1962	15.00
❑ 5816	It Just Ain't Right/It'll Never Happen Again	1963	15.00
❑ 5880	Unchain My Heart/Friends Call Me a Fool	1964	15.00
❑ 6034	Bye Bye Baby/Please Believe in Me	1966	15.00
OKEH			
❑ 7225	Baby, You Turn Me On/Love Don't Grow on Trees	1965	15.00
❑ 7235	I Fall to Pieces/Gotta Get Myself Together	1965	15.00
❑ 7248	I Got Loving/Welcome Home	1966	15.00
❑ 7261	Ain't Gonna Walk Your Dog No More/Your Sweet Love (Rained Over Me)	1966	15.00
SCEPTER			
❑ 12376	Here Lie the Bones of Nellie Jones/When You Turn On the Love	1973	8.00
STOP			
❑ 301	Begging to You/(B-side unknown)	1968	10.00
❑ 306	Begging to You/Everybody's Got a Song But Me	1968	10.00
❑ 346	Jesus Is a Soul Man/Make a Woman Feel Like a Woman	1969	10.00
❑ 360	Ling, Ting, Tong/For the Love	1970	10.00
❑ 388	I Wanna Go Country/Rocky Top	1971	8.00
—As "Otis Williams and the Midnight Cowboys"			
7-Inch Extended Plays			
DELUXE			
❑ EP-385	*That's Your Mistake/Too Late I Learned/Miss the Love/Gum Drop	1956	300.00
❑ EP-385 [PS]	Otis Williams and His Charms	1956	300.00
Albums			
DELUXE			
❑ 570 [M]	Their All Time Hits	1957	1000.
KING			
❑ 570 [M]	Their All Time Hits	1957	600.00
❑ 614 [M]	This Is Otis Williams and His Charms	1959	400.00
STOP			
❑ STLP-1022	Otis Williams and the Midnight Cowboys	1971	25.00

WILLIAMS, PAUL

Number	Title (A Side/B Side)	Yr	NM
45s			
A&M			
❑ 1325	We've Only Just Begun/Waking Up Alone	1972	4.00
❑ 1356	My Love and I/I Never Had It So Good	1972	4.00
❑ 1409	I Won't Last a Day Without You/Little Girl	1973	4.00
❑ 1429	Lady in Waiting/Look What I Found	1973	4.00
❑ 1479	What Would They Say/Inspiration	1973	4.00
❑ 1525	That's What Friends Are For/Dream Away	1974	4.00
❑ 1659	A Little Bit of Love/Nice to Be Around	1975	4.00
❑ 1686	One More Angel/This Is Supposed to Be a Party	1975	4.00
❑ 1797	Don't Call It Love/Time and Tide	1976	4.00
❑ 1853	Even Better Than I Know Myself/Time and Tide	1976	4.00
❑ 1868	Bugsy Malone/Ordinary Fool	1976	4.00
❑ 1961	Love Theme from "A Star Is Born"/Waking Up Alone	1977	4.00
PAID			
❑ 146	Making Believe/Oh, How I Miss You Tonight	1981	4.00
PORTRAIT			
❑ 70029	The Gift/A Little on the Windy Side	1979	4.00
REPRISE			
❑ 0903	Someday/Mornin' I'll Be Movin' On	1970	6.00
Albums			
A&M			
❑ SP-3131	Just an Old Fashioned Love Song	198?	8.00
—Budget-line reissue			
❑ SP-3606	Here Comes Inspiration	1974	10.00
❑ SP-3655	A Little Bit of Love	1974	10.00
❑ SP-4327	Just an Old Fashioned Love Song	1971	10.00
❑ SP-4367	Life Goes On	1972	10.00
❑ SP-4550	Ordinary Fool	1975	10.00
❑ SP-4701	Classics	1977	10.00
PORTRAIT			
❑ JR 35610	Windy Side	1979	10.00
REPRISE			
❑ RS 6401	Someday Man	1970	12.00

WILLIAMS, TIMMY

Number	Title (A Side/B Side)	Yr	NM
45s			
MALA			
❑ 515	Competition/Wipe Away Your Tears	1965	1200.

WILLIAMS, TONY

Also see THE PLATTERS.

Number	Title (A Side/B Side)	Yr	NM
45s			
DOT			
❑ 16806	Endless Street/Smoke, Drink, Play 21	1965	8.00
MERCURY			
❑ 71158	Let's Start All Over Again/When You Return	1957	20.00
❑ 71532	Charmaine/Peg o' My Heart	1959	20.00
PHILIPS			
❑ 40069	Chloe/Second Best	1962	10.00
❑ 40123	Twenty-Four Lonely Hours/Save Me	1963	10.00
❑ 40141	How Come/When I Had You	1963	10.00
REPRISE			
❑ 20019	Sleepless Nights/Movin' In	1961	15.00
❑ 20030	Miracle/My Prayer	1961	15.00
❑ 20067	Come Along Now/That's More Like It	1962	15.00
Albums			
MERCURY			
❑ MG-20454 [M]	A Girl Is a Girl Is a Girl	1959	40.00
❑ SR-60138 [S]	A Girl Is a Girl Is a Girl	1959	50.00
PHILIPS			
❑ PHM 200051 [M]	The Magic Touch of Tony	1962	25.00
❑ PHS 600051 [S]	The Magic Touch of Tony	1962	30.00
REPRISE			
❑ R-6006 [M]	His Greatest Hits	1961	25.00
❑ R9-6006 [S]	His Greatest Hits	1961	30.00

WILLIAMS, WENDY O.

Number	Title (A Side/B Side)	Yr	NM
Albums			
PASSPORT			
❑ PB-6034	W.O.W.	1984	12.00
PROFILE			
❑ PAL 1230	Maggots: The Record	1987	15.00

WILLIAMSON, SONNY BOY (1)

The "original," born John Lee Williamson and murdered in 1948.

Number	Title (A Side/B Side)	Yr	NM
45s			
RCA VICTOR			
❑ 50-0005	Little Girl/Bring Another Half a Pint	1949	300.00
—Orange vinyl			
❑ 50-0030	Southern Dream/I Love You For Myself	1949	300.00
—Orange vinyl			
Albums			
BLUES CLASSICS			
❑ 3	Blues Classics by Sonny Boy Williamson	196?	25.00
❑ 20	Blues Classics by Sonny Boy Williamson, Vol. 2	196?	25.00
❑ BC 24	Blues Classics by Sonny Boy Williamson, Vol. 3	196?	25.00

WILLIAMSON, SONNY BOY (2)

Really Aleck Ford, also known as Alex "Rice" Miller, before taking the name of his predecessor.

Number	Title (A Side/B Side)	Yr	NM
45s			
ACE			
❑ 511	Boppin' with Sonny/No Nights By Myself	1955	120.00
CHECKER			
❑ 824	Don't Start Me Talkin'/All My Love In Vain	1955	100.00
❑ 834	Let Me Explain/Your Imagination	1956	60.00
❑ 847	Keep It To Yourself/The Key to Your Door	1956	50.00
❑ 864	I Don't Know/Fattening Frogs for Snakes	1957	50.00
❑ 883	Born Blind/Ninety-Nine	1958	40.00
❑ 894	Your Funeral & My Trial/Wake Up, Baby	1958	40.00
❑ 910	Cross My Heart/Dissatisfied	1958	40.00
❑ 927	Let Your Conscience Be Your Guide/Unseeing Eye	1959	40.00
❑ 943	The Goat/It's Sad to Be Alone	1960	30.00
❑ 956	Temperature 110/Lonesome Cabin	1960	30.00
❑ 963	Trust My Baby/Too Close Together	1960	30.00
❑ 975	The Hurt/Stop Right Now	1961	30.00

W

Number	Title (A Side/B Side)	Yr	NM
❑ 1003	One Way Out/Nine Below Zero	1962	30.00
❑ 1036	Bye Bye Bird/Help Me	1963	30.00
❑ 1065	Trying to Get Back on My Feet/ Decoration Day	1963	30.00
❑ 1080	My Younger Days/ I Want You Close to Me	1964	30.00
❑ 1134	Bring It On Home/Down Child	1966	25.00
TRUMPET			
❑ 144	West Memphis Blues/ I Cross My Heart	1951	100.00
❑ 145	Sonny Boy's Christmas Blues/ Pontiac Blues	195?	120.00
❑ 166	Nine Below Zero/ Mighty Long Time	1952	100.00
❑ 167	Too Close Together/She Brought Life Back to the Dead	1952	
—Unreleased			
❑ 168	Stop Now Baby/Mr. Downchild	1952	100.00
❑ 212	Cat Hop/Too Close Together	1952	80.00
❑ 215	Gettin' Out of Town/She Brought Life Back to the Dead	1952	80.00
❑ 216	Red Hot Kisses/ Going in Your Direction	1952	80.00
❑ 228	From the Bottom/ Empty Bedroom	1953	70.00
Albums			
ALLIGATOR			
❑ AL-4787	Keep It To Ourselves	1990	12.00
ARHOOLIE			
❑ 2020	King Biscuit Time	197?	12.00
CHECKER			
❑ LP-1437 [M]	Down and Out Blues	1959	320.00
CHESS			
❑ 2ACMB-206 [(2)]	Sonny Boy Williamson	1976	20.00
—Reissue of 50027			
❑ CHV-417	One Way Out	1975	15.00
❑ LP-1503 [M]	The Real Folk Blues	1966	80.00
❑ LP-1509 [M]	More Real Folk Blues	1966	80.00
❑ LPS-1536	Bummer Road	1969	25.00
❑ CH-9116	One Way Out	198?	10.00
❑ CH-9257	Down and Out Blues	1988	10.00
❑ CH-9272	The Real Folk Blues	1988	10.00
❑ CH-9277	More Real Folk Blues	1988	10.00
❑ 2CH-50027 [(2)]	This Is My Story	1972	25.00
GNP CRESCENDO			
❑ GNPS-10003	Sonny Boy Williamson in Chicago	198?	10.00
STORYVILLE			
❑ 4016	A Portrait in Blues	197?	12.00
❑ 4062	The Blues of Sonny Boy Williamson	197?	12.00

WILLIAMSON, SONNY BOY (2), AND THE YARDBIRDS

Number	Title (A Side/B Side)	Yr	NM
Albums			
MERCURY			
❑ MG-21071 [M]	Sonny Boy Williamson and the Yardbirds	1965	80.00
❑ SR-61071 [R]	Sonny Boy Williamson and the Yardbirds	196?	25.00
—Later cover with cartoon artwork on the cover			
❑ SR-61071 [R]	Sonny Boy Williamson and the Yardbirds	1965	50.00
—First cover with a picture of the bluesman and the band			
❑ SR-61271 [R]	Eric Clapton and the Yardbirds Live with Sonny Boy Williamson	1970	20.00
—Reissue			

WILLIE AND THE WHEELS

Still another creation of STEVE BARRI and P.F. SLOAN.

Number	Title (A Side/B Side)	Yr	NM
45s			
DUNHILL			
❑ 4002	Skateboard Craze/ Do What You Do	1965	40.00

WILLING, FOY, AND THE RIDERS OF THE PURPLE SAGE

Number	Title (A Side/B Side)	Yr	NM
45s			
CAPITOL			
❑ F1070	Texas Blues/Sometime	1950	40.00
CHALLENGE			
❑ 1011	Cool Water/No One to Cry To	1958	20.00
DECCA			
❑ 9-46365	Detour/Address Unknown	1951	25.00
Albums			
CROWN			
❑ CST-582	Country & Western Favorites	196?	10.00
❑ CLP-5306 [M]	Cool Water	196?	12.00
CUSTOM			
❑ CS 1017	Cool, Cool Water	197?	10.00
JUBILEE			
❑ JL-5028 [M]	The New Sound of American Folk	1962	20.00

WILLIS, CHUCK

Also see THE ROYALS (2).

Number	Title (A Side/B Side)	Yr	NM
45s			
ATLANTIC			
❑ 1098	It's Too Late/Kansas City Woman	1956	25.00
❑ 1112	Juanita/Whatcha' Gonna Do When Your Baby Leaves You	1956	25.00
❑ 1130	C.C. Rider/Ease the Pain	1957	25.00
❑ 1148	Love Me, Cherry/That Train Has Gone	1957	25.00
❑ 1168	Betty and Dupree/ My Crying Eyes	1958	25.00
❑ 1179	What Am I Living For/Hang Up My Rock And Roll Shoes	1958	30.00
❑ 1192	Thunder and Lightning/My Life	1958	20.00
❑ 2005	You'll Be My Love/Keep a-Driving	1958	20.00
❑ 2029	My Baby/Just One Kiss	1959	20.00
OKEH			
❑ 6810	I Tried/I Rule My House	1951	100.00
❑ 6841	Let's Jump Tonight/ It's Too Late Baby	1951	80.00
❑ 6873	Lud Mouth Lucy/Here I Come	1952	80.00
❑ 6905	My Story/Caldonia	1952	50.00
❑ 6930	Salty Tears/Wrong Lake to Catch a Fish	1953	50.00
❑ 6952	Going to the River/ Baby Has Left Me Again	1953	50.00
❑ 6985	Don't Deceive Me/I've Been Treated Wrong Too Long	1953	50.00
❑ 7004	My Baby's Coming Home/ When My Day Is Over	1953	50.00
❑ 7015	You're Still My Baby/ What's Your Name	1954	50.00
❑ 7029	I Feel So Bad/ Need One More Chance	1954	60.00
❑ 7041	Change My Mind/My Heart's Been Broke Again	1954	40.00
❑ 7048	Give and Take/ I've Been Away Too Long	1954	40.00
❑ 7051	Lawdy Miss Mary/Love-Struck	1955	40.00
❑ 7055	I Can Tell/One More Break	1955	40.00
❑ 7062	Search My Heart/Ring-Ding-Doo	1955	40.00
❑ 7067	Come On Home/It Were You	1956	40.00
❑ 7070	Two Spoons of Tears/ Charged with Cheating	1956	40.00
7-Inch Extended Plays			
ATLANTIC			
❑ EP 591	Juanita/Whatcha' Gonna Do When Your Baby Leaves You//Kansas City Woman/ It's Too Late	1957	200.00
❑ EP 591 [PS]	Chuck Willis	1957	200.00
❑ EP 609	C.C. Rider/Ease the Pain//That Train Has Gone/ Love Me, Cherry	1958	120.00
❑ EP 609 [PS]	Rock with Chuck Willis	1958	120.00
❑ EP 612	What Am I Living For/Hang Up My Rock and Roll Shoes//Betty and Dupree/My Crying Eyes	1958	150.00
❑ EP 612 [PS]	What Am I Living For	1958	200.00
EPIC			
❑ 7070	(contents unknown)	1956	200.00
❑ 7070 [PS]	Chuck Willis Sings the Blues	1956	200.00
Albums			
ATLANTIC			
❑ 8018 [M]	The King of the Stroll	1958	300.00
—Black label			
❑ 8018 [M]	The King of the Stroll	1960	150.00
—Purple and orange label			
❑ 8079 [M]	I Remember Chuck Willis	1963	150.00
❑ SD 8079 [P]	I Remember Chuck Willis	1963	200.00
EPIC			
❑ LN 3425 [M]	Chuck Willis Wails the Blues	1958	500.00
❑ LN 3728 [M]	A Tribute to Chuck Willis	1960	300.00

WILLIS, HAL

Number	Title (A Side/B Side)	Yr	NM
45s			
ATHENS			
❑ 704	Crazy Little Mama/Walkin' Dream	1958	150.00
ATLANTIC			
❑ 1114	Bop-A-Dee, Bop-A-Doo/My Pink Cadillac	1956	200.00
DECCA			
❑ 30949	Poor Little Jimmy/That's the Way It Goes	1959	12.00
MERCURY			
❑ 71933	Bayou Pierre/I Love You (Around the World)	1962	12.00
SIMS			
❑ 207	The Lumberjack/Dig Me a Hole	1964	12.00
❑ 224	The One I Love/What's Left of Me	1965	12.00
❑ 235	Klondike Mike/ So Right But So Wrong	1965	12.00
❑ 243	Thumb and Shoes/ Nopper the Topper	1965	12.00
❑ 250	Creole Rose/When It's Springtime in Alaska	1965	12.00
❑ 288	Doggin' in the U.S. Mail/ The Battle of Viet Nam	1966	12.00
❑ 307	Parson from Paint Rock/ Private Dick	1966	12.00

WILLOWS, THE (1)

Number	Title (A Side/B Side)	Yr	NM
45s			
MELBA			
❑ 102	Church Bells May Ring/ Baby Tell Me	1956	100.00
❑ 102	Church Bells Are Ringing/ Beby Tell Me	1956	300.00
—Original A-side title			
❑ 106	Do You Love Me/My Angel	1956	60.00
❑ 115	Little Darlin'/My Angel	1957	80.00

WILLOWS, THE (2)

Number	Title (A Side/B Side)	Yr	NM
45s			
4-STAR			
❑ 1753	There's a Dance Goin' On/ Now That I Have You	1961	300.00

WILLOWS, THE (3)

Number	Title (A Side/B Side)	Yr	NM
45s			
HEIDI			
❑ 103	It's Such a Shame/Tears in Your Eyes	1964	15.00
❑ 107	Sit by the Fire/Such a Night	1965	15.00

WILLOWS, THE (4)

Number	Title (A Side/B Side)	Yr	NM
45s			
MGM			
❑ 13484	Hurtin' All Over/My Kinda Guy	1966	12.00
❑ 13714	Snow Song/Outside the City	1967	12.00

WILMER AND THE DUKES

Number	Title (A Side/B Side)	Yr	NM
45s			
APHRODISIAC			
❑ 260	Give Me One More Chance/Git It	1968	8.00
❑ 261	Heavy Time/I'm Free	1969	8.00
❑ 261 [PS]	Heavy Time/I'm Free	1969	12.00
❑ 262	Living in the U.S.A./Count on Me	1969	8.00
❑ 263	Get Out of My Life, Women/ I Do Love You	1969	10.00
Albums			
APHRODISIAC			
❑ 6001	Wilmer and the Dukes	1969	20.00

WILSON, AL

Number	Title (A Side/B Side)	Yr	NM
45s			
BELL			
❑ 867	Mississippi Woman/ Sometimes a Man Must Cry	1970	7.00
❑ 909	You Do the Right Thing/ Bachelor Man	1970	7.00
CAROUSEL			
❑ 30051	I Hear You Knocking/ Sugar Cane Girl	1971	6.00
❑ 30052	Falling/Bachelor Man	1971	6.00
PLAYBOY			
❑ 6062	I've Got a Feeling (We'll Be Seeing Each Other Again)/ Be Concerned	1976	5.00
❑ 6076	Baby I Want Your Body/ Stay with Me	1976	5.00
❑ 6076 [PS]	Baby I Want Your Body/ Stay with Me	1976	6.00
❑ 6085	You Did It for Me/Differently	1976	5.00
ROADSHOW			
❑ PB-11583	Count the Days/Is This the End	1979	4.00
❑ PB-11714	Earthquake/You Got It	1979	4.00
ROCKY ROAD			
❑ 30060	Heavy Church/(B-side unknown)	1972	6.00
❑ 30067	Born on the Bayou/(B-side unknown)	1972	6.00
❑ 30073	Show and Tell/Listen to Me	1973	6.00
❑ 30076	Touch and Go/Settle Me Down	1974	6.00
❑ 30200	La La Peace Song/ Keep On Loving You	1974	6.00
❑ 30202	I Won't Last a Day Without You-Let Me Be the One/ Willoughbry Brook Road	1974	6.00
SOUL CITY			
❑ 759	When You Love, You're Loved Too/Who Could Be Lovin' You	1967	10.00

W

Number	Title (A Side/B Side)	Yr	NM
❑ 761	Do What You Gotta Do/Now I Know What Love Is	1968	8.00
❑ 767	The Snake/Getting Ready for Tomorrow	1968	8.00
❑ 771	Poor Side of Town/The Dolphins	1969	8.00
❑ 773	I Stand Accused/Shake Me, Wake Me	1969	8.00
❑ 775	Lodi/By the Time I Get to Phoenix	1969	8.00

WAND

❑ 1135 Help Me/(Instrumental) 1966 30.00

Albums

PLAYBOY

❑ PB 410 I've Got a Feeling 1976 12.00
❑ JZ 34744 I've Got a Feeling 1977 10.00
—Reissue of 410

ROCKY ROAD

❑ RR-3600 Weighing In 1973 15.00
❑ RR-3601 Show and Tell 1973 15.00
❑ 3700 La La Peace Song 1974 15.00

SOUL CITY

❑ SCS-92006 Searching for the Dolphins 1969 25.00

WILSON, ANN, AND THE DAYBREAKS
Ann Wilson was later with Heart.

45s

TOPAZ

❑ 1311 Standin' Watchin' You/Wonder How I Managed 1967 120.00
❑ 1312 Through Eyes and Glass/I'm Gonna Drink My Hurt Away 1967 120.00

WILSON, BENNY

45s

COLUMBIA

❑ 38-04197 Lay Down and Lie/Boy Was I Wrong 1983 4.00
❑ 38-04724 Acres of Diamonds/I Just Don't Love You, That's All 1984 3.00
❑ 38-05829 If You Wanna Talk Love/Where the Light Comes From 1986 3.00

WILSON, BRIAN Also see THE BEACH BOYS.

45s

CAPITOL

❑ 5610 Caroline, No/Summer Means New Love 1966 25.00
—Actually a Beach Boys recording released as a solo Brian record

GIANT

❑ 17216 Your Imagination/Your Imagination (A Cappella) 1998 3.00

SIRE

❑ 27694 Melt Away/Being with the One You Love 1988 20.00
❑ 27787 [DJ] Night Time (same on both sides) 1988 30.00
—Stock copies not known to exist
❑ 27787 [PS] Night Time 1988 60.00
❑ 27814 Love and Mercy/He Couldn't Get His Poor Old Body to Move 1988 10.00
—Promo copies go for 50% of this price
❑ 27814 [PS] Love and Mercy/He Couldn't Get His Poor Old Body to Move 1988 5.00
—Accompanied both stock and promo copies
❑ 28350 Let's Go to Heaven in My Car/Too Much Sugar 1987 10.00
—Promo copies go for 50% of this price
❑ 28350 [PS] Let's Go to Heaven in My Car/Too Much Sugar 1987 5.00
—Accompanied both stock and promo copies

Albums

ARISTA

❑ 82876-70300-1 What I Really Want for Christmas 2005 12.00

RHINO

❑ RI-76471 [(2)] Gettin' In Over My Head 2004 20.00
❑ RI-76582 [(2)] Brian Wilson Presents Smile 2004 25.00

SIRE

❑ PRO-A-3248 [DJ] Words and Music 1988 25.00
—Promo-only music and interview
❑ 25669 Brian Wilson 1988 10.00

WILSON, BRIAN, AND MIKE LOVE Also see THE BEACH BOYS; BRIAN WILSON.

45s

BROTHER

❑ 1002 Gettin' Hungry/Devoted to You 1967 30.00

WILSON, CLARA

45s

HIT

❑ 62 Don't Say Nothin' Bad About My Baby/Pipeline 1963 8.00
—B-side by the Music City Five
❑ 71 Easier Said Than Done/Surf City 1963 8.00
—B-side by Jimmy and Joe
❑ 117 My Guy/Little Children 1964 8.00
—B-side by Ed Hardin

WILSON, CLARA, AND THE CLEFTONES This Cleftones is no relation to the popular vocal group, as this is a studio girl group.

45s

HIT

❑ 55 Our Day Will Come/The End of the World 1963 8.00
—As "Clara and the Cleftones"; B-side by Kathy Taylor
❑ 65 Foolish Little Girl/Da Doo Ron Ron 1963 8.00
—B-side by Alpha Zoe

WILSON, DENNIS

45s

CARIBOU

❑ 9023 You and I/Friday Night 1978 15.00

Albums

CARIBOU

❑ PZ 34354 Pacific Ocean Blue 1977 30.00

WILSON, FLIP

45s

LITTLE DAVID

❑ 721 Don't Fight the Feeling/Geraldine-Killer 1972 5.00
❑ 730 There Oughta Be a Law/Berries in Salinas 1975 5.00
❑ 8113 There Oughta Be a Law/Berries in Salinas 1975 4.00

Albums

ATLANTIC

❑ 8149 [M] Cowboys and Colored People 1967 25.00
❑ SD 8149 [S] Cowboys and Colored People 1967 15.00
—Green and blue label
❑ SD 8149 [S] Cowboys and Colored People 1969 12.00
—Red and green label
❑ SD 8179 You Devil You 1968 15.00
—Green and blue label
❑ SD 8179 You Devil You 1969 12.00
—Red and green label

IMPERIAL

❑ LP-9155 [M] Flippin' 1961 25.00

LITTLE DAVID

❑ LD 1000 The Devil Made Me Buy This Dress 1970 12.00
❑ LD 1001 [M] Geraldine/Don't Fight the Feeling 1972 25.00
—White label promo only; sticker on cover says "Promotional DJ Copy Monaural Not for Sale"
❑ LD 1001 [S] Geraldine/Don't Fight the Feeling 1972 12.00
❑ LD 2000 The Flip Wilson Show 1970 12.00

MINIT

❑ 24012 Flippin' 1968 15.00
—Reissue of Imperial LP

SCEPTER

❑ S-520 Flip Wilson's Pot Luck 1964 20.00

SPRINGBOARD

❑ SPB-4004 Funny and Live at the Village Gate 1972 12.00
—Reissue of Scepter LP

SUNSET

❑ SUS-5297 Flipped Out 1970 12.00
—Reissue of Minit LP

WILSON, FRANK

45s

SOUL

❑ 35019 Do I Love You (Indeed I Do)/Sweeter As the Days Go By 1966 20000.
—VG 10000; VG+ 15000

WILSON, HANK See LEON RUSSELL.

WILSON, J. FRANK, AND THE CAVALIERS

45s

CHARAY

❑ 13 Last Kiss '69/Black Car 1969 6.00

JOSIE

❑ 923 Last Kiss/That's How Much I Love You 1964 12.00
❑ 924 Tears of Happiness/Summertime 1964 10.00
—As "The Cavaliers"
❑ 926 Hey Little One/Speak to Me 1964 10.00
❑ 929 Say It Now/Six Boys 1965 10.00
❑ 931 Dreams of a Fool/Open Your Eyes 1965 10.00
❑ 938 Forget Me Not/A White Sport Coat (And a Pink Carnation) 1965 10.00

LE CAM

❑ 722 Last Kiss/Carla 1964 30.00

SOLLY

❑ 927 Me and My Teardrops/Unmarked and Uncovered with Sand 1966 10.00

TAMARA

❑ 761 Last Kiss/That's How Much I Love You 1964 25.00

VIRGO

❑ 506 Last Kiss/That's How Much I Love You 1973 7.00

Albums

JOSIE

❑ JM-4006 [M] Last Kiss 1964 75.00
❑ JS-4006 [S] Last Kiss 1964 100.00

WILSON, JACKIE Also see THE DOMINOES.

45s

BRUNSWICK

❑ 738105 [S] Please Tell Me Why/Doggin' Around 196? 25.00
—Small hole, plays at 33 1/3 rpm
❑ 9-55024 Reet Petite (The Finest Girl You Ever Want to Meet)/By the Light of the Silvery Moon 1957 30.00
❑ 9-55052 To Be Loved/Come Back to Me 1958 25.00
❑ 9-55070 As Long As I Live/I'm Wanderin' 1958 25.00
❑ 9-55086 We Have Love/Singing a Song 1958 25.00
❑ 9-55105 Lonely Teardrops/In the Blue of Evening 1958 30.00
❑ 55121 That's Why (I Love You So)/Love Is All 1959 25.00
❑ 55121 [PS] That's Why (I Love You So)/Love Is All 1959 60.00
❑ 55136 I'll Be Satisfied/Ask 1959 25.00
❑ 55149 You Better Know It/Never Go Away 1959 20.00
❑ 55165 Talk That Talk/Only You, Only Me 1959 20.00
❑ 55165 [PS] Talk That Talk/Only You, Only Me 1959 60.00
❑ 55166 Night/Doggin' Around 196? 10.00
—Black label, color-bar arrow (reissue pressing)
❑ 55166 Night/Doggin' Around 1960 15.00
—Orange label (standard pressing)
❑ 55166 Night/Doggin' Around 1960 40.00
—Maroon label (scarce original)
❑ 55166 [PS] Night/Doggin' Around 1960 50.00
❑ 55167 (You Were Made for) All My Love/A Woman, A Lover, A Friend 1960 20.00
❑ 55170 Alone at Last/Am I the Man 1960 20.00
❑ 55170 [PS] Alone at Last/Am I the Man 1960 50.00
❑ 55201 My Empty Arms/The Tear of the Year 1961 15.00
❑ 55201 [PS] My Empty Arms/The Tear of the Year 1961 40.00
❑ 55208 Please Tell Me Why/Your One and Only Love 1961 15.00
❑ 55216 I'm Comin' On Back to You/Lonely Life 1961 15.00
❑ 55219 Years from Now/You Don't Know What It Means 1961 15.00
❑ 55220 The Way I Am/My Heart Belongs to Only You 1961 15.00
❑ 55220 [PS] The Way I Am/My Heart Belongs to Only You 1961 40.00
❑ 55221 The Greatest Hurt/There'll Be No Next Time 1962 15.00
❑ 55221 [PS] The Greatest Hurt/There'll Be No Next Time 1962 40.00
❑ 55224 I Found Love/There's Nothing Like Love 1962 12.00
—With Linda Hopkins
❑ 55225 Hearts/Sing (And Tell the Blues So Long) 1962 15.00
❑ 55229 I Just Can't Help It/My Tale of Woe 1962 15.00
❑ 55233 Forever and a Day/Baby That's All 1962 15.00
❑ 55236 What Good Am I Without You/A Girl Named Tamiko 1962 15.00
❑ 55236 [PS] What Good Am I Without You/A Girl Named Tamiko 1962 30.00
❑ 55239 Baby Workout/I'm Going Crazy 1963 20.00
❑ 55243 Shake a Hand/Say I Do 1963 12.00
—With Linda Hopkins
❑ 55246 Shake! Shake! Shake!/He's a Fool 1963 12.00
❑ 55250 Baby Get It (And Don't Quit It)/The New Breed 1963 12.00
❑ 55254 Silent Night/Oh Holy Night 1963 15.00
❑ 55260 Haunted House/I'm Travelin' On 1964 10.00
❑ 55263 Call Her Up/The Kickapoo 1964 10.00
❑ 55266 Big Boss Line/Be My Girl 1964 10.00
❑ 55269 Squeeze Her-Tease Her (But Love Her)/Give Me Back My Heart 1964 10.00
❑ 55273 Watch Out/She's All Right 1964 10.00

W

Number	Title (A Side/B Side)	Yr	NM
❑ 55277	Danny Boy/Soul Time	1965	8.00
❑ 55278	Yes Indeed/When the Saints Go Marching In	1965	8.00
—With Linda Hopkins			
❑ 55280	No Pity (In the Naked City)/I'm So Lonely	1965	8.00
❑ 55283	I Believe I'll Love On/Lonely Teardrops	1965	8.00
❑ 55287	Think Twice/Please Don't Hurt Me	1965	8.00
—With LaVern Baker			
❑ 55289	I've Got to Get Back/3 Days, 1 Hour, 30 Minutes	1966	8.00
❑ 55290	Soul Galore/Brand New Things	1966	8.00
❑ 55294	I Believe/Be My Love	1966	8.00
❑ 55300	Whispers (Gettin' Louder)/The Fairest of Them All	1966	8.00
❑ 55309	I Don't Want to Lose You/Just Be Sincere	1967	8.00
❑ 55321	I've Lost You/Those Heartaches	1967	8.00
❑ 55336	(Your Love Keeps Lifting Me) Higher and Higher/I'm the One to Do It	1967	10.00
❑ 55354	Since You Showed Me How to Be Happy/The Who Who Song	1967	8.00
❑ 55365	For Your Precious Love/Uptight	1968	8.00
❑ 55373	Chain Gang/Funky Broadway	1968	8.00
❑ 55381	I Get the Sweetest Feeling/Nothing But Heartaches	1968	8.00
❑ 55392	For Once in My Life/You Brought About a Change in Me	1968	8.00
❑ 55402	I Still Love You/Hum De Dum De Do	1969	8.00
❑ 55418	Helpless/Do It the Right Way	1969	8.00
❑ 55423	With These Hands/Why Don't You (Do Your Thing)	1969	8.00
❑ 55435	Let This Be a Letter (To My Baby)/Didn't I	1970	6.00
❑ 55435 [PS]	Let This Be a Letter (To My Baby)/Didn't I	1970	12.00
❑ 55443	(I Can Feel Those Vibrations) This Love Is Real/Love Uprising	1970	6.00
❑ 55449	This Guy's in Love with You/Say You Will	1971	6.00
❑ 55454	Say You Will/(B-side unknown)	1971	6.00
❑ 55461	Love Is Funny That Way/Try It Again	1971	6.00
❑ 55467	You Got Me Walking/The Mountain	1972	6.00
❑ 55475	The Girl Turned Me On/Forever and a Day	1972	6.00
❑ 55480	What a Lovely Way/You Left the Fire Burning	1972	6.00
❑ 55490	Beautiful Day/What 'Cha Gonna Do About Love	1973	6.00
❑ 55495	Because of You/Go Away	1973	200.00
❑ 55499	Sing a Little Song/No More Goodbyes	1973	6.00
❑ 55504	It's All Over/Shake a Leg	1973	6.00
❑ 55522	Don't Burn No Bridges/(Instrumental)	1975	6.00
—With the Chi-Lites			
❑ 55536	Nobody But You/I've Learned About Life	1977	6.00
❑ 7-78002 [S]	(You Were Made) For All My Love/One Kiss	196?	40.00
—Jukebox issue; small hole, plays at 33 1/3 rpm			

COLUMBIA

Number	Title (A Side/B Side)	Yr	NM
❑ 38-07329	Reet Petite/You Better Know It	1987	5.00
❑ 38-07329 [PS]	Reet Petite/You Better Know It	1987	5.00

7-Inch Extended Plays

BRUNSWICK

Number	Title (A Side/B Side)	Yr	NM
❑ EB 71040	To Be Loved/Reet Petite//Danny Boy/As Long As I Live	1959	60.00
❑ EB 71040 [PS]	The Versatile Jackie Wilson	1959	60.00
❑ EB 71042	Lonely Teardrops/It's Too Bad We Had to Say Goodbye//Someone to Need Me/Joke	1960	60.00
❑ EB 71042 [PS]	Jumpin' Jack	1960	60.00
❑ EB 71045 [M]	That's Why/Love Is All//You Better Know It/Each Time	1960	60.00
❑ EB 71045 [PS]	That's Why (I Love You So)	1960	60.00
❑ EB 71046	Talk That Talk/Ask//I'll Be Satisfied/Wishing Well	1960	60.00
❑ EB 71046 [PS]	Talk That Talk	1960	60.00
❑ EB 71047	(contents unknown)	1960	60.00
❑ EB 71047 [PS]	Mr. Excitement	1960	60.00
❑ EB 71048	So Much/Only You, Only Me//Happiness/Magic of Love	1960	60.00
❑ EB 71048 [PS]	Jackie Wilson	1960	60.00
❑ EB 71049	Night/Doggin' Around//All My Love/A Woman, a Lover, a Friend	1960	60.00
❑ EB 71049 [PS]	Jackie Wilson	1960	60.00
❑ EB 71101	The Greatest Hurt/I Don't Know You Anymore//Tear of the Year/There'll Be No Next Time	1962	60.00
❑ EB 71101 [PS]	Jackie Wilson	1962	60.00
❑ EB 71102	I Just Can't Help It/My Tale of Woe//Bad News Travels Fast/You Ought to Be Ashamed	1962	60.00
❑ EB 71102 [PS]	Jackie Wilson	1962	60.00
❑ EB 71103	Baby Workout/Say You Will//Kickapoo/Yeah Yeah Yeah	1963	60.00
❑ EB 71103 [PS]	Baby Workout	1963	60.00
❑ EB 71104	(contents unknown)	1963	60.00
❑ EB 71104 [PS]	Shake a Hand	1963	60.00
❑ 7-78009	No Pity (In the Naked City)/Mama of My Song/Soul Time//Danny Boy/She's All Right/No Time Out	196?	50.00
—Jukebox issue; small hole, plays at 33 1/3 rpm			
❑ 7-78009 [PS]	Soul Time	196?	50.00
❑ EB 771045	That's Why/Love Is All//You Better Know It/Each Time	1960	80.00
❑ EB 771045 [PS]	That's Why (I Love You So)	1960	80.00

Albums

BRUNSWICK

Number	Title	Yr	NM
❑ BL 54042 [M]	He's So Fine	1959	120.00
—All-black label			
❑ BL 54042 [M]	He's So Fine	1964	25.00
—Black label with color bars			
❑ BL 54045 [M]	Lonely Teardrops	1959	150.00
—All-black label			
❑ BL 54045 [M]	Lonely Teardrops	1964	25.00
—Black label with color bars			
❑ BL 54050 [M]	So Much	1960	100.00
—All-black label			
❑ BL 54050 [M]	So Much	1964	20.00
—Black label with color bars			
❑ BL 54055 [M]	Jackie Sings the Blues	1960	150.00
—All-black label			
❑ BL 54055 [M]	Jackie Sings the Blues	1964	20.00
—Black label with color bars			
❑ BL 54058 [M]	My Golden Favorites	1960	60.00
—All-black label			
❑ BL 54058 [M]	My Golden Favorites	1964	25.00
—Black label with color bars			
❑ BL 54059 [M]	A Woman, a Lover, a Friend	1961	50.00
—All-black label			
❑ BL 54059 [M]	A Woman, a Lover, a Friend	1964	20.00
—Black label with color bars			
❑ BL 54100 [M]	You Ain't Heard Nothin' Yet	1961	50.00
—All-black label			
❑ BL 54100 [M]	You Ain't Heard Nothin' Yet	1964	20.00
—Black label with color bars			
❑ BL 54101 [M]	By Special Request	1961	50.00
—All-black label			
❑ BL 54101 [M]	By Special Request	1964	20.00
—Black label with color bars			
❑ BL 54105 [M]	Body and Soul	1962	50.00
—All-black label			
❑ BL 54105 [M]	Body and Soul	1964	20.00
—Black label with color bars			
❑ BL 54106 [M]	The World's Greatest Melodies	1962	50.00
—All-black label			
❑ BL 54106 [M]	The World's Greatest Melodies	1964	20.00
—Black label with color bars			
❑ BL 54108 [M]	Jackie Wilson at the Copa	1962	50.00
—All-black label			
❑ BL 54108 [M]	Jackie Wilson at the Copa	1964	20.00
—Black label with color bars			
❑ BL 54110 [M]	Baby Workout	1963	20.00
—Black label with color bars			
❑ BL 54110 [M]	Baby Workout	1963	50.00
—All-black label			
❑ BL 54112 [M]	Merry Christmas from Jackie Wilson	1963	30.00
❑ BL 54113 [M]	Shake a Hand	1964	25.00
❑ BL 54115 [M]	My Golden Favorites, Vol. 2	1964	25.00
❑ BL 54117 [M]	Somethin' Else	1964	25.00
❑ BL 54118 [M]	Soul Time	1965	25.00
❑ BL 54119 [M]	Spotlight on Jackie	1965	25.00
❑ BL 54120 [M]	Soul Galore	1966	25.00
❑ BL 54122 [M]	Whispers	1966	25.00
❑ BL 54130 [M]	Higher and Higher	1967	25.00
❑ BL 54134 [M]	Manufacturers of Soul	1968	50.00
—With Count Basie			
❑ BL 54138 [M]	I Get the Sweetest Feeling	1968	100.00
—Yellow label promo only; "Monaural" sticker over the word "Stereo" on cover			
❑ BL 754050 [S]	So Much	1960	150.00
—All-black label			
❑ BL 754050 [S]	So Much	1964	25.00
—Black label with color bars			
❑ BL 754055 [S]	Jackie Sings the Blues	1960	200.00
—All-black label			
❑ BL 754055 [S]	Jackie Sings the Blues	1964	25.00
—Black label with color bars			
❑ BL 754059 [S]	A Woman, a Lover, a Friend	1961	80.00
—All-black label			
❑ BL 754059 [S]	A Woman, a Lover, a Friend	1964	25.00
—Black label with color bars			
❑ BL 754100 [S]	You Ain't Heard Nothin' Yet	1961	80.00
—All-black label			
❑ BL 754100 [S]	You Ain't Heard Nothin' Yet	1964	25.00
—Black label with color bars			
❑ BL 754101 [S]	By Special Request	1961	80.00
—All-black label			
❑ BL 754101 [S]	By Special Request	1964	25.00
—Black label with color bars			
❑ BL 754105 [S]	Body and Soul	1962	80.00
—All-black label			
❑ BL 754105 [S]	Body and Soul	1964	25.00
—Black label with color bars			
❑ BL 754106 [S]	The World's Greatest Melodies	1962	80.00
—All-black label			
❑ BL 754106 [S]	The World's Greatest Melodies	1964	25.00
—Black label with color bars			
❑ BL 754108 [S]	Jackie Wilson at the Copa	1962	80.00
—All-black label			
❑ BL 754108 [S]	Jackie Wilson at the Copa	1964	25.00
—Black label with color bars			
❑ BL 754110 [S]	Baby Workout	1963	25.00
—Black label with color bars			
❑ BL 754110 [S]	Baby Workout	1963	80.00
—All-black label			
❑ BL 754112 [S]	Merry Christmas from Jackie Wilson	1963	40.00
❑ BL 754113 [S]	Shake a Hand	1964	30.00
❑ BL 754115 [S]	My Golden Favorites, Vol. 2	1964	30.00
❑ BL 754117 [S]	Somethin' Else	1964	30.00
❑ BL 754118 [S]	Soul Time	1965	30.00
❑ BL 754119 [S]	Spotlight on Jackie	1965	30.00
❑ BL 754120 [S]	Soul Galore	1966	30.00
❑ BL 754122 [S]	Whispers	1966	30.00
❑ BL 754130 [S]	Higher and Higher	1967	30.00
❑ BL 754134 [S]	Manufacturers of Soul	1968	20.00
—With Count Basie			
❑ BL 754138 [S]	I Get the Sweetest Feeling	1968	20.00
❑ BL 754140	Jackie Wilson's Greatest Hits	1969	20.00
❑ BL 754154	Do Your Thing	1969	20.00
❑ BL 754158	It's All a Part of Love	1970	20.00
❑ BL 754167	This Love Is Real	1971	20.00
❑ BL 754172	You Got Me Walking	1971	20.00
❑ BL 754185	Beautiful Day	1972	15.00
❑ BL 754199	Nowstalgia	1974	15.00
❑ BL 754212	Nobody But You	1977	15.00

COLUMBIA

Number	Title	Yr	NM
❑ FC 40866	Reet Petite: The Best of Jackie Wilson	1987	12.00

EPIC

Number	Title	Yr	NM
❑ EG 38623 [(2)]	The Jackie Wilson Story	1983	20.00
❑ FE 39408	The Jackie Wilson Story, Vol. 2	1985	12.00
❑ PE 39408	The Jackie Wilson Story, Vol. 2	198?	8.00
—Budget-line reissue			

RHINO

Number	Title	Yr	NM
❑ RNLP-70230	Through the Years: A Collection of Rare Album Tracks and Single Sides	1987	12.00

WILSON, MARTY

45s

DECCA

Number	Title (A Side/B Side)	Yr	NM
❑ 30544	Super Sonic/I'm All Woke Up	1958	30.00
❑ 30644	Po-Go/Hey Eula	1958	30.00

TEL

Number	Title (A Side/B Side)	Yr	NM
❑ 1008	Stroll Me/Hot Foot	1959	25.00

WILSON, MURRY

Father of Brian, Carl and Dennis Wilson of the Beach Boys.

45s

CAPITOL

Number	Title (A Side/B Side)	Yr	NM
❑ 2063	Leaves/Plumber's Tune	1967	12.00

Albums

CAPITOL

Number	Title	Yr	NM
❑ ST 2819 [S]	The Many Moods of Murry Wilson	1967	50.00
❑ T 2819 [M]	The Many Moods of Murry Wilson	1967	60.00

WILSON, NANCY

45s

CAPITOL

Number	Title (A Side/B Side)	Yr	NM
❑ 2061	Ode to Billie Joe/I'm Always Drunk in San Francisco	1967	6.00
❑ 2136	Face It Girl, It's Over/The End of Our Love	1968	6.00
❑ 2283	Peace of Mind/This Bitter Earth	1968	6.00
❑ 2361	In a Long White Room/Only Love	1968	6.00
❑ 2422	You'd Better Go/I'm Your Special Fool	1969	6.00
❑ 2555	Got It Together/One Soft Night	1969	6.00
❑ 2644	Can't Take My Eyes Off You/Do You Know Why	1969	6.00
❑ 2749	Waitin' for Charlie to Come Home/Words and Music	1970	6.00
❑ 2831	This Girl Is a Woman Now/Trip with Me	1970	6.00
❑ 2934	Now I'm a Woman/The Real Me	1970	6.00
❑ 3212	The Greatest Performance of My Life/Everybody Knows	1971	6.00
❑ 3956	Streetrunner/Ocean of Love	1974	5.00
❑ 3973	You're As Right As Rain/There'll Always Be Forever	1974	5.00

Except when noted otherwise, VG = 25% of NM, and VG+ = 50% of NM. (Example: VG = $2.00, VG+ = $4.00 and NM = $8.00.)

Number	Title (A Side/B Side)	Yr	NM
❑ 4117	He Called Me Baby/Like a Circle Never Stops	1975	5.00
❑ 4189	Don't Let Me Be Lonely Tonight/Happy Tears	1975	5.00
❑ 4284	Now/This Mother's Daughter	1976	4.00
❑ 4359	In My Loneliness (When We Were One)/He Never Had It So Good	1976	4.00
❑ 4476	I've Never Been to Me/Here It Comes	1977	4.00
❑ 4509	My Foolish Heart/Seventh Son	1961	15.00
❑ 4558	Next Time You See Him/Give Him Love	1961	10.00
❑ 4578	I'm Gonna Let Ya/Light	1978	4.00
❑ 4647	The Verdict/Guess Who I Saw Today	1961	10.00
❑ 4741	Life, Love and Harmony/Open Up Your Heart and Take Me In	1979	4.00
❑ 4801	Sunshine/This Is Our Song	1979	4.00
❑ 4816	Put On a Happy Face/You Don't Know What Love Is	1962	8.00
❑ 4839	Welcome Home/Let's Hold On to Love	1980	4.00
❑ 4926	You Can Have Him/A Lot of Livin' to Do	1963	8.00
❑ 4991	Tell Me the Truth/My Sweet Thing	1963	8.00
❑ 5084	That's What I Want for Christmas/What Are You Doing New Year's Eve	1963	10.00
❑ 5133	Don't Rain on My Parade/The Grass Is Greener	1964	8.00
❑ 5198	(You Don't Know) How Glad I Am/Never Less Than Yesterday	1964	7.00
❑ 5254	I Wanna Be with You/It's Time for Me	1964	7.00
❑ 5319	And Satisfy/Take What I Have	1964	7.00
❑ 5340	Don't Come Running Back to Me/Love Has Many Faces	1965	7.00
❑ 5340 [PS]	Don't Come Running Back to Me/Love Has Many Faces	1965	12.00
❑ 5408	The Best Is Yet to Come/Welcome, Welcome	1965	7.00
❑ 5455	Where Does That Leave Me/Gentle Is My Love	1965	7.00
❑ 5515	I'll Only Miss Him When I Think of Him/Afterthoughts	1965	7.00
❑ 5564	No One Else But You/Have a Heart	1966	7.00
❑ 5639	The Power of Love/Rain Sometime	1966	7.00
❑ 5673	Uptight (Everything's Alright)/You've Got Your Troubles	1966	7.00
❑ 5720	Go Away/That Special Way	1966	7.00
❑ 5771	Love Can Do Anything/I'll Make a Man of the Man	1966	7.00
❑ 5841	In the Dark/Ten Years of Tears	1967	7.00
❑ 5935	Don't Look Over Your Shoulder/But Only Sometimes	1967	7.00
❑ 6275	That's What I Want for Christmas/What Are You Doing New Year's Eve	197?	5.00
—Starline reissue			
❑ S7-19763	That's What I Want for Christmas/What Are You Doing New Year's Eve	1997	3.00

COLUMBIA

Number	Title (A Side/B Side)	Yr	NM
❑ 07037	Forbidden Lover/A Song for You	1987	3.00
❑ 08058	Quiet Fire/The Power, The Glory	1988	3.00

7-Inch Extended Plays

CAPITOL

Number	Title (A Side/B Side)	Yr	NM
❑ SXA-2351 [PS]	Gentle Is My Love	1965	10.00
❑ SXA-2351 [S]	Who Can I Turn To/Gentle Is My Love/There Will Never Be Another You//Funnier Than Funny/More/If Ever I Would Leave You	1965	10.00
—33 1/3 rpm, small hole			
❑ SU-2555 [PS]	Tender Loving Care	1966	10.00
❑ SU-2555 [S]	Don't Go to Strangers/Like Someone in Love/Tender Loving Care//Gee Baby, Ain't I Good to You/Close Your Eyes/As You Desire Me	1966	10.00
—33 1/3 rpm, small hole			

Albums

CAPITOL

Number	Title (A Side/B Side)	Yr	NM
❑ ST-148	Nancy	1969	15.00
❑ ST-234	Son of a Preacher Man	1969	15.00
❑ SWBB-256 [(2)]	Close-Up	1969	20.00
—Combines 1828 and 1934 into one package			
❑ ST-353	Hurt So Bad	1969	15.00
❑ ST-429	Can't Take My Eyes Off You	1970	15.00
❑ ST-541	Now I'm a Woman	1970	15.00
❑ STBB-727 [(2)]	For Once in My Life/Who Can I Turn To	1971	20.00
❑ ST-763	The Right to Love	1971	15.00
—Retitled reissue of 2757			
❑ SM-798	But Beautiful	197?	10.00
—Reissue			
❑ ST-798	But Beautiful	1971	15.00
❑ ST-842	Kaleidoscope	1971	15.00
❑ ST 1319 [S]	Like in Love	1960	20.00
—Black label with colorband, Capitol logo on top			
❑ ST 1319 [S]	Like in Love	1960	30.00
—Black label with colorband, Capitol logo on left			
❑ T 1319 [M]	Like in Love	1960	15.00
—Black label with colorband, Capitol logo on top			
❑ T 1319 [M]	Like in Love	1960	25.00
—Black label with colorband, Capitol logo on left			
❑ ST 1440 [S]	Something Wonderful	1960	20.00
—Black label with colorband, Capitol logo on top			
❑ ST 1440 [S]	Something Wonderful	1960	30.00
—Black label with colorband, Capitol logo on left			
❑ T 1440 [M]	Something Wonderful	1960	15.00
—Black label with colorband, Capitol logo on top			
❑ T 1440 [M]	Something Wonderful	1960	25.00
—Black label with colorband, Capitol logo on left			
❑ SM-1524 [S]	The Swingin's Mutual	1976	10.00
—With George Shearing; reissue			
❑ ST 1524 [S]	The Swingin's Mutual	1961	20.00
—Black label with colorband, Capitol logo on top			
❑ ST 1524 [S]	The Swingin's Mutual	1961	30.00
—Black label with colorband, Capitol logo on left			
❑ T 1524 [M]	The Swingin's Mutual	1961	15.00
—Black label with colorband, Capitol logo on top			
❑ T 1524 [M]	The Swingin's Mutual	1961	25.00
—Black label with colorband, Capitol logo on left			
❑ ST 1767 [S]	Hello Young Lovers	1962	25.00
❑ T 1767 [M]	Hello Young Lovers	1962	20.00
❑ SM-1828	Broadway My Way	197?	10.00
—Reissue			
❑ ST 1828 [S]	Broadway My Way	1963	20.00
❑ T 1828 [M]	Broadway My Way	1963	15.00
❑ SM-1934	Hollywood My Way	197?	10.00
—Reissue			
❑ ST 1934 [S]	Hollywood My Way	1963	20.00
❑ T 1934 [M]	Hollywood My Way	1963	15.00
❑ ST 2012 [S]	Yesterday's Love Songs/Today's Blues	1964	20.00
❑ T 2012 [M]	Yesterday's Love Songs/Today's Blues	1964	15.00
❑ ST 2082 [S]	Today, Tomorrow, Forever	1964	20.00
❑ T 2082 [M]	Today, Tomorrow, Forever	1964	15.00
❑ KAO 2136 [M]	The Nancy Wilson Show!	1965	15.00
❑ SKAO 2136 [S]	The Nancy Wilson Show!	1965	20.00
❑ ST 2155 [S]	How Glad I Am	1964	20.00
❑ T 2155 [M]	How Glad I Am	1964	15.00
❑ ST 2321 [S]	Today — My Way	1965	20.00
❑ T 2321 [M]	Today — My Way	1965	15.00
❑ ST 2351 [S]	Gentle Is My Love	1965	20.00
❑ T 2351 [M]	Gentle Is My Love	1965	15.00
❑ ST 2433 [S]	From Broadway with Love	1966	20.00
❑ T 2433 [M]	From Broadway with Love	1966	15.00
❑ SM-2495	A Touch of Today	197?	10.00
—Reissue			
❑ ST 2495 [S]	A Touch of Today	1966	20.00
❑ T 2495 [M]	A Touch of Today	1966	15.00
❑ ST 2555 [S]	Tender Loving Care	1966	20.00
❑ T 2555 [M]	Tender Loving Care	1966	15.00
❑ ST 2634 [S]	Nancy — Naturally	1967	20.00
❑ T 2634 [M]	Nancy — Naturally	1967	15.00
❑ ST 2712 [S]	Just for Now	1967	20.00
❑ T 2712 [M]	Just for Now	1967	15.00
❑ ST 2757 [S]	Lush Life	1967	15.00
❑ T 2757 [M]	Lush Life	1967	20.00
❑ ST 2844 [S]	Welcome to My Love	1968	15.00
❑ T 2844 [M]	Welcome to My Love	1968	25.00
❑ ST 2909	Easy	1968	15.00
❑ SKAO 2947	The Best of Nancy Wilson	1968	15.00
❑ ST 2970	The Sound of Nancy Wilson	1968	15.00
❑ SY-4575	Broadway My Way	197?	10.00
—Odd reissue			
❑ ST-11131	I Know I Love Him	1972	12.00
❑ ST-11317	All in Love Is Fair	1974	12.00
❑ ST-11386	Come Get to This	1975	12.00
❑ ST-11518	This Mother's Daughter	1976	12.00
❑ ST-11659	I've Never Been to Me	1977	12.00
❑ SM-11767	How Glad I Am	1978	10.00
—Reissue of 2155			
❑ SMAS-11786	Music on My Mind	1978	12.00
❑ SM-11802	Easy	1978	10.00
—Reissue of 2909			
❑ SM-11819	Come Get to This	1978	10.00
—Reissue of 11386			
❑ SM-11884	Nancy — Naturally	1979	10.00
—Reissue of 2634			
❑ ST-11943	Life, Love and Happiness	1979	12.00
❑ SM-12031	Can't Take My Eyes Off You	1980	10.00
—Reissue of 429			
❑ ST-12055	Take My Love	1980	12.00
❑ SN-16128	The Best of Nancy Wilson	198?	8.00
—Budget-line reissue			

COLUMBIA

Number	Title (A Side/B Side)	Yr	NM
❑ FC 40330	Keep You Satisfied	1986	10.00
❑ FC 40787	Forbidden Lover	1987	10.00
❑ FC 44464	Nancy Now!	1989	10.00

PAUSA

Number	Title (A Side/B Side)	Yr	NM
❑ PR-9041	Nancy — Naturally	1985	10.00

PICKWICK

Number	Title (A Side/B Side)	Yr	NM
❑ SPC-3273	Goin' Out of My Head	197?	10.00
❑ SPC-3348	The Good Life	197?	10.00

WILSON, NANCY, AND CANNONBALL ADDERLEY

45s

CAPITOL

Number	Title (A Side/B Side)	Yr	NM
❑ 4693	Save Your Love for Me/Never Will I Marry	1962	8.00

Albums

CAPITOL

Number	Title (A Side/B Side)	Yr	NM
❑ SM-1657	Nancy Wilson/Cannonball Adderley	197?	10.00
—Reissue			
❑ ST 1657 [S]	Nancy Wilson/Cannonball Adderley	1962	20.00
—Black label with colorband, Capitol logo on top			
❑ ST 1657 [S]	Nancy Wilson/Cannonball Adderley	1962	30.00
—Black label with colorband, Capitol logo on left			
❑ T 1657 [M]	Nancy Wilson/Cannonball Adderley	1962	15.00
—Black label with colorband, Capitol logo on top			
❑ T 1657 [M]	Nancy Wilson/Cannonball Adderley	1962	25.00
—Black label with colorband, Capitol logo on left			

WILSON, PEANUTS

45s

BRUNSWICK

Number	Title (A Side/B Side)	Yr	NM
❑ 55039	Cast Iron Arm/You've Got Love	1957	150.00

WILSON, SONNY

45s

CANDIX

Number	Title (A Side/B Side)	Yr	NM
❑ 327	I Ain't Givin' Up Nothin'/Troubled Time	1962	20.00

SUN

Number	Title (A Side/B Side)	Yr	NM
❑ 341	The Great Pretender/I'm Gonna Take a Walk	1960	20.00

WILSON, TED

45s

SIERRA

Number	Title (A Side/B Side)	Yr	NM
❑ 267	I Can't Take No More/(B-side unknown)	196?	1500.

WILSON, WALLY

45s

SABRE

Number	Title (A Side/B Side)	Yr	NM
❑ 106	If You Don't Love Me/The Hunt	1954	600.00

WIMBERLEY, MAGGIE SUE

45s

SUN

Number	Title (A Side/B Side)	Yr	NM
❑ 229	Daydreams Come True/How Long	1956	60.00

WINCHELL, DANNY

45s

MGM

Number	Title (A Side/B Side)	Yr	NM
❑ 11335	Carolina in the Morning/There Goes My Heart	1952	30.00

RECORTE

Number	Title (A Side/B Side)	Yr	NM
❑ 406	Jeannie/Beware You've Fallen in Love	1959	40.00
❑ 410	We're Gonna Have a Rockin' Party/Don't Say You're Sorry	1959	50.00
❑ 415	Come Back Baby/I've Chosen You	1959	40.00

WINCHESTER, JESSE

45s

AMPEX

Number	Title (A Side/B Side)	Yr	NM
❑ 11004	Yankee Lady/That's the Touch I Like	1970	6.00
❑ 11018	Quiet About It/Biloxi	1970	6.00

BEARSVILLE

Number	Title (A Side/B Side)	Yr	NM
❑ 0311	The Brand New Tennessee Waltz/Let the Rough Side Drag	1976	4.00
❑ 0314	Everybody Knows But Me/Damned If You Do	1976	4.00
❑ 0318	Nothing But a Breeze/Twigs and Seeds	1977	4.00
❑ 0320	Rhumba Man/Twigs and Seeds	1977	4.00
❑ 0332	Sassy/Wintry Feeling	1978	4.00
❑ 49711	Say What/If Only	1981	4.00
❑ 49781	Baby Blue/Sure Enough	1981	4.00

Number	Title (A Side/B Side)	Yr	NM
Albums			
AMPEX			
❑ A 10104	Jesse Winchester	1970	20.00
BEARSVILLE			
❑ PRO 560 [DJ]	The Jesse Winchester Radio Show	1976	40.00
❑ PRO-A-693 [(2)DJ]	Live at the Bijou Café Plus a Live Interview at Media College in Montreal	1977	40.00
❑ BR 2045	Jesse Winchester	1971	15.00
—Reissue of Ampex LP			
❑ BR 2102	Third Down, 110 to Go	1972	15.00
❑ BR 6953	Learn to Love It	1974	12.00
❑ BR 6964	Let the Rough Side Drag	1976	12.00
❑ BR 6968	Nothing But a Breeze	1977	10.00
❑ BRK 6984	A Touch on the Rainy Side	1978	10.00
❑ BRK 6989	Talk Memphis	1981	10.00
RHINO			
❑ R1-70085	The Best of Jesse Winchester	1989	10.00
❑ RNLP-70885	Jesse Winchester	1988	10.00
❑ RNLP-70886	Third Down, 110 to Go	1988	10.00
SUGAR HILL			
❑ SH-1023	Humour Me	1988	12.00

WIND TONY ORLANDO was in this group.

Number	Title (A Side/B Side)	Yr	NM
45s			
FORWARD			
❑ 152	Groovin' with Mr. Bloe/Are You Nuts?	1970	5.00
—As "Cool Heat"			
LIFE			
❑ 200	Make Believe/Groovin' with Mr. Bloe	1969	5.00
❑ 202	Teeny Bopper/I'll Hold Out My Hand	1969	5.00
❑ 203	Groovin' with Mr. Bloe/Are You Nuts?	1970	6.00
—As "Cool Heat"			
Albums			
LIFE			
❑ LLPS-2000	Make Believe	1969	20.00

WIND HARP, THE

Number	Title (A Side/B Side)	Yr	NM
Albums			
UNITED ARTISTS			
❑ UAS-9963 [(2)]	Song from the Hill	1972	20.00

WIND IN THE WILLOWS, THE With Debbie Harry, later of Blondie.

Number	Title (A Side/B Side)	Yr	NM
45s			
CAPITOL			
❑ 2274	Uptown Girl/Moments Spent	1968	20.00
Albums			
CAPITOL			
❑ SKAO 2956	The Wind in the Willows	1968	50.00

WINDING, KAI

Number	Title (A Side/B Side)	Yr	NM
45s			
A&M			
❑ 1035	Wichita Lineman/Betwixt and Between	1969	6.00
COLUMBIA			
❑ 41330	Manhattan/Cha Cha Chicago	1959	10.00
IMPULSE!			
❑ 201	Theme from Picnic/Side by Side	1961	10.00
—With J.J. Johnson			
VERVE			
❑ 10258	Baby Elephant Walk/Experiment in Terror	1963	8.00
❑ 10295	More/Comin' Home Baby	1963	10.00
❑ 10301	Ice Cream Man/The Lonely One	1963	8.00
❑ 10307	Time Is On My Side/Baby Don't Come On with Me	1963	8.00
❑ 10313	Portrait of My Love/Mondo Cane #2	1964	8.00
❑ 10313 [PS]	Portrait of My Love/Mondo Cane #2	1964	12.00
❑ 10328	Don't Blow Your Cool (In the Merry Old Summertime)/New Song of India	1964	8.00
❑ 10334	Theme from The Luck of Ginger Coffey/Do Anything You Wanna	1964	8.00
❑ 10335	Dear Heart/Wolverton Mountain	1964	8.00
❑ 10343	I Will Wait for You/Baker Street Mystery	1965	6.00
❑ 10348	Marriage, Italian Style/My Hands Reach Out to You	1965	6.00
❑ 10355	Singin' in the Rain/Half a Crown	1965	6.00
❑ 10372	A Sign of the Times/You've Lost That Lovin' Feelin'	1965	6.00
❑ 10407	Dirty Dog/Sunrise	1966	6.00
❑ 10433	The Sidewinder/Something You Got	1966	6.00
❑ 10455	All/More	1966	6.00
❑ 10488	Penny Lane/Time	1967	6.00
Albums			
A&M			
❑ SP-3008	Israel	1969	12.00
ABC IMPULSE!			
❑ AS 3 [S]	The Incredible Kai Winding Trombones	1968	12.00
—Black and red label			
COLUMBIA			
❑ CL 936 [M]	Trombone Sound	1956	50.00
❑ CL 999 [M]	Trombone Panorama	1957	50.00
❑ CL 1264 [M]	Swingin' State	1958	50.00
❑ CL 1329 [M]	Dance to the City Beat	1959	40.00
❑ CS 8062 [S]	Swingin' State	1958	40.00
❑ CS 8136 [S]	Dance to the City Beat	1959	30.00
GATEWAY			
❑ 7022	Jazz Showcase	1979	10.00
GLENDALE			
❑ 6003	Danish Blue	1976	10.00
❑ 6004	Caravan	1977	10.00
HARMONY			
❑ HL 7341 [M]	The Great Kai Winding Sound	1962	15.00
IMPULSE!			
❑ A 3 [M]	The Incredible Kai Winding Trombones	1960	30.00
❑ AS 3 [S]	The Incredible Kai Winding Trombones	1960	25.00
—Orange and black label			
MCA			
❑ 29062	Incredible Kai Winding Trombones	198?	10.00
—Reissue of Impulse! 3			
PICKWICK			
❑ SPC-3004	Trombones	196?	12.00
RED RECORD			
❑ VPA-143	Duo Bones	198?	12.00
ROOST			
❑ LP 408 [10]	Kai Winding All Stars	1952	120.00
SAVOY			
❑ MG-9017 [10]	New Trends Of Jazz	1952	120.00
❑ MG-12119 [M]	In the Beginning	196?	15.00
VERVE			
❑ V-8427 [M]	Kai Ole	1962	25.00
❑ V6-8427 [S]	Kai Ole	1962	25.00
❑ V-8493 [M]	Suspense Themes in Jazz	1962	25.00
❑ V6-8493 [S]	Suspense Themes in Jazz	1962	25.00
❑ V-8525 [M]	Kai Winding Solo	1963	25.00
❑ V6-8525 [S]	Kai Winding Solo	1963	25.00
❑ V-8551 [M]	More!!!	1963	25.00
❑ V6-8551 [S]	More!!!	1963	25.00
❑ V-8556 [M]	The Lonely One	1963	25.00
❑ V6-8556 [S]	The Lonely One	1963	25.00
❑ V-8573 [M]	Mondo Cane #2	1964	25.00
❑ V6-8573 [S]	Mondo Cane #2	1964	30.00
❑ V-8602 [M]	Modern Country	1964	15.00
❑ V6-8602 [S]	Modern Country	1964	20.00
❑ V-8620 [M]	Rainy Day	1965	15.00
❑ V6-8620 [S]	Rainy Day	1965	20.00
❑ V-8639 [M]	The "In" Instrumentals	1965	15.00
❑ V6-8639 [S]	The "In" Instrumentals	1965	20.00
❑ V-8657 [M]	More Brass	1966	12.00
❑ V6-8657 [S]	More Brass	1966	15.00
❑ V-8661 [M]	Dirty Dog	1966	12.00
❑ V6-8661 [S]	Dirty Dog	1966	15.00
❑ V-8691 [M]	Penny Lane and Time	1967	15.00
❑ V6-8691 [S]	Penny Lane and Time	1967	12.00
WHO'S WHO IN JAZZ			
❑ 21001	Lionel Hampton Presents Kai Winding	1978	10.00

WINDING, KAI, AND SONNY STITT

Number	Title (A Side/B Side)	Yr	NM
Albums			
HALL OF FAME			
❑ 612	Early Modern	197?	10.00

WINDSORS, THE (1)

Number	Title (A Side/B Side)	Yr	NM
45s			
ABC-PARAMOUNT			
❑ 10563	Keep Away/Fingers and Thumbs	1964	15.00

WINDSORS, THE (2)

Number	Title (A Side/B Side)	Yr	NM
45s			
BACK BEAT			
❑ 506	My Gloria/Cool Seabreeze	1958	8000.
—VG 4000; VG+ 6000			

WINDSORS, THE (U)

Number	Title (A Side/B Side)	Yr	NM
45s			
UNITED ARTISTS			
❑ 128	Saki Rock/Caramba	1958	20.00
WIG WAG			
❑ 203	Carol Ann/Keep Me from Crying	1959	200.00

WINE, TONI

Number	Title (A Side/B Side)	Yr	NM
45s			
ATCO			
❑ 6736	Sisters in Sorrow/Take a Little Time Out for Love	1970	6.00
COLPIX			
❑ 715	My Boyfriend's Coming Home for Christmas/What a Pity	1963	15.00
❑ 732	I Love That Boy/The Thirteenth Hour	1964	12.00
❑ 742	A Boy Like You/Funny Little Heart	1964	12.00
❑ 756	Only Fools/A Girl Is Not a Girl	1964	12.00
SENATE			
❑ 2104	River Deep, Mountain High/Toni's Tune	1967	10.00

WINGFIELD, PETE Also see OLYMPIC RUNNERS.

Number	Title (A Side/B Side)	Yr	NM
45s			
ISLAND			
❑ 026	Eighteen with a Bullet/Shadow of a Doubt	1975	5.00
—Second pressing: Mostly black label with Island logo at bottom			
❑ 026	Eighteen with a Bullet/Shadow of a Doubt	1975	8.00
—First pressing: Mostly yellow label with island scene			
❑ 051	Lovin' As You Wanna Be/Please	1975	4.00
❑ 065	Scratchy 45's/A Whole Pot of Jelly (For a Little Slice of Toast)	1976	4.00
Albums			
ISLAND			
❑ ILPS 9333	Breakfast Special	1975	12.00

WINGS See PAUL McCARTNEY.

WINKLY AND NUTLY

Number	Title (A Side/B Side)	Yr	NM
45s			
MK			
❑ 101	Report to the Nation (Part 1)/Report to the Nation (Part 2)	1960	20.00

WINSTON, GEORGE

Number	Title (A Side/B Side)	Yr	NM
45s			
WINDHAM HILL			
❑ WS-0005	Variations on the Kanon by Johann Pachelbel/Carol of the Bells	1984	5.00
❑ WS-0005 [PS]	Variations on the Kanon by Johann Pachelbel/Carol of the Bells	1984	5.00
Albums			
LOST LAKE ARTS			
❑ LL-0081	Ballads and Blues 1972	1981	10.00
—Reissue of Takoma recordings			
TAKOMA			
❑ 9016	Piano Solos	1973	15.00
WINDHAM HILL			
❑ C-1012	Autumn	1980	12.00
—Original issue			
❑ WH-1012	Autumn	1984	10.00
—Reissue with A&M distribution			
❑ C-1019	Winter Into Spring	1982	12.00
—Original issue			
❑ WH-1019	Winter Into Spring	1984	10.00
—Reissue, distributed by A&M Records			
❑ C-1025	December	1982	15.00
—NOT distributed by A&M Records; "December: in black letters			
❑ WH- 1025	December	1984	10.00
—Distributed by A&M Records; "December" in raised white letters			

WINSTON, HATTIE

Number	Title (A Side/B Side)	Yr	NM
45s			
PARKWAY			
❑ 928	Pictures Don't Lie/"Please Write Back to Me	1964	20.00
❑ 956	Pass Me By/Pictures Don't Lie	1965	80.00

WINSTONS, THE

Number	Title (A Side/B Side)	Yr	NM
45s			
METROMEDIA			
❑ 117	Color Him Father/Amen, Brother	1969	8.00
❑ 142	Love of the Common People/Wheel of Fortune	1969	6.00
❑ 151	Birds of a Feather/The Greatest Love	1969	6.00

Except when noted otherwise, VG = 25% of NM, and VG+ = 50% of NM. (Example: VG = $2.00, VG+ = $4.00 and NM = $8.00.)

Number	Title (A Side/B Side)	Yr	NM
Albums			
METROMEDIA			
❑ MD-1010	Color Him Father	1969	50.00

WINTER, EDGAR

Number	Title (A Side/B Side)	Yr	NM
12-Inch Singles			
BODY ROCK			
❑ BR 5001	Frankenstein 1984 (Monster Version 9:49) (Human Version 4:52) (Monster Rap 9:51)	1984	12.00
45s			
BLUE SKY			
❑ 2758	One Day Tomorrow/ Jasmine Nightdream	1975	4.00
❑ 2761	Outa Control/I Always Wanted You	1975	4.00
❑ 2762	Cool Dance/People Music	1975	4.00
❑ 2763	Diamond Eyes/Infinite Peace in Rhythm	1976	4.00
❑ 2769	Stickin' It Out/Puttin' It Back	1977	4.00
❑ 2780	Forever in Love/ It's Your Life to Live	1979	4.00
❑ 2786	Above and Beyond/ (Instrumental)	1980	4.00
❑ 70068	Love Is Everywhere/ Everyday Man	1981	4.00
EPIC			
❑ JBQ 506 [Q]	Frankenstein/Free Ride	1973	10.00
—"Special Coin Operator Release" in quadraphonic; contains single edit of "Frankenstein" and unknown version of "Free Ride"			
❑ 10618	Tobacco Road/Now Is the Time	1970	8.00
❑ 10740	Good Morning Music/ Where Would I Be	1971	8.00
❑ 10750	Where Would I Be/ Feeling Like a Woman	1971	6.00
—B-side by Patsy Sledd			
❑ 10762	Give It Everything You've Got/ You Were My Light	1971	6.00
❑ 10788	Keep Playin' That Rock 'N' Roll/ Dying to Live	1971	6.00
❑ 10855	I Can't Turn You Loose/Cool Fool	1972	6.00
❑ 10903	Free Ride/Catchin' Up	1972	8.00
❑ 10922	Round and Round/Catchin' Up	1972	8.00
❑ 10945	Frankenstein/Hangin' Around	1973	8.00
❑ 10967	Frankenstein/Undercover Man	1973	4.00
—Orange label			
❑ 10967	Frankenstein/Undercover Man	1973	6.00
—Yellow label			
❑ 11024	Free Ride/When It Comes	1973	4.00
❑ 11069	Hangin' Around/We All Had a Real Good Time	1973	4.00
❑ 11143	River's Risin'/Animal	1974	4.00
❑ 50034	Easy Street/Do Like Me	1974	4.00
❑ 50060	Miracle of Love/Someone Take My Heart Away	1975	4.00
Albums			
BLUE SKY			
❑ PZ 33483	Jasmine Nightdreams	1975	12.00
❑ PZQ 33483 [Q]	Jasmine Nightdreams	1975	20.00
❑ PZ 33798	The Edgar Winter Group with Rick Derringer	1975	12.00
❑ PZQ 33798 [Q]	The Edgar Winter Group with Rick Derringer	1975	20.00
❑ PZ 34858	Re-Cycled	1977	12.00
❑ JZ 35989	The Edger Winter Album	1979	12.00
❑ JZ 36494	Standing on Rock	1981	12.00
EPIC			
❑ BN 26503	Entrance	1970	15.00
—Yellow label			
❑ BN 26503	Entrance	1973	12.00
—Orange label			
❑ E 30512	Edgar Winter's White Trash	1971	15.00
—Yellow label			
❑ KE 30512	Edgar Winter's White Trash	1973	12.00
—Orange label			
❑ PE 30512	Edger Winter's White Trash	1985	8.00
—Budget-line reissue; dark blue label			
❑ EG 31249 [(2)]	Roadwork	1987	10.00
—Budget-line reissue; dark blue labels			
❑ KEG 31249 [(2)]	Roadwork	1972	20.00
—Yellow labels			
❑ KEG 31249 [(2)]	Roadwork	1973	15.00
—Orange labels			
❑ EQ 31584 [Q]	They Only Come Out at Night	1973	25.00
❑ KE 31584	They Only Come Out at Night	1972	15.00
—Yellow label			
❑ KE 31584	They Only Come Out at Night	1973	12.00
—Orange label			
❑ PE 31584	They Only Come Out at Night	197?	10.00
—Reissue with new prefix; orange label			
❑ PE 31584	They Only Come Out at Night	1979	8.00
—Budget-line reissue; dark blue label			
❑ PE 32461	Shock Treatment	1974	15.00
—Orange label			
❑ PE 32461	Shock Treatment	1985	8.00
—Budget-line reissue; dark blue label			
❑ PEQ 32461 [Q]	Shock Treatment	1974	25.00
❑ BG 33770 [(2)]	Entrance/White Trash	1975	15.00
—Combines 26503 and 30512 into one package			
RHINO			
❑ R1-70709	Mission Earth	1989	12.00
❑ R1-70895	The Edger Winter Collection	1989	10.00

WINTER, JOHNNY

Also see JOHNNY AND THE JAMMERS.

Number	Title (A Side/B Side)	Yr	NM
45s			
ATLANTIC			
❑ 2248	Gangster of Love/Eternally	1964	10.00
BLUE SKY			
❑ 2754	Raised on Rock/ Pick Up on My Mojo	1974	4.00
❑ 2756	Golden Olden Days of Rock 'N' Roll/Stranger	1975	4.00
BUDDAH			
❑ 168	Out of Sight/Bad News	1970	10.00
COLUMBIA			
❑ 44900	I'll Drown in My Tears/ I'm Yours and I'm Here	1969	5.00
❑ 45058	Johnny B. Goode/I'm Not Sure	1969	5.00
❑ 45260	Rock and Roll Hoochie Koo/ 21st Century Man	1970	5.00
❑ 45368	Jumpin' Jack Flash/Good Morning, Little Schoolgirl	1971	5.00
❑ 45860	Silver Train/Rock and Roll	1973	5.00
❑ 45899	Can't You Feel It/Rock and Roll	1973	5.00
❑ 46006	Bad Luck Situation/Stone County	1974	5.00
❑ 46036	Boney Moroney/Hurtin' So Bad	1974	5.00
FROLIC			
❑ 501	That's What Love Does/Shed So Many Tears	1962	50.00
❑ 503	Voo Doo Twist/Ease My Pain	1962	100.00
❑ 509	Gangster of Love/Eternally	1963	50.00
❑ 512	Gone for Bad/I Won't Believe It	1963	60.00
GRT			
❑ 9	Gangster of Love/Roadrunner	1969	8.00
IMPERIAL			
❑ 66376	Forty-Four/Rollin' & Tumblin'	1969	8.00
MGM			
❑ 13380	Gone for Bad/I Won't Believe It	1965	8.00
PACEMAKER			
❑ 243	Leavin' Blues/ Birds Can't Row Boats	1966	20.00
TODD			
❑ 1084	Road Runner/The Guy You Left Behind	1963	20.00
Albums			
ACCORD			
❑ SN-7135	Ready for Winter	1981	10.00
ALLIGATOR			
❑ 4735	Guitar Slinger	1984	10.00
❑ 4742	Serious Business	1985	10.00
❑ 4748	Third Degree	1986	10.00
BLUE SKY			
❑ PZ 33292	John Dawson Winter III	1974	12.00
❑ PZQ 33292 [Q]	John Dawson Winter III	1974	20.00
❑ PZ 33944	Captured Live!	1976	12.00
—No bar code on cover			
❑ PZ 33944	Captured Live	198?	8.00
—Budget-line reissue with bar code on cover			
❑ PZ 34813	Nothin' But the Blues	1977	12.00
—No bar code on cover			
❑ PZ 34813	Nothin' But the Blues	198?	8.00
—Budget-line reissue with bar code on cover			
❑ JZ 35475	White, Hot and Blue	1978	12.00
❑ JZ 36343	Raisin' Cain	1980	12.00
BUDDAH			
❑ BDS-7513	First Winter	1969	20.00
COLUMBIA			
❑ CS 9826	Johnny Winter	1969	20.00
—"360 Sound" label			
❑ CS 9826	Johnny Winter	1970	12.00
—Orange label			
❑ PC 9826	Johnny Winter	198?	8.00
—Budget-line reissue			
❑ KCS 9947 [(2)]	Second Winter	1969	25.00
—"360 Sound" labels; record 2 has music on only one side (other side is blank)			
❑ KCS 9947 [(2)]	Second Winter	1970	15.00
—Orange labels			
❑ PC 9947 [(2)]	Second Winter	198?	10.00
—Budget-line reissue			
❑ C 30221	Johnny Winter And	1970	12.00
—Orange labels			
❑ C 30221	Johnny Winter And	1970	20.00
—"360 Sound" label			
❑ PC 30221	Johnny Winter And	198?	8.00
—Budget-line reissue			
❑ C 30475	Live/Johnny Winter And	1971	15.00
❑ PC 30475	Live/Johnny Winter And	198?	8.00
—Budget-line reissue			
❑ CQ 32188 [Q]	Still Alive and Well	1973	25.00
❑ KC 32188	Still Alive and Well	1973	15.00
❑ PC 32188	Still Alive and Well	198?	8.00
—Budget-line reissue			
❑ CQ 32715 [Q]	Saints and Sinners	1974	25.00
❑ KC 32715	Saints and Sinners	1974	15.00
❑ PC 32715	Saints and Sinners	197?	8.00
—Budget-line reissue			
❑ CG 33651 [(2)]	Johnny Winter And//Live/ Johnny Winter And	1975	15.00
GRT			
❑ 10010	The Johnny Winter Story	1969	20.00
IMPERIAL			
❑ LP-12431	The Progressive Blues Experiment	1969	50.00
JANUS			
❑ 3008	About Blues	1970	20.00
❑ 3023	Early Times	1970	25.00
❑ 3056 [(2)]	Before the Storm	197?	20.00
LIBERTY			
❑ LN-10294	The Progressive Blues Experiment	1986	10.00
—Reissue of Imperial LP			
MCA/VOYAGER			
❑ 42241	The Winter of '88	1988	10.00
SONOBEAT			
❑ RS-1002	The Progressive Blues Experiment	1968	300.00
—Released in plain white cardboard jacket			
UNITED ARTISTS			
❑ UA-LA139-F	Austin, Tex.	1974	15.00

WINTER, JOHNNY AND EDGAR

Also see each artist's individual listings.

Number	Title (A Side/B Side)	Yr	NM
45s			
BLUE SKY			
❑ 2764	Soul Man/Let the Good Times Roll	1976	4.00
Albums			
BLUE SKY			
❑ ASZ 242 [DJ]	Johnny and Edgar Winter Discuss Together	1976	25.00
—Promo-only interview album			
❑ PZ 34033	Together	1976	12.00

WINTERS, JONATHAN

Number	Title (A Side/B Side)	Yr	NM
Albums			
COLUMBIA			
❑ CL 2811 [M]	Jonathan Winters Wings It!	1968	25.00
❑ CS 9611 [S]	Jonathan Winters Wings It!	1968	15.00
❑ CS 9799	Stuff 'N' Nonsense	1969	15.00
❑ KG 31985 [(2)]	Jonathan Winters Laughs Live	1972	20.00
—Reissue of 9611 and 9799 in one package			
❑ PG 31985 [(2)]	Jonathan Winters Laughs Live	197?	12.00
—Reissue with new prefix			
VERVE			
❑ MGVS-6099 [S]	The Wonderful World of Jonathan Winters	1960	25.00
❑ MGVS-6155 [S]	Down to Earth	1960	25.00
❑ MGV-15009 [M]	The Wonderful World of Jonathan Winters	1960	25.00
❑ V-15009 [M]	The Wonderful World of Jonathan Winters	1961	20.00
❑ V6-15009 [S]	The Wonderful World of Jonathan Winters	1961	20.00
—Reissue of 6099			
❑ MGV-15011 [M]	Down to Earth	1960	25.00
❑ V-15011 [M]	Down to Earth	1961	20.00
❑ V6-15011 [S]	Down to Earth	1961	20.00
—Reissue of 6155			
❑ V-15025 [M]	Here's Jonathan	1961	25.00
❑ V6-15025 [S]	Here's Jonathan	1961	25.00
❑ V-15032 [M]	Another Day, Another World	1962	25.00
❑ V6-15032 [R]	Another Day, Another World	196?	12.00
❑ V-15035 [M]	Humor As Seen Through the Eyes of Jonathan Winters	1963	25.00
❑ V6-15035 [S]	Humor As Seen Through the Eyes of Jonathan Winters	1963	25.00
❑ V-15037 [M]	Whistle Stopping with Jonathan Winters	1964	20.00
❑ V6-15037 [R]	Whistle Stopping with Jonathan Winters	196?	12.00
❑ V-15041 [M]	Jonathan Winters' Mad, Mad, Mad, Mad World	1964	20.00
❑ V6-15041 [R]	Jonathan Winters' Mad, Mad, Mad, Mad World	196?	12.00
❑ V-15047 [M]	Great Moments in Comedy	1965	20.00
❑ V6-15047 [R]	Great Moments in Comedy	196?	12.00
❑ V-15052 [M]	The Best of Frickert and Suggins	1966	20.00
❑ V6-15052 [R]	The Best of Frickert and Suggins	196?	12.00
❑ V-15057 [M]	Movies Are Better Than Ever	1967	20.00
❑ V6-15057 [R]	Movies Are Better Than Ever	196?	12.00

W

Steve Winwood, "Holding On," Virgin 1457, 1988, **$3.**

WINWOOD, STEVE Also see BLIND FAITH; THE SPENCER DAVIS GROUP; TRAFFIC.

12-Inch Singles

ISLAND

Number	Title (A Side/B Side)	Yr	NM
❑ PRO-A2-940 RE-1 [DJ]	Night Train/I Will Follow	1980	100.00
—B-side by U2			
❑ PRO-A-1054 [DJ]	Still in the Game (same on both sides)	1982	12.00
❑ PRO-A-2507 [DJ]	Higher Love (same on both sides?)	1986	15.00
❑ PRO-A-2540 [DJ]	Split Decision (same on both sides)	1986	10.00
❑ PRO-A-2562 [DJ]	Freedom Overspill (Edit 4:09) (LP Version 5:33)	1986	8.00
❑ PRO-A-2620 [DJ]	Back in the High Life Again (Edit 4:20) (LP Version 5:33)	1986	10.00
❑ PRO-A-2651 [DJ]	The Finer Things (Edit) (LP Version)	1987	12.00
❑ PRO-A-2703 [DJ]	Wake Me Up on Judgment Day (Edit) (LP Version)	1987	10.00
❑ PRO-A-2814 [DJ]	Valerie (same on both sides)	1987	8.00
❑ PRO-A-2908 [DJ]	Talking Back to the Night (same on both sides)	1987	10.00
❑ 20537	Freedom Overspill (Liberty Mix 7:30) (Dub 6:00)/Higher Lover (Extended Remix 7:45)/Help Me Angel (5:05)	1986	10.00

VIRGIN

Number	Title (A Side/B Side)	Yr	NM
❑ DMD 1193 [DJ]	Roll With It (12" Remix) (Steve Testifies Dub) (Dub #2)	1988	8.00
❑ PR 2303 [DJ]	Roll With It (7" Version) (LP Version)	1988	12.00
❑ PR 2427 [DJ]	Don't You Know What the Night Can Do? (Remix) (LP Version)	1988	10.00
❑ PR 2524 [DJ]	Put On Your Dancing Shoes/ Holding On (Instrumental)/ Don't You Know What the Night Can Do? (Instrumental)/Gojuan (Aaghh Mix)	1988	20.00
❑ PR 2637 [DJ]	Hearts on Fire (Remix) (LP Version)	1988	8.00
❑ 96595	Holding On (Dance Mix 9:55)/ Gojuan (Aaghh Mix 5:05) (Groove Mix 4:56)	1988	8.00
❑ 96620	Don't You Know What the Night Can Do? (Extended)/ (Instrumental)	1988	10.00
❑ 96648	Roll With It (12" Remix 9:53) (Steve Testifies Dub 6:44)/ The Morning Side (3:57)	1988	6.00

45s

ISLAND

Number	Title (A Side/B Side)	Yr	NM
❑ 091	Time Is Running Out/Hold On	1977	10.00
❑ 091 [DJ]	Time Is Running Out (same on both sides)	1977	5.00
❑ GIS 0411	While You See a Chance/ Arc of a Diver	198?	3.00
—"Back to Back Hits" reissue			
❑ 7-21932	The Finer Things/Back in the High Life Again	198?	3.00
—"Back to Back Hits" reissue			
❑ 7-21971	Higher Love/Freedom Overspill	198?	3.00
—"Back to Back Hits" reissue			
❑ 7-28122	Talking Back to the Night/ There's a River	1988	4.00
❑ 7-28122 [PS]	Talking Back to the Night/ There's a River	1988	4.00
❑ 7-28231	Valerie/Talking Back to the Night (Instrumental)	1987	3.00
❑ 7-28231 [PS]	Valerie/Talking Back to the Night (Instrumental)	1987	3.00
❑ 7-28472	Back in the High Life Again/ Night Train	1987	3.00
❑ 7-28472 [PS]	Back in the High Life Again/ Night Train	1987	3.00
❑ 7-28498	The Finer Things/Night Train	1987	3.00
❑ 7-28498 [PS]	The Finer Things/Night Train	1987	3.00
❑ 7-28595	Freedom Overspill/Help Me Angel	1986	3.00
❑ 7-28595 [PS]	Freedom Overspill/Help Me Angel	1986	3.00
❑ 7-28710	Higher Love/And I Go	1986	3.00
❑ 7-28710 [PS]	Higher Love/And I Go	1986	3.00
❑ 7-29879	Valerie/Slowdown Sundown	1982	7.00
❑ 7-29940	Still in the Game/Dust	1982	5.00
❑ 49656	While You See a Chance/ Vacant Chair	1981	4.00
❑ 49656 [PS]	While You See a Chance/ Vacant Chair	1981	5.00
❑ 49656 [DJ]	While You See a Chance (Edit)/ (LP Version)	1981	7.00
❑ 49726	Arc of a Diver/Dust	1981	4.00
❑ 49726 [PS]	Arc of a Diver/Dust	1981	5.00
❑ 49773	Night Train (Remix Edit)/ (Instrumental)	1981	8.00

VIRGIN

Number	Title (A Side/B Side)	Yr	NM
❑ 7-98892	One and Only Man/Always	1990	5.00
❑ 7-99234	Hearts On Fire (7" Remix)/ (Instrumental)	1989	3.00
❑ 7-99234 [PS]	Hearts On Fire (7" Remix)/ (Instrumental)	1989	3.00
❑ 7-99261	Holding On/(Instrumental)	1988	3.00
❑ 7-99261 [PS]	Holding On/(Instrumental)	1988	3.00
❑ 7-99290	Don't You Know What the Night Can Do/(Instrumental)	1988	3.00
❑ 7-99290 [PS]	Don't You Know What the Night Can Do/(Instrumental)	1988	3.00
❑ 7-99326	Roll With It/The Morning Side	1988	3.00
❑ 7-99326 [PS]	Roll With It/The Morning Side	1988	3.00

Albums

ISLAND

Number	Title	Yr	NM
❑ ILPS 9387	Go	1976	12.00
—With Stomo Yamahita and Michael Shrieve			
❑ ILPS 9494	Steve Winwood	1977	10.00
❑ ILPS 9576	Arc of a Diver	1981	10.00
❑ ILPS 9777	Talking Back to the Night	1982	10.00
❑ 25448	Back in the High Life	1986	8.00
❑ 25660	Chronicles	1987	8.00
❑ 5317713	Arc of a Diver	2009	20.00

SPRINGBOARD

Number	Title	Yr	NM
❑ SPB-4040	Winwood & Friends	197?	15.00
—Budget release with Winwood material on Side 1 and a collection of Jeff Beck, Yardbirds, Long John Baldry and Jack Bruce/Ginger Baker material on Side 2			

UNITED ARTISTS

Number	Title	Yr	NM
❑ UAS-9950 [(2)]	Winwood	1971	15.00
—Collection of tracks Winwood recorded with the Spencer Davis Group, Traffic and Blind Faith; without booklet			
❑ UAS-9950 [(2)]	Winwood	1971	25.00
—Collection of tracks Winwood recorded with the Spencer Davis Group, Traffic and Blind Faith; with booklet			

VIRGIN

Number	Title	Yr	NM
❑ 90946	Roll With It	1988	8.00
❑ 91405	Refugees of the Heart	1990	15.00
❑ R 154633	Roll With It	1988	10.00
—BMG Direct Marketing edition			

WIPERS, THE

45s

PARK AVE.

Number	Title (A Side/B Side)	Yr	NM
❑ PA-10	Alien Boy//Image of Man/ Telepathic Love/ Voices in the Rain	1980	12.50
❑ PA-10 [PS]	Alien Boy//Image of Man/ Telepathic Love/ Voices in the Rain	1980	12.50

TIM/KERR

Number	Title (A Side/B Side)	Yr	NM
❑ 7064	Silver Sail/Never Win	1993	2.00
❑ 7064 [PS]	Silver Sail/Never Win	1993	2.00

TRAP

Number	Title (A Side/B Side)	Yr	NM
❑ 008	Romeo/No Solution	1982	12.00
❑ 008 [PS]	Romeo/No Solution	1982	12.00
❑ 810x44	Better Off Dead//Up in Flames/ Does It Hurt?	1978	15.00
❑ 810x44 [PS]	Better Off Dead//Up in Flames/ Does It Hurt?	1978	15.00
—Black on orange sleeve, printed on one side, address on rear			
❑ 810x44 [PS]	Better Off Dead//Up in Flames/ Does It Hurt?	1978	25.00
—Red and black on yellow sleeve, printed on both sides			

Albums

PARK AVE.

Number	Title	Yr	NM
❑ (# unknown)	Is This Real?	1980	50.00
❑ 82802	Youth of America	1981	50.00

Except when noted otherwise, VG = 25% of NM, and VG+ = 50% of NM. (Example: VG = $2.00, VG+ = $4.00 and NM = $8.00.)

Number	Title (A Side/B Side)	Yr	NM
RESTLESS			
❑ 72026	Wipers Live	1985	12.00
❑ 72094	Land of the Lost	1986	12.00
❑ 72187	Over the Edge	1987	12.00
—Reissue			
❑ 72194	Follow Blind	1987	12.00
TIM/KERR			
❑ 31	Silver Sail	1993	12.00

WIRE

Number	Title (A Side/B Side)	Yr	NM
12-Inch Singles			
ENIGMA			
❑ EPRO 215 [DJ]	In Vivo (3 versions)	1989	10.00
❑ 75528	In Vivo (3 versions)/Illuminated (Remix)/Finest Drops (Live)	1989	10.00
MUTE/ENIGMA			
❑ 75520	Eardrum Buzz (LP)/Eardrum Buzz (Edit)/The Offer/It's a Boy	1986	6.00
RESTLESS			
❑ 72245	Kidney Bingos/Pieta (2 versions)/Over Theirs (Live)/Drill (Live)	1987	15.00
❑ 72299	Silk Skin Paws/German Shepherds/Ambitious (Remix)/Come Back in Two Halves	1988	10.00
Albums			
HARVEST			
❑ ST-11757	Pink Flag	1977	18.00
MUTE/ENIGMA			
❑ SWAO-73270	The Ideal Copy	1987	12.00
❑ MLP-73273 [EP]	Snakedrill	1987	12.00
❑ D1-73314	A Bell Is a Cup Until It Is Struck	1988	12.00
❑ D1-73516	It's Beginning to and Back Again	1989	12.00
WARNER BROS.			
❑ BSK 3398	154	1979	15.00

WISDOM, BILLY

Number	Title (A Side/B Side)	Yr	NM
45s			
OUT-A-SITE			
❑ 11	Handwriting on the Wall/(B-side unknown)	196?	2500.
—VG 1000; VG+ 1750			

WISDOMS, THE

Number	Title (A Side/B Side)	Yr	NM
45s			
GAITY			
❑ 169	Two Hearts Make One Love/Lost in Dreams	1959	600.00

WISHBONE ASH

Number	Title (A Side/B Side)	Yr	NM
45s			
ATLANTIC			
❑ 3381	Lorelei/Lorelei	1977	5.00
DECCA			
❑ 32826	Blind Eye/Queen of Torture	1971	8.00
❑ 32902	Jail Bait/Vas Dis	1971	8.00
❑ 33004	Blowin' Free/No Easy Road	1972	8.00
MCA			
❑ 40041	Rock and Roll Widow/No Easy Road	1973	6.00
❑ 40362	Persephone/Silver Shoes	1975	6.00
❑ 40829	Front Page News/Goodbye Baby, Hello Friends	1977	4.00
Albums			
ATLANTIC			
❑ SD 18164	Locked In	1976	10.00
❑ SD 18200	New England	1976	10.00
DECCA			
❑ DL 75249	Wishbone Ash	1971	15.00
❑ DL 75295	Pilgrimage	1971	15.00
❑ DL 75437	Argus	1972	15.00
FANTASY			
❑ 9629	Twin Barrels Burning	1983	10.00
I.R.S.			
❑ 42101	Nouveau Calls	1988	12.00
❑ 82006	Here to Hear	1989	12.00
MCA			
❑ 36	Pilgrimage	1973	12.00
—Reissue of Decca 75295			
❑ 49	Argus	1973	12.00
—Reissue of Decca 75437			
❑ 327	Wishbone Four	1973	12.00
❑ 464	There's the Rub	1974	12.00
❑ 769	No Smoke Without Fire	198?	8.00
—Reissue			
❑ 770	Just Testing	198?	8.00
—Reissue			
❑ 786	Wishbone Four	198?	8.00
—Reissue			
❑ 787	Argus	198?	8.00
—Reissue			
❑ 2311	Front Page News	1977	10.00
❑ 2343	Wishbone Ash	1978	10.00
—Reissue of Decca 75249			
❑ 2344	Argus	1978	10.00
—Reissue of MCA 49			
❑ 2348	Wishbone Four	1978	10.00
—Reissue of MCA 327			
❑ 3060	No Smoke Without Fire	1978	10.00
❑ 3221	Just Testing	1980	10.00
❑ 5283	Hot Ash	1981	10.00
❑ 8006 [(2)]	Live Dates	1973	15.00

WISNER, JIMMY

Number	Title (A Side/B Side)	Yr	NM
45s			
ATLANTIC			
❑ 2315	Choppin' Around/Juliet's Theme	1966	30.00
CAMEO			
❑ 373	A Walk in Space/El Senor Jose	1965	15.00
COLUMBIA			
❑ 4-44558	Theme from "The Swimmer"/Music	1967	8.00
❑ 4-44651	Interlude/La Playa	1968	7.00
❑ 4-44727	A Time for Us/Look to the Rainbow	1968	7.00
❑ 4-44959	Manhattan Safari/Quiet Boy	1969	7.00
Albums			
CHANCELLOR			
❑ CHJ-5014 [M]	Apér-Sepshun	1960	25.00
❑ CHJS-5014 [S]	Apér-Sepshun	1960	30.00
COLUMBIA			
❑ CS 9837	Love Theme from "Romeo and Juliet"	1969	10.00
FELSTED			
❑ FL-2509 [S]	Blues for Harvey	1962	25.00
❑ FL-7509 [M]	Blues for Harvey	1962	30.00
WYNCOTE			
❑ SW-9103 [S]	Cast Your Fate to the Wind	1965	12.00
❑ W-9103 [M]	Cast Your Fate to the Wind	1965	10.00

WITHERS, BILL

Number	Title (A Side/B Side)	Yr	NM
12-Inch Singles			
COLUMBIA			
❑ CAS 2112 [DJ]	Something That Turns You On (same on both sides)	1985	8.00
45s			
COLUMBIA			
❑ 02071	I Want to Spend the Night/Memories Are That Way	1981	4.00
❑ 02651	USA/Paint Your Pretty Picture	1981	4.00
❑ 02651 [PS]	USA/Paint Your Pretty Picture	1981	5.00
❑ 04841	Oh Yeah!/Just Like the First Time	1985	4.00
❑ 05424	Something That Turns You On/You Tried to Find a Love	1985	4.00
❑ 05424 [PS]	Something That Turns You On/You Tried to Find a Love	1985	4.00
❑ 05675	We Could Be Sweet Lovers/You Just Can't Smile It Away	1985	4.00
❑ 10255	Make Love to Your Mind/I Love You Dawn	1975	5.00
❑ 10308	I Wish You Well/She's Lonely	1976	5.00
❑ 10357	Family Table/Hello Like Before	1976	5.00
❑ 10420	If I Didn't Mean You Well/My Imagination	1976	5.00
❑ 10459	Close to Me/I'll Be with You	1976	5.00
❑ 10627	Lovely Day/It Ain't Because of Me Baby	1977	5.00
❑ 10702	Lovely Night for Dancing/I Want to Spend the Night	1978	5.00
❑ 10892	Don't It Make It Better/Love Is	1979	4.00
❑ 10958	You Got the Stuff/Look to Each Other for Love	1979	4.00
SUSSEX			
❑ 219	Ain't No Sunshine/Harlem	1971	6.00
❑ 227	Grandma's Hands/Sweet Wanomi	1971	5.00
❑ 227 [DJ]	Grandma's Hands (with Monologue)/(without Monologue)	1971	10.00
❑ 235	Lean On Me/Better Off Dead	1972	6.00
❑ 241	Use Me/Let Me in Your Life	1972	5.00
❑ 247	Let Us Love/The Gift of Giving	1972	5.00
❑ 247 [PS]	Let Us Love/The Gift of Giving	1972	8.00
❑ 250	Kissing My Love/I Don't Know	1973	5.00
❑ 257	Friend of Mine/Lonely Town, Lonely Street	1973	5.00
❑ 513	The Same Love That Made Me Laugh/Make a Smile for Me	1974	5.00
❑ 518	You/Stories	1974	5.00
❑ 629	Heartbreak Road/Ruby Lee	1974	5.00
—"Heartbreak Road" was the side that charted, though at least some copies of the stock 45 have it labeled as the B-side			
❑ 638	Who Is He (And What Is He to You)/Harlem	1975	5.00
Albums			
COLUMBIA			
❑ PC 33704	Making Music	1975	10.00
❑ PC 34327	Naked and Warm	1976	10.00
❑ JC 34903	Menagerie	1977	10.00
❑ JC 35596	'Bout Love	1979	10.00
❑ JC 36877	The Best of Bill Withers	1981	—
—Canceled?			
❑ FC 37199	Bill Withers' Greatest Hits	1981	10.00
—Re-release of 36877 with "Just the Two of Us" added			
❑ FC 39887	Watching You Watching Me	1985	10.00
❑ PC 40177	Still Bill	1985	8.00
—Reissue of Sussex 7014			
❑ PC 40178	Just As I Am	1985	8.00
—Reissue of Sussex 7006			
SUSSEX			
❑ SXBS-7006	Just As I Am	1971	20.00
❑ SXBS-7014	Still Bill	1972	20.00
❑ SXBS-7025-2 [(2)]	Bill Withers Live at Carnegie Hall	1973	20.00
❑ SUX-8032	+'Justments	1974	15.00
❑ SUX-8037	The Best of Bill Withers	1975	15.00

WITHERSPOON, JIMMY

Number	Title (A Side/B Side)	Yr	NM
45s			
ABC			
❑ 11288	Handbags and Gladrags/Stay with Me Baby	1971	6.00
BLUE NOTE			
❑ XW716	Pearly Whites/Sign on the Building	1975	5.00
BLUESWAY			
❑ 61028	Just a Dream/I Don't Know	1969	6.00
CAPITOL			
❑ 3998	Love Is a Five Letter Word/Other Side of Love	1974	5.00
CHECKER			
❑ 798	Big Daddy/When the Lights Go Out	1954	30.00
❑ 810	Time Brings About a Change/Waiting for Your Return	1955	30.00
❑ 826	It Ain't No Secret/Why Do I Love You Like I Do	1955	30.00
FEDERAL			
❑ 12095	Foolish Prayer/Two Little Girls	1952	30.00
❑ 12099	Lucille/Blues in Trouble	1952	30.00
❑ 12107	Don't Tell Me Now/Corn Whiskey	1952	30.00
❑ 12118	Jay's Blues (Part 1)/Jay's Blues (Part 2)	1953	30.00
❑ 12128	One Fine Gal/Back Home	1953	30.00
❑ 12138	Back Door Blues/Last Mile	1953	30.00
❑ 12155	Fast Women and Sloe Gin/Miss Mistreater	1953	30.00
❑ 12156	Sad Life/Move Me Baby	1953	50.00
—With the Lamplighters			
❑ 12173	24 Sad Hours/Just for You	1954	30.00
❑ 12180	It/Highway to Happiness	1954	30.00
❑ 12189	Oh Boy/I Done Told You	1954	30.00
GNP CRESCENDO			
❑ 156	Ain't Nobody's Business/No Rollin' Blues	1959	12.00
HIFI			
❑ 594	Everytime I Feel the Spirit/Oh Mary Don't You Weep	1960	12.00
KENT			
❑ 343	Stormy Monday Blues/Your Cheating Heart	1960	20.00
❑ 4551	Ain't Nobody's Business (Part 1)/Ain't Nobody's Business (Part 2)	1971	6.00
KING			
❑ 5997	Foolish Prayer/Two Little Girls	1965	10.00
MODERN			
❑ 857	The Wind Is Blowin'/My Baby Make a Change	1952	40.00
—Note: Earlier Jimmy Witherspoon 45s on Modern are not known to exist			
❑ 877	Love My Baby/Daddy Pinocchio	1952	40.00
❑ 895	Baby Baby/Slow Your Speed	1953	40.00
❑ 903	Each Step of the Way/Let Jesus Fix It for You	1953	40.00
❑ 909	Oh Mother, Dear Mother/I'll Be Right On Down	1953	40.00
PACIFIC JAZZ			
❑ 327	Ain't Nobody's Business/Times Have Changed	1961	10.00
PRESTIGE			
❑ 266	One Scotch, One Bourbon, One Beer/Baby, Baby, Baby	196?	10.00
❑ 274	Mean Ole Frisco/Sail On Little Girl	196?	10.00

W

Number	Title (A Side/B Side)	Yr	NM
❑ 291	Goin' to Chicago Blues/You Made Me Love You	196?	10.00
❑ 298	I Had a Dream/S.K. Blues	1963	10.00
❑ 307	Money's Gettin' Cheaper/Ever In	1963	10.00
❑ 340	I Never Will Marry/Happy Blues	1964	10.00
❑ 341	Some of My Best Friends Are the Blues/You're Next	1964	10.00
❑ 358	Come On and Walk with Me/Two Hearts Are Better Than One	196?	8.00
❑ 378	Love Me Right/Make This Heart of Mine Smile Again	196?	8.00
❑ 402	I Never Thought I'd See the Day/If There Wasn't Any You	196?	8.00
RCA VICTOR			
❑ 47-6977	Ain't Nobody's Busine ss/Who Baby Who	1957	20.00
❑ 47-7377	Confessin' the Blues/Ooo Wee, Then the Lights Go Out	1958	20.00
REPRISE			
❑ 0275	Key to the Highway/I'd Rather Drink Muddy Water	1964	8.00
❑ 20013	The Masquerade Is Over/ I Don't Know	1961	10.00
❑ 20029	Warm Your Heart/ Hey Mrs. Jones	1961	10.00
VEE JAY			
❑ 322	Everything But You/ I Know, I Know	1959	12.00
VERVE			
❑ 10439	It's All Over But the Crying/ My Blue Tears	1966	8.00
❑ 10495	Fast Forty Blues/ My Baby Quit Me	1967	8.00
WORLD PACIFIC			
❑ 814	Ain't Nobody's Business/There's Good Rockin' Tonight	1960	12.00
Albums			
ABC			
❑ 717	Handbags and Gladrags	1970	25.00
ANALOGUE PRODUCTIONS			
❑ APR 3008	Evenin' Blues	199?	15.00
BLUE NOTE			
❑ BN-LA534-G	Spoonful	1976	12.00
BLUESWAY			
❑ BLS-6026	Blues Singer	1969	25.00
❑ BLS-6040	Hunh	1970	25.00
❑ BLS-6051	The Best of Jimmy Witherspoon	1970	25.00
CAPITOL			
❑ ST-11360	Love Is a Five Letter Word	1975	12.00
CHESS			
❑ CH-93003	Spoon So Easy: The Chess Years	1990	12.00
CONSTELLATION			
❑ CM 1422 [M]	Take This Hammer	1964	50.00
❑ CMS 1422 [R]	Take This Hammer	1964	30.00
CROWN			
❑ CST-215 [S]	Jimmy Witherspoon Sings the Blues	1961	100.00
—Black vinyl; this value assumes that this is in true stereo, as the red vinyl version is, but this has not been confirmed			
❑ CST-215 [S]	Jimmy Witherspoon Sings the Blues	1961	150.00
—Red vinyl; contrary to prior reports, this album — at least the red vinyl version — is in true stereo!			
❑ CLP-5156 [M]	Jimmy Witherspoon	1959	80.00
—Black label, silver print			
❑ CLP-5156 [M]	Jimmy Witherspoon	1961	25.00
—Gray label, black print			
❑ CLP-5192 [M]	Jimmy Witherspoon Sings the Blues	1959	80.00
—Black label, silver print			
❑ CLP-5192 [M]	Jimmy Witherspoon Sings the Blues	1961	25.00
—Gray label, black print			
FANTASY			
❑ OBC-511	Evenin' Blues	1988	12.00
—Reissue of Prestige 7300			
❑ OBC-527	Baby, Baby, Baby	1990	12.00
—Reissue of Prestige 7290			
❑ 9660	Rockin' L.A.	1989	12.00
❑ 24701 [(2)]	The 'Spoon Concerts	1972	20.00
HIFI			
❑ R-421 [M]	At the Monterey Jazz Festival	1959	100.00
❑ SR-421 [S]	At the Monterey Jazz Festival	1959	60.00
❑ R-422 [M]	Feelin' the Spirit	1959	100.00
❑ SR-422 [S]	Feelin' the Spirit	1959	60.00
❑ R-426 [M]	Jimmy Witherspoon at the Renaissance	1959	100.00
❑ SR-426 [S]	Jimmy Witherspoon at the Renaissance	1959	60.00

Number	Title (A Side/B Side)	Yr	NM
JAZZ MAN			
❑ 5013	Jimmy Witherspoon Sings the Blues	1980	12.00
LAX			
❑ PW 37115	Love Is a Five Letter Word	1981	10.00
—Reissue of Capitol LP			
MUSE			
❑ MR-5288	Jimmy Witherspoon Sings the Blues	1983	10.00
❑ MR-5327	Midnight Lady Called the Blues	1986	10.00
PRESTIGE			
❑ PRLP-7290 [M]	Baby, Baby, Baby	1963	40.00
❑ PRST-7290 [S]	Baby, Baby, Baby	1963	40.00
❑ PRLP-7300 [M]	Evenin' Blues	1964	40.00
❑ PRST-7300 [S]	Evenin' Blues	1964	40.00
❑ PRLP-7314 [M]	Blues Around the Clock	1964	40.00
❑ PRST-7314 [S]	Blues Around the Clock	1964	40.00
❑ PRLP-7327 [M]	Blue Spoon	1964	40.00
❑ PRST-7327 [S]	Blue Spoon	1964	40.00
❑ PRLP-7356 [M]	Some of My Best Friends Are the Blues	1965	25.00
❑ PRST-7356 [S]	Some of My Best Friends Are the Blues	1965	25.00
❑ PRLP-7418 [M]	Spoon in London	1966	25.00
❑ PRST-7418 [S]	Spoon in London	1966	25.00
❑ PRLP-7475 [M]	Blues for Easy Livers	1967	25.00
❑ PRST-7475 [S]	Blues for Easy Livers	1967	20.00
❑ PRST-7713	The Best of Jimmy Witherspoon	1969	20.00
❑ 7855	Mean Old Frisco	1974	15.00
RCA VICTOR			
❑ ANL1-1048	Goin' to Kansas City Blues	1976	10.00
—Reissue			
❑ LPM-1639 [M]	Goin' to Kansas City Blues	1957	100.00
REPRISE			
❑ R-2008 [M]	Spoon	1961	40.00
❑ R9-2008 [S]	Spoon	1961	60.00
❑ R-6012 [M]	Hey, Mrs. Jones	1961	40.00
❑ R9-6012 [S]	Hey, Mrs. Jones	1961	60.00
❑ R-6059 [M]	Roots	1962	40.00
❑ R9-6059 [S]	Roots	1962	60.00
UNITED			
❑ 7715	A Spoonful of Blues	197?	12.00
VERVE			
❑ V-5007 [M]	Blue Point of View	1966	20.00
❑ V6-5007 [S]	Blue Point of View	1966	25.00
❑ V-5030 [M]	Blues Is Now	1967	25.00
❑ V6-5030 [S]	Blues Is Now	1967	20.00
❑ V-5050 [M]	A Spoonful of Soul	1968	30.00
❑ V6-5050 [S]	A Spoonful of Soul	1968	20.00
WORLD PACIFIC			
❑ WP-1267 [M]	Singin' the Blues	1959	100.00
❑ WP-1402 [M]	There's Good Rockin' Tonight	1961	60.00
—Reissue of 1267			

WITHERSPOON, JIMMY, AND RICHARD "GROOVE" HOLMES

Number	Title (A Side/B Side)	Yr	NM
Albums			
OLYMPIC GOLD MEDAL			
❑ 7107	Groovin' and Spoonin'	1974	12.00
SURREY			
❑ S-1106 [M]	Blues for Spoon and Groove	1965	25.00
❑ SS-1106 [S]	Blues for Spoon and Groove	1965	30.00

WITHERSPOON, JIMMY, AND GERRY MULLIGAN

Number	Title (A Side/B Side)	Yr	NM
Albums			
EVEREST ARCHIVE OF FOLK & JAZZ			
❑ 264	Jimmy Witherspoon and Gerry Mulligan	197?	12.00

WITHERSPOON, JIMMY, AND BEN WEBSTER

Number	Title (A Side/B Side)	Yr	NM
Albums			
VERVE			
❑ V6-8835	Previously Unreleased Recordings	197?	15.00

WIZARDS FROM KANSAS, THE

Number	Title (A Side/B Side)	Yr	NM
Albums			
MERCURY			
❑ SR-61309	The Wizards from Kansas	1970	200.00

WOLFE, DANNY

Number	Title (A Side/B Side)	Yr	NM
45s			
DOT			
❑ 15591	Pretty Blue Jean Baby/ Once with You	1957	40.00
❑ 15667	Let's Flat Get It/I'm Glad I Waited	1957	60.00
❑ 15715	I'd Rather Be Lucky/Pucker Paint	1958	40.00

WOMACK, BOBBY

Also see THE VALENTINOS.

Number	Title (A Side/B Side)	Yr	NM
12-Inch Singles			
MCA			
❑ L33-17104 [DJ]	Gypsy Woman/Whatever Happened to the Times? (2 versions)	1986	8.00
❑ 23688	(I Wanna) Make Love to You/ Whatever Happened to the Times?	1986	8.00
❑ 23795	Living in a Box (3 versions)	1987	6.00
❑ 23827	Outside Myself (3 versions)	1988	6.00
SOLAR			
❑ ZAS 1923 [DJ]	Save the Children (3 versions)	1989	8.00
45s			
ARISTA			
❑ 0421	How Could You Break My Heart/I Honestly Love You	1979	4.00
❑ 0446	The Roads of Life/Give It Up	1979	4.00
ATLANTIC			
❑ 2388	Night Train/It's Karate Time	1967	10.00
BEVERLY GLEN			
❑ 2000	If You Think You're Lonely Now/ Secrets	1981	4.00
❑ 2001	Where Do We Go from Here/ Just My Imagination	1982	4.00
❑ 2012	Love Has Finally Come at Last/ American Dream	1984	4.00
—With Patti LaBelle			
❑ 2014	Tell Me Why/Through the Eyes of a Child	1984	4.00
—B-side with Patti LaBelle			
❑ 2018	It Takes a Lot of Strength to Say Goodbye/Who's Foolin' Who	1984	4.00
—A-side with Patti LaBelle			
❑ 2021	Someday We'll All Be Free/ I Wish I Had Someone to Go Home To	1985	4.00
❑ 2023	I'm So Proud/Searching for My Love	1985	4.00
CHECKER			
❑ 1122	Lonesome Man/I Found a True Love	1965	15.00
COLUMBIA			
❑ 10437	Home Is Where the Heart Is/ We've Only Just Begun	1976	5.00
❑ 10493	Standing in the Safety Zone/ A Change Is Gonna Come	1977	5.00
❑ 10672	Trust Your Heart/When Love Begins, Friendship Ends	1978	5.00
❑ 10732	Wind It Up/Stop Before We Start	1978	5.00
LIBERTY			
❑ 56186	I'm Gonna Forget About You/ Don't Look Back	1970	8.00
❑ 56206	Something/Everybody's Talkin'	1970	8.00
MCA			
❑ 52624	I Wish He Didn't Trust Me So Much/Got to Be with You Tonight	1985	4.00
❑ 52624 [PS]	I Wish He Didn't Trust Me So Much/Got to Be with You Tonight	1985	4.00
❑ 52709	Let Me Kiss It Where It Hurts/ Check It Out	1985	4.00
❑ 52793	Gypsy Woman/What Evert Happened to the Times	1986	3.00
❑ 52955	(I Wanna) Make Love to You/ The Launch	1986	3.00
❑ 52955 [PS]	(I Wanna) Make Love to You/ The Launch	1986	3.00
❑ 53190	Living in a Box/I Can't Stay Mad	1987	3.00
❑ 53263	Outside Myself/A Woman Likes to Hear Than	1988	3.00
MINIT			
❑ 32024	Baby, I Can't Stand It/Trust Me	1967	10.00
❑ 32030	Somebody Special/ Broadway Walk	1967	10.00
❑ 32037	What Is This/What You Gonna Do (When Your Love Is Gone)	1968	10.00
❑ 32048	Fly Me to the Moon/Take Me	1968	10.00
❑ 32055	California Dreamin'/Baby, You Oughta Think It Over	1968	10.00
❑ 32059	I Left My Heart in San Francisco/ Love, The Time Is Now	1969	8.00
❑ 32071	It's Gonna Rain/Thank You	1969	8.00
❑ 32081	How I Miss You Baby/ Tried and Convicted	1969	8.00
❑ 32093	More Than I Can Stand/ Arkansas State Prison	1970	8.00
SOLAR			
❑ 74006	Save the Children/(Instrumental)	1989	3.00

W

Except when noted otherwise, VG = 25% of NM, and VG+ = 50% of NM. (Example: VG = $2.00, VG+ = $4.00 and NM = $8.00.)

Number	Title (A Side/B Side)	Yr	NM
THE RIGHT STUFF			
❑ 58815	Dear Santa Claus/Dear Santa Claus (Kids Version)	1999	3.00
UNITED ARTISTS			
❑ 0123	That's the Way I Feel About Cha/Woman's Gotta Have It	1973	4.00
—"Silver Spotlight Series" reissue			
❑ XW196	Across 110th Street/Hang On In There	1973	5.00
❑ XW255	Nobody Wants You When You're Down and Out/I'm Thru Trying to Prove My Love	1973	5.00
❑ XW375	Lookin' for a Love/Let It Hang Out	1973	5.00
❑ XW439	You're Welcome, Stop On By/I Don't Want to Be Hurt	1974	5.00
❑ XW525	Lookin' for a Love/Nobody Wants You When You're Down and Out	1974	4.00
—Reissue			
❑ XW526	Harry Hippie/Sweet Caroline	1974	4.00
—Reissue			
❑ XW527	California Dreamin'/Fly Me to the Moon	1974	5.00
❑ XW561	I Don't Know/Yes, Jesus Loves Me	1974	5.00
❑ XW621	Check It Out/Interlude No. 2	1975	5.00
❑ XW674	It's All Over Now/Git It	1975	5.00
❑ XW735	Where There's a Will, There's a Way/Everything's Gonna Be Alright	1975	5.00
❑ XW763	Daylight/Trust Me	1976	5.00
❑ XW804	I Feel a Groove Comin' On/Trust Me	1976	5.00
❑ 50773	The Preacher/More Than I Can Stand	1971	6.00
❑ 50816	Communication/Fire and Rain	1971	6.00
❑ 50847	That's the Way I Feel About 'Cha/Come L'Amore	1971	6.00
❑ 50902	Woman's Gotta Have It/Give It Back	1972	6.00
❑ 50946	Harry Hippie/Sweet Caroline (Good Times Never Seemed So Good)	1972	6.00
❑ 50988 [DJ]	Harry Hippie (mono/stereo)	1972	8.00
—Apparently, no stock copy exists			
Albums			
ARISTA			
❑ AB 4222	Roads of Life	1979	10.00
BEVERLY GLEN			
❑ 10000	The Poet	1981	10.00
❑ 10003	The Poet II	1984	10.00
COLUMBIA			
❑ PC 34384	Home Is Where the Heart Is	1977	10.00
❑ JC 35083	Pieces	1978	10.00
LIBERTY			
❑ LST-7645	The Womack "Live"	1971	12.00
❑ LN-10171	Bobby Womack's Greatest Hits	198?	8.00
—Budget-line reissue of United Artists 346			
MCA			
❑ 5617	So Many Rivers	1985	8.00
MINIT			
❑ 24014	Fly Me to the Moon	1968	30.00
❑ 24027	My Prescription	1969	30.00
UNITED ARTISTS			
❑ UA-LA043-F	Facts of Life	1973	12.00
❑ UA-LA199-G	Lookin' for a Love Again	1974	12.00
❑ UA-LA346-G	Bobby Womack's Greatest Hits	1974	12.00
❑ UA-LA353-G	I Don't Know What the World Is Coming To	1975	12.00
❑ UA-LA544-G	Safety Zone	1975	12.00
❑ UA-LA638-G	B.W. Goes C and W	1976	12.00
❑ LM-1002	Understanding	1980	8.00
—Reissue of 5577			
❑ UAS-5225	Across 110th Street	1972	12.00
❑ UAS-5539	Communication	1971	12.00
❑ UAS-5577	Understanding	1972	12.00

WOMB

Number	Title (A Side/B Side)	Yr	NM
45s			
DOT			
❑ 17250	Hang On/My Baby Thinks About the Good Things	1969	12.00
Albums			
DOT			
❑ DLP-25933	Womb	1969	24.00
❑ DLP-25959	Overdub	1969	24.00

WOMBLES, THE

Number	Title (A Side/B Side)	Yr	NM
45s			
COLUMBIA			
❑ 10013	Wombling Summer Party/Wimbledon Sunset	1974	4.00
❑ 10033	Remember You're a Womble/The Wellington Womble	1974	4.00

Stevie Wonder, *Looking Back*, Motown M-804LP3, 1977, 3-record set, **$25.**

Number	Title (A Side/B Side)	Yr	NM
EPIC			
❑ 11119	Wombling Song/Wombles Everywhere	1974	5.00
Albums			
COLUMBIA			
❑ KC 33140	Remember You're a Womble	1974	12.00

WOMENFOLK, THE

Number	Title (A Side/B Side)	Yr	NM
45s			
RCA VICTOR			
❑ 47-8301	Little Boxes/Love Came a-Tricklin' Down	1964	8.00
❑ 47-8562	My Heart Tells Me to Believe/The Way I Feel	1965	8.00
❑ 47-8782	The Last Thing on My Mind/Meditation	1966	8.00
Albums			
RCA VICTOR			
❑ LPM-2832 [M]	The Womenfolk	1964	12.00
❑ LSP-2832 [S]	The Womenfolk	1964	15.00
❑ LPM-2919 [M]	Never Underestimate the Power of the Womenfolk	1964	12.00
❑ LSP-2919 [S]	Never Underestimate the Power of the Womenfolk	1964	15.00
❑ LPM-2991 [M]	The Womenfolk at the Hungry I	1965	12.00
❑ LSP-2991 [S]	The Womenfolk at the Hungry I	1965	15.00
❑ LPM-3527 [M]	Man Oh Man	1966	12.00
❑ LSP-3527 [S]	Man Oh Man	1966	15.00

WONDER, STEVIE

Also see PAUL McCARTNEY AND STEVIE WONDER.

Number	Title (A Side/B Side)	Yr	NM
12-Inch Singles			
MOTOWN			
❑ PR 161 [DJ]	Love Light in Flight (Special 12" Version 6:30) (Instrumental 7:38)	1984	10.00
❑ L33-1065 [DJ]	Keep Our Love Alive/(Instrumental)	1990	8.00
❑ L33-1093 [DJ]	Gotta Have You (3 versions)	1991	10.00
❑ 37463 1215 1 [DJ]	Tomorrow Robins Will Sing (7 versions)	1995	10.00
❑ 37463 1261 1 [DJ]	For Your Love (Single Version) (LP Version) (Instrumental) (A Cappella)	1995	10.00
❑ 37463 1482 1 [DJ]	Kiss Lonely Goodbye (6 versions)	1996	15.00
❑ L33-1602 [DJ]	Fun Day (Edit) (LP) (Instrumental)	1991	10.00
❑ L33-1690 [DJ]	Fun Day (8 versions)	1991	12.00
❑ 4517 MG	Happy Birthday/Martin Luther King: Excerpts from His Speeches	1984	80.00
❑ 4527 MG	Don't Drive Drunk (12" Version 8:18) (Instrumental 8:27)/Did I Hear You Say You Love Me (8:27)	1984	8.00
❑ 4593 MG	Skeletons (6:43)/(Instrumental)	1987	8.00
❑ MOT-4616	My Eyes Don't Cry (Extended Version 6:30) (Radio Edit 5:18) (Dub Mix 7:21)	1988	8.00
❑ MOT-4626	With Each Beat of My Heart (LP) (Edit) (Instrumental)	1988	8.00
❑ MOT12-4665	Keep Our Love Alive/(Instrumental)	1990	8.00
❑ MOT12-4759	Gotta Have You (3 versions)/Feeding Off the Love of the Land	1991	10.00
❑ L33-17755 [DJ]	With Each Beat of My Heart (LP) (Edit) (Instrumental)	1987	8.00
TAMLA			
❑ PR 61 [DJ]	A Seed's a Star-Tree Medley/Power Flower//Black Orchid/Outside My Window	1979	20.00
—Promo-only sampler for "Journey Through the Secret Life of Plants"			
❑ PR 76 [DJ]	Master Blaster (Jammin') (6:11)/Master Blaster (Dub) (6:27)	1980	70.00

W

Number	Title (A Side/B Side)	Yr	NM
❑ PR 77 [DJ]	I Ain't Gonna Stand For It//All I Do/Did I Hear You Say You Love Me	1980	60.00
—Promo-only sampler for "Hotter Than July"			
❑ PR 98/99 [(2)DJ]	Do I Do (10:27) (Instrumental 10:27)//Front Line (6:01) (Instrumental 6:01)	1982	25.00
—Two-record promo set			
❑ PR 186 [DJ]	Land of La La (8:40)/(Instrumental)	1986	8.00
❑ 4548 TG	Part Time Lover (12-Inch Vocal Version 8:20) (12-Inch Instrumental 8:20)	1985	10.00
❑ 4553 TG	Go Home (12" Version 9:22)/(Radio Edit of 12" Version 6:26) (Instrumental 8:36)	1985	10.00

45s

GORDY

Number	Title (A Side/B Side)	Yr	NM
❑ 7076	Alfie/More Than a Dream	1968	25.00
—As "Eivets Rednow" (read it backwards)			

MOTOWN

Number	Title (A Side/B Side)	Yr	NM
❑ 1745	I Just Called to Say I Love You/(Instrumental)	1984	3.00
❑ 1745 [PS]	I Just Called to Say I Love You/(Instrumental)	1984	40.00
—Sleeve is labeled promo only, though it has been found on the (very) occasional stock copy			
❑ 1769	Love Light in Flight/It's More Than You	1984	3.00
❑ 1769 [PS]	Love Light in Flight/It's More Than You	1984	4.00
❑ 1907	Skeletons/(Instrumental)	1987	3.00
❑ 1907 [PS]	Skeletons/(Instrumental)	1987	4.00
❑ 1919	You Will Know/(Instrumental)	1988	3.00
❑ 1919 [DJ]	You Will Know/You Will Know-Stevie Wonder Interview	1988	6.00
—Promo-only release			
❑ 1919 [PS]	You Will Know/(Instrumental)	1988	4.00
❑ 1919 [PS]	You Will Know/You Will Know-Stevie Wonder Interview	1988	6.00
—Only the promo sleeve mentions the interview			
❑ 1946	My Eyes Don't Cry/(Instrumental)	1988	3.00
❑ 1946 [PS]	My Eyes Don't Cry/(Instrumental)	1988	3.00
❑ 1953	With Each Beat of My Heart/(Instrumental)	1989	3.00
❑ 1990	Keep Our Love Alive/(Instrumental)	1990	5.00
❑ 2081	Gotta Have You/Feeding Off the Love of the Land	1991	4.00
❑ 2127	Fun Day/(Instrumental)	1991	4.00
❑ 2143	These Three Words (same on both sides)	1991	4.00
❑ 860310-7	For Your Love/(Instrumental)	1995	4.00
❑ 860418-7	Tomorrow Robins Will Sing/For Your Love	1995	4.00

MOTOWN YESTERYEAR

Number	Title (A Side/B Side)	Yr	NM
❑ Y 620F	I Wish/Sir Duke	1978	3.00
—Reissue			
❑ Y 621F	Another Star/As	1978	3.00
—Reissue			
❑ Y 646F	Master Blaster (Jammin')/Master Blaster (Dub)	1982	3.00
—Reissue			
❑ Y 647F	I Ain't Gonna Stand For It/Lately	1982	3.00
—Reissue			
❑ Y 657F	That Girl/Do I Do	1983	3.00
—Reissue			
❑ Y 684F	I Just Called to Say I Love You/Love Light in Flight	1985	3.00
—Reissue			
❑ Y 685F	Don't Drive Drunk/(Instrumental)	1985	3.00
—First U.S. edition of this song on 45			

TAMLA

Number	Title (A Side/B Side)	Yr	NM
❑ 1602	That Girl/All I Do	1982	4.00
❑ 1612	Do I Do/Rocket Love	1982	4.00
❑ 1639	Ribbon in the Sky/Black Orchid	1982	4.00
❑ 1639 [PS]	Ribbon in the Sky/Black Orchid	1982	4.00
❑ 1808	Part-Time Lover/(Instrumental)	1985	3.00
❑ 1808 [PS]	Part-Time Lover/(Instrumental)	1985	4.00
❑ 1817	Go Home/(Instrumental)	1985	3.00
❑ 1817 [PS]	Go Home/(Instrumental)	1985	4.00
❑ 1832	Overjoyed/(Instrumental)	1986	3.00
❑ 1832 [PS]	Overjoyed/(Instrumental)	1986	4.00
❑ 1846	Land of La La/(Instrumental)	1986	3.00
❑ 1846 [PS]	Land of La La/(Instrumental)	1986	4.00
❑ 54061	I Call It Pretty Music But The Old People Call It the Blues (Part 1)/I Call It Pretty Music But The Old People Call It the Blues (Part 2)	1962	30.00
❑ 54061 [PS]	I Call It Pretty Music But The Old People Call It the Blues (Part 1)/I Call It Pretty Music But The Old People Call It the Blues (Part 2)	1962	80.00
❑ 54070	Little Water Boy/La La La La La	1962	25.00
❑ 54074	Contract on Love/Sunset	1963	25.00
❑ 54080	Fingertips — Pt. 2/Fingertips — Pt. 1	1963	20.00
❑ 54080 [PS]	Fingertips — Pt. 2/Fingertips — Pt. 1	1963	50.00
❑ 54086	Workout Stevie, Workout/Monkey Talk	1963	15.00
❑ 54090	Castles in the Sand/Thank You (For Loving Me All the Way)	1964	15.00
—Up to and including this, as "Little Stevie Wonder"			
❑ 54096	Hey Harmonica Man/This Little Girl	1964	15.00
❑ 54096 [PS]	Hey Harmonica Man/This Little Girl	1964	40.00
❑ 54103	Sad Boy/Happy Street	1964	20.00
❑ 54108	Pretty Little Angel/Tears in Vain	1964	—
—Unreleased			
❑ 54114	Kiss Me Baby/Tears in Vain	1965	12.00
❑ 54119	High Heel Sneakers/Music Talk	1965	12.00
❑ 54119	High Heel Sneakers/Funny How Time Slips Away	1965	20.00
❑ 54124	Uptight (Everything's Alright)/Purple Rain Drops	1965	15.00
❑ 54130	Nothing's Too Good for My Baby/With a Child's Heart	1966	12.00
❑ 54136	Blowin' in the Wind/Ain't That Asking for Trouble	1966	12.00
❑ 54136 [PS]	Blowin' in the Wind/Ain't That Asking for Trouble	1966	25.00
❑ 54139	A Place in the Sun/Sylvia	1966	12.00
❑ 54139 [PS]	A Place in the Sun/Sylvia	1966	25.00
❑ 54142	Some Day at Christmas/The Miracles of Christmas	1966	15.00
❑ 54147	Travlin' Man/Hey Love	1967	10.00
❑ 54151	I Was Made to Love Her/Hold Me	1967	10.00
❑ 54157	I'm Wondering/Every Time I See You I Go Wild	1967	10.00
❑ 54165	Shoo-Be-Doo-Be-Doo-Da-Day/Why Don't You Lead Me to Love	1968	8.00
❑ 54168	You Met Your Match/My Girl	1968	8.00
❑ 54174	For Once in My Life/Angie Girl	1968	8.00
❑ 54180	My Cherie Amour/Don't Know Why I Love You	1969	8.00
—Re-release with A and B side switched and new title on B-side			
❑ 54180	I Don't Know Why/My Cherie Amour	1969	10.00
❑ 54188	Yester-Me, Yester-You, Yesterday/I'd Be a Fool Right Now	1969	8.00
❑ 54191	Never Had a Dream Come True/Somebody Knows, Somebody Cares	1970	6.00
❑ 54196	Signed, Sealed, Delivered, I'm Yours/I'm More Than Happy	1970	6.00
❑ 54200	Heaven Help Us All/I Gotta Have a Song	1970	6.00
❑ 54202	We Can Work It Out/Never Dreamed You'd Leave in Summer	1971	6.00
❑ 54208	If You Really Love Me/Think of Me As Your Soldier	1971	6.00
❑ 54214	What Christmas Means to Me/Bedtime for Toys	1971	6.00
❑ 54216	Superwoman (Where Were You When I Needed You)/I Love Every Little Thing About You	1972	6.00
❑ 54223	Keep On Running/Evil	1972	6.00
❑ 54226	Superstition/You've Got It Bad Girl	1972	5.00
❑ 54232	You Are the Sunshine of My Life/Tuesday Heartbreak	1973	5.00
❑ 54235	Higher Ground/Too High	1973	5.00
❑ 54242	Living for the City/Visions	1973	5.00
❑ 54245	Don't You Worry 'Bout a Thing/Blame It on the Sun	1974	5.00
❑ 54252	You Haven't Done Nothin'/Big Brother	1974	5.00
❑ 54254	Boogie On Reggae Woman/Seems So Long	1974	5.00
—With correct spelling of A-side			
❑ 54254	Boogie On Raggae Woman/Seems So Long	1974	6.00
—With incorrect spelling of A-side			
❑ 54274	I Wish/You and I	1976	5.00
❑ 54281	Sir Duke/He's Misstra Know-It-All	1977	5.00
❑ 54281 [PS]	Sir Duke/He's Misstra Know-It-All	1977	10.00
❑ 54286	Another Star/Creepin'	1977	5.00
❑ 54291	As/Contusion	1977	5.00
❑ 54303	Send One Your Love/(Instrumental)	1979	4.00
❑ 54303 [PS]	Send One Your Love/(Instrumental)	1979	6.00
❑ 54308	Outside My Window/Same Old Story	1980	4.00
❑ 54308 [PS]	Outside My Window/Same Old Story	1980	6.00
❑ 54317	Master Blaster (Jammin')/(Instrumental)	1980	4.00
❑ 54317 [PS]	Master Blaster (Jammin')/(Instrumental)	1980	6.00
❑ 54320	I Ain't Gonna Stand For It/Knocks Me Off My Feet	1980	4.00
❑ 54323	Lately/If It's Magic	1981	4.00
❑ 54328	Did I Hear You Say You Love Me/As If You Read My Mind	1981	4.00
❑ 54331	Happy Birthday/(Instrumental)	1981	—
—Canceled			

TOPPS/MOTOWN

Number	Title (A Side/B Side)	Yr	NM
❑ 8	Fingertips Part 2	1967	75.00
—Cardboard record			
❑ 10	Uptight (Everything's Alright)	1967	75.00
—Cardboard record			

7-Inch Extended Plays

TAMLA

Number	Title (A Side/B Side)	Yr	NM
❑ T 340EP	Saturn/Ebony Eyes//All Day Sucker/Easy Goin' Evening (My Mama's Call)	1976	4.00
—Called "A Something's Extra for Songs in the Key of Life," this was issued with the 2-LP set of the same name and is sometimes found separately, though it was never sold separately; not issued with picture sleeve			

Albums

GORDY

Number	Title	Yr	NM
❑ GS 932	Eivets Rednow	1968	30.00
—As "Eivets Rednow"			

JOBETE

Number	Title	Yr	NM
❑ JSA-6253 [DJ]	The Wonder of Stevie	1988	20.00
—Publisher's demo with excerpts of 105 (!) Stevie Wonder songs			

MOTOWN

Number	Title	Yr	NM
❑ M5-131V1	Recorded Live/Little Stevie Wonder/The 12 Year Old Genius	1981	12.00
—Reissue of Tamla 240			
❑ M5-150V1	With a Song in My Heart	1981	12.00
—Reissue of Tamla 250			
❑ M5-166V1	Down to Earth	1981	12.00
—Reissue of Tamla 272			
❑ M5-173V1	Tribute to Uncle Ray	1981	12.00
—Reissue of Tamla 232			
❑ M5-176V1	Signed, Sealed and Delivered	1981	12.00
—Reissue of Tamla 304			
❑ M5-179V1	My Cherie Amour	1981	12.00
—Reissue of Tamla 296			
❑ M5-183V1	Up-Tight Everything's Alright	1981	12.00
—Reissue of Tamla 268			
❑ M5-219V1	The Jazz Soul of Little Stevie	1981	12.00
—Reissue of Tamla 233			
❑ 31453 0238-1 [(2)DJ]	Conversation Peace	1995	25.00
—Vinyl is promo only; white cover with custom sticker			
❑ M9-804A3 [(3)]	Looking Back	1977	25.00
—Withdrawn after Stevie Wonder objected to its release			
❑ 5255 ML	Someday at Christmas	1982	10.00
—Reissue of Tamla 281			
❑ 6108 ML	The Woman in Red	1984	10.00
—With sticker at top proclaiming "New Stevie Wonder Album"			
❑ 6108 ML	The Woman in Red	1984	12.00
—With no sticker proclaiming "New Stevie Wonder Album"			
❑ 6248 ML	Characters	1987	10.00
❑ 6291 ML	Music from the Movie Jungle Fever	1991	20.00
❑ 10903141	Music of My Mind	2008	20.00

TAMLA

Number	Title	Yr	NM
❑ T 232 [M]	Tribute to Uncle Ray	1962	150.00
❑ T 233 [M]	The Jazz Soul of Little Stevie	1962	150.00
❑ T 240 [M]	Recorded Live/Little Stevie Wonder/The 12 Year Old Genius	1963	120.00
—The above three LPs as "Little Stevie Wonder"			
❑ T 248 [M]	Workout Stevie, Workout	1963	1000.
—Canceled; test pressings or acetates may exist			
❑ T 250 [M]	With a Song in My Heart	1964	80.00
❑ T 255 [M]	Stevie at the Beach	1964	80.00
❑ T 268 [M]	Up-Tight Everything's Alright	1966	25.00
❑ TS 268 [S]	Up-Tight Everything's Alright	1966	30.00
❑ T 272 [M]	Down to Earth	1966	20.00
❑ TS 272 [S]	Down to Earth	1966	25.00
❑ T 279 [M]	I Was Made to Love Her	1967	20.00
❑ TS 279 [S]	I Was Made to Love Her	1967	25.00
❑ T 281 [M]	Someday at Christmas	1967	30.00
❑ TS 281 [S]	Someday at Christmas	1967	40.00
❑ T 282 [M]	Greatest Hits	1968	30.00
❑ TS 282 [S]	Greatest Hits	1968	20.00
❑ TS 291	For Once in My Life	1968	20.00
❑ TS 296	My Cherie Amour	1969	20.00
❑ TS 298	Stevie Wonder Live	1970	20.00
❑ TS 304	Signed Sealed and Delivered	1970	20.00
❑ TS 308	Where I'm Coming From	1971	20.00
❑ T 313L	Stevie Wonder's Greatest Hits Vol. 2	1971	20.00
—Some, if not all, LP covers have the title mis-punctuated as "Stevie Wonders' Greatest Hits Vol. 2"			
❑ T 314L	Music of My Mind	1972	20.00
❑ T 319L	Talking Book	1972	15.00
—Original pressings have a braille note on cover			

Except when noted otherwise, VG = 25% of NM, and VG+ = 50% of NM. (Example: VG = $2.00, VG+ = $4.00 and NM = $8.00.)

Number	Title (A Side/B Side)	Yr	NM
❑ T 319L	Talking Book	1973	10.00
—No braille note on cover			
❑ T 326L	Innervisions	1973	15.00
❑ T6-332S1	Fulfillingness' First Finale	1974	15.00
❑ T13-340C2 [(2)]	Songs in the Key of Life	1976	20.00
—With booklet and bonus 7-inch EP (deduct 25% if missing)			
❑ T7-362R1	Someday at Christmas	1978	20.00
—Unusual reissue of 281			
❑ T13-371C2 [(2)]	Journey Through the Secret Life of Plants	1979	15.00
❑ T8-373S1	Hotter Than July	1980	12.00
❑ 6002 TL2 [(2)]	Stevie Wonder's Original Musiquarium I	1982	15.00
❑ 6134 TL	In Square Circle	1985	10.00
UNIVERSAL MOTOWN			
❑ 5316422 [(2)]	Songs in the Key of Life	2009	30.00
—Two LP plus 7"			

WONDER, STEVIE, AND MICHAEL JACKSON
Also see each artist's individual listings.

12-Inch Singles

Number	Title (A Side/B Side)	Yr	NM
MOTOWN			
❑ 4606 MG	Get It (6:44) (Instrumental 6:47)	1988	8.00
45s			
MOTOWN			
❑ 1930	Get It/(Instrumental)	1988	3.00
❑ 1930 [PS]	Get It/(Instrumental)	1988	3.00

WONDER WHO?, THE
See THE FOUR SEASONS.

WONDERETTES, THE

45s

Number	Title (A Side/B Side)	Yr	NM
ENTERPRISE			
❑ 5025	Love's Got a Hold on Me/Work Out Fine	1964	25.00
RUBY			
❑ 5065	I Feel Strange/Wait Until Tonight	1965	40.00
UNITED ARTISTS			
❑ 944	I Feel Strange/Wait Until Tonight	1965	25.00
❑ 997	Mend My Broken Heart/And If I Had My Way	1966	20.00
—By "Rose St. John and the Wonderettes"			
VEEP			
❑ 1231	Fool Don't Laugh/I Know the Meeting	1966	25.00
—As "Rose St. John and the Wonderettes"			

WOOD, ANITA

45s

Number	Title (A Side/B Side)	Yr	NM
SUN			
❑ 361	I'll Wait Forever/I Can't Show How I Feel	1961	30.00

WOOD, BOBBY

45s

Number	Title (A Side/B Side)	Yr	NM
CHALLENGE			
❑ 9160	The Day After Forever/Everybody's Searchin'	1962	10.00
CINNAMON			
❑ 790	I'm a Fool for Loving You/Secret Love Affair	1974	4.00
JOY			
❑ 277	I Still Hurt/Just the Same	1963	10.00
❑ 279	Do Darlin' (Do Remember Me)/That's All I Need	1963	10.00
❑ 285	If I'm a Fool for Loving You/My Heart Went Boing! Boing! Boing!	1964	10.00
❑ 288	That's All I Need to Know/This Time	1964	10.00
❑ 291	So Cruel/I'd Do It Again	1964	10.00
❑ 295	Bed of Roses/Show Me	1965	8.00
❑ 298	Human Emotions/When a Lonely Boy Meets a Lonely Girl	1965	8.00
❑ 301	Fool's Paradise/What Am I Gonna Tell Myself	1965	8.00
LUCKY ELEVEN			
❑ 361	One Day Behind/Sound of Sadness	1973	5.00
MALA			
❑ 526	My Special Angel/I'd Rather Forgive You	1966	8.00
MGM			
❑ 13729	My Last Date (With You)/Everybody's Baby	1967	6.00
❑ 13797	Break My Mind/This Thing Called Love	1967	6.00
❑ 13912	Is That All There Is To It/Say It's Not You	1968	6.00
❑ 13952	Mary/Big Buildup	1968	6.00
❑ 14051	(Margie's at the) Lincoln Park Inn/I'm the Name of Her Game	1969	6.00
SUN			
❑ 369 [DJ]	Everybody's Searchin'/Human Emotions	1961	600.00
—No stock copies known; should one be discovered, it would be worth much more			
Albums			
JOY			
❑ JL 1001 [M]	Bobby Wood	1964	40.00

WOOD, BRENTON

45s

Number	Title (A Side/B Side)	Yr	NM
BRENT			
❑ 7052	Good Lovin'/I Want to Love	1966	15.00
❑ 7057	Cross the Bridge/Sweet Molly Malone	1966	25.00
❑ 7068	I Want Love/Sweet Molly Malone	1967	10.00
CREAM			
❑ 7602	All That Jazz/Bless Your Little Heart	1976	4.00
❑ 7716	Come Softly to Me/You're Everything I Need	1977	4.00
❑ 7720	Number One/(B-side unknown)	1977	4.00
❑ 7833	Let's Get Crazy Together/Love Is Free	1978	4.00
DOUBLE SHOT			
❑ 111	The Oogum Boogum Song/I Like the Way You Love Me	1967	10.00
❑ 116	Gimme Little Sign/I Think You've Got Your Fools Mixed Up	1967	10.00
❑ 121	Baby You Got It/Catch You on the Rebound	1967	8.00
❑ 126	Lovey Dovey Kinda Lovin'/Two-Time Loser	1968	8.00
❑ 130	Some Got It, Some Don't/Me and You	1968	8.00
❑ 135	Trouble/It's Just a Game, Love	1968	8.00
❑ 137	Where Are You/A Change Is Gonna Come	1969	8.00
❑ 142	Whoop It On Me/Take a Chance	1969	8.00
❑ 147	Can You Dig It/Great Big Bubble of Love	1970	6.00
❑ 150	Bogaloosa, Lousiana/I Need Your Love So Bad	1970	6.00
❑ 156	Sad Little Song/Who But a Fool	1971	6.00
MIDGET			
❑ 101	Rainin' Love/All That Jazz	197?	5.00
PHILCO-FORD			
❑ HP-38	Gimme Little Sign/Oogum Boogum	1969	20.00
—4-inch plastic "Hip Pocket Record" with color sleeve			
PROPHESY			
❑ 3002	Sticky Boom Boom Too Cold (Part 1)/Sticky Boom Boom Too Cold (Part 2)	1973	5.00
❑ 3003	Another Saturday Night/(B-side unknown)	1973	5.00
WAND			
❑ 145	Mr. Schemer/Hide-A-Way	1963	40.00
WARNER BROS.			
❑ 8079	All That Jazz/Rainin' Love	1975	5.00
❑ 8144	Better Believe It/It Only Makes Me Want It More	1975	5.00
Albums			
BRENT			
❑ S-100 [S]	Introducing Brenton Wood! Boogaloo	1967	60.00
—Four tracks by Brenton Wood, six by other artists			
❑ 5100 [M]	Introducing Brenton Wood! Boogaloo	1967	40.00
CREAM			
❑ 1006	Come Softly	1977	15.00
DOUBLE SHOT			
❑ 1002 [M]	Oogum Boogum	1967	25.00
❑ 1003 [M]	Baby You Got It	1967	25.00
❑ 5002 [S]	Oogum Boogum	1967	30.00
❑ 5003 [S]	Baby You Got It	1967	30.00
—Black vinyl			
❑ 5003 [S]	Baby You Got It	1967	200.00
—Multi-color vinyl			
RHINO			
❑ RNLP-70223	The Best of Brenton Wood	1986	10.00

WOOD, MARTY

45s

Number	Title (A Side/B Side)	Yr	NM
HIT			
❑ 67	18 Yellow Roses/I Love You Because	1963	8.00
❑ 128	Tears and Roses/My Boy Lollipop	1964	8.00
—B-side by Connie Dee			
❑ 140	In the Misty Moonlight/G.T.O.	1964	8.00
—B-side by the Roamers			
❑ 162	Right or Wrong/Just Give Me Time	1964	8.00
—B-side by Bobby and Buddy			
❑ 177	You're Nobody Till Somebody Loves You/Speaking of Broken Hearts	1965	8.00
—B-side by John Preston			
❑ 200	Send Me the Pillow You Dream On/You Can't Trust a Friend	1965	8.00
—B-side by Lisa French			

WOOD, MITCH

45s

Number	Title (A Side/B Side)	Yr	NM
HIT			
❑ 92	500 Miles Away from Home/Walking Proud	1963	8.00
—B-side by John Preston			

WOOD, RONNIE
Also see FACES; THE ROLLING STONES.

45s

Number	Title (A Side/B Side)	Yr	NM
COLUMBIA			
❑ 1-11014	Seven Days/Breakin' My Heart	1979	6.00
WARNER BROS.			
❑ 8036	Breathe on Me/I Can Feel the Fire	1974	6.00
❑ 8131	I Got a Feeling/If You Don't Want My Love	1975	6.00
Albums			
COLUMBIA			
❑ JC 35702	Gimme Some Neck	1979	15.00
❑ PC 35702	Gimme Some Neck	198?	8.00
—Budget-line reissue			
❑ FC 37473	1234	1981	15.00
WARNER BROS.			
❑ BS 2819	I've Got My Own Album to Do	1974	20.00
❑ BS 2872	Now Look	1975	15.00

WOOD, ROY
Also see ELECTRIC LIGHT ORCHESTRA; THE MOVE.

45s

Number	Title (A Side/B Side)	Yr	NM
UNITED ARTISTS			
❑ XW160	Ball Park Incident/Carlsberg Special	1973	10.00
—As "Wizzard"			
❑ XW272	See My Baby Jive/Bend Over Beethoven	1973	10.00
❑ XW320	Dear Elaine/Song of Praise	1973	10.00
❑ XW394	Forever/Woodbe	1974	10.00
❑ XW792	Any Old Time Will Do/Why Does Such a Pretty Girl Sing Those Sad Songs	1976	10.00
Albums			
TOWNHOUSE			
❑ SN-7127	One Man Band	1981	12.00
UNITED ARTISTS			
❑ (# unknown) [DJ]	Boulders Folder	1973	40.00
—Promo version of 168 in 13x13 folder with press kit and postcards			
❑ UA-LA042-F	Wizzard's Brew	1973	10.00
❑ UA-LA168-F	Boulders	1973	10.00
❑ UA-LA219-G	Introducing Eddy and the Falcons	1974	10.00
❑ UA-LA575-G	Mustard	1976	10.00
WARNER BROS.			
❑ BS 3065	Super Active Wizzo	1977	10.00
❑ BSK 3247	On the Road Again	1979	10.00

WOODS, BENNIE

45s

Number	Title (A Side/B Side)	Yr	NM
ATLAS			
❑ 1040	I Cross My Fingers/Wheel Baby Wheel	1955	500.00
—As "Bennie Woods and Rockin' Townies"			
❑ 1040	I Cross My Fingers/Wheel Baby Wheel	1955	800.00
—As "Bennie Woods and the Five Dukes"			

WOODS, BILLY

45s

Number	Title (A Side/B Side)	Yr	NM
DOT			
❑ 16053	Falling Rain/Friendly Mr. Wendley	1960	40.00
SUSSEX			
❑ 213	Let Me Make You Happy/That Was the Love That Was	1971	1500.
VERVE			
❑ 10451	I Don't Want to Lose Your Love/No One to Blame	1966	50.00
❑ 10484	I Found Satisfaction/If I Could Only See	1967	50.00

WOODS, DANNY

Number	Title (A Side/B Side)	Yr	NM
45s			
HIT			
❑ 188	No Arms Can Ever Hold You/ Swinging Spiritual	1965	8.00
—B-side by William Randolph			

WOODS, DONALD

Number	Title (A Side/B Side)	Yr	NM
45s			
ALADDIN			
❑ 3412	Memories of an Angel/ That Much of Your Love	1958	30.00
FLIP			
❑ 306	Death of an Angel/ Man from Utopia	1955	40.00

WOODS, KENNI

Number	Title (A Side/B Side)	Yr	NM
45s			
PHILIPS			
❑ 40112	Can't He Take a Hint/ That Guy Is Mine	1963	10.00
❑ 40156	Back with My Baby/ Do You Really Love Me	1963	10.00

WOODS, MARTY

Number	Title (A Side/B Side)	Yr	NM
45s			
HIT			
❑ 248	Secret Agent Man/ Time Won't Let Me	1966	8.00
—B-side by the Chellows			

WOODS, MICKEY

Number	Title (A Side/B Side)	Yr	NM
45s			
TAMLA			
❑ 54039	They Rode Through the Valley/ Poor Sam Jones	1961	50.00
❑ 54052	Please Mr. Kennedy/ (They Call Me) Cupid	1962	40.00

WOODY, DON

Number	Title (A Side/B Side)	Yr	NM
45s			
DECCA			
❑ 30277	You're Barking Up the Wrong Tree/Bird-Dog	1957	100.00

WOOFERS, THE

Number	Title (A Side/B Side)	Yr	NM
Albums			
WYNCOTE			
❑ SW 9011 [S]	Dragsville	1964	50.00
❑ W 9011 [M]	Dragsville	1964	40.00

WORLD OF OZ, THE

Number	Title (A Side/B Side)	Yr	NM
45s			
DERAM			
❑ 85029	The Muffin Man/Peter's Birthday	1968	10.00
❑ 85034	King Croesus/Jack	1968	10.00
❑ 85043	Mandy-Ann/Beside the Fire	1969	10.00
Albums			
DERAM			
❑ DES 18022	The World of Oz	1969	50.00

WOULD

Number	Title (A Side/B Side)	Yr	NM
Albums			
PERCEPTION			
❑ 24	Would	1972	30.00

WRAY, LINK

Number	Title (A Side/B Side)	Yr	NM
45s			
CADENCE			
❑ 1347	Rumble/The Swag	1958	40.00
EPIC			
❑ 9300	Raw-Hide/Dixie-Doodle	1958	25.00
❑ 9321	Comanche/Lillian	1959	25.00
❑ 9343	Rendezvous/Slinky	1959	25.00
❑ 9343 [PS]	Rendezvous/Slinky	1959	250.00
❑ 9361	Trail of the Lonesome Pine/ Golden Strings	1960	25.00
❑ 9419	Mary Ann/Ain't That Lovin' You Baby	1960	25.00
❑ 9454	El Toro/Tijuana	1961	25.00
HEAVY			
❑ 101	Rumble '68/Blow Your Mind	1968	15.00
KAY			
❑ 3690	I Sez Baby/(B-side unknown)	1958	100.00
MALA			
❑ 458	There's a Hole in the Middle of the Moon/Dancing Party	1963	20.00
MR. G.			
❑ 820	Rumble '69/Mind Blower	1969	10.00
NORTON			
❑ (no #) [PS]	Link Wray and the Wraymen	199?	2.00
—Custom sleeve with large hole to reveal the record label. The same generic sleeve was issued with each of 801-810.			
❑ 801	Jack the Ripper/Bo Diddley	199?	3.00
❑ 802	Ace of Spades/Fat Back	199?	3.00
❑ 803	Hidden Charms/Five and Ten	199?	3.00
❑ 804	The Black Widow/Mustang	199?	3.00
❑ 805	Run Chicken Run/Scatter	199?	3.00
❑ 806	Branded/Law of the Jungle	199?	3.00
❑ 807	Deuces Wild/The Sweeper	199?	3.00
❑ 808	The Shadow Knows/Hang On	199?	3.00
❑ 809	Good Rockin' Tonight/Soul Train	199?	3.00
❑ 810	Batman Theme/Zip Code	199?	3.00
OKEH			
❑ 7166	Rumble Mambo/Ham Bone	1963	20.00
—B-side by Red Saunders			
❑ 7282	Rumble Mambo/Ham Bone	1967	15.00
—B-side by Red Saunders			
POLYDOR			
❑ 14084	Fire and Brimstone/ June Box Mama	1970	8.00
❑ 14096	Fallin' Rain/Juke Box Mama	1971	8.00
❑ 14188	Shine the Light/ Lawdy Miss Clawdy	1973	6.00
❑ 14256	I Got to Ramble/She's That Kind of Woman	1974	6.00
RUMBLE			
❑ 1000	Jack the Ripper/The Stranger	1961	40.00
SWAN			
❑ 4137	Jack the Ripper/ The Black Widow	1963	20.00
❑ 4154	Weekend/Turnpike U.S.A.	1963	20.00
❑ 4163	Run Chicken Run/The Sweeper	1963	20.00
❑ 4171	The Shadow Knows/My Alberta	1964	20.00
❑ 4187	Deuces Wild/Summer Dream	1964	20.00
❑ 4201	Good Rockin' Tonight/ I'll Do Anything for You	1965	25.00
❑ 4211	Branded/Hang On	1965	20.00
❑ 4232	Girl from the North Country/ You Hurt Me So	1965	20.00
❑ 4239	The Fuzz/Ace of Spades	1966	20.00
❑ 4244	Batman Theme/Alone	1966	25.00
❑ 4261	Ace of Spades/Hidden Charms	1966	25.00
❑ 4284	Jack the Ripper/I'll Do Anything for You	1967	15.00
TRANS ATLAS			
❑ 687	Big City Stomp/Poppin' Popeye	1962	20.00
Albums			
EPIC			
❑ LN 3661 [M]	Link Wray and the Wraymen	1960	250.00
NORTON			
❑ 210	Hillbilly Wolf (Missing Links Vol. 1)	199?	10.00
❑ 211	Big City After Dark (Mizssing Links Vol. 2)	199?	10.00
❑ 212	Some Kinda Nut (Missing Links Vol. 3)	199?	10.00
❑ 253	Streets of Chicago (Missing Links Vol. 4)	1995	10.00
POLYDOR			
❑ 24-4064	Link Wray	1971	20.00
❑ PD-5047	Be What You Want To	1972	20.00
❑ PD-6025	The Link Wray Rumble	1974	20.00
RECORD FACTORY			
❑ 1929	Yesterday and Today	1969	80.00
SWAN			
❑ SLP-510 [M]	Jack the Ripper	1963	150.00
VERMILLION			
❑ 1924 [M]	Great Guitar Hits	196?	80.00
❑ 1925 [M]	Link Wray Sings and Plays Guitar	196?	80.00
VISA			
❑ 7009	Bullshot	1979	12.00
❑ 7010	Live at the Paradiso	1980	12.00

WRENS, THE

Number	Title (A Side/B Side)	Yr	NM
45s			
RAMA			
❑ 53	Love's Something That's Made for Two/Beggin' for Love	1955	1500.
❑ 65	Come Back My Love/ Beggin' for Love	1955	150.00
❑ 65	Come Back My Love/ Eleven Roses	1955	400.00
❑ 110	Love's Something That's Made for Two/Eleven Roses	1955	300.00
❑ 174	Hey Girl/Serenade of the Bells	1955	400.00
❑ 184	I Won't Come to Your Wedding/ What Makes You Do the Things That You Do	1956	400.00
❑ 194	C'est La Vie/C'est La Vie	1956	400.00
—B-side by Jimmy Wright and His Orchestra			

WRIGHT, BETTY

Number	Title (A Side/B Side)	Yr	NM
12-Inch Singles			
FIRST STRING			
❑ 268	I Can (2 versions)/Music Street	1986	10.00
JAMAICA			
❑ 9002	One Step Up, Two Steps Back (9:52) (7:57 Dub)	1984	8.00
❑ 9004	Sinderella (6:30) (5:28)	1985	8.00
MS. B.			
❑ 1217	From Pain to Joy (Project Mix)/ From Pain to Joy (Project Mix with Rap)	1989	8.00
❑ 1230	We Down (5 versions)	1989	8.00
T.K. DISCO			
❑ TKD-125	Lovin' Is Really My Game (2 versions)	1979	12.00
VISION			
❑ 7005	After the Pain (6:56)/ After the Pain (Project Mix)	1988	8.00
45s			
ALSTON			
❑ 3711	Shoorah! Shoorah!/ Tonight Is the Night	1974	5.00
❑ 3713	Where Is the Love/My Baby Ain't My Baby Anymore	1975	5.00
❑ 3715	Ooola La/To Love and Be Loved	1975	5.00
❑ 3718	Slip and Do It/I Think I Better Think About It	1975	5.00
❑ 3719	Everybody Was Rockin'/ Show Your Girl	1976	5.00
❑ 3722	If I Ever Do Wrong/Rock On Baby, Rock On	1976	5.00
❑ 3725	Life/If I Was a Kid	1976	5.00
❑ 3734	You Can't See for Lookin'/ Sometime Kind of Thing	1977	5.00
❑ 3736	Man of Mine/Sweet	1978	5.00
❑ 3740	Tonight Is the Night (Part 1)/ Tonight Is the Night (Part 2)	1978	5.00
❑ 3745	Lovin' Is Really My Game/ A Song for You	1979	5.00
❑ 3747	My Love Is/I Believe It's Love	1979	5.00
❑ 3749	Thank You for the Many Things You've Done/Child of the Man	1979	5.00
❑ 4569	Girls Can't Do What the Guys Do/Sweet Lovin' Daddy	1968	8.00
❑ 4571	He's Bad Bad Bad/Watch Out, Love	1968	8.00
❑ 4573	The Best Girls Don't Always Win/Circle of Heartbreaks	1969	8.00
❑ 4575	The Wrong Girl/The Joy of Becoming a Woman	1969	8.00
❑ 4580	I'm Not Free Hearted/A Woman Was Made for One Man	1969	8.00
❑ 4581	Soldier Boy/A Woman Was Made for One Man	1969	8.00
❑ 4587	Pure Love/If You Ain't Got It	1970	7.00
❑ 4589	I Found That Guy/If You Love Like I Love You	1970	7.00
❑ 4594	I Love the Way You Love/When We Get Together Again	1971	7.00
❑ 4601	Clean Up Woman/ I'll Love You Forever	1971	6.00
❑ 4609	If You Love Me Like You Say You Love Me/I'm Gettin' Tired Baby	1972	6.00
❑ 4611	Is It You Girl/Crying in My Sleep	1972	6.00
❑ 4614	Baby Sitter/Outside Woman	1972	6.00
❑ 4617	It's Hard to Stop (Doing Something When It's Good to You)/Who'll Be the Fool	1973	6.00
❑ 4619	Let Me Be Your Lovemaker/ Jealous Man	1973	6.00
❑ 4620	It's Bad for Me to See You/ One Thing Leads to Another	1974	6.00
❑ 4622	Secretary/Value Your Love	1974	6.00
EPIC			
❑ 02143	I Like Your Loving/Body Slang	1981	4.00
❑ 02521	Goodbye Him Hello You/ Make Me Love the Rain	1981	4.00
❑ 03523	He's Older Now/Special Love	1983	4.00
❑ 03954	Burning Desire/Show Me	1983	4.00
❑ 51009	What Are We Gonna Do About It/I Believe in You	1981	4.00
FIRST STRING			
❑ 965	Pain/(B-side unknown)	1985	4.00
❑ 968	The Sun Don't Shine/ Music Street	1986	4.00
JAMAICA			
❑ 3	One Step Up, Two Steps Back/ (B-side unknown)	1984	4.00
MS. B.			
❑ 4501	No Pain, No Gain/(Instrumental)	1988	4.00

Except when noted otherwise, VG = 25% of NM, and VG+ = 50% of NM. (Example: VG = $2.00, VG+ = $4.00 and NM = $8.00.)

Number	Title (A Side/B Side)	Yr	NM
❑ 4503	After the Pain/Love Days	1988	4.00
❑ 4504	A Christmas To Remember/2nd Chapter Of The Book Of Mathew	1988	3.00
❑ 4505	From Pain to Joy/From Pain to Joy (The Project Mix)	1989	4.00
❑ 4508	Quiet Storm/We Down	1989	4.00

Albums

ALSTON

Number	Title (A Side/B Side)	Yr	NM
❑ SD 33-388	I Love the Way You Love	1972	15.00
❑ 4400	Danger High Voltage	1974	12.00
❑ 4406	This Time for Real	1977	12.00
❑ 4408	Betty Wright Live	1978	12.00
❑ 4410	Betty Travelin' in the Wright Circle	1979	12.00
❑ SD 7026	Hard to Stop	1973	15.00

ATCO

Number	Title (A Side/B Side)	Yr	NM
❑ SD 33-260	My First Time Around	1968	25.00

COLLECTABLES

Number	Title (A Side/B Side)	Yr	NM
❑ COL-5118	Golden Classics	198?	10.00

EPIC

Number	Title (A Side/B Side)	Yr	NM
❑ JE 36879	Betty Wright	1981	10.00
❑ FE 38558	Wright Back at You	1983	10.00

FANTASY

Number	Title (A Side/B Side)	Yr	NM
❑ 9644	Sevens	1986	10.00

MS. B.

Number	Title (A Side/B Side)	Yr	NM
❑ 3301	Mother Wit	1988	10.00
❑ 3318	Passion and Compassion	198?	15.00

WRIGHT, CHARLES, AND THE WATTS 103RD STREET RHYTHM BAND

45s

ABC

Number	Title (A Side/B Side)	Yr	NM
❑ 12127	Is It Real/One Lie	1975	4.00
—Charles Wright solo			

ABC DUNHILL

Number	Title (A Side/B Side)	Yr	NM
❑ 4363	Liberated Lady/You Threw It All Away	1973	4.00
❑ 4364	(Well I'm) Doing What Cums Naturally Part 1/Part 2	1973	4.00
❑ 4381	The Weight of Hate/You Threw It All Away	1974	4.00
❑ 15027	Don't Rush Tomorrow/Is It Real	1974	4.00

KEYMEN

Number	Title (A Side/B Side)	Yr	NM
❑ 108	Spreadin' Honey/Charlie	1967	10.00
—As "The Watts 103rd Street Rhythm Band"			

WARNER BROS.

Number	Title (A Side/B Side)	Yr	NM
❑ 7175	Brown Sugar/Caesar's Palace	1968	10.00
—Through 7298, as "The Watts 103rd Street Rhythm Band"			
❑ 7222	Bottomless/65 Bars and a Taste of Soul	1968	10.00
❑ 7250	Do Your Thing/A Dance, a Kiss, and a Song	1969	8.00
❑ 7298	Till You Get Enough/Light My Fire	1969	8.00
❑ 7338	Must Be Your Thing/Comment	1969	6.00
❑ 7365	Love Land/Sorry Charlie	1970	6.00
❑ 7417	Express Yourself/Living on Borrowed Time	1970	6.00
❑ 7475	Your Love (Means Everything to Me)/What Can You Bring Me	1971	5.00
❑ 7504	Nobody/Wine	1971	5.00
❑ 7577	I've Got Love/Let's Make Love — Not War	1972	5.00
❑ 7600	Soul Train/Run Judy Run	1972	5.00
❑ 7630	Here Comes the Sun/You Gotta Know Whatcha Doin'	1972	5.00

Albums

ABC

Number	Title (A Side/B Side)	Yr	NM
❑ D-887	Lil' Encouragement	1975	12.00

ABC DUNHILL

Number	Title (A Side/B Side)	Yr	NM
❑ DS-50162 [(2)]	Doin' What Comes Naturally	1973	15.00
❑ DS-50187	Ninety Day Cycle People	1974	12.00

WARNER BROS.

Number	Title (A Side/B Side)	Yr	NM
❑ WS 1741	The Watts 103rd Street Rhythm Band	1968	20.00
—Green label with "W7" logo			
❑ WS 1761	Together	1969	20.00
—Green label with "W7" logo			
❑ WS 1761	Together	1970	15.00
—Green label with "WB" logo			
❑ WS 1801	In the Jungle, Babe	1969	20.00
—Green label with "W7" logo			
❑ WS 1801	In the Jungle, Babe	1970	15.00
—Green label with "WB" logo			
❑ WS 1864	Express Yourself	1970	15.00
❑ WS 1904	You're So Beautiful	1971	15.00
❑ BS 2620	Rhythm and Poetry	1972	15.00
—Green label with "WB" logo			
❑ BS 2620	Rhythm and Poetry	1973	12.00
—"Burbank" palm-trees logo			

WRIGHT, GARY Also see SPOOKY TOOTH.

45s

A&M

Number	Title (A Side/B Side)	Yr	NM
❑ 1228	Over You Now/Get On the Right Road	1970	5.00
❑ 1267	Stand for Our Rights/I Can't See the Reason	1971	5.00
❑ 1319	Love to Survive/Fascinating Things	1972	5.00
❑ 1344	Two-Faced Man/I Know	1972	5.00

WARNER BROS.

Number	Title (A Side/B Side)	Yr	NM
❑ 8143	Love Is Alive/Much Higher	1975	4.00
—Reissued in 1976 with the same number			
❑ 8167	Dream Weaver/Let It Out	1975	4.00
❑ 8250	Made to Love You/Power of Love	1976	4.00
❑ 8331	Phantom Writer/Child of Light	1977	4.00
❑ 8383	Empty Inside/Water Sign	1977	4.00
❑ 8426	Light of Smiles/Silent Fury	1977	4.00
❑ 8548	Something Very Special/Starry Eyed	1978	4.00
❑ 8598	Can't Get Above Losing You/Starry Eyed	1978	4.00
❑ 8809	Follow Next to You/I'm the One Who'll Be At Your Side	1979	4.00
❑ 49769	Really Wanna Know You/More Than a Heartache	1981	4.00
❑ 49836	Comin' Apart/Heartbeat	1981	4.00
❑ 49879	Got the Feelin'/Close to You	1981	4.00

Albums

A&M

Number	Title (A Side/B Side)	Yr	NM
❑ SP-3528 [(2)]	That Was Only Yesterday	1976	15.00
—By "Gary Wright/Spooky Tooth"			
❑ SP-4277	Extraction	1970	15.00
❑ SP-4296	Footprint	1971	15.00

CYPRESS

Number	Title (A Side/B Side)	Yr	NM
❑ 0111	Who I Am	1988	12.00

WARNER BROS.

Number	Title (A Side/B Side)	Yr	NM
❑ BS 2868	The Dream Weaver	1975	10.00
❑ BS 2951	The Light of Smiles	1976	10.00
❑ BSK 3137	Touch and Gone	1977	10.00
❑ BSK 3244	Headin' Home	1979	10.00
❑ BSK 3511	The Right Place	1981	10.00

WRIGHT, O.V.

45s

ABC

Number	Title (A Side/B Side)	Yr	NM
❑ 12119	What More Can I Do (To Prove My Love to You)/Henpecked Man	1975	6.00
❑ 12154	Nobody But You/Slow and Easy	1976	6.00

BACK BEAT

Number	Title (A Side/B Side)	Yr	NM
❑ 544	Don't Want to Sit Down/Can't Find True Love	1965	10.00
❑ 548	You're Gonna Make Me Cry/Monkey Dog	1965	10.00
❑ 551	I'm In Your Corner/Poor Boy	1965	10.00
❑ 558	Gone for Good/How Long Baby	1966	10.00
❑ 580	Eight Men, Four Women/Fed Up with the Blues	1967	8.00
❑ 583	Heartaches-Heartaches/Treasured Moments	1967	8.00
❑ 586	What About You/What Did You Tell This Girl of Mine	1967	8.00
❑ 591	Oh Baby Mine/Working Your Game	1968	8.00
❑ 597	I Want Everyone to Know/I'm Gonna Forget About You	1968	8.00
❑ 604	Missing You/This Must Be Real	1969	8.00
❑ 607	I'll Take Care of You/Why Not Give Me a Chance	1969	8.00
❑ 611	Love the Way You Love/Blowin' in the Wind	1970	8.00
❑ 615	Ace of Spade/Afflicted	1970	8.00
❑ 620	When You Took Your Love from Me/I Was Born All Over	1971	6.00
❑ 622	A Nickel and a Nail/Pledging My Love	1971	6.00
❑ 625	He Made Woman for Man/Don't Let My Baby Ride	1972	6.00
❑ 626	Drowning on Dry Land/I'm Gonna Forget About You	1973	6.00
❑ 628	I'd Rather Be (Blind, Cripple and Crazy)/Please Forgive Me	1973	6.00
❑ 631	I've Been Searching/I'm Going Home	1974	6.00
❑ 5103	I'm In Your Corner/Poor Boy	1974	6.00

GOLDWAX

Number	Title (A Side/B Side)	Yr	NM
❑ 106	That's How Strong My Love Is/There Goes My Used to Be	1964	12.00

HI

Number	Title (A Side/B Side)	Yr	NM
❑ 2315	Rhymes/Without You	1976	6.00
❑ 77501	Into Something (Can't Shake Loose)/The Time We Have	1977	6.00
❑ 77506	Precious, Precious/You Gotta Have Love	1977	6.00
❑ 78514	I Don't Do Windows/I Feel Love Growin'	1978	6.00
❑ 78521	No Easy Way to Say Goodbye/Bottom Line	1978	6.00
❑ 79531	We're Still Together/I Don't Know Why	1979	6.00

Albums

BACK BEAT

Number	Title (A Side/B Side)	Yr	NM
❑ 61 [M]	If It's Only for Tonight	1965	100.00
❑ S-61 [S]	If It's Only for Tonight	1965	150.00
❑ 66	Eight Men, Four Women	1968	60.00
❑ 67	Nucleus of Soul	1969	60.00
❑ 70	A Nickel and a Nail and Ace of Spade	1971	60.00
❑ 72	Memphis Unlimited	1973	50.00

HI

Number	Title (A Side/B Side)	Yr	NM
❑ 6001	Into Something	1977	25.00
❑ 6008	Bottom Line	1978	25.00
❑ 6011	We're Still Together	1979	25.00

WRIGHT, OSCAR

45s

FAIRMOUNT

Number	Title (A Side/B Side)	Yr	NM
❑ 1011	Fell in Love/Leave Me Alone	1966	50.00

HEMISPHERE

Number	Title (A Side/B Side)	Yr	NM
❑ 100	Fell in Love/Leave Me Alone	1966	200.00

WRIGHT, RANDY

45s

ATLANTIC

Number	Title (A Side/B Side)	Yr	NM
❑ 1115	What My Heart Didn't Know/Snake in the Grass	1956	20.00

MCA

Number	Title (A Side/B Side)	Yr	NM
❑ 52273	There's Nobody Lovin' at Home/Times Like This (Make Me Want Times Like That)	1983	4.00
❑ 52358	If You're Serious About Cheating/Times Like This	1984	4.00

WRIGHT, RICHARD

Albums

COLUMBIA

Number	Title (A Side/B Side)	Yr	NM
❑ JC 35559	Wet Dream	1978	20.00

WRIGHT, RITA Later recorded as SYREETA.

45s

GORDY

Number	Title (A Side/B Side)	Yr	NM
❑ 7064	I Can't Give Back the Love I Feel for You/Something on My Mind	1967	10.00

WRIGHT, RUBY (1)

45s

CANDEE

Number	Title (A Side/B Side)	Yr	NM
❑ 502	This Is Christmas/(B-side unknown)	196?	20.00

COLUMBIA

Number	Title (A Side/B Side)	Yr	NM
❑ 4-41807	Wasn't the Summer Short/Fooled	1960	20.00

FRATERNITY

Number	Title (A Side/B Side)	Yr	NM
❑ 787	Let's Light the Christmas Tree/Merry Merry Christmas	1957	15.00

KING

Number	Title (A Side/B Side)	Yr	NM
❑ 1249	You Walked Out of My Dreams/I Only Have One Lifetime	1953	30.00
❑ 1288	Santa's Little Sleigh Bells/Toodle Oo To You	1953	30.00
❑ 1293	Boy You Got Yourself a Girl/Bimbo	1953	25.00
❑ 1305	Tennessee Churchbells/I Had the Funniest Feeling	1954	25.00
❑ 1411	God Loves You Child/What Have They Told You	1954	25.00
❑ 4850	Do You Believe/I Fall in Love with You Every Day	1955	20.00
❑ 4870	Rummy Dumb Bunny/Don't Take Me for Granted	1956	20.00
❑ 5192	Three Stars/I Only Have One Lifetime	1959	20.00
❑ 5208	Goodbye, Jimmy, Goodbye/Don't Take Me for Granted	1959	20.00
❑ 5225	Don't Take Me for Granted/I Only Have One Lifetime	1959	20.00
❑ 5261	Sweet Night of Love/You're Just a Flower from an Old Bouquet	1959	20.00
❑ 5297	Free-Hearted/When You're Away	1959	20.00

W

Bill Wyman, "(Si Si) Je Suis Un Rock Star," A&M 2367, 1981, **$10.**

Number	Title (A Side/B Side)	Yr	NM
7-Inch Extended Plays			
CANDEE			
❑ EP-50-50	Christmas Is a Birthday Time//Have A Merry Merry Merry Merry Christmas/The Happy Time	196?	8.00
—B-side by Ruth Lyons			

WRIGHT, RUBY (2)

Number	Title (A Side/B Side)	Yr	NM
45s			
EPIC			
❑ 5-10055	A New Place to Hang Your Hat/A Kick in the Conscience	1966	10.00
❑ 5-10150	(I Can Find) A Better Deal Than That/Everything, All the Time	1967	10.00

WRIGHT, SONNY (1) R&B singer, formerly with THE DIAMONDS (2).

Number	Title (A Side/B Side)	Yr	NM
45s			
ATLANTIC			
❑ 45-2045	Heaven Help Me/Lullaby with a Beat	1960	30.00

WRIGHT, SONNY (2)

Number	Title (A Side/B Side)	Yr	NM
45s			
COLUMBIA			
❑ 4-44320	Leftover Love/Running Drunk	1967	8.00
❑ 4-44496	Pain Remover/Hung to Another Man	1968	8.00
COUNTRY INT'L.			
❑ 178	Don't Leave Without Taking Your Silver/(B-side unknown)	1982	5.00
❑ 184	The Ride/Don't Leave Without Taking Your Silver	198?	5.00
CUTLASS			
❑ 126	Gettin' Ready to Die/Here Comes a Million	197?	6.00
❑ 814	Truck Driver's Hymn/Hangout for a Hasbeen	197?	6.00
DOOR KNOB			
❑ 040	Motel Mourning/When I Start Drinking	1977	5.00
❑ 057	Same Old Highway/Motel Mourning	1978	5.00
❑ 100	You Make Me Feel Brand New/If This Isn't It	1979	5.00
❑ 128	Molly (And the Texas Rain)/It Wasn't Me Who Said I Owned a Gold Mine	1980	5.00
KAPP			
❑ 2009	I Love You, Loretta Lynn/Rose	1969	10.00
❑ 2040	Hung Over/The Trash You Threw Away	1969	8.00
❑ 2090	My Long Gone Reason/Mama Didn't Bend the Twig	1970	8.00
PARTHENON			
❑ 002	Gotta Swim the Mississippi/99 Years	198?	6.00
❑ 008	I'll Build Her Up/You're Leaving Me for Him	198?	6.00
Albums			
KAPP			
❑ KS-3614	I Love You, Loretta Lynn	1968	20.00

WRIGLEY, BETTY

Number	Title (A Side/B Side)	Yr	NM
45s			
HIT			
❑ 141	Selfish One/Save It for Me	1964	8.00
—B-side by the Roamers			

WRITIS, ARTHUR, AND THE NAGGING PAINS

Number	Title (A Side/B Side)	Yr	NM
45s			
REPRISE			
❑ 0589	Say What/Welcome to San Francisco	1967	10.00

WYATT, GENE

Number	Title (A Side/B Side)	Yr	NM
45s			
DOLLIE			
❑ 502	Fightin' for the Free Land/Searching for a New Love Affair	1966	10.00
EBB			
❑ 123	Love Fever/Lover Boy	1957	100.00
LUCKY SEVEN			
❑ 101	Prettiest Girl at the Dance/Music and Arithmetic	1959	60.00
MERCURY			
❑ 72752	I Stole the Flowers/I'm a One Woman Man	1967	10.00
PAULA			
❑ 308	I Just Ain't Got (As Much As He's Got Going for Me)/Chains Around My Heart	1968	10.00
❑ 1206	Little Liza Jane/Country Music Peyton Place	1968	10.00
❑ 1211	My Story of Love/Evangeline	1969	10.00
❑ 1216	Milk and Honey Memories/Failure of T Crop	1969	10.00
❑ 1223	Twelve Men/Back Door of My Mind	1970	8.00
❑ 1224	Go Together/As Long As I Live	1970	8.00

WYLIE, RICHARD "POPCORN"

Number	Title (A Side/B Side)	Yr	NM
45s			
ABC			
❑ 12067	Lost Time/Trust in Me	1975	8.00
❑ 12124	Georgia's After Hours/E.S.P.	1975	8.00
CARLA			
❑ 715	Move Over Babe (Here Comes Henry)/(Instrumental)	1973	10.00
❑ 715 [PS]	Move Over Babe (Here Comes Henry)/(Instrumental)	1973	12.00
EPIC			
❑ 5-9543	Come to Me/Weddin' Bells	1962	20.00
❑ 5-9543 [PS]	Come to Me/Weddin' Bells	1962	25.00
❑ 5-9575	Brand New Man/So Much Love in My Heart	1963	20.00
❑ 5-9611	Greater Than Anything/Head Over Heels in Love	1963	20.00
❑ 5-9663	Do You Still Care for Me/Marlene	1964	50.00
KAREN			
❑ 1542	Rosemary, What Happened/(Instrumental)	1968	30.00
MOTOWN			
❑ 1009	Money (That's What I Want)/I'll Be Around	1961	250.00
❑ 1019	Real Good Loving/Have I the Right	1961	200.00
Albums			
ABC			
❑ ABCD-834	E.S.P.	1974	60.00

WYMAN, BILL Also see THE ROLLING STONES.

Number	Title (A Side/B Side)	Yr	NM
12-Inch Singles			
A&M			
❑ SP-12041	(Si Si) Je Suis Un Rock Star (2 versions)/Rio de Janeiro	1981	15.00
—Red label			
❑ SP-12041	(Si Si) Je Suis Un Rock Star (2 versions)/Rio de Janeiro	1981	40.00
—Silver label			
45s			
A&M			
❑ 2367	(Si Si) Je Suis Un Rock Star/Rio De Janeiro	1981	5.00
❑ 2367 [PS]	(Si Si) Je Suis Un Rock Star/Rio De Janeiro	1981	10.00
ROLLING STONES			
❑ 19111	White Lightning/I Wanna Get Me a Gun	1974	5.00
❑ 19119	A Quarter to Three/Soul Satisfying	1975	5.00
❑ 19303	Apache Woman/Soul Satisfying	1975	5.00
Albums			
ROLLING STONES			
❑ COC 59102	Monkey Grip	1974	15.00
❑ COC 79100	Monkey Grip	1974	12.00
—Reissue of 59102			
❑ QD 79100 [Q]	Monkey Grip	1974	20.00
❑ COC 79103	Stone Alone	1976	12.00
❑ QD 79103 [Q]	Stone Alone	1976	20.00

Except when noted otherwise, VG = 25% of NM, and VG+ = 50% of NM. (Example: VG = $2.00, VG+ = $4.00 and NM = $8.00.)

Number	Title (A Side/B Side)	Yr	NM

WYNDER K. FROG

45s

UNITED ARTISTS

Number	Title (A Side/B Side)	Yr	NM
❑ 50156	The Green Door/Dancing Frog	1967	6.00
❑ 50320	I'm a Man/Oh Mary	1968	6.00
❑ 50453	Jumpin' Jack Flash/ I Feel So Bad	1968	6.00

Albums

UNITED ARTISTS

Number	Title (A Side/B Side)	Yr	NM
❑ UAS-5740	Into the Fire	1971	12.00
❑ UAS-6695	Out of the Frying Pan	1970	12.00

WYNTER, MARK

45s

ARLEN

Number	Title (A Side/B Side)	Yr	NM
❑ 744	Running to You/Don't Cry	1964	12.00

GUYDEN

Number	Title (A Side/B Side)	Yr	NM
❑ 2115	Answer Me/Only You	1964	10.00

LONDON

Number	Title (A Side/B Side)	Yr	NM
❑ 1973	Dream Girl/Two Little Girls	1961	15.00
❑ 1997	Exclusively Yours/ Warm and Willing	1961	15.00
❑ 9522	Heaven's Plan/You Are Everything	1962	15.00

SCEPTER

Number	Title (A Side/B Side)	Yr	NM
❑ 1299	Am I Living in a Dream/Can I Get to Know You Better	1965	10.00

X

X

12-Inch Singles

ELEKTRA

Number	Title (A Side/B Side)	Yr	NM
❑ EAOR 4912 [DJ]	Breathless/Riding with Mary	1983	10.00
❑ EAOR 4943 [DJ]	True Love Part II (Club Version Remix) (AOR Edit) (LP Version)	1983	12.00
❑ ED 5068 [DJ]	Burning House of Love (same on both sides)	1985	8.00
❑ ED 5106 [DJ]	Around My Heart (Edit)/ (LP Version)	1985	8.00
❑ ED 5232 [DJ]	4th of July (same on both sides)	1987	8.00
❑ ED 5248 [DJ]	See How We Are (same on both sides)	1987	8.00
❑ ED 5305 [DJ]	Devil Doll/New World/ Burning House of Love	1988	6.00
❑ 66966	Wild Thing (6:18)/True Love Part II (Club Remix)	1984	10.00

45s

CURB

Number	Title (A Side/B Side)	Yr	NM
❑ 10538 [DJ]	Wild Thing/Wild Thing, Part 2	1988	30.00

—Does not exist as stock copy

DANGERHOUSE

Number	Title (A Side/B Side)	Yr	NM
❑ D-88	Adult Books/We're Desperate	1978	40.00
❑ D-88 [PS]	Adult Books/We're Desperate	1978	60.00

—Folded picture sleeve in plastic bag; authentic sleeves are black, white and yellow (photocopies in black and white exist and have no collector value)

ELEKTRA

Number	Title (A Side/B Side)	Yr	NM
❑ 69462	4th of July/Positively 4th Street	1987	4.00
❑ 69462 [PS]	4th of July/Positively 4th Street	1987	4.00
❑ 69626	Burning House of Love/ Love Shack	1985	8.00
❑ 69626 [DJ]	Burning House of Love (edit) (same on both sides)	1985	4.00
❑ 69626 [PS]	Burning House of Love/ Love Shack	1985	4.00
❑ 69709	Wild Thing/Devil Doll	1984	5.00
❑ 69825	Breathless/Riding with Mary	1983	6.00
❑ 69825 [PS]	Breathless/Riding with Mary	1983	6.00
❑ 69885	Blue Spark/Dancing with Tears in My Eyes	1982	12.00
❑ 69885 [PS]	Blue Spark/Dancing with Tears in My Eyes	1982	12.00

SLASH

Number	Title (A Side/B Side)	Yr	NM
❑ SRS-106	White Girl/Your Phone's Off the Hook (But You're Not)	1980	10.00
❑ SRS-106 [PS]	White Girl/Your Phone's Off the Hook (But You're Not)	1980	10.00

—Blue and white sleeve

Number	Title (A Side/B Side)	Yr	NM
❑ SRS-106 [PS]	White Girl/Your Phone's Off the Hook (But You're Not)	1980	20.00

—Green and white sleeve

Albums

ELEKTRA

Number	Title (A Side/B Side)	Yr	NM
❑ 60150	Under the Big Black Sun	1982	15.00
❑ 60283	More Fun in the New World	1983	12.00
❑ 60430	Ain't Love Grand	1985	12.00
❑ 60492	See How We Are	1987	10.00
❑ 60788 [(2)]	Live at the Whiskey A-Go-Go on the Fabulous Sunset Strip	1988	15.00

RHINO

Number	Title (A Side/B Side)	Yr	NM
❑ R1-74370	Los Angeles	2003	18.00

—Reissue on 180-gram vinyl

SLASH

Number	Title (A Side/B Side)	Yr	NM
❑ SR-104	Los Angeles	1980	25.00
❑ SR-107	Wild Gift	1981	20.00
❑ 23930	Los Angeles	1983	12.00

—Reissue of Slash 104

Number	Title (A Side/B Side)	Yr	NM
❑ 23931	Wild Gift	1983	12.00

—Reissue of Slash 107

X-CELLENTS, THE

45s

SMASH

Number	Title (A Side/B Side)	Yr	NM
❑ 1996	Hey Little Willie/I'll Aways Be On Your Side	1965	20.00

X-CITERS UNLIMITED

45s

ABC

Number	Title (A Side/B Side)	Yr	NM
❑ 11029	Soul to Fillie Joe/Hang On Sloopy	1967	10.00

X. LINCOLN

45s

DOT

Number	Title (A Side/B Side)	Yr	NM
❑ 17101	In the Freedom of My Mind/ What Am I Gonna Do Now	1968	10.00
❑ 17170	Anywhere I Happen to Be/ You're Everything	1968	10.00
❑ 17267	You're My Heaven/Mama Was a Proper Lady	1969	10.00

X-TREMES, THE

45s

STAR TREK

Number	Title (A Side/B Side)	Yr	NM
❑ 1221	Substitute/Facts of Life	1966	25.00

X-RAY SPEX

Albums

BLUE PLATE

Number	Title (A Side/B Side)	Yr	NM
❑ CAROL-1813-1	Germ Free Adolescents	1992	18.00

—Recorded in 1978, this is this classic new wave LP's first American issue

EMI

Number	Title (A Side/B Side)	Yr	NM
❑ INS-3023	Germ Free Adolescents	1978	35.00

—British release only, no U.S. version until 1992

XAVIER

12-Inch Singles

LIBERTY

Number	Title (A Side/B Side)	Yr	NM
❑ SP-218	Do It to the Max (5:56)/ Rock Me, Sock Me	1982	20.00
❑ 7200	Work That Sucker to Death/ Love Is on the One	1981	15.00

45s

LIBERTY

Number	Title (A Side/B Side)	Yr	NM
❑ 1445	Work That Sucker to Death/ Love Is on the One	1981	6.00
❑ B-1464	Do It to the Max/(Instrumental)	1982	4.00

Albums

LIBERTY

Number	Title (A Side/B Side)	Yr	NM
❑ LT-51116	Point of Pleasure	1981	15.00

XAVION

12-Inch Singles

ASYLUM

Number	Title (A Side/B Side)	Yr	NM
❑ ED 4999 [DJ]	Eat Your Heart Out (LP Version) (Dance Version) (Dub)	1984	8.00
❑ ED 5029 [DJ]	Get Me Hot (same on both sides)	1984	8.00

45s

ASYLUM

Number	Title (A Side/B Side)	Yr	NM
❑ 69670	Get Me Hot/You're My Type	1984	4.00

Albums

ASYLUM

Number	Title (A Side/B Side)	Yr	NM
❑ 60375	Burnin' Hot	1984	15.00

XIT

45s

MOTOWN

Number	Title (A Side/B Side)	Yr	NM
❑ 1304	I Need Your Love (Git It To Me)/ Movin' from the City	1974	8.00
❑ 1320	Renegade/Cement Prairie	1974	8.00

RARE EARTH

Number	Title (A Side/B Side)	Yr	NM
❑ 5044	Nihaa Shil Hozho (I Am Happy About You)/End	1972	10.00
❑ 5055	Reservation of Education/ Color Nature Gone	1973	10.00

Albums

CANYON

Number	Title (A Side/B Side)	Yr	NM
❑ 7114	Entrance	197?	50.00
❑ C-7121	Relocation	1977	40.00

RARE EARTH

Number	Title (A Side/B Side)	Yr	NM
❑ R-536	Plight of the Redman	1972	30.00
❑ R-545	Silent Warrior	1973	30.00

WARRIOR

Number	Title (A Side/B Side)	Yr	NM
❑ WAR 49	Plight of the Redman	1981	15.00

—Reissue of Rare Earth 536

XTC

12-Inch Singles

GEFFEN

Number	Title (A Side/B Side)	Yr	NM
❑ PRO-A-2117 [DJ]	Great Fire/Love on a Farmboy's Wages//Wonderland/ Funk Pop a Roll	1983	12.00
❑ PRO-A-2214 [DJ]	All You Pretty Girls//Wake Up/ Shake You Donkey Up	1984	15.00
❑ PRO-A-2840 [DJ]	Vanishing Girl (same on both sides)	1987	10.00

—As "The Dukes of Stratosphear"

Number	Title (A Side/B Side)	Yr	NM
❑ PRO-A-3522 [DJ]	King for a Day (Czar Mix 6:30) (I Dub Thee Sir Mix 6:10) (Versailles Mix 5:07)/ Toys/Desert Island	1989	12.00
❑ 20630	Dear God/Extrovert// Earn Enough for Us/Grass	1986	8.00
❑ 21160	The Mayor of Simpleton/One of the Millions//Ella Guru/Living in a Haunted Heart/The Good Things	1989	10.00

VIRGIN/EPIC

Number	Title (A Side/B Side)	Yr	NM
❑ AS 1405 [DJ]	Senses Working Overtime/Ball & Chain	1982	15.00

45s

EVA-TONE

Number	Title (A Side/B Side)	Yr	NM
❑ 113824XS	Blame the Weather/Tissue Tigers	1982	25.00

—Red flexi-disc included in April 1982 edition (#72) of "Trouser Press"; second song by the Arguers

GEFFEN

Number	Title (A Side/B Side)	Yr	NM
❑ 22953	King for a Day/Toys	1989	3.00
❑ 22953 [PS]	King for a Day/Toys	1989	3.00
❑ 27552	The Mayor of Simpleton/One of the Millions	1989	3.00
❑ 27552 [PS]	The Mayor of Simpleton/One of the Millions	1989	3.00
❑ 28394	Dear God/Mermaid Smiled	1987	4.00
❑ 29351	Wonderland/Jump	1984	5.00

VIRGIN

Number	Title (A Side/B Side)	Yr	NM
❑ PR 344	Limelight//Day In Day Out/ Chain of Command	1979	8.00

—7-inch 33 1/3 record with small center hole; only issued with first 15,000 copies of album 13134, though often found separately

Number	Title (A Side/B Side)	Yr	NM
❑ 67004	Ten Feet Tall//Helicopter/The Somnabulist	1980	12.00
❑ 67004 [DJ]	Ten Feet Tall (mono/stereo)	1980	5.00
❑ 67004 [PS]	Ten Feet Tall//Helicopter/ The Somnabulist	1980	5.00

—Sleeve came with both stock and promo copies

Number	Title (A Side/B Side)	Yr	NM
❑ 67009	Making Plans for Nigel//This Is Pop/Meccanik Dancing	1980	12.00
❑ 67009 [DJ]	Making Plans for Nigel (mono/stereo)	1980	5.00
❑ 67009 [PS]	Making Plans for Nigel//This Is Pop/Meccanik Dancing	1980	5.00

—Sleeve came with both stock and promo copies

VIRGIN/EPIC

Number	Title (A Side/B Side)	Yr	NM
❑ 14-02875	Senses Working Overtime/ English Roundabout	1982	10.00

VIRGIN/RSO

Number	Title (A Side/B Side)	Yr	NM
❑ 300	Generals and Majors/Living Through Another Cuba	1981	8.00

Albums

GEFFEN

Number	Title (A Side/B Side)	Yr	NM
❑ GHS 4027	Mummer	1983	10.00
❑ GHS 4032	White Music	1984	10.00

—Reissue of Virgin/Epic 38153

Number	Title (A Side/B Side)	Yr	NM
❑ GHS 4033	Go2	1984	10.00

—Reissue of Virgin/Epic 38152

Number	Title (A Side/B Side)	Yr	NM
❑ GHS 4034	Drums and Wires	1984	10.00

—Reissue of Virgin/Epic 38151

Number	Title (A Side/B Side)	Yr	NM
❑ GHS 4035	Black Sea	1984	10.00

—Reissue of Virgin/Epic 38150

Number	Title (A Side/B Side)	Yr	NM
❑ GHS 4036 [(2)]	English Settlement	1984	15.00

—First release of British version of this album in U.S.

Number	Title (A Side/B Side)	Yr	NM
❑ GHS 4037	Waxworks (Some Singles, 1977-82)	1984	12.00
❑ GHS 24054	The Big Express	1984	10.00

The Yardbirds, "Happenings Ten Years Time Ago," Epic 5-10094, 1966, **$50.**

Number	Title (A Side/B Side)	Yr	NM
❑ GHS 24117	Skylarking	1986	10.00
—Second pressing, with "Dear God" and without "Mermaid Smiled"			
❑ GHS 24117	Skylarking	1986	15.00
—First pressing, with "Mermaid Smiled" and without "Dear God"			
❑ GHS 24169	Psonic Psunspot	1987	15.00
—As "The Dukes of Stratosphear"			
❑ GHS 24218 [(2)]	Oranges and Lemons	1989	15.00
❑ R 201086 [(2)]	Oranges and Lemons	1989	15.00
—BMG Direct Marketing edition			
VIRGIN			
❑ VA 13134	Drums and Wires	1979	20.00
—With bonus 7-inch record (PR 344) enclosed — deduct 40 percent if missing			
❑ VA 13147	Black Sea	1980	30.00
—Promo only; label, jacket and innersleeve ALL must have this number			
VIRGIN INTERNATIONAL			
❑ VI-2095	White Music	1979	15.00
❑ VI-2108	Go2	1979	15.00
VIRGIN/EPIC			
❑ ARE 37943	English Settlement	1982	10.00
—Drastically edited version of U.K. original, which was a 2-record set			
❑ PE 38150	Black Sea	1982	10.00
—Reissue of Virgin/RSO 1001			
❑ PE 38151	Drums and Wires	1982	10.00
—Reissue of Virgin 13134			
❑ PE 38152	Go2	1982	10.00
—Reissue of Virgin International VI-2108			
❑ PE 38153	White Music	1982	10.00
—Reissue of Virgin International VI-2095			
VIRGIN/RSO			
❑ VR-1-1000	Black Sea	1980	12.00
—Without green outer bag; innersleeves may or may not have "VA 13147" reference			
❑ VR-1-1000	Black Sea	1980	20.00
—With green outer bag and "VA 13147" on innersleeve			
WARNER BROS.			
❑ WBMS-146 [DJ]	Skylarking Interview with Andy Partridge	1986	25.00
—Part of "The Warner Bros. Music Show" series			

X

XYMOX

Number	Title (A Side/B Side)	Yr	NM
12-Inch Singles			
WING			
❑ PRO 711-1 [DJ]	Obsession (Edit) (LP Version)/In a City	1989	12.00
❑ PRO 787-1 [DJ]	Blind Hearts (unknown versions)	1989	10.00
❑ PRO 950-1 [DJ]	Phoenix of My Heart (unknown versions)	1991	12.00
❑ 867321-1	At the End of the Day (Endless Day Mix) (7" Remix) (Hutchinson Remix) (Hutchinson Dub)/ Dream House	1991	10.00
❑ 868133-1	Phoenix of My Heart (3 versions)/Love Thy Neighbor	1991	12.00
❑ 871707-1	Obsession (Club Mix) (Edit)/ Hitchhiker's Dance Guide	1989	10.00
❑ 873001-1	Imagination (3 versions)/ Obsession (Club Mix)	1990	15.00
❑ 889633-1	Blind Hearts (2 versions)/Shame	1989	8.00
45s			
WING			
❑ 871707-7	Obsession/(B-side unknown)	1989	5.00
Albums			
RELATIVITY			
❑ EMC 8037	The Clan of Xymox	1985	25.00
WING			
❑ 839233-1	Twist of Shadows	1989	12.00
❑ 848516-1	Phoenix	1991	12.00

XYZ

Number	Title (A Side/B Side)	Yr	NM
12-Inch Singles			
CAPITOL			
❑ SPRO-79913 [DJ]	Face Down in the Gutter (same on both sides?)	1991	8.00
Albums			
ENIGMA			
❑ 7 73525 1	XYZ	1989	10.00

Y

Y KANT TORI READ
Lead singer is Tori Amos.

Number	Title (A Side/B Side)	Yr	NM
12-Inch Singles			
ATLANTIC			
❑ PR 2298 [DJ]	The Big Picture (same on both sides)	1988	120.00
45s			
ATLANTIC			
❑ 89021	Cool on Your Island/ Heart Attack at 23	1988	120.00
—Copies of this have been documented			
❑ 89021 [DJ]	Cool on Your Island (same on both sides)	1988	50.00
❑ 89021 [PS]	Cool on Your Island/Heart Attack at 23	1988	80.00
❑ 89086	The Big Picture/ You Go to My Head	1988	120.00
—Copies of this have been documented			
❑ 89086 [DJ]	The Big Picture (same on both sides)	1988	50.00
—Lead vocal: Tori Amos			
❑ 89086 [PS]	The Big Picture/ You Go to My Head	1988	80.00
Albums			
ATLANTIC			
❑ 81845	Y Kant Tori Read	1989	200.00
—Deduct 20% for albums with a gold promo stamp and cut-out mark. Also, any picture disc of this album is a bootleg, no matter what it claims to be			

YA HO WA 13

Number	Title (A Side/B Side)	Yr	NM
Albums			
HIGHER KEY			
❑ 3301	Kohoutek	1973	300.00
❑ 3302	Contraction	1974	500.00
❑ 3303	Expansion	1974	500.00
❑ 3304	All or Nothing at All	1974	400.00
—Above 4 as "Father Yod and the Spirit of '76"			
❑ 3305	Ya Ho Wa 13	1974	500.00
❑ 3306	The Savage Sons of Ya Ho Wa	1974	400.00
❑ 3307	Penetration: An Aquarian Symphony	1974	400.00
❑ 3308 [(2)]	I'm Gonna Take You Home	1975	800.00
❑ 3309	To the Principles for the Children	1975	800.00

YANCY DERRINGER

Number	Title (A Side/B Side)	Yr	NM
Albums			
HEMISPHERE			
❑ H-15104	Openers	1975	50.00

YANKEE DOLLAR, THE

Number	Title (A Side/B Side)	Yr	NM
45s			
DOT			
❑ 17123	City Sidewalks/Sanctuary	1968	15.00
❑ 17155	Live and Let Live/Sanctuary	1968	15.00
❑ 17213	Mucky Truckee River/Reflections of a Shattered Mind	1969	15.00
Albums			
DOT			
❑ DLP-25874	The Yankee Dollar	1968	120.00

YANOVSKY, ZALMAN
Also see THE LOVIN' SPOONFUL.

Number	Title (A Side/B Side)	Yr	NM
45s			
BUDDAH			
❑ 12	As Long As You're Here/Ereh Er'uoy Sa Gnol Sa	1967	10.00
❑ 12 [PS]	As Long As You're Here/Ereh Er'uoy Sa Gnol Sa	1967	30.00
Albums			
BUDDAH			
❑ BDS-5019	Alive and Well in Argentina	1968	40.00
KAMA SUTRA			
❑ KSBS-2030	Alive and Well in Argentina	1971	20.00

YARDBIRDS, THE
Also see JEFF BECK; ERIC CLAPTON; JIMMY PAGE; KEITH RELF; SONNY BOY WILLIAMSON (2). Ex-members of the group formed LED ZEPPELIN and RENAISSANCE.

Number	Title (A Side/B Side)	Yr	NM
45s			
EPIC			
❑ 5-9709	I Wish You Could/I Ain't Got You	1964	—
—Unreleased?			
❑ 5-9709	I Wish You Could/A Certain Girl	1964	40.00
—With typographical error on A-side			
❑ 5-9709	I Wish You Would/A Certain Girl	1964	50.00
—With correct A-side title; also includes "Radio Station Copy" versions, some of which were used as giveaways in stores			
❑ 5-9709 [PS]	I Wish You Could/A Certain Girl	1964	800.00
—Promo-only picture sleeve used by Esquire Socks, Burlington, N.C.; the back of the sleeve advertises "Denim Tones" by Esquire Socks;			

Except when noted otherwise, VG = 25% of NM, and VG+ = 50% of NM. (Example: VG = $2.00, VG+ = $4.00 and NM = $8.00.)

some copies of the sleeve also contain an insert, through which a store could order multiple copies of the Yardbirds record for use as a giveaway in the store (double the value if included)

Number	Title (A Side/B Side)	Yr	NM
❑ 5-9790	For Your Love/Got to Hurry	1965	15.00
❑ 5-9823	Heart Full of Soul/Steeled Blues	1965	15.00
❑ 5-9823 [PS]	Heart Full of Soul/Steeled Blues	1965	50.00
❑ 5-9857	I'm a Man/Still I'm Sad	1965	15.00
❑ 5-9881	Shapes of Things/I'm Not Talking	1966	15.00
❑ 5-10006	New York City Blues/ You're a Better Man Than I	1966	—

—Unreleased

Number	Title (A Side/B Side)	Yr	NM
❑ 5-10006	Shapes of Things/ New York City Blues	1966	20.00
❑ 5-10035	Over Under Sideways Down/ Jeff's Boogie	1966	15.00
❑ 5-10035 [PS]	Over Under Sideways Down/ Jeff's Boogie	1966	50.00
❑ 5-10094	Happenings Ten Years Time Ago/Psycho Daisies	1966	—

—Unreleased

Number	Title (A Side/B Side)	Yr	NM
❑ 5-10094	Happenings Ten Years Time Ago/The Nazz Are Blue	1966	15.00
❑ 5-10094 [PS]	Happenings Ten Years Time Ago/The Nazz Are Blue	1966	50.00
❑ 5-10156	Little Games/Puzzles	1967	20.00
❑ 5-10204	Ha Ha Said the Clown/ Tinker, Tailor, Soldier, Sailor	1967	20.00
❑ 5-10248	Ten Little Indians/Drinking Muddy Water	1967	20.00
❑ 5-10303	Goodnight Sweet Josephine/ Think About It	1968	50.00

Albums

ACCORD

Number	Title (A Side/B Side)	Yr	NM
❑ SN-7143 [S]	For Your Love	1981	8.00
❑ SN-7237 [R]	Having a Rave Up with the Yardbirds	1981	8.00

COLUMBIA SPECIAL PRODUCTS

Number	Title (A Side/B Side)	Yr	NM
❑ P 13311 [S]	Live Yardbirds Featuring Jimmy Page	1976	80.00

COMPLEAT

Number	Title (A Side/B Side)	Yr	NM
❑ CPL-2-2002 [(2)]	A Compleat Collection	1984	12.00

EPIC

Number	Title (A Side/B Side)	Yr	NM
❑ LN 24167 [DJ]	For Your Love	1965	400.00

—White label promo

Number	Title (A Side/B Side)	Yr	NM
❑ LN 24167 [M]	For Your Love	1965	300.00
❑ LN 24177 [DJ]	Having a Rave Up with the Yardbirds	1965	400.00

—White label promo

Number	Title (A Side/B Side)	Yr	NM
❑ LN 24177 [M]	Having a Rave Up with the Yardbirds	1965	80.00
❑ LN 24210 [DJ]	Over Under Sideways Down	1966	400.00

—White label promo

Number	Title (A Side/B Side)	Yr	NM
❑ LN 24210 [M]	Over Under Sideways Down	1966	60.00
❑ LN 24246 [DJ]	The Yardbirds' Greatest Hits	1966	300.00

—White label promo

Number	Title (A Side/B Side)	Yr	NM
❑ LN 24246 [M]	The Yardbirds' Greatest Hits	1966	50.00
❑ LN 24313 [DJ]	Little Games	1967	300.00
❑ LN 24313 [M]	Little Games	1967	80.00

—Some copies with this number are stereo; look for the "XSB" prefix before the master number

Number	Title (A Side/B Side)	Yr	NM
❑ BN 26167 [P]	For Your Love	1965	200.00

—The album is in true stereo except for "Sweet Music"

Number	Title (A Side/B Side)	Yr	NM
❑ BN 26177 [R]	Having a Rave Up with the Yardbirds	1965	50.00
❑ BN 26177 [R]	Having a Rave Up with the Yardbirds	1973	30.00

—Reissue with orange label

Number	Title (A Side/B Side)	Yr	NM
❑ BN 26210 [P]	Over Under Sideways Down	1966	80.00

—"Over Under Sideways Down" is rechanneled

Number	Title (A Side/B Side)	Yr	NM
❑ BN 26246 [P]	The Yardbirds' Greatest Hits	1966	30.00
❑ BN 26313 [S]	Little Games	1967	50.00
❑ EG 30135 [(2)]	The Yardbirds Featuring Performances by Jeff Beck, Eric Clapton, Jimmy Page	1970	50.00
❑ E 30615 [S]	Live Yardbirds Featuring Jimmy Page	1971	80.00
❑ PE 34490 [P]	Yardbirds Favorites	1977	10.00
❑ PE 34491 [P]	Great Hits	1977	10.00
❑ FE 38455	Yardbirds (Roger the Engineer)	1982	30.00
❑ HE 48455	Yardbirds (Roger the Engineer)	1982	250.00

—"Half-Speed Mastered" edition

PAIR

Number	Title (A Side/B Side)	Yr	NM
❑ PDL2-1151 [(2)]	Best of British Rock	1988	12.00

RHINO

Number	Title (A Side/B Side)	Yr	NM
❑ RNDF 253 [PD]	Afternoon Tea	1982	15.00
❑ RNLP 70128 [M]	Greatest Hits, Vol. 1: 1964-1966	1986	8.00
❑ RNLP 70189 [M]	Five Live Yardbirds	1986	8.00

SPRINGBOARD

Number	Title (A Side/B Side)	Yr	NM
❑ SPB-4036 [R]	Eric Clapton and the Yardbirds	1972	10.00
❑ SPB-4039 [R]	Shapes of Things	1972	10.00

SUNDAZED

Number	Title (A Side/B Side)	Yr	NM
❑ LP 5181	Live! Blueswailing July '64	2004	12.00

YARROW, PETER

Also see PETER, PAUL AND MARY.

45s

WARNER BROS.

Number	Title (A Side/B Side)	Yr	NM
❑ 7236	Don't Remind Me Now of Time/ Teenage Fair	1968	8.00

—B-side by Rosko

Number	Title (A Side/B Side)	Yr	NM
❑ 7567	Don't Ever Take Away My Freedom/Greenwood	1972	5.00
❑ 7587	Weave Me the Sunshine/ Wings of Time	1972	5.00
❑ 7761	Old Father Time/Isn't That So	1973	4.00
❑ 8114	Wanderin'/Another Chain Unbound	1975	4.00

Albums

WARNER BROS.

Number	Title (A Side/B Side)	Yr	NM
❑ BS 2599	Peter	1972	12.00
❑ BS 2730	That's Enough for Me	1973	12.00
❑ BS 2860	Hard Times	1975	12.00
❑ BS 2891	Peter Yarrow	1975	12.00

YATES, BILL

45s

SUN

Number	Title (A Side/B Side)	Yr	NM
❑ 390	Stop, Wait and Listen/ Don't Step on My Dog	1964	15.00
❑ 397	Carleen/Too Late to Right My Wrong	1965	15.00
❑ 399	Big Big World/I Dropped My M & M's	1966	15.00

YATES, TOMMY

45s

VERVE

Number	Title (A Side/B Side)	Yr	NM
❑ 10556	Darling, Something's Gotta Give/ If You're Looking for a Fool	1967	25.00

YELLO

12-Inch Singles

ELEKTRA

Number	Title (A Side/B Side)	Yr	NM
❑ EAOR 4920 [DJ]	I Love You (3 versions)	1983	10.00
❑ 4941 [DJ]	Pumping Velvet/No More Words/Lost Again/Bostich	1983	10.00
❑ ED 5039 [DJ]	Vicious Games (3 versions)	1985	10.00
❑ 5487 [DJ]	Unbelievable (6 versions)	1990	8.00
❑ 67917	I Love You/Heavy Whispers	1983	8.00

FFRR

Number	Title (A Side/B Side)	Yr	NM
❑ 350005-1	Bostich (6 versions)	1992	15.00

—Yellow vinyl

4TH & B'WAY

Number	Title (A Side/B Side)	Yr	NM
❑ PR12 607 [DJ]	Tremendous Pain (4 mixes)	1995	10.00

—Black vinyl

Number	Title (A Side/B Side)	Yr	NM
❑ PR12 609 [DJ]	Tremendous Pain (4 versions)	1995	10.00

—Yellow vinyl

Number	Title (A Side/B Side)	Yr	NM
❑ 445604-1	How How (6 versions)	1994	10.00
❑ 448018-1	Jingle Bells (Single Version)/ Jingle Bells (Movie Version)// Jingle Bells (Santa Club Mix)	1995	10.00

MERCURY

Number	Title (A Side/B Side)	Yr	NM
❑ PRO 744-1 [DJ]	The Race (4 versions)/I Love You	1989	12.00
❑ PRO 768-1 [DJ]	Tied Up (4 versions)	1988	8.00
❑ 872761-1	Tied Up (4 versions)/Oh Yeah	1989	6.00
❑ 874939-1	The Race (3 mixes)/Blazing Saddles (2 mixes)	1989	8.00
❑ 884930-1	Oh Yeah (3 mixes)	1985	8.00
❑ 888994-1	Call It Love (4 versions)	1987	8.00

RALPH

Number	Title (A Side/B Side)	Yr	NM
❑ YL 8209	Bimbo/Smile on You	1982	15.00

SMASH

Number	Title (A Side/B Side)	Yr	NM
❑ 440812-1	Vicious Games (4 new versions)	199?	10.00
❑ 445815-1 [(2)]	Do It (8 versions)	1994	12.00

—Two-record set, stock or promo

Number	Title (A Side/B Side)	Yr	NM
❑ 880003-1	Jungle Bill (4 versions)	1992	10.00

STIFF

Number	Title (A Side/B Side)	Yr	NM
❑ TEES 12-12	You Gotta Say Yes/ Heavy Whispers	1982	15.00

45s

ELEKTRA

Number	Title (A Side/B Side)	Yr	NM
❑ 69656	Vicious Games/Blue Nabou	1985	3.00
❑ 69824	I Love You/Rubber Vest	1983	3.00

MERCURY

Number	Title (A Side/B Side)	Yr	NM
❑ 884935-7	Oh Yeah/Oh Yeah (Indian Summer Music)	1986	3.00
❑ 884935-7 [PS]	Oh Yeah/Oh Yeah (Indian Summer Music)	1986	4.00

—Yellow sleeve with reference to movie "Ferris Bueller's Day Off"

Number	Title (A Side/B Side)	Yr	NM
❑ 884935-7 [PS]	Oh Yeah/Oh Yeah (Indian Summer Music)	1987	3.00

—Multicolored sleeve

Number	Title (A Side/B Side)	Yr	NM
❑ 888311-7	Call It Love/L'Hotel	1987	3.00
❑ 888311-7 [PS]	Call It Love/L'Hotel	1987	3.00

RALPH

Number	Title (A Side/B Side)	Yr	NM
❑ YL 8058	Bimbo/I.T. Splash	1980	4.00
❑ YL 8058 [PS]	Bimbo/I.T. Splash	1980	4.00

Albums

ELEKTRA

Number	Title (A Side/B Side)	Yr	NM
❑ 60271	You Gotta Say Yes to Another Excess	1983	12.00
❑ 60401	Stella	1985	12.00

MERCURY

Number	Title (A Side/B Side)	Yr	NM
❑ 812166-1	You Gotta Say Yes to Another Excess	1988	8.00

—Reissue

Number	Title (A Side/B Side)	Yr	NM
❑ 818339-1	Solid Pleasure	1988	8.00

—Reissue

Number	Title (A Side/B Side)	Yr	NM
❑ 818340-1	Claro Que Si	1988	8.00

—Reissue

Number	Title (A Side/B Side)	Yr	NM
❑ 822820-1	Stella	1988	8.00

—Reissue

Number	Title (A Side/B Side)	Yr	NM
❑ 832675-1	One Second	1987	12.00
❑ 836426-1	Flag	1989	12.00

RALPH

Number	Title (A Side/B Side)	Yr	NM
❑ YL 8059-L	Solid Pleasure	1980	20.00
❑ YL 8159	Claro Que Si	1981	20.00

YELLOW BALLOON, THE

45s

CANTERBURY

Number	Title (A Side/B Side)	Yr	NM
❑ 508	Yellow Balloon/Noollab Wolley	1967	12.00
❑ 513	Good Feeling Time/I've Got a Feeling for Love	1967	10.00
❑ 516	Stained Glass Window/Can't Get Enough of Your Love	1967	10.00

Albums

CANTERBURY

Number	Title (A Side/B Side)	Yr	NM
❑ CLPM-1502 [M]	The Yellow Balloon	1967	25.00
❑ CLPS-1502 [S]	The Yellow Balloon	1967	30.00

YELLOW PAYGES, THE

45s

SHOWPLACE

Number	Title (A Side/B Side)	Yr	NM
❑ 216	Sleeping Minds/Never See the Good in Me	1967	25.00
❑ 217	Love in the Making/Jezebel	1967	20.00

UNI

Number	Title (A Side/B Side)	Yr	NM
❑ .212/3	Finger Poppin' Party/Moonfire	1970	20.00

—Though not marked as such, this appears to be a promo; no regular Uni number; both sides have custom labels

Number	Title (A Side/B Side)	Yr	NM
❑ 55043	Our Time Is Running Out/ Sweet Sunrise	1967	10.00
❑ 55072	Judge Carter/Childhood Friends	1968	10.00
❑ 55089	You're Just What I Was Looking For Today/Crowd Pleaser	1968	10.00
❑ 55107	The Two of Us/Never Put Away My Love for You	1969	10.00
❑ 55153	Would You Mind If I Loved You/ Vanilla on My Mind	1969	10.00
❑ 55176	Slow Down/Fresco Annie	1969	10.00
❑ 55192	Little Women/Follow the Bouncing Ball	1970	10.00
❑ 55225	I'm a Man/Home Again	1970	15.00

Albums

UNI

Number	Title (A Side/B Side)	Yr	NM
❑ 73045	The Yellow Payges, Vol. 1	1969	30.00

YELLOWJACKETS

Albums

MCA

Number	Title (A Side/B Side)	Yr	NM
❑ 5752	Shades	1986	10.00
❑ 5994	Four Corners	1987	10.00
❑ 6236	Politics	1988	10.00
❑ 6304	The Spin	1989	12.00

WARNER BROS.

Number	Title (A Side/B Side)	Yr	NM
❑ BSK 3573	The Yellowjackets	1982	10.00
❑ 23813	Mirage A Trois	1983	10.00
❑ 25204	Samurai Samba	1985	10.00

YELVINGTON, MALCOLM

45s

SUN

Number	Title (A Side/B Side)	Yr	NM
❑ 211	Drinkin' Wine Spo-Dee-O-Dee/ Just Rolling Along	1954	100.00
❑ 246	Rockin' with My Baby /It's Me Baby	1956	100.00

YES

Also see RICK WAKEMAN; JON ANDERSON; STEVE HOWE; ASIA.

12-Inch Singles

ATCO

Number	Title (A Side/B Side)	Yr	NM
❑ PR 529 [DJ]	Owner of a Lonely Heart (Edit)/ Owner of a Lonely Heart (LP Version)	1983	12.00
❑ PR 587 [DJ]	Leave It (3 versions)	1984	8.00

Y

Except when noted otherwise, VG = 25% of NM, and VG+ = 50% of NM. (Example: VG = $2.00, VG+ = $4.00 and NM = $8.00.)

Yes, *Going for the One*, Atlantic SD 19106, 1977, **$10.**

Number	Title (A Side/B Side)	Yr	NM
❑ PR 796 [DJ]	Hold On (Edit 5:10)/(LP Version 6:50)	1985	12.00
❑ PR 1133 [DJ]	Rhythm of Love (3 versions)	1987	10.00
❑ PR 2088 [DJ]	Love Will Find a Way (Edit)/Love Will Find a Way (LP Version)	1987	12.00
❑ 96722	Rhythm of Love (3 versions)/City of Love (Live Edit)	1987	10.00
❑ 96964	Leave It (3 versions)	1984	8.00
❑ 96976	Owner of a Lonely Heart (Special Red & Blue Dance Version)/(Edit)/Our Song	1983	12.00
45s			
ARISTA			
❑ 2218	Lift Me Up/Give and Take	1991	4.00
ATCO			
❑ 99419	Rhythm of Love/City of Love	1987	3.00
❑ 99419 [PS]	Rhythm of Love/City of Love	1987	3.00
❑ 99449	Love Will Find a Way/Holy Lamb	1987	3.00
❑ 99449 [PS]	Love Will Find a Way/Holy Lamb	1987	3.00
❑ 99745	It Can Happen/It Can Happen (Live)	1984	3.00
❑ 99745 [PS]	It Can Happen/It Can Happen (Live)	1984	3.00
❑ 99787	Leave It/Leave It (Acapella)	1984	3.00
❑ 99787 [PS]	Leave It/Leave It (Acapella)	1984	3.00
❑ 99817	Owner of a Lonely Heart/Our Song	1983	3.00
❑ 99817 [PS]	Owner of a Lonely Heart/Our Song	1983	3.00
ATLANTIC			
❑ 2709	Every Little Thing/Sweetness	1970	6.00
❑ 2819	Your Move/Clap	1971	5.00
❑ 2854	Roundabout/Long Distance Runaround	1972	5.00
❑ 2854 [DJ]	Roundabout (mono/stereo)	1972	100.00
—Promo only on yellow vinyl			
❑ 2899	America/Total Mass Retain	1972	5.00
❑ 2920	And You And I (Part 1)/And You And I (Part 2)	1972	5.00
❑ 3242	Sound Chaser/Soon	1975	5.00

Number	Title (A Side/B Side)	Yr	NM
❑ 3416	Awaken (Part 1)/Wonderful Stories	1977	5.00
❑ 3534	Don't Kill the Whale/Release, Release	1978	5.00
❑ 3767	Into the Lens/Does It Really Happen	1980	5.00
❑ 3801	Run Through the Light/White Car	1981	5.00
Albums			
ARISTA			
❑ AL 8643	Union	1991	25.00
—U.S. vinyl available only through Columbia House			
ATCO			
❑ 90125	90125	1983	8.00
❑ 90474	9012Live: The Solos	1985	8.00
❑ 90522	Big Generator	1987	8.00
ATLANTIC			
❑ SD 3-100 [(3)]	Yessongs	1973	18.00
❑ PR 260 [DJ]	Yes Solo LP Sampler	1976	25.00
❑ PR 285 [DJ]	Yes Music: An Evening with Jon Anderson	1977	50.00
❑ SD 2-510 [(2)]	Yesshows	1980	12.00
❑ SD 2-908 [(2)]	Tales from Topographic Oceans	1974	15.00
❑ SD 2-908 [(2)DJ]	Tales from Topographic Oceans	1974	30.00
—Promo copies banded for airplay			
❑ SD 7211	Fragile	1972	12.00
❑ 7244 [DJ]	Close to the Edge	1972	50.00
—White label mono copies banded for airplay			
❑ SD 7244	Close to the Edge	1972	12.00
❑ SD 8243	Yes	1969	12.00
❑ SD 8273	Time and a Word	1970	12.00
❑ 8283 [M]	The Yes Album	1971	40.00
—White label promo only; "DJ Copy Monaural" sticker on cover			
❑ SD 8283	The Yes Album	1971	12.00
❑ SD 16019	Drama	1980	10.00
❑ SD 18103	Yesterdays	1975	10.00
❑ SD 18122	Relayer	1974	10.00
❑ SD 18122 [DJ]	Relayer	1974	20.00
—Promo copies banded for airplay			
❑ SD 19106	Going for the One	1977	10.00

Number	Title (A Side/B Side)	Yr	NM
❑ SD 19131	The Yes Album	1977	8.00
❑ SD 19132	Fragile	1977	8.00
❑ SD 19133	Close to the Edge	1977	8.00
❑ SD 19134	Yesterdays	1977	8.00
❑ SD 19135	Relayer	1977	8.00
❑ SD 19202	Tormato	1978	10.00
❑ SD 19320	Classic Yes	1982	10.00
—With bonus single missing			
❑ SD 19320	Classic Yes	1982	15.00
—Original copies include a bonus 7-inch promo single			
FRIDAY MUSIC			
❑ 219004	Close to the Edge	2008	25.00
MOBILE FIDELITY			
❑ 1-077	Close to the Edge	1982	60.00
—Audiophile vinyl			
RHINO			
❑ R1-73788	The Yes Album	2003	18.00
—Reissue on 180-gram vinyl			

YESTER, JERRY Also see THE LOVIN' SPOONFUL.

Number	Title (A Side/B Side)	Yr	NM
45s			
DUNHILL			
❑ 4042	The Sound of Summer Showers/Ashes Have Turned	1966	10.00
❑ 4061	I Can Live Without You/Garden of Imagining	1967	10.00

YESTERDAY'S CHILDREN

Number	Title (A Side/B Side)	Yr	NM
Albums			
MAP CITY			
❑ 3012	Yesterday's Children	1969	75.00

YESTERDAY'S FOLK

Number	Title (A Side/B Side)	Yr	NM
Albums			
BUDDAH			
❑ BDS-5035	U.S. 69	1969	20.00

YETTI-MEN, THE / THE UPPA TRIO

Number	Title (A Side/B Side)	Yr	NM
Albums			
KAL			
❑ KB-4348	The Yetti-Men/The Uppa Trio	1967	600.00

YOAKAM, DWIGHT

Number	Title (A Side/B Side)	Yr	NM
12-Inch Singles			
REPRISE			
❑ PRO3799 [DJ]	Long White Cadillac (Edit)/Long White Cadillac (FM)	1989	8.00
❑ PRO-A-3799 [DJ]	Long White Cadillac (Edit)/Long White Cadillac (FM)	1989	8.00
45s			
EPIC			
❑ 34-74753	Suspicious Minds/Burning Love	1992	4.00
—B-side by Travis Tritt			
REPRISE			
❑ 15998	You're the One/Turn It On, Turn It Up, Turn Me Loose	1993	3.00
—Reissue			
❑ 7-16938	Crazy Little Thing Called Love/Thinking About Leaving	1999	3.00
❑ 7-17143	These Arms/That's Okay	1998	3.00
❑ 7-17273	Silver Bells/Come On Christmas	1997	3.00
❑ 7-17275	Santa Can't Stay/The Christmas Song (Chestnuts Roasting on an Open Fire)	1997	3.00
❑ 7-17734	Nothing/Gone (That'll Be Me)	1995	3.00
❑ 7-18239	Try Not to Look So Pretty/Wild Ride	1994	4.00
❑ 7-18341	Fast As You/Home for Sale	1993	5.00
❑ 7-18528	A Thousand Miles from Nowhere/Ain't That Lonely Yet	1993	4.00
❑ 7-18590	Ain't That Lonely Yet/Lonesome Roads	1993	4.00
❑ 7-18846	Send a Message to My Heart/Takes a Lot to Rock You	1992	4.00
—A-side with Patti Loveless			
❑ 7-18966	The Heart That You Own/Dangerous Man	1992	4.00
❑ 7-19148	It Only Hurts When I Cry/Let's Work Together	1991	5.00
❑ 7-19256	Nothing's Changed Here/Sad, Sad Music	1991	4.00
❑ 7-19405	You're the One/If There Was a Way	1991	4.00
❑ 7-19543	Turn It On, Turn It Up, Turn Me Loose/Since I Started Drinkin' Again	1990	4.00
❑ 7-21868	I Sang Dixie/Long White Cadillac	1989	3.00
—"Back to Back Hits" reissue			
❑ 7-21898	Streets of Bakersfield/Please Please Baby	198?	3.00
—"Back to Back Hits" reissue; A-side with Buck Owens			
❑ 7-21947	Little Sister/Little Ways	198?	3.00
—"Back to Back Hits" reissue			

Except when noted otherwise, VG = 25% of NM, and VG+ = 50% of NM. (Example: VG = $2.00, VG+ = $4.00 and NM = $8.00.)

Number	Title (A Side/B Side)	Yr	NM
❑ 7-21957	Honky Tonk Man/Guitars, Cadillacs	198?	3.00
—"Back to Back Hits" reissue			
❑ 7-22799	Long White Cadillac/Little Ways	1989	3.00
❑ 7-22799 [PS]	Long White Cadillac/Little Ways	1989	4.00
❑ 7-22944	Buenas Noches from a Lonely Room (She Wore Red Dresses)/What I Don't Know	1989	3.00
❑ 7-27567	I Got You/South of Cincinnati	1989	3.00
❑ 7-27715	I Sang Dixie/Floyd County	1988	3.00
❑ 7-27715 [PS]	I Sang Dixie/Floyd County	1988	4.00
❑ 7-27964	Streets of Bakersfield/One More Name	1988	5.00
—A-side with Buck Owens			
❑ 7-27964 [PS]	Streets of Bakersfield/One More Name	1988	5.00
—With Buck Owens			
❑ 7-27994	Always Late with Your Kisses/1,000 Miles	1988	3.00
❑ 7-27994 [PS]	Always Late with Your Kisses/1,000 Miles	1988	4.00
❑ 7-28156	Santa Claus Is Back in Town/Christmas Eve With The Babylonian Cowboys: Jingle Bells	1987	5.00
❑ 7-28156 [PS]	Santa Claus Is Back in Town/Christmas Eve With The Babylonian Cowboys: Jingle Bells	1987	5.00
❑ 7-28174	Please, Please Baby/Throughout All Time	1987	3.00
❑ 7-28310	Little Ways/Readin', Rightin', Rt. 23	1987	3.00
❑ 7-28310 [PS]	Little Ways/Readin', Rightin', Rt. 23	1987	4.00
❑ 7-28432	Little Sister/This Drinkin' Will Kill Me	1987	3.00
❑ 7-28432 [PS]	Little Sister/This Drinkin' Will Kill Me	1987	4.00
❑ 7-28565	It Won't Hurt/Bury Me (Duet with Maria McKee)	1986	3.00
❑ 7-28688	Guitars, Cadillacs/I'll Be Gone	1986	3.00
❑ 7-28688 [PS]	Guitars, Cadillacs/I'll Be Gone	1986	8.00
❑ 7-28793	Honky Tonk Man/Miner's Prayer	1986	3.00
WARNER BROS.			
❑ PRO2424 [DJ]	This Drinkin' Will Kill Me (Live)/Miner's Prayer (Live)	1985	8.00
❑ PRO-S-2424 [DJ]	This Drinkin' Will Kill Me (Live)/Miner's Prayer (Live)	1985	12.00
Albums			
OAK			
❑ OR 2356 [EP]	Guitars, Cadillacs, Etc., Etc.	1984	80.00
—Six-song EP; cover is in black and white; the song "Guitars, Cadillacs" does NOT appear on this release			
REPRISE			
❑ 25372	Guitars, Cadillacs, Etc., Etc.	1986	10.00
—LP has 10 songs rather than the six on the Oak EP; front cover has color on it			
❑ W1-25372	Guitars, Cadillacs, Etc., Etc.	1986	12.00
—Columbia House edition			
❑ 25567	Hillbilly Deluxe	1987	10.00
❑ W1-25567	Hillbilly Deluxe	1987	12.00
—Columbia House edition			
❑ 25749	Buenas Noches from a Lonely Room	1988	10.00
❑ W1-25749	Buenas Noches from a Lonely Room	1988	12.00
—Columbia House edition			
❑ 25989	Just Lookin' for a Hit	1989	10.00
❑ W1-25989	Just Lookin' for a Hit	1989	12.00
—Columbia House edition			
❑ R 100009	Buenas Noches from a Lonely Room	1988	12.00
—BMG Direct Marketing edition			
❑ R 150223	Guitars, Cadillacs, Etc., Etc.	1986	12.00
—RCA Music Service edition			
❑ R 164146	Hillbilly Deluxe	1987	12.00
—BMG Direct Marketing edition			
❑ R 164310	If There Was a Way	1990	20.00
—BMG Direct Marketing edition; only U.S. vinyl version			
❑ R 174052	Just Lookin' for a Hit	1989	12.00
—BMG Direct Marketing edition			

YORK, BETTY

45s

Number	Title (A Side/B Side)	Yr	NM
HIT			
❑ 174	Downtown/Have You Been There	1965	8.00
—B-side by the Chords (2)			
❑ 238	My Love/Michelle	1966	10.00
—B-side by Bobby and Buddy			

YORK, FRED

45s

Number	Title (A Side/B Side)	Yr	NM
HIT			
❑ 29	Send Me the Pillow You Dream On/Ramblin' Rose	1962	8.00
—B-side by Frank Clark			
❑ 43	Go Away Little Girl/My Coloring Book	1962	8.00
—B-side by Connie Landers			
❑ 59	Don't Be Afraid Little Darling/Puff the Magic Dragon	1963	8.00
—B-side by Jimmy, Joe and Betty			
❑ 82	Blue Velvet/You Can Never Stop Me Loving You	1963	8.00
—B-side by Bill Austin			
❑ 96	There! I've Said It Again/You Don't Have to Be a Baby to Cry	1963	8.00
—B-side by the Belles			
❑ 104	A Fool Never Learns/I Want to Hold Your Hand	1964	12.00
—B-side by the Doodles			
❑ 113	White on White/Can't Buy Me Love	1964	12.00
—B-side by the Beagles			
❑ 139	Clinging Vine/A Broken Hearted Fool Like Me	1964	8.00
❑ 157	Pay It No Mind/Ask Me	1964	8.00
—B-side by Ed Hardin			
❑ 163	Mr. Lonely/Two Plus Two	1964	8.00
—B-side by the Chords (2)			
❑ 179	My Love, Forgive Me/Anything	1965	8.00
—B-side by Joanie Key			
❑ 204	The Race Is On/Uptown, Downtown	1965	8.00
❑ 208	Lonely Girl/10 Little Bottles	1965	8.00
—B-side by Jack White			
❑ 239	Lightnin' Strikes/Crying Time	1966	8.00
—B-side by Leroy Jones			
❑ 249	A Sign of the Times/I'm So Lonesome I Could Cry	1966	8.00
—B-side by Leroy Jones			
❑ 253	Rhapsody in the Rain/Sloop John B	1966	12.00
—B-side by the Jalopy Five			

YORK, RUSTY

45s

Number	Title (A Side/B Side)	Yr	NM
CAPITOL			
❑ 4663	That's What I Need/Just Like You	1961	15.00
CHESS			
❑ 1730	Sugaree/Red Rooster	1959	20.00
GAYLORD			
❑ 6428	Sally Was a Good Old Girl/I Might Just Walk Right Back Again	1962	15.00
KING			
❑ 5103	Peggy Sue/Shake 'Em Up Baby	1958	25.00
❑ 5511	Love Struck/Goodnight Cincinnati, Good Morning Tennessee	1961	15.00
❑ 5587	Tramblin'/Tore Up Over You	1961	15.00
NOTE			
❑ 10021	Sugaree/Red Rooster	1959	25.00
P.J.			
❑ 100	Sugaree/Red Rooster	1959	30.00
SAGE AND SAND			
❑ 266	Sadie May/Margaret Ann	1960	20.00

YOST, DENNIS, AND THE CLASSICS IV

See CLASSICS IV.

YOUNG, BARRY

45s

Number	Title (A Side/B Side)	Yr	NM
COLUMBIA			
❑ 43584	A Heart Without a Home/He'll Have to Go	1966	8.00
❑ 43723	I Love You So Much It Hurts/Cryin' Street	1966	8.00
DOT			
❑ 16756	One Has My Name (The Other Has My Heart)/Show Me the Way	1965	10.00
❑ 16819	Since You Have Gone from Me/Nashville, Tennessee	1966	8.00
Albums			
DOT			
❑ DLP 3672 [M]	One Has My Name	1965	20.00
❑ DLP 25672 [S]	One Has My Name	1965	25.00

YOUNG, BOBBY

45s

Number	Title (A Side/B Side)	Yr	NM
GUYDEN			
❑ 2087	To Each His Own/The Only Girl for Me	1963	250.00

YOUNG, CATHY

45s

Number	Title (A Side/B Side)	Yr	NM
MAINSTREAM			
❑ 703	Spoonful/Circus	1969	15.00
Albums			
MAINSTREAM			
❑ S-6121	A Spoonful of Cathy Young	1968	40.00

YOUNG, COLIN

Formerly of THE FOUNDATIONS.

45s

Number	Title (A Side/B Side)	Yr	NM
UNI			
❑ 55286	You're No Good/Amy Time at All	1971	6.00

YOUNG, DONNY

See JOHNNY PAYCHECK.

YOUNG, GEORGIE

45s

Number	Title (A Side/B Side)	Yr	NM
CAMEO			
❑ 150	Nine More Miles/The Sneak	1958	25.00
❑ 166	Feels So Good/Two Weeks with Pay	1959	20.00
❑ 168	Georgie Porgie/Where Is Your Heart	1959	20.00
CHANCELLOR			
❑ 1066	Autumn Lovers/Indian Summer	1960	15.00
❑ 1069	Birdland Hully Gully/Marie	1961	15.00
COLUMBIA			
❑ 42773	Supercar/Chicken Scratch	1963	30.00
FORTUNE			
❑ 524	Shakin' Shelley/Buggin' Baby	1957	25.00
MERCURY			
❑ 71259	Can't Stop Me/Come Back to Me	1958	80.00
PARKWAY			
❑ 809	Gold Rush/That's Tough	1960	20.00
SWAN			
❑ 4059	Yogi/By George	1960	15.00

YOUNG, JACK AND SHERRY

45s

Number	Title (A Side/B Side)	Yr	NM
HIT			
❑ 296	Jackson/Don't Sleep in the Subway	1967	8.00
—B-side by Kathy Shannon			

YOUNG, JESSE COLIN

Also see THE YOUNGBLOODS.

45s

Number	Title (A Side/B Side)	Yr	NM
ELEKTRA			
❑ 45530	Rave On/Maui Sunrise	1978	4.00
❑ 46026	Sanctuary/City Boy	1979	4.00
WARNER BROS.			
❑ 7404	Peace Song/Pretty in the Fair	1970	6.00
❑ 7581	Good Times/Peace Song	1972	5.00
❑ 7581 [PS]	Good Times/Peace Song	1972	10.00
❑ 7618	It's a Lovely Day/Sweet Little Child	1972	5.00
❑ 7749	Evenin'/Morning Sun	1973	5.00
❑ 7816	Cuckoo/Light Shine	1974	5.00
❑ 8053	Susan/Barbados	1974	5.00
❑ 8106	Songbird/'Til You Come Back Home	1975	5.00
❑ 8129	Sugar Babe/Motorhome	1975	5.00
❑ 8225	Sunlight/Peace Song	1976	5.00
❑ 8352	Love on the Wing/(B-side unknown)	1977	5.00
❑ 8398	Fool/Higher and Higher	1977	5.00
Albums			
CAPITOL			
❑ T 2070 [M]	The Soul of a City Boy	1964	50.00
❑ ST-11267	The Soul of a City Boy	1974	12.00
—Reissue of 2070			
❑ N-16129	The Soul of a City Boy	1981	8.00
—Budget-line reissue			
CYPRESS			
❑ 0103	The Highway Is for Heroes	1987	10.00
ELEKTRA			
❑ 6E-157	American Dreams	1978	10.00
MERCURY			
❑ MG 21005 [M]	Young Blood	1965	30.00
❑ SR 61005 [S]	Young Blood	1965	40.00
RACCOON			
❑ BS 2588	Together	1972	12.00

Y

Neil Young, *Everybody Knows This Is Nowhere*, Reprise RS 6349, 1969, "Reprise/W7" logos on two-tone orange label $30, "Reprise" on one-tone orange label **$15.**

Number	Title (A Side/B Side)	Yr	NM
WARNER BROS.			
❑ BS 2734	Song for Juli	1973	10.00
❑ BS 2790	Light Shine	1974	10.00
❑ BS 2845	Songbird	1975	10.00
❑ BS 2913	On the Road	1976	10.00
❑ BS 3033	Love on the Wing	1977	10.00

YOUNG, KATHY, AND THE INNOCENTS Also see THE INNOCENTS.

Number	Title (A Side/B Side)	Yr	NM
45s			
INDIGO			
❑ 108	A Thousand Stars/ Eddie My Darling	1960	30.00
❑ 115	Happy Birthday Blues/ Someone to Love	1961	20.00
❑ 115 [PS]	Happy Birthday Blues/ Someone to Love	1961	50.00
❑ 121	Our Parents Talked It Over/Just As Though You Were Here	1961	20.00
❑ 125	Magic Is the Night/Du Du'nt Du	1961	20.00
❑ 125 [PS]	Magic Is the Night/Du Du'nt Du	1961	50.00
❑ 137	Baby, Oh Baby/ The Great Pretender	1961	20.00
❑ 141	Time/Dee Dee Di Oh	1962	20.00
❑ 146	Lonely Blue Nights/I'll Hang My Letters Out to Dry	1962	20.00
❑ 147	Send Her Away/Dream Awhile	1962	20.00
MONOGRAM			
❑ 506	Dreamboy/I'll Love That Man	1962	20.00
PORT			
❑ 3025	A Thousand Stars/ Eddie My Darling	196?	5.00
STARFIRE			
❑ 112	Sparkle and Shine/ Please Love Me Forever	1979	5.00
7-Inch Extended Plays			
INDIGO			
❑ 1001	Sparkle and Shine/Eddie My Darling//Happy Birthday Blues/Angel on My Shoulder	1961	200.00
❑ 1001 [PS]	Kathy Young	1961	200.00
Albums			
INDIGO			
❑ LP-504 [M]	The Sound of Kathy Young	1961	300.00

YOUNG, LEON

Number	Title (A Side/B Side)	Yr	NM
45s			
ATCO			
❑ 6274	Sea Winds/Spinning Jenny	1963	8.00
❑ 6301	John, Paul, George and Ringo/ Westward Ho	1964	12.00
Albums			
ATCO			
❑ 33-163 [M]	Liverpool Sound for Strings	1964	25.00
❑ SD 33-163 [S]	Liverpool Sound for Strings	1964	30.00

YOUNG, SHERRY

Number	Title (A Side/B Side)	Yr	NM
45s			
HIT			
❑ 206	Goldfinger/Something's Happened	1965	8.00
—B-side by Fred Hess			
❑ 274	Single Girl/Sugar Town	1966	8.00
—B-side by Connie Dee			

YOUNG AMERICANS, THE

Number	Title (A Side/B Side)	Yr	NM
45s			
ABC			
❑ 10940	Born to Be with You/One by One	1967	6.00
❑ 10977	Beautiful, Beautiful World/ Little Girl	1967	6.00
❑ 10998	Here I Am (Billy Guy)/ As Quiet As It's Kept	1967	6.00
❑ 11044	Happiness/Oh, What a Lovely Day	1968	6.00
❑ 11220	On the Blue Cloud Sky/ Blackberry Organ	1969	6.00
Albums			
ABC			
❑ 586 [M]	While We're Young	1967	15.00
❑ S-586 [S]	While We're Young	1967	12.00
❑ S-626	The Wonderful World of the Young	1968	12.00
❑ S-659	Time for Livin'	1969	12.00

YOUNG BROTHERS, THE

Number	Title (A Side/B Side)	Yr	NM
45s			
SOUL POWER			
❑ 21267	What's Your Name/ (B-side unknown)	196?	1000.

YOUNG GENERATION, THE With Janis Siegel, pre-MANHATTAN TRANSFER.

Number	Title (A Side/B Side)	Yr	NM
45s			
RED BIRD			
❑ 10-065	Hideaway/Hymn of Love	1966	15.00

YOUNG-HOLT UNLIMITED

Number	Title (A Side/B Side)	Yr	NM
45s			
BRUNSWICK			
❑ 55305	Wack Wack/This Little Light of Mine	1966	8.00
—As "The Young-Holt Trio"			
❑ 55317	Ain't There Something Money Can't Buy/Mellow Yellow	1967	8.00
—As "The Young-Holt Trio"			
❑ 55338	The Beat Goes On/ Doin' the Thing	1967	8.00
—As "The Young-Holt Trio"			
❑ 55356	Dig Her Walk/You Gimmie Thum	1967	8.00
❑ 55374	Soul Sister/Give It Up	1968	8.00
❑ 55391	Soulful Strut/Country Slicker Joe	1968	8.00
❑ 55400	Who's Making Love/ Just Ain't No Love	1969	6.00
❑ 55410	Just a Melody/Young and Holtful	1969	6.00
❑ 55417	Straight Ahead/ California Montage	1969	6.00
❑ 55420	Soulful Samba/Horoscope	1969	6.00
COTILLION			
❑ 44092	Mellow Dreaming/Got to Get My Baby Back Home	1970	5.00
❑ 44111	Luv Bugg/Wah Wah Man	1971	5.00
❑ 44120	Hot Pants/I'll Be There	1971	5.00
PAULA			
❑ 380	Superfly/Give Me Your Love	1973	5.00
❑ 382	Could It Be I'm Falling in Love/ HeyPancho	1973	5.00
Albums			
ATLANTIC			
❑ SD 1634	Oh Girl	1973	12.00
BRUNSWICK			
❑ BL 54121 [M]	Wack-Wack	1966	20.00
—As "Young-Holt Trio"			
❑ BL 54125 [M]	On Stage	1967	20.00
—As "Young-Holt Trio"			
❑ BL 54128 [M]	The Beat Goes On	1967	30.00
❑ BL 754121 [S]	Wack-Wack	1966	20.00
—As "Young-Holt Trio"			
❑ BL 754125 [S]	On Stage	1967	20.00
—As "Young-Holt Trio"			
❑ BL 754128 [S]	The Beat Goes On	1967	20.00
❑ BL 754141	Funky But!	1968	20.00
❑ BL 754144	Soulful Strut	1968	15.00
❑ BL 754150	Just a Melody	1969	15.00
CADET			
❑ LP-791 [M]	Feature Spot	1967	30.00
❑ LPS-791 [S]	Feature Spot	1967	20.00
—As "Eldee Young and Red Holt (of the Ramsey Lewis Trio)"			
COTILLION			
❑ SD 18001	Mellow Dreamin'	1971	12.00
❑ SD 18004	Born Again	1972	12.00
PAULA			
❑ LPS-4002	Super Fly	1973	20.00

YOUNG LADS, THE

Number	Title (A Side/B Side)	Yr	NM
45s			
FELICE			
❑ 712	Graduation Kiss/Night After Night	1963	100.00
NEIL			
❑ 100	Moonlight/I'm in Love	1956	70.00

YOUNG LIONS, THE (U)

Number	Title (A Side/B Side)	Yr	NM
45s			
DOT			
❑ 16172	Little Girl/It Would Be	1960	50.00

YOUNG RASCALS, THE See THE RASCALS.

YOUNG WORLD SINGERS, THE

Number	Title (A Side/B Side)	Yr	NM
45s			
DECCA			
❑ 31660	Ringo for President/Like That	1964	12.00

Except when noted otherwise, VG = 25% of NM, and VG+ = 50% of NM. (Example: VG = $2.00, VG+ = $4.00 and NM = $8.00.)

Number	Title (A Side/B Side)	Yr	NM

YOUNG, NEIL Also see BUFFALO SPRINGFIELD; CROSBY, STILLS, NASH AND YOUNG; THE STILLS-YOUNG BAND.

12-Inch Singles

GEFFEN

- ❑ PRO-A-2373 [DJ] Get Back to the Country (Long)/Get Back to the Country (Short) 1985 10.00
- ❑ PRO-A-2528 [DJ] Weight of the World (same on both sides) 1986 10.00
- ❑ PRO-A-2623 [DJ] People on the Street (same on both sides) 1986 10.00
- ❑ PRO-A-2811 [DJ] Too Lonely (Remix Edit) (same on both sides) 1987 10.00

REPRISE

- ❑ PRO2-901 [DJ] Hawks & Doves/Union Man 1980 10.00
  —Blue vinyl
- ❑ 49895 Southern Pacific/Motor City 1982 10.00
  —Black vinyl, triangle-shaped
- ❑ 49895 Southern Pacific/Motor City 1982 10.00
  —Red vinyl, triangle-shaped
- ❑ 49895 Southern Pacific/Motor City 1982 200.00
  —Green vinyl, triangle-shaped
- ❑ 49895 Southern Pacific/Motor City 1982 300.00
  —Picture disc, triangle-shaped

45s

GEFFEN

- ❑ 28196 Mideast Vacation/Long Walk Home 1987 3.00
- ❑ 28623 Weight of the World/Pressure 1986 3.00
- ❑ 28623 [PS] Weight of the World/Pressure 1986 3.00
- ❑ 28753 Old Ways/Once an Angel 1986 3.00
- ❑ 28883 Get Back to the Country/Misfits 1985 3.00
- ❑ 29433 Cry, Cry, Cry/Payola Blues 1983 4.00
- ❑ 29574 Wonderin'/Payola Blues 1983 4.00
- ❑ 29574 [PS] Wonderin'/Payola Blues 1983 4.00
- ❑ 29707 Mr. Soul/Mr. Soul 1983 4.00
- ❑ 29887 Little Thing Called Love/We Are In Control 1982 4.00
- ❑ 29887 [PS] Little Thing Called Love/We Are In Control 1982 4.00

REPRISE

- ❑ 0746 Only Love Can Break Your Heart/Cinnamon Girl 1971 3.00
  —"Back to Back Hits" release
- ❑ 0785 The Loner/Sugar Mountain 1968 120.00
- ❑ 0819 Everyone Knows This Is Nowhere/The Emperor of Wyoming 1969 100.00
- ❑ 0819 [DJ] Everyone Knows This Is Nowhere/The Emperor of Wyoming 1969 30.00
  —Standard version of A-side, with "RE-1" in trail-off wax
- ❑ 0819 [DJ] Everyone Knows This Is Nowhere/The Emperor of Wyoming 1969 500.00
  —Alternate acoustic version of A-side
- ❑ 0836 Down By the River/(When You're On the) Losing End 1969 50.00
- ❑ 0861 Oh, Lonesome Me/Sugar Mountain 1969 50.00
- ❑ 0898 I've Been Waiting for You/Oh, Lonesome Me 1970 50.00
- ❑ 0911 Cinnamon Girl/Sugar Mountain 1970 5.00
- ❑ 0958 Only Love Can Break Your Heart/Birds 1970 5.00
- ❑ 0992 When You Dance I Can Really Love/Sugar Mountain 1971 5.00
- ❑ 1023 Brave Belt/Rock and Roll Band 1971 5.00
  —With Graham Nash
- ❑ 1065 Heart of Gold/Sugar Mountain 1971 4.00
  —Without reference to "Harvest" LP on label
- ❑ 1065 Heart of Gold/Sugar Mountain 1971 5.00
  —With reference to "Harvest" LP on label
- ❑ 1084 Old Man/The Needle and the Damage Done 1972 4.00
- ❑ 1099 War Song/The Needle and the Damage Done 1972 4.00
  —With Graham Nash
- ❑ 1152 Heart of Gold/Old Man 1972 3.00
  —"Back to Back Hits" release
- ❑ 1184 Time Fades Away/The Last Train to Tulsa (Live) 1973 10.00
- ❑ 1209 Walk On/For the Turnstiles 1974 4.00
- ❑ 1209 [DJ] Walk On (same on both sides) 1974 10.00
  —Large hole
- ❑ 1209 [DJ] Walk On (same on both sides) 1974 15.00
  —Small hole
- ❑ 1344 Lookin' for a Love/Sugar Mountain 1976 4.00
- ❑ 1350 Drive Back/Stupid Girl 1976 4.00
- ❑ 1390 Hey Baby/Homegrown 1977 4.00
- ❑ 1391 Like a Hurricane/Hold Back the Tears 1978 4.00
- ❑ 1393 Sugar Mountain/The Needle and the Damage Done 1978 4.00
- ❑ 1395 Comes a Time/Motorcycle Mama 1978 4.00
- ❑ 1395 [PS] Comes a Time/Motorcycle Mama 1978 4.00
- ❑ 1396 Four Strong Winds/Human Highway 1979 4.00
- ❑ 18685 Harvest Moon/Old King 1992 4.00
- ❑ 22776 Rockin' in the Free World/Rockin' in the Free World (Live) 1989 4.00
- ❑ 22776 [DJ] Rockin' in the Free World (same on both sides) 1989 10.00
- ❑ 22776 [PS] Rockin' in the Free World/Rockin' in the Free World (Live) 1989 5.00
- ❑ 27848 This Note's For You (LP Version)/This Note's For You (Edited Live Version) 1988 4.00
- ❑ 27848 [PS] This Note's For You (LP Version)/This Note's For You (Edited Live Version) 1988 4.00
- ❑ 27908 Ten Men Workin'/I'm Goin' 1988 3.00
- ❑ 27908 [PS] Ten Men Workin'/I'm Goin' 1988 8.00
- ❑ 49031 Rust Never Sleeps (Hey Hey, My My [Into the Black])/Rust Never Sleeps (My My, Hey Hey [Out of the Blue]) 1979 4.00
- ❑ 49031 [PS] Rust Never Sleeps (Hey Hey, My My [Into the Black])/Rust Never Sleeps (My My, Hey Hey [Out of the Blue]) 1979 10.00
- ❑ 49189 The Loner/Cinnamon Girl 1980 4.00
- ❑ 49555 Hawks and Doves/Union Man 1980 3.00
- ❑ 49555 [PS] Hawks and Doves/Union Man 1980 3.00
- ❑ 49641 Stayin' Power/Captain America 1980 3.00
- ❑ 49870 Southern Pacific/Motor City 1981 3.00
- ❑ 50014 Opera Star/Surfer Joe and Moe the Sleaze 1982 3.00

7-Inch Extended Plays

REPRISE

- ❑ SR 2032 Old Man/The Needle and the Damage Done/Heart of Gold//Harvest/Alabama 1972 20.00
  —Jukebox issue; small hole, plays at 33 1/3 rpm
- ❑ SR 2032 [PS] Harvest 1972 20.00
  —Part of "Little LP" series (LLP #183)

Albums

GEFFEN

- ❑ GHS 2018 Trans 1982 10.00
  —Later pressings have neither sticker nor title of absent song
- ❑ GHS 2018 Trans 1982 15.00
  —First pressings have a sticker on rear cover explaining the absence of "If You've Got Love"
- ❑ GHS 2018 [DJ] Trans 1982 20.00
  —Promo on Quiex II audiophile vinyl
- ❑ GHS 4013 Everybody's Rockin' 1983 10.00
- ❑ GHS 4013 Everybody's Rockin' 1983 20.00
  —Promo on Quiex II audiophile vinyl
- ❑ GHS 24068 Old Ways 1985 12.00
- ❑ GHS 24109 Landing on Water 1986 12.00
- ❑ GHS 24154 Life 1987 12.00
- ❑ R 134125 Landing on Water 1986 15.00
  —RCA Music Service edition
- ❑ R 144439 Life 1987 15.00
  —BMG Direct Marketing edition
- ❑ R 163233 Old Ways 1985 15.00
  —RCA Music Service edition

MOBILE FIDELITY

- ❑ 1-252 Old Ways 1996 45.00
  —Audiophile vinyl

NAUTILUS

- ❑ NR-44 Harvest 1982 150.00
  —Audiophile vinyl

REPRISE

- ❑ MS 2032 Harvest 1972 10.00
- ❑ MS 2032 Harvest 1972 15.00
  —First pressings have textured cover and lyric insert
- ❑ M 2151 [M] Time Fades Away 1973 100.00
  —Special mono pressing for radio stations only
- ❑ MS 2151 Time Fades Away 1973 10.00
- ❑ MS 2151 [S] Time Fades Away 1973 200.00
  —With a cardboard inner sleeve, withdrawn after the earliest pressing
- ❑ R 2180 On the Beach 1974 20.00
- ❑ MS 2221 Tonight's the Night 1975 10.00
- ❑ MS 2242 Zuma 1975 10.00
- ❑ 3RS 2257 [(3)] Decade 1977 20.00
- ❑ 3RS 2257 [(3)DJ] Decade 1977 500.00
  —Test pressing; "Campaigner" contains extra verse deleted from the final version
- ❑ MSK 2261 American Stars 'N' Bars 1977 10.00
- ❑ MSK 2266 Comes A Time 1978 10.00
  —With "Peace of Mind" as the last song on side 1. Covers can list either "Lotta Love" or "Peace of Mind."
- ❑ MSK 2266 Comes A Time 1978 75.00
  —With "Lotta Love" listed and playing as the last song on side 1
- ❑ MSK 2266 [DJ] Give to the Wind 1978 1000.
  —Test pressing; plain white jacket with inserts and STOCK COPY LABEL. Title changed to "Comes A Time" for commercial release.
- ❑ MSK 2277 Harvest 1978 8.00
  —Brown "Reprise" label; new number
- ❑ MSK 2282 Everybody Knows This Is Nowhere 1978 8.00
  —Brown "Reprise" label; new number
- ❑ MSK 2283 After the Gold Rush 1978 40.00
  —Contains remixed extended version of "When You Dance I Can Really Love." Title on cover in red, "RE 2" in trail-off vinyl
- ❑ HS 2295 Rust Never Sleeps 1979 10.00
- ❑ 2RX 2296 [(2)] Live Rust 1979 15.00
- ❑ HS 2297 Hawks and Doves 1980 10.00
- ❑ HS 2304 Re-Ac-Tor 1981 10.00
- ❑ RS 6317 Neil Young 1968 200.00
  —Brown and orange "Reprise/W7" label, no name on front cover, no "RE-1" in trail-off wax
- ❑ RS 6317 Neil Young 1969 60.00
  —Re-release: Brown and orange "Reprise/W7" label, no name on front cover, four tracks remixed ("RE 1" in trail-off wax)
- ❑ RS 6317 Neil Young 1970 15.00
  —Reissue: Brown "Reprise" label, Neil Young's name is now on front cover
- ❑ RS 6349 Everybody Knows This Is Nowhere 1969 30.00
  —Brown and orange "Reprise/W7" label
- ❑ RS 6349 Everybody Knows This Is Nowhere 1970 15.00
  —Brown "Reprise" label
- ❑ RS 6349 [DJ] Everybody Knows This Is Nowhere 1969 75.00
  —White label promo
- ❑ RS 6383 After the Gold Rush 1970 10.00
  —Brown "Reprise" label
- ❑ RS 6383 After the Gold Rush 1970 15.00
  —Brown and orange label; all photos correct
- ❑ RS 6383 After the Gold Rush 1970 35.00
  —Brown and orange label; photo of Neil Young appears erroneously printed upside down in gatefold
- ❑ RS 6383 After the Gold Rush 1970 40.00
  —Brown and orange label; photo of Marc Bolan (of T. Rex) appears erroneously in gatefold
- ❑ 2XS 6480 [(2)] Journey Through the Past (Soundtrack) 1972 20.00
- ❑ 25719 This Note's for You 1988 12.00
- ❑ 25899 Freedom 1989 15.00
- ❑ 26315 Ragged Glory 1990 20.00
- ❑ 43328 Live at Massey Hall 2008 25.00
- ❑ 44335-1 Living with War 2006 25.00
  —Distributed by Classic Records; 200-gram vinyl
- ❑ 45749 [(2)] Sleeps with Angels 1994 25.00
- ❑ 45934 [(2)] Mirror Ball 1995 15.00
  —With Pearl Jam (uncredited)
- ❑ 46291 [(2)] Broken Arrow 1996 40.00
- ❑ 46652 [(2)] Year of the Horse 1997 40.00
- ❑ 48935-1 [(2)] Greatest Hits 2005 40.00
  —Distributed by Classic Records; 200-gram vinyl; with poster; also includes a bonus 7-inch single of "The Loner"/"Sugar Mountain" on either red, white or blue vinyl (not marked on packaging which color is inside; no difference in value)
- ❑ 49593-1 [(2)] Prairie Wind 2005 40.00
  —Distributed by Classic Records; 200-gram vinyl
- ❑ SMAS-94285 Harvest 1972 25.00
  —Capitol Record Club edition
- ❑ R 113998 Harvest 1972 12.00
  —RCA Music Service edition
- ❑ R 154182 This Note's for You 1987 12.00
  —BMG Direct Marketing edition

VAPOR

- ❑ VAP-1001 [(3)] Greendale 2005 50.00
  —Distributed by Classic Records; 140-gram vinyl with bonus 7-inch single, book, bumper sticker and stage bill
- ❑ VAP-1001 [(3)] Greendale 2005 80.00
  —Distributed by Classic Records; 200-gram vinyl with bonus 7-inch single, book, bumper sticker and stage bill
- ❑ 46171 [(2)] Dead Man (Soundtrack) 1996 12.00
- ❑ 48111 [(2)] Are You Passionate? 2002 25.00

WARNER BROS.

- ❑ WBMS-107 [DJ] The Warner Bros. Music Show 1979 50.00
  —Promo-only interview album

YOUNGBLOOD, LONNIE Also see JIMI HENDRIX AND LONNIE YOUNGBLOOD.

12-Inch Singles

RADIO

- ❑ DMD 272 The Best Way to Break a Habit (same on both sides) 1981 8.00

45s

CALLA

- ❑ 109 Let My Love Bring Out the Woman in You/Right Back Where We Started 1976 40.00

CAMEO

- ❑ 374 Come On Let's Strut/Youngblood Feeling 1965 50.00

EARTH

- ❑ 701 Riverside Rock/Nitty Gritty 196? 50.00

FAIRMOUNT

- ❑ 1002 Go Go Shoes/Go Go Place 1966 50.00
  —Jimi Hendrix plays guitar on this record (both sides)

Y

Number	Title (A Side/B Side)	Yr	NM
❑ 1016	The Grass (Will Sing for You)/ Wooly Bully	1966	40.00
❑ 1022	Soul Food (That's What I Like)/ Goodbye Bessie Mae	1967	60.00

—Jimi Hendrix plays guitar on this record (both sides)

LOMA

Number	Title (A Side/B Side)	Yr	NM
❑ 2081	African Twist Pt. 1/Pt. 2	1967	20.00
❑ 2097	Roll with the Punches/Tomorrow	1968	15.00

RADIO

Number	Title (A Side/B Side)	Yr	NM
❑ 3820	The Best Way to Break a Habit/ Reasons	1981	8.00
❑ 3866	Feelings and Expressions Medley/Try Love	1981	8.00

SHAKAT

Number	Title (A Side/B Side)	Yr	NM
❑ 708	Man to Woman/(Instrumental)	1974	6.00

TURBO

Number	Title (A Side/B Side)	Yr	NM
❑ 013	Let's Party/(B-side unknown)	1971	15.00
❑ 026	Sweet Sweet Tootie/ In My Lonely Room	1972	15.00
❑ 029	Super Cool/Black Is So Bad	1973	15.00
❑ 050	Gonna Fly Now (Rocky Theme)/ Happiness Is You	1977	6.00

VIBRATION

Number	Title (A Side/B Side)	Yr	NM
❑ 568	Reachin' for a Dream/ (Instrumental)	1976	6.00

Albums

RADIO

Number	Title (A Side/B Side)	Yr	NM
❑ RR 16045	Lonnie Youngblood	1981	15.00

TURBO

Number	Title (A Side/B Side)	Yr	NM
❑ TU 7011	Sweet Sweet Tootie	1972	50.00
❑ TU 7019	Lonnie Youngblood	1977	20.00

YOUNGBLOODS, THE
Also see JESSE COLIN YOUNG.

45s

MERCURY

Number	Title (A Side/B Side)	Yr	NM
❑ 72583	Sometimes/Rider	1966	20.00
—As "Jesse Colin and the Youngbloods"			
❑ 73068	Sometimes/Rider	1969	10.00

RCA VICTOR

Number	Title (A Side/B Side)	Yr	NM
❑ 47-9142	Merry-Go-Round/Foolin' Around (The Waltz)	1967	10.00
❑ 47-9222	The Wine Song/Euphoria	1967	10.00
❑ 47-9264	Get Together/ All My Dreams Blue	1967	15.00
❑ 47-9360	Fool Me/I Can Tell	1967	10.00
❑ 47-9422	Dreamer's Dream/Quicksand	1967	10.00
❑ 47-9752	Get Together/Beautiful	1969	8.00
❑ 74-0129	On Sir Francis Drake/ Darkness, Darkness	1969	8.00
❑ 74-0270	Sunlight/Trillium	1969	8.00
❑ 74-0342	On Sir Francis Drake/ Darkness, Darkness	1970	7.00
❑ 74-0380	On Sir Francis Drake/ Darkness, Darkness	1970	6.00
❑ 74-0465	Reason to Believe/Sunlight	1971	6.00
❑ 47-9015	Grizzely Bear/Tears Are Falling	1966	10.00
❑ 47-9015 [PS]	Grizzely Bear/Tears Are Falling	1966	35.00

WARNER BROS.

Number	Title (A Side/B Side)	Yr	NM
❑ 7445	Hippie from Olema/Misty Roses	1970	5.00
❑ 7499	It's a Lovely Day/Ice Bag	1971	5.00
❑ 7563	Will the Circle Be Unbroken/ Light Shine	1972	5.00
❑ 7639	Dreamboat/Kind Hearted Woman	1972	5.00
❑ 7660	Running Bear/Kind Hearted Woman	1972	5.00

Albums

MERCURY

Number	Title (A Side/B Side)	Yr	NM
❑ SR-61273	Two Trips	1970	25.00
—Gold border on cover			
❑ SR-61273	Two Trips	1971	20.00
—Red border on cover			

RACCOON

Number	Title (A Side/B Side)	Yr	NM
❑ WS 1878	Rock Festival	1970	12.00
❑ BS 2563	Ride the Wind	1971	12.00
❑ BS 2566	Good and Dusty	1971	12.00
❑ BS 2653	High on a Ridge Top	1972	12.00

RCA VICTOR

Number	Title (A Side/B Side)	Yr	NM
❑ AYL1-3680	The Best of the Youngbloods	1980	8.00
—"Best Buy Series" reissue			
❑ LPM-3724 [M]	The Youngbloods	1967	40.00
❑ LSP-3724	Get Together	1969	15.00
—Retitled version of "The Youngbloods"			
❑ LSP-3724 [S]	The Youngbloods	1967	25.00
❑ LPM-3865 [M]	Earth Music	1968	50.00
❑ LSP-3865 [S]	Earth Music	1968	25.00
❑ AFL1-4150	Elephant Mountain	1977	10.00
—Reissue of LSP-4150			
❑ LSP-4150	Elephant Mountain	1969	15.00
—Orange label			
❑ LSP-4150	Elephant Mountain	1975	12.00
—Tan label			
❑ AFL1-4399	The Best of the Youngbloods	1977	10.00
—Reissue of LSP-4399			
❑ LSP-4399	The Best of the Youngbloods	1970	15.00
❑ LSP-4561	Sunlight	1971	12.00
❑ VPS-6051 [(2)]	This Is the Youngbloods	1972	15.00

YOUNGTONES, THE

45s

BRUNSWICK

Number	Title (A Side/B Side)	Yr	NM
❑ 55089	Come On Baby/Oh Tell Me	1958	60.00

YUM YUM KIDS, THE

Albums

MGM

Number	Title (A Side/B Side)	Yr	NM
❑ E-4396 [M]	Yummy in Your Tummy	1966	15.00
❑ SE-4396 [S]	Yummy in Your Tummy	1966	20.00

YUM YUMS, THE

45s

ABC-PARAMOUNT

Number	Title (A Side/B Side)	Yr	NM
❑ 10697	Looky, Looky (What I Got)/ Gonna Be a Big Thing	1965	1000.
—Black label stock copy			
❑ 10697 [DJ]	Looky, Looky (What I Got)/ Gonna Be a Big Thing	1965	500.00
—White label promo			

Z

ZABACH, FLORIAN

45s

CADENCE

Number	Title (A Side/B Side)	Yr	NM
❑ 1406	Oceans of Love/ Theme from "Carnival"	1961	8.00

DECCA

Number	Title (A Side/B Side)	Yr	NM
❑ 9-27509	The Hot Canary/Jalousie	1951	15.00
❑ 9-27614	Tea for Two/Running After the Rails	1951	15.00
❑ 9-27729	The Waltzing Cat/ The Whistler and His Dog	1951	15.00
❑ 9-27775	Ida (Sweet as Apple Cider)/ Cold Turkey	1951	15.00
❑ 9-28090	The Happy Whistler/Jazz Legato-Jazz Pizzicato	1952	15.00
❑ 9-28646	Red Canary/April in Portugal	1953	15.00
❑ 9-28781	Red Wing/Pussy Footin'	1953	15.00
❑ 9-28916	The Funny Fiddle/ Plink, Plank, Plunk	1953	15.00
❑ 9-29047	Callaghan's Monkey/Solfaggio	1954	15.00
❑ 9-29497	Nocturne/Poeme by Fibich	1955	12.00

MERCURY

Number	Title (A Side/B Side)	Yr	NM
❑ 70936X45	When the White Lilacs Bloom Again/Fiddler's Boogie	1956	12.00
❑ 70975X45	Petticoats of Portugal/ Rainbow Trail	1956	12.00
❑ 71213X45	Runaway Romance/Two Tickets to Guantanamo	1957	12.00

7-Inch Extended Plays

DECCA

Number	Title (A Side/B Side)	Yr	NM
❑ ED 2154	The Hot Canary/Jalousie//Tea for Two/The Whistler and His Dog	195?	12.00
❑ ED 2154 [PS]	The Hot Canary	195?	12.00

Albums

DECCA

Number	Title (A Side/B Side)	Yr	NM
❑ DL 4425 [M]	The Hot Canary	196?	15.00
❑ DL 5367 [10]	The Hot Canary	1951	50.00
❑ DL 8086 [M]	Hour of Love	195?	25.00
—Black label, silver print			
❑ DL 8158 [M]	Dream of Romance	195?	25.00
—Black label, silver print			
❑ DL 8239 [M]	Hi-Fi Fiddle	195?	25.00
—Black label, silver print			

MERCURY

Number	Title (A Side/B Side)	Yr	NM
❑ MG 20305 [M]	Till the End of Time	1958	15.00
❑ MG 20436 [M]	It's Easy to Dance with Florian Zabach	1959	20.00
❑ MG 20463 [M]	Do-It-Yourself Wedding Album	1959	20.00
❑ SR 60084 [S]	Till the End of Time	1958	20.00
❑ SR 60107 [S]	It's Easy to Dance with Florian Zabach	1959	25.00
❑ SR 60145 [S]	Do-It-Yourself Wedding Album	1959	25.00

VOCALION

Number	Title (A Side/B Side)	Yr	NM
❑ VL 3701 [M]	String Along	196?	12.00

WING

Number	Title (A Side/B Side)	Yr	NM
❑ MGW 12172 [M]	Golden Strings	196?	12.00
❑ MGW 12245 [M]	Till the End of Time	196?	12.00
❑ SRW 16172 [S]	Golden Strings	196?	15.00
❑ SRW 16245 [S]	Till the End of Time	196?	15.00

ZACHARIAS, HELMUT

45s

CAPITOL

Number	Title (A Side/B Side)	Yr	NM
❑ 2415	Respect/Hurdy Gurdy Man	1969	6.00

DECCA

Number	Title (A Side/B Side)	Yr	NM
❑ 9-29632	Under the Linden Tree/Waltzes from "The Merry Widow"	1955	12.00
❑ 9-29849	China-Boogie/The Big Bell and the Little Bell	1956	12.00
❑ 9-30039	When the White Lilacs Bloom Again/Blue Blues	1956	12.00
❑ 9-30102	Spanish Violins/The Whistler and His Dog	1956	10.00
❑ 9-30795	Crazy Violins/The Tipsy Piano	1958	10.00
❑ 9-31101	La Montana/Mare Nostrum	1960	8.00
❑ 31259	Tres Jolie/Innocence Abroad	1961	8.00
❑ 31296	Bermuda Shorts/Adios My Love	1961	8.00
❑ 31715	Tokyo Melody/Teatime in Tokyo	1964	8.00

Albums

CAPITOL

Number	Title (A Side/B Side)	Yr	NM
❑ ST-150	Zacharias Plays the Hits	1969	12.00

DECCA

Number	Title (A Side/B Side)	Yr	NM
❑ DL 4083 [M]	Themes	196?	12.00
❑ DL 8089 [M]	Wine, Women and Waltzes	195?	15.00
❑ DL 8150 [M]	Holiday in Vienna	195?	15.00
❑ DL 8382 [M]	A Million Strings	195?	15.00
❑ DL 8431 [M]	Magic Violins	195?	15.00
❑ DL 8594 [M]	Strings, Moonlight and You	195?	15.00
❑ DL 8753 [M]	Smorgasbord for Strings	195?	15.00
❑ DL 8822 [M]	Hi-Fi Fiddler's Delight	195?	15.00
❑ DL 8926 [M]	2,000,000 Strings	1960	12.00
❑ DL 8949 [M]	Romantic Strings	1960	12.00
❑ DL 8982 [M]	Rendezvous for Strings	1960	12.00
❑ DL 8985 [M]	Strauss Waltzes	1960	12.00
❑ DL 74083 [S]	Themes	196?	15.00
❑ DL 78926 [S]	2,000,000 Strings	1960	15.00
❑ DL 78949 [S]	Romantic Strings	1960	15.00
❑ DL 78982 [S]	Rendezvous for Strings	1960	15.00
❑ DL 78985 [S]	Strauss Waltzes	1960	15.00

PHILIPS

Number	Title (A Side/B Side)	Yr	NM
❑ PHM 200053 [M]	A Violin Sings	196?	12.00
❑ PHS 600053 [S]	A Violin Sings	196?	15.00

RCA VICTOR

Number	Title (A Side/B Side)	Yr	NM
❑ LPM-3597 [M]	Pop Goes Baroque	1966	12.00
❑ LSP-3597 [S]	Pop Goes Baroque	1966	15.00

ZACHARIAS AND THE TREE PEOPLE

45s

VIKING

Number	Title (A Side/B Side)	Yr	NM
❑ 1004	We're All Paul Bearers (Part 1)/ We're All Paul Bearers (Part 2)	1969	20.00

ZACHERLE, JOHN

45s

CAMEO

Number	Title (A Side/B Side)	Yr	NM
❑ 130	Dinner with Drac (Part 1)/ Dinner with Drac (Part 2)	1958	30.00
—Orange label			
❑ 130	Igor/Dinner with Drac	1958	40.00
❑ 130	Dinner with Drac (Part 1)/ Dinner with Drac (Part 2)	1960	20.00
—Red and black label			
❑ 139	Lunch with Mother Goose/82 Tombstones	1958	30.00
❑ 145	I Was a Teenage Caveman/ Dummy Doll	1958	30.00

COLPIX

Number	Title (A Side/B Side)	Yr	NM
❑ 743	Monsters Have Problems Too/ Hello Dolly	1964	25.00

PARKWAY

Number	Title (A Side/B Side)	Yr	NM
❑ 853	Dinner with Drac/ Hurry Bury Baby	1962	25.00
❑ 885	Clementine/Surfboard 109	1963	25.00
—As "Zacherley"			
❑ 888	Scarey Tales from Mother Goose/Monster Monkey	1963	25.00
—As "Zacherley"			

Albums

ELEKTRA

Number	Title (A Side/B Side)	Yr	NM
❑ EKL-190 [M]	Spook Along with Zacherle	1960	60.00
❑ EKS-7190 [S]	Spook Along with Zacherle	1960	80.00

PARKWAY

Number	Title (A Side/B Side)	Yr	NM
❑ P 7018 [M]	Monster Mash	1962	60.00
❑ P 7023 [M]	Scary Tales	1963	60.00

ZACK, EDDIE

45s

COLUMBIA

Number	Title (A Side/B Side)	Yr	NM
❑ 4-21148	Little Donkey/You Knew Men When You Were Lonely	1953	40.00

Y

Except when noted otherwise, VG = 25% of NM, and VG+ = 50% of NM. (Example: VG = $2.00, VG+ = $4.00 and NM = $8.00.)

Number	Title (A Side/B Side)	Yr	NM
DECCA			
❑ 9-28082	Call of the Mountains/Words	1952	40.00
❑ 9-28329	Draggin' the Bow/Lights Out	1952	40.00
❑ 9-46245	Dill Pickles/That Silver Haired Daddy of Mine	1950	40.00
❑ 9-46284	Land Beyond the Sun/ Heaven's TV Screen	1951	40.00
❑ 9-46302	Beautiful Brown Eyes/ Shenandoah Waltz	1951	40.00
❑ 9-46330	The Clouds Will Soon Roll By/ You Remind Me of So Much	1951	40.00

ZACK, EDDIE, AND COUSIN RICHIE

45s

Number	Title (A Side/B Side)	Yr	NM
COLUMBIA			
❑ 4-21199	I've Lost Again/ I Never Saw Her Again	1954	50.00
❑ 4-21261	Positively No Dancing/ Dancing Country Style	1954	50.00
❑ 4-21307	You're Out of My Sight/ Cryin' Tears	1954	150.00
❑ 4-21387	Rocky Road Blues/Lover, Lover	1955	150.00
❑ 4-21441	I'm Gonna Rock and Roll/ Foolish Me	1955	150.00

ZAGER, MICHAEL

12-Inch Singles

Number	Title (A Side/B Side)	Yr	NM
BANG			
❑ B 737 D	Do It with Feeling/This Is the Life	1978	8.00
—As "Michael Zager's Moon Band"; PEABO BRYSON appears on this record			
CBS ASSOCIATED			
❑ 4Z9-05046	Shot in the Dark (6:56) (Breakdown Mix)	1984	8.00
COLUMBIA			
❑ AS 787 [DJ]	Don't Sneak on Me (4:54) (same on both sides)	1980	10.00
MOSAIC			
❑ 4Z9-05371	Like a Tiger (New York Mix) (Uptown Mix) (Bonus Beats) (Downtown Mix)	1985	8.00
—As "Michael Zager from ABC Funfit"			
PRIVATE STOCK			
❑ PS 5104	Let's All Chant/Love Express	1978	8.00
❑ PS 5107	Music Fever/Freak	1978	8.00

45s

Number	Title (A Side/B Side)	Yr	NM
BANG			
❑ 720	Do It with Feeling/This Is the Life	1976	7.00
—As "Michael Zager's Moon Band"; PEABO BRYSON appears on this record			
CBS ASSOCIATED			
❑ ZS4-04546	Shot in the Dark/(Instrumental)	1984	4.00
COLUMBIA			
❑ 1-11080	You Don't Know a Good Thing/ Still Not Over	1979	5.00
❑ 1-11273	Don't Sneak on Me/ Bring Me Love	1980	4.00
PRIVATE STOCK			
❑ 45,184	Let's All Chant/Love Express	1978	5.00
❑ 45,202	Soul to Soul/Freak	1978	5.00

Albums

Number	Title (A Side/B Side)	Yr	NM
COLUMBIA			
❑ JC 35771	Life's a Party	1979	10.00
❑ JC 36348	Zager	1980	10.00
PRIVATE STOCK			
❑ PS 7013	Let's All Chant	1978	10.00

ZAGER AND EVANS

45s

Number	Title (A Side/B Side)	Yr	NM
RCA VICTOR			
❑ 47-9816	Help One Man Today/Year 32	1969	5.00
❑ 74-0174	In the Year 2525 (Exordium & Terminus)/Little Kids	1969	6.00
❑ 74-0246	Mr. Turnkey/Cary Lynn Jones	1969	5.00
❑ 74-0299	Listen to the People/She Never Sleeps Beside Me	1969	5.00
❑ 74-0359	Plastic Park/Crutches	1970	5.00
TRUTH			
❑ (# unknown)	In the Year 2525 (Exordium & Terminus)/Little Kids	1967	20.00
VANGUARD			
❑ 35125	Hydra 15,000/I Am	1971	5.00
❑ 35125 [PS]	Hydra 15,000/I Am	1971	20.00

Albums

Number	Title (A Side/B Side)	Yr	NM
RCA VICTOR			
❑ ANL1-1077	2525 (Exordium and Terminus)	1975	10.00
—Reissue of 4214			
❑ LSP-4214	2525 (Exordium and Terminus)	1969	20.00
❑ LSP-4302	Zager and Evans	1970	20.00

Frank Zappa, *Strictly Commercial: The Best of Frank Zappa*, Ryko Analogue RALP 40500, 1995, 2 records, **$20.**

Number	Title (A Side/B Side)	Yr	NM
VANGUARD			
❑ VSD-6568	Food for the Mind	1971	15.00
WHITE WHALE			
❑ WWS-7123	The Early Writings of Zager and Evans (And Others)	1969	20.00
—Actually doesn't contain any music by Zager or Evans, but only songs they wrote; it remains here as it's usually considered a "Zager and Evans" LP			

ZAHND, RICKY, AND THE BLUE JEANERS

45s

Number	Title (A Side/B Side)	Yr	NM
COLUMBIA			
❑ 4-263	(I'm Getting) Nuttin' For Christmas/Something Barked On Christmas Morning	1955	15.00
—Yellow-label Children's Series edition			
❑ 40576	(I'm Getting) Nuttin' For Christmas/Something Barked On Christmas Morning	1955	15.00
❑ 40670	My Church Is My Palace/ You Got to Go to Church	1956	12.00

ZANIES, THE

45s

Number	Title (A Side/B Side)	Yr	NM
DORE			
❑ 509	The Blob/Do You Dig Me, Mr. Pygmy	1958	25.00
❑ 515	The Mad Scientist/ She's a Winner	1958	25.00
❑ 597	It's Lovely/Saxophone Safari	1961	20.00
❑ 632	Rockin' Chopin/Frustration	1962	20.00
❑ 638	London Rock/Stalled	1962	20.00
❑ 647	Sleepwalker/Alexander's Ragtime Band	1962	20.00
❑ 655	Comin' Down the Track/ Hello Jackie	1962	20.00
❑ 658	Russian Roulette/ Caught in a Ringer1	1963	20.00
❑ 683	Chicken Surfer/London Rick	1963	20.00
❑ 705	Slinky/Camel Walk	1964	15.00
❑ 734	Bless 'Em All/ Last Dance at the Prom	1965	15.00
❑ 853	Will the Real Dr. Frankenstein Please Stand Up/ Frankenstein's Laboratory	1971	15.00
❑ 875	Do the 1-2-3/Mr. President-to-Be	1972	10.00
❑ 889	Let Out a Scream (Part 1)/ Let Out a Scream (Part 2)	1973	8.00
❑ 893	Flakey/(Instrumental)	1974	6.00
❑ 900	Los Angeles, Los Angeles/ Let Out a Scream	1974	6.00
❑ 912	Frustration/Roller Coaster	1975	5.00
❑ 920	Old Man River/Los Angeles, Los Angeles	1976	5.00
❑ 957	Janie for President/ Los Angeles, Los Angeles	1980	4.00
❑ 959	The Song of the Masochist/ Special	1980	4.00
❑ 959	The Song of the Masochist/ What Is a One	1980	4.00
❑ 959	What Is a One/Louie's Market	1980	4.00
❑ 962	Curvacious Cora and Carlos Condo/Percolator	1980	4.00
❑ 963	I Love Life, Men, Candy and Paree/I Love Life, Men, Candy and Paree (X-Rated Adult Version)	1981	4.00
❑ 968	From Peanuts to Jelly Beans/ For He's a Jolly Good Fellow	1981	4.00
❑ 974	I Hate Baseball/Dancing with Ronnie Cey	1982	5.00
—With "A. Player"			
❑ 975	Just Another Day in L.A./ I'll Be Waiting	1983	4.00
❑ 978	Is There An Echo in the Joint/ Doin' the Head	1983	4.00
❑ 979	Gesundheit/Darlin' Come Back	1983	4.00
❑ 980	The Raiders, the Steelers, the Cowboys and Bills (same on both sides)	1984	4.00
❑ 1015	Politics, Religion, and Sin (Part 1)/ Politics, Religion, and Sin (Part 2)	198?	4.00

Z

Number	Title (A Side/B Side)	Yr	NM
Albums			
DORE			
❑ 321	The Zanies	1969	30.00
❑ 337	The Zanies	1979	15.00

ZAPPA, DWEEZIL

Number	Title (A Side/B Side)	Yr	NM
12-Inch Singles			
BARKING PUMPKIN			
❑ AS 1579 [DJ]	My Mother Is a Space Cadet/ Crunchy Water	1982	10.00
CHRYSALIS			
❑ VAS 1015 [DJ]	My Guitar Wants to Kill Your Mama (same on both sides)	1988	8.00
❑ VAS 2676 [DJ]	Havin' a Bad Day (same on both sides?)	1986	8.00
45s			
BARKING PUMPKIN			
❑ WS9-03366	My Mother Is a Space Cadet/ Crunchy Water	1982	4.00
❑ WS9-03366 [PS]	My Mother Is a Space Cadet/ Crunchy Water	1982	4.00
❑ B-74204	Let's Talk About It/ Electric Hoedown	1987	6.00
❑ B-74204 [PS]	Let's Talk About It/ Electric Hoedown	1987	6.00
Albums			
BARKING PUMPKIN			
❑ ST-74204	Havin' a Bad Day	1987	10.00
—Reissue of Chrysalis 41581			
CHRYSALIS			
❑ BFV 41581	Havin' a Bad Day	1986	12.00
❑ BFV 41633	My Guitar Wants to Kill Your Mama	1988	10.00

ZAPPA, FRANK

Includes his work leading The Mothers of Invention. The label credit, if other than "Frank Zappa," is listed under each record. Also see BABY RAY AND THE FERNS; BOB GUY; ADRIAN BELEW.

Number	Title (A Side/B Side)	Yr	NM
12-Inch Singles			
BARKING PUMPKIN			
❑ 4W9-02616	Goblin Girl/Pink Napkins	1982	30.00
—Picture disc			
❑ 4W9-03069	Valley Girl/You Are What You Is	1982	15.00
—Sleeve credit is "Frank and Moon Zappa"			
ZAPPA			
❑ MK 107 [DJ]	Joe's Garage/Central Scrutinizer	1979	40.00
45s			
BARKING PUMPKIN			
❑ WS9-02972	Valley Girl/You Are What You Is	1982	5.00
❑ WS9-02972 [PS]	Valley Girl/You Are What You Is	1982	7.00
—Sleeve credited to "Frank and Moon Zappa"			
BIZARRE			
❑ 0840	My Guitar/Dog Breath	1969	50.00
—The Mothers of Invention			
❑ 0889	Peaches En Regalia/ Little Umbrellas	1970	50.00
❑ 0892	WPLJ/My Guitar	1970	50.00
—The Mothers of Invention			
❑ 0967	Tell Me You Love Me/ Would You Go All the Way for the U.S.A.?	1970	50.00
❑ 1027	Tears Began to Fall/ Junior Mintz Boogie	1971	50.00
—Junior Mintz			
❑ 1052	Tears Began to Fall/ Junior Mintz Boogie	1971	50.00
—Frank Zappa and The Mothers of Invention			
❑ 1127	Cletus Awreetus-Awrightus/ Eat That Question	1972	35.00
—The Mothers			
DISCREET			
❑ PRO 586 [DJ]	Uncle Remus/Cozmik Debris	1974	20.00
❑ 1180	I'm the Slime/Montana	1973	25.00
—The Mothers			
❑ 1312	Don't Eat the Yellow Snow/ Cosmic Debris	1974	15.00
UNITED ARTISTS			
❑ 50857	Magic Fingers/ Daddy, Daddy, Daddy	1971	50.00
VERVE			
❑ 10418	How Could I Be Such a Fool/Help I'm a Rock (3rd Movement: It Can't Happen Here)	1966	200.00
—The Mothers of Invention			
❑ 10418 [DJ]	How Could I Be Such a Fool/Help I'm a Rock (3rd Movement: It Can't Happen Here)	1966	100.00
—The Mothers of Invention			
❑ 10458	Who Are the Brain Police/ Trouble Comin' Every Day	1966	200.00
—The Mothers of Invention			
❑ 10458 [DJ]	Who Are the Brain Police/ Trouble Comin' Every Day	1966	100.00
—The Mothers of Invention			
❑ 10513	Why Don't You Do Me Right/ Big Leg Emma	1967	200.00
—The Mothers of Invention			
❑ 10513 [DJ]	Why Don't You Do Me Right/ Big Leg Emma	1967	100.00
—The Mothers of Invention			
❑ 10570	Mother People/Lonely Little Girl	1967	200.00
—The Mothers of Invention			
❑ 10570 [DJ]	Mother People/Lonely Little Girl	1967	100.00
—The Mothers of Invention			
❑ 10632	Jelly Roll Gum Drop/ Any Way the Wind Blows	1968	150.00
—Ruben & The Jets			
❑ 10632	Jelly Roll Gum Drop/Deseri	1968	150.00
—Ruben & The Jets			
❑ 10632 [DJ]	Jelly Roll Gum Drop/ Any Way the Wind Blows	1968	75.00
—Ruben & The Jets			
❑ 10632 [DJ]	Jelly Roll Gum Drop/Deseri	1968	75.00
—Ruben & The Jets			
WARNER BROS.			
❑ 8296	Find Her Finer/Zoot Allures	1976	25.00
❑ 8342	Disco Boy/Miss Pinky	1977	25.00
ZAPPA			
❑ Z-10	Dancin' Fool/Baby Snakes	1979	10.00
❑ ZRP-21 [DJ]	I Don't Wanna Get Drafted (Stereo)/(Mono)	1980	15.00
—Sold at Zappa concerts around 1980			
❑ Z-31	Joe's Garage/Central Scrutinizer	1979	20.00
❑ ZR 1001	I Don't Wanna Get Drafted/ Ancient Armaments (Live)	1980	5.00
❑ ZR 1001 [PS]	I Don't Wanna Get Drafted/ Ancient Armaments (Live)	1980	10.00
Albums			
ANGEL			
❑ DS-38170	Boulez Conducts Zappa: The Perfect Stranger	1983	12.00
BARKING PUMPKIN			
❑ 7X4-1	The Old Masters Sampler	1984	25.00
❑ AS 995 [DJ]	Tinsel Town Rebellion	1981	20.00
—Promo-only sampler			
❑ BPR-1111	Shut Up 'N' Play Yer Guitar	1981	20.00
—Mail-order item only			
❑ BPR-1112	Shut Up 'N' Play Yer Guitar Some More	1981	20.00
—Mail-order item only			
❑ BPR-1113	Return of the Son of Shut Up 'N' Play Yer Guitar	1981	20.00
—Mail-order item only			
❑ BPRP-1114 [PD]	Zappa	1982	15.00
—Picture disc with two songs			
❑ BPRP-1115 [PD]	Baby Snakes	1983	15.00
—Picture disc			
❑ AS 1294 [DJ]	You Are What You Is Special Clean Cuts Edition	1981	20.00
❑ 7777 [(8)]	The Old Masters, Box 1	1984	60.00
—Boxed set			
❑ 8888 [(8)]	The Old Masters, Box 2	1986	60.00
—Another boxed set			
❑ 8888X	The Old Masters Sampler 2	1986	25.00
❑ 9999 [(8)]	The Old Masters, Box 3	1987	60.00
—Still another boxed set			
❑ PW2 37336 [(2)]	Tinsel Town Rebellion	1981	20.00
❑ PW2 37537 [(2)]	You Are What You Is	1981	20.00
❑ FW 38066	Ship Arriving Too Late to Save a Drowning Witch	1982	12.00
❑ W3X-38289 [(3)]	Shut Up 'N' Play Yer Guitar	1982	25.00
—Box set containing all three "Shut Up 'N' Play Yer Guitar" albums			
❑ FW 38403	Man from Utopia	1983	12.00
❑ FW 38820	London Symphony Orchestra	1983	12.00
❑ SVBO-74200 [(2)]	Them Or Us	1984	15.00
❑ SWCO-74201 [(3)]	Thing-Fish	1984	20.00
❑ ST-74202	Francesco Zappa	1985	10.00
❑ ST-74203	Frank Zappa Meets the Mothers of Prevention	1985	10.00
❑ ST-74205	Jazz from Hell	1986	10.00
❑ 74206 [(3)]	Joe's Garage, Acts 1, 2 and 3	1986	50.00
—Box set, two gatefolds, with insert			
❑ SJ-74207	London Symphony Orchestra, Vol. 2	1987	10.00
❑ D1-74212 [(2)]	Guitar	1988	10.00
❑ D1-74213 [(3)]	You Can't Do That on Stage Anymore Sampler	1988	10.00
❑ R1 74213	You Can't Do That on Stage Anymore Sampler	1988	12.00
❑ D1-74217 [(3)]	You Can't Do That on Stage Anymore Vol. 2	1988	10.00
❑ D1-74218	Broadway the Hard Way	1988	10.00
BIZARRE			
❑ MS-2024 [(2)]	Uncle Meat	1969	35.00
—Originals come with a booklet; blue label			
❑ MS-2024 [(2)]	Uncle Meat	1973	20.00
—Reissue with brown Reprise label			
❑ MS-2028	Weasels Ripped My Flesh	1970	25.00
—Blue label original			
❑ MS-2028	Weasels Ripped My Flesh	1973	15.00
—Reissue with brown Reprise label			
❑ MS 2030 [DJ]	Chunga's Revenge	1970	50.00
—White label promo			
❑ MS-2030	Chunga's Revenge	1970	25.00
—Blue label original			
❑ MS-2030	Chunga's Revenge	1973	15.00
—Reissue with brown Reprise label			
❑ MS-2042	Fillmore East, June 1971	1971	25.00
—Blue label original			
❑ MS-2042	Fillmore East, June 1971	1973	15.00
—Reissue with brown Reprise label			
❑ MS 2075	Just Another Band from L.A.	1972	25.00
—Blue label original			
❑ MS 2075	Just Another Band from L.A.	1973	15.00
—Reissue with brown Reprise label			
❑ MS 2093	The Grand Wazoo	1972	25.00
—Blue label original			
❑ MS 2093	The Grand Wazoo	1973	15.00
—Reissue with brown Reprise label			
❑ MS 2094	Waka/Jawaka	1972	25.00
—Blue label original			
❑ MS 2094	Waka/Jawaka	1973	15.00
—Reissue with brown Reprise label			
❑ RS-6356	Hot Rats	1969	50.00
—Blue label original			
❑ RS-6356	Hot Rats	1973	15.00
—Reissue with brown Reprise label			
❑ RS-6370	Burnt Weenie Sandwich	1970	25.00
—Blue label original; with booklet			
❑ RS-6370	Burnt Weenie Sandwich	1973	15.00
—Reissue with brown Reprise label			
COLUMBIA			
❑ (no #) [(4)DJ]	Lather	1977	750.00
—Test pressing only; parts of this LP are on DSK 2291, 2292 and 2294; released as a whole only after Zappa's death, with vinyl only coming out in Japan			
DISCREET			
❑ MS 2149	Over-Nite Sensation	1973	20.00
❑ MS4 2149 [Q]	Over-Nite Sensation	1973	40.00
❑ DS 2175	Apostrophe (')	1974	15.00
❑ DS 2175	Apostrophe (')	1974	50.00
—White label promo			
❑ DS4 2175 [Q]	Apostrophe (')	1974	35.00
❑ 2DS 2202 [(2)]	Roxy and Elsewhere	1974	25.00
❑ DS 2216	One Size Fits All	1975	15.00
❑ DS 2234	Bongo Fury	1975	15.00
❑ DSK 2288	Over-Nite Sensation	1977	12.00
—Reissue of DiscReet 2149 with new number			
❑ DSK 2289	Apostrophe (')	1977	12.00
—Reissue with new number			
❑ 2D 2290 [(2)]	Zappa in New York	1978	20.00
❑ 2D 2290 [(2)]	Zappa in New York	1978	250.00
—Stock copy with "Punky's Whips" erroneously listed on jacket			
❑ 2D 2290 [(2)DJ]	Zappa in New York	1978	400.00
—Test pressing with "Punky's Whips"			
❑ DSK 2291	Studio Tan	1978	15.00
❑ DSK 2292	Sleep Dirt	1978	15.00
❑ DSK 2294	Orchestral Favorites	1978	15.00
FOO-EEE			
❑ R1-70372 [(11)]	Beat the Boots #2	1992	100.00
—Legitimate box-set release by Rhino of 11 bootlegged concerts			
❑ R1-70907 [(10)]	Beat the Boots	1991	100.00
—Legitimate box-set release by Rhino of eight bootlegged concerts			
MCA			
❑ 4183 [(2)]	200 Motels (movie soundtrack)	1986	15.00
—Reissue			
MGM			
❑ GAS-112	The Mothers of Invention	1970	50.00
❑ GAS-112 [DJ]	The Mothers of Invention	1970	100.00
—Yellow label promo			
❑ SE-4754	The Worst of the Mothers	1971	50.00
❑ SE-4754 [DJ]	The Worst of the Mothers	1971	150.00
—Yellow label promo			
RHINO/DEL-FI			
❑ RNEP-604	Rare Meat: The Early Productions of Frank Zappa	1984	40.00
—With original cover			
RYKO ANALOGUE			
❑ RALP 10503	We're Only in It for the Money	1995	12.00
—Vinyl reissue; Frank Zappa/The Mothers of Invention			
❑ RALP 40500 [(2)]	Strictly Commercial: The Best of Frank Zappa	1995	20.00
—Issued with obi			
UNITED ARTISTS			
❑ UAS-9956 [(2)]	200 Motels (movie soundtrack)	1971	50.00

Except when noted otherwise, VG = 25% of NM, and VG+ = 50% of NM. (Example: VG = $2.00, VG+ = $4.00 and NM = $8.00.)

VERVE

Number	Title (A Side/B Side)	Yr	NM
❑ V-5005-2 [(2)M]	Freak Out!	1966	150.00

—Cover version 2: Has no blurb inside on getting a map of "freak-out hot spots"

Number	Title (A Side/B Side)	Yr	NM
❑ V-5005-2 [(2)M]	Freak Out!	1966	200.00

—Cover version 1: Has blurb on inside gatefold on how to get a map of "freak-out hot spots" in L.A.

Number	Title (A Side/B Side)	Yr	NM
❑ V-5005-2 [(2)M]	Freak Out!	1966	400.00

—White label promo

Number	Title (A Side/B Side)	Yr	NM
❑ V6-5005-2 [(2)S]	Freak Out!	1966	60.00

—Cover version 2: Has no blurb inside on getting a map of "freak-out hot spots"

Number	Title (A Side/B Side)	Yr	NM
❑ V6-5005-2 [(2)S]	Freak Out!	1966	80.00

—Cover version 1: Has blurb on inside gatefold on how to get a map of "freak-out hot spots" in L.A.

Number	Title (A Side/B Side)	Yr	NM
❑ V6-5005-2 [(2)S]	Freak Out!	1966	300.00

—Yellow label promo

Number	Title (A Side/B Side)	Yr	NM
❑ V-5013 [M]	Absolutely Free	1967	120.00
❑ V-5013 [M]	Absolutely Free	1967	200.00

—White label promo

Number	Title (A Side/B Side)	Yr	NM
❑ V6-5013 [S]	Absolutely Free	1967	60.00
❑ V-5045 [M]	We're Only in It for the Money	1968	150.00

—With sheet of cut-outs a la "Sgt. Pepper's Lonely Hearts Club Band"

Number	Title (A Side/B Side)	Yr	NM
❑ V-5045 [M]	We're Only in It for the Money	1968	300.00

—White label promo

Number	Title (A Side/B Side)	Yr	NM
❑ V6-5045 [S]	We're Only in It for the Money	1968	60.00

—Un-censored version, with cut-outs

Number	Title (A Side/B Side)	Yr	NM
❑ V6-5045 [S]	We're Only in It for the Money	1968	150.00

—Censored version: the songs "Who Needs the Peace Corps?" and "Let's Make the Water Turn Black" have lines deleted

Number	Title (A Side/B Side)	Yr	NM
❑ V6-5055	Cruising with Ruben and the Jets	1968	60.00
❑ V6-5055 [DJ]	Cruising with Ruben and the Jets	1968	150.00

—Yellow label promo

Number	Title (A Side/B Side)	Yr	NM
❑ V6-5068	Mothermania — The Best of the Mothers	1969	75.00
❑ V6-5068 [DJ]	Mothermania — The Best of the Mothers	1969	150.00

—Yellow label promo

Number	Title (A Side/B Side)	Yr	NM
❑ V6-5074	The XXXX of the Mothers	1969	50.00
❑ V6-5074 [DJ]	The XXXX of the Mothers	1969	150.00

—Yellow label promo

Number	Title (A Side/B Side)	Yr	NM
❑ V-8741 [M]	Lumpy Gravy	1968	300.00

—Yellow label promo; no stock copies were issued in mono

Number	Title (A Side/B Side)	Yr	NM
❑ V6-8741	Lumpy Gravy	1968	50.00
❑ V6-8741 [DJ]	Lumpy Gravy	1968	200.00

—Yellow label promo

WARNER BROS.

Number	Title (A Side/B Side)	Yr	NM
❑ BS-2970	Zoot Allures	1976	15.00

ZAPPA

Number	Title (A Side/B Side)	Yr	NM
❑ MK-78 [DJ]	Sheik Yerbouti Clean Cuts	1979	35.00
❑ MK-129 [DJ]	Joe's Garage Acts I, II and III Sampler	1980	35.00
❑ SRZ-2-1501 [(2)]	Sheik Yerbouti	1979	20.00
❑ SRZ-2-1502 [(2)]	Joe's Garage, Acts II and III	1980	20.00
❑ SRZ-1-1603	Joe's Garage, Act I	1979	15.00

ZAVARONI, LENA

45s

STAX

Number	Title (A Side/B Side)	Yr	NM
❑ 0206	Ma! (He's Making Eyes at Me)/ Rock-a-Bye Your Baby with a Dixie Melody	1974	6.00

Albums

STAX

Number	Title (A Side/B Side)	Yr	NM
❑ STS-5511	Ma! He's Making Eyes at Me	1974	12.00

ZAWINUL, JOE

Albums

ATLANTIC

Number	Title (A Side/B Side)	Yr	NM
❑ SD 1579	Zawinul	1970	20.00
❑ SD 1694	Concerto	1976	15.00
❑ 3004 [M]	Money in the Pocket	1966	20.00
❑ SD 3004 [S]	Money in the Pocket	1966	25.00

COLUMBIA

Number	Title (A Side/B Side)	Yr	NM
❑ FC 40081	Dialects	1986	10.00
❑ FC 40969	Immigrants	1988	10.00
❑ FC 44316	Black Water	1989	12.00

VORTEX

Number	Title (A Side/B Side)	Yr	NM
❑ 2002 [S]	The Rise and Fall of the 3rd Stream	1968	20.00

ZAZU

Albums

WOODEN NICKEL

Number	Title (A Side/B Side)	Yr	NM
❑ BWL1-0791	Zazu	1975	20.00

ZEBRA

12-Inch Singles

ATLANTIC

Number	Title (A Side/B Side)	Yr	NM
❑ PR 500 [DJ]	Who's Behind the Door? (same on both sides)	1983	8.00
❑ PR 536 [DJ]	La La Song (same on both sides)	1983	10.00
❑ PR 1018 [DJ]	You're Only Losing Your Heart (same on both sides)	1986	6.00

45s

ATLANTIC

Number	Title (A Side/B Side)	Yr	NM
❑ 89276	You're Only Losing Your Heart/ Take Your Fingers from My Hair	1986	4.00
❑ 89592	Lullabye/One More Chance	1984	4.00
❑ 89605	Bears/One More Chance	1984	4.00
❑ 89605 [PS]	Bears/One More Chance	1984	4.00
❑ 89781	Tell Me What You Want/ When You Get There	1983	4.00
❑ 89821	Who's Behind the Door?/ As I Said Before	1983	4.00

Albums

ATLANTIC

Number	Title (A Side/B Side)	Yr	NM
❑ PR 1028 [DJ]	Interview/Questions and Answers	1987	20.00

—Promo-only music and interviews

Number	Title (A Side/B Side)	Yr	NM
❑ 80054	Zebra	1983	8.00
❑ 80159	No Tellin' Lies	1984	8.00
❑ 81692	3.V	1986	10.00

ZEBRA, THE

45s

BLUE THUMB

Number	Title (A Side/B Side)	Yr	NM
❑ 109	Christmas Morning (Part 1)/ Christmas Morning (Part 2)	1969	10.00

PHILIPS

Number	Title (A Side/B Side)	Yr	NM
❑ 40535	Groovy Personality/Miss Ann (Ain't That Kind of Man)	1968	12.00

WHITE WHALE

Number	Title (A Side/B Side)	Yr	NM
❑ 305	Bring Me to My Knees/ (B-side unknown)	1969	10.00

ZEBULONS, THE

45s

CUB

Number	Title (A Side/B Side)	Yr	NM
❑ 9069	Falling Water/Wo-Ho-La-Tee-Da	1960	60.00

ZEE, TOMMY

45s

AMY

Number	Title (A Side/B Side)	Yr	NM
❑ 815	Rebecca, Remember/ Worlds Apart	1961	40.00

ZEKLEY, GARY

Also see THE YELLOW BALLOON.

45s

AVA

Number	Title (A Side/B Side)	Yr	NM
❑ 151	Vagabond/When I Go to Sleep	1963	40.00

—With Dean Torrence on backing vocals

Number	Title (A Side/B Side)	Yr	NM
❑ C151	Other Towns, Other Girls/ When I Go to Sleep	1963	75.00

—($180 on eBay auction 3/2008)

ZELLA, DANNY

45s

DIAL

Number	Title (A Side/B Side)	Yr	NM
❑ 100	Sapphire/You Made Me Blue	1959	200.00

FOX

Number	Title (A Side/B Side)	Yr	NM
❑ F # 1	Black Saxs/Wicked Ruby	1959	30.00
❑ ZTSC 10056/7	Black Saxs/Wicked Ruby	1959	30.00

—Some copies of this 45 do not have a catalog number; these are the master numbers of each side

RED ROCKET

Number	Title (A Side/B Side)	Yr	NM
❑ 475	Black Saxs/Wicked Ruby	1959	40.00

ZENITHS, THE

Albums

ATLANTIC

Number	Title (A Side/B Side)	Yr	NM
❑ 8043 [M]	Makin' the Scene	1960	100.00
❑ SD 8043 [S]	Makin' the Scene	1960	150.00

ZENO

Albums

MANHATTAN

Number	Title (A Side/B Side)	Yr	NM
❑ ST-53025	Zeno	1986	10.00

ZENTNER, SI

45s

LIBERTY

Number	Title (A Side/B Side)	Yr	NM
❑ 55204	Sock Hop/Two Guitars	1959	10.00
❑ 55240	Armen's Theme/ The Swinging Eye	1960	10.00
❑ 55374	Up a Lazy River/Shufflin' Blues	1961	8.00
❑ 55408	Hollywood Twist/Nice 'N Easy	1962	8.00
❑ 55420 [DJ]	The Goulash (Shufflin' Blues)	1962	15.00

—One-sided promo-only release

Number	Title (A Side/B Side)	Yr	NM
❑ 55476	Shadrack/Boogie Woogie Maxine	1962	8.00
❑ 55499	Desafinado/Elephant's Tango	1962	8.00
❑ 55538	Waltz in Jazz Time/A La Mode	1963	8.00
❑ 55609	Broken Date/Fink	1963	8.00
❑ 55648	James Bond Theme/ Classes de Cha-Cha	1963	10.00
❑ 55675	I'm Getting Sentimental Over You/Sentimental Journey	1964	8.00
❑ 55683	From Russia with Love/ James Bond Theme	1964	10.00
❑ 55941	Warning Shot/Mona Lisa	1967	6.00
❑ 55955	Dear John/Haven't Been to Church	1967	6.00

RCA VICTOR

Number	Title (A Side/B Side)	Yr	NM
❑ 47-8454	Theme from Max/Spanish Rice	1964	6.00
❑ 47-8550	Dear Heart/In a Little Spanish Town	1965	6.00
❑ 47-8634	Fat Cat/My Devotion	1965	6.00
❑ 47-8779	Baby, Take Another Bow/ Mr. Nashville	1966	6.00

7-Inch Extended Plays

RCA VICTOR

Number	Title (A Side/B Side)	Yr	NM
❑ VLP 3484	You Were Meant for Me/Fly Me to the Moon (In Other Words)/ Don't Blame Me//Put Your Head on My Shoulder/You're Nobody 'Til Somebody Loves You/Soft Sound of Love	1966	10.00

—Jukebox issue; small hole, plays at 33 1/3 rpm

Number	Title (A Side/B Side)	Yr	NM
❑ VLP 3484 [PS]	Put Your Head on My Shoulder	1966	10.00

SESAC

Number	Title (A Side/B Side)	Yr	NM
❑ AD-78	Oatmeal Stomp/Hollow Horse Hoedown//All-American Scramble/Tigertail	196?	12.00
❑ AD-78 [PS]	Tigertail	196?	12.00

Albums

LIBERTY

Number	Title (A Side/B Side)	Yr	NM
❑ LRP-3197 [M]	Big Band Plays the Big Hits	1961	12.00
❑ LRP-3216 [M]	Up a Lazy River (Big Band Plays the Big Hits: Vol. 2)	1962	12.00
❑ LRP-3247 [M]	The Stripper and Other Big Band Hits	1962	12.00
❑ LRP-3273 [M]	Desafinado	1963	12.00
❑ LRP-3284 [M]	Waltz in Jazz Time	1963	12.00
❑ LRP-3326 [M]	More	1963	12.00
❑ LRP-3350 [M]	Big Big Band Hits	1964	12.00
❑ LRP-3353 [M]	From Russia with Love	1964	12.00
❑ LRP-3457 [M]	The Best of Si Zentner	1966	12.00
❑ LST-7197 [S]	Big Band Plays the Big Hits	1961	15.00
❑ LST-7216 [S]	Up a Lazy River (Big Band Plays the Big Hits: Vol. 2)	1962	15.00
❑ LST-7247 [S]	The Stripper and Other Big Band Hits	1962	15.00
❑ LST-7273 [S]	Desafinado	1963	15.00
❑ LST-7284 [S]	Waltz in Jazz Time	1963	15.00
❑ LST-7326 [S]	More	1963	15.00
❑ LST-7350 [S]	Big Big Band Hits	1964	15.00
❑ LST-7353 [S]	From Russia with Love	1964	15.00
❑ LST-7457 [S]	The Best of Si Zentner	1966	12.00
❑ LMM-13009 [M]	A Great Band with Great Voices	1961	12.00
❑ LMM-13017 [M]	A Great Band with Great Voices Swing the Great Voices of the Great Bands	1962	12.00
❑ LSS-14009 [S]	A Great Band with Great Voices	1961	15.00
❑ LSS-14017 [S]	A Great Band with Great Voices Swing the Great Voices of the Great Bands	1962	15.00

SMASH

Number	Title (A Side/B Side)	Yr	NM
❑ MGS-27007 [M]	Presenting Si Zentner	1961	15.00
❑ MGS-27013 [M]	Swing Fever	1962	15.00
❑ SRS-67007 [S]	Presenting Si Zentner	1961	20.00
❑ SRS-67013 [S]	Swing Fever	1962	20.00

SUNSET

Number	Title (A Side/B Side)	Yr	NM
❑ SUM-1110 [M]	Big Band Brilliance	196?	10.00
❑ SUS-5110 [S]	Big Band Brilliance	196?	12.00

ZENTNER, SI AND MARTIN DENNY

Also see each artist's individual listings.

Albums

LIBERTY

Number	Title (A Side/B Side)	Yr	NM
❑ LMM-13020 [M]	Exotica Suite	1962	15.00
❑ LSS-14020 [S]	Exotica Suite	1962	20.00

ZEPHYR

Also see TOMMY BOLIN.

45s

PROBE

Number	Title (A Side/B Side)	Yr	NM
❑ 475	Sail On/Cross the River	1970	12.00

WARNER BROS.

Number	Title (A Side/B Side)	Yr	NM
❑ 7444	Going Back to Colorado/ Radio Song	1970	10.00

Albums

PROBE

Number	Title (A Side/B Side)	Yr	NM
❑ 4510	Zephyr	1969	50.00

WARNER BROS.

Number	Title (A Side/B Side)	Yr	NM
❑ WS 1897	Goin' Back to Colorado	1971	40.00
❑ BS 2603	Sunset Ride	1972	20.00

Z

ZEPHYRS, THE

45s

ROTATE

Number	Title (A Side/B Side)	Yr	NM
❑ 5006	She's Lost You/There's Something About You	1965	25.00
❑ 5009	Let Me Love You Baby/Wonder What I'm Gonna Do	1965	35.00

ZERFAS

Albums

700 WEST

Number	Title (A Side/B Side)	Yr	NM
❑ 730710	Zerfas	1973	800.00

ZERO BOYS

7-Inch Extended Plays

LOOKOUT!

Number	Title (A Side/B Side)	Yr	NM
❑ LK-251	Livin' in the 80's/Stoned to Death/Stick to Your Guns/I'm Bored/Piece of Me	2000	2.00

—Released at the same time as Panic Button 284

Number	Title (A Side/B Side)	Yr	NM
❑ LK-251 [PS]	Livin' in the 80's	2001	2.00

PANIC BUTTON

Number	Title (A Side/B Side)	Yr	NM
❑ PB 284	Livin' in the 80's/Stoned to Death/Stick to Your Guns/I'm Bored/Piece of Me	2000	2.50

—Reissue of Z-Disk release

Number	Title (A Side/B Side)	Yr	NM
❑ PB 284 [PS]	Livin' in the 80's	2000	2.50

Z-DISK

Number	Title (A Side/B Side)	Yr	NM
❑ (# unknown)	Livin' in the 80's/Stoned to Death/Stick to Your Guns/I'm Bored/Piece of Me	1980	100.00
❑ (# unknown) [PS]	Livin' in the 80's	1980	100.00

—The above has been counterfeited, but it also has been reissued on Lookout and Panic Button

Albums

LOOKOUT!

Number	Title (A Side/B Side)	Yr	NM
❑ LK-253	Vicious Circle	2000	10.00

—Same reissue as on Panic Button except for the label and number

NIMROD

Number	Title (A Side/B Side)	Yr	NM
❑ 1	Vicious Circle	1982	100.00

PANIC BUTTON

Number	Title (A Side/B Side)	Yr	NM
❑ PB 286	Vicious Circle	2000	12.00

—Reissue of Nimrod release with two bonus tracks

TOXIC SHOCK

Number	Title (A Side/B Side)	Yr	NM
❑ TXLP 11	Vicious Circle	1987	30.00

—Reissue of Nimrod release

ZEROES, THE

45s

TY-TEX

Number	Title (A Side/B Side)	Yr	NM
❑ 105	Flossie Mae/Twisting with Crazee Babee	1963	200.00

ZEROS

45s

BOMP!

Number	Title (A Side/B Side)	Yr	NM
❑ 110	Don't Push Me Around/Wimp	1977	40.00
❑ 110 [PS]	Don't Push Me Around/Wimp	1977	40.00
❑ 118	Wild Weekend/Beat Your Heart Out	1978	40.00
❑ 118 [PS]	Wild Weekend/Beat Your Heart Out	1978	40.00

ROCKVILLE

Number	Title (A Side/B Side)	Yr	NM
❑ 6091	Bottoms Up/Sneakin' Out	1992	4.00

—Blue vinyl

Number	Title (A Side/B Side)	Yr	NM
❑ 6091 [PS]	Bottoms Up/Sneakin' Out	1992	4.00
❑ 6187	Knockin' Me Dead/(B-side unknown)	1994	4.00

—Gray vinyl

Number	Title (A Side/B Side)	Yr	NM
❑ 6187 [PS]	Knockin' Me Dead/(B-side unknown)	1994	4.00

—Gray vinyl

SYMPATHY FOR THE RECORD INDUSTRY

Number	Title (A Side/B Side)	Yr	NM
❑ SFTRI 166	I Don't Wanna/Little Latin Lupe Lu	1993	3.00
❑ SFTRI 166 [PS]	I Don't Wanna/Little Latin Lupe Lu	1993	3.00

TEST TUBE

Number	Title (A Side/B Side)	Yr	NM
❑ 003	They Say That Everything's Alright/Getting Nowhere Fast	1980	40.00
❑ 003 [PS]	They Say That Everything's Alright/Getting Nowhere Fast	1980	40.00

Albums

BOMP!

Number	Title (A Side/B Side)	Yr	NM
❑ BLP 4035	Don't Push Me Around	1991	15.00
❑ BLP 4074	Right Now!	1999	10.00

ZEVON, WARREN

12-Inch Singles

ASYLUM

Number	Title (A Side/B Side)	Yr	NM
❑ ED 5185 [DJ]	Werewolves of London (same on both sides)	1986	10.00
❑ AS 11386 [DJ]	Werewolves of London/Roland the Headless Thompson Gunner	1978	60.00

—Promo-only picture disc with die-cut cover

Number	Title (A Side/B Side)	Yr	NM
❑ AS 11395 [DJ]	Nighttime in the Switching Yard (same on both sides?)	1978	30.00

VIRGIN

Number	Title (A Side/B Side)	Yr	NM
❑ DMD 1053 [DJ]	Leave My Monkey Alone (10:31) (5:45) (5:51)	1987	8.00
❑ PR 2033 [DJ]	Sentimental Hygiene (LP Version) (Edit)	1987	10.00
❑ PR 2062 [DJ]	Detox Mansion/Leave My Monkey Alone	1987	8.00
❑ PR 2133 [DJ]	Boom Boom Mancini (same on both sides)	1987	8.00
❑ PR 2216 [DJ]	Reconsider Me (same on both sides)	1988	8.00
❑ 96762	Leave My Monkey Alone (10:31) (5:45) (5:51)	1987	8.00

45s

ASYLUM

Number	Title (A Side/B Side)	Yr	NM
❑ 45356	Hasten Down the Wind/Mohammad's Radio	1976	8.00
❑ 45472	Werewolves of London/Roland the Headless Thompson Gunner	1978	5.00
❑ 45498	Lawyers, Guns and Money/Vera Cruz	1978	7.00
❑ 45526	Johnny Strikes Up the Band/Night Time in the Switching Yard	1978	6.00
❑ 46610	A Certain Girl/Empty-Handed Heart	1980	5.00
❑ 46641	Gorilla, You're a Desperado/Jungle Work	1980	7.00
❑ 47118	Lawyers, Guns and Money/Werewolves of London	1981	5.00
❑ 47118 [DJ]	Lawyers, Guns and Money (Clean)/(Dirty)	1981	10.00
❑ 69509	Werewolves of London/Jesus Mentioned	1986	5.00
❑ 69946	Let Nothing Come Between You/The Hula Hula Boys	1982	6.00
❑ 69966	Looking for the Next Best Thing/The Hula Hula Boys	1982	5.00

ELEKTRA

Number	Title (A Side/B Side)	Yr	NM
❑ 45091	Werewolves of London/Lawyers, Guns and Money	1979	4.00

—"Spun Gold" reissue series

VIRGIN

Number	Title (A Side/B Side)	Yr	NM
❑ 99370	Reconsider Me/Factory	1988	3.00
❑ 99370 [PS]	Reconsider Me/Factory	1988	5.00
❑ 99440	Leave My Monkey Alone/(Latin Rascals Dub)	1987	3.00
❑ 99440 [PS]	Leave My Monkey Alone/(Latin Rascals Dub)	1987	5.00

Albums

ARTEMIS

Number	Title (A Side/B Side)	Yr	NM
❑ 51156	The Wind	2004	20.00

—180-gram version; CD was issued in 2003

ASYLUM

Number	Title (A Side/B Side)	Yr	NM
❑ 6E-118	Excitable Boy	1978	10.00
❑ 5E-509	Bad Luck Streak in Dancing School	1980	10.00
❑ 5E-519	Stand in the Fire	1980	10.00
❑ 7E-1060	Warren Zevon	1976	10.00
❑ 60159	The Envoy	1982	10.00
❑ 60503	A Quiet Normal Life: The Best of Warren Zevon	1987	10.00

IMPERIAL

Number	Title (A Side/B Side)	Yr	NM
❑ LP-12456	Wanted Dead or Alive	1970	50.00

—As "Zevon"

PICKWICK

Number	Title (A Side/B Side)	Yr	NM
❑ SPC-3715	Wanted Dead or Alive	1979	15.00

—Reissue of Imperial album

VIRGIN

Number	Title (A Side/B Side)	Yr	NM
❑ 90603	Sentimental Hygiene	1987	10.00
❑ 91068	Transverse City	1989	10.00

ZILL, PAT

45s

BIG ADD

Number	Title (A Side/B Side)	Yr	NM
❑ 3151	Big Man, Big House/Little Lies	196?	10.00

BIG C

Number	Title (A Side/B Side)	Yr	NM
❑ 119	Air Mail to Heaven/Two Empty Arms	1962	15.00

BOONE

Number	Title (A Side/B Side)	Yr	NM
❑ 1031	All I Have to Do Is Wait/Heartaches by the Number	1965	10.00

CAROL

Number	Title (A Side/B Side)	Yr	NM
❑ 109	It Don't Mean a Thing to Me/I Took the Blues Out	196?	10.00

DOLEJO

Number	Title (A Side/B Side)	Yr	NM
❑ 1002	The Fool/Pretend	196?	10.00

ERA

Number	Title (A Side/B Side)	Yr	NM
❑ 3108	The Key's in the Mailbox/I Couldn't See My Heart Before My Eyes	1963	12.00

INDIGO

Number	Title (A Side/B Side)	Yr	NM
❑ 119	Pick Me Up on Your Way Down/La Marida	1961	15.00
❑ 126	Bouquet of Roses/Hold Tight	1961	15.00

QCA

Number	Title (A Side/B Side)	Yr	NM
❑ 403	Glory of Love/Let's Say Goodbye Like We Said Hello	197?	8.00

SAND

Number	Title (A Side/B Side)	Yr	NM
❑ 336	Pick Me Up on Your Way Down/La Marida	1961	20.00

SIMS

Number	Title (A Side/B Side)	Yr	NM
❑ 234	The Key's in the Mailbox/I Couldn't See My Heart Before My Eyes	1965	10.00

STOP

Number	Title (A Side/B Side)	Yr	NM
❑ 236	The Things You Should Do/Lonesome 7-7203	1969	8.00

ZIMMERMAN, GEORGE, AND THE THRILLS

45s

JAB

Number	Title (A Side/B Side)	Yr	NM
❑ 103	Whose Baby Are You/I Ain't Got the Money to Pay for This Drink	1956	400.00

ZINE, BEN

45s

PARKWAY

Number	Title (A Side/B Side)	Yr	NM
❑ 994	Village of Tears/What the Heck's the Hanky Panky	1966	80.00

ZIP AND THE ZIPPERS

45s

PAGEANT

Number	Title (A Side/B Side)	Yr	NM
❑ 607	Where You Goin' Little Boy/Gig	1963	25.00

ZIP CODES, THE

45s

LIBERTY

Number	Title (A Side/B Side)	Yr	NM
❑ 55703	Run, Little Mustang/Fancy Filly from Detroit City	1964	30.00

Albums

LIBERTY

Number	Title (A Side/B Side)	Yr	NM
❑ LRP-3367 [M]	Mustang	1964	150.00
❑ LST-7367 [S]	Mustang	1964	200.00

ZIPPERS, THE

Albums

RHINO

Number	Title (A Side/B Side)	Yr	NM
❑ RNEP 601 [EP]	Six Song Mini Album	1981	30.00

ZIRCONS, THE

Could be as many as four different groups.

45s

AMBER

Number	Title (A Side/B Side)	Yr	NM
❑ 851	One Summer Night/The Lone Stranger	1966	15.00

BAGDAD

Number	Title (A Side/B Side)	Yr	NM
❑ 1007	Going Places/Surfing in the Sunset	1963	80.00

CAPITOL

Number	Title (A Side/B Side)	Yr	NM
❑ 2667	Finders Keepers/You Ain't Comin' Back	1969	40.00

COOL SOUND

Number	Title (A Side/B Side)	Yr	NM
❑ 1030	Silver Bells/You Are My Sunshine	1964	30.00

DOT

Number	Title (A Side/B Side)	Yr	NM
❑ 15724	Only One Love/I Need It	1958	20.00

FEDERAL

Number	Title (A Side/B Side)	Yr	NM
❑ 12452	No Twistin' on Sunday/Mama Wants to Drive	1962	20.00
❑ 12478	Get Up and Go to School/Mr. Jones	1962	20.00

HEIGH HO

Number	Title (A Side/B Side)	Yr	NM
❑ 607	Where There's a Will/Don't Put Off for Tomorrow	1967	40.00
❑ 608/9	I Couldn't Stop Crying/Sit Down Girl	1967	40.00
❑ 645/6	Go On and Cry/Was It Meant to Be This Way	1967	40.00

MELLOMOOD

Number	Title (A Side/B Side)	Yr	NM
❑ 1000	Lonely Way/Your Way	1963	20.00

OLD TIMER

Number	Title (A Side/B Side)	Yr	NM
❑ 603	Stormy Weather/Sincerely	1964	15.00

Number	Title (A Side/B Side)	Yr	NM
SIAMESE			
❑ 403	Stormy Weather/Sincerely	1964	12.00
WINSTON			
❑ 1020	I Need It/Only One Love	1957	60.00
❑ 1022	Crazy Crazy/Return My Love	1958	80.00
Albums			
SNOWFLAKE			
❑ 1003	The Crown Kings of Acappella	196?	60.00

ZODIAC MINDWARP & THE LOVE REACTION

12-Inch Singles

Number	Title (A Side/B Side)	Yr	NM
VERTIGO			
❑ PRO 553-1 [DJ]	Prime Mover (same on both sides)	1988	10.00
Albums			
VERTIGO			
❑ 832729-1	Tattooed Beat Messiah	1988	12.00

ZODIACS, THE

See MAURICE WILLIAMS AND THE ZODIACS.

ZOE, ALPHA

45s

Number	Title (A Side/B Side)	Yr	NM
HIT			
❑ 31	You Beat Me to the Punch/ Patches	1962	8.00
—B-side by Mitch Lucas			
❑ 41	Keep Your Hands Off My Baby/ You Are My Sunshine	1962	8.00
—B-side by Leroy Jones and Lucille Johns			
❑ 44	Everybody Loves a Lover/ Love Came to Me	1962	8.00
—B-side by Ed Hardin			
❑ 54	Let's Turkey Trot/One Broken Heart for Sale	1963	8.00
—B-side by Ed Hardin			
❑ 65	Da Doo Ron Ron/ Foolish Little Girl	1963	8.00
—B-side by Clara Wilson and the Cleftones			
❑ 70	Hello Stranger/Sukiyaki	1963	8.00
—B-side by the Music City Chorus and Orchestra Featuring Samayami			
❑ 229	A Lover's Concerto/ Keep On Dancing	1965	20.00
—B-side by the Gentrys			

ZOMBIES, THE

Also see ARGENT; COLIN BLUNSTONE.

45s

Number	Title (A Side/B Side)	Yr	NM
COLUMBIA			
❑ 44363	Care of Cell 44/Maybe After He's Gone	1967	100.00
DATE			
❑ 2-1203	Time of the Season/ Imagine the Swan	1970	5.00
—"Hall of Fame" series			
❑ 1604	Time of the Season/ I'll Call You Mine	1968	40.00
❑ 1612	Butcher's Tale (Western Front 1914)/This Will Be Our Year	1968	10.00
❑ 1612 [PS]	Butcher's Tale (Western Front 1914)/This Will Be Our Year	1968	20.00
❑ 1628	Time of the Season/ Friends of Mine	1968	12.00
❑ 1644	Imagine the Swan/ Conversation of Floral Street	1969	10.00
❑ 1648	If It Don't Work Out/ Don't Cry for Me	1969	10.00
EPIC			
❑ 11145	Time of the Season/ Imagine the Swan	1974	5.00
PARROT			
❑ 3004	Indication/How We Were Before	1966	15.00
❑ 9695	She's Not There/You Make Me Feel So Good	1964	15.00
❑ 9723	Tell Her No/Leave Me Be	1965	15.00
❑ 9723 [PS]	Tell Her No/Leave Me Be	1965	30.00
❑ 9747	She's Coming Home/ I Must Move	1965	12.00
❑ 9747 [PS]	She's Coming Home/ I Must Move	1965	30.00
❑ 9769	I Want You Back Again/ Once Upon a Time	1965	12.00
❑ 9786	I Love You/Whenever You're Ready	1965	12.00
❑ 9797	Just Out of Reach/ Remember You	1965	15.00
❑ 9821	Don't Go Away/Is This the Dream	1966	15.00
Albums			
DATE			
❑ TES-4013	Odessey and Oracle	1968	30.00
—With no mention of "Time of the Season" on front cover			
❑ TES-4013	Odessey and Oracle	1969	20.00
—With "Time of the Season" mentioned on front cover			

The Zombies, *Odessey & Oracle*, Date TES 4013, 1968, **$30.**

Number	Title (A Side/B Side)	Yr	NM
EPIC			
❑ KEG 32861 [(2)B]	Time of the Zombies	1974	20.00
—Record 1 is mono; Record 2 is stereo; orange labels			
❑ PEG 32861 [(2)B]	Time of the Zombies	1979	15.00
—Later edition with blue labels			
LONDON			
❑ PS 557 [P]	Early Days	1969	20.00
—All tracks in true stereo except "Tell Her No"			
PARROT			
❑ PA 61001 [M]	The Zombies	1965	60.00
❑ PAS 71001 [R]	The Zombies	1965	40.00
RHINO			
❑ RNLP-120	Live on the BBC, 1965-67	1985	10.00
❑ RNLP 70186 [S]	Odessy and Oracle	1986	8.00

ZOO, THE (1)

45s

Number	Title (A Side/B Side)	Yr	NM
SUNBURST			
❑ 775	One Night Man/(Standing On) The Sunset Strip	1968	10.00
Albums			
MERCURY			
❑ SR-61300	The Zoo	1970	20.00
SUNBURST			
❑ 7500	The Zoo Presents the Chocolate Moose	1968	50.00

ZOO, THE (U)

Could be group (1).

45s

Number	Title (A Side/B Side)	Yr	NM
PARKWAY			
❑ 147	Good Day Sunshine/Where Have All the Good Times Gone	1967	12.00

ZOOM

45s

Number	Title (A Side/B Side)	Yr	NM
MCA			
❑ 52227	Ready to Roll/Sexy Sassy	1983	7.00
POLYDOR			
❑ 2186	Saturday, Saturday Night/ Distant Destiny	1981	8.00
❑ 2197	Love Seasons/Bye Bye Baby	1982	8.00
Albums			
MCA			
❑ 5420	Blasting Off	1983	15.00
POLYDOR			
❑ PD-1-6343	Saturday, Saturday Night	1981	20.00

ZORN, JOHN

Albums

Number	Title (A Side/B Side)	Yr	NM
ELEKTRA			
❑ 60844	Spy vs. Spy	1989	12.00
ELEKTRA/NONESUCH			
❑ 79139	The Big Gundown	1987	10.00
❑ 79172	Spillane/Two-Lane Highway/ Forbidden Fruit	1987	10.00
❑ 79238	Naked City	1990	12.00
HAT ART			
❑ 2034 [(2)]	Cobra	1987	15.00

ZORO AND THE ZIPS

45s

Number	Title (A Side/B Side)	Yr	NM
SPOT			
❑ 1002	The Woodpecker Song/ Frankie and Johnny	196?	15.00

ZWOL

45s

Number	Title (A Side/B Side)	Yr	NM
EMI AMERICA			
❑ 8005	New York City/A Little Bit Crazy	1978	5.00
❑ 8005 [DJ]	New York City/(Long Version)	1978	12.00
—Promo only; square-shaped record on white vinyl			
❑ 8009	Call Out My Name/It's So Real	1979	5.00
❑ 8021	Shaka Shaka/It's a Wonder	1979	5.00
Albums			
EMI AMERICA			
❑ SW-17005	Zwol	1978	10.00

Z

ZZ Top, *Takin' Texas to the People*, London PS-X-1001, 1976, **$50.**

Number	Title (A Side/B Side)	Yr	NM
❑ SW-17014	Effective Immediately	1979	10.00

ZZ TOP Also see MOVING SIDEWALKS.

12-Inch Singles

WARNER BROS.

Number	Title (A Side/B Side)	Yr	NM
❑ PRO-A-877 [DJ]	Cheap Sunglasses (LP Version)/ (Live Version)	1979	20.00
❑ PRO-A-2011 [DJ]	Gimme All Your Lovin/Got Me Under Pressure	1983	15.00
❑ PRO-A-2052 [DJ]	Sharp Dressed Man (same on both sides)	1983	15.00
❑ PRO-A-2094 [DJ]	TV Dinners (same on both sides)	1983	15.00
❑ PRO-A-2124 [DJ]	Legs (Remix 4:31) (same on both sides)	1984	15.00
❑ PRO-A-2146 [DJ]	Legs (Special Dance Mix) (same on both sides)	1983	12.00
❑ PRO-A-2365 [DJ]	Sleeping Bag (same on both sides)	1985	7.00
❑ PRO-A-2404 [DJ]	Can't Stop Rockin' (3:01) (same on both sides)	1985	10.00
❑ PRO-A-2407 [DJ]	Stages (3:32) (same on both sides)	1985	7.00
❑ PRO-A-2432 [DJ]	Delirious (3:41) (same on both sides)	1985	8.00
❑ PRO-A-2456 [DJ]	Rough Boy (same on both sides)	1985	8.00
❑ PRO-A-2494 [DJ]	Woke Up with Wood (same on both sides)	1986	8.00
❑ PRO-A-2529 [DJ]	Velcro Fly (Extended Mix) (Dub Version)	1985	8.00
❑ PRO-A-5483 [DJ]	Viva Las Vegas (5:11) (8:36)	1992	12.00
❑ 20207	Legs (Special Dance Mix)/ La Grange	1984	8.00
❑ 20395	Sleeping Bag (Extended Version)/Party on the Patio	1985	10.00
❑ 20524	Velcro Fly (Extended Mix) (Dub Mix)/Woke Up with Wood	1985	8.00
❑ 21840	Give It Up (2,800 Mile Remix 6:24) (2,800 Mile Dub 5:51) (D.O.R. Remix 6:39) (D.O.R. Dub 5:30)/Concrete and Steel	1990	7.00

45s

LONDON

Number	Title (A Side/B Side)	Yr	NM
❑ 45-131	Salt Lick/Miller's Farm	1970	10.00
❑ 45-138	Neighbor, Neighbor/ (Somebody Else Been) Shakin' Your Tree	1970	10.00
❑ 45-179	Francene/Francene (Spanish)	1972	10.00
❑ 45-203	La Grange/Just Got Paid	1973	8.00
❑ 5N-220	Tush/Blue Jean Blues	1975	8.00
❑ 5N-220 [PS]	Tush/Blue Jean Blues	1975	12.00
❑ 5N-241	It's Only Love/ Asleep in the Desert	1976	8.00
❑ 5N-241 [PS]	It's Only Love/ Asleep in the Desert	1976	10.00
❑ 5N-251	Arrested for Driving While Blind/It's Only Love	1977	7.00
❑ 5N-252	Enjoy and Get It On/El Diablo	1977	10.00

RCA

Number	Title (A Side/B Side)	Yr	NM
❑ 62812	Breakaway/Pincushion	1994	4.00
❑ 62928	Fuzzbox Voodoo/ Girl in a T-Shirt	1994	4.00

SCAT

Number	Title (A Side/B Side)	Yr	NM
❑ 500	Salt Lick/Miller's Farm	1969	200.00

WARNER BROS.

Number	Title (A Side/B Side)	Yr	NM
❑ 18979	Viva Las Vegas/2000 Blues	1992	4.00
❑ 19812	Doubleback/Planet of Women	1990	3.00
❑ 19812 [PS]	Doubleback/Planet of Women	1990	6.00
❑ 28650	Velcro Fly/Woke Up with Wood	1986	3.00
❑ 28733	Rough Boy/Delirious	1986	3.00
❑ 28733 [PS]	Rough Boy/Delirious	1986	3.00
❑ 28810	Stages/Can't Stop Rockin'	1986	3.00
❑ 28810 [PS]	Stages/Can't Stop Rockin'	1986	3.00
❑ 28884	Sleeping Bag/Party on the Patio	1985	3.00
❑ 28884 [PS]	Sleeping Bag/Party on the Patio	1985	3.00
❑ 29272	Legs/Bad Girl	1984	4.00
❑ 29272 [PS]	Legs/Bad Girl	1984	4.00
❑ 29576	Sharp Dressed Man/I Got the Six	1983	4.00
❑ 29693	Gimme All Your Lovin/If I Could Only Flag Her Down	1983	4.00
❑ 29693 [PS]	Gimme All Your Lovin/If I Could Only Flag Her Down	1983	5.00
❑ 49163	I Thank You/Fool for Your Stockings	1980	4.00
❑ 49220	Cheap Sunglasses/ Esther Be the One	1980	4.00
❑ 49782	Leila/Don't Tease Me	1981	4.00
❑ 49865	Tube Snake Boogie/ Heaven, Hell or Houston	1981	5.00

Albums

LONDON

Number	Title (A Side/B Side)	Yr	NM
❑ PS 584	ZZ Top's First Album	1971	12.00
❑ PS 612	Rio Grande Mud	1972	12.00
❑ XPS 631	Tres Hombres	1973	12.00
❑ PS 656	Fandango!	1975	12.00
❑ PS 680	Tejas	1977	12.00
❑ PS 706	The Best of ZZ Top	1977	12.00
❑ PS-X-1001 [DJ]	Takin' Texas to the People	1976	50.00

RHINO/WARNER BROS.

Number	Title (A Side/B Side)	Yr	NM
❑ 306172	Fandango!	2008	22.00

WARNER BROS.

Number	Title (A Side/B Side)	Yr	NM
❑ BSK 3268	ZZ Top's First Album	1979	8.00
❑ BSK 3269	Rio Grande Mud	1979	8.00
❑ BSK 3270	Tres Hombres	1979	8.00
❑ BSK 3271	Fandango!	1979	8.00
❑ BSK 3272	Tejas	1979	8.00
❑ BSK 3273	The Best of ZZ Top	1979	8.00
❑ HS 3361	Deguello	1979	10.00
❑ BSK 3593	El Loco	1981	10.00
❑ 23774	Eliminator	1983	8.00
❑ 25342	Afterburner	1985	8.00
❑ 26265	Recycler	1990	15.00
❑ 26846	Greatest Hits	1992	20.00
—U.S. vinyl available only through Columbia House			
❑ 274492	Tres Hombres	2007	25.00
—Reissue on 180-gram vinyl with gatefold, replica of "Burbank" WB label and insert			

ZZEBRA

Albums

POLYDOR

Number	Title (A Side/B Side)	Yr	NM
❑ PD-6043	Panic	1975	12.00

Except when noted otherwise, VG = 25% of NM, and VG+ = 50% of NM. (Example: VG = $2.00, VG+ = $4.00 and NM = $8.00.)

ORIGINAL CAST RECORDINGS

Number Title (A Side/B Side)	Yr	NM
ALL AMERICAN		
❑ Columbia Masterworks KOS 2160 [S]	1962	30.00
❑ Columbia Masterworks KOL 5760 [M]	1962	25.00
ANKLES AWEIGHT		
❑ Decca DL 9025 [M]	1955	40.00
ANNIE GET YOUR GUN		
❑ Decca DL 8001 [M]	1949	50.00
—Original LP issue of the Broadway cast		
❑ Decca DL 9018 [M]	1955	40.00
—Early reissue of DL 8001; black label with silver print		
❑ Decca DL 79018 [R]	196?	12.00
❑ RCA Victor LOC-1124 [M]	1966	12.00
❑ RCA Victor LSO-1124 [S]	1966	15.00
—Revival cast; black label, dog on top, "Stereo Dynagroove" at bottom		
❑ RCA Victor LSO-1124 [S]	1969	10.00
—Revival cast; orange, tan or black "dog near top" label		
ANYA		
❑ United Artists UAL-4133 [M]	1965	20.00
❑ United Artists UAS-5133 [S]	1965	50.00
APPLAUSE		
❑ ABC ABCS-OC-11	1970	20.00
THE APPLE TREE		
❑ Columbia Masterworks KOS 3020 [S]	1966	25.00
❑ Columbia Masterworks KOL 6620 [M]	1966	20.00
ARABIAN NIGHTS		
❑ Decca DL 9013 [M]	1954	80.00
THE ATHENIAN TOUCH		
❑ Broadway East OCM-101 [M]	1964	150.00
❑ Broadway East OCS-101 [S]	1964	200.00
BAJOUR		
❑ Columbia Masterworks KOS 2700 [S]	1964	30.00
❑ Columbia Masterworks KOL 6300 [M]	1964	25.00
BAKER STREET (A MUSICAL ADVENTURE OF SHERLOCK HOLMES)		
❑ MGM E-7000 [M]	1965	25.00
❑ MGM SE-7000 [S]	1965	30.00
A BALLAD FOR BIMSHIRE		
❑ London AM 48002 [M]	1963	40.00
❑ London AMS 78002 [S]	1963	80.00
THE BALLAD OF BABY DOE		
❑ MGM 3GC-1 [(3)M]	1958	150.00
—Box set		
THE BAND WAGON		
❑ "X" LVA-1001 [M]	1955	70.00
BELLS ARE RINGING		
❑ Columbia Masterworks OS 2006 [S]	1959	25.00
—Re-recording in stereo of OL 5170		
❑ Columbia Masterworks OL 5170 [M]	1957	30.00
—Gray and black label with six "eye" logos		
BEN FRANKLIN IN PARIS		
❑ Capitol SVAS 2191 [S]	1964	30.00
❑ Capitol VAS 2191 [M]	1964	25.00
BEST FOOT FORWARD		
❑ Cadence CLP-4012 [M]	1963	20.00
❑ Cadence CLP-24012 [S]	1963	30.00
—1963 revival of 1941 play		
BEYOND THE FRINGE		
❑ Capitol SW 1792 [S]	1962	30.00
❑ Capitol W 1792 [M]	1962	25.00
BEYOND THE FRINGE '64		
❑ Capitol SW 2072 [S]	1964	25.00
❑ Capitol W 2072 [M]	1964	20.00
THE BOY FRIEND		
❑ RCA Victor LOC-1018 [M]	1954	30.00
—Originals have green labels		
THE BOYS IN THE BAND		
❑ A&M SP-6001 [(2)]	1969	25.00
BRAVO, GIOVANNI		
❑ Columbia Masterworks KOS 2200 [S]	1962	20.00
❑ Columbia Masterworks KOL 5800 [M]	1962	15.00
BRIGADOON		
❑ RCA Victor LOC-1001 [M]	195?	20.00
—Photos of kilted dancers on front cover; black "Long Play" label		
❑ RCA Victor LOC-1001 [M]	1951	30.00
—Green front cover; green label		
❑ RCA Victor LOC-1001 [M]	1963	15.00
—Drawing of kilted dancers on front cover; black "Mono" label		
❑ RCA Victor LSO-1001(e) [R]	1963	12.00
—Black label, dog on top		
BY JUPITER		
❑ RCA Victor LOC-1137 [M]	1967	40.00
❑ RCA Victor LSO-1137 [S]	1967	75.00
—Above is by a revival cast		

Original cast, *Bye Bye Birdie,* Columbia Masterworks KOL 5510, 1960, gatefold cover, "6 eye" label, **$25.**

Number Title (A Side/B Side)	Yr	NM
BY THE BEAUTIFUL SEA		
❑ Capitol S 531 [M]	1954	70.00
BYE BYE BIRDIE		
❑ Columbia Masterworks KOS 2025 [S]	1960	30.00
—Gray and black label with six "eye" logos; with gatefold cover		
❑ Columbia Masterworks OS 2025 [S]	196?	25.00
—Gray and black label with six "eye" logos; with regular cover		
❑ Columbia Masterworks KOL 5510 [M]	1960	25.00
—Gray and black label with six "eye" logos; with gatefold cover		
❑ Columbia Masterworks OL 5510 [M]	196?	20.00
—Gray and black label with six "eye" logos; with regular cover		
CABARET		
❑ Columbia Masterworks KOS 3040 [S]	1966	20.00
❑ Columbia Masterworks KOL 6640 [M]	1966	15.00
CABIN IN THE SKY		
❑ Capitol SW 2073 [S]	1964	50.00
—Above is by a revival cast		
❑ Capitol W 2073 [M]	1964	30.00
CALL ME MADAM		
❑ RCA Victor LOC-1000 [M]	1950	80.00
—Dinah Shore sings Ethel Merman's part for contractual reasons, otherwise it's by the entire original cast		
CAMELOT		
❑ Columbia Masterworks KOS 2031 [S]	1960	25.00
—Gray and black label with six "eye" logos; gatefold cover		
❑ Columbia Masterworks KOL 5620 [M]	1960	20.00
—Gray and black label with six "eye" logos		
CAN-CAN		
❑ Capitol DW 452 [R]	196?	12.00
❑ Capitol S 452 [M]	1953	25.00
—Originals have red labels with Capitol logo at top		
❑ Capitol W 452 [M]	195?	15.00
CANTERBURY TALES		
❑ Capitol SW-229	1969	25.00
CAPTAIN JINKS OF THE HORSE MARINES		
❑ RCA Victor ARL2-1727 [(2)]	1975	30.00
—Box set		

Number Title (A Side/B Side)	Yr	NM
CARMEN JONES		
❑ Decca DL 8014 [M]	1949	40.00
—Black label, gold print		
❑ Decca DL 9021 [M]	1955	20.00
—Reissue of 8014; black label, silver print		
CARNIVAL		
❑ MGM E-3946 [M]	1961	20.00
❑ MGM SE-3946 [S]	1961	25.00
—Black label		
❑ MGM SE-3946 [S]	1968	10.00
—Blue and gold label		
CAROUSEL		
❑ Command RS 33-843 [M]	1962	15.00
—Studio cast		
❑ Command RS-843 SD [M]	1962	20.00
—Studio cast witrh Alfred Drake and Roberta Peters, and Enoch Light's orchestra		
❑ Decca DL 8003 [M]	1949	40.00
—Original LP issue of the Broadway cast		
❑ Decca DL 9020 [M]	1955	30.00
—Early reissue of DL 8003; black label with silver print		
❑ Decca DL 79020 [R]	196?	10.00
❑ MCA 1627 [R]	198?	8.00
—Reissue of MCA 37093		
❑ MCA 2033 [R]	1973	8.00
—Reissue of Decca 79020; black label with rainbow		
❑ MCA 37093 [R]	1980	8.00
—Reissue of MCA 2033		
CHRISTINE		
❑ Columbia Masterworks OS 2026 [S]	1960	100.00
❑ Columbia Masterworks OL 5520 [M]	1960	60.00
CINDY		
❑ ABC-Paramount ABC-OC-2 [M]	1964	30.00
❑ ABC-Paramount ABC-OCS-2 [S]	1964	50.00
CLARA (BEG, BORROW OR STEAL)		
❑ Commentary CYN-02 [M]	1960	60.00
CLOWNAROUND		
❑ RCA Victor LSP-4741	1972	250.00
CLUB 15		
❑ Decca DL 5155 [10]	1949	60.00

Original cast, *Funny Girl,* Capitol SVAS 2059, 1964, gatefold cover, stereo, **$20.**

Number	Title (A Side/B Side)	Yr	NM
THE COACH WITH THE SIX INSIDES			
❑ ESP-Disk' 1019 [M]		1967	25.00
COCO			
❑ Paramount PMS-1002		1969	25.00
THE COMMITTEE			
❑ Reprise F-2023 [M]		1964	30.00
❑ Reprise FS-2023 [S]		1964	40.00
COMPANY			
❑ Columbia Masterworks OS 3550		1970	12.00
❑ Columbia Masterworks SQ 30993 [Q]		1971	30.00
—Quadraphonic version has substantially different mixes than the original stereo LP			
THE CRADLE WILL ROCK			
❑ MGM E-4289-2 [(2)M]		1964	25.00
❑ MGM SE-4289-2 [(2)S]		1964	30.00
—The above is by a revival cast			
THE CRITIC			
❑ Decca DL 9154 [M]		1967	20.00
❑ Decca DL 79154 [S]		1967	20.00
CRY FOR US ALL			
❑ Project 3 TS-1000 SD		1970	40.00
DAMES AT SEA			
❑ Columbia Masterworks OS 3550		1969	20.00
DAMN YANKEES			
❑ RCA Victor LOC-1021 [M]		195?	20.00
—Orange cover			
❑ RCA Victor LOC-1021 [M]		1955	30.00
—Green cover			
❑ RCA Victor LSO-1021(e) [R]		1965	15.00
—Black label, dog on top, "Stereo Electronically Reprocessed" at bottom			
THE DANCERS OF BALI			
❑ Columbia Masterworks ML 4618 [M]		1952	40.00
DARLING OF THE DAY			
❑ RCA Victor LOC-1149 [M]		1968	40.00
❑ RCA Victor LSO-1149 [S]		1968	60.00
DEAR WORLD			
❑ Columbia Masterworks BOS 3260		1969	20.00

Number	Title (A Side/B Side)	Yr	NM
DEATH OF A SALESMAN			
❑ Decca DX 102 [(2)M]		1951	40.00
—Two-record boxed set with contents of 9007 and 9008			
DEATH OF A SALESMAN (PART 1)			
❑ Decca DL 9006 [M]		1951	25.00
—Black label, gold print			
DEATH OF A SALESMAN (PART 2)			
❑ Decca DL 9007 [M]		1951	25.00
—Black label, gold print			
DESTRY RIDES AGAIN			
❑ Decca DL 9075 [M]		1959	30.00
❑ Decca DL 79075 [S]		1959	40.00
DO I HEAR A WALTZ?			
❑ Columbia Masterworks KOS 2770 [S]		1965	20.00
❑ Columbia Masterworks KOL 6370 [M]		1965	15.00
DO RE MI			
❑ RCA Victor LOC-1105 [M]		1965	15.00
—Reissue of 2002 with standard red cover			
❑ RCA Victor LSO-1105 [S]		1965	20.00
—Reissue of 2002 with standard red cover			
❑ RCA Victor LOCD-2002 [M]		1961	30.00
—In black box with orange sleeve			
❑ RCA Victor LSOD-2002 [S]		1961	40.00
—In black box with orange sleeve			
DOCTOR SELAVY'S MAGIC THEATRE			
❑ United Artists UA-LA196-G		1974	30.00
DONNYBROOK!			
❑ Kapp KD-8500-S [S]		1961	25.00
❑ Kapp KDL-8500 [M]		1961	20.00
DRESSED TO THE NINES			
❑ MGM E-3914 [M]		1960	25.00
❑ MGM SE-3914 [S]		1960	40.00
THE EARL OF RUSTON			
❑ Capitol ST-465		1971	40.00
ERNEST IN LOVE			
❑ Columbia Masterworks OS 2027 [S]		1960	100.00
❑ Columbia Masterworks OL 5530 [M]		1960	60.00

Number	Title (A Side/B Side)	Yr	NM
AN EVENING WITH RICHARD NIXON			
❑ Ode SP-77015		1972	30.00
FADE OUT-FADE IN			
❑ ABC-Paramount ABC-OC-3 [M]		1964	25.00
❑ ABC-Paramount ABCS-OC-3 [S]		1964	30.00
A FAMILY AFFAIR			
❑ United Artists UAL-4099 [M]		1962	30.00
❑ United Artists UAS-5099 [S]		1962	50.00
FANNY			
❑ RCA Victor LOC-1015 [M]		1954	25.00
—"Long Play" on label			
❑ RCA Victor LOC-1015 [M]		196?	15.00
—"Mono" on label			
❑ RCA Victor LSO-1015(e) [R]		196?	12.00
—"Stereo Electronically Reprocessed" on label			
THE FANTASTICKS			
❑ MGM E-3872 [M]		196?	10.00
—White gatefold cover			
❑ MGM E-3872 [M]		1963	20.00
—Original non-gatefold cover			
❑ MGM SE-3872 [S]		196?	10.00
—Black gatefold cover			
❑ MGM SE-3872 [S]		196?	12.00
—White gatefold cover			
❑ MGM SE-3872 [S]		1963	25.00
—Original non-gatefold cover			
FIDDLER ON THE ROOF			
❑ RCA Victor LOC-1093 [M]		1964	15.00
❑ RCA Victor LSO-1093 [S]		1964	20.00
—Black label, dog on top			
FINIAN'S RAINBOW			
❑ Columbia Masterworks OS 2080 [R]		1963	12.00
❑ Columbia Masterworks ML 4062 [M]		1948	30.00
—Original cover with no photo; green label			
❑ Columbia Masterworks OL 4062 [M]		196?	12.00
—Reissue cover, either pink or green; gray label			
❑ RCA Victor LOC-1057 [M]		1960	10.00
—Revival cast; cover shows co-stars hiding in the trees			
❑ RCA Victor LOC-1057 [M]		1960	12.00
—Revival cast; "pot of gold" cover			
❑ RCA Victor LSO-1057 [S]		1960	12.00
—Revival cast; cover shows co-stars hiding in the trees			
❑ RCA Victor LSO-1057 [S]		1960	15.00
—Revival cast; "pot of gold" cover			
FIORELLO!			
❑ Capitol SWAO 1321 [S]		1959	25.00
❑ Capitol WAO 1321 [M]		1959	20.00
FIRST IMPRESSIONS			
❑ Columbia Masterworks OS 2014 [S]		1959	60.00
❑ Columbia Masterworks OL 5400 [M]		1959	30.00
FLAHOOLEY			
❑ Capitol S 284 [M]		1951	150.00
FLORA, THE RED MENACE			
❑ RCA Victor LOC-1111 [M]		1965	25.00
❑ RCA Victor LSO-1111 [S]		1965	30.00
FLOWER DRUM SONG			
❑ Columbia Masterworks OS 2009 [S]		1958	25.00
—Gray and black label with six "eye" logos			
❑ Columbia Masterworks OL 5350 [M]		1958	20.00
—Gray and black label with six "eye" logos			
FLY BLACKBIRD			
❑ Mercury OCM-2206 [M]		1962	30.00
❑ Mercury OCS-6206 [S]		1962	60.00
FUNNY GIRL			
❑ Capitol STAO 2059 [S]		196?	12.00
—Only Barbra Streisand is pictured on the back cover			
❑ Capitol SVAS 2059 [S]		1964	20.00
—Both Barbra Streisand and Sydney Chaplin are pictured on the back cover			
❑ Capitol VAS 2059 [M]		1964	15.00
A FUNNY THING HAPPENED ON THE WAY TO THE FORUM			
❑ Capitol SWAO 1717 [S]		1962	20.00
—Gatefold cover			
❑ Capitol WAO 1717 [M]		1962	15.00
—Gatefold cover			
THE GAY LIFE			
❑ Capitol SWAO 1560 [S]		1961	50.00
❑ Capitol WAO 1560 [M]		1961	25.00
GENTLEMEN PREFER BLONDES			
❑ Columbia Masterworks OS 2310 [R]		1963	10.00
—Gray label			
❑ Columbia Masterworks ML 4290 [M]		1949	25.00
—Original with green label			
❑ Columbia Masterworks OL 4290 [M]		196?	15.00
—Reissue with new prefix and various gray labels			
❑ Columbia Masterworks S 32610 [R]		1973	8.00
GEORGE M!			
❑ Columbia Masterworks KOS 3200 [S]		1968	20.00
❑ Columbia Masterworks KOL 6800 [M]		1968	30.00

Number Title (A Side/B Side)	Yr	NM
THE GIRL IN PINK TIGHTS		
❑ Columbia Masterworks ML 4890 [M]	1954	60.00
THE GIRL WHO CAME TO SUPPER		
❑ Columbia Masterworks KOS 2420 [S]	1963	30.00
❑ Columbia Masterworks KOL 6020 [M]	1963	25.00
GIVE 'EM HELL, HARRY!		
❑ United Artists UA-LA540-H2 [(2)]	1975	20.00
THE GOLDEN APPLE		
❑ RCA Victor LOC-1014 [M]	1954	100.00
GOLDEN BOY		
❑ Capitol SVAS 2124 [S]	1964	30.00
❑ Capitol VAS 2124 [M]	1964	25.00
GOLDILOCKS		
❑ Columbia Masterworks OS 2007 [S]	1958	60.00
❑ Columbia Masterworks OL 5340 [M]	1958	25.00
GOODTIME CHARLEY		
❑ RCA Victor ARL1-1011	1975	30.00
GREASE		
❑ MGM 1SE-34	1972	12.00
THE GREAT WALTZ		
❑ Capitol SVAS 2426 [S]	1965	25.00
❑ Capitol VAS 2426 [M]	1965	20.00
GREENWICH VILLAGE U.S.A.		
❑ 20th Fox TCF-105-2 [(2)M]	1960	60.00
—With complete show		
❑ 20th Fox TCF-105-2S [(2)S]	1960	100.00
—With complete show		
❑ 20th Fox FOX-4005 [M]	1960	40.00
—With excerpts from the show		
❑ 20th Fox SFX-4005 [S]	1960	50.00
—With excerpts from the show		
GREENWILLOW		
❑ RCA Victor LOC-2001 [M]	1960	20.00
❑ RCA Victor LSO-2001 [S]	1960	50.00
GUYS AND DOLLS		
❑ Decca DL 8036 [M]	1950	30.00
❑ Decca DL 9023 [M]	1955	20.00
—Reissue of 8036		
❑ Decca DL 79023 [R]	196?	12.00
❑ MCA 2034	1973	10.00
—Reissue of 79023		
GYPSY		
❑ Columbia Masterworks OS 2017 [S]	1959	25.00
—Original covers are white with drawings		
❑ Columbia Masterworks OS 2017 [S]	1962	15.00
—Reissue covers are brown with show photos		
❑ Columbia Masterworks OL 5420 [M]	1959	20.00
—Original covers are white with drawings		
❑ Columbia Masterworks OL 5420 [M]	1962	12.00
—Reissue covers are brown with show photos		
HAIR		
❑ Atco SD 7002	1969	25.00
—Original London cast		
❑ Philips PHS 600329	1969	25.00
—Original French cast		
❑ RCA Victor ABD1-0245 [Q]	1973	20.00
—Broadway cast; quadraphonic remix		
❑ RCA Victor ANL1-0986	1974	10.00
—Off-Broadway cast; reissue with new number		
❑ RCA Victor LOC-1143 [M]	1967	15.00
—Off-Broadway cast		
❑ RCA Victor LSO-1143 [S]	1967	12.00
—Off-Broadway cast; black label, dog at top, "Stereo" at bottom		
❑ RCA Victor LOC-1150 [M]	1968	30.00
—Broadway cast		
❑ RCA Victor LSO-1150 [S]	1968	10.00
—Broadway cast; orange label		
❑ RCA Victor LSO-1150 [S]	1968	20.00
—Broadway cast; black label, dog on top, "Stereo" at bottom		
HALF A SIXPENCE		
❑ RCA Victor LOC-1110 [M]	1965	20.00
❑ RCA Victor LSO-1110 [S]	1965	25.00
HALF PAST WEDNESDAY		
❑ Columbia CL 1917 [M]	1962	30.00
❑ Columbia CS 8717 [S]	1962	40.00
HAMLET		
❑ Columbia Masterworks DOL 302 [(4)M]	1964	25.00
—Boxed set with entire play (Broadway revival)		
❑ Columbia Masterworks DOS 702 [(4)S]	1964	25.00
—Boxed set with entire play (Broadway revival)		
❑ Columbia Masterworks OS 2620 [S]	1964	15.00
—Highlights from the box set		
❑ Columbia Masterworks OL 6220 [M]	1964	15.00
—Highlights from the box set		
THE HAPPIEST GIRL IN THE WORLD		
❑ Columbia Masterworks KOS 2050 [S]	1961	40.00
—Second covers are white		
❑ Columbia Masterworks KOS 2050 [S]	1961	60.00
—Original covers are yellow		
❑ Columbia Masterworks KOL 5650 [M]	1961	30.00
—Second covers are white		

Original cast, *Lost in the Stars,* Decca DL 8028, 1949, mono, **$50.**

Number Title (A Side/B Side)	Yr	NM
❑ Columbia Masterworks KOL 5650 [M]	1961	40.00
—Original covers are yellow		
HAPPY HUNTING		
❑ RCA Victor LOC-1026 [M]	1956	40.00
HEAR! HEAR!		
❑ Decca DL 9031 [M]	1955	50.00
HELLO, DOLLY!		
❑ RCA Victor LOCD-1087 [M]	1964	15.00
—New back cover is in color and has a photo of Carol Channing; "RE" is on cover		
❑ RCA Victor LOCD-1087 [M]	1964	25.00
—Original cover is black and white on back and spotlights "Come and Be My Butterfly"; this song was deleted from the show, so the cover was changed		
❑ RCA Victor LSOD-1087 [S]	1964	20.00
—New back cover is in color and has a photo of Carol Channing; "RE" is on cover; black label, dog on top		
❑ RCA Victor LSOD-1087 [S]	1964	30.00
—Original cover is black and white on back and spotlights "Come and Be My Butterfly"; this song was deleted from the show, so the cover was changed		
❑ RCA Victor LSOD-1087 [S]	1969	10.00
—Orange or tan label		
HENRY, SWEET HENRY		
❑ ABC ABC-OC-4 [M]	1967	30.00
❑ ABC ABCS-OC-4 [S]	1967	50.00
HERE'S LOVE		
❑ Columbia Masterworks KOS 2400 [S]	1963	40.00
❑ Columbia Masterworks KOL 6000 [M]	1963	30.00
HIGH BUTTON SHOES		
❑ RCA Camden CAL-457 [M]	1958	30.00
❑ RCA Victor LOC-1107 [M]	1964	40.00
❑ RCA Victor LSO-1107 [R]	1964	30.00
HIGH SPIRITS		
❑ ABC-Paramount ABC-OC-1 [M]	1964	25.00
❑ ABC-Paramount ABCS-OC-1 [S]	1964	30.00
HOUSE OF FLOWERS		
❑ Columbia Masterworks ML 4969 [M]	1954	40.00
—Blue label original		

Number Title (A Side/B Side)	Yr	NM
❑ United Artists UAS-5180	1968	40.00
—Revival cast		
HOW NOW, DOW JONES		
❑ RCA Victor LOC-1142 [M]	1967	25.00
❑ RCA Victor LSO-1142 [S]	1967	30.00
HOW TO SUCCEED IN BUSINESS WITHOUT REALLY TRYING		
❑ RCA Victor LOC-1066 [M]	1961	20.00
❑ RCA Victor LSO-1066 [S]	1961	25.00
—Black label, dog on top		
❑ RCA Victor LSO-1066 [S]	1969	10.00
—Orange or tan label		
HUGHIE		
❑ Columbia Masterworks OS 2760 [S]	1965	30.00
❑ Columbia Masterworks OL 6260 [M]	1965	25.00
I CAN GET IT FOR YOU WHOLESALE		
❑ Columbia Masterworks KOS 2180 [S]	1962	30.00
❑ Columbia Masterworks KOL 5780 [M]	1962	25.00
I DO! I DO!		
❑ RCA Victor LOC-1128 [M]	1966	15.00
❑ RCA Victor LSO-1128 [S]	1966	20.00
—Black label, dog on top		
I HAD A BALL		
❑ Mercury OCM-2210 [M]	1964	20.00
❑ Mercury OCM-2210 [(2)M]	1964	40.00
—Promo-only two-record set with bonus interview record MGD-2-24		
❑ Mercury OCS-6210 [S]	1964	25.00
ICE FOLLIES		
❑ Dot DLP-3757 [M]	1967	25.00
❑ Dot DLP-25757 [S]	1967	30.00
ILLYA DARLING		
❑ United Artists UAL-8901 [M]	1967	20.00
❑ United Artists UAS-9901 [S]	1967	20.00
IRMA LA DOUCE		
❑ Columbia Masterworks OS 2029 [S]	1960	25.00
❑ Columbia Masterworks OL 5560 [M]	1960	20.00

Number — Title (A Side/B Side) — Yr — NM

J.B.
❑ RCA Victor LD-6075 [(2)M] 1959 60.00
❑ RCA Victor LDS-6075 [(2)S] 1959 70.00

JACQUES BREL IS ALIVE AND WELL AND LIVING IN PARIS
❑ Columbia Masterworks D2S 779 [(2)] 1968 20.00
—Box set; gray "360 Sound" labels

JENNIE
❑ RCA Victor LOC-1083 [M] 1963 25.00
❑ RCA Victor LSO-1083 [S] 1963 50.00

JESUS CHRIST SUPERSTAR
❑ Decca DL 71503 1971 20.00
—From the Broadway production; also see listings for this title in the VARIOUS ARTISTS COLLECTIONS sections.
❑ MCA 5000 1973 12.00
—From the Broadway production; reissue

JOSEPH AND THE AMAZING TECHNICOLOR DREAMCOAT
❑ Scepter SPS-588X 1968 20.00
—With gatefold cover and libretto
❑ Scepter SMAS-93738 197? 25.00
—Capitol Record Club edition

JOY
❑ RCA Victor LSO-1166 1970 20.00

JUNO
❑ Columbia Masterworks OS 2013 [S] 1959 70.00
❑ Columbia Masterworks OL 5380 [M] 1959 40.00

KEAN
❑ Columbia Masterworks KSO 2120 [S] 1961 40.00
❑ Columbia Masterworks KOL 5720 [M] 1961 30.00

THE KING AND I
❑ Decca DL 9008 [M] 195? 12.00
—Drawing of Gertrude Lawrence and Yul Brynner on cover, with title on two lines
❑ Decca DL 9008 [M] 195? 40.00
—Drawing of Gertrude Lawrence and Yul Brynner on cover, with title on three lines
❑ Decca DL 9008 [M] 1951 25.00
—Black label, gold print
❑ Decca DL 79008 [R] 196? 10.00

KWAMINA
❑ Capitol SW 1645 [S] 1962 50.00
❑ Capitol W 1645 [M] 1962 30.00

THE LADY'S NOT FOR BURNING
❑ Decca DL 9508 /9 [(2)M] 1951 50.00
—Oversize box set

LAGINAPPE '59 PRESENTS BE MY GUEST
❑ (no label) XCTV-10303 [M] 1959 250.00
—Custom pressing for New Trier High School, Illinois. Collectible because the future Ann-Margret sings one track on the LP!

LET IT RIDE
❑ RCA Victor LOC-1064 [M] 1961 20.00
❑ RCA Victor LSO-1064 [S] 1961 40.00

LI'L ABNER
❑ Columbia Masterworks OL 5150 [M] 1956 30.00

LITTLE ME
❑ RCA Victor LOC-1078 [M] 1962 20.00
❑ RCA Victor LSO-1078 [S] 1962 25.00

LOOK MA, I'M DANCIN'!
❑ Decca DL 5231 [M] 1950 100.00

LORELEI
❑ MGM M3G-55 1974 30.00
—Second version, recorded with Broadway cast
❑ Verve MV-5097-OC 1974 25.00
—First version, recorded before the show hit Broadway

LOST IN THE STARS
❑ Decca DL 8028 [M] 1949 50.00
❑ Decca DL 9120 [M] 1965 15.00
—Reissue of 8028

THE MAD SHOW
❑ Columbia Masterworks OS 2930 [S] 1965 100.00
❑ Columbia Masterworks OL 6530 [M] 1965 50.00

MAGGIE FLYNN
❑ RCA Victor LSOD-2009 1968 20.00
❑ RCA Victor LSOD-2009 1968 25.00

THE MAGIC SHOW
❑ Bell 9003 1974 20.00

MAKE A WISH
❑ RCA Victor LOC-1002 [M] 1951 150.00

MAME
❑ Columbia Masterworks KOS 3000 [S] 1966 20.00
—Gray label with "360 Sound Stereo"
❑ Columbia Masterworks KOS 3000 [S] 1970 12.00
—Olive label with orange "Columbia" around outside
❑ Columbia Masterworks KOL 6600 [M] 1966 15.00

MAN OF LA MANCHA
❑ Kapp KRL-4505 [M] 1965 15.00
❑ Kapp KRS-4505 [S] 1965 20.00

MARK TWAIN TONIGHT!
❑ Columbia Masterworks OS 2019 [S] 1959 15.00
❑ Columbia Masterworks OL 5440 [M] 1959 12.00

ME AND JULIET
❑ RCA Victor LOC-1012 [M] 1953 70.00

MEDEA
❑ Decca DLP 9000 [M] 1949 30.00

MEGILLA OF ITZIG MANGER
❑ Columbia Masterworks OS 3270 1968 40.00

THE MERRY WIDOW
❑ RCA Victor LOC-1094 [M] 1964 20.00
❑ RCA Victor LSO-1094 [S] 1964 25.00

MEXICAN HAYRIDE
❑ Decca DL 5232 [10] 1950 120.00

MILK AND HONEY
❑ RCA Victor LOC-1065 [M] 1961 20.00
—With picture of Tommy Rall and two dancers on front cover
❑ RCA Victor LOC-1065 [M] 1961 25.00
—With only credits (no picture) on front cover
❑ RCA Victor LSO-1065 [S] 1961 25.00
—With picture of Tommy Rall and two dancers on front cover
❑ RCA Victor LSO-1065 [S] 1961 30.00
—With only credits (no picture) on front cover

MISS LIBERTY
❑ Columbia Masterworks ML 4220 [M] 1949 30.00
—Originals have green labels

THE MOST HAPPY FELLA
❑ Columbia Masterworks O3L 240 [(3)M] 1956 50.00
—Box set with entire show
❑ Columbia Masterworks OS 2330 [R] 196? 15.00
❑ Columbia Masterworks OL 5118 [M] 1956 30.00
—Gray and black label with six "eye" logos

MR. PRESIDENT
❑ Columbia Masterworks KOS 2270 [S] 1962 30.00
—Gatefold with shiny silver cover
❑ Columbia Masterworks KOL 5870 [M] 1962 20.00
—Gatefold with shiny silver cover

MR. WONDERFUL
❑ Decca DL 9032 [M] 1956 50.00

MRS. PATTERSON
❑ RCA Victor LOC-1017 [M] 1954 150.00

THE MUSIC MAN
❑ Capitol SW 990 [S] 196? 15.00
—Regular cover with photo of Robert Preston as Harold Hill
❑ Capitol SWAO 990 [S] 1957 25.00
—Gatefold cover, white with credits and drawing on front; gray label
❑ Capitol W 990 [M] 196? 12.00
—Regular cover with photo of Robert Preston as Harold Hill
❑ Capitol WAO 990 [M] 1957 20.00
—Gatefold cover, white with credits and drawing on front; gray label

MY FAIR LADY
❑ Columbia Masterworks OS 2015 [S] 1959 12.00
—Gray label, "Stereo" at bottom; original London cast
❑ Columbia Masterworks OS 2015 [S] 1959 20.00
—Gray and black label with six "eye" logos; original London cast
❑ Columbia Masterworks PS 2015 [S] 198? 6.00
—Budget-line reissue with new prefix
❑ Columbia Masterworks OL 5090 [M] 1956 10.00
—Gray label, "Mono" at bottom
❑ Columbia Masterworks OL 5090 [M] 1956 25.00
—Gray and black label with six "eye" logos
❑ Columbia Masterworks OL 5090 [M] 1963 15.00
—Gray label with "Guaranteed High Fidelity" at bottom

MY PEOPLE
❑ Contact C-1 [M] 1966 20.00
❑ Contact CS-1 [S] 1966 25.00

THE NERVOUS SET
❑ Columbia Masterworks OS 2018 [S] 1959 60.00
❑ Columbia Masterworks OL 5430 [M] 1959 30.00

NEW FACES OF 1952
❑ RCA Victor LOC-1008 [M] 1952 25.00

NEW FACES OF 1956
❑ RCA Victor LOC-1025 [M] 1956 50.00

NEW FACES OF 1968
❑ Warner Bros. BS 2551 1968 30.00

THE NEW GIRL IN TOWN
❑ RCA Victor LOC-1027 [M] 1957 20.00
❑ RCA Victor LSO-1027 [S] 1958 50.00
❑ RCA Victor LOC-1106 [M] 1965 20.00
❑ RCA Victor LSC-1106 [S] 1965 30.00

THE NINA, THE PINTA AND THE SANTA MARIA
❑ Dot DLP-9009 [M] 1960 40.00
❑ Dot DLP-29009 [S] 1960 50.00

NO STRINGS
❑ Capitol O 1695 [M] 1962 20.00
❑ Capitol SO 1695 [S] 1962 40.00

OF THEE I SING
❑ Capitol S 350 [M] 1952 150.00

OH, KAY!
❑ 20th Fox FOX-4003 [M] 1960 25.00
❑ 20th Fox SFX-4003 [S] 1960 50.00

OKLAHOMA!
❑ Decca DLP 8000 [M] 1949 30.00
—Black label, gold print; the first 12-inch LP on Decca
❑ Decca DL 9017 [M] 1955 20.00
—Reissue of 8000
❑ Decca DL 9017 [M] 196? 20.00
—Reissue with new cover art
❑ Decca DL 79017 [R] 196? 15.00
❑ Decca DL 79017 [R] 1968 20.00
—Special 25th Anniversary edition; cover has yellow drawing, inner sleeve has liner notes
❑ MCA 2030 1973 8.00
—Reissue of 79017; black label with rainbow
❑ MCA 37096 198? 8.00
—Reissue of 2030

OLIVER!
❑ RCA Victor LOCD-2004 [M] 1962 15.00
❑ RCA Victor LSOD-2004 [S] 1962 20.00

ON A CLEAR DAY YOU CAN SEE FOREVER
❑ RCA Victor LOCD-2006 [M] 1965 20.00
❑ RCA Victor LSOD-2006 [S] 1965 25.00

ON YOUR TOES
❑ Decca DL 9015 [M] 1954 75.00

ONCE UPON A MATTRESS
❑ Kapp KDL-7004 [M] 1959 25.00
❑ Kapp KDL-7004-S [S] 1959 30.00

110 IN THE SHADE
❑ RCA Victor LOC-1085 [M] 1963 25.00
❑ RCA Victor LSO-1085 [S] 1963 40.00

ONE TOUCH OF VENUS
❑ Decca DL 9122 [M] 1965 25.00
❑ Decca DL 79122 [R] 1965 25.00

OVER HERE!
❑ Columbia Masterworks KS 32961 1974 20.00
❑ Columbia Masterworks SQ 32961 [Q] 1974 30.00

PAINT YOUR WAGON
❑ RCA Victor LOC-1006 [M] 1951 25.00
—Green label
❑ RCA Victor LOC-1006 [M] 1955 20.00
—Black label, dog on top, "Long Play" at bottom
❑ RCA Victor LOC-1006 [M] 1965 15.00
—Black label, dog on top, "Mono" at bottom
❑ RCA Victor LSO-1006 [R] 1965 12.00
—Black label, dog on top
❑ RCA Victor LSO-1006 [R] 1969 10.00
—Orange or tan label

PARADE
❑ Kapp KDL-7005 [M] 1960 200.00
❑ Kapp KDS-7005 [S] 1960 250.00

PARIS '90
❑ Columbia Masterworks ML 4619 [M] 1952 150.00

PEACE
❑ Metromedia MP-33001 1969 30.00

PETER PAN
❑ RCA Victor LOC-1019 [M] 1954 40.00
❑ RCA Victor LSO-1019 [R] 196? 12.00
❑ RCA Victor AYL1-3762 [R] 1980 8.00

PIPE DREAM
❑ RCA Victor LOC-1023 [M] 1955 50.00
—Without "Special Advance Edition" sticker on cover
❑ RCA Victor LOC-1023 [M] 1955 70.00
—With "Special Advance Edition" sticker on cover

PLAIN AND FANCY
❑ Capitol S 603 [M] 1955 25.00
—Red label

PLAYGIRLS
❑ Warner Bros. W 1530 [M] 1964 25.00
❑ Warner Bros. WS 1530 [S] 1964 30.00

PORGY AND BESS
❑ Decca DL 7006 [10] 1950 30.00
—Reissue of material first released on 78s
❑ Decca DL 8042 [M] 1950 30.00
❑ Decca DL 9024 [M] 1955 25.00
—Reissue of 8042; drawing of Catfish Row on cover
❑ Decca DL 9024 [M] 196? 15.00
—Photo of cast members on cover
❑ Decca DL 79024 [R] 196? 10.00
—Photo of cast members on cover
❑ MCA 1631 [R] 198? 6.00
—Reissue of 2035
❑ MCA 2035 [R] 1973 8.00
—Reissue of 79024; black label with rainbow

THE PREMISE
❑ Vanguard VRS-9092 [M] 1960 40.00

PURLIE
❑ Ampex A-40101 1970 30.00

Number	Title (A Side/B Side)	Yr	NM
RASHOMON			
❑ Carlton LPX-5000 [M]		1959	25.00
❑ Carlton STLPX-5000 [S]		1959	30.00
—Not actually the original cast recording, but the play's incidental music			
REDHEAD			
❑ RCA Victor LOC-1048 [M]		1959	20.00
❑ RCA Victor LSO-1048 [S]		1959	50.00
—Without "Essie's Vision"			
❑ RCA Victor LOC-1104 [M]		1959	15.00
—Reissue of 1048			
❑ RCA Victor LSO-1104 [S]		1965	25.00
—Reissue adds "Essie's Vision" to stereo version			
THE RIVER WIND			
❑ London AM-48001 [M]		1962	40.00
❑ London AMS-78001 [S]		1962	80.00
THE ROAR OF THE GREASEPAINT — THE SMELL OF THE CROWD			
❑ RCA Victor LOC-1109 [M]		1965	15.00
❑ RCA Victor LSO-1109 [S]		1965	20.00
THE ROTHSCHILDS			
❑ Columbia Masterworks S 30337		1970	25.00
SAIL AWAY			
❑ Capitol SWAO 1643 [S]		1961	30.00
❑ Capitol WAO 1643 [M]		1961	20.00
SARATOGA			
❑ RCA Victor LOC-1051 [M]		1959	25.00
❑ RCA Victor LSO-1051 [S]		1959	50.00
SAY, DARLING			
❑ RCA Victor LOC-1045 [M]		1958	40.00
❑ RCA Victor LSO-1045 [S]		1958	60.00
SEVENTEEN			
❑ RCA Victor LOC-1003 [M]		1951	150.00
1776			
❑ Columbia Masterworks BOS 3310		1969	12.00
—Revised (correct) edition has Rex Everhart shown as Ben Franklin in credits and synopsis			
❑ Columbia Masterworks BOS 3310		1969	30.00
—The first edition has Howard DaSilva shown as Ben Franklin in credits and synopsis, though he does not appear on the LP			
SEVENTH HEAVEN			
❑ Decca DL 9001 [M]		1955	150.00
70 GIRLS, 70			
❑ Columbia Masterworks S 30589		1971	50.00
SHE LOVES ME			
❑ MGM E 4118OC-2 [(2)M]		1963	40.00
❑ MGM SE 4118OC-2 [(2)S]		1963	50.00
SHOW BIZ (FROM VAUDE TO VIDEO)			
❑ RCA Victor LOC-1011 [M]		1954	40.00
SHOW BOAT			
❑ Columbia Masterworks ML 4058 [M]		1948	25.00
—From the 1946 revival; paper envelope jacket with its opening on top			
❑ Columbia Masterworks OL 4058 [M]		195?	20.00
—From the 1946 revival; reissue of ML 4058			
SHOW GIRL			
❑ Roulette R-80001 [M]		1961	20.00
❑ Roulette SR-80001 [S]		1961	25.00
SILK STOCKINGS			
❑ RCA Victor LOC-1016 [M]		1955	40.00
❑ RCA Victor LOC-1102 [M]		1965	20.00
—Reissue; regular cover			
❑ RCA Victor LSO-1102 [R]		1965	20.00
SIMPLY HEAVENLY			
❑ Columbia Masterworks OL 5240 [M]		1957	25.00
SING OUT, SWEET LAND!			
❑ Decca DL 4304 [M]		1963	20.00
❑ Decca DL 8023 [M]		1950	50.00
❑ Decca DL 74304 [R]		1963	20.00
SKYSCRAPER			
❑ Capitol SVAS 2422 [S]		1965	25.00
❑ Capitol VAS 2422 [M]		1965	20.00
SONDHEIM: A MUSICAL TRIBUTE			
❑ Warner Bros. 2WS 2705 [(2)]		1973	20.00
SONG OF NORWAY			
❑ Columbia CL 1328 [M]		1959	20.00
—1958 revival cast			
❑ Columbia CS 8135 [S]		1959	50.00
—1958 revival cast			
❑ Decca DL 8002 [M]		1949	30.00
❑ Decca DL 9019 [M]		1955	20.00
❑ Decca DL 79019 [R]		196?	12.00
❑ MCA 2032 [R]		1973	10.00
—Reissue of 79019; black label with rainbow			
THE SOUND OF MUSIC			
❑ Capitol DT 91034 [R]		1966	12.00
—Original London cast; Capitol Record Club exclusive			
❑ Columbia Masterworks KOS 2020 [S]		1959	12.00
—Gray label with "360 Sound Stereo" at bottom			
❑ Columbia Masterworks KOS 2020 [S]		1959	25.00
—Gray and black label with six "eye" logos			
❑ Columbia Masterworks KOL 5450 [M]		1959	20.00
—Gray and black label with six "eye" logos			
❑ Columbia Masterworks KOL 5450 [M]		1963	12.00
—Gray label with "Guaranteed High Fidelity" or "360 Sound Mono" on label			
❑ Columbia Masterworks S 32601 [S]		1973	10.00
—Reissue of 2020			
SOUTH PACIFIC			
❑ Columbia Masterworks OS 2040 [R]		196?	10.00
—Gray label with "360 Sound Stereo"			
❑ Columbia Masterworks ML 4180 [M]		1949	25.00
—Green or blue label; large anchor on front cover			
❑ Columbia Masterworks OL 4180 [M]		195?	12.00
—Gray and black label with six "eye" logos; glossy gatefold cover with Ezio Pinza and Mary Martin pictured			
❑ Columbia Masterworks OL 4180 [M]		195?	15.00
—Gray and black label with six "eye" logos; large anchor on front cover			
❑ Columbia Masterworks OL 4180 [M]		1963	10.00
—Gray label with "Guaranteed High Fidelity" or "360 Sound Mono"			
❑ Columbia Masterworks S 32604 [R]		1973	8.00
—Reissue of 2040			
ST. LOUIS WOMAN			
❑ Capitol L 355 [10]		1952	80.00
STOP THE WORLD-I WANT TO GET OFF			
❑ London AM 58001 [M]		1962	15.00
❑ London AMS 88001 [S]		1962	20.00
STREET SCENE			
❑ Columbia Masterworks ML 4139 [M]		1949	30.00
—Paper envelope jacket with its opening on top			
THE SUBJECT WAS ROSES			
❑ Columbia Masterworks DOL 308 [(3)M]		1964	20.00
❑ Columbia Masterworks DOS 708 [(3)S]		1964	30.00
SUBWAYS ARE FOR SLEEPING			
❑ Columbia Masterworks KOS 2130 [S]		1962	40.00
❑ Columbia Masterworks KOL 5730 [M]		1962	25.00
THE SURVIVAL OF ST. JOAN			
❑ Paramount PAS-9000 [(2)]		1971	25.00
SWEET CHARITY			
❑ Columbia Masterworks KOS 2900 [S]		1966	20.00
❑ Columbia Masterworks KOL 6500 [M]		1966	15.00
TAKE ME ALONG			
❑ RCA Victor LOC-1050 [M]		1959	15.00
❑ RCA Victor LSO-1050 [S]		1959	20.00
—Black label			
TAMALPAIS EXCHANGE			
❑ Atlantic SD 8263		1970	30.00
TAROT			
❑ United Artists UAS-5563		1970	20.00
TENDERLOIN			
❑ Capitol SWAO 1492 [S]		1960	40.00
—With program			
❑ Capitol WAO 1492 [M]		1960	25.00
—With program			
TEVYA AND HIS DAUGHTERS			
❑ Columbia Masterworks OL 5225 [M]		1957	30.00
TEXAS, LI'L DARLIN'			
❑ Decca DL 5188 [10]		1950	80.00
THIS IS THE ARMY			
❑ Decca DL 5108 [10]		1950	100.00
THIS WAS BURLESQUE			
❑ Roulette R-25185 [M]		1962	25.00
❑ Roulette SR-25186 [S]		1962	30.00
THREE TO MAKE MUSIC			
❑ RCA Victor LPM-2012 [M]		1958	25.00
❑ RCA Victor LSP-2012 [S]		1958	30.00
THREE WISHES FOR JAMIE			
❑ Capitol S 317 [M]		1952	120.00
THE THREEPENNY OPERA			
❑ MGM E-3121 [M]		1954	25.00
—Revival cast; yellow label			
❑ MGM E-3121 [M]		1959	15.00
—Revival cast; black label			
❑ MGM SE-3121 [R]		196?	12.00
—Revival cast; rechanneled stereo			
❑ Polydor 820260-1		198?	8.00
—Revival cast; reissue			
TIME CHANGES			
❑ ABC ABCS-681		1969	30.00
A TIME FOR SINGING			
❑ Warner Bros. W 1639 [M]		1966	40.00
❑ Warner Bros. WS 1639 [S]		1966	60.00
A TIME REMEMBERED			
❑ Mercury MG-20380 [M]		1957	25.00
❑ Mercury SR-60023 [S]		1957	40.00
—Music from the dramatic play			
TO BROADWAY WITH LOVE			
❑ Columbia Masterworks OS 2630 [S]		1964	50.00
❑ Columbia Masterworks OL 6030 [M]		1964	25.00
TOP BANANA			
❑ Capitol S 308 [M]		1952	100.00
TOVARICH			
❑ Capitol STAO 1940 [S]		1963	30.00
❑ Capitol TAO 1940 [M]		1963	20.00
A TREE GROWS IN BROOKLYN			
❑ Columbia Masterworks ML 4405 [M]		1951	30.00
—Blue label			
TWO BY TWO			
❑ Columbia Masterworks S 30338		1970	20.00
TWO ON THE AISLE			
❑ Decca DL 8040 [M]		1951	100.00
—Black label, gold print			
❑ Decca DL 8040 [M]		1955	60.00
—Black label, silver print			
❑ Decca DL 8040 [M]		196?	60.00
—Black label with color bars			
TWO'S COMPANY			
❑ RCA Victor LOC-1009 [M]		1952	100.00
THE UNSINKABLE MOLLY BROWN			
❑ Capitol SWAO 1509 [S]		1960	25.00
❑ Capitol WAO 1509 [M]		1960	20.00
UP IN CENTRAL PARK			
❑ Decca DL 8016 [M]		1950	40.00
—Black label, gold print			
❑ Decca DL 8016 [M]		1955	30.00
—Black label, silver print			
WAITING FOR GODOT			
❑ Columbia Masterworks O2L 238 [(2)M]		1956	30.00
WEST SIDE STORY			
❑ Columbia Masterworks OS 2001 [S]		1958	30.00
—Gray and black label with six "eye" logos			
❑ Columbia Masterworks OS 2001 [S]		1963	15.00
—Gray label with "360 Sound Stereo"			
❑ Columbia Masterworks OL 5230 [M]		1958	25.00
—Gray and black label with six "eye" logos			
❑ Columbia Masterworks OL 5230 [M]		1963	12.00
—Gray label with "Guaranteed High Fidelity" or "360 Sound Mono"			
❑ Columbia Masterworks S 32603 [S]		1973	10.00
—Reissue with new number			
WHAT MAKES SAMMY RUN?			
❑ Columbia Masterworks KSO 2440 [S]		1964	40.00
❑ Columbia Masterworks KOL 6040 [M]		1964	30.00
WILDCAT			
❑ RCA Victor LOC-1060 [M]		1961	25.00
❑ RCA Victor LSO-1060 [S]		1961	40.00
WISH YOU WERE HERE			
❑ RCA Victor LOC-1007 [M]		1952	60.00
WONDERFUL TOWN			
❑ Decca DL 9010 [M]		1953	30.00
—Black label, gold print			
YOU'RE A GOOD MAN, CHARLIE BROWN			
❑ MGM 1E-9 [M]		1967	20.00
❑ MGM S1E-9 [S]		1967	20.00
YOUR OWN THING			
❑ RCA Victor LOC-1148 [M]		1968	25.00
❑ RCA Victor LSO-1148 [S]		1968	20.00
ZORBA			
❑ Capitol SO-118		1969	20.00

Number	Title (A Side/B Side)	Yr	NM

SOUNDTRACKS

AARON SLICK FROM PUNKIN CRICK
- ❑ RCA Victor LPM-3006 [10] | 1952 | 150.00

ADVENTURES IN PARADISE
- ❑ ABC-Paramount ABC-329 [M] | 1960 | 30.00
- ❑ ABC-Paramount ABCS-329 [S] | 1960 | 40.00

ADVISE AND CONSENT
- ❑ RCA Victor LOC-1068 [M] | 1962 | 30.00
- ❑ RCA Victor LSO-1068 [S] | 1962 | 60.00

AN AFFAIR TO REMEMBER
- ❑ Columbia CL 1013 [M] | 1957 | 40.00

AFRICA ADDIO
- ❑ United Artists UAL-4141 [M] | 1966 | 20.00
- ❑ United Artists UAS-5141 [S] | 1966 | 25.00

THE AGONY AND THE ECSTASY
- ❑ Capitol MAS 2427 [M] | 1965 | 60.00
- ❑ Capitol SMAS 2427 [S] | 1965 | 80.00

AIRPORT
- ❑ Decca DL 79173 | 1970 | 25.00

ALAKAZAM THE GREAT
- ❑ Vee Jay LP-6000 [M] | 1961 | 80.00

THE ALAMO
- ❑ Columbia CL 1558 [M] | 1960 | 20.00
- ❑ Columbia CS 8358 [S] | 1960 | 25.00

ALBERT PECKINPAW'S REVENGE
- ❑ Sidewalk ST 5907 [S] | 1967 | 30.00
- ❑ Sidewalk T 5907 [M] | 1967 | 30.00

ALEXANDER
- ❑ Polydor 24-7001 | 1970 | 40.00

ALEXANDER THE GREAT
- ❑ Mercury MG-20148 [M] | 1956 | 250.00

ALFIE
- ❑ ABC Impulse! AS-9111 [S] | 1968 | 15.00
- ❑ Impulse! A-9111 [M] | 1966 | 30.00
- ❑ Impulse! AS-9111 [S] | 1966 | 30.00

ALIKI, MY LOVE
- ❑ Fontana MGF-27523 [M] | 1963 | 25.00
- ❑ Fontana SRF-67523 [S] | 1963 | 30.00

ALL NIGHT LONG
- ❑ Epic LA 16032 [M] | 1962 | 40.00
- ❑ Epic BA 17032 [S] | 1962 | 50.00

ALL THE LOVING COUPLES
- ❑ GNP Crescendo GNPS-2051 | 1969 | 40.00

ALL THE RIGHT NOISES
- ❑ Buddah BDS-5132 | 1971 | 30.00

AMERICA, AMERICA
- ❑ Warner Bros. W 1527 [M] | 1963 | 20.00
- ❑ Warner Bros. WS 1527 [S] | 1963 | 25.00

AN AMERICAN IN PARIS
- ❑ MGM E-93 [10] | 1951 | 40.00

THE AMOROUS ADVENTURES OF MOLL FLANDERS
- ❑ RCA Victor LOC-1113 [M] | 1965 | 40.00
- ❑ RCA Victor LSO-1113 [S] | 1965 | 80.00

ANASTASIA
- ❑ Decca DL 8460 [M] | 1956 | 30.00

ANATOMY OF A MURDER
- ❑ Columbia CL 1360 [M] | 1959 | 40.00
- ❑ Columbia CS 8166 [S] | 1959 | 50.00

AND GOD CREATED WOMAN
- ❑ Decca DL 8685 [M] | 1957 | 120.00

THE ANDROMEDA STRAIN
- ❑ Kapp KRS-5513 | 1971 | 40.00
  —Regular cover
- ❑ Kapp KRS-5513 | 1971 | 100.00
  —Hexagonal cover glued onto silver cardboard

ANGEL, ANGEL, DOWN WE GO
- ❑ Tower ST-5161 | 1970 | 25.00

ANGELS DIE HARD
- ❑ Uni 73091 | 1971 | 30.00

ANGELS FROM HELL
- ❑ Tower ST 5128 | 1968 | 60.00

THE ANONYMOUS VENETIAN
- ❑ United Artists UAS-5218 | 1971 | 30.00

ANOTHER TIME, ANOTHER PLACE
- ❑ Columbia CL 1180 [M] | 1958 | 40.00

ANY WEDNESDAY
- ❑ Warner Bros. W 1669 [M] | 1966 | 25.00
- ❑ Warner Bros. WS 1669 [S] | 1966 | 40.00

THE APARTMENT
- ❑ United Artists UAL-3105 [M] | 1960 | 30.00
- ❑ United Artists UAS-6105 [S] | 1960 | 40.00

APRIL LOVE
- ❑ Dot DLP-9000 [M] | 1957 | 20.00

ARMS AND THE GIRL
- ❑ Decca DL 5200 [10] | 1950 | 100.00

AROUND THE WORLD IN 80 DAYS
- ❑ Decca DL 9046 [M] | 1957 | 25.00
  —Black label, silver print
- ❑ Decca DL 79046 [S] | 1959 | 40.00
  —Maroon label, silver print; cover has "Full Stereo" banner
- ❑ Decca DL 79046 [S] | 196? | 12.00
  —Black label with color bars
- ❑ Decca SW-94840 [S] | 1972 | 15.00
  —Capitol Record Club edition
- ❑ MCA 2062 [S] | 1973 | 10.00
  —Reissue of 79046; black label with rainbow
- ❑ MCA 37086 [S] | 198? | 8.00
  —Reissue of 2062

AROUND THE WORLD UNDER THE SEA
- ❑ Monument MLP-8050 [M] | 1966 | 30.00
- ❑ Monument SLP-18050 [S] | 1966 | 50.00

ARRIVIDERCI, BABY!
- ❑ RCA Victor LOC-1132 [M] | 1966 | 20.00
- ❑ RCA Victor LSO-1132 [S] | 1966 | 40.00

AT LONG LAST LOVE
- ❑ RCA Victor ABL2-0967 [(2)] | 1975 | 20.00

ATHENA
- ❑ Mercury MG-25202 [10] | 1954 | 150.00

BABES IN TOYLAND
- ❑ Buena Vista BV-4022 [M] | 1961 | 30.00
- ❑ Buena Vista STER-4022 [S] | 1961 | 40.00

BABY DOLL
- ❑ Columbia CL 958 [M] | 195? | 50.00
  —No ads for LPs on back cover
- ❑ Columbia CL 958 [M] | 1956 | 60.00
  —Ads for other Columbia LPs on back cover

BABY FACE NELSON
- ❑ Jubilee JLP-2021 [M] | 1957 | 120.00

BABY, THE RAIN MUST FALL
- ❑ Ava A-53 [M] | 1965 | 40.00
- ❑ Ava AS-53 [S] | 1965 | 50.00
- ❑ Mainstream S-6056 [S] | 1965 | 40.00
  —Reissue of Ava AS-53
- ❑ Mainstream 56056 [M] | 1965 | 30.00
  —Reissue of Ava A-53

BACK STREET
- ❑ Decca DL 9097 [M] | 1961 | 40.00
- ❑ Decca DL 79097 [S] | 1961 | 80.00

THE BAD SEED
- ❑ RCA Victor LPM-1395 [M] | 1956 | 300.00

BAND OF ANGELS
- ❑ RCA Victor LPM-1557 [M] | 1957 | 100.00

THE BAND WAGON
- ❑ MGM E-3051 [M] | 1953 | 30.00
  —Yellow label
- ❑ MGM E-3051 [M] | 1960 | 20.00
  —Black label

BARABBAS
- ❑ Colpix CP 510 [M] | 1962 | 40.00
- ❑ Colpix SCP 510 [S] | 1962 | 80.00

BARBARELLA
- ❑ Dyno Voice DV-31908 | 1968 | 50.00

THE BARBARIAN AND THE GEISHA
- ❑ 20th Fox FOX-3004 [M] | 1958 | 250.00

BAREFOOT ADVENTURE
- ❑ Pacific Jazz PJ-35 [M] | 1961 | 40.00
- ❑ Pacific Jazz ST-35 [S] | 1961 | 60.00

BAREFOOT IN THE PARK
- ❑ Dot DLP-3803 [M] | 1967 | 20.00
- ❑ Dot DLP-25803 [S] | 1967 | 30.00

THE BARKLEYS OF BROADWAY
- ❑ MGM E-503 [10] | 1949 | 80.00

BATTLE OF THE BULGE
- ❑ Warner Bros. W 1617 [M] | 1965 | 40.00
- ❑ Warner Bros. WS 1617 [S] | 1965 | 40.00

BEACH BLANKET BINGO
- ❑ Capitol ST 2323 [S] | 1965 | 60.00
- ❑ Capitol T 2323 [M] | 1965 | 30.00

BEAU JAMES
- ❑ Imperial LP-9041 [M] | 1957 | 40.00

BECKET
- ❑ Decca DL 9117 [M] | 1964 | 30.00
- ❑ Decca DL 79117 [S] | 1964 | 50.00

BEDAZZLED
- ❑ London MS-82009 | 1967 | 80.00

BEHOLD A PALE HORSE
- ❑ Colpix CP 519 [M] | 1964 | 50.00
- ❑ Colpix SCP 519 [S] | 1964 | 70.00

BELL, BOOK AND CANDLE
- ❑ Colpix CP 502 [M] | 1959 | 60.00

BELLS ARE RINGING
- ❑ Capitol SW 1435 [S] | 1960 | 30.00
- ❑ Capitol W 1435 [M] | 1960 | 25.00

BEN-HUR
- ❑ MGM 1E1 [M] | 1959 | 40.00
  —Boxed edition with hardcover book
- ❑ MGM 1E1 [M] | 196? | 12.00
  —Gatefold cover, no book
- ❑ MGM S-1E1 [S] | 1959 | 50.00
  —Boxed edition with hardcover book
- ❑ MGM S-1E1 [S] | 196? | 10.00
  —Gatefold cover, no book; blue and gold label
- ❑ MGM S-1E1 [S] | 196? | 15.00
  —Gatefold cover, no book; black label

BENEATH THE PLANET OF THE APES
- ❑ Amos AAS-8001 | 1970 | 40.00

BEYOND THE GREAT WALL
- ❑ Capitol T 10401 [M] | 1965 | 50.00

BEYOND THE VALLEY OF THE DOLLS
- ❑ 20th Century Fox TFS-4211 | 1970 | 200.00

THE BIBLE
- ❑ 20th Century Fox TF-3184 [M] | 1966 | 20.00
- ❑ 20th Century Fox TFS-4184 [S] | 1966 | 30.00

THE BIG COUNTRY
- ❑ United Artists UAL-4004 [M] | 1958 | 25.00
- ❑ United Artists UAS-5004 [S] | 1958 | 50.00

THE BIG GUNDOWN
- ❑ United Artists UAS-5190 | 1967 | 40.00

THE BIGGEST BUNDLE OF THEM ALL
- ❑ MGM E-4446 [M] | 1967 | 20.00
- ❑ MGM SE-4446 [S] | 1967 | 25.00

BILLIE
- ❑ United Artists UAL-4131 [M] | 1965 | 20.00
- ❑ United Artists UAS-5131 [S] | 1965 | 25.00

THE BILLION DOLLAR BRAIN
- ❑ United Artists UAL-4174 [M] | 1967 | 15.00
- ❑ United Artists UAS-5174 [S] | 1967 | 20.00

BILLY JACK
- ❑ Warner Bros. BJS-1001 | 1973 | 15.00
  —Reissue; "Burbank" palm trees label
- ❑ Warner Bros. WS 1926 | 1971 | 25.00
  —Original; green "WB" label

THE BIRD WITH THE CRYSTAL PLUMAGE
- ❑ Capitol ST-642 | 1970 | 100.00

BLACK GIRL
- ❑ Fantasy F-9420 | 1973 | 70.00

THE BLACK ORCHID
- ❑ Dot DLP-3178 [M] | 1959 | 40.00
- ❑ Dot SLP-25178 [S] | 1959 | 50.00

BLACK ORPHEUS
- ❑ Epic LN 3672 [M] | 1959 | 40.00
- ❑ Fontana MGF-27520 [M] | 1963 | 20.00
- ❑ Fontana SRF-67520 [R] | 1963 | 15.00

BLACKBIRDS OF 1928
- ❑ Columbia Masterworks OL 6770 [M] | 1968 | 15.00
- ❑ Revue 1 [M] | 196? | 30.00
- ❑ Sutton SSU-270 [R] | 196? | 12.00
- ❑ Sutton SU-270 [M] | 196? | 20.00

BLACULA
- ❑ RCA Victor LSP-4806 | 1972 | 60.00

BLESS THE BEASTS AND CHILDREN
- ❑ A&M SP-4322 | 1971 | 25.00

BLOOD AND SAND
- ❑ Decca DL 5380 [10] | 1952 | 80.00

BLOOMER GIRL
- ❑ Decca DL 8015 [M] | 1950 | 30.00

BLOW-UP
- ❑ MGM E-4447 [M] | 1967 | 40.00
- ❑ MGM SE-4447 [S] | 1967 | 50.00

THE BLUE MAX
- ❑ Mainstream S-6081 [S] | 1966 | 80.00
- ❑ Mainstream 56081 [M] | 1966 | 40.00

BOBO
- ❑ Warner Bros. W 1711 [M] | 1967 | 20.00
- ❑ Warner Bros. WS 1711 [S] | 1967 | 20.00

BOEING, BOEING
- ❑ RCA Victor LOC-1121 [M] | 1965 | 25.00
- ❑ RCA Victor LSO-1121 [S] | 1965 | 30.00

BONNIE AND CLYDE
- ❑ Warner Bros. W 1742 [M] | 1968 | 40.00
- ❑ Warner Bros. WS 1742 [S] | 1968 | 25.00
  —Originals have green labels with "W7" logo in a square at top
- ❑ Warner Bros. ST-91414 [S] | 1968 | 30.00
  —Capitol Record Club issue

Except when noted otherwise, VG = 25% of NM, and VG+ = 50% of NM. (Example: VG = $2.00, VG+ = $4.00 and NM = $8.00.)

Number	Title (A Side/B Side)	Yr	NM
BORA, BORA			
❑ American Int'l. STA-1029		1970	30.00
BORN FREE			
❑ MGM E-4368 [M]		1966	15.00
❑ MGM SE-4368 [S]		1966	20.00
BORSALINO			
❑ Paramount PAS-5019		1970	30.00
THE BOY FRIEND			
❑ MGM 1SE-32		1971	20.00
A BOY NAMED CHARLIE BROWN			
❑ Columbia Masterworks OS 3500		1970	20.00
BOY ON A DOLPHIN			
❑ Decca DL 8580 [M]		1957	60.00
—Black label with silver print, or pink label with black print (promo)			
❑ Decca DL 8580 [M]		196?	20.00
—Black label with color bars			
THE BOYS FROM SYRACUSE			
❑ Capitol STAO 1933 [S]		1963	30.00
❑ Capitol TAO 1933 [M]		1963	25.00
THE BRAVE ONE			
❑ Decca DL 8344 [M]		1956	40.00
BROTHER ON THE RUN			
❑ Perception PLP-45		1973	40.00
BUCCANEER			
❑ Columbia CL 1278 [M]		1958	25.00
❑ Columbia CS 8096 [S]		1958	40.00
BULLITT			
❑ Warner Bros. WS 1777		1968	60.00
BUNDLE OF JOY			
❑ RCA Victor LPM-1399 [M]		1956	40.00
BUNNY LAKE IS MISSING			
❑ RCA Victor LOC-1115 [M]		1965	40.00
❑ RCA Victor LSO-1115 [S]		1965	70.00
BUNNY O'HARE			
❑ American Int'l. STA-1041		1971	20.00
BUONA SERA, MRS. CAMPBELL			
❑ United Artists UAS-5192		1969	30.00
THE BURGLARS			
❑ Bell 1105		1971	40.00
BUTTERFIELD-8			
❑ MGM E-3952 [M]		1960	20.00
❑ MGM SE-3952 [S]		1960	25.00
BYE BYE BIRDIE			
❑ RCA Victor LOC-1081 [M]		196?	15.00
—Third cover with Ann-Margret on front and with credits underneath			
❑ RCA Victor LOC-1081 [M]		196?	20.00
—Second cover with Ann-Margret on front, but with no credits underneath			
❑ RCA Victor LOC-1081 [M]		1963	25.00
—First cover without Ann-Margret on the front			
❑ RCA Victor LSO-1081 [S]		196?	20.00
—Third cover with Ann-Margret on front and with credits underneath			
❑ RCA Victor LSO-1081 [S]		196?	25.00
—Second cover with Ann-Margret on front, but with no credits underneath			
❑ RCA Victor LSO-1081 [S]		1963	30.00
—First cover without Ann-Margret on the front			
C'MON, LET'S LIVE A LITTLE			
❑ Liberty LRP-3430 [M]		1966	25.00
❑ Liberty LST-7430 [S]		1966	30.00
CABARET			
❑ ABC ABCD-752		1972	20.00
❑ MCA 37125		198?	8.00
—Reissue; blue label with rainbow			
THE CAINE MUTINY			
❑ RCA Victor LOC-1013 [M]		1993	200.00
—Very limited edition (100 copies) reproduction of the original LP			
❑ RCA Victor LOC-1013 [M]		1954	10000.
—VG value 4000; VG+ value 7000			
CALL ME MADAM			
❑ Decca DL 5465 [10]		1953	50.00
CALL ME MISTER			
❑ Decca DLP 7005 [10]		1950	100.00
CAMELOT			
❑ Warner Bros. B 1712 [M]		1967	25.00
❑ Warner Bros. BS 1712 [S]		1967	20.00
—Gold label original			
❑ Warner Bros. BS 1712 [S]		1968	15.00
—Green label, "W7" box logo at top			
❑ Warner Bros. BS 1712 [S]		1970	12.00
—Green label, "WB" shield logo at top			
❑ Warner Bros. BS 1712 [S]		1973	10.00
—"Burbank" palm trees label			
❑ Warner Bros. BSK 3102 [S]		1977	8.00
—Reissue with new number			

Soundtrack, *Becket,* Decca DL 9117, 1964, mono, **$30.**

Number	Title (A Side/B Side)	Yr	NM
❑ Warner Bros. SW-91347		1968	25.00
—Capitol Record Club edition			
CAN-CAN			
❑ Capitol SW 1301 [S]		1960	30.00
❑ Capitol W 1301 [M]		1960	20.00
CANDY			
❑ ABC ABCS-OC-9		1968	30.00
THE CARDINAL			
❑ RCA Victor LOC-1084 [M]		1963	40.00
❑ RCA Victor LSO-1084 [S]		1963	60.00
THE CARETAKERS			
❑ Ava A-31 [M]		1963	20.00
❑ Ava AS-31 [S]		1963	25.00
CAROUSEL			
❑ Capitol SW 694 [S]		1962	20.00
—Black colorband label			
❑ Capitol SW 694 [S]		1969	15.00
—Lime green label			
❑ Capitol SW 694 [S]		1973	12.00
—Orange label			
❑ Capitol W 694 [M]		1956	30.00
—Gray label			
❑ Capitol W 694 [M]		1959	20.00
—Black colorband label, logo at left			
❑ Capitol W 694 [M]		1962	15.00
—Black colorband label, logo at top			
THE CARPETBAGGERS			
❑ Ava A-45 [M]		1964	30.00
❑ Ava AS-45 [S]		1964	40.00
CARRY IT ON			
❑ Vanguard VSD-79313		1971	25.00
CASINO ROYALE			
❑ Colgems COMO-5005 [M]		1967	30.00
❑ Colgems COSO-5005 [S]		1967	100.00
❑ Colgems COSO-5005-45 [(4)]		199?	40.00
—Classic Records reissue on four 12-inch 45 rpm records			
A CERTAIN SMILE			
❑ Columbia CL 1194 [M]		1958	40.00
❑ Columbia CS 8068 [S]		1958	80.00

Number	Title (A Side/B Side)	Yr	NM
THE CHAIRMAN			
❑ Tetragrammaton T-5007		1969	30.00
CHARLOTTE'S WEB			
❑ Paramount PAS-1008		1973	30.00
THE CHASE			
❑ Columbia Masterworks OS 2960 [S]		1966	60.00
❑ Columbia Masterworks OL 6560 [M]		1966	40.00
CHINATOWN			
❑ ABC ABDP-848		1974	40.00
CHITTY CHITTY BANG BANG			
❑ United Artists UAS-5188		1968	25.00
THE CHRISTMAS THAT ALMOST WASN'T			
❑ RCA Camden CAL-1086 [M]		1966	25.00
❑ RCA Camden CAS-1086 [S]		1966	40.00
CINDERELLA			
❑ Disneyland DQ-1207 [M]		1959	40.00
—Second issue, white back cover with ads for nine other LPs			
❑ Disneyland DQ-1207 [M]		1963	30.00
—Third issue, pink back cover			
❑ Disneyland WDL-4007 [M]		1957	200.00
—Original issue, gatefold cover			
CINDERFELLA			
❑ Dot DLP-8001 [M]		1960	60.00
❑ Dot SLP-38001 [S]		1960	100.00
—Gatefold cover with many extras including game board, spinner, booklet, music stand.			
CLEOPATRA			
❑ 20th Century Fox FXG-5008 [M]		1963	30.00
❑ 20th Century Fox SXG-5008 [S]		1963	40.00
CLEOPATRA JONES			
❑ Warner Bros. BS 2719		1973	30.00
THE CLOWNS			
❑ Columbia S 30772		1971	40.00
COFFY			
❑ Polydor PD-5048		1973	100.00
THE COLLECTOR			
❑ Mainstream S-6053 [S]		1965	50.00
❑ Mainstream 56053 [M]		1965	30.00

SOUNDTRACKS

Number	Title (A Side/B Side)	Yr	NM
	COLLEGE CONFIDENTIAL		
❑ Chancellor CHL-5016 [M]		1960	40.00
❑ Chancellor CHLS-5016 [S]		1960	50.00
	COMANCHE		
❑ Coral CRL 57046 [M]		1956	400.00
	COME BACK CHARLESTON BLUE		
❑ Atco SD 7010		1972	30.00
	COME BLOW YOUR HORN		
❑ Reprise R-6071 [M]		1963	30.00
❑ Reprise R9-6071 [S]		1963	50.00
	COMETOGETHER		
❑ Apple SW-3377		1971	20.00
	THE CONNECTION		
❑ Charlie Parker PLP-806 [M]		1962	30.00
❑ Charlie Parker PLP-806S [S]		1962	40.00
❑ Felsted 2512 [S]		1960	300.00
❑ Felsted 7512 [M]		1960	200.00
	COOLEY HIGH		
❑ Motown M7-840 R2 [(2)]		1975	20.00
	THE CORRUPT ONES		
❑ United Artists UAL-4158 [M]		1967	40.00
❑ United Artists UAS-5158 [S]		1967	40.00
	COTTON COMES TO HARLEM		
❑ United Artists UAS-5211		1970	30.00
	THE COURT JESTER		
❑ Decca DL 8212 [M]		1956	70.00
—Black label, silver print, or pink label, black print promo copy			
❑ Decca DL 8212 [M]		196?	30.00
—Black label with color bars			
	THE COWBOY		
❑ Decca DL 8684 [M]		1958	60.00
—Black label, silver print, or pink label, black print promo copy			
❑ Decca DL 8684 [M]		196?	20.00
—Black label with color bars			
	CRIME IN THE STREETS		
❑ Decca DL 8376 [M]		1956	60.00
—Black label, silver print, or pink label, black print promo copy			
❑ Decca DL 8376 [S]		196?	30.00
—Black label with color bars			
	THE CROSS AND THE SWITCHBLADE		
❑ Light LS-5550		1970	30.00
	CUSTER OF THE WEST		
❑ ABC ABC-OC-5 [M]		1968	80.00
❑ ABC ABCS-OC-5 [S]		1968	100.00
	CYCLE SAVAGES		
❑ American Int'l. STA-1033		1970	30.00
	CYRANO DE BERGERAC		
❑ Capitol S 283 [M]		1951	30.00
—Originals have red labels with Capitol logo at top			
	DAKTARI		
❑ Leo the Lion CH-1043 [M]		1967	20.00
❑ MGM CH-1043 [M]		1967	20.00
	DAMN THE DEFIANT!		
❑ Colpix CP 511 [M]		1962	30.00
❑ Colpix SCP 511 [S]		1962	60.00
	DAMN YANKEES		
❑ RCA Victor LOC-1047 [M]		1958	40.00
—Original pressing with "Long Play" on label			
	THE DAMNED		
❑ Warner Bros. WS 1829		1969	30.00
	THE DARK OF THE SUN		
❑ MGM SE-4544		1968	40.00
	DARLING LILI		
❑ RCA Victor LSPX-1000		1969	20.00
	DAY OF ANGER		
❑ RCA Victor LSO-1165		1969	20.00
	THE DAY OF THE DOLPHIN		
❑ Avco AV-11014		1973	25.00
	THE DAY THE FISH CAME OUT		
❑ 20th Century Fox TF-3194 [M]		1967	30.00
❑ 20th Century Fox TFS-4194 [S]		1967	40.00
	DAYDREAMER		
❑ Columbia Masterworks OS 2940 [S]		1966	40.00
❑ Columbia Masterworks OL 6540 [M]		1966	30.00
	DE SADE		
❑ Tower ST-5170		1969	30.00
	DEADFALL		
❑ 20th Century Fox S-4203		1968	60.00
	THE DEADLY AFFAIR		
❑ Verve V-8679 [M]		1966	25.00
❑ Verve V6-8679 [S]		1966	30.00
	DEAR JOHN		
❑ Dunhill OCD-55001 [M]		1966	20.00
❑ Dunhill OCDS-55001 [S]		1966	25.00
	DEEP IN MY HEART		
❑ MGM E-3153 [M]		1955	40.00
❑ MGM E-3153 [M]		1955	50.00
	DESIRE UNDER THE ELMS		
❑ Dot DLP-3095 [M]		1958	100.00
	DESTINATION MOON		
❑ Columbia CL 6151 [10]		1950	120.00
❑ Omega OL-3 [M]		1959	40.00
❑ Omega OSL-3 [S]		196?	80.00
	THE DEVIL AT 4 O'CLOCK		
❑ Colpix CP 509 [M]		1962	40.00
❑ Colpix SCP 509 [S]		1962	70.00
	THE DEVIL IN MISS JONES		
❑ Janus JLS-3059		1973	25.00
	THE DEVIL'S BRIGADE		
❑ United Artists UAS-6654		1968	20.00
	DIAMOND HEAD		
❑ Colpix CP-440 [M]		1963	30.00
❑ Colpix SCP 440 [S]		1963	60.00
	DIAMONDS ARE FOREVER		
❑ United Artists UA-LA301-G		1974	12.00
—Reissue of 5520			
❑ United Artists UAS-5520		1971	20.00
	THE DIARY OF ANNE FRANK		
❑ 20th Fox FOX-3012 [M]		1959	50.00
❑ 20th Fox SFX-3012 [S]		1959	80.00
	DIRTY GAME		
❑ Laurie LLP-2034 [M]		1966	25.00
❑ Laurie SLP-2034 [S]		1966	30.00
	DIVORCE AMERICAN STYLE		
❑ United Artists UAL-4163 [M]		1967	20.00
❑ United Artists UAS-5163 [S]		1967	20.00
	DIVORCE ITALIAN STYLE		
❑ United Artists UAL-4106 [M]		1962	40.00
❑ United Artists UAS-5106 [S]		1962	50.00
	DOCTOR DOLITTLE		
❑ 20th Century Fox TCF-5101 [M]		1967	20.00
❑ 20th Century Fox TCS-5101 [S]		1967	20.00
	DOCTOR GOLDFOOT AND THE GIRL BOMBS		
❑ Tower DT 5053 [R]		1966	25.00
❑ Tower T 5053 [M]		1966	20.00
	DOCTOR ZHIVAGO		
❑ MCA 39042		198?	8.00
—Reissue			
❑ MGM 1E-6 [M]		1965	15.00
❑ MGM S1E-6 ST [S]		1965	20.00
❑ MGM SWAE-90620 [S]		1965	20.00
—Capitol Record Club issue			
	A DOG OF FLANDERS		
❑ 20th Fox FOX-3026 [M]		1959	80.00
❑ 20th Fox SFX-3026 [S]		1959	300.00
	$ (DOLLARS)		
❑ Reprise MS 2051		1971	20.00
	DON'T MAKE WAVES		
❑ MGM E-4483 [M]		1967	30.00
❑ MGM SE-4483 [S]		1967	30.00
	DR. NO		
❑ Liberty LT-50275		1981	8.00
—Reissue of United Artists 275			
❑ United Artists UA-LA275-G		1974	10.00
—Reissue of 5108			
❑ United Artists UAL-4108 [M]		1963	40.00
❑ United Artists UAS-5108 [S]		1963	50.00
	DR. PHIBES		
❑ American Int'l. A-1040		1971	60.00
	DRANGO		
❑ Liberty LRP-3036 [M]		1957	150.00
	A DREAM OF KINGS		
❑ National General NG-1000		1969	30.00
	DUCK, YOU SUCKER		
❑ United Artists UAS-5221		1972	40.00
	DUEL AT DIABLO		
❑ United Artists UAL-4139 [M]		1966	25.00
❑ United Artists UAS-5139 [S]		1966	30.00
	DUMBO		
❑ Disneyland 1204 [M]		197?	10.00
—Fourth issue, yellow rainbow label, flying Dumbo on back cover			
❑ Disneyland DQ-1204 [M]		1959	25.00
—Second issue, back cover has ads for nine other LPs			
❑ Disneyland DQ-1204 [M]		1963	15.00
—Third issue, four black & white photos on back cover			
❑ Disneyland WDL-4013 [M]		1957	200.00
—Original issue, gatefold cover			
❑ Disneyland ST-4904 [M]		1963	200.00
—Special issue with pop-up figures in gatefold			
	THE DUNWICH HORROR		
❑ American Int'l. STA-1028		1970	40.00
	EAST SIDE, WEST SIDE		
❑ Columbia CL 2123 [M]		1963	30.00
❑ Columbia CS 8923 [S]		1963	40.00
	EASTER PARADE		
❑ MGM E-502 [10]		1950	80.00
	EASY RIDER		
❑ ABC Dunhill DSX-50063		1969	25.00
	ECCO		
❑ Warner Bros. W 1600 [M]		1965	25.00
❑ Warner Bros. WS 1600 [S]		1965	30.00
	THE EDDY DUCHIN STORY		
❑ Decca DL 8289 [M]		1956	40.00
—Original cover with Tyrone Power and Kim Novak at a piano			
❑ Decca DL 8289 [M]		1959	20.00
—Reissue cover with Tyrone Power and Kim Novak kissing			
❑ Decca DL 9121 [M]		196?	12.00
—Reissue of 8289			
❑ Decca DL 78289 [S]		1959	25.00
—Maroon label, silver print, "Full Stereo" on front cover			
❑ Decca DL 79121 [S]		196?	15.00
—Reissue of 78289			
❑ MCA 2041		1973	10.00
—Reissue of 79121; black label with rainbow			
❑ MCA 37088		198?	8.00
—Reissue of 2041			
	THE EDUCATION OF SONNY CARSON		
❑ Paramount PAS-1045		1974	20.00
	THE EGYPTIAN		
❑ Decca DL 9014 [M]		1954	60.00
❑ Decca DL 79014 [R]		196?	20.00
	EL CID		
❑ MGM E-3977 [M]		1962	40.00
❑ MGM SE-3977 [S]		1962	50.00
	EL DORADO		
❑ Epic FLM-13114 [M]		1967	50.00
❑ Epic LFS-15114 [S]		1967	70.00
	EL TOPO		
❑ Apple SWAO-3388		1972	40.00
	ELECTRA GLIDE IN BLUE		
❑ United Artists UA-LA062-H [(2)]		1973	40.00
—With booklet and two posters			
	ELEPHANT STEPS		
❑ Columbia Masterwords M2X 33044 [(2)]		1975	20.00
	ELMER GANTRY		
❑ United Artists UAL-4069 [M]		1960	40.00
❑ United Artists UAS-5069 [S]		1960	50.00
	ENTER THE DRAGON		
❑ Warner Bros. BS 2727		1973	60.00
	EVERYTHING I HAVE IS YOURS		
❑ MGM E-187 [10]		1953	40.00
	EXODUS		
❑ RCA Victor LOC-1058 [M]		1960	20.00
—"Long Play" on label			
❑ RCA Victor LSO-1058 [S]		1960	25.00
—"Living Stereo" on label			
	THE EXORCIST		
❑ Warner Bros. W 2774		1974	30.00
	A FACE IN THE CROWD		
❑ Capitol W 872 [M]		1957	50.00
	THE FALL OF THE ROMAN EMPIRE		
❑ Columbia Masterworks OS 2460 [S]		1964	60.00
❑ Columbia Masterworks OL 6060 [M]		1964	40.00
	THE FAMILY WAY		
❑ London M 76007 [M]		1967	100.00
—No promo sticker on front cover (deduct 20 percent for promo)			
❑ London ST 82007 [S]		1967	120.00
—No promo sticker on front cover (deduct 20 percent for promo)			
	FANNY		
❑ Warner Bros. W 1416 [M]		1961	25.00
❑ Warner Bros. WS 1416 [S]		1961	30.00
	FANTASIA		
❑ Buena Vista 101 [(2)S]		1982	20.00
—Stereo reissue, two records, no booklet			
❑ Buena Vista STER-101 [(3)S]		1961	40.00
—First stereo issue, black and yellow rainbow labels, includes 24-page booklet			
❑ Buena Vista WDX-101 [(3)M]		1961	30.00
—Second issue, blue labels, includes 24-page booklet			
❑ Disneyland WDX-101 [(3)]		1957	60.00
—Original issue, maroon/red labels, includes 24-page booklet			
	FANTASIA: NIGHT ON BALD MOUNTAIN; PASTORAL SYMPHONY; AVE MARIA		
❑ Disneyland STER-4101C [S]		1958	30.00
❑ Disneyland WDL-4101C [M]		1958	20.00
	FANTASIA: RITE OF SPRING; TOCCATA AND FUGUE		
❑ Disneyland STER-4101A [S]		1959	30.00
❑ Disneyland WDL-4101A [M]		1958	20.00

Except when noted otherwise, VG = 25% of NM, and VG+ = 50% of NM. (Example: VG = $2.00, VG+ = $4.00 and NM = $8.00.)

Number	Title (A Side/B Side)	Yr	NM
FANTASIA: THE NUTCRACKER SUITE; DANCE OF THE HOURS			
❑ Disneyland STER-4101B [S]		1959	30.00
❑ Disneyland WDL-4101B [M]		1958	20.00
THE FANTASTIC PLASTIC MACHINE			
❑ Epic BN 26469		1969	25.00
FAR FROM THE MADDING CROWD			
❑ MGM 1E-11 [M]		1967	15.00
❑ MGM S1E-11 [S]		1967	25.00
A FAREWELL TO ARMS			
❑ Capitol W 918 [M]		1957	50.00
THE FASTEST GUITAR ALIVE			
❑ MGM SE-4475		1968	30.00
FATHOM			
❑ 20th Century Fox TFM-4195 [M]		1967	40.00
❑ 20th Century Fox TFS-4195 [S]		1967	50.00
FELLINI SATYRICON			
❑ United Artists UAS-5208		1969	30.00
FELLINI'S ROMA			
❑ United Artists UA-LA052-F		1972	30.00
THE FEMALE PRISONER			
❑ Columbia Masterworks OS 3320		1969	30.00
FIDDLER ON THE ROOF			
❑ United Artists UAS-10900 [(2)]		1971	20.00
—With booklet			
55 DAYS AT PEKING			
❑ Columbia CL 2028 [M]		1963	40.00
❑ Columbia CS 8828 [S]		1963	70.00
THE FIGHTER			
❑ Decca DL 5414 [10]		1952	80.00
FINIAN'S RAINBOW			
❑ Warner Bros. BS 2550		1968	20.00
FIRE DOWN BELOW			
❑ Decca DL 8597 [M]		1957	70.00
A FISTFUL OF DOLLARS			
❑ RCA Victor LOC-1135 [M]		1967	20.00
❑ RCA Victor LSO-1135 [S]		1967	30.00
—Black label, dog on top			
❑ RCA Victor LSO-1135 [S]		1969	12.00
—Orange label, tan label, or black label with dog at 1 o'clock			
FITZWILLY			
❑ United Artists UAL-4173 [M]		1967	20.00
❑ United Artists UAS-5173 [S]		1967	25.00
FIVE EASY PIECES			
❑ Epic KE 30456		1971	25.00
THE FIVE PENNIES			
❑ Dot DLP-9500 [M]		1959	25.00
❑ Dot DLP-29500 [S]		1959	50.00
A FLEA IN HER EAR			
❑ 20th Century Fox TFS-4200		1968	30.00
FLOWER DRUM SONG			
❑ Decca DL 9098 [M]		1961	20.00
❑ Decca DL 79098 [S]		1961	25.00
❑ MCA 2069		1973	10.00
—Reissue; black label with rainbow			
FOLIES BERGERE			
❑ Decca DL 8571 [M]		1958	25.00
FOLLOW ME			
❑ Uni 73056		1969	30.00
FOR A FEW DOLLARS MORE			
❑ United Artists UAL-3608 [M]		1967	20.00
❑ United Artists UAS-6608 [S]		1967	25.00
FOR LOVE OF IVY			
❑ ABC SOC-7		1968	25.00
FOR THE FIRST TIME			
❑ RCA Victor Red Seal LM-2338 [M]		1959	15.00
❑ RCA Victor Red Seal LSC-2338 [S]		1959	20.00
—"Shaded dog" and smaller "RCA Victor" lettering			
❑ RCA Victor Red Seal LSC-2338 [S]		1965	15.00
—"White dog" and larger "RCA Victor" lettering			
❑ RCA Victor Red Seal LSC-2338 [S]		1969	12.00
—Red label, no dog			
40 POUNDS OF TROUBLE			
❑ Mercury MG-20784 [M]		1963	30.00
❑ Mercury SR-60784 [S]		1963	40.00
THE FOUR HORSEMEN OF THE APOCALYPSE			
❑ MGM E-3993 [M]		1962	20.00
❑ MGM SE-3993 [S]		1962	25.00
FOUR IN THE MORNING			
❑ Roulette OS 805 [M]		1966	40.00
❑ Roulette OSS 805 [S]		1966	50.00
THE FOX			
❑ Warner Bros. W 1738 [M]		1968	40.00
❑ Warner Bros. WS 1738 [S]		1968	25.00

Soundtrack, *Can-Can,* Capitol SW 1301, 1960, stereo, Capitol logo at left on label, **$30.**

Number	Title (A Side/B Side)	Yr	NM
FOXY BROWN			
❑ Motown M7-811		1974	20.00
FRANCIS OF ASSISI			
❑ 20th Fox FOX-3053 [M]		1961	200.00
❑ 20th Fox SFX-3053 [S]		1961	250.00
THE FRENCH LINE			
❑ Mercury MG-25182 [10]		1954	80.00
FRIENDLY PERSUASION			
❑ RKO Unique LP-110 [M]		1956	75.00
FRITZ THE CAT			
❑ Fantasy F-9406		1972	30.00
FROM RUSSIA WITH LOVE			
❑ United Artists UAL-4114 [M]		1964	20.00
❑ United Artists UAS-5114 [S]		1964	25.00
THE FUGITIVE KIND			
❑ United Artists UAL-4065 [M]		1959	50.00
❑ United Artists UAS-5065 [S]		1959	70.00
FUNERAL IN BERLIN			
❑ RCA Victor LOC-1136 [M]		1966	30.00
❑ RCA Victor LSO-1136 [S]		1966	50.00
FUNNY GIRL			
❑ Columbia Masterworks BOS 3220		1968	12.00
—Gray "360 Sound" label; record is removed from inside the gatefold; liner notes on a tan background			
❑ Columbia Masterworks BOS 3220		1968	15.00
—Gray "360 Sound" label; record is removed from inside the gatefold; liner notes on a black background			
❑ Columbia Masterworks BOS 3220		1970	10.00
—Olive label with "Columbia" encircling the edge			
❑ Columbia Masterworks SQ 30992 [Q]		1971	40.00
A FUNNY THING HAPPENED ON THE WAY TO THE FORUM			
❑ United Artists UA-LA284-G		1974	10.00
—Reissue of 5144			
❑ United Artists UAL-4144 [M]		1966	12.00
❑ United Artists UAS-5144 [S]		1966	15.00
GAILY, GAILY			
❑ United Artists UAS 5202		1969	25.00

Number	Title (A Side/B Side)	Yr	NM
THE GAME IS OVER			
❑ Atco 33-205 [M]		1967	20.00
❑ Atco SD 33-205 [S]		1967	25.00
THE GAMES			
❑ Viking LPS-105		1970	200.00
GAY PURR-EE			
❑ Warner Bros. B 1479 [M]		1963	20.00
❑ Warner Bros. BS 1479 [S]		1963	30.00
GEISHA BOY			
❑ Jubilee JGS-1096 [S]		1959	80.00
❑ Jubilee JLP-1096 [M]		1958	50.00
THE GENE KRUPA STORY			
❑ Verve MGVS-6105 [S]		1959	100.00
—Original issue			
❑ Verve MGV-15010 [M]		1959	50.00
❑ Verve V-15010 [M]		1961	20.00
❑ Verve V6-15010 [S]		1963	80.00
—Early reissue			
GENGHIS KHAN			
❑ Liberty LRP-3412 [M]		1965	40.00
❑ Liberty LST-7412 [S]		1965	60.00
THE GENTLE RAIN			
❑ Mercury MG-21016 [M]		1966	20.00
❑ Mercury SR-61016 [S]		1966	25.00
GENTLEMEN MARRY BRUNETTES			
❑ Coral CRL 57013 [M]		1955	70.00
GENTLEMEN PREFER BLONDES			
❑ MGM E-208 [M]		1953	120.00
GET YOURSELF A COLLEGE GIRL			
❑ MGM E-4273 [M]		1965	20.00
❑ MGM SE-4273 [S]		1965	40.00
GETTING STRAIGHT			
❑ Colgems COSO-5010		1970	30.00
GIANT			
❑ Capitol DW 773 [R]		196?	12.00
❑ Capitol W 773 [M]		1956	40.00
—Turquoise or gray label			

SOUNDTRACKS

Except when noted otherwise, VG = 25% of NM, and VG+ = 50% of NM. (Example: VG = $2.00, VG+ = $4.00 and NM = $8.00.)

Soundtrack, *Easy Rider,* ABC-Dunhill DSX-50063, 1969, **$25.**

Number	Title (A Side/B Side)	Yr	NM
❑ Capitol W 773 [M]		1959	25.00
—Black colorband label, logo at left			
❑ Capitol W 773 [M]		1962	15.00
—Black colorband label, logo at top			
GIDGET GOES HAWAIIAN			
❑ Colpix CP 418 [M]		1961	50.00
GIGI			
❑ MGM E-3641 [M]		1958	20.00
—Yellow label			
❑ MGM E-3641 [M]		1960	12.00
—Black label			
❑ MGM SE-3641 [S]		1959	25.00
—Yellow label			
❑ MGM SE-3641 [S]		1960	15.00
—Black label			
❑ MGM SE-3641 [S]		1968	12.00
—Blue and gold label			
❑ MGM SW 90523 [S]		1965	15.00
❑ MGM W 90523 [M]		1965	12.00
—Capitol Record Club edition			
GIGOT			
❑ Capitol SW 1754 [S]		1962	40.00
❑ Capitol W 1754 [M]		1962	30.00
THE GIRL IN THE BIKINI			
❑ Poplar PLP 33-1002 [M]		1952	400.00
THE GIRL MOST LIKELY			
❑ Capitol W 930 [M]		1957	60.00
GIRL ON A MOTORCYCLE			
❑ Tetragrammaton T-5000		1969	30.00
THE GLENN MILLER STORY			
❑ Decca DL 5519 [10]		1954	40.00
❑ Decca DL 8226 [M]		1956	30.00
❑ Decca DL 9123 [M]		196?	20.00
—Reissue of 8226			
❑ Decca DL 79123 [R]		196?	15.00
❑ MCA 1624		198?	15.00
—This reissue is a bit more desirable because it was issued in true stereo			
❑ MCA 2036		1973	10.00

Number	Title (A Side/B Side)	Yr	NM
THE GLORY STOMPERS			
❑ Sidewalk DT 5910 [R]		1968	50.00
GO, GO, GO WORLD			
❑ Musicor MM-2059 [M]		1965	40.00
❑ Musicor MS-3059 [S]		1965	60.00
GO, JOHNNY, GO!			
❑ (no label) (no number) [DJ]		1959	1000.
—Only exists as a promo			
GOD'S LITTLE ACRE			
❑ United Artists UAL-4002 [M]		1958	150.00
THE GODFATHER			
❑ Paramount PAS-1003		1972	20.00
—Original cover with triple gatefold			
THE GODFATHER PART II			
❑ ABC ABDP-856		1975	20.00
GOLD			
❑ ABC ABCD-855		1975	30.00
GOLDEN BOY			
❑ Colpix CP-478 [M]		1964	20.00
❑ Colpix SCP-478 [S]		1964	25.00
THE GOLDEN BREED			
❑ Capitol ST 2886		1967	30.00
THE GOLDEN COACH			
❑ MGM E-3111 [M]		1954	150.00
THE GOLDEN SCREW			
❑ Atco 33-208 [M]		1967	30.00
❑ Atco SD 33-208 [S]		1967	40.00
GOLDFINGER			
❑ United Artists UAL-4117 [M]		1964	15.00
❑ United Artists UAS-5117 [S]		1964	20.00
GOLIATH AND THE BARBARIANS			
❑ American Int'l. 1001-M [M]		1960	40.00
❑ American Int'l. 1001-S [S]		1960	70.00
GONE WITH THE WAVE			
❑ Colpix CP-492 [M]		1965	40.00
❑ Colpix SCP-492 [S]		1965	60.00

Number	Title (A Side/B Side)	Yr	NM
GONE WITH THE WIND			
❑ MGM 1E-10 [M]		1967	20.00
—Gatefold edition with 32-page booklet			
❑ MGM S1E-10 [S]		1967	20.00
—Gatefold edition with 32-page booklet			
GOOD NEWS			
❑ MGM E-504 [10]		1950	50.00
GOODBYE AGAIN			
❑ United Artists UAL-4091 [M]		1961	30.00
❑ United Artists UAS-5091 [S]		1961	40.00
GOODBYE, CHARLIE			
❑ 20th Century Fox TFM-3165 [M]		1964	25.00
❑ 20th Century Fox TFS-4165 [S]		1964	30.00
GOODBYE, MR. CHIPS			
❑ MCA 39006		1986	8.00
—Reissue			
❑ MGM 1SE-19		1969	20.00
GORDON'S WAR			
❑ Buddah BDS-5137		1973	40.00
THE GOSPEL ACCORDING TO ST. MATTHEW			
❑ Mainstream S-4000 [S]		1966	100.00
❑ Mainstream 54000 [M]		1966	25.00
GOYA			
❑ Decca DL 8236 [M]		1959	150.00
THE GRADUATE			
❑ CBS Masterworks JS 3180 [S]		198?	8.00
—"CBS Masterworks" replaces "Columbia" along outer edge of label			
❑ Columbia Masterworks JS 3180 [S]		197?	8.00
—Reissue with new prefix			
❑ Columbia Masterworks OS 3180 [S]		1968	12.00
—Original stereo edition: Gray label, "360 Sound Stereo" in white			
❑ Columbia Masterworks OS 3180 [S]		1971	10.00
—Olive label, "Columbia" along outer edge			
❑ Columbia Masterworks OL 6780 [M]		1968	50.00
—"Mono" on label			
GRAND PRIX			
❑ MGM 1E-8 [M]		1967	20.00
❑ MGM 1SE-8 [S]		1967	25.00
THE GREAT ESCAPE			
❑ United Artists UAL-4107 [M]		1963	25.00
❑ United Artists UAS-5107 [S]		1963	30.00
THE GREAT GATSBY			
❑ Paramount 2-3001 [(2)]		1974	20.00
THE GREATEST SHOW ON EARTH			
❑ RCA Victor LPM-3018 [10]		1952	200.00
THE GREATEST STORY EVER TOLD			
❑ United Artists UAL-4120 [M]		1965	25.00
❑ United Artists UAS-5120 [S]		1965	30.00
GROUNDS FOR MARRIAGE			
❑ MGM E-536 [M]		1950	80.00
GUESS WHO'S COMING TO DINNER			
❑ Colgems COM-108 [M]		1968	30.00
❑ Colgems COS-108 [S]		1968	30.00
GULLIVER'S TRAVELS BEYOND THE MOON			
❑ Mainstream S-4001 [S]		1965	40.00
❑ Mainstream 54001 [M]		1965	30.00
GUNS FOR SAN SEBASTIAN			
❑ MGM SE-4565		1968	60.00
THE GUNS OF NAVARONE			
❑ Columbia CL 1655 [M]		1961	20.00
❑ Columbia CS 8455 [S]		1961	50.00
GURU			
❑ RCA Victor LSO-1158		1969	20.00
GYPSY			
❑ Warner Bros. B 1480 [M]		1962	20.00
❑ Warner Bros. BS 1480 [S]		1962	30.00
GYPSY GIRL			
❑ Mainstream S-6090 [S]		1966	40.00
❑ Mainstream 56090 [M]		1966	30.00
HALLELUJAH THE HILLS			
❑ Fontana MGF-27524 [M]		1964	25.00
❑ Fontana SRF-67524 [S]		1964	30.00
THE HALLELUJAH TRAIL			
❑ United Artists UAL-4127 [M]		1965	20.00
❑ United Artists UAS-5127 [S]		1965	25.00
HAMMERHEAD			
❑ Colgems COS-110		1968	40.00
HAMMERSMITH IS OUT			
❑ Capitol SW-861		1972	30.00
HANG 'EM HIGH			
❑ United Artists UAS-5179		1968	25.00
THE HAPPENING			
❑ Colgems COMO-5006 [M]		1967	30.00
❑ Colgems COSO-5006 [S]		1967	50.00

Except when noted otherwise, VG = 25% of NM, and VG+ = 50% of NM. (Example: VG = $2.00, VG+ = $4.00 and NM = $8.00.)

Number	Title (A Side/B Side)	Yr	NM
THE HAPPIEST MILLIONAIRE			
❑ Buena Vista BV-5001 [M]		1967	15.00
❑ Buena Vista STER-5001 [S]		1967	20.00
THE HARD RIDE			
❑ Paramount PAS-6005		1971	30.00
HARPER			
❑ Mainstream S-6078 [S]		1966	25.00
❑ Mainstream 56078 [M]		1966	20.00
THE HARRAD EXPERIMENT			
❑ Capitol ST-11182		1973	25.00
HARRAD SUMMER			
❑ Capitol ST-11338		1974	25.00
HAWAII			
❑ United Artists UAL-4143 [M]		1966	20.00
❑ United Artists UAS-5143 [S]		1966	25.00
❑ United Artists SW-90935 [S]		1966	30.00
—Capitol Record Club issue			
THE HEART IS A LONELY HUNTER			
❑ Warner Bros. WS 1759		1968	30.00
HEAVY TRAFFIC			
❑ Fantasy F-9436		1973	25.00
THE HELEN MORGAN STORY			
❑ RCA Victor LOC-1030 [M]		1957	60.00
HELL TO ETERNITY			
❑ Warwick W 2030 [M]		1960	120.00
❑ Warwick WST 2030 [S]		1960	200.00
HELL UP IN HARLEM			
❑ Motown M 802V1		1974	30.00
HELL'S ANGELS '69			
❑ Capitol SKAO-303		1969	25.00
HELL'S ANGELS ON WHEELS			
❑ Smash MGS-27094 [M]		1967	25.00
❑ Smash SRS-67094 [S]		1967	30.00
HELL'S BELLS			
❑ Sidewalk ST 5919		1969	30.00
HELLCATS			
❑ Tower ST 5124		1968	30.00
HELLO-GOODBYE			
❑ 20th Century Fox S-4210		1970	40.00
HEMINGWAY'S ADVENTURES OF A YOUNG MAN			
❑ RCA Victor LOC-1074 [M]		1962	40.00
❑ RCA Victor LSO-1074 [S]		1962	70.00
THE HERO			
❑ Capitol SW-11098		1972	20.00
HEROES OF TELEMARK			
❑ Mainstream S-6064 [S]		1965	30.00
❑ Mainstream 56064 [M]		1965	20.00
HEY THERE, IT'S YOGI BEAR!			
❑ Colpix CP-472 [M]		1964	50.00
❑ Colpix SCP-472 [S]		1964	80.00
HEY, LET'S TWIST			
❑ Roulette R-25168 [M]		1962	25.00
❑ Roulette SR-25168 [S]		1962	30.00
HIGH SOCIETY			
❑ Capitol SW 750 [S]		1959	30.00
—Black colorband label, logo at left			
❑ Capitol SW 750 [S]		1962	20.00
—Black colorband label, logo at top			
❑ Capitol W 750 [M]		1956	30.00
—Gray label original			
❑ Capitol W 750 [M]		1959	20.00
—Black colorband label, logo at left			
❑ Capitol W 750 [M]		1962	15.00
—Black colorband label, logo at top			
HOLIDAY INN			
❑ Decca DL 4256		1962	25.00
HOOTENANNY HOOT			
❑ MGM E-4172 [M]		1963	20.00
❑ MGM SE-4172 [S]		1963	25.00
THE HORSE SOLDIERS			
❑ United Artists UAL-4035 [M]		1959	60.00
❑ United Artists UAS-5035 [S]		1959	150.00
THE HORSEMEN			
❑ Sunflower SNF-5007		1971	40.00
THE HOT ROCK			
❑ Prophesy SD 8055		1972	20.00
HOT ROD RUMBLE			
❑ Liberty LRP-3048 [M]		1957	150.00
HOTEL PARADISO			
❑ MGM E-4419 [M]		1966	20.00
❑ MGM SE-4419 [S]		1966	25.00
THE HOUR OF THE GUN			
❑ United Artists UAL-4166 [M]		1967	40.00
❑ United Artists UAS-5166 [S]		1967	70.00

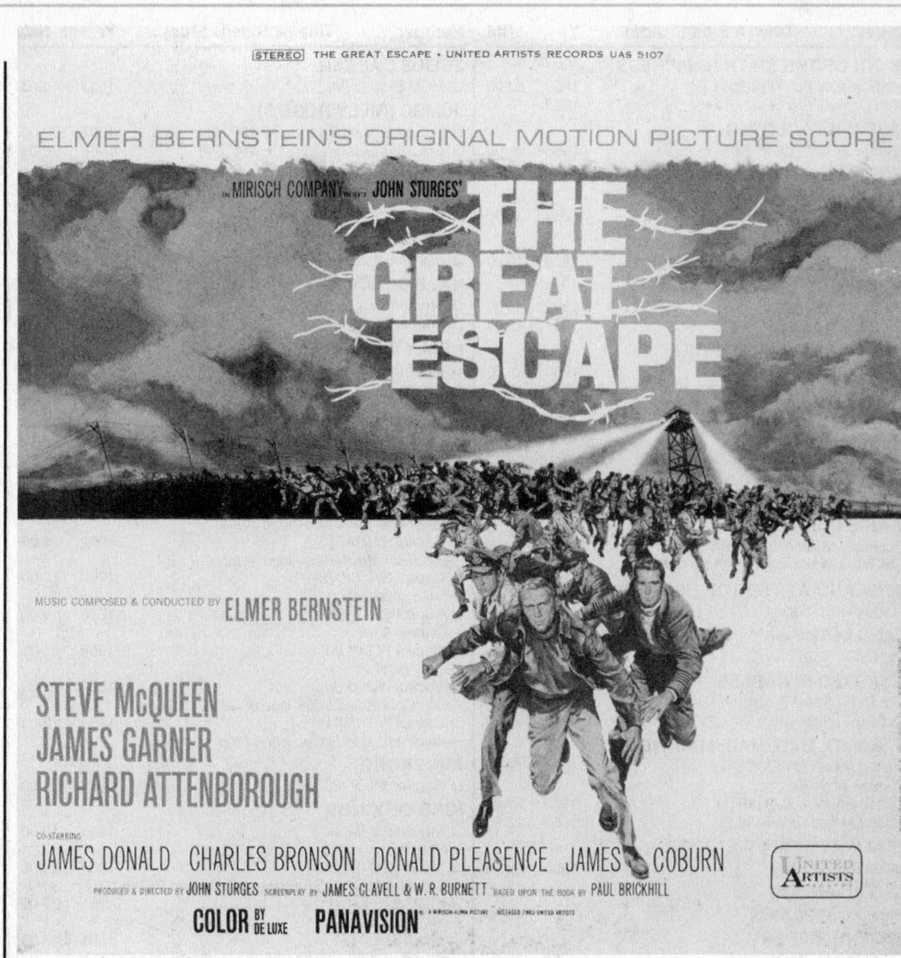

Soundtrack, *The Great Escape*, United Artists UAS 5107, 1963, stereo, **$30.**

Number	Title (A Side/B Side)	Yr	NM
A HOUSE IS NOT A HOME			
❑ Ava A-50 [M]		1964	25.00
❑ Ava AS-50 [S]		1964	30.00
HOUSEBOAT			
❑ Columbia CL 1222 [M]		1958	50.00
HOW SWEET IT IS			
❑ RCA Victor LSP-4037		1968	20.00
HOW THE WEST WAS WON			
❑ MGM 1E-5 [M]		1963	15.00
❑ MGM 1SE-5 [S]		1963	20.00
HOW TO MURDER YOUR WIFE			
❑ United Artists UAL-4119 [M]		1965	15.00
❑ United Artists UAS-5119 [S]		1965	20.00
HOW TO SAVE A MARRIAGE AND RUIN YOUR LIFE			
❑ Columbia Masterworks OS 3140		1968	20.00
HOW TO STEAL A MILLION			
❑ 20th Century Fox TFM-3183 [M]		1966	40.00
❑ 20th Century Fox TFS-4183 [S]		1966	50.00
HOW TO STUFF A WILD BIKINI			
❑ Wand 671 [M]		1965	30.00
❑ Wand S-671 [S]		1965	40.00
HOW TO SUCCEED IN BUSINESS WITHOUT REALLY TRYING			
❑ United Artists UAL-4151 [M]		1967	20.00
❑ United Artists UAS-5151 [S]		1967	25.00
HURRY SUNDOWN			
❑ RCA Victor LOC-1133 [M]		1967	30.00
❑ RCA Victor LSO-1133 [S]		1967	40.00
THE HUSTLER			
❑ Kapp KL-1264 [M]		1961	60.00
❑ Kapp KS-3264 [S]		1961	120.00
I LOVE MELVIN			
❑ MGM E-190 [10]		1953	50.00
I NEVER SANG FOR MY FATHER			
❑ Bell 1204		1970	40.00

Number	Title (A Side/B Side)	Yr	NM
I WANT TO LIVE			
❑ United Artists UXL 1 [(2)M]		1958	60.00
—Combines 4005 and 4006 into one package			
❑ United Artists UXS 51 [(2)S]		1958	80.00
—Combines 5005 and 5006 into one package			
❑ United Artists UAL-4005 [M]		1958	25.00
—Orchestral music by Johnny Mandel			
❑ United Artists UAS-4005 [S]		1958	40.00
—Orchestral music by Johnny Mandel			
❑ United Artists UAL-4006 [M]		1958	30.00
—Jazz music by Gerry Mulligan, Shelly Manne and Art Farmer			
❑ United Artists UAS-4006 [S]		1958	40.00
—Jazz music by Gerry Mulligan, Shelly Mann and Art Farmer			
I'LL NEVER FORGET WHAT'S 'IS NAME			
❑ Decca DL 9163 [M]		1967	25.00
❑ Decca DL 79163 [S]		1967	30.00
ICE STATION ZEBRA			
❑ MGM S1E-14 ST		1968	40.00
IF HE HOLLERS, LET HIM GO			
❑ Tower ST 5152		1968	40.00
IMITATION OF LIFE			
❑ Decca DL 8879 [M]		1959	50.00
❑ Decca DL 78879 [S]		1959	80.00
IN HARM'S WAY			
❑ RCA Victor LOC-1100 [M]		1965	40.00
❑ RCA Victor LSO-1100 [S]		1965	80.00
IN LIKE FLINT			
❑ 20th Century Fox 4193 [M]		1967	40.00
❑ 20th Century Fox S-4193 [S]		1967	80.00
IN SEARCH OF THE CASTAWAYS			
❑ Disneyland ST-3916 [M]		1962	70.00
IN THE GOOD OLD SUMMERTIME			
❑ MGM E-169 [10]		1949	100.00
IN THE HEAT OF THE NIGHT			
❑ United Artists UAL-4160 [M]		1967	15.00
❑ United Artists UAS-5160 [S]		1967	20.00
THE INDISCRETION OF AN AMERICAN WIFE			
❑ Columbia CL 6277 [10]		1954	80.00

Number	Title (A Side/B Side)	Yr	NM
	THE INN OF THE SIXTH HAPPINESS		
❑ 20th Century Fox FOX-3011 [M]		1958	50.00
❑ 20th Century Fox SFX-3011 [S]		1958	70.00
	INSIDE DAISY CLOVER		
❑ Warner Bros. W 1616 [M]		1965	20.00
❑ Warner Bros. WS 1616 [S]		1965	30.00
	INSPECTOR CLOUSEAU		
❑ United Artists UAS-5186		1968	30.00
	INTERLUDE		
❑ Colgems COSO-5007		1968	40.00
	THE INTERNS		
❑ Colpix CP 427 [M]		1962	30.00
❑ Colpix SCP 427 [S]		1962	40.00
	INVITATION TO THE DANCE		
❑ MGM E-3207 [M]		1956	50.00
	THE IPCRESS FILE		
❑ Decca DL 9124 [M]		1965	30.00
❑ Decca DL 79124 [S]		1965	40.00
	IRMA LA DOUCE		
❑ United Artists UAL-4109 [M]		1963	20.00
❑ United Artists UAS-5109 [S]		1963	25.00
	IS PARIS BURNING?		
❑ Columbia Masterworks OS 3030 [S]		1966	40.00
❑ Columbia Masterworks OL 6630 [M]		1966	30.00
	THE ISLAND AT THE TOP OF THE WORLD		
❑ Disneyland ST-3814		1974	25.00
	ISLAND IN THE SKY		
❑ Decca DL 7029 [10]		1953	300.00
	IT STARTED IN NAPLES		
❑ Dot DLP-3324 [M]		1960	60.00
❑ Dot DLP-25324 [S]		1960	100.00
	IT'S A MAD, MAD, MAD, MAD WORLD		
❑ United Artists UA-LA276-G		1974	10.00
—Reissue of 5110			
❑ United Artists UAL-4110 [M]		1963	20.00
❑ United Artists UAS-5110 [S]		1963	25.00
	IT'S ALWAYS FAIR WEATHER		
❑ MGM E-3241 [M]		1955	50.00
	THE ITALIAN JOB		
❑ Paramount PAS-5007		1969	40.00
	JACK THE RIPPER		
❑ RCA Victor LPM-2199 [M]		1960	30.00
❑ RCA Victor LSP-2199 [S]		1960	50.00
	JAMBOREE!		
❑ Warner Bros. (no #) [M]		1957	1200.
—Album has been counterfeited. Originals have front cover slicks and back cover notes printed on the cardboard, and the records have "Jam 1" and "Jam 2" stamped (not etched) in the dead wax.			
	THE JAMES DEAN STORY		
❑ Capitol W 881 [M]		1957	60.00
❑ Kimberly 2016 [M]		1960	40.00
❑ Kimberly 11016 [S]		1960	50.00
—Reissue of World Pacific 2005			
❑ World Pacific P-2005 [M]		1958	100.00
	JAWS		
❑ MCA 2087		1975	20.00
	JEREMIAH JOHNSON		
❑ Warner Bros. BS 2902		1972	20.00
—Green label			
	JESSICA		
❑ United Artists UAL-4096 [M]		1962	20.00
❑ United Artists UAS-5096 [S]		1962	25.00
	THE JOE LOUIS STORY		
❑ MGM E-221 [10]		1953	80.00
	JOHN PAUL JONES		
❑ Warner Bros. W 1293 [M]		1959	60.00
❑ Warner Bros. WS 1293 [S]		1959	120.00
	JOHNNY COOL		
❑ United Artists UAL-4111 [M]		1963	20.00
❑ United Artists UAS-5111 [S]		1963	25.00
	JOHNNY TREMAIN		
❑ Disneyland WDL-4014 [M]		1957	50.00
	JUD		
❑ Ampex A-50101		1971	20.00
	JUDGMENT AT NUREMBERG		
❑ United Artists UAL-4095 [M]		1961	20.00
❑ United Artists UAS-5095 [S]		1961	50.00
	JUDITH		
❑ RCA Victor LOC-1119 [M]		1966	15.00
❑ RCA Victor LSO-1119 [S]		1966	30.00
	JULIET OF THE SPIRITS		
❑ Mainstream S-6062 [S]		1965	60.00
❑ Mainstream 56062 [M]		1965	25.00
	JULIUS CAESAR		
❑ MGM E-3033 [M]		1953	40.00
	JUMBO (BILLY ROSE'S)		
❑ Columbia Masterworks OS 2260 [S]		1962	30.00
❑ Columbia Masterworks OL 5860 [M]		1962	20.00
	THE JUNGLE BOOK		
❑ Buena Vista BV-4041 [M]		1967	15.00
❑ Buena Vista STER-4041 [S]		1967	25.00
	JUSTINE		
❑ Monument SLP-18123		1969	30.00
	KALEIDOSCOPE		
❑ Warner Bros. W 1663 [M]		1966	20.00
❑ Warner Bros. WS 1663 [S]		1966	25.00
	KELLY'S HEROES		
❑ MGM S1E-23		1970	30.00
	THE KEY		
❑ Columbia CL 1185 [M]		1958	80.00
	KILLERS THREE		
❑ Tower ST-5141		1968	20.00
	THE KING AND I		
❑ Capitol SW 740 [S]		1959	20.00
—Black colorband label, logo at left			
❑ Capitol SW 740 [S]		1962	15.00
—Black colorband label, logo at top			
❑ Capitol SW 740 [S]		1969	12.00
—Lime green label			
❑ Capitol SW 740 [S]		1973	10.00
—Orange label			
❑ Capitol W 740 [M]		1956	25.00
—Gray label			
❑ Capitol W 740 [M]		1959	15.00
—Black colorband label, logo at left			
❑ Capitol W 740 [M]		1962	12.00
—Black colorband label, logo at top			
	KING KONG		
❑ Reprise MS 2260		1976	20.00
	KING OF KINGS		
❑ MGM 1E-2 [M]		1961	15.00
—Standard cover			
❑ MGM 1E-2 [M]		1961	30.00
—Boxed version with hardbound book and four 8x10 photos			
❑ MGM S1E-2 [S]		1961	20.00
—Standard cover			
❑ MGM S1E-2 [S]		1961	40.00
—Boxed version with hardbound book and four 8x10 photos			
	KING RAT		
❑ Mainstream S-6061 [S]		1965	50.00
❑ Mainstream 56061 [M]		1965	30.00
	KINGS GO FORTH		
❑ Capitol W 1063 [M]		1958	150.00
	KISMET		
❑ Metro M-526 [M]		1965	12.00
—Reissue of MGM E-3281 with one fewer track			
❑ Metro MS-526 [R]		1955	10.00
—Rechanneled reissue of MGM E-3281 with one fewer track			
❑ MGM E-3281 [M]		1955	20.00
—Yellow label			
❑ MGM E-3281 [M]		1960	15.00
—Black label			
	KISS ME, KATE		
❑ Metro M-525 [M]		1965	12.00
—Reissue of MGM 3077, but with only 10 songs			
❑ Metro MS-525 [R]		1965	10.00
—Rechanneled reissue of MGM 3077, but with only 10 songs			
❑ MGM E-3077 [M]		1953	20.00
—Yellow label			
❑ MGM E-3077 [M]		1959	15.00
—Black label			
	KWAMINA		
❑ Mercury MG-20654 [M]		1961	25.00
❑ Mercury SR-60654 [S]		1961	30.00
	LADY AND THE TRAMP		
❑ Decca DL 5557 [10]		1955	60.00
❑ Decca DL 8462 [M]		1957	70.00
	THE LANDLORD		
❑ United Artists UAS-5209		1970	20.00
	THE LAST OF THE SECRET AGENTS		
❑ Dot DLP-3714 [M]		1966	20.00
❑ Dot DLP-25714 [S]		1966	25.00
	THE LAST RUN		
❑ MGM 1SE-30		1971	25.00
	LAST SUMMER		
❑ Warner Bros. WS 1791		1969	20.00
	THE LAST VALLEY		
❑ ABC-Dunhill DSX-50102		1971	40.00
	LAWRENCE OF ARABIA		
❑ Arista ABM-4009		1975	10.00
—Reissue of Bell 1205			
❑ Bell 1205		1971	10.00
—Reissue of Colgems COSO-5004			
❑ Colgems COMO-5004 [M]		1967	12.00
—Reissue of Colpix CP-514			
❑ Colgems COSO-5004 [S]		1967	15.00
—Reissue of Colpix SCP-514			
❑ Colpix CP-514 [M]		1962	20.00
❑ Colpix SCP-514 [S]		1962	30.00
	LENNY		
❑ United Artists UA-LA359-H [(2)]		1974	20.00
	THE LEOPARD		
❑ 20th Century Fox FXG-5015 [M]		1963	30.00
❑ 20th Century Fox SXG-5015 [S]		1963	40.00
	LES LIAISONS DANGEREUSES		
❑ Charlie Parker PLP-813 [M]		1962	25.00
❑ Charlie Parker PLP-813S [S]		1962	30.00
❑ Epic LA 16022 [M]		1961	40.00
❑ Epic BA 17022 [S]		1961	30.00
❑ Fontana MGF-27539 [M]		1965	20.00
❑ Fontana SRF-67539 [R]		1965	15.00
	LET THE GOOD TIMES ROLL		
❑ Bell 9002 [(2)]		1973	25.00
	LET'S MAKE LOVE		
❑ Columbia CL 1527 [M]		1960	30.00
❑ Columbia CS 8327 [S]		1960	50.00
	LI'L ABNER		
❑ Columbia Masterworks OS 2021 [S]		1959	40.00
—Credits within photo			
❑ Columbia Masterworks OS 2021 [S]		196?	25.00
—Credits in red strip at bottom of photo			
❑ Columbia Masterworks OL 5460 [M]		1959	30.00
—Credits within photo			
❑ Columbia Masterworks OL 5460 [M]		196?	20.00
—Credits in red strip at bottom of photo			
	THE LIFE AND TIMES OF JUDGE ROY BEAN		
❑ Columbia Masterworks S 31948		1972	25.00
	LIGHT FANTASTIC		
❑ 20th Century Fox FXG-5016 [M]		1963	20.00
❑ 20th Century Fox SXG-5016 [S]		1963	25.00
	LILIES OF THE FIELD		
❑ Epic LN 24094 [M]		1964	20.00
❑ Epic BN 26094 [S]		1964	30.00
	THE LION		
❑ London M-76001 [M]		1962	400.00
	THE LION IN WINTER		
❑ Columbia Masterworks OS 3250		1969	20.00
	LITTLE BIG MAN		
❑ Columbia Masterworks S 30545		1970	20.00
	LIVE AND LET DIE		
❑ United Artists UA-LA100-G		1973	10.00
—Tan label; cover corner is clipped			
❑ United Artists UA-LA100-G		1973	20.00
—Tan label; cover corner is not clipped off			
❑ United Artists SWAO-95120		1973	30.00
—Longines (formerly Capitol) Record Club edition			
	LIVE FOR LIFE		
❑ United Artists UAL-4165 [M]		1967	20.00
❑ United Artists UAS-5165 [S]		1967	20.00
	THE LIVELY SET		
❑ Decca DL 9119 [M]		1964	30.00
❑ Decca DL 79119 [S]		1964	40.00
	LOLITA		
❑ MGM E-4050 [M]		1962	20.00
❑ MGM SE-4050 [S]		1962	30.00
	THE LOLLIPOP COVER		
❑ Mainstream S-6067 [S]		1966	30.00
❑ Mainstream 56067 [M]		1966	20.00
	THE LONG HOT SUMMER		
❑ Roulette R-25026 [M]		1958	75.00
	LONG JOHN SILVER		
❑ RCA Victor LPM-3279 [10]		1954	300.00
	THE LONG SHIPS		
❑ Colpix CP-517 [M]		1964	50.00
❑ Colpix SCP-517 [S]		1964	60.00
	THE LONGEST DAY		
❑ 20th Century Fox FXG-5007 [M]		1962	20.00
❑ 20th Century Fox SXG-5007 [S]		1962	25.00
	LORD JIM		
❑ Colpix CP-521 [M]		1965	25.00
❑ Colpix SCP-521 [S]		1965	40.00
	LORD LOVE A DUCK		
❑ United Artists UAL-4137 [M]		1966	20.00
❑ United Artists UAS-5137 [S]		1966	25.00
	THE LORDS OF FLATBUSH		
❑ ABC ABCD-828		1974	30.00
	A LOSS OF INNOCENCE		
❑ Colpix CP-508 [M]		1961	40.00

SOUNDTRACKS

Except when noted otherwise, VG = 25% of NM, and VG+ = 50% of NM. (Example: VG = $2.00, VG+ = $4.00 and NM = $8.00.)

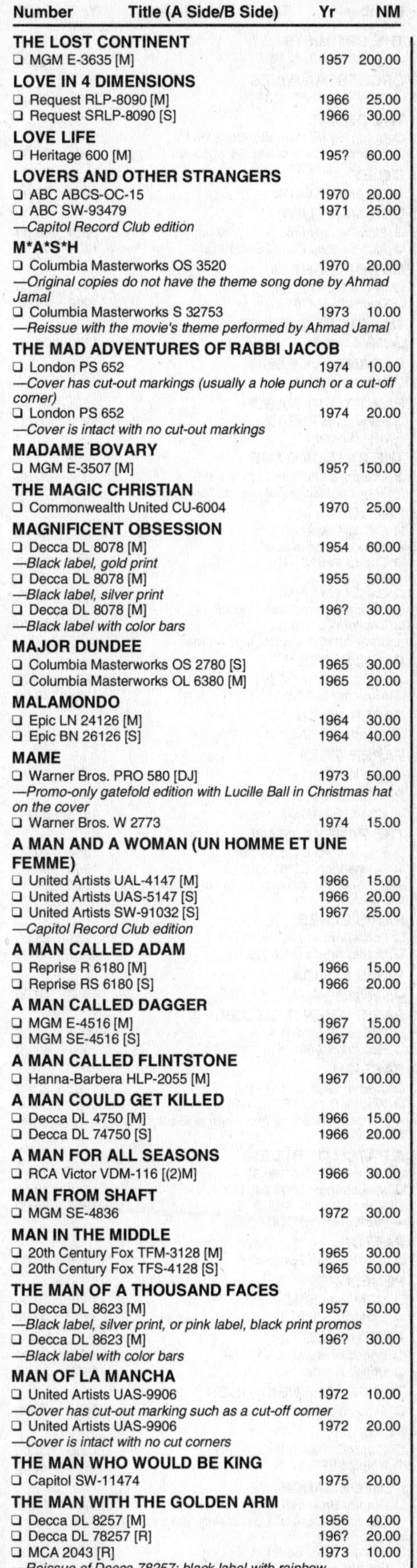

Number	Title (A Side/B Side)	Yr	NM

THE LOST CONTINENT
❑ MGM E-3635 [M] 1957 200.00

LOVE IN 4 DIMENSIONS
❑ Request RLP-8090 [M] 1966 25.00
❑ Request SRLP-8090 [S] 1966 30.00

LOVE LIFE
❑ Heritage 600 [M] 195? 60.00

LOVERS AND OTHER STRANGERS
❑ ABC ABCS-OC-15 1970 20.00
❑ ABC SW-93479 1971 25.00
—Capitol Record Club edition

M*A*S*H
❑ Columbia Masterworks OS 3520 1970 20.00
—Original copies do not have the theme song done by Ahmad Jamal
❑ Columbia Masterworks S 32753 1973 10.00
—Reissue with the movie's theme performed by Ahmad Jamal

THE MAD ADVENTURES OF RABBI JACOB
❑ London PS 652 1974 10.00
—Cover has cut-out markings (usually a hole punch or a cut-off corner)
❑ London PS 652 1974 20.00
—Cover is intact with no cut-out markings

MADAME BOVARY
❑ MGM E-3507 [M] 195? 150.00

THE MAGIC CHRISTIAN
❑ Commonwealth United CU-6004 1970 25.00

MAGNIFICENT OBSESSION
❑ Decca DL 8078 [M] 1954 60.00
—Black label, gold print
❑ Decca DL 8078 [M] 1955 50.00
—Black label, silver print
❑ Decca DL 8078 [M] 196? 30.00
—Black label with color bars

MAJOR DUNDEE
❑ Columbia Masterworks OS 2780 [S] 1965 30.00
❑ Columbia Masterworks OL 6380 [M] 1965 20.00

MALAMONDO
❑ Epic LN 24126 [M] 1964 30.00
❑ Epic BN 26126 [S] 1964 40.00

MAME
❑ Warner Bros. PRO 580 [DJ] 1973 50.00
—Promo-only gatefold edition with Lucille Ball in Christmas hat on the cover
❑ Warner Bros. W 2773 1974 15.00

A MAN AND A WOMAN (UN HOMME ET UNE FEMME)
❑ United Artists UAL-4147 [M] 1966 15.00
❑ United Artists UAS-5147 [S] 1966 20.00
❑ United Artists SW-91032 [S] 1967 25.00
—Capitol Record Club edition

A MAN CALLED ADAM
❑ Reprise R 6180 [M] 1966 15.00
❑ Reprise RS 6180 [S] 1966 20.00

A MAN CALLED DAGGER
❑ MGM E-4516 [M] 1967 15.00
❑ MGM SE-4516 [S] 1967 20.00

A MAN CALLED FLINTSTONE
❑ Hanna-Barbera HLP-2055 [M] 1967 100.00

A MAN COULD GET KILLED
❑ Decca DL 4750 [M] 1966 15.00
❑ Decca DL 74750 [S] 1966 20.00

A MAN FOR ALL SEASONS
❑ RCA Victor VDM-116 [(2)M] 1966 30.00

MAN FROM SHAFT
❑ MGM SE-4836 1972 30.00

MAN IN THE MIDDLE
❑ 20th Century Fox TFM-3128 [M] 1965 30.00
❑ 20th Century Fox TFS-4128 [S] 1965 50.00

THE MAN OF A THOUSAND FACES
❑ Decca DL 8623 [M] 1957 50.00
—Black label, silver print, or pink label, black print promos
❑ Decca DL 8623 [M] 196? 30.00
—Black label with color bars

MAN OF LA MANCHA
❑ United Artists UAS-9906 1972 10.00
—Cover has cut-out marking such as a cut-off corner
❑ United Artists UAS-9906 1972 20.00
—Cover is intact with no cut corners

THE MAN WHO WOULD BE KING
❑ Capitol SW-11474 1975 20.00

THE MAN WITH THE GOLDEN ARM
❑ Decca DL 8257 [M] 1956 40.00
❑ Decca DL 78257 [R] 196? 20.00
❑ MCA 2043 [R] 1973 10.00
—Reissue of Decca 78257; black label with rainbow

THE MAN WITH THE GOLDEN GUN
❑ United Artists UA-LA358-G 1974 20.00

Soundtrack, *Light Fantastic,* 20th Century Fox FXG 5016, 1963, mono, **$20.**

Number	Title (A Side/B Side)	Yr	NM

MARACAIBO
❑ Decca DL 8756 [M] 1958 40.00
—Black label, silver print, or pink label, black print promos
❑ Decca DL 8756 [M] 196? 20.00
—Black label with color bars

MARCO THE MAGNIFICENT
❑ Columbia Masterworks OS 2870 [S] 1966 40.00
❑ Columbia Masterworks OL 6470 [M] 1966 25.00

MARJORIE MORNINGSTAR
❑ RCA Victor LOC-1044 [M] 1958 40.00
—"RE" next to label number
❑ RCA Victor LOC-1044 [M] 1958 60.00
—"An Original Soundtrack Recording" on spine

MARRY ME, MARRY ME
❑ RCA Victor LSO-1160 1969 20.00

MARY POPPINS
❑ Buena Vista BV-4026 [M] 1964 12.00
—Originals have gatefold covers
❑ Buena Vista STER-4026 [S] 1964 15.00
—Originals have gatefold covers
❑ Buena Vista STER-5005 [S] 1973 10.00
—Reissue with new number and no gatefold
❑ RCA Victor COP-111 [M] 1964 15.00
—With gatefold; RCA Record Club edition
❑ RCA Victor CSO-111 [S] 1964 20.00
—With gatefold; RCA Record Club edition

MARY, QUEEN OF SCOTS
❑ Decca DL 79186 1972 30.00

MASKED AND ANONYMOUS
❑ Columbia CSK 90618-1 [(2)] 2006 30.00
—Classic Records issue on 140-gram vinyl; CD issued in 2003

MASTER OF THE WORLD
❑ Vee Jay LP-4000 [M] 1961 25.00
❑ Vee Jay SR-4000 [S] 1961 40.00

MCLINTOCK!
❑ United Artists UAL-4112 [M] 1963 60.00
❑ United Artists UAS-5112 [S] 1963 80.00

ME AND THE COLONEL
❑ RCA Victor LOC-1046 [M] 1958 50.00

MEDITERRANEAN HOLIDAY
❑ London M-76003 [M] 1964 50.00
❑ London MS-82003 [S] 1964 80.00

MEET ME IN ST. LOUIS
❑ Decca DL 8498 [M] 1957 30.00
—LP reissue of 78 rpm album from 1944; B-side of LP is "The Harvey Girls."

MEMORIES AUX BRUXELLES
❑ Carlton LP-112 [M] 1959 25.00
❑ Carlton LP-12112 [S] 1959 40.00

MEN IN WAR
❑ Imperial LP-9032 W [M] 1957 150.00

MERRY ANDREW
❑ Capitol T 1016 [M] 1958 50.00

MICKEY ONE
❑ MGM E-4312 [M] 1965 20.00
❑ MGM SE-4312 [S] 1965 25.00

MIDNIGHT COWBOY
❑ United Artists UAS-5198 1969 20.00

A MILANESE STORY
❑ Atlantic 1388 [M] 1962 20.00
❑ Atlantic SD 1388 [S] 1962 25.00

THE MINX
❑ Amsterdam 12007 1970 120.00

THE MISFITS
❑ United Artists UA-LA273-G [S] 1974 12.00
—Reissue of 5087
❑ United Artists UAL-4087 [M] 1961 50.00
❑ United Artists UAS-5087 [S] 1961 100.00

MISS SADIE THOMPSON
❑ Mercury MG-20123 [M] 1956 150.00
❑ Mercury MG-25181 [10] 1954 75.00

MOBY DICK
❑ RCA Victor LPM-1247 [M] 1956 120.00

MODERN TIMES
❑ United Artists UAL-4049 [M] 1959 25.00
❑ United Artists UAS-5049 [R] 196? 20.00

SOUNDTRACKS

Number	Title (A Side/B Side)	Yr	NM
MODESTY BLAISE			
❑ 20th Century Fox TFM-3182 [M]		1966	30.00
❑ 20th Century Fox TFS-4182 [S]		1966	50.00
MONDO CANE			
❑ United Artists UAL-4105 [M]		1963	15.00
❑ United Artists UAS-5105 [S]		1963	20.00
MONDO CANE NO. 2			
❑ 20th Century Fox TFM-3147 [M]		1964	30.00
❑ 20th Century Fox TFS-4147 [S]		1964	40.00
THE MOON SPINNERS			
❑ Buena Vista BV-3323 [M]		1964	40.00
MR. BUDDWING			
❑ Verve V-8638 [M]		1965	15.00
❑ Verve V6-8638 [S]		1965	25.00
MR. MAGOO: 1001 ARABIAN NIGHTS			
❑ Colpix CP-410 [M]		1959	50.00
❑ Colpix SCP-410 [S]		1959	150.00
MURDER INC.			
❑ Canadian American CALP-1003 [M]		1960	100.00
MUSCLE BEACH PARTY PLUS MERLIN JONES AND THE SCRAMBLED EGGHEAD			
❑ Buena Vista BV-3314 [M]		1964	60.00
❑ Buena Vista STER-3314 [S]		1964	120.00
THE MUSIC MAN			
❑ Warner Bros. B 1459 [M]		1962	15.00
❑ Warner Bros. BS 1459 [S]		1962	20.00
—Gold label originals			
❑ Warner Bros. BS 1459 [S]		1968	12.00
—Green label with "W7" box logo at top			
❑ Warner Bros. BS 1459 [S]		1970	10.00
—Green label with "WB" shield logo at top			
❑ Warner Bros. BS 1459 [S]		1973	8.00
—"Burbank" palm trees label or later white label			
MUTINY ON THE BOUNTY			
❑ MCA 25007		1986	8.00
—Reissue of MGM 1SE-4			
❑ MGM 1E-4 [M]		196?	12.00
—Standard cover			
❑ MGM 1E-4 [M]		1962	30.00
—Boxed set with book and painting			
❑ MGM S1E-4 [S]		196?	15.00
—Standard cover			
❑ MGM S1E-4 [S]		1962	40.00
—Boxed set with book and painting			
MY FAIR LADY			
❑ Columbia Masterworks KOS 2600 [S]		1964	15.00
❑ Columbia Masterworks KOL 8000 [M]		1964	12.00
MY GEISHA			
❑ RCA Victor LOC-1070 [M]		1962	50.00
❑ RCA Victor LSO-1070 [S]		1962	100.00
MY SIDE OF THE MOUNTAIN			
❑ Capitol ST-245		1969	25.00
MY WILD IRISH ROSE			
❑ RCA Victor LPM-3036 [10]		1952	40.00
NAKED ANGELS			
❑ Straight STS-1056		1969	25.00
THE NAKED MAJA			
❑ United Artists UAL-4031 [M]		1959	30.00
❑ United Artists UAS-5031 [S]		1959	40.00
NANCY GOES TO RIO			
❑ MGM E-508 [10]		1950	60.00
NASHVILLE			
❑ ABC ABCD-893		1975	20.00
NAVAJO JOE			
❑ United Artists UA-LA292-G		1974	25.00
NED KELLY			
❑ United Artists UA-LA300-G		1974	12.00
—Reissue of 5213			
❑ United Artists UAS-5213		1970	25.00
NEVADA SMITH			
❑ Dot DLP-3718 [M]		1966	25.00
❑ Dot DLP-25718 [S]		1966	40.00
NEVER ON SUNDAY			
❑ United Artists UAL-4070 [M]		1960	15.00
❑ United Artists UAS-5070 [S]		1960	20.00
❑ United Artists SW-90834 [S]		196?	20.00
—Capitol Record Club edition			
THE NEW INTERNS			
❑ Colpix CP-473 [M]		1964	30.00
❑ Colpix SCP-473 [S]		1964	40.00
A NEW KIND OF LOVE			
❑ Mercury MG-20859 [M]		1963	15.00
❑ Mercury SR-60859 [S]		1963	20.00
THE NEW MESSIAH			
❑ Columbia KC 31713		1972	20.00
NICHOLAS AND ALEXANDRA			
❑ Bell 1103		1971	25.00

Number	Title (A Side/B Side)	Yr	NM
NIGHT OF THE GENERALS			
❑ Colgems COMO-5002 [M]		1967	40.00
❑ Colgems COSO-5002 [S]		1967	70.00
THE NIGHT OF THE HUNTER			
❑ RCA Victor LPM-1136 [M]		1955	250.00
NINE HOURS TO RAMA			
❑ London M-76002 [M]		1963	300.00
NO WAY TO TREAT A LADY			
❑ Dot DLP-25846		1968	25.00
NOT WITH MY WIFE, YOU DON'T			
❑ Warner Bros. W 1668 [M]		1966	15.00
❑ Warner Bros. WS 1668 [S]		1966	20.00
NOTHING BUT THE BEST			
❑ Colpix CP-477 [M]		1964	20.00
❑ Colpix SCP-477 [S]		1964	25.00
A NUN'S STORY			
❑ Warner Bros. B 1306 [M]		1959	60.00
❑ Warner Bros. BS 1306 [S]		1959	100.00
THE ODD COUPLE			
❑ Dot DLP-25862		1968	20.00
ODDS AGAINST TOMORROW			
❑ United Artists UAL-4061 [M]		1959	30.00
❑ United Artists UAS-5061 [S]		1959	50.00
OF LOVE AND DESIRE			
❑ 20th Century Fox FXG-5014 [M]		1963	25.00
❑ 20th Century Fox SXG-5014 [S]		1963	30.00
OH DAD, POOR DAD, MAMMA'S HUNG YOU IN THE CLOSET AND I'M FEELIN' SO SAD			
❑ RCA Victor LPM-3750 [M]		1967	20.00
❑ RCA Victor LSP-3750 [S]		1967	25.00
OH, ROSALINDA!			
❑ Mercury MG-20145 [M]		1957	50.00
OIL TOWN, U.S.A.			
❑ RCA Victor LFM-2000 [10]		1953	60.00
OKLAHOMA!			
❑ Capitol SWAO 595 [S]		1959	20.00
—Black colorband label, logo at left			
❑ Capitol SWAO 595 [S]		1962	15.00
—Black colorband label, logo at top			
❑ Capitol SWAO 595 [S]		1969	12.00
—Lime green label			
❑ Capitol SWAO 595 [S]		1973	10.00
—Orange label			
❑ Capitol WAO 595 [M]		1955	25.00
—Purple or dark red label			
❑ Capitol WAO 595 [M]		1956	20.00
—Gray label			
❑ Capitol WAO 595 [M]		1959	15.00
—Black colorband label, logo at left			
❑ Capitol WAO 595 [M]		1962	12.00
—Black colorband label, logo at top			
THE OLD MAN AND THE SEA			
❑ Columbia CL 1183 [M]		1958	30.00
❑ Columbia CS 8013 [S]		1958	60.00
OLD YELLER			
❑ Disneyland 1024 [M]		1974	25.00
—Reissue with no prefix			
❑ Disneyland WDL-1024 [M]		1960	40.00
—Second edition			
❑ Disneyland WDL-3024 [M]		1957	50.00
—First edition			
ON HER MAJESTY'S SECRET SERVICE			
❑ United Artists UA-LA299-G		1974	12.00
—Reissue of 5204			
❑ United Artists UAS-5204		1969	20.00
ON THE BEACH			
❑ Roulette R-25098 [M]		1959	80.00
❑ Roulette SR-25098 [S]		1959	150.00
ONCE UPON A TIME IN THE WEST			
❑ RCA Victor LSP-4736		1969	30.00
THE ONE AND ONLY, GENUINE, ORIGINAL FAMILY BAND			
❑ Buena Vista BV-5002 [M]		1968	15.00
❑ Buena Vista STER-5002 [S]		1968	20.00
ONE FLEW OVER THE CUCKOO'S NEST			
❑ Fantasy MPF-4531		198?	10.00
—Budget-line reissue of 9500			
❑ Fantasy F-9500		1975	20.00
101 DALMATIONS			
❑ Disneyland DQ-1308 [M]		1966	20.00
❑ Disneyland ST-1908 [M]		1960	25.00
❑ Disneyland ST-3931 [M]		1965	40.00
❑ Disneyland ST-4903 [M]		1963	150.00
—Gatefold cover with pop-up scene in center			
THE ONE-EYED JACKS			
❑ Liberty LOM-16001 [M]		1961	30.00
❑ Liberty LOS-17001 [S]		1961	50.00

Number	Title (A Side/B Side)	Yr	NM
THE OPTIMISTS			
❑ Paramount PAS-1015		1973	30.00
ORCHESTRA WIVES			
❑ RCA Victor LPT-3065 [10]		1954	60.00
THE OSCAR			
❑ Columbia Masterworks OS 2950 [S]		1966	25.00
❑ Columbia Masterworks OL 6550 [M]		1966	20.00
OTLEY			
❑ Colgems COS-112		1969	30.00
OUR MAN FLINT			
❑ 20th Century Fox TFM-3179 [M]		1966	40.00
❑ 20th Century Fox TFS-4179 [S]		1966	60.00
OUT OF SIGHT			
❑ Decca DL 4751 [M]		1966	20.00
❑ Decca DL 74751 [S]		1966	25.00
THE OUTLAW RIDERS			
❑ MGM 1SE-26		1970	20.00
PAGAN LOVE SONG			
❑ MGM E-534 [M]		1950	40.00
PAINT YOUR WAGON			
❑ Paramount PMS-1001		1969	20.00
—With booklet			
THE PAJAMA GAME			
❑ Columbia Masterworks OL 5210 [M]		1957	30.00
—Gray and black label with six "eye" logos			
PAL JOEY			
❑ Capitol DW 912 [R]		196?	10.00
—Black colorband label			
❑ Capitol W 912 [M]		1957	20.00
—Gray label			
❑ Capitol W 912 [M]		1959	15.00
—Black colorband label, logo at left			
❑ Capitol W 912 [M]		1962	12.00
—Black colorband label, logo on top			
PANIC BUTTON			
❑ Musicor MM-2026 [M]		1964	80.00
❑ Musicor MS-3026 [S]		1964	120.00
PAPER MOON			
❑ Paramount PAS-1012		1973	20.00
PAPER TIGER			
❑ Capitol SW-11475		1975	20.00
PAPILLON			
❑ Capitol ST-11260		1973	20.00
THE PARENT TRAP!			
❑ Buena Vista BV-3309 [M]		1961	40.00
❑ Buena Vista STER-3309 [S]		1961	60.00
—B-side of the above two: Camerata Conducts Themes from Great Motion Pictures			
PARIS BLUES			
❑ United Artists UAL-4092 [M]		1961	25.00
❑ United Artists UAS-5092 [S]		1961	30.00
PARIS HOLIDAY			
❑ United Artists UAL-4001 [M]		1958	50.00
PARIS WHEN IT SIZZLES			
❑ Reprise R 6113 [M]		1964	25.00
❑ Reprise RS 6113 [S]		1964	40.00
PARRISH			
❑ Warner Bros. W 1413 [M]		1961	30.00
❑ Warner Bros. WS 1413 [S]		1961	80.00
—B-side of the above two: Popular Piano Concertos by George Greeley			
A PATCH OF BLUE			
❑ Mainstream S-6068 [S]		1965	25.00
❑ Mainstream 56068 [M]		1965	20.00
❑ Mainstream ST-90805 [S]		1965	30.00
—Capitol Record Club edition			
PATTON			
❑ 20th Century Fox S-4208		1970	20.00
PENELOPE			
❑ MGM E-4426 [M]		1966	20.00
❑ MGM SE-4426 [S]		1966	30.00
PENTHOUSE			
❑ United Artists UAL-4170 [M]		1967	20.00
❑ United Artists UAS-5170 [S]		1967	20.00
THE PEOPLE NEXT DOOR			
❑ Avco AV-11002		1970	25.00
PEPE			
❑ Colpix CP-507 [M]		1960	20.00
❑ Colpix SCP-507 [S]		1960	25.00
PERFORMANCE			
❑ Warner Bros. WS 1846		1970	1500.
—Original issue; has a completely different cover to the more common 2554			
❑ Warner Bros. BS 2554		1970	20.00
—Second issue			
PETE KELLY'S BLUES			
❑ Columbia CL 690 [M]		1955	40.00

SOUNDTRACKS

Except when noted otherwise, VG = 25% of NM, and VG+ = 50% of NM. (Example: VG = $2.00, VG+ = $4.00 and NM = $8.00.)

SOUNDTRACKS

Number Title (A Side/B Side)	Yr	NM
❑ Decca DL 8166 [M]	1955	50.00
—Black label, silver print		
PETULIA		
❑ Warner Bros. WS 1755	1968	25.00
PEYTON PLACE		
❑ RCA Victor LOC-1042 [M]	1958	30.00
—"Long Play" at bottom of label		
❑ RCA Victor LOC-1042 [M]	1965	25.00
—"Monaural" at bottom of label		
❑ RCA Victor LSO-1042 [S]	1958	100.00
—"Living Stereo" at bottom of label		
❑ RCA Victor LSO-1042 [S]	1965	60.00
—"Stereo" at bottom of label		
PHAEDRA		
❑ United Artists UAL-4102 [M]	1962	20.00
❑ United Artists UAS-5102 [S]	1962	30.00
PICNIC		
❑ Decca DL 8320 [M]	1956	30.00
—Black label, silver print		
❑ Decca DL 8320 [M]	196?	15.00
—Black label with color bars		
❑ Decca DL 78320 [S]	1959	30.00
—Maroon or all-black label		
❑ Decca DL 78320 [S]	196?	15.00
—Black label with color bars		
❑ MCA 2049	1973	10.00
—Reissue of Decca 78320; black label with rainbow		
PINOCCHIO		
❑ Disneyland DQ-1202 [M]	1959	30.00
—Second edition		
❑ Disneyland DQ-1202MO [M]	1963	20.00
—Third edition		
❑ Disneyland WDL-4002 [M]	1956	250.00
—Original edition		
❑ Disneyland ST-4905 [M]	1963	150.00
—Gatefold cover with pop-up center graphics		
THE PIRATE		
❑ MGM E-21 [10]	1951	70.00
PLANET OF THE APES		
❑ Project 3 PR-5023 SD	1968	20.00
—Regular cover		
❑ Project 3 PR-5023 SD	1968	30.00
—Gatefold cover		
THE PLEASURE SEEKERS		
❑ RCA Victor LOC-1101 [M]	1964	50.00
❑ RCA Victor LSO-1101 [S]	1964	100.00
POLLYANNA		
❑ Disneyland DQ-1307 [M]	1967	25.00
❑ Disneyland ST-1906 [M]	1960	50.00
PORGY AND BESS		
❑ Columbia Masterworks OS 2016 [S]	1959	20.00
❑ Columbia Masterworks OL 5410 [M]	1959	15.00
PRETTY BOY FLOYD		
❑ Audio Fidelity AFLP-1936 [M]	1960	60.00
❑ Audio Fidelity AFSD-5936 [S]	1960	80.00
THE PRIDE AND THE PASSION		
❑ Capitol W 873 [M]	1957	60.00
THE PRISONER OF ZENDA		
❑ United Artists UA-LA374-G	1974	20.00
PRIVATE HELL 36		
❑ Coral CRL 56122 [10]	1954	100.00
THE PRODUCERS		
❑ RCA Victor ANL1-1132	1975	10.00
—Reissue of LSP-4008		
❑ RCA Victor LPM-4008 [M]	1968	50.00
❑ RCA Victor LSP-4008 [S]	1968	30.00
THE PROFESSIONALS		
❑ Colgems COMO-5001 [M]	1966	60.00
❑ Colgems COSO-5001 [S]	1966	150.00
A PROMISE AT DAWN		
❑ Polydor 24-5502	1970	30.00
THE PROPER TIME		
❑ Contemporary M-3587 [M]	1960	30.00
❑ Contemporary S-7587 [S]	1960	40.00
PRUDENCE AND THE PILL		
❑ 20th Century Fox S-4199	1968	20.00
THE QUIET MAN		
❑ Decca DL 5411 [10]	1952	120.00
THE QUILLER MEMORANDUM		
❑ Columbia Masterworks OS 3060 [S]	1966	60.00
❑ Columbia Masterworks OL 6660 [M]	1966	30.00
QUO VADIS?		
❑ MGM E-103 [10]	1951	40.00
—Music soundtrack only		
❑ MGM E-134 [(2)10]	1951	60.00
—Box set of two discs; includes dialogue		
❑ MGM E-3524 [M]	1957	25.00
—Yellow label; has both music and dialogue		

Soundtrack, *The Producers*, RCA Victor LSP-4008, 1968, stereo, **$30.**

Number Title (A Side/B Side)	Yr	NM
THE RAILWAY CHILDREN		
❑ Capitol SW-871	1972	20.00
THE RAINMAKER		
❑ RCA Victor LPM-1434 [M]	1956	100.00
RAINTREE COUNTY		
❑ RCA Victor LOC-1038 [M]	1958	30.00
❑ RCA Victor LSO-1038 [S]	1958	50.00
❑ RCA Victor LOC-6000 [(2)M]	1957	120.00
THE RAT RACE		
❑ Dot DLP-3306 [M]	1960	40.00
❑ Dot DLP-25306 [S]	1960	50.00
RED GARTERS		
❑ Columbia CL 6282 [10]	1954	50.00
THE RED PONY		
❑ Columbia Masterworks ML 5983 [M]	196?	25.00
❑ Columbia Masterworks MS 6583 [R]	196?	25.00
THE RED TENT		
❑ Paramount PAS-6019	1971	25.00
THE REPORTER		
❑ Columbia CL 2269 [M]	1963	30.00
❑ Columbia CS 9069 [S]	1963	40.00
RETURN TO PARADISE		
❑ Decca DL 5489 [10]	1953	200.00
THE REVOLUTION		
❑ United Artists UA-LA296-G	1974	12.00
—Reissue of 5185		
❑ United Artists UAS-5185	1968	25.00
RHAPSODY OF STEEL		
❑ U.S. Steel JB-502/3	1958	100.00
RICH, YOUNG AND PRETTY		
❑ MGM E-86 [10]	1951	40.00
RIDER ON THE RAIN		
❑ Capitol ST-584	1970	25.00
RIOT ON SUNSET STRIP		
❑ Tower DT 5065 [R]	1967	25.00
❑ Tower T 5065 [M]	1967	20.00

Number Title (A Side/B Side)	Yr	NM
ROAD TO HONG KONG		
❑ Liberty LOM-16002 [M]	1962	20.00
❑ Liberty LOS-17002 [S]	1962	40.00
THE ROBE		
❑ Decca DL 9012 [M]	1953	30.00
—Maroon label		
❑ Decca DL 79012 [R]	196?	12.00
❑ MCA 1529	198?	8.00
—Reissue of MCA 2052		
❑ MCA 2052	1973	10.00
—Reissue of Decca 79012; black label with rainbow		
ROBIN AND THE SEVEN HOODS		
❑ Reprise F 2021 [M]	1964	50.00
❑ Reprise FS 2021 [S]	1964	60.00
ROBIN HOOD		
❑ Disneyland ST-3810	1973	25.00
ROCK ALL NIGHT		
❑ Mercury MG-20293 [M]	1957	100.00
ROCK, PRETTY BABY		
❑ Decca DL 8429 [M]	1957	120.00
—Black label, silver print; also includes pink label promo		
❑ Decca DL 8429 [M]	196?	30.00
—Black label with color bars		
ROCK, ROCK, ROCK		
❑ (no label) (no #) [M]	1958	1500.
—Demo version, 20 tracks		
❑ Chess LP-1425 [M]	1958	200.00
ROMANCE OF A HORSETHIEF		
❑ Allied Artists AAS-110-100	1971	50.00
ROME ADVENTURE		
❑ Warner Bros. W 1458 [M]	1962	20.00
❑ Warner Bros. WS 1458 [S]	1962	25.00
ROMEO AND JULIET		
❑ Capitol SWDR-289 [(4)]	1969	30.00
—From the 1968 Franco Zeffirelli remake; contains dialogue and music		
❑ Capitol ST-400	1970	15.00
—From the 1968 Franco Zeffirelli remake; edited version of 289		

Soundtrack, *Quo Vadis,* MGM E-103, 1951, 10-inch LP, **$40.**

Number	Title (A Side/B Side)	Yr	NM
❑ Capitol ST-2993		1968	12.00
—From the 1968 Franco Zeffirelli remake; contains the music; black label with colorband			
❑ Epic LC 3126 [M]		1954	60.00
❑ Epic FLM 13104 [M]		1966	30.00
—Reissue of 3126			
❑ Epic FLS 15104 [R]		1966	25.00
ROOTS OF HEAVEN			
❑ 20th Fox FOX-3005 [M]		1958	300.00
ROSE MARIE			
❑ MGM E-229 [10]		1954	40.00
THE ROSE TATTOO			
❑ Columbia CL 727 [M]		1955	50.00
ROSEMARY'S BABY			
❑ Dot DLP-25875		1968	20.00
THE ROYAL WEDDING			
❑ MGM E-543 [10]		1951	50.00
THE RULING CLASS			
❑ Avco AV-11003		1972	25.00
THE RUN OF THE ARROW			
❑ Decca DL 8620 [M]		1957	60.00
—Black label, silver print, or pink label, black print promo			
❑ Decca DL 8620 [M]		196?	30.00
—Black label with color bars			
RUN WILD, RUN FREE			
❑ SGC SD 5003		1969	20.00
RUN, ANGEL, RUN			
❑ Epic BN 26474		1969	20.00
RYAN'S DAUGHTER			
❑ MGM 1SE-27		1970	25.00
SACCO AND VANZETTI			
❑ RCA Victor LSP-4612		1971	20.00
THE SACRED IDOL			
❑ Capitol ST 1293 [S]		1960	30.00
❑ Capitol T 1293 [M]		1960	25.00
SAINT JOAN			
❑ Capitol W 865 [M]		1957	30.00

Number	Title (A Side/B Side)	Yr	NM
SALLAH			
❑ Philips PHM 200177 [M]		1965	20.00
❑ Philips PHS 600177 [S]		1965	25.00
SALOME			
❑ Decca DL 6026 [10]		1953	120.00
SAMSON AND DELILAH			
❑ Decca DL 6007 [10]		1952	60.00
THE SAND CASTLE			
❑ Columbia CL 1455 [M]		1961	15.00
❑ Columbia CS 8249 [S]		1961	20.00
THE SAND PEBBLES			
❑ 20th Century Fox 3189 [M]		1966	30.00
❑ 20th Century Fox S-4189 [S]		1966	50.00
THE SANDPIPER			
❑ Mercury MG-21032 [M]		1965	25.00
❑ Mercury SR-61032 [S]		1965	30.00
SANTA AND THE 3 BEARS			
❑ Mr. Pickwick SPC 1501		196?	20.00
—With "Santa" cutout intact			
SATAN IN HIGH HEELS			
❑ Charlie Parker PLP-406 [M]		1962	30.00
—Standard cover			
❑ Charlie Parker PLP-406 [M]		1962	50.00
—Gatefold cover			
❑ Charlie Parker PLP-406S [S]		1962	40.00
—Standard cover			
❑ Charlie Parker PLP-406S [S]		1962	60.00
—Gatefold cover			
SATAN'S SADISTS			
❑ Smash SRS-67127		1969	30.00
THE SAVAGE SEVEN			
❑ Atco 33-245 [M]		1968	30.00
❑ Atco SD 33-245 [S]		1968	30.00
SAVAGE WILD			
❑ American Int'l. STA-1032		1970	20.00
SAY ONE FOR ME			
❑ Columbia CL 1337 [M]		1959	40.00
❑ Columbia CS 8147 [S]		1959	80.00

Number	Title (A Side/B Side)	Yr	NM
SAYONARA			
❑ RCA Victor LOC-1041 [M]		1957	50.00
❑ RCA Victor LSO-1041 [S]		1957	70.00
THE SCALPHUNTERS			
❑ United Artists UAL-4176 [M]		1968	30.00
❑ United Artists UAS-5176 [S]		1968	40.00
SCENT OF MYSTERY			
❑ Ramrod ST-6001 [S]		1960	100.00
❑ Ramrod T-6001 [M]		1960	50.00
SCROOGE			
❑ Columbia Masterworks S 30258		1970	30.00
SEARCH FOR PARADISE			
❑ RCA Victor LOC-1034 [M]		1957	40.00
SEASIDE SWINGERS			
❑ Mercury MG-21031 [M]		1965	20.00
❑ Mercury SR-61031 [S]		1965	25.00
SEBASTIAN			
❑ Dot DLP-3845 [M]		1968	50.00
❑ Dot DLP-25845 [S]		1968	20.00
THE SECRET OF SANTA VITTORIA			
❑ United Artists UAS-5200		1969	30.00
SERGEANTS 3			
❑ Reprise R-2013 [M]		1962	30.00
❑ Reprise RS-2013 [S]		1962	50.00
SERPICO			
❑ Paramount PAS-1016		1973	25.00
SEVEN BRIDES FOR SEVEN BROTHERS			
❑ MGM E-244 [10]		1954	40.00
SEVEN GOLDEN MEN			
❑ United Artists UAS-5193		1969	25.00
THE SEVEN LITTLE FOYS			
❑ RCA Victor LPM-3275 [10]		1955	70.00
1776			
❑ Columbia S 31741		1972	20.00
THE 7TH DAWN			
❑ United Artists UAL-4115 [M]		1964	30.00
THE SEVENTH DAWN			
❑ United Artists UAL-4115 [M]		1964	30.00
THE 7TH DAWN			
❑ United Artists UAS-5115 [S]		1964	40.00
THE SEVENTH DAWN			
❑ United Artists UAS-5115 [S]		1964	40.00
THE 7TH VOYAGE OF SINBAD			
❑ Colpix CP-504 [M]		1958	200.00
SEX AND THE SINGLE GIRL			
❑ Warner Bros. W 1572 [M]		1964	15.00
❑ Warner Bros. WS 1572 [S]		1964	20.00
SHAFT IN AFRICA			
❑ ABC ABCX-793		1973	30.00
SHAFT'S BIG SCORE			
❑ MGM 1SE-36		1972	30.00
SHAKE HANDS WITH THE DEVIL			
❑ United Artists UAL-4043 [M]		1959	30.00
❑ United Artists UAS-5043 [S]		1959	50.00
SHALAKO			
❑ Philips PHS 600286		1968	30.00
SHEBA BABY			
❑ Buddah BDS-5634		1975	30.00
SHENANDOAH			
❑ Decca DL 9125 [M]		1965	30.00
❑ Decca DL 79125 [S]		1965	40.00
THE SHOP ON MAIN STREET			
❑ Mainstream S-6082 [S]		1966	40.00
❑ Mainstream 56082 [M]		1966	25.00
SHOW BOAT			
❑ MGM E-559 [10]		1951	30.00
THE SICILIAN CLAN			
❑ 20th Century Fox S-4209		1970	50.00
THE SIDEHACKERS			
❑ Amaret ST-5004		1969	20.00
THE SILENCERS			
❑ RCA Victor LOC-1120 [M]		1966	30.00
❑ RCA Victor LSO-1120 [S]		1966	50.00
SILENT RUNNING			
❑ Decca DL 79188		1972	40.00
SILK STOCKINGS			
❑ MGM E-3542 [M]		1957	30.00
SINGIN' IN THE RAIN			
❑ MCA 39044		198?	10.00
❑ Metro M-599 [M]		1966	15.00
—Reissue of MGM LP			
❑ Metro MS-599 [R]		1966	12.00
❑ MGM E-113 [10]		1952	30.00

Except when noted otherwise, VG = 25% of NM, and VG+ = 50% of NM. (Example: VG = $2.00, VG+ = $4.00 and NM = $8.00.)

Number	Title (A Side/B Side)	Yr	NM
SINGLE ROOM FURNISHED			
❑ Sidewalk ST-5917		1968	40.00
THE 633 SQUADRON			
❑ United Artists UA-LA305-G		1974	25.00
SKATEDANCER			
❑ Mira LP-3004 [M]		1966	20.00
❑ Mira LPS-3004 [S]		1966	25.00
SKI ON THE WILD SIDE			
❑ MGM E-4439 [M]		1967	30.00
❑ MGM SE-4439 [S]		1967	50.00
SLAUGHTER ON 10TH AVENUE			
❑ Decca DL 8657 [M]		1957	25.00
—Black label, silver print			
❑ Decca DL 8657 [M]		1960	12.00
—Black label with color bars			
❑ Decca DL 78657 [S]		1957	30.00
—Black label, silver print			
❑ Decca DL 78657 [S]		1960	15.00
—Black label with color bars			
SLAUGHTERHOUSE-FIVE			
❑ Columbia Masterworks S 31333		1972	25.00
THE SLAVE TRADE IN THE WORLD TODAY			
❑ London M-76006 [M]		1964	200.00
SLAVES			
❑ Skye SK-11		1969	30.00
SLEEPING BEAUTY			
❑ Disneyland STER-4018 [S]		1959	40.00
❑ Disneyland WDL-4018 [M]		1959	30.00
❑ Disneyland STER-4036 [S]		1970	20.00
—Reissue of STER-4018			
SLEUTH			
❑ Columbia Masterworks S 32154		1973	20.00
SLIPPERY WHEN WET			
❑ World Pacific WP-1265 [M]		1959	50.00
A SMASHING TIME			
❑ ABC ABC-OC-6 [M]		1967	20.00
❑ ABC ABCS-OC-6 [S]		1967	25.00
❑ ABC SW-91399 [S]		1967	25.00
—Capitol Record Club edition			
SNOOPY COME HOME			
❑ Columbia Masterworks S 31451		1972	20.00
THE SNOW QUEEN			
❑ Decca DL 8977 [M]		1959	40.00
❑ Decca DL 78977 [S]		1959	60.00
SNOW WHITE AND THE SEVEN DWARFS			
❑ Buena Vista 102 [(3)]		1975	50.00
—Entire movie on three LPs; TV mail-order item			
❑ Disneyland DQ-1201 [M]		1959	50.00
—Reissue of 4005; whirlpool-like designs on cover			
❑ Disneyland DQ-1201 [M]		1968	25.00
—Reissue; with same cover as 4005, but no gatefold			
❑ Disneyland WDL-4005 [M]		1956	200.00
—Gatefold cover			
SNOW WHITE AND THE THREE STOOGES			
❑ Columbia CL 1650 [M]		1961	60.00
❑ Columbia CS 8450 [S]		1961	100.00
SO THIS IS LOVE			
❑ RCA Victor LOC-3000 [10]		1953	80.00
SO THIS IS PARIS			
❑ Decca DL 5553 [10]		1955	50.00
SODOM AND GOMORRAH			
❑ RCA Victor LOC-1076 [M]		1963	80.00
❑ RCA Victor LSO-1076 [S]		1963	100.00
SOL MADRID			
❑ MGM SE-4541 ST		1968	30.00
SOLOMON AND SHEBA			
❑ United Artists UAL-4051 [M]		1959	25.00
—Second, regular cover			
❑ United Artists UAL-4051 [M]		1959	50.00
—First cover with silky finish			
❑ United Artists UAS-5051 [S]		1959	60.00
—Second, regular cover			
❑ United Artists UAS-5051 [S]		1959	120.00
—First cover with silky finish			
SOME CAME RUNNING			
❑ Capitol SW 1109 [S]		1958	80.00
❑ Capitol W 1109 [M]		1958	30.00
SOME LIKE IT HOT			
❑ United Artists UA-LA272-G		1974	12.00
—Reissue of 5030			
❑ United Artists UAL-4030 [M]		1959	50.00
❑ United Artists UAS-5030 [S]		1959	75.00
SOMEBODY LOVES ME			
❑ RCA Victor LPM-3097 [10]		1952	50.00
SONG OF THE SOUTH			
❑ Disneyland WDL-4001 [M]		1956	300.00
—Yellow label (first pressing)			
❑ Disneyland WDL-4001 [M]		1957	200.00
—Red/maroon label (second pressing)			
SONG OF THE SOUTH (UNCLE REMUS)			
❑ Disneyland DQ-1205 [M]		1959	25.00
SONG WITHOUT END			
❑ Colpix CP-506 [M]		1960	20.00
❑ Colpix SCP-506 [S]		1960	25.00
THE SONS OF KATIE ELDER			
❑ Columbia Masterworks OS 2820 [S]		1965	100.00
❑ Columbia Masterworks OL 6420 [M]		1965	50.00
THE SOUL OF NIGGER CHARLEY			
❑ MGM 1SE-46		1973	20.00
THE SOUND AND THE FURY			
❑ Decca DL 8885 [M]		1959	30.00
❑ Decca DL 78885 [S]		1959	70.00
THE SOUND OF MUSIC			
❑ RCA Victor LOCD-2005 [M]		1965	12.00
—With booklet; back cover lists "I Have Confidence" correctly			
❑ RCA Victor LOCD-2005 [M]		1965	15.00
—With booklet; back cover lists "I Have Confidence" as "I Have Confidence in Me"			
❑ RCA Victor LSOD-2005 [S]		1965	15.00
—With booklet; back cover lists "I Have Confidence" correctly			
❑ RCA Victor LSOD-2005 [S]		1965	20.00
—With booklet; back cover lists "I Have Confidence" as "I Have Confidence in Me"			
❑ RCA Victor LSOD-2005 [S]		1969	12.00
—No booklet; gatefold cover, record comes out from inside; orange or tan label			
❑ RCA Victor LSOD-2005 [S]		1977	10.00
—Gatefold cover, record comes out from outside; black label with dog at 1 o'clock			
SOUTH PACIFIC			
❑ RCA Victor LOC-1032 [M]		1958	20.00
—"Long Play" on label; no "Academy Award Winner" on front cover			
❑ RCA Victor LOC-1032 [M]		196?	12.00
—"Long Play" or "Mono" on label; with "Academy Award Winner" on front cover			
❑ RCA Victor LSO-1032 [S]		1958	12.00
—Orange label			
❑ RCA Victor LSO-1032 [S]		1958	25.00
—"Living Stereo" on label; no "Academy Award Winner" on front cover			
❑ RCA Victor LSO-1032 [S]		196?	15.00
—"Living Stereo" or "Stereo" on black label; with "Academy Award Winner" on front cover			
❑ RCA Victor LOCD-2000 [M]		1958	40.00
—Gatefold cover with photos inside			
SOUTHERN STAR			
❑ Colgems COSO-5009		1969	60.00
A SPANISH AFFAIR			
❑ Dot DLP-3078 [M]		1958	100.00
SPARTACUS			
❑ Decca DL 9092 [M]		1960	20.00
—Black label, silver print			
❑ Decca DL 9092 [M]		1961	12.00
—Black label with color bars			
❑ Decca DL 79092 [S]		1960	25.00
—Maroon label, silver print			
❑ Decca DL 79092 [S]		1961	15.00
—Black label with color bars			
❑ MCA 2068		1973	12.00
—Reissue of 79092; black label with rainbow			
THE SPIRIT OF ST. LOUIS			
❑ RCA Victor LPM-1472 [M]		1957	50.00
THE SPY WHO CAME IN FROM THE COLD			
❑ RCA Victor LOC-1118 [M]		1965	20.00
❑ RCA Victor LSO-1118 [S]		1965	40.00
THE SPY WITH A COLD NOSE			
❑ Columbia Masterworks OS 3070 [S]		1966	30.00
❑ Columbia Masterworks OL 6670 [M]		1966	20.00
ST. LOUIS BLUES			
❑ Capitol W 993 [M]		1958	50.00
—Turquoise or gray label			
❑ Capitol W 993 [M]		1959	25.00
—Black colorband label, logo at left			
❑ Capitol W 993 [M]		196?	20.00
—Black colorband label, logo at top			
ST. LOUIS WOMAN			
❑ Capitol L 355 [10]		1955	80.00
STAGECOACH			
❑ Mainstream S-6077 [S]		1966	30.00
❑ Mainstream 56077 [M]		1966	20.00
❑ Mainstream ST-90802 [S]		1966	30.00
—Capitol Record Club edition			
❑ Mainstream T-90802 [M]		1966	25.00
—Capitol Record Club edition			
STAR!			
❑ 20th Century Fox DTCS-5102		1968	20.00
THE STARS AND STRIPES FOREVER			
❑ MGM E-176 [10]		1952	30.00
STATE FAIR			
❑ Dot DLP-9011 [M]		1962	25.00
❑ Dot DLP-29011 [S]		1962	30.00
THE STERILE CUCKOO			
❑ Paramount PAS-5009		1970	20.00
STILETTO			
❑ Columbia Masterworks OS 3360		1969	20.00
THE STING			
❑ MCA 390		1973	12.00
—Original edition			
THE STRANGE ONE			
❑ Coral CRL 57132 [M]		1957	70.00
THE STRAWBERRY STATEMENT			
❑ MGM 2SE-14 [(2)]		1970	25.00
A STREETCAR NAMED DESIRE			
❑ Capitol L 289 [10]		1951	50.00
A STUDY IN TERROR			
❑ Roulette OS-801 [M]		1965	40.00
❑ Roulette OSS-801 [S]		1965	80.00
THE SUBTERRANEANS			
❑ MGM E-3812 ST [M]		1960	40.00
❑ MGM SE-3812 ST [S]		1960	80.00
SUMMER AND SMOKE			
❑ RCA Victor LOC-1067 [M]		1961	50.00
❑ RCA Victor LSO-1067 [S]		1961	70.00
SUMMER HOLIDAY			
❑ Epic LN 24063 [M]		1963	25.00
❑ Epic BN 26063 [S]		1963	30.00
SUMMER LOVE			
❑ Decca DL 8714 [M]		1958	60.00
—Black label, silver print, or pink label, black print promo			
❑ Decca DL 8714 [M]		196?	30.00
—Black label with color bars			
SUMMER MAGIC			
❑ Buena Vista BV-4025 [M]		1963	40.00
❑ Buena Vista STER-4025 [S]		1963	60.00
SUMMER STOCK			
❑ MGM E-519 [10]		1950	40.00
THE SUN ALSO RISES			
❑ Kapp KDL-7001 [M]		1957	60.00
SUN VALLEY SERENADE			
❑ RCA Victor LPT-3064 [10]		1954	60.00
THE SUNNY SIDE OF THE STREET			
❑ Mercury MG-25100 [10]		1951	60.00
SURF PARTY			
❑ 20th Century Fox TFM-3131 [M]		1964	25.00
❑ 20th Century Fox TFS-4131 [S]		1964	30.00
THE SWAN			
❑ MGM E-3399 [M]		1956	70.00
SWEDISH HEAVEN AND HELL			
❑ Ariel ARS-15000		1969	25.00
SWEET CHARITY			
❑ Decca DL 71502		1969	20.00
SWEET LOVE, BITTER			
❑ ABC Impulse! AS-9141 [S]		1968	15.00
❑ Impulse! A-9141 [M]		1967	40.00
❑ Impulse! AS-9141 [S]		1967	30.00
THE SWEET RIDE			
❑ 20th Century Fox S-4198		1968	20.00
THE SWEET SMELL OF SUCCESS			
❑ Decca DL 8610 [M]		1957	60.00
SWEET SWEETBACK'S BADASSSSSS SONG			
❑ Stax STS-3001		1971	30.00
SWEPT AWAY			
❑ Peters International PLD 1005		1957	40.00
THE SWIMMER			
❑ Columbia Masterworks OS 3210		1968	25.00
SWINGER'S PARADISE			
❑ Epic LN 24145 [M]		1965	20.00
❑ Epic BN 26145 [S]		1965	25.00
A SWINGIN' SUMMER			
❑ Hanna-Barbera HLP-8500 [M]		1966	25.00
❑ Hanna-Barbera HST-9500 [S]		1966	30.00
SYLVIA			
❑ Mercury MG-21004 [M]		1965	20.00
❑ Mercury SR-61004 [S]		1965	30.00
TARAS BULBA			
❑ United Artists UAL-4100 [M]		1962	30.00
❑ United Artists UAS-5100 [S]		1962	50.00
TEENAGE REBELLION			
❑ Sidewalk ST-5903 [S]		1967	25.00
❑ Sidewalk T-5903 [M]		1967	20.00
TELL ME THAT YOU LOVE ME, JUNIE MOON			
❑ Columbia Masterworks OS 3540		1970	20.00

SOUNDTRACKS

Number	Title (A Side/B Side)	Yr	NM
THE TEN COMMANDMENTS			
❑ Dot DLP-3054 [M]		1956	40.00
❑ Dot DLP-25054 [S]		1959	25.00
—Re-recording of the original soundtrack in stereo			
❑ Paramount PAS-1006 [(2)]		1973	20.00
—Reissue of Dot 25054			
TENDER IS THE NIGHT			
❑ 20th Century Fox FOX-3054 [M]		1962	150.00
❑ 20th Century Fox SFX-3054 [S]		1962	200.00
THE TENTH VICTIM			
❑ Mainstream S-6071 [S]		1965	50.00
❑ Mainstream 56071 [M]		1965	40.00
THAT DARN CAT			
❑ Buena Vista BV-3334 [M]		1965	20.00
❑ Buena Vista STER-3334 [S]		1965	25.00
THAT MAN IN ISTANBUL			
❑ Mainstream S-6072 [S]		1966	25.00
❑ Mainstream 56072 [M]		1966	20.00
THERE'S NO BUSINESS LIKE SHOW BUSINESS			
❑ Decca DL 8091 [M]		1954	30.00
—Black label with silver print			
❑ Decca DL 8091 [M]		196?	20.00
—Black label with color bars			
THEY SHOOT HORSES, DON'T THEY?			
❑ ABC ABCS-OC-10		1969	20.00
THIS COULD BE THE NIGHT			
❑ MGM E-3530 [M]		1957	50.00
THIS EARTH IS MINE			
❑ Decca DL 8915 [M]		1959	80.00
❑ Decca DL 78915 [S]		1959	100.00
THIS PROPERTY IS CONDEMNED			
❑ Verve V-8664 [M]		1966	20.00
❑ Verve V6-8664 [S]		1966	30.00
THE THOMAS CROWN AFFAIR			
❑ United Artists UA-LA295-G		1974	12.00
—Reissue of 5182			
❑ United Artists UAS-5182		1968	20.00
THOROUGHLY MODERN MILLIE			
❑ Decca DL 1500 [M]		1967	20.00
—With bound-in booklet			
❑ Decca DL 71500 [S]		1967	20.00
—With bound-in booklet			
THOSE GLORIOUS MGM MUSICALS: DEEP IN MY HEART/WORDS AND MUSIC			
❑ MGM 2-SES-54-ST [(2)]		1973	20.00
THOSE GLORIOUS MGM MUSICALS: EVERYTHING I HAVE IS YOURS/SUMMER STOCK/I LOVE MELVIN			
❑ MGM 2-SES-52-ST [(2)]		1973	20.00
THOSE GLORIOUS MGM MUSICALS: GOOD NEWS/IN THE GOOD OLD SUMMERTIME/TWO WEEKS WITH LOVE			
❑ MGM 2-SES-49-ST [(2)]		1973	20.00
THOSE GLORIOUS MGM MUSICALS: LOVELY TO LOOK AT/BRIGADOON			
❑ MGM 2-SES-50-ST [(2)]		1973	20.00
THOSE GLORIOUS MGM MUSICALS: NANCY GOES TO RIO/RICH, YOUNG AND PRETTY/ROYAL WEDDING			
❑ MGM 2-SES-53-ST [(2)]		1973	20.00
THOSE GLORIOUS MGM MUSICALS: ROSE MARIE/SEVN BRIDES FOR SEVEN BROTHERS			
❑ MGM 2-SES-41-ST [(2)]		1973	20.00
THOSE GLORIOUS MGM MUSICALS: SHOW BOAT/ANNIE GET YOUR GUN			
❑ MGM 2-SES-42-ST [(2)]		1973	20.00
THOSE GLORIOUS MGM MUSICALS: SINGIN' IN THE RAIN/EASTER PARADE			
❑ MGM 2-SES-40-ST [(2)]		1973	20.00
THOSE GLORIOUS MGM MUSICALS: THE BAND WAGON/KISS ME, KATE			
❑ MGM 2-SES-44-ST [(2)]		1973	20.00
THOSE GLORIOUS MGM MUSICALS: THE BARKLEYS OF BROADWAY/LES GIRLS			
❑ MGM 2-SES-51-ST [(2)]		1973	20.00
THOSE GLORIOUS MGM MUSICALS: THE PIRATE/PAGAN LOVE SONG/HIT THE DECK			
❑ MGM 2-SES-43-ST [(2)]		1973	40.00
THOSE GLORIOUS MGM MUSICALS: TILL THE CLOUDS ROLL BY/THREE LITTLE WORDS			
❑ MGM 2-SES-45-ST [(2)]		1973	20.00
THREE BITES OF THE APPLE			
❑ MGM E-4444 [M]		1967	25.00
❑ MGM SE-4444 [S]		1967	20.00
THREE FOR THE SHOW			
❑ Mercury MG-25204 [M]		1955	60.00
THREE IN THE ATTIC			
❑ Sidewalk ST-5918		1968	30.00
THREE LITTLE WORDS			
❑ MGM E-516 [10]		1959	60.00
THE THREE WORLDS OF GULLIVER			
❑ Colpix CP-414 [M]		1960	60.00
THE THREEPENNY OPERA			
❑ RCA Victor LOC-1086 [M]		1964	15.00
—Reissue cover: White background, orange drawing, Sammy Davis Jr. in foreground, "RE" at bottom			
❑ RCA Victor LOC-1086 [M]		1964	150.00
—With rare original cover: White background, pink and black drawing, characters underneath			
❑ RCA Victor LSO-1086 [S]		1964	20.00
—Reissue cover: White background, orange drawing, Sammy Davis Jr. in foreground, "RE" at bottom			
❑ RCA Victor LSO-1086 [S]		1964	200.00
—With rare original cover: White background, pink and black drawing, characters underneath			
THUNDER ALLEY			
❑ Sidewalk ST-5902 [S]		1967	25.00
❑ Sidewalk T-5902 [M]		1967	20.00
THUNDERBALL			
❑ United Artists UAL-4132 [M]		1965	20.00
❑ United Artists UAS-5132 [S]		1965	30.00
❑ United Artists SW-90820 [S]		1965	40.00
—Capitol Record Club edition			
TICK...TICK...TICK			
❑ MGM SE-4667 [M]		1970	25.00
TILL THE CLOUDS ROLL BY			
❑ Metro M-578 [M]		1966	12.00
—Reissue of MGM 501			
❑ Metro MS-578 [R]		1966	10.00
❑ MGM E-501 [10]		1950	50.00
A TIME TO LOVE AND A TIME TO DIE			
❑ Decca DL 8778 [M]		1958	100.00
TO BED... OR NOT TO BED			
❑ London M-76005 [M]		1963	40.00
TO KILL A MOCKINGBIRD			
❑ Ava A-20 [M]		1962	25.00
❑ Ava AS-20 [S]		1962	30.00
TO SIR, WITH LOVE			
❑ Fontana MGF-27569 [M]		1967	20.00
❑ Fontana SRF-67569 [S]		1967	25.00
TOKYO OLYMPIAD			
❑ Monument MLP-8046 [M]		1966	15.00
❑ Monument SLP-18046 [S]		1966	20.00
TOM JONES			
❑ United Artists UAL-4113 [M]		1963	20.00
❑ United Artists UAS-5113 [S]		1963	25.00
TOM SAWYER			
❑ United Artists UA-LA057-F		1973	20.00
TOMMY			
❑ Polydor PD 2-9502 [(2)]		1975	20.00
TOO MUCH TOO SOON			
❑ Mercury MG-20381 [M]		1958	30.00
❑ Mercury SR-60019 [S]		1958	80.00
TOPKAPI			
❑ United Artists UAL-4118 [M]		1964	20.00
❑ United Artists UAS-5118 [S]		1964	30.00
THE TOUCHABLES			
❑ 20th Century Fox S-4206		1969	20.00
THE TRAIN			
❑ United Artists UAL-4122 [M]		1965	20.00
❑ United Artists UAS-5122 [S]		1965	40.00
THE TRAP			
❑ Atco 33-204 [M]		1966	40.00
❑ Atco SD 33-204 [S]		1966	70.00
TRAPEZE			
❑ Columbia CL 870 [M]		1956	25.00
THE TRAPP FAMILY			
❑ 20th Fox FOX-3044 [M]		1961	25.00
❑ 20th Fox STX-3044 [S]		1961	40.00
THE TREASURE OF SAN GENNARO			
❑ Buddah BDS-5011		1968	40.00
THE TRIP			
❑ Sidewalk ST-5908 [S]		1967	40.00
❑ Sidewalk T-5908 [M]		1967	30.00
TRIPLE CROSS			
❑ United Artists UAL-4162 [M]		1967	20.00
❑ United Artists UAS-5162 [S]		1967	30.00
THE TROUBLE WITH ANGELS			
❑ Mainstream S-6073 [S]		1966	80.00
❑ Mainstream 56073 [M]		1966	40.00
TRUE GRIT			
❑ Capitol ST-263		1969	30.00
❑ Capitol ST-8-0263		1969	40.00
—Capitol Record Club edition			
TRUE LIFE ADVENTURES			
❑ Disneyland WDL-4011 [M]		1957	70.00
THE TRUE STORY OF THE CIVIL WAR			
❑ Coral CRL 59100 [M]		1958	80.00
TWO MULES FOR SISTER SARA			
❑ Kapp KRS-5512		1970	25.00
TWO WEEKS WITH LOVE			
❑ MGM E-530 [10]		1950	40.00
ULYSSES			
❑ RCA Victor LOC-1138 [M]		1967	25.00
❑ RCA Victor LSO-1138 [S]		1967	30.00
THE UMBRELLAS OF CHERBOURG (LES PARAPLUIES DE CHERBOURG)			
❑ Philips PCC 216 [M]		1965	20.00
❑ Philips PCC 616 [S]		1965	30.00
UNCLE TOM'S CABIN			
❑ Philips PHS 600272		1968	40.00
THE UNFORGIVEN			
❑ United Artists UAL-4068 [M]		1960	40.00
❑ United Artists UAS-5068 [S]		1960	70.00
THE UNSINKABLE MOLLY BROWN			
❑ MGM E-4232 [M]		1964	15.00
❑ MGM SE-4232 [S]		1964	20.00
❑ MGM SW-90048 [S]		1964	15.00
—Capitol Record Club edition			
❑ MGM W-90048 [M]		1964	12.00
—Capitol Record Club edition			
UP IN THE CELLAR			
❑ American Int'l. A-1036		1970	20.00
UP THE DOWN STAIRCASE			
❑ United Artists UAL-4169 [M]		1967	20.00
❑ United Artists UAS-5169 [S]		1967	40.00
UP THE JUNCTION			
❑ Mercury SR-61159		1968	25.00
THE V.I.P.S			
❑ MGM E-4184 [M]		1963	20.00
❑ MGM SE-4184 [S]		1963	25.00
—Music by Bill Evans			
VALLEY OF THE DOLLS			
❑ 20th Century Fox TF-4196 [M]		1968	30.00
❑ 20th Century Fox TFS-4196 [S]		1968	30.00
❑ 20th Century Fox SW-91374 [S]		1968	30.00
—Capitol Record Club edition			
THE VANISHING POINT			
❑ Amos AAS-8002		1971	20.00
THE VANISHING PRAIRIE			
❑ Columbia CL 6332 [10]		1954	80.00
VERTIGO			
❑ Mercury MG-20384 [M]		1958	150.00
THE VICTORS			
❑ Colpix CP-516 [M]		1963	20.00
❑ Colpix SCP-516 [S]		1963	30.00
THE VIKINGS			
❑ United Artists UAL-4003 [M]		1958	30.00
❑ United Artists UAS-5003 [S]		1958	40.00
VILLA RIDES!			
❑ Dot DLP-25870		1968	40.00
VIVA MARIA!			
❑ United Artists UAL-4135 [M]		1965	20.00
❑ United Artists UAS-5135 [S]		1965	30.00
VIVA MAX!			
❑ RCA Victor LSP-4275		1969	20.00
THE VIXEN			
❑ Beverly Hills BHS-22		1968	50.00
VOYAGE EN BALLON			
❑ Philips PHM 200029 [M]		1960	30.00
❑ Philips PHS 600029 [S]		1960	40.00
W.W. AND THE DIXIE DANCEKINGS			
❑ 20th Century ST-103		1975	25.00
WALK DON'T RUN			
❑ Mainstream S-6080 [S]		1966	40.00
❑ Mainstream 56080 [M]		1966	20.00
WALK ON THE WILD SIDE			
❑ Ava A-4-ST [M]		1962	20.00
❑ Ava AS-4-ST [S]		1962	40.00
❑ Choreo A-4-ST [M]		1962	30.00
❑ Choreo AS-4-ST [S]		1962	50.00
WAR AND PEACE			
❑ Columbia CL 930 [M]		1956	25.00
❑ Melodiya/Capitol SWAO 2918		1968	40.00
THE WAR LORD			
❑ Decca DL 9149 [M]		1965	25.00
❑ Decca DL 79149 [S]		1965	50.00

Except when noted otherwise, VG = 25% of NM, and VG+ = 50% of NM. (Example: VG = $2.00, VG+ = $4.00 and NM = $8.00.)

Number	Title (A Side/B Side)	Yr	NM
WARNING SHOT			
❑ Liberty LRP-3498 [M]		1967	30.00
❑ Liberty LST-7498 [S]		1967	40.00
WATERLOO			
❑ Paramount PAS-6003		1971	30.00
❑ Paramount SW-93729		1971	30.00
—Capitol Record Club edition			
WATERMELON MAN			
❑ Beverly Hills BHS-26		1970	30.00
WAY...WAY OUT			
❑ 20th Century Fox 3192 [M]		1966	30.00
❑ 20th Century Fox S-4192 [S]		1966	40.00
WEDDING IN MONACO			
❑ Mercury MG-20149 [M]		1956	250.00
WEST SIDE STORY			
❑ Columbia Masterworks OS 2070 [S]		196?	12.00
—Regular cover; gray "360 Sound Stereo" label			
❑ Columbia Masterworks OS 2070 [S]		1961	25.00
—Originals have gatefold covers and gray and black labels with six "eye" logos			
❑ Columbia Masterworks OS 2070 [S]		1963	15.00
—Gatefold cover; gray "360 Sound Stereo" label			
❑ Columbia Masterworks OS 2070 [S]		1971	10.00
—Regular cover; olive label with "Columbia" continuously around edge			
❑ Columbia Masterworks OL 5670 [M]		196?	10.00
—Regular cover; gray "360 Sound Stereo" label			
❑ Columbia Masterworks OL 5670 [M]		1961	20.00
—Originals have gatefold covers and gray and black labels with six "eye" logos			
❑ Columbia Masterworks OL 5670 [M]		1963	12.00
—Gatefold cover; gray "360 Sound Stereo" label			
WHAT A WAY TO GO!			
❑ 20th Century Fox TFM-3143 [M]		1964	20.00
❑ 20th Century Fox TFS-4143 [S]		1964	40.00
WHAT'S NEW PUSSYCAT?			
❑ United Artists UA-LA278-G		1974	12.00
—Reissue of 5128			
❑ United Artists UAL-4128 [M]		1965	20.00
❑ United Artists UAS-5128 [S]		1965	25.00
WHEN THE BOYS MEET THE GIRLS			
❑ MGM E-4334 [M]		1965	15.00
❑ MGM SE-4334 [S]		1965	30.00
WHERE EAGLES DARE			
❑ MGM S1E-16 ST		1969	30.00
WHERE'S JACK?			
❑ Paramount PAS-5005		1969	25.00
WHERE'S POPPA?			
❑ United Artists UAS-5216		1970	25.00
THE WHISPERERS			
❑ United Artists UAL-4161 [M]		1967	20.00
❑ United Artists UAS-5161 [S]		1967	30.00
WHITE CHRISTMAS			
❑ Decca DL 8083		1954	50.00
WHO'S AFRAID OF VIRGINIA WOOLF?			
❑ Warner Bros. B 1656 [M]		1966	25.00
❑ Warner Bros. BS 1656 [S]		1966	30.00
❑ Warner Bros. 2B 1657 [(2)M]		1966	40.00
—Above (1657) is the complete film, not just the music and some dialogue			
THE WILD BUNCH			
❑ Warner Bros. WS 1814		1969	100.00
THE WILD EYE			
❑ RCA Victor LSP-4003		1968	25.00
WILD IN THE STREETS			
❑ Tower SKAO 5099		1968	30.00
WILD IS THE WIND			
❑ Columbia CL 1090 [M]		1957	25.00
WILD ON THE BEACH			
❑ RCA Victor LPM-3441 [M]		1965	25.00
❑ RCA Victor LSP-3441 [S]		1965	40.00
THE WILD ONE			
❑ Decca DL 5515 [10]		1954	80.00
❑ Decca DL 8349 [M]		1956	40.00
THE WILD RACERS			
❑ Sidewalk ST-5914		1968	25.00
WILD WHEELS			
❑ RCA Victor LSO-1156		1969	20.00
WILD, WILD WINTER			
❑ Decca DL 4699 [M]		1966	20.00
❑ Decca DL 74699 [S]		1966	30.00
WILLIE DYNAMITE			
❑ MCA 393		1974	20.00
WILLY WONKA AND THE CHOCOLATE FACTORY			
❑ Paramount PAS-6012		1971	40.00
WITH A SONG IN MY HEART			
❑ Capitol L 309 [10]		1952	40.00
❑ Capitol T 309 [M]		195?	25.00
THE WIZARD OF OZ			
❑ MGM E-3464 [M]		1956	50.00
—Yellow label			
❑ MGM E-3996 [M]		1962	15.00
—Gatefold cover, black label			
❑ MGM SE-3996 [R]		196?	15.00
—Gatefold cover, black label			
WOMEN OF THE WORLD			
❑ Decca DL 9112 [M]		1963	20.00
❑ Decca DL 79112 [S]		1963	30.00
WONDERFUL COUNTRY			
❑ United Artists UAL-4050 [M]		1959	50.00
❑ United Artists UAS-5050 [S]		1959	100.00
WONDERFUL TO BE YOUNG			
❑ Dot DLP-3474 [M]		1962	25.00
❑ Dot DLP-25474 [S]		1962	40.00
THE WONDERFUL WORLD OF THE BROTHERS GRIMM			
❑ MGM 1E-3 [M]		1962	25.00
—With box and hardback book			
❑ MGM S1E-3 [S]		1962	40.00
—With box and hardback book			
WORDS AND MUSIC			
❑ Metro M-580 [M]		1966	12.00
❑ Metro MS-580 [R]		1966	10.00
❑ MGM E-505 [10]		1950	50.00
THE WORLD OF SUZIE WONG			
❑ RCA Victor LOC-1059 [M]		1960	20.00
❑ RCA Victor LSO-1059 [S]		1960	50.00
WRITTEN ON THE WIND			
❑ Decca DL 8424 [M]		1956	40.00
—Black label, silver print, or pink label, black print promo			
❑ Decca DL 8424 [M]		196?	20.00
—Black label with color bars			
THE WRONG BOX			
❑ Mainstream S-6088 [S]		1966	150.00
❑ Mainstream 56088 [M]		1966	100.00
WUTHERING HEIGHTS			
❑ American Int'l. A-1039		1971	30.00
THE YELLOW CANARY			
❑ Verve V-8548 [M]		1963	20.00
❑ Verve V6-8548 [S]		1963	25.00
THE YELLOW ROLLS-ROYCE			
❑ MGM E-4292 [M]		1965	20.00
❑ MGM SE-4292 [S]		1965	30.00
❑ MGM ST 90424 [S]		1965	15.00
—Capitol Record Club edition			
❑ MGM T 90424 [M]		1965	15.00
—Capitol Record Club edition			
YESTERDAY, TODAY AND TOMORROW			
❑ Warner Bros. W 1552 [M]		1964	40.00
❑ Warner Bros. WS 1552 [S]		1964	50.00
YOJIMBO			
❑ MGM E-4096 [M]		1962	100.00
❑ MGM SE-4096 [S]		1962	150.00
YOU ARE WHAT YOU EAT			
❑ Columbia Masterworks OS 3240		1968	20.00
YOU ONLY LIVE TWICE			
❑ United Artists UA-LA289-G		1974	12.00
—Reissue of 5155			
❑ United Artists UAL-4155 [M]		1967	20.00
❑ United Artists UAS-5155 [S]		1967	25.00
YOUNG BILLY YOUNG			
❑ United Artists UAS-5199		1969	25.00
YOUNG FRANKENSTEIN			
❑ ABC ABCD-870		1975	20.00
THE YOUNG GIRLS OF ROCHEFORT			
❑ Philips PCC 2-226 [(2)M]		1968	20.00
❑ Philips PCC 2-626 [(2)S]		1968	30.00
THE YOUNG LIONS			
❑ Decca DL 8719 [M]		1958	30.00
❑ Decca DL 78719 [S]		1958	80.00
YOUNG LOVERS			
❑ Columbia Masterworks OS 2510 [S]		1964	25.00
❑ Columbia Masterworks OL 7010 [M]		1964	20.00
YOUNG MAN WITH A HORN			
❑ Columbia CL 582 [M]		1950	40.00
❑ Columbia CL 6106 [10]		1950	100.00
THE YOUNG SAVAGES			
❑ Columbia CL 1672 [M]		1961	30.00
❑ Columbia CS 8472 [S]		1961	100.00
YOUNG WINSTON			
❑ Angel SFO-36901		1972	25.00
YOURS, MINE AND OURS			
❑ United Artists UAS-5181		1968	20.00
Z			
❑ Columbia Masterworks OS 3370		1970	20.00
ZABRISKIE POINT			
❑ MGM SE-4468		1970	20.00
ZACHARIAH			
❑ ABC ABCS-OC-13		1970	25.00
ZORBA THE GREEK			
❑ 20th Century T-903		1973	12.00
—Reissue of 20th Century Fox 4167			
❑ 20th Century Fox TFM-3167 [M]		1965	20.00
❑ 20th Century Fox TFS-4167 [S]		1965	25.00
ZULU			
❑ United Artists UAL-4116 [M]		1964	40.00
❑ United Artists UAS-5116 [S]		1964	70.00

Number | Title (A Side/B Side) | Yr | NM

TELEVISION RECORDS

THE ADDAMS FAMILY
❑ RCA Victor LPM-3421 [M] 1965 80.00
❑ RCA Victor LSP-3421 [S] 1965 150.00

AFRICA
❑ MGM E-4462 [M] 1967 50.00
❑ MGM SE-4462 [S] 1967 60.00

THE AGE OF TELEVISION — A CHRONICLE OF THE FIRST 25 YEARS
❑ RCA Victor LL-8 1972 20.00
—With booklet
❑ Warner Bros. BS 2670 1972 30.00
—With booklet; this version seems to be much rarer than the RCA issue

ALADDIN
❑ Columbia CL 1117 [M] 1958 50.00

ALICE THROUGH THE LOOKING GLASS
❑ RCA Victor LOC-1130 [M] 1966 25.00
❑ RCA Victor LSO-1130 [S] 1966 30.00

AMAHL AND THE NIGHT VISITORS
❑ RCA Red Seal LM-1701 [10] 1952 50.00
—Soundtrack of the 1951 NBC-TV production
❑ RCA Red Seal LM-1701 [M] 1952 40.00
—Soundtrack of the 1951 NBC-TV production; 12-inch record in box with booklet
❑ RCA Red Seal LM-2762 [M] 1964 15.00
—Soundtrack of the 1963 NBC Opera Company TV production
❑ RCA Red Seal LSC-2762 [S] 1964 15.00
—Large "RCA Victor" and dog at top of label
❑ RCA Red Seal LSC-2762 [S] 1969 12.00
—Stereo reissue on red label without dog; no bar code on back cover

ANDROCLES AND THE LION
❑ RCA Victor LOC-1141 [M] 1967 25.00
❑ RCA Victor LSO-1141 [S] 1967 25.00

ANNIE GET YOUR GUN
❑ Capitol W 913 [M] 1957 30.00
—Los Angeles/San Francisco production aired on NBC-TV

AT HOME WITH THE MUNSTERS
❑ Golden LP-139 [M] 1964 200.00

ATOM ANT IN MUSCLE MAGIC
❑ Hanna-Barbera HLP-2041 [M] 1966 150.00

THE AVENGERS
❑ Hanna-Barbera HLP-8506 [M] 1966 60.00
❑ Hanna-Barbera HST-9506 [S] 1966 80.00

BATMAN
❑ 20th Century Fox TFM-3180 [M] 1966 60.00
❑ 20th Century Fox TFS-4180 [S] 1966 100.00

THE BEVERLY HILLBILLIES
❑ Columbia CL 2402 [M] 1965 40.00
❑ Columbia CS 9202 [S] 1965 60.00

THE BIG VALLEY
❑ ABC-Paramount ABC-527 [M] 1965 40.00
❑ ABC-Paramount ABCS-527 [S] 1965 50.00

THE BORN LOSERS
❑ Tower DT 5082 [R] 1967 20.00
❑ Tower T 5082 [M] 1967 25.00

THE BORROWERS
❑ Stanyan SRQ-4014 [Q] 1973 50.00

BOURBON STREET BEAT
❑ Warner Bros. W 1321 [M] 1960 25.00
❑ Warner Bros. WS 1321 [S] 1960 30.00

BRIGADOON
❑ Columbia Special Products CSM 385 1968 20.00
—Sold through the mail by broadcast sponsor Armstrong

BURKE'S LAW
❑ Liberty LRP-3374 [M] 1964 60.00
❑ Liberty LST-7374 [S] 1964 80.00

CAROUSEL
❑ Columbia Special Products CSM 479 1969 20.00
—Sold through the mail by broadcast sponsor Armstrong

CHECKMATE
❑ Columbia CL 1591 [M] 1960 40.00
❑ Columbia CS 8391 [S] 1960 60.00

CINDERELLA
❑ Columbia Masterworks OS 2005 [S] 1959 40.00
—Stage presentation for TV starring Julie Andrews
❑ Columbia Masterworks OS 2730 [S] 1965 30.00
—Stage presentation for TV starring Lesley-Ann Warren
❑ Columbia Masterworks OL 5190 [M] 1957 30.00
❑ Columbia Masterworks OL 6330 [M] 1965 25.00

THE COMING OF CHRIST
❑ Decca DL 9093 [M] 1960 40.00
❑ Decca DL 79093 [S] 1960 50.00

THE CRICKET ON THE HEARTH
❑ RCA Victor LOC-1140 [M] 1967 20.00
❑ RCA Victor LSO-1140 [S] 1967 30.00

DANGER
❑ MGM E-111 [10] 1951 120.00

THE DANGEROUS CHRISTMAS OF RED RIDING HOOD
❑ ABC-Paramount ABC-536 [M] 1965 15.00
❑ ABC-Paramount ABCS-536 [S] 1965 25.00

DARK SHADOWS
❑ Philips PHS 600314 1969 30.00
—With poster

DAVID COPPERFIELD
❑ GRT 10008 1970 150.00

DENNIS THE MENACE SONGS
❑ Golden LP-59 [M] 1960 80.00
—Black label original

DOGGIE DADDY TELLS AUGGY DOGGIE THE STORY OF PINOCCHIO
❑ Hanna-Barbera HLP-2028 [M] 1965 100.00

EAST SIDE, WEST SIDE
❑ Columbia CL 2123 [M] 1963 30.00
❑ Columbia CS 8923 [S] 1963 40.00

ELEVEN AGAINST THE ICE
❑ RCA Victor LPM-1618 [M] 1958 60.00

ELIZABETH TAYLOR IN LONDON
❑ Colpix CP 459 [M] 1963 30.00
❑ Colpix SCP 459 [S] 1963 50.00

EXCITING HONG KONG
❑ ABC-Paramount ABC-367 [M] 1961 40.00
❑ ABC-Paramount ABCS-367 [S] 1961 50.00

FELIX THE CAT
❑ Cricket CR-28 [M] 1958 100.00

FENWICK
❑ Fenwick FLP-621 1968 20.00
—Soundtrack to TV special; packaged in oversize (13 1/2 x 13 1/2) sleeve with color cartoon booklet; made especially for Motorola

THE FLINTSTONES
❑ Colpix CP-302 [M] 1961 200.00

THE FLINTSTONES AND JOSE JIMENEZ IN THE TIME MACHINE
❑ Hanna-Barbera HLP-2052 [M] 1966 80.00

THE FLINTSTONES IN S.A.S.F.A.T.P.O.G.O.B.S.O.A.L.T.
❑ Hanna-Barbera HLP-2047 [M] 1966 100.00

THE FLINTSTONES' FLIP FABLES: GOLDI-ROCKS AND THE THREE BEAROSAURUSES
❑ Hanna-Barbera HLP-2021 [M] 1965 100.00

THE FORD 50TH ANNIVERSARY TELEVISION SHOW
❑ Decca DL 7027 [10] 1953 40.00

FOUR ADVENTURES OF ZORRO
❑ Disneyland WDA-3601 [M] 1958 80.00
—Gatefold with booklet

FRED FLINTSTONE AND BARNEY RUBBLE SING SONGS FROM MARY POPPINS
❑ Hanna-Barbera HLP-2035 [M] 1965 100.00

FROSTY THE SNOWMAN
❑ MGM SE-4733 1970 60.00

GENERAL ELECTRIC THEATER
❑ Columbia CL 1395 [M] 1959 40.00
❑ Columbia CS 8190 [S] 1959 50.00

GENERAL MOTORS' 50TH ANNIVERSARY SHOW
❑ RCA Victor LOC-1037 [M] 1958 100.00

GET SMART
❑ United Artists UAL-3533 [M] 1965 40.00
❑ United Artists UAS-6566 [S] 1965 60.00

THE GIFT OF LOVE
❑ Columbia CL 1113 [M] 1958 30.00

THE GIFT OF THE MAGI
❑ United Artists UAL-4013 [M] 1959 40.00
❑ United Artists UAS-5103 [S] 1959 50.00

THE GIRL FROM U.N.C.L.E.
❑ MGM E-4410 [M] 1966 40.00
❑ MGM SE-4410 [S] 1966 60.00

GOOFY'S TV SPECTACULAR
❑ Disneyland DQ-1252 [M] 1964 20.00

THE GREEN HORNET
❑ 20th Century Fox S-3186 [S] 1966 250.00
❑ 20th Century Fox TF-3186 [M] 1966 200.00

HANS BRINKER
❑ Dot DLP-9001 [M] 1958 40.00

HANSEL AND GRETEL STARRING THE FLINTSTONES
❑ Hanna-Barbera HLP-2038 [M] 1965 100.00

HAWAII FIVE-O
❑ Capitol ST-410 1969 40.00

HAWAIIAN EYE
❑ Warner Bros. W 1355 [M] 1959 30.00
❑ Warner Bros. WS 1355 [S] 1959 40.00

HECTOR, THE STOWAWAY PUP
❑ Disneyland ST-1921 [M] 1964 30.00

HEIDI
❑ Capitol SKAO 2995 1968 40.00

HENNESSEY
❑ Signature 1049 [M] 1959 60.00
❑ Signature SS-1049 [S] 1959 80.00

HERE COMES HUCKLEBERRY HOUND
❑ Colpix CP-207 [M] 1961 180.00

HEY THERE, IT'S YOGI BEAR
❑ Golden LP-124 [M] 1964 40.00

HIGH TOR
❑ Decca DL 8272 [M] 1956 400.00

THE HILLBILLY BEARS IN HILLBILLY SHINDIG
❑ Hanna-Barbera HLP-2044 [M] 1966 150.00

HOGAN'S HEROES SING THE BEST OF WWII
❑ Sunset SUM-1137 [M] 1967 30.00
❑ Sunset SUS-5137 [S] 1967 40.00

HONEY WEST
❑ ABC-Paramount ABC-532 [M] 1965 40.00
❑ ABC-Paramount ABCS-532 [S] 1965 50.00

HOW THE GRINCH STOLE CHRISTMAS
❑ Leo LE-901 [M] 1966 50.00
❑ Leo LES-901 [S] 1966 70.00

HOWL ALONG WITH HUCKLEBERRY HOUND AND YOGI BEAR
❑ Golden LP-55 [M] 1959 150.00
—Black label original

HUCKLEBERRY HOUND AND THE GHOST SHIP
❑ Colpix CP-210 [M] 1962 100.00

HUCKLEBERRY HOUND FOR PRESIDENT
❑ Golden LP-60 [M] 1960 100.00
—Black label original

HUCKLEBERRY HOUND TELLS STORIES OF UNCLE REMUS
❑ Hanna-Barbera HLP-2022 [M] 1965 100.00

HUCKLEBERRY HOUND, THE GREAT KELLOGG'S TV SHOW
❑ Colpix CP-202 [M] 1959 200.00

I SPY
❑ Warner Bros. W 1637 [M] 1965 30.00
❑ Warner Bros. WS 1637 [S] 1965 40.00

I SPY, VOL. 2
❑ Capitol ST 2839 1968 30.00

IT'S HOWDY DOODY TIME
❑ RCA Victor LSP-4546 1971 25.00

JAMES BOMB STARRING SUPER SNOOPER AND BLABBER MOUSE
❑ Hanna-Barbera HLP-2036 [M] 1965 100.00

JANE EYRE
❑ Capitol SW-749 1971 30.00

THE JETSONS
❑ Colpix CP-213 [M] 1962 250.00
❑ Golden LP-98 [M] 1963 200.00
—Red cover original
❑ Golden LP-98 [M] 1964 120.00
—Blue cover reissue

THE JETSONS IN FIRST FAMILY ON THE MOON
❑ Hanna-Barbera HLP-2037 [M] 1965 150.00

THE JIMMY DURANTE TV SHOW
❑ Royale 1812 [10] 1955 100.00

JONNY QUEST IN 20,000 LEAGUES UNDER THE SEA
❑ Hanna-Barbera HLP-2030 [M] 1965 150.00

KING KONG
❑ Golden LP-151 [M] 1965 40.00

KISS ME, KATE
❑ Columbia Special Products CSS 645 1968 25.00
—Sold through the mail by broadcast sponsor Armstrong

A LOOK AT MONACO
❑ Columbia CL 2019 [M] 1963 50.00
❑ Columbia CS 8819 [R] 1963 50.00

LOVE, AMERICAN STYLE
❑ Capitol ST-11250 1973 40.00

MAGILLA GORILLA AND HIS PALS
❑ Golden LP-120 [M] 1964 50.00

MAGILLA GORILLA TELLS OGEE THE STORY OF ALICE IN WONDERLAND
❑ Hanna-Barbera HLP-2024 [M] 1965 100.00

Except when noted otherwise, VG = 25% of NM, and VG+ = 50% of NM. (Example: VG = $2.00, VG+ = $4.00 and NM = $8.00.)

Number	Title (A Side/B Side)	Yr	NM
THE MAN FROM INTERPOL			
❑ Top Rank RM-327 [M]		1962	50.00
❑ Top Rank RS-627 [S]		1962	60.00
THE MAN FROM U.N.C.L.E.			
❑ RCA Victor LPM-3475 [M]		1965	60.00
❑ RCA Victor LSP-3475 [S]		1965	80.00
THE MAN FROM U.N.C.L.E. VOL. 2			
❑ RCA Victor LPM-3574 [M]		1966	40.00
❑ RCA Victor LSP-3574 [S]		1966	50.00
MARK TWAIN TONIGHT!			
❑ Columbia Masterworks OS 3080 [S]		1967	20.00
❑ Columbia Masterworks OL 6680 [M]		1967	15.00
MERRY CHRISTMAS FROM KUKLA, FRAN AND OLLIE			
❑ Decca DL 8192 [M]		1955	80.00
MICKEY MOUSE CLUB MOUSEKEDANCES AND OTHER MOUSEKETEER FAVORITES			
❑ Disneyland DQ-1362 [M]	*—With booklet*	1974	20.00
❑ Disneyland STER-1362 [S]	*—With booklet*	1974	25.00
MICKEY MOUSE CLUB SONG HITS			
❑ Disneyland ST-3815	*—With 16-page photo album*	1975	40.00
MICKEY MOUSE CLUB: 27 NEW SONGS FROM THE MICKEY MOUSE CLUB TV SHOW			
❑ Mickey Mouse Club MM-14		1958	50.00
MICKEY MOUSE CLUB: A WALT DISNEY SONG FEST			
❑ Mickey Mouse Club MM-20		1958	40.00
MICKEY MOUSE CLUB: FUN WITH MUSIC — 30 FAVORITE DISNEY SONGS			
❑ Disneyland DQ-1209 [M]		1959	25.00
MICKEY MOUSE CLUB: HOLIDAYS WITH THE MOUSEKETEERS (A SONG FOR EVERY HOLIDAY)			
❑ Mickey Mouse Club MM-22		1958	40.00
MICKEY MOUSE CLUB: HOW TO BE A MOUSEKETEER			
❑ Disneyland ST-3918		1962	40.00
MICKEY MOUSE CLUB: MOUSEKETEERS TALENT ROUNDUP			
❑ Mickey Mouse Club MM-16		1958	40.00
MICKEY MOUSE CLUB: MUSICAL HIGHLIGHTS FROM THE MICKEY MOUSE CLUB			
❑ Disneyland DQ-1227 [M]		1962	30.00
MICKEY MOUSE CLUB: MUSICAL HIGHLIGHTS FROM THE MICKEY MOUSE CLUB TV SHOW			
❑ Mickey Mouse Club MM-12		1958	80.00
MICKEY MOUSE CLUB: SONGS FROM ANNETTE AND OTHER WALT DISNEY SERIALS			
❑ Mickey Mouse Club MM-24		1958	120.00
MICKEY MOUSE CLUB: SONGS FROM THE MICKEY MOUSE CLUB SERIALS			
❑ Disneyland DQ-1229 [M]		1962	40.00
MICKEY MOUSE CLUB: WE'RE THE MOUSEKETEERS			
❑ Mickey Mouse Club MM-18		1957	40.00
THE MIGHTY HERCULES			
❑ Golden LP-109 [M]		1963	200.00
MIKADO			
❑ Columbia Masterworks OS 2022 [S]		1960	100.00
❑ Columbia Masterworks OL 5480 [M]		1960	30.00
THE MISADVENTURES OF DENNIS THE MENACE			
❑ Colpix CP-204 [M]		1960	200.00
MR. BROADWAY			
❑ RCA Victor LPM-1520 [M]		1957	30.00
MR. ED, THE TALKING HORSE			
❑ Colpix CP-209 [M]		1962	300.00
MR. ED: STRAIGHT FROM THE HORSE'S MOUTH			
❑ Golden LP-88 [M]		1962	200.00
MR. JINKS, PIXIE AND DIXIE			
❑ Colpix CP-208 [M]		1961	100.00
THE MUNSTERS			
❑ Decca DL 4588 [M]		1964	60.00
❑ Decca DL 74588 [S]		1964	100.00
THE MUSIC FROM M SQUAD			
❑ RCA Victor LPM-2062 [M]		1959	30.00
❑ RCA Victor LSP-2062 [S]		1959	40.00
THE MUSIC FROM MARLBORO COUNTRY			
❑ United Artists SP-107		1967	50.00
MUSIC FROM SHUBERT ALLEY			
❑ Sinclair OSS-2250 [M]	*—From the NBC TV program, November 13, 1959*	1959	40.00
NAKED CITY — A MUSICAL PORTRAIT			
❑ Colpix CP-505 [M]		1958	40.00
❑ Colpix SCP-505 [S]		1959	60.00
OF THEE I SING			
❑ Columbia S 31763		1972	20.00
THE OFFICIAL ALBUM OF NBC'S BAT MASTERSON			
❑ Sea Horse/Chancellor CSH-7002 [M]		1960	80.00
ON THE FLIP SIDE			
❑ Decca DL 4836		1966	25.00
❑ Decca DL 74836 [S]		1966	30.00
ONE STEP BEYOND			
❑ Decca DL 8970 [M]		1960	30.00
❑ Decca DL 78970 [S]		1960	40.00
ORIGINAL AMATEUR HOUR 25TH ANNIVERSARY ALBUM			
❑ United Artists UXL 2 [(2)M]		1960	40.00
THE ORIGINAL TV ADVENTURES OF KING KONG			
❑ Epic LN 24231 [M]		1966	25.00
❑ Epic BN 26231 [S]		1966	30.00
THE OTHER WORLD OF WINSTON CHURCHILL			
❑ Mercury MG-21033 [M]		1965	30.00
❑ Mercury SR-61033 [S]		1965	40.00
OZZIE AND HARRIET			
❑ Imperial LP-9049 [M]		1957	200.00
PEYTON PLACE			
❑ Epic LN 24147 [M]		1965	30.00
❑ Epic BN 26147 [S]		1965	40.00
THE PIED PIPER OF HAMELIN			
❑ RCA Victor LPM-1563 [M]		1957	50.00
PINOCCHIO			
❑ Columbia CL 1055 [M]		1957	40.00
PIXIE AND DIXIE WITH MR. JINKS TELL THE STORY OF CINDERELLA			
❑ Hanna-Barbera HLP-2025 [M]		1965	100.00
PRECIOUS PUPP IN HOT ROD GRANNY			
❑ Hanna-Barbera HLP-2045 [M]		1966	150.00
QUICK DRAW MCGRAW			
❑ Colpix CP-203 [M]		1960	80.00
QUICK DRAW MCGRAW AND HUCKLEBERRY HOUND			
❑ Golden LP-51 [M]	*—Black label original*	1959	150.00
QUICK DRAW MCGRAW: THE TREASURE OF SARAH'S MATTRESS			
❑ Colpix CP-211 [M]		1962	120.00
THE REPORTER			
❑ Columbia CL 2269 [M]		1964	30.00
❑ Columbia CS 9069 [S]		1964	40.00
RICHARD DIAMOND			
❑ EmArcy MG-36162 [M]		1959	50.00
❑ EmArcy SR-80045 [S]		1959	80.00
THE RISE AND FALL OF THE THIRD REICH			
❑ MGM 1SE-12		1968	30.00
ROBIN HOOD STARRING TOP CAT			
❑ Hanna-Barbera HLP-2031 [M]		1965	100.00
ROCKY AND HIS FRIENDS			
❑ Golden LP-64 [M]	*—Gold label original*	1961	200.00
THE ROGUES			
❑ RCA Victor LPM-2976 [M]		1964	20.00
❑ RCA Victor LSP-2976 [S]		1964	30.00
RUDOLPH THE RED-NOSED REINDEER			
❑ Decca DL 4815 [M]		1964	60.00
❑ Decca DL 34327 [M]	*—Same as DL 4815; custom products reissue*	1965	40.00
❑ Decca DL 74815 [S]		1964	80.00
❑ MCA 15003	*—Reissue; black rainbow label*	1973	20.00
RUFF AND READY ADVENTURES IN SPACE			
❑ Colpix CP-201 [M]		1959	200.00
RUGGLES OF RED GAP			
❑ Verve MGV-15000 [M]		1957	50.00
THE SAINT			
❑ RCA Victor LPM-3631 [M]		1966	120.00
❑ RCA Victor LSP-3631 [S]		1966	200.00
SANTA CLAUS IS COMIN' TO TOWN			
❑ MGM SE-4732		1970	60.00
SATINS AND SPURS			
❑ Capitol L 547 [10]		1954	70.00
SECRET AGENT			
❑ RCA Victor LPM-3630 [M]		1966	250.00
❑ RCA Victor LSP-3630 [S]	*—With incorrect title, "Danger Man," on label*	1966	250.00
❑ RCA Victor LSP-3630 [S]	*—With correct title on label*	1966	300.00
SECRET AGENT MEETS THE SAINT			
❑ RCA Victor LPM-3467 [M]		1965	200.00
❑ RCA Victor LSP-3467 [S]	*—Music from both TV shows; pre-dates the individual albums*	1965	220.00
SECRET SQUIRREL AND MOROCCO MOLE IN SUPER SPY			
❑ Hanna-Barbera HLP-2046 [M]		1966	150.00
77 SUNSET STRIP			
❑ Warner Bros. W 1289 [M]		1959	30.00
❑ Warner Bros. WS 1289 [S]		1959	40.00
SHOTGUN SLADE			
❑ Mercury MG-20575 [M]		1960	40.00
❑ Mercury SR-60235 [S]		1960	60.00
SINBAD JR. IN TREASURE ISLAND			
❑ Hanna-Barbera HLP-2039 [M]		1965	120.00
67 MELODY LANE			
❑ Columbia CL 724 [M]		1955	30.00
SNAGGLEPUSS TELLS THE STORY OF THE WIZARD OF OZ			
❑ Hanna-Barbera HLP-2026 [M]		1965	100.00
SONGS OF THE FLINTSTONES			
❑ Golden LP-66 [M]	*—Gold label original*	1961	250.00
SONGS OF YOGI BEAR AND HIS PALS			
❑ Golden LP-70 [M]	*—Gold label original*	1961	80.00
THE SOUND OF JAZZ			
❑ Columbia CL 1098 [M]		1958	25.00
❑ Columbia CS 8040 [S]		1958	40.00
SPACE: 1999			
❑ RCA Victor ABL1-1422		1975	20.00
SQUIDDLEY DIDDLEY IN SURFIN' SAFARI			
❑ Hanna-Barbera HLP-2043 [M]		1966	150.00
STACCATO (MUSIC FROM JOHNNY STACCATO)			
❑ Capitol ST 1287 [S]		1959	50.00
❑ Capitol T 1287 [M]		1959	30.00
THE STINGIEST MAN IN TOWN			
❑ Columbia CL 950	*—Music from a television play first aired on The Alcoa Hour*	1956	20.00
❑ Columbia Special Products P 12637	*—Reissue of Columbia LP; same contents*	1975	10.00
SUPER SNOOPER AND BLABBER MOUSE IN MONSTER SHINDIG			
❑ Hanna-Barbera HLP-2020 [M]		1965	100.00
THRILLER			
❑ Time S-2034 [S]		1960	40.00
❑ Time 52034 [M]		1960	30.00
TOM SAWYER			
❑ Decca DL 8432 [M]	*—First aired on the U.S. Steel Hour, starring Jimmy Boyd*	1957	40.00
TOP CAT			
❑ Colpix CP-212 [M]		1963	300.00
TOUCHE TURTLE AND DUM-DUM IN THE RELUCTANT DRAGON			
❑ Hanna-Barbera HLP-2029 [M]		1965	100.00
THE UNTOUCHABLES			
❑ Capitol ST 1430 [S]		1960	50.00
❑ Capitol T 1430 [M]		1960	40.00
UP WITH PEOPLE!			
❑ Pace 1101	*—Among the many people on this LP is a young Glenn Close (first name misspelled "Gleen")*	1965	20.00
THE VALIANT YEARS			
❑ ABC-Paramount ABC-387 [M]		1962	30.00
❑ ABC-Paramount ABCS-387 [S]		1962	40.00
VICTORY AT SEA			
❑ RCA Victor LM-1779 [M]	*—Original recording*	1954	25.00
❑ RCA Victor LM-2335 [M]	*—Re-recording of 1779*	1959	20.00
❑ RCA Victor LSC-2335 [S]	*—Re-recording of 1779 in stereo*	1959	20.00
VICTORY AT SEA, VOL. 2			
❑ RCA Victor LM-2226 [M]		1958	20.00
❑ RCA Victor LSC-2226 [S]	*—Original with "shaded dog" label*	1958	25.00
VICTORY AT SEA, VOL. 3			
❑ RCA Victor LM-2523 [M]		1961	20.00
❑ RCA Victor LSC-2523 [S]		1961	25.00
WAGON TRAIN			
❑ Mercury MG-20502 [M]		1959	50.00
❑ Mercury SR-60179 [S]		1959	80.00
WALT DISNEY'S WONDERFUL WORLD OF COLOR			
❑ Disneyland DQ-1245 [M]		1963	30.00
WIDE, WIDE WORLD			
❑ RCA Victor LPM-1280 [M]		1956	40.00
WILMA FLINTSTONE TELLS THE STORY OF BAMBI			
❑ Hanna-Barbera HLP-2027 [M]		1965	100.00

Number	Title (A Side/B Side)	Yr	NM
WINSOME WITCH IN IT'S MAGIC			
❑ Hanna-Barbera HLP-2042 [M]		1966	150.00
WONDERFUL TOWN			
❑ Columbia Masterworks OS 2008 [S]		1958	25.00
❑ Columbia Masterworks OL 5360 [M]		1958	20.00
YOGI BEAR AND BOO-BOO			
❑ Colpix CP-205 [M]		1961	120.00
YOGI BEAR AND BOO-BOO TELL STORIES OF LITTLE RED RIDING HOOD AND JACK AND THE BEANSTALK			
❑ Hanna-Barbera HLP-2023 [M]		1965	100.00
YOGI BEAR AND THE THREE STOOGES IN THE MAD, MAD, DR. NO-NO			
❑ Hanna-Barbera HLP-2050 [M]		1966	100.00
YOGI BEAR: HOW TO BE A BETTER THAN AVERAGE CHILD			
❑ Golden LP-90 [M]		1962	80.00

VARIOUS ARTISTS COLLECTIONS

Number	Title (A Side/B Side)	Yr	NM
ACCENT ON PIANO			
❑ Urania UJLP-1207 [M]		1955	—
—See WILLIE "THE LION" SMITH.			
ACCENT ON TROMBONE			
❑ Urania UJLP-1205 [M]		1955	30.00
ADD-A-PART JAZZ			
❑ Columbia CL 908 [M]		1956	25.00
THE ADVANCE GUARD OF THE '40S			
❑ EmArcy MG-36016 [M]		1955	50.00
AFRO SUMMIT			
❑ BASF 20675		197?	20.00
AFRO-COOL			
❑ GNP Crescendo GNP-48 [M]		1959	20.00
AFTER HOUR JAZZ			
❑ Epic LN (# unk) [M]		1955	30.00
AFTER HOURS			
❑ King 395-528 [M]		1956	500.00
❑ King KLP-528		1987	12.00
—With "Highland Music" on label			
AFTER HOURS BLUES, 1949			
❑ Biograph 12010		1969	12.00
AIN'T THAT GOOD NEWS			
❑ Specialty SPS-2115		1969	20.00
ALAN FREED'S GOLDEN PICS			
❑ End LP-313 [M]		1961	60.00
ALAN FREED'S MEMORY LANE			
❑ End LP-314 [M]		1962	60.00
ALAN FREED'S TOP 15			
❑ End LP-315 [M]		1962	60.00
❑ Roulette SR 42042 [R]		1970	15.00
—Reissue of End LP-315			
ALL DAY LONG			
❑ Prestige PRLP-7081 [M]		1957	100.00
—Reissued as Prestige 7277; see KENNY BURRELL.			
ALL GIRL MILLION SELLERS			
❑ Ascot AM-13007 [M]		1964	40.00
❑ Ascot AS-16007 [P]		1964	40.00
ALL MEAT			
❑ Warner Bros. PRO 604 [(2)]		1975	20.00
ALL NIGHT LONG			
❑ Prestige PRLP-7073 [M]		1957	100.00
—Reissued as Prestige 7289; see KENNY BURRELL.			
ALL SINGING — ALL TALKING — ALL ROCKING			
❑ Warner Bros. PRO 573 [(2)]		1973	25.00
ALL STAR JAZZ			
❑ Halo 50223 [M]		195?	30.00
ALL STAR ROCK AND ROLL REVUE			
❑ King 395-513 [M]		1956	400.00
❑ King 638 [M]		1959	200.00
—Reissue of King 395-513			
ALL STAR SESSIONS			
❑ Capitol M-11031		1973	12.00
ALL STAR TRIBUTE TO TATUM			
❑ American Recording Society G-424 [M]		1957	30.00
ALL THE HITS BY ALL THE STARS			
❑ Parkway P 7013 [M]		1962	40.00
ALL THE HITS BY ALL THE STARS, VOL. 2			
❑ Parkway P 7016 [M]		1963	30.00
ALL THE STARS' BIGGEST HITS			
❑ Parkway P-7033 [M]		1963	50.00
—With "pull-off pix" still intact on cover			
ALL THE STARS' BIGGEST HITS, VOL. 2			
❑ Parkway P-7034 [M]		1963	50.00
—With "pull-off pix" still intact on cover			
ALL THESE THINGS			
❑ Instant LP-71000		1969	30.00
ALL-TIME ALL-STAR COUNTRY HITS: 48 HISTORIC PERFORMANCES			
❑ RCA Victor CWS 0002 [(4)]		196?	30.00
—Box set			
ALL TIME COUNTRY AND WESTERN HITS			
❑ King 537 [M]		1956	150.00
❑ King 710 [M]		1961	100.00
—Not a reissue of King 537, but a different collection			
ALL TIME HIT SACRED AND GOSPEL SONGS			
❑ King 1023 [M]		1967	30.00
ALL-STAR DATES			
❑ RCA Victor LPT-21 [10]		1951	50.00
ALL-TIME CHRISTMAS FAVORITES			
❑ Capitol Special Markets SL-6931		1973	12.00
—Sold only at Sylvania dealers			
ALTERNATIVES			
❑ Warner Bros. BS 1873		1970	12.00
ALTO ALTITUDE			
❑ EmArcy MG-36018 [M]		1955	50.00
ALTO SAXES			
❑ Norgran MGN-1035 [M]		1955	80.00
❑ Verve MGV-8126 [M]		1957	30.00
❑ Verve V-8126 [M]		1961	20.00
ALTO SUMMIT			
❑ Prestige PRLP-7684		1969	15.00
THE AMAZING METS			
❑ Buddah 1969		1969	25.00
AMERICA'S GREATEST JAZZMEN PLAY COLE PORTER			
❑ Moodsville MVLP-34 [M]		1963	40.00
—Green label			
❑ Moodsville MVLP-34 [M]		1965	20.00
—Blue label, trident logo at right			
❑ Moodsville MVST-34 [S]		1963	40.00
—Green label			
❑ Moodsville MVST-34 [S]		1965	20.00
—Blue label, trident logo at right			
AMERICA'S GREATEST JAZZMEN PLAY GEORGE GERSHWIN			
❑ Moodsville MVLP-33 [M]		1963	40.00
—Green label			
❑ Moodsville MVLP-33 [M]		1965	20.00
—Blue label, trident logo at right			
❑ Moodsville MVST-33 [S]		1963	40.00
—Green label			
❑ Moodsville MVST-33 [S]		1965	20.00
—Blue label, trident logo at right			
AMERICA'S GREATEST JAZZMEN PLAY RICHARD RODGERS			
❑ Moodsville MVLP-35 [M]		1963	40.00
—Green label			
❑ Moodsville MVLP-35 [M]		1965	20.00
—Blue label, trident logo at right			
❑ Moodsville MVST-35 [S]		1963	40.00
—Green label			
❑ Moodsville MVST-35 [S]		1965	20.00
—Blue label, trident logo at right			
AMERICA'S GREATEST JAZZMEN PLAY THE BROADWAY SCENE			
❑ Moodsville MVLP-38 [M]		1963	40.00
—Green label			
❑ Moodsville MVLP-38 [M]		1965	20.00
—Blue label, trident logo at right			
❑ Moodsville MVST-38 [S]		1963	40.00
—Green label			
❑ Moodsville MVST-38 [S]		1965	20.00
—Blue label, trident logo at right			
AMERICAN FOLK BLUES FESTIVAL			
❑ Excello LPS-8029		1972	20.00
❑ Exodus EX-302 [M]		1966	20.00
❑ Exodus EXS-302 [S]		1966	25.00
AMERICAN JAZZ FESTIVAL AT NEWPORT '56, NO. 1			
❑ Columbia CL 931 [M]			—
—See LOUIS ARMSTRONG.			
AMERICAN JAZZ FESTIVAL AT NEWPORT '56, NO. 2			
❑ Columbia CL 932 [M]			—
—See DAVE BRUBECK.			
AMERICAN JAZZ FESTIVAL AT NEWPORT '56, NO. 3			
❑ Columbia CL 933 [M]			—
—See DUKE ELLINGTON.			
AMERICAN JAZZ FESTIVAL AT NEWPORT '56, NO. 4			
❑ Columbia CL 934 [M]			—
—See DUKE ELLINGTON.			
AMERICANS ABROAD, VOL. 1			
❑ Pax LP-6009 [10]		1955	40.00
AMERICANS ABROAD, VOL. 2			
❑ Pax LP-6015 [10]		1955	40.00
AMERICANS IN EUROPE, VOL. 1			
❑ ABC Impulse! AS-36 [S]		1968	12.00
❑ Impulse! A-36 [M]		1963	20.00
❑ Impulse! AS-36 [S]		1963	25.00
AMERICANS IN EUROPE, VOL. 2			
❑ ABC Impulse! AS-37 [S]		1968	12.00
❑ Impulse! A-37 [M]		1963	20.00
❑ Impulse! AS-37 [S]		1963	25.00
THE ANATOMY OF IMPROVISATION			
❑ Verve MGV-8230 [M]		1958	30.00
❑ Verve V-8230 [M]		1961	20.00
ANOTHER MONDAY NIGHT AT BIRDLAND			
❑ Roulette R 52022 [M]		1959	30.00
❑ Roulette SR 52022 [S]		1959	30.00
AN ANTHOLOGY OF BRITISH BLUES, VOL. 1			
❑ Immediate Z12 52006		1968	30.00
AN ANTHOLOGY OF BRITISH BLUES, VOL. 2			
❑ Immediate Z12 52014		1968	30.00
AN ANTHOLOGY OF CALIFORNIA MUSIC			
❑ Jazz: West Coast JWC-500 [M]		1955	150.00
AN ANTHOLOGY OF CALIFORNIA MUSIC, VOL. 2			
❑ Jazz: West Coast JWC-501 [M]		1956	150.00
APOLLO SATURDAY NIGHT			
❑ Atco 33-159 [M]		1964	40.00
❑ Atco SD 33-159 [S]		1964	50.00
APPETIZERS			
❑ Warner Bros. PRO 569 [(2)]		1973	25.00
APPROVED BY 10,000,000			
❑ Teem LP-5004 [M]		196?	30.00
AROUND THE CHRISTMAS TREE			
❑ Decca DL 38170 [M]		196?	12.00
THE ART OF JAZZ PIANO			
❑ Epic LN 3295 [M]		1956	30.00
THE ART OF THE BALLAD			
❑ Verve VSP-17 [M]		1966	15.00
❑ Verve VSPS-17 [R]		1966	10.00
THE ART OF THE BALLAD 2			
❑ Verve VSP-38 [M]		1966	15.00
❑ Verve VSPS-38 [R]		1966	10.00
ASSORTED FLAVORS OF PACIFIC JAZZ			
❑ Pacific Jazz HFS-1 [M]		1956	50.00
AT THE HOOTENANNY			
❑ Kapp KL-1330 [M]		1963	20.00
❑ Kapp KS-3330 [S]		1963	25.00
AT THE HOOTENANNY, VOL. 2			
❑ Kapp KL-1343 [M]		1963	20.00
❑ Kapp KS-3343 [S]		1963	25.00
AT THE HOOTENANNY, VOL. 3			
❑ Kapp KL-1344 [M]		1963	20.00
❑ Kapp KS-3344 [S]		1963	25.00
AUTOBIOGRAPHY IN JAZZ			
❑ Debut DEB-198 [M]		1955	150.00
AWARD ALBUM JAZZ VOCALS			
❑ Bethlehem BCP-6060 [M]		1961	25.00
BACKGROUNDS OF JAZZ, VOL. 1: THE JUG BANDS			
❑ "X" LX-3009 [10]		1954	80.00
BACKGROUNDS OF JAZZ, VOL. 2: COUNTRY & URBAN BLUES			
❑ "X" LVA-3016 [10]		1954	80.00
BACKGROUNDS OF JAZZ, VOL. 3: KINGS OF THE BLUES			
❑ "X" LVA-3032 [10]		1955	80.00
BACKWOOD BLUES			
❑ Riverside RLP-1039 [10]		1954	80.00
BALLADS AND BREAKDOWNS OF THE GOLDEN ERA			
❑ Columbia CS 9660		1968	20.00
BALLROOM BANDSTAND			
❑ Columbia CL 611 [M]		1955	25.00
BANG AND SHOUT SUPER HITS			
❑ Bang BLPS-220 [P]		1969	20.00
BANJO COUNTRY STYLE			
❑ Audio Lab AL-1569 [M]		1962	80.00
BARGAIN DAY			
❑ EmArcy MG-36087 [M]		1956	40.00
BARREL HOUSE PIANO			
❑ Brunswick BL 58022 [10]		1951	60.00
A BARREL OF OLDIES			
❑ Del-Fi DFLP-1219 [M]		1961	50.00

Except when noted otherwise, VG = 25% of NM, and VG+ = 50% of NM. (Example: VG = $2.00, VG+ = $4.00 and NM = $8.00.)

Number | Title (A Side/B Side) | Yr | NM

BARRY MANN AND CYNTHIA WEIL: SOLID GOLD
❑ Screen Gems/Columbia CPL-712 [DJ] 1975 20.00
—Promo-only compilation of oldies sent to radio to spur airplay on songs owned by this publishing house

THE BASS
❑ ABC Impulse! AS-9284 [(3)] 197? 20.00

BATTLE OF BANDS
❑ Capitol H 235 [10] 1950 50.00

BATTLE OF JAZZ, VOL. 3
❑ Brunswick BL 58039 [10] 1953 50.00

BATTLE OF THE BIG BANDS
❑ Capitol T 667 [M] 1956 30.00

BATTLE OF THE GROUPS
❑ End LP-305 [M] 1960 60.00

BATTLE OF THE GROUPS, VOL. 2
❑ End LP-309 [M] 1960 60.00

BATTLE OF THE SAXES
❑ Aladdin LP-701 [10] 1950 —
—See LESTER YOUNG AND ILLINOIS JACQUET.

BATTLE OF THE SAXES-TENOR ALL STARS
❑ EmArcy MG-36023 [M] 1955 50.00

BE OUR GUEST
❑ Gene Norman GNP-20 [M] 1955 25.00

THE BE-BOP ERA
❑ RCA Victor LPV-519 1965 20.00

BE-BOP SINGERS
❑ Prestige PRST-7828 1971 12.00

THE BELLS OF CHRISTMAS
❑ Book-of-the-Month Club 90-5677 [(3)] 1973 20.00
—Sold through Book-of-the-Month Records; secondary number is "P3 11972"

BEST COAST JAZZ
❑ EmArcy MG-36039 [M] 1955 80.00

BEST FROM THE WEST: MODERN SOUNDS FROM CALIFORNIA, VOL. 1
❑ Blue Note BLP-5059 [10] 1955 200.00

BEST FROM THE WEST: MODERN SOUNDS FROM CALIFORNIA, VOL. 2
❑ Blue Note BLP-5060 [10] 1955 200.00

THE BEST OF ARGO JAZZ
❑ Argo ALPS-1 [M] 1961 30.00

THE BEST OF BLUE NOTE, VOL. 1
❑ Blue Note BST-84429 [(2)] 197? 20.00

THE BEST OF BLUE NOTE, VOL. 2
❑ Blue Note BST-84433 [(2)] 197? 20.00

THE BEST OF CHRISTMAS
❑ Capitol STBB 2979 [(2)] 1968 20.00

THE BEST OF DIXIELAND
❑ RCA Victor LPM-2982 [M] 1965 20.00
❑ RCA Victor LSP-2982 [R] 1965 12.00

BEST OF RHYTHM AND BLUES
❑ Jubilee JLP-1014 [M] 1956 150.00
—Blue label, black vinyl
❑ Jubilee JLP-1014 [M] 1956 200.00
—Pink label, black vinyl
❑ Jubilee JLP-1014 [M] 1956 500.00
—Pink label, red vinyl

THE BEST OF RHYTHM AND BLUES
❑ Warwick W 2026 [M] 1961 80.00

BEST OF THE BIG NAME BANDS
❑ RCA Camden CAL-368 [M] 1958 25.00

BEST OF THE BLUES, VOL. 1
❑ Imperial LP-9257 [M] 1964 25.00
❑ Imperial LP-12257 [R] 1964 20.00

BEST OF THE BLUES, VOL.E 2
❑ Imperial LP-9259 [M] 1964 25.00
❑ Imperial LP-12259 [R] 1964 20.00

BEST OF THE GREAT SONGS OF CHRISTMAS (ALBUM 10)
❑ Columbia Special Products CSS 1478 1970 12.00
—Sold only at Goodyear tire dealers

BEST OF THE MUSICAL SOUNDS OF CHRISTMAS
❑ Capitol Creative Products SL-6713 1971 12.00

THE BEST OF THE R AND B GROUPS
❑ Warwick W 2025 [M] 1961 100.00

BEST OF THE SOUNDTRACKS
❑ Tower ST-5148 1969 25.00

THE BEST VOCAL GROUPS IN ROCK 'N' ROLL
❑ Dooto DL-224 [M] 1957 100.00
—Yellow label
❑ Dooto DL-224 [M] 196? 30.00
—Multi-color label

BETHLEHEM'S BEST
❑ Bethlehem EXLP-6 [(3)M] 1958 70.00
—Box set of 82, 83, and 84

BETHLEHEM'S BEST, VOL. 1
❑ Bethlehem BCP-82 [M] 1958 30.00

BETHLEHEM'S BEST, VOL. 2
❑ Bethlehem BCP-83 [M] 1958 30.00

BETHLEHEM'S BEST, VOL. 3
❑ Bethlehem BCP-84 [M] 1958 30.00

BETHLEHEM'S GRAB BAG
❑ Bethlehem EXLP-2 [M] 1958 40.00

THE BIG BALL
❑ Warner Bros. PRO 358 [(2)] 1970 25.00
—Originals have green labels

BIG BAND CONTRAST
❑ Bethlehem BCP-6037 [M] 1960 30.00

BIG BAND JAZZ
❑ Brunswick BL 58050 [10] 1953 50.00

BIG BAND STEREO
❑ Capitol SW 1055 [S] 1959 25.00

BIG BANDS
❑ Capitol STFL-293 [(6)] 1969 30.00
—One album each by Les Brown, Glen Gray, Duke Ellington, Benny Goodman, Harry James and Woody Herman

THE BIG BANDS 1933
❑ Prestige PRLP-7645 1969 15.00

BIG BANDS UPTOWN, VOL. 1
❑ Decca DL 79242 1969 12.00

BIG BANDS' GREATEST HITS
❑ Columbia CG 30009 [(2)] 197? 12.00
—"CG" prefix is a reissue of "G"
❑ Columbia G 30009 [(2)] 1970 15.00
—Orange labels
❑ Columbia G 30009 [(2)] 1970 20.00
—Red "360 Sound" labels

BIG BANDS' GREATEST HITS, VOL. 2
❑ Columbia CG 31213 [(2)] 197? 12.00
—"CG" prefix is a reissue of "G"
❑ Columbia G 31213 [(2)] 1972 15.00

BIG COUNTRY HITS
❑ Pickwick JS-6166 1975 30.00

THE BIG HITS
❑ Columbia CL 1353 [M] 1959 30.00
❑ Columbia CS 8161 [S] 1959 40.00

THE BIG HITS OF MID-AMERICA
❑ Soma MG-1245 [M] 1965 80.00

THE BIG HITS OF MID-AMERICA, VOL. 2
❑ Soma MG-1246 [M] 1965 80.00

BIG NAME DIXIE
❑ Score SLP-4024 [M] 1958 50.00

THE BIG ONES FROM DUKE AND PEACOCK RECORDS
❑ Peacock PLP-2000 [M] 1967 20.00

THE BIG SOUNDS OF THE DRAGS!
❑ Capitol ST 2001 [S] 1963 25.00
❑ Capitol T 2001 [M] 1963 20.00

BIG SUR FESTIVAL/ONE HAND CLAPPING
❑ Columbia KC 31138 1972 20.00

BIG SURF HITS
❑ Del-Fi DFLP-1249 [M] 1964 50.00
❑ Del-Fi DFST-1249 [S] 1964 75.00

BILLIE HOLIDAY REVISITED
❑ Mainstream MRL-409 197? 12.00

BIRD'S NIGHT — THE MUSIC OF CHARLIE PARKER
❑ Savoy MG-12138 [M] 1958 50.00

BIRDLAND ALL STARS AT CARNEGIE HALL
❑ Roulette RE-127 [(2)] 197? 12.00

THE BIRDLAND STARS ON TOUR, VOL. 1
❑ RCA Victor LPM-1327 [M] 1956 40.00

THE BIRDLAND STARS ON TOUR, VOL. 2
❑ RCA Victor LPM-1328 [M] 1956 40.00

THE BIRDLAND STORY
❑ Roulette RB-2 [(2)M] 1961 40.00
❑ Roulette SRB-2 [(2)S] 1961 40.00

THE BIRTH OF BOP, VOL. 1
❑ Savoy MG-9022 [10] 1953 150.00

THE BIRTH OF BOP, VOL. 2
❑ Savoy MG-9023 [10] 1953 150.00

THE BIRTH OF BOP, VOL. 3
❑ Savoy MG-9024 [10] 1953 150.00

THE BIRTH OF BOP, VOL. 4
❑ Savoy MG-9025 [10] 1953 150.00

THE BIRTH OF BOP, VOL. 5
❑ Savoy MG-9026 [10] 1953 150.00

BIRTH OF SOUL
❑ Decca DL 79245 1969 12.00

BLACK AND WHITE RAGTIME, 1921-39
❑ Biograph 12047 197? 12.00

BLOWIN' SESSIONS
❑ Blue Note BN-LA521-H2 [(2)] 1975 20.00

BLOWOUT AT MARDI GRAS
❑ Cook LP-1084 [M] 1955 40.00

BLUE NOTE CLASSICS
❑ Blue Note B-6509 [M] 1969 15.00

BLUE RIBBON COUNTRY
❑ Capitol STBB 2969 [(2)] 1968 25.00

BLUE RIBBON COUNTRY, VOL. 2
❑ Capitol STBB-217 [(2)] 1969 25.00

THE BLUES
❑ Vee Jay VJS-2-1007 [(2)] 1974 20.00
❑ Vee Jay LP-1020 [M] 1960 40.00

BLUES 'N' FOLK
❑ Bethlehem BCP-6071 [M] 1963 60.00

BLUES FOR TOMORROW
❑ Riverside RLP 12-243 [M] 1957 40.00

BLUES FROM BIG BILL'S COPACABANA
❑ Chess LP 1533 [M] 1969 25.00
—Possibly a reissue of "Folk Festival of the Blues," Argo 4031

THE BLUES IN MODERN JAZZ
❑ Atlantic 1337 [M] 1961 20.00
—Multicolor label, white "fan" logo at right
❑ Atlantic 1337 [M] 1963 15.00
—Multicolor label, black "fan" logo at right
❑ Atlantic SD 1337 [R] 1969 12.00

THE BLUES IN STEREO
❑ World Pacific ST-1021 [S] 1959 30.00

BLUES LIVE IN BATON ROUGE
❑ Excello LPS-8021 1971 25.00

THE BLUES PROJECT
❑ Elektra EKL-264 [M] 1964 25.00
❑ Elektra EKS-7264 [S] 1964 30.00
—No relation to the band of the same name; on one track, Bob Dylan plays piano under the name "Bob Landy"

BLUES THAT GAVE AMERICA SOUL
❑ ABC Duke DLPX-82 [S] 1974 15.00
❑ Duke DLP-82 [M] 1966 20.00
❑ Duke DLPS-82 [S] 1966 25.00

BLUES UPTOWN: URBAN BLUES, VOL. 1
❑ Imperial LP-94002 1968 20.00

THE BLUES, VOL. 2
❑ Pacific Jazz JWC-502 [M] 1956 50.00
❑ World Pacific JWC-502 [M] 1958 40.00

THE BLUES, VOL. 2: HAVE BLUES, WILL TRAVEL
❑ World Pacific JWC-509 [M] 1958 40.00

THE BLUES, VOL. 3: BLOWIN' THE BLUES
❑ World Pacific JWC-512 [M] 1958 40.00
❑ World Pacific ST-1029 [S] 1959 30.00

THE BLUES, VOL. 1
❑ Argo LP-4026 [M] 1963 25.00

THE BLUES, VOL. 2
❑ Argo LP-4027 [M] 1963 25.00

THE BLUES, VOL. 3
❑ Argo LP-4034 [M] 1964 25.00

THE BLUES, VOL. 4
❑ Argo LP-4042 [M] 1964 25.00

THE BLUES, VOL. 5
❑ Cadet LP-4051 [M] 1966 25.00

BLUESVILLE
❑ Bethlehem BCP-6038 [M] 1960 30.00

BODY AND SOUL
❑ RCA Victor LPV-501 1964 20.00

BONING UP ON 'BONES
❑ EmArcy MG-36038 [M] 1955 50.00

BOOGIE WOOGIE
❑ Decca DL 5248 [10] 1950 50.00

BOOGIE WOOGIE KINGS AND QUEENS
❑ Decca DL 5249 [10] 1950 50.00

BOOGIE WOOGIE PIANO
❑ Brunswick BL 58018 [10] 1950 60.00

BOOGIE WOOGIE PIANOS
❑ Columbia KC 32708 197? 10.00

BOOTY
❑ Mainstream MRL-413 1974 30.00

BOPPIN'
❑ Jubilee JGM-1118 [M] 1960 150.00

Number	Title (A Side/B Side)	Yr	NM
BOSS GOLDIES — SOUNDS FROM THE GROOVEYARD			
❑ Columbia CL 2559 [M]		1966	20.00
❑ Columbia CS 9339 [S]		1966	25.00
BOY MEETS GIRL			
❑ Stax STS 2-2024 [(2)]		1969	20.00
THE BRIGHTEST STARS OF CHRISTMAS			
❑ RCA Special Products DPL1-0086		1974	20.00
—Sold only at JCPenney department stores			
BRITISH FESTIVAL OF JAZZ CONCERT			
❑ Decca DL 5422 [10]		1952	50.00
BRITISH JAZZ FESTIVAL			
❑ Decca DL 5424 [10]		1952	50.00
BRUNSWICK'S GREATEST HITS			
❑ Brunswick BL 754186		1973	20.00
BUBBLE GUM MUSIC IS THE NAKED TRUTH, VOL. 1			
❑ Buddah BDA 5032		1969	25.00
BUDDAH'S 360 DEGREE DIAL-A-HIT			
❑ Buddah BDA 5039		1969	30.00
—With rotating wheel under the front LP cover			
A BUMPER CROP OF ALL STARS			
❑ King 753 [M]		1961	100.00
BUNCH OF GOODIES			
❑ Chess LP 1441 [DJ]		1960	600.00
—Multi-color splash vinyl			
❑ Chess LP 1441 [M]		1960	120.00
—Black vinyl			
BURBANK			
❑ Warner Bros. PRO 529 [(2)]		1972	25.00
—Originals have green labels			
BURBANK'S GREATEST HITS			
❑ Warner Bros. PRO 548		1973	20.00
BUSHKIN-SAFRANSKI-WILSON GROUPS			
❑ Allegro 1590 [10]		1955	50.00
BYE BYE BIRDIE			
❑ Colpix CP-454 [M]		1963	80.00
❑ Colpix SCP-454 [S]		1963	100.00
—Studio version performed by Paul Petersen, Shelley Fabares, James Darren, the Marcels and others			
THE CAPITOL DISC JOCKEY ALBUM MARCH 1967			
❑ Capitol SPRO-4291/2 [DJ]		1967	12.00
THE CAPITOL DISC JOCKEY ALBUM APRIL 1967			
❑ Capitol SPRO-4316/7 [DJ]		1967	12.00
THE CAPITOL DISC JOCKEY ALBUM JUNE 1967			
❑ Capitol SPRO-4344/5 [DJ]		1967	12.00
THE CAPITOL DISC JOCKEY ALBUM JULY 1967			
❑ Capitol SPRO-4359/60 [DJ]		1967	12.00
THE CAPITOL DISC JOCKEY ALBUM AUGUST 1967			
❑ Capitol SPRO-4370/1 [DJ]		1967	12.00
THE CAPITOL DISC JOCKEY ALBUM JANUARY 1968			
❑ Capitol SPRO-4469/70 [DJ]		1968	12.00
THE CAPITOL DISC JOCKEY ALBUM APRIL 1968			
❑ Capitol SPRO-4520/1 [DJ]		1968	12.00
THE CAPITOL DISC JOCKEY ALBUM SEPTEMBER 1968			
❑ Capitol SPRO-4621/2 [DJ]		1968	12.00
THE CAPITOL DISC JOCKEY ALBUM JULY 1969			
❑ Capitol SPRO-4774/5 [DJ]		1969	12.00
—Label calls this "Disc Jockey Sampler"			
THE CAPITOL DISC JOCKEY ALBUM NOVEMBER 1969			
❑ Capitol SPRO-4883/4 [DJ]		1969	12.00
THE CAPITOL DISC JOCKEY ALBUM JANUARY 1970			
❑ Capitol SPRO-4920/1 [DJ]		1970	12.00
THE CAPITOL DISC JOCKEY ALBUM FEBRUARY 1970			
❑ Capitol SPRO-4934/5 [DJ]		1970	12.00
THE CAPITOL DISC JOCKEY ALBUM FOR CHRISTMAS 1967			
❑ Capitol SPRO-4456/7 [DJ]		1967	15.00
CARLOAD O' HITS			
❑ Muse M-500 [M]		1959	200.00
A CARNIVAL OF SONGS			
❑ King 819 [M]		1963	100.00
CAROLS AND CANDLELIGHT			
❑ Columbia Special Products P 12525		1974	10.00
—Sold only at Goodyear tire dealers			
THE CATS			
❑ New Jazz NJLP-8217 [M]		1959	80.00
—Purple label			
❑ New Jazz NJLP-8217 [M]		1965	30.00
—Blue label, trident logo at right			
CATS AND JAMMER KIDS			
❑ Angel ANG-60007 [10]		1955	50.00
CATS VS. CHICKS			
❑ MGM E-255 [10]		1954	50.00
CBS TWO-FERS ARE GREAT MUSICAL VALUES!			
❑ CBS A2S 143/4 [(2)DJ]		1975	20.00
CHA CHA CHA CARNIVAL			
❑ Forum F 9051 [M]		196?	10.00
❑ Forum FS 9051 [S]		196?	12.00
—Caney; Neil Lewis; Joe Lustig; Machito; Tito Puente; Tito Rodriguez; Pete Terrace			
CHARLIE PARKER 10TH MEMORIAL CONCERT			
❑ Limelight LM-82017 [M]		1965	15.00
❑ Limelight LS-86017 [S]		1965	20.00
CHARLIE PARKER MEMORIAL CONCERT			
❑ Cadet 2CA-60002 [(2)]		1971	20.00
CHART BUSTERS '62			
❑ Capitol ST 1837 [S]		1963	40.00
❑ Capitol T 1837 [M]		1963	30.00
CHARTBUSTERS, VOL. 2			
❑ Capitol ST 1945 [S]		1963	40.00
❑ Capitol T 1945 [M]		1963	30.00
CHARTBUSTERS, VOL. 3			
❑ Capitol ST 2006 [S]		1963	40.00
❑ Capitol T 2006 [M]		1963	30.00
CHARTBUSTERS, VOL. 4			
❑ Capitol ST 2094 [S]		1964	60.00
❑ Capitol T 2094 [M]		1964	40.00
CHICAGO / AUSTIN HIGH SCHOOL			
❑ RCA Victor LPM-1508 [M]		1957	30.00
CHICAGO AND ALL THAT JAZZ!			
❑ Verve V-8441 [M]		1961	25.00
❑ Verve V6-8441 [S]		1962	30.00
CHICAGO BLUES ANTHOLOGY			
❑ Chess 2CH-60012 [(2)]		1972	20.00
CHICAGO JAZZ ALBUM			
❑ Decca DL 8029 [M]		1954	40.00
CHICAGO JAZZ, 1923-29			
❑ Biograph 12005		1968	12.00
CHICAGO JAZZ, VOL. 2, 1925-29			
❑ Biograph 12043		197?	12.00
CHICAGO SOUTH SIDE			
❑ Historical 10		1968	10.00
CHICAGO SOUTH SIDE, VOL. 2			
❑ Historical 30		1969	10.00
CHICAGO STYLE JAZZ			
❑ Columbia CL 632 [M]		1955	—
—See EDDIE CONDON.			
CHICAGO'S BOSS TENORS			
❑ Chess CHV-414		1970	15.00
CHICAGO: THE LIVING LEGENDS, VOL. 1			
❑ Riverside RLP-389 [M]		196?	20.00
❑ Riverside RS-9389 [R]		196?	12.00
CHICAGO: THE LIVING LEGENDS, VOL. 2			
❑ Riverside RLP-390 [M]		196?	20.00
❑ Riverside RS-9390 [R]		196?	12.00
THE CHICAGOANS			
❑ Decca DL 79231		1968	12.00
A CHILD'S CHRISTMAS			
❑ Harmony HS 14563		197?	12.00
CHRISTMAS — A GIFT OF MUSIC			
❑ Capitol Special Markets SL-6687		197?	12.00
—Reissue of "Zenith Presents Chrisrmas, A Gift of Music, Vol. 4" with almost identical cover			
CHRISTMAS — THE SEASON OF MUSIC			
❑ Capitol Creative Products SL-6679		1970	12.00
—Reissue of "Zenith Presents Christmas, A Gift of Music, Vol. 3" with almost identical cover			
THE CHRISTMAS ALBUM			
❑ Columbia G 30763 [(2)]		1972	15.00
CHRISTMAS AMERICA			
❑ Capitol Special Markets SL-6884		1973	12.00
—Sold only at Firestone tire dealers (add 50% for sticker that says "Season's Greetings Firestone")			
CHRISTMAS AMERICA, ALBUM TWO			
❑ Capitol Special Markets SL-6950		1974	12.00
—Sold only at Firestone tire dealers (add 50% for sticker that says "Season's Greetings Firestone")			
CHRISTMAS AS IT HAPPENED			
❑ Mennonite Hour TR4H-5299/5300 [DJ]		1966	12.00
—"A series of seven 'newscasts' of the memorable events leading up to the birth of Jesus Christ"; tracks have locked grooves; possibly issued without a cover			
CHRISTMAS AT HOME			
❑ Capitol Creative Products SL-6530		1967	12.00
CHRISTMAS AT OUR HOUSE			
❑ Impact R 3381		1975	12.00
—Also contains narration by John T. Benson			
CHRISTMAS CAROUSEL			
❑ Capitol SQBE-94406 [(2)]		1972	15.00
—Available only through the Capitol Record Club			
CHRISTMAS CHORUS			
❑ Columbia Special Products CSS 932/3 [(2)]		1969	15.00
—Produced for NORM/A Step Ahead			
CHRISTMAS CLASSICS 1963			
❑ E.F. MacDonald EFMX-63		1963	20.00
—Special album done by the E.F. MacDonald Company, Dayton, Ohio			
CHRISTMAS DAY IN THE COUNTRY			
❑ Columbia Special Products P 11887		1973	10.00
CHRISTMAS DAY WITH COLONEL SANDERS			
❑ RCA Victor PRS-274		1968	20.00
—Sold only at Kentucky Fried Chicken restaurants			
CHRISTMAS EVE WITH COLONEL SANDERS			
❑ RCA Victor PRS-256		1967	20.00
—Sold only at Kentucky Fried Chicken restaurants			
CHRISTMAS FAVORITES			
❑ RCA Victor PR-115-A [M]		1961	15.00
—Sold only at Acme markets (Mid-Atlantic states)			
A CHRISTMAS FESTIVAL			
❑ RCA Record Club CCS-0145 [(2)]		1970	15.00
A CHRISTMAS FESTIVAL OF SONGS AND CAROLS			
❑ RCA Victor PRM-170 [M]		1964	12.00
—Sold only at JCPenney department stores			
❑ RCA Victor PRS-170 [S]		1964	15.00
—Sold only at JCPenney department stores			
A CHRISTMAS FESTIVAL OF SONGS AND CAROLS, VOL. 2			
❑ RCA Victor PRM-195 [M]		1965	12.00
—Sold only at JCPenney department stores			
❑ RCA Victor PRS-195 [S]		1965	15.00
—Sold only at JCPenney department stores			
CHRISTMAS GIFT 'RAP			
❑ Motown MS-725		1970	20.00
—Reissue of "Merry Christmas from Motown," MS-681			
A CHRISTMAS GIFT FOR YOU FROM PHILLES RECORDS			
❑ Philles PHLP-4005 [M]		1963	150.00
—First edition of this group of songs; blue and black labels			
❑ Philles PHLP-4005 [M]		1964	80.00
—Second edition of this group of songs; yellow and red labels; both first and second editions have "Marshmellow [sic] World" typo on front cover; also see PHIL SPECTOR'S CHRISTMAS ALBUM			
CHRISTMAS GREETINGS			
❑ Columbia Special Products CSS 1433		1970	10.00
❑ Columbia Special Products CSS 1499		1970	10.00
—Sold only at A&P grocery stores			
CHRISTMAS GREETINGS FROM NASHVILLE			
❑ RCA Victor APL1-0262		1973	12.00
CHRISTMAS GREETINGS, VOL. 2			
❑ Columbia Special Products C 10399		1971	10.00
—Sold only at A&P grocery stores			
CHRISTMAS GREETINGS, VOL. 3			
❑ Columbia Special Products P 11383		1972	10.00
—Sold only at A&P grocery stores			
CHRISTMAS GREETINGS, VOL. 4			
❑ Columbia Special Products P 11987		1973	12.00
—Sold only at A&P grocery stores			
CHRISTMAS HITS FROM WARNER BROS.			
❑ Warner Bros. 8467/8 [DJ]		1959	50.00
CHRISTMAS IN CALIFORNIA			
❑ RCA Victor PRS-276		1968	12.00
—Available only from Bank of America			
CHRISTMAS IN ENGLAND			
❑ Capitol T 10097 [M]		195?	15.00
CHRISTMAS IN ITALY			
❑ Capitol SM-10093 [R]		197?	10.00
❑ Capitol T 10093 [M]		196?	15.00
CHRISTMAS IN NEW YORK			
❑ RCA Victor PRM-257 [M]		1967	12.00
❑ RCA Victor PRS-257 [S]		1967	15.00
CHRISTMAS IN NEW YORK VOL. 2			
❑ RCA Victor PRS-270		1968	12.00
CHRISTMAS IN NORWAY			
❑ Capitol T 10377 [M]		196?	15.00
CHRISTMAS IN SAN FRANCISCO			
❑ Embarcadero Center EC-101		1974	15.00
—Featuring members of the San Francisco, Oakland ans San Jose Symphonies, the San Francisco and Western Operas, etc.; not all tracks have artists identified			

Except when noted otherwise, VG = 25% of NM, and VG+ = 50% of NM. (Example: VG = $2.00, VG+ = $4.00 and NM = $8.00.)

Number | Title (A Side/B Side) | Yr | NM

CHRISTMAS IN THE AIR
❑ RCA Special Products DPL1-0133 1975 10.00

CHRISTMAS IS...
❑ Columbia Special Products P 11417 1972 12.00
—Sold only at Goodyear tire dealers

A CHRISTMAS MUSIC FESTIVAL
❑ Capitol Creative Products SL-6688 1970 10.00

CHRISTMAS NIGHT IN BETHLEHEM: THE MIDNIGHT CEREMONY AT ST. CATHERINE'S CHURCH
❑ ABC Dunhill DS-55002 1968 15.00
—Recording of the 1967 midnight Mass in the Holy Land; with 24-page booklet

CHRISTMAS PROGRAMMING FROM RCA VICTOR
❑ RCA Victor SP-33-66 [DJ] 1959 1000.
—Promo-only collection; has been counterfeited, but originals have color covers

THE CHRISTMAS SONG AND OTHER FAVORITES
❑ Columbia Special Products P 12446 1974 10.00

THE CHRISTMAS SOUND OF MUSIC
❑ Capitol Special Markets SL-6996 1975 10.00

THE CHRISTMAS SOUNDS OF MUSIC
❑ Capitol Creative Products SL-6643 1969 12.00
—Sold only at B.F. Goodrich tire dealers

CHRISTMAS STARS: SUTHERLAND/TEBALDI/PRICE SING BEST LOVED CHRISTMAS FAVORITES
❑ London OS 26408 1974 12.00

CHRISTMAS STOCKING
❑ Capitol NP 90494 [M] 1965 15.00
—Available only through the Capitol Record Club
❑ Capitol SNP 90494 [S] 1965 15.00
—Available only through the Capitol Record Club

CHRISTMAS THROUGH THE YEARS
❑ MCA Special Markets DL 734596 197? 12.00
—Produced for First Financial Marketing Group

CHRISTMAS TIME
❑ Decca DL 34037 [M] 196? 15.00

CHRISTMAS TRIMMINGS
❑ Columbia Special Products P 12795 1975 10.00

CHRISTMAS WITH ANDY WILLIAMS AND THE WILLIAMS BROTHERS
❑ Columbia Special Products C 10105 1971 10.00

CHRISTMAS WITH COLONEL SANDERS
❑ RCA Victor PRS-291 1969 20.00
—Sold only at Kentucky Fried Chicken restaurants

CHRISTMAS WITH EDDY ARNOLD/CHRISTMAS WITH HENRY MANCINI
❑ RCA Special Products DPL1-0079 1974 12.00

CHRISTMAS WITH GLEN CAMPBELL AND THE HOLLYWOOD POPS ORCHESTRA
❑ Capitol Creative Products SL-6699 1971 12.00
❑ Capitol Special Markets SL-6699 197? 10.00
—Reissue on renamed label

CHRISTMAS WITH JOHNNY MATHIS AND PERCY FAITH
❑ Columbia Special Products P 11805 1973 10.00

CHRISTMAS WITH JULIE ANDREWS (FEATURING THE YULETIDE CHORISTERS)
❑ RCA Victor PRS-290 1969 12.00

CHRISTMAS WITH NAT KING COLE AND FRED WARING & THE PENNSYLVANIANS
❑ Capitol Special Markets SL-6883 197? 10.00

CHRISTMAS WITH THE STARS
❑ Capitol Special Markets SL-6931 1973 10.00

CHRISTMASTIME IN CAROL AND SONG
❑ RCA Victor PRM-271 [M] 1968 20.00
❑ RCA Victor PRS-271 [S] 1968 12.00
❑ RCA Victor PRS-289 1969 12.00

CLAMBAKE ON BOURBON STREET
❑ Cook LP-1085 [10] 1955 50.00

CLASSIC BLUES ACCOMPANISTS
❑ Riverside RLP-1052 [10] 1955 80.00

THE CLASSIC COLLECTION — TRADITIONAL: THE GREAT JAZZ MEN/VOL. 1
❑ Dot DLP-25878 1968 15.00

CLASSIC JAZZ PIANO STYLES
❑ RCA Victor LPV-544 [M] 1967 20.00

CLASSICS IN JAZZ
❑ Capitol T 320 [M] 1954 40.00

CLASSICS IN JAZZ: COOL AND QUIET
❑ Capitol H 371 [10] 1953 50.00

CLASSICS IN JAZZ: DIXIELAND STYLISTS
❑ Capitol H 321 [10] 1952 50.00

CLASSICS IN JAZZ: SMALL COMBOS
❑ Capitol H 322 [10] 1952 50.00

Number | Title (A Side/B Side) | Yr | NM

CLAY COLE PRESENTS BLASTS FROM THE PAST
❑ Blast BLP 6803 [M] 196? 50.00

CLAY COLE'S BIN OF ORIGINAL GOLDEN OLDIES
❑ Jubilee JGM-5026 [M] 1964 100.00

A COLLECTION OF 16 ORIGINAL BIG HITS, VOL. 10
❑ Motown MS 684 1969 20.00

A COLLECTION OF 16 ORIGINAL BIG HITS, VOL. 11
❑ Motown MS 693 1969 20.00

A COLLECTION OF 16 ORIGINAL BIG HITS, VOL. 3
❑ Motown MS 624 [S] 1966 25.00

A COLLECTION OF 16 ORIGINAL BIG HITS, VOL. 5
❑ Motown MS 651 [S] 1966 20.00

A COLLECTION OF 16 ORIGINAL BIG HITS, VOL. 6
❑ Motown MS 655 [S] 1967 20.00
❑ Motown MT 655 [M] 1967 20.00

A COLLECTION OF 16 ORIGINAL BIG HITS, VOL. 7
❑ Motown M 661 [M] 1967 20.00
❑ Motown MS 661 [S] 1967 20.00

A COLLECTION OF 16 ORIGINAL BIG HITS, VOL. 8
❑ Motown MS 666 [S] 1967 20.00
❑ Motown MT 666 [M] 1967 20.00

A COLLECTION OF 16 ORIGINAL BIG HITS, VOL. 9
❑ Motown MS 668 [S] 1968 20.00
❑ Motown MT 668 [M] 1968 50.00
—Mono is white label promo only; "Monaural Record DJ Copy" sticker on stereo cover

COLLECTORS ITEMS, VOL. 2
❑ Riverside RLP-1040 [10] 1954 80.00

COLLECTORS' CHOICE
❑ Verve V-8408 [M] 1961 —
—Canceled

COLLECTORS' ITEMS, 1922-30
❑ Historical 11 1967 10.00

COLLECTORS' ITEMS, 1925-29
❑ Historical 20 1968 10.00

COLLEGE ALBUM
❑ Verve MGV-8341 [M] 1959 —
—Canceled

COLLEGE JAZZ: DIXIELAND
❑ Columbia CL 736 [M] 1956 20.00

COLOR ME OBG: STATION WDRC
❑ Roulette R 25347 [M] 1967 20.00

COLORADO JAZZ PARTY
❑ BASF 25099 [(2)] 197? 20.00

COLUMBIA JAZZ FESTIVAL
❑ Columbia JJ-1 [M] 1959 25.00

COMBO JAZZ
❑ Jazztone J-1221 [M] 1956 30.00

COME CLOSER TO GOD
❑ Vee Jay LP-5061 [M] 1964 30.00

COMPARATIVE BLUES
❑ Jazztone J-1258 [M] 1957 30.00

COMPOSERS AT PLAY: HAROLD ARLEN AND COLE PORTER
❑ "X" LVA-1003 [M] 1955 40.00

THE COMPOSITIONS OF BENNY GOLSON
❑ Riverside RLP-3505 [M] 1962 15.00
❑ Riverside RS-93505 [S] 1962 20.00

THE COMPOSITIONS OF BOBBY TIMMONS
❑ Riverside RLP-3512 [M] 1962 15.00
❑ Riverside RS-93512 [S] 1962 20.00

THE COMPOSITIONS OF CHARLIE PARKER
❑ Riverside RLP-3506 [M] 1962 15.00
❑ Riverside RS-93506 [S] 1962 20.00

THE COMPOSITIONS OF COLE PORTER
❑ Riverside RM-3515 [M] 1963 15.00
❑ Riverside RS-93515 [S] 1963 20.00

THE COMPOSITIONS OF DIZZY GILLESPIE
❑ Riverside RLP-3508 [M] 1962 15.00
❑ Riverside RS-93508 [S] 1962 20.00

THE COMPOSITIONS OF DUKE ELLINGTON
❑ Riverside RLP-3507 [M] 1962 15.00
❑ Riverside RS-93507 [S] 1962 20.00

THE COMPOSITIONS OF DUKE ELLINGTON, VOL. 2
❑ Riverside RLP-3510 [M] 1962 15.00
❑ Riverside RS-93510 [S] 1962 20.00

THE COMPOSITIONS OF GEORGE GERSHWIN
❑ Riverside RM-3517 [M] 1963 15.00
❑ Riverside RS-93517 [S] 1963 20.00

THE COMPOSITIONS OF HAROLD ARLEN
❑ Riverside RM-3518 [M] 1963 15.00
❑ Riverside RS-93518 [S] 1963 20.00

THE COMPOSITIONS OF HORACE SILVER
❑ Riverside RLP-3509 [M] 1962 15.00

Number | Title (A Side/B Side) | Yr | NM

❑ Riverside RS-93509 [S] 1962 20.00

THE COMPOSITIONS OF IRVING BERLIN
❑ Riverside RM-3519 [M] 1963 15.00
❑ Riverside RS-93519 [S] 1963 20.00

THE COMPOSITIONS OF JEROME KERN
❑ Riverside RM-3516 [M] 1963 15.00
❑ Riverside RS-93516 [S] 1963 20.00

COMPOSITIONS OF LIONEL HAMPTON
❑ Crown CLP-5107 [M] 195? 25.00

THE COMPOSITIONS OF MILES DAVIS
❑ Riverside RLP-3504 [M] 1962 15.00
❑ Riverside RS-93504 [S] 1962 20.00

THE COMPOSITIONS OF RICHARD RODGERS
❑ Riverside RM-3514 [M] 1963 15.00
❑ Riverside RS-93514 [S] 1963 20.00

THE COMPOSITIONS OF TADD DAMERON
❑ Riverside RLP-3511 [M] 1962 15.00
❑ Riverside RS-93511 [S] 1962 20.00

THE COMPOSITIONS OF THELONIOUS MONK
❑ Riverside RLP-3503 [M] 1962 15.00
❑ Riverside RS-93503 [S] 1962 20.00

CONCEPTION
❑ Prestige PRLP-7013 [M] 1956 100.00

CONCERT IN JAZZ
❑ Tops L-1532 [M] 1958 20.00

CONCERT JAZZ
❑ Brunswick BL 54027 [M] 1956 30.00

COOL AND CAREFREE
❑ Columbia Special Products CSP 119 [M] 1963 12.00
—Sold only by Carrier air conditioner dealers

COOL EUROPE
❑ MGM E-3157 [M] 1955 30.00

COOL GABRIELS
❑ Groove LG-1003 [M] 1956 60.00

COOL JAZZ
❑ Seeco CELP-465 [M] 1960 20.00

COOL JAZZ FROM HOLLAND
❑ Epic LN 1126 [10] 1955 40.00

COOLIN'
❑ New Jazz NJLP-8216 [M] 1959 60.00
—Purple label
❑ New Jazz NJLP-8216 [M] 1965 30.00
—Blue label, trident logo at right

THE CORE OF JAZZ
❑ MGM SE-4737 1970 12.00

COUNTRY & WESTERN CLASSICS 1955
❑ Economic Consultants 1955 1973 20.00

COUNTRY & WESTERN CLASSICS 1956
❑ Economic Consultants 1956 1973 20.00

COUNTRY & WESTERN CLASSICS 1957
❑ Economic Consultants 1957 1973 20.00

COUNTRY & WESTERN CLASSICS 1958
❑ Economic Consultants 1958 1973 20.00

COUNTRY AND WESTERN JAMBOREE
❑ King 697 [M] 1961 150.00

COUNTRY CHRISTMAS
❑ Columbia CS 9888 1968 15.00
❑ King 811 [M] 1962 100.00
❑ Monument SLP-18125 1969 20.00

A COUNTRY CHRISTMAS
❑ Columbia Special Products CSS 1434 1970 12.00

COUNTRY CHRISTMAS FAVORITES
❑ Columbia Special Products C 10876 1972 10.00

COUNTRY CREAM
❑ QMO Q-110 197? 10.00
—Alternate number is Columbia Special Products C 10422

COUNTRY FAIR
❑ Capitol SWBB-562 [(2)] 1970 25.00

COUNTRY HITS PARADE
❑ RCA Victor LPM-3452 [M] 1966 15.00
❑ RCA Victor LSP-3452 [S] 1966 20.00

COUNTRY HOLIDAY
❑ Columbia Musical Treasury DS 467 1968 15.00

COUNTRY MUSIC BY THE WAYSIDE
❑ Wayside 1013 1968 20.00

COUNTRY MUSIC HOOTENANNY
❑ Capitol ST 2009 [S] 1963 30.00
❑ Capitol T 2009 [M] 1963 25.00

COUNTRY MUSIC STAR SPECTACULAR
❑ Hickory LPM-116 [M] 1963 25.00

THE COUNTRY SIDE OF CHRISTMAS/ALL-TIME FAVORITES IN THE TRADITIONAL STYLE
❑ Capitol Creative Products SL-6586 1968 12.00

Number	Title (A Side/B Side)	Yr	NM
COUNTRY SPECIAL			
❑ Capitol STBB-402 [(2)]		1969	25.00
A COUNTRY STYLE CHRISTMAS			
❑ Columbia Musical Treasury 3P 6316 [(3)]		1975	15.00
CRITICS' CHOICE			
❑ Dawn DLP-1123 [M]		1958	80.00
CRUISIN'			
❑ Jazzland JLP-7 [M]		1960	25.00
❑ Jazzland JLP-97 [S]		1960	30.00
D'OES CRAZY OLDIES			
❑ Oldies 33 OL-8007 [M]		1964	25.00
DANCE BAND HITS			
❑ RCA Victor LPT-2 [10]		1951	40.00
DANCE DISCOTHEQUE			
❑ Decca DL 4556 [M]		1964	15.00
❑ Decca DL 74556 [S]		1964	20.00
DANCE ON THE WILD SIDE			
❑ Chancellor CHL-5028 [M]		1962	25.00
❑ Chancellor CHLS-5028 [S]		1962	30.00
DANCE THE ROCK & ROLL			
❑ Atlantic 8013 [M]		1957	80.00
DANCE TO THE BANDS			
❑ Capitol TBO 727 [(2)M]		1956	40.00
❑ Capitol T 977 [M]		1958	20.00
DANCE TUNES FROM THE VAULT, VOL. 2			
❑ Chess LP 1476 [M]		1962	40.00
DANCE, BE HAPPY!			
❑ Columbia CL 967 [M]		1957	20.00
DANCING WITH THE STARS			
❑ Epic LN 3136 [M]		1955	30.00
DARK MUDDY BOTTOM BLUES			
❑ Specialty SPS-2149		1971	20.00
DAS IS JAZZ!			
❑ Decca DL 8229 [M]		1956	30.00
A DATE WITH GREATNESS			
❑ Imperial LP-9188A [M]		1962	50.00
—Features Aladdin tracks by Coleman Hawkins, Howard McGhee and Lester Young			
❑ Imperial LP-12188A [R]		1962	25.00
A DATE WITH RIVERSIDE			
❑ Riverside S-4 [M]		195?	40.00
A DAY IN THE COUNTRY			
❑ Audio Lab AL-1519 [M]		1959	80.00
DAYS OF WINE AND VINYL			
❑ Warner Bros. PRO 540 [(2)]		1973	30.00
DECADE OF JAZZ, VOL. 1, 1939-49			
❑ Blue Note BN-LA158-G2 [(2)]		1974	15.00
DECADE OF JAZZ, VOL. 2, 1949-59			
❑ Blue Note BN-LA159-G2 [(2)]		1974	15.00
DECADE OF JAZZ, VOL. 3, 1959-69			
❑ Blue Note BN-LA160-G2 [(2)]		1974	15.00
DEEP EAR			
❑ Warner Bros. PRO 591 [(2)]		1974	25.00
THE DEFINITIVE JAZZ SCENE, VOL. 1			
❑ ABC Impulse! AS-99 [S]		1968	12.00
❑ Impulse! A-99 [M]		1966	15.00
❑ Impulse! AS-99 [S]		1966	20.00
THE DEFINITIVE JAZZ SCENE, VOL. 2			
❑ ABC Impulse! AS-100 [S]		1968	12.00
❑ Impulse! A-100 [M]		1966	15.00
❑ Impulse! AS-100 [S]		1966	20.00
THE DEFINITIVE JAZZ SCENE, VOL. 3			
❑ ABC Impulse! AS-9101 [S]		1968	12.00
❑ Impulse! A-9101 [M]		1966	15.00
❑ Impulse! AS-9101 [S]		1966	20.00
DEL-FI ALBUM SAMPLER			
❑ Del-Fi (no #) [DJ]		1959	500.00
—Green vinyl, promo only, with paper sleeve			
DEL-FI RECORD HOP			
❑ Del-Fi DFLP-1210 [M]		1959	80.00
DEMAND PERFORMANCES			
❑ Monument MLP-8010 [M]		1963	25.00
❑ Monument SLP-18010 [S]		1963	40.00
DEMONSTRATION RECORD — DISC JOCKEYS — JAN.-FEB. 1955			
❑ Capitol PRO-213 [DJ]		1955	40.00
DIAL A HIT			
❑ Bell 6030		1969	20.00
DICK CLARK: 20 YEARS OF ROCK N' ROLL			
❑ Buddah BDS 5133 [(2)]		1973	20.00
—Gatefold cover with booklet and bonus 7-inch cardboard record			
❑ Buddah BDS 5133 [(2)]		1974	10.00
—With none of the extras			
DISCO-TEEN '66			
❑ Columbia Record Club D 155 [M]		1966	20.00
❑ Columbia Record Club DS 155 [S]		1966	50.00
—Sought-after for its otherwise unavailable extended stereo mix of Bob Dylan's "Positively 4th Street"			
DISCOTHEQUE AU GO GO			
❑ Design DLP-194 [M]		1964	12.00
—Cover calls this "Johnny Rivers Discotheque Au Go Go," but only one Johnny Rivers song is on the LP			
❑ Design SDLP-194 [R]		1964	10.00
—Cover calls this "Johnny Rivers Discotheque Au Go Go," but only one Johnny Rivers song is on the LP			
DISPLAY CASE #10			
❑ Warner Bros. PRO 542 [(3)]		1973	30.00
DISPLAY CASE #8			
❑ Warner Bros. PRO 532 [(2)]		1972	30.00
DISPLAY CASE #9			
❑ Warner Bros. PRO 538 [(2)]		1972	30.00
DIXIE LAND U.S.A.			
❑ Promenade 2134 [M]		195?	15.00
DIXIE, LONDON STYLE			
❑ London LL 1337 [M]		1956	20.00
DIXIELAND — NEW ORLEANS			
❑ Mainstream S-6003 [R]		1965	12.00
❑ Mainstream 56003 [M]		1965	25.00
DIXIELAND AT CARNEGIE HALL			
❑ Forum F-9011 [M]		196?	20.00
❑ Forum SF-9011 [S]		196?	25.00
❑ Roulette R 25038 [M]		1958	30.00
—Originals have a black label			
❑ Roulette R 25038 [M]		1959	20.00
—Second pressings have a white label with colored spokes			
DIXIELAND AT ITS BEST			
❑ RCA Camden CAL-838 [M]		1964	12.00
❑ RCA Camden CAS-838 [R]		1964	10.00
DIXIELAND AT JAZZ, LTD.			
❑ Atlantic 1261 [M]		1957	40.00
—Black label			
❑ Atlantic 1261 [M]		1961	25.00
—Multicolor label, white "fan" logo at right			
DIXIELAND AT JAZZ, LTD., VOL. 1			
❑ Atlantic ALS-139 [10]		1952	60.00
DIXIELAND AT JAZZ, LTD., VOL. 2			
❑ Atlantic ALS-140 [10]		1952	60.00
DIXIELAND CLASSICS			
❑ Jazztone J-1216 [M]		1956	30.00
DIXIELAND CONTRASTS			
❑ Jazzman LJ-334 [M]		1954	30.00
DIXIELAND DETOUR			
❑ Capitol H 312 [10]		1952	—
—See PEE WEE HUNT.			
DIXIELAND FESTIVAL, VOL. 1			
❑ Vik LX-1057 [M]		1956	30.00
DIXIELAND HITS			
❑ Swingville SVLP-2040 [M]		1962	40.00
—Purple label			
❑ Swingville SVLP-2040 [M]		1965	20.00
—Blue label, trident logo at right			
DIXIELAND IN OLD NEW ORLEANS			
❑ Golden Crest GC-3021 [M]		1958	20.00
DIXIELAND JAZZ			
❑ Audiophile XL-325 [M]		1954	30.00
❑ Audiophile XL-330 [M]		1954	30.00
❑ Grand Award GA 33-310 [M]		1955	25.00
—Without wrap-around outer cover			
❑ Grand Award GA 33-310 [M]		1955	60.00
—With wrap-around outer cover			
DIXIELAND JAZZ GEMS			
❑ Commodore FL-20010 [10]		1950	50.00
DIXIELAND MAIN STREAM			
❑ Savoy MG-12213 [M]		196?	20.00
DIXIELAND RHYTHM KINGS			
❑ Paradox LP-6002 [10]		1951	50.00
DIXIELAND SERIES, VOL. 1			
❑ Savoy MG-15005 [10]		1952	80.00
DIXIELAND SERIES, VOL. 2			
❑ Savoy MG-15009 [10]		1952	80.00
DIXIELAND VS. BIRDLAND			
❑ MGM E-231 [10]		1954	80.00
DIZZY ATMOSPHERE			
❑ Specialty LP-2110 [M]		1957	40.00
—Original edition, heavier vinyl			
DO IT NOW - 20 GIANT HITS			
❑ Ronco LP-1001		1971	20.00
DOO WOP			
❑ Specialty SPS-2114		1969	20.00
DOUBLE BARREL JAZZ			
❑ Bethlehem BCP-87 [M]		1958	30.00
DOWN BEAT CRITICS POLL WINNERS			
❑ Clef MGC-742 [M]		1955	—
—Canceled			
DOWN BEAT JAZZ CONCERT			
❑ Dot DLP-9003 [M]		1958	30.00
❑ Dot DLP-29003 [S]		1958	25.00
DOWN BEAT JAZZ CONCERT, VOL. 2			
❑ Dot DLP-3188 [M]		1959	30.00
❑ Dot DLP-25188 [S]		1959	25.00
DOWN BEAT'S HALL OF FAME, VOL. 1			
❑ Verve MGV-8320 [M]		1959	50.00
❑ Verve V-8320 [M]		1961	20.00
DOWN HOME STOMP: RURAL BLUES, VOL. 3			
❑ Imperial LP-94006		1968	20.00
DREAMING ON THE RIVER TO NEW ORLEANS			
❑ Southland SLP-238		1963	15.00
THE DRUMS			
❑ ABC Impulse! AS-9272 [(3)]		197?	20.00
DRUMS ON FIRE			
❑ World Pacific WP-1247 [M]		1958	40.00
THE DUTCH EXPLOSION			
❑ White Whale WWS-7130		1970	30.00
DYNAMITE			
❑ K-Tel TU 2360		1974	10.00
EARLY AND RARE: CLASSIC JAZZ "COLLECTORS ITEMS"			
❑ Riverside RLP 12-134 [M]		1957	40.00
EARLY JAZZ GREATS, VOL. 1			
❑ Jazztone J-1249 [M]		1957	30.00
EARLY JAZZ GREATS, VOL. 2			
❑ Jazztone J-1252 [M]		1957	30.00
EARTHY!			
❑ Prestige PRLP-7102 [M]		1957	100.00
THE EAST COAST JAZZ SCENE, VOL. 1			
❑ Coral CRL 57035 [M]		1956	50.00
EASY LISTENING			
❑ Audiophile AP-27 [M]		1953	30.00
❑ Audiophile AP-38 [M]		1953	30.00
❑ Audiophile XL-327 [M]		1954	30.00
ECHOES OF NEW ORLEANS			
❑ Southland SLP-239		1963	15.00
EIGHT WAYS TO JAZZ			
❑ Riverside RLP 12-272 [M]		1958	30.00
18 ALL TIME COUNTRY AND WESTERN HITS			
❑ King 1027 [M]		1968	30.00
18 ALL TIME RHYTHM 'N' BLUES HITS			
❑ King 1026 [M]		1968	30.00
18 KING-SIZE COUNTRY HITS			
❑ Columbia CL 2668 [M]		1967	20.00
❑ Columbia CS 9468 [R]		1967	20.00
18 KING-SIZE RHYTHM AND BLUES HITS			
❑ Columbia CL 2667 [M]		1967	30.00
❑ Columbia CS 9467 [R]		1967	20.00
ELEKTRA NEW FOLK SAMPLER			
❑ Elektra SMP 2 [M]		1956	30.00
ELEKTRA'S BEST, VOL. 1: 1966-1968			
❑ Elektra EB-1 [(2)]		1969	25.00
—Promo only, red labels			
ENCYCLOPEDIA OF JAZZ IN THE '60'S, VOL. 1			
❑ Verve V-8677 [M]		1966	15.00
❑ Verve V6-8677 [S]		1966	20.00
THE ENCYCLOPEDIA OF JAZZ ON RECORDS			
❑ Decca DXF 140 [(4)M]		1957	100.00
—Box set; individually issued as Decca 8398, 8399, 8400 and 8401			
THE ENCYCLOPEDIA OF JAZZ ON RECORDS, VOL. 1: JAZZ OF THE TWENTIES			
❑ Decca DL 8398 [M]		1957	20.00
THE ENCYCLOPEDIA OF JAZZ ON RECORDS, VOL. 2: JAZZ OF THE THIRTIES			
❑ Decca DL 8399 [M]		1957	20.00
THE ENCYCLOPEDIA OF JAZZ ON RECORDS, VOL. 3: JAZZ OF THE FORTIES			
❑ Decca DL 8400 [M]		1957	20.00
THE ENCYCLOPEDIA OF JAZZ ON RECORDS, VOL. 4: JAZZ OF THE FIFTIES			
❑ Decca DL 8401 [M]		1957	20.00
END OF AN ERA: RHYTHM 'N' BLUES, VOL. 1			
❑ Imperial LP-94003		1968	20.00
ENERGY ESSENTIALS			
❑ ABC Impulse! ASD-9228 [(3)]		197?	20.00

Except when noted otherwise, VG = 25% of NM, and VG+ = 50% of NM. (Example: VG = $2.00, VG+ = $4.00 and NM = $8.00.)

Number	Yr	NM
ENGLAND'S GREATEST HIT MAKERS		
❑ London PS 430 [R]	1965	20.00
❑ London LL 3430 [M]	1965	25.00
ENGLAND'S GREATEST HITS		
❑ Fontana MGF 27570 [M]	1967	40.00
—Without poster		
❑ Fontana MGF 27570 [M]	1967	50.00
—With poster		
❑ Fontana SRF 67570 [R]	1967	20.00
—Without poster		
❑ Fontana SRF 67570 [R]	1967	30.00
—With poster		
ERA OF THE CLARINET		
❑ Mainstream S-6011 [R]	1965	12.00
❑ Mainstream 56011 [M]	1965	25.00
ESCAPADE REVIEWS THE JAZZ SCENE		
❑ Liberty SL-9005 [M]	1957	30.00
ESCAPE		
❑ Gene Norman GNP-27 [M]	1958	25.00
ESQUIRE'S ALL-AMERICAN HOT JAZZ		
❑ RCA Victor LPV-544 [M]	1967	20.00
ESQUIRE'S WORLD OF JAZZ		
❑ Capitol STBO 1970 [(2)S]	1963	20.00
❑ Capitol TBO 1970 [(2)M]	1963	20.00
THE ESSENTIAL JAZZ VOCALS		
❑ Verve V-8505 [M]	1963	20.00
❑ Verve V6-8505 [R]	1963	12.00
AN EVENING OF JAZZ		
❑ Norgran MGN-1065 [M]	1956	80.00
❑ Verve MGV-8155 [M]	1957	30.00
❑ Verve V-8155 [M]	1961	20.00
EVERYBODY ROCKS!		
❑ Capitol T 1025 [M]	1957	40.00
—Turquoise label		
EVERYBODY'S FAVORITE BLUES		
❑ King 875 [M]	1963	70.00
EVERYBODY'S GONE SURFIN'		
❑ Parkway P-7035 [M]	1963	50.00
THE EXCELLO STORY		
❑ Excello LPS-8025 [(2)]	1972	25.00
THE EXCITING NEW LIVERPOOL SOUND		
❑ Columbia CL 2172 [M]	1964	30.00
EXPLOSIVE!		
❑ Liberty MM-412 [DJ]	1962	50.00
—Promo-only release		
FABULOUS FAVORITES OF OUR TIME		
❑ Liberty LRP-3223 [M]	1962	20.00
❑ Liberty LST-7223 [S]	1962	25.00
FAMILY CHRISTMAS FAVORITES FROM BING CROSBY AND THE COLUMBUS BOYCHOIR		
❑ Decca DL 34487	1967	15.00
—Sold only at Safeway grocery stores		
FAMILY PORTRAIT		
❑ A&M SP-19002	1968	20.00
FANFARE OF HITS		
❑ Argo LP-656 [M]	1960	25.00
FAVORITE CHRISTMAS CAROLS FROM THE VOICE OF FIRESTONE		
❑ Firestone MLP 7005 [M]	1962	12.00
—Sold only at Firestone tire dealers; actually Volume 1 of the "Firestone Presents..." series		
FAVORITE SACRED SONGS		
❑ King 556 [M]	1956	150.00
THE FEMININE TOUCH		
❑ Decca DL 5486 [10]	1953	50.00
❑ Decca DL 8316 [M]	1956	30.00
15 FAVORITES		
❑ Hickory LPM-105 [M]	1962	25.00
15 GOLDEN HITS		
❑ United Artists UAL-3192 [M]	1962	25.00
❑ United Artists UAS-6192 [S]	1962	30.00
15 HITS: THE ORIGINAL RECORDINGS (THE ORIGINAL HITS, VOL. 5)		
❑ Liberty LRP-3235 [M]	1962	20.00
FIFTEEN STAR SAXOPHONES		
❑ Bethlehem BCP-6035 [M]	1959	30.00
FIFTY CHRISTMAS FAVORITES		
❑ RCA Camden CXS-9025 [(2)]	1972	15.00
50 YEARS OF FILM		
❑ Warner Bros. 3XX 2737 [(3)]	1973	25.00
—Box set with 60-page booklet		
50 YEARS OF FILM MUSIC		
❑ Warner Bros. 3XX 2736 [(3)]	1973	25.00
—Box set with 28-page booklet		

Various artists, *Elektra New Folk Sampler,* Elektra SMP-2, 1956, mono, **$30.**

Number	Yr	NM
50 YEARS OF JAZZ GREATS		
❑ Columbia Musical Treasury P3S 5932 [(3)]	197?	20.00
52ND STREET JAZZ		
❑ Waldorf Music Hall MH 33-148 [10]	195?	100.00
FILL YOUR HEAD WITH JAZZ		
❑ Columbia G 30217 [(2)]	1971	15.00
FILLET OF SOUL		
❑ Stax STS 3021	1972	20.00
FILM MUSIC FROM FRANCE		
❑ Philips PHM 200071 [M]	1962	20.00
❑ Philips PHS 600071 [S]	1962	30.00
FINK ALONG WITH MAD		
❑ Big Top 12-1306 [M]	1962	100.00
FIRESTONE PRESENTS YOUR CHRISTMAS FAVORITES, VOL. 3		
❑ Firestone MLP 7008 [M]	1964	10.00
—Sold only at Firestone tire dealers		
❑ Firestone SLP 7008 [S]	1964	10.00
—Sold only at Firestone tire dealers		
FIRESTONE PRESENTS YOUR CHRISTMAS FAVORITES, VOL. 7		
❑ Firestone CSLP 7015	1968	10.00
—Sold only at Firestone tire dealers		
FIRESTONE PRESENTS YOUR FAVORITE CHRISTMAS CAROLS, VOL. 2		
❑ Firestone MLP 7006 [M]	1963	10.00
—Sold only at Firestone tire dealers		
❑ Firestone SLP 7006 [S]	1963	10.00
—Sold only at Firestone tire dealers		
FIRESTONE PRESENTS YOUR FAVORITE CHRISTMAS MUSIC, VOL. 4		
❑ Firestone MLP 7011 [M]	1965	10.00
—Sold only at Firestone tire dealers		
❑ Firestone SLP 7011 [S]	1965	10.00
—Sold only at Firestone tire dealers		

Number	Yr	NM
FIRESTONE PRESENTS YOUR FAVORITE CHRISTMAS MUSIC, VOL. 5		
❑ Firestone MLP 7012 [M]	1966	10.00
—Sold only at Firestone tire dealers		
❑ Firestone SLP 7012 [S]	1966	10.00
—Sold only at Firestone tire dealers		
FIRESTONE PRESENTS YOUR FAVORITE CHRISTMAS MUSIC, VOL. 6		
❑ Firestone MLP 7014 [M]	1967	10.00
—Sold only at Firestone tire dealers		
❑ Firestone SLP 7014 [S]	1967	10.00
—Sold only at Firestone tire dealers		
FIRST ALBUM OF JAZZ		
❑ Folkways FP-712 [10]	1951	50.00
FIRST CHRISTMAS RECORD FOR CHILDREN		
❑ Harmony HS 14554	197?	12.00
THE FIRST GREAT ROCK FESTIVALS OF THE SEVENTIES: ISLE OF WIGHT/ATLANTA POP FESTIVAL		
❑ Columbia G3X 30805 [(3)]	1971	25.00
FIVE FEET OF SWING		
❑ Decca DL 8045 [M]	1954	40.00
5-STRING BANJO PICKIN' AND SINGIN'		
❑ King 994 [M]	1966	40.00
THE FOLK BOX		
❑ Elektra EKL-9001 [(4)]	1964	50.00
FOLK FESTIVAL OF THE BLUES		
❑ Argo LP-4031 [M]	1964	40.00
FOLK POPS 'N JAZZ SAMPLER		
❑ Elektra SMP 3 [M]	1957	25.00
FOLK SAMPLER FIVE		
❑ Elektra SMP 5 [M]	196?	25.00
THE FOLK SCENE		
❑ Elektra SMP 6 [M]	196?	25.00
FOLKSONG '65		
❑ Elektra SMP 8 [M]	1965	20.00
❑ Elektra S 78 [S]	1965	25.00

Various artists, *50 Years of Film,* Warner Bros. 3XX 2737, 1973, 3 records, **$25.**

Number	Title (A Side/B Side)	Yr	NM
FOOTNOTES TO JAZZ, VOL. 2: ANATOMY OF A JAZZ COMPOSITION			
❑ Folkways FP-31 [10]		1951	50.00
FOOTPRINTS IN TIME			
❑ White Whale WWS-7125		1970	25.00
FOR A MUSICAL MERRY CHRISTMAS			
❑ RCA Victor PR-149A [M]		1963	12.00
—Sold only at Acme Markets (Mid-Atlantic states)			
❑ RCA Victor PRM-163 [M]		1964	12.00
—Sold at B.F. Goodrich dealers			
❑ RCA Victor PRS-163(e) [S]		1964	12.00
—Sold at B.F. Goodrich dealers			
FOR A MUSICAL MERRY CHRISTMAS, VOL. TWO			
❑ RCA Victor PRM 189 [M]		1965	12.00
—Sold at B.F. Goodrich dealers			
❑ RCA Victor PRS 189 [S]		1965	15.00
—Sold at B.F. Goodrich tire dealers			
FOR A MUSICAL MERRY CHRISTMAS, VOL. 3			
❑ RCA Victor PRM-221 [M]		1966	12.00
—Sold at B.F. Goodrich dealers			
❑ RCA Victor PRS-221 [S]		1966	15.00
—Sold at B.F. Goodrich dealers			
FOR A MUSICAL MERRY CHRISTMAS, VOL. 4			
❑ RCA Victor PRS-253		1967	12.00
—Sold at B.F. Goodrich dealers			
FOR DANCERS ONLY			
❑ Epic LN 3120 [M]		1955	30.00
FOR JAZZ LOVERS			
❑ EmArcy MG-36086 [M]		1956	40.00
FOR TWISTERS ONLY			
❑ Ace LP-1020 [M]		1962	70.00
THE FORCE			
❑ Warner Bros. PRO 593		1974	20.00
❑ Warner Bros. PRO 596 [(2)]		1974	25.00
FORD HOOTENANNY			
❑ RCA Victor PRM-152 [M]		1964	20.00
—Sold only at Ford dealers			

Number	Title (A Side/B Side)	Yr	NM
FORGOTTEN MILLION SELLERS			
❑ King 792 [M]		1962	100.00
FORTY GOSPEL GREATS			
❑ Vee Jay VJS-2-19000 [(2)]		1975	25.00
FOUR ALTOS			
❑ Prestige PRLP-7116 [M]		1957	100.00
FOUR FRENCH HORNS			
❑ Savoy MG-12173 [M]		1961	50.00
THE FOUR MOST GUITARS			
❑ ABC-Paramount ABC-109 [M]		1956	30.00
❑ Paramount LP-109 [10]		1954	60.00
THE FOUR ROSES DANCE PARTY			
❑ Columbia Special Products XTV 68933/4 [M]		1961	15.00
FOUR TO GO			
❑ Columbia CL 2018 [M]		1963	20.00
❑ Columbia CS 8818 [S]		1963	25.00
14 GOLDEN RECORDINGS FROM THE HISTORIC VAULTS OF DUKE-PEACOCK RECORDS			
❑ ABC ABCX-784		1973	20.00
14 GOLDEN RECORDINGS FROM THE HISTORIC VAULTS OF DUKE-PEACOCK RECORDS, VOL. 2			
❑ ABC ABCX-789		1973	20.00
14 GREAT ALL TIME C&W WALTZES			
❑ King 890 [M]		1964	70.00
14 HIT FLASHBACKS FROM THE GOLDEN GROUP ERA			
❑ King 893 [M]		1964	70.00
14 MORE NEWIES BUT GOODIES			
❑ Mercury MG-20493 [M]		1960	30.00
❑ Mercury SR-60241 [S]		1960	40.00
14 NEWIES BUT GOODIES			
❑ Mercury MG-20493 [M]		1960	30.00
❑ Mercury SR-60172 [S]		1960	40.00

Number	Title (A Side/B Side)	Yr	NM
14 OF THE WORLD'S BEST-LOVED CHRISTMAS SONGS			
❑ Columbia Special Products CSP 122 [M]		1963	15.00
—Sold only at Walgreens drug stores. Title on record is "Music of Christmas"; number on record is "XTV 88672" on Side 1, "XTV 88673" on Side 2			
FRANK BULL AND GENE NORMAN PRESENT DIXIELAND JUBILEE			
❑ Decca DL 7022 [10]		1952	50.00
FRENCH TOAST			
❑ Angel ANG-60009 [10]		1956	50.00
FROM DAVID FROST AND BILLY TAYLOR...MERRY CHRISTMAS			
❑ Bell 6053		1970	15.00
FROM UNDER THE CHRISTMAS TREE			
❑ Capitol Creative Products SL-6589		1968	12.00
FUNKY BLUES NO. 2			
❑ American Recording Society G-404 [M]		1956	30.00
GARDEN OF DELIGHTS			
❑ Elektra S3 10 [(3)]		1971	20.00
—Butterfly labels, possibly promo only			
GARY MOORE PRESENTS "MY KIND OF MUSIC"			
❑ Columbia CL 717 [M]		1956	25.00
GEMS OF JAZZ, VOL. 1			
❑ Decca DL 5133 [10]		1950	50.00
❑ Decca DL 8039 [M]		1954	40.00
GEMS OF JAZZ, VOL. 2			
❑ Decca DL 5134 [10]		1950	50.00
❑ Decca DL 8040 [M]		1954	40.00
GEMS OF JAZZ, VOL. 3			
❑ Decca DL 5383 [10]		1952	50.00
❑ Decca DL 8041 [M]		1954	40.00
GEMS OF JAZZ, VOL. 4			
❑ Decca DL 5384 [10]		1952	50.00
❑ Decca DL 8042 [M]		1954	40.00
GEMS OF JAZZ, VOL. 5			
❑ Decca DL 8043 [M]		1954	40.00
GENE NORMAN PRESENTS JUST JAZZ			
❑ RCA Victor LPT-3102 [10]		1952	—
—See LES THOMPSON.			
GERRY GOFFIN AND CAROLE KING: SOLID GOLD			
❑ Screen Gems/Columbia CPL-713 [DJ]		1975	20.00
—Promo-only compilation of oldies sent to radio to spur airplay on songs owned by this publishing house			
GET IT TOGETHER			
❑ Mainstream MRL-350		197?	12.00
GIANTS OF BOOGIE WOOGIE			
❑ Riverside RLP 12-106 [M]		1956	40.00
GIANTS OF JAZZ			
❑ American Recording Society G-401 [M]		1956	30.00
THE GIANTS OF JAZZ			
❑ Columbia CL 1970 [M]		1963	30.00
GIANTS OF JAZZ ORGAN			
❑ King 837 [M]		1963	120.00
GIANTS OF JAZZ VOL. 2			
❑ American Recording Society G-444 [M]		1957	30.00
GIANTS OF SMALL BAND SWING, VOL. 1			
❑ Riverside RLP 12-143 [M]		1957	40.00
GIANTS OF SMALL BAND SWING, VOL. 2			
❑ Riverside RLP 12-145 [M]		1957	40.00
THE GIFT OF CHRISTMAS			
❑ Columbia Special Products C 10018		1971	12.00
—Sold only at Ace hardware stores (sticker on lower right front cover)			
❑ Columbia Special Products P 11648		1973	10.00
—Same contents and order as "The Gift of Christmas," C 10018; oddly, the record calls this "The Gift of Christmas — Volume II"!			
THE GIFT OF CHRISTMAS, VOL. I			
❑ Columbia Special Products CSS 706		1968	12.00
—Produced for First Financial Marketing Group			
THE GIRLS SING			
❑ Savoy MG-12220 [M]		196?	20.00
THE GLORY OF CHRISTMAS			
❑ Columbia Musical Treasury P3S 5356 [(3)]		196?	15.00
—Performed by anonymous musicians			
GOIN' UP THE COUNTRY: RURAL BLUES, VOL. 1			
❑ Imperial LP-94000		1968	20.00
GOLD HITS			
❑ Warwick W 2008 [M]		1959	80.00
—Reissue of "Goodies But Oldies, Volume 2"; this title still appears on the label			
GOLD SOUL			
❑ Stax STS 2031		1970	20.00
THE GOLDEN AGE OF RHYTHM AND BLUES			
❑ Chess 2CH-50030 [(2)]		1972	25.00

Except when noted otherwise, VG = 25% of NM, and VG+ = 50% of NM. (Example: VG = $2.00, VG+ = $4.00 and NM = $8.00.)

Number	Title (A Side/B Side)	Yr	NM
GOLDEN ECHOES			
❑ Arvee A-433 [M]		1962	25.00
❑ Arvee SA-433 [S]		1962	30.00
GOLDEN ENCORES			
❑ Cadence CLP-3043 [M]		1960	40.00
THE GOLDEN ERA OF JAZZ, VOL. 1			
❑ Savoy MG-15015 [10]		1952	80.00
THE GOLDEN ERA OF JAZZ, VOL. 2			
❑ Savoy MG-15018 [10]		1952	80.00
GOLDEN GASSERS			
❑ Chess LP 1458 USA [M]		1961	120.00
—National version; see listings in this section under "KYA," "Murray the K" and "WAMO" for regional releases			
THE GOLDEN GLOW OF CHRISTMAS			
❑ Columbia Special Products C 10925		1972	12.00
—Sold only at JCPenney department stores			
GOLDEN GOODIES OF 1963, VOL. 18			
❑ Roulette R 25247 [M]		1964	20.00
GOLDEN GOODIES, VOL. 1			
❑ Roulette R 25207 [M]		1963	25.00
GOLDEN GOODIES, VOL. 2			
❑ Roulette R 25210 [M]		1963	25.00
GOLDEN GOODIES, VOL. 3			
❑ Roulette R 25218 [M]		1963	25.00
GOLDEN GOODIES, VOL. 4: GOODIES FOR A DANCE PARTY			
❑ Roulette R 25209 [M]		1963	25.00
GOLDEN GOODIES, VOL. 5			
❑ Roulette R 25215 [M]		1963	25.00
GOLDEN GOODIES, VOL. 6			
❑ Roulette R 25216 [M]		1963	25.00
GOLDEN GOODIES, VOL. 7			
❑ Roulette R 25212 [M]		1963	25.00
GOLDEN GOODIES, VOL. 8			
❑ Roulette R 25214 [M]		1963	25.00
GOLDEN GOODIES, VOL. 9			
❑ Roulette R 25213 [M]		1963	25.00
GOLDEN GOODIES, VOL. 10			
❑ Roulette R 25217 [M]		1963	25.00
GOLDEN GOODIES, VOL. 11			
❑ Roulette R 25219 [M]		1963	25.00
GOLDEN GOODIES, VOL. 12			
❑ Roulette R 25211 [M]		1963	25.00
GOLDEN GOODIES, VOL. 14			
❑ Roulette R 25239 [M]		1964	20.00
GOLDEN GOODIES, VOL. 15			
❑ Roulette R 25240 [M]		1964	20.00
GOLDEN GOODIES, VOL. 16			
❑ Roulette R 25241 [M]		1964	20.00
GOLDEN GOODIES, VOL. 17			
❑ Roulette R 25242 [M]		1964	20.00
GOLDEN GREATS			
❑ Liberty LRP-3500 [M]		1967	15.00
❑ Liberty LST-7500 [P]		1967	20.00
THE GOLDEN GROUPS			
❑ Specialty SPS-2155		1972	20.00
GOLDEN HITS FROM THE GANG AT BANG			
❑ Bang BLP-215 [M]		1967	20.00
❑ Bang BLPS-215 [P]		1967	25.00
GOLDEN INSTRUMENTALS			
❑ Dot DLP-3820 [M]		1967	25.00
❑ Dot DLP-25820 [S]		1967	25.00
GOLDEN JAZZ INTRSUMENTALS			
❑ Bethlehem BCP-6065 [M]		1962	25.00
GOLDEN MOMENTS IN COUNTRY AND WESTERN MUSIC			
❑ Capitol SQBO-90985 [(2)S]		196?	20.00
—Capitol Record Club exclusive			
GOLDEN SOUVENIRS			
❑ United Artists UAL-3317 [M]		1963	25.00
❑ United Artists UAS-6317 [S]		1963	30.00
GOLDEN TEEN HITS			
❑ Liberty L-5505 [M]		1962	40.00
GOLDEN TREASURE CHEST			
❑ United Artists UAL-3314 [M]		1963	25.00
❑ United Artists UAS-6314 [S]		1963	30.00
GONE BUT NOT FORGOTTEN			
❑ Class LP-5004 [M]		1959	100.00
❑ Rendezvous M-1314 [M]		196?	40.00
—Reissue of Class 5004			
GOOD GUY JACK SPECTOR PRESENTS 22 ORIGINAL WINNERS			
❑ Roulette R 25254 [M]		1964	20.00

Various artists, *Golden Treasure Chest,* United Artists UAL 3314, 1963, mono, **$25.**

Number	Title (A Side/B Side)	Yr	NM
THE GOOD OLD 50'S			
❑ Atco 33-118 [M]		1960	60.00
GOODIES BUT OLDIES VOL. 2			
❑ Warwick W 2008 [M]		1959	120.00
—Original title of LP appears on both cover and label; reissued as "Gold Hits" — and there was no Volume 1!			
GOOFY GREATS			
❑ K-Tel NU 9030 [(2)]		1975	12.00
GOSPEL HOOTENANNY			
❑ Imperial LP-9240 [M]		1963	20.00
❑ Imperial LP-12240 [S]		1963	25.00
GOSPEL STARS IN CONCERT			
❑ Specialty SPS-2153		1971	20.00
GRAFFITI GOLD			
❑ Vee Jay VJS-2-9000 [(2)]		1974	20.00
THE GREAT BAND ERA			
❑ Reader's Digest RD-25 [(10)M]		1965	20.00
—Box set with flip-open top			
❑ Reader's Digest RD-25 [(10)R]		1965	15.00
—Box set with flip-open top			
THE GREAT BANDS			
❑ Columbia Musical Treasury P2M 5267 [(2)]		1968	20.00
GREAT BLUES			
❑ Riverside RLP-1074 [10]		1955	80.00
GREAT BLUES SINGERS			
❑ Riverside RLP 12-121 [M]		1957	40.00
THE GREAT BLUES SINGERS			
❑ Riverside RLP-1032 [10]		1954	80.00
THE GREAT GROUP GOODIES			
❑ Atco 33-143 [M]		1962	80.00
GREAT GROUP OLDIES			
❑ Oldies 33 OL-8003 [M]		1963	25.00
GREAT GROUP OLDIES, VOL. 2			
❑ Oldies 33 OL-8006 [M]		1964	25.00
GREAT GROUPS, GREAT RECORDS			
❑ Laurie LLP-2010 [M]		1961	30.00

Number	Title (A Side/B Side)	Yr	NM
GREAT GUITARS OF JAZZ			
❑ MGM SE-4691		1970	12.00
THE GREAT HITS OF 1964 AND SOME GOLDEN OLDIES			
❑ Vee Jay LP-1112 [M]		1965	30.00
—Not known to exist in stereo			
GREAT INSTRUMENTAL R&B HITS			
❑ Imperial LP-9271 [M]		1964	25.00
❑ Imperial LP-12271 [R]		1964	20.00
GREAT JAZZ			
❑ Rondo-lette A-31 [M]		195?	25.00
GREAT JAZZ BRASS			
❑ RCA Camden CAL-383 [M]		1958	25.00
GREAT JAZZ PIANISTS			
❑ RCA Camden CAL-328 [M]		1958	25.00
GREAT JAZZ PIANISTS OF OUR TIME			
❑ RCA Camden CAL-882 [M]		1965	15.00
❑ RCA Camden CAS-882 [R]		1965	10.00
GREAT JAZZ REEDS			
❑ RCA Camden CAL-339 [M]		1958	25.00
THE GREAT JAZZ SINGERS			
❑ Halo 50269 [M]		1957	15.00
GREAT MOTION PICTURE THEMES			
❑ United Artists UAL-3122 [M]		1960	15.00
❑ United Artists UAS-6122 [S]		1960	20.00
GREAT MOTION PICTURE THEMES (MORE ORIGINAL SOUND TRACKS AND HIT MUSIC)			
❑ United Artists UAL-3158 [M]		1961	15.00
❑ United Artists UAS-6158 [S]		1961	20.00
THE GREAT SONGS OF CHRISTMAS			
❑ Columbia Special Products XTV 69406/7 [M]		1961	15.00
—Sold only at Goodyear tire dealers			
❑ Columbia Special Products XTV 69406/7 [M]		1962	12.00
—Reissue with no reference to Goodyear on the cover			
THE GREAT SONGS OF CHRISTMAS, ALBUM TWO			
❑ Columbia Special Products XTV 86100/1 [M]		1962	15.00
—Sold only at Goodyear tire dealers			

Number	Title (A Side/B Side)	Yr	NM
THE GREAT SONGS OF CHRISTMAS, ALBUM THREE			
❑ Columbia Special Products CSP 117 [M]		1963	15.00
—Sold only at Goodyear tire dealers. The number listed is on the jacket; on the record, the number is "XTV 86656" on Side 1 and "XTV 86657" on Side 2			
THE GREAT SONGS OF CHRISTMAS, ALBUM FOUR			
❑ Columbia Special Products CSP 155M [M]		1964	15.00
—Sold only at Goodyear tire dealers			
❑ Columbia Special Products CSP 155S [S]		1964	18.00
—Sold only at Goodyear tire dealers			
THE GREAT SONGS OF CHRISTMAS, ALBUM FIVE			
❑ Columbia Special Products CSP 238M [M]		1965	12.00
—Sold only at Goodyear tire dealers			
❑ Columbia Special Products CSP 238S [S]		1965	15.00
—Sold only at Goodyear tire dealers			
THE GREAT SONGS OF CHRISTMAS, ALBUM SIX			
❑ Columbia Special Products CSM 388 [M]		1966	12.00
—Sold only at Goodyear tire dealers			
❑ Columbia Special Products CSS 388 [S]		1966	15.00
—Sold only at Goodyear tire dealers			
THE GREAT SONGS OF CHRISTMAS, ALBUM SEVEN			
❑ Columbia Special Products CSS 547		1967	12.00
—Sold only at Goodyear tire dealers			
GREAT SONGS OF CHRISTMAS, ALBUM EIGHT			
❑ Columbia Special Products CSS 888		1968	12.00
—Sold only at Goodyear tire dealers			
GREAT SONGS OF CHRISTMAS, ALBUM NINE			
❑ Columbia Special Products CSS 1033		1969	12.00
—Sold only at Goodyear tire dealers; version 1 has a 10 1/2-inch flap on right inner gatefold (part of record is exposed)			
❑ Columbia Special Products CSS 1033		1969	12.00
—Sold only at Goodyear tire dealers; version 2 has a 12 1/4-inch flap on right inner gatefold (record is completely covered)			
THE GREAT SOUL HITS			
❑ Brunswick BL 54129 [M]		1968	25.00
❑ Brunswick BL 754129 [S]		1968	15.00
THE GREAT SWING BANDS			
❑ Jazztone J-1245 [M]		1957	30.00
GREAT SWING BANDS OF THE FORTIES			
❑ Audio Lab AL-1530 [M]		1959	80.00
THE GREAT TENOR JAZZMEN			
❑ Allegro 1634 [M]		195?	40.00
GREAT TRUMPET ARTISTS			
❑ RCA Victor LPT-26 [10]		1951	50.00
❑ RCA Victor LPT-35 [10]		1952	50.00
THE GREATEST 15 HITS ON ACE RECORDS			
❑ Ace LP-1012 [M]		1960	70.00
GREATEST COUNTRY AND WESTERN HITS NO. 3			
❑ Columbia CL 1816 [M]		1962	20.00
❑ Columbia CS 8616 [S]		1962	25.00
GREATEST COUNTRY AND WESTERN HITS NO. 4			
❑ Columbia CL 2081 [M]		1963	20.00
❑ Columbia CS 8881 [S]		1963	25.00
THE GREATEST GOLDEN GOODIES			
❑ Laurie LLP-2014 [M]		1962	30.00
❑ Laurie SLP-2014 [R]		196?	15.00
GREATEST GOSPEL SONGS OF OUR TIMES			
❑ Vee Jay LP-5043 [M]		1963	30.00
GREATEST GOSPEL SONGS, VOL. 1			
❑ Specialty SPS-2144		1970	20.00
GREATEST GOSPEL SONGS, VOL. 2			
❑ Specialty SPS-2145		1970	20.00
GREATEST HITS			
❑ Harmony HL 7255 [M]		1960	15.00
THE GREATEST HITS FROM ENGLAND			
❑ Parrot PA 61010 [M]		1967	25.00
❑ Parrot PAS 71010 [R]		1967	20.00
THE GREATEST HITS FROM ENGLAND, VOL. 2			
❑ Parrot PA 61017 [M]		1968	25.00
❑ Parrot PAS 71017 [R]		1968	20.00
THE GREATEST NAMES IN JAZZ			
❑ Verve PR2-3 [(3)]		196?	20.00
—Box set			
THE GREATEST ROCK & ROLL			
❑ Atlantic 8001 [M]		1956	120.00
THE GREATEST SONGS OF WOODY GUTHRIE			
❑ Vanguard VSD-35/36 [(2)]		1972	15.00
THE GREATEST TEENAGE HITS OF ALL TIME!			
❑ Teem LP-5003 [M]		196?	30.00
GREATEST WESTERN HITS			
❑ Columbia CL 1257 [M]		1959	30.00
❑ Columbia CS 8776 [R]		1963	20.00
GREATEST WESTERN HITS NO. 2			
❑ Columbia CL 1408 [M]		1960	30.00
❑ Columbia CS 8777 [R]		1963	20.00
GRETSCH DRUM NIGHT AT BIRDLAND			
❑ Roulette R 52049 [M]		1960	30.00
❑ Roulette SR 52049 [S]		1960	30.00
GRETSCH DRUM NIGHT, VOL. 2			
❑ Roulette R 52067 [M]		1961	30.00
❑ Roulette SR 52067 [S]		1961	30.00
GROOVY GOODIES			
❑ Colpix CP-466 [M]		1964	80.00
❑ Colpix SCP-466 [S]		1964	100.00
GROUP OF GOODIES			
❑ Chess LP 1478 [M]		1963	50.00
❑ Chess LPS 1478 [R]		196?	20.00
GROUP OF GOODIES, VOL. 2			
❑ Chess LP 1491 [M]		1965	50.00
GUARANTEED TO PLEASE			
❑ Teem LP-5002 [M]		196?	30.00
GUIDE TO JAZZ			
❑ RCA Victor LPM-1393 [M]		1956	30.00
GUITAR BOOGIE			
❑ Pickwick ACL-7041		197?	10.00
—Reissue of RCA Victor LSP-4624(e)			
❑ RCA Victor AYL1-3768(e)		1980	8.00
—Another reissue of RCA Victor LSP-4624(e)			
❑ RCA Victor LSP-4624(e)		1971	15.00
—Includes tracks by Eric Clapton, Eric Clapton and Jimmy Page, The Allstars Featuring Jeff Beck, The Allstars Featuring Jimmy Page; orange label original			
GUITAR PLAYERS			
❑ Mainstream MRL-410		197?	12.00
HANDFUL OF COOL JAZZ			
❑ Bethlehem BCP-90 [M]		1959	30.00
HAPPY HOLIDAYS			
❑ Columbia Special Products CSP 242 [M]		1965	15.00
—Sold only at True Value Hardware stores			
HAPPY HOLIDAYS, VOL. II			
❑ Columbia Special Products CSM 348 [M]		1966	15.00
—Sold only at True Value Hardware stores			
❑ Columbia Special Products CSS 348 [S]		1966	12.00
—Sold only at True Value Hardware stores			
HAPPY HOLIDAYS, VOL. III			
❑ RCA Victor PRS-255		1967	15.00
—Sold only at True Value Hardware stores			
HAPPY HOLIDAYS, VOL. IV			
❑ RCA Victor PRS-267		1968	15.00
—Sold only at True Value Hardware stores			
HAPPY HOLIDAYS, VOL. 5			
❑ Capitol Creative Products SL-6627		1969	12.00
—Sold only at True Value Hardware stores			
HAPPY HOLIDAYS, ALBUM 6			
❑ Capitol Creative Products SL-6669		1970	12.00
—Sold only at True Value Hardware stores			
HAPPY HOLIDAYS, ALBUM SEVEN			
❑ Capitol Creative Products SL-6730		1971	12.00
—Sold only at True Value Hardware stores			
HAPPY HOLIDAYS, ALBUM 8			
❑ Columbia Special Products C 11086		1972	10.00
—Sold only at True Value Hardware stores			
HAPPY HOLIDAYS, ALBUM NINE			
❑ Columbia Special Products P 11793		1973	10.00
—Sold only at True Value Hardware stores			
HAPPY HOLIDAYS, ALBUM 10			
❑ Columbia Special Products P 12344		1974	10.00
—Sold only at True Value Hardware stores			
HAPPY HOLLY DAYS			
❑ Capitol Creative Products SL-6654		1969	12.00
❑ Capitol Creative Products SL-6761		1971	10.00
HAPPY JAZZ			
❑ Jazztone J-1215 [M]		1956	30.00
HARD GOODS			
❑ Warner Bros. PRO 583 [(2)]		1974	25.00
THE HARD SWING			
❑ Pacific Jazz JWC-508 [M]		1957	50.00
❑ World Pacific JWC-508 [M]		1958	40.00
HARLEM JAZZ 1930			
❑ Brunswick BL 58024 [10]		1951	50.00
HAVE A HAPPY HOLIDAY			
❑ Columbia Special Products CSS 1432		1970	10.00
HAVE A JEWISH CHRISTMAS...?			
❑ Tower T-5081 [M]		1967	15.00
—Comedy sketches narrated by Lennie Weinrib and acted by Christine Nelson, Benny Rubin, Reginald X. Carlisle and Naomi Lewis			
HAVE YOURSELF A MERRY LITTLE CHRISTMAS			
❑ Reprise 50001 [M]		1963	25.00
—Red and green cover with ornaments at top; titled on back cover "Top Hollywood Stars Want You to..."			
❑ Reprise R 50001 [M]		1963	25.00
—Christmas tree cover; titled "Frank Sinatra and His Friends Want You to..."			
❑ Reprise R 50001 [M]		1963	25.00
—Wreath cover; titled on back cover "Top Hollywood Stars Want You to..."			
❑ Reprise R9-50001 [S]		1963	30.00
—Christmas tree cover; titled "Frank Sinatra and His Friends Want You to..."; stereo version of above			
HAVING A BALL			
❑ End LP-302 [M]		1958	500.00
—Original cover with groups pictured on a record			
HEAVY HEADS			
❑ Chess LP 1522 [M]		1967	25.00
❑ Chess LPS 1522 [P]		1967	25.00
HEAVY HEADS, VOYAGE 2			
❑ Chess LP 1528 [M]		1969	20.00
HEAVY HITS!			
❑ Columbia CS 9840		1969	15.00
HEAVY METAL (SUPERSTARS OF THE 70S, VOL. 2)			
❑ Warner Special Products SP-2001		1974	20.00
HEAVY SOUNDS			
❑ Columbia CS 9952		1970	15.00
HENRY MANCINI SELECTS GREAT SONGS OF CHRISTMAS			
❑ RCA Special Products DPL1-0148		1975	10.00
—Sold only at Goodyear tire dealers			
HERALD THE BEAT			
❑ Herald HLP-0110 [M]		195?	150.00
—Yellow label			
❑ Herald HLP-0110 [M]		1957	300.00
—Black label			
HERE ARE THE HITS!			
❑ Fire FLP-100 [M]		1959	400.00
—Reissued as "Memory Lane, Hits by the Original Groups" with the same label and number			
HERE COME THE GIRLS			
❑ Verve MGV-2036 [M]		1956	40.00
❑ Verve V-2036 [M]		1961	20.00
HERE COME THE SWINGING BANDS			
❑ Verve MGV-8207 [M]		1957	30.00
❑ Verve V-8207 [M]		1961	20.00
HI-FI JAZZ			
❑ Brunswick BL 58058 [10]		1954	50.00
HI-FI JAZZ SESSION			
❑ Masterseal MSLP 5013 [M]		1957	25.00
A HI-FI SALUTE TO THE GREAT ONES			
❑ MGM E-3325 [M]		1956	30.00
A HI-FI SALUTE TO THE GREAT ONES, VOL. 2			
❑ MGM E-3354 [M]		1956	30.00
HILLBILLY HOUSE PARTY			
❑ Imperial LP-9214 [M]		1963	25.00
❑ Imperial LP-12214 [R]		1963	20.00
HISTORIC JAZZ CONCERT AT MUSIC INN			
❑ Atlantic 1298 [M]		1958	40.00
—Black label			
❑ Atlantic 1298 [M]		1961	25.00
—Multicolor label, white "fan" logo at right			
❑ Atlantic 1298 [M]		1963	20.00
—Multicolor label, black "fan" logo at right			
HISTORY OF BRITISH BLUES, VOL. 1			
❑ Sire SASH-3701 [(2)]		1973	20.00
HISTORY OF BRITISH ROCK			
❑ Sire SASH-3702 [(2)]		1974	20.00
HISTORY OF BRITISH ROCK, VOL. 2			
❑ Sire SASH-3705 [(2)]		1974	20.00
HISTORY OF BRITISH ROCK, VOL. 3			
❑ Sire SASH-3712 [(2)]		1975	20.00
HISTORY OF CLASSIC JAZZ			
❑ Riverside SDP-11 [(5)M]		1956	300.00
—Five-record set in leatherette album with booklet; records were available separately as Riverside 112, 113, 114, 115 and 116.			
HISTORY OF CLASSIC JAZZ, VOL. 1			
❑ Riverside RLP 12-112 [M]		1957	40.00
HISTORY OF CLASSIC JAZZ, VOL. 2			
❑ Riverside RLP 12-113 [M]		1957	40.00
HISTORY OF CLASSIC JAZZ, VOL. 3			
❑ Riverside RLP 12-114 [M]		1957	40.00
HISTORY OF CLASSIC JAZZ, VOL. 4			
❑ Riverside RLP 12-115 [M]		1957	40.00
HISTORY OF CLASSIC JAZZ, VOL. 5			
❑ Riverside RLP 12-116 [M]		1957	40.00
HISTORY OF JAZZ, VOL. 1: NEW ORLEANS ORIGINS			
❑ Capitol T 793 [M]		1956	25.00
HISTORY OF JAZZ, VOL. 1: THE SOLID SOUTH			
❑ Capitol H 239 [10]		1950	50.00

VARIOUS ARTISTS COLLECTIONS

Except when noted otherwise, VG = 25% of NM, and VG+ = 50% of NM. (Example: VG = $2.00, VG+ = $4.00 and NM = $8.00.)

Number Title (A Side/B Side)	Yr	NM
HISTORY OF JAZZ, VOL. 2: THE GOLDEN ERA		
❑ Capitol H 240 [10]	1950	50.00
HISTORY OF JAZZ, VOL. 2: THE TURBULENT '20S		
❑ Capitol T 794 [M]	1956	25.00
HISTORY OF JAZZ, VOL. 3: EVERYBODY SWINGS		
❑ Capitol T 795 [M]	1956	25.00
HISTORY OF JAZZ, VOL. 3: THEN CAME SWING		
❑ Capitol H 241 [10]	1950	50.00
HISTORY OF JAZZ, VOL. 4: ENTER THE COOL		
❑ Capitol H 242 [10]	1950	50.00
❑ Capitol T 796 [M]	1956	25.00
HISTORY OF RHYTHM & BLUES, VOL. 1/ THE ROOTS 1947-52		
❑ Atlantic SD 8161	1968	20.00
HISTORY OF RHYTHM & BLUES, VOL. 2/ THE GOLDEN YEARS 1953-55		
❑ Atlantic 8162 [M]	1968	40.00
❑ Atlantic SD 8162 [S]	1968	20.00
HISTORY OF RHYTHM & BLUES, VOL. 3/ ROCK & ROLL 1956-57		
❑ Atlantic SD 8163	1968	20.00
HISTORY OF RHYTHM & BLUES, VOLU. 4/ THE BIG BEAT 1958-60		
❑ Atlantic SD 8164	1968	20.00
HISTORY OF RHYTHM & BLUES, VOL. 5/ THE BEAT GOES ON, 1961-62		
❑ Atlantic 8193 [M]	1968	40.00
—Mono is promo only; "DJ Copy Monaural" sticker on front cover		
❑ Atlantic SD 8193 [S]	1968	20.00
THE HIT MAKERS AND THEIR RECORD BREAKERS		
❑ King 737 [M]	1961	100.00
HIT SOUNDS OF MERRIE MELODIES		
❑ Warner Bros. PRO 550 [(2)]	1973	25.00
THE HITS ARE ON VERVE		
❑ Verve V-201 [M]	1964	15.00
❑ Verve V6-201 [S]	1964	20.00
HITS FROM THE SOUTH PRESENTED BY NICK CHARLES		
❑ Stax 702 [M]	1962	100.00
—Has the same number as "Walk Right In" by Gus Cannon, but this LP doesn't have any mention of Atlantic distribution		
HITS I FORGOT TO BUY		
❑ Swan SLP-512 [M]	1963	50.00
HITS OF THE HOPS		
❑ Warner Bros. W 1448 [M]	1962	30.00
❑ Warner Bros. WS 1448 [S]	1962	40.00
HITS THAT JUMPED		
❑ Checker LP 2975 [M]	1959	120.00
HITSVILLE		
❑ Coral CRL 57269 [M]	1959	80.00
❑ Coral CRL 757269 [S]	1959	100.00
HITSVILLE U.S.A.		
❑ Imperial LP-9084 [M]	1959	40.00
HITSVILLE U.S.A., VOL. 2		
❑ Imperial LP-9099 [M]	1960	40.00
HOLIDAY IN SAX		
❑ EmArcy MG-26019 [10]	1954	80.00
HOLIDAY IN TRUMPET		
❑ EmArcy MG-26015 [10]	1954	80.00
HOLIDAY MAGIC		
❑ Capitol Creative Products SL-6728	1971	12.00
❑ Capitol Special Markets SL-6728	197?	10.00
—Same as above, but reissue on renamed label		
HOME FOR CHRISTMAS		
❑ Columbia Musical Treasury P3S 5608 [(3)]	1971	15.00
HOME FOR THE HOLIDAYS		
❑ Columbia Special Products P 12014	1973	10.00
—Sold only at Big N discount department store		
HOME OF THE BLUES		
❑ Minit LP-0001 [M]	1961	50.00
HOME OF THE BLUES, VOL. 2		
❑ Minit LP-0004 [M]	1963	50.00
❑ Minit LP-24004 [R]	1964	20.00
❑ Minit LP-40004 [M]	1964	25.00
—Reissue of 0004		
HOMESPUN HUMOR		
❑ King 726 [M]	1961	100.00
HOT CANARIES		
❑ Columbia CL 2534 [10]	1954	30.00
HOT CLARINETS		
❑ Historical 25	1969	10.00
THE HOT ONES		
❑ Columbia Special Products CSP-107 [M]	1963	20.00
—Available only from Johnson Sea Horse boat dealers		

Number Title (A Side/B Side)	Yr	NM
HOT PIANOS		
❑ Historical 29	1969	10.00
HOT PLATTERS		
❑ Warner Bros. PRO 474 [(2)]	1971	25.00
—Originals have green labels		
HOT TRUMPETS		
❑ Historical 28	1969	10.00
HOT VS. COOL: A BATTLE OF JAZZ		
❑ MGM E-211 [10]	1953	50.00
HOUSE RENT PARTY		
❑ Savoy MG-12199 [M]	1961	50.00
HOW HIGH THE MOON		
❑ Clef MGC-Vol. 1 [M]	1955	50.00
—Reissue of 608		
❑ Clef MGC-608 [M]	1955	40.00
—Reissue of Mercury 608		
❑ Mercury MGC-Vol. 1 [10]	1951	60.00
—Reissue of 35001		
❑ Mercury MGC-608 [M]	1953	80.00
—Reissue of Vol. 1		
❑ Mercury MG-35001 [10]	1950	80.00
❑ Verve MGV-Vol. 1 [M]	1957	30.00
—Reissue of 12-inch Clef Vol. 1		
HOW THE GRINCH STOLE CHRISTMAS		
❑ Random House/Scholastic 0-394-05008-8	1975	15.00
—Not the original soundtrack, but placed here to avoid confusion (we hope). B-side is a condensation of Folkways FC-7750 (1956).		
HUM-N-STRUM: THE BEST OF FOLK AND COUNTRY		
❑ Columbia Special Products CSP 309 [M]	1966	15.00
—For General Electric		
HYMNS OF FAITH		
❑ Colpix CP-408 [M]	1959	30.00
I DIDN'T KNOW THEY STILL MADE RECORDS LIKE THIS		
❑ Warner Bros. PRO 608 [(2)]	1975	20.00
I DIG ROCK AND ROLL		
❑ Score SLP-4002 [M]	1957	200.00
—Reissue of "Rock & Roll with Rhythm & Blues," Aladdin 710		
I LIKE JAZZ!		
❑ Columbia JZ 1 [M]	1955	30.00
I'M WILD ABOUT MY LOVIN'		
❑ Historical 32	1969	10.00
IMAGINE THE JOYS OF CHRISTMAS. PRESENTED BY SYLVANIA.		
❑ Capitol Creative Products SL-6700	1971	12.00
—Sold only at Sylvania dealers; label calls this "A Sylvania Christmas"		
IMPERIAL MOVES		
❑ Imperial MM-428 [DJ]	1966	40.00
IMPERIAL SAMPLER		
❑ Imperial DJLP-1 [10]	195?	100.00
—Promo-only item		
IMPULSE ARTISTS ON TOUR		
❑ ABC Impulse! AS-9264	197?	12.00
IMPULSIVELY!		
❑ ABC Impulse! AS-9266 [(2)]	197?	15.00
IN CONCERT		
❑ RCA Victor CPL2-1014 [(2)]	1975	20.00
IN LOVING MEMORY		
❑ Motown M 642 [DJ]	1969	500.00
—With custom silver cover; Loucye Gordy Wakefield Scholarship Fund benefit giveaway		
❑ Motown M 642 [M]	1968	150.00
—With song titles on cover		
❑ Motown M 642 [M]	1968	250.00
—Without song titles on cover		
❑ Motown MS 642 [S]	1968	150.00
—With song titles on cover		
❑ Motown MS 642 [S]	1968	250.00
—Without song titles on cover		
INCENSE AND OLDIES		
❑ Buddah BDS 5014	1969	20.00
INFORMAL SESSION AT SQUIRREL'S BY THE SONS OF BIX		
❑ Paramount LP-104 [(2)10]	1954	80.00
THE INSTRUMENTAL CHRISTMAS FAVORITES		
❑ Capitol STBB-349 [(2)]	1969	15.00
INSTRUMENTAL GOLDEN GOODIES, VOL. 13		
❑ Roulette R 25238 [M]	1964	20.00
INTERCOLLEGIATE MUSIC FESTIVAL, VOL. 1		
❑ ABC Impulse! AS-9145 [S]	1968	12.00
❑ Impulse! A-9145 [M]	1967	20.00
❑ Impulse! AS-9145 [S]	1967	15.00
INTERNATIONAL JAZZ WORKSHOP		
❑ EmArcy MGE-26002 [M]	1964	25.00
❑ EmArcy SRE-66002 [S]	1964	30.00

Number Title (A Side/B Side)	Yr	NM
INTERPLAY FOR TWO TRUMPETS AND TWO TENORS		
❑ Fantasy OJC-292	1988	10.00
❑ Prestige PRLP-7112 [M]	1957	100.00
INTRODUCTION TO JAZZ		
❑ Decca DL 8244 [M]	1956	30.00
INTRODUCTION TO RARE EARTH RECORDS		
❑ Rare Earth RS-505 to 509 [(5)DJ]	1969	200.00
—Promo-only box set with rounded top; contains the first five LPs on the Rare Earth label		
IRREPRESSIBLE IMPULSES		
❑ ABC Impulse! IMP-1972	1972	15.00
ISLES OF JAZZ		
❑ Discovery DL-2010 [10]	1954	50.00
IT'S CHRISTMAS		
❑ Columbia Special Products C 10040	1971	12.00
IT'S CHRISTMASTIME!		
❑ Columbia Special Products CSM 429 [M]	1966	12.00
—Sold only at A&P grocery stores		
IT'S DANCE TIME		
❑ Cameo C-1068 [M]	1964	30.00
ITALIAN JAZZ STARS		
❑ Angel ANG-60001 [10]	1955	50.00
IVY LEAGUE JAZZ		
❑ Decca DL 8282 [M]	1956	30.00
❑ Golden Crest GC-3039 [M]	1958	20.00
JACKPOT OF HITS		
❑ Apollo LP-490 [M]	1959	150.00
JAM SESSION		
❑ Clef MGC-4001/7 [(7)M]	1953	300.00
—Boxed set containing 4001-4007		
❑ EmArcy MG-36002 [M]	1954	50.00
JAM SESSION #1		
❑ Clef MGC-601 [M]	1954	40.00
❑ Clef MGC-651 [M]	1955	40.00
—Reissue of 4001		
❑ Clef MGC-4001 [M]	1953	50.00
❑ Mercury MGC-601 [M]	1953	80.00
❑ Verve MGV-8049 [M]	1956	30.00
—Reissue of Clef 651		
JAM SESSION #2		
❑ Clef MGC-602 [M]	1954	40.00
❑ Clef MGC-652 [M]	1955	40.00
—Reissue of 4002		
❑ Clef MGC-4002 [M]	1953	50.00
❑ Mercury MGC-602 [M]	1953	80.00
❑ Verve MGV-8050 [M]	1956	30.00
—Reissue of Clef 652		
JAM SESSION #3		
❑ Clef MGC-653 [M]	1955	40.00
—Reissue of 4003		
❑ Clef MGC-4003 [M]	1953	50.00
❑ Verve MGV-8051 [M]	1956	30.00
—Reissue of Clef 653		
JAM SESSION #4		
❑ Clef MGC-654 [M]	1955	40.00
—Reissue of 4004		
❑ Clef MGC-4004 [M]	1953	50.00
❑ Verve MGV-8052 [M]	1956	30.00
—Reissue of Clef 654		
JAM SESSION #5		
❑ Clef MGC-655 [M]	1955	40.00
—Reissue of 4005		
❑ Clef MGC-4005 [M]	1953	50.00
❑ Verve MGV-8053 [M]	1956	30.00
—Reissue of Clef 655		
JAM SESSION #6		
❑ Clef MGC-656 [M]	1955	40.00
—Reissue of 4006		
❑ Clef MGC-4006 [M]	1953	50.00
❑ Verve MGV-8054 [M]	1956	30.00
—Reissue of Clef 656		
JAM SESSION #7		
❑ Clef MGC-677 [M]	1955	40.00
❑ Verve MGV-8062 [M]	1957	30.00
—Reissue of Clef 677		
JAM SESSION #8		
❑ Clef MGC-711 [M]	1955	40.00
❑ Verve MGV-8094 [M]	1957	30.00
—Reissue of Clef 711		
JAM SESSION #9		
❑ Verve MGV-8196 [M]	1957	30.00
JAM SESSION AT CARNEGIE HALL		
❑ Columbia CL 557 [M]	1954	30.00
JAM SESSION AT COMMODORE		
❑ Commodore FL-30006 [M]	1951	40.00
JAM SESSION COAST TO COAST		
❑ Columbia CL 547 [M]	1954	30.00

Number | Title (A Side/B Side) | Yr | NM

JAMES BOND — 10TH ANNIVERSARY
❑ United Artists UXS-91 [(2)] 1972 30.00

THE JATP ALL STARS: HOW HIGH THE MOON
❑ Verve VSP-15 [M] 1966 15.00
❑ Verve VSPS-15 [R] 1966 10.00

THE JATP ALL STARS: PERDIDO
❑ Verve VSP-16 [M] 1966 15.00
❑ Verve VSPS-16 [R] 1966 10.00

THE JATP ALL-STARS AT THE OPERA HOUSE
❑ Verve MGVS-6029 [S] 1960 30.00
❑ Verve MGV-8267 [M] 1958 40.00
❑ Verve V-8267 [M] 1961 20.00
❑ Verve V6-8267 [S] 1961 15.00
❑ Verve MGV-8284 [M] 1959 —
—Canceled
❑ Verve V-8489 [M] 1962 25.00
❑ Verve V6-8489 [S] 1962 30.00

THE JATP ALL-STARS: FUNKY BLUES
❑ Verve V-8486 [M] 1962 25.00
❑ Verve V6-8486 [S] 1962 30.00

JAZZ
❑ Halo 50242 [M] 1957 15.00
❑ Mainstream MRL-408 197? 12.00
❑ Royale 1883 [10] 195? 30.00

JAZZ — WEST COAST VOL. III
❑ Jazztone J-1274 [M] 195? 30.00

JAZZ A LA MIDNIGHT
❑ Jazztone J-1282 [M] 1957 30.00

JAZZ A LA MOOD
❑ Jazztone J-1254 [M] 1957 30.00

JAZZ AMERICANA
❑ Tampa TP-11 [M] 1957 100.00
—Colored vinyl
❑ Tampa TP-11 [M] 1958 40.00
—Black vinyl

JAZZ ANTHOLOGY OF WEST COAST JAZZ
❑ Jazztone J-1243 [M] 1957 30.00

JAZZ AT CARNEGIE HALL
❑ Arco AL-4 [10] 1950 80.00
❑ Mercury MG-35002 [10] 1950 80.00
—Reissue of Arco 4

JAZZ AT CARNEGIE HALL, VOL. 2
❑ Arco AL-8 [10] 195? 80.00

JAZZ AT COLUMBIA — COLLECTORS ITEMS
❑ Columbia CB-16 [M] 195? 20.00
—Columbia Record Club "bonus record" in generic sleeve with die-cut circle in middle

JAZZ AT COLUMBIA — DIXIELAND
❑ Columbia CB-8 [M] 195? 20.00
—Columbia Record Club "bonus record" in generic sleeve with die-cut circle in middle

JAZZ AT JAZZ LTD.
❑ Atlantic 1338 [M] 1961 25.00
—Multicolor label, white "fan" logo at right

JAZZ AT PRESERVATION HALL
❑ Atlantic 1408 [M] 1964 12.00
❑ Atlantic SD 1408 [S] 1964 15.00

JAZZ AT PRESERVATION HALL, VOL. 2
❑ Atlantic 1409 [M] 1964 12.00
❑ Atlantic SD 1409 [S] 1964 15.00

JAZZ AT PRESERVATION HALL, VOL. 3
❑ Atlantic 1410 [M] 1964 12.00
❑ Atlantic SD 1410 [S] 1964 15.00

JAZZ AT STORYVILLE
❑ Paradox LP-6003 [10] 1951 50.00
❑ Savoy MG-15001 [10] 1952 80.00
❑ Savoy MG-15014 [10] 1952 80.00
❑ Storyville STLP-319 [10] 1955 80.00

JAZZ AT STORYVILLE, VOL. 2
❑ Savoy MG-15016 [10] 1952 80.00

JAZZ AT STORYVILLE, VOL. 3
❑ Savoy MG-15019 [10] 1953 80.00

JAZZ AT STORYVILLE, VOL. 4
❑ Savoy MG-15020 [10] 1953 80.00

JAZZ AT THE BOSTON ARTS FESTIVAL
❑ Storyville STLP-311 [10] 1954 80.00

JAZZ AT THE HOLLYWOOD BOWL
❑ Verve MGV-8231-2 [(2)M] 1958 50.00
❑ Verve V-8231-2 [(2)M] 1961 25.00

JAZZ AT THE PHILHARMONIC
❑ Stinson SLP-23 [10] 195? 80.00
—Black vinyl
❑ Stinson SLP-23 [10] 195? 80.00
—Opaque red vinyl
❑ Stinson SLP-23 [10] 1950 120.00
—See-through red vinyl; the first pressing of the first volume to be issued
❑ Stinson SLP-23 [M] 195? 20.00

JAZZ AT THE PHILHARMONIC ALL STARS
❑ American Recording Society G-416 [M] 1957 30.00

JAZZ AT THE PHILHARMONIC IN EUROPE
❑ Verve V6-8823 [(2)] 197? 20.00

JAZZ AT THE PHILHARMONIC IN EUROPE, VOL. 1
❑ Verve V-8539 [M] 1963 20.00
❑ Verve V6-8539 [S] 1963 25.00

JAZZ AT THE PHILHARMONIC IN EUROPE, VOL. 2
❑ Verve V-8540 [M] 1963 20.00
❑ Verve V6-8540 [S] 1963 25.00

JAZZ AT THE PHILHARMONIC IN EUROPE, VOL. 3
❑ Verve V-8541 [M] 1963 20.00
❑ Verve V6-8541 [S] 1963 25.00

JAZZ AT THE PHILHARMONIC IN EUROPE, VOL. 4
❑ Verve V-8542 [M] 1963 20.00
❑ Verve V6-8542 [S] 1963 25.00

JAZZ AT THE PHILHARMONIC, NEW VOL. 2
❑ Clef MGC-Vol. 2 [M] 1955 50.00
—Side 1 is the 10-inch Vol. 2; Side 2 is the 10-inch Vol. 3

JAZZ AT THE PHILHARMONIC, NEW VOL. 3
❑ Clef MGC-Vol. 3 [M] 1955 50.00
—Side 1 is the 10-inch Vol. 4; Side 2 is the 10-inch Vol. 5

JAZZ AT THE PHILHARMONIC, NEW VOL. 4
❑ Clef MGC-Vol. 4 [M] 1955 50.00
—Combines the 10-inch Vol. 6 and Vol. 14 on one record

JAZZ AT THE PHILHARMONIC, NEW VOL. 5
❑ Clef MGC-Vol. 5 [M] 1955 50.00
—Combines the 10-inch Vol. 7, 10 and 11 on one record

JAZZ AT THE PHILHARMONIC, NEW VOL. 6
❑ Clef MGC-Vol. 6 [M] 1955 50.00
—Combines the 10-inch Vol. 8 and Vol. 9 on one record

JAZZ AT THE PHILHARMONIC, NEW VOL. 7
❑ Clef MGC-Vol. 7 [M] 1955 50.00
—Combines the 10-inch Vol. 12 and 13 on one record

JAZZ AT THE PHILHARMONIC, VOL. 10
❑ Verve MGV-Vol. 10 [(3)M] 1957 60.00
—Reissue of Clef Vol. 17

JAZZ AT THE PHILHARMONIC, VOL. 11
❑ Verve MGV-Vol. 11 [(3)M] 1957 60.00
—Reissue of Clef Vol. 18

JAZZ AT THE PHILHARMONIC, VOL. 12
❑ Verve MGV-Vol. 12 [(2)M] 195? —
—Advertised, but unreleased?

JAZZ AT THE PHILHARMONIC, VOL. 2
❑ Verve MGV-Vol. 2 [M] 1957 30.00
—Reissue of 12-inch Clef Vol. 2

JAZZ AT THE PHILHARMONIC, VOL. 3
❑ Verve MGV-Vol. 3 [M] 1957 30.00
—Reissue of 12-inch Clef Vol. 3

JAZZ AT THE PHILHARMONIC, VOL. 4
❑ Verve MGV-Vol. 4 [M] 1957 30.00
—Reissue of 12-inch Clef Vol. 4

JAZZ AT THE PHILHARMONIC, VOL. 5
❑ Verve MGV-Vol. 5 [M] 1957 30.00
—Reissue of 12-inch Clef Vol. 5

JAZZ AT THE PHILHARMONIC, VOL. 6
❑ Verve MGV-Vol. 6 [M] 1957 30.00
—Reissue of 12-inch Clef Vol. 6

JAZZ AT THE PHILHARMONIC, VOL. 7
❑ Verve MGV-Vol. 7 [M] 1957 30.00
—Reissue of 12-inch Clef Vol. 7

JAZZ AT THE PHILHARMONIC, VOL. 8
❑ Verve MGV-Vol. 8 [(3)M] 1957 60.00
—Reissue of Clef Vol. 15

JAZZ AT THE PHILHARMONIC, VOL. 9
❑ Verve MGV-Vol. 9 [(3)M] 1957 60.00
—Reissue of Clef Vol. 16

JAZZ AT THE PHILHARMONIC, VOL. 10
❑ Clef MGC-Vol. 10 [10] 1953 60.00
—Reissue of Mercury Vol. 10
❑ Mercury MGC-Vol. 10 [10] 1951 60.00
—Reissue of 35010
❑ Mercury MG-35010 [10] 1950 100.00

JAZZ AT THE PHILHARMONIC, VOL. 11
❑ Clef MGC-Vol. 11 [10] 1953 60.00
—Reissue of Mercury Vol. 11
❑ Mercury MGC-Vol. 11 [10] 1951 60.00
—Reissue of 35011
❑ Mercury MG-35011 [10] 1950 80.00

JAZZ AT THE PHILHARMONIC, VOL. 12
❑ Clef MGC-Vol. 12 [10] 1953 60.00
—Reissue of Mercury Vol. 12
❑ Mercury MGC-Vol. 12 [10] 1951 60.00

JAZZ AT THE PHILHARMONIC, VOL. 13
❑ Clef MGC-Vol. 13 [10] 1953 60.00
—Reissue of Mercury Vol. 13
❑ Mercury MGC-Vol. 13 [10] 1951 60.00

JAZZ AT THE PHILHARMONIC, VOL. 14
❑ Clef MGC-Vol. 14 [10] 1953 60.00
—Reissue of Mercury Vol. 14
❑ Mercury MGC-Vol. 14 [10] 1951 60.00

JAZZ AT THE PHILHARMONIC, VOL. 15
❑ Clef MGC-Vol. 15 [10] 1953 60.00
—Reissue of Mercury Vol. 15
❑ Clef MGC-Vol. 15 [(3)M] 1954 80.00
—Boxed set of new material with program
❑ Mercury MGC-Vol. 15 [10] 1951 60.00

JAZZ AT THE PHILHARMONIC, VOL. 16
❑ Clef MGC-Vol. 16 [(3)M] 1954 80.00
—Boxed set of new material with program

JAZZ AT THE PHILHARMONIC, VOL. 17
❑ Clef MGC-Vol. 17 [(3)M] 1955 80.00
—Boxed set of new material with photo booklet

JAZZ AT THE PHILHARMONIC, VOL. 18
❑ Clef MGC-Vol. 18 [(3)M] 1955 80.00
—Boxed set of new material with booklet

JAZZ AT THE PHILHARMONIC, VOL. 2
❑ Arco AL-1 [10] 1950 80.00
❑ Clef MGC-Vol. 2 [10] 1953 60.00
—Reissue of Mercury Vol. 2
❑ Mercury MGC-Vol. 2 [10] 1951 60.00
—Reissue of 35003
❑ Mercury MG-35003 [10] 1950 80.00
—Reissue of Arco 1

JAZZ AT THE PHILHARMONIC, VOL. 3
❑ Arco AL-2 [10] 1950 80.00
❑ Clef MGC-Vol. 3 [10] 1953 60.00
—Reissue of Mercury Vol. 3
❑ Mercury MGC-Vol. 3 [10] 1951 60.00
—Reissue of 35004
❑ Mercury MG-35004 [10] 1950 80.00
—Reissue of Arco 2

JAZZ AT THE PHILHARMONIC, VOL. 4
❑ Clef MGC-Vol. 4 [10] 1953 60.00
—Reissue of Mercury Vol. 4
❑ Mercury MGC-Vol. 4 [10] 1951 60.00
—Reissue of 35005
❑ Mercury MG-35005 [10] 1950 80.00

JAZZ AT THE PHILHARMONIC, VOL. 5
❑ Clef MGC-Vol. 5 [10] 1953 60.00
—Reissue of Mercury Vol. 5
❑ Mercury MGC-Vol. 5 [10] 1951 60.00
—Reissue of 35006
❑ Mercury MG-35006 [10] 1950 80.00

JAZZ AT THE PHILHARMONIC, VOL. 6
❑ Clef MGC-Vol. 6 [10] 1953 60.00
—Reissue of Mercury Vol. 6
❑ Mercury MGC-Vol. 6 [10] 1951 60.00
—Reissue of 35007
❑ Mercury MG-35007 [10] 1950 80.00

JAZZ AT THE PHILHARMONIC, VOL. 7
❑ Clef MGC-Vol. 7 [10] 1953 60.00
—Reissue of Mercury Vol. 7
❑ Mercury MGC-Vol. 7 [10] 1951 60.00
—Reissue of 35008
❑ Mercury MG-35008 [10] 1950 80.00

JAZZ AT THE PHILHARMONIC, VOL. 8
❑ Clef MGC-Vol. 8 [10] 1953 60.00
—Reissue of Mercury Vol. 8
❑ Mercury MGC-Vol. 8 [10] 1951 60.00
—Reissue of 35000
❑ Mercury MG-35000 [10] 1950 80.00

JAZZ AT THE PHILHARMONIC, VOL. 9
❑ Clef MGC-Vol. 9 [10] 1953 60.00
—Reissue of Mercury Vol. 9
❑ Mercury MGC-Vol. 9 [10] 1951 60.00
—Reissue of 35009
❑ Mercury MG-35009 [10] 1950 80.00

JAZZ BAND BALL
❑ Good Time Jazz L-12005 [M] 1954 20.00

JAZZ BANDS 1926-30
❑ Historical 16 1967 10.00

JAZZ CITY PRESENTS
❑ Bethlehem BCP-80 [M] 1957 30.00

JAZZ COMMITTEE FOR LATIN AMERICAN AFFAIRS
❑ FM LP-303 [M] 1963 50.00
❑ Vee-Jay LP-303 [S] 196? 20.00
—All-black label with Vee Jay "brackets" logo and "STEREO" on label; most likely a reissue

JAZZ CONCERT
❑ Jazztone J-1219 [M] 1956 30.00
❑ Mercury MGJC-1 [(2)M] 1953 120.00
—Combines 601 and 602 in a box
❑ Norgran MGN-3501-2 [(2)M] 1956 120.00
—Reissue of Mercury MGJC-1

JAZZ CONCERT WEST COAST
❑ Savoy MG-12012 [M] 1955 80.00
❑ Savoy MG-12196 [M] 1961 50.00

Except when noted otherwise, VG = 25% of NM, and VG+ = 50% of NM. (Example: VG = $2.00, VG+ = $4.00 and NM = $8.00.)

Number	Title (A Side/B Side)	Yr	NM
	JAZZ CONFIDENTIAL		
❑ Crown CLP-5056 [M]		1959	20.00
	JAZZ CORNUCOPIA		
❑ Coral CRL 57149 [M]		1958	30.00
	JAZZ CRITICS' CHOICE: GREAT JAZZ CRITICS CHOOSE HISTORIC PERFORMANCES		
❑ Columbia CL 2126 [M]		1964	12.00
	JAZZ DANCE		
❑ Jaguar JP-801 [10]		1954	50.00
	JAZZ DUPLEX		
❑ Pax LP-6006 [10]		1954	30.00
	JAZZ FESTIVAL		
❑ Imperial LP-9233 [M]		1963	20.00
❑ Imperial LP-12233 [S]		1963	25.00
❑ Kapp KS-1 [M]		1956	20.00
	JAZZ FESTIVAL IN HI-FI: NEAR IN AND FAR OUT		
❑ Warner Bros. W 1281 [M]		1959	25.00
	JAZZ FESTIVAL IN STEREO: NEAR IN AND FAR OUT		
❑ Warner Bros. WS 1281 [S]		1959	30.00
	JAZZ FESTIVAL, VOL. 2		
❑ Imperial LP-9238 [M]		1963	20.00
❑ Imperial LP-12238 [S]		1963	25.00
	JAZZ FOR A SUNDAY AFTERNOON		
❑ Solid State SS-18027		1968	15.00
	JAZZ FOR A SUNDAY AFTERNOON, VOL. 2		
❑ Solid State SS-18028		1968	15.00
	JAZZ FOR A SUNDAY AFTERNOON, VOL. 3		
❑ Solid State SS-18037		1968	15.00
	JAZZ FOR A SUNDAY AFTERNOON, VOL. 4		
❑ Solid State SS-18052		1969	15.00
	JAZZ FOR ART'S SAKE		
❑ Dotted Eighth 101 [M]		195?	40.00
	JAZZ FOR HI-FI LOVERS		
❑ Dawn DLP-1124 [M]		1958	80.00
	JAZZ FOR LOVERS		
❑ Riverside RLP 12-244 [M]		1957	40.00
	JAZZ FOR PEOPLE WHO HATE JAZZ		
❑ RCA Victor LJM-1008 [M]		1954	50.00
	JAZZ FOR SURF-NIKS		
❑ Bethlehem BCP-6073 [M]		1961	30.00
	JAZZ FROM DOWN UNDER		
❑ Jaguar JP-803 [10]		1954	50.00
	JAZZ FROM NEW YORK, 1928-32		
❑ Historical 33		1969	10.00
	JAZZ FROM SWEDEN		
❑ Discovery DL-2002 [10]		1953	50.00
	JAZZ GIANTS		
❑ Biograph 3002		196?	12.00
	THE JAZZ GIANTS		
❑ Norgran MGN-1056 [M]		1956	80.00
	THE JAZZ GIANTS '56		
❑ Verve MGV-8146 [M]		1957	30.00
❑ Verve V-8146 [M]		1961	20.00
	JAZZ GIANTS '58		
❑ Verve MGV-8248 [M]		1958	50.00
❑ Verve V-8248 [M]		1961	25.00
	JAZZ GIANTS, VOL. 1		
❑ EmArcy MG-36048 [M]		1955	40.00
	JAZZ GIANTS, VOL. 2: THE PIANO PLAYERS		
❑ EmArcy MG-36049 [M]		1955	40.00
	JAZZ GIANTS, VOL. 3: REEDS, PART 1		
❑ EmArcy MG-36050 [M]		1955	40.00
	JAZZ GIANTS, VOL. 3: REEDS, PART 2		
❑ EmArcy MG-36051 [M]		1955	40.00
	JAZZ GIANTS, VOL. 4: FOLK BLUES		
❑ EmArcy MG-36052 [M]		1955	40.00
	JAZZ GIANTS, VOL. 5: BRASS		
❑ EmArcy MG-36053 [M]		1955	40.00
	JAZZ GIANTS, VOL. 6: MODERN SWEDES		
❑ EmArcy MG-36054 [M]		1955	40.00
	JAZZ GIANTS, VOL. 7: DIXIELAND		
❑ EmArcy MG-36055 [M]		1955	40.00
	JAZZ GIANTS, VOL. 8: DRUM ROLE		
❑ EmArcy MG-36071 [M]		1956	40.00
	JAZZ GOES TO BROADWAY		
❑ Kapp KL-1007 [M]		1956	20.00
	JAZZ GREATS		
❑ Tops L-1508 [M]		1958	20.00
	JAZZ GREATS!		
❑ Allegro 737 [M]		1958	30.00

Number	Title (A Side/B Side)	Yr	NM
	JAZZ HALL OF FAME, VOL. 2		
❑ Design DLP-113 [M]		196?	20.00
	A JAZZ HOLIDAY		
❑ MCA MCA2-4018 [(2)]		1973	15.00
—Black label with rainbow			
	THE JAZZ HOUR		
❑ Savoy MG-12126 [M]		1957	50.00
	JAZZ IN HOLLYWOOD		
❑ Liberty LJH-6001 [M]		1955	30.00
	JAZZ IN TRANSITION		
❑ Transition TRLP-30 [M]		1956	200.00
—With booklet (deduct 1/4 if missing)			
	JAZZ INTERPLAY		
❑ Prestige PRLP-7341 [(2)M]		1964	40.00
❑ Prestige PRLP-7341 [(2)R]		1964	25.00
	JAZZ IS BUSTING OUT ALL OVER		
❑ Savoy MG-12123 [M]		1957	50.00
	JAZZ JAMBOREE		
❑ Halo 50229 [M]		1957	20.00
	JAZZ LAB		
❑ Starlite ST-7003 [M]		1955	50.00
	THE JAZZ LIFE		
❑ Candid CD-8019 [M]		1960	40.00
❑ Candid CS-9019 [S]		1960	30.00
	JAZZ LTD.		
❑ Regal LP-11 [10]		1951	50.00
	THE JAZZ MAKERS		
❑ Columbia CL 1036 [M]		1957	20.00
	JAZZ MONTAGE		
❑ Liberty LRP-3292 [M]		1963	15.00
❑ Liberty LST-7292 [S]		1963	20.00
	JAZZ MUSIC FOR BIRDS		
❑ Bethlehem BCP-6039 [M]		1959	30.00
	JAZZ MUSIC FOR PEOPLE WHO DON'T CARE ABOUT MONEY		
❑ Bethlehem BCP-88 [M]		1958	30.00
	JAZZ ODYSSEY: THE SOUND OF CHICAGO		
❑ Columbia C3L 32 [(3)M]		1964	40.00
	JAZZ ODYSSEY: THE SOUND OF HARLEM		
❑ Columbia C3L 33 [(3)M]		1964	40.00
	JAZZ ODYSSEY: THE SOUND OF NEW ORLEANS		
❑ Columbia C3L 30 [(3)M]		1964	40.00
	JAZZ OF THE FORTIES, VOL. 1		
❑ Folkways FJ-2841		197?	12.00
	JAZZ OF THE ROARING 20'S		
❑ Riverside RLP 12-801 [M]		195?	50.00
	JAZZ OF THE ROARING TWENTIES: DANCE MUSIC OF THE CHARLESTON ERA		
❑ Riverside RLP 12-108 [M]		1956	40.00
	JAZZ OF THE SIXTIES		
❑ Vee Jay VJS-2-1008 [(2)]		1974	20.00
	JAZZ OF TWO DECADES		
❑ EmArcy DEM-2 [M]		1956	40.00
	JAZZ OFF THE AIR, VOL. 1		
❑ Esoteric ESJ-2 [10]		1952	80.00
	JAZZ OFF THE AIR, VOL. 2		
❑ Esoteric ESJ-3 [10]		1952	80.00
	JAZZ OMNIBUS		
❑ Columbia CL 1020 [M]		1957	20.00
	JAZZ ON THE AIR		
❑ Brunswick BL 58048 [10]		1953	50.00
	JAZZ ON THE SCREEN		
❑ Fontana MGF-27532 [M]		1965	40.00
❑ Fontana SRF-67532 [S]		1965	40.00
	JAZZ PIANISTS GALORE		
❑ Jazz: West Coast JWC-506 [M]		1956	150.00
	THE JAZZ PIANO		
❑ RCA Victor LPM-3499 [M]		1966	20.00
❑ RCA Victor LSP-3499 [S]		1966	25.00
	A JAZZ PIANO ANTHOLOGY		
❑ Columbia PG 32355 [(2)]		197?	15.00
	JAZZ PIANO GREATS		
❑ Folkways FJ-2852		197?	12.00
	JAZZ PIONEERS 1933-36		
❑ Prestige PRLP-7647		1969	15.00
	JAZZ POLL WINNERS		
❑ Columbia CL 1610 [M]		1960	20.00
	JAZZ POTPOURRI		
❑ Audiophile AP-24 [M]		1953	30.00
	THE JAZZ ROUND		
❑ Verve VSP-24 [M]		1966	15.00
❑ Verve VSPS-24 [R]		1966	10.00

Number	Title (A Side/B Side)	Yr	NM
	A JAZZ SALUTE TO FREEDOM		
❑ Core 100 [(2)M]		196?	25.00
	THE JAZZ SCENE		
❑ American Recording Society G-419 [M]		1957	30.00
❑ Clef MGC-674 [M]		1955	40.00
—Reissue of 4007			
❑ Clef MGC-4007 [M]		1953	50.00
❑ Clef Special Edition (no #) [(2)10]		1953	100.00
—Two 10-inch LPs in box. Buyers had the option of purchasing a collection of photos that had been used in the original 78 rpm album; add another 50 percent if these photos are included			
❑ Verve MGV-8060 [M]		1957	30.00
—Reissue of Clef 674			
❑ Verve V-8060 [M]		1961	20.00
	JAZZ SET		
❑ Columbia Special Products CSP-217M [M]		1965	12.00
❑ Columbia Special Products CSP-217S [S]		1965	10.00
—Special item for Zenith			
	JAZZ SOUL OF "CLEOPATRA"		
❑ New Jazz NJLP-8292 [M]		1962	40.00
—Purple label			
❑ New Jazz NJLP-8292 [M]		1965	20.00
—Blue label, trident logo at right			
	THE JAZZ SOUND		
❑ Columbia Special Products CSP 298 [M]		1966	10.00
	JAZZ SOUTH PACIFIC		
❑ Regent MG-6001 [M]		1956	—
—See J.J. JOHNSON.			
	THE JAZZ STORY		
❑ Coral CJE-100 [(3)M]		195?	100.00
—Box set; narrated by Steve Allen			
	JAZZ SUPER HITS		
❑ Atlantic SD 1528		1969	25.00
	JAZZ SUPER HITS, VOL. 2		
❑ Atlantic SD 1559		1970	20.00
	JAZZ SURPRISE		
❑ Crown CLP-5008 [M]		1957	20.00
	JAZZ SWINGS BROADWAY		
❑ Pacific Jazz PJM-404 [M]		1956	50.00
❑ World Pacific PJM-404 [M]		1958	40.00
	JAZZ TIME U.S.A. — VOL. 1		
❑ Brunswick BL 54000 [M]		1952	30.00
	JAZZ TIME U.S.A. — VOL. 2		
❑ Brunswick BL 54001 [M]		1953	30.00
	JAZZ TIME U.S.A. — VOL. 3		
❑ Brunswick BL 54002 [M]		1954	30.00
	JAZZ VARIATIONS, VOL. 1		
❑ Stinson SLP-20 [10]		195?	60.00
❑ Stinson SLP-20 [M]		196?	25.00
	JAZZ VARIATIONS, VOL. 2		
❑ Stinson SLP-29 [M]		196?	25.00
	JAZZ VIOLINS OF THE 40S		
❑ Folkways FJ-2854		197?	12.00
	JAZZ VOCALS AWARD ALBUM		
❑ Bethlehem BCP-6068 [M]		1963	25.00
	JAZZ WEST COAST, VOL. 1		
❑ Pacific Jazz JWC-500 [M]		1956	50.00
❑ World Pacific JWC-500 [M]		1958	40.00
	JAZZ WEST COAST, VOL. 2		
❑ Pacific Jazz JWC-501 [M]		1956	50.00
❑ World Pacific JWC-501 [M]		1958	40.00
	JAZZ WEST COAST, VOL. 3		
❑ Pacific Jazz JWC-507 [M]		1957	50.00
❑ World Pacific JWC-507 [M]		1958	40.00
	JAZZ WEST COAST, VOL. 4		
❑ World Pacific JWC-510 [M]		1958	40.00
❑ World Pacific ST-1009 [S]		1959	30.00
	JAZZ WEST COAST, VOL. 5		
❑ World Pacific JWC-511 [M]		1958	40.00
	THE JAZZ WORLD		
❑ Columbia Special Products CSS 524 [S]		1967	10.00
	JAZZ, VOL. 1: THE SOUTH		
❑ Folkways FP-53/4 [M]		1951	25.00
❑ Folkways FJ-2801 [M]		197?	12.00
	JAZZ, VOL. 10: BOOGIE WOOGIE, JUMP, KANSAS CITY		
❑ Folkways FP-73/4 [M]		1951	25.00
❑ Folkways FJ-2810 [M]		197?	12.00
	JAZZ, VOL. 11: ADDENDA		
❑ Folkways FP-75/6 [M]		1951	25.00
❑ Folkways FJ-2811 [M]		197?	12.00
	JAZZ, VOL. 2: THE BLUES		
❑ Folkways FP-55/6 [M]		1951	25.00
❑ Folkways FJ-2802 [M]		197?	12.00
	JAZZ, VOL. 3: NEW ORLEANS		
❑ Folkways FP-57/8 [M]		1951	25.00

Number	Title (A Side/B Side)	Yr	NM
❑ Folkways FJ-2803 [M]		197?	12.00
JAZZ, VOL. 4: JAZZ SINGERS			
❑ Folkways FP-59/60 [M]		1951	25.00
❑ Folkways FJ-2804 [M]		197?	12.00
JAZZ, VOL. 5: CHICAGO			
❑ Folkways FP-63/4 [M]		1951	25.00
❑ Folkways FJ-2805 [M]		197?	12.00
JAZZ, VOL. 6: CHICAGO #2			
❑ Folkways FP-65/6 [M]		1951	25.00
❑ Folkways FJ-2806 [M]		197?	12.00
JAZZ, VOL. 7: NEW YORK 1922-1934			
❑ Folkways FP-67/8 [M]		1951	25.00
❑ Folkways FJ-2807 [M]		197?	12.00
JAZZ, VOL. 8: BIG BANDS BEFORE 1938			
❑ Folkways FP-69/70 [M]		1951	25.00
❑ Folkways FJ-2808 [M]		197?	12.00
JAZZ, VOL. 9: PIANO			
❑ Folkways FP-71/2 [M]		1951	25.00
❑ Folkways FJ-2809 [M]		197?	12.00
JAZZMEN — DETROIT			
❑ Savoy MG-12083 [M]		1956	80.00
JAZZTONE SAMPLER			
❑ Jazztone J-SPEC-100 [10]		1955	50.00
—With booklet			
JAZZVILLE, VOL. 1			
❑ Dawn DLP-1101 [M]		1956	80.00
JESUS CHRIST SUPERSTAR			
❑ Decca DXA 7206 [(2)]		1970	30.00
—Box set with booklet			
❑ Decca DXSA 7206 [(2)]		1970	25.00
—Gatefold cover with booklet			
❑ Decca MCA 2-10000 [(2)]		1973	12.00
—Gatefold cover with booklet; reissue; same custom labels as Decca issue			
❑ MCA 10000 [(2)]		197?	12.00
—Gatefold cover with booklet; reissue; generic MCA labels			
JINGLE BELL JAZZ			
❑ Columbia CL 1893 [M]		1962	20.00
❑ Columbia CS 8693 [S]		1962	15.00
❑ Harmony KH 32529		1973	12.00
—Reissue of CS 8693 with one track changed			
JOHN COLTRANE IN THE WINNER'S CIRCLE			
❑ Bethlehem BCP-6066 [M]		1961	25.00
—Reissue of 6024 with new title			
JOHN HAMMOND PRESENTS "FROM SPIRITUALS TO SWING" AT CARNEGIE HALL 1938			
❑ Vanguard VRS-8523 [M]		1959	40.00
JOHN HAMMOND PRESENTS "FROM SPIRITUALS TO SWING" AT CARNEGIE HALL 1939			
❑ Vanguard VRS-8524 [M]		1959	40.00
THE JOY OF CHRISTMAS			
❑ Capitol SP 8693		1968	12.00
❑ Capitol Creative Products SL-6580		1968	12.00
❑ Columbia Special Products P 12042		1973	12.00
—Sold only at Strawbridge & Clothier stores (Philadelphia area)			
❑ RCA Victor PRM-197 [M]		1965	15.00
—Created for the National Tea Company			
❑ RCA Victor PRS-429		1972	12.00
THE JOY OF CHRISTMAS, FEATURING MARTY ROBBINS AND HIS FRIENDS			
❑ Columbia Special Products C 11087		1972	15.00
THE JOY OF CHRISTMAS, VOL. II			
❑ RCA Victor PRM-230 [M]		1966	15.00
—Created for the National Tea Company			
❑ RCA Victor PRM-230-A [M]		1966	15.00
—Sold only at Acme markets (Mid-Atlantic area); same contents as PRM-230			
JOY TO THE WORLD			
❑ Columbia Special Products P 11647		1973	10.00
THE JOYFUL SOUND OF CHRISTMAS			
❑ RCA Record Club CSP-0601 [(2)]		1969	20.00
—Available only through the RCA Record Club			
JOYOUS CHRISTMAS, VOL. 2			
❑ Columbia Special Products CSS 808		1968	12.00
—Produced for the Beneficial Finance System			
JOYOUS CHRISTMAS, VOL. 4			
❑ Columbia Special Products CSS 1485		1970	12.00
—Produced for the Beneficial Finance System			
JOYOUS CHRISTMAS, VOL. 6			
❑ Columbia Special Products C 11083		1972	10.00
—Produced for the Beneficial Finance System			
JOYOUS CHRISTMAS, VOL. V			
❑ Columbia Special Products C 10398		1971	10.00
—Produced for the Beneficial Finance System			
JOYOUS MUSIC FOR CHRISTMAS TIME			
❑ Reader's Digest RD 45-M [(4)M]		1963	20.00
❑ Reader's Digest RD 45-S [(4)S]		1963	20.00
—Available only through Reader's Digest magazine by mail order			

Number	Title (A Side/B Side)	Yr	NM
JOYOUS NOEL			
❑ Reader's Digest RDA-57A [(4)]		1966	20.00
—Available only through Reader's Digest magazine by mail order			
THE JOYOUS SONGS OF CHRISTMAS			
❑ Columbia Special Products C 10400		1971	10.00
—Sold only at Goodyear tire dealers			
JOYS OF CHRISTMAS			
❑ Capitol Creative Products SL-6610		1969	12.00
❑ Capitol Special Markets SL-6610		197?	10.00
—Reissue with revised label name			
JUBILEE MONAURAL SAMPLER: VOCALS AND INSTRUMENTALS			
❑ Jubilee MSJLP-803 [M]		1959	30.00
JUBILEE STEREOSONIC VOCAL SAMPLER, VOL. 2			
❑ Jubilee SSJLP-802 [S]		1959	40.00
JUBILEE SURPRISE PARTY			
❑ Jubilee JGM-1107 [M]		1959	150.00
❑ Jubilee JGS-1107 [S]		1959	200.00
JUST FOUR LAUGHS VOL. I			
❑ Scepter SPS 5104		1972	12.00
—Contains routines by Bill Cosby, Dick Gregory, Redd Foxx and Flip Wilson			
JUST FOUR LAUGHS VOL. II			
❑ Scepter SPS 5105		1972	12.00
—Contains routines by Bill Cosby, Dick Gregory, Redd Foxx and Flip Wilson			
JUST JAZZ			
❑ Imperial LP-9246 [M]		1963	20.00
❑ Imperial LP-12246 [S]		1963	25.00
K-BOX DUSTY DISCS			
❑ Roulette R 25338 [M]		1966	20.00
KANSAS CITY IN THE '30S			
❑ Capitol T 1057 [M]		1958	25.00
KANSAS CITY JAZZ			
❑ Decca DL 8044 [M]		1954	40.00
KANSAS CITY PIANO			
❑ Decca DL 9226 [M]		1967	30.00
❑ Decca DL 79226 [R]		1967	12.00
KATS KARAVAN (OLD FAVORITES WITH JIM LOWE)			
❑ Vee Jay LP-100 [M]		1957	50.00
—Gold label, black print			
KBIG CHOICES			
❑ World Pacific KBIG-1 [S]		1964	25.00
KEYBOARD KINGS			
❑ MGM E-100 [10]		1951	50.00
KEYBOARD KINGS OF JAZZ			
❑ RCA Victor LPT-4 [10]		1951	40.00
KGFJ SOUNDS OF SUCCESS			
❑ Roulette R 25349 [M]		1967	20.00
KINGS OF CLASSIC JAZZ			
❑ Riverside RLP 12-131 [M]		1957	40.00
KINGS OF THE KEYBOARD			
❑ American Recording Society G-406 [M]		1956	30.00
THE KINGS SING THE BLUES			
❑ Teem LP-5005 [M]		196?	30.00
KNOW YOUR JAZZ			
❑ ABC-Paramount ABC-115 [M]		1956	30.00
KPOI'S BATTLE OF THE SURFING BANDS			
❑ Del-Fi DFLP-1235 [M]		1964	60.00
❑ Del-Fi DFST-1235 [S]		1964	100.00
—Honolulu version of the above LP			
KTLA'S BATTLE OF THE SURFING BANDS			
❑ Del-Fi DFLP-1235 [M]		1964	50.00
❑ Del-Fi DFST-1235 [S]		1964	80.00
—Los Angeles version of the above LP			
KYA GOLDEN GATE GREATS			
❑ Chess LP 1458 SF [M]		1961	150.00
—San Francisco version of "Golden Gassers," Chess 1458			
KYA'S BATTLE OF THE SURFING BANDS			
❑ Del-Fi DFLP-1235 [M]		1964	50.00
❑ Del-Fi DFST-1235 [S]		1964	80.00
—San Francisco version of the above LP, with slightly different contents			
KYA'S MEMORIES OF THE COW PALACE			
❑ Autumn LP 101 [M]		1963	70.00
LATE MUSIC, VOL. I			
❑ Columbia CL 541 [M]		1954	25.00
LATE MUSIC, VOL. II			
❑ Columbia CL 542 [M]		1954	25.00
LATE MUSIC, VOL. III			
❑ Columbia CL 543 [M]		1954	25.00
LAURIE GOLDEN GOODIES			
❑ Laurie LLP-2041 [M]		1967	15.00
❑ Laurie SLLP-2041 [P]		1967	25.00

Number	Title (A Side/B Side)	Yr	NM
LEONARD FEATHER'S ENCYCLOPEDIA OF JAZZ OF THE '60S: BLUES BAG			
❑ Vee Jay LP-2506 [M]		1964	20.00
LEONARD FEATHER'S ENCYCLOPEDIA OF JAZZ, VOL. ONE: GIANTS OF THE SAXOPHONE			
❑ Vee Jay LP-2501 [M]		1964	20.00
❑ Vee Jay VJS-2501 [S]		1964	25.00
LESTORIAN MODE			
❑ Savoy MG-12105 [M]			—
—See STAN GETZ.			
LET'S CELEBRATE CHRISTMAS			
❑ Capitol Special Markets SL-6923		1973	12.00
LET'S HAVE A DANCE PARTY			
❑ Ace LP-1019 [M]		1961	70.00
LET'S SING ABOUT FREEDOM			
❑ Vee Jay LP-5044 [M]		1963	30.00
LIBERTY PREMIER SERIES SPECTACULAR			
❑ Liberty L-5504 [M]		1962	20.00
❑ Liberty S-6604 [S]		1962	30.00
LIBERTY PROUDLY PRESENTS STEREO — THE VISUAL SOUND			
❑ Liberty LST-100 [S]		1959	40.00
THE LIFE TREASURY OF CHRISTMAS MUSIC			
❑ Project/Capitol TL 100 [M]		1963	20.00
—Designed as a supplement to the Life Book of Christmas; selections performed by anonymous chorus and orchestra and Boy Choristers from the Church of the Transfiguration (NY)			
LIGHTS OUT SAN FRANCISCO			
❑ Blue Thumb BT 6004		1970	25.00
LIKE 'ER RED HOT			
❑ ABC Duke DLPX-73 [M]		1974	15.00
❑ Duke DLP-73 [M]		196?	30.00
—Green label, "Distributed by ABC-Dunhill"			
❑ Duke DLP-73 [M]		196?	50.00
—Orange label			
❑ Duke DLP-73 [M]		1960	120.00
—Purple and yellow label			
LISTEN TO OUR STORY			
❑ Brunswick BL 59001 [10]		1950	60.00
A LITTLE ROCK AND ROLL FOR EVERYBODY			
❑ Audio Lab AL-1567 [M]		1960	200.00
THE LITTLEST ANGEL/LULLABY OF CHRISTMAS			
❑ Decca DLP 8009 [M]		1949	40.00
LIVE AT BILL GRAHAM'S FILLMORE WEST			
❑ Columbia CS 9893		1969	15.00
LIVE AT THE WHISKEY A-GO-GO			
❑ Vee Jay LP-1100 [M]		1964	30.00
—Not known to exist in stereo			
THE LIVELY SOUND OF UNIVERSITY			
❑ Capitol Custom (no #) [M]		1966	20.00
—"Mustang Sweepstakes Prize Winner" on front cover			
LOADED			
❑ Savoy MG-12074 [M]		1956	50.00
LONDON BROIL			
❑ Angel ANG-60004 [10]		1955	50.00
A LOOK AT YESTERDAY			
❑ Mainstream S-6025 [R]		1965	12.00
❑ Mainstream 56025 [M]		1965	25.00
LOOK WHO'S SURFIN' NOW!			
❑ King 882 [M]		1964	150.00
LOONEY TUNES AND MERRIE MELODIES			
❑ Warner Bros. PRO 423 [(3)]		1970	100.00
—Box set with booklet of liner notes; originals have green labels			
A LOT OF YARN BUT A WELL-KNITTED JAZZ ALBUM			
❑ Bethlehem BCP-91 [M]		1958	30.00
LOVE THOSE GOODIES			
❑ Checker LP 2973 [DJ]		1959	500.00
—White label, multi-color splash vinyl			
❑ Checker LP 2973 [M]		1959	120.00
LULLABY OF BIRDLAND			
❑ RCA Victor LPM-1146 [M]		1955	50.00
LUSTY MOODS			
❑ Moodsville MVLP-37 [M]		1963	40.00
—Green label			
❑ Moodsville MVLP-37 [M]		1965	20.00
—Blue label, trident logo at right			
❑ Moodsville MVST-37 [S]		1963	40.00
—Green label			
❑ Moodsville MVST-37 [S]		1965	20.00
—Blue label, trident logo at right			
❑ New Jazz NJLP-8319 [M]		1963	—
—Canceled			
❑ Status ST-8319 [M]		1965	30.00
MAD "TWISTS" ROCK 'N' ROLL			
❑ Big Top 12-1305 [M]		1962	100.00

Except when noted otherwise, VG = 25% of NM, and VG+ = 50% of NM. (Example: VG = \$2.00, VG+ = \$4.00 and NM = \$8.00.)

Number	Yr	NM
THE MAGIC HORN		
❑ RCA Victor LPM-1332 [M]	1956	40.00
THE MAGIC OF CHRISTMAS		
❑ Capitol SWBB-93810 [(2)]	1971	15.00
—Available only through the Capitol Record Club		
❑ Columbia Musical Treasury P2M 5245	196?	15.00
—No artists mentioned		
❑ Columbia Musical Treasury P3S 5806 [(3)]	1972	20.00
THE MAGIC OF CHRISTMAS WITH CHILDREN		
❑ Capitol Creative Products L 6517 [M]	196?	15.00
—Sold only at Safeway stores (In Association with Jon M. Huntsman Inc., Continental Production Company)		
MAGNAVOX ALBUM OF CHRISTMAS MUSIC		
❑ Columbia Special Products CSQ 11093 [Q]	1972	20.00
—Sold only at Magnavox dealers; yes, this is in quadraphonic!		
MAGNAVOX PRESENTS A REPRISE OF GREAT HITS		
❑ Reprise PRO 578	1973	10.00
MAHALIA (JACKSON) AND FRIENDS AT CHRISTMASTIME		
❑ Columbia Special Products P 11804	1973	12.00
—Side 2 is all rechanneled stereo; Side 1 is true stereo		
MAMBO JAZZ		
❑ Prestige PRLP-135 [10]	1952	150.00
THE MAN WITH A HORN		
❑ Decca DL 5191 [10]	1950	50.00
THE MANY FACES OF THE BLUES		
❑ Savoy MG-12125 [M]	1957	50.00
THE MANY MOODS OF CHRISTMAS		
❑ Columbia Special Products P 12013	1973	12.00
—Sold only at Goodyear tire dealers		
❑ RCA Special Products DPL1-0085	1974	10.00
MAR Y SOL		
❑ Atco SD-2-705 [(2)]	1972	15.00
THE MELLOW MOODS		
❑ RCA Victor LPM-1365 [M]	1956	40.00
MELLOW THE MOOD/JAZZ IN A MELLOW MOOD		
❑ Blue Note BLP-5001 [10]	1951	200.00
MEMORABLE SESSIONS IN JAZZ		
❑ Blue Note BLP-5026 [10]	1953	200.00
MEMORIES ARE MADE OF HITS		
❑ Liberty LRP-3200 [M]	1961	25.00
—Reissued as "The Original Hits, Volume 4"		
MEMORY LANE, HITS BY THE ORIGINAL GROUPS		
❑ Fire FLP-100 [M]	1959	200.00
—Reissue of "Here Are the Hits!" with the same label and number		
MEMPHIS COUNTRY		
❑ Sun 120	1970	15.00
MEMPHIS GOLD		
❑ Stax 710 [M]	1966	25.00
❑ Stax S710 [S]	1966	30.00
MEMPHIS GOLD VOL. 2		
❑ Stax 726 [M]	1967	20.00
❑ Stax S726 [S]	1967	25.00
MEMPHIS MILLIONS		
❑ Stax STS 3023	1973	15.00
MERRY CHRISTMAS		
❑ Columbia Musical Treasury 3P 6306 [(3)]	1975	15.00
❑ Coral CRL 56080 [10]	1952	80.00
❑ RCA Victor PRS-168	1964	15.00
MERRY CHRISTMAS BABY (CHRISTMAS MUSIC FOR YOUNG LOVERS)		
❑ Hollywood HLP 501 [M]	1956	120.00
MERRY CHRISTMAS FROM CORAL RECORDS		
❑ Coral CRL 57355 [M]	1960	20.00
MERRY CHRISTMAS FROM MOTOWN		
❑ Motown MS-681	1968	30.00
MERRY CHRISTMAS FROM SESAME STREET		
❑ CRA CTW 25516	1975	12.00
MERRY CHRISTMAS FROM...		
❑ King 680 [M]	1959	200.00
MERRY CHRISTMAS MUSIC/CHRISTMAS FAVORITES		
❑ Plymouth P12-59 [M]	1952	20.00
—Artists not mentioned on jacket or label		
MERRY CHRISTMAS TO YOU		
❑ Capitol T 9030 [M]	1955	50.00
MERRY CHRISTMAS WITH NAT KING COLE/FRED WARING AND THE PENNSYLVANIANS		
❑ Capitol Special Markets SL-6883	1973	10.00
A MERRY MERRY CHRISTMAS		
❑ Columbia Special Products CSP 161	1964	15.00
—Number on record is "XTV 86094" on Side 1 and "XTV 86095" on Side 2		
METRONOME ALL STARS 1956		
❑ Clef MGC-743 [M]	1956	40.00
❑ Verve MGV-8030 [M]	1957	40.00
❑ Verve V-8030 [M]	1961	20.00
METRONOME ALL-STARS		
❑ Harmony HL 7044 [M]	1957	25.00
❑ RCA Camden CAL-426 [M]	1958	25.00
THE METRONOME ALL-STARS		
❑ Columbia CL 2528 [10]	1954	30.00
MGM RECORDS PARADE OF STARS		
❑ MGM NP 90569 [M]	1965	20.00
—Capitol Record Club sampler of 12 MGM artists and soundtracks		
MICKEY MOST PRESENTS BRITISH GO-GO		
❑ MGM E 4306 [M]	1965	30.00
❑ MGM SE 4306 [R]	1965	30.00
MICKEY MOST PRESENTS ENGLISH IN-GROUPS		
❑ Metro M-577 [M]	1966	20.00
❑ Metro MS-577 [R]	1966	20.00
MIDDLE OF THE ROAD		
❑ Warner Bros. PRO 525 [(2)]	1972	30.00
—Originals have green labels		
MIDNIGHT JAZZ AT CARNEGIE HALL		
❑ Verve MGV-8189-2 [(2)M]	1957	50.00
❑ Verve V-8189-2 [(2)M]	1961	25.00
A MILLION OR MORE		
❑ ABC-Paramount ABC-216 [M]	1959	80.00
MILLION SELLER DANCE HITS		
❑ Parkway P-7028 [M]	1963	30.00
THE MILLION-AIRS		
❑ Coral CRL 57310 [M]	1959	25.00
MISS AMERICA PRESENTS A COLLECTOR'S ALBUM		
❑ Columbia Special Products XTV 68873/4	1961	15.00
—With photo of Nancy Anne Fleming, Miss America 1961, on the cover; specially pressed for Philco		
THE MODERN IDIOM		
❑ Capitol H 325 [10]	1952	60.00
MODERN JAZZ		
❑ London LL 1185 [M]	1955	20.00
❑ Tops L-1521 [M]	1958	20.00
MODERN JAZZ CONCERT		
❑ Adventures in Sound WL-127 [M]	1958	40.00
MODERN JAZZ FESTIVAL		
❑ Harmony HL 7196 [M]	1958	20.00
MODERN JAZZ GALLERY		
❑ Kapp KXL-5001 [M]	195?	20.00
MODERN JAZZ GREATS		
❑ Crown CLP-5212 [M]	196?	15.00
MODERN JAZZ GREATS, VOL. 2		
❑ Crown CLP-5220 [M]	196?	—
—See THE CONTINENTAL OCTETTE.		
MODERN JAZZ HALL OF FAME		
❑ Design DLP-29 [M]	196?	12.00
❑ Design DLPS-29 [R]	196?	8.00
MODERN JAZZ PIANO		
❑ RCA Camden CAL-384 [M]	1958	25.00
MODERN JAZZ SPECTACULAR		
❑ Jazztone J-1231 [M]	1956	30.00
MODERN JAZZ TRUMPETS		
❑ Prestige PRLP-113 [10]	1951	200.00
MODERN MOODS		
❑ Moodsville MVLP-2 [M]	1961	40.00
—Green label		
❑ Moodsville MVLP-2 [M]	1965	20.00
—Blue label, trident logo at right		
MONARCH ALL STAR JAZZ, VOL. 1		
❑ Monarch LP-201 [10]	1952	50.00
MONARCH ALL STAR JAZZ, VOL. 2		
❑ Monarch LP-202 [10]	1952	50.00
MONARCH ALL STAR JAZZ, VOL. 3		
❑ Monarch LP-203 [10]	1952	50.00
MONARCH ALL STAR JAZZ, VOL. 4		
❑ Monarch LP-204 [10]	1952	50.00
MONARCH ALL STAR JAZZ, VOL. 5		
❑ Monarch LP-205 [10]	1952	50.00
MONDAY NIGHT AT BIRDLAND		
❑ Roulette R 52015 [M]	1958	30.00
❑ Roulette SR 52015 [S]	1959	30.00
MONTAGE		
❑ Savoy MG-12029 [M]	1955	80.00
MONTGOMERY WARD PRESENTS A CHRISTMAS TO REMEMBER		
❑ Capitol Creative Products SL-6573	1968	12.00
—Sold only at Montgomery Ward stores		
MONTGOMERY WARD PRESENTS A CHRISTMAS TO REMEMBER VOL. 2		
❑ Capitol Creative Products SL-6610	1969	12.00
—Sold only at Montgomery Ward stores		
MONTGOMERY WARD PRESENTS A CHRISTMAS TO REMEMBER VOL. 3		
❑ Capitol Creative Products SL-6681	1970	10.00
—Sold only at Montgomery Ward stores		
MONTGOMERY WARD PRESENTS CHRISTMAS FAVORITES		
❑ Montgomery Ward W-101	1965	15.00
—No artists mentioned on label or jacket		
MONUMENTAL COUNTRY HITS		
❑ Monument SLP-18095	1968	20.00
MONUMENTAL POP HITS		
❑ Monument SLP-18096	1968	20.00
MOOD IN BLUE		
❑ Urania UJLP-1209 [M]	1955	30.00
MOOD TO BE WOOED		
❑ Cadet LP-784 [M]	1967	20.00
❑ Cadet LPS-784 [S]	1967	15.00
MORE DRUMS ON FIRE		
❑ World Pacific ST-1022 [S]	1960	30.00
❑ World Pacific WP-1261 [M]	1960	40.00
MORE FOR YOUR MONEY		
❑ Bell 6009	1968	20.00
MORE GOLD HITS, VOL. 2		
❑ Warwick W 2044 [M]	1961	80.00
MORE GOLDEN GREATS		
❑ Liberty LRP-3548 [M]	1967	20.00
❑ Liberty LST-7548 [P]	1967	15.00
MORE GREAT HITS OF 1964 AND OTHER GOLDEN GOODIES		
❑ Vee Jay LP-1136 [M]	1965	30.00
—Not known to exist in stereo		
MORE LIVE ECHOES OF THE SWINGING BANDS		
❑ RCA Victor LPM-1983 [M]	1959	40.00
❑ RCA Victor LSP-1983 [S]	1959	50.00
MORE SOLID GOLD PROGRAMMING		
❑ Screen Gems/Columbia CPL-716/7 [(2)DJ]	1975	30.00
—Promo-only compilation of oldies sent to radio to spur airplay on songs owned by this publishing house; contains three Beatles recordings		
THE MOST		
❑ Forum Circle FC-9079 [M]	1963	12.00
❑ Forum Circle FCS-9079 [S]	1963	12.00
THE MOST OF THE TWIST		
❑ Roulette R 25176 [M]	1962	25.00
—Originals have a white label with colored spokes		
THE MOST, VOL. 1		
❑ Roulette R 52050 [M]	1960	20.00
❑ Roulette SR 52050 [S]	1960	25.00
THE MOST, VOL. 2		
❑ Roulette R 52053 [M]	1960	20.00
❑ Roulette SR 52053 [S]	1960	25.00
THE MOST, VOL. 3		
❑ Roulette R 52057 [M]	1961	20.00
❑ Roulette SR 52057 [S]	1961	25.00
THE MOST, VOL. 4		
❑ Roulette R 52062 [M]	1961	20.00
❑ Roulette SR 52062 [S]	1961	25.00
THE MOST, VOL. 5		
❑ Roulette R 52075 [M]	1961	20.00
❑ Roulette SR 52075 [S]	1961	25.00
MOTOR CITY SCENE		
❑ Bethlehem BCP-6056 [M]	1961	50.00
THE MOTOR-TOWN REVIEW, VOL. 1		
❑ Motown MT 609 [M]	1963	40.00
THE MOTOR-TOWN REVIEW, VOL. 2		
❑ Motown MT 615 [M]	1964	30.00
THE MOTORTOWN REVIEW IN PARIS		
❑ Tamla T 264 [M]	1965	25.00
❑ Tamla TS 264 [S]	1965	30.00
THE MOTORTOWN REVUE LIVE!		
❑ Motown MS-688	1969	25.00
MOTOWN AT THE HOLLYWOOD PALACE		
❑ Motown MS 703	1970	15.00
❑ Motown MS-703	1970	15.00
MOTOWN CHARTBUSTERS, VOL. 1		
❑ Motown MS-707	1970	15.00
MOTOWN CHARTBUSTERS, VOL. 2		
❑ Motown MS-715	1970	15.00
A MOTOWN CHRISTMAS		
❑ Motown M-795V2 [(2)]	1973	20.00

Number	Title (A Side/B Side)	Yr	NM

MOTOWN SPECIAL
❑ Motown M 603 [M] 1962 80.00
THE MOTOWN STORY: THE FIRST DECADE
❑ Motown MS-726 [(5)] 1971 30.00
MOTOWN WINNER'S CIRCLE: #1 HITS, VOL. 1
❑ Gordy GS-935 1969 25.00
MOTOWN WINNER'S CIRCLE: #1 HITS, VOL. 2
❑ Gordy GS-936 1969 25.00
MOTOWN WINNER'S CIRCLE: #1 HITS, VOL. 3
❑ Gordy GS-943 1969 25.00
MOTOWN WINNER'S CIRCLE: #1 HITS, VOL. 4
❑ Gordy GS-946 1969 25.00
MOTOWN WINNER'S CIRCLE: #1 HITS, VOL. 5
❑ Gordy GS-950 1970 25.00
MOUNTAIN FROLIC
❑ Brunswick BL 59000 [10] 1950 60.00
MURRAY THE "K'S" SING ALONG WITH THE ORIGINAL GOLDEN GASSERS
❑ Roulette R 25159 [M] 1961 30.00
MURRAY THE K — LIVE FROM THE BROOKLYN FOX
❑ KFM 1001 [M] 1963 40.00
MURRAY THE K PRESENTS GOLDEN GASSERS FOR A DANCE PARTY
❑ Roulette R 25192 [M] 1962 25.00
MURRAY THE K PRESENTS GOLDEN GASSERS FOR HAND HOLDERS
❑ Roulette R 25191 [M] 1962 25.00
MURRAY THE K'S BLASTS FROM THE PAST
❑ Chess LP 1461 [M] 1961 40.00
MURRAY THE K'S GASSERS FOR SUBMARINE RACE WATCHERS
❑ Chess LP 1470 [M] 1962 40.00
MURRAY THE K'S GOLDEN GASSERS
❑ Chess LP 1458 NYC [M] 1961 150.00
—New York version of "Golden Gassers," Chess 1458
MURRAY THE K'S NINETEEN-SIXTY TWO BOSS GOLDEN GASSERS
❑ Scepter SP-510 [M] 1963 20.00
❑ Scepter SPS-510 [P] 1963 25.00
MUSIC BOX
❑ A&M SP-19006 196? 12.00
—Created for BankAmericard
MUSIC FOR THE BOY FRIEND...HE REALLY DIGS JAZZ
❑ Decca DL 8314 [M] 1956 30.00
MUSIC FROM THE DANCING YEARS
❑ RCA Victor PR-112 [M] 1961 15.00
—Created for Dole Pineapple
MUSIC FROM THE SOUTH, VOL. 1: COUNTRY BRASS BANDS
❑ Folkways FA-2650 [M] 195? 20.00
THE MUSIC OF NEW ORLEANS, VOL. 1
❑ Folkways FA-2461 [M] 1959 20.00
THE MUSIC OF NEW ORLEANS, VOL. 2
❑ Folkways FA-2462 [M] 1959 20.00
THE MUSIC OF NEW ORLEANS, VOL. 3: DANCE HALLS
❑ Folkways FA-2463 [M] 1959 20.00
THE MUSIC OF NEW ORLEANS, VOL. 4: THE BIRTH OF JAZZ
❑ Folkways FA-2464 [M] 1959 20.00
THE MUSIC OF NEW ORLEANS, VOL. 5: NEW ORLEANS JAZZ
❑ Folkways FA-2465 [M] 1959 20.00
THE MUSIC PEOPLE
❑ Columbia C3X 31280 [(3)] 1972 25.00
MUSIC TO READ JAMES BOND BY
❑ United Artists UAL-3415 [M] 1965 20.00
❑ United Artists UAS-6415 [S] 1965 25.00
MUSIC TO READ JAMES BOND BY, VOL. 2
❑ United Artists UAL-3541 [M] 1966 20.00
❑ United Artists UAS-6541 [S] 1966 25.00
MUSIC TO TRIM YOUR TREE BY
❑ RCA Victor PRM 225 [M] 1966 12.00
❑ RCA Victor PRS 225 [S] 1966 15.00
A MUSICAL HISTORY OF JAZZ
❑ Grand Award GA 33-322 [M] 1955 20.00
MY FAIR LADY
❑ New Jazz NJLP-8315 [M] 1963 —
—Canceled
❑ Status ST-8315 [M] 1965 30.00
MY SON THE SURF NUT
❑ Capitol ST 1939 [S] 1963 60.00
❑ Capitol T 1939 [M] 1963 50.00

THE NAMES OF DIXIELAND
❑ Baronet B-108 [M] 195? 20.00
NASCAR GOES COUNTRY
❑ MCA 474 1975 30.00
NASHVILLE BANDSTAND
❑ King 813 [M] 1962 100.00
NASHVILLE BANDSTAND, VOL. 2
❑ King 847 [M] 1963 80.00
NATIVE NEW ORLEANS JAZZ
❑ Dot DLP-3009 [M] 1956 30.00
NEW BLUE HORNS
❑ Riverside RLP 12-294 [M] 1958 30.00
NEW CHAMBER JAZZ
❑ Epic LN 1124 [10] 1955 30.00
NEW FACES AT NEWPORT
❑ Metrojazz E-1005 [M] 1958 50.00
❑ Metrojazz SE-1005 [S] 1958 40.00
NEW ORLEANS BOUNCE: URBAN BLUES, VOL. 2
❑ Imperial LP-94004 1968 20.00
NEW ORLEANS DIXIELAND
❑ Southland SLP-216 [M] 1955 25.00
NEW ORLEANS ENCORE
❑ Riverside RLP-2503 [10] 1954 80.00
NEW ORLEANS EXPRESS
❑ EmArcy MG-36022 [M] 1955 50.00
NEW ORLEANS HORNS
❑ Riverside RLP-1005 [10] 1953 80.00
NEW ORLEANS JAZZ
❑ Decca DL 5483 [10] 1953 50.00
❑ Decca DL 8283 [M] 1956 30.00
NEW ORLEANS JAZZ BABIES
❑ Southland SLP-214 [M] 1955 25.00
NEW ORLEANS JAZZ KINGS
❑ Southland SLP-217 [M] 1955 25.00
NEW ORLEANS JAZZ STARS
❑ Southland SLP-211 [M] 1955 25.00
NEW ORLEANS LEGENDS
❑ Riverside RLP 12-119 [M] 1957 40.00
NEW ORLEANS REVIVAL
❑ Riverside RLP-1047 [10] 1954 80.00
NEW ORLEANS STYLE
❑ "X" LVA-3029 [10] 1954 80.00
NEW ORLEANS TO LOS ANGELES
❑ Southland SLP-215 [M] 1955 25.00
NEW ORLEANS, OUR HOME TOWN
❑ Imperial LP-9260 [M] 1964 25.00
❑ Imperial LP-12260 [R] 1964 20.00
NEW ORLEANS: THE LIVING LEGENDS
❑ Riverside RLP-356/7 [(2)M] 196? 50.00
—Two records in gatefold jacket
NEW ORLEANS: THE LIVING LEGENDS, VOL. 1
❑ Riverside RLP-356 [M] 196? 20.00
❑ Riverside RS-9356 [R] 196? 12.00
NEW ORLEANS: THE LIVING LEGENDS, VOL. 2
❑ Riverside RLP-357 [M] 196? 20.00
❑ Riverside RS-9357 [R] 196? 12.00
NEW SOUNDS FROM SWEDEN, VOL. 1: THE DARING YOUNG SWEDES
❑ Prestige PRLP-119 [10] 1951 400.00
THE NEW SPIRIT OF CAPITOL
❑ Capitol SNP-6 1970 12.00
NEW VOICES
❑ Dawn DLP-1125 [M] 1956 80.00
THE NEW WAVE IN JAZZ
❑ ABC Impulse! AS-90 [S] 1968 12.00
❑ Impulse! A-90 [M] 1966 15.00
❑ Impulse! AS-90 [S] 1966 20.00
NEW YORK JAZZ OF THE TWENTIES
❑ Riverside RLP-1048 [10] 1954 80.00
NEWPORT JAZZ FESTIVAL
❑ RCA Victor LPM-3369 [M] 1965 15.00
❑ RCA Victor LSP-3369 [S] 1965 20.00
NEWPORT JAZZ FESTIVAL ALL STARS
❑ Atlantic SD 1331 [S] 1961 30.00
—Multicolor label, white "fan" logo at right
NEWPORT JAZZ FESTIVAL ALL-STARS
❑ Atlantic 1331 [M] 1961 25.00
—Multicolor label, white "fan" logo at right
A NIGHT AT THE BOULEVARD
❑ Felsted FL-7503 [M] 1960 40.00
1966 COUNTRY & WESTERN AWARD WINNERS
❑ Decca DL 4837 [M] 1967 20.00
❑ Decca DL 74837 [S] 1967 20.00

THE 1969 WARNER/REPRISE RECORD SHOW
❑ Warner Bros. PRO 336 [(2)] 1969 30.00
—Originals have "W7" logos on labels
❑ Warner Bros. PRO 336 [(2)] 197? 15.00
—With "WB" logos on labels
THE 1969 WARNER/REPRISE SONGBOOK
❑ Warner Bros. PRO 331 [(2)] 1969 30.00
—The first of the famous Warner/Reprise "Loss Leaders" mail-order series; originals have "W7" logos on labels
❑ Warner Bros. PRO 331 [(2)] 197? 15.00
—With "WB" logos on labels
THE NITTY GRITTY
❑ Vee Jay LP-1084 [M] 1964 30.00
—Not known to exist in stereo
NO 'COUNT
❑ Savoy MG-12078 [M] 1956 60.00
NO ENERGY CRISIS
❑ ABC Impulse! AS-9267 [(2)] 1974 20.00
NO SOUR GRAPES, JUST PURE JAZZ
❑ Bethlehem BCP-92 [M] 1958 30.00
NON DAIRY CREAMER
❑ Warner Bros. PRO 443 1971 25.00
—Originals have green labels
NORMAN GRANZ JAZZ CONCERT
❑ Norgran MGN-2501 [M] 1954 80.00
❑ Norgran MGN-2502 [M] 1954 80.00
NOTHING CHEESY ABOUT THIS JAZZ
❑ Bethlehem BCP-85 [M] 1958 30.00
NOVA SCOTIA FOLK SONGS
❑ Elektra EKL-23 [10] 1954 40.00
NUGGETS
❑ Elektra 7E-2006 [(2)] 1972 40.00
O. HENRY'S THE GIFT OF THE MAGI
❑ E.F. MacDonald EFMX-62 1962 20.00
—Special album done by the E.F. MacDonald Company, Dayton, Ohio
OCTOBER '61 POP SAMPLER
❑ RCA Victor SPS-33-141 [DJ] 1961 600.00
—Promo-only collection.
OCTOBER 1960 POPULAR STEREO SAMPLER
❑ RCA Victor SPS-33-96 [DJ] 1960 600.00
—Promo-only collection
OCTOBER CHRISTMAS SAMPLER 59-40-41
❑ RCA Victor SPS-33-54 [DJ] 1959 600.00
—Promo-only collection
OLD 'N GOLDEN
❑ Jamie JLPS-3031 1968 20.00
OLD AND HEAVY GOLD 1955
❑ Economic Consultants 1955 1973 20.00
OLD AND HEAVY GOLD 1956
❑ Economic Consultants 1956 1973 30.00
OLD AND HEAVY GOLD 1957
❑ Economic Consultants 1957 1973 30.00
OLD AND HEAVY GOLD 1958
❑ Economic Consultants 1958 1973 30.00
OLD AND HEAVY GOLD 1959
❑ Economic Consultants 1959 1973 20.00
OLD AND HEAVY GOLD 1960
❑ Economic Consultants 1960 1973 30.00
OLD AND HEAVY GOLD 1961
❑ Economic Consultants 1961 1973 30.00
OLD AND HEAVY GOLD 1962
❑ Economic Consultants 1962 1973 30.00
OLD AND HEAVY GOLD 1963
❑ Economic Consultants 1963 1973 20.00
OLD AND HEAVY GOLD 1964
❑ Economic Consultants 1964 1973 20.00
—Original magazine ads claimed that six Beatles tracks would appear on this LP; they were replaced before release
OLD AND HEAVY GOLD 1965
❑ Economic Consultants 1965 1973 20.00
—Original magazine ads claimed that three Beatles tracks would appear on this LP; they were replaced before release
OLD AND HEAVY GOLD 1966
❑ Economic Consultants 1966 1973 20.00
OLD AND HEAVY GOLD 1967
❑ Economic Consultants 1967 1973 20.00
—Original magazine ads claimed that a Beatles track would appear on this LP; it was replaced with another track before release
OLD AND HEAVY GOLD 1968
❑ Economic Consultants 1968 1973 20.00
—Original magazine ads claimed that a Beatles track would appear on this LP; it was replaced with another track before release

VARIOUS ARTISTS COLLECTIONS

Number | Title (A Side/B Side) | Yr | NM

OLD AND HEAVY GOLD 1969
❑ Economic Consultants 1969 — 1973 — 20.00
—Original magazine ads claimed that a Beatles track would appear on this LP; it was replaced with another track before release

OLD AND HEAVY GOLD 1970
❑ Economic Consultants 1970 — 1973 — 20.00
—Original magazine ads claimed that a Beatles track would appear on this LP; it was replaced with another track before release

OLD AND HEAVY GOLD 1971
❑ Economic Consultants 1971 — 1973 — 20.00
—Original magazine ads claimed that a Paul McCartney track would appear on this LP; it was replaced with another track before release

OLD TIME BANJO PROJECT
❑ Elektra EKL-276 [M] — 1964 — 20.00
❑ Elektra EKS-7276 [S] — 1964 — 25.00

OLDIES BUT GOODIES
❑ Original Sound LPM-5001 [M] — 1959 — 50.00
—Original pressing with no reference to other volumes on the back cover
❑ Original Sound LPM-5001 [M] — 1960s — 12.00
—Later editions with later volumes in the series on the back cover

OLDIES BUT GOODIES, VOL. 2
❑ Original Sound LPM-5003 [M] — 1960 — 40.00
—Original pressing with no reference to later volumes on the back cover
❑ Original Sound LPM-5003 [M] — 1960s — 12.00
—Later editions with later volumes in the series on the back cover

OLDIES BUT GOODIES, VOL. 3
❑ Original Sound LPM-5004 [M] — 1960s — 12.00
—Later editions with later volumes in the series on the back cover
❑ Original Sound LPM-5004 [M] — 1961 — 30.00
—Original pressing with no reference to later volumes on the back cover

OLDIES BUT GOODIES, VOL. 4
❑ Original Sound LPM-5005 [M] — 1960s — 12.00
—Later editions with later volumes in the series on the back cover
❑ Original Sound LPM-5005 [M] — 1962 — 30.00
—Original pressing with no reference to later volumes on the back cover

OLDIES BUT GOODIES, VOL. 5
❑ Original Sound LPM-5007 [M] — 1960s — 12.00
—Later editions with later volumes in the series on the back cover
❑ Original Sound LPM-5007 [M] — 1963 — 20.00
—Original pressing with no reference to later volumes on the back cover

OLDIES BUT GOODIES, VOL. 6
❑ Original Sound LPM-5011 [M] — 1960s — 12.00
—Later editions with later volumes in the series on the back cover
❑ Original Sound LPM-5011 [M] — 1963 — 20.00
—Original pressing with no reference to later volumes on the back cover

OLDIES BUT GOODIES, VOL. 7
❑ Original Sound LPM-5012 [M] — 1960s — 12.00
—Later editions with later volumes in the series on the back cover
❑ Original Sound LPM-5012 [M] — 1964 — 20.00
—Original pressing with no reference to later volumes on the back cover

OLDIES BUT GOODIES, VOL. 8
❑ Original Sound LPM-5014 [M] — 1960s — 10.00
—Later editions with later volumes in the series on the back cover
❑ Original Sound LPM-5014 [M] — 1966 — 15.00
—Original pressing with no reference to later volumes on the back cover

OLDIES BY THE DOZEN
❑ Parkway P-7035 [M] — 1963 — 30.00

OLDIES BY THE DOZEN, VOL. 2
❑ Parkway P-7041 [M] — 1964 — 50.00
—With bonus 45 of "The Twist" by Chubby Checker on one side and "Mashed Potato Time" by Dee Dee Sharp on the other; deduct 40 percent if missing

OLDIES DANCE PARTY, VOL. 1
❑ Oldies 33 OL-8001 [M] — 1963 — 20.00

OLDIES DANCE PARTY, VOL. 2
❑ Oldies 33 OL-8002 [M] — 1963 — 20.00

OLDIES IN HI-FI
❑ Chess LP 1439 [DJ] — 1959 — 600.00
—Multi-color splash vinyl
❑ Chess LP 1439 [M] — 1959 — 300.00
—Black vinyl

OLIO
❑ Prestige PRLP-7084 [M] — 1957 — 250.00
—Yellow label with W. 50th St. address

ON-THE-ROAD JAZZ
❑ Riverside RLP 12-127 [M] — 1957 — 40.00

ONE DOZEN GOLDIES
❑ Carlton LP 12-121 [M] — 1960 — 50.00

ONE WORLD JAZZ
❑ Adventures in Sound WL-162 [M] — 1959 — 50.00
❑ Adventures in Sound WS-314 [S] — 1959 — 40.00

OPUS DE BLUES
❑ Savoy MG-12142 [M] — 1959 — 60.00

OPUS DE BOP
❑ Savoy MG-12114 [M] — —
—See STAN GETZ.

OPUS DE JAZZ
❑ Savoy MG-12036 [M] — 1955 — 80.00

OPUS IN SWING
❑ Savoy MG-12085 [M] — 1956 — 60.00

THE ORCHESTRA "HOUSE OF SOUND"
❑ Brunswick BL 54003 [M] — 1954 — 30.00

THE ORGAN PLAYS MUSIC FOR A MERRY CHRISTMAS
❑ Reader's Digest RDA 42-A [(4)] — 1966 — 20.00
—Available only through Reader's Digest magazine by mail order

ORIGINAL BLUE NOTE JAZZ, VOL. 1
❑ Blue Note B-6504 — 1969 — 20.00

ORIGINAL BLUE NOTE JAZZ, VOL. 2
❑ Blue Note B-6506 — 1970 — 20.00

THE ORIGINAL COUNTRY HITS #1
❑ Liberty LRP-3305 [M] — 1963 — 20.00

THE ORIGINAL COUNTRY HITS #2
❑ Liberty LRP-3345 [M] — 1964 — 20.00

THE ORIGINAL COUNTRY HITS #3
❑ Liberty LRP-3382 [M] — 1964 — 20.00

ORIGINAL GOLDEN BLUES GREATS, VOL. 1
❑ Liberty LST-7572 [R] — 1968 — 12.00
—Reissue of "The Original R&B Hits, Volume 1," Liberty 3381, in rechanneled stereo

ORIGINAL GOLDEN COUNTRY GREATS, VOL. 1
❑ Liberty LST-7569 [R] — 1968 — 12.00
—Reissue of "The Original Country Hits #1," Liberty 3305, in rechanneled stereo

ORIGINAL GOLDEN COUNTRY GREATS, VOL. 2
❑ Liberty LST-7570 [R] — 1968 — 12.00
—Reissue of "The Original Country Hits #2," Liberty 3345, in rechanneled stereo

ORIGINAL GOLDEN COUNTRY GREATS, VOL. 3
❑ Liberty LST-7571 [R] — 1968 — 12.00
—Reissue of "The Original Country Hits #3," Liberty 3382, in rechanneled stereo

ORIGINAL GOLDEN GREATS, VOL. 3
❑ Liberty LST-7573 [R] — 1968 — 12.00
—Reissue of "The Original Hits, Volume 7," Liberty 3274, in rechanneled stereo

ORIGINAL GOLDEN GREATS, VOL. 4
❑ Liberty LST-7574 [R] — 1968 — 12.00
—Only one track, "Surf City" by Jan and Dean, is true stereo

ORIGINAL GOLDEN GREATS, VOL. 5
❑ Liberty LST-7575 [R] — 1968 — 12.00
—Three tracks are in true stereo: "Hurt" (Timi Yuro), "Tower of Strength" (Gene McDaniels) and "The Night Has a Thousand Eyes" (Bobby Vee)

ORIGINAL GOLDEN GREATS, VOL. 6
❑ Liberty LST-7576 [R] — 1968 — 12.00
—Four tracks are in true stereo

ORIGINAL GOLDEN GREATS, VOL. 7
❑ Liberty LST-7577 [R] — 1968 — 12.00
—Three tracks are in true stereo

ORIGINAL GOLDEN GREATS, VOL. 8
❑ Liberty LST-7578 [R] — 1968 — 12.00

ORIGINAL GOLDEN GREATS, VOL. 9
❑ Liberty LST-7579 [R] — 1968 — 12.00

ORIGINAL GOLDEN GREATS, VOL. 10
❑ Liberty LST-7619 — 1969 — 15.00

ORIGINAL GOLDIES FROM THE FABULOUS '50S, VOL. 1
❑ Josie JM-4002 [M] — 1963 — 60.00

ORIGINAL GOLDIES FROM THE FABULOUS '50S, VOL. 2
❑ Josie JM-4003 [M] — 1963 — 60.00

ORIGINAL GOLDIES FROM THE FABULOUS '50S, VOL. 3
❑ Josie JM-4004 [M] — 1963 — 60.00

ORIGINAL HIT RECORDS
❑ Roulette R 25106 [M] — 1960 — 30.00
—Originals have a white label with colored spokes

THE ORIGINAL HITS, PAST & PRESENT
❑ Liberty LRP-3178 [M] — 1960 — 20.00

THE ORIGINAL HITS, VOL. 10
❑ Liberty LRP-3344 [M] — 1964 — 20.00

THE ORIGINAL HITS, VOL. 11
❑ Liberty LRP-3418 [M] — 1965 — 20.00
❑ Liberty LST-7418 [P] — 1965 — 20.00

THE ORIGINAL HITS, VOL. 3: PAST & PRESENT
❑ Liberty LRP-3187 [M] — 1961 — 20.00

THE ORIGINAL HITS, VOL. 4
❑ Liberty LRP-3200 [M] — 1962 — 20.00
—Reissue of "Memories Are Made of Hits"; for "The Original Hits, Volume 5," see "15 Hits: The Original Recordings"

THE ORIGINAL HITS, VOL. 6
❑ Liberty LRP-3260 [M] — 1962 — 20.00

THE ORIGINAL HITS, VOL. 7: ALL-TIME HIT INSTRUMENTALS
❑ Liberty LRP-3274 [M] — 1963 — 20.00

THE ORIGINAL HITS, VOL. 8
❑ Liberty LRP-3288 [M] — 1963 — 20.00

THE ORIGINAL HITS, VOL. 9
❑ Liberty LRP-3325 [M] — 1963 — 20.00

THE ORIGINAL HITS, VOL. TWO: PAST & PRESENT
❑ Liberty LRP-3180 [M] — 1961 — 20.00

THE ORIGINAL HOOTENANNY
❑ Crestview CRV 806 [M] — 1963 — 20.00
❑ Crestview CRS 7806 [S] — 1963 — 25.00

ORIGINAL MEMPHIS ROCK AND ROLL, VOL. 1
❑ Sun 116 — 1970 — 20.00

ORIGINAL MOTION PICTURE HIT THEMES
❑ United Artists UAL-3197 [M] — 1962 — 15.00
❑ United Artists UAS-6197 [S] — 1962 — 20.00

THE ORIGINAL R&B HITS, VOL. 1
❑ Liberty LRP-3381 [M] — 1964 — 20.00

ORIGINAL ROCK OLDIES, VOL. 1
❑ Specialty SPS-2129 — 1970 — 20.00

ORIGINAL ROCK OLDIES, VOL. 2
❑ Specialty SPS-2130 — 1970 — 20.00

THE ORIGINAL SOUND OF THE 20'S
❑ Columbia C3L 35 [(3)] — 1965 — 40.00

ORIGINAL SURFIN' HITS
❑ GNP Crescendo GNP-84 [M] — 1963 — 40.00
—With bonus photos; deduct 25-50 percent if missing
❑ GNP Crescendo GNPS-84 [S] — 1963 — 50.00
—With bonus photos; deduct 25-50 percent if missing

OUR BEST
❑ Clef MGC-639 [M] — 1955 — 50.00
❑ Norgran MGN-1021 [M] — 1955 — 80.00

OUR BEST TO YOU
❑ Everlast ELP-201 [M] — 1960 — 200.00

OUR SIGNIFICANT HITS
❑ Specialty SP-2112 [M] — 1960 — 120.00
—Gold and black label

OUR SINGING HERITAGE, VOL. 1
❑ Elektra EKL-151 [M] — 1958 — 25.00

OUR SINGING HERITAGE, VOL. 2
❑ Elektra EKL-152 [M] — 1958 — 25.00

OUTSTANDING JAZZ COMPOSITIONS OF THE 20TH CENTURY
❑ Columbia C2L 31 [(2)M] — 1964 — 20.00

A PACKAGE OF 16 BIG HITS
❑ Motown MS 614 [S] — 1966 — 30.00
—No "package" on cover; contains alternate stereo versions of "Please Mr. Postman" by the Marvelettes and "Do You Love Me" by the Contours
❑ Motown MT 614 [M] — 1964 — 100.00
—"Package" cover
❑ Motown MT 614 [M] — 1966 — 20.00
—No "package" on cover

PAJAMA PARTY
❑ Forum F-9006 [M] — 196? — 30.00
—Reissue of Roulette 25021
❑ Forum SF-9006 [R] — 196? — 20.00
❑ Gee GLP-703 [M] — 1959 — —
—Canceled; released as Roulette R-25021 instead
❑ Roulette R 25021 [M] — 1958 — 40.00
—Originals have a black label
❑ Roulette R 25021 [M] — 1959 — 25.00
—Second pressings have a white label with colored spokes
❑ Roulette SR 25021 [R] — 196? — 12.00

PANORAMA OF BRITISH JAZZ
❑ Discovery DL-2001 [10] — 1953 — 50.00

PARTY AFTER HOURS
❑ Aladdin LP-703 [10] — 1950 — 4000.
—Black vinyl
❑ Aladdin LP-703 [10] — 1950 — 8000.
—Red vinyl

PEACE ON EARTH
❑ Capitol S?B?-585 [(2)] — 1970 — 15.00

PERCUSSION UNABRIDGED
❑ Kimberly 2022 [M] — 1963 — 20.00
❑ Kimberly 11022 [S] — 1963 — 25.00

Number	Title (A Side/B Side)	Yr	NM
PERFECT FOR DANCING: ALL TEMPOS			
❑ RCA Victor LPM-1072 [M]		1954	30.00
PERFECT FOR DANCING: FOX TROTS			
❑ RCA Victor LPM-1070 [M]		1954	30.00
PERFECT FOR DANCING: JITTERBUG OR LINDY			
❑ RCA Victor LPM-1071 [M]		1954	30.00
PERIOD'S JAZZ DIGEST			
❑ Period SPL-302 [M]		1956	50.00
PERIOD'S JAZZ DIGEST VOL. 2			
❑ Period SPL-304 [M]		1955	50.00
PETAL PUSHERS			
❑ Chess LP 1520 [M]		1967	25.00
❑ Chess LPS 1520 [S]		1967	25.00
THE PHIL SPECTOR SPECTACULAR			
❑ Philles PHLP 100 [DJ]		1972	1500.
—Not issued with cover			
PHIL SPECTOR'S CHRISTMAS ALBUM			
❑ Apple SW 3400 [M]		1972	30.00
—Reissue of A CHRSTMAS GIFT FOR YOU FROM PHILLES RECORDS; third edition of this group of songs; completely different cover with Phil Spector dressed as Santa Claus and wearing a "Back to Mono" button			
❑ Warner/Spector SP 9103 [S]		1974	20.00
—Fourth edition of this group of songs; similar cover to third edition; despite the cover's "Authentic Mono" statement and Phil Spector-as-Santa Claus' "Back to Mono" button, this album is in true stereo!			
PHIL SPECTOR'S GREATEST HITS			
❑ Warner/Spector 2SP 9104 [(2)]		1977	40.00
THE PHILCO ALBUM OF HOLIDAY MUSIC			
❑ Columbia Special Products CSM 431		1966	15.00
—Sold only at Philco dealers			
PIANISTS GALORE			
❑ Pacific Jazz JWC-506 [M]		1957	50.00
❑ World Pacific JWC-506 [M]		1958	40.00
PIANO ARTISTRY			
❑ Audiophile AP-28 [M]		1953	30.00
PIANO INTERPRETATIONS			
❑ Norgran MGN-1036 [M]		1955	80.00
❑ Verve MGV-8125 [M]		1957	30.00
❑ Verve V-8125 [M]		1961	20.00
PIANO JAZZ, VOL. 1			
❑ Brunswick BL 54014 [M]		1955	30.00
PIANO JAZZ, VOL. 2			
❑ Brunswick BL 54015 [M]		1955	30.00
PIANO MODERN			
❑ Verve VSP-13 [M]		1966	15.00
❑ Verve VSPS-13 [R]		1966	10.00
PIANO MUSIC FOR PARTIES			
❑ Columbia CL 603 [M]		1955	25.00
PIANO MUSIC FOR TWO			
❑ Columbia CL 602 [M]		1955	25.00
PIANO ROLL HALL OF FAME			
❑ Sounds 1202		196?	12.00
PIANO ROLL TRANSCRIPTIONS			
❑ Riverside RLP 12-110 [M]		1956	40.00
❑ Riverside RLP 12-126 [M]		1957	40.00
PIANO STYLISTS			
❑ Capitol H 323 [10]		1952	50.00
PIANO VARIATIONS			
❑ King 540 [M]		1956	—
—See ERROLL GARNER.			
PICK HITS OF THE RADIO GOOD GUYS			
❑ Laurie LLP-2021 [M]		1963	30.00
❑ Laurie SLP-2021 [R]		196?	15.00
PICK HITS OF THE RADIO GOOD GUYS, VOL. 2			
❑ Laurie LLP-2026 [M]		1964	25.00
❑ Laurie SLP-2026 [R]		196?	15.00
PICK UP THE BEAT			
❑ Epic LN 3127 [M]		1955	30.00
PIONEERS OF BOOGIE WOOGIE			
❑ Riverside RLP-1009 [10]		1953	80.00
PIONEERS OF BOOGIE WOOGIE, VOL. 2			
❑ Riverside RLP-1034 [10]		1954	80.00
PLAYBOY ALL STARS VOL. 1			
❑ Playboy PB-1957 [(2)M]		1957	40.00
PLAYBOY ALL STARS VOL. 2			
❑ Playboy PB-1958 [(2)M]		1958	40.00
PLAYBOY ALL STARS VOL. 3			
❑ Playboy PB-1959 [(3)M]		1959	60.00
PLAZA HOUSE PRESENTS MUSIC HALL			
❑ Capitol Creative Products SL-6719		1971	12.00
—One side by Merle Haggard; one side by Sonny James			
POLKAS			
❑ Audio Lab AL-1543 [M]		1959	40.00
POP HIT PARTY			
❑ Columbia CL 1237 [M]		195?	20.00
POP ORIGINS			
❑ Chess LP 1544 [M]		1969	25.00
POP PARADE			
❑ MGM E-194 [10]		1953	50.00
POPULAR FAVORITES			
❑ Columbia CL 6057 [10]		1949	40.00
THE POPULAR GOLD ALBUM			
❑ Capitol T 972 [M]		1958	30.00
PORGY AND BESS			
❑ Bethlehem EXLP-1 [(3)M]		1956	70.00
❑ Bethlehem BCP-6040 [M]		1959	30.00
PORTRAITS IN JAZZ			
❑ Reprise R-6084 [M]		1963	12.00
❑ Reprise R9-6084 [S]		1963	15.00
A POT OF FLOWERS			
❑ Mainstream S-6100 [S]		1967	100.00
❑ Mainstream 56100 [M]		1967	80.00
POT OF GOLDEN GOODIES			
❑ Herald HLP-1015 [M]		1962	150.00
A POTPOURRI OF JAZZ			
❑ Verve MGV-2032 [M]		1956	40.00
❑ Verve V-2032 [M]		1961	20.00
PRESTIGE GROOVY GOODIES, VOL. 1			
❑ Prestige PRLP-7298 [M]		1964	30.00
❑ Prestige PRST-7298 [R]		1964	20.00
PRIMITIVE PIANO			
❑ Tone 1 [M]		195?	30.00
PROGRESSIVE PIANO			
❑ RCA Victor LJM-3001 [10]		1952	50.00
THE PROGRESSIVES			
❑ Columbia CG 31574 [(2)]		197?	12.00
—"CG" prefix is a reissue of "KG"			
❑ Columbia KG 31574 [(2)]		1973	20.00
RADAR BLUES			
❑ King KLP-1050 [M]		1969	30.00
RADIO SMASH FLASHBACKS: DRIVE TIME			
❑ Laurie LLP-2028 [M]		1964	25.00
❑ Laurie SLP-2028 [R]		196?	15.00
RADIO SMASH FLASHBACKS: PRIME TIME			
❑ Laurie LLP-2029 [M]		1964	25.00
❑ Laurie SLP-2029 [R]		196?	15.00
RAGTIME PIANO ROLL, VOL. 1			
❑ Riverside RLP-1006 [10]		1953	100.00
RAGTIME PIANO ROLL, VOL. 2			
❑ Riverside RLP-1025 [10]		1954	80.00
RAGTIME PIANO ROLL, VOL. 3			
❑ Riverside RLP-1049 [10]		1954	80.00
RAGTIMERS' IMMORTAL PERFORMANCES			
❑ RCA Victor LPT-1000 [M]		1954	30.00
RAILROAD SONGS			
❑ King 869 [M]		1963	70.00
RARE BANDS OF THE 20S, VOL. 1			
❑ Historical ASC-3		1966	12.00
RARE BANDS OF THE 20S, VOL. 2			
❑ Historical ASC-6		1966	12.00
RARE BANDS OF THE 20S, VOL. 3			
❑ Historical ASC-7		1966	12.00
RARE VERTICAL JAZZ			
❑ Historical ASC-8		1966	12.00
THE RCA VICTOR ENCYCLOPEDIA OF RECORDED JAZZ, ALBUM 1			
❑ RCA Victor LEJ-1 [10]		1956	40.00
THE RCA VICTOR ENCYCLOPEDIA OF RECORDED JAZZ, ALBUM 2			
❑ RCA Victor LEJ-2 [10]		1956	40.00
THE RCA VICTOR ENCYCLOPEDIA OF RECORDED JAZZ, ALBUM 3			
❑ RCA Victor LEJ-3 [10]		1956	40.00
THE RCA VICTOR ENCYCLOPEDIA OF RECORDED JAZZ, ALBUM 4			
❑ RCA Victor LEJ-4 [10]		1956	40.00
THE RCA VICTOR ENCYCLOPEDIA OF RECORDED JAZZ, ALBUM 5			
❑ RCA Victor LEJ-5 [10]		1956	40.00
THE RCA VICTOR ENCYCLOPEDIA OF RECORDED JAZZ, ALBUM 6			
❑ RCA Victor LEJ-6 [10]		1956	40.00
THE RCA VICTOR ENCYCLOPEDIA OF RECORDED JAZZ, ALBUM 7			
❑ RCA Victor LEJ-7 [10]		1956	40.00
THE RCA VICTOR ENCYCLOPEDIA OF RECORDED JAZZ, ALBUM 8			
❑ RCA Victor LEJ-8 [10]		1956	40.00
THE RCA VICTOR ENCYCLOPEDIA OF RECORDED JAZZ, ALBUM 9			
❑ RCA Victor LEJ-9 [10]		1956	40.00
THE RCA VICTOR ENCYCLOPEDIA OF RECORDED JAZZ, ALBUM 10			
❑ RCA Victor LEJ-10 [10]		1956	40.00
THE RCA VICTOR ENCYCLOPEDIA OF RECORDED JAZZ, ALBUM 11			
❑ RCA Victor LEJ-11 [10]		1956	40.00
THE RCA VICTOR ENCYCLOPEDIA OF RECORDED JAZZ, ALBUM 12			
❑ RCA Victor LEJ-12 [10]		1956	40.00
RCA VICTOR PRESENTS MUSIC FOR THE TWELVE DAYS OF CHRISTMAS			
❑ RCA Victor PRS-188 [S]		1965	12.00
THE REAL AMBASSADORS			
❑ Columbia OS 2250 [S]		1962	25.00
❑ Columbia CL 5850 [M]		1962	20.00
THE REAL BLUES			
❑ Excello LPS-8011 [R]		1969	20.00
RECORD HOP			
❑ Decca DL 8067 [M]		1955	30.00
RECORDED IN NEW ORLEANS, VOL. 1			
❑ Good Time Jazz L-12019 [M]		1955	20.00
RECORDED IN NEW ORLEANS, VOL. 2			
❑ Good Time Jazz L-12020 [M]		1955	20.00
RECORDED ON LOCATION AT THE FIVE SPOT CAFE IN NEW YORK CITY...A MEMORIAL CONCERT DEDICATED TO THE MUSIC OF CHARLIE PARKER			
❑ Signal S-1204 [M]		1957	200.00
RED BIRD GOLDIES			
❑ Red Bird LP 20-102 [M]		1965	80.00
RED HOT AND BLUE JAZZ			
❑ Waldorf Music Hall MH 33-141 [10]		195?	200.00
RELAXED SAXOPHONE MOODS			
❑ Prestige PRLP-141 [10]		1953	100.00
REMEMBER HOW GREAT, VOL. 1			
❑ Roulette SR 42027 [R]		1968	12.00
REMEMBER HOW GREAT, VOL. 2			
❑ Roulette SR 42028 [R]		1968	12.00
REMEMBER HOW GREAT, VOL. 3			
❑ Roulette SR 42029 [R]		1968	12.00
REMEMBER HOW GREAT, VOL. 4			
❑ Roulette SR 42031 [R]		1969	12.00
REMEMBER HOW GREAT, VOL. 5			
❑ Roulette SR 42032 [R]		1969	12.00
REMEMBER THE OLDIES			
❑ Argo LP-649 [M]		1963	40.00
❑ Argo LP-649 [M]		1963	400.00
—Multi-color splash vinyl; white label promo			
REPRISE ALL STAR SPECTACULAR!			
❑ Reprise R-6028 [M]		1962	40.00
REQUESTED BY YOU			
❑ Columbia CL 607 [M]		1955	25.00
RHYTHM & BLUES			
❑ RCA Camden CAL-371 [M]		1958	25.00
RHYTHM AND BLUES			
❑ Savoy MG-15008 [10]		1952	80.00
RHYTHM PLUS ONE			
❑ Epic LN 3297 [M]		1956	30.00
THE RHYTHM SECTION			
❑ Epic LN 3271 [M]		1956	30.00
RHYTHM, BLUES AND BOOGIE-WOOGIE			
❑ Decca DL 4011 [M]		1960	30.00
RICHARD NADER/LET THE GOOD TIMES ROLL			
❑ Bell 9002 [(2)]		1973	20.00
RINGSIDE AT CONDON'S			
❑ Savoy MG-15029 [10]		1954	80.00
RINGSIDE AT CONDON'S VOL. 2			
❑ Savoy MG-15030 [10]		1954	80.00
RIVERBOAT JAZZ			
❑ Brunswick BL 58026 [10]		1951	50.00
RIVERSIDE DRIVE			
❑ Riverside RLP 12-267 [M]		1958	30.00
RIVERSIDE MODERN JAZZ SAMPLER			
❑ Riverside S-3 [M]		1956	40.00

Except when noted otherwise, VG = 25% of NM, and VG+ = 50% of NM. (Example: VG = $2.00, VG+ = $4.00 and NM = $8.00.)

Number	Title (A Side/B Side)	Yr	NM
ROBERT W. SARNOFF — 25 YEARS OF RCA LEADERSHIP			
❑ RCA Victor RWS-0001 [DJ]		1973	2000.
—Souvenir record handed out at Sarnoff's retirement party; VG value 1000; VG+ value 1500			
ROCK & ROLL FOREVER			
❑ Atlantic 1239 [M]		1956	150.00
ROCK & ROLL WITH RHYTHM & BLUES			
❑ Aladdin LP-710 [M]		195?	1500.
ROCK 'N' ROLL SOCK HOP			
❑ Score SLP-4018 [M]		1958	200.00
ROCK AND ROLL BANDSTAND			
❑ Roulette R 25093 [M]		1959	30.00
—Originals have a white label with colored spokes			
ROCK AND ROLL DANCE PARTY			
❑ King 536 [M]		1956	300.00
❑ RPM LRP-3001		195?	500.00
ROCK AND ROLL RECORD HOP			
❑ Roulette R 25059 [M]		1959	30.00
—Originals have a white label with colored spokes			
ROCK AND ROLL REVUE, VOL. 2			
❑ King 654 [M]		1959	150.00
ROCK AND ROLL VS. RHYTHM AND BLUES			
❑ Dooto DTL-223 [M]		1957	100.00
ROCK N' ROLL JAMBOREE			
❑ End LP-302 [M]		1959	120.00
—Second cover and title with puppet and a guitar			
ROCK'S GREATEST HITS			
❑ Columbia GP 11 [(2)]		1969	20.00
ROCK-A-BALLADS			
❑ Cadence CLP-3041 [M]		1960	40.00
ROCK-A-HITS			
❑ Cadence CLP-3042 [M]		1960	40.00
ROCK-O-RAMA			
❑ Abkco AB 4222 [(2)]		1972	20.00
ROCK-O-RAMA, VOL. 2			
❑ Abkco AB 4223 [(2)]		1972	20.00
A ROCKIN' CHRISTMAS			
❑ Columbia Special Products P 12445		1974	15.00
ROCKIN' SLUMBER PARTY			
❑ Famous LP-501 [M]		1961	30.00
ROCKIN' TOGETHER			
❑ Atco 33-103 [M]		1958	100.00
RODGERS AND HART GEMS			
❑ Pacific Jazz JWC-504 [M]		1956	50.00
❑ World Pacific JWC-504 [M]		1958	40.00
RONCO PRESENTS A CHRISTMAS GIFT			
❑ Ronco/CSP P 12430		1974	15.00
—Gatefold with pop-up manger scene			
RONCO PRESENTS A CHRISTMAS PRESENT			
❑ Ronco/CSP P 11772		1973	15.00
—Gatefold with pop-up North Pole scene			
ROOST 5TH ANNIVERSARY ALBUM			
❑ Roost RST-1201 [M]		1955	50.00
ROOTS OF BRITISH ROCK			
❑ Sire SASH-3711 [(2)]		1975	20.00
ROULETTE PRESENTS A DEMONSTRATION OF THE NEW DIMENSIONAL SOUND OF DYNAMIC STEREO			
❑ Roulette SR-100 [S]		1958	30.00
RUMBLE			
❑ Jubilee JGM-1114 [M]		1959	150.00
SATURDAY NIGHT AT THE UPTOWN			
❑ Atlantic 8101 [M]		1964	25.00
❑ Atlantic SD 8101 [S]		1964	30.00
SATURDAY NIGHT FUNCTION: RURAL BLUES, VOL. 2			
❑ Imperial LP-94001		1968	20.00
SATURDAY NIGHT MOOD			
❑ Columbia CL 599 [M]		1954	25.00
THE SAX SECTION			
❑ Epic LN 3278 [M]		1956	40.00
SAX STYLISTS			
❑ Capitol H 328 [10]		1952	50.00
SAXES, INC.			
❑ Warner Bros. W 1336 [M]		1959	50.00
❑ Warner Bros. WS 1336 [S]		1959	80.00
SAXOMANIAC			
❑ Apollo LP-477 [M]		1958	100.00
THE SAXOPHONE			
❑ ABC Impulse! AS-9253 [(3)]		197?	20.00
SAXOPHONE REVOLT			
❑ Riverside RLP 12-284 [M]		1958	150.00

Various artists, *Schlagers!*, Warner Bros. PRO 359, 1970, 2 records, green labels, **$30.**

Number	Title (A Side/B Side)	Yr	NM
SCHLAGERS!			
❑ Warner Bros. PRO 359 [(2)]		1970	30.00
—Originals have green labels			
A SCRAPBOOK OF BRITISH JAZZ, 1926-1956			
❑ London LL 1444 [M]		1956	20.00
SEASON'S GREETINGS FROM BARBRA STREISAND...AND FRIENDS			
❑ Columbia Special Products CSS 1075		1969	20.00
—Created exclusively for Maxwell House Coffee			
SEASONS GREETINGS (A CHRISTMAS FESTIVAL OF STARS)			
❑ Columbia CL 1394 [M]		1959	20.00
❑ Columbia CS 8189 [S]		1959	25.00
SECOND SESSION AT SQUIRREL'S			
❑ Paramount LP-108 [10]		1954	60.00
SELECTIONS FROM APRIL 1956 ALBUMS FOR RADIO-TV PROGRAM USE			
❑ Capitol PRO-252/3 [DJ]		1956	40.00
SELECTIONS FROM FEBRUARY 1956 POPULAR ALBUMS FOR RADIO-TV PROGRAM USE			
❑ Capitol PRO-240/1 [DJ]		1956	40.00
SELECTIONS FROM JANUARY 1956 ALBUMS FOR RADIO-TV PROGRAM USE			
❑ Capitol PRO-238/9 [DJ]		1956	40.00
SELECTIONS FROM MARCH 1956 ALBUMS FOR RADIO-TV PROGRAM USE			
❑ Capitol PRO-246/7 [DJ]		1956	40.00
SELECTIONS FROM THE VINTAGE SERIES			
❑ RCA Victor SP-33-322 [DJ]		196?	15.00
—Promo-only sampler from albums issued in the LPV-500 series			
SESSION AT MIDNIGHT			
❑ Capitol T 707 [M]		1956	30.00
SESSION AT RIVERSIDE			
❑ Capitol T 761 [M]		1956	30.00
THE SEVEN AGES OF JAZZ			
❑ Metrojazz 2-E-1009 [(2)M]		1959	60.00

Number	Title (A Side/B Side)	Yr	NM
❑ Metrojazz 2-SE-1009 [(2)S]		1959	50.00
SHADES OF GOSPEL SOUL			
❑ Motown MS-701		1970	15.00
SHADES OF NEW ORLEANS			
❑ Southland SLP-240		1963	15.00
SHOUTIN', SWINGIN' AND MAKIN' LOVE			
❑ Chess CHV-412		1970	15.00
SHUT DOWN			
❑ Capitol DT 1918 [R]		1963	40.00
❑ Capitol T 1918 [M]		1963	40.00
SHUT DOWNS AND HILL CLIMBS			
❑ Liberty LRP-3366 [M]		1964	40.00
❑ Liberty LST-7366 [S]		1964	50.00
THE SINATRA FAMILY WISH YOU A MERRY CHRISTMAS			
❑ Reprise FS-1026		1969	50.00
SING A SONG OF SOUL			
❑ Checker LP 2998 [M]		1966	80.00
❑ Checker LPS 2998 [S]		1966	100.00
THE SINGER-SONGWRITER PROJECT			
❑ Elektra EKL-299 [M]		1965	20.00
—With 11 tracks, though the label and cover claim there are 13			
❑ Elektra EKL-299 [M]		1965	25.00
—With 13 tracks			
❑ Elektra EKS-7299 [S]		1965	20.00
—With 11 tracks, though the label and cover claim there are 13			
❑ Elektra EKS-7299 [S]		1965	30.00
—With 13 tracks			
SINGIN' AND SWINGIN'			
❑ Savoy MG-12217 [M]		196?	20.00
SITTIN' IN			
❑ Verve MGV-8225 [M]		1958	50.00
❑ Verve V-8225 [M]		1961	25.00
16 GOODIES — BLASTS FROM THE PAST			
❑ Blast BLP-6803 [M]		1964	40.00
16 ORIGINAL BIG HITS, VOL. 2			
❑ Tamla TM 256 [M]		1964	20.00

Various artists, *Sounds in Space*, RCA Victor SP-33-13, 1958, stereo, **$20.**

VARIOUS ARTISTS COLLECTIONS

Number	Title (A Side/B Side)	Yr	NM
16 ORIGINAL BIG HITS, VOL. 3			
❑ Motown MT 624 [M]		1965	20.00
16 ORIGINAL BIG HITS, VOL. 4			
❑ Motown M 633 [M]		1965	15.00
❑ Motown MS 633 [S]		1965	20.00
16 ORIGINAL BIG HITS, VOL. 5			
❑ Motown M 651 [M]		1966	15.00
60 YEARS OF MUSIC AMERICA LOVES BEST			
❑ RCA Victor LM-6074 [(2)]		1959	30.00
60 YEARS OF MUSIC AMERICA LOVES BEST, VOL. II			
❑ RCA Victor LM-6088 [(2)]		1960	30.00
60 YEARS OF MUSIC AMERICA LOVES BEST, VOL. III (POPULAR)			
❑ RCA Victor LOP-1509		1961	20.00
$64,000 JAZZ			
❑ Columbia CL 777 [M]		1955	50.00
A SLICE OF LEMON			
❑ Columbia Special Products CSM-389 [M]		1966	25.00
—Manufactured for Dr. Pepper; contains a spoken-word introduction by Dick Clark, plus tracks by Bob Dylan, Simon & Garfunkel, the Dave Clark Five, the Brothers Four, Percy Faith, Dave Brubeck, the New Christy Minstrels, Tony Bennett and Doris Day			
SMALL COMBO HITS			
❑ RCA Victor LPT-3 [10]		1951	40.00
SMART, LUSCIOUS, BEAUTIFUL			
❑ Bethlehem BCP-6034 [M]		1960	30.00
THE SMITHSONIAN COLLECTION OF CLASSIC JAZZ			
❑ Smithsonian/CSP P6 11891 [(6)]		1973	40.00
SMOKE RINGS			
❑ RCA Victor LPT-13 [10]		1951	40.00
SMOOTH & SWINGING JAZZ			
❑ Verve PM-12 [M]		1964	15.00
—Custom edition for Whyte & Mackay's Blended Scotch Whiskey			
SOFT PEDAL			
❑ Columbia CL 2511 [10]		1954	30.00

Number	Title (A Side/B Side)	Yr	NM
SOLID GOLD HITS			
❑ Imperial LP-9230 [M]		1963	25.00
❑ Imperial LP-12230 [R]		1963	20.00
SOLID GOLD PROGRAMMING			
❑ Screen Gems/Columbia CPL-711 [DJ]		1975	20.00
—Promo-only compilation of oldies sent to radio to spur airplay on songs owned by this publishing house			
❑ Screen Gems/Columbia CPL-715 [DJ]		1975	20.00
—Same concept as above album, but completely different contents, and mostly in stereo			
SOLID GOLD SONGS INSTRUMENTALLY			
❑ Screen Gems/Columbia CPL-714 [DJ]		1975	20.00
—Promo-only compilation of oldies sent to radio to spur airplay on songs owned by this publishing house			
SOLID GOLD SOUL			
❑ Atlantic 8116 [M]		1966	15.00
❑ Atlantic SD 8116 [S]		1966	20.00
SOLID STATE DEMONSTRATION RECORD			
❑ Solid State SS 93 [DJ]		1966	15.00
—Sampler from six Solid State LP releases			
SOLO FLIGHT			
❑ Pacific Jazz JWC-505 [M]		1956	50.00
❑ World Pacific JWC-505 [M]		1958	40.00
SOLO SPOTLIGHTS			
❑ King 745 [M]		1961	100.00
SOME LIKE IT COOL			
❑ United Artists SX-71 [S]		1959	40.00
❑ United Artists X-71 [M]		1959	40.00
SOMETHING FESTIVE!			
❑ A&M SP-19003		1968	15.00
—Sold only at B.F. Goodrich tire dealers			
SOMETHING FOR BOTH EARS			
❑ World Pacific HFS-2 [S]		1958	40.00
—Stereo sampler			
SOMETHING NEW, SOMETHING BLUE			
❑ Columbia CL 1388 [M]		1959	20.00

Number	Title (A Side/B Side)	Yr	NM
SONGS BY RODGERS AND HART AND JOHNNY GREEN			
❑ Discovery DL-3014 [10]		1951	50.00
SONGS FOR A SUMMER NIGHT			
❑ Columbia PM 2 [(2)M]		1963	20.00
❑ Columbia PMS 2 [(2)S]		1963	25.00
SONGS FOR CHRISTMAS — THE OLD AND THE NEW			
❑ RCA Victor PR-132-A [M]		1962	15.00
—Sold only at Jewel food stores			
SONGS FOR THE CHRISTMAS SEASON			
❑ Capitol Creative Products SL-6541		1967	12.00
SONGS OF FAITH			
❑ Audio Lab AL-1504 [M]		1959	80.00
SONGS OF FAITH VOL. 2			
❑ Audio Lab AL-1523 [M]		1959	80.00
SONGS OF RIVERS, OCEANS AND SEAS			
❑ King 871 [M]		1963	70.00
SONGS OF THE HILLS			
❑ Audio Lab AL-1515 [M]		1959	80.00
SOUL CHRISTMAS			
❑ Atco SD 33-269		1968	30.00
SOUL EXPLOSION			
❑ Stax STS 2-2007 [(2)]		1969	20.00
SOUL JAZZ GIANTS			
❑ Prestige PRST-7791		1970	15.00
SOUL JAZZ, VOL. 1			
❑ Bluesville BVLP-1009 [M]		1960	50.00
—Blue label, silver print			
❑ Bluesville BVLP-1009 [M]		1965	25.00
—Blue label, trident logo at right			
SOUL JAZZ, VOL. 2			
❑ Bluesville BVLP-1010 [M]		1960	50.00
—Blue label, silver print			
❑ Bluesville BVLP-1010 [M]		1965	25.00
—Blue label, trident logo at right			
SOUL MEETING SATURDAY NIGHT HOOTENANNY STYLE			
❑ Vee Jay LP-1074 [M]		1963	30.00
—Not known to exist in stereo			
THE SOUL OF JAZZ			
❑ Riverside S-5 [M]		1957	40.00
❑ World Wide MGS-20002 [S]		1958	80.00
THE SOUL OF JAZZ PERCUSSION			
❑ Warwick W 5003 [M]		1961	30.00
❑ Warwick W 5003ST [S]		1961	40.00
THE SOUL OF JAZZ PIANO			
❑ Riverside 9S-7 [S]		196?	30.00
SOUL OLDIES VOL. I			
❑ Unart M 20022 [M]		1967	15.00
❑ Unart S 21022 [S]		1967	12.00
SOUL OLDIES VOL. II			
❑ Unart M 20023 [M]		1967	15.00
❑ Unart S 21023 [S]		1967	12.00
SOULED OUT			
❑ Chess LPS 1546 [S]		1969	50.00
SOULFUL OLDIES			
❑ Oldies 33 OL-8005 [M]		1964	25.00
THE SOUND OF BIG BAND JAZZ IN HI-FI			
❑ World Pacific WP-1257 [M]		1960	40.00
THE SOUND OF BIG BAND JAZZ IN STEREO			
❑ World Pacific ST-1015 [S]		1960	30.00
THE SOUND OF CHRISTMAS			
❑ Capitol Creative Products SL-6515 [S]		1966	12.00
THE SOUND OF CHRISTMAS, VOL. 2			
❑ Capitol Creative Products SL-6534		1967	12.00
THE SOUND OF CHRISTMAS, VOL. 3			
❑ Capitol Creative Products SL-6680		1970	12.00
THE SOUND OF GENIUS			
❑ Columbia Masterworks SGM 1 [(2)M]		1963	20.00
❑ Columbia Masterworks SGS 1 [(2)S]		1963	25.00
THE SOUND OF JAZZ			
❑ Columbia CL 1098 [M]		1957	20.00
SOUNDS IN SPACE			
❑ RCA Victor SP-33-13 [S]		1958	20.00
—Narrated by Ken Nordine with songs by various artists			
SOUNDS OF CHRISTMAS			
❑ Columbia Special Products P 12474		1974	12.00
—Sold only through Amway dealers			
THE SOUNDS OF CHRISTMAS			
❑ Capitol STBB-93245 [(2)]		1970	15.00
—Available only through the Capitol Record Club			
❑ MCA Special Markets DL 734735		197?	12.00
SOUNDS OF SUCCESS			
❑ Jamie JLP-3017 [M]		1961	25.00
❑ Jamie JLPS-3017 [S]		1961	30.00

Except when noted otherwise, VG = 25% of NM, and VG+ = 50% of NM. (Example: VG = $2.00, VG+ = $4.00 and NM = $8.00.)

Number	Title (A Side/B Side)	Yr	NM
SOUTH SIDE JAZZ			
❑ Chess CHV-415		1971	12.00
SOUTHERN MEETIN'			
❑ Kimberly 2017 [M]		1963	20.00
❑ Kimberly 11017 [S]		1963	25.00
SOUVENIR/PROGRAMMING RECORD — DEALERS/ DISC JOCKEYS — OCT.-NOV. 1955			
❑ Capitol PRO-232 [DJ]		1955	40.00
THE SPANISH SIDE OF JAZZ			
❑ Roulette SR-42001		1968	20.00
SPECIAL CHRISTMAS LP FOR DISC JOCKEYS			
❑ Capitol PRO-201 [DJ]		1954	50.00
SPIN TIME WITH LIBERTY			
❑ Liberty MM-417 [DJ]		1962	50.00
—Promo-only release			
THE SPIRIT OF CHRISTMAS			
❑ Capitol Creative Products SL-6516		1966	15.00
❑ Columbia Musical Treasury DS 453		1968	12.00
—Columbia Record Club exclusive			
❑ Columbia Special Products CSP 249 [M]		1965	15.00
—Sold only at A&P grocery stores			
❑ Columbia Special Products P 11403		1972	10.00
—Sold only by The Treasury family store and supermarket			
THE SPIRIT OF CHRISTMAS, VOL. II			
❑ Columbia Special Products CSS 889		1969	12.00
—Distributed by TG&Y			
THE SPIRIT OF CHRISTMAS, VOL. III			
❑ Columbia Special Products CSS 1463		1970	12.00
SPIRITUALS			
❑ King 951 [M]		1966	50.00
—Reissue of "Spirituals, Volume 5," King 576			
SPIRITUALS TO SWING: JOHN HAMMOND'S 30TH ANNIVERSARY CONCERT 1967			
❑ Columbia CG 30776 [(2)]		197?	12.00
—"CG" prefix is a reissue of "G"			
❑ Columbia G 30776 [(2)]		1971	15.00
SPIRITUALS, VOL. 5			
❑ King 576 [M]		1957	150.00
STABLE MATES			
❑ Savoy MG-12115 [M]		1957	50.00
STARS FOR A SUMMER NIGHT			
❑ Columbia PM 1 [(2)M]		1961	25.00
❑ Columbia PMS 1 [(2)S]		1961	30.00
THE STARS OF HEE HAW			
❑ Capitol ST-437		1970	20.00
STARS OF JAZZ '61			
❑ Jazzland JLP-1001 [M]		1961	25.00
STARS OF THE APOLLO			
❑ Columbia CG 30788 [(2)]		197?	12.00
—"CG" prefix is a reissue of "G"			
❑ Columbia G 30788 [(2)]		1971	15.00
STARS OF THE GRAND OLE OPRY 1926-1974			
❑ RCA Victor CPL2-0466 [(2)]		1974	20.00
THE STAX/VOLT REVUE — LIVE IN LONDON			
❑ Stax 721 [M]		1967	20.00
❑ Stax S721 [S]		1967	25.00
THE STAX/VOLT REVUE — LIVE IN LONDON, VOL. 2			
❑ Stax 722 [M]		1967	20.00
❑ Stax S722 [S]		1967	25.00
STAX...ONCE YOU'VE BEEN THERE, YOU KNOW YOU'RE HOME			
❑ Stax STS 1 [(2)DJ]		1971	40.00
—Promo only in blank white gatefold cover			
STAY IN SCHOOL — DON'T BE A DROP OUT			
❑ Stax A-11 [DJ]		1967	500.00
STEREOSONIC JUBILEE SAMPLER, VOL. 1			
❑ Jubilee SSJLP-801 [S]		1959	40.00
STERLING BALL 1971			
❑ Motown M 739 [DJ]		1971	250.00
—Loucye Gordy Wakefield Scholarship Fund benefit giveaway			
STILL MORE GOLD HITS, VOL. 3			
❑ Warwick W 2048 [M]		1962	80.00
STRETCHING OUT			
❑ United Artists UAL-4023 [M]		1959	400.00
❑ United Artists UAS-5023 [S]		1959	300.00
STRICTLY BEBOP			
❑ Capitol M-11059		1973	12.00
STRICTLY FROM DIXIE			
❑ MGM E-3262 [M]		1956	30.00
THE STRING BAND PROJECT			
❑ Elektra EKL-292 [M]		1965	20.00
❑ Elektra EKS-7292 [S]		1965	25.00
A STRING OF SWINGIN' PEARLS			
❑ RCA Victor LPM-1373 [M]		1956	30.00

Number	Title (A Side/B Side)	Yr	NM
SUMMER SOUVENIRS			
❑ Bell 6035		1969	20.00
SUMMIT MEETING			
❑ Vee Jay LP-3026 [M]		1961	20.00
❑ Vee Jay SR-3026 [S]		1961	25.00
SUN'S GOLD HITS			
❑ Sun LP-1250 [M]		1961	200.00
SUNDAY MORNING			
❑ Vee Jay LP-5016 [M]		1961	30.00
SUPER GOLDEN HITS			
❑ Jubilee JGS-8019		1968	100.00
—Despite the stereo prefix, this LP is mono			
SUPER GOLDEN HITS, VOL. 2			
❑ Jubilee JGS-8023		1969	100.00
—Reissue of "Clay Cole's Bin of Original Golden Oldies," Jubilee 5026; again, despite the stereo prefix, this LP is mono			
THE SUPER GROUPS			
❑ Atco SD 33-279		1969	20.00
THE SUPER GROUPS FROM HOLLAND			
❑ White Whale WWS-7129		1970	25.00
THE SUPER HITS, VOL. 2			
❑ Atlantic 8188 [M]		1968	40.00
—Mono is white label promo only; cover has "d/j copy monaural" sticker on it			
❑ Atlantic SD 8188 [S]		1968	20.00
THE SUPER HITS, VOL. 3			
❑ Atlantic 8203 [M]		1968	40.00
—Mono is white label promo only			
❑ Atlantic SD 8203 [S]		1968	20.00
THE SUPER HITS, VOL. 4			
❑ Atlantic SD 8224		1969	20.00
THE SUPER HITS, VOL. 5			
❑ Atlantic 8274 [M]		1970	50.00
—Mono is white label promo only			
❑ Atlantic SD 8274 [S]		1970	20.00
—This was the first album to contain "Ohio" by Crosby, Stills, Nash and Young and the only LP to contain the 3:11 version of "Whole Lotta Love" by Led Zeppelin			
SUPER OLDIES/VOL. 1			
❑ Capitol ST 2562 [S]		1966	25.00
❑ Capitol T 2562 [M]		1966	20.00
SUPER OLDIES/VOL. 2			
❑ Capitol ST 2565 [S]		1966	25.00
❑ Capitol T 2565 [M]		1966	20.00
SUPER OLDIES/VOL. 3			
❑ Capitol STBB 2910 [(2)]		1968	20.00
SUPER OLDIES/VOL. 4			
❑ Capitol STBB-149 [(2)]		1969	20.00
SUPER OLDIES/VOL. 5			
❑ Capitol STBB-216 [(2)]		1969	20.00
SUPER ROCK			
❑ Columbia G 30121 [(2)]		1970	15.00
THE SUPER SOUL-DEES			
❑ Capitol ST 2798 [S]		1967	20.00
❑ Capitol T 2798 [M]		1967	20.00
THE SUPER SOUL-DEES, VOL. 2			
❑ Capitol STBB-2911 [(2)]		1968	20.00
THE SUPER SOUL-DEES, VOL. 3			
❑ Capitol STBB-178 [(2)]		1969	20.00
SUPERSTARS OF THE '70S			
❑ Warner Special Products SP-4000 [(4)]		1973	40.00
—Box set with booklet of liner notes			
SURF'S UP AT BANZAI PIPELINE			
❑ Northridge NM-101 [M]		1963	200.00
—Original pressing of LP reissued on Reprise			
❑ Reprise R 6094 [M]		1963	100.00
❑ Reprise RS 6094 [S]		1963	150.00
SURFIN' ON WAVE NINE			
❑ King 855 [M]		1963	80.00
SWAMP BLUES VOL. 1			
❑ Excello LPS-8015 [R]		1970	20.00
SWAMP BLUES VOL. 2			
❑ Excello LPS-8016 [R]		1970	20.00
SWEDES FROM JAZZVILLE			
❑ Epic LN 3309 [M]		1957	50.00
SWEDISH PASTRY			
❑ Discovery DL-2008 [10]		1954	50.00
SWEET 'N GREASY: RHYTHM 'N' BLUES, VOL. 2			
❑ Imperial LP-94005		1968	20.00
SWEET ADELINES MEDALIST QUARTETS OF 1958			
❑ Cadence CLP-3018 [M]		1959	40.00
SWEET ADELINES MEDALISTS OF 1957			
❑ Cadence CLP-3009 [M]		1958	40.00
SWING 1946			
❑ Prestige PRLP-7604		1969	15.00

Number	Title (A Side/B Side)	Yr	NM
SWING AGAIN!			
❑ Capitol DT 1386 [R]		196?	12.00
❑ Capitol T 1386 [M]		1960	20.00
SWING BILLIES			
❑ Audio Lab AL-1546 [M]		1960	120.00
SWING BILLIES VOL. 2			
❑ Audio Lab AL-1566 [M]		1960	120.00
SWING CLASSICS 1935			
❑ Prestige PRLP-7646		1969	15.00
THE SWING ERA, VOL. 1			
❑ "X" LVA-3030 [10]		1955	80.00
SWING GOES DIXIE			
❑ American Recording Society G-420 [M]		1957	30.00
SWING GUITARS			
❑ Norgran MGN-1033 [M]		1955	80.00
❑ Verve MGV-8124 [M]		1957	30.00
❑ Verve V-8124 [M]		1961	20.00
SWING HI, SWING LO			
❑ Blue Note BLP-5027 [10]		1953	200.00
❑ Blue Note B-6507 [M]		1969	15.00
SWING LIGHTLY			
❑ Jazztone J-1265 [M]		1957	30.00
SWING POTPOURRI			
❑ Audiophile AP-23 [M]		1953	30.00
SWING... NOT SPRING!			
❑ Savoy MG-12062 [M]		1956	50.00
A SWINGIN' GIG			
❑ Tampa TP-2 [M]		1957	100.00
—Colored vinyl			
❑ Tampa TP-2 [M]		1958	50.00
—Black vinyl			
SWINGIN' LIKE SIXTY, VOL. 1			
❑ World Pacific ST-1289 [S]		1960	30.00
❑ World Pacific WP-1289 [M]		1960	30.00
SWINGIN' LIKE SIXTY, VOL. 2			
❑ World Pacific ST-1290 [S]		1960	30.00
SWINGIN' LIKE SIXTY, VOL. 3			
❑ World Pacific ST-1291 [S]		1960	30.00
SWINGIN' SOUNDS			
❑ Columbia Special Products XTV 82030 [M]		1962	25.00
—Issued for the W.A. Sheaffer Pen Co.			
SWINGIN': BIG BAND SWING AND JAZZ FROM THE 1930S AND 1940S			
❑ Folkways FJ-2861		1986	12.00
SWINGING BROADWAY			
❑ Kimberly 2024 [M]		1963	20.00
❑ Kimberly 11024 [S]		1963	25.00
SWINGING FOR THE KING			
❑ Mercury MG-20133 [M]		1956	50.00
SWINGING SOUNDTRACK			
❑ Kimberly 2016 [M]		1963	20.00
❑ Kimberly 11016 [S]		1963	25.00
THE SWINGVILLE ALL-STARS			
❑ Swingville SVLP-2010 [M]		1960	40.00
—Purple label			
❑ Swingville SVLP-2010 [M]		1965	20.00
—Blue label, trident logo at right			
SWITCHED ON BLUES			
❑ Soul SS-720		1969	150.00
TAKE THE LIBERTY			
❑ Liberty MM-427 [DJ]		1966	40.00
TAMLA SPECIAL #1			
❑ Tamla TM 224 [M]		1962	150.00
—White label			
❑ Tamla TM 224 [M]		1963	70.00
—Yellow label			
TEEN DELIGHTS			
❑ Vee Jay LP-1021 [M]		1960	30.00
TEEN DELIGHTS, VOL. 2			
❑ Vee Jay LP-1036 [M]		1961	30.00
THE TEEN SOUND			
❑ Columbia Special Products CSS 523		1967	12.00
TEENAGE PARTY			
❑ Gee GLP-702 [M]		1958	200.00
—Red label			
❑ Gee GLP-702 [M]		196?	60.00
—Gray label			
TEENSVILLE			
❑ Liberty L-5503 [M]		1962	40.00
TENNESSEE			
❑ Design DLP-611 [M]		1962	20.00
TENOR CONCLAVE			
❑ Prestige PRLP-7074 [M]		1957	100.00
—Reissued as Prestige 7249; see JOHN COLTRANE.			

Various artists, *20 Original Winners of 1964*, Roulette R-25293, 1965, mono, **$20.**

VARIOUS ARTISTS COLLECTIONS

Number	Title (A Side/B Side)	Yr	NM
TENOR JAZZ			
❑ Mercury MG-20016 [10]		1950	100.00
—Issued in a paper sleeve			
TENOR SAX			
❑ Concord 3012 [M]		195?	40.00
TENOR SAX SOLOS, VOL. 1			
❑ Savoy MG-9008 [10]		1952	150.00
TENOR SAX SOLOS, VOL. 2			
❑ Savoy MG-9013 [10]		1952	150.00
TENOR SAX SOLOS, VOL. 3			
❑ Savoy MG-9021 [10]		1953	150.00
TENOR SAXES			
❑ Norgran MGN-1034 [M]		1955	80.00
❑ Verve MGV-8127 [M]		1957	30.00
❑ Verve V-8127 [M]		1961	20.00
TENORS ANYONE?			
❑ Dawn DLP-1126 [M]		1958	120.00
TERRITORY BANDS 1926-31			
❑ Historical 26		1969	10.00
TERRITORY BANDS 1929-33			
❑ Historical 24		1968	10.00
THAT CHRISTMAS FEELING			
❑ Columbia Special Products P 11853		1973	12.00
—Sold only at JCPenney department stores			
THAT CHRISTMAS FEELING!			
❑ Columbia Special Products CSS 1429		1970	10.00
THAT'S TRUCKDRIVIN'			
❑ Starday DT-90617 [R]		196?	20.00
—Capitol Record Club edition			
❑ Starday T-90617 [M]		196?	30.00
—Capitol Record Club edition			
THEME SONGS			
❑ Columbia CL 6016 [10]		1949	40.00
❑ RCA Victor LPT-1 [10]		1951	40.00
THEMES LIKE OLD TIMES			
❑ Viva 36018 [(2)]		1969	20.00

Number	Title (A Side/B Side)	Yr	NM
THESAURUS OF CLASSIC JAZZ			
❑ Columbia C4L 18 [(4)]		1961	50.00
3RD ANNIVERSARY ALBUM — 25 COUNTRY MUSIC GREATS			
❑ Homestead AC-1		196?	12.00
A THIRD SESSION AT SQUIRREL'S			
❑ Paramount LP-110 [10]		1954	60.00
30 FAVORITE SONGS OF CHRISTMAS WITH CHIMES AND CHORUS			
❑ Disneyland DQ-1329 [M]		1963	20.00
—Performed by anonymous musicians			
THIS COULD LEAD TO LOVE			
❑ Riverside RLP 12-808 [M]		195?	50.00
THIS IS CHRISTMAS			
❑ RCA Victor VPS-6046 [(2)]		1971	15.00
THIS IS HOW IT ALL BEGAN: THE SPECIALTY STORY, VOL. 1			
❑ Specialty SPS-2117		1970	20.00
THIS IS HOW IT ALL BEGAN: THE SPECIALTY STORY, VOL. 2			
❑ Specialty SPS-2118		1970	20.00
THIS IS SOUL			
❑ Atlantic 8170 [M]		1968	40.00
❑ Atlantic SD 8170 [S]		1968	20.00
THIS IS STEREO			
❑ Liberty LST-101 [S]		1960	40.00
—Black vinyl			
❑ Liberty LST-101 [S]		1960	120.00
—Red vinyl			
THIS IS THE BIG BAND ERA			
❑ RCA Victor VPM-6043 [(2)]		197?	15.00
THIS IS THE BLUES			
❑ Kimberly 2020 [M]		1963	20.00
❑ Kimberly 11020 [S]		1963	25.00
THIS IS THE BLUES, VOL. 1			
❑ Pacific Jazz PJ-13 [M]		1961	30.00

Number	Title (A Side/B Side)	Yr	NM
THIS IS THE BLUES, VOL. 2			
❑ Pacific Jazz PJ-30 [M]		1962	25.00
❑ Pacific Jazz ST-30 [M]		1962	30.00
THREADS OF GLORY — 200 YEARS OF AMERICA IN WORDS & MUSIC			
❑ London Phase 4 6SP 14000 [(6)]		1975	30.00
THREE DECADES OF MUSIC, 1939-49, VOL. 1			
❑ Blue Note BST-89902 [(2)]		1969	25.00
THREE DECADES OF MUSIC, 1949-59, VOL. 1			
❑ Blue Note BST-89903 [(2)]		1969	25.00
THREE DECADES OF MUSIC, 1959-69, VOL. 1			
❑ Blue Note BST-89904 [(2)]		1969	25.00
THREE ROADS TO JAZZ			
❑ American Recording Society LP-100 [M]		1956	30.00
A TIME FOR PRAYER			
❑ Audio Lab AL-1518 [M]		1959	80.00
'TIS THE SEASON			
❑ Columbia Special Products C 10874		1972	10.00
TODAY'S HITS			
❑ Philles PHLP 4004 [M]		1963	400.00
—First pressings have blue and black labels			
❑ Philles PHLP 4004 [M]		1964	200.00
—Second pressings have yellow and red labels			
TOGETHER			
❑ Warner Bros. PRO 486		1972	20.00
—Originals have green labels			
TOGETHER AT CHRISTMAS (READER'S DIGEST FAMILY ALBUM OF CHRISTMAS MUSIC)			
❑ Reader's Digest RDA 151-A [(5)]		1974	20.00
—Available only through Reader's Digest magazine by mail order			
TOMORROW'S HITS			
❑ Vee Jay LP-1042 [M]		1962	30.00
TOP HITS OF '54 VOL. II			
❑ Capitol H 9119 [10]		1954	50.00
TOP R&B ARTISTS SING COUNTRY SONGS			
❑ King 884 [M]		1964	80.00
TOWN HALL CONCERT			
❑ Mainstream S-6004 [R]		1965	12.00
❑ Mainstream 56004 [M]		1965	25.00
TRADITIONAL CHRISTMAS SONGS			
❑ Audio Lab AL-1517 [M]		1959	80.00
TRADITIONAL JAZZ			
❑ London LL 1242 [M]		1955	20.00
TRADITIONAL JAZZ AT THE ROYAL FESTIVAL HALL			
❑ London LL 1184 [M]		1955	20.00
TREASURE ALBUM			
❑ Hickory LPS-154		1970	40.00
TREASURE CHEST GOODIES			
❑ Stax 703 [M]		1963	40.00
—National version of "Hits from the South Presented by Nick Charles" with rearranged contents			
TREASURE CHEST OF HITS			
❑ Swan LP-501 [M]		1960	80.00
A TREASURE CHEST OF SONG HITS			
❑ Columbia CL 613 [M]		1955	25.00
TREASURE TUNES FROM THE VAULT (AS ADVERTISED ON WLS)			
❑ Chess LP 1474 [M]		1962	40.00
A TREASURY OF CHRISTMAS			
❑ Columbia Record Club P4S 5022 [(4)]		1965	30.00
A TREASURY OF GOLDEN CHRISTMAS SONGS			
❑ Vee Jay LP-5045 [M]		1963	30.00
TRIBUTE TO CHARLIE PARKER FROM THE NEWPORT JAZZ FESTIVAL			
❑ RCA Victor LPM-3738 [M]		1967	30.00
❑ RCA Victor LSP-3738 [S]		1967	20.00
TROMBONE BAND STAND			
❑ Bethlehem BCP-6036 [M]		1960	30.00
TROMBONE SCENE			
❑ Vik LX-1087 [M]		1957	30.00
TROMBONES			
❑ Savoy MG-12086 [M]		1956	60.00
TRUCK DRIVER SONGS			
❑ King 866 [M]		1963	70.00
TRUMPET BLUES 1925-29			
❑ Historical 27		1969	10.00
TRUMPET INTERLUDE			
❑ EmArcy MG-36017 [M]		1955	50.00
TRUMPET STYLISTS			
❑ Capitol H 326 [10]		1952	50.00
TRUMPETER'S HOLIDAY			
❑ Epic LN 3252 [M]		1956	30.00

Except when noted otherwise, VG = 25% of NM, and VG+ = 50% of NM. (Example: VG = $2.00, VG+ = $4.00 and NM = $8.00.)

Number	Title (A Side/B Side)	Yr	NM
TRUMPETS ALL OUT			
❑ Savoy MG-12096 [M]		1957	60.00
TUNES TO BE REMEMBERED			
❑ Excello LP-8001 [M]		1960	150.00
—Original cover is green with black records that list the title and artist of each selection			
TURN BACK THE CLOCK			
❑ King 859 [M]		1963	70.00
THE 12 GREATEST OLDIES IN THE WHOLE WORLD, EVER			
❑ Parkway P-7031 [M]		1963	30.00
12 MILLION SELLERS			
❑ Forum F-9057 [M]		1963	20.00
❑ Forum SF-9057 [R]		1963	15.00
12 + 3 = 15 HITS			
❑ End LP 310 [M]		1961	60.00
12 SONGS OF CHRISTMAS			
❑ Reprise F-2022 [M]		1964	20.00
❑ Reprise FS-2022 [S]		1964	15.00
12 TOP TEEN DANCES 1961-1962			
❑ Cameo C-1016 [M]		1962	30.00
20 ALL TIME NO. 1 HITS			
❑ Roulette R 25290 [M]		1965	20.00
❑ Roulette SR 25290 [R]		1965	12.00
20 BIG BOSS FAVORITES: 10 GREAT HITS OF 1964 — 10 GREAT OLDIES HITS			
❑ Roulette R 25304 [M]		1965	20.00
❑ Roulette SR 25304 [R]		1965	15.00
—Of the 20 tracks, only "Laugh, Laugh" by the Beau Brummels and "El Watusi" by Ray Barretto are true stereo			
20 ORIGINAL WINNERS OF 1964			
❑ Roulette R 25293 [M]		1965	20.00
❑ Roulette SR 25293 [R]		1965	12.00
20 ORIGINAL WINNERS, VOL. 1			
❑ Roulette R 25249 [M]		1964	20.00
20 ORIGINAL WINNERS, VOL. 2			
❑ Roulette R 25251 [M]		1964	20.00
20 ORIGINAL WINNERS, VOL. 3			
❑ Roulette R 25263 [M]		1965	20.00
20 ORIGINAL WINNERS, VOL. 4			
❑ Roulette R 25264 [M]		1965	20.00
20 POWER HITS, VOL. 2			
❑ K-Tel TU 222		1971	10.00
20 SOULFUL OLDIES, VOL. 1			
❑ Vee Jay VJVS-1001 [R]		1972	20.00
20 SOULFUL OLDIES, VOL. 2			
❑ Vee Jay VJVS-1002 [R]		1972	20.00
20 SOULFUL OLDIES, VOL. 3			
❑ Vee Jay VJVS-1003 [R]		1972	20.00
20 SOULFUL OLDIES, VOL. 4			
❑ Vee Jay VJVS-73-1006/7 [R]		1973	20.00
20 SOULFUL OLDIES, VOL. 5			
❑ Vee Jay VJVS-73-1008/9 [R]		1973	20.00
20 SOULFUL OLDIES, VOL. 6			
❑ Vee Jay VJVS-73-1010/11 [R]		1973	20.00
24 KARAT GOLD FOR GROOVIN'			
❑ Verve V6-6654 [(2)]		1968	20.00
24 SACRED SONGS			
❑ King 965 [M]		1966	50.00
25 YEARS OF C&W HITS			
❑ King 1006 [M]		1966	30.00
25 YEARS OF COUNTRY AND WESTERN SACRED SONGS			
❑ King 807 [M]		1962	100.00
25 YEARS OF POPULAR MUSIC			
❑ King 1008 [M]		1966	30.00
25 YEARS OF R&B HITS			
❑ King 1004 [M]		1966	30.00
25 YEARS OF R&B HITS, VOL. 1			
❑ King 725 [M]		1961	100.00
25 YEARS OF R&B HITS, VOL. 2			
❑ King 749 [M]		1961	100.00
TWISTIN' ALL NIGHT LONG			
❑ Swan LP-506 [M]		1962	120.00
THE UNAVAILABLE 16			
❑ Vee Jay LP-1051 [M]		1962	40.00
UNDER ONE ROOF			
❑ EmArcy MG-36088 [M]		1956	40.00
UNDERGROUND GOLD			
❑ Liberty LST-7625		1969	15.00
UNEXPURGATED JAZZ			
❑ Audiophile AP-43 [M]		1953	30.00

Number	Title (A Side/B Side)	Yr	NM
UNFORGETTABLE OLDIES			
❑ Unart M 20014 [M]		1967	15.00
❑ Unart S 21014 [S]		1967	12.00
UNFORGETTABLE OLDIES — VOL. II			
❑ Unart M 20027 [M]		1968	15.00
❑ Unart S 21027 [S]		1968	12.00
UNFORGETTABLE PERFORMANCES BY THE JAZZ IMMORTALS			
❑ Dot DLP-3444 [M]		196?	12.00
UP SWING			
❑ RCA Victor LPT-12 [10]		1951	40.00
UPRIGHT AND LOWDOWN			
❑ Columbia CL 685 [M]		1955	20.00
A VARIETY OF COUNTRY SACRED SONGS			
❑ Audio Lab AL-1557 [M]		1960	60.00
THE VERVE COMPENDIUM OF JAZZ, NO. 1			
❑ Verve MGV-8194 [M]		1957	30.00
❑ Verve V-8194 [M]		1961	20.00
THE VERVE COMPENDIUM OF JAZZ, NO. 2			
❑ Verve MGV-8195 [M]		1957	30.00
❑ Verve V-8195 [M]		1961	20.00
A VERY MERRY CHRISTMAS			
❑ Columbia Special Products CSS 563		1967	20.00
—Sold only at Grants stores			
A VERY MERRY CHRISTMAS, VOL. TWO			
❑ Columbia Special Products CSS 788		1968	12.00
—Sold only at Grants stores			
A VERY MERRY CHRISTMAS, VOL. 3			
❑ Columbia Special Products CSS 997		1969	12.00
—Sold only at Grants stores			
A VERY MERRY CHRISTMAS, VOL. IV			
❑ Columbia Special Products CSS 1464		1970	15.00
—Sold only at Grants stores			
A VERY MERRY CHRISTMAS, VOL. 5			
❑ RCA Special Products PRS-343		1971	10.00
—Sold only at Grants stores			
A VERY MERRY CHRISTMAS, VOL. VI			
❑ RCA Special Products PRS-427		1972	10.00
—Sold only at Grants stores			
A VERY MERRY CHRISTMAS, VOL. VII			
❑ RCA Special Products DPL1-0049		1973	10.00
—Sold only at Grants stores			
A VERY MERRY CHRISTMAS, VOL. VIII			
❑ Capitol Special Markets SL-6954		1974	10.00
—Sold only at Grants stores			
A VERY MERRY CHRISTMAS TO ALL			
❑ Columbia Special Products CSP 159		1964	15.00
—Sold only at Acme markets (Mid-Atlantic states)			
VERY SAXY			
❑ Prestige PRLP-7167 [M]		1959	60.00
❑ Prestige PRST-7790		1971	20.00
—Reissue of 7167			
VICEROY CIGARETTES CAMPUS JAZZ FESTIVAL			
❑ RCA Custom KO7P-1544 [M]		1959	30.00
—Available thoruigh Viceroy cigarettes			
THE VIOLIN SUMMIT			
❑ Prestige PRLP-7631		1969	15.00
VOICES OF HAITI			
❑ Elektra EKL-5 [10]		1953	40.00
VOODOO DRUMS IN HI-FI			
❑ Atlantic 1296 [M]		1958	40.00
—Black label			
❑ Atlantic 1296 [M]		1961	25.00
—Multicolor label, white "fan" logo at right			
❑ Atlantic 1296 [M]		1963	20.00
—Multicolor label, black "fan" logo at right			
WALKIN' BY MYSELF			
❑ Chess LP 1446 [M]		1960	80.00
THE WALTONS' CHRISTMAS ALBUM			
❑ Columbia KC 33193		1974	15.00
—Only one of the actors who appeared on the show appears on the album, thus it's listed here under Various Artists rather than Soundtracks or Television Albums			
WAMO'S GOLDEN GASSERS			
❑ Chess LP 1458 PGH [M]		1961	150.00
—Pittsburgh version of "Golden Gassers," Chess 1458			
THE WARNER/REPRISE RADIO SHOW			
❑ Warner Bros. PRO 463		1971	25.00
—Originals have green labels			
WASHBOARD RHYTHM KINGS, VOL. 1			
❑ "X" LVA-3021 [10]		1954	80.00
WE CUT THIS ALBUM FOR BREAD			
❑ Bethlehem BCP-86 [M]		1958	30.00
WE LIKE BANDS			
❑ Coral CRL 57229 [M]		195?	12.00

Number	Title (A Side/B Side)	Yr	NM
WE LIKE BOYS/GREAT BOY OLDIES			
❑ Oldies 33 OL-8004 [M]		1964	25.00
WE SING THE BLUES			
❑ Minit LP-0003 [M]		1962	50.00
WE WISH YOU A MERRY CHRISTMAS			
❑ Harmony KH 31536		1972	10.00
❑ RCA Victor PRS-277 [Picture Sleeve]		1968	10.00
—Sleeve says the number is "68-1968"			
❑ Warner Bros. W 1337 [M]		1960	25.00
❑ Warner Bros. WS 1337 [S]		1960	30.00
WE'VE BUILT A JAZZ ALBUM FOR YOU			
❑ Bethlehem BCP-89 [M]		1958	30.00
WEST COAST JAZZ, VOL. 2			
❑ Jazztone J-(# unk) [M]		1957	30.00
WEST COAST VS. EAST COAST			
❑ MGM E-3390 [M]		1956	30.00
WESTERN SWING			
❑ King 876 [M]		1963	70.00
WFUN GOOD GUYS			
❑ Roulette R 25273 [M]		1965	20.00
WHAT'S NEW? ON CAPITOL STEREO, VOL. 1			
❑ Capitol SN-1 [S]		1959	25.00
WHAT'S SHAKIN'			
❑ Elektra EKL-4002 [M]		1966	40.00
—Deduct 25 percent if booklet is missing			
❑ Elektra EKS-74002 [S]		1966	50.00
—Deduct 25 percent if booklet is missing			
WHEELIN' AND DEALIN'			
❑ Prestige PRLP-7131 [M]		1957	100.00
—Reissued as Status 8327; see JOHN COLTRANE.			
WHK GOOD GUYS			
❑ Roulette R 25295 [M]		1965	20.00
THE WHO'S WHO OF COUNTRY AND WESTERN MUSIC			
❑ Capitol ST 2538 [S]		1966	20.00
❑ Capitol T 2538 [M]		1966	20.00
THE WHOLE BURBANK CATALOG			
❑ Warner Bros. PRO 512 [(2)]		1972	20.00
—Originals have green labels			
A WHOLE LOT OF BLOWIN'			
❑ Audio Lab AL-1539 [M]		1959	60.00
WHOPPERS			
❑ Jubilee JGM-1119 [M]		1960	100.00
—Reissue of "Best of Rhythm and Blues," Jubilee 1014			
THE WIDE, WIDE WORLD OF JAZZ			
❑ RCA Victor LPM-1325 [M]		1956	30.00
WILD WILDWOOD RECORDED LIVE			
❑ Chancellor CHL-5017 [M]		1960	25.00
❑ Chancellor CHLS-5017 [S]		1960	30.00
WILDFLOWERS: NEW YORK LOFT JAZZ 1			
❑ Douglas 7045		1976	12.00
WILDFLOWERS: NEW YORK LOFT JAZZ 2			
❑ Douglas 7046		1976	12.00
WILDFLOWERS: NEW YORK LOFT JAZZ 3			
❑ Douglas 7047		1976	12.00
WILDFLOWERS: NEW YORK LOFT JAZZ 4			
❑ Douglas 7048		1976	12.00
WILDFLOWERS: NEW YORK LOFT JAZZ 5			
❑ Douglas 7049		1976	12.00
WING LIVELY GUYS			
❑ Roulette R 25307 [M]		1965	20.00
WINNER'S CIRCLE			
❑ Bethlehem BCP-6024 [M]		1958	40.00
WINNERS ALL! THE DOWN BEAT JAZZ POLL '64			
❑ Verve V-8579 [M]		1964	20.00
❑ Verve V6-8579 [S]		1964	25.00
WINNERS CIRCLE LIMITED EDITION			
❑ Columbia GB-4 [M]		1959	25.00
WINTER'S WARMTH			
❑ Columbia Special Products CSP 315/6 [(2)]		1965	15.00
—Produced for NORM/A Step Ahead			
WISHING YOU A MERRY CHRISTMAS			
❑ RCA Victor LSP-4793		1972	12.00
WMAK JET SET-22 WINNERS			
❑ Roulette R 25291 [M]		1965	20.00
WOL SOUL BROTHERS			
❑ Roulette R 25337 [M]		1966	20.00
—Same LP as "WWIN Astro Jocks"			
THE WOMEN IN JAZZ			
❑ Storyville STLP-916 [M]		1956	50.00
WONDERFUL MEMORIES FROM THE FAMILY PRAYER BOOK			
❑ Vee Jay LP-5066 [M]		1964	30.00

Number	Title (A Side/B Side)	Yr	NM
THE WONDERFUL WORLD OF CHRISTMAS			
❑ Capitol Special Markets SL-8000		1975	12.00
—Sold only at Firestone tire dealers (add 50% for sticker that says "Season's Greetings Firestone")			
WONDROUS WINTER			
❑ Columbia Special Products CSS 708/9 [(2)]		1968	15.00
—Produced for NORM/A Step Ahead			
WOODSTOCK			
❑ Cotillion SD 3-500 [(3)]		1970	20.00
—Pale blue labels			
WOODSTOCK TWO			
❑ Cotillion SD 2-400 [(2)]		1971	20.00
THE WORKS			
❑ Warner Bros. PRO 610 [(2)]		1975	25.00
A WORLD OF BLUES			
❑ Imperial LP-9210 [M]		1963	30.00
❑ Imperial LP-12210 [R]		1963	20.00
THE WORLD OF COUNTRY MUSIC			
❑ Capitol NPB-5 [(3)]		1965	30.00
THE WORLD OF SWING			
❑ Columbia KG 32945 [(2)]		1974	15.00
THE WORLD'S GREATEST MUSIC SERIES 'POP' — JAZZ			
❑ Artia-Parliament WGM(S)-2A [(5)S]		196?	60.00
❑ Artia-Parliament WGM-2A [(5)M]		196?	50.00
❑ Artia-Parliament WGM 2AB [(10)]		196?	100.00
—Box set of material from the Roulette label; also issued as two five-record boxes			
❑ Artia-Parliament WGM 2B [(5)]		196?	50.00
—Second of two five-record sets			
WWIN ASTRO JOCKS			
❑ Roulette R 25337 [M]		1966	20.00
—Same LP as "WOL Soul Brothers"			
YESTERDAY			
❑ Mainstream MRL-364		197?	12.00
YOU'VE GOT TO HEAR IT TO BELIEVE IT			
❑ Solid State SS-94		1966	20.00
THE YOUNG AT BOP			
❑ EmArcy MG-26001 [10]		1954	80.00
THE YOUNG ONES OF JAZZ			
❑ EmArcy MG-36085 [M]		1956	40.00
YOUR FAVORITE GROUPS AND THEIR GOLDEN GOODIES, VOL. 19			
❑ Roulette R 25248 [M]		1964	20.00
YOUR FAVORITE SINGING GROUPS			
❑ Hull 1002 [M]		1962	1500.
YOUR INTRODUCTION TO THE SOUND OF THE 'SIXTIES			
❑ Liberty MM-403 [DJ]		1960	30.00
—Promo-only release			
YOUR OLD FAVORITES ON OLD TOWN			
❑ Old Town LP-101 [M]		1959	200.00
YOURS			
❑ Harmony HL 7042 [M]		1957	20.00
ZENITH PRESENTS ALL STAR HOOTENANNY			
❑ Columbia Special Products CSP 149 [M]		1963	50.00
—With three early Bob Dylan tracks credited to "Bobby Dylan." Also has tracks by Pete Seeger (2), Orriel Smith (2) and The Clancy Brothers with Tommy Makem (3)			
ZENITH PRESENTS CHRISTMAS, A GIFT OF MUSIC			
❑ Capitol Creative Products SL-6544 [S]		1967	12.00
—Sold only at Zenith dealers			
ZENITH PRESENTS CHRISTMAS, A GIFT OF MUSIC VOL. 2			
❑ Columbia Special Products CSS 834		1968	12.00
—Sold only at Zenith dealers			
ZENITH PRESENTS CHRISTMAS, A GIFT OF MUSIC VOL. 3			
❑ Capitol Creative Products SL-6659		1969	12.00
—Sold only at Zenith dealers; reissued as "Christmas — The Season of Music" for general release			
ZENITH PRESENTS CHRISTMAS, A GIFT OF MUSIC VOL. 4			
❑ Capitol Creative Products SL-6687		1970	12.00
—Sold only at Zenith dealers; reissued as "Christmas -- A Gift of Music" for general release			
ZENITH PRESENTS CHRISTMAS, A GIFT OF MUSIC VOL. 5			
❑ Columbia Special Products C 10395		1971	10.00
—Sold only at Zenith dealers			
ZENITH PRESENTS CHRISTMAS, A GIFT OF MUSIC, VOL. 6 (THE CHRISTMAS HIT PARADE)			
❑ Longines Symphonette SYS 5562		1972	10.00
—Sold only at Zenith dealers			
ZENITH PRESENTS HOOTENANNY SPECIAL			
❑ Columbia Special Products CSP 216M [M]		1965	25.00
❑ Columbia Special Products CSP 216S [S]		1965	30.00
ZENITH SALUTES THE SWINGIN' BANDS			
❑ Columbia Special Products CSS 525 [M]		1967	15.00
—Available from Zenith dealers			
ZIG ZAG FESTIVAL			
❑ Mercury SRD-2-29 [DJ]		1970	25.00